DICCIONARIO

ESPAÑOL-INGLÉS

ENGLISH-SPANISH

DICTIONARY

GRAN DICCIONARIO ESPAÑOL-INGLÉS ENGLISH-SPANISH DICTIONARY

Unabridged edition

DIRIGIDO Y REALIZADO POR

Ramón García-Pelayo y Gross

Professor de la Universidad de Paris (Sorbona) y del Instituto
de Estudios Políticos
Miembro c. de la Academia Argentina de Letras,
de la Academia de San Dionisio de Ciencias, Artes y Letras
de la Academia Boliviana de la Historia
y de la Real Academia de Bellas Artes de San Telmo

CON LA COLABORACIÓN DE

Micheline Durand

Licenciada en Letras, intérprete de Conferencia
Profesora de la Escuela Superior de Intérpretes y Traductores
de la Universidad de París y del Instituto de Ciencias Políticas

Barry Tulett

Alan Biggins, Carol Cockburn, Barbara Penick,
Della Roberts, Alan Taylor, Gary D. Wright

David E. Warham

y de

Fernando García-Pelayo

Pilar Andrés Solana, Trinidad Fungairiño,
Elena Real Carbonell, Carmen Warren

José Pau Andersen

LAROUSSE

21 Rue du Montparnasse
75298 París Cedex 06

Dinamarca 81
México 06600, D. F.

Elsley House 24-30
Londres WIP 7AD

Av. Diagonal 407 Bis-10
08008 Barcelona

95 Madison Aveneu
Nueva York 10016

Valentín Gómez 3530
1191 Buenos Aires

PRIMERA EDICIÓN — 13ª reimpresión

ISBN 2-03-420200-7
Distribution/Sales Larousse Kingfisher Chambers Inc., New York

Library of Congress Catalog Card Number
93-086201

ISBN 970-607-937-8 (Ediciones Larousse)

Impreso en México — Printed in Mexico

Esta obra se terminó de imprimir y encuadernar en diciembre de 2000 en Encuadernación Ofgloma, S. A. Rosa Blanca núm. 12, Col. Santiago Acahualtepec, México, D. F.

La edición consta de 6 000 ejemplares

NUEVA EDICIÓN

POR LA REDACCIÓN
LAROUSSE BILINGÜES

NEW EDITION

BY LAROUSSE STAFF

Béatrice Cazalaà
Paloma Cabot
Anna Jené Palat

COORDINACIÓN EDITORIAL
EDITORIAL MANAGEMENT

Ralf Brockmeier
Elvira de Moragas Maragall

COLABORADORES
CONTRIBUTORS

Leslie Gallmann
Monica Henry
Jacqueline Minett
Victoria Ordóñez Diví

CORRECCIÓN
PROOFREADING

Jean-Jacques Carreras, Pierre Coët

INFORMÁTICA EDITORIAL
DATA MANAGEMENT

Gabino Alonso

CARTOGRAFÍA
CARTOGRAPHY

Dominique Cormier
Krystyna Mazoyer
Catherine Zacharopoulou

FOREWORD

THE CHIEF AIM of the authors of the first edition of this dictionary was to address all those aspects of language confronting users in their daily lives. This radically new approach successfully catered to the needs of both the scholar and the general reader.

In order to provide full coverage of a language in all its complexity it is essential to consult the widest possible range of texts, and in compiling this dictionary the authors have drawn extensively from many sources, including newspapers and periodicals of both general and specialist nature, as well as literary works by the major authors writing in Spanish and English. Numerous new entries in this edition bear witness to the many recent advances in science and technology. Whilst the editors have been careful not to sacrifice tradition to modernity, ample space is given to current developments in the idiomatic and colloquial use of both languages, with particular attention to Spanish and English usage in the Americas, as distinct from European Spanish and British English. Some entries include special comments where the authors have felt this to be useful. The result is a reference work which will prove to be an invaluable tool for the many thousands of users who, for purposes of work or study, may wish to consult this dictionary.

The profound changes in contemporary society in terms of the creative media, cultural exchange and communication, are reflected in the 8 000 new items which have been added to the original text. Thus, while remaining faithful to the high ideals and quality of the first edition, this new edition constitutes a comprehensive and up-to-date reference work, indispensable to the understanding of current Spanish and English. Vocabulary from fields of knowledge such as nuclear energy and environmental studies appears in this edition for the first time, whilst the number of entries relating to other areas such as information technology, telecommunications, economics, medicine, biology and sport has greatly increased. Nevertheless, the aim of this work is not to provide a specialized dictionary, but rather to record, through the inclusion of new technical and scientific terms, the ways in which both Spanish and English are evolving as they become permeated by specialized vocabulary. Other, more general terms drawn from contemporary life and culture add a new, fully modern dimension to the dictionary. The reader will find in these pages the familiar, colloquial words and expressions, including slang, used in everyday life. The number of acronyms, abbreviations and geographical names, which appear for the first time in the main body of the dictionary, has been very considerably enlarged.

There have been a number of modifications in the presentation and layout of the text. For instance, any change in grammatical category under a particular entry is now preceded by a lozenge. The dictionary has also been set in a new, clear type which makes it even more user-friendly.

We are confident that, like the parent edition, this revised and enlarged edition will meet with the approval and satisfaction of our readers, and we remind users that their comments and observations on the dictionary are, as always, most welcome.

THE EDITORS

PRÓLOGO

La principal preocupación de los autores de la primera edición de esta obra fue abarcar en todas sus manifestaciones la realidad lingüística con que el usuario pudiera llegar a encontrarse en su quehacer cotidiano y profesional, ambición no poco revolucionaria en aquella época. Este nuevo planteamiento supo responder a las expectativas de los estudiosos de la lengua inglesa y supuso un éxito indiscutible.

¿Cómo captar la totalidad de una realidad lingüística sin contar con un corpus lo más amplio posible? Para la constitución de dicho corpus se acudió a diarios y revistas de carácter general o especializadas, y a extractos de obras literarias de los más señalados autores en lengua española y en lengua inglesa. De los progresos realizados por la ciencia y la técnica dejan constancia los numerosos términos de especialidad recogidos en esta obra, en la que también tienen cabida los giros y expresiones coloquiales cuyo carácter y sabor propios se intenta conservar en las traducciones. Las variantes americanas tanto del español como del inglés, fiel reflejo de la importancia de la realidad americana, ocupan aquí un lugar por derecho propio. En algunos artículos, los autores ofrecen observaciones sobre dificultades de uno u otro idioma. El resultado de todo ello es una inapreciable herramienta de trabajo que ha servido a miles de usuarios en su estudio de la lengua inglesa.

Pero la sociedad de nuestro tiempo está experimentando una profunda transformación en cuanto a medios de creación, intercambio y comunicación. Movidos por la fidelidad a los principios de calidad que hicieron posible su éxito inicial, hemos enriquecido el texto de partida con 8 000 nuevas voces a fin de ofrecer una obra de consulta indispensable para la comprensión del español y el inglés de nuestros días. Algunas áreas de conocimiento — energía nuclear, medio ambiente — aparecen por primera vez en este diccionario, mientras que otras, informática, telecomunicaciones, economía, medicina, biología y deportes, ven ampliados sus horizontes terminológicos. Sin embargo, esta obra no trata de convertirse en un diccionario de especialidad; al introducir los nuevos términos técnicos y científicos sólo pretende dar testimonio de la evolución de la lengua y de su mayor permeabilidad y receptividad frente a los vocablos especializados. Sin pertenecer a ninguna materia en particular, algunas de las voces incorporadas confieren a esta obra una dimensión plenamente contemporánea. Ciertamente, el usuario podrá encontrar palabras familiares, incluso de argot, las mismas que puede oír en su entorno habitual. El número de siglas, abreviaturas y nombres geográficos, que a partir de ahora integran el cuerpo del diccionario, se ha visto considerablemente aumentado.

También la presentación del texto ha sufrido modificaciones: cualquier cambio de categoría gramatical va ahora precedido de un rombo. Por si esto fuese poco, la nitidez de la tipografía y la elección de un tipo de letra de sobria elegancia y más legibilidad ofrecen una lectura cómoda y agradable.

Estamos persuadidos de que, al consultar la presente edición corregida y aumentada, los usuarios se sentirán tan satisfechos como con la anterior y confiamos en que nos comuniquen cuantos comentarios y observaciones consideren oportunos.

LOS EDITORES

EXPLANATORY NOTES

Order of material

1. The material has been arranged in alphabetical order, except where two words are equivalent in meaning and spelt similarly. The latter are entered at the same entry (e.g. **estancación; estancamiento**).
2. English compound words also appear alphabetically. For instance, **dress circle** is listed as a separate entry following and not included under the headword **dress**.
3. Variant British and American spellings are indicated (see **behaviour**).
4. No provision is made for regular adverbs, diminutives and augmentatives whose meaning is obvious from the stem word (e.g. **fortunately**).
5. Preterites, past participles and contracted forms are also listed in their own alphabetical order (see **I'm**). In the two former instances the user is referred to the infinitive of the verb (e.g. **got** *pret/pp* See **get**).

Phonetic transcription

Phonetic transcription, in square brackets after the headword, appears only in the English-Spanish part as, with very few exceptions, the pronunciation of Spanish is well represented by normal orthography (see chapter on PRONUNCIATION in the *Summary of Spanish grammar*). The symbols used are those of the International Phonetic Alphabet (see table on page VI, part II). Where British and American pronunciation differ, British comes first followed, after *US*, by American (e.g. **schedule**).

Grammatical information

1. The grammatical function of the headword is made clear using the abbreviations listed in full on pages VIII (part I) and V (part II).
2. Genders of Spanish nouns are printed in both parts of the dictionary and English nouns of common gender are translated into both masculine and feminine forms (e.g. **baker** *n* panadero, ra). Number is indicated only when it differs in translation (e.g. **clothes** *pl n* ropa *f sing*).

Number and gender are also recorded in the phrases at the end of entries (e.g. *disturbance of the peace* alteración *f* del orden público) except where the word treated has already been translated or where context suffices (e.g. *disturbance in the night* escándalo nocturno).

3. English irregular noun plurals are indicated at the end of entries in the English-Spanish part and Spanish plurals in the other part.
4. Words which can assume various functions (adjective, noun, adverb, etc.) are contained in the same article and appear preceded by a black lozenge (◆). Verbs, however, are treated separately (e.g. under **right** the adjective followed by the noun and adverb come under subheadings while the verb is covered in a separate entry).
5. Irregular verbs bear asterisks referring the reader to the Grammar Section which discusses conjugation of modes and tenses. Irregular forms of English verbs, chiefly preterites and past participles, are indicated where necessary at the end of the entries in the English-Spanish part.
6. When verbs, nouns or adjectives take different prepositions in the two languages, an indication is given in parenthesis or in the form of an example (see **desdecir**).

Differentiation of meanings

1. Translations of diverse meanings of headwords in all entries are separated by the symbol || and, in some cases, cross-references to relevant subject matter are provided (see lists of ABREVIATURAS on page VIII of part I and of ABBREVIATIONS on page V of part II). Where a word has several meanings pertaining to a single discipline, that discipline is indicated by an abbreviation only once at the beginning and the meanings are separated out using | symbol. Search lists are located before words with many meanings, to simplify use. To find the translation of *estar para* the user only need consult subheading 6 of the entry on **estar** (headed FOLLOWED BY A PREPOSITION) without having to read through the preceding items. The more common meanings are listed at the beginning of the entry.
2. Phrases and expressions are placed, in alphabetical order, immediately ofter the various meanings and are preceded by the || — symbol. The dash is omitted when there is only one phrase or expression.
3. Common English verbs that change their meaning when accompanied by some particles are printed in boldface in the same paragraph preceded by a black lozenge (◆) at the end of entries and placed between ||. Meanings are marked off with | and followed by phrases and expressions after || — (see the verb **to go**).
4. By way of guidance to the user on social usage of words and phrases, we have drawn a distinction between colloquial or familiar but acceptable terms FAM and vulgar or common parlance POP. These abbreviations are placed before the translation if they pertain to the word treated and after it if they apply to the equivalent word. For instance, the third application of the Spanish word **jeta** carries FAM to denote its colloquial nature. As a general rule, wherever possible, care has been taken in translation to reflect social register.

Clarification of meanings

Where words can assume several meanings each one is defined. Parentheses are used for definitions written in the language of the headword and square brackets for those which appear in the language of translations (see **descubrimiento**). The same procedure has been adopted when phrases have diverse meanings (e.g. *to get sick* would usually be the equivalent of «ponerse enfermo» but, when the reference is to travel sickness, the translation is «marearse»). As well as indications, which should be seen as such and not as synonyms, numerous examples are used. Where examples and phrases begin with the same words the latter are entered once only, the variant part following after the word «or» o «*o*» (e.g. *edad de la razón* or *del juicio* age of reason; *to get* o *to come to the point* ir al grano). Some expressions are not always used in full, in which case the words that can be omitted are placed in parentheses (e.g. *hablando del rey de Roma por la puerta asoma* talk of the devil (and he will appear)).

Additional notes

Additional explanatory notes are provided, in Spanish or in English as appropriate, to clarify the meaning of some words further, or peculiar usage, semantic evolution, irregular plurals, irregular verb forms or any other point requiring explanation (see **menor**).

Americanisms

In the light of the importance and growing influence today of the English- and Spanish-speaking nations of the New World, numerous Americanisms have been included in both parts of the dictionary. The abbreviations used are *AMER* before Latin American words or phrases and *US* before North American ones.

CÓMO USAR ESTE DICCIONARIO

Orden de las palabras

1. Las palabras siguen siempre un riguroso orden alfabético, pero, cuando dos voces tienen igual sentido y parecida ortografía, se reseñan en el mismo artículo (por ej., **estancación; estancamiento**).

2. Las palabras compuestas inglesas se registran también alfabéticamente. Así, **dress circle** figura a continuación de **dress** y no en el interior de este artículo.

3. Se indican las ortografías existentes en Gran Bretaña y los Estados Unidos (véase **behaviour**).

4. Los adverbios, diminutivos y aumentativos de formación regular, cuyos significados son fácilmente deducibles a partir de las palabras de las que se derivan, no se han estudiado (por ej. **fortunately**).

5. Se hace mención de los pretéritos y participios pasivos irregulares, lo mismo que de las contracciones, en el orden alfabético que les corresponde (véase **I'm**). En los dos primeros casos se remite al infinitivo del verbo (p. ej. **got** *pret/pp* See **get**).

Pronunciación figurada

La pronunciación figurada, colocada entre corchetes después del artículo, se indica solamente en la parte inglés-español y no en la otra, ya que las palabras se pronuncian en castellano tal y como se escriben, salvo contadas excepciones (véase PRONUNCIATION en *Summary of Spanish grammar*). Se ha utilizado el Alfabeto Fonético Internacional (véase pág. VI, 2.ª parte). Cuando la pronunciación difiere entre Gran Bretaña y Estados Unidos, se ha transcrito primero la inglesa y luego, tras *US*, la americana (por ej. **schedule**).

Indicaciones gramaticales

1. La naturaleza morfológica de cada palabra se señala con abreviaturas cuyas listas detalladas se encuentran en las págs. VIII (1.ª parte) y V (2.ª parte).

2. El género de los sustantivos españoles figura tanto en la primera como en la segunda parte y las palabras inglesas que son a la vez masculinas y femeninas están traducidas en las dos formas (por ej. **baker** equivale a **panadero, ra**). El número se precisa en la traducción únicamente si es diferente al de la palabra estudiada (por ej. **clothes** *pl n* ropa *f sing*).

Estas indicaciones existen igualmente en la traducción de las expresiones que vienen al final del artículo, por ej. *disturbance of the peace* alteración *f* del orden público, a menos que sea una palabra que ya figure en las acepciones o si el género y el número no ofrecen dudas gracias al contexto (por ej. *disturbance in the night* escándalo nocturno).

3. Una observación al final del artículo señala el plural irregular de ciertos sustantivos. En la parte español-inglés se encuentran los plurales españoles y en la otra los ingleses.

4. Cuando un mismo vocablo tiene varias funciones en la oración (adjetivo, sustantivo, adverbio, etc.), éstas van reunidas en el mismo artículo, precedidas de un rombo negro (◆), excepto en el caso del verbo que se trata separadamente (por ej. en **right** se estudia en primer lugar el adjetivo, el sustantivo y el adverbio, en varios apartados, y el verbo tiene otra entrada aparte).

5. Los verbos irregulares llevan un asterisco que remite al compendio de gramática en el que se da la conjugación de los distintos modos y tiempos. En la parte inglés-español, las irregularidades de los verbos ingleses, que se limitan generalmente al pretérito y participio pasivo, se indican en una observación al final del artículo.

6. Si el régimen de los verbos, sustantivos o adjetivos varía de un idioma a otro se señala entre paréntesis o mediante un ejemplo (véase **desdecir**).

Diferenciación de los sentidos

1. El signo ‖ separa, en todos los artículos, las traducciones de cada acepción y existen a veces rúbricas para determinar las materias a las que pertenecen (véase lista de ABREVIATURAS, en la pág. VIII de la 1.ª parte, y la de ABBREVIATIONS en la pág. V de la 2.ª). Si un vocablo tiene varios sentidos correspondientes a una misma rúbrica, ésta figura solamente al principio y las acepciones sólo están separadas por el signo |. Las palabras que poseen numerosos significados van precedidas por un cuadro destinado a clasificar las diversas acepciones y facilitar así la tarea del lector. Si se intenta traducir *estar para*, basta consultar el párrafo 6 del artículo **estar** (que figura con el título SEGUIDO DE UNA PREPOSICIÓN), sin necesidad de recorrer todo lo que precede. Las acepciones más usuales aparecen al comienzo del artículo.

2. Las locuciones y expresiones, siguiendo el orden alfabético, se encuentran siempre después de las diferentes acepciones y tras el signo ‖ —. Se prescinde del guión cuando sólo existe una locución o expresión.

3. Los verbos ingleses de uso corriente, que adquieren un sentido particular al ser acompañados por ciertas partículas, figuran en negritas al final del artículo en un solo bloque precedido de un rombo negro (◆) y van separados entre sí por el signo ‖. Las diferentes acepciones tienen entre ellas | y van seguidas de las locuciones o expresiones después de ‖ — (véase **to go**).

4. Con objeto de orientar al lector y darle el nivel lingüístico de la palabra o expresión empleada se han distinguido dos grados de familiaridad: FAM, es decir «familiar, pero admitido», y POP, que corresponde a «popular» y «vulgar». Si estas rúbricas preceden a la traducción, se refieren a la palabra estudiada, mientras que si están a continuación se aplican al término dado como equivalente. Así el vocablo español **jeta** ha sido considerado familiar en la tercera acepción, al intercalarse la rúbrica FAM. En general, al escoger la traducción, se ha puesto el mismo grado de familiaridad, salvo cuando era completamente imposible.

Diferenciación de las acepciones

Cuando una palabra tiene varias acepciones, cada una de ellas va seguida de una explicación. Ésta se coloca entre paréntesis, si está redactada en la lengua de la que se traduce, y entre corchetes, si está escrita en la otra (véase **descubrimiento**). Se procede del mismo modo con las expresiones que tienen diversos significados (por ej. *to get sick* quiere decir «ponerse enfermo» en el sentido más general y «marearse» al tratarse de un malestar producido por un viaje en coche, barco o avión). Las explicaciones, que no son más que meras orientaciones y no han de considerarse nunca como sinónimos, se sustituyen frecuentemente por ejemplos. Si diferentes ejemplos o expresiones tienen una primera parte común, ésta se indica sólo una vez y las variantes están unidas por «or» o por «*o*» (por ej. *edad de la razón* or *del juicio* age of reason; *to get* o *to come to the point* ir al grano). En los casos en que se puede conservar u omitir una parte de la oración, ésta se pone entre paréntesis (por ej. *hablando del rey de Roma por la puerta asoma* talk of the devil (and he will appear)).

Observaciones

Ciertos artículos tienen al final algunas observaciones, escritas en español o en inglés según el lector a quien van dirigidas, para precisar aún más el sentido de una palabra, el uso especial de la misma, su evolución, las irregularidades del plural o verbales o cualquier otra aclaración que se juzgue útil (véase **menor**).

Americanismos

Se ha procurado también, dada la importancia que siempre tuvieron y la pujanza que cobran en la actualidad las naciones de lengua castellana e inglesa en el Nuevo Mundo, incluir incontables americanismos en ambas partes del diccionario. Los empleados en Hispanoamérica van precedidos de la abreviatura *AMER* y los utilizados en Norteamérica de las letras *US*.

ABREVIATURAS

abrev	abreviatura	abbreviation
adj	adjetivo	adjective
adv	adverbio	adverb
AGR	agricultura, economía rural	agriculture, rural economy
AMER	americanismo	americanism
ANAT	anatomía	anatomy
ant	anticuado	antiquated, obsolete
ARQ	arquitectura, construcción	architecture, building
art	artículo	article
ARTES	artes	arts
ASTR	astronomía	astronomy
AUT	automóvil	automobile
aux	auxiliar	auxiliary
AVIAC	aviación	aviation
BIOL	biología	biology
BOT	botánica	botany
CINEM	cinematografía	cinematography
COM	comercio, finanzas	commerce, finance
comp	comparativo	comparative
compl	complemento	complement
conj	conjunción	conjunction
CULIN	culinario, cocina	culinary, cooking
def	definido	definite
dem	demostrativo	demonstrative
DEP	deportes	sports
dim	diminutivo	diminutive
ECON	economía	economics
ELECTR	electricidad	electricity
exclamat	exclamativo	exclamatory
f	femenino	feminine
FAM	familiar	familiar, colloquial
FIG	figurado	figurative
FIL	filosofía	philosophy
FÍS	física	physics
FOT	fotografía	photography
GEOGR	geografía	geography
GEOL	geología	geology
GRAM	gramática	grammar
HERÁLD	heráldica	heraldry
HIST	historia	history
impers	impersonal	impersonal
IMPR	imprenta	printing
indef	indefinido	indefinite
INFORM	informática	computing
interj	interjección	interjection
interr	interrogativo	interrogative
inv	invariable	invariable
JUR	jurisprudencia	jurisprudence
loc adv	locución adverbial	adverbial phrase
loc lat	locución latina	latin phrase
m	masculino	masculine
MAR	marítimo	maritime
MAT	matemáticas	mathematics
MED	medicina	medicine
MIL	militar	military
MIN	minería, mineralogía	mining, mineralogy
MIT	mitología	mythology
MÚS	música	music
n	nombre	noun
n pr	nombre propio	proper noun
num	numeral	numeral
NUCL	nuclear	nuclear
o.s.	se	oneself
pers	personal	personal
pl	plural	plural
POÉT	poético	poetry
POP	popular	popular
pos	posesivo	possessive
pp	participio pasivo	past participle
pref	prefijo	prefix
prep	preposición	preposition
pret	pretérito	preterite
pron	pronombre	pronoun
p us	poco usado	infrequent
QUÍM	química	chemistry
RAD	radio, televisión	radio, television
rel	relativo	relative
REL	religión	religion
s	sustantivo	substantive
s.o.	alguien, uno	someone
sth.	algo	something
superl	superlativo	superlative
TAUR	tauromaquia	tauromachy
TEATR	teatro	theatre
TECN	tecnología, mecánica, industria	technology, mechanical engineering, industry
US	Estados Unidos	United States
v	verbo	verb
vi	verbo intransitivo	intransitive verb
vpr	verbo pronominal	pronominal verb
vt	verbo transitivo	transitive verb
VET	veterinaria	veterinary science
ZOOL	zoología	zoology

ESPAÑOL - INGLÉS
SPANISH - ENGLISH

SUMMARY OF SPANISH GRAMMAR

The Spanish alphabet

The Spanish alphabet is made up of the following 28 letters:

a	**b**	**c**	**ch**	**d**	**e**	**f**	**g**	**h**	**i**	**j**	**k**
a	be	ce:	che	de:	e	efe	ge	hache	i	jota	ka
l	**ll**	**m**	**n**	**ñ**	**o**	**p**	**q**	**r**	**s**	**t**
ele	elle	eme	ene	eñe	o	pe	cu	erre	ese	te
u	**v**	**x**	**y**	**z**						
u	uve	equis	i griega	zeta						

Note: The Spanish alphabet contains three letters which are not found in the English alphabet: **ch** (che), **ll** (elle), **ñ** (eñe). The letter **w** (uve doble *or* ve doble) exists in Spanish only in words of foreign origin, and is therefore not considered part of the Spanish alphabet. All Spanish letters are feminine in gender (*una s mayúscula* a capital «s»; *la jota* the «j»).

Pronunciation

The Spanish-English half of this dictionary contains no phonetic transcription of the Spanish for the simple reason that Spanish spelling is an exact reflection of the pronunciation of the language. The pronunciation of each individual letter in Spanish is subject to certain strict rules (see below), and a word is pronounced simply by adding together the sounds of the individual letters which make up the word.

Every letter is pronounced in Spanish with the exception of the inaspirate **h** as in *hacha* ['atʃa], and the **u** in the groups *-qu-*, *-gue-*, *-qui-*, which is silent unless it bears a diaeresis (*guerra* ['gerra], *paragüero* [para'gwero]).

Consonants

Consonants are never doubled in Spanish, except **c**, **r**, and **n** (a**c**ción, ca**rr**o, i**nn**ovación). **Ll** is considered a letter in its own right.

1. **b** and **v**. These two letters represent the same sound in Spanish. They are less explosive than the English **b**.
In an initial position and after certain consonants, especially *m* and *n*, the sound is similar to that of the English **b** (**b**rillo, **v**aca, con**v**oy).
Elsewhere the sound is softer. It is a bilabial fricative, similar to the English **v** but pronounced between the upper and lower lip rather than between the lower lip and the upper teeth (a**v**e, la**b**or).

2. **c.** Before *e* or *i* it is pronounced like the **th** in *thirst* (**c**iudad, **c**eguera). In certain regions (See **seseo**) this **c** is pronounced as **s**.
Elsewhere it is like the hard **c** in *cat* (**c**asco, lo**c**ura, a**c**to).
Note that words like *acción, reducción* contain both sounds, the **cc** being pronounced *kth* [kθ].

3. **ch.** Like the English **ch** [tʃ] in *church* (co**ch**e, mu**ch**a**ch**o).

4. **d.** In an initial position and after *l* or *n* the sound is similar to that of the English **d**, but pronounced with the tip of the tongue touching the back of the upper front teeth (**d**ebo, con**d**e, cal**d**o).
Elsewhere the sound is similar to that of the **th** [ð] in *though* (ar**d**uo, cua**d**ra, bo**d**a). This sound varies in intensity and is particularly weak in the verb ending *-ado* and at the end of certain words where it is often scarcely perceptible (ciuda**d**, Madri**d**).

5. **f.** Like the English **f** in *for* (**f**atal, o**f**erta).

6. **g.** Before *e* or *i* like the guttural **ch** in Scottish *loch* (**g**estión, ele**g**ir).
In an initial position of after a nasal consonant the **g** is like the hard English **g** in *gate* (**g**arbo, pon**g**o). In other positions the pronunciation is basically similar to this hard **g**, with the difference that the back of the tongue does not quite touch the velum, making the sound more fricative than occlusive (a**g**ua, la**g**o, al**g**o).

7. **h.** The **h** is mute (**h**ombre, **h**eno).

8. **j.** Like the guttural **ch** in Scottish *loch* (o**j**o, in**j**erto, pa**j**a).

9. **k.** Pronounced as in English and found only in words of foreign origin (**k**ilo).

10. **l.** Like the English **l** (**l**obo, o**l**mo, paño**l**, per**l**a).

11. **ll.** Somewhat similar to the **lli** in *million* or the [-lj-] sound in *failure* ['feiljə*], but with the two elements, *l* and *y*, pronounced so closely as to become one sound (va**ll**e, **ll**orar, **ll**amar). See *yeísmo*.

12. **m.** Like the English **m** (**m**ármol, a**m**ar).

13. **n.** Pronounced as in English, but with the tip of the tongue touching the back of the upper front teeth (**n**o, cá**n**dido, comú**n**).
Before hard *c* and *g* and before *j* and soft *g* the Spanish **n** tends to nasalize the preceding vowel and is itself pronounced like the **n** in the English words *song* and *thank* (co**n**goja, ca**n**je).
Before a bilabial consonant (*b, v*) the sound of the **n** approaches that of the **m** (co**n**vidar).

14. **ñ.** Pronounced like the **ni** in *onion* (**ñ**ame, ni**ñ**o).

15. **p.** Slightly less explosive than the English **p**, but more explosive than the English **b** (**p**ara, com**p**rar).

16. **q.** Found only in the groups *-que* and *-qui* in which the two letters *q* and *u* together have the sound of the English **k** (**q**uedar [ke'ðar], **q**uitar [ki'tar]).

17. **r** and **rr**. The Spanish **r** is always «rolled» or «trilled», the tip of the tongue vibrating against the hard palate.
Between two vowels or after a consonant other than *l, n, s*, a single **r** is pronounced with only one «trill».
In an initial position, and after *l, n,* or *s*, the **r** requires two or three «trills», as does the double **r** (**rr**) whatever its position.
Note: The **rr** may never be split at the end of a line in written Spanish.

18. **s.** Similar to the English **s** in *soap* (pa**s**o, e**s**perar).
Note: Only words borrowed from other languages begin with **s** followed by a consonant in Spanish. Such words are usually pronounced as if there were an *e* before the **s** (starter [es'tarter]).

19. **t.** Slightly less aspirate than in English, and with the tip of the tongue against the back of the upper front teeth (**t**on**t**o, con**t**ra).

20. **v.** See **b**.

21. **w.** Broadly speaking the **w** is pronounced like the **v** in Spanish. In certain foreign words the sound is that of the Spanish **u** (**W**aterloo, **w**hisky).

22. **x.** Similar to the **ks** in *thinks*, although the *k* sound is very weak when this letter precedes a consonant (éxito ['eksito], exponer [expo'ner]).

23. **y.** As a consonant is stronger than the English **y** in *yonder*.

24. **z.** Pronounced like the **th** [θ] in *think*.
Note: This letter is not used before *e* or *i*, except in certain words of foreign origin and in the name of the letter itself (zeta). This implies the substitution of *c* for *z* in certain verb forms and in the plural of words ending in **z** (pe**z**, pe**c**es; empe**z**ar, empe**c**emos).

Vowels

Spanish vowels are pure sounds, the position of the mouth remaining the same throughout the pronunciation of the vowel. They are pronounced clearly even in unstressed positions, unlike English vowels, and are not subject to diphthongization (e.g. *lumbago* in English [lʌm'beigəu], in Spanish [lum'bago]).

1. **a.** An open vowel, similar to but shorter than the **a** in the English *father*. The sound is like the Northern English **a** in *hat*.

2. **e.** Pronounced like the first **e** in *element*.

3. **i.** A sound shorter than the **ee** in *seen*, and longer than the **i** in *hit*.

4. **o.** Similar to the **o** in *hot*.

5. **u.** Similar to the **oo** in *boot*.
Note: The **u** is mute in the groups *-que, -qui* (**qu**erer, e**qu**ipo), and also in the groups *-gue*, and *-gui* (**gu**erra, **gu**itarra), unless it bears a diaeresis (a**gü**ero).

6. **y.** Pronounced like the Spanish **i** at the end of a word and when it stands alone as a conjunction. In certain Latin American countries, especially Argentina, Chile and Uruguay, this letter is pronounced like the **si** in *decision*.

Diphtongs and triphthongs

A *diphthong* is one syllable made up of two vowels each of which conserves its own sound. In speaking or writing Spanish one must take care never to divide a diphthong. Spanish diphthongs contain either one strong vowel (**a, e, o**) and one weak vowel (**u, i** and final **y**), e.g. **ai, au; ei, eu; oi, ou; ia, ie, io; ua, ue, uo,** or two weak vowels (**iu, ui**). Unless otherwise indicated by a written accent, the stress automatically falls on the strong vowel if there is one, or on the final vowel of the diphthong if both are weak (c**ai**go, g**ua**nte, r**ui**do).

A triphthong (three vowels in the same syllable) is always formed in Spanish by a strong vowel placed between two weak vowels (**iai, iei; uai, uei**). The stress falls on the strong vowel (no os ri**á**is).

Note: Two strong vowels which occur together are considered as two separate syllables and as such conform to the following rules for tonic stress. In order to put the stress on a vowel other than that on which it would naturally fall, it is necessary to mark the stressed vowel with a written accent (pa**í**s).

Tonic stress and the written accent

The stress falls on the **penultimate syllable** if the word ends in *a vowel, -n* or *-s* (es**cri**bo, es**cri**bes, es**cri**ben).

The stress falls on the **final syllable** if the word ends in a *consonant* other than -n or -s or in *y* (agili**dad**, man**tel**, a**mor**, Para**guay**).

Any deviation from the above rules is indicated by means of a written accent (**ár**bol, can**ción**, jaba**lí**), even if the stressed letter is a capital (**Á**frica).

A written accent on the *u* or *i* in a diphthong changes the diphthong into two separate syllables (descon**fí**o, ata**úd**). When an accent is needed to stress a syllable containing a diphthong or a triphthong, it must be placed over the strong vowel (averi**guáis**, tam**bién**).

In general the stress remains on the same syllable in the plural as in the singular (esta**ción**, esta**cio**nes). It may therefore be necessary to add or remove a written accent according to the above rules. There are three exceptions (**ré**gimen, re**gí**menes; ca**rá**cter, carac**te**res; es**pé**cimen, espe**cí**menes).

Note: The written accent is also used to distinguish between words which are spelt alike but have different grammatical functions, such as the article *el* and the pronoun *él*, the conjunction *si* and the adverb or the reflexive *sí*, the pronoun *tú* and the possessive adjective *tu*, the conjunction *mas* and the adverb *más*, the adjective *solo* and the adverb *sólo*, the demonstrative adjectives *este, esta, etc.* and the demonstrative pronouns *éste, ésta, etc.*, the relative pronouns *que, quien, etc.* and the interrogative and exclamative pronouns *qué, quién, etc.*, *dé*, 1st and 3rd person of the present subjunctive of the verb «dar», and the preposition *de*, *sé*, 1st person present indicative of «saber» and 2nd person singular of the imperative of «ser», and the reflexive pronoun *se*.

The first element of a compound word is written without an accent (*decimosexto*), unless the word is an adverb formed by an adjective and the adverbial suffix **-mente** (*fácilmente*) or two adjectives joined by a hyphen (*histórico-crítico*).

SPELLING RULES ESTABLISHED BY
THE SPANISH ACADEMY IN 1952

Words ending in **-oo** have no written accent (*Feijoo*).

The infinitive ending in **-uir** has no written accent (*huir*).

Monosyllabic verb forms have no written accent (*fue, fui, dio, vio*).

Other monosyllables (*ni*) bear no written accent, except to avoid confusion with similar words (*si*, conjunction, *sí* adverb).

Accents are not added to foreign names unless they have passed into the Spanish language under a hispanicized form.

Capital letters

Capitals are very seldom used in Spanish. Nouns and adjectives of nationality, the days of the week, the months, titles and names of society members or doctrine followers are always written with a small initial letter (*un argentino, la bandera mexicana, martes, febrero, el duque de Rivas, los laboristas*).

The article

	Definite article		*Indefinite article*	
	Singular	*Plural*	*Singular*	*Plural*
Masculine	el	los	un	unos
Feminine	la	las	una	unas

The definite article

The prepositions *a* and *de* combine with the masculine singular definite article *el* to give **al** and **del** respectively (*al chico, del hombre* but *a los chicos, de la(s) mujer(es)*). Immediately before a feminine singular noun beginning with stressed *a* or *ha* the definite article *la* is replaced by **el** (*el agua, el hambre*). Descriptive adjectives take the usual feminine endings (*el agua fría*). The article **la** is used before unstressed *a* or *ha*, and also before feminine proper nouns beginning with stressed *a* or *ha* (*la antítesis, la Ángela, La Haya*).

The definite article is used more frequently in Spanish than in English:

— when the noun is qualified (*la Andalucía oriental* eastern Andalusia; *la España de la posguerra* postwar Spain; *la Europa del siglo veinte* twentieth-century Europe);

— with most names of rivers, seas and mountains;

— before titles (*el rey Arturo* King Arthur; *el doctor Pérez* Doctor Pérez; *llame al teniente García* call Lieutenant García; *el Presidente Roosevelt* President Roosevelt; *el señor Hernández* Mr. Hernández; *la señora de Hernández* Mrs. Hernández; *la señora ha salido* madam is out), except with *don, doña, santo, santa* (*me lo dijo don Ramón; Santa Bárbara*), in direct address (*¿Ud. qué opina, doctor Pérez?; buenas tardes, señora*), when the title is in apposition (*el señor X, presidente del club; el presidente del club, señor X*), before foreign titles such as Herr, Lord, etc.;

— with parts of the body and articles of clothing where in English the possessive adjective is frequently used (*levantó la mano* he raised his hand; *llevaba la chaqueta en el brazo* he carried his jacket over his arm). The idea of possession is often conveyed by a weak object pronoun (*me lavé la cara* I washed my face).

Note the use of the singular in Spanish (*se pusieron la chaqueta* they put on their jackets);

— in certain expressions of time (*eran las cinco* it was five o'clock; *es la hora de cenar* it is dinner time; *se fue el jueves y volvió el domingo* he left on Thursday and came back on Sunday; *los domingos se aburría* he used to get bored on Sundays; *la semana que viene* next week; *el mes, el año, el jueves pasado* last month, year, Thursday);

— with the seasons (*cuando llegó el invierno* when winter arrived). After *en* the article is not essential (*en (el) invierno*);

— with certain institutions (*la cárcel, la ciudad, el colegio, el instituto, el mercado, la universidad*);

— with nouns used generically (*los profesores están mal pagados* teachers are underpaid; *el azúcar es dulce* sugar is sweet);

— before terms of quantity (*una libra la docena* a pound a dozen);

— before infinitives (*el comer* eating);

— to express a percentage (*el diez por ciento* ten percent).

The names of countries are not generally preceded by the definite article. In case of doubt, however, it is advisable to omit the article with the name of a country.

The definite article is omitted:

— before an unqualified name of a country (*España, México*), with the exceptions mentioned above;

— before certain words (*casa, caza, misa, palacio, paseo, pesca, presidio*) when used with verbs of motion;

— between the name and number of a ruler (*Enrique cuatro*).

The indefinite article

Before feminine nouns beginning with stressed *a* or *ha* the singular indefinite article *una* is replaced by **un** (*un hacha, un ala, un alma*, but *una alumna*).

The plural forms *unos* and *unas* mean *some*, although the English *some* is frequently omitted in Spanish (*unos guantes preciosos* some lovely gloves; *compré pan también* I bought some bread too).

Unos and *unas* also indicate approximate quantity (*unos diez días* about ten days; *tendrá unos cuarenta años* he must be about forty).

The indefinite article, which is used less in Spanish than in English, is omitted:

— with *ciento* (a hundred), *cierto* (a certain), *igual* (such a), *medio* (half a), *mil* (a thousand), *otro* (another), *semejante* (such a), *tal* (such a), *tan* (such a);

— before an unqualified noun indicating rank, occupation or nationality used after the verbs *ser* or *parecer* (*era oficial de marina* he was a naval officer, *quiere ser doctor* he wants to be a doctor). If the noun is qualified the article is used (*es un doctor excelente* he is an excellent doctor);

— before most nouns in apposition (*Paraguay, país que...*);

— before an unqualified noun dependent on a negative (*no tengo coche* I haven't got a car; *sin chaqueta ni corbata* without a jacket or tie; *no dijo palabra* he did not say a word). The use of the indefinite article in such cases adds emphasis (*no tiene un coche sino tres* he hasn't got one car, but three; *no dijo ni una palabra* he did not say a single word);

— after *qué* (*¡qué mujer más guapa!* what a lovely woman!).

Note: The indefinite article is used in Spanish before an abstract noun followed by a qualifying adjective (*reinaba un silencio total* total silence reigned).

The English construction *a shirt and tie*; omitting the second article, in impossible in Spanish; the article must be repeated (*una camisa y una corbata*).

The neuter article *lo* serves to substantivize adjectives, adverbs and participles (*lo interesante del caso* the interesting thing; *lo dicho* what has been said; *lo antes posible* as soon as possible). It also intensifies adjectives and adverbs in the construction *lo... que* (*por lo inteligente que es* because he is so intelligent). [See **lo**.]

The noun

Gender

Apart from the straightforward masculine and feminine, the following genders are found in the Spanish language: **ambiguo** which denotes a word that can be either masculine or feminine (*el mar, la mar*), **común** which applies to nouns that change gender according to the sex of the being they represent (*el joven, la joven*), **epiceno** which applies to words having only one form and gender for both the male and the female of the species (*el leopardo, la perdiz*). To distinguish between the male and the female in this case one must add «macho» or «hembra» respectively (*el leopardo hembra*).

Masculine nouns

— Those ending in **-o** (except *la mano, la moto, la foto, la dinamo, la radio, la nao, la seo*).

— Those ending in **-or** (except *la flo***r**, *la coliflo***r**, *la labor. la sor*).

— Names of men, male animals, jobs and titles concerning men, seas, rivers, mountains, trees, metals, languages, days, months, colours, and infinitives used as nouns.

Feminine nouns

— Those ending in **-a** (except *el día, el albacea, el mapa, el monarca, el Papa, el patriarca, el planeta, el cometa, el poeta, el tranvía*, words of Greek origin ending in *-ma*, such as *el diploma, el problema, el idioma*, words ending in *-ista*, such as *dentista, turista*, which can be masculine or feminine, and word usually denoting male beings, such as *el guardia, el cura*).

— Those ending in **-ción** (*la canción*), **-sión** (*la profesión*), **-d** (*la verdad, la red, la virtud*), except *el almud, el alud, el ardid, el ataúd, el césped, el laúd, el sud, el talmud*.

— Names of female beings, jobs and titles concerning women, and the letters of the alphabet.

Formation of the feminine

The general rules are as follows:

— for masculine nouns ending in **-o**, replace the **-o** by **-a** (*el abuelo, la abuela; el gato, la gata*);

— for masculine nouns ending in a consonant, add **-a** (*el director, la directora; el león, la leona*);

— for masculine nouns ending in **-ante**, **-ente**, **-ote**, replace the final **-e** by **-a** (*el presidente, la presidenta*);

— other feminine ending are **-esa** (*el conde, la condesa*), **-isa** (*el poeta, la poetisa*), **-triz** (*el actor, la actriz*);

— some nouns have a completely different feminine equivalent (*hombre, mujer*).

Formation of the plural

The general rules are as follows:

— for words ending in an **unstressed vowel** or a **stressed -e** add **-s** (*los niños, los cafés*);

— for words ending in a **consonant, -y** or a **stressed vowel** other than *-e*, add **-es** (*las paredes, los reyes, los alelíes*). There are numerous exceptions in this category, such as *mamás, papás, sofás, dominós*. Note also that, in words ending in **-z**, the **-z** changes to **-c** before the ending **-es** (*voz, voces; luz, luces*);

— for words ending in **-s**, which are monosyllabic or stressed on the final syllable, add **-es** (*mes, meses; inglés, ingleses*);

— words ending in **-s** or **-x**, which are not stressed on the final syllable, have the same form in the plural as in the singular (*las crisis; los fénix*). [See ***tonic stress and the written accent above.***]

Diminutives and augmentatives

The use of diminutive and augmentative suffixes is widespread in Spanish. More often than not they indicate the favourable or unfavourable disposition of the user. They are added to nouns and adjectives, the same rules applying to both.

The general rules for the formation of DIMINUTIVES are as follows:

Word endings	*Suffixes*	*Examples*
-a, -o, consonant (except **-n** or **-r**)	-ito, a -illo, a -uelo, a	cas*ita* carte*lillo* moz*uela*
-e, -n, -r	-cito, a -cillo, a -zuelo, a	nube*cita* cancion*cilla* pastor*zuelo*
monosyllables, words containing a diphthong	-ecito, a -ezuelo, a	pan*ecito* rey*ezuelo*
monosyllables ending in a vowel	-cecito, a -cecillo, a -cezuelo, a	pie*cecito*

The forms **-ito**, **-cito**, **-ecito** and **-cecito** are by far the most common and usually suggest endearment as well as smallness. The suffixes **-uelo**, **-zuelo**, **-ezuelo**, **-cezuelo** are often used with pejorative connotations (*mujerzuela*).

The suffixes **-ico**, **-ín**, **-ino**, **-iño** also exist and are used to varying degrees in different regions.

AUGMENTATIVE SUFFIXES are used to a lesser extent than diminutive suffixes, and, are often pejorative.

They often suggest clumsiness or coarseness.

The commonest augmentative suffix is **-ón**, **-ona** (*solterón, solterona*). Some others are **-azo, -a**; **-acho, -a**; **-achón, -ona**; **-ote, -a** (*manaza, populacho, corpachón, librote*).

Many augmentatives and diminutives derived in this way have become nouns in their own right (*la silla; el sillín; el sillón*).

Other suffixes worth mentioning here are **-azo** (*cañonazo*) and **-ada** (*pedrada*), which mean *blow* or *shot*, and **-al**, **-aje**, **-ar**, **-edo**, **-eda** which indicate a plantation or an area where a certain plant abounds, and also a place covered with or abundant in a certain thing (*pedregal* stony ground; *ramaje* branches; *olivar* olive grove; *viñedo* vineyard; *arboleda* copse).

The adjective

Position of adjectives

The position of adjectives in Spanish is a complicated subject, but the following outline of basic principles should prove helpful.

1. Adjectives which describe the noun, distinguishing it from others in its class, are usually placed after it (*un libro rojo; una casa enorme; una pregunta indiscreta*). They are called descriptive adjectives.

2. Adjectives which limit rather than describe are placed before the noun. This category includes the cardinal numbers (*once jugadores*), adjectives of quantity such as *mucho, poco, demasiado, tanto, varios, cuanto*, demonstrative and possessive adjectives (*este profesor; mi lápiz*), *cada, demás, mero, otro, tal*.

3. Ordinal numbers usually precede the noun (*el primer punto* the first point, though *el punto primero* is also possible; *su último hijo* his youngest son).

4. The following common adjectives frequently precede the noun: *bueno, malo, nuevo, viejo, joven, pequeño, hermoso*, though this is not a steadfast rule. Broadly speaking, if the adjective precedes the noun, the emphasis falls on the noun (*un buen* **libro** as opposed to *una buena* **revista**). If it follows the noun, more emphasis falls on the adjective (*un libro* **bueno** as opposed to *un libro* **malo**).

5. The meanings of certain common adjectives change according to their position before of after the noun (*distintas* or *diferentes personas* different (sundry, various, several) people, but *personas distintas* or *diferentes* different (from one another) people; *varias personas* several people, but *personas varias* various (sundry) people; *un nuevo coche* a new (another) car, but *un coche nuevo* a (brand-) new car; *un pobre hombre* a poor (pitiful) man, but *un hombre pobre* a poor (impecunious) man; *un gran hombre* a great (important) man, but *un hombre grande* a tall man).

6. Note the following possibilities when more than one adjective qualifies the same noun (*un pequeño coche rojo* a small, red car; *sus ojos alegres y sonrientes, sus alegres y sonrientes ojos* her happy, smiling eyes; *la situación económica americana* the American economic situation. Here the adjective *americana* might be said to describe the noun *situación económica*).

Formation of the feminine

For adjectives which end in **-o** in the masculine singular form, change **-o** to **-a** (*cansado, cansada*);

— for adjectives ending in **-án**, **-ín**, **-ón**, **-or** and those indicating nationality add **-a** and remove the written accent where necessary (*holgazán, holgazana; cantarín, cantarina; gordinflón, gordinflona; trabajador, trabajadora; portugués, portuguesa*). Note that comparatives ending in **-or** remain the same in the masculine and feminine (*la mejor manera*), as do certain adjectives of nationality such as *árabe, marroquí, etíope* and all those ending in **-a** (*belga, persa, etc.*);

— for adjectives ending in **-ete** or **-ote** replace the final **-e** by **-a** (*regordete, regordeta; vulgarote, vulgarota*);

— other adjectives have the same form in both genders (*agrícola, azul, cursi, gris, verde, feliz, etc.*).

Formation of the plural

The same rules apply to the formation of the plural of adjectives as to the formation of the plural of nouns. [See **lo**.]

Agreement of adjectives

The adjective agrees in number and gender with the noun or pronoun it modifies (*dos muchachas encantadoras*).

When it precedes more than one noun the adjective agrees with the first of them (*en sosegada paz y reposo*).

When the adjective follows the nouns the following five rules apply:

1. If the nouns are all singular or all plural and of the same gender, the adjective takes the plural form and agrees in gender with the nouns (*historia y geografía colombianas*).

2. If the nouns differ in gender but are all in the singular, the adjective either agrees in number and gender with the last of the nouns (*el hombre y la mujer española*) or takes the masculine plural form (*el hombre y la mujer españoles*), which is the better solution.

3. If the nouns are all plural but different in gender, the adective may agree with the last noun, though it is preferable to use the masculine plural form of the adjective (*bailes y canciones americanas* or *bailes y canciones americanos*).

4. If the nouns differ in number and gender, the adjective takes the masculine plural form (*la ciudad y los suburbios adormecidos*).

5. If the noun is singular when taken with each adjective separately, the adjective takes the singular form (*los ministros español y argentino*).

Comparatives

A comparison of **equality** is expressed by **tan** (with adjectives) or **tanto** (with nouns)... **como** (*ella es tan alta como yo* she is as tall as I; *tenías tanto tiempo como yo* you had as much time as I; *tiene tantos hermanos como tú* he has as many brothers as you).

A comparison of **inequality** is expressed by **más... que** and **menos... que** (*ella es más simpática que su hermana* she is more friendly (*or* friendlier) than her sister; *es menos inteligente que tú* he is not so intelligent as you; *menos exigente que* less demanding than).

Note: More than and *less than* before a number or an expression of quantity are translated by **más de** and **menos de** (*tengo más que tú* but *tengo más de cien*).

More than and *less than* are translated by **más** and **menos de lo que** (or **de los que**, etc.) when the second member of the comparison is a clause (*tienen más empleados de los que necesitan; era más fácil de lo que pensaba*).

For **irregular** comparatives see below.

Number table

Cardinal		*Ordinal*
0	cero	
1	uno, una	primero, ra
2	dos	segundo, da
3	tres	tercero, ra
4	cuatro	cuarto, ta
5	cinco	quinto, ta
6	seis	sexto, ta
7	siete	séptimo, ma
8	ocho	octavo, va
9	nueve	noveno, na
10	diez	décimo, ma
11	once	undécimo, ma
12	doce	duodécimo, ma
13	trece	decimotercero, ra
14	catorce	decimocuarto, ta
15	quince	decimoquinto, ta
16	dieciséis	decimosexto, ta
17	diecisiete	decimoséptimo, ma
18	dieciocho	decimoctavo, va
19	diecinueve	decimonoveno, na
20	veinte	vigésimo, ma
21	veintiuno, na	vigésimo (-ma) primero, ra
22	veintidós	vigésimo (-ma) segundo, da
30	treinta	trigésimo, ma
31	treinta y uno	trigésimo (-ma) primero, ra
40	cuarenta	cuadragésimo, ma
50	cincuenta	quincuagésimo, ma
60	sesenta	sexagésimo, ma
70	setenta	septuagésimo, ma
80	ochenta	octogésimo, ma
90	noventa	nonagésimo, ma
100	cien *or* ciento	centésimo, ma
101	ciento uno	centésimo (-ma) primero, ra
134	ciento treinta y cuatro	centésimo (-ma) trigésimo (-ma) cuarto, ta
200	doscientos, tas	ducentésimo, ma
300	trescientos, tas	tricentésimo, ma
400	cuatrocientos, tas	cuadringentésimo, ma
500	quinientos, tas	quingentésimo, ma
600	seiscientos, tas	sexcentésimo, ma
700	setecientos, tas	septingentésimo, ma
800	ochocientos, tas	octingentésimo, ma
900	novecientos, tas	noningentésimo, ma
1000	mil	milésimo, ma
1001	mil uno	milésimo (-ma) primero, ra
2034	dos mil treinta y cuatro	dos milésimo (-ma) trigésimo (-ma) cuarto, ta
1 000 000	un millón	millonésimo, ma
1 000 000 000	mil millones	mil millonésimo, ma
1 000 000 000 000	un billón	billonésimo, ma

Superlatives

The **absolute** superlative is formed by placing **muy** before the adjective or adding the suffix **-ísimo** to the adjective (*alto, muy alto, altísimo*). The latter method is more difficult to use since not all adjectives can take the suffix **-ísimo**, e.g. *arduo*. **Muy** should not however be used with *mucho*, the superlative of which is *muchísimo*. The suffix **-ísimo** also makes certain spelling changes necessary: adjectives ending in **-co** take the suffix **-quísimo** (*rico, riquísimo*), those ending in **-go** take the suffix **-guísimo** (*largo, larguísimo*), those ending in **-n** or **-z** take the suffix **-císimo** (*joven, jovencísimo*), those containing a diphthong usually lose it in the superlative (*valiente, valentísimo*), although in many cases both forms are possible (*bueno, buenísimo, bonísimo; fuerte, fuertísimo, fortísimo*), adjectives ending in **-io** change this ending to **-ísimo** (*limpio, limpísimo*), but **-ío** becomes **-iísimo** (*pío, piísimo*), adjectives ending in **-ble** take **-bilísimo** (*agradable, agradabilísimo*), those ending in **-bre**, **-cre**, **-ero**, take **-érrimo** (*célebre, celebérrimo; acre, acérrimo; áspero, aspérrimo*), **pobre** and **pulcro** have two superlative forms, one regular (*pobrísimo, pulcrísimo*), the other of Latin origin (*paupérrimo, pulquérrimo*).

The **relative** superlative is formed as follows: *la más simpática de las mujeres; la mujer más simpática que conozco.*

Irregular comparatives and superlatives

Positive	*Comparative*	*Superlative*
bueno	*mejor*	óptimo
malo	*peor*	pésimo
grande	*mayor*	máximo
pequeño	*menor*	mínimo
alto	*superior*	supremo
bajo	*inferior*	ínfimo

Note: that *más grande, más pequeño, más alto* and *más bajo* and the regular superlatives *buenísimo, malísimo, grandísimo, pequeñísimo, altísimo* and *bajísimo* also exist (*es más grande que el otro* or *es mayor que el otro*).

Cardinal numbers

They are invariable except *uno*, the multiples of *ciento, ciento* and *mil* in certain cases, *millón* and its multiples. Numbers 16 to 19 and 21 to 29 inclusive may be written as one word or three (*diecinueve, diez y nueve; veintitrés, veinte y tres*). They are usually written as one word with an accent where necessary to conserve the stress (*veintidós*).

The conjunction **y** is only placed between the tens and the units (*mil treinta y dos* one thousand and thirty-two).

Uno changes to **una** before a feminine singular noun (*una mujer*), and to **un** before a masculine singular noun (*un hombre*).

Ciento changes to **cien** before a common noun or a number it multiplies (*cien mujeres, cien millones de habitantes, cien mil hombres*). It is never preceded by the indefinite article. Multiples of a hundred are written as one word and agree in number and gender with the noun they multiply (*doscientos hombres, doscientas mil mujeres, quinientas treinta y ocho páginas*). *Cientos de* may be used to mean «hundreds of».

Millón is a masculine noun (*un millón de pesetas, dos millones de pesetas, cuatrocientos veintiún millones de pesetas*).

Mil is used without the article (*cuarenta mil kilómetros*). It has a plural form when used to mean «thousands of» (*miles de víctimas* thousands of victims; *miles y miles de* thousands and thousands of).

For numbers eleven hundred and above Spanish uses the formula *mil cien* or *mil ciento, mil doscientos, etc.* (*en el año mil setecientos* in (the year) seventeen hundred).

Ordinal numbers

They agree with the noun they qualify (*las primeras personas*).

Primero and **tercero** become **primer** and **tercer** in the cases described under the heading APOCOPATION (below).

In everyday Spanish the ordinal numbers are used from one to nine inclusive (*Felipe Segundo*). From ten to twelve inclusive the cardinal or the ordinal is used (*la fila duodécima* or *la fila doce*), and for thirteen and above the cardinal number is used (*el siglo veinte*). There are two forms of the ordinal *ninth* in Spanish, *noveno* and *nono*. The latter is generally used only with the name of the Pope *Pío IX* (*nono*).

There are several ways of conveying the idea of approximate quantity in Spanish. The most common uses the plural indefinite article *unos, unas* (*unas treinta personas* about thirty people; *unos sesenta kilos* some sixty kilos). The suffix **-ena** may be used in *docena, quincena* and with numbers which are multiples of ten, such as *veintena, cuarentena*, etc. (*compré una docena de huevos, debe de tener una treintena de diccionarios*).

Adjectives and pronouns

Possessive adjectives and pronouns

		One possessor	
		Singular noun	*Plural noun*
1st pers	*adj*	**mi; mío, mía** (my)	**mis; míos, mías** (my)
	pron	**mío, mía** (mine)	**míos, mías** (mine)
2nd pers	*adj*	**tu; tuyo, a** (your)	**tus; tuyos, as** (your)
	pron	**tuyo, a** (yours)	**tuyos, as** (yours)
3rd pers	*adj*	**su; suyo, a** (his, her, its)	**sus; suyos, as** (his, her, its)
	pron	**suyo, a** (his, hers)	**suyos, as** (his, hers)
		Several possessors	
		Singular noun	*Plural noun*
1st pers	*adj*	**nuestro, a** (our)	**nuestros, as** (our)
	pron	**nuestro, a** (ours)	**nuestros, as** (ours)
2nd pers	*adj*	**vuestro, a** (your)	**vuestros, as** (your)
	pron	**vuestro, a** (yours)	**vuestros, as** (yours)
3rd pers	*adj*	**su; suyo, a** (their)	**sus; suyos, as** (their)
	pron	**suyo, a** (theirs)	**suyos, as** (theirs)

Indefinite adjectives

The main ones are *alguno, ninguno, cierto, varios, cualquiera, poco, bastante, mucho, demasiado, demás, cuanto, todo, cada, tal, otro, uno, tanto.* They are variable in gender except for *bastante, cualquiera, cada, demás* and *tal*, and variable in number except for *cada, demás* and *varios*.

The interrogative adjective

Qué is an invariable interrogative adjective (*¿qué día es?* what day is it?; *¿qué chaqueta te vas a poner?* which jacket are you going to wear?).

Cuánto varies in number and gender according to the noun it accompanies (*¿cuántas personas vinieron?* how many people came?; *¿cuánto tiempo nos queda?* how much time do we have left?).

The above adjectives are used in direct and indirect questions (*no sabía qué decir* he did not know what to say). They are also used exclamatively (*¡qué calor!* isn't it hot!; *¡cuánta gente!* what a lot of people!).

Apocopation

Apocopation is the dropping of the final vowel or syllable of a word. The following words lose their final **-o** before a masculine singular noun: *uno, veintiuno, alguno, ninguno, primero, tercero, postrero, bueno* and *malo* (*un buen hombre, de ningún modo, el primer alumno, el tercer libro, ayer hizo mal tiempo, etc.*). In the case of *veintiuno, alguno, ninguno* a written accent is added to the apocopated form (*veintiún, etc.*).

Santo becomes *san* before the name of a canonized saint (*San Miguel*), except before *Tomás, Tomé, Toribio* and *Domingo* (*Santo Tomás, Santo Tomé, Santo Toribio, Santo Domingo*).

Ciento becomes *cien* before a common noun or a number which it multiplies (*cien dólares, cien mil casas*).

Grande becomes *gran* before a masculine singular noun beginning with a consonant (*un gran ruido*). This apocopation is optional before a feminine noun or a masculine noun beginning with a vowel (*una gran mujer, un gran automóvil*).

There are other cases of apocopation. The adverbs **tanto** and **cuanto** become *tan* and *cuan* before and adjective or another adverb (*cuan largo, tan pronto ríe como llora*).

Recientemente becomes *recién* before a past participle (*recién llegado*). **Cualquiera** loses its final **-a** before a masculine singular noun (*cualquier hombre*); this apocopation is also possible before a feminine singular noun (*me parece que cualquier mujer es capaz de hacerlo*).

They agree in number and gender with the thing or things possessed and not with the possessor.

The adjectives **mi, tu, su** are always placed before the noun they modify (*mi casa*). **Mío, tuyo, suyo**, however, follow the noun (*la casa mía*). Ambiguity may arise from the use of the adjective **su**, which means «your», «his», «her», «its», «their», and of the pronoun **suyo**. This ambiguity may be avoided by replacing them by *el ... de ella, etc.* (*el coche de ellos* their car), or by adding *de usted, de ella, etc.* (*su libro de usted* your book).

The possessive is used to a lesser extent in Spanish than in English and is often replaced by the article. In such a case the idea of possession is often conveyed by a verb in the reflexive form (*se quitó el abrigo* he took off his coat) or by the indirect object pronoun (*me vendaron la herida* they bandaged my wound).

Demonstrative adjectives and pronouns

Degree of remoteness (adverbs of place)		Masculine and feminine: Singular	Masculine and feminine: Plural	Neuter: Singular
aquí here	*adj*	**este, esta** this	**estos, estas** these	
	pron	**éste, ésta** this (one)	**éstos, éstas** these (ones)	**esto** this
ahí there	*adj*	**ese, esa** that	**esos, esas** those	
	pron	**ése, ésa** that (one)	**ésos, ésas** those (ones)	**eso** that
allí, allá there	*adj*	**aquel, aquella** that	**aquellos, aquellas** those	
	pron	**aquél, aquélla** that (one)	**aquéllos, aquéllas** those (ones)	**aquello** that

The written accent on the demonstrative pronoun distinguishes it from the demonstrative adjective. Since there are no neuter demonstrative adjectives in Spanish, the neuter demonstrative pronouns bear no written accent.

The three forms **este, ese** and **aquel** correspond to different degrees of remoteness in time and space.

Éste is the least remote and denotes the same degree of closeness as *this* in English. **Aquel** indicates the greatest degree of remoteness (*aquella mañana hacía mucho frío* it was very cold that morning). **Ese** describes an intermediate or an undetermined degree of remoteness (*esa tienda está lejos de casa* that shop is a long way from home). **Ese** can also have pejorative overtones (*no me gusta nada que salgas con esa gente* I don't like you going around with the likes of them). When the demonstrative pronouns refer to nouns mentioned in immediately preceding clauses, **éste**, etc. usually means «the latter» and **aquél**, etc. «the former». Demonstrative pronouns are often replaced by *el de, la de, los de, las de* (that of, those of, the one of, the one with, those with, the one in, those in) or by *el que, la que, los que, las que* (the one that, those that, the one which, those which, the one who, those who).

Pronouns

Personal pronouns

Spanish subject pronouns are usually omitted unless a certain emphasis is required (*no vamos* we're not going; *nosotros no vamos* we aren't going). The subject pronoun is normally omitted when it is implicit in the verb ending (*canto* I sing). It is sometimes necessary to include the pronoun to avoid ambiguity (*cuando él llegó yo cantaba*).

The subject pronoun is used in the second half of a comparison (*la conoces mejor que yo* you know her better than I) and immediately after *según, salvo, excepto* and sometimes *entre* (*según él* according to him).

In certain regions of Spain and Latin America there are variations in the usage of the object pronoun *la, le* and *lo*: **laísmo** is the use of *la* and *las* instead of *le* and *les* as the feminine indirect object pronouns; **leísmo** is the use of *le* and never *lo* as the masculine singular direct object pronoun; **loísmo** is the use of *lo* instead of *le* as the masculine singular direct and indirect object pronoun. These variations are frowned upon by the Spanish Academy, which recommends the use of *lo* as the masculine direct object pronoun (*lo veo* I see him), and *le* as the indirect object pronoun (*le dije* I told him). Literary style tends to prefer *le* when reference is made to a person, reserving *lo* for objects.

The object pronoun always precedes the verb (*te hablo* I am speaking to you), except when the verb is in the infinitive, the gerund or the imperative, in which case the pronoun is enclitic (*mirarle, mirándole, mírale*).

This enclitic use of the pronoun is also found in literary style when a verb in the indicative or the conditional is initial in a main or independent clause (*diríale la verdad si la ocasión se me presentase* I should tell him the truth were the opportunity to arise; *mirábanle con admiración* they contemplated him in admiration). When there are two pronouns, the indirect object pronoun is placed before the direct object pronoun (*me lo dio* he gave it to me; *dámelo* give it to me). When both pronouns are in the third person *le* or *les* (to him, to her, to them) are replaced by **se** (*se lo diré* I shall tell him; *dáselo* give it to him).

Usted (*Ud.* or *Vd.*) and **ustedes** (*Uds.* or *Vds.*) are the polite forms of address used with strangers and people to whom one owes a certain amount of respect (as opposed to the familiar forms of address *tú* and *vosotros*). Personal and possessive pronouns and adjectives related to *usted* and *ustedes* respectively assume the form of the third person singular and the third person plural (*si usted me lo pide, le llevaré a su casa* if you wish, I shall take you home).

Vos is used instead of *usted* in poetic or oratorial style, in addressing God or an eminent person. (See **vos**.)

The reflexive pronoun is used when the action of a verb refers back to the subject (*nos levantamos tarde* we got up late). The position of reflexive pronouns is the same as that of object pronouns. With *nos* and *os* in the first and second person plural of the imperative the verb loses its final *-s* and *-d* respectively before the pronouns (*sentémonos, sentaos*).

Himself, herself, itself, themselves preceded by a preposition are translated by **sí** when they refer back to the subject of the verb (*esa mujer siempre habla de sí* that woman is always talking about herself). If the preposition is *con* it joins with *mí, ti, sí* to form *conmigo, contigo, consigo*.

Relative pronouns

The relative pronoun must never be omitted in Spanish (*el perro que vimos* the dog (which) we saw).

Within its own clause the relative pronoun may be *a*) the subject, *b*) the direct object, *c*) the prepositional object. Its antecedent (the part of the main clause to which it refers) may be *a*) a person, *b*) a thing, *c*) a clause or verb (*la chica que llamó dejó su número; el coche que conducía era nuevo; no pudo contestar, de lo cual deduje que...*).

Que, the most common relative pronoun, can be a subject or a direct object pronoun when the antecedent is a person or a thing (*el amigo que me presentó, el coche que pasó*).

Subject	Objects: No preposition: Direct	Objects: No preposition: Indirect	Objects: After preposition	Objects: Reflexive
yo (I)	**me** (me, to me, etc.)		**mí** (me)	**me** (myself)
tú (you)	**te** (you, to you, etc.)		**ti** (you)	**te** (yourself)
él (he)	**le, lo** (him)	**le** (to him, etc.)	**él** (him)	**se** (himself)
ella (she)	**la** (her)	**le** (to her, etc.)	**ella** (her)	**se** (herself)
ello (neuter: it)	**lo** (it)	**le** (to it, etc.)	**ello** (it)	**se** (itself)
nosotros, as (we)	**nos** (us, to us, etc.)		**nosotros, as** (us)	**nos** (ourselves)
vosotros, tras (you)	**os** (you, to you, etc.)		**vosotros, as** (you)	**os** (yourselves)
ellos (they)	**los** (them)	**les** (to them, etc.)	**ellos** (them)	**se** (themselves)
ellas (they)	**las** (them)	**les** (to them, etc.)	**ellas** (them)	**se** (themselves)

Quien (pl *quienes*) is used only for persons and agrees in number with its antecedent. It can be the subject, the direct object or the prepositional object in its clause (*fue él quien lo dijo* it was he who said it; *las mujeres a quienes miraba* the women (whom) he was watching). Used without an antecedent *quien* means «he who», «anyone who», «whoever», etc. (*quien no estudia no aprende* he who does not study learns nothing). It can also mean «someone who» (*necesita quien le proteja* she needs someone to protect her; *no hubo quien me ayudase* there was no one who would help me).

El que (**la, los, las que**) and **el cual** (**la cual, los, las cuales**) sometimes replace *que* and *quien* as the subject pronoun, when the antecedent is a person and the relative clause gives added information about the subject (*encontré a sus hermanas, las cuales iban al colegio*). They may also be used as direct object pronouns in the same kind of clause if the antecedent is a person (*ésta es la muchacha a la que mandaron* this is the girl they sent), and as prepositional object pronouns applying to persons or things (*el hijo para el que lo compré* the child for whom I bought it; *la sala por la cual pasamos* the room we passed through). **Lo que** and **lo cual** are used when the antecedent is a verb or clause (*lo que más me molesta es el calor* what bothers me most is the heat; *no veo lo que haces* I cannot see what you are doing; *llegó tarde, lo cual* (or *lo que*) *era de esperar* he was late, which was to be expected; *nos despedimos de él, con lo cual* (or *lo que*) *subió al tren* we said good-bye to him, whereupon he boarded the train). Note that *lo cual* may only be used to refer back to something already mentioned.

Cuyo (whose, of whom, of which) agrees in number and gender with the *object possessed* (*la casa cuyo tejado es rojo* the house with the red roof (the roof of which is red); *el chico cuyas gafas se rompieron* the boy whose glasses broke).

Interrogative pronouns

These differ from the relative pronouns only in that they bear a written accent, both in direct and indirect questions. They are: **qué** (what), **quién** (who, whom), and **cuál** (which, which one).

Qué is invariable in number and gender; **quién** and **cuál** add **-es** in the plural without loss of the written accent (*¿qué ocurre?* what's happening?; *¿quién fue?* who was it?; *no sé quien habrá sido* I don't know who it could have been; *¿a cuáles te refieres?* to which are you referring?).

Note that in Spanish a question is always introduced by an inverted question mark.

Indefinite pronouns

These are **alguien** (someone), **nadie** (no one), **quienquiera** and **cualquiera** (anyone), which become *quienesquiera* and *cualesquiera* in the plural, **uno** (one), **alguno** (someone, some), **ninguno** (no one, none), **se** (one), **algo** (something), **nada** (nothing).

Cualquiera, uno, alguno and *ninguno* do not apocopate when used as pronouns.

Remember that all the indefinite adjectives may also be used as pronouns.

The adverb

Adverbs **of manner** are formed by adding the suffix **-mente** to the feminine singular form of the adjective (*blando, blandamente; fácil, fácilmente*). Note that if an adjective carries a written accent the corresponding adverb bears the same accent. When several adverbs appear consecutively the suffix *-mente* is added only to the last one, the others taking the form of the feminine singular adjective (*lentea y perezosamente* slowly and lazily).

Adverbs **of quantity** may be simple words such as *más* (more), *menos* (less), *bastante* (enough), *demasiado* (too much), *poco* (little), *mucho* (a lot), *tanto* (so much), *cuanto* (as much), or adverbial phrases such as *poco más o menos* (about), *al menos* (at least), *etc.* These words are invariable when used as adverbs.

Common adverbs **of place** are *abajo, acá, adelante, adentro, ahí, alrededor, allá, allí, aquí, arriba, atrás, cerca, debajo, delante, dentro, detrás, donde, dondequiera, encima, enfrente, fuera, lejos, etc.*

Adverbs **of time** include *ahora, anoche, antaño, antes, aún, ayer, ¿cuándo?, después, entonces, hoy, jamás, luego, mañana, nunca, pronto, siempre, tarde, temprano, todavía, ya, etc.*

In the compound tenses in Spanish the adverb must not be placed between the auxiliary and the main verb (*siempre lo hemos hecho así* we have always done it that way), unless the auxiliary is *ser*.

The main adverbs **of negation** are *ni, no, no ... más, no ... más que, no ... sino, ya no.* **No** on its own translates the English *no* (*¿lo harás? — no* will you do it? — no). Before a verb it is equivalent to *not* in English (*no vinieron* they did not come).

If the negatives *nunca, jamás, nada, nadie, ninguno, tampoco,* and expressions such as *en mi vida, en mis días, etc.* precede the verb, the word **no** is omitted (*nunca lo haré* I shall never do it). If they follow the verb, **no** must be used (*no lo haré nunca* I shall never do it).

The comparative of adverbs is formed with **tan**, **más** or **menos** (*tan despacio como puedas* as slowly as you can; *más rápido que yo* faster than I). Four adverbs are compared irregularly: *bien* (mejor), *mal* (peor), *mucho* (más), *poco* (menos).

The superlative of adverbs may fe formed with the neuter article *lo* followed by a word or phrase expressing possibility (*lo más pronto posible* as soon as possible).

The verb

Classification

The different types of verb are:

— **transitive**, which have a direct object (*comía cerezas* I was eating cherries);

— **intransitive**, which have an indirect object or none at all (*voy al cine* I am going to the pictures; *comía* I was eating);

— **reflexive**, when the subject and the object of the action are the same person. This verb form uses the reflexive pronouns *me, te, se, nos, os, se,* which are usually placed before the verb (*el niño se lavó* the child washed (himself); *el niño se durmió* the child fell asleep). These pronouns are, however, enclitic in the infinitive (*dormirse*), the imperative (*duérmete*) and the gerund (*durmiéndose*). Compound tenses are formed with the auxiliary **haber**, and the past participle remains invariable (*tu madre se ha dormido* your mother has fallen asleep). Reciprocity is also expressed in Spanish by the reflexive (*no se conocían antes* they did not know each other before, they did not know one another before);

— **impersonal**, when they are used only in the third person singular with an indeterminate subject (*llueve* it is raining). Note that the pronoun *it* is not translated into Spanish. In expressions such as *es tarde* (it is late), *es de noche* (it is dark), *es de desear* (it is desirable), the verb **ser** is impersonal and invariable in number. In telling the time, however, **ser** agrees in number with the hour (*es la una* it is one o'clock; *son las dos* it is two o'clock). **Haber** is used impersonally to mean «there is», «there are», etc. (*hay sitio para cien coches* there is room for a hundred cars; *había cien coches* there were a hundred cars). When used with *que* and an infinitive it denotes obligation or necessity (*hay que comer* it is necessary to eat). **Hacer** is used impersonally to describe certain weather conditions (*hace frío, calor* it is cold, hot) and to indicate the lapse of time (*hace un mes que ocurrió* it happened a month ago; *hace un mes que no lo veo* I have not seen him for a month; *está en Madrid desde hace una semana* he has been in Madrid for a week);

— **defective**, which do not exist in all the normal tenses and persons (like the English verb *must,* which has no past tense, no conditional, etc.). Such verbs in Spanish are *abolir, atañer, concernir, soler, etc.*;

— **auxiliary**, when they are used to conjugate certain tenses of other verbs (see AUXILIARY VERBS below).

Note that a transitive verb in Spanish is not necessarily translated by a transitive English verb (*la bala traspasó la pared* the bullet went right through the wall). Spanish reflexive verbs are often intransitive verbs in English (*vestirse* to dress, to get dressed).

Verbs do not necessarily govern the same preposition in the two languages (*depender de* to depend on). Such differences are indicated in the corresponding entries in the body of the dictionary.

Personal A

An important feature of Spanish syntax is the use of the preposition **a** before a direct object (noun or pronoun) representing a person or a personified object or being (*no conozco a su padre* I do not know his father; *mató al toro* he killed the bull; *esperar a la muerte* to await death).

The **a** is placed before the direct object of a verb which usually has a person for its object (*amar a su país* to love one's country; *temer a la oscuridad* to be afraid of the dark).

Nothe that, when a verb has a direct object and an indirect object, both of which are persons, the **a** is usually omitted before the direct object (*dejó su hijo a su madre* she left her son with her mother).

The preposition **a** avoids possible confusion of the subject with the object (*ayer encontró Pedro a mi padre* Peter met my father yesterday), and also of the direct object with the complement (*nombraron director a mi padre* they made my father director). It also clarifies the order of succession or of superiority one wishes to express (*el adjetivo posesivo precede al sustantivo* the possessive adjective precedes the noun; *a la tempestad siguió la calma* calm followed the storm; *al padre le supera en mucho el hijo* the son is far superior to the father).

The presence or absence of **a** causes certain verbs to change their meaning (*querer* to want; *querer a* to love).

Voices, moods and tenses

The Passive Voice

The passive voice is conjugated with the auxiliary verb **ser** and the past participle of the verb which agrees in number and gender with the subject (*las alumnas fueron expulsadas* the pupils were expelled). The agent is introduced by **por** (*fueron expulsadas por el director* they were expelled by the headmaster).

Use of the passive is far more common in English than in Spanish. When the agent is expressed it is often preferable to use an active construction in Spanish (*las expulsó el director*). Where no agent is expressed the most common way to avoid the passive in Spanish is to use the reflexive form of the verb (*se comen crudos* they are eaten raw) or a verb in the third person plural (*los venden en el mercado* they are sold *o* they sell them in the market).

The Infinitive

Use of the infinitive differs considerably in English and Spanish (*me permitió salir* he allowed me to *or* he let me go out; *se puso a cantar* he started singing *o* to sing; *insiste en venir* he insists on coming; *siento no haberle visto* I am sorry I didn't see him; *¿has oído hablar de?* have you heard of?).

A must precede the infinitive used after verbs of motion (*fueron a trabajar* they went to work), of exhorting (*animar a*), inviting (*convidar a*), forcing (*obligar a*), impelling (*mover a*), beginning (*empezar a*), deciding and refusing in their reflexive forms (*decidirse a, negarse a*).

Al followed by an infinitive expresses simultaneity (*al llegar vino a verme* when he arrived *o* on arriving he came to see me); **con** followed by an infinitive expresses manner or concession (*con hacer un esfuerzo lo conseguirás* if you make an effort you will succeed; *con ser tan tonto es el que más éxito ha tenido* despite his stupidity he is the one who has been most successful); **de** followed by an infinitive expresses condition (*de haberlo pensado lo hubiera hecho* if I had thought about it I should have done it); **por** followed by an infinitive expresses cause (*no le dejaron entrar por ir mal vestido* they did not let him in because he was unsuitably dressed); **sin** followed by an infinitive gives a negative idea (*me quedé sin comer* I didn't eat; *está sin resolver* it is unsolved); *quedar por* or *estar por hacer, terminar, etc.*, mean «to remain to be done, finished, etc.».

Most Spanish infinitives can be used as nouns (*en un abrir y cerrar de ojos* in the twinkling of an eye, in a wink). If they play the role of subject in the sentence they may usually be translated by the English gerund (*el andar es muy saludable* walking is very healthy). When the infinitive used thus is preceded by a word other than the definite article it often means «the way of doing something» (*su andar gracioso* her graceful gait *or* walk).

The infinitive can also be the object of a preposition (*le escribiré antes de venir* I shall write to you before I come *o* before coming).

In spoken Spanish *a* followed by the infinitive is often used as a command or an exhortation (*¡a trabajar!* (get *o* let's get) to work!).

The Gerund

The Spanish gerund is formed by adding **-ando** or **-iendo** to the stem of the verb and is invariable.

Used without a preposition it indicates manner (*le esperaba leyendo* he read as he waited for him; *fui corriendo* I ran), duration and cause (*estando con él no tenía miedo* when (or because) I was with him I was not afraid).

En followed by the gerund indicates an action immediately prior to that of the main verb (*en llegando se lo diré* I'll tell him as soon as I arrive).

Estar with the gerund gives the idea of action in progress (*está leyendo* he is reading) and will be dealt with below (see *The Progressive Tenses* below). **Ir** with the gerund indicates progression (*iba creciendo* it grew and grew). **Seguir** with the gerund indicates continued action (*sigue trabajando* he is still working).

Llevar with the gerund gives the idea of an action which started at some time in the past and continues at the moment under consideration (*lleva* (*llevaba*) *tres horas esperando* he has (he had) been waiting for three hours).

The Spanish gerund may not refer to the object of a verb, unlike the English present participle (*vi a un muchacho que corría* (not *corriendo*) I saw a boy running). When the English *-ing* has an adjectival function it is usually translated into Spanish by an adjective or an adjectival phrase (*a flickering light* una luz vacilante *or* que vacilaba).

The *-ing* form in English is often translated by the Spanish infinitive when it follows a preposition or when it has the function of a noun (*after meeting him* después de haberle encontrado; *upon meeting him* al encontrarle; *by trying* con intentarlo; *walking is very healthy* el andar es muy saludable; *the singing of the birds* el cantar de los pájaros).

The Progressive Tenses

The Spanish progressive tenses, which correspond to the English *to be ...-ing*, are formed with the appropriate tense of **estar** and the **gerund** of the verb in question (*está leyendo*). The progressive tenses convey an idea of the continuity of an action taking place at any given moment. This idea is also conveyed in Spanish by the simple present tense and the imperfect (*¿adónde vas?* where are you going?; *caminaba lentamente* he was walking slowly). Consequently, the progressive tenses are less frequently used in Spanish than in English, and when used tend to emphasize the idea that the action is in the process of being performed at the moment under consideration (*estaba leyendo cuando llegue* she was (in the act of) reading when I arrived). In some cases the progressive tense would never be used, namely when there is no real stress on the continuity of the action (*llevaba un vestido rojo*), and with verbs of motion (*vamos al colegio* we are going to school).

In certain cases the two forms are more or less interchangeable (*está lloviendo* or *llueve*). In other cases each form would convey a slightly different emphasis (*cuando la encontraron cantaba en un bar* when they found her she was singing (she was a singer) in a bar *or* when they found her she was (in the act of) singing in a bar; *cuando la encontraron estaba cantando en un bar* when they found her she was (in the act of) singing in a bar).

The preterite of *estar* with the gerund conveys an idea which is more difficult to express in English — that of continuing action during a limited time in the past (*estuvieron hablando durante dos horas* they talked for two (whole) hours, they spent two hours talking).

The Indicative

The **present tense** in Spanish corresponds to the simple present (*dice* he says), the progressive tense (*llueve* it is raining) and the form with *do* (*no voy a menudo, pero cuando voy...* I don't go very often, but when I do (go)...).

It is used when asking for instructions (*¿dónde pongo este libro?* where shall I put this book?), to describe an action beginning in the past and continuing to the present (*llevo aquí un mes, hace un mes que estoy aquí* I have been here for a month), and also with the expressions *por poco* and *casi* (*por poco me caigo* I almost fell).

The Spanish **imperfect** and **preterite** both correspond to the English preterite, but they are not interchangeable. The **imperfect** describes an action that was going on at some time in the past or when something else happened (*almorzaba* or *estaba almorzando cuando llegaron* I was having lunch when they arrived) or a customary state or action in the past (*en aquel entonces era muy caro* it was very expensive in those days; *antes leía mucho pero ya no* I used to read a lot, but I don't any more). It is also used in telling the time in the past (*eran las ocho de la mañana* it was 8 a.m.).

The **preterite** stresses the momentariness or the completeness of an action at a definite time in the past (*llovió aquel día* it rained that day; *a pesar de los esfuerzos que hizo no pudo abrir la puerta* despite all his efforts he did not manage to open the door).

The **future** is used to describe future action (*iré mañana* I shall go tomorrow), and also to express probability or supposition (see *Conjecture and Doubt* below). The idea of willingness sometimes present in the English future tense with *will* must be conveyed in Spanish by the present tense of the verb *querer*.

The Subjunctive

This mood is used to present things as possible or doubtful in subordinate and independent clauses. In the first case, the subject in the main clause must be different from the subject of the verb in the subordinate clause (*no quiero que vayas* I don't want you to go). It is compulsory in a subordinate clause dependent on:

— verbs or other words expressing desire (*quiero que lo hagas* I want you to do it), request (*me pidió que lo hiciese* he asked me to do it), command (*me ha mandado que la mate* he has ordered me to kill her), permission (*no permitieron que saliera* they did not allow him to go out), prohibition (*les prohibieron que se viesen* they were forbidden from seeing each other), advice (*te aconsejo que llegues temprano* I advise you to arrive early), causation (*esto hizo que se perdiesen* this made them lose their way), necessity (see ***Obligation*** below), emotions, such as regret, fear our surprise (*siento que no le hayamos podido ayudar* I am sorry we were unable to help you; *es extraño que no haya llamado* it is strange that he has not called), uncertainty or negation (*parece dudoso que vaya* it seems unlikely that he will go; *negó que estuviera casado* he denied that he was married), preference (*prefiero que tomes la decisión* I would rather that you took the decision) and evaluation (*es inútil que grites* it is no good your shouting);

— impersonal expressions of probability (*puede ser que lo consigas* you might succeed);

— conjunctions which introduce future or hypothetical action (*cuando termines llámame* call me when you finish; *por mucho que insistas no iré* I shall not go, however much you insist), including *antes (de) que* (before), *para que* (in order that), *con tal que* (provided that), *a no ser que* (unless), *no porque* (not because), *como si* (as if), *etc.*;

— a relative pronoun with a negative or indefinite antecedent (*no hay excusa que valga* no excuses; *haré lo que pueda* I shall do my best). In the latter case the statement expresses hypothesis because of the future tense;

— conditional clauses (*¿dónde estaría ahora si no te hubiera conocido?* where should I be now had I never met you?; *si tuviera bastante dinero me compraría una casa* if I had enough money I should buy a house).

Note: The imperfect of the subjunctive has two endings, **-ra** and **-se**; the former sometimes replaces the conditional (*hubiera* instead of *habría, quisiera* instead of *querría*).

There is strict correspondence between the tense of the subjunctive used in the subordinate clause and that of the main verb. The present or perfect subjunctive are used after a verb in the present, future or future perfect (*es inútil que llores; es extraño que no haya llamado*). The imperfect or pluperfect subjunctive are used when the main verb is in the imperfect, preterite, conditional, pluperfect or conditional perfect (*habría sido inútil que gritaras; era inútil que gritaras; fue extraño que no viniese*).

The Imperative

The true imperative is restricted in Spanish to the singular and plural of the second person in affirmative commands (*canta, bebed*). The present subjunctive must be used for the other persons in the affirmative (*cantemos, suban*) as well as for all persons in the negative (*no cantes, no mintamos*).

Object pronouns are enclitic in the affirmative (*cántamelo, subámoslo*). The first and the second person plural of reflexive verbs drop respectively the final *-s* and *-d* before enclitic *nos* and *os* (*levantémonos; sentaos*). *Vamos a* followed by an infinitive is another common command form; it is translated by «let us» (*vamos a ver* let's see).

The Participle

There are two kinds of participle, past and present.

The **past participle** obeys the following rules of agreement:

— used *without an auxiliary* it agrees with the noun in the same way as any adjective (*las casas edificadas* the houses built);

— used *with the auxiliary «haber»* it never agrees with the noun (*las he visto*), and the auxiliary and the past participle must not be separated by anything other than an object pronoun (*ha terminado ya* he has already finished; but *habiéndolo hecho* having done it);

— used *with the auxiliary «ser»* and the *semi-auxiliaries* (andar, encontrarse, estar, hallarse, ir, llevar, quedar, resultar, tener, venir, etc.), it agrees with the noun in number and gender (*fueron tomados por asesinos* they were taken for murderers; *iban muy bien vestidos* they were very well dressed; *cuando las tenga hechas* when you have done them).

The past participle is also used in constructions analogous to the Latin ablative absolute (*acabado el trabajo, saldremos* when the work is finished we shall go out). In this case it always precedes the noun and agrees with it in number and gender.

Certain verbs have an irregular past participle, such as *abrir* (abierto), *cubrir* (cubierto), *decir* (dicho), *escribir* (escrito), *hacer* (hecho), *imprimir* (impreso), *morir* (muerto), *poner* (puesto), *resolver* (resuelto), *romper* (roto), *ver* (visto), *volver* (vuelto) and their derivatives, such as *descubrir* (descubierto), *entreabrir* (entreabierto), *etc.* Others have two past participles, one regular, the other irregular: *concluir* (concluido, concluso), *despertar* (despertado, despierto), *elegir* (elegido, electo), *eximir* (eximido, exento), *soltar* (soltado, suelto), *sujetar* (sujetado, sujeto), *etc.* Most of these irregular past participles have become simple adjectives. The main exceptions are *frito, impreso, preso, provisto* and *roto*, which have either replaced the regular forms or developed a meaning different from their *roto* has replaced *rompido*; *prender* gives *prendido*, which means «fastened», and *preso* which means «taken prisoner».

The **present participle** is formed with the suffixes **-ante, -ente, -iente**.

It exists for a very limited number of verbs and has become an adjective (*referente*) or a noun (*amante*). In its verbal function it has been replaced by the gerund (see ***The Progressive Tenses*** above).

Conjecture and Doubt

The Spanish future indicative can be used to express conjecture in the present (*tendrá unos cuarenta años* he must be about forty years old). Conjecture in the past is expressed by the conditional (*tendría unos cuarenta años* he must have been about forty). The same idea can be conveyed by **deber de** with an infinitive (*debe* or *debía de tener cuarenta años*). For the use of the subjunctive in expressions of uncertainty (see ***The Subjunctive*** above).

Obligation

General obligation is expressed by **hay que** with the infinitive (*hay que trabajar para vivir* one must work to live) or by the phrases **es preciso**, **es necesario**, **es menester** and **hace falta** also followed by the infinitive (*es preciso trabajar, hace falta trabajar*).

Personal obligation is expressed by **tener que** with the infinitive (*tengo que verte* I must see you; *tuve que disculparme* I had to apologize) or by **es preciso que**, **es menester que**, **es necesario que** and **hace falta que** followed by the subjunctive (*es preciso que cooperemos todos* we must all cooperate).

Auxiliary verbs

Haber. This auxiliary is used to form the compound tenses of all Spanish verbs, transitive, intransitive and reflexive (*he comido una manzana* I have eaten an apple; *hemos ido a España* we have been to Spain; *se habían caído* they had fallen). The past participle remains invariable.

Note: Haber is also an impersonal verb (*hay* there is, there are; *había* there was, there were; *hubo* there was, there were).

Ser. Like the English *to be*, **ser** is used to form the passive voice in Spanish (*es apreciada por todos* she is appreciated by all). The past participle used with the auxiliary **ser** agrees in number and gender with the subject.

Note: Ser is also an intransitive verb which, like the English *to be*, introduces a definition or a description of the subject.

There are other verbs in Spanish which occasionally serve as auxiliaries: *estar, tener, andar, encontrarse, hallarse, ir, llevar, quedar, resultar, venir,* etc.

Ser and **estar.** For information about the correct use of these verbs consult the English-Spanish half of the dictionary under BE.

HABER

The compound tenses are in italics

Infinitive: haber
Gerund: habiendo
Participle: habido

INDICATIVE

present	**perfect**
Yo he	*Yo he habido*
Tú has	*Tú has habido*
Él ha	*Él ha habido*
Nosotros hemos	*Nosotros hemos habido*
Vosotros habéis	*Vosotros habéis habido*
Ellos han	*Ellos han habido*
imperfect	**past anterior**
Yo había	*Yo hube habido*
Tú habías	*Tú hubiste habido*
Él había	*Él hubo habido*
Nosotros habíamos	*Nosotros hubimos habido*
Vosotros habíais	*Vosotros hubisteis habido*
Ellos habían	*Ellos hubieron habido*
preterite	**pluperfect**
Yo hube	*Yo había habido*
Tú hubiste	*Tú habías habido*
Él hubo	*Él había habido*
Nosotros hubimos	*Nosotros habíamos habido*
Vosotros hubisteis	*Vosotros habíais habido*
Ellos hubieron	*Ellos habían habido*

future
Yo habré
Tú habrás
Él habrá
Nosotros habremos
Vosotros habréis
Ellos habrán

future perfect
Yo habré habido
Tú habrás habido
Él habrá habido
Nosotros habremos habido
Vosotros habréis habido
Ellos habrán habido

CONDITIONAL

simple
Yo habría
Tú habrías
Él habría
Nosotros habríamos
Vosotros habríais
Ellos habrían

perfect
Yo habría habido
Tú habrías habido
Él habría habido
Nosotros habríamos habido
Vosotros habríais habido
Ellos habrían habido

IMPERATIVE

He tú
Habed vosotros
(The remaining forms are borrowed from the present subjunctive).

SUBJUNCTIVE

present
Yo haya
Tú hayas
Él haya
Nosotros hayamos
Vosotros hayáis
Ellos hayan

imperfect
Yo hubiera *o* hubiese
Tú hubieras *o* hubieses
Él hubiera *o* hubiese
Nosotros hubiéramos *o* hubiésemos
Vosotros hubierais *o* hubieseis
Ellos hubieran *o* hubiesen

future
Yo hubiere
Tú hubieres
Él hubiere
Nosotros hubiéremos
Vosotros hubiereis
Ellos hubieren

perfect
Yo haya habido
Tú hayas habido
Él haya habido
Nosotros hayamos habido
Vosotros hayáis habido
Ellos hayan habido

pluperfect
Yo hubiera o *hubiese habido*
Tú hubieras o *hubieses habido*
Él hubiera o *hubiese habido*
Nosotros hubiéramos o *hubiésemos habido*
Vosotros hubierais o *hubieseis habido*
Ellos hubieran o *hubiesen habido*

SER

The compound tenses are in italics

Infinitive: ser
Gerund: siendo
Participle: sido

INDICATIVE

present
Yo soy
Tú eres
Él es
Nosotros somos
Vosotros sois
Ellos son

imperfect
Yo era
Tú eras
Él era
Nosotros éramos
Vosotros erais
Ellos eran

preterite
Yo fui
Tú fuiste
Él fue
Nosotros fuimos
Vosotros fuisteis
Ellos fueron

perfect
Yo he sido
Tú has sido
Él ha sido
Nosotros hemos sido
Vosotros habéis sido
Ellos han sido

past anterior
Yo hube sido
Tú hubiste sido
Él hubo sido
Nosotros hubimos sido
Vosotros hubisteis sido
Ellos hubieron sido

pluperfect
Yo había sido
Tú habías sido
Él había sido
Nosotros habíamos sido
Vosotros habíais sido
Ellos habían sido

future
Yo seré
Tú serás
Él será
Nosotros seremos
Vosotros seréis
Ellos serán

future perfect
Yo habré sido
Tú habrás sido
Él habrá sido
Nosotros habremos sido
Vosotros habréis sido
Ellos habrán sido

CONDITIONAL

simple
Yo sería
Tú serías
Él sería
Nosotros seríamos
Vosotros seríais
Ellos serían

perfect
Yo habría sido
Tú habrías sido
Él habría sido
Nosotros habríamos sido
Vosotros habríais sido
Ellos habrían sido

IMPERATIVE

Sé tú
Sed vosotros
(The remaining forms are borrowed from the present subjunctive).

SUBJUNCTIVE

present
Yo sea
Tú seas
Él sea
Nosotros seamos
Vosotros seáis
Ellos sean

imperfect
Yo fuera *o* fuese
Tú fueras *o* fueses
Él fuera *o* fuese
Nosotros fuéramos *o* fuésemos
Vosotros fuerais *o* fueseis
Ellos fueran *o* fuesen

future
Yo fuere
Tú fueres
Él fuere
Nosotros fuéremos
Vosotros fuereis
Ellos fueren

perfect
Yo haya sido
Tú hayas sido
Él haya sido
Nosotros hayamos sido
Vosotros hayáis sido
Ellos hayan sido

pluperfect
Yo hubiera o *hubiese sido*
Tú hubieras o *hubieses sido*
Él hubiera o *hubiese sido*
Nosotros hubiéramos o *hubiésemos sido*
Vosotros hubierais o *hubieseis sido*
Ellos hubieran o *hubiesen sido*

Regular verbs groups

AMAR (stem *am-*)

The endings are in bold type and the compound tenses in italics

Infinitive: am**ar**
Gerund: am**ando**
Participle: am**ado**

INDICATIVE

present
Yo am**o**
Tú am**as**
Él am**a**
Nosotros am**amos**
Vosotros am**áis**
Ellos am**an**

imperfect
Yo am**aba**
Tú am**abas**
Él am**aba**
Nosotros am**ábamos**
Vosotros am**abais**
Ellos am**aban**

preterite
Yo am**é**
Tú am**aste**
Él am**ó**
Nosotros am**amos**
Vosotros am**asteis**
Ellos am**aron**

perfect
*Yo he am**ado***
*Tú has am**ado***
*Él ha am**ado***
*Nosotros hemos am**ado***
*Vosotros habéis am**ado***
*Ellos han am**ado***

past anterior
*Yo hube am**ado***
*Tú hubiste am**ado***
*Él hubo am**ado***
*Nosotros hubimos am**ado***
*Vosotros hubisteis am**ado***
*Ellos hubieron am**ado***

pluperfect
*Yo había am**ado***
*Tú habías am**ado***
*Él había am**ado***
*Nosotros habíamos am**ado***
*Vosotros habíais am**ado***
*Ellos habían am**ado***

future
Yo am**aré**
Tú am**arás**
Él am**ará**
Nosotros am**aremos**
Vosotros am**aréis**
Ellos am**arán**

future perfect
*Yo habré am**ado***
*Tú habrás am**ado***
*Él habrá am**ado***
*Nosotros habremos am**ado***
*Vosotros habréis am**ado***
*Ellos habrán am**ado***

CONDITIONAL

simple
Yo am**aría**
Tú am**arías**
Él am**aría**
Nosotros am**aríamos**
Vosotros am**aríais**
Ellos am**arían**

perfect
*Yo habría am**ado***
*Tú habrías am**ado***
*Él habría am**ado***
*Nosotros habríamos am**ado***
*Vosotros habríais am**ado***
*Ellos habrían am**ado***

IMPERATIVE

Am**a** tú
Am**ad** vosotros
(The remaining forms are borrowed from the present subjunctive).

SUBJUNCTIVE

present
Yo am**e**
Tú am**es**
Él am**e**
Nosotros am**emos**
Vosotros am**éis**
Ellos am**en**

imperfect
Yo am**ara** *o* am**ase**
Tú am**aras** *o* am**ases**
Él am**ara** *o* am**ase**
Nosotros am**áramos** *o* am**ásemos**
Vosotros am**arais** *o* am**aseis**
Ellos am**aran** *o* am**asen**

future
Yo am**are**
Tú am**ares**
Él am**are**
Nosotros am**áremos**
Vosotros am**areis**
Ellos am**aren**

perfect
*Yo haya am**ado***
*Tú hayas am**ado***
*Él haya am**ado***
*Nosotros hayamos am**ado***
*Vosotros hayáis am**ado***
*Ellos hayan am**ado***

pluperfect
Yo hubiera o *hubiese am**ado***
Tú hubieras o *hubieses am**ado***
Él hubiera o *hubiese am**ado***
Nosotros hubiéramos o *hubiésemos am**ado***
Vosotros hubierais o *hubieseis am**ado***
Ellos hubieran o *hubiesen am**ado***

TEMER (stem *tem-*)

The endings are in bold type and the compound tenses in italics

Infinitive: tem**er**
Gerund: tem**iendo**
Participle: tem**ido**

INDICATIVE

present
Yo tem**o**
Tú tem**es**
Él tem**e**
Nosotros tem**emos**
Vosotros tem**éis**
Ellos tem**en**

imperfect
Yo tem**ía**
Tú tem**ías**
Él tem**ía**
Nosotros tem**íamos**
Vosotros tem**íais**
Ellos tem**ían**

preterite
Yo tem**í**
Tú tem**iste**
Él tem**ió**
Nosotros tem**imos**
Vosotros tem**isteis**
Ellos tem**ieron**

perfect
*Yo he tem**ido***
*Tú has tem**ido***
*Él ha tem**ido***
*Nosotros hemos tem**ido***
*Vosotros habéis tem**ido***
*Ellos han tem**ido***

past anterior
*Yo hube tem**ido***
*Tú hubiste tem**ido***
*Él hubo tem**ido***
*Nosotros hubimos tem**ido***
*Vosotros hubisteis tem**ido***
*Ellos hubieron tem**ido***

pluperfect
*Yo había tem**ido***
*Tú habías tem**ido***
*Él había tem**ido***
*Nosotros habíamos tem**ido***
*Vosotros habíais tem**ido***
*Ellos habían tem**ido***

future
Yo tem**eré**
Tú tem**erás**
Él tem**erá**
Nosotros tem**eremos**
Vosotros tem**eréis**
Ellos tem**erán**

future perfect
*Yo habré tem**ido***
*Tú habrás tem**ido***
*Él habrá tem**ido***
*Nosotros habremos tem**ido***
*Vosotros habréis tem**ido***
*Ellos habrán tem**ido***

CONDITIONAL

simple
Yo tem**ería**
Tú tem**erías**
Él tem**ería**
Nosotros tem**eríamos**
Vosotros tem**eríais**
Ellos tem**erían**

perfect
*Yo habría tem**ido***
*Tú habrías tem**ido***
*Él habría tem**ido***
*Nosotros habríamos tem**ido***
*Vosotros habríais tem**ido***
*Ellos habrían tem**ido***

IMPERATIVE

Tem**e** tú
Tem**ed** vosotros
(The remaining forms are borrowed from the present subjunctive).

SUBJUNCTIVE

present
Yo tem**a**
Tú tem**as**
Él tem**a**
Nosotros tem**amos**
Vosotros tem**áis**
Ellos tem**an**

imperfect
Yo tem**iera** *o* tem**iese**
Tú tem**ieras** *o* tem**ieses**
Él tem**iera** *o* tem**iese**
Nosotros tem**iéramos** *o* tem**iésemos**
Vosotros tem**ierais** *o* tem**ieseis**
Ellos tem**ieran** *o* tem**iesen**

future
Yo tem**iere**
Tú tem**ieres**
Él tem**iere**
Nosotros tem**iéremos**
Vosotros tem**iereis**
Ellos tem**ieren**

perfect
*Yo haya tem**ido***
*Tú hayas tem**ido***
*Él haya tem**ido***
*Nosotros hayamos tem**ido***
*Vosotros hayáis tem**ido***
*Ellos hayan tem**ido***

pluperfect
Yo hubiera o *hubiese tem**ido***
Tú hubieras o *hubieses tem**ido***
Él hubiera o *hubiese tem**ido***
Nosotros hubiéramos o *hubiésemos tem**ido***
Vosotros hubierais o *hubieseis tem**ido***
Ellos hubieran o *hubiesen tem**ido***

PARTIR (stem *part-*)

The endings are in bold type and the compound tenses in italics

Infinitive: part**ir**
Gerund: part**iendo**
Participle: part**ido**

INDICATIVE

present
Yo part**o**
Tú part**es**
Él part**e**
Nosotros part**imos**
Vosotros part**ís**
Ellos part**en**

imperfect
Yo part**ía**
Tú part**ías**
Él part**ía**
Nosotros part**íamos**
Vosotros part**íais**
Ellos part**ían**

preterite
Yo part**í**
Tú part**iste**
Él part**ió**
Nosotros part**imos**
Vosotros part**isteis**
Ellos part**ieron**

perfect
*Yo he part**ido***
*Tú has part**ido***
*Él ha part**ido***
*Nosotros hemos part**ido***
*Vosotros habéis part**ido***
*Ellos han part**ido***

past anterior
*Yo hube part**ido***
*Tú hubiste part**ido***
*Él hubo part**ido***
*Nosotros hubimos part**ido***
*Vosotros hubisteis part**ido***
*Ellos hubieron part**ido***

pluperfect
*Yo había part**ido***
*Tú habías part**ido***
*Él había part**ido***
*Nosotros habíamos part**ido***
*Vosotros habíais part**ido***
*Ellos habían part**ido***

future
Yo part**iré**
Tú part**irás**
Él part**irá**
Nosotros part**iremos**
Vosotros part**iréis**
Ellos part**irán**

future perfect
*Yo habré part**ido***
*Tú habrás part**ido***
*Él habrá part**ido***
*Nosotros habremos part**ido***
*Vosotros habréis part**ido***
*Ellos habrán part**ido***

CONDITIONAL

simple
Yo part**iría**
Tú part**irías**
Él part**iría**
Nosotros part**iríamos**
Vosotros part**iríais**
Ellos part**irían**

perfect
*Yo habría part**ido***
*Tú habrías part**ido***
*Él habría part**ido***
*Nosotros habríamos part**ido***
*Vosotros habríais part**ido***
*Ellos habrían part**ido***

IMPERATIVE

Part**e** tú
Part**id** vosotros
(The remaining forms are borrowed from the present subjunctive).

SUBJUNCTIVE

present
Yo part**a**
Tú part**as**
Él part**a**
Nosotros part**amos**
Vosotros part**áis**
Ellos part**an**

imperfect
Yo part**iera** *o* part**iese**
Tú part**ieras** *o* part**ieses**
Él part**iera** *o* part**iese**
Nosotros part**iéramos** *o* part**iésemos**
Vosotros part**ierais** *o* part**ieseis**
Ellos part**ieran** *o* part**iesen**

future
Yo part**iere**
Tú part**ieres**
Él part**iere**
Nosotros part**iéremos**
Vosotros part**iereis**
Ellos part**ieren**

perfect
*Yo haya part**ido***
*Tú hayas part**ido***
*Él haya part**ido***
*Nosotros hayamos part**ido***
*Vosotros hayáis part**ido***
*Ellos hayan part**ido***

pluperfect
Yo hubiera o *hubiese part**ido***
Tú hubieras o *hubieses part**ido***
Él hubiera o *hubiese part**ido***
Nosotros hubiéramos o *hubiésemos part**ido***
Vosotros hubierais o *hubieseis part**ido***
Ellos hubieran o *hubiesen part**ido***

The three different groups of verbs in Spanish can be distinguished by the last two letters of the infinitive.

The *first group* includes verbs ending in **-ar** in the infinitive (am**ar**).

The *second group* includes verbs ending in **-er** in the infinitive (tem**er**).

The third group includes verbs ending in **-ir** in the infinitive (part**ir**).

The only differences between groups two and three lie in the infinitive, the first and second person plural of the present indicative (tem**emos**, tem**éis**; part**imos**, part**ís**) and the imperative second person plural (tem**ed**; part**id**).

The future and conditional are formed by adding the appropriate endings to the infinitive (amar **é**; amar **ía**), and the imperfect subjunctive and the future subjunctive by replacing the third person plural preterite ending *-ron* with the appropriate subjunctive endings (ama **ra**; ama **se**; ama **re**).

Spelling changes in certain verbs

Spanish rules for spelling and pronunciation (see above) give rise to the following irregularities in the spelling of certain verbs.

Verbs in -eír, -chir, -llir, -ñer, -ñir

Infinitive		*Gerund*	*Preterite*	*Imperfect subjunctive*	*Future subjunctive*
-eír	desleír	desliendo	deslió..., deslieron	desliera..., desliese...	desliere...
-chir	henchir	hinchendo	hinchó..., hincheron	hinchera..., hinchese...	hinchere...
-llir	engullir	engullendo	engulló..., engulleron	engullera..., engullese...	engullere...
-ñer	atañer	atañendo	atañó..., atañeron	atañera..., atañese...	atañere...
-ñir	astriñir	astriñendo	astriñó..., astriñeron	astriñera..., astriñese...	astriñere...

The **unstressed «i»** in the verbs disappears between *ch, ll, ñ* and a vowel, i.e. in the gerund, the 3rd person singular and plural of the preterite and tenses derived from these. *Desleír* is included in this category because its stem is to all intents and purposes *desli-*, and the «i» is not doubled in the tenses mentioned above as it should be in theory. All these verbs appear in the list of irregular verbs.

Verbs in -aer, -eer, -oer, -oír, -uir

Infinitive		*Gerund*	*Preterite*	*Imperfect subjunctive*	*Future subjunctive*
-aer	raer	rayendo	rayó..., rayeron	rayera..., rayese...	rayere...
-eer	creer	creyendo	creyó..., creyeron	creyera..., creyese...	creyere...
-oer	corroer	corroyendo	corroyó..., corroyeron	corroyera..., corroyese...	corroyere...
-oír	oír	oyendo	oyó..., oyeron	oyera..., oyese...	oyere...
-uir	concluir	concluyendo	concluyó..., concluyeron	concluyera..., concluyese...	concluyere...

The common feature of the above verbs is that the **unstressed «i»** between two vowels changes to **y**.

All these verbs appear in the list of irregular verbs.

Verbs in -car, -gar, -guar, -zar

	Infinitive	*Present subjunctive*	*Preterite*
-car : c → *qu*	tocar	toque...	toqué
-gar : g → *gu*	pagar	pague...	pagué
-guar: gu → *gü*	amortiguar	amortigüe...	amortigüé
-zar : z → *c*	alcanzar	alcance...	alcancé

Here the final consonant of the stem changes before endings beginning with **-e**, i.e. in the present subjunctive and the first person singular of the preterite of **-ar** verbs.

Verbs in -cer, -cir, -ger, -gir, -guir, -quir

	Infinitive	*Present indicative*	*Present subjunctive*
-cer, -cir: c → *z*	mecer	mezo	meza, mezas...
	resarcir	resarzo	resarza, resarzas...
-ger, -gir: g → *j*	proteger	protejo	proteja, protejas...
	dirigir	dirijo	dirija, dirijas...
-guir: gu → *g*	distinguir	distingo	distinga, distingas...
-quir: qu → *c*	delinquir	delinco	delinca, delincas...

Here the final consonant of the stem changes before an ending beginning with **-o** or **-a**, i.e. in the first person singular of the present indicative and in the present subjunctive of **-er** and **-ir** verbs.

Tonic stress on verbs in «-iar» and «-uar»

These verbs take a written accent on the **i** or the **u** of the stem in the singular and the 3rd person plural of the present indicative (*confío, confías, confía..., confían*), of the present subjunctive (*gradúe, gradúes, gradúe..., gradúen*) and in the 2nd person singular of the imperative (*confía*).

There are exceptions to this rule, notably certain verbs ending in **-iar** (*abreviar, acariciar, apreciar, copiar, estudiar,* etc.) and all verbs ending in **-cuar** and **-guar**.

Groups of irregular verbs

The following pages contain a list of irregular Spanish verbs. Since certain irregularities are common to large groups of verbs, here is a summary of the most common changes which affect irregular verbs:

— **o** and **e** in the stem change to **ue** and **ie** respectively. *Volar, helar, poder, perder, concernir* and *discernir* are examples of verbs which undergo this change. The **o** and **e** become diphthongs when in a stressed position, i.e. in the 1st, 2nd and 3rd person singular and the 3rd person plural of the present indicative (*vuelo, vuelas, vuela..., vuelan*) and of the present subjunctive (*pierda, pierdas, pierda..., pierdan*), and also in the 2nd person singular of the imperative;

— **e** in the stem changes to **i**. This change affects all **-ir** verbs with an *e* in the stem which is not followed by *r* or *nt,* and also the verb *servir.* The *e* remains only when the ending of the verb begins with *stressed i.* It changes to *i* in all other cases, namely in the 1st, 2nd and 3rd person singular and the 3rd person plural of the present indicative (*pido, pides, pide..., piden*), in the 3rd person singular and plural of the preterite (*pidió, pidieron*), in the 2nd person singular of the imperative (*pide*), in the present subjunctive (*pida, pidas, etc.*), the imperfect subjunctive (*pidiera* or *pidiese, etc.*), the future subjunctive (*pidiere, pidieres, etc.*), and the gerund (*pidiendo*);

— **e** in the stem becomes **i** in certain cases and **ie** in others. Verbs in **-ir** with an *e* in the stem followed by *r* or *nt* (except *servir*) fall into this category. These verbs undergo the same changes as the preceding group, except in the present indicative, the imperative and the present subjunctive where the diphthong *ie* replaces *i* in stressed positions (*miento, mientes, miente..., mienten; miente; mienta, mientas, mienta..., mientan*);

— **o** in the stem becomes **u** in certain cases and **ue** in others according to the same rules as for the above group. The main verbs in this class are *morir* and *dormir;*

— when the stem of a verb ends in vowel followed by **c** this **c** changes to **zc** before endings beginning with *o* or *a.* This category includes verbs ending in **-acer, -ecer, -ocer, -ucir**, except *hacer, cocer, escocer* and *mecer.* This change affects the first person singular of the present indicative (*reconozco*) and the present subjunctive (*reconozca, reconozcas, etc.*).

An added irregularity of verbs ending in **-ducir** is the preterite tense which ends in **-duje, -dujiste**, etc. (*conduje, etc.*), and consequently the imperfect and future subjunctive forms which end in **-dujera** or **-dujese**, etc. (*condujera* or *condujese, etc.*) and **-dujere**, etc. (*condujere, etc.*).

— verbs ending in **-uir** add a **y** after the *u* before the vowels *a, o, e,* that is in the 1st, 2nd and 3rd person singular and the 3rd person plural of the present indicative (*huyo, huyes, huye..., huyen*), in the 2nd person singular of the imperative (*huye*), in the 3rd person singular and plural of the preterite (*huyó, huyeron*), and in all forms of the subjunctive (*huya, huyas, etc.; huyera, huyeras, etc.; huyere, huyeres, etc.*).

Note: Some verbs combine several irregularities (*despliegue, elija, persigo, etc.*).

List of irregular verbs

A

abastecer conjugated like *parecer*.
abnegarse like *comenzar*.
abolir defective. Conjugated only in those forms which have endings beginning in *i*. *Pres. ind.:* abolimos, abolís. *Imperf.:* abolía, abolías... *Pret.:* abolí, aboliste, abolió... *Fut.:* aboliré, abolirás... *Cond.:* aboliría, abolirías... *Imper.:* abolid. *Pres. subj.:* (does not exist); *Imperfect subj.:* aboliera, abolieras... (first form); aboliese, abolieses... (second form). *Fut. subj.:* aboliere, abolieres... *Ger.:* aboliendo. *Past. part.:* abolido.
aborrecer like *parecer*.
absolver like *volver*.
abstenerse like *tener*.
abstraer like *traer*.
abuñolar like *contar*.
acaecer like *parecer*. Defective. Conjugated only in 3rd pers. sing.
acertar like *comenzar*.
acollar like *contar*.
acontecer like *parecer*. Defective. Conjugated only in 3rd pers. sing. and pl.
acordar like *contar*.
acostar like *contar*.
acrecentar like *comenzar*.
acrecer like *nacer*.
adherir like *sentir*.
adir defective. Conjugated only in the infinitive, the gerund and the past participle.
adolecer like *parecer*.
adormecer like *parecer*.
adquirir *Pres. ind.:* adquiero, adquieres... *Pres. subj.:* adquiera, aquiramos, adquiráis... *Imper.:* adquiere, adquiera... (regular in the remaining tenses).
aducir *Pres. ind.:* aduzco, aduces, aduce... *Pret.:* adujimos, adujisteis... *Imper.:* aduce, aduzca, aducid... *Pres. subj.:* aduzca, aduzcas, aduzcáis... *Imperf. subj.:* adujera, adujeras, adujerais... (first form); adujese, adujeses, adujeseis... (second form). *Fut. subj.:* adujere, adujeres... *Ger.:* aduciendo. *Past part.:* aducido.
advenir like *venir*.
advertir like *sentir*.
aferrar like *comenzar*.
afluir like *huir*.
afollar like *contar*.
aforar like *contar* (when it means «to grant a privilege»).
agorar like *contar* (with diaeresis on diphthong *-üe*).
agradecer like *parecer*.
agredir like *abolir*.
aguerrir like *abolir*. Defective.
alentar like *comenzar*.
aliquebrar like *comenzar*.
almorzar like *contar*.
amanecer like *parecer*. Impersonal.
amarillecer like *parecer*.
amolar like *contar*.
amorecer like *parecer*.
amortecer like *parecer*.
andar *Pret.:* anduve, anduviste, anduvo, anduvimos, anduvisteis, anduvieron. *Imperf. subj.:* anduviera, anduvieras... (first form); anduviese, anduvieses... (second form). *Fut. subj.:* anduviere, anduvieres...
anochecer like *parecer*. Impersonal.
antedecir like *decir*.
anteponer like *poner*.
apacentar like *comenzar*.
aparecer like *parecer*.
apercollar like *contar*.
apetecer like *parecer*.
apostar like *contar* (when it means «to bet»).
apretar like *comenzar*.
aprobar like *contar*.
arborecer like *parecer*.
argüir like *huir*.
aridecer like *parecer*.
arrecirse like *abolir*. Defective.
arrendar like *comenzar*.
arrepentirse like *sentir*.
ascender like *hender*.
asentar like *comenzar*.
asentir like *sentir*.
aserrar like *comenzar*.
asir *Pres. ind.:* asgo, ases, asimos, asís... *Imper.:* ase, asga, asgamos, asid... *Pres. subj.:* asga, asgáis...
asolar like *contar*.
asonar like *contar*.
astreñir like *teñir*.
astriñir like *mullir*.
atañer like *tañer*. Defective. Conjugated only in 3rd pers. sing. and pl.
atardecer like *parecer*. Impersonal.
atender like *hender*.
atenerse like *tener*.
aterirse like *abolir*. Defective.
aterrar like *comenzar* (but regular when it means «to terrify»).
atestar like *comenzar* (when it means «to fill up»).
atraer like *traer*.
atravesar like *comenzar*.
atribuir like *huir*.
atronar like *contar*.
avenir like *venir*.
aventar like *comenzar*.
avergonzar like *contar*.
azolar like *contar*.

B

balbucir like *abolir*. Defective.
beldar like *comenzar*.
bendecir like *decir* (but regular in future indicative, conditional and past participle).
bienquerer like *querer*.
blandir like *abolir*. Defective.
blanquecer like *parecer*.
bruñir like *mullir*.
bullir like *mullir*.

C

caber *Pres. ind.:* quepo, cabes, cabe, cabéis... *Pret.:* cupe, cupiste, cupo, cupimos, cupisteis, cupieron. *Fut.:* cabré, cabrás, cabrá, cabréis... *Cond.:* cabría, cabrías... *Imper.:* cabe, quepa, quepamos... *Pres. subj.:* quepa, quepas, quepáis... *Imperf. subj.:* cupiera, cupieras, cupierais... (first form); cupiese, cupieses, cupieseis... (second form); *Fut. subj.:* cupiere, cupieres...
caer *Pres. ind.:* caigo. *Pret.:* caí, caíste, cayó, cayeron... *Pres. subj.:* caiga, caigas, caiga, caigamos, caigáis, caigan.
calentar like *comenzar*.
carecer like *parecer*.
cegar like *comenzar*.
ceñir like *teñir*.
cerner like *hender*.
cernir like *sentir*.
cerrar like *comenzar*.
cimentar like *comenzar*.
circunferir like *sentir*.
clarecer like *parecer*. Defective. Impersonal.
cocer like *volver*.
colar like *contar*.
colegir like *pedir*.
colgar like *contar*.
colorir like *abolir*.
comedirse like *pedir*.
comenzar *Pres. Ind.:* comienzo, comienzas, comienza, comenzamos... *Pres. subj.:* comience, comiences, comencemos... *Imper.:* comienza, comience, comencemos....
compadecer like *parecer*.
comparecer like *parecer*.
competir like *pedir*.
complacer like *parecer*.
componer like *poner*.
comprobar like *contar*.
concebir like *pedir*.
concernir like *discernir*.

concertar like *comenzar.*
concluir like *huir.*
concordar like *contar.*
condescender like *hender.*
condolerse like *volver.*
conducir like *aducir.*
conferir like *sentir.*
confesar like *comenzar.*
confluir like *huir.*
conmover like *volver.*
conocer *Ind. pres.:* conozco... *Imper.:* conoce, conozca, conozcamos, conozcan. *Pres. subj.:* conozca, conozcas, conozcan.
conseguir like *pedir.*
consentir like *sentir.*
consolar like *contar.*
consonar like *contar.*
constituir like *huir.*
constreñir like *teñir.*
construir like *huir.*
contar *Pres. ind.:* cuento, cuentas, cuenta, contamos, contáis, cuentan. *Pres. subj.:* cuente, cuentes, contemos... *Imper.:* cuenta, cuente, contemos...
contender like *hender.*
contener like *tener.*
contradecir like *decir.*
contraer like *traer.*
contrahacer like *hacer.*
contramanifestar like *comenzar.*
contraponer like *poner.*
contravenir like *venir.*
contribuir like *huir.*
controvertir like *sentir.*
convalecer like *parecer.*
convenir like *venir.*
convertir like *sentir.*
corregir like *pedir.*
corroer like *roer.*
costar like *contar.*
crecer like *parecer.*
creer *Pret.:* creyó, creyeron. *Imperf. subj.:* creyera, creyeras... (1st form); creyese, creyeses... (2nd form). *Fut. subj.:* creyere, creyeres... *Ger.:* creyendo.

D

dar *Pres. ind.:* doy, das, dais... *Pret.:* di, diste, dio, disteis... *Subj. pres.:* dé, des, dé, demos... *Imperf. subj.:* diera, dieras, dierais... (1st form); diese, dieses... (2nd form). *Fut. subj.:* diere, dieres... *Imper.:* da, dé, demos...
decaer like *caer.*
decentar like *comenzar.*
decir *Pres. ind.:* digo, dices, decimos, decís... *Pret.:* dije, dijiste, dijo... *Fut.:* diré, dirás, diréis... *Pres. subj.:* diga, digas, digáis... *Imperf. subj.:* dijera, dijeras... (1st form); dijese, dijeses... (2nd form); *Fut. subj.:* dijere, dijeres... *Cond.:* diría, dirías... *Imper.:* di, diga, digamos, decid... *Ger.:* diciendo. *Past part.:* dicho.
decrecer like *parecer.*
deducir like *aducir.*
defender like *hender.*
deferir like *sentir.*
degollar like *contar.*
demoler like *volver.*
demostrar like *contar.*
denegar like *comenzar.*
denostar like *contar.*
dentar like *comenzar.*
deponer like *poner.*
derretir like *pedir.*
derruir like *huir.*
desacertar like *comenzar.*
desacordar like *contar.*
desadvertir like *sentir.*
desaforar like *contar.*
desagradecer like *parecer.*
desalentar like *comenzar.*
desandar like *andar.*
desaparecer like *parecer.*
desapretar like *comenzar.*
desaprobar like *contar.*
desarrendar like *comenzar.*
desasentar like *comenzar.*
desasir like *asir.*
desasosegar like *comenzar.*
desatender like *hender.*
desavenir like *venir.*
desbravecer like *parecer.*
descaecer like *parecer.*
descender like *hender.*
desceñir like *teñir.*
descolgar like *contar.*
descollar like *contar.*
descomedirse like *pedir.*
descomponer like *poner.*
desconcertar like *comenzar.*
desconocer like *parecer.*
desconsolar like *contar.*
descontar like *contar.*
desconvenir like *venir.*
descordar like *contar.*
descornar like *contar.*
desdecir like *decir.*
desdentar like *comenzar.*
desembravecer like *parecer.*
desempedrar like *comenzar.*
desencordar like *contar.*
desenfurecer like *parecer.*
desengrosar like *contar.*
desenmohecer like *parecer.*
desenmudecer like *parecer.*
desensoberbecer like *parecer.*
desentenderse like *hender.*
desenterrar like *comenzar.*
desentorpecer like *parecer.*
desentumecer like *parecer.*
desenvolver like *volver.*
desfallecer like *parecer.*
desfavorecer like *parecer.*
desflorecer like *parecer.*
desgobernar like *comenzar.*
desguarnecer like *parecer.*
deshacer like *hacer.*
deshelar like *comenzar.*
desherbar like *comenzar.*
desherrar like *comenzar.*
deshumedecer like *parecer.*
desleír like *reír.*
deslucir like *lucir.*
desmajolar like *contar.*
desmedirse like *pedir.*
desmembrar like *comenzar.*
desmentir like *sentir.*
desmerecer like *parecer.*
desobedecer like *parecer.*
desobstruir like *huir.*
desoír like *oír.*
desolar like *contar.*
desoldar like *contar.*
desollar like *contar.*
desosar *Pres. ind.:* deshueso, deshuesas, deshuesa... *Imper.:* deshuesa, deshuese... *Pres. subj.:* deshuese, deshueses...
despavorirse like *abolir.*
despedir like *pedir.*
desperecer like *parecer.*
despernar like *comenzar.*
despertar like *comenzar.*
desplacer like *placer.*
desplegar like *comenzar.*
despoblar like *contar.*
desteñir like *teñir.*
desterrar like *comenzar.*
destituir like *huir.*
destorcer like *volver.*
destruir like *huir.*
desvanecer like *parecer.*
desvergonzarse like *contar.*
desvestir like *pedir.*
detener like *tener.*
detraer like *traer.*
devenir like *venir.*
devolver like *volver.*
diferir like *sentir.*
difluir like *huir.*
digerir like *sentir.*
diluir like *huir.*

discernir *Pres. ind.:* discierno, disciernes, discierne, discernimos, discernís, disciernen. *Pres. subj.:* discierna, disciernas, discernamos... *Imper.:* discierne, discierna, discernid...
disconvenir like *venir.*
discordar like *contar.*
disentir like *sentir.*
disminuir like *huir.*
disolver like *volver.*
disonar like *contar.*
displacer like *placer.*
disponer like *poner.*
distender like *hender.*
distraer like *traer.*
distribuir like *huir.*
divertir like *sentir.*
doler like *mover.*
dormir *Pres. ind.:* duermo, duermes, duerme, dormís... *Pret.:* dormí, dormiste, durmió, durmieron. *Imper.:* duerme, duerma, durmamos, dormid... *Pres. subj.:* duerma, duermas, duerma... *Imperf. subj.:* durmiera, durmieras... (1st form); durmiese, durmieses... (2nd form). *Fut. subj.:* durmiere, durmieres... *Ger.:* durmiendo.

E

educir like *aducir.*
elegir like *pedir.*
embaír like *abolir.* Defective.
embastecer like *parecer.*
embebecer like *parecer.*
embellaquecerse like *parecer.*
embellecer like *parecer.*
embermejecer like *parecer.*
embestir like *pedir.*
emblandecer like *parecer.*
emblanquecer like *parecer.*
embobecer like *parecer.*
embosquecer like *parecer.*
embravecer like *parecer.*
embrutecer like *parecer.*
emparentar like *comenzar.*
empecer like *parecer.*
empedernir like *abolir.* Defective.
empedrar like *comenzar.*
empequeñecer like *parecer.*
empezar like *comenzar.*
emplumecer like *parecer.*
empobrecer like *parecer.*
empodrecer like *parecer.*
enaltecer like *parecer.*
enardecer like *parecer.*
encalvecer like *parecer.*
encallecer like *parecer.*
encandecer like *parecer.*
encanecer like *parecer.*
encarecer like *parecer.*
encarnecer like *parecer.*
encender like *hender.*
encentar like *comenzar.*
encerrar like *comenzar.*
enclocar like *contar.*
encloquecer like *parecer.*
encomendar like *comenzar.*
encontrar like *contar.*
encordar like *contar.*
encrudecer like *parecer.*
encruelecer like *parecer.*
endentar like *comenzar.*
endentecer like *parecer.*
endurecer like *parecer.*
enflaquecer like *parecer.*
enfurecer like *parecer.*
engrandecer like *parecer.*
engreír like *reír.*
engrosar like *contar.*
engrumecerse like *parecer.*
engullir like *mullir.*
enloquecer like *parecer.*
enlucir like *lucir.*
enmarillecerse like *parecer.*
enmendar like *comenzar.*
enmohecer like *parecer.*
enmudecer like *parecer.*
ennegrecer like *parecer.*
ennoblecer like *parecer.*
enorgullecer like *parecer.*
enrarecer like *parecer.*
enriquecer like *parecer.*
enrojecer like *parecer.*
enronquecer like *parecer.*
ensangrentar like *comenzar.*
ensoberbecer like *parecer.*
ensombrecer like *parecer.*
ensordecer like *parecer.*
entallecer like *parecer.*
entender like *hender.*
entenebrecer like *parecer.*
enternecer like *parecer.*
enterrar like *comenzar.*
entesar like *comenzar.*
entontecer like *parecer.*
entorpecer like *parecer.*
entrecerrar like *comenzar.*
entreoír like *oír.*
entretener like *tener.*
entrever like *ver.*
entristecer like *parecer.*
entullecer like *parecer.*
entumecer like *parecer.*
envanecer like *parecer.*
envejecer like *parecer.*
envilecer like *parecer.*
envolver like *volver.*
equivaler like *valer.*
erguir *Pres. ind.:* irgo *or* yergo, irgues *or* yergues, irgue *or* yergue, erguimos, erguís, irguen *or* yerguen. *Pret.:* erguí, erguiste, irguió, erguimos, erguisteis, irguieron. *Imper.:* irgue *or* yergue, irga *or* yerga, irgamos... *Pres. subj.:* irga *or* yerga, irgas *or* yergas, irga *or* yerga, irgamos... *Imperf. subj.:* irguiera, irguieras... (1st form); irguiese, irguieses... (2nd form). *Fut. subj.:* irguiere, irguieres... *Ger.:* irguiendo.
errar *Pres. ind.:* yerro, yerras, yerra, erramos... *Pres. subj.:* yerre, yerres... *Imper.:* yerra, yerre, erremos...
escabullirse like *mullir.*
escarmentar like *comenzar.*
escarnecer like *parecer.*
esclarecer like *parecer.*
escocer like *cocer.*
esforzar like *contar.*
establecer like *parecer.*
estar *Pres. ind.:* estoy, estás... *Pret.:* estuve, estuviste, estuvo, estuvimos... *Imper.:* está, esté... *Pres. subj.:* esté, estés... *Imperf. subj.:* estuviera, estuvieras... (1st form); estuviese, estuvieses... (2nd form). *Fut. subj.:* estuviere, estuvieres...
estatuir like *huir.*
estregar like *comenzar.*
estremecer like *parecer.*
estreñir like *teñir.*
excluir like *huir.*
expedir like *pedir.*
exponer like *poner.*
extender like *hender.*
extraer like *traer.*

F

fallecer like *parecer.*
favorecer like *parecer.*
fenecer like *parecer.*
florecer like *parecer.*
fluir like *huir.*
follar like *contar.*
fortalecer like *parecer.*
forzar like *contar.*
fosforecer like *parecer.*
fregar like *comenzar.*
freír like *reír.*

G

gañir like *mullir.*
garantir like *abolir.* Defective.
gemir like *pedir.*
gobernar like *comenzar.*

gruir like *huir*.
gruñir *Pres. ind.:* gruñí, gruñiste, gruñó, gruñeron... *Imperf. subj.:* gruñera, gruñeras... *or* gruñese, gruñeses... *Fut. subj.:* gruñere, gruñeres... *Ger.:* gruñendo.
guarecer like *parecer*.
guarnecer like *parecer*.
guarnir like *abolir*. Defective.

H

haber see AUXILIARY VERBS.
hacendar like *comenzar*.
hacer *Pres. ind.:* hago, haces, hace... *Pret.:* hice, hiciste, hizo... *Fut.:* haré, harás, hará... *Imper.:* haz, haga, hagamos... *Cond.:* haría, harías... *Pres. subj.:* haga, hagas... *Imperf. subj.:* hiciera, hicieras... (1st form); hiciese, hicieses... (2nd form). *Fut. subj.:* hiciere, hicieres... *Ger.:* haciendo. *Past part.:* hecho.
heder like *hender*.
helar like *comenzar*.
henchir like *pedir*.
hender *Pres. ind.:* hiendo, hiendes, hiende, hendemos, hendéis, hienden. *Imper.:* hiende, hienda, hendamos... *Pres. subj.:* hienda, hiendas...
hendir like *sentir*.
herbecer like *parecer*.
herir like *sentir*.
herrar like *comenzar*.
hervir like *sentir*.
holgar like *contar*.
hollar like *contar*.
huir *Pres. ind.:* huyo, huyes, huye, huimos, huis, huyen. *Pret.:* hui, huiste, huyó... *Imper.:* huye, huya, huid... *Pres. subj.:* huya, huyas, huya...
humedecer like *parecer*.

I

imbuir like *huir*.
impedir like *pedir*.
imponer like *poner*.
incensar like *comenzar*.
incluir like *huir*.
incoar like *amar*, but defective like *abolir*.
incumbir like *partir*. Defective. Conjugated only in the infinitive, the gerund, the past participle and the 3rd persons sing. and pl. of all tenses.
indisponer like *poner*.
inducir like *aducir*.
inferir like *sentir*.
influir like *huir*.
ingerir like *sentir*.
inquirir like *adquirir*.
instituir like *huir*.
instruir like *huir*.
interferir like *sentir*.
interponer like *poner*.
intervenir like *venir*.
introducir like *aducir*.
intuir like *huir*.
invernar like *comenzar*.
invertir like *sentir*.
investir like *pedir*.
ir *Pres. ind.:* voy, vas, va, vamos, vais, van. *Pret.:* fui, fuiste, fue... *Imperf.:* iba, ibas... *Imper.:* ve, vaya, vayamos, id, vayan. *Pres. subj.:* vaya, vayas... *Imperf. subj.:* fuera, fueras... (1st form); fuese, fueses... (2nd form). *Fut. subj.:* fuere, fueres, fuere, fuéremos... *Ger.:* yendo. *Past part.:* ido.

J

jugar like *contar*.

L

languidecer like *parecer*.
lobreguecer like *parecer*. Impersonal.
lucir *Pres. ind.:* luzco, luces, luce... *Imper.:* luce, luzca, luzcamos, lucid... *Pres. subj.:* luzca, luzcas...

LL

llover like *volver*. Impersonal.

M

maldecir like *decir*.
malherir like *sentir*.
malquerer like *querer*.
maltraer like *traer*.
manifestar like *comenzar*.
manir like *abolir*. Defective.
mantener like *tener*.
medir like *pedir*.
mentar like *comenzar*.
mentir like *sentir*.
merecer like *parecer*.
merendar like *comenzar*.
moblar like *contar*.
moler like *volver*.
morder like *volver*.
morir like *dormir*.
mostrar like *contar*.
mover *Pres. ind.:* muevo, mueves, mueve, movemos, movéis, mueven. *Pres. subj.:* mueva, muevas... *Imper.:* mueve, mueva, movamos... *Ger.:* moviendo. *Past part.:* movido.
mullir *Pret.:* mullí, mulliste, mulló... *Imperf. subj.:* mullera, mulleras... (1st form); mullese, mulleses... (2nd form). *Fut. subj.:* mullere, mulleres... *Ger.:* mullendo.

N

nacer *Pres. ind.:* nazco, naces, nace... *Pres. subj.:* nazca, nazcas... *Imper.:* nace, nazcamos...
negar like *comenzar*.
nevar like *comenzar*. Impersonal.

O

obedecer like *parecer*.
obscurecer like *parecer*.
obstruir like *huir*.
obtener like *tener*.
ofrecer like *parecer*.
oír *Pres. ind.:* oigo, oyes, oye, oímos, oís, oyen. *Pres. subj.:* oiga, oigas... *Imper.:* oye, oiga. *Pret.:* oí, oíste, oyó... *Ger.:* oyendo. *Past part.:* oído.
oler *Pres. ind.:* huelo, hueles, huele, olemos, oléis, huelen. *Pres. subj.:* huela, huelas... *Imper.:* huele, huela, olamos, oled, huelan.
oponer like *poner*.
oscurecer like *parecer*.

P

pacer like *nacer*.
padecer like *parecer*.
palidecer like *parecer*.
parecer *Pres. ind.:* parezco, pareces... *Imper.:* parece, parezca... *Pres. subj.:* parezca, parezcas...
pedir *Pres. ind.:* pido, pides, pide, pedimos, pedís, piden. *Pret.:* pedí, pediste, pidió... *Imper.:* pide, pida, pidamos... *Pres. subj.:* pida, pidas... *Imperf. subj.:* pidiera, pidieras (1st form); pidiese, pidieses... (2nd form). *Fut. subj.:* pidiere, pidieres... *Ger.:* pidiendo.
pensar like *comenzar*.
perder like *hender*.
perecer like *parecer*.
permanecer like *parecer*.
perniquebrar like *comenzar*.
perquirir like *adquirir*.
perseguir like *pedir*.
pertenecer like *parecer*.
pervertir like *sentir*.
placer *Pres. ind.:* plazco, places, place... *Pret.:* plací, placiste, plació *or* plugo, placimos, placisteis... *Imper.:* place, plazca, placed... *Pres. subj.:* plazca, plazcas, plazca *or* plegue *or* plega... *Imperf. subj.:* placiera, placieras, placiera *or* pluguiera... (1st form); placiese, placieses, placiese *or* pluguiese... (2nd form). *Fut. subj.:* placiere, placieres, placiere *or* pluguiere...
plañir like *mullir*.
plegar like *comenzar*.
poblar like *contar*.
poder *Pres. ind.:* puedo, puedes, puede, podemos, podéis, pueden. *Pret.:* pude, pudiste, pudo... *Fut.:* podré, podrás, podrá... *Cond.:* podría, podrías... *Imper.:* puede, pueda, podamos... *Pres. subj.:* pueda, puedas, pueda... *Imperf. subj.:* pudiera, pudieras... (1st form); pudiese, pudieses... (2nd form). *Ger.:* pudiendo.

podrir like *pudrir.*
poner *Pres. ind.:* pongo, pones, pone... *Pret.:* puse, pusiste, puso... *Fut.:* pondré, pondrás... *Cond.:* pondría, pondrías... *Imper.:* pon, ponga, pongamos... *Pres. subj.:* ponga, pongas... *Imperf. subj.:* pusiera, pusieras... (1st form); pusiese, pusieses... (2nd form). *Fut. subj.:* pusiere, pusieres... *Ger.:* poniendo. *Past part.:* puesto.
poseer like *creer.*
posponer like *poner.*
preconcebir like *pedir.*
predecir like *decir.*
predisponer like *poner.*
preelegir like *pedir.*
preferir like *sentir.*
preponer like *poner.*
presentir like *sentir.*
presuponer like *poner.*
preterir like *abolir.* Defective.
prevalecer like *parecer.*
prevaler like *valer.*
prevenir like *venir.*
prever like *ver.*
probar like *contar.*
producir like *aducir.*
proferir like *sentir.*
promover like *volver.*
proponer like *poner.*
proseguir like *pedir.*
prostituir like *huir.*
provenir like *venir.*
pudrir *Past part.:* podrido.

Q

quebrar like *comenzar.*
querer *Pres. ind.:* quiero, quieres, quiere, queremos, queréis, quieren. *Pret.:* quise, quisiste, quiso... *Fut.:* querré, querrás, querrá... *Imper.:* quiere, quiera... *Cond.:* querría, querrías... *Pres. subj.:* quiera, quieras... *Imperf. subj.:* quisiera, quisieras... (1st form); quisiese, quisieses... (2nd form). *Fut. subj.:* quisiere, quisieres...

R

raer *Pres. ind.:* raigo *or* rayo, raes... *Imper.:* rae, raiga *or* raya, raigamos *or* rayamos... *Pres. subj.:* raiga *or* raya, raigas *or* rayas...
rarefacer like *parecer.*
reaparecer like *parecer.*
reblandecer like *parecer.*
rebullir like *mullir.*
recaer like *caer.*
recalentar like *comenzar.*
recentar like *comenzar.*
recluir like *huir.*
recocer like *volver.*
recolar like *contar.*
recomendar like *comenzar.*
recomponer like *poner.*
reconducir like *aducir.*
reconocer like *conocer.*
reconstituir like *huir.*
reconstruir like *huir.*
recontar like *contar.*
reconvenir like *venir.*
reconvertir like *sentir.*
recordar like *contar.*
recostar like *contar.*
recrecer like *parecer.*
recrudecer like *parecer.*
reducir like *aducir.*
reelegir like *pedir.*
reexpedir like *pedir.*
referir like *sentir.*
reflorecer like *parecer.*
refluir like *huir.*
reforzar like *contar.*
refregar like *comenzar.*
refreír like *reír.*
regar like *comenzar.*
regimentar like *comenzar.*
regir like *pedir.*
rehacer like *hacer.*
rehuir like *huir.*
rehumedecer like *parecer.*
reír *Pres. ind.:* río, ríes, ríe, reímos, reís, ríen. *Pret.:* reí, reíste, rió... *Imper.:* ríe, ría, reíd... *Pres. subj.:* ría, rías, ría, riamos... *Imperf. subj.:* riera, rieras... (1st form); riese, rieses... (2nd form). *Fut. subj.:* riere, rieres... *Ger.:* riendo.
rejuvenecer like *parecer.*
relucir like *lucir.*
remendar like *comenzar.*
remoler like *volver.*
remorder like *volver.*
remover like *volver.*
renacer like *nacer.*
rendir like *pedir.*
renegar like *comenzar.*
renovar like *contar.*
reñir like *teñir.*
repetir like *pedir.*
replegar like *comenzar.*
repoblar like *contar.*
reponer like *poner.*
reprobar like *contar.*
reproducir like *aducir.*
requebrar like *comenzar.*
requerir like *sentir.*
resalir like *salir.*
resentirse like *sentir.*
resolver like *volver.*
resollar like *contar.*
resonar like *contar.*
resplandecer like *parecer.*
restablecer like *parecer.*
restituir like *huir.*
restregar like *comenzar.*
restriñir like *mullir.*
retemblar like *comenzar.*
retener like *tener.*
retoñecer like *parecer.*
retorcer like *volver.*
retostar like *contar.*
retraer like *traer.*
retribuir like *huir.*
retrotraer like *traer.*
reventar like *comenzar.*
reverdecer like *parecer.*
revertir like *sentir.*
revestir like *pedir.*
revolcar like *contar.*
revolver like *volver.*
robustecer like *parecer.*
rodar like *contar.*
roer *Pres. ind.:* roo *or* roigo *or* royo... *Imper.:* roe, roa *or* roiga *or* roya... *Pres. subj.:* roa, roas... *or* roiga, roigas... *or* roya, royas... *Ger.:* royendo.
rogar like *contar.*

S

saber *Pres. ind.:* sé, sabes, sabe... *Pret.:* supe, supiste, supo... *Fut.:* sabré, sabrás, sabrá... *Imper.:* sabe, sepa, sepamos... *Cond.:* sabría, sabrías... *Pres. subj.:* sepa, sepas... *Imperf. subj.:* supiera, supieras... (1st form); supiese, supieses... (2nd form). *Fut. subj.:* supiere, supieres... *Ger.:* sabiendo. *Past part.:* sabido.
salir *Pres. ind.:* salgo, sales, sale... *Fut.:* saldré, saldrás, saldrá... *Imper.:* sal, salga, salgamos... *Cond.:* saldría, saldrías... *Pres. subj.:* salga, salgas... *Ger.:* saliendo. *Past part.:* salido.
salpimentar like *comenzar.*
satisfacer *Pres. ind.:* satisfago, satisfaces, satisface... *Pret.:* satisfice, satisficiste, satisfizo... *Fut.:* satisfaré, satisfarás, satisfará... *Imper.:* satisfaz *or* satisface, satisfaga, satisfagamos... *Cond.:* satisfaría, satisfarías... *Pres. subj.:* satisfaga, satisfagas... *Imperf. subj.:* satisficiera, satisficieras... (1st form); satisficiese, satisficieses... (2nd form). *Fut. subj.:* satisficiere, satisficieres... *Past part.:* satisfecho.
seducir like *aducir.*
segar like *comenzar.*
seguir like *pedir.*
sembrar like *comenzar.*
sentar like *comenzar.*

sentir *Pres. ind.:* siento, sientes, siente, sentimos, sentís, sienten. *Pret.:* sentí, sentiste, sintió, sentimos, sentisteis, sintieron. *Imper.:* siente, sienta, sintamos... *Pres. subj.:* sienta, sientas... *Imperf. subj.:* sintiera, sintieras... (1st form); sintiese, sintieses... (2nd form). *Fut. subj.:* sintiere, sintieres... *Ger.:* sintiendo.
ser see AUXILIARY VERBS.
serrar like *comenzar.*
servir like *pedir.*
sobreentender or **sobrentender** like *hender.*
sobreponer like *poner.*
sobresalir like *salir.*
sobrevenir like *venir.*
sobrevolar like *contar.*
sofreír like *reír.*
solar like *contar.*
soldar like *contar.*
soler like *volver.* Defective.
soltar like *contar.*
sonar like *contar.*
sonreír like *reír.*
soñar like *contar.*
sosegar like *comenzar.*
sostener like *tener.*
soterrar like *comenzar.*
subarrendar like *comenzar.*
subseguir like *pedir.*
substituir like *huir.*
substraer like *traer.*
subvenir like *venir.*
subvertir like *sentir.*
sugerir like *sentir.*
superponer like *poner.*
suponer like *poner.*
sustituir like *huir.*
sustraer like *traer.*

T

tallecer like *parecer.*
tañer *Pret.:* tañí, tañiste, tañó... *Imperf. subj.:* tañera, tañeras... (1st form); tañese, tañeses... (2nd form). *Fut. subj.:* tañere, tañeres... *Ger.:* tañendo. *Past part.:* tañido.
tardecer like *parecer.* Impersonal.
temblar like *comenzar.*
tender like *hender.*
tener *Pres. ind.:* tengo, tienes, tiene, tenemos, tenéis, tienen. *Pret.:* tuve, tuviste, tuvo... *Fut.:* tendré, tendrás... *Imper.:* ten, tenga, tengamos... *Cond.:* tendría, tendrías... *Pres. subj.:* tenga, tengas... *Imperf. subj.:* tuviera, tuvieras... (1st form); tuviese, tuvieses... (2nd form). *Fut. subj.:* tuviere, tuvieres... *Ger.:* teniendo. *Past part.:* tenido.
tentar like *comenzar.*
teñir *Pres. ind.:* tiño, tiñes, tiñe, teñimos, teñís, tiñen. *Pret.:* teñí, teñiste, tiñó... *Imper.:* tiñe, tiña, tiñamos... *Pres. subj.:* tiña, tiñas... *Imperf. subj.:* tiñera, tiñeras... (1st form); tiñese, tiñeses... (2nd form). *Fut. subj.:* tiñere, tiñeres... *Ger.:* tiñendo. *Past part.:* teñido.
torcer like *volver.*
tostar like *contar.*
traducir like *aducir.*
traer *Pres. ind.:* traigo, traes, trae... *Pret.:* traje, trajiste, trajo... *Imper.:* trae, traiga, traigamos... *Pres. subj.:* traiga, traigas... *Imperf. subj.:* trajera, trajeras... (1st form); trajese, trajeses... (2nd form). *Fut. subj.:* trajere, trajeres... *Ger.:* trayendo. *Past part.:* traído.
transcender like *hender.*
transferir like *sentir.*
transgredir like *abolir.*
transponer like *poner.*
trascender like *querer.*
trascolar like *contar.*
trascordarse like *contar.*
trasegar like *comenzar.*
trasgredir like *abolir.*
traslucirse like *lucir.*
trasoñar like *contar.*
trastocar like *contar.*
trastrocar like *contar.*
trasver like *ver.*
trasverter like *hender.*
trasvolar like *contar.*
travestir like *pedir.*
trocar like *contar.*
tronar like *contar.*
tropezar like *comenzar.*
tullir like *mullir.*

U

usucapir defective. Conjugated chiefly in the infinitive.

V

valer *Pres. ind.:* valgo, vales, vale... *Fut.:* valdré, valdrás, valdrá... *Imper.:* val *or* vale, valga, valgamos... *Cond.:* valdría, valdrías... *Pres. subj.:* valga, valgas... *Ger.:* valiendo. *Past part.:* valido.
venir *Pres. ind.:* vengo, vienes, viene, venimos, venís, vienen. *Pret.:* vine, viniste, vino... *Fut.:* vendré, vendrás... *Imper.:* ven, venga, vengamos... *Cond.:* vendría, vendrías... *Pres. subj.:* venga, vengas... *Imperf. subj.:* viniera, vinieras... (1st form); viniese, vinieses... (2nd form). *Fut. subj.:* viniere, vinieres... *Ger.:* viniendo. *Past part.:* venido.
ver *Pres. ind.:* veo, ves, ve... *Imperf.:* veía, veías... *Imper.:* ve, vea... *Pres. subj.:* vea, veas... *Ger.:* viendo. *Past part.:* visto.
verter like *hender.*
vestir like *pedir.*
volar like *contar.*
volcar like *contar.*
volver *Pres. ind.:* vuelvo, vuelves, vuelve... *Pret.:* volví, volviste... *Imper.:* vuelve, vuelva... *Pres. subj.:* vuelva, vuelvas... *Ger.:* volviendo. *Past part.:* vuelto.

Y

yacer *Pres. ind.:* yazco *or* yazgo *or* yago, yaces, yace... *Imper.:* yace *or* yaz, yazca *or* yazga *or* yaga, yazcamos *or* yazgamos *or* yagamos, yaced... *Pres. subj.:* yazca *or* yazga *or* yaga, yazcas, yazca... *Ger.:* yaciendo. *Past part.:* yacido.
yuxtaponer like *poner.*

Z

zaherir like *sentir.*
zambullir like *mullir.*

A

a *f* a; *una a minúscula* a small a || *a por a y be por be* in detail, point by point.

— OBSERV The pronunciation of the Spanish *a* corresponds to the sound midway between the *a* in *at* and the *a* in *are*.

a *prep*

1. COMPLEMENTO INDIRECTO — **2.** ENTRE DOS VERBOS — **3.** VERBOS DE EXHORTACIÓN, INVITACIÓN, ETC. — **4.** TIEMPO — **5.** SITUACIÓN, LUGAR — **6.** PRECIO — **7.** EVALUACIÓN — **8.** MODO — **9.** EXPRESIONES DIVERSAS.

1. COMPLEMENTO INDIRECTO to (destinación); *escribí a mi abuela* I wrote to my grandmother; *dar el libro al maestro* to give the book to the teacher || from (procedencia); *se lo compré a Juan* I bought it from John.
2. ENTRE DOS VERBOS to; *voy a escribir* I'm going to write; *se sentó a comer* he sat down to eat; *empezó a llover* it began to rain; *le ayudaron a hacer la maleta* they helped him to pack his suitcase.
3. VERBOS DE EXHORTACIÓN, INVITACIÓN, ETC. to; *los agitadores nos incitaron a la rebelión* the agitators incited us to rebellion; *nos obligó a salir* he obliged us to go out.
4. TIEMPO at (momento concreto); *a las dos de la tarde* at two o'clock in the afternoon; *al principio* at the beginning; *a los veinte años* at twenty || after (después); *a los seis meses de su llegada* six months after his arrival || later, afterwards (más tarde); *a los diez minutos volvió* ten minutes later he came back.
5. SITUACIÓN, LUGAR to; *ir a Inglaterra* to go to England; *voy al peluquero* I'm going to the hairdresser's || at; *a la puerta* at the door; *sentarse a la mesa* to sit down at the table; *mi casa está al final de esta calle* my house is at the end of this street || on; *llevaba un cesto al brazo* he carried a basket on his arm; *a orillas del Támesis* on the banks of the Thames; *a la derecha, izquierda* on the right left; *a este lado* on this side || to; *el pueblo está al norte de Madrid* the town is to the North of Madrid; *llegar a Inglaterra* to arrive to England || not translated; *la fábrica está a dos kilómetros de su casa* the factory is two kilometres from his house || into, in (dentro); *cayó al pozo* he fell into the well; *échalo al fuego* throw it in the fire || in; *mirarse al espejo* to look at o.s. in the mirror; *a lo lejos* in the distance; *a los ojos de todos* in everybody's eyes; *sentarse al sol* to sit in the sun.
6. PRECIO at; *patatas a* or *de a cinco pesetas el kilo* potatoes at five pesetas a kilogramme.
7. EVALUACIÓN to; *de tres a cinco años* from three to five years || in, by (distributivo); *a docenas* in dozens, by the dozen; *a millares* in thousands, by the thousand || a, per; *gano veinte libras a la semana* I earn twenty pounds a week || at; *a cien kilómetros por hora* at a hundred kilometres an hour.
8. MODO by; *a mano* by hand || in; *escribir a lápiz* to write in pencil; *a sangre fría* in cold blood || with; *a duras penas* with great difficulty || on; *a pie* on foot; *a petición suya* on his request; *acompañar al piano* to accompany on the piano || — *escrito a máquina* typewritten || *hecho a máquina* machine-made.
9. EXPRESIONES DIVERSAS *a caballo* on horseback || *a casa* home || *a casa de Pérez* to Pérez's house, to Pérez's || *¡a comer!* lunch (breakfast, dinner, etc.) is ready! || *¿a cuánto es esto? — a veinte pesetas* how much is this? — twenty pesetas (precio) || *¿a cuántos estamos? — a veinte de junio* what is the date?, what date is it? — it's the twentieth of June (fecha) || *¡a dormir!, ¡a la cama!* to bed!, bedtime! || *a eso de las dos* (at) about two o'clock || *a la francesa* in the French way, in the French fashion, à la française || *al día siguiente* the next day, the following day, the day after || *a lo caballero* like a gentleman || *a lo grande* in a big way || *a los quince años* at fifteen, at the age of fifteen (edad), fifteen years later (quince años más tarde), fifteen years after (quince años después de) || *amor a la verdad* love of the truth || *a no ser por* but for, if it were not for || *a que* I bet; *a que llego más pronto que tú* I bet I get there before you || *¿a qué viene Vd.?* what do you want here? || *a su llegada* on his arrival || *a tiempo* in time || *a ver* let's see, let's have a look || *cercano a* near to, close to || DEP *empatar a dos* to draw two all | *ganar tres a dos* to win three-two || FAM *ir a por vino* to go for some wine, to go and fetch some wine || *ir en fila de a dos* to go in twos || *Madrid, a 10 de febrero* Madrid, 10th February || *matar a alguien a puñaladas* to stab s.o. to death || *miedo al lobo* fear of the wolf || *olor a rosas* smell of roses || *subir al autobús* to get on the bus || *torcer a la derecha* to turn right, to turn to the right.

— OBSERV The preposition *a* introduces the direct object of transitive verbs when the object is a person or, in certain cases, an animal, a town, a country or a personified noun. It can also be used to avoid possible ambiguity. It is not translated in English: *oigo a mi madre* I can hear my mother; *este libro describe a Inglaterra* this book describes England; *llama casa a este tugurio* he calls this slum a house.

— OBSERV The preposition *a* must introduce the emphatic pronoun in Spanish: *a éste le conozco bien* I know him very well; *me dio el libro a mí* he gave the book to me, he gave me the book.

— OBSERV When the preposition *a* directly precedes the article *el*, *a el* is contracted to *al*.

abacá *m* abaca (árbol de Manila) || Manilla hemp (tejido).

abacería *f* grocer's, grocer's shop.

abacero, ra *m/f* grocer.

abacial *adj* abbatial.

abaco *m* abacus, counting frame || ARQ abacus.

abad *m* abbot (de un monasterio).

abadejo *m* codfish, cod (bacalao) || fire-crested wren (ave) || spanish fly, cantharides (insecto).

abadengo, ga *adj* abbatial; *tierras abadengas* abbatial lands.

abadesa *f* abbess.

abadía *f* abbey (convento) || abbacy (dignidad) || parsonage, rectory, vicarage (casa del cura).

abajeño, ña; abajero, ra; abajino, na *adj* AMER lowland.
◆ *m/f* AMER lowlander.

abajero, ra *adj* AMER bottom; *sábana abajera* bottom sheet.

abajo *adv* below; *abajo hay gente esperando* there are people waiting below || down here, down below; *estoy abajo* I am down here *o* down below || down there, down here, down below, downstairs (en una casa); *el cartero está abajo* the postman is down here *o* down below *o* downstairs (si el que habla está también abajo), the postman is down there *o* down below *o* downstairs (si el que habla está arriba) || down, down below, downstairs; *vete abajo a abrir la puerta* go down and open the door || down with; *¡abajo el tirano!* down with the tyrant! || — *aquí abajo* down here, here below || *calle abajo* down the street || *cuesta abajo* downhill || *de arriba abajo* from top to bottom || *desde abajo* from below || *echar abajo* to pull down, to demolish (derribar), to ruin (reputación), to bring down, to overthrow (un gobierno), to break down (una puerta) || *el abajo firmante* the undersigned || *escaleras abajo* downstairs || *ir hacia abajo* to go down || *los vecinos de abajo* the neighbours below || *más abajo* below; *el pasaje citado más abajo* the passage quoted below; lower down (en un lugar inferior), further down; *cinco casas más abajo* five houses further down || *por abajo* underneath || *río* or *aguas abajo* downstream || *tirar abajo* to pull down, to knock down, to demolish (un edificio), to break down (una puerta) || *venirse abajo* to fall down, to collapse (un edificio), to fall through, to collapse (un proyecto).

abalanzar *vt* to balance (la balanza) || to throw (lanzar).
◆ *vpr* to rush; *abalanzarse sobre su adversario* to rush (at) one's enemy; *abalanzarse hacia las lanchas de salvamento* to rush towards the lifeboats || to swoop; *el águila se abalanzó sobre el cordero* the eagle swooped on the lamb || to pounce; *los niños se abalanzaron sobre los pasteles* the children pounced on the cakes || AMER to rear (el caballo).

abalaustrado, da *adj* balustered.

abalear *vt* AMER to shoot (fusilar).

abaleo *m* broom (escoba y planta).

abalizamiento *m* MAR marking with buoys *o* beacons, buoying.

abalizar *vt* MAR to buoy, to mark with buoys *o* beacons.

abalorio *m* glass bead (cuenta) || glass beads *pl*, glass beadwork.

abaluartar *vt* to fortify with bastions *o* with a bulwark.

abancaino, na; abancayno, na *adj* [from *o* of] Abancay (Perú).
◆ *m/f* native *o* inhabitant of Abancay.

abanderado *m* MIL standard bearer || FIG champion (defensor de una causa).

abanderamiento *m* MAR registering (de un barco).

abanderar *vt* MAR to register || FIG to champion || *AMER* to draw up a programme for [politics, etc.] || *barco abanderado en España* ship flying Spanish colours.

abanderizar *vt* to divide, to cause discord in *o* between.
◆ *vpr* to join (un partido).

abandonado, da *adj* abandoned || neglected; *tener un jardín muy abandonado* to have a very neglected garden || FIG negligent, neglectful (desidioso) | untidy; *una chica abandonada* an untidy girl || *AMER* depraved (depravado).

abandonar *vt* to leave (un lugar, algo); *abandonar la casa de sus padres* to leave home *o* one's parent's house || to abandon; *abandonar el barco* to abandon ship || to abandon, to desert; *abandonar a sus hijos* to abandon one's children || to desert, to forsake; *no me abandones* don't desert me; *la suerte nunca nos abandona* luck never forsakes us || to give up; *abandonar la carrera* to give up one's studies; *abandonar una idea* to give up an idea || FIG to neglect; *abandonar sus deberes* to neglect one's duties || to renounce, to relinquish (un privilegio, etc.).
◆ *vi* to give up, to withdraw (un deportista).
◆ *vpr* FIG to give way, to give in, to succumb, to yield; *abandonarse a la tentación* to give way to temptation | to give o.s. over to (al alcohol, al vicio, etc.) | to confide, to open one's heart; *abandonarse a su madre* to confide in one's mother, to abandon one's heart to one's mother.

abandonismo *m* defeatism.

abandonista *adj/s* defeatist; *política abandonista* defeatist policy.

abandono *m* abandoning, abandonment; *el abandono de un niño* the abandoning of a child || giving up; *el abandono de una idea, de una carrera* the giving up of an idea, of one's studies || neglect, dereliction; *el abandono de sus deberes* the neglect of one's duties || neglect (de uno mismo) || abandon, derelict state (de un edificio) || retirement; *el abandono de un ciclista* the retirement of a cyclist || FIG abandon (despreocupación) || — *con abandono* nonchalantly, casually || *ganar por abandono* to win by default.

abanicar *vt* to fan.
◆ *vpr* to fan o.s.

abanico *m* fan || tail [of a peacock] (del pavo real) || MAR derrick (cabria) || FIG range (de salarios) || — *en abanico* fan-shaped || *poner los naipes en abanico* to fan out one's cards.

abaniquear *vt* to fan.

abaniqueo *m* fanning.

abaniquero *m* fan manufacturer (fabricante) || fan dealer (vendedor).

abanto *m* ZOOL African vulture.
◆ *adj* simple, stupid (necio) || cowardly (toro).

abaratado, da *adj* cut-price, reduced in price; *géneros abaratados* cut-price goods, goods reduced in price.

abaratamiento *m* reduction in price; *el abaratamiento de un producto* the reduction in price of a product || *el abaratamiento de la vida* the fall in the cost of living.

abaratar *vt* to reduce *o* to cut the price of, to make cheaper, to reduce; *abaratar las frutas* to reduce the price of fruit || to reduce, to cut, to lower; *abaratar los precios* to lower prices.
◆ *vpr* to become cheaper, to come down in price (la vida) || to come down (precios).

abarca *f* sandal [worn by peasants].

abarcamiento *m* embracing.

abarcar *vt* to get *o* to put one's arms round, to embrace; *no puedo abarcar esta columna* I cannot get my arms round this column || FIG to embrace, to cover (comprender) || to be able to see *o* to take in; *desde la torre abarco todo el paisaje* from the tower I can see all the countryside || to undertake, to take on (varios trabajos) || *AMER* to monopolize (acaparar) || *quien mucho abarca poco aprieta* do not bite off more than you can chew.

abaritonado, da *adj* MÚS baritone.

abarloar *vt* MAR to bring alongside.

abarquillado, da *adj* warped (madera) || curled up, wrinkled (papel, cartón) || blistered (pintura) || buckled (chapa).

abarquillamiento *m* warping (de madera) || curling up, wrinkling (de papel, cartón) || blistering (de pintura) || buckling (de chapa).

abarquillar *vt* to warp (madera) || to curl up, to wrinkle (papel, cartón) || to blister (pintura) || to buckle (chapa).
◆ *vpr* to warp (madera) || to curl up, to wrinkle (papel, cartón).

abarraganamiento *m* concubinage.

abarraganarse *vpr* to live together.

abarrajado, da *adj* *AMER* shameless (desvergonzado) | debauched (disoluto).

abarrancamiento *m* bogging down (enlodamiento).

abarrancar *vt* to bog down.
◆ *vi* MAR to go *o* to run aground.
◆ *vpr* to get bogged down, to get stuck in the mud (atascarse) || FIG to get bogged down, to get *o* to be stuck (en un asunto).

abarrotado, da *adj* packed, full, crammed (atestado); *un autobús abarrotado* a packed bus; *una carta abarrotada de disparates* a letter full of *o* packed with nonsense.

abarrotar *vt* to put bars on (con barrotes) || MAR to stow (la carga) || to cram, to pack, to overload (atestar) || *AMER* to buy up (acaparar).
◆ *vpr* to fill up, to become packed || *AMER* to become cheaper, to go down in price (abaratarse) | to be over-plentiful (superabundar).

abarrote *m* MAR bundle.
◆ *pl* *AMER* groceries (artículos) | grocer's (shop) *sing*, grocery *sing* (tienda) | ironmonger's (shop) *sing*, ironmongery *sing* (ferretería).

abarrotería *f* *AMER* ⟶ **abarrote** *pl.*

abarrotero, ra *m/f* *AMER* grocer.

abasí *adj/s* Abbasid.

Abasidas *npr pl* HIST Abbasids.

abastardar *vi* to degenerate, to become bastardized.

abastecedor, ra *adj* providing, supplying.
◆ *m/f* supplier, purveyor || *AMER* butcher (carnicero).

abastecer* *vt* to supply, to provide; *abastecer un ejército de víveres* to supply an army with provisions, to supply provisions to an army.

abastecido, da *adj* supplied, provisioned; *un ejército bien abastecido* a well-supplied army || stocked; *una tienda bien abastecida* a well-stocked shop.

abastecimiento *m* provisioning, supplying (avituallamiento) || supply; *abastecimiento de aguas* supply of water, water supply.

abastero *m* *AMER* wholesale supplier, wholesaler.

abastionar *vt* to bastion.

abasto *m* provisioning, supplying (abastecimiento) || abundance, great amount || *AMER* slaughterhouse, abattoir (matadero) || — *dar abasto a* to supply || *no poder dar abasto* not to be able to keep up (sentido general); *tengo tantas cosas que hacer que no puedo dar abasto* I have so many things to do that I cannot keep up; not to be able to satisfy (demanda).
◆ *pl* provisioning *sing.*

abatanado, da *adj* fulled (el paño).

abatanador *m* fuller.

abatanar *vt* to full (el paño) || FIG to beat (golpear).

abatatar *vt* *AMER* FAM to intimidate, to frighten (amedrentar).
◆ *vpr* FAM to become lethargic (aplatanarse) || *AMER* FAM to become intimidated *o* frightened (acobardarse).

abate *m* (p us) father; *el abate Grégoire* father Grégoire.

abatí *m* *AMER* maize [*US* corn] | drink distilled from maize (bebida).

abatible *adj* folding (asiento, mesa).

abatido, da *adj* downcast, dejected, depressed, disheartened (desanimado); *estaba muy abatido por su desgracia* he was very depressed by his misfortune || abject, despicable (despreciable) || drooping; *párpados abatidos* drooping eyelids.

abatimiento *m* dejection, low spirits *pl*, depression (desánimo) || shame (cosa afrentosa) || MAR *abatimiento del rumbo* leeway.

abatir *vt* to knock *o* to pull down, to demolish (destruir); *abatir un edificio* to knock down a building || to fell, to cut down (árbol) || to take down (desmontar); *abatió la tienda de campaña* he took down the tent || to shoot down, to bring down (un pájaro, un avión) || FIG to depress, to dishearten, to get down (deprimir); *la adversidad nos abate a todos* adversity depresses us all *o* gets us all down | to lay low (por una enfermedad, de dolor) | to humiliate, to humble (una persona), to lower, to humble (orgullo, soberbia) || MAR to strike, to lower; *abatir banderas, velas* to strike the colours, the sails || to lay on the table, to show (juegos de naipes) || MAT *abatir una perpendicular* to drop *o* to draw a perpendicular.
◆ *vpr* to swoop, to sweep down (arrojarse); *el águila se abatió sobre su presa* the eagle swooped on its prey || FIG to humble o.s., to lower o.s. (humillarse) | to fall; *la desgracia se abatió sobre su familia* misfortune fell upon his family | to become disheartened *o* depressed *o* dejected *o* downcast, to lose heart (desanimarse).

abayado, da *adj* BOT bacciform, berry-shaped.

abazón *m* cheek pouch (de monos).

abdicación *f* abdication.

abdicar *vt* to abdicate, to abdicate from; *abdicó el trono en su hijo* he abdicated the throne *o* he abdicated from the throne in favour of his son || to give up (la corona) || to give up, to surrender (derechos) || to give up (ideas, principios).
◆ *vi* to abdicate (el rey).

abdomen *m* ANAT abdomen.

abdominal *adj* abdominal; *músculos abdominales* abdominal muscles.

abducción *f* abduction.

abductor *adj* ANAT abducent.
◆ *m* abductor.

abecé *m* ABC, alphabet (alfabeto) || FIG rudiments *pl*, basic steps *pl* || FIG *eso es el abecé* that's child's play | *no saber el abecé* not to know A from B.

abecedario *m* alphabet (alfabeto) || primer, spelling book (libro).

abedul *m* birch (árbol).

abeja *f* bee || — *abeja carpintera* carpenter bee || *abeja maesa* or *maestra* or *reina* queen bee || *abeja neutra* or *obrera* worker, worker bee.

abejarrón *m* bumblebee, humble-bee.

abejaruco *m* bee-eater (pájaro).

abejera *f* apiary (colmenar) || BOT balm.

abejero, ra *m/f* beekeeper, apiculturist, apiarist.
◆ *m* bee-eater (pájaro).

abejón *m* bumblebee, humble-bee (abejorro) || drone (zángano).

abejorreo *m* FAM buzzing, bumbling.

abejorro *m* bumblebee, humble-bee (insecto himenóptero) || cockchafer (insecto coleóptero) || FIG & FAM *ser un abejorro* to be a nuisance.

Abel *npr m* Abel.

abellacado, da *adj* wicked, mean, villainous.

abellacar *vt* to debase, to degrade.
◆ *vpr* to degrade o.s.

abellotado, da *adj* acorn-shaped.

abemolar *vt* to soften (la voz) || MÚS to flatten, to mark with a flat.

aberenjenado, da *adj* violet, egg-plant coloured (color) || egg-plant shaped (forma).

aberración *f* aberration.

aberrante *adj* aberrant.

aberrar *vi* to be mistaken.

abertura *f* opening, gap (boquete) || hole (agujero) || cove, creek (ensenada) || slit, crack (grieta) || pass (entre dos montañas) || aperture (del diafragma) || vent; *chaqueta con aberturas laterales* jacket with side vents || FIG openness, frankness (franqueza) || FIG *abertura de espíritu* broad-mindedness.

abertzale *m/f* Basque nationalist.

abestiarse *vpr* to become an animal *o* a brute.

abetal; abetar *m* fir wood (pequeño), fir forest (grande).

abeto *m* fir (árbol) || — *abeto blanco* or *albar* silver fir || *abeto falso* or *rojo* spruce.

abetunado, da *adj* very brown.

abetunar *vt* to polish, to clean (zapatos).

abierto, ta *adj* open; *el niño dormía con la boca abierta* the child was sleeping with his mouth open; *flor abierta* open flower || open, clear (terreno) || GRAM open; *vocal abierta* open vowel || INFORM open (fichero, etc.) || FIG open, frank, sincere; *una persona muy abierta* a very open person || — *abierto de par en par* wide-open, open wide || *a cielo abierto* open-cast (mina) || *a tumba abierta* flat out, a top speed (conducir) || MIL *ciudad abierta* open *o* unfortified city || *con las piernas abiertas* with one's legs apart || *con los brazos abiertos* with one's arms open wide || *dejar el grifo abierto* to leave the tap running, to leave the tap on || *herida abierta* open *o* gaping wound || FIG *quedarse con la boca abierta* to gape in amazement | *ver el cielo abierto* to see a way out.
◆ *m* AMER reclaimed land.

abigarrado, da *adj* multicoloured [US multicolored]; *una tela abigarrada* a multicoloured cloth || FIG motley, mixed; *una multitud abigarrada* a motley crowd.

abigarramiento *m* multicolouring [US multicoloring] || FIG motleyness, mixture.

abigarrar *vt* to mottle, to variegate.

abigeato *m* rustling, rustle.

ab intestato *loc lat* intestate.

abintestato *m* JUR intestate estate.

abisagrar *vt* to hinge.

abisal *adj* abyssal.

abiselar *vt* to bevel.

Abisinia *npr f* GEOGR Abyssinia.

abisinio, nia *adj/s* Abyssinian.

abismal *adj* abysmal.

abismar *vt* to throw into an abyss || FIG to humiliate, to humble (confundir).
◆ *vpr* to sink (en el mar) || FIG to get absorbed (en los pensamientos, en el trabajo) | to be plunged (en el dolor) || AMER to be amazed *o* astonished (asombrarse).

abismático, ca *adj* abysmal.

abismo *m* abyss, gulf || hell (infierno) || FIG abyss; *un abismo de dolor* an abyss of suffering | world of difference; *hay un abismo entre tus ideas y las mías* there is a world of difference between your ideas and mine | depth; *desde los abismos de la historia* from the depths of history | gulf; *la guerra abrió un abismo entre las dos naciones* the war opened a gulf between the two nations || FIG *estar al borde del abismo* to be on the brink of ruin.

abitar *vt* MAR to bitt.

Abiyán *n pr* GEOGR Abidjan.

abizcochado, da *adj* spongy.

abjuración *f* abjuration.

abjurar *vt/vi* to abjure, to forswear; *abjurar de su fe* to abjure one's faith.

ablación *f* MED ablation || GEOL wearing away, ablation.

ablandabrevas *m/f* FIG & FAM good-for-nothing.

ablandador, ra *adj* softening || FIG soothing.

ablandadura *f*; **ablandamiento** *m* softening || FIG soothing (acción de calmar) | dropping (del viento) | softening; *el ablandamiento de una dictadura* the softening of a dictatorship | moderation.

ablandar *vt* to soften; *ablandar cera* to soften wax || to melt (nieve) || to make tender (la carne) || to loosen (con un laxante) || FIG to soothe (calmar) | to move, to touch (conmover) | to soften up; *ablandó a sus padres* he softened his parents up | to moderate (harshness) || AMER AUT to run in.
◆ *vi* to drop (el viento) || to get milder (el tiempo).
◆ *vpr* to soften, to go soft || to get milder (el tiempo) || to drop (el viento) || to melt (nieve) || FIG to become *o* to turn soft, to soften.

ablande *m* AMER AUT running-in.

ablandecer *vt* to soften.

ablativo *m* GRAM ablative; *ablativo absoluto* ablative absolute.

ablepsia *f* MED ablepsia [loss of eyesight].

ablución *f* ablution (lavatorio).

ablusado, da *adj* bloused.

abnegación *f* abnegation, self-denial.

abnegado, da *adj* self-sacrificing, unselfish.

abnegarse* *vpr* to sacrifice o.s., to deny o.s.

abobado, da *adj* silly, stupid (tonto).

abobamiento *m* stupefaction (asombro) || silliness, stupidity (tontería).

abobar *vt* to stupefy (asombrar) || to make stupid (atontar).
◆ *vpr* to become stupid.

abocado, da *adj* medium-dry (jerez) || *estar abocado a la ruina* to be heading for *o* destined for ruin.

abocar *vt* to bring together the mouths [of two recipients] || to seize in one's mouth (coger con la boca).
◆ *vi* to arrive at, to come to; *abocar a una solución* to arrive at a solution.
◆ *vpr* to meet, to confer (reunirse).

abocardado, da *adj* bell-shaped, funnel-shaped, wide-mouthed.

abocardar *vt* to widen the mouth of, to widen the opening of.

abocardo *m* drill (barrena grande).

abocatero *m* avocado tree (aguacate).

abocelado, da *adj* torus-shaped.

abocetado, da *adj* rough (pintura) || rough-hewn (escultura).

abocetar *vt* to sketch; *abocetar un dibujo* to sketch a drawing.

abocinado, da *adj* trumpet-shaped (como una trompeta) || ARQ splayed (arco).

abocinamiento *m* widening.

abocinar *vt* to widen (un orificio).

abochornado, da *adj* FIG ashamed; *estoy abochornado con tu conducta* I am ashamed of your conduct.

abochornar *vt* to suffocate; *el calor nos abochorna* the heat is suffocating us || FIG to put to shame, to show up; *siempre intentas abochornarme delante de todos* you always try to show me up in front of everyone.
◆ *vpr* FIG to be ashamed (avergonzarse) || to blush (ruborizarse) || AGR to parch, to become parched (las plantas).

abofeteamiento *m* slapping || FIG insult.

abofetear *vt* to slap (dar bofetadas) || FIG to insult; *abofetear la moralidad* to insult morality.

abogacía *f* legal profession.

abogada *f* (woman) lawyer || FIG mediatrix, mediatress, patron saint (mediadora) | advocate (defensora).

abogaderas *f pl* AMER FAM irrational arguments.

abogadesco, ca; abogadil *adj* FAM characteristic of lawyers | pettifogging (despectivo).

abogadete; abogadillo *m* FAM pettifogger.

abogado *m* JUR lawyer, solicitor (consejero) | barrister [US attorney, lawyer] (en el tribunal) || FIG advocate, defender (defensor) | mediator, patron saint (intercesor) || — *abogado consultor* counsel || *abogado defensor* counsel for the defence, defending counsel, defence lawyer || *abogado del diablo* Devil's advocate || *abogado del Estado* public prosecutor [US attorney general] || *abogado de oficio* court-appointed counsel || FAM *abogado de secano* quack lawyer, pettifogger || *abogado fiscal* prosecuting counsel [US district attorney] || *ejercer de abogado* to be a lawyer, to practise law || *hacerse el abogado de* to advocate, to defend || *pasante de abogado* assistant lawyer.

abogar *vi* to plead; *abogar por* or *en* or *a favor de uno* to plead on s.o.'s behalf *o* for s.o. || FIG to mediate (mediar) | to advocate, to champion (defender).

abolengo *m* lineage, ancestry || *de abolengo* of noble *o* proud lineage (ilustre).

abolición *f* abolition.

abolicionismo *m* abolitionism.

abolicionista *adj/s* abolitionist.

abolir* *vt* to abolish.
— OBSERV *Abolir* is a defective verb used only in the forms whose endings begin with *i*: *abolí, aboliendo, abolido, aboliste, abolía, aboliera, aboliré, etc.*

abolsado, da *adj* baggy.

abolsarse *vpr* to pouch (la piel) || to be *o* to go baggy (tejido).

abollado, da *adj* dented; *una carrocería abollada* a dented bodywork || FIG penniless.

abolladura *f* bump (hacia afuera), dent (hacia adentro).

abollar *vt* to dent (chapa, etc.) || to emboss (como adorno).

abollonar *vt* to emboss.

abombado, da *adj* convex; *cristal abombado* convex pane of glass || AMER stupefied, stunned (atontado) || tipsy, fuddled (achispado).

abombar *vt* to make convex, to convex || FIG & FAM to stupefy, to stun (aturdir).
◆ *vpr* AMER to get tipsy *o* fuddled (emborracharse) | to stagnate (el agua) | to curdle (la leche) | to rot (pudrirse).

abominable *adj* abominable; *el abominable hombre de las nieves* the abominable snowman.

abominación *f* abomination.

abominar *vt* to detest, to abominate, to loathe; *abomino la injusticia* I detest injustice.
◆ *vi* to curse; *abominar de su suerte* to curse one's luck || to detest, to loathe.

abonable *adj* payable (pagadero) || AGR improvable (tierras).

abonado, da *adj* paid (pagado) || fertilized, manured || *abonado en cuenta* credited.
◆ *m/f* subscriber (de teléfono, de revista) || season ticket holder (para un espectáculo).
◆ *m* AGR fertilizing, manuring, manure spreading (estercolado) || INFORM subscriber.

abonador, ra *m/f* guarantor.
◆ *m* auger (de tonelero).
◆ *f* AGR fertilizer spreading machine, manure spreader.

abonamiento *m* → **abono.**

abonanzar *vi* MAR to abate, to calm down (calmarse).
◆ *vpr* to calm down.

abonar *vt* to pay; *abonar una gran cantidad* to pay a large amount; *abonar sus deudas* to pay one's debts || to credit (*en* to), to pay (*en* to) || to pay for (pagar una compra) || to take out a subscription for (s.o.) (a uno a un periódico, etc.) || to vouch for, to be guarantor of (salir fiador) || to vouch for, to guarantee (dar por cierto); *abono la certeza de lo que dijo* I vouch for the truth of what he said || to improve (mejorar) || AGR to fertilize, to manure, to dress (la tierra) || — FIG *abonar el terreno* to prepare the ground, to make the ground ready || *abonar en cuenta de* to pay into the account of, to credit to (s.o.'s account).
◆ *vi* to calm down (el mar).
◆ *vpr* to subscribe (a un periódico) || to buy a season ticket for (a un espectáculo).

abonaré *m* COM promissory note, I. O. U. (pagaré).

abonero *m* AMER hanker, pedlar.

abono; abonamiento *m* payment (pago) || AGR fertilizer (palabra general); *abonos nitrogenados* nitrate fertilizers | manure, muck (estiércol) | fertilizing, manuring, manure spreading (esparcimiento del abono) || subscription (a un periódico) || season ticket (para una temporada); *sacar un abono para las corridas* to buy *o* to take out a season ticket for the bullfights || guarantee (fianza) || improvement (mejora) || credit (en una cuenta) || AMER instalment, term payment || *en abono de* in support of (una idea).

aboquillado, da *adj* with a mouthpiece | widemouthed (abocardado) || bevelled, chamfered (achaflanado).

aboquillar *vt* to fit a mouthpiece to || to widen the mouth *o* opening of (abocardar) || to bevel, to chamfer (achaflanar).

abordable *adj* within everyone's means, reasonable; *precio abordable* price within everyone's means || which can be tackled (asunto) || approachable (persona) || accessible (lugar).

abordaje *m* MAR boarding || FIG approach || MAR *saltar al abordaje* to board a ship.

abordar *vt* to tackle, to approach (un asunto, problema) || to undertake, to get down to (tarea) || to approach, to accost (una persona) || MAR to come alongside (acercarse a) | to run foul of (chocar con) | to board (al enemigo).
◆ *vi* MAR to put in, to dock (llegar a puerto); *abordamos a Bilbao* we put in at Bilbao | to land (desembarcar); *abordar a* or *en una isla* to land on an island | to come alongside; *abordar al muelle* to come alongside the quay.
◆ *vpr* MAR to board (atacar) | to come alongside | to run foul of (chocar con).

aborigen *adj/s* native (indígena).
— OBSERV Las palabras inglesas *aborigine* y *aboriginal*, a pesar de tener los mismos sentidos que la palabra española *aborigen*, se emplean principalmente con relación a los indígenas de Australia.

aborrajarse *vpr* to dry prematurely (mieses).

aborrascado, da *adj* stormy (tiempo).

aborrascarse *vpr* to turn *o* to become stormy (el tiempo).

aborrecer* *vt* to hate, to abhor, to loathe, to detest; *aborrecer a su vecino* to hate one's neighbour || to abandon [nest or young] (los pájaros) || to annoy, to get on s.o.'s nerves (molestar).

aborrecible *adj* detestable, abhorrent, despicable, loathesome (detestable).

aborrecido, da *adj* detestable, loathed, hated || FIG bored, fed up (aburrido).

aborrecimiento *m* hatred, hate, loathing, abhorrence (odio) || disgust (repugnancia) || boredom (aburrimiento).

aborregado, da *adj* mackerel, covered with fleecy clouds || FIG like sheep.

aborregarse *vpr* to become covered with fleecy clouds (el cielo) || AMER FIG to get frightened (acobardarse).

aborricarse *vpr* to become coarse (embrutecerse).

abortar *vi* MED to miscarry, to have a miscarriage, to abort || FIG to fail, to abort, to miscarry; *la conspiración abortó* the conspiracy failed || *hacerse abortar* to have an abortion.
◆ *vt* FIG & FAM to come up with (algo extraordinario).

abortista *m/f* abortionist.

abortivo, va *adj* abortive.
◆ *m* abortifacient.

aborto *m* miscarriage (involuntario), abortion (voluntario) || FIG failure, miscarriage (fracaso) || FIG & FAM freak (persona) | abortion (cosa) || — *aborto ilegal* illegal abortion || *aborto provocado* induced abortion.

abotagado, da; abotargado, da *adj* swollen (hinchado); *me levanté con la cara abotargada* I got up with a swollen face.

abotagamiento; abotargamiento *m* swelling.

abotagarse; abotargarse *vpr* to swell, to swell up.

abotinado, da *adj* high-fronted (zapatos).

abotonador *m* buttonhook.

abotonadura *f* buttoning, fastening.

abotonar *vt* to button, to button up.
◆ *vi* to bud (plantas).
◆ *vpr* to do one's buttons up, to fasten one's buttons (persona) || to button (ropa).

abovedado, da *adj* vaulted, arched.
◆ *m* vaulting.

abovedar *vt* to arch, to vault.

aboyar *vt* MAR to buoy, to mark with buoys || to put floats on (las redes).

abozalar *vt* to muzzle, to put a muzzle on.

abra *f* MAR cove, bay, creek (ensenada) || dale (valle) || fissure, cleft (en el suelo) || AMER leaf (de puerta o ventana) | clearing (en un bosque).

abracadabrante *adj* strange, unusual, extravagant.
— OBSERV This word is a Gallicism and can be replaced by *extraordinario* or *extravagante*.

Abrahán *npr m* Abraham.

abrasado, da *adj* burnt.

abrasador, ra *adj* burning; *una pasión abrasadora* a burning passion.

abrasar *vt* to burn; *el sol abrasa* the sun is burning; *las llamas lo abrasaron todo* the flames burnt everything || AGR to scorch, to dry up (las plantas) || FIG to squander, to waste (la fortuna) | to shame, to put to shame, to make ashamed (avergonzar) || — *me abrasa la sed* I'm parched, I'm dying of thirst || *morir abrasado* to be burnt to death.
◆ *vpr* to burn; *el guisado se abrasó* the stew burnt; *abrasarse de* or *en amor* to burn with love || to be scorched (plantas) || — *abrasarse de calor* to be sweltering || *abrasarse de sed* to be dying of thirst.

abrasilado, da *adj* deep red.

abrasión *f* abrasion, graze || erosion (por el mar).

abrasivo, va *adj/sm* abrasive.

abrazadera *f* bracket, clasp.

abrazar *vt* to take in one's arms, to embrace || to hug, to clasp in one's arms; *el padre abrazó al niño* the father hugged the child, the father clasped the child in his arms || to enclose (rodear) || FIG to embrace, to comprise, to cover (comprender) | to embrace, to adopt (una causa, una religión).
◆ *vpr* to embrace.

abrazo *m* hug (con amistad), hug, embrace (con ternura) || — *abrazos* with love (en una carta) || *dar un abrazo* to hug, to embrace || *un (fuerte) abrazo de* best wishes from, kind regards (entre amigos), with love from, love (entre un hombre y una mujer o entre mujeres), with all my love (entre íntimos).

abreboca *m/f* AMER daydreamer, absent-minded person.

abrebotellas *m inv* bottle-opener.

abrecartas *m inv* letter opener, paper knife.

abrecoches *m inv* person who opens the car door for s.o. [doorman].

ábrego *m* south wind (viento del sur).

abrelatas *m inv* tin opener [US can opener].

abrevadero *m* drinking trough, water trough || watering place (natural) || AMER flooded mine.

abrevador, ra *adj* who waters, who gives water.
◆ *m* water trough, drinking trough (abrevadero).

abrevar *vt* to water, to give water to || TECN to soak [skins] || to water (regar).
◆ *vpr* to drink, to water (el ganado).

abreviación *f* shortening, abridgement (acción) || abridged text (texto abreviado).

abreviadamente *adv* in short, briefly.

abreviado, da *adj* abridged, shortened (un texto) || brief, short; *ésta es una explicación abreviada* this is a brief explanation.

abreviar *vt* to abridge, to shorten (un texto) || to shorten, to cut short (un plazo) || to cut short (una estancia) || to abbreviate (una palabra).

◆ *vi* to take less time || to be brief, to make it short (ser breve); *abrevia, que no tengo mucho tiempo* be brief, I have not got much time.

abreviatura *f* abbreviation; *cuadro de abreviaturas* table of abbreviations || *en abreviatura* abbreviated.

abriboca *adj inv* AMER open-mouthed, agape (boquiabierto).

abribonarse *vpr* to become a rascal *o* a scoundrel.

abridor, ra *adj* who opens (persona) || which opens (cosa).

◆ *m* opener || sleeper (arete de oro para las orejas) || freestone peach (melocotón).

abrigada *f*; **abrigadero** *m* shelter || MAR natural harbour, sheltered cove || AMER hideout (guarida).

abrigado, da *adj* sheltered, protected; *un lugar abrigado del viento* a place sheltered from the wind || wrapped up (persona); *iba muy abrigado para no coger frío* he was well wrapped up so as not to catch cold || cosy (confortable).

abrigaño *m* shelter || AGR matt, matting.

abrigar *vt* to shelter, to protect, to shield (proteger); *abrigar del viento* to shelter from the wind || FIG to harbour, to cherish, to foster; *abrigar una esperanza* to harbour a hope | to have, to harbour (una sospecha, duda) || to be warm, to keep one warm; *este jersey abriga mucho* this sweater is very warm *o* keeps one very warm || to wrap up; *abrígalo bien que hace mucho frío* wrap him up well because it is very cold || MAR to shelter.

◆ *vpr* to take shelter, to shelter; *abrigarse de la lluvia* to take shelter from the rain || to wrap o.s. up, to wrap up, to cover o.s. up (con prendas de vestir); *abrígate bien* wrap up well.

abrigo *m* shelter (refugio) || overcoat (prenda de hombre) || coat (de mujer); *abrigo de pieles* fur coat || FIG protection, shield, shelter (protección) || MAR natural harbour || — *al abrigo de* sheltered from, protected from (del viento, frío, etc.), safe from (del peligro), with *o* under the protection of (de la ley) || *de abrigo* warm; *prendas de abrigo* warm clothes; first-class, proper; *un tonto de abrigo* a first-class fool; to be avoided (de cuidado) || *fugarse al abrigo de la noche* to flee under cover of darkness.

ábrigo *m* south wind (viento sur).

abril *m* April || FIG springtime, youth || — *en abril, aguas mil* April showers bring May flowers || *una muchacha de quince abriles* a young girl of fifteen.

abrileño, ña *adj* April, spring; *una mañana abrileña* an April morning.

abrillantador *m* lapidary, polisher (persona) || polishing tool, burnisher (instrumento) || polish (producto).

abrillantar *vt* to polish, to burnish (pulir) || to cut (piedras preciosas) || FIG to enhance.

abrir *vt* to open (la puerta, un libro, los ojos, una carta, una cuenta, una herida, una negociación, el fuego) || to make; *abrir un hueco* to make a hole || to build, to make; *abrir una carretera, un túnel* to build a road, a tunnel || to dig, to make; *abrir un surco* to dig a trench || to lance (un absceso) || to dig, to sink (un pozo) || to split open; *abrir la cabeza a alguien con la espada* to split s.o.'s head open with one's sword || to put up, to open (paraguas) || COM to open; *abrir una cuenta* to open an account || to open (un establecimiento, un curso escolar, una suscripción) || to turn on (grifos) || FIG to open (la frontera, la universidad) | to whet (el apetito) | to head, to lead; *abrir el desfile* to head the procession || — FIG *abrir el ojo* to keep one's eyes open, to be careful || *abrir en canal un animal* to slit an animal open || FIG *abrir la mano* to be more lenient | *abrir los ojos* to keep one's eyes open (vigilante), to open one's eyes (*ante* to) (percatarse de algo) | *abrir un abismo entre* to open a gulf between || *abrir una puerta de par en par* to open a door wide || *abrir un libro* to cut the pages of a book (con cortapapel) || *a medio abrir* half-open || *en un abrir y cerrar de ojos* in the twinkling of an eye, in a wink, in a jiffy.

◆ *vi* to open up; *¡abre!* ¡open up!

◆ *vpr* to open (las flores, un paracaídas, las tiendas, la puerta) || to clear (el tiempo) || to burst (un absceso) || to sprain; *abrirse el tobillo* to sprain one's ankle || to split open; *abrirse la cabeza* to split open one's head || to look, to open (ventana) || to open (puerta); *puertas que se abren a la calle* doors which open onto the street || to confide (sincerarse); *abrirse con uno* to confide in s.o. || to open up (la tierra) || to spread out, to open out, to unfold (extenderse); *el paisaje se abría ante nosotros* the countryside spread out before us || AMER to leave, to go away (largarse) | to back down, to give up (rajarse) || — *abrirse camino* to make one's way, to force one's way (al andar), to go places, to get on well (en la vida) || *abrirse paso entre* to force *o* to fight one's way through (en una muchedumbre, etc.), to break through (las tropas) || *abrirse paso a codazos, a tiros* to elbow, to shoot one's way through || *abrirse paso en la vida* to make one's way in life (triunfar).

— OBSERV The past participle of *abrir* is irregular (*abierto, ta*).

abrochador *m* buttonhook.

abrochadura *f*; **abrochamiento** *m* buttoning (con botones) || fastening (con broches).

abrochar *vt* to button, to button up, to do up (cerrar con botones) || to fasten (con broche) || to tie (up), to do up (los zapatos) || to lace up (un corsé) || AMER to seize, to grasp (agarrar).

abrogación *f* abrogation, repeal.

abrogar *vt* to abrogate, to repeal (anular).

abrojal *m* thistle patch.

abrojo *m* BOT thistle || MIL caltrop.

◆ *pl* MAR reef *sing* || FIG pains (dolores).

abroncar *vt* FAM to tear a strip off [US to bawl out, to get mad at] (un superior a un inferior) | to boo, to whistle (abuchear) | to shame (avergonzar).

◆ *vpr* FAM to be ashamed (avergonzarse) | to get annoyed, to loose one's temper (enfadarse).

abroquelado, da *adj* shield-shaped || BOT peltate.

abroquelarse; embroquelarse *vpr* to shield o.s. || FIG to shield o.s., to defend o.s. (escudarse).

abrótano *m* BOT southernwood.

abrumado, da *adj* overwhelmed; *abrumado por tantas atenciones* overwhelmed by so much attention; *abrumado de trabajo* overwhelmed with work.

abrumador, ra *adj* overwhelming, exhausting (trabajo, calor) || overwhelming, crushing (derrota, mayoría) || overwhelming, damning (testimonio).

abrumar *vt* to overwhelm, to get on top of, to overcome (trabajo, preocupaciones, carga, años) || to overwhelm; *su noticia me abrumó* his news overwhelmed me; *abrumar a preguntas* to overwhelm with questions; *abrumar con atenciones* to overwhelm with attention.

◆ *vpr* to become foggy *o* misty.

abrupción *f* MED abruption [detachment].

abrupto, ta *adj* craggy, rugged (roca) || steep, sheer, abrupt (pendiente) || abrupt; *tono abrupto* abrupt tone.

abrutado, da *adj* brutish.

Abruzos *npr mpl* GEOGR Abruzzi.

absceso *m* MED abscess; *el absceso se ha abierto* the abscess has burst.

abscisa *f* MAT abscissa.

abscisión *f* MED abscission.

absentismo *m* absenteeism (de trabajadores) || landlord absenteeism (de terratenientes).

absentista *m* absentee landlord (terrateniente) || absentee (obrero).

ábsida *f*; **ábside** *m/f* ARQ apse || ASTR apsis.

absidal *adj* apsidal; *ornamentos absidales* apsidal decorations.

absidiola *f*; **absidiolo** *m* ARQ apsidiole, absidiole.

absintio *m* absinthe, absinth.

absolución *f* REL absolution (perdón); *el sacerdote me dio la absolución* the priest granted me absolution || JUR acquital (de un reo).

absoluta *f* dogmatic statement *o* assertion || MIL discharge (del servicio militar).

absolutamente *adv* absolutely, completely; *absolutamente absurdo* absolutely absurd || not at all (de ninguna manera) || *absolutamente nada* nothing at all.

absolutismo *m* absolutism.

absolutista *adj/s* absolutist.

absoluto, ta *adj* absolute; *poder absoluto* absolute power; *valor absoluto* absolute value || — *en absoluto* absolutely (enteramente); *está prohibido en absoluto* it is absolutely forbidden; not at all; *¿le gusta esta película? — en absoluto* do you like this film? — not at all || *nada en absoluto* nothing at all, not anything || *obtener la mayoría absoluta* to obtain an absolute majority.

absolutorio, ria *adj* JUR of not guilty, of acquittal; *veredicto absolutorio* verdict of acquittal.

absolvederas *f pl* FAM excessive leniency *sing* of a confessor || *tener buenas* or *bravas absolvederas* to be over-lenient.

absolver* *vt* REL to absolve (a un pecador) | JUR to declare not guilty, to acquit (declarar no culpable).

— OBSERV The past participle of *absolver* is *absuelto*.

absorbencia *f* absorbency.

absorbente *adj* absorbent || FIG absorbing, engrossing (trabajo, conversación) | demanding (que exige mucho tiempo).

◆ *m* absorbent.

absorber *vt* to absorb, to soak up; *la esponja absorbe el agua* sponge absorbs water || to suck in (aspiradora) || to attract, to catch; *este tejido absorbe mucho polvo* this material attracts a lot of dust || FIG to absorb, to take up (consumir); *la lectura absorbe todo mi tiempo* reading absorbs all my time || FIG *sus estudios le absorben tanto que nunca sale* he becomes so absorbed *o* engrossed in his studies that he never goes out, he spends so much time studying that he never goes out.

— OBSERV This verb has two past participles: *absorbido* and *absorto*. The first is used in compound tenses and the second as an adjective.

absorción *f* absorption || FIG engrossment, absorption || QUÍM absorption.

absortó, ta *adj* absorbed, engrossed; *absorto en su trabajo, en la lectura* absorbed in one's work, in a book || astonished, astounded; *estoy absorto ante sus progresos* I'm astonished at his progress || *absorto en sus pensamientos* deep in thought.

abstemio, mia *adj* temperate, teetotal, abstemious (p us) || *soy abstemio* I am a teetotaller.

◆ *m/f* teetotaller, abstainer.

abstención *f* abstention.

abstencionismo *m* abstentionism.

abstencionista *adj/s* abstentionist.

abstenerse* *vpr* to refrain; *abstenerse de intervenir* to refrain from intervening || to abstain; *abstenerse del vino, del tabaco* to abstain from wine, from smoking || to abstain (en una votación) || to give up, to stop; *abstente de decir tonterías* stop talking nonsense || *en la duda abstente* when in doubt, don't.

abstinencia *f* abstinence || REL fasting.

abstinente *adj* abstinent.

abstracción *f* abstraction || concentration, engrossment (concentración mental) || *hacer abstracción de* to leave aside.

abstracto, ta *adj* abstract; *pintura abstracta* abstract painting || GRAM abstract || — *en abstracto* in the abstract || *lo abstracto* the abstract.

abstraer* *vt* to abstract, to consider apart.

◆ *vi* *abstraer de* to leave aside.

◆ *vpr* to absorb o.s., to engross o.s.

— OBSERV This verb has two past participles: *abstraído* and *abstracto*. Only the first is used in compound tenses.

abstraído, da *adj* absorbed, engrossed; *estar abstraído por la lectura* to be engrossed in a book || FIG absentminded (distraído) || isolated (aislado).

abstruso, sa *adj* abstruse.

absuelto, ta *adj* REL absolved; *absuelto de todo pecado* absolved from all sin || JUR acquitted (un reo); *salir absuelto* to be acquitted.

absurdidad *f* absurdity.

absurdo, da *adj* absurd || — *lo absurdo* absurdity; *el colmo de lo absurdo* the height of absurdity; the realm of the absurd; *caer en lo absurdo* to fall into the realm of the absurd || *lo absurdo sería perder esta oportunidad* it would be absurd to waste this opportunity.

◆ *m* absurd thing, absurdity (disparate); *decir absurdos* to say absurd things.

abubilla *f* hoopoe (pájaro).

abuchear *vt* to boo, to jeer at; *los actores fueron abucheados* the actors were booed.

abucheo *m* FAM booing, jeering; *salió bajo un abucheo* he left amidst booing.

Abu Dhabi *n pr* GEOGR Abu Dhabi.

abuela *f* grandmother || FIG old woman (mujer vieja) || — FIG & FAM *¡cuéntaselo a tu abuela!* pull the other leg!, it's got bells on! [US tell it to the marines!] | *¡éramos pocos y parió la abuela!* that's all we needed! | *no tener* or *no necesitar abuela* not to be afraid of blowing one's own trumpet.

abuelastro, tra *m/f* father *o* mother of one's father-in-law *o* mother-in-law || stepgrandfather, step-grandmother.

abuelita *f* granny, grandma, nanny || *AMER* baby's bonnet.

abuelito *m* grandpa, grandad.

abuelo *m* grandfather; *sólo me queda un abuelo* I only have one grandfather left || FIG old man (anciano).

◆ *pl* grandparents || ancestors (antepasados); *nuestros abuelos eran muy valientes* our ancestors were very brave || FAM short hairs on the back of the neck (pelo).

abuhardillado, da *adj* with an attic *o* garret.

abulense *adj* [of *o* from] Ávila.

◆ *m/f* native *o* inhabitant of Ávila.

abulia *f* lack of willpower, abulia.

abúlico, ca *adj* lacking in willpower, abulic, weak-willed.

abulomanía *f* MED abulomania.

abultado, da *adj* bulky, big; *este paquete es muy abultado* this parcel is very bulky || thick; *labios abultados* thick lips || swollen; *tengo los labios abultados porque me ha picado una avispa* my lips are swollen because a wasp stung me || FIG exaggerated (exagerado) | overwhelming (abrumador).

abultamiento *m* bulkiness (bulto) || swelling (hinchazón) || enlargement (crecimiento) || FIG exaggeration.

abultar *vt* to enlarge (aumentar) || to swell (hinchar) || FIG to exaggerate; *abultar una historia* to exaggerate a story.

◆ *vi* to be bulky; *este ropero abulta mucho* this wardrobe is very bulky.

abundamiento *m* abundance || *a mayor abundamiento* furthermore (además), with all the more reason, with greater justification (con mayor razón).

abundancia *f* abundance, plenty || — *cuerno de la abundancia* horn of plenty || *de la abundancia del corazón habla la boca* what the heart feels the mind speaks || *en abundancia* in abundance, in plenty || FIG *nadar en la abundancia* to be rolling in money.

abundante *adj* abundant, in abundance, plentiful || *abundante en* abounding in.

abundar *vi* to be plentiful, to abound; *la plata abunda en México* silver is plentiful in Mexico || to be rich in; *México abunda en plata* Mexico is rich in silver || — *abundar en la opinión de* to share the opinion of, to agree completely with, to be in complete agreement with || *lo que abunda no daña* store is no sore.

abuñolar*; abuñuelar *vt* to make fritter-shaped || to deep-fry (huevos, buñuelos).

¡abur! *interj* FAM cheerio!, bye-bye!

aburguesado, da *adj* middle-class, bourgeois.

aburguesamiento *m* adoption of a bourgeois way of life.

aburguesarse *vpr* to become bourgeois.

aburrido, da *adj* bored, weary; *estoy aburrido* I am bored || boring, tiresome, tedious (que aburre); *es una película aburrida* it is a boring film || tired, sick, fed up (*fam*); *aburrido de la vida* tired of *o* sick of *o* fed up with life.

aburrimiento *m* boredom, weariness (estado de aburrido); *cara de aburrimiento* look of boredom || bore (cosa, persona) || — *¡qué aburrimiento!* what a bore! || *ser un aburrimiento* to be a bore, to be boring; *esta conferencia es un aburrimiento* this lecture is boring.

aburrir *vt* to bore, to weary; *aburrir con un largo discurso* to bore with a long speech.

◆ *vpr* to be *o* to get bored, to be *o* to get weary || FIG & FAM *aburrirse como una ostra* to be *o* to get bored to death, to be *o* to get bored stiff.

abusado, da *adj* *AMER* shrewd (astuto).

abusar *vi* to go too far || — *abusar de* to take advantage of; *abusar de un empleado* to take advantage of an employee; to abuse, to misuse (la autoridad), to abuse, to make unfair demands on, to impose upon (la amabilidad, la hospitalidad), to betray (la confianza de alguien), to waste (el tiempo), to go beyond the limits of (los derechos) || *abusar de la bebida, del tabaco,...* to drink, to smoke,... too much.

Abu Simbel *n pr* GEOGR Abu Simbel (emplazamiento).

abusivo, va *adj* excessive, exorbitant, extortionate; *precio abusivo* excessive price || wrong, improper (impropio).

abuso *m* abuse, misuse (de autoridad) || betrayal (de confianza) || misuse, improper use (de palabra) || — *abuso de la amabilidad de alguien* unfair demand on *o* imposition on s.o.'s kindness || *abuso deshonesto* indecent assault || *es un abuso cobrar tanto dinero* it is disgraceful to charge so much money.

abusón, ona *adj* FAM selfish (aprovechado) || barefaced, shameless (descarado).

◆ *m/f* selfish person, person who takes unfair advantage of others (aprovechado) || barefaced *o* shameless person (descarado).

abyección *f* abjection, wretchedness.

abyecto, ta *adj* abject, wretched; *condición abyecta* abject condition.

acá *adv* here, over here; *ven acá* come here; *vente para acá* come over here || — *acá y allá* or *acullá* here and there; *poner unas citas acá y allá* to put a few quotations in here and there || *¿de cuándo acá?* since when?, how long? || *de acá para allá* to and fro, up and down; *anduve de acá para allá* I walked up and down || *de ayer acá* since yesterday (desde ayer), recently, lately (recientemente) || *de... para acá* from here to; *de Londres para acá hay veinte millas* it is twenty miles from here to London || *desde entonces acá, de cuando acá* since then, from then on || *más acá* nearer (véase OBSERV); *ven más acá* come nearer || *más acá de* on this side of || *muy acá* very near || *no tan acá* not so near.

— OBSERV *Acá* is less precise than *aquí*; thus *acá* has degrees of comparison not possible with *aquí*. — In certain Latin American countries (Argentina, for example) *acá* is almost always used to translate *here*.

acabable *adj* finishable, which can be finished.

acabado, da *adj* finished, completed (concluido); *tenemos que devolver el trabajo acabado lo más pronto posible* we must give back the finished work as soon as possible || finished; *producto acabado* finished product || perfect (perfecto) || accomplished (persona); *un historiador acabado* an accomplished historian || spent, worn-out (viejo, agotado) || ruined (salud) || *yo, acabado de llegar, dije...* no sooner had I arrived than I said...

◆ *m* finish; *el acabado de un coche, de un cuadro* the finish of a car, of a picture.

acaballadero *m* stud farm.

acaballado, da *adj* horselike, horsy; *cara acaballada* horselike face.

acaballar *vt* to cover (el caballo).

acaballonador *m* AGR ridger.

acaballonar *vt* AGR to ridge (un campo).

acabamiento *m* finishing, completion (acción de acabar) || end, finish (término) || TECN finish.

acabañar *vi* to build a hut (los pastores).

acabar *vt* to finish, to complete (terminar); *he acabado el libro* I've finished the book || to finish off (rematar) || to put the finishing touches to (perfilar) || to finish; *no ha acabado de tomarse la leche* he has not finished drinking his milk || to complete; *acabar su ruina* to complete one's ruin || *AMER* to speak badly of, to gossip about (murmurar de) || *acabar sus días* to end one's days, to die.

◆ *vi* to finish, to end; *acabar en punta* to end *o* to finish in a point || to finish; *ven cuando acabes* come when you finish || to end up, to finish up; *acabar agotado* to end up exhausted || — FAM *¡acaba de parir!* let's have it!, spit it out! | *¡acabáramos!* at last!, finally! || *acabar con* to end with, to finish with (terminar con), to put paid to, to finish off; *por fin he acabado con este trabajo* I've finally put paid to this work; to finish with, to break with; *acabar con su no-*

vía to finish with one's fiancée; to get rid of, to finish with, to put an end to; *acabar con la influencia extranjera* to get rid of foreign influence; to be the end of, to finish, to kill; *este clima va a acabar conmigo* this climate will be the end of me || *acabar de* to have just; *acaba de morir* he has just died; *acababa de terminar su trabajo cuando...* he had just finished his work when...; to finish; *cuando acabe de hacer esto* when I finish doing this || *acabar de una vez* to finish once and for all || *acabar diciendo* to finish by saying (al final), to end up saying (en fin) || *acabar en* to end in || *acabar mal* to come to a nasty end || *acabar por* (seguido de infinitivo) in the end, finally, eventually; *acabó por reconocerlo* in the end he recognized him || *cuenta y no acaba* he never stops talking about it || *es cosa* or *es el cuento de nunca acabar* there's no end to it, it goes on and on || *no acabo de comprender* I don't quite *o* fully understand.

◆ *vpr* to finish, to end, to come to an end (terminarse); *se acabó el programa a las ocho* the programme finished at eight o'clock || to run out (gastarse); *se acabó el carbón* the coal has run out || to die (morirse) || — *se acabó* that's it, that's all || *se le acabó el dinero* his money ran out, he ran out of money || *se me acabó la paciencia* my patience has run out, I've lost my patience || *y san se acabó* and that's all there is to it, and that's the end of it.

acabestrar *vt* to accustom to a halter.

acabildar *vt* to rally together.

acabóse *m* FAM end, limit (el colmo); *esto fue el acabóse* this was the end.

acacalote *m* AMER cormorant (ave).

acacia *f* acacia || *acacia blanca* or *falsa* locust tree.

acacóyotl *m* AMER BOT Job's tears.

achachetear *vt* to slap.

acachetar *vt* TAUR to finish off [with a dagger].

academia *f* academy; *academia militar, naval* military, naval academy || academy, school; *academia de baile, de idiomas* dancing, language school || ARTES nude study || — *academia de música* conservatoire || *la Real Academia Española* the Spanish Academy.

academicismo *m* academicism.

académico, ca *adj* academic, academical || university; *título académico* university degree.

◆ *m/f* academician, member of an academy; *académico correspondiente* corresponding academician.

acaecer* *vi* to happen, to occur, to take place (ocurrir).

— OBSERV This verb is defective and exists only in the third person.

acaecimiento *m* event, happening, occurrence.

acalabazado, da *adj* pumpkin-shaped.

acalabrotar *vt* MAR to braid, to twist [into a cable].

acalefo *m* ZOOL acaleph.

◆ *pl* acalepha.

acalenturarse *vpr* to become feverish.

acalia *f* BOT marshmallow (malvavisco).

acaloradamente *adv* FIG heatedly, fiercely; *discutir acaloradamente* to argue heatedly || eagerly, keenly, enthusiastically; *defender acaloradamente un proyecto* to defend a plan keenly.

acalorado, da *adj* hot; *estoy acalorado por tanto esfuerzo* all this exertion has made me hot || FIG excited, worked up; *acalorado por la disputa* worked up by the argument | heated; *una discusión acalorada* a heated argument | eager, keen, enthusiastic; *es un defensor acalorado de mis ideas* he is a keen supporter of my ideas.

acaloramiento *m* heat (del tiempo, por el esfuerzo) || FIG enthusiasm, eagerness, keenness; *defender una causa con mucho acaloramiento* to defend a cause with great enthusiasm | heat; *en el acaloramiento de la pelea* in the heat of the battle.

acalorar *vt* to warm up, to make warm; *el correr me acalora* running makes me warm || FIG to excite, to arouse, to inflame; *acalorar a las masas* to excite the masses.

◆ *vpr* to get warm *o* hot || FIG to get excited, to get worked up (airarse) | to become enthusiastic, to become eager (entusiasmarse) | to become heated (una discusión).

acallar *vt* to quieten, to silence; *el orador no consiguió acallar a la multitud* the speaker was unable to quieten the crowd || FIG to ease (el dolor, la conciencia) | to appease (el hambre) | to silence (la crítica) | to pacify (a alguien que está enfadado).

acamar *vt* to flatten (las plantas).

acamastronarse *vpr* AMER to become sly *o* crafty.

acamellado, da *adj* camel-like.

acamellonar *vt* AMER AGR to ridge.

acampanado, da *adj* bell-shaped || wide-mouthed (vasija) || flared (ropa); *falda acampanada* flared skirt; *pantalones acampanados* flared trousers.

acampanar *vt* to shape like a bell || to flare (costura).

◆ *vpr* to become bell-shaped.

acampar *vt* to encamp, to camp; *acampar tropas en el valle* to encamp troops in the valley.

◆ *vi* to camp, to encamp; *acampar en la playa* to camp on the beach.

◆ *vpr* to camp, to encamp.

acanalado, da *adj* grooved (con estrías) || ARQ fluted; *columna acanalada* fluted column || ribbed; *calcetines acanalados* ribbed socks.

◆ *m* → **acanaladura.**

acanalador *m* TECN grooving plane (de carpintero).

acanaladura *f*; **acanalado** *m* groove (ranura) || ARQ fluting, flute.

acanalar *vt* to groove || ARQ to flute.

acanallado, da *adj* base, low, disreputable.

acanallar *vt* to debase, to drag down (*fam*).

◆ *vpr* to become debased, to go to the dogs (*fam*).

acanelado, da *adj* cinnamon-coloured (color) || cinnamon-flavoured (sabor).

acantilado, da *adj* steep, sheer, precipitous (abrupto) || shelving (fondo del mar) || rocky (rocoso).

◆ *m* cliff; *los acantilados de Dover* the cliffs of Dover || steep slope (pendiente).

acanto *m* ARQ & BOT acanthus.

acantonamiento *m* MIL cantonment, quarters *pl* (sitio) | quartering (acción).

acantonar *vt* MIL to quarter.

acantopterigios *m pl* ZOOL acanthopterygii.

acantosis *f* MED acanthosis.

acaobado, da *adj* mahogany (color).

acaparador, ra *adj* monopolistic || FIG acquisitive (instinto).

◆ *m/f* monopolist, monopolizer || hoarder (de géneros).

acaparamiento *m* monopolizing || monopolizing, cornering (mercado, ventas) || hoarding (existencias) || monopolizing, commanding (de la atención).

acaparar *vt* to monopolize || to monopolize, to corner (el mercado, las ventas) || to hoard (las existencias) || to monopolize, to command (la atención).

acaparrosado, da *adj* copper-coloured, coppery.

acápite *m* AMER paragraph || AMER *punto acápite* full stop, new paragraph [US period, new paragraph].

acaponado, da *adj* effeminate; *voz acaponada* effeminate voice || castrated (capado).

acaramelado, da *adj* caramelled, caramel-covered || caramel-coloured (color) || FIG overpolite (obsequioso) | syrupy, sugary, sickly; *una voz acaramelada* a syrupy voice || FIG *estar acaramelados* to be starry-eyed (novios).

acaramelar *vt* to caramel, to coat with caramel.

◆ *vpr* FIG & FAM to be sugar-sweet (ser muy obsequioso) | to gaze lovingly at each other (mirar con cariño).

acardenalar *vt* to beat black and blue, to cover with bruises, to bruise.

◆ *vpr* to become covered with bruises, to turn black and blue, to get bruised.

acardenillarse *vpr* to become covered with verdigris.

acariciante *adj* caressing.

acariciar *vt* to caress, to fondle (personas) || to stroke (animales) || to brush (rozar) || FIG to cherish, to harbour; *acariciar grandes ambiciones* to cherish great ambitions | to have in mind (proyectos, ideas).

acáridos *m pl* ZOOL acaridae.

acarminado, da *adj* crimson, carmine.

acarnerado, da *adj* with a sheep-like head (caballo).

acarralar *vt* to catch (un hilo, una tela) || to ladder (una media).

acarreador, ra *adj* transporting, conveying.

◆ *m/f* transporter, conveyor.

◆ *m* haulage, contractor, haulier.

acarreamiento *m* → **acarreo.**

acarrear *vt* to transport, to convey, to carry, to haul (llevar) || to carry (arrastrar) || to carry along (un río) || FIG to cause, to bring about, to bring; *el terremoto acarreó la ruina del país* the earthquake brought about the country's ruin.

acarreo; acarreamiento *m* transporting, conveying, carrying (transporte) || haulage, transport costs *pl* (precio de transporte) || AGR bringing-in (cosechas) || GEOL alluvium (arrastre) || *tierras de acarreo* alluvium.

acarroñarse *vpr* (ant) to decay || AMER FAM to get scared, to turn chicken (acobardarse).

acartonado, da *adj* cardboard-like || FIG & FAM wizened; *una cara acartonada* a wizened face.

acartonarse *vpr* to go stiff *o* hard || FIG & FAM to become wizened.

acasamatado, da *adj* casamated.

acaso *m* chance.

◆ *adv* perhaps, maybe; *acaso venga* perhaps he will come || (ant) by chance (por casualidad) || — *¿acaso...?* by any chance...?; *¿acaso ha sido él?* was it he by any chance? || *al acaso* to chance; *esta decisión no hay que dejarla al acaso* this decision must not be left to chance || *por si acaso* in case, just in case; *me llevo el paraguas por si acaso* I am taking my umbrella just in case || *si acaso* if; *si acaso llueve, espérame dentro* if it rains *o* if it should rain, wait for me inside || *probablemente no podré ir de veraneo, si acaso en septiembre* I shall probably not be able to take any summer holidays, but if I do, it will be in September.

acatable *adj* worthy of respect.

acatadamente *adv* with respect.

acatador, ra *adj* respectful.

acatamiento *m* respect (a una persona) || observance, respect; *acatamiento de las leyes* observance of the law.

acatar *vt* to respect, to heed; *acatar los consejos de los mayores* to respect the advice of one's elders || to observe, to respect; *acatar la ley* to observe the law || AMER to notice (notar).

acatarrarse *vpr* to catch a cold || AMER FAM to get drunk.

acaudalado, da *adj* rich, wealthy (rico).

acaudalar *vt* to accumulate, to amass.

acaudillador, ra *adj* (p us) commanding.
◆ *m/f* leader, commander.

acaudillamiento *m* leadership, command.

acaudillar *vt* to lead, to command.

acaule *adj* BOT acaulescent, acauline.

acayú *m* AMER mahogany (caoba).

acceder *vi* to agree, to accede, to consent; *accedió a recibirnos* he agreed to receive us || to accede (al trono, a los honores).

accesibilidad *f* accessibility.

accesible *adj* accessible; *montaña accesible* accessible mountain || approachable; *un jefe muy accesible* a very approachable boss.

accesión *f* agreement, consent (consentimiento) || accession (al poder) || JUR accession || MED attack (de fiebre).

accésit *m* honourable mention, accessit.
— OBSERV According to the Spanish Academy the plural of this word is *accésit,* but *accésits* is often found.

acceso *m* access; *tener acceso al jardín* to have access to the garden || accession (al poder) || access, approach (camino) || approach (de un avión) || sexual intercourse || MED access (de fiebre) || fit, attack (de tos, de locura, de ira) || FIG fit, moment (de generosidad) | outburst, fit, outbreak; *acceso de fanatismo* outburst of fanaticism || — INFORM *acceso aleatorio* random access | *acceso directo* direct access | *acceso secuencial* sequential access.

accesoria *f* outbuilding, annexe.

accesorio, ria *adj* accessory || *gastos accesorios* incidental expenses, contingencies.
◆ *m* accessory; *accesorios de automóvil* car accessories.
◆ *pl* TEATR props, properties.

accesorista *m/f* TEATR property man, property woman.

accidentado, da *adj* uneven (terreno) || FIG troubled, agitated; *una vida accidentada* a troubled life | eventful (complicado) || injured (persona) || damaged (coche).
◆ *m/f* accident victim.

accidental *adj* accidental, unintentional (involuntario) || chance, fortuitous, unexpected (casual).
◆ *m* MÚS accidental.

accidentarse *vpr* to have an accident, to be involved in an accident.

accidente *m* accident; *accidente de carretera* road accident; *sufrir un accidente* to have an accident || GEOGR unevenness, irregularity (del terreno) || MED faint (desmayo) || GRAM accidence || MÚS accidental || accident (cosa no esencial) || — *accidente de trabajo* or *laboral* industrial accident || *por accidente* by accident, accidentally.

acción *f* action (en general); *la acción del ácido sobre los metales* the action of acid on metals || deed, act; *ejecutar una buena acción* to do a good deed || COM share; *acción nominal, al portador* registered, bearer share || JUR action || TEATR acting (de un actor) | action (de una obra) || MIL action, fighting (combate) || — *acción de gracias* thanksgiving || *de acción retardada* delayed-action (mecanismo) || JUR *ejercitar una acción* to bring an action || *esfera de acción* field of action || *ganar a uno la acción* to beat s.o. to it || *hombre de acción* man of action || *radio de acción* range of action, operating range || *unir la acción a la palabra* to suit the action to the word.
◆ *pl* COM shares, stock *sing,* stocks; *tengo acciones en una compañía* I hold stock in a company.
◆ *interj* CINEM action!

accionamiento *m* working.

accionar *vt* to work, to actuate (una palanca) || to drive, to work (una máquina) || AMER JUR to bring an action against.
◆ *vi* to gesticulate.

accionariado *m* shareholders *pl,* stockholders *pl.*

accionista *m/f* COM shareholder, stockholder; *accionista beneficiario* preference shareholder.

Accra *n pr* GEOGR Accra.

acebal *m;* **acebada** *f;* **acebado** *m* holly thicket.

acebo *m* BOT holly, holly tree.

acebollado, da *adj* affected with ring shake (madera).

acebolladura *f* ring shake, cup shake.

acebrado, da *adj* striped.

acebuchal *m* grove of wild olive trees.

acebuche *m* wild olive tree.

acebuchina *f* wild olive.

acecinar *vt* to cure (la carne).
◆ *vpr* FIG to become wizened.
— OBSERV Do not confuse with *asesinar* (to assasinate).

acechadera *f* hiding place.

acechanza *f* → **acecho.**
— OBSERV Do not confuse with *asechanza* (ambush).

acechar *vt* to watch (observar) || to lie in wait for (esperar) || to stalk (un animal).

acecho *m;* **acechanza** *f* watching, observation || — *cazar al acecho* to stalk || *estar al acecho* to be on the watch *o* on the lookout.

acedar *vt* to turn sour, to sour (agriar) || FIG to sour, to embitter.
◆ *vpr* to turn sour, to become sour (ponerse agrio) || to wither (ajarse).
— OBSERV Do not confuse with *asedar* (to soften).

acedera *f* BOT sorrel.

acederaque *m* cinnamon tree (árbol).

acederón *m* type of sorrel (planta).

acedía *f* sourness || acidity (en el estómago) || FIG sourness, harshness, unpleasantness (desabrimiento) || withered state (de las plantas) || ZOOL plaice (pez).

acedo, da *adj* sour (ácido) || FIG sour, harsh, unpleasant (carácter).

acéfalo, la *adj* acephalous (sin cabeza) || FIG leaderless.

aceitada *f* olive oil cake (torta de aceite).

aceitado *m* oiling.

aceitar *vt* to oil || CULIN to add oil to.

aceitazo *m* thick oil.

aceite *m* oil; *aceite de oliva, de cacahuete* olive, groundnut oil; *aceite de motor* engine oil || — *aceite alcanforado* camphorated oil || *aceite bruto* crude oil (petróleo) || *aceite de germen de trigo* wheat-germ oil || *aceite de hígado de bacalao* cod-liver oil || *aceite de linaza* linseed oil || *aceite de ricino* castor oil || *aceite de vitriolo* oil of vitriol || *aceite lampante* paraffin oil [*US* kerosene] || *aceite pesado* heavy oil || *aceite secante* siccative oil || *aceite vegetal* vegetable oil || FIG *balsa de aceite* millpond | *echar aceite al fuego* to add fuel to the fire, to pour oil on the flames | *extenderse como mancha de aceite* to spread like wildfire.

aceitera *f* oil bottle (vasija para el aceite) || oilcan (alcuza).

aceitería *f* oilshop.

aceitero, ra *adj* oil; *producción aceitera* oil production.
◆ *m* oil seller.

aceitón *m* thick oil || oil sediment, dregs *pl* (impurezas).

aceitoso, sa *adj* oily || *lo aceitoso* oiliness.

aceituna *f* olive; *aceituna rellena* stuffed olive || — *aceituna gordal* queen olive || *aceituna picudilla* crescent olive.

aceitunada *f* olive harvest.

aceitunado, da *adj* olive; *tiene una tez aceitunada* he has an olive complexion.

aceitunero, ra *m/f* olive seller (que las vende) || olive harvester (que coge aceitunas).
◆ *m* olive store.

aceituno, na *adj* AMER olive, olive-coloured.
◆ *m* olive tree (árbol) || *aceituno silvestre* wild olive tree.

aceleración *f* acceleration || FIG speeding up || AUT *poder de aceleración* acceleration.

aceleradamente *adv* quickly, rapidly, speedily.

acelerado, da *adj* quick, rapid, fast; *paso acelerado* fast pace || FÍS accelerated; *movimiento acelerado* accelerated movement.
◆ *f* acceleration.
◆ *m* CINEM quick motion.

acelerador, ra *adj* accelerating.
◆ *m* accelerator || *acelerador nuclear* or *de partículas* nuclear *o* particle accelerator.

aceleramiento *m* acceleration.

acelerar *vt/vi* to accelerate || FIG to speed up || *acelerar el paso* to quicken one's pace.
◆ *vpr* to hurry, to hasten.

aceleratriz *adj f* accelerating; *fuerza aceleratriz* accelerating force.

acelerón *m* sudden acceleration || — *dar acelerones al motor* to rev the engine || *dar un acelerón* to put one's foot down.

acelga *f* beet (planta) || FAM *cara de acelga* dismal face, face a mile long (mal humor), washed-out face (por falta de salud).

acémila *f* mule, pack animal || FAM ass (persona ruda).

acemilero *m* mule driver, muleteer.

acemita *f* bran bread.

acemite *m* bran mixed with flour.

acendrado, da *adj* pure, untarnished; *amor acendrado* pure love.

acendramiento *m* refining, purifying.

acendrar *vt* to refine (metales) || FIG to purify (purificar).

acento *m* accent; *«ático» lleva acento ortográfico* «ático» has a written accent || accent, stress, emphasis; *el acento cae en la última sílaba* the stress is on the last syllable || accent (manera de pronunciar); *acento andaluz* Andalusian accent || MÚS accent || — *acento agudo* acute accent || *acento circunflejo* circumflex accent || *acento grave* grave accent || *acento ortográfico* written accent || *acento tónico* tonic accent, stress.

acentuación *f* accentuation, stress.

acentuadamente *adv* markedly, clearly; *tendencia acentuadamente conservadora* clearly conservative tendency.

acentuado, da *adj* accentuated, with an accent (con acento gráfico); *letra acentuada* accentuated letter, letter with an accent || stressed, accentuated (con acento tónico); *sílaba acentuada* stressed syllable || marked, strong, notable, emphasized; *una tendencia social muy acentuada* a very marked social tendency.

acentuar *vt* to accent, to put an accent on (con acento gráfico) || to stress, to accentuate, to accent (con acento tónico) || FIG to accentuate, to accent, to emphasize, to highlight; *acentuar el carácter español de algo* to emphasize the Spanish character of sth.
◆ *vpr* to have the accent, to be stressed *o* accentuated || FIG to become noticeable, to increase (aumentar) || to be heightened (*con* by).

aceña *f* watermill.

aceñero *m* miller.

acepar *vi* to take root (arraigar).

acepción *f* meaning, sense, acceptation (significado); *una palabra con muchas acepciones* a word with many meanings || preference (de personas) || *sin acepción de personas* without respect of persons.

acepilladora *f* TECN planing machine, planer (máquina).

acepilladura *f* ⟶ **cepillado.**

acepillar *vt* ⟶ **cepillar.**

aceptabilidad *f* acceptability.

aceptable *adj* acceptable; *una proposición aceptable* an acceptable suggestion || passable, acceptable; *un producto aceptable* a passable product.

aceptación *f* acceptance (acción de aceptar) || approval (aprobación) || success; *tener poca aceptación* to have little success.

aceptador, ra; aceptante *adj* who accepts, accepting.
◆ *m/f* COM acceptor.

aceptar *vt* to accept; *aceptar una invitación* to accept an invitation; *aceptar una letra de cambio* to accept a bill of exchange || *aceptar hacer algo* to agree to do sth., to undertake to do sth.

aceptor *m* COM acceptor.

acequia *f* irrigation ditch, irrigation channel (para el riego) || *AMER* stream (arroyo).

acera *f* pavement [*US* sidewalk] || side of the street; *la acera derecha* the right-hand side of the street || ARQ face (paramento) || FAM *ser de la acera de enfrente* to be queer, to be gay (ser homosexual).

acerado, da *adj* steel (de acero) || steely (parecido al acero) || cutting (cortante) || FIG biting, cutting, caustic (mordaz); *una frase acerada* a biting phrase.
◆ *m* TECN steeling.

acerar *vt* to steel (cubrir de acero) || to turn into steel; *acerar el hierro* to turn iron into steel || FIG to strengthen (fortalecer) | to put an edge on, to make biting (hacer mordaz) || to build a pavement on (poner acera) || ARQ to face.

acerbidad *f* harshness, acerbity.

acerbo, ba *adj* sour (sabor) || bitter, scathing, harsh (mordaz); *tono acerbo* harsh tone.

acerca de *adv* about; *ha escrito un libro acerca de Cervantes* he has written a book about Cervantes.

acercamiento *m* approach || bringing together, reconciling (de dos personas) || coming together || nearness, closeness (de dos cosas) || rapprochement (entre estados).

acercar *vt* to draw up, to bring near, to bring up; *acerca tu silla a la mesa* bring your chair near to the table || to bring nearer (poner más cerca); *acerca tu silla a la mía* bring your chair nearer to mine || to bring over; *acerca aquella silla* bring that chair over || FIG to draw *o* to bring together; *las medidas acercarán a los pueblos* the measures will bring the nations together | to bring nearer; *esto nos acerca a la solución* this brings us nearer to the solution || FAM to pass, to give; *acércame ese libro* pass me that book | to drop; *¿puedes acercarme a mi casa?* can you drop me at my house?
◆ *vpr* to approach, to draw near; *el ejército se acercó a la ciudad* the army approached the city; *acercarse a la edad del retiro* to approach retirement age || to go up, to go over; *me acerqué a él* I went up to him || to come over, to come up, to approach; *se acercó a mí en la calle* he came up to me in the street || to lean towards (aproximarse mucho) || FIG to approach, to border on; *una doctrina que se acerca al existencialismo* a doctrine which approaches existentialism || FAM to drop in; *acércate a mi casa esta tarde* drop in at my house this evening.

acería *f* steelworks *pl*, steel mill.

acerico; acerillo *m* pincushion (almohadilla para alfileres).

acerino, na *adj* POÉT steellike, steely.

acero *m* steel; *acero inoxidable* stainless steel; *acero colado* cast steel || FIG sword, steel (espada) || — *acero dulce, duro* soft, hard steel || FIG *cruzar el acero* to cross swords.

acerola *f* BOT haw (fruto).

acerolo *m* BOT hawthorn.

acérrimo, ma *adj* FIG staunch, out-and-out; *un acérrimo partidario* a staunch supporter.
— OBSERV This adjective is the superlative form of *acre*, and is used only in its figurative sense.

acerrojar *vt* to bolt.

acertado, da *adj* right, correct (opinión) || wise, fitting; *no sería muy acertado que fueses a verle ahora* it wouldn't be very wise for you to go and see him now || fitting, apt (comentario) || skilful, clever (hábil); *decisión acertada* clever decision || good; *una idea muy acertada* a very good idea || well chosen (color) || well done; *es muy acertada la disposición de este libro* the layout of this book is very well done || *lo acertado es marcharse ahora* it is best to leave now.

acertante *adj* winning; *quiniela acertante* winning coupon.
◆ *m/f* winner; *ha habido cuatro acertantes* there were four winners.

acertar* *vt* to hit (el blanco) || to guess, to get right (adivinar); *a que no lo aciertas* I bet you don't get it right || to find (encontrar).
◆ *vi* to guess right, to get right; *no acierto con la solución* I can't get the answer right || to be right, to hit the nail on the head, to guess right; *has acertado* you are right || to succeed, to manage; *acertó a abrir la puerta* he succeeded in opening the door, he managed to open the door || to find, to hit on; *has acertado con el color que quería* you've hit on the colour I wanted || to do right, to do the right thing; *acertaste en marcharte* you did right in leaving || to happen; *acertó a pasar un soldado* a soldier happened to pass.

acertijo *m* riddle.

aceruelo *m* pincushion (acerico) || small saddle (silla de montar).

acervo *m* pile, heap (montón) || common property; *el acervo familiar* the common property of the family || FIG wealth, riches *pl*, patrimony; *el acervo cultural* cultural wealth.

acetato *m* QUÍM acetate.

acético, ca *adj* QUÍM acetic; *ácido acético* acetic acid.

acetificar *vt* QUÍM to acetify.

acetileno *m* QUÍM acetylene.

acetilo *m* QUÍM acetyl.

acetona *f* QUÍM acetone.

acetonuria *f* MED acetonuria.

acetosa *f* BOT sorrel.

acetre *m* (p us) small bucket || REL portable stoup (para agua bendita).

acetrinar *vt* to make sallow.

aciago, ga *adj* unlucky, fateful, black; *aquél fue un día aciago para mí* that was a black day for me || ill-fated, unlucky; *una persona aciaga* an ill-fated person.

acial *m* barnacle (para caballos) || *AMER* whip.

aciano *m* BOT cornflower.

acíbar *m* BOT aloe || aloes *pl* (jugo) || FIG bitterness || FIG *amargo como el acíbar* as bitter as gall.

acibarar *vt* to add aloes to || FIG to embitter, to make bitter (a una persona) | to make bitter, to make unpleasant, to make a misery; *acibararle a uno la vida* to make s.o.'s life a misery.

acicalado, da *adj* polished (armas) || dressed up, smart, dressed to kill (*fam*), dressed up to the nines (*fam*) (muy vestido); *siempre va muy acicalado* he's always dressed up || well groomed (pelo, etc.) || done up; *el burro está acicalado para la feria* the donkey is done up for the fair.
◆ *m* polishing.

acicalamiento *m* polishing (armas) || dressing up (vestido) || grooming (del pelo).

acicalar *vt* to polish (armas) || FIG to dress up, to deck out (en el vestido) | to groom (el pelo) | to do up (animales y cosas) | to sharpen (el espíritu).
◆ *vpr* to get dressed up, to deck o.s. out (vestirse) || to groom o.s. (el pelo).

acicate *m* spur || FIG stimulus, incentive, spur; *el premio le sirve de acicate* the prize is an incentive to him.

acicatear *vt* to stimulate, to spur on (animar).

acíclico, ca *adj* acyclic.

acidez *f* sourness, tartness || MED acidity (del estómago) || QUÍM acidity.

acidificación *f* acidification.

acidificar *vt* to acidify.
◆ *vpr* to acidify.

acidímetro *m* acidimeter.

ácido, da *adj* sour, tart; *sabor ácido* sour flavour || FIG bitter, harsh; *hablar en un tono ácido* to speak in a harsh tone.
◆ *m* QUÍM acid; *ácido carbónico* carbonic acid; *ácido cianhídrico* hydrocyanic acid; *ácido clorhídrico* hydrochloric acid; *ácido desoxirribonucleico* desoxirribonucleic acid; *ácido lisérgico* lysergic acid; *ácido nítrico* nitric acid; *ácido nucleico* nucleic acid; *ácido sulfúrico* sulphuric acid; *ácido sulfuroso* sulphurous acid; *ácidos grasos insaturados* unsaturated fatty acids.

acidómetro *m* FÍS acidometer.

acidosis *f* MED acidosis.

acidular *vt* to acidulate.

acierto *m* success; *esta idea ha sido un acierto* this idea has been a success || good choice; *el título de este libro fue un acierto* the title of this book was a good choice || right answer (en un cuestionario) || good idea; *ha sido un acierto el haber venido hoy* it was a good idea to come today || coincidence (casualidad) || wisdom (cordura) || skill (habilidad); *el delantero remató con mucho acierto* the forward shot with great skill || *obrar con acierto* to do well.

ácigos *adj/sf* ANAT azygous.

acije *m* QUÍM vitriol, copperas.

ácimo *adj* unleavened; *pan ácimo* unleavened bread.

acimut *m* ASTR azimuth.

ación *m* stirrup strap.

acionera *f* AMER stirrup strap ring.

acirate *m* ridge of earth (caballón entre dos campos).

aclamación *f* acclamation, acclaim.

aclamar *vt* to acclaim, to applaud; *aclamar al rey* to acclaim the king || to acclaim, to name (nombrar); *le aclamaron jefe* they acclaimed him leader.

aclaración *f* explanation; *al día siguiente, el autor publicó una aclaración a su artículo* the next day the author published an explanation of his article || note, explanation; *una aclaración al margen* a note in the margin.

aclarado *m* rinsing, rinse.

aclarar *vt* to make lighter, to lighten (un color, un líquido) || to thin out (un bosque, las filas) || to rinse (la ropa) || to clear (la voz) || to thin down (una salsa) || FIG to throw light on, to clarify, to make clear; *un ejemplo aclarará el problema* an example will throw light on the problem *o* will make the problem clear | to resolve, to remove (dudas) | to explain, to make clear; *voy a aclarar lo dicho anteriormente* I am going to explain what was said before | to make it clear; *te aclaro que ya no debes salir* I'm making it clear that you must not go out.
◆ *vi* to clear (el tiempo) || to break (el día) || AMER to clear (un líquido).
◆ *vpr* to clear (la voz, el tiempo, líquidos) || to become clear (ideas, dudas, problemas, etc.) || FIG to explain o.s.; *aclárate* explain yourself | to understand each other; *estas dos personas no se aclaran* these two people do not understand each other | to recover, to come round; *después del puñetazo que había recibido tardó mucho en aclararse* after the punch he had received he took a long time to come round | to make out, to understand; *no consigo aclararme en este asunto* I can't make this matter out || AMER to be broke (no tener dinero).

aclaratorio, ria *adj* explanatory; *nota aclaratoria* explanatory note.

aclavelado, da *adj* carnation-like.

aclimatable *adj* able to be acclimatized [US able to be acclimated].

aclimatación *f* acclimatization [US acclimation].

aclimatar *vt* to acclimatize [US to acclimate].
◆ *vpr* to become acclimatized [US to become acclimated].

aclorhidria *f* MED achlorhydria.

aclorhídrico, ca *adj* achlorhydric.

acné *f* MED acne.

acobardamiento *m* loss of nerve.

acobardar *vt* to intimidate, to frighten, to unnerve || to discourage, to dishearten (abatir).
◆ *vpr* to lose one's nerve, to become frightened *o* intimidated.

acobijar *vt* AGR to mulch, to earth up.

acobrado, da *adj* copper-coloured, coppery (color).

acocil; acocili *m* AMER freshwater shrimp || AMER FIG *estar como un acocili* to be as red as a lobster.

acocote *m* AMER gourd used for collecting maguey juice.

acochambrar *vt* AMER to dirty, to soil.

acochinar *vt* FAM to murder, to kill, to bump off [s.o. unable to defend himself].

acodado, da *adj* elbowed (doblado); *un tubo acodado* an elbowed pipe || leaning (on one's elbows); *acodado en la barra* leaning on the bar || AGR layered.

acodadura *f* leaning on one's elbows || AGR layering (de una planta) || elbow (incurvación).

acodalamiento *m* ARQ propping, shoring.

acodalar *vt* ARQ to prop up, to shore up.

acodamiento *m* leaning on one's elbows.

acodar *vt* ARQ to prop up, to shore up (apuntalar) || to bend (doblar) || AGR to layer.
◆ *vpr* to lean; *acodarse en la barra* to lean on the bar.

acoderar *vt* MAR to turn (a ship) broadside on.

acodillar *vt* to bend.

acodo *m* AGR layer (esqueje) | layering (acodadura).

acogedor, ra *adj* welcoming, hospitable (persona); *un pueblo muy acogedor* a very hospitable people || welcoming, inviting; *un saloncito muy acogedor* a very inviting little sitting room || warm, friendly; *un ambiente muy acogedor* a very warm atmosphere.

acoger *vt* to welcome, to make welcome; *acoger a los amigos* to make one's friends welcome || to take in (a un huérfano, etc.) || to shelter, to protect (proteger) || FIG to receive, to take; *acoger las peticiones* to receive requests | to receive; *el actor fue acogido con una ovación* the actor was received with great applause; *la proposición fue acogida con cierta frialdad* the proposal was rather coolly received.
◆ *vpr* to take refuge; *se acogió a la corte del rey* he took refuge in the king's court || to resort to (recurrir a) || to have recourse to (la ley) || to base o.s.; *acogerse al artículo 13 de la ley* to base o.s. on article 13 of the law || to avail o.s. of (una promesa) || *acogerse a* or *bajo sagrado* to take holy sanctuary || *acogerse a uno* to seek s.o.'s help (pedir auxilio), to seek s.o.'s protection (pedir protección).

acogida *f* welcome, greeting; *una acogida calurosa* a warm welcome; *una acogida triunfal* a triumphal welcome || FIG refuge, shelter (refugio) || reception; *la proposición tuvo una acogida favorable* the proposal had a favourable reception.

acogido, da *adj* welcomed || *acogido a la ley* protected by the law.
◆ *m/f* inmate (de un hospicio).

acogimiento *m* welcome, greeting || refuge, shelter (refugio).

acogollar *vi* AGR to bud.
◆ *vt* AGR to cover up.

acogotar *vt* to kill [with a rabbit punch] (matar) || to knock down (derribar) || FIG to oppress (oprimir a alguien) | to intimidate (asustar) || AMER to have at one's mercy (vencer).

acojinamiento *m* TECN cushioning.

acojinar *vt* to pad (acolchar).

acojonamiento *m* POP jitters *pl.*

acojonar *vt* POP to put the wind up.
◆ *vpr* POP to get the wind up.

acolada *f* accolade (al armar caballero) || hug, embrace (abrazo).

acolar *vt* HERÁLD to join, to unite [two coats of arms].

acolchado, da *adj* padded; *pared acolchada* padded wall || quilted; *bata acolchada* quilted dressing-gown || upholstered (muebles).
◆ *m* padding (relleno) || AMER mattress (colcha).

acolchar *vt* to pad || to upholster (muebles) || to quilt; *acolchar un tejido* to quilt material || FIG to muffle, to deaden; *la nieve acolcha el ruido* the snow deadens noise.

acolchonar *vt* AMER to quilt.

acolitado *m* acolyteship.

acolitar *vi* AMER to serve as acolyte | FIG & FAM to share s.o.'s meal.

acolitazgo *m* acolyteship.

acólito *m* REL acolyte (ministro) | altar boy, server (monaguillo) || FIG acolyte.

acollador *m* MAR lanyard (cuerda).

acolladura *f* earthing up, covering up.

acollar* *vt* AGR to earth up, to cover up || MAR to caulk (calafatear) | to haul (cuerdas).

acollarado, da *adj* ZOOL ring-necked; *mirlo acollarado* ring-necked blackbird.

acollarar *vt* to put a collar on (un animal) || to yoke (bueyes) || AMER to couple (unir).
◆ *vpr* AMER POP to live together (amancebarse), to get hitched (casarse).

acomedirse *vpr* AMER to volunteer, to offer o.s.

acometedor, ra *adj* enterprising (atrevido) || aggressive; *un delantero acometedor* an aggressive forward.

acometer *vt* to attack; *acometer al enemigo* to attack the enemy || to undertake; *acometer una reforma* to undertake a reform || to come over, to overcome; *me acometieron ganas de llorar* a desire to cry came over me || to fill; *estaba acometido por el miedo* he was filled with fear || to occur to, to come to; *le acometió la idea de irse* the idea of going away came to him || to connect with, to join (galería, cañería, etc.) || FAM to attack, to get down to; *acometer un trabajo* to attack a job || *me acometieron dudas* I was filled with doubts, I began to have doubts.

acometida *f* attack || connection (de una cañería, de tubos).

acometimiento *m* attack || undertaking; *el acometimiento de un trabajo* the undertaking of a job || connection (de cañería).

acometividad *f* aggression, aggressiveness (agresividad) || enterprise (de un vendedor).

acomodación *f* arrangement (arreglo) || accommodation (del ojo, de un anteojo) || preparation (de un piso).

acomodadamente *adv* conveniently, suitably (convenientemente) || easily, with ease (fácilmente) || *vivir acomodadamente* to live comfortably.

acomodadizo, za *adj* adaptable (que se aviene a todo) || obliging, accommodating (complaciente).

acomodado, da *adj* suitable, convenient (conveniente) || arranged, prepared; *un piso bien acomodado* a well arranged flat || well-to-do, well-off, comfortable; *una familia acomodada* a well-to-do family || comfort-loving (comodón) || moderate; *un precio acomodado* a moderate price.

acomodador, ra *m/f* usher (hombre), usherette (mujer) (en un espectáculo).

acomodamiento *m* convenience, suitability (comodidad) || arrangement (convenio) || preparation (de un sitio).

acomodar *vt* to place, to arrange (ordenar) || to settle, to make comfortable; *acomodar al niño en un sillón* to settle the child in an armchair, to make the child comfortable in an armchair || to accommodate (en casa) || to adjust (ajustar) || to provide, to supply (proveer) || to adapt, to suit; *acomodar su conducta con* to adapt one's conduct to || to prepare, to get ready (preparar) || to accommodate (el ojo, una lente) || to show to one's seat (en el teatro, cine) || FIG to reconcile, to bring together again (conciliar) || to apply; *acomodar una norma a un*

caso to apply a rule to a particular case || AMER to offer work to, to take on (ofrecer trabajo) | to repair, to mend (reparar) || *haga usted lo que le acomode* do as you please, please yourself, do whatever suits you.
◆ *vi* to be suitable (convenir).
◆ *vpr* to sit down, to take one's seat (en un espectáculo) || to settle down, to make o.s. comfortable (cómodamente); *acomodarse en un sillón* to settle down in an armchair || to stay (alojarse) || to accommodate (el ojo) || to go into service, to take a job; *acomodarse de criada* to go into service as a maid || to find work (lograr empleo) || to adapt o.s., to conform; *acomodarse con todo* to adapt o.s. to *o* to conform with everything || to comply, to conform; *acomodarse a una norma* to comply with a rule || AMER to dress up (componerse) | to look after o.s., to fend for o.s. (amañarse).

acomodaticio, cia *adj* adaptable (que se adapta a todo) || obliging, accommodating (complaciente).

acomodo *m* room (sitio) || accommodation, lodgings *pl* (habitación) || job, position (empleo) || convenience (conveniencia) || AMER toilet, dress (compostura).

acompañado, da *adj* accompanied; *ir acompañado* to be accompanied || FAM busy, frequented (concurrido) ||— *estar bien, mal acompañado* to be in good, in bad company || *más vale estar solo que mal acompañado* better alone than in bad company.
◆ *adj/s* assistant.
◆ *m* AMER sewage pipe.

acompañador, ra *adj* accompanying.
◆ *m/f* companion.

acompañamiento *m* accompaniment || retinue, escort (comitiva) || funeral procession (cortejo) || TEATR supporting cast || MÚS accompaniment || FIG trail, sequel; *la guerra y su acompañamiento de horrores* war and its trail of horrors || *sin acompañamiento* unaccompanied.

acompañanta *f* companion.

acompañante *adj* accompanying.
◆ *m* companion || MÚS accompanist.
◆ *pl* retinue *sing*, escort *sing*; *el ministro y sus acompañantes* the minister and his retinue.

acompañar *vt* to go with, to accompany; *acompañar a su hijo al cine* to go to the pictures with one's son || to attend; *la Reina iba acompañada por dos damas de honor* the Queen was accompanied by two ladies-in-waiting || to escort (a una señorita) || to keep company; *acompañar a un enfermo* to keep a sick person company || to take, to see; *le acompañaré a su casa porque es tarde* I'll take you home because it's late || to see; *le acompañé hasta la puerta* I saw him to the door || to follow; *acompañar a un entierro* to follow a funeral || to enclose (adjuntar) || to eat with, to accompany; *yo acompaño el jamón con piña* I accompany ham with pineapple || to go with, to accompany; *el vino tinto acompaña bien el queso* red wine goes well with cheese || MÚS to accompany; *acompañar con el piano* to accompany on the piano || to join; *mañana organizamos un bridge en casa ¿quiere usted acompañarnos?* tomorrow we're having a game of bridge at home, would you like to join us? || to share; *le acompaño en sus ideas* I share your views ||— *le acompaño en su sentimiento* my condolences || *no quiero que me acompañen* I would rather go alone.
◆ *vpr* to accompany o.s.; *acompañarse con el piano* to accompany o.s. on the piano.

acompasadamente *adv* rhythmically || calmly, regularly, steadily, slowly; *hablar acompasadamente* to speak slowly.

acompasado, da *adj* rhythmic; *el ruido acompasado de las olas* the rhythmic sound of the waves || measured; *paso acompasado* measured step || FIG calm, steady.

acompasar *vt* to keep in time; *el jinete debe acompasar su movimiento al del caballo* the rider must keep his movement in time with the horse's || MÚS to mark the rhythm of, to mark the time of || FIG to adjust; *hay que acompasar las exportaciones con las importaciones* exports must be adjusted according to imports.

acomplejado, da *adj* with a complex || *está acomplejado por su estatura* he has a complex about his size.

acomplejar *vt* to make feel inferior, to give a complex; *me acomplejas con todos tus éxitos* you make me feel inferior with all your successes.
◆ *vpr* to get a complex.

Aconcagua *npr m* GEOGR Aconcagua (cima).

aconcagüino, na *adj* from Aconcagua (Chile).

aconchabamiento *m* ganging together.

aconchabarse *vpr* FAM to gang up, to gang together; *aconchabarse con malhechores* to gang up with ruffians.

aconchar *vt* to shelter, to protect || MAR to run aground, to beach.
◆ *vpr* MAR to run aground.

acondicionado, da *adj* equipped, fitted-out; *un hospital bien acondicionado* a well-equipped hospital ||— *aire acondicionado* air conditioning || *hotel con aire acondicionado* air-conditioned hotel, hotel with air conditioning || *poner aire acondicionado* to air-condition.

acondicionador *m* conditioner (de aire) || *acondicionador de escaparates* window dresser.

acondicionamiento *m* fitting out, fitting up; *el acondicionamiento de un palacio en museo* the fitting out of a palace as a museum || preparation; *acondicionamiento de alimentos para la venta* preparation of foodstuffs for sale || conditioning (del aire) || improvement; *acondicionamiento de la red de carreteras* improvement of the road network.

acondicionar *vt* to fit out, to fit up, to set up; *acondicionar un sótano para tienda* to fit out a basement as a shop || to prepare; *acondicionar mercancías* to prepare merchandise || to improve; *acondicionar las carreteras* to improve the roads || to condition (el aire).

acongojar *vt* to distress, to make anxious (angustiar).
◆ *vpr* to become anxious, to become distressed.

aconitina *f* QUÍM aconitine.

acónito *m* BOT aconite.

aconsejable *adj* advisable; *poco aconsejable* not very advisable.

aconsejado, da *adj* advised ||— *bien aconsejado* well-advised || *mal aconsejado* ill-advised.

aconsejador, ra *adj* advisory, advising, who advises.
◆ *m/f* adviser, counsellor.

aconsejar *vt* to advise, to counsel; *le aconsejo viajar* or *que viaje* I advise you to travel || to advise, to recommend (la moderación, etc.).
◆ *vpr* to seek advice, to consult; *aconsejarse con* or *de su médico* to seek advice from *o* to consult one's doctor.

aconsonantar *vt* to rhyme, to make rhyme.
◆ *vi* to rhyme.

acontecedero, ra *adj* possible.

acontecer* *vi* to happen, to occur, to take place; *todo aconteció conforme a lo previsto* everything happened as planned.
◆ *m* *el acontecer cotidiano* everyday life, the normal course of events.

acontecimiento *m* event, happening (suceso).

acopiamiento *m* store, stock.

acopiar *vt* to store, to collect (amontonar) || to collect (reunir).

acopio *m* store, stock (provisión) || storing (acción de acopiar) || abundance || *hacer acopio de* to store up, to stock up.

acoplado, da *adj* matched; *un matrimonio bien acoplado* a well-matched couple || coordinated; *un equipo bien acoplado* a well-coordinated team || adjusted; *un horario mal acoplado* a badly adjusted timetable.
◆ *m* AMER trailer (vehículo).

acopladura *f* assembly.

acoplamiento *m* connecting, coupling, joining (acción de acoplar) || connection, joint (unión de piezas) || engaging (de engranajes) || assembly (ensambladura) || coordination (de un equipo) || docking (de naves espaciales) ||— ELECTR *acoplamiento en serie* connection in series || TECN *acoplamiento universal* universal joint | *manguito de acoplamiento* sleeve coupling.

acoplar *vt* to fit; *acoplar una rueda al eje* to fit a wheel to the axle || ELECTR to connect || to fit together, to join; *acoplar dos vigas* to fit two beams together || to fit, to adapt; *acoplar un motor de coche a una lancha* to fit a car engine to a launch || to couple; *acoplar otro vagón al tren* to couple another carriage to the train || to coordinate; *acoplar un equipo* to coordinate a team || to fit in, to coordinate; *tengo que acoplar el horario de clases con mis días de trabajo* I have to fit my timetable in with my working days || to yoke (bueyes) || to make, to pair (parear animales).
◆ *vpr* to mate, to pair (animales) || to dock (naves espaciales).

acoquinamiento *m* fear, intimidation (miedo) || loss of heart (desánimo).

acoquinar *vt* FAM to scare, to frighten, to intimidate (asustar).
◆ *vpr* to become scared *o* frightened *o* intimidated; *acoquinarse ante el enemigo* to become scared in the face of the enemy || to lose heart, to lose courage, to become disheartened (desanimarse).

acorazado, da *adj* armoured, armour-plated; *buque acorazado* armoured ship || FIG hardened; *persona acorazada contra el dolor* person hardened to pain ||— *cámara acorazada* strongroom, safe || MIL *división acorazada* armoured division.
◆ *m* MAR battleship.

acorazamiento *m* armouring, armour-plating.

acorazar *vt* to armour, to armour-plate.
◆ *vpr* FIG to harden o.s.

acorazonado, da *adj* heart-shaped.

acorchado, da *adj* cork-like (como el corcho) || spongy (correoso) || numb (los miembros) || *boca acorchada* numb mouth (insensibilizada), furry mouth, mouth like sandpaper (por el alcohol).

acorchamiento *m* sponginess || FIG numbness (de los miembros).

acorchar *vt* to cover with cork.
◆ *vpr* to become corky *o* cork-like || to become spongy (fruta) || FIG to go numb; *se me acorcharon las piernas* my legs went numb.

acordada *f* decree, order (de un tribunal).

acordadamente *adv* unanimously, by common consent (de común acuerdo) || with much thought (con reflexión).

acordado, da *adj* sensible, wise (prudente) || agreed upon *o* agreed to || *lo acordado* that which has been agreed upon.

acordar* *vt* to agree, to resolve; *ambos estadistas han acordado estrechar la cooperación* both statesmen have agreed to increase cooperation || to decide (decidir) || to agree upon; *acordar un precio* to agree upon a price || to remind (recordar a uno) || ARTES to match, to harmonize (colores) || MÚS to tune (afinar) || *AMER* to grant (otorgar).
◆ *vpr* to remember; *no me acuerdo de la guerra* I don't remember the war || to agree, to come to an agreement || — *no se acuerda ni del santo de su nombre* he can hardly remember his own name || *si mal no me acuerdo* if I remember rightly || FAM *¡te acordarás de mí!* you haven't seen the last of me, you'll be hearing from me.

acorde *adj* in agreement; *las diversas informaciones están acordes* the different reports are in agreement || according (*con, a* to), in agreement (*con, a* with); *construir un edificio acorde con las tendencias actuales* to construct a building according to present trends || identical, same; *sentimientos acordes* the same feelings, identical feelings || MÚS in tune.
◆ *m* MÚS chord; *acorde perfecto* common chord | tune; *cantar algo a los acordes de* to sing sth to the tune of | strain; *hacer algo a los acordes de* to do sth. to the strains of.

acordelado, da *adj* perfectly straight.

acordelar *vt* to measure with a string || to mark out in straight lines (tirar a cordel) || to mark the boundary of [with string].

acordeón *m* MÚS accordion || *plisado de acordeón* accordion pleating.

acordeonista *m/f* accordionist.

acordonado, da *adj* corded, ribbed (en figura de cordón) || cordoned off, surrounded; *el barrio estaba acordonado por la policía* the district was cordoned off by the police || milled (monedas) || *AMER* thin (animales).

acordonamiento *m* lacing, lacing up (lazada) || cordon (de policía) || milling (de las monedas).

acordonar *vt* to lace, to lace up, to tie up (los zapatos) || to pipe (poner un cordón) || to mill (las monedas) || to cordon off, to surround; *la policía acordona la universidad* the police surround the university || *AMER* to prepare [the ground] (para la siembra).

acornar; acornear *vt* ⟶ **cornear.**

acorralado, da *adj* cornered (sin salida) || at bay; *un ciervo acorralado* a stag at bay.

acorralamiento *m* cornering || enclosing, penning (de vacunos), folding (de ovinos).

acorralar *vt* to enclose, to pen (vacunos), to fold (ovinos) || to put at bay (ciervos) || to corner; *acorralar al enemigo* to corner the enemy.

acorrer *vt* to help.
◆ *vi* to run up.

acortamiento *m* shortening; *acortamiento de una falda* shortening of a skirt || reduction.

acortar *vt* to shorten || FIG to reduce; *acortar el racionamiento* to reduce rationing | to cut down, to reduce (distancia) | to abridge, to shorten (un cuento).
◆ *vpr* to become shorter, to shorten; *en agosto los días empiezan a acortarse* in August the days start to become shorter || to be shy (intimidarse).

acosador, ra *adj/s* pursuer.

acosamiento *m* pursuit.

acosar *vt* to pursue, to hound; *acosado por los perros* hounded by the dogs || to run to earth, to put at bay (acorralar) || FIG to hound, to pursue; *acosar a un deudor* to hound a debtor | to pester, to hound, to harass; *acosar con preguntas* to pester with questions || to urge on (un caballo).

acoso *m* pursuit (acosamiento) || hunting down (caza) || FIG hounding || *acoso sexual* sexual harassment.

acostar* *vt* to put to bed (en la cama) || to lay down, to lay (poner en posición horizontal) || MAR to bring alongside.
◆ *vi* MAR to touch land, to reach land.
◆ *vpr* to go to bed; *voy a acostarme porque es muy tarde* I'm going to bed because it is very late || to lie down (tumbarse) || to sleep; *por falta de sitio, los niños se acostaron juntos* because of the lack of room the children slept together || to lean over, to bend over; *el trigo se acostó por el viento* the wheat leant over in the wind || MAR to come alongside (arrimarse) || — FAM *acostarse con las gallinas* to go to bed very early || *la hora de acostarse* bedtime.

acostumbrado, da *adj* usual, customary (que se hace por costumbre) || used, accustomed; *una persona acostumbrada al trabajo* a person used to work.

acostumbrar *vt* to accustom, to get used; *me han acostumbrado al trabajo* they've got me used to working || to be used to, to be accustomed to, to be in the habit of, to usually; *acostumbro levantarme temprano* I am used to getting up early, I usually get up early.
◆ *vpr* to become accustomed, to get used; *acostumbrarse al clima de un país* to get used to the climate of a country || to get into the habit; *se acostumbró a fumar después de comer* he got into the habit of smoking after a meal || to be usual, to be customary; *ahora no se acostumbra llevar miriñaque* it is no longer usual to wear a crinoline.

acotación *f* demarcation (acción de limitar) || boundary mark (señal) || note (nota) || GEOGR elevation mark (en topografía) || TEATR stage direction.

acotado, da *adj* enclosed (terreno) || annotated (texto).

acotamiento *m* demarcation (acción de limitar) || boundary mark (señal) || note, annotation (en un texto) || GEOGR elevation mark (topografía) || FIG outline || *AMER* roadside, hard shoulder (arcén).

acotar *vt* to mark the boundary of, to demarcate, to delimit, to enclose (un terreno) || to reserve, to fence in, to preserve (para la caza) || FIG to delimit, to outline, to define (limitar) | to accept (aceptar) | to vouch for (atestiguar) || to add notes to, to annotate (anotar) || GEOGR to mark with elevations (poner cotas).

acotejar *vt* *AMER* to arrange (acomodar).

acotiledón, ona; acotiledóneo, a *adj* BOT acotyledonous.
◆ *m/f* acotyledon.

acotillo *m* blacksmith's hammer.

acoyundar *vt* to yoke (bueyes).

acoyuntar *vt* to yoke together [beasts of different owners].

acracia *f* anarchy.

ácrata *adj/s* anarchist.

acrático, ca *adj* anarchic, anarchical.

acre *m* acre (medida).

acre *adj* pungent, acrid (olor) || sharp, tart, bitter (sabor) || FIG biting, caustic, bitter (mordaz); *palabras acres* biting words | bitter, crabby (desabrido).

acrecencia *f* increase || JUR accretion.

acrecentamiento *m* increase.

acrecentar* *vt* to increase, to augment.
◆ *vpr* to increase, to augment.

acrecer* *vt* to increase.
◆ *vi* to increase, to grow || JUR *derecho de acrecer* right of accretion.

acrecimiento *m* JUR accretion.

acreción *f* BIOL & GEOL accretion.

acreditado, da *adj* COM credited || reputable; *una marca acreditada* a reputable make || accredited (embajador).

acreditar *vt* to accredit; *el gobierno le ha acreditado embajador en España* the government has accredited him as ambassador to Spain || to prove, to support, to give proof of; *esto acredita lo que le decía* this proves what I was saying to you || to vouch for, to guarantee; *acreditar una firma* to vouch for a signature || to authorize, to sanction; *este documento me acredita para entrar* this paper authorizes me to enter || to be a credit to, to give credit to, to add to the reputation of; *un producto que acredita al fabricante* a product which adds to the manufacturer's reputation || COM to credit || *acreditar como* to prove to be, to prove that; *la carta me acredita como propietario* the letter proves me to be the owner, the letter proves that I am the owner; *esta medida le acredita de loco* this measure proves him to be mad *o* proves that he is mad.
◆ *vpr* to present one's credentials (un embajador) || to gain a reputation, to make one's name; *antes de que este bar se acredite habrá que esperar mucho tiempo* we shall have to wait a long time before this bar gains a reputation *o* makes its name.

acreditativo, va *adj* which proves, which gives proof.

acreedor, ra *adj* deserving, worthy; *acreedor a mi cariño* worthy of *o* deserving my affection.
◆ *m/f* creditor; *tiene muchos acreedores* he has many creditors || *acreedor hipotecario* mortgagee.

acribadura *f* sifting, riddling, sieving (acción).
◆ *pl* siftings, riddlings, sievings (desperdicios).

acribar *vt* to sift, to riddle, to sieve || FIG to riddle.

acribillar *vt* to riddle, to pepper; *acribillar a balazos* to riddle with bullet holes || to cover; *acribillar de picaduras* to cover with stings || FIG to pester, to harass; *me acribillaron a preguntas* they pestered me with questions.

acrílico, ca *adj* QUÍM acrylic.

acriminar *vt* to charge, to accuse, to incriminate.

acrimonia; acritud *f* pungency, acridity (olor) || sharpness, tartness, bitterness (sabor) || FIG acrimony, bitterness.

acrimonioso, sa *adj* acrimonious.

acriollarse *vpr* *AMER* to go native.

acrisolado, da *adj* purified (metales) || proven, tested (la verdad, el amor).

acrisolar *vt* to purify (los metales) || to prove, to test (la verdad, el amor).

acritud *f* ⟶ **acrimonia.**

acrobacia *f* feat of acrobatics.
◆ *pl* acrobatics || *acrobacias aéreas* aerobatics.

acróbata *m/f* acrobat.

acrobático, ca *adj* acrobatic.

acrobatismo *m* acrobatics.

acrocefalia *f* MED acrocephaly.

acrocéfalo, la *adj* MED acrocephalic, acrocephalous.

acromegalia *f* MED acromegaly, acromegalia.

acrónimo *m* GRAM acronym.

acroparestesia *f* MED acroparaesthesia.

Acrópolis *npr f* Acropolis.

acróstico, ca *adj/sm* acrostic.

acrotera; acrótera *f* ARQ acroter.

acta *f* minutes *pl*, record (de una reunión) || certificate of election (en elecciones) || official document, deed || *AMER* act, law || — *acta de acusación* bill of indictment || *acta de bautismo* certificate of baptism || *acta de calidad* quality control certificate || *acta de defunción* death certificate || *acta de nacimiento, de matrimonio* birth, marriage certificate || *acta de peritaje* technichal inspection certificate || *acta de recepción* bill of receipt || *acta notarial* notarial deed || *levantar acta* to draw up the minutes, to take the minutes (de una reunión) || *tomar acta* to take note.
◆ *pl* REL life *sing*, acts (de los santos) || minutes, record *sing* || register *sing* (para las notas de un examen) || *actas taquigráficas* or *literales* verbatim record *sing*.

actinia *f* ZOOL actinia, sea anemone (anémona de mar).

actínico, ca *adj* FÍS & QUÍM actinic.

actinio *m* QUÍM actinium (metal).

actinomorfo, fa *adj* ZOOL actinomorphic.

actitud *f* posture, pose, position, attitude (postura del cuerpo); *adoptar una actitud pensativa* to strike a pensive pose || FIG attitude, position; *ha adoptado una actitud rebelde* he has adopted *o* has taken up a rebellious attitude.

activación *f* speeding-up, quickening || QUÍM activation.

activador *m* QUÍM activator.

activamente *adv* actively, energetically || GRAM actively, with an active meaning.

activar *vt* to speed up, to quicken; *activar el trabajo* to speed up the work || to activate, to stimulate; *activar el mercado* to stimulate the market || QUÍM to activate; *carbón activado* activated carbon || INFORM to activate || to stir up (el fuego).
◆ *vpr* to hurry, to hurry up.

actividad *f* activity; *la actividad de un volcán, de un ácido* the activity of a volcano, of an acid; *esfera de actividad* field of activity || bustle, activity (en la calle) || activity (ocupación); *cada uno tiene una actividad distinta* each one has a different activity || — *desplegar una actividad* to work as (seguido de un sustantivo) || *tiene una actividad enorme* he is very active *o* energetic || *volcán en actividad* active volcano.

activismo *m* activism.

activista *adj/s* activist.

activo, va *adj* active || energetic, active; *una persona muy activa* a very energetic person || GRAM active; *verbo activo* active verb || GEOL active (volcán) || — *dividendo activo* dividend || *en activo* on active service; *militar en activo* soldier on active service || GRAM *participio activo* present participle.
◆ *m* COM assets *pl* (haber); *activo y pasivo* assets and liabilities; *activo circulante* current assets; *activo fijo* fixed assets; *activo neto* net worth, net assets.

acto *m* act, action, deed (hecho); *se conoce un hombre por sus actos* a man is known by his acts || act; *acto de fe, de contricción* act of faith, of contrition || ceremony; *mañana se celebrará el acto de clausura* the closing ceremony will take place tomorrow || TEATR act; *comedia en dos actos* two-act play, play in two acts || — *acto carnal* sexual intercourse, carnal act || *acto continuo* or *seguido* immediately, immediately afterwards, straight away, at once || *acto reflejo* reflex action || *acto sexual* sexual intercourse || *Actos de los Apóstoles* Acts of the Apostles || JUR *actos de violencia* assault and battery || *en el acto* immediately, on the spot || *en el acto de* in the act of || *hacer acto de presencia* to be present, to put in an appearance || *muerto en acto de servicio* killed in active service, killed in action || *salón de actos* assembly hall.

actor, ra *m/f* JUR plaintiff, claimant.
◆ *adj f* JUR *parte actora* prosecution.

actor, triz *m/f* actor, actress || — *primer actor* leading actor, star || *primera actriz* leading lady *o* actress, star.

actuación *f* behaviour, conduct (conducta) || action, intervention; *la actuación de la policía fue muy dura* the police's action was very severe || performance; *la actuación de un artista* an artist's performance || — *actuación pericial* expert valuation.
◆ *pl* JUR proceedings.

actual *adj* present, present-day, modern; *la técnica actual* present-day technology || topical; *un problema muy actual* a very topical problem.
◆ *m* this month; *el 12 del actual* the 12th of this month.

actualidad *f* present, present time || topicality, current importance; *la actualidad de un problema* a problem's topicality || — *en la actualidad* at the present time, nowadays, at the moment || *un tema de gran actualidad* a very topical subject, a subject of great importance today.
◆ *pl* current events || CINEM newsreel *sing*.

actualización *f* bringing up to date, modernization || FIL actualization.

actualizador, ra *adj* modernizing.

actualizar *vt* to bring up to date, to modernize; *actualizar un texto* to bring a text up to date || FIL to actualize.

actualmente *adv* at present, at the moment, at the present time (en este momento) || nowadays (hoy día).

actuante *adj* acting.
◆ *m/f* performer || defender [of a thesis] || candidate [in an examination].

actuar *vi* to act; *una medicina que actúa como calmante* a medicine which acts as a sedative; *actuar de secretario* to act as a secretary || CINEM & TEATR to act, to play, to perform || to perform (un cantante, músico) || to behave; *ha actuado muy mal en este asunto* he has behaved very badly in this matter || to defend a thesis (en la universidad) || to take; *actuar en un ejercicio oral* to take an oral examination || JUR to take proceedings || TAUR to fight.
◆ *vt* to operate, to work (un mecanismo).

actuariado *m* position of actuary *o* of clerk of the court.

actuarial *adj* actuarian, actuarial.

actuario *m* JUR clerk of the court, actuary || actuary (de seguros).

acuache *m* *AMER* mate, pal, chum (amigo).

acuadrillar *vt* to band together, to form into a band || to lead [a band].

acuafortista *m* ARTES aquafortist.

acuaplano *m* aquaplane.

acuarela *f* ARTES watercolour [*US* watercolor].

acuarelista *m* watercolourist [*US* watercolorist].

acuario *m* aquarium (de peces) || ASTR Aquarius.

acuartelado *adj* HERÁLD quartered.

acuartelamiento *m* MIL billeting, quartering || confinement to barracks (en previsión de disturbios).

acuartelar *vt* MIL to quarter, to billet || to confine to barracks (en previsión de disturbios) || to divide into quarters.
◆ *vpr* MIL to withdraw to barracks.

acuartillar *vi* to bend its knees (caballo).

acuático, ca *adj* aquatic; *ave acuática* aquatic bird || *esquí acuático* water-skiing.

acuátil *adj* aquatic.

acuatinta *f* ARTES aquatint.

acuatizar *vi* to land on the water (un hidroavión).

acucia *f* haste (prisa) || longing, desire (anhelo) || diligence (diligencia).

acuciador, ra *adj* pressing, urgent (urgente) || desirous (ansioso) || stimulating (estimulante).

acuciamiento *m* stimulation, urging on (estímulo) || desire (deseo, ansia) || diligence (diligencia).

acuciante *adj* pressing, urgent.

acuciar *vt* to urge on (estimular); *estar acuciado por la necesidad* to be urged on by necessity || to hound, to pester, to harass; *acuciar a alguien con preguntas* to hound s.o. with questions || to desire, to long for (anhelar) || *no me acucia marcharme* there is no hurry for me to leave.

acucioso, sa *adj* diligent, keen || urgent, pressing (urgente) || desirous (ansioso).

acuclillarse *vpr* to crouch down, to squat down.

acucharado, da *adj* spoon-shaped.

acuchillado, da *adj* knifed, slashed, stabbed || FIG experienced || slashed; *mangas acuchilladas* slashed sleeves.
◆ *m* surfacing (de madera).

acuchillador, ra *adj* quarrelsome (pendenciero).
◆ *m/f* quarrelsome person || slasher, knifer, stabber || floor dresser (de suelos).
◆ *m* bully (espadachín).

acuchillamiento *m* surfacing (de madera).

acuchillar *vt* to knife, to stab, to slash (apuñalar) || to slash (vestidos) || to slash, to cleave (el aire) || to surface (la madera).
◆ *vpr* to fight with knives, to hack at one another.

acudir *vi* to come (venir); *ayer no acudió a la oficina* yesterday he didn't come to the office; *el perro acude cuando le llaman* the dog comes when they call him; *acudir a la mente* to come to one's mind || to go (ir); *mucha gente acudió al espectáculo* a lot of people went to the show; *acudir a la puerta* to go to the door || to keep; *acudir a una cita* to keep an appointment || to take; *acudir a un examen* to take an examination || to answer; *¿quién acudió al teléfono?* who answered the telephone? || to happen (sobrevenir); *siempre le acuden desdichas* misfortunes always happen to him || to carry out, to obey (una orden) || to see, to attend; *no pudo acudir a todo lo que tenía que hacer* he couldn't see to everything he had to do || to come forward; *pidió ayuda y muchos acudieron* he asked for help and many came forward || to help, to give aid *o* help; *acudir a alguien* to give help to *o* to help s.o. || to come up: *acudieron a tiempo con la solución* they came up with the solution in time || to resort (recurrir); *sin acudir a las armas* without resorting to weapons || to consult (al médico) || to call, to turn (recurrir a una persona); *si es necesario, acudiré al ministro* if it's necessary I'll turn to *o* call on the minister || to obey (el caballo) || — *acudir a la huida* to take flight || *acudir en ayuda de alguien* to come to s.o.'s aid *o* rescue || *no saber a quién acudir* not to know where to turn, to be at one's wits' end.

acueducto *m* aquaduct.

ácueo, a *adj* aqueous; *humor ácueo* aqueous humour.

acuerdo *m* agreement, understanding; *tienen un acuerdo entre ellos* they have an agreement between themselves; *llegar a un acuerdo* to come to an agreement || agreement; *acuerdo general sobre tarifas arancelarias y comercio* general agreement on tariffs and trade; *concertar un acuerdo* to conclude an agreement || harmony; *el acuerdo de dos colores* the harmony of two colours || resolution (en el Parlamento) || sense, wisdom (cordura) || advice, opinion (consejo) || memory (recuerdo) || — *acuerdo bilateral* bilateral agreement || *acuerdo de crédito* credit arrangement || JUR *acuerdo de las partes* agreement between the parties || *acuerdo marco* blueprint agreement || *acuerdo multilateral* multilateral agreement || *acuerdo tripartito* tripartite agreement || *acuerdo verbal* verbal agreement, gentleman's agreement || *¡de acuerdo!* right!, O. K.!, all right!, alright! || *de acuerdo con* in accordance with; as laid down in, in accordance with (una ley) || *de común acuerdo* by common consent || *estar de acuerdo con una persona* to agree with a person, to be in agreement with a person || *estar de acuerdo en* to agree with, to be in agreement about; *estoy de acuerdo en el aumento del capital* I agree with the increase in capital; *estoy de acuerdo en aumentar el capital* I agree with increasing the capital || *estar en su acuerdo* to have one's wits about one, to be in one's right mind || *llegar a un acuerdo* to come to an agreement, to reach (an) agreement || *poner de acuerdo* to make agree, to bring to an agreement; *nos puso de acuerdo* he made us agree, he brought us to an agreement || *ponerse de acuerdo* to come to an agreement, to agree || *volver a su acuerdo* to come back to one's senses.

acuicultivo *m* AGR aquaculture, aquiculture.

acuidad *f* sharpness, acuity.

acuífero, ra *adj* aquiferous, water-bearing; *capa acuífera* aquiferous layer.

acuitadamente *adv* sorrowfully, with grief.

acuitar *vt* to grieve.

◆ *vpr* to grieve; *acuitarse por algo* to grieve at sth., to grieve sth.

aculado, da *adj* HERÁLD sejant.

acular *vt* to back up, to drive back (arrimar) || FAM to corner (acosar, arrinconar).

◆ *vpr* MAR to run aground.

acullá *adv* there, over there || *acá y acullá* here and there.

acumulación *f*; **acumulamiento** *m* accumulation (acción) || store, accumulation; *acumulación de recuerdos* store of memories || plurality (de empleos) || JUR non-concurrence (de penas).

acumulador, ra *adj* accumulative.

◆ *m* TECN storage battery, accumulator || INFORM accumulator.

acumular *vt* to accumulate, to store up, to amass (amontonar); *acumular riquezas* to accumulate riches || to store up, to collect; *acumular recuerdos* to store up memories || to accumulate; *acumular intereses al capital* to accumulate interest on capital || to pile, to heap, to load; *acumular preocupaciones sobre alguien* to pile worries onto s.o. || *acumular vapor* to get up steam.

◆ *vpr* to accumulate, to build up (cosas) || to gather, to collect; *la gente se acumuló delante del escaparate* the people gathered in front of the window.

acumulativamente *adv* JUR non-concurrently, cumulatively.

acumulativo, va *adj* accumulative, which accumulates || JUR non-concurrent, cumulative.

acunar *vt* to rock; *acunar a un niño* to rock a child.

acuñación *f* minting, striking, coining (de monedas).

acuñador *m* minter.

acuñar *vt* to strike, to mint, to coin (monedas) || to strike (medallas) || to wedge (poner cuñas) || *expresión acuñada* set phrase.

◆ *vi* to mint *o* to strike *o* to coin money.

acuosidad *f* wateriness (de fruta) || aqueousness (de humor).

acuoso, sa *adj* aqueous; *humor acuoso* aqueous humour || watery; *fruta acuosa* watery fruit.

acuotubular *adj* TECN watertube; *caldera acuotubular* watertube boiler.

acupuntor, ra *m/f* MED acupuncturist.

acupuntura *f* MED acupuncture.

acure *m* ZOOL agouti.

acurrucarse *vpr* to curl up, to nestle, to snuggle up; *se acurrucó en el sillón* he curled up in the armchair || to huddle (por el frío).

acurrullar *vt* MAR to lower [sails].

acusación *f* accusation; *lo que ha dicho es una acusación contra mi primo* what he said is an accusation against my cousin || — JUR *acta de acusación* indictment | *cargo de acusación* count of indictment.

acusado, da *adj* accused (inculpado) || marked, clear, outstanding, pronounced (saliente).

◆ *m/f* accused, defendant.

acusador, ra *adj* accusing; *en tono acusador* in an accusing tone.

◆ *m/f* accuser || *acusador público* public prosecutor.

acusar *vt* to accuse, to charge; *acusar de robo* to accuse of robbery, to charge with robbery || to point to; *todas las pruebas le acusan* all the evidence points to him || to blame; *le acuso de todas nuestras desdichas* I blame him for all our misfortunes || to show, to indicate; *el termómetro acusa un cambio de temperatura* the thermometer shows a change in temperature || to show, to reveal, to register, to reflect; *su cara acusa gran dolor* his face reflects great pain || to declare, to announce (naipes) || to denounce, to give away, to inform on; *su antiguo amigo le acusó* his old friend gave him away || to tell tales about; *es una mala costumbre acusar a los demás* it is a bad habit to tell tales about others || — *acusar alegría, cansancio* to look happy, tired || *acusar el golpe* to feel the blow || FIG *acusar las cuarenta a uno* to tell s.o. a few home truths || COM *acusar recibo de una cosa* to acknowledge receipt of sth.

◆ *vpr* to confess (confesar); *acusarse de un crimen* to confess to a crime; *acusarse de un pecado* to confess a sin || to become clear *o* pronounced *o* marked.

acusativo, va *adj/sm* GRAM accusative.

acusatorio, ria *adj* accusatory.

acuse *m* acknowledgement; *acuse de recibo* acknowledgement of receipt || winning card (naipes).

acusetas; acusete *m* AMER FAM telltale, tattletale (niño) || sneak (adulto).

acusica *m/f* FAM telltale, tattletale (niño) | sneak (adulto).

acusón, ona *adj* FAM fond of telling tales (niño) || sneaky (adulto).

◆ *m/f* FAM telltale, tattletale (niño) || sneak (adulto).

acústico, ca *adj* acoustic || *trompetilla acústica* ear trumpet.

◆ *f* acoustics; *la acústica es la ciencia del sonido* acoustics is the science of sound.

acutángulo, la *adj* acute-angled.

acutí *m* AMER ZOOL agouti (roedor).

achabacanar *vt* to make vulgar *o* crude.

◆ *vpr* to become vulgar *o* crude.

achacable *adj* attributable.

achacar *vt* to attribute; *me achacan unas frases que nunca he dicho* they attribute statements to me that I have never made; *achacarle a uno una falta* to attribute a fault to s.o. || to put on, to lay on; *me achacaron la culpa* they laid the blame on me || *achacar a uno la responsabilidad de* to hold s.o. responsible for.

achacosamente *adv* weakly, in a sickly fashion || with difficulty; *andar achacosamente* to walk with difficulty.

achacoso, sa *adj* sickly, ailing (enfermizo) || ill, unwell, indisposed (ligeramente enfermo) || faulty, defective (una cosa).

achaflanar *vt* to chamfer, to bevel.

¡achalay! *interj* AMER how lovely!, how nice!

achampanado, da; achampañado, da *adj* champagne-type; *vino achampanado* champagne-type wine || sparkling (espumoso) || *sidra achampanada* champagne cider.

achantar *vt* FAM to frighten (asustar) | to shut up (dejar desarmado) || POP *¡achanta la muí!* shut your face!, shut up!

◆ *vpr* FAM to hide [during danger] | to climb down; *cuando saqué mi pistola se achantó* when I got my gun out he climbed down.

achaparrado, da *adj* small and thick (árbol) || FIG stocky, squat, stumpy; *un viejo achaparrado* a stocky old man | crushed, flattened (aplastado).

achaparrarse *vpr* to grow thick [without getting taller] (los árboles) || FIG to get chubby (personas).

achapinarse *vpr* AMER to adopt the way of life of Guatemala.

achaque *m* ailment, complaint (enfermedad ligera) || FIG excuse, pretext; *con el achaque de* on the pretext of, with the excuse of || *achaques de la vejez* old age complaints.

achaquiento, ta *adj* sickly, ailing (enfermizo) || ill, indisposed, unwell (ligeramente enfermo).

achares *m pl* jealousy *sing* || *dar achares a* to make jealous.

acharolado, da *adj* varnished.

acharolar *vt* to patent (la piel).

acharramarse *vpr* FAM to become crude *o* vulgar.

achatamiento *m* flattening.

achatar *vt* to flatten, to squash.

◆ *vpr* AMER to become frightened, to lose heart.

achicado, da *adj* childish (aniñado).

achicador *m* MAR baler.

achicamiento *m* reduction || MAR baling || draining (en una mina) || FIG humiliation (humillación) | feeling of inferiority.

achicar *vt* to reduce; *achicar sus pretensiones* to reduce one's claims || to make smaller; *han achicado los jardines* they have made the gardens smaller || to take in (la ropa) || MAR to bale out || to drain (en una mina) || DEP to throw (un balón, una pelota, una bola) || FIG to humiliate, to belittle (humillar) | to bring down, to kill (matar).

◆ *vpr* FIG to back down, to lose heart (amilanarse); *no te achiques ante el enemigo* don't lose heart in the face of the enemy | to humble o.s. (humillarse).

achicoria *f* BOT chicory.

achicharradero *m* furnace, inferno (sitio caluroso).

achicharrante *adj* burning.

achicharrar *vt* to burn (asar demasiado) || FIG to roast, to burn (calentar con exceso) | to pester, to annoy (molestar) | to bombard, to

plague; *le achicharraron a preguntas* they bombarded him with questions || AMER to flatten, to crush (estrujar).
◆ *vpr* to burn (un guiso) || to roast, to burn (con el sol).

achicharronar *vt* AMER → **achicharrar.**

achichinque *m* AMER miner, mine worker (obrero) | flatterer (adulador) | minion (servidor).

achiguarse *vpr* AMER to bulge (pared, tabla, etc.) | to put on weight (una persona).

achinado, da *adj* slanting (los ojos) || oriental, eastern; *tiene una cara achinada* he has an oriental face || AMER half-caste (mestizo) | vulgar, low.

achinar *vt* FAM to intimidate, to scare, to frighten (acoquinar).

achinelado, da *adj* slipper-shaped.

achique *m* MAR baling || draining (en una mina).

achiquillado, da *adj* childish.

achiquitar *vt* AMER FAM to make smaller.
◆ *vpr* AMER FAM to back down, to lose heart (amilanarse).

achira *f* AMER BOT canna (cañacoro).

achispado, da *adj* tipsy, tight, merry (medio ebrio).

achispar *vt* to make tipsy *o* tight *o* merry (embriagar).
◆ *vpr* to get tipsy *o* merry *o* tight.

achocar *vt* to throw *o* to dash against the wall (contra la pared) || to throw to the floor (contra el suelo).

achocolatado, da *adj* chocolate-brown.

achocharse *vpr* FAM to become senile, to begin to dote, to become doddery.

acholado, da *adj* AMER half-caste, half-breed (cobrizo) | ashamed (avergonzado) | scared (con miedo).

acholar *vt* AMER to shame, to make ashamed (avergonzar).
◆ *vpr* AMER to be ashamed (avergonzarse) | to get scared (amedrentarse) | to get sunstroke (insolarse) | to adopt half-breed ways (volverse mestizo).

achubascarse *vpr* to become threatening *o* overcast (cielo).

achucutar; achucuyar *vt* AMER to shame, to make ashamed.

achuchado, da *adj* FAM hard, difficult; *la vida está muy achuchada* life is very hard.

achuchar *vt* FAM to squash, to flatten (aplastar) | to push, to jostle (empujar); *me achucharon por todos lados* I was pushed from all sides | to press (down) on (apretar) || to excite, to rouse (un perro).
◆ *vpr* FAM to jostle, to push (empujarse).

achucharrar *vt* AMER to flatten.
◆ *vpr* AMER to back down, to lose heart (amilanarse).

achuchón *m* FAM push, shove; *me tiró al agua de un achuchón* with a push he threw me into the water || flattening, squashing (aplastamiento) || *dar un achuchón* to push, to shove, to give a push *o* a shove.
◆ *pl* pushing *sing*; *no voy al desfile porque detesto los achuchones* I'm not going to the parade because I hate pushing.

achulado, da; achulapado, da *adj* vulgar, crude, coarse (grosero) || funny, comical (gracioso) || hard-faced, shameless (descarado) || cocky (presumido).

achuncharse *vpr* AMER to be ashamed (avergonzarse) || to get scared (asustarse).

achura *f* AMER offal.

achurar; achurear *vt* AMER to gut, to eviscerate | to knife *o* to stab to death.

achurruscar *vt* AMER to squash, to flatten.
◆ *vpr* to curl up (ensortijarse).

adagio *m* proverb, adage || MÚS adagio.
◆ *adj/adv* MÚS adagio.

adala *f* MAR scupper.

adalid *m* leader || champion; *adalid de la democracia* champion of democracy.

adamado, da *adj* effeminate (afeminado) || refined, fine, delicate (fino) || pretentious (pretencioso).

adamantino, na *adj* diamond-like, adamantine; *brillo adamantino* diamond-like glitter.

adamarse *vpr* to become effeminate (afeminarse).

adamascado, da *adj* damask.

adamascar *vt* to damask (tejidos).

adán *m* FIG & FAM sloven (descuidado) || lazy bones, idler (haragán) || *ir hecho un adán* to be dressed in rags, to be slovenly dressed.

Adán *npr m* Adam || — *ir en el traje de Adán* to be in one's birthday suit || ANAT *manzana* or *nuez de Adán* Adam's apple.

adaptable *adj* adaptable.

adaptación *f* adaptation; *la adaptación de una novela al teatro* the adaptation of a novel for the theatre || fitting; *la adaptación de un segundo carburador a un motor* the fitting of a second carburettor to an engine.

adaptador, ra *adj* adapting, fitting.
◆ *m* adapter, adaptor || INFORM *adaptador de interfaz* interface adaptor.

adaptar *vt* to adapt; *adaptar una novela al teatro* to adapt a novel for the theatre || to adjust, to fit; *adaptar un sombrero a la cabeza de alguien* to adjust a hat to s.o.'s head || to adapt, to make suitable; *adaptar algo para otro uso* to adapt sth. for a different use || to model; *adaptar su conducta a la de su hermano* to model one's conduct on one's brother's.
◆ *vpr* to adapt o.s.; *adaptarse a la vida del campo* to adapt o.s. to country life.

adaraja *f* ARQ toothing stone.

adarga *f* shield, targe (escudo).

adarme *m* (ant) dram [measurement of weight] || FIG trace, grain; *no tiene un adarme de bondad* there isn't a grain of goodness in him || FIG *no me importa ni un adarme* I couldn't care less, I don't give a hang.

adarve *m* parapet walk (fortificación).

addenda *m inv* addenda *pl.*

Addis Abeba *n pr* GEOGR Addis Ababa.

adecentamiento *m* tidying-up.

adecentar *vt* to tidy up, to clean up (ordenar); *adecentar una ciudad* to tidy up a city.
◆ *vpr* to make o.s. decent, to tidy o.s. up.

adecuación *f* fitting, adjusting.

adecuadamente *adv* appropriately, suitably (convenientemente) || sufficiently, adequately (suficientemente).

adecuado, da *adj* appropriate, suitable (conveniente); *vehículo adecuado para este tipo de terreno* vehicle appropriate for this kind of land || adequate, sufficient (suficiente).

adecuar *vt* to make appropriate *o* suitable, to adapt.

adefesio *m* FAM ridiculously-dressed person, gaudily-dressed person || ridiculous *o* gaudy outfit (traje) || absurdity, piece of nonsense (disparate) || — FAM *estar hecho un adefesio* to look a sight, to be dressed like a clown, to be outrageously dressed | *poner como un adefesio* to dress up like a clown.

adehala *f* tip, gratuity (propina) || bonus (suplemento de sueldo).

adehesamiento *m* converting (of land) into pasture.

adehesar *vt* to convert into pasture.

adelantadamente *adv* beforehand, in advance.

adelantado, da *adj* advanced, precocious (niño) || early; *la vendimia está adelantada* the grape harvest is early || in advance; *pago adelantado* payment in advance || developed, advanced; *un país adelantado* a developed country || excellent, first-class (excelente) || forward, bold (atrevido) || — *eso tenemos* or *llevamos adelantado* that's one thing we've got done || *pase adelantado* long forward pass (en fútbol) || *por adelantado* in advance || *tengo el reloj adelantado* my watch is fast.
◆ *m* HIST «adelantado», governor (of a province) || FIG pioneer (precursor) || *adelantado de mar* captain of an expedition.

— OBSERV The *adelantado* was the person with highest political, military and judicial powers in America at the time of the Spanish conquest and colonization.

adelantamiento *m* advance (adelanto) || overtaking (de un coche) || HIST office of «adelantado» | district under an «adelantado» (territorio).

adelantar *vt* to advance, to move forward, to go forward; *adelantar cuatro pasos* to advance four steps || to put on, to put forward; *adelantar el reloj* to put one's watch forward || to go up, to advance; *adelantar cuatro puestos en la clase* to go up four places in the class || to speed up, to hurry along; *adelantar un trabajo* to speed up a job || to overtake; *adelantar un vehículo, a un atleta* to overtake a car, an athlete || DEP to pass forward (el balón) || to advance; *adelantar dinero* to advance money || to get, to win, to gain; *no adelantas nada gritando* you don't get anywhere by shouting, you don't win *o* gain anything by shouting || FIG to further, to promote (una idea).
◆ *vi* to go forward, to advance; *el ejército adelanta rápidamente* the army is advancing quickly || to progress, to make headway, to make progress; *ha adelantado mucho en matemáticas* he has progressed a lot in mathematics, he has made a lot of progress in mathematics || to be fast, to gain; *tu reloj adelanta mucho* your watch is very fast, your watch gains a lot || — *adelantar en edad* to be getting on || AUT *prohibido adelantar* no overtaking.
◆ *vpr* to go forward, to advance; *adelantarse al encuentro de alguien* to go forward to meet s.o. || to be early; *el verano se ha adelantado este año* summer was early this year || to be first; *yo me adelanté a recibirle* I was first to meet him || to go ahead; *me adelanto un momento a comprar tabaco* I'm going ahead a moment to buy some cigarettes || to go earlier; *él se adelantó un día para buscar alojamiento* he went a day earlier to look for lodgings || to anticipate; *me adelanté a sus deseos* I anticipated his wishes || to be ahead; *adelantarse a su época* to be ahead of one's time || to gain (un reloj) || to overtake (un coche) || — *adelantarse a la acción* to be one step ahead || *adelantarse a uno* to steal a march on s.o., to beat s.o. to it.

adelante *adv* further, ahead, forward; *marchemos adelante* let us go forward || — *camino adelante* further on || *de aquí en adelante, de hoy en adelante, en adelante* from now on, henceforth, in future || *de diez libras en adelante* from ten pounds up *o* upwards || *ir adelante* to make progress, to progress || *llevar adelante* to go ahead with, to carry out; *el general insiste en llevar adelante la ofensiva* the general insists on going ahead with the attack; to keep going,

to maintain (una familia), to carry on (un negocio) || *más adelante* late, later on, afterwards (luego), further on, later on (en textos) || *para más adelante* for later, for afterwards || *sacar adelante* to give a good education to, to bring up well; *el padre sacó adelante a sus diez hijos* the father gave a good education to his ten children; to make prosper (un negocio) || *salir adelante* to get on *o* by, to make out, to manage || *seguir adelante* to go on, to carry on (en un trabajo), to go straight on (en un camino).
◆ *interj* come in! (voz para que alguien entre), go on, carry on (siga) || FAM *¡adelante con los faroles!* carry on!, keep it up!, come on then!

adelanto *m* advance, step forward; *el descubrimiento de la luz eléctrica fue un gran adelanto* the discovery of electric light was a great step forward || improvement, advance, innovation; *el aparato lleva incorporados los últimos adelantos técnicos* the machine incorporates the latest technical advances || lead; *este ciclista tiene veinte minutos de adelanto sobre los otros* this cyclist has twenty minutes' lead over the others || advancement, progress; *el adelanto de las obras* the advancement of the work || advance (de dinero); *pedir un adelanto* to ask for an advance || — *el reloj tiene un adelanto de cinco minutos* the clock is five minutes fast || *los adelantos de la ciencia* the progress of science || *llegar con un adelanto de media hora* to arrive half an hour early || *tener un adelanto en su trabajo* to be ahead with one's work.

adelfa *f* BOT rosebay, common oleander.

adelfal *m* oleander grove.

adelgazador, ra *adj* slimming; *un régimen adelgazador* a slimming diet.

adelgazamiento *m* slimming (pérdida de peso); *cura, régimen de adelgazamiento* slimming cure, diet || thinning (de una cosa) || tapering (de una punta).

adelgazar *vt* to make thin, to thin (la madera, etc.) || to taper (una punta) || to lose; *he adelgazado tres kilos* I have lost three kilogrammes || to slim, to make slim (quitar peso a una persona); *esta medicina te adelgazará* this medicine will make you slim || to make thin (poner flaco) || to make look slim; *ese vestido la adelgaza mucho* that dress makes her look very slim || to scrimp (escatimar).
◆ *vi* to get thin, to lose weight (ponerse flaco) || to slim, to lose weight (ponerse delgado); *he adelgazado mucho* I've lost a lot of weight, I have slimmed a lot.
◆ *vpr* to slim, to lose weight.

ademán *m* expression, look; *ademán severo* severe look || gesture, movement (de las manos); *con un ademán amenazador* with a threatening gesture || position, posture (del cuerpo) || — *en ademán de* as if to, with the intention of (con intención de), as a sign of, as a token of; *en ademán de respeto* as a sign of respect || *hacer ademán de* to make a move to, to look as if one is going to *o* about to; *hizo ademán de marcharse* he made a move to go, he looked as if he was about to go; to signal to, to motion to (mandar); *me hizo ademán de que me callase* he signalled me to be quiet.
◆ *pl* manners, ways (modales); *tiene ademanes muy groseros* he has very crude manners || signs (manifestaciones).

además *adv* besides, in addition, also, as well (formas corrientes), moreover, furthermore (formas cultas) || *además de esto* besides this, on top of this, in addition of this, as well as this, furthermore.

adenoideo, a *adj* ANAT adenoid.

adenomatosis *f* MED adenomatosis.

adenotomía *f* MED adenotomy.

adentellar *vt* to bite || ARQ to leave toothing stones in [a wall].

adentrarse *vpr* to penetrate *o* to go *o* to enter deep *o* deeply; *adentrarse en un bosque* to penetrate deep into a wood || to go deeply, to study thoroughly; *adentrarse en un asunto* to go deeply into a subject, to study a subject thoroughly || *adentrarse en uno mismo* to become absorbed in thought, to become deep in thought.

adentro *adv* inside; *vamos adentro* let's go inside || far in; *la espina estaba tan adentro que no pude sacarla* the thorn was so far in that I couldn't get it out || — *mar adentro* out to sea, towards the open sea || *tierra adentro* inland.
◆ *m pl* heart *sing* || — *decir para sus adentros* to say to o.s. || *en* or *para sus adentros no quiere venir* in his heart he does not want to come, deep down he does not want to come || *hablar para sus adentros* to talk to o.s.
◆ *interj* come in!
— OBSERV In Latin America the interjection *¡adentro!* is often used in singing and dancing to encourage the singers to begin singing again and the dancers to begin dancing.

adepto, ta *adj* who supports, in favour, supporting.
◆ *m/f* supporter, adept, follower; *adepto del gobierno* government supporter || member, adept (afiliado).

aderezamiento *m* → **aderezo.**

aderezar *vt* to adorn, to decorate (adornar) || to beautify (hermosear) || to deck out, to dress up (ataviar) || CULIN to cook, to prepare, to get ready | to dress (la ensalada) | to season (aliñar); *limón para aderezar* lemon juice for seasoning | to flavour (bebidas) || to prepare, to get ready (disponer) || to dress, to give a finish to (dar apresto a las telas) || to guide (guiar) || FIG to season.
◆ *vpr* to get ready (prepararse) || to deck o.s. out, to dress up (ataviarse).

aderezo; aderezamiento *m* dressing, toilet (acción de embellecerse) || ornament, adornment, decoration (adorno) || set of jewellery (joyas) || CULIN cooking, preparation (de la comida) | dressing (de ensalada) | seasoning (con especias, etc.) | flavouring (de bebidas) || finishing, dressing (de las telas).

adeudado, da *adj* owing (cantidad que se debe) || in debt (persona que debe dinero).

adeudar *vt* to owe, to have a debt of; *adeudar un millón de pesetas* to owe *o* to have a debt of a million pesetas || COM to charge, to debit (en una cuenta).
◆ *vpr* to get *o* to run into debt.

adeudo *m* COM debit, charge (de una cuenta) || duty (en las aduanas) || debt (deuda).

adherencia *f* sticking, adhesion (acción de pegar) || adherence (acción de adherir) || roadholding (de un coche) || MED adhesion || *tener buena adherencia* to have good roadholding, to hold the road well (un coche).

adherente *adj* adherent.
◆ *m/f* adherent, follower.
◆ *pl* accessories.

adherir* *vt* to stick on; *adherir un sello* to stick a stamp on.
◆ *vi* to stick; *este parche no adhiere* this patch will not stick.
◆ *vi/vpr* to adhere, to follow (una doctrina, un partido); *no se adhiere a ningún partido* he does not adhere to any party, he does not follow any party || to join (afiliarse).

adhesión *f* adhesion, adherence (de algo pegado) || adherence (a una doctrina, etc.) || membership (afiliación) || support (apoyo); *espero poder contar con su adhesión* I hope to be able to count on your support.

adhesivo, va *adj/sm* adhesive.

adiabático, ca *adj* FÍS adiabatic.

adiamantado, da *adj* diamond-like.

adiar *vt* to fix, to appoint.

adicción *f* addiction.

adición *f* addition; *hacer adiciones a un texto* to make additions to a text || MAT addition || JUR acceptance; *adición de una herencia* acceptance of an inheritance || AMER bill [US check] (cuenta).

adicional *adj* additional, supplementary; *poner una cláusula adicional en un contrato* to put an additional clause in a contract.

adicionar *vt* to add; *adicionar un párrafo a un artículo* to add a paragraph to an article || MAR to add (up).

adicto, ta *adj* devoted, faithful; *un amigo adicto* a devoted friend || addicted (a drogas) || *ser muy adicto a una causa* to be very devoted to a cause.
◆ *m/f* follower, supporter (partidario) || addict (a drogas).

adiestrado, da *adj* trained, instructed || HERÁLD dexterwise.

adiestrador, ra *adj* who trains *o* instructs.
◆ *m/f* trainer, instructor.

adiestramiento *m* training (de un animal) || training, instruction; *adiestramiento de las tropas* troop training.

adiestrar *vt* to train (un animal) || to train, to instruct (una persona) || to guide, to lead (guiar).
◆ *vpr* to train o.s., to practise, to instruct o.s.; *adiestrarse en el uso de la espada* to train o.s. to use a sword, to practise using a sword, to instruct o.s. in the use of the sword.

adietar *vt* to put on a diet.

Adigio *npr m* GEOGR Adige.

adinerado, da *adj* rich, wealthy, well-off, well-to-do.
◆ *m/f* rich *o* wealthy person.

adinerarse *vpr* FAM to get rich *o* wealthy, to make one's fortune.

adintelado, da *adj* ARQ flat (arco).

¡adiós! *interj* good-bye, farewell, adieu (véase OBSERV) || hello (al cruzarse con alguien) || — FAM *¡adiós mi dinero!* that's good-bye to my money!, there went my money! | *decir adiós a sus pretensiones* to give up one's ambitions, to say good-bye to one's ambitions.
◆ *m* good-bye, farewell.
— OBSERV En inglés las interjecciones *farewell* y *adieu* son antiguas y sólo se emplean para una despedida definitiva.

¡adiosito! *interj* AMER cheerio!

adiposidad *f* MED adiposity, obesity.

adiposo, sa *adj* ANAT fatty, adipose; *tejido adiposo* fatty tissue || obese, fat (persona).

adir *vt* JUR to accept [an inheritance].

aditamento *m* addition (añadido) || accessory (accesorio).

aditivo *m* additive; *aditivos alimentarios* food additives.

adivinable *adj* forseeable (previsible) || guessable (por conjeturas).

adivinación *f*; **adivinamiento** *m* divination (de los adivinos) || solution (de un enigma o acertijo) || guessing (descubrimiento por conjeturas) || *adivinación del pensamiento* thought reading, mind reading.

adivinador, ra *m/f* fortune-teller (adivino).

adivinanza *f* riddle, puzzle, conundrum.

adivinar *vt* to divine, to prophesy, to foretell (el porvenir, etc.) || to guess (acertar por conjeturas) || to read; *adivinar el pensamiento de alguien* to read s.o.'s mind || to solve; *adivinar* *un acertijo* to solve a riddle || — *¡adivina quién soy!* guess who! || *adivina quién te dio* blindman's buff (juego infantil) || *¡a que no lo adivina!* I bet you can't guess || *dejar adivinar* to hint at (con sustantivo), to hint that (con locución verbal); *dejó adivinar su descontento* he hinted at his unhappiness, he hinted that he was unhappy.

adivinatorio, ria *adj* divinatory.

adivino, na *m/f* fortune-teller.

adjetivación *f* adjectival use, use as an adjective.

adjetivamente *adv* adjectivally.

adjetival *adj* adjectival.

adjetivar *vt* to use as an adjective, to use adjectivally || to describe; *lo adjetivaron de inmenso* they described it as immense.

adjetivo, va *adj* adjectival, adjective; *expresión adjetiva* adjectival expression.
◆ *m* adjective.

adjudicación *f* award, awarding || sale (subasta).

adjudicador, ra *adj* awarding.
◆ *m/f* awarder.

adjudicar *vt* to award (conceder); *le adjudicaron el primer premio* they awarded him first prize || to sell, to knock down (algo en una subasta) || *¡adjudicado!* sold! (en una subasta).
◆ *vpr* to appropriate (apropiarse).

adjudicatario, ria *m/f* awardee || successful bidder (en una subasta).

adjuntar *vt* to attach, to append (a un documento) || to enclose; *le adjunto un sobre con un sello* I enclose a stamped adressed envelope || to give; *le van a ajuntar un auxiliar* they are going to give him an assistant.

adjunto, ta *adj* attached (a un texto, documento, etc.) || enclosed, attached (en una carta); *la tarifa adjunta* the enclosed price list || assistant; *profesor adjunto* assistant teacher || *remitir algo adjunto* to enclose sth.
◆ *m/f* assistant.

adjuración *f* adjuration.

adjurar *vt* to adjure.

adjutor, ra *adj/s* assistant.

adlátere *m* inseparable companion, lapdog.

adminículo *m* thing, gadget; *la patilla de las gafas tenía un adminículo para mejorar la audición* the spectacles had a thing on the arm to improve one's hearing.

administración *f* administration || management, running, administration (gestión) || management (los gerentes) || administrative centre, headquarters *pl* (oficina) || — *administración de Correos* Post Office || *administración pública* public administration, civil service *Consejo de administración* board of directors.

administrado, da *adj* under administration.
◆ *m/f* person under administration.

administrador, ra *adj* administrating.
◆ *m/f* administrator || manager, administrator (de una finca) || — *administrador de aduanas* customs officer || *administrador de Correos* postmaster || *es buena administradora* she is a good housewife.

administrar *vt* to administer, to run, to manage, to administrate (regir) || to administer (sacramentos, medicamentos) || FAM to hand out, to dish out (dar); *administrar una paliza* to hand out a beating || *administrar (la) justicia* to administer *o* to dispense justice.

administrativo, va *adj* administrative.
◆ *m* office worker, white-collar worker.

admirable *adj* admirable.

admiración *f* admiration; *causar admiración* to inspire admiration || surprise, wonder, astonishment; *su llegada puntual me llenó de admiración* his punctual arrival filled me with wonder || GRAM exclamation mark || — *ser la admiración de alguien* to be the object of s.o.'s admiration, to be admired by s.o. || *tener* or *sentir admiración por alguien* to feel admiration for s.o., to admire s.o.

admirador, ra *adj* admiring.
◆ *m/f* admirer.

admirar *vt* to admire; *admiro su valor* I admire his courage || to surprise, to astonish, to amaze (sorprender); *tanta generosidad me admira* such generosity amazes me || *quedarse admirado* to be astonished *o* astounded (maravillarse).
◆ *vpr* to be amazed *o* surprised *o* astonished; *me admiro de su insolencia* I am amazed at his insolence || to admire, to have great admiration for, to marvel at; *me admiro de los progresos científicos* I have great admiration for scientific progress.

admirativamente *adv* admiringly, with admiration, in admiration || amazedly, in wonderment (con asombro).

admirativo, va *adj* admiring (que admira); *hablar en tono admirativo* to speak in an admiring tone || amazed (asombrado).

admisibilidad *f* admissibility.

admisible *adj* admissible, acceptable, permissible; *tal conducta no es admisible* such behaviour is not permissible || acceptable (excusa).

admisión *f* admission || acceptance (aceptación) || TECN induction, intake (en un motor de explosión) || — *examen de admisión* entrance examination || *reservado el derecho de admisión* the management reserves the right to refuse admission || TECN *válvula de admisión* inlet valve.

admitancia *f* ELECTR admittance.

admitir *vt* to admit; *admitir a uno en una sociedad* to admit s.o. to a society || to accept, to admit; *en correos no admiten paquetes voluminosos* bulky parcels are not accepted by the post office || to accept for, to allow to sit (un examen) || to allow, to permit; *yo no puedo admitir esto* I can't allow this || to acknowledge, to admit, to recognize, to agree; *admito que estaba equivocado* I admit I was wrong || to suppose; *admitamos que tenga razón* supposing he is right, let us suppose he is right || to hold; *el estadio admite quinientos espectadores* the stadium holds five hundred spectators || to allow (explicación) || to lend o.s. to, to be open to; *esta frase admite varias interpretaciones* this sentence lends itself to several interpretations || — *este asunto no admite dilación* this matter must be deal with immediately || *esto no admite duda* there is no doubt about this, this leaves no room for doubt || *no se admiten propinas* no tipping.

admonición *f* rebuke, admonition, reprimand.

admonitorio, ria *adj* admonitory, reprimanding.

adobado, da *adj* CULIN marinated.
◆ *m* CULIN marinated meat.

ADN *abrev de ácido desoxirribonucleico* DNA, deoxyribonucleid acid.

adobador, ra *m/f* pickler (de carnes) || tanner (de pieles).

adobadura *f*; **adobamiento** *m* CULIN pickling, marinating (de la carne) | dressing, seasoning (de ciertos platos) || tanning (de las pieles).

adobar *vt* CULIN to pickle, to marinate (la carne, el pescado) | to season, to dress (sazonar) | to cook (guisar) || to tan (las pieles) || FIG to twist, to turn round; *adobar un relato* to twist a story.

adobe *m* sun-dried brick, adobe (ladrillo secado al sol) || AMER big foot (pie).

adobera *f* brick mould || adobe yard, brickyard (adobería) || AMER cheese mould | rectangular cheese (queso).

adobería *f* adobe yard, brickyard || tannery (curtiduría).

adobo *m* CULIN seasoning, dressing (aderezamiento) | cooking (acción de guisar) || pickling sauce, marinade (para carne y pescado) || tanning (de pieles) || tanning mixture (mezcla para las pieles) || (p us) makeup (afeite) || *carne, pescado en adobo* marinated meat, fish.

adocenado, da *adj* commonplace, ordinary, common or garden (*fam*).

adocenar *vt* to divide into dozens.
◆ *vpr* to become commonplace *o* ordinary.

adoctrinamiento *m* indoctrination || teaching (enseñanza).

adoctrinar *vt* to indoctrinate (condicionar) || to teach (enseñar).

adolecer* *vi* to fall ill (caer enfermo) || to suffer, to have; *adolecer de reúma* to suffer from *o* to have rheumatism || FIG to have, to suffer; *adolecer de ciertos defectos* to suffer from certain faults || — FIG *adolece de ser apático* his fault *o* failing is that he is apathetic, his fault *o* failing is his apathy | *el libro adolece de monotonía* the book's fault *o* failing is its monotony.

adolescencia *f* adolescence.

adolescente *adj/s* adolescent.

Adolfo *npr m* Adolph.

adonde *adv* where, whither (ant) || *el lugar adonde voy* the place where I am going, the place I am going to.

— OBSERV *Where* without the idea of movement is usually translated by *donde: la casa donde vivo* the house where I live. *Adonde* is also sometimes seen where no movement is involved, but this usage is now obsolete. In an interrogative sentence, *adonde* has a written accent: *¿adónde va?* where is he going?

adondequiera *adv* wherever, wheresoever (movimiento); *adondequiera que vayamos* wherever we (may) go.

Adonis *npr m* Adonis.

adonizarse *vpr* to beautify o.s., to tittivate o.s.

adopción *f* adoption; *país de adopción* country of adoption.

adoptar *vt* to adopt (un hijo, una costumbre, una actitud, una resolución) || to assume, to adopt; *adoptar la nacionalidad británica* to assume British nationality.

adoptivo, va *adj* adopted, adoptive (hijo) || adoptive (padres) || — FIG *hijo adoptivo* honorary citizen (de una ciudad) || *patria adoptiva* country of adoption.

adoquín *m* paving stone (piedra) || FIG & FAM numbskull, dunce, dimwit (necio); *eres un adoquín* you're a numbskull || AMER wooden paving block (tarugo) || FIG & FAM *me comería hasta adoquines* I could eat a horse.

adoquinado, da *adj* paved.
◆ *m* paving.

adoquinador *m* paver.

adoquinar *vt* to pave.

adorable *adj* adorable.

adoración *f* worship, adoration (de Dios) || adoration, idolization, worshipping (de una persona) || *Adoración de los Reyes* Epiphany.

adorador, ra *adj* worshipping, adoring (que adora a Dios) || adoring, idolizing (que adora a otra persona).

◆ *m/f* worshipper, adorer (de Dios) ‖ adorer, idolizer (de una persona).

adorar *vt* to worship, to adore (a Dios) ‖ to adore, to worship, to idolize (a una persona).
◆ *vi* to pray (orar).

adoratorio *m* portable retable ‖ AMER Indian temple.

adormecedor, ra *adj* soporific, sleep-inducing ‖ FIG sedative (sedante).

adormecer* *vt* to make sleepy, to send to sleep; *esta música me adormece* this music is sending me to sleep ‖ FIG to calm, to soothe; *el opio adormece los dolores* opium soothes pain.
◆ *vpr* to fall asleep (dormirse) ‖ to grow drowsy, to drowse, to doze (amodorrarse) ‖ FIG to go to sleep, to turn numb (un miembro) ‖ to give o.s. up to; *adormecerse en un vicio* to give o.s. up to a vice.

adormecido, da *adj* sleepy, drowsy ‖ numb, asleep (un miembro).

adormecimiento *m* drowsiness, sleepiness ‖ numbness (de un miembro) ‖ FIG calmness.

adormidera *f* BOT poppy ‖ narcotic, drug (estupefaciente).

adormilarse; adormitarse *vpr* to become drowsy, to drowse, to doze.

adornamiento *m* decoration, adornment ‖ finery (atavío).

adornar *vt* to decorate, to adorn; *adornar con* or *de flores* to decorate with flowers ‖ to trim (trajes, etc.) ‖ FIG to elaborate on, to embellish; *adornar una historia* to embellish a story ‖ to garnish (la comida) ‖ FIG *las virtudes que le adornan* the virtues with which he is endowed *o* blessed.
◆ *vpr* to be decorated *o* adorned ‖ to dress up (ataviarse).

adorno *m* decoration, adornment ‖ trimming (de trajes) ‖ CULIN garnishing ‖ TAUR «adorno» (véase OBSERV) ‖ *de adorno* decorative.
◆ *pl* BOT balsamine *sing.*
— OBSERV The *adorno* is a gesture made by the bullfighter (turning his back on the bull, stroking the bull's head, touching its horns, etc.) which «adorns» his performance and is intended to show his domination of the bull.

adosamiento *m* leaning.

adosar *vt* to lean; *adosar una silla a la pared* to lean a chair against the wall ‖ ARQ *columna adosada* embedded column.

adovelado, da *adj* ARQ voussoir.

adquirente *adj/s* ⟶ **adquisidor.**

adquirido, da *adj* acquired; *velocidad adquirida* acquired speed; *hábito adquirido* acquired habit ‖ purchased, bought, acquired (comprado).

adquiridor, ra *adj/s* ⟶ **adquisidor.**

adquirir* *vt* to acquire; *adquirir un hábito* to acquire a habit ‖ to purchase, to buy, to acquire; *he adquirido una bicicleta* I have purchased a bicycle.

adquisición *f* acquisition ‖ acquisition, purchase (compra) ‖ INFORM *adquisición de datos* data acquisition.

adquisidor, ra; adquiridor, ra; adquirente *adj* acquiring ‖ purchasing, buying, acquiring.
◆ *m/f* purchaser, buyer (comprador).

adquisitivo, va *adj* acquisitive ‖ — *poder adquisitivo* purchasing power ‖ JUR *prescripción adquisitiva* positive prescription.

adragante; adraganto *m* tragacanth (goma) ‖ BOT tragacanth.

adral *m* rail, rave, rack (de un carro).

adrede *adv* on purpose, deliberately, purposely.

adrenalectomía *f* MED adrenalectomy.

adrenalina *f* BIOL adrenalin.

Adrián *npr m* Adrian.

Adriano *npr m* Hadrian.

Adriático *npr m* GEOGR Adriatic.

adrizamiento *m* MAR righting.

adrizar *vt* MAR to right.

adscribir *vt* to attribute, to ascribe (atribuir) ‖ to assign, to appoint (destinar); *le adscribieron al servicio de ventas* they assigned him to the sales department.
— OBSERV The past participle of *adscribir* is irregular (*adscrito, ta*, or the less common *adscripto, ta*).

adscripción *f* attribution (atribución) ‖ appointment, assignment (destino).

adscripto, ta; adscrito, ta *adj* attributed, ascribed ‖ appointed, assigned (destinado).

adsorbente *adj/sm* QUÍM adsorbent.

adsorber *vt* QUÍM to adsorb.

adsorción *f* QUÍM adsorption.

aduana *f* customs *pl*; *derechos de aduana* customs duty; *pasar por la aduana* to go through customs ‖ customhouse, customs building (oficina) ‖ — *oficial de aduana(s)* customs officer ‖ *sin aduana* duty-free.

aduanar *vt* to pay customs duty on.

aduanero, ra *adj* customs; *tarifa aduanera* customs tariff.
◆ *m* customs officer.

aduar *m* douar, dowar (de beduinos) ‖ encampment, camp (de gitanos).

aducción *f* adduction.

aducir* *vt* to allege, to plead (razones) ‖ to adduce, to produce (pruebas) ‖ to advance, to bring forward (disculpas) ‖ to cite, to quote (un texto).

aductor *adj* ANAT adductive.
◆ *m* ANAT adductor.

adueñarse *vpr* to take possession of, to appropriate; *se adueñó de mi coche* he appropriated my car.

aduja *f* coil (de un cable).

adujar *vt* MAR to coil.
◆ *vpr* to curl up.

adulación; adulonería *f* flattery, adulation (lisonja).

adulador, ra *adj* flattering, adulating.
◆ *m/f* flatterer, adulator.

adular *vt* to flatter, to adulate.

adulatorio, ria *adj* flattering, adulating.

adulón, ona *adj* grovelling, fawning.
◆ *m/f* crawler, toady.

adulonería *f* ⟶ **adulación.**

adulteración *f* adulteration.

adulterado, da *adj* adulterated, adulterate.

adulterador, ra *adj* adulterating.
◆ *m/f* adulterator.

adulterar *vt* to adulterate; *adulterar la verdad* to adulterate the truth; *adulterar la leche con agua* to adulterate milk with water.
◆ *vi* to commit adultery.

adulterinamente *adv* adulterously.

adulterino, na *adj* adulterine; *hijo adulterino* adulterine child.

adulterio *m* adultery (acto).

adúltero, ra *adj* adulterous.
◆ *m/f* adulterer, adulteress.

adulto, ta *adj/s* adult, grown-up ‖ *una nación adulta* a mature nation.

adulzar *vt* TECN to soften.

adustez *f* severity, austerity, harshness.

adusto, ta *adj* (p us) scorching hot (muy caliente) ‖ FIG severe, austere, harsh; *rostro adusto* harsh expression.

advenedizo, za *adj/s* upstart, parvenu; *en aquella época pululaban los advenedizos* at that time there were swarms of upstarts.

advenimiento *m* coming (llegada) ‖ advent (del mesías) ‖ arrival, coming, advent (de una época) ‖ accession (de un soberano) ‖ FIG & FAM *parece que estás esperando el santo Advenimiento* you look as if you're waiting for Christmas.

advenir* *vi* to come, to arrive.
— OBSERV This verb is used only in the third person of the past historic.

adventicio, cia *adj* accidental, adventitious (ocasional) ‖ BOT adventitious.

adventista *adj/s* Adventist.

adverado, da *adj* certified, legalized (certificado).

adverar *vt* to certify, to legalize.

adverbial *adj* adverbial; *locución adverbial* adverbial phrase.

adverbializar *vt* to use as an adverb.

adverbio *m* GRAM adverb.

adversario, ria *adj* opposing; *el equipo adversario* the opposing team.
◆ *m/f* opponent, adversary; *derribar al adversario* to knock down one's opponent.

adversativo, va *adj* GRAM adversative.

adversidad *f* adversity, misfortune, setback; *sufrió muchas adversidades* he suffered many setbacks ‖ *se conoce a los amigos en la adversidad* a friend in need is a friend indeed.

adverso, sa *adj* adverse, unfavourable; *situación adversa* unfavourable situation ‖ bad; *suerte adversa* bad luck ‖ opposing (adversario); *el equipo adverso* the opposing team ‖ opposite (opuesto materialmente).

advertencia *f* warning; *después de repetidas advertencias se negaron a dispersarse* after repeated warnings they refused to disperse ‖ piece of advice (consejo) ‖ explanation (explicación) ‖ note, explanation, observation (nota) ‖ foreword (prólogo) ‖ MAR call ‖ — JUR *advertencia conminatoria* summons ‖ *hacer una advertencia a un niño* to correct a child, to tell a child off.

advertidamente *adv* knowingly.

advertido, da *adj* informed, warned (avisado) ‖ experienced; *una secretaria muy advertida* a very experienced secretary.

advertidor *adj* warning.

advertimiento *m* warning (advertencia).

advertir* *vt* to warn, to inform; *te advierto que mañana no vendré* I warn you that I'm not coming tomorrow ‖ to warn of, to give warning of; *una señal de tráfico advertía el peligro* a road sign gave warning of the danger ‖ to tell, to recommend, to advise; *adviértele que no llegue tarde a la reunión* advise him not to arrive late at the meeting ‖ to warn; *te advierto que es la última vez que lo tolero* I warn you that it's the last time I'll stand for it ‖ to point out (señalar); *le advierto algunos errores* I will point out a few mistakes to you ‖ to notice, to observe, to see, to realize; *he advertido que había muchas faltas* I noticed that there were many mistakes ‖ to tell; *te advierto que soy el menos interesado en esta reforma* I tell you I am the least interested in this reform.
◆ *vi* to realize, to understand (comprender).

Adviento *m* Advent; *el cuarto domingo de Adviento* the fourth Sunday of Advent.

advocación *f* REL invocation ‖ — REL *bajo la advocación de la Virgen* dedicated to the Virgin ‖ *poner bajo la advocación de* to dedicate to.

adyacente *adj* adjacent.

adyuvante *adj* helping, assisting.

AEB *abrev de Asociación Española de Banca Privada* Spanish Private Banking Association.

aedo *m* bard (poeta).

Aenor *abrev de Asociación Española para la Normalización y Racionalización* Spanish industrial standards authority.

aeración *f* QUÍM aeration ‖ ventilation (ventilación).

aéreo, a *adj* aerial; *fotografía aérea* aerial photography ‖ air; *tráfico aéreo* air traffic ‖ flimsy, light (ligero) ‖ — *compañía aérea* airline company ‖ *ferrocarril aéreo* overhead *o* elevated railway ‖ *línea aérea* airline ‖ *toma aérea* aerial ‖ *transportador aéreo* cableway.

aereofotografía *f* ⟶ **aerofotografía.**

aerífero, ra *adj* air.

aerobic *m* aerobics.

aerobio, bia *adj* BIOL aerobic.
◆ *m* BIOL aerobe.

aeroclub *m* flying club.

aerodeslizador *m* hovercraft.

aerodinámico, ca *adj* aerodynamic ‖ streamlined; *la forma aerodinámica de un avión* the streamlined shape of a plane ‖ — *freno aerodinámico* air brake ‖ *túnel aerodinámico* wind tunnel.
◆ *f* aerodynamics.

aerodino *m* aerodyne.

aeródromo *m* aerodrome [US airdrome], airfield.

aerofagia *f* aerophagia.

aerofaro *m* runway beacon, aerial beacon.

aerofotografía; aereofotografía *f* aerial photography (arte) ‖ aerial photograph (foto).

aerógrafo *m* ARTES airbrush.

aerograma *m* aerogram.

aerolito *m* ASTR aerolite, meteorite.

aeromarítimo, ma *adj* aeromarine.

aerometría *f* aerometry.

aerómetro *m* aerometer.

aeromodelismo *m* aeromodelling, aeroplane modelling [US airplane modeling].

aeromodelista *adj* aeroplane modelling, aeromodelling [US airplane modeling].
◆ *m/f* aeroplane modeller [US airplane modeler].

aeromodelo *m* model aeroplane [US model airplane].

aeromotor *m* aeromotor.

aeromoza *f* AMER air hostess, stewardess (azafata).

aeromozo *m* AMER steward.

aeronauta *m/f* aeronaut.

aeronáutico, ca *adj* aeronautical, aeronautic.
◆ *f* aeronautics.

aeronaval *adj* sea and air, aeromarine; *batalla aeronaval* sea and air battle.

aeronave *f* airship ‖ *aeronave espacial* spaceship.

aeronavegación *f* aerial navigation.

aeroplano *m* aeroplane [US airplane] (avión).

aeropostal *adj* airmail.

aeropuerto *m* airport.

aerosol *m* aerosol.

aerostación *f* balloon-flying, aerostation.

aerostático, ca *adj* aerostatic.
◆ *f* aerostatics.

aeróstato *m* aerostat (globo).

aerotaxi *m* taxi-plane.

aerotecnia; aerotécnica *f* aeronautics.

aerotécnico, ca *adj* aerotechnical.

aeroterapia *f* aerotherapy, aerotherapeutics.

aerotermodinámica *f* aerothermodynamics.

afabilidad *f* affability, geniality, pleasantness (amabilidad).

afabilísimo, ma *adj* very affable, very pleasant.

afable *adj* affable, pleasant, genial; *afable con* or *para con todos* affable with everyone.

afabulación *f* moral of a fable.

afacetado, da *adj* in facets.

afamado, da *adj* famous, renowned (famoso).

afamar *vt* to make famous, to bring renown to.
◆ *vpr* to win fame, to become famous.

afán *m* toil, labour (trabajo penoso); *los afanes cotidianos* the daily toils ‖ enthusiasm, zeal, eagerness, fervour; *trabajar con afán* to work with enthusiasm ‖ desire, urge (deseo) ‖ anxiety (preocupación) ‖ — *afán de lucro* profit motive ‖ *cada día trae su afán* sufficient unto the day is the evil thereof ‖ *con afán* enthusiastically, zealously, keenly ‖ *poner todo su afán en* to put all one's efforts into, to put everything one has into.

afanador, ra *adj* enthusiastic, zealous, fervent.
◆ *m/f* enthusiastic *o* zealous *o* eager *o* fervent person ‖ POP thief ‖ AMER labourer.

afanar *vi* to toil (en trabajos penosos).
◆ *vt* to work hard, to press hard (cansar con mucho trabajo) ‖ FAM to pinch, to swipe, to steal (robar) ‖ AMER to make, to earn [money].
◆ *vpr* to toil, to labour ‖ to do one's utmost, to strive; *afanarse por* or *en conseguir un buen puesto* to do one's utmost to get a good job, to strive to get a good job.

afanosamente *adv* enthusiastically, zealously, fervently ‖ laboriously (con mucho trabajo) ‖ *desear afanosamente* to want desperately *o* urgently.

afanoso, sa *adj* laborious, hard, wearying, heavy (trabajoso) ‖ enthusiastic, industrious, hard-working, keen (concienzudo) ‖ worried, anxious (preocupado) ‖ hectic, feverish (la búsqueda).

afantasmado, da *adj* FAM big-headed, conceited, vain (presumido).

afarolado, da *adj* AMER worked up, excited (emocionado) ‖ angry (enfadado) ‖ TAUR *pase afarolado* «afarolado» pass [when the bullfighter swings his cape above his head].
◆ *m* «afarolado» pass.

afarolarse *vpr* AMER to get excited *o* worked up (conturbarse) ‖ to get angry (enfadarse).

afasia *f* MED aphasia.

afásico, ca *adj/s* MED aphasic.

afeador, ra *adj* disfiguring, which makes ugly ‖ reproachful, condemning, censuring (que censura).

afeamiento *m* disfigurement ‖ censure, condemnation.

afear *vt* to make ugly, to disfigure; *este maquillaje le afea* this makeup makes her ugly ‖ to reproach, to censure; *afear mucho a uno su conducta* to reproach s.o. severely for his behaviour.

afección *f* affection (cariño) ‖ MED affection, complaint, disease; *afección cardíaca* heart disease; *afección hepática* liver disease.

afeccionarse *vpr* to become attached, to grow fond; *afeccionarse por uno* to become attached to s.o., to grow fond of s.o.

afectación *f* affectation.

afectado, da *adj* affected, unnatural (amanerado) ‖ damaged, spoiled; *finca afectada por la inundación* farm damaged by the flood ‖ upset; *está muy afectado por la muerte de su madre* he is very upset over the death of his mother ‖ — *estar afectado del corazón* to have a heart complaint ‖ *estar afectado de un ataque gripal* to be suffering from an attack of influenza.

afectar *vt* to affect, to put on a show of; *afectar suma elegancia* to affect great elegance, to put on a show of great elegance ‖ to pretend, to feign; *afectó un dolor de cabeza para salir de la conferencia* he pretended to have a headache *o* he feigned a headache as an excuse to leave the lecture ‖ to adopt, to take on; *afectar la forma de estrella* to adopt the shape of a star ‖ to concern, to affect (atañer); *esta ley afecta a todos los ciudadanos* this law concerns all citizens ‖ to damage (dañar); *las tormentas han afectado las cosechas* the storms have damaged the crops ‖ to upset, to make sad, to trouble; *la enfermedad de su madre le afecta mucho* his mother's illness upsets him a lot ‖ to affect, to have an effect on; *su pulmonía le ha afectado mucho* his pneumonia has affected him seriously.
◆ *vi* to affect, to concern; *un problema que afecta a la economía* a problem which affects the economy.

afectísimo, ma *adj* my dear; *afectísimo amigo* my dear friend ‖ COM sincerely, faithfully (al final de cartas); *suyo afectísimo* yours sincerely, sincerely yours ‖ *su afectísimo servidor* your devoted servant.

afectividad *f* affectivity ‖ sensitivity, sensitiveness (sensibilidad).

afectivo, va *adj* affective (referente a las emociones) ‖ sensitive (sensible) ‖ affectionate (cariñoso).

afecto, ta *adj* dear; *un amigo afecto* a dear friend ‖ — *afecto a* fond of, attached to (alguien), subject to, liable to (los impuestos) ‖ MED *afecto de* suffering from, afflicted with.
◆ *m* affection, fondness (cariño) ‖ *tomar afecto a alguien* to become attached to *o* fond of s.o.

afectuosidad *f* affection, fondness.

afectuoso, sa *adj* affectionate.

afeitado *m* shave ‖ TAUR blunting of the horns, shaving.

afeitadora *f* razor, shaver.

afeitar *vt* to shave ‖ (ant) to make up, to put makeup on (poner afeites) ‖ to trim (los animales) ‖ to cut, to trim (césped, plantas) ‖ TAUR to blunt the horns of, to shave ‖ FIG & FAM to graze, to brush (rozar).
◆ *vpr* to shave, to have a shave (la barba, etc.) ‖ to make up, to make o.s. up (ponerse afeites).

afeite *m* (ant) makeup, cosmetics *pl* (cosmético).

afelio *m* ASTR aphelion.

afelpado, da *adj* plush, velvety.

afelpar *vt* to make velvety *o* plush.

afeminación *f* effeminacy.

afeminadamente *adv* in an effeminate way, effeminately.

afeminado, da *adj* effeminate.
◆ *m* effeminate person, sissy, cissy (*fam*).

afeminamiento *m* effeminacy.

afeminar *vt* to make effeminate.
◆ *vpr* to become effeminate.

aferente *adj* ANAT afferent.

aféresis *f* GRAM aphaeresis.

aferrado, da *adj* obstinate, stubborn (obstinado) || FIG established; *una idea bien aferrada* a well established idea || *seguir aferrado a* to stand by, to stick to.

aferramiento *m* seizing-grasping (acción de agarrar) || MAR mooring, anchoring (acción de anclar) || FIG obstinacy, stubbornness.

aferrar* *vt* to seize, to grasp, to clutch (agarrar) || MAR to anchor, to moor (anclar) | to take in, to furl (las velas) | to hook, to grapple (con un garfio).
◆ *vi* MAR to bite, to grip (el ancla) | to anchor (el barco).
◆ *vpr* to cling || MAR to anchor || FIG to stick, to cling (obstinarse); *aferrarse a* or *en una idea, una opinión* to cling to an idea, an opinion.

afestonado, da *adj* festooned (festonado) || scalloped (labrado en forma de festón).

affaire *m* case, affair (caso).

Afganistán *npr m* GEOGR Afghanistan.

afgano, na *adj/s* Afghan.

afianzador, ra *adj* guaranteeing.

afianzamiento *m* guarantee (garantía) || surety, bond (fianza) || strengthening, reinforcement; *el afianzamiento de las estructuras* the reinforcement of structures || establishment, consolidation; *el afianzamiento de un régimen* the establishment of a régime || building up, restoring; *el afianzamiento de la salud* the building up of one's health.

afianzar *vt* to guarantee (garantizar) || to strengthen, to reinforce; *afianzar las patas de una silla* to strengthen the legs of a chair || to establish, to make secure; *su éxito le ha afianzado en su puesto* his success has established him in his job || to build up, to restore; *tienes que afianzar tu salud* you must build up your health || to make sure of, to fix in one's mind; *estudio un poco para afianzar lo que he oído en la conferencia* I am studying a little to fix in my mind what I heard in the lecture, I'm studying a little to make sure of what I heard in the lecture || to support, to back (sostener) || to grasp, to seize (agarrar).
◆ *vpr* to seize, to grasp (agarrar) || to cling (agarrarse) || FIG to establish o.s., to secure o.s.; *afianzarse en un puesto* to secure o.s. in a job | to steady o.s. (afirmarse) | to become established (establecerse) | to set in (reacción, etc.).

afición *f* liking, love; *afición a la lectura* liking for reading, love of reading || taste; *su empleo está de acuerdo con sus aficiones* his job suits his tastes || fans *pl*, public; *la afición está satisfecha con el programa de corridas* the fans are satisfied with the programme of bullfights || hobby, interest (interés) || affection, fondness (cariño) || — *cobrar* or *tomar afición a* to acquire a taste for, to take a liking to || *por afición* as a hobby; *pintar por afición* to paint as a hobby; amateur; *pintor por afición* amateur painter || *tener afición a* to have a liking for, to like, to be fond of (cosas); *tengo afición al estudio* I like studying; to be fond of, to be attached to; *tener afición a una persona* to be fond of a person.

aficionado, da *adj* enthusiastic, keen (entusiasta) || fond, keen; *aficionado a la pintura* fond of *o* keen on painting || amateur (no profesional); *un ciclista aficionado* an amateur cyclist.
◆ *m/f* fan, enthusiast (a los deportes, al cine, etc.) || amateur (no profesional); *los Juegos Olímpicos están reservados a los aficionados* the Olympic Games are reserved for amateurs || lover (de las artes) || *partido de aficionados* amateur game.
— OBSERV When used by itself *aficionados* usually applies to *fans of bullfighting*, and it can be used with this meaning in English.

aficionar *vt* to make fond (inducir a amar) || to give a liking, to interest, to make fond; *me ha aficionado a la pintura* he has interested me in painting, he has given me a liking for painting.
◆ *vpr* to become fond *o* attached; *aficionarse a una persona* to become fond of a person, to become attached to a person || to take a liking, to become fond; *aficionarse a la pintura* to take a liking to painting, to become fond of painting.

afiche *m* AMER poster, bill.

afidávit *m* sworn statement.

áfido *m* aphid (insect).

afiebrarse *vpr* AMER to have a fever.

afijo, ja *adj* GRAM affixed.
◆ *m* GRAM affix.

afiladera *adj f* *piedra afiladera* hone, whetstone.
◆ *f* hone, whetstone.

afilado, da *adj* sharp; *cuchillo afilado* sharp knife || sharpened, sharp; *lápiz afilado* sharpened pencil || sharp, pointed; *diente afilado* pointed tooth || slender, slim; *dedos afilados* slender fingers || sharp, high-pitched, piercing; *voz afilada* high-pitched voice || — *cara afilada* long, thin face || FIG *tener las uñas afiladas* to be light-fingered.
◆ *m* sharpening (de un cuchillo, un lápiz).

afilador, ra *adj* sharpening.
◆ *m* knifegrinder (hombre) || strop (correa) || AMER Don Juan, Casanova.
◆ *f* AGR grinding machine, sharpening machine.

afiladura *f* sharpening (acción de afilar).

afilalápices *m inv* pencil sharpener (sacapuntas).

afilamiento *m* slenderness (de los dedos) || sharpness, pointedness (de la nariz, la cara).

afilar *vt* to sharpen, to grind; *afilar un cuchillo en una piedra* to sharpen a knife on a stone || to sharpen, to put an edge on (la hoja de algo) || to sharpen, to put a point on, to taper (sacar punta) || to sharpen (un lápiz) || to strop (la navaja) || to sharpen (la voz) || AMER FAM to court (cortejar) | to flatter (adular) || *piedra de afilar* whetstone, hone.
◆ *vpr* FIG to become peaked *o* drawn, to sharpen (la cara) || to grow pointed *o* sharp *o* thin; *su nariz se ha afilado* his nose has become pointed || to be slender, to taper (los dedos) || AMER to get ready (prepararse).

afiliación *f* affiliation.

afiliado, da *adj* affiliated || member; *los países afiliados* the member countries || subsidiary (una empresa).
◆ *m/f* member, affiliate; *afiliado a un partido* member of a party.

afiliar *vt* to affiliate.
◆ *vpr* to become affiliated to, to join, to become a member of; *afiliarse a un partido* to join a party.

afiligranado, da *adj* filigreed, filagreed || FIG delicate, fine (cosas) | delicate, dainty (personas).

afiligranar *vt* to filigree, to filagree || FIG to polish (pulir) | to adorn, to decorate (hermosear).

afilosofado, da *adj* pseudo-philosophical.

afín; afine *adj* adjacent; *campos afines* adjacent fields || similar; *temperamentos, gustos, tendencias afines* similar temperaments, tastes, tendencies || related; *palabras afines* related words || similar, kindred; *ideas afines* kindred ideas || *la economía y los problemas afines* economics and the problems related to it, economics and the problems connected with it, economics and its related problems.

◆ *m pl* relatives, relations (parientes).

afinación *f* TECN refining (afinado) || FIG refining, polishing (de una persona) || MÚS tuning (de un instrumento) | intonation (en el canto) || completion, perfection (acción de acabar).

afinadamente *adv* in tune (cantar) || delicately (delicadamente).

afinado, da *adj* in tune, tuned; *piano afinado* tuned piano, piano in tune || purified, refined (metales) || finished, polished (acabado).
◆ *m* refining (depuración) || tuning (de un piano).

afinador, ra *m/f* MÚS tuner (persona que afina).
◆ *m* tuning key (para afinar).

afinadura *f*; **afinamiento** *m* TECN refining (depuración) || tuning (de un piano) || intonation (en el canto) || FIG refinement, polish (de una persona).

afinar *vt* TECN to refine; *afinar el oro* to refine gold || FIG to refine, to polish; *su estancia en la ciudad le ha afinado mucho* his stay in the city has refined him a great deal || MÚS to tune; *afinar un piano* to tune a piano | to sing in tune (cantar) | to play in tune (tocar) || to complete, to finish, to perfect (acabar) || to sharpen, to improve; *afinar la puntería* to sharpen one's aim.
◆ *vi* to be exact; *no hemos afinado en la definición* we have not been exact in the definition || MÚS to sing in tune (cantar) | to play in tune (tocar).
◆ *vpr* to become slimmer *o* thinner (adelgazar) || FIG to become refined *o* polished (pulirse).

afincar *vi* to come into property.
◆ *vpr* to settle down, to establish o.s.; *afincarse en Madrid* to settle down in Madrid.

afine *adj* → **afín.**

afinidad *f* similarity, likeness, affinity, resemblance (semejanza); *hay cierta afinidad entre estas dos personas* there is a certain likeness between these two people || BOT & QUÍM affinity || — *las afinidades electivas* elective affinities || *parentesco por afinidad* relationship by marriage.

afino *m* TECN refining (de metales).

afirmación *f* statement, affirmation, assertion; *afirmación atrevida* daring statement || securing, strengthening (acción de sostener).

afirmado *m* road surface [US roadbed] (firme de la carretera).

afirmar *vt* to secure, to strengthen, to make firm; *poner unos clavos para afirmar un estante* to put in a few nails to secure a shelf || to assure; *le afirmo que es verdad* I assure you that it is true || to state, to say (decir); *un portavoz del gobierno ha afirmado que habrá elecciones* a spokesman for the government has stated that there will be elections || to declare (la lealtad).
◆ *vpr* to steady o.s. (apoyarse) || *afirmarse en lo dicho* to confirm one's statement.

afirmativo, va *adj* affirmative, positive; *respuesta afirmativa* affirmative reply || *en caso afirmativo* if that is the case.
◆ *f* affirmative answer || *contestar con la afirmativa* to answer in the affirmative, to give an affirmative answer.

afistolarse; afistularse *vpr* MED to fistulate.

aflamencado, da *adj* flamenco-like.

aflatarse *vpr* AMER to be sad *o* gloomy *o* down-hearted.

aflautado, da *adj* flute-like || high-pitched, piercing, fluty; *voz aflautada* high-pitched voice.

aflautar *vt* AMER to make high-pitched *o* piercing (la voz, un sonido).

aflicción *f* affliction, grief, sorrow, sadness (pesar); *esta noticia me ha dado mucha aflicción* this news has caused me great affliction.

aflictivo, va *adj* JUR corporal; *pena aflictiva* corporal punishment || distressing, troubling (que causa aflicción); *una noticia aflictiva* a distressing piece of news.

afligidamente *adv* sadly, sorrowfully (con tristeza) || llorar afligidamente to weep bitterly.

afligido, da *adj* distressed, troubled, grieved; *afligido con la noticia* distressed by the news || suffering, afflicted; *afligido de sordera* suffering from *o* afflicted by deafness || bereaved (por una muerte).
◆ *m* afflicted; *los afligidos* the afflicted || bereaved (por una muerte).

afligimiento *m* affliction.

afligir *vt* to afflict, to grieve, to distress (entristecer) || to afflict, to make suffer (causar molestia física) || to afflict, to trouble, to beset; *la desgracia que nos aflige* the misfortune which afflicts us || AMER to beat, to thrash (apalear).
◆ *vpr* to be distressed, to be grieved, to grieve; *afligirse con* or *de algo* to be distressed about sth., to be grieved by sth., to grieve over sth.

aflojamiento *m* loosening, slackening (de una cuerda) || relaxing, relaxation (de la disciplina) || loosening (de vínculos) || abatement (de tormenta).

aflojar *vt* to loosen, to slacken; *aflojar un nudo, la corbata, una tuerca* to loosen a knot, one's tie, a nut || to release (un muelle) || to relax, to ease (la severidad) || to moderate, to reduce (pretensiones) || to release, to take off (el freno) || FAM to fork out, to cough up; *aflojar dinero* to fork money out || — *aflojar el paso* to slow down || POP *aflojar la bolsa* or *la mosca* to fork out, to cough up.
◆ *vi* to let up, to die down; *el calor, la tormenta ha aflojado* the heat, the storm has let up || to slacken, to grow slack (cuerda) || to weaken, to give in, to relent (ceder) || to grow lax, to slack; *alumno que afloja en el estudio* pupil who is slacking in his studies || to grow weak, to fail; *fe que afloja* faith which is failing || to flag; *la conversación afloja* conversation is flagging || to abate (fiebre) || POP to fork out, to cough up (pagar).
◆ *vpr* to grow slack, to slacken (cuerda) || to loosen, to come loose, to grow slack (la corbata, el cinturón, una tuerca) || to grow lax, to slack (en la aplicación) || to ease (un dolor) || to flag (interés, conversación) || to go down (los precios) || to let up, to die down (el calor, la fiebre).

afloramiento *m* MIN outcrop.

aflorar *vi* to outcrop, to crop out (minerales) || to spring (agua) || FIG to appear, to arise (surgir).
◆ *vt* to sift, to sieve (cerner).

afluencia *f* crowd, flow; *afluencia de espectadores* flow of spectators || rush (tropel) || inflow, influx; *la afluencia de refugiados al país* the influx of refugees into the country || afflux, flow (de sangre) || abundance (abundancia) || eloquence (facundia).

afluente *adj* flowing, inflowing (que afluye) || eloquent (facundo).
◆ *m* tributary; *el Segre es afluente del Ebro* the Segre is a tributary of the Ebro.

afluir* *vi* to flow; *la sangre afluye al cerebro* the blood flows to the brain || FIG to flow, to flock; *los turistas afluyen a Madrid* the tourists flock to *o* flow into Madrid || to be a tributary, to flow; *este río afluye al Támesis* this river is a tributary of the Thames, this river flows into the Thames || to flow; *afluir al mar* to flow into the sea || to open, to lead; *esta calle afluye a la que buscas* this street leads into *o* opens onto the one you are looking for.

aflujo *m* MED afflux, flow.

afluxionarse *vpr* AMER to catch a cold (resfriarse) | to swell (abotargarse).

afofado, da *adj* soft.

afofarse *vpr* to turn soft (ponerse fofo).

afollar* *vt* (p us) to blow [with bellows] || to pleat (plegar); *un cuello afollado* a pleated collar.
◆ *vpr* to blister (avejigarse) || to hollow out (ahuecarse).

afonía *f* MED aphony, aphonia, loss of voice.

afónico, ca; áfono, na *adj* aphonic (término médico) || hoarse, voiceless (término común) || — *estar afónico* to have lost one's voice, to be hoarse || *volverse afónico* to lose one's voice, to become hoarse.

aforado, da *adj* privileged, which has a «fuero» [a royal privilege granted to city or province in the Middle Ages].

aforador *m* gauge (instrumento) || gauger (obrero).

aforamiento *m* gauging, measuring (de un barco, de un tonel) || valuation (evaluación) || appraisal, assessment (en las aduanas) || privilege, exemption (fuero).

aforar* *vt* to gauge, to measure the capacity of (un tonel) || to gauge, to measure the tonnage of (un barco) || to gauge, to measure; *aforar una corriente de agua* to gauge a stream of water || to appraise, to value, to assess (valorar) || to grant a privilege *o* a «fuero» to (una ciudad).
◆ *vpr* FAM to cough up, to fork out (pagar) | to beat it, to make tracks (irse).

aforismo *m* aphorism (máxima).

aforístico, ca *adj* aphoristic.

aforo *m* gauging, measuring, measurement; *el aforo de un barco* the gauging of a boat || appraisal, assessment, valuation (evaluación) || flow; *el aforo de un río* the flow of a river || *este teatro tiene un aforo de dos mil personas* this theatre holds two thousand people, this theatre has a seating capacity of two thousand.

afortunado, da *adj* fortunate, lucky; *una coincidencia afortunada* a fortunate coincidence; *¡qué afortunado eres!* how lucky you are! || happy; *fue una época afortunada* those were happy times || fortunate (que tiene buena fortuna); *un pueblo afortunado* a fortunate nation || MAR stormy (tiempo) || — *los afortunados por la lotería* the winners of the lottery || *poco afortunado* unsuccessful; *una reforma poco afortunada* an unsuccessful reform; unpleasant; *una cara poco afortunada* an unpleasant face; not very successful, not very good; *la decoración de este piso es poco afortunada* the décor of this flat is not very successful || *un estilo afortunado en imágenes* a style with good imagery || *un hombre afortunado en amores* a man who is lucky in love.

afoscarse *vpr* MAR to become misty (la atmósfera).

afrailado, da *adj* parsonic, parsonical || IMPR with a friar, with a defect [page].

afrailar *vt* AGR to trim, to cut off the branches of.

afrancesado, da *adj* Francophile (francófilo) || FAM Gallicized, Frenchified || supporting the French, pro-French.
◆ *m* person with French tastes and culture, francophile [especially in the eighteenth century] || HIST supporter of Napoleon in the Peninsular War, French sympathizer.

afrancesamiento *m* Frenchification, Gallicization.

afrancesar *vt* to frenchify, to gallicize, to make French.
◆ *vpr* to become gallicized (cosas) || to adopt French tastes *o* ways, to become gallicized (personas) || HIST to become a supporter of the French.

afrecho *m* bran.

afrenillar *vt* MAR to tie up.

afrenta *f* affront, insult; *aguantar una afrenta* to suffer an insult || disgrace, shame; *es la afrenta de la familia* he is the disgrace of the family || *hacer afrenta a alguien* to insult *o* affront s.o.

afrentar *vt* to insult, to affront (ultrajar) || to offend (ofender) || to disgrace, to dishonour, to shame (ser la vergüenza de) || to humiliate (humillar).
◆ *vpr* to be ashamed *o* embarrassed; *afrentarse de* or *por su pobreza* to be ashamed of *o* embarrassed by one's poverty.

afrentoso, sa *adj* insulting (insultante) || offensive, offending (que ofende) || humiliating (humillador) || disgraceful, shameful, outrageous, dishonourable (deshonroso); *una acción afrentosa* a shameful action.

afretar *vt* MAR to scrub, to clean (limpiar el casco).

África *npr f* GEOGR Africa; *África del Sur* South Africa.

africado, da *adj* GRAM affricative.
◆ *f* affricate (consonante).

africanista *adj/s* Africanist.

africanización *f* Africanization.

africanizar *vt* to Africanize.

africano, na *adj/s* African.

áfrico *m* South wind.

afrikaans *m* Afrikaans.

afrikánder *m* Afrikaner, Afrikander.

afroamericano, na *adj/s* Afro-American.

afroasiático, ca *adj/s* Afro-Asian.

afrodisiaco, ca *adj/sm* aphrodisiac.

Afrodita *npr f* Aphrodite.

afrontamiento *m* facing (acción de arrostrar) || confrontation, confronting; *el afrontamiento de los manifestantes con la policía* the confrontation of the demonstrators with the police; *el afrontamiento de dos ideologías* the confrontation of two ideologies.

afrontar *vt* to face, to confront, to face up to; *afrontar al enemigo* to face the enemy || to confront, to bring face to face (dos cosas o dos personas); *afrontar dos testigos* to confront two witnesses || to place opposite each other; *afrontar dos cuadros* to place two paintings opposite each other.

afta *f* MED aphtha.

aftoso, sa *adj* aphthous || *fiebre aftosa* foot-and-mouth disease.

afuera *adv* out, outside; *váyase afuera* get out; *afuera hace más frío* it is colder outside || outside; *vengo de afuera* I have been outside, I have come from outside || — *de puertas afuera* on the outside || *la parte de afuera* the outside || *más afuera* further out || *por afuera* outside, on the outside.
◆ *f pl* outskirts; *las afueras de Madrid* the outskirts of Madrid.
◆ *interj* get out! (¡salga de aquí!) || off! (abucheando).

afuereño, ña; afuerino, na *adj* AMER strange, foreign (forastero).

afuerita *adv* AMER FAM outside (fuera).

afusilar *vt* AMER to shoot (fusilar).

afusión *f* MED affusion (ducha).

afuste *m* MIL gun carriage (de cañón).

agabachar *vt* FAM to Frenchify, to Gallicize.
◆ *vpr* to become Frenchified.

agachada *f* FAM trick, dodge (astucia) || bending over (acción de agacharse).
◆ *pl* excuses, pretexts (pretextos).

agachadiza *f* snipe (ave) || FAM *hacer la agachadiza* to duck, to try to hide.

agachado, da *adj* AMER low (servil) || sly, underhand (disimulado).

agachaparse *vpr* to bend over, to lean over (inclinarse) || to crouch (ponerse en cuclillas) || FIG & FAM to hide (ocultarse).

agachar *vt* to lower, to bow, to bend; *agachar la cabeza* to lower one's head.
◆ *vpr* to lean over, to bend down; *agáchate para que te pueda peinar* lean over so that I can comb your hair || to crouch, to squat (ponerse en cuclillas) || to duck (para evitar algo) || FIG to grin and bear it; *más vale agacharse* it's better to grin and bear it | to lie low, to hide away (retirarse) || AMER to give in, to yield (someterse) | to get ready (prepararse).

agalbanado, da *adj* FAM lazy, idle (perezoso).

agalerar *vt* MAR to tilt (las velas).

agalla *f* BOT gall, gallnut || ANAT tonsil || gill (de los peces) || temple, side of head (de las aves) || AMER pole with hooked end (gancho) | BOT *agalla de roble* oak apple, oak gall.
◆ *pl* sore throat *sing* (angina) || FIG & FAM pluck *sing*, guts; *hay que tener muchas agallas para hacer frente a ciertas personas* it takes a lot of pluck to face some people.

agallegado, da *adj* like a Galician || AMER Spanish-sounding.

agallón *m* hollow silver bead (de collar) || large bead (de rosario) || ARQ gadroon, godroon || AMER gall, gallnut (agalla).
◆ *pl* AMER ganglions (cuerpos glandulosos) | mumps (paperas).

agalludo, da *adj* AMER FAM plucky, daring (valiente) | stingy, miserly (roñoso) | cheeky, bold (desvergonzado).

agamí *m* AMER trumpeter (ave).

ágamo, ma *adj* BOT agamic, agamous.

agamuzado, da *adj* chamois-coloured.

agamuzar *vt* to chamois.

agangrenarse *vpr* to become gangrenous, to gangrene (una herida).

ágape *m* agape, love feast (convite entre los primeros cristianos) || banquet (banquete).

agar agar *m* agar-agar, agar.

agarbanzado, da *adj* beige (color).

agarbillar *vt* AGR to sheave, to sheaf.

agareno, na *adj/s* Mohammedan, Muslim, Moslem [specially in Spain].

agárico *m* BOT agaric || *agárico mineral* agaric mineral.

agarrada *f* FAM quarrel, row (pelea); *tuvieron una agarrada* they had a quarrel.

agarradera *f* AMER handle (mango) || FAM *tener buenas agarraderas* to have friends in the right places, to have connections.

agarradero *m* handle (asa) || curtain hook (de las cortinas) || FIG & FAM excuse (excusa) || FIG & FAM *tener agarraderos* to have friends in the right places, to have connections.

agarrado, da *adj* FAM stingy, miserly, mean; *es un hombre muy agarrado* he is a very stingy man || — *agarrados del brazo* arm in arm || FAM *baile agarrado* dance in couples || FIG & FAM *ser más agarrado que un chotis* or *que el pasamanos de una escalera* to be a tightfisted so-and-so.

agarrador, ra *adj* AMER strong (bebida).
◆ *m* handle (de la plancha) || FAM cop, copper (guardia).

agarrar *vt* to grasp, to seize, to grab, to clutch; *agarrar a una persona de* or *por la manga* to grasp s.o. by the sleeve; *agarrar un palo* to seize a stick || FAM to get, to land s.o. (obtener); *agarrar una buena colocación* to get a good job | to get, to hook; *agarrar un marido* to get a husband | to get, to win; *agarró dos puntos en el partido* he got two points in the game | to grasp, to get (comprender) | to get, to cop; *agarrar un bofetón* to get a good hiding | to catch; *agarrar un resfriado* to catch a cold | to catch, to get hold of; *si lo agarro lo mato* if I catch him I'll kill him | to take (tomar); *no se sabe por donde agarrarlo* you don't know how to take him || — *agarrar del brazo* to take by the arm || FIG *agarrar el sueño* to fall asleep, to be overcome by sleep || *agarrar un autobús* to catch a bus || FAM *agarrar un buen susto* to have a fright | *agarrar una rabieta* to go into a tantrum.
◆ *vi* to take (vacuna, tinte, planta) || to stick; *el arroz ha agarrado en la sartén* the rice has stuck to the frying pan || AMER to take (dirección); *agarró por esta calle* he took this street || — FAM *como no venga, agarro y me voy* if he doesn't come, then I'm going || FIG *estar siempre agarrado a las faldas de su madre* to be tied to one's mother's apron strings.
◆ *vpr* to grasp, to hold on, to cling; *agarrarse a las ramas de un árbol* to cling to *o* to hold on to the branches of a tree || to cling; *la hiedra se agarra a las paredes* ivy clings to walls || to stick; *el arroz se ha agarrado a la sartén* the rice has stuck to the frying pan || to stick; *el humo se me agarra a la garganta* smoke sticks in my throat || to hold on; *agárrate a la barra* hold on to the bar || FIG to use; *se agarra a cualquier pretexto para no hacer lo que le mando* he uses any excuse not to do as I tell him || FAM to quarrel, to row, to argue (pelearse) || — AUT *agarrarse al camino* to hold the road || FIG *agarrarse a un clavo ardiendo* to clutch at a straw *o* at straws | *agarrarse a* or *de un palo* to use the least excuse || *agarrarse del brazo* to link arms || FIG *agarrarse del moño* to pull each other's hair, to tear each other's hair out || *agarrarse una fiebre* to catch a fever || AMER *se agarraron a tiros* they fought it out with pistols.

agarrochar *vt* to goad (el picador) || MAR to brace.

agarrón *m* FAM quarrel, row, argument (agarrada) | jerk, tug, pull (tirón).

agarrotado, da *adj* tightly bound (fardo) || stiff (tieso) || seized up (un motor) || FIG tied down (atado, restringido) || *tener los músculos agarrotados* to be stiff.

agarrotamiento *m* binding, tying up (acción de atar) || seizing up, seizing (de un motor) || stiffening, tightening (de un músculo) || garotting, garrotting, garroting (de un reo).

agarrotar *vt* to bind tightly, to tie up tightly (atar) || to stiffen, to tighten; *el agua muy fría agarrota los músculos* very cold water stiffens one's muscles || to garrote, to garrotte, to garotte (a un reo) || FIG to tie down (poniendo restricciones).
◆ *vpr* to seize (up) (un motor) || to stiffen, to go numb (un músculo), to get *o* to have (a) cramp (una persona).

agasajado, da *m/f* guest of honour.

agasajador, ra *adj* welcoming, cordial, warm.

agasajar *vt* to receive warmly (acoger); *he sido muy agasajado durante mi estancia en Madrid* I was very warmly received during my stay in Madrid || to shower attentions on, to overwhelm with attentions (tener muchas atenciones con); *agasajar a sus convidados* to overwhelm one's guest with attentions || to wine and dine (dar muy bien de comer a).

agasajo *m* warm reception, royal *o* warm welcome (acogida calurosa) || present, gift (regalo).
◆ *pl* hospitality *sing* (hospitalidad) || *me paso la vida en agasajos* my life is one long round of parties and receptions.

ágata *f* agate.

agauchado, da *adj* AMER like the gauchos.

agaucharse *vpr* to assume a gaucho's way of life.

agavanza *f*; **agavanzo** *m* wild rose, dogrose.

agave *f* BOT agave (pita).

agavillador, ra *m/f* binder, person who binds.
◆ *f* AGR binder (machine).

agavillar *vt* to bind, to sheave, to sheaf; *agavillar la mies* to sheave the harvest.
◆ *vpr* to band *o* to get together (personas).

agazapar *vt* to catch, to get hold of.
◆ *vpr* FIG to crouch, to duck (agacharse); *el niño se agazapó detrás de la puerta* the child crouched behind the door.

agencia *f* agency; *agencia de viajes* travel agency; *agencia inmobiliaria* estate agency, real estate agency || bureau, agency; *agencia de colocaciones* employment bureau || agency [which carries out official business for its clients] (gestoría) || FIG step (trámite) || AMER pawnshop || — *agencia de patentes* patents office || *agencia de prensa* news agency || *agencia de publicidad* advertising agency || *agencia de transportes* haulage contracting company || *agencia funeraria* undertaker's || *agencia matrimonial* marriage bureau.

agenciar *vt* to get, to find; *te voy a agenciar una colocación muy buena* I'll get you a very good job || to engineer (conseguir que suceda algo) || FAM to wangle (conseguir).
◆ *vpr* FAM to look after o.s., to manage, to send for o.s.; *sabe agenciárselas* he knows how to *o* he can look after himself || to get o.s.; *agenciarse una buena colocación* to get o.s. a good job; *se ha agenciado un piso magnífico* he has got himself a marvellous flat || *no te preocupes, yo me las agenciaré* don't worry, I'll think of sth. *o* I'll manage.

agenciero *m* AMER agent | pawnbroker.

agenda *f* diary || *agenda de entrevistas* appointment book.

agente *m* agent; *agente químico* chemical agent || agent (persona); *agente de seguros* insurance agent; *agente secreto* secret agent || policeman (policía) || GRAM agent || — *agente comercial* or *de negocios* business agent || *agente de bolsa* or *de cambio* or *de cambio y bolsa* stockbroker || *agente de colocaciones* manager of an employment agency || *agente de compras* purchasing agent || *agente de policía* policeman || *agente de transportes* carrier || *agente de ventas* selling agent || *agente ejecutivo* bailiff || *agente inmobiliario* estate agent [US real estate broker *o* manager] || *agente provocador* agent provocateur || *agente secreto* secret agent.

agermanado, da *adj* Germanized.

agibílibus *m* FAM know-how, knack (habilidad).

agible *adj* feasible (factible).

agigantado, da *adj* huge, gigantic || *a pasos agigantados* with giant strides (con paso largo), by leaps and bounds (muy rápidamente).

agigantar *vt* to exaggerate; *no hay que agigantar lo que pasó* you should not exaggerate what happened || to enlarge *o* to increase considerably, to make much greater; *este acontecimiento agiganta el problema* this event makes the problem much greater, this event enlarges the problem considerably.
◆ *vpr* to take on huge proportions.

ágil *adj* agile, nimble; *está todavía muy ágil a pesar de su edad* he is still very agile in spite of his age || FIG agile, nimble, alert; *es muy ágil de pensamiento* he has a very agile mind | flexible, nimble (estilo).

agílibus *m* FAM know-how, knack (habilidad).

agilidad *f* agility; *para dar este salto hace falta mucha agilidad* you need a great deal of agility to manage this jump || FIG head; *tener mucha agilidad en los negocios* to have a good head for business.

agilitar; agilizar *vt* to make agile (persona) || to facilitate (cosa) || AMER to activate.

agio *m* COM agio (beneficio) | agiotage, speculation, stockjobbing (especulación).

agiotador *m* COM speculator, stockjobber.

agiotaje *m* COM agiotage, speculation, stockjobbing | agio (beneficio).

agiotar *vi* COM to speculate, to gamble.

agitación *f* shaking, agitation (de un líquido, etc.) || bustle, jostle; *la agitación de la muchedumbre* the bustle of the crowd || roughness (de las olas) || movement roll (de un barco) || sway, swaying (de un árbol) || waving, flapping (de una bandera) || agitation, restlessness (nervios) || excitement (emoción) || agitation (política) || FIG *sembrar la agitación en el ánimo de alguien* to cause s.o. unrest, to trouble s.o.

agitado, da *pp* → **agitar.**
◆ *adj* rough, choppy (el agua) || turbulent (el aire) || FIG upset, worried (preocupado) | hectic (la vida).

agitador, ra *m/f* agitator.
◆ *m* QUÍM stirring rod || shaker (máquina).

agitanado, da *adj* gipsy-like.

agitar *vt* to shake; *agitar una botella antes de abrirla* to shake a bottle before opening it || to wave (un pañuelo, una bandera, los brazos, etc.) || to flap (el ala) || FIG to upset, to disturb; *agitar el ánimo de uno* to upset *o* disturb s.o. | to stir up, to excite, to agitate (excitar) || to brandish (un arma) || to stir, to stir up; *agitar un líquido con una cuchara* to stir a liquid with a spoon.
◆ *vpr* to sway; *los árboles se agitan con el viento* the trees sway in the wind || to fidget; *el niño se agita en su silla* the baby is fidgeting in its chair || to flutter, to flap (una bandera) || to get rough *o* choppy (el mar) || to roll, to toss (un barco) || FIG to become agitated (personas).

aglomeración *f* agglomeration, mass || — *aglomeración de tráfico* traffic jam || *aglomeraciones de gente* crowds of people.

aglomerado *m* briquette, briquet (combustible) || agglomerate (conglomerado).

aglomerar *vt* to amass (amontonar).
◆ *vpr* to amass, to pile up, to agglomerate (amontonarse) || to form a crowd, to crowd round; *curiosos que se aglomeran* inquisitive people who crowd round || to crowd; *la gente se aglomera en las ciudades* people are crowding the towns.

aglutinación *f* agglutination.

aglutinante *adj* agglutinant, adhesive, binding || *lengua aglutinante* agglutinative language.
◆ *m* agglutinant.

aglutinar *vt* to agglutinate, to bind.
◆ *vpr* to agglutinate.

agnación *f* agnation.

agnado *m* JUR agnate.

agnosia *f* ignorance.

agnosticismo *m* agnosticism.

agnóstico, ca *adj/s* agnostic.

agobiado, da *adj* bent, bent over, bowed, weighed down; *agobiado por* or *con el peso de una carga, de los años* bowed under the weight of a burden, of the years || overwhelmed, overburdened; *agobiado de trabajo* overwhelmed with work || exhausted (cansado) || round-shouldered (cargado de espaldas).

agobiador, ra *adj* exhausting, backbreaking (trabajo) || crushing, backbreaking (carga) || oppressive (calor) || overwhelming (dolor, responsabilidad).

agobiante *adj* exhausting, backbreaking; *una tarea agobiante* an exhausting job || oppressive; *calor agobiante* oppressive heat || overwhelming (dolor, responsabilidad) || tiresome; *es un niño agobiante* he is a tiresome child || *es agobiante ir ahora allí* it is a nuisance *o* it is annoying to have to go there now.

agobiar *vt* to burden, to weigh down (recargar) || FIG to overwhelm, to burden; *le agobian las penas* he is overwhelmed by worry | to overwhelm; *tanta bondad me agobia* such kindness overwhelms me | to get down, to tire; *me agobias con tus preguntas* you get me down with your questions | to depress, to dishearten (desanimar) | to humiliate (rebajar).

agobio *m* burden, weight (carga, peso) || exhaustion (cansancio) || anguish, worry (angustia) || oppression (sofocación) || boredom (aburrimiento) || *soportar el agobio de tanta responsabilidad* to bear the burden of so much responsibility.

agolpamiento *m* accumulation, pile (de cosas) || crowd, throng, rush, flood (de gente).

agolparse *vpr* to crowd, to rush, to throng; *la gente se agolpó en el lugar del accidente* people crowded to the scene of the accident || FIG to accumulate, to amass, to pile up (cosas) | to come all together, to come in one fell swoop (problemas) || *se agolparon las lágrimas en sus ojos* tears welled up *o* gathered in his eyes.

agonía *f* death, last throes *pl*, last *o* death agony (de un moribundo) || knell (de las campanas por un moribundo) || FIG death, last throes *pl* (de una civilización, una sociedad) | desire, yearning (deseo) | agony, anguish (angustia) || *acortar la agonía a un animal* to put an animal out of its misery.
◆ *pl* FAM misery *sing* (persona).

agónico, ca *adj* death; *estertores agónicos* death rattle || moribund, dying; *está agónico* he is dying.

agonioso, sa *adj* FAM selfish (egoísta) | worrisome, anxious (angustiado) || FAM *¡no seas tan agonioso!* don't be such a nuisance *o* a pest!

agonizante *adj* moribund, dying (moribundo) || FIG failing, dying; *luz agonizante* failing light.
◆ *m/f* moribund, dying person.
◆ *m* monk who helps the dying.

agonizar *vi* to be dying *o* moribund || FIG to fail, to falter; *luz que agoniza* failing light | to annoy, to pester, to bother (molestar) | to be dying; *agonizo por salir* I'm dying to go out | to be in agony (sufrir mucho).

ágora *f* agora.

agorafobia *f* MED agoraphobia.

agorar* *vt* to auger, to predict, to forecast.

agorero, ra *m/f* soothsayer, fortune-teller.
◆ *adj* of ill omen; *ave agorera* bird of ill omen || ominous (que predice la desdicha) || prophetic (profético).

agorgojarse *vpr* to be weevilled *o* weevilly *o* weevileaten.

agostadero *m* summer pasture (sitio) || summer pasture season (temporada).

agostamiento *m* AGR withering.

agostar *vt* to wither, to fade; *el sol agosta las flores* the sun withers the flowers || to plough in August (arar) || to hoe in August (desherbar).
◆ *vi* to graze [in the dry season] (los animales) || to wither, to fade (secarse).

agosteño, ña *adj* August, of August; *el calor agosteño* the August heat, the heat of August.

agostero, ra *adj* August || grazing (animales).

agostizo, za *adj* August || weak (débil).

agosto *m* August (mes); *el 15 de agosto* the 15th of August, August the fifteenth || harvest (cosecha) || FIG & FAM *hacer su agosto* to make a fortune *o* a packet, to feather one's nest.

agotador, ra *adj* exhausting.

agotamiento *m* exhaustion.

agotar *vt* to empty *o* to drain [completely]; *agotar una cisterna* to drain a tank || to exhaust, to deplete; *agotar las existencias, los recursos* to exhaust the stocks, one's resources || to exhaust (la tierra, un tema) || to exhaust, to tire out (cansar) || — *agotar la paciencia de uno* to try *o* to exhaust s.o.'s patience || *edición agotada* edition out of print || *estar agotado* to be exhausted.
◆ *vpr* to run out, to become exhausted (existencias) || to exhaust o.s., to wear o.s. out (persona) || to go out of print (un libro) || *se me ha agotado la paciencia* my patience has run out, I'm at the end of my tether.

agracejo *m* barberry, berberry || unripe grape (uva).

agraciado, da *adj* pretty, attractive; *un rostro agraciado* a pretty face || graceful (gracioso) || favoured; *agraciado por la suerte* favoured by luck || winning; *el billete agraciado* the winning ticket || — *no agraciado* losing (billete) || *poco agraciado* unattractive, plain; *una cara poco agraciada* a plain face || *salir agraciado* to be lucky.
◆ *m/f* lucky winner; *los agraciados recibirán su premio* the lucky winners will receive their prize.

agraciar *vt* to enhance s.o.'s looks (a una persona); *este vestido la agracia* that dress enhances her looks || to enhance (un vestido, etc.) || to award, to reward with; *agraciar a uno con un premio, una condecoración* to award s.o. a prize, a decoration || to pardon (a un condenado).

agradable *adj* pleasant, agreeable, nice, pleasing; *agradable al tacto* pleasant to the touch; *agradable de sabor* pleasant tasting || — *el accidente no era muy agradable a la vista* the accident was not a pretty sight || *es difícil ser agradable con* or *para todos* it is hard to please everyone || *ha sido una velada muy agradable* it has been a very enjoyable *o* pleasant evening || *unir lo útil con lo agradable* to combine *o* to mix business and pleasure.

agradar *vi* to please; *agradar a todos* to please everyone; *un regalo que siempre agrada* a present which is sure to please || — *a mí este espectáculo me agrada mucho* I like this show very much || *si le agrada* if you wish, if you feel like it, if you want.
◆ *vpr* to like each other (dos personas).
— OBSERV En inglés se suele emplear el verbo *to like*. En este caso el sujeto del verbo español viene a ser el complemento del verbo inglés: *esto me agrada* I like this.

agradecer* *vt* to thank; *le agradezco su oferta* I thank you for your offer || to be grateful *o*

obliged; *si pudiera usted venir, se lo agradecería mucho* if you could come, I should be very grateful || *se lo agradezco mucho* I'm very grateful to you, thank you very much.
◆ *vpr* to be welcome; *una copa de vino siempre se agradece* a glass of wine is always welcome || *se agradece* thank you very much, much obliged.

agradecido, da *adj* grateful; *agradecido a su bienhechor* grateful for one's benefactor; *agradecido por un favor* grateful for a favour ||— *le estaría muy agradecido si me dejara el coche* I should be very grateful *o* I should be much obliged if you would lend me your car || *me miró agradecido* he looked at me gratefully || *¡muy agradecido!* much obliged.

agradecimiento *m* gratitude, appreciation, gratefulness.

agrado *m* pleasure; *hallar agrado en hacer algo* to take pleasure in doing sth || liking, taste; *no es de mi agrado* it is not to my liking || affability, friendliness (afabilidad) ||— *con agrado* with pleasure, willingly || *recibí con agrado sus noticias* I was pleased to receive your news.

agrafe *m* MED agraffe, clip (grapa).
— OBSERV This word is a Gallicism widely used in medicine.

agramadera *f* brake.

agramado *m* braking.

agramador, ra *adj* braking.
◆ *m/f* braker.
◆ *m* brake.

agramaduras *f pl* boon *sing*, stalk *sing*.

agramar *vt* to brake (el cáñamo).

agramilar *vt* to even out (ladrillos, etc.) || to face (a wall) in imitation brickwork (simular hileras de ladrillos).

agramiza *f* boon, stalk.

agrandamiento *m* enlargement, enlarging.

agrandar *vt* to enlarge, to make larger; *agrandar una casa* to enlarge a house; *agrandar un boquete* to enlarge a hole || to exaggerate, to magnify; *agrandar los defectos de alguien* to exaggerate s.o.'s faults || to increase; *esto agranda la diferencia de opinión que existe entre nosotros* this increases the difference of opinion that exists between us.
◆ *vpr* to increase (una diferencia) || to grow larger, to expand (un boquete, etc.).

agranujado, da *adj* grained, rough || pimply, spotty; *una cara agranujada* a spotty face || FAM coarse (grosero) | roguish (pícaro).

agranujarse *vpr* to become a rogue.

agrario, ria *adj* agrarian, land; *ley, reforma agraria* land law, reform || agrarian, agricultural (política) || *la clase agraria* the agricultural community.

agravación *f*; **agravamiento** *m* aggravation, worsening (empeoramiento).

agravante *adj* aggravating ||— JUR *circunstancias agravantes* aggravating circumstances || *robo con agravante* aggravated theft.
◆ *f* JUR aggravating circumstance || further *o* added difficulty.

agravar *vt* to aggravate, to worsen (hacer más grave) || to increase (una pena, un impuesto).
◆ *vpr* to worsen, to get worse.

agraviador, ra *adj* offensive, insulting.
◆ *m/f* insulter, offender.

agraviamiento *m* insult.

agraviante *m* offender.
◆ *adj* offensive, insulting.

agraviar *vt* to offend (ofender) || to insult (insultar) || to wrong, to do wrong (perjudicar) || JUR to appeal (apelar) || *agraviar de palabra* to insult.
◆ *vpr* to take offence, to be offended.

agravio *m* insult, offence (injuria) || affront (afrenta) || wrong, harm, damage (perjuicio) || JUR injustice || *deshacer agravios* to right wrongs (defender a los otros), to avenge o.s. (vengarse).

agravioso, sa *adj* insulting, offensive.

agraz *m* verjuice grape, sour grape (uva sin madurar) || verjuice (zumo de uva en agraz) || BOT barberry, berberry (agracejo) || FIG & FAM bitterness (amargura) || *en agraz* prematurely.

agrazón *m* verjuice grape (uva) || gooseberry bush (grosellero) || FIG annoyance.

agredir* *vt* to attack || *agredir de palabra* to insult.

agregable *adj* aggregable, which may be added.

agregación *f* aggregation.

agregado *m* aggregate (conjunto) || addition (añadidura) || assistant (adjunto) || attaché; *agregado comercial, cultural, naval* commercial, cultural, naval attaché || AMER métayer, farmer who pays rent in kind.

agregaduría *f* office of attaché.

agregar *vt* to incorporate, to aggregate, to admit || to join (unir) || to aggregate, to amass (reunir) || to add; *agregar cinco a diez* to add five to ten || to appoint; *ha sido agregado a la dirección* he has been appointed to the managerial staff.
◆ *vpr* to be added; *agregarse a* or *con* to be added to || to be incorporated.

agremán *m* insertion.

agremiación *f* forming into a guild.

agremiar *vt* to form into a guild.
◆ *vpr* to form a guild.

agresión *f* aggression || attack, assault (ataque).

agresividad *f* aggressiveness.

agresivo, va *adj* aggressive; *tono agresivo* aggressive tone.

agresor, ra *adj* attacking; *el ejército agresor* the attacking army.
◆ *m/f* aggressor.

agreste *adj* country, rustic, rural (campestre) || wild, uncultivated (inculto) || FIG uncouth (tosco).

agrete *adj* sour; *vino agrete* sour wine.

agriado, da *adj* sour; *vino agriado* sour wine || FIG embittered, made bitter; *persona agriada por las injusticias* person embittered by injustice.

agriamente *adv* FIG sharply, sourly (con aspereza); *me contestó muy agriamente* he answered me very sharply || bitterly (amargamente).

agriar *vt* to sour, to turn sour || FIG to embitter, to make bitter (amargar) | to annoy (enfadar).
◆ *vpr* to turn sour; *el vino se ha agriado* the wine has turned sour || to go sour *o* off (la leche) || FIG to become embittered *o* bitter, to turn sour; *desde su última enfermedad se ha agriado mucho* since his last illness he has become very bitter.

agrícola *adj* agricultural, farming.

agricultor, ra *adj* farming, agricultural.
◆ *m/f* farmer.

agricultura *f* agriculture, farming.

agridulce *adj* bittersweet || CULIN *cerdo agridulce* sweet and sour pork.

agriera *f*; **agrieras** *f pl* AMER heartburn, acidity of the stomach.

agrietamiento *m* cracking (en el suelo, una pared, un plato, etc.) || chapping (en la piel).

agrietar *vt* to crack, to make cracks in || to chap (la piel, los labios, etc.).
◆ *vpr* to crack || to get chapped (la piel, los labios).

Agrigento *n pr* GEOGR Agrigento.

agrilla *f* sorrel (acedera).

agrimensor *m* surveyor.

agrimensura *f* surveying.

agrimonia; agrimoña *f* agrimony (planta).

agringarse *vpr* AMER to behave like a gringo *o* foreigner.

agrio, gria *adj* sour, tart; *esta naranja está agria* this orange is sour; *agrio de gusto* sour-tasting || FIG sour, bitter (carácter) || short, brittle (metal).
◆ *m* acidity, sourness (sabor) || sour juice (zumo).
◆ *pl* citrus fruits.

agrior *m* AMER heartburn, acidity of the stomach.

agripalma *f* BOT motherwort.

agriparse *vpr* AMER to catch flu.

Agripina *npr f* Agrippina.

agrisado, da *adj* grey, greyish.

agrisar *vt* to grey, to gray.
◆ *vpr* to grey, to go *o* to become grey, to gray, to become gray.

agro *m* agriculture || *los problemas del agro* agricultural problems.

agronomía *f* agronomy, agriculture.

agronómico, ca *adj* agronomic, agronomical.

agrónomo *adj m* agricultural; *ingeniero agrónomo* agricultural expert.
◆ *m* agronomist.

agropecuario, ria *adj* agricultural, farming ||— *ingeniero agropecuario* veterinarian, veterinary surgeon || *productos agropecuarios* agricultural products.

agrupación *f*; **agrupamiento** *m* grouping (acción) || group (grupo) || association, society; *agrupación de jóvenes* association of young people || *agrupación coral* choral society *o* group.

agrupar *vt* to group, to assemble.
◆ *vpr* to form a group, to crowd *o* to group together.

agrura *f* tartness, sourness.

agua *f* water (líquido); *dame agua* give me some water || rain (lluvia) || slope; *tejado de dos aguas* roof with two slopes || tears *pl* (lágrimas) || MAR leak (agujero) | tide, water (flujo o reflujo) ||— *agua* or *aguas abajo* downstream, downriver || *agua* or *aguas arriba* upstream, upriver || *agua bendita* holy water || *agua calcárea* hard water || *agua cibera* irrigation water || *agua con gas* sparkling water || *agua corriente* running water || *agua cruda* hard water || *agua de azahar* orange-flower water || *agua de cal* lime water || FAM *agua de cepas* wine || *agua de colonia* cologne || *agua de espliego* lavender water || *agua de fregar* dishwater || *agua de lejía* bleach || *agua delgada* soft water || *agua del grifo* tap water || *agua de limón* lemonade || *agua de lluvia* or *llovediza* rainwater || *agua de manantial* spring water || *agua de mar* seawater || *agua de olor* toilet water || *agua de pie* spring water || *agua de Seltz* soda *o* Seltzer water || *agua de sifón* soda *o* Seltzer water || *agua de socorro* emergency baptism (bautismo) || *agua de soda* soda *o* Seltzer water || *agua destilada* distilled water || *agua dulce* fresh water || *agua dura* hard water || *agua estancada* stagnant water || *agua fuerte* nitric acid, aqua fortis (ácido nítrico) || *agua gorda* hard water || *agua mineral* mineral water || *agua natural* tapwater || *agua oxigenada* hydrogen peroxide, oxygenated water || FIG *agua pasada no mueve molino* it's no use crying over spilt milk || *agua pesada* heavy water || *agua potable* drinking water || FIG *agua que no has de beber* it's none of your business || *agua regia* aqua regia || *agua salada* salt water || *agua salobre* brackish *o* briny water || *agua viento* squall || *agua viva* springwater || FIG *ahogarse en un vaso de agua* to make a mountain out of a molehill | *algo tendrá el agua cuando la bendicen* there must be sth. in it (in him, in her, etc.) || FIG & FAM *bailarle a uno el agua* to lick s.o.'s boots | *bañarse en agua de rosas* to see the world through rose-coloured glasses || AMER *capa de agua* raincoat || *como pez en el agua* in one's element || *dar agua a la ropa* to wet the washing || AMER *dar agua a uno* to kill s.o. || *del agua mansa me libre Dios, que de la brava me guardaré yo* or *me libro yo* still waters run deep || FIG *echar agua en el mar* to carry coals to Newcastle || *echar el agua a* to baptize (bautizar) || FIG *echarse al agua* to take the plunge || *es agua sucia* it's like dishwater (café) || AMER *estar como agua para chocolate* to be hopping mad || FIG *estar con el agua al cuello* to have the noose round one's neck, to be in deep water, to be up to one's neck in it | *estar entre dos aguas* to be in two minds, to be undecided | *estar hecho un agua* to be dripping with sweat | *gastar dinero como agua* to spend money like water || MAR *hacer agua* to leak, to have sprung a leak || *hacerse una cosa agua en la boca* to melt in one's mouth || AMER *hay agua puesta* it is going to rain, it looks like rain || FIG *irse al agua* to fall through, to fail (fracasar) | *llevar el agua a su molino* to look after number one | *nadar entre dos aguas* to run with the hare and hunt with the hounds | *nadie diga de este agua no beberé* we never know what the future has in store, don't be too sure! || *parecerse como dos gotas de agua* to be as like as two peas in a pod || *pescar en agua turbia* to fish in troubled waters || AMER *ponerse al agua* to turn rainy, to turn to rain (el tiempo) || *quedar en agua de borrajas* to fizzle out, to peter out || FIG & FAM *sacar agua de las piedras* to get blood out of stone || *se me hace la boca agua al ver ese pastel* the sight of that cake makes my mouth water || *se mete en agua el tiempo* it looks like rain || *ser como el agua por San Juan* to be harmful, to be unwelcome || FIG *ser más claro que el agua* to be as clear as crystal *o* as a bell, to be crystal clear || FIG & FAM *sin decir agua va* without warning || FAM *venir como agua de mayo* to be a godsend, to come *o* to happen just at the right moment.

◆ *pl* FIG water *sing* (de una piedra preciosa) | water *sing*, moiré *sing* (en las telas) || MAR waters; *aguas jurisdiccionales* territorial waters || wake *sing* (estela) || waters, watercures; *tomar las aguas* to take the waters || — *aguas de creciente* flow, rising tide || *aguas de menguante* ebb, ebbing tide || *aguas llenas* high tide || *aguas madres* mother water *o* liquor || *aguas mayores* motion of the bowels, stool || *aguas menores* urine || *aguas muertas* neap tide || *aguas sucias* or *residuales* sewage *sing* || *aguas termales* thermal spring, hot spring (caldas) || *aguas vivas* spring tide (marea) || *cubrir aguas* to put the roof on a building (poner el techo) || *hacer aguas* to urinate, to pass water || *romper aguas* to break one's water bag (una parturienta) || *tomar las aguas* to take the waters (enfermo), to roof (arquitectura).

◆ *interj* man overboard! (¡hombre al agua!) || *¡agua va!* look out below!

aguacatal *m* avocado plantation.

aguacate *m* BOT avocado (árbol) || avocado, avocado pear (fruto) || AMER FAM drip, fool (tonto).

aguacero *m* downpour, shower; *cayó un aguacero* there was a shower || AMER glowworm (luciérnaga).

aguacibera *f* AGR irrigation water.

aguacil *m* ⟶ **alguacil.**

aguacha *f* stagnant water.

aguachar *m* puddle (charco).

aguachar *vt* to flood || AMER to tame (amansar).

◆ *vpr* AMER to get fat (un caballo) | to get attached (*de* to) (encariñarse).

aguachento, ta *adj* AMER watery, full of water.

aguachirle *m* dishwater (bebida o sopa sosa); *este café es aguachirle* this coffee is like dishwater.

aguada *f* MAR fresh water supply | water; *hacer aguada* to take on water || watering place (sitio) || flooding, flood (inundación en las minas) || gouache (pintura) || AMER drinking trough (abrevadero).

aguaderas *f pl* packsaddle *sing* [for carrying jars].

aguadero *m* drinking trough.

aguado, da *adj* watered-down; *vino aguado* watered-down wine || FIG troubled (trastornado).

◆ *m* watering (del vino).

aguador *m* water bearer *o* carrier.

aguaducho *m* refreshment stand (puesto de agua) || noria, Persian wheel (noria) || aqueduct.

aguadura *f* VET founder, laminitis.

aguafiestas *m/f* wet blanket, killjoy, spoilsport.

aguafuerte *f* etching (grabado) || nitric acid (ácido) || *grabar al aguafuerte* to etch.

— OBSERV *Aguafuerte* meaning *etching* is often used as a masculine noun.

aguafuertista *m/f* etcher.

aguaitar *vt* AMER to watch, to be on the watch for (acechar, mirar).

aguaje *m* MAR sea current | unusually high tide, spring tide (marea) | wake (estela) | fresh water supply (aguada) || watering place (abrevadero) || AMER heavy shower, downpour (aguacero) | dressing down, telling off, talking-to (reprimenda).

aguamala *f* ZOOL jellyfish.

aguamanil *m* water jug (jarro) || washbasin, washbowl (palangana) || ewer (lavamanos).

aguamanos *m inv* water jug.

aguamar *m* jellyfish.

aguamarina *f* MIN aquamarine.

aguamiel *f* mead || AMER agave juice [from which *pulque* is made].

aguanieve *f* sleet.

aguanieves *f inv* wagtail (ave).

aguanoso, sa *adj* waterlogged, sodden; *terreno aguanoso* sodden ground || watery (fruto, etc.) || AMER FAM wet (persona).

aguantable *adj* bearable, tolerable.

aguantaderas *f pl* patience *sing*; *para no enfadarse conmigo hace falta que tenga muchas aguantaderas* he has to have a lot of patience not to get angry with me || endurance *sing*, stamina *sing*.

aguantar *vt* to put up with, to bear, to stand, to tolerate (soportar); *aguantar el dolor* to stand the pain || to stand, to tolerate, to bear; *no aguanto las impertinencias* I will not tolerate insolence; *no poder aguantar a alguien* not to be able to stand s.o. || to weather, to ride out, to withstand (una tempestad, un huracán) || to keep *o* to hold back (contener); *aguantar la risa* to keep back laughter || to hold; *aguantar la respiración* to hold one's breath || to wait (esperar); *aguanté tres horas y luego me fui* I waited three hours and then I went || to hold; *aguanta el cuadro mientras yo lo cuelgo* hold the picture while I hang it || to hold up, to support (sostener) || to be good for, to last (durar); *este abrigo aguantará otro invierno* this overcoat is good for *o* will last another winter || TAUR to take (the bull's attack at the kill) without moving || — *aguantar mucho bebiendo* to be able to take *o* to hold one's drink || *no aguanto más* I've had enough || *sabe aguantar bromas* he can take a joke || *su marido aguanta mucho* her husband is very patient || *yo no lo aguanto* I can't bear it *o* stand it.

◆ *vi* to hold out; *el enemigo aguantó tres horas* the enemy held out for three hours || to resist (resistir).

◆ *vpr* to keep quiet; *él se aguanta, no dice ni pío* he keeps quiet, he doesn't say a word || to put up with, to hold o.s. back; *hace tiempo que me aguanto pero ya no puedo más* I have put up with this for some time, but now I've had enough || to resign o.s.; *aguantarse con una cosa* to resign o.s. to sth. || FIG & FAM *¡pues aguántate!* well, you'll just have to put up with it! | *¡que se aguante!* that's his hard luck!

aguante *m* endurance, stamina (resistencia) || patience (paciencia) || *tener mucho aguante* to be very patient, to have a lot of patience (paciencia), to have a lot of stamina (resistencia).

aguapié *m* weak *o* watery wine (vino malo).

aguar *vt* to dilute *o* to water down, to water, to add water to (un líquido); *aguar el vino* to water down the wine || FIG to spoil, to ruin; *la discusión le aguó la noche* the argument ruined her evening; *aguó la fiesta al armar una bronca* he ruined the party by kicking up a fuss || AMER to water || FIG *aguar la fiesta a uno* to spoil s.o.'s enjoyment *o* fun.

◆ *vpr* to be flooded (una casa, etc.) || FIG to be ruined, to be spoilt *o* spoiled; *se aguó la fiesta* the party was ruined || to be exhausted, to founder (un caballo).

aguaraibá *m* AMER terebinth, turpentine tree (árbol).

aguardada *f* wait, waiting (en la caza).

aguardar *vt* to wait for, to await (esperar); *aguardar a alguien, otro día* to wait for s.o., until another day || *no sabes lo que te aguarda* you don't know what is in store for you *o* what awaits you.

◆ *vi* to wait, to hold on; *aguarda, ya voy* hold on, I'm coming.

aguardentería *f* AMER liquor store.

aguardentoso, sa *adj* alcoholic, which contains spirits || — *bebidas aguardentosas* spirits || *voz aguardentosa* husky *o* rough voice.

aguardiente *m* liquor, eau-de-vie (licor) || *aguardiente de caña* tafia, rum.

aguaribay *m* AMER terebinth, turpentine tree (árbol).

aguarrás *m* turpentine.

— OBSERV pl *aguarrases*.

aguasal *f* pickling brine.

aguasarse *vpr* AMER to become coarse *o* rough (volverse rústico).

aguate *m* AMER thorn, prickle.

aguatero *m* AMER water bearer *o* carrier (aguador).

aguaturma *f* BOT Jerusalem artichoke.

aguaverde *f* ZOOL jellyfish.

aguaviento *m* squall.

aguavientos *m* BOT phlomis.

aguazal *m* mire.

aguazar *vt* to flood (encharcar).

agudamente *adv* shrewdly || subtly || wittily (ingeniosamente).

agudeza *f* sharpness, keenness (de un instrumento, de los sentidos) || sharpness, acuteness (del dolor) || FIG insight, shrewdness (de ingenio) | wit, wittiness (ingenio) | bite, sting (de la sátira) | wittiness (de un chiste) | flash of wit (rasgo de ingenio) | witticism (palabra chistosa) || *es una persona muy graciosa, tiene mucha agudeza* he's a very funny person, he is very witty.

agudizamiento *m* aggravation, worsening; *agudizamiento de la situación social* aggravation of the social situation || increase (aumento); *agudizamiento de la tensión internacional* increase in international tension.

agudizar *vt* to sharpen || to worsen, to make worse *o* more acute; *esto no hará más que agudizar la crisis* that will only make the crisis worse.
◆ *vpr* to worsen, to become *o* to get worse (una enfermedad) || FIG to intensify, to become more intense *o* acute; *el conflicto político se ha agudizado* the political conflict has become more intense | to get worse, to worsen, to become more pronounced; *con la edad sus manías se agudizan* his idiosyncracies get worse as he gets older.

agudo, da *adj* sharp (afilado) || acute (ángulo y acento) || FIG sharp, shrewd (listo) | witty, clever (gracioso); *una persona aguda* a witty person || sharp, acute (dolor) || acute (enfermedad, crisis) || sharp (crítica) || high-pitched, shrill, piercing (voz) || searching (pregunta) || keen, sharp (vista) || MÚS high (nota) | treble (tono en el magnetófono, etc.) || GRAM oxytone, with the accent on the last syllabe || — *dicho agudo* witticism || *ser agudo de ingenio* to be witty.
◆ *m pl* treble *sing* (botón del magnetófono, etc.).

Águeda *npr f* Agatha.

agüero *m* augury, omen, presage || — *de buen agüero* lucky, propitious || *pájaro de mal agüero* bird of ill omen.

aguerrido, da *adj* hardened, veteran, trained || FIG experienced.

aguerrir* *vt* to harden, to season, to train.
— OBSERV This is a defective verb used only in the forms whose endings begin with *i*.

aguijada *f* goad (de boyero) || ploughstaff [*US* plowstaff] (de labrador).

aguijar *vt* to goad || FIG to goad, to spur on, to urge on.
◆ *vi* to hurry along.

aguijón *m* spike of a goad || sting (del escorpión, de la avispa, etc.) || prickle, thorn, sting (de las plantas) || FIG prick, sting; *el aguijón de los celos* the prick of jealousy | stimulus, spur; *la gloria es un poderoso aguijón* glory is a powerful stimulus || *cocear contra el aguijón* to struggle *o* to kick in vain.

aguijonada *f*; **aguijonazo** *m* jab, prick || sting (de un insecto).

aguijonear *vt* to goad (a los animales) || FIG to goad, to spur on || — *aguijonear la curiosidad de uno* to arouse *o* to prick one's curiosity || *me aguijoneaba el deseo de decirle algo* I was dying *o* itching to tell him sth.

águila *f* eagle (ave) || eagle (condecoración); *el águila negra de Prusia* the Black Eagle of Prussia || eagle, standard (estandarte) || ASTR Aquila, Eagle (constelación) || eagle (moneda) || FIG crack, ace; *ser un águila para los negocios* to be a crack *o* an ace businessman || *AMER* FAM cheat, swindler (petardista) | kite (cometa) || — HERÁLD *águila agrifada* griffin, griffon, gryphon || *águila barbuda* lammergeyer, bearded vulture || *águila blanca* kind of osprey *o* sea eagle || *águila caudal* or *real* royal *o* golden eagle || *águila de mar* eagle ray (pez) || *águila imperial* Imperial Eagle || HERÁLD *águila pasmada* eagle with wings folded || *águila pescadora* sea eagle, osprey, erne || *águila ratonera* buzzard || FIG *mirada de águila* penetrating glance.

aguileña *f* columbine (planta).

aguileño, ña *adj* aquiline (nariz) || sharp-featured (rostro).

aguilera *f* eyrie (nido del águila).

aguilón *m* jib, arm (de una grúa) || ARQ draintile, chimney-flue tile (caño) | gable (parte superior del muro).

aguilucho *m* eaglet, young eagle.

agüilla *f* water, fluid, watery liquid.

aguinaldo *m* Christmas box, tip; *dar el aguinaldo al cartero* to give the postman his Christmas box || *AMER* Christmas carol (canción).

agüista *m/f* person taking water cures.

aguja *f* needle (de coser, etc.) || needle, stylus (de gramófono) || hand (del reloj) || pointer, needle (de un indicador) || needle (de la brújula) || needle beam (de un puente) || ARQ spire, steeple (de un campanario) || ZOOL pipefish, needlefish (pez) || firing pin (de arma de fuego) || AGR graft (púa) || BOT needle (de pino) || MED needle (de inyección) || ARTES etcher's needle (de grabador) || — *aguja colchonera* tufting needle || *aguja de gancho* crochet hook *o* needle || *aguja de hacer punto* or *de hacer media* knitting needle || AUT *aguja de la cuba del carburador* float needle *o* spindle || *aguja de marear* compass (brújula) || *aguja de pastor* or *de Venus* scandix, Venus's comb, shepherd's needle (planta) || *aguja de zurcir* darning needle || *aguja hipodérmica* hypodermic needle || *aguja imantada* or *magnética* magnetic needle || *aguja mechera* larding needle *o* pin || *aguja paladar* garfish, hornfish (pez) || FIG *buscar una aguja en un pajar* to look for a needle in a haystack || FIG *conocer la aguja de marear* to be able to look after o.s. | *meter aguja por sacar reja* to throw out a sprat to catch a mackerel.
◆ *pl* points [*US* switches] (de ferrocarril); *entrar en agujas* to approach the points; *dar agujas* to change the points || ribs (de un animal) || *carne de agujas* clod, shoulder.

agujazo *m* prick *o* jab [with a needle].

agujerar; agujerear *vt* to make holes in; *agujerear una pared* to make holes in a wall || to perforate.

agujereado, da *adj* *está agujereado* it has a hole in it (con un solo agujero), it has holes in it, it is full of holes (con varios).

agujero *m* hole (abertura); *tapar un agujero* to plug a hole || needle maker (fabricante), needle seller (vendedor) || pincushion (alfiletero) || — ASTR *agujero negro* black hole || *tiene más agujeros que un colador* it is like a sieve, it is riddled with holes.

agujeta *f* *AMER* large needle.
◆ *pl* stiffness *sing* (dolor) || *estar lleno de agujetas* to be stiff all over.

agujón *m* hairpin (pasador) || large needle.

aguosidad *f* water, fluid, watery liquid.

aguoso, sa *adj* watery.

¡agur! *interj* cheerio!, bye-bye!

agusanado, da *adj* maggoty, wormy (fruto) || worm-eaten (madera).

agusanarse *vpr* to become maggoty *o* wormy (frutos) || to become worm-eaten *o* rotten (madera).

Agustín *npr m* Augustine.

agustinianismo *m* Augustinianism, Augustinism.

agustiniano, na *adj* Augustinian.

agustino, na *adj/s* Augustinian.

agutí *m* ZOOL agouti, agouty.

aguzadero, ra *adj* sharpening || *piedra aguzadera* whetstone.

aguzado, da *adj* sharpened || sharp (puntiagudo).

aguzador, ra *adj* sharpening.
◆ *f* whetstone (piedra).

aguzamiento *m* sharpening.

aguzanieves *f inv* wagtail (ave).

aguzar *vt* to sharpen; *aguzar un cuchillo, un lápiz* to sharpen a knife, a pencil || FIG to goad, to spur on (estimular) | to whet (el apetito) | to sharpen (la inteligencia, etc.) || — *aguzar el ingenio, el entendimiento* to sharpen one's wits (mostrarse ingenioso), to concentrate very hard (concentrarse) || *aguzar el oído* to prick up one's ears || *aguzar las orejas* to prick up its *o* his ears (un perro, etc.) || *aguzar la vista* to look closely *o* attentively.

¡ah! *interj* oh! || *AMER* eh?, what? || *¡ah del barco!* ship ahoy!

ahebrado, da *adj* fibrous.

ahechaduras *f pl* siftings, chaff *sing*.

ahechar *vt* to sift, to sieve, to winnow.

ahecho *m* sifting, winnowing.

aherrojamiento *m* chaining.

aherrojar *vt* to chain, to shackle, to put in irons (cargar de cadenas) || FIG to oppress (oprimir).

aherrumbrar *vt* to turn rusty red (color) || to give a rusty taste to (sabor).
◆ *vpr* to rust, to rusty (oxidarse) || to become rusty red (color) || to taste of rust (sabor).

ahí *adv* there; *ahí está el hombre que buscamos* there's the man we are looking for || — *ahí está* there he (it, etc.) is, here he (it, etc.) is || *ahí está la dificultad* that's the problem, that is where the difficulty lies || *ahí fue ello* or *ella* that was where it all started, that's when the trouble started || FAM *ahí me las den todas* that's the least of my worries, I couldn't care less | *¡ahí es nada!* fancy that!, just fancy! || *AMER* *ahí no más* right here || FAM *ahí será ello* there will be trouble || *ahí tienes lo que querías* there's what you wanted || *¡ahí va!* there it is!, there he is! (allí está), goodness me! (sorpresa) || *ahí viene* here he comes || *¿de ahí?* so what?, well? || *de ahí que* so that, with the result that || *de ahí se deduce que* from that we can deduce that || *¡hasta ahí podíamos llegar!* not so likely! || *he ahí* there is, there's; *he ahí lo que buscaba* there's what I was looking for || *por ahí* there, that way; *ha pasado por ahí* he went that way; for a walk; *me voy un rato por ahí* I'm going for a little walk || *por ahí, por ahí; por ahí va la cosa* something like that, more or less, thereabouts || FAM *vete por ahí* get away with you, go on, tell us another one.

ahidalgado, da *adj* noble.

ahijado, da *m/f* godson (chico), goddaughter (chica), godchild || adopted child || FIG protégé (protegido).

ahijamiento *m* adoption.

ahijar *vt* to adopt || FIG to attribute, to impute.

¡ahijuna! *interj* *AMER* POP well, I'll be!, stone me!

ahilado, da *adj* light, soft (viento) || thin, weak (voz).

ahilamiento *m* faint (desmayo).

ahilar *vi* to go in single file.
◆ *vpr* to faint (desmayarse) || to go off, to go bad (vino, etc.) || FIG to lose weight (adel-

gazar) || to droop, to wilt (ajarse) || to grow tall and thin (los árboles).

ahílo *m* faint.

ahincadamente *adv* insistently (con insistencia) || tenaciously, earnestly, religiously.

ahincado, da *adj* insistent || eager, enthusiastic.

ahincar *vt* to urge.
◆ *vpr* to hurry (darse prisa).

ahínco *m* insistence; *pedir con ahínco* to ask with insistence || enthusiasm, eagerness || *trabajar con ahínco* to work eagerly *o* hard.

ahitar *vt* to give indigestion || to stake *o* to mark out; *ahitar un terreno* to mark out a piece of ground.
◆ *vpr* to gorge o.s., to stuff o.s. (*fam*); *ahitarse de caramelos* to stuff o.s. with sweets || to have *o* to get indigestion.

ahíto, ta *adj* who has indigestion (malucho) || full, satiated; *quedarse ahíto después de una buena comida* to be full after a good meal || FIG fed up (*de* with) (harto de una cosa) || FAM *estar ahíto* to have had enough, to have had one's fill.

ahocicar *vt* FIG & FAM to shut (s.o.) up, to show (s.o.) (en una discusión).
◆ *vi* FIG & FAM to give in, to yield, to admit defeat; *al final no tuvo más remedio que ahocicar* he had to admit defeat in the end || to fall flat on one's face (caer de bruces) || to dip the bows (barco).

ahogadero *m* Turkish bath, hothouse; *esta sala es un ahogadero* this room is like a Turkish bath || hangman's rope (del ahorcado) || throatlash, throatlatch (arreo del caballo).

ahogadilla *f* ducking || *darle a uno una ahogadilla* to duck s.o., to give s.o. a ducking.

ahogadizo, za *adj* bitter, sharp, tarty (fruta) || which does not float (madera).

ahogado, da *adj* drowned (en el agua); *en ese naufragio hubo diez personas ahogadas* in that shipwreck ten people were drowned || asphyxiated, gassed (por el gas) || strangled (estrangulado) || suffocated (por falta de aire, en general) || restricted; *respiración ahogada* restricted breathing || pent-up (emoción) || muffled, smothered (grito) || stuffy, close (sin ventilación) || stalemated (en ajedrez) || overcrowded (atestado) || harassed, at the end of one's tether (apurado) || AMER stewed (rehogado) || — FIG *ahogado de deudas* up to one's neck in debt | *estar* or *verse ahogado* to have the noose round one's neck, to be in a tight spot || *morir* or *perecer ahogado* to drown (en agua), to suffocate (por falta de aire).

ahogador, ra *adj* suffocating.
◆ *m* choker (collar).

ahogamiento *m* suffocation (asfixia) || drowning (en agua).

ahogar *vt* to drown; *ahogar a un gato* to drown a cat || to suffocate (impedir la respiración) || to asphyxiate, to gas (por el gas) || to strangle; *ahogar a uno con una cuerda* to strangle s.o. with a rope || to flood (encharcar, inundar) || to drown (regar con exceso) || to smother, to put out; *ahogar la lumbre con ceniza* to smother the fire with ashes || to choke (las plantas, sembrándolas muy apretadas) || FIG to stifle, to quell, to suppress, to put down; *ahogar una rebelión* to suppress a rebellion | to kill (un proyecto, etc.) | to overwhelm; *la pena le ahogaba* he was overwhelmed by grief | to stifle (los sollozos) | to keep *o* to hold back; *ahogar el llanto* to hold back one's tears || to stalemate (en ajedrez) || — FIG *ahogar en germen* to nip in the bud, to strangle at birth || *ahogar los remordimientos* to clear *o* to ease one's conscience || *ahogar su pena embriagándose* to drown one's sorrows.
◆ *vpr* to drown, to be drowned; *se ahogó en el río* he drowned in the river || to drown o.s. (suicidarse) || to suffocate, to be smothered (asfixiarse); *el niño se ahogó bajo la almohada* the child suffocated under the pillow || to go out (incendio) || to strangle o.s. (ahorcándose por accidente) || to suffocate; *ahogarse de calor* to suffocate with heat || — FIG *ahogarse en poca agua* or *en un vaso de agua* to make a mountain out of a molehill | *uno se ahoga aquí* it is stifling in here.

ahogo *m* MED breathing trouble, breathlessness (dificultad para respirar) || FIG distress (angustia) | financial difficulties *pl*; *pasar un ahogo* to experience *o* to be in financial difficulties || — *me dio un ahogo* I could not breathe || *perecer por ahogo* to drown (en agua), to suffocate (por falta de aire).

ahoguío *m* MED breathing trouble, breathlessness.

ahombrado, da *adj* FAM masculine (hombruno).

ahondamiento *m* deepening, digging, excavation || FIG investigation.

ahondar *vt* to deepen; *ahondar un pozo* to deepen a well || to drive (una cosa en otra) || FIG to go deeply into, to investigate thoroughly.
◆ *vi* to go deep; *las raíces ahondan en la tierra* the roots go deep in the ground || FIG to investigate thoroughly, to examine in depth, to go deeply into; *ahondar en una cuestión* to examine a question in depth.
◆ *vpr* to get deeper.

ahonde *m* deepening.

ahora *adv* now, right now; *ahora no puedo ir* I can't go now || FIG in a moment (dentro de un momento) | right away *o* now (en seguida) || — *ahora me lo han dicho* they've just told me || *ahora (que)* mind you; *ahora (que) tampoco me disgustaría hacer ese trabajo* mind you, I wouldn't mind doing that job || *ahora mismo* right away *o* now; *lo haré ahora mismo* I'll do it right away; just; *ha salido ahora mismo* he has just gone out || *ahora o nunca* it's now or never || *ahora sí que me voy* this time I really am going || *¡ahora vengo!* coming! || *de ahora en adelante, desde ahora* from now on, in future, in the future || *hasta ahora* see you later, see you soon (hasta luego), up till now, until now, to date (hasta la fecha) || *por ahora* for the moment, at the moment, for the time being.
◆ *conj* now, now then; *lo hemos discutido, ahora, ¿qué hacemos?* we have talked about it, now, what shall we do? || but; *es perezoso, ahora, si le haces trabajar* he is lazy, but if you make him work || — *ahora... ahora* either... or; *ahora vengas, ahora no vengas* either you come or you don't come; one minute... the next minute..., now... now; *ahora corre, ahora anda* one minute he's running, the next minute he's walking || *ahora, ahora bien* now; *ahora bien, su padre ha vuelto* now, his father has come back; but, however; *no me gusta, ahora bien, si lo quieres absolutamente* I don't like it, but if you really insist; come now; *ahora bien, ¡qué te crees!* come now, do you really think so? || *ahora que* but; *es inteligente, ahora que es perezoso* he is intelligent, but (he is) lazy.

ahorca *f* AMER present, gift.

ahorcado, da *m/f* hanged person, dead man.

ahorcadura *f* hanging.

ahorcajarse *vpr* to sit astride, to straddle; *ahorcajarse en una silla* to sit astride a chair.

ahorcar *vt* to hang || — *ahorcar los hábitos* to give up the cloth || FIG *a la fuerza ahorcan* I (you, etc.) have no choice *o* alternative | *¡que me ahorquen si lo cuento!* cross my heart and hope to die! | *¡que me ahorquen si lo sé!* I'm hanged if I know.
◆ *vpr* to hang o.s.; *ahorcarse de* or *en una rama de árbol* to hang o.s. from the branch of a tree.

ahorita *adv* FAM right now, this very minute.

ahormar *vt* to form (los zapatos, los sombreros) || to fit (un vestido) || to break in (los zapatos al andar) || to wear in (un vestido, un traje, al llevarlo) || FIG to mould (el carácter) || TAUR to manoeuvre (the bull) into a good position for the kill.
◆ *vpr* FIG to conform, to yield | to mould o.s. to, to get used to; *ahormarse a una nueva vida* to mould o.s. to a new life, to get used to a new life.

ahornagarse *vpr* to become parched (tierra) || to dry up (tierra, frutos, etc.).

ahornar *vt* to put in an oven.
◆ *vpr* to bake on the outside only.

ahorquillado, da *adj* forked.

ahorquillar *vt* to prop up [with forks] || to shape like a fork (dar forma de horquilla).
◆ *vpr* to fork.

ahorrador, ra *adj* thrifty.
◆ *m/f* thrifty person; *sus padres son unos ahorradores* his parents are thrifty people || saver; *el Estado estimula a los ahorradores* the government encourages savers.

ahorrar *vt* to save, to put aside; *la sociedad ahorró dinero* the society saved money; *he ahorrado unos cuartos para irme de vacaciones* I've put aside some money to go on holiday || FIG to save; *esto me ahorra hacerlo* that saves me doing it; *ahorrar sus fuerzas* to save one's strenght; *ahorrar saliva* to save one's breath || to free (un esclavo) || *no ahorraremos sacrificios para mantener la paz* there is no sacrifice we would not make to keep the peace.
◆ *vi* to save, to save up.
◆ *vpr* to save *o* to spare o.s.; *ahorrarse un trabajo penoso* to spare o.s. a difficult job || to save; *ahorrarse trabajo, tiempo* to save work, time || to save, to save o.s.; *fue andando para ahorrarse el billete* he went on foot to save himself the fare || to avoid, to save; *así se ahorra usted discusiones* that way you avoid arguments.

ahorrativo, va *adj* thrifty.

ahorro *m* saving; *tener algunos ahorros* to have a few savings || saving, thrift; *hay que fomentar el ahorro* saving must be encouraged || FIG saving; *es un ahorro de tiempo* it's a saving of time || — *esos son ahorros de chicha y nabo* this is cheeseparing economy || *hacer ahorros de chicha y nabo* to count every penny, to overeconomize || *caja postal de ahorros* Post Office savings bank.

ahuate *m* AMER thorn.

ahuecado, da *adj* deep (voz) || hollow (hueco) || bouffant (vestido).

ahuecador *m* bustle, crinoline (miriñaque).

ahuecamiento *m* hollowing-out, scooping-out (acción de dejar hueco) || loosening; *ahuecamiento del suelo* loosening of the soil || fluffing-up (de un colchón, etc.) || inflation (inflado) || FIG vanity.

ahuecar *vt* to hollow *o* to scoop out; *ahuecar un tronco de árbol* to hollow out a tree trunk || to loosen (la tierra) || to fluff up (lana, etc.) || to expand (un vestido) || — FAM *¡ahueca!* beat it!, clear off! | *ahuecar* or *ahuecar el ala* to take off, to make o.s. scarce (largarse) || *ahuecar la voz* to deepen one's voice, to put on a solemn *o* sanctimonious voice.
◆ *vpr* to become hollow || to fluff up (hacerse menos compacto) || to bubble, to blister

(el enlucido, etc.) || FIG & FAM to puff o.s. up, to put on airs.

ahuehué; ahuehuete *m* mexican coniferous tree.

ahuesado, da *adj* bone-coloured, bone, yellowish (amarillento) || bone-hard (duro).

ahuesarse *vpr* AMER to be spoilt (cosas) | to lose weight (personas).

ahuevado, da *adj/s* AMER FAM stunned, dazed (atontado).

ahuizote *m* AMER nuisance, bore (pesado) | witchcraft (brujería).

ahulado *m* AMER oilcloth, oilskin.

ahumado, da *adj* smoke-filled, smoky (lleno de humo) || smoked; *salmón ahumado* smoked salmon; *gafas ahumadas* smoked glasses || smoky; *cuarzo ahumado* smoky quartz || FIG tipsy, merry; *cuando salió del casino estaba algo ahumado* when he left the casino he was a bit tipsy || *arenque ahumado* smoked herring, kipper.

◆ *m* smoking; *el ahumado de la carne* the smoking of meat || smoking-out (de las abejas, etc.).

ahumar *vt* to smoke; *ahumar el jamón* to smoke ham || to cure (acecinar) || to smoke (una superficie) || to fill with smoke (llenar de humo) || to smoke out (las abejas, etc.).

◆ *vi* to smoke || to intoxicate, to be intoxicating; *los licores ahuman* drink intoxicates.

◆ *vpr* to acquire a smoky taste || to blacken, to get black (ennegrecerse) || FAM to get sozzled *o* tipsy (emborracharse) || FAM *ahumársele a uno el pescado* to get all steamed up, to get annoyed; *se le ahumó el pescado* he got all steamed up.

ahusado, da *adj* streamlined || fine, thin, tapered (dedos).

ahusar *vt* to taper.

◆ *vpr* to taper.

ahuyentar *vt* to scare *o* to drive away; *el perro ahuyentó a los ladrones* the dog scared the thieves away || to drive out *o* away; *el fuego ahuyentó las fieras de la selva* the fire drove the animals out of the forest || to keep at bay, to keep off (mantener a distancia) || FIG to dimiss, to dispel, to banish; *ahuyentar un pensamiento* to dimiss a thought || FIG *ahuyentar las penas con vino* to drown one's sorrows in wine.

◆ *vpr* to run away, to flee (huir).

aijada *f* goad.

ailanto *m* BOT ailanthus (árbol).

aíllo; ayllu *m* AMER line, race (entre los quechuas) | agricultural community.

aimara; aimará *adj* Aymaran.

◆ *m/f* Aymara (raza andina).

◆ *m* Aimara, Aymaran (lengua).

aindiado, da *adj* Indian-like, Indian.

airado, da *adj* angry, annoyed; *con gesto airado* with an angry look on his face; *respondió con un tono airado* he replied in an angry voice || in a temper *o* rage, seething; *salió airado* he left in a temper || immoral, loose (la vida) || *mujer de vida airada* loose woman.

airamiento *m* anger, annoyance.

airampo *m* cactus found in Peru and northern Argentina.

airar *vt* to annoy, to anger.

◆ *vpr* to get annoyed *o* angry.

aire *m* ZOOL solenodon (animal de Cuba).

aire *m* air (fluido); *bocanada de aire* breath of air || air; *el avión vuela por los aires* the aeroplane flies through the air || draught (corriente); *¿de dónde viene este aire?* where is this draught coming from? || FIG likeness (parecido); *aire de familia* family likeness | look, appearance (aspecto); *con un aire triste* with a sad look; *tiene un aire severo* he has a severe appearance, he has a severe look about him | allure, bearing (porte); *aire marcial* soldierly bearing || MÚS movement | tune, air (música); *aire bailable* dance tune | tune, song (canción); *un aire popular* a folk song || AUT choke (estrangulador) || gait (del caballo) || FAM attack; *le dio un aire que le dejó paralizado* he had an attack which left him paralyzed || — *aire acondicionado* air conditioning || *aire colado* draught || *aire comprimido* compressed air || *aire de suficiencia* conceited air || MIN *aire detonante* firedamp || *aire líquido* liquid air || *al aire* into the air; *disparar al aire* to shoot into the air || *al aire libre* in the open air; *dormir al aire libre* to sleep in the open air; open air; *la vida al aire libre* open-air life || FIG *beber el aire por* to be madly in love with || *cambia el aire* the wind is changing || FIG & FAM *cogerlas* or *matarlas en el aire* to be quick on the uptake || *con aire acondicionado* air-conditioned || *corriente de aire* draught || *dar aire a uno* to fan s.o. (airear) || *dar buen aire al dinero* to spend money freely, to spend money like mad || *darse aires* to put on airs and graces, to put on airs || *darse aires de intelectual* to put on intellectual airs, to play the intellectual || FAM *darse aires de suficiencia* to get on one's high horse || *darse un aire a* to look rather like, to resemble || FIG *de buen aire* willingly | *dejar en el aire* to leave pending *o* in the air | *de mal aire* reluctantly, unwillingly || *echar al aire* to uncover (desnudar), to throw into the air || FIG *estar de buen aire* to be in a good mood | *estar en el aire* to be in the air (un negocio), to be on the air (un programa de radio) | *hablar al aire* to talk idle rubbish || *hacer aire* it's windy || *hacer aire con un abanico* to fan o.s. || FIG *herir el aire* to rend the air | *levantar castillos en el aire* to build castles in the air *o* in Spain || FIG *mudar a cualquier aire* to be fickle, to change with the wind || *mudar* or *cambiar de aires* to have a change of air (enfermo) || *nivel de aire* spirit level || FIG *promesas en el aire* worthless *o* idle promises | *¿qué aires le traen por aquí?* what brings you here?, to what do we owe your visit?, to what do we owe the honour? | *seguir el aire a alguien* to do s.o.'s every wish | *ser aire* to be worthless | *sustentarse del aire* to live on next to nothing, to live on fresh air (vivir con poco) || *tener aires de gran señor* to have the air of *o* to look like a gentleman || FIG *tiene la cabeza llena de aire* he is empty-headed || *tomar el aire* to go out for a breath of air (pasearse) || FIG *¡vete a tomar el aire!* clear off!, get out!

◆ *interj* FAM clear off!

aireación *f* ventilation.

aireado, da *adj* ventilated (ventilado) || sour, bitter; *vino aireado* bitter wine.

airear *vt* to air || to ventilate (ventilar) || FIG to air (discutir) | to make public, to air || *airear la atmósfera* to clear the air.

◆ *vpr* to catch a cold (coger un resfriado) || *ha salido para airearse* he has gone out for a breath of fresh air.

airón *m* heron (ave) || crest, tuft, aigrette (penacho) || panache, crest (de cascos) || *pozo airón* very deep well.

airosamente *adv* gracefully, elegantly (con elegancia); *andar airosamente* to walk gracefully || *salir airosamente de algo* to come out of sth. with flying colours.

airosidad *f* gracefulness, grace, elegance.

airoso, sa *adj* ventilated (ventilado) || windy (ventoso) || FIG graceful, elegant (garboso); *una postura airosa* a graceful pose | neat; *una respuesta airosa* a neat reply || *quedar* or *salir airoso de algo* to come out of sth. with flying colours.

aislable *adj* isolable || ELECTR insulatable.

aislacionismo *m* isolationism.

aislacionista *adj/s* isolationist.

aisladamente *adv* on one's own, alone, by o.s.

aislado, da *adj* alone, by o.s., on one's own (solo); *vivir aislado* to live alone || remote, isolated (casa, aldea, sitio) || isolated (apartado) || ELECTR insulated || — *con inodoro aislado* with separate W. C. || *se les estropeó la radio dejándoles aislados de la civilización* their radio broke down cutting them off from civilization.

aislamiento *m* isolation; *vivir en el aislamiento* to live in isolation || ELECTR insulation || *aislamiento de sonido* soundproofing.

aislante *adj* insulating; *cinta aislante* insulating tape.

◆ *m* insulator.

aislar *vt* to isolate; *aislar un edificio* to isolate a building || ELECTR to insulate || FIG to isolate (dejar solo).

◆ *vpr* to isolate o.s., to go into seclusion.

¡ajá!; ¡ajajá!; ¡ajajay! *interj* FAM fine! good! (aprobación) | aha! (sorpresa).

Ajaccio *n pr* GEOGR Ajaccio.

ajado, da *adj* shabby, crumpled, creased (vestido, etc.) || withered (flor) || aged, drawn (persona) || wrinkled (piel).

¡ajajá!; ¡ajajay! *interj* → **¡ajá!**

ajamiento *m* shabbiness; *el ajamiento de una tela* the shabbiness of a piece of material || wrinkling (de la piel).

ajamonado, da *adj* FAM plump, sout; *una mujer ajamonada* a plump woman.

ajamonarse *vpr* FAM to get plump (una mujer).

ajar *m* garlic field, garlic patch.

ajar *vt* to crumple, to mess up (telas, etc.); *ajar un vestido* to crumple a dress || to fade; *flores ajadas* faded flowers || to make fade; *el sol aja las cortinas* sunlight makes the curtains fade || to wrinkle; *tez ajada* wrinkled complexion || FIG to age; *los sufrimientos la han ajado prematuramente* her suffering has aged her prematurely | to hurt; *ajar el amor propio de alguien* to hurt s.o.'s pride | to abuse, to disparage (rebajar).

◆ *vpr* to fade, to wither (flores) || to get crumpled *o* creased *o* shabby (un vestido) || to wrinkle (la piel).

ajardinado, da *adj* laid out with gardens, landscaped (arreglado como un jardín).

aje *m* AMER yam (planta) | kind of cochineal.

ajebe *m* alum (alumbre).

ajedrecista *m/f* chess player.

ajedrez *m* chess (juego) || chess set (piezas y tablero) || MAR grating (enjaretado).

ajedrezado, da *adj* check (tejido) || chequered; *escudo ajedrezado* chequered coat of arms.

ajengibre *m* ginger.

ajenjo *m* wormwood, absinth, absinthe (planta) || absinthe, absinth (bebida).

ajeno, na *adj* other people's, other's, of other people, of others (de otros, de los demás); *las desgracias ajenas* other people's misfortunes, the misfortunes of others; *los bienes ajenos* other people's property || someone else's (de otro); *vive con un corazón ajeno* he is living with someone else's heart || unaware of, out of; *yo era completamente ajeno a* or *de lo que ocurría* I was completely unaware of what was happening || irrelevant; *pregunta ajena al tema* question irrelevant to the subject || detached; *vivía completamente ajeno a las cosas de este mundo* he lived completely detached from the things of this world || free (libre); *ajeno de prejuicios* free from prejudice || different; *mis* *preocupaciones son muy ajenas a las tuyas* my worries are very different from yours || not in keeping with, inconsistent with; *ajeno de su estado, a su carácter* not in keeping with his position, his character || outside; *eso es ajeno a su especialidad* that is outside his speciality *o* field || strange, alien; *este asunto me es completamente ajeno* this matter is completely strange to me || without, devoid of; *ajeno de sentido común* devoid of common sense || — *estar ajeno de sí* to be beside o.s. || DEP *este equipo va a jugar en campo ajeno* this team is going to play away [from home] || *lo ajeno, el bien ajeno* other people's property || *persona ajena a un asunto* person who has nothing to do with a matter, outsider to a matter || *por razones ajenas a nuestra voluntad* for reasons beyond our control || *prohibida la entrada a las personas ajenas al servicio* staff only || *ser ajeno a un crimen* to have no part in a crime || *vivir a costa ajena* to live off other people, to live at other people's expense.

ajerezado, da *adj* sherry-like.

ajete *m* young garlic || garlic sauce (salsa).

ajetreado, da *adj* busy; *una persona, una vida muy ajetreada* a very busy person, life.

ajetrearse *vpr* to be busy (atarearse) || to wear o.s. out, to exhaust o.s.; *me he ajetreado mucho para nada* I've worn myself out for nothing || to rush, to hurry (darse prisa).

ajetreo *m* activity (actividad) || rush; *¡qué ajetreo!, no paré ni un momento* what a rush! I didn't stop for a second || rushing about, hard work; *la preparación de un viaje acarrea mucho ajetreo* preparing for a journey involves a lot of rushing about || bustle, life, movement; *hay mucho ajetreo en la calle* there's a lot of bustle in the street || hustle and bustle, bustle; *el ajetreo de la vida en la ciudad* the hustle and bustle of town life || exhaustion, weariness (cansancio).

ají *m* red pepper, chili || chili sauce (salsa) || — AMER FAM *ponerse como un ají* to go as red as a beetroot (sonrojarse), to go up the wall, to lose one's temper (enfadarse) | *ser más bravo que el ají* to have a nasty character.

ajiaceite *m* garlic sauce (salsa).

ajiaco *m* chili sauce (salsa) || AMER chili stew.

ajilimoje; ajilimójili *m* piquant sauce.
◆ *pl* FIG & FAM bits and pieces || FIG & FAM *y con todos sus ajilimójilis* and the whole bag of tricks, and the whole caboodle.

ajipuerro *m* wild leek.

ajo *m* garlic; *ristra de ajos* string of garlics || clove of garlic (diente de ajo) || garlic sauce (salsa) || — *ajo blanco* garlic soup || *ajo cañete* or *castañete* garlic with reddish skin || *ajo cebollino* chive, chives || *ajo chalote* shallot || *ajo porro* or *puerro* leek || *ajo tierno* fresh garlic || FIG *bueno anda el ajo* things are really looking bad, things are really in a state || *diente de ajo* clove of garlic || FIG & FAM *estar en el ajo* to be in on it (saber lo que sucede), to be involved, to be mixed up in it | *estar harto de ajos* to be ill-bred *o* uncouth | *quien se pica, ajos come* if the cap fits, wear it | *revolver el ajo* to stir up trouble, to add fuel to the fire | *soltar ajos* to swear, to curse.

¡ajo!; ¡ajó! *interj* coo coo!, goo goo! [talking to a baby].

ajoarriero *m* dish prepared with cod, eggs and garlic.

ajobar *vt* to carry on one's back.

ajofaina *f* washbowl, washbasin (palangana).

ajolín *m* kind of bedbug.

ajolote *m* axolotl (animal anfibio).

ajomate *m* conferva (alga).

ajonjolí *m* BOT sesame (alegría).

ajorca *f* bracelet (pulsera).

ajornalar *tr* to employ by the day.

ajuanetado, da *adj* deformed by a bunion (pie) || with prominent cheekbones (rostro).

ajuar *m* furnishings *pl* (de una casa) || trousseau (de novia) || *ajuar de niño* layette.

ajuglarado, da *adj* minstrel-like.

ajuiciado, da *adj* wise, sensible (juicioso).

ajuiciar *vt* to bring to one's senses (volver juicioso) || to judge (juzgar).

ajumado, da *adj* FAM canned, tight, sozzled.
◆ *m* FAM drunk.

ajumarse *vpr* FAM to get sozzled *o* drunk *o* canned.

ajustado, da *adj* adjusted || correct, right; *una solución ajustada* a correct answer || tight, clinging; *un vestido muy ajustado* a very tight dress || close; *resultados ajustados* close results || *bien ajustado, mal ajustado* well-fitting, badly-fitting.
◆ *m* fitting; *el ajustado de las piezas del motor* the fitting of engine parts.

ajustador *m* (ant) jerkin (prenda de vestir) || corselet (ropa interior) || fitter (obrero) || IMPR compositor, maker-up.

ajustamiento *m* ⟶ **ajuste.**

ajustar *vt* to fit; *ajustar un vestido* to fit a dress || to make fit; *ajustar una tapa a una caja* to make a lid fit a box || to arrange; *ajustar un matrimonio* to arrange a marriage || to work out, to arrange; *ajustar un horario* to work out a timetable || to reconcile (enemigos) || to take on, to employ (un criado, un empleado) || to settle, to pay (una cuenta) || to draw up (un tratado) || to fix; *hemos ajustado el alquiler en 2 000 pesetas* we have fixed the rent at 2, 000 pesetas || to give (un golpe) || to adapt; *ajustar su conducta a* to adapt one's conduct to || IMPR to make up || TECN to fit; *ajustar dos piezas* to fit two parts | to adjust, to regulate (una máquina) || AMER to catch (una enfermedad) || — FIG *ajustar el paso al de alguien* to keep pace with s.o. || COM *ajustar las cuentas* to balance the accounts || FIG *ajustar las cuentas a uno* to settle accounts with s.o. | *ajustarle las clavijas a uno* to put the pressure on s.o., to tighten up on s.o., to put the screws on s.o.
◆ *vi* to fit; *esta tapadera no ajusta* this lid doesn't fit || to cling, to be tight (un vestido) || FIG to fit in; *esto ajusta con lo que te dije* that fits in with what I said.
◆ *vpr* to adjust *o* to adapt o.s.; *me ajusto a todo* I adapt myself to everything || to conform; *ajústate exactamente a mis instrucciones* conform exactly with my instructions || to be consistent, to fit in; *lo que me dices se ajusta a la verdad* what you say is consistent with the truth || to cling, to be tight (un vestido) || to tighten; *ajustarse el cinturón* to tighten one's belt || to come to an agreement (llegar a un acuerdo) || to agree; *se ajustaron en que iban a venir* they agreed to come || — *ajustarse a razones* to yield to reason || *ajustarse en sus costumbres* to settle down.

ajuste; ajustamiento *m* fitting (acción de ajustar un vestido, etc.) || adjustment (encaje, adaptación) || agreement, compromise (acuerdo); *llegar a un ajuste* to come to an agreement || engagement, hiring, employment (de un criado, obrero) || fixing (del precio) || TECN fitting, assembly (ensamblaje) | adjustment (arreglo) || IMPR composition, makeup || COM settlement, payment (de una cuenta) || CINEM splicing || FOT framing, centring || bonus (sobre el sueldo) || — FIG *ajuste de cuentas* settling of accounts || *ajuste de la paz* peace talks || *anillo de ajuste* bush || *carta de ajuste* test card (en la televisión) || *más vale mal ajuste que buen pleito* a poor agreement is better than a good court case || *tornillo de ajuste* adjusting screw.

ajusticiado, da *m/f* executed person.

ajusticiamiento *m* execution (de un reo).

ajusticiar *vt* to execute.

al contraction of the preposition *a* and the masculine definite article *el*.
1. SEGUIDO DE UN SUSTANTIVO (véase A, preposición) || into; *traducir al italiano* to translate into italian || — *al mediodía* at midday, at noon || *al menos* at least || *dar la vuelta al mundo* to go round the world.
2. SEGUIDO DEL INFINITIVO when, on; *al llegar se cayó* when he arrived, he fell over; on arriving, he fell over; *al entrar vio a su tío* when he came in *o* on entering he saw his uncle || — *al dar las cinco* on the stroke of five, when the clock struck five || *al anochecer* at nightfall || *al salir el sol* at sunrise.

ala *f* wing (de ave, insecto, avión, edificio, ejército, partido político) || brim; *sombrero de ala ancha* widebrimmed hat || lobe (del hígado) || wing, ala (de nariz) || eave (del techo) || leaf, flap (de mesa) || blade (de hélice) || sail (de molino) || DEP wing (parte del campo) | winger (jugador) || — FIG & FAM *ahuecar el ala* to take off, to make o.s. scarce (marcharse) || *ala del corazón* auricle || DEP *ala delta* hang-gliding || FIG *caérsele a uno las alas del corazón* to lose heart || *con alas en delta* delta-winged || *con alas de flecha* swept-wing || FIG *cortarle las alas a uno* to clip s.o.'s wings (estorbar), to take the wind out of s.o.'s sails (desanimar) | *dar alas a alguien* to encourage s.o. || FAM *del ala* peseta; *veinte del ala* twenty pesetas || *ser como ala de mosca* to be paper-thin || *volar con sus propias alas* to stand on one's own two feet.

¡ala! *interj* come on! (para incitar) || hey! (para llamar).

Alá *npr m* Allah.

alabado, da *adj* praised || *¡alabado sea Dios!* God be praised!, praise be to God!
◆ *m* eulogy (motete) || AMER dawn call [of night watchman] || AMER *al alabado* at dawn.

alabamiento *m* praise || boasting (jactancia).

alabanza *f* praise (*a, de* of); *cantar las alabanzas de* to sing the praises of || boasting, boastfulness (jactancia) || *en alabanza de* in praise of.

alabar *vt* to praise, to laud (celebrar) || *alabar a uno de discreto* or *por su discreción* to praise s.o. for his discretion, to praise s.o.'s discretion.
◆ *vi* AMER to call dawn.
◆ *vpr* to boast (jactarse) || to be glad *o* pleased; *me alabo de tu triunfo* I am pleased about your triumph.

alabarda *f* halberd.

alabardado, da *adj* halberd-shaped.

alabardazo *m* blow with a halberd.

alabardero *m* halberdier.
◆ *pl* claque *sing*, hired applauders (en el teatro).

alabastrado, da *adj* alabastrine, alabaster.

alabastrino, na *adj* alabastrine, alabaster.
◆ *f* thin sheet of alabaster.

alabastrita; alabastrites *f* translucent gypsum.

alabastro *m* alabaster || *alabastro yesoso* translucent gypsum.

álabe *m* TECN paddle, blade (de rueda hidráulica) | tooth [of a cog] || drooping branch (de un árbol).

alabeado, da *adj* warped; *una tabla alabeada* a warped plank.

alabear *vt* to warp.
◆ *vpr* to warp.

alabeo *m* warp, warping (torcedura).

alacena *f* cupboard [*US* closet].

alacrán *m* scorpion (arácnido) ‖ s-shaped hook (de un corchete) ‖ cheek (del bocado) ‖ *AMER* scandalmonger, gossip (maldiciente) ‖ — *alacrán cebollero* mole cricket ‖ *alacrán marinero* angler (pez).

alacranado, da *adj* stung by a scorpion ‖ FIG rotten, corrupt (viciado).

alacranera *f* scorpiurus (planta).

alacridad *f* alacrity, readiness ‖ brickness (vivacidad) ‖ *con alacridad* with alacrity, readily.

alacha *f*; **alache** *m* ZOOL (fresh) anchovy.

alada *f* flap *o* stroke of the wing.

aladares *m pl* hair *sing* on the temples, hair *sing* that falls over the temples.

aladierna *f*; **aladierno** *m* buckthorn (arbusto).

Aladino *npr m* Aladdin.

alado, da *adj* winged, flying; *hormiga alada* winged ant ‖ BOT wing-shaped ‖ FIG swift, rapid, quick (ligero).

alagartado, da *adj* motley.

alajú *m* kind of gingerbread.

alalia *f* MED aphasia.

alalimón *m* a children's game ‖ ⟶ **alimón (al).**

alamar *m* decorative clasp (presilla) ‖ frog (adorno de casaca) ‖ fringe (fleco) ‖ tassel (en el traje del torero).

alambicado, da *adj* FIG elaborate, subtle, intricate; *una teoría alambicada* an elaborate theory | restricted, minimal, reduced to the bare minimum (escaso) | precious, subtle (estilo) | affected (afectado) ‖ FIG *precios alambicados* rock-bottom prices, cheapest possible prices.

alambicamiento *m* distillation ‖ FIG excessive subtlety; *el alambicamiento de un razonamiento* the excessive subtlety of an argument | affectation (afectación) | preciosity (del lenguaje, etc.).

alambicar *vt* to distil, to distill (destilar) ‖ FIG to subtilize (sutilizar) | to overrefine (pulir excesivamente) | to complicate, to make over-intricate (complicar) | to elaborate (precisar) | to minimize, to keep to a minimum, to bring down to the lowest possible level (precio, etc.).

alambique *m* still ‖ — FIG *pasar algo por el alambique* to scrutinize sth., to go through sth. with a fine toothcomb.

alambrada *f* barbed-wire barrier *o* entanglement (en la guerra) ‖ wire netting (reja) ‖ wire fence (valla).

alambrado *m* wire netting (alambrera) ‖ wire fence *o* fencing (valla) ‖ ELECTR wiring, wiring system.

alambrar *vt* to enclose with wire netting (una ventana) ‖ to fence, to enclose with wire fencing (un terreno).

alambre *m* wire (de metal) ‖ bells *pl* (del ganado) ‖ — *alambre de púas* or *de espino* or *espinoso* barbed wire ‖ FIG & FAM *piernas de alambre* matchstick *o* skinny legs ‖ FAM *ser un alambre* to be as thin as a rake.

alambrera *f* wire netting (red de alambre) ‖ wire gauze (red muy fina) ‖ wire cover ‖ food safe (alacena) ‖ fireguard (en el brasero o chimenea).

alambrista *m/f* tightrope walker.

alameda *f* tree-lined avenue, boulevard (avenida) ‖ poplar grove (plantío de álamos).

alamín *m* (ant) inspector of wheights and measures | surveyor of buildings (de obras arquitectónicas) | irrigation superintendant (de los riegos).

álamo *m* BOT poplar; *álamo blanco, negro* white, black poplar ‖ *álamo temblón* aspen.

alampar *vi* to long, to be longing *o* dying; *alampar por ir al cine, por un coche* to be longing to go to the cinema, for a car.

alanceado, da *adj* BOT lanceolate.

alancear *vt* to lance, to spear.

alano *adj m* *perro alano* mastiff.
◆ *m pl* alans, alani.

Alano *npr m* Alan, Allen, Allan.

alantoides *f* ANAT allantois.

alar *m* eaves *pl* (alero).

alarde *m* MIL review, parade, match past ‖ FIG show, display; *un alarde de buen gusto* a display of good taste ‖ *hacer alarde de* to display, to show off, to boast of; *hacer alarde de su riqueza* to show off one's wealth; to put on a show of, to display; *hacer alarde de indiferencia* to put on a show of indifference, to display indifference.

alardear *vi* to boast, to brag, to show off; *alardear de sus conocimientos* to boast *o* to brag about one's knowledge, to show off one's knowledge ‖ to boast, to brag; *alardea de tener influencia con el ministro* he boasts that he has influence with the Minister ‖ *alardea de buen mozo* he thinks he is good-looking.

alardeo *m* show, display (alarde) ‖ boasting, bragging (jactancia).

alargadera *f* extension piece, extension (de un compás, de un goniómetro) ‖ adapter (retorta).

alargado, da *adj* elongated, lengthened, long; *forma alargada* elongated shape.

alargador, ra *adj* lengthening, extending.

alargamiento *m* lengthening ‖ extension; *el alargamiento de una calle* the extension of a street ‖ prolongation (en el tiempo) ‖ TECN elongation ‖ stretch, stretching; *el alargamiento de un elástico* the stretch of an elastic band.

alargar *vt* to lengthen, to let down; *alargar un vestido* to lengthen a dress ‖ to lengthen (en longitud) ‖ to prolong (en el tiempo); *alargar su estancia, un discurso* to prolong one's stay, a speech ‖ to spin out (un cuento) ‖ to put off, to defer (diferir) ‖ to raise (un sueldo) ‖ to extend, to lengthen; *alargar un plazo* to extend a time limit ‖ to pass, to reach, to hand (dar); *alárgame ese libro* pass me that book ‖ to hold out, to stretch out (la mano) ‖ to crane, to stretch (el cuello) ‖ FIG to make stretch, to stretch out; *no puede alargar más su paga* he cannot make his wages stretch any further ‖ to let *o* to pay out; *alarga un poco de cuerda* pay some rope out ‖ FIG & FAM to make drag on, to draw out; *la indecisión del general alargó la guerra* the general's indecision made the war drag on *o* drew the war out ‖ to increase (aumentar) ‖ — *alargarle el camino a uno* to take s.o. out of one's way ‖ *alargar el paso* to lengthen one's stride, to step *o* to stride out.
◆ *vpr* to lengthen, to grow *o* to get longer ‖ to grow longer, to draw out; *en marzo los días se alargan* in March the days get longer ‖ to get longer, to stretch; *este traje se alarga al lavarse* this dress gets longer when it is washed ‖ to drag on *o* out (un discurso) ‖ FIG to get carried away, to be longwinded, to go on; *me he alargado mucho en mi carta* I went on a lot in my letter ‖ FIG & FAM to carry on; *alargarse a* or *hasta la ciudad* to carry on to the town | to nip round, to pop over *o* round; *alárgate a casa de tu hermano* nip round to your brother's ‖ MAR to change (el viento) ‖ to enlarge; *alargarse en un tema* to enlarge upon a theme.

Alarico *npr m* Alaric.

alarido *m* (ant) war cry of the Moors ‖ howl, yell, shriek (grito fuerte) ‖ *dar alaridos* to howl, to yell, to shriek.

alarifazgo *m* position of master builder.

alarife *m* master builder (maestro albañil) ‖ bricklayer (albañil) ‖ *AMER* clever *o* crafty one.

alarije *m* variety of grape.

alarma *f* alarm; *dar la alarma* to raise *o* to give the alarm ‖ emergency; *proclamar* or *declarar el estado de alarma* to declare a state of emergency ‖ anxiety; *vivir en alarma* to live in anxiety ‖ — *alarma aérea* air-raid siren, air-raid warning ‖ *con creciente alarma* with increasing concern, with increasing alarm ‖ *dar un toque de alarma* to sound the alarm ‖ *falsa alarma* false alarm ‖ *señal de alarma* alarm, alarm signal ‖ *voz de alarma* alarm, alarm call.

alarmado, da *adj* alarmed.

alarmante *adj* alarming.

alarmar *vt* to alarm, to frighten; *me alarma la gravedad de la situación* the seriousness of the situation alarms me ‖ to alert, to rouse (dar la alarma a) ‖ to call to arms (incitar a tomar las armas).
◆ *vpr* to be *o* to get alarmed, to be frightened ‖ *no alarmarse por nada* not to be alarmed by anything.

alarmista *m/f* alarmist (que hace cundir las noticias alarmantes) ‖ nervous *o* jumpy *o* easily-frightened person (persona inclinada a alarmarse).

Alaska *n pr* GEOGR Alaska.

a latere *m* FIG & FAM lapdog, inseparable companion (compañero).

alaterno *m* BOT buckthorn (aladierna).

Álava *n pr* GEOGR Alava [one of the Basque provinces in Spain].

alavense; alavés, esa *adj* [of *o* from] Alava.
◆ *m/f* native *o* inhabitant of Alava.

alazán, ana; alazano, na *adj/s* chestnut ‖ *alazán dorado, tostado* golden, burnt chestnut (caballo).

alba *f* dawn, daybreak; *me levanté al alba* I got up at dawn ‖ alb (de los sacerdotes) ‖ — *al rayar el alba* at dawn, at daybreak; *levantarse al rayar el alba* to get up *o* to rise at daybreak ‖ *clarea* or *raya* or *rompe el alba* dawn is breaking ‖ *misa del alba* early morning mass.

albacea *m/f* executor (hombre), executrix (mujer).

albaceazgo *m* executorship.

albaceteño, ña; albacetense *adj* [of *o* from] Albacete [Spanish town].
◆ *m/f* native *o* inhabitant of Albacete.

albacora *f* early fig (breva) ‖ ZOOL tunny, tunny fish [*US* tuna, tuna fish] (bonito).

albahaca *f* basil (planta).

albalá *m or f* letters patent *pl* ‖ document (documento).
— OBSERV pl *albalaes.*

albanegra *f* hairnet (para el pelo) ‖ net (para cazar).

albanés, esa *adj/s* Albanian.

Albania *npr f* GEOGR Albania.

albañal; albañar *m* sewer, drain (alcantarilla).

albañil *m* bricklayer ‖ — *oficial de albañil* master bricklayer ‖ *peón de albañil* hodman, bricklayer's labourer.

albañila *adj f* *abeja albañila* mason-bee.

albañilería *f* bricklaying (arte) ‖ masonry, brickwork ‖ *pared de albañilería* brick wall.

albar *adj* white; *conejo albar* white rabbit.
◆ *m* dry, white land (terreno).

albarán *m* «to let» sign || letters patent *pl* (albalá) || delivery note, invoice (lista de mercancías entregadas).

albarazado, da *adj* leprous (gafo) || whitish (blanquecino) || motley (abigarrado) || AMER Chinese and Indian half-breed.

albarda *f* packsaddle (de una caballería) || AMER saddle (silla de montar) || slice of bacon fat (albardilla de tocino).

albardado, da *adj* with the back of a different colour from the rest of the body (animal).

albardar *vt* to put a packsaddle on, to saddle.

albardería *f* saddler's shop, saddlery (talabartería).

albardero *m* saddler and harness maker.

albardilla *f* saddle for breaking horses (silla de montar) || ARCH coping (tejadillo) || small cushion (almohadilla) || mound of earth (en un huerto) || slice of bacon fat, lard (de tocino).

albardón *m* large saddle || AMER mound of earth (de tierra).

albareque *m* sardine net (red).

albaricoque *m* apricot (fruta) || apricot, apricot tree (árbol).

albaricoquero *m* apricot, apricot tree (árbol).

albarillo *m* white apricot (fruto y árbol) || lively guitar tune.

albariza *f* lagoon (laguna) || dry, white land (terreno).

albarizo, za *adj* whitish (blanquecino).
◆ *m* dishcloth (paño).

albarrada *f* dry-stone wall (muro) || terrace (en una pendiente) || mud wall (tapia) || defensive wall (defensa) || clay jar (alcarraza).

albarrana *adj f* flanking (torre) || *cebolla albarrana* scilla (planta).

albatros *m* albatross.

albayaldado, da *adj* covered in white lead.

albayalde *m* white lead.

albazano, na *adj* bay (caballo).

albazo *m* AMER dawn attack (acción de guerra) | dawn music, aubade (música) | early riser (madrugón).

albeador *m* AMER early riser.

albear *m* clay track.

albear *vi* to turn white, to whiten || AMER to get up early (madrugar).

albedrío *m* will; *libre albedrío* free will || whim, fancy (capricho) || custom (costumbre) || *hazlo a tu albedrío* do it as you like *o* as the fancy takes you, do it at your pleasure.

albéitar *m* veterinary surgeon, vet [*US* veterinarian].

albeitería *f* veterinary surgery.

alberca *f* tank, (small) reservoir (estanque) || retting pit, rettery (poza para cáñamo) || AMER swimming pool (piscina) || *en alberca* roofless.

albérchigo *m* clingstone peach (melocotón) || clingstone apricot (albaricoque) || clingstone-peach tree (melocotonero) || clingstone-apricot tree (albaricoquero).

alberchiguero *m* clingstone-peach tree (melocotonero) || clingstone-apricot tree (albaricoquero).

albergador, ra *adj* (p us) accommodating.
◆ *m* host (anfitrión) || landford (ventero).
◆ *f* hostess (anfitriona) || landlady (ventera).

albergar *vt* to give shelter to (servir de albergue) || to accommodate, to house, to lodge; *el bloque de viviendas albergará a doscientas familias* the block of flats will house two hundred families; *la compañía alberga a los trabajadores extranjeros* the company houses its foreing workers || to accommodate, to house; *el viejo edificio no albergaba todos los ministerios* the old building did not house all the ministries || to accommodate, to take in, to put up; *una familia me alberga cuando voy a España* a family puts me up when I go to Spain || FIG to cherish, to harbour, to foster; *alberga la esperanza de ir a México* he cherishes hopes of going to Mexico | to harbour (odio) | to experience; *albergar cierta inquietud* to experience a certain anxiety.
◆ *vi/vpr* to stay; *nos albergamos en el mismo hotel* we are staying at the same hotel || to shelter (refugiarse).

albergue *m* accommodation, lodgings *pl* (alojamiento); *tengo un albergue en un barrio central* I have got accommodation in the town centre || hostel (posada); *albergue de juventud* youth hostel || lair, den (de animales) || shelter, refuge (refugio); *encontrar albergue en casa de un amigo* to find shelter in a friend's house || — *albergue de carretera* (roadside) inn, roadhouse || *dar albergue a alguien* to give s.o. lodgings, to take s.o. in.

albero, ra *adj* (p us) white (albar).
◆ *m* dishcloth (paño) || dry, white land (terreno).

Alberto *npr m* Albert.

albigense *adj* [of *o* from] Albi || Albigensian (de los albigenses).
◆ *m/f* native *o* inhabitant of Albi || — HIST *la cruzada de los albigenses* the Albigensian Crusade | *los albigenses* the Albigenses.

albillo, lla *adj/sf* *uva albilla* white grape.

albina *f* salt lake *o* marsh.

albinismo *m* albinism.

albino, na *adj/s* albino; *una niña albina* an albino girl || AMER half-caste.

Albión *npr f* GEOGR Albion.

albis (in) *adv* FAM *quedarse in albis* not to have a clue, not to understand a thing, to be completely flummoxed, to be left in the dark.

albita *f* MIN albite.

albitana *f* fence to protect plants (para las plantas).
◆ *m* MAR apron (en la proa) | inner sternpost (en la popa).

albo, ba *adj* POÉT white.

albóndiga; albondiguilla *f* meatball, rissole (de carne).

albor *m* whiteness (blancura) || dawn, daybreak (alba) || FIG beginning (principio) || — *albores de la vida* springtime of life || *a los albores* at dawn.

alborada *f* dawn, daybreak (alba) || MÚS aubade, dawn song || MIL reveille.

alborear *v impers* to break, to dawn [the day] (amanecer); *ya alborea* day is dawning *o* breaking, dawn is breaking.

alborno *m* BOT alburnum, sapwood.

albornoz *m* burnous (de los árabes) || bathrobe (para el baño).

alboronía *f* stew (guiso).

alboroque *m* gratuity, tip (agasajo).

alborotadamente *adv* noisily, boisterously.

alborotado, da *adj* agitated, excited, worked up; *los ánimos están alborotados* people are excited || FIG eventful, full, busy; *hoy ha sido un día alborotado* today has been an eventful day || rough, choppy (el mar) || mutinous (amotinado) || hasty, rash, reckless (aturdido).

alborotador, ra *adj* rowdy, noisy, boisterous; *alumnos alborotadores* rowdy schoolchildren || rebellious (rebelde) || seditious; *ideas alborotadoras* seditious ideas.
◆ *m/f* agitator, troublemaker; *siempre hay alborotadores en las manifestaciones* there are agitators in every demonstration || subversive element (sedicioso) || unruly *o* noisy child (en un colegio).

alborotamiento *m* → **alboroto.**

alborotapueblos *m inv* agitator, troublemaker.

alborotar *vi* to make a din *o* racket, to kick up a row (hacer ruido) || to create *o* to cause disorder (causar desorden) || to move about (agitarse) || — *él no deja de alborotar* he won't keep still || *¡no alborotéis más, niños!* children, behave yourselves!
◆ *vt* to upset, to cause a stir in *o* among, to agitate; *un acontecimiento que ha alborotado a toda la familia* an event which has upset the whole family || to stir up; *alborotar el barrio* to stir up the district || to upset, to turn upside down; *lo has alborotado todo* you've upset everything || to ruffle; *el viento alborota el pelo* the wind ruffles one's hair || to arouse the curiosity of (excitar la curiosidad de) || FIG & FAM *alborotar el gallinero* or *el cotarro* to cause trouble *o* a stir.
◆ *vpr* to get upset *o* agitated (perturbarse) || to get excited (excitarse) || to riot (una multitud) || to lose one's temper, to get angry (encolerizarse) || to get worked up, to lose one's head; *no te alborotes por tan poca cosa* don't get worked up over such a little thing || to get rough *o* choppy (el mar).

alborotero, ra; alborotista *adj* AMER noisy, rowdy (que mete jaleo) | troublesome, rebellious (rebelde).

alboroto; alborotamiento *m* uproar, disturbance (jaleo) || din, racket, row (ruido); *hubo tal alboroto que la gente salió a ver lo que ocurría* there was such a din that people came out to see what was happening || disturbance, riot (disturbio) || scare, fright (susto) || *alboroto nocturno* disturbance of the peace at night.
◆ *pl* AMER roasted grains of maize || *alborotos públicos* public disturbances.

alborotoso, sa *adj* AMER troublesome, rebellious (rebelde) | rowdy, noisy (que mete jaleo) || — AMER *ideas alborotosas* seditious ideas | *persona alborotosa* agitator (dispuesta a promover disturbios).

alborozadamente *adv* joyfully, merrily.

alborozado, da *adj* joyful, overjoyed.

alborozador, ra *adj* cheering, heartening.

alborozar *vt* to make laugh; *los payasos alborozan a la chiquillería* clowns make children laugh || to delight, to gladden, to make happy, to fill with joy (llenar de alegría); *la noticia me alborozó* the news delighted me.
◆ *vpr* to be overjoyed, to rejoice.

alborozo *m* joy, gaiety, merriment.

albricias *f pl* reward *sing*, gift *sing* (regalo) || AMER air holes (en metalurgia) || *dar albricias* to congratulate.
◆ *interj* great!, good!, smashing!

albufera *f* lagoon, pool, «albufera» [especially in Valencia].

álbum *m* album; *álbum de fotografías* photograph album || *álbum de recortes* scrapbook.
— OBSERV The plural of *álbum* is *álbumes*.

albumen *m* BOT albumen, endosperm.

albúmina *f* BIOL albumin, albumen.

albuminoide *m* QUÍM albuminoid.

albuminoideo, a *adj* QUÍM albuminoid.

albuminosis *f* MED albuminosis.

albuminoso, sa *adj* albuminous.

albuminuria *f* MED albuminuria.

albur *m* bleak (pez) ‖ first draw in the game of monte (en el juego) ‖ FIG hazard, risk; *los albures de la vida* the hazards of life ‖ *jugar* or *correr un albur* to run a risk.
◆ *pl* card game.

albura *f* whiteness (blancura) ‖ white [of an egg] (de huevo) ‖ BOT alburnum, sapwood.

alburno *m* BOT alburnum, sapwood (albura).

alca *f* ZOOL razorbill (ave).

alcabala *f* (ant) sales tax.

alcabalero *m* tax collector (recaudador).

alcacel; alcacer *m* BOT green barley ‖ barley field (terreno).

alcací; alcacil *m* (wild) artichoke.

alcachofa *f* artichoke (planta) ‖ head of thistle (del cardo) ‖ rose (de regadera) ‖ sprinkling nozzle, sprinkler (de la ducha) ‖ strainer, rose (de un tubo).

alcachofado, da *adj* artichoke-shaped.
◆ *m* dish of artichokes.

alcachofero, ra *adj* producing artichokes.
◆ *f* artichoke (planta).

alcade *m* → **alcalde.**

alcahueta *f* procuress, bawd, go-between (celestina) ‖ FIG & FAM scandalmonger, gossip (chismosa).

alcahuete *m* procurer, pimp (proxeneta) ‖ FIG & FAM scandalmonger, gossip (chismoso) | receiver (de cosas robadas) ‖ TEATR draw curtain ‖ *AMER* informer (soplón).

alcahuetear *vi* to procure, to pimp (el proxeneta) ‖ to gossip (chismorrear) ‖ to be a receiver (de cosas robadas).

alcahuetería *f* procuring, pimping ‖ FIG & FAM complicity | trap (artimaña).

alcaicería *f* (ant) customs house for silk (aduana) ‖ silk merchant's district (sitio con tiendas de seda).

alcaico, ca *adj/m* POÉT Alcaic.

alcaide *m* (ant) governor (de una fortaleza) ‖ prison governor (de una prisión).

alcaidesa *f* governor's wife, governess.

alcaidía *f* governorship (cargo de alcaide) ‖ governor's house (casa del alcaide).

alcalaíno, na *adj* [of *o* from] Alcalá [especially Alcalá de Henares].
◆ *m/f* native *o* inhabitant of Alcalá.

alcaldada *f* abuse of authority.

alcalde; alcade *m* mayor; *el alcalde de Madrid* the mayor of Madrid ‖ card game (juego de cartas) ‖ justice of the peace (juez) ‖ — *alcalde de barrio, teniente de alcalde* deputy mayor ‖ FAM *alcalde de monterilla* village mayor ‖ *alcalde mayor* magistrate.

alcaldesa *f* mayoress.

alcaldía *f* mayorship, mayoralty (dignidad de alcalde) ‖ mayor's office (oficina).

alcalemia *f* MED alcalaemia.

alcalescencia *f* QUÍM alkalescence.

alcalescente *adj* QUÍM alkalescent.

álcali *m* QUÍM alkali ‖ *álcali volátil* ammonia.

alcalimetría *f* QUÍM alkalimetry.

alcalímetro *m* QUÍM alkalimeter.

alcalinidad *f* QUÍM alkalinity.

alcalinización *f* QUÍM alkalinization, alkalization.

alcalinizar *vt* alkalize.

alcalino, na *adj* QUÍM alkaline.

alcalinotérreo, a *adj* QUÍM alkaline-earth.
◆ *m* QUÍM alkaline earth.

alcalizar *vt* QUÍM to alkalize, to alkalify, to alkalinize.

alcaloide *adj/sm* QUÍM alkaloid.

alcaloideo, a *adj* QUÍM alkaloid.

alcalometría *f* QUÍM alkalometry.

alcalosis *f* MED alkalosis.

alcance *m* reach; *libro que está a mi alcance* book which is within my reach; *póngalo fuera del alcance de los niños* put it out of the children's reach *o* out of reach of the children ‖ range (de telescopio, arma de fuego, emisora de radio, etc.); *cañón de largo alcance* long-range gun; *estar al alcance* to be within range ‖ FIG importance, significance; *noticia de mucho alcance* news of great importance | scope; *un proyecto de mucho alcance* a plan with great scope ‖ deficit (en las cuentas) ‖ stop press (en los periódicos) ‖ pastern tumour (del caballo) ‖ — *afirmación de mucho alcance* far-reaching statement ‖ *al alcance de la mano* within reach, handy ‖ *al alcance de la vista* in sight ‖ *al alcance de la voz* within call ‖ *al alcance del oído* within earshot ‖ *buzón de alcance* late collection box ‖ FIG *dar alcance a uno* to catch up with s.o. | *estar fuera del alcance de uno* to go over s.o.'s head (demasiado complicado), to be inaccessible (demasiado caro) | *ir al alcance de uno* to chase s.o., to pursue s.o. (perseguir), to shadow s.o. (espiar) | *persona de pocos* or *cortos alcances* unintelligent person | *política de largo alcance* far-reaching policy | *poner algo al alcance de todos* to put sth. within everybody's reach | *ser corto de alcances, tener pocos* or *cortos alcances* to be unintelligent, not to be very bright.

alcancía *f* money box (hucha).

alcándara *f* perch (cetrería) ‖ clothes rack (para la ropa).

alcandía *f* BOT Indian millet.

alcanfor *m* camphor.

alcanforar *vt* to camphorate.
◆ *vpr* *AMER* to disappear, to vanish.

alcanforero *m* camphor tree (árbol).

alcantarilla *f* sewer (cloaca); *las alcantarillas de una ciudad* a town's sewers ‖ culvert (paso dejado por debajo de los caminos) ‖ drain (boca de alcantarilla) ‖ small bridge (puentecillo) ‖ *AMER* fountain.

alcantarillado *m* sewers *pl*, drains *pl*.

alcantarillar *vt* to lay sewers in; *alcantarillar una calle* to lay sewers in a street.

alcantarillero *m* sewerman.

alcantarino, na *adj* [of *o* from] Alcántara.
◆ *m/f* native *o* inhabitant of Alcántara.
◆ *m* knight of the order of Alcántara ‖ reformed Franciscan.

alcanzable; alcanzadizo, za *adj* attainable, accessible, within reach.

alcanzado, da *adj* reached; *el nivel alcanzado* the level reached ‖ — *ir alcanzado* to be short [of money], to be broke ‖ *salir alcanzado* to make a loss.

alcanzadura *f* pastern tumour (del caballo).

alcanzar *vt* to reach; *alcanzar con la mano el techo* to reach the ceiling with one's hand ‖ to catch up, to catch up with; *alcanzar a los que van en cabeza* to catch up with the leaders ‖ to understand, to grasp; *no alcanzo lo que me dices* I can't grasp what you're saying ‖ to reach, to come to, to join; *allí alcanzas la carretera* there you come to the road ‖ FIG to live through (una guerra, etc.) | to live in the time of (a una persona) ‖ to hit; *la bala le alcanzó en la frente* the bullet hit him in the forehead ‖ to reach, to attain; *alcanzar su objetivo* to reach one's goal ‖ to reach, to amount to; *la producción alcanza tanto* production reaches so much ‖ to affect; *ley que alcanza a todos los damnificados* law which affects all the victims ‖ to see; *desde la ventana se alcanzaba la torre de la iglesia* from the window you could see the church tower ‖ to make out, to perceive (con los sentidos) ‖ to run to; *este libro ha alcanzado tres ediciones* this book has run to three editions ‖ to get, to obtain; *siempre alcanza lo que quiere* he always gets what he wants ‖ to rise to (la montaña) ‖ to catch up with; *le he alcanzado en sus estudios* I've caught up with him in his studies ‖ to have, to enjoy; *la película alcanzó gran éxito* the film enjoyed great success ‖ to be able to get *o* to catch; *todavía alcanzas el tren de las siete* you can still catch the seven o'clock train ‖ to pass; *alcánzame el pan* pass me the bread ‖ to knock down; *el coche alcanzó al peatón* the car knocked the pedestrian down.
◆ *vi* to succeed, to manage; *por fin alcanzó a comprenderlo* he finally succeeded in understanding *o* managed to understand ‖ to fall, to be left; *a mí me alcanzó una finca inmensa* a huge estate was left *o* fell to me ‖ to be enough *o* sufficient; *la gasolina alcanza para el camino* the petrol will be sufficient for the journey; *el sueldo no me alcanza para todo el mes* my wage is not sufficient for the whole month ‖ to last (durar) ‖ to have a range, to carry; *los cañones modernos alcanzan muy lejos* modern guns have a very long range *o* carry a long way ‖ — *no alcanzo a comprenderle* I just can't understand him ‖ *no creo que una sola tortilla alcance para todos* I don't think one omelette will be enough to go round.
◆ *vpr* to catch one another up, to meet ‖ to overreach (caballos).

alcaparra *f* caper bush (arbusto) ‖ caper (flor y condimento).

alcaparrado, da *adj* dressed with capers.

alcaparral *m* caper plantation.

alcaparrera *f*; **alcaparrero** *m* caper bush.

alcaparrón *m* caper.

alcaraván *m* stone curlew (ave).

alcaravea *f* caraway.

alcarraza *f* clay jar.

alcarria *f* barren plateau.

alcatifa *f* carpet (alfombra).

alcatraz *m* gannet (ave) ‖ arum (planta).

alcaucí; alcaucil *m* BOT wild artichoke (silvestre) | artichoke (comestible).

alcaudón *m* shrike, butcher-bird (ave).

alcayata *f* hook (escarpia).

alcazaba *f* citadel, fortress, castle ‖ casbah (en África del Norte).

alcázar *m* palace (palacio) ‖ citadel, fortress (fortaleza) ‖ MAR quarterdeck.

alce *m* ZOOL elk, moose ‖ cut (naipes) ‖ *AMER* rest, respite (tregua) | gathering [of sugar cane].

alcedo *m* maple tree grove.

Alcestes *npr m* Alcestis.

Alcibíades *npr m* Alcibiades.

alcino *m* wild basil.

alción *m* kingfisher (ave) ‖ halcyon (ave fabulosa) ‖ alcyonium (pólipo).
◆ *f* alcyone.

alcista *m/f* bull (en la Bolsa).
◆ *adj* rising, upward; *tendencia alcista* upward tendency ‖ *mercado alcista* bull market (en la Bolsa).

alcoba *f* bedroom (dormitorio) ‖ bedroom suite (muebles) ‖ FIG *secretos de alcoba* intimacies [of married life].

alcohol *m* alcohol; *alcohol absoluto* pure alcohol ‖ spirit, spirits *pl*; *alcohol de quemar* or *desnaturalizado* or *metílico* methylated spirits ‖ alcohol, spirits *pl* (bebida) ‖ galena (mineral) ‖ kohl (afeite) ‖ — *alcohol etílico* ethyl alcohol ‖ *lámpara de alcohol* spirit lamp.

alcoholar *vt* to alcoholize || to make up with kohl (pintarse) || to clean with alcohol || MAR to tar.

alcoholato *m* spirit, alcoholate.

alcoholaturo *m* MED alcoholature [solution made from medicinal herbs and alcohol].

alcoholero, ra *adj* alcohol, of alcohol.
◆ *f* distillery.

alcohólico, ca *adj/s* alcoholic || *bebida no alcohólica* non-alcoholic drink, soft drink.

alcoholificación *f* alcoholic fermentation.

alcoholímetro *m* alcoholometer.

alcoholismo *m* alcoholism.

alcoholización *f* alcoholization.

alcoholizado, da *adj* poisoned by alcohol || *está alcoholizado* he has alcohol poisoning.
◆ *m/f* alcoholic.

alcoholizar *vt* to alcoholize.
◆ *vpr* to become an alcoholic.

alcohómetro *m* breathalyser.

alcohotest *m* breathalyser (instrumento).

alcor *m* hill (colina).

Alcorán *npr m* Koran.

alcoránico, ca *adj* Koranic.

alcornocal *m* cork oak grove.

alcornoque *m* cork oak || FIG dimwit, dope; *¡qué alcornoque es!* what a dope he is!

alcornoqueño, ña *adj* cork oak.

alcorza *f* icing.

alcotán *m* ZOOL lanner.

alcotana *f* pickaxe || ice axe (de alpinista).

alcubilla *f* tank, reservoir.

alcurnia *f* ancestry, lineage (estirpe) || — *familia de alcurnia* old family, family with long history || *ser de alta alcurnia* to come from a good *o* noble family, to have noble ancestry, to be of noble birth (ser noble).

alcuza *f* oil bottle, cruet (aceitera).

alcuzcuz *m* couscous (plato árabe).

aldaba *f* doorknocker (llamador) || latch, bolt, bar (de puerta o de ventana) || FAM *tener buenas aldabas* to have friends in the right places, to have contacts.

aldabada *f* knock || *dar aldabadas en* to knock at.

aldabazo *m* loud knock.

aldabear *vi* to knock at *o* on the door.

aldabeo *m* knocking at *o* on the door.

aldabilla *f* hook, catch, latch (de cerradura).

aldabón *m* large doorknocker (aldaba) || handle (asa).

aldabonazo *m* loud knock, bang || FIG shock, warning (advertencia).

aldea *f* village, hamlet.

aldeaniego, ga *adj* ⟶ **aldeano.**

aldeano, na *adj* village (de aldea) || rustic, country (campesino) || FIG peasant.
◆ *m/f* villager (que vive en una aldea) || peasant, rustic.

aldehído *m* QUÍM aldehyde.

aldehuela *f* small village, hamlet.

aldeorrio; aldehorro *m* backwater (poblacho).

ale *m* ale (cerveza).

¡ale! *interj* come on!

álea *m* risk (riesgo).

aleación *f* alloy.

alear *vi* to flap its wings (aletear) || to convalesce, to recover (convalecer).
◆ *vt* to alloy; *alear el cobre con el oro* to alloy copper with gold.

aleatorio, ria *adj* aleatory, contingent.

alebrarse; alebrestarse; alebronarse *vpr* to lie down flat (agazaparse) || FIG to cower; to lose heart.

aleccionador, ra *adj* instructive, enlightening; *una historia muy aleccionadora* a very instructive story || exemplary, which serves as an example, which teaches one a lesson; *un castigo aleccionador* an exemplary punishment, a punishment which serves as an example.

aleccionamiento *m* instruction.

aleccionar *vt* to instruct, to teach; *aleccionar a un aprendiz en el uso de un torno* to instruct an apprentice in the use of a lathe, to teach an apprentice to use a lathe || to lecture; *su madre le aleccionó para que no volviera a hacer lo mismo* his mother lectured him so that he would not do it again || to train; *aleccionar a un criado* to train a servant || to teach; *esto te aleccionará para no volver a caer en los mismos errores* that will teach you not to make the same mistakes again || *estar aleccionado* to have learnt one's lesson.

aleche *m* (fresh) anchovy (boquerón).

alechugar *vt* to goffer, to crimp, to pleat, to flute || *cuello alechugado* ruff.

aledaño, ña *adj* bordering, adjacent; *región aledaña del* or *al Támesis* region bordering on *o* adjacent to the Thames.
◆ *m pl* outskirts, surrounding district *sing*, surroundings.

alegación *f* assertion || JUR allegation || *alegación de falsedad* plea of forgery.

alegar *vt* to allege (menos usado en inglés que en español), to say, to claim; *para disculparse de no haber venido alegó que había estado enfermo* as an excuse for not having come, he claimed that he had been ill || to point out, to emphasize, to stress (méritos, etc.) || to quote (una autoridad, un dicho) || to put forward; *alegar razones* to put forward reasons || JUR to allege, to plead, to claim || AMER to dispute.
◆ *vi* AMER to argue.

alegato *m* JUR allegation, plea; *el alegato del abogado defensor* the allegation of the counsel for the defence || FIG statement, declaration; *pronunció un alegato en defensa de su postura* he made a declaration in defence of his position.

alegoría *f* allegory.

alegórico, ca *adj* allegorical, allegoric.

alegorizar *vt* to allegorize.

alegrar *vt* to make happy, to cheer up, to gladden; *la noticia me alegra* the news make me happy || FIG to brighten up, to liven up; *unos cuadros alegran las paredes* a few pictures brighten up the walls; *para alegrar la fiesta vamos a cantar* let's sing to liven up the party || to make merry *o* tipsy; *este vinillo me ha alegrado* this wine has made me merry || FIG to be pleasing to; *ramillete de flores que alegra la vista* bouquet of flowers which is pleasing to the eye | to poke, to stir (la lumbre) || to make brighter, to brighten up; *alegrar los colores* to brighten up the colours || TAUR to rouse *o* to excite (the bull) into attacking || MAR to slack [a rope] (aflojar) || — *me alegra verte* I'm glad *o* happy to see you || *tu venida me alegra* I am glad *o* happy that you have come.
◆ *vpr* to be happy *o* glad; *me alegro por* or *de* or *con la noticia* I am happy to hear the news, I am happy about the news || to cheer up; *alégrate, no pongas esa cara de duelo* cheer up, don't pull such a long face || to light up (los ojos, la cara) || FAM to get merry *o* tipsy (achisparse) || — *¡aquí está! — me alegro* here he is! — I'm glad *o* Good || *me alegro de verte* I am glad *o* happy to see you.

alegre *adj* happy, joyful, cheerful; *un niño alegre* a happy child; *una cara alegre* a cheerful face || happy, glad; *alegre con la noticia* happy with *o* about *o* glad about the news || good, happy; *una noticia alegre* good news || pleasant, bright (tiempo) || gay, lively; *música alegre* lively music || bright, gay (color) || tipsy, merry (achispado) || spicy, naughty (chiste) || daring, rash (atrevido) || loose, loose-living (mujer) || fast, immoral (vida) || — *alegre como unas pascuas* or *como unas castañuelas* as happy as a lark, as chirpy as a cricket || *alegre como un niño con zapatos nuevos* as happy as a dog with two tails, as pleased as Punch || *alegre de cascos* scatterbrained, harebrained || *alegre de corazón* lighthearted.

alegremente *adv* gaily, merrily, happily.

alegreto *adv/s m* MÚS allegretto.

alegría *f* joy; *la alegría de vivir* the joy of living || gaiety, cheerfulness, joy, happiness (buen humor) || merriment, gaiety (regocijo) || happiness, joyfulness (de una ocasión) || brightness (de colores, etc.) || BOT sesame (ajonjolí) || — *¡qué alegría!* that's marvellous!, that's great! || *saltar de alegría* to jump for joy || *tener mucha alegría* to be very happy *o* glad; *tengo mucha alegría en anunciarte esta noticia* I am very happy to give you this news.
◆ *pl* «alegrías», song and dance from Cádiz || public festivities (fiestas).

alegro *adv/s m* MÚS allegro.

alegrón *m* FAM great joy *o* happiness || FIG flare-up, blaze (llamarada breve) || *me dio un alegrón con su éxito* his success gave me a great thrill, I was thrilled to bits about his success.
◆ *adj* AMER flirtatious, gallant (enamoradizo) | tipsy, merry (medio ebrio).

alejado, da *adj* far away, faraway, remote; *un lugar alejado de todo* a place far away from everything, a faraway *o* remote place || a long way from; *su casa está muy alejada de la mía* his house is a very long way from mine || aloof, apart; *alejado de los intereses del mundo* aloof from worldly interests || *está alejado de la política* he takes no part in politics.

alejamiento *m* absence (ausencia) || estrangement (enfriamiento entre novios, amigos, etc.) || withdrawal (acción de alejarse) || removal (acción de alejar).

Alejandría *n pr* GEOGR Alexandria.

alejandrino, na *adj/m* Alexandrine (verso).
— OBSERV The Spanish *alejandrino* has 14 syllabes, divided into two hemistiches.
— OBSERV El *alexandrine* inglés tiene 12 sílabas y dos hemistiquios.

alejandrita *f* alexandrite.

Alejandro *npr m* Alexander; *Alejandro Magno* Alexander the Great.

alejar *vt* to move away, to remove; *si no lo alejas del fuego se quemará* if you don't move it away from the fire it will burn || to keep away; *hay que alejarle de las malas compañías* he must be kept away from bad company || to remove (una cosa, una persona, peligro) || to avert; *alejar las sospechas* to avert suspicion || to get rid of; *aleja de ti esa idea* get rid of that idea || to remove; *alejar a alguien del poder* to remove s.o. from power || to separate (separar).
◆ *vpr* to go away (marcharse) || to move away *o* off; *el tren se alejó* the train moved off || to move *o* to go off into the distance (en la distancia) || to keep away; *alejarse de las malas compañías* to keep away from bad company || to go off, to leave; *alejarse del buen camino* to go off the right road || to give up, to relinquish; *alejarse del poder* to relinquish one's power || *alejarse cada vez más* to grow more and more distant.

alelado, da *adj* bewildered, stupefied (atontado) || stupid (lelo).

alelamiento *m* bewilderment, stupefaction.

alelar *vt* to stupefy, to bewilder.
◆ *vt* to be stupefied *o* bewildered.

alelí *m* BOT wallflower (amarillo) ‖ BOT *alelí de Mahón* Virginian stock.
— OBSERV pl *alelíes*.

aleluya *m/f* hallelujah, alleluia (canto religioso).
◆ *m* Easter (Pascuas).
◆ *f* small religious print (estampita) ‖ small print depicting a story explained by rhyming couplets ‖ rhyming couplet (pareado) ‖ wood sorrel (planta) ‖ FAM bad painting (cuadro malo) | joy (alegría) ‖ *estar de aleluya* to rejoice.
◆ *m pl* FIG & FAM doggerel (versos malos).

alemán, ana *adj/s* German ‖ *plata alemana* German silver, nickel silver.

Alemania *npr f* GEOGR Germany.

alemánico, ca *adj* Germanic.

alemanisco, ca *adj* Germanic ‖ damask (mantel).

alentada *f* breath; *de una alentada* in one breath.

alentado, da *adj* encouraged; *alentado por sus éxitos* encouraged by his success ‖ brave (valiente) ‖ haughty, proud (orgulloso).

alentador, ra *adj* encouraging; *palabras alentadoras* encouraging words; *noticia alentadora* encouraging news.

alentar* *vi* to breathe ‖ FIG to burn, to glow; *en su pecho alienta el amor a la patria* his love for his country glows in his heart.
◆ *vt* to encourage (animar); *alentar a uno para que siga adelante* to encourage s.o. to continue; *alentar la rebelión* to encourage rebellion ‖ to raise (las esperanzas, los ánimos) ‖ *AMER* to clap, to applaud (palmotear) | to give birth to (dar a luz).
◆ *vpr* to pluck up courage (envalentonarse) ‖ to cheer up, to take heart (alegrarse) ‖ MED to get better, to recover (reponerse) ‖ *AMER* to give birth.

aleonado, da *adj* tawny.

alerce *m* larch (árbol).

alergia *f* allergy.

alérgico, ca *adj* allergic; *alérgico a los gatos* allergic to cats.
◆ *m/f* person suffering from an allergy.

alergista; alergólogo, ga *m/f* MED allergist.

alergodermia *f* MED allergodermia.

alergología *f* MED study of allergies.

alergólogo, ga *m/f* MED ⟶ **alergista.**

alergosis *f* MED allergosis.

alero *m* ARQ eaves *pl* (tejado) ‖ AUT mudguard [*US* fender] ‖ FIG *estar en el alero* to be in the balance, to be uncertain.

alerón *m* aileron.

alerta *adv* alertly ‖ on the alert, alert ‖ — *estar alerta* or *ojo alerta* to be on the alert *o* on one's guard, to watch out, to be alert ‖ *ponerse alerta* to become alert.
◆ *adj* alert ‖ agile (estilo).
◆ *f* alert; *dar la alerta* to give the alert ‖ — *alerta roja* red alert ‖ *dar la voz de alerta* to give the alert, to raise the alarm ‖ *poner en alerta* to put on alert.
◆ *interj* look out!, watch out!

alertar *vt* to alert, to put on one's guard, to give the alert to (poner en guardia) ‖ to alert, to warn (avisar).
◆ *vi* to keep one's eyes open, to keep a lookout, to keep watch.

alerto, ta *adj* (p us) ⟶ **alerta.**

aleta *f* ZOOL fin (de los peces) | flipper (de la foca) ‖ wing (de la nariz, de un coche) ‖ ala (de la nariz) ‖ fin, rib, gill (de radiador) ‖ vane (de una bomba) ‖ blade (de hélice) ‖ aileron (alerón) ‖ flipper (para nadar) ‖ MAR fashion piece (de la popa).

aletada *f* flap of the wing.

aletargado, da *adj* lethargic ‖ numb (pierna, etc.) ‖ FIG drowsing, dozing; *aletargado en un rincón* dozing in a corner.

aletargamiento *m* lethargy (letargo) ‖ drowsiness (adormecimiento) ‖ numbness (de una pierna, etc.).

aletargar *vt* to make drowsy *o* sleepy (una persona) ‖ to numb, to send to sleep (una pierna, etc.).
◆ *vpr* to become sleepy, to grow drowsy.

aletazo *m* flap of the wing, wingbeat (de un ave) ‖ flick of the fin (del pez) ‖ *AMER* FAM slap (bofetada).

aletear *vi* to flap its wings, to flutter (las aves) ‖ to wave *o* to flap one's arms (un niño).

aleteo *m* flapping *o* beating of the wings, fluttering ‖ FIG beating (del corazón).

aleto *m* osprey (ave).

aleudar *vt* to leaven.
◆ *vpr* to rise.

aleurona *f* BOT aleurone.

aleve *adj* treacherous, perfidious.

alevín; alevino *m* fry, young fish (pez).

alevosa *f* ranula (del ganado).

alevosamente *adv* treacherously ‖ in cold blood (fríamente).

alevosía *f* treachery (traición) ‖ premeditation (premeditación) ‖ caution [before committing crime] (cautela) ‖ *con* or *por alevosía* treacherously (a traición), in cold blood (fríamente).

alevoso, sa *adj* treacherous, perfidious.
◆ *m* traitor.
◆ *f* traitess.

alexia *f* MED alexia.

alezo *m* MED abdominal belt.

alfa *f* alpha (letra griega) ‖ *rayos alfa* alpha rays.

alfabéticamente *adv* alphabetically.

alfabético, ca *adj* alphabetical, alphabetic; *por orden alfabético* in alphabetical order.

alfabetización *f* teaching to read and write, education ‖ *campaña de alfabetización* literacy campaign.

alfabetizado, da *adj* literate.

alfabetizar *vt* to make literate, to teach to read and write (a una persona) ‖ to alphabetize, to arrange in alphabetical order (poner en orden alfabético).

alfabeto *m* alphabet ‖ *alfabeto Morse* Morse code.

alfaguara *f* abundant spring (manantial).

alfajía *f* ⟶ **alfarjía.**

alfajor *m* kind of gingerbread (alajú) ‖ *AMER* macaroon (dulce redondo).

alfalfa *f* BOT lucerne, alfalfa [*US* alfalfa].

alfalfal; alfalfar *m* alfalfa field, lucerne field [*US* alfalfa field].

alfandoque *m* *AMER* a paste made from treacle and cheese with aniseed or ginger | nougat | maraca (instrumento).

alfaneque *m* ZOOL kestrel.

alfanje *m* scimitar (sable) ‖ swordfish (pez).

alfanumérico, ca *adj* INFORM alphanumeric.

alfañique *m* *AMER* stick of barley sugar (alfeñique).

alfaque *m* MAR bar, sand bank (banco de arena).

alfaquí *m* ulema, ulama.

alfar *m* potter's workshop, pottery (el taller) ‖ clay (arcilla).

alfaraz *m* charger (caballo).

alfarda *f* ARQ rafter ‖ tax [formerly paid by Moors and Jews].

alfardilla *f* gold *o* silver braid.

alfarería *f* pottery (arte) ‖ potter's workshop, pottery (taller).

alfarero *m* potter.

alfarje *m* oil-mill stone ‖ ARQ panelled ceiling.

alfarjía; alfajía *f* timber [for door or window frame] (madero).

alfayate *m* (ant) tailor.

alfeiza; alféizar *m* ARQ embrasure (de puerta o de ventana) | windowsill (en la parte inferior).

alfénido *m* britannia metal (metal blanco).

alfeñicarse *vpr* FIG & FAM to lose weight, to get thin | to make a fuss, to stand on ceremony (remilgarse).

alfeñique *m* stick of barley sugar ‖ almond paste (de almendra) ‖ FIG & FAM weakling; *su hijo es un alfeñique* his son is a weakling | affectation, fuss (remilgo).

alferazgo *m* rank of standard-bearer (oficio de abanderado) ‖ rank of second lieutenant.

alferecía *f* MED epilepsy | epileptic fit; *darle a uno una alferecía* to have an epileptic fit.

alférez *m* second lieutenant (oficial) ‖ standard-bearer (abanderado) ‖ *AMER* person responsible for the expenses of a party ‖ — MAR *alférez de fragata* commissioned officer [*US* ensign] | *alférez de navío* sub-lieutenant [*US* lieutenant Junior Grade].

alfil *m* bishop (en el ajedrez).

alfiler *m* pin (en costura) ‖ pin, brooch (joya) ‖ — *alfiler de corbata* tiepin ‖ *alfiler de la ropa* clothespeg [*US* clothespin] ‖ *AMER alfiler de nodriza* or *de criandera* safety pin ‖ *alfiler de sombrero* hatpin ‖ FIG & FAM *aquí no cabe un alfiler* it's packed tight *o* out, it's crammed full | *el alumno lleva la lección prendida con alfileres* the pupil has learnt the lesson very sketchily | *estar de veinticuatro alfileres* to be dressed up to the nines, to be dressed to kill ‖ *estar prendido con alfileres* to be pinned (up) (vestido, etc.), to be rather shaky (poco seguro) ‖ *AMER no caberle un alfiler de gusto* to be beside o.s. with joy ‖ FIG & FAM *para alfileres* as a tip (propina), for pocket money (a un niño), for pin money (a una mujer) ‖ *sujetar con un alfiler* to pin (up).

alfilerar *vt* to pin; *alfilerar un vestido* to pin a dress.

alfilerazo *m* pinprick ‖ FIG & FAM dig; *siempre me está tirando alfilerazos* he's always having digs at me.

alfilerillo *m* *AMER* fodder plant, erodium | cactus (pita) | parasitic insect [found on tobacco].

alfiletero; alfilerero *m* pin box, pin case.

alfolí *m* public granary (granero) ‖ salt warehouse.

alfombra *f* carpet (grande); *alfombra persa* Persian carpet ‖ rug, mat (más pequeña) ‖ FIG carpet; *alfombra de flores* carpet of flowers ‖ *alfombra de baño* bathmat ‖ *alfombra voladora* flying carpet.

alfombrado, da *adj* carpeted; *salón alfombrado* carpeted drawing room.
◆ *m* carpeting, carpets *pl* (conjunto de alfombras) ‖ carpeting, laying carpets (acción) ‖ *el alfombrado de la escalera* the stair carpet.

alfombrar *vt* to carpet ‖ FIG to carpet; *calles alfombradas de flores* streets carpeted with flowers.

alfombrero, ra *m/f* carpet maker (fabricante) || carpet dealer (vendedor).

alfombrilla *f* rug (alfombra pequeña) || doormat (esterilla en las puertas) || MED German measles || *alfombrilla de cama* bedside rug.

alfombrista *m* carpet dealer (vendedor) || carpet fitter (que instala alfombras).

alfóncigo *m* pistachio (árbol) || pistachio nut (fruto).

alfonsí; alfonsino, na *adj* Alphonsine [concerning one of the Spanish kings called Alfonso] || *tablas alfonsinas* Alphonsine tables [of Alfonso X].

alfónsigo *m* pistachio (árbol).

alfonsismo *m* Alphonsism.

Alfonso *npr m* Alfonso (King).

alforfón *m* buckwheat.

alforjas *f pl* saddlebags (sobre las caballerías) || knapsack *sing* (colgadas al hombro) || provisions, supplies (provisión) || — FIG & FAM *para este viaje no se necesitan alforjas* a fat lot of good that is || AMER FIG & FAM *pasarse a la otra alforja* to go too far (excederse) | *sacar los pies de las alforjas* to go off on a different track.

alforza *f* tuck (en costura) || scar (cicatriz).

alforzar *vt* to tuck, to put tucks in; *alforzar la manga de una camisa* to put tucks in *o* to tuck a shirt sleeve.

Alfredo *npr m* Alfred.

alga *f* BOT alga || *había algas en la playa* there was seaweed on the beach.

— OBSERV En inglés el plural de *alga* es *algae* o *algas*.

algaida *f* thicket, bush || dune, sand hill (duna).

algalia *f* civet (perfume) || abelmosk (planta) || MED catheter || *gato de algalia* civet cat (animal).

algara *f* MIL raid | raiding party (tropa) || skin (de la cebolla).

algarabía *f* (ant) arabic (lengua) || FIG Greek; *para mí esto es algarabía* this is Greek for me | double Dutch, gibberish; *hablar en algarabía* to speak double Dutch | racket, row; *los niños armaban una algarabía tremenda* the children were kicking up a terrible row || BOT broom.

algarada *m* MIL raid (ataque) | raiding party (tropa) || FIG racket, din, row (jaleo).

algarroba *f* BOT vetch (planta forrajera) | vetch, vetch seed (semilla) | carob bean (fruto del algarrobo).

algarrobal *m* vetch plantation (de algarroba) || carob tree plantation (de algarrobo).

algarrobera *f;* **algarrobero** *m* carob tree (árbol).

algarrobilla *f* vetch (algarroba) || alga, seaweed (*fam*) (alga).

algarrobillo *m* AMER carob bean (fruto).

algarrobo *m* carob tree (árbol) || *algarrobo loco* Judas tree.

algazara *f* Arab war cry || racket, din, row, uproar (jaleo).

algazul *m* carpetweed (planta).

álgebra *f* MAT algebra || MED bonesetting.

algebraico, ca; algébrico, ca *adj* algebraic, algebraical.

algebrista *m/f* MAT algebraist || MED bonesetter.

algecireño, ña *adj* [of *o* from] Algeciras.
◆ *m/f* native *o* inhabitant of Algeciras.

algidez *f* MED algidity.

álgido, da *adj* MED algid; *fiebre álgida* algid fever || FIG decisive, critical (decisivo) || FIG *punto álgido* height.

— OBSERV The figurative use of this word, though frequent, is considered incorrect.

algo *pron indef* something; *aquí hay algo que no entiendo* there is something here which I don't understand; *quiero algo original* I want something original || anything (cualquier cosa); *yo daría algo por tenerlo* I'd give anything to have it || anything, something (véase OBSERV) (en interrogación); *¿ha pasado algo?* has something happened?, has anything happened? || — *algo así* something like that || *algo así como* a sort of, a kind of, a type of (una especie de), something like, about; *vive a algo así como a tres quilómetros de aquí* he lives something like three kilometres from here || *algo de* some (véase OBSERV); *algo de vino* some wine || *algo es algo* or *ya es algo* it is better than nothing, it's a start || FAM *creerse algo* to think one is something *o* somebody || *de hacer algo me iría de vacaciones* if anything I'd go on holiday || *más vale algo que nada* something is better than nothing || *por algo lo hice* I had my reason for doing it, I didn't do it for nothing || *por algo será* there's bound to be *o* there must be a reason for it || FAM *si no se callan me va a dar algo* I'll go mad if they don't shut up || *tener algo que ver con* to have something to do with || *tomar algo* to have a drink (de beber), to have a bite to eat, to have something to eat (de comer).
◆ *adv* rather, quite, somewhat; *algo lejos* quite far, quite a long way; *algo tímido* rather shy || a little, slightly, a bit, somewhat; *el enfermo está algo mejor* the patient is a little better; *anda algo escaso de dinero* he's somewhat short of money || at all, any (en preguntas); *¿te ha dolido algo?* did it hurt you at all?; *¿estás algo mejor?* are you any better?
◆ *m* snack, something to eat; *tomé un algo antes de salir* I had a snack before I left || something; *tiene un algo de su madre* there is something of his mother in him || — *tiene un algo* he has that certain something, there is something about him (encanto) || *tiene un algo de egoísmo* he is rather selfish.

— OBSERV En las oraciones interrogativas, *something* se convierte generalmente en *anything* (*¿encontraste algo nuevo?* did you find anything new?) y *some* en *any* (*¿tiene algo de vino?* have you any wine?).

algodón *m* BOT cotton plant (planta) || cotton; *algodón hidrófilo, en rama* cotton wool, raw cotton || cotton (tejido); *vestido de algodón* cotton dress || cotton wool (hidrófilo) || candy floss [US cotton candy] (golosina de azúcar) || MED swab || — *algodón pólvora* guncotton || FIG & FAM *criado entre algodones* mollycoddled, pampered.

algodonal *m* cotton plantation.

algodonar *vt* to pad *o* to pack with cotton wool.

algodoncillo *m* BOT milkweed.

algodonero, ra *adj* cotton; *industria algodonera* cotton industry.
◆ *m/f* cotton worker (obrero) || cotton dealer (comerciante).
◆ *m* cotton plant (planta).
◆ *f* cotton mill (fábrica).

algodonoso, sa *adj* cottony || downy (fruta).
◆ *f* cottonweed (planta).

algorín *m* olive bin.

algoritmia *f* algorithmics.

algoritmo *m* MAT & INFORM algorithm.

algoso, sa *adj* full of seaweed.

alguacil; aguacil *m* alguazil (en España) || sheriff, constable || governor (gobernador) || TAUR alguazil || ZOOL jumping spider || AMER dragonfly (insecto).

alguacilazgo *m* position of alguazil.

alguacilesco, ca *adj* alguazil's, of the alguazil.

aguacilillo *m* alguazil (en las corridas de toros).

alguien *pron indef* somebody, someone; *alguien llama a la puerta* someone is knocking at the door || anybody, anyone (interrogación); *¿hay alguien en casa?* is there anybody at home? || — *creerse alguien* to think one is somebody || *para alguien que haya hecho esto* for anybody *o* anyone who has done this || *ser alguien* to be somebody || *si llama alguien* if anyone *o* anybody calls, if someone *o* somebody calls.

algún *adj* some, any (véase OBSERV en ALGUNO); *algún pobre niño* some poor child || some or *other, some, a, a certain; algún hombre* some man or *other, a man* || — *algún que otro* one or two, the odd, a few, some; *algún que otro libro* one or two books, the odd book || *algún tanto* a little, a bit || *algún tiempo* some time || *en algún sitio* somewhere.

alguno, na *adj* a, some, some or other, a certain; *vino alguna mujer* a woman came, some woman or other came || some; *alguna pobre niña* some poor child; *quiere algunos libros* he wants some books || any; *si viene alguna carta para mí, avísame* if any letters come for me, let me know; *¿necesitas alguna ayuda?* do you need any help? || any, a (interrogación); *¿hay alguna traducción para esto?* is there a translation for this? || — *alguna cosa* something || *alguna que otra vez* from time to time, now and again || *algunas veces* sometimes || *alguna vez* occasionally, sometimes; *alguna vez voy al teatro* I sometimes go to the theatre; ever (interrogación); *¿vas alguna vez al teatro?* do you ever go to the theatre? || *no... alguno* not... any, not... any at all, no... at all; *no tengo dinero alguno* I haven't any money, I have no money at all || *no he visto cosa alguna* I haven't seen anything at all || *por alguna razón que otra* for some reason or other || *sin prisa alguna* without hurrying.
◆ *pron* one *sing*, some *pl*; *alguno de ellos me lo preguntó* one of them asked me || someone, somebody (alguien) (véase OBSERV) || — *alguno que otro* one or two, some, a few || *algunos piensan* some (people) think, certain people think || *hacer alguna* to be up to one's tricks; *el niño habrá hecho alguna (de las suyas)* the child will have been up to his tricks again.

— OBSERV En las oraciones interrogativas, *some* suele ser sustituido por *any* (*¿quieres algunos libros?* do you want any books?) y *somebody* o *someone* por *anybody* o *anyone* (*¿ha quedado alguno sin entrada?* is anyone without a ticket?).

— OBSERV The adjective *alguno* is apocopated to *algún* before masculine singular nouns: *algún pobre niño* some poor child.

alhaja *f* jewel, gem, piece of jewellery; *una alhaja de oro* a piece of gold jewellery || jewel; *las alhajas de la corona* the crown jewels || FIG jewel, treasure, gem; *nuestra criada es una alhaja* our maid is a jewel; *la catedral es una verdadera alhaja del arte gótico* the cathedral is a real gem of Gothic art | darling, gem, jewel; *este niño es una alhaja* this child is a darling || FIG *¡buena alhaja!* he's (she's, etc.) a fine one *o* a right one!
◆ *pl* jewels, gems, jewellery *sing* [US jewelry *sing*].

alhajar *vt* to deck with jewels; *alhajar a una chica* to deck a girl with jewels || to furnish (amueblar).

alhajera *f;* **alhajero** *m* AMER jewel box, jewel case.

alharaca *f* fuss, fuss and bother || *a pesar de sus alharacas* despite all the fuss he makes.

alharma *f* BOT harmal, harmala, harmel.

alhelí *f* wallflower (amarillo) || BOT *alhelí de Mahón* Virginian stock.
— OBSERV pl *alhelíes.*

alheña *f* privet (arbusto) || henna (polvo y arbusto) || privet blossom (flor) || blight, mildew, rust (de las mieses) || *estar hecho una alheña* or *molido como una alheña* to be exhausted (agotado).

alheñar *vt* to dye with henna (teñir).
◆ *vpr* to wither, to dry up (secarse) || to become mildewed (tener añublo).

alhóndiga *f* corn exchange.

alhucema *f* lavender (espliego).

aliabierto, ta *adj* with its wings spread *o* open.

aliacán *m* jaundice.

aliado, da *adj* allied.
◆ *m/f* ally || *los Aliados* the Allies.

aliadófilo, la *adj* allied.

aliaga *f* BOT furze, gorse (aulaga).

alianza *f* alliance (unión); *pacto de alianza* alliance treaty || wedding ring (anillo) || covenant (en la Biblia) || — *la Alianza Atlántica* the Atlantic Alliance || *la Santa Alianza* the Holy Alliance.

aliar *vt* to combine, to ally; *aliar el valor a* or *con la inteligencia* to combine courage with intelligence || to ally (un país).
◆ *vpr* to be combined || to become allies, to form an alliance (dos países).

alias *adv* alias, otherwise known as; *Antonio López alias el Cojo* Antonio López alias Hopalong.
◆ *m* alias.

alibí *m* alibi (coartada).

alicaído, da *adj* with drooping wings || FIG & FAM weak, frail; *el enfermo anda alicaído* the patient is a bit weak | depressed, crestfallen, dejected; *desde que ha recibido la noticia anda muy alicaído* ever since he received the news he has been very depressed || *tener la moral alicaída* to be depressed *o* crestfallen.

alicante *m* cerastes, horned viper (víbora) || nougat (dulce).

Alicante *n pr* GEOGR Alicante.

alicantino, na *adj* [of *o* from] Alicante.
◆ *m/f* native *o* inhabitant of Alicante.

alicatado, da *adj* tiled, decorated with glazed tiles.
◆ *m* glazed tiling.

alicatar *vt* to tile, to decorate with glazed tiles || to shape, to cut, to work (los azulejos).

alicates *m pl* pliers, pincers; *alicates universales* multipurpose pliers || *alicates de uñas* nail clippers.

Alicia *npr f* Alice || — *Alicia en el país de las maravillas* Alice in Wonderland || *Alicia en el país del espejo* Alice through the looking glass.

aliciente *m* attraction, lure; *los alicientes del campo* the attractions of the countryside || interest; *este viaje no tiene aliciente para mí* this journey has no interest for me || encouragement, incentive, inducement (incentivo); *las primas son un aliciente para el trabajador* bonuses are an incentive for the worker || *un aliciente para que trabajen más* an inducement *o* an incentive for them to work harder.

alicortar *vt* to clip the wings of (cortar) || to wing, to wound in the wing (herir) || FIG to clip s.o.'s wings (a uno).

alicuanta *adj f/sf* aliquant; *parte alicuanta* aliquant part.

alícuota *adj* aliquot; *parte alícuota* aliquot part.

alidada *f* alidade, alidad (regla).

alienable *adj* alienable.

alienación *f* JUR alienation || MED *alienación mental* alienation, mental derangement.

alienado, da *adj* mentally ill, insane.
◆ *m/f* lunatic || *los alienados* the mentally ill, the insane.

alienar *vt* to alienate (enajenar).
— OBSERV *Alienar* is used less frenquently than *enajenar.*

alienígeno, na *adj* alien, strange, unnatural.

alienista *m/f* psychiatrist, alienist.

aliento *m* breath; *perder el aliento* to get out of breath || FIG encouragement; *su apoyo es un aliento para mí* his support is an encouragement for me | enthusiasm, vitality; *ya no tiene los alientos de su juventud* he no longer has the enthusiasm of his youth || — *aguantar* or *contener el aliento* to hold one's breath || *cobrar aliento* to catch one's breath, to get one's breath back || *dejar sin aliento* to leave breathless, to wind || *de un aliento* in one breath || *estar sin aliento* to be out of breath (jadeante), to be depressed, to be dejected (desanimado) || *exhalar el postrer aliento* to breath one's last, to draw one's last breath || *tener mal aliento* to have bad breath || *tomar aliento* to catch one's breath, to get one's breath back.

alifafe *m* windgall (de las caballerías) || FAM ailment, complaint; *mi abuelo tiene muchos alifafes* my grandfather has always got some ailment or other.

aliforme *adj* aliform, wing-shaped.

aligación *f* bond, tie || MAT alligation.

aligátor *m* alligator.

aligeramiento *m* lightening (de una carga, etc.) || cutting-down, reduction (de un programa, etc.) || lessening, reduction (de una obligación) || alleviation, relief, easing (alivio).

aligerar *vt* to lighten, to make lighter; *aligerar una carga* to lighten a burden || to cut down, to reduce; *aligerar un programa* to cut down a programme || to shorten (abreviar); *aligerar un discurso* to shorten a speech || FIG to relieve, to alleviate; *la morfina aligera el dolor* morphine relieves pain | to alleviate, to lessen, to relieve; *su presencia aligeraba mi tristeza* his presence lessened my sadness || to quicken; *aligerar el paso* to quicken one's pace.
◆ *vi/vpr* to hurry, to get a move on (*fam*); *aligera* or *aligérate que hay que irse* get a move on, we've got to go || to lighten, to get lighter (la carga) || *aligerarse de ropa* to put lighter clothes on (cuando hace calor), to take a garment *o* an article of clothing off (quitar).

aligero, ra *adj* POÉT winged; *Mercurio aligero* winged Mercury | swift, rapid.

aligustre *m* privet (alheña).

alijador *m* MAR barge, lighter (barcaza) | docker, stevedore (descargador) || smuggler (matutero).

alijar *m* waste land (terreno) || tile (azulejo).
◆ *pl* common land *sing.*

alijar *vt* to lighten (aligerar) || to smuggle (contrabando) || to unload (descargar un barco) || to gin (el algodón) || to sandpaper (pulir con lija).

alijarar *vt* to share out (waste land for cultivation).

alijo *m* unloading (de un barco) || smuggling (contrabando) || contraband (géneros de contrabando) || — *alijo de drogas* illegal consignment of drugs || *alijo de whisky* consignment *o* load of smuggled whisky.

alimaña *f* vermin, pest, noxious animal.

alimañero *m* gamekeeper, pest controller.

alimentación *f* food; *la higiene de la alimentación* food hygiene; *una región donde la alimentación es excelente* a region where the food is excellent || feeding, nourishment (acción de alimentar) || TECN feed; *la alimentación de un alto horno* the feed of a blast furnace || — *alimentación de energía* power supply || *alimentación equilibrada* balanced diet || *alimentación por gravedad* gravity feed || *ramo de la alimentación* food trade || *tubo de alimentación* feed pipe.

alimentador, ra *adj* feeding.
◆ *m* TECN feeder || INFORM *alimentador de papel* paper bin.

alimentar *vt* to feed; *alimentar a su familia* to feed one's family || to be nourishing; *las patatas alimentan poco* potatoes are not very nourishing || TECN to feed; *alimentar una computadora con datos* to feed data into a computer, to feed a computer with data || to supply; *mineral que alimenta la industria siderúrgica* mineral which supplies the iron and steel industry || FIG to feed; *la lectura alimenta el espíritu* reading feeds the mind | to foster, to encourage; *hay libertades que alimentan toda clase de disturbios* certain kinds of freedom foster all sorts of disturbances | to feed (las pasiones) | to cherish, to feed (esperanzas) | to put fuel on (un fuego).
◆ *vpr* to feed, to live; *alimentarse con* or *de arroz* to feed *o* to live on rice || TECN to be fed (una máquina, etc.) || to be supplied (una industria, etc.) || FIG *alimentarse de quimeras* to live in a dream world.

alimenticio, cia *adj* food; *la industria alimenticia* the food industry || nourishing; *los huevos son muy alimenticios* eggs are very nourishing || — *pastas alimenticias* pasta || *pensión alimenticia* alimony, allowance || *productos alimenticios* foodtuffs, food products || *valor alimenticio* food value, nutritional value.

alimentista *m/f* person receiving alimony *o* an allowance.

alimento *m* food; *el pan es un alimento* bread is a food || FIG food; *la lectura es un alimento del espíritu* reading is food for the mind | fuel (para las pasiones) || *de mucho alimento* very nourishing.
◆ *pl* JUR alimony *sing*, maintenance, allowance *sing.*

alimentoso *adj* nourishing, nutritive.

alimoche *m* ZOOL Egyptian volture.

alimón (al) *loc adv* together; *lo han hecho al alimón* they did it together || — *hacer un trabajo al alimón* to share a piece of work || TAUR *torear al alimón* to fight a bull together [two toreros holding the cape].

alimonarse *vpr* to yellow, to turn yellow (las hojas de un árbol).

alindado, da *adj* dandified (afectadamente pulcro) || conceited (presumido).

alindamiento *m* marking out [of boundaries].

alindar *vt* to mark out the boundaries of; *alindar dos fincas* to mark out the boundaries of two estates || to embellish, to beautify, to make beautiful, to make pretty (embellecer).
◆ *vi* to border on, to be adjacent *o* next to; *tu campo alinda con el mío* your fiel borders on mine *o* is adjacent to mine || to be next to one another, to be adjacent; *nuestras casas alindan* our houses are next to one another.

alinderar *vt* AMER to mark out the boundaries of (deslindar).

alineación *f* alignment, lining up || DEP line-up; *la alineación de un equipo* the line-up of a team || — *fuera de alineación* out of alignment, out of true || *política de no alineación* nonalignment policy.

alineado, da *adj* aligned, lined-up || *país no alineado* nonaligned country.

alineamiento *m* alignment, lining up || *política de no alineamiento* nonalignment policy.

alinear *vt* to align, to line up, to put in line ‖ MIL to form up (tropas) ‖ FIG to bring into line.
◆ *vpr* to join; *me he alineado en el equipo de España* I have joined the Spanish team ‖ to line up; *se alinearon contra la pared* they lined up against the wall ‖ MIL to fall in, to form up.

aliñado, da *adj* neat (aseado).

aliñador, ra *adj* decorative ‖ CULIN seasoning.
◆ *m/f* AMER bonesetter.

aliñar *vt* CULIN to season, to flavour (condimentar) | to dress; *aliñar la ensalada* to dress the salad ‖ to set [a bone] (arreglar los huesos dislocados) ‖ to adorn (adornar) ‖ to prepare (preparar) ‖ TAUR to prepare (the bull) for a quick kill.

aliño *m* CULIN seasoning (con condimentos) | dressing (para la ensalada) ‖ preparation (preparación) ‖ neatness (aseo) ‖ adornment (adorno) ‖ TAUR *faena de aliño* short «faena» performed in orden to kill the bull quickly.

alioli *m* garlic and oliveoil sauce.

alionín *m* ZOOL blue tit.

alípede; alípedo *adj m* POÉT with winged feet.

aliquebrado, da *adj* broken-winged, with a broken wing ‖ FIG & FAM depressed, dejected, crestfallen (desanimado) | weak, weakened (débil).

¡alirón! *interj* come on! [shout of exhortation during a football match].

alisado *m* smoothing.

alisador, ra *adj* smoothing.
◆ *m* smoother (instrumento) ‖ polisher (persona) ‖ AMER toothcomb.

alisadura *f* smoothing, polishing (acción de alisar).
◆ *pl* shavings (de madera).

alisar *m* alder grove.

alisar *vt* to smooth, to polish (pulir) ‖ to flatten, to level (allanar) ‖ to smooth (el pelo).
◆ *vpr* to smooth ‖ *alisarse el pelo* to smooth one's hair (arreglarse el pelo).

aliseda *f* alder grove.

alisios *adj mpl* MAR trade; *los vientos alisios* the Trade Winds.
◆ *m pl* Trade Winds.

aliso *m* alder (árbol) ‖ *aliso negro* black alder.

alistado, da *adj* enlisted, enrolled; *alistado en el ejército* enlisted in the army ‖ striped (listado).
◆ *m* volunteer.

alistador *m* recruiting officer.

alistamiento *m* MIL enlistment, recruitment | enlistment; *alistamiento voluntario* voluntary enlistment ‖ joining, enrolment [US enrolment] (en un partido político, etc.) ‖ annual contingent (quinta).

alistar *vt* to enlist, to recruit (reclutar) ‖ to list, to put on a list (registrar) ‖ to prepare, to make ready (preparar).
◆ *vpr* to enroll, to enrol ‖ to enlist, to enroll, to enrol (en el ejército) ‖ to prepare, to make ready (prepararse) ‖ FIG to rally; *alistarse en las filas monárquicas* to rally to the royalist flag.

aliteración *f* alliteration.

aliterado, da *adj* alliterative.

alitierno *m* buckthorn (aladierna).

alitranca *f* AMER brake (retranca).

aliviadero *m* overflow channel, spillway (desaguadero).

aliviador, ra *adj* comforting, consoling.
◆ *m* lever for raising or lowering a millstone.

alivianar *vt* AMER ⟶ **aliviar.**

aliviar *vt* to lighten, to make lighter; *aliviar una carga* to make a burden lighter ‖ to help (out) (ayudar); *aliviarle a uno en el trabajo* to help s.o. out with his work ‖ to give relief; *esta medicina le aliviará* this medicine will give you relief ‖ to relieve, to alleviate, to soothe; *aliviar el dolor* to relieve the pain ‖ to comfort, to console, to soothe (consolar) ‖ to lessen, to relieve (una pena) ‖ to quicken (el paso) ‖ — *aliviar el luto* to go into half mourning ‖ FIG & FAM *aliviar la cartera a uno* to relieve s.o. of his wallet (robar).
◆ *vpr* to be better, to feel better, to recover (un enfermo) ‖ to diminish, to ease up (un dolor) ‖ *¡que se alivie!* get better soon!, get well soon!

alivio *m* lightening (de una carga) ‖ relief; *con estas inyecciones sentirá pronto un alivio* with these injections you will soon feel relief ‖ relief; *su marcha fue un alivio para mí* his departure was a relief for me ‖ comfort, consolation; *tus palabras son un alivio* your words are a comfort to me ‖ relief, mitigation, alleviation (pena, sufrimiento) ‖ — *alivio de luto* half mourning ‖ FAM *de alivio* a hell of a; *un catarro de alivio* a hell of a cold; *un susto, un pesado de alivio* a hell of a fright, of a bore; horrible; *él es muy simpático, pero su mujer es de alivio* he is very nice, but his wife is horrible.

aljaba *f* quiver (para las flechas) ‖ AMER fuchsia (planta).

aljama *f* synagogue (sinagoga) ‖ mosque (mezquita) ‖ assembly of Moslems or Jews ‖ Arab quarter (barrio de moros) ‖ Jewish quarter (barrio judío).

aljamía *f* Spanish [name given to Spanish by the Arabs] ‖ Spanish text written in Arabic characters.

aljamiado, da *adj* written in Spanish with Arabic characters ‖ Spanish-speaking (que habla español).

aljez *m* gypsum.

aljibe *m* tank, cistern (de agua) ‖ MAR tanker ‖ AMER spring (manantial) | well (pozo) ‖ dungeon (cárcel) ‖ *barco aljibe* tanker.

aljofaina *f* washbowl, washbasin (jofaina).

aljófar *m* (small) pearl (perla) ‖ dewdrop (gota de rocío).

aljofarar *vt* to moisten, to pearl (el rocío).

aljofifa *f* floorcloth.

aljofifado *m* wash, washing.

aljofifar *vt* to clean with a floorcloth, to mop.

aljuba *f* (ant) Jubbah.

alma *f* soul ‖ spirit, heart; *alma noble* noble spirit; *tener el alma destrozada* to have a broken heart ‖ soul; *es un alma inocente* he is an innocent soul ‖ FIG soul, living soul; *no hay ni un alma* there is not a soul | soul, person; *ciudad de cien mil almas* town with a hundred thousand people *o* persons | lifeblood, moving spirit, heart and soul; *es el alma de la rebelión* he is the lifeblood of the rebellion | life and soul; *es el alma de la fiesta* he is the life and soul of the party ‖ scaffold pole (de un andamio) ‖ bore (de cañón) ‖ core (de cable, de estatua) ‖ BOT pith ‖ MÚS sound post (de un violín) ‖ — *alma de Caín* or *de Judas* devil, fiend ‖ FIG & FAM *alma de cántaro* fathead, drip ‖ *alma de Dios* good soul, good-hearted person ‖ *alma en pena* soul in Purgatory; lost *o* poor soul (sentido figurado) ‖ *alma gemela* kindred spirit ‖ *alma mía* my dear, my darling (querido), for heaven's sake! (por Dios) ‖ *alma viviente* living soul ‖ *arrancarle el alma a alguien* to shock s.o. deeply ‖ *con el alma, con toda el alma* out of the goodness of one's heart; *me lo ofreció con el alma* he offered it to me out of the goodness of his heart; with all one's heart; *siente con toda su alma no poder hacerlo* he regrets with all his heart that he cannot do it ‖ *con el alma y la vida* with heart and soul, with all one's heart ‖ *dar el alma* to pass away, to give up the ghost ‖ *de mi alma* dear, darling; *hijo de mi alma* my dear *o* my darling son ‖ *dolerle a uno en el alma* to break one's heart, to hurt one; *me duele en el alma que no me haya escrito* it hurts me to think that she hasn't written ‖ FAM *echarse el alma a las espaldas* to do just as one pleases (no preocuparse nada) ‖ *encomendar el alma a Dios* to commend one's soul to God ‖ *en cuerpo y alma* body and soul ‖ *en lo más hondo de mi alma* deep down, in my heart of hearts, in the depth of my heart ‖ *entregar* or *rendir uno el alma (a Dios)* to pass away, to give up the ghost ‖ *estar como el alma de Caribay* not to be able to make up one's mind ‖ *estar como un alma perdida* to be undecided, to be lost ‖ *estar con el alma en la boca* to be at death's door, to have one foot in the grave ‖ *estar con el alma en un hilo* to be worried stiff, to be on tenterhooks (estar inquieto), to be scared stiff, to have one's heart in one's mouth (de miedo) ‖ *hablar al alma* to speak in earnest ‖ FAM *ir como alma que lleva el diablo* to run hell for leather, to run like hell ‖ *llegarle al alma a uno* to move s.o., to touch s.o. ‖ *llevar la música en el alma* to have music in one's blood ‖ *me da en el alma que no volverá* I have a feeling that he will not come back ‖ FIG *no tener alma* to have a heart of stone, to have no heart (ser duro) ‖ *partir* or *romper el alma a uno* to break s.o.'s heart ‖ FAM *romperse el alma* to break one's neck ‖ *se le cayó el alma a los pies* his heart sank ‖ *sentir en el alma* to be deeply sorry ‖ *tener su alma en el almario* to have a heart (ser sensible), to have a lot of pluck ‖ *tocar en el alma a uno* to touch s.o.'s heart ‖ *vender el alma al diablo* to sell one's soul to the devil ‖ *volverle a uno el alma al cuerpo* to calm down (tranquilizarse).

almacén *m* warehouse (depósito) ‖ department store; *los grandes almacenes* the big department stores ‖ magazine (de un arma) ‖ IMPR magazine ‖ AMER grocer's shop (tienda de comestibles) ‖ — *almacén de consignación* consignment stock ‖ *almacén de depósito* bonded warehouse (de la aduana) ‖ *almacén nevera* cold store.

almacenaje *m* warehouse dues *pl*, storage charges *pl* (gastos) ‖ storage, warehousing ‖ *almacenaje frigorífico* cold storage.

almacenamiento *m* storage, warehousing; *estar encargado del almacenamiento de las mercancías* to be in charge of the storage of the goods ‖ stock, supply; *hay almacenamientos de víveres aquí* there are stocks of food here ‖ INFORM storage.

almacenar *vt* to store, to warehouse ‖ to store, to store up; *almacenar recuerdos* to store memories ‖ to keep, to hoard; *¿por qué almacenas tantas porquerías?* why do you keep so much rubbish?

almacenero *m* storekeeper, warehouseman ‖ AMER grocer, shopkeeper.

almacenista *m* warehouseman (dueño de un almacén).

almáciga *f* mastic (resina) ‖ AGR seedbed, nursery (semillero).

almácigo *m* BOT mastic tree, lentiscus ‖ AGR plantation, nursery (semillero).

almádana; almádena *f* sledgehammer, large hammer (de cantero).

almadraba *f* mandrague, tunny net (red) ‖ tunny fishing (pesca) ‖ tunny-fishing ground (lugar de pesca).

almadrabero *m* tunny fisherman.

almadreña *f* clog, sabot (zueco).

almagesto *m* almagest.

almagra *f* red ochre.

almagradura *f* red ochre colouring.

almagral *m* ochre deposit.

almagrar *vt* to dye with red ochre.

almagre *m* red ochre.

almagrero, ra *adj* red-ochre bearing (terreno).

almajal *m* → **almarjal.**

almajaneque *m* HIST mangonel, catapult (máquina de guerra).

almalafa *f* haik, haick.

alma máter *f* alma mater.

almanaque *f* almanac || diary (agenda) || calendar; *almanaque de taco* tear-off calendar.

almandina *f* almandite, almandine.

almarjal; almajal *m* field of barilla *o* saltwort || marsh.

almarjo *m* barilla, saltwort (planta).

almazara *f* oil mill.

almea *f* BOT water plantain (azúmbar) || storax bark (corteza).

almecina *f* hackberry, fruit of the nettle tree.

almecino *m* BOT nettle tree.

almeja *f* clam (molusco).

almejar *m* clam bed.

almena *f* merlon (de piedra) || crenel (hueco).
◆ *pl* battlements.

almenado, da *adj* battlemented, crenellated.

almenaje *m* battlements *pl.*

almenar *vt* to build battlements on, to crenellate.

almenara *f* beacon, signal fire || candelabrum, candelabra (candelero).

almendra *f* almond; *almendra amarga* bitter almond || FIG & FAM pebble (guijarro).
◆ *pl* pendants, drops, crystals (de araña) || — *almendras garapiñadas* pralines || *almendras tostadas* burnt almonds.

almendrada *f* almond milk (bebida) || almond paste (salsa).

almendrado *m* almond paste.

almendral *m* almond grove.

almendrera *f* almond tree.

almendrilla *f* gravel (grava) || TECN round-ended file (lima).

almendro *m* almond tree (árbol).

almenilla *f* scalloping (en la ropa).

almeriense *adj* [from *o* of] Almería [Spain].
◆ *m/f* native *o* inhabitant of Almería.

almete *m* helmet (casco).

almez *m* nettle tree, hackberry (árbol).

almeza *f* hackberry, fruit of the nettle tree.

almezo *m* nettle tree, hackberry (árbol).

almiar *m* AGR haystack, hayrick (pajar).

almíbar *m* syrup; *melocotones en almíbar* peaches in syrup || FAM *estar hecho un almíbar* to be as sweet as can be *o* to be as sweet as sugar pie.

almibarado, da *adj* syrupy (muy dulce) || FIG & FAM sugary, syrupy (meloso).

almibarar *vt* to preserve [in syrup] (confitar) || to cover in syrup || FIG to sweeten [one's words].

almidón *m* starch || *dar almidón a una camisa* to starch a shirt.

almidonado, da *adj* starched; *un cuello almidonado* a starched collar || FIG & FAM dressed up to the nines, dressed to kill (muy compuesto).
◆ *m* starching.

almidonar *vt* to starch.

almidonería *f* starch factory *o* works.

almijar *m* place for drying olives or grapes.

almilla *f* jerkin, (tight-fitting) jacket || TECN tenon (espiga) || breast of pork (carne).

almimbar *m* mimbar, minbar, almemor, almemar (de mezquita).

alminar *m* minaret.

almiranta *f* viceadmiral's ship (barco) || admiral's wife.

almirantazgo *m* admiralty || admiralty court (tribunal) || admiral's jurisdiction.

almirante *m* admiral.

almirez *m* mortar (mortero).

almizcate *m* space between two houses.

almizcle *m* musk.

almizcleña *f* BOT grape hyacinth.

almizcleño, ña *adj* musky, scented with musk.

almizclero, ra *adj* musky, scented with musk || — *lirón almizclero* dormouse || *ratón almizclero* muskrat.
◆ *m* musk deer (rumiante).
◆ *f* desman (roedor).

almocadén *m* (ant) commander.

almocafre *m* spud, weeding hoe.

almocárabes; almocarbes *m pl* interlaced desing *sing.*

almocela *f* hood.

almocrí *m* reader of the Koran [in a mosque].

almogávar *m* raiding soldier, raider.

almogavaría *f* raiding party, body of raiding troops.

almohada *f* pillow (de la cama) || cushion (para sentarse) || pillowslip, pillowcase (funda) || ARQ boss, bossage (almohadilla) || FIG & FAM *hay que consultar con la almohada* I'll (you'll, etc.) have to sleep on it.

almohadado, da *adj* ARQ bossed, with a bossage.

almohadazo *m* blow with a pillow.

almohadilla *f* small cushion (cojincillo) || harness pad (en los arreos) || inkpad (para sellar) || ARQ boss (piedra) | coussinet, cushion (de la voluta jónica) || AMER pincushion (acerico) | holder (de la plancha).

almohadillado, da *adj* padded (acolchado) || ARQ bossed, with a bossage.
◆ *m* ARQ boss, bossage || padding (relleno).

almohadillar *vt* ARQ to boss, to decorate with bosses *o* bossage || to pad (acolchar).

almohadón *m* cushion; *almohadones de pluma* feather cushions || ARQ coussinet, cushion (de un arco) || REL hassock (cojín).

almohaza *f* currycomb (para los caballos).

almohazar *vt* to curry, to brush down.

almojarifazgo *m* (ant) former duty on imports and exports.

almojarife *m* (ant) king's tax collector (recaudador) || (ant) customs officer (aduanero).

almóndiga *f* meatball, rissole.

almoneda *f* auction (subasta) || (clearance) sale (a bajo precio) || *vender en almoneda* to auction (el subastador), to put up for auction (el vendedor), to sell off (a bajo precio).

almonedear *vt* to auction (el subastador) || to put up for auction (el vendedor) || to sell of (a bajo precio).

almorávide *adj/s* Almoravid, Almoravide.

almorranas *f pl* MED haemorrhoids, piles.

almorta *f* vetchling, vetch (planta).

almorzada *f* cupped handful, handful.

almorzado, da *adj* viene almorzado he has already eaten.

almorzar* *vi* to lunch, to have lunch (al mediodía) || to have breakfast, to breakfast (desayunar).
◆ *vt* to have for lunch, to lunch on (al mediodía) || to have for breakfast, to breakfast on (desayuno).

almotacén *m* inspector of weights and measures.

almotacenazgo *m* office of the inspector of weights and measures (cargo u oficina).

almozárabe *adj/s* → **mozárabe.**

almud *m* almud, almude (medida).

almudí; almudín *m* corn exchange (alhóndiga).

almuecín; almuédano *m* muezzin.

almuerzo *m* lunch (al mediodía) || breakfast (por la mañana).

¡alo!; ¡aló! *interj* hello?, hullo? (teléfono).

alocación *f* allocation; *alocación de créditos* allocation of credits.

alocadamente *adv* foolishly, hastily, thoughtlessly.

alocado, da *adj* scatterbrained (distraído); *es un niño alocado, lo olvida todo* he's a scatterbrained child, he forgets everything || irresponsible; *es una persona demasiado alocada para que le confíes algo importante* he is too irresponsible a person to be trusted with anything important || mad, crazy (loco) || thoughtless, hasty; *un gesto alocado* a hasty gesture || strange (extraño).
◆ *m/f* madcap.

alocar *vt* to drive mad.
◆ *vpr* to go *o* to become mad (volverse loco) || FIG to lose one's head; *no hay que alocarse por tan poca cosa* you shouldn't lose your head over such a trivial matter.

alocución *f* allocution, speech, address.

alodial *adj* JUR alodial, allodial.

alodio *m* JUR alodium, allodium.

áloe; aloe *m* aloe (planta) || MED aloes.

aloja *f* a sort of mead || AMER a refreshing drink made from fermented carob beans.

alojado, da *adj* housed, lodged.
◆ *m* soldier billeted in a privated house.
◆ *m/f* AMER guest, lodger (persona hospedada).

alojamiento *m* accommodation, lodging (acción) || accommodation, lodgings *pl* (sitio); *buscar alojamiento* to look for lodgings || MIL quartering, billeting (acción) | billet, quarters *pl* (sitio) | camp (campamento) || — MIL *boleta de alojamiento* billeting order || *dar alojamiento a* to accommodate, to take in, to put up.

alojar *vt* to accommodate, to house, to lodge (hospedar) || to house, to accommodate (albergar); *el nuevo edificio alojará a doscientas familias* the new block of flats will house two hundred families || MIL to billet, to quarter || FIG to fit in; *no puedo alojar tantos libros aquí* I can't fit so many books in here || *tiene una bala alojada en el brazo* he has a bullet lodged in his arm.
◆ *vpr* to put up, to stay, to lodge; *alojarse en un hotel* to put up at a hotel, to stay *o* to lodge in a hotel || to lodge; *la bala se le alojó en el brazo* the bullet lodged in his arm || MIL to take up position (situarse) | to be billeted (vivir).

alomado, da *adj* high-backed (caballo, mulo) || AGR ridged.

alomar *vt* AGR to ridge.

alomorfo, fa *adj* QUÍM allomorphic.
◆ *m/f* QUÍM allomorph.

◆ *m* GRAM allomorph.

alón *m* wing (de ave).
◆ *adj m* AMER large-winged.

alondra *f* lark (pájaro).

Alonso *npr m* Alphonse.

alópata *adj* allopathic.
◆ *m* allopath, allopathist (médico).

alopatía *f* MED allopathy.

alopecia *f* MED alopecia.

aloque *adj* light-red || rosé (vino).
◆ *m* rosé wine.

alotropía *f* allotropy.

alotrópico, ca *adj* allotropic.

alpaca *f* alpaca (animal, tejido); *un traje de alpaca* a suit made of alpaca || German *o* nickel silver (metal).

alpargata *f* canvas shoe, rope-soled shoe.

alpargatazo *m* *como sigas así te doy un alpargatazo* if you carry on like that you'll get a taste of my slipper *o* you'll get a slippering.

alpargate *m* canvas shoe, rope-soled shoe.

alpargatería *f* canvas shoe factory (fábrica) || shoe shop (tienda).

alpargatero, ra *m/f* manufacturer of canvas shoes (fabricante) || canvas shoe dealer (vendedor).

alpargatilla *m/f* FIG schemer, crafty person.

alpechín *m* foul-smelling liquid which runs from piled-up olives.

alpechinera *f* pit in which olive juice is collected.

alpenstock *m* alpenstock (bastón de alpinista).

Alpes *npr mpl* GEOGR Alps.

alpestre *adj* Alpine (de los Alpes) || FIG mountainous.

alpinismo *m* mountaineering, climbing (montañismo).

alpinista *m/f* mountaineer, climber.

alpino, na *adj* Alpine; *raza alpina* alpine race || *cordillera alpina* Alpine range.

alpiste *m* BOT alpist, canary grass || FAM drink, booze (la bebida) | dough, brass (dinero) || FAM *gustarle a uno mucho el alpiste* to be a boozer.

alpistelarse *vpr* FAM to get sozzled, to get drunk.

alpistera *f* small cake [made from flour, eggs and sesame].

alpujarreño, ña *adj* from the Alpujarras [South Andalusian mountains].

alquequenje *m* winter cherry, strawberry tomato, husk tomato (planta).

alquería *f* farmstead, farm (granja) || hamlet (aldea).

alquilable *adj* rentable, which can be rented (piso, televisor, etc.) || which can be hired, for hire (coche, barca, etc.).

alquilar *vt* to rent (piso, etc.); *alquilar un piso en 1000 pesetas* to rent a flat for 1, 000 pesetas || to hire, to hire out (dar en alquiler un coche, una barca, etc.); *alquilar por horas, por meses* to hire by the hour, by the month || to hire (tomar en alquiler un coche, una barca, etc.) || to charter (avión) || — *es cosa de alquilar balcones* it's sth. worth seeing, it's a must || *piso por alquilar* flat to let.
◆ *vpr* to be let (casa) || to be for hire (coche, taxi) || to hire o.s. out (persona) || *se alquila* to let (casa), for hire (taxi, coche).

alquiler *m* renting, letting (acción de alquilar un piso, un televisor) || hiring (acción de alquilar otra cosa) || rent; *hay que pagar el alquiler del piso* we must pay the rent for the flat || hire charge, rental (de un coche, barca, etc.) || — *alquiler con opción a compra* hire with option of purchase || *alquiler trimestral* quarterly rent (de una casa) || *casa en alquiler* block of flats || *de alquiler* to let (pisos), for rent (televisor), for hire (coches, animales, etc.) || *exento de alquiler* rent-free.
◆ *pl* rent || *control de alquileres* rent control.

alquimia *f* alchemy.

alquimista *m* alchemist.

alquitara *f* still (alambique).

alquitarar *vt* to distil (destilar) || FIG *estilo alquitarado* over-refined *o* precious style.

alquitrán *m* tar; *alquitrán de hulla* coal tar.

alquitranado, da *adj* tarred, tarry.
◆ *m* MAR tarpaulin (lienzo) || tarring (acción de alquitranar); *el alquitranado de las carreteras* the tarring of the roads || tarmac, tar (revestimiento).

alquitranador, ra *adj* tarring.
◆ *m/f* tar spreader.
◆ *f* tar-spreading machine (máquina).

alquitranar *vt* to tar || *máquina de alquitranar* tar-spreading machine.

alrededor *adv* round, around; *girar alrededor de la mesa* to go round the table || FAM about, around, round about; *alrededor de mil pesetas* about a thousand pesetas; *llegó alrededor de las nueve* he arrived around nine o'clock || — *alrededor suyo* around him || *todo alrededor* all around.
◆ *m pl* surrounding districts, outskirts; *los alrededores de París* the outskirts of Paris || surroundings (ambiente) || *mirar a su alrededor* to look around one, to look all around.

Alsacia *npr f* GEOGR Alsace.

alsaciano, na *adj/s* Alsatian.

alta *f* discharge; *ya tengo el alta del hospital* my hospital discharge has come through || enrollment (ingreso) || army enlistment from (documento) || — *dar de alta* to pass as fit (un militar enfermo), to enrol (incorporar los militares a sus unidades), to discharge (a un enfermo) || *darse de alta* to enrol || MIL *ser alta* to enrol into active service.

altaico, ca *adj* Altaic (raza).

altamente *adv* highly, extremely.

altanería *f* high flight (de pájaros) || falconry (forma de caza) || pride, haughtiness, arrogance (orgullo).

altanero, ra *adj* proud, haughty, arrogant (orgulloso) || high-flying (pájaro).

altar *m* altar || MIN furnace bridge, fire bridge (de horno) || — *altar mayor* high altar || FIG *llevar a una mujer al altar* to lead a woman to the altar | *poner en un altar* to put on a pedestal, to praise to the skies | *quedarse para adornar altares* to be left on the shelf.

altaverapacense *adj* [of *o* from] Alta Verapaz (Guatemala).
◆ *m/f* native *o* inhabitan of Alta Verapaz.

altavoz *m* loudspeaker; *altavoces potentes* powerful loudspeakers.

alterabilidad *f* changeability.

alterable *adj* changeable (que cambia o puede ser cambiado) || perishable, prone to deterioration (que se pudre rápidamente).

alteración *f* alteration; *alteración del horario* alteration of the timetable || change for the worse, deterioration; *alteración de la salud* deterioration in health || irregularity (del pulso) | argument, quarrel, upset (altercado) || *alteración del orden público* breach of the peace, disturbance of the peace.

alterado, da *adj* altered || disturbed (orden, etc.) || FIG changed (voz, cara) || agitated, upset, disturbed (una persona) || upset (estómago, etc.) || angry (enfadado).

alterante *adj* MED alterative.

alterar *vt* to alter, to change; *el acontecimiento alteró mis proyectos* the event changed my plans || to change for the worse (empeorar) || FIG to disturb; *alterar el orden público* to disturb the peace | to upset, to disturb; *mis palabras le alteraron* my words upset him | to annoy, to anger (enfadar) | to frighten (asustar) | to spoil, to make go bad, to cause to go bad; *el calor altera los alimentos* heat makes food go bad || *alterar la verdad* to distort the truth.
◆ *vpr* to change, to alter (cambiar) || to go bad *o* off (la comida) || to go sour *o* off (la leche) || to be disturbed *o* upset; *no alterarse por nada* not to be upset by anything || to falter (la voz) || to get angry, to lose one's temper (enojarse) || to get excited (emocionarse) || — *¡no te alteres!* there's no need to lose your temper! || *se altera con la humedad* store in a dry place (medicina, etc.).

altercación *f*; **altercado** *m* argument, quarrel, altercation.

altercante *adj* quarrelsome, argumentative.

altercar *vi* to quarrel, to argue.

alternación *f* alternation.

alternado, da *adj* alternate.

alternador *m* ELECTR alternator.

alternancia *f* alternation.

alternante *adj* alternating.

alternar *vt* to alternate; *alternar trabajos* to alternate jobs || AGR *alternar cultivos* to rotate the crops.
◆ *vi* to alternate || to relieve one another, to take turns, to work in relays; *alternar en un trabajo* to take turns on a job || to mix, to associate, to go around; *alternar con poetas* to mix with poets || to go out, to mix with people; *a María le gusta mucho alternar* Mary loves to go out || MAT to interchange [the terms of two fractions].
◆ *vpr* to take turns; *nos alternamos en el volante* we took turns at the wheel.

alternativa *f* alternation (sucesión) || alternative, option, choice; *no dejar una alternativa* to leave no option || shift work (trabajo en turnos) || AGR rotation (de las cosechas) || TAUR ceremony in which the senior matador confers professional status on the novice (novillero), thus accepting him as a professional equal capable of dispatching any bull in the proper manner || — TAUR *tomar la alternativa* to become a qualified bullfighter || *tomar una alternativa* to make a decision *o* a choice.

alternativamente *adv* alternately.

alternativo, va *adj* alternating; *el movimiento alternativo del péndulo* the alternating swing of the pendulum || *huelga alternativa* staggered strike.

alterno, na *adj* alternating; *corriente alterna* alternating current || alternate; *hojas alternas* alternate leaves; *ángulos alternos* alternate angles || *clases alternas* lessons on alternate days.

alteza *f* Highness (tratamiento); *Su Alteza Real* His *o* Her Royal Highness; *en seguida, Alteza* at once, your Highness || height (altura) || sublimity, grandeur (de sentimientos) || *alteza de miras* highmindedness.

altibajo *m* downward thrust (esgrima)
◆ *pl* bumps, roughness *sing* (de un terreno) || FIG & FAM ups and downs, vicissitudes; *los altibajos de la política* the ups and downs of politics.

altilocuencia *f* grandiloquence.

altilocuente; altílocuo, cua *adj* grandiloquent.

altillano *m*; **altillanura** *f* AMER plateau (meseta).

altillo *m* hill, hillock (cerrillo) || attic (desván).

altimetría *f* altimetry.

altímetro *m* altimeter.

altiplanicie *f* high plateau (meseta).

altiplano *m* AMER high plateau (altiplanicie).

altísimo, ma *adj* very high; *una torre altísima* a very high tower || very tall; *un hombre altísimo* a very tall man.
◆ *m el Altísimo* the Almighty.

altisonancia *f* grandiloquence.

altisonante; altísono, na *adj* grandiloquent, pompous, bombastic (estilo, discurso, etc.) || highsounding, pompous (apellido).

altitonante *adj* thundering; *Júpiter altitonanté* thundering Jove.

altitud *f* AVIAC altitude, height || GEOGR height, elevation.

altivarse; altivecerse *vpr* to be haughty, to put on airs.

altivez; altiveza *f* arrogance, haughtiness.

altivo, va *adj* arrogant, haughty.

alto, ta *adj* tall; *una mujer alta, un árbol alto* a tall woman, a tall tree || high (edificio, puesto, frecuencia, cuello, precio, río, porcentaje, mando) || upper; *el Alto Rin* the Upper Rhine; *el Alto Egipto* Upper Egypt || upper; *los pisos altos* the upper floors || loud (fuerte); *voz alta* loud voice || MÚS alto (instrumento) | high (de sonido agudo) || rough (mar) || GRAM high; *alto alemán* High German || advanced; *altos estudios de matemáticas* advanced studies in mathematics || FIG high, lofty; *tener alta idea de sus méritos* to have a high opinion of one's merits | highly-placed (personaje) | noble, lofty; *altos sentimientos* noble sentiments | fine; *el más alto ejemplo de patriotismo* the finest example of patriotism | AMER short (vestido) || — *a altas horas de la noche* late at night || *alta presión* high pressure || *alta sociedad* high society || *alta traición* high treason || *alto horno* blast furnace || *alto personal* high officials || *cámara alta* upper chamber || *clase alta* upper class || *desde lo alto de* from the top of || *en alta mar* on the high seas || *en las altas esferas* in high places *o* circles || *en lo alto de* on the top of || *en lo alto del árbol* at the top of the tree || *en voz alta* in a loud voice || *estar en lo alto* to be high up || *hacer algo por (todo) lo alto* to do sth. in style || *lo alto* the top || || *pasar por lo alto* to pass overhead || *tener tantos metros de alto* to be so many metres high *o* in height.
◆ *m* height (altura) | hill (elevación del terreno) || high floor; *vivir en un alto* to live on a high floor || MÚS viola (instrumento) | contralto (voz) || MIL halt || stop (parada) || AMER pile (montón) || — MIL *dar el alto a uno* to challenge s.o., to order s.o. to halt | *hacer alto* to halt || *los altos y bajos* the ups and downs || *un alto el fuego* a cease-fire.
◆ *adv* high, high up; *poner un libro muy alto* to put a book very high up || out loud; *gritar alto* to shout out loud || loudly, loud; *hablar alto* to speak loudly || — *de alto abajo* from top to bottom || *mantener en alto* to hold up high || *pasar por alto* to pass over, to ignore || FIG *picar alto* to aim high || *poner la radio más alto* to turn the radio up || *poner muy alto* to praise to the skies to put on a pedestal (alabar) || *se me pasó por alto* it completely slipped my mind || *tirando por lo alto* at the outside, at the most || *tirar por alto* to throw away (tirar) || *ver las cosas de alto* to look at things on a lofty plane.
◆ *interj* halt! || — *¡alto ahí!* halt! || *¡alto el fuego!* cease fire!, cease firing!

altoparlante *m* AMER loudspeaker (altavoz).

altozano *m* hill, hillock (cerro) || AMER parvis (de iglesia).

altramuz *m* lupin (planta).

altruismo *m* altruism.

altruista *adj* altruistic.
◆ *m/f* altruist.

altura *f* height, altitude; *las nubes circulan a gran altura* the clouds go by at a very great height || height; *la altura de un peldaño, de una persona* the height of a step, of a person || depth (del agua) || MAT height; *altura de un triángulo* height of a triangle || GEOGR latitude; *a la altura de* on the same latitude as || level (nivel); *estar a la misma altura* to be on the same level || FIG merit, worth || nobleness, loftiness (de sentimiento) || MÚS pitch || ASTR elevation || — *a la altura del corazón* in the region of the heart || *a la altura de la tarea* equal to the task, up to the task || *altura de caída* fall (de catarata) || *altura de la vegetación* timber line || *altura del barómetro* barometer reading || *altura de miras* high-mindedness || *barco de altura* oceangoing *o* seagoing ship || *estar a la altura de las circunstancias* to rise to the occasion || *estar a la altura del tiempo* to be abreast of the times || *navegación de altura* ocean navigation || *no llega a la altura de su padre* he does not measure up to his father || *pesca de altura* deep-sea fishing || FIG *poner a alguien a la altura del betún* or *de una zapatilla* to make s.o. feel very small | *quedar a la altura del betún* or *de una zapatilla* to give a poor show, to do very badly || *rayar a gran altura* to shine || *salto de altura* high jump || *tomar altura* to climb (avión) || *un poste de cinco metros de altura* a post five metres high *o* in height || FIG *un programa de altura* a first-rate programme.
◆ *pl* heights (cumbres); *hay nieve en las alturas* there is snow on the heights || REL heaven *sing* || — *a estas alturas* at this hour, at this stage, as late as this || *gloria a Dios en las alturas* glory to God in the highest.

alúa *f* AMER pyrophorus, firefly (insecto).

aluato *m* ZOOL howler monkey.

alubia *f* bean (judía).

alucinación *f* hallucination.

alucinamiento *m* hallucination (alucinación) || delusion (error) || deceit (engaño).

alucinante *adj* hallucinating, hallucinatory || FIG & FAM incredible.

alucinar *vt* to hallucinate || to delude, to deceive (engañar) || to fascinate (fascinar).
◆ *vpr* to delude o.s.

alucinógeno, na *adj* hallucinogenic.
◆ *m* hallucinogen.

alud *m* avalanche.

aluda *f* ZOOL winged ant, flying ant.

aludido, da *adj* in question, above-mentioned, being talked about; *la persona aludida* the person in question || FIG *darse por aludido* to take the hint (cuando es una indirecta), to feel as though one is being got at (*fam*), to take it personally || *no darse por aludido* to turn a deaf ear.

aludir *vi* to allude to, to mention (hablar de); *no ha aludido a este negocio* he has not mentioned this deal || to allude to (referirse indirectamente) || to refer (referirse en un texto).

alumbrado, da *adj* lighted, lit; *alumbrado con gas* lighted by gas, gas-lit || illuminated (calle, parque, etc.) || FAM tipsy, merry (achispado).
◆ *m/f* alumbrado, perfectibilist (de la secta española), iluminist.
◆ *m* lighting; *alumbrado eléctrico* electric lighting || lights *pl* (de un coche).

alumbramiento *m* lighting, lighting-up (acción de alumbrar) || illumination (de una calle) || child-birth, confinement (parto).

alumbrante *adj* lighting, illuminating || FIG enlightening, illuminating.

alumbrar *vt* to light; *cuando la sala estaba alumbrada con gas* when the room was lit by *o* with gas || to illuminate, to light up (en gran escala); *aquella noche la luna alumbraba los campos* that night the moon lit up the fields || to give light; *el Sol nos alumbra* the Sun gives us light || to light the way; *voy a alumbrarte para ir a la bodega* I'll light your way down to the cellar || to restore the sight of (a un ciego) || FIG to strike, to find, to discover [underground streams] || to shed light on (un asunto) || to enlighten (enseñar) || FIG & FAM to beat (golpear) || TECN to treat with alum, to aluminate.
◆ *vi* to give birth (parir) || to give light, to give off a light; *la lámpara alumbra bien* the lamp gives off a good light || to give light; *alumbra aquí para que vea bien* give me some light here so that I can see properly || to shine (brillar).
◆ *vpr* FAM to get tipsy *o* merry.

alumbre *m* alum.

alúmina *f* QUÍM alumina.

aluminar *vt* TECN to treat with alumina, to aluminate.

aluminio *m* aluminium [*US* aluminum].

aluminoso, sa *adj* aluminous.

aluminotermia *f* aluminothermy.

alumnado *m* pupils *pl* (de colegio) || student body (de universidad).

alumno, na *m/f* pupil; *un alumno modelo* a model pupil || student (en la universidad) || — *alumno externo* day pupil || *alumno interno* boarder || *antiguo alumno* old boy (chico), old girl (chica), former pupil.

alunado, da *adj* whimsical, capricious (lunático) || mad, insane (loco).

alunarado, da *adj* spotted, mottled (res).

alunarse *vpr* to spoil, to go off (la carne) || to fester (las heridas).

alunita *f* alunite (mineral).

alunizaje *m* landing on the moon, moon landing.

alunizar *vi* to land on the moon.

alusión *f* allusion (referencia) || mention, reference.

alusivo, va *adj* allusive (*a* to).

aluvial *adj* alluvial.

aluvión *m* flood (inundación) || alluvium, alluvion (depósito) || FIG flood (gran cantidad) || — *terrenos de aluvión* alluvial land, alluvium || FAM *un aluvión de improperios* a shower of insults, a torrent of abuse.

alveario *m* external auditory duct.

álveo *m* bed (madre de un río).

alveolado, da *adj* honeycombed, alveolate.

alveolar *adj* alveolar.

alveolo; alvéolo *m* ANAT alveolus || cell (de panal) || *alveolos pulmonares* alveoli, air cells of the lungs.

alverja; alverjana *f* ⟶ **arveja.**

alverjilla; alverjita *f* AMER sweet pea (guisante de olor).

alza *f* rise; *el alza de los precios* the rise in prices || back sight, sight (de un arma de fuego) || IMPR underlay || sluice gate (de presa) || extension (para suplir falta de altura) || — COM *en alza* rising (precios) || FAM *estar en alza* to be coming up, to be rising [in popularity, etc.] || COM *jugar al alza* to speculate on a rising market, to bull the market (en la Bolsa) || FAM *un joven autor en alza* an up-and-coming writer.

alzacuello *m* bands *pl*, collar (corbatín de eclesiástico).

alzada *f* height at the withers (de los caballos) || summer pasture (pasto) || JUR appeal (apelación) || *caballo de mucha, de poca alzada* horse long in the leg, short in the leg.

alzado, da *adj* fraudulently bankrupt || fixed (precio) || AMER wild, runaway (montaraz) || in rut, on heat (en celo) || insolent (insolente) || rebellious (rebelde) || — *a tanto alzado* by the job (trabajar), in a lump sum (pagar) || *precio a tanto alzado* fixed price.
◆ *m* ARQ elevation (proyección) || IMPR gathering || *máquina de alzado* gatherer.

alzador *m* IMPR gathering room (taller) || gatherer (obrero).

alzamiento *m* raising, lifting (levantamiento) || uprising; *un alzamiento popular* a popular uprising || increase, rise (de precios) || higher bid (puja) || IMPR gathering || COM *alzamiento de bienes* fraudulent bankruptcy.

alzapaño *m* curtain holder (para cortinas).

alzaprima *f* crowbar, lever (palanca) || wedge (calce) || AMER timber cart (para transportar árboles) || MÚS bridge.

alzaprimar *vt* to lever up (con una palanca).

alzar *vt* to raise, to lift (up); *alzar la mano* to raise one's hand || to raise (la voz, los precios) || to make higher (pared, etc.) || to turn up (el cuello de un abrigo) || to remove, to take off (quitar) || to draw up, to make out; *alzar un plano* to draw up a plan || to raise, to put up (la caza) || FIG to lift (un castigo, el embargo, etc.) || AGR to gather, to bring in; *alzar la cosecha* to bring in the harvest | to plough for the first time (arar) || REL to elevate (la hostia) || IMPR to gather || to cut (una baraja) || — *¡alza!* bravo! || *alzar con una cosa* to carry off *o* to lift sth. || *alzar el vuelo* to take off (empezar a volar), to clear off, to beat it (*fam*) (irse) || *alzar los ojos* to look up || *alzar velas* to hoist sail.
◆ *vpr* to get up, to rise (levantarse) || to stand out (sobresalir) || to run off with, to carry off, to lift (*fam*); *alzarse con los fondos* to run off with the funds || FIG to rise; *el ejército se ha alzado contra el gobierno* the army has risen against the government | to rebel; *alzarse contra el orden establecido* to rebel against the established order || to leave the table when one is in pocket (en el juego) || COM to go bankrupt fraudulently (quebrar) || JUR to lodge an appeal || AMER to go back to the wild, to run away (un animal) || — *alzarse con la victoria* to carry off the victory || *se alzó con el santo y la limosna* he cleared off with everything.

allá *adv* over there, there (lugar) || long ago, back (tiempo); *allá en mis mocedades* long ago in my youth || — *allá abajo* down there || *allá arriba* up there (arriba), in Heaven, above (en el Cielo) || *allá cada uno* that is for each one to decide || *allá él* it's his business, it's his affair, that's his funeral || *allá en esos tiempos* back in those days || *allá en mis tiempos* in my day || *allá por el año 1980* around about 1980 || *allá se las componga* let him get on with it || *allá se va* there's not much difference, it's more or less the same thing || *allá usted* that's your lookout, it's up to you || *allá voy* I'm coming || *de Madrid para allá* from Madrid onwards *o* on || *el más allá* the beyond || *más allá* further on || *no más allá de* not any more than, not beyond || *no ser muy allá* not to be up to much, not to be very good (no ser muy bueno) || *no tan allá* not so far (away) || *vamos allá* let's go.
— OBSERV *Allá* (which is less precise than *allí*) can be modified to express certain degrees of comparison: *tan allá* so far; *no tan allá* not so far; *más allá* further away *o* on; *muy allá* a long way away. When *allá* is followed by an adverbial phrase of time or place, it is, in many cases, not translated: *allá en América* in America.

allanador, ra *adj* which levels, levelling.
◆ *m/f* leveller || JUR burglar, housebreaker (de morada).

allanamiento *m* levelling, smoothing, flattening (acción de poner llano) || FIG smoothing-out; *el allanamiento de las dificultades* the smoothing-out of difficulties || JUR submission [to a legal decision] || JUR *allanamiento de morada* housebreaking, breaking and entering.

allanar *vt* to level (out), to flatten (out), to smooth (out); *allanar el suelo* to level the ground || FIG to smooth out, to overcome, to iron out (una dificultad) || JUR to break into, to burgle (una casa) || FIG *allanar el terreno* to clear the way.
◆ *vpr* to collapse (derrumbarse) || to level out (nivelarse) || to submit, to give in (darse por vencido) || to agree, to comply, to submit (conformarse); *éste se allana a todo* he agrees to *o* he complies with everything.

allegado, da *adj* close; *la gente allegada al Presidente* those close to the President || supporting (partidario).
◆ *m/f* (close) relation, relative (pariente) || supporter, follower (partidario) || close friend (a una casa, etc.).
◆ *m pl* entourage *sing*, suite *sing*; *los allegados al rey* the king's entourage || *los allegados al Ministro* those closest to the Minister.

allegador, ra *adj* gathering, collecting.
◆ *m* rake (rastro) || poker (hurgón).

allegamiento *m* collection, gathering together, raising (de fondos).

allegar *vt* to collect, to raise (recoger); *allegar fondos* to raise money *o* funds || to bring closer, to bring near (acercar) || AGR to pile up (la parva trillada) || to add (añadir).
◆ *vi* to arrive (llegar).
◆ *vpr* to approach, to come near (acercarse) || to conform (conformarse).

allegretto *adv/s m* MÚS allegretto.

allegro *adv/s m* MÚS allegro.

allende *adv* beyond; *allende el estrecho de Gibraltar está África* beyond the straits of Gibraltar lies África || besides (además) || *allende los mares* overseas, beyond the seas.

allí *adv* there; *voy allí todos los días* I go there every day; *allí arriba* up there || then (entonces) || — *allí dentro* in there || *allí donde* wherever || *allí están* there they are || *aquí y allí* here and there || *hasta allí* as far as that || *por allí* over there, that way.

ama *f* lady of the house (señora de la casa) || owner (dueña) || mistress (para los criados) || housekeeper (de un soltero, de un clérigo) || wet nurse (ama de leche) || — AMER *ama de brazos* nursemaid || *ama de casa* housewife || *ama de cría* or *de leche* wet nurse || *ama de gobierno, ama de llaves* housekeeper || *ama seca* dry nurse.

amabilidad *f* kindness; *le estoy agradecido por su amabilidad* I am grateful for your kindness || amiability, affability || — *es de una gran amabilidad* he is an extremely nice person || *tenga la amabilidad de pasar* would you be so kind as to come in || *tuvo la amabilidad de traerme un regalo* he was kind enough to bring me a present.

amabilísimo, ma *adj* very kind (servicial) || very nice *o* friendly (afable).

amable *adj* kind, nice, pleasant, amiable (afable); *es un profesor muy amable* he is a very nice teacher; *el ministro ha sido muy amable conmigo* the minister has been very kind to me || — *amable con* or *para con todos* kind to everybody || *es amable de carácter* he has a pleasant character || *ha sido usted muy amable viniendo* it was very kind *o* good of you to come || *¿sería usted tan amable de...?* would you be so kind as to...?

amachetar; amachetear *vt* to hack with a machete.

amadamado, da *adj* effeminate (amanerado).

Amadeo *npr m* Amadeus.

amado, da *adj* dear, beloved.
◆ *m/f* dear one, sweetheart.

amadrigarse *vpr* to go to ground (en la madriguera).

amadrinamiento *m* yoking in pairs (de caballos) || FIG sponsorship (apadrinamiento).

amadrinar *vt* to yoke together (dos caballos) || FIG to sponsor (apadrinar).

amaestrado, da *adj* trained (animal) || performing; *pulga amaestrada* performing flea.

amaestrador, ra *adj* who trains, training.
◆ *m/f* trainer.

amaestramiento *m* training.

amaestrar *vt* to train.

amagar *vi* to promise to be; *amaga un día hermoso* it promises to be a fine day || to threaten; *amaga una tempestad* a storm is threatening; *está amagando con golpearle* he is threatening to hit him || to appear the first signs; *amagó una epidemia de cólera en la ciudad* the first signs of a cholera epidemic appeared in the town || DEP to feint (boxeo, esgrima) || — *amaga (con) llover* it looks like rain || *amagar una sonrisa* to smile weakly || *amagar y no dar* to make a threat and not carry it out.
◆ *vpr* FAM to hide (esconderse).

amago *m* threat (amenaza) || sign (señal) || MED symptom, sign (de una enfermedad) || DEP feint (finta) || beginning (comienzo) || attempt; *sólo hemos oído hablar de amagos de industrialización* we have only heard talk about attempts at industrialization || *hizo un amago de sacar su pistola* he made a move to draw his revolver.

amainar *vt* MAR to lower, to take in (las velas) || FIG to moderate, to calm.
◆ *vi/vpr* to die down; *amaina el temporal* the storm is dying down || to drop, to die down; *el viento amaina* the wind is dropping || FIG to moderate; *amainar en sus pretensiones* to moderate one's claims | to calm down (los ánimos).

amaine *m* MAR lowering, taking in [of the sails] || dying-down (del viento, etc.) || FIG moderation | calming down (de la furia, etc.).

amajadar *vt* AGR to pen, to put in the fold (rebaños).
◆ *vi* to return to the fold.

amalgama *f* QUÍM amalgam || FIG amalgam, combination.

amalgamiento *m* QUÍM amalgamation || FIG amalgamation, amalgam, combination.

amalgamar *vt* QUÍM to amalgamate || FIG to amalgamate, to combine.
◆ *vpr* QUÍM to amalgamate || FIG to amalgamate, to combine.

amamantamiento *m* suckling, breast-feeding.

amamantar *vt* to suckle, to breast-feed.

amán *m* pardon (amnistía).

amancebamiento *m* living together, cohabitation, living in sin (ant).

amancebarse *vpr* to live together, to cohabit, to live in sin (ant).

amanecer* *v impers* to dawn, to break [day *o* dawn]; *amanece tarde en invierno* day breaks late in winter, it dawns late in winter || *amaneciendo* at dawn, at daybreak.
◆ *vi* to be at dawn *o* daybreak; *amanecimos en París* we were in Paris at dawn; *el jardín*

amaneció cubierto de nieve at dawn the garden was covered in snow ‖ to arrive at dawn *o* at daybreak (llegar) ‖ to wake up [in the morning]; *ayer amanecí con mucha fiebre* yesterday I woke up with a high temperature ‖ to appear, to begin to show ‖ *el día amaneció nublado* the sky was cloudy at dawn.

amanecer *m*; **amanecida** *f* dawn, daybreak; *al amanecer* at daybreak, at dawn.

amanerado, da *adj* affected, mannered; *una persona amanerada* an affected person.

amaneramiento *m* affectation.

amanerarse *vpr* to become affected *o* mannered, to adopt an affected style.

amanita *f* BOT amanita (hongo).

amanojar *vt* to gather into bundles.

amansador, ra *m/f* horsebreaker (de caballos) ‖ tamer (de fieras).

amansamiento *m* breaking (de caballos) ‖ taming (de fieras).

amansar *vt* to break in; *amansar un caballo* to break in a horse ‖ to tame; *amansar una fiera* to tame a wild animal ‖ FIG to case (dolor, pena) | to calm (tranquilizar) | to tame (el carácter).
◆ *vpr* to tame o.s. ‖ to calm down (los ánimos).

amante *adj* fond; *amante de la buena mesa* fond of good food; *amante de la belleza* fond of beauty.
◆ *m/f* lover; *un amante de la gloria* a lover of glory; *Romeo y Julieta eran amantes* Romeo and Juliette were lovers.
◆ *m* lover (querido) ‖ MAR runner.
◆ *f* mistress, lover (querida).

amantillo *m* MAR topping lift.

amanuense *m* scribe, clerk (escribiente) ‖ copyist (copista).

amanzanar *vt* AMER to parcel out [a piece of ground].

amañado, da *adj* skilful [US skillful] (hábil) ‖ fake (falso) ‖ rigged, fixed (elecciones).

amañar *vt* to fix, to arrange ‖ to fix, to rig (las elecciones) ‖ to alter (falsificar) ‖ to fake (una foto, un documento) ‖ to cook (cuentas).
◆ *vpr* to arrange things, to fix things; *siempre te las amañas para conseguir lo que quieres* you always arrange things to get what you want ‖ to be skilful (ser habilidoso).

amaño *m* skill, cleverness (maña) ‖ scheme, trick, ruse (ardid, arreglo).
◆ *pl* tools (herramientas, aperos).

amapola *f* BOT poppy ‖ *ponerse rojo como una amapola* to turn as red as a beetroot.

amar *vt* to love; *amar al prójimo* to love one's neighbour; *amar con locura* to love madly.
— OBSERV *To love* is usually expressed in Spanish by *querer*. *Amar* is more poetic and tends to define more abstract or lofty sentiments to love one's country, etc.). It never means *to find pleasing*: *I love apples* me encantan las manzanas.

amaraje *m* landing [on the sea] (de un hidroavión) ‖ splashdown (de astronave).

amaranto *m* BOT amaranth.

amarar *vi* to land [on the sea] (un hidroavión) ‖ to splash down (astronave).

amargado, da *adj* FIG embittered, bitter; *amargado por su fracaso* embittered by his failure, bitter from his failure.
◆ *m/f* bitter *o* embittered person, person with a grudge.

amargar *vi* to be bitter, to taste bitter; *esta fruta amarga* this fruit is bitter.
◆ *vt* to make bitter (dar sabor amargo) ‖ FIG to grieve (afligir) | to make bitter, to embitter; *los reveses de la fortuna le han amargado* reverses of fortune have made him bitter | to get down; *me amarga la vida* life is getting me down ‖ — *amargarle la vida a alguien* to make s.o.'s life a misery ‖ *a nadie le amarga un dulce* a gift is always welcome.
◆ *vpr* to become bitter (una cosa) ‖ FIG to become bitter, to become embittered (una persona).

amargo, ga *adj* bitter; *almendra amarga* bitter almond ‖ FIG bitter; *un recuerdo amargo* a bitter memory | bitter, embittered (persona, carácter).
◆ *m* bitterness (sabor amargo) ‖ bitters *pl* (licor) ‖ AMER bitter maté.

amargón *m* BOT dandelion.

amargor *m* bitterness.

amargoso, sa *adj* AMER bitter (amargo).

amargura *f* bitterness (sabor) ‖ FIG bitterness; *sus fracasos le han llenado de amargura* his failures have filled him with bitterness | grief (pena) ‖ — *¡qué amargura!* what a pity! ‖ FIG *traer* or *llevar a uno por la calle de la amargura* to give s.o. a hard time.

amariconado, da *adj* FAM queer, effeminate.

amarilis *f* BOT amaryllis.

amarillar; amarillear; amarillecer* *vi* to go yellow, to yellow; *en otoño las hojas amarillean* the leaves go yellow in autumn ‖ to be yellowish (tirar a amarillo).

amarillento, ta *adj* yellowish ‖ sallow, yellowish; *tener la tez amarillenta* to have a sallow complexion.

amarilleo *m* yellowing.

amarillo, lla *adj* yellow; *raza amarilla* yellow race ‖ — *amarillo como la cera* as yellow as a guinea ‖ MED *fiebre amarilla* yellow fever ‖ *ponerse amarillo* to turn yellow.
◆ *m* yellow (color); *amarillo claro* light yellow.

Amarillo *adj m* GEOGR *mar Amarillo, río Amarillo* Yellow Sea, Yellow River.

amarilloso, sa *adj* AMER yellowish (amarillento).

amariposado, da *adj* BOT papilionaceous, butterfly-like.

amaro *m* BOT clary, clary sage (planta).

amaromar *vt* to moor, to tie up (atar).

amarra *f* MAR mooring rope *o* line (cabo) ‖ martingale (de un arnés).
◆ *pl* FIG & FAM connections; *tener buenas amarras* to have good connections ‖ — MAR *largar amarras* to set sail, to cast off ‖ *soltar las amarras* to let go, to cast off (un barco), to break loose (quedar libre).

amarradero *m* MAR bollard (poste) | mooring ring (argolla) | mooring, berth (sitio donde se amarran los barcos).

amarrado, da *adj* FIG tied down (sujeto).

amarradura *f* mooring.

amarraje *m* MAR mooring charge (impuesto).

amarrar *vt* MAR to make fast, to tie up, to moor (un barco) ‖ to tie, to fasten; *amarra tus zapatos* fasten your shoes ‖ to tie up; *amarrar un paquete* to tie up a parcel ‖ to tie, to bind; *le amarraron a una silla* they tied him to a chair ‖ to stack (las cartas al barajarlas) ‖ — FIG *jugar muy amarrado* to play safe (en el póker) | *lo lleva bien amarrado* he knows it back to front (un alumno).
◆ *vi* FAM to study hard, to swot (empollar).
◆ *vpr* to fasten, to tie (los zapatos) ‖ AMER POP *amarrársela* to get sozzled *o* sloshed, to get drunk.

amarre *m* stacking (al barajar las cartas) ‖ MAR mooring.

amarrete *adj* AMER stingy, tight (tacaño).
◆ *m/f* AMER stingy person.

amartelado, da *adj* in love, infatuated; *están muy amartelados* they are very much in love, they are completely infatuated with each other.

amarteladamente *adv* madly, passionately.

amartelamiento *m* infatuation, passionate love ‖ *ya no está en edad de amartelamientos* he is past it, a man of his age doesn't go falling head over heels in love.

amartelar *vt* to make jealous (dar celos) ‖ to make fall in love (enamorar).
◆ *vpr* to fall madly in love (enamorarse).

amartillar *vt* to hammer (golpear) ‖ to cock (un arma de fuego).

amasadera *f* kneading trough.

amasadero *m* kneading room.

amasador, ra *adj* kneading ‖ MED massaging (masajista).
◆ *m/f* kneader.
◆ *m* MED masseur.
◆ *f* MED masseuse ‖ kneading machine (máquina).

amasadura *f* → **amasamiento.**

amasamiento *m* kneading (del pan) ‖ MED massage (masaje) ‖ mixing (de yeso, mortero, etc.).

amasar *vt* to knead (el pan) ‖ TECN to mix (yeso, mortero) ‖ MED to massage (dar masajes) ‖ FIG to amass; *amasar una fortuna* to amass a fortune ‖ FIG & FAM to cook up (tramar); *están amasando algo* they're cooking sth. up.

amasia *f* AMER lover (querida, amante).

amasiato *m* AMER pickup, one-right stand (ligue).

amasijo *m* dough (masa de harina) ‖ kneading (amasamiento) ‖ mixture (de yeso, cal, etc.) ‖ FIG & FAM jumble, hotchpotch, mixture (mezcolanza); *este libro es un amasijo de tópicos* this book is a jumble of clichés.

amateur *adj/s* amateur.

amatista *adj/sf* MIN amethyst.

amatorio, ria *adj* love; *cartas amatorias* love letters.

amaurosis *f* MED amaurosis (ceguera).

amauta *m* AMER Indian sage (sabio).

amazacotado, da *adj* hard (un colchón, etc.) ‖ FIG clumsy, heavy, stodgy (estilo); *autor con un estilo amazacotado* author with a heavy style | stodgy; *un arroz con leche amazacotado* stodgy rice pudding | crammed; *libro amazacotado de fechas* book crammed with dates | over-ornate; *una fachada amazacotada* an over-ornate façade.

amazona *f* Amazon (mujer guerrera) ‖ FIG Amazon, mannish woman (mujer varonil) ‖ horsewoman (mujer que monta a caballo) ‖ FIG lady's riding habit (traje) ‖ *montar en amazona* or *a la amazona* to ride sidesaddle.

Amazonas *npr m* GEOGR Amazon.

amazónico, ca *adj* Amazonian, Amazon.

ambages *m pl* FIG circumlocution *sing*, ambages ‖ — *andarse con ambages* to beat around the bush ‖ *hablar sin ambages* to speak frankly, to get straight to the point, to speak in plain language.

ámbar *m* amber ‖ — *ámbar gris* or *pardillo* ambergris ‖ *ámbar negro* jet (azabache) ‖ *de ámbar* perfumed with ambergris (perfumado).

ambarino, na *adj* amber.

Amberes *n pr* GEOGR Antwerp.

amberino, na *adj* [of *o* from] Antwerp.
◆ *m/f* inhabitant *o* native of Antwerp.

ambición *f* ambition.

ambicionar *vt* to strive after, to seek, to want; *ambiciona el poder* he is striving after power ‖ to want; *ambiciona que su hijo se haga profesor de inglés* he wants his son to become an English teacher ‖ *ambicionar hacer algo* to have an ambition to do sth.

ambicioso, sa *adj* ambitious ‖ self-seeking (egoísta).
◆ *m/f* ambitious person.

ambidextro, tra *adj* ambidextrous.
◆ *m/f* ambidextrous person.

ambientación *f* atmosphere (ambiente) ‖ setting (marco) ‖ RAD sound effects *pl* ‖ *ruido de ambientación* background noises *pl*.

ambiental *adj* environmental.

ambientar *vt* to give atmosphere to; *ambientar una exposición* to give atmosphere to an exhibition ‖ to bring to life (dar vida) ‖ to set; *la obra está ambientada en una cárcel* the play is set in prison ‖ *un cuadro bien ambientado* a painting with a lot of atmosphere.
◆ *vpr* to adapt o.s.; *se ambienta rápidamente en todos los países* he adapts himself quickly to every country.

ambiente *adj* ambient; *la temperatura ambiente* the ambient temperature ‖ *medio ambiente* environment.
◆ *m* atmosphere; *ambiente cargado de humo* smoky atmosphere ‖ environment (medio ambiente); *contaminación del ambiente* pollution of the environment ‖ FIG environment, milieu (medio); *un ambiente intelectual* an intellectual environment | atmosphere; *un ambiente optimista* an optimistic atmosphere; *no hay ambiente para trabajar* the atmosphere is not conducive to work; *no entres en esa sala de fiestas, que no hay ambiente* don't go into that nightclub, there is no atmosphere ‖ AMER room (habitación) ‖ — *ambiente rural* country atmosphere ‖ *cambiar de ambiente* to change one's surroundings ‖ *dar ambiente a* to give atmosphere to.

ambigú *m* buffet (comida, lugar donde se sirve).

ambiguamente *adv* ambiguously.

ambigüedad *f* ambiguity.

ambiguo, gua *adj* ambiguous; *una contestación ambigua* an ambiduous answer ‖ effeminate (afeminado) ‖ GRAM of either gender.

ámbito *m* environment, atmosphere (ambiente) ‖ scope, compass; *en el ámbito de la ley* within the scope of the law ‖ field, world, sphere; *en el ámbito artístico* in the field of art ‖ enclosure (recinto) ‖ expanse (extensión) ‖ MÚS compass ‖ — *empresa constructora de ámbito nacional* nationwide building firm ‖ *en el ámbito nacional* throughout the whole country.

ambivalencia *f* ambivalence.

ambivalente *adj* ambivalent.

amblador, ra pacing, ambling (caballo).

amblar *vi* to amble, to pace.

ambliopía *f* MED amblyopia.

ambón *m* ambo (púlpito).

ambos, bas *adj* both; *llegaron ambos hermanos* both brothers came ‖ — *de ambas partes* on both sides ‖ *por ambos lados* from both sides.
◆ *pron pl* both ‖ *ambos vinieron* they both came, both of them came.
— OBSERV This word is used when referring to people or things which usually go in pairs: *con ambas manos* with both hands.

ambrosía *f* ambrosia.

ambrosiaco, ca *adj* ambrosial; *perfume ambrosiaco* ambrosial perfume.

ambrosiano, na *adj* ambrosian; *rito, canto ambrosiano* ambrosian rite, chant.

Ambrosio *npr m* Ambrose.

ambulancia *f* ambulance ‖ field ambulance, field hospital (hospital móvil) ‖ *ambulancia de correos* travelling post office.

ambulanciero, ra *m/f* ambulance man, ambulance woman.

ambulante *adj* travelling; *circo ambulante* travelling circus ‖ strolling, itinerant; *actor ambulante* strolling player; *trovador ambulante* strolling troubador ‖ walking (que anda) ‖ — *biblioteca ambulante* mobile library ‖ *vendedor ambulante* pedlar, street salesman, hawker (en la calle), travelling salesman (representante).
◆ *m ambulante de correos* travelling post office worker (en los trenes).

ambulatorio, ria *adj* ambulatory.
◆ *m* national health clinic.

ameba *f* ZOOL amoeba, ameba.

amedrentador, ra *adj* terrifying, frightening.

amedrentamiento *m* fright, terror.

amedrentar *vt* to scare, to frighten, to terrify, to intimidate; *no amedrento a nadie* I don't frighten anyone ‖ to terrify, to frighten; *los gritos amedrentaron a los vecinos* the shouting terrified the neighbours.
◆ *vpr* to be frightened, to be scared, to be terrified; *se amedrenta por cualquier cosa* he is frightened by the slightest thing ‖ to become nervous *o* intimidated; *se amedrentaba ante el profesor* he became nervous in front of the teacher.

amelar *vi* to make honey (las abejas).

amelcochar *vt* AMER to thicken (un dulce).

amelga *f* AGR land (sembrado).

amelgado, da *adj* unevenly sown (el trigo).

amelgar *vt* AGR to furrow (surcar).

amelocotonado, da *adj* peachlike.

amelonado, da *adj* melon-shaped.

amén *m inv* amen ‖ — FAM *decir amén a todo* to agree with everything, to be a yes-man | *en un decir amén, en un amén* in the twinkling of an eye, before you can say Jack Robinson.
◆ *interj* amen; *líbranos del mal, amén* deliver us from evil, amen.
◆ *prep* FAM *amén de* except for (excepto), besides; *amén de lo dicho* besides what has been said.

amenaza *f* threat, menace; *amenazas vanas* vain threats.

amenazador, ra; amenazante *adj* threatening, menacing; *mirada amenazadora* menacing look.

amenazar *vt* to threaten, to menace; *amenazar a uno con una pistola* to threaten s.o. with a revolver; *nos amenaza una gran catástrofe* we are menaced by a terrible catastrophe ‖ to threaten; *la casa amenaza derribarse* or *amenaza ruina* the house is threatening to fall down *o* into ruins ‖ FIG to threaten, to be imminent (estar inminente); *amenaza nieve* it is threatening to snow, snow is imminent ‖ *amenazar a alguien de muerte* to threaten to kill s.o.

amenguar *vt* to lessen ‖ FIG to defame, to denigrate (deshonrar).

amenidad *f* pleasantness, agreeableness, amenity.

amenizar *vt* to brighten up, to liven up; *amenizar la conversación* to brighten up the conversation; *amenizar la fiesta* to liven up the party ‖ to make more interesting *o* more entertaining; *amenizar un discurso con citas* to make a speech more interesting by addings quotations ‖ to make pleasanter, to make more agreeable; *un poco de música de fondo para amenizar la comida* a little background music to make the meal pleasanter.

ameno, na *adj* pleasant, nice, agreeable (agradable) ‖ charming; *es un hombre muy ameno, siempre tiene algo gracioso que contar* he is a very charming man, he always has sth. amusing to say.

amenorrea *f* MED amenorrhoea.

amentáceo, a; amentífero, ra *adj* BOT amentaceous, amentiferous.

amento *m* BOT ament, catkin.

amerengado, da *adj* meringue-like ‖ FIG sugary (remilgado).

América *npr f* GEOGR America; *América del Norte, Central, del Sur* North, Central, South America ‖ Latin America (Iberoamérica).
— OBSERV On its own, the Spanish word *América* often refers solely to Latin America, although it can also mean the United States.
— OBSERV En inglés, la palabra *America*, empleada a solas, se refiere normalmente a los Estados Unidos.

americana *f* jacket, coat; *una americana cruzada* a double-breasted jacket; *su americana no es del mismo color que su pantalón* his coat isn't the same colour as his trousers ‖ American phaeton (faetón).

americanismo *m* Americanism.

americanista *m/f* Americanist.

americanización *f* Americanization.

americanizar *vt* to Americanize.
◆ *vpr* to become Americanized.

americano, na *adj/s* American (del continente) ‖ Latin American (de Iberoamérica) ‖ American (de EE.UU.).
— OBSERV Traditionally the adjective *americano* refers to a person or a thing from Latin America, but owing to the modern influence of the United States of America it is often the equivalent of *estadounidense* or *norteamericano*.
— OBSERV En inglés *American*, sin otra indicación, significa normalmente *estadounidense*.

americio *m* QUÍM americium (metal).

amerindio, dia *adj* Amerindian.
◆ *m/f* Amerind.

ameritar *vt* AMER to deserve (merecer).

amerizaje *m* landing [on the sea] ‖ splashdown (de astronave).

amerizar *vi* to land [on the sea] (amarar) ‖ to splash down (un astronave).

amestizado, da *adj* like a half-breed.

ametrallador, ra *adj* *fusil ametrallador* automatic rifle.
◆ *m* machine gunner.
◆ *f* machine gun.

ametrallar *vt* to machine-gun.

ametropía *f* MED ametropia.

amianto *m* MIN amianthus, asbestos.

amiba *f* ZOOL amoeba, ameba.

amida *f* QUÍM amide.

amidol *m* QUÍM amidol.

amiga *f* friend ‖ mistress (amante) ‖ girlfriend, sweetheart (de un joven) ‖ schoolmistresss (maestra) ‖ girls' school (escuela).

amigable *adj* friendly, amicable; *contrato amigable* friendly contract ‖ *amigable componedor* arbitrator.

amigablemente *adv* amicably, in a friendly way.

amigacho, cha *m/f* FAM pal, mate.

amigar *vt* to make friends (hacer amigos).
◆ *vpr* to live together ‖ to make friends.

amígdala *f* ANAT tonsil, amygdala ‖ *ser operado de amígdalas* to have one's tonsils out.

amigdalectomía *f* MED tonsillectomy.

amigdalitis *f* MED tonsillitis.

amigo, ga *adj* friendly; *una voz amiga* a friendly voice || fond, given; *es más amigo de salir que de quedarse en casa* he is more fond of *o* given to going out than staying in || fond; *ser amigo de las cosas buenas* to be fond of good things.
◆ *m/f* friend; *amigo de siempre* or *de toda la vida* lifelong friend; *es un amigo mío* he is a friend of mine; *amigo íntimo* close friend || supporter (partidario) || lover (amante).
◆ *m* boyfriend, sweetheart (novio) || — FAM *amigo del asa* close *o* intimate friend || *amigo de la casa* friend of the family || *amigo de lo ajeno* thief || *bueno es tener amigos hasta en el infierno* it's worth having friends anywhere || *como amigos* like friends, as friends || *en el peligro se conoce al amigo* a friend in need is a friend indeed || *es muy amigo mío* he is a very good friend of mine || *ganar amigos* to make friends || *hacerse amigo de* to make friends with || *hacerse amigos* to become friends || *poner cara de pocos amigos* to pull a long face || *seguir siendo amigo de* to keep friends with || *son muy amigos* they are very good friends || *soy amigo de decir las cosas claramente* I'm one for *o* I'm all for *o* I'm in favour of saying things frankly || *tener cara de pocos amigos* to look unfriendly, to have an unfriendly face.
◆ *f* ⟶ **amiga.**
◆ *interj ¡amigo, qué alegre vienes hoy!* I say, you're happy today! || *¡pero no es lo mismo, amigo!* but it's not the same thing, old boy! || *vaya en paz, amigo* go in peace, my friend.

amigote *m* FAM mate, chum, friend [US buddy].

amiláceo, a *adj* QUÍM starchy, amylaceous.

amilanamiento *m* fear (miedo) || discouragement (desánimo).

amilanar *vt* to frighten, to terrify, to intimidate (asustar) || FIG to discourage (desanimar).
◆ *vpr* to be frightened, to get frightened (acobardarse) || to be discouraged (desanimarse).

amilasa *f* BIOL amylase.

amileno *m* QUÍM amylene.

amílico, ca *adj* QUÍM amyl, amylic; *alcohol amílico* amyl alcohol.

amilo *m* QUÍM amyl.

amiloide *adj* BIOL amyloid.

amiloide *adj* BIOL amyloid.

amilosis *f* MED amyloidosis.

amillaramiento *m* cadastre, tax assessment.

amillarar *vt* to register in the cadastre.

amina *f* QUÍM amine.

aminado, da *adj* QUÍM amino.

aminoácido *m* QUÍM amino acid.

aminoración *f* lessening, decrease; *una aminoración de los intercambios comerciales* a decrease in trade || reduction, cut; *la aminoración de los precios* the reduction of prices, the cut in prices || slackening; *la aminoración del ritmo de los negocios* the slackening of business || *aminoración de la velocidad* decrease in speed, slowing down.

aminorar *vt* to reduce, to decrease, to cut, to lessen || — *aminorar el paso* to slow down, to walk more slowly || *aminorar la velocidad* to slow down.

amiotrofia *f* MED amyotrophia.

amistad *f* friendship; *granjearse la amistad de alguien* to win s.o.'s friendship || — *contraer* or *trabar amistad con alguien* to make friends with s.o.
◆ *pl* friends; *tener amistades poco recomendables* to have rather undesirable friends || — *estar en buenas amistades* to be on friendly terms || *hacer las amistades* to make it up || *romper las amistades* to fall out, to break up.

amistar *vt* to make friends, to bring together || to make it up between, to reconcile (reconciliar).
◆ *vpr* to become friends || to make it up (reconciliarse).

amistosamente *adv* amicably, in a friendly way.

amistoso, sa *adj* friendly, amicable; *un consejo amistoso* a friendly piece of advice.

amito *m* amice (paño sacerdotal).

amnesia *f* MED amnesia.

amnésico, ca *adj* amnesic.
◆ *m/f* amnesiac.

amnios *f* ANAT amnion.

amniótico, ca *adj* ANAT amniotic.

amnistía *f* amnesty || ECON *amnistía fiscal* fiscal amnesty.

amnistiar *vt* to amnesty, to grant an amnesty to.

amo *m* master; *el amo del perro* the dog's master || master, head of the family (cabeza de familia) || landlord (propietario de una casa) || owner (de una finca, coche, etc.) || employer, boss (de un taller) || — *el ojo del amo engorda al caballo* it is the master's eye that makes the mill go || AMER *Nuestro Amo* the Blessed Sacrament || FIG *perro de muchos amos* Jack of all trades || FIG & FAM *ser el amo del cotarro* to be the boss, to rule the roost.

amodita *f* ZOOL cerastes, horned viper (víbora) | ammodyte (pez).

amodorrado, da *adj* drowsy, sleepy, dozy.

amodorramiento *m* drowsiness, sleepiness, doziness.

amodorrarse *vpr* to get drowsy *o* sleepy, to doze.

amohinar *vt* to annoy, to irritate, to vex.
◆ *vpr* to get annoyed, to sulk.

amojamado, da *adj* wizened, dried up (flaco).

amojamar *vt* to dy and salt [tuna].
◆ *vpr* to become wizened (apergaminarse).

amojonamiento *m* marking out.

amojonar *vt* to mark out, to mark the boundaries of; *amojonar un campo* to mark out a field.

amoladera *adj f piedra amoladera* whetstone, grindstone.
◆ *f* grindstone (rueda) || grindstone, whetstone (piedra).

amolador *m* grinder || FIG & FAM nuisance (latoso).

amoladura *f* grinding, sharpening.
◆ *pl* grinding dust *sing* (arenilla).

amolar* *vt* to sharpen, to grind (un cuchillo, etc.) || FIG & FAM to annoy, to pester, to get on s.o.'s nerves (fastidiar).

amoldamiento *m* fitting, adapting, adjusting (ajuste) || FIG adaptation; *amoldamiento a* adaptation to.

amoldar *vt* to mould || to fit; *amoldar un zapato a la forma del pie* to fit a shoe to the shape of the foot || FIG to mould, to shape; *amoldar su conducta a los principios cristianos* to mould one's conduct according to Christian principles.
◆ *vpr* to adapt (o.s.), to adjust (o.s.); *amoldarse a las costumbres locales* to adapt o.s. to the local customs; *amoldarse a las circunstancias* to adapt o.s. to the circumstances.

amondongado, da *adj* flabby (rechoncho).

amonedar *vt* to coin, to mint.

amonestación *f* reprimand, admonition, rebuke (reprensión) || warning (advertencia) || bann (anuncio de bodas); *correr las amonestaciones* to publish the banns.

amonestador, ra *adj* reprimanding (reprensivo) || warning; *en tono amonestador* in a warning tone.

amonestar *vt* to reprimand, to admonish (reprender) || to warn (advertir) || to publish the banns of (anunciar la boda).

amoniacal *adj* QUÍM ammoniacal.

amoniaco, ca; amoníaco, ca *adj* QUÍM ammoniac; *sal amoniaca* sal ammoniac.
◆ *m* QUÍM ammonia || gum ammoniac (goma).

amonio *m* QUÍM ammonium.

amonita *f* ZOOL ammonite (fósil).

amontillado, da *adj* «amontillado».
◆ *m* «amontillado», pale dry sherry.

amontonadamente *adv* in a pile, in a heap.

amontonador, ra *adj* heaping.
◆ *f* heaper, heaping machine.

amontonamiento *m* piling, heaping (acción de apilar) || hoarding (de riquezas) || gathering, collection (de datos) || crowding (de gente) || pile, heap (montón).

amontonar *vt* to pile up, to heap up, to put in a pile (poner en montón); *amontonaron todos los libros* they piled up all the books, they put all the books in a pile || FIG to accumulate, to hoard (riquezas) | to collect, to gather; *amontonó datos, pruebas* he collected data, proof | to accumulate; *amontonar conocimientos* to accumulate knowledge.
◆ *vpr* to crowd together; *se amontonaba la gente en la plaza* the people crowded together in the square || to pile up, to heap up; *las pruebas contra él se amontonaban* proof against him was piling up || to gather (nubes) || FIG & FAM to get angry, to fly into a temper (enfadarse) | to live together (amancebarse).

amor *m* love; *el amor de un padre a su hijo* a father's love for his son; *amor a la música* love of music; *amor materno* motherly love || devotion; *trabajó con amor* he worked with devotion || loving care; *limpió con amor los vasos* he cleaned the glasses with loving care || love (persona o cosa amada); *eres mi amor* you are my love; *su gran amor es la pintura* painting is his great love || lover (amante) || — *al amor de la lumbre* by the fireside, by the fire || *amor con amor se paga* one good turn deserves another (en buen sentido), an eye for an eye and a tooth for a tooth (irónicamente) || *amor correspondido* requited love || BOT *amor de hortelano* cleavers || *amor interesado* love for money || *amor pasajero* passing fancy || *amor propio* self-respect, self-esteem, amour propre || *en amor y compañía* peacefully || *hacer el amor* to court (cortejar), to make love (tener relaciones sexuales) || *por amor al arte* for the love of it || *por el amor de* for the love of, for the sake of || *por (el) amor de Dios* for the love of God.
◆ *pl* loves, love affairs; *los amores de Luis XV* the love affairs of Louis XV || — *con* or *de mil amores* with pleasure, with the greatest pleasure || *requerir de amores* to court || *tener amores con* to have a love affair with.

amoral *adj* amoral.

amoralidad *f* amorality.

amoralismo *m* amoralism.

amoratado, da *adj* purple, blue; *tengo las manos amoratadas de frío* my hands are blue with cold || black and blue, badly bruised; *un rostro amoratado de golpes* a badly bruised face.

amoratar *vt* to make blue *o* purple (el frío) || to make black and blue, to bruise (golpes).
◆ *vpr* to turn blue *o* purple (por el frío) || to turn black and blue, to bruise (por golpes).

amorcillo *n* cupid (figura) || FIG affair, flirtation.

amordazar *vt* to gag; *los ladrones le amordazaron* the thieves gagged him || to muzzle; *amordazar un perro* to muzzle a dog || FIG to gag, to silence; *amordazar la prensa* to gag the press.

amorecer* *vt* to mate with (the ewe) (el morueco).

amorfismo *m* amorphism.

amorfo, fa *adj* amorphous.

amoricones *m pl* FAM caresses.

amorío *m* FAM flirtation, affair.

amoriscado, da *adj* Moorish || ARQ Moresque, mauresque.

amoroso, sa *adj* affectionate, loving; *un padre amoroso* a loving father || amorous; *miradas amorosas* amorous glances || love; *cartas amorosas* love letters || AGR workable (tierra) || FIG mild (tiempo).

amortajador, ra *m/f* shrouder, person who puts on the shroud.

amortajamiento *m* shrouding.

amortajar *vt* to shroud, to wrap in a shroud || TECN to join (tenon and mortise) | to box (the tenon in the mortise).

amortecer* *vt* to muffle, to deaden (ruido) || to subdue, to soften, to dim (la luz) || to absorb (golpe).
◆ *vpr* to faint.

amortiguación *f*; **amortiguamiento** *m* muffling, deadening (del ruido) || subduing, softening, dimming (de la luz) || damping, sushioning (de un golpe) || damping (del fuego) || FIG lessening, reduction | toning down (de colores).

amortiguador, ra *adj* muffling, deadening (del sonido) || subduing, softening (de la luz) || absorbing, cushioning (de un golpe).
◆ *m* TECN shock absorber, damper.

amortiguar *vt* to muffle, to deaden (el ruido) || to subdue, to soften, to dim (la luz) || to absorb, to cushion (un golpe) || to damp (down) (el fuego) || FIG to alleviate, to mitigate (mitigar) | to tone down (colores).
◆ *vpr* to die down (el ruido) || to grow dim, to soften (la luz).

amortizable *adj* COM redeemable; *renta amortizable* redeemable annuity.

amortización *f* COM paying-off, amortization; *la amortización de una deuda* the paying-off of a debt | depreciation (de máquina, etc.) | writing off (de capital) || JUR amortization || abolition (de un empleo) || COM *fondo de amortización* sinking fund.

amortizar *vt* COM to pay off, to repay, to amortize; *amortizar una deuda* to pay off a debt | to depreciate (una máquina, etc.) | to write off (capital) || JUR to amortize || to abolish (un empleo).

amoscamiento *m* anger, temper.

amoscarse *vpr* FAM to get cross, to get into a huff.

amostazar *vt* FAM to make cross.
◆ *vpr* FAM to get into a huff, to get cross (enfadarse) || AMER to get embarrassed (avergonzarse).

amotinado, da *adj* insurgent, riotous (insurrecto) || rebellious (rebelde) || mutinous (soldado, marinero).
◆ *m/f* insurgent, rioter (insurrecto) || rebel (rebelde) || mutineer (soldado, marinero).

amotinador *m* → **amotinado.**

amotinamiento *m* riot (motín) || uprising, insurrection (rebelión) || mutiny (motín de soldados o de marineros).

amotinar *vt* to stir to rebellion, to incite to revolt (incitar a la rebelión) || to incite to riot (incitar a motín); *el aumento de impuestos amotinó a los habitantes* the increase in taxes incited the inhabitants to riot || to incite to mutiny (soldados, marineros) || FIG to upset, to disturb.
◆ *vpr* to rise up, to revolt, to rebel (rebelarse) || to riot (promover un motín); *los estudiantes se amotinaron porque la policía entró en la universidad* the students rioted because the police entered the university || to mutiny; *los marineros se amotinaron* the sailors mutinied || FIG to become upset *o* disturbed.

amovible *adj* removable, detachable || revocable (empleo).

amovilidad *f* detachability, removability || revocability (de un empleo).

amparador, ra *adj* protecting, defending.
◆ *m/f* protector, defender.

amparar *vt* to aid, to help (ayudar) || to protect, to harbour, to shelter; *amparar a un criminal* to protect a criminal || to protect; *esta ley ampara nuestros derechos* this law protects our rights || *¡Dios le ampare!* God help you!
◆ *vpr* to seek help (buscar ayuda) || to shelter, to take shelter; *ampararse de la lluvia* to shelter from the rain || to seek protection; *ampararse en la ley* to seek protection in the law; *ampararse en una persona* to seek s.o.'s protection.

amparo *m* protection; *al amparo de alguien, de la ley* under s.o.'s protection, under the protection of the law || shelter; *ponerse al amparo de la lluvia* to take shelter from the rain || help, assistance, protection; *puedo contar con su amparo* I can count on his help || refuge; *la Iglesia ha sido siempre el amparo de los desdichados* the Church has always been a refuge for the unfortunate.

amperaje *m* TECN amperage.

amperímetro *m* TECN ammeter.

amperio *m* ELECTR ampere, amp || — ELECTR *amperio hora* ampere-hour | *amperio segundo* ampere-second | *amperio vuelta* ampere-turn.

ampliable *adj* which can be enlarged, enlargeable.

ampliación *f* extension, enlargement; *la ampliación de una tienda* the extension of a shop || extension; *la ampliación de las actividades, de un acuerdo, de un plazo* the extension of activities, of an agreement, of a time limit || FOT enlargement || amplification, development (de una explicación) || widening (de una calle) || — COM *ampliación de capital* increase of capital || *ampliación de estudios* furthering of studies.

ampliado, da *adj* enlarged, extended || extended; *un programa ampliado de asistencia técnica* an extended programme of technical aid.

ampliador, ra *adj* enlarging, extending.
◆ *f* enlarger (de fotos).

ampliar *vt* to enlarge, to extend; *ampliar un almacén, un acuerdo* to extend a store, an agreement || to lengthen, to elaborate on, to amplify on; *ampliar una explicación* to lengthen an explanation || to develop; *ampliar su argumento* to develop one's argument || to extend, to increase; *ampliar los poderes del gerente* to extend the manager's powers || to expand (el comercio, un negocio) || to increase; *ampliar el número de accionistas, el capital* to increase the number of shareholders, the capital || to widen; *ampliar una carretera* to widen a road || FOT to enlarge.

amplificación *f* amplification; *la amplificación del sonido* sound amplification || amplification (de una idea).

amplificador, ra *adj* amplifying.
◆ *m* amplifier, amp (*fam*).

amplificar *vt* to amplify; *amplificar un sonido* to amplify a sound || to amplify (una idea) || to magnify; *el microscopio amplifica los pequeños cuerpos* the microscope magnifies small bodies.

amplio, plia *adj* wide, full; *una falda amplia* a wide skirt || wide, big; *este pantalón te está un poco amplio* these trousers are rather big for you || wide, extensive; *tener amplios poderes* to have extensive powers; *tener un conocimiento amplio de la historia* to have an extensive knowledge of history; *un amplio cambio de impresiones* a wide exchange of views || vast, extensive; *una finca muy amplia* a very vast estate || considerable, extensive, great; *el amplio desarrollo de la economía* the considerable development of the economy || roomy, spacious; *un comedor muy amplio* a very spacious dining room || *el sentido amplio de una palabra* the broad sense of a word.

amplísimo, ma *adj* very extensive, very wide.

amplitud *f* width, fullness; *la amplitud de una falda* the width of a skirt || extent; *la amplitud de sus poderes, de sus conocimientos, de un desastre* the extent of one's powers, of one's knowledge, of a disaster || expanse, size, extent; *la amplitud de una finca* the expanse of an estate || spaciousness (de una habitación, etc.) || room, space (espacio); *quitamos la mesa para dar más amplitud* we removed the table to make more room || FÍS amplitude (de una oscilación) || — *amplitud de ideas, de miras* broadmindedness, broad outlook || *con amplitud* easily; *aquí caben con amplitud veinte personas* twenty people fit in here easily, there is easily room for twenty people here || *de gran amplitud* far-reaching, with a large scope; *un proyecto de gran amplitud* a far-reaching plan, a plan with a large scope.

ampo *m* brilliant whiteness; *el ampo de la nieve* the brilliant whiteness of the snow || snowflake (copo de nieve).

ampolla *f* MED blister; *tengo ampollas en las manos* I have blisters on my hands || phial, ampoule (de medicamento) || flask, bottle (frasco).

ampollar *vt* to blister.
◆ *vpr* to blister; *se me ampollaron los pies* my feet blistered.

ampolleta *f* hourglass (reloj) || bulb [of an hourglass] || time taken by sand to pour through an hourglass (tiempo).

ampón, ona *adj* wide, baggy.

ampulosidad *f* FIG bombast, pomposity (estilo).

ampuloso, sa *adj* FIG bombastic, pompous (estilo) || *tener un nombre muy ampuloso* to have a highsounding name.

ampurdanés, esa *adj* [from *o* of] Ampurdán (Cataluña).
◆ *m/f* native *o* inhabitant of Ampurdán.

amputación *f* amputation; *amputación de un miembro* amputation of a limb || FIG cutting-out, deletion (en un texto) | curtailment, curtailing (de créditos).

amputar *vt* to amputate; *amputar un miembro* to amputate a limb || FIG to cut out, to delete (un párrafo, etc.) | to curtail (créditos).

Amsterdam *n pr* GEOGR Amsterdam.

amueblado *m* AMER apartment let for assignations (casa de citas).

amueblar *vt* to furnish || *piso amueblado* furnished flat.

amuelar *vt* to collect into a pile [grain].

amugronar *vt* AGR to provine, to layer.

amujerado, da *adj* effeminate (afeminado).

amulatado, da *adj* like a mulatto, mulatto-like.

amuleto *m* amulet.

amunicionar *vt* to supply with munitions.

amuñecado, da *adj* doll-like; *rostro amuñecado* doll-like face.

amura *f* MAR tack (cabo) | bow (proa).

amurada *f* MAR ceiling.

amurallar *vt* to wall, to fortify.

amurar *vt* MAR to haul in (velas).

amurrarse; amurriarse *vpr* AMER to become sad, to get depressed.

amusgar *vt* to put back, to throw back (las orejas) || to screw up (los ojos).
◆ *vi* to put *o* to throw back its ears (toro, caballo).
◆ *vpr* AMER to give way, to back down.

amustiar *vt* to wither.

ana *f* ell [measurement of lenght approximately equivalent to a metre].

Ana *npr f* Ann, Anne.

anabaptismo *m* REL Anabaptism.

anabaptista *adj/s* REL Anabaptist.

anabolismo *m* BIOL anabolism.

anabolizante *adj* anabolic.
◆ *m* anabolic steroid.

anacarado, da *adj* pearly, mother-of-pearl.

anacardo *m* cashew tree (árbol) || cashew nut (fruto).

anacoluto *m* GRAM anacoluthon.

anaconda *f* ZOOL anaconda (serpiente).

anacora *f* horn (clarín).

anacoreta *m/f* anchoret, anchorite.

Anacreonte *npr m* Anacreon.

anacreóntico, ca *adj* Anacreontic.

anacrónico, ca *adj* anachronic, anachronistic.

anacronismo *m* anachronism.

anacrusis *f* anacrusis (métrica).

ánade *m/f* duck (pato).

anadear *vi* to waddle.

anadeo *m* waddle.

anadino, na *m/f*; **anadón** *m* duckling (patito).

anaerobio, bia *adj* BIOL anaerobic.
◆ *m* BIOL anaerobe.

anafe *m* portable stove (hornillo).

anafiláctico, ca *adj* MED anaphylactic.

anafilaxia; anafilaxis *f* MED anaphylaxis.

anáfora *f* anaphora (repetición).

anafre *m* portable stove (hornillo).

anafrodisia *f* anaphrodisia.

anafrodisiaco, ca *adj/sm* anaphrodisiac.

anáglifo *m* ARTS & PHOT anaglyph.

anagoge *m*; **anagogía** *f* REL anagoge, anagogy.

anagrama *m* anagram.

anagramático, ca *adj* anagrammatic, anagrammatical.

anal *adj* ANAT anal.

analectas *f pl* analects, analecta, florilegium *sing*.

analéptico, ca *adj/sm* MED analeptic.

anales *m pl* annals.

analfabetismo *m* illiteracy.

analfabeto, ta *adj/s* illiterate.

analgesia *f* MED analgesia.

analgésico, ca *adj/sm* MED analgesic.

análisis *m* analysis; *análisis cuantitativo* quantitative analysis || MED test; *análisis de sangre* blood test | analysis; *análisis de orina* urine analysis || INFORM *análisis de memoria* dump.

analista *m/f* analyst (el que hace análisis) || annalist (escritor de anales) || — INFORM *analista de sistemas* systems analyst || ECON *analista financiero* financial analyst || INFORM *analista programador* programmer analyst.

analítico, ca *adj* analytic, analytical.
◆ *f* analytics.

analizador, ra *adj* analysing, analyzing, who analyses.
◆ *m* FÍS analyser, analyzer || INFORM analyzer, scanner.

analizar *vt* to analyse, to analyze.

análogamente *adv* similarly, analogously, in a similar way, likewise.

analogía *f* similarity, analogy (semejanza) || analogy (relación); *establecer una analogía entre dos cosas* to draw an analogy between two things || GRAM analogy.

analógico, ca *adj* analogical.

analogismo *m* analogism.

análogo, ga *adj* similar, analogous.

Anam *npr m* GEOGR Annam.

anamita *adj/s* Annamite (de Anam).

ananá; ananás *m* BOT pineapple (planta y fruto).
— OBSERV The plural is either *ananaes* or *ananases*

anapelo *m* BOT monkshood (acónito).

anapéstico, ca *adj* anapaestic [*US* anapestic].

anapesto *m* anapaest [*US* anapest].

anaquel *m* shelf (estante).

anaquelería *f* shelves *pl*, shelving.

anaranjado, da *adj/sm* orange (color).

anarquía *f* anarchy.

anárquico, ca *adj* anarchic, anarchical.

anarquismo *m* anarchism.

anarquista *adj/s* anarchist.

anarquizante *adj* anarchic.

Anastasio, sia *n pr m y f* Anastasius, Anastasia || FIG & FAM *Doña Anastasia* the censorship of the press.

anastigmático, ca *adj* anastigmatic; *objetivo anastigmático* anastigmatic lens.

anastomosarse *vpr* BIOL to anastomose.

anastomosis *f* BIOL anastomosis.

anatema *m* REL anathema || FIG *lanzar* or *fulminar un anatema contra alguien* to put a curse on s.o., to curse s.o.

anatematización *f* REL anathematization || FIG cursing.

anatematizar *vt* REL to anathematize || to curse.

anatife *m* ZOOL barnacle (percebe).

Anatolia *npr f* GEOGR Anatolia.

anatomía *f* anatomy (ciencia) || anatomy (cuerpo); *varias partes de su anatomía* various parts of his anatomy || dissection; *hacer la anatomía de un cadáver* to do a dissection on a body.

anatómico, ca *adj* anatomic, anatomical.

anatomista *m/f* anatomist.

anatomizar *vt/vi* to anatomize, to dissect.

anatoxina *f* MED toxoid, anatoxin.

anátropo, pa *adj* BOT anatropous, anatropal.

Anaxágoras *npr m* Anaxagoras.

anca *f* haunch (parte posterior lateral del caballo) || crupper, rump (parte posterior superior).
◆ *pl* FAM bottom *sing*, behind *sing* (nalgas) || — *a ancas* behind another person; *montar a ancas* to ride behind another person || *ancas de rana* frogs' legs.

ancestral *adj* ancestral.

ancianidad *f* old age.

anciano, na *adj* old, elderly, aged (de edad).
◆ *m* old *o* elderly man || REL elder.
◆ *f* old *o* elderly lady.
◆ *pl* old men, old ladies, old people.
— OBSERV *Anciano* is the polite term for *old man*, whilst *viejo* is usually derogatory.

ancla *f* MAR anchor || — FIG *ancla de salvación* last hope, sheet anchor || MAR *echar anclas* to cast anchor, to anchor | *levar anclas* to weigh anchor.

ancladero *m* MAR anchorage (fondeadero).

anclaje *m* MAR anchorage (acción de anclar, fondeadero, derechos que se pagan).

anclar *vt/vi* to anchor.

anclote *m* MAR grapnel, small anchor.

ancolía *f* BOT columbine.

ancón *m*; **anconada** *f* MAR cove, inlet, small bay (bahía pequeña) || AMER corner (rincón).

áncora *f* MAR & TECN & ARQ anchor || FIG *áncora de salvación* sheet anchor, last hope.

ancoraje *m* MAR anchorage (acción de anclar, fondeadero, derechos).

ancorar *vi* MAR to anchor, to cast anchor.

ancho, cha *adj* broad, wide; *una carretera ancha* a broad road || wide, full; *falda ancha* wide skirt || thick (espeso); *una pared ancha* a thick wall || too wide (demasiado grande); *esta mesa es ancha para la habitación* this table is too wide for the room || big, large; *el abrigo te está ancho* the overcoat is big for you; *el piso nos viene ancho* the flat is big for us || FIG relieved; *se quedó ancho después de acabar el trabajo* he was relieved after finishing the work | satisfied with o.s., smug, self-satisfied (satisfecho) || — *a lo largo y a lo ancho* lengthwise and breadthwise || FIG *a mis, a tus, a sus anchas* at ease, comfortable | *ancha es Castilla* everything is yours, the future is yours | *la independencia le viene un poco ancha al país* the country is not yet ready for independance | *le viene un poco ancho su cargo* his job is too much for him | *ponerse a sus anchas* to make o.s. comfortable, to make o.s. at home | *quedarse tan ancho* to behave as if nothing had happened || *ser ancho de espaldas* to be broad-shouldered, to have broad shoulders || FIG *tener la conciencia ancha* not to be overscrupulous | *tener miras anchas* or *tener la manga ancha* to be broad-minded.
◆ *m* width, breadth (anchura); *el ancho de la acera* the width of the pavement; *estos dos objetos tienen lo mismo de ancho* these two objects are the same width || width; *una falda plegada necesita tres anchos* a pleated skirt takes three widths || gauge (ferrocarril); *el ancho de vía* the gauge of the rails || — *tener menos ancho que* to be narrower than || *tener un metro de ancho* to be one metre wide.

anchoa *f* anchovy (pescado).
— OBSERV *Anchovy* can be translated two ways: *boquerón* is used for the live or fresh fish and *anchoa* for the salted fish packed in tins.

anchova; anchoveta *f* anchovy (pez).

anchura *f* width, breadth (dimensión); *la anchura de un libro* the width of a book; *la anchura de un río* the width of a river || measurement (medida); *anchura de pecho, de cintura* chest, waist measurement || fullness; *la anchura de una falda* the fullness of a skirt || FIG cheek (frescura) || IMPR justification ||— *a mis anchuras* at ease, comfortable || FIG *anchura de miras* broad-mindedness.

anchuroso, sa *adj* wide, large; *un campo anchuroso* a large field || spacious; *una habitación anchurosa* a spacious room.

anda *f* AMER stretcher (para enfermos) | bier (féretro) | portable platform (para una imagen).

andada *f* AMER long walk (caminata).
◆ *pl* tracks (huellas) ||— FIG *cuéntame tus andadas por Londres* tell me what you've been up to in London | *volver a las andadas* to fall back into one's old ways *o* habits, to revert to one's old habits *o* ways (reincidir en un vicio).

andaderas *f pl* baby walker *sing* (para niños).

andado, da *adj* busy; *calle andada* busy street || ordinary, everyday, common (corriente) || worn, threadbare (vestidos).

andador, ra *adj* good at walking (capaz de andar mucho) || who walks quickly, quick, fast-walking (veloz) || fond of wandering about, wandering (andariego).
◆ *m/f* good walker (que anda mucho) || quick *o* fast walker (veloz) || wanderer (andariego).
◆ *m* baby walker (andaderas) || (p us) messenger (recadero) || (p us) path (senda).
◆ *m pl* reins, harness *sing* (de niño) || FIG *ese chico no necesita andadores* that boy can look after himself.

andadura *f* walking (acción) || walk, gait (manera de andar) || pace, gait (del caballo) || *paso de andadura* amble.

Andalucía *npr f* Andalusia.

andalucismo *m* Andalusian word *o* expression (expresión) || Andalusian way of speaking (modo de hablar) || love of things typical of Andalusia (amor a lo andaluz).

andaluz, za *adj/s* Andalusian.

andaluzada *f* FAM tall story; *decir andaluzadas* to tell tall stories.

andaluzarse *vpr* to become Andalusian.

andamiaje *m* TECN scaffolding.

andamio *m* TECN scaffold || stage, platform (tablado) || FAM *flor de andamio* old rope, bad tobacco, third-rate tobacco.
◆ *pl* scaffolding *sing*; *andamios suspendidos* or *colgantes* hanging scaffolding.

andana *f* row, line (hilera) || FAM *llamarse andana* to go back on one's word, to break a promise (no cumplir su promesa), to wash one's hands of the matter (hacerse el desentendido).

andanada *f* broadside (descarga); *soltar una andanada* to fire a broadside || FAM scolding, telling off (reprimenda) | shower; *una andanada de injurias* a shower of insults || covered stand (gradería) || FAM *soltarle a uno una andanada* to give s.o. a rocket *o* a tongue-lashing (echar una bronca).

andancia *f*; **andancio** *m* AMER mild epidemic (epidemia).
◆ *pl* AMER adventures (andanzas).

¡andandito!; ¡andando! *interj* FAM come on!, let's go, let's get a move on!

andante *adv/s m* MÚS andante || errant; *caballero andante* knight-errant.

andantino *adv/ s m* MÚS andantino.

andanza *f* adventure; *a su regreso de América me contó todas sus andanzas* on his return from America he told me all about his adventures || event, occurrence (suceso) || luck, fortune; *buena, mala andanza* good, bad luck || AMER *volver a las andanzas* to fall back into one's old ways *o* habits, to revert to one's old habits *o* ways (reincidir en un vicio).

andar* *vi* to walk; *andar de prisa* to walk quickly; *andar a gatas, con las manos* to walk on all fours, on one's hands || to move; *los planetas andan* the planets move; *los peces andan por el mar* fish move about the sea || to go, to work, to function; *mi reloj anda bien* my watch works well || to go; *el negocio anda mal estos días* business is going badly these days || to be; *anda alguien por el jardín* there is s.o. in the garden; *anda un poco malo estos días* he is not very well these days; *anda tras un empleo* he's after a job; *¿dónde andan mis guantes? — por ahí andarán* where are my gloves? — they will be over there somewhere; *¿estás leyendo mi libro?, ¿por dónde andas?* are you reading my book?, where are you up to?; *ando muy ocupado* I am very busy; *ando escaso de dinero* I am short of money || to be (con el gerundio); *andaba escribiendo* he was writing || to pass (el tiempo) ||— *¡anda!* come on! (para animar), go on!, get away with you! (desconfianza), my word! (admiración), come on now (para rechazar); *¡anda, déjame en paz!* come on now, leave me alone!; so there! (triunfo); *me han puesto mejor nota que a ti, ¡anda!* they've given me a better mark than you, so there!; what! (sorpresa); *¡anda, si estás tú aquí!* what, you're here! || *¡anda, anda!* don't be silly! || *andar a* to go on, to ride; *andar a caballo* to go on horseback, to ride a horse || *andar a golpes* to fight, to come to blows || *andar a gusto* to be comfortable || *andar a la greña* to tear each other's hair out || *andar a la que salta* to live from day to day || *andar bien de salud* to be in good health || *andar como alma en pena* to wander about like a lost soul || *andar con* to be (con adjetivo en inglés); *andar con miedo* to be afraid; *andar con cuidado* or *con ojo* to be careful; to mess about with, to play about with; *andar con pólvora* to mess about with gunpowder; to wear, to have on; *andar con un traje nuevo* to have a new suit on; to have; *andar con ojos enrojecidos* to have red eyes || FIG *andar con cumplidos* to stand on ceremony | *andar con pies de plomo* to tread carefully | *andar con rodeos* to beat about the bush | *andar con secreteos* to be secretive || *andar de acá para allá* to wander about *o* from place to place || FIG *andar de cabeza* to be in a flurry *o* a fluster *o* a tizzy | *andar de Herodes a Pilato* to fall out of the frying pan into the fire || *andar de puntillas* to tiptoe, to walk on tiptoe || *andar en* to rummage in; *andar en un cajón* to rummage in a drawer; to be mixed up in; *andar en negocios raros* to be mixed up in strange business; to be almost *o* nearly; *andar en los treinta años* to be almost thirty || FIG *andar en dimes y diretes* to bicker | *andar en boca de todos* or *en lenguas* to be on everyone's lips, to be the talk of the town | *andar en tratos* to be negotiating, to be in negotiations | *andar mal de la cabeza* not to be right in the head | *andar por* to be about; *andar por los siete años* to be about seven | *andar por las nubes* to have one's head in the clouds || *andar tras* to be after (desear, perseguir) || FIG *ande yo caliente, ríase la gente* I'm all right Jack | *a todo* or *a más andar* at full speed | *¿cómo anda eso?* how are things going? | *¿cómo andamos de dinero, de tiempo?* how are we (off) for money, for time? | *dime con quién andas y te diré quién eres* a man is known by the company he keeps || *ir andando* to go on foot, to walk || FIG *más viejo que andar a pie* or *para adelante* as old as the hills | *no andar por las nubes* to have one's feet firmly planted on the ground | *quien mal anda, mal acaba* those who fall into bad ways will come to a bad end | *¡vamos, anda!* come on, hurry up! (date prisa), come on, do something! (haz algo), come now!, go on!, come off it! (incredulidad).
◆ *vt* to walk (a pie); *andar diez millas en un día* to walk ten miles in a day || to cover, to travel, to go (recorrer); *andar tres kilómetros* to cover three kilometres || to travel, to go along (un camino) || AMER to wear, to have (llevar, llevar puesto).
◆ *vpr* to leave, to go away (marcharse) ||— FIG *andarse con* or *en* to be mixed up in; *siempre te andas en negocios raros* you are always mixed up in strange business; to use; *siempre se anda con los mismos cuentos* he always uses the same stories; *andarse con paños calientes* to use half measures | *andarse con bromas* to joke, to make jokes | *andarse por las ramas* or *por las márgenes* to beat about the bush | *dejar los años que se anduvo a gatas* to leave one's childhood behind || FIG & FAM *no andarse con chiquitas* not to beat about the bush, not to mess about, not to hem and haw (no vacilar), to be generous (no escatimar nada) || FIG *no andarse con rodeos* not to beat about the bush, to get straight to the point | *todo se andará* all in good time, everything comes to him who waits.

andar *m* walk, gait (acción).
◆ *pl* walk *sing*, gait *sing*; *con sus andares femeninos* with her feminine walk.

andariego, ga *adj* fond of walking, good at walking (que anda mucho) || fond of gadding about, fond of wandering (callejero) || wandering, roving, roaming (errante).
◆ *m/f* good walker (de mucho andar) || gadabout (callejero) || wanderer, rover, roamer (errante).

andarín, ina *adj* good at walking.
◆ *m/f* good walker.
◆ *f* ZOOL swallow (golondrina).

andarivel *m* cable ferry (en un río) || MAR lifeline (pasamanos) || AMER ferryboat (barco).

andas *f pl* stretcher *sing* (para enfermos) || bier *sing* (féretro) || portable platform *sing* (para una imagen).

andén *m* platform (de estación) || side, side of the road (de carretera) || hard shoulder (de autopista) || shelf (anaquel) || quayside (muelle) || AMER footpath, pavement [*US* sidewalk] (acera) | cultivation terrace (bancal de tierra).

Andes *npr mpl* GEOGR Andes || *Cordillera de los Andes* the Andes Mountain Ranges.

andesita *f* andesite.

andinismo *m* AMER mountaineering [in the Andes].

andinista *m/f* AMER mountaineeer [in the Andes].

andolina *f* ZOOL swallow (golondrina).

andorga *f* FAM belly (barriga).

andorina *f* ZOOL swallow (golondrina).

Andorra *npr f* GEOGR Andorra.

Andorra la Vella *n pr* GEOGR Andorra la Vella.

andorrano, na *adj/s* Andorran.

andrajo *m* rag, tatter; *ir vestido de andrajos* to be dressed in rags || FIG rag (cosa de poco valor) ||— *estar hecho un andrajo* to be in rags (cosa), to be in rags and tatters (persona) || FIG *ser un andrajo humano* to be a (physical) wreck.

andrajoso, sa *adj* ragged, tattered.

Andrés *npr m* Andrew.

Andrinópolis *n pr* GEOGR Adrianople.

androceo *m* BOT androecium.

androfobia *f* MED androphobia [fear of man].

androgénesis *m* MED androgenesis [development from male cells].

andrógeno *m* BIOL androgen.

andrógino, na *adj* BIOL androgynous, androgyne.
◆ *m/f* BIOL androgyne.

androide *m* android.

andrología *f* MED andrology.

Andrómaca *npr f* Andromache.

Andrómeda *npr f* ASTR Andromeda.

andrómina *f* FAM tall story, tale, fib (embuste).

andullo *m* rolled tobacco-leaf (hoja de tabaco) ‖ plug (para masticar) ‖ MAR fender.

andurriales *m pl* FAM out-of-the-way place *sing*, parts; *¿qué haces por estos andurriales?* what are you doing in this out-of-the-way place?

anea; enea *f* BOT cat's-tail, reed mace, bulrush ‖ *silla de anea* rush-bottomed chair.

anécdota *f* anecdote.

anecdotario *m* collection of anecdotes.

anecdótico, ca *ajd* anecdotal, anecdotic, anecdotical.

anegadizo, za *adj* subject to flooding; *terreno anegadizo* land subject to flooding.

anegamiento *m* flooding.

anegar *vt* to flood; *anegar un campo* to flood a field ‖ to drown (ahogar) ‖ *anegado en sangre* bathed in blood.
◆ *vpr* to drown ‖ to flood (inundarse) ‖ MAR to sink (un navío) ‖ — *anegarse en llanto* to fill with tears (los ojos), to be bathed in tears (el rostro), to dissolve into tears (una persona).

anejar *vt* to annex (un territorio) ‖ to annex, to append (un documento).

anejo, ja *adj* dependent, attached ‖ — *anejo a* joined to, attached to; *edificio anejo a la fábrica* building attached to the factory ‖ *edificios anejos* outbuildings ‖ *escuela aneja* school annex.
◆ *m* annex, annexe (edificio) ‖ dependency (parroquia dependiente de otra) ‖ annex, annexe, appendix (de un texto).

anélido *m* ZOOL annelid, annelide.

anemia *f* MED anaemia, anemia.

anemiante *adj* debilitating; *un clima anemiante* a debilitating climate.

anémico, ca *adj* anaemic, anemic.
◆ *m/f* anaemia sufferer.

anemófilo, la *adj* BOT anemophilous.

anemógrafo *m* FÍS anemograph.

anemometría *f* FÍS anemometry.

anemómetro *m* FÍS anemometer.

anémona; anemone *f* BOT anemone (planta) ‖ *anémona de mar* sea anemone (actinia).

aneroide *adj* FÍS aneroid (barómetro).

anestesia *f* MED anaesthesia [*US* anesthesia]; *anestesia local* local anaesthesia.

anestesiar *vt* MED to anaesthetize [*US* to anesthetize], to give an anaesthetic to.

anestésico, ca *adj/sm* MED anaesthetic [*US* anesthetic].

anestesista *m/f* anaesthetist [*US* anesthetist].

aneurisma *m* MED aneurysm, aneurism.

anexar *vt* to annex (un territorio) ‖ to annex, to append (un documento).

anexidades *f pl* JUR annexes, appurtenances.

anexión *f* annexation.

anexionar *vt* to annex.

anexionismo *m* annexationism, annexionism.

anexo, xa *adj* dependent, annexed, attached (edificio) ‖ attached (documento) ‖ *anexo a* joined to, attached to.
◆ *m* annex, annexe; *el anexo de un hotel* a hotel annex ‖ annex, annexe, appendix (documento).
◆ *pl* ANAT adnexa.

anfeta *f* FAM amphetamine, speed.

anfetamina *f* amphetamine.

anfibio, bia *adj* amphibious (que vive dentro y fuera del agua) ‖ amphibian (vehículo).
◆ *m* amphibian.
◆ *pl* ZOOL amphibia.

anfíbol *m* MIN amphibole.

anfibolita *f* MIN amphibolite.

anfibología *f* amphibology (ambigüedad).

anfibológico, ca *adj* amphibological.

anfictión *m* HIST amphictyon (diputado griego).

anfictionía *f* HIST amphictyony.

anfioxo *m* ZOOL amphioxus.

anfisbena *f* ZOOL amphisbaena.

anfiteatro *m* amphitheatre [*US* amphitheater] ‖ lecture theatre (de una universidad) ‖ TEATR gallery ‖ *anfiteatro anatómico* dissecting room.

Anfitrión *npr m* Amphitryon.

anfitrión, ona *m/f* host, hostess.

Anfitrite *npr f* MIT Amphitrite.

ánfora *f* amphora (cántaro).

anfractuosidad *f* roughness, cragginess (desigualdad) ‖ twisting, turning, winding (cualidad de torcido) ‖ ANAT anfractuosity, convolution, fold.
◆ *pl* roughness *sing*, cragginess *sing*; *las anfractuosidades de las montañas* the roughness of the mountains ‖ twisting *sing*, turning *sing*, winding *sing*; *las anfractuosidades de la carretera* the twisting of the road.

anfractuoso, sa *adj* rough, craggy (desigual) ‖ twisting, winding, anfractuous (torcido).

angaria *f* angaria.

angarillas *f pl* stretcher *sing* (para enfermos) ‖ portable platform *sing* (para llevar imágenes) ‖ handbarrow *sing* (para piedras) ‖ panniers (de las caballerías) ‖ cruet set *sing* (vinagreras).

ángel *m* angel; *ángel de la guarda, ángel custodio* guardian angel ‖ FIG charm (encanto) ‖ — *ángel caído* fallen angel ‖ *ángel malo* or *de las tinieblas* Devil ‖ *bueno como un ángel* as good as gold, like a little angel ‖ *cantar como los ángeles* to sing like an angel ‖ *no tener ángel, tener mal ángel* to be dull, to have no charm ‖ *salto del ángel* swallow dive ‖ *ser como un ángel* to be extremely good-looking (hermoso), to be as good as gold, to be a little angel (bueno) ‖ *tener ángel* to have charm, to be charming.

angélica *f* BOT angelica.

angelical *adj* angelic, angelical; *mirada angelical* angelic look.

angélico, ca *adj* angelic, angelical ‖ REL *la salutación angélica* the Hail Mary.
◆ *m* little angel, cherub.

angelito *m* little angel, cherub ‖ FIG & FAM *estar con los angelitos* to be miles away, to be asleep (estar distraído).

angelote *m* angel (estatua) ‖ FIG & FAM chubby child (niño gordinflón) | good type, good sort, decent sort (persona sencilla) ‖ ZOOL angelfish (pez) ‖ BOT type of clover.

Angelus *m* Angelus.

angevino, na *adj/s* Angevin, Angevine.

angina *f* MED angina ‖ — *angina de pecho* angina pectoris ‖ *angina diftérica* diphteria.

angiocardiopatía *f* MED angiocardiopathy.

angiocolitis *f* MED angiocholitis.

angiografía *f* MED angiography.

angiograma *m* angiogram.

angioleucitis *f* MED angioleucitis [inflammation of the lymph gland].

angiología *f* MED angiology.

angiólogo, ga *m/f* angiologist.

angioma *m* MED angioma.

angiospasmo *m* MED angiospasm.

angiospermas *f pl* BOT angiospermae.

angiospermo, ma *adj* BOT angiospermous.

angitis *f* MED angitis.

anglicanismo *m* REL Anglicanism.

anglicanizar *vt* to anglicize.

anglicano, na *adj/s* REL Anglican ‖ *La Iglesia Anglicana* the Anglican Church, the Church of England.

anglicismo *m* Anglicism (giro inglés).

anglicista *m/f* Anglicist.

anglo, gla *adj* Anglian.
◆ *m/f* Angle, Anglian.

angloamericano, na *adj/s* Anglo-American ‖ American (de los Estados Unidos).

angloárabe *adj* Anglo-Arabian.
◆ *m/f* Anglo-Arab.

anglofilia *f* Anglophilia.

anglófilo, la *adj/s* Anglophile, Anglophil.

anglofobia *f* Anglophobia.

anglófobo, ba *adj/s* anglophobe.

anglohablante *adj* English speaking.
◆ *m/f* English speaker.

anglomanía *f* Anglomania.

anglómano *adj* anglomaniacal.
◆ *m/f* Anglomaniac.

anglonormando, da *adj/s* Anglo-Norman ‖ *las Islas Anglonormandas* the Channel Islands.

anglosajón, ona *adj/s* Anglo-Saxon.

Angola *n pr* GEOGR Angola.

angolés, esa *adj/s* Angolese.

Angora *n pr* HIST Angora (Ankara) ‖ *gato, cabra de Angora* Angora cat, goat.

angostar *vt* to narrow.
◆ *vpr* to narrow; *allí el camino se angosta* the road narrows there.

angosto, ta *adj* narrow.

angostura *f* narrowness (estrechez) ‖ narrow part (parte estrecha) ‖ GEOGR narrow pass (entre montañas) | narrows *pl* (de un río) ‖ BOT angostura.

angra *f* MAR creek, cove (ensenada).

angrelado, da *adj* HERÁLD engrailed.

angström *m* FÍS angstrom (unidad de longitud de onda).

anguila *f* ZOOL eel (pez) ‖ — *anguila de cabo* whip (rebenque) ‖ ZOOL *anguila de mar* conger eel (pez).
◆ *pl* MAR slipway *sing* (maderos).

anguilazo *m* whiplash, lash of a whip (latigazo).

anguílula *f* ZOOL anguillule, vinegar eel.

anguina *f* ZOOL inguinal vein.

angula *f* elver (cría de anguila).

angular *adj* angular ‖ — FOT *objetivo gran angular* wide-angle lens ‖ *piedra angular* cornerstone.
◆ *m* TECN angle iron.

angularidad *f* angularity.

ángulo *m* angle; *ángulo agudo* acute angle; *ángulo obtuso* obtuse angle; *ángulo recto* right angle; *ángulo interno, externo* internal, external angle ‖ corner (rincón, esquina) ‖ bend (curva) ‖ TECN angle iron (angular) ‖ — MIL *ángulo de* *mira* angle of sight || FÍS *ángulo de reflexión* angle of reflection || MIL *ángulo de tiro* elevation || ANAT *ángulo facial* facial angle || *ángulos adyacentes* adjacent angles || *ángulos alternos* alternate angles || *ángulos correspondientes* corresponding angles || FIG *desde este ángulo* from this angle || *en* or *de ángulo recto* right-angled || *estar en ángulo* to be at an angle || *formar ángulo con* to be at an angle to || *formar un ángulo de 10°* to be at 10°.

anguloso, sa *adj* angular; *cara angulosa* angular face || twisting, winding; *camino anguloso* winding road.

angurria *f* MED & FAM strangury || *AMER* FAM starvation, hunger (hambre) | miserliness, stinginess (avaricia).

angurriento, ta *adj* *AMER* FAM gluttonish, gluttonous, greedy (glotón) | miserly, stingy (avaro).

angustia *f* anguish, distress; *vivir en la angustia* to live in anguish || FIL anguish || anguish (malestar físico) || — *angustia vital* anxiety || *dar angustia a* to trouble, to distress, to worry, to grieve; *me da angustia verlo tan enfermo* it troubles me to see him so ill; to make ill; *me da angustia presenciar una operación* it makes me ill to see an operation.
◆ *pl* throes, pangs, agonies; *angustias de la muerte* death throes.

angustiado, da *adj* anguished, distressed; *están angustiados con la desaparición de su hijo* they are distressed by the disappearance of their son || narrow (estrecho) || miserable, wretched (apocado) || worried, anxious (preocupado); *a finales de mes está siempre angustiado porque no le queda dinero* he's always worried at the end of the month because he has no money left.

angustiar *vt* to distress, to anguish || to worry (inquietar).
◆ *vpr* to become distressed || to worry, to get anxious (inquietarse).

Angustias *npr f* Angustias.
— OBSERV This name is derived from *María de las Angustias*, and has no English equivalent.

angustiosamente *adv* with anguish, in an anguished way (con angustia) || in a distressing way, distressingly (causando angustia) || anxiously (con preocupación).

angustioso, sa *adj* distressing; *una situación angustiosa* a distressing situation || agonizing; *es angustioso esperar el resultado de los exámenes* it is agonizing waiting for the exam results || anguished, distressed (angustiado); *con voz angustiosa* in a distressed voice || *un momento angustioso* a moment of anguish, a moment's anguish.

angustura *f* BOT angostura.

anhelante *adj* panting, out of breath, gasping; *estar anhelante* to be out of breath || longing, eager, yearning (deseoso) || *esperar anhelante una cosa* to long for *o* to yearn for sth.

anhelar *vi* to pant, to gasp || FIG *anhelar por algo* to long for sth.
◆ *vt* FIG to long for, to yearn for; *anhelo su regreso* I am longing for his return || to long, to yearn (con infinitivo); *anhela vivir en el campo* he longs to live in the country || to aspire to, to crave; *anhelar la gloria, dignidades* to aspire to glory, honours.

anhelo *m* (p us) panting, gasping || FIG yearning, longing, craving (deseo).
◆ *pl* aspirations; *sus anhelos de gloria* his aspirations to glory || yearning *sing*, craving *sing*, longing *sing* (deseos).

anheloso, sa *adj* panting, gasping (persona) || laboured (respiración) || FIG longing, eager, yearning (deseoso).

anhídrido *m* QUÍM anhydride.

anhidrita *f* MIN anhydrite.

anhidro, dra *adj* QUÍM anhydrous.

anhidrosis *f* MED anidrosis, anhidrosis.

Aníbal *npr m* Hannibal.

anidar *vi* to nest, to make one's nest; *el águila anida en los altos peñascos* the eagle nests on high rocks, the eagle makes its nest on high rocks || FIG *el odio anida en su alma* his soul is filled with hate.
◆ *vt* FIG to take in, to shelter (acoger).
◆ *vpr* to nest, to make one's nest (las aves) || FIG *no dejes que la avaricia se anide en tu alma* harbour *o* nurture no avarice in your bosom, drive all avarice from your soul.

anilina *f* QUÍM aniline, anilin.

anilla *f* ring || curtain ring (de cortinas) || ring (de un ave).
◆ *pl* rings (de gimnasia).

anillado, da *adj* ZOOL annelid (gusano) || ringed (ave) || ring-like, annular (en forma de anillo) || curly (pelo).
◆ *m/f* ZOOL annelid.

anillar *vt* to ring, to put rings on (poner anillas) || to fasten with a ring, to ring (sujetar) || to make into a ring (dar forma de anillo) || to ring (poner anillas a las aves).

anillo *m* ring; *anillo de boda* wedding ring; *los anillos de Saturno* the rings of Saturn; *anillo de pedida* or *de compromiso* or *de comprometida* engagement ring || ARQ annulet (de una columna) | circular base (de cúpula) || ZOOL annulus; *los anillos de un gusano* the annuli of a worm | coil; *los anillos de la culebra* the coils of a snake || HERÁLD annulet || TAUR bullring, ring (redondel) || BOT ring (de los árboles) || — *anillo pastoral* bishop's ring || *sentar como anillo al dedo* to fit like a glove (estar bien ajustado), to suit down to the ground (convenir o favorecer mucho) || *viene como anillo al dedo* it's just what the doctor ordered (adecuado), it's come just at the right time (oportuno).

ánima *f* soul [in Purgatory] || bore (de un cañón) || *ánima bendita* soul in Purgatory.
◆ *pl* evening bell (campana).

animación *f* animation (acción y efecto de animar) || life, vivacity (de una persona); *tener mucha animación* to be full of life || liveliness; *la animación de una discusión* the liveliness of an argument || life (de un cuadro) || movement, bustle, life, activity; *había mucha animación en la calle* there was a lot of activity in the street || activity; *ha habido mucha animación en la Bolsa* there has been a lot of activity on the Stock Exchange || CINEM animation || starting (de un mecanismo) || *dar animación a* to put life into, to enliven, to liven up.

animadamente *adv* in a lively way.

animado, da *adj* prompted, moved, animated; *animado de buenas intenciones* prompted by good intentions || busy, lively, bustling; *una calle muy animada* a very busy street || lively, full of life, animated; *la fiesta estuvo muy animada* the party was very lively; *una persona muy animada* a very lively person, a person full of life || encouraged, inspired; *animado por sus primeros éxitos, siguió cantando* encouraged by his first successes, he continued to sing || on form, in high spirits; *hoy no estoy nada animado* I'm not at all on form today || animate; *seres animados* animate beings || *dibujos animados* (animated) cartoons.

animador, ra *adj* encouraging, inspiring; *noticia animadora* encouraging news.
◆ *m/f* entertainer [in bar, café, etc.] || compère (presentador), hostess (presentadora).

animadversión *f* ill will; *tener animadversión hacia alguien* to bear s.o. ill will.

animal *adj* animal; *el reino animal* the animal kingdom || FIG & FAM rough, brutish; *es tan animal que lo rompe todo* he is so rough that he breaks everything || stupid, daft (estúpido).
◆ *m* animal; *animales domésticos* domestic animals; *animal de asta* or *cornudo* horned animal || FIG blockhead, fool, dunce (persona estúpida) | brute, lout, animal, beast (persona tosca en sus maneras) || — *animal de bellota* pig (cerdo), blockhead, fool, dunce (persona estúpida) || *animal de carga* pack animal, beast of burden || *animales vivos* animals on the hoof || *animal salvaje* wild animal || FIG *comer como un animal* to eat like a horse | *es un animal* he's as strong as an ox (persona robusta).

animalada *f* FAM stupid thing, piece of nonsense (burrada) | piece of coarse language (grosería) | disgrace (conducta); *el bombardeo fue una animalada* the bombing was a disgrace | piece of gluttonous behaviour (gula) || — FAM *decir animaladas* to speak *o* to talk nonsense, to speak *o* to talk rubbish (tonterías), to be crude, to be vulgar (groserías) | *¡qué animalada comerse dos pollos enteros!* what a pig, eating two whole chickens! | *¡qué animalada haber venido andando desde tan lejos!* fancy walking all that way!

animálculo *m* ZOOL animalcule.

animalejo *m* nasty animal, creepy-crawly.

animalidad *f* animality.

animalismo *m* animalism.

animalista *adj/s* animalist (pintor o escultor de animales).

animalizar *vt* to animalize.
◆ *vpr* to become animalized || FIG to become brutish.

animalucho *m* nasty beast (repugnante) || creepy-crawly (pequeño).

animar *vt* to animate, to give life to; *el alma anima al cuerpo* the soul animates the body || to encourage; *animar a los soldados al combate* to encourage the soldiers to fight; *no animo a nadie a seguir mi ejemplo* I encourage no one to follow my example || to liven up, to put life into, to enliven (la conversación, la reunión, etc.) || to brighten up, to liven up; *para animar las calles han puesto guirnaldas* they've put up garlands to brighten up the streets || to cheer up, to buck up (*fam*); *estaba muy decaído pero conseguí animarle* he was very depressed but I managed to cheer him up || to give new life to; *una mano de pintura animará este cuarto* a coat of paint will give new life to this room || to move, to prompt, to activate, to inspire (mover); *no le anima ningún deseo de riqueza* he is not prompted by any desire for riches || to intensify (dar intensidad).
◆ *vpr* to pluck up courage, to regain courage, to take heart (cobrar ánimo) || to brighten up, to light up; *sus ojos se animan cuando habla* his eyes brighten up when he speaks || to liven up, to get livelier (conversación, reunión, etc.) || to cheer up, to liven up; *cuando ha tomado unas copas siempre se anima* when he's had a few drinks he always cheers up || to make up one's mind, to decide (decidirse); *al final me animé y me fui de excursión* in the end I made up my mind and went on a trip || — *¡anímate!* cheer up! (para dar ánimo), make up your mind! (¡decídete!) || *¿te animas?* are you game? || *¿te animas a dar un paseo?* do you fancy going out for a stroll?

anímico, ca *adj* psychic.

animismo *m* animism.

animista *adj* animistic.
◆ *m/f* animist.

ánimo *m* soul (alma) || spirit (espíritu) || spirit, heart; *hombre de ánimo valiente* man with a brave heart || mind; *quiero grabar esto en el ánimo de todos* I want to fix this in everyone's mind ‖ intention; *mi ánimo no es hacerte daño* it is not my intention to hurt you ‖ FIG courage (valor); *cobrar ánimo* to pluck up courage; *recobrar ánimo* to pluck up courage again ‖ — *¡ánimo!* come on! ‖ *con ánimo de* in *o* with the intention of ‖ *dar ánimos a* to encourage, to give encouragement to ‖ *está en mi ánimo vender el coche, tengo el ánimo de vender el coche, mi ánimo es vender el coche* I intend to sell the car, it is my intention to sell the car ‖ *estado de ánimo* state of mind, mood, spirits *pl*; *estoy en buen estado de ánimo* I'm in a good mood, I'm in good spirits ‖ *estar sin ánimo* to be in low spirits ‖ *hacerse el ánimo* to get used to the idea; *tengo que hacerme el ánimo de que se ha ido* I must get used to the idea that he has left ‖ *levantar el ánimo* to cheer up, to buck up ‖ *presencia de ánimo* presence of mind ‖ *tener ánimos de* or *estar con ánimos de* or *sentirse con ánimos de hacer algo* to feel like doing sth., to be in the mood for doing sth. ‖ *tener muchos ánimos* to have a lot of spirit; *a pesar de sus años tiene muchos ánimos* in spite of his age he has a lot of spirit.

animosidad *f* animosity, enmity (antipatía).

animoso, sa *adj* brave, daring, spirited; *animoso en la lucha* brave in battle ‖ determined (decidido).

aniñado, da *adj* childlike; *una cara aniñada* a childlike face ‖ childish; *comportamiento aniñado* childish behaviour.

aniñarse *vpr* to become childish.

anión *m* FÍS anion.

aniquilación *f* annihilation, destruction.

aniquilador, ra *adj* annihilating, destructive.

aniquilamiento *m* annihilation, destruction.

aniquilar *vt* to annihilate, to destroy, to wipe out; *el ejército enemigo fue aniquilado* the enemy army was wiped out ‖ to destroy, ton ruin (acabar con); *esto aniquila todas mis esperanzas* this destroys all my hopes; *este trabajo aniquilará tu salud* this work will ruin your health ‖ to crush, to defeat (en una discusión) ‖ to overwhelm, to overcome (anonadar).
◆ *vpr* to deteriorate (la salud) ‖ to vanish, to disappear (la fortuna).

anís *m* BOT anise (planta); *anís estrellado* star anise | aniseed (grano) ‖ anissed balls *pl* (confite) ‖ aniseed oil (esencia) ‖ anisette (licor) ‖ FIG & FAM *no ser grano de anís* to be no small matter, to be no trifle.

anisado, da *adj* flavoured with aniseed.
◆ *m* anisette (licor).

anisar *vt* to flavour with aniseed.

anisete *m* anisette.

anisopétalo, la *adj* BOT anisopetalous.

anisotropía *f* anisotropy.

anisótropo, pa *adj* anisotropic.

Anita *npr f* Annie.

aniversario, ria *adj/sm* anniversary; *el primer aniversario del final de la guerra* the first anniversary of the end of the war | anniversary of (s.o.'s) death; *hoy es el décimo aniversario de su padre* today is the tenth anniversary of his father's death ‖ *aniversario de boda* wedding anniversary.

Ankara *npr f* GEOGR Ankara.

ano *m* ANAT anus.

anoche *adv* last night, yesterday evening; *anoche fui al teatro* yesterday evening I went to the theatre ‖ last night; *anoche no pude dormir* I couldn't sleep last night ‖ *antes de anoche* the night before last.

anochecedor, ra *adj* fond of *o* in the habit of going to bed late.
◆ *m/f* late bird, night owl.

anochecer* *v impers* to get dark; *anochece* it's getting dark ‖ — *anocheció despejado* the sky was clear at nightfall *o* at dusk, the sky was clear when it got dark ‖ *cuando anochezca* at nightfall, at dusk ‖ *me anocheció mientras estaba buscando su casa* night fell while I was looking for his house.
◆ *vi* to be at nightfall, to be at dusk (estar); *anocheció en París* he was in Paris at nightfall ‖ to arrive at nightfall *o* at dusk (llegar); *anochecí en Londres* I arrived in London at dusk.

anochecer *m*; **anochecida** *f* · nightfall, dusk; *al anochecer* at nightfall.

anochecido *adv* night, dark; *era ya anochecido y no pudo distinguir el número de la casa* it was already dark and he couldn't make out the number of the house.

anódico, ca *adj* FÍS anodic.

anodinia *f* MED anodynia.

anodino, na *adj* MED anodyne ‖ insignificant, insubstantial (insubstancial) ‖ uninteresting, anodyne (sin interés); *una película anodina* an anodyne film.
◆ *m* anodyne (medicina).

ánodo *m* FÍS anode.

anodonte *m* ZOOL anodont, anodon.

anodontia *f* MED anodontia.

anofeles *m* ZOOL anopheles (mosquito).

anomalía *f* anomaly.

anómalo, la *adj* anomalous.

anona *f* BOT anona, annona, soursop (arbusto y fruto).

anonadamiento *m* annihilation, destruction (aniquilación).

anonadar *vt* to annihilate, to destroy (aniquilar) ‖ to overcome, to overwhelm (apocar); *me anonadó esa noticia* that news overwhelmed me ‖ to crush, to defeat (en una discusión, en una lucha) ‖ to astound, to dumbfound, to flabbergast (pasmar).

anonimato *m* anonimity.

anónimo, ma *adj* anonymous; *carta anónima* anonymous letter; *un admirador anónimo* an anonymous admirer ‖ *sociedad anónima* limited company [*US* incorporated company].
◆ *m* anonimity (anonimato) ‖ anonymous person (persona) ‖ anonymous letter (carta) ‖ anonymous work (obra) ‖ *conservar* or *guardar el anónimo* to remain anonymous *o* nameless.

anorak *m* anorak (chaqueta impermeable).

anorexia *f* MED anorexy.

anormal *adj* abnormal, irregular (no normal); *una situación anormal* an irregular situation ‖ MED subnormal (deficiente mentalmente).
◆ *m/f* abnormal person ‖ subnormal *o* mentally deficient person.

anormalidad *f* abnormality.

anosmia *f* anosmia.

anotación *f* noting, jotting down (acción de apuntar) ‖ annotation (acción de poner notas) ‖ note (nota).

anotador, ra *adj* who takes note (que apunta) ‖ who annotates (que pone anotaciones).
◆ *m/f* note taker (que toma apuntes) ‖ annotator (que pone anotaciones).
◆ *f* CINEM continuity girl.

anotar *vt* to make a note of, to jot down (*fam*), to note down (apuntar); *voy a anotar su dirección* I'm going to make a note of your address ‖ to put down, to put down the name of, to register; *me han anotado en la lista de candidatos* they have put me down on the list of candidates, they have put down my name on the list of candidates ‖ to annotate, to add notes to (poner notas); *anotar un texto* to annotate a text.

anoxemia *f* anoxemia.

anquilosamiento *m* MED anchylosis, ankylosis ‖ FIG paralysing, paralysis; *el anquilosamiento de la economía* the paralysing of the economy.

anquilosar *vt* to anchylose, to ankylose.
◆ *vpr* to anchylose ‖ FIG to be paralysed; *se está anquilosando la economía* the economy is being paralysed.

anquilosis *f* MED anchylosis, ankylosis.

anquilostoma *m* ZOOL hookworm.

anquilostomiasis *f* MED anchylostomiasis, ankylostomiasis.

ansa *f* HIST hanse (confederación).

ánsar *m* ZOOL goose (oca).

ansarino, na *adj* anserine.

ansarino; ansarón *m* gosling (pollo del ánsar).

anseático, ca *adj* HIST Hanseatic; *Liga anseática* Hanseatic League.

ansí *adv* (ant) thus, in this way.

ansia *f* anxiety (ansiedad) ‖ anguish (angustia) ‖ longing, yearning; *satisfacer el ansia de libertad* to satisfy one's longing for freedom ‖ — *con ansia* longingly ‖ *desear con ansia* to long for, to yearn for.
◆ *pl* pangs, throes; *las ansias de la muerte* death pangs ‖ nausea *sing* ‖ *tener ansias* to feel sick.

ansiar *vt* to long for, to yearn for; *ansiar la tranquilidad* to yearn for peace ‖ — *ansiar hacer algo* to long to do sth., to yearn to do sth. ‖ *el día tan ansiado* the much longed-for day.

ansiedad *f* anxiety, worry (estado de agitación) ‖ longing, yearning (deseo) ‖ MED anxiety.

ansiosamente *adv* longingly, yearningly (anhelosamente) ‖ anxiously (con inquietud).

ansioso, sa *adj* anxious, worried, uneasy (inquieto) ‖ eager (deseoso); *ansioso de gloria* eager for glory ‖ greedy (avaricioso); *es muy ansioso y lo quiere todo para él* he's very greedy and wants everything for himself ‖ *estamos ansiosos por saber dónde está* we are ansious *o* eager to know where he is.

anta *f* ZOOL elk, moose (rumiante) ‖ menhir (menhir) ‖ ARQ anta (pilastra) ‖ *AMER* ZOOL tapir.

antagónico, ca *adj* antagonistic.

antagonismo *m* antagonism.

antagonista *adj* antagonistic, antagonist.
◆ *m/f* antagonist.

antaño *adv* last year (el año pasado) ‖ formerly, in days gone by, in the past (antiguamente) ‖ *un libro de antaño* an ancient book (muy antiguo).

antañón, ona *adj* ancient, very old.

antártico, ca; antárctico, ca *adj/sm* Antarctic.

Antártida *f* GEOGR Antarctica.

ante *m* ZOOL elk, moose (ciervo) ‖ suède [*US* suede]; *un abrigo de ante* a suède overcoat ‖ bubal, bubale (antílope) ‖ buff (color) ‖ (ant) first course (primer plato) ‖ *AMER* cold fruit drink (bebida) | almond cake (pastel) | broth made from cereals and honey.

ante *prep* in front of, before; *comparecer ante un tribunal* to appear before the court; *ante él se extendía un paisaje hermoso* a beautiful landscape stretched out before him ‖ with regard to; *ante este asunto* with regard to this question ‖ before, in the presence of; *se prosternó* *ante la reina* he prostrated himself before the queen || in the face of (el peligro, el enemigo) || to, in the face of; *se rindió ante mis razones* he gave way to my reasoning || next to, compared with; *ante ella yo soy fea* I'm ugly compared with her || — *ante el juez* before the judge, in the presence of the judge || *ante el temor de que* for fear that || *ante las circunstancias* under the circumstances || *ante los ojos* before one's eyes || *ante notario* in the presence of the notary || *ante tantas posibilidades* faced with all these possibilities || *ante todo* above all, first of all.

— OBSERV *Ante* usually indicates an abstract relationship (in the presence of, compared with) as opposed to *delante de*, which indicates a position in space, and to *antes de* which indicates time.

antealtar *m* chancel, choir.

anteanoche *adv* the night before last, two nights ago.

anteayer *adv* the day before yesterday, two days ago; *le vi anteayer* I saw him two days ago.

antebrazo *m* forearm.

anteburro *m* AMER tapir.

antecama *f* bedside mat, bedside rug (alfombra).

antecámara *f* antechamber, anteroom, lobby (vestíbulo).

antecambriano, na *adj/sm* GEOL Precambrian.

antecapilla *f* antechapel.

antecedencia *f* antecedence.

antecedente *adj* antecedent, previous, preceding.

◆ *m* antecedent; *los antecedentes y las consecuencias* the antecedents and the consequences || cause, antecedent (causa); *los antecedentes del accidente* the causes of the accident || antecedent (matemáticas, gramática, música).

◆ *pl* history *sing*, background *sing*; *¿cuáles son sus antecedentes?* what is his background? || — JUR *antecedentes penales* criminal record; *persona con antecedentes penales* person with a criminal record || *estar en antecedentes* to be in the picture || *no tener antecedentes penales* to have a clean record || *poner una persona en antecedentes* to put s.o. in the picture || *tener malos antecedentes* to have a bad record.

anteceder *vt/vi* to precede, to go before.

antecesor, ra *m/f* predecessor; *he sido tu antecesor en este despacho* I was your predecessor in this office || ancestor, forebear, forefather (antepasado).

antecocina *f* scullery, pantry.

antecristo *m* Antichrist.

antedata *f* JUR antedate || *poner antedata en una carta* to put an antedate on a letter, to antedate a letter.

antedatar *vt* to antedate.

antedecir* *vt* to predict, to foretell.

antedía *adv* before the appointed day (antes del día previsto) || the day before (la víspera).

antedicho, cha *adj* aforementioned, aforesaid.

antediluviano, na *adj* antediluvian, before the flood || FIG antiquated, antediluvian (muy antiguo).

antefijo *m* ARQ antefix.

antefirma *f* title of the signatory (título) || formal ending to a letter (fórmula).

anteiglesia *f* porch.

antelación *f* time in advance, advance || — *con antelación* in advance, beforehand || *con antelación a* before || *con cinco días de antelación* five days in advance *o* beforehand || *con la debida antelación* in due time.

antelina *f* suède [*US* suede], suède cloth.

antemano (de) *loc adv* in advance, beforehand; *lo preparó de antemano* he prepared it beforehand.

antemeridiano, na *adj* antemeridian.

antena *f* RAD aerial, antenna || MAR latten yard || ZOOL antenna, feeler || — *antena colectiva* communal aerial || *antena emisora, receptora* transmitting, receiving aerial || *antena interior* indoor aerial || *antena parabólica* satellite dish || *estar en antena* to be on the air.

antenatal *adj* antenatal, prenatal.

antenombre *m* title [used before the Christian name] (e. g. *san, don, etc.*).

anteojera *f* blinker [*US* blinder] (de caballo) || spectacle case (estuche).

anteojo *m* telescope (telescopio) || — *anteojo de larga vista* telescope || *serpiente de anteojo* cobra.

◆ *pl* opera glasses (gemelos) || binoculars, field glasses (prismáticos) || blinkers [*US* blinders] (de caballo) || spectacles, glasses (gafas).

antepalco *m* vestibule of a box [in the theatre].

antepasado, da *adj* before last, previous.

◆ *m* ancestor, forefather, forebear (ascendiente).

antepatio *m* forecourt.

antepecho *m* handrail, guardrail, parapet (de escalera, de puente, de balcón) || sill (de ventana) || narrow balcony, ledge (balcón) || breast collar (de las caballerías) || MIN stratum, layer (banco).

antepenúltimo, ma *adj/s* antepenultimate, last but two.

anteponer* *vt* to place in front, to put in front || FIG to put before; *el chico antepone el deber al interés personal* the boy puts duty before personal interest.

anteportada *f* IMPR half title, bastard title.

anteportal *m* porch.

anteposición *f* placing in front, anteposition || preference (preferencia).

anteproyecto *m* preliminary plan, draft || FIG blueprint.

antepuerto *m* MAR outer harbour.

antepuesto, ta *adj* placed in front *o* before || put before, preferred (preferido).

Antequera *n pr* GEOGR Antequera || *que salga el sol por Antequera* come what may.

antequerano, na *adj* [from *o* of] Antequera.

◆ *m/f* native *o* inhabitant of Antequera.

antera *f* BOT anther.

anteridia *f* BOT antheridium.

anterior *adj* front, anterior, fore (pierna, parte) || previous, before; *el año anterior* the previous year, the year before; *la página anterior* the previous page, the page before || earlier; *ese éxito fue anterior al que digo* that success was earlier than the one I'm talking about || — *anterior a* previous to, before, prior to; *el hombre anterior a mí en la lista* the man before me on the list || *el nuevo es mejor que el anterior* the new one is better than the last *o* the old *o* the previous one.

anterioridad *f* anteriority (de tiempo) || priority (prioridad) || — *con anterioridad* before, formerly, previously (antes), in advance, beforehand (con antelación) || *con anterioridad a* prior to.

anteriormente *adv* before, previously (antes); *esto no había ocurrido nunca anteriormente* this had never happened before || beforehand, in advance (con antelación); *su secretaria había ido anteriormente para preparar el despacho* his secretary had gone beforehand to get the office ready || *véase anteriormente* see above.

antes *adv* before; *cuatro días antes* four days before; *antes que llegue* before I arrive; *antes todo era distinto* before, everything was different || first; *yo lo vi antes* I saw it first || earlier; *no quise hacerlo antes* I didn't want to do it earlier || rather, better; *antes morir que faltar a su deber* rather die than fail in one's duty || — *antes de* before; *la última calle antes de los semáforos* the last street before the traffic lights || *antes de anoche* the night before last || *antes de ayer* the day before yesterday || *antes de Jesucristo* before Christ || *antes de que me vaya* before I leave || *antes hoy que mañana* the sooner the better || *antes que* before; *lo he visto antes que tú* I saw it before you || *antes que nada* above all, more than anything else || *cuanto antes* or *lo antes posible* as soon as possible || *cuanto antes mejor* the sooner the better || *de antes de la guerra* pre-war (sentido literal), something else, first-rate (muy bueno) || *mucho antes* a long time before, long before || *poco antes* a short time before, not long before, shortly before.

◆ *conj* on the contrary (más bien); *no teme la muerte, antes la desea* he does not fear death, on the contrary, he longs for it || *antes bien, antes al contrario* on the contrary.

◆ *adj* before, previous; *el día antes* the previous day, the day before.

antesala *f* anteroom, antechamber || — FIG *estar en la antesala de* to be on the verge of || *hacer antesala* to wait to be received, to cool one's heels (*fam*).

antevíspera *f* two days before.

anti *pref* anti [indicating «against» or «opposite»] (the following list of words constructed with this prefix is by no means complete).

antiabortista *m/f* antiabortionist.

antiácido, da *adj/sm* antiacid.

antiaéreo, a *adj* antiaircraft (cañón, etc.).

antialcohólico, ca *adj* teetotal.

◆ *m/f* teetotaller.

antialcoholismo *m* antialcoholism, anti-alcoholism.

antiamericano, na *adj* anti-American.

antiarrugas *adj* antiwrinkle.

antiatómico, ca *adj* *refugio antiatómico* fallout shelter.

antibiótico, ca *adj/sm* MED antibiotic.

anticanceroso, sa *adj* anticancerous.

anticatarral *adj* MED anticatarrhal.

anticátodo *m* FÍS anticathode.

anticiclón *m* anticyclone.

anticiclonal *adj* anticyclonic.

anticipación *f* bringing forward (de una fecha, etc.) || COM advance (de dinero) || prediction, anticipation (predicción) || — *con anticipación* in advance; *pagar con anticipación* to pay in advance; early; *la nieve ha venido este año con anticipación* the snow has come early this year || *con bastante anticipación* in good time, well in advance || *con cinco minutos de anticipación* five minutes early || *llegar con anticipación* to arrive early, to arrive in good time.

anticipadamente *adv* in advance.

anticipado, da *adj* advance, in advance; *pago anticipado* payment in advance, advance payment || — *gracias anticipadas* thanks in advance *o* in anticipation || *por anticipado* in advance.

anticipamiento *m* bringing forward (de una fecha, etc.) || advancing, advance (de dinero) || prediction, anticipation (predicción) || time in advance, anticipation (tiempo).

anticipante *adj* bringing forward, advancing.

anticipar *vt* to bring forward, to advance; *anticipar su viaje, la fecha de los exámenes* to bring forward one's journey, the date of the examinations || to advance, to lend (dinero) || to predict, to foretell (predecir) || to pay in advance; *anticipar el alquiler* to pay the rent in advance || FIG to anticipate (prever) || *anticipar las gracias* to thank in advance.
◆ *vpr* to be early; *se anticipa la primavera* spring is early || to arrive before; *se anticipó a la carta en que anunciaba su llegada* he arrived before the letter in which he announced his arrival || to get there before, to beat (s.o.) to it; *fui a coger un trabajo pero se me anticiparon* I went for a job but s.o. got there before me *o* s.o. beat me to it || to anticipate, to be one step ahead of; *anticiparse a un rival* to be one step ahead of a rival || to be premature, to be born prematurely; *el niño se anticipó* the child was born prematurely || FIG to see sth. coming, to foresee; *me anticipé a la lluvia y cogí el paraguas* I saw the rain coming and took my umbrella | to predict, to foretell (predecir) | to anticipate (adivinar) || — *anticiparse a* (con infinitivo) to... before; *anticiparse a pagar* to pay before; *se me anticipó a decir el final del chiste* he told the end of the joke before me || *anticiparse a su época* to be ahead of one's time.

anticipo *m* advance (sobre un sueldo) || advance payment, payment on account (sobre una deuda) || FIG foretaste; *esto es sólo un anticipo de lo que te podría pasar* this is merely a foretaste of what could happen to you || JUR retainer, retaining fee; *el anticipo de un abogado* a lawyer's retainer || *llegar con anticipo* to arrive early *o* in advance.

anticlerical *adj/s* anticlerical.

anticlericalismo *m* anticlericalism.

anticlinal *adj* GEOL anticlinal.
◆ *m* anticline.

anticoagulante *adj/sm* anticoagulant.

anticolonialismo *m* anticolonialism.

anticolonialista *adj/s* anticolonialist.

anticomunista *adj/s* anticommunist.

anticoncepción *f* contraception.

anticoncepcional; anticonceptivo, va *adj* contraceptive, birth-control.
◆ *m* contraceptive.

anticoncepcionista *adj* contraceptive.

anticonformismo *m* non-conformism.

anticonformista *adj/s* non-conformist.

anticongelante *m* AUT antifreeze (de radiador) || de-icer (de parabrisas).

anticonstitucional *adj* unconstitutional, contrary to the constitution.

anticorrosivo, va *adj* anticorrosive, anti-rust.

anticresis *f* JUR antichresis (contrato).

anticristo *m* Antichrist.

anticuado, da *adj* antiquated, obsolete, out-of-date (máquina, palabra, uso) || outdated, out-of-date, old-fashioned (fuera de moda) || antiquated, old-fashioned (persona) || old, ancient, out-of-date (película) || *quedarse anticuado* to go out of fashion, to date; *este vestido se ha quedado anticuado* this dress has gone out of fashion *o* has dated.

anticuar *vt* to declare obsolete *o* out-of-date.
◆ *vpr* to date, to go out of fashion (vestido) || to become obsolete, to go out of use (máquina, uso) || to go out of use, to become obsolete *o* antiquated (palabra).

anticuario *m* antique dealer (vendedor de antigüedades) || anticuary, anticuarian (aficionado) || antique shop (tienda).

anticuerpo *m* BIOL antibody.

antidemócrata *m/f* antidemocrat.

antidemocrático, ca *adj* antidemocratic, undemocratic.

antideportivo, va *adj* unsportsmanlike, unsporting.

antideslizante *adj* nonskid, antiskid (neumático).
◆ *m* antiskid device.

antideslumbrante *adj/sm* antiglare, anti-dazzle.

antidetonante *adj/sm* antiknock.

antidiabético, ca *adj* antidiabetic.
◆ *m* diabetic preparation.

antidopaje *adj/sm* anti-doping || *control antidopaje* dope test.

antídoto *m* antidote (*contra* to, for, against).

antidroga *adj* anti-drug.

antidumping *adj* *medidas antidumping* anti-dumping measures, measures against dumping.

antieconómico, ca *adj* uneconomical.

antiemético, ca *adj/sm* antiemetic, antemetic.

antier *adv* FAM the day before yesterday.

antiesclavista *adj* antislavery.
◆ *m* abolitionist.

antiescorbútico, ca *adj/sm* MED antiscorbutic.

antiespasmódico, ca *adj/sm* MED antispasmodic.

antiestético, ca *adj* unsightly, ugly.

antifascismo *m* antifascism.

antifascista *adj/s* antifascist.

antifaz *m* mask.

antifebrífugo, ga *adj* MED antifebrile.

antifederalista *m/f* antifederalist.

antifeminismo *m* antifeminism.

antifeminista *adj/s* antifeminist.

antifermento *m* antiferment.

antifilosófico, ca *adj* anti-philosophic, anti-philosophical.

antiflogístico, ca *adj/sm* MED antiphlogistic.

antífona *f* REL antiphon.

antifonario *m* antiphonary.

antifonero *m* precentor.

antífrasis *f* antiphrasis.

antifricción *f* antifriction.

antigás *adj inv* gas; *careta antigás* gas mask.

antigénico, ca *adj* MED antigenic.

antígeno *m* MED antigen.

Antígona *npr f* Antigone.

antigripal *adj* *vacuna antigripal* flu vaccine.

Antigua y Barbuda *npr f* GEOGR Antigua and Barbuda.

antigualla *f* old relic; *su coche es una antigualla* his car is an old relic || has-been, relic (persona) || old story (cuento) || old news, stale news, old hat (noticia) || *vestirse de antiguallas* to dress in old rags.

antiguamente *adv* before, formerly (antes) || in former times, in olden days (en la Antigüedad).

antiguar *vt* to declare out of use *o* obsolete (una palabra).
◆ *vi/vpr* to gain seniority (en un empleo).
◆ *vpr* to go out of fashion, to date, to become old-fashioned (anticuarse).

antigubernamental *adj* anti-government.

antigüedad *f* antiquity (época antigua) || seniority; *ascenso por antigüedad* promotion by seniority || antiquity, age (cualidad de antiguo) || — *de toda antigüedad* from time immemorial || *tener mucha antigüedad* to have great seniority, to have held a post for a long time.
◆ *pl* antiques (objetos antiguos) || antiquities (monumentos, etc.); *las antigüedades de Roma* the antiquities of Rome || *tienda de antigüedades* antique shop.

antiguo, gua *adj* antique, ancient (de la Antigüedad) || old (viejo); *tradición antigua* old tradition; *porcelana antigua* old porcelain || old (ya pasado); *una herida antigua* an old wound || former, old; *es el antiguo presidente* he is the former president; *antiguos alumnos* old pupils || old-fashioned, out-of-date, out-dated (pasado de moda); *un traje antiguo* an old-fashioned suit || — *a la antigua, a lo antiguo* in an old-fashioned way || *Antiguo testamento* Old Testament || *de antiguo* for a long time || *desde muy antiguo* from time immemorial || *en lo antiguo* formerly, in olden times || *estar chapado a la antigua* to be old-fashioned [in one's ways] || *más antiguo* senior; *es más antiguo que yo* he is senior to me, he is my senior || *venir de antiguo* to be ancient.
◆ *m* antiquity.
◆ *pl* Ancients; *los antiguos eran supersticiosos* the Ancients were superstitious.

antihalo *adj/sm* non-helation (fotografía).

antihemorroidal *adj* anti-haemorrhoid.
◆ *m* haemorrhoidal.

antihéroe *m* anti-hero.

antihigiénico, ca *adj* unsanitary, unhygienic, unhealthy.

antihipertensivo *adj/s* MED antihypertensive.

antihistamínico, ca *adj/sm* MED antihistamine.

antihistérico, ca *adj* antihysteric.

antiimperialista *adj/s* anti-imperialist.

antiinflacionista *adj* anti-inflationary.

antiinflamatorio, ria *adj* anti-inflammatory.
◆ *m* anti-inflammatory treatment.

antilogaritmo *m* MAT antilogarithm.

antilogía *f* antilogy (contradicción).

antilógico, ca *adj* illogical.

antílope *m* ZOOL antelope.

antillano, na *adj/s* West Indian, Antillean.

Antillas *npr fpl* GEOGR West Indies, Antilles.

antimacasar *m* antimacassar (cubierta de una butaca).

antimagnético, ca *adj* antimagnetic.

antimasónico, ca *adj* antimasonic.

antimateria *f* antimatter.

antimilitarismo *m* antimilitarism.

antimilitarista *adj/s* antimilitarist.

antimisil *adj/sm* antimissile.

antimonárquico, ca *adj* antimonarchical.

antimoniado, da *adj* QUÍM antimoniated.

antimonial *adj* QUÍM antimonial.

antimoniato *m* QUÍM antimoniate.

antimonio *m* QUÍM antimony (metal).

antimonopolio *adj* ECON antitrust.

antimonopolista *adj* antitrust; *ley antimonopolista* antitrust law.

antinacional *adj* antinational.

antinatural *adj* unnatural, contrary to nature.

antineurálgico, ca *adj* MED antineuralgic.

antiniebla *adj* *faro antiniebla* fog light *o* lamp ‖ *sirena antiniebla* foghorn.

antinodo *m* antinode (en acústica).

antinomia *f* antinomy.

antinómico, ca *adj* antinomic, antinomical.

Antíoco *npr m* Antiochus.

antioqueno, na *adj* [from *o* of] Antioch [in Syria].
◆ *m/f* native *o* inhabitant of Antioch.

antioqueño, ña *adj* [from *o* of] Antioquia [in Colombia].
◆ *m/f* native *o* inhabitant of Antioquia.

Antioquía *npr f* GEOGR Antioch.

antioxidante *adj* antirust, rustproof.

antipalúdico, ca *adj* antimalarial.

antipapa *m* antipope.

antipara *f* screen (biombo) ‖ gaiter (polaina).

antiparásito, ta; antiparasitario, ria *adj/sm* suppressor (radio).

antiparlamentario, ria *adj* antiparliamentary.

antiparlamentarismo *m* antiparliamentarianism.

antiparras *f pl* FAM glasses, specs (gafas).

antipartícula *f* FÍS antiparticle.

antipatía *f* dislike; *los niños han cogido antipatía al nuevo profesor* the children have taken a dislike to the new teacher ‖ unpleasantness, antipathy (cualidad de antipático) ‖ antipathy, opposition (entre dos cosas) ‖ *le tengo antipatía a tu primo* I dislike your cousin, I do not like your cousin.

antipático, ca *adj* disagreeable, unpleasant; *es un chico muy antipático* he's a very unpleasant boy ‖ unfriendly, uncongenial (ambiente) ‖ *su hermana me cae antipática* I don't like his sister, I find his sister unpleasant.
◆ *m/f* unpleasant *o* disagreeable person.

antipatriota *adj* unpatriotic (sin patriotismo) ‖ antipatriotic (perjudicial a la patria).
◆ *m/f* unpatriotic person ‖ antipatriotic person.

antipatriótico, ca *adj* unpatriotic (sin patriotismo) ‖ antipatriotic (perjudicial a la patria).

antipatriotismo *m* lack of patriotism (falta de patriotismo) ‖ antipatriotism.

antiperistáltico, ca *adj* antiperistaltic.

antipersonal *adj* MIL antipersonnel.

antipirético, ca *adj/sm* MED antipyretic.

antipirina *f* MED antipyrine.

antípoda *adj* antipodal.
◆ *m* antipode.

antipoético, ca *adj*. unpoetical.

antiprogresista *adj/s* antiprogressive.

antiprohibicionista *adj/s* antiprohibitionist.

antiproteccionista *adj/s* antiprotectionist.

antiprotón *m* FÍS antiproton.

antipútrido, da *adj/sm* BIOL antiputrefactive.

antiquísimo, ma *adj* very old, ancient.

antirrábico, ca *adj* MED antirabic; *vacuna antirrábica* antirabic vaccine.

antirradar *adj* anti-radar.

antirraquítico, ca *adj* MED antirachitic.

antirreflectante *adj* nonreflecting.

antirreglamentario, ria *adj* against the rules, unlawful.

antirreligioso, sa *adj* antireligious.

antirrepublicano, na *adj/s* antirepublican.

antirrevolucionario, ria *adj/s* antirevolutionary.

antirrobo *m* antitheft device (para vehículos, etc.) ‖ burglar alarm (para casas, etc.).

antiscios *m pl* antiscians.

antisemita *adj* anti-Semitic.
◆ *m/f* anti-Semite.

antisemítico, ca *adj* anti-Semitic.

antisemitismo *m* anti-Semitism.

antisepsia *f* MED antisepsis.

antiséptico, ca *adj/sm* MED antiseptic.

antisifilítico, ca *adj* MED antisyphilitic.

antisociable *adj* unsociable.

antisocial *adj* antisocial.

antistrofa *f* POÉT antistrophe.

antisubmarino, na *adj* antisubmarine.

antitanque *adj* antitank.

antítesis *f* antithesis.

antitetánico, ca *adj* MED antitetanic.

antitético, ca *adj* antithetic, antithetical.

antitipo *m* antitype.

antitóxico, ca *adj* antitoxic.

antitoxina *f* MED antitoxin.

antituberculoso, sa *adj* MED antitubercular.

antitusígeno, na *adj* MED antitussive.
◆ *m* antitussive, cough remedy.

antivenenoso, sa *adj* antitoxic.

antivenéreo, a *adj* MED antivenereal.

antivirus *m* MED antiviral (drug) ‖ INFORM antivirus.

antojadizo, za *adj* whimsical, capricious, fanciful (caprichoso) ‖ unpredictable, fickle (cambiadizo).

antojarse *vpr* to fancy, to feel like; *no hace más que lo que se le antoja* he does just as he fancies; *se le antojó un pastel* he fancied a cake ‖ to take it into one's head, to have the idea; *se le antojó dar la vuelta al mundo* he took it into his head to go round the world, he had the idea of going round the world ‖ to have a feeling, to fancy; *se me antoja que va a llover* I have a feeling it is going to rain.
— OBSERV The subject of the verb in English becomes the indirect object in Spanish: *se me antoja un helado* I feel like an ice cream.

antojitos *m pl* AMER savoury titbits (tapas).

antojo *m* whim, (passing) fancy, caprice, fad; *no es más que un antojo* it is only a whim ‖ sudden craving; *los antojos son un síntoma del embarazo* sudden cravings are a symptom of pregnancy ‖ birthmark (mancha en la piel) ‖ — *cada uno a su antojo* each to his own ‖ *manejar a uno a su antojo* to twist s.o. round one's little finger ‖ *no obrar sino a su antojo* to like to have one's own way, to do exactly as one pleases ‖ *seguir sus antojos* to do as one's fancy takes one ‖ *vivir a su antojo* to live as one pleases, to live one's own life.

antología *f* anthology ‖ FAM *de antología* fantastic, terrific, great; *Rodríguez marcó un gol de antología* Rodríguez scored a fantastic goal.

antológico, ca *adj* anthological.

antónimo *m* antonym (contrario).

Antonino *npr m* Antoninus.

Antonia *npr f* Antoinette.

Antonio *npr m* Anthony.

antonomasia *f* antonomasia.

antorcha *f* torch ‖ FIG guiding light (persona).

antozoarios *m pl* ZOOL anthozoans.

antraceno *m* anthracene.

antracita *f* anthracite.
◆ *adj* black (color).

ántrax *m inv* MED anthrax; *ántrax maligno* malignant anthrax.

antreno *m* ZOOL anthrenus (insecto).

antro *m* cavern, cave (cueva) ‖ ANAT antrum ‖ FIG & FAM hole, dump; *no me gusta trabajar en ese antro* I don't like working in that hole ‖ FIG *antro de corrupción* or *de perdición* den of iniquity, den of vice.

antropocéntrico, ca *adj* anthropocentric.

antropocentrismo *m* anthropocentrism.

antropofagia *f* anthropophagy, cannibalism.

antropófago, ga *adj* anthropophagous.
◆ *m/f* anthropophagite, anthropophagus, cannibal.

antropoide; antropoideo, a *adj/sm* anthropoid.

antropología *f* anthropology.

antropológico, ca *adj* anthropological, anthropologic.

antropologista; antropólogo, ga *m/f* anthropologist.

antropometría *f* anthropometry.

antropométrico, ca *adj* anthropometric, anthropometrical.

antropomorfismo *m* anthropomorphism.

antropomorfita *m/f* anthropomorphist, anthropomorphite.

antropomorfo, fa *adj* anthropomorphous.
◆ *m/f* anthropomorph.

antroponimia *f* anthroponymy.

anthropopiteco *m* anthropopithecus.

antruejo *m* Carnival.

antucá *m* parasol, sunshade (sombrilla).

antuerpiense; antuerpino, na *adj* [of *o* from] Antwerp (de Amberes).
◆ *m/f* native *o* inhabitant of Antwerp.

anual *adj* annual; *planta anual* annual plant ‖ *trescientas mil pesetas anuales* three hundred thousand pesetas per annum *o* a year.

anualidad *f* annuity, annual payment; *pagar las anualidades* to pay the annuities ‖ annual occurrence *o* event (acontecimiento).

anualmente *adv* annually, yearly.

anuario *m* yearbook, annual ‖ *anuario telefónico* telephone directory.

anubarrado, da *adj* cloudy, overcast; *cielo anubarrado* cloudy sky.

anublar *vt* to cloud (el cielo) ‖ to cover, to hide, to cloud over (los astros) ‖ FIG to tarnish (la fama) | to cloud over (la alegría) ‖ AGR to wither (las plantas).
◆ *vpr* to cloud over, to become overcast; *el cielo se va anublando* the sky is clouding over ‖ to wither (plantas) ‖ FIG to fade away (desvanecerse).

anublo *m* blight (añublo).

anudadura *f*; **anudamiento** *m* knotting ‖ fastening, tying (de zapatos) ‖ tying (de corbata) ‖ knot (nudo).

anudar *vt* to knot, to tie [in a knot] (hilo, cinta) ‖ to tie (la corbata) ‖ to tie, to fasten (los zapatos) ‖ FIG to join, to unite (unir) | to begin (empezar) ‖ *anudamos nuestra amistad en Londres* our friendship began *o* we became friends in London.
◆ *vpr* to get tied up, to get into knots ‖ AGR to remain stunted (las plantas) ‖ to remain underdeveloped (las personas, los animales) ‖ FIG *se le anudó la voz* he got a lump in his throat.

anuencia *f* consent.

anuente *adj* consenting, who gives consent.

anulable *adj* revocable, that can be annulled *o* repealed (ley) ‖ that can be annulled *o* nullified *o* cancelled (contrato).

anulación *f* repeal, revocation, annulment (de ley) ‖ cancellation, annulment, invalidation (de contrato) ‖ cancellation (de cheque, encargo, etc.) ‖ annulment (de testamento) ‖ repeal, rescission (de fallo).

anular *adj* annular, ring-shaped.
◆ *m* ring finger.

anular *vt* to repeal, to revoke (ley) ‖ to invalidate, to cancel, to annul (un contrato) ‖ to cancel (un cheque) ‖ to cancel out (un efecto) ‖ to disallow (un gol) ‖ to annul, to declare void (un testamento) ‖ to cancel; *anular un encargo* to cancel an order ‖ to repeal (fallo) ‖ FIG to overshadow, to dominate (hacer perder personalidad) ‖ MAT to cancel out.
◆ *vpr* FIG to give up everything; *vivir en ese pueblo equivale a anularse* living in that town is like giving up everything ‖ to be overshadowed *o* diminished (perder autoridad) ‖ MAT & FÍS to cancel out.

anulativo, va *adj* annulling, cancelling.

anunciación *f* announcement (anuncio).

Anunciación *npr f* Annunciation (de la Virgen).

anunciador, ra *adj* who announces ‖ who advertises ‖ advertising; *empresa anunciadora* advertising company.
◆ *m/f* advertiser (en un periódico) ‖ announcer.

anunciante *m/f* advertiser.

anunciar *vt* to announce; *anunciar una noticia* to announce a piece of news; *anunciar al presidente* to announce the president ‖ to forebode (augurar) ‖ to tell, to announce; *me ha anunciado que se va a Inglaterra* he told me that he is going to England ‖ to announce, to advertise; *anunciar una subasta* to announce an auction ‖ to advertise; *es un producto que han anunciado mucho* it's a product that has been advertised a lot ‖ to be a sign of; *las golondrinas anuncian la primavera* swallows are a sign of Spring ‖ *el tiempo anuncia lluvia* it looks like rain.
◆ *vpr* to promise to be, to look like being; *la cosecha se anuncia buena* the harvest promises to be a good one.

anuncio *m* announcement; *hacer un anuncio* to make an announcement ‖ sign, omen (presagio) ‖ advertisement; *los anuncios de un diario* the advertisements in a daily paper ‖ notice, bill, poster (cartel) ‖ hoarding, billboard; *había un gran anuncio de madera al borde de la carretera* there was a large wooden hoarding at the side of the road ‖ — *anuncio mural* hoarding ‖ *anuncio publicitario* advertisement ‖ *anuncios por palabras* classified advertisements (en un periódico) ‖ *hombre anuncio* sandwichman ‖ *prohibido fijar anuncios* stick no bills ‖ *tablón* or *tablilla de anuncios* notice board.

anuo, nua *adj* annual; *planta anua* annual plant.

anuria *f* MED anury.

anuro, ra *adj* ZOOL anurous, anuran.
◆ *m* ZOOL anuran.

anverso *m* obverse, head (de moneda) ‖ recto (de una página).

anzuelo *m* fishhook, hook ‖ FIG lure (aliciente) ‖ FIG *tragar el anzuelo, picar en el anzuelo* to take *o* to swallow the bait; to be taken in; to be taken in hook, line and sinker; to fall for it.

añada *f* year; *una añada de lluvias* a year of rain ‖ AGR break, strip of land.

añadido, da *adj* added ‖ *lo añadido* what is added, the additions *pl*.
◆ *m* false piece, switch, hairpiece (de cabello) ‖ addition; *hacer un añadido a un texto* to make an addition to a text ‖ extra leaf (de una mesa) ‖ piece added on; *llevaba un añadido en la manga* he had a piece added on to his sleeve.

añadidura *f* addition (en un texto) ‖ extra weight *o* measure (suplemento) ‖ piece added on (de un vestido) ‖ *por añadidura* besides, in addition, into the bargain (además).

añadir *vt* to add; *añadir agua al vino* to add water to the wine ‖ to increase (aumentar) ‖ to add, to lend (interés, etc.).
◆ *vi* to make additions (a un texto).

añafea *f* rough brown paper.

añagaza *f* decoy, stool pigeon, lure (pájaro que atrae a los demás) ‖ FIG trick, ruse, scheme (ardid).

añal *adj* annual (anual) ‖ year-old (las reses).
◆ *m* year-old lamb, yearling (cordero) ‖ year-old kid, yearling (cabrito) ‖ offering made on the first anniversary of a death.

añalejo *m* REL liturgical calendar, ordo.

añejar *vt* to mature, to age.
◆ *vpr* to mature, to age (el vino).

añejo, ja *m* mature; *vino añejo* mature wine ‖ cured; *jamón añejo* cured ham ‖ old; *colonia añeja* old cologne ‖ FIG & FAM stale, old (noticia).

añicos *m pl* bits, fragments, pieces ‖ — FIG *estar hecho añicos* to be worn out (una persona) ‖ *hacer añicos* to smash to smithereens (jarrón, objeto), to tear to shreds (papel).

añil *m* BOT indigo plant, indigo (arbusto) ‖ indigo (color) ‖ blue (para el lavado).

añinos *m pl* lambskin *sing* (piel) ‖ lamb's wool *sing* (lana).

año *m* year; *tener veinte años* to be twenty years old; *durante todo el año* all the year round; *el año que viene* next year; *año bisiesto, civil, académico, escolar* leap, civil, academic, school year; *cada año, todos los años* every year ‖ — *al año de casado* within a year of getting married, after a year of marriage ‖ *año de gracia* year of grace ‖ *año del Señor* year of our Lord ‖ ASTR *año de luz, año luz* light year ‖ *año económico* financial year ‖ *año entrante* coming year ‖ ECON *año fiscal* tax *o* fiscal year ‖ *Año Nuevo* New Year ‖ *año tras año* year after year; year in, year out ‖ *¡Buen año!, ¡Feliz Año Nuevo!* Happy New Year! ‖ *el año antepasado* the year before last ‖ *estar de buen año* to be in good health ‖ *felicitar el día de Año Nuevo, felicitar por Año Nuevo* to wish a Happy New Year ‖ FIG *ser del año de la nana* or *del rey que rabió* to be as old as the hills, to be ancient ‖ *un año con otro* taking one year with another ‖ *un año sí y otro no* every other year ‖ *una vez al año por año* or once a year.
◆ *pl* days; *en aquellos años felices de nuestra juventud* in those happy days of our youth ‖ — *cada dos años* every other year ‖ *con los años que tiene* at his age ‖ *en los años cuarenta* in the forties ‖ *en los años que corren* at the present time, nowadays ‖ *en mis últimos años* in my later years ‖ *en sus años mozos* in his youth, in his younger days ‖ *entrado en años* elderly ‖ *hace años* years ago, ages ago; *le conocí hace años* I met him years ago; for years, for ages; *hace años que está así* he has been like that for years ‖ *no hay quince años feos* youth is beauty in itself ‖ *no pasan los años por él* he doesn't seem to get any older ‖ *¡qué años aquellos!* those were the days! ‖ *¿qué* or *cuántos años tienes?* how old are you? ‖ *tardará años y años* it will take years ‖ *tener muchos años* to be very old.

añojal *m* AGR break, strip of land.

añojo *m* yearling (becerro).

añoranza *f* longing, yearning, nostalgia (nostalgia) ‖ grief, sense of loss (dolor) ‖ *tener añoranza de su país* to be homesick.

añorar *vt* to miss, to long for, to yearn for (el pasado) ‖ to grieve, to mourn (una persona muerta).
◆ *vi* to pine, to grieve.

añoso, sa *adj* old, aged (viejo).

añublo *m* AGR blight (enfermedad) | rust (tizón).

añusgar *vi* to choke.

aojador, ra *adj* who casts the evil eye.
◆ *m/f* hexer.

aojadura *f*; **aojamiento** *m* evil eye, curse, jinx (mal de ojo).

aojar *vt* to cast the evil eye on, to put a curse on, to jinx.

aojo *m* evil eye, curse, jinx.

aoristo *m* GRAM aorist.

aorta *f* ANAT aorta.

aórtico, ca *adj* aortic.

aortitis *f* MED aortitis.

aovado, da *adj* oval, egg-shaped.

aovar *vi* to lay eggs.

apabullar *vt* FAM to squash, to flatten (aplastar) ‖ FIG & FAM to crush, to silence (callar); *lo apabulló con sus argumentos* he silenced him with his arguments.

apacentadero *m* AGR pasture.

apacentador, ra *m/f* shepherd (hombre), shepherdess (mujer).

apacentamiento *m* AGR pasturing, grazing (acción) ‖ pasture (pasto).

apacentar* *vt* AGR to pasture, to graze, to put to graze *o* to pasture (los rebaños) ‖ FIG to feed (el intelecto) | to minister to, to teach (discípulos) | to gratify, to satisfy (deseos, pasiones).
◆ *vpr* to pasture, to graze (comer) ‖ FIG to feed (*con* on), to be nourished (*con* with).

apacibilidad *f* gentleness, mildness, even temper, placidity (de persona) ‖ calmness, peacefulness (de vida) ‖ calmness (del tiempo, del mar).

apacible *adj* gentle, mild, even-tempered, placid (persona) ‖ calm, peaceful (vida) ‖ calm (tiempo, mar).

apaciguador, ra *adj* calming, pacifying.
◆ *m/f* pacifier.

apaciguamiento *m* appeasement, calming, pacifying.

apaciguar *vt* to calm, to pacify, to appease, to calm down, to quieten down (a personas) ‖ to relieve, to soothe (un dolor).
◆ *vpr* to calm down, to become calm (el mar) ‖ to die down, to abate; *la tempestad se apaciguó* the storm died down ‖ to calm down, to quieten down (personas).

apache *m* Apache (piel roja) ‖ FIG Apache, tough, thug (malhechor).

apacheta *f* AMER barrow, shrine (túmulo funerario en los Andes).

apadrinado *m* sponsored person, protégé (protegido).

apadrinador, ra *adj* sponsoring, who sponsors.
◆ *m/f* sponsor (protector).
◆ *m* second (en un desafío).

apadrinamiento *m* function of best man (en una boda) ‖ function of godfather (en un bautizo) ‖ function of second (en un desafío) ‖ sponsorship, sponsoring, patronage (de un escritor, etc.).

apadrinar *vt* to be *o* to stand godfather to; *apadrinar a un niño en un bautizo* to be godfather to a child at a baptism ‖ to be best man for (en una boda) || to act as second for (en un desafío) || to sponsor; *apadrinar a un escritor joven* to sponsor a young writer || to support, to defend; *apadrina todas las ideas humanitarias* he supports all humanitarian ideas.

apagado, da *adj* extinguished, that has been put out, that is out; *fuego apagado* extinguished fire, fire that has been put out || out; *el fuego está apagado* the fire is out || dull, lifeless (color) || weak (voz) || muffled, muted (sonido) || lifeless, listless (mirada, persona) || FIG dull; *una mujer muy apagada* a very dull woman || — *cal apagada* slaked lime || *volcán apagado* extinct volcano.

apagador, ra *adj* which extinguishes, extinguishing.
◆ *m/f* extinguisher.
◆ *m* extinguisher (útil para apagar) || fire extinguisher (de incendio) || candle snuffer (apagavelas) || MÚS damper (del piano).

apagamiento *m* extinction, extinguishing, putting-out (del fuego) || switching-off, turning-off, putting-out (de la luz) || muffling, deadening (de un sonido).

apagar *vt* to put out, to extinguish (un fuego, un incendio) || to turn *o* to switch off, to put out (luz) || to switch off, to turn off (la radio, etc.) || to muffle, to deaden (sonido) || to fade; *el sol apaga los colores* the sun fades colours || to quench (la sed) || to slake (cal) || to soften (color) || FIG to calm, to soothe; *apagar su ira* to calm one's anger | to deaden, to kill, to soothe (el dolor) | to calm down, to quieten (disturbios) || MÚS to mute, to damp (sonido) || MIL to silence (la artillería enemiga) || FAM *apaga y vámonos* that's enough, let's leave it at that.
◆ *vpr* to go out (fuego) || to go out *o* off (la luz) || to fade *o* to die away (sonido) || FIG to pass away (morir) | to subside (la ira).

apagavelas *m inv* candle snuffer.

apagón *m* blackout.

apainelado, da *adj* ARQ basket-handle (arco).

apaisado, da *adj* oblong; *formato apaisado* oblong format.

apajarado, da *adj* AMER silly, stupid.

apalabrar *vt* to make a verbal agreement on, to agree to; *apalabrar una compra con un amigo* to make a verbal agreement with a friend on a purchase || to engage, to take on; *apalabrar una criada* to engage a maid.
◆ *vpr* to make *o* to come to a verbal agreement.

Apalaches *npr mpl* GEOGR Appalachian Mountains.

apalancamiento *m* leverage.

apalancar *vt* to lever up, to lift with a lever (levantar) || to lever open, to pry open [with a lever] (abrir) || to lever, to move with a lever (mover) || FIG to support (apoyar).

apaleado, da *adj* beaten.

apaleador, ra *adj* who beats, which beats, beating.
◆ *m/f* winnower, thresher || beater, thrasher (de frutos).

apaleamiento *m* winnowing, threshing (del grano) || beating (de alfombras, etc.) || beating, thrashing (de los frutos) || beating, thrashing, striking (de personas).

apalear *vt* to winnow, to thresh (el grano) || to beat (alfombras) || to beat, to thrash (los frutos) || to beat, to thrash (maltratar) || FIG to be rolling in; *apalear dinero* to be rolling in money.

apaleo *m* beating, thrashing || AGR threshing, winnowing (del trigo) | thrashing, beating (de los frutos).

apamparse *vpr* to become confused.

apanalado, da *adj* faveolate, alveolate, honey-combed.

apanojado, da *adj* BOT panicled.

apantanar *vt* to flood (un terreno).

apañado, da *adj* FIG & FAM handy, clever, skilful; *es muy apañado para toda clase de cosas* he's very handy at all kinds of things | handy, practical; *me he comprado un vestido muy apañado* I've bought myself a very practical dress | dolled up; *esta chica va siempre bien apañada* this girl is always well dolled up || — FIG & FAM *¡estamos apañados!* that's all we needed!, we're really in it now! | *¡vas apañado si crees que te van a hacer caso!* if you think they are going to take any notice of you you've got another think coming!

apañamiento *m* repairing, mending (arreglo).

apañar *vt* FAM to get ready (preparar) | to patch up, to mend, to repair; *apañar unos pantalones* to mend a pair of trousers | to suit, to be all right for; *¿te apaña coger el avión de la noche?* does it suit you *o* is it all right for you to catch the night plane? | to dress up (ataviar) | to wrap up (abrigar, arropar) | to pick up, to grab (coger) | to swipe, to lift (robar) || AMER to cover up for (un criminal) | to excuse, to forgive (disculpar) || FAM *ya le apañaré* I'll fix him, I'll sort him out (amenaza).
◆ *vpr* FAM to fix things, to arrange things, to contrive; *yo me apaño siempre para conseguir lo que quiero* I always fix things to get what I want | to get o.s.; *me apañé un coche muy bonito para irme de vacaciones* I got myself a very nice car to go on holiday || FAM *apañárselas* to manage, to get by; *me las apañaré* I'll manage, I'll get by.

apaño *m* FAM repair, mend (arreglo) | skill, knack (habilidad) | mistress (concubina) || — FAM *esta maleta es de mucho* or *de gran apaño* this case is very handy *o* useful | *no tiene apaño* there's no way out, there's nothing I (we, etc.) can do about it.

apañuscar *vt* FAM to pinch, to swipe (robar) | to crumple (apretujar y ajar).

apapachado, da *adj* AMER pampered (mimado).

apapachador, ra *adj* AMER soothing, comforting (reconfortante).

apapachar *vt* AMER to pamper, to cuddle (mimar, abrazar).

apapacho *m pl* AMER cuddles, caresses (caricias).

aparador *m* sideboard (mueble) || workshop (taller) || shopwindow, window (escaparate).

aparato *m* pomp, show, fuss; *la corte está rodeada de mucho aparato* the court is surrounded by a great deal of pomp || set; *aparato de radio, de televisión* radio, television set || instrument (brújula, reloj, velocímetro) || device (dispositivo) || FAM telephone, phone (teléfono) | plane (avión) || ANAT system, apparatus; *aparato digestivo, circulatorio* digestive, circulatory system || MED brace (para los dientes) | bandage (vendaje) || QUÍM & FÍS apparatus || AMER ghost || — *aparato auditivo* or *del oído* hearing aid || *aparato electrodoméstico* domestic appliance || *aparato escénico* staging || *aparatos de gimnasia* gymnastic apparatus || *aparatos de mando* controls (en un avión) || *aparatos sanitarios* bathroom fittings || *ponerse al aparato* to come to the phone || *¿quién está en el aparato?* who's speaking? (teléfono).

aparatosamente *adv* ostentatiously, pretentiously (con ostentación) || spectacularly (espectacularmente).

aparatosidad *f* ostentation, show (ostentación).

aparatoso, sa *adj* pompous (pomposo) || spectacular; *accidente aparatoso* spectacular accident || showy, flashy, ostentatious (vistoso); *un traje aparatoso* a showy dress.

aparcamiento *m* parking (acción de aparcar) || car park [US parking lot] (sitio reservado) || lay-by (en la carretera).

aparcar *vt* to park; *aparcar su coche* to park one's car.
◆ *vi* to park; *en esta calle nunca puede uno aparcar* you can never park in this street || — *aparcar en batería* to park obliquely, to park at a slant to the kerb || *prohibido aparcar* no parking.

aparcería *f* AGR partnership, métayage | contract of métayage, partnership contract (contrato).

aparcero, ra *m/f* AGR métayer, tenant farmer || part owner (copropietario) || AMER companion.

apareamiento *m* pairing off, matching up (de cosas) || mating (de animales).

aparear *vt* to match up, to pair off (cosas) || to mate (animales) || to make equal (hacer igual).
◆ *vpr* to mate (animales) || to match, to go together (cosas).

aparecer* *vi* to appear; *apareció un barco en el horizonte* a boat appeared on the horizon || to come out, to be published (un libro) || to be, to appear (en una lista) || FAM to show up, to turn up; *no suele aparecer por la oficina* he doesn't usually turn up at the office; *el mechero perdido no ha aparecido* the lost lighter has not turned up || — *aparecer como* to look like; *el río Amazonas aparece como un mar inmenso* the Amazon river looks like an immense sea || *aparecer en escena* to appear on the stage.
◆ *vpr* to appear; *Dios se apareció a Moisés* God appeared to Moses.

aparecido *m* ghost.

aparejado, da *adj* ready, fit (preparado) || convenient, suitable, fitting, apt (adecuado) || — *ir aparejado con* to go hand in hand with; *su ignorancia va aparejada con una irresponsabilidad absoluta* his ignorance goes hand in hand with complete irresponsability || *traer aparejado* to entail, to lead to, to involve, to mean; *la no asistencia a clase trae aparejada la expulsión* absence from school leads to *o* involves *o* means *o* entails expulsion.

aparejador *m* quantity surveyor (ayudante de arquitecto) || MAR rigger.

aparejar *vt* to get ready, to prepare (preparar) || to harness, to saddle (los caballos) || MAR to rig out || to prime (un cuadro).
◆ *vpr* to get ready, to get o.s. ready.

aparejo *m* preparation (preparativo) || equipment, gear, tackle (conjunto de cosas) || harness (arreo) || ARQ bond || MAR rigging (jarcia) || TECN block and tackle (poleas) || priming (de un cuadro) || *aparejo de pescar* fishing tackle.
◆ *pl* equipment *sing*, materials, gear *sing* || tools (herramientas).

aparentador, ra *adj* who pretends.
◆ *m/f* pretender.

aparentar *vt* to feign, to affect (simular) || to pretend; *aparentó desvanecerse* she pretended to faint || — *aparentar* (con sustantivo) to pretend to be (con adjetivo) (simular); *aparentar alegría* to pretend to be happy; to look *o* to seem (con adjetivo) (parecer); *aparentar tristeza* to seem sad || *aparentar trabajar* or *que se trabaja* to pretend to be working || *aparentar treinta años* to look thirty years old || *no aparentar la edad que se tiene* not to look one's age.
◆ *vi* to show off; *a esta mujer le gusta aparentar* this woman likes to show off.

aparente *adj* apparent; *un éxito aparente* an apparent success || suitable (adecuado) || visible, apparent (visible) || evident (patente) || *un vestido muy aparente* a very showy dress.

aparición *f* appearance (acción de aparecer) || apparition (visión) || publication, appearance, issue (publicación) || *de próxima aparición* forthcoming (libro).

apariencia *f* appearance, outward appearance; *fiarse de las apariencias* to trust outward appearances || FIG & FAM show; *un vestido con mucha apariencia* a dress with a lot of show || — *apariencia falsa* false appearance || *tener apariencia de* to look like, to have the appearance of; *tiene apariencia de gran señor* he looks like an important gentleman.
◆ *pl* appearances; *según todas las apariencias ganará las elecciones* to all appearances he will win the election; *a juzgar por las apariencias* judging by appearances || — *cubrir* or *guardar* or *salvar las apariencias* to save *o* to keep up appearances, to save face || *en apariencia* apparently, seemingly || *las apariencias engañan* appearances are deceptive.

aparroquiar *vt* (p us) COM to provide with customers.
◆ *vpr* to become a customer.

apartadamente *adv* apart.

apartadero *m* siding (vía muerta) || lay-by (en el camino) || TAUR yard where bulls are selected [for bullfights].

apartado, da *adj* remote, isolated; *un pueblo apartado* a remote town || aloof, solitary (persona) || — *mantenerse apartado* to keep to o.s., to remain in the background || FIG *vivir apartado* to live in a world apart.
◆ *m* paragraph, section (párrafo) || MIN refining (del oro) || TAUR penning [of bulls before the bullfight] || TEATR aside (aparte) || spare room (habitación) || — *apartado de correos* post-office box || *apartado de localidades* ticket agency.

apartador, ra *adj* who separates, which separates, separating (que aparta).
◆ *m/f* sorter (que selecciona) || *AMER* goad, stick (para el ganado).

apartamento *m* flat [*US* apartment].
— OBSERV The word *apartamento* is applied to a *small flat*.

apartamiento *m* separation, putting aside (acción de apartar) || extraction (del mineral) || flat [*US* apartment] (piso) || remoteness, seclusion, isolation (lejanía) || remote *o* secluded *o* isolated place (lugar apartado) || JUR withdrawal.

apartar *vt* to remove, to move away; *apartar el armario de la pared* to move the wardrobe away from the wall || to put aside; *he apartado todo lo que tengo que llevar* I've put aside everything that I have to take || to separate, to part; *apartar a dos personas que riñen* to separate two people who are arguing || to take aside; *apartar a alguien para hablar con él* to take s.o. aside to talk to him || to turn away; *apartar la atención de un tema* to turn one's attention away from a subject || FAM to begin, to start; *apartó a correr* he began to run | to keep, to save; *apártame la cena* keep my dinner for me || to extract (el mineral) || to separate (separar) || to put off, to dissuade (disuadir) || to shunt (vagones de ferrocarril) || to push *o* knock aside; *apartó el perro con el pie* he pushed the dog aside with his foot || — *apartar a alguien de un tema* to turn s.o. off a subject, to change the subject || *apartar de sí una idea* to put an idea out of one's mind || *apartar la vista* or *la mirada (de)* to look away (from) || *no apartar la mirada de* not to take one's eyes off, to keep one's eyes glued to.
◆ *vpr* to go away, to leave (irse) || to part, to separate (separarse) || to move over *o* up (correrse) || to move aside *o* away, to stand aside (quitarse de en medio) || to stray, to move away; *apartarse del cristianismo* to stray from Christianity || to withdraw, to cut o.s. off, to retire; *apartarse del mundo* to withdraw from the world || to fail in; *apartarse de su deber* to fail in one's duty || to wander off, to go off, to stray from; *apartarse del tema* to wander off the subject || to turn off, to stray from (de un camino) || JUR to withdraw an action || — *apartarse de los peligros de* to flee *o* to avoid the dangers of || *¡apártate!* get out of the way!, move out of the way! || *¡apártate de mi vista!* get out of my sight!

aparte *adv* separated; *las pesetas y los chelines están aparte* the pesetas and the shillings are separated || aside, apart; *poner aparte* to put aside; *bromas aparte* joking aside || apart; *es una niña aparte* she's a child apart || besides (además); *aparte recibe ayuda del exterior* besides he receives help from outside || separately (por separado) || separately, on one's own; *me habló aparte* he spoke to me on my own || TEATR aside || — *aparte de* apart from; *aparte del estilo la obra no vale nada* apart from the style the work is of no value; as well as (además de); *aparte del estilo, el tema de esta obra vale mucho* as well as the style, the subject-matter of this work is of great value || *conversación aparte* private conversation || *dejando aparte* leaving aside, not to mention || *eso aparte* apart from that; besides that (además) || *eso es capítulo aparte* that's another story, that's beside the point || *hacer párrafo aparte* to begin a new paragraph || *hacer rancho aparte* to keep to o.s. || *llamar aparte* to call aside || *poner aparte* to separate (separar); *poner aparte las patatas y el arroz* to separate the potatoes and the rice; to put aside (poner de lado) || *tener aparte* to exclude, to leave out; *sus amigos siempre le tienen aparte* his friends always leave him out; to keep apart *o* separate (separar).
◆ *m* TEATR aside || new paragraph (párrafo) || *punto y aparte* full stop, new paragraph [*US* period, new paragraph].

apartheid *m* apartheid.

apartijo *m* small share *o* portion.

aparvadera *f* wooden rake (rastrillo).

aparvar *vt* to spread out on the threshing floor (el trigo).

apasionado, da *adj* extremely *o* passionately fond, very keen; *apasionado por la caza* extremely fond of *o* very keen on hunting || impassioned, intense, fervent (discusión, etc.) || madly in love; *estar apasionado por una chica* to be madly in love with a girl || passionate; *amor apasionado* passionate love || partial, biassed, prejudiced; *un juicio muy apasionado* a very partial judgement || passionate, keen, fervent, enthusiastic; *es un defensor apasionado de* he is a keen defender of.
◆ *m/f* admirer, enthusiast, devotee (de un autor) || enthusiast, lover (de la música, etc.).

apasionamiento *m* passion (amor intenso) || great fondness, passion, enthusiasm; *mostrar apasionamiento por el arte* to show great fondness for art || rousing, stirring, excitement (acción de apasionar); *el apasionamiento de los ánimos* the rousing of one's spirits || *con apasionamiento* passionately (con amor), enthusiastically, keenly (con entusiasmo).

apasionante *adj* exciting, thrilling.

apasionar *vt* to rouse, to stir, to excite, to work up; *la discusión apasionó los ánimos* the discussion stirred people's spirits || — *es un tema que apasiona* it is a thrilling *o* a enthralling *o* an exciting subject || *le apasiona el fútbol, la música* he's very keen on *o* he's mad on *o* he's very fond of football, of music || *me apasiona esa mujer* I'm mad about *o* crazy about her.
◆ *vpr* to get excited, to get worked up (excitarse) || to get very keen, to become very interested; *apasionarse por cualquier cosa* to get very keen on anything, to become very interested in anything || to fall madly in love (*por* with) (enamorarse).

apaste; apastle *m* *AMER* bowl.

apatía *f* apathy, indifference || listlessness (pereza).

apático, ca *adj* apathetic, indifferent (*a, en* towards) || listless (perezoso).

apatito *m* MIN apatite.

apátrida *adj* stateless.
◆ *m/f* stateless person.

apeadero *m* halt (ferrocarriles); *la línea cuenta con cuarenta estaciones y once apeaderos* the line has forty stations and eleven halts || halt, stopping place (en el camino) || horse block (poyo) || small flat, pied-à-terre (casa).

apeador *m* surveyor (agrimensor).

apealar *vt* *AMER* to hobble (trabar).

apeamiento *m* dismounting (de un caballo) || alighting, getting off (de un autobús, de un tren) || getting out (de un coche).

apear *vt* to help down (de un carruaje, un caballo, un vagón) || to help out (de un coche) || to tie the legs of, to hobble (trabar un caballo) || to chock (un vehículo) || to take down (un objeto); *apear una estatua* to take down a statue || to fell (un árbol) || ARQ to prop up (apuntalar) || to survey (medir) || FIG & FAM to dissuade, to make back down; *no pude apearlo* I couldn't dissuade him *o* make him back down || *apear el tratamiento a uno* to drop s.o.'s formal title, to address s.o. informally.
◆ *vpr* to dismount, to get off *o* down (bajarse de un caballo) || to get off, to alight; *apearse de un autobús* to get off a bus, to alight from a bus || to get out (de un coche) || FIG & FAM to back down; *no quiere apearse* he won't back down || *AMER* to put up (en un hotel) || — FAM *apearse por las orejas* to be thrown over the horse's head | *no apearse del burro* not to back down, not to climb down, to refuse to back down, to refuse to recognize one's mistake.

apechugar *vi* to push with one's chest (empujar) || FIG & FAM *apechugar con* to shoulder, to take on; *siempre tengo que apechugar con todo el trabajo* I always have to take on *o* to shoulder all the work; to face, to put up with; *hay que apechugar con las consecuencias de su acción* you have to face the consequences of your action.

apedreado, da *adj* stoned || variegated, mottled (abigarrado) || pock-marked (de viruelas) || *San Esteban murió apedreado* Saint Stephen was stoned to death.

apedreamiento *m* stoning.

apedrear *vt* to throw stones at (lanzar piedras contra) || to stone to death, to stone (ejecutar).
◆ *v impers* to hail (granizar).
◆ *vpr* to be damaged by hail (cosechas).

apedreo *m* stoning || damage by hail (de las cosechas).

apegadamente *adv* devotedly.

apegado *adj* attached, devoted; *está muy apegado a las costumbres* he is very attached to *o* very devoted to tradition.

apegarse *vpr* to become attached *o* devoted, to grow fond; *apegarse a una persona* to become attached to *o* devoted to a person, to grow fond of a person || *AMER* to approach (acercarse).

apego *m* affection, attachment; *apego a una persona, a la patria* affection for a person, for one's country, attachment to a person, to one's country || interest; *el chico demuestra poco apego a los estudios* the boy shows little interest in his studies || — *tener apego a* to be fond of *o* attached to; *tengo mucho apego a este vestido* I'm very fond of *o* I'm very attached to this dress; to value; *tiene apego a su reputación* he values his reputation || *tomar* or *cobrar apego a* to become attached to *o* fond of.

apegualar *vt* AMER to hobble, to tie the legs of.

apelación *f* JUR appeal; *presentar* or *interponer una apelación* to make an appeal || consultation (entre médicos) || — JUR *juicio sin apelación* judgment without appeal, final judgment || *médico de apelación* consultant doctor || *recurso de apelación* appeal || FIG *sin apelación* irremediable, hopeless (sin arreglo) || *tribunal de apelación* court of appeal.

apelambrar *vt* to remove the hair from [skins by soaking].

apelante *adj/s* JUR appellant.

apelar *vi* JUR to appeal; *apelar de una sentencia* to appeal against a sentence || FIG to appeal; *apelo a su buena voluntad* I appeal to your good will | to resort to, to have recourse to; *apelar a la violencia* to resort to violence.

apelativo, va *adj/sm* appellative.

apelmazado, da *adj* soggy, stodgy; *arroz apelmazado* soggy rice || compact, solid, compressed (compacto) || matted (pelo) || FIG clumsy, heavy, stodgy (estilo).

apelmazamiento *m* sogginess, stodginess (de la comida) || flattening, compressing (de la tierra).

apelmazar *vt* to make soggy *o* stodgy || to compress (la tierra).
◆ *vpr* to go soggy *o* stodgy.

apelotonar *vt* to roll into a ball.
◆ *vpr* to go lumpy; *el colchón se ha apelotonado* the mattress has gone lumpy || to form balls (la lana) || to crowd together, to gather together (personas).

apellidar *vt* to call by one's surname (llamar por su apellido) || to call; *a este indio le apellidan Toro Sentado* they call this Indian Sitting Bull || FIG to call; *yo a esto lo apellido una broma pesada* I call this a bad joke.
◆ *vpr* to be called || *se apellida López* his surname is López, he is called López.

apellido *m* surname, last name; *me acuerdo de su nombre pero no de su apellido* I can remember his Christian name but not his surname || nickname (apodo); *le han dado un apellido muy feo* they've given him a horrible nickname || shout, call (llamamiento) || *apellido de soltera* maiden name.

apenado, da *adj* AMER ashamed.

apenar *vt* to grieve, to pain; *su conducta ha apenado mucho a su madre* his behaviour has greatly grieved his mother.
◆ *vpr* to be grieved *o* pained, to grieve, to distress o.s.

apenas *adv* hardly, scarcely; *apenas se mueve* he is hardly moving || with difficulty (penosamente) || as soon as; *apenas llegó se puso a trabajar* as soon as he arrived he began to work || — *apenas... cuando* no sooner... than; *apenas había llegado Juan cuando entró la policía* no sooner had John arrived than the police came in; only just... when; *apenas había llegado Juan cuando lo vi* John had only just arrived when I saw him || *apenas si* hardly, scarcely; *apenas si me tenía de pie* I could hardly stand up.

apencar *vi* FAM to take on, to shoulder; *apenca con el trabajo más pesado* he takes on the hardest work | to face, to put up with; *apencar con las consecuencias* to face the consequences.

apéndice *m* ANAT appendix (del intestino grueso) | appendage (protuberancia) || appendix (de un libro) || FIG lapdog (persona que acompaña).

apendicectomía *f* MED appendicectomy, appendectomy.

apendicitis *f* MED appendicitis.

apendicular *adj* appendicular.

Apeninos *npr mpl* GEOGR Apennines.

apeñuscar *vt* to press together, to pack, to cram together.

apeo *m* surveying (de tierras) || felling (de árboles) || ARQ propping up (con puntales) | prop, support (puntal) | scaffolding (andamiaje).

apeonar *vi* to run (las aves).

apepsia *f* MED apepsy.

aperar *vt* to make (hacer) || to provide, to equip (*de* with) (proveer).

apercibimiento *m* warning (aviso) || preparation.

apercibir *vt* to prepare, to get ready (preparar) || to provide, to equip (proveer); *apercibir de ropa* to provide with clothing || to warn (advertir); *nos apercibieron de la presencia de lobos en el bosque* they warned us about the presence of wolves in the woods || to threaten; *le han apercibido con una sanción si sigue llegando tarde* they have threatened him with punishment if he continues to arrive late || JUR to warn.
◆ *vpr* to get ready; *apercibirse para un viaje* to get ready for a journey || *apercibirse de* to provide o.s. with, to equip o.s. with.

apercollar* *vt* to grab by the neck (agarrar) || FAM to kill with a rabbit punch *o* with a blow on the back of the neck (matar) || FIG & FAM to swipe, to snatch (coger).

apergaminado, da *adj* parchment-like || FIG wizened; *rostro apergaminado* wizened face | wrinkled, dried (la piel) || *papel apergaminado* parchment paper.

apergaminarse *vpr* FIG & FAM to become wizened, to wrinkle, to dry up.

aperiódico, ca *adj* aperiodic.

aperitivo, va *adj* MED aperitive, aperient.
◆ *m* «apéritif», appetizer (bebida) || MED aperitive, aperient.

apero *m* AGR agricultural implements *pl*, farm equipment || draught animals *pl* (animales) || tools *pl*, equipment, gear (utensilios) || AMER fancy harness, trappings *pl* (guarniciones).
◆ *pl* implements, equipment *sing* (herramientas); *aperos de labranza* farm equipment, farming implements.

aperreado, da *adj* FAM lousy, wretched || *una vida aperreada* a dog's life.

aperreador, ra *adj* tiresome (cargante).

aperrear *vt* to set the dog's on || FIG & FAM to tire *o* to wear out (cansar) | to plague, to pester (molestar).
◆ *vpr* FAM to wear *o* to tire o.s. out (trabajar demasiado) | to insist; *¿por qué te aperreas en ir tan lejos?* why do you insist on going so far?

aperreo *m* FAM nuisance (molestia); *¡qué aperreo tener que ir a trabajar!* what a nuisance it is having to go to work! | exhaustion (cansancio) | rage, anger (ira) || — FAM *el niño cogió un aperreo* the child flew into a rage | *¡qué aperreo de vida!* it's a dog's life!

apersogar *vt* to tether, to tie.

apersonado, da *adj* *bien apersonado* presentable || *mal apersonado* not presentable, scruffy.

apersonamiento *m* JUR appearance.

apersonarse *vpr* to appear, to appear in person.

apertura *f* opening; *apertura de la pesca, del congreso, de la sesión* opening of the fishing season, of the congress, of the session || reading; *la apertura de un testamento* the reading of a will || opening (de una calle) || beginning; *apertura de hostilidades* beginning of hostilities || opening move, gambit (ajedrez) || — *apertura de crédito* opening of credit || *apertura de curso* beginning of term || *medio de apertura* standoff half, fly-half (rugby).
— OBSERV Unlike its paronym *abertura, apertura* often has an abstract meaning: *apertura de las hostilidades*.

apesadumbrar; apesarar *vt* to grieve, to trouble, to upset.
◆ *vpr* to be grieved *o* troubled *o* upset; *apesadumbrarse con* or *de* or *por una noticia* to be grieved by a piece of news.

apestado, da *adj* pestilential, foul (olor) || plague-stricken, suffering from the plague (que tiene peste) || FIG infested; *la ciudad está apestada de pordioseros* the city is infested with beggars.
◆ *m/f* plague-stricken person, person suffering from the plague || *hospital para apestados* pesthouse.

apestar *vt* to infect with the plague || FIG & FAM to plague; *me apesta con sus quejas* he plagues me with his complaints | to stink out; *apestas el cuarto con esa pipa* you're stinking the room out with that pipe.
◆ *vi* to smell, to stink; *apestar a ajo* to smell of garlic; *aquí apesta* it smells here.
◆ *vpr* to catch the plague || AMER to catch a cold.

apestoso, sa *adj* stinking, foul-smelling (hediondo) || foul, awful; *un olor apestoso* a foul smell || FIG annoying, sickening (enojoso) || *bolas apestosas* stink bombs.

apétalo, la *adj* BOT apetalous.

apetecedor, ra *adj* tempting; *lo que me propones es muy apetecedor* your proposition is very tempting || desirable.

apetecer* *vt* to long for, to crave for, to yearn for; *apetezco la llegada de la primavera* I am longing for Spring to arrive.
◆ *vi* to be welcome; *una taza de té siempre apetece* a cup of tea is always welcome || to tempt, to fancy; *esta tarta con nata me apetece* this cream cake tempts me, I fancy this cream cake || — *esto no me apetece nada* I don't feel like it at all, I don't fancy it at all || *hoy no me apetece salir* I don't feel like going out today || *me apetece un helado* I feel like an ice cream, I fancy an ice cream || *si le apetece, podemos ir al cine* if you feel like it *o* if you like, we can go to the cinema.

apetecible *adj* tempting, attractive.

apetecido, da *adj* desired; *puede que la búsqueda de petróleo no dé el resultado apetecido* it is possible that the search for oil will not give the desired result.

apetencia *f* longing, yearning, desire, craving, hunger; *apetencia de riquezas* longing for riches || appetite (ganas de comer).

apetito *m* appetite; *tener apetito* to have an appetite; *tener mucho apetito* to have a good *o* a big appetite || FIG yearning, desire, hunger; *el apetito de riquezas* the desire for riches || — *abrir* or *dar* or *despertar el apetito* to whet one's appetite || *apetito carnal* sexual appetite *o* desire || *comer con mucho apetito* to eat heartily.

apetitoso, sa *adj* appetizing, tempting; *este pastel parece muy apetitoso* this cake looks appetizing || tasty; *hemos comido un plato muy apetitoso* we ate a tasty dish || FIG & FAM tempting, attractive.

ápex *m* ASTR apex.

apezonado, da *adj* mamillated.

Apia (Vía) *npr f* Appian Way.

apiadar *vt* to move to pity; *su desgracia apiada a sus amigos* his misfortune moves his friends to pity.
◆ *vpr* to take pity, to pity; *apiadarse de uno* to take pity on s.o., to pity s.o.

apical *adj* apical.

apicararse *vpr* to take up bad ways.

ápice *m* apex, tip, point (extremo) || end, tip (de la lengua) || accent (signo gráfico) || FIG height (apogeo) | crux (de un problema) | iota (cosa muy pequeña) || — FIG *no ha cedido ni un ápice* he hasn't given an inch | *no ha perdido ni un ápice de su prestigio* he hasn't lost an ounce of his prestige.

apícola *adj* apicultural (de las abejas).

apicultor, ra *m/f* beekeeper, apiarist, apiculturist.

apicultura *f* beekeeping, apiculture.

apilador, ra *adj* piling.
◆ *m/f* piler.

apilamiento; apilado *m* piling up, heaping up.

apilar, apilarse *v tr y pr* to pile up, to heap up.

apimplarse *vpr* FAM to get tipsy, to get merry (emborracharse).

apimpollarse *vpr* AGR to bud.

apiñado, da *adj* packed, crammed, jammed (apretado) || cone-shaped, conical (de figura de piña).

apiñamiento *m* packing, cramming, jamming.

apiñar *vt* to pile up, to heap up (amontonar) || to pack, to cram, to jam (apretar).
◆ *vpr* to pack together, to cram together, to crowd together, to jam together; *la gente se apiñaba ante los escaparates* the people packed together in front of the windows || to press; *la gente se apiñaba alrededor del orador* the people pressed round the speaker.

apiñonado, da *adj* AMER brown-skinned, with a brown complexion (moreno).

apio *m* BOT celery.

apiolar *vt* FIG & FAM to do in, to bump off (matar) | to nab, to catch (prender).

apiparse; apiporrarse *vpr* to guzzle, to stuff o.s. (atracarse).

apirético, ca *adj* MED apyretic.

apirexia *f* MED apyrexy.

apisonadora *f* steamroller, road roller.

apisonamiento *m* rolling (con la apisonadora) || ramming (con el pisón).

apisonar *vt* to roll (la apisonadora) || to ram (el pisón).

apitonar *vi* to begin to grow (los cuernos) || to begin to grow horns (los animales) || BOT to sprout (los brotes).
◆ *vt* to pierce, to crack (el huevo).
◆ *vpr* FIG & FAM to get into a huff (amostazarse).

apizarrado, da *adj* slate-coloured.

aplacamiento *m* appeasement, placation, calming.

aplacar *vt* to appease, to placate, to calm; *aplacar la ira* to placate one's anger || to quench; *aplacar la sed* to quench one's thirst || to satisfy (el hambre).
◆ *vpr* to calm down, to die down; *la tempestad se aplacó* the storm calmed down.

aplanacalles *m inv* idler, loafer, loiterer (paseante).

aplanadera *f* TECN rammer (para apisonar).

aplanador, ra *adj* levelling, flattening, smoothing.
◆ *f* AGR leveller.

aplanamiento *m* smoothing || levelling; *el aplanamiento del suelo* the levelling of the ground || collapse (derrumbamiento).

aplanar *vt* to smooth, to flatten (allanar) || to level off, to make level (suelo) || FIG & FAM to knock out, to bowl over; *la noticia le aplanó* the news bowled him over *o* knocked him out | to overcome, to knock out; *estar aplanado por el calor* to be overcome *o* to be knocked out by the heat || AMER *aplanar las calles* to loiter about the streets, to hang about the streets, to loaf about.
◆ *vpr* to fall down, to collapse (edificio) || FIG to grow weak, to lose one's strength (perder el vigor).

aplanético, ca *adj* FÍS aplanatic.

aplastador, ra; aplastante *adj* overwhelming, crushing; *un triunfo aplastante* an overwhelming triumph.

aplastamiento *m* squashing, flattening, crushing || squashing; *aplastamiento de un tomate* squashing of a tomato || FIG crushing (de argumentos, críticas, etc.) | dumbfounding (confusión) | crushing, flattening, defeat (en una discusión, una lucha); *el aplastamiento de las tropas* the crushing of the troops.

aplastar *vt* to squash, to flatten, to crush; *aplastar un sombrero* to flatten a hat || to squash; *aplastar un tomate* to squash a tomato || FIG to crush, to destroy; *sus argumentos aplastan las críticas* his arguments destroy any criticism | to leave speechless, to floor, to dumbfound (dejar confuso) | to crush, to flatten, to overwhelm (en una discusión, una lucha); *aplastar al ejército enemigo* to crush the enemy army || AMER to overwork (una caballería).
◆ *vpr* to be crushed *o* flattened *o* squashed; *el sombrero se aplastó* the hat was crushed || to crash, to smash; *el coche se aplastó contra el árbol* the car crashed against the tree || FIG to flatten o.s.; *se aplastó contra el suelo para no ser alcanzado por las balas* he flattened himself against the ground so that he wouldn't be hit by the bullets || AMER to collapse (en un sillón) | to lose heart (desanimarse).

aplatanado, da *adj* FAM lethargic, listless.

aplatanarse *vpr* FAM to get listless, to become lethargic || *uno se aplatana con este clima* this climate makes one very listless.

aplaudidor, ra *m/f* applauder.

aplaudir *vt/vi* to applaud, to clap; *aplaudir a un artista* to applaud an artist || FIG to applaud (aprobar); *aplaudo tu decisión* I applaud your decision.

aplauso *m* applause (ovación) || applause, praise, acclaim; *su obra merece el mayor aplauso* his work is worthy of the greatest praise || *con el aplauso de* to the applause of.
◆ *pl* applause *sing*; *una salva de aplausos* thunderous applause.

aplazamiento *m* postponement, adjournment; *el aplazamiento de una reunión* the postponement of a meeting || deferment (de un pago).

aplazar *vt* to postpone, to adjourn; *aplazar una reunión* to postpone a meeting || to defer; *aplazar un pago* to defer a payment || to call, to summon (convocar).

aplebeyamiento *m* degradation; *el aplebeyamiento de las costumbres* the degradation of customs.

aplebeyar *vt* to demean, to degrade.
◆ *vpr* to lower o.s., to degrade o.s.

aplicabilidad *f* applicability.

aplicable *adj* applicable (*a* to).

aplicación *f* application; *la aplicación de una teoría* the application of a theory; *la aplicación de una pomada* the application of an ointment || fixing, attaching (de una cosa sobre otra) || putting into practice, application; *la aplicación del plan de desarrollo* the putting into practice of the development plan || use, application; *el acero tiene muchas aplicaciones* steel has many applications || application, diligence, industry (esmero) || appliqué; *mueble con aplicaciones de marfil* piece of furniture with ivory appliqués || INFORM application || MIL *escuela de aplicación* school of instruction.

aplicado, da *adj* diligent, industrious, painstaking; *un trabajador muy aplicado* a very industrious worker || studious; *un alumno aplicado* a studious pupil.

aplicar *vt* to apply; *aplicar una capa de pintura* to apply a coat of paint; *aplicar un criterio a un problema* to apply a criterion to a problem || to put into effect, to apply (ley) || to attach, to fix; *aplicar algo a la pared* to attach sth. to *o* to fix sth. on the wall || to put into practice, to use, to apply; *aplicar un método empírico* to use an empirical method || to put on; *aplicar un ribete a una chaqueta* to put an edging on a jacket || to assign (dinero, hombres, recursos) || *aplicar el oído* to put one's ear (sentido propio), to listen carefully *o* attentively (escuchar).
◆ *vpr* to work hard, to be devoted; *aplicarse en el estudio* to work hard at one's studies, to be devoted in one's studies || to devote o.s.; *aplicarse en hacer algo* to devote o.s. to doing sth || to be used for; *el agua se aplica al riego* the water is used for irrigation || to apply, to be applicable to; *la ley se aplica a todos* the law applies to everyone || to come into effect, to take effect (entrar en vigor) || *aplíquese el cuento* you might take a lesson from it yourself.

— OBSERV En inglés, *to apply* significa frecuentemente *solicitar*: *to apply for a job* solicitar un puesto.

aplique *m* wall lamp, wall light (lámpara).

aplomado, da *adj* leaden, lead-coloured (plomizo) || vertical; *un muro bien aplomado* a completely vertical wall || FIG cool, level-headed, self-assured; *una persona muy aplomada* a very cool person || TAUR which refuses to move (toro).

aplomar *vt* to test with a plumb line, to plumb (comprobar la verticalidad) || to plumb, to make vertical (poner vertical).
◆ *vpr* to gain self-assurance (cobrar aplomo) || to collapse, to fall down (desplomarse) || AMER to be ashamed, to be embarrassed.

aplomo *m* verticality || sense, aplomb (sensatez) || aplomb, assurance, self-assurance, level-headedness (serenidad) || set of the legs (del caballo) || *hacer que alguien pierda el aplomo* to rattle *o* to rile s.o.

apnea *f* MED apnoea, apnea.

apocado, da *adj* diffident, timid (tímido, sin ánimo) || lowly (bajo).

apocalipsis *m* Apocalypse || *el Libro del Apocalipsis* the Book of Revelation, the Apocalypse.

apocalíptico, ca *adj* apocalyptic, apocalyptical.

apocamiento *m* diffidence, timidity (timidez) || lowliness (bajeza).

apocar *vt* to make smaller, to diminish, to reduce (disminuir) || FIG to belittle, to humiliate (humillar) | to intimidate (intimidar).
◆ *vpr* FIG to humble o.s. (humillarse) | to feel small (sentirse humillado) | to be frightened *o* scared; *no me apoco por nada* I'm not scared of anything.

apócopa *f* GRAM apocopation, apocope.

apocopar *vt* GRAM to apocopate.

apócope *f* GRAM apocopation, apocope.

apócrifo, fa *adj* apocryphal (supuesto).

apodar *vt* to nickname (dar un apodo a).

apoderado *m* agent, representative (que tiene poder) || manager (de deportista) || JUR proxy (poderhabiente).

apoderamiento *m* empowering, granting of powers (acción de apoderar) || seizure, seizing (acción de apoderarse).

apoderar *vt* to empower, to authorize || JUR to grant power of attorney to.
◆ *vpr* to seize; *apoderarse del poder* to seize power || to take possession, to seize; *se apoderaron de la casa* they took possession of *o* they seized the house || FIG to take hold of, to grip; *el miedo se apoderó de ellos* fear took hold of them.

apodíctico, ca *adj* apodictic (indiscutible).

apodo *m* nickname (mote).

ápodo, da *adj* ZOOL apodal.
◆ *m* ZOOL apod.

apódosis *f* apodosis.

apófisis *f* ANAT apophysis.

apofonía *f* ablaut.

apogeo *m* ASTR apogee || FIG height, summit, acme; *el apogeo de la gloria* the acme of glory || *estar en todo su apogeo* to be on one's best form; *este artista está ahora en todo su apogeo* this artist is now on his best form; at one's height; *la temporada turística está en todo su apogeo en el mes de agosto* the tourist season is at its height in August.

apolillado, da *adj* moth-eaten (ropa) || worm-eaten (madera).

apolilladura *f* moth hole (en la ropa) || woodworm hole (en la madera).

apolillamiento *m* damage done by moths (en las telas) || woodworm (en la madera).

apolillar *vt* to eat, to make holes in (la polilla) || *AMER* POP *estarla apolillando* to be snoozing (dormir).
◆ *vpr* to get worm-eaten (la madera) || to get moth-eaten (la ropa).

apolíneo, a *adj* Apollonian (relativo a Apolo) || FAM Apollonian (esbelto).

apolítico, ca *adj* apolitical.

apolitismo *m* apoliticism.

Apolo *npr m* MIT Apollo.

apologético, ca *adj* apologetic.
◆ *f* apologetics (en teología).

apología *f* vindication, defence, apology, justification || *hacer la apología de uno, de algo* to defend *o* to justify *o* to vindicate s.o., sth.

apologista *m/f* apologist.

apólogo *m* apologue.

apoltronado, da *adj* lazy, idle.

apoltronarse *vpr* to get lazy *o* idle, to let o.s. go (hacerse poltrón).

apomazar *vt* to smooth with a pumice stone.

aponeurosis *f* aponeurosis.

aponeurótico, ca *adj* aponeurotic.

apoplejía *f* MED apoplexy || *ataque de apoplejía* stroke.

apoplético, ca *adj/s* apoplectic.

apoquinar *vt/vi* POP to fork out, to cough up (pagar).

aporca; aporcadura *f* AGR earthing-up.

aporcar *vt* AGR to earth up.

aporco *m* *AMER* earthing-up.

aporía *f* FIL aporia.

aporrar *vi* to get stuck for words, to dry up.
◆ *vpr* to become a bore.

aporreado, da *adj* beaten (golpeado) || miserable, wretched; *llevar una vida aporreada* to lead a miserable life || rascally (pícaro).

aporreadura *f*; **aporreamiento** *m* beating, thumping.

aporrear *vt* to hit, to thump, to give a beating to; *aporrear a uno* to hit s.o., to give s.o. a beating || to bang on, to hammer on; *aporrear la puerta* to bang on the door || to thump, to pound, to hammer away on; *aporrear el piano* to thump the piano || FIG *aporrearle a uno los oídos* to go right through one, to get on one's nerves (un ruido).
◆ *vpr* to fight, to hit each other (pelearse) || FIG to slave, to slog, to wear o.s. out (trabajar).

aporreo *m* beating, thumping (golpeo).

aportación *f* contribution; *la aportación de este país ha sido considerable* the contribution of this country has been considerable; *la aportación de fondos* the contribution of funds.

aportar *vi* MAR to reach port (tocar tierra) || FIG to arrive (llegar) | to be; *hace mucho tiempo que no aporta por aquí* it's a long time since he was here, he hasn't been here for a long time.
◆ *vt* to contribute (contribuir) || to bring forward, to provide; *aportar pruebas* to bring forward evidence.

aporte *m* *AMER* contribution.

aportillar *vt* to breach, to break open, to make a breach in (un muro).
◆ *vpr* to collapse.

aportuguesado, da *adj* who seems Portuguese.

aposentador, ra *adj* lodging || MIL *partida aposentadora* quartering party.
◆ *m* landlord, person who gives lodgings || MIL quartermaster.
◆ *f* landlady, person who gives lodgings.

aposentamiento *m* lodging, putting-up (acción).

aposentar *vt* to lodge, to put up, to give lodgings to.
◆ *vpr* to put up, to lodge, to stay; *aposentarse en un hotel* to put up at a hotel, to lodge *o* to stay in *o* at a hotel.

aposento *m* room (habitación) || lodgings *pl* (hospedaje) || *tomar aposento* to put up, to stay; *tomar aposento en una fonda* to put up at an inn, to stay at *o* in an inn.

aposición *f* GRAM apposition; *en aposición* in apposition.

apósito *m* MED dressing; *poner un apósito* to put on a dressing.

aposta; apostas *adv* on purpose, deliberately, purposely; *lo hizo aposta para molestarme* he did it on purpose to annoy me.

apostadero *m* MIL post, station || MAR military port, naval station.

apostador, ora; apostante *adj* betting.
◆ *m/f* better.

apostar* *vt* to bet, to stake, to lay; *apostar mil pesetas a un caballo* to bet a thousand pesetas on a horse || to post, to station (colocar a gente en un sitio); *apostar a un centinela* to post a sentry.
◆ *vi* to bet; *apostar en las carreras de caballos* to bet on horse races; *apuesto a que no lo haces* I bet you don't.
◆ *vpr* to bet; *me he apostado mil pesetas con él* I have bet him a thousand pesetas || to take up one's post *o* one's station (en un lugar) || — FIG *apostarse la cabeza a que* to bet anything that || *¿qué te apuestas a que se rompe?* what do you bet that it breaks?, I bet you it breaks, what's the betting it breaks? (*fam*).
— OBSERV This verb is irregular in the sense *to bet*, and is conjugated like *contar*. It is regular when it means *to post*.

apostasía *f* apostasy.

apóstata *adj/s* apostate.

apostatar *vi* to apostatize || FIG to change sides.

apostema *f* MED aposteme.

apostemar *vt* MED to apostemate.

apostilla *f* note.

apostillar *vt* to add notes to (anotar).
◆ *vpr* MED to scab over; *la herida se ha apostillado* the wound has scabbed over.

apóstol *m* apostle; *los Hechos de los Apóstoles* the Acts of the Apostles || FIG champion, apostle; *apóstol de la paz* champion of peace.

apostolado *m* apostolate.

apostólico, ca *adj* apostolic || papal, apostolical (del Papa) || *nuncio apostólico* papal nuncio.

apostrofar *vt* to apostrophize.

apóstrofe *m* apostrophe.

apóstrofo *m* apostrophe (signo ortográfico).

apostura *f* bearing (aspecto); *de buena apostura* of good bearing; *una noble apostura* noble bearing || elegance, grace (elegancia).

apotegma *m* apothegm, apophtegm.

apotema *f* MAT apothem.

apoteósico, ca *adj* tremendous; *un triunfo apoteósico* a tremendous triumph.

apoteosis *f* apotheosis || TEATR *apoteosis final* grand finale.

apotrerar *vt* *AMER* to divide (land) into pastures.

apoyar *vt* to lean; *apoyar el armario en la pared* to lean the wardrobe against the wall || to rest; *apoyar la cabeza en las manos* to rest one's head in one's hands || to put, to rest; *apoyar los codos en la mesa* to rest one's elbows on the table; *apoyar el pie en un escalón* to put one's foot on a step || FIG to support, to back up; *sus discursos apoyan su decisión* his speeches support his decision; *apoyar a un candidato* to support a candidate | to base, to found; *apoya su teoría en hechos concretos* he bases his theory on concrete facts | to second (una moción) | to confirm (confirmar) || MIL to support || ARQ & TECN to support, to hold up.
◆ *vi* to rest; *la viga apoya en una columna* the beam rests on a column.
◆ *vpr* to lean; *apoyarse en un bastón* to lean on a walking stick || to rest, to be supported; *la viga se apoya en una columna* the beam rests on *o* is supported by a column || FIG to be based on, to rest on; *un argumento que se apoya en la realidad* an argument which is based on reality | to base o.s. on; *me apoyo en las estadísticas oficiales* I am basing myself on official statistics | to rely; *puedo apoyarme en Rodríguez para esta empresa* I can rely on Rodriguez for this job || *apoyarse demasiado en sus padres* to be overdependent on one's parents.

apoyatura *f* MÚS appoggiatura.

apoyo *m* support; *una columna que sirve de apoyo* a column which acts as a support || FIG support, backing (protección, ayuda) | approval (aprobación) || MIL support || — TECN *cigüeñal de cinco apoyos* five main bearing crankshaft || *punto de apoyo* fulcrum (física), base; *establecer un punto de apoyo para una red* *comercial* to set up a base for a commercial network.

apreciable *adj* appreciable; *una diferencia apreciable* an appreciable difference || audible, sensible (ruido) || FIG worthy, estimable; *una persona apreciable* a worthy person.

apreciación *f* appreciation || appraisal (valoración).

apreciador *adj* who appreciates.
◆ *m/f* person who appreciates.

apreciar *vt* to appraise, to value (valorar), to price, to value (poner precio a) || to register; *este cronómetro aprecia centésimas de segundos* this cronometer registers hundredths of a second || to make out; *desde lejos no puedo apreciar los detalles* from afar I can't make out the details || to see, to notice (percibir) || FIG to appreciate; *apreciar la cocina francesa* to appreciate French cooking | to have esteem for, to hold in esteem; *apreciar mucho a un muchacho* to have great esteem for a boy, to hold a boy in high esteem || — *apreciar algo en su justo valor* to appreciate sth. for its true value || *el médico le apreció una doble fractura* the doctor observed that he was suffering from a double fracture.
◆ *vpr* to be observed *o* registered *o* noted; *se aprecia un alza en el costo de la vida* a rise in the cost of living is observed.

apreciativo, va *adj* appreciative.

aprecio *m* appraisal, valuation (evaluación) || FIG esteem, regard, appreciation; *tener gran aprecio a uno* to have great esteem for s.o. || *es una persona de mi mayor aprecio* he is a person that I hold in the highest esteem *o* regard.

aprehender *vt* to seize; *aprehender contrabando* to seize contraband || to apprehend, to arrest (apresar) || to conceive of, to imagine (concebir) || to understand (comprender).

aprehensible *adj* conceivable, understandable.

aprehensión *f* apprehension, capture, arrest; *la aprehensión de un ladrón* the apprehension of a thief || seizure (de contrabando) || comprehension, understanding (comprensión) || conception.

aprehensivo, va *adj* perceptive (perspicaz).

apremiable *adj* JUR coercible.

apremiador, ra; apremiante *adj* urgent, pressing; *trabajo apremiante* urgent work.

apremiantemente *adv* urgently.

apremiar *vt* to urge, to press; *aprémialo para que termine* urge him to finish || to compel, to oblige, to force (obligar) || to hurry (up) (dar prisa).
◆ *vi* to be urgent (ser urgente); *apremia dar salida a la mercancía* it is urgent that we sell the merchandise || *el tiempo apremia* time is pressing *o* short.

apremio *m* hurry, haste, urgency (prisa) || obligation, compulsion (obligación) || JUR writ; *comisionado de apremios* writ server || — *por apremio de tiempo* because time is (was) pressing || JUR *por vía de apremio* under duress.

aprender *vt* to learn; *aprender de memoria* to learn by heart || — FIG *aprender en cabeza ajena* to learn from other people's mistakes | *para que aprenda* that will teach him (her, you), he (she, you) asked for that.
◆ *vpr* to learn; *aprenderse la lección* to learn one's lesson.

aprendiz, za *m/f* beginner, novice, learner (principiante) || apprentice, trainee; *aprendiz de pastelero* confectioner's apprentice, apprentice confectioner || learner; *aprendiz de conductor* learner driver || — *colocar de aprendiz* to apprentice, to find an apprenticeship for || FIG *ser aprendiz de todo y oficial de nada* to be a Jack of all trades and master of none.

aprendizaje *m* apprenticeship, traineeship || *hacer su aprendizaje* to serve one's apprenticeship.

aprensión *f* apprehension, fear (miedo); *aunque está sano tiene la aprensión de que se va a morir* although he is healthy he has the apprehension that he is going to die || good manners *pl*, courtesy (delicadeza) || — *me da aprensión aceptar este trabajo porque se lo quito a otro* I don't like *o* I hesitate to accept this job because I'm taking it from s.o. else || *me da aprensión beber en su vaso porque está acatarrado* I'm afraid to drink *o* I hesitate to drink *o* I'm apprehensive about drinking from his glass because he has a cold.
◆ *pl* strange ideas, strange notions.

aprensivo, va *adj* fearful, apprehensive, squeamish; *es tan aprensivo que nunca va a ver a los enfermos* he is so apprehensive that he never goes to see sick people || worried, anxious; *está muy aprensivo con su tos* he is very worried about his cough || FIG *ser aprensivo* to be a hypochondriac.

apresador, ra *adj* capturing, who captures.
◆ *m/f* captor.

apresamiento *m* capture, seizure.

apresar *vt* to catch, to seize [with teeth or claws]; *el lobo apresó el cordero* the wolf seized the lamb || MAR to capture, to seize; *apresar un barco enemigo* to capture an enemy ship || (ant) to imprison, to put in prison (aprisionar).

aprestador, ra *m/f* sizer (de tela).

aprestar *vt* to prepare, to get ready (preparar) || TECN to size (telas) || — *aprestar el oído* to lend an ear, to listen || *aprestar la atención* to pay attention, to give one's attention.
◆ *vpr* to make *o* to get ready, to prepare; *aprestarse para salir* to get ready to go out.

apresto *m* preparation (preparación) || TECN size (substancia) | sizing (acción).

apresuradamente *adv* hurriedly, in a hurry (con prisa) || FIG hastily.

apresurado, da *adj* in a hurry; *que las personas apresuradas pasen primero* let those who are in a hurry go first || hurried, hasty (hecho con prisa); *un viaje apresurado* a hurried journey || FIG hasty; *conclusión apresurada* hasty conclusion.

apresuramiento *m* hurry, haste (prisa) || FIG haste.

apresurar *vt* to quicken up, to speed up, to hurry up, to accelerate; *apresurar el trabajo* to quicken up the work || to hurry, to rush; *si me apresuras no lo haré bien* if you hurry me I shan't do it well || *apresurar el paso* to walk more quickly, to go faster, to quicken one's pace.
◆ *vpr* to hurry, to make haste, to hurry up; *hay que apresurarse, ya es muy tarde* we'll have to hurry, it's late || — *apresurarse a hacer algo* to hurry *o* to hasten to do sth., to do sth. at once *o* straight away || *apresurarse en contestar* to waste no time in replying, to reply as quickly as possible || *apresurémonos por llegar* let's hurry up and get there, let's get there as soon as we can || *no apresurarse* to take one's time; *no se apresure* take your time.

apretadamente *adv* tightly || (only) just; *ganó apretadamente* he (only) just won || — *con su sueldo vive muy apretadamente* his wage gives him just enough to live on || *llegar muy apretadamente al final del mes* to just manage to the end of the month.

apretadera *f* strap (correa).

apretado, da *adj* tight; *el corcho de la botella está muy apretado* the cork of the bottle is very tight; *un lío muy apretado* a very tight bundle; *un vestido apretado* a tight dress; *un nudo apretado* a tight knot || close; *los codos apretados al cuerpo* with one's elbows close to one's body; *un tejido apretado* a close weave || hard; *un colchón apretado* a hard mattress || crowded together, squashed together, tightly packed (la gente) || cluttered; *con tantos muebles el cuarto está muy apretado* with so much furniture the room is very cluttered || compact, dense (compacto) || FIG difficult, tricky; *asunto, lance apretado* difficult matter, moment | cramped (escritura) | tight (los labios) | tightfisted, miserly, stingy (tacaño) || — FIG & FAM *estar muy apretado* to be very hard up, to be very short of money (de dinero), to have problems (tener problemas) || *la gente iba muy apretada en el tren* the train was packed *o* very crowded || *vivir muy apretado en un piso* not to have much room in a flat, to be cramped in a flat.

apretador, ra *adj* which tightens.
◆ *m* corset (corsé) || jerkin (almilla) || body bandage (faja de niños) || clamp (grapa).

apretamiento *m* squeezing || tightening (de un tornillo, de un cinturón, etc.) || crowding (de la gente) || difficult situation, tight spot (situación).

apretar* *vt* to squeeze, to hug; *apretar entre los brazos* to squeeze in one's arms || to grip, to grasp; *me apretó el brazo* he gripped my arm || to tighten; *apretar un tornillo, un cinturón* to tighten a screw, a belt || to press; *apretar el botón* to press the button || to pinch, to be too tight for; *me aprietan los zapatos* my shoes pinch, my shoes are too tight for me || to pull (el gatillo) || to press down (comprimir) || to shake; *apretar la mano a alguien* to shake s.o.'s hand || to quicken up, to quicken, to speed up (acelerar); *apretar el paso* to quicken up one's pace || to pack, to squeeze; *apretar cosas en una caja* to pack *o* to squeeze things into a box || to put pressure on; *le están apretando para que dimita* they are putting pressure on him to resign || — FIG *apretar la mano* or *las clavijas a alguien* to clamp down on s.o., to tighten up on s.o. || *apretar los dientes* to grit *o* to clench one's teeth || *apretarse el cinturón* to tighten one's belt || *me aprieta el tiempo* time is running out, I'm short of time.
◆ *vi* to get worse (frío, dolor) || to get heavier (lluvia) || to get stronger *o* worse (calor) || to be too tight (un vestido) || to hurt, to pinch (zapatos) || to make an effort, to pull one's socks up; *tienes que apretar, si quieres sacar buenas notas* you've got to make an effort if you want to get good marks || to hurry up; *¡apriete!* hurry up! || to be strict (ser exigente) || *apretar a correr* to break into a run.
◆ *vpr* to crowd, to crowd together (apiñarse) || to huddle together (para entrar en calor, etc.).

apretón *m* squeeze (presión fuerte y rápida) || FAM call of nature, urgent need (necesidad natural) || FIG & FAM difficult *o* awkward situation, fix, tight spot (aprieto) || FAM dash (carrera) || dash of dark colour (pintura) || — *apretón de manos* handshake || *me dio un apretón de manos* he shook my hand, we shook hands || *odio los apretones de los transportes públicos* I hate the crush of public transport || *reciba un apretón de manos* best wishes (en una carta).

apretujar *vt* FAM to squeeze hard.
◆ *vpr* FAM to squash up together, to squeeze together, to cram together (las personas por falta de espacio).

apretujón *m* FAM crush, crowding (de las personas) | hard squeeze (apretón).

apretura *f* scarcity (escasez) || hurrying (prisa) || FIG difficult *o* awkward situation, tight spot, fix, jam (apuro).

◆ *pl* crowds, crush *sing; no me gustan las apreturas del autobús* I don't like the crush on the bus.

aprieto *m* difficult *o* awkward situation, tight spot, tight corner, fix, jam; *estar* or *hallarse* or *verse en un aprieto, pasar un aprieto* to be in a tight spot ‖ — *poner en un aprieto* to put into a difficult situation *o* in a tight corner *o* in a tight spot ‖ *salir del aprieto* to get out of trouble.

a priori *adj/adv* a priori.

apriorismo *m* apriority.

aprisa *adv* quickly; *se fue muy aprisa* he left very quickly ‖ *¡aprisa!* quick!, quickly!, be quick!

apriscar *vt* to fold, to put in a fold [sheep].
◆ *vpr* to go into a fold (el ganado).

aprisco *m* fold.

aprisionar *vt* to imprison, to put into prison (encarcelar) ‖ to trap; *la carrocería le aprisionó una pierna* the bodywork trapped one of his legs ‖ FIG to clasp, to grasp; *aprisionar a alguien en los brazos* to clasp s.o. in one's arms | to tie down; *estoy aprisionado en el engranaje administrativo* I am tied down by red tape.

aproar *vi* MAR to head, to steer.

aprobación *f* approval, approbation; *dar su aprobación* to give one's approval ‖ passing (de una ley).

aprobado, da *adj* approved; *aprobado por el Ministerio de Educación Nacional* approved by the Ministry of Education ‖ passed (una ley) ‖ *salir aprobado* to pass (en un examen).
◆ *m* pass, passing grade; *tuvo tres aprobados* he got three passes.

aprobar* *vt* to approve; *aprobar un proyecto* to approve a plan ‖ to approve of; *su padre no aprueba sus amistades* his father doesn't approve of his friends ‖ to pass; *he aprobado el examen de matemáticas* I have passed the mathematics examination ‖ to pass (una ley) ‖ *aprobar por unanimidad* to approve unanimously.
◆ *vi* to pass; *ha aprobado en español* he has passed in Spanish.

aprobatorio, ria *adj* approving, approbative, approbatory.

aproches *m pl* MIL approaches ‖ *AMER* surrounding districts, environs (cercanías) | neighbourhood (vecindad).

apropiación *f* appropriation (robo) ‖ adaptation (adecuación) ‖ JUR *apropiación indebida* embezzlement (de fondos).

apropiado, da *adj* appropriate, suitable.

apropiar *vt* to adapt, to fit; *apropiar las leyes a las costumbres* to adapt laws to customs.
◆ *vpr* to appropriate, to take; *siempre se apropia de lo que no le pertenece* he always takes what doesn't belong to him.

apropincuarse *vpr* to approach; *apropincuarse a algo* to approach sth.

apropósito *m* TEATR skit.

aprovechable *adj* usable, serviceable ‖ wearable; *tu vestido es aún aprovechable* your dress is still wearable ‖ *estos restos son todavía aprovechables* these leftovers can still be used.

aprovechadamente *adv* profitably.

aprovechado, da *adj* thrifty, economical; *una ama de casa muy aprovechada* a very thrifty housewife ‖ resourceful (apañado) ‖ diligent, studious (estudioso) ‖ industrious (trabajador) ‖ planned; *casa bien aprovechada* well-planned house ‖ selfish (egoísta) ‖ spent; *dinero, tiempo bien aprovechado* money, time well spent ‖ FAM *es un tipo muy aprovechado* he's a real sponger.
◆ *adj/s* opportunist.

aprovechador, ra *adj/s* opportunist.

aprovechamiento *m* advantage; *sacaron el máximo aprovechamiento de ello* they used it to the greatest advantage, they took the greatest advantage of it ‖ exploitation, tapping, use; *el aprovechamiento de los recursos naturales* the exploitation of natural resources ‖ use; *aprovechamiento en común de un bosque* joint use of a wood ‖ development, improvement; *el aprovechamiento de las tierras* land development ‖ harnessing; *el aprovechamiento de un río* the harnessing of a river.
◆ *pl* products.

aprovechar *vi* to be helpful, to be useful, to be a help; *les aprovechará mucho a tus hermanos* it will be a great help to *o* it will be very helpful to your brothers ‖ to take advantage of it, to make the most of it, to seize the opportunity; *como hacía buen tiempo, aprovecharon y se fueron al campo* as the weather was fine, they took advantage of it and went into the country ‖ FIG to make progress, to progress; *no hemos aprovechado en esa clase* we have made no progress *o* we haven't progressed in that class ‖ MAR to haul as close as possible ‖ — *no aprovechar para nada* to be of no use at all ‖ *¡que aproveche!* (I hope you) enjoy your meal, bon appétit (véase OBSERV).
◆ *vt* to take advantage of, to make the most of; *aprovechar el tiempo, la situación* to take advantage of the weather, of the situation ‖ to make good use of, to put to good use; *un cocinero que sabe aprovechar toda clase de alimentos* a cook who can make good use of any kind of food, a cook who can put any kind of food to good use ‖ to use; *no aprovecho nunca los restos* I never use the leftovers ‖ to take (unfair) advantage of (de una manera egoísta) ‖ to exploit (los recursos naturales) ‖ to develop, to improve (tierras) ‖ to harness (curso de agua) ‖ to take advantage of, to take up (una oferta) ‖ *aprovechar la ocasión* to take *o* to seize the opportunity, to make the most of the opportunity.
◆ *vpr* to take advantage, to use to one's advantage (sacar provecho) ‖ to make the most of it, to take advantage; *aprovéchate ahora, luego será demasiado tarde* make the most of it now, before it is too late ‖ to take advantage of; *aprovecharse de uno, de un momento de descuido* to take advantage of s.o., of a moment's negligence.

— OBSERV *¡Que aproveche!* is a polite expression used by one person to others who are already eating. As no fixed expression is used in these circumstances in English, only an approximate translation can be given.

aprovechón, ona *adj* selfish, opportunist (que saca provecho de todo).
◆ *m/f* advantage-taker, selfish person, opportunist.

aprovisionamiento *m* supply, supplying, provision (acción de abastecer) ‖ supply, provision (vituallas).

aprovisionar *vt* to supply, to give supplies to, to give provisions to.

aproximación *f* approximation; *cálculo con aproximación* calculation by approximation ‖ prize for runners-up, consolation prize (en la lotería) ‖ proximity, closeness, nearness (proximidad) ‖ bringing together (de dos personas) ‖ rapprochement (de dos países) ‖ approximation (acercamiento) ‖ — *con una aproximación del uno por ciento* to the nearest one per cent ‖ *sólo es una aproximación* it is only a rough estimate *o* an approximation.

aproximadamente *adv* approximately.

aproximado, da *adj* approximate, rough; *valor, cálculo aproximado* approximate value, calculation.

aproximar *vt* to bring nearer; *aproxima tu silla a la mía* bring your chair nearer to mine ‖ to draw up; *aproximar una silla a la mesa* to draw a chair up to the table ‖ to put nearer; *aproxima la mesa a esa pared* put the table nearer to that wall ‖ to pass; *aproxímame el libro* pass me the book ‖ to bring together (dos personas).
◆ *vpr* to move nearer; *aproximarse al fuego* to move nearer to the fire ‖ to draw near, to approach; *se aproxima su cumpleaños* his birthday is drawing near ‖ to be nearly; *se aproxima a los veinte* he is nearly twenty ‖ to be near *o* close; *me aproximé bastante a la solución* I was quite near to the answer ‖ to approach, to near; *aproximarse a su destino* to approach *o* to near one's destination ‖ FIG to approach ‖ *¡ni se le aproxima!* it's nothing like it! (es completamente distinto).

aproximativo, va *adj* approximate, rough (aproximado).

ápside *m* ASTR apsis; *los ápsides* the apsides.

aptamente *adv* conveniently.

ápterix *m* ZOOL apteryx.

áptero, ra *adj* ZOOL apterous (sin alas).

aptitud *f* suitability, aptness, aptitude (de una cosa) ‖ capacity, ability (capacidad) ‖ — *aptitud para los negocios* business sense ‖ *prueba de aptitud* aptitude test.
◆ *pl* gift *sing*, aptitude *sing*; *tiene aptitudes para la pintura* he has a gift for painting ‖ *aptitudes físicas* physical capacities.

apto, ta *adj* capable; *un obrero muy apto* a very capable worker ‖ suitable, fitted; *apto para ocupar este cargo* suitable for this post ‖ fit (*para* to) (en condiciones de) ‖ — MIL *apto para el servicio* fit for service ‖ *película apta para todos los públicos* U-certificate film ‖ *película no apta para menores* X-certificate film, film unsuitable for children.

apuesta *f* bet, wager ‖ *apuestas mutuas* pari-mutuel.

apuesto, ta *adj* spruce, neat, smart (elegante).

Apuleyo *npr m* Apuleius.

apulgarar *vt* to press with one's thumb, to thumb.
◆ *vpr* to get mildewed, to become spotted with mildew (la ropa blanca).

apunar *vt* *AMER* to give mountain sickness.
◆ *vpr* *AMER* to have mountain sickness.

apuntación *f* note (nota) ‖ aiming (de armas) ‖ MÚS notation.

apuntado, da *adj* pointed, sharp (puntiagudo) ‖ ARQ gothic, pointed (arco).

apuntador, ra *adj* who makes notes (que apunta) ‖ aiming, who aims (artillería).
◆ *m* aimer (artillería) ‖ TEATR prompter; *concha del apuntador* prompter's box ‖ FIG *en esta película muere hasta el apuntador* there's not a soul left alive at the end of the film.

apuntalamiento *m* propping-up, shoring-up ‖ spragging, propping-up, shoring-up (de minas).

apuntalar *vt* to prop up, to shore up ‖ to sprag, to prop up, to shore up (una mina).

apuntamiento *m* aiming (de un arma) ‖ note (nota) ‖ JUR records *pl* of the proceedings.

apuntar *vt* to aim, to point (un arma) ‖ to point at (señalar); *apuntar a uno con el dedo* to point at s.o. with one's finger ‖ to point out (sugerir); *el ministro apuntó la necesidad de una reforma* the minister pointed out the need for a reform ‖ to show; *este principiante apunta excelentes cualidades* this beginner shows excellent qualities ‖ to take *o* to note down, to make a note of (anotar); *apunta sus señas* take down his address ‖ to put down, to put; *apúntelo en mi cuenta* put it on my account; *me apuntó en la lista* he put me on the list ‖ to put

a mark on (señalar un escrito) || to sharpen (sacar punta); *apuntar un lápiz* to sharpen a pencil || to bet, to stake (jugar); *apuntar mil pesetas* to bet a thousand pesetas || to score (en deportes, juegos) || to tack (en costura) || to fasten *o* to fix temporarily (fijar provisionalmente) || FAM to darn, to mend (zurcir) || to sketch out (bosquejar) || TEATR to prompt || to prompt with, to whisper; *le apuntaron la solución* they prompted him with the answer, they whispered the answer to him || — FAM *apúntalo en la barra de hielo* you can forget it, you can give it up as lost || *apuntar presente* to mark present.
◆ *vi* to aim; *apuntar a uno a la cabeza* to aim at s.o.'s head; *apuntar a un blanco con un arma* to aim a weapon at a target; *objetivos que apuntan a la supresión de los privilegios* objectives which aim at the suppression of privileges || to dawn, to break (el día) || to sprout, to begin to grow (la barba) || to sprout to come through; *la hierba apunta* the grass is sprouting || TEATR to prompt || to point; *la proa de la nave apuntaba al sur* the bow of the ship pointed towards the south || MIL *¡apunten!* take aim!
◆ *vpr* to begin to turn sour (el vino) || to put one's name; *me apunté en la lista* I put my name on the list || FAM to enrol, to enroll; *me apunté en el colegio* I enrolled in the school | to get tipsy (embriagarse) || — FIG *apuntarse un tanto, un triunfo* to chalk up *o* to score a point, a victory | *yo me apunto* I'm with you, I'm game, count me in.

apunte *m* note (nota) || sketch (dibujo) || TEATR prompter (apuntador) | prompt (voz del apuntador) | prompter's script, promptbook (texto) || staker (jugador) || stake, bet (puesta en juego) || COM entry || AMER *llevar el apunte a uno* to respond to s.o. (corresponder).
◆ *pl* notes; *tomar apuntes* to take notes || ARTES *sacar apuntes* to do some sketches.

apuntillar *vt* TAUR to deal the coup de grâce (to the bull) with a dagger.

apuñalar *vt* to stab; *lo apuñaló por la espalda* he stabbed him in the back || FIG *apuñalar con la mirada* to look daggers at.

apuñar *vt* to take in one's fist.

apuracabos *m inv* save-all (palmatoria).

apuradamente *adv* with difficulty || in want, in need; *vivir apuradamente* to live in want || FAM exactly || *vino a decírmelo muy apuradamente* he was very embarrassed when he came to tell me.

apurado, da *adj* hard up; *estar apurado de dinero* to be hard up for money || difficult, awkward; *estoy en una situación apurada* I'm in an awkward situation || worn-out, tired-out, exhausted (agotado) || embarrassed (avergonzado); *me vi apurado cuando tuve que pedirle dinero* I was embarrassed when I had to ask him for money || exact (preciso) || AMER in a hurry (apresurado) || — *estar apurado de tiempo* to be short of time, not to have much time || *estar apurado por uno* to be annoyed by s.o. || *verse apurado* to be in a jam *o* a fix (estar en un apuro).

apurador, ra *adj* tiring, exhausting (que agota).

apuramiento *m* purification (acción de purificar) || exhaustion (agotamiento) || FIG clarification (aclaración).

apurar *vt* to purify (purificar) || to exhaust; *apurar todos los medios para conseguir algo* to exhaust every means of obtaining sth. || to drain; *apurar una copa* to drain a glass || to use up, to finish off; *apurar la pintura* to use up the paint || to exhaust, to wear *o* to tire out (abrumar); *los padres apuraron al niño* the parents exhausted the child || to examine thoroughly *o* in detail (examinar a fondo) || to embarrass (causar vergüenza); *me apura pedirle dinero* it embarrasses me to ask him for money || to exhaust the patience of, to make lose one's patience; *si me apuras, sufrirás las consecuencias* if you make me lose *o* if you exhaust my patience, you will suffer the consequences || to rush, to hurry (dar prisa); *no me apures tanto* don't rush me so || — *apurándolo mucho* at the most (como mucho); *apurándolo mucho esta casa le ha costado tres mil libras* this house cost him three thousand pounds at the most || *apurar el cáliz hasta las heces* to drain the cup to the dregs || *me apura tener que decirle esto* I don't like having to tell you this, I hate to have to tell you this || *si me apura mucho, se lo vendería por mil libras* at a push I would sell it to him for a thousand pounds.
◆ *vi* to be unbearable; *el calor apuraba* the heat was unbearable.
◆ *vpr* to worry, to get worried; *no se apure por eso* don't worry about that || to hurry, to hurry up (apresurarse); *apúrate o llegaremos tarde* hurry up or we'll be late || *apurarse la barba* to have a close shave.

apuro *m* difficult situation, tight spot, trouble, mess, jam, fix; *estar en un apuro* to be in a fix *o* in trouble; *sacar a alguien de un apuro* to get s.o. out of a mess || difficulty, hardship; *al principio pasé muchos apuros en este país* at first I had a lot of difficulties in this country || embarrassment (vergüenza) || AMER hurry (prisa) || — *estar en apuros, estar en un apuro de dinero, tener apuros de dinero* to be short of money, to be hard up || *me da apuro hacer eso* I'm afraid of doing that, I don't like to do that || *pasar un apuro* to be embarrassed || *salir de apuro* to get out of trouble *o* out of a tight spot *o* out of a difficult situation.

aquaplaning *m* aquaplaning.

aquejado, da *adj* suffering (de una enfermedad).

aquejar *vt* to trouble || — FIG *estar* or *encontrarse aquejado de* to be suffering from; *la economía se encuentra aquejada de falta de mano de obra* the economy is suffering from a lack of manpower || *le aqueja una grave enfermedad* he is suffering from a serious illness.

aquel *m* FAM certain something, special something; *no es guapa pero tiene un aquel* she is not pretty but she has a certain something.

aquel, aquella *adj dem* that; *aquel sombrero* that hat; *aquella casa* that house; *aquellos años de mi juventud* those years of my youth; *las mujeres aquellas* those women || the former; *Juana y Diana son hermanas, aquella hermana tiene veinte años y ésta treinta* Joan and Diana are sisters, the former (sister) is twenty and the latter thirty (véase OBSERV en AQUÉL).
◆ *pron* the one, that one; *aquel que ves allí* the one you can see there; *aquellos de quienes te hablo* the ones *o* those I am talking about || *todo aquel que* anyone who.

— OBSERV pl *those.*

aquél, aquélla *pron dem* that one; *éste es más barato que aquél, que aquéllos* this one is cheaper than that one, than those || the former; *Juan y Pedro se han casado, aquél con una chica inglesa y éste con una española* John and Peter got married, the former to an English girl and the latter to a Spaniard.

— OBSERV pl *those.*

— OBSERV *Aquel* and *aquél* denote remoteness from both the speaker and the person spoken to, and remoteness in time either in the past or in the future. They are often opposed to *este* and *éste.* The pronouns *aquél* and *aquélla* have accents to distinguish them from the adjectives when they are not followed by a relative pronoun.

aquelarre *m* (nocturnal) witches' sabbath || FIG uproar, din (ruido).

aquella *adj dem* —> **aquel.**

aquélla *pron dem* —> **aquél.**

aquello *pron dem* that; *esto no es tan bueno como aquello* this is not as good as that || the former (anterior) || that affair, that business, that matter; *aquello del ministro y la empresa* that affair about the minister and the firm || — *¡aquello fue para morirse de risa!* it was hilarious! || *por aquello del orgullo* because of pride, out of pride || *por aquello de no quedar mal* so as not to look bad.

aquende *adv* on this side of; *aquende los Pirineos* on this side of the Pyrenees.

aquenio *m* BOT achene.

aqueo, a *adj/s* Achaean.

aquerenciarse *vpr* to become fond of *o* attached to.

aquese, sa, so *adj dem* POÉT —> **ese, esa, eso.**

aqueste, ta, to *adj dem* POÉT —> **este, esta, esto.**

aquí *adv* here; *aquí abajo* down here; *aquí dentro* in here; *ven aquí* come here || then, at that moment, here (entonces); *aquí no pudo contenerse* then he could not restrain himself || now, here; *aquí viene lo mejor del caso* now comes the good part || POP he, she || — *andar de aquí para allá* to come and go, to walk up and down, to walk to and fro || *aquí está* here it is, here he is, here she is (como interjección), here is; *aquí está tu libro* here is your book || *¡aquí fue Troya!* then the trouble began, that was when it started || *aquí presente* present || *aquí y allí, aquí y allá* here and there || *aquí yace* here lies || *de aquí* hence; *de aquí los males que venimos padeciendo* hence the evils which plague us; from here; *de aquí arranca la evolución de la economía española* from here stems the development of the Spanish economy || *de aquí a* or *en ocho días* in eight days, within eight days, in *o* within a week (plazo), a week today (fecha) || *de aquí a poco* in a short time, soon || *de aquí en adelante* from now on, henceforth || *de aquí hasta entonces* until then || *de aquí que* hence; *es muy tímido, de aquí que no le guste ir a la escuela* he is very shy, hence he does not like going to school || *hasta aquí* this far, as far as here (lugar), so far, until now (tiempo) || *he aquí* here is || *heme aquí* here I am || *por aquí* round here; *no ha pasado por aquí* he hasn't been round here; this way; *por aquí por favor* this way please; somewhere round here, near here; *vive por aquí* he lives somewhere round here; through here; *la autopista va a pasar por aquí* the motorway is going to pass through here || *por aquí y por allá* here and there.

aquiescencia *f* acquiescence, assent.

aquietador, ra *adj* soothing, calming (que calma) || soothing, which eases (que alivia).

aquietar *vt* to calm down, to calm; *aquietar a un caballo* to calm a horse down || to ease, to soothe (el dolor) || to calm (el temor).
◆ *vpr* to calm down (calmarse) || to ease (el dolor).

aquilatado, da *adj* proven, tested; *hombre de aquilatada virtud* man of proven virtue || *precio aquilatado* rock-bottom price, lowest possible price.

aquilatamiento *m* assay.

aquilatar *vt* to assay (el oro) || to value (piedras preciosas) || FIG to purify (purificar) | to make as cheap as possible, to reduce as much as possible (precio).

Aquiles *npr m* Achilles || — *talón de Aquiles* Achilles heel || *tendón de Aquiles* Achilles tendon.

aquilino, na *adj* aquiline (aguileño); *nariz aquilina* aquiline nose.

aquilón *m* north wind.

aquillado, da *adj* keel-shaped.

Aquisgrán *n pr* GEOGR Aachen ‖ HIST Aix-la-Chapelle.

Aquitania *npr f* GEOGR Aquitaine ‖ HIST Aquitania.

ara *f* altar (altar) ‖ altar stone (piedra) ‖ *en aras de* for the sake of, for, in honour of; *en aras de nuestra amistad* for the sake of our friendship.
◆ *m* ZOOL ara, macaw (guacamayo) ‖ ASTR Altar, Ara (constelación).

árabe *adj* Arab, Arabic, Arabian.
◆ *m/f* Arab, Arabian.
◆ *m* Arabic (lengua) ‖ FAM *eso es árabe para mí* that's Greek *o* double Dutch to me.

arabesco, ca *adj* arabesque.
◆ *m* arabesque.

arabia *f* AMER blue and white checked cotton material.

Arabia *npr f* GEOGR Arabia; *Arabia Saudí, Arabia Saudita* Saudi Arabia.

arábico, ca; arábigo, ga *adj* Arabic; *número arábigo* Arabic numeral; *goma arábiga* gum arabic ‖ *Golfo Arábico* Arabian Gulf.
◆ *m* Arabic (lengua).

arabismo *m* Arabicism, Arabic expression [used in another language].

arabista *m/f* Arabist, student of Arabic.

arabización *f* Arabicization.

arabizar *vt* to Arabicize.

arable *adj* Arable.

arácnido, da *adj/sm* ZOOL arachnid, arachnidan.

aracnoideo, a *adj* arachnoid.

aracnoides *f* ANAT arachnoid.

arada *f* AGR ploughing [US plowing, ploughing] (acción de arar) | farming (labranza) | ploughed land [US plowed *o* ploughed land] (tierra arada) | day's ploughing (jornal).

arado *m* AGR plough [US plow, plough]; *arado bisurco* double-furrow plough ‖ AMER farming (labranza) ‖ AGR *arado de balancín* balance plough.

arador, ra *adj* who ploughs, ploughing.
◆ *m* ploughman [US plowman, ploughman] (labrador) ‖ ZOOL Itch mite.

aradura *f* ploughing [US plowing, ploughing].

Aragón *npr m* GEOGR Aragon.

aragonés, esa *adj/s* Aragonese ‖ FIG *testarudo* or *terco como un aragonés* as stubborn as a mule.

aragonito *m* MIN aragonite.

araguato *m* ursine howler (mono).

Aral (mar de) *npr m* GEOGR the Aral Sea.

arambel *m* hangings *pl* (colgadura) ‖ FIG rag, tatter (andrajo).

arameo, a *adj/s* Aramaean.
◆ *m* Aramaean, Aramaic (lengua).

arana *f* trick, swindle.

arancel *m* customs tariff *o* duty (tarifa) ‖ *Arancel Aduanero Comunitario* E.C. Customs Duty.

arancelario, ria *adj* tariff; *barreras arancelarias* tariff barriers ‖— *derechos arancelarios* customs duties ‖ *leyes arancelarias* customs laws.

arándano *m* BOT bilberry, whortleberry.

arandela *f* washer (para tornillos) ‖ candle ring (de bujía) ‖ frill, flounce (chorrera) ‖ guard (de lanza) ‖ candlestick (candelabro).

arandillo *m* ZOOL marsh warbler (pájaro).

araña *f* ZOOL spider ‖ BOT love-in-a-mist (arañuela) ‖ chandelier (lámpara de techo) ‖ bird net (red) ‖ MAR clew (de hamaca) ‖ FIG & FAM resourceful *o* thrifty person ‖ whore (prostituta) ‖— *araña de agua* water spider ‖ *araña de mar* sea spider, spider crab ‖ *red* or *tela de araña* spider's web.

arañadura *f* scratch.

arañar *vt* to scratch; *el gato me ha arañado* the cat has scratched me ‖ to scratch, to scrape; *arañar la pared con algo* to scratch the wall with sth. ‖ FIG to scrape together (recoger) | to scrape (un instrumento de cuerda).
◆ *vi* to scratch; *este cepillo araña* this brush scratches.
◆ *vpr* to scratch o.s.

arañazo *m* scratch (rasguño) ‖ scratch, scrape (en la pared, en un metal).

arañero *m* ZOOL creeper (pájaro).

arañuela *f* ZOOL small spider | insect's larva (larva) ‖ BOT love-in-a-mist, nigella.

arañuelo *m* ZOOL insect's larva | tick (garrapata).

arar *m* BOT juniper (enebro) | larch (alerce).

arar *vt* AGR to plough [US to plow, to plough] ‖ FIG to plough through (surcar) | to furrow, to wrinkle; *rostro arado por el sufrimiento* face furrowed by suffering ‖ FIG *arar en el mar* to plough the sands.

araucano, na *adj/s* Araucanian.

araucaria *f* BOT araucaria.

aravico *m* AMER bard [amongst the Indians of Peru].

arbitrable *adj* submissible to arbitration.

arbitraje *m* arbitration ‖ DEP refereeing (en fútbol, boxeo, etc.) | umpirage (en críquet, tenis, béisbol) ‖— ECON *arbitraje de divisas* exchange arbitrage | *arbitraje monetario* monetary arbitrage.

arbitral *adj* JUR by arbitration; *sentencia arbitral* judgement by arbitration ‖ DEP of the referee (del árbitro).

arbitrar *vt/vi* JUR to arbitrate (*en* in; *entre* between) ‖ DEP to referee; *arbitrar un partido de fútbol* to referee a football match | to umpire (en tenis, críquet, béisbol) ‖ to find, to work out; *arbitrar los medios para lograr algo* to work out the means of achieving sth. ‖ to raise, to get together (fondos, recursos).
◆ *vpr* to manage (arreglárselas).

arbitrariedad *f* arbitrariness (cualidad de arbitrario) ‖ outrage, abuse, arbitrary action; *la sanción que me impusieron fue una arbitrariedad* the sanction that they imposed on me was an outrage.

arbitrario, ria *adj* arbitrary; *una orden arbitraria* an arbitrary order.

arbitrio *m* will, wishes *pl* (voluntad); *seguir el arbitrio de sus padres* to obey the will of one's parents ‖ free will (albedrío) ‖ fancy (capricho) ‖ means, expedient (recurso) ‖ JUR judgement, judgment ‖ *dejar al arbitrio de alguien* to leave to s.o.'s discretion.
◆ *pl* taxes (impuestos).

arbitrista *m/f* armchair politician, political dreamer, soapbox politician ‖ idealist (idealista).

árbitro *m* JUR arbitrator, arbiter ‖ DEP umpire (en tenis, críquet, béisbol) | referee (en fútbol, boxeo, etc.) ‖ *Petronio, árbitro de la elegancia* Petronious, arbiter of elegance.

árbol *m* tree; *árbol frutal* fruit tree ‖ body (de la camisa) ‖ newel (de escalera) ‖ IMPR shank (del tipo) ‖ MAR mast (palo) ‖ TECN shaft; *árbol motor* drive *o* driving shaft ‖— BOT *árbol de la cera* wax myrtle, candleberry ‖ MAR *árbol de la hélice* propeller shaft ‖ BOT *árbol del diablo* sandbox tree ‖ AUT *árbol de levas* camshaft ‖ BOT *árbol del pan* breadfruit tree | *árbol de Navidad* Christmas tree ‖ BOT *árbol desmochado* pollard ‖ *árbol genealógico* family tree, genealogical tree (de una persona), pedigree (de un animal) ‖ ANAT *árbol respiratorio* respiratory system ‖ FIG *del árbol caído todos hacen leña* a fallen man is everybody's prey | *por el fruto se conoce el árbol* a tree is known by its fruits.

arbolado, da *adj* wooded; *región arbolada* wooded area.
◆ *m* trees *pl*, woodland (conjunto de árboles).

arboladura *f* MAR masts and spars *pl*.

arbolar *vt* MAR to mast (poner mástiles) ‖ to hoist; *arbolar bandera española* to hoist the Spanish flag ‖ to brandish (un arma).
◆ *vpr* to rear up (encabritarse).

arboleda *f* wood, copse, spinney.

arborecer* *vi* to grow [into a tree].

arbóreo, a *adj* arboreal, sylvan (de árboles) ‖ arboreal (animal) ‖ arborescent, treelike (de forma de árbol) ‖ *vegetación arbórea* woodland, trees *pl*.

arborescencia *f* BOT arborescence.

arborescente *adj* BOT arborescent.

arborícola *adj* ZOOL tree-dwelling, arboreal.

arboricultor *m* arboriculturist, nurseryman.

arboricultura *f* arboriculture, cultivation of trees.

arborización *f* MIN arborization.

arbotante *m* ARQ flying buttress ‖ MAR outrigger.

arbustivo, va *adj* BOT shrublike, bushlike.

arbusto *m* BOT shrub, bush.

arca *f* chest (cofre) ‖ safe, strongbox (caja de caudales) ‖ Ark; *Arca de Noé* Noah's Ark ‖ TECN tempering oven [for blown glass] ‖— *arca de agua* water tower ‖ *arca de la Alianza* Ark of the Covenant ‖ *Arca del cuerpo* (human) trunk.
◆ *pl* vaults (en tesorerías) ‖ ANAT flanks, sides (debajo de las costillas) ‖ *arcas públicas* Treasury *sing*, public coffers.

arcabucero *m* arquebusier, harquebusier.

arcabuz *m* arquebus, harquebus ‖ arquebusier, harquebusier (arcabucero).

arcada *f* arcade (arcos) ‖ arches *pl* (de un puente) ‖ *puente de una sola arcada* single-span bridge.
◆ *pl* retching (náuseas).

Arcadia *npr f* GEOGR Arcadia.

arcadio, dia *adj/s* Arcadian.

arcaduz *m* pipe, conduit (caño) ‖ scoop, bucket (de noria).

arcaico, ca *adj* archaic (primitivo).

arcaísmo *m* archaism.

arcaísta *m/f* archaist.

arcaizante *adj* archaistic.

arcaizar *vi* to archaize, to imitate the archaic.
◆ *vt* to archaize, to make archaistic.

arcángel *m* archangel.

arcangélico, ca *adj* archangelic.

arcano, na *adj* arcane.
◆ *m* mystery, secret; *los arcanos del universo* the secrets of the universe.

arce *m* BOT maple.

arcedianato *m* archdeaconship (cargo) ‖ archdeaconry (jurisdicción).

arcediano *m* archdeacon.

arcén *m* hard shoulder (de autopista) ‖ verge, side of the road (de una carretera) ‖ curb, kerb (de la acera).

arcilla *f* clay (greda) || matter, substance (materia) || — *arcilla cocida* baked clay || *arcilla figulina* potter's clay.

arcillar *vt* AGR to clay, to dress with clay.

arcilloso, sa *adj* clayey, argillaceous.

arciprestal *adj* of an archpriest, archpriest's.

arciprestazgo *m* archpriesthood, archpriestship.

arcipreste *m* archpriest.

arco *m* MAT arc; *arco de círculo* arc of a circle || bow (arma) || MÚS bow (de violín) || hoop (de tonel) || ANAT arch; *arco alveolar* dental arch || ARQ arch || ELECTR arc || *AMER* DEP goal, goalmouth (portería) || — ARQ *arco abocinado* splayed arch | *arco adintelado* or *a nivel* flat arch | *arco apuntado* pointed arch | *arco capialzado* splayed arch | *arco carpanel* or *apainelado* or *rebajado* basket-handle arch | *arco conopial* ogee arch | *arco de cortina* inflected arch | *arco de herradura* or *morisco* or *arábigo* horseshoe *o* Moorish arch | *arco de medio punto* semicircular arch | *arco de todo punto* or *ojival* Gothic arch, ogive | *arco de triunfo* or *triunfal* triumphal arch | *arco escarzano* segmental arch || *arco iris* rainbow || ARQ *arco lanceolado* lancet arch | *arco peraltado* stilted arch | *arco por tranquil* flying arch | *arco tercelete* tierceron | *arco trebolado* or *trilobulado* trefoil arch || ELECTR *arco voltaico* electric arc || *tirar con arco* to shoot with bow and arrow || DEP *tiro con arco* or *de arco* archery.

arcón *m* large chest.

arcontado *m* archonship, archontate.

arconte *m* archon (magistrado griego).

archi *pref* FAM this prefix is often added to an adjective in Spanish to intensify it: *architonto* extremely stupid.

archicofradía *f* archconfraternity.

archiconocido, da *adj* FAM known by everyone, extremely well-known.

archidiácono *m* archdeacon.

archidiocesano, na *adj* archdiocesan.

archidiócesis *f* archbishopric, archdiocese.

archiducado *m* archduchy.

archiduque, quesa *m/f* archduke (hombre), archduchess (mujer).

archifamoso, sa *adj* FAM world famous.

archimandrita *m* archimandrite (sacerdote griego).

archimillonario, ria *m/f* multimillionaire (hombre), multimillionairess (mujer).

archipámpano *m* FAM *se cree el archipámpano de las Indias* or *de Sevilla* he thinks he's a big shot *o* the Great Panjandrum.

archipiélago *m* archipelago.

archisabido, da *adj* FAM very well-known || *eso es una cosa archisabida* that's common knowledge.

archivador, ra *m/f* archivist, keeper of records (persona).
◆ *m* filing cabinet (mueble).

archivar *vt* to file, to file away (clasificar) || to put into the archives, to archive || INFORM to file || FIG to shelve; *han archivado los mayores problemas* they have shelved the main problems || FIG *archivar algo en su cabeza* to make a mental note of sth.

archivero, ra; archivista *m/f* archivist.

archivo *m* file; *buscaré su dirección en su archivo personal* I shall look for his adress in his personal file || archives *pl*, files *pl* (conjunto de documentos custodiados); *el archivo de una casa editorial* the archives of a publishing company || filing cabinet (mueble) || FIG soul of discretion | example, model, paragon (dechado) || *Archivo Nacional* Public Records Office [*US* National Archives].
◆ *pl* archives; *los archivos de la biblioteca municipal* the town library's archives.

archivolta *f* ARQ archivolt.

ardentía *f* heat (ardor) || phosphorescence (en el mar) || MED *sentir ardentía* or *ardentías* to have heartburn.

arder *vi* to burn; *la leña seca arde bien* dry wood burns well || FIG to seethe, to boil, to burn; *arder de* or *en ira* to seethe with anger | to burn; *arder en deseos de* to burn with desire to | to burn, to be consumed; *arder en celos* to be consumed by jealousy, to burn with jealousy || AGR to decompose (el estiércol) || — *arder sin llama* to smoulder || FIG *el país entero arde en guerra* war is raging throughout the country | *la ciudad arde en fiestas* celebrations in the town are in full swing | *la cosa está que arde* the situation is very tense, things are getting very hot | *me arde la boca* my mouth is on fire | *toma un duro, y vas que ardes* take five pesetas, and that's more than enough.
◆ *vt* to burn (quemar).
◆ *vpr* to burn, to burn up || AGR to scorch, to parch (quemarse).

ardid *m* ruse, scheme, trick || *valiéndose de ardides* by trickery.

ardido, da *adj* (ant) bold, brave.

ardiente *adj* hot, scalding || FIG ardent, passionate, fervent; *ardiente partidario* fervent supporter | burning, keen; *deseo ardiente* burning desire | ardent, passionate (muy amoroso) | blazing, flaming (color) || *capilla ardiente* mortuary chapel [lit with tapers].

ardientemente *adv* ardently, passionately, fervently.

ardilla *f* ZOOL squirrel || — ZOOL *ardilla rayada* chipmunk | *ardilla terrestre* gopher.

ardimiento *m* burning (ardor) || FIG fervour [*US* fervor], keenness (fervor) | bravery, boldness (valor).

ardite *m* (ant) «ardite» [old Spanish coin of very little value] || — FAM *me importa un ardite* I don't give a damn *o* two hoots *o* a hang | *no vale un ardite* it's not worth a brass farthing.

ardor *m* heat; *el ardor del Sol* the heat of the sun; *en el ardor de la batalla* in the heat of the battle || burn (quemazón), burning (sensación de quemarse) || FIG ardour [*US* ardor], keenness, enthusiasm, fervour [*US* fervor]; *ardor en el trabajo* keenness in one's work || *ardor de estómago* heartburn.

ardorosamente *adv* ardently.

ardoroso, sa *adj* hot, burning (ardiente) || feverish, fevered (febril) || passionate, fervent.

arduo, dua *adj* arduous, difficult.

área *f* area (superficie); *el área de un triángulo* the area of a triangle || ARQ plot area, area (de un edificio) || are [100 square metres] (medida agraria) || AGR bed (de flores) | patch (de hortalizas) || — DEP *área de castigo* penalty area | *área de gol* goal area (fútbol), in-goal (rugby) || ECON *área de libre cambio* free trade area || *área de servicios* service area (en una autopista) || *área metropolitana* or *urbana* metropolitan area || *área metropolitana de Londres, de Nueva York* Greater London, metropolitan New York.

areca *f* BOT areca palm, betel palm (palmera) | areca nut, betel nut (fruto).

arena *f* sand; *la arena de la playa está mojada* the sand on the beach is wet; *las arenas del desierto* the sands of the desert || arena (en el circo romano) || TAUR bullring (ruedo) || — *arena movediza* quicksand || FIG *edificar sobre arena, sembrar en arena* to build on sand || *reloj de arena* hourglass, sandglass; egg-timer (en la cocina) || *una playa de arena* a sandy beach.
◆ *pl* MED stones, gravel *sing* (en el riñón) || dust *sing*; *arenas de oro* gold dust.

arenáceo, a *adj* arenaceous.

arenal *m* large expanse of sand || quicksand (arena movediza).

arenar *vt* to sand, to sprinkle with sand (enarenar) || to sand, to abrade with sand (frotar con arena).

arenero *m* sand dealer, sand merchant (vendedor) || sandbox (de locomotora) || TAUR sand boy [who keeps the surface smooth in the bullring].

arenga *f* harangue, sermon; *dirigir una arenga* to give a harangue.

arengar *vt* to harangue.

arenícola *adj* arenicolous, sand-dwelling.
◆ *f* lugworm.

arenilla *f* blotting powder (para la tinta).
◆ *pl* MED stones, gravel *sing* (en el riñón) || granulated saltpetre *sing* (salitre).

arenillero *m* powder sprinkler [for drying ink].

arenisco, ca *adj* sandy (arenoso) || stoneware; *vaso arenisco* stoneware vase || *piedra arenisca* sandstone.
◆ *f* sandstone (piedra).

arenoso, sa *adj* sandy; *playa arenosa* sandy beach.

arenque *m* ZOOL herring || — *arenque ahumado* kippered herring, kipper || FIG & FAM *seco como un arenque* as dry as a bone.

arenquera *f* herring net (red) || FIG & FAM fishwife (vendedora de pescado).

areola; aréola *f* MED & ANAT areola, areole.

areometría *f* areometry.

areómetro *m* areometer, hydrometer.

areópago *m* areopagus.

arepa *f* *AMER* round maize loaf || FAM *ganar la arepa* to earn one's bread and butter.

arepero, ra *adj* *AMER* loutish.

arepita *f* *AMER* fried maize cake.

arestín *m* BOT eryngium || VET thrush (enfermedad de los caballos).

arete *m* small ring (anillo) || *AMER* earring (pendiente).

arfada *f* MAR pitch, pitching.

arfar *vi* MAR to pitch.

argadijo; argadillo *m* winding frame (devanadera).

argallera *f* croze.

argamasa *f* mortar.

argamasar *vt* to mortar (trabar con argamasa).
◆ *vi* to make *o* to mix mortar (hacer argamasa).

argamasón *m* large piece of dried mortar (pedazo) || rubble (conjunto de pedazos).

árgana *f* crane (grúa).

árganas *f pl* baskets, panniers [used on pack animals].

arganeo *m* MAR anchor ring.

árgano *m* crane (grúa).

Argel *n pr* GEOGR Algiers.

Argelia *npr f* GEOGR Algeria.

argelino, na *adj/s* Algerian.

argén *m* HERÁLD argent.

argentado, da *adj* silver-plated, silvered (bañado de plata) || silvery, silver (de color de plata).

argentar *vt* to silver-plate, to silver (platear) || to adorn with silver (guarnecer) || to give a silvery shine to (hacer brillar).

argénteo, a *adj* silver (de plata) || silver-plated (bañado de plata) || silvery (semejante a la plata) || HERÁLD argent.

argentería *f* gold embroidery, orphrey (bordado de oro) ‖ silver embroidery, orphrey (bordado de plata) ‖ silversmith's shop (tienda) ‖ silversmithing (oficio de platero).

argentero *m* silversmith (platero).

argentífero, ra *adj* argentiferous.

argentina *f* BOT silverweed.

Argentina *npr f* GEOGR Argentina, the Argentine.

argentinismo *m* Argentine expression *o* word.

argentinizarse *vpr* to adapt to Argentine life.

argentino, na *adj* silvery, argentine (de aspecto de plata) ‖ crystal-clear, silvery; *voz argentina* crystal-clear voice ‖ Argentinean, Argentine (de la República Argentina).
◆ *m/f* Argentinean, Argentine.

argento *m* POÉT silver, argent.

argentoso, sa *adj* argentiferous.

argivo, va *adj/s* argive (de Argos).

argólico, ca *adj* argive (argivo).

argolla *f* ring (aro de metal) ‖ (type of) croquet (juego) ‖ carcan, iron collar (castigo público) ‖ collar (adorno de mujer) ‖ bracelet (pulsera) ‖ FIG shackles *pl* (sujeción) ‖ *AMER* wedding *o* engagement ring (de matrimonio).

árgoma *f* BOT furze, gorse, whin (aulaga).

argón *m* QUÍM argon (gas).

argonauta *m* MIT argonaut ‖ ZOOL argonaut, paper nautilus (molusco).

argos *m* FIG argus, watchful person (persona muy vigilante) ‖ ZOOL argus.

Argos *n pr* MIT Argus.

argot *m* jargon; *argot médico* medical jargon ‖ slang (lenguaje familiar).

argucia *f* sophism, fallacy (argumento falso).

árguenas; árgueñas *f pl* handbarrow *sing* (angarillas) ‖ saddlebags (alforjas).

argüir* *vt* to argue (alegar) ‖ to deduce, to infer, to conclude; *de esto arguyo que vendrá* from this I deduce that he will come ‖ to indicate (indicar) ‖ to demonstrate (demostrar) ‖ to prove, to show (probar) ‖ to reproach, to accuse (echar en cara).
◆ *vi* to argue.

argumentación *f* argumentation, arguing (acción de argumentar) ‖ argument (argumento).

argumentador, ra *adj* argumentative (aficionado a discutir).
◆ *m/f* arguer, debater (el que argumenta) ‖ arguer (el que discute).

argumentar *vi* to argue, to dispute.
◆ *vt* to conclude, to deduce (concluir) ‖ to indicate (indicar) ‖ to demonstrate (demostrar) ‖ to prove, to show (probar) ‖ to argue, to claim, to say; *argumenta que las mujeres tienen que trabajar en casa* she argues that women have to work at home ‖ to say, to put forward an argument; *no tiene nada que argumentar para su defensa* he has nothing to say in his defence, he has no argument to put forward in his defence.

argumentista *m/f* scenarist.

argumento *m* argument, reasoning; *no sigo tu argumento* I cannot follow your reasoning ‖ plot (de una obra literaria) ‖ story, plot (de una película) ‖ scenario, summary, synopsis (resumen) ‖ *argumento cornuto* dilemma.

arguyente *adj* arguing.

aria *f* MÚS aria.

Ariana *npr f* MIT Ariadne.

aricar *vt* to plough roughly (arar).

aridecer* *vt* to make arid, to dry up.
◆ *vi* to become arid, to dry up.

aridez *f* aridity ‖ FIG aridity, dryness.

árido, da *adj* arid; *terreno árido* arid land ‖ FIG dull, arid, dry; *asunto árido* dull subject.
◆ *m pl* COM dry commodities ‖ TECN aggregate *sing* ‖ *medida de áridos* dry measure.

Aries *npr m* ASTR Aries, the Ram (constelación).

ariete *m* MIL battering ram (máquina de guerra) ‖ centre forward (en fútbol) ‖ *ariete hidráulico* hydraulic ram.

arije *adj* *uva arije* black grape.

arijo, ja *adj* light, loose (tierra).

arilo *m* BOT aril, seed coat (tegumento).

arillo *m* wooden hoop [used to stiffen priest's bands] ‖ earring (pendiente).

arimez *m* ARQ projection, ledge.

ario, a *adj/s* Aryan.

arisco, ca *adj* unfriendly, surly, unsociable (huraño) ‖ unfriendly, vicious (animales) ‖ shy (tímido) ‖ *AMER* frightened, fearful (miedoso).

arista *f* BOT beard (del trigo) ‖ MAT edge; *arista de un cubo* edge of a cube ‖ ARQ arris, edge (de una viga) | groin (de una bóveda) ‖ boon (parte leñosa del cáñamo) ‖ arête (de montaña).

aristado, da *adj* with prominent edges ‖ bearded (trigo).

Arístides *npr m* Aristides.

aristocracia *f* aristocracy ‖ nobility, distinction (en las maneras).

aristócrata *adj* aristocratic.
◆ *m/f* aristocrat.

aristocrático, ca *adj* aristocratic ‖ aristocratic, distinguished, noble (maneras, aspecto).

aristocratizar *vt* to make aristocratic.

Aristófanes *npr m* Aristophanes.

aristoloquia *f* BOT aristolochia.

Aristóteles *npr m* Aristotle.

aristotélico, ca *adj/s* Aristotelian.

aritmética *f* arithmetic.

aritmético, ca *adj* arithmetic, arithmetical; *progresión aritmética* arithmetical progression; *media aritmética* arithmetic mean.
◆ *m/f* arithmetician.

arlequín *m* TEATR harlequin ‖ harlequin's mask (máscara) ‖ clown, fool, buffoon (persona ridícula y despreciable) ‖ FIG & FAM Neapolitan ice cream (helado).

arlequinada *f* FAM clowning, buffoonery, fooling.

arlequinesco, ca *adj* harlequin ‖ FIG & FAM ridiculous, buffoonish, foolish.

arma *f* weapon, arm; *el arcabuz es un arma antigua* the arquebus is an ancient weapon ‖ arm; *armas portátiles* small arms ‖ MIL arm; *arma de caballería* cavalry arm ‖ means of defence, weapon (de los animales) ‖ FIG weapon, arm; *su pluma es su única arma* his pen is his only weapon ‖ — *arma arrojadiza* missile, projectile [weapon which is thrown] ‖ *arma blanca* steel, cold steel ‖ *arma de depósito* magazine-loading weapon ‖ *arma de fuego* firearm ‖ FIG *arma de dos filos* or *de doble filo* argument which cuts both ways (argumento), double-edged sword ‖ *arma de repetición* repeater, repeating firearm ‖ *arma de retrocarga* breech-loading firearm ‖ *arma homicida* murder weapon ‖ *rendir el arma* to present arms to the Holy Sacrament ‖ MIL *¡sobre el hombro, arma!* slope arms! ‖ *tocar el arma* to sound the call to arms ‖ FIG *volver el arma contra alguien* to give s.o. a taste of his own medecine, to turn the tables on s.o.
◆ *pl* MIL forces; *las armas aliadas* the allied forces | army *sing* (carrera militar); *mi hijo ha elegido la carrera de las armas* my son has chosen the army as his career | weapons; *armas nucleares* nuclear weapons ‖ HERÁLD coat *sing* of arms, arms (escudo) | arms (blasones) ‖ — *¡a las armas!, ¡a formar con armas!, ¡arma, arma!* to arms! ‖ *alzarse* or *levantarse en armas* to rise up in arms ‖ *con las armas en la mano* weapon in hand, armed ‖ MIL *¡cuelguen armas!* sling arms! ‖ FIG *dar armas contra sí mismo* to make a rod for one's own back | *de armas tomar* formidable (temible) ‖ MIL *descansar las armas* to order arms | *¡descansen armas!* order arms! ‖ HERÁLD *escudo de armas* coat of arms ‖ *estar en arma* or *en armas* to be up in arms ‖ FIG *hacer sus primeras armas* to make one's début, to take one's first steps; *hizo sus primeras armas en el foro* he made his début at the bar ‖ *hecho de armas* feat of arms ‖ HERÁLD *libro de armas* armorial, book of heraldry ‖ *licencia de armas* firearm licence (autorización legal) ‖ *llegar a las armas* to take up arms ‖ *medir las armas* to cross swords, to fight ‖ MIL *pasar por las armas* to shoot, to execute ‖ *poner en armas* to arm (armar), to rouse up (sublevar) ‖ MIL *presentar las armas* to present arms | *¡presenten armas!* present arms! ‖ *rendir las armas* to surrender one's arms, to lay down one's arms (entregar las armas), to give in, to surrender (rendirse) ‖ *sobre las armas* under arms ‖ *tomar (las) armas* to take up arms (armarse), to present arms (hacer los honores militares) ‖ *velar las armas* to carry out the vigil of arms.

armada *f* navy, neet, naval forces *pl* (conjunto de fuerzas navales) ‖ fleet, squadron (escuadra) ‖ *AMER* preparation of a lasso [for throwing] ‖ *la Armada Invencible* the Spanish Armada.

armadía *f* raft.

armadijo *m* trap (trampa).

armadillo *m* ZOOL armadillo.

armado, da *adj* armed (en armas) ‖ loaded; *una pistola armada* a loaded gun ‖ reinforced; *hormigón armado* reinforced concrete ‖ provided (provisto) ‖ assembled (montado) ‖ *AMER* stubborn (terco).
◆ *m* man dressed as a Roman soldier [in processions] ‖ *AMER* hand-rolled cigarette.

armador *m* MAR shipowner (naviero) ‖ jerkin (jubón) ‖ fitter (de máquinas, coches, etc.) ‖ *AMER* waistcoat (chaleco) | hanger (percha).

armadura *f* armour [*US* armor] ‖ suit of armour (para proteger el cuerpo) ‖ frame; *armadura de las gafas* spectacle frame ‖ skeleton, framework (del tejado) ‖ skeleton (esqueleto) ‖ assembly, fitting (montaje) ‖ fitting together (en costura) ‖ casing (de neumático) ‖ FÍS armature (de imán) | plate (de condensador) ‖ reinforcement (del hormigón) ‖ MÚS key signature ‖ *armadura de la cama* bedstead.

armajo *m* saltwort (almarjo).

armamentista *adj* arms, armaments; *carrera armamentista* arms race.

armamento *m* arms *pl*, armaments *pl* (de un país) ‖ armament (de un barco, un cuerpo militar) ‖ arms *pl* (de un soldado) ‖ *carrera de armamentos* arms race.

Armando *npr m* Herman.

armar *vt* to arm; *armado con un fusil* armed with a rifle; *armar a cien mil hombres* to arm a hundred thousand men ‖ to prepare for war, to arm; *armar a un país* to prepare a country for war ‖ to load (un arma de fuego) ‖ to fix (una bayoneta) ‖ to brace (un arco) ‖ MAR to fit out, to equip (un navío) ‖ to assemble, to fit together, to mount (una máquina) ‖ to pitch (una tienda de campaña) ‖ to put up (una cama) ‖ to set (una trampa) ‖ to fit together (en costura) ‖ to reinforce (reforzar) ‖

FIG to provide; *le han armado de una buena educación* they have provided him with a good education | to arrange, to prepare, to get ready (preparar) || FIG & FAM to arrange, to organize (organizar) | to make, to kick up; *armar jaleo, ruido* to kick up a fuss, a noise | to cause, to create; *armar dificultades a uno* to cause s.o. difficulties || *AMER* to roll [a cigarette] || — *armar caballero* to knight || FIG & FAM *armarla, armar una, armarla buena, armar un escándalo* to kick up a rumpus *o* a fuss *o* a stink || *armar una intriga* or *una cábala* to hatch a plot, to scheme, to intrigue || *armar un lío* to make a fuss, to kick up a rumpus || *armar pendencia* to look for fight *o* for trouble || FIG & FAM *¡buena la has armado!* you've really done it now!
◆ *vpr* to arm o.s. (un soldado) || to arm, to prepare for war (un país) || FIG to arm o.s., to provide o.s.; *armarse de una escoba* to provide o.s. with a broom | to break out; *se armó una riña* an argument broke out || *AMER* to stop dead (plantarse) | to balk, to shy (un caballo, etc.) | to be obstinate *o* stubborn (obstinarse) || — *armarse de paciencia* to muster one's patience || *armarse de valor* to pluck up courage, to summon one's courage || FIG & FAM *¡qué lío se armó!* what a fuss there was!, what a rumpus there was! || FIG *se está armando una tempestad* a storm is brewing, a storm is imminent || FIG & FAM *se va a armar la de Dios es Cristo* or *la gorda* or *la de San Quintín* there's going to be a tidy row *o* a hell of a row, there's going to be real trouble.

armario *m* cupboard (para cosas) || wardrobe (para ropa); *armario de luna* wardrobe with a mirror || — *armario botiquín* first-aid cabinet || *armario empotrado* built-in wardrobe, fitted wardrobe || *armario frigorífico* refrigerator || *armario para libros* bookcase.

armatoste *m* monstrosity (cosa grande y fea) || FIG & FAM big oaf, great brute (persona corpulenta).

armazón *f* frame, framework; *armazón de una pantalla* frame of a lampshade || timberwork (maderamen) || FIG framework, outline (de una obra) || chassis (bastidor) || rib (de un violín).
◆ *m* skeleton (esqueleto) || *AMER* set of shelves (estantería) | bookcase (para libros).

armella *f* eyebolt (tornillo) || staple, socket (de cerrojo).

Armenia *npr f* GEOGR Armenia.

arménico, ca *adj* Armenian; *bol arménico* Armenian bole.

armenio, nia *adj/s* Armenian.

armería *f* gunsmith's shop (tienda del armero) || museum of arms, military *o* war museum (museo) || gunsmith's craft (oficio de armero) || heraldry (heráldica).

armero *m* gunsmith (fabricante de armas de fuego) || armourer [*US* armorer] (fabricante de armas) || weapon rack (para colocar las armas).

armilar *adj* ASTR armillary (esfera).

armilla *f* ARQ astragal (de columna) || ASTR armillary sphere.

arminiano, na *adj/s* Arminian.

armiñado, da *adj* ermine-trimmed, trimmed with ermine || HERÁLD ermine.

armiño *m* ZOOL ermine (animal).

armisticio *m* armistice.

armón *m* limber (del cañón).

armonía; harmonía *f* MAT & MÚS harmony || FIG harmony; *vivir en armonía* to live in harmony.

armónicamente; harmónicamente *adv* harmoniously, in harmony.

armónico, ca; harmónico, ca *adj* harmonic.
◆ *m* harmonic (sonido).
◆ *f* harmonica, mouth organ (instrumento de música).

armonio; harmonio *m* MÚS harmonium.

armonioso, sa; harmonioso, sa *adj* harmonious, tuneful.

armonista *m* MÚS harmonist.

armonización; harmonización *f* MÚS harmonizing || harmonizing, reconciliation (de personas) || matching, harmonizing (de colores).

armonizar; harmonizar *vt* MÚS to harmonize || to reconcile (reconciliar) || to match, to harmonize (colores).
◆ *vi* to harmonize (al cantar) || to be in harmony, to harmonize (sonidos) || to match, to harmonize (colores) || to be in harmony (personas).

armorial *m* armorial, book of heraldry (libro de armas).

armuelle *m* BOT orach (planta).

arnés *m* armour, harness (armadura).
◆ *pl* harness *sing*, trappings (de las caballerías) || FIG & FAM things, gear *sing*, equipment *sing*.

árnica *f* BOT arnica || *tintura de árnica* arnica tincture, arnica.

aro *m* hoop (de tonel) || hoop; *los niños ya no juegan al aro* children do not play hoop any more || iron ring (argolla) || BOT cuckoopint, lords-and-ladies || *AMER* ring (sortija) | earring (pendiente) || — *aro para las servilletas* napkin *o* serviette ring || FIG & FAM *tener que pasar* or *tener que entrar por el aro* to knuckle under.

aroma *m* aroma, perfume, fragrance || aroma; *el aroma del café* the aroma of coffee || bouquet (del vino).

aromático, ca *adj* fragrant, sweet-smelling, aromatic (oloroso) || aromatic; *bebida aromática* aromatic drink.

aromatización *f* perfuming || CULIN flavouring [*US* flavoring].

aromatizador *m* *AMER* spray.

aromatizante *adj* perfuming || CULIN flavouring [*US* flavoring].

aromatizar *vt* to perfume, to scent (dar aroma) || CULIN to flavour [*US* to flavor], to aromatize.

aron *m* BOT cuckoopint, lords-and-ladies.

arpa *f* MÚS harp; *arpa eolia* Aeolian harp; *tocar* or *tañer el arpa* to play the harp.

arpado, da *adj* serrated, saw-edged || POÉT sweet-sounding, melodious (pájaros).

arpar *vt* to scratch (rasguñar) || to rip up, to tear up (desgarrar).

arpegiar *vi* MÚS to arpeggio.

arpegio *m* MÚS arpeggio.

arpeo *m* MAR grapnel.

arpía; harpía *f* MIT harpy (ave) || FIG hussy, old witch, harpy (mujer mala) | hag (mujer fea).

arpillar *vt* *AMER* to wrap in sackcloth *o* sacking.

arpillera *f* sackcloth, sacking (tela).

arpista *m/f* harpist.

arpón *m* harpoon, gaff (para pescar) || ARQ cramp, cramp iron (grapa).

arponado, da *adj* harpoon-like.

arponar; arponear *vt* to harpoon.

arponeo *m* harpooning.

arponero *m* harpooner.

arqueado, da *adj* bow-shaped, curved, arched || *piernas arqueadas* bow legs, bandy legs.

arqueador *m* ship gauger (de las embarcaciones) || beater (de la lana).

arqueaje; arqueamiento *m* gauging (acción de arquear) || tonnage (cabida).

arquear *vt* to arch, to curve (curvar) || TECN to beat (la lana) || MAR to gauge, to measure the tonnage of (un navío) || COM to check (los caudales) || *arquear el lomo* to arch one's back.
◆ *vi* FAM to retch.
◆ *vpr* to curve, to arch || to arch one's back (persona).

arquegonio *m* BOT archegonium.

arqueo *m* arching, curving (acción de arquear) || arching (del cuerpo) || MAR gauging (acción de medir la capacidad) | tonnage (tonelaje); *arqueo neto, de registro, bruto* net, registered, gross tonnage || beating (de la lana) || COM checking, cashing up || COM *hacer el arqueo* to cash up.

arqueolítico, ca *adj* stone-age.

arqueología *f* archaeology.

arqueológico, ca *adj* archaeological.

arqueólogo *m* archaeologist.

arqueoptérix *m* archaeopteryx (ave fósil).

arquería *f* arcade, series of arches.

arquero *m* archer, bowman (soldado) || (p us) COM cashier (cajero) || hoopmaker (para toneles) || *AMER* goalkeeper (en fútbol).

arqueta *f* small chest.

arquetipo *m* archetype, prototype (prototipo) || archetype, perfect example; *este chico es el arquetipo del estudiante moderno* this boy is the archetype of the modern student.

arquidiócesis *f* archbishopric, archdiocese.

arquiepiscopal *adj* archiepiscopal.

arquillo *m* MÚS bow.

Arquímedes *npr m* Archimedes.

arquípteros *m pl* ZOOL archips.

arquita *f* small chest.

arquitecto *m* architect || *arquitecto paisajista* landscape architect.

arquitectónico, ca *adj* architectonic, architectural.
◆ *f* architectonics.

arquitectura *f* architecture || INFORM *arquitectura de red* network architecture.

arquitectural *adj* architectural.

arquitrabe *m* ARQ architrave.

arquivolta *f* ARQ archivolt.

arrabal *m* suburb.
◆ *pl* outskirts, suburbs (afueras) || slums (tugurios).

arrabalero, ra; arrabalesco, ca *adj* suburban || common, coarse, rough (de modales groseros).
◆ *m/f* suburbanite (que vive en las afueras) || coarse person (persona tosca).

arrabio *m* cast iron (hierro colado) || *lingote de arrabio* pig iron.

arracacha *f* *AMER* arracacha, Peruvian carrot || *AMER* FIG & FAM stupid thing (tontería).

arracada *f* pendant earring.

arracimado, da *adj* in a bunch (en forma de racimo) || clustered together, bunched together (apiñado).

arracimarse *vpr* to form a bunch, to bunch together, to cluster together.

arraclán *m* BOT buckthorn (árbol) || ZOOL scorpion (alacrán).

arraigamiento *m* → **arraigo.**

arraigadamente *adv* staunchly; *arraigadamente protestante* staunchly protestant || firmly, securely (fijamente).

arraigado, da *adj* deeply rooted, deep-rooted; *costumbres, ideas arraigadas* deeply rooted customs, ideas || influential, respected (persona).

◆ *m* MAR mooring || landowner (propietario).

arraigar *vi* to take root (plantas) || FIG to take root (costumbres, vicios, etc.) | to settle down (establecerse).

◆ *vpr* BOT to take root || FIG to settle down; *se arraigó en París* he settled down in Paris | to take root, to take hold, to become fixed (costumbres, etc.).

arraigo; arraigamiento *m* rootedness (situación de arraigado) || rooting (acción de arraigar) || FIG roots *pl*; *tener arraigo en una ciudad* to have roots in a city | property (bienes raíces) | influence (influencia) || FIG *tener mucho arraigo* to be very respected *o* influential, to have great influence (ser estimado).

arramblar; arramplar *vt* to cover with sand (cubrir de arena).

◆ *vi* FIG & FAM to make off with, to pinch, to carry off (robar, coger); *arrambló con todos mis lápices* he made off with *o* he carried off all my pencils.

◆ *vpr* to be covered with sand, to become covered with sand.

arrancaclavos *m inv* nail puller, nail claw.

arrancada *f* sudden start (de un coche) || dart forward, dash forward (de una persona o cosa que se mueve) || start (de una carrera, de un corredor) || sudden acceleration (aceleración repentina) || jerk, jolt (sacudida) || track (de la res) || snatch (halterofilia) || MAR starting, setting off.

arrancado, da *adj* uprooted (árboles, plantas) || FIG & FAM penniless, broke (arruinado) || HERÁLD erased || FAM *es más malo que arrancado* he's a little devil (un niño).

arrancador *m* grubber (herramienta) || AUT starter (de un motor).

arrancadora *f* AGR lifter, picker; *arrancadora de patatas* potato lifter.

arrancadura *f*; **arrancamiento** *m* pulling up, uprooting (de plantas) || uprooting (de árboles) || extraction, pulling out (de un diente) || snatching, grabbing (acción de coger) || picking (de patatas).

arrancar *vt* to pull up, to uproot; *arrancar una planta* to pull up a plant || to uproot; *la tormenta arrancó el árbol* the storm uprooted the tree || to extract, to pull out (un diente) || to pull, to tear; *arrancar una rama del árbol* to pull a branch off a tree | to tear off (una página, un botón) || to pull out, to tear out (el pelo) || to cough up, to hawk (las flemas) || to heave (un suspiro) || to snatch, to grab (coger); *arrancó al niño de los brazos de su madre* he snatched the child from his mother's arms || to wrest (con dificultad); *lograron arrancarle la pistola* they managed to wrest the pistol from him || FIG to drive out; *han arrancado a los extranjeros que vivían allí* they have driven out the foreigners who lived there | to drag away; *es imposible arrancarle de una fiesta* it is impossible to drag him away from a party | to wipe out, to put an end to, to eradicate (suprimir) | to wean, to stop; *no hay quien le arranque del tabaco* no one can wean him away from smoking, no one can stop him smoking | to get, to force, to wangle; *le arrancaron la verdad, una promesa* they got the truth out of him, a promise out of him | to draw; *arrancar aplausos* to draw applause | to snatch; *el equipo arrancó un punto, la victoria* the team snatched a point, victory || AUT to start; *a ver si podemos arrancar este motor* let's see if we can start this engine || AGR to lift, to pick (patatas) || — *arrancar de raíz* or *de cuajo* to uproot (un árbol), to wrench off (puerta, etc.), to wipe out, to eradicate, to uproot (suprimir completamente), to nip in the bud (hacer abortar) || *es una película que arranca lágrimas* the film is a tearjerker.

◆ *vi* to start (un coche) || to set off, to start out; *el tren arrancó en seguida* the train set off at once || to set sail (un barco) || to make a move, to leave (marcharse); *no arrancan aunque hace horas que están aquí* they're not making a move although they've been here ages || to begin; *la carretera arranca de San Sebastián* the road begins in San Sebastián || FIG to stem, to arise, to originate; *dificultades que arrancan de su mala gestión* difficulties which stem from his bad management | to date back to (remontar a) || to begin (empezar); *arrancó a hablar* he began speaking || to set off at a run, to start running, to break into a run (echar a correr) || *arrancar contra* to charge at; *el toro arrancó contra el matador* the bull charged at the matador.

◆ *vpr* to begin (empezar) || to start to charge; *el toro se arrancó en dirección del hombre* the bull started to charge at the man || to tear o.s. away (tener que irse) || — *arrancarse a cantar, a llorar* to burst into song, into tears || FAM *se arrancó con mil pesetas* or *dándome mil pesetas* he suddenly gave me a thousand pesetas.

arranchar *vt* MAR to hug, to sail close to (la costa, etc.) | to brace (las velas).

◆ *vpr* to get together (reunirse, juntarse).

arranque *m* starting (de un coche, de una máquina) || start (de un atleta, de una carrera) || beginning (de una carretera) || dash forward, sudden spurt (de una persona que echa a correr) || jump, start, jerk (arrebato) || FIG beginning; *el arranque de la película es bueno* the beginning of the film is good | outburst, fit, attack; *arranque de ira, de locura* fit of anger, of madness | burst; *arranque de energía* burst of energy | origin, root; *el arranque de las dificultades* the origin of the difficulties | impulse; *en un arranque decidió comprar un coche* on an impulse he decided to buy a car | thrust, drive, go (ímpetu, pujanza) | flash of wit (ocurrencia) || ANAT start, beginning || ARQ foot; *el arranque de una escalera* the foot of a staircase | spring (de bóveda o de arco) || BOT base || TECN starter (de un motor) || MIN ragging || — *esperando el arranque del tren* waiting for the train to start *o* to move *o* to leave || *motor de arranque* starting motor.

arrapiezo *m* rag, tatter (harapo) || FIG & FAM scallywag (niño).

arras *f pl* security *sing*, earnest *sing*, pledge *sing* (prenda) || thirteen coins given by bridegroom to bride (monedas).

arrasadura *f* smoothing, levelling (allanamiento) || striking (de los granos).

arrasamiento *m* smoothing, levelling (allanamiento) || devastation, ravaging (de un terreno) || demolition, razing, destruction (de un edificio).

arrasar *vt* to smooth, to level (allanar) || to fill to the brim (llenar hasta el borde) || to demolish, to raze to the ground (un edificio) || to devastate, to ravage; *el ciclón ha arrasado la región* the cyclone has devastated the area || to strike (los granos) || *ojos arrasados en lágrimas* eyes brimming with tears.

◆ *vi/vpr* to clear (el cielo) || *arrasarse en lágrimas* to fill with tears (los ojos).

arrastradero *m* TECN timber slide (camino) || TAUR place where dead bulls are left when dragged from the ring || AMER gambling den (garito).

arrastrado, da *adj* FIG & FAM miserable, wretched; *llevar una vida arrastrada* to lead a miserable life | rascally, roguish (bribón) | hard-up (mal de dinero) || in which one must follow suit (juegos).

◆ *m/f* FIG & FAM rogue, rascal (bribón).

◆ *f* FIG & FAM whore, prostitute (mujer pública).

arrastramiento *m* dragging, trailing.

arrastrar *vt* to pull, to haul; *el caballo arrastraba el carruaje* the horse was pulling the carriage || to drag, to trail; *arrastrar los pies* to drag one's feet || to haul, to transport (una mercancía) || to drag along, to trail, to drag; *la niña arrastraba la muñeca detrás de ella* the child was dragging the doll along behind her || to sweep away *o* along, to carry away *o* along; *la corriente arrastró el barco* the current swept the boat away || to blow away, to carry off; *el viento arrastró las hojas* the wind blew the leaves away || FIG to lead; *su éxito como ladrón arrastró a sus hermanos a cometer crímenes* his success as a criminal lead his brothers to commit crimes | to lead to, to give rise to; *eso arrastró muchas dificultades* it gave rise to many difficulties | to win over; *su discurso arrastró a la multitud* his speech won over the crowd | to lead; *arrastra una vida miserable* he leads a miserable life || — FIG *dejarse arrastrar* to get carried away (por el juego, etc.) | *un déficit que arrastramos desde hace mucho tiempo* a deficit which has been hanging over us for a long time.

◆ *vi* to trail, to trail on the ground (una cortina, un vestido) || to lead (juegos).

◆ *vpr* to crawl, to creep (reptar) || to drag o.s.; *el herido se arrastró hasta la puerta* the injured man dragged himself to the door || to drag, to trail (una cosa) || FIG to grovel (humillarse).

arrastre *m* dragging || haulage, transportation, transport (de una mercancía) || lead (juegos) || AVIAC drag (fricción) || AMER ore crusher || — FIG & FAM *estar para el arrastre* to have had it, to be worn out (persona), to have had it (cosa) | *ser de mucho arrastre* to be very influential, to have a lot of influence.

arrayán *m* myrtle.

arrayanal *m* myrtle patch.

¡arre! *interj* gee up!, giddy up! (a los caballos) || FAM come on then!

arrea *f* AMER packtrain (recua).

¡arrea! *interj* come on!, hurry up! (para meter prisa), get away! (para manifestar sorpresa).

arreador *m* AMER whip (látigo).

arrear *vt* to spur on, to urge on (a las caballerías) || to harness (poner los arreos) || to decorate, to adorn (adornar) || to hurry, to rush (dar prisa) || FAM to deal, to fetch; *arrear un golpe* to deal a blow.

◆ *vi* to hurry, to go quickly (ir de prisa) || *irse arreando* to rush off, to hurry away.

arrebañaduras *f pl* leftovers, remains.

arrebañar *vt* FAM to scrape together (juntar) | to make off with (arramblar) || to eat up, to finish off (comida) || to clean up, to clean (un plato).

arrebatadamente *adv* in a hurry, hurriedly (con prisa) || impulsively (irreflexivamente).

arrebatadizo, za *adj* FIG irritable, short-tempered, quick-tempered (carácter).

arrebatado, da *adj* enraged, carried away (de ira) || impulsive, impetuous, rash (irreflexivo) || violent, sudden, hasty, rash (con prisa) || very red, flushed (rostro).

arrebatador, ra *adj* which snatches || FIG captivating; *una sonrisa arrebatadora* a captivating smile | catchy (ritmo) | devouring (pasión).

arrebatamiento *m* snatch, seizure, snatching (acción de quitar) || ecstasy (éxtasis) || rage, fury (furor).

arrebatar *vt* to snatch, to wrench; *arrebatar algo de las manos de alguien* to snatch sth. from s.o.'s hands; *arrebatarle la victoria a alguien* to snatch victory from s.o. || to blow away, to carry off, to snatch up; *el viento le arrebató el sombrero* the wind blew his hat away || to sweep away, to carry away; *la corriente arrebató a los nadadores* the current swept the swimmers away || to take; *arrebatar la vida a alguien* to take s.o.'s life || to tear *o* to rip off (una página, un botón) || to win, to win over; *arrebataba los corazones con su elocuencia* he won people's hearts with his eloquence || to sweep off one's feet, to captivate; *arrebata a las chicas con su manera de hablar* he sweeps girls off their feet with the way he speaks || to force (las plantas) || to cook too quickly (en cocina) || to enrage, to make furious (de ira) || AMER to knock down (atropellar).
◆ *vpr* to get carried away (de emoción) || to burn (en cocina) || *arrebatarse en cólera* or *de ira* to lose one's temper, to fly into a rage.

arrebato *m* rage, fury (furor); *hablar con arrebato* to speak with rage || fit, attack, outburst; *lo hizo en un arrebato de cólera* he did it in a fit of anger || flurry, sudden fit (de entusiasmo) || ecstasy (éxtasis) || JUR alienation || JUR *con arrebato y obcecación* without malice aforethought.

arrebol *m* red glow; *el sol poniente tiene arreboles magníficos* the sun gives off a magnificent red glow at sunset || rouge (colorete) || rosiness, ruddiness (en las mejillas).

arrebolada *f* red clouds *pl* [at sunrise or at sunset].

arrebolar *vt* to redden, to give a red glow to; *la aurora arrebolaba el cielo* the dawn gave a red glow to the sky || *tener el rostro arrebolado* to have a red face.
◆ *vpr* to go red, to flush || to glow red (el cielo) || to put on rouge (con colorete).

arrebolera *f* rouge jar || BOT marvel of Peru [US pretty-by-night] (dondiego de noche).

arrebozar *vt* to coat, to roll (con harina, etc.).
◆ *vpr* to wrap o.s. up, to muffle o.s.; *arrebozarse en la capa* to wrap o.s. up in one's cape || to swarm (las abejas).

arrebozo *m* —→ **rebozo.**

arrebujar; rebujar *vt* to crumple up, to crease (arrugar) || to wrap up (envolver) || to muddle up, to jumble (enredar).
◆ *vpr* to wrap o.s. up; *arrebujarse en una capa* to wrap o.s. up in a cape || to muffle o.s. up; *arrebujarse en una manta* to muffle o.s. up in a blanket.

arreciar *vi* to get worse, to get heavier; *arrecia la lluvia* the rain is getting heavier || to get stronger (el viento).

arrecife *m* MAR reef; *arrecife de coral* coral reef.

arrecirse* *vpr* to be frozen stiff, to be frozen to the bone.

arrecharse *vpr* AMER FAM to get mad (encolerizarse) | to get horny *o* randy (excitarse).

arrecho, cha *adj* AMER FAM horny, randy (cachondo).

arrechucho *m* FAM fit, outburst, attack; *arrechucho de cólera* fit of anger | turn, bad turn (indisposición); *le dio un arrechucho* he had a bad turn.

arredramiento *m* fear, fright (miedo).

arredrar *vt* to move away (apartar) || FIG to frighten away (hacer retroceder) || to frighten (asustar).
◆ *vpr* to move away (apartarse) || to be frightened, to be afraid; *no se arredra por nada* he's not afraid of anything.

arredro *m* backwards, back (hacia atrás).

arregazado, da *adj* tucked up (faldas) || turned-up (nariz).

arregazar *vt* to tuck up.

arreglado, da *adj* regulated (sujeto a regla) || settled, fixed (un asunto) || FIG moderate (moderado) | neat, tidy (limpio y ordenado) | reasonable, sensible (razonable) | smart, well-dressed (bien vestido) | arranged, set out; *una casa que está bien arreglada* a house that is nicely set out | well-ordered (ordenado) | orderly; *vida arreglada* orderly life | good (conducta) | reasonable; *me ha hecho un precio muy arreglado* he sold it to me for a very reasonable price || — *arreglado a la ley* in accordance with the law || FAM *¡estamos arreglados!* that's all we needed!, a fine mess we're in! | *estar arreglado con alguien* to be in a fine mess *o* pickle with s.o.; *¡arreglados estamos con estos invitados!* we're a fine mess with these guests! | *¡pues estaría yo arreglado si lo tuviera que pagar!* I'd be in a fine spot if I had to pay it, it would be a fine thing if I had to pay it | *va arreglado si cree que...* he's got another think coming if he thinks that...

arreglar *vt* to regulate, to organize (someter a una regla) || to arrange, to lay *o* to set out (disponer); *no sé cómo arreglar este cuarto* I can't think how to arrange this room || to tidy up, to put straight, to put in order (poner en orden); *arreglar la casa* to tidy up the house || to repair, to mend; *arreglar un mueble roto* to repair a damaged piece of furniture || to settle, to sort out, to fix; *arreglaré este asunto* I will settle this matter || to get ready, to fix up; *arreglar todo para una fiesta* to get everything ready for a party || to arrange, to fix up (una entrevista, una cita) || to get in order; *arreglar los papeles para un viaje* to get one's papers in order for a journey || to get ready (preparar); *tenemos que arreglar a los niños para salir* we'll have to get the children ready to go out || to put right, to right (rectificar) || to settle; *esta taza de caldo te arreglará el estómago* this cup of broth will settle your stomach || to dress (los escaparates) || to prepare, to dress (una comida) || to pack (una maleta) || AMER to castrate || — *arreglar el cuello* to trim one's hair || *le han arreglado el pelo muy bien* they've done your hair very well *o* very nicely || FAM *lo han arreglado de lo lindo* they've made a fine mess of him, they've fixed him up good and proper | *no te preocupes, yo te lo arreglo* don't worry, I'll fix it *o* I'll arrange it for you *o* I'll see to it | *¡ya te arreglaré!* I'll fix you!, I'll show you!, I'll teach you!
◆ *vpr* to make do, to be content *o* satisfied; *me tendré que arreglar con lo que me han dado* I'll have to make do with what they've given me || to get ready; *me voy a arreglar para salir* I'm going to get ready to go out || to dress; *esa mujer se arregla muy bien* that woman dresses very well || to arrange things, to come to an agreement; *arréglate con tu madre para salir esta tarde* arrange things with your mother so that you can come out this afternoon || to work sth. out, to manage; *ya nos arreglaremos* we'll work sth. out || to improve, to clear up (el tiempo) || to work out right; *si se arreglan mis asuntos...* if things work out right... || to improve, to get better; *espero que se arreglará tu situación* I hope your situation will improve || to get by, to manage; *no sabe arreglarse sin teléfono* he can't get by without a telephone || to manage; *no sé cómo se arregla para llegar siempre tarde* I don't know how he always manages to be late || to agree, to come to an agreement (ponerse de acuerdo) || to agree, to come to terms; *arreglarse en el precio* to come to terms on the price || — *arreglarse el pelo* to have one's hair done (por otro), to do one's hair (uno mismo) || FAM *arreglárselas* to manage, to get by; *¡que se las arregle como pueda!* let him get by as best as he can! | *arreglárselas para* to manage to || *arreglarse muy bien con alguien* to get on very well with s.o. || *arreglarse por las buenas* to come to a friendly agreement || *espero que se arreglarán tus problemas* I hope your problems will sort themselves out || FAM *saber arreglárselas* to be able to look after o.s., to know what one is doing.

arreglo *m* agreement, arrangement (acuerdo); *llegar a un arreglo* to come to an arrangement, to reach an agreement || settlement, arrangement (acción y efecto); *el arreglo de un asunto* the settlement of a matter || repair, reparation, repairing; *el arreglo de algo roto* the repairing of sth. broken || order (orden) || MÚS arrangement || FAM relationship, affair (amancebamiento) || — *arreglo personal* personal appearance || *con arreglo a* in accordance with, according to; *con arreglo a la ley* in accordance with the law; in comparison with, compared with (en comparación) || *el asunto no tiene arreglo* there's no way out, there's no solution, there's nothing we can do about it || *este coche no tiene arreglo* this car is beyond repair || FAM *este hombre ya no tiene arreglo* he is a hopeless case.

arrellanarse *vpr* to sit back, to lounge, to make o.s. comfortable; *arrellanarse en un sillón* to sit back in an armchair.

arremangar *vt* to tuck *o* to hitch up (falda), to roll up (mangas, pantalones) || FIG *nariz arremangada* turned-up *o* snub nose.
◆ *vpr* to roll up one's shirt sleeves.

arremetedor, ra *adj* attacking.
◆ *m/f* attacker.

arremeter *vi* to attack, to charge, to rush; *arremeter al* or *contra el enemigo* to attack the enemy, to rush at the enemy || FIG to attack; *arremeter contra la Constitución* to attack the Constitution | to offend (a la vista).
◆ *vpr* to attack (atacar) || to spur on (un caballo).

arremetida *f* attack, assault (acción de atacar) || rush, crush (empujón) || FIG attack.

arremolinadamente *adv* in confusion || *las cabras entraron arremolinadamente en el redil* the goats scrambled into the pen.

arremolinarse *vpr* to whirl (about), to swirl; *las hojas se arremolinan en el suelo* the leaves whirl about on the ground || to swirl, to eddy (el agua) || FIG to mill, to rush, to scramble (la gente).

arrendable *adj* rentable (alquilable) || JUR leasable (contrato legal).

arrendadero *m* ring for tethering horses.

arrendado, da *adj* obedient [to the reins] || rented (alquilado) || JUR leased (por contrato legal).

arrendador, ra *m/f* JUR lessor (que da en arriendo), lessee (que toma en arriendo) || landlord (hombre), landlady (mujer) (que da en alquiler), tenant, renter (que toma en alquiler) || tenant farmer (de finca rústica).
◆ *m* ring for tethering horses (anillo).

arrendajo *m* ZOOL jay (pájaro europeo) | American oriole || FIG & FAM mimic, ape (persona que remeda a otra).

arrendamiento *m* JUR leasing (cuando hay contrato legal) || renting (acción de alquilar) || JUR lease (contrato legal) || rent (cantidad que se paga) || *tomar en arrendamiento* to lease, to rent.

arrendar* *vt* JUR to lease (ceder y tomar en arriendo); *arrendar tierras* to lease land || to rent (alquilar) ‖ to tether, to tie up (un caballo) ‖ FIG *no le arriendo la ganancia* I wouldn't like to be in his shoes, rather him than me, I don't envy him.

arrendatario, ria *adj* leasing ‖ *Compañía Arrendataria de Tabacos* state-owned tobacco company.
◆ *m/f* JUR lessee (con contrato legal) ‖ tenant (que alquila) ‖ JUR tenant farmer (de una finca rústica).

arrendaticio, cia *adj* lease, of a lease.

arrenquín *m* AMER muleteer's horse (caballo) | assistant, helper (ayudante).

arreo *m* adornment, ornament (adorno) ‖ AMER drove, herd (recua).
◆ *pl* harness *sing*, trappings (para los caballos) ‖ FIG & FAM trappings, stuff *sing*, gear *sing*; *llegó a casa con todos sus arreos* he arrived at our house with all his gear.

arrepanchigarse; arrepanchingarse *vpr* to sit back, to loll, to lounge (arrellanarse).

arrepentido, da *adj* repentant, regretful, sorry ‖ *estar arrepentido de algo* to regret sth., to be sorry about *o* for sth.
◆ *m/f* penitent.
◆ *f* magdalen, reformed prostitute.

arrepentimiento *m* repentance (contrición), regret (pesar) ‖ ARTES alteration ‖ *tener arrepentimiento por haber hecho algo* to repent of having done sth.

arrepentirse* *vpr* to repent; *arrepentirse de sus pecados* to repent one's sins; *se arrepintió de haberlo robado* he repented of having stolen it ‖ to be sorry, to regret; *me arrepiento de haber venido* I'm sorry I came, I regret having come ‖ *¡ya se arrepentirá usted!* you'll be sorry!, you'll regret it!

arrequesonarse *vpr* to curdle (la leche).

arrequives *m pl* FAM Sunday best *sing*, best clothes, finery *sing*; *Juana iba con todos sus arrequives* Joan was decked out in all her finery ‖ requirements (requisitos).

arrestado, da *adj* imprisoned (preso) ‖ bold, daring (audaz).

arrestar *vt* to put under arrest, to detain, to arrest.
◆ *vpr* to rush boldly; *arrestarse a hacer algo* to rush boldly into sth.

arresto *m* MIL arrest; *arresto mayor, menor* or *simple* close arrest, open arrest ‖ arrest (civil); *bajo arresto domiciliario* under house arrest ‖ detention under remand (provisional) ‖ imprisonment (reclusión).
◆ *pl* boldness *sing*, daring *sing* (arrojo) ‖ *tener arrestos para hacer algo* to be bold enough to do sth.

arretranca *f* AMER brake.

arrezagar *vt* to lift up (falda) ‖ to roll up (mangas, pantalón) ‖ to lift up, to raise (el brazo).

arriada *f* overflowing, flood (riada) ‖ MAR lowering of the sails.

arrianismo *m* Arianism (herejía).

arriano, na *adj/s* Arian (hereje).
— OBSERV No hay que confundir la palabra inglesa *Arian* con *Aryan*, que significa *ario*, de la raza aria.

arriar *vt* MAR to strike, to lower; *arriar bandera* to strike the flag | to lower (vela) | to slacken (un cable).
◆ *vpr* to be flooded (inundarse).

arriata *f*; **arriate** *m* flower bed, border ‖ road (camino).

arriba *adv* upstairs (en casa); *Pepe está arriba* Pepe is upstairs; *vete arriba* go upstairs ‖ up there; *¿dónde está? — arriba, en el árbol* where is he? — up there, in the tree ‖ above (encima) ‖ above; *lo arriba mencionado* the above mentioned ‖ up, upwards (dirección); *ir arriba* to go up ‖ — *aguas* or *río arriba* upstream, upriver ‖ *allá arriba* up there ‖ *arriba del todo* right on the top, on the very top ‖ *arriba mencionado* aforesaid ‖ *calle arriba* up the street ‖ *cuesta arriba* uphill ‖ *de arriba* from above, from up there; from above, from on high, from God (del cielo), free, for nothing (gratuito) ‖ *de arriba abajo* from top to bottom; up and down, from head to foot (personas); *mirar a uno de arriba abajo* to looks s.o. up and down, to eye s.o. from head to foot ‖ *de la cintura para arriba* from the waist up ‖ *hacia arriba* upwards ‖ *lo de arriba* what is on top, the top part ‖ *¡manos arriba!* hands up! ‖ *más arriba* above (en una carta), higher up, further up (más alto) ‖ *más arriba de* more than; *más arriba de cincuenta años* more than fifty years ‖ *para arriba* upwards; *gana de veinte libras para arriba* he earns upwards of twenty pounds; *hay artículos que cuestan de mil pesetas para arriba* there are items which cost from a thousand pesetas upwards ‖ *patas arriba* on one's back; *caerse patas arriba* to fall flat on one's back; back to front, upside down, muddled; *ponerlo todo patas arriba* to get everything muddled ‖ *peñas arriba* towards the summit ‖ FAM *que si arriba que si abajo* this that and the other, and so on and so forth ‖ *véase más arriba* see above.
◆ *interj* get up!, stand up!, up you get! (levántate) ‖ come on! (ánimo) ‖ — *¡arriba España!* long live Spain! ‖ *¡arriba los corazones!* don't lose heart! chin up!

arribada *f* MAR arrival (llegada de un barco) | tack (bordada) ‖ arrival; *arribada de mercancías* arrival of goods ‖ *arribada forzosa* unscheduled stop.

arribaje *m* MAR arrival.

arribano *m/f* AMER inhabitant of the northern coast of Peru | inhabitant of the southern provinces of Chile.

arribar *vi* MAR to arrive (llegar) | to put into port (hacer escala) | to drift with the wind (derivar) ‖ to arrive (por tierra) ‖ *arribar a buen puerto* to arrive safely.

arribazón *m* large shoals *pl* of fish.

arribeño, ña *adj* AMER highland.
◆ *m/f* AMER highlander.

arribismo; arrivismo *m* arrivism.

arribista; arrivista *adj* self-seeking.
◆ *m/f* arriviste, arrivist.

arribo *m* MAR arrival (de un barco, de mercancías).

arricés *m* stirrup strap buckle.

arriendo *m* JUR leasing (cuando hay contrato legal) ‖ renting (acción de alquilar) ‖ rent (cantidad que se paga) ‖ JUR lease (contrato legal) ‖ *tomar en arriendo* to lease.

arriero *m* muleteer, mule driver.

arriesgadamente *adv* riskily, hazardously (con riesgo) ‖ dangerously; *vivir arriesgadamente* to live dangerously ‖ boldly, bravely (con valor).

arriesgado, da *adj* risky, hazardous, dangerous (peligroso) ‖ risky, rash; *una empresa arriesgada* a risky venture ‖ daring, bold, brave (audaz).

arriesgar *vt* to risk, to endanger; *arriesgar la vida* to risk one's life ‖ to risk, to stake; *arriesgar dinero, su buena fama* to risk money, one's good name ‖ to venture; *arriesgar una nueva hipótesis* to venture a new theory ‖ FAM *arriesgar el pellejo* to risk one's neck *o* skin.
◆ *vpr* to take a risk (correr un riesgo) ‖ to risk; *arriesgarse a perderlo todo* to risk losing everything; *arriesgarse a salir* to risk going out ‖ *quien no se arriesga no pasa el río* or *la mar* nothing ventured, nothing gained.

arrimadero *m* support (apoyo) ‖ horse block (para montar a caballo).

arrimador *m* log (leña).

arrimadura *f* approach (acción de acercarse) ‖ leaning (acción de apoyarse).

arrimar *vt* to bring closer, to draw up; *arrima tu silla a la mía* bring your chair closer to mine ‖ to bring together (juntar) ‖ to put; *arrima tu silla a la pared* put your chair against the wall ‖ to lean (*a* against) (apoyar) ‖ to put away (arrinconar) ‖ to ignore (a una persona) ‖ — POP *arrimar candela a uno* to thrash s.o., to give s.o. a good thrashing *o* beating ‖ FIG *arrimar el hombro* to put one's shoulder to the wheel (trabajar mucho), to lend a hand (ayudar) | *arrimarle un golpe a uno* to hit s.o. | *arrimarle a uno un palo* to hit s.o. with a stick ‖ *estar arrimado a alguien* to live off s.o. (parásito) ‖ *vivir arrimado con una mujer* to live with a woman (sin estar casados).
◆ *vpr* to come *o* to go *o* to get close *o* near, to draw up, to approach; *arrimarse al fuego* to draw up to the fire ‖ to gather; *se arrimó mucha gente* many people gathered ‖ to lean (apoyarse); *arrimarse a la pared* to lean against the wall ‖ FIG to join together (juntarse) | to seek the protection (*a* of), to lean (*a* on) (buscar apoyo) | to live together (amancebarse) ‖ FIG *arrimarse al sol que más calienta* to get on the winning side.

arrimo *m* FIG support, protection, help (apoyo) | attachment (inclinación) ‖ dividing wall (pared) ‖ living together (amancebamiento) ‖ — FIG *hacer algo al arrimo de alguien* to do sth. with s.o.'s support *o* help | *tener buen arrimo* to have good support (gozar de apoyo).

arrinconado, da *adj* forgotten, neglected, laid aside; *un objeto arrinconado* a forgotten object ‖ forsaken, deserted, abandoned; *un hombre arrinconado y solitario* a lonely and forsaken man.

arrinconamiento *m* discarding, laying aside.

arrinconar *vt* to put in a corner ‖ to corner (perseguir y acorralar); *arrinconé al ladrón* I cornered the thief ‖ to discard, to put aside *o* away; *arrinconar un mueble desvencijado* to discard a rickety piece of furniture ‖ to ignore, to leave out (apartar a alguien).
◆ *vpr* FIG & FAM to withdraw from the world, to live in isolation (vivir solo).

arriñonado, da *adj* kidney-shaped, reniform.

arriostrar *vt* ARQ to shore up, to prop up, to stay.

arriscado, da *adj* rough, uneven, craggy (terreno) ‖ bold, daring (audaz) ‖ reckless (temerario) ‖ AMER *nariz arriscada* turned-up nose, snub nose (nariz respingona).

arriscador, ra *m/f* olive picker, olive gleaner.

arriscamiento *m* boldness, daring.

arriscar *vt* to risk ‖ AMER to lift up, to turn up (levantar).
◆ *vi* AMER to come (*a* to) (ascender) ‖ *no arrisca a cien pesos* it is less than a hundred pesos, it does not come to a hundred pesos.
◆ *vpr* to fall headlong (las reses) ‖ AMER to dress elegantly (vestirse con esmero) | to get angry (enfurecerse).

arritmia *f* MED arrhythmia.

arrítmico, ca *adj* MED arrhythmic.

arritranca *f* breeching (correa).

arrivismo *m* → **arribismo.**

arrivista *adj/s* → **arribista.**
— OBSERV *Arrivismo* and *arrivista* are barbarisms better replaced by *arribismo* and *arribista*.

arrizar *vt* MAR to reef, to take in a reef (tomar rizos) | to lash, to tie down (atar).

arroba *f* «arroba», 25 pounds [11. 5 kg] || «arroba», about 28. 5 pints [16. 1 litres of wine] || «arroba», about 22 pints [12. 6 litres of oil] || — FIG *por arrobas* in abundance, galore || *tiene gracia por arrobas* he's extremely witty, he's full of wit.

arrobado, da *adj* in ecstasy, in transports, in raptures (sumo placer) || in a trance (fuera de sí).

arrobamiento *m* ecstasy, rapture, transports *pl* (sumo placer) || trance (de un místico).

arrobar *vt* to entrance, to send into raptures.
◆ *vpr* to go into raptures, to go into transports, to go into ecstasies || to go into a trance (los místicos).

arrobo *m* ecstasy, rapture (sumo placer) || trance (de un místico).

arrocero, ra *adj* rice; *industria arrocera* rice industry || *molino arrocero* rice mill.
◆ *m/f* rice grower.

arrodillamiento *m* kneeling.

arrodillar *vt* to make kneel down || *estar arrodillado* to be kneeling, to be on one's knees.
◆ *vi/vpr* to kneel, down, to go down on one's knees.

arrodrigar; arrodrigonar *vt* AGR to prop, to stake (la vid).

arrogación *f* arrogation.

arrogancia *f* arrogance, arrogancy (soberbia) || bravery, boldness (valor) || pride (orgullo).

arrogante *adj* arrogant (altanero) || proud (airoso) || bold, brave (valiente).

arrogantemente *adv* arrogantly || bravely (con valor) || proudly, with bearing (airosamente).

arrogarse *vpr* to arrogate to o.s., to assume; *se arrogó el derecho de castigar a los presos* he assumed the right to punish the prisoners.

arrojadizo, za *adj* throwable || *arma arrojadiza* projectile, missile.

arrojado, da *adj* FIG brave, bold (valiente) || rash, daring (temerario).

arrojador, ra *adj* throwing, projectile.

arrojar *vt* to throw; *arrojar una piedra, una pelota* to throw a stone, a ball; *arrojar algo por la borda* to throw sth. overboard || to fling, to hurl (con fuerza) || to throw out, to belch out *o* forth; *volcán que arroja lava* volcano belching out lava || to belch, to send out (humo) || to drop; *arrojar bombas* to drop bombs || to give out *o* off, to emit; *arrojar rayos* to give out rays || to cast (el sedal) || to indicate, to show; *el balance arroja un beneficio* the balance shows a profit || FAM to throw up, to vomit (vomitar) || BOT to sprout (flores, brotes) | to put out (raíces) || to throw out; *le arrojaron del bar* they threw him out of the bar || — *los tres diamantes arrojan un valor de 1000 dólares* the three diamonds are worth a total of 1000 dollars || *prohibido arrojar basuras* no tipping || *según lo que arrojan las estadísticas* according to statistics.
◆ *vi* FAM to be sick, to vomit (vomitar).
◆ *vpr* to throw o.s., to fling o.s., to hurl o.s., to rush, to plunge; *arrojarse al agua* to throw o.s. into the water; *arrojarse al combate* to hurl o.s. into the fray || to jump; *el perro se arrojó sobre el hombre* the dog jumped at *o* on the man || — *arrojarse a los pies de uno* to throw o.s. at s.o.'s feet || — *arrojarse de cabeza* to throw o.s. headlong *o* headfirst || *arrojarse por la ventana* to throw o.s. out of the window.

arrojo *m* courage, daring, boldness; *hace falta mucho arrojo para obrar de esta manera* you need a lot of courage to do that.

arrollado *m* AMER dressed pork.

arrollador, ra *adj* rolling (que enrolla) || FIG sweeping, devastating; *un viento arrollador* a devastating wind | irresistible; *argumentos arrolladores* irresistible arguments | resounding, overwhelming; *éxito arrollador* overwhelming success; *una mayoría arrolladora* a resounding majority.
◆ *m* windlass (cilindro).

arrollamiento *m* rolling, rolling-up (acción de arrollar) || ELECTR winding.

arrollar *vt* to roll, to roll up, to coil (enrollar) || to sweep away, to carry off; *el agua de la crecida lo arrolló* the floodwater swept it away || to run over, to knock down; *el coche arrolló a un peatón* the car ran over a pedestrian || FIG to rout, to crush; *arrollar los batallones enemigos* to rout the enemy battalions | to squash, to leave speechless, to silence; *en la discusión le arrolló en seguida* he immediately squashed him in the discussion | to have no respect for, to trample over; *arrollar los derechos ajenos* to trample over other people's rights.

arromanzar *vt* to translate into Castilian Spanish.

arropamiento *m* wrapping up, covering up.

arropar *vt* to wrap up; *en invierno hay que arropar mucho a los niños* in winter you must wrap the children up well || to tuck up (a alguien en una cama) || to add grape syrup [to wine] || FIG to shelter; *dos montañas arropan la bahía* two mountains shelter the bay || *estar muy arropado en la cama* to be well tucked up in bed.
◆ *vpr* to wrap o.s. up; *arrópate bien que hace mucho frío* wrap yourself up well, it's very cold || to tuck o.s. up (en la cama).

arrope *m* boiled must || syrup (jarabe).

arropía *f* taffy (melcocha).

arrorró *m* lullaby (canción de cuna) || *arrorró mi nene* hushaby baby.

arrostrar *vt* to face, to face up to, to brave; *arrostrar el frío, un peligro* to brave the cold, a danger || to face, to face up to; *arrostrar la muerte* to face up to death; *arrostrar las consecuencias de una acción* to face the consequences of an action.
◆ *vpr* to stand up, to face up; *arrostrarse con uno* to stand up to s.o.

arroyar *vt* to channel, to hollow out || to form channels in (la lluvia).
◆ *vpr* to be channelled, to be hollowed out || AGR to mildew.

arroyo *m* stream, brook (riachuelo) || gutter (en una calle) || FIG street, gutter (calle); *tirar al arroyo, plantar* or *poner en el arroyo* to throw into the street | stream, flood; *arroyos de lágrimas* streams *o* floods of tears || AMER river (río) || FIG *sacar del arroyo* to drag from the gutter.

arroyuelo *m* streamlet, rivulet, rill, brooklet.

arroz *m* rice; *arroz descascarillado* husked rice || — *arroz a la italiana* risotto || *arroz blanco* or *en blanco* boiled rice || *arroz con leche* rice pudding, creamed rice || AMER *arroz de leche* rice pudding, creamed rice || *arroz picón* or *quebrantado* broken rice || *más pesado que el arroz con leche* as heavy as lead (comida), as dull as dishwater, as boring as can be (aburrido) || *polvos de arroz* face powder || FIG & FAM *tener arroz y gallo muerto* to have a meal fit for a king, to have a slap-up meal.

arrozal *m* rice field, rice plantation || rice paddy, paddy (en China).

arrufadura *f* MAR sheer (curvatura del puente del navío).

arrufar *vt* MAR to build with a sheer.
◆ *vpr* FAM to fly off the handle, to lose one's temper.

arrufianado, da *adj* rascally, vulgar, coarse.

arrufo *m* MAR sheer (curvatura del puente del navío).

arruga *f* wrinkle, line; *una cara surcada de arrugas* a face furrowed with wrinkles || crease (en la ropa) || AMER fraud, swindle (estafa) || *mi vestido tiene muchas arrugas* my dress is very creased.

arrugamiento *m* wrinkling (de la piel) || creasing (de la ropa).

arrugar *vt* to wrinkle, to line (hacer arrugas) || to crumple up, to screw up; *con rabia arrugó la carta que tenía en la mano* he furiously crumpled up the letter that he held in his hand || to crease (la ropa) || AMER to annoy, to bother || — *arrugar el ceño* or *el entrecejo* to frown || *arrugar la cara* to screw one's face up.
◆ *vpr* to shrink (encogerse) || to wrinkle (la cara) || to crease (la ropa).

arruinar *vt* to ruin; *la guerra arruinó a mucha gente* the war ruined many people || to destroy, to lay waste (destruir) || FIG to ruin, to wreck; *arruinar la salud* to ruin one's health | to ruin; *arruinar la reputación* to ruin one's reputation.
◆ *vpr* to be ruined (perder la fortuna) || to fall into ruins, to fall down (un edificio) || to go to rack and ruin (estropearse).

arrullador, ra *adj* cooing (de las palomas) || lulling (voz, canto) || FIG cajoling, coaxing.

arrullar *vt* to coo at (una paloma) || FIG to lull, to sing to sleep (dormir a un niño cantándole) || FIG & FAM to say sweet nothings to, to bill and coo to (enamorar).
◆ *vpr* FIG & FAM to bill and coo (los enamorados).

arrullo *m* cooing; *el arrullo de las palomas* the cooing of the doves || FIG billing and cooing (de los enamorados) | lullaby (canción de cuna).

arrumaco *m* FAM cajolery, flattery (zalamería) || fondling, caressing || trinket, frill (adorno ridículo) || — *andar con arrumacos* to flatter || *no me vengas con arrumacos* don't try and get round me.

arrumaje *m* MAR stowing, stowage.

arrumar *vt* MAR to stow. || AMER to pile up
◆ *vpr* MAR to cloud over.

arrumazón *f* MAR stowing | clouds *pl* (nublado).

arrumbador *m* wine-cellar worker.

arrumbamiento *m* MAR course, direction (rumbo).

arrumbar *vt* to discard, to lay aside, to put away (arrinconar) || FIG to ignore, to exclude (a una persona).
◆ *vi* MAR to head, to set course (hacia for).
◆ *vpr* MAR to take one's bearings (determinar la situación del barco).

arrume *m* AMER heap (montón).

arrurruz *m* arrowroot (fécula).

arsenal *m* shipyard (astillero) || naval dockyard (para buques de guerra) || arsenal (de armas) || FIG store, storehouse, arsenal.

arseniato *m* QUÍM arsenate, arseniate.

arsenical *adj* QUÍM arsenical.

arsénico, ca *adj/sm* QUÍM arsenic.

arsenioso, sa *adj* QUÍM arsenious, arsenous.

arseniuro *m* QUÍM arsenide.

arsina *f* QUÍM arsine.

arta *f* BOT plantain (llantén).

Artajerjes *npr m* Artaxerxes.

artanica; artanita *f* BOT cyclamen.

arte *m o f* art; *una obra de arte* a work of art; *no comprendo el arte abstracto* I do not understand abstract art; *el arte culinario* (the art of) cooking || skill (habilidad) || artistry, workmanship; *mira con qué arte está hecho* just look at the workmanship || cunning (astucia) || rules *pl* (reglas) || arts *pl*; *dedicarse al arte* to dedicate o.s. to the arts || — *arte cisoria* art of carving [meat] || *arte plumaria* embroidery with feathers || *arte poética* art of poetry || *artes de pesca* fishing tackle *sing* || *artes domésticas* domestic science *sing* || *artes liberales* liberal arts || DEP *artes marciales* martial arts || *bellas artes* fine arts || *con arte* skilfully || *con todas las reglas del arte* according to the book *o* to the rules || *el arte por el arte* art for art's sake || *escuela de artes y oficios* school of arts and crafts || *no tener arte ni parte en una cosa* to have nothing to do with sth. || *por amor al arte* for the love of it || *por arte de birlibirloque, por arte de magia* as if by magic || *por buenas o malas artes* by fair means or foul || *sin arte* clumsily.

— OBSERV The word *arte* is always feminine in the plural (*las artes gráficas* the graphic arts) and usually masculine in the singular except when it is followed by certain adjectives (*arte cisoria, poética, plumaria,* etc.).

artefacto *m* device, contrivance, appliance; *un extraño artefacto* a strange device || *artefacto nuclear* nuclear device.

artejo *m* ANAT knuckle || ZOOL article (de los insectos).

arteramente *adv* cunningly, slyly, craftily.

arteria *f* ANAT artery || FIG artery (vía de comunicación).

artería *f* cunning, slyness, craftiness.

arterial *adj* arterial.

arteriectomía *f* MED arterectomy, arteriectomy.

arteriola *f* ANAT arteriole.

arteriopatía *f* MED arteriopathy.

arterioplastia *f* MED arterioplasty.

arteriosclerosis *f* MED arteriosclerosis.

arteriostenosis *f* MED arteriostenosis

arteritis *f* MED arteritis.

artero, ra *adj* cunning, sly, crafty.

artesa *f* trough.

artesanado *m* craftsmen *pl.*

artesanía *f* handicrafts *pl*, crafts *pl*; *artesanía mexicana* Mexican crafts || craftsmanship (habilidad); *está realizado con gran artesanía* it is made with great craftsmanship || *objeto de artesanía* handmade article.

artesano, na *m/f* artisan, craftsman (hombre), artisan, craftswoman (mujer).

artesiano, na *adj* artesian; *pozo artesiano* artesian well.

artesilla *f* small trough.

artesón *m* tub (cubo) || ARQ coffer (de un techo) | coffered ceiling (techo).

artesonado, da *adj* ARQ coffered.
◆ *m* coffered ceiling (techo).

artesonar *vt* ARQ to coffer.

ártico, ca *adj* Arctic || — *Círculo Polar Ártico* Arctic Circle || *Océano Ártico* Arctic Ocean.
◆ *m* Arctic.

articulación *f* ANAT articulation, joint || articulation (pronunciación) || TECN joint; *articulación universal* universal joint.

articuladamente *adv* articulately, distinctly.

articulado, da *adj* articulate; *lenguaje articulado* articulate speech || articulated; *camión articulado* articulated lorry || ANAT jointed, articulated.
◆ *m* articles *pl* (de una ley).

articular *adj* articular; *reúma articular* articular rheumatism.

articular *vt* to articulate, to join together, to joint; *articular dos piezas de una máquina* to articulate two parts of a machine || to articulate (las sílabas) || JUR to write in separate articles.

articulista *m* contributor, writer of articles (periodista).

artículo *m* article; *un artículo de periódico* a newspaper article || entry (en un diccionario) || JUR article || article, item (mercancía); *artículo de primera calidad* top-quality article || ZOOL article (de los insectos) || GRAM article; *artículo definido, indefinido, partitivo* definite, indefinite, partitive article || — ECON *artículo básico* base item || *artículo de fe* article of faith (afirmación religiosa), gospel truth (verdad) || *artículo de fondo* leader, leading article, editorial || *como artículo de fe* as though it were gospel truth || *en el artículo de la muerte* in the article of *o* at the point of death || *hacer el artículo a* to boost, to plug (*fam*).
◆ *pl* goods; *artículos de consumo* consumer goods || — *artículos alimenticios* foodstuffs, food products || *artículos de caballero* men's accessories || *artículos de escritorio* stationery || *artículos de fantasía* fancy goods || *artículos de primera necesidad* basic commodities *o* necessities || *artículos de tocador* cosmetics.

artífice *m/f* FIG author; *Dios es el artífice de la Creación* God is the author of Creation || maker, artificer (hacedor) || craftsman, artificer (artesano) || — *el Artífice Supremo* the Maker (Dios) || *ha sido el artífice de su fortuna* he is a self-made man.

artificial *adj* artificial; *inseminación artificial* artificial insemination; *pierna artificial* artificial leg; *una sonrisa artificial* an artificial smile || *fuegos artificiales* fireworks.

artificiero *m* firework maker, pyrotechnist (de fuegos artificiales) || MIL artificer.

artificio *m* skill, ingenuity (habilidad) || device (aparato) || FIG trick, artifice; *emplea muchos artificios para disimular su edad* he uses lots of tricks to hide his age || firework (pirotecnia) || *fuegos de artificio* fireworks.

artificioso, sa *adj* crafty, cunning; *conducta artificiosa* crafty behaviour || skilful, clever (hecho con habilidad).

artilugio *m* FAM device, contraption, gadget (cosa) || FIG scheme, trick (trampa).

artillar *vt* to arm with artillery.

artillería *f* MIL artillery; *artillería pesada* heavy artillery || armament (de un buque) || MIL *artillería antiaérea* antiaircraft guns *pl.*

artillero *m* MIL artilleryman || gunner (en barcos, aviones).

artimaña *f* trick, scheme (astucia) || trap (trampa).

artimón *m* MAR mizzen, mizen (vela) | mizzenmast, mizenmast (palo).

artista *m/f* artist (escultor, pintor, etc.) || artist, artiste (espectáculos) || TEATR actor (actor), actress (actriz) || — *artista de cine* film actor (actor), film actress (actriz) || FIG *es un artista conduciendo* he makes driving an art.

artísticamente *adv* artistically.

artístico, ca *adj* artistic.

artralgia *f* MED arthralgia.

artrítico, ca *adj/s* MED arthritic.

artritis *f* MED arthritis.

artritismo *m* MED arthritism.

artrópodo, da *adj* ZOOL arthropodal, arthropodous.
◆ *m* arthropod.
◆ *pl* arthropoda.

artuña *f* ewe which has lost its lamb.

arturiano, na; artúrico, ca *adj* Arthurian.

Arturo *npr m* Arthur.

Artús *npr m* Arthur (rey).

aruco *m* AMER ZOOL horned screamer (ave).

arúspice *m* HIST haruspex.

— OBSERV El plural de *haruspex* es *haruspices.*

arveja; alverja; alverjana *f* BOT vetch, tare || AMER pea (guisante) || *arveja silvestre* everlasting pea.

arvejal *m* vetch field, tare field || AMER pea field.

arvejana *f* BOT ⟶ **arveja.**

arvejera *f* BOT vetch, tare.

arvejo *m* BOT pea (guisante).

arvejona *f* BOT vetch, tare.

arzobispado *m* archbishopric (dignidad, territorio) || archiepiscopate (dignidad, duración).

arzobispal *adj* archiepiscopal || *palacio arzobispal* archbishop's palace.

arzobispo *m* archbishop.

arzolla *f* BOT centaury.

arzón *m* saddletree (de la silla de montar) || *potro con arzón* pommelled horse, side horse.

as *m* ace (carta y dado); *pareja de ases* pair of aces; *un as de diamantes* an ace of diamonds || as (moneda romana) || FIG ace, star; *un as del volante* an ace driver; *ser un as* to be an ace.

asa *f* handle (de una vasija, cesta, etc.) || bend (del intestino) || BOT juice (jugo) || — *asa dulce* benzoin, asa dulcis || *asa fétida* asafetida, asafoetida || *los brazos en asa* hands on hips.

asá *adv* FAM *así que asá* either way; *a mí se me da así que asá* I don't mind either way.

asadero, ra *adj* roasting, for roasting.
◆ *m* spit roaster.

asado, da *adj* roast, roasted; *carne asada* roast meat.
◆ *m* roast || AMER barbecued beef || AMER *asado con cuero* joint roasted in its skin.

asador *m* spit (varilla para asar) || spit roaster (aparato para asar).

asadura *f* liver (hígado) || FAM sluggishness, slowness (pachorra).
◆ *m* sluggish person, big lump (*fam*).
◆ *f pl* offal *sing*, innards || FIG & FAM *echar las asaduras* to slog one's heart out.

asaetear *vt* to shoot *o* to wound with arrows (herir o matar con flechas) || to fire *o* to shoot arrows at (disparar contra) || FIG to pester, to badger; *asaetear a* or *con preguntas* to pester with questions.

asalariado, da *adj* salaried.
◆ *m/f* salary earner.

asalariar *vt* to pay a salary to.

asalmonado, da *adj* salmon-like (salmonado) || salmon pink (color) || *trucha asalmonada* salmon trout.

asaltador, ra; asaltante *adj* attacking, assaulting.
◆ *m/f* attacker, assailant (de una persona, de un sitio) || robber, raider (de un banco).

asaltar *vt* to storm, to attack, to assault (soldados) || to assault, to attack; *el ladrón le asaltó* the thief assaulted him || to raid, to rob (un banco) || to assail; *los mendigos le asaltaron* the beggars assailed him || FIG to cross one's mind, to come to one; *una idea me asaltó* an idea crossed my mind | to afflict, to assail (las dudas).

asalto *m* assault, attack, raid; *dar asalto a* to make an assault on || DEP round (boxeo) | bout (esgrima) || FAM party (fiesta) || *tomar por asalto* to take by storm.

asamblea *f* assembly (reunión) || congress, conference (congreso) || MIL assembly (toque).

asambleísta *m/f* member of an assembly || member of a congress, congressist (congresista).

asao *adv* FAM *lo mismo me da así que asao* I don't mind either way, it's all the same to me, I'm easy.

asar *vt* to roast || FIG to annoy, to pester, to plague; *me asaron a preguntas* they pestered me with questions || — *asar a la plancha* to griddle || *asar en* or *a la parrilla* to grill || *eso no se le ocurre ni al que asó la manteca* only a fool would think of doing that.
◆ *vpr* to be roasted *o* roasting, to be boiling hot; *me aso en este abrigo* I'm roasting in this overcoat || FIG *asarse vivo* to be roasted alive.

asargado, da *adj* twilled, serge-like.

asaz *adv* rather, quite (bastante) || very, exceedingly (muy).

asbesto *m* MIN asbestos.

asca *f* BOT ascus.

ascalonia *f* BOT shallot (chalote).

ascáride *f* ZOOL threadworm.

ascendencia *f* descent, ancestry, origin; *es de ascendencia americana* he is of American descent || ascendancy, ascendency, influence (predominio).

ascendente *adj* ascending, upward, rising || *marea ascendente* incoming *o* rising tide.

ascender* *vi* to go up, to rise, to ascend; *ascender por los aires* to rise into the air; *la temperatura ha ascendido durante la mañana* the temperature has risen during the morning || to come to, to amount to, to add up to; *la cuenta asciende a tres libras* the bill amounts to three pounds || to climb (montaña) || to reach; *la producción de acero asciende a cinco mil toneladas* steel production reaches five thousand tons || FIG to be promoted, to be raised, to rise; *ascender a capitán* to rise to the rank of captain || — *ascender a la primera división* to be promoted to the first division || *ascender al trono* to ascend (to) the throne.
◆ *vt* to promote, to raise; *ser ascendido a jefe por antigüedad* to be promoted to boss by seniority.

ascendido, da *adj* promoted.

ascendiente *adj* ascending, upward, rising.
◆ *m* influence, ascendancy, ascendency.
◆ *pl* ancestors, ancestry *sing* (parientes).

ascensión *f* ascent, climbing; *la ascensión del Everest* the ascent of Everest || promotion (de grado, de división) || ascension; *día de la Ascensión* Ascension Day || accession (al pontificado, al trono).

ascensional *adj* upward, ascendant, ascendent.

ascensionista *m/f* mountaineer (alpinista) || balloonist.

ascenso *m* ascent, climbing, climb (subida) || FIG promotion (en un empleo); *conseguir un ascenso* to obtain promotion; *el ascenso a capitán* promotion to captain || — *ascenso por antigüedad, por méritos* promotion by seniority, on merit || *lista de ascenso* promotion list.

ascensor *m* lift [*US* elevator]; *el hueco del ascensor* the lift shaft || *ascensor de subida y bajada* two-way lift.

ascensorista *m/f* lift attendant [*US* elevator operator].

ascesis *f* ascesis.

asceta *m/f* ascetic.

ascético, ca *adj* ascetic.
◆ *f* asceticism.

ascetismo *m* asceticism.

asco *m* disgust, repulsion (repugnancia) || — FIG *canta que da asco* he's an awful singer || *coger* or *cobrar* or *tomar asco a algo* to take a dislike to sth. || *¡da asco!* it's revolting *o* horrible *o* disgusting! || *da asco que no se pueda salir por la noche* it makes you sick not being able to go out at night || *dar asco* to make sick, to disgust; *le da asco* it makes him sick || FAM *está hecho un asco* he's disgusting, he's disgustingly filthy, it makes you feel sick to look at him | *hacer asco (a todo)* to turn one's nose up (at everything), to pull a face (at everything) | *le da asco la carne* he can't stand meat, he loathes meat | *le tengo asco* I can't stand the sight of him (le odio), he makes me sick (me da asco) | *le tiene asco al agua* he can't bear water, he can't stand the sight of water | *me da asco verlo* it makes me feel sick to see it || *poner cara de asco* to look disgusted || *¡qué asco!* how revolting! || FIG & FAM *ser un asco* to be worthless (no tener valor), to be filthy, to be disgusting (estar sucio) | *tener asco a la vida* to be disgusted with life.

ascomiceto *m* BOT ascomycete (hongo).

ascua *f* ember, live coal || — FIG *arrimar uno el ascua a su sardina* to look after number one | *estar echando ascuas* to be furious *o* livid | *estar en* or *sobre ascuas* to be on tenterhooks || *hierro hecho ascua* red-hot iron || FIG *pasar como sobre ascuas por un asunto* to touch lightly on *o* to skim over a subject | *ser un ascua de oro* to glitter like a diamond | *tener ojos como ascuas* to have eyes which sparkle like diamonds.

aseadamente *adv* cleanly (limpiamente) || neatly, tidily (arregladamente).

aseado, da *adj* clean (limpio) || neat, tidy (arreglado).

asear *vt* to wash (lavar) || to clean (limpiar) || to tidy up (arreglar) || to decorate (adornar).
◆ *vpr* to have a wash (and brush up), to wash o.s. (lavarse) || to tidy o.s. up, to get ready (componerse).

asechamiento *m*; **asechanza** *f* trap (trampa).

asechar *vt* to set a trap for.

asecho *m* trap (trampa).

asedar *vt* to make as soft as silk (suavizar) || to hackle (el cáñamo).

asediador, ra *adj* besieging || FIG annoying (importuno).
◆ *m/f* besieger.

asediar *vt* to besiege, to lay siege to (sitiar) || FIG to snow under, to besiege, to bombard; *estaba asediado de solicitudes* he was snowed under with requests; *los periodistas le asediaron a preguntas* the reporters bombarded him with questions.

asedio *m* siege (cerco) || FIG nuisance, annoyance.

asegurado, da *adj* insured, assured; *casa asegurada de incendio* house insured against fire; *asegurado en un millón de pesetas* insured for one million pesetas.
◆ *m/f* insured, policyholder.

asegurador, ra *adj* insurance, assurance; *compañía aseguradora* insurance company.
◆ *m* insurer, underwriter.

aseguramiento *m* securing, fastening (acción de fijar) || assurance (afirmación) || insurance, assurance (seguro).

asegurar *vt* to secure, to fix, to make safe (sujetar) || to put in a safe place (poner en sitio seguro) || to safeguard, to keep secure (preservar) || to strengthen, to make secure (consolidar) || to reassure (tranquilizar) || to insure, to assure; *asegurar contra incendio* or *de incendio* to assure against fire || to assure; *le aseguro que...* I assure you that...
◆ *vpr* to make sure; *asegúrate de que esté bien cerrada la puerta* make sure that the door is properly closed || to insure *o* to assure o.s., to take out an insurance [policy].

asemejar *vt* to make alike *o* like *o* similar (hacer parecido) || to liken, to compare (comparar).
◆ *vpr* to resemble each other, to be alike (parecerse) || *asemejarse a* to resemble, to be like.

asendereado, da *adj* FIG overworked, overwhelmed (agobiado) || beaten, well-trodden (camino) || FIG experienced (experto).

asenderear *vt* to open paths through; *asenderear un bosque* to open paths through a forest || to bother, to annoy (acosar) || to chase, to pursue (perseguir).

asenso *m* consent, approbation, assent.

asentada *f* session, sitting; *de una asentada* at one sitting.

asentaderas *f pl* FAM buttocks, behind *sing*, bottom *sing*.

asentado, da *adj* situated; *San Sebastián está asentado a orillas del Urumea* San Sebastian is situated on the banks of the Urumea || FIG settled, stable (estable) | established; *reputación muy asentada* well-established reputation.

asentador *m* wholesale merchant (de un mercado al por mayor) || TECN chisel (de herrero) || strop (suavizador) || *AMER* planer (en la imprenta) || *asentador de vías* tracklayer.

asentamiento *m* sitting (down) (acción de sentarse) || establishment, settling (de personas) || emplacement (emplazamiento) || COM entry, registration || FIG wisdom, common sense (juicio).

asentar* *vt* to seat, to sit (down) (sentar) || to place (colocar) || to settle; *la lluvia ha asentado el polvo* the rain has settled the dust || to lay; *asentar los cimientos* to lay the foundations || to found; *asentar una ciudad* to found a city || to pitch, to set up; *asentar un campamento* to pitch camp || to hone, to sharpen (afilar) || to level, to flatten down (la tierra) || TECN to seat (una válvula) || to note, to enter (anotar) || to affirm, to assure, to assert (afirmar) || to establish (establecer) || FAM to land, to give, to fetch (una bofetada, etc.) || to agree; *se asentó que* it was agreed that || to draw up (un contrato, un convenio) || to steady, to calm down; *asentar a una persona inestable* to calm an unstable person down || to set down (principio, argumento) || JUR to award || *asentar el juicio* to come to one's senses.
◆ *vi* to be suitable (ir o sentar bien) || to be steady (una mesa, etc.).
◆ *vpr* to sit down, to seat o.s. || to alight, to land (los pájaros) || to settle (los líquidos, el polvo, el tiempo, un edificio) || to sink, to subside (la tierra) || to rub (arreos) || to be situated (estar situado) || FIG to establish o.s. (en un empleo) | to settle down (establecerse) | to develop, to settle down (el carácter) || *asentarse en el estómago* to lie (heavily) on one's stomach (los alimentos).

asentimiento *m* consent, assent (aprobación).

asentir* *vi* to agree, to assent, to approve (aprobar) || — *asentir a* to agree to, to approve || *asentir con la cabeza* to nod [one's approval] || *asentir con un gesto* to signal one's approval.

asentista *m* supplier (suministrador) || contractor (contratista).

aseñorado, da *adj* haughty, pompous, stuck-up (*fam*), toffee-nosed (*fam*).

aseo *m* cleanliness (limpieza) || tidiness, neatness (pulcritud) || washing and dressing, toilet || (small) bathroom, toilet (cuarto) ||— *aseo personal* personal toilet (acción), personal cleanliness (efecto) || *cuarto de aseo* (small) bathroom, toilet.
◆ *pl* toilets [*US* rest room *sing*] (en un restaurante, etc.).

asépalo, la *adj* BOT having no sepals.

asepsia *f* asepsis (saneamiento).

aséptico, ca *adj* aseptic.

aseptizar *vt* to asepticize.

asequible *adj* reasonable; *precio asequible* reasonable price || obtainable, accessible (alcanzable) || practicable, feasile (proyecto) || easy to get on with, affable, easily-approached, approachable; *una persona asequible* an affable *o* approachable person, a person easy to get on with || comprehensible, understandable (entendible) || *libros asequibles a todos* books within everybody's reach.

aserción *f* assertion, affirmation.

aserradero *m* sawmill.

aserrado, da *adj* serrated.
◆ *m* sawing.

aserrador, ra *adj* sawing.
◆ *m* sawyer, sawer.
◆ *f* power saw.

aserradura *f* sawing (acción) || saw cut (corte que hace la sierra).
◆ *pl* sawdust *sing* (serrín).

aserrar* *vt* to saw.

aserruchar *vt* AMER to saw.

aserto *m* assertion, affirmation (aserción).

asertorio, ria *adj* assertory, affirmatory (juicio).

asesinar *vt* to murder || to assassinate || FIG to murder (una obra, etc.).
— OBSERV Cuando *asesinar* significa matar por motivos políticos, y especialmente a una persona destacada, se suele traducir por *to assassinate*.

asesinato *m* murder, assassination (véase OBSERV en ASESINAR).

asesino, na *adj* murderous; *mano asesina* murderous hand.
◆ *m* murderer, killer, assassin ||— *asesino pagado* hired assassin || *asesino profesional* professional *o* hired killer.
◆ *f* murderess, killer, assassin.
— OBSERV Véase OBSERV en ASESINAR.

asesor, ra *adj* advisory.
◆ *m* consultant, adviser, advisor; *asesor jurídico* legal adviser || *asesor agrónomo* agricultural advisor, farming expert.

asesoramiento *m* advising (acción de asesorar) || opinion (de asesor jurídico) || advice (consejo); *con el asesoramiento técnico de* with the technical advice of.

asesorar *vt* to advise, to counsel.
◆ *vpr* to consult, to take advice; *asesorarse con* or *de un letrado* to consult a lawyer, to take legal advice.

asesoría *f* consultantship (cargo del asesor) || consultant's office (oficina) || consultant's fee (estipendio).

asestadura *f* aiming, levelling, pointing.

asestar *vt* to aim, to level, to point (un arma) || to give, to deliver, to fetch, to land (un golpe) || to fire; *asestar un tiro* to fire a shot ||— *asestar una puñalada* to stab || *asestar un puñetazo* to land a punch, to punch.

aseveración *f* assertion, contention, asseveration, affirmation.

aseverar *vt* to assert, to affirm, to asseverate.

asexual; asexuado, da *adj* asexual.

asfaltado, da *adj* asphalted, asphalt, covered with asphalt.
◆ *m* asphalting (acción de asfaltar) || asphalt (pavimento de asfalto).

asfaltar *vt* to asphalt, to cover with asphalt.

asfalto *m* asphalt.

asfixia *f* asphyxia, suffocation.

asfixiado, da *adj* asphyxiated, suffocated.

asfixiante; asfixiador, ra *adj* asphyxiating, suffocating; *gas asfixiante* asphyxiating gas || FIG suffocating, stifling; *calor asfixiante* suffocating heat.

asfixiar *vt* to asphyxiate, to suffocate || FIG to stifle; *la miseria asfixia muchos talentos* a great deal of talent is stifled by poverty.
◆ *vpr* to suffocate, to asphyxiate.

asfódelo *m* BOT asphodel.

así *adv* thus, so, in this way, in that way, like this, like that; *yo lo hago así* I do it like this || like that, such; *un amigo así no se encuentra todos los días* you don't find a friend like that *o* such a friend every day || like that; *quiero un coche así* I want a car like that || so, then; *¿así me dejas?* so you're leaving me?, you're leaving me, then? || thereabouts; *cuesta 200 pesetas o así* it costs 200 pesetas or thereabouts || in such a way; *así lo dijo que toda la gente se lo creyó* he said it in such a way that everybody believed it || therefore, consequently, so; *se resfrió, así no pudo venir* he caught a cold, so he couldn't come || — *así* (con el subjuntivo) even if; *iremos así llueva a cántaros* we'll go even if it pours with rain; I hope (ojalá); *¡así llegue pronto!* I hope it comes soon! || *así, así; así como así* so-so, middling || *así como* as well as; *estaban sus padres así como sus hermanas* his parents were there as well as his sisters; as soon as; *así como llegue, le hablaré* as soon as he arrives I shall speak to him; (just) like; *así como lo hiciste, lo hice yo* I did it just like you || *así... como* both... and, as well as, alike; *así los buenos como los malos* both the good and the bad, the good as well as the bad, the good and the bad alike || *así como así* just like that; *me pidieron así como así que les prestara un millón de pesetas* they asked me to lend them a million pesetas just like that; anyhow, anyway (de todos modos) || *así como... así* in the same way that (so), as... so; *así como los sordos no oyen, así los ciegos no ven* in the same way that the deaf cannot hear, (so) the blind cannot see || FAM *así de* so, as... as that, that; *así de grande* so big, as big as that, that big || *así Dios te ayude* (may) God help you || *así es* that's how it is, that's how it goes || *así es* or *fue como* that is *o* was how; *así fue como se nos escapó* that was how he escaped from us || *así es la vida* that's life, such is life, life's like that || *¡así me gusta!* well done!, bravo!, that's the way I like it! || *así mismo* likewise, in the same way || AMER *así no más* so-so || *así o asá* either way || *así pues* so, then; *nos están esperando, así pues date prisa* they're waiting for us, so hurry up || *así que* as soon as; *así que amanezca, me levantaré* as soon as it's dawn, I shall get up; so, consequently, therefore; *llovía, así que no salimos* it was raining, so we didn't go out || *así... que* so much... that; *así había trabajado que estaba agotado* he had worked so much that he was exhausted || FAM *así que asá* or *así que asao lo mismo me da* either way, it's all the same to me || *así sea* so be it, let it be so || *así te mueras* on your own head be it (allá tú) || *así y todo* even so, in spite of everything, just the same || *¿cómo así?* how's that?, what was that? || *es hombre bueno y así honrado* he's a good man and honest as well || *¿no es así?* isn't it so?, isn't that so?, isn't that the case? || *no es así como hay que hacerlo* that's not the way to do it, that's not how it should be done || *por decirlo así* so to speak, as it were || *puesto que así es* since that is so, since that is the case || *si así como* instead of; *si así como lo hicieron ellos lo hubiéramos hecho nosotros* if we had done it instead of them || *y así* so, and so, so that; *¡y así ya puedes devolvérmelo!* so you can just give it back to me! || *y así (sucesivamente)* and so on.

Asia *npr f* GEOGR Asia || *Asia Menor* Asia Minor.

asiático, ca *adj/s* Asiatic, Asian.

asidera *f* AMER saddle horn.

asidero *m* handle (agarradero) || FIG excuse, pretext (pretexto) || FIG *tengo un buen asidero en el ministerio* I've got a good connection in the ministry.

asido, da *adj* grasped || *asidos del brazo* arm in arm.

asidonense *adj* from Medina Sidonia [Andalusian town, formerly called «Asido»].

asiduamente *adv* assiduously || regularly, frequently (frecuentemente).

asiduidad *f* assiduity || regularity, frequency (frecuencia).

asiduo, dua *adj* assiduous, industrious, hard-working (porfiado) || regular, frequent (frecuente).
◆ *m/f* regular, habitué; *un asiduo del café* a regular of the café || *un asiduo del cine* a regular cinemagoer [*US* a regular moviegoer].

asiento *m* seat, chair; *estos asientos no son muy confortables* these seats are not very comfortable || seat (de un coche, un tren, etc.); *asiento delantero, trasero* front, rear seat || place, seat; *déjame tu asiento* let me have your place || seat (localidad en un espectáculo); *reservar un asiento* to book a seat || site (sitio en que está un pueblo o un edificio) || hold; *ese partido político no tiene asiento en este país* that political party does not have a hold in this country || bottom, base (de botellas, vasijas, etc.) || sediment (poso) || ARQ settling (de un edificio) || trading contract (contrato para aprovisionamiento) || treaty (tratado) || COM entry, registry (en un libro); *asiento contable* bookkeeping entry | item (de un presupuesto, en una cuenta, etc.) || establishment (del impuesto, hipotecas) || note (anotación) || mouthpiece (del freno del caballo) || bars *pl* (de la boca del caballo) || TECN seating; *asiento de válvula* valve seating | layer (de argamasa) || FIG permanence (estabilidad) | common sense; *persona de asiento* person with common sense || AMER mining area | farm buildings *pl*, centre of a farm (centro de hacienda) ||— *asiento abatible* reclining seat || *asiento de colmenas* apiary || *asiento de estómago* attack of indigestion || BOT *asiento de pastos* kind of broom (*Erinacea pungens*) || *asiento de rejilla* wickerwork *o* cane seat || COM *asiento duplicado* duplication || *asiento giratorio* revolving *o* swivel chair || AVIAC *asiento proyectable* ejector seat | *avión de un solo asiento* single-seater plane || *baño de asiento* hip bath || *estar de asiento* to reside || *tomar asiento* to sit down, to take a seat; *tome usted asiento* sit down, take a seat.
◆ *pl* seat *sing*, bottom *sing* (asentaderas).

asignación *f* appointment, rendezvous (cita) || assigning, allocation, assignment (atribución); *la asignación de fondos* the allocation of funds || allowance, grant (subsidio) || pension (pensión) || salary, wages *pl*, remuneration (sueldo) || INFORM *asignación de fichero* file allocation.

asignar *vt* to assign (valor, trabajo, papel, cualidad, plazo, misión); *le han asignado una tarea difícil* they have assigned him a difficult task || to ascribe, to attribute, to assign (valor, papel, nombre, cualidad) || to allot, to give, to allocate (trabajo, número, pensión, tiempo); *me han asignado una semana para terminar el trabajo* they have allotted me a week to finish off the work || to grant, to award (pensión, salario, derecho) || to allocate (fondos).

asignatario, ria *m/f* AMER legatee, heir.

asignatura *f* subject (disciplina); *me aprobaron en seis asignaturas y me suspendieron en una* I passed six subjects and failed one || FIG *asignatura pendiente* matter pending, outstanding matter.

asilado, da *m/f* inmate || *asilado político* political refugee.

asilar *vt* to put in a home (a un anciano, a un pobre, etc.) || to take in, to give shelter (albergar) || *asilar a un extranjero* to grant asylum to a foreigner.
◆ *vpr* to take refuge.

asilo *m* home; *asilo de ancianos* old people's home || sanctuary, asylum; *derecho de asilo* right of asylum || FIG refuge, shelter; *nos dieron asilo por la noche* they gave us shelter for the night | haven; *asilo de la paz* haven of peace || ZOOL asilus, hornet fly (insecto) || — *buscar* or *pedir* or *solicitar asilo (político)* to seek (political) asylum || *dar* or *conceder asilo (político)* to grant (political) asylum.

asimetría *f* asymmetry.

asimétrico, ca *adj* asymmetrical, asymmetric.

asimiento *m* grasping, holding (acción de asir) || FIG attachment (afecto).

asimilable *adj* assimilable || comparable (equiparable).

asimilación *f* assimilation || comparison (equiparación).

asimilar *vt* to assimilate || to compare (equiparar) || to put on the same footing; *a este efecto los residentes extranjeros están asimilados a los nacidos en territorio nacional* for this purpose foreign residents are put on the same footing as those born in the country.
◆ *vi* to assimilate.
◆ *vpr* to be assimilated, to assimilate || to resemble, to be like (asemejarse); *esto se asimila a mi trabajo* this resembles my work || to be alike (dos cosas).

asimismo *adv* in like manner, in the same way, likewise (del mismo modo) || also, too (también).

asimplado, da *adj* simple, foolish.

asincrónico, ca *adj* asynchronous.

asíndeton *m* asyndeton (supresión de conjunciones).

asíntota *f* MAT asymptote.

asintótico, ca *adj* asymptotic, asymptotical.

asir* *vt* to get hold of, to grasp, to take, to seize; *asir del brazo* to get hold of by the arm || to grip; *asió el puñal con los dientes* he gripped the dagger between his teeth || — *asidos del brazo* arm in arm || *asir la ocasión por los cabellos* to seize the opportunity by the scruff of the neck.
◆ *vi* to take root (las plantas).
◆ *vpr* to take hold, to get hold, to grab hold; *asirse a* or *de algo* to take hold of sth. || FIG to seize, to avail o.s.; *se asió del primer pretexto* he seized (upon) the first pretext, he availed himself of the first pretext || FIG & FAM to fight, to quarrel (reñir).

Asiria *npr f* GEOGR Assyria.

asirio, ria *adj/s* Assyrian.

asiriología *f* Assyriology.

asisito *adv* AMER FAM just like that.

asistencia *f* audience (en el teatro, etc.) || crowd; *la asistencia al estadio fue numerosa* there was a large crowd in the stadium || attendance; *la asistencia es obligatoria* attendance is compulsory; *la reunión se celebró con mediana asistencia* there was a moderate attendance at the meeting || assistance, help; *prestar asistencia a uno* to give s.o. assistance *o* help || care, aid; *asistencia médica* medical care *o* aid || presence; *con asistencia de* in the presence of || TAUR staff [of bullring] || DEP pass (baloncesto) || AMER private drawing room (saloncito) || — *asistencia facultativa* medical treatment (tratamiento), medical staff (médicos) || *asistencia pública* public health system, national health service || *asistencia social* social welfare || *asistencia técnica* technical assistance || AMER *casa de asistencia* boardinghouse.
◆ *pl* allowance *sing*, maintenance *sing* (pensión alimenticia).

asistenta *f* charwoman, charlady, daily help (criada no permanente) || assistant (en un convento) || chambermaid (en un palacio) || *asistenta social* welfare worker.

asistente *adj* assistant, assisting, helping.
◆ *m* assistant (de obispo, etc.) || MIL orderly || person present, member of the audience (que está presente).
◆ *pl* audience *sing* (en el teatro, etc.), crowd *sing* (en un estadio, etc.); *había numerosos asistentes* there was a large audience | those present; *entre los asistentes se encontraban varios artistas* among those present were several artists.

asistido, da *adj* assisted (socorrido) || — *dirección asistida* power steering || *frenos asistidos* power brakes.

asistir *vt* to assist, to help; *le asiste en su trabajo* he assists him in his work || to treat, to attend; *le asiste un buen médico* he is being treated by a good doctor || to serve, to attend (servir) || to help out; *como estoy sin criada me asiste Pepe* I have no maid at the moment so Joe is helping me out || *me asiste el derecho* the law is on my side, I have the law on my side.
◆ *vi* to attend, to be present, to come, to go; *no asiste nunca a esta clase* he never attends *o* comes to *o* goes to this lesson, he is never present at this lesson || to be (present); *asistía una multitud impresionante* there was an impressive crowd (present) || to witness, to be present at the time of; *asistir a un accidente* to witness an accident || to follow suit (en los naipes).

asma *f* MED asthma.

asmático, ca *adj* MED asthmatic, asthmatical.

asna *f* she-ass (hembra del asno).
◆ *pl* rafters (vigas).

asnada *f* FIG & FAM stupid thing, silly thing.

asnería *f* FAM herd of asses *o* donkeys || FIG & FAM stupid thing, silly thing (tontería) || *decir asnerías* to talk nonsense.

asno *m* donkey, ass (animal) || FIG & FAM ass, fool, dunce, dimwit, twit (torpe) | boor, pig, lout (grosero) || — FIG *al asno muerto, la cebada al rabo* it's no good closing the stable door after the horse has bolted || FIG & FAM *apearse* or *caer uno de su asno* to back down, to climb down, to give in | *no ver tres en un asno* to be as blind as a bat || *parecerse al asno de Buridán* to be in two minds, to be like Buridan's ass || FIG *puente de los asnos* pons asinorum.

asociable *adj* associable.

asociación *f* association; *Asociación Europea de Libre Cambio* European Free Trade Association || COM partnership || — *asociación de consumidores* consumer council || *asociación de ideas* association of ideas.

asociacionismo *m* associationism.

asociado, da *adj* associate, associated; *miembro asociado* associate member.
◆ *m* associate, member || COM associate, partner.

asociamiento *m* association, partnership.

asociar *vt* to associate || COM to take into partnership; *asoció a su hijo al negocio* he took his son into partnership in the business || to pool, to put together (esfuerzos) || to bracket (en categoría, etc.).
◆ *vpr* to associate, to join forces, to team up || COM to enter into partnership, to become partners || FIG to share; *asociarse a la alegría de uno* to share s.o.'s joy || — *el granizo y las heladas se han asociado para destruir la cosecha* between them the hail and ice have ruined the harvest || *su recuerdo se asocia con mi estancia en Inglaterra* he reminds me of when I was in England, I associate him with the time I was in England.

asocio *m* AMER association || *en asocio de* in collaboration with, in association with.

asolador, ra *adj* devastating, destructive.

asolamiento *m* devastation, destruction.

asolar* *vt* to devastate, to destroy (destruir); *el granizo ha asolado las viñas* the hail has devastated the vines || to raze, to flatten (arrasar); *el terremoto asoló la ciudad* the earthquake flattened the city || AGR to scorch, to dry up, to parch (el sol, el calor) || to ravage (una epidemia).
◆ *vpr* to be devastated, to be destroyed || to settle (los líquidos).

asoleada *f* AMER sunstroke (insolación).

asolear *vt* to put in the sun, to isolate, to expose to the sun.
◆ *vpr* to sunbathe (tomar el sol) || to tan, to become tanned, to get a tan (tostarse al sol) || VET to suffocate (los animales).

asomada *f* brief appearance.

asomar *vi* to show, to appear; *la torre de la iglesia asomaba en el horizonte* the church tower showed on the horizon || to loom up; *asomó una figura en la niebla* a figure loomed up in the fog || to come out; *hoy el sol no asoma* the sun is not coming out today || to break; *asoma el día* day is breaking || to show; *su vestido asomaba debajo del abrigo* her dress was showing below her coat || to hang out; *un pañuelo asomaba fuera de su bolsillo* a handkerchief was hanging out of his pocket.
◆ *vt* to put out, to stick out; *asomar la cabeza a* or *por la ventana* to put one's head out of the window || to show, to reveal; *asomar la punta de la oreja* to reveal one's real self *o* one's true colours.
◆ *vpr* to lean out; *prohibido asomarse al exterior* do not lean out of the window || FAM to become tipsy (achisparse) || to take a brief look; *si nos asomamos al panorama de la situación económica española* if we take a brief look at the Spanish economic panorama || to glance, to look; *usted no se ha asomado siquiera a la lección* you haven't even glanced at the lesson || to show one's face (negativo); *no me asomé a la reunión* I didn't show my face at the meeting || to look in, to pop in (positivo); *no hice más que asomarme a la reunión* I only popped in to the meeting.

asombradizo, za *adj* easily astonished (asombro) || easily scared (espanto).

asombrado, da *adj* surprised || astonished, amazed (pasmado).

asombrar *vt* to shade (dar sombra) || to deepen, to darken (color) || to surprise (sorprender) || to astonish, to amaze (pasmar) || to frighten, to scare (asustar).
◆ *vpr* FIG to be frightened *o* scared (asustarse) | to be surprised; *no se asombra de* or *por* or *con nada* he is not surprised at *o* by anything; *me asombro de verte aquí* I'm surprised to find you here | to be amazed *o* astonished (quedarse pasmado); *asombrarse de algo* to be amazed at sth., to be astonished by sth.

asombro *m* fright, fear (susto) ‖ surprise, astonishment, amazement (sorpresa); *con gran asombro de mi madre* to my mother's great amazement ‖ amazement, wonder (estupefacción) ‖ FAM ghost, phantom, apparition (aparecido) ‖ — *de asombro* astonishing, surprising ‖ *¡no salgo de mi asombro!* I can't get over it!, it's amazing!

asombrosamente *adv* wonderfully, amazingly.

asombroso, sa *adj* amazing, astonishing (sorprendente) ‖ bewildering, stupefying (estupefaciente).

asomo *m* appearance (apariencia) ‖ shadow; *sin el menor asomo de duda* without the shadow of a doubt ‖ hint, sign, trace, indication (indicio); *sin un asomo de cansancio* without a trace of tiredness ‖ suspicion, supposition (sospecha) ‖ — *ni por asomo* by no means, not in the least ‖ *no le conozco ni por asomo* I don't know him from Adam, I don't know him at all.

asonada *f* riot, disturbance (motín).

asonancia *f* assonance (poesía, retórica) ‖ consonance, harmony (entre sonidos) ‖ relation, connection (entre dos cosas).

asonantado, da *adj* assonated.

asonantar *vi* to assonate.
◆ *vt* to make assonant.

asonante *adj/s* assonant.

asonar* *vi* to assonate.

asorocharse *vpr* AMER to get mountain sickness ‖ FAM to blush, to go red (ruborizarse).

aspa *f* St-Andrew's cross, an X-shaped cross ‖ MAT multiplication sign ‖ reel, winding frame (devanadera) ‖ arms *pl* (armazón de molino) ‖ arm (ala de molino) ‖ — HERÁLD saltire ‖ AMER horn (asta) ‖ *colocado en aspa, en forma de aspa* X-shaped, cross-shaped.

aspadera *f* reel, winding frame (devanadera).

aspado, da *adj* with the arms extended like a cross (los penitentes de una procesión) ‖ FIG & FAM awkward, stiff (llevando ropa estrecha) ‖ X-shaped, cross-shaped.

aspar *vt* to reel, to wind (hilo) ‖ to crucify (crucificar) ‖ FIG & FAM to mortify (mortificar) ‖ to vex, to annoy (vejar) ‖ *¡que me aspen si...!* I'll be hanged if...!
◆ *vpr* FIG *asparse a gritos* to shout o.s. hoarse (desgañitarse).

asparagus *m* BOT asparagus (planta ornamental).

aspaventero, ra *adj* theatrical, given to making extravagant gestures.

aspaviento *m* fuss, extravagant behaviour, theatricality.

aspecto *m* look, appearance; *no me gusta el aspecto de la herida* I don't like the look of the wound; *la casa tenía un aspecto austero* the house had an austere appearance; *este hombre tiene un aspecto elegante* this man has a smart appearance ‖ ASTR aspect ‖ aspect, side; *el problema tiene varios aspectos* the problem has several aspects, there are several sides to the problem ‖ — *al* or *a primer aspecto* at first sight ‖ *bajo este aspecto* from this point of view, viewed from this angle, in this respect ‖ *en ciertos aspectos* in some respects ‖ *en todos los aspectos* in every respect, in all respects; on every account, in every way ‖ *persona de aspecto salubre, perverso* a healthy-looking, evil-looking person ‖ *tener buen aspecto* to look nice (cosas), to look well (personas).

aspereza; asperidad *f* roughness, asperity (al tacto) ‖ tartness, sourness (al gusto) ‖ harshness, roughness, gruffness (de la voz) ‖ roughness, ruggedness, unevenness (del terreno) ‖ rudeness, brusqueness, gruffness, harshness (del carácter, de una respuesta) ‖ — FIG *limar asperezas* to smooth things over ‖ *un terreno lleno de asperezas* a very uneven piece of ground.

asperges *m* REL asperges, sprinkling.

aspergilo *m* BOT aspergillus (hongo).

asperidad *f* ⟶ **aspereza.**

asperilla *f* BOT woodruff.

asperillo *m* sour *o* bitter taste (de fruta no madura, etc.).

asperjar *vt* to sprinkle (rociar) ‖ REL to sprinkle with holy water.

áspero, ra *adj* rough, asperous (al tacto) ‖ tart, sour (al gusto) ‖ harsh, gruff, brusque, rude (carácter, respuesta) ‖ harsh, rough, gruff (voz) ‖ rough, rugged, uneven (terreno) ‖ harsh, hard (clima) ‖ *ser áspero de condición* or *de genio* to be bad-tempered.

asperón *m* sandstone (piedra).

aspersión *f* aspersion, sprinkling ‖ AGR spraying.

aspersorio *m* REL aspergillum.

áspid; áspide *m* ZOOL asp, aspic.

aspidistra *f* BOT aspidistra.

aspillera *f* loophole.

aspiración *f* inhalation, breathing in (respiración) ‖ GRAM aspiration ‖ TECN intake; *aspiración de aire* intake of air ‖ FIG aspiration, desire (deseo) ‖ MÚS pause.

aspirado, da *adj* aspirate; *hache aspirada* aspirate aitch.

aspirador, ra *adj* suction; *bomba aspiradora* suction pump.
◆ *m/f* vacuum cleaner (aparato doméstico).

aspirante *adj* suction; *bomba aspirante* suction pump ‖ FIG aspiring.
◆ *m/f* candidate, applicant, aspirant (p us).

aspirar *vt* to inhale, to breathe in (respirar) ‖ to suck, to suck up (máquina) ‖ GRAM to aspirate.
◆ *vi* to inhale, to breathe in ‖ to suck (máquina) ‖ FIG to aspire; *aspirar a altos cargos* to aspire to high positions.

aspiratorio, ria *adj* aspiratory.

aspirina *f* aspirin.

asquear *vt* to sicken, to nauseate, to turn (s.o.'s) stomach; *las ostras me asquean* oysters turn my stomach ‖ to disgust, to nauseate, to sicken; *su conducta me asquea* his behaviour disgusts me ‖ *esta vida me asquea, estoy asqueado de la vida* I'm sick of this life.
◆ *vi* to be sickening *o* nauseating *o* disgusting.
◆ *vpr* to be disgusted *o* nauseated *o* sickened ‖ *asquearse de la vida* to become sick of life.

asquerosamente *adv* dirtily, filthily, disgustingly.

asquerosidad *f* dirtiness, filthiness, filth ‖ obscenity ‖ dirty trick (mala jugada) ‖ mess; *este niño siempre hace asquerosidades en la mesa* this child always makes a mess at the table.

asqueroso, sa *adj* revolting, foul, sickening, nauseating, nasty, awful, vile; *una comida asquerosa* a revolting meal; *un olor asqueroso* a foul smell ‖ dirty, filthy; *tiene las manos asquerosas* his hands are filthy ‖ dirty, squalid; *vive en una habitación asquerosa* he lives in a squalid room ‖ disgusting (conducta) ‖ dirty, filthy (obsceno) ‖ vile, loathsome (muy malo) ‖ repulsive, disgusting (aspecto) ‖ squeamish (que siente asco).
◆ *m/f* vile *o* disgusting person (obsceno) ‖ vile *o* loathsome person (muy malo).

asta *f* lance, spear, pike (arma) ‖ shaft (palo de la lanza) ‖ staff, pole (de la bandera) ‖ handle, haft, helve (mango) ‖ handle (del pincel) ‖ horn (cuerno) ‖ antler (del ciervo) ‖ horn (materia); *gafas con montura de asta* horn-rimmed spectacles ‖ — *a media asta* at half-mast (bandera) ‖ FIG & FAM *dejar a uno en las astas del toro* to leave s.o. in the lurch, to leave s.o. high and dry, to leave s.o. stranded.

astado, da *adj* BOT hastate ‖ horned (animal).
◆ *m* bull (toro) ‖ pike bearer (soldado).

astático, ca *adj* FÍS astatic.

astenia *f* MED asthenia.

asténico, ca *adj/s* asthenic.

aster *m* BOT aster.

asterisco *m* asterisk ‖ *poner asterisco a* to asterisk.

asterismo *m* ASTR & MIN asterism.

astero *m* pike bearer (soldado romano).

asteroide *adj/sm* ASTR asteroid.

astifino, na *adj* narrow-horned (toro).

astigitano, na *adj/s* Ecijan [from Ecija, town in Andalusia, formerly «Astigi»].

astigmático, ca *adj* astigmatic.
◆ *m/f* astigmat.

astigmatismo *m* MED astigmatism.

astil *m* handle, helve, haft (mango de instrumento) ‖ shaft (de la flecha) ‖ arm, beam (de la balanza) ‖ quill (de la pluma).

astilla *f* splinter, chip (de madera, leña, hueso, piedra, etc.) ‖ — *de tal palo, tal astilla* like father, like son ‖ *no hay peor astilla que la del mismo palo* former friends can be dangerous enemies.
◆ *pl* chips, firewood *sing* (leña menuda) ‖ *hacer astillas* to smash into fragments, to splinter, to smash to smithereens (*fam*).

astillar *vt* to splinter, to smash, to break (hacer pedazos) ‖ to splinter [wood].
◆ *vpr* to splinter, to split [wood].

Astillejos *npr mpl* ASTR Gemini *sing*, the Twins (estrellas).

astillero *m* MAR shipyard, dockyard (taller) ‖ rack (de armas).

astilloso, sa *adj* splintery, easily splintered.

astracán *m* astrakhan, astrachan.

astracanada *f* FAM farce.

astrágalo *m* BOT astragalus ‖ ARQ astragal ‖ ANAT astragalus, astragal.

astral *adj* astral; *influencia astral* astral influence; *cuerpos astrales* astral bodies.

astreñir* *vt* to astringe (los tejidos orgánicos) ‖ FIG to bind (sujetar).

astricto, ta *adj* obliged, compelled, bound, forced; *astricto a un servicio* obliged *o* forced to do a duty, duty bound ‖ astricted, bound; *astricto al respeto de la ley* bound to observe the law.

astringencia *f* astringency.

astringente *adj/sm* astringent.

astringir; astriñir* *vt* to astringe, to contract (los tejidos) ‖ FIG to bind (sujetar).

astro *m* ASTR heavenly body, star (estrella) ‖ FIG star (de cine, etc.) ‖ *el astro rey* or *del día* the sun (el sol).

astrobiología *f* astrobiology.

astrocompás *m* TECN astrocompass.

astrofísico, ca *m/f* astrophysicist.
◆ *f* astrophysics.

astrolabio *m* ASTR astrolabe.

astrología *f* astrology.

astrológico, ca *adj* astrological, astrologic.

astrólogo *m* astrologer.

astronauta *m/f* astronaut.

astronáutica *f* astronautics.

astronave *f* spaceship, spacecraft.

astronomía *f* astronomy.

astronómico, ca *adj* astronomical, astronomic || FIG & FAM astronomical (cifra); *un precio astronómico* an astronomical price.

astrónomo *m* astronomer.

astroso, sa *adj* dirty, unclean (sucio) || shabby, slovenly, untidy (desaseado) || unfortunate, wretched, unhappy (desgraciado) || despicable, contemptible, vile (despreciable).

astucia *f* cleverness, astuteness (habilidad) || cunning, craftiness, artfulness (peyorativo) || trick, ruse, artifice; *las astucias del ratero* the tricks of the pickpocket || *obrar con astucia* to act cunningly *o* astutely *o* with cunning, to be cunning.

astucioso, sa *adj* —> **astuto.**

astur; asturiano, na *adj/s* Asturian.

asturianismo *m* asturianism.

Asturias *npr fpl* GEOGR Asturias || *el príncipe de Asturias* the prince of Asturias [crown prince of Spain].

astuto, ta; astucioso, sa *adj* astute, clever (hábil); *un abogado astuto* an astute lawyer || cunning, crafty, artful, foxy, sly; *un ladrón astuto* a crafty thief || *astuto como un zorro* as sly as a fox.

Asuán *n pr* GEOGR Aswan; *la presa de Asuán* the Aswan Dam.

asueto *m* short vacation, time off, holiday (vacación corta); *un día de asueto* a day off, a day's holyday || school holiday.

asumir *vt* to assume, to take on, to take upon o.s.; *asumir una responsabilidad* to assume a responsibility || to adopt (una actitud) || *asumir la dirección* to take control.

asunceno, na *adj* [of *o* from] Asunción.
◆ *m/f* native *o* inhabitant of Asunción.

asunción *f* assumption, taking-on (acción de asumir) || FIG accession, ascension (al trono) || rising, promotion (a un cargo) || elevation (a una dignidad).

Asunción *npr f* REL Assumption || GEOGR Asunción (capital del Paraguay).

asunto *m* theme, subject, subject matter (tema) || question, matter, issue; *asuntos de orden económico* economic questions || affair, business; *esto es asunto mío* that's my business; *un asunto peliagudo* a tricky business; *un asunto sucio* a dirty business || matter, affair; *trataré el asunto* I shall deal with the matter || fact (caso); *el asunto es que* the fact is that || affair (sentimental, etc.); *tuvo un asunto con María* he had an affair with Mary || — *asunto concluido* closed affair *o* matter; *es asunto concluido* the matter is closed; let that be the end of the matter; *toma esto y asunto concluido* take this and let that be the end of the matter || *asuntos exteriores* or *extranjeros* foreign affairs || *asuntos pendientes* unsolved matters, matters in hand *o* not yet settled (sin resolver), outstanding matters, matters in abeyance (sin estudiar) || *conocer el asunto* to know what's what || *eso es otro asunto* that's another matter, that's another story || *ir al asunto* to get down to the heart of the matter || *Ministerio de Asuntos Exteriores* Foreign Office [*US* State Department] || *no me gusta el asunto* I don't like the look of it || AMER *poner el asunto* to watch one's step, to take care || *suspendiendo todos los demás asuntos* to the exclusion of all other matters || *volvamos a nuestro asunto* let's get back to the subject in hand.

asustadizo, za *adj* easily frightened *o* scared, timid, timorous, fearful || shy, skittish (caballo) || FAM *más asustadizo que una mona* as timid as a mouse.

asustar *vt* to frighten, to alarm, to scare; *le asusta el trueno* thunder frightens him || to scare away (ahuyentar) || FIG to horrify; *me asusta su conducta* I'm horrified at his behaviour, his behaviour horrifies me.
◆ *vpr* to be frightened *o* scared; *se asusta por* or *de* or *con nada* he is frightened *o* scared by *o* of the slightest thing || FIG to be horrified || *nada le asusta* nothing can scare *o* frighten him.

atabacado, da *adj* tobacco-coloured.

atabal *m* MÚS kettledrum.

atabalear *vi* to stamp (el caballo) || to drum, to tap [the fingers] (tamborilear).

atabalero *m* kettledrummer (timbalero).

atabanado, da *adj* spotted white (caballo).

atabe *m* vent (para la ventilación de una cañería) || peephole (para la inspección de una cañería).

atacable *adj* attackable, assailable.

atacador, ra *adj* attacking, assailing (que ataca).
◆ *m/f* attacker, assailant.
◆ *m* ramrod (de cañón).

Atacama *npr m* GEOGR Atacama (desierto).

atacante *adj* attacking, assailing (que ataca).
◆ *m* attacker, assailant.

atacar *vt* to attack, to assail; *atacar a un adversario* to attack an adversary || to attack; *las langostas han atacado las cosechas* the locusts have attacked the crops || to attack, to seize, to affect (una enfermedad) || to overcome (el sueño) || MÚS to attack (un instrumento, una pieza) | to strike (una nota) | to strike up; *la banda atacó una marcha* the band struck up a march || to pack, to cram, to stuff (recalcar) || to ram home, to ram (carga de arma de fuego) || to fasten, to button, to do up (una prenda de vestir) || QUÍM to attack, to corrode, to eat away *o* into, to erode (corroer); *el ácido ataca el metal* acid attacks metal || FIG to begin, to start upon; *atacar la ascensión del Aconcagua* to begin the ascent of Aconcagua | to grapple with, to tackle (una dificultad, un problema, etc.) || — JUR *atacar de falsedad* to deny, to contradict || *atacar los nervios* to get on the nerves; *este ruido me ataca los nervios* this noise gets on my nerves.

atacola *f* tail strap (arreo).

ataderas *f pl* FAM garters (ligas).

atadero *m* tether, rope, cord (cuerda) || hitching ring *o* hook (sitio donde se ata) || FIG tie, bond (vínculo).

atadijo *m* FAM bundle.

atado, da *adj* FIG timid, bashful, shy, diffident (apocado).
◆ *m* bundle (paquete); *un atado de ropa* a bundle of clothing || AMER *atado de cigarrillos* packet [*US* pack] of cigarettes.

atador, ra *adj* binding, bundling.
◆ *m/f* binder, bundler.
◆ *f* AGR binding machine, (sheaf) binder.
◆ *m* AMER halter, tether, headrope, lunge.

atadura *f* tying, binding, attaching, fastening (acción de atar) || string, rope, cord (para atar) || binding (de esquís) || FIG tie, bond (vínculo) | tie (traba); *ataduras matrimoniales* marriage ties.

atafagar *vt* to stifle, to suffocate (olor) || to pester (molestar).

atafetanado, da *adj* resembling taffeta.

atagallar *vi* MAR to crowd sail.

ataguía *f* cofferdam.

ataharre *m* crupper (para sujetar la silla).

ataire *m* moulding.

atajadero *m* stemming ridge [for irrigation].

atajador, ra *adj* barring, checking, damming, stemming, stopping.
◆ *m/f* interceptor.
◆ *m* AMER muleteer, mule driver (arriero).

atajar *vi* to take a shortcut; *atajar por los campos* to take a shortcut across the fields.
◆ *vt* to cut off, to head off, to intercept; *atajaron al fugitivo* they intercepted the fugitive || to bar, to block, to obstruct; *atajar un camino* to block a road || to divide (dividir) || to partition (off) (separar) || FIG to cut (suprimir) | to stop from spreading, to check; *atajar un incendio, una enfermedad* to stop a fire, a disease from spreading | to stop, to check, to put an end to, to stem; *hay que atajar el aumento de la delincuencia juvenil* the rise in juvenile delinquency must be checked | to cut short; *atajar los comentarios* to cut short criticism | to interrupt, to cut short; *atajar al orador* to interrupt the speaker | to cross out, to strike out (tachar).
◆ *vpr* FIG to stop short (turbarse, cortarse) || FAM to get drunk (emborracharse).

atajea; atajía *f* drain, sewer.

atajo *m* shortcut (camino); *tirar por un atajo* to take a shortcut || division (separación) || cut (en un escrito) || — FIG *no hay atajo sin trabajo* no gains without pains | *tirar* or *tomar por el atajo* to take the easiest way out.
— OBSERV Do not confuse *atajo* with *hatajo*, meaning *heap, bunch, lot.*

atalaya *f* watchtower, observation tower (torre) || vantage point (lugar elevado).
◆ *m* lookout (el que vigila).

atalayar *vt* to watch, to observe (vigilar) || FIG to spy on (espiar).

atalayero *m* scout, lookout.

atanasia *f* BOT sisymbrium || IMPR English type [14 points].

atañer* *vi* to concern, to have to do with; *este asunto no te atañe* this matter has nothing to do with you || to be incumbent on (incumbir) || *en* or *por lo que atañe a* with respect to, with regard to, as far as... is concerned; *en lo que atañe a mi viaje, todavía no he decidido nada* as far as my trip is concerned, I still haven't decided anything.

ataque *m* attack; *ataque por sorpresa* surprise attack; *ataque al corazón* heart attack || fit; *ataque epiléptico, de apoplejía* epileptic, apoplectic fit || fit, attack; *ataque de nervios, de risa, de tos* fit of hysterics, of laughter, of coughing || — *ataque aéreo* air raid || MIL *iniciar un ataque* to launch an attack.

atar *vt* to tie, to bind; *atar a un árbol* to tie to a tree || to tie, to do up, to fasten, to knot (los cordones del zapato, etc.) || to tether, to tie up (un animal) || CULIN to truss (un ave) || FIG to bind; *estas obligaciones me atan* I am bound by these obligations | to tie down; *este trabajo me ata mucho* this work ties me down a lot || — FIG & FAM *átame esta mosca por el rabo* you will have your work cut out || FIG *atar cabos* to put two and two together || *atar corto a un perro* to keep a dog on a short lead || FIG & FAM *atar corto a uno* to keep a tight rein over s.o. | *atar de pies y manos* to bind hand and foot | *atar la lengua a uno* to silence s.o. || *el poder de atar y desatar* the power to bind and to loose || *no atar ni desatar* to lead nowhere, to settle *o* to decide nothing (no decidir nada) || *ser un loco de atar* to be as mad as a hatter.
◆ *vpr* FIG to get tied up (crearse trabas) | to become involved (en un asunto) | to stick to (a una opinión) | to limit o.s. (limitarse) || *es hombre que no se ata por tan poco* he doesn't let such things hinder him.

atarantado, da *adj* bitten by a tarantula || FIG & FAM restless (bullicioso) | stunned, dazed, stupefied (aturdido) | terrified, frightened (espantado).

atarantamiento *m* dizziness, giddiness.

atarantar *vt* to daze, to stun (aturdir) || FIG to stun, to bewilder, to dumbfound.

ataraxia *f* ataraxia, ataraxy (impasibilidad).

atarazana *f* shipyard (astillero) || ropemaker's workshop (taller del cordelero) || wine store || *AMER* pointed roof.

atardecer* *v impers* to get late, to get *o* to grow dark.

atardecer *m* late afternoon, evening, dusk || *al atardecer* at dusk.

atareado, da *adj* busy; *un hombre muy atareado* a very busy man.

atarear *vt* to assign work *o* a job to.
◆ *vpr* to busy o.s.; *atarearse en hacer algo* to busy o.s. doing sth.

atarjea *f* culvert (bóveda) || sewer, drain (alcantarilla) || *AMER* water conduit (conducto de agua).

atarquinar *vt* to cover with mud *o* with slime.
◆ *vpr* to cover o.s. with mud *o* with slime.

atarugamiento *m* pegging, pinning (acción de poner cuñas) || plugging (acción de tapar con tarugos) || FIG & FAM confusion | stuffing, gorging, guzzling (acción de atracarse) | stuffing, packing, cramming (atestamiento).

atarugar *vt* to peg, to pin (fijar con tarugos) || to plug (tapar con tarugos) || FIG & FAM to silence, to shut up (hacer callar) | to stuff, to pack, to cram (llenar) || to stuff, to cram [with food] (atracar).
◆ *vpr* FIG & FAM to stop short (quedar sin saber qué responder) | to become confused (turbarse) | to stuff o.s., to gorge o.s., to guzzle (atracarse).

atascadero *m* bog, mire, mudhole || FIG stumbling block (estorbo).

atascar *vt* to obstruct, to block (up), to choke (up), to clog (up) (una cañería) || to plug, to stop up (un agujero) || to jam, to make stick (un mecanismo) || FIG to hinder, to impede (a una persona).
◆ *vpr* to get *o* to become stuck, to get bogged down (un coche) || to become obstructed *o* blocked (up)*o* choked [up] *o* clogged (up) (atorarse una cañería) || to jam, to stick, to become *o* to get jammed *o* stuck (un mecanismo) || FIG to get into a muddle *o* into a tangle, to get all mixed up *o* tangled up (embrollarse) | to get bogged down (en un asunto).

atasco *m* obstruction, blockage (cosa que atasca) || obstruction, blocking, choking, clogging (acción de atascar) || bogging down (de un coche) || traffic jam; *siempre hay atascos en las horas punta* there are always traffic jams in the rush hour || jamming, sticking (de un mecanismo) || FIG stumbling block (obstáculo) | muddle, tangle (en un discurso, etc.).

ataúd *m* coffin [*US* casket].

ataujía *f* inlaid work, damascene work.

ataviar *vt* to dress (up), to array, to adorn, to deck (out) (adornar).
◆ *vpr* *ataviarse con* or *de* to dress o.s. up in, to array o.s. in, to adorn o.s. with, to deck o.s. out in.

atávico, ca *adj* atavistic, atavic.

atavío *m* dressing, adornment (acción de ataviar) || dress, attire (vestidos) || garb, getup, rig (peyorativo).

atavismo *m* atavism.

ataxia *f* MED ataxia, ataxy.

ate *m* *AMER* quince jelly (dulce de membrillo).

ateísmo *m* atheism.

ateísta *adj* atheistic (ateo).
◆ *m/f* atheist (ateo).

atelaje *m* team (caballos) || harness (arreos).

atelanas *f pl* atellans (comedia latina).

ateles *m* ZOOL ateles (mono).

atemorizar *vt* to frighten, to scare (asustar).
◆ *vpr* *atemorizarse de* or *por algo* to be frightened of *o* at sth.

atemperación *f* moderation, restraint.

atemperar *vt* to moderate, to restrain (moderar) || to adjust, to accomodate (*a* to).
◆ *vpr* to restrain o.s. || to adjust o.s., to accomodate o.s.; *la formación profesional debe atemperarse al ritmo de la industria* vocational training should adjust itself to the pace of industry.

Atenas *n pr* GEOGR Athens.

atenazar *vt* to tear (the flesh) with red-hot pincers (suplicio) || FIG to torture, to torment (un pensamiento, los remordimientos) || FIG *estar atenazado* to be held in a vice-like grip.

atención *f* attention; *prestar atención a* to pay attention to || courtesy, politeness (cortesía) || care, attention; *hacer un trabajo con mucha atención* to do a job with great care || interest; *su atención por estos problemas ha sido muy grande* he has taken a great interest in these problems || — *a la atención de* for the attention of || *en atención a* in view of, considering, taking into consideration; *en atención a sus méritos* in view of his merits, taking his merits into consideration || *llamar la atención* to be conspicuous, to attract attention || *llamar la atención a alguien* to attract s.o.'s attention (llamar), to tell s.o. off, to tick s.o. off (reprender), to catch s.o.'s eye, to attract s.o.'s attention (despertar la curiosidad) || *llamar la atención de alguien sobre algo* to draw s.o.'s attention to sth. || *no me llamó la atención* I didn't notice || *poner atención* to pay attention.
◆ *pl* respect *sing*, consideration *sing*; *tener atenciones con las personas de edad* to have *o* to show respect for old people, to show consideration towards old people || affairs, duties, obligations (ocupaciones) || *deshacerse en atenciones* or *tener atenciones delicadas* or *tener mil atenciones con* or *para uno* to be very nice to s.o., to shower attention on s.o., to make a great fuss over s.o.
◆ *interj* look out! (¡cuidado!) || your attention, please! (para que la gente escuche) || beware! (en letreros).

atendedor, ra *m/f* IMPR copyholder.

atender* *vt* to attend to; *atiendo mis negocios* I attend to my business || to serve, to see to, to attend to (en una tienda); *¿le atienden?* are you being served? || to look after, to tend; *el médico atiende al enfermo* the doctor looks after *o* tends the patient || to take care of, to attend to; *el propio director atendió al visitante* the manager himself attended to the visitor || to service (una máquina) || to take charge of (un servicio) || to heed, to listen to (un aviso, un consejo) || to meet, to satisfy; *atender una petición* to meet a request || (ant) to wait (esperar).
◆ *vi* to pay attention, to mind, to be careful; *atiende a lo que haces* pay attention to *o* mind *o* be careful what you're doing || to pay attention, to be attentive; *atender a una lección* to pay attention to a lesson, to be attentive to a lesson || IMPR to follow a galley proof as the proofreader reads aloud || — *atender al nombre de, atender por* to answer to the name of || *atender a lo más urgente* to attend to what is most urgent *o* pressing || *atender al teléfono* to answer the telephone || *atender a sus necesidades* to meet *o* to satisfy one's needs || *atendiendo a las circunstancias* in view of the circumstances || *el servicio postal, este hotel, está mal atendido* the postal service, this hotel, is badly run *o* organized || *este almacén está muy bien atendido* this store is very well staffed, customers are very well attended to in this store || *iglesia bien atendida* well-administered church || *no atender a razones* not to listen to reason.

ateneísta *m/f* member of an athenaeum.

ateneo, a *adj/s* POÉT Athenian.
◆ *m* athenaeum (sociedad científica o literaria).

atenerse* *vpr* to abide, to adhere, to hold, to stick; *me atengo a lo que él me dijo* I am abiding by what he told me, I am sticking to what he told me; *atenerse a las reglas* to abide by the rules || to rely on (a una persona) || — *atenerse a su promesa* to stand by one's promise, to keep one's word || *aténgase a las consecuencias* be prepared to meet *o* to face the consequences || *no saber a qué atenerse* not to know what to think *o* to believe, not to know where *o* how one stands || *querer saber a qué atenerse* to want to know where *o* how one stands; to want to know how matters stand, to want to know what is going on.

ateniense *adj/s* Athenian.

atentado, da *adj* moderate, prudent (prudente) || discreet, cautious (hecho sin ruido).
◆ *m* attempted murder, attempt upon s.o.'s life (contra personas) || attack (ataque); *atentado con bomba* bomb attack || offence [*US* offense], transgression (contra la ley) || — *atentado contra las buenas costumbres* indecent behaviour, immoral offence || *atentado contra la seguridad del Estado* treason.

atentamente *adv* attentively (con atención) || courteously, politely || *le saluda atentamente* I remain, yours faithfully; Yours faithfully (en una carta).

atentar *vi* to make an attempt, to attempt; *atentar contra* or *a la vida de su hermano* to make an attempt on one's brother's life, to attempt one's brother's life || to offend; *atentar contra la moralidad pública* to offend public decency || to commit an offence *o* a crime || *atentar contra la honra de alguien* to indecently assault s.o. (atacar), to cast a slur on s.o.'s honour (difamar).

atentatorio, ria *adj* which constitutes an attempt; *medida atentatoria a la libertad* measure which constitutes an attempt on liberty.

atento, ta *adj* attentive, heedful; *atento al menor ruido* attentive to *o* heedful of the slightest sound || attentive; *un alumno muy atento* a very attentive pupil || thoughtful, considerate, attentive; *este hombre es atento con todos* this man is thoughtful *o* considerate towards everyone || mindful, aware; *atento a los peligros* mindful of *o* aware of the danger || kind, nice; *es usted muy atento* you're very kind || careful, mindful; *atento a hablar bien* careful to speak well || special; *su atenta atención a los problemas árabes* his special attention to Arab problems || — *contesto a su atenta del 13 de febrero* in reply to your letter of the 13th February (véase OBSERV) || *su atento y seguro servidor* [abbreviated to s. a. s. s.] yours truly, yours faithfully (fórmula de correspondencia).
◆ *adv* considering, in view of, taking into consideration (en atención a).

— OBSERV *Su atenta* is a commercial term widely used in Spanish with the meaning *your letter*; it is often abbreviated to *su atta.*

atenuación *f* attenuation, diminishing (disminución) || litotes (retórica) || JUR extenuation.

atenuante *adj* extenuating, extenuatory, palliative || JUR extenuating; *circunstancia atenuante* extenuating circumstance.
◆ *m* extenuating circumstance.

atenuar *vt* to attenuate (poner tenue) || JUR to extenuate, to mitigate (el suplicio, la sentencia) || to diminish, to lessen, to reduce (disminuir) || to dim, to subdue (la luz) || to tone down (los colores).
◆ *vpr* to attenuate.

ateo, a *adj* atheistic, atheistical.
◆ *m/f* atheist.

aterciopelado, da *adj* velvety, velvet-like; *cutis, papel aterciopelado* velvety skin, paper.

aterido, da *adj* frozen [stiff], perished [with cold].

aterimiento *m* stiffness (de frío).

aterirse* *vpr* to be frozen, to be perished [with cold].
— OBSERV This verb is used only in the infinitive and past participle forms.

atérmano, na *adj* FÍS athermanous.

aterrador, ra *adj* terrifying, terrible, frightening, frightful, fearful, dreadful.

aterrajado *m* threading (de un tornillo) || tapping (de una tuerca).

aterrajar *vt* to thread (tornillo) || to tap (tuerca).

aterrar* *vt* to knock down (echar por tierra) || to demolish, to pull down (abatir) || MIN to dump || to terrify, to frighten, to scare; *me aterra pensar que* it terrifies me to think that || *AMER* to fill with earth (llenar) || *quedó aterrado por la noticia* he was horror-stricken at the news.
◆ *vi* MAR to keep *o* to stand inshore || AVIAC to land, to touch down (aterrizar).
◆ *vpr* to be horror-stricken *o* terrified *o* frightened.

aterrizaje *m* AVIAC landing, touchdown ||— *aterrizaje forzoso, de emergencia* forced, emergency landing || *aterrizaje sin visibilidad* or *a ciegas* blind landing || *tren de aterrizaje plegable* retractable undercarriage.

aterrizar *vi* AVIAC to land, to touch down.

aterrorizador, ra *adj* terrifying, frightening, fearful, frightful.

aterrorizar *vt* to terrify, to frighten, to score || to terrorize; *los bandidos aterrorizaron a la población* the bandits terrorized the population.
◆ *vpr* to be *o* to become terrified *o* frightened.

atesoramiento *m* hoarding, amassing, accumulation (acción de atesorar).

atesorar *vt* to hoard, to accumulate, to amass (acumular) || FIG to possess; *Juan atesora muchas cualidades* John possesses many qualities.

atestación *f* attestation (escrita) || testimony, evidence, statement, deposition (más bien oral).

atestado *m* JUR attestation, constat (documento) || report (relato); *hacer un atestado* to make a report.

atestado, da *adj* full up, crammed, stuffed (lleno) || crammed, crowded, packed, full up (lugar público) || obstinate, stubborn, pigheaded (*fam*) (testarudo).

atestadura *f*; **atestamiento** *m* cramming, stuffing, packing (acción de atestar) || must [for filling up casks] (mosto) || ullage (de una cuba).

atestar* *vt* to fill up, to cram, to stuff, to pack (llenar) || to fill up, to cram, to crowd, to pack; *un tren atestado* a crowded train || to clutter up; *atestar un piso con muebles* to clutter up a flat with furniture || to fill up (las cubas de vino) || JUR to attest, to testify, to bear witness (atestiguar).
◆ *vpr* FIG & FAM to stuff o.s., to cram o.s., to gorge o.s.; *atestarse de pasteles* to stuff *o* to cram o.s. with cakes, to gorge o.s. on cakes.

atestiguar *vt* to attest, to testify, to give evidence of, to bear witness to || FIG to prove, to bear witness to, to give a clear indication of; *esto atestigua el valor de estas medidas* this proves the worth of these measures.

atezado, da *adj* brown, bronzed, tanned (piel) || black, blackened (negro) || polished, smooth (pulido).

atezar *vt* to brown, to bronze, to tan (la piel) || to blacken || to polish, to smooth (pulir).
◆ *vpr* to become brown *o* tanned, to tan.

atiborrar *vt* to cram, to stuff, to pack (llenar).
◆ *vpr* to stuff *o* to cram o.s. (*de* with), to gorge o.s. (*de* on).

Ática *npr f* GEOGR Attica.

aticismo *m* atticism (delicadeza).

ático, ca *adj/s* attic || Athenian.
◆ *m* ARQ attic (buhardilla) || top flat (piso último) || penthouse (lujoso).

atigrado, da *adj* striped, marked like a tiger's skin || skewbald (caballo).

Atila *npr m* Attila.

atildado, da *adj* elegant, neat, smart || FIG elegant; *prosa atildada* elegant prose | affected, recherché; *estilo atildado* affected style.

atildamiento *m* criticism, censure || elegance, neatness, smartness, tidiness (del vestido) || punctuation (puntuación) || *vestido con atildamiento* elegantly dressed.

atildar *vt* (p us) to put a tilde *o* an accent on *o* over [a letter] || FIG to criticize, to censure.
◆ *vpr* FIG to smarten o.s. (up), to spruce o.s. (up), to titivate o.s. (up).

atinadamente *adv* wisely, cleverly, sensibly (con sagacidad) || correctly, accurately, precisely (acertadamente).

atinado, da *adj* sensible, wise, sound; *una observación atinada* a sensible remark || apt, fitting, relevant, felicitous; *una contestación atinada* an apt reply || opportune, timely, appropriate; *una medida atinada* an opportune measure || wise, sensible (una persona) || correct, accurate (acertado).

atinar *vi* to find, to discover, to hit upon; *atinar con la solución* to hit upon the solution || to guess right (acertar) || to be right; *has atinado en coger el paraguas* you were right in bringing your umbrella || to succeed; *atinó a encontrar la solución* he succeeded in finding the solution || to hit the mark (dar en el blanco).

atingencia *f* *AMER* connection, relation (relación) || remark (observación, puntualización).

atípico, ca *adj* atypical.

atiplado, da *adj* high-pitched, shrill; *una voz atiplada* a high-pitched voice.

atiplar *vt* to raise the pitch of.
◆ *vpr* to become sharp, to rise in pitch.

atirantar *vt* to tighten, to tauten || ARQ to stay, to brace with ties.

atisbadero *m* lookout post.

atisbadura *f* watch, watching, lookout.

atisbar *vt* to watch for, to be on the lookout for (acechar) || to spy on, to watch, to observe (mirar) || to distinguish, to make out, to see faintly *o* indistinctly (vislumbrar).

atisbo *m* spying, watching (acecho) || FIG hint, sign, trace, indication (asomo) | flash, spark; *no es muy astuto pero a veces tiene atisbos de inteligencia* he is not very smart, but at times he has flashes of intelligence.

¡atiza! *interj* goodness me!, oh, my word!, good Lord! (¡arrea!).

atizador, ra *adj* stirring, inciting, rousing (que atiza).
◆ *m* poker (instrumento).

atizar *vt* to poke (up), to stir (el fuego) || FIG to stir up; *atizar la discordia* to stir up discord | to excite, to rouse, to fan (las pasiones) || FIG & FAM to give, to land; *atizar un puntapié a uno* to give s.o. a kick.
◆ *vpr* FAM to swig, to knock back; *se atizó el vaso de un trago* he knocked the glassful back in one gulp.

atizonar *vt* to embeb, to set [in a wall] (una viga).
◆ *vpr* to blight (el trigo).

atlante *m* ARQ atlas, telamon.

Atlántico *npr m* GEOGR Atlantic.

atlántico, ca *adj* GEOGR Atlantic.

Atlántida *npr f* Atlantis.

atlas *m* atlas.

atleta *m/f* athlete.
◆ *m* FIG muscleman (hombre fuerte).

atlético, ca *adj* athletic.

atletismo *m* athletics; *practicar el atletismo* to do *o* to practise athletics.

atmósfera; atmosfera *f* atmosphere; *atmósfera cargada de humo* smoke-laden atmosphere || FIG atmosphere; *en la reunión la atmósfera estaba muy cargada* the atmosphere was electric at the meeting.

atmosférico, ca *adj* atmospheric.

atoaje *m* MAR towing, warping.

atoar *vt* to tow, to warp.

atocinado, da *adj* FIG & FAM fat, fleshy.

atocinar *vt* to cut up [a pig] (partir un cerdo) || to cure (preparar el tocino) || FIG & FAM to do in, to knock off, to bump off (matar).
◆ *vpr* FAM to get mad (amostazarse) | to fall madly in love (enamorarse).

atocha *f* esparto [grass].

atochar *vt* to fill with esparto || to stuff, to pack (rellenar) || MAR to jam (una vela).

atol; atole *m* *AMER* drink made from cornflour.

atolón *m* atoll (arrecife).

atolondradamente *adv* thoughtlessly, recklessly, foolishly || bewilderedly, confusedly.

atolondrado, da *adj* thoughtless, reckless, scatterbrained || bewildered, confused.

atolondramiento *m* thoughtlessness, recklessness, foolishness (irreflexión) || bewilderment, confusion (aturdimiento) || *obrar con atolondramiento* to act thoughtlessly.

atolondrar *vt* to stun, to daze, to make (s.o.) dizzy *o* giddy || to bewilder, to confuse.
◆ *vpr* FIG to lose one's head, to become *o* to get bewildered *o* confused (turbarse).

atolladero *m* bog, mire, slough, mudhole (atascadero) || FIG impasse, deadlock; *las negociaciones están ahora en un atolladero* the negociations are now in an impasse, the negociations have now reached a deadlock ||— FIG *cada sendero tiene su atolladero* every path has a pudddle | *estar en un atolladero* to be in a tight corner *o* in a fix *o* in a jam (*fam*), *o* in the soup (*fam*) | *sacar del atolladero* to get (s.o.) out of trouble *o* out of a scrape | *salir del atolladero* to get out of difficulty *o* out of trouble *o* out of a jam (*fam*).

atollar, atollarse *vi/vpr* to get bogged down, to stick *o* to get stuck in the mud.

atomicidad *f* QUÍM atomicity.

atómico, ca *adj* atomic; *bomba, cabeza, energía, pila atómica* atomic bomb, warhead, energy, pile; *número, peso atómico* atomic number, weight; *masa atómica* atomic mass.

atomismo *m* atomism.

atomista *m/f* atomist.

atomístico, ca *adj* atomistic.
◆ *f* FÍS atomics.

atomización *f* atomization, spraying.

atomizador *m* atomizer, spray.

atomizar *vt* to atomize, to spray.

átomo *m* atom || — *átomo-gramo* gram atom || FIG & FAM *ni un átomo de* not an ounce of, not a grain of, not an atom of.

atonal *adj* MÚS atonal, toneless.

atonalidad *f* MÚS atonality, tonelessness.

atonía *f* MED atony.

atónico, ca *adj* atonic.

atónito, ta *adj* astonished, amazed, astounded (estupefacto) || aghast, dumbfounded, flabbergasted (boquiabierto); *quedarse atónito* to be aghast.

átono, na *adj* atonic, unstressed.

atontado, da *adj* stupid, dimwitted (tonto) || stunned, dazed (por el asombro, un golpe, un ruido) || dumbfounded, flabbergasted (boquiabierto) || dulled, stupefied (embrutecido); *atontado por un trabajo monótono* dulled by monotonous work || dopey, stupefied (por una medicina, por las drogas) || *atontado por el alcohol* sodden with drink, groggy.

atontamiento; entontecimiento *m* dazed *o* stunned state (por el asombro, un golpe, un ruido) || astoundment, dumbfoundedness (por la sorpresa) || dullness, stupefaction (embrutecimiento) || dopiness (por una medicina, las drogas) || grogginess, stupor (por las bebidas).

atontar; entontecer* *vt* to stun, to daze (un ruido, un golpe, el asombro) || to dumbfound, to flabbergast (la sorpresa) || to dull, to deaden, to stupefy (embrutecer) || to make (s.o.) giddy *o* dizzy, to go to s.o.'s head (un perfume, una bebida) || to make stupid *o* dopey (una medicina, las drogas) || to drive (s.o.) mad *o* insane (volver loco).
◆ *vpr* to become stunned *o* dazed || to become dull *o* stupid.

atontolinamiento *m* FAM stunned state, stupor, daze (atontamiento) | dullness, stupidity (embrutecimiento).

atontolinar *vt* FAM to stun, to daze, to stupefy (atontar) || *estar atontolinado* to be all at sea (aturdido), to be groggy (por un golpe, las bebidas).

atoramiento *m* blockage, obstruction, clogging, choking (atascamiento).

atorar *vt* to block (up), to obstruct, to clog (up), to choke (up) (una cañería, etc.).
◆ *vi/vpr* to get blocked (up) *o* obstructed *o* clogged (up) *o* choked (up) || FAM to choke (o.s.) (atragantarse).

atormentadamente *adv* painfully || sorrowfully, grievously.

atormentador, ra *adj* tormenting, distressing, troubling, worrying (una persona, una cosa).
◆ *m/f* torturer.

atormentar *vt* to torture (al reo) || to torment, to trouble, to distress (causar dolor físico) || FIG to torment, to torture; *¿por qué me atormentas con estos recuerdos?* why do you torment me with these memories?
◆ *vpr* to torment o.s., to worry || *no atormentarse por nada* not to worry about anything.

atornillar *vt* to screw in (introducir un tornillo) || to screw down (sujetar) || to screw on (fijar con tornillos); *atornillar algo a la pared* to screw sth. onto the wall.

atoro *m* AMER obstruction, blockage (atascamiento) || FIG difficulty, jam, fix.

atorón *m* AMER trafic jam, blockage.

atorrante *m* AMER tramp, vagabond, vagrant [US bum, hobo].

atorrantismo *m* AMER vagrancy.

atorrar *vi* AMER to live as a vagabond *o* as a tramp.

atortolar *vt* FAM to rattle, to disquiet (turbar) || FIG *estar muy atortolados* to be like two turtledoves.

atosigador, ra *adj* poisonous (envenenador) || harassing, harrying, pestering, pressing (que apremia).
◆ *m/f* poisoner (envenenador) || harasser, tormentor (que apremia).

atosigamiento *m* poisoning (envenenamiento) || harassing, harrying, pestering.

atosigar *vt* to poison (envenenar) || FIG to harass, to harry, to pester, to press (dar prisa) || FAM to badger, to pester, to annoy, to bother (molestar).
◆ *vpr* to toil away (atarearse).

atrabiliario, ria; atrabilioso, sa *adj* irritable, irascible, atrabilious.

atrabilis *f* MED black bile || FIG ill humour, irascibility.

atracada *f* MAR coming alongside (al lado de otra embarcación) | docking (en el muelle) || AMER gorging, stuffing (atracón) | brawl, scuffle, fight (pelea).

atracadero *m* MAR landing stage, quay.

atracador *m* bandit, robber, raider (ladrón) || pipe cleaner (para la pipa)

atracar *vt* MAR to bring alongside || FAM to stuff, to gorge (hartar) || to hold up, to rob, to raid (robar).
◆ *vi* MAR to come alongside || *atracar en el muelle* to dock, to berth.
◆ *vpr* FAM to stuff o.s., to gorge o.s. (hartarse); *atracarse de melocotones* to stuff o.s. with *o* to gorge o.s. on peaches || AMER to adhere, to follow; *atracarse a una teoría* to adhere to *o* to follow a theory | to fight, to brawl (reñir).

atracción *f* attraction; *atracción molecular* molecular attraction || attraction (espectáculo); *la atracción principal de la feria* the main attraction at the fair || — *atracción universal* gravity || *sentir atracción por una persona* to be attracted to a person.
◆ *pl* entertainment *sing*, floor show *sing*, cabaret *sing* (en una sala de fiestas) || *parque de atracciones* fairground.

atraco *m* holdup, robbery, raid || *ser víctima de un atraco* to be held up.

atracón *m* FAM gorging, stuffing || AMER fight, brawl (riña) || *darse un atracón de caramelos* to gorge (o.s.) on sweets, to stuff o.s. with sweets.

atractivo, va *adj* attractive, of attraction (fuerza) || gravitational (de la gravitación) || attractive (persona, cosa); *es una idea atractiva* it is an attractive idea.
◆ *m* attractiveness, attraction, charm, appeal (encanto) || Lure, attraction; *el atractivo de la ganancia* the lure of profit.

atractriz *adj* FÍS attractive (fuerza).

atraer* *vt* to attract; *el imán atrae el hierro* a magnet attracts iron || FIG to attract, to draw; *atraer las miradas* to attract attention | to attract, to lure; *el clima atrae a los turistas* the climate attracts the tourists.

atragantamiento *m* choking (ahogo).

atragantarse *vpr* to choke (o.s.); *come tan de prisa que se atraganta* he eats so quickly that he chokes || to stick in s.o.'s throat; *se me ha atragantado una espina* a bone has stuck in my throat, I have a bone stuck in my throat || FIG & FAM to get mixed up (turbarse) | to stop short, to become tongue-tied (cortarse) || — FIG & FAM *atragantársele (algo* or *alguien) a uno* to sicken s.o., to make s.o. sick | *se me atraganta este tío* I can't stomach this fellow, this fellow makes me sick.

atraillar *vt* to leash (perros).

atramojar *vt* AMER to leash.

atramparse *vpr* to become blocked (up) *o* choked *o* clogged (up) (cegarse un conducto) || to become jammed, to stick (un pestillo).

atrancar *vt* to bar; *atrancó la puerta por miedo a los bandidos* he barred the door through fear of the bandits || to block (up), to choke, to clog (up) (obstruir).
◆ *vpr* to become blocked (up) *o* choked *o* clogged (up) (obstruirse) || to become jammed, to jam, to stick (un mecanismo) || to get *o* to become stuck (atascarse) || to get muddled *o* mixed up *o* confused (al hablar) || AMER to be obstinate *o* stubborn (empeñarse).

atranco; atranque *m* bog, mire, slough, mudhole (atasco) || FIG difficulty, fix, jam (apuro) || FIG *no hay barranco sin atranco* no gains without pains.

atrapamoscas *m inv* BOT Venus's-flytrap.

atrapar *vt* FAM to catch, to trap || to land; *atrapar un empleo* to land a job || to catch (un constipado).

atrás *adv* behind; *quedar atrás* to stay behind || behind, in the rear, at the back; *ir atrás* to walk in the rear || rear, back (de un coche); *los asientos de atrás* the rear seats || backwards, back; *dar un paso atrás* to step backwards || back, at the back; *en las filas de atrás* in the back rows, in the rows at the back || ago, back; *algunos días atrás* a few days back (hace algunos días) || earlier, previously; *dos semanas atrás* two weeks earlier (hacía dos semanas) || — *cuenta (hacia) atrás* countdown || *dejar atrás* to leave behind || *echado para atrás* thrown *o* flung back; *la cabeza echada para atrás* (with) one's head thrown back || *el de atrás* the one behind || *el pelo echado para atrás* (with) one's hair brushed back || *estos problemas vienen de muy atrás* these problems date back a long time || *hacia atrás, para atrás* backwards; *mirar hacia atrás* or *para atrás* to look backwards || AUT *marcha atrás* reverse || *quedarse atrás* to fall *o* to lag behind || *volverse atrás* to go back || FIG *volverse* or *echarse para atrás* to go back on *o* to break one's word, to change one's mind.
◆ *interj* back!, get back!, go back!, back up!

atrasado, da *adj* late; *llegué atrasado* I arrived late || behind; *está atrasado en los estudios* he is behind in his studies; *estar atrasado en el pago del alquiler* to be behind with one's rent; *este país está mucho más atrasado que sus vecinos* this country is far behind its neighbours || in arrears, outstanding, overdue; *pago atrasado* payment in arrears, outstanding *o* overdue payment || backward; *pueblo atrasado* backward nation || FIG in debt, in the red (entrampado) || slow (reloj) || — *¡andas atrasado de noticias!* you're behind the times! || *lo atrasado* arrears, back payments; *saldar lo atrasado* to make up arrears *o* back payments || *número atrasado* back number (de una revista) || *tener trabajo atrasado* to be behind with one's work || *un atrasado mental* a mentally retarded person, a mental defective.

atrasar *vt* to put back, to set back; *atrasar un reloj* to put a clock back || to retard, to slow down *o* up (algo que adelanta) || to postpone, to delay (diferir).
◆ *vi* to lose; *mi reloj atrasa* my watch loses || to be slow; *atrasar cinco minutos* to be five minutes slow.
◆ *vpr* to stay *o* to remain behind, to lag (behind) (quedarse atrás) || to be late (llevar atraso) || to be retarded (mentalmente) || to be

slow (reloj) || *atrasarse en el pago del alquiler* to get into arrears with the rent.

atraso *m* slowness (de un reloj) || backwardness (mental, cultural) || lateness, delay (retraso de tiempo) || — *con atraso* late; *con cinco minutos de atraso* five minutes late || *mi reloj tiene un atraso de diez minutos* my watch is ten minutes slow || *su hija tiene mucho atraso en los estudios* his daughter is a long way behind in her studies.
◆ *pl* arrears; *tener atrasos* to be in arrears.

atravesado, da *adj* lying across; *había un árbol atravesado en la carretera* there was a tree lying across the road || pierced, transfixed; *atravesado por flechas* pierced with arrows || cross-eyed (bizco) || crossbred, mongrel (animales) || FIG wicked, evil; *una persona atravesada* a wicked person || — *poner atravesado* to place *o* to lay across || FIG *tener a alguien atravesado* not to be able to stand *o* to bear *o* to abide s.o.; *le tengo atravesado* I can't stand him || *tener el genio atravesado* to be bad-humoured *o* bad-tempered || *tener la cara atravesada* to be grim-faced *o* glum-faced *o* surly.

atravesar* *vt* to place *o* to put *o* to lay across (poner) || to pass *o* to go through, to penetrate; *el agua atraviesa este impermeable* water goes through this mackintosh || to pierce (traspasar); *un balazo le atravesó el pecho* a bullet pierced his chest; *atravesar de parte a parte* to pierce right through || to run through (con una espada, una lanza) || to cross, to go across (cruzar); *atravesar los Alpes, la calle* to cross the Alps, the road || to cross, to span; *el puente atraviesa el río* the bridge spants the river || FIG to go *o* to pass through; *la economía atraviesa un período difícil* the economy is going through a difficult period | to cross; *atravesar el pensamiento* to cross one's mind || to bet, to wager, to stake (apostar) || MAR to heave to || FIG *atravesar el Rubicón* to cross the Rubicon.
◆ *vpr* to lie across (una cosa) || to stand across, to bar; *se atravesó en mi camino* he stood across *o* barred my path || to stick, to get stuck; *se le atravesó una espina en la garganta* a bone (got) stuck in his throat || FIG to interfere, to butt in, to meddle (entrometerse) | to quarrel, to argue, to dispute (tener pendencia) || FAM *atravesársele a uno una persona* not to be able to stand *o* to bear *o* to abide s.o.; *se me atraviesa* I cannot bear him.

atrayente *adj* attractive.

atreverse *vpr* to dare; *hazlo, si te atreves* do it, if you dare; *no me atrevería a salir sola* I wouldn't dare to go out alone || to venture, to dare; *atreverse a hablar* to venture to speak || to be insolent *o* disrespectful; *atreverse con un superior* to be disrespectful towards one's superior || FIG to manage; *¿te atreves con un pastel?* could you manage a cake? || — *atreverse con un adversario* to take on an opponent || *¡atrévete!* just you dare!

atrevidamente *adv* boldly, daringly || insolently, disrespectfully (con insolencia).

atrevido, da *adj* daring, bold, adventurous; *una política atrevida* an adventurous policy || insolent, disrespectful, impertinent, cheeky (descarado) || daring, bold; *una película atrevida* a daring film || forward, bold; *atrevido con las mujeres* forward with women.
◆ *m/f* audacious *o* bold *o* daring person, daredevil || insolent *o* disrespectful *o* impertinent *o* cheeky person.

atrevimiento *m* boldness, daring (osadía) || audacity, effrontery; *tiene el atrevimiento de interrumpirme* he has the audacity to interrupt me || insolence, disrespectfulness, impertinence, cheekiness (insolencia).

atribución *f* attribution; *la atribución de una obra a Bacon* the attribution of a work to Bacon || duty, function (función).
◆ *pl* authority *sing*, jurisdiction *sing*; *esto se sale de mis atribuciones* this does not come within my authority.

atribuir* *vt* to attribute, to credit; *le atribuyen palabras que nunca ha dicho* they attribute him with words he has never uttered || to attribute, to put down; *atribuye su fracaso a una falta de experiencia* he puts his failure down to inexperience || to confer; *atribuir una función a alguien* to confer authority on s.o.
◆ *vpr* to (lay) claim, to take the credit; *se atribuyó el éxito de la producción* he laid claim to *o* he took the credit for the success of the production || *se atribuye la culpa* he blames himself.

atribulado, da *adj* full of tribulation; *una vida atribulada* a life full of tribulation.

atribular *vt* to afflict, to grieve, to distress.
◆ *vpr* to be afflicted *o* grieved *o* distressed; *se atribuló con la noticia de su muerte* he was grieved at the news of his death.

atributivo, va *adj* attributive.

atributo *m* attribute; *uno de sus muchos atributos es la generosidad* generosity is one of his many attributes || GRAM attribute (predicado) || symbol (símbolo).

atrición *f* attrition.

atril *m* bookrest || lectern (facistol) || MUS music stand (con pie), music rest (sin pie).

atrincheramiento *m* MIL entrenchment.

atrincherar *vt* to entrench (fortificar).
◆ *vpr* to entrench (o.s.), to dig in || FIG to entrench o.s.; *atrincherarse en su silencio* to entrench o.s. in one's silence.

atrio *m* ARQ atrium (de la casa romana) | portico (de un templo, un palacio) | cloister (claustro) | vestibule, entrance (zaguán).

atrito, ta *adj* attrite (arrepentido).

atrocidad *f* atrocity, outrage; *los invasores hicieron atrocidades por todo el país* the invaders committed atrocities throughout the country.

atrochado *adj m* mottled (hierro).

atrochar *vi* to take a shortcut.

atrofia *f* MED atrophy.

atrofiar *vt* to atrophy.
◆ *vpr* to atrophy, to become atrophied.

atrompetado, da *adj* funnel-shaped, trumpet-shaped, bell-mouthed || *nariz atrompetada* turned-up nose, snub nose.

atronado, da *adj* thoughtless, reckless (irreflexivo).

atronador, ra *adj* deafening, thundering, thunderous; *un ruido atronador* a deafening noise; *una voz atronadora* a thundering voice || *unos aplausos atronadores, una atronadora ovación* thunderous applause, a thunder of applause.

atronar *vt* to deafen, to stun, to daze (con el ruido) || to stun, to daze (con un golpe) || TAUR to kill (a bull) by a stab in the back of the neck.

atropar *vt* to gather (together), to assemble.

atropelladamente *adv* hurriedly, hastily (con descuido) || helter-skelter, pell-mell (en desorden) || *hablar atropelladamente* to gabble.

atropellado, da *adj* hasty, precipitate.
◆ *f* AMER hustle, scuffle, scurry (atropello).

atropellador, ra *adj* brusque, impetuous, hasty, precipitate.
◆ *m/f* hothead, tearaway.

atropellamiento *m* → **atropello**.

atropellaplatos *adj inv* FAM clumsy, careless.
◆ *m/f inv* FAM clumsy *o* careless person, butterfingers.

atropellar *vt* to knock *o* to run down *o* over; *fue atropellado por un coche* he was knocked down by a car || to trample on (pisotear); *fue atropellado por la muchedumbre* he was trampled on by the crowd || to hustle, to jostle (empujar con violencia) || to push past, to push aside (para abrirse paso) || to knock down *o* over, to push over (derribar) || FIG to ignore, to disregard, to brush aside; *atropellar todo principio moral* to disregard all moral principles | to outrage, to offend (ultrajar) | to oppress, to bully (agraviar) | to rush, to hurry, to scamp (un trabajo) | to crush, to overwhelm (las desgracias).
◆ *vi* *atropellar por* to ignore, to disregard.
◆ *vpr* to rush, to hurry (empujarse) || to splutter, to gabble (al hablar).

atropello; atropellamiento *m* pushing, hustling, jostling (acción de empujar) || push (empujón) || accident, running over, knocking down (por un vehículo) || FIG violation, infraction (de las leyes) | violation, breach (de los principios) | outrage, offence [*US* offense] (insulto) | abuse, outrage, high-handed behaviour (agravio) || FIG *hablar con atropello* to gabble.

atropina *f* QUÍM atropine.

atroz *adj* atrocious, cruel, inhuman (cruel) || FAM enormous, huge (enorme). | atrocius, dreadful, awful; *tiempo atroz* atrocious weather.

atrozmente *adv* atrociously || FIG awfully, dreadfully, terrible; *me duele atrozmente* it hurts terribly.

ATS *abrev de ayudante técnico sanitario* medical auxiliary.

attrezzista *m* TEATR property man.

attrezzo; atrezo *m* TEATR properties *pl*, props *pl*.

atuendo *m* dress, attire (vestidos) || getup, rig (extravagante) || (p us) pomp, ostentation.

atufado, da *adj* irritated, angry (irritado) || offended, bothered (por el tufo) || overcome, choked (ahogado) || AMER reckless, scatterbrained (atolondrado).

atufamiento *m* anger, irritation.

atufar *vt* FIG to anger, to irritate (enfadar) || to overcome, to choke (un olor).
◆ *vi* to smell bad, to stink (oler mal).
◆ *vpr* FIG to become angry *o* irritated; *se atufa por* or *con* or *de nada* he becomes angry *o* irritated over the slightest thing || to be offended *o* bothered (por un olor) || to be overcome *o* choked (por el tufo) || to turn sour *o* acid (vino).

atufo *m* anger, irritation.

atún *m* tunny, tunnyfish, tuna, tuna fish || FIG & FAM *pedazo de atún* fool, nitwit, idiot, nincompoop.

atunara *f* madrague, tunny net (red) || tunny fishery, tunny-fishing ground (lugar).

atunero, ra *m/f* tunny seller, tuna seller (que vende atún).
◆ *m* tunny fisher, tuna fisher (pescador) || tunny boat (barco).
◆ *f* tuna hook (anzuelo).
◆ *adj* tunny, tuna; *industria atunera* tuna industry; *barco atunero* tunny boat.

aturdido, da *adj* reckless, scatterbrained, thoughtless (imprudente) || dazed, bewildered (confuso).

aturdidor, ra *adj* deafening; *un ruido aturdidor* a deafening noise.

aturdimiento *m* daze, stunned state (por un golpe) || dizziness, giddiness (mareo) || amazement, bewilderment (sorpresa) || FIG carelessness, thoughtlessness, recklessness; *a causa de su aturdimiento no se puede uno fiar de él* because of his carelessness he cannot be trusted | clumsiness, awkwardness (torpeza).

aturdir *vt* to daze, to stun, to make dizzy *o* giddy (el ruido, un golpe, etc.) || to make dizzy *o* giddy (un movimiento, el vino) || FIG to amaze, to bewilder, to stun; *su éxito me aturde* his success amazes *o* stuns me, I'm amazed at *o* stunned by his success.
◆ *vpr* FIG to try to forget.

aturquesado, da *adj* turquoise (color).

aturrullamiento; aturullamiento *m* FAM confusion, bewilderment.

aturrullar; aturullar *vt* FAM to confound, to bewilder, to fluster.
◆ *vpr* FAM to become *o* to get confused *o* flustered (turbarse) | to become frantic, to panic; *aturrullarse por el tráfico* to panic over the traffic.

atusar *vt* to trim (cortar el pelo) || to smooth (el pelo, el bigote) || to stroke; *atusarle el cuello a un caballo* to stroke a horse's neck || *AMER* to cut *o* to trim the mane and tail [of an animal] (de un animal).
◆ *vpr* FIG to titivate o.s., to smarten *o* to spruce o.s. up (componerse mucho) || *AMER* to become angry (enfadarse).

atutía *f* tutty (óxido de zinc).

audacia *f* audacity, boldness, daring (valentía); *demostrar audacia* to show *o* to display audacity || audacity, cheek, impudence (desfachatez).

audaz *adj* audacious, bold, daring (valiente) || audacious, cheeky, impudent (descarado).
◆ *m/f* audacious *o* bold *o* daring person, daredevil || audacious *o* cheeky *o* impudent person || *la fortuna es de los audaces* fortune favours the brave.

audibilidad *f* audibility.

audible *adj* audible.

audición *f* audition, hearing (acción de oír) || audition (prueba) || concert (concierto).

audiencia *f* audience; *conceder audiencia* to grant an audience || hearing (audición); *audiencia pública* public hearing || court (tribunal de justicia); *audiencia arbitral* Arbitration; *Audiencia Nacional* National High Court; *Audiencia Provincial* Provincial High Court; *Audiencia Territorial* Territorial High Court || lawcourt, court of law (palacio de justicia) || (ant) audiencia [in Spain and South America].

audífonos *m pl* *AMER* earphones.

audímetro *m* audience-monitoring device.

audio *m* audio.

audiofrecuencia *f* audio frequency.

audiograma *m* audiogram.

audiometría *f* audiometry.

audiómetro *m* FÍS audiometer.

auditivo, va *adj* auditory.

audiovisual *adj* audio-visual; *enseñanza audiovisual* audio-visual teaching; *medios audiovisuales* audio-visual aids.

auditor *m* judge advocate || auditor (interventor de cuentas).

auditoría *f* office of judge advocate (cargo del auditor) || judge advocate's court (tribunal) || judge advocate's office (despacho) || auditorship (empleo de interventor de cuentas) || ECON *auditoría externa* field audit .

auditorio *m* audience (público) || FIG public; *persona que tiene mucho auditorio* person with a large public || auditorium (sala).

auditorium *m* auditorium.

auge *m* peak, climax (punto máximo) || prosperity, development, progress, expansion (progreso) || ASTR apogee || — *auge económico* economic boom *o* expansion || *en período de* or *en pleno auge* progressing *o* developing *o* expanding rapidly.

augur *m* augur (adivino).

augurador, ra *adj* who predicts, who foretells.

augural *adj* augural.

augurar *vt* to predict, to foresee, to foretell, to prophesy; *le auguro a la chica un futuro feliz* I foresee a happy future for the girl || to augur; *las nubes auguran lluvia* the clouds augur rain; *augurar bien, mal* to augur well, ill.

augurio *m* augury, omen, sign.

augusto *m* auguste (payaso).

Augusto *npr m* Augustus.

augusto, ta *adj* august, illustrious.

aula *f* lecture hall (grande), lecture room (pequeña) || classroom (de una escuela) || POÉT palace (palacio) || *aula magna* main lecture theatre *o* amphitheatre.

aulaga *f* BOT gorse, furze.

áulico, ca *adj* palace, court.
◆ *m* courtier.

aullador, ra *adj* howling.
◆ *m* howler monkey, howler (mono).

aullar *vi* to howl.

aullido; aúllo *m* howl.

aumentación *f* increase (aumento) || progression (en retórica).

aumentador, ra *adj* increasing, which increases.

aumentar *vt* to increase; *aumentar la velocidad* to increase speed; *aumentar el tamaño de algo* to increase the size of sth || to raise, to increase (el sueldo) || to put up, to raise (el precio) || to augment, to add to; *trabaja para aumentar los ingresos familiares* she works to augment the family income || to magnify; *el microscopio aumenta los objetos* the microscope magnifies the objects || *aumentar la producción, el voltaje* to step up production, the voltage.
◆ *vi* to increase, to rise; *los precios han aumentado en un diez por ciento* prices have risen by ten per cent; *el ruido aumenta* the noise is increasing || to get worse (empeorar); *el frío va aumentando* the cold is getting worse || to get better (mejorar) || — *aumentar de peso* to put on weight || *aumentar de velocidad* to increase one's speed.
◆ *vpr* to increase, to augment.

aumentativo, va *adj/sm* augmentative.

aumento *m* increase, rise; *aumento de precio* price increase || addition (acción de añadir, cosa añadida) || magnification (de microscopio) || *AMER* postscript (posdata) || — *aumento de sueldo* wage increase, rise (*fam*) || *ir en aumento* to be on the increase.

aun *adv* even; *te daría mil libras y aun dos mil* I would give you a thousand pounds or even two thousand; *aun en verano, siempre lleva un abrigo* he always wears an overcoat, even in summer || — *aun* (con gerundio) although, even though (with indicative); *aun siendo viejo, trabaja mucho* although he is old he works a lot || *aun así, ni aun así* even so, all the same; *aun así no llegaré a tiempo* all the same I shan't arrive in time; *ni aun así tendré el tiempo de verte* even so, I'm not going to have time to see you || *aun cuando, aun si* even if; *aun cuando quisiera ir, no podría* even if I wanted to go, I could not || *ni aun* (con gerundio) not even if (with indicative), not even by (with gerund); *ni aun amenazándole le harás confesar* not even if you threaten him will you make him confess, not even by threatening him will you make him confess.

aún *adv* still, yet; *no ha llegado aún* he still hasn't arrived, he has not yet arrived; *yo tengo más aun* I have still more || still; *aún está aquí* he is still here || *aún no* not yet.
— OBSERV *Aún* is written with an accent when it means *todavía*.

aunar *vt* to join, to unite; *aunar esfuerzos* to join forces.
◆ *vpr* to unite, to join together.

aunche; aunchi *m* *AMER* remains *pl*.

aunque *conj* although, though, even though; *aunque estoy malo, no faltaré a la cita* although I am ill I shall keep the appointment || even if, even though; *aunque no venga nadie, debes quedarte aquí* even if no one comes *o* even though no one may come you must stay here; *iré aunque llueva* I will go even if it rains.
— OBSERV *Aunque* is followed by the subjunctive when the clause it introduces expresses a hypothesis. It is used with the indicative when the clause expresses a fact.
— OBSERV En inglés se puede utilizar el subjuntivo después de *though* o *although* pero se emplea más frecuentemente el indicativo.

¡aúpa! *interj* hup!, hup la! || — FAM *de aúpa* fantastic, great, terrific (magnífico), terrible (malo) || *los de aúpa* the picadors.
— OBSERV The expression *de aúpa* is used to intensify the meaning of the word it qualifies: *una bofetada de aúpa* a tremendous wallop.

aupar *vt* FAM to lift up (levantar) | to help up (ayudar) || FIG to praise, to praise to the skies (ensalzar).

aura *f* ZOOL urubu (buitre de América) || POÉT zephyr, breeze (viento apacible) || FIG general approval (aceptación) || aura, atmosphere (atmósfera inmaterial) || MED aura; *aura epiléptica* epileptic aura.

áureo, a *adj* gold (de oro) || golden, aureate (parecido al oro) || golden; *edad áurea* golden age || *número áureo* golden number.

aureola *f* REL aureole (gloria) || halo, aureole, nimbus (en la cabeza de imágenes sagradas) || ASTR aureole || FIG reputation, aureole (fama).

aureolar *vt* to aureole, to halo.

áurico, ca *adj* auric, gold.
◆ *adj f* MAR fore-and-aft (vela).

aurícula *f* ANAT auricle (del corazón) | pinna, auricle (de la oreja) || BOT auricle, auricula.

auriculado, da *adj* auriculate.

auricular *adj* auricular.
◆ *m* little finger (dedo meñique) || earpiece, receiver (de teléfono).
◆ *pl* earphones, headphones, headset *sing*.

aurífero, ra *adj* auriferous, gold-bearing.

auriga *m* POÉT coachman (cochero) || ASTR wagoner, Auriga (constelación).

auroch *m* aurochs, urus.

aurora *f* dawn, daybreak (amanecer) || FIG dawn, beginning (principio) || — *aurora austral* aurora australis || *aurora boreal* aurora borealis, northern lights || *despunta* or *rompe la aurora* day *o* dawn is breaking.

auscultación *f* MED auscultation, sounding.

auscultar *vt* MED to auscultate, to sound.

ausencia *f* absence (de una persona, de una cosa) || — FAM *brillar por su ausencia* to be conspicuous by one's absence || *en ausencia de* in the absence of.

ausentarse *vt* to leave, to absent o.s., to take one's leave (irse) || to be absent, to stay away (no volver).

ausente *adj* absent (alumno) || away, out; *está ausente de la capital* he is away from *o* he

is out of the capital || JUR missing || — FIG *estar ausente* to be in a dream, to be distracted *o* inattentive, to be woolgathering || *estar ausente de su domicilio* to be away from home.
◆ *m/f* absentee, person absent || JUR missing person || *ni ausente sin culpa, ni presente sin disculpa* the absent are always in the wrong.

ausentismo *m* absenteeism (absentismo).

auspiciar *vt* AMER to patronize, to favour [US to favor].

auspicio *m* omen, auspice; *con buenos auspicios* with good omens || *bajo los auspicios de* under the auspices of, under the patronage of, sponsored by.

auspicioso, sa *adj* AMER auspicious, favourable [US favorable].

austeridad *f* austerity || severity (severidad).

austero, ra *adj* austere; *lleva una vida austera* he leads an austere life.

austral *adj* southern, austral.

Australasia *npr f* GEOGR Australasia.

Australia *npr f* GEOGR Australia.

australiano, na *adj/s* Australian.

Austrasia *npr f* GEOGR Austrasia.

Austria *npr f* GEOGR Austria.

austríaco, ca *adj/s* Austrian.

austro *m* south wind (viento del sur).

autarquía *f* national self-sufficiency, autarky (económica) || autarchy (gobierno).

autárquico, ca *adj* autarkic, autarkical (economía) || autarchic, autharchical (gobierno).

auténtica *f* certificate, attestation (certificado) || legal *o* certified copy (copia).

autentificación *f* certification, authentication, legalization.

autenticar *vt* JUR to authenticate, to legalize.

autenticidad *f* authenticity, genuineness.

auténtico, ca *adj* genuine, authentic, real; *joya auténtica* genuine jewel; *un gitano auténtico* a real gipsy || MÚS authentic (modo) || JUR authentic || *una auténtica tormenta* a real storm.

autentificar; autentizar *vt* JUR to authenticate, to legalize.

autillo *m* ZOOL tawny owl || judgement of the Inquisition (auto particular del tribunal de la Inquisición).

auto *m* JUR judgement, sentence (sentencia) | judgement (de un pleito) || «auto», mystery play [mainly in the 16th and 17th centuries] || — *auto de comparecencia* summons || *auto de fe* auto-da-fé || *auto de prisión* warrant for arrest || *auto de procesamiento* indictment || *auto sacramental* «auto sacramental», mystery play.
◆ *pl* proceedings || *el día de autos* the day of the crime.

auto *m* FAM car (coche) || *autos de choque* dodgems, bumper cars.

autoacusación *f* self-accusation.

autoacusarse *vpr* to accuse o.s.

autoadhesivo, va *adj* self-adhesive, stick-on.

autoametralladora *f* light armoured car.

autoanálisis *m* self-analysis.

autoarranque *m* TECN automatic starting.

autobiografía *f* autobiography.

autobiográfico, ca *adj* autobiographical, autobiographic.

autobiógrafo *m* autobiographer.

autobombo *m* FAM self-praise || FAM *hacerse el autobombo* to blow one's own trumpet, to praise o.s.

autobús *m* bus || — *autobús de dos pisos* double-decker bus || *autobús de línea* long-distance bus.

autocamión *m* lorry [US truck].

autocar *m* coach, motor coach [US bus]; *viaje en autocar* coach trip.

autocarril *m* AMER railcar.

autocine *m* drive-in cinema.

autoclave *f* autoclave (cámara hermética) || sterilizer (para esterilizar).

autoconsumo *m* ECON self-supply.

autocontrol *m* self-control.

autocracia *f* autocracy.

autócrata *m/f* autocrat.

autocrático, ca *adj* autocratic, autocratical.

autocrítica *f* self-criticism || criticism by the author (de una obra).

autóctono, na *adj* autochthonous, autochthonic.
◆ *m/f* authochthon.

autodefensa *f* self-defence [US self-defense].

autodegradación *f* self-abasement.

autodeterminación *f* self-determination.

autodeterminado, da *adj* self-determining.

autodidáctico, ca; autodidacto, ta *adj* self-taught, autodidactic.
◆ *m/f* self-taught person, autodidact.
— OBSERV According to the Real Academia de la Lengua, *autodidacto, ta* exists in both masculine and feminine forms. In practice, however, the form *autodidacta* is applied to both masculine and feminine nouns.

autodirigido, da *adj* self-directing.

autodisciplina *f* self-discipline.

autódromo *m* motor-racing track, racing circuit.

autoedición *f* INFORM desktop publishing, DTP.

autoencendido *m* AUT self-ignition.

autoescuela *f* driving school.

autoestima *f* self-esteem.

autoestop; autostop *m* hitchhiking, hitching || *hacer autoestop* to hitchhike, to hitch.

autoestopismo; autostopismo *m* hitchhiking.

autoestopista; autostopista *m/f* hitchhiker.

autoexcitación *f* ELECTR self-excitation.

autofecundación *f* self-fertilization.

autofinanciación *f*; **autofinanciamiento** *m* self-financing.

autogamia *f* BOT autogamy.

autogénesis *f* BIOL autogenesis, autogeny.

autógeno, na *adj* autogenous || *soldadura autógena* autogenous welding, fusion welding.

autogiro *m* autogiro, autogyro.

autografía *f* autography.

autográfico, ca *adj* autographic, autographical.

autógrafo, fa *adj* autographic, autographical.
◆ *m* autograph.

autoinducción *f* self-induction.

autoinfección *f* MED autoinfection.

autoinoculación *f* MED autoinoculation.

autointoxicación *f* autointoxication.

autólisis *f* autolysis.

automación *f* automation.
— OBSERV *Automación* is an Anglicism which it is usually considered preferable to replace by *automatización*.

autómata *m* automaton, robot.

automaticidad *f* automaticity, automatic working.

automático, ca *adj* automatic.
◆ *m* press stud [US snap fastener].

automatismo *m* automatism.

automatización *f* automation || — *automatización de fábricas* factory automation || *automatización doméstica* domestic automation [integrated home system].

automatizar *vt* to automate.

automotor, ra *adj* self-propelled, self-driven, automotive.
◆ *m* railcar.

automotriz *adj f* self-propelled, self-driven, automotive.

automóvil *adj* self-propelled, self-driven, automotive || motor; *vehículo automóvil* motor vehicle.
◆ *m* car, motorcar [US automobile] (coche) || — *automóvil de carreras* racing car || *automóvil eléctrico* electromobile || *automóvil todo terreno* Land-Rover || *ir en automóvil* to go by car.

automovilismo *m* motoring, driving.

automovilista *m/f* motorist, driver.

automovilístico, ca *adj* motoring || — *accidente automovilístico* road accident, car crash || *carrera automovilística* motor race.

autonomía *f* autonomy, self-government || MIL & AVIAT range.

autonómico, ca *adj* autonomous, self-governing.

autonomista *adj* autonomous.
◆ *m/f* autonomist.

autónomo, ma *adj* autonomous || autonomous, self-governing (país).

autopista *f* motorway [US freeway, superhighway] || *autopista de peaje* toll-paying motorway [US turnpike].

autoplastia *f* MED autoplasty.

autoplástico, ca *adj* MED autoplastic.

autopropulsado, da *adj* self-propelled; *cohete autopropulsado* self-propelled rocket.

autopropulsión *f* self-propulsion.

autopropulsor *adj* self-propelling.

autopsia *f* MED autopsy, postmortem.

autopsiar *vt* MED to autopsy, to carry out an autopsy on *o* a postmortem on.

autopullman *m* pullman.

autor, ra *m/f* author (hombre o mujer) || authoress (mujer) || author, perpetrator (de un crimen) || author, originator, creator (de una idea) || TEATR treasurer || JUR *autor material del hecho* perpetrator of the deed.

autoría *f* TEATR treasurership.

autoridad *f* authority; *tener autoridad sobre sus empleados* to have authority over one's employees || official; *las autoridades que acompañan al jefe del Estado* the officials who accompany the Head of State || authority, expert; *es una autoridad en literatura griega* he is an authority on Greek literature || authorities *pl*; *entregarse a la autoridad* to give o.s. up to the authorities || — *con plena autoridad* with complete authority || *por su propia autoridad* on one's own authority, on one's own account || *tener autoridad para* to have the authority to (con verbo).

autoritariamente *adv* in an authoritarian way.

autoritario, ria *adj* authoritarian.

autoritarismo *m* authoritarianism.

autorización *f* authorization, permission (permiso); *pedir autorización para salir* to ask permission to go out.

autorizadamente *adv* with authority (con autoridad) ‖ with authorization *o* permission (con permiso).

autorizado, da *adj* legal, authorized, official; *precio autorizado* official price ‖ authoritative, reliable; *opinión autorizada* authoritative opinion; *fuente autorizada* reliable source.

autorizar *vt* to authorize, to give permission to; *autorizar a uno para salir* to authorize s.o. to go out, to give s.o. permission to go out ‖ to authorize, to give permission for; *autorizar una manifestación* to authorize *o* to give permission for a demonstration ‖ to give (the) authority to, to give (the) power to, to authorize, to empower; *el ser capitán no le autoriza a insultar a sus soldados* the fact that he is captain does not give him the authority *o* does not authorize him to insult his soldiers ‖ to authorize, to legalize (un documento) ‖ to accept; *palabra autorizada por su uso constante* word accepted through its constant use.

autorradio *m* car radio.

autorregulación *f* self-regulation.

autorregulador, ra *adj* self-regulating.

autorretrato *m* self-portrait.

autorriel *m* AMER railcar.

autorzuelo *m* hack, poor writer.

autoservicio *m* self-service store, supermarket (tienda) ‖ self-service [restaurant] (restaurante).

autostop *m* ⟶ **autoestop.**

autostopismo *m* ⟶ **autoestopismo.**

autostopista *m/f* ⟶ **autoestopista.**

autosuficiencia *f* self-sufficiency.

autosuficiente *adj* self-sufficient.

autosugestión *f* autosuggestion.

autotomía *f* autotomy.

autovacuna *f* autovaccine, autogenous vaccine.

autovía *f* railcar.

autrigones *m pl* former inhabitants of the western Basque provinces.

autumnal *adj* autumnal, autumn.

Auvernia *npr f* GEOGR Auvergne.

auxiliador, ra *adj* helping, assisting.
◆ *m/f* helper.

auxiliar *adj* assistant; *catedrático auxiliar* assistant lecturer ‖ auxiliary; *servicios auxiliares* auxiliary services ‖ GRAM auxiliary.
◆ *m/f* assistant, auxiliary ‖ MED *auxiliar sanitario* nursing auxiliary.
◆ *m* assistant teacher (de instituto, etc.) ‖ assistant lecturer (de universidad) ‖ GRAM auxiliary, auxiliary verb ‖ — *auxiliar de contabilidad* assistant accountant ‖ *auxiliar de farmacia* assistant chemist *o* pharmacist ‖ *auxiliar de laboratorio* laboratory assistant ‖ *auxiliar de vuelo* steward (avión).

auxiliar *vt* to help, to assist, to give help *o* aid to; *auxiliar a uno con donativos* to help s.o. *o* to give help to s.o. with donations ‖ to attend [a dying person].

auxiliaría *f* assistant professorship.

auxilio *m* help, aid, assistance; *con el auxilio de* with the help of ‖ — *auxilio en carretera* breakdown service ‖ *auxilios espirituales* last rites ‖ *darle* or *prestarle auxilio a una persona* to give aid *o* help *o* assistance to a person, to help *o* to aid *o* to assist a person ‖ *en auxilio de* in aid of ‖ *pedir auxilio* to cry for help ‖ *primeros auxilios* first aid.
◆ *interj* help!

Av.; Avda. *abrev de avenida* Av, Ave, Avenue.

aval *m* guarantor's signature (firma) ‖ guarantee (garantía); *aval crediticio* or *de crédito* guarantee of credit ‖ — *dar su aval a* to act as guarantor to (persona), to guarantee (cosa) ‖ *por aval* as a guarantee.

avalancha *f* avalanche.

avalar *vt* COM to guarantee (un documento) ‖ to be the guarantor of, to answer for (a una persona).

avalentonado, da *adj* boastful, arrogant (valentón).

avalorar *vt* to enhance (realzar) ‖ FIG to encourage, to inspire.

avaluación *f* evaluation, appraisal, valuation.

avaluar *vt* to evaluate, to appraise, to value (valuar).

avalúo *m* evaluation, appraisal, valuation.

avance *m* advance (acción de avanzar) ‖ advance (espacio avanzado) ‖ FIG step forward, advance; *un avance en el campo de la ciencia* a step forward in the field of science ‖ advance, progress (progreso) ‖ advance (de dinero) ‖ budget (presupuesto de un Estado) ‖ COM balance (balance) ‖ MIL advance ‖ TECN feed ‖ ELECTR lead ‖ CINEM trailer ‖ *avance al encendido* ignition advance.

avant *m* DEP knock-on (al caerse la pelota) ‖ forward pass (pase).

avante *adv* MAR forward, ahead.

avantrén *m* MIL limber.

avanzada *f* MIL advance guard *o* party, outpost.

avanzadilla *f* MIL advance guard *o* party, outpost (avanzada) ‖ pier (muelle).

avanzado, da *adj* advanced, progressive; *ideas avanzadas* advanced ideas ‖ advanced; *fase avanzada de desarrollo* advanced stage of development ‖ prominent (saliente) ‖ — *avanzado de* or *en edad* advanced *o* well on in years ‖ *una hora muy avanzada* a very late hour.

avanzar *vt* to move forward; *hay que avanzar su silla* you must move your chair forward ‖ to put forward; *avanzar un pie* to put one foot forward ‖ to advance; *avanzar una pieza de ajedrez* to advance a chessman.
◆ *vi* to advance; *el ejército avanzó rápidamente* the army advanced swiftly ‖ to progress, to advance (progresar) ‖ to draw on; *avanzaba el verano* summer was drawing on ‖ *avanzar en edad* to be getting on in years.

avanzo *m* COM balance sheet, balance (balance) ‖ estimate (presupuesto).

avaricia *f* avarice, miserliness (tacañería) ‖ avarice, greed, greediness (codicia) ‖ *la avaricia rompe el saco* a rich man and his money are soon parted.

avaricioso, sa; avariento, ta *adj* miserly, avaricious, mean (tacaño) ‖ greedy, avaricious (codicioso) ‖ REL *la parábola del rico avariento* the parable of Lazarus and the rich man.
◆ *m/f* miser (tacaño) ‖ greedy *o* avaricious person (codicioso).

avariosis *f* MED syphilis.

avaro, ra *adj* miserly, avaricious, mean (tacaño) ‖ greedy, avaricious (codicioso) ‖ — *hombre avaro de palabras* a man of few words ‖ *ser avaro de alabanzas* to be sparing *o* mean with one's praise.
◆ *m/f* miser (tacaño) ‖ greedy *o* avaricious person (codicioso).

avasallador, ra *adj* domineering ‖ FIG overpowering, overwhelming; *la fuerza avasalladora de su discurso* the overpowering force of his speech.
◆ *m/f* enslaver.

avasallamiento *m* enslavement.

avasallar *vt* to enslave, to subjugate ‖ to dominate (dominar).
◆ *vi* FAM to throw one's weight about; *¡sin avasallar!* there's no need to throw your weight about!
◆ *vpr* to become a slave ‖ to submit, to yield (someterse).

avatar *m* avatar (de Visnú) ‖ reincarnation (reincarnación) ‖ change, transformation (cambio).
◆ *pl* ups and downs; *los avatares de su vida* the ups and downs of his life.

ave *f* ZOOL bird ‖ AMER chicken (pollo) ‖ — *ave canora* or *cantora* songbird ‖ *ave de corral* fowl ‖ *ave del Paraíso* bird of paradise ‖ FIG *ave del mal agüero* bird of ill omen ‖ *ave de presa* or *de rapiña* bird of prey ‖ *ave lira* lyre bird ‖ *ave nocturna* night bird (animal), night bird, night rake (persona) ‖ *ave pasajera* or *de paso* migratory bird, bird of passage (sentido propio), rolling stone, bird of passage (sentido figurado) ‖ *ave zancuda* wader.
— OBSERV *Ave* is used mainly for large birds, whereas *pájaro* indicates smaller birds.

AVE *abrev de Alta Velocidad Española* Spanish high-speed train.

avecasina *f* AMER woodcock.

avecilla *f* small bird ‖ *avecilla de las nieves* wagtail.

avecinarse *vpr* to approach, to get nearer; *se avecina la tormenta* the storm is approaching ‖ to take up residence, to settle (establecerse).

avecindamiento *m* settling (en un lugar) ‖ residence, domicile (lugar).

avecindar *vt* to domicile, to give residence to.
◆ *vpr* to take up residence, to settle.

avechucho *m* ugly bird (pájaro) ‖ FIG ragamuffin, pest (persona despreciable).

avefría *f* ZOOL lapwing ‖ FIG & FAM wet blanket, drip (persona).

avejentar *vt* to age.
◆ *vi/vpr* to age, to get old; *Felipe se ha avejentado mucho* Philip has aged a lot.

avejigar *vt* to blister.
◆ *vpr* to blister.

avellana *f* hazelnut ‖ — *color de avellana, color avellana* hazel, hazel-coloured; *ojos color de avellana* hazel eyes ‖ *más seco que una avellana* parched, wizened, shrivelled (rostro).

avellanado, da *adj* wizened, shrivelled, parched (seco y arrugado) ‖ hazel, hazel-coloured (color).
◆ *m* TECN countersinking.

avellanador *m* TECN countersink.

avellanal; avellanar *m* hazel grove.

avellanar *vt* TECN to countersink.
◆ *vpr* to become wizened, to shrivel up, to wrinkle (envejecer).

avellaneda *f*; **avellanedo** *m* hazel grove.

avellanera *f* BOT hazel tree (avellano) ‖ hazelnut seller (vendedora).

avellano *m* hazel tree.

avemaría *f* Ave Maria, Hail Mary (oración) ‖ Ave Maria, small rosary bead (cuenta del rosario) ‖ Ave Maria, Angelus ‖ — FIG *al avemaría* in a wink, in the twinkling of an eye ‖ *saber algo como el avemaría* to know sth. by heart, to know sth. backwards.

¡ave María! *interj* goodness gracious!, good Lord! ‖ *¡Ave María!, ¡ave María Purísima!* God bless this house [said on entering a house].

avena *f* BOT oats *pl*; *la avena sirve para la alimentación de los animales* oats are used for feeding animals ‖ POÉT Pipe (zampoña) ‖ *avena loca* wild oats *pl*.

avenado, da *adj* touched (algo loco) || drained; *terreno avenado* drained land.

avenal *m* oat field.

avenamiento *m* drainage || *tubos de avenamiento* drainage pipes.

avenar *vt* to drain.

avenate *m* oatmeal drink (bebida) || fit of madness (ataque de locura).

avenencia *f* agreement (acuerdo) || compromise (arreglo) || COM deal (transacción) || *más vale mala avenencia que buena sentencia* a poor agreement is better than a good court case.

avenida *f* swell, swelling, freshet (crecida) || flood (desbordamiento) || avenue (calle).

avenido, da *adj estar bien, mal avenido con* to be on good, bad terms with.

avenimiento *m* agreement (acuerdo).

avenir* *vt* to bring to an agreement, to bring into agreement, to reconcile, to bring together.
◆ *vi* to happen (suceder).
◆ *vpr* to agree, to come to an agreement; *avenirse en el precio* to agree about *o* on the price || to get on, to agree; *no puede avenirse con su hermano* he cannot agree with *o* get on with his brother || to adapt *o* to adjust o.s.; *una persona que se aviene a* or *con todo* a person who adjusts himself to everything || to correspond to, to be in agreement with (corresponder) || — FAM *allá se las avenga* that's his look-out, let him get on with it || *avenirse a razones* to listen to reason.

aventador, ra *adj* winnowing.
◆ *m/f* winnower (persona).
◆ *m* fan (para el fuego) || winnowing fork (bieldo) || leather valve (de tubo de aspiración).
◆ *f* winnowing machine (máquina).

aventadura *f* windgall (de los caballos).

aventajado, da *adj* outstanding (notable) || advantageous, favourable (ventajoso).

aventajamiento *m* advantage (ventaja).

aventajar *vt* to come *o* to finish ahead of *o* in front of; *le aventajó en la carrera* he came ahead of him in the race || to lead, to be ahead of; *el piloto inglés aventaja al francés* the English driver leads the French one || to surpass, to excel, to outstrip, to be superior to; *aventaja a todos en los deportes* he surpasses everyone in sports || to give an advantage to, to be to the advantage of (dar ventaja) || to better, to improve (mejorar) || to prefer, to put before (preferir) || *aventaja a todos en simpatía* he beats everyone for friendliness.

aventamiento *m* AGR winnowing.

aventar* *vt* to blow away (el viento) || to expose to the wind (exponer al viento) || to fan, to blow (el fuego) || AGR to winnow || to throw *o* to cast to the winds (las cenizas) || *AMER* to expose (sugar) to the sun and air || FIG & FAM to throw out (expulsar).
◆ *vpr* to swell in the wind (llenarse de aire) || FIG & FAM to dash off, to rush off, to beat it (marcharse).

aventura *f* adventure; *novela de aventuras* adventure novel || risk (riesgo) || chance (casualidad) || affair (de amor) || — FIG *a la aventura* at random || *nos contaba las aventuras de su juventud* he would tell us about his youthful adventures *o* exploits *o* escapades.

aventurado, da *adj* risky, hazardous, dangerous (peligroso); *empresa aventurada* risky undertaking || venturesome, risky; *proyecto aventurado* risky plan || *no es aventurado decir que* one can say that, it can be said that, it is safe to say that.

aventurar *vt* to risk, to venture, to chance; *aventurar su vida* to risk one's life || FIG to venture, to hazard; *aventurar una teoría* to hazard a theory.
◆ *vpr* to venture, to dare || *el que no se aventura no pasa la mar* nothing ventured, nothing gained.

aventurero, ra *adj* adventurous, venturesome (que busca aventura) || *AMER* produced out of season (maíz, arroz).
◆ *m* adventurer || *AMER* hired mule driver (arriero).
◆ *f* adventuress.

avergonzado, da *adj* ashamed || embarrassed (confuso).

avergonzar* *vt* to shame, to put to shame (escarnecer); *el orador avergonzó públicamente a su rival* the speaker shamed his rival publicly || to embarrass (poner en un apuro).
◆ *vpr* to be ashamed; *me avergüenzo de tu conducta* I am ashamed of your conduct || to be embarrassed (pasar un apuro).

avería *f* breakdown (en un coche); *tuvimos una avería* we had a breakdown || damage (daño) || — *avería con compensación* breakdown with compensation || *avería general* general breakdown || *avería parcial* partial breakdown || *avería sin compensación* breakdown without compensation || MAR *avería gruesa* general average || AUT *el coche tiene una avería* there is sth. wrong with the car.

averiado, da *adj* AUT broken down (un automóvil, un motor) || damaged (estropeado) || spoilt, spoiled (echado a perder) || *está averiado* it has broken down, there is sth. wrong with it.

averiar *vt* to damage (estropear) || to spoil (echar a perder).
◆ *vpr* to break down (un coche) || to fail (los frenos, etc.) || to be *o* to get damaged (estropearse) || to spoil (echarse a perder) || to be *o* to get damaged (un buque).

averiguable *adj* verifiable || ascertainable.

averiguación *f* verification (examen) || ascertainment || investigation, inquiry (investigación).

averiguador, ra *adj* inquiring, investigating.
◆ *m/f* investigator, inquirer (el que investiga).

averiguar *vt* to check, to verify (examinar) || to ascertain, to find out (enterarse de); *voy a averiguar lo que ha sucedido* I am going to ascertain what has happened || to investigate, to ascertain, to inquire into (investigar); *hay que averiguar las causas del accidente* we must investigate the causes of the accident || to guess (adivinar) || to look up, to check; *averígualo en el diccionario* look it up *o* check it in the dictionary || *¡averígüelo Vargas!* find out for yourself!, make your own inquiries!
◆ *vi AMER* to quarrel, to argue (andarse en disputas).

averno *m* POÉT Hades, the nether regions *pl*, the underworld.

Averroes *n pr* Averroes, Averrhoes.

averrugado, da *adj* warty.

aversión *f* aversion, loathing, abhorrence; *aversión al trabajo* aversion for work || — *cobrarle* or *cogerle aversión a uno* to develop an aversion *o* a loathing for s.o., to take an extreme dislike to s.o. || *tenerle aversión a uno* to have an aversion *o* a loathing for s.o., to loathe *o* to hate s.o.

avestruceras *f pl* «bolas» [weapon consisting of several ropes tied together, each with a metal ball at the end, and used by Argentinian «gauchos» for catching ostriches].

avestruz *m* ostrich (ave) || — *avestruz de América* rhea, nandu, nandow || FIG *política del avestruz* ostrich policy.

avetado, da *adj* veined.

avetoro *m* ZOOL bittern.

avezado, da *adj* used, accustomed (acostumbrado) || hardened, inured; *avezado a la lucha* hardened against *o* to strife || experienced, inured; *avezado en los negocios* experienced in business.

avezar *vt* to accustom, to get used, to inure; *avezar a una persona al trabajo* to get a person used to work || to harden, to inure; *avezar a un soldado al frío* to harden a soldier against the cold.
◆ *vpr* to get used, to become accustomed; *avezarse a todo* to get used to everything || to become *o* to be hardened (al frío, a las desgracias, etc.).

aviación *f* aviation; *aviación civil* civil aviation || MIL air force; *capitán de aviación* air force captain.

Aviaco *abrev de Aviación y Comercio, S.A.* Spanish commercial airline company.

aviado, da *adj* ready; *aviado para salir* ready to go out || *¡aviado estoy* or *voy!* I'm in a real mess!, I'm done for!

aviador, ra *m/f* aviator, flyer, flier (que tripula un avión) || pilot (piloto) || MIL *mi padre era aviador* my father was in the air force.

aviar *adj* avian || *peste aviar* fowl pest.

aviar *vt* to prepare, to get ready; *aviar una comida* to get a meal ready || to tidy; *aviar una habitación* to tidy a room || to mend, to repair (reparar) || to equip, to supply, to provide (equipar) || to fit out, to equip; *aviarle a uno de ropa* to fit s.o. out with clothes || FAM to help out; *¿me puedes prestar mil pesetas para aviarme?* can you lend me a thousand pesetas to help me out? | to help; *¿te avía si te llevo en coche?* will it help you if I take you by car? || — *dejar a alguien aviado* to leave s.o. stranded || FAM *ir aviando* to get a move on, to hurry up; *vamos aviando* let's get a move on.
◆ *vpr* to get ready; *aviarse para ir a cenar* to get ready to go to dinner || FAM to manage; *se avía con muy poca cosa* he manages with very little | to hurry up, to get a move on (darse prisa); *¡avíate!* hurry up!, get a move on!

aviario, ria *adj* → **aviar.**

avícola *adj* poultry.

avicultor, ra *m/f* poultry keeper.

avicultura *f* poultry keeping (aves de corral) || aviculture (de otras aves).

avidez *f* avidity, greed, greediness (ansia) || eagerness (ganas).

ávido, da *adj* avid, greedy (*de* for) (ansioso) || eager, avid (*de* for) (con ganas) || *ávido de sangre* bloodthirsty.

aviejar *vt* → **envejecer.**

aviesamente *adv* perversely.

avieso, sa *adj* perverse, wicked, depraved; *espíritu avieso* perverse character.

avilés, esa *adj* [of *o* from] Avila [in Spain].
◆ *m/f* native *o* inhabitant of Avila.

avilesino, na *adj* [of *o* from] Avilés [in Asturias].
◆ *m/f* native *o* inhabitant of Avilés.

avillanado, da *adj* common (no noble).

avillanamiento *m* lowering, debasing.

avillanar *vt* to lower, to debase.

avinado, da *adj* drunken.
— OBSERV This word is a Gallicism.

avinagrado, da *adj* sour, vinegary || FIG sour, bitter; *carácter avinagrado* sour character.

avinagrar *vt* to turn to vinegar, to turn sour, to sour || FIG to sour, to embitter, to make sour.
◆ *vpr* to turn sour, to turn to vinegar (el vino) || FIG to turn bitter *o* sour, to become bitter *o* sour.

Aviñón *n pr* GEOGR Avignon.

avío *m* preparation || provisions *pl* (de un pastor) || AMER loan [made to farmer or miner] ||— *¡al avío!* let's get cracking!, down to work!, let's get down to it! || *hacer avío* to be a help; *esta bicicleta me hace un avío imponente* this bicycle is a great help to me; *hace mi avío* it is a help to me || FAM *ir a su avío* to think only of o.s., to be selfish.
◆ *pl* FAM things (cosas) || equipment *sing*, materials; *avíos de coser, de escribir* sewing, writing equipment || tackle *sing*; *avíos de pesca* fishing tackle || gear *sing*; *avíos de afeitar* shaving gear || ingredients (de cocina) || TAUR *tomar los avíos de matar* to take the muleta and the sword.

avión *m* aeroplane [US airplane], plane, aircraft; *avión de reacción, de carga, de reconocimiento, sin piloto, supersónico* jet, cargo, reconnaissance, remote-controlled, supersonic plane ||— *avión de bombardeo* bomber || *avión de caza* fighter (plane) || *avión de distancias medias* or *continental* medium-haul aircraft || *avión de larga distancia* or *transcontinental* long-range *o* long-haul aircraft || *avión de pasajeros* or *de línea* airliner, passenger aircraft || *avión sin motor* glider || *ir* or *viajar en avión* to fly, to go by air *o* by plane || *por avión* (by) air mail (una carta), by air (viaje).
◆ *pl* aircraft, planes; *la compañía tiene veinte aviones* the company has twenty aircraft.

avion *m* ZOOL martin (pájaro).

avioneta *f* light aircraft *o* plane.

avisacoches *m inv* person tipped to tell chauffeur that the owner requires the car.

avisadamente *adv* wisely, prudently, sensibly.

avisado, da *adj* wise, circumspect, prudent || TAUR experienced [bull] || *mal avisado* rash, thoughtless.

avisador, ra *adj* warning.
◆ *m* TECN warning device (alarma) | fire alarm (contra incendios) || errand boy (chico de los recados).

avisar *vt* to warn; *me avisó que me llevara el paraguas* he warned me to take my umbrella || to let know, to tell, to notify, to warn; *le han avisado que llegarán tarde* they have warned him that they will arrive late; *me acaba de avisar que se tiene que ir* he has just told me that he has to go || to send for, to call; *avisar al médico* to send for the doctor || to notify, to warn; *avisar a la policía* to notify the police || *hacer algo sin avisar* to do sth. without warning.

aviso *m* warning; *darle un aviso a uno por sus retrasos repetidos* to give s.o. a warning about repeatedly being late; *el ataque del país es un aviso* the attack on the country is a warning || announcement (anuncio); *dar un aviso al público* to make an announcement to the public || note (nota) || MAR dispatch boat, aviso || TAUR warning [given by the president of the bullfight to the bullfighter when the bull has not been killed within the time laid down by the rules] ||— *andar* or *estar sobre aviso* to be on one's guard, to be on the alert || *aviso de crédito* credit memorandum, credit note || *aviso de débito* debit note || *aviso de vencimiento* notice to pay || *aviso por escrito* written notice || *aviso telefónico* call from the operator || *carta de aviso* advice note || *conferencia telefónica con aviso* person-to-person call || *dar previo aviso de un mes* to give a month's notice || *hasta nuevo aviso* until further notice || *poner a uno sobre aviso* to alert s.o., to put s.o. on his guard || *salvo aviso en contrario* unless otherwise informed || *sin el menor aviso* without the slightest *o* least warning; *le han echado sin el menor aviso* they have thrown him out without the slightest warning || *sin previo aviso* without previous warning, without notice.

avispa *f* wasp (insecto) || *cintura de avispa* wasp waist.

avispado, da *adj* FIG & FAM sharp, quick, bright, clever (despabilado) | sly, crafty (astuto).

avispar *vt* to spur on (a los caballos) || FIG & FAM to liven up, to quicken up, to prod (espabilar).
◆ *vpr* FIG & FAM to brighten up, to liven up, to quicken up (espabilarse) | FIG to get worried, to worry (preocuparse).

avispero *m* wasps' nest (nido de avispas) || comb (panal) || FIG & FAM mess, tight spot, jam; *meterse en un avispero* to get o.s. into a mess || MED carbuncle.

avispón *m* hornet (insecto).

avistar *vt* to sight, to glimpse; *por la tarde avistamos la costa* in the afternoon we sighted the coast.
◆ *vpr* to meet [to discuss business], to have a business interview.

avitaminosis *f* avitaminosis, vitamin deficiency.

avituallamiento *m* provisioning || MAR victualling.

avituallar *vt* to provision, to supply with food || MAR to victual.

avivado, da *adj* FIG quicker, livelier, brighter (espíritu) | brighter, livelier (color) | quicker, livelier (paso) | excited, roused (ira).

avivador, ra *adj* livening, quickening, enlivening || exciting, rousing (que excita).
◆ *m* ARQ quirk (espacio entre dos molduras) || TECN rabbet plane (cepillo).

avivamiento *m* livening, quickening, enlivening (del espíritu) || brightening, livening (de un color) || quickening, livening (del paso) || rousing, excitement (de la ira).

avivar *vt* to revive, to arouse, to stimulate (estimular) || to stoke, to stoke up (el fuego) || FIG to enliven, to liven up, to quicken (el espíritu) || to brighten (up), to liven up, to enliven (los colores) || to quicken, to liven up, to enliven (el paso) || to excite, to stir, to arouse (una pasión, una cólera) || to intensify (el dolor) || to stir up; *avivar el fuego de la insurrección* to stir up the flames of insurrection.
◆ *vi/vpr* to come back to life, to revive || to hatch (gusanos de seda) ||— FAM *¡avívate!* get a move on!, look lively! (date prisa), snap out of it!, cheer up! (anímate).

avizor *adj* *estar ojo avizor* to be on one's guard, to keep one's eyes open, to keep a sharp look out || *¡ojo avizor!* look out!, be careful!

avizorar *vt* to spy on, to watch, to keep watch on (acechar) || to foresee (ver).

avo, va MAT suffix added to cardinal numbers to indicate fractions whose denominators are greater than ten; *un onzavo* an eleventh; *un quinzavo* a fifteenth; *tres dieciseisavos* three sixteenths; *una treintava parte* a thirtieth.

— OBSERV *Octavo* [eighth] is an exception to this rule, its denominator being smaller than ten.

avoceta *f* ZOOL avocet, avoset.

avulsión *f* MED extraction.

avutarda *f* ZOOL bustard (ave zancuda).

axial; axil *adj* axial; *líneas axiales* axial lines.

axila *f* BOT axil || ANAT axilla, armpit (sobaco).

axilar *adj* axillary, axillar.

axiología *f* axiology.

axioma *m* axiom.

axiomático, ca *adj* axiomatic.

axis *m* ANAT axis (vértebra).

axolotl *m* ZOOL axolotl.

ay *m* ZOOL ai, three-toed sloth (perezoso).

¡ay! *interj* ouch! (dolor físico) || oh!, oh dear! (aflicción) || (followed by *de* and a noun or pronoun *¡ay!* expresses pain, threat, fear or pity); *¡ay de mí!* poor me!, why me?, woe is me! (dolor); *¡ay de él!* poor thing! (compasión); *¡ay de Pedro!* woe betide Peter! (amenaza) ||— *¡ay de los vencidos!* woe unto the vanquished || *¡ay del que...!* woe betide the man who...!, beware he who...! (amenaza), pity on him who...! (compasión) || *¡ay, Dios mío!* my goodness!, goodness me!
◆ *m* moan, lament; *se oían tristes ayes* sad moans could be heard || *dar ayes* to moan, to lament.

aya *f* governess.

ayacuá *f* AMER little invisible devil [in South America Indian mythology].

ayahasca; ayahuasa *f* AMER narcotic plant.

ayatollah *m* ayatollah.

ayer *adv* yesterday; *ayer por la tarde* yesterday afternoon; *ayer hizo un año que nos encontramos* it was a year ago yesterday that we met || FIG yesterday (poco tiempo ha); *parece que fue ayer* it seems like yesterday | before, formerly (en tiempo pasado); *ella ya no es lo que era ayer* she is not what she was before, she is not like she was before ||— *antes de ayer* the day before yesterday || *ayer noche* last night || FIG *de ayer acá, de ayer a hoy* lately; *de ayer a hoy la aviación se ha desarrollado mucho* aviation has developed a great deal lately || *el Madrid de ayer* the Madrid of yesteryear || *lo que va de ayer a hoy* things aren't what they used to be, things have changed a lot || *no es cosa de ayer* it is nothing new || *no ha nacido ayer* he was not born yesterday.
◆ *m* past (pasado).

ayllu *m* —› **AÍLLO.**

ayo *m* (private) tutor.

ayocote *m* AMER kidney bean.

ayote *m* AMER gourd, pumpkin (fruto).

ayotera *f* AMER gourd, pumpkin (planta).

ayuda *f* help, aid, assistance; *hacer el trabajo con ayuda de alguien* to do the work with s.o.'s help; *acudir en ayuda de uno* to come to s.o.'s assistance || aid, assistance (económica); *ayuda estatal* state aid || MED enema (lavativa) ||— *ayuda crediticia* credit aid || *ayuda extranjera* foreign aid || *ayuda financiera* financial aid || *ayuda mutua* mutual aid *o* assistance || FAM *no necesitar ayuda del vecino* not to need anyone's help, to need no one's help || *prestar ayuda* to give help *o* aid, to help, to aid.
◆ *m* valet, manservant ||— *ayuda de cámara* valet || *no hay hombre grande para su ayuda de cámara* no man is great in the eyes of his manservant.
◆ *f pl* aids.

ayudado *m* TAUR pass holding the cape in both hands.

ayudante *m* assistant || MIL adjutant ||— *ayudante de campo* aide-de-camp || *ayudante de laboratorio* laboratory assistant *o* technician || *ayudante de obras públicas* assistant civil engineer || CINEM *ayudante de operador* assistant cameraman || *ayudante de peluquería* apprentice hairdresser.

ayudantía *f* assistantship || MIL adjutancy, adjutant's rank.

ayudar *vt* to help, to aid, to assist; *ayudar a uno con consejos* to help s.o. with some advice; *ayudar a los pobres* to help the poor || to help, to assist; *ayudar a uno a llevar una maleta* to help s.o. to carry a suitcase || — *ayudar a misa* to serve at Mass || *ayudar a uno a bajar* to help s.o. down.
◆ *vpr* to help *o* to aid *o* to assist each other; *en la vida hay que ayudarse* we have to help each other in life || to use, to make use of (valerse); *ayudándose con los dientes, desató la cuerda* using his teeth he undid the string || *ayúdate y ayudarte he, ayúdate y el cielo te ayudará, ayúdate y Dios te ayudará* God helps those who help themselves.

ayunante *m/f* faster.

ayunar *vi* to fast; *ayunar en cuaresma* to fast during Lent || FIG to go without.

ayunas (en) *loc adv* fasting (abstinencia) || without breakfast (sin desayunar) || — *estar en ayunas* not ot have eaten breakfast (sin desayunar), to be in the dark, to have no idea (no saber) || *quedarse en ayunas* not to understand a thing.

ayuno, na *adj* FIG deprived, completely lacking; *estar ayuno en educación moral* to be deprived of *o* completely lacking in moral education || FIG *estar ayuno de un asunto* to know nothing about a matter, to have no idea about a matter (no saber), not to understand a matter (no entender).
◆ *m* fasting, fast || *guardar ayuno* to fast.

ayuntamiento *m* town council, city council (institución) || town hall, city hall (edificio) || meeting (reunión) || copulation (cópula) || *ayuntamiento carnal* sexual intercourse.

ayuntar *vt* MAR to splice.

azabachado, da *adj* jet black.

azabache *m* jet (variedad de lignito) || coal tit (pájaro).

azacán, ana *adj* hard-working.
◆ *m* slave, drudge || water carrier (aguador) || FIG & FAM *estar hecho un azacán* to work like a slave, to be overworked.

azacanear *vi* FAM to slave away, to toil.

azache *m* rough silk (seda basta).

azada *f* AGR hoe.

azadada *f*; **azadado** *m* stroke of *o* blow with a hoe.

azadilla *f* small hoe, gardener's hoe (escardillo).

azadón *m* hoe (instrumento agrícola) || *azadón de peto* or *de pico* mattock.

azadonar *vt* to hoe.

azadonazo *m* stroke of *o* blow with a hoe.

azafata *f* lady-in-waiting (en palacio) || air hostess, stewardess (en avión) || *azafata de exposiciones y congresos* hostess.

azafate *m* AMER tray (bandeja).

azafrán *m* saffron.

azafranado, da *adj* saffron-flavoured, saffroned (guiso) || saffron, saffron-coloured (color).

azafranal *m* saffron plantation.

azafranar *vt* to add saffron to, to saffron || to colour saffron.

azafranero, ra *m/f* saffron grower (cultivador).

azagaya *f* assegai, assagai, light javelin.

azahar *m* orange blossom, lemon blossom || — *agua de azahar* orange-flower water || *corona de azahar* orange-blossom wreath.

azalea *f* BOT azalea.

azar *m* chance (casualidad); *por puro azar encontré a mi amigo* by pure chance I met my friend || accident, misfortune (desgracia) || — *al azar* at random || *juego de azar* game of chance || *los azares de la vida* the ups and downs of life.

azarado, da; azorado, da *adj* embarrassed, flustered.

azaramiento; azoramiento *m* frightening (acción de dar miedo) || fright (susto) || fear (miedo) || embarrassment, fluster (confusión).

azarar; azorar *vt* to embarrass, to fluster (avergonzar).
◆ *vpr* to be embarrassed (turbarse); *se azara fácilmente* she is easily embarrassed || to get flustered (perder la serenidad) || to go wrong, to turn out badly (malograrse).

azarosamente *adv* with difficulty.

azaroso, sa *adj* risky, dangerous, hazardous (arriesgado) || difficult; *una vida azarosa* a difficult life.

Azerbaián; Azerbayán *n pr* GEOGR Azerbaijan.

azerbayano, na *adj* Azerbaijani.

ázimo *adj m* unleavened || *pan ázimo* unleavened bread, azyme, azym.

azimut *m* ASTR azimuth (acimut).

azoado, da *adj* QUÍM (p us) nitrogenous.

azoar *vt* QUÍM (p us) to nitrogenate.

azoato, ta *adj* QUÍM (p us) nitrate.

ázoe *m* QUÍM (p us) nitrogen, azote (nitrógeno).

azofaifo *m* jujube (fruto).

azófar *m* brass (latón).

azogado, da *adj* quicksilvered, silvered (espejos) || MED suffering from mercurialism, mercurial || FIG restless, fidgety (agitado).
◆ *m/f* MED person with mercurialism || FIG restless *o* fidgety person.
◆ *m* silvering, quicksilvering (de un espejo) || FIG *temblar como un azogado* to shake like a leaf.

azogador *m* silverer.

azogamiento *m* quicksilvering, silvering (de los espejos) || FIG restlessness, fidgetiness (agitación) || MED mercurialism, mercury poisoning.

azogar *vt* to quicksilver, to silver (los espejos) || to slake (la cal viva).
◆ *vpr* MED to contract mercurialism *o* mercury poisoning || FIG & FAM to be restless *o* fidgety (agitarse mucho).

azogue *m* quicksilver, mercury (metal) || — FIG *ser un azogue, tener azogue en las venas* to be always on the move, to never keep still for a minute | *temblar como el azogue* to shake like a leaf.

azoico, ca *adj* QUÍM nitric || GEOL azoic.

azolar* *vt* to adze, to adz, to dress with an adze *o* adz (la madera).

azor *m* goshawk (ave).

azorado, da *adj* ⟶ **azarado.**

azoramiento *m* ⟶ **azaramiento.**

azorar *vt* ⟶ **azarar.**

Azores (islas) *npr fpl* GEOGR Azores.

azorrarse *vpr* to get drowsy.

azotacalles *m/f inv* FAM idler, loafer.

azotado, da *adj* beaten || whipped, lashed, flogged (con un látigo) || whipped (por el viento) || lashed (por la lluvia) || variegated (flor) || AMER striped (acebrado).
◆ *m* criminal condemned to be whipped (reo) || penitent (disciplinante).

azotador, ra *adj* lashing (lluvia, viento).

azotaina *f* spanking, smacking (a los niños) || beating (paliza); *dar una azotaina* to give a beating || whipping, lashing, flogging (con un látigo).

azotamiento *m* whipping, lashing, flogging.

azotar *vt* to whip, to lash, to flog (con un látigo) || to spank, to smack (a los niños) || to beat (pegar) || to whip (el viento) || to beat against, to lash; *el mar azotaba las rocas* the sea beat against the rocks || to beat down on, to lash; *la tormenta azotó la isla* the storm lashed the island || FIG to scourge (la peste, una calamidad) || — *azotar las calles* to loaf about *o* to roam about *o* to idle about the streets || FIG *azotar el aire* to waste one's efforts, to flog a dead horse.
◆ *vpr* AMER to idle, to loaf.

azotazo *m* smack (a un niño) || lash (con un látigo).

azote *m* whip (látigo) || cat-o'-nine tails (con nueve cuerdas) || stroke [of the whip], lash [of the whip] (latigazo); *veinte azotes* twenty lashes || spanking, smacking (golpes en las nalgas) || FIG lash, beating (del viento, del mar) | scourge; *la peste es un azote* the plague is a scourge; *Atila, el Azote de Dios* Attila, the scourge of God.
◆ *pl* public whipping *o* flogging (suplicio antiguo) || *dar azotes* or *de azotes* to whip, to flog, to lash.

azotea *f* flat roof (terraza) || AMER flat-roofed house || FIG & FAM *estar mal de la azotea* to have bats in the belfry.

azotina *f* FAM spanking, smacking.

azteca *adj/s* aztec.

azúcar *m o f* sugar; *un terrón de azúcar* a lump of sugar || — *azúcar blanco* or *de flor* or *florete* or *refinado* refined sugar || *azúcar cande* or *candi* sugar candy || *azúcar de caña* cane sugar || *azúcar de cortadillo* or *en terrones* lump sugar || *azúcar de pilón* loaf sugar || *azúcar de quebrados* rough lump sugar || *azúcar en polvo* powdered sugar || *azúcar extra fina* castor sugar || *azúcar mascabada* inferior cane sugar || *azúcar morena* or *negra* brown *o* Demerara sugar || *azúcar terciada* brown *o* Demerara sugar || *echar azúcar a* to put sugar in, to sugar (el café, el té) || *¿le pongo dos azúcares?* would you like two lumps *o* two sugars?

azucarado, da *adj* sugared, sweetened; *café azucarado* sugared coffee || sweet (dulce); *sabor azucarado* sweet taste || FIG sugary, sweet (almibarado).

azucarar *vt* to sugar, to put sugar in, to sweeten; *azucarar el té* to put sugar in one's tea || FIG to sweeten.

azucarera *f* sugar bowl (vasija para el azúcar) || sugar factory (fábrica).

azucarería *f* sugar refinery *o* factory (fábrica) || AMER sugar shop (tienda).

azucarero, ra *adj* sugar; *industria azucarera* sugar industry.
◆ *m* sugar bowl (recipiente) || tree creeper (ave).

azucarillo *m* lemon candy used to flavour drinks.

azucena *f* BOT white *o* Madonna lily || *azucena de agua* water lily.

azud *m*; **azuda** *f* waterwheel (rueda) || dam (presa).

azuela *f* adz, adze.

azufaifa *f* jujube (fruto).

azufaifo *m* jujube tree (árbol).

azufrado, da *adj* sulphured (plantas, toneles) || sulphurated (impregnado de azufre) || sulphur-coloured.
◆ *m* sulphuring.

azuframiento *m* sulphuring.

azufrar *vt* to sulphur (toneles, plantas) || to sulphurate (impregnar de azufre).

azufre *m* sulphur || *flor de azufre* flower of sulphur.

azufrera *f* sulphur mine (mina).

azufroso, sa *adj* sulphurous.

azul *adj* blue || AMER indigo (añil) || — *azul celeste, claro, oscuro, de cobalto, marino, de Prusia, de ultramar, verdoso* sky, light *o* pale, dark *o* deep, cobalt, navy, Prussian, ultramarine, petrol blue || *azul turquí* indigo || *el príncipe azul* Prince Charming || *enfermedad azul* blue disease, cyanosis || GEOGR *la Costa Azul* the Riviera || *sangre azul* blue blood.
◆ *m* blue (color) || blue, blueness (del cielo, del mar).

azulado, da *adj* bluish, blue.
◆ *m* blueing.

azulaque *m* lute.

azular *vt* to colour blue, to blue.
◆ *vpr* to turn blue.

azulear *vi* to look blue (mostrarse azul) || to be bluish, to have a bluish cast (tirar a azul).
◆ *vpr* to turn blue.

azulejar *vt* to tile.

azulejería *f* tiling, tiles *pl* (revestimiento) || tile manufacturing (fabricación) || tile works *pl*, tile factory (fábrica).

azulejo *m* tile || glazed tile (con dibujos) || BOT bluebottle, cornflower (aciano) || ZOOL bee-eater (abejaruco) | bluebird (pájaro).
◆ *adj* bluish (azulado).

azulenco, ca *adj* bluish.

azuleo *m* blueing.

azulete *m* blue (para la ropa blanca) || *dar azulete a* to blue, to colour blue.

azulgrana *adj inv* blue and scarlet.

azulillo *m* indigo dye.

azuloso, sa *adj* bluish.

azumar *vt* to dye, to tint (los cabellos).

azúmbar *m* BOT water plantain.

azumbrado, da *adj* FIG tipsy (borracho).

azumbre *f* «azumbre» [liquid measure approximately equal to half a gallon].

azuquita *m* sugar.

azur *adj/s* HERÁLD azure.

azurita *f* MIN azurite.

azurronarse *vpr* to remain in the husk [grain of wheat].

azuzador, ra *adj* teasing, who teases || FIG troublesome (molesto).
◆ *m/f* troublemaker.

azuzar *vt* to set (a dog) on s.o. (a los perros) || FIG to incite, to urge (incitar).
◆ *vi* to cause trouble, to stir things up.

B

b *f* b; *una b mayúscula, minúscula* a capital, small b || *probar por a más b* to prove conclusively, to demonstrate clearly.

— OBSERV When the Spanish *b* comes at the beginning of a word or after the letters *m* or *n* it is pronounced rather like the English *b*. In all other cases the pronunciation is less explosive than that of the English b.

baalita *adj/s* baalite.

baba *f* dribble (de niños), spittle, slobber (de adultos) || froth, foam (de animales) || sap (de plantas) || slime (de caracoles) || — FIG *caérsele a uno la baba* to be charmed, to be delighted (estar embelesado), to be an idiot | *se le cae la baba con su niño* she dotes on her child || FAM *tener mala baba* to be bad tempered.

babada *f* stifle.

babadero; babador *m* AMER bib.

babaza *f* slime (de caracoles).

babear *vi* to dribble (niños), to slobber (adultos) || to foam *o* to froth at the mouth (animales) || FIG to drool [over a woman].

babel *m o f* bedlam; *la casa es una babel* it is bedlam in the house.

Babel *n pr* HIST Babel; *Torre de Babel* Tower of Babel.

babeo *m* dribbling (de niños), slobbering (de adultos) || foaming, frothing (de animales) || slime (de caracoles) || FIG drooling.

babera *f* beaver (de la armadura) || bib (de niño).

babero *m* bib; *los niños llevan un babero para comer* children wear a bib for eating || overall [US frock] (bata) || smock (para el colegio).

Babia *n pr* FIG & FAM *estar en Babia* to have one's head in the clouds.

babieca *adj* FAM simple, silly.
◆ *m/f* simpleton, fool.

Babieca *n pr* Babieca [El Cid's horse].

babilonia *f* FIG & FAM bedlam, mess.

Babilonia *npr f* GEOGR Babylon (ciudad) | Babylonia (reino).

babilónico, ca *adj* Babylonian.

babilonio, nia *adj/s* Babylonian.

babilla *f* stifle.

babirusa *f* ZOOL babiroussa, babirusa, wild hog (cerdo salvaje).

bable *m* Asturian dialect.

babor *m* MAR port, port side, larboard || — *a babor* to port, on the port side || *de babor a estribor* athwartships || *¡tierra a babor!* land to port!

babosa *f* ZOOL slug.

babosada *f* AMER rubbish, stupid thing.

babosear *vt* to dribble over (niños), to slobber over (adultos).
◆ *vi* FIG to drool.

baboso, sa *adj* slimy (caracoles) || dribbly (niños), slobbery (adultos) || FIG runny, lightly done (tortilla) || FIG & FAM sloppy, maudlin (sentimental) || AMER FAM foolish, silly.
◆ *m* FAM bore (empalagoso) | drip (mocoso); *este chico es un baboso* this boy is a drip || FAM *viejo baboso* dirty old man.
◆ *m/f* AMER FAM fool, silly person.

babucha *f* babouche, baboush, slipper, mule (zapatilla).

babuino *m* ZOOL baboon (mono).

baby *m* FAM overall [US frock] (bata) | smock (de niños) || AMER baby.

baca *f* top, roof (de la diligencia) || AUT roof *o* luggage rack || tarpaulin, rainproof cover (lona).

bacalada *f* cured cod, stockfish.

bacaladero, ra; bacalaero, ra *adj* cod-fishing || *industria bacaladera* cod industry.
◆ *m* cod-fishing boat (barco) || codfisherman (pescador).

bacalao *m* cod, codfish; *bacalao seco* cured cod || — FIG & FAM *cortar* or *partir el bacalao* to be the boss | *te conozco bacalao aunque vienes* or *vengas disfrazado* I can see straight through you, you can't fool me.

bacán *m* AMER posh person [US swank].

bacanal *f* orgy (orgía).
◆ *pl* bacchanalia.

bacante *f* bacchanal, bacchante.

bacarrá; bacará *m* Baccarat (juego).

Baccarat *n pr* GEOGR baccarat || *cristal de Baccarat* baccarat glass.

bacía *f* barber's bowl (de barbero) || basin (recipiente).

bacilar *adj* MED bacillary, bacillar.

bacilemia *f* MED bacillaemia.

baciliforme *adj* bacilliform, rod-shaped.

bacilo *m* MED bacillus; *bacilo de Koch* Koch's bacillus.

bacilosis *f* MED bacillus infection (tuberculosis).

baciluria *f* MED bacilluria.

bacín *m* chamber pot (orinal) || alms plate (para pedir limosna) || FIG cur (persona despreciable).

bacineta *f* alms plate (para limosna) || small chamber pot (orinal).

bacinete *m* basinet (de armadura) || ANAT pelvis.

bacinica; bacinilla *f* alms plate (para limosna) || small chamber pot (orinal).

Baco *npr m* Bacchus.

bacteria *f* bacterium.

— OBSERV En inglés el plural de *bacterium* es *bacteria.*

bacteriano, na *adj* bacterial.

bactericida *adj* bactericidal, germ-killing.
◆ *m* bactericide, germicide.

bacteriología *f* bacteriology.

bacteriológico, ca *adj* bacteriological; *guerra bacteriológica* bacteriological warfare.

bacteriólogo *m* bacteriologist.

báculo *m* walking stick, staff (bastón) || crosier, crozier, staff (de obispo) || staff (de peregrino) || FIG staff, support (apoyo) || FIG *báculo de la vejez* comfort *o* help in one's old age.

bache *m* hole, pothole (en una carretera) || air pocket (en avión) || FIG bad patch; *los baches de la vida* the bad patches in life | slump (depresión).

bachicha; bachiche *m* AMER FAM eyetie [italiano].

bachiller *m/f* holder of the General Certificate of Education [US holder of a high school diploma] || HIST bachelor (de una universidad).

bachiller, ra *m/f* FIG & FAM chatterbox (hablador).
◆ *f* FIG & FAM bluestocking.

bachillerato *m* HIST bachelor's degree ⟶ **BUP.**

bachillerear *vi* FAM to prattle away (charlar).

bachillería *f* FAM prattle (charla).

badajada *f*; **badajazo** *m* stroke of a bell (de campana) || FIG & FAM rubbish, sth. stupid; *soltar una badajada* to talk rubbish, to come out with sth. stupid.

badajear *vi* to prattle away.

badajo *m* clapper (de campana) || FIG & FAM chatterbox (charlatán).

badajocense; badajoceño, ña *adj* [of *o* from] Badajoz.
◆ *m/f* native *o* inhabitant of Badajoz.

badana *f* sheepskin, basan, bazan (piel) || FIG & FAM *zurrarle a uno la badana* to tan s.o.'s hide (pegar), to give s.o. a dressing down (reprender).

badén *m* furrow drain (para las aguas de lluvia) || pothole, hole (en una carretera) || uneven road surface (señal de tráfico).

baderna *f* MAR nipper.

badián *m* anise (árbol).

badiana *f* aniseed (fruto).

badil *m*; **badila** *f* fire shovel || FIG & FAM *darle a uno con la badilla en los nudillos* to rap s.o.'s knuckles.

bádminton *m* badminton (juego del volante).

badulacada *f* FAM silly *o* stupid thing.

badulaque *m/f* fool, nincompoop (idiota) || AMER rogue (pillo).

baffle *m* RAD baffle (caja de resonancia).

baga *f* flaxseed head, boll.

bagaje *m* MIL baggage || AMER luggage [US baggage] (equipaje) || beast of burden (acémila) || FIG stock of knowledge (intelectual).

— OBSERV This word is a Gallicism in the sense of *luggage.*

bagar *vi* to go to seed (lino).

bagatela *f* knick-knack (objeto pequeño) || trifle; *no hay por qué enfadarse por bagatelas* it is not worth getting angry over such trifles || triviality; *no gastemos el tiempo en bagatelas* let us not waste time with trivialities.

bagazo *m* waste pulp (de la caña de azúcar) || husk (del lino) || marc (de aceitunas, uvas, etc.) || AMER cur (persona despreciable).

bagre *m* catfish (pez) || AMER FIG & FAM crafty one, sly one (persona lista) || hag (mujer fea) | unfriendly person (persona antipática).

bagual *adj* AMER wild (animal) | rough (persona).
◆ *m* AMER wild horse (caballo) | FIG bumpkin, yokel [*US* hick].

bagualada *f* AMER herd of wild horses || — FAM *decir bagualadas* to talk rubbish | *decir una bagualada* to come out with a stupid remark.

bagualón *m* half-tamed horse.

baguarí *m* AMER type of white stork.

baguío *m* hurricane [in the Philippines].

¡bah! *interj* bah!

Bahamas *npr fpl* GEOGR the Bahamas.

bahareque *m* AMER → **bajareque.**

baharí *m* hobby (halcón).

bahía *f* GEOGR bay; *la bahía de Málaga* the bay of Malaga.

Baikal (lago) *npr m* GEOGR Lake Baikal.

bailable *adj* for dancing, dance; *música bailable* music for dancing, dance music || — *esta música no es bailable* you can't dance to this music || AMER *té bailable* tea dance.
◆ *m* ballet (ballet).

bailador, ra *m/f* dancer.
— OBSERV This word applies to Spanish folk dancers, especially Flamenco dancers. It is usually written *bailaor.* In the more general sense, dancer is translated by *bailarín.*

bailaor, ra *m/f* Flamenco dancer.

bailar *vi* to dance || to spin (el trompo) || FIG to dance || FIG & FAM to swim; *mis pies bailan en los zapatos* my feet swim in these shoes || — *bailar agarrado* to dance close together || FIG *bailar al son que tocan* to toe the line, to run with the pack || *bailar como una peonza* or *un trompo* to spin like a top || FIG & FAM *bailar con la más fea* to get the short end of the stick || *bailar de puntas* to dance on points || FIG *bailar en la cuerda floja* to walk the tightrope || FIG & FAM *le bailaban los ojos de alegría* his eyes sparkled with joy || FIG *no saber a qué son bailar* not to know what road to take, to be in a quandary || FIG & FAM *otro que tal baila* they are two of a kind | *¡que me quiten lo bailado!* nothing can take away the good times I've had || *sacar a bailar a una chica* to ask a girl to dance.
◆ *vt* to dance; *bailar un vals* to dance a waltz || to spin (el trompo).

bailarín, ina *adj* dancing.
◆ *m/f* dancer || ballet dancer (de baile clásico).
◆ *f* ballerina (de baile clásico).

baile *m* dance; *música de baile* dance music || dancing (acción); *me gusta el baile* I like dancing || dance, ball (véase OBSERV); *voy al baile* I am going to the dance || ballroom, dance hall (lugar) || TEATR ballet || — *baile clásico* ballet || FAM *baile de candil* or *de botón gordo* local hop, public dance || *baile de etiqueta* ball, formal dance || *baile de gala* gala ball || *baile de máscaras* or *de disfraces* masked ball, fancy dress ball || *baile de piñata* carnival ball || *baile de San Vito* Saint Vitus's dance || *baile de trajes* fancy dress ball || *baile folklórico* folk dancing || FIG *dirigir el baile* to rule the roost, to run the show.
— OBSERV La palabra inglesa *ball* se refiere sobre todo a los bailes de etiqueta.

baile *m* bailiff (magistrado).

bailete *m* TEATR ballet.

bailía *f* bailiwick.

bailío *m* knight commander of Malta || bailiff (magistrado).

bailón, ona *m/f* FAM dancing enthusiast, keen dancer.

bailongo *m* AMER public dance.

bailotear *vi* to jig about, to dance about.

bailoteo *m* jigging about, dancing about; *le gusta mucho el bailoteo* he loves dancing about.

baivel *m* bevel (escuadra falsa).

baja *f* fall, drop, decrease (de los precios, de la temperatura) || drop (en la Bolsa) || ebb (de la marea) || MIL loss, casualty; *el ejército tuvo muchas bajas en el combate* the army suffered many losses in the battle || — *baja por enfermedad* sick leave || *dar de baja* to report missing (a un soldado muerto, un desertor), to discharge as unfit (en el servicio militar), to lay off (a un obrero, un empleado), to give notice to (despedir), to strike off the list (echar de una sociedad) || *darse de baja* to resign, to drop out (dejar de pertenecer, dimitir), to take sick leave (declararse enfermo) || *darse de baja en una suscripción* to withdraw one's subscription || *estar dado de baja* to be on sick leave, to be off sick (por enfermedad) || *estar de* or *en baja* to be dropping *o* falling *o* going down (perder valor) || *jugar a la baja* to bear (en la Bolsa) || *ser baja* to be reported missing (un soldado), to be struck off the list (en una sociedad, etc.).

bajá *m* pasha (dignatario turco).

bajada *f* ebb (de las aguas) || slope (pendiente) || descent, going down (descendimiento) || way down; *la bajada hacia el río* the way down to the river || drop (caída) || — *bajada de aguas* down pipe, down spout || *bajada de bandera* minimum fare (en un taxi) || *bajada del telón* fall *o* lowering of the curtain (teatro).

bajamar *m* low tide, low water.

bajante *f* AMER low tide, low water.

bajapieles *m inv* orange stick (de manicura).

bajar *vi* to go down, to descend, to sink; *el sol bajaba detrás de las colinas* the sun went down behind the hills || to come down; *bajaré a verte ahora mismo* I'll come down and see you right away || to go down; *no bajaré a verle* I will not go down and see him || to get off (de una bicicleta, un caballo, un autobús); *bajar del autobús* to get off the bus || to get out (de un coche) || to ebb, to go out *o* down (la marea) || to go down, to drop, to fall (los precios, la temperatura) || to fall (ventas, compras); *nuestros pedidos no han bajado de quinientos* our orders have not fallen below five hundred || to fail (la vista) || FIG to go down; *Miguel ha bajado en mi estima* Michael has gone down in my esteem || — *bajar de tono* to lower one's tone || *no bajará de dos horas* it will take at least two hours.
◆ *vt* to get *o* to bring *o* to take down; *bájame este libro de la repisa* get that book down from the shelf for me; *baja esta botella a la bodega* take this bottle down to the cellar; *bájame la maleta del desván* bring me the suitcase down from the attic || to lower (down); *bajar el cubo al pozo* to lower the bucket (down) into the well || to go down, to come down; *para ir a la cocina hay que bajar la escalera* to get to the kitchen you have to go down the stairs; *baja la escalera para que te hable* come down the stairs so that I can speak to you || to bow, to bend; *bajar la cabeza en signo de deferencia* to bow one's head in deference || to lower, to bend; *bajó la cabeza para pasar por la puerta* he lowered his head to go through the door || to put down; *baja el brazo* put your arm down || to turn down; *bajar las alas de un sombrero* to turn down the brim of a hat || to lower (cortina, párpados, voz, precios) || to give *o* to make a reduction; *me ha bajado la cuenta* he has given me a reduction on the bill || to turn down (radio, etc.) || to lessen (reducir) || — FIG *bajar el orgullo a uno* to take s.o. down a peg or two || *bajar el tono* to lower one's tone || FIG *bajarle los humos a uno* to put s.o. in his place, to take s.o. down a peg or two || *bajar sus pretensiones* to lower one's aspirations.
◆ *vpr* to stoop, to bend over *o* down (inclinarse) || to get off (de una bicicleta, un autobús, un caballo) || to get out (de un coche).
— OBSERV The verb *bajar* in the reflexive form can mean «to go or to come down with a certain effort»: *me bajo la escalera veinte veces al día* I go up and down the stairs twenty times a day.

bajareque; bahareque *m* AMER wattle and daub wall (pared) | hut, hovel (choza).

bajel *m* vessel, ship.

bajero, ra *adj* bottom, lower; *sábana bajera* bottom sheet.

bajete *m* MÚS baritone.

bajeza *f* baseness, lowness (del carácter, de los sentimientos) || vile deed *o* action (acción) || vulgarity (de una expresión).

bajial *m* AMER lowland, flood plain (tierra baja que se inunda).

bajines (por); bajini (por lo) *adv* FAM on the sly, on the quiet, in an underhand way; *hacer algo por bajines* to do sth. in an underhand way | in a whisper; *hablar por bajines* to speak in a whisper || FAM *reírse por lo bajini* to laugh up one's sleeve.

bajío *m* sandbank, shoal || AMER lowland.

bajista *m* bear.

bajito *adv* quietly, softly; *le gusta hablar bajito* he likes to speak quietly.

bajo, ja *adj* low; *una silla baja* a low chair || small, short (estatura); *una mujer muy baja* a very small woman || downcast, lowered, on the ground; *con los ojos bajos* with downcast eyes, with one's eyes on the ground || bowed, lowered; *con la cabeza baja* with bowed head || low (cifra, precios) || pale, pallid (color); *azul bajo* pale blue || base (metal) || low; *bajo latín* low Latin || lower (en comparación con algo más alto); *el Bajo Rin* the lower Rhine; *en la parte baja de la casa* in the lower part of the house || soft (sonido) || low (voz); *en voz baja* in a low voice || humble, low (nacimiento) || menial (tarea) || MÚS deep (sonido, voz) || FIG degrading (degradante) | vile, low (acción) | disgraceful, base (conducta) | lowly (de condición) | lower; *clase baja* lower class | base, contemptible (motivo) | overcast, low (cielo) || — *baja temporada* off season, slack season || *bajo relieve* low relief, bas-relief || FIG *bajos fondos* scum, dregs, depths (de la sociedad), low district *sing* (de una ciudad) || IMPR *caja baja* lower case || *de baja ralea* low-class || *en este bajo mundo* here below || *golpe bajo* low punch, blow below the belt || *los barrios bajos* the lower-class districts || *monte bajo* bush || *tierras bajas* lowlands.
◆ *adv* low; *este avión vuela bajo* this aeroplane flies low || in a low voice, softly; *hablar bajo* to speak in a low voice || quietly, softly; *cantar bajo* to sing quietly || *¡más bajo!* not so loud!
◆ *prep* under; *bajo la dominación romana* under Roman rule || under, underneath, beneath; *bajo el árbol* under the tree || on; *bajo palabra* on one's word || in; *bajo la lluvia* in the rain || below; *dos grados bajo cero* two degrees below zero || — *bajo el reinado de* in the reign of, under the reign of || *bajo juramento* under oath, on oath || *bajo mano* secretly, sneakily || *bajo pena de muerte* under penalty of death || *bajo tutela* under guardianship (un menor de edad), under trusteeship (un país) || *echando por bajo* at the very least, at the lowest estimate || *por lo bajo* in secret, on the quiet (*fam*) (en secreto), in a whisper, under one's breath

(en voz baja), at the very least (por lo menos) ‖ *tirando por lo bajo* at the very least, at the lowest estimate.
◆ *m* lowland (terreno) ‖ MAR shoal, sandbank ‖ hollow (hondonada) ‖ ground floor [*US* first floor] (piso) ‖ MÚS cellist (artista) | cello (instrumento) | bass (cantante, voz).
◆ *pl* underclothes (ropa interior) ‖ bottoms (de pantalones) ‖ hem *sing* (de una falda) ‖ ground floor *sing* [*US* first floor *sing*] (piso).

bajón *m* MÚS bassoon (instrumento) | bassoonist (músico) ‖ COM slump ‖ FIG & FAM great drop, fall (bajada brusca) | turn for the worse (salud, situación); *dar un bajón* to take a turn for the worse | fall, slump (de la moral).

bajonazo *m* TAUR ⟶ **golletazo.**

bajonista *m* MÚS bassoonist.

bajorrelieve *m* low relief, bas-relief.

bajura *f* *navegación de bajura* coasting ‖ *pesca de bajura* inshore fishing, coastal fishing.

bakelita *f* ⟶ **baquelita.**

bala *f* bullet (de escopeta, de pistola); *a prueba de balas* bullet-proof ‖ cannonball (de cañón) ‖ bale (de algodón) ‖ bale, pack (de lana) ‖ — *bala fría* spent bullet ‖ *bala perdida* stray bullet ‖ *bala trazadora* tracer bullet ‖ FIG *como una bala* like a shot ‖ *¿cuántas balas te quedan?* how many shots have you left? ‖ *AMER ni a bala* by no means ‖ FAM *salir como una bala* to shoot out.
◆ *m* FAM hooligan (golfo) ‖ — FIG & FAM *bala perdida* scatterbrain | *bala rasa* hothead, daredevil.

balacear *vt* *AMER* to shoot, to fire (tirotear).

balacera *f* *AMER* shoot-out (tiroteo).

balada *f* ballad (canción) ‖ ballade, ballad (poema).

baladí *adj* trivial, trifling; *asuntos baladíes* trivial matters.

baladronada *f* brag, boast (bravuconería) ‖ bravado, piece of bravado (acción) ‖ *decir* or *soltar baladronadas* to brag, to boast.

baladronear *vi* to brag, to boast.

balagar *m* haystack, hayrick.

bálago *m* grain stalk, straw (paja).

balaj; balaje *m* balas (rubí).

balalaica *f* MÚS balalaika.

balance *m* COM balance sheet (declaración); *hacer el balance* to draw up the balance sheet | stocktaking (inventario) | balance (de una cuenta) ‖ FIG result ‖ *hacer el balance (de)* to take stock (of), to make an inventory (of) (en una empresa), to weigh up, to take stock (of) (la situación).

balancé *m* balancing (paso de baile).

balancear *vt* to balance.
◆ *vi* FIG to hesitate (vacilar) ‖ to roll (un barco).
◆ *vpr* to rock (en una mecedora) ‖ to swing (en un columpio, etc.) ‖ to roll (un barco) ‖ to oscillate, to swing to and fro (un péndulo).

balanceo *m* swinging (de un columpio) ‖ rocking (de una mecedora) ‖ rolling, roll (barco) ‖ to-and-fro motion, oscillation (de un péndulo) ‖ *AMER* wheel balancing (equilibrado de ruedas).

balancín *m* swingletree (de vehículo) ‖ rudder bar (de avión) ‖ beam (de máquina) ‖ rocker, rocker arm (de motor) ‖ balance pole (de volatinero) ‖ seesaw [*US* seesaw, teeter-totter] (columpio) ‖ rocking chair (mecedora) ‖ outrigger (para dar estabilidad a una barca) ‖ coining press (para acuñar monedas).

balandra *f* MAR sloop (barco).

balandrista *m/f* MAR yachtsman (hombre), yachtswoman (mujer).

balandro *m* MAR yacht (de vela).

bálano; balano *m* ANAT glans penis ‖ acorn barnacle, balanus (molusco).

balanza *f* scales *pl*, balance (para pesar) ‖ COM balance; *balanza comercial, de cuentas, de pagos* balance of trade, of accounts, of payments ‖ comparison (confrontación) ‖ *AMER* balance pole (de volatinero) ‖ — *balanza de cocina* kitchen scales ‖ *balanza de precisión* precision balance ‖ *balanza romana* steelyard ‖ FIG *estar en la balanza* to be in the balance | *inclinar el fiel de la balanza* to tip the balance *o* the scales | *poner en balanza* to weigh up, to compare (comparar), to put in the balance (poner en juego).

Balanza *npr f* ASTR the Scales, Libra.

balar *vi* to bleat, to baa (las ovejas).

balarrasa *m* FIG hothead, daredevil.

balastar *vi* to ballast.

balasto; balastro *m* ballast (grava).

balata *f* ballade, ballad (poesía).

balaustrada *f* balustrade, railing.

balaustrar *vt* to build a balustrade on.

balaustre; balaústre *m* banister, baluster (columnita).

balay *m* *AMER* wicker basket.

balazo *m* shot (tiro) ‖ bullet wound (herida); *murió de un balazo* he died of a bullet wound ‖ *le dieron un balazo en el pecho* he was shot in the chest.

balboa *m* balboa [Panamanian currency].

balbucear; balbucir* *vt/vi* to stammer, to stutter ‖ to babble (un niño).

balbuceo *m* stammering, stuttering ‖ babble, babbling (de un niño).

balbuciente *adj* stammering, stuttering ‖ babbling (niño).

balbucir* *vt/vi* ⟶ **balbucear.**

Balcanes *npr mpl* GEOGR Balkans.

balcánico, ca *adj* Balkan.

balcón *m* balcony; *asomarse al balcón* to look over the balcony ‖ FIG & FAM *es cosa de alquilar balcones* it is sth. not to be missed, it is sth. worth seeing.

balconada *f*; **balconaje** *m* row of balconies.

balconcillo *m* enclosure over the bullpen (en la plaza de toros) ‖ TEATR dress circle.

balconear *vt* *AMER* to watch out of the window.
◆ *vi* *AMER* to talk at the window.

balda *f* shelf (de un armario).

baldada *f* *AMER* bucket.

baldado, da *adj* crippled, disabled ‖ FIG & FAM shattered (cansado).
◆ *m/f* cripple (inválido).

baldaquín; baldaquino *m* baldachin, canopy.

baldar *vt* to cripple, to maim, to disable ‖ to trump (en los naipes) ‖ FAM to beat up (dar una paliza) | to inconvenience (molestar) | to cripple; *este impuesto le ha baldado* this tax has crippled him ‖ FAM *estar* or *quedarse baldado* to be shattered [*US* to be bushed] (estar cansado).
◆ *vpr* FIG & FAM to wear o.s. out, to break one's back.

balde *m* MAR pail (cubo de madera) ‖ bucket (de metal) ‖ — FIG & FAM *caerle a uno como un balde de agua fría* to hit s.o. like a ton of bricks ‖ FIG *de balde* free of charge, free; *viajar de balde* to travel free of charge ‖ *en balde* in vain, for nothing; *tanto esfuerzo en balde* so much effort in vain.

baldear *vt* to swill down, to wash down (lavar) ‖ to bale out (achicar).

baldeo *m* swilling.

baldíamente *adv* in vain, fruitlessly, for nothing.

baldío, a *adj* waste, uncultivated (sin cultivo); *terreno baldío* waste land ‖ AGR uncultivated ‖ FIG useless, fruitless, vain; *esfuerzos baldíos* vain efforts.
◆ *m* waste *o* uncultivated land.

baldón *m* insult (afrenta); *esto es un baldón para nosotros* this is an insult to us ‖ shame, disgrace; *este hijo es el baldón de la familia* this son is the shame of the family.

baldonar *vt* to insult ‖ to disgrace, to shame.

baldosa *f* tile ‖ flagstone (de mayor tamaño).

baldosar *vt* to tile (con baldosas pequeñas) ‖ to flag (con baldosas grandes).

baldosín *m* tile.

baldragas *adj* FAM spineless, meek.
◆ *m inv* FAM mouse.

balduque *m* tape (cinta) ‖ FIG red tape (papeleo).

balear *vt* *AMER* to shoot (matar a balazos, disparar contra).

balear *adj* Balearic; *islas Baleares* Balearic Islands.
◆ *m/f* native *o* inhabitant of the Balearic Islands.
◆ *f pl* GEOGR Balearics.

baleárico, ca *adj* Balearic.

balénidos *m pl* ZOOL whales.

baleo *m* mat (estera) ‖ *AMER* exchange of shots (tiroteo).

balido *m* bleat (grito de las ovejas) ‖ bleating (varios gritos) ‖ *dar balidos* to bleat, to baa.

balín *m* small bullet (pequeña bala) ‖ shot (perdigón).

balista *m* MIL ballista.

balístico, ca *adj* ballistic; *proyectiles balísticos* ballistic missiles.
◆ *f* ballistics.

balita *f* *AMER* marble (canica).

balitar *vi* to bleat continually.

baliza *f* MAR buoy, beacon ‖ AVIAC beacon.

balizar *vt* MAR to mark out with buoys, to beacon ‖ AVIAC to mark out with beacons, to beacon.

balneario, ria *adj* *estación balnearia* spa, watering place (medicinal), seaside resort (con playa).
◆ *m* spa, watering place (medicinal), seaside resort (con playa).

balneoterapia *f* balneotherapy.

balompédico, ca *adj* of football, football [*US* of soccer, soccer].

balompié *m* football [*US* soccer].

balón *m* ball, football (pelota) ‖ QUÍM bag ‖ bale (fardo) ‖ — *balón alto* lob [*US* fly ball] (fútbol), up-and-under (rugby) ‖ *balón de fútbol* football ‖ *balón de oxígeno* oxigen cylinder ‖ *balón muerto* dead ball.

balonazo *m* blow [from a ball].

baloncesto *m* basketball; *jugador de baloncesto* basketball player.

balonmano *m* handball (juego).

balonvolea *m* volleyball (juego).

balota *f* ballot (para votar).

balotada *f* ballotade (salto del caballo).

balotaje *m* *AMER* voting (votación) | tie (empate en una elección).

balotar *vi* *AMER* to ballot, to vote by ballot papers.

balsa *f* raft (embarcación); *balsa insuflable* inflatable raft ‖ pond, pool (charca) ‖ BOT balsa (árbol y madera) || AMER ferry || — FIG *como una balsa (de aceite)* as calm as a millpond (mar) | *este lugar es una balsa de aceite* this is a very quiet place.

balsadera *f*; **balsadero** *m* ferry crossing.

balsamera *f* flask for balsam.

balsamero *m* balsam fir (árbol).

balsámico, ca *adj* balsamic, balmy, soothing || BOT *álamo balsámico* balsam poplar.

balsamina *f* balsam apple (planta).

bálsamo *m* balm, balsam || BOT balsam || FIG balm.

balsar *m* AMER overgrown marshland.

balsero *m* ferryman.

Baltasar *npr m* Balthasar || Belshazzar (de Babilonia).

báltico, ca *adj* Baltic; *el mar Báltico* the Baltic Sea.
◆ *m* Baltic language (lengua).

Báltico *npr m* GEOGR Baltic Sea.

balto, ta *adj/s* Baltic.

baluarte *m* bastion, bulwark || FIG bastion, bulwark, stronghold; *esta provincia es un baluarte del Cristianismo* this province is a bulwark of Christianity.

baluma; balumba *f* bulk (bulto) || pile (montón) || racket, din (barullo) || mess (desorden).

ballena *f* whale (mamífero) || stay, bone (de corsé) || bone (de cuello) || ASTR whale.

ballenato *m* whale calf, young whale.

ballenero, ra *adj* whaling.
◆ *m* whaler (pescador) || whaler, whaling ship (barco).
◆ *f* whaler, whaling ship (barco).

ballesta *f* crossbow (arma antigua) || ballista (máquina de guerra) || spring (de coche).

ballestero *m* crossbowman || maker of crossbows.

ballestilla *f* swingletree (balancín pequeño) || fleam (navajilla de veterinario).

ballet *m* ballet (baile y música); *los ballets rusos* the Russian ballets.

ballico *m* BOT rye grass.

ballueca *f* wild oats *pl* (gramínea).

bamba *f* fluke (en el billar) || AMER name of several currencies | knar (en un árbol) | «bamba» [popular Mexican dance] (baile).

bambalear *vi* ⟶ **bambolear.**

bambalina *f* TEATR border || — FIG *actor nacido entre bambalinas* actor born into the profession, actor born on the stage | *detrás de las bambalinas* behind the scenes.

bambalinón *m* TEATR valance.

bambarria *m/f* FAM dumb (tonto).
◆ *f* fluke (en el billar).

bambino, na *m/f* AMER child.

bamboche *m* FAM plump person.

bambolear (se); bambalear (se) *vi/vpr* to swing || to sway, to reel (titubear al andar, etc.) || to sway; *el árbol se bambolea* the tree sways || to wobble; *la mesa se bambolea* the table wobbles || to rock, to roll; *el barco se bambolea* the ship is rolling || to sway, to rock (vehículo) || *hacer bambolear* to rock.

bamboleo *m* swinging || rocking, rolling (de un barco) || swaying, rocking (de un coche) || wobble; *el bamboleo de la mesa me impide escribir* the wobble of the table prevents me from writing || swaying, reeling (de una persona) || swaying (de un árbol, etc.).

bambolla *f* FAM sham, show (fachada) | show, fuss; *una fiesta con mucha bambolla* a party with lots of show || AMER chatter (charla) | bragging (fanfarronería).

bambollero, ra *adj* FAM bragging (fanfarrón) | showy (aparatoso).

bambú *m* BOT bamboo.
— OBSERV The plural form of *bambú* is *bambúes.*

banal *adj* banal, commonplace.

banalidad *f* banality || triviality (palabra).

banana *f* banana (fruto) || banana tree (árbol).
— OBSERV In Spain the usual word for *banana* or *banana tree* is *plátano. Banana* or *banano* is usually employed in Latin America.

bananal; bananar *m* AMER banana plantation.

bananero, ra *adj* banana; *producción bananera* banana production.
◆ *m* banana tree (árbol) || banana boat (barco).

banano *m* banana (fruto) || banana tree (árbol).

banasta *f* hamper, large basket (cesto).

banastero, ra *m/f* basket maker (fabricante) || basket dealer (vendedor).

banasto *m* large round basket (cesto).

banca *f* bench (asiento) || bank (juegos); *hacer saltar la banca* to break the bank || COM banking; *el sector de la banca* the banking sector | bank (establecimiento de crédito) || stand (de lavandera) || type of Philippine canoe || AMER bench (asiento, escaño en el Parlamento) || — COM *banca oficial* official banks, state banking institution | *banca privada* private banks || *copar la banca* to hold the bank (bacarrá) || AMER *tener banca* to have connections (tener influencias) || *tener la banca* to be banker.
— OBSERV At present the word *banca* or *casa de banca* is rarely used to mean a banking establishment, the usual term being *banco,* but, when referring to the banking profession or to all the banks as a whole, *banca* is commonly employed: *la nacionalización de la banca, la banca hace jornada intensiva.*

bancada *f* stone bench (banco) || large table (mesa) || thwart (de un bote de remos) || TECN bed (soporte) || MIN step.
◆ *pl* litter *sing* (en una cuadra).

bancal *m* patch, bed (de verduras); *bancal de lechugas* lettuce patch || terrace (en una montaña) || bench cover (tapete) || *campo de bancales* terraced field.

bancario, ria *adj* bank; *descuento bancario* bank discount; *cheque bancario* bank check || banking; *sistema bancario* banking system.

bancarrota *f* bankruptcy || FIG bankruptcy, complete failure || *hacer bancarrota* to go bankrupt.

banco *m* bench (de piedra, de madera, de carpintero) || settee (en un salón, en una antesala) || pew (en una iglesia) || form, desk (en el colegio) || COM bank (establecimiento de crédito) (véase OBSERV en BANCA) || bank, shoal (de arena) || thwart (de una barca) || shoal, school (de peces) || JUR box [US seat] (de los testigos) || ARQ attic, garret (sotabanco) || GEOL layer (estrato) || AMER dock (de los acusados) | bank (juego) || — *banco agrícola* farmer's bank || *banco azul* front bench (en las Cortes) || *banco comercial* commercial *o* trade bank || *banco de ahorros* savings bank || *banco de arena* sandbank || MAR *banco de coral* coral reef || *banco de crédito* credit bank || INFORM *banco de datos* data bank || *banco de emisión* or *emisor* issuing bank || *banco de hielo* ice floe || *banco del Comercio* bank of Commerce || *banco de liquidación* clearing house || *banco de nieve* snowbank || *banco de negocios* merchant bank || *banco de préstamos* lending bank [US loans bank] || *banco de pruebas* testing bench || *banco de sangre* blood bank || *banco de semen* sperm bank || *banco hipotecario* mortgage bank || *Banco Mundial* World Bank || *banco por acciones* joint-stock bank || *billete de banco* bank note || *empleado de banco* bank clerk.

banda *f* sash, band (faja) || ribbon (cinta, condecoración) || strip (de una momia) || party, group (grupo de personas) || throng (multitud de personas) || gang, pack (de ladrones, de gente desordenada) || group (de animales en general) || flock (de pájaros) || covey (de perdices) || side (lado); *de la banda de acá de la montaña* on this side of the mountain || bank (orilla); *de la banda de allá del río* on the opposite bank of the river || lane (de una carretera) || strip (de tierra) || wing (de un partido político) || cushion (billar); *jugar por la banda* to play off the cushion || MÚS band || RAD band; *banda de frecuencia* frequency band || MAR side; *de banda a banda* from side to side || HERÁLD bend || REL humerus || AMER leaf (de puerta) | flap (de ventana) || — MAR *arriar en banda* to cast off || MAR *banda de estribor* starboard side || *banda de rodadura* tread (de una rueda) || *banda de tambores* drum corps || *banda magnética* magnetic tape (para grabar) || CINEM *banda sonora* sound track || *banda transportadora* conveyor belt || ECON *bandas de fluctuación* (exchange rates) band || FIG & FAM *cerrarse en banda* to stick to one's guns || MAR *dar a la banda* to lie alongside ship || DEP *fuera de banda* in touch || MAR *irse a la banda* to list || DEP *juez de banda* linesman (fútbol, tenis), touch judge (rugby) | *línea de banda* sideline, touchline | *quedarse en la banda* to stay on the sideline | *saque de banda* throw-in (fútbol), line-out (rugby).

bandada *f* flock (de pájaros) || covey (de perdices) || shoal, school (de peces) || party (de personas).

bandazo *m* MAR violent roll || FAM stroll (paseo) || *dar bandazos* to swerve, to lurch (coche).

bandear *vt* AMER to cross (cruzar) | to shoot through (traspasar de un balazo) | to pursue (perseguir) | to wound (herir) | to court (a una mujer).
◆ *vpr* to manage, to look after o.s., to get by; *sabe bandearse* he knows how to manage, he can look after himself.

bandeja *f* tray || AMER dish (fuente) || — *bandeja para los cubiletes de hielo* ice tray || FIG *en bandeja de plata* on a silver platter *o* plate | *poner* or *traer algo en bandeja a alguien* to hand sth. to s.o. on a plate.

bandera *f* flag; *la bandera española* the Spanish flag; *bandera blanca* white flag || flag, colours *pl* [US colors]; *izar la bandera* to hoist the flag *o* the colours; *la bandera del regimiento* the regimental colours || banner (estandarte); *la bandera de una cofradía* the banner of a guild || (ant) MIL company (compañía) || — FIG *a banderas desplegadas* in the open, openly || MAR *afianzar* or *afirmar* or *asegurar la bandera* to enforce the colours by a shot || MIL *alzar* or *levantar (la) bandera* to raise men || MAR *arriar (la) bandera* to haul down the flag, to strike one's colours || *bajada de bandera* minimum fare (taxi) || MAR *bandera amarilla* quarantine flag || *bandera de Gran Bretaña* Union Jack, British flag || MAR *bandera de inteligencia* answering flag || *bandera de los Estados Unidos de América* Stars and Stripes, American flag || *bandera de parlamento* or *de paz* flag of truce || MAR *bandera de popa* ensign | *bandera de práctico* pilot flag | *bandera de proa* jack || *bandera a media asta* flag at half-mast || MIL *batir banderas* to salute with the colours || FIG & FAM *de bandera* terrific || *jurar la bandera* to swear allegiance *or* to take the pledge of allegiance to the flag || FIG & FAM *lleno hasta la bandera* full to the brim, packed full || *militar bajo* or *seguir la bandera de uno* to follow s.o.'s flag || MAR *rendir la bandera* to salute with the colours || MIL *salir con banderas desplegadas* to come out with flying colours.

bandería *f* faction, party (partido).

banderilla *f* TAUR «banderilla» || IMPR sticker indicating a correction || cocktail snack on a stick (tapa) || *AMER* FIG & FAM tapping, touching (sablazo) || — TAUR *banderilla de fuego* banderilla with fireworks attached || FIG & FAM *clavar* or *plantar* or *poner banderillas a uno* to taunt s.o., to goad s.o.

banderillazo *m* *AMER* FAM tapping, touching (sablazo).

banderillear *vt* TAUR to stick the «banderillas» in (a bull).

banderillero *m* TAUR «banderillero».

banderín *m* MIL pennant (bandera) | pennant bearer (soldado) || signal flag (ferrocarriles) || DEP flag (de un juez de línea) || *banderín de enganche* recruiting office.

banderita *f* little flag || *fiesta de la banderita* flag day.

banderizo, za *adj* factious, seditious || FIG turbulent, fiery.

banderola *f* banderole || MIL pennant (con dos o varias puntas) || *AMER* transom (de una puerta).

bandidaje *m* banditry, brigandage.

bandido *m* bandit, outlaw, brigand || FIG crook, bandit; *este comerciante es un bandido* this shopkeeper is a crook.

bando *m* edict, proclamation; *echar un bando* to proclaim an edict, to make a proclamation || decree; *bando de policía, de la alcaldía* police decree, mayor's decree || party, faction (facción) || flock (de pájaros) || shoal, school (de peces) || FIG *pasarse al otro bando* to go over to the other side.
◆ *pl* marriage banns (amonestaciones).

bandola *f* MÚS mandolin, mandoline || MAR jurymast.

bandolera *f* (woman) bandit (mujer) || bandoleer, bandolier (correa) || — *a la* or *en bandolera* over one's shoulder || *a la bandolera* in a sling (brazo).

bandolerismo *m* banditry, brigandage.

bandolero *m* brigand, bandit, highwayman (bandido).

bandolina *f* MÚS mandolin, mandoline (bandola).

bandolinista *m/f* mandoline player.

bandoneón *m* MÚS concertina.

bandullo *m* FAM paunch, belly (vientre).

bandurria *f* MÚS mandola, mandora.

Bangkok *n pr* GEOGR Bangkok.

Bangla Desh *n pr* GEOGR Bangladesh.

Bangui *n pr* GEOGR Bangui.

baniano *m* banian (miembro de una secta brahmánica).

banjo *m* MÚS banjo.

Banjul *n pr* GEOGR Banjul.

banquear *vt* *AMER* to level.

banquero, ra *m/f* banker.

banqueta *f* bench, long seat, form (banco corrido) || wall seat (de restaurante, etc.) || stool (taburete) || footstool (para los pies) || banquette, bank (terraplén) || MIL berm, banquette || pavement [*US* sidewalk] (acera).

banquetazo *m* slap-up meal, huge feast.

banquete *m* banquet, feast (festín); *banquete de boda* wedding banquet.

banquetear *vt/vi* to banquet.

banquillo *m* JUR dock || stool, footstool (taburete) || bench (de zapatero) || FIG *colocar* or *sentar a uno en el banquillo de los acusados* to have s.o. on the carpet.

banquisa *f* ice floe, ice field.

bántam *m* DEP bantamweight || *gallina bántam* bantam.

banzo *m* frame, edge (del bastidor para bordar) || upright (de una escalera de mano, de una silla).

baña *f* → **bañadero.**

bañada *f* *AMER* swim (baño).

bañadera *f* *AMER* bath, bathtub (bañera).

bañadero *m*; **baña** *f* lair (de un jabalí).

bañado *m* *AMER* marsh, bog, swamp (pantano).

bañador, ra *m/f* bather, swimmer (que se baña).
◆ *m* bathing costume, swimsuit, bathing suit (traje de baño de mujer y de hombre), bathing trunks *pl* (de hombre) || — *bañador de dos piezas* two-piece swimsuit, two-piece bathing costume || *bañador de una pieza* one-piece swimsuit.

bañar *vt* to bath, to bathe (a un niño) || to dip, to bathe, to immerse (un cuerpo) || to wash (el mar); *costas bañadas por el mar* coasts washed by the sea || to water, to wash (un río); *el arroyo bañaba hermosas huertas* the brook watered some beautiful gardens || to coat, to cover; *un pastel bañado en chocolate* a cake coated in chocolate || to bathe, to flood (luz, sol, etc.); *el sol baña la habitación de una luz cruda* the sun floods the room with *o* bathes the room in a harsh light || FIG *bañado en llanto* or *en lágrimas, en sangre, en sudor* bathed in tears, in blood, in sweat.
◆ *vpr* to bathe, to have a swim, to go swimming (en el mar) || to take *o* to have a bath (en la bañera).

bañera *f* bath, bathtub (baño).

bañil *m* lair (de un jabalí).

bañista *m/f* bather, swimmer (en el mar) || patient at a spa (en un balneario).

baño *m* bath || swim, dip (de mar, de río) || bath, bathtub (bañera) || coat (capa); *un baño de pintura* a coat of paint || coating, covering (de chocolate, etc.) || FIG smattering; *allí reciben un baño de formación militar* there they receive a smattering of military training | touch; *tiene un cierto baño de distinción* he has a touch of class || QUÍM bath || — *baño de asiento, de vapor* hip bath, steam bath || *baño (de) maría* bain-marie || FIG *baño de sangre* bloodbath || *baño de sol* sunbath || *baño turco* Turkish bath; *esta habitación es un baño turco* it is like a Turkish bath in here || *darse un baño* to take a bath || FIG *darse un baño de francés, de matemáticas, etc.* to brush up one's French, mathematics, etc. || FAM *dar un baño a uno* to outshine s.o. (superar), to beat s.o. hollow; *el equipo rojo ha dado un baño al equipo verde* the read team beat the green team hollow || *tomar un baño* to take a bath || *tomar un baño de mar* to go for a swim, to take a dip, to bathe in the sea || *tomar un baño de sol* to sunbathe.
◆ *pl* baths || — *baños de mar* sea bathing || *casa de baños* public baths || *ir a los baños* to take the waters, to go for a water cure.

bao *m* MAR beam.

baobab *m* BOT baobab.

baptista *m/f* baptist.

baptisterio *m* baptistry, baptistery (edificio) || font (pila).

baque *m* bang, bump (golpe) || fall (caída).

baqueano, na *adj/s* → **baquiano.**

baquear *vi* MAR to drift with the current.

baquelita; bakelite *f* bakelite.

baqueta *f* cleaning rod, ramrod (de fusil) || ARQ beading || FIG & FAM *llevar* or *mandar* or *tratar a la baqueta* to rule with an iron hand, to treat harshly.
◆ *pl* drumsticks (de tambor).

baqueteado, da *adj* hardened (avezado) || experienced (experimentado).

baquetear *vt* FIG to treat harshly (tratar mal) | to train, to harden, to season (ejercitar) | to bother, to put out (incomodar).

baqueteo *m* bother (molestia) || hardening, seasoning, training (ejercitación) || jolting, shaking (traqueteo).

baquía *f* local knowledge, local expertise (conocimiento de una región) || *AMER* skill, expertise (habilidad).

baquiano, na; baqueano, na *adj* experienced, expert (experto); *ser baquiano en el comercio* to be experienced in commerce.
◆ *m/f* guide (guía) || *AMER* local expert.

báquira; baquira *f* *AMER* ZOOL peccary.

bar *m* bar, café, snack bar || bar (unidad de presión atmosférica).

baraca *f* luck (suerte).

baracuda *f* barracuda (pez).

barahúnda; baraúnda *f* uproar, row, din (alboroto) || confusion, chaos, uproar (confusión); *meterse en la barahúnda* to get mixed up in the confusion.

baraja *f* pack [of cards], deck [of cards] (de naipes) || FIG quarrel, argument (disputa) || FIG & FAM *jugar con dos barajas* to double-deal.
— OBSERV The Spanish *pack* is composed of 48 cards.
— OBSERV La baraja *inglesa* consta de 52 cartas.

barajar *vi* to fall out (enemistarse).
◆ *vt* to shuffle (naipes) || FIG to mix up, to shuffle around (mezclar, revolver) | to juggle with, to play with (cifras, nombres) | to be in the balance; *barajaron varios nombres para esta colocación* several names were in the balance for this job || *AMER* FIG to catch (agarrar al vuelo) | to hinder, to obstruct, to get in the way of (estorbar) || FIG *barajar ideas* to toy with ideas.

baranda *f* handrail, banister (de escalera) || balustrade, handrail, railing (de un balcón) || cushion (de billar).

barandal *m* base (larguero inferior de una balaustrada) || rail, handrail (larguero superior) || banister (barandilla).

barandilla *f* handrail, banister (de una escalera) || balustrade (balaustrada) || handrail, balustrade, railing (de un balcón) || bar (de un tribunal) || *AMER* rail (de un carro).

baratear *vt* to sell off cheap, to sell at a loss (saldar).

baratería *f* JUR barratry || fraud, fraudulence (fraude) || MAR barratry.

baratía *f* *AMER* cheapness, low price.

baratija *f* trinket, bauble (fruslería).
◆ *pl* rubbish *sing*, junk *sing* (cosas sin valor).

baratillero *m* secondhand dealer, junk dealer.

baratillo *m* secondhand shop, junk shop (tienda) || secondhand sale, jumble sale (subasta) || secondhand goods *pl*, jumble, junk (conjunto de cosas).

barato, ta *adj* cheap, inexpensive (no caro); *una falda barata* a cheap skirt || — *lo barato es* or *sale caro* cheap things are dear in the long run || *salir barato* to turn out cheap.
◆ *m* sale, bargain sale, clearance sale (venta).

◆ *adv* cheap, cheaply; *vender barato* to sell cheap *o* cheaply.

báratro *m* POÉT kingdom of the dead, Hades (infierno).

baratura *f* cheapness, low price.

baraúnda *f* —→ **barahúnda.**

barba *f* beard (pelo); *barba cerrada* or *bien poblada* thick beard (véase OBSERV) || beard (de cabra, etc.) || wattle (de ave) || chin (parte de la cara) || whalebone (de ballena) || AGR swarm (enjambre) | upper part of beehive (de la colmena) || — *barba corrida* full beard || FAM *con toda la barba* for good || *hacer la barba* to shave (afeitar), to butter up (adular) || FIG *hazme la barba, hacerte he el copete* you scratch my back and I will scratch yours || *llevar* or *gastar barba* to have a beard || FIG & FAM *nos salió a tanto por barba* it cost us so much per head | *tener pelos en la barba* to be old enough to look after o.s.
◆ *pl* barbs (de pluma, flecha, planta, papel) || beard *sing*; *barbas enmarañadas* bushy beard || — *barbas de chivo* goatee || FIG *cuando las barbas del vecino veas pelar, echa las tuyas a remojar* when the next house is on fire, it's high time to look to your own || FAM *echar a las barbas de uno* to throw in s.o.'s face | *en las barbas de uno* to *o* in s.o.'s face; *reírse en las barbas de uno* to laugh to *o* in s.o.'s face || *subirse a las barbas de* to treat disrespectfully || *tener pocas barbas* to be wet behind the ears || *tirarse de las barbas* to tear one's hair out.
— OBSERV *Barba* is also expressed in the plural form in Spanish, usually to indicate a thick or bushy beard.

barba *m* TEATR old man's part (comediante).

Barba Azul *npr m* Bluebeard.

barbacana *f* barbican (fortificación, tronera).

barbacoa *f* barbecue (parrilla) || barbecued *o* grilled meat (carne asada) || AMER litter, rough bed [made from a mat of rushes fastened to four stakes] | hut [built on stilts or in a tree] (choza) | loft (para guardar los granos).

barbada *f* lower jaw (de un caballo) || curb (cadenilla del freno) || brill (pez) || AMER chin strap.

barbado, da *adj* bearded.
◆ *m* shoot (sarmiento) || cutting (esqueje) || shoot, sucker (rama que brota al pie de un árbol).

Barbados *n pr* GEOGR Barbados.

Bárbara *npr f* Barbara.

barbaridad *f* barbarity, cruelty (crueldad) || outrage, atrocity; *durante la guerra se cometieron barbaridades* during the war outrages were committed || FIG nonsense (palabra); *decir barbaridades* to talk *o* to speak nonsense | terrible thing (acción) || — FAM *comer una barbaridad* to eat an awful lot *o* like a horse | *costar una barbaridad* to cost a fortune | *habla una barbaridad* she goes on and on, she never stops talking || FIG & FAM *hacer barbaridades* to act the fool | *me divertí una barbaridad* I had a marvellous time | *¡qué barbaridad!* how awful!, how terrible! (¡qué vergüenza!), good grief!, fancy that! (de asombro), it's amazing *o* incredible; *¡qué barbaridad, hay que ver cómo las ciencias adelantan!* it's incredible the way science progresses | *se ve una barbaridad* it is terribly obvious (es evidente), you see them everywhere (se ven mucho) | *una barbaridad* an awful lot, a lot, lots; *bebe una barbaridad* he drinks an awful lot; *una barbaridad de libros* lots of books, an awful lot of books.

barbarie *f* FIG barbarism, barbarity.

barbarismo *m* GRAM barbarism || FIG barbarity (crueldad).

bárbaro, ra *adj* HIST barbarian || FIG barbaric, barbarous (cruel, grosero); *un soldado bárbaro* a barbarous *o* barbaric soldier | daring, bold, reckless (temerario) || rough, uncouth (bruto) || FAM fantastic, terrific, fabulous, marvellous (muy bueno); *esta película es bárbara* this film is fantastic | massive (muy grande) || — FAM *hace un calor bárbaro* it is terribly hot | *hacer un efecto bárbaro* to have a tremendous effect | *lo he pasado bárbaro* I had a great *o* a fantastic time | *¡qué bárbaro!* fantastic!, great!
◆ *m/f* barbarian || FIG lout, brute.
◆ *interj* FAM great!, fantastic!

barbarote, ta *adj* FAM brutish, savage.
◆ *m/f* FAM brute.

barbear *vt* AMER to shave (afeitar) | to butter up (adular) | to throw (un animal).

barbechar *vt* AGR to leave fallow (dejar descansar la tierra) | to fallow, to plough (arar).

barbechera *f*; **barbecho** *m* AGR fallow land, fallow || *estar en barbecho* to be left fallow, to be in fallow.

barbería *f* barber's shop, barber's.

barberil *adj* FAM barber's.

barbero, ra *adj* *navaja barbera* cutthroat razor [US straight razor].
◆ *m* barber.

barbeta *f* barbette (fortificación).

barbián *m* FAM gay dog.

barbicano *adj m* with a white *o* grey beard, white-bearded, grey-bearded; *un hombre barbicano* a white-bearded man, a man with a white beard.

barbicastaño *adj m* with a brown beard, brown-bearded.

barbiespeso *adj m* with a bushy beard, thick-bearded.

barbijo *m* AMER —→ **barboquejo.**

barbilampiño *adj m* smoothfaced, beardless (sin barba) || with a scanty beard (con poca barba).
◆ *m* FIG greenhorn, novice (novicio).

barbilindo; barbilucio *m* dandy.

barbilla *f* ANAT chin || barb, barbel (de pez) || TECN tenon || VET ranula.

barbillas *m* AMER scantily bearded man.

barbillera *f* chin strap.

barbinegro *adj m* black-bearded.

barbiquejo *m* chin strap (barboquejo) || AMER halter (cabestro) || MAR *barbiquejo de bauprés* bobstay.

barbirrojo *adj m* red-bearded, ginger-bearded.

barbirrubio *adj m* fair-bearded, blond-bearded.

barbirrucio *adj m* grey-bearded.

barbitúrico *adj/sm* QUÍM barbiturate.

barbo *m* barbel (pez) || *barbo de mar* red mullet (salmonete).

barbón *m* bearded man || he-goat, billy goat (macho cabrío).

barboquejo; barbuquejo *m* chin strap.

barbotar; barbotear *vt/vi* to mumble, to mutter.

barboteo *m* mumbling, muttering.

barbotina *f* TECN barbotine, slip (cerámica).

Barbuda *npr f* GEOGR Barbuda.

barbudo, da *adj* bearded.
◆ *m* AMER shoot, sucker (de árbol).

barbulla *f* FAM din, row.

barbullador, ra *m/f* stammerer.

barbullar *vi* to stammer.

barbullón, ona *m/f* stammerer.

barbuquejo *m* —→ **barboquejo.**

barca *f* boat; *barca de pesca* fishing boat || *barca de pasaje* ferryboat.

barcada *f* boatload (carga de una barca) || crossing (viaje).

barcaje *m* ferrying, transport (transporte) || fare (lo que se paga).

barcarola *f* MÚS barcarolle, barcarole.

barcaza *f* lighter, barge (embarcación) || ferryboat, ferry (transbordador) || MIL *barcaza de desembarco* landing craft.

Barcelona *n pr* GEOGR Barcelona.

barcelonés, esa *adj* [of *o* from] Barcelona.
◆ *m/f* native *o* inhabitant of Barcelona.

barceo *m* BOT esparto, esparto grass.

barcia *f* chaff (del trigo).

barcino, na *adj* reddish, rust-coloured (color).
◆ *m/f* AMER FIG & FAM turncoat (que muda de partido).

barco *m* boat; *ir en barco* to go by boat || ship, vessel (grande) || car, nacelle (de un globo) || cockpit, capsule (de nave espacial) || gully, shallow ravine (barranco) || — *barco aljibe* or *cisterna* tanker || *barco bomba* fireboat || *barco de guerra* warship || *barco del práctico* pilot boat || *barco de pasajeros* liner, passenger liner || *barco de recreo* pleasure boat || *barco de vapor* steamer, steam boat (pequeño), steam ship, steamer (grande) || *barco de velas* sailing boat (pequeño), sailing ship (grande), yacht (yate) || *barco escuela* training ship || *barco faro* lightship || *barco mercante* or *de carga* merchant boat, cargo boat (pequeño), merchant ship, cargo ship (grande) || *barco náufrago* wreck, wrecked ship || *barco ómnibus* pleasure boat, pleasure steamer || *barco patrullero* patrol boat.
— OBSERV *Barco* is a very general term: *buque* and *navío* are only used for vessels of large tonnage; *nave* is a poetic or archaic word (*las naves de Cristóbal Colón*).

barchilón, ona *m/f* AMER nurse (de un hospital) | quack (curandero).

barda *f* bard (armadura de caballo) || protective covering of brambles [on a wall] (de una tapia) || MAR low black cloud (nubarrón oscuro).

bardado, da *adj* barded (caballo).

bardal *m* bramble-topped wall (tapia) || fence (vallado).

bardana *f* BOT burdock (lampazo).

bardar *vt* to top with brambles (una tapia) || to bard (con una armadura).

bardo *m* bard (poeta).

baremo *m* scale, schedule (de impuestos, de precios) || ready reckoner (libro para hacer cálculos).

bargueño *m* decorated Spanish cabinet.
— OBSERV The *bargueño*, a typically Spanish piece of furniture, is a richly decorated cabinet which stands on legs and has a large number of small drawers.

baria *f* barye (unidad de presión).

baricentro *m* barycentre.

bario *m* barium (metal).

barita *f* QUÍM baryta.

baritina *f* MIN barytes.

barítono *m* MÚS baritone.

barloa *f* MAR mooring rope.

barloar *vt* MAR to moor (a un muelle) | to moor alongside (un barco con otro).

barloventear *vi* MAR to tack to windward || FIG & FAM to wander about (vagabundear).

barlovento *m* MAR windward; *banda de barlovento* windward side; *estar a barlovento* to be to windward || GEOGR *islas de Barlovento* Windward Isles.

barman *m* barman.
— OBSERV In Spanish the plural of *barman* is *barmans*.

barn *m* FÍS barn (unidad de superficie).

barnabita *adj/s* barnabite.

barnacla *m* barnacle goose (pato marino).

barnio *m* FÍS barn.

barniz *m* varnish (muebles) || glaze (cerámica) || makeup (afeite) || nail varnish (para las uñas) || FIG veneer; *sólo tiene un barniz de cultura* he only has a veneer of culture | smattering (conocimiento superficial) || BOT *barniz del Japón* laquer tree, varnish tree.

barnizado *m* varnishing, varnish (madera) || glazing, glaze (cerámica).

barnizador *m* varnisher (madera) || glazer (cerámica).

barnizar *vt* to varnish (madera) || to glaze (cerámica).

barógrafo *m* barograph.

barométrico, ca *adj* barometric, barometrical.

barómetro *m* barometer; *barómetro aneroide, registrador, de mercurio, de cubeta* aneroid, recording, mercury, cistern barometer.

barón *m* baron (título).

baronesa *f* baroness (título).

baronet *m* baronet (título).

baronía *f* barony (dignidad, territorio).

baroscopio *m* FÍS baroscope.

barquear *vt* to cross in a boat, to sail across || to row across (remando).

barquero, ra *m/f* boatman (hombre), boatwoman (mujer) || FIG *decirle* or *cantarle a uno las verdades del barquero* to give s.o. a piece of one's mind, to tell s.o. a few home truths.

barqueta *f*; **barquete** *m*; **barquichuelo** *m* small boat (barco pequeño).

barquilla *f* MAR log chip, log ship || basket, nacelle, car (de un globo) || nacelle (de un motor de avión).

barquillero, ra *m/f* wafer seller.

barquillo *m* rolled wafer.

barquín *m* large bellows (fuelle).

barquinazo *m* jolt (tumbo) || overturning, roll (vuelco) || *dar barquinazos* to jolt (dar tumbos), to overturn, to turn over (volcar).

barquito *m* soldier, finger (de pan).

barra *f* bar (de madera, metal, chocolate, jabón de lavar) || rod (vara delgada y redonda) || rod (de cortinas) || ingot, bar (de plata, de oro) || lever, crowbar (palanca) || stick (de lacre, de jabón de afeitar) || crossbar (de bicicleta) || pin (joya) || french loaf (pan de forma alargada) || block (de hielo) || bar (banco de arena) || bar (mostrador); *tomar una cerveza en la barra* to have a beer at the bar || HERÁLD bar || JUR witness box (de los testigos) | dock (de los acusados) | bar (que separa el público del tribunal) || MAR tiller, bar (de barca), helm (de barco grande) || MÚS bar || DEP kind of javelin || *AMER* audience (público) || — AUT *barra de acoplamiento* track rod || *barra de labios* or *de carmín* lipstick || INFORM *barra espaciadora* or *de espacios* space bar || DEP *barra fija* horizontal bar || *barra para cortinas* curtain rod || *ejercicios en la barra* bar exercises || JUR *llevar a la barra* to impeach, to bring to court.

◆ *pl* bars (de la quijada del caballo) || — *barras asimétricas* asymmetric bars || *barras paralelas* parallel bars || FIG *no pararse en barras* not to stop at anything, to stop at nothing.

barrabás *m* FIG & FAM rascal, little scamp (niño) | scamp, rogue, villain (tunante).

Barrabás *npr m* Barabbas.

barrabasada *f* FAM dirty *o* low trick (mala jugada) || — FAM *decir barrabasadas* to talk nonsense || *hacer barrabasadas* to get up to mischief, to play up (ser malo), to play the fool (hacer tonterías).

barraca *f* hut, cabin || stand, stall (en las ferias) || thatched house [in the Valencian and Murcian «huertas»] || *AMER* shed | stall (en un mercado) | barracks *pl* (militar).

barracón *m* large hut *o* cabin || large stand *o* stall || *barracón de tiro al blanco* shooting gallery, rifle range.

barracuda *f* barracuda.

barrado, da *adj* striped, streaked; *tela barrada* striped material || HERÁLD barred.

barragana *f* concubine.

barraganería *f* concubinage.

barraganete *m* MAR stanchion, futtock.

barranca *f* ravine, gully (barranco).

barrancal *m* ravinated land.

barranco *m* ravine, gully || precipice, cliff (precipicio) || FIG obstacle, difficulty || FIG *salir del barranco* to get out of trouble.

barranquera *f* ravine, gully (barranco).

barredero, ra *adj* sweeping || MAR *red barredera* trawl.

◆ *f* sweeper (máquina); *barredera de alfombras* carpet sweeper || road sweeper (de calles).

barredor, ra *adj* sweeping.

◆ *f* road sweeper (municipal) || *barredora-regadora* road cleaner.

barredura *f* sweeping.

◆ *pl* sweepings (basura).

barreminas *m inv* minesweeper.

barrena *f* drill, bit (sin mango) || auger, gimlet, drill (con mango) || jumper, jumper bar (de minero) || — *barrena de mano* gimlet || *entrar en barrena, hacer la barrena* to go into a spin (un avión).

barrenado, da *adj* FAM barmy, daft, dotty (loco).

barrenador *m* person who lays explosive charges, blaster.

barrenadora *f* drill, boring machine.

barrenar *vt* to drill, to bore (abrir agujeros) || to mine (una roca, etc.) || MAR to scuttle (un barco) || FIG to undermine, to frustrate (un proyecto, una empresa) | to infringe, to break, to violate (las leyes, los reglamentos) || TAUR to twist the pikehead in the bull's wound.

barrendero, ra *m/f* sweeper.

barrenero *m* driller, borer (minero).

barrenillo *m* ZOOL borer.

barreno *m* large mechanical drill *o* borer (barrena grande) || bore, borehole, drill hole (agujero) || MIN charge (de pólvora) || blasthole (taladro) || FIG constant worry (preocupación) | vanity, presumptuousness (vanidad) || *AMER* idiosyncrasy, mania (manía) || MAR *dar barreno a un barco* to scuttle a ship.

barreño *m* earthenware bowl (de barro) || bowl (metálico, de plástico).

barrer *vt* to sweep (limpiar) | to sweep, to rake (con un arma) || FIG to sweep, to trail on; *su abrigo era tan largo que barría el suelo* his overcoat was so long that it swept the floor | to sweep away; *el viento barre las hojas secas* the wind sweeps the dead leaves away | to sweep aside (un adversario) || — FIG *barrer con todo* to make a clean sweep, to take everything away | *barrer para adentro* to look after number one.

barrera *f* barrier, gate (cierre de un camino) || gate (de paso a nivel) || FIG barrier; *los Pirineos sirven de barrera natural entre España y Francia* the Pyrenees act as a natural barrier between Spain and France | obstacle, barrier (obstáculo) || claypit (de arcilla) || MIL barricade (barricada) | barrage (de tiros) || TAUR barrier, fence (para saltar el torero) | ringside seat, seat in the first row (localidad) || defensive wall (fútbol); *formar barrera* to form a defensive wall || — *barrera coralina* coral reef || *barrera de contención* retaining wall || *barrera del sonido* sound barrier || *barrera racial* colour bar || *barreras arancelarias* customs barriers || FIG *poner barreras a* to obstruct, to hinder.

barrero *m* potter (alfarero) || claypit (de arcilla) || mire, bog (barrizal) || *AMER* saltpetrous land (terreno salitroso).

barreta *f* small bar (barra pequeña) || jumper bar (de minero, albañiles) || bar (de turrón, etc.) || *AMER* pickaxe (pico).

barretear *vt* to bar, to fasten with bars || *AMER* to jump, to drill (abrir agujeros con la barrena).

barretero *m* MIN miner, drill runner.

barretina *f* Catalan cap (gorro).

— OBSERV The *barretina* resembles the Phrygian cap.

barretón *m* pickaxe.

barriada *f* quarter, district [in the suburbs].

barrial *m* claypit (gredal) || mire, quagmire (barrizal).

barrica *f* barrel, cask (tonel).

barricada *f* barricade (obstáculo); *levantar una barricada* to put up *o* to erect a barricade.

barrida *f*; **barrido** *m* sweeping || swoop, raid (de la policía) || INFORM scanning || — *dar un barrido ligero* to run the broom round || FIG *lo mismo sirve para un barrido que para un fregado* he is a jack-of-all-trades.

◆ *pl* sweepings, swept-up rubbish (barreduras).

barriga *f* belly (vientre) || FAM paunch, potbelly, corporation; *tiene mucha barriga* he has quite a paunch | belly, bulge (de una vasija) || bulge (de una pared) || — *dolor de barriga* bellyache || *echar barriga* to get a paunch, to get fat || POP *hacer una barriga a una chica* to get a girl pregnant || FIG *llenar el ojo antes que la barriga* to have eyes bigger than one's belly || FAM *llenarse la barriga* to fill one's belly | *rascarse la barriga* to laze about, to lounge about, to twiddle one's thumbs.

barrigón, ona; barrigudo, da *adj* FAM potbellied.

◆ *m/f* FAM tiny tot, kiddy, little child (niño).

barriguera *f* bellyband, girth (arreo).

barril *m* barrel, cask (tonel); *un barril de vino* a barrel of wine || keg (de pólvora) || keg, herring barrel (para pescado salado) || small earthenware jug (de barro) || — *barril de cerveza* beer keg || *cerveza de barril* draught beer || FIG *este país es un barril de pólvora* this country is a powder keg.

barrilaje *m*; **barrilamen** *m*; **barrilería** *f* *AMER* stock of barrels *o* casks.

barrilero *m* cooper.

barrilete *m* small barrel || clamp, dog (de carpintero) || fiddler crab (crustáceo) || chamber (de un revólver) || barrel (de un clarinete) || *AMER* kite (cometa) | tubby person (persona gorda) | junior barrister (pasante de abogado).

barrilla *f* BOT saltwort, barilla.

barrillar *m* place covered with saltwort.

barrillo *m* blackhead (en la piel).

barrio *m* district, area; *una ciudad se divide en varios barrios* a city is divided in several districts; *un barrio residencial* a residential district || quarter (véase OBSERV) || suburb (arrabal) || — *barrio comercial* shopping district || *barrio chino* red-light district || *barrio de las latas* shantytown, slums *pl*, slum area || *barrio latino* Latin quarter || *barrio periférico* outlying district || FIG & FAM *el otro barrio* the other world | *irse al otro* *barrio* to kick the bucket || *los barrios bajos* the lower-class districts || FAM *mandar a uno al otro barrio* to do s.o. in, to bump s.o. off | *ser el hazmerreír de todo el barrio* to be the laughingstock of the whole neighbourhood.

— OBSERV En inglés, la palabra *quarter* se emplea hoy día sobre todo para designar un barrio donde viven extranjeros: *the Chinese quarter* el barrio chino.

barriobajero, ra *adj* vulgar, low-class, common; *acento barriobajero* vulgar *o* low-class accent.

barrista *m* gymnast who works on the horizontal bar.

barrizal *m* mire, quagmire (lodazal).

barro *m* mud (lodo); *después de un aguacero los caminos están llenos de barro* after a shower the paths are covered with mud || clay (arcilla) || earthenware, clay; *jarro de barro* earthenware jar || earthenware (objetos de barro) || FIG trifle, mere nothing (cosa sin importancia) || MED blackhead (granillo) | pustule (pústula) || AMER blunder, clanger (metedura de pata) || — *barro cocido* baked earth || *barro de alfareros* modelling clay, potters' clay || *barro esmaltado* glazed terra-cotta || *barro refractario* fireclay || *Dios hizo al hombre de barro* God made man from dust || FIG & FAM *estar comiendo* or *mascando barro* to be pushing up daisies (estar enterrado) | *estar de barro hasta los ojos* to be up to one's eyes in mud || *mancharse de barro* to spatter o.s. with mud, to get mud on o.s.

barroco, ca *adj* baroque || FIG ornate, extravagant (con adornos superfluos).

◆ *m* baroque period (período) || baroque style (estilo).

barroquismo *m* baroque style || FIG extravagance.

barroso, sa *adj* clayish (con arcilla) || muddy (lleno de barro) || earth-coloured, brownish (de color rojizo) || pimply, spotty; *rostro barroso* pimply face.

barrote *m* bar; *barrotes de hierro* iron bars || crosspiece (entre las patas de un mueble) || rung (peldaño).

barruntador, ra *adj* prophetic; *signos barruntadores* prophetic signs.

barruntamiento *m* presentiment.

barruntar *vt* to have a feeling; *barrunto que me va a dar un sablazo* I have a feeling that he is going to touch me for a loan || to suppose, to guess (suponer).

barrunte; barrunto *m* sign, indication (indicio) || feeling, presentiment (presentimiento) || suspicion (sospecha) || guess (suposición) || *tener barruntos de que* to have a feeling that.

bartola (a la) *loc adv* FIG & FAM carelessly, nonchalantly || — FAM *echarse* or *tenderse* or *tumbarse a la bartola* to put one's feet up, to idle away one's time; *este alumno se ha tumbado a la bartola durante el segundo semestre* this student idled his time away during the second term.

bartolillo *m* type of small meat pie.

Bartolomé *npr m* Bartholomew.

bártulos *m pl* things, odds and ends, bits and pieces; *preparar todos los bártulos para un viaje* to get all the things ready for a trip; *llévate tus bártulos de aquí* take your odds and ends away from here; *compró todos los bártulos para pintar* he bought all the bits and pieces he needs for painting || FIG & FAM *liar los bártulos* to pack one's bags.

barullero, ra *adj/s* riotous.

barullo *m* FAM confusion, hubbub, din, racket | hell (alboroto); *armar barullo* to raise hell | confusion; *tengo tal barullo en la cabeza que no comprendo nada* there is so much confusion in my head that I cannot understand a thing || — FAM *a barullo* galore; *había pasteles a barullo* there were cakes galore | *armarse* or *hacerse un barullo* to get into a muddle.

barzón *m* walk, stroll (paseo) || *dar barzones* to wander *o* to walk about aimlessly.

barzonear *vi* to wander *o* to walk about aimlessly.

basa *f* base (de una columna) || FIG basis.

basada *f* cradle (de un barco).

basal *adj* basal; *metabolismo basal* basal metabolism.

basáltico, ca *adj* basaltic.

basalto *m* basalt.

basamento *m* plinth, base (de una columna) || FIG basis, foundation.

basar *vt* to base; *basar una opinión en* to base an opinion on.

◆ *vpr* to base o.s. || to be based on.

basca *f* sick feeling, nausea || *este olor da bascas* this smell is nauseating, this smell makes you feel sick.

bascosidad *f* repugnance (asco) || nausea || filth (suciedad) || obscenity (grosería) || *dar bascosidad a uno* to make one feel sick.

bascoso *adj* queasy (que tiene bascas) || filthy, disgusting (repugnante) || obscene (grosero).

báscula *f* scales *pl* (peso); *báscula de baño* bathroom scales || TECN weighbridge (para camiones).

basculador *m* tilter.

basculante *adj* bascule; *puente basculante* bascule bridge.

bascular *vi* to tilt.

base *f* base, basis || base; *una inscripción en la base de una estatua* an inscription on the base of a statue || QUÍM & MAT base || main ingredient (de una receta de comida) || MIL base; *base aérea, naval* air, naval base || DEP base (en béisbol) || FIG foundation, basis; *este argumento carece de base* this argument has no foundation | basis, grounds *pl*; *base de comparación* basis for comparison | cornerstone; *Juan es la base del grupo* John is the cornerstone of the group | foundation; *sentar las bases de* to lay the foundations for || — *a base de* by; *a base de no hacer nada* by doing nothing; with the help of, by means of; *traducir a base de diccionarios* to translate with the help of a dictionary; thanks to; *a base de muchos esfuerzos* thanks to all his efforts || FAM *a base de bien* extremely well || *alimento base* staple food || INFORM *base de datos* database | *base de datos relacional* relational database || MIL *base de lanzamiento* launch basis | *base de operaciones* operations base || *base espacial* space station || *base imponible* taxable income || *bebida a base de ron* rum-based drink || *de base* basic || *pelota base* baseball || *salario* or *sueldo base* minimum wage, basic wage || *teniendo como base, si tomamos como base* taking as a basis || *una comida a base de productos españoles* a meal based on Spanish products || *un jarrón de poca base se cae fácilmente* a narrow-based vase falls over easily.

basic *m* INFORM basic, Basic [Beginner's All-purpose Symbolic Instruction Code].

basicidad *f* QUÍM basicity.

básico, ca *adj* basic, essential; *un hecho básico* a basic fact || QUÍM basic, basal || *industrias básicas* basic industries.

basidio *m* basidium (hongo).

basidiomiceto *adj* basidiomycetous.

◆ *m* basidiomycete.

basilar *adj* ANAT basilary, basilar.

Basilea *n pr* GEOGR Basle, Bale, Basel.

basileense; basilense; basiliense *adj* [of *o* from] Basle.

◆ *m/f* native *o* inhabitant of Basle.

basílica *f* basilica.

basílico, ca *adj* ANAT basilic; *vena basílica* basilic vein.

basiliense *adj/s* ⟶ **basileense.**

Basilio *npr m* Basil.

basilisco *m* basilisk (animal fabuloso, reptil) || FIG & FAM *estar hecho un basilisco, ponerse como un basilisco* to be furious, to become furious.

basquear *vi* to feel sick.

◆ *vt* to nauseate, to make sick.

basquilla *f* a disease of sheep.

basquiña *f* outer skirt, skirt (falda).

basta *f* coarse stitching, tacking, basting (hilvanado) || quilting (en los colchones).

bastante *adv* quite, rather, fairly; *es bastante viejo* he is quite old; *habla bastante bien francés* she speaks fairly good French || enough; *no hemos comido bastante* we have not eaten enough; *bastante grande, rápido* large fast enough || long enough (mucho tiempo); *ya ha trabajado bastante* he has worked long enough || *lo bastante para* enough to, sufficiently to (con verbo); *es lo bastante rico para comprar un coche* he is rich enough to buy a car, he is sufficiently rich to buy a car; enough for, sufficiently for (con sustantivo o pronombre); *lo bastante salado para mí* salty enough for me.

◆ *adj* enough (suficiente); *no tengo bastante tiempo* I have not got enough time; *no tengo bastantes textos para todos* I have not got enough texts for everyone || quite a lot of, enough (mucho); *parece tener bastante dinero* he seems to have quite a lot of money || quite a lot of, quite a few, quite a number of, enough (muchos); *tiene bastantes amigos* he has quite a few friends || quite a lot (mucho, muchos); *¿había mucha gente? sí, bastante* were there many people there? yes, quite a lot.

bastanteo *m* JUR recognition, validation (de un documento).

bastar *vi* to be sufficient, to be enough, to suffice; *basta pulsar el botón para que el motor arranque* it suffices to push the button for the motor to start || — *¡basta!, ¡basta ya!* that's enough! || *basta con decir* suffice it to say || *basta con escribirlo* you need only write it down || *¡basta de bromas!* that's enough joking, joking aside || *¡basta de tonterías!* enough of your nonsense! || *basta y sobra* that's more than enough || *con eso basta* that will do, that's enough || *eso te basta* that's enough for you || *hasta decir basta* until one has had enough || *me basta con tu palabra* your word is good enough for me || *me basta y me sobra* I have more than enough.

◆ *vpr* to be self-sufficient (a sí mismo) || to do sth. by o.s., to rely only on o.s. (valerse por sí mismo).

bastarda *f* bastard file (lima) || slanting hand (letra) || MAR lateen mainsail.

bastardear *vi* to degenerate, to decline || FIG to degenerate.

◆ *vt* to bastardize, to degrade || FIG to bastardize, to distort; *bastardear una doctrina política* to bastardize a political doctrine.

bastardeo *m* bastardization, degeneration.

bastardía *f* bastardy || FIG meanness, baseness (bajeza) | villainous *o* infamous deed *o* action; *cometer una bastardía* to commit a villainous deed.

bastardillo, lla *adj* italic.

◆ *f* italics *pl*, italic type; *escrito en bastardilla* written in italics || type of flute (flauta) || *poner en bastardilla* to italicize.

bastardo, da *adj* bastard || crossbred, mongrel (perro) || hybrid (plant) || FIG hybrid, mixed

(híbrido) | mean, base (bajuno) || *letra bastarda* slanting hand.
◆ *m/f* bastard (persona) || mongrel (perro) || hybrid (planta).

baste *m* coarse stitch, tacking, basting (hilván) || saddle pad (de la silla de montar).

bastear *vt* to tack, to baste (hilvanar).

bastedad *f* coarseness, rudeness.

basteza *f* coarseness, rudeness (de una persona) || coarseness (de una cosa).

bastida *f* MIL small moving fortress.

bastidor *m* frame; *bastidor de una puerta* door frame || stretcher, frame (de lienzo para pintar) || sash; *bastidor de una ventana* window sash || embroidery frame (para bordar) || chassis (de vagón, de coche) || frame (de una máquina) || MAR frame of a screw propeller (de la hélice) || *AMER* latticework (celosía) | box-spring mattress (colchón de muelles).
◆ *pl* TEATR flats (decorado) | wings (partes laterales del escenario) || — *entre bastidores* behind the scenes || *estar entre bastidores* to be offstage (un actor).

bastilla *f* hem (dobladillo).

bastillado, da *adj* HERÁLD embattled.

bastimentar *vt* to supply, to provision.

bastimento *m* vessel (barco) || supply (abastecimiento) || supplies *pl*, provisions *pl* (provisiones).

bastión *m* bastion.

basto *m* packsaddle (arnés) || saddle pad (de la silla de montar) || ace of clubs (as de bastos).
◆ *pl* clubs (naipes).

basto, ta *adj* coarse, rough; *una tela basta* a coarse material || FIG rude, coarse; *un hombre basto* a rude man.

bastón *m* stick, cane, walking stick (para apoyarse); *un bastón con contera de plata* a cane with a silver knob || baton (insignia); *bastón de mariscal* field marshall's baton || HERÁLD baton || — *bastón alpino* alpenstock || *bastón de mando* staff of command || *bastón de montañero* ice axe || FIG *empuñar el bastón* to take command | *no hay razón como la del bastón* might makes right.

bastonada *f*; **bastonazo** *m* blow *o* hit with a cane (golpe) || *dar un bastonazo a alguien* to hit s.o. with a stick *o* a cane.

bastoncillo *m* small cane || ANAT rod (de la retina) || BIOL rod bacterium (bacteria).

bastonera *f* umbrella stand.

bastonero *m* cane manufacturer *o* merchant || maitre de ballet || caller (en ciertas danzas) || master of ceremonies.

basura *f* rubbish, refuse [*US* trash, garbage]; *tirar la basura* to throw out the rubbish || litter (en la calle) || FIG rubbish, trash; *esa película es una basura* that film is rubbish || — *cubo de la basura* rubbish bin [*US* trash can] (en la casa), dustbin [*US* trash can, garbage can] (en la calle) || *prohibido arrojar basuras* no tipping || *vertedero* or *colector de basuras* rubbish chute [*US* garbage disposal].

basurero *m* dustman [*US* garbage colletor] (el que recoge la basura) || rubbish dump [*US* garbage dump] (sitio donde se amontona la basura) || rubbish bin [*US* trash can] (cubo de la basura).

bata *f* dressing gown (salto de cama) || housecoat (traje de casa) || overall [*US* frock] (de un alumno) || white coat (de farmacéutico, médico, etc.) || *bata de cola* Ladies' dress with train such as is worn by Sevillanas dancers.
◆ *m* young native of the Philippines.

batacazo *m* crash, bump, bang (ruido) || fall (caída) || *AMER* unexpected win of a horse || FAM *darse un batacazo* to come a cropper.

batahola; bataola *f* FAM row, din, rumpus; *armar una batahola infernal* to make *o* to kick up an infernal row.

batalla *f* battle; *batalla campal* pitched battle || battle order, battle formation; *formar en batalla* to line up in battle order || FIG inner struggle, agitation (en el espíritu) || seat (de la silla de montar) || wheelbase (de un coche, etc.) || bout (esgrima) || ARTES battle scene || groove (de la ballesta) || — *dar batalla* to give battle || FIG *de batalla* everyday; *traje de batalla* everyday suit | *estos niños dan mucha batalla* these children are a real handful *o* cause a lot of trouble *o* get up to all kinds of mischief || *librar* or *trabar batalla* to do *o* to join battle || *presentar batalla* to draw up in battle array || FIG *quedar sobre el campo de batalla* to pass away.

batallador, ra *adj* fighting, battling; *un equipo batallador* a fighting team.
◆ *m/f* fighter, battler (persona animosa) || fencer (esgrimidor).

batallar *vi* to battle, to make war (guerrear) || FIG to fight, to quarrel (disputar); *batallar por pequeñeces* to fight over trifles | to battle, to struggle, to fight (esforzarse); *he tenido que batallar mucho para sacar adelante a mi familia* I've had to battle a lot to get my family ahead || to fence (en esgrima).

batallola *f* MAR rail, rails *pl*.

batallón, ona *adj* FAM quarrelsome (una persona) || boisterous, unruly, wild (un niño) || — *cuestión batallona* vexed *o* much-debated question, moot point || FAM *traje batallón* everyday suit.
◆ *m* MIL battalion.

batán *m* fulling mill (máquina para el paño) || *tierra de batán* fuller's earth.
◆ *pl* children's game.

batanadura *f* fulling (del paño).

batanar *vt* to full, to beat.

batanear *vt* FIG & FAM to give (s.o.) a thrashing, to beat.

batanero *m* fuller.

batanga *f* outrigger (de algunas embarcaciones filipinas).

bataola *f* ⟶ **batahola.**

batasuno, na *adj* pro-Herri Batasuna [Basque Separatist party].
◆ *m/f* Herri Batasuna supporter [Basque Separatist]

batata *f* BOT sweet potato, «batata» || *AMER* bashfulness (timidez).
◆ *m* spineless person, mouse (apocado).

batatar; batatal *m* sweet potato plantation.

batatazo (dar un) *loc AMER* to win the race (un caballo) | to play a fluky *o* lucky shot (billar).

bátavo, va *adj/s* Batavian (holandés).

batayola *f* MAR rail, rails, *pl*.

bate *m* bat (béisbol, cricket).

batea *f* tray (bandeja) || wicker tray (de mimbre) || flat-bottomed boat (barco) || flatcar (vagón descubierto) || MIN washing trough || *AMER* washtub (para lavar), pail (cubeta).

bateador *m* DEP batsman (cricket) | batter (béisbol).

batear *vt AMER* to bat, to hit.
◆ *vi* to bat.

batel *m* small boat, dinghy, dingey.

batelero, ra *m/f* boatman (hombre), boatwoman (mujer); *los bateleros del Volga* the Volga boatmen.

batería *f* MIL battery; *batería antiaérea* antiaircraft battery | artillery; *batería contracarro* antitank artillery | breach (brecha) || MAR gundeck (entrepuente) || ELECTR battery; *batería de acumuladores* storage battery || MÚS percussion (en una orquesta) | drums *pl* (en un conjunto) || TEATR footlights *pl* || — *aparcar en batería* to park obliquely *o* at an angle to the kerb (automóviles) || *batería de cocina* kitchen utensils || TEATR *batería de luces* footlights || MIL *entrar en batería* to prepare for action.
◆ *m* drummer (músico).

batey *m AMER* sugar refinery (fábrica de azúcar) | machinery in a refinery (maquinaria).

batiborrillo; batiburrillo *m* FAM mess, jumble; *había un batiburrillo terrible en sus papeles* his papers were in a terrible mess; *esta novela es un batiborrillo de ideas inconexas* this novel is a jumble of incoherent ideas.

baticola *f* crupper (arnés).

batida *f* beat, battue (cacería) || searching, combing (acción de registrar) || MIL reconnaissance || *batida de la policía* police raid.

batidera *f* larry, mortar hoe (de albañil) || honey-comb cutter (de apicultor).

batidero *m* banging (golpes seguidos) || stony ground (terreno).

batido, da *adj* beaten (camino, tierra) || shot (tejido) || whipped; *nata batida* whipped cream.
◆ *m* beaten egg (de huevos) || white of egg beaten stiff (clara de huevos a punto de nieve) || milk shake (de leche); *batido de fresa* strawberry milk shake || beating (acción de batir) || churning (de la mantequilla) || batter (para hacer un dulce) || battu (danza).

batidor, ra *adj* which beats, beating.
◆ *m* MIL scout (explorador) || large-toothed comb (peine) || beater (cacería) || plunger, dasher (para la mantequilla) || beater; *batidor de oro, de plata* gold, silver beater || *amer* chocolate pot (chocolatera) | informer (soplón).
◆ *f* mixer (aparato de cocina).

batiente *adj* banging || FIG *reírse a mandíbula batiente* to laugh till one's sides ache, to laugh one's head off, to laugh until one's jaws ache.
◆ *m* leaf (hoja de la puerta) || jamb (marco de puerta o de ventana) || MAR place where waves break || MÚS damper.

batifondo *m AMER* rumpus, uproar.

batiesfera *f* bathysphere.

batihoja *m* gold *o* silver beater (batidor).

batimento *m* ARTES shading.

batimetría *f* bathymetry.

batimiento *m* beating.

batín *m* short dressing gown.

batintín *m* gong.

batiporte *m* MAR sill.

batir *vt* to beat (los huevos, el metal) || to hammer (el metal) || to beat against; *las olas baten el acantilado* the waves beat against the cliff || to beat down on (el sol) || to break down, to knock down; *la artillería batió las murallas enemigas* the artillery broke down the enemy walls || to take down (desmontar) || to flap (los pájaros pequeños); *el ruiseñor bate las alas* the nightingale flaps its wings || to beat (ave grande); *el águila bate las alas* the eagle beats its wings || to clap (las manos) || to mix, to beat (la leche) || to cream (la mantequilla) || to whip (la nata) || DEP to beat (la caza) || to coin, to mint (monedas), to strike (medalla) || to beat, to defeat (vencer) || to backcomb (el pelo) || MIL to reconnoitre (registrar una región) || to sweep; *el viento batió la región durante tres días* the wind swept the region for three days || to beat (tambor) || *AMER* to rinse (la ropa) || — FIG *al hierro candente batir de repente* strike while the iron is hot || FIG & FAM *batir el cobre* to go hard at it, to buckle down to it, to get on with one's work || *batir en brecha* to batter (sentido militar), to attack (sentido figurado) || *batir palmas* to clap one's

hands || *batir una mayonesa* to beat a mayonnaise || *batir un récord* to break a record.
◆ *vpr* to fight; *batirse en duelo* to fight a duel || — FIG & FAM *batirse el cobre por hacer algo* to go all out to do sth., to buckle down to doing sth. || *batirse en retirada* to beat a retreat.

batiscafo *m* bathyscaphe.

batisfera *f* bathysphere.

batista *f* cambric, batiste (tela).

batitú *m* AMER snipe.

bato *m* peasant, country bumpkin (rústico) || simpleton (tonto) || POP old man (padre); *mi bato me dijo que* my old man told me that.

batojar *vt* to beat, to thrash (varear).

batómetro *m* bathometer.

batracio, cia *adj/m* ZOOL batrachian.

Batuecas *npr fpl* FIG & FAM *estar en las Batuecas* to be daydreaming, to be woolgathering.

batueco, ca *adj* [of *o* from] Batuecas.
◆ *m/f* inhabitant *o* native of Batuecas.

batuque *m* AMER row, uproar, racket (ruido) | FAM mess, shambles, jumble (confusión).

baturrada *f* act *o* saying of Aragonese peasants.

baturrillo *m* FIG & FAM jumble, hotchpotch, mess (mezcla) || gibberish, double Dutch (galimatías).

baturro, rra *m/f* Aragonese peasant.

batuta *f* MÚS baton (de un director de orquesta) || *llevar la batuta* to direct *o* to conduct the orchestra (una orquesta), to be the boss, to rule the roost (dirigir un asunto).

baúl *m* trunk (maleta grande) || boot (de un automóvil) || FIG & FAM paunch, potbelly (barriga) || *baúl mundo* Saratoga trunk.

baumé *m* baumé (grado).

bauprés *m* MAR bowsprit.

bausa *f* AMER FAM laziness, idleness (pereza).

bautismal *adj* baptismal; *pila bautismal* baptismal font.

bautismo *m* baptism, christening || — *bautismo de fuego* baptism of fire (de soldado) || *bautismo del aire* first flight || *fe de bautismo* baptismal certificate, certificate of baptism || *pila del bautismo* baptismal font || FIG & FAM *romper el bautismo a uno* to smash s.o.'s head in.

bautista *m* Baptist (miembro de una secta protestante) || *San Juan Bautista* Saint John the Baptist.

bautisterio *m* baptistry, baptistery.

bautizar *vt* to baptize, to christen || FIG to name; *bautizar una calle* to name a street || FAM to water down (aguar el vino, la leche) | to drench, to soak (mojar).

bautizo *m* baptism, christening (ceremonia) || christening party (fiesta).

bauxita *f* bauxite.

bauza *f* log, billet (madero).

bávaro, ra *adj/s* Bavarian.

Baviera *npr f* GEOGR Bavaria.

baya *f* BOT berry (fruto) | type of hyacinth (planta) || AMER fermented grape drink (bebida).

bayadera *f* bayadere.

Bayardo *npr m* Bayard.

bayeta *f* flannel (tejido de lana) || floorcloth (para fregar el suelo) || AMER FAM *este chico es una bayeta* this boy is a weakling, this boy has no backbone || *bayeta de gamuza* shammy leather, chamois.

bayetón *m* duffle, duffel, thick woollen cloth (tejido).

bayo, ya *adj* bay (caballo).
◆ *m* silkworm moth (mariposa) || bay (caballo) || AMER coffin (féretro).

Bayona *n pr* GEOGR Bayonne.

bayonés, esa *adj* [of *o* from] Bayonne.
◆ *m/f* inhabitant *o* native of Bayonne.

bayoneta *f* MIL bayonet; *ataque a la bayoneta* bayonet charge || — *armar* or *calar la bayoneta* to fix the bayonet || *con bayonetas caladas* with fixed bayonets || *hacer frente con la bayoneta* to resist with fixed bayonet.

bayonetazo *m* bayonet thrust (golpe) || bayonet wound (herida).

bayú *m* AMER brothel.

baza *f* trick (en el juego); *una baza de menos* one trick less || FIG asset; *tiene muchas bazas para conseguir lo que quiere* he has many assets to help him get what he wants || — FIG *jugar otra baza* to try a new tack | *meter baza en* to poke one's nose into, to interfere in (un asunto), to butt into, to intervene in, to interrupt (la conversación) | *no me dejó meter baza* he did not let me get a word in edgeways | *sentada esta baza* having established this point | *tiene todas las bazas en su mano* he's holding all the trumps.

bazar *m* bazar, bazaar.

bazo, za *adj* brown, wholemeal (pan) || brownish, fawn (tela).
◆ *m* ANAT spleen.

bazofia *f* leftovers *pl* (de comida) || FIG filth, rubbish (cosa sucia) | pigswill, slop (mala comida).

bazooka; bazuca *m* MIL bazooka.

be *f* b [name of the letter b] || — FIG *be por be, be por be y ce por ce* in detail, down to the last detail || FAM *tener (una cosa) las tres bes* to have everything [to have three advantages: *bonita* pretty, *barata* cheap, *buena* good]; *esta casa tiene las tres bes* this house has everything.

be *m* bleat, bleating (balido).

beata *f* very devout woman || lay sister, Beguine sister (mujer que vive en comunidad) || FAM sanctimonious woman, bigot (mojigata) || POP peseta.

beatería *f* religious bigotry.

beaterio *m* Beguine convent.

beatificación *f* beatification.

beatíficamente *adj* blissfully.

beatificar *vt* to beatify.

beatífico, ca *adj* beatific; *visión beatífica* beatific vision || blissful; *una sonrisa beatífica* a blissful smile.

beatísimo, ma *adj* *Beatísimo Padre* Holy Father (el Papa).

beatitud *f* REL beatitude || bliss (placidez).

beatnik *m/f* beatnik.

beato, ta *adj* REL blessed (beatificado) || devout (piadoso) || FAM sanctimonious (exageradamente devoto) || blessed, happy (feliz).
◆ *m/f* REL blessed person || devout person (piadoso) || FAM (religious) bigot, sanctimonious person.
◆ *m* lay brother (religioso) || devout man.

beatón, ona; beatuco, ca *adj/s* FAM → **beato.**

Beatriz *npr f* Beatrice, Beatrix.

bebé *m* baby || *bebé probeta* test-tube baby.
— OBSERV In Argentina the forms *bebe* (niño) and *beba* (niña) also exist.

bebedero, ra *adj* drinkable (que se puede beber) || tasty (sabroso).
◆ *m* water trough, drinking trough (de animales) || watering place (donde beben los animales y los pájaros) || lip, spout (de algunas vasijas).

bebedizo, za *adj* drinkable (bebedero).
◆ *m* MED potion || philtre, love potion (filtro mágico) || poisonous drink (veneno).

bebedor, ra *adj* drinking, hard-drinking.
◆ *m/f* drinker; *es buen bebedor* he is a good drinker.

beber *m* drinking; *el beber en exceso puede tener malas consecuencias* excessive drinking can have bad consequences.

beber *vi/vt* to drink; *beber agua* to drink water; *beber de la botella* to drink from the bottle; *beber en un vaso* to drink out *o* from a glass || to drink (bebida alcohólica); *este hombre bebe demasiado* this man drinks too much || to drink (brindar); *beber por* or *a la salud de alguien* to drink to s.o.'s health, to drink to s.o. || FIG to drink in; *estaba bebiendo tus palabras mientras hablabas* he was drinking in your words as you spoke || — *beber a chorro* to pour drink into one's mouth (de bota, etc.) || *beber a sorbos* to sip || *beber a tragos* to gulp || FIG & FAM *beber como una esponja* or *como un cosaco* to drink like a fish || *beber de un trago* to down in one, to drink down in one || FIG *beber en buenas fuentes* to have reliable sources of information | *beber en las fuentes* to draw upon the sources; *beber en las fuentes latinas* to draw upon Latin sources || FIG & FAM *beberle los sesos a uno* to have s.o. bewitched *o* under one's spell | *beber los vientos por* to be dying to (con verbo), to be dying for (con sustantivo), to be head over heels in love with (una mujer) || *dar de beber* to give a drink (a personas, a animales), to water (animales) || *echar de beber* to pour a drink (a personas), to give water (a animales) || FIG *esto es como quien se bebe un vaso de agua* this is as easy as A B C *o* as pie | *sin comerlo ni beberlo* without asking for it, for no apparent reason, through no fault of one's own.
◆ *vpr* to drink || FIG to drink; *beberse todo lo que se gana* to drink one's wages || *bébete eso, que nos vamos* drink up, we're leaving.

bebezón *m* AMER drunkenness (borrachera) | drink (bebida).

bebible *adj* FAM drinkable.

bebida *f* drink; *sirven bebidas en el avión* they serve drinks on the plane || drink, beverage; *bebida alcohólica* alcoholic beverage || drinking, drink; *no se puede vivir sin bebida ni comida* one cannot live without drinking and eating, one cannot live without food and drink || AMER potion (potingue) || — *dado a la bebida* given to drink || *darse a la bebida* to take to drinking, to take to drink, to indulge in drinking || *tener mala bebida* to turn nasty with drink, to be quarrelsome in one's cups.

bebido, da *adj* tipsy, merry.

bebistrajo *m* concoction, nasty drink, foul drink (bebida desagradable) || strange concoction, strange mixture (mezcla extraña de bebidas).

bebito *m* AMER little baby (nenito, niñito).

be-bop *m* MÚS be-bop.

beborrotear *vi* FAM to tipple.

beca *f* grant, scholarship; *beca de investigación* research grant.

becacina *f* snipe (agachadiza).

becada *f* woodcock (pájaro).

becado, da *m/f* AMER scholarship holder || *los alumnos becados* the scholarship holders.

becafigo *m* ZOOL beccafico (pájaro).

becardón *m* snipe (agachadiza).

becario, ria *m/f* scholarship holder.

becasina *f* → **becacina.**

becerra *f* yearling calf (animal) || snapdragon (planta).

becerrada *f* fight with yearling bulls.

becerril *adj* of a calf, calf.

becerrillo *m* calfskin, calf (cuero).

becerrista *m* bullfighter who fights very young bulls.

becerro *m* yearling calf || calfskin (cuero); *botas de becerro* calfskin boots || cartulary (libro para la Iglesia) || register of landed property (para la nobleza) || — *becerro de oro* golden calf || *becerro marino* sea calf, seal (foca) || FAM *no seas becerro* don't be stupid | *sangrar como un becerro* to bleed freely.

becuadro *m* MÚS natural sign.

bechamel *f* white sauce, béchamel sauce (salsa).

bedano *m* chisel (cincel).

bedel *m* beadle, porter (en la Universidad).

bedelía *f* beadleship.

beduino, na *adj/s* Bedouin, Beduin (árabe nómada).
◆ *m* FIG brute (hombre brutal).

befa *f* jeering, scoffing, mockery (acción y efecto) || *hacer befa de* to jeer at, to mock, to scoff at.

befar *vi* to move the lips [horses] (los caballos).
◆ *vt* to mock, to jeer at, to scoff at.

befo, fa *adj* thick-lipped, blubber-lipped (de labio grueso) || knock-kneed (zambo).
◆ *m* pendulous lips (de mono, perro, gato), chops (de rumiantes) || thick lower lip (labio inferior grueso) || ape (mico).

begonia *f* BOT begonia.

beguina *f* Beguine (religiosa).

begum *f* begum.

behaviorismo *m* behaviourism [*US* behaviorism].

behetría *f* HIST free town whose inhabitants had the right to elect their own master || FIG confusion, bedlam.

beige *adj/sm* beige (color).

Beirut *n pr* GEOGR Beirut, Beyrouth.

béisbol *m* baseball; *jugador de béisbol* baseball player.

bejucal *m* rattan field.

bejuco *m* liana, rattan, reed.

bejuquear *vt* AMER to thrash (un árbol) | to hit with a cane (una persona).

bel *m* bel (unidad de intensidad sonora).

Belcebú *npr m* Beelzebub.

belcho *m* BOT ephedra, horsetail.

beldad *f* beauty || beauty (mujer bella); *ella es una beldad* she is a beauty.

beldar* *vt* AGR to winnow (grain) whith a fork.

belemnita *f* belemnite, finger stone (fósil).

belén *m* Nativity scene, crib (del niño Jesús) || FIG & FAM bedlam, mess (confusión) | madhouse, bedlam (lugar donde hay desorden) || FIG & FAM *meterse en belenes* to stir up a hornet's nest.

Belén *n pr* GEOGR Bethlehem || FIG *estar en Belén* to daydream.

beleño *m* BOT henbane.

belérico *m* BOT myrobalan.

belesa *f* BOT leadwort.

belfo, fa *adj* thick-lipped, blubber-lipped (de labio grueso).
◆ *m* pendulous lips (de mono, perro, gato), chops (de rumiantes) || thick lower lip (labio inferior grueso).

belga *adj/s* Belgian.

Bélgica *npr f* GEOGR Belgium.

Belgrado *n pr* GEOGR Belgrade.

Belice *npr m* GEOGR Belize.

belicismo *m* warmongering, militarism.

belicista *adj* warmongering, bellicist.
◆ *m/f* warmonger, militarist.

bélico, ca *adj* warlike, bellicose; *espíritu bélico* warlike spirit || *preparativos bélicos* preparations for war.

belicosidad *f* bellicosity, aggressiveness.

belicoso, sa *adj* bellicose, warlike (nación) || aggresive (persona).

beligerancia *f* belligerency || — FIG *no dar beligerancia a uno* to pay no attention to s.o., to take no notice of s.o. || *política de no beligerancia* policy of non-aggression.

beligerante *adj/s* belligerent.

belígero, ra *adj* POÉT bellicose.

belinograma *m* belinogram.

belio *m* FÍS bel (unidad de intensidad sonora).

Belisario *npr m* Belisarius.

belísono, na *adj* POÉT with warlike sound, with martial sound.

belitre *adj* foolish (bobo) || vile (vil).
◆ *m/f* fool (bobo) || knave, scoundrel (granuja).

Beltrán *npr m* Bertrand.

beluario *m* animal tamer.

beluza *f* ZOOL beluza (esturión, cetáceo).

belvedere *m* belvedere.

bellaco, ca *adj* sly, cunning (astuto) || roguish, wicked, evil (malo) || AMER restive, vicious (caballo).
◆ *m/f* sly dog (astuto) || rogue, villain (malo) || *mentir como un bellaco* to lie one's head off.

belladona *f* BOT belladona, deadly nightshade.

bellaquear *vi* to do evil || to cheat, to play a sly trick (obrar con astucia) || AMER to buck, to rear (los caballos).

bellaquería *f* fiendish trick (acción) || knavery, roguery (carácter) || cunning (astucia).

belleza *f* beauty || — *concurso de belleza* beauty contest || *crema de belleza* beauty cream || *diplomada en belleza* qualified beautician || *es una belleza* it's beautiful (cosa) || *tratamiento de belleza* beauty treatment || *una belleza* a beauty (mujer).

bellísimo, ma *adj* ravishing, gorgeous, very beautiful || *una bellísima persona* an extremely nice person, a wonderful person.

bello, lla *adj* beautiful (mujer), handsome (hombre), fair (término poético) || noble, fine (sentimiento) || — *bello como un sol* fine-looking, extremely hand-some (adolescente), as pretty as a picture, divine (niño, chica) || *el bello sexo* the fair sex || *la bella durmiente del bosque* Sleeping Beauty || *la bella y la bestia* Beauty and the Beast || *las bellas artes* the fine arts || FIG & FAM *por su bella cara* for love, for s.o.'s pretty face.

bellota *f* BOT acorn (de la encina) || ANAT glans penis (bálano) || tassel (adorno) || carnation bud (del clavel) || *animal de bellota* pig (cerdo), blockhead, fool, dunce (persona estúpida).

bellotero, ra *m/f* gatherer *o* seller of acorns.
◆ *f* crop of acorns, mast (cosecha).

bembo, ba *adj* AMER FAM thick-lipped (de labios gruesos) | foolish, silly, simple (bobo).
◆ *m/f* AMER thick lower tip (labio grueso) | snout (hocico).

bembón, ona; bembudo, da *adj* AMER thick-lipped.
◆ *m/f* AMER thick-lipped person.

bemol *adj/sm* MÚS flat; *si bemol* B flat || — FIG *esto tiene bemoles* or *muchos bemoles* or *tres bemoles* this is not an easy job at all, this is a tough one || MÚS *hacer bemol* to flatten.

bemolado, da *adj* flat.

ben *m* ben (hijo de) || BOT horseradish.

bencedrina *f* MED benzedrine.

benceno *m* QUÍM benzene.

bencílico, ca *adj* benzilic.

bencina *f* QUÍM benzine.

bendecidor, ra *adj* benedictory.
◆ *m/f* person who blesses.

bendecir* *vt* to bless; *estar bendecido por los dioses* to be blessed by the gods || — *bendecir la mesa* to say grace || *¡Dios le bendiga!* God bless you!

— OBSERV The Spanish verb *bendecir* has two past participles: *bendecido* and *bendito*. The former is the regular form and is used to denote an action or its result: *esta iglesia fue bendecida por* this church was blessed by. The latter, which is irregular, is used as an adjective. *Bendito* is currently used in prayers and invocations: *bendita eres entre todas las mujeres, bendito sea tu nombre* blessed art Thou amongst women, blessed be Thy name.

bendición *f* blessing; *el padre dio su bendición a su hijo* the father gave his blessing to his son || REL benediction; *la bendición papal* or *del Papa* the Pope's benediction || — *bendición de la mesa* grace || *bendición nupcial* blessing [in marriage ceremony] || FAM *echar la bendición a uno* to give one's blessing to s.o. | *es una bendición de Dios* it is a blessing, it is a Godsend | *la cosecha este año es una bendición* the harvest is magnificent this year | *toca que es una bendición* he plays extremely well *o* divinely *o* marvellously | *ya nos echaron las bendiciones* the knot has been tied (matrimonio) | *y llovió que era una bendición* and it really rained, and you should have seen it rain.

bendito, ta *adj* blessed || holy; *agua bendita* holy water; *la bendita Virgen María* the holy Virgin Mary || joyful (dichoso) || lucky (que tiene suerte) || simple, silly (de poco alcance) || — FAM *¡bendita la madre que te hizo!* what a child for a mother to have! || *¡bendito sea Dios!* good God! (de disgusto), thank goodness!, thank heavens! (de alivio).
◆ *m* saint (santo) || simpleton (bobo) || good sort *o* soul (bonachón) || prayer which begins with the words «bendito y alabado, etc.» || AMER niche for a statue (hornacina) | type of tent (tienda de campaña) || — FIG & FAM *dormir como un bendito* to sleep like a baby | *reír como un bendito* to laugh one's head off.

— OBSERV Cuando *blessed* expresa una acción o su resultado, por ejemplo en la frase *the church was blessed by*, se pronuncia «blest». Cuando se utiliza como adjetivo (*the blessed martyrs, blessed be Thy name*) se pronuncia «blesid».

benedícite *m* benedicite, grace (oración).

benedictino, na *adj/s* Benedictine || FIG *obra de benedictinos* task requiring a great deal of patience.
◆ *m* Benedictine (licor).

Benedicto *npr m* Benedict (solamente los Papas).

benefactor, ra *adj* beneficent.
◆ *m/f* benefactor (hombre), benefactress (mujer).

beneficencia *f* beneficence, benevolence, charity || welfare, public welfare (organización pública) || — *sección de beneficencia* charity board || *vivir de la beneficencia* to be on relief, to live on public welfare.

beneficiado, da *m/f* beneficiary.
◆ *m* beneficiary (eclesiástico).

beneficiar *vt* to benefit (hacer bien); *beneficiar al género humano* to benefit humanity || to exploit (una cosa, un terreno, una mina) ||

to cultivate (la tierra) || to reduce (un mineral) || to favour [*US* to favor] (favorecer) || *AMER* to slaughter (matar una res) | to quarter, to cut into pieces (descuartizar).
◆ *vi* to benefit; *beneficiar de una ley* to benefit from *o* by a law; *beneficiar de la ayuda de* to benefit from the help to || to profit (*de* from) (sacar provecho).
◆ *vpr* to benefit || to profit (sacar provecho).

beneficiario, ria *m/f* beneficiary || — *beneficiario del cheque* payee || *beneficiario de patente* patentee.

beneficio *m* profit (ganancia); *los beneficios anuales* yearly profits || advantage; *los beneficios del empleo* the advantages of the job || benefit; *beneficios sociales* social benefits || FIG favour (bien); *colmar a uno de beneficios* to heap favours on s.o. | benefit, behalf (provecho); *trabajar para el* or *a* or *en beneficio de la humanidad* to labour for the benefit of *o* on behalf of humanity || REL benefice || exploitation (explotación) || AGR cultivation (cultivo) || MIN reduction (de un mineral) || benefit (en el teatro) || *AMER* slaughter (matanza) | quartering (descuartizamiento) | rural development (hacienda) | manure (abono) || — *a beneficio de* for the benefit of || *a beneficio de inventario* under beneficium inventarii, under the benefit of inventory (sentido jurídico), with reservations (con reservas) || *beneficio bruto* gross profit || *beneficio neto* net profit || *beneficios adicionales* fringe benefits || *en beneficio propio* to one's own advantage, in one's own interest || *margen de beneficio* profit margin || FIG *no tener oficio ni beneficio* to have no job, to be out of a job || *vender con beneficio* to sell at a profit *o* at a premium.

beneficioso, sa *adj* beneficial, advantageous || profitable (provechoso).

benéfico, ca *adj* beneficent, charitable; *obras benéficas* charitable works || beneficial; *lluvia benéfica* beneficial rain || favourable; *influencia benéfica de los planetas* favourable influence of the planets || — *función benéfica* charity performance || *obra benéfica* charity || *una cena benéfica* a charity dinner.

Benelux *npr m* the Benelux countries.

benemérito, ta *adj* meritorious, worthy (muy bueno) || distinguished; *el benemérito profesor* the distinguished professor || *los hijos beneméritos de la patria* the glorious sons of the motherland.
◆ *f* *la Benemérita* the Spanish Civil Guard.

beneplácito *m* blessing, approval, consent; *negar el beneplácito* to refuse to give one's blessing; *di mi beneplácito* I gave my consent.

benévolamente *adv* benevolently, kindly.

benevolencia *f* benevolence, kindness.

benevolente; benévolo, la *adj* benevolent, kind.

bengala *f* BOT rattan || Bengal light, flare.

Bengala *npr m* GEOGR Bengal || *luz de Bengala* Bengal light, flare.

bengali *adj/s* Bengali, Bengalese.
◆ *m* waxbill (pájaro) || Bengali (lengua).

benignamente *adv* benignly, kindly || mildly (sin gravedad).

benignidad *f* benignancy, benignity, kindness || mildness (falta de gravedad).

benigno, na *adj* benign, kindly (amable) || mild (sin gravedad, templado); *enfermedad benigna* mild illness; *invierno benigno* mild winter || benign, nonmalignant; *tumor benigno* benign tumour, non-malignant tumour.

Benito *npr m* Benedict.

benjamín *m* youngest son (hijo menor).

Benjamín *npr m* Benjamin.

benjuí *m* benjamin, benzoin (bálsamo).

bentonita *f* GEOL bentonite (arcilla).

benzoato *m* QUÍM benzoate.

benzoico, ca *adj* QUÍM benzoic.

benzoína *f* QUÍM benzoin.

benzol *m* QUÍM benzol.

Beocia *npr f* GEOGR Boetia.

beocio, cia *adj/s* Boeotian.

beodez *f* drunkenness.

beodo, da *adj* drunk, drunken (borracho).
◆ *m/f* drunk, drunkard.

berberecho *m* cockle (molusco).

berberí *adj/s* ⟶ **beréber.**

Berbería *npr f* GEOGR Barbary.

berberidáceas *f pl* BOT berberidaceae.

berberisco, ca *adj* Barbaresque, Berber.
◆ *m* Berber.

berbiquí *m* brace, carpenter's brace.

beréber; berebere; berberí *adj/s* Berber.

berenjena *f* BOT aubergine, eggplant; *berenjenas rellenas* stuffed aubergines.

berenjenal *m* field of aubergines *o* eggplants || FIG & FAM mess, confusion; *armar un berenjenal* to make a mess || FIG & FAM *meterse en un berenjenal* to get into a fine mess *o* a fine pickle *o* a fine predicament.

bergamota *f* BOT bergamot.

bergamoto *m* BOT bergamot.

bergante *m* FAM scoundrel, rascal, knave.

bergantín *m* MAR brig, brigantine.

berginización *f* berginization.

beri *m* FAM *con las del beri* maliciously.

beriberi *m* MED beriberi.

berilio *m* QUÍM beryllium.

beriliosis *f* MED berylliosis.

berilo *m* MIN beryl.

berkelio *m* berkelium.

berlanga *f* three of a kind (trío de cartas).

Berlín *n pr* GEOGR Berlin; *Berlín Occidental* West Berlin || *el muro de Berlín* the Berlin wall.

berlina *f* saloon (vehículo) || berlin, berline (coche cerrado de dos asientos).

berlinés, esa *adj* [of *o* from] Berlin.
◆ *m/f* Berliner, inhabitant *o* native of Berlin.

berma *f* Berm, foreland (fortificación).

bermejear *vi* to be reddish.

bermejizo, za *adj* reddish.

bermejo, ja *adj* red, vermilion (rojo) || red, ginger (cabellos).

bermellón *m* vermilion.

bermudas *m pl* Bermuda shorts.

Bermudas *npr fpl* GEOGR Bermuda *sing.*

Berna *n pr* GEOGR Bern, Berne.

Bernabé *npr m* Barnabas, Barnaby.

bernabita *m* Bernabite (monje).

bernardo, da *adj/s* Bernardine (religiosos).

Bernardo, da *npr m/f* Bernard, Bernadette.

bernés, esa *adj/s* Bernese (de Berna).

berra; berraza *f* cress.

berraco *m* FIG & FAM Noisy brat, squalling brat (niño).

berrear *vi* to low (los becerros) || FIG & FAM to bawl, to howl (gritar, cantar o llorar) | to lose one's temper, to fly off the handle (enfadarse).

berrenchín *m* foul-smelling breath of the wild boar || FIG & FAM ⟶ **berrinche.**

berrendo, da *adj* mottled, speckled; *berrendo en negro* mottled with black (toro).
◆ *m* *AMER* type of cereal with a blue stalk (trigo) | type of antelope.

berrido *m* lowing (del becerro) || FIG shout, bellow, howl (grito).

berrinche *m* FAM temper, rage (rabieta); *mi padre ha cogido un berrinche* my father flew into a temper | tantrum (disgusto de los niños); *el niño cogió un berrinche* the child threw a tantrum || *como sigas así me vas a dar un berrinche* if you carry on like that you are going to make me cross.

berrinchudo, da *adj* *AMER* quick-tempered, irascible, choleric.

berrizal *m* watercress bed *o* pond.

berro *m* BOT cress, watercress.

berrocal *m* rocky ground, craggy place.

berroqueña *adj f* *piedra berroqueña* granite.

berrueco *m* granite rock (roca) || baroque, baroque pearl (perla) || MED tumour of the eye.

Berta *npr f* Bertha.

berza *f* cabbage (col).

berzal *m* cabbage field (grande), cabbage patch (pequeño).

berzas; berzotas *m/f inv* FAM twerp, drip.

besalamano *m* card, unsigned note with the abbreviation B. L. M [*besa la mano* kisses your hand].

besamanos *m inv* royal audience (recepción de los reyes) || hand kissing (modo de saludar).

besamela; besamel *f* white sauce, béchamel sauce (salsa).

besana *f* AGR ploughed field (surcos paralelos) | first furrow (primer surco) | Catalan agricultural measure [21. 87 ares].

besante *m* besant, bezant (moneda) || HERÁLD besant, bezant.

besar *vt* to kiss (dar un beso); *le besé en las mejillas* I kissed him on the cheeks || FIG to touch, to graze, to brush against (rozar) || — FAM *aquello fue llegar y besar el santo* it was as easy as pie, it was a piece of cake, it was like taking candy from a baby | *besa la tierra que pisa su amada* he worships the ground his loved one walks on | *hacer besar la lona* to floor s.o. (boxeo), to bring s.o. down (humillar).
◆ *vpr* to kiss, to kiss each other; *se besaron al verse* they kissed each other when they met || to brush, to touch *o* to graze *o* to brush against each other (rozarse).

besico; besito *m* little kiss, peck; *dar un besito* to give a little kiss *o* a peck || BOT *besico de monja* campanula.

beso *m* kiss; *beso de paz* kiss of peace || FIG clash, bump, blow (golpe) || — FIG & FAM *comerse a besos* to kiss each other passionately, to eat each other (dos personas), to smother in kisses (a uno) || *tirar un beso* to blow a kiss.

besotear *vt* FAM to kiss, to cover with kisses.

bestezuela *f* creepy-crawly, beastie.

bestia *f* beast, animal.
◆ *m/f* FIG beast, brute, animal (persona ruda); *¡vaya bestia!* what a brute!, what an animal! | ignoramus, dunce, idiot (ignorante) || — *bestia de albarda* pack animal || *bestia de carga* beast of burden || *gran bestia* elk (anta), tapir || FIG & FAM *mala bestia* nasty piece of work, brute (persona muy mala), dunce (ignorante).

bestial *adj* animal, bestial, beastly (irracional); *instintos bestiales* animal instincts || FIG & FAM terrific, great, fabulous, smashing (magnífico) | huge, big, enormous (enorme); *tiene un apetito bestial* he has a huge appetite.

bestialidad *f* bestiality, beastliness || FAM stupidity (estupidez) | horrible thing (acción mala) || — FAM *decir bestialidades* to say horrible things (cosas malas), to speak *o* to talk nonsense (tonterías) | *¡qué bestialidad!* how awful!, how terrible! (disgusto), good grief! (asombro) | *una bestialidad de* piles *o* stacks of, a great number of, lots and lots of.

bestiario *m* bestiary.

best seller *m* best seller.

besucar *vt* FAM to kiss, to cover with kisses.

besucón, ona *adj* FAM fond of kissing. ◆ *m/f* person fond of kissing.

besugo *m* sea bream (pez) || FIG & FAM idiot, drip, twerp || FAM *ojos de besugo* bulging eyes.

besuguera *f* sea bream seller || fish pan (recipiente para el pescado).

besuguete *m* sea bream (pez).

besuquear *vt* FAM to kiss, to cover with kisses. ◆ *vpr* FAM to smooch, to kiss and cuddle.

besuqueo *m* FAM smooching, kissing and cuddling.

beta *f* beta (letra griega) || piece of rope *o* string (cuerda) || MAR rope, cable (cable) || *rayos beta* beta rays.

betarraga; betarrata *f* beetroot [*US* beet] (remolacha).

betatrón *m* FÍS betatron.

betel *m* BOT betel.

Bética *npr f* Andalusia.

bético, ca *adj* Andalusian.

betún *m* asphalt, bitumen || shoe polish, polish (para el calzado) || — *betún de Judea* asphalt || FIG *negro como el betún* as black as coal || FAM *quedar a la altura del betún* to be the lowest of the low (ser el peor de todos), to do badly *o* poorly (en una competición).

betunero *m* bootblack, shoeblack, shoeshine boy (limpiabotas).

bevatrón *m* FÍS bevatron.

bezaar *m* bezoar.

bezante *m* HERÁLD besant, bezant.

bezar *m* ⟶ **bezdar.**

bezo *m* thick lip (labio grueso) || lip (de una herida).

bezoar *m* bezoar.

bezoácico *m* antidote (contraveneno).

bezote *m* Indian lip ring.

bezudo, da *adj* thick-lipped.

biaba *f* AMER FAM slap, smack (bofetada) | spanking, thrashing, beating (zurra).

biácido, da *adj* QUÍM biacid, diacid.

bianual *adj* biennial.

biatómico, ca *adj* QUÍM diatomic.

biaxial *adj* biaxial.

bíbaro *m* beaver (castor).

bibásico, ca *adj* QUÍM bibasic, dibasic.

bibelot *m* bibelot, curio, trinket.

biberón *m* baby's bottle, feeding bottle || *dar el biberón al niño* to give the baby his bottle, to feed the baby.

bibijagua *f* AMER type of large ant found in Cuba (hormiga) | FIG busy bee.

bibijaguera *f* AMER anthill.

biblia *f* bible; *la Santa Biblia* the Holy Bible || — *papel biblia* Bible paper || FIG *saber más que la Biblia* to know everything.

bíblico, ca *adj* Biblical.

bibliofilia *f* bibliophilism.

bibliófilo, la *m/f* bibliophile, booklover.

bibliografía *f* bibliography.

bibliográfico, ca *adj* bibliographical, bibliographic.

bibliógrafo, fa *m/f* bibliographer.

bibliomanía *f* bibliomania.

bibliorato *m* AMER file, folder (archivo).

biblioteca *f* library; *biblioteca de consulta, de préstamo* reference, lending library; *biblioteca circulante* mobile library; *biblioteca pública* public library; *biblioteca universitaria* university library || bookcase, bookshelves *pl* (mueble) || INFORM *library* || FIG *es un biblioteca viviente* he is a walking encyclopedia.

bibliotecario, ria *m/f* librarian.

bicameral *adj* bicameral, two-chamber.

bicameralismo *m* bicameralism, bicameral system, two-chamber system.

bicarbonatado, da *adj* containing bicarbonate.

bicarbonato *m* QUÍM bicarbonate; *bicarbonato de sosa* or *sódico* bicarbonate of soda (nombre corriente), sodium bicarbonate (nombre científico).

bicarburo *m* QUÍM bicarbide.

bicéfalo, la *adj* bicephalous, two-headed; *águila bicéfala* two-headed eagle.

bicentenario *m* bicentennial, bicentenary.

bíceps *m inv* ANAT biceps.

bici *f* FAM bike (bicicleta).

bicicleta *f* bicycle; *ir en bicicleta* to go by bicycle; *no sabe montar en bicicleta* he doesn't know how to ride a bicycle.

biciclo *m* velocipede.

bicipital *adj* bicipital (de los biceps).

bicípite *adj* bicephalous, two-headed.

bicloruro *m* QUÍM dichloride, bichloride.

bicoca *f* FIG & FAM trinket, knick-knack (fruslería) | bargain (ganga) || trifle (casi nada) | cushy job (puesto ventajoso) || small fort (fortificación) || *AMER* calotte, skullcap (de los clérigos) | flick (capirotazo) || FIG & FAM *por una bicoca* for a song (muy barato).

bicolor *adj* two-tone, two-colour, bicolour [*US* bicolor] || *un coche bicolor* a two-tone car.

bicóncavo, va *adj* biconcave.

biconvexo, xa *adj* biconvex.

bicorne *adj* two-cornered (sombrero).

bicornio *m* two-cornered hat (sombrero).

bicromato *m* QUÍM dichromate, bichromate.

bicromía *f* two-colour print.

bicuadrado, da *adj* MAT biquadratic (ecuación).

bicúspide *adj/sm* bicuspid.

bicha *f* (ant) little animal, tiny creature *o* beast (bicho) || snake (culebra) || ARQ mask, mascaron.

bichear *vt* AMER to spy on, to keep watch on.

bichero *m* MAR boathook (para barco).

bicho *m* little animal, tiny beast (animal pequeño) || bug, creepy-crawly (insecto) || FAM bull (toro de lidia) || INFORM bug || FIG queer specimen, queer card (persona extraña) | ugly person, freak (persona fea) || — *AMER bicho colorado* harvest bug, harvest louse || FIG & FAM *bicho malo, mal bicho* swine, nasty piece of work (hombre), bitch (mujer) | *bicho malo nunca muere* bad pennies always turn up | *no hay bicho viviente que no lo sepa* it is common knowledge | *todo bicho viviente* every Tom, Dick and Harry, every living soul.

bichoco, ca *adj* AMER old, no longer fit for work (caballo) | old, decrepit (persona).

bidé *m* bidet (mueble).

bidentado, da *adj* bidentate, double-toothed. ◆ *m* AGR pitchfork.

bidón *m* can; *bidón de gasolina* petrol can, can of petrol.

biela *f* AUT connecting rod (biela de conexión) || — *biela de acoplamiento* drag link || AUT *cabeza de biela* big end | *pie de biela* small end | *una biela se ha fundido* a big end has gone.

bielda *f* AGR winnowing fork | winnowing (acción de bieldar).

bieldar *vt* to winnow (los cereales).

bieldo *m* AGR winnowing fork | pitchfork (con dos dientes).

bien *m* good; *lo hice por tu bien* or *en bien tuyo* I did it for your good; *el bien de la patria* the good of the country; *el bien público* the common good || interest, benefit, good (provecho); *hacer algo por el bien común* to do sth. in the common interest *o* for the common good || property; *bienes comunes* public property || right, good; *discernir el bien del mal* to tell right from wrong *o* good from evil || *devolver bien por mal* to repay evil with good || *en bien de* for the good of, for the benefit of || *hacer bien* or *el bien* to do good || *haz bien y no mires a quien* do well and dread no shame || *hombre de bien* upright *o* honest man || *mi bien* my darling || *no hay mal que por bien no venga* every cloud has a silver lining || *para* or *por el bien de* for the good of, in the interest of. ◆ *pl* goods; *bienes de consumo* consumer goods || — *bienes de consumo duraderos* consumer durables ||bienes de equipo capital goods || *bienes fungibles* fungible goods || *bienes gananciales* acquest, property acquired in married life || *bienes inmuebles* real estate || *bienes mal adquiridos a nadie han enriquecido* ill-gotten gains seldom prosper || *bienes mostrencos* ownerless property || *bienes muebles* personal property, movables || *bienes públicos* public property || *bienes raíces, bienes sedientes* real estate *sing* || *bienes semovientes* livestock *sing* || *bienes terrestres* worldly goods || *bienes y personas* all hands and goods (en un naufragio) || *comunidad de bienes gananciales* joint estate, community of property acquired during marriage || FAM *decir mil bienes de* to speak highly of.

bien *adv* well; *hablar bien un idioma* to speak a language well; *bien criado* well brought-up; *el negocio marcha bien* the business is going well || properly (de acuerdo con los principios); *obrar bien* to act properly || properly, right, well (según las reglas); *lo has hecho bien* you did it right || correctly, right (exactamente); *respondió bien* he answered correctly || soundly; *razonar bien* to reason soundly || comfortably, well; *vivo bien* I live comfortably || good; *oler bien* to smell good || willingly, gladly, with pleasure; *bien le ayudaría si* I would help you with pleasure if || quite, pretty, very; *está bien cansado* he is quite tired; *es bien cruel* he is very cruel; *es bien tarde* it is quite late || a lot; *hemos caminado bien* we have walked a lot || all right, okay (de acuerdo) || — *ahora bien* now, now then || *¡bien!* good!, great! || *bien es verdad que* it is quite *o* very true that || *bien... o bien, bien sea... o bien* either... or; *bien en coche o bien andando* either by car or on foot || *bien se ve que* it is quite plain that, it is easy to see that || *bien te lo dije* I told you so || *como bien te parezca* as you wish, as you want || *de bien en mejor* better and better || *¡está bien!* fine!, al right (de acuerdo), that's enough! (¡basta!) || *está bien que lo haga* is it all right for me (*o* him, etc.) to do it || *estar bien con* to be well in with || *estar bien de dinero* to be well off || *estar bien de salud* to be well || *estar bien en un sitio* to feel comfortable *o* happy in a place || *gente bien* the best people (de la alta sociedad), nice people (respetable) || *hacer bien en* to do well to, to be right to || *lo bien fundado* the grounds || *mal que bien* as best as one can (lo mejor posible), one way or another (de cualquier manera) || *más bien* rather

|| *más o menos bien* quite well || *¡muy bien!* hear, hear! (asentimiento) || *no bien* as soon as, no sooner... than; *no bien vio el relámpago, echó a correr* as soon as he saw the lightning he started to run, no sooner did he see the lightning than he started to run || *no sentar bien a* not to suit, not to become (favorecer); *no te sienta nada bien el amarillo* yellow doesn't suit you at all; *esa actitud no te sienta nada bien* that attitude doesn't become you at all; || not to fit (las medidas de la ropa, etc.) || not to agree with (dirigirse bien) || *o bien* or, or else || *¡pues bien!* well, well then || FAM *¡qué bien!* oh, good!, great! || *quien bien te quiere te hará llorar* you have to be cruel to be kind, spare the rod and spoil the child || *sentar bien* to do good, to be good for (hacer buen efecto); *bébete este té, que te sentará bien para el dolor de vientre* drink his tea, it will be good for your tummy ache *o* it will do your tummy good; to like, to appreciate (gustar a uno); *los cumplidos siempre sientan bien* people always like to be flattered; to take well (tomar a bien); *le sentó bien lo que le dije* he took what I said well || *si bien* while, although || *tener a bien* to be so kind *o* so good as to; *tenga usted a bien decirme* be so kind as to tell me; to think it better, to see fit; *tuve a bien quedarme más tiempo* I thought it better to stay longer || *tomar a bien* to take well; *tomar a bien una broma* to take a joke well || *¡ya está bien!* that's enough! || *y bien* now then.

bienal *adj/sf* biennial.

bienandante *adj* happy (feliz) || prosperous.

bienandanza; buenandanza *f* happiness (felicidad) || success (éxito) || prosperity (prosperidad).

bienaventurado, da *adj* happy, fortunate || REL blessed || FIG simple, naïve.
◆ *m/f* FIG simpleton, naïve person (inocente) || fortunate person (feliz).

bienaventuranza *f* well-being (bienestar) || happiness (felicidad) || bliss (suma felicidad) || REL blessedness.
◆ *pl* REL beatitudes.

bienestar *m* well-being, welfare.

bienhablado, da *adj* well-spoken.

bienhadado, da *adj* fortunate, lucky.

bienhechor, ra *adj* beneficent, beneficial.
◆ *m/f* benefactor (hombre), benefactress (mujer).

bienintencionado, da *adj* well-meaning.

bienio *m* biennium, two-year period.

bienmandado, da *adj* obedient.

bienoliente *adj* fragrant, sweet-smelling.

bienquerencia *f*; **bienquerer** *m* affection || goodwill (buena voluntad).

bienquerer* *vt* to appreciate, to like.

bienquistar *vt* to reconcile, to bring together.
◆ *vpr* to make it up, to become reconciled.

bienquisto, ta *adj* well-liked.
— OBSERV This word is the irregular past participle of *bienquerer*.

bienteveo *m* lookout post [hut built on piles for watching vineyards] || observation post, lookout post (mirador).

bienvenida *f* welcome || *dar la bienvenida a* to welcome, to bid welcome to.

bienvenido, da *adj* welcome || *¡que sea usted bienvenido!* welcome!

bienvivir *vi* to live well *o* comfortably (con holgura) || to live honestly *o* decently (decentemente).

bies *m* bias binding, band cut on the cross (trozo de tela) || *al bies* on the bias, on the cross.

bifásico, ca *adj* two-phase (corriente).

bife *m* AMER steak; *bife a caballo* steak with two fried eggs | slap (bofetada).

bífido, da *adj* BOT bifid.

bifocal *adj* bifocal || *lentes bifocales* bifocal glasses, bifocals.

biftec *m* steak.

bifurcación *f* bifurcation || fork (de la carretera, etc.) || junction (en ferrocarriles).

bifurcarse *vpr* to fork, to bifurcate (dividirse en dos); *la carretera se bifurca en Soria* the road forks at Soria || to branch off (separarse).

bigamia *f* bigamy.

bígamo, ma *adj* bigamous.
◆ *m/f* bigamist.

bigardear *vi* FAM to roam idly (vagar).

bigardo, da; bigardón, ona *adj* idle, lazy (vago) || licentious.
◆ *m/f* idler, lazybones (vago) || libertine.

bígaro *m* winkle (molusco).

bigarrado, da *adj* variegate, mottled.

bigarro *m* winkle (molusco).

bignoniáceas *f pl* BOT bignoniaceae.

bigorneta *f* small anvil, small beakiron, small bickiron.

bigornia *f* beakiron, bickiron, two-beaked anvil.

bigote *m* moustache [*US* mustache]; *bigote retorcido* handlebar moustache; *bigote con guías* curled-up moustache || whiskers *pl* (de un gato) || IMPR rule || tap *o* tapping hole (en un horno) || — FAM *de bigote* great, terrific (bien); *estar de bigote* to be terrific | *tener bigotes, ser un hombre de bigotes* to be a man of energy.

bigotera *f* moustache support (para el bigote) || flap seat, folding seat (en los coches) || bow compass (compás) || toe-cup (del zapato) || slag tap (en un horno).
◆ *pl* moustache *sing* [*US* mustache] (bocera en los labios).

bigotudo, da *adj* moustached [*US* mustached].

bigudí *m* curler.

bikini *m* bikini (bañador).

bilabarquín *m* AMER brace and bit.

bilabiado, da *adj* BOT bilabiate.

bilabial *adj/sf* bilabial.

bilarciasis; bilharciasis *f* MED bilharziasis, bilharziosis, bilharzia.

bilateral *adj* bilateral; *acuerdo bilateral* bilateral agreement.

bilbaína *f* beret (boina).

bilbaíno, na *adj* [of *o* from] Bilbao.
◆ *m/f* native *o* inhabitant of Bilbao.

bilbilitano, na *adj* [of *o* from] Calatayud [city in Aragon formerly «*Bibbilis*»].
◆ *m/f* native *o* inhabitant of Calatayud.

bilharciasis *f* MED → **bilarciasis.**

biliar; biliario, ria *adj* biliary || — MED *cálculo biliar* bile stone || ANAT *conducto biliar* bile duct.

bilingüe *adj* bilingual.

bilingüismo *m* bilingualism.

bilioso, sa *adj* bilious.

bilirrubina *f* bilirubin.

bilis *f* bile (humor) || FIG bile, bad temper || — FIG *descargar la bilis contra uno* to rail at s.o. | *exaltar la bilis a uno* to rile s.o.

bilobulado, da *adj* bilobed, bilobate.

bilocular *adj* BOT bilocular.

bilongo *m* AMER evil eye; *echar bilongo a* to cast the evil eye on.

billa *f* billiard ball.

billar *m* billiards; *jugar al billar* to play billiards || — *billar americano* pool || *billar automático* pinball (juego), pinball machine (aparato) || *billar ruso* snooker || *bola, mesa, taco de billar* billiard ball, table, cue.

billarista *m* billiard player.

billetaje *m* tickets *pl* (de un espectáculo).

billete *m* note (carta) || note [*US* bill] (de banco) || ticket (de tren, de lotería, de espectáculo, etc.); *sacar un billete* to buy *o* to get a ticket; *billete circular* round-trip ticket || Note; *billete al portador* note payable to bearer || HERÁLD billet || — *billete a mitad de precio* half-price ticket || *billete amoroso* love letter || *billete de andén* platform ticket || *billete de banco* banknote || *billete de ida* single ticket || *billete de ida y vuelta* return ticket [*US* round-trip ticket] || *billete kilométrico* mileage ticket || *billete postal* lettercard || *billete semanal* weekly ticket || *billete sencillo* single o one-wau ticket || *billete tarifa completa* full fare ticket || *dar una función con el cartel de «no hay billetes»* to give a sell-out performance || *medio billete* half, half-price ticket, half fare || *no hay billetes* sold out, house full.

billetera *f*; **billetero** *m* wallet [*US* pocketbook, billfold].

billón *m* billion [*US* trillion] (millón de millones).
— OBSERV En los Estados Unidos la palabra *billion* equivale a mil millones.

billonésimo, ma *adj/s* billionth [*US* trillionth].

bimano, na *adj* bimanous, bimanal, two-handed.
◆ *m* bimane.

bimba *f* FAM topper (chistera) | punch (puñetazo) || AMER FAM beanpole (persona alta) | drunkenness (borrachera).

bimbalete *m* AMER seesaw (columpio) | shadoof, shaduf (para extraer agua).

bimensual *adj* twice-monthly, fortnightly, bimonthly.

bimestral *adj* bimonthly, bimestrial.

bimestre *m* two months.

bimetálico, ca *adj* bimetallic.

bimotor, ra *adj* twin-engine, twin-engined.
◆ *m* twin-engine plane, twin-engined plane.

bina *f* AGR second ploughing.

binadera *f* AGR hoe.

binador *m* AGR hoer | hoe (herramienta).

binadora *f* AGR second ploughing.

binar *vt* AGR to plough for the second time (arar) | to hoe for the second time (cavar).

binario, ria *adj* binary || MÚS two-four (compás) || INFORM binary; *cifra binaria* binary digit || MAT *sistema binario* binary system.

binazón *f* AGR second ploughing.

bincha *f* AMER hairband.

bingarrote *m* AMER agave liquor.

binocular *adj* binocular.

binóculo *m* pince-nez.

binomio, mia *adj/sm* MAT binomial.

binza *f* membrane (telilla) || skin (de cebolla).

biobibliografía *f* biobibliography.

biodegradable *adj* biodegradable.

bioenergética *f* bioenergetics.

biofísica *f* biophysics.

biofísico, ca *adj* biophysical.
◆ *m/f* biphysicist.

biogénesis *f* biogenesis.

biogenético, ca *adj* biogenetic, biogenetical.

biogeografía *f* biogeography.
biografía *f* biography.
biografiar *vt* to write (s.o.'s) biography.
biográfico, ca *adj* biographic, biographical.
biógrafo, fa *m/f* biographer.
◆ *m* AMER cinema.
bioingeniería *f* bioengineering.
biología *f* biology.
biológico, ca *adj* biological; *guerra biológica* biological warfare.
biólogo *m* biologist.
biombo *m* folding screen.
biomecánica *f* biomechanics.
biometría *f* biometry.
biopsia *f* MED biopsy.
bioquímico, ca *adj* biochemical.
◆ *m/f* biochemist.
◆ *f* biochemistry.
biorritmo *m* MED biorhythm.
bioscopio *m* bioscope.
biosfera *f* biosphere.
biosíntesis *f* biosynthesis.
biotecnia *f* biotechnics.
bioterapia *f* MED biotherapy.
biótico, ca *adj* biotic.
biotipo *m* biotype.
biotita *f* MIN biotite.
bióxido *m* QUÍM dioxide.
bipartición *f* bipartition.
bipartido, da *adj* bipartite.
bipartito, ta *adj* bipartite; *acuerdo bipartito* bipartite agreement.
bípedo, da *adj/sm* biped.
biplano *m* biplane (avión).
biplaza *adj/sm* two-seater.
bipolar *adj* bipolar, two-pole.
bipolaridad *f* bipolarity.
bipolarización *f* bipolarization.
biricú *m* sword belt.
birimbao *m* MÚS jew's-harp.
birla *f* skittle, ninepin (bolo).
birlar *vt* to bowl a second time (en el juego de los bolos) ‖ FIG & FAM to pinch (robar, quitar) | to bump off (matar).
birlibirloque (por arte de) *loc adv* as if by magic.
birlocha *f* kite (cometa).
birlocho *m* open carriage.
birlonga *f* brelan (juego).
Birmania *npr f* GEOGR Burma.
birmano, na *adj/s* Burmese.
birome *f* AMER Biro, ball-point pen (bolígrafo).
birreactor *adj* twin-jet.
◆ *m* twin-jet plane.
birrefringencia *f* FÍS birefringence.
birrefringente *adj* FÍS birefringent.
birreme *f* MAR bireme.
birreta *f* biretta.
birrete *m* biretta (birreta) ‖ cap (de un magistrado) ‖ bonnet (gorro) ‖ mortarboard (de catedrático).
birretina *f* MIL hussar's cap.
birria *f* FAM horror (cosa o persona fea) | piece of junk *o* trash *o* rubbish (cosa mala o sin valor) ‖ AMER mania (capricho) ‖ *ser una birria* to be horrible.
bis *adv* A (número); *vivo en el 22 bis* I live at 22 A ‖ MÚS bis ‖ twice, bis (dos veces).
◆ *m* encore.
◆ *interj* encore!
bisabuelo, la *m/f* great-grandfather, great-grandmother.
◆ *m pl* great-grandparents.
bisagra *f* hinge (de puerta, etc.).
bisanual; bisanuo, nua *adj* biennial.
bisar *vt* to encore [an actor], to call [an actor], to give an encore ‖ to repeat (una canción).
bisbisar; bisbisear *vt* FAM to mutter, to mumble (decir entre dientes) | to whisper (al oído).
bisbiseo *m* whisper, whispering (susurro) ‖ muttering, mumbling (murmullo).
biscote *m* rusk, toast; *biscote integral* wholewheat toast.
biscuit *m* biscuit (porcelana).
— OBSERV The Spanish translation of *biscuit* (pastry) is *galleta*.
bisección *f* MAT bisection.
bisector, triz *adj* MAT bisecting.
◆ *f* MAT bisector, bisectrix.
bisel *m* bevel, bevel edge ‖ — *el espejo tiene el borde en bisel* the mirror has a bevelled edge ‖ *tallar en bisel* to bevel.
biselado *m* bevelling.
biselar *vt* to bevel.
bisemanal *adj* twice-weekly, biweekly; *una revista bisemanal* a biweekly magazine.
bisemanario *m* AMER twice-weekly *o* biweekly magazine.
bisexual *adj* bisexual.
bisexualidad *f* bisexuality.
bisiesto *adj* bissextile ‖ *año bisiesto* leap year.
bisilábico, ca; bisílabo, ba *adj* two-syllabled.
bismuto *m* bismuth.
bisnieto, ta; biznieto, ta *m/f* great-grandchild (chico o chica), great-grandson (chico), great-granddaughter (chica).
◆ *m pl* great-grandchildren.
bisojo, ja *adj* cross-eyed, squinting (bizco) ‖ *un chico bisojo* a cross-eyed boy, a boy with a squint.
bisonte *m* ZOOL bison.
bisoñada; bisoñería *f* FIG & FAM beginner's mistake, blunder.
bisoñé *m* toupee.
bisoño, ña *adj* green, inexperienced (principiante) ‖ MIL raw (recluta).
◆ *m/f* greenhorn, novice.
◆ *m* MIL raw recruit, rookie (*fam*).
bistec; bisté *m* steak.
bistorta *f* BOT bistort.
bistre *m* bistre [US bister] (color).
bisturí *m* MED bistoury, scalpel.
bisulco, ca *adj* ZOOL bisulcate, cloven-hoofed.
bisulfato *m* bisulphate.
bisulfito *m* QUÍM bisulphite.
bisurco *adj m* *arado bisurco* double-furrow plough.
bisutería *f* imitation jewellery, paste ‖ *una joya de bisutería* a piece of imitation jewellery.
bit *m* INFORM bit.
bita *f* MAR bitt, bollard.
bitácora *f* MAR binnacle ‖ *cuaderno de bitácora* logbook.
Bitinia *npr f* Bithynia.
bitongo *adj m* FAM *niño bitongo* young upstart.
bitoque *m* spigot, spile (de barril) ‖ AMER tap (grifo) | cannula (de una jeringa) | sewer, drain (sumidero).
bitter *m* bitters *pl* (aperitivo).
bituminoso, sa *adj* bituminous; *carbón bituminoso* bituminous coal.
bivalencia *f* QUÍM bivalence.
bivalente *adj* QUÍM bivalent, divalent.
bivalvo, va *adj/sm* bivalve.
Bizancio *n pr* GEOGR Byzantium.
bizantinismo *m* Byzantinism.
bizantino, na *adj/s* Byzantine ‖ *discusiones bizantinas* hairsplitting.
bizarrear *vi* to show courage (valor) ‖ to show generosity (generosidad).
bizarría *f* bravery, gallantry (valor) ‖ generosity (generosidad) ‖ dash (gallardía).
bizarro, rra *adj* brave, gallant; *un bizarro coronel* a brave colonel ‖ generous ‖ dashing (gallardo).
bizaza *f*; **bizazas** *f pl* double bag *sing*.
bizcar *vi* to squint, to be cross-eyed.
bizco, ca *adj* cross-eyed, squinting ‖ — FIG & FAM *dejar bizco* to dumbfound, to flabbergast ‖ *ponerse bizco* to squint (ojos), to be dumbfounded, to be flabbergasted (pasmado).
◆ *m/f* cross-eyed person, person with a squint.
bizcochar *vt* to warm up; *pan bizcochado* warmed-up bread ‖ to bake (porcelana).
bizcochería *f* AMER confectioner's shop, confectioner's.
bizcocho *m* CULIN sponge (masa) | sponge cake (pastel) ‖ TECN biscuit (de porcelana) ‖ *bizcocho borracho* rum baba.
bizcotela *f* iced cake.
biznaga *f* BOT bishop's weed ‖ small bouquet of jasmine (ramillete).
biznieto, ta *m/f* → **bisnieto.**
bizquear *vi* FAM to squint, to be cross-eyed.
bizquera *f* squint (estrabismo).
black-rot *m* black rot (enfermedad de la vid).
blanca *f* ancient coin (antigua moneda) ‖ MÚS minim ‖ ZOOL magpie (urraca) ‖ — *blanca doble* double blank (dominós) ‖ FIG & FAM *no tener blanca, estar sin blanca* to be stony broke, not to have two halfpennies to rub together.
Blancanieves *npr f* Snow White.
blanco, ca *adj* white; *pan, vino blanco* white bread, wine ‖ white, light (piel) ‖ white (raza) ‖ fair (tez) ‖ FIG & FAM yellow, cowardly (cobarde) ‖ — *arma blanca* knife ‖ *bandera blanca* white flag ‖ *blanco como el papel* as white as a sheet, as white as a ghost ‖ *darle carta blanca a uno* to give s.o. a free hand ‖ FIG *estar en blanco* not to have a clue ‖ *manjar blanco* blancmange (natilla) ‖ *más blanco que la nieve* as white as snow ‖ *ropa blanca* linen, drapery (sábanas, etc.), lingerie (de mujer), underwear (de hombre).
◆ *m/f* white man, white woman, white person, white (de raza blanca).
◆ *m* white (color) ‖ interval, interlude (intervalo) ‖ gap (en un fila) ‖ blank (espacio) ‖ target (de tiro) ‖ white patch (mancha de un animal) ‖ FIG goal, aim, target (objetivo) ‖ — *blanco de ballena* spermaceti ‖ *blanco de cinc* zinc white ‖ *blanco de España* whiting ‖ *blanco de la uña* half-moon ‖ *blanco del ojo* white of the eye ‖ *blanco de plomo* white lead ‖ *calentar al blanco* to bring to white heat, to make white-hot (metal) ‖ *caseta de tiro al blanco* shooting gallery ‖ *como de lo blanco a lo negro* as different as chalk and cheese ‖ *dar en el*

blanco, hacer blanco to hit the mark, to hit the bull's eye || *dejar algo en blanco* to leave sth. blank || *en blanco* blank (papel), useless; *ha sido un día en blanco* it has been a useless day; disappointed; *quedarse en blanco* to be disappointed || *mirarle a uno en el blanco de los ojos* to look s.o. in the face || *no distinguir lo blanco de lo negro* not to distinguish black from white || *pasar una noche en blanco* to spend a sleepless night || *ser el blanco de las burlas* to be a laughingstock, to be the object of ridicule || *ser el blanco de las miradas* to be the centre of attention || *tirar al blanco* to shoot at a target || *tiro al blanco* target shooting || *votar en blanco* to vote blank.

blancor *m* whiteness (blancura).

blancote, ta *adj* sickly white || FAM yellow (cobarde).

blancura *f* whiteness || FIG purity (del alma).

blancuzco, ca *adj* whitish.

blandear *vi* to weaken, to yield.
◆ *vt* to convince || to brandish (blandir).
◆ *vpr* to weaken, to yield.

blandengue *adj* FAM weak, feeble, soft.
◆ *m/f* softy, weakling (débil).
◆ *m* soldier who protected the frontiers of Argentina.

blandenguería *f* weakness, feebleness, softness.

blandicia *f* softness (molicie) || flattery (lisonja).

blandir* *vt* to brandish (un arma).

blando, da *adj* soft; *este colchón es blando* this mattress is soft || tender (carne, etc.) || FIG gentle (mirada, palabras, etc.) | weak; *carácter blando* weak character | soft; *un profesor blando con sus alumnos* a teacher who is soft with his pupils | easy, cushy (*fam*); *una vida blanda* an easy life | soft, gentle; *blando murmullo de las olas* soft murmuring of the waves | mild (clima) | cowardly (cobarde) || — *blando de carnes* flabby || *blando de corazón* tender-hearted, soft-hearted || FIG & FAM *ojos blandos* watery eyes (llorosos).
◆ *adv* softly, gently.

blandón *m* torch (hachón) || candlestick (candelero).

blanducho, cha; blandujo, ja *adj* FAM softish | flabby (carne, cuerpo).

blandura *f* softness (cualidad) || tenderness (de los alimentos) || FIG gentleness (de la mirada, las palabras, etc.) | weakness (de carácter) | ease, easiness (de vida) | flabbiness (de carne) | mildness (del tiempo) | blandishment (lisonja) | endearment (amabilidad).

blanduzco, ca *adj* FAM softish.

blanqueado *m* ⟶ **blanqueo.**

blanqueador, ra *m/f* whitewasher.

blanqueamiento *m* ⟶ **blanqueo.**

blanquear *vt* to whiten (volver blanco) || to whitewash (encalar las paredes) || to bleach (tejidos, etc.) || to blanch (almendras, metales) || to wax [the honeycomb after winter] (las abejas) || IMPR to space out || to refine (azúcar) || ECON to launder (dinero) || *sepulcro blanqueado* whited sepulchre.
◆ *vi* to turn white, to whiten || to show white, to appear white; *blanquean algunas manchas de nieve en la ladera* a few patches of snow show white on the hillside || to be whitish (tirar a blanco).

blanquecer* *vt* to whiten || to blanch (metales).

blanquecimiento *m* blanching (metales).

blanquecino, na *adj* whitish.

blanqueo *m*; **blanqueado** *m*; **blanqueamiento** *m* whitening || whitewashing (encalado) || bleaching (con lejía) || TECN blanching | refining (del azúcar).

blanquete *m* whiting (sustancia para blanquear) || white cosmetic (afeite).

blanquición *f* blanching (metales).

blanquillo, lla *adj* *trigo blanquillo* white wheat.
◆ *m* AMER white-skinned peach (durazno) | white-fish (pez) | egg (huevo).

blanquinegro, gra *adj* black and white.

blanquinoso, sa *adj* whitish.

blanquizco, ca *adj* whitish.

Blas *npr m* Blase || *díjolo* or *lo dijo Blas, punto redondo* you're always right, whatever you say [said ironically].

blasfemador, ra *adj* blasphemous.
◆ *m/f* blasphemer.

blasfemar *vi* to blaspheme || FIG to curse.

blasfematorio, ria *adj* blasphemous.

blasfemia *f* blasphemy || FIG curse.

blasfemo, ma *adj* blasphemous.
◆ *m/f* blasphemer.

blasón *m* heraldry (heráldica) || coat of arms, armorial bearings *pl*, blazon (escudo de armas) || bearing, device (divisa) || FIG honour, glory || *hacer blasón de* to boast of *o* about, to brag of *o* about.
◆ *pl* noble ancestry *sing*; *está orgulloso de sus blasones* he is proud of his noble ancestry.

blasonador, ra *adj* boasting, bragging.
◆ *m/f* boaster, braggart.

blasonar *vt* to emblazon.
◆ *vi* FIG to boast of *o* about, to brag of *o* about; *blasonar de rico* to boast of being rich.

blasonería *f* boasting, bragging.

blastema *m* BIOL blastema.

blastodermo *m* BIOL blastoderm.

blastómero *m* BIOL blastomere.

blastomicetos *m pl* blastomycetes (hongos).

blastomicosis *f* MED blastomycosis.

blástula *f* BIOL blastula.

bledo *m* blite (planta) || FIG & FAM *me importa un bledo, no se me da un bledo* I don't care two hoots, I don't give a damm.

blenda *f* MIN blende.

blenorragia *f* MED blennorrhagia.

blindado, da *adj* MIL armoured, armour-plated || TECN shielded.

blindaje *m* MIL blindage (fortificación) | armour plate, armour (revestimiento de tanques, etc.) | armour plating (operación) || TECN shield.

blindar *vt* to armour, to armour-plate || TECN to shield.

bloc *m* pad (para apuntes) || writing pad (para cartas).

blocao *m* blockhouse.

block-system *m* TECN block system.

blonda *f* Spanish lace, blond lace.

blondo, da *adj* blond, fair (rubio).

bloom *m* bloom (lingote bruto).

bloque *m* block; *un bloque de mármol* a block of marble || bloc (política); *el bloque atlántico* the Atlantic Bloc || block, brick (de helado) || — TECN *bloque de cilindros* cylinder block | *bloque del motor* engine block | *bloque de matrizar* female die || *bloque de viviendas* block of flats || *bloque diagrama* block diagram || *de un solo bloque* in one piece || FIG *en bloque* en bloc | *formar bloque con* to form a block with.

bloqueador, ra *adj* blocking, which blocks || blockading; *armada bloqueadora* blockading fleet || besieging (sitiador).
◆ *m/f* besieger.

bloquear *vt* MIL & MAR to blockade || COM to freeze, to block || DEP to block; *bloquear una pelota* to block a ball || to block, to jam (un mecanismo, etc.) || to obstruct, to block (obstruir) || FIG to block (un proyecto de ley, etc.) || *estar bloqueado por la tormenta* to be cut off by the storm.

bloqueo *m* MIL & MAR blockade; *levantar un bloqueo* to raise a blockade; *romper un bloqueo* to run a blockade || COM freezing, blocking || — *bloqueo económico* economic blkockade || *bloqueo mental* mental block.

blue-jean *m* jeans *pl* (pantalón vaquero).

blues *m* MÚS blues.

bluff *m* bluff.

blúmers *m pl* AMER knickers (bragas).

blusa *f* blouse (de mujer) || overall [*US* frock] (guardapolvo).

blusón *m* long *o* loose shirt (blusa larga) || sailor blouse (de mujer).

bluyines *m pl* AMER jeans (vaqueros).

boa *f* boa (reptil) || boa (adorno de pieles *o* de plumas).

boardilla *f* attic, garret (buhardilla).

boato *m* show, ostentation (ostentación) || pomp (pompa).

bobada; bobería *f* stupid *o* silly thing; *decir, hacer una bobada* to say, to do sth. stupid || — *déjate de bobadas* that's enough of your nonsense || *¡qué bobadas dices!* you're talking nonsense.

bobalicón, ona *adj* FAM simple, stupid, idiotic.
◆ *m/f* FAM simpleton, idiot, nincompoop.

bobear *vi* to talk nonsense, to be silly (decir tonterías) || to be stupid *o* silly, to play the fool (hacer el tonto).

bobería *f* ⟶ **bobada** || **silliness, stupidity.**

bobeta *adj/s* AMER ⟶ **bobalicón.**

bóbilis bóbilis (de) *adv* FAM without lifting a finger (sin esfuerzo) | for nothing (de balde).

bobina *f* reel; *las bobinas de una máquina de escribir* the reels on a typewriter || bobbin, reel, spool (de hilo) || spool, reel (de fotos) || ELECTR coil; *bobina de sintonía, de encendido* tuning, ignition coil.

bobinado *m* winding.

bobinador, ra *m/f* winder (operario).
◆ *f* winding machine (máquina).

bobinar *vt* to wind.

bobito *m* ZOOL cuban flycatcher.

bobo, ba *adj* stupid, silly, foolish (tonto) || naïve, simple (candoroso).
◆ *m/f* dunce, fool.
◆ *m* TEATR buffoon || Central American fresh water fish || — FIG *a los bobos se les aparece la Madre de Dios* fortune favours fools | *el bobo de Coria* the village idiot | *entre bobos anda el juego* they are as thick as thieves.

bobsleigh *m* bobsleigh (trineo).

boca *f* ANAT mouth || pincers *pl*, nippers *pl* (de crustáceo) || lip, mouth (de vasija) || muzzle (de cañón) || entrance, mouth (de puerto, metro, túnel) || TECN opening (de un horno) | mouth, throat (de alto horno) | cutting edge (de una herramienta cortante) | jaws *pl* (de las pinzas) | peen (de un martillo) || entry, entrance (de una calle) || aroma, bouquet (del vino) || opening (en el teatro) || FIG mouth; *tener seis bocas que alimentar* to have six mouths to feed || — *a boca de cañón* point-blank (desde muy cerca), suddenly (repentinamente) || FIG *a boca de jarro* point-blank (a quemarropa) | *a*

boca de noche at dusk, at twilight | *a boca llena* without mincing one's words, straight out | *abrir boca* to give an appetite || FAM *¡a callarse la boca* shut up!, shut your mouth! || *ancho de boca* wide-mouthed (vasija) || FIG *andar de boca en boca* to be on everyone's lips | *andar en boca de las gentes* to be the main talking point | *a pedir de boca* to one's heart's content, for the asking || *blando de boca* soft-mouthed, tender-mouthed (un caballo) || *boca abajo* face down, on one's stomach || *boca a boca* mouth-to-mouth respiration, kiss of life || *boca arriba* face up, on one's back (una persona); *le volvieron boca arriba* they turned him onto his back; face up (una cosa) || FIG *boca de escorpión* evil tongue (maldiciente) | *boca de espuerta* big mouth || MIL *boca de fuego* piece of artillery, gun || *boca de incendio* fire hydrant || *boca del estómago* pit of the stomach || *boca de metro* underground station entrance, tube station entrance [US subway entrance] || FIG *boca de oro* silver tongue || *boca de riego* hydrant || FIG *buscarle a uno la boca* to try to pick a quarrel with s.o. | *calentársele a uno la boca* to get carried away (hablar con extensión), to get heated, to lose one's temper (enfadarse) | *callar la boca* to keep quiet, to keep one's mouth shut | *cerrarle a uno la boca* to shut s.o. up || *con la boca abierta* gaping, agape, openmouthed; *quedarse con la boca abierta* to stand gaping || *con toda la boca* in one mouthful || FAM *darle a uno en la boca* to smash s.o.'s face in (romper las narices), to leave s.o. speechless (dejar asombrado) || FIG *decir algo con la boca chica* or *chiquita* to say one thing and mean another || *decir uno lo que le viene a la boca* to say whatever comes into one's head || *de la mano a la boca se pierde la sopa* there's many a slip 'twixt the cup and the lip || *despegar la boca* to open one's mouth || *duro de boca* hard-mouthed (caballo) || FIG *echar por aquella boca* to spit out (insultos) | *el que tiene boca se equivoca* anyone can make a mistake | *en boca cerrada no entran moscas* silence is golden | *estar colgado de la boca de uno* to hang on to s.o.'s every word | *estar oscuro como boca de lobo* to be pitch dark, to be pitch black (túnel, noche, etc.) | *estar uno a qué quieres boca* to be well off, to be comfortable | *estar uno con la boca a la pared* to be down and out | *hablar uno por boca de ganso* to speak from hearsay | *hablar por boca de uno* to have s.o. as spokesman | *hacer boca* to give an appetite | *hacer una promesa de boca para fuera* to make a half-hearted promise | *írsele la boca a uno* to let the cat out of the bag, not to be able to keep one's mouth shut | *meterse en la boca del lobo* to put one's head into the lion's mouth | *no abrir* or *descoser la boca* not to open one's mouth | *no caérsele a uno algo de la boca* to always have sth. on one's lips | *no decir esta boca es mía* not to say a word | *¡no me busques la boca!* you're asking for it! | *no tener nada que llevarse a la boca* not to have a bite to eat | *poner boca de corazoncito* to pout | *poner en boca de* to put into the mouth of || *poner* or *volver las cartas boca arriba* to lay one's cards face up (sentido propio), to put one's cards on the table (descubrir sus intenciones) | FIG *por la boca muere el pez* the least said the better, silence is golden, least said is soonest mended | *por una boca* in one voice, in unison | *¡punto en boca!* mum's the word!, don't say a word! | *quitarle a uno las palabras de la boca* to take the words right out of s.o.'s mouth | *quitarse algo de la boca por otra persona* to deprive o.s. of sth. for the sake of s.o. else | *respira este chico por boca de su padre* in this boy's eyes his father cannot do a thing wrong | *salir a pedir de boca* to turn out perfectly | *se me hace la boca agua al ver este pastel* that cake makes my mouth water || FAM *taparle la boca a uno* to shut s.o. up (hacer callar), to shut s.o. up, to keep s.o. quiet (sobornar) || *telón de boca* drop curtain || FIG *torcer la boca* to grimace | *venir a pedir de boca* to come at the right moment, to come at an opportune moment.
◆ *pl* mouth *sing*; *las bocas del Nilo* the mouth of the Nile.

bocacalle *f* intersection || *tuerza a la tercera bocacalle a la izquierda* take the third turning *o* street on your left.

bocacaz *f* outlet to irrigation ditch.

bocacha *f* big mouth | MIL blunderbuss (trabuco).

bocadear *vt* to divide into pieces.

bocadillo *m* sandwich (emparedado); *un bocadillo de queso* a cheese sandwich || snack, bite to eat (comida ligera); *tomar un bocadillo* to have a snack || fancy ribbon (cinta) || *AMER* guava or coconut sweet.

bocado *m* mouthful; *un bocado de pan* a mouthful of bread || snack, bite to eat; *comer* or *tomar un bocado* to have a snack *o* a bite to eat || beakful, billful (lo que coge el ave de una vez con el pico) || bite (mordisco); *el niño me dio un bocado* the child gave me a bite || bit (freno del caballo) || — *bocado de Adán* Adam's apple || FAM *bocado de cardenal* choice morsel | *comer algo en un bocado* to eat sth. in one mouthful | *con el bocado en la boca* having scarcely finished eating | *me la comería a bocados* I could eat her | *no hay para un bocado* there's not enought to feed a sparrow || *no pruebo bocado desde ayer* I haven't had a bite to eat since yesterday.

bocajarro (a) *adv* point-blank.

bocal *m* jar, pitcher.

bocamanga *f* cuff, wristband.

bocamina *f* pithead, mine entrance.

bocana *f* *AMER* mouth (de un río).

bocanada *f* puff, whiff (de humo) || blast, whiff (de olor desagradable) || mouthful, swallow; *una bocanada de vino* a swallow of wine || — FIG *bocanada de aire* some air; *abrió la ventana para que entrara una bocanada de aire* he opened the window to let some air in; rush of air; *al abrir la ventana entró una bocanada de aire* when he opened the window there was a rush of air into the room | *bocanada de gente* crowd, throng of people | *bocanada de viento* gust of wind.

bocarte *m* MIN ore crusher, stamp mill.

bocateja *f* front tile [of a roof].

bocatijera *f* futchel, futchell (de carruaje).

bocaza *f* FAM big mouth.

bocazas *m inv* FAM big mouth (que habla demasiado).

bocazo *m* fizzle, dud explosion (de mina, de cohete).

bocel; bocelete *m* ARQ torus || *cuarto bocel* quarter round, ovolo.

bocelar *vt* ARQ to make mouldings on.

bocelete *m* —> **bocel**.

bocera *f* moustache [smear left on lips after eating or drinking]; *boceras de chocolate* moustache of chocolate || MED lip sore [in the corners of the mouth].

boceras *m inv* big mouth (que habla demasiado).

boceto *m* sketch (dibujo) || rough study (escultura) || rough draught, outline (escrito).

bocina *f* MÚS horn || megaphone (para hablar desde lejos) || AUT horn; *tocar la bocina* to sound one's horn || horn (de los gramófonos) || ASTR Ursa Minor, the Little Bear || ZOOL whelk || *AMER* hubcap (de rueda) | ear trumpet (aparato para los sordos).

bocinar *vi* MÚS to play the horn || to sound one's horn (un automóvil).

bocinazo *m* hoot, toot, honk || FAM telling off, scolding.

bocio *m* MED goitre [US goiter].

bock *m* tankard, beer mug (de cerveza).

bocón, ona *adj* FAM big-mouthed || FIG & FAM big-mouthed (fanfarrón).
◆ *m* FIG & FAM braggart (fanfarrón) || ZOOL species of Antillian sardine || *AMER* MIL blunderbuss.

bocoy *m* hogshead, cask (tonel).
— OBSERV pl *bocoyes*.

bocudo, da *adj* big-mouthed.

bocha *f* bowl.
◆ *pl* bowls (juego).

bochar *vt* to displace, to send flying (en el juego de bochas) || FIG & FAM to snub (desairar) | to fail (en un examen) | to reject (rechazar).

bochazo *m* blow of one bowl against another.

boche *m* small hole (agujero) || *AMER* blow of one bowl against another | quarrel (pendencia) | din, uproar, row (jaleo) | executioner (verdugo) || *AMER* *dar boche a uno* to snub s.o.

bochinche; buchinche *m* FAM row, din, uproar (alboroto); *armar un bochinche* to kick up a row, to cause uproar | dive (taberna, cafetucho).

bochinchero, ra *adj/s* FAM rowdy.

bochorno *m* sultry *o* heavy weather (tiempo) || stifling atmosphere (atmósfera) || warm breeze (viento) || FIG shame (vergüenza) | blushing (rubor) | dizziness, giddiness (mareo corto) || MED flush || — FIG *¡qué bochorno!* how embarrassing! | *sufrir un bochorno* to feel so embarrassed *o* ashamed (estar avergonzado).

bochornoso, sa *adj* sultry, heavy; *un día bochornoso* a sultry day || stifling (atmósfera) || FIG shameful (vergonzoso); *una acción bochornosa* a shameful action | embarrassing (molesto).

boda *f* wedding, marriage || — FIG *boda de negros* rowdy party | *bodas de Camacho* banquet || *bodas de plata, de oro, de diamante* silver, golden, diamond wedding.

bodega *f* wine cellar (para guardar y criar el vino) || cellar (en una casa) || wine shop (tienda) || hold (de un barco) || warehouse (almacén en un puerto) || *AMER* grocery store, grocer's (tienda de abarrotes) | restaurant.

bodegaje *m* *AMER* storage.

bodegón *m* cheap restaurant (restaurante malo) || dive (tabernucho) || still life (pintura) || FIG *¿en qué bodegón hemos comido juntos?* please remember whom you are talking to.

bodeguero, ra *m/f* owner of a wine cellar.

bodijo *m* unequal marriage, misalliance (boda desigual) || quiet wedding (sin aparato).

bodoque *m* pellet (de ballesta) || FIG & FAM dunce, blockhead (persona tonta) || *AMER* lump (chichón).

bodoquera *f* pellet mould (molde) || blowpipe (cerbatana).

bodorrio *m* FAM —> **bodijo**.

bodrio *m* hotchpotch (comida) || muddle, mess (de cosas).

bóer *adj/s* boer.

bofe *m*; **bofes** *m pl* lights *pl*, lungs *pl* (de ternera, etc.).
◆ *m sing* *AMER* child's play (cosa muy fácil) || FIG & FAM *echar el bofe* or *los bofes* to slog away, to go at it hammer and tongs (trabajar), to pant heavily, to blow like a grampus (jadear).

bofetada *f*; **bofetón** *m* slap (guantazo) || FIG blow; *fue una bofetada para su orgullo* it was a blow to his pride || — FIG *darse de bofetadas* *por una cosa* to come to blows over sth || *dar una bofetada a alguien* to slap s.o. [in the face], to slap s.o.'s face || FIG *esos dos colores se dan de bofetadas* these two colours clash horribly.

boga *f* MAR rowing || FIG fashion, vogue; *estar en boga* to be in fashion.
◆ *m/f* MAR rower.

bogada *f* stroke of the oar.

bogador, ra *m/f* rower.

bogar *vi* to row (remar) || to sail (navegar) || TECN to skim (metal fundido).

bogavante *m* ZOOL lobster || MAR stroke (primer remero).

bogie; boggie *m* bogie, bogy, bogey (carretón).

Bogotá *n pr* GEOGR Bogota.

bogotano, na *adj* [of *o* from] Bogotá.
◆ *m/f* native *o* inhabitant of Bogotá.

Bohemia *npr f* GEOGR Bohemia.

bohémico, ca *adj* Bohemian.

bohemio, mia *adj* Bohemian; *vida bohemia* Bohemian life.
◆ *adj/s* Bohemian || gipsy (gitano).
◆ *f* Bohemianism, Bohemian life.

bohemo, ma *adj/s* Bohemian.

bohío *m* AMER cabin, hut.

bohordo *m* scape, stem (tallo).

boicot; boycot *m* boycott.

boicotear; boycotear *vt* to boycott.

boicoteo; boycoteo *m* boycott, boicotting.

boíl *m* cowshed.

boina *f* beret (vasca).

boite *f* nightclub.

boj; boje *m* BOT box (árbol) | boxwood (madera).

bojar; bojear *vt* MAR to measure the perimeter of [an island].
◆ *vi* MAR to have a perimeter of [an island] | to coast (costear).

boje *m* —> **boj.**

bojeo *m* MAR measurement of the perimeter of an island (acción de medir) | perimeter (medida) | coasting (acción de costear).

bol *m* bowl || dragnet (red) || *bol arménico* Armenian bole (barro rojo).

bola *f* ball (cuerpo esférico); *bola de billar* billiard ball || marble (canica) || slam (bridge); *media bola* little slam || shoe polish (betún) || FIG & FAM ball (fútbol) | lie, fib (cuento); *contar* or *meter bolas* to tell fibs | globe (del mundo) || AMER round kite (cometa) | rowdy party (reunión ruidosa) || — *bola de cristal* crystal ball || *bola de naftalina* mothball || *bola de nieve* snowball || *bola negra* blackball (en una votación) || *carbón de bola* ovoid || FAM *¡dale bola!* what, again?, come off it! || *dar bola* to polish, to clean [US to shine] || AMER *dar en bola* to hit the bull's-eye || FIG *dejar que ruede la bola* to let things take their course | *echar bola negra* to blackball, to turn down || *el Niño de la Bola* Baby Jesus || FIG & FAM *no da pie con bola* he can't do a thing right! | *no rascar bola* not to lift a finger, not to do a stroke of work | *¡ruede la bola!* let us chance it!, here goes!
◆ *pl* POP balls (testículos) || — *cojinete de bolas* ball bearing || FAM *ir en bolas* to be starkers || —> **boleadoras.**

bolada *f* throw (lanzamiento) || stroke (en el billar) || AMER opportunity, chance (oportunidad) | sweet [US candy] (golosina) | dirty trick (jugarreta) | witticism, witty remark [US wisecrack] || AMER *estar de bolada* to be in luck.

bolardo *m* MAR bollard (noray).

bolazo *m* blow (golpe) || AMER silly remark (tontería) | fib, lie (mentira).

bolchevique *adj/s* Bolshevik.

bolchevismo *m* Bolshevism.

boleada *f* AMER hunting with «boleadoras».

boleadoras *f pl* bolas [weapon used by Argentine gauchos which consists of several ropes tied together with metal balls at the ends].

bolear *vi* to knock the balls about (al billar) || FIG to lie, to fib (mentir).
◆ *vt* FAM to throw (arrojar) || AMER to throw the bolas at | to blackball (en una votación) | to fail (en un examen) | to mix up, to confuse (enredar) | to polish, to clean [US to shine] (el calzado) | to play a dirty trick on (hacer una jugarreta).
◆ *vpr* AMER to be wrong *o* mistaken (equivocarse) | to get mixed up *o* confused (enredarse) | to rear (un potro).

bolera *f* skittles (juego de bolos) || bowling alley (local) || skittle alley (en un bar, etc.) || *bolera americana* bowling alley.

bolero, ra *adj* lying, fibbing (mentiroso) || who plays truant [US who plays hookey] (estudiante) || *escarabajo bolero* dung beetle.
◆ *m/f* FIG & FAM fibber (embustero).
◆ *m* bolero (baile y chaquetilla) || AMER top hat (sombrero de copa) | bootblack, shoeblack [US shoeshine boy] (limpiabotas).

boleta *f* ticket (billete) || MIL billet || pass (permiso) || voucher (vale) || ballot paper, voting paper (de votación) || AMER bulletin, report; *boleta de sanidad* health bulletin.

boletería *f* AMER ticket office, box office (en un teatro) | ticket office, booking office (en una estación, un estadio, etc.).

boletero, ra *m/f* AMER ticket seller.

boletín *m* bulletin; *boletín informativo* or *de noticias* news bulletin || report (de los alumnos) || journal (publicación de una sociedad) || form (para suscribirse a algo) || ticket (billete) || MIL billet || — *boletín de suscripción* subscription form || *boletín meteorológico* weather forecast, weather report || *Boletín Oficial del Estado* Official Gazette.

boleto *m* BOT boletus (hongo) || ticket (de lotería) || AMER ticket (billete de ferrocarril, de teatro, etc.) | coupon (de quinielas) | FAM fib (embuste) || FAM *boleto de apuestas* betting slip.

bolichada *f* FIG & FAM lucky break.

boliche *m* jack (en la petanca) || skittles (juego de bolos) || bowling alley (bolera americana) || cup-and-ball (juego de niños) || small dragnet (red) || small fry (morralla) || small furnace (horno) || AMER small grocery store (tenducho) | dive (taberna).

bolichear *vi* AMER to potter about, to tinker about [US to putter].

bolichero, ra *m/f* bowling alley manager || fishmonger (pescadero) || AMER grocer.

bólido *m* ASTR bolide, meteorite || racing car (coche de carreras) || FAM *ir como un bólido* to go like a bat out of hell.

bolígrafo *m* ball-point pen.

bolilla *f* small ball || *bolilla pestosa* stink bomb.

bolillo *m* bobbin; *encaje de bolillos* bobbin lace || fetlock (de las caballerías) || AMER bread roll.
◆ *pl* lollipops (caramelos) || AMER drumsticks.

bolina *f* MAR sounding line (sonda) | bowline (cuerda) || FIG & FAM din, row (alboroto) || MAR *ir* or *navegar de bolina* to sail close-hauled *o* close to the wind.

bolista *adj* FAM lying, fibbing.
◆ *m/f* FAM fibber (mentiroso).

bolitas *f pl* AMER marbles.

bolívar *m* bolivar [monetary unit of Venezuela].

Bolivia *npr f* GEOGR Bolivia.

boliviano, na *adj/s* Bolivian.
◆ *m* boliviano [currency of Bolivia].

bolo *m* skittle, ninepin (juego) || newel (de una escalera) || slam (en los naipes) || capot (el que no hace baza en el juego) || bolus (píldora) || FAM clod, dimwit (persona torpe) || — *bolo alimenticio* alimentary bolus | *bolo arménico* Armenian bole.
◆ *pl* skittles *sing* || bowling alley *sing* (bolera) || *jugador de bolos* skittles player.

bolo, la *adj* AMER drunk (ebrio) | tailless (sin cola).

bolómetro *m* bolometer.

bolón *m* ARQ quarry stone.

Bolonia *n pr* GEOGR Bologna (Italia) | Boulogne (Francia).

bolonio, nia *m/f* FIG & FAM dunce, ignoramus.

boloñés, esa *adj/s* Bolognan, Bolognian, Bolognese.

bolsa *f* purse (para el dinero); *tener la bolsa repleta* to have a well-lined purse; *tener la bolsa vacía* to have a light *o* empty purse || bag (para objetos en general); *bolsa del cartero, de papel* postman's bag, paper bag || pouch (para el tabaco) || foot muff (para los pies) || pucker, bag (de un vestido) || COM exchange; *Bolsa de Comercio* Commodity Exchange; *Bolsa de Valores* Stock Exchange; *operaciones de Bolsa* exchange transactions || ANAT bursa; *bolsas sinoviales* synovial bursae | sac (lagrimal) || bag (bajo los ojos) || bag (de abeja, de serpiente), pouch (de canguro, de calamares) || MED ice bag (de hielo) | hot-water bottle (de agua caliente) || MIN pocket (de mineral, de gas) || DEP purse (de un boxeador) || AMER pocket (bolsillo) || — AVIAT *bolsa de aire* air pocket || AMER *bolsa de dormir* sleeping bag || *bolsa de herramientas* toolbag || *bolsa de labores* workbag || *bolsa de compra* shopping bag || MED *bolsa de las aguas* bag of waters || *bolsa del automóvil, de la propiedad inmobiliaria* vehicles for sale, property for sale || BOT *bolsa de pastor* shepherd's purse || *Bolsa de Trabajo* Labour Exchange, Employment Exchange [US Employment Bureau] || *bolsa de viaje* travelling bag || *bolsa negra* black market || FIG *bolsa rota* spendthrift || *jugar a la Bolsa* to speculate, to play the market || COM *la Bolsa* the Stock Exchange || *la Bolsa baja* there is a drop on the Stock Exchange || *¡la bolsa o la vida!* your money or your life! || FIG *sin aflojar la bolsa* without spending a penny.
◆ *pl* ANAT scrotum *sing* (escroto) || *se me han hecho bolsas en el pantalón* my trousers have gone baggy at the knees.

bolsear *vi* to bag, to pucker (los vestidos).
◆ *vt* AMER FAM to send packing (echar) | to tap s.o. for (pedir) | to pick *o* to steal (sth.) from the pocket of (robar).

bolsero, ra *m/f* maker (fabricante) *o* seller (vendedor) of purses.
◆ *m* AMER sponger, parasite (gorrón) | pickpocket (ratero).

bolsico *m* AMER pocket.

bolsicón *m* AMER thick petticoat.

bolsillo *m* pocket (de un vestido); *bolsillo de parche, con cartera* patch pocket, flap pocket || fob (para el reloj) || purse [US pocketbook] (monedero) || — *bolsillo de pecho* breastpocket || *consultar con el bolsillo* to see whether one has enough money || *de bolsillo* pocket; *edición de bolsillo* pocket edition || FIG & FAM *meterse a alguien en el bolsillo* to win s.o. over to one's side | *pagar a alguien de su bolsillo* to pay s.o. out of one's own pocket | *poner de su bolsillo* to dip into one's own pocket | *rascarse el bolsillo* to dig deep | *sin echarse la mano al bolsillo* without spending a penny | *tener a uno en el bolsillo* to have s.o. in one's pocket.

bolsín *m* COM outside market.

bolsiquear *vt* AMER to pick (sth.) from the pocket of.

bolsista *m* COM stockbroker || AMER pickpocket (ladrón).

bolsita *f* small bag.

bolso *m* handbag, bag [US purse, pocketbook] (de mujer) || purse [US pocketbook] (portamonedas) || pocket (bolsillo) || *bolso de mano* handbag [US purse, pocketbook].

bolsón *m* handbag [US purse, pocketbook] (bolso) || AMER school satchel (de colegial) | ore pocket (mineral) | hollow [ground] (en una zona desértica) | lagoon (lago) || AMER FAM dunce (alumno malo).

boludo, da *adj* AMER POP bloody stupid.
◆ *m/f* AMER POP arsehole (gilipollas).

bolladura *f* dent (hacia dentro) || bump (hacia fuera).

bollar *vt* to dent (hacia dentro) || to bump (hacia fuera).

bollería *f* bakery, baker's shop.

bollero, ra *m/f* baker.

bollo *m* bun, roll (panecillo) || dent (abolladura) || bump, swelling (bulto, chichón) || puff (en una tela) || AMER punch (puñetazo) || — FIG & FAM *no está el horno para bollos* the time is not right, this is not the right time || FIG *perdonar el bollo por el coscorrón* to realize that it is not worth the effort || FIG & FAM *¡se va a armar un bollo!* there is going to be trouble *o* a rumpus!

bollón *m* stud (tachuela) || button earring (pendiente) || BOT bud (de la vid).

bollonado, da *adj* studded.

bomba *f* TECN pump; *bomba aspirante* suction pump; *bomba impelente* force pump; *bomba aspirante impelente* suction and force pump; *bomba de bicicleta* bicycle pump; *bomba de aire* air pump || MIL bomb; *bomba atómica, de efecto retardado, termonuclear* atomic bomb, time bomb, thermonuclear bomb || globe (de lámpara) || MÚS slide || FIG bombshell (noticia inesperada) || improvised poem (poema) || AMER round kite (cometa) | soap bubble (burbuja) | ladle (cucharón) | top hat (chistera) | lie (mentira) | hoax (noticia falsa) | aerostatic balloon [globe] | drunkenness (borrachera) | petrol pump, filling station [US gas station] (gasolinera) || — AMER FIG & FAM *agarrar una bomba* to get plastered *o* canned *o* drunk (emborracharse) || *a prueba de bombas* bombproof, shellproof || MED *bomba de cobalto* cobalt bomb || *bomba de hidrógeno* hydrogen bomb || *bomba de humo* or *fumígena* smoke bomb || *bomba de incendios* fire engine || *bomba de inyección* injection pump || MIL *bomba de mano* hand grenade, grenade | *bomba de relojería* time bomb || *bomba fétida* stink bomb || MED *bomba gástrica* stomach pump || *bomba lacrimógena* tear-gas bomb || *bomba volcánica* or *de lava* volcanic bomb || FIG *caer como una bomba* to drop *o* to burst like a bomb *o* a bombshell || *dar a la bomba* to pump || FIG & FAM *estar echando bombas* to be boiling hot | *éxito bomba* fantastic success | *pasarlo bomba* to have a great time *o* a ball *o* a whale of a time.

bombacha *f* AMER baggy trousers *pl* || knickers *pl* (de niño, de mujer).
— OBSERV The word *bombacha* is usually used in the plural form *bombachas*.

bombacho *adj m/sm* *pantalón bombacho* knicker-bockers *pl* (de hombre), knickers *pl* (de niño), plus fours *pl* (de jugador de golf, etc.), baggy trousers *pl* (de zuavo, etc.).

bombarda *f* MIL bombard || MÚS bombardon.

bombardear *vt* MIL to bomb, to bombard, to shell || FÍS to bombard.

bombardeo *m* MIL bombing, bombardment; *bombardeo de una ciudad* bombing of a city || FÍS bombardment || — *bombardeo aéreo* air raid, aerial bombing || *bombardeo en picado* dive bombing.

bombardero, ra *adj* bombing, bomber || *lancha bombardera* gunboat.
◆ *m* bombardier (soldado) || bomber (avión).

bombardino *m* MÚS saxhorn.

bombardón *m* MÚS bombardon.

bombástico, ca *adj* bombastic.

bombazo *m* explosion [of a bomb].

bombeador *m* AMER fireman (bombero) | spy (espía).

bombear *vt* to pump, to pump up (recoger); *bombear agua* to pump water || to pump out (sacar el agua) || to bend (arquear) || to warp (alabear) || FIG & FAM to puff up (dar bombo) || AMER to spy on (espiar) | to scout, to spy out, to reconnoitre (explorar) | to fire (despedir) || DEP to lob (la pelota) || *un balón bombeado* a lob.
◆ *vpr* to warp (alabearse).

bombeo *m* bulge, convexity (convexidad) || warp (alabeo) || camber (de la calzada) || *estación de bombeo* pumping station.

bombero *m* fireman (de incendios) || MIL mortar (cañón) || AMER scout (explorador) | spy (espía) | petrol-pump attendant (vendedor de gasolinera) || *cuerpo de bomberos* fire brigade.

bómbice; bómbix *m* bombix, silkworm.

bombilla *f* ELECTR bulb; *el casquillo de una bombilla* the socket of a bulb; *se ha fundido la bombilla* the bulb has gone || MAR lantern (farol) || AMER small pipe for drinking maté | ladle (cucharón).

bombillo *m* U-bend, trap (sifón) || pipette (para sacar líquidos) || MAR small pump || AMER bulb (bombilla).

bombín *m* FAM bowler [US derby] (sombrero) || pump (de bicicleta).

bombo, ba *adj* dumbfounded, stunned (atolondrado) || — FAM *ponerle la cabeza bomba a uno* to make s.o.'s head split | *tengo la cabeza bomba* my head is splitting.
◆ *m* bass drum (tambor) || bass-drum player (músico) || barge, lighter (barco) || lottery drum (de lotería) || FIG song and dance (publicidad); *dar mucho bombo a una novela* to make a great song and dance about a novel || — FAM *anunciar a bombo y platillos* or *a todo bombo* to announce with a lot of ballyhoo | *darse bombo* to boast, to blow one's own trumpet || FIG & FAM *estar con bombo* to be in the club, to have a bun in the oven | AMER *irse al bombo* to fail || *publicidad a bombo y platillos* noisy *o* loud publicity || *sin bombo ni platillos* quietly, without fuss.

bombón *m* chocolate; *una caja de bombones* a box of chocolates || Philippine bamboo container (recipiente) || AMER type of ladle (cucharón) || FIG & FAM *ser un bombón* to be gorgeous (una mujer), to be cute enough to eat (un niño).

bombona *f* carboy || gas cylinder (de butano).

bombonera *f* chocolate box (caja) || FIG cosy little place (casita, teatro).

bombonería *f* confectioner's shop, sweetshop.

Bona *n pr* GEOGR Bonn.

bonachón, ona *adj* FAM easy going (acomodadizo) | good-natured (bueno) | naïve (cándido).
◆ *m/f* good soul.

bonachonería *f* good nature (bondad) naïveté (candidez).

bonaerense *adj* [from *o* of] Buenos Aires.
◆ *m/f* inhabitant *o* native of Buenos Aires.

bonancible *adj* calm (mar) || fair (tiempo).

bonanza *f* MAR fair weather, calm at sea || FIG prosperity, bonanza (prosperidad) | peacefulness (tranquilidad) || AMER MIN bonanza (en una mina).

bonapartista *adj/s* Bonapartist.

bondad *f* goodness (benevolencia); *la bondad es una virtud rara* goodness is a rare virtue || kindness, kindliness (generosidad); *se le conoce por su extrema bondad* he is known for his extreme kindliness || *tenga la bondad de* be kind enough to, be good enough to; *tenga la bondad de ayudarme* be kind enough to help me; please; *tenga la bondad de no escupir en el suelo* please do not spit on the floor.

bondadosamente *adv* kindly.

bondadoso, sa *adj* king, good, goodnatured.

bonderización *f* bonderizing (protección contra la herrumbre).

boneta *f* MAR bonnet.

bonete *m* cap (de eclesiástico, colegiales, graduados, etc.) || biretta (de cardenal) || FIG secular priest (clérigo) || fruit dish (tarro) || bonnet (fortificación) || ZOOL bonnet (de un rumiante) || — FIG & FAM *a tente bonete* doggedly | *tirarse los bonetes* to bicker, to quarrel, to squabble.

bonetería *f* hat factory (fábrica) || AMER haberdashery.

bonetero, ra *m/f* hatter || AMER haberdasher.
◆ *m* spindle tree (arbusto).

bongo *m* AMER barge (barco) | canoe (canoa).

bongó *m* bongo drum, bongo.

boniato *m* sweet potato (buniato).

bonico, ca *adj* FAM cute, sweet.

Bonifacio *npr m* Boniface.

bonificación *f* improvement (mejora) || COM allowance, discount (descuento).

bonificar *vt* to improve; *bonificar la tierra* to improve the land || COM to allow, to discount (descontar).

bonísimo, ma *adj* very good.

bonitamente *adv* nicely || artfully, craftly (con habilidad) || slowly, little by little (despacio).

bonito, ta *adj* pretty (persona) || nice, pretty (sitio) || pretty, nice (cantidad) || *¡muy bonito!* that's nice!, very nice!
◆ *m* tuna (fish) (atún); *bonito en aceite* tuna fish in oil.

bono *m* voucher (papeleta) || bond; *bonos del Tesoro* Treasury bonds; *bono del Estado* Government bond [US State bond].

bonsai *m* BOT bonsai.

bonzo *m* bonze (monje budista).

boñiga *f*; **boñigo** *m* cow dung.

bookmaker *m* bookie, bookmaker (corredor de apuestas).

boom *m* boom.

boomerang *m* boomerang.

Bootes *npr m* ASTR Bootes.

bootlegger *m* bootlegger (contrabandista de licores).

boqueada *f* last breath || *dar las últimas boqueadas* to be at one's last gasp, to be on one's last legs (persona), to be on its last legs (cosa).

boquear *vt* to say, to utter, to mouth (palabras).

◆ *vi* to gape, to gasp ‖ to be at one's last gasp (persona) ‖ FIG & FAM to be on one's last legs (cosa y persona).

boquera *f* MED lip sore ‖ sluice [in an irrigation channel] (para regar) ‖ window in a hayloft (del pajar) ‖ sore mouth (de animal).

boquerón *m* anchovy (pez) ‖ wide opening, large breach (abertura).
— OBSERV *Boquerón* is used only to denote *fresh anchovy. Canned anchovy* is called *anchoa.*

boquete *m* narrow opening (paso angosto) ‖ hole (agujero) ‖ breach (brecha).

boquiabierto, ta *adj* agape, gaping, open-mouthed; *me quedé boquiabierto cuando la vi* I stood agape *o* gaping when I saw her.

boquiancho, cha *adj* wide-mouthed.

boquiangosto, ta *adj* narrow-mouthed.

boquiblando, da *adj* soft-mouthed, tender-mouthed (caballo).

boquiduro, ra *adj* hard-mouthed (caballo).

boquifresco, ca *adj* tender-mouthed (caballo) ‖ FIG & FAM cheeky, shameless, impudent (descarado).

boquilla *f* cigarette holder (para fumar cigarrillos) ‖ cigar holder (para fumar cigarros puros) ‖ tip; *boquilla con filtro* filter tip ‖ mouthpiece (de pipa) ‖ sluice in irrigation channel (para regar) ‖ MÚS mouthpiece (de varios instrumentos) ‖ mortise, mortice (escopleadura) ‖ opening (orificio) ‖ clasp (de un bolso) ‖ teat [US nipple] (de biberón) ‖ metal mouth (de la funda de la espada) ‖ burner (de lámpara) ‖ nozzle (de tobera) ‖ coupling, joint (de dos tubos) ‖ *decir algo de boquilla* to say one thing and mean another.

boquirroto, ta *adj* FAM loose-tongued, talkative (parlanchín).
◆ *m/f* FAM chatterbox.

boquirrubio, bia *adj* loose-tongued, talkative (parlanchín) ‖ naïve, innocent (candoroso).
◆ *m/f* chatterbox (parlanchín).
◆ *m* FAM dandy.

boquiseco, ca *adj* dry-mouthed (caballo).

boquituerto, ta *adj* wry-mouthed.

borato *m* QUÍM borate.

bórax *m* QUÍM borax.

borbollar; borbollear *vi* to bubble ‖ FIG to stammer, to stutter (hablar mal).

borbolleo *m* → **borboteo.**

borbollón *m* → **borbotón.**

borbollonear *vi* to bubble (borbollar).

Borbón *n pr* Bourbon.

borbónico, ca *adj* Bourbon ‖ *nariz borbónica* Bourbon nose.

borbor *m* bubbling.

borborigmo *m* MED rumblings *pl* [in the bowels].

borboritar; borbotar; borbotear *vi* to bubble.

borboteo; borbolleo *m* bubbling.

borbotón; borbollón *m* bubbling ‖ — *el agua hierve a borbotones* the water is boiling furiously ‖ *hablar a borbotones* to gabble ‖ *la sangre corre a borbotones* the blood gushes out ‖ *salir a borbotones* to gush forth.

borceguí; brodequín *m* half boot (calzado).

borda *f* MAR gunwale, rail | mainsail (de una galera) ‖ hut, cabin (choza) ‖ — FIG & FAM *arrojar* or *echar* or *tirar por la borda* to throw overboard ‖ *motor de fuera borda* outboard motor.

bordada *f* MAR tack, board ‖ *dar una bordada* to tack, to make a board.

bordado, da *adj* embroidered ‖ FIG *salir bordado* to turn out perfectly.
◆ *m* embroidery; *bordado de realce* raised embroidery.

bordador, ra *m/f* embroiderer, embroideress.

bordar *vt* to embroider ‖ FIG to perform perfectly; *este actor bordó su papel* this actor performed his role perfectly | to do perfectly (un trabajo) ‖ *bordar en calado* to do drawnwork.

borde *m* edge; *al borde del abismo, de la mesa* on the edge of the abyss, of the table ‖ hem, edge (de un vestido) ‖ border (banda) ‖ brim (de un sombrero) ‖ brim, rim (de una vasija) ‖ side (de una carretera) ‖ lip (de una herida) ‖ — *al borde de* on the edge of (en la linde de), on the brink of, on the verge of; *estar al borde de la ruina* to be on the brink of ruin ‖ *al borde del mar* at the seaside ‖ AVIAC *borde de ataque, de salida* leading, trailing edge ‖ *borde de acera* kerb [US curb] ‖ FIG *estar al borde de la tumba* to be at death's door, to have one foot in the grave.

bordear *vi* MAR to tack ‖ *el agua del vaso bordeaba* the glass was full to overflowing.
◆ *vt* to border; *bordear una foto con una lista blanca* to border a photo with a white band ‖ to border on; *mi campo bordea el tuyo* my field borders on yours ‖ FIG to border on, to verge on; *esto bordea el ridículo* this borders on the ridiculous | MAR to skirt; *bordear una isla* to skirt an island.

bordelés, esa *adj* [of *o* from] Bordeaux; *un vino bordelés* a Bordeaux wine.
◆ *m/f* inhabitant *o* native of Bordeaux.

bordillo *m* kerb [US curb] (de la acera).

bordo *m* MAR board; *subir a bordo* to go on board | side (lado) | tack (bordada) ‖ — MAR *a bordo del barco* on board (the) ship | *barco de alto bordo* seagoing vessel | *diario de a bordo* ship's log, logbook ‖ COM *franco a bordo* free on board ‖ MAR *los hombres de a bordo* the ship's company, the crew | *segundo de a bordo* first mate | *virar de bordo* to put round.

bordón *m* pilgrim's staff (de peregrino) ‖ refrain (estribillo) ‖ FIG pet phrase (repetición) | helping hand (ayuda) ‖ IMPR omission, out ‖ MÚS bass string (cuerda) | bourdon (de un órgano).

bordoncillo *m* pet phrase.

bordonear *vi* to buzz, to hum (zumbar).
◆ *vt* MÚS to strum (la guitarra).

bordoneo *m* buzz, buzzing, hum, humming.

bordura *f* HERÁLD bordure.

boreal *adj* northern, boreal ‖ *aurora boreal* aurora borealis, northern lights.

bóreas *m* boreas, the north wind.

borgoña *m* Burgundy (vino).

Borgoña *npr f* GEOGR Burgundy.

borgoñón, ona *adj/s* Burgundian.

bórico, ca *adj* boric, boracic.

borinqueño, ña *adj/s* Puerto Rican (puertorriqueño).

borla *f* tassel (adorno) ‖ tassel, pompon (del gorro militar) ‖ puff; *borla para polvos* powder puff ‖ tassel [on doctor's cap] (insignia) ‖ FIG *tomar la borla* to graduate as a doctor.

borlarse; borlearse *vpr* AMER to graduate as a doctor.

borne *m* ELECTR terminal.

Borneo *n pr* GEOGR Borneo.

bornear *vt* to look along with one eye (para comprobar la rectitud de algo) ‖ to bend (doblar) ‖ ARQ to put in place.
◆ *vi* MAR to swing at anchor.
◆ *vpr* to warp (madera).

boro *m* QUÍM boron.

borona *f* millet (mijo) ‖ maize [US corn] (maíz) ‖ maize bread [US corn bread] (pan de maíz) ‖ AMER crumb (migaja).

borra *f* flock (para rellenar colchones, etc.) ‖ floss (de seda) ‖ fluff (pelusa de suciedad) ‖ sediment, lees *pl* (de la tinta, etc.) ‖ FIG padding ‖ FIG *meter borra* to pad (out).

borrachera *f* drunkenness (ebriedad) ‖ FIG rapture, ecstasy; *la borrachera de los triunfos* the rapture of victories ‖ — *agarrar* or *coger una borrachera* to get drunk ‖ *ir de borrachera* to go on a binge, to go on a drinking spree [US to go on a drunk].

borrachín *m* FAM drunkard, soak.

borracho, cha *adj* drunk; *está borracho* he is drunk ‖ hard-drinking (aficionado a beber) ‖ FIG drunk; *borracho de ira* drunk with rage ‖ violet (morado) ‖ — *bizcocho borracho* rum baba ‖ FAM *borracho como una cuba* drunk as a lord | *estar borracho perdido* to be paralytic, to be blind drunk.
◆ *m/f* drunkard, drunk ‖ *ser un borracho perdido* to be an inveterate drunkard.

borrador *m* rough copy [US first draft] (texto) ‖ rough notebook [US scratch pad] (cuaderno) ‖ rough paper [US scratch paper] (papel) ‖ COM daybook ‖ eraser, rubber (goma de borrar) ‖ board rubber, rubber (de la pizarra).

borradura *f* erasure, crossing-out.

borraja *f* BOT borage ‖ FIG *quedar en agua de borrajas* to fizzle out, to come to nothing, to peter out.

borrajear *vt* to scribble (palabras) ‖ to scribble on (papel).

borrar *vt* to cross out (tachar) ‖ to cross (*de* off), to cross (suprimir) ‖ to clean (la pizarra) | to rub off; *borrar algo de la pizarra* to rub sth. off the board ‖ to rub out, to erase (con una goma) ‖ to blurr (dejar borroso) ‖ INFORM to erase ‖ FIG to erase, to wipe away; *el tiempo todo lo borra* time erases everything ‖ *goma de borrar* eraser, rubber.
◆ *vpr* FIG to fade, to disappear, to be erased; *esta historia se borró de mi memoria* this story faded from my memory | to resign; *me he borrado del club* I have resigned from the club.

borrasca *f* storm (tormenta) ‖ squall (chubasco) ‖ flurry (de nieve) ‖ FIG peril, hazard (riesgo); *las borrascas de la vida* the perils of life | orgy, spree (orgía).

borrascoso, sa *adj* stormy (lugar, mar, etc.) ‖ gusty, squally (viento) ‖ FIG & FAM stormy, tumultuous (vida, conducta, reunión).

borregada *f* flock of lambs.

borrego, ga *m/f* lamb [one or two years old] ‖ FIG & FAM simpleton, dope (tonto) ‖ AMER hoax (noticia falsa).

borreguil *adj* *tener un espíritu borreguil* to follow the crowd.

borrica *f* donkey, she-ass (asna) ‖ FIG & FAM dunce, dimwit, ass (mujer ignorante).

borricada *f* drove of asses ‖ donkey ride; *dar una borricada* to go for a donkey ride ‖ FIG & FAM nonsense, stupid thing; *soltar borricadas* to talk nonsense, to say stupid things ‖ *hacer borricadas* to act the goat, to do stupid things.

borrical *adj* of an ass, of a donkey.

borrico *m* donkey, ass (asno) ‖ sawhorse, trestle (de carpintero) ‖ FIG & FAM ass, dimwit, dunce (necio) ‖ — FIG *apearse de su borrico, caerse de su borrico* to climb down, to back down | *ser muy borrico* to be a real ass *o* dunce.

borricón; borricote *adj* FIG & FAM dense, stupid, dim (necio) ‖ — FIG & FAM *ser borricón* to be as strong as an ox (fuerte) | *ser muy bo-*

rricote para las matemáticas to be hopeless at mathematics.
◆ *m* FAM dunce, ass, dimwit.

borrilla *f* fur, fuzz (de las frutas).

borriquero *adj m* *cardo borriquero* cotton thistle.
◆ *m* donkey driver.

borriquillo; borriquito *m* donkey || *el borriquito por delante, para que no se espante* it is impolite to put one's own name first.

borro *m* lamb [one or two years old].

Borromeas (islas) *npr fpl* GEOGR Borromean Islands.

borrón *m* blot, blotch, smudge (de tinta) || rough copy (texto) || scribbling pad [*US* scratch pad] (cuaderno) || rough sketch (de una pintura) || FIG blemish (defecto) | blot, blemish (deshonor); *este acto es un borrón en su vida* this deed is a blemish on his life | scrawl, scribble (escrito) || FIG & FAM *borrón y cuenta nueva* let's forget about it, let's wipe the slate clean, let's start afresh.

borronear *vt* to scribble (palabras) || to scribble on; *borronear el papel* to scribble on the paper.

borroso, sa *adj* muddy (líquido) || confused (escritura) || blurred, fuzzy (fotografía, pintura) || indistinct (contornos) || hazy, vague (ideas) || IMPR blurred, mackled.

borujo *m* marc (orujo) || lump (bulto) || cattle cake made of olives or grapes (para el ganado).

borujón *m* large lump (bulto).

boscaje *m* grove, thicket, copse (bosque pequeño) || woodland scene (pintura).

boscoso, sa *adj* wooded.

Bósforo *npr m* GEOGR Bosphorus.

Bosnia *npr f* GEOGR Bosnia.

bosniaco, ca; bosnio, nia *adj/s* Bosnian.

bosorola *f* sediment, dregs *pl* (poso).

bosque *m* wood (pequeño), forest (más grande); *un bosque de pinos* a pine wood; *bosque comunal* communal wood; *bosque del Estado* State wood; *bosque maderable* timber-yielding wood.
— OBSERV En inglés *wood* y *forest* difieren sólo por la extensión. La primera palabra se aplica a un sitio poblado de árboles generalmente menos extenso que *forest. Forest* no corresponde al español *selva* sino cuando se trata de superficies arboladas muy extensas y de carácter salvaje: *the Black Forest* la Selva Negra.

bosquecillo *m* grove, small wood, copse.

bosquejar *vt* to sketch; *bosquejar un retrato* to sketch a portrait || to roughhew (una escultura) || FIG to draft (proyecto) || FIG *bosquejar un cuadro de* to outline, to give an outline of; *bosquejar un cuadro de la situación* to give an outline of the situation.

bosquejo *m* sketch (de una pintura) || study, rough shape (de una escultura) || FIG outline, draft (de un proyecto).

bosquete *m* grove, thicket, copse.

bosquimano, na *adj/s* Bushman.

bosta *f* dung (de los bovinos, de los caballos).

bostezar *vi* to yawn.

bostezo *m* yawn.

bostón *m* boston (juego, baile).

bota *f* wineskin (para el vino) || barrel (cuba) || boot; *botas de agua* waders; *botas de goma* Wellington *o* rubber boots; *botas de campaña* top boots; *botas altas* or *de montar* riding boots || — *El Gato con botas* Puss-in-Boots || FIG *estar con las botas puestas* to be ready to go out | *morir con las botas puestas* to die with one's boots on || FIG & FAM *ponerse las botas* to feather one's nest (ganar mucho dinero), to have one's fill (beber o comer mucho).

botada *f* launching (botadura).

botadero *m* AMER ford (vado) | tip, rubbish dump (vertedero).

botado, da *adj* AMER foundling (expósito) | cheeky, saucy, bold (descarado) | dirt cheap (barato) | spendthrift (derrochador) | blind drunk (borracho).
◆ *m/f* AMER foundling (expósito) | cheeky person (descarado) | cheap thing (barato) | spendthrift (derrochador) | drunk, drunkard (borracho).

botador *m* MAR pole (palo para impulsar un barco) || nail puller, claw hammer (para sacar clavos) || forceps (de un dentista) || IMPR shooting stick.
◆ *adj m/sm* AMER spendthrift (derrochador).

botadura *f* launching (of a ship).

botafuego *m* MIL linstock || FIG firebrand (persona que provoca alborotos) | quick-tempered person (persona irritable).

botafumeiro *m* censer, incense burner (en Santiago de Compostela).

botalón *m* MAR boom || stake, post (estaca).

botana *f* patch [of a wineskin] || cork, stopper (tapón), bung (de un tonel) || FIG & FAM plaster (con que se cubre una herida) | scar (cicatriz) || AMER leather hood [used in cockfighting] | cocktail snack (tapa).

botánico, ca *adj* botanical, botanic || *jardín botánico* botanical garden.
◆ *m/f* botanist.
◆ *f* botany (ciencia).

botanista *m/f* (p us) botanist.

botar *vt* to throw out (arrojar) || MAR to launch (barco) | to turn the helm; *botar a babor* to turn the helm to port || FAM to chuck out (echar); *lo botaron del colegio* they chucked him out of school || to take (fútbol); *botar un córner* to take a corner || AMER to throw away (tirar) | to squander (malgastar).
◆ *vi* to bounce, to rebound (una pelota, una piedra) || to jolt, to bounce (pegar botes) || to jump; *botar de alegría* to jump for joy || to buck (un caballo) || FIG *está que bota* he is hopping mad.
◆ *vpr* AMER to become (volverse).

botaratada *f* FAM stupid thing, foolish thing, piece of nonsense || — *decir botaratadas* to talk nonsense || *hacer botaratadas* to act the fool.

botarate *m* FAM fool, idiot; *no seas botarate* don't be a fool || AMER spendthrift (manirroto).

botarel *m* ARQ flying buttress.

botarete *adj* ARQ *arco botarete* flying buttress.

botarga *f* motley, jester's outfit.

botasillas *f pl* MIL boots and saddles (toque de clarín).

botavara *f* MAR spanker boom.

bote *m* jump, leap, bound (salto) || bounce, rebound (de una pelota) || bump, jolt (sacudida) || tin, can; *bote de leche condensada* tin of condensed milk || jar (de farmacia, etc.); *bote de tabaco* tobacco jar || MAR boat; *bote de remos* rowing boat || thrust, lunge (de pico o de lanza) || hole (boche) || jump, prance (caballo) || FAM pocket (bolsillo) || box for tips (en un bar) || jackpot (en el juego) || — *bote de carnero* buck (de caballo) || DEP *bote neutro* bounce-up || MAR *bote salvavidas* lifeboat || *dar botes de alegría* to jump for joy, to jump with happiness || FIG & FAM *dar el bote* to chuck out (echar) | *darse el bote* to beat it | *de bote en bote* packed, full to overflowing; *el cuarto está de bote en bote* the room is packed | *estar en el bote* to be in the bag || *pegar un bote* to jump || FIG & FAM *tener a uno metido en el bote* to have won s.o. over, to have s.o. in one's pocket; *tenemos a mi padre metido en el bote* we have won my father over.

botella *f* bottle; *beber de la botella* to drink from the bottle || — FÍS *botella de Leiden* Leyden jar || *botella termo* thermos flask, thermos, thermos bottle || *en botella* bottled.

botellazo *m* blow with a bottle.

botellero *m* bottle rack (estante) || bottle basket (cesta) || bottle maker (fabricante) || bottle seller (comerciante).

botellín *m* small bottle.

botellón *m* large bottle || AMER demijohn (damajuana).

botepronto *m* dropkick (rugby) || half volley (fútbol).

botería *f* MAR casks *pl* || wineskin workshop (taller del botero) || AMER cobbler's shop, shoemaker's shop (zapatería).

botero *m* wineskin maker || skipper, master (de un bote) || cobbler, shoemaker (zapatero) || FAM *Pedro Botero* Satan, the Fiend.

botica *f* chemist's shop, pharmacy [*US* drugstore] (farmacia) || FIG medicine cabinet (botiquín) | medicines *pl* (medicamentos) || (p us) shop (tienda) || — *hay de todo como en botica* there is everything under the sun || FAM *oler a botica* to smell like a chemist's shop.

boticaria *f* chemist's *o* pharmacist's wife (esposa) || chemist, pharmacist [*US* druggist].

boticario *m* chemist, pharmacist, apothecary (ant) [*US* druggist] || FIG *venir como pedrada en ojo de boticario* to come in the nick of time, to come just right.

botija *f* earthenware pitcher || AMER buried treasure.

botijero, ra *m/f* pitcher maker (el que hace botijos) || pitcher seller (vendedor).

botijo *m* earthenware pitcher [with spout and handle] || — FAM *cara de botijo* face like a full moon || *tren botijo* excursion train.

botilla *f* ankle boot, bootee (de señora) || half boot (borceguí).

botillería *f* refreshment bar.

botín *m* spat, legging (polaina) || bootee, ankle boot (calzado) || MIL booty, loot || AMER sock (calcetín).

botina *f* bootee, ankle boot.

botinería *f* cobbler's shop, shoemaker's shop (zapatería).

botinero *m* cobbler, shoemaker (zapatero).

botiquín *m* medicine chest (maletín) || first-aid kit (estuche) || medicine cabinet (mueble) || sick room, sick bay (enfermería) || AMER wine shop.

botivoleo *m* striking a ball on the bounce *o* rebound [in ball games].

boto *m* boot (calzado) || wineskin (odre).

boto, ta *adj* blunt || FIG dull, dense (torpe).

botón *m* button (en los vestidos) || BOT bud (de una planta) || button [*US* bell push] (de timbre); *pulsar el botón* to press the button || handle, knob (de puerta, etc.) || DEP button (del florete) || MÚS key (de instrumento de viento) || RAD knob; *botón de sintonización* tuning knob || buttons, bellboy (muchacho en un hotel) || AMER FAM copper [*US* cop] (poli) || — AMER *al botón* in vain (en vano), at random (al buen tuntún) || *botón automático* press stud [*US* snap fastener] || AUTOM *botón de arranque* starter button || *botón de fuego* ignipuncture || FIG *botón de muestra* sample; *como botón de muestra* as a sample || MED *botón de Oriente* oriental sore || *botón de oro* buttercup (planta) || *dar al botón* to turn the knob; to press the button || FAM *de* *botones adentro* deep down, in one's heart of hearts.

botonadura *f* buttons *pl*, set of buttons.

botonazo *m* touché (en la esgrima).

botones *m inv* buttons, bellboy (de un hotel) || messenger, errand boy (recadero).

bototo *m* AMER calabash (calabaza).
◆ *pl* AMER heavy shoes *o* boots (zapatos).

Botsuana *n pr* GEOGR Botswana.

botulismo *m* MED botulism.

botuto *m* war trumpet of the Orinoco Indians (trompeta) || BOT stalk of pawpaw.

bou *m* seine fishing (pesca) || seiner (barco).

bóveda *f* ARQ vault | crypt (cripta) || — *bóveda celeste* heaven vault, celestial vault || *bóveda craneana* or *craneal* cranial cavity || *bóveda de cañón* barrel vault || *bóveda de crucería* groined *o* ribbed vault || *bóveda de medio punto* semicircular arch || *bóveda palatina* palate, roof of the mouth || *bóveda por arista* or *claustral* or *esquifada* groined *o* cloister vault || *clave de bóveda* keystone.

bovedilla *f* ARQ small vault (bóveda pequeña) | space between girders (parte del techo entre vigas) || MAR curved part of the stern.

bóvidos *m pl* ZOOL bovidae, bovines.

bovino, na *adj* bovine.
◆ *m pl* bovines, bovidae.

box *m* AMER DEP boxing.

boxcalf *m* box calf (cuero).

boxeador *m* boxer (deportista).

boxear *vi* to box.

boxeo *m* boxing.

bóxer *m* boxer (perro).

boy *m* boy (criado indígena).

boya *f* MAR buoy; *boya luminosa* light buoy || float (de una red) || *boya de salvamento* or *salvavidas* lifebuoy.

boyada *f* drove of oxen.

boyante *adj* TAUR easy to fight (toro) || prosperous, successful (próspero) || happy, buoyant (feliz) || MAR buoyant.

boyar *vi* to float (flotar).

boyardo *m* boyar.

boycot *m* → **boicot.**

boycotear *vt* → **boicotear.**

boycoteo *m* → **boicoteo.**

boyera; boyeriza *f* cowshed.

boyerizo *m* cowherd.

boyero *m* cowherd || ASTR Bootes, the Wagoner, the Waggoner.

boyezuelo *m* young bullock [*US* steer].

boy-scout *m* boy scout (explorador).

boyuno, na *adj* bovine.

boza *m* MAR stopper (cable).

bozal *adj* (ant) pure (negro) || FIG & FAM green, raw (novicio) | daft, stupid, silly (tonto) || wild, untamed; *caballo bozal* wild horse || AMER who speaks bad *o* broken Spanish.
◆ *m/f* pure negro (negro) || FIG & FAM greenhorn, novice (novato) | fool, idiot, clod (tonto) || AMER foreigner who speaks bad *o* broken Spanish.
◆ *m* muzzle (para los animales) || AMER halter (cabestro).

bozo *m* down, fuzz (vello) || mouth (parte exterior de la boca) || halter (cabestro) || *a este niño ya le apunta el bozo* the boy is already starting to get fuzz on his upper lip.

Brabante *npr m* GEOGR Brabant.

braceada *f* violent waving of the arms.

braceador, ra *adj* high-stepping (caballo).

braceaje *m* minting (de las monedas) || MAR depth (profundidad en brazas).

bracear *vi* to wave *o* to swing one's arms (agitar los brazos) || to swim (nadar) || FIG to strive, to struggle (luchar) || to step high (un caballo) || MAR to brace (las velas).

braceo *m* waving of the arms || stroke (natación).

bracero *m* labourer.

bracmán *m* Brahman, Brahmin.

bráctea *f* BOT bract.

bradicardia *f* MED bradycardia [slow breathing].

bradipnea *f* MED bradypnoea.

braga *f* panties *pl*, knickers *pl* (de mujer) || napkin, nappy [*US* diaper] (de niño de pecho) || guy (cuerda).
◆ *pl* breeches (calzón ancho) || panties, knickers (de mujer) || FIG *no se pescan truchas a bragas enjutas* nothing ventured, nothing gained (no se consigue nada sin correr riesgos).

bragado, da *adj* FIG & FAM resolute, tough (decidido) | wicked (malintencionado) || FIG & FAM *hay que ser muy bragado para hacer algo tan peligroso* it takes a lot of guts to do such a dangerous thing.

bragadura *f* crutch, crotch (entrepierna).

bragapañal *m* shaped nappy [*US* diaper].

bragazas *m inv* FAM henpecked man.

braguero *m* truss (ortopédico).

bragueta *f* flies *pl*, fly (de pantalón) || — *casamiento de bragueta* marriage of convenience || *hidalgo de bragueta* one who becomes a nobleman by siring seven successive sons.

braguetazo *m* FIG & FAM marriage of convenience || FIG & FAM *dar un braguetazo* to marry money.

braguetón *m* AMER tierceron (de bóveda).

Brahma *npr m* Brahma.

brahmán *m* Brahmin, Brahman.

brahmánico, ca *adj* Brahminic, Brahminical, Brahmanic, Brahmanical.

brahmanismo *m* Brahminism, Brahmanism.

brahmín *m* Brahmin, Brahman.

braille *m* Braille (sistema de escritura para ciegos).

brama *f* rut, rutting (de los ciervos, etc.) || rutting season, rut (época).

bramadero *m* rutting place (de los ciervos, etc.) || tethering post (poste).

bramador, ra *adj* lowing (vacas) || bellowing, roaring (toros).

bramante *m* string, cord (cuerda) | twine (especialmente de cáñamo).

bramar *vi* to low (vacas) || to roar, to bellow (toros) || to bell, to troat (el venado) || to trumpet (el elefante) || FIG to howl, to roar (el viento) | to roar; to thunder (el mar) | to rumble, to roll (el trueno) | to roar, to bellow, to thunder (de ira) || FAM to bawl, to bellow, to howl (gritar).

bramido *m* lowing (de la vaca) || bellowing, bellow, roar (del toro) || bell, troat (del venado) || trumpeting (del elefante) || FIG howling, roaring (del viento) | roaring, thundering (del mar) | rumbling, rolling (del trueno) | roaring, bellowing, thundering (de ira) || FAM howl (grito) | bawling, howling, bellowing (gritos) || FAM *dar bramidos de dolor* to bellow *o* to howl with pain.

brancada *f* trammel net, trammel (red).

brancal *m* side members *pl* (de un carro).

brandal *m* MAR backstay.

Brandeburgo; Brandenburgo *npr m* GEOGR Brandenburg.

brandy *m* brandy (coñac).

branquia *f* branchia, gill (del pez).
— OBSERV El plural de la palabra inglesa *branchia* es *branchiae*.

branquial *adj* branchial.

branquiópodos *m pl* ZOOL branchiopodes.

braquial *adj* ANAT brachial.

braquicefalismo *m* brachycephalism.

braquicéfalo, la *adj* brachycephalic.

braquiópodos *m pl* brachiopodes (gusanos).

braquiuro *m* brachyuran (crustáceos).

brasa *f* ember (ascua) || — *carne a la brasa* braised meat || FIG *estar como en brasas* or *en brasas* to be on tenterhooks | *pasar como sobre brasas por un asunto* to touch lightly on *o* to skim over a subject.

brasca *f* lute.

braseado, da *adj* braised.

braserillo *m* small brazier.

brasero *m* brazier || stake (hoguera) || AMER hearth (hogar).
— OBSERV In Spain a *brasero* is a kind of brazier used for heating the house. It is frequently placed under a table which is called a *camilla*.

brasier *m* AMER bra (sostén).

brasil *m* brazilwood, brazil (palo brasil).

Brasil *npr m* GEOGR Brazil || — BOT *nuez del Brasil* Brazil nut || *palo del Brasil* brazilwood, brazil.

brasileño, ña *adj/s* Brazilian.

brasilero, ra *adj/s* AMER Brazilian.

brasilete *m* BOT brazilette.

Brasilia *n pr* GEOGR Brasilia.

Bratislava *n pr* GEOGR Bratislava.

bravata *f* swanking, boasting, bragging (jactancia) || boast, brag (fanfarronada) || piece of bravado (acción descarada) || *decir bravatas* to swank, to boast, to brag.

bravear *vi* to swank, to boast, to brag || to cheer (aplaudir).

bravera *f* vent (de un horno).

braveza *f* bravery, valour (bravura) || fury (de los elementos).

bravío, a *adj* wild, untamed (salvaje) || wild (silvestre) || FIG uncouth, coarse (rústico).
◆ *m* wildness, ferocity, fierceness.

¡bravísimo! *interj* well done!, wonderful!

bravo, va *adj* brave, courageous, valiant (valeroso) || fierce, ferocious (feroz) || TAUR brave (toro) || wild (salvaje); *un paisaje muy bravo* a very wild countryside || rugged (accidentado) || uncivilized; *indio bravo* uncivilized Indian || wild, furious (los elementos) || rough (mar) || good, excellent (excelente) || FAM boastful, swaggering (valentón) || FIG & FAM rough, churlish, rude (de mal carácter) | magnificent, superb, marvellous (magnífico) | wild, angry (enfadado) | hot (picante) || *toros bravos* fighting bulls.
◆ *m* cheer (aplauso).
◆ *interj* well done!, bravo!

bravucón, ona *adj* boastful, boasting, swaggering.
◆ *m* boaster, braggart, swaggerer.

bravuconada; bravuconería *f* bragging, boasting (jactancia) || brag, boast, swagger (fanfarronada).

bravura *f* ferocity, fierceness (de los animales) || fighting spirit, bravery (de un toro) || bravery, courage, valour (valor) || boasting, bragging (jactancia).

braza *f* MAR fathom (medida) | brace (cuerda) || breaststroke (modo de nadar); *nadar a la braza* to swim breaststroke || — *braza de espalda* backstroke || *braza mariposa* butterfly.
— OBSERV The Spanish *braza* equals 1.671 metres, and the English *fathom* 6 feet (1.83 metres).

brazada *f* stroke (del nadador, de un remo) || armful (lo que abarcan los brazos) || AMER fathom (medida).

brazado *m* armful.

brazal *m* brassard (de la armadura) || armband (en la manga) || irrigation ditch (de un río).

brazalete *m* armband (en la manga) || bracelet (pulsera).

brazo *m* ANAT arm || foreleg (de un caballo, etc.) || arm (de palanca, balanza, ancla, sillón, tocadiscos) || boom (del micrófono) || branch (de candelabro, de río) || arm (de mar) || jib, arm (de grúa) || limb (de la cruz) || limb, branch (de árbol) || handle (de herramienta) || sail arm (pala de molino) || leg (de tijera para podar) || FIG arm (fuerza) || estate (en las Cortes) || — *a brazo* by hand || *a brazo partido* hand to hand (sin armas), tooth and nail (con violencia), for all one is worth, with all one's might (con empeño) || FIG *brazo de gitano* swiss roll, roly-poly (pastel) | *brazo derecho* right hand, right arm || *dar el brazo a uno* to give s.o. one's arm || FIG *dar su brazo a torcer* to give in || *del brazo* arm in arm || *entregar al brazo secular* to hand over to the secular arm || FIG *estar atado de brazos* to be bound hand and foot | *estar hecho un brazo de mar* to be dressed up to the nines, to be dressed to kill || *ir del brazo* or *dándose el brazo* or *cogidos del brazo* to walk arm in arm || *ser el brazo derecho de alguien* to be s.o.'s right arm.
◆ *pl* hands; *aquí hacen falta brazos* more hands are needed here || protectors (ayudas) || — *a fuerza de brazos* by hard work || *con los brazos abiertos* with open arms || *con los brazos cruzados* with one's arms folded (con los brazos en el pecho), twiddling one's thumbs (sin hacer nada) || *cruzarse de brazos* to fold one's arms; to sit back and do nothing, to twiddle one's thumbs (no obrar) || *echar los brazos al cuello de alguien* to throw one's arms around s.o.'s neck || FIG *echarse* or *entregarse en brazos de uno* to put o.s. into s.o.'s hands || *en brazos* in one's arms || *huelga de brazos caídos* down tools, sit-down strike || FIG *levantar los brazos al cielo* to throw one's arms in the air.

brazola *f* MAR coaming [of the hatches].

brazolargo *m* AMER spider monkey.

brazuelo *m* forearm (de caballo) || shoulder (de carnero) || knuckle (del cerdo).

Brazzaville *n pr* GEOGR Brazzaville.

brea *f* pitch, tar; *brea mineral* mineral pitch || tarpaulin (tela embreada).

break *m* brake, shooting brake, estate car [*US* station wagon] (coche).

brear *vt* FIG & FAM to thrash, to beat (pegar) | to ill-treat (maltratar) || — FIG & FAM *le brearon a palos* they showered him with blows | *le brearon a preguntas* they bombarded him with questions.
◆ *vpr* FAM *brearse de trabajar* to wear one's fingers to the bone.

brebaje *m* concoction, brew.

brebajo *m* drink of bran, salt and water for animals.

breca *f* ZOOL bleak (albur) | sea bream (pagel).

brecol *m*; **brecolera** *f* BOT broccoli, brocoli.

brecha *f* MIL breach; *abrir una brecha en la muralla* to make a breach in the wall || opening, gap, break (en muro, vallado, etc.) || FIG breach || — *batir en brecha* to batter (una muralla), to attack (atacar) || FIG *estar siempre en la brecha* to be always at it | *hacer brecha en* to make an impression on || *hacerse una brecha en la frente* to open a gash in one's forehead || FIG *morir en la brecha* to die in harness.

brega *f* struggle, fight (pelea); *la brega de la vida* the struggle for life || quarrel, row (pendencia) || hard task, arduous work (trabajo) || practical joke, trick (burla) || — FIG *andar a la brega* to slog away || TAUR *capote de brega* cape used by the matador for his passes with the bull before taking the cape used for the kill || *en brega con* struggling with, fighting against.

bregar *vi* to struggle, to fight; *bregar con* to struggle with *o* against, to fight with *o* against || to quarrel (reñir) || FIG to slog away, to toil away, to slave away (trabajar) | to wear o.s. out (cansarse).
◆ *vt* to knead (amasar) || TAUR to make passes with (the bull).

brema *f* bream (pez).

Brema; Bremen *n pr* GEOGR Bremen.

breña *f* scrub.

breñal *m* scrub.

breñoso, sa *adj* scrubby, bushy.

breque *m* sea bream (pez) || AMER handbrake (freno) | luggage van (vagón de equipajes) | brake (coche).

Bretaña *npr f* GEOGR Britain; *Gran Bretaña* Great Britain | Brittany (provincia francesa).

brete *m* shackles *pl*, fetters *pl* [of prisoners] || — FIG *estar en un brete* to be in a tight spot | *poner a uno en un brete* to put s.o. in a tight spot.

breteles *m pl* AMER braces (tirantes).

bretón, ona *adj/s* breton.
◆ *m* Breton (lengua) || BOT tree cabbage (col).

breva *f* early fig (higo) || FIG & FAM stroke of luck; *cogió* or *le cayó una buena breva* he had a real stroke of luck | cushy *o* soft job (buena colocación) || flat cigar (puro) || AMER chewing tobacco (tabaco) || — FIG & FAM *de higos a brevas* once in a blue moon | *¡no caerá esa breva!* no such luck!

breve *adj* brief, short (corto) || a few; *me lo dijo en breves palabras* he told me so in a few words || GRAM short || *en breve* shortly, soon (pronto).
◆ *m* papal brief (bula apostólica).
◆ *f* MÚS breve (nota) || GRAM breve (sílaba, vocal).

brevedad *f* briefness, brevity, shortness || — *con brevedad* concisely, briefly || *con la mayor brevedad* as soon as possible || *para la mayor brevedad* to be brief.

brevete *m* heading (membrete).

breviario *m* breviary (libro de rezos) || compendium (compendio) || IMPR brevier.

brezal *m* moor, moorland, heath.

brezo *m* heather, heath.

briba *f* vagabond's *o* tramp's life || *andar* or *vivir a la briba* to loaf around, to idle around.

bribón, ona *adj* roguish, rascally (pícaro).
◆ *m/f* rascal, rogue (pícaro) || beggar, vagabond, tramp (mendigo).

bribonada; bribonería *f* roguishness (cualidad de bribón) || rascally trick (acción).

bribonear *vi* to lead a rascally *o* roguish life || to play roguish *o* rascally tricks (hacer bribonadas).

bribonería *f* ⟶ **bribonada.**

bricbarca *f* MAR bark, barque.

brida *f* bridle (freno, correaje y riendas) || rein (rienda) || clamp, clip (para apretar) || flange (de un tubo) || MED. bride [*US* adhesion] || FIG *a toda brida* at full gallop.

bridge *m* bridge (naipes); *jugar al bridge* to play bridge.

bridón *m* snaffle || MIL bridoon || POÉT steed (caballo).

brigada *f* MIL brigade || squad (de policías); *brigada antidisturbios* riot squad; *brigada antidroga* drug squad; *brigada móvil* flying squad || gang (de obreros) || MIL *general de brigada* brigadier [*US* brigadier general].
◆ *m* MIL warrant officer.

brigadier *m* (ant) brigadier.

Bright (mal de) *m* MED Bright's disease (nefritis).

Brígida *npr f* Bridget.

Briján *n pr* FIG & FAM *saber más que Briján, ser más listo que Briján* to have all one's wits about one.

brillante *adj* brilliant || sparkling, glittering, bright (luz, piedra preciosa) || brilliant, bright (color) || sparkling, scintillating (conversación, estilo, ojos) || bright (acero) || bright, brilliant; *es el alumno más brillante* he is the brightest pupil || shining (ejemplo) || radiant; *estaba brillante de juventud* she was radiant with youth || glittering, brilliant (reunión) || brilliant (grupo) || lustrous, shimmering (seda).
◆ *m* brilliant, diamond (diamante) || *un collar de brillantes* a diamond necklace.

brillantez *f* brightness, brillance (de un metal, del sol, etc.) || splendour (de una ceremonia) || brilliance (del estilo) || *terminó sus estudios con gran brillantez* he finished his studies brilliantly.

brillantina *f* brilliantine.

brillar *vi* to shine (en general) || to glisten, to glint (el acero) || to glitter, to glisten (el oro, etc.) || to sparkle (los ojos) || to glimmer (una vela, el agua) || to glitter, to sparkle, to twinkle, to shine (las joyas, las estrellas) || to shine (la luna) || to blaze (las llamas) || to shimmer (la seda) || to glare (los faros de un coche) || to glow (las ascuas) || FIG to stand out (sobresalir por su inteligencia, etc.) | to shine (en la conversación) || FIG *brillar por su ausencia* to be conspicuous by one's absence.

brillazón *f* AMER mirage (en la pampa).

brillo *m* sheen (del cabello, del agua, de una tela) || lustre, sheen (de la seda) || shine, polish (del betún, del barniz) || brilliance (de un color, de la inteligencia, del estilo) || sparkle (de un diamante, de los ojos) || sparkling, shimmer (de las estrellas) || light, brightness, shimmer (de la luna) || brightness (del sol) || gloss, shine (del papel de una fotografía) || gloss, sheen, shine (de una superficie) || shine, glint (de un metal) || glow (de las ascuas) || FIG brilliance, splendour; *le gusta el brillo de la vida pública* he likes the brilliance of public life || *dar* or *sacar brillo a* to polish, to shine.

brilloso, sa *adj* AMER shining (brillante).

brin *m* coarse linen cloth.

brincar *vi* to jump, to hop (saltar) || to jump up and down, to jump about, to leap about (saltar repetidamente) || to gambol (las ovejas, etc.) || FIG to explode, to flare up (enfadarse) | to jump; *brincaron de alegría* they jumped for joy || FIG & FAM *está que brinca* he's hopping mad.

brinco *m* jump, hop, leap (salto) || bound, jump (de un caballo, de una cabra, etc.) || — *dar* or *pegar un brinco* to jump, to hop || *de un brinco* in one leap || FIG *en un brinco, en dos brincos* before you can say Jack Robinson, in no time at all.

brindar *vi* to drink, to drink a toast, to toast; *brindemos por nuestra amistad* let us drink to our friendship, let us toast our friendship || to touch *o* to clink glasses (chocar las copas).
◆ *vt* to offer; *le brindo la oportunidad de...* I am offering you the opportunity to... || — TAUR *brindar el toro* to dedicate the bull || *esto nos brinda la ocasión de hablar* this affords us the opportunity to talk.
◆ *vpr* to offer; *se brindó a pagar* he offered to pay.

brindis *m* toast || TAUR «brindis» [the matador's dedication of the bull he is about to kill] || *echar un brindis* to toast, to drink a toast.

brío *m* energy (energía) || determination (decisión) || spirit; *hablar con brío* to speak with spirit || dash, go, fire (empuje); *lleno de brío* full of go || elegance (gracia) || — FIG *cortar a uno los bríos* to clip s.o.'s wings || *hombre de bríos* man of spirit.

briofita *f* BOT bryophyte.

briol *m* MAR buntline (cabo).

briología *f* BOT bryology.

brionia *f* BOT bryony.

bríos! (¡voto a) *interj* FAM damn!

briosamente *adv* courageously, bravely (con valor) || resolutely (con determinación) || vigorously, energetically (con ardor) || with spirit (con brío).

brioso, sa *adj* energetic, vigorous (enérgico) || resolute, determined (determinado) || fiery, spirited (caballo) || elegant (garboso).

briozoario; briozoo *m* BOT bryozoan, bryozoon.

briqueta *f* briquette, briquet (carbón).

brisa *f* breeze; *brisa marina* sea breeze.

brisca *f* card game (juego de naipes) || brisques (as).

briscar *vt* to brocade.

brístol *m* bristol board.

británico, ca *adj* British; *las islas Británicas* the British Isles || *Su Majestad Británica* Her Britannic Majesty (reina), His Britannic Majesty (rey).
◆ *m/f* Britisher || *los británicos* the British.

britano, na *adj* British.
◆ *m/f* HIST Briton.

brizna *f* blade (de hierba) || string (de judía) || bit, piece (trozo).

broca *f* drill, bit (taladro) || tack (clavo) || bobbin (de bordadora).

brocado, da *adj* brocaded.
◆ *m* brocade (tela).

brocal *m* curb (de un pozo).

brocamantón *m* large jewelled brooch.

brocatel *m* brocatelle (tela) || brocatello (mármol).

bróculi *m* brocoli, broccoli.

brocha *f* paintbrush (pincel grande) || powder puff (para polvos) || shaving brush (de afeitar) || — *pintor de brocha gorda* painter and decorator (de casa), dauber (mal pintor) || *versos de brocha gorda* doggerel.

brochada *f*; **brochazo** *m* brushstroke, stroke of the brush.

broche *m* brooch [*US* breastpin] (joya) || fastener, clip, clasp (de un vestido) || AMER paper clip (para sujetar papeles) || FIG *el broche final* or *de oro* grand finale, finishing flourish.
◆ *pl* AMER cuff links (gemelos).

brocheta *f* CULIN skewer.

brocho *adj m* TAUR with horns close together.

brodequín *m* → **borceguí.**

broma *f* joke; *¡no es ninguna broma!* it is no joke! || joke, prank, trick, practical joke; *gastar bromas a* to play jokes on || ZOOL shipworm (gusano) || — *¡basta de bromas!, dejémonos de bromas* that's enough joking, joking aside || *broma aparte* joking apart, seriously || *broma de mal gusto* joke in bad taste || *broma pesada* practical joke || *dar una broma a* to play a joke on || *en broma* in fun, jokingly, as a joke || *entre bromas y veras* half jokingly, half in earnest || *es pura broma* it's a big *o* a huge joke || *estar de broma* to be in a joking mood || *fuera de broma* joking apart, seriously || *lo decía en broma* I was only joking || *medio en broma, medio en serio* half jokingly || *ni en broma* not on any account, not on your life || *no estar para bromas* not to be in the mood for joking, to be in no mood for joking || *saber (cómo) tomar una broma* to be able to take a joke || FIG *salir por la broma de* to cost a mere, to cost the huge amount of || *ser amigo de bromas* to like a joke, to like joking || *sin broma* joking apart, seriously || *tienda de bromas y engaños* joke shop || *tomar a broma* to make fun of, to deride (ridiculizar), to take as a joke (tomar a guasa).

bromar *vt* to gnaw (roer).

bromato *m* QUÍM bromate.

bromazo *m* stupid joke, stupid trick; *dar un bromazo a* to play a stupid trick on.

bromear *vi* to joke; *no estoy bromeando* I am not joking.

bromhídrico, ca *adj* QUÍM hydrobromic.

brómico, ca *adj* QUÍM bromic.

bromista *adj* fond of joking.
◆ *m/f* practical joker (que gasta bromas) || joker (que cuenta chistes) || funny person, laugh (persona graciosa).

bromo *m* QUÍM bromine.

bromuro *m* QUÍM bromide || FOT *papel de bromuro* bromide paper.

bronca *f* quarrel, row, fight (riña) || telling off, ticking off (represión) || scuffle, brawl, fight (pelea) || jeering, jeers *pl*, boos *pl* (gritos de desagrado) || — *armarle una bronca a uno* to boo *o* to jeer s.o. (abuchearle), to give s.o. hell (reprenderle) || *armar una bronca* to kick up a rumpus || *buscar bronca* to look for a fight || *echar una bronca* to tell off, to tick off, to haul over the coals || *ganarse una bronca* to be booed, to be jeered (ser abucheado) || *llevarse una bronca* to be told off *o* ticked off, to be hauled || over the coals || AMER *me da bronca* it makes me mad || *se armó una bronca* there was a tremendous quarrel *o* row.

bronce *m* bronze (metal y objeto de arte) || copper coin (moneda de cobre) || FIG *ser de bronce* to have a heart of stone.

bronceado, da *adj* bronze, bronze coloured (color) || tanned, brown, sunburnt (tostado por el sol).
◆ *m* bronzing; *el bronceado de las medallas* the bronzing of medals || suntanning (acción de broncearse) || tan, suntan (piel tostada).

bronceador *m* suntan oil.

bronceadura *f* bronzing.

broncear *vt* to bronze (un metal, una estatua) || to tan, to bronze (la piel).
◆ *vpr* to tan, to get brown, to get a suntan (la piel) || TECN to bronze.

broncíneo, a *adj* bronze (del color del bronce) || bronze, bronzed (de bronce).

broncista *m* bronzesmith.

bronco, ca; brozno, na *adj* rough, coarse (tosco) || brittle (metales) || raucous, harsh, rough (voz, sonido) || FIG surly (carácter).

broncofonía *f* MED broncophony.

bronconeumonía *f* MED bronchopneumonia.

broncopatía *f* MED bronchopathy.

broncoscopio *m* bronchoscope.

bronquedad; bronquera *f* roughness, coarseness (tosquedad) || brittleness (metales) || harshness, roughness (voz, sonido) || FIG surliness (carácter).

bronquial *adj* ANAT bronchial.

bronquio *m* ANAT bronchus.
◆ *pl* ANAT bronchi, bronchia.

bronquiolos *m pl* ANAT bronchioles.

bronquítico, ca *adj* MED bronchitic.

bronquitis *f* MED bronchitis.

broquel *m* shield.

broquelarse *vpr* to shield o.s. || FIG to defend o.s., to protect o.s.

broqueta *f* skewer || *riñones en broqueta* kidney kebab.

brotadura *f* budding, shooting (de una planta) || gushing (de una fuente).

brotar *vi* to sprout, to come up, to spring up; *ya ha brotado el trigo* the wheat has come up || to bud, to shoot (echar renuevos); *el árbol empieza a brotar* the tree is starting to bud || to sprout, to come out; *los renuevos han brotado* the buds have sprouted || to gush forth, to spring up (las fuentes) || to rise (los ríos) || to shoot out; *brotaron chispas* sparks shot out || to well up; *brotaron las lágrimas de sus ojos* tears welled up in his eyes || to appear, to break out (erupción cutánea) || FIG to spring up; *brotó una llamarada* a flame sprang up | to appear; *en mi mente brotó una duda* a doubt appeared in my mind || *hacer brotar chispas* to make sparks fly.
◆ *vt* to produce.

brote *m* BOT bud, shoot (renuevo) | budding (brotadura) || gushing (del agua) || welling-up (de lágrimas) || MED rise (de fiebre) | appearance (de erupción cutánea) || FIG outbreak; *los primeros brotes de una epidemia* the first outbreaks of an epidemic.

browniano *adj m* FIG Brownian (movimiento).

browning *m* Browning (pistola).

broza *f* dead leaves *pl* (hojas muertas) || dead wood (ramas) || rubbish (desechos) || thicket, undergrowth, brushwood (matorrales) || FIG rubbish; *en su libro había mucha broza* there was a lot of rubbish in his book || IMPR printer's brush (bruza).

brozno, na *adj* → **bronco.**

bruces (de) *loc adv* face downwards || *caer de bruces* to fall flat on one's face, to fall headlong.

bruja *f* witch (hechicera) || barn owl (lechuza) || FIG old witch, hag (mujer fea) | witch (mujer mala) || AMER *estar bruja* to be poverty-stricken, to be penniless.

Brujas *n pr* GEOGR Bruges.

brujear *vi* to practise witchcraft.

brujería *f* witchcraft, sorcery.

brujidor *m* glass cutter (herramienta).

brujir *vt* to trim [glass].

brujo *m* sorcerer, wizard || witch doctor (en las tribus primitivas) || AMER medicine man || *El aprendiz de brujo* The Sorcerer's Apprentice.

brújula *f* compass; *brújula marina* mariner's compass || (p us) sight (mira) || FIG *perder la brújula* to lose one's bearings.

brujulear *vt* FIG & FAM to guess (adivinar) | to plot, to scheme (tramar) || to uncover (las cartas).
◆ *vi* FIG & FAM to loaf about (vagar).

brujuleo *m* FIG & FAM guessing.

brulote *m* MAR fire ship || AMER insult (insulto) | scorching article (escrito incendiario).

bruma *f* mist (niebla) || haze (de calor).
◆ *pl* FIG confusion *sing*, fog *sing*, haze *sing*.

brumazón *f* fog.

brumoso, sa *adj* misty, hazy (ligeramente neblinoso), foggy (muy neblinoso).

bruno, na *adj* dark brown.
◆ *m* BOT black plum (ciruela, ciruelo).

bruñido *m* polishing, burnishing (acción) || polish, burnish (resultado).

bruñidor, ra *m/f* polisher, burnisher.
◆ *m* polisher, burnisher (herramienta).

bruñir* *vt* to polish, to burnish || AMER to pester (fastidiar).
◆ *vpr* FIG & FAM to make up (maquillarse).

brusco, ca *adj* brusque, abrupt; *una persona brusca* a brusque person || sudden, abrupt (repentino); *un cambio brusco* a sudden change || sharp (curva) || sharp (cambio de temperatura).
◆ *m* butcher's broom (arbusto).

brusela *f* periwinkle (flor).

bruselas *f pl* jeweller's tweezers.

Bruselas *n pr* GEOGR Brussels || *coles de Bruselas* Brussels sprouts.

bruselense *adj* [of *o* from] Brussels.
◆ *m/f* native *o* inhabitant of Brussels.

brusquedad *f* brusqueness, abruptness (de una persona) || suddenness, abruptness (de cosas).

brutal *adj* brutal, rough; *hombres brutales* brutal men || FIG sudden, abrupt (repentino) || FAM terrific (formidable) | colossal, huge, gigantic (enorme).

brutalidad; bruteza *f* brutality, savagery (crueldad) || brutality, brutishness (de una persona) || brutal *o* savage act (salvajada) || FAM foolish act (acción estúpida) | foolishness (estupidez).

brutalizar *vt* to brutalize.

bruteza *f* → **brutalidad.**

bruto, ta *adj* stupid, dense (estúpido); *este chico es muy bruto* this boy is very dense || ignorant (sin cultura) || uncouth, coarse, rough (tosco) || brutal, brutish (brutal) || crude; *petróleo bruto* crude oil || rough, uncut (piedra, diamante) || unworked (madera) || — AMER *a la bruta, a lo bruto* crudely || *en bruto* gross; *peso en bruto* gross weight; rough, uncut; *diamante en bruto* uncut diamond; unworked (madera) || FIG & FAM *¡pedazo de bruto!* stupid brute! || *producto nacional bruto* gross national product.
◆ *m/f* brute (estúpido, cruel) || lout, country, bumpkin (rústico).
◆ *m* brute, beast (animal) || *el noble bruto* the noble beast (el caballo).

bruza *f* scrubbing brush (para restregar) || brush (para caballos) || IMPR printer's brush.

bruzar *vt* to clean with a brush, to brush.

bu *m* bogeyman.

buarillo; buaro *m* scops owl.

bubi *m* bubi (de Fernando Poo).

bubón *m* MED bubo.

bubónico, ca *adj* MED bubonic; *peste bubónica* bubonic plague.

bucal *adj* ANAT buccal; *órganos bucales* buccal organs || oral.

bucanero *m* buccaneer.

bucarán *m* buckram (tela).

Bucarest *n pr* GEOGR Bucharest.

búcaro *m* odoriferous clay (arcilla) || jar made of (odoriferous) clay (vasija) || vase (florero).

buccinador *m* ANAT buccinator.

buccino *m* whelk (molusco).

buceador *m* diver (buzo) || pearl diver (de perlas).

bucear *vi* to dive (el buzo) || to swim under water (nadar) || FIG to investigate, to explore, to sound (un asunto).

bucéfalo *m* FIG & FAM blockhead, jackass (tonto).

Bucéfalo *npr m* Bucephalus.

buceo *m* diving (de buzo, de nadador) || skin diving (natación submarina) || dive (zambullida) || FIG investigation.

bucero *m* griffon (perro).

bucle *m* ringlet, curl (de cabellos) || INFORM *bucle de iteración* iteration loop | *bucle de programa* program loop.

bucólica *f* bucolic (composición poética) || FAM grub, chow (comida).

bucólico, ca *adj* bucolic.

buchaca *f* AMER bag.

buchada *f* mouthful [of liquid].

buche *m* crop, craw (de aves), maw (de animales) || pucker, bag (que hace la ropa) || mouthful (de líquido) || FIG & FAM belly, stomach (estómago); *llenarse el buche* to fill one's belly | bosom (fuero interno) || newly-born donkey (borrico) || AMER top hat (chistera) | goitre [US goiter] (bocio) || FAM *no le cupo en el buche esa broma* he couldn't stomach *o* take the joke.

buchinche *m* → **bochinche.**

buchón, ona *adj* potbellied (barrigón) || *paloma buchona* pouter [pigeon].

Buda *npr m* Buddha.

Budapest *n pr* GEOGR Budapest.

budare *m* AMER dish for baking corn bread.

budín *m* CULIN pudding.

budinadora *f* TECN extruder.

budinera *f* pudding bowl, pudding basin.

budión *m* ZOOL wrasse (pez).

budismo *m* Buddhism.

budista *adj/s* Buddhist.

buen *adj* (apocopated form of *bueno*) → **bueno.**
— OBSERV The adjective *bueno* is apocopated to *buen* when it precedes the word it qualifies, whether it is a masculine noun (*un buen libro* a good book; *un buen hombre* a good man, etc.) or a verb in the infinitive used as a noun (*un buen andar* a good pace, etc.).

Buena Esperanza (cabo de) *n pr* GEOGR Cape of Good Hope.

buenamente *adv* simply (sencillamente) || easily, effortlessly (fácilmente) || readily, happily, unthinkingly; *cree buenamente cualquier cosa que se le diga* he readily believes everything he is told || willingly (de buen grado).

buenandanza *f* → **bienandanza.**

buenaventura *f* good fortune, good luck (suerte) || fortune; *echar* or *decir la buenaventura a uno* to tell s.o.'s fortune.

Buenaventura *npr m* Bonaventura.

buenazo, za *adj* good-natured.
◆ *m/f* good-natured person, good soul.

bueno, na; buen *adj* good; *es un hombre muy bueno* he is a very good man; *¡qué niño más bueno!* there's a good boy!; *buena conducta* good behaviour; *ser de buena familia* to be from a good family; *un buen obrero* a good worker; *dele una buena paliza* give him a good beating; *una buena ocasión* a good opportunity || good, fine, fair (tiempo) || bad, nasty; *un buen constipado* a bad cold || strong, sound (constitución física) || nice, pleasant (agradable); *es bueno pasearse en el jardín* it is nice to walk in the garden || good (deseable, útil); *sería bueno que acabaras esto muy pronto* it would be good if you finished this as soon as possible; *este barco es bueno para pescar* this boat is good for fishing; *este jarabe es bueno para la tos* this syrup is good for coughs || sound (doctrina, argumento) || nice, kind, good (amable); *una buena chica* a nice girl; *eres muy bueno conmigo* you are very kind to me || good, fine, beautiful; *tiene buena voz* he has a fine voice || polite, good (sociedad) || FAM considerable; *una buena cantidad* a considerable amount || real, proper; *¡buen sinvergüenza estás hecho!* you are a real good-for-nothing! | fine; *en buen lío nos hemos metido!* a fine mess we have got ourselves into || — *¿adónde* or *a dónde bueno?* where are you going? || *a la buena de Dios* in a slapdash way, any old how (a lo que salga) || FAM *¡buena es ésa!* that's a good one! || *buena jugada* a good move (buena táctica), a nice piece of play, a nice move (en deportes), a dirty trick (jugarreta) || FAM *¡buena la has hecho!, ¡buena la has armado!* that's done it!, you've done it now! | *¡buenas!* hello! || *buenas noches* good evening (al atardecer), good night (al acostarse) || *buenas tardes* good afternoon (después del mediodía), good evening (al atardecer) || *bueno de comer* good to eat || *¡bueno está!* that's enough!, that will do! (¡basta!) || *¡bueno está lo bueno!* enough is enough || *buenos días* good morning || *dar por bueno* to approve, to accept || *darse buena vida* to have a good life, to live well *o* comfortably || *de buena gana* willingly, gladly || *de buenas a primeras* all at once, without warning (de repente), at first sight, from the very start, right from the start (a primera vista), straight away (en seguida) || *¿de dónde bueno?* where did you spring from? || *de las buenas* first-rate || *de verdad de la buena* really and truly || *el buen camino* the straight and narrow || *en el buen momento* at the proper time, at the right time || *es bueno saberlo* it is nice *o* good to know || FAM *¡estamos buenos!* we're in a fine mess! || *estar a buenas con uno* to be on good terms with s.o. || FAM *estar buena* to be hot stuff, to be gorgeous (mujer) || *estar bueno* to be well, to be in good health || FAM *estar de buenas* to be in a good mood (de buen humor), to be in luck (tener suerte) || FIG *estaría bueno (que)...* it would be just fine (if)..., it would be the last straw (if)... || *hace buen tiempo* the weather is good || *ir por buen camino* to be on the right road || FAM *librarse de una buena* to have a narrow escape *o* a close call || *los buenos tiempos* the good old days, the good times || *¡pero bueno!* come off it! || *por las buenas* willingly || *por las buenas o por las malas* willy-nilly (de buen grado o por fuerza), by fair means or foul (de cualquier modo) || *¡qué buena!, ¡muy buena!* that's a good one! (historia) || *¡qué bueno!, ¡muy bueno!* bravo!, very good! (excelente) || *¿qué dice de bueno?* what's new? || *ser bueno como un ángel* to be as good as gold || *ser más bueno que el pan* to be kindness *o* goodness itself || *ser muy buena persona* to be very nice *o* kind || FAM *tirarse una buena vida* to lead a soft life || *verás lo que es bueno* you will see sth. really good (sentido propio), just you wait (sentido irónico).
◆ *m* good one (persona) || quality; *preferir lo bueno a lo bello* to put quality before looks || — FAM *lo bueno es que...* the good part about it is that..., the strange thing is that... || *lo bueno, si breve, dos veces bueno* brevity is the soul of wit, the shorter the better.
◆ *pl* the good (ones); *los buenos y los malos* the good (ones) and the bad (ones).
◆ *interj* well! || very well!, all right!, O. K.! (de acuerdo) || that's enough, that'll do! (¡basta!) || come on!, come off it! (con incredulidad).

Buenos Aires *n pr* GEOGR Buenos Aires.

buey *m* ZOOL bullock, ox (toro castrado) || ox (animal de tiro) || — *buey marino* manatee, sea cow || FIG *el buey suelto bien se lame* there is nothing like freedom | *habló el buey y dijo mu* what can you expect from a pig but a grunt?

bueyada *f* drove of oxen (boyada).

bueyecillo; bueyezuelo *m* little bullock, steer.

bueyuno, na *adj* bovine, of oxen.

bufa *f* joke (broma) || jest, piece of bufoonery (bufonada) || *AMER* drunkenness (borrachera).

bufado, da *adj* blown (vidrio).

búfalo, la *m/f* ZOOL buffalo.

bufanda *f* scarf, muffler.

bufar *vi* to snort (el toro, etc.) || to spit (el gato) || to neigh (el caballo) || FIG to snort [with rage] (persona) || FIG & FAM *está que bufa* he is hopping mad.

bufete *m* writing table, writing desk (mesa) || lawyer's office (despacho) || practice (clientela).

buffer *m* INFORM buffer (memoria intermedia).

buffet *m* buffet.

bufido *m* snort (del toro) || roar (del león, etc.) || hiss (del gato) || neigh (del caballo) || FIG & FAM outburst (de ira) | telling-off, bawling-out (reprimenda); *recibir un bufido* to get a telling-off | yell (grito) || FIG & FAM *dar bufidos de rabia* to bellow with rage.

bufo, fa *adj* comic; *actor bufo* comic actor || *ópera bufa* opera bouffe, comic opera.
◆ *m* buffoon.

bufón, ona *adj* farcical, comical.
◆ *m* buffoon, fool || HIST jester.

bufonada *f* piece of buffoonery, jest.

bufonearse *vpr* to play the fool (hacer bufonadas) || to laugh at, to make fun of (burlarse de).

bufonesco, ca *adj* farcical, comical.

buganvilla *f* BOT bougainvillea.

buggy *m* buggy (coche).

bugle *m* MÚS bugle.

buglosa *f* bugloss (planta).

buharda; buhardilla *f* attic, garret || dormer (window) (ventana).

buharro *m* scops owl.

búho *m* owl || FIG recluse, unsociable person || *búho real* eagle owl.

buhonería *f* pedlar's wares, hawker's wares (objetos) || peddling, hawking (oficio).

buhonero *m* pedlar [*US* peddler], hawker.

buido, da *adj* sharp (afilado) || grooved (acanalado) || *estilo buido* easy *o* fluent style.

buitre *m* ZOOL vulture (ave) || FIG vulture (persona).

buitrear *vt* *AMER* to hunt (vultures) | to vomit (vomitar).

buitrón *m* fish trap (para pescar).

buje *m* axle box, bushing (de un eje).

bujería *f* knick-knack (fruslería).

bujía *f* candle (vela) || candlepower (unidad de intensidad luminosa) || sparking plug [*US* spark plug] (del encendido).

bula *f* bull (del papa) || bulla (adorno romano) || — *bula de oro* golden bull || FIG *no poder con la bula* to be finished, to have had it.

bulbo *m* BOT bulb || ANAT & ARQ bulb || *bulbo raquídeo* rachidian bulb.

bulboso, sa *adj* bulbous.

buldog; bulldog *m* bulldog (perro).

buldozer; bulldozer *m* bulldózer (excavadora).

bulerías *f pl* bulerias [Andalusian song and dance].

buleto *m* papal brief.

bulevar *m* boulevard (alameda).

Bulgaria *npr f* GEOGR Bulgaria.

búlgaro, ra *adj/s* Bulgarian.

bulín *m* *AMER* FAM bachelor pad (piso de soltero).

bulo *m* FAM hoax, false report, false piece of news.

bulto *m* volume, size, bulk (volumen) || shape, form (objeto o persona de aspecto confuso); *he visto dos bultos cerca de la casa* I saw two shapes near the house || bump (chichón) || lump, swelling (protuberancia) || parcel, package (paquete) || piece of luggage (equipaje) || bundle; *un bulto de ropa* a bundle of clothes || body; *el toro busca el bulto* the bull goes for the body || *AMER* satchel (cartapacio) || — *a bulto* roughly, approximately || *bultos de mano* hand luggage || FIG & FAM *buscar a uno el bulto* to hound s.o., to try to rile s.o. || *cuanto menos bulto, más claridad* good riddance to bad rubbish || *de bulto* obvious, striking, glaring || *de mucho bulto* bulky || *de poco bulto* small || *escoger a bulto* to choose at random || FAM *escurrir el bulto* to get out of it, to dodge it || *hacer (de) bulto* to help to make up a crowd, to swell the numbers || *hacer mucho bulto* to be very bulky, to be cumbersome, to take up a lot of space.

bulla *f* uproar, noise, racket, row; *armar* or *meter bulla* to make a racket || crowd, mob (muchedumbre) || bustling, jostling; *hay mucha bulla en las tiendas* there is a lot of bustling in the shops || confusion || — *meter bulla* to hurry (meter prisa) || *tener bulla* to be in a hurry.

bullabesa *f* bouillabaisse.

bullanga *f* tumult, disturbance, racket, riot (tumulto).

bullanguero, ra *adj* riotous, noisy, uproarious.
◆ *m/f* noisy person (persona ruidosa) || rioter, troublemaker (persona alborotadora).

bullaranga *f* *AMER* —> **bullanga.**

bullebulle *m/f* busybody.

bullicio *m* hubbub, noise, din (ruido) || bustle, hustle and bustle; *retirarse al campo para huir del bullicio de la ciudad* to retire to the country to escape from the hustle and bustle of the city || crush (muchedumbre); *ser cogido en el bullicio* to be caught in the crush || confusion.

bullicioso, sa *adj* busy, bustling; *una calle bulliciosa* a busy street || boisterous, restless (turbulento); *un niño bullicioso* a boisterous child || noisy (ruidoso) || riotous (alborotador).

bullidor, ra *adj* restless, bustling (que se mueve mucho) || active (que tiene muchas actividades).

bullir* *vi* to boil (hervir) || to bubble, to bubble up (a borbotones) || to swarm, to teem (pulular) || FIG to boil (la sangre, de enfado) | to seethe; *bullía de ira* he was seething with rage | to bustle about (agitarse) | to bustle; *bullir de actividad* to bustle with activity || — FIG *le bullen los pies al ver bailar a los demás* he is itching to dance as he watches the others | *me bulle la lengua* I am dying to talk.
◆ *vt* to stir, to move; *no bullía pie ni mano* he did not stir hand or foot.
◆ *vpr* to move (moverse).

bullón *m* stud (adorno de metal) || puff (en un vestido).

bulterrier *m* bull terrier (perro).

bumerang *m* boomerang.

bungalow *m* bungalow.

buniato *m* BOT sweet potato (boniato).

bunker *m* bunker.

buñolada *f* fair.

buñolería *f* doughnut shop.

buñuelo *m* doughnut || FIG & FAM mess, botch; *esa película es un buñuelo* that film is a botch || — *buñuelo de viento* fritter || FIG & FAM *hacer un buñuelo* to make a botch *o* a mess.

BUP *abrev de Bachillerato Unificado Polivalente* Secondary school course and qualification.

buque *m* ship, boat, vessel || *buque aljibe* tanker || *buque carguero* or *de carga* or *mercante* cargo boat, freighter, merchant ship || *buque costanero* or *de cabotaje* coasting vessel, coaster || *buque de desembarco* landing craft || *buque de guerra* warship || *buque de pasajeros* passenger ship || *buque de ruedas* paddle steamer || *buque de vapor* steamship, steamer || *buque de vela* sailing ship || *buque escuela* training ship || *buque insignia* flagship || *buque nodriza* mother ship.

buqué *m* bouquet (del vino).

burbuja *f* bubble || *hacer burbujas* to bubble, to make bubbles.

burbujear *vi* to bubble || to sparkle, to fizz (champán, agua mineral).

burbujeo *m* bubbling || fizz, sparkle (de champán, de agua mineral).

burda *f* MAR backstay.

burdégano *m* ZOOL hinny.

burdel *m* brothel.

burdeos *adj/sm* Bordeaux (vino).

Burdeos *n pr* GEOGR Bordeaux.

burdo, da *adj* clumsy (torpe); *una excusa burda* a clumsy excuse || coarse, rough (tosco); *paño burdo* coarse cloth; *modales burdos* rough manners.

bureo *m* FAM pastime, amusement (diversión) || FAM *estar* or *irse de bureo* to go on a spree *o* on a binge.

bureta *f* QUÍM burette.

burgalés, esa *adj* [of *o* from] Burgos.
◆ *m/f* native *o* inhabitant of Burgos.

burgo *m* (ant) hamlet, borough (población pequeña) || *burgo podrido* rotten borough.

burgomaestre *m* burgomaster.

burgrave *m* burgrave.

burgués, esa *adj* bourgeois, middle class.
◆ *m/f* bourgeois, middle-class man *o* woman.

burguesía *f* bourgeoisie, middle class || *alta burguesía* upper middle class.

burí *m* BOT sago palm.

buril *m* burin.

burilada; buriladura *f* burin stroke.

burilado *m* engraving.

burilar *vt* to engrave (with a burin).

burjaca *f* (pilgrim's) scrip.

burla *f* gibe, jeer, taunt (mofa) || joke (broma) || — *burla burlando* without noticing it, merrily (sin darse cuenta), jokingly (bromeando), on the quiet, craftily (disimuladamente) || *de burlas, en son de burlas* in fun || *entre burlas y veras* half jokingly || *gastar burlas* to play tricks || *hacer burla a uno* to mock s.o., to make fun of s.o. (mofarse) || *hacer burla de uno con la mano* to thumb one's nose at s.o. (un palmo de narices).

burladero *m* TAUR refuge [in a bullring].

burlador, ra *adj* mocking.
◆ *m/f* mocker.
◆ *m* seducer, Don Juan.

burlar *vt* to deceive, to trick, to take in (engañar) || to outwit (chasquear) || to deceive (a una mujer) || FIG to flout; *burlar las leyes* to flout

the law | to frustate (una esperanza, etc.) | to evade (la vigilancia).
◆ *vpr* to mock, to ridicule, to make fun of.

burlería *f* mockery (mofa) || deceit (engaño) || tall story (cuento fabuloso).

burlesco, ca *adj* burlesque; *el género burlesco* the burlesque style || FIG funny, comic; *una situación muy burlesca* a very funny situation.

burlete *m* draught excluder.

burlón, ona *adj* mocking; *un aire burlón* a mocking air.
◆ *m/f* joker.

buró *m* bureau, writing desk (mesa de escribir) || executive committee (junta directiva) || AMER bedside table.

burocracia *f* bureaucracy.

burócrata *m/f* bureaucrat.

burocrático, ca *adj* bureaucratic.

burra *f* she-ass (hembra del burro) || FIG & FAM dunce, ass (ignorante) | hard worker (mujer trabajadora).

burrada *f* drove of donkeys || FIG & FAM stupid *o* foolish remark (necedad); *dijo una burrada* he made a stupid remark | stupid *o* foolish thing (acción estúpida); *hizo una burrada* he did a stupid thing | vulgar *o* rude remark, vulgarity (grosería) | atrocity (atrocidad) || — FIG & FAM *decir burradas* to talk nonsense | *una burrada* a lot, an awful lot; *una burrada de gente* a lot of people; *me gusta una burrada* I like it a lot.

burrero *m* donkey driver.

burriciego, ga *adj* FAM as blind as a bat.

burrillo *m* FAM liturgical calendar, ordo.

burrito *m* young donkey, foal || AMER fringe (flequillo).

burro *m* ZOOL donkey, ass || sawhorse (para serrar) || FIG & FAM ass, dunce, fool; *este chico es muy burro* this boy is a real dunce | lout, brute (tosco) || AMER stepladder, folding ladder (escalera de tijera) || — FIG *a burro muerto cebada al rabo* it is no good shutting the stable door after the horse has bolted | *apearse* or *caerse del burro* to back down, to climb down | *bajar del burro* to give in | *burro cargado de letras* pompous ass | *burro de carga* hard worker (que trabaja mucho), dogsbody, person who does the donkey work, drudge (que carga con todo el trabajo) || *ir en burro* to ride on a donkey || FIG & FAM *no ver tres en un burro* to be as blind as a bat.

bursátil *adj* stock-exchange; *información bursátil* stock-exchange news.

burujo *m* lump (en una masa) || knot, tangle (en la lana, etc.) || cattle cake made of olives or grapes (para el ganado).

burujón *m* bump, lump (chichón).

bus *m* INFORM bus.

busca *f* search; *ir en* or *a la busca de* to go in search of || party of hunters (cacería).
◆ *pl* AMER perks (*fam*).

buscador, ra *adj* seeking, searching || *cabeza buscadora* homing device (de un cohete).
◆ *m/f* seeker, searcher || prospector.
◆ *m* TECN finder (de telescopio).

buscaniguas *m inv* AMER jumping jack, firecracker (petardo).

buscapié *m* feeler [in conversation].

buscapiés *m inv* jumping jack, firecracker (petardo).

buscapleitos *m inv* troublemaker.

buscar *vt* to search for, to look for; *lo busqué en toda la casa sin encontrarlo* I looked for it all over the house without finding it; *buscar una solución a un problema* to search for a solution to a problem || to seek; *buscar ayuda, un consejo, la amistad* to seek help, advice, friendship || to be after, to be out for (perseguir); *sólo busca su propio beneficio* he is only after what he can gain || to look for; *buscar un trabajo* to look for work || to look up (en un libro) || to fumble for (con dificultad); *buscar sus palabras, el ojo de la cerradura* to fumble for words, for the keyhole || FIG & FAM to ask for, to look for (provocar) || — FIG & FAM *buscarle las cosquillas a uno* to rub s.o. up the wrong way | *buscarle tres pies al gato* to split hairs (hilar muy fino), to make life more difficult than it is, to complicate matters (complicarse la vida) | *buscar una aguja en un pajar* to look for a needle in a haystack || *ir a buscar* to fetch, to go and get, to bring || *pasaré a buscarte a las tres* I'll pick you up at three o'clock.
◆ *vi* to look, to search || *quien busca halla* seek and ye shall find.
◆ *vpr* FIG *buscarse la vida* to try to earn one's living || FIG & FAM *buscársela* to ask for it || *buscarse la ruina* to be on the road to ruin.

buscarruidos *m/f inv* FIG & FAM troublemaker, quarrelsome person (pendenciero).

buscavidas *m/f inv* hustler (persona muy activa) || go-getter (ambicioso) || busybody (entrometido).

buscón, ona *m/f* (p us) searcher (que busca).
◆ *m* pickpocket (ratero) || petty thief (ladrón) || crook, swindler (estafador).
◆ *f* POP streetwalker, prostitute.

buseta *f* AMER minibus.

busilis *m* snag, hitch (dificultad) || core (parte central) || *allí está el busilis* that's the rub, that's the catch.

búsqueda *f* search.

busto *m* bust.

butaca *f* seat (en un teatro) || easy chair, armchair (en una casa) || — *butaca de patio* seat in the stalls [*US* seat in the orchestra] || *patio de butacas* stalls [*US* orchestra].
◆ *pl* stalls (en un teatro).

butadieno *m* QUÍM butadiene.

butano *m* QUÍM butane; *bombona de butano* butane cylinder; *gas butano* butane gas.

buten (de) *loc adv* FAM first-rate, fabulous, terrific.

butifarra *f* Catalan sausage.

butileno *m* QUÍM butylene.

butilo *m* QUÍM butyl.

butírico, ca *adj* QUÍM butyric; *ácido butírico* butyric acid.

buyo *m* betel.

buzamiento *m* MIN dip (del filón).

buzar *vi* MIN to dip.

buzo *m* diver || AMER sweat shirt (sudadera) | track suit (chándal) || — *campana de buzo* diving bell || *enfermedad de los buzos* the bends, caisson disease, diver's paralysis.

buzón *m* letter box [*US* mailbox] (en general) || sluice (de un estanque) || stopper, plug, bung (tapón) || *echar una carta a* or *en el buzón* to post a letter.

buzonero *m* AMER postmanr.

C

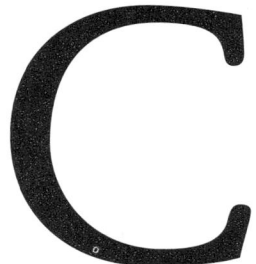

c *f* c; *una c mayúscula* a capital c.
— OBSERV Before *e* or *i* the *c* has the same sound as the Spanish *z* (an interdental fricative) and it is pronounced with the tip of the tongue between the teeth, as in the English *th* sound [θ]. In other cases the *c* is a voiceless velar occlusive like the *k*. The first of these sounds is often confused with the *s* sound in Latin American and Andalusian pronunciation.

¡ca! *interj* FAM not at all!, never! (indicates negation).

cabal *adj* exact, right, accurate; *una cuenta cabal* an exact sum; *una definición cabal* an exact definition || perfect (sin defecto); *un hombre cabal* a perfect man || whole, full; *el peso cabal* the full weight || complete, total; *un cabal fracaso* a total defeat || exactly; *duró tres horas cabales* it lasted exactly three hours || — *es hermosa a carta cabal* she is beauty itself || *estar en sus cabales* to be in one's right mind || *no estar en sus cabales* not to be in one's right mind, to be out of one's mind; *cuando hiciste eso, no estabas en tus cabales* you must have been out of your mind to do that || *por sus cabales* properly (perfectamente), at a fair price (precio).

cábala *f* cabala, cabbala (doctrina) || FIG intrigue, cabal; *andar metido en una cábala* to be mixed up in an intrigue || FIG *hacer cábalas sobre algo* to speculate *o* to make guesses about sth.

cabalgada *f* troop of cavalry (tropa de jinetes) || cavalry raid (correría).

cabalgadura *f* mount (bestia de silla) || pack animal, beast of burden (bestia de carga).

cabalgar *vi* to ride; *cabalgar en un burro* to ride an ass, to ride on an ass || to straddle (sentarse a horcajadas); *el niño cabalgaba sobre la tapia* the child straddled the wall.
◆ *vt* to ride || to cover, to mount (cubrir una hembra).

cabalgata *f* cavalcade, procession (desfile) || ride (correría a caballo) || *la cabalgata de los Reyes Magos* the procession of the Three Wise Men.

cabalista *adj/s* cabalist, cabbalist || intriguer (intrigante).

cabalístico *adj* cabalistic, cabbalistic || FIG occult.

cabalmente *adv* exactly (exactamente, precisamente) || at a fair price (a su precio) || completely, entirely (completamente) || properly (perfectamente).

caballa *f* mackerel (pescado).

caballada *f* herd of horses || AMER blunder (acción desacertada); *hacer una caballada* to make a blunder | stupid thing (necedad) || AMER *hacer caballadas* to make an ass of o.s., to act the goat.

caballar *adj* equine; *raza caballar* equine race || — *cara* or *perfil caballar* horses *pl.*

caballejo *m* FAM nag.

caballeresco, ca *adj* chivalrous, knightly (propio de un caballero andante) || FIG chivalrous, gentlemanly; *conducta caballeresca* chivalrous conduct | chivalrous, noble; *sentimientos caballerescos* chivalrous feelings || *literatura caballeresca* books of chivalry.

caballerete *m* FAM young dandy.

caballería *f* mount, steed (bestia de silla) || cavalry (cuerpo militar); *una carga de caballería* a cavalry charge || chivalry (orden) || AMER name of different types of land measurements [1,343 ares in Cuba, 7,858 ares in Puerto Rico and 4,279 ares in Mexico and Guatemala] || — FIG & FAM *andarse en caballerías* to overdo the compliments || *caballería andante* knight-errantry || MIL *caballería ligera* light cavalry, light horse.

caballeriza *f* stable (cuadra) || stud (para la cría de caballos) || grooms *pl*, stable hands *pl* (personal).

caballerizo *m* groom, stableman (de caballeriza) || *caballerizo mayor del rey* Master of the King's Horse.

caballero, ra *adj* mounted, riding; *caballero en un asno* mounted on an ass || FIG firm (porfiado).
◆ *m* sir (sólo en el singular); *caballero, por favor* please, sir || gentleman; *traje de caballero* gentleman's suit || FIG gentleman; *es un verdadero caballero* he is a real gentleman || noble, nobleman (noble) || knight (de una orden); *el Caballero de la Triste Figura* the Knight of the Sorrowful Countenance || MIL cavalry man || — *armar caballero a uno* to knight s.o., to dub s.o. knight || *caballero andante* knight-errant || *caballero de industria* swindler || TAUR *caballero en plaza* bullfighter on horseback || *poderoso caballero es don Dinero* money talks.
◆ *pl* gentlemen; *¡entren señoras y caballeros!* come in ladies and gentlemen!

caballerosamente *adv* chivalrously.

caballerosidad *f* chivalry.

caballeroso, sa *adj* noble, chivalrous (noble); *una acción caballerosa* a noble action || chivalrous, gentlemanly (galante, cortés); *un hombre caballeroso* a chivalrous man.

caballete *m* ridge (del tejado) || rack (de tortura) || trestle (soporte) || cowl (de una chimenea) || bridge (de la nariz) || AGR ridge (caballón) || ARTES easel (de pintor) || *caballete de aserrar* sawhorse.

caballista *m/f* rider, horseman, horsewoman.

caballito *m* small horse || AMER bridge (de la nariz) | nappy [US diaper] (metedor de niños) | raft (balsa) || toy horse (caballo de juguete) || hobbyhorse (juguete en el cual se monta el niño) || type of roulette (juego) || — *caballito de balancín* rocking horse || ZOOL *caballito del diablo* dragonfly | *caballito de mar* or *marino* sea horse || AMER *caballito de totora* small reed raft.
◆ *pl* round-about, merry-go-round [US carrousel] (en las ferias).

caballo *m* ZOOL horse; *montar a caballo* to ride a horse || knight (juego de ajedrez) || «caballo» [the «caballo» in the Spanish pack of cards corresponds to the queen in the English pack] (en la baraja) || sawhorse (burro de serrar) || MIN mass of rock || MIL horse soldier, cavalryman (soldado de a caballo) || — *a caballo* on horseback || FIG *a caballo regalado no le mires el diente* don't look a gift horse in the mouth | *a uña de caballo* at full gallop *o* speed || *caballo blanco* backer || *caballo castrado* gelding || FIG *caballo de batalla* hobbyhorse | *caballo de buena boca* obliging person || *caballo de carga* packhorse || *caballo de carrera* racehorse || MIL *caballo de frisa* cheval-de-frise (defensa) || TECN *caballo de fuerza* horsepower || *caballo del diablo* dragonfly || *caballo de mar* sea horse || *caballo de montar* or *de silla* saddle horse || *caballo de tiro* cart horse || *caballo de Troya* Trojan horse, wooden horse (of Troy) || FIG *caballo de vapor* horsepower || *caballo entero* stallion || FIG *caballo fiscal* treasury horsepower || *caballo padre* or *semental* stallion || FIG *como caballo desbocado* hastily | *fuerte como un caballo* strong as an ox || *soldado de a caballo* horse soldier, cavalryman || *subir* or *montar a caballo* to get on *o* to mount a horse || *tropas de a caballo* mounted troops || *un coche de diez caballos* a ten horsepower car.
— OBSERV El *horsepower* (H. P.) difiere ligeramente del *caballo de vapor* (C V). Un H. P. equivale a 1,0138 C V

caballón *m* AGR ridge.

caballuno, na *adj* horsy, horse-like; *una cara caballuna* a horse-like face.

cabaña *f* cabin, hut, shack (choza de ramas) || livestock (conjunto del ganado); *la cabaña nacional* the national livestock || *cabaña alpina* Alpine chalet.

cabañal *adj* animal; *camino cabañal* animal track *o* path.
◆ *m* hamlet.

cabañero, ra; cabañil *adj* livestock (del ganado) || *perro cabañero* sheep dog.
◆ *m* shepherd (pastor) || mule driver, muleteer (arriero).

cabañuela *f* small cabin *o* hut.
◆ *pl* weather forecast [according to observations made during the first 24 days of August, September or January, depending on the region] || AMER first summer rains (lluvias de verano), first winter rains (lluvias de invierno).

cabaret *m* night club, cabaret.

cabaretera *f* cabaret entertainer.

cabe *prep* (ant) POÉT next to; *cabe la casa* next to the house.

cabeceada *f* AMER butt (golpe dado con la cabeza) | nod (al dormitar) || *dar cabeceadas* to nod (el que duerme sentado).

cabecear *vi* to shake *o* to nod one's head (balancear) || to shake one's head (negar) || to nod (durmiéndose) || to head the ball (fútbol) || to toss its head (caballo) || MAR to pitch (los barcos) || to lurch, to jolt (carruajes) || to slip (moverse una carga, etc.).
◆ *vt* to blend (vino) || to bind (los tapices) || to put a headband on (un libro) || to foot, to put a new foot in (las medias viejas) || to head (el balón) || AGR to plough [US to plow]

|| AMER to bind together by the stalks [tobacco leaves].

cabeceo *m* nodding, nod, shaking (de la cabeza) || nodding (oscilación ligera) || lurch, jolt (de un carruaje) || toss of the head (de un caballo) || MAR pitching || slipping (de una carga, etc.).

cabecera *f* top (parte principal) || head, bedhead (de la cama) || headboard (pieza que limita la cama) || bedside; *estar a la cabecera del enfermo* to be at the invalid's bedside; *libro de cabecera* bedside book || place of honour, head (plaza de honor en la mesa) || source, headwaters *pl* (fuente de un río) || county town [US county seat] (capital de distrito o de territorio) || head (persona principal); *la cabecera del partido* the head of the party || IMPR frontispiece, headband (de un libro) | headline (en un periódico) || (p us) pillow (almohada) || headland (extremo de un campo) || sanctuary (de una iglesia) || — *cabecera del reparto* top of the bill || *cabecera de puente* bridgehead || *estar a la cabecera de la mesa* to be at the head of the table || *médico de cabecera* family doctor.

cabecero *m* headrest.

cabecilla *m* leader (jefe).

cabellera *f* hair, head of hair; *una hermosa cabellera negra* beautiful black hair, a beautiful head of black hair || tail (de cometa) || — *Cabellera de Berenice* Coma Berenices || *cabellera postiza* wig.

cabello *m* hair (pelo); *cabellos postizos* false hair; *tenía el cabello rubio* she had blond hair || *asirse de un cabello* to clutch at a straw || *cabello de ángel* vermicelli (fideos) || *cabello lacio* straight hair || BOT *cabello de Venus* maidenhair || FIG *cortar* or *partir un cabello en el aire* to split hairs | *estar pendiente de un cabello* to be hanging by a thread.
◆ *pl* corn silk *sing*, beard *sing* (del maíz) || — FIG *agarrar la ocasión por los cabellos* to seize the opportunity by the scruff of the neck || FIG *llevar por los cabellos* to twist round one's little finger || *mesarse los cabellos* to tear one's hair || FIG *se le pusieron los cabellos de punta* his hair stood on end | *traído por los cabellos* farfetched; *explicación traída por los cabellos* far-fetched explanation.

cabelludo, da *adj* hairy (persona) || shaggy (animal) || BOT downy || *cuero cabelludo* scalp.

caber* *vi* to fit, to go; *mi chaqueta no cabe en la maleta* my jacket does not fit *o* will not go in the suitcase || there is room for, to hold; *caben seis personas en el coche* there is room for six people in the car, the car holds six people; *en este local no caben tantas personas* there is not room for so many people in this place || to go, to fit; *el armario no cabe por la puerta* the wardrobe will not go through the door || to be possible; *cabía que viniese más tarde, pero no tanto* it was possible that he would come late, but not this late; *cabe decir que...* it is possible to say that... || to have; *me cabe la satisfacción de anunciarle esta noticia* I have the pleasure of announcing this news to you || to go; *veinte entre tres caben a seis y sobran dos* three into twenty goes six and two over || to be for; *no me cabe decirlo* it is not for me to say || — *¿cabe mayor disparate que...?* can you imagine anything more stupid than...? || *cabe pensar que...* one might think that... || *caber a uno* to fall to s.o.; *me cupo ir a decírselo* it fell to me to go and tell him || *dentro de* or *en lo que cabe* as far as possible || *¡esto no me cabe en la cabeza!* it is beyond me! || *no cabe duda* there is no doubt || *no cabe más* it is full, there is no more room (lleno), that is the last straw, that's the lot, that beats all (el colmo) || *no cabe más holgazán* they don't come any lazier || *no cabe perdón* it is inexcusable || *no caber en el pellejo* to be bursting || *no caber en sí* to be swollen-headed || *no caber en sí de gozo* or *de júbilo* or *de contento* to be beside o.s. with enjoyment *o* joy *o* happiness || *no caberle a uno el corazón en el pecho* to have a heart of gold (ser bueno), to be beside o.s. with joy (estar muy contento) || *no cabe un alfiler* it is full to overflowing, it is packed || *no me cabe en la cabeza (la idea) que...* I cannot believe *o* get it into my head that... || *¿quepo yo?* is there room for me? || *si cabe* if one might say so || FAM *todo cabe en él* he is capable of anything || *todo cabe en lo humano* everything is possible, nothing is impossible.

— OBSERV When *caber* is translated by *to hold, to have,* the subject of the Spanish verb becomes the object of the English verb and vice versa.

cabestrante *m* capstan (cabrestante).

cabestrar *vt* to halter.

cabestrillo *m* sling; *brazo en cabestrillo* arm in a sling.

cabestro *m* halter (rienda) || leading ox (buey guía).

cabeza *f* ANAT head || head (individuo); *pagar tanto por cabeza* to pay so much per head, to pay so much a head || head (res); *rebaño de cien cabezas* a hundred head of sheep || FIG good judgment (juicio); *un hombre de cabeza* a man with good judgment | head (mente); *tener algo metido en la cabeza* to have sth. in one's head | head, life (vida); *pedir la cabeza del reo* to ask for the head of the accused | head; *estar en cabeza de una cola* to be at the head of a queue | front; *el ciclista que está en cabeza en la carrera* the cyclist who is at the front of the race | top; *estar a la cabeza de la clase* to be at the top of the class || GEOGR summit, top (de una montaña) || head (de un alfiler, de un clavo, de ajo, de procesión, de un rotor, etc.) || MAR head || end (de una viga) || head (de magnetófono); *cabeza sonora, auditiva* or *lectora, supresora* recording, playback, erasing head || AMER source (de un río) || — *agachar la cabeza* to lower one's head (bajar), to give in, to back down (humillarse) || *alzar* or *levantar cabeza* to raise one's head (sentido propio), to pick up (recuperarse) || FIG *andar* or *ir de cabeza* to be in a flurry *o* in a fluster *o* in a tizzy (estar muy ocupado) | *andar mal de la cabeza* to be weak in the head, to have a screw loose | *apostar* or *apostarse la cabeza* to bet one's life *o* shirt, to stake one's life *o* shirt || *asentir con la cabeza* to nod || TECN *cabeza atómica* atomic warhead | *cabeza buscadora* homing device (de un cohete) || FIG *cabeza caliente* hothead || TECN *cabeza de biela* big end || INFORM *cabeza de borrado* erase *o* erasing head || FIG *cabeza de cordada* leader (alpinismo) | *cabeza de chorlito* scatterbrain || *cabeza de espárrago* asparagus tip || FIG *cabeza de hierro* stubborn person || INFORM *cabeza de lectura* read *o* reading head || *cabeza de línea* terminus || *cabeza de lista* main *o* leading candidate (elecciones) || IMPR *cabeza de muerto* turning || *cabeza de partido* county town || *cabeza de playa* beachhead || MIL *cabeza de puente* bridgehead || *cabeza de serie* seeded player, seed (tenis) || FIG *cabeza de turco* scapegoat | *cabeza dura* stubborn person (testarudo) | *cabeza hueca* or *sin seso* idiot, blockhead | *cabeza loca* scatterbrain | *cabeza redonda* roundhead || FIG *calentarle a uno la cabeza con* to pester s.o. with | *calentarse la cabeza* to get worked up (perder la calma), to rack one's brains (estudiar) || *con la cabeza alta* with one's head held high || *con la cabeza baja* head down || *darle a uno dolores de cabeza* to make s.o.'s head ache (dolor físico), to get headaches; *cuando me dan estos dolores de cabeza me tengo que acostar* when I get these headaches I have to lie down; to be a pain in the neck (dar la lata) || FIG *dar en la cabeza* to rub up the wrong way (contrariar) || *darle uno vueltas la cabeza* one's head to be swimming, to feel dizzy; *la cabeza me da vueltas* my head is swimming, I feel dizzy | *darse de cabeza en la pared* to beat one's head against a brick wall || FIG & FAM *dar un buen lavado de cabeza* to haul s.o. over the coals || *de cabeza* by heart (de memoria), like a flash (con rapidez), headfirst; *caerse de cabeza* to fall headfirst || *de pies a cabeza* from head to foot, from top to toe || FIG *de mi (tu etc.) cabeza* out of my (your, etc.); own head || *dolor de cabeza* headache || FIG *estar de cabeza* to have a lot on (muy ocupado) || FIG & FAM *estar mal de la cabeza* to be weak in the head, to be dotty *o* daft | *estar tocado de la cabeza* to be off one's rocker, to be touched [US to be nuts *o* goofy] || *ganar por una cabeza* to win by a head || FIG *hinchar la cabeza a uno* to stuff s.o. with || *ir en cabeza* to be in the lead || FIG & FAM *írsele a uno la cabeza* to lose one's head (perder la cabeza), to feel giddy (marearse) || FIG *írsele a uno de la cabeza* to slip s.o.'s mind; *se me fue de la cabeza* it slipped my mind | *jugarse la cabeza* to bet one's life *o* shirt, to stake one's life *o* shirt || *lavarse la cabeza* to wash one's hair || *llevarle a uno la cabeza* to be taller than s.o. by a head || FIG *llevarse las manos a la cabeza* to throw one's hands to one's head | *más vale ser cabeza de ratón que cola de león* it is better to reign in Hell than to serve in Heaven | *meter la cabeza en alguna parte* to get a look in somewhere | *meterle a uno en la cabeza* to put into s.o.'s head | *meterse de cabeza en algo* to plunge headfirst into sth. | *metérsele a uno en la cabeza hacer algo* to take it into one's head to do sth. (ocurrírsele); *se le metió en la cabeza ir solo* he took it into his head to go alone; to set one's mind on doing sth. (empeñarse) | *nadie escarmienta en cabeza ajena* one only learns by one's own mistakes || *negar con la cabeza* to shake one's head || FIG *no levantar cabeza* not to lift one's head (trabajar), not to pick up (no recuperarse) | *no se me va* or *no se me puede ir de la cabeza la muerte de mi amigo* I can't get my friend's death off my mind | *no tener cabeza* to be forgetful, to be absentminded | *no tener ni pies ni cabeza* to be ridiculous *o* absurd, to be nonsense | *pasarle a alguien por la cabeza* to occur to s.o., to cross s.o.'s mind | *perder la cabeza* to lose one's head, to panic | *poner la cabeza bomba* or *tarumba a alguien* to drive s.o. mad || *poner la cabeza de uno a precio* to put a price on s.o.'s head || *por una cabeza* by a head (ganar o perder una carrera) | FIG *quebradero de cabeza* headache | *quebrarse* or *romperse la cabeza* to rack one's brains | *¡quítate eso de la cabeza!* get that out of your head || *sacar la cabeza* to put one's head out || *sacarle la cabeza a uno* to be taller by a head than s.o. || FIG *se le subieron los humos a la cabeza* he got on his high horse, he became conceited | *sentar cabeza* to calm down, to settle down | *ser duro de cabeza* to be slow on the uptake, to be thick-headed | *subirse a la cabeza* to go to one's head | *tener algo metido en la cabeza* to have sth. on the brain | *tener la cabeza a las once* to be brainless (tonto), to be miles away (distraído) | *tener la cabeza en su sitio* to have one's head screwed on | *tener la cabeza loca* to be in a whirl | *tener la cabeza llena de pájaros, tener pájaros en la cabeza, tener la cabeza a pájaros* to have bats in the belfry (ser tonto), to be a scatterbrain (ser distraído) | *tener mala cabeza* to be absentminded | *tengo la cabeza como un bombo* my head is splitting || *tirarse de cabeza* to dive (de un trampolín, etc.) || FIG *traer a uno de cabeza* to worry s.o. (preocupar), to get on s.o.'s nerves (molestar), to be on s.o.'s mind (ocupar los pensamientos), to drive s.o. mad (volver loco) | *venir a la cabeza* to come to mind || *volver la cabeza* to turn one's head.
◆ *m* head; *cabeza de familia* head of a family.

cabezada *f* butt (golpe dado con la cabeza) || blow *o* bump on the head (golpe recibido en la cabeza) || nod (al dormirse, saludo) || vamp (de bota) || headband (encuadernación) || MAR pitching, pitch || cavesson (del caballo) || *AMER* saddlebow (arzón) || — FIG & FAM *dar cabezadas* to nod (persona), to pitch (barco) | *darse de cabezadas* to rack one's brains | *echar una cabezada* to have a nap *o* a snooze.

cabezal *m* pillow (almohada) || bolster (almohada larga) || headrest (de un sillón) || MED compress || TECN front carriage (de coche) | poppet, latherhead (de torno).

cabezazo *m* butt (golpe dado con la cabeza) || blow on the head (golpe recibido en la cabeza) || header (fútbol) || *dar un cabezazo* to head the ball.

cabezón, ona *adj* FAM bigheaded, with a big head || FIG & FAM stubborn, pigheaded, obstinate; *ser cabezón como un aragonés* to be as stubborn as a mule.

◆ *m/f* FAM big head || FIG & FAM stubborn *o* pigheaded *o* obstinate person, mule.

cabezonada *f* FIG & FAM obstinacy, stubbornness, pigheadedness || obstinate *o* stubborn *o* pigheaded action (capricho).

cabezonería *f* FIG & FAM obstinacy, stubbornness, pigheadedness.

cabezota *f* FAM big head.

◆ *m/f* obstinate *o* stubborn *o* pigheaded person.

cabezudo, da *adj* bigheaded with a big head || FIG & FAM stubborn, obstinate, pigheaded (terco) || heady (bebidas).

◆ *m* ZOOL mullet (mújol) || carnival figure with a huge head (en algunas fiestas).

cabezuela *f* small head || third flour (harina) || fungoid growth (del vino) || BOT capitulum, flower head (inflorescencia) | rose bud (de rosa) | tip (de espárrago) || FIG scatterbrain, birdbrain (alocado).

cabiai *m* ZOOL capybara.

cabida *f* capacity; *esta sala tiene cabida para cien personas* this hall has a capacity of a hundred people || place; *estas ideas no tienen cabida en una mente equilibrada* these ideas have no place in a balanced mind || — *dar cabida a* to leave room *o* space for || FIG *dar cabida a circunstancias imprevistas* to leave room for unforeseen circumstances.

cabila *adj/s* Kabyle.

cabildada *f* FAM abuse of authority.

cabildante *m* *AMER* town councillor.

cabildear *vi* to scheme (intrigar) || to lobby (influir en las autoridades).

cabildeo *m* scheming (intriga) || speculation, surmise (suposiciones) || lobbying (para ejercer presión) || *andar de cabildeos* to scheme.

cabildero *m* schemer (intrigante) || lobbyist (que ejerce presión sobre las autoridades).

cabildo *m* chapter (de iglesia) || chapter house (sala) || chapter (reunión de canónigos) || town council (ayuntamiento) || town hall (sala del ayuntamiento) || council meeting (reunión del ayuntamiento) || organization formed in the Canary Islands of representatives from all the towns of the Islands.

cabilla *f* MAR treenail (clavo grueso) | belaying pin (de los cabos).

cabillo *m* BOT stalk of a peduncle || end (extremo).

cabina *f* kiosk, box [*US* booth] (telefónica) || cabin (en un barco) || cab (de camión grúa) || AVIAC cabin, cockpit || room, booth (en un cine); *cabina de proyección* projection room *o* booth || booth (de intérpretes) || car (de ascensor) || bathing hut (caseta de baños) || — *cabina de cambio de agujas* signal box || *cabina electoral* polling booth, voting booth.

cabinera *f* *AMER* air hostess.

cabio *m* ARQ joist, beam (viga) | lintel (de ventana o de puerta) || *cabio bajo* lower transom (de ventana).

cabizbajo, ja *adj* crestfallen; *iba cabizbajo y meditabundo* he was crestfallen and pensive.

cable *m* cable (maroma, de electricidad) || cable (cablegrama) || MAR cable length (medida de 185,19 metros) || — *cable de remolque* towline, towrope || FIG & FAM *echar un cable* to give a hand.

cablear *vt* to twist (alambres).

cablegrafiar *vt/vi* to send a cable, to cable.

cablegrama *m* cablegram, cable.

cablero *m* MAR cable ship (barco).

cabo *m* end (extremidad) || end, stub, stump (pedazo que queda); *cabo de vela* stub of a candle || handle (de herramienta) || bit, piece (trozo); *un cabo de hilo* a piece of thread || GEOGR cape || parcel (paquete) || MAR rope, line (cuerda) || MIL corporal (de escuadra de caballería) || sergeant (de policía) || — *al cabo* in the end || *al cabo de* after, in; *al cabo de un año* after a year, in a year || *al fin y al cabo* after all, when all is said and done (no obstante) || *cabo de fila* leading man in a line (soldado), leading ship (barco) || MAR *cabo de la Marina* leading seaman || *cabo de vara* prison guard || FIG *cabo suelto* loose end; *en la novela quedan muchos cabos sueltos* there are a lot of loose ends in the novel || *dar cabo a una cosa* to finish sth. off || *dar cabo de* to put an end to || *de cabo a cabo, de cabo a rabo* from beginning to end || *en mi, en tu, en su solo cabo* by myself, by yourself, by himself (a solas) || FIG *estoy al cabo (de la calle)* I'm well up on this, I'm well acquainted with this || *llevar a cabo* to carry out (ejecutar, efectuar), to conclude (concluir) || FIG *no dejar cabo suelto* not to leave any loose ends || *por ningún cabo* by no means, in no way.

◆ *pl* accessories [of clothing] || ANAT ankle *sing* (tobillo) || wrist *sing* (muñeca) || tail and mane *sing* (del caballo) || FIG *atar* or *juntar cabos* to put two and two together.

Cabo (El) *npr m* GEOGR Cape Town, Capetown.

Cabo Verde (islas de) *npr m* GEOGR Cape Verde Islands.

cabotaje *m* MAR coastal traffic, cabotage || *barco de cabotaje* coaster, coasting vessel.

cabra *f* ZOOL goat || *AMER* loaded dice (dado cargado) | type of sulky (carruaje) || — *cabra de almizcle* muskdeer || *cabra de los Alpes* ibex || *cabra montés* chamois, wild goat || FAM *estar como una cabra* to be daft *o* dotty *o* stupid || FIG *la cabra siempre tira al monte* what's bred in the bone will come out in the fresh.

cabrahigadura *f* AGR caprification.

cabrahigal; cabrahigar *m* plantation of wild fig trees.

cabrahigo *m* BOT wild fig tree, caprifig (árbol) | wild fig (fruto).

cabrajo *m* lobster (bogavante).

cabreado, da *adj* FAM in a foul *o* filthy mood (de muy mal humor) | livid (enfadado).

cabrear *vt* FAM to get one's goat, to get worked up (enojar).

◆ *vi* *AMER* to leap *o* to prance about (jugar).

◆ *vpr* FAM to get worked up, to see red (irritarse) | to get furious, to fly off the handle (ponerse furioso).

cabreo *m* FAM *coger* or *pillar* or *agarrar un cabreo* to fly off the handle | *dar un cabreo a uno* to get one's goat, to get s.o. worked up | *tener un cabreo* to be really annoyed *o* worked up.

cabreriza *f* goatherd (pastora) || goatherd's hut (choza del cabrero) || goat shed (para las cabras).

cabrerizo, za *adj* goatish, caprine.

◆ *m* goatherd (cabrero).

cabrero, ra *m/f* goatherd (pastor).

cabrestante *m* MAR capstan.

cabria *f* TECN gin.

cabrilla *f* TECN sawyer's trestle, sawhorse.

◆ *pl* ASTR The Pleiades || white horses, foam-crested waves (olas en el mar) || scorches on the legs (producidas por el brasero) || ducks and drakes (juego) || *jugar al juego de cabrillas* to play ducks and drakes.

cabrillear *vi* to form white crests, to break into white horses (las olas) || to glisten, to sparkle, to shimmer (rielar).

cabrilleo *m* breaking, foaming, white horses (en el mar) || shimmer (centelleo).

cabrio *m* ARQ joist || HERÁLD chevron.

cabrío, a *adj* caprine; *raza cabría* caprine race || *macho cabrío* he-goat, billy goat.

◆ *m* herd of goats.

cabriola *f* jump, skip, leap (salto) || capriole (de caballo) || FIG trick, device, dodge || *hacer cabriolas* to romp, to scamper about, to gambol, to frisk, to caper about (los niños), to capriole (el caballo).

cabriolar; cabriolear *vi* to romp, to scamper about, to gambol, to frisk, to caper about (los niños) || to capriole (un caballo).

cabriolé; cabriolet *m* cabriolet.

cabriolear *vi* ⟶ **cabriolar.**

cabrita *f* small goat, kid (cabra pequeña) || *AMER* POP corn (palomita de maíz).

cabritilla *f* kid; *guantes de cabritilla* kid gloves.

cabrito *m* kid || POP bastard, swine, bugger (canalla).

◆ *pl* *AMER* popcorn (rosetas de maíz).

cabro, bra *m/f* *AMER* FAM kid (chico).

cabrón *m* he-goat, billy goat || POP bastard, swine, bugger (canalla) | deceived husband, cuckold (cornudo) || *AMER* pimp (rufián).

cabronada *f* FAM dirty trick; *hacerle a uno una cabronada* to play a dirty trick on s.o.

cabruno, na *adj* caprine.

cabuchón; cabujón *m* cabochon (piedra).

cabuya *f* BOT agave || aloe fibre, Mexican hemp (fibra) || MAR rope || — *AMER dar cabuya* to moor | *ponerse en la cabuya* to cotton on.

cabuyera *f* crowfoot, clew (de la hamaca).

caca *f* FAM duty, business; *hacer caca* to do one's business | muck, cack (excremento, suciedad) || — FAM *eso es una caca* this is rubbish | *tira eso, es una caca* throw that away, it's dirty *o* nasty.

cacahual *m* AGR cacao plantation.

cacahuate *m* ⟶ **cacahuete.**

cacahué; cacahuey *m* peanut, monkey nut.

cacahuete; cacahuate *m* monkey nut, peanut || *aceite de cacahuete* groundnut oil [*US* peanut oil].

cacahuetero *m* peanut seller.

cacalote *m* *AMER* crow (cuervo) | popcorn (rosetas).

cacao *m* cacao (árbol y grano) || cocoa (en el comercio) || *AMER* chocolate || *manteca de cacao* cocoa butter, cacao butter.

cacaotal *m* AGR cacao plantation.

cacarañar *vt* to pockmark (la viruela) || *AMER* to pinch (pellizcar).

cacareado, da *adj* hackneyed, trite; *un éxito muy cacareado* a very hackneyed success.

cacareador, ra *adj* clucking (que cacarea) || boastful, bragging, crowing (que presume).

cacarear *vi* to cluck (las gallinas).
◆ *vt* FIG & FAM to make a big noise about, to boast about (presumir); *¡cómo cacarea las pocas cosas buenas que ha hecho!* what a big noise he is making about the few good things he has done!

cacareo *m* clucking (de la gallina) || FIG shower of praises (alabanzas) | bragging, boasting, crowing (presunción).

cacatúa *f* ZOOL cockatoo (ave).

cacera *f* irrigation ditch.

cacería *f* hunting; *ir de cacería* to go hunting || hunt (partida de caza); *cacería de leones* lion hunt.

cacerola *f* casserole.

cacillo *m* ladle (cucharón) || small saucepan (cacerola).

cacique *m* cacique, Indian chief (jefe indio) || FIG & FAM local political boss, cacique | despot, tyrant.

caciquismo *m* caciquism || FIG caciquism, despotism.

cacle *m* AMER leather sandal.

caco *m* thief, crook (ladrón).

cacodilato *m* QUÍM cacodylate.

cacofonía *f* cacophony.

cacofónico, ca *adj* cacophonous.

cacoquimia *f* cacochymy.

cacosmia *f* MED cacosmia.

cacotimia *f* MED cacotimia.

cacotrofia *f* MED cacotrophy.

cactáceo, a; cácteo, a *adj* BOT cactaceous.
◆ *f pl* cactaceae.

cacto; cactus *m* BOT cactus.

cacumen *m* FIG & FAM acumen, brains *pl.*

cacha *f* handle (mango) || butt (de una pistola) || FAM cheek (nalga) || AMER horn (cuerno) | money (dinero) | leg (anca) || — AMER *hacer la cacha* to joke || FIG & FAM *hasta las cachas* up to the hilt; *se ha metido en el asunto hasta las cachas* he's got himself up to the hilt in the affair.

— OBSERV The word *cacha* is usually used in the plural.

cachaciento, ta *adj* AMER calm, phlegmatic (cachazudo) | lazy, idle, loafing (perezoso).

cachada *f* AMER gore, butt (cornada) | joke (burla).

cachafaz *m* AMER rogue, scoundrel (pillo).

cachalote *m* ZOOL sperm whale, cachalot.

cachar *vt* to break, to smash (romper) || to split (la madera) || AGR to plough up, to break up || AMER FAM to get, to obtain (obtener) | to seize (asir) | to surprise, to catch (sorprender) | to ridicule (ridiculizar) | to catch (el autobús, el tranvía, etc.) | to butt, to gore (con los cuernos).

cacharpari *m* AMER farewell celebration.

cacharpas *f pl* AMER things, bits and pieces (cosas).

cacharrazo *m* FAM blow (porrazo) | fall (caída) || AMER FAM drink (trago).

cacharrería *f* pottery shop.

cacharrero, ra *m/f* pottery dealer.

cacharro *m* earthenware vessel (recipiente tosco) || vase (vasija) || piece of broken pottery, potsherd (tiesto) || FAM thing (chisme) | boneshaker (bicicleta) | old tub (barco) | wreck (máquina) | joanna (piano) | old crock, jaloppy (coche) || AMER prison (cárcel).
◆ *pl* things; *llegó con todos sus cacharros* he came with all his things || utensils; *los cacharros de la cocina* the kitchen utensils || *lavar los cacharros* to do the washing up, to wash the dishes (fregar los platos).

cachava *f* shinny (juego y bastón).

cachavazo *m* blow with a shinny.

cachaza *f* sluggishness, slowness (lentitud) || phlegm, forbearance (flema); *hombre que tiene mucha cachaza* man who has a lot of phlegm || tafia, rum (aguardiente) || AMER froth from cane [when making sugar] (impurezas).

cachazo *m* AMER butt, gore (cornada).

cachazudo, da *adj* phlegmatic, calm (flemático) || slow, sluggish (lento).
◆ *m/f* slow coach (lento) || phlegmatic person (flemático).

cachear *vt* to search, to frisk (registrar) || AMER to gore (cornear).

cachemir *m*; **cachemira** *f* cashmere (tela).

Cachemira *npr f* GEOGR Kashmir.

cacheo *m* search, searching, frisking (registro).

cachería *f* AMER FAM small shop (cambalache) | lack of dress sense, bad taste (falta de gusto en el vestir).

cachetada *f*; **cachetazo** *m* slap, whack; *dar una cachetada a uno* to give s.o. a slap.

cachete *m* FAM cheek (carrillo) | cheek (nalga) | swollen cheek (mejilla abultada) || punch, blow (golpe) | slap, whack (bofetada) || dagger (puñal) || FAM *pegar un cachete a uno* to slap *o* to whack *o* to wallop s.o.

cachetear *vt* to whack, to slap.

cachetero *m* dagger || TAUR bullfighter who finishes off the bull with a dagger.

cachetudo, da; cachetón, ona *adj* FAM chubby-faced, chubby-cheeked (mofletudo).

cachicamo *m* AMER armadillo (animal).

cachicuerno, na *adj* with a horn handle, horn-handled (cuchillo).

cachifollar *vt* FAM to foil (un plan) | to squash, to flatten (apabullar) | to spoil, to ruin (estropear).

cachimba *f*; **cachimbo** *m* pipe; *fumar en cachimba* to smoke a pipe || AMER *chupar cachimbo* to smoke a pipe (fumar en pipa), to suck one's thumb (un niño).

cachipolla *f* mayfly, ephemera (insecto).

cachiporra *f* club, truncheon.

cachiporrazo *m* blow with a club.

cachirulo *m* flask [for spirits] || earthenware jar (botijo) || small ship with three masts (embarcación) || FAM lid, hat (sombrero) || reinforcement on jodhpurs (de pantalón de montar).
◆ *pl* things.

cachito *m* small piece, little bit (trocito) || *a cachitos* in bits.

cachivache *m* utensil (utensilio) || pot, pan (recipiente) || thing (chisme) || bauble, knick-knack (fruslería).

cacho, cha *adj* bent (encorvado).
◆ *m* piece, bit; *un cacho de pan* a piece of bread || brelan (juego de cartas) || AMER horn (cuerno) || — FIG & FAM *¡cacho bestia!* you beast! | *ella es un cacho de pan* she is a darling *o* an angel.

cachondearse *vpr* FIG & FAM to take the mickey out of; *cachondearse de alguien* to take the mickey out of s.o. | to treat as a joke; *se cachondea de todo* he treats everything as a joke.

cachondeo *m* FAM ragging, jeering, leg-pulling (burla), skylarking, messing about (jarana), joking (guasa) || — FAM *armar cachondeo* to lark about | *la fiesta fue un cachondeo* the party was a scream | *te lo digo sin cachondeo* I mean it, no messing about | *tomar a cachondeo* to treat as a joke.

cachondez *f* heat (de perra), rut (de perro) || lust, randiness, sensuality (de persona).

cachondo, da *adj* on heat (perra), in rut, rutting (perro) || POP randy (sensual) | hilarious (gracioso).

cachopín *m* AMER ⟶ **cachupín.**

cachorrillo *m* small pistol (arma).

cachorro, rra *m/f* pup, puppy (del perro) || cub (del león, del tigre, del oso, del lobo) || kitten (de gato) || young (de otros mamíferos).
◆ *adj* AMER ill-mannered, uncouth (malcriado).

cachú *m* catechu (extracto vegetal) || cachou (pastilla).

cachucha *f* MAR small rowing boat (bote) || cap (gorra).

cachuchear *vt* to fondle, to caress (acariciar).

cachucho *m* pin box, pin case (alfiletero) || jar (vasija tosca) || pitcher (botijo) || MAR small rowing boat (bote).

cachudo, da *adj* AMER horned, long-horned.

cachuela *f* stew (guiso).

cachumbo *m* AMER husk, shell.

cachunde *m* catechu (pasta aromática).

cachupín, ina *m/f* AMER FAM spanish immigrant.

cachureco, ca *adj* AMER conservative (en política) | deformed (deformado).

cada *adj inv* every, each; *cada día* every day || every (con un sustantivo en plural); *cada tres días* every three days, every third day || each (cuando se trata de dos cosas); *cada uno de los dos chicos tiene su coche* each one of the two boys has his car || — *a cada paso* at every step *o* turn || *cada cierta distancia* every so often, at intervals || *cada cierto tiempo* every so often || *cada cual; cada uno, una* each one, everyone || *¿cada cuánto?* how often? || *cada dos días* every other day, every two days || *cada dos por tres* every five minutes || FAM *cada hijo de vecino, cada quisque* everyone || FIG *cada oveja con su pareja* every Jack his Jill | *cada uno en su casa y Dios en la de todos* every man for himself and God for us all | *cada uno es rey en su casa* every man's home is his castle || *cada vez* every time, each time || *cada vez más* more and more || *cada vez menos* (seguido de un adjetivo o de un sustantivo en singular) less and less; *es cada vez menos difícil* it gets less and less difficult; (seguido de un sustantivo en plural) less and less, fewer and fewer; *hay cada vez menos oportunidades* there are fewer and fewer opportunities || *cada vez peor* from bad to worse, worse and worse || *el pan nuestro de cada día* our daily bread || FAM *¡le dio cada bofetada!* he gave him such a slap! || *¡se veían señoras con cada sombrero!* you should have seen the hats the women were wearing! || *uno de cada diez* one in ten *o* one out of ten.

cadalso *m* scaffold, scaffolding (patíbulo).

cadáver *m* corpse, body, dead body; *hacer la autopsia de un cadáver* to do an autopsy on a corpse || body, carcass (de un animal) || — *antes pasarán por encima de mi cadáver* over my dead body! || *ingresó cadáver* he was dead on arrival || *rígido como un cadáver* as stiff as a corpse.

cadavérico, ca *adj* cadaverous (relativo al cadáver) || cadaverous, deathly pale (muy pálido) || *rigidez cadavérica* rigor mortis.

caddy *m* caddie (en el juego de golf).

cadena *f* chain (de hierro, de bicicleta, etc.) || MAR cablechain || chain (de presidiarios) || chain gang (cuerda de presos) || JUR imprison-

ment; *cadena perpetua* life imprisonment || FIG chains *pl*, bondage; *la cadena de la esclavitud* the chains of slavery | chain, sequence (sucesión de hechos) || ARQ shoring || chain (de periódicos, de cines, etc.) || channel (de televisión) || QUÍM chain || — *cadena alimenticia* food chain || *cadena antirrobo* anti-theft chain, chain-lock || *cadena de agrimensor* surveyor's chain, land chain, measuring chain || *cadena de enganche* chain coupling || *cadena de fabricación* production line || *cadena de hoteles* chain of hotels || *cadena de montaje* assembly line || GEOGR *cadena de montañas* mountain chain *o* range || *cadena de seguridad* safety chain (de pulsera) || *cadena de tiendas* chain of shops || *cadena de transmisión* drive chain || *hacer cadena* to form *o* to make a chain || *reacción en cadena* chain reaction || *tirar de la cadena* to pull the chain, to flush || *trabajar en cadena* to work on the production line || *trabajo en cadena* assembly line work [US serial production].
◆ *pl* chains.

cadencia *f* rhythm, cadence (ritmo) || MÚS cadence.

cadencioso, sa *adj* rhythmic, rhythmical (verso) || measured (pasos) || melodious (voz).

cadeneta *f* headband (encuadernación) || paper chain (adorno de papel) || *punto de cadeneta* chain stitch.

cadenilla; cadenita *f* small chain.

cadera *f* ANAT hip; *con las manos en las caderas* with one's hands on one's hips.

cadete *m* MIL cadet.

cadí *m* cadi (juez musulmán).

Cádiz *n pr* GEOGR Cádiz.

cadmio *m* QUÍM cadmium.

caducar *vi* to expire, to become invalid, to lapse (perder su validez); *su pasaporte ha caducado* his passport has expired || to become senile, to be in one's dotage (una persona).

caduceo *m* caduceus, Mercury's wand (emblema).

caducidad *f* JUR expiration, expiry, lapse || senility, dotage, decrepitude (de un anciano).

caduco, ca *adj* decrepit, senile (viejo) || FIG expired, invalid | gone by; *tiempos caducos* times gone by || BOT deciduous (hojas) || JUR null and void; *testamento caduco* null and void will || transitory (bienes) || fleeting (placer).

caer* *vi* to fall, to fall down *o* over (las personas); *el niño ha caído a tierra* or *por tierra* the child has fallen on the ground *o* to the ground; *caer de cabeza* to fall head first *o* on one's head; *caer de espaldas, de rodillas* to fall on one's back, on one's knees; *cayó muerto* he fell dead || to fall (las cosas); *las hojas de los árboles caían lentamente* the leaves fell slowly from the trees; *la nieve cae* the snow falls || to crash, to come down (un avión) || FIG to fall; *caer en la trampa* to fall into the trap; *caer en desgracia* to fall into disgrace; *caer en desuso* to fall into disuse | to make; *caer en un error* to make a mistake | to fall (imperio, ministerio, precio, temperatura, etc.) | to fall (la noche) | to set (el sol) | to drop, to die down (el viento) | to draw in; *al caer el día* when day draws in | to fall (morir); *el capitán cayó al frente de sus tropas* the captain fell at the head of his troops | to fall; *nuestras ilusiones caen una tras otra* our illusions fall one after another; *su cumpleaños cae en domingo* his birthday falls on a Sunday | to find, to hit upon; *he caído en la solución* I have found the solution | to be; *la puerta cae a la derecha* the door is on the right; *este detalle cae en el capítulo 10* this point is in chapter 10; *ese pueblo cae dentro de esta provincia* that village is in this province | to look onto; *una ventana que cae a la calle* a window which looks onto the street | to come; *al final de esta calle cae usted en el parque* at the end of this street you come to the park | to come, to fall; *esto no cae dentro de la jurisdicción del gobierno* this does not come within the jurisdiction of the government | to fall; *me cayó en suerte hacerlo* it fell on me *o* to my lot *o* to me to do it | to lapse (costumbre) | to fall; *caer entre* or *en las manos de alguien* to fall into s.o.'s hands | to end (la conversación) | to lapse; *relato que cae a veces en lo vulgar* story which at times lapses into vulgarity || to fall, to hang; *los pelos le caen en la espalda* her hair falls down her back || to strike; *un rayo cayó en su casa* lightning struck his house || to dip; *la falda te cae por un lado* your skirt dips at one side || FIG to fall, to be taken; *caer enfermo* to fall ill; *cayó la ciudad en la batalla* the town was taken in the battle | to drop; *cayó por mi casa cuando menos lo esperaba* he dropped by my house when I was least expecting him | to win; *le cayó el premio gordo en la lotería* he won first prize in the lottery | to give in; *caer en la tentación* to give in to temptation | to fail; *caí en matemáticas* I failed in mathematics | to be due; *el pago cae al final del mes* payment is due at the end of the month | to get (entender); *ahora caigo en lo que dices* now I get what you mean | to think, to imagine; *no caigo en la persona de quien me hablas* I can't think who (it is) you are talking about | to be able to remember; *no caigo en cuál es su nombre* I can't remember what his name is | to pounce, to descend; *cayeron sobre él como lobos* they pounced on him like wolves || — *al caer la noche* at nightfall || FIG *caer a mano* to be near at hand | *caer a tiempo* to be well-timed | *caer como chinches* or *moscas* to fall *o* to drop like flies | *caer como un jarro de agua fría* to fall like a ton of bricks | *caer como un muerto* to fall in a heap, to fall like a log | *caer de bruces* to fall flat on one's face | *caer de las nubes* to come down to earth | *caer de perlas* to be perfect | *caer de pie* to fall on one's feet | *caer de su peso* or *de suyo* to go without saying | *caer encima de* or *sobre uno* to fall on s.o.'s head (cosa, falta), to fall on s.o.'s shoulders (responsabilidad) | *caer en el garlito* or *en el lazo* to fall into the trap | *caer en la cuenta* to realize (darse cuenta), to remember (acordarse) | *caer en saco roto* to go in one ear and out the other, to fall upon deaf ears | *caer en suerte* to fall to one's lot | *caer en un grupo simpático* to fall in with a friendly group of people || FIG *caer gordo* or *pesado a uno* to get on s.o.'s nerves || *caer hecho jirones* to fall in rags || FIG *caerle a uno seis meses de cárcel* to get six months in prison || *caer(le) bien, mal a alguien* to suit, not to suit s.o.; *no le cae bien esta chaqueta* this jacket does not suit him; to like, not to like; *lo que Juan dijo me cayó mal* I did not like what John said || *caerle bien, mal uno a alguien* to get on well, badly with s.o.; *me cae bien Miguel* I get on well with Michael || *caer patas arriba* to fall with one's feet in the air || *cayó cuan largo era* or *de plano* he fell full length, he fell flat || *dejar caer* to drop || *dejarse caer* to let o.s. go || FIG *dejarse caer con* to come out with (decir, pedir), to come up with (dar) || *dejarse caer en la cama* to lie down on *o* to drop onto the bed || *dejarse caer en un sillón* to drop into an armchair || FIG *estar al caer* to be about to happen, to be due || *hacer caer* to knock over || *hacer caer el gobierno* to bring about the fall of the government, to bring down the government || FIG *hacerle caer a uno la venda de los ojos* to open s.o.'s eyes | *Juan me cae simpático* or *en gracia* I like John, I think John is nice | *tomar las cosas cuando caen* to take things as they come | *¡ya caigo (en la cuenta)!* I've got it!, the penny has dropped!
◆ *vpr* to fall, to fall down *o* over; *caerse de espaldas* to fall on one's back || to drop, to fall; *el dinero se me cayó del bolsillo* the money dropped out of my pocket || to fall out; *se me cae el pelo* my hair is falling out || to fall; *caerse del caballo* to fall off one's horse || to fall down, to collapse (hundirse); *la casa se cayó* the house fell down || to fall out; *se le cayó un diente* one of his teeth fell out || to come off; *se cayó un botón* a button came off || to drop; *se caía de cansancio* he was dropping with tiredness || to fall in (paredes) || to crash, to come down (avión) || — *caerse al agua* to fall into the water || *caerse a pedazos* to fall to pieces || FIG *caerse de debilidad* to fall with weakness | *caerse de risa, de miedo* to be helpless with laughter, with fear | *caerse de sueño* to be falling asleep [on one's feet] | *caerse de tonto* to be a complete fool | *caerse de viejo* to be falling apart with age | *caérsele a uno la cara de vergüenza* to die of shame | *caerse redondo* or *en redondo* to collapse, to fall in a heap (caerse de repente), to drop dead (morir) | *no se cayó de la cuna* he wasn't born yesterday | *no tener dónde caerse muerto* not to have a penny to one's name.

Cafarnaum *n pr* HIST Capernaum.

café *m* coffee (planta, grano y bebida); *café solo, con leche* black, white coffee || café, coffee bar, coffee shop, coffee house (establecimiento) || AMER FAM scolding, telling off (regañina) || — *café americano* large black coffee || *café cantante* bar with cabaret || *café instantáneo* or *soluble* instant coffee || *café irlandés* Irish coffee || *café molido* ground coffee || *café teatro* café where plays are put on || *café torrefacto* roasted coffee || FAM *estar de mal café* to be in a foul mood || *grano de café* coffee bean || FIG *los estrategas de café* the armchair strategists || FAM *tener mal café* to be a nasty piece of work.
◆ *adj* *color café* coffee-coloured; *un vestido de color café* a coffee-coloured dress.

cafeína *f* QUÍM caffeine, caffein.

cafetal *m* AGR coffee plantation.

cafetalero, ra *adj* coffee; *producción cafetalera* coffee production.
◆ *m* coffee planter *o* grower.

cafetera *f* coffeepot || FAM old crock, heap, jaloppy (coche) | piece of junk, wreck (aparato que funciona mal) || — *cafetera exprés* expresso-coffee machine || FIG & FAM *estar como una cafetera* to be daft *o* batty *o* nuts.

cafetería *f* snack bar, coffee house.
— OBSERV The *cafetería* is a café which serves food and drink. The *cafeteria* in England is essentially a self-service restaurant.

cafetero, ra *adj* coffee || FAM *Juan es muy cafetero* John loves a cup of coffee.
◆ *m/f* café proprietor, café owner (dueño de un café) || coffee grower (cafetalero) || coffee merchant (comerciante).

cafetín; cafetucho *m* FAM third-rate café (establecimiento) || *cafetucho cantante* third-rate concert hall.

cafeto *m* BOT coffee.

cafiche *m* AMER FAM pimp (alcahuete).

cáfila *m* FAM crowd (de personas) | line (de coches, etc.) || FIG & FAM string; *soltar una cáfila de mentiras* to tell a string of lies.

cafre *adj* kaffir || FIG barbarous, brutal (cruel y bárbaro) | wild (zafio).
◆ *m/f* kaffir | FIG savage, beast (bruto).

caftán *m* caftan, kaftan.

cagaaceite *m* missel thrush (ave).

cagachín *m* small red fly (mosquito) || finch (pájaro).

cagada *f* flyspeck (de mosca) || droppings *pl* (de ave) || POP shit (de persona) || FIG & POP a load of crap; *su última película es una cagada* his latest film is a load of crap.

cagadero *m* POP bog, loo [US head, john].

cagado, da *adj* POP yellow, cowardly || POP *estar cagado* to be shit-scared.

◆ *m/f* POP chicken.

cagafierro *m* slag (escoria).

cagajón *m* dung.

cagalaolla *m/f* FAM masquerader, harlequin (mamarracho).

cagalera; cagaleta *f* POP diarrhoea, the runs *pl* || FIG & POP *tener cagalera* to be scared stiff *o* shit-scared (tener miedo).

cagar *vi* POP to shit.
◆ *vt* FIG & FAM to bungle (chapucear).
◆ *vpr* POP to shit || FIG & POP to be scared stiff, to be shit-scared || FIG & POP *¡me cago en la mar!* stone me!, shit!, goddamn!

cagarria *f* morel (seta).

cagarruta *f* pellet, dropping (bolita de excremento).

cagatinta; cagatintas *m* FAM penpusher (chupatintas, oficinista).

cagatorio *m* POP bog, loo [*US* head, john].

cagón, ona; cagueta *adj* POP yellow (cobarde) | diarrhoeic (que hace de vientre).
◆ *m/f* POP chicken (cobarde) | diarrhoeic child.

caid *m* kaid (gobernador musulmán).

caída *f* falling, fall (acción de caer); *la caída de las hojas, de la nieve* the falling of the leaves, of the snow || fall; *después de su caída, le dolía la pierna* after his fall he had a sore leg || tumble, spill (de una motocicleta, etc.) || crash, crashing (de un avión) || loss (de pelo, dientes) || slope, drop (declive); *aquí hay una caída muy brusca del terreno* there is a very steep slope here || slope, tilt (inclinación); *la mesa de billar tiene mucha caída* the billiard table has a lot of slope || setting (del sol) || drawing-in, close, closing (del día) || hangings *pl* (tapicería colgante) || body (peso); *esta tela tiene mucha caída* this material has a lot of body || hang (manera de caer un vestido, etc.) || width (ancho); *la falda lleva tres caídas* the skirt has three widths || length (longitud de tela); *una caída de mangas* a sleeve length || GEOL dip || ELECTR drop (de potencia, de voltaje, etc.) || DEP landing (de un salto) || FIG sin (pecado) | fall, drop (de precio, de temperatura) | mistake, slip (equivocación) | fall, downfall; *la caída del gobierno* the fall of the government | witticism, flash of wit (ocurrencia) || MAR rake (de una vela) || — *a la caída de la tarde* at nightfall, at the close of day || *a la caída de la hoja* in autumn [*US* in the fall] || *a la caída del sol* at sunset || TEATR *caída del telón* curtain || *caída en desuso* disappearance, falling into disuse (de una cosa) || *caída libre* free fall (paracaidista) || *caída vertical de los precios* sudden drop in prices || *hacerle a uno una caída de ojos* to make goo-goo eyes at s.o. || *ir de caída* to ease off, to let up (fiebre, calor), to be on the decline (una persona) || *la caída del primer hombre* the Fall of Man.

caído, da *adj* fallen; *un árbol caído* a fallen tree || FIG faint, weak (desfallecido) | downcast, dejected, low-spirited (abatido) || turned-down (cuello de vestido) || drooping; *tener los hombros caídos* to have drooping shoulders || FIG *caído del cielo* out of the blue (inesperado), heaven-sent (oportuno).
◆ *m pl* dead, fallen (en la guerra) || oblique lines (de un cuaderno) || *monumento a los Caídos* war memorial.

Caifás *npr m* Caiaphas || FIG bully, brute.

caimacán *m* FAM big shot (pez gordo).

caimán *m* cayman, caiman (reptil) || FIG sly old fox.

Caín *npr m* Cain || — FIG & FAM *ir con* or *tener las de Caín* to have evil intentions, to be up to no good | *pasar las de Caín* to go through murder.

Cairo (El) *npr m* GEOGR Cairo.

cairel *m* wig (peluca) || fringe (pasamanería).

cairelar *vt* to trim with a fringe.

caja *f* box (pequeña o de cartón); *una caja de bombones* a box of chocolates || case, crate (de gran tamaño y de madera); *una caja de uva* a case of grapes || box, case, crate, boxful (contenido) || till; *ayer robaron la caja* they robbed the till yesterday || cashdesk, cashbox (donde se efectúan los pagos) || cash, funds *pl*; *ocuparse de la caja* to take charge of the cash || coffin [*US* casket] (ataúd) || cabinet (de radio) || TECN housing, casing | watch case (de reloj) || MÚS drum (tambor) | case (estuche) | body (de violín) | case (de piano) || AUT body (carrocería) | interior (interior) || ARQ well (de escalera) | well, shaft (de ascensor) || stock (de un arma de fuego) || IMPR case; *caja alta* upper case; *caja baja* lower case || BOT capsule (fruto) || AMER bed (de un río) || — ANAT *caja craneana* skull, cranium || *caja de ahorros* savings bank || TECN *caja de cambios* or *de velocidades* gearbox || *caja de caudales* or *fuerte* safe, strongbox || *caja de colores* paintbox || *Caja de Depósitos y Consignaciones* Deposit and Consignment Office || TECN *caja de empalmes* junction box | *caja de engrase* journal box, axle box | *caja de fusibles* fuse box | *caja de herramientas* toolbox | *caja de humos* smokebox || *caja de jubilaciones* pension fund || *caja de la cama* bedstead || FAM *caja de las muelas* mouth, gob || TECN *caja del cigüeñal* crankcase || ANAT *caja del cuerpo* rib cage || *caja del tímpano* eardrum || *caja de música* musical box || MIL *caja de recluta* recruiting office || *caja de registro* manhole || MÚS *caja de resonancia* sounding board, soundbox || MIL *caja de respetos* spares kit || *caja de seguridad* safe || *caja de sorpresa* jack-in-the box || AVIAC *caja negra* black box || *caja postal de ahorros* post office savings bank || *caja registradora* cash register || ANAT *caja torácica* thoracic cage || FAM *echar* or *despedir a uno con cajas destempladas* to throw s.o. out by the scruff of the neck, to send s.o. packing || *entrar en caja* to be called up (militar), to settle down (una persona) || *hacer caja* to cash up || *ingresar en caja* to take (un almacén, etc.), to deposit (en un banco) || *libro de caja* cash book || *valores en caja* cash in hand.

cajel *adj* *naranja cajel* Seville orange.

cajero, ra *m/f* cashier (encargado de la caja).
◆ *m* box *o* case maker (fabricante de cajas) || *cajero automático* (automatic) cash dispenser.
◆ *f* MAR sheave channel (de polea).

cajetilla *f* packet [*US* pack] (de cigarrillos, de tabaco) || box; *una cajetilla de cerillas* a box of matches.
◆ *m* AMER FAM dandy, dude.

cajetín *m* small box (cajita) || hole (en el marco de la puerta) || ELECTR rod || IMPR box.

cajiga *f* gall oak.

cajigal *m* gall oak grove.

cajista *m/f* IMPR compositor, typesetter.

cajón *m* chest, case, crate (caja grande) || drawer (de mueble) || shelf space (en los estantes) || stall (puesto en el mercado) || shop (tienda) || IMPR half-case || caisson (obras públicas) || AMER gorge, gulley (cañada) | coffin [*US* casket] (ataúd) || — *cajón de herramientas* toolbox, toolchest || FIG *cajón de sastre* or *de turco* muddle, jumble, mess (objetos en desorden) || FIG & FAM *ser de cajón* to be obvious, to go without saying (ser evidente) | *un reloj de cajón* an ordinary watch.

cajuela *f* AMER boot (maletero del automóvil).

cake *m* fruit cake.

cal *f* lime; *cal apagada* or *muerta, hidráulica* slaked, hydraulic lime || — FIG & FAM *a* or *de cal y canto* solidly built *o* made (cosa), very strong (persona) || *cal viva* quicklime || FIG *cerrar a cal y canto* to shut tight *o* firmly || *lechada de cal* milk of lime || FIG *una de cal y otra de arena* six of one and half a dozen of the other.

cala *f* sample slice [to taste a fruit] (primer trozo) || MED suppository (supositorio) | probe (sonda) || MAR hold (de un barco) | fishing ground (sitio para pescar) || GEOGR creek, cove, bight || test boring (agujero para explorar) || BOT arum || FIG opinion poll (sondeo de opinión) || *vender a cala y cata* to allow the customer to taste the merchandise.

calabacear *vt* FAM to fail, to plough (en un examen) | to send packing, to jilt (a un pretendiente).

calabacín *m* marrow (fruto) || FIG & FAM fathead, dope.

calabacino *m* gourd, calabash (recipiente).

calabaza *f* BOT gourd | pumpkin (de gran tamaño) || gourd, calabash (recipiente) || FIG & FAM fathead, dolt (persona tonta) | big tub (buque pesado) || — FIG & FAM *dar calabazas a uno* to fail s.o., to plough s.o. (en un examen), to jilt, to send s.o. packing, to reject (a un pretendiente) | *recibir* or *llevarse calabazas* to get the brush-off, to be jilted (un pretendiente), to fail (en un examen).

calabazada *f* FAM butt (golpe dado con la cabeza) | bump *o* blow on the head (golpe en la cabeza).

calabazar *m* AGR gourd field, pumpkin field.

calabazazo *m* blow with a gourd *o* pumpkin || FAM bump, blow on the head.

calabazo *m* pumpkin, gourd.

calabobos *m inv* FAM drizzle (lluvia).

calabocero *m* gaoler, jailer (carcelero).

calabozo *m* gaol, jail, prison (prisión); *meter en el calabozo* to put in prison || MIL FAM glasshouse [*US* calaboose] || cell (celda de cárcel).

calabrés, esa *adj/s* Calabrian.

calabrote *m* MAR hawser, warp.

calada *f* soaking (en o con un líquido) || puff (de cigarrillo) || swoop, dive (vuelo de ave hacia abajo), soar (hacia arriba).

calado *m* openwork embroidery (bordado) || perforation, openwork (perforado de papel, tejidos, etc.) || MAR depth (de agua) | draught (del barco) || TECN stalling (de un motor).

calador *m* MED probe || AMER borer, probe [for taking samples].

calafate *m* MAR caulker.

calafateado *m*; **calafateadura** *f* MAR caulking.

calafatear *vt* MAR to caulk (barcos) || to fill in *o* up (cualquier juntura).

calafateo *m*; **calafatería** *f* caulking.

calamar *m* squid, calamary (molusco).

calambre *m* cramp; *calambre de estómago* stomach cramp; *me ha dado un calambre en la pierna* I got cramp in my leg || electric shock, shock; *si tocas ese enchufe te dará calambre* if you touch that socket you'll get a shock || — *calambre del escribiente* writer's cramp || *ese hilo da calambre* that wire is live.

calamidad *f* calamity, disaster (desastre) || upset, problem (desgracia); *ha pasado muchas calamidades* he has had a lot of upsets || — FIG & FAM *estar hecho una calamidad* to look a sight | *ser una calamidad* to be useless, to be a dead loss (un incapaz), to be jinxed (desgraciado).

calamina *f* calamine (carbonato de cinc).

calamita *f* MIN lodestone (piedra imán).

calamitoso, sa *adj* calamitous, disastrous.

cálamo *m* MÚS reed, reed pipe || POÉT reed, stalk (planta) | pen (para escribir) || *cálamo currente* hastily.

calamocano, na *adj* FAM tipsy, merry (borracho).

calamoco *m* icicle (carámbano).

calamón *m* sultana bird, purple gallinule (ave) || stud (clavo).

calamorra *f* FAM head, nut.

calandrado *m* TECN calendering (de telas, de papel).

calandrajo *m* FAM rag (jirón) | rag, tatter (harapo) || FIG & FAM drip, dope (persona despreciable).

calandrar *vt* to calender (tela, papel).

calandria *f* calandra lark (ave) || TECN calender (para lustrar) | treadmill (torno) || AUT radiator grille || FIG & FAM malingerer (enfermo fingido).

calaña *f* sample, pattern (muestra) || FIG nature, disposition (personas), quality (cosas) || stamp, kind (sentido despectivo); *estos dos chicos son de la misma calaña* these two boys are of the same stamp || cheap fan (abanico) || *gente de mala calaña* undesirable people.

calañés *adj m* *sombrero calañés* Andalusian hat with an upturned brim.

calar *adj* calcareous, lime.
◆ *m* limestone quarry (cantera).

calar *vt* to soak through, to soak, to drench (un líquido); *la lluvia ha calado el abrigo* the rain has soaked through the coat || to penetrate, to pierce; *calar una tabla con la barrena* to pierce a board with the drill || to do openwork embroidery on (bordar) || to pierce, to perforate (agujerear) || to sample, to plug (la fruta) || to jam on (un sombrero) || FIG to rumble, to find out; *me han calado* they've found me out; *te caló las intenciones* he found out your intentions | to probe; *calar hondamente en un asunto* to probe deeply into a matter || MAR to strike (una vela) | to lower (las redes) || MIL to fix (la bayoneta) || AMER to humiliate (humillar) | to take a sample || FIG *te tengo calado* I am wise to you, I've got your number.
◆ *vi* MAR to draw || to swoop (el ave).
◆ *vpr* to get soaked *o* drenched; *se caló hasta los huesos* he got soaked to the skin || to soak in (un líquido) || to leak, to let in water (zapatos) || to jam on; *calarse el sombrero* to jam on one's hat || to come through; *la lluvia se cala por el tejado* the rain comes through the roof || to swoop (el ave) || FAM to push one's way into (introducirse) || TECN to stall; *se me caló el motor* my engine stalled || *calarse las gafas* to put on one's spectacles.

calato, ta *adj* AMER naked (desnudo) | broke (sin dinero).

calatravo, va *adj* of Calatrava.
◆ *m* knight of the order of Calatrava.

calavera *f* skull (cráneo) || ZOOL death's-head hawk moth (mariposa).
◆ *m* FIG gay dog (juerguista) | madcap (cabeza loca).
◆ *f pl* AMER AUT rear lights.

calaverada *f* revel, spree, binge (juerga) || foolish stunt *o* trick (acción insensata).

calcado *m* tracing.

calcador, ra *m/f* tracer.

calcáneo *m* calcaneus (hueso).

calcañal; calcañar; calcaño *m* heel.

calcar *vt* to trace (un dibujo, etc.) || FIG to copy (imitar) || to tread on (pisar) || FIG *calcar una cosa en otra* to model one thing on another.

calcáreo, a *adj* calcareous.

Calcas *npr m* Calchas.

calce *m* rim (de rueda) || metal cutting edge (de instrumentos cortantes) || wedge (cuña, alza); *poner un calce a una mesa coja* to put a wedge under a wobbly table || AMER foot (de un documento).

calcedonia *f* MIN chalcedony.

calceolado, da *adj* BOT calceolate.

calceolaria *f* calceolaria (planta).

calcés *m* MAR masthead.

calceta *f* stocking (media) || fetters *pl*, shackles *pl* (de preso) || *hacer calceta* to knit.

calcetería *f* hosier's, hosiery shop (tienda) || hosiery (oficio).

calcetero, ra *m/f* hosier (comerciante) || knitter (que hace punto).

calcetín *m* sock || FIG *volverle a uno como a un calcetín* to change s.o.'s mind.

calcetón *m* long heavy sock (polaina).

cálcico, ca *adj* QUÍM calcic || *óxido cálcico* calcium oxide.

calcicosis *f* MED calcicosis.

calcífero, ra *adj* calciferous.

calciferol *m* QUÍM calciferol.

calcificación *f* calcification.

calcificar *vt* to calcify.

calcina *f* concrete (hormigón).

calcinación *f* calcination.

calcinar *vt* to calcine || to roast, to burn; *piedras calcinadas por el sol* stones roasted by the sun || FIG & FAM *este hombre me calcina* this fellow gets on my nerves (fastidiar).
◆ *vpr* to calcine.

calcinosis *f* MED calcinosis.

calcio *m* calcium (metal).

calcita *f* MIN calcite, calcspar.

calciterapia *f* calcitherapy.

calco *m* tracing (acción de calcar) || tracing (dibujo calcado) || FIG copy (copia) || *papel de calco* tracing paper.

calcografía *f* chalcography.

calcógrafo *m* chalcographer (grabador).

calcomanía *f* transfer.

calcopirita *f* MIN chalcopyrite.

calculable *adj* calculable.

calculador, ra *adj* calculating.
◆ *m/f* calculator, calculating machine (máquina) || FIG calculator (interesado) || — *calculadora de bolsillo* pocket calculator || *calculadora electrónica* (electronic) computer.

calcular *vt* to calculate, to work out; *calcular una raíz cuadrada* to calculate a square root || to do the calculations for; *calcular un puente* to do the calculations for a bridge || to compute (una calculadora) || FIG to calculate; *calcular los gastos del viaje* to calculate the cost of the journey | to think, to reckon; *calculo que lo terminaré mañana* I think I shall finish it tomorrow || — *calculando por bajo* or *por lo bajo* at the lowest estimate || *le calculo siete años* I should say he is seven years old || *máquina de calcular* calculating machine.

cálculo *m* calculation; *el cálculo de una raíz cuadrada* the calculation of a square root || estimation, calculation (acción); *cálculo de gastos* estimation of costs || estimate (resultado); *hizo un cálculo de gastos* he made an estimate of costs || MAT calculus; *cálculo diferencial, integral* differential, integral calculus || FIG reckoning (conjetura, reflexión); *según tus cálculos* by your reckoning | caution, care; *obrar con cálculo* to act with caution || MED calculus, stone (piedra) || — *cálculo de costo* costing || *cálculo mental* mental arithmetic || *regla de cálculo* slide rule.
◆ *pl* MED gallstones.

calculoso, sa *adj* MED calculous.

calcha *f* AMER fetlock (del caballo), leg feather (de ciertas aves) | clothes *pl*, clothing (prendas de vestir).

calda *f* heating (acción de calentar) || stoking (introducción del combustible) || TECN heat (metal).
◆ *pl* thermal springs (baños).

caldaico, ca *adj* Chaldaic.

Caldea *npr f* GEOGR Chaldea.

caldeamiento *m* heating, warming.

caldear *vt* to heat, to warm (calentar) || to bring to red heat (los metales) || FIG to heat up, to warm up (el ambiente, etc.).
◆ *vpr* to become warm *o* hot; *en cinco minutos se caldeó la habitación* the room became warm in five minutes || to be heated *o* warmed; *la habitación se caldea con el sol* the room is heated by the sun || to become red-hot (metales) || FIG to warm up (el ambiente).

caldeo *m* heating, warming (caldeamiento); *el caldeo de una habitación* the heating of a room.

caldeo, a *adj/s* Chaldean (de Caldea).

caldera *f* boiler; *caldera de vapor* steam boiler || cauldron, caldron (caldero) || boilerful, cauldronful (calderada) || MIN sump (pozo) || AMER coffee-pot (para café), teapot (para té) | crater || FIG & FAM *las calderas de Pedro Botero* Hell.

calderada *f* boilerful, cauldronful.

calderería *f* boilermaking (oficio) || boilermaker's shop (taller).

calderero *m* boilermaker.

caldereta *f* small boiler, small cauldron (caldera) || REL holy-water vessel (de agua bendita) || CULIN fish soup (sopa de pescado) | lamb stew (guiso).

calderilla *f* coppers *pl*, small change (moneda fraccionaria) || REL holy-water vessel (de agua bendita).

caldero *m* cauldron, boiler (recipiente) || cauldronful (contenido) || TECN ladle (para la colada).

calderón *m* large cauldron *o* boiler (recipiente) || IMPR paragraph mark (signo) || MÚS pause (signo).

calderoniano, na *adj* Calderonian [of the playwright Calderón].

caldibache *m* FAM dishwater (caldo malo).

caldillo *m* thin sauce, gravy (salsa).

caldo *m* stock, broth; *caldo de gallina, de pescado* chicken, fish stock || soup (sopa) || dressing [of salad] || AMER sugar-cane juice (jugo de caña) || — FIG *al que no quiere caldo, la taza llena* or *taza y media* or *tres tazas* things have a way of turning out just the way you don't want them to || *caldo bordelés* Bordeaux mixture || *caldo corto* stock of wine and spice [for cooking fish] || *caldo de carne* beef tea || QUÍM *caldo de cultivo* culture medium || FIG *gallina vieja da* or *hace buen caldo* there's many a good tune played on an old fiddle || FIG & FAM *hacerle a uno el caldo gordo* to make it easy for s.o.
◆ *pl* liquid foodstuffs (vinagre, aceite, etc.) || wines; *los caldos de Jerez* the wines of Jerez.

caldoso, sa *adj* with a lot of stock *o* dressing.

calducho *m* FAM dishwater (caldo malo).

calé *m* gypsy (gitano) || copper coin (moneda).

Caledonia *npr f* GEOGR Caledonia || *Nueva Caledonia* New Caledonia.

calefacción *f* heating; *calefacción central* central heating; *calefacción por fuel-oil* oil heating || calefaction (acción de calentarse) || TECN *superficie de calefacción* heating surface.

calefactor *m* heating engineer (encargado de la calefacción).

caleidoscópico, ca *adj* kaleidoscopic.

caleidoscopio *m* kaleidoscope.

calendario *m* calendar; *calendario gregoriano, juliano* Gregorian, Julian calendar ‖ almanac (con varios datos) ‖ — *calendario americano* or *exfoliador* or *de taco* tear-off calendar, day calendar ‖ *calendario escolar* school calendar ‖ *calendario laboral* work schedule ‖ FIG *hacer calendarios* to make hasty forecasts (pronósticos), to be woolgathering (estar pensativo).

calendas *f pl* calends (día del mes).

caléndula *f* BOT calendula, marigold.

calentador, ra *adj* heating, warming.
◆ *m* heater (aparato) ‖ water heater (para calentar agua) ‖ geyser (de baño) ‖ warming pan, bed warmer (de cama) ‖ TECN superheater (de locomotora) ‖ FIG & FAM large clumsy pocket watch (reloj muy grueso).

calentamiento *m* heating ‖ DEP *ejercicios de calentamiento* warming-up exercises.

calentar* *vt* to heat (up), to warm (up); *calentar un horno* to heat an oven; *caliéntame un poco de agua* heat me a drop of water ‖ to warm (up) (habitación, cuerpo, comida) ‖ to heat (metales); *calentar al rojo blanco* to heat until white hot ‖ FIG to tone up, to warm up; *calentar los músculos* to tone up one's muscles ‖ FIG & FAM to warm; *calentar el asiento* to warm the seat | to liven up (animar); *el vino nos calentó los ánimos* the wine livened up our spirits ‖ FAM to tan, to warm (azotar) | to inflame, to excite (pasiones) ‖ — FIG *calentar a alguien la cabeza* or *los cascos con* to pester s.o. with | *calentar las orejas a alguien* to get on s.o.'s nerves (fastidiar), to box s.o.'s ears (pegar), to send s.o. away with a flea in his ear (reprender) | *calentarle la sangre a alguien* to rub s.o. up the wrong way, to irritate s.o.
◆ *vpr* to warm o.s. (el que tiene frío); *nos calentamos alrededor de la chimenea* we warmed ourselves round the fire ‖ to get hot *o* warm (una cosa) ‖ to be on heat (animales hembras), to be in rut (animales machos) ‖ POP to get randy (personas) ‖ FIG & FAM to become inflamed *o* excited (pasiones) | to pick up (excitarse); *se nos calentaron los ánimos* our spirits picked up | to get annoyed *o* irritated (irritarse) | to get heated, to get excited (en una discusión) ‖ — FIG *las manos se le calientan* his fingers are itching | *no calentarse los cascos* not to worry.

calentón, ona *adj* POP randy.
◆ *m darse un calentón* to overheat (un motor).
◆ *m/f* POP randy person.

calentura *f* MED fever, temperature; *tener calentura* to have a fever ‖ AMER type of asclepias (planta) | phthisis, consumption, tuberculosis (tisis) | anger (ira).

calenturiento, ta *adj* MED feverish ‖ AMER consumptive, tuberculous ‖ FIG feverish, restless; *tener la mente calenturienta* to have a feverish mind.

calenturón *m* MED very high fever *o* temperature.

calero, ra *adj* limestone.
◆ *m* lime burner.
◆ *f* limestone quarry (cantera) ‖ lime kiln (horno).

calesa *f* calèche, calash (carruaje).

calesera *f* bolero jacket [worn by carriage driver] (chaqueta) ‖ Andalusian folk song (cante).

calesero *m* caleche driver (cochero).

calesita *f* AMER merry-go-round [US carousel] (tiovivo).

caleta *f* creek, cove (ensenada) ‖ AMER small coaster (barco).

caletero *m* AMER stevedore, docker (descargador de barcos) | coaster (barco).

caletre *m* FAM common sense, gumption (seso); *tener poco caletre* to have little common sense ‖ — FAM *de su propio caletre* out of one's own little head | *no le cabe en el caletre* it's too much for him.

calibración *f* calibration.

calibrado *m* TECN boring (de un tubo o un cilindro) ‖ gauging (medición).

calibrador *m* gauge, gage; *calibrador de mordazas* calliper gauge; *calibrador de profundidades* depth gauge ‖ borer (de un tubo) ‖ *calibrador micrométrico* vernier calliper.

calibrar *vt* to gauge, to gage, to measure (medir) ‖ to bore (mandrilar) ‖ to calibrate (un termómetro) ‖ FIG to size up, to judge (juzgar) ‖ *máquina de calibrar* boring machine.

calibre *m* MIL calibre [US caliber], bore; *de grueso calibre* large calibre ‖ TECN bore (diámetro interior) | gauge (de alambre) ‖ FIG importance; *un asunto de mucho calibre* a matter of great importance.

calicata *f* MIN bore.

calicó *m* calico (tejido de algodón).

caliche *m* AMER saltpetre [US saltpeter] (nitrato) | bruise (maca) | flake [of paint, etc.] (de pintura, de cal) | crack (en una vasija).

calidad *f* quality; *tela de buena calidad* good quality material ‖ capacity (condición); *por su calidad de ciudadano* in his capacity as a citizen ‖ class (categoría); *naranjas de primera, de segunda calidad* first-class, second-class oranges ‖ class, nobility, quality (nobleza); *una persona de calidad* a person of class ‖ FIG importance; *asunto de calidad* matter of importance ‖ condition (cláusula de contrato) ‖ — *calidad de vida* quality of life ‖ *control de calidad* quality control ‖ *en calidad de* as; *en calidad de amigo* as a friend ‖ FIG *de dinero y calidad la mitad de la mitad* believe only half of what you hear of a man's wealth and goodness ‖ *voto de calidad* casting vote.
◆ *pl* qualities ‖ conditions, rules (de juego).

cálido, da *adj* warm; *colorido cálido* warm tone ‖ hot, warm; *clima cálido* hot climate.

calidoscópico, ca *adj* kaleidoscopic.

calidoscopio *m* kaleidoscope.

calientapiés *m inv* foot warmer.

calientaplatos *m inv* chafing dish, hot plate.

caliente *adj* warm, hot (véase OBSERV); *agua caliente* hot water; *la sopa está caliente* the soup is hot ‖ warm; *colorido caliente* warm tone ‖ FIG angry (enfadado) | heated; *discusión caliente* heated argument | fiery, spirited (apasionado) | hot, randy (ardiente sexualmente) ‖ — FIG *caliente, caliente* now you're hot (en juegos de niños) | *en caliente* there and then, straight away, on the spot (en el acto) ‖ *estar caliente* to be on heat (los animales), to be in the mood (personas) ‖ *mantener caliente* to keep warm (un guiso) ‖ FIG *ser caliente de cascos* to be hotheaded.

— OBSERV El primer significado de *caliente* se traduce por dos palabras en inglés según la intensidad sea mayor (*hot*) o menor (*warm*).

califa *f* caliph.

califato *m* caliphate.

calificable *adj* qualifiable.

calificación *f* qualification ‖ assessment (evaluación) ‖ mark (de un ejercicio).

calificado, da *adj* qualified ‖ skilled (obrero) ‖ eminent (científico) ‖ necessary (pruebas) ‖ proven [theft].

calificador, ra *adj* examining; *el jurado calificador* the examining jury.
◆ *m* examiner, marker (de exámenes, de ejercicios) ‖ REL qualificator.

calificar *vt* to describe, to qualify; *la crítica califica la obra de atrevida* the critics describe the work as daring ‖ to assess (evaluar) ‖ to mark (un examen, un ejercicio) ‖ GRAM to qualify ‖ to label; *esas palabras le califican de orgulloso* those words label him as proud ‖ to call (tratar); *le calificó de mentiroso* he called him a liar ‖ FIG to make famous (ilustrar) ‖ *yo le calificaría de estafador* I think *o* say he's a swindler.
◆ *vpr* to give proof of nobility.

calificativo, va *adj* qualifying; *adjetivo calificativo* qualifying adjective.
◆ *m* epithet; *un calificativo injurioso* an insulting epithet ‖ GRAM qualifier.

California *npr f* GEOGR California.

californiano, na; californio, nia *adj/s* Californian (de California).

californio *m* QUÍM californium.

calígine *f* POÉT darkness, gloom.

caliginoso, sa *adj* dark, gloomy, caliginous (oscuro) ‖ misty, caliginous (brumoso).

caligrafía *f* calligraphy.

caligrafiar *vt* to write ornamentally, to calligraph.

caligráfico, ca *adj* calligraphic.

calígrafo, fa *m/f* calligrapher, calligraphist.

calilla *f* small suppository (supositorio) ‖ AMER FAM pest, bore (cargante) | nuisance (molestia).

calina *f* haze, mist (niebla) ‖ heat (calor).

calinoso, sa *adj* hazy, misty (brumoso) ‖ hot, warm (caluroso).

Calíope *npr f* MIT Calliope.

calipso *m* calypso (baile).

Calipso *npr f* MIT Calypso.

calistenia *f* callisthenics.

Calixto *npr m* Calixtus.

cáliz *m* REL chalice (copa) ‖ BOT calyx ‖ POÉT cup, chalice, goblet ‖ ANAT calyx (del riñón) ‖ FIG *apurar el cáliz hasta las heces* to drain the cup to the dregs, to drain the bitter cup.

caliza *f* limestone (roca sedimentaria) ‖ *caliza litográfica* lithographic stone.

calizo, za *adj* calcareous, lime.

calma *f* calm, calmness, tranquility (tranquilidad) ‖ FIG calm; *la calma de la noche* the calm of the night | lull (de una tormenta) | lull, slack period; *el negocio está en calma* business is going through a slack period | abatement, lull (de dolor) | composure (serenidad de una persona); *perder la calma* to lose one's composure | calm, phlegm (flema); *lo hace todo con una calma increíble* he does everything with incredible calm ‖ — MAR *calma chicha* dead calm ‖ *con calma* calmly, with composture ‖ *después de la tempestad viene la calma* it's the calm after the storm ‖ COM *el mercado está en calma* the market is steady *o* calm ‖ *en calma* calm ‖ *todo está en calma* all is calm.

calmante *adj* MED sedative, tranquillizing, calmative.
◆ *m* MED sedative, tranquillizer.

calmar *vt* to calm, to calm down (tranquilizar) ‖ to soothe, to relieve; *esta medicina calma el dolor* this medicine soothes pain ‖ to soothe, to steady (los nervios).
◆ *vi/vpr* to calm down ‖ to drop, to abate (el viento) ‖ to let up, to die down (el calor) ‖ *¡cálmate!* calm down!

calmazo *m* MAR dead calm ‖ lull, short period of calm (calma momentánea).

calmo, ma *adj* AGR uncultivated (erial) | fallow (en barbecho).

calmoso, sa *adj* calm, quiet, tranquil (tranquilo) ‖ FAM nonchalant, phlegmatic (indolente) | sluggish (lento).

calmuco, ca *adj/s* Kalmuck.

caló *m* Gypsy dialect.

— OBSERV Since certain words or expressions of this dialect are now used in everyday speech, the word *caló* often means *slang*.

calofrío *m* shiver (escalofrío).

calomel *m*; **calomelanos** *m pl* calomel *sing* (cloruro de mercurio).

calor *m* FÍS heat; *calor específico, latente* specific, latent heat ‖ heat, warmth (véase OBSERV); *el calor del verano* the heat of summer; *el calor del fuego* the warmth of the fire ‖ FIG heat; *en el calor de la batalla, de la discusión* in the heat of the battle, of the argument | ardour (de sentimientos) | warmth; *acoger con calor* to welcome with warmth | enthusiasm; *tomar las cosas con demasiado calor* to take things with too much enthusiasm | passion (pasión) ‖ — FIG & FAM *asarse* or *morirse de calor* to be boiling (hot) *o* roasting ‖ *calor animal* animal heat ‖ *calor blanco* white heat ‖ *calor natural* natural heat ‖ *calor rojo* red heat ‖ *dar calor* to encourage (animar), to keep warm ‖ *darse calor* to keep warm ‖ *entrar en calor* to get warm (cuando se tiene frío), to warm up (los deportistas) ‖ *hace calor* it is warm *o* hot ‖ *hacer entrar en calor* to warm up ‖ *¡qué calor!* isn't it hot! ‖ *tener calor* to be hot.

— OBSERV Ciertos significados de *calor* se traducen por dos palabras en inglés según la intensidad sea mayor (*hot, heat*) o menor (*warm, warmth*).

caloría *f* FÍS calorie, calory; *caloría grande* large calorie; *caloría pequeña* small calorie; *caloría gramo* gramme calorie.

calórico, ca *adj* caloric.

calorífero, ra *adj* heat-producing.
◆ *m* radiator, heater.

calorífico, ca *adj* calorific; *potencia calorífica* calorific value *o* power.

calorífugo, ga *adj* heat-resistant (mal conductor del calor) ‖ uninflammable.

calorimetría *f* calorimetry.

calorimétrico, ca *adj* calorimetric, calorimetrical.

calorímetro *m* calorimeter.

calostro *m* colostrum (primera leche).

calote *m* AMER fraud, swindle (estafa) ‖ AMER *dar calote* to cheat, to swindle.

calotear *vt* AMER to cheat, to swindle (estafar).

calpense *adj/s* Gibraltarian (de Gibraltar).

calta *f* BOT marsh marigold.

caluma *f* AMER pass (entre los Andes).

calumet *m* calumet, peace pipe (pipa de la paz).

calumnia *f* calumny, false accusation (acusación falsa) ‖ calumniation (acción) ‖ JUR slander (oral) | libel (*de* on), libel (escrita).

calumniador, ra *adj* calumniatory, slanderous.
◆ *m/f* calumniator, slanderer.

calumniar *vt* to calumniate, to slander ‖ to libel (por escrito).

calumnioso, sa *adj* calumnious, calumniatory, slanderous.

calurosamente *adv* warmly; *el Presidente fue recibido calurosamente* the President was warmly received; *felicitar calurosamente* to congratulate warmly.

caluroso, sa *adj* warm, hot; *un día caluroso* a warm day (véase OBSERV en CALIENTE) ‖ FIG warm; *un recibimiento caluroso* a warm reception.

calva *f* bald patch *o* pate (calvicie) ‖ bald *o* bare patch (de una piel) ‖ clearing (en un bosque).

calvario *m* REL calvary | stations *pl* of the Cross (vía crucis) ‖ FIG & FAM cross, tribulations *pl*, ordeal, suffering (adversidades) ‖ *tener un calvario de deudas* to be head over heels in debt, to be crippled with debt.

calvero *m* clearing (en un bosque) ‖ claypit (yacimiento de arcilla).

calvicie *f* baldness.

calvinismo *m* Calvinism.

calvinista *adj* Calvinist, Calvinistic.
◆ *m/f* Calvinist.

Calvino *npr m* HIST Calvin.

calvo, va *adj* bald (cabeza, persona); *quedarse calvo* to go bald ‖ barren, desert (terreno) ‖ bald, threadbare (tejido) ‖ — FIG *a la ocasión la pintan calva* make hay while the sun shines, strike while the iron is hot | *ni tanto ni tan calvo* neither one extreme nor the other.
◆ *m/f* bald *o* bald-headed person (persona).
◆ *f* → **calva.**

calza *f* wedge, scotch (cuña) ‖ FAM stocking (media) ‖ ring (señal que se pone a ciertos animales) ‖ AMER filling [of a tooth].
◆ *pl* breeches (vestido antiguo) ‖ — *medias calzas* knee socks ‖ FAM *verse en calzas prietas* to be in a fix *o* in a tight spot.

calzada *f* road, roadway.

calzado, da *adj* wearing shoes, with shoes on (que lleva zapatos); *un niño calzado* a child with shoes on ‖ wearing [on one's feet]; *calzado con zapatos rojos* wearing red shoes ‖ shod; *los pies calzados con sandalias* feet shod in sandals; *calzado por el mejor zapatero del pueblo* shod by the best shoemaker in the town ‖ calced (religioso) ‖ with feet of a different colour (animales) ‖ *caballo calzado de blanco* horse with white stockings.
◆ *m* footwear, shoe; *industria del calzado* footwear industry ‖ shoe; *una tienda de calzado* a shoe shop.

calzador *m* shoehorn ‖ AMER penholder (portaplumas) | pencil (lápiz).

calzadura *f* wedging (con calce) ‖ wooden tyre *o* rim (llanta).

calzapiés *m inv* toe clip (de pedal).

calzar *vt* to put on shoes for; *hay que calzar a los niños porque no pueden hacerlo solos* you have to put children's shoes on for them because they cannot do it themselves ‖ to wear; *calzar nuevos zapatos* to wear new shoes ‖ to take, to wear; *calzo un 43* I take size 43 ‖ to make the shoes of; *le calza un zapatero inglés* an English shoemaker makes his shoes ‖ to wedge, to scotch (poner un calce) ‖ to wear [gloves, spurs] (guantes, espuelas) ‖ to take (armas de fuego) ‖ to put on tyres (poner neumáticos) ‖ AMER to fill [a tooth].
◆ *vi* to wear shoes; *calza bien* he wears good shoes.
◆ *vpr* to put one's shoes on ‖ to put on (ponerse); *calzarse las sandalias* to put on one's sandals.

calzo *m* wedge, scotch (calce) ‖ dangerous kicking (en fútbol) ‖ TECN brake shoe (del freno) ‖ MAR skid.

calzón *m* trousers *pl* (prenda); *calzón bombacho* baggy trousers ‖ TECN safety belt (para sujetarse) ‖ AMER panties *pl*, knickers *pl* (de mujer), underpants *pl* [US shorts *pl*] (de hombre) | pork stew (guiso) | disease affecting sugarcane ‖ — FIG & FAM *hablar a calzón quitado* to speak frankly, to speak one's mind.
◆ *pl* trousers ‖ FIG *llevar los calzones* or *tener los calzones bien puestos* to wear the trousers (en un matrimonio).

calzonarias *f pl* AMER braces (tirantes).

calzonarios *m pl* AMER pants (bragas).

calzonazos *m inv* FAM henpecked husband.

calzoncillos *m pl* underpants, pants [US shorts].

calzoneras *f pl* AMER trousers buttoned up the sides.

calzonudo *adj m* AMER FAM henpecked [husband].

calzorras *m inv* FAM henpecked husband.

calla *f* AMER dibble.

callada *f* silence (silencio) ‖ — *a la callada, de callada* on the quiet, on the sly ‖ *dar la callada por respuesta* to say nothing in reply, not to deign to answer.

calladamente *adv* silently, without saying a word.

callado, da *adj* silent, quiet; *esos niños están demasiado callados* those children are too quiet ‖ reserved, quiet; *un chico muy callado* a very reserved boy ‖ secret (secreto) ‖ — *de callado* quietly, discreetly ‖ FIG *más callado que un muerto* as close as a clam, as quiet as a mouse ‖ *no se queda nunca callado* he always has an answer, he has an answer to everything ‖ *tener a alguien callado* to keep s.o. quiet ‖ *tener algo callado* to keep sth. quiet.

callampa *f* AMER mushroom (hongo) | FAM felt hat (sombrero) | umbrella (paraguas).

callana *f* AMER dish [used by Indians for roasting maize].

callandico; callandito *adv* FAM on the quiet, on the sly (en secreto) | quietly, silently (en silencio).

callar *vi/vpr* to be quiet, to keep quiet; *los niños deben callar cuando hablan las personas mayores* children should be quiet when adults are speaking ‖ to remain silent, to shut up (*fam*); *dicho esto, calló* having said this, he remained silent ‖ to stop (ruido) ‖ to stop, to fall silent (un motor) ‖ to be stilled (el mar, el viento) ‖ — FIG *al buen callar llaman Sancho* discretion is the better part of valour ‖ *a la chita callando* on the quiet, on the sly ‖ FIG *¡calla!* or *¡calle!* never!, go on!, no! (de asombro) | *calla callando* discreetly, quietly ‖ *¡cállate!* keep quiet!, be quiet! ‖ FAM *cállate la boca* shut up!, shut your mouth! ‖ *¡cállense!* keep quiet!, be quiet! ‖ *hacer callar a uno* to silence s.o., to shut s.o. up (*fam*) ‖ *quien calla otorga* silence gives consent ‖ *sería mejor callarse* it would be best to say nothing.
◆ *vt* to silence, to shut up (a una persona) ‖ to keep (un secreto) ‖ not to mention, to say nothing about, to keep to o. s; *he callado su nombre* I have not mentioned his name ‖ to hush up, to keep quiet about (un asunto vergonzoso).

calle *f* street, road; *calle mayor* main *o* high street; *en la calle* in the street ‖ lane (de autopista, de piscina, en atletismo) ‖ IMPR river ‖ — FIG & FAM *abrir calle* to clear the way, to make way | *azotar calles* to roam the streets ‖ *calle abajo* down the street ‖ *calle arriba* up the street ‖ *calle de dirección única* one-way street ‖ *calle peatonal* pedestrian street ‖ *calle pública* public thoroughfare ‖ FAM *coger la calle* to clear off | *dejar en la calle* to throw out, to turn (s.o.) out onto the street (despedir), to leave destitute (arruinar) ‖ *doblar la calle* to turn the corner ‖ FIG *echar* or *tirar por la calle de en medio* to forge ahead *o* to go ahead regardless | *echarse a la calle* to go out into the street (salir), to riot (sublevarse) | *el hombre de la calle* the man in the street | *estar en la calle* to be out (haber salido), to be destitute (ser pobre) | *hacer calle* to line the streets | *llevarse de calle a uno* to win s.o. over (despertar simpatía, etc.), to defeat (en una discusión) | *pasear* or *rondar la calle* to court ‖ FIG & FAM *plantar en la* *calle, echar a la calle* to throw *o* to turf out | *poner de patitas en la calle* to throw *o* to turf out | *quedarse en la calle* to be homeless, to be in the street (sin casa), to be left jobless (sin empleo).

calleja *f* alley, narrow street (calle pequeña).

callejear *vi* to wander *o* to stroll about the streets (deambular) || to loiter about (vagar).

callejeo *m* strolling *o* wandering about (paseo) || loitering (vagabundeo).

callejero, ra *adj* fond of wandering about (amigo de callejear) || in the street; *la animación callejera* animation in the street || street; *festejo callejero* street festivity; *venta callejera* street sale || popular; *obra callejera* popular work || stray; *perro callejero* stray dog.
◆ *m* street guide *o* map (guía de calles) || directory classified by streets (guía telefónica).

callejón *m* alley, narrow street || TAUR barricaded passage around the edge of bullring || — *callejón sin salida* cul-de-sac, blind alley (calle) || FIG *en un callejón sin salida* at an impasse, deadlocked, at a stalemate.

callejuela *f* back street, back alley (calle) || FIG way out, loophole (evasiva).

callicida *m* MED corn remover, corn plaster, corn cure.

callista *m/f* chiropodist.

callo *m* MED corn (en los pies), callus, callous (en los pies o en las manos) | callus (de una fractura) || caulk, calk (de herradura) || FIG & FAM horror sight (persona fea).
◆ *pl* tripe *sing* (plato) || *callos a la madrileña* tripe speciality of Madrid.

callosidad *f* callosity, callus.

calloso, sa *adj* callous, hard; *manos callosas* callous hands || ANAT *cuerpo calloso* corpus callosum.

cama *f* bed; *cama de campaña* camp bed; *cama de matrimonio* double bed; *camas separadas* or *gemelas* twin beds; *destapar la cama* to throw the covers off the bed; *ir a la cama* to go to bed || bedstead (armadura del lecho) || bed; *hospital de cien camas* hundred-bed hospital || form (de la liebre) || harbour [*US* harbor] (del ciervo) || lair (de otros animales salvajes) || litter (camada de perros, de gatos, etc.) || brood (camada de aves) || floor (suelo de la carreta) || part of melon which touches the ground || FIG layer; *una cama de tierra* a layer of earth || AGR beam (del arado) || MAR bed (hoyo del casco en la arena) || — FIG *caer en (la) cama* to fall ill || *cama de paja* litter || DEP *cama elástica* trampolin || *cama individual* single bed || FAM *cama redonda* group sex || *cama turca* couch, divan || *echarse en la cama* to lie down on the bed || *estar en cama, guardar* or *hacer cama* to be confined to bed, to stay in bed || *hacer la cama a la inglesa* to straighten the bed || *hacer las camas* to make the beds || FIG & FAM *hacerle* or *ponerle a uno la cama* to put the skids under s.o. (causar perjuicio) || *meterse en la cama* to go to bed (acostarse), to get into bed (entre las sábanas).

camada *f* litter (de animales) || brood (de pájaros) || layer; *caja con dos camadas de huevos* box with two layers of eggs || FIG & FAM band, gang (de ladrones) || FAM *son lobos de la misma camada* they're tarred with the same brush, they are birds of a feather.

camafeo *m* cameo (piedra grabada, pintura).

camagua *f* AMER ripening maize, ripening corn (maíz).

camal *m* halter (cabestro) || AMER slaughterhouse, abattoir.

camaleón *m* chameleon (reptil) || FIG chameleon (persona).

camamila *f* camomile.

camándula *f* rosary || FAM cunning, slyness (astucia) | trick (treta) | hypocrisy (hipocresía).

camandulero, ra *adj* FAM sly, cunning (astuto) | hypocritical (hipócrita).
◆ *m/f* FAM sly *o* cunning dog (persona astuta) | hypocrite (hipócrita) | trickster (tramposo) || sanctimonious person (beato).
◆ *m* bigot, hypocrite (mojigato).

cámara *f* room (habitación) || (ant) royal chamber (dormitorio) || council, board, chamber (consejo) || house, chamber; *cámara alta, baja* upper, lower house || inner tube (neumático) || loft (desván) || ANAT cavity (de la boca) | socket (del ojo) || CINEM camera || AGR granary || MAR wardroom (de los oficiales) | saloon (de los pasajeros) || MIL breech, chamber (de las armas de fuego) || TECN chamber (de un horno, de un motor, de una esclusa) || — CINEM *a cámara lenta* slow-motion (cine), in slow motion (rodar) || *ayuda de cámara* valet || *cámara acorazada* strongroom, vault || *cámara de cine* cinecamera || *cámara de comercio* chamber of commerce || *cámara de compensación* clearinghouse || *cámara de compresión* compression chamber || *Cámara de Diputados* Chamber of Deputies || *cámara de gas* gas chamber || *Cámara de los Comunes, de los Lores* House of Commons, of Lords || *Cámara de Representantes* House of Representatives (en los Estados Unidos) || *cámara de resonancia* echo chamber || *cámara de televisión* television camera || *cámara fotográfica* camera, still camera || *cámara frigorífica* cold-storage room || *cámara mortuoria* funeral chamber, chapelle ardente || *cámara nupcial* bridal suite || *cámara oscura* camera obscura || *de cámara* royal, court; *médico de cámara* royal doctor || *gentilhombre de cámara* gentleman-in-waiting || *música de cámara* chamber music.
◆ *pl* faeces (excremento), diarrhoea *sing* (diarrea).
◆ *m* CINEM cameraman.

camarada *m* colleague; *mi camarada el Doctor Blanco* my colleague, Doctor Blanco || comrade (en política) || — *camarada de colegio* classmate, fellow pupil, schoolfellow; *somos camaradas de colegio* we are classmates || *camarada de trabajo* workmate, fellow worker, workfellow.

camaradería *f* comradeship, friendship, companionship, camaraderie (relación entre camaradas) || team spirit (de un equipo).

camarera *f* waitress (en un café, restaurante) || stewardess (en un barco, avión) || chambermaid (que arregla las habitaciones en un hotel) || servant, maid (sirvienta) || headmaid (en casa principal) || lady-in-waiting (de una reina) || — *camarera de teatro* wardrobe mistress || *camarera mayor de la Reina* the Queen's first lady-in-waiting.

camarería *f* position of head maid.

camarero *m* waiter (en un café, un restaurante) || steward (en un barco, un avión) || valet (de un rey) || wardrobe master (en el teatro) || (ant) chamberlain (del papa) || *camarero de piso* boots (en un hotel).
◆ *interj* waiter!

camareta *f* MAR deck cabin || AMER type of gun for shooting fireworks.

camarilla *f* clique, camarilla, cabal, pressure group (grupo) || lobby (en el Parlamento).

camarín *m* dressing room (de los actores, tocador) || alcove, niche (para las estatuas) || room (donde se guarda una colección) || study (despacho).

camarista *f* lady-in-waiting.

camarlengo *m* camerlingo, camerlengo (dignidad eclesiástica).

camarón *m* shrimp (de mar) || camaron (de agua dulce) || AMER tip (propina).

camaronero, ra *m/f* shrimp fisher, shrimp catcher (pescador) || shrimp seller (vendedor).

camarote *m* MAR cabin.

camarotero *m* AMER steward.

camastro *m* rough old bed, makeshift bed (cama mala).

camastrón, ona *m/f* FAM sly *o* cunning dog, crafty person, sly old fox (astuto).

cambalache *m* FAM swap, exchange || AMER secondhand shop.

cambalachear *vt* FAM to swap, to exchange.

cámbaro *m* crayfish, crawfish (cangrejo de mar).

cambiable *adj* changeable (susceptible de ser alterado) || exchangeable (susceptible de ser cambiado por otra cosa).

cambiadiscos *m inv* record changer.

cambiador, ra *m/f* moneychanger.
◆ *m* control, control switch (mando) || AMER pointsman [*US* switchman] (guardagujas) || TECN *cambiador de calor* heat exchanger.

cambiante *adj* changing (que altera) || exchanging || changeable, inconsistent (carácter).
◆ *m* watered effect, iridescence (de tela) || lustre, glitter, gleam (used mainly in the plural) (visos) || money changer (de monedas).

cambiar *vt* to change; *cambiar una rueda* to change a wheel; *han cambiado el horario* they have changed the timetable || to exchange; *cambiar sellos con un filatelista* to exchange stamps with a stamp collector; *cambiar impresiones* to exchange views; *he cambiado mi pluma por otra* I've exchanged my pen for another; *nos cambiamos los libros* we exchanged books || to move; *lo cambié a otro sitio* I moved it to another place || to change; *cambiar pesetas en libras* to change pesetas into pounds; *la noticia cambió la tristeza en alegría* the news changed sadness into joy || to change, to give change for; *¿me puede cambiar un billete de mil pesetas?* can you change a thousand peseta note for me?, can you give me change for a thousand peseta note? || to change (devolver a una tienda) || to alter (un vestido) || to reverse; *cambiar los papeles* to reverse the roles || — FIG *cambiar el disco* to change the record | *cambiar la chaqueta* to turn one's coat, to change sides.
◆ *vi* to change; *no has cambiado nada* you haven't changed a bit; *ha cambiado el tiempo* the weather has changed; *cambiar de libros, de costumbres* to change books, one's habits || to veer, to change round (el viento) || to give change (dar cambio) || to get some change (pedir cambio) || AUT to change gear, to change (de velocidad) || — *cambiar de casa* to move || *cambiar de dueño* to change hands (una cosa) || *cambiar de idea* to change one's mind || *cambiar de manos* or *de mano* to change hands || MAR *cambiar de rumbo* to come about || *cambiar de sitio* to move, to change places || FIG *cambiar más que una veleta* to change with the wind || AMER FAM *mandarse cambiar* to get out.
◆ *vpr* to change (de ropa) || to change; *se cambió de zapatos* he changed his shoes || to change, to change round (el viento) || — *cambiarse de ropa* to change one's clothes, to get changed || FIG *cambiarse la chaqueta* to turn one's coat, to change sides.

cambiazo *m* switch || FAM *dar el cambiazo a uno* to do a switch on s.o. || *dar un cambiazo* to do a switch.

cambio *m* changing; *el cambio de una rueda* the changing of a wheel; *cambio de guardia* changing of the guard || exchanging; *el cambio de una cosa por otra* the exchanging of one thing for another || reversal; *el cambio de papeles* the reversal of roles || turn (de la marea) || shift, move (de sitios) || change (modificación); *cambio de tiempo* change in the weather; *cambio de plan* change of plan; *cambio de política* change of policy || COM rate of exchange; *¿a cuánto está el cambio de la peseta hoy?* what is the rate of exchange of the peseta today? || changeover; *el cambio al sistema decimal* the changeover to the decimal system || price, quotation; *el cambio de acciones* the price of shares || change (moneda fraccionaria); *¿tiene usted cambio?* have you any change? || exchange (trueque); *perder con el cambio* to lose in the exchange || gear change [US gearshift] (de velocidad) || FIG change, reversal (en su opinión) || — *a cambio de* in exchange for || COM *agente de Cambio y Bolsa* stockbroker || FIG *a las primeras de cambio* at the first opportunity || AUT *caja de cambios* gearbox | *cambio automático* automatic transmission || *cambio de impresiones* exchange of views || AUT *cambio de marcha* or *de velocidades* gear change [US gearshift] || *cambio de vía* points || *cambio escénico* scene change (teatro) || *casa de cambio* foreign exchange office || *caseta* or *cabina de cambio de agujas* signal box || *en cambio* on the other hand, however (al contrario), in return; *hazme este favor y en cambio te haré otro* do me this favour and in return I'll do you one || *en cambio de* instead of, in the place of, in place of || *letra de cambio* bill of exchange || *libre cambio* free trade || *zona de libre cambio* free-trade area.

cambista *m* cambist (de letras de cambio) || money changer (de moneda).

Camboya *npr f* GEOGR Cambodia.

camboyano, na *adj/s* Cambodian.

cambriano, na; cámbrico, ca *adj* GEOL Cambrian.

cambrón *m* BOT buckthorn (espino cerval) | bramble (zarza) | Christ's thorn (espina santa).

cambronal *m* bramble patch.

cambujo, ja *adj* AMER swarthy, dark (muy moreno).

cambullón *m* AMER trick (trampa) | swap, exchange (cambalache) | intrigue (intriga).

cambur *m* AMER banana (fruta) | state employee (funcionario).

camelador, ra *adj* flattering (halagador).
◆ *m/f* flatterer.

camelar *vt* FAM to flatter, to butter up, to get round (halagar); *hace lo que puede para camelar al jefe* he does what he can to flatter the boss || to woo, to court (enamorar) || AMER to watch, to look at (mirar).
◆ *vpr* to flatter, to butter up, to get round.

cameleo *m* FAM flattery.

camelia *f* BOT camellia (planta).

camélidos *m pl* ZOOL camelidae.

camelista *m/f* FAM joker (cuentista) | flatterer (el que halaga).
◆ *adj* FAM would-be, sham; *un pintor camelista* a would-be artist.

camelo *m* FAM flattery, flirting (galanteo) | cock-and-bull story (cuento) | joke, hoax; *es puro camelo* it's a big hoax | con (timo) || — FAM *dar el camelo a uno* to take s.o. in, to pull a fast one on s.o., to diddle s.o. | *de camelo* would-be, sham; *un escritor de camelo* a would-be writer | *me huele a camelo* it smells fishy to me.

camella *f* she-camel (rumiante) || AGR ridge (caballón) || trough (artesa).

camellero *m* cameleer.

camello *m* camel (rumiante) || MAR camel (pontón).

camellón *m* AGR ridge (caballón) || trough (artesa, bebedero) || AMER central grass walkway [in road] [US median strip].

cameraman *m* cameraman.
— OBSERV pl *cameramen* en ambos idiomas.
— OBSERV *Cameraman* is an Anglicism which can be replaced by the Spanish word *cámara* masculine.

camerino *m* TEATR dressing room.

camero, ra *adj* double bed, double; *manta camera* double-bed blanket || *cama camera* double bed.

Camerún *npr m* GEOGR Cameroons *pl* (antiguo protectorado) | Cameroun (estado actual).

Camila *npr f* Camilla, Camille.

Camilo *npr m* Camillus.

camilla *f* small bed (cama para descansar) || stretcher (para enfermos) || round table under which a brazier is placed || — *camilla de ruedas* hospital trolley || *mesa camilla* round table under which a brazier is placed.

camillero *m* stretcher-bearer.

caminante *m/f* traveller.

caminar *vi* to travel (viajar); *caminar de noche* to travel by night || to walk (andar) || to move (desplazarse) || FIG to make its way, to move (un río, un astro) | to head; *caminar a su perdición* to be heading for ruin || FIG *caminar derecho* to keep to the straight and narrow.
◆ *vt* to travel, to go, to cover (recorrer); *hemos caminado tres kilómetros* we have covered three kilometres.

caminata *f* FAM long walk (paseo largo); *darse una caminata* to go for *o* to take a long walk | trek, hike (largo y fatigoso) || distance, stretch (distancia).

caminero, ra *adj* road || *peón caminero* navvy, roadman.

camino *m* path, track (vía); *camino de cabaña* animal path || road (carretera); *camino vecinal* local road || route, itinerary (itinerario) || way; *te vi en el camino de casa al colegio* I saw you on the way to school || journey; *hizo dos veces el camino al despacho* he made the journey to the office twice || FIG path, road (*de* to) (del honor, de la gloria, de la virtud, etc.) | way (medio); *el camino para hacerse rico* the way to make o.s. rich || — *abrir camino* to make *o* to clear a way || *abrirse camino* to make one's way, to force one's way (al andar), to go places, to get on well (en la vida) || *a camino largo paso corto* slow and steady wins the race || *allanar el camino* to smooth the way || *a medio camino, a la mitad del camino* halfway || *camino adelante* straight on || *camino carretero* or *de ruedas* road || *camino de* towards; *vamos camino de España* we are going towards Spain; on the way to; *camino del colegio le encontramos* we met him on the way to school || *camino de entrada* approach road || *camino de herradura* bridle path || *camino de hierro* railway || *camino de ronda* parapet walk, rampart walk || FIG & FAM *camino de rosas* bed of roses || ASTR *Camino de Santiago* the Milky Way || *camino de sirga* towpath || *camino forestal* forest track || *camino real* main road (carretera), the shortest way (lo más corto) || *caminos, canales y puertos* civil engineering (carrera) || FIG *camino trillado* or *trivial* the beaten track || *¿cuánto camino hay de aquí a Madrid?* how far is it from here to Madrid? || *de camino* on the way, on one's way; *su casa nos coge de camino* his house is on the way *o* on our way; travelling; *traje de camino* travelling clothes; at the same time (al mismo tiempo) || FIG *dejar en el camino* to leave unfinished || *después de un día de camino* after a day's travelling || FIG *echar camino adelante* to strike out | *en camino de desaparecer* on its way out | *errar el camino* to go the wrong way, to mistake the way | *escoger el buen camino* to make the right choice || *hacerse su camino* to go places, to get on well || *ir de camino por un sitio* to pass through *o* to travel through a place || *ir fuera de camino* to go the wrong way || *ir por buen camino* to be on the right road, to be going the right way (seguir la buena dirección), to follow the straight and narrow (obrar como es debido) || *ir por mal camino* to be going the wrong way (dirección), to go astray (conducta) || FIG *ir por su camino* to go one's own sweet way | *llevar a alguien por mal camino* to lead s.o. astray | *llevar buen camino* to be on the right track, to be going the right way, to be doing well *o* getting along well | *llevar camino de* to be on the way to, to look as if; *lleva camino de ganar* he is on the way to victory *o* to winning, he looks as if he will win; to look as if; *el trabajo lleva camino de no acabarse nunca* it looks as if this job will never be finished || *pillarle de camino a uno* to be on the way || *ponerse en camino* to set off || *por buen camino* along the right road || *salirle a uno al camino* to go to meet s.o. || *¡siga usted su camino!* on your way!, pass along! || *si te quieres matar vas por buen camino* if you want to kill yourself you're going the right way about it || FIG *todos los caminos van a Roma* all roads lead to Rome || *tomar el camino más largo* to go the long way round || FIG *traer a uno al buen camino* to put s.o. right, to put s.o. on the right track.

camión *m* lorry [US truck] (vehículo) || AMER bus (autobús) || — *camión cisterna* tanker || *camión de bomberos* fire engine || *camión de carga pesada* heavy lorry, heavy goods vehicle || *camión de la basura* dustcart, refuse lorry || *camión de mudanzas* removal van || *camión de riego* water cart, water wagon || *camión remolque* articulated lorry *o* truck, trailer truck || FIG & FAM *está como un camión* she's a bit of all right, she's gorgeous || *transportar en camión* to ship *o* to haul by lorry.

camionaje *m* haulage, cartage (transporte y precio pagado).

camionero *m* lorry driver [US truck driver, teamster].

camioneta *f* van.

camisa *f* shirt (ropa) || skin (de ciertas semillas) || slough (de las serpientes) || folder (envoltura de papel) || jacket, dust jacket (de un libro) || TECN lining (de horno) | sleeve (de cilindro) | gas mantle (manguito) | facing (enlucido de cemento y yeso) | jacket; *camisa de agua* water jacket || — FAM *cambiar de camisa* to turn one's coat, to change sides (chaquetear) || *camisa de dormir* nightdress, nightgown, nightie (de mujer), nightshirt (de hombre) || *camisa de fuerza* straightjacket, straitjacket || FAM *dejarle a uno sin camisa* to ruin s.o., to leave s.o. penniless || *estar en mangas de camisa* to be in one's shirt-sleeves || FAM *jugarse uno hasta la camisa* to stake one's shirt | *meterse en camisa de once varas* to poke one's nose in other people's business (entrometerse), to bite off more than one can chew (abarcar demasiado) | *no llegar a uno la camisa al cuerpo* to be scared stiff | *¡no te metas en camisa de once varas!* mind your own business! | *perder hasta la camisa* to lose one's shirt.

camisería *f* shirt shop, outfitter's (tienda) || shirt industry (industria).

camisero, ra *m/f* shirt maker, outfitter (persona).
◆ *adj* *blusa camisera* shirt blouse, shirtwaist || *vestido camisero* shirtwaist dress.

camiseta *f* T-shirt (camisa corta) || vest [US undershirt] (de ropa interior) || shirt (de rugby, de fútbol) || singlet, vest (para el atletismo) || *camiseta de punto* vest [US undershirt].

camisola *f* camisole (blusa, camisa) || shirt (camisa, camiseta).

camisolín *m* dicky, dickey.

camisón *m* nightgown, nightdress, nightie (de mujer) || nightshirt (de hombre) || AMER lady's shirt.

camoatí *m* AMER wasp (avispa).

camomila *f* BOT camomile (manzanilla).

camorra *f* FAM quarrel, fight, trouble; *buscar camorra* to be asking for trouble, to be looking for a fight *o* a quarrel | row; *armar camorra* to kick up a row.

camorrero, ra; camorrista *adj* quarrelsome, rowdy.
◆ *m/f* troublemaker, rowdy.

camote *m* AMER sweet potato (batata) | bulb (bulbo) | love, infatuation (enamoramiento) | lover, mistress (querida) | fool, simpleton (tonto) | AMER FIG & FAM *tragar camote* to stammer, to stutter.

campal *adj f* *batalla campal* pitched battle.

campamento *m* encampment, camping (acción de acampar) || camp, encampment (lugar) || camp (tropa acampada); *campamento volante* temporary camp || — *campamento de trabajo* workcamp || *campamento de verano* summer camp.

campana *f* bell; *las campanas de la iglesia* the church bells || mantelpiece (parte exterior de la chimenea), hood (parte interior) || TECN caisson (obras públicas) || bell (objeto de forma de campana) || parish (parroquia) || parish church (iglesia) || curfew (queda) || — *campana de buzo* or *de inmersión* diving bell || *campana de cristal* bell jar, bell glass || *campana extractora de humos* cooker hood || *campana mayor* great bell || *dar la vuelta de campana* to overturn (un coche) || *echar las campanas a vuelo* to set all the bells ringing, to ring all the bells full peal (sentido propio), to shout from the rooftops (cacarear), to be overcome with joy, to rejoice (alegrarse) || *Por quién doblan las campanas* For Whom the Bell Tolls (obra) || *tañer las campanas, tocar las campanas* to peal the bells, to ring the bells || *un toque de campana* a peal *o* a stroke of the bell || FIG *usted ha oído campanas y no sabe dónde* you don't really know what you are talking about.

campanada *f* peal *o* stroke *o* ring of a bell (toque) || FIG scandal, sensation (escándalo); *dar una* or *la campanada* to cause a scandal, to cause a sensation.

campanario *m* belfry, bell tower (de iglesia).

campanear *vi* to ring the bells (tañer) || AMER to spy (espiar) || FAM *allá se las campanee* let him look after himself.

campaneo *m* peal *o* chime of bells (de campana) || FIG & FAM swagger (contoneo).

campanero *m* bell founder (fundidor) || bellringer (el que tañe).

campaniforme *adj* campanulate.

campanil *adj* bell; *metal campanil* bell metal.
◆ *m* belfry, bell tower (campanario), campanile (campanilo).

campanilo *m* bell tower, campanile (en Italia).

campanilla *f* small bell (campana) || electric bell (eléctrica) || handbell (para llamar) || bubble (burbuja) || tassel (adorno de pasamanería) || ANAT uvula (úvula) || BOT bellflower (flor) || FIG *de muchas campanillas* of great importance.

campanillazo *m* ring *o* tinkle of a bell || clang (ruido fuerte).

campanillear *vi* to tinkle, to ring (campanillas).

campanilleo *m* tinkling, ringing (tintineo).

campanillero *m* bellringer.

campanología *f* campanology.

campante *adj* FAM unruffled, relaxed, cool (tranquilo); *había perdido todo su dinero, pero se quedó tan campante* he had lost all his money, but he remained quite cool *o* but he was completely unruffled || proud, pleased; *va tan campante con sus nuevos zapatos* he is so proud of *o* pleased with his new shoes.

campanudo, da *adj* bell-shaped || FIG high-sounding, bombastic, pompous (lenguaje), pompous, grandiloquent (orador).

campánula *f* BOT campanula (farolillo) || *campánula azul* bluebell.

campanuláceas *f pl* BOT campanulaceae.

campaña *f* plain; *campaña fértil* fertile plain || MIL campaign || FIG campaign; *campaña publicitaria, parlamentaria, electoral* advertising, parliamentary, electoral campaign || AMER countryside || — *cama de campaña* camp bed || MAR *campaña de pesca* fishing trip || *campaña de publicidad* advertising campaign || *campaña electoral* electoral *o* election campaign || MIL *de campaña* field || *misa de campaña* open-air mass || *tienda de campaña* tent.

campañol *m* vole (animal).

campar *vi* to stand out, to excel (sobresalir) || to camp (acampar) || FIG *campar por sus respetos* to do as one pleases.

campeador *adj m* valiant, extremely brave.
◆ *m* warrior.

campear *vi* AGR to graze in the fields (los animales) || FIG to abound; *en su prosa campea la ironía* irony abounds in his prose || to turn *o* to show green (los sembrados) || AMER to search *o* to scour the countryside.

campechanía *f* FAM good nature, geniality (bondad) || openness, straightforwardness.

campechano, na *adj* FAM good-natured, genial (bonachón) | straightforward, open (sin cumplidos).
◆ *f* AMER whore (prostituta).

campeche *m* BOT *palo (de) campeche* logwood, campeachy wood.

campeón, ona *adj* champion.
◆ *m/f* champion; *un campeón ciclista* a champion cyclist || FIG *hacerse el campeón de una causa* to champion a cause.

campeonato *m* championship || FIG & FAM *de campeonato* terrific, fantastic, great; *una paliza de campeonato* a terrific beating; absolute, out-and-out; *un tonto de campeonato* an absolute idiot.

campero, ra *adj* country, rural (relativo al campo) || open-air (al aire libre) || not brought in at night (ganado) || AMER with experience of the country || *traje campero* outfit worn by Andalusian herdsmen.
◆ *m* jeep (coche).
◆ *f* AMER blouson, jacket (cazadora).

campesinado *m* peasants *pl*, peasantry.

campesino, na *adj* country, rural, rustic (del campo); *costumbres campesinas* rural customs || *ratón campesino* field mouse.
◆ *m/f* peasant, countryman, countrywoman.

campestre *adj* rural, country, rustic.

camping *m* camping (actividad) || camping ground, camping site (terreno) || *hacer camping* to camp, to go camping.
— OBSERV The plural of the Spanish word *camping* is *campings*.

campiña *f* stretch of cultivated land || countryside; *la campiña española* the Spanish countryside.

campista *m* camper || AMER herdsman (ganadero).

campito *m* AMER farm (finca).

campo *m* field; *un campo de trigo* a field of wheat || open country (en contraposición a montaña); *desde mi ventana se ve un trozo de campo* from my window you can see a stretch of open country || country; *pasar las vacaciones en el campo* to spend one's holidays in the country || countryside (paisaje); *el campo está hermoso después de la lluvia* the countryside is beautiful after the rain || FIG field; *campo de actividad, de la medicina* field of activity, of medicine | camp (facción); *el campo carlista* the Carlist camp || DEP pitch (terreno de juego, en fútbol), ground (conjunto de terreno y tribunas) | course (de golf) | court (de tenis) | side (lado del terreno) || HERÁLD field || background (fondo) || MIL field | camp; *campo atrincherado* entrenched camp | army (ejército) || — *a campo raso* open to the sky (sin techo), in the open air, under the stars; *dormir a campo raso* to sleep in the open air || *a campo traviesa* across country || *batir* or *descubrir* or *reconocer el campo* to scour the countryside || *campo aurífero* goldfield || *campo de aterrizaje* landing field || *campo de aviación* airfield || MIL *campo de batalla* battlefield || *campo de concentración* concentration camp || *campo deportivo* or *de deportes* sports ground, playing field || MIL *campo de minas* minefield || *campo de trabajo* work camp || ELECTR & FÍS *campo de microscopio* field of a microscope | *campo eléctrico, magnético, óptico* electric, magnetic, optic field || MED *campo operatorio* operative field || *campo petrolífero* oilfield || *campo raso* open country || *campo santo* cemetery || GRAM *campo semántico* semantic field || MIT *Campos Elíseos* Elysian Fields || *campo visual* field of vision || *carrera a campo través* or *traviesa* cross-country (race) || *casa de campo* country house || *conejo de campo* wild rabbit || FIG *creer que todo el campo es orégano* to think that life is just a bowl of cherries || *dejar el campo libre* to leave the field open || *en campo raso* in the open country || *feria del campo* agricultural show || *hacer campo* to clear a space || *levantar el campo* to strike *o* to break camp (sentido propio), to leave (largarse), to give up (abandonar el campo) || *montar el campo* to pitch camp || FOT *profundidad de campo* depth of field || *retirarse al campo* to retire to the country || FIG *tener campo libre* to have a clear field, to have an open hand || *trabajo de campo* fieldwork.

camposanto *m* cemetery.

campus *m* campus (recinto universitario).

camuesa *f* pippin (manzana).

camueso *m* apple tree || FIG fool, idiot.

camuflaje *m* MIL camouflage.

camuflar *vt* MIL to camouflage || FIG to hide, to cover up.

can *m* dog (perro) || ARQ corbel | modillion (modillón) || MIL trigger (gatillo) || — ASTR *Can, Can Mayor* Greater Dog | *Can Menor* Lesser Dog.
— OBSERV The word *can* is used especially in poetry. *Perro* is the usual word for *dog*.

cana *f* white *o* grey hair || — FIG & FAM *echar una cana al aire* to have a fling, to cut loose, to let one's hair down | *peinar canas* to be getting old, to be going grey.

canaca *m* AMER Chinese, Chinaman (chino) | brothel keeper (dueño de un burdel).

canaco, ca *adj* Kanaka (de Nueva Caledonia) || AMER yellowish.

Canadá *npr m* GEOGR Canada.

canadiense *adj/s* Canadian.
◆ *f* fur-lined lumber jacket (pelliza).

canal *m* canal; *canal navegable* navigable canal; *canal de Panamá* Panama canal || channel, ditch; *canal de riego* irrigation channel ||

channel; *el canal del puerto* the channel of the port; *el canal de la Mancha* the English Channel || channel (de televisión) || FIG channel (vía); *canales comerciales* commercial channels || pipe; *el agua pasa por canales de plomo* the water flows through lead pipes || ANAT canal || ARQ gutter tile (del tejado) || INFORM channel || — *canal de desagüe* sewer || MAR *canal de experiencia* experimental tank.
◆ *f* carcass, carcase, dressed body (de un animal) || fluting, canal (de una columna) || front edge (de un libro) || — *abrir en canal* to slit from top to bottom || *canal maestra* gutter || FAM *mojar la canal maestra* to wet one's whistle.
◆ *adj* FÍS *rayos canales* canal rays.

canaladura *f* ARQ flute.

canalera *f* ARQ guttering.

canaleta *f* AMER gutter.

canalete *m* paddle (remo).

canalizable *adj* canalizable (río).

canalización *f* canalization || TECN piping (tubería) || AMER sewage system, sewers *pl*.

canalizar *vt* to canalize (un río) || to channel (agua) || to pipe (por tuberías) || FIG to channel; *canalizar ideas* to channel ideas.

canalizo *m* MAR fairway, navigable channel.

canalón *m* fallpipe, drainpipe (conducto vertical) || gutter (conducto en el borde del tejado) || shovel hat.

canalones *m pl* cannelons, canneloni (pasta alimenticia).

canalla *f* mob, rabble, riffraff.
◆ *m* FAM swine, rotter; *¡qué canalla!* the swine!

canallada *f* vile trick, dirty trick.

canallesco, ca *adj* vile, dirty, rotten; *acción canallesca* vile deed || rascally, roguish; *risa canallesca* roguish laughter.

canana *f* cartridge belt || AMER goitre (bocio).

cananeo, a *adj/s* Canaanite.

canapé *m* sofa, couch, settee || CULIN aperitive snack, canapé.

Canarias (islas) *npr fpl* GEOGR Canary Islands.

canario, ria *adj/s* Canarian (de las islas Canarias).
◆ *m* ZOOL canary.

canasta *f* basket (cesta); *canasta para ropa* clothes basket || hamper (cesta muy grande) || canasta (juego de cartas) || basket (en el baloncesto).

canastero *m* basket maker (fabricante) || basket dealer (vendedor) || AMER barrow boy.

canastilla *f* basket; *la canastilla de la costura* the sewing basket || layette (ropa para recién nacido).

canastillo *m* small basket (canasto pequeño) || basket; *un canastillo de flores* a basket of flowers.

canasto *m* basket (canasta) || hamper (cesta muy grande).
◆ *interj* *¡canastos!* dash! (disgusto, enfado), good grief!, my goodness! (sorpresa).

Canberra *n pr* GEOGR Canberra.

cáncamo *m* eyebolt (armella).

cancamurria *f* FAM misery, blues, gloom || AMER FAM *tener cancamurria* to be fed up, to be down in the dumps.

cancamusa *f* FAM trick, fraud.

cancán *m* cancan (baile) || frilly petticoat (ropa interior).

cáncana *f* large brown spider (araña).

cancanear *vi* FAM to lounge about, to loaf about, to laze about (vagar) || AMER to stutter, to stammer (tartamudear).

cancaneo *m* AMER stuttering, stammering (tartamudeo).

cáncano *m* FAM louse (piojo).

cancel *m* storm door (puerta) || screen partition (mámpara) || AMER folding screen (biombo).

cancela *f* iron gate.
— OBSERV In Andalusian houses, the *cancela* separates the porch from the yard.

cancelación *f* cancellation.

cancelar *vt* to cancel (anular); *cancelaron el contrato* they cancelled the contract || to settle, to pay (una deuda).

cancelaría *f* papal chancery.

cáncer *m* MED cancer || FIG cancer (de la sociedad, etc.).

Cáncer *npr m* ASTR Cancer.

cancerarse *vpr* MED to become cancerous (un tumor) | to get cancer (persona) || FIG to become corrupt (corromperse).

cancerbero *m* FIG ogre (portero antipático) | goalkeeper (guardameta).

Cancerbero *npr m* MIT Cerberus.

canceriforme *adj* cancriform.

cancerígeno, na *adj* MED cancerigenic, cancerogenic.

cancerólogo *m* MED cancerologist.

canceroso, sa *adj* MED cancerous; *tumor canceroso* cancerous tumour.

cancilla *f* gate (puerta).

canciller *m* chancellor (alto funcionario) || AMER Minister of Foreign Affairs (ministro de Asuntos Exteriores).

cancilleresco, ca *adj* diplomatic; *lenguaje cancilleresco* diplomatic language || of chancellors (propio del canciller).

cancillería *f* chancellory, chancellery || AMER Ministry of Foreign Affairs (ministerio de Asuntos Exteriores).

canción *f* song || — *canción báquica* drinking song || *canción cuartelera* barrack-room song || *canción de cuna* lullaby || *canción de gesta* chanson de geste, epic poem || *canción infantil* nursery rhyme || FIG *volver siempre a* or *estar siempre con la misma canción* to harp on the same old story.

cancionero *m* collection of lyrical poems || song-writer (cancionista) || song book (libro de canciones).

cancioneta *f* short song.

cancionista *m/f* songwriter (compositor).

canco *m* earthenware pot (olla) || FAM buttocks *pl* (nalgas) || queer (marica).

cancro *m* MED cancer || BOT & VET canker.

cancroide *m* MED cancroid.

cancroideo, a *adj* cancroid.

cancha *f* DEP ground (de fútbol) | court (de tenis, de pelota vasca) | cockpit (de peleas de gallo) | racecourse (hipódromo) || AMER open space (terreno libre) | yard; *cancha de maderas* timber yard | wide part (en un río) || roasted maize *o* beans (maíz, habas) || — AMER FIG *abrir cancha* to make way, to clear a path | *dar cancha a uno* to give s.o. an advantage | *estar en su cancha* to be in one's element | *tener cancha* to be experienced.
◆ *interj* AMER make away!, gangway!

canchal *m* rocky place (peñascal).

canchar *vi* AMER to spar, to pretend to fight | to fight with bare fists | to do business (negociar) | to earn a lot of money (ganar).

canchear *vi* AMER to mess about.

canchero, ra *adj* AMER expert, skilled.
◆ *m* groundsman (dueño de una cancha) || expert (experto) || grasping priest (párroco).

cancho *m* boulder, rock || AMER fees *pl* (emolumentos) | tip (propina).

candado *m* padlock || AMER goatee beard (perilla).

candaliza *f* MAR brail.

candanga *f* AMER devil.

cande *adj* candied, crystalized || *azúcar cande* candy, sugar candy.

candeal *adj* *pan, trigo candeal* white bread, wheat.
◆ *m* AMER egg flip.

candela *f* candle (vela de sebo) || fire (fuego) || blossom (de encina, de castaño) || FÍS candle, candela (unidad de intensidad) || FAM light; *pedir, dar candela para un cigarrillo* to ask for, to give a light for a cigarette || — FIG & FAM *acabarse la candela* to kick the bucket, to snuff it | *arrimar candela a uno* to give s.o. a beating || MAR *en candela* on end.

candelabro *m* candelabrum, candelabra || BOT type of cactus.

candelada *f* bonfire (hoguera).

Candelaria *f* Candlemas (fiesta).

candelecho *m* vineyard guard's hut.

candelero *m* candlestick (utensilio) || oil lamp (velón) || fishing torch (para la pesca) || MAR stanchion || — FIG *estar en el candelero* to be at the top, to be high up (en un lugar destacado), to be very popular (ser popular) | *poner en el candelero* to put at the top (en lugar destacado), to make popular (hacer popular).

candelilla *f* small candle (candela pequeña) || MED bougie (sonda) || BOT catkin (inflorescencia) || AMER will-o'-the-wisp (fuego fatuo) | glowworm (luciérnaga) | type of euphorbia (planta) || — BOT *echar candelillas* to sprout catkins || FIG & FAM *se le hacen candelillas los ojos* he's tipsy *o* merry.

candente *adj* candescent, white-hot (blanco) || incandescent, red-hot (rojo) || FIG burning; *problema, cuestión candente* burning problem, question | electric (atmósfera).

candi *adj* crystalized, candied || *azúcar candi* candy, sugar candy.

Candía *n pr* GEOGR Canea.

candidato, ta *m* candidate; *candidato a* or *para un puesto* candidate for a post.

candidatura *f* candidature, candidacy; *presentar su candidatura* to put forward one's candidature || list of candidates (conjunto de candidatos).

candidez *f* frankness, candour || FIG naïvety, ingenuousness (ingenuidad) | silly remark, stupidity (tontería).

cándido, da *adj* POÉT white, snowy (blanco) | innocent, pure || FIG naïve, ingenuous, gullible (ingenuo) | frank, candid (franco).

candil *m* oil lamp (lámpara) || tine (cuerno) || FIG & FAM point [of cocked hat] (de sombrero) || AMER chandelier (araña) || — *baile de candil* local hop || FIG *ni buscado con candil* it couldn't be better, it's just what the doctor ordered || *pescar al candil* to fish by torchlight.

candileja *f* small lamp || BOT nigella (neguilla).
◆ *pl* TEATR footlights.

candombe *m* AMER south American Negro dance | drum (tambor).

candombear *vi* AMER to engage in underhand dealings [in politics].

candonga *f* FAM blarney (zalamería) | joking, teasing (burla) | draught mule (mula) || AMER stomach band (de recién nacido).
◆ *pl* AMER earrings.

candongo, ga *adj* FAM wheedling, coaxing (zalamero) | sly, crafty (astuto) | lazy, idle (holgazán).

◆ *m/f* FAM wheedler, coaxer (zalamero) | crafty, devil, sly one (astuto) | shirker, layabout, lazybones (holgazán).

candonguear *vt* FAM to tease (burlarse de).
◆ *vi* FAM to shirk (ser holgazán).

candor *m* innocence; *el candor de un niño* the innocence of a child || naïvety, ingenuousness, gullibility, credulity (ingenuidad) || frankness, candidness (candidez) || POÉT whiteness.

candoroso, sa *adj* innocent; *un niño candoroso* an innocent child || naïve, gullible, ingenuous, credulous (ingenuo) || frank, candid (franco).

caneca *f* earthenware bottle (vasija de barro) || *AMER* wooden bucket (cubo).

canecillo *m* ARQ corbel | modillion (modillón).

caneco, ca *adj* *AMER* tipsy, merry (ebrio).

canela *f* cinnamon (especia) || FIG *ser canela fina* to be exquisite (cosa), to be wonderful (persona).

canelé *m* rib (de los calcetines).

canelero *m* BOT cinnamon [tree] (árbol).

canelo, la *adj* cinnamon, cinnamon-coloured (color).
◆ *m* BOT cinnamon (árbol) || FAM *hacer el canelo* to be a mug.

canelón *m* drainpipe, fallpipe (canalón) || icicle (carámbano) || curl (de pelo) || cord (pasamanería).
◆ *pl* cannelons, canneloni (pastas alimenticias).

canesú *m* bodice (de vestido de mujer) || yoke (de camisa).

canevá *m* *AMER* canvas (cañamazo).

caney *m* *AMER* hut, cabin (bohío) | bend (de un río).

cangalla *m/f* *AMER* coward (cobarde).

cangilón *m* bucket (de rueda hidráulica) || scoop, bucket (de una draga) || earthenware jug *o* jar (vasija) || goffering, gauffering (pliegue) || *AMER* rut (carril) | pothole (hoyo).

cangreja *f* MAR brig sail, fore-and-aft sail (vela).

cangrejero, ra *m/f* crab seller, crayfish seller (vendedor).
◆ *f* nest of crabs (nido).

cangrejo *m* ZOOL crab (de mar) | crayfish (de río) || MAR gaff (verga) || truck (ferrocarril) || ASTR Cancer || — FIG & FAM *andar* or *ir para atrás como los cangrejos* to be slipping | *rojo como un cangrejo* as red as a lobster, as red as a beetroot.

canguelo *m* FAM funk || FAM *tener canguelo* to have the wind up.

canguro *m* ZOOL kangaroo.

caníbal *adj* cannibal, cannibalistic (antropófago) || FIG savage, fierce (cruel).
◆ *m/f* cannibal.

canibalismo *m* cannibalism.

canica *f* marble; *jugar a las canicas* to play marbles.

canicie *f* whiteness, greyness (de los cabellos).

canícula *f* dog days *pl*.

canicular *adj* canicular || *calor canicular* midsummer heat.
◆ *m pl* dog days.

caniche *m* poodle (perro).

cánidos *m pl* ZOOL canidae.

canijo, ja *adj* FAM weak, puny (enclenque).

canilla *f* ANAT long bone, slender bone (hueso) || wing bone (de ave) || TECN bobbin, reel, spool (para el hilo) | tap, spout, faucet (caño) || *AMER* tap (grifo) | strength (fuerza) || rib (defecto de tela) || — *canilla de la pierna* shinbone || FIG & FAM *irse de canilla* to have diarrhoea (padecer diarrea), to spout, to babble (hablar sin ton ni son).

canillera *f* shin guard (para deportes) || greave (de armadura).

canillero *m* tap hole (piquera).

canillita *m* *AMER* news boy, newspaper boy.

canillón, ona; canilludo, da *adj* *AMER* long-legged.

canino, na *adj* canine; *raza canina* canine race || — MED *hambre canina* ravenous hunger || FIG *tener hambre canina* to be starving.
◆ *m* canine [tooth].

canje *m* exchange; *canje de prisioneros, de notas diplomáticas* exchange of prisoners, of diplomatic notes.

canjeable *adj* exchangeable.

canjear *vt* to exchange; *canjear los bonos por premios* to exchange the vouchers for prizes.

cannabis *m* cannabis.

cano, na *adj* white, grey (el cabello); *un anciano de pelo cano* an old man with white hair || white-haired, grey-haired; *un viejo cano* a white-haired old man || FIG old (viejo) || POÉT snowy, snow-white (blanco) || *ponerse cano* to go grey.

canoa *f* canoe (piragua) || boat (bote de remo o con motor) || motor boat (con motor) || launch (lancha).

canódromo *m* greyhound track, dog track.

canoero; canoísta *m* canoeist.

canon *m* REL & MÚS canon || canon, norm (regla, precepto) || model, perfect example (tipo perfecto) || canon (pago) || COM rent (renta) | tax, levy (tributo) || IMPR *doble canon* canon.
◆ *pl* REL canon law || — *como mandan los cánones* according to the rules || *no estar de acuerdo con los cánones* to be unorthodox, not to be in accordance with the rules.

canonesa *f* canoness.

canónico, ca *adj* canon; *derecho canónico* canon law || — *horas canónicas* canonical hours || *matrimonio canónico* canonical marriage.

canóniga *f* nap before a meal.

canónigo *m* canon || FIG & FAM *vivir como un canónigo, llevar una vida de canónigo* to live like a lord.

canonista *m* canonist, canon lawyer.

canonización *f* canonization.

canonizar *vt* to canonize || FIG to sing the praises of (alabar).

canonjía *f* canonry (beneficio de canónigo) || FIG & FAM sinecure, cushy job (sinecura).

canoro, ra *adj* musical, melodious (melodioso) || *ave canora* songbird.

canoso, sa *adj* white-haired, grey-haired; *anciano canoso* white-haired old man; *estar canoso* to be grey-haired || — *barba canosa* white *o* grey beard || *pelo canoso* grey *o* white hair || *sienes canosas* greying *o* grey temples.

canotié; canotier *m* straw hat, boater (sombrero).

canquén *m* *AMER* wild duck found in Chili.

cansado, da *adj* tired, weary; *cansado por un largo viaje* tired by a long journey; *con voz cansada* in a weary voice || tired, strained (los ojos) || FIG tiring (fatigoso); *un viaje muy cansado* a very tiring journey | tiresome, tedious (fastidioso); *es cansado oír todos los días la misma canción* it's tiresome to hear the same song every day || AGR exhausted || — *marfil cansado* old ivory || *nacer cansado* to be permanently tired || *tener la cara cansada* to look drawn, to look peaked.

cansador, ra *adj* *AMER* tiresome, tiring, tedious (aburrido).

cansancio *m* tiredness, weariness || MED exhaustion || FIG *estar muerto de cansancio* to be dead tired.

cansar *vt* to tire, to make tired, to weary (causar cansancio); *este trabajo nos cansa muchísimo* this work tires us a lot, this work makes us very tired || MED to exhaust || to tire, to strain (los ojos) || FIG to bore, to make bored; *el discurso me cansó* the speech bored me || AGR to exhaust || — FIG *estar cansado* to be tired, to be fed up (*fam*); *estoy cansado de verlo* I'm tired of seeing him | *me cansa ir al cine todos los días* I get tired of going to the cinema every day, I get fed up going to the pictures every day (*fam*).
◆ *vi* to be tiring; *este trabajo cansa mucho* this work is very tiring || FIG to be *o* to get boring *o* tedious *o* tiresome (fastidiar); *la misma comida todos los días acaba por cansar* the same meal day after day gets boring in the end.
◆ *vpr* to get tired, to tire; *se cansa fácilmente* he gets tired easily, he tires easily || FIG to get tired, to get fed up (*fam*); *me canso de repetir tantas veces la misma cosa* I get tired of saying the same thing over and again.

cansera *f* FAM nuisance, bother (molestia) || tiredness (cansancio).

cansino, na *adj* tired (animales) || weary, tired, lifeless; *paso cansino* weary pace; *voz cansina* lifeless voice.

cantábile *adj* cantabile.

cantable *adj* which can be sung, singable; *un trozo cantable* a piece which can be sung, a singable piece.
◆ *m* MÚS cantabile (trozo lento y fácil de cantar) | singing part (de la zarzuela).

Cantabria *n pr* GEOGR Cantabria.

cantábrico, ca *adj* Cantabrian || — GEOGR *Cordillera Cantábrica* Cantabrian Mountains | *mar Cantábrico* Bay of Biscay.

cántabro, bra *adj/s* Cantabrian.

cantador, ra *m/f* singer; *cantador de baladas* ballad singer.

cantaleta *f* *AMER* boring chorus (estribillo).

cantaletear *vt* *AMER* to harp on, to repeat (repetir).

cantalupo *m* BOT cantaloup, cantaloupe (melón).

cantante *adj* singing, who sings (que canta) || *café cantante* bar with cabaret.
◆ *m/f* singer || opera singer (en la ópera).

cantaor, ra *m/f* flamenco singer.

cantar *m* ballad, song || song (canto) || — *cantar de gesta* chanson de geste || *Cantar del Mío Cid* Poem of the Cid || REL *el Cantar de los Cantares* the Canticles, the Song of Songs || FIG *¡ese es otro cantar!* that's a different kettle of fish!, that's different!

cantar *vt* to sing; *cantar una canción muy corta* to sing a very short song || to sing, to sing of; *cantar la gloria de una nación* to sing the glory of a nation || *cantar misa* to sing *o* to say one's first mass (después de la ordenación), to say *o* to sing mass.
◆ *vi* to sing; *canta muy bien* he sings very well; *cantar a dos voces* to sing a duet | to sing, to chirp (los pájaros) || to chirp (el grillo) || to call (naipes) || FIG & FAM to creak (rechinar) | to talk, to squeal, to sing (confesar) || MÚS to play a solo || — *al cantar el gallo* at cockcrow, at daybreak || FIG & FAM *cantar de plano* to talk, to spill the beans, to sing (confesar) || *cantar entonado* to sing in tune || FAM *cantarlas claras a uno* to give s.o. a piece of one's mind | *cantarle a uno las cuarenta* to tell s.o. a few home truths, to give s.o. a piece of one's mind | *en menos que canta un gallo* in a flash, before you

can say Jack Robinson | *eso es coser y cantar* it's as easy as pie *o* as A. B. C., it's child's play.

cántara *f* pitcher || churn (metálica) || liquid measure [16.13 litres, approximately 3.5 gallons].

cantarela *f* MÚS first *o* highest string of a violin.

cantarera *f* shelf for pitchers.

cantarería *f* pottery shop.

cantarero, ra *m/f* potter (alfarero).

cantárida *f* ZOOL Spanish fly, cantharis || MED cantharides *pl.*

cantarín, ina *adj* singsong; *voz cantarina* singsong voice || singing (cantador).
◆ *m/f* singer.

cántaro *m* pitcher || pitcherful (contenido) || — FIG & FAM *alma de cántaro* dimwit, blockhead || FIG *llover a cántaros* to rain cats and dogs, to pour down | *tanto va el cántaro a la fuente que al fin se rompe* the pitcher goes so often to the well that in the end it breaks.

cantata *f* cantata.

cantatriz *f* opera singer.

cantazo *m* blow with a stone.

cante *m* folk song.
— OBSERV One must not confuse *cante* with *canto.* The former applies only to *cante hondo* or *jondo* and *cante flamenco,* which are types of Andalusian folk music.

cantegril *m* AMER shantytown.

cantera *f* quarry (de piedra) || FIG breeding ground, nursery; *Sevilla es una cantera de toreros* Seville is a nursery for bullfighters || AMER freestone, ashlar, hewn stone (cantería).

cantería *f* hewing of stones (labra de piedras) || ARQ building made of hewn stone (obra) | freestone, ashlar, hewn stone (sillar).

cantero *m* stonemason (que labra las piedras) || plot *o* strip of land (haza) || crust (de pan).

cántico *m* MÚS canticle || song (canción).

cantidad *f* quantity; *una gran cantidad* a large quantity || sum; *abonar una cantidad de mil pesetas* to pay a sum of a thousand pesetas || a lot (mucho) || — *adjetivo, adverbio de cantidad* quantitative *o* quantitive adjective, adverb || *cantidad alzada* inclusive price (tanto alzado) || *cantidad de electricidad* amperage || FIG *en cantidades industriales* in massive *o* huge amounts || *¡había una cantidad* or *cantidad de gente!* there were loads of people!

cántiga; cantiga *f* (ant) song, poem, ballad.

cantil *m* cliff (acantilado) || shelf (en el fondo del mar) || AMER cliff edge (borde de un despeñadero).

cantilena; cantinela *f* cantilena, ballad (composición poética) || FIG & FAM *siempre la misma cantilena* always the same old story.

cantiléver *adj/sm* TECN cantilever.

cantillo *m* small stone, pebble (piedra pequeña).
◆ *pl* jacks (juego de las tabas).

cantimpla *adj* simple, stupid.
◆ *m/f* simpleton, stupid person.

cantimplora *f* canteen (para llevar líquidos) || AMER goitre (bocio).

cantina *f* buffet (en una estación) || wine cellar (sótano) || canteen (comedor) || picnic basket (fiambrera) || AMER bar (taberna).
◆ *pl* AMER saddlebags (en un caballo).

cantinela *f* → **cantilena.**

cantinera *f* barmaid (en un bar) || camp follower (en la guerra).

cantinero *m* bar attendant, barman.

canto *m* song; *canto de victoria* victory song || canto (de un poema) || singing; *me gusta el canto* I like singing || — *al canto del gallo* at cockcrow, at daybreak || *canto gregoriano* or *llano* Gregorian chant, plain song || FIG *el canto del cisne* the swan song.

canto *m* edge (de moneda, etc.) || blunt edge, back (de cuchillo) || corner (ángulo) || crust (pedazo de pan) || pebble, stone (guijarro) || — FAM *al canto* in support; *pruebas al canto* evidence in support; for sure; *si se entera tu padre, disgusto al canto* if your father finds out, there will be trouble for sure; *cada vez que voy a Bilbao, lluvia al canto* every time I go to Bilbao, it rains for sure || *canto rodado* boulder (grande), pebble (pequeño) || FIG & FAM *darse con un canto en los dientes* to be thankful for small mercies || *de canto* on edge || FIG & FAM *le faltó el canto de un duro* he had a narrow escape, he escaped by the skin of his teeth || *libro de canto dorado* gilt-edged book || *tiene dos centímetros de canto* it is two centimetres thick.

cantón *m* corner (esquina) || HERÁLD canton || canton; *Suiza se divide en cantones* Switzerland is divided into cantons || MIL cantonment || *cantón redondo* rasp (lima de grano grueso).

cantonal *adj* cantonal.

cantonera *f* corner piece (encuadernación) || butt plate (de arma) || corner cabinet *o* table (rinconera).

cantonero, ra *adj* idling, loafing.
◆ *m/f* idler, loafer.

cantor, ra *adj* singing || *ave cantora* songbird.
◆ *m/f* singer; *cantor callejero* street singer || FIG bard, songster (poeta).

cantoral *m* choir book.

Cantorbery *n pr* GEOGR Canterbury.

cantueso *m* type of red lavender (espliego).

canturrear; canturriar *vi* to hum, to sing softly.

canturreo *m* humming, soft singing.

cánula *f* MED cannula.

canutero *m* pin case, pin box (alfiletero) || AMER pen holder | fountain pen.

canutillo *m* golden *o* silver purl (hilo de oro o de plata) || *pana de canutillo* corduroy.

canuto; cañuto *m* BOT internode || pin case, pin box (canutero) || tube (tubo) || blowpipe (cerbatana) || FAM demobbing (licencia del soldado).

canzonetista *f* singer.

caña *f* BOT cane, stem (tallo) | reed; *caña común* common reed | rattan (caña de Indias) || ANAT shinbone (hueso de la pierna), arm bone (hueso del brazo) | cannon bone (del caballo) | marrow (tuétano) || leg (de la bota) || glass; *una caña de cerveza* a glass of beer || rod; *pescar con caña* to fish with a rod || stock (de un fusil) || MIN gallery || ARQ shaft (de una columna) || shank (del ancla) || MAR helm (del timón) || MÚS Andalusian folk song || AMER sugar cane | tafia (aguardiente de caña) | boasting (bravata) || — *caña de azúcar* sugar cane || ARQ *media caña* gorge (moldura semicircular).
◆ *pl* jousting *sing* (torneo).

cañabrava *f* AMER giant reed (especie de caña muy fuerte).

cañacoro *m* BOT canna.

cañada *f* gorge, ravine (entre dos montañas) || cattle track (camino) || AMER stream (arroyo).

cañaduz *f* sugar cane.

cañafístola; cañafístula *f* BOT cassia (árbol, fruto).

cañamazo *m* tow (estopa) || tow cloth, burlap (tela) || canvas (para bordar) || sketch (de pintura); *sólo está hecho el cañamazo del cuadro* only the sketch of the painting is done || FIG rough draft *o* outline (de una novela, etc.).

cáñamo *m* hemp (planta y fibra); *cáñamo de Manila* Manila hemp || *cáñamo indio* or *índico* or *de Indias* Indian hemp, cannabis.

cañamón *m* BOT hempseed.

cañaveral *m* cane plantation (plantación de cañas) || sugar-cane plantation (de caña de azúcar) || reedbed (sitio poblado de cañas).

cañazo *m* blow with a cane (golpe) || AMER tafia (aguardiente de caña).

cañería *m* piping (tubería) || pipe, length of pipe (tubo).

cañí *adj/s* gipsy.
— OBSERV pl *cañís.*

cañizal; cañizar *m* cane plantation (plantación de cañas) || sugar-cane plantation (cañaveral).

cañizo *m* wattle screen.

caño *m* pipe (tubo) || jot (de una fuente) || sewer (albañal) || gallery (de una mina) || cellar (sótano) || MAR navigable channel.

cañón *m* pipe (de órgano) || flue (de chimenea) || flute (pliegue de la ropa) || tube, pipe (tubo) || shaft (de una pluma de ave) || whisker (de la barba) || MIL gun, cannon (ant); *cañón antiaéreo* anti-aircraft gun | barrel (de fusil) || trunk (tronco de árbol) || GEOGR canyon (desfiladero) || — *bóveda de cañón* barrel vault || FÍS *cañón de electrones* or *electrónico* electron gun || MIL *cañón rayado* rifled barrel || *escopeta de dos cañones* double-barrelled rifle || FIG *estar siempre al pie del cañón* to be always on the job || *morir al pie del cañón* to die with one's boots on, to die in harness.
◆ *adj* FAM terrific, great.
◆ *adv* *lo pasé cañón* I had a marvellous time.

cañonazo *m* gunshot (tiros y ruido) || shot (fútbol).
◆ *pl* gunfire, shellfire || *salva de 21 cañonazos* 21-gun salute.

cañonear *vt* to shell; *el acorazado cañoneó la costa* the battleship shelled the coast.

cañoneo *m* gunfire, shellfire.

cañonera *f* MIL embrasure (tronera) || MAR gun port (porta) || gunboat (lancha) || AMER holster (funda para la pistola).
◆ *adj* MAR *lancha cañonera* gunboat.

cañonería *f* artillery (conjunto de cañones) || pipes *pl* (de un órgano).

cañonero *m* MAR gunboat.

cañuto *m* → **canuto.**
— OBSERV The term *cañuto* is rarely used; *canuto* is preferred. This preference also applies to the derivaties of the two words.

caoba *f* mahogany (árbol y madera).

caolín *m* kaolin.

caos *m* chaos.

caótico, ca *adj* chaotic.

cap *m* cup (bebida).

capa *f* cape, cloak (vestido sin mangas) || cape (de torero) || coat (de pintura) || layer (de aire, de tierra) || GEOL stratum, layer (de roca, etc.) || pall (de humo) || outer leaf (de cigarro) || film, layer (de polvo) || FIG stratum, layer, sector (social) | cloak, sheet, layer (de nieve, etc.) | mask; *bajo una capa de humildad* behind a mask of humility || coat (color del pelaje) || CULIN coating, coat || QUÍM shell (de átomo) || wealth (bienes) || — FIG *andar de capa caída* to be in a bad way (estar mal), to have come down in the world, to have seen better days (decaer) || *capa del cielo* celestial vault || *capa de ozono* ozone layer || *capa freática* water table || REL *capa pluvial* pluvial, cope || *de capa y espada* cloak-and-dagger || FIG *echar una capa a alguien* to cover up for s.o. | *hacer de su capa un sayo* to do as one pleases || *madera de cuatro capas* 4-ply wood || *primera capa* undercoat (de pintura) || FIG *so capa de* on *o* under the pretext of

| *una buena capa todo lo tapa* you cannot judge a book by its cover.

capacidad *f* capacity; *capacidad de trabajo* work capacity; *la capacidad de un tonel* the capacity of a barrel || JUR capacity || FIG capacity, ability (mental) || ELECTR capacity || — *capacidad adquisitiva* purchasing power || *capacidad de arrastre* pulling power || *capacidad de decisión* decision-making power || INFORM *capacidad de memoria* memory capacity | *capacidad de proceso* or *de tratamiento* data handling capacity || *capacidad financiera* financial status || *tener capacidad para* to be capable of (ser capaz de), to have talent for (tener talento para) || *un avión con capacidad para 300 pasajeros* a plane which seats 300 passengers, a plane with room for 300 passengers.

capacitación *f* training (formación) || qualification (capacidad de un obrero) || *escuela de capacitación profesional* technical school.

capacitado, da *adj* qualified (obrero, persona) || JUR qualified, competent; *capacitado para suceder* qualified to succeed || *capacitado para* capable of.

capacitancia *f* ELECTR capacitance.

capacitar *vt* to train (instruir) || to qualify, to entitle; *este título me capacita para ejercer* this diploma entitles me to practise || JUR to capacitate, to entitle.

capacha *f* shopping basket, basket.

capacho *m* shopping basket, basket || hemp pressing bag (para la aceituna) || AMER old hat (sombrero) || TECN dipper (de pala mecánica).

capador *m* castrator, gelder.

capadura *f* castration (castradura).

capar *vt* to castrate (castrar) || FIG to curtail.

caparazón *m* shell (de tortuga, de crustáceo) || HIST caparison || FIG cover (cubierta) || nosebag (para el pienso del caballo) || *quitar el caparazón* to shell (un cangrejo).

caparrosa *f* vitriol; *caparrosa azul* blue vitriol.

capataz *m* foreman (en una empresa) || *capataz de campo* overseer.

capaz *adj* capable, able, competent; *un gobernante capaz* a capable ruler || qualified (para un trabajo) || capable; *este hombre es capaz de todo* this man is capable of anything || which holds; *estadio capaz para cien mil personas* stadium which holds a hundred thousand people || spacious, roomy; *una sala muy capaz* a very spacious hall || enough; *este frío es capaz de matarme* this cold is enough to kill me || JUR qualified, competent || *¿serías capaz?* you wouldn't dare!

capazo *m* shopping basket || carrycot (para un niño).

capcioso, sa *adj* captious, insidious, artful || *pregunta capciosa* catch question, captious question.

capciosidad *f* captiousness, insidiousness, artfulness.

capea *f* TAUR amateur bullfight using young bulls (lidia con novillos) | cape work, passes *pl* with the cape (toreo con la capa).

capeador *m* TAUR amateur *o* novice bullfighter (de novillos) | cape man (torero con capa).

capear *vt* TAUR to make passes with a cape || FIG & FAM to stall, to put off (entretener con promesas, etc.) | to take in, to fool (engañar); *a mí no me capea nadie* you can't fool me | to get round (s.o.) (embaucar) || MAR to ride out; *capear el temporal* to ride out the storm || FIG to brave, to ride out; *ha capeado las consecuencias del accidente* he has braved the consequences of the accident | to shirk, to dodge (una dificultad) | to avoid, to dodge (evitar).

capelina *f* MED capeline (vendaje).

capelo *m* cardinal's hat (sombrero) || cardinalship (dignidad de cardenal) || AMER bell glass (fanal).

capellán *m* REL chaplain; *capellán castrense* army chaplain.

capellanía *f* REL chaplaincy.

capellina *f* capeline (sombrero) || MED capeline (vendaje).

capeo *m* TAUR passes with the cape, cape work | amateur bullfight using young bulls.

caperucita *f* small hood || *Caperucita Roja* Little Red Riding Hood.

caperuza *f* pointed hood *o* cap (gorro terminado en punta) || hood, cowl (de chimenea, etc.) || cap; *la caperuza de una pluma* the cap of a pen.

Capeto *npr m* HIST Capetian.

capialzado *m* ARQ splay.

capibara *f* ZOOL capybara.

capicúa *f* palindrome, reversible word *o* number; *el número 1991 es capicúa* the number 1991 is a palindrome.

capilar *adj* hair; *loción capilar* hair lotion || ANAT capillary (vaso) || FÍS capillary (tubo).
◆ *m* ANAT capillary.

capilaridad *f* capillarity.

capilla *f* chapel (pequeña iglesia); *capilla ardiente* funeral chapel || MÚS chapel, choir; *maestro de capilla* chapel *o* choir master || hood, cowl (capucha) || FIG & FAM clan (camarilla) || IMPR proof, proof sheet || *estar en capilla* to be awaiting execution (condenado a muerte), to be like a cat on hot bricks, to be on tenterhooks (esperar con ansia).

capillita *f* clan (camarilla).

capillo *m* hood (capucha) || bonnet (de niño) || christening *o* baptism cape (para bautizo) || toe lining (del calzado) || coffee strainer (para colar el café).

capirotazo *m* flip, fillip.

capirote *adj* with the head of a different colour from the rest of the body (res).
◆ *m* hennin (para mujeres) || hood (gorro puntiagudo) || hood (de doctores) || penitent's hood (de penitente) || flip, fillip (con los dedos) || FIG & FAM *tonto de capirote* dunce, nitwit, nincompoop, ass.

capirucho *m* FAM hood (capuchón).

capisayo *m* hooded cape || mantelletta (episcopal).

capitación *f* capitation, poll tax (impuesto).

capital *adj* capital, chief, principal (principal); *error capital* capital mistake || main (rasgo) || capital; *ciudad capital* capital city || — IMPR *letra capital* capital letter || *pecado capital* deadly sin || *pena* or *sentencia capital* death sentence, capital punishment.
◆ *m* capital (dinero); *capital activo, social, suscrito* working, share, subscribed capital; *capital de riesgo* risk *o* venture capital; *capital fijo* fixed capital; *capital líquido* net capital.
◆ *f* capital (sede del gobierno) || IMPR capital (letra) || — *capital del condado* county town (en Inglaterra) || *capital de provincia* county town [US county seat].

capitalino, na *adj* of the capital.
◆ *m/f* inhabitant of the capital.

capitalismo *m* capitalism.

capitalista *adj* capitalist, capitalistic.
◆ *m/f* capitalist.

capitalización *f* capitalization.

capitalizar *vt* to capitalize.

capitán *m* MAR & MIL captain (oficial) || shipmaster (mercante) || captain, skipper (de un equipo) || FIG chief, leader, commander (jefe) || — MAR *capitán de corbeta* lieutenant commander | *capitán de fragata* commander | *capitán de navío* captain || MIL *capitán general* field marshal.

capitana *f* flagship (buque principal de la escuadra).

capitanear *vt* to lead, to command (mandar); *capitanear una banda de ladrones* to lead a band of robbers || to captain (un equipo deportivo) || to command, to captain (un barco).

capitanía *f* captaincy, captainship (empleo) || harbour dues *pl* (derechos que se pagan para fondear) || *Capitanía General* military headquarters (oficina), Captaincy General (dependencia de un virreinato); *la Capitanía General de Guatemala* the Captaincy General of Guatemala.

capitel *m* ARQ capital.

capitolio *m* capitol || imposing building (edificio majestuoso).

capitoné *m* removal van, furniture van (para mudanzas).
◆ *adj* upholstered (acolchado).
— OBSERV The word *capitoné* is a Gallicism.

capitoste *m* FAM big wheel, big boss.

capitulación *f* capitulation, surrender (rendición); *capitulación sin condiciones* unconditional surrender || agreement, pact (convenio).
◆ *pl* marriage settlement *o* contract *sing*.

capitular *adj* capitular, capitulary || REL chapter; *sala capitular* chapter house.
◆ *m* capitular, capitulary (miembro de un cabildo).
◆ *f pl* HIST capitulars, capitularies (ordenanzas de los francos).

capitular *vi* to capitulate, to surrender (rendirse) || to make *o* to reach an agreement (pactar).
◆ *vt* to charge.

capítulo *m* chapter (de un libro) || REL reproof, reprimand (reprensión) || subject, matter (tema) || chapter (de una orden militar, de una congregación) || ANAT & BOT capitulum || — *capítulos matrimoniales* marriage settlement *o* contract *sing* || FIG *eso es otro capítulo* that is another story | *llamar a alguien a capítulo* to call s.o. to account.

capitulum *m* ANAT capitulum.

capó *m* AUT bonnet [US hood].

capoc *m*; **capoca** *f* kapok (fibra).

capón *m* capon (pollo) || rap with the knuckles (golpe) || AMER sheep (carnero).
◆ *adj* castrated, gelded (capado).

caponada *f* AMER flock of sheep.

caponera *f* coop (jaula para cebar capones) | caponier (fortificación) || open house (lugar donde se recibe buen trato) || FAM nick, clink (cárcel).

caporal *m* farm manager (capataz) || MIL corporal (cabo) || FIG chief, leader.

capot *m* AUT bonnet [US hood].

capota *f* bonnet (de mujer) || hood (de automóvil y de coche de niños) || AUT *capota plegable* folding hood *o* top.

capotar *vi* to overturn (automóvil) || to nosedive (avión).

capotazo *m* TAUR pass with a cape.

capote *m* capote, cape (prenda de abrigo) || MIL greatcoat || TAUR cape; *lucirse con el capote* to be brilliant with the cape; *capote de paseo* ceremonial cape || slam (en el juego de naipes) || AMER hiding, beating, thrashing (paliza) || — AMER *capote de monte* poncho || *dar capote* to win all the tricks (naipes) || FIG & FAM *echar un capote a uno* to give s.o. a helping hand, to help s.o. out || *para mí, tu, su capote* to myself, yourself, himself.

capotear *vt* TAUR to make passes using the cape || FIG & FAM to stall, to put off (entretener con promesas, etc.) | to get out of, to dodge (dificultades).

capoteo *m* TAUR cape work, passes with the cape || FIG & FAM trickery (engaño) | shirking (escamoteo).

capotera *f* AMER coat hanger.

capotillo *m* short cape || TAUR *capotillo de paseo* ceremonial cape.

Capricornio *npr m* ASTR Capricorn.

capricho *m* whim, fancy, caprice; *los caprichos de la moda* the whims of fashion || fancy (deseo) || frill (adorno) || MÚS caprice, capriccio || — *hacer algo a capricho* to do sth. as the fancy takes one || *le dio el capricho de tomar fresas* she suddenly fancied some strawberries.

caprichoso, sa *adj* whimsical, fanciful, capricious; *un niño muy caprichoso* a very whimsical child.

cápsico *m* BOT capsicum (planta).

cápsula *f* capsule (de un cohete, de las plantas, de medicamentos) || top, cap (de botella, de envase) || MIL cap (de proyectil) || QUÍM dish || ANAT capsule; *cápsulas suprarrenales* suprarenal capsules || *poner cápsulas a* to cap.

capsulado *m* capping.

capsuladora *f* capping machine.

capsular *adj* ANAT & BOT capsular.

capsular *vt* to cap.

captación *f* harnessing (de aguas) || reception (de ondas) || grasping, comprehension (comprensión) || *captación de partidarios* winning *o* convincing of supporters.

captar *vt* to harness (aguas) || RAD to pick up, to receive (ondas) || to grasp; *captar el sentido de una palabra* to grasp the meaning of a word || to hold; *captar la atención del oyente* to hold the attention of the listener || to win, to get (la confianza, etc.) || to win over (partidarios, etc.).

◆ *vpr* to win, to gain, to capture; *captarse la amistad de todos* to win everyone's friendship.

captura *f* capture; *la captura de un criminal* the capture of a criminal.

capturar *vt* to capture, to seize.

capucha *f* hood || IMPR circumflex accent || pouch (de pulpo).

capuchino, na *adj* Capuchin.

◆ *m* Capuchin monk || Capuchin monkey (mono).

◆ *f* Capuchin nun (monja) || BOT nasturtium || small lamp.

capuchón *m* hood (de abrigo) || capuchin (capa) || cap (de pluma estilográfica) || TECN valve cap (válvula).

capullo *m* cocoon (de insecto) || BOT bud (de flor) | cup (de bellota) || coarse spun silk (tela de seda) || ANAT prepuce.

capuz *m* hood (capuchón) || type of cloak *o* cape (capa).

caquéctico, ca *adj* MED cachectic.

caquexia *f* MED cachexy, cachexia.

caqui *m* BOT persimmon (árbol y fruto) || khaki (color) || FIG & FAM *ponerse el caqui* to dress in khaki (soldado).

◆ *adj inv* khaki; *una camisa caqui* a khaki shirt.

cara *f* face; *la cara de un niño* a child's face; *asomar la cara* to show one's face || expression, face; *juzgar por la cara* to judge by one's expression; *me recibió con buena cara* he received me with a friendly face || head (de una moneda); *si sale cara ganas tú* if it's heads you win || side; *las dos caras de una hoja, de un disco* the two sides of a sheet, of a record || face, surface (superficie) || FIG side; *las dos caras de un asunto* the two sides of a matter || right side (anverso) || MAT & ARQ face || FIG & FAM nerve, cheek; *ese tío tiene mucha cara* that fellow has got a lot of cheek || FIG look (cariz); *no me gusta la cara de este asunto* I do not like the look of this affair || — FIG *a cara descubierta* openly | *caérsele a uno la cara de vergüenza* to die of shame, to blush with shame || *cara a* facing (hacia); *cara a la pared, al sol* facing the wall, the sun; into, towards; *andar cara al viento* to walk into the wind || *cara a cara* face to face; *a la vuelta de la esquina se encontraron cara a cara* round the corner they met face to face; in private; *tener una conversación cara a cara* to hold a conversation in private; to one's face; *decir algo a alguien cara a cara* to say sth. to s.o.'s face || *cara adelante, atrás* forwards, backwards || FIG *cara de circunstancias* serious look | *cara de Cuaresma* or *de viernes* sad *o* dismal face | *cara de perro* scowling face | *cara de pascua* or *de risa* cheerful *o* smiling face | *cara de pocos amigos* or *de vinagre* sour *o* grim *o* unfriendly face | *cara dura* nerve, cheek (descaro) | *cara larga* long face || FAM *cruzar la cara a uno* to hit s.o. across the face, to slap s.o.'s face || *dar con la puerta en la cara a uno* to shut the door in s.o.'s face || FIG *dar la cara* to face up to things (afrontar) | *dar la cara por uno* to stand up for s.o., to defend s.o. (defender), to answer for s.o., to vouch for s.o. (salir fiador) || *decir algo a uno en su cara* to say sth. to s.o.'s face || INFORM *doble cara* double-sided (disquete) || FIG *echar algo en cara a uno* to throw sth. in s.o.'s face || *echar* or *jugarse algo a cara o cruz* to toss (up) for sth. || *en la cara se le conoce* one can see it in his face || *hacer cara a* to face (afrontar) || FAM *no lo hice por tu bella* or *linda cara* I didn't do it because I like your face *o* for your pretty face || FIG *no mirar la cara a alguien* not to be on speaking terms with s.o. || *no saber qué cara poner* not to know what to do with o.s. *o* where to put o.s. || FAM *nos veremos las caras* I'll see you later (amenaza) || FIG *no tener cara para hacer algo* not to dare to do sth., not to have the nerve to do sth. || *no volver la cara atrás* not to look back || FIG *plantar cara a alguien* to face up to s.o. | *poner a mal tiempo buena cara* to keep a stiff upper lip, to keep one's chin up, to look on the bright side || *poner buena cara* to look happy *o* pleased || FIG *poner buena cara a algo* to take sth. well | *poner buena cara a alguien* to be nice to s.o. || *poner cara de* to look like (con sustantivo), to look as if (con verbo) || *poner cara de asco* to look disgusted || FIG *poner mala cara* or *cara larga* to pull a face *o* a long face || *reírse en la cara de alguien* to laugh in s.o.'s face || FAM *romper la cara* to smash s.o.'s face (in) || FIG *sacar la cara por alguien* to stick up for s.o. || *tener cara de* to look; *tener cara de tristeza* to look sad || *tener cara de alma en pena* or *de duelo* to have a face as long as a fiddle || FIG *tener dos caras* to be two-faced || *tener el sol de cara* to be facing the sun || *tener el viento de cara* to be facing into the wind || *tener mala cara* to look bad || FIG & FAM *tener más cara que un buey con paperas* to have a lot of cheek, to be a cheeky devil || *terciar la cara a uno* to slash s.o.'s face || *tiene cara de no haber dormido* he looks as if he hasn't slept || *volver la cara* to turn away, to look the other way.

caraba *f* FAM *éste es la caraba* he's the limit | *esto es la caraba* this is the end *o* the limit *o* the last straw.

carabao *m* carabao (buffalo).

cárabe *m* amber (ámbar).

carabela *f* MAR caravel, carvel.

carabina *f* carbine, rifle (arma) || FIG chaperon, chaperone (que acompaña) || — FAM *eso es la carabina de Ambrosio* that's as much good as a poultice on a wooden leg || FIG & FAM *ir* or *hacer de carabina* to be chaperon (vigilar a una pareja), to play gooseberry (llevar la cesta).

carabinero *m* customs officer || large prawn (crustáceo).

◆ *m pl* AMER the police.

— OBSERV In Spain the name *carabineros* was given to the body of armed policemen whose main function is the suppression of smuggling.

cárabo *m* carabus, carabid beetle (coleóptero) || tawny owl (autillo).

caracará *f* AMER caracara (bird of prey).

Caracas *npr f* GEOGR Caracas.

caracol *m* ZOOL snail (molusco terrestre) | winkle (de mar) || sea shell, conch (concha) || CULIN snail; *purgar los caracoles* to purge the snails || kiss-curl (rizo) || snail wheel (de reloj) || ANAT cochlea || *escalera de caracol* spiral staircase.

◆ *pl* Andalusian folk song || *hacer caracoles* to caracol, to caracole (el caballo).

◆ *interj* ¡*caracoles!* goodness me! (asombro, sorpresa), damn it! (enfado).

caracola *f* ZOOL conch.

caracolada *f* dish made from snails.

caracolear *vi* to caracole, to prance (hacer caracoles un caballo).

caracoleo *m* caracole.

caracolillo *m* BOT snail-flowered kidney bean (judía) || pea-bean coffee (café) || densely grained mahogany (caoba).

carácter *m* character (genio, personalidad); *una pintura, un hombre de mucho carácter* a painting, a man with a lot of character || kind, nature (índole) || characteristic (característica) || IMPR & INFORM character || handwriting (letra manuscrita) || character (personaje de un libro) || — *caracteres de imprenta* type, typeface || *con carácter de* as; *con carácter de embajador* as an ambassador || *escribir en caracteres de imprenta* to write in block letters || *persona de poco carácter* person with a weak character || *tener buen carácter* to be good-natured || *tener mal carácter* to be bad-tempered.

— OBSERV pl *caracteres.* (Note the transferring of the stress in the plural.).

característico, ca *adj* characteristic, typical; *una cualidad característica* a characteristic quality.

◆ *m/f* TEATR character actor (actor, actriz).

◆ *f* characteristic, feature (particularidad); *la cortesía es una característica de los japoneses* politeness is a characteristic of the Japanese; *las características de un avión* the characteristics of a plane || MAT characteristic (del logaritmo).

caracterización *f* characterization.

caracterizado, da *adj* characterized || special, peculiar (especial) || distinguished (notable); *un científico caracterizado* a distinguished scientist.

caracterizar *vt* to characterize (distinguir) || to portray, to capture, to characterize; *el escritor ha caracterizado brillantemente el ambiente* the writer portrays the atmosphere brilliantly || TEATR to play well.

◆ *vpr* to be characterized || to make up (un actor).

caracterología *f* characterology.

caracú *m* AMER marrow (tuétano).

caracul *m* caracul, karakul (piel y carnero).

caradura *m/f* FAM cheeky devil (fresco).

◆ *f* FAM nerve, cheek; *tener mucha caradura* to have a lot of cheek || ¡*qué caradura es!* he's got a nerve!, of all the nerve!

◆ *adj* FAM cheeky, shameless || ¡*qué tío más caradura!* what a nerve!, he's got a nerve!

carajillo *m* FAM coffee with brandy.

carajo *m* POP prick ‖ — POP *carajo!* bloody hell! | *¡vete al carajo!* go to hell!, get stuffed!

caramanchel *m* MAR hatch cover (escotillón) ‖ slum, hovel (tugurio) ‖ AMER snack bar, cheap restaurant, eating house (figón).

¡caramba! *interj* goodness me! (asombro, sorpresa), damn it! (enfado) ‖ *¡caramba con él!* to hell with him!

carámbano *m* icicle.

carambola *f* cannon [US carom] (billar) ‖ FIG & FAM fluke; *he aprobado por carambola* I passed by a fluke | trick (faena hecha a alguien).

carambolear *vt* to cannon [US to carom] (billar).

caramelizar *vt* to caramel, to caramelize.

caramelo *m* sweet [US candy] (golosina) ‖ caramel (azúcar fundida y pasta de azúcar) ‖ — *a punto de caramelo* syrupy (el azúcar), tasty (sabroso) ‖ *caramelo blando* caramel, toffee ‖ FAM *de caramelo* excellent.

caramillo *m* MÚS pipe, shawm (ant) ‖ pile, heap (montón) ‖ FIG piece of gossip, tale (chisme) | fuss (enredo).

carancho *m* AMER owl (búho) | caracara (caracará).

carángano *m* AMER louse (piojo).

carantoña *f* FIG & FAM mutton dressed as lamb (mujer vieja y presumida).
◆ *pl* flattery *sing*, soft soap *sing (fam)*, coaxing *sing* (zalamerías) ‖ caresses (caricias) ‖ *hacerle carantoñas a alguien* to caress s.o. (acariciar), to butter s.o. up, to soft-soap s.o. (para conseguir algo).

carantoñero, ra *m/f* coaxer, flatterer.

caraota *f* AMER bean (judía).

carapacho *m* carapace (de tortuga, de cangrejo, etc.).

¡carape! *interj* goodness me! (asombro, sorpresa), damn it! (enfado).

caraqueño, ña *adj* [from *o* of] Caracas (Venezuela).
◆ *m/f* inhabitant *o* native of Caracas.

carátula *f* mask (careta) ‖ FAM theatre, stage (teatro); *dejó la espada por la carátula* he left the army for the theatre ‖ AMER title page (de un libro) | dial, face (de reloj).

caravana *f* caravan (de camellos, de peregrinos) ‖ long line *o* queue (de coches, etc.) ‖ caravan [US trailer] (remolque).
◆ *pl* AMER earrings (pendientes) | courtesies, compliments ‖ *en caravana* in Indian file, in single file.

caravanero *m* caravaneer (de camellos).

caravaning *m* caravanning.

caravanseray; caravasar; caravaserrallo *m* caravanserai, caravansary.

¡caray! *interj* goodness me!, good Lord! (asombro, sorpresa), damn it! (enfado).

carbohidrato *m* carbohydrate (hidrato de carbono).

carbón *m* coal (combustible) ‖ carbon paper (para reproducir) ‖ charcoal (para dibujar) ‖ ELECTR carbon ‖ — *carbón de bola* ovoid ‖ *carbón de gas* gas coal ‖ *carbón de leña* or *vegetal* charcoal ‖ *carbón de piedra* or *mineral* coal ‖ *carbón en polvo* coal dust ‖ *carbón vegetal* charcoal ‖ *copia al carbón* carbon copy ‖ *cubo del carbón* coal scuttle ‖ *negro como el carbón* black as coal ‖ *papel carbón* carbon paper ‖ FAM *se acabó el carbón* that's that, that's it.

carbonada *f* load of coal (paletada de carbón) ‖ dish made of stewed meat which is then grilled (plato de carne) ‖ AMER stew [made from meat, potatoes, maize, rice and marrow] (guisado).

carbonado *m* MIN black diamond, carbonado (diamante negro).

carbonar *vt* to turn into charcoal.

carbonario *m* HIST carbonaro.

carbonatación *f* carbonation, carbonatation.

carbonatar *vt* QUÍM to carbonate.

carbonato *m* QUÍM carbonate.

carboncillo *m* charcoal; *dibujo al carboncillo* charcoal drawing ‖ AUT carbon.

carbonear *vt* to turn into charcoal.

carboneo *m* charcoal making.

carbonera *f* charcoal stack *o* pile (para hacer carbón) ‖ coal cellar *o* bunker (para guardar carbón) ‖ MAR coal bunker, bunker ‖ coalmine (mina) ‖ AMER coal tender (de locomotora).

carbonería *f* coal merchant's yard, coalyard.

carbonero, ra *adj* coal; *industria carbonera* coal industry ‖ charcoal ‖ *barco carbonero* collier.
◆ *m* coal merchant, coalman, coalheaver ‖ collier (barco) ‖ FIG *la fe del carbonero* simple faith.

carbónico, ca *adj* QUÍM carbonic; *gas, ácido carbónico* carbonic gas, acid ‖ *anhídrido carbónico* carbon dioxide, carbonic acid gas.

carbonífero, ra *adj* carboniferous ‖ GEOL *el período carbonífero* the Carboniferous, the Carboniferous Period.

carbonilla *f* coaldust (polvo de carbón) ‖ soot (de la locomotora) ‖ AMER charcoal (carboncillo).

carbonizar *vt* to carbonize (transformar en carbón) ‖ to burn, to char (quemar) ‖ *quedar carbonizado* to be burnt to a cinder (una cosa), to be electrocuted (electrocutarse), to be burnt down (un edificio).
◆ *vpr* to carbonize.

carbono *m* QUÍM carbon; *ciclo del carbono* carbon cycle ‖ *bióxido* or *dióxido de carbono* carbon dioxide.

carbonoso, sa *adj* carbonaceous.

carbunclo; carbunco *m* MED carbuncle (tumor) | anthrax (enfermedad).

carbunclo; carbúnculo *m* carbuncle (piedra preciosa).

carburación *f* carburation [US carburetion] (de un motor) ‖ carburization (en metalurgia) ‖ QUÍM carburetting.

carburador *m* carburettor *o* carburetter [US carburetor, carbureter].

carburante *m* fuel.

carburar *vt* to carburate, to carburet (un motor) ‖ FIG & FAM to go strong, to go well.

carburo *m* QUÍM carbide; *carburo de calcio* calcium carbide.

carca *adj/s* FAM carlist ‖ FIG & FAM reactionary (reaccionario) | square (chapado a la antigua).

carcaj *m* quiver (caja de las flechas) ‖ standard holder (de la bandera) ‖ AMER holster (de arma de fuego).

carcajada *f* burst of laughter, guffaw ‖ — *reír a carcajadas* to split one's sides laughing ‖ *soltar la carcajada* to burst out laughing.

carcajear *vi* to laugh heartily, to roar with laughter.
◆ *vpr* to laugh heartily, to roar with laughter ‖ FIG *me carcajeo de tus principios* I laugh at your principles, your principles make me laugh, principles be damned.

carcamal *m* FAM old fogy *o* old fogey (persona vieja).

cárcel *f* prison, gaol, jail; *salir de la cárcel* to come out of prison ‖ TECN clamp (herramienta) | groove (ranura) ‖ *cárcel de alta seguridad* high *o* top security wing.

carcelario, ria *adj* prison, gaol, jail; *la vida carcelaria es dura* prison life is hard.

carcelero, ra *adj* prison, gaol, jail (carcelario).
◆ *m/f* gaoler, jailer, warder.
◆ *f* Andalusian folk song.

carcinogénesis *f* MED carcinogenesis.

carcinógeno, na *adj* MED carcinogen.

carcinoide *m* MED carcinoid.

carcinoma *m* MED carcinoma, cancer.

carcinomatoso, sa *adj* carcinomatous.

cárcola *f* pedal (del telar).

carcoma *f* ZOOL woodworm ‖ wood dust (polvo de la madera) ‖ FIG & FAM anxiety, grief (preocupación) | spendthrift (persona gastosa).

carcomer *vt* to eat away, to eat into (la madera) ‖ FIG to gnaw (at), to eat up, to consume; *le carcomía la envidia* he was gnawed *o* eaten up by envy | to undermine (la salud).
◆ *vpr* to become eaten away, to become worm-eaten ‖ FIG to waste away, to decay.

carcomido, da *adj* eaten away, worm-eaten (madera) ‖ FIG eaten away, rotten (podrido) | undermined (salud).

carda *f* carding (acción) ‖ teasel (cabeza de la cardencha) ‖ card, teasel (instrumento) ‖ FIG & FAM telling off, dressing down, scolding (reprimenda).

cardado *m* TECN carding ‖ back-combing (del pelo).

cardador, ra *m/f* TECN carder (persona).
◆ *m* ZOOL millepede.
◆ *f* TECN carder, carding machine (máquina).

cardadura *f* carding.

cardamomo *m* cardamom (planta).

cardán *f* TECN cardan, cardan joint (articulación).

cardar *vt* to card (la lana) ‖ to back-comb (el pelo) ‖ FIG *unos cobran la fama y otros cardan la lana* some people do all the work while others get the credit.

cardenal *m* cardinal (prelado, pájaro) ‖ bruise (equimosis) ‖ AMER geranium.

cardenalato *m* cardinalate, cardinalship.

cardenalicio, cia *adj* of a cardinal, cardinal's; *la púrpura cardenalicia* cardinal's purple ‖ *colegio cardenalicio* college of cardinals.

cardencha *f* BOT card thistle ‖ TECN card, teasel (carda).

cardenillo *m* verdigris ‖ *criar cardenillo* to become covered with verdigris.

cárdeno, na *adj* cardinal red (color) ‖ black and white (color de reses) ‖ opaline blue (líquidos) ‖ livid (lívido).

cardiáceo, cea *adj* heart-shaped.

cardiaco, ca; cardíaco, ca *adj* cardiac, heart; *enfermedad cardiaca* cardiac illness ‖ — *ataque cardiaco* heart attack ‖ *tónico cardiaco* heart tonic.
◆ *m/f* heart sufferer, sufferer of a heart disease.

cardias *m* ANAT cardia (del estómago).

cardillo *m* BOT golden thistle.

cardinal *adj* cardinal; *los puntos cardinales* the cardinal points; *las virtudes cardinales* the cardinal virtues; *número cardinal* cardinal number.

cardioangiología *f* MED cardioangiology.

cardiografía *f* MED cardiography.

cardiográfico, ca *adj* MED cardiographic.

cardiógrafo *m* MED cardiograph (instrumento).

cardiograma *m* MED cardiogram.

cardiología *f* MED cardiology.

cardiológico, ca *adj* cardiological.

cardiólogo, ga *m/f* cardiologist.

cardiomegalia *f* MED cardiomegaly.

cardiópata *adj* MED cardiopathic.
◆ *m/f* MED heart patient.

cardiotónico *m* MED heart tonic.

cardioversión *f* MED cardioversion, defibrillation.

carditis *f* MED carditis.

cardizal *m* land covered with thistles.

cardo *m* cardoon (planta comestible) || thistle (planta espinosa) || — *cardo borriquero* cotton thistle || FIG *ser un cardo (borriquero)* to be a prickly customer.

cardón *m* card, teasel (instrumento para cardar) || carding (acción de cardar) || *AMER* type of giant cactus.

Cardona *n pr* *más listo que Cardona* as sharp as a needle.

cardoncillo *m* BOT milk thistle.

cardume; cardumen *m* shoal of fish (banco de peces) || *AMER* abundance, great quantity.

carear *vt* JUR to confront, to bring face to face; *carear a dos personas* to bring two people face to face || FIG to compare (cosas).
◆ *v pr* to come face to face (entrevistarse).

carecer* *vi* to lack; *carecer de los recursos necesarios* to lack the necessary resources || — *carecer de sentido* to make no sense, not to make sense, to lack meaning || *no podemos empezar careciendo de tantas cosas* we can't start with so many things lacking *o* missing.

carena; carenadura *f* MAR careening || AUT & AVIAC streamlining.

carenar *vt* MAR to careen || AUT & AVIAC to streamline.

carencia *f* lack, shortage; *carencia de datos* lack of data || deficiency; *enfermedad por carencia* deficiency disease.

carenero *m* MAR careenage (lugar).

carente *adj* lacking; *carente de datos* lacking (in) data.

careo *m* JUR confrontation (de personas) | comparison (de cosas).

carero, ra *adj* expensive, dear; *este carnicero es muy carero* this butcher is very expensive.
◆ *m/f* expensive *o* dear shopkeeper.

carestía *f* shortage, scarcity (escasez) || high price, high cost (precio subido); *la carestía de la vida* the high cost of living.

careta *f* mask || — *careta antigás* or *contra gases* gasmask || FIG *quitarle la careta a uno* to unmask s.o.

carey *m* sea turtle (tortuga) || turtleshell (caparazón) || tortoiseshell; *un peine de carey* a tortoiseshell comb.

carga *f* load (peso y cosas llevadas) || loading (acción); *la carga de un camión* the loading of a lorry || refill (de bolígrafo, de estilográfica) || MAR cargo (lo contenido) || charge (de pólvora) || ELECTR charge (de un condensador) | load (en un circuito) || INFORM loading || FOT magazine || DEP charge (en fútbol) || MIL charge; *carga de caballería* cavalry charge || FIG burden; *la carga de los años* the burden of the years | liability, obligation (obligación) | responsibility; *las cargas de un ministro* the responsibilities of a minister | tax, duty, charge (impuesto); *propiedad libre de cargas* property free from taxes | contribution, payment; *cargas sociales* social contributions || — *andén de carga* loading platform || MIL *a paso de carga* at the double || MAR *barco de carga* cargo boat, freighter || *bestia de carga* beast of burden || *carga de familia* dependent relative || *carga de pólvora* blasting powder || *carga de profundidad* depth charge || *carga máxima* maximum load, peak load || *carga útil de un vehículo* carrying capacity *o* payload of a vehicle || FIG *llevar la carga de algo* to be responsible for sth., to be in charge of sth. || *permitido carga y descarga* loading and unloading || MIL *tocar paso de carga* to sound the charge || *tomar carga* to load up (un camión, etc.) || *volver a la carga* to renew the attack *o* the assault, to charge again (las tropas), to keep at it (insistir).

cargadero *m* loading base || loading platform (de estación) || ARQ lintel (dintel).

cargado, da *adj* loaded || FIG burdened, weighed down (de penas, de problemas, etc.) || heavy (tiempo) || MIL live (bala) || ELECTR charged (pila), live (hilo) || heavy, dense; *ambiente cargado* heavy atmosphere || stuffy; *tener la cabeza cargada* to have a stuffy head || strong; *un whisky muy cargado* a very strong whisky || — *cargado de años* burdened by the years || *cargado de espaldas* round-shouldered || FIG & FAM *estar un poco cargado* to be tipsy (borracho) | *tener los ojos cargados* to have heavy eyes || *un árbol cargado de fruto* a tree laden with fruit.

cargador, ra *adj* *pala cargadora* mechanical digger.
◆ *m* loader (sentido general) || docker, stevedore (de los muelles) || stoker (de alto horno) || MIL chamber | ramrod (de cañones) || TECN charger (de acumuladores, etc.) || filler (de bolígrafo, de pluma) || *AMER* porter || FOT cartridge.
◆ *f* mechanical digger.

cargamento *m* MAR cargo || load, shipment (de camión).

cargante *adj* FIG & FAM annoying, tiresome.

cargar *vt* to load (una acémila, un barco, un arma de fuego, una máquina de foto) || to fill (una pluma estilográfica) || to hold; *este depósito carga mil litros* this reservoir holds a thousand litres || to stoke (un horno) || FIG to charge (un precio) || JUR to charge, to accuse || ELECTR to charge (batería) || INFORM to load || FIG to burden, to weigh down (con penas, impuestos, deudas) | to fill (la imaginación, etc.) | to levy, to impose (un impuesto) || FIG & FAM to annoy, to get on one's nerves (molestar); *este niño me carga* this child annoys me | to load with; *me han cargado este trabajo* they've loaded me with this work | to place (la responsabilidad) | to put, to lay; *le cargaron la culpa* they put the blame on him || to trump (naipes) || to load (dados) || MAR to take in (las velas) || MIL to charge; *cargar al enemigo* to charge the enemy || *AMER* to wear (ropa) | to carry (llevar consigo) || — COM *cargar algo en cuenta a uno* to debit s.o.'s account with sth; *le hemos cargado esta cantidad en cuenta* we have debited your account with this amount; to charge sth. to s.o.'s account (en un almacén, etc.) || FAM *cargar la cuenta* to overcharge, to add to the bill || *cargar la mano* to insist, to lay stress (*de* on) (insistir), to put one's foot down, to crack down (tener rigor), to be too strict (ser demasiado severo), to overcharge (*en* on) (en los precios), to add too much, to go heavy on [a certain ingredient to a stew, etc.] (con un ingrediente, etc.) | *cargar las tintas* to lay it on || FIG *cargar una salsa de especias* to put too much spice in a sauce, to overdo the spice in a sauce | *me cargaron de menos* they undercharged me.
◆ *vi* to load (up) (un camión, etc.) || to rest; *el peso del arco carga sobre el contrafuerte* the weight of the arch rests on the buttress || to come down on, to sweep down on (tempestad, ejército) || to take charge (encargarse) || to take, to pick up; *yo he cargado con el paquete* I have taken the parcel || FIG to take, to shoulder; *cargar con la responsabilidad, con la culpa* to take the responsibility, the blame | to rest, to fall; *los impuestos cargan sobre el pueblo* the taxes rest on the people | to bear (the burden of); *el pueblo carga con los impuestos* the people bear the burden of the taxes | to be annoying, to be a nuisance; *este niño carga* this child is annoying || GRAM to fall (el acento) || — FAM *cargar con las consecuencias* to suffer the consequences | *cargar con uno* to take charge of s.o. | *cargar sobre alguien* to press s.o., to pester s.o.
◆ *vpr* to become overcast (el cielo, el tiempo) || to become oppressive (la atmósfera) || to fill; *se le cargaron los ojos de lágrimas* his eyes filled with tears || to load o.s., to burden o.s.; *cargarse de preocupaciones* to load o.s. with worries || to overburden o.s.; *me cargué de deudas* I overburdened myself with debts || ELECTR to become charged (pila), to become live (cable) || FAM to smash; *me he cargado este reloj* I have smashed this watch | to get o.s.; *se cargó seis meses de cárcel* he got himself six months in prison | to bump off, to knock off (matar) | to bring (about) the downfall of, to topple (derribar); *cargarse a un gobierno* to bring about the downfall of a government | to fail, to plough (suspender); *cargarse a un alumno* to fail a pupil | to get bored (fastidiarse) || — *cargarse de años* to get very old || *cargarse de paciencia* to summon up *o* to muster up one's patience || FAM *cargársela* to get into trouble.

cargazón *f* MAR cargo (cargamento) || heavy feeling (del estómago, de la cabeza) || overcast sky (de nubes) || *AMER* good harvest (de frutos) || *cargazón de espaldas* stoop.

cargo *m* post; *desempeñar un cargo de profesor* to have a teacher's post || charge, accusation; *formular graves cargos* to make serious charges || charge (responsabilidad); *tener alguien a su cargo* to have s.o. in one's charge || COM charge, debit || MAR cargo boat, freighter (buque de carga) || — *a cargo de uno* in one's charge || *con cargo a* charged to; *gastos con cargo a mi cuenta* expenses charged to my account || *correr a cargo de* it is the responsability of (incumbir a), it is to be paid by (estar pagado por), it is in the hands of (depender de) || *cuenta a cargo* charge account || *es un cargo de conciencia* it is a weight on one's conscience || *girar* or *librar a cargo de* to draw on || *hacerse cargo de* to take charge of || *hacerse cargo de la gravedad de la situación* to realize the gravity of the situation || *hacerse cargo de la situación* to understand the situation || *jurar un cargo* to take an oath || *las tropas se hicieron cargo del poder* the troops took over power, the troops seized power || JUR *testigo de cargo* witness for the prosecution.

cargosear *vt* *AMER* to pester (molestar).

carguero *m* *AMER* beast of burden (acémila) | cargo boat, freighter (barco) | transport plane (avión).

cari *adj* *AMER* lead grey (gris plomo).
◆ *m* curry (especia).

cariacontecido, da *adj* down in the mouth, dejected, crestfallen.

cariado, da *adj* decayed, carious (dientes).

cariancho, cha *adj* broad-faced, with a broad face.

cariar *vt* to cause to decay (dientes).
◆ *vpr* to decay.

cariátide *f* ARQ caryatid.

Caríbdis *n pr* → **escila.**

caribe *adj* Caribbean || *mar Caribe* Caribbean Sea.
◆ *m/f* Carib.
◆ *m* Carib (lengua).

caribú *m* ZOOL caribou.

caricato *m* comedian (actor cómico).

caricatura *f* caricature.

caricaturesco, ca *adj* caricatural.

caricaturista *m/f* caricaturist.

caricaturizar *vt* to caricature.

caricia *f* stroke; *hacer una caricia al gato* to give the cat a stroke || caress (muestra de cariño) || *hacer caricias a* to stroke, to caress.

caridad *f* charity (virtud, limosna); *vivir de la caridad* to live on charity || — REL *Hermana de la Caridad* sister of charity || FIG *la caridad bien entendida comienza por uno mismo* charity begins at home || *¡por caridad!* for pity's sake!

caries *f inv* decay, caries.

carilampiño, ña *adj* beardless, smooth-faced.

carilargo, ga *adj* FAM long-faced, with a long face.

carilla *f* side, page (de una hoja de papel) || mask (de colmenero).

carillón *m* MÚS carillon (campanas y sonido).

carimba *f*; **carimbo** *m* brand (marca con hierro candente) || branding iron (hierro candente).

cariñito *m* FAM caress (caricia) | little darling (apelativo cariñoso).

cariño *f* affection; *tener mucho cariño a alguien* to have a lot of affection for s.o. || loving care (esmero); *hacer una cosa con cariño* to do sth. with loving care || FIG caress (caricia) || — *¡cariño mío!* my darling! || *sentir cariño por alguien, tener cariño a alguien* to be fond of s.o. || *tener cariño a una cosa* to be attached to sth., to cherish sth. || *tomar cariño a* to get attached to, to take a liking to (a uno, a una cosa).
◆ *pl* love (en una carta).

cariñoso, sa *adj* affectionate, loving (afectuoso); *una carta muy cariñosa* a very affectionate letter || nice; *estuvieron muy cariñosos conmigo* they were very nice to me || *recibir a alguien con un cariñoso saludo* to greet s.o. warmly *o* fondly.

carioca *adj* from Rio de Janeiro, of Rio de Janeiro.
◆ *m/f* person from *o* inhabitant of Rio de Janeiro.

carioplasma *m* karyoplasm.

cariópside *f* BOT caryopsis.

carisma *m* charisma, charism.

carismático, ca *adj* charismatic.

caritativo, va *adj* charitable; *caritativo con los pobres* charitable towards the poor.

carite *m* AMER edible fish from Venezuela.

cariz *m* look; *no me gusta el cariz de este asunto* I don't like the look of this business || look of the weather (del tiempo) || *la situación presenta mal cariz* the situation looks bad.

carlanca *f* mastiff's collar (collar con púas para el perro).

carlinga *f* MAR & AVIAC cockpit (del piloto) | cabin (de los pasajeros).

carlismo *m* Carlism.

carlista *adj/s* Carlist; *guerras carlistas* Carlist Wars.

Carlomagno *npr m* Charlemagne.

Carlos *npr m* Charles.

Carlota *npr f* Charlotte.

carmañola *f* carmagnole.

carmelita *adj/s* REL Carmelite; *la orden carmelita* the Carmelite order || *un carmelita, una carmelita* a Carmelite monk, nun.
◆ *adj/sf* light brown (color).
◆ *f* flower of a type of cress.

carmelitano, na *adj* REL Carmelite.

Carmelo *npr m* Carmel (monte de Palestina).

carmen *m* villa [in Granada] || POÉT verse (verso).

Carmen *npr m* REL Carmelite order (orden).
◆ *f* Carmen [girl's name].

carmenador *m* large-toothed comb (peine) || carder (para la lana).

carmenadura *f* combing, disentangling (el pelo) || carding (la lana).

carmenar; escarmenar *vt* to comb, to disentangle (el pelo) || to card (la lana) || FIG & FAM to fleece, to rob (robar).

carmesí *adj/sm* crimson (color).
◆ *m* cochineal powder.

carmín *adj inv* carmine, crimson (color).
◆ *m* carmine, crimson (color) || BOT wild rose || *carmín de labios* lipstick.

carminativo, va *adj/sm* carminative.

carmíneo, a *adj* carmine, crimson.

carnación *f* flesh colour.

carnada *f* bait [meat] (cebo).

carnadura *f* robustness (de una persona) || healing capacity (disposición para cicatrizar).

carnal *adj* carnal || sensual (sensual) || full, blood; *hermano carnal* full brother || FIG material.

carnauba *f* BOT carnauba.

carnaval *m* carnival || REL shrovetide || *Martes de Carnaval* Shrove Tuesday.

carnavalesco, ca *adj* carnivalesque || FIG ludicrous, absurd, farcical (grotesco).

carnaza *f* (p us) derma (cara interior de las pieles) || meat (carne) || AMER bait [meat] (cebo) | scapegoat (cabeza de turco).

carne *f* ANAT flesh (tejidos) || FIG flesh (cuerpo); *la carne es flaca* the flesh is weak || meat (comestible); *carne poco hecha, congelada* rare, frozen meat || flesh (de los frutos) || heart (de un árbol) || — FIG *abrírsele las carnes a uno* to be frightened to death || *carne de cañón* cannon fodder (soldados) || FIG *carne de gallina* goosflesh, goose pimples, *pl*; *me pone la carne de gallina* it gives me goose pimples | *carne de horca* gallows bird || *carne de membrillo* quince preserve *o* jelly || FIG *carne de mi carne* flesh of my flesh || *carne de pelo* ground game || *carne de pluma* winged game || *carne de ternera* veal || *carne de vaca* beef || *carne magra* or *mollar* lean meat || *carne picada* mince, minced meat || *carne sin hueso* boned meat || *carne viva* raw flesh || *color carne* flesh colour || *criar* or *echar carnes* to put on weight || *de abundantes* or *muchas carnes* fat || *de pocas carnes* thin || FIG *echar* or *poner toda la carne en el asador* to put everything into it, to give it everything one has || *en carnes, en carne viva* naked, in the raw (*fam*) || *en carne y hueso* in the flesh || *en carne viva* red raw (la espalda, la piel etc.), like an unhealed wound; *el recuerdo de la guerra está todavía en carne viva* the memory of the war is still like an unhealed wound || FIG *herir en carne viva* to touch *o* to cut to the quick (ofender), to rub salt in a wound (volver a herir) || FAM *metido* or *metidito en carnes* plump, chubby || FIG *no ser ni carne ni pescado* to be neither fish nor fowl | *ser de carne y hueso* to be only human, to be flesh and blood | *ser uña y carne* to be inseparable, to be hand in glove || *temblarle a uno las carnes* to tremble with fright.

carné; carnet *m* card; *carné de identidad* identity card || pocket notebook (librito) || *carné de conducir* driving licence.
— OBSERV pl *carnés*.

carneada *f* AMER slaughtering.

carnear *vt* AMER to slaughter (matar reses) | to cheat, to trick (engañar) | to butcher, to slaughter (matar).

carnecería *f* butcher's shop, butcher's.
— OBSERV This word is sometimes used in Castile and Aragon instead of *carnicería*.

carnerada *f* flock of sheep.

carnero *m* sheep (animal vivo) || ram (macho de la oveja) || mutton (carne del animal) || sheepskin (piel) || cemetery (cementerio) || charnel house, ossuary (osario) || AMER llama | FIG sheep (sin voluntad) || — *carnero marino* seal (foca) || *carnero padre* or *morueco* ram || FIG *no hay tales carneros* it can't be true, there's no such thing.

carneruno, na *adj* sheep-like.

Carnestolendas *f pl* Carnival (época) || REL Shrovetide.

carnet *m* —> **carné.**

carnicería *f* butcher's shop, butcher's (tienda) || FIG massacre, slaughter, carnage (matanza); *la batalla de Stalingrado fue una carnicería* the battle of Stalingrad was a massacre || AMER slaughterhouse, abattoir (matadero).

carnicero, ra *adj* carnivorous (que mata para alimentarse); *el lobo es carnicero* the wolf is carnivorous || FAM fond of meat (person) || FIG & FAM blood-thirsty (cruel).
◆ *m* butcher || FIG butcher (hombre sanguinario) || carnivore (animal).

cárnico, ca *adj* meat; *industrias cárnicas* meat industries.

carnicol *m* hoof (pezuña).

carnívoro, ra *adj* carnivorous; *el hombre y el gato son carnívoros* man and the cat are carnivorous.
◆ *m* carnivore.

carnosidad *f* MED outgrowth (excrecencia) | proud flesh (en una herida) || fatness, plumpness (gordura).

carnoso, sa; carnudo, da *adj* fleshy; *fruto carnoso* fleshy fruit; *parte carnosa del brazo* fleshy part of the arm.

caro, ra *adj* expensive, dear; *hotel caro* expensive hotel; *la langosta es cara* lobster is expensive || dear; *caro amigo* dear friend.
◆ *adv* *pagar caro* to pay a high price, to pay a lot || *salir caro* to work out *o* to turn out dear *o* expensive || FIG *su error le costó caro* his mistake cost him dearly || *vender caro* to sell at a high price.
— OBSERV When used as an adverb, *caro* may or may not agree with the subject, whereas with the verbs *resultar, quedar, permanecer, seguir,* there must be agreement: *la casa me resultó cara* the house worked out expensive for me.

carocha *f* eggs *pl* (de algunos insectos).

Carolina *npr f* Caroline (nombre de mujer) || GEOGR Carolina; *Carolina del Norte* North Carolina.

carolingio, gia *adj/s* Carlovingian, Carolingian (de Carlomagno).

carolino, na *adj* caroline || GEOGR *islas Carolinas* Caroline Islands.

carota *m/f* FAM cheeky devil (caradura).

caroteno *m* QUÍM carotene, carrotene, carotin, carrotin.

carotenoide *m* QUÍM carotenoid, carotinoid.

carótida *f* ANAT carotid.

carotídeo, a *adj* ANAT carotid.

carozo *m* cob (de la mazorca de maíz) || stone (de aceituna, de melocotón, etc.).

carpa *f* carp (pez) || part of a bunch of grapes, small bunch of grapes (racimillo) || AMER tent (de camping) | big top (de circo) |

awning (toldo) | stall (en la feria) || — DEP *en carpa* pike (salto) | *salto de la carpa* jackknife.

carpanel *adj* MAT & ARQ basket-handle.

carpanta *f* FAM ravenous hunger (hambre) || AMER band *o* gang of rowdies (pandilla) || FAM *tener carpanta* to be ravenous *o* famished.

Cárpatos *npr mpl* Carpathian Mountains.

carpelo *m* BOT carpel (del pistilo).

carpeta *f* portfolio (cartones con cintas) || folder, file (cartón doblado); *ordenar los documentos en una carpeta* to arrange documents in a folder || briefcase (cartera) || table cover (de mesa) || blotting pad (para escribir) || *cerrar la carpeta* to close the file (de una investigación).

carpetazo (dar) *loc* FIG to shelve; *dar carpetazo a un asunto* to shelve a matter.

carpetovetónico, ca *adj* FIG & FAM Spanish to the core.

carpiano, na *adj* ANAT carpal.

carpincho *m* ZOOL capybara (capibara).

carpintería *f* carpentry, joinery (oficio y elementos de madera en una construcción) || carpenter's *o* joiner's shop (taller) || *carpintería metálica* metal structural work.

carpintero, ra *adj* carpenter; *abeja, hormiga, polilla carpintera* carpenter bee, ant, moth || *pájaro carpintero* woodpecker.
◆ *m* carpenter, joiner.

carpo *m* ANAT carpus.

carpología *f* BOT carpology (estudio de las frutas).

carpológico, ca *adj* BOT carpological.

carpólogo *m* BOT carpologist.

carraca *f* MAR carack, carrack (navío) || FIG old tub (barco viejo) | old crock (coche viejo) | decrepit old person (persona vieja) || (ant) shipyard || TECN ratchet brace (trinquete) || MÚS rattle (instrumento) || AMER jaw (quijada).

carraco, ca *adj* FAM decrepit.

Carracuca *n pr estar más perdido que Carracuca* to have no way out, to be doomed, to be hopelessly lost.

carrada *f* cartload (carga de un carro) || FAM heaps *pl*, loads *pl* (cantidad grande) || *ganar dinero a carradas* to rake in money.

carraleja *f* ZOOL black beetle with yellow stripes.

carrasca *f* BOT holm oak (encina pequeña).

carrascal *m* holm-oak forest || AMER stony ground (pedregal).

carraspear *vi* to clear one's throat (aclararse la voz) || to speak with a hoarse voice (hablar con voz ronca).

carraspeo *m*; **carraspera** *f* clearing of the throat || hoarseness (aspereza en la garganta) || *tener carraspera* to have a hoarse voice, to have a frog in one's throat (*fam*).

carrasposo, sa *adj* very hoarse (ronco) || AMER rough (áspero).

carrasqueño, ña *adj* rough (áspero).

carrera *f* DEP race; *carrera ciclista, de caballos, de sacos, de fondo* cycling, horse, sack, long-distance race; *carrera pedrestre* footrace | run (béisbol, cricket) || run (acción) || route; *la carrera de una procesión* the route of a procession || ride (de taxi) || TECN stroke (de émbolo) || FIG row, line; *carrera de árboles* row of trees | ladder (en la media) | life; *una carrera bien aprovechada* a life well spent || career; *la carrera diplomática, militar* the diplomatic, military career || profession (profesión) || course (de estudios) || ARQ girder, beam (viga) || avenue, boulevard (calle) || parting (raya del pelo) || ASTR course || — *abrir carrera* to set the pace || *a carrera tendida* at full speed || *a la carrera* at full speed || *carrera a campo traviesa* or *a campo través* cross-country running (deporte), cross-country race (una competición) || *carrera contra el reloj* race against the clock, race against time (en deporte), race against time (prisa) || *carrera de armamentos* arms race || *carrera de obstáculos* obstacle race (atletas), steeplechase (caballos) || *carrera sin obstáculos* flat race || *carrera de relevos* relay race || *carrera de vallas* hurdle race (atletas, caballos) || *cubrir la carrera* to line the route || *dar carrera a uno* to pay for s.o.'s studies, to send s.o. to university || *dar carrera libre a* to give free rein to || *darse una carrera* to hurry, to rush || FIG *de carrera* parrot-fashion; *recitar de carrera* to recite parrot-fashion || *exámenes de fin de carrera* finals, final examinations || FIG *hacer carrera* to get on; *este hombre ha hecho carrera en Australia* this man has got on in Australia || FAM *hacer la carrera* to solicit, to streetwalk (prostituta) || *hacer la carrera de derecho* to study law || *hacer una cosa a la carrera* to race through sth. || FAM *no puedo hacer carrera con* or *de mi hijo* I can't get anywhere with this son of mine, I am getting nowhere with this son of mine || *tener la carrera de derecho* to have a degree in law || *tomar carrera* to take a run (para saltar).
◆ *pl* DEP races.

carrerilla *f* MÚS run || ladder (en una media); *coger una carrerilla* to mend a ladder || — *saber de carrerilla* to have at one's fingertips, to know by heart, to know backwards || *tomar carrerilla* to take a run (para saltar).

carrerista *m* racegoer (aficionado a las carreras) || rider (ciclista) || runner (a pie) || punter (persona que apuesta).
◆ *f* FAM street prostitute, street-walker (ramera).

carreta *f* cart || — FIG *andar como una carreta* to go at a snail's pace || *carreta de bueyes* oxcart || *carreta de mano* barrow, handcart || FAM *tren carreta* slow train.

carretada *f* cartload (carga de una carreta) | FIG & FAM load, heap (gran cantidad) || FIG & FAM *naranjas a carretadas* loads of oranges.

carrete *m* bobbin, reel (de hilo) || spool (de película) || reel (de caña de pescar) || ELECTR coil; *carrete de inducción* induction coil || — *dar carrete* to pay out the line (pesca) || FIG *dar carrete a uno* to keep s.o. on a string.

carretear *vt* to cart (transportar en carro).

carretel *m* reel (de caña de pescar) || MAR winch (de la corredera) || AMER bobbin, reel (carrete).

carretera *f* road; *carretera secundaria* or *comarcal* B road [US secondary road]; *carretera de acceso* approach road || — *albergue de carretera* roadside hotel || *carretera de circunvalación* bypass, ring road || AMER *carretera de cuota* toll-road || *carretera general* or *nacional* A *o* arterial road [US arterial highway] || *carretera radial* radial road || *estrechamiento de carretera* road narrows (señal de tráfico) || *mapa de carreteras* road map || *por carretera* by road || *red de carreteras* road network.

carretería *f* cartwright's work (oficio) || cartwright's shop (taller).

carretero *adj* for vehicles || *camino carretero* cart track.
◆ *m* cartwright (constructor) || cart driver, carter (conductor) || AMER road (carretera) || FIG *blasfemar* or *jurar como un carretero* to swear like a trooper.

carretilla *f* wheelbarrow, barrow (de jardinero, etc.) || trolley [US pushcart] (en tiendas, estaciones, etc.) || baby walker (para los niños) || banger, cracker, squib (cohete) || AMER jaw (quijada) || — *carretilla eléctrica* electric truck *o* trolley || *carretilla elevadora* forklift truck || *de carretilla* by heart.

carretón *m* small cart (carro) || handcart (tirado a mano) || cart (del afilador) || bogie, bogy, bogey (ferrocarril) || AMER bobbin, reel (de hilo).

carricoche *m* FAM old crock, jalopy (coche malo) || caravan (de gitanos).

carricuba *f* water cart.

carril *m* rut (huella) || furrow (surco) || track (camino) || lane (de una autopista) || rail (de vía férrea) || AMER railway (ferrocarril), train (tren) || *carril de aceleración* slip road.

carrilano; carrilero *m* AMER railway man (que trabaja en los ferrocarriles) | robber (ladrón).

carrilera *f* rut (huella) || AMER siding (apartadero).

carrillada *f* chop, cheek (de un cerdo).

carrillera *f* jaw (quijada) || chin strap (barboquejo).

carrillo *m* cheek (parte de la cara) || trolley (mesa para servir) || trolley [US pushcart] (en las tiendas, estaciones, etc.) || pulley (garrucha) || carrier tricycle (triciclo de reparto) || FIG *comer a dos carrillos* to guzzle, to gobble (comer con gula).

carrilludo, da *adj* fat-cheeked, chubby-cheeked.

carrito *m* trolley (para servir la mesa) || trolley [US pushcart] (en tiendas, estaciones, etc.) || shoe (en juegos de cartas).

carrizal *m* reedbed.

carrizo *m* reed (caña).

carro *m* cart (vehículo de dos ruedas) || cartload (carga) || IMPR press carriage || carriage (de máquina de escribir) || MIL tank (carro de combate) || AMER car (automóvil) || tram [US streetc.ar] (tranvía) | carriage (vagón) || — FAM *aguantar* or *tragar carros y carretas* to put up with murder || MIL *carro blindado* armoured car [US armored car] || AMER *carro comedor* buffet car || *carro cuba* water car || MIL *carro de combate* tank || AMER *carro dormitorio* sleeper, sleeping car || ASTR *Carro Mayor* or *de David* Great Bear | *Carro Menor* Little Bear || FIG *empujar el carro* to put one's shoulder to the wheel | *parar el carro a alguien* to calm s.o. down (calmar), to put s.o. in his place (hacer callar) | *poner el carro delante de las mulas* to put the cart before the horse | *tirar del carro* to pull all the weight, to do all the donkey work | *untar el carro a uno* to bribe s.o., to grease s.o.'s palm.

carrocería *f* body, bodywork (de automóvil) || *taller de carrocería* bodywork *o* coachwork *o* coachbuilding shop.

carrocero *m* coachbuilder, body-builder (constructor de carrocería) || panel beater (chapista).

carrocha *f* eggs *pl* (de insectos).

carrochar *vi* to lay eggs (los insectos).

carromato *m* covered wagon *o* cart (carro) || caravan (de gente de circo, gitanos).

carroña *f* decaying carcass, carrion || FIG trash (gente despreciable).

carroño, ña *adj* decayed (podrido).

carroza *f* coach, carriage (coche antiguo de lujo) || float (en carnaval) || MAR awning || *carroza fúnebre* hearse.

carruaje *m* carriage.

carrusel *m* horse tattoo (ejercicio hípico) || round-about, merry-go-round [US carrousel].

carta *f* letter (misiva); *carta certificada* registered letter; *echar una carta* to post a letter || card (naipe); *baraja de cartas* pack of cards || JUR deed || menu (lista de platos) (véase OBSERV) || list (de vinos) || charter (ley); *carta del Atlántico* Atlantic charter || MAR chart; *carta de marear* or *marina* maritime chart || — *a carta cabal* completely, totally, perfectly, one hundred per cent; *un hombre honrado a carta cabal* a perfectly honest man; perfect (con sustantivo); *un caballero a carta cabal* a perfect gentleman ‖ *a cartas vistas* with the cards on the table; *jugar a cartas vistas* to play with the cards on the table ‖ *a la carta* a la carte (en un restaurante) ‖ *carta abierta* open letter ‖ *carta adjunta* covering letter ‖ *carta aérea* air-mail letter ‖ *carta blanca* carte blanche, free hand; *dar carta blanca a alguien* to give s.o. a free hand ‖ *carta de ajuste* test card (televisión) ‖ *carta de crédito* letter of credit ‖ *carta de despido* letter of dismissal ‖ *carta de hidalguía* letters patent of nobility ‖ *carta de llamada* letter of sponsorship (para un emigrante) ‖ *carta de naturaleza* or *de ciudadanía* naturalization papers ‖ *carta de origen* pedigree (de un animal) ‖ COM *carta de pago* receipt | *carta de pedido* order ‖ *carta de pésame* letter of condolence ‖ *carta de porte* consignment paper [US waybill] ‖ *carta de presentación* or *de recomendación* letter of introduction ‖ *carta de solicitud* application ‖ *carta de vecindad* certificate of residence ‖ *carta franqueada* postage-paid letter ‖ *Carta Magna* Magna Carta ‖ *carta pastoral* pastoral letter ‖ AUT *carta verde* green card ‖ *cartas al director* letters to the editor (en un periódico) ‖ *cartas credenciales* letter *sing* of credence, letters credential, credential letters ‖ *carta urgente* express letter, special delivery letter ‖ AUT *carta verde* green card ‖ *echar las cartas* to read the cards ‖ FIG *jugar bien sus cartas* to play one's cards right *o* well | *jugarse la última carta* to play one's last card | *jugárselo todo a una carta* to put all one's eggs in one basket | *mostrar* or *enseñar las cartas* to show one's hand, to put one's cards on the table | *no saber a qué carta quedarse* to be all at sea, to be in a dilemma | *poner las cartas sobre la mesa* or *boca arriba* to put *o* to lay one's cards on the table *o* face upwards | *tener* or *tomar cartas en un asunto* to intervene in an affair.

— OBSERV En inglés *menú* significa tanto el menú fijo como la carta. Sin embargo la expresión *comer a la carta* se traduce por *to eat à la carte.*

cartabón *m* set square, triangle (de dibujante, de agrimensor) ‖ foot gauge (de zapatero) ‖ AMER measuring apparatus, measure (talla).

cartaginense; cartaginés, esa *adj/s* Carthaginian.

Cartago *n pr* GEOGR Carthage.

cartapacio *m* portfolio (para libros, dibujos, etc.) ‖ writing pad (para escribir) ‖ notebook (cuaderno).

cartearse *vpr* to correspond, to write to each other.

cartel *m* poster, bill (anuncio) ‖ wall chart (en la escuela) ‖ (ant) cartel (de desafío) ‖ pasquinade (pasquín) ‖ — *colgar el cartel de «no hay billetes»* to put up the «house full» sign *o* the «sold out» sign ‖ *de cartel* celebrated; *un equipo, un torero de cartel* a celebrated team, bullfighter ‖ *obra que continúa en cartel* a work which is still on *o* still running ‖ *pegar* or *fijar carteles* to put up *o* to stick up *o* to post bills ‖ *se prohibe* or *prohibido fijar carteles* post *o* stick no bills ‖ FIG *tener buen* or *mucho cartel* to be very successful, to be a hit, to be good box office.

cártel *m* cartel, trust; *cártel industrial* industrial cartel ‖ coalition; *el cártel de las izquierdas* the coalition of the left.

— OBSERV pl *cárteles.*

cartelera *f* billboard, hoarding (para carteles) ‖ entertainments *pl* (en el periódico) ‖ *llevar mucho tiempo en cartelera* to run *o* to be on for a long time.

cartelista *m/f* poster designer (dibujante).

cartelón *m* large poster, large bill.

carteo *m* exchange of letters, correspondence.

cárter *m* TECN housing (en general) | crankcase (de automóvil) | chain guard (de bicicleta).

cartera *f* wallet (de bolsillo) ‖ purse [US pocketbook] (monedero) ‖ briefcase, document case (portadocumentos) ‖ satchel (de colegial) ‖ bag (de cobrador) ‖ saddlebag, pannierbag (de bicicleta) ‖ flap (pieza que cubre el bolsillo) ‖ FIG portfolio; *ministro sin cartera* minister without portfolio ‖ COM portfolio (de valores) ‖ — *cartera de pedidos* order book ‖ FAM *echar mano a la cartera* to dip into one's pocket (para pagar) ‖ FIG *en cartera* planned (un proyecto) | *tener en cartera* to have plans for, to be planning ‖ *valores en cartera* holdings, stocks.

cartería *f* postman's job *o* work ‖ sorting office (en correos).

carterilla *f* flap (de un bolsillo).

carterista *m* pickpocket.

carterita *f* book (de cerillas).

cartero *m* postman [US mailman].

cartesianismo *m* Cartesianism.

cartesiano, na *adj/s* Cartesian.

cartilagíneo, a; cartilaginoso, sa *adj* ANAT cartilaginous, cartilaginoid; *tejido cartilaginoso* cartilaginous tissue.

cartílago *m* ANAT cartilage.

cartilla *f* first reader, first reading book (libro) ‖ FIG primer (tratado elemental) ‖ book; *cartilla de ahorros, de racionamiento* savings, ration book ‖ MIL record; *cartilla militar* military record ‖ REL ordo, liturgical calendar (añalejo) ‖ certificate of ordination (de un sacerdote) ‖ — *cartilla de parado* unemployment card ‖ FIG & FAM *leerle a uno la cartilla* to give s.o. a lecture | *no saber ni la cartilla* not to have the faintest *o* the slightest idea.

cartografía *f* cartography.

cartográfico, ca *adj* cartographic, cartographical.

cartógrafo, fa *m/f* cartographer.

cartograma *m* cartogram.

cartomancia; cartomancía *f* cartomancy, fortune telling.

cartomántico, ca *adj* fortune telling.
◆ *m/f* fortune teller.

cartón *m* cardboard; *caja de cartón* cardboard box ‖ ARTES cartoon, sketch ‖ board (de un libro) ‖ carton (de cigarrillos) ‖ — *cartón ondulado* corrugated cardboard ‖ *cartón piedra* papier mâché.

cartonaje *m* cardboard box industry *o* trade.

cartoné (en) *adj* in boards ‖ *un libro en cartoné* a book bound in boards.

cartonería *f* cardboard box industry *o* trade.

cartonero, ra *adj* cardboard; *industria cartonera* cardboard industry.
◆ *m/f* cardboard maker.

cartuchera *f* MIL cartridge holder (en general), cartridge belt (cinturón).

cartuchería *f* cartridge factory.

cartucho *m* MIL cartridge; *cartucho de fogueo* or *de salvas* blank cartridge | cartridge bag (saquete de pólvora) ‖ paper cone (de papel grueso) ‖ roll (de moneda) ‖ — FIG *luchar hasta quemar el último cartucho* to fight to the bitter end | *quemar el último cartucho* to play one's last card.

cartuja *f* REL Carthusian order (orden) | charterhouse, chartreuse (monasterio).

cartujano, na *adj/s* Carthusian ‖ *caballo cartujano* breed of horse found in Jerez [Andalusia].

cartujo *adj m/sm* Carthusian ‖ FIG & FAM *vivir como un cartujo* to live like a hermit.

cartulario *m* cartulary.

cartulina *f* bristol board.

carúncula *f* ANAT & ZOOL caruncle; *carúncula lagrimal* lachrymal caruncle.

carvallar; carvalledo *m* (p us) oak grove *o* wood.

casa *f* house; *casa de campo* country house; *casa de juego* gambling house ‖ flat [US apartment] (piso) ‖ building (edificio) ‖ home (hogar); *quedarse en casa* to stay at home; *me gusta mi casa* I like my home ‖ house (familia); *la casa de los Estuardos* the house of Stuart ‖ household, family (habitantes de una casa) ‖ firm, company (empresa) ‖ branch (sucursal) ‖ square (casilla); *el tablero de ajedrez tiene 64 casas* the chessboard has 64 squares ‖ ASTR House ‖ — *a casa* home (de uno mismo); *irse a casa* to go home ‖ *a casa de Pedro* to Peter's house, to Peter's ‖ *aquí está usted en su casa* make yourself at home ‖ *aquí tiene usted su casa* you are always welcome here ‖ *buscar casa* to look for somewhere to live ‖ FIG *cada uno en su casa y Dios en la de todos* every man for himself and God for us all | *cada uno es rey en su casa* a man's home is his castle ‖ *casa adosada* semi-detached house ‖ *casa central* head office, main branch ‖ *casa civil* household (del rey o del jefe de Estado) ‖ *casa comercial* business firm ‖ *casa consistorial* town hall ‖ *casa cuna* nursery ‖ *casa de banca* bank ‖ *casa de baños* public baths, bathhouse ‖ *casa de bebidas* bar ‖ *casa de beneficencia* poorhouse ‖ *casa de cambio* exchange office ‖ *casa de citas* house of call ‖ *casa de comidas* eating house ‖ *casa de correos* general post office ‖ *casa de Dios* House of God ‖ *casa de empeños* or *de préstamos* pawnbroker's (shop) *o* pawnshop ‖ *casa de fieras* zoo, menagerie ‖ *casa de huéspedes* boarding house ‖ *casa de labor* or *de labranza* farmhouse ‖ *Casa de la Villa* Town Hall ‖ *casa de lenocinio* brothel ‖ *casa de locos* lunatic asylum (manicomio) ‖ *casa de maternidad* maternity hospital *o* home ‖ *Casa de la Moneda* mint, Royal Mint ‖ *casa de modas* fashion house ‖ *casa de pisos* block of flats [US apartment building] ‖ *casa de recreo* country house ‖ *casa de reposo* rest home ‖ *casa de socorro* emergency *o* casualty hospital, first-aid post ‖ *casa de trato* licensed brothel ‖ *casa de vecindad* or *de vecinos* block of flats [US apartment building] ‖ *casa discográfica* record company ‖ *casa editorial* publishing house ‖ REL *casa matriz* mother house ‖ *casa militar* Royal Guard ‖ *casa mortuoria* house of the deceased ‖ *casa paterna* parent's house ‖ *casa pública* brothel ‖ *casa real* Royal Family ‖ *casa religiosa* convent (de monjas), monastery (de frailes) ‖ *casa remolque* caravan [US trailer] ‖ *casa solariega* ancestral home, family seat, country seat ‖ *casa y comida* board and lodging ‖ FIG & FAM *como Pedro por su casa* as if he owned the place ‖ FIG *de* or *para andar por casa* ordinary, everyday (insignificante) | *echar* or *tirar la casa por la ventana* to spare no expense, to go overboard, to lash out (*fam*) | *empezar la casa por el tejado* to put the cart before the horse | *en casa del herrero cuchillo de palo* the shoemaker's wife is always worst shod | *es mi segunda casa* it is my home from home ‖ *estar de casa* to be dressed casually ‖ *estar en casa* to be at home, to be in ‖ *estar fuera de casa* to be out, not to be in ‖ *hacer la casa* to do the housework ‖ *inaugurar la casa* to have a house-warming ‖ DEP *jugar en casa* to play at home ‖ FAM *la casa de Tócame Roque* bear garden, bedlam ‖ *levantar casa* to move house ‖ *llevar la casa* to run the house ‖ *marcharse de casa* to leave home ‖ *mujer de su casa* good housekeeper ‖ *no parar en casa* to be never at home, to be always out ‖ *no salir de casa* not to go out ‖ *no tener ni casa* *ni hogar* to have neither house nor home || *ofrecer la casa* to offer one's house || *pasar por casa de alguien* to call on s.o. || *poner casa* to settle down, to set up house (instalarse) || FIG & FAM *se me cae la casa encima* I can't stand being in the house, the house is getting me down || *sentirse como en casa* to feel at home || *tener casa abierta* to keep open house || *un amigo de (la) casa* a friend of the family.

casabe *m* cassava flour (harina) || cassava bread (pan).

Casablanca *n pr* GEOGR Casablanca.

Casa Blanca *npr f* White House.

casaca *f* dress coat (vestido) || FIG *volver casaca* or *la casaca* to turn one's coat, to change sides.

casación *f* JUR cassation, annulment.

casacón *m* greatcoat.

casadero, ra *adj* old enough to marry, marriageable, of marrying age; *una muchacha casadera* a marriageable girl, a girl old enough to marry.

casado, da *adj* married; *hombre casado* married man; *una mujer recién casada* a newly-married woman || — *estar casado* to be married (*con* to) || *mal casado* unhappily married.
◆ *m/f* married man, woman || — *el casado casa quiere* everyone wants his own home || *los recién casados* the newlyweds.
◆ *m* IMPR imposition.

casamata *f* MIL casemate.

casamentero, ra *adj* matchmaking; *una mujer casamentera* a matchmaking woman.
◆ *m/f* matchmaker.

casamiento *m* marriage; *un casamiento ventajoso* a marriage for money || — *casamiento desigual* misalliance, unequal marriage || *casamiento por amor* love match.

Casandra *npr f* Cassandra.

casapuerta *f* porch, entrance (zaguán).

casaquilla *f* short cassock.

casar *vt* to marry (unir en matrimonio) || to marry off; *ha casado muy bien a sus hijas* she has married off her daughters quite well || FIG to match (poner en armonía) | to join (unir) || IMPR to impose || JUR to annul, to quash.
◆ *vi* to marry, to get married; *Fernando II de Aragón casó con Isabel I de Castilla* Fernando II of Aragon married Isabel I of Castile *o* got married to Isabel I of Castile || to match, to go together (armonizar); *estos colores no casan bien* these colours do not match || to balance, to tally; *las cuentas no casan* the accounts do not tally || to fit together; *estas dos piezas no casan* these parts do not fit together || to tally; *esas dos versiones no casan* those two versions do not tally.
◆ *vpr* to marry, to get married; *casarse con una hermosa mujer* to get married to *o* to marry a beautiful woman || — FIG *antes que te cases mira lo que haces* look before you leap || *casarse en segundas nupcias* to remarry, to marry again || *casarse por detrás de la iglesia* to live together [as a married couple] || *casarse por interés* to marry (for) money || *casarse por lo civil* to get married in a registry office || *casarse por poderes* to get married by proxy || FAM *¡cásate y verás!* live and learn! || FIG *no casarse con nadie* to keep o.s. to o.s.

casca *f* skin of pressed grapes (piel de la uva) || marc (orujo) || bark, tan, tanning bark (para curtir).
◆ *pl* rind *sing*, peel *sing* (fruta confitada).

cascabel *m* bell (campanilla) || — FIG & FAM *de cascabel gordo* cheap (obra) | *poner el cascabel al gato* to stick one's neck out, to bell the cat || *serpiente de cascabel* rattlesnake.

cascabelear *vt* FIG & FAM to lure, to take in.
◆ *vi* to tinkle, to jingle (hacer ruidos como cascabeles) || FIG & FAM to act recklessly || AMER to grumble (refunfuñar).

cascabeleo *m* jingling, tinkling.

cascabelero, ra *adj* tinkling, jingling.

cascada *f* waterfall, cascade || FIG cascade.

cascado, da *adj* broken-down, broken, worn-out; *un anciano muy cascado* a very broken-down old man || harsh, cracked; *tener la voz cascada* to have a harsh voice || broken-down (desvencijado) || cracked; *el jarrón, el vaso está cascado* the vase, the glass is cracked.

cascadura *f* crack.

cascajal; cascajar *m* pebbly ground.

cascajo *m* gravel (guijo), grit (guijarrillo) || screenings *pl* (escombros) || broken pieces *pl*, fragments *pl* (de vasijas, etc.) || nut (fruto) || FIG & FAM decrepit old man (viejo) | old crock (coche) | old scrap, junk (trastos viejos) || FAM *estar hecho un cascajo* to be a wreck.

cascanueces *m inv* nutcrackers *pl*, nutcracker; *¿dónde está el cascanueces?* where are the nutcrackers? || ZOOL nutcracker (pájaro) || *un cascanueces* a pair of nutcrackers.

cascapiñones *m inv* nutcrackers *pl*, nutcracker.

cascar *vt* to crack (una vasija, un huevo, una nuez) || FAM to beat up, to give a beating to; *le han cascado en el mitin* they beat him up at the meeting | to blow; *hoy casqué mil pesetas en el juego* today I blew a thousand pesetas gambling | to cough up (pagar) | to give (poner); *le han cascado un cero en matemáticas* they've given him a goose egg in mathematics.
◆ *vi* FAM to chatter; *esta mujer está siempre cascando* this woman is always chattering | to swot up; *cascarle fuerte al latín* to swot up Latin hard | to kick the bucket (morir).
◆ *vpr* to crack, to become harsh (la voz) || to crack, to split (romperse).

cáscara *f* shell (del huevo, de los frutos secos) || bark (de los troncos) || husk (de cereales) || skin, peel (de las frutas) || peel (de naranja o de limón) || rind (del queso) || — *¡cáscaras!* damn!, dash! || FAM *ser de la cáscara amarga* to be a queer (ser homosexual).

cascarilla *f* husk (corteza) || metal covering (de un botón) || flake (fragmento desprendido del enlucido) || cocoa (del cacao) || FAM *el hermanito jugó de cascarilla* their little brother played but they didn't count him.

cascarillo *m* cascarilla (árbol).

cascarón *m* shell, eggshell (de huevo) || — FIG & FAM *aún no ha salido del cascarón* he is still a baby || *cascarón de nuez* nutshell (barco).

cascarrabias *m/f inv* grouse, irritable *o* crabby *o* grumpy person.

casco *m* helmet (de soldado, de bombero, de aviador) || crown (del sombrero) || headband (del auricular) || skull, cranium (cráneo) || FAM nut, head (cabeza) || broken piece, fragment (de botella, de vidrio) || piece of shrapnel (de metralla, de obús) || BOT coat, skin (de la cebolla) | segment (de naranja) || barrel (tonel) || empty (botella vacía) || central area (de población) || MAR hull (del barco) || ZOOL hoof (de las caballerías) || *casco protector* crash helmet || *el casco antiguo de una ciudad* the old part of a city.
◆ *pl* head *sing* of sheep *o* calf [without brain and tongue] (cabeza de res) || — FIG & FAM *alegre* or *ligero de cascos* scatterbrained | *calentarle a alguien los cascos con* to pester s.o. with | *estar mal de los cascos* to be dotty, to be off one's rocker | *romperse* or *calentarse los cascos* to rack one's brains | *sentar los cascos* to settle down.

cascotes *m pl* rubble *sing*.

caseína *f* QUÍM casein.

cáseo, a *adj* caseous, cheesy.
◆ *m* curd (requesón).

caseoso, sa *adj* caseous, cheesy.

caserío *m* hamlet, small village (pueblecito) || country house and its outbuildings (de un cortijo).

casero, ra *adj* domestic (animal); *conejo casero* domestic rabbit || home-made; *tarta casera* home-made tart || family; *una reunión casera* a family gathering || indoor, everyday (ropa) || home-loving, stay-at-home (amante del hogar) || household (medicina) || *cocina casera* home cooking.
◆ *m/f* proprietor, owner, landlord (hombre), landlady (de casa alquilada) || keeper (de finca rústica) || stay-at-home, home-lover (amante del hogar) || house agent (administrador de casa).

caserón *m* big rambling house.

caseta *f* small house, cottage (casita) || booth, stall (de feria) || bathing cabin, bathing hut [*US* bathhouse] (de bañista) || stand, stall (de exposición) || cubicle (en la piscina) || pavilion (en otros deportes) || — *caseta de cambios de agujas* signal box (ferrocarriles) || MAR *caseta del timón* wheelhouse || *caseta de perro* kennel, doghouse.

casi *adv* almost, nearly; *tiene casi cien años* he is almost a hundred years old || — *casi, casi* very nearly; *eran casi, casi las doce* it was very nearly twelve o'clock || *casi nada* hardly any; *¿cuánto queda de azúcar? casi nada* how much sugar is there left? hardly any; hardly anything; *no dijo casi nada* he hardly said anything; hardly at all; *la vacuna no me ha dolido casi nada* the vaccination hardly hurt me at all || *¡casi nada!* (irónicamente) is that all!; *le ha tocado el gordo de la lotería ¡casi nada!* he has won first prize in the lottery is that all! || *casi no* hardly; *casi no me duele ya* it hardly hurts now; hardly any; *casi no tiene amigos* he has hardly any friends || *casi nunca* hardly ever; *casi nunca pasa por casa* he hardly ever comes round || *casi prefiero el otro modelo* I think I prefer the other model || *casi sin* without hardly; *se fue casi sin decir adiós* he left without hardly saying goodbye || *es casi tonto sin casi* he's almost stupid more than almost.

casia *f* BOT cassia (arbusto).

casicontrato *m* JUR quasi-contract, implied contract.

casilla *f* small house, cottage (casita) || lodge, hut (de guarda) || cabin, hut (de madera) || stall, booth (puesto de venta) || ticket office, box office (taquilla) || square (de papel rayado, de crucigrama, de ajedrez) || pigeonhole (de estante) || FAM clink (prisión) || AMER toilet, lavatory (excusado) | bird trap, snare (trampa) || — AMER *casilla postal* post-office box (apartado) || FIG *sacar a uno de sus casillas* to shake s.o. up, to bring s.o. out of his shell (trastornar), to make s.o. mad, to infuriate s.o. (enfurecer) | *salir de sus casillas* to come out of one's shell (cambiar de costumbres), to lose one's temper, to fly off the handle (enfurecerse).

casillero *m* set of pigeonholes, pigeonholes *pl*.

casimir *m*; **casimira** *f* cashmere (tela).

Casimiro *npr m* Casimir.

casino *m* casino (casa de recreo) || club, circle (asociación y lugar donde se reúne).

Casio *npr m* Cassius.

Casiopea *f* ASTR Cassiopeia.

casis *m* blackcurrant liqueur (licor).

casita *f* small house, little house || *vámonos a casita* let's go home.

casiterita *f* MIN cassiterite, tinstone.

caso *m* case (circunstancia) || event, happening (suceso) || case, instance; *fue un caso de falta de cuidado* it was an instance of carelessness || affair; *el caso Dreyfus* the Dreyfus affair || MED case; *un caso de meningitis* a case of meningitis || GRAM case || case, subject (de un experimento, etc.) || — *caso clínico* clinical case || *caso de conciencia* case of conscience || *caso de fuerza mayor* case of dire necessity (necesidad), force majeure (término jurídico) || *caso fortuito* accidental case, accident (imprevisto), act of God (jurídico) || *caso perdido* hopeless case || *caso que* or *en caso de que ganemos* in case we win, if we should win || *dado el caso de que* supposing (that) || *el caso es que...* the fact is that... || *en caso de incendio* in the event of *o* in case of fire || *en caso de necesidad* should the need arise, if need be || *en el mejor de los casos* at best || *en el peor de los casos* if the worst comes to the worst, at worst || *en este* or *en tal caso* in this case, in such a case || *en todo caso* in any case, anyway, at all events || *en último caso* as a last resort || *¡es un caso!* he is a case, he's a right one || *eso no viene* or *no hace al caso* that is beside the point, that has nothing to do with it, that is irrelevant || *hacer caso a* to take notice of || *hacer caso de algo* to take notice of sth., to take sth. into account || *hacer caso de alguien* to look after s.o., to pay attention to s.o.; *haz caso del niño* look after the child || *hacer caso omiso de* to take no notice of, to pay no attention to, to ignore || *lo mejor del caso* the best part || *llegado* or *si llega el caso* if the case arises, if need be || *maldito el caso que me hace* a fat lot of attention he pays to me || *no hacerle caso a uno* to pay no attention to s.o., not to look after s.o. (no ocuparse), to take no notice of s.o., not to listen to s.o. (desobedecer) || *no hizo caso* he didn't pay attention, he wasn't careful || *no sea caso que...* in case... || *para el caso es igual* it's all the same, it makes no difference || *poner por caso* to suppose, to assume || *según el caso* as the case may be || *según lo requiera el caso* as the case may be *o* require || *servir para el caso* to serve one's purpose || *vamos al caso* let's come *o* get to the point || *venir* or *hacer al caso* to be relevant || *verse en el caso de* to be compelled to || *y en el caso contrario* and if not, otherwise.

casón *m*; **casona** *f* big rambling house.

casorio *m* FAM wedding.

caspa *f* dandruff (del pelo) || scurf (de la piel).

caspera *f* toothcomb.

¡cáspita! *interj* my goodness! (sorpresa, asombro), damn it! (enfado).

casposo, sa *adj* full of *o* covered in dandruff.

casquería *f* tripe shop.

casquero *m* tripe seller (tripicallero).

casquete *m* skullcap, toque (sombrero) || toupée (peluca) || MED cataplasm (de tiñoso) || MIL helmet || — *casquete esférico* segment of a sphere || *casquete glaciar* or *polar* ice cap.

casquillo *m* TECN collar, ferrule, tip (anillo) || cap; *casquillo de bayoneta, de rosca* bayonet cap, screw cap || case (de cartucho) || metal base (parte metálica de un cartucho) || head (de saeta) || AMER horseshoe (herradura) | penholder (portaplumas).

casquivano, na *adj* FAM scatterbrained, dizzy (atolondrado).

cassette *f* cassette (de cinta magnetofónica).

casta *f* breed (de animales) || lineage, descent (de personas) || caste (en la India) || FIG clan, circle (mundo cerrado) | class (clase) || IMPR fount (fundición) || — *de casta* thoroughbred (animal), of breeding (persona), real (torero, bailarín, etc.) || *de casta le viene al galgo (el ser rabilargo)* like father, like son || *le viene de casta* it runs in the family.

castaña *f* chestnut (fruto) || demijohn (botella) || bun (peinado de mujer) || FIG & FAM punch, thump; *arrear una castaña* to land a punch | booze-up [US drunk] (borrachera) || — *castaña apilada* or *maya* or *pilonga* dried chestnut || *castaña confitada* glacé chestnut || *castaña de Indias* horse chestnut || *¡castañas calentitas!* hot chestnuts! (pregón) || FIG & FAM *parecerse como un huevo a una castaña* to be as different as chalk and cheese | *sacar las castañas del fuego a uno* to pull s.o.'s chestnuts out of the fire for him.

castañal *m*; **castañar** *m*; **castañeda** *f* chestnut grove.

castañazo *m* FAM punch, thump (puñetazo) || FAM *pegarse un puñetazo contra* to crash into.

castañero, ra *m/f* chestnut seller.

castañeta *f* snap *o* click of the fingers (chasquido) || MÚS castanet (castañuela).

castañetazo *m* cracking *o* crackling of chestnuts (de la castaña en el fuego) || snap *o* click of the fingers || crack (de los huesos) || FAM punch, thump (golpe) || FAM *pegarse un castañazo contra* to crash into.

castañetear *vt* to play (the castanets) (con castañuelas) || to snap (los dedos).
◆ *vi* to chatter (los dientes) || to snap (los dedos) || to crack (los huesos) || to cry (las perdices) || to play the castanets (con las castañuelas).

castañeteo *m* clacking *o* clicking of castanets || chattering (de los dientes) || cracking (de los huesos) || snapping (de los dedos).

castaño, ña *adj* chestnut-brown, chestnut (color); *una cabellera castaña* chestnut-brown hair.
◆ *m* chestnut tree, chestnut (árbol) || chestnut (madera, color) || — *castaño de Indias* horse chestnut (tree) || FIG & FAM *pasar de castaño oscuro* to be going too far, to be a bit much.

castañuela *f* MÚS castanet || type of cyperus (planta) || FIG & FAM *alegre como unas castañuelas* as happy as a lark, as chirpy as a cricket.

castellanía *f* castellany.

castellanismo *m* word *o* expression common to Castile.

castellanizar *vt* to make Spanish, to hispanicize, to castilianize.

castellano, na *adj/s* Castilian (de Castilla) || *a la castellana* in the Castilian way.
◆ *m/f* Castilian, Spaniard.
◆ *m* Spanish, Castilian (lengua).

castellonense *adj* [from *o* of] Castellón de la Plana.
◆ *m/f* native *o* inhabitant of Castellón de la Plana.

casticidad *f*; **casticismo** *m* correction, purity (en el lenguaje) || traditionalism (de las costumbres) || genuineness, authenticity (de personas).

casticista *adj/s* purist.

castidad *f* chastity.

castigador, ra *adj* castigatory (que castiga).
◆ *m/f* punisher, chastiter, castigator.
◆ *m* FIG & FAM lady-killer, Don Juan.

castigar *vt* to punish, to chastise, to castigate; *castigado por su temeridad* punished for his rashness || DEP to penalize (a un jugador) || FIG to make suffer (hacer sufrir) | to mortify (mortificar) | to afflict (por una enfermedad) | to correct (un escrito) | to reduce, to cut (los gastos) | to cause damage to *o* in; *las inundaciones castigaron mucho la región* the floods caused a lot of damage in the area | to ride hard (un caballo) || FIG & FAM to lead on (a las mujeres) || TAUR to wound [the bull in order to excite it] || FIGR *la vida le ha castigado mucho* life has been very hard on him, he has suffered a lot.

castigo *m* punishment, chastisement, castigation; *infligir un duro castigo* to inflict a harsh punishment || punishing, punishment, chastising, chastisement (acción de castigar); *castigo ejemplar* exemplary punishment || penalty; *la pena capital es el castigo para los traidores* the death sentence is the penalty for traitors || correction (de un escrito) || MIL punishment || TAUR wound [in order to excite the bull] || — DEP *área de castigo* penalty area | *castigo máximo* penalty (fútbol), penalty kick (rugby) || *levantar el castigo* to withdraw the punishment.

Castilla *npr f* GEOGR Castile; *Castilla la Vieja* Old Castile || FIG *¡ancha es Castilla!* come on, we've got nothing to lose!

Castilla-La Mancha *npr f* GEOGR Castile La Mancha.

Castilla-León *n pr* GEOGR Castile and Leon.

castillejo *m* baby walker (para enseñar a andar a los niños) || scaffold, scaffolding (andamio).

castillete *m* small castle (pequeño castillo) || MIN headgear, derrick || MIN *castillete de extracción* headframe, gallows.

castillo *m* castle (edificio); *en Segovia hay un castillo* there is a castle in Segovia || — *castillo de fuego* firework display (pirotecnia) || FIG *castillo de naipes* house of cards || MAR *castillo de popa* quarterdeck || *castillo de proa* forecastle, fo'c'sle || *castillo en la arena* sandcastle || FIG *levantar* or *hacer castillos en el aire* to build *o* to make castles in the air *o* in Spain.

castina *f* limestone flux (fundente).

castizo, za *adj* true, through and through, pure-blooded, genuine (puro); *un madrileño castizo* a true Madrilenian, a Madrilenian through and through || pure (lenguaje); *estilo castizo* pure style || typical, traditional (típico).

casto, ta *adj* chaste, pure.

castor *m* beaver, castor (p us).

Cástor *m* ASTR Castor; *Cástor y Pólux* Castor and Pollux.

castoreño *m* beaver hat || felt hat || TAUR picador's hat | picador.

castóreo *m* castor, castoreum.

castorina *f* castor, beaver (tejido).

castra; castración *f* castration || gelding (de caballos) || pruning (poda de árboles) || uncapping (de la colmena).

castradera *f* uncapping knife (de apicultor).

castrado, da *adj* castrated || gelded (caballo).
◆ *m* eunuch (eunuco).

castrador *m* castrator || gelder (de caballos).

castrar *vt* to castrate (capar) || to doctor (un gato) || to geld (los caballos) || to uncap (las colmenas) || FIG to weaken (debilitar) || AGR to prune (podar).

castrazón *f* uncapping (de las colmenas).

castrense *adj* military; *vida, costumbre, capellán castrense* military life, custom, chaplain.

castrismo *m* Castroism [Castro's doctrine *o* policy].

castrista *adj* Castroist.
◆ *m/f* Castroite, Castroist [supporter of Castro].

casual *adj* accidental, fortuitous, casual, chance; *un encuentro casual* an accidental meeting.

casualidad *f* chance, accident; *por* or *de casualidad* by chance || coincidence (coincidencia); *una verdadera casualidad* a real coincidence || — *dar la casualidad* to (just) happen; *dio la casualidad que...* it (just) happened that... || *el otro día entré por casualidad* the other day I just happened to drop in || *¿tiene por casualidad un peine?* have you a comb by any chance?

casualmente *adv* by chance, by accident.

casuario *m* cassowary (ave).

casuca *f*; **casucha** *f*; **casucho** *m* hovel, shabby little house.

casuista *m* casuist.

casuístico, ca *adj* casuistical, casuistic.
◆ *f* casuistry.

casulla *f* REL chasuble.

casullero *m* chasuble maker.

cata *f* tasting (acción de catar) || sample (porción para probar) || *AMER* parakeet (cotorra).

catabólico, ca *adj* BIOL katabolic, catabolic.

catabolismo *m* BIOL katabolism, catabolism.

catacaldos *m inv* FIG & FAM dabbler (persona inconstante) | busybody, nosey parker (persona entrometida).

cataclismo *m* cataclysm.

catacresis *f inv* catachresis (extensión del sentido de una palabra).

catacumba *m* catacomb (cementerio).

catador *m* taster, sampler (que prueba alimentos) || FIG connoisseur || *catador de vinos* wine taster (persona).

catadura *f* tasting, sampling || FIG & FAM *un individuo de mala catadura* a nasty-looking type.

catafalco *m* cataphalque, catafalque.

catafaro; catafoto *m* reflector (de automóviles).

catalán, ana *adj/s* Catalan, Catalonian.
◆ *m* Catalan (lengua).

catalanismo *m* Catalan expression used in Spanish, Catalanism || quality of being Catalan || Catalan separatist sympathies *pl*.

catalanista *adj* in favour of regional autonomy for Catalonia.
◆ *m/f* Catalanist.

catalejo *m* telescope (anteojo).

catalepsia *f* MED catalepsy.

cataléptico, ca *adj/s* cataleptic.

catalicores *m inv* wine taster || sampling tube (pipeta).

catalina *f* FAM dirt, droppings *pl* (excremento) || *rueda catalina* balance wheel (de un reloj).

Catalina *npr f* Catherine, Catharine, Katherine, Kathleen.

catálisis *f* QUÍM catalysis.

catalítico, ca *adj* catalytic.

catalizador, ra *adj* QUÍM catalytic.
◆ *m* catalyst.

catalizar *vt* to catalyse || FIG to act as a catalyst for.

catalogación *f* cataloguing.

catalogar *vt* to catalogue || FIG to classify, to class; *catalogar a uno de conservador* to classify s.o. as conservative.

catálogo *m* catalogue [*US* catalog].

Cataluña *npr f* GEOGR Catalonia.

catamarán *m* MAR catamaran.

catanga *f* *AMER* dung beetle, dor (escarabajo).

cataplasma *f* cataplasm, poultice (pasta medicinal) || FIG & FAM bore, drag.

¡cataplum!; ¡cataplún! *interj* crash!, bang!

cataplexia *f* MED cataplexy.

catapulta *f* catapult.

catapultar *vt* to catapult.

catapún (el año) *loc* FAM the year dot || *ser del año catapún* to be as old as the hills, to be ages old.

catar *vt* to sample, to taste (probar) || (ant) to look at (mirar) | to inspect, to examine (examinar) || to uncap (colmenas).

catarata *f* waterfall (de agua), cataract (muy grande) || MED cataract (del ojo); *tener una catarata* to have a cataract || — MED *batir la catarata* to perform cataractopiesis || *las cataratas del Niágara* Niagara Falls || *operar de catarata* to remove a cataract from s.o.'s eye || FIG *se abrieron las cataratas del cielo* the heavens opened, it poured down.

cátaro, ra *adj* catharian (hereje).

catarral *adj* MED catarrhal; *afección catarral* catarrhal infection.

catarro *m* cold (palabra usual), catarrh (p us); *coger un catarro* to catch a cold || *catarro pradial* hay fever.

catarsis *f* FIL catharsis, catharses, katharsis, katharses.

catártico, ca *adj* cathartic, kathartic.

catastral *adj* cadastral; *levantamiento catastral* cadastral survey.

catastro *m* official land register, cadastre.

catástrofe *f* catastrophe, disaster (desastre).

catastrófico, ca *adj* catastrophic, disastrous.

catastrofismo *m* undue pessimism (actitud) || catastrophism (teoría).

catatonía *f* MED catatonia.

cataviento *m* MAR dogvane (grímpola).

catavino *m* wine taster (copa).

catavinos *m inv* wine taster (persona) || FIG & FAM drunkard, boozer (borracho).

catch *m* DEP wrestling || *luchador de catch* wrestler.

catchup *m* ketchup.

cate *m* FAM punch (puñetazo) | thump, blow (golpe) | slap, smack (bofetada) || FAM *le han dado un cate en física* they failed him in physics (en un examen).

cateador *m* *AMER* prospector.

catear *vt* to look for, to search for (buscar) || FAM to fail (suspender); *me han cateado* they failed me || *AMER* to prospect (minas).

catecismo *m* catechism.

catecú *m* catechu.

catecúmeno, na *m/f* catechumen.

cátedra *f* chair (puesto de catedrático) || senior teaching post (en un colegio) || lecture room (aula) || FIG chair || — *cátedra del Espíritu Santo* pulpit || *cátedra de San Pedro* Holy See || *hablar ex cátedra* to speak ex cathedra || *hacer oposiciones a cátedra, opositar a una cátedra* to compete for a chair || FIG *poner* or *sentar cátedra de algo* to give a lesson in sth., to show how to do sth.

catedral *adj/sf* cathedral || FIG & FAM *como una catedral* massive, huge, enormous.

catedralicio, cia *adj* cathedral; *iglesia catedralicia* cathedral church.

catedrático, ca *m/f* professor (de universidad), teacher, head of department (de instituto).

categoría *f* category || class; *hotel de primera categoría* first-class hotel || class, type, category (clase); *de la misma categoría* of the same type || rank (graduación) || class; *categoría social* social class; *un equipo de gran categoría* a first-class team || FIL category || — *dar categoría* to give prestige; *una sortija de brillantes da categoría* a diamond ring gives prestige || FAM *de categoría* important (notable), luxury (de lujo); *un coche de categoría* a luxury car; standing; *persona de cierta categoría* person of some standing; serious; *un sarampión de categoría* a serious bout of measles; real good; *le han dado una paliza de categoría* they gave him a real good beating || *de segunda categoría* second-rate.

categórico, ca *adj* categoric, categorical || strict, express (orden) || *negativa categórica* flat refusal.

catenario, ria *adj/sf* TECN catenary.

catequesis *f*; **catequismo** *m* catechesis, catechizing || catechism (catecismo).

catequista *m/f* catechist.

catequización *f* catechization, catechizing.

catequizar *vt* to catechize || FIG to preach to (predicar) | to talk round, to convince (convencer).

caterva *f* host, crowd, band; *caterva de pillos* crowd of rascals || load, heap; *una caterva de cosas viejas* a load of old things.

catéter *m* MED catheter (sonda).

cateterismo *m* MED catheterism (sondaje).

cateto, ta *adj/s* FAM peasant, yokel (palurdo).
◆ *m* MAT side of right-angled triangle [adjacent to the right angle].

catetómetro *m* cathetometer.

catgut *m* MED catgut.

catilinaria *f* outburst of criticism (sátira).

catinga *f* *AMER* bad smell (mal olor) | forest (bosque) | soldier (soldado).

catión *m* FÍS cation.

catire; catiro, ra *adj* redheaded, redhaired, ginger-haired.
◆ *m/f* redhead.

catite *m* loaf of best refined sugar (azúcar) || slap (golpe o bofetada) || — FAM *dar catite a uno* to slap s.o. (golpear) || *sombrero de catite* sugarloaf hat.

cato *m* catechu (pasta aromática).

catódico, ca *adj* cathodic, cathode.

cátodo *m* cathode.

catolicidad *f* catholicity (universalidad y cualidad de católico) || Catholicism (mundo católico).

catolicismo *m* Catholicism, Roman Catholicism.

católico, ca *adj/s* Roman Catholic, Catholic || — FIG & FAM *no estar muy católico* to feel under the weather (pachucho), to be a bit off (alimento) | *no ser muy católico* to sound fishy (asunto).

catolizar *vt* to catholicize.

catón *m* FIG severe critic || first reading book (libro).

Catón *npr m* Cato.

catóptrica *f* FÍS catoptrics.

catorce *adj* fourteen; *catorce lápices* fourteen pencils || fourteenth (decimocuarto); *Luis XIV* (catorce) Louis XIV [the fourteenth]; *el siglo XIV* (catorce) the fourteenth century.
◆ *m* fourteen (número) || fourteenth (fecha); *el 14 (catorce) de febrero* 14 February, February 14th [the fourteenth] (encabezamiento de una carta), February the fourteenth, the fourteenth of February (en la conversación) || *el catorce* fourteen, number fourteen.

catorceno, na *adj* fourteenth.

catre *m* FAM bed (cama) || *catre de tijera* or *de viento* camp bed.

catrecillo *m* folding chair (asiento).

catrera *f* AMER FAM bed (cama).

catrín *m* AMER beau, toff [US dude].

Cátulo *npr m* Catullus.

caucasiano, na; caucásico, ca *adj/s* Caucasian.

Cáucaso *npr m* GEOGR Caucasus.

cauce *m* bed [of a river] || ditch, trench (acequia) || FIG way, channel; *los cauces constitucionales* constitutional channels *o* ways | course; *las cosas han vuelto a su cauce* things have resumed their course.

caución *f* guarantee, security (fianza) || cover (en Bolsa) || caution (precaución) || JUR bail.

caucionar *vt* to guarantee || to stand bail for (alguien en la cárcel).

caucho *m* rubber; *caucho vulcanizado* vulcanized rubber || *industria del caucho* rubber industry.

cauchutado *m* rubberizing, treating with rubber.

cauchutar *vt* to rubberize, to treat with rubber.

caudado, da *adj* ZOOL caudate.

caudal *adj* caudal; *plumas caudales* caudal feathers.
◆ *m* fortune, wealth (riqueza) || flow (de un río) || FIG wealth, great amount, abundance (abundancia) || COM assets *pl*.

caudaloso, sa *adj* mighty, swift, large (río) || rich, wealthy (rico) || copious, abundant (abundante).

caudatario *m* train bearer.

caudillaje; caudillismo *m* government by a caudillo || AMER bossism, tyranny || *bajo el caudillaje de* under the leadership of.

caudillo *m* leader || caudillo [in Spain] || AMER FIG boss.

caulescente *adj* BOT caulescent.

cauri *m* cowrie, cowry.

causa *f* cause; *causa y efecto* cause and effect; *causa eficiente* efficient cause; *causa final* final cause; *causa primera* prime cause || reason, cause, motive; *hablar sin causa* to speak without reason || cause, side, sake; *luchar por la causa de la libertad* to fight for the cause of liberty || JUR case, suit, cause, lawsuit (pleito) | trial (proceso) || AMER snack (comida ligera) || — *a causa de, por causa de* because of, on account of || JUR *causa pública* public good || JUR *entender* or *conocer una causa* to hear a case || *fuera de causa* irrelevant || *hacer causa común con* to make common cause with, to side with || JUR *instruir causa* to take legal proceedings || FIG *no hay efecto sin causa* there's no smoke without fire || *por causa tuya* for your sake, because of you || *por cuya causa* on account of which, because of which || *por esta causa* on this account, because of this || *¿por qué causa?* for what reason?, why? || *sin causa* for no reason, without reason (adverbio), caseless, groundless (adjetivo).

causahabiente *m* JUR assignee, executor, trustee.

causal *adj* GRAM causal.
◆ *f* reason, cause.

causalidad *f* causality, causation; *el principio de causalidad* the principle of causality || origin (origen).

causante *adj* causing, which caused; *la acción causante del alboroto* the action which caused the disturbance.
◆ *m/f* person who caused, cause; *el causante del accidente* the person who caused the accident.

causar *vt* to cause, to be the cause of (ser causa); *causar perjuicio* to cause damage || to make (una impresión) || to provoke (ira, etc.) || — *causar placer* to give pleasure || *causar risa a uno* to make s.o. laugh.

causticidad *f* causticity || FIG causticity.

cáustico, ca *adj* caustic || *sosa cáustica* caustic soda.
◆ *m* FIG caustic.

cautela *f* caution, cautiousness; *obrar con cautela* to act with caution || *tener la cautela de hacer algo* to take the precaution of doing sth.

cautelarse *vpr* to guard (*de* against), to take precautions (*de* against).

cautelosamente *adv* cautiously, warily.

cauteloso, sa *adj* cautious, wary; *un hombre muy cauteloso* a very cautious man.

cauterio *m* cautery (instrumento) || FIG drastic measure.

cauterización *f* cauterization.

cauterizador, ra *adj* cauterizing, cauterant.
◆ *m* person who cauterizes || cautery (cosa).

cauterizar *vt* to cauterize || FIG to apply drastic measures to.

cautivador, ra *adj* captivating; *una sonrisa cautivadora* a captivating smile.

cautivar *vt* to take prisoner, to capture (a un enemigo) || FIG to hold, to capture (la atención, a un auditorio) | to captivate, to charm (fascinar).

cautiverio *m*; **cautividad** *f* captivity; *vivir en cautividad* to live in captivity.

cautivo, va *adj/s* captive || *globos cautivos* barrage balloons, captive balloons.

cauto, ta *adj* cautious, wary.

cava *adj f* ANAT *vena cava* vena cava.
◆ *f* digging || dressing of vines (de las viñas) || TECN banking up.
◆ *m* Catalan wine similar to champagne.

cavador *m* digger.

cavadura *f* digging || AGR dressing.

cavar *vt* to dig (excavar) || to dig, to sink (un pozo) || AGR to dress || TECN to bank up || FIG *cavar su (propia) fosa* or *sepultura* to dig one's own grave.
◆ *vi* to dig || FIG to examine closely, to go thoroughly into (ahondar) | to meditate on, to ponder on; *cavar en los misterios de la fe* to meditate on the mysteries of faith.

cavatina *f* MÚS cavatina.

cavazón *m* digging || AGR dressing.

caverna *f* cave, cavern || cavity (en el pulmón).

cavernario, ria *adj* cave, cavern.

cavernícola *adj* cave-dwelling (personas, animales) || FIG reactionary (en política) || *hombre cavernícola* caveman, troglodyte.
◆ *m/f* cave dweller, caveman, troglodyte || FIG reactionary (en política).

cavernoso, sa *adj* cavernous || FIG deep, hollow; *voz cavernosa* deep voice.

caveto *m* ARQ cavetto (moldura).

caviar *m* caviar, caviare (hueva de esturión).

cavidad *f* cavity.

cavilación *f* pondering, meditation, deep thought.

cavilar *vi* to ponder, to meditate, to think deeply (pensar mucho).

caviloso, sa *adj* pensive (pensativo) || worried, troubled (preocupado).

cavitación *f* MAR & AVIAC cavitation.

cayado *m* shepherd's crook (de pastor) || crozier (de obispo) || ANAT *cayado de la aorta* arch of the aorta.

Cayena *n pr* GEOGR Cayenne.

cayo *m* key; *Cayo Hueso* Key West.

cayuco *m* AMER small Indian boat.

caz *m* millrace (de molino) || irrigation canal (acequia).

caza *f* hunting; *ir de caza* to go hunting || shooting (con arma de fuego) || trapping (con trampas) || game (animales que se cazan); *caza mayor, menor* big, small game || hunt (partida de caza) || shoot (partida con arma de fuego) || trapping (con trampas) || open season, hunting season (temporada) || MAR chase || — FIG *andar a la caza de* to be in search of, to be hunting for || *caza a la espera* or *al aguardo* or *en puesto* still hunt, stalking || *caza con hurón* ferreting || *caza de cabezas* headhunting || *caza del tesoro* treasure hunt || *caza furtiva* poaching || *caza submarina* underwater fishing || *dar caza* to give chase, to pursue || FIG *ir a la caza del hombre* to go on a manhunt || *levantar la caza* to put up the game (los cazadores), to let the cat out of the bag (figurado) || *partida de caza* hunting party (gente), hunt (actividad) || *permiso de caza* hunting licence || *vedado de caza* game preserve.
◆ *m* AVIAC fighter, pursuit plane, fighter plane || *piloto de caza* fighter pilot.

cazabe *m* cassava flour (harina) || cassava bread (pan).

cazabombardero *m* fighter bomber.

cazador, ra *adj* hunting (que caza) || *Diana Cazadora* Diana the Huntress.
◆ *m/f* hunter (en general), huntsman (cazador de zorros) || — *cazador de cabezas* headhunter || FIG *cazador de dotes* fortune hunter || *cazador furtivo* poacher || *cazador de pieles* trapper.
◆ *f* jerkin (chaqueta).

cazadotes *m inv* fortune hunter.

cazalla *f* aniseed spirit [made in Cazalla (Sevilla)].

cazar *vt* to hunt (los animales); *han ido a cazar conejos* they are out hunting rabbits || to catch, to bag; *hemos cazado diez conejos* we have bagged ten rabbits || FIG to hunt down, to track down (a una persona) || FIG & FAM to get, to land; *cazar un buen destino* to land a good job | to pick out (una falta) | to catch, to surprise (sorprender) | to catch, to trap, to land (un marido) || MAR to haul taut (una vela) || — *cazar furtivamente* to poach || FIG & FAM *cazar una cosa al vuelo* to catch on to sth. quickly | *cogerlas* or *cazarlas al vuelo* to catch on quickly, to be quick on the uptake.

cazasubmarinos *m inv* MAR submarine chaser.

cazatorpedero *m* MAR destroyer, torpedo-boat destroyer.

cazcarria *f* splash *o* spatter of mud || AMER sheep dung.

cazo *m* ladle (cucharón) || saucepan (para calentar el agua) || glue pot (de carpintero) || — TECN *cazo de colada* casting ladle || *cazo eléctrico* electric kettle.

cazolada *f* panful.

cazolero; cazoletero *adj/s* sissy (hombre entrometido en cosas de mujeres).

cazoleta *f* small saucepan || bowl (de pipa) || hand guard (de la espada) || boss (del escudo) || pan (de arma de chispa) || TECN housing.

cazoletear *vi* to meddle, to interfere.

cazón *m* dogfish (pez).

cazuela *f* casserole (de arcilla) || stewpan (metálico) || casserole, stew (guiso) || TEATR gods *pl* (gallinero) || cup (de un sostén).

cazumbre *m* hemp cord.

cazurro, rra *adj* taciturn, sullen (huraño) || obstinate, stubborn (obstinado) || stupid (bruto).

CC.OO. *abrev de Comisiones Obreras* Spanish trade union [with Communist affiliations].

ce *f* c (letra) || psst (llamando a alguien) || *por ce o por be* for one reason or another.

ceba *f* fattening [of animals] || stoking (de un horno) || AMER primer (de un arma).

cebada *f* barley (planta, semilla); *cebada perlada* pearl barley || FIG *a burro muerto cebada al rabo* it is no good shutting the stable door after the horse has bolted.

cebadal *m* barley field.

cebadera *f* nosebag || barley hopper (cajón para la cebada) || TECN hopper (de un horno).

cebadero *m* barley dealer (el que vende) || TECN mouth [of a furnace] || lead mule (mula que va delante).

cebadilla *f* wild barley.

cebado, da *adj* fattened (un animal) || FIG & FAM very fat || (ant) fatted (becerro en la Biblia).

cebadura *f* fattening (de un animal) || stoking (de un horno) || priming (de un arma) || AMER quantity of mate leaves [used at one time].

cebar *vt* to fatten (engordar un animal) || to bait (con un anzuelo, una trampa) || FIG to feed; *cebar el fuego* to feed the fire || MIL to prime (armas) || TECN to stoke (un horno) | to prime (una bomba, un sifón) || AMER *cebar mate* to prepare maté.
◆ *vi* to go in, to grip (un tornillo) || to grip, to bite (un tuerco) || to go in (un clavo).
◆ *vpr* to set upon; *se cebó en su víctima, conmigo* he set upon his victim, upon me || to rage (incendio, plaga).

cebellina *adj f/sf* sable.

cebiche *m* AMER dish of marinated raw fish.

cebo *m* feed, food (para los animales) || bait (para atraer los peces, etc.) || primer (de un arma) || charge, fuel (horno) || FIG bait, lure, incentive (señuelo) | food, fuel (pábulo) || — *cebo artificial* artificial bait || *cebo artificial de cuchara* spoon bait (para la pesca).

cebo *m* sajou, sapajou (mono).

cebolla *f* onion (planta y bulbo); *una ristra de cebollas* a string of onions || bulb (de tulipán) || rose, nozzle (de ducha) || AMER FAM power (mando); *agarrar la cebolla* to seize power || — BOT *cebolla albarrana* squill | *cebolla escalonia* shallot.

cebollar *m* onion patch.

cebollero, ra *adj* *alacrán cebollero* mole cricket.
◆ *m* onion seller.

cebolleta *f* BOT chive || tender onion.

cebollino *m* small onion || FIG & FAM *mandar a alguien a escardar cebollinos* to tell s.o. to jump in the lake, to send s.o. packing.

cebollón *m* large sweet onion || AMER FAM confirmed bachelor.

cebollona *f* AMER FAM old maid, confirmed spinster (solterona).

cebolludo, da *adj* bulbaceous (plantas) || coarse (personas).

cebón, ona *adj* fattened.
◆ *m* fattened pig (puerco) || fattened animal (otro animal).

cebra *f* zebra (animal) || *paso de cebra* zebra crossing.

cebrado, da *adj* striped.

cebú *m* zebu (animal).

ceca *f* (ant) Royal Mint (Casa de la Moneda) || FIG & FAM *ir de la Ceca a la Meca* to chase about, to dash all over the place, to go from place to place.

cecal *adj* ANAT caecal, cecal.

cecear *vi* to lisp (tener frenillo) || to pronounce the Spanish *s* as a Spanish *z* (característica regional).
◆ *vt* to call, to call (s.o.) over (llamar).

ceceo *m* lisp (frenillo).
— OBSERV *Ceceo* is a linguistic feature whereby the Spanish *s* is pronounced as the Spanish *z* [θ]. It is common in southern Andalusia, especially in Seville and Cadiz, and also in certain parts of Latin America.

cecidia *f* BOT cecidium, gall.

Cecilia *npr f* Cecily.

Cecilio *npr m* Cecil.

cecina *f* cured meat || AMER jerked meat (tasajo).

cecinar *vt* to jerk, to cure.

ceda *f* z (letra).

cedacear *vi* to fail (la vista).

cedacero *m* sieve maker *o* seller.

cedacillo *m* quaking grass.

cedazo *m* sieve.

ceder *vt* to transfer, to make over; *ceder un comercio* to transfer a business || to give up, to hand over (entregar) || to give; *ceder el paso* to give way; *ceder el sitio a una señora* to give one's seat to a lady || to cede (un territorio) || to pass (el balón) || — *ceda el paso* give way (señal de tráfico) || *ceder terreno* to give way, to yield ground.
◆ *vi* to yield, to give in (no poder resistir) || to collapse, to give way; *el puente ha cedido* the bridge has given way || to drop, to ease off, to let up (el viento) || to let up, to lull (la tormenta) || to let up (el frío) || to abate, to ease off (el dolor) || to slacken (aflojarse) || MED to yield || — *ceder a* to yield to, to give way to, to submit to (alguien), to yield to (una solicitud, al miedo), to succumb to (el sueño), to yield to, to bow to (voluntad) || *ceder en un derecho* give up a right || *la puerta cedió* the door gave way || *no cederle a alguien en algo* to match s.o. at *o* for sth., to hold one's own to s.o. in sth. || *obligar a ceder* to bring to terms.

cedilla *f* cedilla.
— OBSERV The *cedilla* is no longer used in Spanish.

cedrino, na *adj* cedrine.

cedro *m* cedar (árbol, madera).

cédula *f* document || I. O. U. (de reconocimiento de deuda) || index card (ficha de catálogo) || COM warrant (catálogo) || — JUR *cédula de citación* summons | *cédula hipotecaria* mortgage bond || (ant) *cédula personal* identity card || (ant) *cédula real* royal warrant.

CEE *abrev de Comunidad Económica Europea* EEC, European Economic Community.

cefalalgia *f* MED cephalalgia, headache.

cefalea *f* MED migraine.

cefálico, ca *adj* cephalic.

cefalitis *f* MED encephalitis.

cefalópodo, da *adj/sm* cephalopod.

cefalotórax *m* ZOOL cephalothorax.

céfiro *m* zephyr (viento).

cefo *m* sajou, sapajou (mono).

cegado, da *adj* blinded || blocked (cerrado).

cegador, ra *adj* blinding.

cegar* *vi* to go blind (perder la vista).
◆ *vt* to blind (quitar la vista) || FIG to blind, to dazzle (deslumbrar) | to block up; *cegar un pozo* to block up a well | to wall up (puerta, ventana) | to blind; *le ciega la ira* anger blinds him.
◆ *vpr* to be blinded.

cegarra; cegarrita *adj* short-sighted || *a cegarritas* blindly.
◆ *m/f* short-sighted person.

cegato, ta; cegatón, ona *adj* short-sighted.
◆ *m/f* short-sighted person.

cegesimal *adj* C. G. S.; *sistema cegesimal* C. G. S. system.

cegetista *adj* C. G. T. (de la Confederación General del Trabajo).
◆ *m/f* member of the C. G. T.

ceguedad; ceguera *f* blindness || FIG shortsightedness, blindness || MED *ceguera verbal* word blindness.

ceiba *f* ceiba, silk-cotton tree, bombax (árbol).

ceibo *m* BOT ceibo.

Ceilán *n pr* GEOGR Ceylon.

ceilanés, esa *adj/s* Ceylonese.

ceja *f* eyebrow (del ojo) || projecting edge (borde saliente de un objeto) || piping, edging (en la ropa) || joint (de un libro) || summit, top (cumbre de una sierra) || cap of clouds [on a hill] || TECN rim, flange || MÚS nut (de la guitarra) | capotasto (abrazadera) || AMER track, path (vereda) || — *arquear* or *enarcar las cejas* to raise one's eyebrows (gesto de sorpresa o de asombro) || FIG & FAM *estar hasta las cejas de* to be fed up to the teeth of, to have had enough of || *fruncir las cejas* to frown || FIG & FAM *quemarse las cejas* to burn the midnight oil | *tener a uno entre ceja y ceja* or *entre cejas* not to be able to stand s.o. | *tener* or *meterse una cosa entre ceja y ceja* to get sth. into one's head || *tener la ceja abierta* to have a cut above the eye (en boxeo).

cejar *vi* to go *o* to move backwards, to back up (andar hacia atrás) || FIG to slack, to let up, to relax; *no cejes en tu esfuerzo* don't slack in your effort | to back down, to climb down (ceder en un argumento).

cejijunto, ta *adj* bushy-browed, with thick eyebrows || FIG frowning (ceñudo).

cejilla *f* MÚS nut (en la guitarra) | capotasto (abrazadera).

cejudo, da *adj* bushy-browed, with thick eyebrows.

celacanto *m* ZOOL coelacanth.

celada *f* sallet, helmet (de la armadura) || FIG ambush; *caer en una celada* to fall into an ambush | trap (trampa) || *celada borgoñota* burgonet.

celador, ra *m/f* monitor (en un colegio) || guard, warden (en una cárcel) || attendant, curator (de museo) || attendant (de biblioteca) || maintenance man (que arregla máquinas).

celaje *m* coloured cloud effect (en pintura) || coloured clouds *pl* (en el cielo) || skylight (claraboya) || FIG presage, indication, foreboding (presagio).

celar *vt* to supervise (en un colegio) || to guard, to keep watch over (en una cárcel) || to observe closely (las leyes) || to hide, to conceal (ocultar).
◆ *vi* *celar por* or *sobre* to watch over.

celda *f* cell; *celda de castigo* solitary confinement cell || INFORM cell; *celda de memoria* memory cell.

celdilla *f* cell (de una colmena) || niche (hornacina).

cele *adj* AMER unripe, green (no maduro).

celebérrimo, ma *adj* most famous, renowned, illustrious.

celebración *f* celebration (de un acto solemne) || holding (de una reunión).

celebrado, da *adj* popular.

celebrante *adj* REL celebrant.
◆ *m* celebrant priest (oficiante).

celebrar *vt* to praise, to extol; *celebrar su belleza* to praise her beauty || to sing (las haza-

ñas) || to celebrate (una fiesta, una ceremonia) || to perform, to celebrate (una boda) || to say, to celebrate (la misa) || to hold (reunión, conversaciones) || to be glad *o* happy (alegrarse); *celebro que no sea grave* I am glad that it is not serious || to laugh at; *celebrar las gracias del niño* to laugh at the child's remarks || to welcome; *celebraron la mejoría del enfermo* they welcomed the patient's recovery || to reach (un acuerdo).
◆ *vi* to say mass (misa).
◆ *vpr* to take place; *ayer se celebró la ceremonia de clausura* the closing ceremony took place yesterday || to fall on, to be celebrated on; *mi cumpleaños se celebra el dos de marzo* my birthday falls on the second of March || *se celebró ayer un consejo de administración* there was a meeting of the board of directors yesterday, a meeting of the board of directors was held yesterday.

célebre *adj* famous, renowned, noted, celebrated || FAM funny (gracioso).

celebridad *f* fame, renown, celebrity; *ganar celebridad* to win fame || celebrity (persona célebre).

celemín *m* dry measure of about a half-peck (para áridos) || Castilian land measure of about an eighth of an acre (medida agraria).

celentéreo *m* ZOOL coelenterate.

celeridad *f* speed, swiftness, quickness, celerity, rapidity (velocidad) || *con toda celeridad* as quickly as possible, in all haste, at full speed.

celeste *adj* celestial, heavenly (del cielo); *los espacios celestes* the celestial spaces || — *bóveda celeste* vault of heaven || *cuerpo celeste* heavenly body || *el Celeste Imperio* the Celestial Empire.
◆ *adj/sm* sky blue (color).

celestial *adj* celestial, heavenly (del cielo); *música celestial* celestial music || FIG divine (don) | delightful, heavenly (delicioso) || FIG & FAM stupid, daft (bobo).

celestina *f* FIG procuress, bawd (alcahueta).

Celestina *npr f* Celestine.

celestino *m* celestine (monje).

celiaco, ca; celíaco, ca *adj* coeliac, celiac (intestinal).
◆ *f* MED coeliac disease, celiac disease.

celibato *m* celibacy; *el celibato eclesiástico* ecclesiastical celibacy.

célibe *adj* celibate, unmarried, single.
◆ *m/f* celibate, single person (hombre o mujer), bachelor (hombre), spinster (mujer).

celidonia *f* BOT celandine.

celinda *f* syringa (planta).

celo *m* zeal, fervour [*US* fervor] (cuidado) || REL religious fervour, piety || ZOOL oestrus, heat (de la hembra) | rut (del macho) || *estar en celo* to be on heat (animal hembra), to be in rut (animal macho).
◆ *pl* jealousy *sing* || — *dar celos* to make jealous || *entrar en celos* to come on heat (animal hembra), to come into rut (animal macho) || *tener celos* to be jealous.

celofán *m*; **celófana** *f* cellophane.

celosamente *adv* enthusiastically, zealously || fervently || jealously (con envidia).

celosía *f* lattice window (ventana) || lattice (enrejado).

celoso, sa *adj* enthusiastic, zealous (esmerado) || jealous (que tiene celos); *un hombre celoso* a jealous man || jealous (que mantiene algo con rigor); *es muy celoso de sus derechos* he is very jealous of his rights || MAR light and unsteady (embarcación).

celsitud *f* sublimity, grandeur (elevación).

celta *m/f* Celt, Kelt (persona).
◆ *m* Celtic, Keltic (lengua).
◆ *adj* Celtic, Keltic.

Celtiberia *npr f* Celtiberia.

celtibérico, ca; celtiberio, ria *adj/s* Celtiberian.

celtíbero, ra; celtibero, ra *adj/s* Celtiberian.

céltico, ca *adj/sm* Celtic, Keltic.

célula *f* cell (celda) || BIOL & ZOOL cell; *célula nerviosa* nerve cell || INFORM cell || FIG cell (política) || — *célula fotoeléctrica* photoelectric cell || *célula solar* solar cell.

celular *adj* ANAT cellular; *tejido celular* cellular tissue || *coche celular* police van, Black Maria (*fam*).

celulitis *f* MED cellulitis.

celuloide *m* celluloid || — FIG *celuloide rancio* old film | *llevar al celuloide* to make a film of (obra de teatro, novela, etc.).

celulosa *f* QUÍM cellulose.

celulósico, ca *adj* cellulose.

cella *f* ARQ cella, body [of temple].

cellisca *f* sleetstorm, sleet.

cellisquear *v impers* to sleet.

cello *m* hoop (de tonel).

cementación *f* TECN case hardening, cementation (de metales).

cementador *m* cement maker *o* mixer (obrero).

cementar *vt* TECN to case harden, to cement, to face-harden.

cementerio *m* cemetery, graveyard || — *cementerio de coches* wrecked-car dump, wrecker's yard, breaker's yard || *cementerio nuclear* or *radioactivo nuclear o* radioactive dump.

cemento *m* cement || concrete (hormigón); *cemento armado* reinforced concrete || cement (de los dientes) || FAM *tener una cara de cemento armado, tener la cara como cemento* to have a lot of cheek (ser muy descarado).

cena *f* dinner, supper (véase OBSERV); *cena con baile* dinner dance, dinner and dance; *cena de despedida* farewell dinner || *la Última* or *la Santa Cena* The Last Supper.

— OBSERV *Supper* suele ser una comida más ligera que *dinner*.

cenáculo *m* cenacle (de la Última Cena) || FIG cenacle, coterie (reunión literaria).

cenacho *m* basket (de esparto); *un cenacho de legumbres* a basket of vegetables.

cenado, da *adj* who has eaten dinner *o* supper || *estar cenado* to have dined, to have eaten dinner *o* supper.

cenador, ra *m/f* diner, person eating dinner *o* supper.
◆ *m* bower, arbour [*US* arbor] (en un jardín) || loggia (galería).

cenagal *m* bog, marsh, swamp (sitio pantanoso) || FIG & FAM mess, jam, tight spot; *estar metido en un cenagal* to be in a mess.

cenagoso, sa *adj* muddy; *camino cenagoso* muddy road.

cenar *vi* to dine, to have dinner *o* supper (véase OBSERV en CENA) || — *invitar a uno a cenar* to invite s.o. to dinner || *quedarse sin cenar* to go without dinner *o* supper.
◆ *vt* to have for dinner *o* supper, to dine on; *cenó una tortilla* he had an omelette for supper.

cenceño, ña *adj* thin, slim.

cencerrada *f* din, racket, row (alboroto); *dar una cencerrada* to make a row || noisy serenade [given to a widow who remarries].

cencerrear *vi* to ring bells continually (agitar una campanilla) || to jingle, to jangle, to clang (campanillas, etc.) || FIG & FAM to scrape a violin (violín) | to strum, to twang away (con guitarra, laúd) | to rattle (puerta, ventana).

cencerreo *m* jingling *o* ringing *o* clanging of bells (de campanillas) || row, din (ruido) || rattle (de puerta, de ventana) || twang (de guitarra).

cencerro *m* cowbell (campanilla de los animales) || — FIG *a cencerros tapados* on the quiet, on the sly | *estar más loco que un cencerro* to be completely mad.

cencuate *m* poisonous snake [from Mexico].

cendal *m* veil (velo) || sendal (tela) || REL humeral veil.
◆ *pl* barbs (de la pluma).

cenefa *f* border, edging (de alfombra, de toalla, de jardín, etc.) || frieze, ornamental border (en una pared) || skirting board [*US* baseboard] (zócalo).

cenicero *m* ashtray.

Cenicienta *npr f* Cinderella.

ceniciento, ta *adj* ash, ashen, ashy (color).

cenit *m* ASTR zenith.

cenital *adj* zenithal.

ceniza *f* ash; *reducir a cenizas* to reduce to ashes || — *Miércoles de Ceniza* Ash Wednesday.
◆ *pl* ashes, mortal remains (restos mortales) || dust *sing*; *cenizas radiactivas* radioactive dust || FIG *reducir a cenizas* to burn to ashes, to reduce to ashes || *remover las cenizas* to rake up the past.

cenizo, za *adj* ash-grey, ashen, ashy (ceniciento).
◆ *m* FAM wet blanket, spoilsport, killjoy (aguafiestas) | jinx (mala suerte); *tiene el cenizo* he has a jinx on him || FIG & FAM *ser un cenizo* to be a jinx (ser gafe).

cenobial *adj* cenobitic, coenobitic, cenobitical, coenobitical.

cenobio *m* monastery (monasterio).

cenobita *m/f* cenobite, coenobite.

cenobítico, ca *adj* cenobitic, coenobitic, cenobitical, coenobitical.

cenobitismo *m* cenobitism, coenobitism.

cenotafio *m* cenotaph.

cenote *m* AMER natural well.

cenozoico, ca *adj* GEOL Cenozoic, Caenozoic.

censar *vt* to take a census of.

censo *m* census (empadronamiento); *hicieron el censo de* they took a census of || JUR tax (tributo) | annuity, pension, allowance (renta); *censo muerto* perpetual annuity | ground rent (sobre una casa) | lease, agreement (arrendamiento); *constituir un censo* to draw up a lease *o* an agreement || FIG burden (carga); *la educación de su hijo es un censo* his son's education is a burden || — *censo electoral* electorate (número de electores), electoral roll *o* register (lista de electores) || *censo enfitéutico* long lease || FIG & FAM *ser un censo para uno* to be a constant drain on s.o.'s money (costarle dinero), to be a burden on s.o. (pesarle).

censor *m* censor || auditor (de cuentas) || FIG critic.

censual *adj* census, censual (del empadronamiento) || pertaining to an annuity.

censualista *m/f* annuitant (que percibe una renta) || lessor (arrendador).

censura *f* censure (acción); *moción de censura* motion of censure || censorship (de prensa, de espectáculos) || censure, criticism, disapproval (reproche) || — *digno de censura* censurable || *pa-*

sar por la censura to go through the censor, to undergo censorship.

censurable *adj* censurable, blameworthy.

censurador, ra *adj* censorious.

censurar *vt* to censor; *censurar una película* to censor a film || to censure, to condemn, to criticize, to disapprove of; *censurar a* or *en uno su conducta* to disapprove of s.o.'s conduct.

centaura; centaurea *f* BOT centaury.

centauro *m* centaur.

centavo, va *adj* hundredth (centésimo).
◆ *m* hundredth, hundredth part || AMER cent, «centavo» [one hundredth part of peso, etc.] || FAM *estar sin un centavo* not to have two halfpennies to rub together, to be broke.

centella *f* flash (rayo) || lightning, flash of lightning (relámpago); *cayó una centella sobre la torre* the tower was struck by lightning || spark (chispa) || FIG spark || FIG *raudo como la centella* as quick as lightning *o* as a flash.

centellar *vi* —> **centellear.**

centelleador, ra; centellante; centelleante *adj* sparkling, flashing || twinkling (las estrellas) || flickering (fuego, llamas).

centellear; centellar *vi* to sparkle, to flash || to twinkle (las estrellas) || to flicker (un fuego).

centelleo *m* sparkling, flashing || twinkling (de las estrellas).

centena *f* hundred.

centenada *f* hundred || *a centenadas* by the hundred, in hundreds.

centenal; centenar *m* rye field.

centenar *m* hundred (centena); *centenares de hombres* hundreds of men || centenary, centennial (centenario) || *a* or *por centenares* by the hundred, in hundreds.

centenario, ria *adj* hundred-year-old, centenarian (persona) || centennial, centenary (fecha).
◆ *m/f* centenarian (persona).
◆ *m* centenary, centennial (aniversario).

centenaza *adj f* *paja centenaza* rye straw.

centeno *m* BOT rye.

centesimal *adj* centesimal.

centésimo, ma *adj* hundredth || *la centésima parte* a hundredth, one hundredth part.
◆ *m* hundredth, hundredth part || «centésimo», cent (centavo en Uruguay y Panamá).

centiárea *m* square metre, centiare.

centígrado, da *adj* centigrade; *escala centígrada* centigrade scale.

centigramo *m* centigramme [US centigram].

centilitro *m* centilitre [US centiliter].

centímetro *m* centimetre [US centimeter]; *centímetro cuadrado, cúbico* square, cubic centimetre.

céntimo, ma *adj* hundredth (centésimo).
◆ *m* cent, centime [one hundredth part of peseta, peso, etc.] || — *no tener un céntimo* not to have a penny || FIG *no valer un céntimo* not to be worth a brass farthing.

centinela *m* MIL sentry, guard || look-out, look-out man (persona que vigila) || FIG watch, look-out; *hacer centinela* to keep watch, to keep a look-out || MIL *estar de centinela, hacer centinela* to mount guard, to be on guard, to stand sentry.
— OBSERV The word *centinela* is used both as a masculine and a feminine noun. Common usage gives preference to the masculine form.

centinodia *f* knotgrass (planta).

centolla *f*; **centollo** *m* spider crab.

centón *m* cento (poesía) || patchwork quilt (colcha).

centrado, da *adj* centred [US centered] || FIG balanced; *una persona bien centrada* a well-balanced person.
◆ *m* centring [US centering].

centrador *m* TECN centring device *o* tool [US centering device *o* tool].

central *adj* central, centric; *punto central* central point || *casa central* head office.
◆ *f* power station; *central eólica, hidráulica, hidroeléctrica, nuclear, térmica* wind, hidraulic, hydroelectric, nuclear, thermal power station || switchboard (teléfono interior) || head office (casa matriz) || plant, station (industrial) || — *central azucarera* sugar mill, sugar refinery || *central de correos* central post office || *central telefónica* telephone exchange (de una ciudad).

centralismo *m* centralism.

centralista *adj/s* centralist.

centralita *f* switchboard (teléfono).

centralización *f* centralization, centralizing.

centralizador, ra *adj* centralizing.
◆ *m/f* centralizer.

centralizar *vt* to centralize.
◆ *vpr* to be centralized.

centrar *vt* to centre [US to center] (colocar bien) || to aim, to point (arma de fuego) || to focus (rayos de luz) || FIG to centre [US to center] (*en* on, around), to focus (*en* on), to focus (la atención, la discusión, etc.) | to base, to centre [US to center] (basar); *centra su vida en la política* he centres his life around politics; *centrar una novela sobre las cuestiones sociales* to base a novel on social questions.
◆ *vt/vi* to centre [US to center] (en deportes).
◆ *vpr* to centre [US to center] (*en* on, around); *la discusión se centró en la política* the discussion centred on politics || to be based (*en* on), to be based (basarse) || to find one's feet (orientarse una persona).

céntrico, ca *adj* central; *barrios céntricos* central districts.

centrifugador, ra *adj* centrifugal.
◆ *f* centrifugal machine, centrifuge (máquina).

centrifugar *vt* to centrifuge.

centrífugo, ga *adj* centrifugal; *bomba centrífuga* centrifugal pump.

centrípeto, ta *adj* centripetal; *aceleración centrípeta* centripetal acceleration.

centrista *m/f* centrist [US middle-of-the-roader] (en política).
◆ *adj* centre [US center], of the centre; *partido político centrista* Centre political party.

centro *m* centre [US center] (medio); *el centro del círculo* the centre of the circle || town centre, city centre; *comprar algo en el centro* to buy sth. in the town centre || FIG aim, goal, objective (objeto principal) || middle; *en el centro de la calle* in the middle of the street || circle; *en los centros diplomáticos* in diplomatic circles || FIG heart, centre; *el centro de la rebelión* the heart of the rebellion || centre (club) || centre (en el fútbol) || ANAT & MAT centre || MED root, origin (de una enfermedad) || — *centro comercial* shopping centre || DEP *centro chut* centre || *centro de atracción, de gravedad* centre of attraction, of gravity || INFORM *centro de cálculo* computer centre || *centro de desintoxicación* detoxification centre || *centro de interés* centre of interest || *centro de masa* centre of mass || *centro de mesa* centrepiece (en la mesa) || *centro docente* educational institution || *centro nervioso* or *neurálgico* nerve centre || *delantero centro* centre forward || *en el mismísimo centro* right in the centre, in the very centre || FIG *estar en su centro* to feel at home, to be in one's element || *medio centro* centre half || *partido del centro* Centre party.

Centroamérica *npr f* GEOGR Central America.

centroamericano, na *adj/s* Central American.

Centroeuropa *npr f* GEOGR Central Europe.

centroeuropeo, a *adj/s* Central European.

centrosfera *f* BIOL centrosphere.

centrosoma *m* BIOL centrosome.

centuplicar *vt* to increase a hundredfold, to centuple, to centuplicate, to multiply by one hundred.

céntuplo, a *adj* hundredfold, centuple.
◆ *m* hundredfold, centuple, centuplicate.

centuria *f* century.

centurión *m* HIST centurion.

cénzalo *m* mosquito.

ceñido, da *adj* tight-fitting, close-fitting, figure-hugging, clinging; *un vestido muy ceñido* a very tight-fitting dress || tight (una curva) || close (cerca) || pediculate, pedicellate (los insectos).

ceñidor *m* belt (cinturón), girdle (cordón).

ceñir *vt* to be tight for; *ese vestido te ciñe demasiado* that dress is too tight for you || to wreath, to crown (con flores) || to gird, to circle, to encircle, to surround; *el mar ciñe la isla* the sea circles the island; *las murallas ciñen la ciudad* the walls encircle the city || to frame; *cabellos negros que ciñen un rostro* black hair which frames a face || to cling to, to be tight on; *el jersey la ciñe mucho* the pullover is very tight on her || to get hold of *o* to grip round the waist (abrazar); *ceñir a un adversario* to get hold of an opponent round the waist || to gird (la espada) || to shorten, to cut down (una narración) || to take in (estrechar un vestido) || *ceñir la cabeza con una corona* to crown s.o. *o* to put a crown on s.o.'s head.
◆ *vpr* to limit o.s., to cut down; *tenemos que ceñirnos en los gastos* we have to cut down on spending *o* limit our spending || to stich, to keep; *ceñirse al tema* to stick to the subject || to keep to; *ceñirse a la derecha* to keep to the right || to adapt o.s., to conform (amoldarse); *hay que ceñirse al reglamento de la universidad* you have to conform to the university rules || to cling; *este traje se ciñe al cuerpo* this dress clings to the body || TAUR to get very close [to the bull] || — *ceñirse a la curva* to take the bend tightly (un coche) || *ceñirse a un sueldo modesto* to live with a modest salary || *ceñirse la espada* to gird one's sword, to put on one's sword.

ceño *m* scowl, frown || *fruncir el ceño* to scowl, to frown, to knit one's brow.

ceñudo, da *adj* frowning, scowling.

cepa *f* stock, vine (vid) || stump (tronco de árbol) || FIG stock, origin (origen de una persona); *de pura* or *de vieja cepa* of pure stock || pillar (de un puente) || — *de buena cepa* of good stock || FIG *de pura cepa* real, genuine, authentic (de verdad).

cepillado *m*; **cepilladura** *f*; **acepilladura** *f* planing (carpintería) || brushing, brush (de un vestido).
◆ *pl* shavings.

cepillar; acepillar *vt* to brush (los trajes, etc.) || to plane (carpintería).
◆ *vpr* FAM to fail (en un examen); *cepillarse a uno en física* to fail s.o. in physics | to kill, to polish off (matar) | to polish off, to brush off (comiendo) || POP to lay (acostarse con).

cepillo *m* brush; *cepillo para el suelo, las uñas, los zapatos* scrubbing brush, nail brush, shoe brush || collecting box, poor box, alms box (en las iglesias) || plane (carpintería) || — *cepillo bocel* moulding plane (herramienta) || *cepillo de dientes* toothbrush || *cepillo para el pelo* hairbrush || *tener el pelo al cepillo* to have a crew cut.

cepo *m* branch, bough (rama) || block, stock (para el yunque) || stocks *pl*, pillory (instrumento de tortura) || trap (trampa) || collecting box, poor box, alms box (en las iglesias) || fetters *pl*, shackles *pl* (grilletes) || TECN clamp (objeto para sujetar) || ZOOL sajou, sapajou (mono) || — FIG *caer en el cepo* to fall into the trap || MAR *cepo del ancla* anchor stock.

cepón *m* large vine.

ceporro *m* old vine used for fuel || FIG & FAM fat lump, fatty (persona muy gruesa) | thickhead, blockhead (estúpido) || FIG *dormir como un ceporro* to sleep like a log.

cequí *m* sequin (moneda antigua).

cequía *f* irrigation ditch *o* channel (acequia).

cera *f* wax; *cera amarilla, mineral* yellow, mineral wax || AMER candle (vela) || — FIG *amarillo como la cera* as yellow as a guinea || *cera de abejas* beeswax || MED *cera de los oídos* earwax, cerumen || *cera para suelos* floor polish || FIG *estar pálido como la cera* to be as white as a sheet | *no hay más cera que la que arde* that is all there is there is nothing more than what you see.
◆ *pl* honeycomb *sing* (alveolos).

cerámica *f* ceramics (arte) || pottery (cosas).

cerámico, ca *adj* ceramic || *gres cerámico* stoneware.

ceramista *m/f* ceramist, potter.

cerapez *f* → **cerote.**

cerasta *f*; **cerastes** *m* cerastes, horned viper (víbora).

cerato *m* cerate, ointment (ungüento).

cerbatana *f* blowpipe || peashooter (de niños) || ear trumpet (para los sordos).

Cerbero *npr m* MIT Cerberus.

cerca *f* fence (valla) || hedge (seto).

cerca *adv* near, nearby, close; *vivimos muy cerca* we live very nearby || near, close; *no te pongas tan cerca* do not get so near || — *aquí cerca* near here, nearby || *cerca de* about; *cerca de mil muertos* about a thousand dead; nearly, almost (casi); *son cerca de las diez* it is nearly ten o'clock; with; *medié cerca del director para que no le expulsasen* I had a word with the boss so that they would not sack him || *cerca de mí, de ti, etc.* near me, you, etc. || *de cerca* closely, from close up || *embajador cerca de la Santa Sede* Ambassador to the Holy See || *estar cerca de hacer algo* to be near to doing sth., to be on the point of doing sth. || *mirar de cerca* to look closely, to take a close look || *muy de cerca* very closely, from very close quarters || *por aquí cerca* nearby, somewhere round here || *ya están cerca las Navidades* Christmas is nearly *o* almost here, it will soon be Christmas, Christmas will soon be here.
◆ *m pl* ARTES foreground *sing*.

cercado *m* enclosed garden, fenced-in garden (huerto) || enclosure (terreno cercado) || enclosure, fence (valla) || enclosure (terreno) || AMER territorial division, district (distrito).

cercanía *f* proximity, nearness || — *trabaja en la cercanía de su casa* he works near his house, he works in his neighbourhood.
◆ *pl* outskirts (alrededores); *vive en las cercanías de Leeds* he lives in the outskirts of Leeds || suburbs (afueras) || *tren de cercanías* suburban train.

cercano, na *adj* near, close (próximo, inmediato) || close; *un pariente cercano* a close relative || nearby, neighbouring; *ir a un pueblo cercano* to go to a neighbouring village || FIG impending (muerte) || — *cercano a su fin* nearing *o* near one's end || *Cercano Oriente* Near East.

cercar *vt* to enclose, to fence, to wall in (rodear con una cerca) || MIL to besiege, to surround, to encircle (sitiar) | to surround, to hem in (al enemigo) || to surround, to crowd round, to encircle; *la muchedumbre cercaba al rey* the crowd surrounded the King.

cercén (a) *loc adv* close, flush, right down to the roots; *cortar a cercén* to cut close.

cercenador, ra *adj* cutting, trimming.
◆ *m/f* trimmer, cutter.

cercenadura *f*; **cercenamiento** *m* cutting, trimming, clipping (parte cortada, acción de cercenar) || abridgement, shortening (de un texto, de un discurso) || reduction, curtailment (de gastos).

cercenar *vt* to cut, to trim (cortar el borde) || to cut down, to reduce, to curtail (disminuir, suprimir una parte de); *cercenar los gastos* to cut down expenditure || to shorten, to abridge, to cut down (un texto) || to cut off, to amputate (amputar) || to cut off (quitar algo cortando).

cerceta *f* garganey (ave).
◆ *pl* first antlers (del ciervo).

cerciorar *vt* to assure (asegurar) || to convince (convencer).
◆ *vpr* to make sure; *cerciorarse de un hecho* to make sure of a fact.

cerco *m* circle, ring (lo que rodea) || hoop (aro de tonel) || group (corrillo) || magic circle (figura mágica) || ring, circle (de una marcha) || ASTR halo (corona, halo) || TECN rim (de una rueda) || frame (marco de puerta, etc.) || MIL siege (asedio); *alzar* or *levantar el cerco* to raise the siege || AMER enclosure (cercado) | fence (cerca) | quickset hedge (seto vivo) || — *cerco policíaco* police cordon || MIL *poner cerco a* to besiege, to lay siege to.

cercopiteco *m* ZOOL cercopithecus (mono).

cerchar *vt* AGR to layer (la vid).

cerchearse *vpr* to warp (alabearse).

cerchón *m* ARQ truss (cimbra).

cerda *f* bristle (del cerdo) || horsehair (del caballo) || sow (hembra del cerdo) || noose, snare (lazo para cazar) || (harvested) corn (mies segada) || — *cepillo de cerda* bristle brush || *ganado de cerda* pigs.

cerdada *f* FAM foul *o* lousy trick (acción que perjudica a uno) | mess; *el niño está haciendo cerdadas en la mesa* the child is making a mess on the table.

cerdamen *m* tuft of bristle *o* horsehair.

Cerdaña *npr f* GEOGR Cerdagne Valley.

cerdear *vi* to be lame *o* weak in the forelegs (los animales) || MÚS to be out of tune (un instrumento) || FIG & FAM to play a foul *o* a lousy trick (jugar una mala pasada) | to back out *o* down (esquivar) | to play up, to give trouble; *este coche empieza a cerdear* this car is starting to play up | to put things off, to hedge (aplazar) || AMER to cut the hair of a horse (cortar la cerda a un caballo).

Cerdeña *npr f* GEOGR Sardinia.

cerdo *m* pig (puerco) || FIG & FAM pig (persona sucia, etc.) || — FIG *a cada cerdo le llega su San Martín* every dog has his day || *carne de cerdo* pork || *cerdo marino* porpoise || *cerdo salvaje* wild boar.

cerdoso, sa *adj* bristly; *barba cerdosa* bristly beard.

cereal *m* cereal.
◆ *pl* celebration *sing* in honour of Ceres || cereals, grain *sing* || *mercado de cereales* corn exchange.

cerealista *adj* cereal (de los cereales) || cereal-producing; *región cerealista* cereal-producing district.
◆ *m* cereal farmer (productor) *o* dealer (comerciante).

cerebelo *m* ANAT cerebellum.

cerebral *adj* cerebral.

cerebro *m* ANAT cerebrum (parte del encéfalo) | brain (encéfalo) || FIG brains *pl* (inteligencia) || — *cerebro electrónico* electronic brain || FIG *torturar su cerebro* to rack one's brains.

cerebroespinal *adj* cerebrospinal.

cereceda *f* cherry orchard (cerezal).

ceremonia *f* ceremony || fuss, ceremony (cumplidos); *andarse con* or *hacer ceremonias* to stand on ceremony, to make a fuss || REL ceremony, service || — *ceremonia civil* registry-office wedding || *con gran ceremonia* with great ceremony, ceremoniously, with a lot of fuss *o* of to-do (*fam*) || *hablar sin ceremonia* to speak informally || *maestro de ceremonias* master of ceremonies || *traje de ceremonia* formal dress.

ceremonial *adj/sm* ceremonial.

ceremonioso, sa *adj* ceremonious, formal.

céreo, a *adj* wax, waxen.

cerería *f* chandler's shop, chandlery.

cereza *f* cherry (fruta) || AMER husk of coffee bean (de café) | coffee cherry *o* berry (fruto del café) || — *cereza gordal* or *garrafal* white-heart cherry, bigarreau || *cereza pasa* dried cherry || *cereza silvestre* wild cherry, gean, merry || *rojo cereza* cherry-red.

cerezal *m* cherry orchard (plantío de cerezos).

cerezo *m* cherry tree (árbol) || *cerezo silvestre* wild cherry tree, gean tree, merry tree.

cerífero, ra *adj* ceriferous.

cerilla *f*; **cerillo** *m* match (fósforo); *una caja de cerillas* a box of matches || small wax taper (vela) || earwax (cera de los oídos).

cerillera *f*; **cerillero** *m* matchbox (caja) || match vendor (vendedor) || match pocket (bolsillo).

cerillo *m* → **cerilla.**

cerina *f* cerin (del alcornoque) || MIN cerium silicate || QUÍM cerin, cerotic acid (ácido cerótico).

cerio *m* QUÍM cerium (metal raro).

cerita *f* MIN cerite.

cermeño *m* boor, lout, uncouth chap (tosco).

cernada *f* leached ashes *pl* (de lejía) || ARTES primer (para imprimar los lienzos).

cerne *adj* hard, strong.
◆ *m* heart of the tree (parte más dura).

cernedera *f* bolter, bolting machine (tamiz).

cernedero *m* bolting cloth, sifter's apron (tela) || bolting mill (sitio).

cernedor *m* sieve, bolter (cedazo) || sifter (persona).

cerneja *f* fetlock (del caballo).

cerner*; cernir *vt* to bolt, to sieve, to sift (la harina) || to sieve, to sift (cualquier materia) || FIG to scan; *cerner el horizonte* to scan the horizon | to sift, to clear, to purge (los pensamientos).
◆ *vi* to bloom (florecer) || to drizzle (llover muy fino).
◆ *vpr* to hover (los pájaros) || to circle (los aviones) || FIG to hang, to loom; *se cernía sobre Europa la amenaza de la guerra* the threat of war hung over Europe || to swing *o* to sway one's hips, to wiggle (al andar).

cernícalo *m* kestrel (pájaro) || FIG & FAM lout, brute (bruto) || FAM *coger, pillar un cernícalo* to get sozzled, drunk.

cernidillo *m* drizzle (lluvia fina) || FIG swing of one's hips, wiggle (al andar).

cernido *m* sifting, sieving (acción de cerner) || sifted flour (harina).

cernidor *m* sieve.

cernidura *f* sifting, sieving (cernido).
◆ *pl* siftings, sievings, residue *sing* (residuos del cernido).

cernir* *vt* ⟶ **cerner.**

cero *m* MAT & FÍS zero; *cero absoluto* absolute zero; *seis grados bajo cero* six degrees below zero || nil (fútbol, rugby, etc.); *tres a cero* three nil || love (tenis); *cuarenta a cero* forty-love || nought, nothing (la cifra 0) || — *me pusieron un cero en inglés* I got a nought in *o* for English || FIG *partir de cero* to start from scratch || FIG & FAM *ser un cero* or *un cero a la izquierda* to be a nobody.

cerón *m* wax residue.

ceroso, sa *adj* waxen, waxy, ceraceous || *tez cerosa* waxy *o* sallow complexion.

cerote *m*; **cerapez** *f* cobbler's wax || FIG & FAM funk, fear (miedo).

cerotear *vt* to wax (los hilos).

cerquillo *m* fringe (de monje) || welt (del calzado) || AMER fringe (flequillo).

cerquita *adv* very near.

cerrado, da *adj* shut, closed; *la puerta está cerrada* the door is shut || shut in, enclosed; *un lugar cerrado de árboles* a place shut in by trees || FIG hidden (oculto); *el sentido cerrado de una carta* the hidden meaning of a letter || clenched, closed (puño) || dark, black (la noche) || overcast, dark (cielo) || heavy (lluvia) || sharp, tight (curva) || obstinate (obstinado) || thick, bushy; *una barba cerrada* a thick beard || FIG & FAM reticent, uncommunicative, secretive (poco expansivo) | thick, dense, dim (muy torpe) | typical; *es un alemán cerrado* he's a typical German || GRAM close; *vocales cerradas* close vowels || broad, with a marked accent; *hablar un andaluz cerrado* to speak broad Andalusian, to speak with a marked Andalusian accent || — *a ojos cerrados* with one's eyes closed, blindfold || *a puerta cerrada* in camera (jurisprudencia), behind closed doors || FAM *cerrado de mollera* thick, dim, dense || *descarga cerrada* volley, salvo (de armas de fuego) || FAM *oler a cerrado* to smell stuffy || *ovación cerrada* thunderous ovation || *pliego* or *sobre cerrado* sealed letter || *tomar una curva muy cerrada* to take a bend very tightly.
◆ *m* enclosure (cercado) || FIG & FAM blockhead, dunce, dimwit (poco inteligente).

cerrador *m* catch, fastener.

cerradura *f* lock (para cerrar); *cerradura de seguridad* safety lock || closing, shutting (acción de cerrar) || — *cerradura antirrobo* antitheft lock || *cerradura de combinación* combination lock.

cerraja *f* lock (cerradura) || BOT sow thistle || FIG *volverse* or *quedar en agua de cerrajas* to fizzle out, to come to nothing, to peter out.

cerrajería *f* locksmith's trade (oficio) || locksmith's (shop) (taller).

cerrajero *m* locksmith.

cerrar* *vt* to shut, to close (caja, puerta, etc.); *cierra la ventana* close the window || to close the entrance to; *la puerta cierra el jardín* the gate closes the entrance to the garden || to bolt (con cerrojo) | to enclose (cercar) || to close (los ojos, las piernas, etc.) || to clench, to close (el puño) || to seal (una carta) || to close (abanico) || to close, to shut, to put down (paraguas) || ELECTR to close, to complete (el circuito) || FIG to rule out; *este fracaso cierra otra posibilidad* this failure rules out any other possibility || to close (puerto, universidad, frontera) || to block, to close; *cerrar el camino* to block the road || FIG to bar; *me cerraron el paso* they barred my way || to block up, to stop, to plug (abertura, conducto) || to fasten (cinturón) || to turn off; *cerrar un grifo* to turn off a tap || to turn out *o* off (el gas) || to close (unir estrechamente); *cerrar las filas* to close the ranks || to stitch up (un ojal, etc.) || to block (en dominó) || to end, to finish (discusión) || to clinch; *cerrar un trato* to clinch a deal || to conclude (contrato, negocio) || to close (cuenta, etc.) || to shut, to close (una tienda) || to close down (cerrar definitivamente) || — *cerrar con dos vueltas* to double-lock || *cerrar con llave* to lock || FIG & FAM *cerrar con siete llaves* to lock and double-lock || FAM *cerrar el pico* to belt up, to shut one's trap, to shut one's mouth | *cerrarle el pico a uno* to shut s.o. up || *cerrar la marcha* to bring up the rear || *cerrar la puerta en las narices de alguien* to shut the door in s.o.'s face || *cerrar los puños* to clench one's fists.
◆ *vi* to close, to shut; *ventana que cierra mal* window which closes badly || to close with (con el enemigo) || to cast off (géneros de punto) || to come down (la noche) || to close, to heal (una herida) || — *dejar una ventana sin cerrar* to leave a window open || *la noche está cerrada* it is a dark night.
◆ *vpr* to close, to shut (puerta, flor, etc.) || to close up, to heal (una herida) || to cut in on; *el camión se me ha cerrado* the lorry cut in on me || MIL to close ranks || FIG to persist; *se cierra en callar* he persists in keeping quiet | to become overcast, to cloud over (el cielo, el horizonte) || FIG & FAM *cerrarse a la* or *por* or *en banda* to stick to one's guns.

cerrazón *f* dark *o* overcast sky, storm clouds *pl* (cielo nublado) || FIG denseness, slowness (torpeza) | obstinacy (obstinación) || GRAM closeness (de vocales) || AMER spur (de montañas).

cerrejón *m* hillock, small hill.

cerrero, ra *adj* wild, roaming (salvaje, vagabundo) || wild, untamed (caballo, mula) || FIG loutish, uncouth, rough, coarse (bruto) || AMER bitter; *café cerrero* bitter coffee.

cerril *adj* hilly, uneven, rough (terreno) || wild (animal), wild, untamed (caballo, mula) || FIG & FAM uncouth, rough, coarse, loutish (bruto) | dense, dim, slow (torpe).

cerrillo *m* hillock (colina) || BOT couch grass (grama).

cerro *m* hill (colina) || — FIG & FAM *echar* or *irse por los cerros de Úbeda* to wander from the subject, to go off at a tangent (salirse del tema) || *montar en cerro* to ride bareback.

cerrojazo *m* FIG *dar cerrojazo* to shut up shop (una tienda, empresa), to drop everything (dejar lo que se hacía) || *dar un cerrojazo* to shoot a bolt roughly.

cerrojillo *m* coal titmouse (pájaro).

cerrojo *m* bolt (de puerta, etc.) || bolt (del fusil) || blanket defence (en fútbol) || — *cerrar con cerrojo, echar* or *correr el cerrojo* to bolt (the door, etc.), to shoot the bolt || *descorrer el cerrojo* to unbolt (the door).

certamen *m* contest (desafío) || tournament, contest, competition (torneo) || (literary) competition; *participar en un certamen* to take part in a competition.

certero, ra *adj* good, accurate; *tiro certero* good shot || good, crack (tirador); *un tirador certero* a crack shot || good, skilful; *un cazador certero* a skilful hunter || well-founded, sound; *juicio certero* well-founded judgment.

certeza; certidumbre; certitud *f* certainty, certitude (cualidad de cierto) || accuracy (exactitud); *la certeza de la noticia* the accuracy of the news || — *saber algo con certeza* to be certain of sth || *tener la certeza (de) que...* to be quite sure that..., to be certain that..., to know for certain that....

certificación *f* certification (acción de certificar) || registration, registering (de carta o de paquete) || certificate (certificado).

certificado, da *adj* registered (carta, paquete) || certified.
◆ *m* certificate || registered letter *o* package || — *certificado de calidad* certificate of quality || ECON *certificado de depósito* certificate of deposit || *certificado de favor* certificate delivered as a favour || *certificado de penales* copy of one's police record || *certificado de vacuna* vaccination certificate || *certificado médico* medical certificate.

certificador *m* certifier.

certificar *vt* to certify, to guarantee (asegurar) || to register (carta, paquete).

certificatorio, ria *adj* which certifies, certifying.

certitud *f* ⟶ **certeza.**

cerúleo, a *adj* cerulean, azure, deep-blue.

cerumen *m* cerumen, earwax (cerilla de los oídos).

cerusa *f* ceruse.

cerusita *f* MIN cerussite.

cerval *adj* cervine, deer || — *gato cerval* lynx || *lobo cerval* kind of lynx (lince), shark, profiteer (estafador) || FIG *tener un miedo cerval* to be scared stiff.

cervantesco, ca; cervántico, ca; cervantino, na *adj* Cervantic, Cervantine, of Cervantes.

cervantista *adj* Cervantist.
◆ *m/f* Cervantist, expert of Cervantes.

cervantófilo, la *adj* of a person who admires *o* collects Cervantes' works.
◆ *m/f* person who admires *o* collects Cervantes' works.

cervatillo *m* ZOOL musk deer.

cervato *m* fawn (ciervo).

cerveceo *m* beer fermentation.

cervecería *f* brewery (fábrica) || public house, bar.

cervecero *m* brewer (fabricante).

cerveza *f* beer, ale; *cerveza dorada* light *o* pale ale, light beer || — *cerveza de barril* draught beer || *cerveza de botella* bottled beer || *cerveza negra* stout, brown ale.

cervical *adj* cervical.

cérvido *m* ZOOL cervid.

cervigón *m* thick *o* fat neck.

cerviguillo *m* thick *o* fat neck.

cervino, na *adj* cervine.

cerviz *f* nape of the neck, cervix (nuca) || — FIG *bajar* or *doblar* or *humillar la cerviz* to bow one's head, to humble o.s. | *levantar la cerviz* to lift one's head high | *ser de dura cerviz* to be pigheaded *o* to be stubborn.

cervuno, na *adj* cervine.

cesación *f*; **cesamiento** *m* cessation, discontinuation, suspension; *cesación de pagos* suspension of payments || *cesación a divinis* interdict.

cesante *adj* dismissed, removed from office, suspended (funcionario), recalled (embajador), jobless (empleado) || MIL unattached, on half-pay || — *dejar a uno cesante* to relieve s.o. of his office, to dismiss s.o. || *lucro cesante* lucrum cessans.
◆ *m/f* suspended official.

cesantear *vt* AMER to dismiss (despedir).

cesantía *f* suspension (sin trabajo) || pension [of suspended official] || leave of absence (descanso).

cesar *vi* to stop, to cease (parar); *no cesó de reír* he never stopped laughing || to leave, to

quit, to give up (en el trabajo) || — *cesar en el cargo* to cease one's functions || *cesar en sus quejas* to stop complaining, to cease one's complaints || *sin cesar* unceasingly, ceaselessly, nonstop.
◆ *vt* to stop, to suspend (los pagos).

César *m* Caesar (emperador) || FIG *hay que dar a Dios lo que es de Dios y al César lo que es del César* render therefore unto Caesar the things which are Caesar's and unto God the things that are God's.

cesaréo, a *adj* Caesarean, Caesarian.
◆ *adj f* Caesarean (operación).
◆ *f* Caesarean section *o* operation.

cesariano, na *adj* Caesarean, Caesarian (relativo a Julio César).
◆ *m* follower of Julius Caesar.

cesarismo *m* Caesarism.

cese *m* cessation, ceasing, discontinuation (suspensión) || order for the suspension of payments || dismissal (revocación de un oficial) || *dar el cese a alguien* to dismiss s.o.

cesibilidad *f* JUR transferability, assignability.

cesible *adj* JUR transferable, assignable.

cesio *m* caesium, cesium (metal).

cesión *f* cession (acción de ceder); *cesión de territorios* cession of territories || JUR transfer, assignment; *cesión de tierras, de bienes* assignment of land, of property.

cesionario, ria *m/f* JUR cessionary, transferee, assignee.

cesionista *m/f* grantor, transferor, transferer, assignor (que hace cesión de bienes).

césped *m* lawn, grass; *cortar el césped* to mow the lawn, to cut the grass || pitch (para juegos) || green (en las bochas) || turf, sod (trozo de tierra con hierba).

cesta *f* basket (recipiente de mimbre, etc.); *cesta de la compra* shopping basket; *cesta de costura* sewing basket; *cesta de los papeles* wastepaper basket || cesta, chistera, jai-alai basket [used in the Basque game of jai-alai] || basket (en el juego del baloncesto) || — *cesta de labores* workbasket, sewing basket || *cesta de Navidad* Christmas hamper || FIG & FAM *llevar la cesta a uno* to play gooseberry (to s.o.) (acompañar a dos enamorados).

cestada *f* basketful.

cestería *f* basketwork, wickerwork, basketmaking (trabajo) || basketworks *pl* (fábrica) || basketwork shop (tienda).

cestero, ra *m/f* basketmaker.

cestillo *m* small basket || basket (de globo).

cesto *m* basket (grande o pequeño); *cesto de los papeles* wastepaper basket || hamper (con asas y tapa) || cestus (guante de atletas romanos) || — FIG *echar una carta al cesto de los papeles* to discard a letter | *quien hace un cesto, hará ciento* once a thief, always a thief.

cestodo *m* ZOOL cestode.

cestón *m* MIL gabion.

cestonada *f* MIL gabionade, line of gabions.

cesura *f* POÉT caesura, cesura (pausa).

ceta *f* → **zeta.**

cetáceo *m* ZOOL cetacean.

cetonia *f* ZOOL cetonia.

cetona *f* QUÍM ketone.

cetrería *f* falconry, hawking.

cetrero *m* falconer || REL verger.

cetrino, na *adj* sallow || FIG melancholy, despondent.

cetro *m* sceptre [US scepter] (insignia de mando) || perch (para los halcones) || FIG power, dominion (poder) || FIG sceptre (reinado) || — *cetro de bufón* fool's sceptre, jester's bauble || *empuñar el cetro* to ascend the throne.

CEU *abrev de Centro de Estudios Universitarios* Centre where university degree can be obtained.

ceugma *f* GRAM zeugma.

ceutí *adj* [of *o* from] Ceuta.
◆ *m/f* inhabitant *o* native of Ceuta.

Cía. *abrev de Compañía* Co, Company.

cía *f* ANAT hipbone.

ciaboga *f* MAR turn.

cianhídrico, ca *adj* QUÍM hydrocyanic.

cianita *f* MIN cyanite.

cianógeno *m* QUÍM cyanogen.

cianosis *f* MED cyanosis.

cianotipo *m* blueprint, cyanotype.

cianuro *m* QUÍM cyanide.

ciar *vi* to back up, to walk backwards (retroceder) || MAR to backwater, to back the oars || FIG to give up, to drop; *ciar en sus pretensiones* to give up *o* to drop one's claims | to back down (rajarse) || to reverse (el vapor).

ciático, ca *adj* MED sciatic.
◆ *f* MED sciatica.

Cibeles *npr f* MIT Cybele.

cibelina *f* ZOOL sable.

cibera *adj f* feeding.
◆ *f* food, feed (pienso) || load, primer (de un molino) || marc (residuos).

cibernético, ca *adj* cybernetic, cybernetical.
◆ *f* cybernetics.

ciborio *m* ARQ ciborium (baldaquino) || goblet (copa).

cicatear *vi* FAM to be stingy, to be tightfisted, to be closefisted, to be mean.

cicatería *f* stinginess, meanness.

cicatero, ra *adj* stingy, mean, tightfisted, closefisted.
◆ *m/f* miser, skinflint, stingy *o* tightfisted person.

cicatrícula *f* cicatricle, tread (de huevo).

cicatriz *f* scar, cicatrice, cicatrix || FIG scar.

cicatrizable *adj* likely to heal.

cicatrización *f* healing, cicatrization.

cicatrizar *vt/vi* to heal, to cicatrize.
◆ *vpr* to heal, to cicatrize.

cícero *m* IMPR pica, twelve-point type.

Cicerón *npr m* Cicero.

cicerone *m* guide, cicerone (guía).

cicindela *f* cicindela, tiger beetle.

ciclamen; ciclamino *m* BOT cyclamen.

ciclamor *m* BOT Judas tree.

cíclico, ca *adj* cyclic, cyclical.

ciclismo *m* cycling || cycle racing (carrera).

ciclista *adj* cycle, cycling; *carrera ciclista* cycling race, cycle race.
◆ *m/f* cyclist.

ciclo *m* cycle (lunar, vital, etc.) || course, series (de conferencias) || ECON *ciclos económicos* economic cycles.

ciclocrós *m* DEP cyclo-cross.

cicloidal; cicloideo, a *adj* MAT cycloidal.

cicloide *f* MAT cycloid.

ciclomotor *m* autocycle, moped.

ciclón *m* cyclone (huracán), || — FIG *entrar como un ciclón* to burst in | *llegar como un ciclón* to arrive like a whirlwind.

ciclonal; ciclónico, ca *adj* cyclonal.

cíclope *m* cyclops.

ciclópeo, a; ciclópico, ca *adj* cyclopean, gigantic.

ciclorama *m* cyclorama.

ciclostilo *m* cyclostyle, mimeograph.

ciclóstomos *m pl* cyclostomes, cyclostomi (peces).

cicloterapia *f* MED cyclotherapy.

ciclotimia *f* MED cyclothymia.

ciclotrón *m* FÍS cyclotron.

cicloturismo *m* touring by bicycle.

CICR *abrev de Comité Internacional de la Cruz Roja* IRCC, International Red Cross Committee.

cicuta *f* conium, cicuta, hemlock (planta) || *cicuta menor* fool's parsley.

Cid *npr m* The Cid || FIG brave man || FAM *se cree descendiente de la pata del Cid* he thinks he's the cat's whiskers, he thinks he's the Lord God Almighty.

cidra *f* BOT citron (fruta).
— OBSERV Not to be confused with *sidra*, cider [drink].

cidracayote *m* AMER gourd, calabash.

cidrada *f* citron preserve *o* jam.

cidro *m* BOT melissa.

ciegamente *adv* blindly || fearlessly; *los soldados atacaron ciegamente* the soldiers attacked fearlessly || *confiar ciegamente en* to have blind faith in, to trust implicitly.

ciego, ga *adj* blind (que no ve); *quedarse ciego* to go blind; *ciego de nacimiento* blind from birth || FIG blinded, blind (cegado); *ciego de ira* blinded by anger, blind with anger || blocked up, plugged, stopped (cañería) || closely baked (pan) || with no holes (pan, queso) || — FIG & FAM *está ciego con los naipes* he is mad about cards | *estar ciego* to be blind drunk, to be sozzled, to be paralytic (borracho) || FIG *fe ciega* blind faith || FIG & FAM *más ciego que un topo* blind as a bat | *para los defectos de su marido está ciega* she is blind to her husband's faults || ANAT *punto ciego del ojo* blind spot || FIG *tan ciego el uno como el otro* it's like the blind leading the blind || — *a ciegas* blindly || *andar a ciegas* to go blindly on (en la vida), to grope one's way along (en la oscuridad) || *comprar a ciegas* to buy haphazardly *o* blindly *o* at random || *jugar a la ciega* to play blindfold (ajedrez).
◆ *m/f* blind man, blind woman || *coplas de ciego* trashy verse || FIG *dar palos de ciego* to lash out wildly (golpear sin cuidado), to grope about in the dark (tantear) | *en tierra* or *en país de ciegos el tuerto es rey* in the land of the blind the one-eyed man is king || FAM *hacerse el ciego* to turn a blind eye || *los ciegos* the blind || FIG *un ciego lo ve* it's staring you in the face, it stands out a mile.
◆ *m* ANAT caecum (intestino).

cielito *m* AMER popular Argentinian song and dance.

cielo *m* sky; *cielo azul, sereno, encapotado* blue, calm, overcast sky || REL heaven | God (Dios) || prosperity (bienaventuranza) || roof (de la boca) || canopy (de la cama) || ARQ ceiling (techo) || — *a cielo abierto* opencast [US opencut] (minas) || *a cielo descubierto* in the open (air) || *a cielo raso* in the open (air), under the stars (al aire libre) || FIG *bajado del cielo* heaven-sent (muy oportuno), out of the blue (inesperado) || *cerrarse* or *entoldarse el cielo* to become overcast, to cloud over [the sky] || *cielo aborregado* mackerel sky || ARQ *cielo raso* ceiling || *¡cielos!, ¡cielo santo!* good heavens! || *clamar al cielo* to cry out to heaven || *con paciencia se gana el cielo* all things come to him who waits || *desencapotarse el cielo* to brighten up [the weather], to clear [the sky] || *el reino de los cielos* the kingdom of heaven || FIG *estar en el séptimo cielo* to be in the seventh heaven | *estar hecho un cielo* to be an angel | *esto va al cielo* his word is law, what he says goes || *ganar el cielo* to go to heaven || *ir al cielo* to go to heaven || FAM *juntársele a uno el cielo con la tierra* to be in a fix, to be in a tight spot || FIG *llovido del cielo* heaven-sent (oportuno), out of the blue (inesperado) | *¡mi cielo!, ¡cielo mío!* my darling!, my dear! | *mover* or *revolver cielo y tierra* to move heaven and earth | *poner a uno por los cielos* to praise s.o. to the skies | *poner el grito en el cielo* to raise the roof, to raise an outcry, to kick up a fuss || FIG & FAM *se me ha ido el santo al cielo* I clean *o* completely forgot | *ser un cielo* to be an angel || FIG *se vino el cielo abajo* the heavens opened (llovió mucho) || FIG *si escupes al cielo, en la cara te caerá* chickens and curses come home to roast || *subir al cielo* to ascend to heaven (Cristo), to go to heaven (los hombres) || *un aviso del cielo* a warning from heaven || FIG *ver el cielo abierto* to see a way out, to see one's chance (para salir de un apuro).

ciempiés *m inv* centipede.

cien *adj* a hundred || — *cien por cien* one hundred per cent, completely || *de cien en cien* in hundreds, by the hundred.

— OBSERV *Ciento* is apocopated to *cien* before nouns (*cien años, cien pesetas* a hundred years, a hundred pesetas), and before numbers which it multiplies (*cien mil pesetas* a hundred thousand pesetas).

ciénaga *f* marsh, bog, swamp (zona pantanosa).

ciencia *f* science; *los adelantos de la ciencia* the progress of science || FIG learning, knowledge; *un pozo de ciencia* a well of knowledge || — *ciencia ficción* science fiction || *ciencia infusa* intuition, mystical vision (comunicada directamente por Dios), intuitive *o* innate knowledge (saber intuitivo) || *ciencias naturales, exactas* natural, exact *o* pure sciences || *ciencias ocultas* occult sciences || *creer algo a ciencia cierta* to firmly believe sth. || *hombre de ciencia* scientist || FIG *no tener ciencia, tener poca ciencia* to be as easy as pie *o* as ABC || *saber a* or *de ciencia cierta* to know for certain *o* for a fact.

cienmilésimo, ma *adj/s* hundred thousandth || *la cienmilésima parte* one hundred thousandth, the hundred thousandth part.

cienmilímetro *m* hundredth of a millimetre.

cienmillonésimo, ma *adj/s* hundred millionth || *la cienmillonésima parte* one hundred millionth.

cieno *m* mud, mire, muck (fango).

científico, ca *adj* scientific.

◆ *m/f* scientist.

cientifismo *m* scientism.

cientista; cientista social *m/f* AMER sociologist (sociólogo).

ciento *adj/s* a hundred, one hundred; *ciento veinticuatro* one hundred and twenty-four || hundredth (centésimo).

◆ *m* hundred; *un ciento de ostras* a hundred oysters || about a hundred, a hundred-odd; *un ciento de huevos* about a hundred eggs || — *ciento diez* a hundred and ten || FIG & FAM *ciento y la madre* a crowd, a whole string of people || FIG *darle ciento y raya a uno* to run rings round s.o., to knock spot off s.o. || *devolver ciento por uno* to repay a hundredfold || *veinte por ciento* twenty per cent.

◆ *pl* piquet *sing* (juego de naipes) || *por cientos* in hundreds, by the hundred.

— OBSERV Véase *hundred*.

cierne *m* blossoming, blooming || *en cierne, en ciernes* in flower, in blossom, in bloom (la vid), green, unripe, in the blade (el trigo), budding, in the making (persona, cosa), in embryo, in its infancy (una cosa).

cierre *m* closing, shutting || shutdown, shutting-down; *el cierre temporal de la fábrica* the temporary shutdown of the factory || close-down (de una emisión de radio, etc.) || closing (de la Bolsa, de una sesión) || closure (de un debate) || end (de inventario) || end, close; *cierre de ejercicio* end of the financial year || fastener (de un vestido) || clasp, fastener (de un bolso) || buckle, clasp (de un cinturón) || shutter, blind (de una tienda, un escaparate, etc.) || catch (de puerta) || choke (de un automóvil) || binding (de los esquís) || — *cierre centralizado* centralised locking system || *cierre de cremallera* zip, zip fastener [*US* zipper] || *cierre patronal* lockout || AMER *cierre relámpago* zip fastener.

cierro *m* closing, shutting (cierre) || AMER enclosure, fence (vallado) | envelope (sobre) || *cierro de cristales* bay window.

cierto, ta *adj* certain, some (algún, alguno); *ciertos escritores* certain writers; *cierto tiempo* a certain time, some time || sure, certain (seguro); *estar cierto de tener razón* to be sure of being right || true (verdad); *eso es cierto* that's true || correct (exacto) || definite, sure; *hay indicios ciertos de mejoría* there are definite signs of improvement || — *estar en lo cierto* to be right || *lo cierto es que...* the fact is that... || *persona de cierta edad* elderly person.

◆ *pl* some, certain; *en ciertos casos* in some cases.

◆ *adv* of course, certainly || — *de cierto* for certain || *lo que hay de cierto es que...* the truth *o* the fact is that... || *no por cierto* of course not, certainly not || *por cierto* of course, indeed, certainly || *por cierto* by the way; *por cierto ayer fui a verte y no te encontré* by the way I went to see you yesterday and you weren't in || *por cierto que* of course || *saber por cierto* to know for sure *o* for certain || *si es cierto que...* if it is true that... || *tan cierto como dos y dos son cuatro* as sure as eggs are eggs.

— OBSERV In Spanish, the indefinite article is omitted when *cierto* is placed before a noun (*cierto día* a certain day), but is used in cases such as *un dato cierto* a definite fact.

cierva *f* hind (rumiante).

ciervo *m* ZOOL deer (macho y hembra), stag, hart (macho) || — *ciervo común* red deer || *ciervo volante* stag beetle (coleóptero).

cierzo *m* north wind.

cifosis *f* cyphosis.

cifra *f* figure; *un número de tres cifras* a three-figure number || figure, number, numeral; *en nuestro sistema empleamos diez cifras* in our system we use ten numbers || code (escritura secreta); *en cifra* in code || monogram (monograma) || quantity, amount (cantidad) || number; *la cifra de muertos* the number of dead || — *cifra global* lump sum || *cifra de mortalidad* mortality rate || ECON *cifra de negocios* turnover || *cifra romana* Roman numeral || FIG *en cifra* obscurely (ininteligiblemente), briefly, in brief (a' eviadamente).

cifrado, da *adj* in code, coded; *carta cifrada* letter in code || MÚS *bajo cifrado* figured bass.

◆ *m* putting into code.

cifrar *vt* to write in code, to code, tu put into code (un mensaje) || to summarize, to resume (resumir) || COM to evaluate || — *cifra la felicidad en el dinero* for him money is happiness || *cifrar en* to place in, to put in; *cifrar la esperanza en Dios* to place one's hope in God || *cifro mi placer en la lectura* my only pleasure is reading.

◆ *vpr* to amount, to come; *cifrarse en* to come to.

cigala *f* Norway lobster.

cigarra *f* cicada (insecto).

cigarral *m* country house [on the outskirts of Toledo].

cigarrera *f* cigarette manufacturer (que fabrica cigarros) || cigarette seller (que vende cigarrillos) || tobacconist (que tiene un estanco) || cigar case (para puros) || tobacco pouch (petaca).

cigarrería *f* AMER tobacconist's, tobacconist's shop.

cigarrillo *m* cigarette; *liar un cigarrillo* to roll a cigarette; *una cajetilla* or *un paquete de cigarrillos* a packet of cigarettes || *cigarrillo con filtro* filter cigarette, filter-tip cigarette, tipped cigarette.

cigarro *m* cigar (puro) || cigarette (cigarrillo) || AMER dragonfly || — *cigarro de papel* cigarette || *cigarro puro* or *habano* cigar.

cigarrón *m* grasshopper (saltamontes).

cigomático, ca *adj* ANAT zygomatic.

cigoñal *m* shadoof, shaduf (para sacar agua).

cigoñino *m* young stork (cría de la cigüeña).

cigoto *m* BIOL zygote.

cigüeña *f* stork (ave) || TECN crank, winch || AMER barrel organ (órgano de manubrio) || FIG *lo trajo la cigüeña* the stork brought him (un niño).

cigüeñal *m* crank (manubrio) || TECN crankshaft (de motor).

cilantro *m* BOT coriander.

ciliado, da *adj* ciliated, ciliate.

◆ *m* BOT ciliate.

ciliar *adj* ANAT ciliary.

cilicio *m* cilice, hair shirt.

cilindrada *f* cylinder capacity; *gran cilindrada* large cylinder capacity.

cilindrado *m* TECN rolling (de acero, etc.) | mangling, calendering (de tejido).

cilindrar *vt* to roll (acero, etc.) || to mangle, to calender (tejido).

cilíndrico, ca *adj* cylindrical, cylindric.

cilindro *m* MAT cylinder || TECN cylinder; *cilindro maestro* master cylinder || roller (de máquina de escribir) || IMPR cylinder, drum (para los tipos) | roller (para la tinta) || AMER top hat (sombrero) | barrel organ (organillo) || *cilindro compresor* steamroller, road roller (rodillo).

cilindroeje *m* ANAT axis cylinder.

cilio *m* BIOL cilium; *cilio vibrátil* vibratile cilium.

cillerero *m* cellarer (de un monasterio).

cillero *m* granary keeper.

cima *f* summit, top (de una montaña) || top (de un árbol) || BOT cyme | stalk (tallo) || crest (de una ola) || FIG summit, height, peak (apogeo) | end (fin) || — FIG *dar cima a* to finish off, to crown, to complete || *por cima* on top, at the top.

— OBSERV Do not confuse with *sima*, precipice.

cimacio *m* ARQ cyma, ogee moulding, dado (moldura).

cimarra (hacer la) *loc* AMER to play truant [*US* to play hookey].

cimarrón, ona *adj* AMER runaway, fugitive, wild [formerly «slave» in America, but now an animal which has run wild] | wild (animal, planta) | lazy, idle (vago).

◆ *m* AMER fugitive slave (esclavo) | unsweetened maté *o* Paraguay tea (mate).

cimarronada *f* AMER herd of wild animals.

cimarronear *vi* AMER to take maté *o* Paraguay tea without sugar || to run away, to escape, to flee (huir).

cimbalillo *m* small bell.

címbalo *m* small bell (campanita) || MÚS cymbal.

cimbel *m* rope for tying decoy pigeons || decoy bird (pájaro que sirve de señuelo) || FIG lure, enticement (añagaza) || FIG & FAM telltale (soplón).

cimborio; cimborrio *m* ARQ dome, cupola (en el crucero).

cimbra *f* ARQ centering (armazón) | soffit (curvatura interior) || MAR curvature, sweep || *AMER* trap (trampa).

cimbrado, da *adj* centred.
◆ *m* bend from the waist (en el baile).

cimbrar *vt* to waggle, to shake, to make quiver [a flexible object] || FIG & FAM to bash, to hit (golpear); *cimbrar de un bastonazo* to bash with a stick || ARQ to erect the centering for (una bóveda).

cimbreante *adj* supple, flexible || waving (ondulante) || swaying (al andar) || quivering (vara, etc.).

cimbrear *vt* to waggle, to shake, to make quiver (un objeto flexible) || to bend (curvar).
◆ *vpr* to sway (con el viento) || to move gracefully (al andar) || to bend (doblarse).

cimbreño, ña *adj* supple, flexible.

cimbreo *m* bending || quivering (de vara o de junco) || swaying (al andar).

címbrico, ca *adj* HIST Cimbric, Cimbrian.

cimentación *f* laying of foundations (acción de cimentar) || foundation, foundations *pl* (resultado).

cimentar* *vt* ARQ to lay the foundations of (un edificio) || to cement (fijar con cemento) || to case harden, to face-harden (hacer la cementación) || to refine [gold] || FIG to strengthen, to consolidate (la amistad, las relaciones, la paz) | to found, to lay the foundations of (una sociedad, etc.).

cimera *f* crest (del casco).

cimero, ra *adj* highest, uppermost, top, topmost || FIG dominant, dominating.

cimiento *m* ARQ foundations *pl*, foundation; *abrir, echar los cimientos* to dig, to lay the foundations || FIG origin, source (origen) | foundation; *su autoridad tiene sólidos cimientos* his authority has solid foundations *o* a solid foundation || — FIG *desde los cimientos* from the very start | *echar los cimientos de un acuerdo* to lay the foundations for an agreement | *echar los cimientos de una sociedad* to found a company.

cimitarra *f* scimitar (arma).

cinabrio *m* MIN cinnabar || ARTES vermilion.

cinámico, ca *adj* QUÍM cinnamic.

cinamomo *m* BOT cinnamon.

cinc *m* zinc.
— OBSERV pl *cincs*.
— OBSERV In Spanish, the spelling *zinc* is also correct.

cincel *m* chisel.

cincelado, da *adj* chiselled.
◆ *m* chiselling.

cincelar *vt* to chisel, to carve with a chisel.

cincelete *m* TECN graver, small chisel.

cinco *adj* five; *los cinco dedos* the five fingers || fifth, five; *el capítulo V (cinco)* chapter five, the fifth chapter || fifth (la fecha).
◆ *m* five (cifra) || fifth; *el 5 (cinco) de septiembre* September the fifth, the fifth of September (en la conversación), 5 September, September 5th (encabezamiento de una carta) || *AMER* five-stringed guitar (guitarrilla) || — FIG & FAM *decir a uno cuántas son cinco* to tell s.o. a few home truths | *esos cinco* that paw *o* mitt *o* fist *o* hand | *estar sin cinco* to be broke | *no tener los cinco sentidos* to be off one's rocker, not to be all there | *saber cuántas son cinco* to know what's what || *son las cinco* it is five o'clock || FIG & FAM *vengan* or *choca esos cinco* done!, let's shake on it (para concluir un acuerdo), shake!, let's shake (para reconciliarse) || *vivo en el cinco* I live at number five.

cincoenrama *f* BOT cinquefoil, cinqfoil.

cincograbado *m* zincograph.

cincografía *m* zincography.

cincuenta *adj/sm* fifty || fiftieth (quincuagésimo) || *los cincuenta* fifty; *andar por los cincuenta* to be getting on for fifty, to be pushing fifty (*fam*).

cincuentavo, va *adj/s* fiftieth.

cincuentenario *m* quinquagenary, fiftieth anniversary.

cincuenteno, na *adj* fiftieth.
◆ *f* fifty.

cincuentón, ona *adj* fifty-year-old, in one's fifties.
◆ *m/f* fifty-year-old, person in his *o* her, etc. fifties.

cincha *f* girth, cinch || FIG *a revienta cinchas* at full speed, at full tilt, hell for leather.

cinchada *f* *AMER* ⟶ **cinchadura.**

cinchadura *f* girthing, cinching.

cinchar *vt* to girth (la cincha) || to hoop (un tonel).

cinchazo *m* *AMER* blow with the flat of the sword.

cinchera *f* belly (de caballo) || girth gall (desolladura).

cincho *m* belt (cinturón) || hoop (para los toneles) || *AMER* girth (cincha).

cine *m* cinema, pictures [*US* movies]; *ir al cine* to go to the pictures || cinema (arte) || cinema, picture house [*US* movie theater] (edificio) || — *cine de estreno* first-run cinema || *cine de sesión continua* continous performance cinema || *cine en colores* films in colour || *cine mudo* silent cinema *o* films || *cine sonoro* talking cinema, talkies || *hacer cine* to make films.

cineasta *m* (film) actor.
◆ *m/f* person who works in the film industry (en general) || film director (director).

cineclub *m* film society [*US* film club].

cinéfilo, la *m/f* cinema enthusiast.

cinegético, ca *adj* cynegetic.
◆ *f* cynegetics, hunting.

Cinemascope *m* (nombre registrado) Cinemascope.

cinemateca *f* film library.

cinemática *f* FÍS kinematics, cinematics.

cinematografía *f* cinematography, films *pl*, film-making.

cinematografiar *vt* to film.

cinematográfico, ca *adj* cinematographic, film.

cinematógrafo *m* cinematograph (arte y actividad) || cinema (espectáculo) || film projector, projector (máquina).

cinerama *m* cinerama.

cinerario, ria *adj* cinerary; *urna cineraria* cinerary urn.
◆ *f* BOT cineraria.

cinéreo, a; cinericio, cia *adj* cinereous, ash-grey, ashen, ashy.

cinestesia *f* kinaesthesis, kinesthesis.

cinético, ca *adj* kinetic.
◆ *f* kinetics.

cingalés, esa *adj* Singhalese, Cingalese, Cinghalese.

cíngaro, ra *adj* Tzigane, Hungarian gypsy.
◆ *m/f* Tzigane, Hungarian gypsy.
◆ *m* gypsy.

cingiberáceas *f pl* BOT zingiberaceae.

cinglar *vi* MAR to scull.
◆ *vt* TECN to puddle (el hierro).

cíngulo *m* REL cord (para ceñir el alba).

cínico, ca *adj* FIL cynical || hard-faced, brazen, shameless.
◆ *m/f* FIG cynic || hard-faced *o* brazen *o* shameless person.

cínife *m* mosquito (insecto).

cinismo *m* FIL cynicism || shamelessness, brazenness || *¡qué cinismo!* what a nerve!

cinocéfalo *m* cynocephalus, dog-faced baboon.

cinódromo *m* greyhound track (canódromo).

cinoglosa *f* BOT cynoglossum, hound's tongue.

cinorexia *f* MED cynorexia.

cinquero *m* zinc worker.

cinta *f* band (en general) || ribbon (para adornar, envolver, etc., para el pelo) || braid, edging (para adornar una prenda de vestir) || film (película) || tape (magnética) || ribbon (de máquina de escribir) || shoelace (cordón de zapato) || ARQ fillet || MAR bend, wale || kerb, curb [*US* curb] (de la acera) || coronet (del casco de las caballerías) || skirting board [*US* baseboard] (que rodea una habitación) || TECN belt; *cinta transportadora* conveyor belt || MIL loading belt (de ametralladora) || — *cinta adhesiva* adhesive tape || *cinta autoadhesiva* self-adhesive tape || *cinta aisladora* insulating tape || *cinta cinematográfica* film || *cinta de freno* brake lining || *cinta de llegada* finishing tape (en una carrera) || *cinta de vídeo* video tape || INFORM *cinta magnética* magnetic tape || *cinta magnetofónica* magnetic tape, recording tape || *cinta métrica* tape measure || INFORM *cinta (de papel) perforada* punched tape, paper tape || *cinta para el pelo* hairband, ribbon.
— OBSERV *En cinta* when used to mean *encinta* (pregnant) is a barbarism.

cintarazo *m* blow with the flat of the sword.

cinteado, da *adj* decorated with ribbons, ribboned, beribboned (guarnecido de cintas).

cintería *f* ribbons *pl* (cintas) || ribbon industry (industria) || ribbon shop, haberdasher's (tienda).

cintilar *vi* to scintillate, to twinkle, to sparkle.

cinto, ta *adj* encircled.
◆ *m* swordbelt (para el sable) || belt (cinturón) || waist (cintura).
— OBSERV The adjective *cinto* is the irregular past participle of *ceñir*.

cintra *f* ARQ arch, curvature.

cintrado, da *adj* ARQ arched.

cintura *f* ANAT waist (talle); *coger por la cintura* to get hold of (s.o.) round the waist || waist, waistline (medida); *tiene poca cintura* she has a slim waist || belt (ceñidor) || throat (de chimenea) || — ANAT *cintura pelviana* pelvic girdle *o* arch || FIG *doblarse por la cintura* to be in stitches || FIG & FAM *meter a uno en cintura* to make s.o. behave || *tener una cintura de avispa* to have a wasp waist.

cinturón *m* belt (de cuero, etc.); *un cinturón de lagarto* a lizard-skin belt || swordbelt (para el sable) || FIG circle, belt, cordon (de murallas, etc.) || belt, zone; *cinturón industrial* industrial belt || belt (de montañas) || belt (en judo); *cinturón negro* black belt || — FIG *apretarse el cinturón* to tighten one's belt || *cinturón de castidad* chastity belt || *cinturón de seguridad* safety belt, seat belt || *cinturón salvavidas* life belt.

cipayo *m* sepoy.

cipo *m* ARQ cippus, memorial stone || milestone (en los caminos).

cipolino *m* cipolin, onion marble (mármol).

cipote *m/f* AMER kid, nipper, youngster (chiquillo).
◆ *m* POP tool (miembro viril).

ciprés *m* cypress (tree).

ciprino *m* cyprinid (pez).
◆ *pl* cyprinidae.

ciprino, na; ciprio, pria; cipriota *adj/s* Cypriot.

circense *adj* circus.

circo *m* circus (espectáculo) || amphitheatre, circus || GEOL cirque (entre montañas).

circón *m* zircon (piedra preciosa).

circona *f* QUÍM zirconia (óxido).

circonio *m* zirconium (metal).

circonita *f* QUÍM zirconite.

circuito *m* ELECTR circuit || DEP circuit, track, course (sitio) || circumference (contorno) || tour (viaje); *circuito organizado* organized tour || circuit (con vuelta al punto de partida) || — ELECTR *circuito cerrado* closed circuit || *circuito cerrado de televisión, televisión por circuito cerrado* closed-circuit television || *circuito impreso* printed circuit || *circuito integrado* integrated circuit || *circuito magnético* magnetic circuit || TECN *circuito precintado* sealed system || ELECTR *circuito primario, secundario* primary, secundary coil.

circulación *f* circulation (de savia, de sangre, de ideas, de vehículos, de artículos de comercio, etc.) || traffic (conjunto de vehículos) || — *billetes en circulación* notes in circulation || *calle de mucha circulación* busy street || *cerrado a la circulación rodada* closed to traffic || BIOL *circulación de la sangre* or *sanguínea* circulation of the blood, blood circulation || COM *circulación fiduciaria* banknotes in circulation, paper currency || *circulación rodada* traffic *o* vehicular traffic || *código de la circulación* highway code || *la circulación es por la izquierda* they drive on the left || *poner en circulación* to put into circulation || *retirar de la circulación* to withdraw from circulation.

circulante *adj* circulating || working (capital) || *biblioteca circulante* mobile library.

circular *adj* circular; *movimiento circular* circular motion || circular (carta) || *viaje circular* round trip, circular tour.

circular *vi* to flow, to circulate (corriente eléctrica, sangre, agua); *la corriente circula por el circuito* the current flows through the circuit; *el agua circula por la cañería* water flows through the pipes || to drive (automóviles); *circular por la derecha* to drive on the right || to use; *muchos coches circulan por esta calle* many cars use this street || to walk about; *circulaba mucha gente por la calle* there were a lot of people walking about in the street || to run (trenes y autobuses); *por esta vía ya no circulan trenes* trains no longer run on this line || to keep (ceñirse); *circulen por la derecha* keep to the right || FIG to go around, to spread; *el rumor circuló rápidamente* the rumour spread quickly || to circulate (cartas) || to circulate; *el dinero circula* money circulates || — *al abrir esta ventana circula mucho aire* if you open this window there is a big draught || *¡circulen, por favor!* move along, please! || *hacer circular* to keep moving (coches), to move along (gente), to circulate (una cosa); *hicieron circular un documento* they circulated a document.
◆ *vt* to circulate; *circular una orden* to circulate an order.

circulatorio, ria *adj* circulatory.

círculo *m* MAT circle || FIG circle, club; *círculo de juego* gambling club || circle, clique (cenáculo) || clubhouse (sitio de reunión de un club) || circle (extensión) || GEOGR circle; *círculo polar* polar circle || FIG environment (medio) | scope, extent || — MAR *círculo acimutal* azimuth circle || *círculo familiar* family circle || MAT *círculo máximo, menor* great, small circle || *círculo polar Antártico, Ártico* Antarctic, Arctic Circle || FIG *círculo vicioso* vicious circle || *en círculo* in a circle || *formar un círculo alrededor de alguien* to form a circle around s.o.
◆ *pl* circles (medios); *en los círculos bien informados* in well-informed circles | suite *sing*; *en los círculos allegados al rey* in the king's suite.

circumpolar *adj* circumpolar.

circuncidar *vt* to circumcise.

circuncisión *f* circumcision.

circunciso, sa *adj* circumcised.
◆ *m* circumcised man.

circundante *adj* surrounding.

circundar *vt* to surround.

circunferencia *f* circumference.

circunferir* *vt* to circumscribe, to surround (rodear) || to limit (limitar).

circunflejo *adj/sm* circumflex.

circunlocución *f*; **circunloquio** *m* circumlocution.

circunnavegar *vt* to circumnavigate, to sail round.

circunscribir *vt* to circumscribe || FIG to confine, to limit, to circumscribe.
◆ *vpr* to confine o.s., to limit o.s., to restrict o.s.; *circunscribirse a algo* to confine o.s. to sth.

circunscripción *f* circumscription, circumscribing || district, area (distrito) || *circunscripción electoral* electoral constituency, electoral district.

circunscrito, ta; circunscripto, ta *adj* circumscribed || FIG limited (limitado).

circunspección *f* circumspection.

circunspecto, ta *adj* circumspect || carefully chosen (palabras).

circunstancia *f* circumstance; *adaptarse a las circunstancias* to adapt o.s. to the circumstances || — JUR *circunstancia agravante, atenuante* aggravating, extenuating circumstance || *de circunstancias* out of necessity, for a reason; *estaba en un viaje de circunstancias* he was making a journey for a reason *o* out of necessity; improvised; *una silla de circunstancias* an improvised chair || *en estas circunstancias, en las circunstancias presentes* under *o* in the circumstances || *estar a la altura de las circunstancias* to rise to the occasion.

circunstancial *adj* incidental, circumstantial || GRAM adverbial; *complemento circunstancial* adverbial complement.

circunstancialmente *adv* temporality.

circunstante *m/f* person present, bystander.

circunvalación *f* circumvallation || — *carretera de circunvalación* ring road, bypass (en una ciudad) || *línea de circunvalación* circular line (de ferrocarril), circular route (de autobús) || *tren, ferrocarril de circunvalación* circular train, railway line.

circunvalar *vt* to surround, to circumvallate.

circunvecino, na *adj* surrounding, neighbouring, adjacent.

circunvolar *vt* to fly around.

circonvolución *f* circumvolution || *circunvoluciones cerebrales* cerebral convolutions.

circunyacente *adj* circumjacent.

Cirenaica *npr f* GEOGR Cyrenaica.

cirial *m* church candlestick (candelero) || processional candlestick (en las procesiones).

cirílico, ca *adj* Cyrillic (alfabeto).

Cirilo *npr m* Cyril.

cirineo, a *adj/s* Cyrenian.

cirio *m* wax candle || BOT cereus || *cirio pascual* paschal candle.

Ciro *npr m* Cyrus.

cirrípedo *m* ZOOL cirriped.

cirro *m* cirrus (nube) || MED scirrhus (tumor) || BOT & ZOOL cirrus.

cirrocúmulo *m* cirrocumulus.

cirroestrato *m* cirrostratus.

cirrópodo *m* ZOOL cirriped.

cirrosis *f* MED cirrhosis.

cirroso, sa *adj* MED cirrhotic || BOT & ZOOL cirrous.

ciruela *f* BOT plum (fruta) || — *ciruela amarilla* mirabelle plum || *ciruela claudia* greengage || *ciruela damascena* damson || *ciruela pasa* prune.

ciruelo *m* BOT plum tree (árbol).

cirugía *f* surgery || *cirugía estética* or *plástica* plastic surgery.

cirujano *m* surgeon || *cirujano dentista* dental surgeon.

cisalpino, na *adj* cisalpine.

cisca *f* BOT sedge.

ciscar *vt* FAM to dirty, to soil (ensuciar).
◆ *vpr* FAM to soil o.s.

cisco *m* slack (carbón muy menudo) || FIG & FAM row, din; *meter* or *armar cisco* to kick up a row | chaos (jaleo) || — FIG & FAM *estar hecho cisco* to be in a sorry state, to be all in | *hacer cisco* to smash, to smash to pieces | FIG *hacer cisco a uno* to knock s.o. out, to exhaust s.o. (agotarle).

ciscón *m* clinker, ashes *pl*.

cisión *f* incision.

cisma *m* schism || FIG disagreement, discord (desacuerdo) | split (en política).

cismático, ca *adj/s* schismatic, schismatical, dissident.

cisne *m* swan (ave) || ASTR swan, the northern constellation, cygnus || FIG swan, bard (poeta, músico) || AMER powder puff (para polvos).

cisoide *f* MAT cissoid.

cisoria *adj f* *arte cisoria* art of carving.

cisquero *m* pounce bag (para el dibujo).

cista *f* cist.

Cistel; Cister *npr m* Cistercian Order (orden religiosa).

cisterciense *adj/s* Cistercian (de la orden del Cister).

cisterna *f* cistern, tank, reservoir || cistern (de retrete) || *vagón, buque cisterna* tanker.

cisternilla *f* cistern.

cisticerco *m* cysticercus (larva de la tenia).

cístico, ca *adj* cystic.

cistitis *f* MED cystitis.

cisto *m* BOT cistus.

cistopatía *f* MED cystopathy.

cistotomía *f* cystotomy.

cisura *f* incision (incisión).

cita *f* appointment; *arreglar una cita con el médico* to make an appointment with the doctor; *el médico me ha dado cita a las seis* I have an appointment with the doctor at six o'clock || date (entre chico y chica); *tengo una cita con Juan* I've got a date with John || meeting (de amantes) || quotation, quote (nota sacada de una obra) || — *casa de citas* house of call || *cita espacial* space link-up || *con motivo de la Exposición se han dado cita unos mil científicos* on the occasion of the Exhibition some thousand scientists have come together || *darle cita a un amigo* to arrange to meet a friend || *darse cita* to arrange to meet (one another) (sentido general), to make a date (chica y chico) || *tengo cita con un amigo* I've got to go and see a friend.

citación *f* JUR writ of summons, citation || quotation, quote (de un escritor).

citadino, na *adj* AMER urban.
◆ *m/f* city dweller.

citado, da *adj* aforementioned; *el citado libro* the aforementioned book.

citar *vt* to arrange to meet, to make an appointment with; *citar a uno en un café* to arrange to meet s.o. in a café; *le cité para* or *a las cinco* I arranged to meet him at five o'clock || to quote, to cite (hacer una cita literaria) || JUR to summon (llamar el juez a una persona) | to call; *citar a juicio* to call to witness | to subpoena (a un testigo) | to summon; *citar ante un consejo de guerra* to summon before a court martial || TAUR to attract the attention of [the bull], to call [the bull] || to mention (mencionar) || — JUR *citar ante la justicia* to sue, to prosecute, to indict, to arraign || *para no citar otros* to mention but a few, to mention only a few.
◆ *vpr* to arrange to meet (one another) (sentido general), to make a date (chica y chico).

citara *f* brick partition (tabique de ladrillos).

cítara *f* MÚS zither.

citerior *adj* hithermost, hither.

citiso *m* BOT cytisus.

citodiagnosis *f* MED cytodiagnosis.

cítola *f* millclapper.

citología *f* BIOL cytology.

citológico, ca *adj* cytological.

citoplasma *m* ANAT cytoplasm.

citrato *m* QUÍM citrate.

cítrico, ca *adj* QUÍM citric || *productos cítricos* citric produce.
◆ *m pl* citrus fruits (agrios); *exportación de cítricos* export of citrus fruits.

citrón *m* (p us) lemon (limón).

citronela *f* BOT citronella.

ciudad *f* town, city (véase OBSERV) || — *Ciudad del Cabo* Cape Town || *ciudad de lona* canvas town || *Ciudad del Vaticano* Vatican City || *Ciudad de México* Mexico City || *ciudad hermana* twin town || *ciudad hongo* boom town || *Ciudad Imperial* Toledo [in Spain] || *ciudad jardín* garden city || *ciudad obrera* worker's housing estate || *ciudad satélite* satellite town || *ciudad universitaria* university campus || *ir a la ciudad* to go to town *o* into town || *la Ciudad Eterna* the Eternal City, Rome || *Sr. don Juan Ruiz, Ciudad* (en cartas) Mr. Juan Ruiz, local [on an envelope].

— OBSERV *Ciudad* se traduce por dos palabras en inglés según que el tamaño sea más grande (city) o menos grande (town).

ciudadanía *f* citizenship || — *ciudadanía de honor* freedom of the city || *derechos de ciudadanía* citizen's rights.

ciudadano, na *m/f* citizen, townsman, townswoman (de una ciudad) || citizen (de un estado) || — *ciudadano de honor* freeman of the city || *los ciudadanos* (the) townspeople, (the) city dwellers.
◆ *adj* civic, city.

ciudadela *f* citadel, fortress.

civeta *f* (p us) ZOOL civet.

civeto *m* civet.

cívico, ca *adj* civic || FIG public-spirited; *un acto cívico* a public-spirited act.
◆ *m* AMER policeman | tankard (de cerveza).

civil *adj* civil; *guerra, matrimonio civil* civil war, marriage || lay, secular (no eclesiástico) || civilian, civil (no militar); *población civil* civilian population || civil (sociable) || — *administración civil* civil service || *casarse por lo civil* to get married in a registry office *o* in a register office (en Inglaterra), to get married by a civil ceremony, to have a civil marriage *o* wedding (en los demás países) || JUR *derecho civil* civil law || *derechos civiles* civil rights || *incorporado a la vida civil* reinstated in civilian life || *ingeniería civil* civil engineering || *muerte civil* civil death || *por lo civil* in a civil court.
◆ *m* FAM civil guard, guardia civil [type of policeman] (guardia civil) || civilian (paisano).

civilidad *f* civility (cortesía).

civilista *m* person versed in civil law (jurisconsulto).

civilización *f* civilization.

civilizado, da *adj* civilized.
◆ *m/f* civilized person.

civilizador, ra *adj* civilizing.
◆ *m/f* civilizer.

civilizar *vt* to civilize.
◆ *vpr* to become civilized.

civismo *m* civism, good citizenship, community spirit (cualidad de buen ciudadano) || civility (cualidad de cortés).

cizalla *f*; **cizallas** *f pl* shears *pl*, metal clippers *pl* (tijeras) || shearing machine *sing* (máquina) || metal parings *pl*, metal clippings *pl*, metal cuttings *pl* (cortaduras de metal).

cizalladura *f*; **cizallamiento** *m* shearing, cutting.

cizallar *vt* to shear, to cut.

cizaña *f* BOT bearded darnel || FIG discord, trouble (enemistad); *meter* or *sembrar cizaña* to sow discord, to cause *o* to make trouble || *separar la cizaña del buen grano* to separate the chaff from the grain.

cizañar; cizañear *vi* to sow discord, to cause *o* to make trouble.

cizañero, ra *m/f* troublemaker.

clac *m* opera hat, crush hat (sombrero de copa plegable) || cocked hat (sombrero de tres picos).
◆ *interj* crack!, bang!

clachique *m* AMER unfermented pulque.

clamar *vt* to cry out, to clamour [*US* to clamor]; *clamar su inocencia, su indignación* to cry out one's innocence, one's indignation || to beseech (implorar); *clamar a Dios* to beseech God || *clamar venganza* to cry out for revenge, to clamour for vengeance.
◆ *vi* to cry out, to clamour [*US* to clamor]; *clamar por la paz* to cry out for peace; *clamar contra una injusticia* to cry out against an injustice || FIG to cry out; *la tierra clama por agua* the land is crying out for water || FIG *esto clama al cielo* or *a Dios* this cries out to heaven.

clámide *f* chlamys (abrigo griego).

clamor *m* shout, cry, scream (grito) || clamour [*US* clamor], noise (ruido) || groan, moan (voz lastimosa) || cheer (vítores) || knell, toll (toque de campana fúnebre) || FIG outcry, protest (protesta).

clamorear *vt* to appeal for, to cry out for, to clamour for (con instancia) || to beseech (suplicar) || to complain (quejarse) || to cry out for (clamar).
◆ *vi* to toll (las campanas).

clamoreo *m* shouting, clamour [*US* clamor] (clamor) || FAM pestering (ruego).

clamoroso, sa *adj* resounding; *éxito clamoroso* resounding success || loud, clamorous (ruidoso) || complaining (quejoso).

clan *m* clan.

clandestinidad *f* secrecy || *en la clandestinidad* in secret, in secrecy.

clandestino, na *adj* secret, clandestine; *reunión clandestina* secret meeting || clandestine, underground (actividades políticas) || secret (casamiento, policía).

claque *f* FIG & FAM claque, paid applauders *pl*.

claqueta *f* clapper boards *pl* (de cine).
◆ *pl* clapper *sing* (tablillas).

clara *f* white of the egg (del huevo) || clearness (claridad) || bright interval (del tiempo) || threadbare *o* thin *o* bald patch (en una tela) || bald patch (en el cráneo) || AMER nun of the order of Saint Clare (monja) || *levantarse con las claras del día* to get up with the larks, to get up at daybreak.

Clara *npr f* Clara, Clare.

claraboya *f* skylight (tragaluz) || hinged skylight (en el tejado) || clerestory (en una iglesia).

clarear *vt* to light up, to illuminate (dar claridad) || to brighten, to make lighter (aclarar); *clarear un color* to brighten a colour, to make a colour lighter || AMER to go through (una bala).
◆ *vi* to dawn, to break (el día) || to clear up, to brighten up; *el cielo va clareando* the sky is clearing up || *al clarear el día* at dawn, at daybreak.
◆ *vpr* to wear thin *o* threadbare; *el codo de la chaqueta se clarea* the elbow of the jacket is wearing thin || to be transparent, to let the light through (ser transparente) || FIG & FAM to give o.s. away; *este chico se ha clareado sin querer* that boy has given himself away unintentionally || — *sus intenciones se clarean* his intentions are clear *o* evident, his intentions are plain to see || *tu vestido es tan fino que se clarea* your dress is so thin you can see through it.

clarecer* *vi* to dawn.

clareo *m* clearing (de un bosque).

clarete *adj/sm* claret (vino).

claridad *f* light, brightness; *la claridad del día* the light of day || clearness, clarity, lucidity (lucidez) || fame (fama) || FIG home truth (verdad desagradable); *decir claridades a uno* to tell s.o. a few home truths || — *claridad de vista* clear-sightedness, perspicacity || *con claridad* clearly; *me lo explicó con mucha claridad* he explained it to me very clearly || FIG *cuanto menos bulto, más claridad* good riddance, good riddance to bad rubbish | *ser de una claridad meridiana* to be as clear as day *o* as clear as crystal *o* crystal clear | *con claridad meridiana* with striking clarity, very clearly || *todavía hay claridad* it is still light.

clarificación *f* clarification, clearing (de un líquido) || illumination, lighting (acción de iluminar) || FIG explanation, clarification (explicación).

clarificador *m* clarifier (para el vino).

clarificadora *f* clarifier (de azúcar).

clarificar *vt* to clarify, to clear; *clarificar vino* to clarify wine || to light up, to illuminate (iluminar) || FIG to clarify, to explain.

clarín *m* MÚS bugle (instrumento); *toque de clarín* bugle call || bugler (músico) || clarion stop, clarion (del órgano) || kind of batiste *o* cambric (tela) || FIG clarion || AMER ZOOL *clarín de la selva* solitaire (Myadestes unicolor), mockingbird (sinsonte).

clarinazo *m* bugle call (toque) || FIG warning signal; *el resultado de las elecciones fue un clarinazo* the result of the elections was a warning signal.

clarinete *m* MÚS clarinet (instrumento) || clarinettist [*US* clarinetist] (instrumentalista).

clarinetista *m* MÚS clarinettist [*US* clarinetist].

clarión *m* chalk.

clarisa *f* nun of the order of St. Clare, Poor Clare, Clare (monja).

clarividencia *f* clairvoyance || FIG farsightedness.

clarividente *adj* clairvoyant || FIG farsighted.

claro, ra *adj* bright, well-lit (con mucha luz); *una habitación clara* a bright room || bright (ojos, día, luz, etc.) || clear; *agua, voz clara* clear water, voice; *letra clara* clear handwriting || clear (prueba, explicación, lenguaje); *que quede esto bien claro* let this be quite clear || thin, sparse (poco abundante); *pelo claro* thin hair || illustrious, famous (ilustre); *claros varones de Castilla* famous men of Castile || light; *azul claro* light blue; *una tela azul claro* a light blue cloth || threadbare (tela) || light (cerveza) || weak (café, chocolate, té, etc.) || thin (puré, líquido, etc.) || straight (que obra sin disimulo) || TAUR predictable (toro) || — *claro que* of course || *claro que no* of course not, certainly not || *claro que sí* of course, certainly || *¿está claro?* is that clear? || *está claro que...* it is plain that..., evidently..., of course || FIG *¡las cosas claras y el chocolate espeso!* let's get things clear || *más claro que el agua* as clear as crystal || *más claro que el Sol* as clear as daylight || *tan claro como la luz del día* as clear as daylight, as plain as a pikestaff.
◆ *m* opening, crack (agujero) || space, gap (entre dos palabras escritas, en una multitud) || light (porción luminosa en una pintura o una fotografía) || bald patch (en el pelo) || opening (entre las nubes) || clearing (en un bosque, etc.) || ARQ space (entre columnas) || pause (en un discurso, en la caída de la nieve) || bright interval, break in the rain (en la lluvia) || opening (entre las nubes) || — *claro de luna* moonlight || *llenar un claro* to fill in *o* to stop a gap.
◆ *adv* clearly; *hablar claro* to speak clearly || — *a las claras* openly || *de claro en claro* from dusk till dawn || *pasar en claro una noche* to spend a sleepless night || *poner en claro* to clear up, to clarify, to get *o* to make clear || *por lo claro* clearly || *sacar en claro* to get out of, to solve; *hablé con él pero no saqué nada en claro* I talked with him but got nothing out of him *o* but solved nothing; to clear up (aclarar) || *ver poco claro* not to be able to see very clearly *o* very well.
◆ *interj* of course!, obviously! || — *¡claro está!* of course || *¡pues claro!* of course!

claroscuro *m* light and shade, chiaroscuro.

clarucho, cha *adj* very thin (tela) || watery, thin (con mucha agua); *sopa clarucha* watery soup || weak (café, té, etc.).

clascal *m* AMER maize omelette.

clase *f* class; *la clase media* the middle class || class (escuela); *está en la clase de los párvulos* he is in the infant's class || classroom (aula) || lecture room (en la universidad) || class; *clase nocturna* evening class || lesson; *dar clases particulares* to give private lessons; *clase de conducir* driving lesson || class (en un tren, un barco, un avión); *primera clase* first class || sort, kind; *¿qué clase de cosas me traes ahí?* what sort of things are you bringing me?; *cosas de toda clase* all sorts of things; *de una misma clase* of the same kind || quality, class (calidad); *lana de buena clase* good quality wool || class; *esta persona tiene mucha clase* this person has a lot of class || BOT & ZOOL class || — *clase alta, baja, dirigente, obrera* or *trabajadora* upper, lower, governing, working class || *clases de recuperación* remedial classes || *clases pasivas* pensioners || || AVIAC *clase preferente* business class || *clase social* social class || AVIAC *clase turista* tourist class || *dar clase* to teach (el profesor), to lecture (en la universidad) || *dar clase a alguien* to teach s.o., to give a lesson *o* lesson to s.o. (en general), to lecture s.o., to give lectures to s.o. (en la universidad) || *dar clase con alguien* to take lessons from s.o. (solo), to attend s.o.'s lessons (en general), to attend s.o.'s lectures (en la universidad) || *es un modelo en su clase* he is perfect example of his class || *faltar a clase* to miss school || FAM *fumarse una clase* to skip a class (escuela), to skip a lecture (universidad) || *gente de toda clase* all sorts of people || *la clase agraria* the agricultural community || *sin ninguna clase de dudas* without a shadow of doubt, without any doubt whatsoever || *te deseo toda clase de felicidades* I wish you every kind of happiness.
◆ *pl* MIL N. C. O. 's, non-commissioned officers || *la lucha de clases* the class struggle, class warfare.

clasicismo *m* classicism.

clasicista *adj* classicistic.
◆ *m/f* classicist.

clásico, ca *adj* classical, classic; *obras, lenguas clásicas* classical works, languages || FIG classic, typical (típico) || *el remedio clásico* the time-honoured remedy.
◆ *m* classic (escritor, obra literaria).

clasificable *adj* classifiable.

clasificación *f* classification, classing (acción de asignar a una clase) || sorting (del correo, de carbones, etc.) || order (alfabética, etc.) || DEP league, table || INFORM filing, ordering, sorting || *clasificación nacional del disco* top twenty, hit parade.

clasificado, da *adj* classified.

clasificador, ra *m/f* classifier.
◆ *m* filing cabinet (mueble) || MIN classifier.

clasificar *vt* to class, to classify (asignar a una clase) || to sort (seleccionar) || to grade, to class (según la calidad).
◆ *vpr* to come; *él se clasificó después de mi hermano* he came after my brother || to qualify; *el equipo se clasificó para la final* the team qualified for the final.

clástico, ca *adj* GEOL clastic.

claudia *adj f* *ciruela* or *reina claudia* greengage.

Claudia *npr f* Claudia, Claudette.

claudicación *f* shirking [of duty, responsibility, etc.] (incumplimiento de los deberes) || submission (acción de ceder) || giving up (acción de abandonar un esfuerzo) || limp, lameness (cojera).

claudicante *adj* who shirks one's duty (que deja de cumplir deberes) || yielding, who gives in (que cede) || who gives up easily (que abandona un esfuerzo) || limping, lame (que cojea) || failing, faltering; *sus fuerzas claudicantes* his failing strength.

claudicar *vi* (p us) to limp (cojear) || FIG to shirk [one's duty, responsibility, etc.] (dejar de cumplir deberes) | to abandon one's principles (no seguir sus principios) | to give in, to yield (ceder) | to give up (abandonar un esfuerzo) || to falter, to fail (disminuir).

Claudio *npr m* Claud, Claude.

claustral *adj* claustral, cloistral, monastic.

claustrar *vt* to enclose, to shut in.

claustro *m* cloister (de un convento) || FIG monastic life, cloister | staff (conjunto de profesores en la universidad), senate (junta de profesores) || ANAT *claustro materno* womb.

claustrofobia *f* claustrophobia.

cláusula *f* clause (de un contrato) || GRAM clause || — *cláusula absoluta* ablative absolute (en latín), absolute construction (en inglés) || *cláusula adicional* additional clause || *cláusula de escape* escape clause || *cláusula del país más favorecido* most-favoured-nation clause || *cláusula de salvaguardia* saving *o* escape clause.

clausura *f* enclosure (religiosa) || closure (de debates) || closing, closure (cierre) || — *monja de clausura* enclosed nun || *sesión de clausura* closing session.

clausurar *vt* to conclude, to close, to bring to a close (una sesión, un debate) || to adjourn (el parlamento) || to shut, to close (cerrar).

clava *f* club (porra).

clavadista *m/f* AMER diver [from a cliff].

clavado, da *adj* nail-studded, studded (guarnecido con clavos) || pinned, fixed; *quedó clavado en la pared* it remained fixed to the wall || — FIG *clavado en la cama* tied to one's bed, bedridden, confined to one's bed | *con la mirada clavada en el cielo* staring up at the sky | *dejar clavado a uno* to leave s.o. dumb-founded | *es clavado el retrato de su padre, es su padre clavado* he is the spitting image of his father | *es la traducción clavada* it's the exact translation | *este traje le está clavado* this suit fits him like a glove *o* fits him perfectly | *llegó a las siete clavadas* he arrived dead on *o* bang on seven o'clock, he arrived at seven o'clock on the dot.
◆ *m* nailing.

clavadura *f* prick (en el casco de un caballo).

clavar *vt* to nail (poner con clavos); *clavar algo a* or *en la pared* to nail sth. to the wall || to knock in, to bang in (un clavo) || to nail together (dos cosas) || to drive, to stick (introducir una cosa con punta); *clavar un palo en el suelo* to drive a stake into the ground || to spike (un cañón) || to pierce, to prick (el casco del caballo) || FIG to fix; *clavar la atención en* to fix one's attention on || to set (piedras preciosas) || FIG & FAM to cheat (engañar) | to get right (acertar exactamente) || — FIG *clavar los ojos en* to stare at, to rivet one's eyes on || FIG & FAM *en ese restaurante te clavan* they sting *o* they fleece you in that restaurant.
◆ *vpr* to get (pincharse); *me clavé una astilla en el pie* I got a splinter in my foot || AMER to dive [from a cliff] || — *clavarse un pincho* to prick o.s. on a thorn || *se clavó un puñal en el corazón* he plunged *o* thrust a dagger into his heart.

clave *f* key, clew, clue (explicación) || key, cipher, code (de un texto cifrado) || ARQ keystone; *clave de arco* keystone of an arch || MÚS clef; *clave de sol* treble clef; *clave de fa* bass clef; *clave de do* tenor *o* alto clef || FIG key; *la clave de su actitud* the key to his attitude || — *escribir en clave* to write in code || *la clave del enigma* the key *o* the clue to the riddle.
◆ *m* MÚS harpsichord.
◆ *m pl* claves (instrumento de música).
◆ *adj* key; *una posición clave* a key position; *la palabra clave* the key word.

clavecín *m* MÚS clavecin, harpsichord.

clavel *m* carnation (flor).

clavelito *m* pink (flor).

clavelón *m* African marigold.

clavellina *f* carnation (clavel) || *clavellina de pluma* cottage pink.

clavero *m* clove tree, clove (árbol) || keeper of the keys (persona).

clavete *m* small nail, tack (clavo pequeño) || MÚS plectrum || stud (adorno).

claveteado *m* studding.

clavetear *vt* to stud [with nails].

clavicémbalo *m* MÚS clavicymbal, harpsichord (instrumento).

clavicordio *m* MÚS clavichord (instrumento).

clavícula *f* ANAT clavicle (voz culta), collar bone (palabra usual).

clavija *f* pin, peg, dowel (de madera o de metal) || plug (eléctrica); *clavija de dos contactos* or *de enchufe* two-pin plug; *clavija banana* banana plug || plug (de central telefónica) || MÚS peg (de guitarra, de violín, etc.) || — FIG & FAM *ajustar las clavijas a uno* to put the pressure on s.o., to put the screws on s.o. ‖ *clavija de escalada* piton, peg (alpinismo) ‖ *clavija hendida* split pin, cotter pin ‖ *clavija maestra* kingpin, kingbolt.

clavijero *m* MÚS pegbox ‖ ELECTR plug ‖ clothes hook (percha).

clavillo *m* pivot, pin (pasador) ‖ clove (especia) ‖ MÚS wrest pin (del piano) ‖ plug (que obstruye un orificio).

clavo *m* nail ‖ stud (de adorno) ‖ BOT clove (especia) ‖ MED boil, carbuncle (furúnculo) | corn (callo) | migraine (jaqueca) | scab (de absceso) ‖ FIG grief ‖ VET pastern tumour ‖ FAM debt; *dejar un clavo en la tasca* to chalk up a debt at the pub ‖ *AMER* piece of junk | rich vein (veta) ‖ — FIG & FAM *agarrarse a un clavo ardiendo* to clutch at a straw ‖ *clavo de especia* clove ‖ *clavo de herrar* horseshoe nail ‖ FIG *dar en el clavo* to hit the nail on the head, to put one's finger on it | *dar una en el clavo y ciento en la herradura* to be wrong more times than one is right, to miss nine times out of ten ‖ *¡por los clavos de Cristo!* for Christ's sake! ‖ FIG *por un clavo se pierde una herradura* for the want of a nail the shoe is lost | *remachar el clavo* to keep on about it, to go on | *ser capaz de clavar un clavo con la cabeza* to be pigheaded o stubborn | *ser de clavo pasado* to stick out a mile | *tener un clavo en el corazón* to have a heavy heart | *un clavo saca otro clavo* the new nail drives out the old.

claxon *m* AUT horn, hooter ‖ *tocar el claxon* to sound one's horn, to hoot, to toot.

claxonazo *m* hoot of a horn, toot.

clazol *m* *AMER* bagasse (bagazo).

clearing *m* clearing (compensación financiera).

clemátide *f* BOT clematis.

clemencia *f* mercy, clemency.

clemente *adj* merciful, clement.

Clemente *npr m* Clement.

clementina *f* tangerine (mandarina).

Clementina *npr f* Clementine.

Cleopatra *npr f* Cleopatra.

clepsidra *f* clepsydra, water clock (reloj de agua).

cleptomanía *f* kleptomania.

cleptómano, na *adj/s* kleptomaniac.

clerecía *f* clergy (cuerpo eclesiástico) ‖ priesthood (estado de clérigo).

clergyman *m* clergyman (clérigo protestante) ‖ *traje de clergyman* clergyman's suit [as opposed to cassock] (traje seglar).

clerical *adj* clerical.
◆ *m* clericalist.

clericalismo *m* clericalism.

clericato *m*; **clericatura** *f* priesthood.

clerigalla *f* FAM the clergy, the priests *pl*.

clérigo *m* priest, clergyman (anglicano) ‖ priest (católico) ‖ clerk, scholar (hombre letrado en la Edad Media).

clero *m* clergy.

clerofobia *f* anticlericalism.

clerófobo, ba *adj/s* anticlerical.

¡clic! *interj* click!

cliché *m* negative (fotografía) ‖ plate, stereotype (imprenta) ‖ cliché (frase hecha).

cliente, ta *m/f* customer, client (comprador, persona que utiliza los servicios de otra) ‖ JUR client ‖ patient (de un médico).

clientela *f* clients *pl*, clientele, customers *pl* ‖ practice (de abogado, etc.) ‖ practice, patients *pl* (de médico).
— OBSERV *Clientele* se usa sobre todo para tiendas de cierta categoría : *tenemos una clientela muy distinguida* we have a very distinguished clientele.

clima *m* climate (condiciones atmosféricas) ‖ zone, clime (zona de la tierra) ‖ FIG climate; *el clima internacional* the international climate.

climatérico, ca *adj* climacterical, climacteric ‖ FIG & FAM *estar climatérico* to be in a bad mood.

climaterio *m* climacteric, climacterium.

climático, ca *adj* climatic.

climatización *f* air conditioning.

climatizado, da *adj* air-conditioned.

climatizar *vt* to air-condition.

climatología *f* climatology.

climatológico, ca *adj* climatological.

clímax *m inv* climax.

clin *f* ⟶ **crin.**

clínica *f* clinic.

clínico, ca *adj* clinical; *termómetro clínico* clinical thermometer.
◆ *m* clinician.

clinómetro *m* FÍS clinometer.

clip *m* paper clip, clip (sujetapapeles) ‖ hairclip, clip (para sujetar el pelo) ‖ earring [*US* earclip] (pendiente) ‖ clip (joya).

clíper *m* clipper (barco y avión).

clisado *m* IMPR stereotyping, plating (estereotipado).

clisador *m* IMPR stereotyper (estereotipador).

clisar *vt* IMPR to stereotype, to plate (estereotipar).

clisé *m* IMPR stereotype, plate ‖ FOT negative ‖ FIG cliché (frase hecha).

clisos *m pl* FAM peepers, blinkers (ojos).

clistel; clister *m* enema, clyster (lavativa).

clítoris *m* ANAT clitoris.

clivoso, sa *adj* POÉT sloping.

clo *m* cluck (de la gallina).

cloaca *f* drain, sewer (alcantarilla).

Clodoveo *npr m* Clovis, Clodowig.

Cloe *npr f* Chloe.

cloque *m* gaff (instrumento de pesca).

cloquear *vi* to cluck (las gallinas).

cloqueo *m* cluck, clucking (de una gallina).

cloral *m* QUÍM chloral.

clorato *m* QUÍM chlorate.

clorhidrato *m* QUÍM hydrochlorate (sal).

clorhídrico, ca *adj* QUÍM hydrochloric (ácido).

clórico *adj m* QUÍM chloric.

cloro *m* QUÍM chlorine.

clorofila *f* BOT chlorophyl, chlorophyll.

clorifílico, ca *adj* chlorophyllous, chlorophyllian, chlorophyllose ‖ *función clorofílica* chlorophyllian function.

cloroformar; cloroformizar *vt* MED to chloroform.

cloroformo *m* QUÍM chloroform.

cloromicetina *f* MED chloromycetin.

cloroplasto *m* BOT chloroplast.

clorosis *f* MED & BOT chlorosis.

clorótico, ca *adj* chlorotic.

clorurar *vt* to chlorate.

cloruro *m* QUÍM chloride; *cloruro de cal* chloride of lime; *cloruro sódico* or *de sodio* sodium chloride.

Clotilde *npr f* Clothilda, Clotilda.

clown *m* clown (payaso).

club *m* club ‖ *club de noche* night club.
— OBSERV pl *clubs* or *clubes*.

clueca *adj f* broody (gallina).
◆ *f* broody hen.

cluniacense *adj/sm* Cluniac.

coa *f* *AMER* hoe (azada) | slang (argot).

coacción *f* coercion, compulsion.

coaccionar *vt* to coerce, to compel, to force (forzar).

coactivo, va *adj* coercive, compelling.

coacusado, da *m/f* JUR codefendant.

coadjutor, ra *m/f* coadjutor.

coadquiridor *m* joint purchaser.

coadyutor *m* coadjutor.

coadyuvante *adj* helping, coadjutant.

coadyuvar *vt* to help.
◆ *vi* to contribute; *coadyuvar al bien público* to contribute to the common good ‖ to help, to aid; *glándulas que coadyuvan a la digestión* glands which aid digestion.

coagente *m* assistant, helper.

coagulación *f* coagulation ‖ clotting (de la sangre).

coagulador, ra *adj* coagulative.
◆ *m* coagulator, coagulant.

coagulante *adj* coagulative.
◆ *m* coagulant, coagulator.

coagular, coagularse *v tr y pr* to coagulate, to congeal ‖ to curdle (la leche) ‖ to clot (la sangre en las arterias) ‖ to coagulate (la sangre en una herida).

coágulo *m* coagulum (de sustancia coagulada) ‖ clot (de sangre).

coaitá *f* ZOOL sapajou, spider monkey.

coalición *f* coalition.

coalicionista *m/f* coalitionist.

coaligarse *vpr* ⟶ **coligarse.**

coartación *f* hindrance (impedimento) ‖ restriction.

coartada *f* JUR alibi; *alegar* or *presentar una coartada* to produce an alibi.

coartar *vt* to hinder (estorbar); *estas medidas coartan el desarrollo natural* these measures hinder natural development ‖ to prevent (impedir); *su presencia me coartó para decírselo* his presence prevented me from telling you ‖ to restrict, to limit (limitar); *coartar la autoridad de uno* to limit s.o.'s authority.

coatí *m* ZOOL coati.

coautor, ra *m/f* joint author, coauthor.

coaxial *adj* MAT & TECN coaxial, coaxal; *cilindros coaxiales* coaxial cylinders.

coba *f* FAM flattery (adulación) ‖ FAM *darle coba a uno* to lick s.o.'s boots, to play up to s.o., to butter s.o. up, to suck up to s.o.

cobáltico, ca *adj* cobaltic.

cobalto *m* cobalt (metal).

cobarde *adj* cowardly.
◆ *m/f* coward.

cobardear *vi* to be a coward.

cobardía *f* cowardice.

cobardón, ona *adj* FAM yellow, chicken.
◆ *m/f* FAM chicken.

cobaya *f*; **cobayo** *m* ZOOL guinea pig (conejillo de Indias).

cobear *vt* FAM to play up to, to butter up, to suck up to.

cobero, ra *adj* FAM ⟶ **cobista.**

cobertera *f* lid, cover, top (tapadera) ‖ procuress (alcahueta) ‖ BOT white water lily.

cobertizo *m* shelter (techo sobre soportes) ‖ garage (cochera) ‖ shed, outhouse (para guardar herramientas) ‖ lean-to (construido contra una pared) ‖ covered passage (paso cubierto).

cobertor *m* blanket (manta) || bedspread, counterpane (colcha).

cobertura *f* covering (acción de cubrir) || *cobertura publicitaria* advertising coverage .

cobija *f* ridge tile (teja) || AMER blanket (manta) | thatched roof (tejado).
◆ *pl* coverts (plumas de ave) || AMER bedclothes (ropa de la cama).

cobijamiento; cobijo *m* protection (protección) || lodging (albergue) || hospitality (hospitalidad) || refuge, shelter (refugio).

cobijar *vt* to cover (cubrir) || FIG to shelter, to receive, to give shelter to (albergar) | to harbour (a un criminal) | to harbour, to cherish; *cobijar una ambición muy grande* to cherish a great ambition | to shelter (proteger); *cobijado bajo un paraguas* sheltered under an umbrella.
◆ *vpr* to take shelter, to shelter.

cobijo *m* → **cobijamiento.**

cobista *m/f* FAM toady, crawler, bootlicker (pelotillero).

cobla *f* brass band (en Cataluña).

cobol *m* INFORM Cobol, COBOL.

cobra *f* cobra (serpiente) || rope for yoking oxen (coyunda) || retrieval (del perro de caza).

cobrable; cobradero, ra *adj* cashable (cheque), chargeable (precio), recoverable (suma).

cobrador, ra *m/f* conductor (hombre), conductress (mujer) (de un autobús o de un tranvía) || collector (recaudador) || retriever (perro).

cobranza *f* → **cobro.**

cobrar *vt* to earn (ganar); *¿cuánto cobras por* or *al mes?* how much do you earn a month? || to cash; *cobrar un cheque* to cash a cheque || to collect, to receive (recibir una cantidad) || to draw, to collect (retirar dinero) || to collect; *cobrar una deuda* to collect a debt || to charge; *¿cuánto te ha cobrado?* how much did he charge you? || to be paid, to get paid (ser pagado); *cobro a finales de mes* I am paid at the end of the month || to take; *cobra lo que te debo* take what I owe you || to recuperate, to recover, to retrieve (recuperar) || to take; *cobrarle cariño, odio a alguien* to take a liking, a strong dislike to s.o. || to get back (recobrar); *cobrar aliento* to get one's breath back || to gain (adquirir); *el asunto cobra importancia* the matter is gaining importance || to gain, to earn, to get; *cobrar buena fama* to get a good reputation || to gather (fuerzas) || to pull *o* to haul in (una cuerda) || to retrieve (en la caza) || FAM to get; *vas a cobrar una torta* you're going to get a slap || — *cantidades por cobrar* amounts due || *cobrar ánimo* or *valor* to pluck up courage, to summon up one's courage, to take heart || *cobrar conciencia* to become conscious *o* aware (*de* of) (darse cuenta), to regain consciousness, to come to (volver en sí) || *cuenta por cobrar* unpaid bill || *ir a cobrar* to collect one's pay.
◆ *vi* to get paid || FIG & FAM *¡vas a cobrar!* you're for it!, you're in for it!
◆ *vpr* to take; *cóbrate lo que te debo* take what I owe you || to recover (recuperar) || to recover, to come to (volver en sí).

cobratorio, ria *adj* collecting.

cobre *m* copper || copper pans *pl* (cacerolas, etc.) || AMER copper (monedas) || — FIG & FAM *batir el cobre* to go hard at it, to buckle down to it, to get on with one's work | *batirse el cobre por hacer algo* to go all out to do sth., to buckle down to doing sth.
◆ *pl* MÚS brass (instrumentos).

cobreño, ña *adj* copper (con cobre).

cobrizo, za *adj* copper-coloured [US copper-colored].

cobro *m*; **cobranza** *f* collection (cobranza) || cashing; *el cobro de un cheque* the cashing of a cheque || payment (pago) || retrieval, recovery (de la caza) || — *cobro indebido* overpayment || *poner al cobro* to make payable || *poner algo en cobro* to put sth. in a safe place || *ponerse en cobro* to go into hiding, to take refuge || *presentar al cobro* to cash, to hand in for payment.

coca *f* BOT coca (arbusto) || coca (hojas) || berry (baya) || indian berry (planta) || kink, bend (retorcimiento de cable, etc.) || bun (moño de pelo) || FAM nut, head (cabeza) | rap on the head (coscorrón) | coke (bebida) || AMER cup-and-ball (juguete) || AMER *de coca* for nothing, for free (de balde).

cocada *f* AMER coconut jam (dulce) | lump of coca for chewing (de coca) | nougat (turrón).

cocaína *f* QUÍM cocaine.

cocainomanía *f* cocaine addiction.

cocainómano, na *m/f* cocaine addict.

cocal *m* AMER coca plantation (de cocas) | coconut grove (cocotal).

coccígeo, a *adj* coccygeal.

cocción *f* boiling (acción de hervir) || cooking (acción de cocer) || baking (del pan, de ladrillos).

cóccix *m inv* ANAT coccyx.

coceamiento *m* kick (de caballería).

cocear *vi* to kick.

cocer* *vt/vi* to boil (hervir) || to cook (preparar para comer); *cocer a fuego lento* to cook slowly || to bake (pan, ladrillos).
◆ *vi* to ferment (vino) || to boil (hervir) || to cook (cocinar).
◆ *vpr* to cook; *legumbres que se cuecen mal* vegetables which cook badly || FIG to be boiling (tener mucho calor) | to cook; *no sé lo que se está cociendo en esa reunión* I don't know what's cooking in that meeting.

cocido, da *adj* boiled, cooked.
◆ *m* stew || FIG & FAM *ganarse el cocido* to earn one's bread and butter.
— OBSERV The *cocido* is similar to *stew* except that a large quantity of chick-peas are added.

cociente *m* MAT quotient || DEP goal average || *cociente intelectual* intelligence quotient, I. Q.

cocimiento *m* boiling (acción de hervir) || cooking (cocción) || baking (del pan, de ladrillos) || decoction, infusion (tisana).

cocina *f* cooking; *la cocina francesa* French cooking; *cocina casera* home cooking || kitchen (cuarto) || cooker, stove (aparato); *cocina eléctrica* electric cooker || — *cocina de gas* gas stove (pequeña), gas cooker (grande) || *cocina de mercado* cuisine based on fresh ingredients in season || *cocina económica* stove (fogón de cocina) || *de cocina* kitchen || *hacer la cocina* to cook, to do the cooking (guisar) || *libro de cocina* cookery book *o* cookbook.

cocinar *vt* to cook.
◆ *vi* to cook, to do the cooking (guisar) || FAM to poke one's nose into other people's business, to meddle (entremeterse).

cocinero, ra *m/f* cook || FIG *haber sido cocinero antes que fraile* to know what one is talking about, to speak from experience (saber lo que uno dice), to know what one is doing (saber lo que hace).

cocinilla *f* (small portable) stove; *cocinilla de alcohol* spirit stove || small kitchen (cuarto) || FAM sissy (afeminado).

cocker *m* cocker spaniel, cocker (perro).

cóclea *f* ZOOL cochlea.

coclear *adj* ANAT cochleate, cochleated, cochlear || BOT cochleariform, spoon-shaped.

coco *m* coconut palm, cocoanut palm (árbol) || coconut, cocoanut (fruto) || coccus (microbio) || grub, larva, worm (de las frutas) || FAM bogeyman (bu) | bun (moño de pelo) | rosary bead (cuenta de rosario) | face (mueca); *hacer cocos* to make faces | nut, head (cabeza) || FAM *comer el coco* to mix up | *ser un coco* to be ugly (ser muy feo).

cococha *f* barbel (de la merluza o del bacalao).

cocodrilo *m* crocodile (reptil) || FIG *lágrimas de cocodrilo* crocodile tears.

cocodriloideos *m pl* ZOOL crocodilians.

cocoliche *m* AMER jargon spoken by Italians in Argentina and Uruguay || FAM Italian (italiano).

cócora *m/f* FAM nuisance, bore.

cocoricó; cocorocó *m* cock-a-doodle-doo (canto del gallo).

cocotal *m* coconut *o* cocoanut grove.

cocotero *m* BOT coconut *o* cocoanut palm.

cóctel *m* cocktail (bebida) || cocktail [party] (reunión) || — *cóctel de mariscos* seafood cocktail || *cóctel molotov* molotov cocktail.

coctelera *f* cocktail shaker (recipiente) || FIG mixture (mezcla).

cocha *f* water tank (para los metales) || AMER pool (laguna) | pampa, large open plain (pampa).

cochambre *f* FAM filth, grime (suciedad) | rubbish [US garbage] (basura) | filthy object (porquería).

cochambrería *f* FAM rubbish (basura), filth (suciedad).

cochambriento, ta; cochambroso, sa *adj* FAM filthy, grimy, dirty.

cochayuyo *m* AMER seaweed.

coche *m* car, motorcar, automobile (automóvil); *ir en coche* to go by car || carriage (de caballos) || coach, carriage (de tren) || — *coche blindado* armoured car || || *coche bomba* car bomb || *coche cama* sleeping car *o* sleeper || *coche celular* police van, Black Maria (*fam*), paddy wagon (*fam*) || *coche cerrado* saloon car || *coche comedor* dining car || *coche de alquiler* hire car (alquilado), self-drive car (sin conductor) || *coche de bomberos* fire engine || *coche de carreras* racing car || *coche de correos* mail van || *coche de plaza* or *de punto* or *de sitio* taxi || *coche deportivo* sports car || *coche de turismo* private car || *coche fúnebre* hearse || *coche patrulla* patrol car || *coche restaurante* restaurant car, dining car, luncheon car || *coche silla* pushchair || *coche simón* hackney carriage, cab || *coches literas* sleepers with couchettes (tren) || *coches que chocan* dodgems || FIG & FAM *esto va en coche* this will do | *ir en el coche de San Fernando* to go on Shanks's pony *o* mare.

cochecito *m* toy car (juguete) || bath chair (para inválidos) || pram, perambulator (de niño) || FIG & FAM *coger el cochecito de San Fernando* to go on Shanks's pony *o* mare.

cochera *adj f* carriage; *puerta cochera* carriage entrance.
◆ *f* garage (para los coches) || coach house (para carruajes) || depot; *cochera de autobuses* bus depot.

cochería *f* AMER garage.

cochero *m* coachman, coach drive || — *cochero de punto* cabman, cabby || FIG & FAM *hablar como un cochero* to swear like a trooper.

Cochero *npr m* ASTR the Waggoner, the Charioteer, Auriga (constelación).

cochevis *f* crested lark (pájaro).

cochifrito *m* goat stew (cabrito), mutton stew (cordero).

cochina *f* sow.

cochinada; cochinería *f* FIG & FAM dirty *o* filthy thing, filth (objeto) | obscenity, foul thing (cosa dicha) | dirty trick (acto) | filth, filthiness (suciedad) || — FIG & FAM *decir cochinadas* to use foul language, to say foul *o* obscene things | *estaba diciendo unas cochinadas* you should have heard the language he was using | *hacerle una cochinada a uno* to play a dirty trick on s.o.

Cochinchina *npr f* GEOGR Cochin-China.

cochinera *f* Pigsty.

cochinería *f* FIG & FAM —> **cochinada.**

cochinero, ra *adj* fit for the pigs, poor quality || FAM *trote cochinero* slow *o* gentle trot.

cochinilla *f* woodlouse (bicho) || cochineal (insecto utilizado en tintorería).

cochinillo *m* sucking pig, young pig, piglet.

cochinito de San Antón *m* Ladybird (insecto).

cochino *m* pig.

cochino, na *m/f* FIG & FAM pig, swine.
◆ *adj* FIG & FAM dirty, filthy, disgusting (sucio) | bloody, flipping, lousy; *este cochino despertador funciona muy mal* this bloody alarm clock is always going wrong | revolting; *una comida cochina* a revolting meal | lousy, rotten; *hace un tiempo cochino* the weather is lousy || *¡este cochino dinero!* damm money!

cochiquera *f*; **cochitril** *m* FAM pigsty.

cocho, cha *adj* cooked (cocido).
— OBSERV This adjective is the irregular past participle of the verb *cocer*.

cochura *f* cooking (cocción) || baking (cocción de pan, de ladrillos, etc.) || batch (conjunto de panes) || kiln (conjunto de ladrillos, etc.).

coda *f* MÚS coda || wedge (cuña).

codadura *f* layer (de la vid).

codal *adj* one cubit long (medida) || bent, elbow-shaped (forma).
◆ *m* elbow piece [of armour] (de la armadura) || layer of vine (de la vid) || ARQ prop, shore (puntal) || frame (de una sierra, nivel de albañil) || AMER large candle (vela).

codaste *m* MAR sternpost.

codazo *m* nudge *o* dig with one's elbow, jab, poke || — *abrirse paso* or *camino a codazos* to elbow one's way through || *dar codazos a uno* to nudge s.o., to dig s.o. with one's elbow (para advertir) || *darle un codazo a alguien* to elbow s.o. (para hacerle daño).

codeador, ra *adj* AMER sponging, cadging, scrounging.
◆ *m/f* AMER sponger, scrounger, cadger.

codear *vi* to elbow, to jostle, to nudge; *abrirse paso codeando* to elbow one's way through || AMER to sponge, to cadge, to scrounge (pedir).
◆ *vpr* to rub shoulders, to hobnob, to mix; *codearse con príncipes* to rub shoulders with princes; *se codea con la alta sociedad* he mixes with high society.

codeína *f* MED codeine.

codelincuencia *f* complicity.

codelincuente *adj* accessory.
◆ *m/f* accomplice.

codemandante *m/f* JUR co-plaintiff, joint plaintiff.

codeo *m* elbowing || AMER sponging, cadging (sablazo).

codera *f* elbow patch || MAR mooring hawser (cabo).

codeso *m* BOT cytisus, laburnum.

codetenido, da *m/f* JUR fellow, prisoner.

codeudor, ra *m/f* JUR joint debtor.

códice *m* codex.

codicia *f* greed, cupidity (ambición de riquezas) || FIG envy, covetousness (envidia) | thirst, greed (deseo vehemente); *codicia de saber* thirst for knowledge || TAUR & DEP fighting spirit.

codiciable *adj* desirable, covetable.

codiciado, da *adj* much desired, coveted.

codiciar *vt* to crave for, to covet, to desire.

codicilar *adj* JUR codicillary.

codicilio; codicilo *m* JUR codicil.

codiciosamente *adv* greedily, covetously.

codicioso, sa *adj* greedy (*de* for), covetous (*de* of) || FIG & FAM hardworking (laborioso) || *mirada codiciosa* greedy *o* covetous look.
◆ *m/f* greedy person || FIG & FAM hard worker, slogger (laborioso).

codificación *f* codification || INFORM coding, code.

codificar *vt* to codify || INFORM to code.

codificador, ra *m/f* codifier.
◆ *m* INFORM coder.

código *m* code; *código de carreteras* or *de la circulación* highway code || — INFORM *código ASCII* ASCII code [American National Standard Code for Information Interchange] || *código de barras* bar code || *código de comercio* or *mercantil* commercial law || *código del honor* code of honour || *código deontológico* professional code of ethics || MAR *código de señales* signal code || INFORM *código EBCDIC* EBCDIC code [Extended Binary Coded Decimal Interchange Code] || *código Morse* Morse code.

codillear *vi* TAUR to keep one's elbows close to the body whilst making a pass with the cape.

codillera *f* tumour (de las caballerías).

codillo *m* elbow (de los caballos) || forearm (brazuelo) || CULIN shoulder; *codillo de cordero* shoulder of mutton || stump (gancho) || knee (caza) || elbow, pipe elbow (tubo acodado) || MAR end of keel || FIG & FAM *tirar a uno al codillo* to have it in for s.o.

codirección *f* co-direction (cine) || joint management (administración).

codirector, ra *m/f* co-director, co-directress (cine) || co-manager, co-manageress (administración).

codo *m* elbow (parte del brazo); *apoyar los codos en la mesa* to lean *o* to rest one's elbows on the table || elbow (de los caballos) || knee (caza) || elbow, pipe elbow (tubo acodado) || cubit (medida) || bend, turn, turning (en el camino, etc.) || — FIG & FAM *alzar* or *empinar el codo* to drink a lot, to tipple (beber mucho) | *aprobar un examen a base de codos* to pass an exam by sheer slogging *o* by sheer hard work || *codo con codo, codo a codo* neck and neck (en una carrera), side by side (juntos) || FIG & FAM *comerse los codos de hambre* to be starving (to death) | *dar con el codo* to nudge | *hablar por los codos* to be a real chatterbox | *mentir por los codos* to be an awful liar | *meterse hasta los codos en un asunto* to get into sth. up to one's neck | *romperse* or *clavar* or *hincar los codos* to slog away, to swot (estudiar mucho).

codoñate *m* quince marmalade.

codorniz *f* quail (ave).

coeducación *f* coeducation.

coeducacional *adj* coeducational.

coeficiencia *f* contribution.

coeficiente *m* coefficient || constant || degree; *coeficiente de invalidez* degree of disablement || rate; *coeficiente de incremento* rate of increase || — *coeficiente de inteligencia* intelligence quotient, I. Q. || ECON *coeficiente de caja* cash ratio | *coeficiente de inversión* investment ratio.

coendú *m* ZOOL coendou.

coenzima *f* QUÍM coenzyme.

coercer *vt* to coerce.

coercible *adj* coercible.

coerción *f* coercion.

coercitividad *f* coercivity.

coercitivo, va *adj* coercive.

coetáneo, a *adj* contemporary, coetaneous.
◆ *m/f* contemporary.

coeterno, na *adj* coeternal.

coexistencia *f* coexistence; *coexistencia pacífica* peaceful coexistence.

coexistente *adj* coexistent, coexisting.

coexistir *vi* to coexist.

cofa *f* MAR top || *cofa mayor* maintop.

cofia *f* hairnet (red para el pelo) || lining (del casco) || breech cover (de proyectil) || coif, cap (de las enfermeras, de las monjas, etc.) || BOT coif, calyptra.

cofrade *m/f* brother (hombre), sister (mujer), sister (de una cofradía).

cofradía *f* brotherhood, confraternity (hermandad) || society (sociedad) || association (asociación) || guild (gremio) || union (unión) || gang (de ladrones).

cofre *m* chest, trunk (grande para guardar ropa, etc.) || coffer (grande para dinero) || box, case (pequeño para dinero, joyas) || IMPR coffin || boxfish, cofferfish (pez).

cofrecillo *m* casket, small box.

cofrero *m* packing-case maker, boxmaker.

cofto, ta *adj/s* —> **copto.**

cogedera *f* fruit picker (para coger los frutos).

cogedor, ra *adj* picking, gathering.
◆ *m/f* picker, gatherer (que coge o recoge).
◆ *m* shovel (instrumento de limpieza).

coger *vt* to get hold of, to take, to grasp (tomar); *coger a uno del* or *por el brazo* to get hold of s.o. by the arm, to get hold of s.o.'s arm || to catch, to get; *coger el tren* to get the train || to go by, to travel by (viajar); *no me gusta coger el avión* I don't like going by aeroplane || to catch; *ha cogido el sol, un catarro* he's caught the sun, a cold || to pick up; *no ha cogido un libro en su vida* he hasn't picked up a book in his life || to pick (plantas, verduras, frutas en el árbol); *coger manzanas* to pick apples || to gather (en el suelo); *coger nueces* to gather nuts || to take; *han cogido la ciudad* they have taken the town || to take, to catch; *coger desprevenido* or *descuidado* to take unawares || to take; *siempre me coge la pluma* he is always taking my pen || to catch (oír) || to take, to take down (notas) || to cover (un área) || to surprise; *le cogió la noche en la selva* night surprised him in the forest || to take; *ha cogido un trabajo* he has taken a job; *no sé cómo cogerá la noticia* I don't know how he'll take the news || to catch (la pelota) || to pick up (algo caído) || to catch, to capture (animales) || to begin; *coger una época difícil* to begin a difficult period || to take; *ha cogido cariño, aversión al perro* he has taken a liking, a dislike to the dog || to catch; *dejarse coger por la lluvia* to be caught in the rain || to choose (elegir) || to get (un billete, un puesto, etc.) || to pick up (una costumbre, un acento) || to catch (pescar) || RAD to get, to pick up; *coger la BBC* to get the BBC || to take on (contratar); *voy a coger cocinero nuevo* I'am going to take on a new cook || FAM to catch; *¡a que no me coges!* I bet you can't catch me! || to knock over *o* down; *le cogió un coche* a car knocked him down || to catch up with (alcanzar en una carrera) || TAUR to gore; *le cogió el toro* he was gored by the bull || to cover (el animal macho a la hembra) || FIG to catch; *coger a un ladrón* to catch a thief | to copy, to pick up; *los niños cogen las expresiones de los mayores* children copy adults' expressions | to take up; *esto coge*

mucho sitio this take up a lot of room | to hold, to use (herramientas) | to get, to understand; *no cojo lo que me dices* I don't get what you're saying || *AMER* POP to fuck || — *antes que nos coja la noche* before night falls || FIG *coger bajo su manto* to take under one's wing || *coger celos, miedo a alguien* to become jealous, afraid of s.o. || FIG *coger con las manos en la masa* to catch red-handed | *coger en flagrante delito* or *in fraganti* to catch red-handed | *cogerlas al vuelo* to be quick on the uptake | *cogerle la palabra a uno* to take s.o. at his word || *coger los puntos* or *las carreras a una media* to mend the ladders in a stocking || *coger por su cuenta* to take charge of || FIG *coger una borrachera* to get drunk || FIG & FAM *coger una liebre* to come a cropper | *coger una mona* to get sozzled || *cogí en Inglaterra el final de la guerra* I was in England when the war ended || *cogí la conferencia en la mitad* I went into the lecture halfway through || *cogió la puerta y se fue* he opened the door and walked out || *dejarse coger* to be *o* to get caught (ser agarrado), to be caught up (ser alcanzado), to be taken in, to let o.s. be taken in (ser engañado) || *ir cogidos de* or *por la mano* to go hand in hand || *le cogió de buen humor* it (impersonal) *o* he (personal) caught him in a good mood || *me ha cogido muy mal tiempo* I had very bad weather || *no hay* or *no se sabe por dónde cogerle* you don't know where to get hold of him (agarrar), you don't know how to take him (abordar) || *no me cogerán otra vez* I won't be caught again, they won't catch me again || FIG *no se cogen truchas a bragas enjutas* nothing ventured, nothing gained || *tengo que coger hora para el dentista* I have to make an appointment with the dentist.
◆ *vi* to turn; *coger a la derecha* to turn to the right || to take; *el tinte no ha cogido* the dye has not taken; *los geranios han cogido bien* the geraniums have taken well || FAM to fit, to have room; *el coche no coge en el garaje* the car doesn't fit in *o* into the garage || FAM *coger y* (verbo), to up and (para indicar resolución o determinación); *como no venga, cojo y me voy* if he doesn't come I'll up and go.
◆ *vpr* to trap, to catch (pillarse); *cogerse los dedos con la puerta* to trap one's fingers in the door || to clutch (s.o.), to cling (to s.o.) (agarrarse) || to steal (robar).
— OBSERV In some Latin American countries *coger* is not in decent use. It is replaced by either *tomar* or *agarrar*.

cogerencia *f* joint management (dirección), co-administration (administración).

cogestión *f* co-partnership.

cogida *f* picking (de frutas, etc.) || TAUR gore, goring || — *cogida de los puntos* or *de las carreras de las medias* mending of ladders in stockings || TAUR *sufrir una cogida* to be gored.

cogido, da *adj* gored (un torero) || — *cogidos del brazo* arm-in-arm || FAM *estar cogido* to be busy, to be tied down.
◆ *m* gather (frunce) || pleat (pliegue).

cogitación *f* cogitation.

cogitativo, va *adj* cogitative.

cognación *f* JUR cognation, kinship (parentesco).

cognado, da *adj* cognate.
◆ *m* cognate (pariente).

cognición *f* FIL cognition.

cognomen *m* cognomen.

cognoscitivo, va *adj* FIL cognitive.

cogollo *m* heart (de una lechuga, una col, etc.) || BOT shoot (tallo nuevo), bud (botón); *echar cogollos* to sprout shoots | top (del pino) || FIG & FAM centre, heart, core (centro) | cream (lo mejor) || *AMER* end (de la caña de azúcar) | large cicada (chicharra).

cogorza *f* FAM *agarrar una cogorza* to get drunk, to get sozzled.

cogotazo *m* FAM rabbit punch, blow on the back of the neck.

cogote *m* nape of the neck, back of the neck.

cogotera *f* neck cover.

cogujada *f* crested lark (ave).

cogulla *f* habit (de monje y de monja), frock (de monje) || cowl (hábito con capucha) || cowl (capucha) || *tomar la cogulla* to take the habit (monje), to take the veil (monja).

cogullada *f* (pig's) dewlap (papada del cerdo).

cohabitación *f* cohabitation.

cohabitar *vi* to cohabit, to live together (compartir la vivienda).

cohechar *vt* to bribe, to suborn (sobornar) || AGR to plough for the last time prior to sowing.

cohecho *m* bribery, subornation (soborno) || AGR time for final ploughing.

coheredar *vt* to inherit jointly.

coheredero, ra *m* coheir, joint heir.
◆ *f* coheiress, joint heiress.

coherencia *f* coherence, coherency.

coherente *adj* coherent.

cohesión *f* cohesion.

cohesivo, va *adj* cohesive.

cohesor *m* RAD coherer.

cohete *m* rocket, sky rocket (de fuegos artificiales) || rocket; *cohete espacial* space rocket; *cohete de tres cuerpos* three-stage rocket || *AMER* mine (barreno) || — *AMER* FAM *al cohete* in vain, all for nothing || *avión cohete* rocket || *cohete de señales* flare, signal flare || AGR *cohete paragranizo* cloud cannon || FIG *salir como un cohete* to shoot out *o* off like a rocket (salir corriendo).

cohetero *m* firework maker.

cohibición *f* restriction, restraint (precaución) || inhibition (por timidez).

cohibidor, ra *adj* restraining || intimidating, inhibiting (que intimida).

cohibir *vt* to restrain, to inhibit; *su presencia le cohíbe* his presence restrains him || to restrict, to hinder (estorbar) || *estar cohibido* to feel inhibited *o* uneasy *o* embarrassed.
◆ *vpr* to feel inhibited (inhibirse) || to feel uneasy (no encontrarse a gusto).

cohombro *m* cucumber (planta) || kind of fritter (churro) || *cohombro de mar* sea cucumber (molusco).

cohonestar *vt* to gloss over, to palliate (una acción) || to reconcile; *cohonestar la alegría con la virtud* to reconcile happiness and virtue.

cohorte *f* cohort || FIG host (de personas, animales, cosas), crowd (de personas) || *cohortes celestiales* heavenly hosts.

COI *abrev de Comité Olímpico Internacional* IOC, International Olympic Committee.

coihué *m* *AMER* coigue (árbol).

coima *f* rake-off (del garitero) || concubine (manceba) || *AMER* gratuity, tip (gratificación).

Coimbra *n pr* GEOGR Coimbra.

coincidencia *f* coincidence; *fue una coincidencia que yo estuviese allí al mismo tiempo que él* it was a coincidence that I was there at the same time as him || — *dio la coincidencia de que su amigo era también amigo mío* it just happened that his friend was also a friend of mine || *en coincidencia con* in agreement with || *la coincidencia de nuestros gustos es perfecta* we have exactly the same tastes, our tastes coincide perfectly.

coincidente *adj* coincident, coinciding, coincidental.

coincidir *vi* to coincide (cosas); *mi cumpleaños coincide con el tuyo* my birthday coincides with yours || to meet; *ayer coincidimos en el teatro* we met at the theatre yesterday || to agree; *coincido contigo* I agree with you || to be at the same time as (al mismo tiempo); *coincidí con él en París* I was in Paris at the same time as him || — *coincidimos los dos en ir al cine* we agree to *o* we both wanted to go to the cinema || *coincidir en la misma opinión* to share the same view, to have the same opinion.

coinquilino, na *m/f* joint tenant, co-tenant.

cointeresado, da *adj* jointly interested.
◆ *m/f* party having joint interest, partner.

coipo; coipu *m* coypu, coypou.

coito *m* coitus; *coito interrupto* coitus interruptus.

cojear *vi* to limp, to hobble, to be lame (personas, animales) || to wobble (los muebles); *mesa que cojea* table which wobbles || FIG & FAM to slip up, to act wrongly (obrar mal) | to falter, to totter; *negocio que cojea* faltering business || — FIG & FAM *los dos cojean del mismo pie* they both have the same faults | *el que no cojea renquea* nobody is perfect | *saber de qué pie cojea uno* to know s.o.'s weak spots || *salió cojeando* he limped out.

cojera *f* limp, lameness.

cojetada *f* limp || *dar cojetadas* to limp, to hobble.

cojín *m* cushion (almohadón).

cojinete *m* small cushion (cojín pequeño) || TECN bearing (de rodamiento) | rail chair, chair (de ferrocarril) || TECN *cojinete de agujas, de bolas, de empuje, de rodillos* needle, ball, thrust, roller bearing.

cojitranco, ca *adj* lame.
◆ *m/f* cripple.

cojo, ja *adj* lame, limping (que cojea) || wobbly (mueble); *una silla coja* a wobbly chair || FIG faulty (razonamiento, etc.) | incomplete; *la frase está coja* the sentence is incomplete || — *andar a la pata coja* to hop (along) || FIG & FAM *no ser cojo ni manco* to be all there, to have one's head screwed on right.
◆ *m/f* cripple, lame person.

cojón *m* POP ball || — POP *ponérsele a uno los cojones de corbata* to have butterflies | *tener cojones* to have guts.

cojonudo, da *adj* POP great, fantastic.

cojudear *vi* *AMER* POP to trick (engañar) || to mess about, to fool around (hacer tonterías).

cojudez *f* *AMER* POP nonsense (tontería).

cojudo, da *adj* uncastrated (no castrado) || *AMER* simple (bobo).

cojuelo, la *adj* slightly lame || *el diablo cojuelo* The Devil on Two Sticks (título de una obra literaria).

cok *m* coke (carbón).

col *f* BOT cabbage; *col lombarda* red cabbage || *coles de Bruselas* Brussels sprouts || *col rizada* kale || FIG *el que quiere la col, quiere las hojas de alrededor* love me, love my dog | *entre col y col, lechuga* a change is as good as a rest.

cola *f* tail (de cuadrúpedos, aves, peces, aviones) || train (de un vestido); *la cola del traje de novia* the train of the wedding dress || tail (de chaqué, frac, etc.) || tail (de una cometa) || queue [*US* line, queue] (de gente); *ponerse en la cola* or *en cola* to get into the queue || glue (sustancia gelatinosa); *cola de pescado* fish glue || BOT kola, cola || INFORM queue || — *a la cola* behind, at the rear || *cola de caballo* horsetail, shave grass (planta), pony tail (peinado) || TECN *cola de milano* or *de pato* dovetail joint (ensambladura) || *cola de zorra* foxtail (planta)

|| *cola fuerte* glue || FIG *estar en la cola* to be the last (ser el último) | *estar en la cola de la clase* to be at the bottom of the class || *hacer cola* to queue (up), to line up || *llevar la cola* to carry the train (en una boda) || *montar en cola* to get in at the back end (tren) || FIG *no pegar ni con cola* to have nothing to do with it || *piano de cola* grand piano || FIG *tener* or *traer cola* to have serious consequences, to bring trouble || *vagón de cola* rear coach || *venir en cola* to come last, to bring up the rear.

colaboración *f* collaboration || contribution (en un periódico).

colaboracionismo *m* collaborationism.

colaboracionista *m/f* collaborator.

colaborador, ra *adj* collaborating || contributing (de un periódico).
◆ *m/f* collaborator, associate || contributor (de un periódico) || *colaboradores de un libro* joint authors of a book.

colaborar *vi* to collaborate || *colaborar en un periódico* to contribute to *o* to write for a newspaper.

colación *f* REL collation (de un beneficio) || conferring (de título universitario) || collation, collating, comparison (comparación) || snack, light meal, collation (ant) || AMER sweet || — JUR *colación de bienes* collation of property || *sacar* or *traer a colación* to bring up, to mention; *siempre traes a colación lo mismo* you're always bringing up the same thing || JUR *traer a colación* to collate (en una sucesión), to give in support, to prove one's point with (un ejemplo).

colacionar *vt* REL to collate, to confer (un beneficio eclesiástico) || to collate, to compare (confrontar) || JUR to collate.

colada *f* washing (lavado); *día de colada* washing day || washing, wash (ropa colada) || bleaching (acción de blanquear) || outflow (de lava) || TECN tapping (del alto horno) || filtering (filtrado) || cattle track (para los rebaños) || (difficult) pass (entre dos montañas) || FIG sword [of El Cid] || — *hacer la colada* to wash, to do the washing || TECN *lecho de colada* pig bed | *orificio de colada* taphole, drawhole || FAM *todo saldrá en la colada* it will all come out in the wash.

coladera *f* strainer (tamiz pequeño) || AMER plughole (sumidero).

coladero *m* strainer, sieve (tamiz) || filter (filtro) || narrow pass || MIN winze || FIG & FAM school where examinations are very easy to pass (enseñanza).

colado, da *adj* *aire colado* draught || FIG & FAM *estar colado por* to be mad *o* crazy about, to have a crush on || *hierro colado* cast iron.

colador *m* REL patron, collator || strainer (para té, café, etc.) || colander (para alimentos mayores) || IMPR leach || — FIG *estos calcetines están como un colador* these socks are full of holes | *tener más agujeros que un colador* to be like a sieve, to be riddled with holes.

coladora *f* washerwoman.

coladura *f* straining (filtración) || MED straining, filtration (filtración) || (used) tea leaves *pl* (de té), coffee grounds *pl*, dregs *pl* (de café), residue, dregs *pl* (en general) || FIG & FAM clanger (metedura de pata) | mistake (equivocación) || FIG & FAM *ésta fue una coladura mía* I put my foot in it, I dropped a clanger *o* a brick.

colapez; colapiscis *f* fish glue, isinglass.

colapsar *vt* to bring sth. to a standstill.
◆ *vi* to collapse.

colapso *m* MED collapse, breakdown || FIG stoppage (paralización) || FIG *la industria sufre un colapso por falta de materias primas* the industry is paralysed through lack of raw materials.

colar* *vt* to strain; *colar la leche* to strain milk; *colar el té* to strain the tea || to filter (el café) || to wash (la ropa) || to confer, to collate (conferir un beneficio) || to cast (los metales) || FIG & FAM to pass, to slip; *trató de colar la pulsera por la aduana* he tried to pass the bracelet through the customs | to pass off; *colar una moneda falsa* to pass off a forged coin || FIG & FAM *es demasiado listo para que le cueles esa historia* he's too clever to swallow *o* to believe that tale.
◆ *vi* to filter (filtrarse) || to squeeze, to slip (por un sitio estrecho) || FIG & FAM to drink wine (beber vino) || FIG to wash; *la mentira era demasiado ridícula para colar* the lie was too ridiculous to wash || — FIG *esto no cuela* that won't wash | *por si cuela* to see if it will wash.
◆ *vpr* FAM to slip; *colarse en la primera fila* to slip into the front row | to gatecrash; *colarse en una fiesta* to gatecrash a party | to jump the queue (en una cola); *haga el favor de no colarse* please don't jump the queue | to make a mistake, to make a boob *o* bloomer (equivocarse) || to put one's foot in it (meter la pata) || FAM *colarse con* or *por alguien* to fall for s.o.

colateral *adj* collateral || collateral (pariente) || *nave colateral* aisle (de iglesia).
◆ *m/f* collateral (pariente).

colcótar *m* colcothar, rouge.

colcha *f* bedspread, counterpane (de cama).

colchón *f* mattress || — *colchón de aire* cushion of air, air cushion (del aerodeslizador) || *colchón de muelles* spring mattress, spring interior mattress (colchón), springs *pl* (bastidor) || *colchón de plumas* feather bed || *colchón de tela metálica* springs *pl* || *colchón neumático* air bed || FIG *dormir en un colchón de plumas* to have it easy, to have an easy life.

colchonería *f* mattress maker's, upholsterer's.

colchonero, ra *m/f* mattress maker || *aguja colchonera* tufting needle.

colchoneta *f* small mattress (colchón estrecho) || long cushion (cojín) || TECN *colchoneta de aire* cushion of air.

cold cream *m* cold cream.

cole *m* FAM school.

coleada *f* ⟶ **coletazo.**

colear *vi* to wag its tail (un perro, gato, etc.) || to swish *o* to switch its tail (caballo, vaca, etc.) || to wriggle (un pez) || to sway (moverse de un lado para otro) || — AMER *colea en los sesenta* he's bordering on sixty, he's getting on for sixty || FAM *todavía colea el asunto* we haven't heard the last of the affair | *vivito y coleando* alive and kicking.
◆ *vt* to throw (a bull) by the tail.

colección *f* collection; *una colección de cuadros* a collection of paintings || range, collection; *esta tienda tiene una colección impresionante de corbatas* this shop has an impressive range of ties || FIG load; *dijo una colección de tonterías* he said a load of rubbish | string (de mentiras).

coleccionador, ra *m/f* collector.

coleccionar *vt* to collect.

coleccionista *m/f* collector.

colecta *f* collection (de un impuesto) || collection (de donativos o limosnas); *hacer una colecta* to make a collection || REL collect (oración de la misa).

colectar *vt* to collect; *colectar los impuestos* to collect the taxes.

colectividad *f* collectivity || community (grupo social); *hay que sacrificar algo a la colectividad* sth. must be sacrified for the community.

colectivismo *m* collectivism.

colectivista *m/f* collectivist.

colectivización *f* collectivization.

colectivizar *vt* to collectivize.

colectivo, va *adj* collective || — *contrato colectivo* collective bargaining || *convenio colectivo* collective agreement || *garantía colectiva* collective security || *granja colectiva* collective farm.
◆ *m* GRAM collective noun || AMER minibus.

colector *m* collector (recaudador) || ELECTR collector, commutator || main sewer (sumidero) || — TECN *colector de admisión* induction manifold || *colector de basuras* rubbish shoot || *colector de drenaje* drainpipe || TECN *colector de escape* exhaust manifold.

colédoco *adj m/sm* choledoch.

colega *m* colleague || counterpart, opposite number; *el primer ministro inglés recibió a su colega español* the English Prime Minister received his Spanish counterpart.

colegatario, ria *m/f* co-legatee, joint legatee.

colegiación *f* membership of a college.

colegiadamente *adv* as a body.

colegiado, da *adj* collegiate (socio).
◆ *m/f* collegian.

colegial *adj* collegial, collegiate (relativo al colegio de médicos, etc.) || schoolboy, schoolgirl (relativo a los colegiales); *costumbres colegiales* schoolboy customs || school; *la vida colegial* school life.
◆ *m/f* collegian (de un Colegio Mayor).
◆ *m* schoolboy.
◆ *f* collegiate church (iglesia).

colegiala *f* schoolgirl.

colegiarse *vpr* to enroll in a college.

colegiata *f* collegiate church (iglesia).

colegiatura *f* grant.

colegio *m* primary school (de enseñanza primaria) || independant secondary school, fee-paying school (de enseñanza media) || college; *colegio de abogados, de médicos* college of barristers, of doctors || — *colegio de cardenales* or *cardenalicio* College of Cardinals, Sacred College || *colegio de internos* boarding school || *colegio de pago* fee-paying school || *colegio de párvulos* infant school || *colegio electoral* electoral college || *colegio mayor* students' hall of residence (residencia), university college (facultad).

colegir* *vt* to collect, to gather (juntar) || to deduce, to infer (inferir); *colegir algo de lo dicho* to deduce sth. from what has been said.

coleo *m* wagging of the tail.

coleóptero *m* ZOOL coleopteron.

cólera *f* anger, fury, rage (ira) || bile (bilis) || — *descargar su cólera en alguien* to vent one's anger *o* one's spleen on s.o., to let fly at s.o. *(fam)* || *montar en cólera* to fly into a temper, to flare up.
◆ *m* MED cholera; *cólera morbo* cholera morbus, malignant Asiatic cholera; *cólera nostras* or *esporádico* sporadic cholera.

colérico, ca *adj* angry, furious, in a bad temper (encolerizado); *estar colérico* to be angry || bad-tempered, choleric, irascible (irascible); *ser colérico* to be bad-tempered.

colesterina *f* BIOL cholesterine.

colesterol *m* BIOL cholesterol.

coleta *f* pigtail [worn by bullfighters] (de los toreros) || plait (de pelo trenzado) || tail (de pelo sin trenzar) || FIG *cortarse la coleta* to retire from bullfighting (torero), to retire (oficio), to give up a habit (costumbre).

coletazo *m*; **coleada** *f* wag of the tail (de perro) || swish *o* flick of the tail (de vaca, caballo, pez) || sway (de un vehículo) || FIG death throe; *los últimos coletazos del régimen* the death throes of the regime || *dar coletazos* to wag its tail.

coletilla *f* FIG postscript, addition; *poner una coletilla a un texto* to make an addition to a text, to put a postscript on a text.

coleto *m* jerkin (casaca) || — FIG & FAM *decir para su coleto* to say to o.s. | *echarse un libro al coleto* to read a book from beginning to end *o* right through | *echarse un vaso al coleto* to have a quick one, to put one away | *para su coleto* to o.s.

colgadero, ra *adj* which can be hung up, hangable.
◆ *m* hook (garfio) || peg, hanger (percha).

colgadizo, za *adj* hanging.
◆ *m* lean-to (tejadillo).

colgado, da *adj* hanging, hung up || pending (sin resolver) || hung (ahorcado) || FIG & FAM disappointed (burlado) || FIG & FAM *dejar a uno colgado* to leave s.o. in the lurch.

colgador *m* IMPR peel || hook (gancho) || coat hanger (percha).

colgadura *f* hangings *pl*, drapes *pl* (cortinas) || tapestry (tapiz).

colgajo *m* rag, torn piece [hanging from garment] || bunch of grapes [hung up to dry] (racimo de uvas) || MED flap (de piel).

colgamiento *m* hanging.

colgante *adj* hanging; *jardín colgante* hanging garden || *puente colgante* suspension bridge.
◆ *m* ARQ festoon || pendant (joya).

colgar* *vt* to hang (up); *colgar un abrigo de un clavo* to hang a coat (up) on a nail || to hang up; *cuelga la gabardina* hang your raincoat up || to hang (un cuadro) || to hang (out); *colgar la ropa en la cuerda* to hang (out) the washing on the line || to drape, to hang [with hangings or drapes] (adornar) || FIG & FAM to hang (ahorcar); *colgar a una persona de un árbol* to hang a person from a tree | to fail, to plough (en un examen) | to palm off; *me colgó un trabajo muy duro* he palmed off a very hard job on me, he palmed me off with a very hard job || — FIG *colgar a uno el sambenito de ladrón, de embustero* to brand s.o. a thief, a liar | *colgar las botas, los guantes* to hang up one's boots, one's gloves (abandonar una profesión) | *colgar los hábitos* to give up the cloth | *colgar los libros* to put away one's books (abandonar los estudios) || MIL *¡cuelguen armas!* sling arms! || FAM *quedarse con dos asignaturas colgadas* to fail in two subjects.
◆ *vi* to hang; *la lámpara cuelga del techo* the lamp hangs from the ceiling; *el sombrero cuelga en la percha* the hat is hanging on the hook || to dip; *un vestido que cuelga de un lado* a dress which dips on one side || to hang up (teléfono) || *¡no cuelgue!* hold on!, don't hang up! (el teléfono).
◆ *vpr* to hang o.s. (ahorcarse).

colibrí *m* hummingbird, colibri (pájaro).

cólico, ca *adj* colic (relativo al colon).
◆ *m* colic || — *cólico hepático, nefrítico* hepatic, nephritic colic || *cólico miserere* ileus || *cólico saturnino* lead colic, painter's colic.

colicuación *f* smelting (de metales).

coliflor *f* cauliflower.

coligación *f* association || alliance (alianza) || coaligation (para gobernar).

coligado, da *adj* associated || allied (aliado) || coalesced (para gobernar).
◆ *m/f* ally (aliado) || associate.

coligarse; coaligarse *vpr* to associate, to form an association (asociarse) || to ally, to unite (aliarse) || to coalesce, to form a coalition (para gobernar).

colilla *f* cigarette end, cigarette butt, butt, stub.

colillero *m* person who picks up cigarette ends.

colimación *f* FÍS collimation.

colimador *m* FÍS collimator.

colimba *f* AMER FAM military service (servicio militar).

colimbo *m* grebe (ave).

colín *adj* bobtail (caballo).
◆ *m* bread stick (pan).

colina *f* hill, rise (elevación de terreno).

colinabo *m* kohlrabi, turnip cabbage.

colindante *adj* adjacent, adjoining; *un campo colindante con otro* a field adjacent to *o* adjoining another.

colindar *vi* to be adjacent, to adjoin; *esta casa colinda con el jardín* this house is adjacent to the garden.

colino *m* cabbage plantation *o* patch || cabbage seed (semilla).

colipavo, va *adj* fantail (palomas).

colirio *m* MED collyrium, eyewash.

colirrojo *m* redstart (ave).

Coliseo *npr m* Coliseum.

colisión *f* collision || FIG clash; *una colisión entre la policía y unos manifestantes* a clash between the police and some demonstrators; *una colisión de ideas* a clash of ideas.

colitigante *adj/s* co-litigant.

colista *m* last, last person.

colitis *f* MED colitis.

colmado, da *adj* full, filled; *una vida colmada de satisfacciones* a life full of *o* filled with satisfaction || *una cucharada colmada* a heaped spoonful.
◆ *m* snack bar, café (tasca) || wine store (tienda de vinos) || grocer's, grocery store (tienda de comestibles).

colmar *vt* to fill to the brim, to fill right up; *colmar un vaso* to fill a glass to the brim || to fill; *colmar una cesta de naranjas* to fill a basket with oranges || FIG to lavish (on), to heap (on), to shower (on); *colmarle a uno de alabanzas* to shower s.o. with praise, to lavish *o* to heap praise on s.o. | to overwhelm, to lavish; *me colmó de favores* he overwhelmed me with favours | to fulfil, to satisfy; *colmar sus ambiciones* to fulfil one's ambitions || FIG *eso colma la medida* that's the last straw.

colmena *f* beehive, hive || FIG hive; *una colmena humana* a human hive.

colmenar *m* apiary.

colmenero, ra *m/f* beekeeper, apiarist.
◆ *m* AMER honey bear (oso).

colmenilla *f* BOT morel (cagarria).

colmillada *f*; **colmillazo** *m* bite, snap (de perros) || blow with a tusk (del elefante, del jabalí).

colmillo *m* ANAT eye tooth, canine tooth, canine || tusk (de jabalí, elefante, morsa) || fang (de un monstruo, lobo, perro, etc.) || — *enseñar los colmillos* to bare its teeth (los animales), to show one's teeth (amenazar) || FIG & FAM *escupir por el colmillo* to boast, to brag, to talk big | *tener el colmillo retorcido* to be a sly old fox, to be crafty.

colmilludo, da *adj* with long canine teeth *o* fangs *o* tusks || FIG crafty, shrewd (astuto).

colmo *m* height, summit; *el colmo de la locura* the height of madness || thatched roof (techo de paja) || — *a colmo* in abundance || *¡eso es el colmo!* that's the limit, that's the last straw, that tops it all || *llegar al colmo* to reach the limit || *para colmo, para colmo de desgracias* to top it all, to make matters worse, on top of everything else || *sería el colmo si* it would be the end if || *una cucharada con colmo* a heaped spoonful.

colmo, ma *adj* full to the top, filled || heaped (cucharada, etc.) || brimming, overflowing (que rebosa).

colocación *f* employment; *agencia* or *oficina de colocaciones* employment office *o* exchange *o* agency || job; *ha encontrado una buena colocación* he has found a good job || positioning, position (posición); *no me gusta la colocación de estos cuadros* I don't like the positioning of these pictures || laying (de una moqueta) || hanging (de un cuadro) || investment (de dinero) || — *colocación de la primera piedra* laying of the first stone || *colocación del marco* framing.

colocar *vt* to place, to put; *colocar los libros en un estante* to place the books on a shelf; *colocar con orden* to put in order || to invest, to place (dinero) || MIL to position (tropas, artillería) || to put; *me colocó en la primera fila* he put me in the first row || FIG to put, to find work for; *sus padres le han colocado en una panadería* his parents have put him in a bakery | to give work *o* a job to; *el director le colocó en su despacho* the manager gave him work in his office | to marry off; *ha colocado bien a sus dos hijas* he has married off his two daughters well | to give; *me colocó la historia de siempre* he gave me the same old story || — *estar colocado* to have a job || *estar muy bien colocado* to have a good job.
◆ *vpr* to take a job; *se ha colocado de criada, en un banco* she has taken a job as a maid, in a bank || to find work, to find a job; *no es tan fácil colocarse* it's not so easy to find a job || to put o.s., to station o.s.; *se colocó detrás de la puerta* he put himself behind the door || to be; *el equipo se ha colocado en sexto lugar* the team is in sixth place.

colocolo *m* AMER wild cat.

colodión *m* QUÍM collodion.

colofón *m* IMPR colophon || appendix, addition (en un libro) || star turn, high spot; *fue el colofón del espectáculo* he was the star turn of the show | climax, height; *el brillante colofón de su carrera* the brilliant climax of his career.

colofonia *f* QUÍM colophony, rosin (resina).

cologaritmo *m* MAT cologarithm.

coloidal *adj* QUÍM colloidal; *metaloides coloidales* colloidal metalloids.

coloide *adj/sm* QUÍM colloid.

coloideo, a *adj* QUÍM colloid, colloidal.

Colombia *npr f* GEOGR Colombia.

colombiano, na *adj/s* Colombian.

colombino, na *adj* of Christopher Columbus.

Colombo *n pr* GEOGR Colombo.

colombofilia *f* pigeon breeding.

colombófilo, la *adj* pigeon fancying *o* breeding.
◆ *m/f* pigeon fancier *o* breeder.

colon *m* colon (intestino) || GRAM main clause (período) | colon (dos puntos), semicolon (punto y coma).

colón *m* colón [unit of currency used in Costa Rica and El Salvador].

Colón *n pr* Columbus; *Cristóbal Colón* Christopher Columbus.

colonato *m* tenant farming.

colonia *f* colony (país, reunión de personas, de animales, de células, etc.) || eau de Cologne (agua de Colonia) || silk ribbon (cinta) || AMER district (barrio) || — *colonia de vacaciones* (children's) holiday camp || *colonia de verano* summer camp || *colonia obrera* worker's housing estate || *colonia penitenciaria* labour *o* prison camp || AMER *colonia proletaria* shanty town.

Colonia *n pr* GEOGR Cologne.

coloniaje *m* colonial period | colonial government.

colonial *adj* colonial; *época colonial* colonial period || imported, overseas; *productos coloniales* imported goods.
◆ *m pl* imported *o* overseas foodstuffs || groceries (comestibles).

colonialismo *m* colonialism.

colonialista *adj/s* colonialist.

colonización *f* colonization.

colonizador, ra *adj* colonizing.
◆ *m/f* colonizer, colonist (persona que coloniza).

colonizar *vt* to colonize.

colono *m* colonist, colonial (habitante de una colonia) || tenant farmer (el que cultiva una granja).

coloquial *adj* colloquial.

coloquio *m* discussion, conversation || dialogue, colloquy (diálogo).

color *m* colour [US color]; *colores complementarios* complementary colours; *ese traje tiene un color muy bonito* this dress is a nice colour || colour, complexion (tez) || colour (raza) || ARTES colouring [US coloring], colour [US color] (colorido) || FIG tone (de una conversación, etc.) | leaning, tendency; *el color de un periódico* a newspaper's tendency || — *a todo color* in full colour, all in colour || *color butano* orange || *color de rosa, de aceituna* pink, olive; *seda de color de rosa* pink silk || FIG *color local* local colour || *color primario* primary colour || *color sólido* fast colour (tejido) || FIG *dar color a algo* to liven sth. up || *de color* coloured; *hombre de color* coloured man; brown; *zapatos de color* brown shoes || *de color vino* wine-coloured || FIG *mudar* or *cambiar de color* to change colour, to turn pale || FIG *so color de* on pretext of, under the pretext of, under colour of | *subido de color, de color subido* strong in colour (un cuadro), off-colour, strong (chiste, etc.) | *tomar color* to ripen (frutas), to take colour (una tela al teñirse) || FIG & FAM *un color se le iba y otro se le venía* he turned all the shades of red || FIG *ver las cosas de color de rosa* to see everything through rose-coloured spectacles.
◆ *pl* colours (bandera); *colores nacionales* national colours || colours (de un equipo deportivo) || — *en colores* in colour || FIG *pintar algo con colores trágicos* to give a tragic impression of sth. | *pintar con negros colores* to paint black || FAM *ponerse de mil colores* to go as red as a beetroot || FIG *sacarle a uno los colores (al rostro)* to make s.o. blush | *salirle a uno los colores a la cara* to blush | *se le suben los colores a la cara* he blushes, he goes red.

coloración *f* colouration [US coloration], colouring [US coloring].

colorado, da *adj* coloured [US colored] || red (rojo); *la flor colorada de la amapola* the red flower of the poppy || red, ruddy (cara) || — FIG *estar colorado* to be red in the face (de vergüenza) | *más vale ponerse una vez colorado que ciento amarillo* it's better to be ashamed once than to have regrets for ever more || *poner colorado a alguien* to make s.o. go red, to make s.o. blush | *ponerse colorado* to go red, to blush | *ponerse más colorado que un pavo* or *que un tomate* to turn *o* to go as red as a beetroot, to turn all the shades of red.
◆ *m* red (color).

Colorado *npr m* GEOGR Colorado || *el Gran Cañón (del Colorado)* the Grand Canyon.

coloradote, ta *adj* FAM red-faced, ruddy || *cara coloradota* ruddy face.

colorante *adj* colouring [US coloring].
◆ *m* colouring [US coloring].

colorar *v tr* to colour [US to color] || to dye, to colour (teñir) || *la clorofilia colora de verde las hojas* chlorophyll colours the leaves green, chlorophyll gives the leaves their green colour.

colorear *vt* to colour [US to color] || to dye, to colour (teñir) || FIG to palliate (un vicio, etc.).
◆ *vi* to ripen, to take on colour (ciertos frutos) || to be reddish, to verge on red (tirar a rojo) || to redden (ponerse rojo).

colorete *m* rouge (afeite).

colorido *m* colour, colouring, colours *pl* [US color, coloring, colors *pl*] || FIG colour.

colorímetro *m* colorimeter, chromometer.

colorín *m* goldfinch (pájaro) || FAM measles *pl* (sarampión) || FAM *y colorín, colorado, este cuento se ha acabado* and they all lived happily ever after (final de un cuento), and that's the end of the story.
◆ *pl* bright *o* vivid *o* loud colours.

colorinche *m* AMER gaudy *o* loud colours *pl* (colores llamativos).

colorir* *vt* to colour [US to color] (dar color) || to colour, to dye (teñir).

colorista *m y f* colourist [US colorist].

colosal *adj* colossal, gigantic, huge; *edificio colosal* huge building || FIG & FAM colossal, fantastic, terrific (extraordinario).

colosalmente *adv* FIG & FAM marvellously || FIG & FAM *lo hemos pasado colosalmente* we had a marvellous time.

colosenses *m pl* REL Colossians; *Epístola a los colosenses* Epistle to the Colossians.

coloso *m* colossus || *Coloso de Rodas* Colossus of Rhodes.

colostro *m* colostrum (calostro).

colpa *f* colcothar.

cólquico *m* BOT colchicum.

Cólquida *npr f* GEOGR Colchis.

colt *m* colt (revólver).

columbario *m* columbarium.

columbear *vt* AMER to swing (columpiar).

Columbia *npr f* GEOGR Columbia.

columbino, na *adj* dovelike, columbine (perteneciente a la paloma), dove-coloured (color).

columbrar *vt* to be able to make out, to be able to see, to make out, to see (ver de lejos); *a lo lejos se columbra una casa* in the distance you can make out a house || to begin to see; *columbro una solución* I begin to see a solution || FIG to foresee (prever).

columbres *m pl* FAM peepers, eyes (ojos).

columelar *adj* *diente columelar* canine tooth.

columna *f* ARQ column; *columna corintia* Corinthian column || FIG pillar, mainstay, prop, support (apoyo) || column (en un periódico o un libro) || MIL column; *columna cerrada* close column || pile, column (pila) || cable (en punto) || — AUT *columna de dirección* steering column || TECN *columna de fraccionamiento* fractionating column || *columna miliar* milestone || ARQ *columna rostrada* or *rostral* rostral column || ANAT *columna vertebral* vertebral *o* spinal column, spine, backbone (espinazo) || FIG *quinta columna* fifth column.

columnata *f* ARQ colonnade.

columnista *m/f* columnist (periodista).

columpiar *vt* to swing, to push [on a swing].
◆ *vpr* to swing (mecerse) || FIG & FAM to sway along (al andar) | to swing (de un lado para otro) | to put one's foot in it, to make a mistake (equivocarse).

columpio *m* swing (juego) || AMER rocking chair (silla).

coluria *f* MED choluria.

colusión *f* JUR collusion.

colusorio, ria *adj* JUR collusive.

colza *f* BOT colza.

colla *f* throatpiece, gorget (de la armadura) || fish trap, line of fishing nets (nasa) || leash (traílla) || team of dockers (en un puerto) || storm (tempestad).

colla *m/f* inhabitant of the Argentinian *o* Bolivian Andes.

collado *m* hill (cerro) || pass (entre dos montañas).

collage *m* collage (pintura).

collar *m* necklace (adorno) || collar (de animales domésticos) || chain (de una condecoración) || iron collar (de los esclavos) || TECN collar, ring (abrazadera) || collar, ruff (de plumas) || *collar de fijación* collar.

collarín *m* bands *pl* (alzacuello) || collar (sobrecuello) || flange (de un tubo) || annulet (de una columna) || *collarín de la botella* lable on the neck of a bottle.

collarino *m* ARQ gorgerin.

collera *f* collar (parte de los arreos) || FIG chain gang (de presidiarios) || AMER pair (de animales).
◆ *pl* AMER cuff links (gemelos).

coma *f* comma (signo ortográfico) || misericord (en las sillas del coro) || MÚS comma (intervalo) || BOT coma (de hojas, etc.) || coma (imperfección en una lente) || point (decimal) || — INFORM *coma fija* fixed point | *coma flotante* floating point || *sin faltar (ni) una coma* down to the last detail, in the minutest detail.
◆ *m* MED coma.

comadre *f* midwife (partera) || godmother (madrina) (véase OBSERV) || FAM procuress (alcahueta) | neighbour [US neighbor] (vecina) | old wife, gossip (mujer murmuradora) | peasant woman (palurda) || *cuentos* or *chismes de comadre* old wive's tales.

— OBSERV The *comadre* is the godmother seen from the point of view of the child's godfather or parent. Thus, if I am the child's godfather, *mi comadre* is *my fellow godparent* and, if I am the child's parent, *mi comadre* is *my child's godmother.*

comadrear *vi* FAM to gossip.

comadreja *f* weasel (animal).

comadreo *m* FAM gossip, gossiping, tittle-tattle.

comadrería *f* AMER gossip, gossiping, tittle-tattle.

comadrero, ra *adj* gossiping.
◆ *m/f* gossip, gossipmonger.

comadrón *m* FAM male midwife (partero).

comadrona *f* FAM midwife (partera).

comal *m* AMER earthenware dish [for baking maize tortilla].

comalia *f* VET sheep dropsy.

comanche *adj/s* Comanche (indio).

comandancia *f* MIL command (grado, distrito) | military headquarters *pl* (edificio).

comandanta *f* FAM commander's wife || flagship (navío).

comandante *m* MIL commander, commanding officer, commandant (jefe) | major (grado) || *comandante en jefe* commander-in-chief.

comandita *f* COM limited partnership [US silent partnership] || *sociedad en comandita* limited partnership [US silent partnership].

comanditar *vt* to enter as a sleeping partner [US to enter as a silent partner].

comanditario, ria *adj* sleeping [US silent]; *socio comanditario* sleeping partner.

comando *m* MIL commando (grupo) | commando raid (operación) | command (mando).

comarca *f* region, area; *La Mancha es una comarca del centro de España* La Mancha is a region of central Spain.

comarcal *adj* regional; *delegación comarcal* regional delegation || local (carretera, emisora).

comatoso, sa *adj* MED comatose || *estar en estado comatoso* to be in coma.

comba *f* curve, bend (de una cuerda) || skipping rope (juguete) || skipping (juego) || camber (de una carretera) || sag, bulge (de una viga) || — *dar a la comba* to twirl the rope || *hacer combas* to swing, to sway || FAM *no perder comba* not to miss a chance || *saltar a la comba* to skip.

combadura *f* curve, bend (de una cuerda) || camber (de una carretera) || bulge, sag (de una pared, de una viga, etc.).

combar *vt* to bend; *combar un hierro* to bend a piece of iron.
◆ *vpr* to bend, to curve (una cuerda) || to bulge, to sag (una pared) || to warp (alabearse).

combate *m* battle (batalla) || combat, fight (lucha) || contest, fight (de boxeo); *combate en quince asaltos* fifteen round contest || FIG struggle, conflict, fight (lucha) || — *combate desigual* unequal *o* uneven fight || *combate naval* sea battle, naval engagement || *combate nulo* draw || *combate singular* single combat || *empeñar el combate* to go into action || *fuera de combate* knocked out (boxeo), out of action (en cualquier batalla) || *ganar por fuera de combate* to win by a knockout (boxeo) || *librar combate por* to do *o* to wage battle for.

combatiente *adj* fighting.
◆ *m/f* fighter, combattant || soldier (soldado) || — *ex combatiente* veteran || *los combatientes de la última guerra* those who fought in the last war, the veterans of the last war.

combatir *vi* to fight.
◆ *vt* to fight, to combat (al enemigo, un incendio) | FIG to combat, to fight; *combatir los prejuicios* to combat prejudice | to beat, to lash (el viento, las olas, etc.).

combatividad *f* aggressiveness, fighting spirit.

combativo, va *adj* full of fighting spirit, aggressive.

combi; combina *f* FAM wangle, fiddle (chanchullo) | setup, scheme (arreglo) || *amigo de combinas* wangler, fiddler, schemer.

combinación *f* combination || QUÍM combination (acción), compound (resultado) || petticoat, slip (prenda femenina) || permutation (matemáticas, quinielas) || cocktail (bebida) || connection (de trenes) || FIG wangle, fiddle (chanchullo) || setup, scheme (arreglo) || — *combinación de colores* colour scheme || *combinación métrica* rhyme scheme.

combinado, da *adj* MIL combined (operación).
◆ *m* QUÍM compound, combination || cocktail (bebida) || combine (industrial) || *AMER* radiogram (radiogramola).

combinador *m* ELECTR controller.

combinar *vt* to combine; *combinó el negocio con la diversión* he combined business with pleasure || to arrange, to plan (out); *combinar las vacaciones para que quede abierta la fábrica* to arrange the holidays so that the factory stays open || to match (colores) || QUÍM to combine.
◆ *vi* to go; *zapatos que combinan con el vestido* shoes which go with the dress.
◆ *vpr* to combine || to get together (ponerse de acuerdo) || to conspire (conspirar) || QUÍM to combine.

combinatorio, ria *adj* MAT combinatorial.

combustible *adj* combustible.
◆ *m* fuel, combustible (p us).

combustión *f* combustion; *combustión orgánica* organic combustion.

combustóleo *m* fuel oil.

comedero, ra *adj* edible, eatable.
◆ *m* feeding trough (para animales) || dining room (comedor) || FIG & FAM *limpiarle a uno el comedero* to deprive s.o. of his livelihood (quitarle el empleo o cargo).

comedia *f* play; *representar una comedia* to perform a play || comedy (de desenlace feliz) || theatre [*US* theater]; *ir a la comedia* to go to the theatre || FIG farce || — *comedia de capa y espada* cloak-and-dagger play || *comedia de carácter* or *de figurón* comedy of character || *comedia de costumbres* comedy of manners || *comedia de enredo* comedy of intrigue || *comedia de magia* fairy play || *comedia en un acto* one-act play || *comedia ligera* light comedy || *comedia musical* musical, musical comedy || FIG *¡eso es pura comedia!* it's just an act, he (you, she, etc.) is just putting it on | *hacer la comedia* to put on an act, to pretend, to make believe.

comediante, ta *m/f* actor (hombre), actress (mujer) || FIG hypocrite.

comedido, da *adj* reserved, moderate, restrained (moderado) || calm, quiet (tranquilo) || polite, courteous (cortés) || *AMER* obliging (servicial).

comedimiento *m* reserve, moderation, restraint (moderación) || politeness, courtesy (cortesía) || *AMER* helpfulness.

comediógrafo *m* playwright, dramatist.

comedirse* *vpr* to be restrained, to be moderate, to restrain *o* to moderate o.s.

comedón *m* MED blackhead.

comedor, ra *adj* big-eating.
◆ *m/f* big eater (persona que come mucho).
◆ *m* dining room (pieza) || dining-room suite (muebles) || canteen (en las fábricas) || refectory, dining hall (en los conventos, en la universidad) || restaurant, café (restaurante) || — *coche comedor* dining car || *jefe de comedor* headwaiter, maître d'hôtel.

comején *m* termite, white ant.

comejenera *f* termitary || *AMER* FIG & FAM dive.

comendador *m* knight commander.

comendadora *f* mother superior (de ciertos conventos).

comendatario *adj m* REL commendatory.

comensal *m* companion at table || *había diez comensales* there were ten people dining together.

comentador, ra *m/f* commentator.

comentar *vt* to comment on (hacer comentarios sobre) || to discuss, to talk about (hablar sobre).

comentario *m* commentary (sobre un texto, etc.) || comment (sobre un acontecimiento) || RAD commentary.
◆ *pl* gossip *sing*; *dar lugar a comentarios* to cause gossip || — *huelgan los comentarios* no comment (is necessary) || *sin comentarios* no comment.

comentarista *m/f* commentator.

comenzar* *vt/vi* to start, to begin; *comenzar a hablar* to begin to speak, to begin speaking; *comenzar bien el día* to start the day well || — *comenzar con* to begin with || *comenzar por el principio* to begin *o* to start at the beginning || *comenzó diciendo que...* he started by saying... || *comenzó por el primero* he started with the first one || *comenzó por insultarle* he began by insulting him.

comer *m* eating; *el comer y el beber* eating and drinking || — FIG *el comer y el rascar, todo es empezar* the first step is the hardest || *ser de buen comer* to have a good *o* a hearty appetite.

comer *vt* to eat; *comer carne, frutas* to eat meat, fruit || to have for lunch, to lunch (al mediodía), to have for dinner, to dine (cenar); *comimos pescado* we had fish for lunch, we lunched fish || to eat, to use, to burn; *la estufa come mucho carbón* the stove burns a lot of coal || to eat away, to corrode; *el orín come el hierro* rust eats away iron || to erode, to swallow up (un río, un mar, etc.) || to take, to capture (ajedrez o damas); *comer un peón* to take a pawn || to fade; *el sol come el color de las telas* the sun fades the colour of materials || to itch (sentir comezón); *la pierna me come* my leg is itching || — FIG *le come la envidia* he is eaten up with envy | *¡parece que ha comido lengua!* he is very talkative today | *sin comerlo ni beberlo* for no apparent reason, through no fault of one's own.
◆ *vi* to eat; *hay que comer para vivir* one must eat to live || to lunch, to have lunch (al mediodía), to dine, to have dinner (cenar), to eat (en un caso u otro) || to take, to capture (ajedrez o damas); *comer al paso* to take (in the same move) || — FIG *come con los ojos* his eyes are bigger than his belly *o* stomach || FAM *comer a dos carrillos* to eat like a horse (comer mucho), to gulp down one's food, to gobble up one's food (con gula) || FIG & FAM *comer como un pajarito* not to eat enough to feed a sparrow | *comer como un sabañón* or *como un regimiento* or *por cuatro* to eat like a horse || *comer con muchas ganas* to eat heartily *o* with a good appetite || *comer de vigilia* to abstain from meat || *comer hasta hartarse* to eat one's fill || *comer sin ganas* to pick at one's food, to nibble || *dar de comer a* to feed (animales, personas hambrientas), to feed, to give a meal to (convidados) || FAM *¿desde cuándo hemos comido en el mismo plato?, ¿en qué plato hemos comido juntos?* please remember whom you are talking to [reproof of familiarity] | *comer en el mismo plato* to be very close friends | *donde comen dos comen tres* there is always enough for one more, an extra mouth makes no difference || *echar de comer* to feed || FIG *no comer ni dejar comer* to be a dog in a manger || *nos dieron de comer pollo* they gave us chicken for lunch *o* for dinner || *ser de buen comer* to have a good *o* a hearty appetite, to be a good eater || FIG *tener qué comer* to have enough to get by *o* enough to live on.
◆ *vpr* to eat, to eat up; *comerse un pollo entero* to eat a whole chicken || FIG to skip, to leave out, to omit; *comerse un párrafo* to skip a paragraph | to swallow, to slur (una letra al hablar) | to fade; *el sol se come los colores* the sun fades colours || to swallow up (el mar, la tierra, etc.); *el mar se lo comió* the sea swallowed him up || to devour, to eat up; *comerse el capital* to eat up one's money || — *AMER* POP *comerse a uno* to screw s.o. || FIG & FAM *comerse a uno a besos* to smother s.o. with kisses | *comerse a uno por los pies* to twist s.o. around one's little finger | *comerse con los ojos a uno* to stare *o* to gaze at s.o. (fijamente), to look daggers at s.o. (con enojo) | *comerse de envidia por hacer algo* to be dying to do sth. | *comerse la risa* to stifle one's laugh || *comerse las uñas* to bite one's nails || FIG & FAM *comerse los codos de hambre* to be starving | *comerse los higadillos* to pull each other to pieces, to quarrel || *comerse los niños crudos* to eat up little children, to eat little children alive | *comerse una cosa con la vista* or *los ojos* to devour sth. with one's eyes, to look greedily at sth., to gloat over sth. | *comerse unos a otros* to pull each other to pieces, to quarrel, to be always at loggerheads | *comerse vivo a uno* to eat s.o. alive, to nearly swal-

low s.o. (de enojo) | *¡con su pan se lo coma!* good luck to him! | *está para comérsela* she is good enough to eat | *se lo come la envidia* he is green with envy | *¿y eso con qué se come?* what on earth is that?

comercial *adj* commercial; *banco comercial* commercial bank; *tratado comercial* commercial treaty || shopping; *centro comercial* shopping centre || *valor comercial* market value.
◆ *m* AMER commercial.

comercialización *f* commercialization || marketing (mercadeo).

comercializar *vt* to commercialize.

comerciante *m* merchant, tradesman || shopkeeper (tendero) || — *comerciante al por mayor* wholesaler || *comerciante al por menor* retailer || *ser comerciante* to be in business.

comerciar *vi* to trade; *comerciar con* or *en naranjas* to trade in oranges; *España comercia con el mundo entero* Spain trades with the whole world || to have dealings (dos personas) || to do business (*con* with) (otra persona) || *comerciar al por mayor, al por menor* to wholesale, to retail.

comercio *m* commerce || trade; *comercio entre dos países* trade between two countries; *comercio exterior* foreign trade, external trade; *comercio interior* domestic trade || business world, big business (las grandes empresas) || shop; *hay buenos comercios en el barrio* there are some good shops in the district || FIG intercourse, dealings *pl* (trato) | sexual intercourse (relaciones sexuales) || — *Cámara de Comercio* Chamber of Commerce || *código de comercio* commercial law || *comercio al por mayor, al por menor* wholesale, retail trade || *comercio de esclavos* slave trade || *libre comercio* free trade; *zona de libre comercio* free-trade area || *viajante de comercio* commercial traveller [US traveling salesman].

comestible *adj* edible, eatable.
◆ *m* food, foodstuff.
◆ *pl* food *sing*, foodstuffs || groceries, provisions (sentido comercial) || *tienda de comestibles* grocer's shop *o* store [US grocery].

cometa *m* ASTR comet.
◆ *f* kite (juguete).

cometer *vt* to commit (un crimen) || to make; *cometió cinco faltas de ortografía* he made five spelling mistakes || to entrust, to charge; *cometerle a uno la ejecución de algo* to entrust s.o. with the execution of sth.

cometido *m* task, assignment; *cumplir su cometido* to carry out one's task || mission (mandato) || duty; *desempeñar su cometido* to do one's duty.

comezón *f* itch, itching || — FIG *sentía comezón por decir algo* he was itching to say sth., he was dying to speak || *sentir comezón* to have an itch, to itch.

cómic *m* comic (tebeo).

comible *adj* eatable, edible.

comicastro *m* ham, third-rate actor.

comicidad *f* comicality, funniness.

comicios *m pl* comitia (de los romanos) || electoral meetings || elections, voting *sing* (elecciones).

cómico, ca *adj* comedy; *actor cómico* comedy actor || comic, comical, funny (divertido) || *autor cómico* playwright.
◆ *m/f* TEATR actor (hombre), actress (mujer) (actor) || comedian, comic (de cabaret, etc.) || comedian, comic (persona graciosa) || — *cómico de la legua* strolling player || FIG *¡es un cómico!* he's a comic! || *lo cómico* the funny part, the comedy.

comida *f* food (alimento) || eating (acción de comer) || meal; *hacemos tres comidas al día* we have three meals a day || lunch (almuerzo); *la comida es a las dos* lunch is at two o'clock (véase OBSERV) || *comida campestre* picnic.
— OBSERV In certain regions the evening meal may be called *comida* and the midday meal *cena*.

comidilla *f* FIG & FAM hobby (pasatiempo) | talk, topic of conversation; *es la comidilla del pueblo* he is the talk of the village.

comido, da *adj* *comido de gusanos* worm-eaten || FIG & FAM *estar comido* to have eaten (una persona) | *lo comido por lo servido* he only just breaks even (una persona) | *sin haberlo comido ni bebido* for no apparent reason, through no fault of one's own.

comienzo *m* beginning, start || birth, conception (de un plan) || onset (de una enfermedad) || — *al comienzo* at first || *dar comienzo* to begin, to start || *en los comienzos del año* at the beginning of the year || *estar en sus comienzos* to be in its early stages.

comilitona *f* FAM feast, big meal, spread.

comilón, ona *adj* FAM greedy, gluttonous.
◆ *m/f* FAM big eater, glutton, guzzler.

comilona *f* FAM feast, big meal, spread; *darse una comilona* to have a feast.

comillas *f pl* inverted commas; *entre comillas* in inverted commas || quotation marks (para palabras citadas) || *abrir, cerrar las comillas* to open, to close the inverted commas *o* the quotation marks.

comino *m* BOT cumin || — FIG & FAM *no me importa un comino* I couldn't care less, I don't give a damn | *no valer un comino* not to be worth bothering about, not to be worth twopence *o* tuppence.

comis *m* waiter (ayudante de camarero).

comisar *vt* to confiscate, to seize (confiscar).

comisaría *f* commissariat || *comisaría de policía* police station.

comisario *f* commissary, commissioner (persona que desempeña una función por comisión) || commissar (en la URSS) || AMER police inspector || — *comisario de policía* police superintendent || *comisario político* political commissioner.
◆ *m* Commissioner.

comiscar *vt* to nibble, to pick at.

comisión *f* commission, assignment, mission (encargo) || commission (delegación) || COM commission (porcentaje); *cobrar una comisión* to get a commission || committee (en el parlamento, etc.); *comisión permanente* standing committee; *comisión conjunta* or *paritaria* joint committee || perpetration, committing (acción de cometer) || — ECON *comisión bancaria* service charge, bank commission || *comisión de servicios* service commission || *Comisión Europea* European Commission || ECON *comisión fija* set commission || *en comisión* on sale or return || *trabajar a* or *con comisión* to work on a commission basis.

comisionado, da *m/f* commissioner || committee member (miembro de un comité).

comisionar *vt* to commission.

comisionista *m* COM commission agent.

comiso *m* JUR confiscation, seizure.

comisorio, ria *adj* JUR binding over a period.

comisquear *vt* → **comiscar.**

comistrajo *m* FAM pigswill, swill (comida mala).

comisura *f* corner, commissure (p us) (de los labios).

comité *m* committee; *comité de honor* committee of honour || *Comité económico y social* Economic and Social Committee.

comitente *m* principal.

comitiva *f* retinue, followers *pl*, suite || *comitiva fúnebre* funeral procession.

cómitre *m* galley sergeant.

Commonwealth *npr f* Commonwealth.

como

1. ADVERBIO *a)* MANERA *b)* INTERROGACIÓN *c)* EXCLAMACIÓN *d)* COMPARACIÓN *e)* EN CALIDAD DE *f)* LOCUCIONES 2. CONJUNCIÓN *a)* TEMPORAL *b)* CAUSAL *c)* CONDICIONAL *d)* COPULATIVA *e)* LOCUCIONES.

1. ADVERBIO

a) manera how; *hazlo como quieras* do it like you like || as; *haz como quieras* do as you like.

b) interrogación how; *¿cómo está su padre?* how is your father?; *¿cómo le va?, ¿cómo está?, ¿cómo anda?* how are you?; *¿cómo es de ancho?* how wide is it?; *no sé cómo agradecerle* I don't know how to thank you || what; *¿cómo te llamas?* what is your name? || why, how come; *¿cómo no me lo dijiste antes?* why didn't you tell me sooner?

c) exclamación how; *¡hay que ver cómo corren los niños!* you should see how the children run!

d) comparación as; *blanco como la nieve* as white as snow || as (después de tan, tanto, tal); *es tan alto como yo* he is so tall as I || like; *lo hace como su padre* he does it like his father.

e) en calidad de as; *asistió a la ceremonia como testigo* he attended the ceremony as a witness; *tratar como amigo* to treat as a friend || like; *como buen francés que era* like the good Frenchman he was || in the role (en el papel de).

f) locuciones *así fue como* that was how || *¡cómo!* what! (sorpresa, indignación) || *¿cómo?* pardon?, sorry?, I beg your pardon?, excuse me? || *¿cómo así?, ¿cómo es posible?, ¿cómo es posible?* how's that?, never!, what? || *como es lógico* or *natural* naturally, of course || *¿cómo es que?* how come?, how is it that? || *¿cómo está usted?* how are you?, how do you do? || *¡cómo llueve!* just look at the rain!, it's pouring down! || AMER *¡cómo no!* of course! (por supuesto) || *como no sea para* what do you mean, nothing? || *¡cómo que no!* of course! (por supuesto) || *cómo quien dice, como si dijéramos* as it were, so to speak || *como sea* any way at all, any way you like, any way you like, one way or another || *como y cuando quieras* as and when you like || *está como para que lo tire* it's fit for the dustbin, it's ready to be thrown out || *había como veinte personas* there were some twenty people *o* about twenty people *o* something like twenty people || *hacer como quien* to pretend to; *hace como quien escribe* he is pretending to write || *quedó como muerto* he lay as if *o* as though dead, he lay like a corpse || *su enfermedad no es grave como para renunciar a su viaje* his illness is no serious enough for him to cancel his journey || *un como, una como* a sort of; *un como gemido* a sort of groan || *¡y cómo!* and how!

2. CONJUNCIÓN

a) temporal as; *como bajaba la cuesta* as he was going down the hill; *como daban las once* as it struck eleven.

b) causal as, since, seeing as; *como recibí tarde tu invitación, no pude venir* as I received your invitation late, I could not come.

c) condicional if; *como no lo hagas, te castigaré* if you do not do it, I shall punish you || if, as long as; *como me lo devuelva mañana no diré nada* as long as you give me back tomorrow I shall not say anything.

d) copulativa that; *sabrás cómo me encontré ayer con el* you no doubt know that i met him yesterday.

e) *locuciones así como* as soon as (en seguida que), in the same way that (del mismo modo que) || *¡como lo hagas otra vez!* if you do it again! || *como no sea que* unless; *como no sea que llueva* unless it rains || *como quiera que contestes, te criticará* no matter how you answer you give him, he will criticize you || *como quiera que no me interrogaba, yo me callé* as *o* since I was not being questioned, I kept quiet || *como quiera que sea* one way or another || *como si nada hubiera ocurrido* as if nothing had happened || *de tanto calor como hacía no pudimos trabajar* it was so hot that we couldn't work || *hacer como si* to pretend to; *hace como si escribiera* he is pretending to write || *parece como que...* it seems that... || *tan pronto como* as soon as.

cómo *m* *el cómo y el porqué* the how and the why.

cómoda *f* chest of drawers (mueble).

cómodamente *adv* comfortably.

comodato *m* JUR free loan.

comodidad *f* comfort, convenience; *esta casa tiene muchas comodidades* this house has many comforts || convenience; *la comodidad de vivir en la ciudad* the convenience of living in the city || well-being, welfare; *sólo piensa en su comodidad* he only thinks of his own well-being || advantage (ventaja) || — *casa con todas las comodidades* house with all mod. cons. *o* amenities (en los anuncios) || *con comodidad* comfortably; *vivir con comodidad* to live comfortably.

comodín *m* wild card (naipes) || substitute, standby (para sustituir) || weak excuse (pretexto) || utility player (fútbol).

cómodo, da *adj* comfortable; *un sillón cómodo* a comfortable armchair; *póngase cómodo* make yourself comfortable; *sin la chaqueta trabajarás más cómodo* you will be more comfortable working without your jacket || easy-going, easy; *carácter cómodo* easy-going character || cosy, snug (habitación) || handy, convenient, useful (útil); *una herramienta muy cómoda* a very handy tool.

comodón, ona *adj* FAM comfort-loving (aficionado a su comodidad).

comodoro *m* commodore.

comoquiera *adv* anyway, anyhow (de cualquier manera) || *comoquiera que* since, in view of the fact that.

compa *m/f* AMER FAM mate (amigo, compañero).

compacidad *f* compactness.

compact disk *m* compact disk.

compactar *vt* AMER to compact, to compress.

compacto, ta *adj* compact || dense (denso) || close (apretado, junto) || *polvos compactos* face powder.

compadecer* *vt* to sympathize with; *compadezco las desgracias ajenas* I sympathize with other people's misfortunes; *te compadezco* I sympathize with you || to pity, to feel sorry for; *compadece a los pobres* he pities the poor; *Pedro no es de compadecer* Peter is not to be pitied.

◆ *vpr* to sympathize with; *compadecerse del* or *con el dolor ajeno* to sympathize with other people's troubles || to pity, to feel sorry for (tener lástima) || to go, to agree, to be in keeping (concordar) || *compadecerse mal con* to be out of keeping with (no concordar).

compadrazgo; compadraje *m* conspiracy (confabulación) || status of godfather.

compadre *m* godfather (padrino) (véase OBSERV) || friend (vecino o amigo) || old man, friend, man (dirigiéndose a uno) || AMER braggart, show-off.

— OBSERV The *compadre* is the godfather seen from the pount of view of the child's godmother or parent. Thus, if I am the child's godmother, *mi compadre* is *my fellow godparent* and if I am the child's parent, *mi compadre* is *my child's godfather.*

compadrear *vi* to be friends || AMER FAM to brag, to boast, to swank (presumir).

compadrito *m* AMER FAM show-off.

compaginación *f* IMPR makeup.

compaginador *m* IMPR maker-up.

compaginar *vt* FIG to reconcile, to make compatible; *compaginar los intereses de las dos partes* to reconcile the interests of both parties | to combine; *puede compaginar todas sus actividades* he can combine all his activities || IMPR to make up.

◆ *vpr* to go together, to be compatible (ir juntos) || to be in keeping, to tally, to agree (concordar) || to match, to go together (colores) || *tanta generosidad no se compagina con su reputación* such generosity is out of keeping with his reputation.

compaña *f* company || *¡adiós a la compaña!* good-bye everybody!, good-bye all!

compañerismo *m* fellowship, comradeship || team spirit (en deportes de equipo).

compañero, ra *m/f* companion; *tiene muchos compañeros* he has many companions; *compañero de viaje* travelling companion; *compañero de desgracias* companion in misfortune || friend (amigo); *es su mejor compañero* he is his best friend || colleague; *compañero de oficina* office colleague || associate (miembro de una corporación, en los negocios) || partner (en el juego, en los negocios) || twin, other one (de una pareja) || — *compañero de armas* comrade-in-arms || *compañero de colegio* schoolmate || *compañero de cuarto* roommate || *compañero de equipo* teammate || *compañero de fatigas* fellow sufferer || FIG *estos zapatos no son compañeros* these shoes are not a pair, these shoes do not match.

compañía *f* company; *hacer compañía a uno* to keep s.o. company; *ser buena compañía* to be good company || company (sociedad); *compañía de seguros* insurance company; *y compañía (y Cía)* and Company (and Co.) || company (of actors) || company; *las malas compañías* bad company || MIL company || — *Compañía de Jesús, la Compañía* Society of Jesus || *compañía de la legua* company of strolling players || ECON *compañía multinacional* multinational company || *en compañía de* with, accompanied by, in the company of || *señora de compañía* lady companion.

comparable *adj* comparable.

comparación *f* comparison || — *en comparación con* in comparison with *o* to, compared with *o* to || *ni punto de comparación* there is no comparison || *sin comparación* beyond all comparison, beyond compare || *todas las comparaciones son odiosas* all comparison is false.

comparador *m* FÍS comparator.

comparar *vt* to compare, to liken; *comparar una persona con otra* to compare one person with *o* to another, to liken one person to another.

comparativo, va *adj/sm* comparative.

comparecencia *f* JUR appearance; *no comparecencia* non-appearance || *orden de comparecencia* summons.

comparecer* *vi* JUR to appear || *orden de comparecer* summons.

compareciente *adj* JUR appearing.

◆ *m/f* person appearing before the court.

comparencia *f* AMER appearance (comparecencia).

comparendo *m* JUR summons.

comparición *f* JUR appearance || *orden de comparición* summons.

comparsa *f* TEATR supernumeraries *pl*, extras *pl* (acompañamiento) || procession, group of people in fancy dress (en el carnaval).

◆ *m/f* TEATR supernumerary, extra.

comparsería *f* TEATR supernumeraries *pl*, extras *pl* (comparsas).

compartimentado, da *adj* FIG partitioned.

compartimento *m* → **compartimiento.**

compartimiento; compartimento *m* compartment; *un compartimiento de primera clase* a first-class compartment || division, sharing (acción) || — *compartimiento de bombas* bomb bay || *compartimiento estanco* watertight compartment.

compartir *vt* to divide (up), to share (out); *ha compartido su herencia entre varias personas* he has divided his inheritance (up) amongst several people, he has shared his inheritance (out) amongst several people || to share; *compartimos el mismo piso* we share the same flat || FIG to share; *compartir una opinión* to share an opinion; *compartir el poder* to share power.

compás *m* compass, pair of compasses; *trazar un círculo con compás* to draw a circle with a compass || volt (esgrima) || MAR compass || MÚS rhythm (ritmo) | bar (división) | time; *compás mayor* two-four time; *compás menor* common *o* four-four time || — TAUR *abrir el compás* to stand with one's legs apart (el torero) || *a compás* in time || *al compás de* in time to *o* with || MÚS *compás binario* binary time || *compás de calibre* calipers *pl* || *compás de corredera* slide calipers *pl* || *compás de cuadrante* quadrant compass || *compás de división* dividers *pl* || *compás de espera* bar rest (música), time lag, delay (pausa) || *compás de espesores* or *de gruesas* outside calipers *pl* || *compás de interiores* inside calipers *pl* || *compás de reducción* proportional dividers *pl* || *compás de dos por cuatro, de tres por cuatro, de seis por ocho* two-four, three-four, six-eight time || *compás de vara* beam compass, trammel || *fuera de compás* out of step (andando), out of time (en la música) || *guardar el compás* to keep time (música), to keep a sense of proportion (ser comedido) || *llevar el compás* to beat time (con la mano), to keep time (bailando) || *perder el compás* to lose the beat || *salió a los compases de un himno bien conocido* he went out to the strains of a well-known hymn.

compasado, da *adj* measured, moderate (mesurado).

compasar *vt* to measure with compasses || MÚS to divide into bars.

compasillo *m* MÚS common *o* four-four time.

compasión *f* compassion, pity || — *llamar* or *mover a uno a compasión* to move s.o. to pity || *¡por compasión!* for pity's sake! || *sin compasión* merciless (adjetivo), mercilessly (adverbio) || *tener compasión de* to take pity on, to feel sorry for.

compasivo, va *adj* compassionate, sympathetic, understanding; *compasivo con los demás* understanding towards other people || merciful (clemente).

compatibilidad *f* compatibility || INFORM compatibility.

compatible *adj* compatible || INFORM compatible.

compatiblemente *adv* compatibly.

compatriota *m/f* compatriot, fellow countryman (hombre), fellow countrywoman (mujer).

compeler *vt* to force, to compel; *le compelieron a hablar* they forced him to speak.

compendiar *vt* to summarize, to abridge.

compendio *m* résumé, précis, summary, synopsis, outline; *compendio de gramática francesa* summary of French grammar || compendium (breve tratado) || — *compendio de historia* short history || *compendio de química* synopsis of chemistry || *en compendio* in brief, in short.

compendioso, sa *adj* concise, compendious.

compenetración *f* compenetration, interpenetration || FIG (mutual) understanding (entre personas).

compenetrarse *vpr* QUÍM to compenetrate, to interpenetrate || FIG to share each other's feelings, to understand each other (dos personas) || *compenetrarse con su papel* to identify o.s. with one's role (actor).

compensación *f* compensation || compensation, damages *pl* (pago) || — COM *cámara de compensación* clearing house || *compensación bancaria* clearing || *en compensación* in payment, in compensation; *reciben cinco libras en compensación a su asistencia* they receive five pounds in payment for their attendance; in return, in exchange; *tú me enseñas español y en compensación yo te enseñaré inglés* you teach me Spanish and in return I'll teach you English.

compensador, ra *adj* compensating; *péndulo compensador* compensating pendulum.
◆ *m* compensator.

compensar *vt* to compensate, to make up for; *compensar las pérdidas con las ganancias* to compensate *o* to make up for the losses with the gains || to make amends for, to make up for (un error) || to indemnify, to compensate; *compensar a uno de algo* to compensate s.o. for sth. || TECN to balance, to compensate || to be worthwhile; *trabajo que compensa* work which is worthwhile || — *me compensó con cien francos por el tiempo perdido* he gave me a hundred francs compensation for lost time || *no me compensa hacer esto* it's not worth my while doing it || *resultados que compensan* worthwhile results.

compensativo, va; compensatorio, ria *adj* compensatory, in compensation.

competencia *f* scope field, province (incumbencia); *esto no es de mi competencia* or *no cae dentro de mi competencia* this is outside my scope, this is not in my field, this is not my province || competence, ability (capacidad) || competition (rivalidad); *la competencia frena la subida de los precios* competition checks rising prices; *competencia desleal* unfair competition || JUR competence || — *en competencia con* in competition with || *hacer la competencia a* to compete with *o* against.

competente *adj* competent; *tribunal competente* competent court; *persona muy competente* very competent person || appropriate; *el departamento competente* the appropriate department.

competer *vi* to be in the field of, to come under the jurisdiction of, to be the business of; *eso compete al ayuntamiento* that comes under the town council's jurisdiction, that is in the town council's field || to be up to; *a él no le compete castigar a los empleados* it is not up to him to punish the employees || to concern, to have to do with; *no me compete* it has nothing to do with me, it doesn't concern me.

competición *f* competition (deportes, comercio).

competido, da *adj* hard-fought, tough (partido, campeonato, etc.).

competidor, ra *adj* competing (que compete) || rival (oponente) || competitive; *espíritu competidor* competitive spirit.
◆ *m/f* competitor (en el comercio, los deportes) || contestant (participante) || candidate (en los exámenes) || rival (rival).

competir* *vi* to compete; *muchas personas compiten para esta colocación* many people are competing for this job || to compete, to contend, to vie; *competir para el título* to vie for the title || to compete; *este almacén compite con aquél* this shop competes with that one.

competitivo, va *adj* competitive.

compilación *f* compiling (acción de compilar) || compilation, collection (obra) || INFORM compilation.

compilador, ra *m/f* compiler || INFORM compiler.

compilar *vt* to compile || INFORM to compile.

compinche *m/f* FAM pal, chum (amigote) | accomplice (cómplice).

complacencia *f* pleasure, satisfaction; *tener complacencia en ayudar a los demás* to find pleasure in helping others || indulgence (indulgencia) || *tener excesivas complacencias hacia alguien* to be over-indulgent towards s.o.

complacer* *vt* to please, to be pleasant to; *los cortesanos procuran complacer al rey* the courtiers try to please the king || to gratify (un deseo, etc.) || to oblige, to please; *le gusta complacer a sus amigos* he likes to oblige his friends || — *¿en qué puedo complacerle?* can I help you?, what can I do for you? || *me complace su éxito* I am happy about his success || *nos complace que haya usted venido* we are pleased *o* glad that you have come.
◆ *vpr* to take pleasure, to delight; *complacerse en su desdicha* to take pleasure in one's misfortune; *complacerse en criticar* to delight in criticizing || to have (the) pleasure, to be pleased; *me complazco en saludar al señor X* I have the pleasure to greet Mr. X, I have pleasure in greeting Mr. X.

complacido, da *adj* satisfied, content, happy, pleased; *complacido con su suerte* satisfied with one's lot.

complaciente *adj* obliging, accommodating, helpful (que ayuda) || complaisant (marido).

complejidad; complexidad *f* complexity.

complejo, ja; complexo, xa *adj* complex, complicated, involved || GRAM complex || MAT compound (número).
◆ *m* complex || — *complejo industrial* industrial complex || complejo de inferioridad inferiority complex || *complejo de Edipo* Oedipus complex.

complementar *vt* to complement, to complete.
◆ *vpr* to be complementary (to each other), to complement each other || *caracteres que se complementan* complementary characters.

complementario, ria *adj* complementary; *ángulos complementarios* complementary angles.

complemento *m* complement || GRAM object, complement; *el complemento del verbo* the object of the verb; *complemento directo, indirecto* direct, indirect object; *complemento circunstancial* adverbial complement [of place, time, etc.] || MAT complement || — MIL *oficial de complemento* reserve officer || *sería el complemento de su felicidad* it would make his happiness complete.

completar *vt* to complete; *completar una suma* to complete an amount.

completas *f pl* REL compline *sing.*

completivo, va *adj* GRAM object; *oración completiva* object clause.

completo, ta *adj* full; *el autobús está completo* the bus is full || complete; *un estudio completo* a complete study || completed, finished (acabado) || — *pensión completa* full board || *por completo* completely || *registrar una casa por completo* to search a house from top to bottom || *terminar algo por completo* to finish sth. off, to completely finish sth.

complexidad *f* —→ **complejidad.**

complexión *f* constitution, disposition, nature.

complexo, xa *adj* —→ **complejo.**

complicación *f* complication.

complicado, da *adj* complicated, complex, intricate (intrincado); *sistema complicado* complicated system || complicated (carácter) || implicated, involved; *persona complicada en una conspiración* person involved in a conspiracy || MED compound (fractura) || elaborate (decorado, etc.).

complicar *vt* to complicate, to make complicated; *complicar una cosa sencilla* to make a simple thing complicated; *esto vino a complicar las cosas* this just complicated matters || *complicar en* to involve in; *complicado en un robo* involved in a theft.
◆ *vpr* to get complicated (volverse complicado) || to make difficult *o* to complicate for o.s., to make complicated for o.s. (hacer más difícil); *complicarse la vida* to make life difficult for o.s. || to get involved *o* mixed up; *complicarse en un negocio ilegal* to get involved in an illegal business || *esto se complica* it's getting serious!

cómplice *m/f* accomplice || *cómplice de un crimen* accomplice in a crime, party to a crime.

complicidad *f* complicity; *está demostrada su complicidad en el robo* his complicity in the theft has been proved.

complot *m* FAM plot, conspiracy.

complotar *vi* to plot, to conspire.

complutense *adj* of *o* from Alcalá de Henares || *Biblia Políglota Complutense* Bible written in Hebrew, Chaldean, Greek and Latin and published in Alcalá de Henares in the 16th century.
◆ *m/f* inhabitant *o* native of Alcalá de Henares.

componedor, ra *m/f* AMER bonesetter (algebrista) || IMPR compositor (obrero) || JUR *amigable componedor* arbitrator.
◆ *m* IMPR setting stick, composing stick.

componenda *f* compromise, arrangement, settlement, agreement (expediente de conciliación) || FAM trick (combinación) || *componendas electorales* electoral scheming.

componente *adj* component.
◆ *m* component, part, constituent (de un todo) || ingredient (de un plato de cocina, bebida) || member (miembro) || INFORM component || *viento de componente sur* south *o* southerly wind.

componer* *vt* to form, to make up, to compose (formar); *componer un ramillete con diversas flores* to make up a bouquet with different flowers; *los once jugadores componen el equipo* the eleven players make up the team || to repair, to mend (arreglar lo que está roto) || to compose (música, versos) || to write (novelas, etc.) || to settle (resolver); *componer un asunto* to settle a matter || to prepare, to decorate, to arrange; *están componiendo la casa para la fiesta* they are preparing the house for the celebration || to settle (desacuerdo) || to reconcile; *componer a dos enemigos* to reconcile two enemies || to adjust (ajedrez) || FAM to settle; *una buena taza de té te compondrá el estómago* a nice cup of tea will settle your stomach || IMPR to set || MED to set (hueso) || AMER to castrate (castrar).
◆ *vpr* to be made up, to consist, to be composed; *el equipo se compone de once jugadores* the team is made up of eleven players || to get ready, to smarten o.s. up (una mujer) || to

agree, to come to an agreement (ponerse de acuerdo) || — FAM *componérselas* to manage; *compóntelas como puedas* manage as best you can | *no sabía cómo componérselas* he didn't know what to do, he didn't know how to get out of it.

comportamiento *m* behaviour [US behavior], conduct.

comportar *v tr* to involve, to entail (contener) || to bear, to put up with (aguantar).
◆ *v pr* to behave (o.s.) (conducirse); *compórtate como es debido* behave properly || to behave, to act; *se comporta como un niño mimado* he acts like a spoilt child || *comportarse mal* to misbehave, to behave badly.

composición *f* composition; *la composición del agua* the composition of water || composición (obra) || composition (ejercicio de redacción) || mixture (medicamento) || agreement (acuerdo) || arrangement, settlement (arreglo) || IMPR setting, composition || GRAM & MÚS composition || — JUR *composición amigable* arbitration || *hacer composición de lugar* to size up the situation (considerar una situación), to decide on one's plan of action (determinar lo que uno va a hacer).

compositivo, va *adj* which can be used to form compound words.

compositor, ra *m/f* MÚS composer.
◆ *m* AMER horse trainer.

compostelano, na *adj* of *o* from Santiago de Compostela.
◆ *m/f* inhabitant *o* native of Santiago de Compostela.

compostura *f* composition, structure (disposición de las partes de una cosa) || repair, repairing, mending (arreglo); *la compostura de un reloj* the repair of a watch || bearing, demeanour, comportment (manera de comportarse) || moderation, restraint (moderación) || composure (dignidad) || arrangement, agreement (convenio); *hacer una compostura con sus acreedores* to come to an arrangement with *o* to make an agreement with one's creditors || CULIN seasoning (condimento) || *¡Juan, las composturas!* John, behave yourself!

compota *f* compote; *una compota de manzanas* an apple compote || FAM *un ojo en compota* a black eye.

compotera *f* compote dish.

compound *m* TECN compound.

compra *f* buy, purchase; *una compra ventajosa* an advantageous buy || — *compra al contado* cash purchase || *compra a plazos* hire-purchase, buying on credit [US installment plan] || *hacer compras* to shop, to go shopping || *hacer la compra, ir a la compra* to do the shopping, to go shopping || *ir de compras* to go shopping || *jefe de compras* chief buyer || *precio de compra* purchase price.

comprador, ra *m/f* buyer, purchaser || shopper, customer (en una tienda).

comprar *vt* to buy, to purchase; *lo volví a comprar* I bought it back || FIG to bribe, to buy (sobornar); *comprar a uno* to bribe s.o. || — *comprar al contado* to pay cash || *comprar algo al contado* to pay cash for sth., to buy sth. for cash, to purchase sth. for cash || *comprar al por mayor, al por menor* to buy wholesale, retail || *comprar con pérdida, en firme* to buy at a loss, firm || *comprar fiado* to buy on credit.

compraventa *f* buying and selling || *contrato de compraventa* contract of sale and purchase.

comprender *vt* to understand (entender); *no comprendo el alemán* I don't understand German || to comprise, to include (componerse de); *esta obra comprende cuatro tomos* this work comprises four volumes || to include (incluir); *servicio no comprendido* service not included || to realize (darse cuenta) || to see (ver) || — *compréndame* try to understand me || *comprender mal* to misunderstand; *has comprendido mal lo que he dicho* you have misunderstood what I said || *¿comprendes?* you see? || *comprendida la suma de...* including the sum of... || *hacerse comprender* to make o.s. understood || *todo comprendido* all-in, inclusive; *viaje todo comprendido* all-in trip || *¡ya comprendo!* I see!, I get it!
◆ *vpr* to understand one another || *se comprende* it is understandable.

comprensibilidad *f* comprehensibility.

comprensible *adj* comprehensible, understandable.

comprensión *f* comprehension, understanding (entendimiento) || understanding (tolerancia) || intension (en lógica) || *ser tardo de comprensión* to be slow in understanding *o* in picking things up.

comprensivo, va *adj* understanding; *hombre comprensivo* understanding man.

compresa *f* MED compress (debajo de un vendaje) | sanitary towel (de mujer).

compresibilidad *f* compressibility.

compresible *adj* compressible.

compresión *f* compression || GRAM synaeresis [US syneresis].

compresivo, va *adj* compressive.

compreso, sa *adj* compressed.
— OBSERV The adjective *compreso* is the irregular past participle of *comprimir.*

compresor *m* compressor || *cilindro compresor* steamroller.

comprimible *adj* compressible.

comprimido, da *adj* compressed || *escopeta de aire comprimido* air rifle.
◆ *m* MED tablet (tableta).

comprimir *vt* to compress || FIG to keep back (lágrimas, una sonrisa) | to stifle (la risa) | to cram together, to pack; *viven comprimidos en una sola habitación* they live crammed together in a single room.
◆ *vpr* to be compressed || to restrict o.s. (en los gastos) || to restrain o.s. (refrenarse) || *me comprimí la risa* I stifled a laugh, I managed not to laugh.

comprobable *adj* provable, verifiable (que se puede verificar).

comprobación *f* verification, check, checking, proof (acción de comprobar) || proof (prueba) || *de fácil comprobación* easy to prove *o* to ascertain.

comprobante *adj* in proof.
◆ *m* proof (justificación) || JUR document in proof || guarantee, warrant, voucher (lo que garantiza) || receipt (recibo) || *comprobante de compra* or *de caja* receipt.

comprobar* *vt* to check (averiguar); *hay que comprobar la marca antes de comprar* you must check the make before buying || to see, to observe (observar); *pudiste comprobar tú mismo que había dicho la verdad* you could see for yourself that he had told the truth || to prove (demostrar) || to confirm (confirmar).

comprometedor, ra *adj* compromising; *situación comprometedora* compromising situation.

comprometer *vt* to endanger, to jeopardize, to put in jeopardy; *comprometer sus intereses* to jeopardize one's interests || to compromise (a una persona) || to commit; *esto no te compromete a nada* this does not commit you to anything || to implicate, to mix up, to involve; *comprometer a uno en un robo* to involve s.o. in a theft || to impair (la salud).
◆ *vpr* to compromise o.s. || to commit o.s.; *comprometerse a defender una causa* to commit o.s. to the defence of a cause || to get involved (meterse) || AMER to get engaged || — *comprometerse a hacer algo* to engage to do sth., to undertake to do sth. || *se compromete a todo* he will agree to anything.

comprometido, da *adj* involved, implicated, mixed up (en un mal negocio) || embarrassing, compromising (situación) || committed (escritor) || — *estar comprometido para hacer algo* to be obliged to do sth., to have an obligation to do sth. || *política no comprometida* non-committal policy.

compromisario *m* representative, delegate.

compromiso *m* obligation, commitment; *hacer honor a sus compromisos, cumplir sus compromisos* to meet one's obligations || commitment; *hoy tengo muchos compromisos* I have many commitments today || engagement, date (cita) || agreement (acuerdo) || compromising *o* difficult situation; *poner en un compromiso* to put in a difficult situation || JUR arbitration, compromise || — *compromiso matrimonial* engagement || *compromiso verbal* verbal agreement || *libre de compromiso* without obligation || *política sin compromisos* non-committal policy || *poner en el compromiso de tener que hacer algo* to put in the position of having to do sth. || *por compromiso* out of a sense of duty || *¡qué compromiso!* what a nuisance! || *sin compromiso por su parte* without obligation, without committing himself || *soltero y sin compromiso* single and fancy-free.

comprovinciano, na *m/f* person from the same province as another.

compuerta *f* sluice, floodgate (de presa o esclusa) || *compuerta de esclusa* sluice gate, lock gate.

compuesto, ta *adj* compound (cuerpo químico, tiempo, nombre, etc.) || mended, repaired (arreglado) || dressed up, smart, elegant (muy bien vestido) || BOT composite || ARQ composite; *orden compuesto* composite order.
◆ *m* QUÍM compound.
◆ *f pl* BOT compositae.

compulsa *f* JUR certified true copy (de un documento) || collation, comparison (cotejo).

compulsación *f* collation, comparison (cotejo).

compulsar *vt* JUR to compare, to collate || to make a certified true copy of (sacar una compulsa) || to oblige, to compel (compeler).

compulsión *f* constraint, compulsion (apremio).

compulsivo, va *adj* compulsive, compelling (que compele) || compulsory (obligatorio).

compunción *f* compunction, remorse (remordimiento) || sorrow, sadness (tristeza).

compungido, da *adj* sad, sorrowful (dolorido); *voz compungida* sad voice || remorseful, regretful.

compungir *vt* to make remorseful.
◆ *vpr* to be sad, to feel remorseful, to be grieved (entristecerse); *compungirse por* to be grieved about.

computable *adj* computable.

computación *f* → **cómputo.**

computador *m* computer.

computadora *f* computer; *computadora electrónica* electronic computer.

computar *vt* to compute, to calculate.

cómputo *m*; **computación** *f* computation, calculation (cálculo) || REL computation.

comulgante *adj/s* communicant.

comulgar *vt* to administer Holy Communion to.
◆ *vi* to receive Holy Communion || FIG to share || *comulgar por Pascua Florida* to take the Sacrament at Easter, to do one's Easter duty.

comulgatorio *m* Communion rail.

común *adj* common (corriente); *una flor muy común* a very common flower; *sentido común* common sense || common, commonplace; *expresión común* common expression || common, widespread (opinión, costumbre) || common, vulgar (vulgar); *modales comunes* common manners || communal, shared, common; *cuarto de baño común* communal bathroom || mutual; *amigos comunes* mutual friends || GRAM common; *nombre común* common noun || MAT common; *denominador común* common denominator || — *bien común* public interest, common interest *o* good || *de común acuerdo, por acuerdo común* by common consent *o* agreement || *en común* in common || *fuera de lo común* out of the ordinary || *gastos comunes* shared expenses || *hacer algo en común* to do sth. jointly *o* together || *la voz común* rumour, hearsay || *lugar común* cliché, commonplace, hackneyed expression || *Mercado Común* Common Market || *poco común* unusual || *por lo común* generally, normally || *tener en común* to have in common (semejante), to have together, to share (compartir).
◆ *m* REL *común de mártires* common of martyrs || *el común* the community, the public || *el común de la gente* or *de los mortales* most people, the majority of people || *la Cámara de los Comunes* the House of Commons || *los Comunes* the Commons.

comuna *f* AMER commune [smallest territorial division].

comunal *adj* municipal, community, communal.

comunalista *m/f* communalist.

comunalmente *adv* generally, usually (generalmente) || communally || together (juntos).

comunero, ra *adj* HIST of the «comuneros» (relativo a las antiguas comunidades de castilla, etc.).
◆ *m* joint owner (copropietario) || HIST «comunero» [supporter of the «Comunidades» in Castile, of independence in Colombia and Paraguay].

comunicabilidad *f* communicability.

comunicable *adj* communicable || sociable, communicative (persona).

comunicación *f* communication (acción de comunicar) || communication, message (aviso, informe) || communiqué (oficial) || transmission (de un movimiento) || connection (por teléfono) || — *estar* or *ponerse en comunicación con* to be *o* to get in touch with, to be *o* to get in contact with (tener relaciones), to be *o* to get through to (por teléfono) || *Palacio de Comunicaciones* (en Madrid) (equivalent of) General Post Office (en Londres) || *poner en comunicación con* to connect with, to link with (carretera), to put in touch with (poner en relación), to connect with, to put through to (por teléfono) || *puerta de comunicación* communicating door || *vía de comunicación* thoroughfare.
◆ *pl* communications; *las comunicaciones entre las dos ciudades son muy malas* communications between the two towns are very poor.

comunicado, da *adj* served; *barrio bien comunicado* well-served district.
◆ *m* communiqué, communication (aviso) || *comunicado a la prensa* press release, official statement to the press.

comunicador, ra *adj* transmitting (que transmite) || communicating (puerta, etc.).

comunicante *adj* communicating; *vasos comunicantes* communicating vessels.
◆ *m/f* communicant.

comunicar *vt* to communicate, to convey; *nos comunicó a todos su alegría* he conveyed his joy to us all || to pass on, to give, to communicate, to convey (información) || to communicate, to inform of, to make known, to convey, to tell; *me comunicó sus ideas, un secreto* he communicated his ideas to me, he told me a secret || to transmit, to communicate, to pass on, to give (enfermedad) || to transmit, to communicate, to impart (movimiento) || to transmit (calor) || to pass on (miedo) || to join, to connect (dos habitaciones).
◆ *vi* to communicate; *comunicamos por medio de gestos* we communicated by sign language || to correspond (por carta); *comunicar con alguien* to correspond with s.o. || to call (por teléfono); *comunicar con alguien* to call s.o. || to communicate; *cuartos que comunican* rooms which communicate || to be engaged (el teléfono); *está comunicando* it's engaged || to report; *comunican de Madrid que* it is reported from Madrid that.
◆ *vpr* to communicate || to spread (propagarse); *enfermedad que se comunica* disease which spreads || to keep in touch with one another (por carta, por teléfono, etc.), to correspond, to communicate (por carta) || to pass, to be transmitted (el temor, etc.) || to communicate (dos casas, habitaciones, lagos, etc.) || to exchange; *nos comunicamos nuestras ideas* we exchanged ideas.

comunicativo, va *adj* communicative, talkative (una persona) || infectious, catching; *risa comunicativa* infectious laugh || *poco comunicativo* not very talkative, reticent.

comunicatoria *adj f* *letra comunicatoria* testimonial.

comunidad *f* COM community (de intereses, ideas, etc.); *Comunidad Económica Europea* European Economic Community || REL community (de religiosos) || (ant) parish (vecinos de un municipio) || — *comunidad autónoma* autonomous region || *Comunidad Británica de Naciones* British Commonwealth of Nations || *comunidad de bienes* co-ownership (entre esposos) || *comunidad de propietarios* owners' association || *en comunidad* together.
◆ *pl* HIST «Comunidades» [popular uprising in the time of Charles V].

comunión *f* fellowship, communion; *comunión de ideas* fellowship of ideas || Holy Communion, Communion, sacrament of the Lord's Supper (sacramento).

comunismo *m* communism.

comunista *adj/s* communist.

comunitario, ria *adj* of the community || *centro comunitario* community center.

comunizar *vt* to communize.

comúnmente *adv* normally, generally, usually (generalmente) || commonly, frequently (frecuentemente).

comuña *f* AGR mixture of wheat and rye (trigo mezclado con cebada).

con *prep*

> **1.** WITH **2.** IN **3.** TO **4.** CON EL INFINITIVO
> **5.** LOCUCIONES.

1. WITH *comer con una cuchara* to eat with a spoon; *un anciano con gafas de oro* an old man with gold spectacles; *contento con las noticias* happy with the news; *estar disgustado con uno* to be annoyed with s.o.; *hacer una cosa con la idea de...* to do sth. with the idea of...; *con las manos juntas* with one's hands together.
2. IN *hablar con voz ronca* to speak in a raucous voice; *con buena salud* in good health; *con toda franqueza* in all frankness; *estás muy bien con ese sombrero* you look nice in that hat; *no puedo salir con este frío* I can't go out in this cold; *con ira, con enojo* in anger.
3. TO *amable con todos* nice to everybody; *disculparse con* to apologize to; *escribirse con alguien* to write to s.o.; *antipático con todos* unfriendly to everyone.
4. CON EL INFINITIVO by (con el gerundio), if; *con pulsar este botón se enciende la luz* by pressing this switch you put the light on, if you press this switch the light goes on || as, since; *con llegar muy tarde, se quedó sin comer* as he arrived very late, he had no lunch || even though, in spite of the fact that, in spite of; *con ser tan inteligente no ha conseguido triunfar* even though *o* in spite of the fact that he is very intelligent, he has not been able to succeed || provided that, as long as; *con escribirme mañana* as long as you write to me tomorrow.
5. LOCUCIONES *con arreglo a la ley* in accordance with *o* according to the law || *con ello* for that || *con el título de* under the title of || *con esto y con todo* however, nevertheless || *con mucho gusto* with (great) pleasure || *con objeto de* in order to, to, with the aim of || *con que* so, then || *con tal que* or *con que* or *con sólo que* so long as, provided that || *con todo* or *con todo y con eso* in spite of everything, nevertheless, even so || *con todos los requisitos* in due form || *están todos con gripe* they have all got the flu || *salvó al niño con gran admiración de los que le rodeaban* he rescued the child to thet great admiration of those around him || FAM *¡vaya con el niño!* that child!

conato *m* (p us) effort, endeavour (empeño) | intention, purpose (propósito) || beginnings *pl* (principio); *conato de incendio* beginnings of a fire || attempt; *hizo un conato de* he made an attempt to || *conato de revolución* attempted revolution.

conca *f* shell.

concadenar *vt* → **concatenar.**

concatenación *f* concatenation, chain, linking; *concatenación de ideas* chain of ideas.

concatenado, da *adj* concatenate, linked up.

concatenar; concadenar *vt* to link, to link up, to concatenate.

concausa *f* cause, factor (causa).

concavidad *f* concavity || hollow, cavity (hoyo).

cóncavo, va *adj* concave; *espejo cóncavo* concave mirror.

concavoconvexo, xa *adj* FÍS concavo-convex.

concebible *adj* conceivable, thinkable, imaginable.

concebir* *vt* to conceive (una mujer) || to understand, to conceive; *eso se concibe fácilmente* that is easily understood || to imagine (imaginar) || to conceive (idea, amistad, amor, proyecto, esperanzas) || to view (un asunto) || to form (un proyecto) || to take; *concibió antipatía hacia su vecino* he took a dislike to his neighbour || *hacer concebir esperanzas a uno* to give s.o. hope, to raise s.o.'s hopes.
◆ *vi* to conceive, to become pregnant (quedar encinta) || to conceive, to imagine (imaginar).

conceder *vt* to grant, to concede (otorgar); *conceder una gracia, un privilegio* to grant a favour, a privilege || to allow, to give, to grant (crédito, plazo, etc.) || to pay (atención) || to spare, to give; *no puedo concederle sino algunos minutos* I can only spare you a few minutes || to award; *conceder una indemnización, un premio* to award damages, a prize || to admit, to agree (reconocer); *concedo que tiene usted razón* I admit that you are right || to confer (*a* on) (honores) || *conceder importancia, valor* to give *o* to attach importance, value.

concejal *m* town councillor, councillor.

concejala *f* town councillor's wife || (female) councillor, councilwoman.

concejero *m* AMER town councillor.

concejil *adj* municipal.

concejo *m* town council (ayuntamiento).
— OBSERV This word must not be confused with *consejo*.

conceller *m* town councillor in Catalonia.

concentrable *adj* concentrative.

concentración *f* concentration; *la concentración de un producto químico* the concentration of a chemical; *campo de concentración* concentration camp || — *concentración parcelaria* (land) consolidation || *llevar a cabo la concentración parcelaria* to consolidate land.

concentrado, da *adj* concentrated || FIG absorbed (absorto).
◆ *m* concentrate; *concentrado de tomates* tomato concentrate || *concentrado de carne* meat extract.

concentrar *vt* to concentrate (tropas, rayos, etc.) || to focus (la observación, los sonidos, etc.) || FIG to concentrate; *concentrar la atención en* to concentrate one's attention on | to concentrate, to centre (los esfuerzos).
◆ *vpr* FIG to concentrate (abstraerse) || to concentre [US to concenter] (rayos) || to concentrate, to be concentrated (tropas, rayos, etc.).

concéntrico, ca *adj* concentric.

concentricidad *f* concentricity.

concepción *f* conception (de un niño) || FIG conception, idea; *tener una curiosa concepción de la vida* to have a strange conception of life || — INFORM *concepción asistida por ordenador* computer-aided design || *Inmaculada Concepción* Immaculate Conception.

Concepción *npr f* girl's name derived from María de la Concepción [there is no equivalent in English].

concepcional *adj* conceptional.

conceptismo *m* conceptism (estilo literario).

concepto *m* concept; *el concepto del tiempo* the concept of time || idea, notion, conception; *no tengo un concepto claro de lo que es esta doctrina* I haven't got a clear idea of what this doctrine is || opinion (juicio) || witticism, pun (agudeza) || reason (razón) || (ant) conceit || heading, section (de una cuenta) || — *en concepto de* as, by way of || *en mi concepto* in my opinion || *en ningún concepto* on no account, under no circumstances || *en su amplio concepto* in its broad *o* broadest sense || *formarse un concepto de* to form *o* to get an idea of, to see (la forma de algo), to form an opinion of (hacerse una opinión) || *perdí el concepto que tenía de él* I have changed my opinion of him || *por* or *bajo todos los conceptos* from every point of view, in every respect || *por ningún concepto* by no means, in no way || *tener buen concepto de* or *tener en buen concepto a alguien* to have a high opinion of s.o., to think well *o* highly of s.o. (tener buena opinión).

conceptual *adj* conceptual.

conceptualismo *m* conceptualism.

conceptuar *vt* to consider, to deem, to think; *conceptuar a uno de* or *por* or *como inteligente* to consider s.o. intelligent || *bien, mal conceptuado* well, badly thought of.

conceptuoso, sa *adj* affected, forced, laboured (estilo) || affected (escritor) || witty (agudo).

concerniente *adj* concerning, regarding, about, dealing with; *los reglamentos concernientes a los transportes* the regulations concerning transport || *en lo concerniente a* with regard to.

concernir* *vi* to concern, to regard (afectar) || to be up to (corresponder); *no me concierne decidir* it's not up to me to decide || — *en lo que a mí concierne* as for me, for my part, as far as I am concerned || *en lo que concierne a* as for, with regard to, with respect to, concerning.
— OBSERV This is a defective verb; it is only used in the third persons singular and plural of the present and imperfect indicative and subjunctive.

concertadamente *adv* of a common accord, together (puestos de acuerdo) || systematically, methodically (con orden).

concertado, da *adj* concerted (acción).

concertador, ra *adj* conciliatory, conciliating (conciliador) || coordinating.
◆ *m/f* peacemaker, appeaser || *concertador de privilegios* issuer of royal privileges.

concertante *adj* MÚS concerted.

concertar* *vt* to concert, to plan (proyectar en común) || to coordinate (coordinar) || to arrange; *concertar una venta* to arrange a sale || to agree on *o* upon, to fix; *concertar un precio* to agree on *o* upon a price || to settle, to conclude, to clinch; *concertar un negocio* to clinch a deal || to agree, to arrange; *hemos concertado reunirnos el sábado* we have agreed to meet on Saturday || to arrive at, to come to, to conclude, to reach; *concertar un acuerdo* to reach an agreement || to conclude (un tratado) || to tune (instrumentos de música) || to harmonize (voces) || to concert, to coordinate; *concertar los esfuerzos* to concert one's efforts || to reconcile (reconciliar).
◆ *vi* to agree, to tally; *dos pasajes que no conciertan* two passages which do not tally || GRAM to agree (las palabras) || MÚS to harmonize, to be in tune.
◆ *vpr* to plot (conchabarse) || to come to *o* to arrive at an agreement, to agree (llegar a un acuerdo).

concertina *f* MÚS concertina.

concertino *m* MÚS first violin [US concertmaster].

concertista *m/f* concert performer, soloist.

concesión *f* granting, concession (acción de conceder) || grant (cosa concedida); *concesión perpetua* grant in perpetuity || awarding; *la concesión de un premio* the awarding of a prize || FIG concession; *hacer concesiones* to make concessions.

concesionario, ria *adj* concessionary.
◆ *m* licence holder, licensee (de bebidas) || concessionaire, concessionnaire (obras, etc.).

conciencia; consciencia *f* consciousness, awareness (conocimiento) || conscience (moralidad); *tener la conciencia limpia* or *tranquila* to have a clear conscience; *caso de conciencia* matter of conscience || mind; *tener la conciencia deformada* to have a twisted *o* warped mind || — *a conciencia* conscientiously; *trabajo hecho a conciencia* work done conscientiously || *acusar a uno la conciencia* to have a guilty conscience, to have pangs of conscience || *cargar la conciencia* to burden *o* to prick one's conscience || *conciencia de clase* class-consciousness || *conciencia sucia* guilty conscience || *en conciencia* in all conscience || FAM *gusanillo de la conciencia* remorse (remordimiento) || *libertad de conciencia* freedom of worship || *objetor de conciencia* conscientious objector || *para descargar la conciencia* to ease one's conscience || *remorderle a uno la conciencia* to have a guilty conscience || *ser ancho, estrecho de conciencia* to be unscrupulous, scrupulous || *tener conciencia de* to be aware *o* conscious of || *tener un peso en la conciencia* to have sth. *o* a burden on one's conscience || *tomar conciencia de* to become aware of.

concienzudo, da *adj* conscientious.

concierto *m* agreement (acuerdo) || MÚS concert (función); *concierto al aire libre* open-air concert | concerto (obra); *concierto de piano* piano concerto || FIG concord, harmony, concert (armonía) | chorus (de alabanzas); *concierto de elogios* chorus of praise || — *concierto económico* flat rate (impuesto) || *de concierto* in concert, together, in unison || *sin orden ni concierto* without rhyme or reason; *hablar sin orden ni concierto* to talk without rhyme or reason; any old how (desordenado).

conciliable *adj* reconcilable, conciliable.

conciliábulo *m* secret meeting (reunión) || confabulation (entrevista) || REL conciliabule.

conciliación *f* conciliation, reconciliation, reconcilement || — *espíritu de conciliación* conciliatory spirit || *tribunal de conciliación* conciliation court || *tribunal de conciliación laboral* conciliation board.

conciliador, ra *adj* conciliatory, conciliating.
◆ *m/f* conciliator.

conciliar *adj* conciliar.
◆ *m* councillor.

conciliar *vt* to reconcile, to conciliate; *conciliar a dos enemigos* to reconcile two enemies || to reconcile, to harmonize (textos, ideas, etc.) || *conciliar el sueño* to get to sleep.
◆ *vpr* to win, to gain; *conciliarse la amistad de todo el mundo* to gain everybody's friendship.

conciliativo, va; conciliatorio, ria *adj* conciliatory, conciliative.

concilio *m* council || *el Concilio Vaticano Segundo* the Second Vatican Council.

concisamente *adv* concisely, tersely, briefly.

concisión *f* concision, conciseness, succinctness.

conciso, sa *adj* concise, terse, brief.

concitar *vt* to stir up; *concitó contra su amigo la ira de su padre* he stirred up his father's anger against his friend.

conciudadano, na *m/f* fellow citizen (en general) || fellow townsman (hombre de la misma ciudad) || fellow townswoman (mujer) || fellow countryman (hombre del mismo país) || fellow countrywoman (mujer).

cónclave; conclave *m* conclave.

conclavista *m* conclavist.

concluir* *vt* to finish (acabar) || to close (un trato) || to conclude, to deduce, to infer (deducir) || to settle, to solve (solucionar) || to convince (convencer) || to put the finishing touches to (una obra de arte).
◆ *vi* to finish, to end; *es tiempo de concluir* it is time to finish || — *concluir con un trabajo* to finish *o* to finish with a piece of work || *concluir haciendo algo* or *por hacer algo* to finish by *o* to end up (by) doing sth. || *concluyeron por pedir un armisticio* they decided to seek an armistice, they eventually requested an armistice.
◆ *vpr* to come to an end, to finish, to end.

conclusión *f* concluding, settlement (de un negocio) || conclusion (de un razonamiento) || conclusion, close (fin) || — *en conclusión* in conclusion || *llegar a la conclusión de que...* to come to the conclusion that...

conclusivo, va *adj* conclusive.

concluso, sa *adj* JUR closed pending sentence.
— OBSERV This adjective is the irregular past participle of the verb *concluir*.

concluyente *adj* conclusive, decisive; *una prueba concluyente* conclusive evidence || categorical.

concoide *adj* conchoidal (en forma de concha).

◆ *f* MAT conchoid (curva).

concoideo, a *adj* conchoidal (en forma de concha).

concomer *vt* FIG to gnaw at, to corrode.
◆ *vpr* to wriggle one's back, to squirm || — FIG & FAM *concomerse de envidia* to be green with envy, to squirm with envy | *concomerse de impaciencia* to itch with impatience | *concomerse de rabia* to be hopping mad, to be seething.

concomitancia *f* concomitance, concomitancy.

concomitante *adj* concomitant.

concordancia *f* concordance, agreement || GRAM agreement (entre sustantivo y adjetivo, etc.), sequence (de los tiempos) || MÚS harmony.

concordante *f* concordant.

concordar* *vt* to reconcile, to bring into agreement; *concordar a dos enemigos* to reconcile two enemies || GRAM to make agree.
◆ *vi* to agree; *los médicos concuerdan en que* the doctors agree that || to agree, to tally; *mi versión no concuerda con la tuya* my version does not tally with yours || GRAM to agree; *el verbo concuerda con el sujeto* the verb agrees with the subject || — *las opiniones concuerdan en que* there is a consensus of opinion that || *los indicios concuerdan en que* the signs all point to the fact that.

concordato *m* concordat.

concorde *adj* in agreement || — *estamos concordes en la necesidad de marcharnos* we all agree that we must leave, we all recognize the need for us to leave || *estar concorde en hacer algo* to be for doing sth., to agree to doing sth. || *poner concordes a dos personas* to make two people agree *o* see eye to eye.

concordemente *adv* together, of a common accord.

concordia *f* harmony, concord, concordance (armonía) || double ring (sortija) || *de concordia* together, of a common accord.

concreción *f* concretion || MED stone.

concretamente *adv* concretely || in particular, specifically; *referirse concretamente a alguien* to refer to s.o. in particular || specifically; *me dijo concretamente que lo hiciera* he specifically told me to do it || exactly; *no sé concretamente lo que significa esto* I don't know exactly what this means || *se lo dije a uno de vosotros, concretamente a Juan* I said it to one of you, to John to be exact *o* to John in fact.

concretar *vt* to state explicitly; *concretar una idea* to state an idea explicitly || to limit (limitar) || to specify (precisar) || *concretemos* let us sum up (al final), let us be more specific (precisemos) || *concretó sus esperanzas en...* he set his hopes on...
◆ *vpr* to confine o.s. to; *me concretaré a hablar de...* I shall confine myself to speaking about... || to become definite, to come out, to be established; *su desacuerdo se concretó durante la última asamblea* their disagreement came out during the last meeting || to take shape; *el proyecto parece concretarse* the project seems to be taking shape || to keep; *concrétese usted al tema* keep to the subject.

concreto, ta *adj* concrete || actual, particular, specific (caso) || — *algo concreto* something concrete || *en concreto* definite (seguro), in short, in brief (en resumen) || *en el caso concreto de* in the particular case of, in the specific case of || *lo concreto* the concrete aspect || *nada se ha dicho hasta ahora en concreto, nada concreto se ha dicho hasta ahora* up to now nothing definite has been said.
◆ *m* concretion || AMER concrete (hormigón).

concubina *f* concubine.

concubinato *m* concubinage.

conculcación *f* infringement, violation.

conculcar *vt* to infringe, to violate, to break (infringir); *conculcar la ley* to break the law.

concuñada *f* sister of one's brother-in-law or sister-in-law.

concuñado *m* brother of one's brother-in-law or sister-in-law.

concupiscencia *f* concupiscence, lustfulness, lust of the flesh || greed (avaricia).

concupiscente *adj* concupiscent, lustful (sensual) || greedy (avaro).

concurrencia *f* audience (en un espectáculo); *una concurrencia numerosa* a large audience || crowd, gathering (muchedumbre) || concurrence, conjunction (simultaneidad); *la concurrencia de dos muertes* the conjunction of two deaths || — *divertir a la concurrencia* to keep the audience amused || *hasta concurrencia de* up to, to the amount of, not exceeding.

concurrente *adj* concurrent (que coincide) || competing, contending (participante en un concurso).
◆ *m/f* competitor (competidor, participante en un concurso) || candidate (en un examen) || member of the audience (en el teatro, etc.) || spectator (en espectáculos deportivos) || *los concurrentes* those present, the audience.

concurrido, da *adj* popular, well-attended (exposición, museo, etc.) || busy, crowded (calle) || much frequented (muy frecuentado).

concurrir *vi* to go (a un lugar) || to converge, to meet (converger) || to attend (presenciar) || to coincide, to concur (en el tiempo) || to contribute; *concurrir al éxito de* to contribute to the success of || to concur (en un dictamen) || to compete, to take part (*a* in) (tomar parte en un concurso o una competición) || to be a candidate (examen) || *concurren en él todas las cualidades* he combines *o* has all the qualities.

concursante *m/f* competitor, participant (en un concurso) || candidate (para un empleo) || DEP contestant.

concursar *vi* to compete (en un concurso) || to be a candidate (en un examen, para un empleo).

concurso *m* concourse (concurrencia) || gathering, crowd (muchedumbre) || help, aid, assistance (ayuda); *prestar su concurso* to lend assistance, to give one's help || cooperation || competition; *un concurso literario* a literary competition || contest; *concurso de tiro con arco, de belleza, de pesca* archery, beauty, fishing contest || show; *concurso hípico* horse show || meeting; *concurso de atletismo* athletics meeting || tender (de una obra, servicio) || competitive examination, competition (examen) || coincidence, concurrence (de hechos) || FIG combination; *concurso de circunstancias* combination of circumstances || — JUR *concurso de acreedores* meeting of creditors || ECON *concurso público* official submission || *concurso radiofónico* radio quiz programme || *fuera de concurso* out of the running || *se ha anunciado concurso para proveer una plaza de médico en el hospital* applications are invited to fill a post of doctor at the hospital.

concusión *f* MED concussion || peculation, extortion (de un funcionario).

concusionario, ria *m/f* extortioner, extortionist, peculator.

concha *f* shell (de molusco, tortuga) || tortoiseshell (carey); *peine de concha* tortoiseshell comb || bay, cove (pequeña bahía) || chip (de porcelana) || nether millstone (de molino) || ANAT concha, conch (de la oreja) || AMER POP cunt || — TEATR *concha del apuntador* prompt box || *concha de peregrino* scallop, scallop shell || *concha de perla* pearl oyster (madreperla) || FIG *meterse en su concha* to withdraw into one's shell || FIG & FAM *tener muchas conchas* or *más conchas que un galápago* to be reserved (reservado), to be a sly one (taimado).

conchabamiento *m*; **conchabanza** *f* plot, conspiracy.

conchabar *vt* to gather together (unir) || to mix (mezclar) || AMER to take on, to hire [mainly servants].
◆ *vpr* to join *o* to band together || to gang up, to join up; *conchabarse con malhechores* to join up with evildoers || *estar conchabado con* to be in league with, to be hand in glove with.

conchífero, ra *adj* GEOL conchiferous.

concho *m* AMER corn husk (del maíz) | sediment, dregs *pl*, deposit (poso) | end (final).
◆ *pl* AMER leftovers (sobras).
◆ *interj* AMER FAM damn!

conchudo, da *adj* AMER POP bloody stupid.
◆ *m/f* wanker (gilipollas).

condado *m* county, shire (territorio) || countship, earldom (dignidad).

condal *adj* of a count, count's || *la Ciudad Condal* Barcelona.

conde *m* count, earl (título) || *el señor conde* his lordship.

condecoración *f* decoration, medal (insignia) || decoration (acción de condecorar) || *imponer una condecoración a uno* to decorate s.o.

condecorado, da *adj* decorated.
◆ *m/f* holder of a decoration *o* of decorations.

condecorar *vt* to decorate; *condecorar con una cruz* to decorate with a cross.

condena *f* JUR conviction, sentence (sentencia) | condemnation (a muerte) || condemnation (acción de reprochar, censurar) || sentence; *el penado cumplió* or *sufrió su condena* the prisoner served his sentence || — *condena a perpetuidad* life sentence || *condena condicional* suspended sentence.

condenable *adj* condemnable, reprehensible, blameworthy (que merece ser condenado) || damnable, heinous (digno de condenación divina).

condenación *f* JUR conviction, sentence (acción de condenar) | condemnation (a muerte) || REL damnation (al infierno) || condemnation (censura).

condenadamente *adv* FAM darned, damned (muy).

condenado, da *adj* condemned, convicted (por un tribunal) || condemned, damned (al infierno) || condemned (puerta, etc.) || hopeless, beyond help (enfermo) || doomed; *una raza condenada* a doomed race || FIG damned, wretched; *este condenado Pablo siempre nos está dando la lata* that damned Paul is always annoying us; *este condenado trabajo* this damned job || *condenado a muerte* condemned to death.
◆ *m/f* condemned person (a muerte) || convicted person, prisoner (a otra pena) || reprobate, damned person (al infierno) || wretch; *¡como vuelva a ver a ese condenado...!* if I see the wretch again...! || — FIG & FAM *correr como un condenado* to run like a hare, to run for dear life | *forcejear como un condenado* to struggle for dear life | *sufrir como un condenado* to go through hell | *trabajar como un condenado* to work like a horse, to slave away.

condenar *vt* to convict, to find guilty; *condenar por ladrón* to find guilty of theft || to condemn, to sentence; *condenar a cinco años, a muerte* to condemn to five years imprisonment, to death || to condemn, to censure, to blame (una doctrina, una conducta) || to condemn, to doom (obligar) || to condemn, to damn (al infierno) || MED to give up (a un en-

fermo) || AMER to annoy, to irritate || — *condenar a una multa* to fine || *condenar en costas* to order to pay costs || *condenar en rebeldía* to judge by default || *condenar una puerta* to condemn a door, to brick up *o* to board up *o* to wall up a door (tabicarla).
◆ *vpr* to condemn o.s., to be damned, to doom o.s. (al infierno) || to condemn o.s. || to get annoyed (irritarse).

condenatorio, ria *adj* JUR condemnatory.

condensabilidad *f* condensability.

condensable *adj* condensable.

condensación *f* condensation (acción y resultado) || condensing (acción).

condensado, da *adj* condensed; *leche condensada* condensed milk.

condensador *m* ELECTR condenser, capacitor || condenser (de gases, máquinas de vapor).

condensar *vt* to condense.
◆ *vpr* to condense, to become condensed.

condesa *f* countess (título) || *la señora condesa* her ladyship.

condescendencia *f* condescension, condescendence (deferencia) | complaisance, indulgence (amabilidad).

condescender* *vi* to yield, to comply (avenirse a, ceder); *condescender a los deseos de uno* to yield to s.o.'s wishes || to condescend (dignarse); *condescender en ir a verle* to condescend to go and see him.

condescendiente *adj* condescending || obliging, complaisant, indulgent (amable).

condestable *m* High Constable.

condición *f* nature, condition (naturaleza de las cosas); *la condición humana* the human condition || quality; *mercancía de mala condición* poor quality goods || condition, state (estado); *en buenas condiciones* in a good condition || character, nature, disposition; *ser áspero de condición* to have a surly character *o* nature, to be a surly disposition || rank, status, position, condition (situación social); *de humilde condición* of modest status || sort, kind (clase) || capacity; *en mi condición de ministro* in my capacity as minister || condition, circumstance (circunstancia); *en estas condiciones* under these circumstances, in these conditions || condition; *condiciones de pago* conditions of payment || condition; *condiciones de trabajo* working conditions || condition (en una promesa); *imponer condiciones* to lay down *o* to impose conditions || JUR condition; *condición casual, tácita* contingent, implicit *o* tacit condition || — *a condición de tener tiempo, lo haré* I shall do it, provided that *o* as long as I have time || *a condición (de) que* or *con la condición de que no llueva* on condition that *o* provided that *o* as long as it does not rain || *condición sine qua non* prerequisite, essential condition || *con esta condición* on this condition || *de buena condición* good-tempered || *de mala condición* ill-tempered, bad-tempered || *persona de condición* person of rank *o* importance, high-class person || *tener condición* to have character, to have a backbone || *tener mala condición* to be evil-minded.
◆ *pl* aptitude *sing*, talent *sing*, capacity *sing*; *tener condiciones para el dibujo* to have an aptitude for drawing || conditions, terms (de un contrato) || state *sing*; *condiciones de salud* state of health || *condiciones requeridas* requirements, requisites || *en condiciones de marcha* in working order || *en iguales condiciones* in the same conditions || *estar en condiciones de hacer algo* to be in a fit state to do sth. (físicamente), to be in a position to do sth. (legalmente, moralmente, etc.) || *estar en malas condiciones* to be off || *poner en condiciones* to prepare, to get ready || *rendición sin condiciones* unconditional surrender || *rendirse sin condiciones* to surrender unconditionally.

condicionado, da *adj* conditioned (acondicionado); *reflejo condicionado* conditioned reflex || conditional (condicional) || *la oferta está condicionada a* or *por la demanda* supply is conditioned by demand.

condicional *adj* conditional.

condicionamiento *m* conditioning.

condicionar *vi* to fit, to agree.
◆ *vt* to suit, to adapt (*a* to), to make depend (*a* on); *ha condicionado su decisión a la opinión de los demás* he suited his decision to the opinion of the others || to condition (temperature, etc.) || to condition (poner condiciones) || to test (las fibras) || *su aceptación condiciona la mía* his acceptance determines mine, my acceptance depends on his.

cóndilo *m* ANAT condyle.

condiloideo, a *adj* BOT condyloid.

condiloma *m* MED condyloma.

condimentación *f* seasoning.

condimentar *vt* to season, to flavour (sazonar) || FIG to spice, to flavour.

condimento *m* condiment, seasoning (aliño) || dressing (de ensalada).

condiscípulo, la *m/f* fellow student, schoolmate, classmate.

condolencia *f* condolence, sympathy.

condolerse* *vpr* to feel pity (*de* for), to pity, to sympathize (*de* with), to feel sorry (*de* for) (compadecerse); *condolerse de los miserables* to feel sorry for the unfortunate.

condominio *m* condominium (de un territorio) || joint ownership (de una cosa).

condón *m* POP French letter.

condonación *f* remission, condonation (de una pena, de una deuda) || remission (de contribuciones).

condonar *vt* to condone, to pardon || to cancel (una deuda).

cóndor *m* condor (ave, moneda).

condritis *f inv* MED chondritis.

condrodisplasia *f* MED chondrodysplasia.

condromalacia *f* MED chondromalacia.

conducción *f* driving; *la conducción de un coche* the driving of a car || FÍS conduction || leading (guía) || transportation (transporte) || pipe (tubería) || piping (por tubos) || wiring (cables) || — *conducción por la izquierda* driving on the left || *permiso de conducción* driving licence.

conducente *adj* conducive, leading.

conducir* *vt* to drive; *conducir un coche* to drive a car || to lead; *conducir un ejército* to lead an army || to convey (un líquido) || to carry (electricidad) || to lead (a una persona) || to manage (un negocio) || to conduct (una encuesta, etc.) || to accompany (acompañar) || to transport, to carry (transportar) || *conducir a la ruina a alguien* to bring s.o. to his ruin, to bring about s.o.'s ruin.
◆ *vi* to drive; *no sabe conducir* he cannot drive || to lead (llevar); *eso no conduce a nada* that leads nowhere *o* to nothing.
◆ *vpr* to behave, to conduct o.s. (portarse).

conducta *f* conduct, behaviour [*US* behavior] (manera de comportarse); *tiene siempre malas notas de conducta* he always has bad marks for conduct || management (dirección) || convoy (de mulas, etc.) || — *cambiar de conducta* to change one's ways || *mala conducta* misconduct, misbehaviour.

conductancia *f* ELECTR conductance.

conductibilidad *f* FÍS conductivity.

conductible *adj* FÍS conductive.

conductividad *f* ELECTR conductivity.

conductivo, va *adj* conductive.

conducto *m* pipe, conduit (cañería) || ELECTR cable, lead, culvert || ANAT duct; *conducto auditivo, lagrimal* auditory, tear duct || — ANAT *conducto alimenticio* alimentary canal || *conducto de desagüe* drain || *conducto de humos* flue || *por conducto de* through, via || *por conducto oficial* or *regular* or *reglamentario* through official channels.

conductor, ra *adj* who drives (de automóvil, etc.) || ELECTR conductive || FIG leading, guiding.
◆ *m/f* driver (de coche, autobús, etc.) || FIG leader (jefe) || *conductor suicida* reckless driver (who travels on a motorway in the opposite direction).
◆ *m* ELECTR conductor || IMPR machine minder [*US* pressman] || inspector (coche cama) || AMER conductor (cobrador).

condueño, ña *m/f* joint owner.

condumio *m* FAM grub, food (comida).

conectado, da *adj* connected.

conectador *m* TECN connector, connecter.

conectar *vt/vi* TECN to connect (up) | to plug in (enchufar) | to switch on (poner) || TECN to couple (acoplar) || — *conectar a alguien* to put s.o. in touch || ELECTR *conectar a tierra* to earth || RAD *conectar con* to tune in with (dar), to tune in to (coger) | *conectamos con Madrid* over to you, Madrid || ELECTR *conectar con la red* to connect to the mains || *conectar un golpe en la mandíbula* to land a punch on the jaw (boxeo) || *estar conectado con* to be in touch with || FAM *estar mal conectados* not to be on the same wavelength.

conector *m* INFORM connector.

coneja *f* doe (hembra del conejo) || FAM *esa mujer es una coneja* she breeds like a rabbit.

conejal; conejar *m* rabbit hutch.

conejera *f* rabbit warren, rabbit burrow (de los conejos en libertad) || rabbit hutch (conejal) || FIG cave (cueva) | den, dive (de gente de mal vivir) | rabbit hutch *o* warren (lugar donde viven muchos).

conejero, ra *adj* rabbit-hunting.
◆ *m/f* rabbit breeder.

conejillo *m* young rabbit || bunny (en lenguaje infantil) || *conejillo de Indias* guinea pig.

conejo *m* rabbit (mamífero); *conejo casero* tame rabbit || — *conejo de Angora* Angora rabbit || *conejo de campo* or *de monte* wild rabbit.
— OBSERV In South America, the word *conejo* is applied to several rodents. One of the most common is the *tapetí* or *tapití* of Brazil.

conejuno, na *adj* of a rabbit, rabbit.

conexión *f* connection, connexion || — *estar en conexión con* to be connected to || *vuelo de conexión* liaison flight.

conexionarse *vpr* to make connections.

conexo, xa *adj* connected, related.

confabulación *f* conspiracy, plot, collusion.

confabular *vi* to converse.
◆ *vpr* to conspire, to plot (conspirar).

confalón *m* gonfalon, banner, standard (estandarte).

confalonier; confaloniero *m* gonfalonier, standard bearer.

confección *f* tailoring, making-up, confection (de traje) || ready-made *o* ready-to-wear *o* off-the-peg clothes *pl* || clothing; *ramo de la confección* clothing industry || making, making-up (realización) || mixing (de un cóctel) || drawing up (de una lista) || IMPR makeup || *tienda, traje de confección* ready-made *o* off-the-peg shop, suit.

confeccionado, da *adj* ready-made, ready-to-wear, off-the-peg (ropa) ‖ *confeccionado a la medida* made to measure.

confeccionador, ra *m/f* ready-made outfitter ‖ maker-up (en la redacción).

confeccionar *vt* to make up (traje, lista, etc.) ‖ CULIN to make (pasteles) ‖ IMPR to make up.

confederación *f* confederacy, alliance, confederation.

confederado, da *adj/s* confederate.

confederal *adj* confederal.

confederar *vt* to confederate.
◆ *vpr* to confederate.

confer confer.
— OBSERV The Spanish abbreviations of *confer* are: *cf., conf., cof.*
— OBSERV La abreviatura inglesa de *confer* es: *cf.*

conferencia *f* conference, meeting (política) ‖ lecture, talk; *dar una conferencia* to give a talk ‖ call; *conferencia interurbana* long-distance call, trunk call ‖ — *conferencia a cobro revertido* reverse-charge call [*US* collect telephone call] ‖ *conferencia de prensa* press conference ‖ *conferencia en la cumbre* or *de alto nivel* summit conference ‖ *poner una conferencia a Madrid* to make a call to Madrid.

conferenciante *m/f* lecturer, speaker.

conferenciar *vi* to hold a conversation, to converse, to talk, to discuss.

conferencista *m/f* *AMER* lecturer.

conferir* *vt* to confer, to bestow (conceder una dignidad, etc.) ‖ to give; *conferir a uno nuevas responsabilidades* to give s.o. new responsibilities ‖ to award (premio).
◆ *vi* to confer, to consult.

confesante *adj* JUR who confesses.

confesar* *vt* to admit, to confess; *confesar su ignorancia* to confess one's ignorance ‖ to own to, to acknowledge (un error) ‖ to own up to (un crimen) ‖ to confess (proclamar); *confesar la fe* to confess one's faith ‖ REL to confess, to hear in confession (oír en confesión) | to confess (los pecados) ‖ *confesar de plano* to own up, to admit everything.
◆ *vpr* to go to confession, to confess ‖ — *confesarse con el párroco* to confess to the parish priest ‖ *confesarse culpable, vencido* to admit one's guilt, to admit defeat ‖ *confesarse de un pecado* to confess a sin ‖ *ir a confesarse* to go to confession.
— OBSERV *Confesar* has two past participles: *confesado* is regular and *confeso* irregular, the latter being used as an adjective.

confesión *f* confession, admission (admisión) ‖ REL confession (acto de confesarse) | confession, faith, avowal (credo religioso) ‖ *oír en confesión* to confess, to hear in confession.

confesional *adj* confessional ‖ denominational (disputas, escuela, etc.), doctrinal (disputas, etc.).

confesionario *m* confessional [box].

confeso, sa *adj* self-confessed ‖ converted (judío).
◆ *m* brother (lego) ‖ converted Jew (judío convertido).

confesonario *m* confessional [box].

confesor *m* confessor.

confesorio *m* confessional [box].

confeti *m pl* confetti *sing* (papelillos).

confiadamente *adv* confidently (con confianza) ‖ conceitedly (con presunción).

confiado, da *adj* trusting (que se fía) ‖ gullible, unsuspecting (crédulo) ‖ confident, self-confident (seguro de sí mismo) ‖ conceited (presumido) ‖ *estamos muy confiados en el resultado* we are very confident about the result.

confianza *f* confidence; *tener confianza en el porvenir* to have confidence in the future; *hacerlo con confianza* to do it with confidence ‖ trust, confidence (en alguien) ‖ intimacy, familiarity (intimidad) ‖ conceit (presunción) ‖ — *amigo de confianza* close friend ‖ *con toda confianza* in all confidence ‖ *creía que teníamos bastante confianza para que te dijese la verdad* I thought we were sufficiently good friends for me to tell the truth, I thought we were close enough for me to tell you the truth ‖ *de confianza* trustworthy, reliable; *él es de confianza* he is reliable; of trust, confidential (puesto, empleo) ‖ *defraudar la confianza de alguien* to betray s.o.'s confidence ‖ *en confianza* confidentially, in confidence ‖ *estar en confianza* to be among friends ‖ *plantear la cuestión de confianza* to ask for a vote of confidence ‖ *poner toda su confianza en una persona* to trust s.o. implicitly ‖ *tener confianza en sí mismo* to be self-confident ‖ *tener mucha confianza con alguien* to be on very close *o* intimate terms with s.o. ‖ *tomarse demasiadas confianzas* to take liberties ‖ *tratar a uno con confianza* to treat s.o. informally *o* like a friend.

confiar *vt* to entrust (encargar); *confiar un trabajo a alguien* to entrust s.o. with a job ‖ to commit; *confiar algo a la memoria* to commit sth. to memory ‖ to confide, to tell in confidence (decir en confianza) ‖ *confiar a uno sus problemas* to tell s.o. about one's problems.
◆ *vi* to put one's trust *o* one's faith in, to have trust *o* faith in; *confiar en Dios* to put one's trust in God ‖ to trust; *confío en mi amigo* I trust my friend, I trust in my friend ‖ to count, to rely; *confío en su discreción* I am counting on your discretion; *confiar en sus fuerzas* to count on one's strength ‖ to be *o* to feel confident; *confío en que esta obra será un éxito* I am confident that this work will be a success ‖ to hope (esperar); *confío en que no le pasará nada* I hope nothing will happen to him.
◆ *vpr* to put o.s.; *me confié en sus manos* I put myself in his hands ‖ to put one's trust (*en* in) ‖ to confide (hacer confidencias); *confiarse a un amigo* to confide in a friend.

confidencia *f* secret, confidence ‖ *hacer confidencias a uno* to confide in s.o. (confiarse a), to reveal secrets to s.o. (revelar secretos a).

confidencial *adj* confidential ‖ *de modo confidencial* confidentially, in confidence.

confidencialidad *f* confidentiality.

confidenta *f* TEATR confidante.

confidente *adj* faithful (fiel).
◆ *m/f* confidant (hombre), confidante (mujer) ‖ informer (de policía).
◆ *m* sociable (canapé).

confidentemente *adv* confidentially.

configuración *f* shape, form, configuration ‖ — INFORM *configuración básica* basic configuration | *configuración del sistema* system configuration ‖ *configuración del terreno* lie of the land.

configurar *vt* to shape, to form ‖ INFORM to configure.

confín *adj* bordering.
◆ *m pl* border *sing*; *los confines de España y Francia* the border between Spain and France, the border of Spain with France ‖ boundaries, limits, confines (límites) ‖ — *en los confines del horizonte* as far as the eye can see ‖ *por todos los confines del mundo* to the four corners of the earth.

confinación *f*; **confinamiento** *m* exile, banishment (destierro) ‖ confinement (encarcelamiento).

confinado *m* exile (exilado) ‖ prisoner (preso).

confinar *vi* to border, to be contiguous (*con* to); *Francia confina con España* France borders on Spain ‖ FIG to border; *su estado confina con la locura* his condition borders on madness.
◆ *vt* to confine; *confinar a uno en un monasterio* to confine s.o. in a monastery ‖ to banish, to exile (desterrar).
◆ *vpr* to shut o.s. away, to shut o.s. up.

confinidad *f* adjacency, nearness (proximidad).

confirmación *f* confirmation, corroboration; *la confirmación de una noticia* the confirmation of a piece of news ‖ REL confirmation.

confirmado, da *adj* confirmed.
◆ *m/f* confirmed man, woman.

confirmador, ra *adj* confirming, confirmative.
◆ *m/f* confirmer.

confirmando, da *m/f* REL confirmand.

confirmar *vt* to confirm; *confirmar una noticia* to confirm a piece of news; *su actitud confirma mis sospechas* his attitude confirms my suspicions ‖ to uphold (una decisión, un veredicto) ‖ to bear out, to corroborate (un testimonio) ‖ to establish, to confirm; *esta nueva novela le confirma como uno de nuestros mejores novelistas* this new novel confirms him as one of our best novelists ‖ REL to confirm ‖ *la excepción confirma la regla* the exception proves the rule.
◆ *vpr* to be confirmed.

confirmativo, va; confirmatorio, ria *adj* confirmative, confirmatory.

confiscable *adj* confiscable, liable to be confiscated.

confiscación *f* confiscation.

confiscador, ra *m/f* confiscator.

confiscar *vt* to confiscate.

confitado, da *adj* glacé, candied, crystallized; *peras confitadas* glacé pears ‖ — *castañas confitadas* iced chestnuts ‖ *frutas confitadas* comfits.

confitar *vt* to preserve in syrup (conservar) ‖ to coat with sugar, to candy.

confite *m* sweet [*US* candy].

confíteor *m* confiteor (oración) ‖ FIG full confession.

confitera *f* sweet box [*US* candy box] (caja de confites).

confitería *f* sweetshop, confectionery, confectioner's [*US* candy shop] (tienda) ‖ *AMER* tea room, tea shop (salón de té).

confitero, ra *m/f* confectioner.

confitura *f* jam, preserve (mermelada) ‖ crystallized fruit (fruta escarchada).

conflagración *f* blaze, conflagration ‖ FIG war (guerra) | flare-up (estallido de la guerra).

conflictivo, va *adj* of conflict (tiempos, etc.) ‖ conflicting (que están en conflicto).

conflicto *m* conflict, struggle; *conflicto entre dos naciones* conflict between two nations ‖ conflict, clash; *conflicto de ideas, opiniones* clash of ideas, opinions ‖ FIG quandary, dilemma (apuro) ‖ *conflicto laboral* industrial dispute, trade dispute.

confluencia *f* MED confluence ‖ confluence, concourse (de los ríos) ‖ FIG *punto de confluencia* common ground, meeting point.

confluente *adj* confluent.
◆ *m* confluence (de dos ríos).

confluir* *vi* to converge, to meet, to come together (ríos, caminos, etc.) ‖ to converge, to gather, to flock together (personas).

conformación *f* conformation, shape, structure || *vicio de conformación* malformation, defect in shape.

conformar *vt* to shape (dar forma a) || to adapt, to adjust, to conform; *conformar los gastos con los ingresos* to adjust spending to income || to reconcile (enemigos).
◆ *vi* to agree, to be of the same opinion (estar conformes) || *ser de buen conformar* to be easy going, to be easy to get on with (una persona).
◆ *vpr* to conform, to comply; *conformarse con la voluntad de Dios* to conform to *o* to comply with God's will || to agree; *sus ideas se conforman con las mías* his ideas agree with mine || to resign o.s. to the fact, to get used to the idea; *no iremos de vacaciones, hay que conformarse* we shan't go on holiday, we'll have to get used to the idea || to resign o.s.; *conformarse con su suerte* to resign o.s. to one's fate || to make do; *como no había carne se conformó con las verduras* as there was no meat he made do with vegetables || *conformarse con el parecer de uno* to agree with s.o.

conforme *adj* in keeping with; *el resultado está conforme con nuestras esperanzas* the result is in keeping with our hopes || in accordance with; *es conforme a la ley* it is in accordance with the law || satisfied; *se mostró conforme con la propuesta* he was satisfied with the suggestion || according; *conforme con la razón* according to reason || in agreement with; *declararse conforme con* to declare o.s. in agreement with || resigned; *conforme con su suerte* resigned to one's fate || seen and approved (un documento) || *estar* or *quedar conforme* to agree || *estar conformes con el precio* to be agreed on the price (las dos partes).
◆ *conj* as; *te describo la escena conforme la vi* I am describing the scene as I saw it || as soon as; *conforme amanezca, iré* as soon as day breaks, I shall go || as; *colocar a la gente conforme llegue* to seat the people as they arrive || — *conforme a* in accordance with, according to; *pagar a uno conforme a su trabajo* to pay s.o. according to his work; *conforme a lo establecido en la ley* according to what is laid down in the law || *según y conforme* it (all) depends (depende).
◆ *interj* okay, all right.
◆ *m* approval, endorsement.

conformemente *adv* in accordance, according; *conformemente con* in accordance with, according to.

conformidad *f* conformity, similarity (parecido) || consent, approval; *me ha dado su conformidad* he has given me his consent || agreement (acuerdo) || resignation, patience (tolerancia); *aceptar con conformidad las pruebas de la vida* to accept life's trials with resignation || — *conformidad en* conformity of || *cuente usted con mi conformidad* you can count on my agreement *o* approval || *de* or *en conformidad con* according to, in accordance *o* agreement with || *en esta* or *en tal conformidad* in that case || *no conformidad* nonconformity.

conformismo *m* conformism, orthodoxy, conventionalism || REL conformism.

conformista *adj* conformist, orthodox || REL conformist.
◆ *m/f* conformist.

confort *m* comfort; *esta casa tiene gran confort* this house has every comfort || *todo confort* all mod. cons. (en anuncios).

confortable *adj* comfortable (cómodo); *un sillón muy confortable* a very comfortable armchair.

confortablemente *adv* comfortably.

confortador, ra *adj* strengthening (que fortalece) || FIG comforting, cheering.

confortante *adj* strengthening (que fortalece) || FIG comforting, cheering.

confortar *vt* to strengthen, to give strength to (fortalecer) || to comfort, to console (consolar); *confortar a un desgraciado* to console an unhappy person || to cheer, to encourage (animar).

confortativo, va *adj* comforting, consoling || strengthening.

confraternal *adj* fraternal, brotherly.

confraternidad *f* brotherhood, confraternity, fellowship, fraternity (unión) || brotherliness, fellowship (amistad).

confraternizar *vi* to fraternize.

confrontación *f* confrontation, confronting || comparison, collation (de textos, etc.).

confrontar *vt* to confront (dos personas) || to face, to confront (afrentar) || to compare, to collate (comparar).
◆ *vi* *confrontar con* to be next to, to border on.
◆ *vpr* to confront, to face || *nos confrontamos con una gran dificultad* we are faced with a great difficulty.

confundible *adj* confusing, easily confused || *fácilmente confundible* easily confused.

confundido, da *adj* embarrassed (confuso) || mistaken, confused (equivocado).

confundir *vt* to blur (borrar los perfiles) || to confuse, to mistake (equivocarse); *confundir una calle con otra* to confuse one street with another, to mistake a street for another || to confuse, to confound (no distinguir) || to confuse; *me confundió con sus teorías* he confused me with his theories || to mix up, to jumble, to confound (mezclar) || to confound, to crush, to floor (dejar sin argumentos) || to humble, to humiliate (humillar) || to embarrass, to confuse, to confound (avergonzar) || to disconcert, to confuse, to perplex, to bewilder (turbar) || *hemos confundido la carretera* we took the wrong road.
◆ *vpr* to be embarrassed (avergonzarse) || to be perplexed *o* disconcerted *o* bewildered (turbarse) || to be mistaken, to make a mistake (equivocarse); *me he confundido* I have made a mistake || to be blurred (ponerse borroso) || to disappear; *se confundió con la muchedumbre* he disappeared into the crowd || to blend; *su ropa se confundía con los árboles* his clothes blended with the trees || to mingle (mezclarse); *los actores se confundían con el público* the actors mingled with the audience || to get mixed up; *los papeles se han confundido* the papers have got mixed up || *confundirse de número* to dial the wrong number (teléfono).

confusión *f* confusion, chaos, disorder (desorden); *en esta casa reina la mayor confusión* this house is in great confusion || embarrassment, shame (vergüenza) || confusion, perplexity, bewilderment (turbación) || mistake (equivocación) || JUR *confusión de penas* concurrency of sentences.

confusionismo *m* confusion.

confuso, sa *adj* mixed up, jumbled up (mezclado) || indistinct (ruido) || obscure (discurso, estilo, etc.) || blurred (recuerdo) || confused; *ideas confusas* confused ideas || embarrassed, confused (avergonzado) || perplexed, confused, disconcerted, bewildered (turbado) || blurred (imagen).

confutar *vt* to refute, to confute (impugnar).

congelable *adj* congealable.

congelación *f*; **congelamiento** *m* freezing, congelation || deep freezing (a temperatura muy baja) || COM freeze (en el sector económico); *congelación de salarios* wage freeze || MED frostbite.

congelado, da *adj* frozen || MED frostbitten.

congelador *m* freezer.

congelamiento *m* → **congelación.**

congelar *vt* to freeze; *carne congelada* frozen meat || to deep freeze (a temperatura muy baja) || to congeal (la sangre) || COM to freeze; *créditos, fondos congelados* frozen credits, funds || MED to affect with frostible.
◆ *vpr* to freeze (agua, etc.) || to congeal (aceite, grasas, sangre, etc.) || MED to become frostbitten.

congénere *adj* congenerous (músculo) || congeneric, of the same species (planta) || cognate (palabra).
◆ *mpl/fpl* sort, kind; *el ladrón y sus congéneres* the thief and his kind.

congeniar *vi* to get on; *congeniar con* to get on with.

congénitamente *adv* fundamentally.

congénito, ta *adj* congenital; *defecto congénito* congenital defect || FIG deep-seated, innate; *una mala fe congénita* innate dishonesty.

congestión *f* MED congestion || FIG congestion (de tráfico) || — *congestión cerebral* stroke, apoplexy || *congestión pulmonar* pneumonia.

congestionado, da *adj* congested || flushed (la cara).

congestionar *vt* to congest, to produce congestion in || *congestionar a uno* to make s.o. flush, to make s.o. go red [in the face].
◆ *vpr* MED to become congested || to turn purple *o* red in the face (una persona) || to flush, to go red (la cara) || to become congested (las calles).

congestivo, va *adj* congestive.

conglobar *vt* to conglobate.

conglomeración *f* conglomeration.

conglomerado, da *adj* conglomerate.
◆ *m* conglomerate || TECN cemented gravel || FIG collection, conglomeration.

conglomerar *vt* to conglomerate.
◆ *vpr* to conglomerate.

conglutinación *f* conglutination.

conglutinar *vt* to conglutinate.
◆ *vpr* to conglutinate.

Congo *npr m* GEOGR Congo.

congoja *f* anguish, distress (angustia) || grief, sorrow, affliction (tristeza).

congojoso, sa *adj* distressed (angustiado) || sad (triste) || distressing, afflicting (que causa congoja).

congoleño, ña; congolés, esa *adj/s* Congolese (del Congo).

congraciar *vt* to win over.
◆ *vpr* to ingratiate o.s. (*con* with).

congratulación *f* congratulation.

congratular *vt* to congratulate (felicitar); *congratular por un éxito* to congratulate on a success.
◆ *vpr* to be pleased, to congratulate o.s.; *congratularse de* or *por algo* to be pleased about *o* with sth., to congratulate o.s. on sth.

congratulatorio, ria *adj* congratulatory.

congregación *f* REL congregation || congregation, gathering, assembly (reunión) || *la congregación de los fieles* the Catholic Church, Christendom.

congregacionalismo *m* REL congregationalism.

congregacionalista *adj* REL congregationalist || *la Iglesia Congregacionalista* the Congregational Church.

congregado, da *adj* congregate.

congregante, ta *m/f* member of a congregation.

congregar, congregarse *v tr y pr* to congregate, to assemble.

congresal *m/f* AMER congress member.

congresista *m/f* delegate, congress member.

congreso *m* congress (conferencia, etc.) || Congress (del gobierno estadounidense).

congrio *m* conger eel, conger (pez).

congrua *f* extra emolument (para funcionarios) || adequate emolument (para eclesiásticos).

congruamente *adv* congruously, appropriately, fittingly.

congruencia *f* congruity || congruity, appropriateness, suitability || MAT congruence.

congruente *adj* suitable, fitting, appropriate (apropiado) || pertinent (pertinente) || MAT congruent.

congruo, grua *adj* congruous, fitting, suitable, appropriate || MAT congruent || *porción congrua* adequate emolument.

cónico, ca *adj* conical (de forma de cono) || conic (proyección, sección).
◆ *f* conic section, conic.

conidio *m* BOT conidium.

conífero, ra *adj* BOT coniferous.
◆ *f* conifer.

coniforme *adj* coniform, cone-shaped.

conjetura *f* conjecture, surmise; *hacer conjeturas sobre el futuro* to make conjectures about the future.

conjeturable *adj* supposable, presumable.

conjetural *adj* conjectural.

conjeturar *vt* to conjecture, to surmise.

conjugable *adj* GRAM that can be conjugated, conjugable.

conjugación *f* GRAM & BIOL conjugation.

conjugado, da *adj* conjugated || FIG combined.

conjugar *vt* GRAM to conjugate || FIG to combine.
◆ *vpr* GRAM to be conjugated, to conjugate || FIG to fit together.

conjunción *f* conjunction.

conjuntado, da *adj* coordinated; *un equipo bien conjuntado* a well-coordinated team.

conjuntamente *adv* jointly, together.

conjuntar *vt* to coordinate; *conjuntar un equipo* to coordinate a team.

conjuntiva *f* ANAT conjunctiva.

conjuntivitis *f* MED conjunctivitis.

conjuntivo, va *adj* GRAM & MED conjunctive.

conjunto, ta *adj* combined, joint, conjoint; *esfuerzos conjuntos* combined efforts || joint; *la base aérea conjunta de Torrejón* the joint air force base at Torrejón.
◆ *m* collection; *un conjunto de casas* a collection of houses || whole; *el conjunto de sus obras* the whole of his works; *un conjunto decorativo* a decorative whole || suit, outfit, ensemble (vestido) || twinset (de jerseys) || MÚS ensemble; *conjunto vocal* vocal ensemble | group (de música pop) || set (de cosas diversas) || suite (de muebles) || — *conjunto urbanístico* or *residencial* housing estate || *de conjunto* overall || *en conjunto* on the whole, altogether || *en su conjunto* as a whole || *formar un conjunto* to form a whole.

conjura; conjuración *f* conspiracy, plot.

conjurado, da *m/f* conspirator, plotter.

conjurador *m* exorcist.

conjurar *vi* to plot, to conspire.
◆ *vt* to exorcise (exorcizar) || to beg; *os conjuro que vengáis* I beg you to come || to stave off, to avert, to ward off (un peligro) || to get rid of (pensamientos).
◆ *vpr* to conspire, to plot; *conjurarse contra la República* to conspire against the Republic.

conjuro *m* exorcism (exorcismo) || plea, entreaty, supplication (ruego) || incantation, spell (encantamiento).

conllevar *vt* to put up with, to bear, to endure; *conllevar una enfermedad, una persona* to put up with an illness, with s.o. || to bear (una pena) || to assist, to help (ayudar).

conmemorable *adj* memorable, noteworthy.

conmemoración *f* commemoration, remembrance || *conmemoración de los difuntos* All Souls' Day.

conmemorar *vt* to commemorate.

conmemorativo, va; conmemoratorio, ria *adj* commemorative || memorial (monumento).

conmensurable *adj* commensurable.

conmigo *pron pers* with me; *ven conmigo* come with me || to me; *es muy amable conmigo* he is very kind to me || — *no tengo dinero conmigo* I haven't got any money on me || *tendrá que habérselas conmigo* he'll have me to deal with.

conminación *f* commination, threat.

conminador, ra *adj* threatening, menacing.

conminar *vt* to threaten, to menace (amenazar) || to warn (avisar).

conminativo, va; conminatorio, ria *adj* threatening, menacing, comminatory || coercive (sentencia).

conmiseración *f* commiseration, pity, sympathy.

conmoción *f* shock || tremor, earthquake (terremoto) || FIG shock; *la noticia de su muerte me produjo una gran conmoción* the news of his death was a great shock to me | upheaval; *una conmoción política* a political upheaval | commotion, disturbance (trastorno) || MED *conmoción cerebral* concussion.

conmocionar *vt* MED to concuss | to shock || FIG to upset, to disturb, to trouble.

conmovedor, ra *adj* moving, touching, poignant; *un discurso, un espectáculo conmovedor* a moving speech, scene.

conmover* *vt* to move, to touch (enternecer, emocionar, impresionar, etc.); *su desgracia me conmovió mucho* his misfortune touched me deeply || to shake; *un terremoto conmovió la ciudad* an earthquake shook the town || FIG to shake; *conmover la fe de uno* to shake s.o.'s faith || *me conmovió mucho ver cómo se ocupaba de mí* I was really touched by the way he took care of me.
◆ *vpr* to be touched, to be moved, to be affected; *no se conmovió* he was not moved || to be shaken (un edificio, etc.).

conmutabilidad *f* commutability.

conmutable *adj* commutable.

conmutación *f* commutation; *conmutación de pena* commutation of sentence || pun, play on words (figura retórica).

conmutador *m* ELECTR switch, commutator.

conmutar *vt* JUR to commute; *conmutar la pena de muerte por la de cadena perpetua* to commute the death sentence to life imprisonment || to exchange; *conmutar una cosa por otra* to exchange one thing for another || ELECTR to commutate, to commute.

conmutativo, va *adj* commutative.

connatural *adj* connatural, innate, inherent, inborn.

connaturalización *f* adaptation, adjustment.

connaturalizarse *vpr* to adjust o.s., to adapt o.s. (*con* to) (adaptarse) || to become accustomed (*con* to) (acostumbrarse).

connivencia *f* connivance, complicity || *estar en connivencia con* to be in league *o* in collusion with.

connotación *f* connotation || distant relationship (connotado).

connotado *m* distant relationship.

connotar *vt* to connote.

connubial *adj* POÉT connubial, conjugal.

connubio *m* POÉT matrimony, marriage.

cono *m* BOT & ANAT cone || MAT cone; *cono circular* circular cone; *cono recto* right cone; *cono truncado* truncated cone || ASTR *cono de sombra* umbra.

conocedor, ra *adj* expert, skilled || *ser conocedor de las últimas noticias* to be well up on the latest news.
◆ *m/f* expert, connoisseur; *ser conocedor de caballos* to be an expert on horses, to be a connoisseur of horses.
◆ *m* head herdsman.

conocer* *vt* to know; *le conozco sólo de vista* I only know him by sight || to know; *conocer el latín* to know Latin; *no conoce nada de pintura* he knows nothing about painting || to know, to recognize (distinguir); *conocer a uno por la voz* to recognize s.o. by his voice || to meet, to make the acquaintance of, to get to know; *le conocí en Londres el año pasado* I met him last year in London || to be (estar); *cuando conocí Londres por primera vez* the first time I was in London || to get to know; *ir a conocer un país* to go to get to know a country || to know (en el sentido bíblico) || *dar algo a conocer a uno* to make sth. known to s.o., to inform s.o. of sth., to tell s.o. sth., to let s.o. know sth. || — *darse a conocer* to make o.s. known || *no conocer a uno ni por asomo* not to know s.o. from Adam.
◆ *vi* *conocer de* to know about (saber) || JUR *conocer de* or *en* to try, to hear (una causa).
◆ *vpr* to know o.s.; *conócete a ti mismo* know yourself || to know each other (dos personas) || to meet, to get to know each other; *se conocieron en un bar* they met in a bar || — *se conoce a la legua* it stands out a mile || *se conoce que* apparently; *se conoce que no puede venir* he can't come apparently; you can tell; *se conoce que el motor está estropeado por el ruido que hace* you can tell that there is sth. wrong with the motor by the noise it makes.

conocible *adj* knowable.

conocidamente *adv* evidently, clearly, obviously.

conocido, da *adj* known || well-known; *un abogado conocido* a well-known lawyer || *el tema no me es conocido* I am not familiar with the subject.
◆ *m/f* acquaintance; *un conocido mío* an acquaintance of mine.

conocimiento *m* knowledge; *tener un conocimiento profundo del inglés* to have a thorough knowledge of English || consciousness (sentido); *perder, recobrar el conocimiento* to lose, to regain consciousness || good sense, sensibleness (sensatez) || acquaintance (conocido) || COM bill of lading (de la carga de un buque) | proof of identity (del portador de una letra de cambio, etc.) || — *con conocimiento de causa* with full knowledge of the facts || *dar conocimiento de algo a uno* to make sth. known to s.o., to inform s.o. of sth. || *habla con conocimiento de causa* he knows perfectly what he is talking about || *ha perdido el conocimiento* he is unconscious, he has lost consciousness || *lo hizo con conocimiento de causa* he was perfectly aware of what he was doing || *poner algo en conocimiento de uno* to make sth. known to

s.o., to inform s.o. of sth. || *venir en conocimiento* or *llegar al conocimiento de uno* to come to s.o.'s knowledge *o* notice *o* attention.
◆ *pl* knowledge *sing.*

conoidal *adj* MAT conoid.

conoide *m* MAT conoid.

conopeo *m* canopy (del sagrario).

conopial *adj* *arco conopial* ogee arch.

conque *conj* FAM so; *tú eres un ignorante, conque cállate* you don't know anything, so be quiet; *¿conque sigue convencido?* so you're still convinced (then)?; *¿conque te mudas de casa?* so you're moving house (then)? || so, whereupon; *conque fuimos a la cama* so we went to bed.

conquense *adj* [of *o* from] Cuenca.
◆ *m/f* inhabitant *o* native of Cuenca.

conquista *f* conquest || FIG *hacer una conquista* to make a conquest, to win s.o.'s heart (enamorar a alguien).

conquistador, ra *adj* conquering || FIG *tiene un aire conquistador* he looks a real lady-killer.
◆ *m/f* conqueror.
◆ *m* conqueror; *Guillermo el Conquistador* William the Conqueror || conquistador (de América) || FIG & FAM Don Juan, lady-killer, Casanova.

conquistar *vt* to conquer; *conquistar un reino* to conquer a kingdom || to win (un puesto, el mercado) || FIG to win over; *por su simpatía nos ha conquistado a todos* he won us all over by his kindness | to win the heart of, to win (a una mujer) || *conquistar laureles* to win glory.

Conrado *npr m* Conrad.

consabido, da *adj* usual, traditional; *el consabido discurso inaugural* the usual opening speech || well-known (muy conocido) || abovementioned (anteriormente citado).

consagración *f* consecration (del pan y del vino, de un obispo) || consecration, dedication (dedicación) || FIG establishment; *la consagración de una costumbre* the establishment of a custom || recognition (de un escritor, de un artista, etc.) || *la consagración de la Primavera* the Rite of Spring (de Stravinsky).

consagrado, da *adj* consecrated || dedicated, consecrated (dedicado) || recognized (artista, escritor) || time-honoured, stock, household (frase, etc.) || time-honoured (costumbre).

consagrante *adj m* consecrating.
◆ *m* consecrating priest, consecrator.

consagrar *vt* REL to consecrate (una iglesia, un obispo, el pan y el vino) || FIG to dedicate, to devote; *consagrar su vida a* to dedicate one's life to | to accept, to recognize; *consagrar una nueva palabra* to accept a new word | to confirm as (un escritor, un artista) || *vino de consagrar* communion wine.
◆ *vpr* to dedicate o.s., to devote o.s.; *consagrarse al estudio* to dedicate o.s. to studying || to establish o.s., to prove o.s. (como artista, etc.).

consanguíneo, a *adj* consanguineous | *hermano consanguíneo, hermana consanguínea* half brother, half sister || *matrimonio consanguíneo* intermarriage.
◆ *m/f* blood relation.

consanguinidad *f* consanguinity, blood relationship.

consciencia *f* → **conciencia.**

consciente *adj* conscious, aware; *consciente de sus derechos* aware of one's rights || of sound mind (sano de juicio) || MED conscious || reliable, responsible (responsable).

conscientemente *adv* knowingly, consciously.

conscripción *f* AMER conscription (reclutamiento).

conscripto *adj m* conscript; *padre conscripto* conscript father (en la antigua Roma).
◆ *m* AMER conscript (quinto).

consecución *f* obtaining; *la consecución de un premio literario* the obtaining of a literary prize || realization; *la consecución de un deseo* the realization of a wish || success (de un proyecto) || attainment (de un objetivo) || consecution (encadenamiento) || *de difícil consecución* hard to obtain, difficult to obtain.

consecuencia *f* consequence || result, outcome (resultado) || consistency (firmeza) || — *a* or *como consecuencia de* as a result of, as a consequence of || *atenerse a* or *aceptar las consecuencias* to suffer the consequences || *en consecuencia* consequently, therefore || *por consecuencia* consequently, therefore || *sacar en consecuencia* to conclude, to come to the conclusion || *ser de consecuencia* to be of importance *o* of consequence || *sufrir las consecuencias* to suffer the consequences || *tener* or *traer buenas consecuencias* to do good, to be beneficial || *tener* or *traer malas consecuencias* to have unfortunate consequences, to do harm || *traer como consecuencia* to result in.

consecuente *adj* consistent || FIL consequent.
◆ *m* consequent.

consecuentemente *adv* consistently || consequently, therefore (por consiguiente).

consecutivo, va *adj* consecutive.

conseguir* *vt* to obtain, to come by; *consiguió un permiso* he obtained a licence || to get, to get hold of; *conseguir billetes para el partido de fútbol* to get hold of tickets for the football match || to obtain, to find, to get; *le consiguió una buena colocación* he found a good job for him || to win (una victoria, fama) || to manage; *conseguí ver al ministro* I managed to see the minister || to attain, to reach, to achieve (un objetivo) || — *conseguir la mayoría* to gain *o* to secure *o* to win a majority (en una votación) || *dar por conseguido* to take for granted || *una cosa muy conseguida* a very successful thing.

conseja *f* legend, tale, fable.

consejería *f* counsellorship (cargo) || autonomous government division (administración).

Consejería *f* Council (establecimiento).

consejero, ra *m/f* adviser, counsellor (persona que aconseja) || adviser, consultant; *consejero técnico* technical adviser || member (de un consejo de administración, etc.) || councillor (miembro de un consejo); *consejero en Corte* Court councillor || — *consejero delegado* managing director || FIG & FAM *ser buen consejero* to give sound advice.

consejo *m* advice, counsel; *me pidió consejo* he asked me for advice, he sought my advice; *tomar consejo de uno* to take s.o.'s advice || piece of advice; *me dio un consejo* he gave me a piece of advice || hint, tip; *le di un consejo muy útil para preparar un buen té* I gave her a very useful hint for making a good cup of tea || council; *Consejo de Estado* Council of State || — *celebrar consejo* to hold council || ECON *consejo de administración* board of directors (cuerpo), board meeting, meeting of the board of directors (reunión) || *Consejo de Ciento* (formerly) the town council of Barcelona || *consejo de disciplina* disciplinary council || JUR *consejo de familia* board of guardians || *consejo de guerra* court-martial || HIST *consejo de la Inquisición* Inquisitional Court || *consejo de ministros* council of ministers, cabinet (cuerpo), cabinet meeting (reunión) || *Consejo europeo* European Council.
◆ *pl* advice *sing*; *hay que seguir los consejos del médico* you must follow the doctor's advice.
— OBSERV This word must not be confused with *concejo*.

consenso *m* consent (consentimiento); *de mutuo consenso* by common consent || consensus (opinión general).

consensual *adj* JUR consensual (contrato).

consentido, da *adj* spoilt, spoiled, pampered (mimado); *niño consentido* spoilt child || easy going, indulgent (demasiado tolerante) || complaisant (marido).

consentidor, ra *adj* tolerant, acquiescent (tolerante) || complaisant (marido) || indulgent (madre).

consentimiento *m* consent.

consentir* *vi* to consent; *consentir en algo* to consent to sth.; *consentir en hacer algo* to consent to do sth.
◆ *vt* to allow, to tolerate (tolerar); *no consiento que le ridiculicen* I cannot tolerate their ridiculing him *o* his being ridiculed, I won't allow them to ridicule him || to let, to allow; *no tienes por qué consentirle que traiga a todos sus amigos a tu casa* there's no reason why you should let him bring all his friends to your house || to spoil, to pamper (mimar) || to stand, to bear (soportar); *el estante no consiente más peso* the shelf won't stand any more weight.
◆ *vpr* to break, to give way.

conserje *m* porter (en una empresa, un ministerio) || hall porter (de un hotel).

conserjería *f* porter's lodge || reception desk (de un hotel).

conserva *f* preserve, preserves *pl*; *conserva de fresas* strawberry preserve || preserving (acción) || — *carne en conserva* canned *o* pickled meat || MAR *navegar en conserva* to sail in convoy.
◆ *pl* tinned *o* canned food *sing*.

conservación *f* preservation (de alimentos, etc.) || conservation (del calor, de la energía) || upkeep, maintenance (de un edificio) || *instinto de conservación* instinct of self-preservation.

conservador, ra *adj* conservative; *partido conservador* conservative party.
◆ *m/f* conservative (en política) || curator (de museo).

conservaduría *f* curatorship (cargo) || curator's office (oficina).

conservadurismo *m* conservatism.

conservar *vt* to keep (un secreto, sus amigos, etc.) || to preserve (la salud, un edificio, etc.) || to preserve; *el frío conserva los alimentos* cold preserves food || to keep in, to retain; *la lana conserva el calor* wool keeps in the warmth || to tin, to can (en lata), to bottle (en bocal); *conservar los tomates* to tin tomatoes || to retain, to have; *conserva un buen recuerdo de su viaje* he retains a pleasant memory of his journey || — *bien conservado* well-preserved || *conserva la costumbre de levantarse muy temprano* he still gets up very early || *conserva una cicatriz de la guerra* he still has a scar from the war || *conserve su derecha* keep to the right || *el ejercicio conserva la salud* exercise keeps one fit.
◆ *vpr* to keep; *conservarse con* or *en salud* to keep fit || to save *o* to conserve one's strength; *me conservo para mañana* I am conserving my strength for tomorrow || to remain (ruinas, etc.) || to keep (alimentos).

conservatismo *m* AMER conservatism.

conservatorio, ria *adj* conservatory.
◆ *m* conservatory, conservatoire, academy, school (de música, etc.) || AMER greenhouse (invernadero).

conservería *f* canning industry, tinned-food industry (industria) || cannery (fábrica).

conservero, ra *adj* canning, tinned-food; *industria conservera* canning industry, tinned-food industry.
◆ *m/f* tinned-food manufacturer, canner (fabricante).

considerable *adj* considerable.

consideración *f* consideration, regard, esteem; *un hombre que merece nuestra mayor consideración* a man worthy of our highest consideration || attention; *un asunto digno de la mayor consideración* a matter that deserves the greatest attention || reason, consideration, motive (motivo) || consideration, respect; *tratarle a uno sin consideración* to treat s.o. without consideration || consideration, deliberation (deliberación) || — *de consideración* considerable, great; *daños de consideración* considerable damage; serious; *quemaduras de consideración* serious burns || AMER *de mi consideración, de nuestra consideración* Dear Sir, Dear Sirs [beginning of a letter] || *en consideración a* considering, in consideration of || *falta de consideración* lack of consideration || *por consideración a* out of consideration for, out of respect for, out of regard for; *no le echan por consideración a su padre* they do not sack him out of consideration for his father || *ser de consideración* to be worthy of consideration || *sin consideración a* irrespective of, regardless of || *tener consideraciones con* to be considerate *o* thoughtful towards || *tomar* or *tener en consideración* to take into consideration, to take into account || *tratar una cosa con consideración* to treat sth. with care.

considerado, da *adj* respected (respetado) || considerate, thoughtful (atento) || considered; *los puntos considerados* the items considered || *bien considerado* all things considered.

considerando *m* whereas (de una resolución).

considerar *vt* to consider, to ponder, to weigh up; *considerar un asunto en* or *bajo todos sus aspectos* to consider every aspect of a matter || to give consideration; *le pido que considere mi propósito con la debida atención* I ask you to give my proposal all due consideration || to think about, to consider; *estoy considerando las ventajas y desventajas de su oferta* I am thinking about the advantages and disadvantages of your offer || to bear in mind, to remember; *tienes que considerar que aún es un niño* you have to bear in mind that he is still a child || to consider, to think; *no le considero capaz de tal acción* I do not consider him capable *o* think he is capable of doing such a thing || to consider, to esteem, to regard, to respect; *se le considera mucho en los círculos literarios* he is highly considered in literary circles || — *considerando que* bearing in mind that, considering that || *considerar a alguien con desprecio* to look down on s.o. || *considerar a alguien responsable* to hold s.o. responsible.
◆ *vpr* to consider o.s. (uno mismo) || to be considered; *se considera grosero* it is considered rude.

consigna *f* orders *pl*, instructions *pl* || watchword, slogan (slogan) || left-luggage office [US check-room] (en las estaciones) || *violar la consigna* to disobey orders.

consignación *f* allocation; *consignación de créditos* allocation of credits || COM consignment (de mercancías) || deposit (de dinero) || noting down, recording (citación) || — *caja de depósitos y consignaciones* Deposit and Consignment Office || *mercancías en consignación* goods on consignment.

consignador *m* COM consignor, consigner.

consignar *vt* to allocate, to assign, to earmark; *consignar créditos* to allocate credits || to consign (mercancías) || to deposit (dinero) || to send (enviar) || to note down, to record (citar) || to write in (escribir).

consignatario *m* COM consignee || JUR depositary, trustee || MAR *consignatario de buques* ship broker, shipping agent.

consigo *pron pers* with him, with her; *se lo llevó consigo* he took it with him || with you (only used with *usted* and *ustedes*); *¿ha traído usted dinero consigo?* have you brought any money with you? || with them; *se llevaron a sus hijos consigo* they took their children with them || — *consigo mismo* with himself, with herself, with o.s; *está rabioso consigo mismo* he is furious with himself; with yourself, with yourselves (only used with *usted* and *ustedes*); *tienen que entrar en cuentas consigo mismos* you have to reckon with yourselves; with themselves; *están muy contentos consigo mismos* they are very pleased with themselves || FAM *no tenerlas todas consigo* not to rate one's chances, to have one's doubts (no estar muy seguro de algo), to have the wind up (tener miedo) || FIG *traer consigo* to entail, to involve, to bring about; *esta medida traerá consigo numerosas dificultades* this measure will entail many difficulties.

consiguiente *adj* resulting, arising; *los gastos consiguientes a mi viaje* the expenses resulting from my trip || consequent; *mi viaje y los gastos consiguientes* my trip and its consequent expenses || *por consiguiente* consequently, therefore.

consiguientemente *adv* consequently, accordingly, therefore.

consistencia *f* consistency, consistence || — *sin consistencia* insubstantial; *argumento sin consistencia* insubstantial argument; without body, thin; *una salsa sin consistencia* a sauce without body, a thin sauce || *tomar consistencia* to materialize, to take form (una idea), to thicken (crema, mayonesa).

consistente *adj* firm, solid (firme) || thick (salsa, crema, etc.) || sound, solid (argumento) || consisting; *una cena consistente en platos exóticos* a dinner consisting of exotic dishes.

consistir *vi* to lie in; *la felicidad consiste en la virtud* happiness lies in virtue || to consist of, to be composed of; *su fortuna consiste en acciones* his fortune consists of stocks || to be up to; *en ti consiste el hacerlo* it is up to you to do it || *el truco consiste en hacerlo rápido* the trick is to do it quickly.

consistorial *adj* REL consistorial || *casa consistorial* town hall.

consistorio *m* consistory (de cardenales) || town council (concejo) || town hall (casa consistorial).

consocio, cia *m/f* fellow member || COM copartner, joint partner.

consola *f* console table (mueble) || console (de órgano, de ordenador).

consolación *f* consolation.

consolador, ra *adj* consoling, comforting.
◆ *m/f* consoler, comforter.

consolar* *vt* to console, to comfort; *consolar a los desgraciados* to console the unfortunate || to console; *consolar a uno por la pérdida de su padre* to console s.o. for the loss of his father.
◆ *vpr* to console o.s., to comfort o.s. || to get over (reponerse); *consolarse de una pérdida* to get over a loss.

consolidación *f* bracing, strengthening, consolidation (de una construcción) || FIG consolidation, strengthening (fortalecimiento) || consolidation (unificación) || consolidation (de una deuda) || MIL strengthening.

consolidar *vt* to brace, to strengthen, to consolidate; *consolidar una pared* to brace a wall || FIG to consolidate, to strengthen; *consolidar los poderes presidenciales* to consolidate presidential powers || to consolidate (unificar); *consolidar las posesiones del rey* to consolidate the king's possessions || COM to consolidate (una deuda flotante) || MIL to strengthen, to consolidate; *consolidar el frente oriental* to consolidate the eastern front.
◆ *vpr* to consolidate.

consomé *m* consommé (caldo).

consonancia *f* MÚS consonance || consonance (rima) || FIG agreement, harmony (similitud) || *en consonancia con* in harmony with.

consonante *adj* consonant (que consuena) || GRAM consonantal.
◆ *f* consonant (letra).

consonántico, ca *adj* consonantal.

consonantismo *m* consonantism.

consonar* *vi* to rhyme (rimar) || MÚS to be harmonious || FIG to agree, to harmonize.

consorcio *m* association (asociación) || consortium (comercial); *consorcio bancario* banking consortium || conjunction (de circunstancias) || fellowship, harmony (unión) || *vivir en buen consorcio* to live *o* to get on well together.

consorte *m/f* spouse, consort (cónyuge) || companion (persona que comparte la existencia de otra) || *príncipe consorte* prince consort.
◆ *pl* JUR joint litigants (que litigan juntos) || accomplices.

conspicuo, cua *adj* illustrious, prominent, eminent.

conspiración *f* conspiracy, plot; *conspiración contra el Estado* conspiracy against the State.

conspirador, ra *m/f* conspirator, plotter.

conspirar *vi* to conspire, to plot; *conspirar contra el Estado* to conspire against the State || FIG to conspire (*a* to).

constancia *f* constancy || perseverance; *trabajar con constancia* to work with perseverance || certainty (certeza) || proof, evidence (prueba); *no hay constancia de ello* there is no proof of that || *dejar constancia de* to put on record (en un acta), to demonstrate, to prove (atestiguar).

constante *adj* constant (que no cambia) || steadfast (friend, love).
◆ *f* MAT constant || MED *constantes vitales* vital signs.

constantemente *adv* constantly.

Constantino *npr m* Constantine.

Constantinopla *n pr* GEOGR Constantinople.

Constanza *n pr* GEOGR Constance || *lago de Constanza* Lake Constance.

constar *vi* to consist, to be composed; *este informe consta de tres partes* this report consists of three parts || to be established *o* stated; *consta por este documento que* it is established by this document that || to be included, to be stated; *esto consta en el contrato* this is stated in the contract || to be listed; *no consta en los archivos* it is no listed in the archives || to appear, to figure; *palabra que no consta en un diccionario* word which does not appear in a dictionary || — *hacer constar* to point out; *el periodista hace constar el incremento de la producción* the journalist points out the increase in production; to mention, to state, to include (en un informe) || *hacer constar por escrito* to register, to write down (en general), to put on record (en un acta) || *me consta que* I am certain *o* sure that, I feel certain *o* sure that || *que conste que* let be clearly understood that || *y para que así conste* and for the record.

constatación *f* verification (verificación) || recording (consignación).

constatar *vt* to verify (averiguar) || to note, to find (encontrar) || to record (consignar).
— OBSERV *Constatar* and *constatación* are Gallicisms.

constelación *f* ASTR constellation.

constelado, da *adj* star-spangled, starry (estrellado); *cielo constelado* star-spangled sky || FIG strewn, bespangled, studded (sembrado); *manto constelado de pedrerías* mantle strewn with precious stones.

constelar *vt* to constellate, to spangle; *las estrellas que constelan la bóveda celeste* the stars that spangle the canopy of heaven.
— OBSERV *Constelado* and *constelar* are Gallicisms.

consternación *f* consternation, dismay (desolación); *producir consternación* to cause dismay.

consternar *vt* to dismay.
◆ *vpr* to be dismayed; *se consternó con la muerte de...* he was dismayed by the death of...

constipación *f* cold (resfriado) || constipation (estreñimiento).

constipado, da *adj* *estar constipado* to have a cold.
◆ *m* cold (catarro); *tengo un constipado muy fuerte* I have a bad cold.

constipar *vt* to give a cold to.
◆ *vpr* to catch a cold (acatarrarse).

constitución *f* constitution (acción) || setting up, constitution (establecimiento) || ANAT & JUR constitution.

constitucional *adj* constitutional; *ley constitucional* constitutional law.

constitucionalidad *f* constitutionality.

constitucionalismo *m* constitutionalism.

constitucionalizar *vt* to constitutionalize.

constituir* *vt* to constitute, to form; *esta molécula está constituida por tres átomos* this molecule is constituted by three atoms || to constitute; *las autoridades oficialmente constituidas* the duly constituted authorities; *la discreción constituye su encanto* discretion constitutes her charm || to set up, to establish, to create (crear) || to make; *Kubitschek constituyó Brasilia en capital del Brasil* Kubitschek made Brasilia the capital of Brazil || to be; *esto no constituye obstáculo* this is no obstacle || *lo constituyen cinco partes* it consists of *o* it is composed of *o* it is made up of five parts.
◆ *vpr* to constitute o.s., to set o.s. up as; *me constituyo en juez* I constitute myself judge || to be established (establecerse) || — JUR *constituirse parte civil* to bring a civil action || *constituirse por* or *en fiador de* to answer for || *constituirse prisionero* to give o.s. up.

constitutivo, va *adj* constitutive (*de* of) || constituent, component (constituyente).

constituyente *adj* constituent; *asamblea constituyente* constituent assembly || constituent, component (componente).
◆ *m* constituent; *el hidrógeno es un constituyente del agua* hydrogen is one of the constituents of water.

constreñimiento *m* constraint, compulsion || restriction (restricción).

constreñir; costreñir* *vt* to constrain, to compel, to force (obligar); *constreñir a uno a que salga* to constrain s.o. to leave || MED to constrict (apretar) || to restrict (restringir).

constricción *f* constriction.

constrictor, ra *adj* constricting, constrictive || ZOOL *boa constrictor* boa constrictor.
◆ *m* constrictor (músculo).

constringente *adj* constringent.

construcción *f* construction, building; *la construcción de un puente* the construction of a bridge || construction, building industry; *trabaja en la construcción* he works in construction || building; *una construcción elevada* a tall building || GRAM construction || — *construcción de buques* or *naval* shipbuilding || *en* or *en vías de construcción* under construction || *solar para construcción* building site.

constructivo, va *adj* constructive; *crítica constructiva* constructive criticism.

constructor, ra *adj* building, construction; *empresa constructora* building firm, construction company.
◆ *m/f* manufacturer (de automóviles), builder (de edificios), constructor (de maquinaria) || *constructor de buques* or *naval* shipbuilder.

construir* *vt* to manufacture (automóviles), to build, to construct (edificios, barcos) || MAT to construct || GRAM to construe.

consubstanciación *f* consubstantiation.

consubstancial *adj* consubstantial.

consubstancialidad *f* consubstantiality.

consuegro, gra *m/f* father-in-law, mother-in-law of one's child.

consuelo *f* solace, consolation, comfort; *la lectura es su único consuelo* reading is his only solace || relief (alivio); *su marcha ha sido un consuelo para mí* his departure has been a relief for me.

consuetudinario, ria *adj* consuetudinary, customary (habitual) || *derecho consuetudinario* Common Law (en Inglaterra), Consuetudinary Law (en otros países).

cónsul *m* consul.

cónsula *f* FAM consul (mujer cónsul).

consulado *m* consulate (oficina) || consulship (cargo).

consular *adj* consular.

consulta *f* consultation (acción) || opinion, advice (dictamen) || consultation, conference (de varios médicos) || consulting room, surgery (consultorio de un médico) || — *consulta a domicilio* home visit || *consulta previa petición de hora* consultation by appointment || *horas de consulta* consulting hours, surgery hours || *obra de consulta* reference book || *pasar la consulta, tener la consulta* to hold surgery (un médico), to have consultation (un especialista) || REL *sacra consulta* judiciary court.

consultación *f* consultation (entre abogados o médicos).

consultar *vt/vi* to consult; *tengo que consultar con mis amigos* I must consult with my friends || to consult; *consultar el diccionario* to consult the dictionary || to look up, to check; *consultar una palabra en el diccionario* to look up a word in the dictionary || — *consultar con un abogado* to consult a lawyer, to take legal advice || *consultar con un médico* to consult a doctor, to take medical advice || FIG *consultarlo con la almohada* to sleep on it.

consultivo, va *adj* advisory, consultative.

consultor, ra *adj* consultant, consulting (médico).
◆ *m* advisor (dignatario de la Corte de Roma); *consultor del Santo Oficio* advisor of the Holy Office || Consultant (asesor) || *ingeniero consultor* engineering consultant, consulting engineer.

consultorio *m* consulting room, surgery (de un médico), surgery (de un dentista), office (de un abogado) || outpatients' department (dispensario) || technical advice bureau (consejos técnicos) || information bureau (de información) || *consultorio sentimental* problem page *o* column, advice page *o* column (en una revista).

consumación *f* consummation, completion; *la consumación de su obra* the consummation of his work || perpetration (de un crimen) || consummation (del matrimonio) || *hasta la consumación de los siglos* to the end of time.

consumado, da *adj* consummated || FIG consummate, perfect; *sabiduría consumada* consummate wisdom | accomplished; *bailarín consumado* accomplished dancer || FAM absolute, perfect; *un bribón, un imbécil consumado* a perfect scoundrel, an absolute fool || *hecho consumado* accomplished fact.

consumar *vt* to complete (terminar) || to carry out (hacer) || to perpetrate (un crimen) || to consummate (el matrimonio, un sacrificio) || to carry out (sentencia).

consumición *f* drink (bebida) || consumption (acción) || *consumición mínima* cover charge (en un club).

consumido, da *adj* FIG emaciated, wasting away (flaco) | exhausted (agotado) | consumed (atormentado); *consumido por los celos* consumed with jealousy | undermined; *su salud consumida por la fiebre* his health undermined by fever.

consumidor, ra *m/f* consumer.

consumir *vt* to consume, to destroy (destruir); *el fuego consumió todos los edificios* the blaze consumed all the buildings || to dry up, to evaporate (un líquido) || to consume, to eat (comestibles, bebidas) || to consume (gastar); *consumir gasolina* to consume petrol || to use (utilizar) || FIG to take up; *esta tarea consumía todo su tiempo* this task took up all his time | to wear away; *las preocupaciones le consumían* worry was wearing him away | to wear out (agotar); *tanto viajar lo consume* all that travelling wears him out | to undermine, to sap, to consume; *su pasión le consumía las fuerzas* his passion undermined his strength | to gnaw at (carcomer) | to wear down, to try (paciencia) | to get on one's nerves (poner nervioso) || — FIG *el tiempo lo consume todo* time is all-consuming | *estar consumido por* to be eaten up *o* consumed with (celos, envidia), to be consumed with, to be tormented with (una pasión), to be tormented by (el dolor).
◆ *vpr* to waste away, to pine (away); *consumirse de pena* to waste away with grief || to wear o.s. out; *se consumió en esfuerzos inútiles* he wore himself out in useless efforts || to boil away (líquido) || to waste away; *este anciano se está consumiendo* this old man is wasting away || to burn itself out; *la vela se ha consumido* the candle has burnt itself out || — *consumirse con la fiebre* to waste away with fever || *consumirse de envidia* to be eaten up with jealousy || *consumirse de fastidio* to be bored to death || *consumirse de impaciencia* to be burning with impatience.

consumo *m* consumption (de víveres, etc.) || — *bienes de consumo* consumer goods || *sociedad de consumo* consumer society.
◆ *pl* toll *sing.*

consunción *f* MED consumption.

consuno (de) *adv* with one accord, by common consent (decidir), in concert (actuar).

consuntivo, va *adj* consuming.

contabilidad *f* bookkeeping, accounting (tiendas y firmas); *contabilidad por partida doble, simple* double-entry bookkeeping, single-entry bookkeeping || accountancy (profesión); *contabilidad mecanizada* machine accountancy || *contabilidad de costos* cost accounting.

contabilizar *vt* COM to enter [in the books].

contable *adj* countable (calculable) || relatable (decible).
◆ *m* bookkeeper (en una empresa) || accountant (de varias empresas).

contacto *m* contact; *ciertas enfermedades se transmiten por simple contacto* certain diseases are transmitted by simple contact || AUT contact || FIG contact, touch; *poner en contacto a dos personas* to put two people in touch with each other | contact; *establecer contactos radiofónicos* to establish radio contact || — *contacto sexual* sexual contact, sexual intercourse || *entrar* or *ponerse en contacto con, establecer contacto con* to get in *o* into contact with, to get in touch with, to contact || *lentes de contacto* contact lenses || *mantenerse en contacto con* to keep in contact with, to keep in touch with.

contadero, ra *adj* countable || beginning, starting (empezando) || *dentro de un plazo de diez días contaderos desde esta fecha* within ten days (beginning) from this date.

contado, da *adj* counted || told, said, related (dicho) || scarce (escaso) || few and far between; *son contados los que saben el griego* people who know Greek are few and far between || — *en contadas ocasiones* seldom, rarely || *tiene contados los días, sus días están contados* his days are numbered.
◆ *m* AMER instalment [US installment]; *pagar una deuda en tres contados* to pay off a debt in three instalments || *al contado* cash; *pagar al contado* to pay cash; *pago al contado* cash payment.

contador, ra *adj* counting (para contar).
◆ *m* counter, checker (que cuenta) || bookkeeper, accountant (contable) || meter (instrumento); *contador de agua, de gas* water meter, gas meter || — *contador de aparcamiento* parking meter || *contador Geiger* Geiger counter.
◆ *m/f* AMER moneylender (prestamista).

contaduría *f* bookkeeping, accounting (contabilidad) || accountant's office (oficina) || accountancy (oficio) || box office, booking office (teatro) || *contaduría general* Audit Office.

contagiar *vt* to contaminate; *contagiar a un país* to contaminate a country || to infect, to give; *me ha contagiado su enfermedad* he has infected me with his disease || FIG to infect, to contaminate.
◆ *vpr* to be communicable, to be infectious, to be contagious, to be catching; *enfermedad que no se contagia* disease that is not communicable || to be infected (*de* with) || FIG to be contagious *o* infectious *o* catching; *el bostezar se contagia fácilmente* yawning is very contagious.

contagio *m* MED contagion || FIG contagion.

contagioso, sa *adj* contagious, infectious, communicable, catching; *una enfermedad contagiosa* an infectious disease || infectious (persona) || FIG contagious, infectious; *risa muy contagiosa* very infectious laugh.

contaminación *f* contamination || pollution (del agua, del aire, etc.) || corruption (corrupción).

contaminante *adj* polluting.
◆ *m* polluting agent.

contaminar *vt* to contaminate || to pollute, to contaminate (el agua, el aire, etc.) || FIG to contaminate, to infect | to corrupt (corromper).
◆ *vpr* FIG to be contaminated, to be corrupted, to be infected; *contaminarse con el mal ejemplo* to be corrupted by a bad example.

contante *adj m* cash (dinero) || *dinero contante y sonante* hard cash.

contar* *vt* to count (numerar); *contar dinero* to count money || to count, to consider; *te cuento entre mis amigos* I count you among my friends, I consider you one of my friends || to talk *o* to tell about; *cuando ha bebido, siempre me cuenta su vida* when he is drunk, he always tells me about his life || to tell, to recount (un cuento) || to include, to count (incluir) || to take into account, to bear in mind (tener en cuenta) || — *contar una cosa por hecha* to consider sth. as good as done || *cuenta ochenta años de edad* he is eighty years old || *¡cuéntamelo a mí!* you're telling me!, you can say that again! || FAM *¡cuénteselo a su abuela!* tell that to the marines! | *me lo contó un pajarito* a little bird told me || *¿qué cuentas?* how is it going?, what's new?, how are things? (saludo) || *¿qué cuentas de nuevo?* what's new? || *se dejó contar la otra versión del suceso por su amigo* he let his friend tell him the other side of the story || *se pueden contar con los dedos* you can count them on your fingers || *si me lo cuentan no lo creo* I can hardly believe my own eyes || *sin contar* not counting, not to mention, excluding; *éramos siete sin contar los niños* there were seven of us, not to mention the children || *tener mucho que contar* to have a lot *o* a great deal to say.
◆ *vi* to count; *contar hasta diez* to count up to ten; *contar con los dedos* to count on one's fingers || to count; *estos puntos no cuentan* these points don't count || to be fitted with, to be equipped with; *el barco cuenta con un motor eléctrico* the boat is equipped with an electric motor || to command, to have at one's disposal *o* at one's command; *cuento con un capital considerable* I have a substantial capital at my disposal || to have (tener) || — *contar con uno* to count on s.o., to rely on s.o. || *¡cuenta con ello!* you can count on it! || *cuenta conmigo* you can rely on me || *es largo de contar* it is a long story || *hay que contar con que siempre pueden ocurrir desgracias* one must always allow for mishaps || *no contaba con encontrar tantos problemas* he didn't bargain for so many problems || *no contaba con que podía llover* I did not think it was going to rain, I did not foresee the possibility of rain.
◆ *vpr* to be said; *se cuenta que lo mataron* it is said that he was killed; *¡se cuentan tantas cosas de su vida!* so many things are said about his life! || to rank (*entre* among); *se cuenta entre los partidarios del proyecto* he ranks among the plan's supporters || FAM *¿qué te cuentas?* how's it going?, how's things?

contemplación *f* contemplation || meditation (meditación).
◆ *pl* indulgence *sing* || ceremony *sing*; *no andar con contemplaciones* not to stand on ceremony || *tener demasiadas contemplaciones con alguien* to be overindulgent with s.o.

contemplar *vt* to contemplate (mirar, meditar) || to be pleasant to, to be considerate towards (complacer).
◆ *vi* to contemplate, to meditate.

contemplativo, va *adj* contemplative; *vida contemplativa* contemplative life || obliging, indulgent (amable).
◆ *m/f* contemplative person || REL contemplative.

contemporaneidad *f* contemporaneity || *obra literaria de constante contemporaneidad* literary work of timeless significance.

contemporáneo, a *adj* contemporary; *historia contemporánea* contemporary history || contemporaneous (*de* with).
◆ *m/f* contemporary.

contemporización *f* temporization, compliance.

contemporizador, ra *adj* temporizing, compliant.
◆ *m/f* temporizer.

contemporizar *vi* to temporize, to comply; *contemporizar con alguien* to temporize with s.o.

contención *f* contention (contienda) || JUR suit || *muro de contención* retaining wall.

contencioso, sa *adj* contentious || JUR litigious || *lo contencioso* contentious business, matters in dispute.

contender* *vi* to contend, to fight, to struggle (batallar) || FIG to quarrel (disputar) | to compete (competir).

contendiente *adj* contending, opposing.
◆ *m/f* contender, contestant (contrincante).

contenedor, ra *adj* containing.
◆ *m* container || *contenedor de basura* rubbish skip.

contener* *vt* to contain; *este libro contiene muchos ejemplos* this book contains many examples || to hold; *le contuvo por el brazo* he held him by the arm || to restrain, to control; *contuvo su cólera* he restrained his anger || to hold (la respiración) || to hold back (lágrimas) || to suppress (risa) || to check, to curb (una tendencia) || to keep in check; *un cordón de policía contuvo a la muchedumbre* a line of policeman kept the crowd in check || MIL to contain, to keep in check || to stop; *contener la sangre de una herida* to stop the flow of blood from a wound || — *el decalitro contiene diez litros* there are ten litres in one decalitre || *no pude contener la risa* I couldn't refrain from laughing, I couldn't help laughing.
◆ *vpr* to control o.s., to restrain o.s., to check o.s.

contenido, da *adj* contained, restrained, pent-up (reprimido) || contained, suppressed; *risa contenida* contained laughter || reserved (circunspecto).
◆ *m* contents *pl* || contents *pl*, subject matter, content (de una carta, de un informe) || content (proporción); *contenido en carbono* carbon content.

contentadizo, za *adj* easily pleased *o* satisfied || *mal contentadizo* hard to please.

contentamiento *m* contentment.

contentar *vt* to content, to satisfy, to please || COM to endorse || AMER to reconcile || — FAM *ser de buen contentar* to be easily pleased *o* satisfied | *ser de mal contentar* to be hard to please *o* to satisfy.
◆ *vpr* to be content, to be satisfied; *conténtate con lo que tienes* be content with what you have || to content o.s., to make do; *se contentó con un bocadillo* he contented himself *o* he made do with a sandwich.

contento, ta *adj* happy, pleased; *estaban muy contentos con sus regalos* they were very happy with their presents || glad, pleased; *¡estoy tan contento de verte!* I am so glad to see you! || satisfied, pleased; *estoy muy contento con mi nuevo coche* I am very satisfied with my new car || content (en estilo literario); *estoy contento con mi suerte* I am content with my lot || — FIG *darse por contento* to consider o.s. lucky | *más contento que unas Pascuas* as happy as a lark, as pleased as Punch | *para dejarlo contento* in order to please him || *vivir contento* to live happily.
◆ *m* contentment, happiness, joy || — FIG *no caber en sí de contento* to be beside o.s. with joy || *sentir gran contento* to be extremely happy.

contera *f* ferrule, tip (de bastón, de paraguas), chape (de la vaina de una espada) || cap (de lápiz) || FIG *por contera* to top it all, to cap it all.

contertuliano, na; contertulio, lia *m/f* participant in a social gathering || *uno de los contertulianos* one of the people present.

contesta *f* AMER talk (conversación) | answer (contestación).

contestación *f* answer, reply (respuesta) || dispute, argument (debate) || JUR plea (del demandado) || — JUR *contestación a la demanda* defendant's plea || *dejar sin contestación* to leave unanswered || *en contestación a su carta del 13* *del corriente* in reply to your letter of the 13th inst. || *escribir cuatro letras de contestación* to drop s.o. a line in reply || *mala contestación* wrong answer (equivocada), retort (irrespetuosa).

contestador *m* *contestador automático* answerphone [US answering service].

contestar *vt/vi* to answer, to reply to; *contestar una carta, una pregunta* to answer a letter, a question; *no contestó* he did not reply *o* answer || to answer (el teléfono) || to return (saludo) || to answer back; *¡no contestes a tu madre!* do not answer your mother back! || to contest, to impugn (impugnar) || JUR to corroborate || AMER to talk (conversar).

contexto *m* context.

contextura *f* contexture, texture (de tejidos, etc.) || build, physique (constitución del cuerpo).

contienda *f* war, conflict (guerra) || FIG dispute, altercation (disputa) | struggle, fight, battle (lucha).

contigo *pron pers* with you; *¿tienes dinero contigo?* have you any money with you? || with Thee (refiriéndose a Dios).

— OBSERV *Contigo* is only used in conjunction with *tu*.

contigüidad *f* contiguity.

contiguo, gua *adj* contiguous (*a* to), adjoining, adjacent (adyacente) || — *la casa contigua* the house next door || *la habitación contigua* the adjoining room.

continencia *f* continence.

continental *adj* continental.

◆ *m* (p us) letter sent by messenger (carta).

continente *adj* containing (que contiene) || continent (moderado).

◆ *m* GEOGR continent || container (lo que contiene); *el continente y el contenido* the container and the contents || countenance, bearing (actitud).

contingencia *f* FIL contingency || possibility, eventuality, contingency; *prever cualquier contingencia* to provide for all eventualities.

contingente *adj* FIL contingent.

◆ *m* quota (cupo) || MIL contingent.

contingentemente *adv* fortuitously, by chance.

continuación *f* continuation || prolongation (prolongación) || — *a continuación* next, immediately after (seguidamente), below (en un escrito) || *a continuación de* after, following.

continuadamente *adv* —> **continuamente.**

continuador, ra *m/f* continuator.

continuamente; continuadamente *adv* continuously, continually, unceasingly.

continuar *vt* to continue, to carry on, to go on, to keep on; *continuar hablando* to continue talking || to continue on, to go on, to proceed on; *continuó su camino* he continued on his way || to extend (carretera).

◆ *vi* to continue, to go on; *la lucha continúa* the struggle continues; *el coche continuó hasta Soria* the car continued on to Soria || to continue, to go on, to keep on, to carry on; *continuar con su trabajo* to continue with one's work; *continuaron en sus pesquisas* they continued with their enquiries || — *continuará* to be continued (revista) || *continuar con buena salud* to keep in good health, to be still in good health || TEATR *continuar en cartel* to be still running || *continuar en el mismo sitio* to be still in the same place || *continuar en vigor* to remain in force.

continuativo, va *adj* continuative.

continuidad *f* continuity || *solución de continuidad* interruption, solution of continuity (interrupción).

continuo, nua *adj* continuous, unbroken (no dividido en el espacio); *línea continua* continuous line || continual, continuous, constant, never-ending; *un temor continuo* a continual fear || — ELECTR *corriente continua* direct current || *movimiento continuo* perpetual motion || *ondas continuas* undampened *o* continuous waves.

◆ *adv* continuously, continually || *de continuo, a la continua* continually, ceaselessly, unceasingly, constantly.

contonearse *vpr* to sway one's hips, to wiggle (una mujer) || to swagger (un hombre).

contoneo *m* swaying of the hips, wiggle (de mujer) || swagger (de hombre).

contornar; contornear *vt* to sketch *o* to trace the outline of (perfilar) || to skirt, to pass round; *contornear una montaña* to skirt a hill || TECN to saw round a curved outline.

contorno *m* outline, contour (línea que perfila) || periphery (perímetro) || edge (de una moneda) || girth (medida) || *contorno de cintura* waist measurement.

◆ *pl* outskirts, environs, surroundings (de una ciudad).

contorsión *f* contortion || *hacer contorsiones* to contort one's body, to writhe.

contorsionista *m/f* contortionist.

contra *prep* against; *lucha contra el enemigo* fight against the enemy || for; *remedio contra la tos* remedy for coughs || over; *alcanzar una victoria contra el enemigo* to win a victory over the enemy || opposite, facing (enfrente); *su casa está contra la iglesia* his house is opposite the church || — *contra todos* despite everyone (a pesar de todos) || *diez contra uno* ten to one || *en contra* against; *en contra suya* against him || *en contra de* against; *hablar en contra de uno* to speak against s.o. || *en contra de lo que pensaban* contrary to what they thought || *ir en contra de la opinión pública* to run counter to *o* against public opinion || *opinar en contra* to disagree || *salvo prueba en contra* unless otherwise proved || *tengo a todo el mundo en contra* everyone is against me || *viento en contra* head wind.

◆ *m* cons *pl*; *el pro y la contra* the pros and the cons || MÚS organ pedal.

◆ *f* FAM rub, catch, hitch; *ahí está la contra* there's the rub || counter (esgrima) || AMER free gift [given to a customer with every purchase] (adehala) || — FAM *hacerle* or *llevarle la contra a uno* to contradict s.o. || *jugar a la contra* to play (a game) on the defensive.

◆ *m pl* lowest bass stops of an organ.

contraalmirante *m* rear admiral.

contraamura *f* MAR preventer tack.

contraatacar *vt* MIL to counterattack.

contraataque *m* MIL counterattack.

contraaviso *m* countermand (contraorden).

contrabajo *m* MÚS contrabass, double bass (instrumento) | contrabass player, double pass player, contrabassist (músico) | bass (voz y cantante).

contrabalancear *vt* to counterbalance, to counterpoise || FIG to counterbalance, to compensate; *sus buenas cualidades contrabalancean sus defectos* his good qualities counterbalance his defects.

contrabandear *vi* to smuggle.

contrabandista *m/f* contrabandist, smuggler || *contrabandista de armas* gunrunner.

contrabando *m* smuggling (actividad); *vivir del contrabando* to live by smuggling || contraband, smuggled goods *pl* (mercancías) || — *de contrabando* contraband || *pasar algo de contrabando* to smuggle sth. in.

contrabarrera *f* TAUR second row of seats [in the bullring].

contracaja *f* IMPR right upper case.

contracarril *m* check rail, guard rail (ferrocarriles).

contracción *f* contraction.

contracepción *f* MED contraception.

contraceptivo, va *adj/sm* contraceptive.

contracifra *f* key (clave de signos).

contraclave *f* ARQ voussoir next to the keystone.

contracorriente *f* countercurrent, crosscurrent || *ir a contracorriente* to go against the current.

contractabilidad *f* contractility.

contráctil *adj* contractile.

contractilidad *f* contractility.

contractivo, va *adj* contractive.

contracto, ta *adj* GRAM contracted; *artículo contracto* contracted article.

contractual *adj* contractual.

contracultura *f* counterculture.

contrachapado; contrachapeado *m* plywood.

contradanza *f* contra dance, contredanse.

contradecir* *vt* to contradict; *siempre me estás contradiciendo* you are always contradicting me || FIG to be inconsistent with, to be at variance with; *su conducta contradice sus palabras* his behaviour is inconsistent with his words.

◆ *vpr* to contradict o.s., to be inconsistent.

contradeclaración *f* counterstatement.

contradenuncia *f* JUR counterclaim.

contradicción *f* contradiction; *lleno de contradicciones* full of contradictions || inconsistency, contradiction; *las contradicciones de la mente humana* the inconsistencies of the human mind || contradiction, discrepancy; *existe una contradicción entre las dos versiones del asunto* there is a discrepancy between the two accounts of the affair || — *espíritu de contradicción* contrariness || *estar en contradicción con* to be contradictory to *o* inconsistent with, to be at variance with || *pruebas que no admiten contradicción* incontrovertible proofs.

contradictoriamente *adv* contradictorily.

contradictorio, ria *adj* contradictory, conflicting.

◆ *f* contradictory proposition (lógica).

contradique *m* strengthening dike.

contradriza *f* MAR auxiliary halyard.

contraenvite *m* bluff call (cartas).

contraer* *vt* to contract; *el frío contrae los metales* cold contracts metals || FIG to contract, to catch (una enfermedad) | to acquire, to develop (un hábito) || GRAM to contract || — *contraer amistad* to make friends || *contraer deudas* to incur *o* to contract debts || *contraer matrimonio* to contract marriage || *contraer matrimonio con* to marry || *contraer obligaciones* to enter into obligations.

◆ *vpr* to contract; *su cara se contrajo en una mueca de dolor* his features contracted into a pained grimace || AMER to apply o.s. (al estudio, al trabajo).

contraescarpa *f* counterscarp.

contraespionaje *m* counterespionage.

contraestay *m* MAR preventer stay.

contrafagot *m* MÚS double bassoon, contrabassoon.

contrafallar *vt* to overtrump (en los naipes).

contrafallo *m* overtrumping.

contrafilo *m* sharpened back (de una espada).

contrafirma *f* countersignature.

contrafirmar *vt* to countersign.

contrafoque *m* MAR fore staysail.

contrafoso *m* TEATR below-stage.

contrafuego *m* backfire.

contrafuero *m* violation of a privilege.

contrafuerte *m* ARQ buttress || spur (de una montaña) || stiffener, reinforcement (del calzado).

contrafuga *f* MÚS counterfugue.

contragolpe *m* MED counterstroke || TECN kickback || FIG counterblow.

contraguerrilla *f* anti-guerrilla warfare (sistema) || anti-guerrilla force (tropas).

contrahacer* *vt* to fake (en general), to counterfeit (la moneda), to forge (un documento, una escritura) || to plagiarize (plagiar) || to imitate; *contrahacer el canto del gallo* to imitate the crowing of the cock.

contrahecho, cha *adj* fake (falso) || counterfeit (moneda) || forged (documento, escritura) || hunchbacked (jorobado).
◆ *m/f* hunchback.

contrahechura *f* fake (en general), counterfeit (de moneda), forgery (de documentos).

contrahílo (a) *adv* against the grain.

contrahuella *f* riser (de un escalón).

contraindicación *f* MED contraindication.

contraindicado, da *adj* contraindicated.

contraindicante *adj* MED contraindicative.

contraindicar *vt* MED to contraindicate; *tratamiento contraindicado* contraindicated treatment.

contralmirante *m* rear admiral.

contralor *m* AMER controller, comptroller (inspector de gastos públicos).

contraloría *f* AMER Office of the Comptroller.

contralto *m/f* MÚS contralto.

contraluz *m* back lighting (en fotografía, pintura) || *fotografiar a contraluz* to take pictures against the light.

contramaestre *m* foreman || MAR boatswain || *contramaestre de segunda* chief petty officer.

contramandar *vt* to countermand.

contramandato *m* countermand.

contramanifestación *f* counter-demonstration.

contramanifestar* *vi* to counter-demonstrate.

contramano (a) *adv* the wrong way [in a one-way street, etc.]; *circulación a contramano* traffic going the wrong way.

contramarca *f* COM countermark || customs duty (impuesto).

contramarcha *f* MIL countermarch || AUT reverse.

contramina *f* MIL countermine.

contraminar *vt* MIL countermine || FIG to frustrate, to thwart, to countermine (frustrar).

contramuralla *f*; **contramuro** *m* ARQ countermure, outer wall.

contraofensiva *f* MIL counteroffensive.

contraorden *f* countermand.

contrapartida *f* compensation (compensación) || *la contrapartida de la gloria* the price of glory.

contrapaso *m* back step || MÚS counterpart.

contrapelo (a) *adv* the wrong way; *acariciar un perro a contrapelo* to stroke a dog the wrong way || against the nap *o* pile, the wrong way (un tejido) || FIG counter to the general trend (contra la tendencia general), against one's will, unwillingly (contra la inclinación personal).

contrapesar *vt* to counterbalance, to counterpoise || FIG to compensate, to offset, to counterbalance (equilibrar).

contrapeso *m* counterpoise, counterweight, counter-balance || balancing pole (balancín de equilibrista) || FIG counterbalance.

contraponer* *vt* to oppose; *contraponer su voluntad a la de alguien* to oppose one's will to s.o. else's || to compare, to contrast (cotejar).
◆ *vpr* to oppose, to be opposed (oponerse) || to contrast (*a* with), to contrast (contrastar).

contraposición *f* opposition || comparison (cotejo) || conflict; *contraposición de intereses* conflict of interests || contrast (contraste).

contraprestación *f* JUR contractual obligation.

contraproducente *adj* self-defeating, counterproductive; *esta medida es contraproducente* this measure is self-defeating || contraindicative; *medicina contraproducente* contraindicative medicine.

contraproposición *f* counterproposal.

contrapropuesta *f* counterproposal.

contraproyecto *m* counterplan, alternative project.

contraprueba *f* second proof (imprenta) || counterproof (grabado).

contrapuerta *f* storm door || second gate, inner door (fortaleza).

contrapuesto, ta *pp* —→ **contraponer.**

contrapunta *f* TECN tailstock (de un torno).

contrapuntista *m* MÚS contrapuntist.

contrapunto *m* MÚS counterpoint || AMER poetry contest (concurso de poesía).

contrariamente *adv* contrarily || *contrariamente a lo que puedas creer* contrary to what you may think.

contrariar *vt* to vex, to annoy, to upset; *esto me contraría mucho* this upsets me a great deal || to contradict (contradecir) || to hinder, to hamper, to interfere with (obstaculizar); *contrariar un proyecto* to interfere with a plan.

contrariedad *f* annoyance, vexation (disgusto) || disappointment (desengaño) || obstacle; *tropezar con una contrariedad* to encounter an obstacle || setback (contratiempo) || mishap (desgracia); *he tenido una contrariedad, he pinchado al cabo de algunos kilómetros* I had a mishap; after a few miles I got a puncture.

contrario, ria *adj* opposite, contrary (opuesto); *correr en sentido contrario* to run in the opposite direction; *sostener opiniones contrarias* to hold contrary opinions || opposed; *es contrario a todo cambio* he is opposed to any change || opposing (gustos) || FIG harmful; *el tabaco es contrario a la salud* tobacco is harmful to the health || adverse, bad; *suerte contraria* adverse fortune || *la parte contraria* the opposing party (en un pleito), the opposing team (en deportes).
◆ *m/f* opponent, rival (adversario) || — *al contrario* on the contrary || *al contrario de lo que pensaban* contrary to what they thought || *de lo contrario* otherwise || *eso es lo contrario de lo que me dijo ayer* that is the opposite of what you told me yesterday || *llevar la contraria a uno* to oppose s.o., to get in s.o.'s way (poner obstáculo), to contradict s.o. (contradecir) || *llevar siempre la contraria* to always contradict s.o., to be contrariness personified || *por el contrario* on the contrary || *salvo prueba en contrario* unless otherwise proved, unless proved to the contrary, unless the contrary be proved || *todo lo contrario* quite the opposite *o* the contrary.

Contrarreforma *f* Counter Reformation.

contrarregistro *m* second examination.

contrarreguera *f* AGR transversal irrigation ditch.

contrarreloj *adj* DEP against the clock.
◆ *f* DEP race against the clock.

contrarréplica *f* rejoinder.

contrarrestar *vt* to counteract, to check, to block, to oppose (oponerse) || to resist (resistir) || to counteract (un efecto) || to return (the ball).

contrarresto *m* counteraction, opposition (oposición) || resistance (resistencia) || return (en el frontón de pelota) || player who returns the ball (jugador).

contrarrevolución *f* counterrevolution.

contrarrevolucionario, ria *adj/s* counterrevolutionary.

contrarriel *m* guard rail, check rail (contracarril).

contrarroda *m* MAR apron.

contraseguro *m* counterinsurance.

contrasello *m* counterseal.

contrasentido *m* mistranslation (en una traducción) || misinterpretation (interpretación mala) || contradiction (contradicción) || nonsense (disparate); *lo que has dicho es un contrasentido* what you said is nonsense.

contraseña *f* countersign (seña) || countermark (contramarca) || MIL countersign, watchword, password || pass out (en un teatro).

contrastar *vt* to resist, to repel (oponerse a); *contrastar el ataque* to resist the attack || to assay and hallmark (metales preciosos) || to check, to verify (averiguar).
◆ *vi* to contrast (formar contraste); *colores que contrastan* contrasting colours; *su conducta actual contrasta con su moderación habitual* his present behaviour contrasts with his usual restraint || to be different; *dos personas que contrastan mucho entre sí* two persons who are very different || *hacer contrastar* to contrast.

contraste *m* resistance, opposition || contrast; *formar contraste* to form a contrast || hallmark (en metales preciosos) || verification, inspection (de pesos y medidas) || assay (acción de controlar) || assay officer (el que controla) || inspector of weights and measures (que comprueba la exactitud de pesas y medidas) || hallmarker (de metales preciosos) || MAR sudden change of the wind || — *en contraste con* in contrast to || *por contraste* in contrast.

contrata *f* (written) contract (obligación por escrito); *firmar una contrata* to sign a contract || hiring (obreros), taking-on, engagement (empleados y artistas) || lump sum contract (contrato a tanto alzado).

contratación *f* contract (contrato) || hiring; *la contratación del personal temporero* the hiring of seasonal workers || engagement, taking-on (de un maestro, etc.) || (ant) trade (comercio) || HIST *casa de contratación* chamber of commerce set up by Isabella I and Ferdinand V in Seville.

contratante *adj* contracting; *las partes contratantes* the contracting parties.
◆ *m* (ant) trader || contracting party.

contratar *vt* to sign a contract for (firmar un contrato por) || to engage (empleados), to hire (obreros), to sign up (deportistas), to engage, to book (artistas); *contratado al mes* engaged by the month.

contratiempo *m* setback, difficulty; *los contratiempos que sufrió le obligaron a vender sus propiedades* as a result of the setbacks he suffered, he had to sell his possessions || mishap; *tuve un pequeño contratiempo en el camino* I had a slight mishap on the way || MÚS syncopation

|| *a contratiempo* on the offbeat (en música), untimely, inopportunely (inoportunamente).

contratista *m/f* contractor; *contratista de obras* building contractor; *contratista de obras públicas* public works contractor.

contrato *m* contract; *contrato gratuito, oneroso* gratuitous, onerous contract || contract (en bridge) || — *contrato administrativo* administrative contract || *contrato de arrendamiento* lease || *contrato de compraventa* bill *o* contract of sale || *contrato de obra* contract to do work, manufactoring contract || *contrato de trabajo* work contract || *contrato enfitéutico* long lease || *contrato temporal* short-term *o* temporary contract || *contrato verbal* parol contract.

contratorpedero *m* destroyer.

contratuerca *f* TECN locknut.

contravención *f* JUR infringement, contravention (infracción).

contraveneno *m* antidote.

contravenir* *vi* JUR to infringe, to contravene; *contravenir a la ley* to infringe the law.

contraventana *f* shutter.

contraventor, ra *adj* JUR contravening, infringing.
◆ *m/f* contravener, infringer.

contraviento *m* ARQ windbrace.

contravisita *f* MED consultation for a second opinion.

contrayente *adj* contracting (person).
◆ *m/f* contracting party [in a marriage].

contribución *f* contribution; *la contribución de la tecnología al progreso* technology's contribution to progress || tax; *contribuciones directas, indirectas* direct, indirect taxes || — *contribución municipal* rates || *contribución territorial* land tax || *recaudador de contribuciones* tax collector.

contribuir* *vt/vi* to pay taxes (pagar) || to contribute; *contribuyó con una suma considerable a la construcción del hospital* he contributed a substantial amount to the construction of the hospital; *contribuir en* or *por una tercera parte* to contribute one third.

contributivo, va *adj* contributive.

contribuyente *adj* taxpaying (que paga impuestos) || contributing.
◆ *m/f* taxpayer (de impuestos) || contributor.

contrición *f* contrition; *acto de contrición* act of contrition.

contrincante *m* rival, opponent, competitor.

contristar *vt* to sadden, to grieve.
◆ *vpr* to become sad *o* unhappy, to be saddened *o* grieved.

contrito, ta *adj* contrite, repentant.

control *m* check, checking (comprobación) || examination (inspección) || control; *pasar por el control de pasaportes* to go through passport control || control; *botón de control* control knob; *punto de control* control point; *sala de control* control room; *control automático* automatic control; *torre de control* control tower; *control de natalidad* birth control || checkpoint (de un rally) || — *bajo control* under control || DEP *control antidopaje* or *antidoping* dope test || *control de calidad* quality control || *control de frontera* or *fronterizo* frontier checkpoint || *control de seguridad* security check || *control de sí mismo* self-control || *control remoto* remote control || *fuera de control* out of control, beyond control || *perder el control* to lose control.

controlador *m* *controlador del tráfico aéreo* air traffic controller || INFORM controller.

controlar *vt* to control (dominar, regular) || to check, to verify (comprobar) || to inspect, to examine (examinar).

controversia *f* controversy, dispute (discusión) || *mantener una controversia* to dispute.

controversista *m/f* controversialist, disputant.

controvertible *adj* controversial (que provoca controversias) || questionable, debatable (discutible).

controvertir* *vt* to controvert, to debate, to discuss, to dispute (discutir) || *es un punto controvertido* it is a controversial point.
◆ *vi* to argue.

contubernio *m* (p us) concubinage, cohabitation || FIG base alliance, collusion.

contumacia *f* JUR contumacy || *juzgar en contumacia* to sentence (a prisoner) in his absence *o* in default.

contumaz *adj* contumacious, insubordinate (insubordinado) || stubborn, obstinate (obstinado) || JUR guilty of default, contumacious.
◆ *m/f* JUR defaulter.

contumelia *f* contumely, insult.

contumelioso, sa *adj* contumelious, insulting.

contundencia *f* contusive properties *pl* [of a blunt weapon] || FIG weight (de un argumento).

contundente *adj* blunt, offensive; *un arma contundente* a blunt weapon || blunt (instrumento) || FIG impressive, forceful, convincing; *argumento contundente* forceful argument | overwhelming, conclusive; *prueba contundente* overwhelming proof.

contundir *vt* to bruise, to contuse.

conturbación *f* restlessness, uneasiness, anxiety.

conturbado, da *adj* restless, uneasy, perturbed.

conturbar *vt* to trouble, to perturb, to disturb.
◆ *vpr* to be perturbed *o* disturbed, to become uneasy.

contusión *f* bruise, contusion || *estar lleno de contusiones* to be bruised all over.

contusionar *vt* to bruise, to contuse.
— OBSERV This verb is a barbarism used instead of *contundir*.

contuso, sa *adj* MED bruised, contused.

conurbación *f* conurbation.

convalecencia *f* convalescence || *casa de convalecencia* convalescent home, sanatorium.

convalecer* *vi* to convalesce, to recover; *convalecer de una enfermedad* to recover from an illness.

convaleciente *adj/s* convalescent.

convalidación *f* ratification || authentication (de un documento).

convalidar *vt* to ratify (ratificar) || to authenticate (dar por válido).

convección *f* FÍS convection.

convecino, na *adj* neighbouring [*US* neighboring].
◆ *m/f* neighbour [*US* neighbor].

convencer *vt* to convince; *intenté convencerle para que viniera* I tried to convince him to come || FIG *ese hombre no me convence* I don't like that man.
◆ *vpr* to be *o* to become convinced; *convencerse de la verdad de la afirmación* to become convinced of the truth of the assertion.

convencido, da *adj* convinced.

convencimiento *m* convincing (acción) || conviction (seguridad) || — *llegar al convencimiento de* to become convinced of || *tener el convencimiento de que...* to be convinced that...

convención *f* convention.

convencional *adj* conventional; *signos convencionales* conventional signs.

convencionalismo *m* conventionality, conventionalism.

convencionalista *m/f* conventionalist.

convenible *adj* fair (precio) || accommodating (persona) || → **conveniente.**

convenido *adv* agreed, settled.

conveniencia *f* conformity, agreement (de gustos, de opinión, etc.), compatibility (de caracteres) || suitability (lo apropiado) || advisability, desirability; *la conveniencia de esa gestión* the advisability of that move || convenience; *a su conveniencia* at your convenience || agreement (acuerdo) || place, position (acomodo de un criado); *buscar conveniencia* to look for a place [as a servant] || — *matrimonio de conveniencia* marriage of convenience || *ser de la conveniencia de uno* to be convenient to s.o., to suit s.o.
◆ *pl* a servant's perquisites || property *sing*, income *sing* || *según sus conveniencias* at your convenience.

conveniente *adj* convenient || suitable (adecuado) || advisable (aconsejable) || desirable (deseable) || proper; *una conducta conveniente* proper behaviour; *no es la respuesta conveniente* that is not the proper answer || — *creer* or *juzgar conveniente* to think fit, to see fit || *es conveniente hacer esto* it is advisable to do this || *ser conveniente* to suit; *este trabajo es conveniente para mí* this job suits me.

convenio *m* agreement; *convenios colectivos, comerciales* collective, trade agreements; *llegar a un convenio* to reach an agreement || covenant (pacto) || convention; *convenio postal internacional* international postal convention || *vinculado por un convenio* bound by an agreement.

convenir* *vt/vi* to arrange, to agree (estar de acuerdo); *hemos convenido (en) irnos mañana* we have agreed to leave tomorrow; *convino con su amigo que vendría a la fiesta* he arranged with his friend to come to the party || to agree, to come to an agreement; *convenir en una cuestión, en el precio* to come to an agreement about a question, about the price || to be worth one's while (ser rentable) || to be convenient for, to suit; *hágalo cuando le convenga* do it whenever it is convenient for you *o* whenever it suits you || to suit (ser adecuado); *me convendría mucho esta casa* this house would suit me well *o* fine || to be advisable (ser aconsejable); *no nos conviene actuar ahora* it is not advisable for us to act now || — *convengo en ello* I agree to that || *cuando más le convenga* at your convenience || *el día convenido* (on) the appointed day || *eso me convendrá mucho* that will suit me well *o* fine, that will be just right for me || *no te conviene tomar este trabajo* that job is not right for you, you should not take that job || *según le convenga* as you see fit || *sueldo a convenir* salary to be arranged *o* to be agreed || *te convendría más olvidarlo* you would do better to forget it, it is best that you forget it.
◆ *v impers* to be fitting, to be advisable; *conviene que vayas* it is advisable for you to go || *conviene olvidar que* it is as well to forget that.
◆ *vpr* to agree (*en* on).

conventillo *m* AMER tenement house.

convento *m* convent (de monjas o monjes), nunnery (de monjas), monastery (de monjes).

conventual *adj/sm* conventual; *vida conventual* conventual life.

convergencia *f* convergence, convergency.

convergente *adj* convergent, converging; *sistema de lentes convergentes* system of converging lenses || MIL *tiro convergente* cross fire.

converger; convergir *vi* to converge || FIG to unite (unirse).

conversación *f* conversation (plática) || talk; *el ministro ha tenido conversaciones con el presidente* the minister has had talks with the President || colloquy (coloquio) || — *conversación a solas* private talk *o* conversation || *dar conversación a uno* to chat with s.o., to entertain s.o. || *sacar la conversación de* to turn the talk to, to bring the conversation round to (a subject) || *tener mucha conversación* to have always plenty to say || *tener poca conversación* not to be very talkative || *trabar conversación con* to strike up a conversation with.

conversacional *adj* INFORM conversational, interactive.

conversada *f* AMER chat (charla)

conversador, ra *adj* talkative.
◆ *m/f* conversationalist, talker.

conversar *vi* to converse, to chat, to talk; *siguió conversando con nosotros* he went on conversing with us || to talk; *conversar sobre varios asuntos* to talk about several matters.

conversión *f* conversion || MIL wheel || conversion (de monedas).

converso, sa *adj* converted.
◆ *m/f* convert (persona convertida a una religión) || lay brother, lay sister (lego, lega).

conversor *m* FÍS converter.

convertibilidad *f* convertibility.

convertible *adj* convertible, transformable || convertible; *moneda convertible* convertible currency || AMER convertible (coche).
◆ *m* convertible (coche).

convertidor *m* TECN converter || *convertidor de frecuencia* frequency changer.

convertir* *vt* to turn, to change, to transform, to convert (p us) (en este sentido); *convertir el agua en vino* to turn water into wine || to exchange, to change, to convert; *convertir dólares en oro* to exchange dollars for gold, to convert *o* to change dollars into gold || to convert; *San Pablo convirtió a los gentiles al cristianismo* St Paul converted the gentiles to Christianity.
◆ *vpr* to convert, to be converted (al catolicismo, etc.) || to turn, to change; *el vino se convirtió en vinagre* the wine turned into vinegar || FIG to become (llegar a ser); *con el tiempo, se convirtió en mi mejor amigo* as time went by, he became my best friend.

convexidad *f* convexity.

convexo, xa *adj* convex.

convicción *f* conviction.

convicto, ta *adj* JUR convicted || *convicto y confeso* guilty in fact and in law.
◆ *m* convict (en los países anglosajones).

convidada *f* FAM round of drinks; *dar* or *pagar una convidada* to stand *o* to pay for a round of drinks.

convidado, da *m/f* dinner guest (que asiste a un convite) || guest (invitado) || *estar como el convidado de piedra* to be as silent as the grave.

convidar *vt* to invite; *me ha convidado a cenar* he has invited me to dinner || to offer; *convidar a uno con algo* to offer sth. to s.o., to offer s.o. sth. || FIG to cause; *los alimentos salados convidan a beber* salty food causes one to drink | to be conducive to; *un ambiente que convida al estudio* an atmosphere which is conducive to study || *convidar a tomar una copa* to treat s.o. to a drink, to offer s.o. a drink.

convincente *adj* convincing || *testimonios convincentes* conclusive evidence.

convite *m* invitation (acción de invitar); *rehusar un convite* to turn down an invitation || feast, party, banquet [in which one is a guest].

convivencia *f* cohabitation, living together || coexistence.

convivir *vi* to live together, to cohabit || to coexist.

convocación *f* convocation, convening, calling together, summoning (de una asamblea, etc.).

convocar *vt* to summon, to call together, to convoke, to convene (una reunión) || to acclaim, to hail (aclamar) || to call (una huelga).

convocatoria *f* convocation, convening, calling together, summoning (de una asamblea, etc.) || convocation notice for an examination (escrito con que se convoca a un examen) || examination session; *convocatoria de septiembre* autumn examination session [US fall examination session] || notice (anuncio).

convolvuláceo, a *adj* BOT convolvulaceous.
◆ *f pl* BOT convolvulaceae.

convoy *m* convoy (de buques y escolta) || escort (escolta) || train (tren) || FIG & FAM retinue (acompañamiento) || cruet (vinagrera) || FAM cowboy.

convoyar *vt* to convoy || to escort (escoltar).

convulsión *f* convulsion, spasm (de los músculos) || tremor (de la tierra) || FIG upheaval; *convulsiones políticas* political upheavals.

convulsionar *vt* to convulse || to throw into confusion; *las actividades subversivas que han convulsionado el país* the subversive activities that have thrown the country into confusion.

convulsivo, va *adj* convulsive.

convulso, sa *adj* convulsed; *rostro convulso de terror* face convulsed by *o* with terror.

conyugal *adj* conjugal || married; *vida conyugal* married life.

cónyuge *m/f* spouse.
◆ *pl* (married) couple *sing.*

coña *f* POP joke; *tomar a coña* to take it as a joke || POP *estar siempre de coña* to be always joking.

coñac *m* brandy, cognac.

coño *m* POP cunt.
◆ *interj* POP shit! (enfado) | Christ! (asombro).

coolí *m* coolie (trabajador chino o indio).

cooperación *f* cooperation.

cooperador, ra *adj* collaborating || cooperative.
◆ *m/f* collaborator, cooperator.

cooperante *adj* contributory || cooperating.

cooperar *vi* to cooperate || to collaborate (colaborar) || — *cooperar al buen éxito de* to contribute to the success of || *cooperar a un mismo fin* to work for a common purpose *o* cause.

cooperativo, va *adj/sf* cooperative; *cooperativa agrícola* agricultural cooperative; *cooperativa de consumidores* consumers' cooperative.

coopositor, ra *m/f* rival, competitor (rival) || candidate (candidato).

cooptación *f* co-optation, co-option.

cooptar *vt* to co-opt.

coordenada *f* MAT coordinate || *coordenadas geográficas* geographic coordinates.

coordinación *f* coordination.

coordinado, da *adj* coordinated.

coordinador, ra *adj* coordinating.
◆ *m/f* coordinator.

coordinamiento *m* coordination.

coordinar *vt* to coordinate; *coordinar (los) esfuerzos* to coordinate efforts || to classify (ordenar).

coordinativo, va *adj* coordinative, coordinating.

copa *f* glass (véase OBSERV); *copa de champaña* champagne glass || (ant) goblet || glass, glassful; *tomar una copa de jerez* to have a glass of sherry || drink; *convidar a una copa* to treat to a drink || cup (trofeo) || top, crown (de un árbol) || crown (del sombrero) || cup (del sostén) || brazier (brasero) || measure of volume (1/8 of a litre) || — FIG *apurar la copa del dolor* to drain the cup of sorrow || *copa del horno* dome *o* crown of a furnace || *copa graduada* measuring cup || *llevar una copa de más* to have had one over the eight || *sombrero de copa* or *de copa alta* top hat [US derby hat] || *tomar una copa* to have a drink.
◆ *pl* «copas» [a suit in Spanish playing cards] || bit bosses (del bocado del caballo) || FAM *estar de copas* to be out drinking.
— OBSERV *Copa* applies only to glasses having stems.

copaiba *f* copaiba (árbol).

copal *m* copal (resina y barniz).

copante *m* AMER stepping stones *pl.*

copaquira *f* AMER blue copperas.

copar *vt* to win; *copar todos los puestos en una elección* to win all the posts in an election || MIL to corner, to cut off the retreat of (un ejército) || — *copar la banca* to go banco (naipes) || *copar los primeros puestos* to win the first places, to sweep the board (en deportes) || FAM *estar copado* to be up a gum tree.

coparticipación *f* joint partnership, copartnership.

copartícipe *m/f* co-participant, fellow participant (que participa) || copartner (que comparte).

copayero *m* copaiba (árbol).

copear *vi* to have a few drinks || FAM to tipple, to booze (beber mucho).

copec *m* kopeck (moneda rusa).

copela *f* cupel (crisol).

copelación *f* TECN cupellation.

Copenhague *n pr* GEOGR Copenhagen.

copeo *m* pub crawl || *estar* or *irse de copeo* to be *o* to go out drinking *o* on a pub crawl.

Copérnico *npr m* Copernicus.

copero *m* cupbearer; *copero mayor* chief cupbearer || cabinet for glasses (armario).

copete *m* tuft [of hair] || topknot (peinado) || crest (de un pájaro) || forelock (del caballo) || top (de un helado) || top, summit (de una montaña) || ornamental top (de un mueble) || haughtiness, arrogance (altanería) || — FIG *de alto copete* highclass, upper-crust (*fam*); *una familia de alto copete* a high-class family | *estar hasta el copete* to be completely fed up.

copetín *m* small glass || AMER cocktail.

copetón *adj* AMER crested.
◆ *m* crested sparrow (gorrión).

copetuda *f* lark, skylark (alondra).

copetudo, da *adj* crested (que tiene copete) || high-class, high-ranking (encumbrado) || haughty, disdainful, arrogant (presumido).

copia *f* profusion, abundance, plethora (gran cantidad) || duplicate, copy (de una carta) || copy (de una obra de arte) || copy; *cien copias de este libro* one hundred copies of this book; *copia legalizada* certified true copy || imitation, copy (imitación) || print; *hacer una copia de una fotografía* to make a print of a photograph; *copia por contacto* contact print || FIG image; *es una copia de su madre* she is the image of her mother || — *copia al carbón* carbon copy || *copia en limpio* fair copy || CINEM *copia intermedia* lavender print || *máquina para sacar copias* printer, copying machine || *sacar una copia* to make a copy.

copiador, ra *adj* copying (máquina) || *libro copiador* letter book.

copiar *vt* to copy; *copiar del natural* to copy from nature || to copy down (escribir) || to imitate (imitar) || *copiar al pie de la letra* to copy word for word.

copiloto *m* copilot (de avión) || co-driver (de un coche).

copinar *vt* to skin (un animal).

copión, ona *m/f* FAM copycat.

copiosidad *f* abundance.

copioso, sa *adj* copious, plentiful; *una comida copiosa* a copious meal || heavy; *lluvias copiosas* heavy rains || large; *copioso botín* large booty || *copiosa cabellera* long *o* flowing hair.

copista *m* copyist.

copla *f* verse, stanza (combinación métrica) || song (canción) || ballad (balada).
◆ *pl* FAM poetry *sing* || — FAM *andar en coplas* to be on everyone's lips, to be the talk of the town || *coplas de ciego* doggerel *sing* || FAM *echar coplas a uno* to speak ill of s.o.

coplanarias *adj f pl* MAT coplanar; *fuerzas coplanarias* coplanar forces.

coplear *vi* to compose *o* to write verse *o* songs || to recite verse || to sing.

coplero; coplista *m* FIG poetaster.

copo *m* flake (de nieve, de maíz, etc.) || small bundle (cáñamo, lino, seda, etc.) || ball (de algodón) || flock, tuft (de lana) || clot, curd (coágulo) || lump (de harina) || MIL cornering, trapping (del enemigo) || bottom of a seine (de una red) || AMER cloud, raincloud (nube) || MAR *sacar el copo* to haul the seine.

copón *m* large cup || REL ciborium, pyx.

coposesión *f* joint ownership.

coposo, sa *adj* thick-topped, bushy (árbol).

copra *f* copra [dried kernel of the coconut].

coprocesador *m* INFORM coprocessor.

coproducción *f* CINEM coproduction, joint production.

coprolito *m* GEOL coprolite.

copropiedad *f* joint ownership.

copropietario, ria *m/f* joint owner, co-owner, coproprietor.

copto, ta; cofto, ta *adj* Coptic.
◆ *m/f* Copt (persona) || Coptic (lengua).

copudo, da *adj* thick-topped, bushy (árbol).

cópula *f* copulation, sexual intercourse || ANAT copula || copula (en la lógica).

copulación *f* copulation.

copular *vt* (ant) to link.
◆ *vpr* to copulate (aparearse).

copulativo, va *adj* copulative.

coque *m* coke (carbón).

coquear *vi* AMER to chew coca.

coquefacción *f* coking.

coqueluche *m* MED whooping cough.

coquera *f* head of a spinning top (del trompo) || coal scuttle (para el coque) || hollow in a stone (en una piedra) || AMER coca store (lugar) | coca bag (bolsa).

coquería *f* TECN coking plant.

coquero, ra *m/f* coca addict (aficionado a la coca).

coqueta *adj f* coquettish, flirtatious.
◆ *f* coquette, flirt || dressing table (tocador).

coquetear *vi* to flirt.

coqueteo *m* flirtation, flirting.

coquetería *f* coquetry, flirtatiousness (de una persona) || flirtation (flirteo).

coqueto *adj/sm* ⟶ **coquetón.**

coquetón, ona *adj* FAM cute, charming; *un apartamento coquetón* a charming apartment | coquettish (persona).
◆ *m* FAM philanderer.
◆ *f* FAM coquette.

coquificación *f* coking.

coquificar *vt* to coke.

coquina *f* small cockle (molusco comestible).

coquito *m* face [to amuse children] || ringlet, small curl (rizo) || AMER type of small coconut (coco) | turtle dove (tórtola mejicana).

coquización *f* coking.

coquizar *vt* to coke.

coracero *m* cuirassier (soldado) || FIG & FAM bad cigar.

coracha *f* leather bag.

coraje *m* anger, rage (ira) || courage, valour, bravery (valor) || — FAM *dar coraje* to make livid (poner furioso) | *echarle coraje a algo* to put some life *o* spirit into sth. | *¡qué coraje!* how annoying!

corajina *f* FAM fit of anger.

corajinoso, sa; corajoso, sa *adj* angry, irate.

corajudo, da *adj* quick-tempered (que tiene mal genio) || AMER courageous; *un hombre corajudo* a courageous man.

coral *adj* choral; *música coral* choral music.
◆ *m* ZOOL coral || MÚS chorale, choral (composición) || wattle and comb (del pavo) || FIG *fino como un coral, más fino que un coral* as sharp as a needle.
◆ *f* coral snake (serpiente) || MÚS choir, choral society.
◆ *pl* coral beads (collar).

Coral (la Gran Barrera del) *n pr* GEOGR the Great Barrier Reef.

coralero *m* worker *o* dealer in coral.

coralífero, ra *adj* coralliferous.

coralillo *m* coral snake (serpiente).

coralino, na *adj* coralline, coral-red (color) || coralline.
◆ *f* coralline (alga).

corambre *f* hides *pl*, skins *pl* (curtidos) || wineskin (odre).

corán *m* Koran (alcorán).

coránico, ca *adj* Koranic.

coraza *f* cuirass || MAR armour plate [*US* armor plate] || ZOOL shell, carapace (de la tortuga) || FIG armour, protection.

corazón *m* heart (víscera) || FIG core, heart (centro) || FIG heart, courage (valor) | heart (afecto); *te amo de todo corazón* I love you with all my heart || heart (naipe) || HERÁLD heart || — FIG *blando de corazón* soft-hearted | *con el corazón en un puño* with one's heart in one's mouth | *con todo mi corazón* wholeheartedly, with all my heart || *corazón artificial* artificial heart || *corazón, corazón mío* my love, my heart || *corazón de alcachofa* artichoke heart || *de corazón* in all honesty, in all sincerity || *dedo del corazón* middle finger || *duro de corazón* hardhearted || *hablar al corazón* to appeal to s.o.'s heart || *hablar con el corazón en la mano* to speak from the heart, to speak sincerely || *llegar al corazón de alguien* to touch s.o.'s heart || *llevar el corazón en la mano* to wear one's heart on one's sleeve || *me da* or *me dice el corazón que...* something tells me that..., I have a hunch that... || *morir con el corazón destrozado* to die of a broken heart || *no caberle a uno el corazón en el pecho* to have a heart of gold (ser bueno), to be beside o.s. with joy (estar muy contento) || *no tener corazón* to have no heart || *no tener corazón para hacer algo* not to have the heart to do sth. || *ojos que no ven, corazón que no siente* out of sight, out of mind || FIG *partir* or *traspasar el corazón* to break s.o.'s heart, to rend s.o.'s heart | *poner el corazón en algo* to set one's heart on sth. | *salir* or *brotar del corazón* to come from the bottom of one's heart | *ser uno todo corazón* to be the soul of kindness | *sin corazón* heartless | *tener buen corazón* to be kind-hearted *o* good-hearted || FIG *tener el corazón que se sale del pecho* to have a heart of gold | *tener mal corazón* to have no heart.
◆ *pl* ARQ hearts.

corazonada *f* hunch, feeling; *tengo la corazonada de que vendrá* I have a hunch he will come || impulse.

corazoncillo *m* BOT St. -John's-wort.

corbata *f* tie [*US* necktie] (prenda de vestir); *ponerse la corbata* to put one's tie on || cravat (banda de tela) || bow and tassels (de la bandera) || insignia || — *con corbata* with a tie on, wearing a tie || *corbata de lazo* bow tie.

corbatería *f* tie shop [*US* necktie shop].

corbatín *m* bow tie || bow and tassels (de la bandera).

corbeta *f* corvette (embarcación).

Córcega *npr f* GEOGR Corsica.

corcel *m* steed, charger, courser.

corcino *m* fawn (corzo pequeño).

corcova *f* hump, hunch (joroba, jiba).

corcovado, da *adj* humpbacked, hunchbacked.
◆ *m/f* hunchback.

corcovar *vt* to bend, to crook, to curve (encorvar).

corcovear *vi* to buck, to curvet (caballería).

corcoveta *m/f* FAM hunchback.

corcovo *m* caper, prance (salto) || buck, curvet (de caballo) || FIG crookedness.

corchea *f* MÚS quaver.

corchera *f* line of cork floats (en una piscina) || wine cooler (recipiente de corcho).

corchero, ra *adj* cork.

corcheta *f* eye [of a clasp].

corchete *m* clasp (para sujetar) || hook [of the hook and eye of a clasp] (que se engancha en la hembra) || bench hook (de carpintería) || square bracket (signo tipográfico) || (ant) FIG constable (alguacil).

corchetera *f* AMER stapler (grapadora).

corcho *m* cork, cork bark (corteza de alcornoque) || cork (tapón) || float [of a fishing line] (para pescar) || wine cooler (corchera) || beehive (colmena) || fireguard made of cork.
◆ *pl* floats (para nadar).

corcholata *f* AMER metal bottle-top.

¡córcholis! *interj* heavens!, good heavens!, gosh!, goodness! [*US* holy smoke!, gee!, gee-whizz!].

corchoso, sa *adj* corklike.

corchotaponero, ra *adj* cork, cork stopper.

cordado, da *adj* HERÁLD with strings in a different coloured enamel || ZOOL chordate.
◆ *m* ZOOL chordate.
◆ *f* rope (alpinismo) || *primero* or *cabeza* or *jefe de cordada* leader, first on the rope, head of the rope.

cordaje *m* ropes *pl*, cordage (conjunto de cuerdas) || MAR rigging, cordage (jarcia).

cordal *adj* *muela cordal* wisdom tooth.
◆ *m* tailpiece (del violín).

cordel *m* thin rope, cord, line (cuerda) || length of five paces (distancia) || cattle path (cañada) || *a cordel* in a straigth line.

cordelería *f* rope manufacturing (oficio) || rope trade (comercio) || ropes *pl* (cuerdas) || MAR rigging, cordage.

cordelero, ra *m/f* ropemaker (fabricante) || rope dealer (comerciante).

cordera *f* ewe lamb (ovejita) || FIG meek and gentle woman, lamb.

cordería *f* ropes *pl*, cordage.

corderillo *m* little lamb || dressed lambskin (piel).

cordero *m* lamb (cría de la oveja) || lamb (carne de cordero menor), mutton (carne de cordero mayor) || lambskin (piel) || FIG lamb; *manso como un cordero* as gentle as a lamb ||— FIG *ahí está* or *ésa es la madre del cordero* that is the crux of the matter (lo esencial), there's the rub (dificultad), that is the key to it (causa) || *cordero lechal* sucking lamb || *cordero pascual* paschal lamb || FIG *el Divino Cordero* or *Cordero de Dios* the Lamb of God.

cordial *adj* stimulating, tonic (reconfortante); *remedio cordial* stimulating medicine || FIG cordial, hearty, warm; *una cordial bienvenida* a warm welcome || — *dedo cordial* middle finger || *saludos cordiales* cordially yours (en una carta).
◆ *m* tonic (bebida reconfortante) || MED cordial.

cordialidad *f* cordiality, warmth; *la cordialidad con que recibió a sus amigos* the cordiality with which he received his friends.

cordialmente *adv* cordially, warmly, heartily || sincerely (al final de una carta).

cordillera *f* mountain range, cordillera, chain || AMER *por cordillera* through a third party.

cordillerano, na *adj* AMER from the Andes.

córdoba *m* córdoba [the basic monetary unit of Nicaragua].

Córdoba *n pr* GEOGR Cordova (en España), Córdoba (en Argentina).

cordobán *m* Cordoban leather (cuero de Córdoba).

cordobés, esa *adj/s* Cordovan (de Córdoba).

cordón *m* string (cuerda pequeña) || braid, cord, cordon (de carácter ornamental) || ribbon (cinta) || cord (de algunos religiosos) || ELECTR flex, wire || lace, string (para los zapatos) || ANAT cord (umbilical) || ARQ cable moulding, twisted fillet, cordon (bocel) || MAR strand (de cable) || FIG cordon; *cordón sanitario* sanitary cordon; *cordón de policía, de tropas* cordon of police, of troops || AMER curb, kerb (de la acera).
◆ *pl* aglets, shoulder braids (de uniforme militar).

cordonazo *m* lash with a cord (golpe).

cordoncillo *m* small cord || rib, cord (de tela) | milling (de una moneda) || piping, braid (costura) || IMPR ornamental border of a page.

cordura *f* good sense, wisdom, sensibleness (sensatez) || sanity (estado de cuerdo).

corea *f* MED chorea, St. Vitus's dance.

Corea *npr f* GEOGR Korea; *Corea del Norte* North Korea; *Corea del Sur* South Korea.

coreano, na *adj/s* Korean.

corear *vt* MÚS to chorus || FIG to chorus.
◆ *vi* to sing in chorus.

coreo *m* trochee (poesía griega) || MÚS chorus.

coreografía *f* choreography.

coreógrafo *m* choreographer.

coriáceo, a *adj* coriaceous.

coriambo *m* choriamb (poesía).

coriana *f* AMER blanket, rug (cobertor).

corifeo *m* coryphaeus || FIG leader.

corimbo *m* BOT corymb.

corindón *m* corundum (piedra fina).

corintio, tia *adj/s* Corinthian.

Corinto *n pr* GEOGR Corinth.

corion *m* chorion (membrana del huevo).

corista *m* chorister (en una iglesia).
◆ *m/f* chorus singer (ópera).
◆ *f* chorus girl (revista, music-hall).

coriza *f* MED coryza (resfriado).

cormorán *m* cormorant (cuervo marino).

cornac; cornaca *m* elephant keeper, mahout.

cornada *f* goring (herida) || butt (golpe) || — *dar cornadas a* to gore, to butt || FAM *más cornadas da el hambre* I'd rather have this than starve, it's better than nothing.

cornadura *f* horns *pl* (de toro, etc.) || antlers *pl* (de ciervo).

cornalina *f* cornelian, carnelian (piedra).

cornalón *adj m* long-horned [bull].
◆ *m* serious goring.

cornamenta *f* horns *pl* (de toro) || antlers *pl* (de ciervo).

cornamusa *f* MÚS bagpipe.

córnea *f* ANAT cornea (del ojo) || — *córnea opaca* sclera (esclerótica) || *córnea transparente* cornea || *de la córnea* corneal.

cornear; acornar; acornear *vt* to butt, to gore (dar cornadas).

corneja *f* ZOOL crow (cuervo) | scops owl (búho).

cornejal *m* dogwood field.

cornejo *m* dogwood (arbusto).

córneo, a *adj* corneous, horny (sustancia), hornlike (hoja, etc.).
◆ *f pl* BOT cornaceae.

córner *m* corner, corner kick (saque de esquina); *tirar un córner* to take a corner.

cornerina *f* carnelian, cornelian.

corneta *f* MÚS bugle (militar) || pennant (bandera de un regimiento) || coif, cornet (de monjas) || — *a toque de corneta* under the bugle call || *corneta acústica* ear trumpet || *corneta de llaves* cornet || *corneta de monte* hunting horn (trompa) || *toque de corneta* bugle call.
◆ *m* MIL bugler (persona que toca la corneta).

cornete *m* turbinate, turbinate bone (de la nariz).

cornetilla *f* hot pepper.

cornetín *m* cornet (instrumento) | cornet player, cornetist, cornettist (instrumentista) || MIL bugler (soldado).

corneto, ta *adj* AMER bow-legged | with downturned horns (res).

cornezuelo *m* ergot (del centeno) || crescent-shaped olive (aceituna) || VET horn.

corniabierto, ta *adj* wide-horned.

corniapretado, da *adj* having *o* with close-set horns.

cornigacho, cha *adj* with downturned horns.

cornijal *m* corner.

cornijón *m* entablature (cornisamiento) || corner (esquina).

cornisa *f* ARQ & GEOGR cornice.

cornisamiento; cornisamiento *m* entablature.

corniveleto, ta *adj* having *o* with straight and upturned horns.

corno *m* BOT dogwood (cornejo) || MÚS *corno inglés* English horn, tenor oboe, cor anglais.

Cornualles *n pr* GEOGR Cornwall.

cornucopia *f* cornucopia, horn of plenty (emblema decorativo) || small mirror (espejo).

cornudo, da *adj* horned (con cuernos) || FIG & FAM deceived (marido).
◆ *m* FIG & FAM deceived husband, cuckold (p us) (marido) || *tras cornudo apaleado* adding insult to injury *o* insult on top of injury.

cornúpeta; cornúpeto *m* bull (toro).

coro *m* MÚS chorus, choir; *cantar a* or *en coro* to sing in chorus || choir, chancel (en las iglesias) || TEATR chorus || — *hablar a coro* to speak all at the same time *o* all together *o* all at once || *hacer coro, repetir a coro* to chorus || *hacer coro a alguien* to back s.o. up || *niño de coro* choirboy.

corografía *f* chorography.

coroideo, a *adj* choroid, chorioid.

coroides *f inv* ANAT choroid, chorioid (del ojo).

corojo *m* BOT corozo, corojo.

corola *f* corolla (de flor).

corolario *m* corollary.

corona *f* crown (de rey, de gloria, de martirio, etc.); *corona de espinas* crown of thorns || halo (halo) || wreath, crown, garland (de flores, de laurel) || coronet (de duque, de marqués, de conde, de vizconde) || crown [of the head] (coronilla) || tonsure (de clérigos) || crown (moneda) || wreath; *corona mortuoria* funeral wreath || FIG crown (reino, soberanía); *ceñirse la corona* to take over the crown || ZOOL coronet (del casco) || ANAT crown (de un diente) || ASTR corona; *corona solar* solar corona || MAT annulus, ring || ARQ corona, crown || BOT corona || TECN washer (arandela) | rim (de una polea, de una rueda) | winder (del reloj) || — *media corona* half crown, half-a-crown (moneda) || *muela con una corona* crowned tooth || *poner una corona a una muela* to crown a tooth || *rey sin corona* uncrowned king.

coronación *f* coronation, crowning (de un soberano) || FIG crowning, culmination || ARQ crown.

coronado, da *adj* crowned.
◆ *m* cleric.

coronar *vt* to crown (poner una corona) || to crown (en el juego de damas) || FIG to crown, to top (acabar, rematar); *una estatua corona el edificio* a statue crowns the building | to crown (colmar).
◆ *vpr* to crown (el niño en el parto).

coronario, ria *adj* coronary; *la arteria coronaria* the coronary artery.

corondel *m* IMPR reglet | vertical watermark lines *pl* (rayas).

coronel *m* MIL colonel || AVIAC group captain [*US* colonel].

coronela *f* FAM colonel's wife.

coronilla *f* crown of the head || tonsure (de los sacerdotes) || BOT coronilla || — FIG & FAM *andar* or *ir de coronilla* to bend over backwards [to please s.o.] | *estar uno hasta la coronilla* to be fed up, to be sick and tired.

corosol *f* BOT custard apple (fruto) | custard-apple tree (árbol).

corotos *m pl* AMER odds and ends, stuff *sing*, things (trastos).

coroza *f* cone-shaped hat [formerly worn by convicts].

corozo *m* BOT corojo, corozo.

corpachón; corpanchón; corpazo *m* FAM big body, carcass || carcass of a fowl (del ave).

corpiño *m* sleeveless bodice || AMER bra, brassière (sostén).

corporación *f* corporation.

corporal *adj* corporal, bodily || *pena corporal* corporal punishment.
◆ *m* REL corporal, corporale.

corporalidad *f* corporality.

corporativismo *m* corporativism.

corporativista *adj/s* corporativist.

corporativo, va *adj* corporate, corporative.

corporeidad *f* corporeity.

corpóreo, a *adj* corporeal.

corps *m* *guardia de corps* royal guard || *sumiller de corps* Lord chamberlain of the royal guard.

corpulencia *f* corpulence, stoutness.

corpulento, ta *adj* corpulent, stout.

Corpus *npr m* REL Corpus Christi.

corpuscular *adj* corpuscular.

corpúsculo *m* corpuscle, corpuscule; *los microbios son corpúsculos* microbes are corpuscles.

corral *m* poultry yard (para aves) || pen, run (para otros animales) || yard, courtyard (junto a una casa) || weir, corral (de pesca) || playpen (para niños) || (ant) playhouse (teatro) || AMER corral (redil) || — *aves de corral* poultry || FIG & FAM *corral de vacas* pigsty.

corralera *f* Andalusian song.

corralero, ra *m/f* poulterer (de aves de corral) || manure dealer (de estiércol).

corraliza *f* poultry yard (para aves).

corralón *m* yard || inner yard (de una casa de vecindad) || AMER warehouse (almacén).

correa *f* leather strip, thong, strap (tira de cuero) || leash, lead (del perro) || TECN belt; *correa de transmisión* drive belt, driving belt; *correa conductora* or *transportadora* conveyor belt; *correa sin fin* continuous *o* endless belt || belt (cinturón) || watchband, watchstrap (de un reloj) || FIG pliability, give, elasticity (flexibilidad) || ARQ purlin || — *correa de ventilación* fan belt || *correa extensible* expanding bracelet (de reloj) || FIG & FAM *tener correa* to have a lot of patience.

correaje *m* leather equipment (de un soldado) || harness (arnés).

correazo *m* blow *o* lash with a belt.

correcalles *m inv* FAM loiterer, loafer (holgazán).

corrección *f* correction (enmienda) || rebuke, reprimand (reprensión) || propriety, politeness, good manners *pl* (buenos modales) || correctness (del lenguaje, etc.) || IMPR proofreading || — *corrección de pruebas* proofreading || *corrección modelo* answers *pl*, solutions *pl*.

correccional *adj* correctional; *establecimiento correccional* correctional institution.
◆ *m* reformatory || *correccional de menores* borstal.

correctivo, va *adj/sm* corrective.

correcto, ta *adj* correct; *su conducta correcta* his correct behaviour; *la contestación correcta* the correct answer || polite, courteous, well-mannered; *no estuviste muy correcto conmigo* you were not very polite to me.

corrector, ra *m/f* corrector || IMPR proofreader.

corredero, ra *adj* sliding; *puerta corredera* sliding door.
◆ *f* runner, groove (de puerta o de ventana) || runner (muela superior de un molino) || ZOOL cockroach (cochinilla) || DEP racetrack || road, street (calle) || MAR log || TECN slide, slide valve (de la máquina de vapor) || FIG & FAM procuress (alcahueta) || FAM diarrhoea, the runs || *de corredera* sliding; *puerta de corredera* sliding door.

corredizo, za *adj* running, slip; *nudo corredizo* slip knot || — *puerta corrediza* sliding door || *techo corredizo* sunshine roof, sliding roof (de los coches).

corredor, ra *adj* running || racing, race (de carreras) || ZOOL ratite (ave que no puede volar).
◆ *m/f* runner (que corre); *corredor de fondo* long-distance runner.
◆ *m* COM broker, agent || MIL scout (soldado) || corridor, gallery, hall (pasillo) || covered way (fortificación) || — *corredor de Bolsa* or *de cambio* stockbroker || *corredor de coches* racing driver || *corredor de fincas* land agent || *corredor de seguros* insurance broker.
◆ *f* ratite [*pl* ratitae] (ave).

corredura *f* overflow [of liquid].

correduría *f* brokerage.

corregidor *m* corregidor (antiguo magistrado español) || mayor (antiguo alcalde).

corregidora *f* corregidor's wife.

corregir* *vt* to correct (una falta, un defecto físico, un vicio) || to correct, to rectify (la conducta de alguien) || to correct, to adjust (un instrumento) || to admonish, to scold (reprender); *hay que corregir a los niños para que se porten bien* children have to be admonished so that they behave || to chastise, to punish (castigar) || IMPR to read (pruebas) || — *corregir a alguien* to set s.o. straight || MIL *corregir el tiro* to correct the range.
◆ *vpr* to correct o.s. (de una equivocación) || to reform, to mend one's ways (manera de comportarse) || *corregirse de una mala costumbre* to break o.s. of a bad habit.

correinado *m* joint reign *o* rule.

correinante *adj* jointly reigning.

correlación *f* correlation.

correlacionar *vt* to correlate.
◆ *vpr* to be correlated *o* correlative.

correlativo, va *adj/sm* correlative.

correligionario, ria *m/f* coreligionist.

correntada *f* AMER strong current.

correntío *adj* flowing, running (corriente).

correntón, ona *adj* gadabout (trotacalles) || lively, jolly, sociable (festivo).
◆ *m/f* gadabout || joker (bromista).

correntoso, sa *adj* AMER rapid, swift, having *o* with a strong current (río).

correo *m* courier (mensajero) || post, post office, mail, mail services *pl* (servicio postal) || MIL dispatch rider || post office (oficina); *voy a correo* I'm going to the post office || mail, post (cartas); *hoy no hay mucho correo* there isn't much mail today || mail train (tren correo) || postman [US mailman] (cartero) || JUR accomplice (cómplice) || — *a vuelta de correo* by return of post || *correo aéreo* air mail, airmail || *correo certificado* resgistered post *o* mail || INFORM *correo electrónico* electronic mail || *correo urgente* special delivery || *echar una carta al correo* to post a letter [US to mail a letter] || *por correo* by post || *sello de correo* postage stamp.
◆ *pl* post office *sing*; *voy a correos* I'm going to the post office || — *apartado de correos* post-office box || *casa de correos* post office || *Central de Correos* central post office || *Director general de Correos* Postmaster General || *estafeta de Correos* sub-post office [US branch post office] || *la Administración de Correos* the General Post Office [US the Post Office Administration] || *lista de Correos* «poste restante» [US General Delivery]; *escribir a lista de Correos* to write care of «poste restante».

correón *m* large leather strap.

correosidad *f* flexibility (flexibilidad) || toughness, leatheriness (de la carne).

correoso, sa *adj* flexible || doughy (el pan) || tough, leathery (la carne).

correr *vi* to run; *correr tras uno* to run after s.o; *correr en busca de uno* to run in search of s.o. || to rush, to hurry (apresurarse) || FIG to run; *la senda corre entre las viñas* the path runs through the vineyards; *la sangre corrió en la batalla* blood ran in the fray | to flow (agua, electricidad); *el río corre entre los árboles* the river flows through the trees | to blow (el viento) | to play (una fuente) | to fly, to pass (el tiempo); *¡cómo corre el tiempo!* how time flies! || to go fast, to be fast; *este coche corre mucho* this car goes really fast || FIG to be legal tender; *esta moneda corre* this coin is legal tender; *esta moneda no corre* this coin is not legal tender | to be payable, to run (interés, sueldo, renta, etc.); *correrá tu sueldo desde el primero de marzo* your wages will run from the 1st of March | to circulate (noticia, rumor) | to slide (puerta corrediza) | to run; *los cajones corren gracias a un sistema de rodamiento de bolas* the drawers run on ball bearings | to run (extenderse) || — *al correr de la pluma* as one writes || *a todo* or *a más correr* at full *o* top speed || *¡corre!, ¡corre!* hurry up!, hurry, hurry!, be quick! || *corre a cargo de* it is the responsability of (incumbir a), it is to be paid by (estar pagado por), it is in the hands of (depender de) || *corre a su perdición* he is heading for his downfall || *corre la voz que...* rumour has it that... || *corre el peligro de que...* there is a risk *o* a danger that... || *correr como un gamo* to run like a hare || *correr con alguna cosa* to be in charge of sth., to be responsible for sth., to take care of sth. || *correr con los gastos* to foot the bill, to meet the expenses || *correr en una carrera* to run in a race, to run a race || *correr prisa* to be urgent || FAM *correr uno que se las pela* to run like mad || *dejar correr las cosas* to let things take their course || *de prisa y corriendo* in a hurry, with utmost speed, at full speed || *el mes que corre* this month, the present month, the current month || *en las cunetas corría agua* the gutters were running with water || *en lo que corre del año* so far this year || *en los tiempos que corren* nowadays || FIG *este hombre ha corrido mucho* this man has been around || *esto corre de* or *por mi cuenta* I'm taking charge of this, I'm seeing to this (encargarse de), I'm bearing the cost of it (pagar), this one's on me (pagar una copa) || *ir corriendo* to run along || *por debajo de la puerta corre mucho aire* there is a considerable draught under the door.
◆ *vt* to race, to run; *correr un caballo* to race a horse || to hunt, to run; *correr un jabalí* to run a wild boar || to fight (los toros) || to cover, to travel (una distancia) || to make run (un color) || to run; *correr la milla* to run the mile || to visit, to travel through (recorrer) || to move; *correr los botones de un vestido* to move the buttons on a dress || to overrun (en una guerra) || to pull up, to move; *correr una silla* to move a chair || to draw; *correr las cortinas* to draw the curtains || to untie, to undo (desatar) || to tip (la balanza) || to have (una aventura) || to put to confusion, to make blush (avergonzar) || — *correr el cerrojo* to bolt the door, to shoot the bolt || FAM *correrla* to go on a spree, to paint the town red (ir de juerga), to live it up, to have one's fling (llevar una vida airada) || *correr las amonestaciones* to publish the banns || FIG *correr las mozas* to be a one for the girls | *correr mundo* to roam the world over, to travel far and wide, to see the world || *correr parejas* to be on an equal footing || *correr peligro* to be in danger || *correr peligro de...* to run the risk of... || *correr un peligro* to run *o* to take a risk || FIG *correr un tupido velo sobre algo* to hush sth. up, to draw a veil over sth., to keep sth. quiet | *estar corrido* to be ashamed.
◆ *vpr* FIG to move over, to move up; *córrase un poco* move over a bit || to slide (un objeto) || to shift (una carga) || FAM to blush; *correrse de vergüenza* to blush with shame | to get em-

barrassed (estar confuso) || to melt (hielo) || to gutter (vela) || to run (tinta, color, maquillaje) || POP to come, to have an orgasm (tener orgasmo) || — FAM *correrse una juerga* to go on a binge || *se le ha corrido la media* her stocking has a ladder, there is a run in her stocking.

correría *f* incursion, raid (en país enemigo) || trip (viaje).

correspondencia *f* correspondence (relación) || correspondence (por escrito) || letters *pl* (cartas) || mail, post; *llevar* or *encargarse de la correspondencia* to be in charge of the mail || communication (comunicación) || interchange, connection (en el metro) || — *curso por correspondencia* correspondence course || *mantener correspondencia con alguien* to correspond with s.o., to be in correspondence with s.o.

corresponder *vi* to return (un favor, el amor, etc.) || to repay (amabilidad) || to tally; *esta cifra no corresponde con esa* this figure doesn't tally with that one || to belong; *este mueble no corresponde a esta habitación* this piece of furniture does not belong in this room || to correspond, to match; *estos botones no corresponden* these buttons don't match || to become, to befit (ser propio de); *esa conducta no corresponde a una persona bien educada* that behaviour does not become an educated person || to fit; *el lugar correspondía a la descripción* the place fitted the description; *la llave no correspondía a la cerradura* the key didn't fit the keyhole || to be the job *o* the responsibility of, to fall to (incumbir); *corresponde al Estado velar por la salud pública* it falls to the State *o* it is responsibility of the State to look after public health || to be the job of (ser el trabajo de) || to come up to, to meet; *el éxito no correspondió a mis esperanzas* the success did not come up to my expectations || ARQ to communicate || — *ahora te corresponde a ti saltar* now it is your turn to jump || *amor no correspondido* unrequited love || *a quien corresponda* to whom it may concern || *correspondió a sus atenciones* she responded to his attentions || *le correspondió con un bolso nuevo* he gave her a new handbag in return || *le contesté como correspondía* I gave him a suitable reply || *les correspondió una libra a cada uno* each one got a pound || *te corresponde a ti hacer este trabajo* that is your job, it is for you to do that job || *toma la parte que te corresponde y vete* take your share and go.

◆ *vpr* to love one another (amarse) || to go together; *las cortinas y los muebles no se corresponden* the curtains and the furniture don't go together || to correspond (cartearse).

correspondiente *adj* corresponding; *ángulos correspondientes* corresponding angles || *miembro correspondiente* corresponding member (academia).

corresponsal *m* correspondent; *corresponsal de periódico* newspaper correspondent || correspondent, agent (de un banco, etc.) || news correspondent (en radio y televisión).

corresponsalía *f* post of a newspaper correspondent (cargo) || correspondent's office (oficina) || *jefe de corresponsalía* chief correspondent.

corretaje *m* COM brokerage.

corretear *vi* to loiter about the streets (vagar) | to run about (ir de un sitio para otro).

◆ *vt* AMER to pursue, to chase (perseguir).

correteo *m* loitering about the streets (del vago) || running about, games *pl*, frolic (de los niños) || running about (acción de ir de un sitio para otro).

corretón, ona *adj* fidgety (inquieto) || FIG gadabout.

correvedile; correveidile *m/f* FIG & FAM gossip (chismoso) | go-between, pimp (alcahuete).

corrida *f* race, run (carrera) || bullfight, corrida (de toros) || AMER outcrop (minas) | spree (juerga) || — *de corrida* hastily (apresuradamente), fluently (hablar), at sight (traducción) || *voy en una corrida a la tienda* I'll run straight round to the shop.

◆ *pl* popular Andalusian song *sing* (playera).

corrido *m* AMER fugitive (fugitivo) | Mexican ballad.

corrido, da *adj* good; *una libra corrida* a good pound || cursive (escritura) || FIG abashed, ashamed, embarrassed (avergonzado) | experienced, sharp (experimentado) || — *balcón corrido* continous balcony || *barba corrida* bushy beard || *de corrido* fluently; *leer de corrido* to read fluently; *hablar un idioma de corrido* to speak a language fluently; at sight; *traducir de corrido* to translate at sight || FAM *mujer corrida* woman who has been around || *pesar corrido* to give good weight || *saber de corrido* to have sth. at one's fingertips || *trece días corridos* thirteen days running.

corriente *adj* running (que corre) || common, usual (común) || current, valid (dinero, etc.) || current, present (año) || ordinary; *un hombre corriente* an ordinary man || fluent, flowing (estilo) || average; *el inglés corriente* the average Englishman || — *agua corriente* running water || *corriente y moliente* ordinary, run-of-the-mill, common of garden; *una cena corriente y moliente* an ordinary dinner || *cuenta corriente* current account [US checking account] || FIG *es cosa corriente, es moneda corriente* it's everyday stuff, it's run-of-the-mill stuff || *lo corriente* the usual thing, the normal thing || *salirse de lo corriente* to be out of the ordinary, to be unusual.

◆ *f* current (movimiento de un fluido); *corriente marina, submarina, de aire* ocean, underwater, air current || stream, current (curso); *seguir la corriente de un río* to follow the stream, to sail with the current; *navegar contra la corriente* to go against the stream, to sail against the current || stream, flow (de lava) || draught [US draft] (en una habitación) || FIG trend; *las últimas corrientes de la moda* the latest fashion trends || ELECTR current; *corriente alterna, continua, de alta frecuencia, trifásica* alternating, direct, high frequency, three-phase current || — FIG *abandonarse a la corriente* to drift with the tide *o* the current || *corriente sanguínea* bloodstream || FIG *dejarse llevar de* or *por la corriente* to follow the herd | *la corriente de la opinión* the current of opinion || GEOGR *la corriente del Golfo, la corriente de Humboldt* the Gulf Stream, the Humboldt Current || FIG *llevarle* or *seguirle la corriente a uno* to humour s.o. [US to humor s.o.] | *seguir la corriente* to swim with the stream, to follow the tide *o* the crowd (ser conformista).

◆ *m* current month || — *al corriente* aware (al tanto), up-to-date (sin atraso) || *el diez del corriente* the tenth inst., the tenth of the current month || *estar al corriente de...* to be aware of..., to know about... || *mantenerse al corriente* to keep up-to-date || *poner al corriente* to inform || *tener al corriente* to keep informed *o* posted.

corrientemente *adv* usually (normalmente) || fluently (con soltura).

corrillo *m* small group *o* knot of people talking (grupo) || round enclosure (en la Bolsa) || FIG clique (círculo de gente).

corrimiento *m* GEOL landslide || slipping, sliding || AGR failure of a vine crop (de la uva) || MED discharge || FIG embarrassment (vergüenza) || AMER rheumatism (reumatismo).

corro *m* circle, ring (de personas) || circle (espacio circular) || ring-a-ring-a-roses (baile de niños) || FIG round enclosure (en la Bolsa) | stocks *pl*; *el corro bancario* bank stocks || — *bailar en corro* to dance in a ring || *entrar en el corro* to join in the circle || *hacer corro* to stand in a ring *o* circle || *hacer corro aparte* to keep to o.s. || *hacerle corro a alguien* to stand *o* to gather round s.o.

corroboración *f* corroboration.

corroborante *adj* corroborating.

◆ *m* (ant) MED tonic.

corroborar *vt* (ant) to strengthen, to fortify (fortificar) || to corroborate; *corroborar con hechos* to corroborate with facts.

corroer* *vt* to corrode, to eat away, to wear away (carcomer) || GEOL to erode || FIG to consume, to eat away || FIG *las preocupaciones le corroen* he is beset by worries.

◆ *vpr* to become corroded, to corrode.

corromper *vt* to corrupt, to pervert (gente, lenguaje, costumbres, etc.) || to bribe (sobornar) || to rot (madera) || to turn bad (alimentos).

◆ *vpr* to become corrupted (personas, etc.) || to rot (madera) || to go bad (alimentos).

corrompido, da *adj* rotten (cosas) || corrupt (personas).

corrosión *f* corrosion.

corrosivo, va *adj/sm* corrosive.

corrupción *f* corruption || rot (de la madera) || FIG corruption, vitiation (de voces, de costumbres) || bribery (soborno) || *corrupción de menores* corruption of minors.

corruptela *f* corruptness, corruption.

corrupto, ta *adj* corrupt.

— OBSERV This adjective is the irregular past participle of *corromper*.

corruptor, ra *adj* corruptive, corrupting.

◆ *m/f* corrupter.

corrusco *m* FAM stale bread crust.

corsario, ria *adj* *buque corsario, nave corsaria* privateer || *capitán corsario* privateer.

◆ *m* corsair, privateer (pirata).

corsé *m* stays *pl*, corset || *corsé ortopédico* corset.

corsetería *f* corset factory, corset shop.

corsetero, ra *m/f* corsetier, corsetière.

corso, sa *adj* Corsican.

◆ *m* MAR privateering || AMER parade (desfile).

◆ *m/f* Corsican (de Córcega).

corta *f* felling (of trees) (tala).

cortaalambres *m inv* wire cutters *pl*.

cortable *adj* that can be cut.

cortabolsas *m inv* FAM pickpocket (ratero).

cortacallos *m inv* corn cutter *o* parer.

cortacésped *m* lawnmower.

cortacigarros *m inv* cigar cutter.

cortacircuitos *m inv* ELECTR circuit breaker.

cortacorriente *m* ELECTR switch, current breaker.

cortada *f* AMER cut (herida).

cortadillo *m* tumbler (vaso) || *azúcar de cortadillo* lump sugar.

cortado, da *adj* cut || FIG embarrassed (confuso); *se quedó cortado* he became embarrassed | ashamed (avergonzado) | tongue-tied (sin poder hablar) | sour; *leche cortada* sour milk | jerky (estilo) || HERÁLD parted in the middle || — AMER *andar cortado* to be broke || *cortado a pico* sheer, steep || *dejar cortado* to cut short; *eso lo dejó cortado* that cut him short || FIG *tener el cuerpo cortado* to feel queer.

◆ *m* coffee with cream, coffee with only a little milk (café con muy poca leche) || caper, leap (paso de baile).

cortador, ra *adj* cutting (que corta).
◆ *m/f* cutter (que corta) || cutter (sastre).
◆ *f* TECN cutting machine [for trimming velvet] || *cortadora de césped* lawnmower.

cortadura *f* cut (incisión) || slit (corte largo) || gorge, pass (entre montañas) || clipping, cutting (de un periódico) || *hacerse una cortadura en la cara con la cuchilla de afeitar* to cut *o* to nick one's face with the razor.
◆ *pl* clippings, cuttings (de periódico) || trimmings (recortes).

cortafierro *m* AMER cold chisel.

cortafrío *m* TECN cold chisel.

cortafuego *m* AGR firebreak || ARQ fire wall.

cortahierro *m* TECN cold chisel.

cortalápices *m inv* pencil sharpener.

cortalegumbres *m inv* vegetable cutter.

cortante *adj* cutting, sharp (utensilio), cutting, keen (filo) || bitter (frío) || biting (viento).
◆ *m* chopper, cleaver.

cortapapel *m*; **cortapapeles** *m inv* paper knife || letter opener (para abrir cartas).

cortapicos *m inv* ZOOL earwig.

cortapiés *m inv* FAM slash at the legs.

cortapisa *f* condition, restriction; *poner cortapisas a...* to impose conditions on..., to make restrictions on... || obstacle, impediment (traba) || trimming, border, edging (guarnición) || FIG charm, spice (gracia) || — *hablar sin cortapisas* to talk freely || *sin cortapisas* with no strings attached.

cortaplumas *m inv* penknife.

cortapuros *m inv* cigar cutter.

cortar *vt* to cut; *cortar un papel con las tijeras* to cut a paper with scissors; *cortarle el pelo a alguien* to cut s.o.'s hair; *cortar una película* to cut a film || to cut out, to cut; *cortar un vestido* to cut a dress out || to cut out (suprimir); *cortar un capítulo de un libro* to cut out a chapter of a book || to crack, to chap, to split; *el frío corta la piel* the cold cracks the skin || to cut *o* to chop down, to fell; *cortar un árbol* to cut a tree down || to cut off; *cortarle la cabeza a alguien* to cut s.o.'s head off || MAT to cut || to carve, to cut up (carne) || to cut off (teléfono, gas, etc.) || FIG to cleave, to cut; *la flecha cortó el aire* the arrow clove the air | to cut through, to slice through; *el navío cortaba las olas* the ship cut through the waves | to cut (el vino, un líquido) | to cut off, to divide (separar) | to cut (los naipes) | to seal off, to bar (una calle) | to cut short (una discusión) | to cut off, to interrupt (una comunicación, la inspiración) | to settle once and for all (decidir) | to curdle (la leche, etc.) || DEP to cut, to slice (una pelota) || — FAM *¡corta!; ¡corta el rollo!* give over!, knock it off! || FIG *cortar algo de raíz* to nip sth. in the bud | *cortar bien una poesía* to recite a poem well | *cortar el apetito* to ruin *o* to take away one's appetite | *cortar el bacalao* to be the boss | *cortar el camino a alguien* to bar s.o.'s way, to cut s.o. off | *cortar el hilo del discurso* to cut the thread of the argument || *cortar el pelo al cepillo* to give a crew cut || FIG *cortar en seco* to cut short || *cortar la digestión* to upset one's digestion || *cortar la fiebre* to bring down the fever || *cortar la palabra* to interrupt || MIL *cortar la retirada* to cut off the retreat || FAM *cortarle a uno un vestido* to slate s.o., to pull s.o. to pieces, to run s.o. down | *cortar vestidos* to gossip, to criticize people, to tittle-tattle, to backbite.
◆ *vi* to cut; *un cuchillo que corta bien* a knife that cuts well || to bite (el viento) || to cut off (teléfono) || to cut (en los naipes) || — *cortar con el pasado* to break with the past || FIG *cortar por lo sano* to take drastic action, to settle things once and for all.
◆ *vpr* to cut o.s.; *me corté con un cuchillo* I cut myself with a knife || to cut; *esta madera se corta fácilmente* this wood cuts easily || to be embarrassed (estar confuso) | to become tongue-tied (no poder hablar) || to curdle, to turn sour; *la leche se ha cortado* the milk has turned sour || to get chapped *o* cracked (la piel) || to have cut; *me corto el pelo en la peluquería* I have my hair cut at the hairdresser's || AMER FAM to peg out (morir) || *cortarse las uñas, la mano* to cut one's nails, one's hand.

cortarraíces *m inv* root slicer.

cortatubos *m inv* pipe cutter.

cortaúñas *m inv* nail clipper.

cortavidrios *m inv* glass cutter.

cortaviento *m* windbreak, windshield.

corte *m* cutting (acción de cortar) || felling (de árboles) || cut (de corriente eléctrica) || cutting edge (filo); *el corte de una espada* the cutting edge of a sword || cut (en un periódico, una película, etc.) || cut, haircut (del pelo); *corte con navaja* razor cut || cut (de un traje) || length (tela de vestido) || cutting (del heno) || cut (herida) || cut (de la cara) || wafer [US ice-cream sandwich] (helado) || cut (en los naipes) || edge (de un libro) || cross section (dibujo de una sección) || cut (trozo de carne) || cut (en el tenis) || FIG squelch (réplica) || AMER harvest, harvesting (siega) || — *corte y confección* dressmaking || FIG *darle un corte a uno* to cut s.o. short || FAM *darse corte* to put on airs (darse tono) | *¡qué corte le di!* he didn't know what to say.
◆ *f* court (residencia de los reyes) || court (familia real y gentes de palacio) || retinue, suite (acompañamiento) || AMER court; *corte suprema* supreme court || — *hacer la corte a...* to court..., to woo... || *la corte celestial* the Heavenly Host.

cortedad *f* smallness (poca extensión), brevity, shortness (brevedad) || FIG lack, dearth [of means, education, courage]; *cortedad de ánimo* lack of courage | shyness, bashfulness, timidity (timidez) || *cortedad de genio* faintheartedness.

cortejar *vt* to court, to woo (galantear) || to court, to curry favour with (halagar).

cortejo *m* courting, wooing (acción de cortejar) || train, retinue, suite, cortège (séquito) || — *cortejo fúnebre* funeral procession, funeral cortège || *cortejo nupcial* wedding party.

Cortes *npr fpl* HIST States General of Spain || Cortes [Spanish parliament] || *Cortes Constituyentes* constituent assembly.

cortés *adj* courteous, polite || FAM *lo cortés no quita lo valiente* courtesy and valour are not mutually exclusive.

cortesanesco, ca *adj* of courtiers.

cortesanía *f* courtesy, politeness.

cortesano, na *adj* of the court, court (de la corte) || courteous, courtly, polite (cortés) || *literatura cortesana* court literature.
◆ *m/f* courtier.
◆ *f* courtezan, courtesan (mujer de mala vida).

cortesía *f* courtesy, politeness; *rivalizar en cortesía* to vie with each other *o* outdo each other in courtesy || formal ending (en las cartas) || bow, curtsy (reverencia) || present (regalo) || COM grace [for redeeming a debt] || grace (merced) || title (tratamiento) || IMPR blank || — *Cortesía de la Dirección General de Turismo* courtesy of the General Office of Tourism || *visita de cortesía* courtesy call.

cortésmente *adv* courteously, politely.

corteza *f* bark (del árbol) || rind, peel (de naranja o de limón) || crust (del pan) || rind (del queso, del tocino) || ZOOL sandgrouse (ave) || BOT cortex || FIG appearance, façade (apariencia) | rudeness, uncouthness (rusticidad) || — ANAT *corteza cerebral* cerebral cortex || *la corteza terrestre* the Earth's crust.

cortical *adj* ANAT cortical.

cortijada *f* farm, farmhouse (finca) || farm buildings *pl*, farmhouses *pl* (edificios).

cortijero, ra *m/f* farmer (granjero) || foreman (capataz).

cortijo *m* farm [especially in Andalusia] (finca) || country home (casa de campo).

cortina *f* curtain; *correr la cortina* to draw the curtain || canopy (dosel) || FIG curtain, screen (lo que oculta); *cortina de humo* smoke curtain || curtain (fortificación) || retaining wall of a pier (muelle) || — MIL *cortina de fuego* barrage || *cortina de gases* gas screen.

cortinado; cortinaje *m* drapery, set of curtains, hangings *pl*.

cortinilla *f* small lace curtain (visillo).

cortisona *f* MED cortisone.

corto, ta *adj* short; *una falda muy corta* a very short skirt || scant, lacking (escaso) || short, brief; *un discurso corto* a short speech || FIG shy, bashful, timid (apocado) || — *a corta distancia* a short distance away || *a la corta, a la larga* sooner or later || *caldo corto* sauce prepared from wine and spices for cooking fish || *corto de alcances* dull-witted || *corto de estatura* very small || *corto de medios* of scant means || *corto de oído* hard of hearing || *corto de vista* shortsighted || *el abrigo se me ha quedado corto* my coat has become too short for me, I have grown out of my coat || *el chico va de corto* the boy is in short trousers || *ni corto ni perezoso* without thinking twice || *novela corta* short story || *onda corta* short wave || *quedarse corto* to fall short (un tiro), to be *o* to go short (de dinero), to underestimate, to miscalculate (calcular mal), not to say all one could, to be unable to say enough (en un relato) || *ser corto de genio* to be fainthearted || *tonelada corta* short ton || *y me quedo corto* and that's only half of it (en un relato), and that's a conservative estimate *o* an underestimation (en cifras).

cortocircuito *m* ELECTR short circuit || *poner en cortocircuito* to short-circuit.

cortometraje *m* CINEM short film.

Coruña (La) *npr f* GEOGR Corunna.

coruñés, esa *adj* [of *o* from] Corunna.
◆ *m/f* native *o* inhabitant of Corunna.

coruscante *adj* (p us) gleaming, shining (que brilla) || dazzling (que deslumbra).

coruscar *vi* to shine.

corva *f* ANAT back of the knee, ham.

corvadura *f* curvature || ARQ curve, arch.

corvar *vt* (ant) to bend.

corvejón *m* hock (de animal) || spur (espolón de las aves) || ZOOL cormorant (cuervo marino) || FAM *meter la pata hasta el corvejón* to put one's foot right in it, to make a huge blunder.

corvejos *m pl* hock *sing*.

corveta *f* DEP curvet (en equitación).

corvetear *vi* to curvet.

corvina *f* corvina (pez).

corvo, va *adj* crooked, bent, curved || hooked; *nariz corva* hooked nose.

corzo, za *m/f* roe deer (nombre genérico), roebuck (macho), doe (hembra).

cosa *f* thing; *llévese sus cosas de aquí* take your things away from here; *toma las cosas demasiado en serio* he takes things too seriously || affair, business (asunto); *meterse en cosas ajenas* to poke one's nose into other people's business *o* affairs || — *a cosa hecha* on purpose (adrede) || *alguna cosa* something || *¿alguna cosa más?* anything else? || *así están las cosas* that's how *o* the way things are || *así las cosas que un día* and so it was that one day || *cada cosa en* *su tiempo, y los nabos en adviento* there is a time and place for everything || *como cosa tuya* as if it were your idea || *como si tal cosa* just like that || *cosa de* about; *cosa de dos horas, de cinco millas* about two hours, about five miles || *cosa igual* such a thing, anything like it || *cosa nunca vista* something unheard of, something surprising || AMER *cosa que* so that (no vaya a ser que); *iré a verle mañana cosa que no vaya a pensar que lo he olvidado* I'll go and see him tomorrow so that he won't think I've forgotten him || *cualquier cosa* anything || *decirle a uno cuatro cosas* to tell s.o. a thing or two || *decir una cosa por otra* to say one thing and mean another || *dejar como cosa perdida* to give up as lost || *dos semanas o cosa así* two weeks or thereabouts || *entre unas cosas y otras* what with one thing and another || *esa es la cosa* that's the crux of the matter || *es cosa de empezar a hacer las maletas* it's time to start packing the cases || *es cosa de unos meses, de unos años* it is a matter of a few months, a few years || *es cosa de ver, de oír* you must see it, hear it; it's worth seeing, hearing || *es cosa fácil* it's easy || *eso es otra cosa* that's another matter || *este niño es una cosa mala* this boy is a little horror || *esto es cosa mía* this is my business || *la cosa es que...* the thing is that... || *las cosas de la vida* that's life, such is life || FIG *las cosas de palacio van despacio* it all takes time || *lo que son las cosas* much to my surprise || *ni cosa que valga* nothing of the kind || *no es cosa de broma* it's no laughing matter || *no es cosa del otro jueves* or *del otro mundo* it's nothing to write home about, it's nothing to make a fuss about (no es ninguna maravilla), there's nothing to it (no es difícil) || *no es cosa de que dejes de ir tú* it doesn't mean you don't have to go || *no es gran cosa* it's not important || *no hace cosa buena* he doesn't do anything worthwhile || *¡no hay tal cosa!* nothing of the sort! || *no sea cosa que* in case || *no vale gran cosa* it's not worth much || *otra cosa* something else || *otra cosa sería si...* things would be different if... || *poquita cosa* nothing much || *por una cosa o por otra* for one reason or another || *¿qué cosa?* what's that?, what did you say? || *¡qué cosa más estúpida!* how utterly stupid! || *¡qué cosas tienes!* the things you come out with! || *ser cosas de* to be just like; *son cosas de Juan* that's just like John || *ser poca cosa* not to be much || *tengo otras cosas en que pensar* I have other things on my mind || *¡vaya una cosa!* marvellous!, wonderful! (irónico) || *y, cosa rara, nadie lo había hecho* and, oddly enough, nobody had done it.

cosaco, ca *adj/sm* cossack || FIG *beber como un cosaco* to drink like a fish.

cosario, ria *adj* beaten (camino).
◆ *m* carrier (paquetes), messenger (mensajes).

coscoja *f* BOT kermes *o* scarlet oak (encina) | dry leaf of the kermes oak (hoja).

coscojal; coscojar *m* oak grove.

coscojo *m* kermes berry, kermes-oak gall.

coscorrón *m* blow on the head || FIG *darse coscorrones* to suffer hard knocks (reveses).

cosecante *f* MAT cosecant.

cosecha *f* AGR harvest, harvesting (recolección) | crop, harvest (lo recogido) | yield (producción) | harvest, harvest time (temporada) || vintage (del vino) || FIG collection, crop (acopio) || — *de su (propia) cosecha* home-grown (comestibles), of his own invention (ideas, pensamientos) || *es de la última cosecha* it's the latest || *hacer la cosecha* to harvest (general), to reap (cereales).

cosechador, ra *m/f* harvester, reaper.

cosechadora *f* combine harvester, combine (máquina).

cosechar *vi* AGR to harvest, to reap.
◆ *vt* to harvest (general), to reap, to gather (cereales) || to pick (frutas, flores) || to grow; *aquí cosechan manzanas* they grow apples here || FIG to win, to reap; *cosechar laureles* to reap *o* to win laurels *o* glory; *cosechó innumerables galardones* he won innumerable awards.

cosechero, ra *m/f* harvester, reaper.

cosedora *f* sewing machine (máquina de coser) || stitching machine (máquina de coser libros).

coselete *m* corslet, corselet (armadura, tórax de los insectos).

coseno *m* MAT cosine.

cosepapeles *m inv* stapler.

coser *vt* to sew (up); *coser un vestido* to sew a dress || to sew on; *coser un botón* to sew on a button || to stitch (dar puntadas en) || MED to stitch up || FIG to join, to unite (reunir) || — *coser a balazos* to riddle with bullets || FIG & FAM *coser a puñaladas* to cut s.o. to pieces || *coser con grapas* to staple (papeles) || FIG & FAM *eso es coser y cantar* it's as easy as pie *o* as A. B. C., it's child's play || *máquina de coser* sewing machine.
◆ *vi* to sew.
◆ *vpr* FIG *coserse a uno* to stick (close) to s.o.

cosi *adv* AMER that is, I mean.

cosido, da *adj* sewn || *cosido a mano* handsewn.
◆ *m* sewing.

cosijoso, sa *adj* AMER grumpy, grouchy, peevish.

cosmético, ca *adj/sm* cosmetic.

cósmico, ca *adj* cosmic; *rayos cósmicos* cosmic rays.

cosmogonía *f* cosmogony.

cosmogónico, ca *adj* cosmogonic.

cosmografía *f* cosmography.

cosmográfico, ca *adj* cosmographic.

cosmógrafo *m/f* cosmographer.

cosmología *f* cosmology.

cosmológico, ca *adj* cosmological.

cosmonauta *m/f* astronaut, cosmonaut.

cosmonáutico, ca *adj* cosmonautic, cosmonautical.
◆ *f* cosmonautics.

cosmonave *f* spaceship, spacecraft.

cosmopolita *adj/s* cosmopolitan, cosmopolite.

cosmopolitismo *m* cosmopolitanism.

cosmorama *m* cosmorama.

cosmos *m inv* cosmos.

coso *m* enclosure (recinto) || bullring (plaza de toros) || street (calle) || ZOOL deathwatch beetle, woodworm (insecto).

cospel *m* blank (de moneda).

cosque; cosqui *m* FAM blow on the head.

cosquillar *vt* to tickle.

cosquillas *f pl* tickles, tickling *sing* || — FIG *buscarle a uno las cosquillas* to rub s.o. up the wrong way || *hacer cosquillas* to tickle (físicamente), to tickle s.o.'s fancy (gustarle a alguien algo) || *tener cosquillas* to be ticklish || *tener malas cosquillas* to be touchy.

cosquillear *vt* to tickle.

cosquilleo *m* tickling (sensation).

cosquilloso, sa *adj* ticklish || FIG touchy, easily offended.

costa *f* coast; *la costa cantábrica* the Cantabrian coast || — GEOGR *Costa de Marfil* Ivory Coast | *Costa de Oro* Gold Coast | *la Costa Azul* the French Riviera, the Côte d'Azur | *la costa Brava* the Costa Brava || *navegar costa a costa* to coast.

costa *f* cost (gasto) || — *a costa ajena* at someone else's expense || *a costa de* at the expense of; *a costa de su familia* at his family's expense; by dint of, by means of, by, through; *se hizo rico a costa de mucho trabajo* he became rich by dint of hard work; at the cost of; *a costa de su salud* at the cost of his health; to one's cost; *me enteré a costa mía de que...* I found out to my cost that... || *a costa de su vida* at the cost of his life || *a poca costa* with little effort || *a toda costa* at all costs || *vivir a costa de uno* to life off s.o.
◆ *pl* JUR costs (gastos judiciales); *reserva de costas* award of costs; *condenar en* or *a costas* to order to pay costs.

costado *m* side; *tendido de costado* lying on his side || MIL flank (de un ejército) || MAR side (de un barco) || — *dar el costado* to be broadside on (en un combate), to careen, to heave over (para carenar o limpiar un barco) || *dolor* or *punto de costado* stitch || *por los cuatro costados* through and through a hundred percent.
◆ *pl* lineage *sing*, ancestry *sing* (genealogía).

costal *m* costal, pertaining to the ribs (de las costillas).
◆ *m* sack || frame [of an adobe wall] || FIG & FAM *el costal de los pecados* the human body | *eso es harina de otro costal* that's another kettle of fish | *ser un costal de huesos* to be nothing but skin and bone, to be a bag of bones | *vaciar el costal* to unburden o.s.

costalada *f*; **costalazo** *m* fall, sidelong fall (caída) || bump (golpe) || *pegarse una costalada* to fall flat (on one's side).

costalero *m* porter (mozo de cordel) | bearer [of «pasos» in Holy Week].

costana *f* steep hill (cuesta) || MAR & AVIAC rib (cuaderna).

costanera *f* slope (cuesta) || AMER promenade (paseo marítimo).
◆ *pl* ARQ rafters (vigas).

costanero, ra *adj* sloping (inclinado) || coastal; *navegación costanera* coastal navegation.

costanilla *f* steep little street.

costar* *vt/vi* to cost; *cuesta cien pesetas* it costs a hundred pesetas || FIG to cost; *las promesas cuestan poco* promises cost nothing; *este trabajo me ha costado muchos esfuerzos* this work has cost me a great deal of effort | to be difficult, to find it difficult; *me cuesta mucho confesarlo* it is very difficult to me to confess it, I find it very difficult to confess; *cuesta creerlo* it is difficult to believe || — *costar barato* to be cheap, not to cost much; *este libro cuesta barato* this book is cheap, this book does not cost much || *costar caro* to be expensive, to cost a lot; *esta sortija cuesta muy cara* this ring is very expensive; to pay dearly for; *esta tontería le costará cara* he will pay dearly for this foolishness || *costarle la vida a uno* to cost s.o. his life || *costar trabajo* to take a lot, to be difficult, to find it difficult; *me ha costado trabajo rehusar* it took a lot to refuse it, it was difficult for me to refuse; *me cuesta trabajo creerlo* it takes a lot of believing, I find it difficult to believe || FIG & FAM *costar un ojo de la cara* or *un riñón* to cost a fortune *o* a mint || *¿cuánto cuesta?* how much is it?, how much does it cost? || *cueste lo que cueste* at all costs, at any cost, whatever the cost || *el trabajo me costó dos horas* the job took me two hours || FIG & FAM *nos costó Dios y ayuda echarle fuera* we had terrible trouble getting rid of him.

Costa Rica *npr f* GEOGR Costa Rica.

costarricense; costarriqueño, ña *adj/s* Costa Rican.

costarriqueñismo *m* word or expression typical of Costa Rica.

coste *m* cost, price; *el coste de un coche* the price of a car || — *coste, seguro y flete* CIF [cost, insurance, freight] || *coste de la vida* cost of living || *coste de producción* production cost || *precio de coste* cost price.

— OBSERV *Coste* and *costo* are often confused. *Coste* represents the money price: *el coste de un mueble* the price of a piece of furniture. *Costo* is applied to large undertakings and is a term used in economics: *el costo de un puente, de una carretera* the cost of a bridge, of a road.

costear *vt* to pay for, to defray the expenses of; *costear los estudios a un niño* to pay for a child's education || to finance (financiar) || MAR to coast || *AMER* to graze (el ganado).
◆ *vpr* to pay for itself; *este negocio apenas se costea* this business hardly pays for itself || FAM to buy o.s. (sth.); *costearse un coche* to buy o.s. a car || *AMER* to pull s.o.'s leg (burlarse).

costeño, ña *adj* coastal.

costeo *m* financing || *AMER* grazing (del ganado) | banter, leg-pulling (burla).

costero, ra *adj* coastal.
◆ *m* flitch [of timber] (tabla) || MAR coaster (barco) || TECN wall.
◆ *f* side (de paquete) || coast (costa) || fishing season (temporada de pesca) || slope (pendiente).

costilla *f* ANAT rib; *costilla verdadera, falsa, flotante* rue, false, floating rib || chop, cutlet (chuleta) || MAR & AVIAC rib || FIG & FAM better half, wife; *ven a cenar con tu costilla* come to dinner and bring your better half.
◆ *pl* FAM back *sing*, shoulders (espalda) || — FIG *a las costillas de...* at the expense of... | *llevar sobre las costillas* to carry on one's shoulders | *medirle a uno las costillas* to give s.o. a good hiding.

costillaje; costillar *m* ribs *pl*.

costo *m* cost; *costo de la vida* cost of living.

— OBSERV Véase OBSERV en COSTE.

costoso, sa *adj* costly, expensive.

costra *f* crust (corteza) || scab (en las heridas) || snuff (de una vela) || MED *costra láctea* milk crust.

costreñir *vt* → **constreñir.**

costroso, sa *adj* crusty || scabby (herida) || FAM scruffy (sucio).

costumbre *f* custom, habit; *cada país tiene sus usos y costumbres* every country has its manners and customs || habit, custom, practice; *tiene la costumbre de levantarse temprano* he is in the habit of getting up early, it is his custom *o* practice to get up early || JUR usage || — *como de costumbre* as usual (como siempre) || *de costumbre* usual (adjetivo), usally, generally (adverbio) || *la costumbre es una segunda naturaleza* habit is second nature || *la costumbre tiene fuerza de ley* or *hace ley* custom has the force of law || *mujer de malas costumbres* loose woman || *novela de costumbres* novel of manners || *perder la costumbre* to lose the habit || *persona de buenas costumbres* respectable person || *por costumbre* through force of habit, out of habit || *según costumbre* according to custom, in accordance with usual practice.

costumbrismo *m* literature of manners.

costumbrista *adj* of manners (literatura).
◆ *m/f* writer of literature of manners.

costura *f* sewing (acción y efecto) || seam; *la costura está deshecha* the seam is undone; *sentar las costuras* to press the seams || dressmaking; *se gana la vida con la costura* she makes her living from dressmaking || scar (cicatriz) || — *alta costura* haute couture, high fashion || *cesto de la costura* sewing basket || *medias sin costura* seamless stockings || FIG *meter a uno en costura* to bring s.o. to reason, to make s.o. see reason.

costurera *f* seamstress, dressmaker (modista).

costurero *m* sewing case, sewing kit (estuche) || workbox (mueble).

costurón *m* heavy stitching || FIG noticeable scar.

cota *f* doublet (vestido antiguo) || tabard (túnica de los heraldos) || bench mark (cifra) || height above sea level (altura) || *cota de mallas* coat of mail.

cotangente *f* MAT cotangent.

cotarro *m* night lodging for the poor and destitute, night shelter, doss house [*US* flophouse (*fam*)] || side [of a ravine] (ladera) || — FIG & FAM *alborotar el cotarro* to cause trouble, to cause a stir | *dirigir el cotarro* to rule the roost.

cotejar *vt* to compare; *si cotejamos las dos situaciones* if we compare both situations || to compare, to collate (textos).

cotejo *m* comparison || collation, comparison (textos).

coterráneo, a *adj* from the same country or region.
◆ *m/f* fellow countryman, fellow countrywoman, compatriot.

cotí *m* ticking (tela para colchones).

cotidianamente *adv* daily, everyday.

cotidiano, na *adj* daily, everyday.

cotila *f* ANAT socket (de un hueso).

cotiledón *m* BOT cotyledon.

cotilla *f* stays *pl*, corset (faja antigua).
◆ *m/f* FAM gossip, tattler (chismoso).

cotillear *vi* FAM to gossip.

cotilleo *m* FAM gossip, gossiping (habladuría).

cotillero, ra *m/f* gossip, tattler (chismoso).

cotillo *m* hammerhead (del martillo).

cotillón *m* cotillion (baile).

cotizable *adj* quotable.

cotización *f* quotation, price (en la Bolsa) || dues *pl* (cuota) || *cotización al cierre* closing price.

cotizado, da *adj* quoted (en la Bolsa) || FIG esteemed, valued (apreciado) | sought-after (que tiene mucha demanda) | popular.

cotizante *adj* subscription-paying.
◆ *m* subscription-paying member.

cotizar *vt* to quote, to price (en la Bolsa) || to pay (pagar) || to fix (fijar) || FIG *estar cotizado* to be highly valued (valorarse).
◆ *vi* to pay a subscription.
◆ *vpr* to be quoted; *valores que se cotizan* stocks that are quoted || to sell for, to fetch; *éstas son las manzanas que se cotizan más* these are the apples which fetch the highest price || FIG to be valued, to be highly esteemed.

— OBSERV The use of *cotizar* in the intransitive form is a Gallicism.

coto *m* enclosure (terreno) || preserve (terreno acotado) || boundary mark, boundary stone (mojón) || limit (límite) || rate, price (precio) || ZOOL miller's thumb (pez) || FIG stop, end; *tengo que poner coto a sus excesos* I have to put a stop to his excesses || *AMER* MED goitre (bocio) || *coto de caza* game preserve.

cotón *m* printed cotton (tela) || *AMER* work shirt (camisa) | vest, undershirt (camiseta).

cotona *f* *AMER* chamois *o* leather jacket (chaqueta) | cotton shirt (camisa) | cotton vest, undershirt (camiseta).

cotonada *f* cotton fabric (tejido).

cotorra *f* ZOOL parrot (loro) | magpie (urraca) || FIG & FAM chatterbox, windbag (persona habladora) || FAM *hablar como una cotorra* to chatter like a magpie.

cotorrear *vi* FIG & FAM to chatter, to prattle away.

cotorreo *m* FIG & FAM chatter, prattle, chattering.

cotorro *m* *AMER* → **cotarro.**

cotorrón, ona *m/f* old person affecting youthfulness *o* pretending to be young.

cotúa *m* *AMER* cormorant (mergo).

cotudo, da *adj* fluffy, furry, cottony || FAM mean, tightfisted (tacaño) | stubborn, pigheaded, obstinate (cabezón) || *AMER* goitrous (con bocio).

cotufa *f* BOT tuber of the Jerusalem artichoke || titbit, delicacy (golosina) || chufa, earth almond.

coturno *m* buskin, cothurnus (zapato) || — FIG *calzar el coturno* to put on the buskin || *de alto coturno* of high degree, lofty.

cotutela *f* JUR joint guardianship.

cotutor *m* JUR joint guardian.

COU *abrev de Curso de Orientación Universitaria* pre-university, secondary school course and qualification.

covacha *f* small cave (cueva pequeña) || FAM shanty, hut (zaquizamí) || *AMER* greengrocer's shop (tienda) | stone bench (poyo) | cubbyhole under the stairs, boxroom (aposento).

covachuela *f* FAM ministry | office (oficina) || small cellar (bodega pequeña).

— OBSERV The first meaning derives from the fact that the offices of the former «Secretariats of the Universal Office» the equivalent of modern ministries were situated in the cellars (*covachas*) of the Royal Palace in Madrid.

covachuelista; covachuelo *m* FAM penpusher, office worker (chupatintas).

covadera *f* *AMER* guano deposit.

cow-boy *m* cowboy (vaquero).

coxalgia *f* MED coxalgia.

coxcojilla; coxcojita *f* hopscotch || *a coxcojita* on one foot.

coxis *m inv* ANAT coccyx.

coy *m* MAR hammock.

coyote *m* coyote, prairie wolf (lobo americano).

coyunda *f* strap *o* rope for yoking oxen, tether (del yugo) || FIG yoke, subjection (sujeción) || FAM bonds *pl* of marriage, yoke.

coyuntura *f* ANAT joint, articulation (articulación) || FIG opportunity (oportunidad) | occasion, moment, juncture (circunstancia) | situation, circumstances *pl* (situación).

coyuntural *adj* of the situation, in the context of the situation, arising from the situation.

coz *f* kick (de un caballo) || backward kick (de una persona) || recoil, kick (de un arma de fuego) || butt (culata de fusil) || — FIG *dar* or *tirar coces contra el aguijón* to kick *o* to struggle in vain || *tirar* or *dar* or *pegar coces* to kick, to lash out || FIG *tratar a la gente a coces* to kick people around.

crac *m* crash, bankruptcy (quiebra comercial).
◆ *interj* crack! snap!

cráking *m* QUÍM cracking (del petróleo).

Cracovia *n pr* GEOGR Cracow.

crampón *m* crampon, climbing iron (de alpinista).

cran *m* IMPR nick (de un carácter).

craneal; craneano, na *adj* cranial; *bóveda craneana* cranial vault.

cráneo *m* ANAT cranium, skull || FAM *¡vas de cráneo!* you are fighting a losing battle.

craneoestenosis *f inv* MED craniostenosis.

craneólogo, ga *m/f* craniologist.

craneopatía *f* MED craniopathy.

craneotabes *f* MED craniotabes.

craneotomía *f* MED craniotomy.

craniectomía *f* MED craniectomy.

crápula *f* debauchery, dissipation (libertinaje) || drunkenness, crapulence (borrachera).

crapuloso, sa *adj* debauched, dissipated (libertino) || drunken, crapulous (borracho).
◆ *m* debauchee, dissipated person (libertino) || drunkard (borracho).

craquear *vt* QUÍM to crack.

craqueo *m* QUÍM cracking.

crascitar *vi* to caw, to croak (graznar).

crasis *f inv* GRAM crasis.

craso, sa *adj* greasy (lleno de grasa) || fat (gordo) || crass, gross; *ignorancia crasa* crass ignorance.

cráter *m* crater (de un volcán, etc.); *cráter de explosión* breached crater.

crátera *f* crater (vasija).

cratícula *f* small window [through which nuns receive Holy Communion].

crawl *m* crawl (natación).

creación *f* creation || INFORM *creación de fichero* file creation.

creador, ra *adj* creative.
◆ *m/f* creator (que crea) || inventor (que inventa) || *el Creador* the Creator.

crear *vt* to create || to make; *ser creado cardenal* to be made a cardinal || to invent (inventar) || to establish, to set up, to institute (establecer) || to found (un hospital, una institución).
◆ *vpr* to make, to make for o.s., to create for o.s.; *crearse enemigos* to make enemies for o.s.; *crearse una posición* to make a position for o.s.; *te estás creando problemas por gusto* you are creating problems for yourself for no reason || to create for o.s. (in the imagination), to imagine; *los niños se crean un mundo imaginario* children create an imaginary world for themselves.

creativo, va *adj* creative.

crecer* *vi* to grow (personas, plantas, etc.); *su hija ha crecido mucho* his daughter has grown a lot; *la hierba ha crecido mucho* the grass has grown very high; *le ha empezado a crecer el pelo* his hair has begun to grow || to grow, to increase, to become *o* get bigger; *crece el malestar general* the general uneasiness is growing; *crecía la mancha* the stain got bigger; *crece la fuerza del viento* the force of the wind is increasing || to wax (la luna) || to draw out, to get longer (días) || to rise, to swell; *crece el río* the river is rising || — FIG *crecer como hongos* to spring up *o* to grow like mushrooms, to mushroom | *crecer como la cizaña* to grow like weeds || *dejar crecer el bigote* to grow a moustache.
◆ *vpr* FIG to become vain *o* conceited, to become too sure of o.s. (engreírse) | to take courage (from sth.), to be encouraged (by sth.), to be braced (by sth.); *los revolucionarios, crecidos por su victoria, atacaron la ciudad* the revolutionaries, encouraged by their victory, attacked the city.

creces *f pl* increase *sing* in volume || FIG interest *sing*; *pagar con creces* to pay with interest || — *con creces* amply, more than, with interest; *su éxito compensó con creces a su madre por los sacrificios que había hecho* his success more than repaid his mother for her self-sacrifice || *devolver con creces* to repay *o* to return a hundredfold.

crecida *f* spate, flood, freshet (de un río).

crecido, da *adj* large, considerable; *una cantidad crecida* a large amount || high, large (proporción, porcentaje); *una crecida proporción* a high proportion || grown; *un niño crecido* a grown boy || in flood, in spate (río) || FIG proud, conceited (engreído).

creciente *adj* growing (que crece) || increasing (que aumenta) || — *cuarto creciente* first quarter (de la Luna) || *luna creciente* crescent *o* waxing moon.
◆ *m* HERÁLD crescent.
◆ *f* spate, flood, freshet (crecida) || yeast (levadura).

crecimiento *m* growth (acción de crecer) || increase (aumento) || waxing (de la luna) || flooding, rising (de un río) || ECON *crecimiento económico* economic growth.

credencial *adj* credential || *cartas credenciales* letter *sing* of credence, letters credential, credential letters.
◆ *f pl* credentials.

credibilidad *f* credibility.

crediticio, cia *adj* credit.

crédito *m* credit, credence; *dar crédito a* to give credit to || FIG reputation; *goza de gran crédito* he has a very good reputation | authority (autoridad) | prestige (prestigio) || COM credit; *crédito a corto plazo, a largo plazo* short-term, long-term credit; *apertura de crédito* opening of credit || — *abrir un crédito a uno* to open a credit account in s.o.'s favour || *a crédito* on credit || *carta de crédito* letter of credit || *crédito hipotecario* debt secured by a mortgage || *crédito inmobiliario* credit on real estate *o* property || *dar crédito* to give credit, to credit (acreditar) || FIG *no doy crédito a mis ojos, mis oídos* I can't believe my eyes, my ears | *tener crédito* to have a good reputation.

credo *m* creed (oración) || FIG creed (convicción) || FIG *en menos que se dice un credo* in a jiffy, before you can say Jack Robinson.

credulidad *f* credulity.

crédulo, la *adj* credulous.
◆ *m/f* dupe.

creederas *f pl* FAM credulity *sing* || FAM *tener buenas creederas* to be credulous, to believe everything | *tener malas creederas* to be incredulous.

creencia *f* belief (pensamiento) || belief, conviction (convicción) || belief, faith (religión) || *en la creencia de que...* in the belief that...

creer* *vt/vi* to believe; *creer en Dios* to believe in God; *creer en la virtud* to believe in virtue || to believe; *creo de mi deber hacerlo* I believe it is my duty to do it; *créame* believe me || to think (pensar); *así lo creo* that is what I think; *cree saberlo todo* he thinks he knows everything || — *creer a ciencia cierta* to be convinced of... || *creer a pies juntillas, a ojos cerrados* to believe firmly, blindly || *creer bajo* or *sobre palabra* to take s.o.'s word for it; *lo creo bajo* or *sobre tu palabra* I take your word for it || *creo que no* I don't think so || *creo que sí* I think so || *cualquiera creería que...* anyone would think that... || *hacer creer algo a uno* to make s.o. believe sth. || *hay que verlo para creerlo* you have to see it to believe it, it has to be seen to be believed || *no vayas a creer que...* don't go thinking that... || *¡quién lo hubiera creído!* who would have thought it! || *según yo creo* to the best of my belief || *si se le cree* according to him || FAM *¡ya lo creo!* of course!, naturally!, I should say so!, I should think so!
◆ *vpr* to believe *o* to think (o.s.) to be; *se cree un escritor* he thinks he is a writer || — *creérselas* to be self-satisfied || *¡es para no creérselo!* it's unbelievable! || *no me lo creo* I don't *o* I can't believe it || FAM *¿qué se cree?* who does he think he is? | *¡qué te crees!, ¡que te crees tú eso!, ¡que te lo has creído!* that's what you think! | *¿qué te has creído?* who do you think you are?

creíble *adj* credible, believable.

creído, da *adj* confident (confiado) || credulous (crédulo) || conceited, arrogant, vain (presumido) || *creído de sí mismo* self-satisfied, complacent.

crema *f* cream (nata, cosmético, licor); *crema hidratante* moisturizing cream; *crema de belleza* beauty cream || custard (relleno de pastelería) || (shoe) cream, shoe polish (betún) || FIG cream, élite (lo mejor) || GRAM diaeresis || — *crema batida* whipped cream || *crema catalana* egg custard dessert [with a crisp topping of burnt sugar] || *crema de chocolate* chocolate cream || *crema dental* dental cream, toothpaste.
◆ *adj* cream (color).

cremación *f* cremation (incineración).

cremallera *f* TECN rack || zip, zip fastener [US zipper] (para abrochar la ropa) || *ferrocarril de cremallera* rack railway.

crematístico, ca *adj* monetary, chrematistic.
◆ *f* political economy, chrematistics *pl* || FAM money matters *pl*, money (dinero).

crematorio, ria *adj* crematory || *horno crematorio* crematorium, crematory.

cremería *f* AMER creamery, dairy.

crémor; crémor tartárico *m* cream of tartar.

cremoso, sa *adj* creamy.

crencha *f* parting (raya del cabello) || hair on each side of parting (pelo).

creosol *m* QUÍM creosol (aceite de creosota).

creosota *f* QUÍM creosote || *aceite de creosota* creosol.

creosotado *m* TECN creosoting.

creosotar *vt* TECN to creosote.

crepe *f* CULIN pancake.

crepé *m* crêpe paper (papel) || crêpe, crape (tela) || crêpe [rubber]; *suelas de crepé* crêpe soles.

crepitante *adj* crackling, crepitant.

crepitar *vi* to crackle, to crepitate || MED to crepitate.

crepuscular *adj* twilight, crepuscular.

crepúsculo *m* twilight, dusk.

cresa *f* eggs *pl* of queen bee || larva (de cualquier insecto) || maggot (larva de la moscarda).

crescendo *adv/sm* MÚS crescendo.

Creso *npr m* Croesus.

cresol *m* QUÍM cresol.

crespo, pa *adj* frizzy, fuzzy, kinky (pelo) || crinkled, curly (hojas) || FIG involved, obscure (estilo) | irritated, angry (enfadado).

crespón *m* crêpe, crape (tela); *crespón de China* crêpe de Chine || *crespón tupido* crepon.

cresta *f* crest, comb (de las aves) || tuft (copete) || crest (de las montañas, de las olas) || MED crest; *cresta occipital* occipital crest || — FIG & FAM *alzar* or *levantar la cresta* to give o.s. airs || *cresta de explanada* crest of the glacis (de fortificación) || BOT *cresta de gallo* cockscomb || FIG & FAM *dar a alguien en la cresta* to take s.o. down a peg or two (humillarle).

crestería *f* ARQ battlements *pl*, crenellation (de fortificación) | crenellation (remate calado).

crestomatía *f* anthology, chrestomathy.

crestón *m* crest (de la celada) || MIN outcrop (de un filón).

creta *f* chalk (carbonato de cal).

Creta *npr f* GEOGR Crete.

cretáceo, a *adj/sm* GEOL cretaceous.
— OBSERV El sustantivo se escribe siempre con mayúscula en inglés.

cretense; crético, ca *adj/s* Cretan.

cretinismo *m* cretinism (enfermedad) || cretinism, idiocy, stupidity (estupidez).

cretino, na *adj* cretinous.
◆ *m/f* cretin.

cretona *f* cretonne (tela).

creyente *adj* believing.
◆ *m/f* believer.

cría *f* breeding; *cría intensiva* intensive breeding || litter (camada de mamíferos), brood (de ovíparos) || infant, baby (niño de pecho) || young (de un animal); *la cría de la loba se llama el lobezno* the young of the wolf is called a (wolf) cub.

criada *f* maid, maidservant || — *criada para todo* all-purpose *o* general-purpose maid || *le salió la criada respondona* he got more than he bargained for.

criadero *m* nursery (de plantas) || breeding place (para animales) || hatchery (de peces) || MIN seam, vein (yacimiento) || *criadero de ostras* oyster bed.

criadilla *f* CULIN bull's testicle | (ant) small round roll (panecillo) || *criadilla de tierra* truffle (trufa).

criado *m* servant, manservant.

criado, da *adj* brought up, bred; *bien, mal criado* well, badly brought up (niño) || bred, reared (animal).

criadona; criadota *f* FAM skivvy, drudge.

criador *m* breeder (de animales) || — *criador de vino* winegrower, viniculturist || *el Criador* the Creator, God (el Creador).

criandera *f* AMER wet nurse (nodriza).

crianza *f* breeding (de animales) || nursing, suckling (de niños de pecho) || FIG upbringing, breeding; *buena, mala crianza* good, bad upbringing.

criar *vt* to suckle, to nurse (amamantar) || to feed (niño de pecho) || to rear, to breed, to raise (animales) || to grow (plantas) || to bring up, to rear, to educate (educar) || to produce, to grow; *la tierra cría plantas* the earth produces plants || to have, to grow; *los gatos crían pelo y las aves plumas* cats have fur and birds have teathers || to elaborate (el vino) || FIG to engender, to beget (engendrar) | to create, to cause, to bring about, to provoke (ocasionar) || — FIG *cría buena fama y échate a dormir* build yourself a good reputation and you can sit back and relax || *criar al pecho* to breast-feed || *criar con biberón* to bottle-feed || FAM *criar grasas* to get fat, to become fat || *Dios los cría y ellos se juntan* birds of a feather flock together || *los alimentos tapados crían moho* covered food goes mouldy || *no críes motivos para que te castigue* do not give me cause to punish you, don't provoke me || *zapatos que crían ampollas* shoes that give blisters.
◆ *vpr* to be brought up, to grow up (niños); *los niños que se crían al aire libre* children that are brought up in the open air || to feed o.s. (alimentarse) || to be reared, to be raised (animales) || to grow (plantas) || to form, to take form (cosas) || FIG *criarse en buena cuna* to be born with a silver spoon in one's mouth.

criatura *f* creature (cosa creada) || infant, baby (niño de pecho) || FIG child, baby, kid (*fam*); *llorar como una criatura* to cry like a baby.

criba *f* sieve, screen || — FIG & FAM *estar como una criba* to be riddled like a sieve | *pasar por la criba* to screen (seleccionar).

cribado *m* sieving, sifting, screening || AMER openwork embroidery (bordado calado).

cribar *vt* to sieve, to sift, to screen.

cric *m* TECN jack (gato).

cricket *m* DEP cricket.

cricoides *adj/sm inv* ANAT cricoid (cartílago de la laringe).

Crimea *npr f* GEOGR Crimea.

crimen *m* crime.

criminación *f* crimination (acusación).

criminal *adj/s* criminal.

criminalidad *f* criminality || crime rate; *la criminalidad aumenta muy rápidamente* the crime rate is increasing very rapidly.

criminalista *m* criminologist (especialista) || criminal lawyer (abogado).

criminar *vt* to criminate, to accuse, to charge (incriminar) || to censure (censurar).

criminología *f* criminology.

criminológico, ca *adj* criminological.

criminologista; criminólogo, ga *m/f* criminologist.

crin; clin *f* mane (del caballo) || horsehair (relleno de colchones, etc.) || *crin vegetal* vegetable fibre.

crineja *f* AMER plait, tress (trenza).

crinoideo *m* ZOOL crinoid.

crinolina *f* crinoline.
— OBSERV This word is a Gallicism for *miriñaque*.

crío *m* FAM baby (niño de pecho) | child, kid, little one; *vino con todos sus críos* he came with all his children.

criógeno *m* cryogen.

criolita *f* MIN cryolite.

criollo, lla *adj/s* creole.
— OBSERV In Latin America the noun and the adjective *criollo* often denote what is indigenous and national as opposed to what is foreign. Thus *un manjar criollo* is a typical dish; *un caballo criollo* is a native horse of a breed peculiar to the country in question. In Argentina *un buen criollo* means a good Argentinian, an Argentinian of good stock.

crioscopia *f* FÍS cryoscopy, cryometry.

cripta *f* crypt.

criptógamo, ma *adj* BOT cryptogamous.
◆ *f* cryptogam.

criptografía *f* cryptography (escritura secreta).

criptográfico, ca *adj* cryptographic.

criptógrafo, fa *m/f* cryptographer.

criptograma *m* cryptogram.

criptón *m* QUÍM krypton (gas).

criptorquidia *f* MED cryptorchidism, cryptorchism.

criquet *m* DEP cricket.

cris *m* kris, creese (puñal malayo).

crisálida *f* ZOOL chrysalis.

crisantemo *m* BOT chrysanthemum.

crisis *f* crisis (de una enfermedad) || fit (ataque); *crisis de llanto, de furia* fit of weeping, of rage || crisis (momento decisivo); *crisis financiera, ministerial* financial, cabinet crisis || — *crisis de la vivienda* housing shortage || ECON *crisis del petróleo* oil crisis | *crisis económica* economic crisis || *crisis nerviosa* nervous breakdown || *hacer crisis* to reach crisis point (una enfermedad) || *llegar a una crisis* to reach crisis point.

crisma *m* chrism (aceite consagrado) || FAM head || — FAM *romper la crisma a alguien* to smash s.o.'s head in | *romperse la crisma* to crack *o* to split one's head open.

crismas *m* christmas card.

crisol *m* TECN crucible, melting pot | hearth (de un horno) || FIG melting pot.

crisólito *m* chrysolite (piedra preciosa).

crispadura *f*; **crispamiento** *m* muscular contraction.

crispar *vt* to contract, to tense (músculo) || to twitch (inconscientemente) || to contort; *tenía el rostro crispado por el dolor* his face was contorted with pain || to irritate, to get on s.o.'s nerves; *este niño me crispa* this child gets on my nerves || *crispar los nervios* to get on s.o.'s nerves.
◆ *vpr* to contract, to tense, to twitch (músculos) || to contort (cara) || to get all on edge (nervios).

cristal *m* crystal (cuerpo cristalizado); *cristal de roca* rock crystal || crystal (vidrio fino); *cristal de Bohemia* Bohemian crystal || pane of glass (de una ventana, etc.) || glass (vidrio); *el cristal de un reloj* the glass of a watch; *cristal ahumado* smoked glass; *cristal tallado* cut glass; *cristal esmerilado* ground glass || lens (lente); *cristal de contacto* contact lens || AUT window || mirror, looking glass (espejo) || FIG & POÉT water; *el cristal de la fuente* the water of the fountain || AMER (drinking) glass (vaso) || — *cristal de aumento* magnifying glass || *cristal trasero* rear window (automóvil) || *de cristal* glass.
◆ *pl* windows (ventanas) || — *limpiar los cristales* to clean the windows || *puerta de cristales* glass door.

cristalera *f* display cabinet (armario con cristales) || glazed door (puerta) || window (ventana).

cristalería *f* glasswork, glass making (arte) || glassworks (fábrica) || glass shop, glassware shop (tienda de vasos, etc.) || glass service (juego de vasos, etc.) || glassware (objetos de cristal).

cristalero, ra *m/f* glazier (que arregla los cristales) || glassworker, glassmaker (que trabaja en cristal) || glassblower (soplador de vidrio).

cristalino, na *adj* FÍS crystalline || FIG limpid, clear.
◆ *m* ANAT crystalline lens (del ojo).

cristalización *f* crystallization.

cristalizador, ra *adj* crystallizing.
◆ *m* crystallizer.

cristalizar *vt/vi* to crystallize || FIG to crystallize (concretarse); *el descontento de los trabajadores cristalizó en una huelga general* the workers' discontent crystallized into a general strike.
◆ *vpr* to crystallize.

cristalografía *f* crystallography.

cristalográfico, ca *adj* crystallographic.

cristaloide *adj/sm* crystalloid.

cristaloideo, a *adj* crystalloidal.

cristianar *vt* FAM to christen || FAM *los trapitos de cristianar* one's Sunday best, one's Sunday clothes (los vestidos más elegantes).

cristiandad *f* Christendom (conjunto de los cristianos) || Christianity (fe cristiana).

cristianía *m* christiania, christy (esquí).

cristianismo *m* Christianity.

cristianización *f* christianization.

cristianizar *vt* to christianize.

cristiano, na *adj/s* Christian || — *cristiano nuevo* Moor, Jew, etc. converted to Christianity || *cristiano viejo* Christian having no Moorish or Jewish ancestors || FIG *hablar en cristiano* to speak plain Spanish, to speak clearly | *vino cristiano* unwatered wine (sin agua).
◆ *m* FAM soul, person; *por la calle no pasa un cristiano* there's not a soul in the street || FAM *no hay cristiano que lo entienda* no one could understand it, it's utterly incomprehensible.

Cristina *npr f* Christine.

cristino, na *adj/s* supporter of Isabel II against the Carlists, under the regency of Maria Cristina.

Cristo *m* Christ || crucifix; *un cristo de marfil* an ivory crucifix || — FAM *allá donde Cristo perdió el gorro* or *la boina* in the back of beyond, out in the sticks || *antes de Cristo* before Christ, B. C. || *después de Cristo* A. D., anno domini (en las fechas) || FIG & FAM *donde Cristo dio las tres voces* miles from anywhere, at the back of beyond | *estar hecho un Cristo* to be a pitiful sight | *¡ni Cristo que lo fundó!* impossible! | *¡voto a Cristo!* by the Lord! (exclamación de enfado).

Cristóbal *npr m* Christopher || *Cristóbal Colón* Christopher Columbus.

cristus *m* christ cross, crisscross (cruz que se ponía al principio del abecedario) || alphabet (abecedario) || primer (librito para aprender a leer).

criterio *m* criterion (regla o norma) || discernment, judgment (discernimiento) || point of view, viewpoint (punto de vista); *juzgó los cuadros con un criterio clásico* he judged the paintings from a classical point of view || approach (enfoque) || opinion; *en mi criterio* in my opinion.

crítica *f* criticism (evaluación de calidades) || review, notice, critique (reseña) || the critics (conjunto de los críticos) || criticism, faultfinding, censure (censura) || *dirigir* or *hacer críticas* to criticize || *¿qué crítica puedes hacerme?* what can you reproach me?

criticable *adj* criticizable, open to criticism.

criticar *vt* to criticize.

criticastro *m* criticaster, petty critic.

criticismo *m* FIL critical philosophy [of Kant].

crítico, ca *adj* critical (propio de la crítica) || critical (propio de la crisis) || critical, crucial (decisivo); *en el momento crítico* at the crucial moment.
◆ *m* critic; *crítico de arte* art critic.

criticón, ona *adj* critical, faultfinding, hypercritical.
◆ *m/f* faultfinder, criticizer.

crizneja *f* plait, braid (de pelo) || rope, plait of esparto (de soga).

croar *vi* to croak (las ranas).

croata *adj/s* Croatian, Croat.

crocitar *vi* to croak, to crow, to caw (el cuervo).

croché; crochet *m* crochet (ganchillo).

croissant *m* CULIN croissant.

croissantería *f* croissant shop.

crol *m* DEP crawl.

cromado *m* TECN chromium-plating.

cromar *vt* TECN to chromium-plate, to chrome || *cromado* chromium-plated, chrome.

cromático, ca *adj* FÍS & MÚS chromatic; *escala cromática* chromatic scale.

cromatina *f* BIOL chromatin.

cromatismo *m* chromatism (defecto de los instrumentos ópticos) || MÚS chromaticism.

cromato *m* QUÍM chromate.

crómico, ca *adj* QUÍM chromic.

crómlech; crónlech *m* cromlech (monumento megalítico).

cromo *m* chromium, chrome (metal) || chromo, chromolithograph, coloured print (cromolitografía) || picture card; *coleccionar cromos* to collect picture cards || FAM *estar hecho un cromo* to look very smart.

cromolitografía *f* chromolithography (imprenta) || chromolithograph (estampa).

cromolitógrafo *m* chromolithographer.

cromosfera *f* ASTR chromosphere.

cromosoma *m* BIOL chromosome.

crónica *f* chronicle (anales) || page (en un periódico); *crónica teatral* theatre page || — *crónica de sociedad* society *o* social column || *crónica de sucesos* «news in brief».

cronicidad *f* chronicity.

cronicismo *m* MED chronicity (de una enfermedad).

crónico, ca *adj* chronic.

cronicón *m* short chronicle.

cronista *m* chronicler (autor de anales) || columnist (periodista que escribe crónicas).

crónlech *m* —> **crómlech.**

cronógrafo *m* chronographer (persona) || chronograph (aparato).

cronología *f* chronology.

cronológico, ca *adj* chronological.

cronologista; cronólogo *m* chronologist, chronologer.

cronometrador *m* timekeeper.

cronometraje *m* timing, timekeeping.

cronometrar *vt* to time.

cronometría *f* chronometry.

cronométrico, ca *adj* chronometric, chronometrical.

cronómetro *m* chronometer || DEP stopwatch.

croquet *m* croquet (juego).

croqueta *f* CULIN croquette, rissole; *croqueta de pescado* fish croquette.

croquis *m* sketch (dibujo).

cros *m* DEP cross-country race (carrera).

crótalo *m* crotalum (castañuela antigua) || ZOOL rattlesnake (serpiente de cascabel).
◆ *pl* POÉT castanets.

croupier *m* croupier (en el juego).

cruce *m* crossing (acción de cruzar) || crisscross, crisscrossing (acción de cruzarse en varios sentidos) || junction, crossroads *pl* [US intersection] (de calles), crossroads *pl* [US intersection] (de carreteras) || pedestrian crossing (paso) || crossed line (interferencia en las comunicaciones telefónicas) || crossing, crossbreeding (de razas diferentes) || cross, crossbreed (ser híbrido) || ELECTR short circuit (cortocircuito)
|| — *hay un cruce* the lines are crossed (teléfono) || AUT *luces de cruce* dipped headlights.

cruceiro *m* cruzeiro (moneda brasileña).

crucería *f* ARQ ogives *pl*, ribs *pl* || *bóveda de crucería* groined *o* ribbed vault.

crucero *m* ARQ transept (en los templos) || junction [US intersection] (de calles), crossroads *pl* [US intersection] (de carreteras) || MAR cruiser (barco de guerra) | cruise (viaje por mar) | cruiser, passenger cruiser (navío) || crossbearer (en las procesiones) || ASTR Southern Cross (constelación) || IMPR fold (de una hoja) | crossbar (listón que divide el molde) || ARQ crossbeam, crosspiece | window bar (de ventana) || cleavage (de un mineral) || *velocidad de crucero* cruising speed.

cruceta *f* cross [in cross-stitch] (punto de cruz, de cruceta) || MAR crosstree || ARQ crossbeam, crosspiece (crucero) || TECN crosshead.

crucial *adj* crucial, cross-shaped; *incisión crucial* crucial incision || FIG crucial, critical (decisivo); *momento crucial* crucial moment.

cruciferario *m* crossbearer (el que lleva la cruz) || member of the religious order of the Holy Cross.

crucífero, ra *adj* BOT cruciferous.
◆ *f* BOT crucifer.
◆ *pl* BOT cruciferae.

crucificado, da *adj* crucified.
◆ *m* *el Crucificado* the Crucified, Jesus Christ.

crucificar *vt* to crucify || FIG & FAM to torment, to torture.

crucifijo *m* crucifix.

crucifixión *m* crucifixion.

cruciforme *adj* cruciform.

crucigrama *m* crossword (puzzle).

crucigramista; cruciverbista *m/f* person who does crosswords.

crudeza *f* coarseness, crudeness (realismo brutal) || rude thing (palabra grosera) || harshness (rigor); *la crudeza del clima, del invierno* the harshness of the climate, of the winter | severity; *la crudeza de las heladas* the severity of the frost || hardness (del agua) || bluntness (franqueza, brusquedad) || rawness (de lo que no está cocido) || unripeness (de lo que no está maduro).
◆ *pl* undigested food *sing*.

crudo, da *adj* raw (no cocido) || unripe, green (no maduro) || crude; *petróleo crudo* crude oil || hard (agua) || hard to digest (difícil de digerir) || unbleached (sin blanquear) || untreated (no elaborado) || raw; *seda cruda* raw silk || FIG coarse, crude (excesivamente realista); *un chiste crudo* a coarse joke || harsh, severe (tiempo, clima) || harsh, cruel (cruel) || inexperienced, raw (torero, artista, etc.) || beige (beige) || AMER suffering from a hangover (después de una borrachera) || *en crudo* raw; *tomate en crudo* raw tomato; bluntly (bruscamente).

cruel *adj* cruel; *un tirano cruel* a cruel tyrant || *mostrarse cruel* to be cruel; *el destino se muestra cruel con él* fate is cruel to him.

crueldad *f* cruelty.

cruentamente *adv* bloodily.

cruento, ta *adj* bloody.

crujía *f* ARQ bay, space between two walls | corridor, gallery (pasillo) || MAR midship gangway || ward (sala de hospital) || passage between choir and sanctuary (en algunas catedrales) || FIG & FAM *pasar* or *sufrir una crujía* to be going through a bad time *o* a rough patch.

crujido *m* rustle (de la seda, de las hojas secas) || creak (de una puerta, de una rama gruesa, de los muelles de un sillón, etc.) || grinding, gnashing (de los dientes) || crackle (de la madera al arder, del papel al arrugarse) || crack (de los nudillos).

crujiente *adj* rustling (seda, hojas secas) || creaky (puerta, rama gruesa, muelles de un sillón, etc.) || grinding, gnashing (dientes) || crackling (madera al arder, papel al arrugarse) || cracking (nudillos) || crusty, crisp (pan) || crisp, crunchy (galleta).

crujir *vi* to rustle (seda, hojas secas) || to creak (puerta, rama gruesa, muelles de un sillón, etc.) || to grind, to gnash (dientes) || to crackle (madera al arder, papel al arrugarse) || to crunch (grava) || to crack (nudillos) || *allí será el llorar y el crujir de dientes* there will be weeping and gnashing of teeth.

crúor *m* POÉT blood || MED cruor, blod clot (sangre coagulada).

crup *m* croup (enfermedad).

crural *adj* ANAT crural (del muslo).

crustáceo, a *adj/sm* ZOOL crustacean.
◆ *pl* ZOOL crustacea.

cruz *f* cross (patíbulo, figura) || cross (condecoración); *gran cruz de Isabel la Católica* grand cross of Isabella I || MAR crown (del ancla) || tails *pl* (de la moneda); *¿cara o cruz?* heads or tails? || withers *pl* (de los caballos) || fork (de un árbol) || ASTR cross; *Cruz del Sur* Southern Cross (constelación) || crotch (de los pantalones) || hilt (de una espada) || HERÁLD cross || FIG cross (carga); *cada uno lleva su cruz* everyone has his own cross to bear || — *con los brazos en* *cruz* with one's arms outstreched, with one's arms spreadeagled || *Cruz de San Andrés* Saint Andrew's Cross || *Cruz de Lorena* Cross of Lorraine || *cruz de los Caídos* monument to the dead, war memorial || *Cruz de Malta* Maltese cross || *cruz gamada* swastika || *cruz griega, latina* Greek, Latin cross || HERÁLD *cruz potenzada* cross potent || *Cruz Roja* Red Cross || FIG & FAM *cruz y raya* that's the end of that, that's that | *de la cruz a la fecha* from beginning to end || *en cruz* crosswise, crossed; *dos espadas en cruz* two crossed swords; cross-shaped (que tiene forma de cruz) || FIG *es la cruz y los ciriales* one has the devil's own job || *firmar con una cruz* to make one's mark || *hacerse cruces* to cross o.s. (santiguarse), to be speechless, to be dumbfounded (quedarse perplejo) || FIG *llevar la cruz a cuestas* to have one's cross to bear || *por esta cruz, por éstas que son cruces* I swear by this cross *o* by all that is holy || *quedarse en cruz y en cuadro* to be reduced to poverty || *señal de la cruz* sign of the cross.

cruza *f* AMER crossbreed (híbrido) || crossbreeding (cruce de razas diferentes).

cruzada *f* HIST crusade || (p us) crossroads *pl* (encrucijada) || FIG crusade, campaign, drive; *una cruzada contra la ignorancia* a crusade against ignorance; *cruzada antialcohólica* temperance campaign.

cruzado, da *adj* crossed || double-breasted; *abrigo cruzado* double-breasted coat || twilled; *tela cruzada* twilled cloth || COM crossed; *cheque cruzado* crossed cheque || crossbred (animales, plantas) || MIL *fuegos cruzados* cross fire || *palabras cruzadas* crossword (puzzle) *sing*.
◆ *m* crusader (participante en una cruzada) || cross, crossbreed (animal) || twill weave (de una tela) || cross (en la danza).
◆ *pl* hatching *sing* (en el dibujo).

cruzamiento *m* crossing (acción de cruzar) || crossing, crossbreeding (de animales).

cruzar *vt* to cross; *cruzar las piernas* to cross one's legs || to cross (atravesar); *cruzar la calle* to cross the street; *el puente cruza el río aquí* the bridge crosses the river here || to lay *o* to place across; *cruzar el camino con un árbol* to lay a tree across the road || to draw across; *cruzar la página con una raya* to draw a line across the page || to lie across (estar cruzado) || COM to cross (un cheque) || to invest [with the insignia of an order] || AGR to plough a second time || to cross, to crossbreed (plantas y animales) || — *cruzar a nado* to swim across || *cruzar apuestas* to make a bet, to bet || FIG & FAM *cruzar a uno la cara* to hit s.o. across the face, to slap s.o.'s face || MIL *cruzar la espada con* to cross swords with (pelearse) || *cruzar los brazos* to fold one's arms || FIG *cruzar unas palabras con uno* to exchange a few words with s.o. (conversar brevemente), to have words with s.o. (disputar) || *cruzar por la imaginación* to cross one's mind || *nunca había cruzado una palabra con él* I had never exchanged a word with him.
◆ *vi* MAR to cruise.
◆ *vpr* to cross; *nuestras cartas se han cruzado* our letters crossed || to exchange (palabras, regalos, etc.) || to pass; *me crucé con él por la calle* I passed him in the street || to intersect, to cross; *dos carreteras que se cruzan* two roads which cross || — *cruzarse de brazos* to fold one's arms || *cruzarse de palabras* to quarrel, to have words (disputar) || *cruzarse de piernas* to cross one's legs || FIG *cruzarse en el camino de alguien* to cross s.o.'s path.

cruzeiro *m* cruzeiro (moneda brasileña).

CTNE *abrev de Compañía Telefónica Nacional de España* Spanish State telephone company.

cu *f* Q, name of the letter *q*.

cuaba *f* AMER torchwood, candlewood (árbol).

cuacar *vi* AMER to please, to suit.

cuácara *f* AMER jacket (chaqueta) | workman's blouse (blusa de mahón) || flock coat (levita).

cuaco *m* AMER horse (caballo).

cuaderna *f* double fours [in game resembling backgammon] || MAR & AVIAC frame; *cuaderna maestra* midship frame || MAR rib || *cuaderna vía* verse form with four alexandrines (estrofa).

cuadernal *m* MAR block and tackle.

cuadernillo *m* IMPR quinternion (cinco pliegos de papel) || booklet (cuaderno pequeño) || liturgical calendar (añalejo) || packet of cigarette paper (de papel de fumar) || *cuadernillo de sellos* book of stamps.

cuaderno *m* exercise book, copy book || FAM pack of cards (baraja) || MAR *cuaderno de bitácora* logbook.

cuadra *f* stable (caballeriza) || stable (conjunto de caballos o de automóviles de un propietario) || FIG pigsty (lugar muy sucio) || croup, rump (grupa) || large hall (sala grande) || ward (de hospital) || hut (de cuartel) || AMER block [of houses] (manzana de casas); *vivo a tres cuadras* I live three blocks away || quarter of a Roman mile (medida itineraria) || MAR quarter || MAR *navegar a la cuadra* to sail with the wind on the quarter.

cuadrada *f* MÚS breve (nota).

cuadradillo *m* square-sectioned ruler (regla) || square-sectioned iron bar (barra de hierro) || gusset (de camisa) || lump, cube [of sugar]; *azúcar de cuadradillo* lump sugar.

cuadrado, da *adj* square; *una vela cuadrada* a square sail; *raíz cuadrada* square root || stocky, broad-shouldered (persona) || full-face (retrato) || perfect, complete (perfecto, cabal).
◆ *m* MAT square (figura) | square; *el cuadrado de la hipotenusa, de un número* the square of the hypotenuse, of a number || square-sectioned iron bar (barra de hierro) || square-sectioned ruler (regla) || gusset (de camisa) || IMPR quadrat, quad (para espacios) || die (para monedas).

cuadrafonía *f* quadrophony, quadraphony.

cuadrafónico, ca *adj* quadrophonic, quadraphonic.

cuadragenario, ria *adj/s* quadragenarian.

Cuadragésima *f* Quadragesima; *domingo de la Cuadragésima* Quadragesima Sunday.

cuadragesimal *adj* lenten (relativo a la cuaresma).

cuadragésimo, ma *adj/s* fortieth.

cuadrangular *adj* quadrangular.

cuadrángulo, la *adj* quadrangular.
◆ *m* quadrangle.

cuadrante *m* quadrant (de círculo) || sundial (reloj de sol) || dial (dispositivo indicador) || face (del reloj) || quadrant (instrumento) || MAR quarter (del horizonte) || list of masses (tablilla de las misas).

cuadrar *vt* to square, to make square (dar forma cuadrada) || MAT to square (un número, una figura) || IMPR to lay out || to divide into squares (cuadricular un dibujo) || TAUR to line up (the bull) || AMER to park (aparcar).
◆ *vi* to agree, to tally, to square; *nuestras cuentas no cuadran con las suyas* our accounts do not tally with yours || to suit, to go with; *esta alfombra cuadra con los muebles* this carpet suits the furniture || to suit (convenir); *esa hora no me cuadra* that time doesn't suit me || to suit (la ropa) || AMER to park (aparcar).
◆ *vpr* MIL to stand to attention || to stop short (el caballo) || FIG & FAM to dig one's heels in; *se ha cuadrado y no hay nada que hacer* he has dug his heels in and there is nothing we can do.

cuadrático, ca *adj* MAT quadratic.

cuadratín *m* IMPR quadrat, quad.

cuadratura *f* quadrature.

cuadrero, ra *adj* AMER fast, quick (caballo).
◆ *f* AMER stable (cuadra).

cuadriceps *adj/sm* quadriceps (músculo).

cuadrícula *f* grid, cross ruling.

cuadriculado, da *adj* grid; *mapa cuadriculado* grid map || *papel cuadriculado* squared paper, graph paper.
◆ *m* grid, cross ruling.

cuadricular *adj* gridded, squared.

cuadricular *vt* to grid, to square, to divide into squares.

cuadridimensional *m* FÍS four-dimensional.

cuadrienal *adj* quadrennial.

cuadrienio *m* quadrennium.

cuadriga *f* quadriga.

cuadrigémino *adj m* ANAT quadrigeminal.

cuadril *m* ANAT hip bone (hueso) | hip, haunch (cadera) | rump (de los animales).

cuadrilátero, ra *adj* MAT quadrilateral.
◆ *m* quadrilateral (polígono) || ring (boxeo).

cuadrilongo, ga *adj* MAT rectangular, oblong.
◆ *m* rectangle, oblong (rectángulo).

cuadrilla *f* TAUR «cuadrilla» [team assisting the matador in the bullright] || gang, band (de malhechores) || gang, party (de amigos) || team, gang (de obreros) || quadrille (baile) || HIST company of bowmen of the «Santa Hermandad» [in charge of hunting criminals].

cuadrillero *m* foreman (capataz) || HIST bowman of the «Santa Hermandad».

cuadrimotor *m* four-engined.
◆ *m* four-engined plane (avión).

cuadripartido, da; cuadripartito, ta *adj* quadripartite; *convenio cuadripartito* quadripartite convention.

cuadriplicado, da *adj* quadruplicate.

cuadriplicar *vt/vi* to quadruplicate, to quadruple.

cuadrisílabo, ba *adj* quadrisyllabic.
◆ *m* quadrisyllable.

cuadrito *m* CULIN cube || *cortar en cuadritos* to dice.

cuadrivalente *adj* QUÍM tetravalent, quadrivalent.

cuadrivio *m* quadrivium.

cuadro, dra *adj* (p us) square (cuadrado).
◆ *m* square (cuadrado) || picture, painting (pintura) || IMPR platen || patch, bed (de un jardín); *cuadro de flores* flower bed || TEATR scene || sight, scene; *la ciudad bombardeada ofrecía un cuadro desolador* the bombed city was a sorry sight || description, picture (descripción) || staff (conjunto del personal) || table, chart (gráfico) || MIL officers and noncommissioned officers | square (formación) || frame (de una bicicleta) || AMER slaughterhouse (matadero) || — *cuadro clínico* clinical pattern || *cuadro de costumbres* study of manners || *cuadro de distribución* switchboard || *cuadro de instrumentos* or *de mandos* dashboard, instrument panel (de un coche), instrument panel (de un avión) || *cuadro facultativo* or *médico* medical staff || *cuadro sinóptico* chart, diagram || *cuadro sueco* crossbeam for attaching gymnastic apparatus || *cuadro vivo* tableau vivant || *dentro del cuadro de* in the framework of || *en cuadro* in a square; *sillas dispuestas en cuadro* chairs arranged in a square || FIG *quedarse en cuadro* to be left friendless (estar abandonado), to be greatly reduced in numbers (de un conjunto de per-

sonas), to be left with officers only (de una unidad militar) || *tela de cuadros* check *o* checked cloth || FAM *¡vaya un cuadro!* what a sight!

cuadrumano, na *adj* ZOOL quadrumanous.
◆ *m* quadrumane.

cuadrupedal *adj* quadrupedal.

cuadrúpedo, da *adj/s* quadruped.

cuádruple *adj* quadruple, fourfold.

cuadruplicación *f* quadruplication.

cuadruplicado, da *adj* quadruplicate || *por cuadruplicado* in quadruplicate.

cuadruplicar *vt/vi* to quadruple.

cuádruplo, pla *adj* quadruple, fourfold.
◆ *m* quadruple.

cuaima *f* AMER poisonous snake of Venezuela || FIG & FAM snake, viper (persona astuta y cruel).

cuajada *f* curd (de la leche) || cottage cheese (requesón).

cuajado, da *adj* curdled (leche) || clotted (sangre) || FIG dumbfounded, astonished (asombrado) | asleep (dormido); *quedarse cuajado* to fall asleep || *cuajado de* full of; *Londres está cuajado de extranjeros* London is full of foreigners; covered with; *un balcón cuajado de flores* a balcony covered with flowers; bursting with; *un libro cuajado de ilustraciones* a book bursting with illustrations; studded with; *un cielo cuajado de estrellas* a sky studded with stars, a star-studded sky.
◆ *m* CULIN mincemeat dish.

cuajadura *f* curdling (de la leche) || clotting (de la sangre) || coagulation, congealing || curd (cuajada) || solidification.

cuajaleche *m* BOT cheese rennet, yellow bedstraw.

cuajamiento *m* curdling || clotting, coagulation.

cuajar *m* ZOOL abomasum, rennet stomach.

cuajar *vt* to coagulate, to congeal (en general) || to clot (la sangre) || to curdle (la leche) || to set (la gelatina) || to congeal (las grasas) || to cover; *cuajar un vestido de perlas* to cover a dress with pearls || to fill with; *cuajar un libro de ilustraciones* to fill a book with illustrations.
◆ *vi* to settle (nieve) || FIG & FAM to work out; *su negocio no cuajó* his business didn't work out | to catch on; *esta moda no cuajó* this fashion did not catch on | to fit in (en un trabajo) | to get away with; *tales mentiras no cuajan* one cannot get away with lies like that | to come off (planes) | to materialize (concretarse) | to develop, to grow; *sus ideas cuajaron en una gran obra* his ideas grew into a great work | to become; *no cabe duda de que algún día cuajará en un gran artista* there is no doubt that some day he will become a great artist | to be acceptable (propuesta) || — *cuajado de* full of; *Londres está cuajado de extranjeros* London is full of foreigners; covered with; *un balcón cuajado de flores* a balcony covered with flowers; bursting with; *un libro cuajado de ilustraciones* a book bursting with illustrations; studded with; *un cielo cuajado de estrellas* a sky studded with stars, a star-studded sky.
◆ *vpr* to coagulate, to congeal (ponerse gelatinoso) || to curdle (leche) || to clot, to congeal (sangre) || to set (gelatina) || to take (mayonesa, etc.) || FIG to fill up (llenarse) | to go to sleep (dormirse).

cuajarón *m* clot.

cuajo *m* rennet (sustancia que cuaja la leche) || curdling (de la leche) || clotting (de la sangre) || ZOOL abomasum, rennet stomach (cuajar del rumiante) || FIG & FAM patience, phlegm (calma) || — *añadir cuajo* to add rennet, to curdle || *arrancar de cuajo* to uproot (un árbol), to wrench off (una puerta, etc.), to uproot, to eradicate (cosas malas) || FIG *tener cuajo* to be sluggish (ser lento), to be patient (paciente).

cuakerismo *m* Quakerism (cuaquerismo).

cuákero, ra *m/f* Quaker.

cual *pron rel*
PRECEDIDO DE ARTÍCULO who, whom (personas), which (cosas); *llamó al portero, el cual dormía* he called the porter, who was asleep; *quitó las piedras, las cuales le obstruían el camino* he removed the stones which were obstructing his path || — *al cual, a la cual, a los cuales, a las cuales* to whom (personas), to which (cosas) (complemento indirecto); *la mujer a la cual mandé la carta* the woman to whom I sent the letter; whom (personas) (complemento directo); *el hombre al cual yo vi esta mañana* the man whom I saw this morning || *bajo el cual* under whom (persona), under which (cosa) || *con lo cual* at *o* upon which, whereupon (entonces), with which (con lo que) || *del cual, de la cual, de los cuales, de las cuales* of whom (personas), of which (cosas); *el hombre del cual hablé* the man of whom I spoke; *cinco chicos dos de los cuales son bandidos* five boys two of whom are bandits; *nueve planetas de los cuales la Tierra es uno* nine planets of which the Earth is one || *de lo cual* which; *ha conseguido lo que quería, de lo cual me alegro mucho* he got what he wanted which makes me very glad; from which; *de lo cual podemos inferir que...* from which we can infer that...; whereof; *en fe de lo cual* in witness whereof || *después de lo cual* after which || *en el cual* in which, where; *el sitio en el cual nací* the place where I was born || *lo cual* which; *ya no nos habla, lo cual indica que está enfadado con nosotros* he no longer speaks to us, which means he is angry with us || *por lo cual* for which reason, because of which, whereby || *sin lo cual* without which.
SIN ARTÍCULO such as; *epidemias cuales se propagaban en la Edad Media ya no habrá más* there will be no more epidemics such as those which were rife in the Middle Ages || POÉT like; *cual las flores del naranjo* like orange blossoms || — *allá cada cual* every man to his own taste || *cada cual* everyone (todos); *cada cual tiene sus problemas* everyone has his problems; each, each one; *a cada cual lo suyo* to each his own || *cual o cual* a few; *entre la asistencia había cual o cual aficionado* among the audience there were a few devotees.
◆ *adv* like, as (como) || just as; *cual se lo cuento* just as I am telling you || *cual... tal* like... like; *cual el padre, el hijo* like father, like son.

cuál *adj y pron interrog* which, what; *no sé cual será su decisión* I do not know what his decision will be; *¿cuál es el camino más corto?* which is the shortest way? || which, which one; *¿cuál de los tres llegará primero?* which of the three will arrive first? || — *estaban gritando a cual más* they were trying to outshout each other || *los dos trabajan a cuál mejor* the two work equally well, it is hard to say which of the two works better || *son a cuál más estúpidos* they are each as stupid as the other.
◆ *pron indef* some; *todos se quejaban, cuáles de la comida, cuáles de la cama* they all complained, some about the food, some about the beds || *todos contribuyeron, cuál más, cuál menos, a su éxito* they all contributed in varying degrees to his success.
◆ *adv* imagine!; *¡cuál fue su sorpresa!* imagine his surprise! || how; *¡cuál gritan!* how they shout!
— OBSERV pl *cuales.*

cualesquier, cualesquiera *pron indef pl* ⟶ **cualquier, cualquiera.**

cualidad *f* quality, attribute (de personas) || property (de cosas) || quality; *la generosidad es una cualidad* generosity is a quality.

cualificado, da *adj* skilled (obrero).

cualitativo, va *adj* qualitative.

cualquier *adj indef* (apocope of cualquiera) ⟶ **cualquiera.**
— OBSERV The apocope of *cualquiera* is used before a masculine or feminine noun in the singular, even if the noun is preceded by an adjective: *cualquier hombre, cualquier otra mujer.* The form *cualquiera* is sometimes used before a feminine noun in the singular.

cualquiera *pron indef* anyone, anybody; *cualquiera haría lo mismo* anyone would do the same || any one, one (interrogativo), any one (afirmativo); *cualquiera de ustedes* any one of you || whatever; *cualquiera que sea su excusa no le perdono* whatever his excuse may be, I will not forgive him || nobody (nadie); *¡cualquiera lo creería!* nobody would believe that! || whichever, whichever one (personas y cosas); *cualquiera que quieras* whichever you like || whoever (personas); *cualquiera que lo diga* whoever says so || — *cualquiera que sea* whoever he is (persona), whichever it is (cosa) || *cualquiera lo diría* one would think so, anyone would say so || *una cualquiera* a loose woman (mujer desvergonzada), a woman of no account, a nobody (mujer sin importancia) || *un cualquiera* a man of no account, a nobody || *unos cualquieras* people of no account, nobodies.
◆ *adj indef* any; *en cualquier momento y a cualquier hora* at any moment, at any time; *cualquier hombre inteligente lo sabe* any intelligent man knows that || whatever; *cualquier excusa que me des, no te creo* I won't believe you whatever excuse you give me || whichever, any (cosas y personas); *puedes escoger cualquier plato (que quieras)* you can choose any *o* whichever dish you like, you can choose any dish || ordinary; *un día cualquiera* an ordinary day || — *cualquier cosa* anything; *es capaz de hacer cualquier cosa* he is capable of anything || *cualquier cosa que* whatever; *cualquier cosa que haga* whatever he does || *cualquier otro* anyone else (personas); *cualquier otro menos yo* anyone else but me; any other one (cosas) || *cualquier persona que* anybody who, whoever, anyone who; *cualquier persona que lo diga es un embustero* anybody who says that is a fibber, whoever says that is a fibber; anyone who, anybody who; *admiro a cualquier persona que sepa hacerlo* I admire anyone who can do it || *en cualquier otra parte* anywhere else || *en cualquier sitio* anywhere || *por cualquier parte que vaya* wherever he goes.
— OBSERV pl *cualesquiera* (*cualesquiera de ustedes* any of you).

cuan *adv* how; *no puedes imaginarte cuán cansada estoy* you cannot imagine how tired I am || how (exclamativo); *¡cuán pronto pasan los años!* how quickly the years go by! || — *cayó cuan largo era* he fell full length || *tan... cuan* as... as; *el castigo será tan grande cuan grave fue la culpa* the punishment will be as severe as the offence was serious; *cuan bueno era el padre, tan malo es el hijo* the son is as bad as the father was good.
— OBSERV *Cuan* is de apocope of *cuanto* and is only used before adjectives and adverbs. It is accented in exclamatory and interrogative sentences.

cuando *conj* when (en el tiempo en que); *será de noche cuando lleguemos a casa* it will be night when we arrive home; *cuando era joven, yo creía...* when I was young, I believed... || whenever (en cualquier momento); *estoy dispuesto a ayudarte cuando quieras* I am ready to help you whenever you like || even though, even if, although (aunque); *cuando lo dijeras* *mil veces* even if you said it a thousand times || since (puesto que); *cuando lo dices será verdad* it must be true since you say so || if; *cuando llueve llevo paraguas, cuando no, lo dejo en casa* if it rains I take an umbrella, if not I leave it at home || — *aun cuando* even if; *aun cuando llueva* even if it rains; *aun cuando lo supiese me callaría* even if I knew it I would not say anything || *cuando más, cuando mucho* at the most (a lo sumo) || *cuando mayor* when I am (you are, he is, etc.) grown up *o* old enough; *cuando mayor compraré un coche* when I am old enough I shall buy a car || *cuando menos* at least; *tiene treinta años cuando menos* he is thirty at least || *cuando no* if not, otherwise (si no) || *cuando quiera que* whenever; *cuando quiera que venga me regala algo* whenever he comes he brings me a present || *de cuando en cuando, de vez en cuando* from time to time, now and again || *entonces es cuando...* it was then that..., that was when... || *hasta cuando* until.

◆ *adv* when; *vendrás, pero ¿cuándo?* you will come, but when?; *no sé cuándo iré* I don't know when I shall go || — *cuándo... cuándo* at times... at times || *cuando quiera* whenever you like || *¿de cuándo acá?, ¿desde cuándo?* since when? || *¿para cuándo?* when?

◆ *prep* during; *cuando la guerra* during the war || at the time of; *cuando la última huelga* at the time of the last strike.

◆ *m* *el cómo y el cuándo* the why and the wherefore.

— OBSERV There is an accent on *cuando* in exclamatory and interrogative sentences.

cuanta *m pl* quanta.

— OBSERV En inglés el singular de *quanta* es *quantum*.

cuantía *f* quantity (cantidad) || extent (extensión, alcance); *desconocemos la cuantía de los daños* we don't know the extent of the damage || amount (importe) || distinction, importance (de una persona) || importance (importancia) || *persona de mayor, de menor cuantía* distinguished *o* important person, undistinguished *o* unimportant person.

cuántico, ca *adj* quantum, quantic; *teoría cuántica* quantum theory.

cuantificación *f* FIL quantification || FÍS quantization.

cuantificar *vt* FIL to quantify || FÍS to quantize.

cuantimás *adv* FAM all the more (so).

cuantioso, sa *adj* abundant (abundante) || numerous (numeroso) || considerable, substantial (grande).

cuantitativo, va *adj* quantitative; *análisis cuantitativo* quantitative analysis.

cuanto, ta *adj* how much; *¿cuánto dinero tiene?* how much money has he? || what a lot of; *¡cuánta gente!* what a lot of people! || — *cuanto más... más* the more... the more; *cuanto más dinero tiene, más quiere* the more money he has the more he wants || *cuanto más frío hace, menos salgo* the colder it is, the less I go out || *cuanto menos trabajo tiene, más se aburre* the less work he has, the more bored he is || *tanto cuanto* as much as; *tiene tanto cuanto dinero necesita* he has as much money as he needs || *tanto más... cuanto que* all the more... since *o* because || *tanto más... cuanto más* the more... the more.

◆ *adj pl* how many; *¿cuántas manzanas quieres?* how many apples do you want? || what, so many, what a lot of (exclamación); *¡cuántos problemas!* what problems!, so many problems! || all; *empeñó cuantos libros tenía* he pawned all his books || — *cuantos... tantos* as many... as; *cuantas cabezas, tantos pareceres* as many opinions as there are individuals || *perdió no sé cuántos libros* he lost I don't know how many books || *unos cuantos, unas cuantas* a few; *tengo unos cuantos amigos* I have a few friends.

◆ *pron* how much; *¿cuánto queda?* how much is left? || all, as much as; *tome cuanto quiera* take as much as you like || all, everything; *¡si supieras cuánto me contó!* if you knew all he told me! || *todo cuanto* everything (cosas); *te dará todo cuanto quieras* he will give you everything you want.

◆ *pron pl* all who, everybody who; *cuantos vayan allí serán castigados* all who go *o* everybody who goes there will be punished || how many; *¿cuántos han muerto?* how many have died? || — *cuantos más, mejor* the more the merrier || *el señor no sé cuantos* Mr. So-and-So || *tenemos que vender cuantos nos mandan* we must sell all they send us *o* as many as they send us || *todos cuantos* everybody, everyone, all (personas), all (cosas); *el cuadro les gusta a todos cuantos lo ven* everybody who sees the painting likes it || *unos cuantos, unas cuantas* a few, some.

◆ *adv* how much (de qué manera); *no sabes cuánto le odio* you do not know how much I hate him || how; *¡cuánto ha cambiado!* how he has changed! || how much (cantidad); *¿cuánto vale eso?* how much is this worth? || how long; *¿cuánto dura este disco?* how long does this record play? || — *¿a cuánto estamos?, ¿a cuántos estamos?* what date is it? (fecha) || *¿cada cuánto?* every how often? || *cuanto a, en cuanto a* as for; *en cuanto a mí* as for me || *cuanto antes* as soon as possible || *cuanto más* all the more (a mayor abundamiento), at the most; *esto vale cuanto más cien pesetas* this is worth a hundred pesetas at the most || *cuanto más... más* the more... the more; *cuanto más le conozco, más le quiero* the more I know him the more I like him || *cuanto más mejor* the more the better *o* the merrier || *cuanto más... menos* the more... the less; *cuanto más lo miro, menos lo comprendo* the more I look at it the less I understand it || *en cuanto* as soon as; *en cuanto le vi le sonreí* as soon as I saw him I smiled at him; as; *ella, en cuanto estudiante* she, as a student || *por cuanto* since, inasmuch as.

— OBSERV *Cuanto, cuanta* are written with an accent in exclamatory and interrogative sentences.

cuanto *m* FÍS quantum.

cuaquerismo *m* Quakerism (doctrina religiosa).

cuáquero, ra *m/f* Quaker.

cuarcita *f* MIN quartzite.

cuarenta *adj* forty; *tengo cuarenta alumnos* I have forty pupils.

◆ *m* forty || fortieth; *es el cuarenta de la clase* he is the fortieth in the class.

◆ *f pl* forty points gained by a player in the game of «tute» when he has the «rey» and the «caballo» of trumps || FAM *cantar a uno las cuarenta* to tell s.o. a few home truths, to give s.o. a piece of one's mind.

cuarentavo, va *adj/s* fortieth.

cuarentena *f* forty || lent (cuaresma) || quarantine (medida de sanidad) || — *poner en cuarentena* to quarantine, to put in quarantine (sentido propio), to send to Coventry (no hablar a) || *una cuarentena de* about forty, forty-odd, some forty.

cuarentón, ona *adj* forty-year-old, in one's forties.

◆ *m/f* forty-year-old, person in his (her, etc.) forties.

cuaresma *m* lent.

cuaresmal *adj* lenten.

cuarta *f* quarter, fourth (cuarta parte) || point (de la brújula) || span (palmo) || quart, quarte (en naipes) || ASTR quadrant || quarte, quart (en esgrima) || MÚS fourth || AMER whip (látigo) || FAM *no levanta una cuarta del suelo* he's a shorty.

cuartana *f* MED quartan.

cuartanal *adj* MED quartan.

cuartear *vt* to divide into four, to quarter (dividir en cuatro) || to cut into joints, to quarter (descuartizar) || to crack (fragmentar) || to zigzag along (carretera).

◆ *vi* TAUR to arch one's body [to put in the banderillas].

◆ *vpr* to crack, to split (agrietarse) || FIG to crack, to weaken suddenly; *las estructuras de esta organización se han cuarteado* the structures of this organization have suddenly weakened || AMER to go back on one's word.

cuartel *m* MIL quarters *pl* (provisional) | barracks *pl* (permanente) || quarter (gracia concedida al vencido); *dar cuartel a* to give quarter to || (p us) quarter (cuarta) || quarter, district, area (barrio) || bed (cuadro de jardín) || lot, plot (de terreno) || HERÁLD quarter || MAR hatch || — *cuartel general* headquarters || MIL *estar de cuartel* to be unassigned and on half pay || AMER *golpe de cuartel* putsch || *guerra sin cuartel* all out war || FIG *no dar cuartel a* to be merciless to || *sin cuartel* merciless; *lucha sin cuartel* merciless fight.

cuartelada *f* putsch.

cuartelado, da *adj* HERÁLD quartered.

cuartelar *vt* HERÁLD to quarter.

cuartelazo *m* putsch.

cuartelero *adj m* barracks.

◆ *m* MIL soldier on dormitory guard duty, orderly.

cuarteo *m* side step (del cuerpo) || crack (grieta).

cuarterón, ona *m/f* quadroon (mulato).

◆ *m* fourth, quarter (cuarta parte) || quarter of a pound (peso de 125 gramos) || shutter (de ventana) || panel (de puerta).

cuarteta *f* quatrain (redondilla).

cuartete; cuarteto *m* quatrain (poema) || MÚS quartet, quartette; *cuarteto de cuerda* string quartet.

cuartilla *f* sheet (de papel) || pastern (de un animal).

cuartillo *m* half litre (1/2 litro) || quarter of a «real» (antigua moneda).

cuartilludo, da *adj* long-pasterned [horse].

cuarto, ta *adj* fourth (que sigue al tercero) || fourth; *Enrique IV* (cuarto), Henry IV [the fourth] || — *cuarta parte* quarter, fourth part; *tres es la cuarta parte de doce* three is a quarter *o* the fourth part of twelve || *en cuarto lugar* fourthly, in fourth place.

◆ *m* quarter; *un cuarto de hora* a quarter of an hour; *son las dos y cuarto* it's a quarter past two; *las ocho menos cuarto* a quarter to eight || room; *estoy en mi cuarto* I'm in my room; *este piso tiene dos cuartos y una cocina* this flat has two rooms and a kitchen, this is a three-room flat || flat [US apartment] (piso); *cuarto amueblado* furnished flat || line, ancestors *pl* (línea de descendencia) || quarter (de un vestido) || quarter (de un animal) || portion, plot (de un terreno) || ASTR quarter; *cuarto creciente* first quarter; *cuarto menguante* last quarter || MIL watch; *estar de cuarto* to be on watch || VET crack (del casco del caballo) || — *botella de a cuarto* quarter-litre bottle || *cuarto de banderas* guardroom || *cuarto de baño* bathroom || *cuarto de dormir* bedroom || *cuarto de estar* living room [US living room, family room] || *cuarto delantero* forequarter || *cuarto delantero derecho* right front (de un vestido) || *cuarto de prevención* detention room || *cuarto oscuro* darkroom (de fotógrafo) || *cuarto trasero* hindquarter || *cuarto trastero* or *de los trastos* lumber room || FAM *dar un cuarto al pregonero* to shout it from the rooftops | *de-*

jar sin un cuarto to leave broke | *de tres al cuarto* cheap, of little value; *un vestido de tres al cuarto* a cheap dress; third-rate; *un político de tres al cuarto* a third-rate politician | *echar su cuarto a espadas* to butt in, to put one's oar in || *en cuarto* quarto (encuadernación) || *poner a uno las peras a cuarto* to clamp down on s.o.
◆ *pl* FAM cash *sing*, dough *sing*; *tener muchos cuartos* to have a lot of dough || — FAM *afloja los cuartos* cough up, fork up || DEP *cuartos de final* quarter finals || *cuatro cuartos* very little; *ganó cuatro cuartos* he won very little; a bit of money; *la gente cuando tiene cuatro cuartos* people, when they get a bit of money; a song; *lo vendió por cuatro cuartos* he sold it for a song || FAM *manejar los cuartos* to hold the purse strings | *no andar bien de cuartos* to be hard up for money | *¡qué... ni qué ocho cuartos!* my foot!; *¡qué fantasmas ni qué ocho cuartos!* ghosts my foot! || *tres cuartos* three-quarter-length; *manga, abrigo tres cuartos* three-quarter-length sleeve, overcoat; three-quarter [back] (rugby) || *tres cuartos de hora* three quarters of an hour || FAM *tres cuartos de lo mismo* or *de lo propio* exactly the same; *hizo tres cuartos de lo mismo* he did exactly the same.

cuartogénito, ta *adj* fourth-born.
◆ *m/f* fourth-born, fourth child.

cuartucho *m* FAM hovel (habitación mala).

cuarzo *m* quartz (piedra) || — *cuarzo ahumado* smoky quartz || *cuarzo hialino* rock crystal.

cuarzoso, sa *adj* GEOL quartzous, quartzose.

cuasi *adv* (p us) almost, quasi.

cuasia *f* BOT quassia.

cuasicontrato *m* JUR quasi contract.

cuasidelito *m* JUR technical offence, quasi delict.

Cuasimodo *npr m* Quasimodo Sunday.

cuate, ta *adj* AMER twin (gemelo) | similar (semejante).
◆ *m y s* AMER twin (gemelo) | mate; *¿qué me cuentas, cuate?* whats new, mate?

cuaternario, ria *adj/sm* Quaternary; *era cuaternaria* Quaternary era.

cuaternio; cuaternión *m* MAT quaternion.

cuatralbo, ba *adj* with four white feet (caballo).

cuatreño, ña *adj* four-year-old (toro).

cuatrero, ra *m/f* horse thief (de caballos), cattle thief (de vacas) || AMER rascal (bribón) || AMER FAM jester, joker (guasón).

cuatrienal *adj* quadrennial.

cuatrifolio *m* ARQ quatrefoil.

cuatrillizos, zas *mpl/fpl* quadruplets (niños).

cuatrillo *m* quadrille (juego de naipes).

cuatrillón *m* quadrillion [*US* septillion].

cuatrimestral *adj* four-monthly (que ocurre cada cuatro meses) || four-month (que dura cuatro meses).

cuatrimestre *m* four-month period.

cuatrimotor *adj m* four-engined.
◆ *m* four-engined plane.

cuatrirreactor *adj m* four-engined.
◆ *m* four-engined jet.

cuatrisílabo, ba *adj* four-syllable, quadrisyllabic.
◆ *m* quadrisyllable.

cuatro *adj* four; *cuatro pesetas* four pesetas || fourth; *Alejandro nació el día cuatro de marzo* Alexander was born on the fourth of March.
◆ *m* four (número) || fourth (fecha); *el 4 (cuatro) de enero* the fourth of January, January the fourth; 4 January, January 4th (encabezamiento de cartas) || four (naipes); *el cuatro de corazones* the four of hearts || MÚS vocal quartet || AMER four-string guitar (guitarra) | blunder (disparate) || — FAM *cuatro gatos* hardly a soul (casi nadie) || *cuatro ojos ven más que dos* two heads are better than one || *de cuatro en cuatro* every four (cada cuatro), four at a time (en grupos de a cuatro) || MÚS *de cuatro por ocho* four-eight || *las cuatro* four o'clock; *son las cuatro* it's four o'clock || FIG & FAM *más de cuatro* several people, lots of people; *más de cuatro se equivocan* lots of people make mistakes | *trabajar por cuatro* to work like a slave.

cuatrocientos, tas *adj/sm* four hundred.

cuba *f* vat, tub (tina) || barrel, cask (barril) || FIG & FAM potbelly (barrigón) | drunkard (borracho) || — FIG & FAM *beber como una cuba* to drink like a fish | *cada cuba huele al vino que tiene* every tub smells of the wine it holds | *estar (borracho) como una cuba* to be plastered, to be sozzled, to be sloshed.

Cuba *n pr* GEOGR Cuba || FIG *más se perdió en Cuba* worse things have happened at sea.

cubaje *m* AMER cubage (cubicación).

cubalibre; cuba libre *m* rum *o* gin and Coke.

cubanismo *m* cubanism.

cubano, na *adj/s* Cuban.
◆ *f* loose-fitting shirt (guayabera).

cubero *m* cooper || FIG & FAM *a ojo de buen cubero* by guesswork, by rule of thumb (sin medir), in a rough and ready way (sin precisión) || *a ojo de buen cubero debe de pesar diez kilos* at a rough estimate it must weigh about ten kilos.

cubertería *f* cutlery.

cubeta *f* small cask (tonel) || pail, bucket (cuba pequeña) || FÍS bulb (del barómetro) || tank, dish, tray (de laboratorio).

cubicación *f* cubage (acción de cubicar).

cubicar *vt* MAT to cube (elevar al cubo) | to cube (evaluar el volumen).

cúbico, ca *adj* cubic; *metro cúbico* cubic metre || cube; *raíz cúbica* cube root.

cubículo *m* cubicle.

cubierta *f* cover, covering || cover (de libro) || cover, covering (funda) || tyre, casing (del neumático) || roof (tejado) || bedspread (de la cama) || MAR deck; *cubierta de popa* poop deck; *cubierta de proa* front deck; *cubierta de vuelos* flight deck || cover, wrapping (de un cable) || FIG pretext, cover || AMER envelope (de una carta).

cubierto, ta *adj* covered || overcast (cielo) || filled (una vacante).
◆ *m* place setting (para comer) || menu; *cubierto turístico* tourists' menu || cover (abrigo); *ponerse a cubierto* to take cover || — *a cubierto, bajo cubierto* under cover; *ponerse a cubierto* to get under cover || *a cubierto de* safe from || *precio del cubierto* cover charge.
◆ *pl* cutlery *sing* || — *juego de cubiertos* canteen of cutlery || *poner los cubiertos* to set the table.

cubil *n f* den, lair (de animales salvajes).

cubilete *m* mould (molde) || ice cube (hielo) || goblet (vaso de metal) || conjurer's goblet (de prestidigitador) || dicebox (para guardar los dados) || cup (para echar los dados) || AMER top hat (sombrero de copa) | plot, scheme (intriga) || *bandeja para los cubiletes de hielo* ice tray.

cubiletear *vi* to scheme, to intrigue.

cubileteo *m* scheming, shady dealing.

cubilote *m* cupola (crisol).

cubismo *m* cubism (pintura y escultura).

cubista *adj/s* cubist.

cubital *adj* ANAT cubital (del codo).

cubito *m* cube; *cubito de hielo* ice cube || bucket (de niño).

cúbito *m* ANAT cubitus, ulna (hueso).

cubo *m* pail, bucket (recipiente portátil) || small vat *o* tank (cuba pequeña) || socket, holder (de bayoneta) || hub (de rueda) || millpond (de un molino) || drum, barrel (de reloj) || round tower (de fortaleza) || MAT cube || — *cubo de la basura* rubbish bin [*US* trash can] (en la casa), dustbin [*US* trash can, garbage can] (en la calle) || *elevar al cubo* to cube.

cuboflash *m* FOT flashcube.

cuboides *adj inv* cuboid (hueso).

cubrecadena *m* chain guard [of a bicycle].

cubrecama *m* counterpane, bedspread, coverlet.

cubrecorsé *m* camisole.

cubrefuego *m* curfew (queda).

cubrejuntas *m inv* TECN butt strap.

cubrepiés *m inv* foot coverlet [*US* foot blanket].

cubrerradiador *m* radiator muff.

cubretetera *m* tea cosy.

cubretiestos *m inv* flowerpot cover.

cubrir *vt* to cover; *cubrir algo con un velo* to cover sth. with a veil || to shroud, to cloak (la niebla, etc.) || to roof, to put a roof on (una casa) || FIG to satisfy, to meet; *cubrir las necesidades* to satisfy needs || to cover, to meet (sufragar los gastos) | to cover; *los ingresos cubren los gastos* the returns cover the expenses | to drown; *su voz cubre todas las demás* his voice drowns all the others | to cover, to do (una distancia) | to repay (una deuda) | to fill; *cubrir una vacante* to fill a vacancy | to shield, to cover, to protect; *está cubierto por una persona importante* he is being shielded by an important person | to cover up, to hide, to mask (ocultar) || MIL to cover (proteger); *cubrir la retirada* to cover the retreat || to cover, to mate with (un animal) || — *cubrir carrera* to line the route || *cubrir de besos* to smother with kisses || *cubrir de gloria* to cover with glory || *cubrir de alabanzas, de improperios* to shower praise, insults on || *cubrir las apariencias* or *las formas* to keep up appearances || *cubrir una demanda* to meet a demand.
◆ *vpr* to put on one's hat (ponerse el sombrero) || to cloud over, to become overcast (el cielo) || FIG to cover o.s.; *cubrirse de un riesgo con un seguro* to cover o.s. for a risk with an insurance policy | to be filled; *sólo pudieron cubrirse dos vacantes* only two vacancies could be filled || *cubrirse de gloria* to cover o.s. with glory.

cuca *f* BOT ground almond, chufa (chufa) || ZOOL caterpillar (cuco) || sweet (confite) || AMER kind of heron (zancuda).

cucamonas *f pl* FAM cajolery *sing*, sweet talk *sing* (carantoñas).

cucaña *f* greasy pole (diversión) || FIG & FAM cinch, easy job (cosa fácil de conseguir).

cucañero, ra *adj* smart, resourceful.
◆ *m/f* smart customer, resourceful person.

cucar *vt* to wink (guiñar).

cucaracha *f* cockroach, blackbeetle (*fam*) || snuff (tabaco) || AMER trailer (de tranvía) | old crock, jalopy (coche viejo).

cucarachero *m* AMER smart customer, resourceful person.

cuclillas (en) *loc adv* crouching, squatting || *ponerse en cuclillas* to crouch, to squat.

cuclillo *m* cuckoo (ave).

cuco, ca *adj* FIG & FAM nice, cute, pretty (mono) || crafty, sly, cunning (astuto).
◆ *m/f* crafty *o* cunning person, wily bird || cheat, trickster (jugador tramposo).

◆ *m* ZOOL cuckoo (pájaro) | caterpillar (oruga) || *reloj de cuco* cuckoo clock.
◆ *pl* panties (prenda de mujer).

cucú *m* cuckoo (canto del cuco).

cucufato *m* AMER sanctimonious person, bigot.

cucuiza *f* AMER agave fibre.

cuculí *m* AMER wild pigeon.

cucúrbita *f* BOT cucurbit || QUÍM retort (retorta).

cucurbitáceo, a *adj* cucurbitaceous.

cucurucho *m* cone, cornet (envase) || penitent's hood (caperuza) || AMER peak, summit, top.

cuchara *f* spoon (de mesa); *cuchara de café* coffee spoon; *cuchara sopera* soup spoon; *cuchara de palo* wooden spoon; *cuchara de postre* dessert spoon || ladle (cucharón para servir) || ladle (para metales) || spoon bait, trolling spoon (para la pesca) || MAR bailing scoop (achicador) || TECN bucket, scoop (de pala mecánica) || AMER trowel (llana) || — *cuchara autoprensora* grab bucket || FIG & FAM *meterle a alguien una cosa con cuchara* to drum something into s.o. *o* into s.o.'s head | *meter su cuchara* to put one's oar in.

cucharada *f* spoonful (cabida de la cuchara).

cucharadita *f* teaspoonful, teaspoon; *una cucharadita de café* a teaspoonful of coffee.
— OBSERV El plural de *teaspoonful* es *teaspoonfuls* o *teaspoonsful*.

cucharetear *vi* FAM to stir (with a spoon); *cucharetear en algo* to stir sth (with a spoon) || FIG to poke one's nose into other people's affairs, to meddle in other people's affairs (entremeterse).

cucharilla *f* teaspoon (cuchara pequeña) || MIN fluke (para barrenos) || *cucharilla de café* coffee spoon.

cucharón *m* ladle (para servir) || TECN bucket, scoop.

cuche *m* AMER pig.

cuché *adj m* *papel cuché* surface-coated paper, art paper.

cuchí *m* AMER pig.

cuchichear *vi* to whisper.

cuchicheo *m* whispering.

cuchichiar *vi* to call, to cry (la perdiz).

cuchifrito *m* roast piglet.

cuchilla *f* kitchen knife (cuchillo grande) || chopper, cleaver (de carnicero) || blade (de guillotina) || guillotine (del encuadernador) || razor blade (hoja de afeitar) || blade (de un arma blanca, de patín) || coulter [US colter] (de arado) || POÉT sword, blade (espada) || AMER mountain crest (cumbre) | knife-edged ridge (montaña abrupta) | mountain range (cadena) | line of hills (colinas) || — FIG *cara cortada con una cuchilla* hatchet face || *patines de cuchilla* ice skates.

cuchillada *f* slash (golpe) || stab wound (herida profunda) || slash, gash (herida larga) || slash (de vestidos) || — FIG *andar a cuchilladas* to be at daggers drawn || *dar una cuchillada* to stab || *dar de cuchilladas a uno* to stab s.o. || *matar a alguien a cuchilladas* to stab s.o. to death.

cuchillazo *m* knife wound (herida) || *dar un cuchillazo a alguien* to stab s.o., to knife s.o.

cuchillería *f* cutlery (oficio) || cutler's shop (tienda).

cuchillero *m* cutler || AMER wrangler, troublemaker, quarrelsome person.

cuchillo *m* knife (instrumento cortante); *cuchillo de monte, de trinchar, de postre* hunting knife, carving knife, dessert knife || knife-edge (de la balanza) || ZOOL lower tusk (del jabalí) || gore (de un vestido) || FIG power, authority (jurisdicción) || ARQ gable frame || MAR lateen sail || — *cuchillo bayoneta* bayonet || FIG *cuchillo de aire* draught || *cuchillo de guillotina* guillotine blade || *cuchillo eléctrico* electric carving knife || *pasar a cuchillo a alguien* to put s.o. to the sword || FIG *tener el cuchillo en la garganta* to have the knife at one's throat.

cuchipanda *f* FAM feed (comilona) | spree (juerga) || FAM *ir de cuchipanda* to go on a spree (ir de juerga), to have a good feed (darse una comilona).

cuchitril *m* hovel, hole, squalid room (habitación sucia) || den, hole, cubbyhole (habitación pequeña).

cuchufleta *f* FAM joke (broma) || *gastar cuchufletas a uno* to pull s.o.'s leg.

cuchufletear *vi* FAM to tell *o* to crack jokes.

cuchufletero, ra *m/f* FAM joker, tease, legpuller.

cueca *f* popular dance of Chile.

cuelgacapas *m inv* coat rack (en la pared), coat stand (en un soporte).

cuelgaplatos *m inv* plate rack.

cuellicorto, ta *adj* short-necked.

cuellilargo, ga *adj* long-necked.

cuello *m* neck (del cuerpo); *alargar el cuello* to stretch *o* to crane one's neck || throat; *cortar el cuello a uno* to cut s.o.'s throat || neck (de botella, de retorta, etc.) || collar (de un vestido, de una camisa); *cuello almidonado, duro* starched, stiff collar || neck (de un diente) || collar size (número de cuello de una camisa) || collar, collarette (de encaje) || — *agarrar* or *agarrarse a uno del cuello* or *por el cuello* to grab *o* to seize s.o. by the scruff of the neck || *cuello alechugado* or *escarolado* ruff || FIG *cuello de botella* bottleneck || *cuello de pajarita* or *de palomita* wing collar || *cuello de pico* V-neck || *cuello postizo* detachable collar || *cuello vuelto* roll neck, polo neck [US turtleneck] || FIG *estar metido en algo hasta el cuello* to be in it up to one's neck | *hablar para el cuello de su camisa* to talk to o.s. || FIG & FAM *me juego el cuello a que...* I bet anything you like that... | *meter el cuello* to put one's nose to the grindstone, to put one's back into it.

cuenca *f* wooden bowl (escudilla) || socket (del ojo) || GEOGR basin; *la cuenca del Ebro* the Ebro basin | valley (valle) | field; *cuenca petrolífera* oil field.

cuenco *m* earthenware bowl (recipiente de barro).

cuenta *f* account || counting (acción de contar) || count (resultado de contar) || bill [US check] (factura); *la cuenta de la electricidad* the electricity bill; *¡mozo, traiga la cuenta, por favor!* waiter, the bill, please! || DEP count (boxeo) || COM account; *cuenta bancaria* bank account || bead (de rosario o collar) || FIG affair, business (cuidado); *eso es cuenta tuya* that's your affair || — *abonar en cuenta de* to pay into the account of, to credit to (s.o.'s account) || *abrir una cuenta* to open an account || *a cuenta, a buena cuenta* on account; *dar cierta cantidad a cuenta* to give a certain amount on account; *cien pesetas a cuenta de las mil que usted me debe* a hundred pesetas on account of the thousand that you owe me || *¿a cuenta de qué?* why on earth?, why?, for what reason? || *a fin de cuentas* when all is said and done, all things considered, taking everything into account (finalmente) || *caer en la cuenta de que* to realize that || COM *cargar algo en cuenta a uno* to debit s.o.'s account with sth.; *valor que le hemos cargado en cuenta* and we have debited your account with this amount; to charge sth. to s.o.'s account (en un almacén, etc.) || *cerrar una cuenta* to close an account || *con cuenta y razón* carefully || *cuenta atrás* countdown || *cuenta corriente* current account [US checking account] || *cuenta de ahorros* savings account || *cuenta de crédito* credit *o* charge account || *cuenta de efectos impagados* bills payable account || FAM *cuenta de la vieja* counting on one's fingers || *cuenta pendiente* outstanding account || *cuenta redonda* round sum || FIG *cuentas galanas* or *del Gran Capitán* exorbitant and fictitious accounts || *dar buena cuenta de sí* to give a good account of o.s. || *dar cuenta de* to give an account of (dar a conocer), to give account of (explicar), to tell about, to inform of (comunicar), to polish off; *dar cuenta de una tortilla* to polish off an omelette || *dar en la cuenta* to realize || *darse cuenta de* to realize || *de cuenta* of importance, important || *dejar de cuenta* to ignore || *echar la cuenta* or *las cuentas* to reckon up | *en resumidas cuentas* in short, in a word || *entrar en cuenta* to come into it, to enter into account || *estar fuera de cuenta* to have reached one's time (una mujer) || *estar lejos de la cuenta* to be wide of the mark, to be very much mistaken || *esto corre de* or *por mi cuenta* I'm taking charge of this, I'm seeing to this (encargarse de), I'm bearing the cost of it (pagar), this one's on me (pagar una copa) || *habida cuenta de* taking into account || FIG *hacer las cuentas de la lechera* to count one's chickens before they are hatched || *hacerse cuenta de* to imagine, to think, to suppose || *hacer sus cuentas* to do one's accounts || FIG *las cuentas claras y el chocolate espeso* let's keep the books straight || *las cuentas son las cuentas* business is business || FIG *le voy a ajustar las cuentas* I've a bone to pick with him || *llevar las cuentas* to keep the accounts || *más de la cuenta* too much, too many || *me salen mal las cuentas* I've miscalculated (por calcular mal), my figures don't tally (por olvidar una cifra, etc.) || FIG *no querer cuentas con uno* to want nothing to do with s.o. | *no tener que dar cuentas a nadie* not to be answerable to anyone || *pasar las cuentas del rosario* to tell one's beads || *pedir cuentas a uno* to call s.o. to account (preguntar), to have it out with s.o. (reprender) || *perder la cuenta de* to lose count of || *por cuenta de* on behalf of (en nombre de), for (para) || *por cuenta y riesgo de uno* at one's own risk || *por la cuenta que le trae* in his own interest; *ya se preocupará de llegar a tiempo, por la cuenta que le trae* he'll make sure he gets here on time in his own interest || *por mi cuenta* for my part, as for me || *por su propia cuenta* for o.s. (para sí), by o.s. (solo) || *saldar una cuenta* to pay s.o. back, to get even with s.o. || *salirle a cuenta a uno* to be worth one's while || *si echamos la cuenta* all things considered, taking everything into account || *tener cuenta* to be advantageous *o* profitable (provechoso), to be worthwhile (conveniente) || *tener en cuenta* to bear in mind, to consider, to take into account *o* consideration; *tengamos en cuenta sus proposiciones* let us take his proposals into consideration; *tenga usted en cuenta que...* bear in mind that... || COM *tomar cuentas* to audit the accounts || *tomar en cuenta* to take into account, to bear in mind (tomar en consideración), to mind; *no tomes en cuenta que no venga a visitarte* don't mind if I don't come and visit you || *trabajar por cuenta de alguien* to work for s.o. || *trabajar por su cuenta* or *por cuenta propia* to work for o.s., to be self-employed, to be one's own boss || *traer cuenta a uno* to be to one's advantage, to be profitable (provechoso), to be worth one's while (conveniente) || *vamos a cuentas* let's settle the matter, let's get things straight, let's clear this up || *vivir a cuenta de* to live at the expense of || *ya caigo en la cuenta* now I get it, the penny has dropped.

cuentagotas *m inv* dropper || FIG *dar una cosa con cuentagotas* to give sth. little by little.

cuentahílos *m inv* counting glass, thread counter.

cuentakilómetros *m inv* AUT mileage recorder, milometer (para contar la distancia recorrida) | speedometer (velocímetro).

cuentarrevoluciones; cuentavueltas *m inv* revolution counter, rev. counter.

cuentista *adj* story-writing (autor de cuentos) || FIG & FAM gossipy (chismoso) | storytelling, fibbing (mentiroso) | exaggerating (exagerado).
◆ *m/f* storywriter (autor de cuentos) || FIG & FAM gossip (chismoso) | fibber, storyteller (mentiroso) | exaggerator (exagerado).

cuento *m* story, tale (relato); *contar un cuento de hadas* to tell a fairy tale || tip (de bastón, etc.) || FAM gossip, tittle-tattle (chisme) | fib, story (mentira); *no me vengas con cuentos* don't come to me with fibs | tall story, yarn (cosa increíble) | trouble (disgusto) | fuss (exageración) || — *a cuento de* with regard to, concerning || *¿a cuento de qué?* why? || *¡aplíquese el cuento!* you might take a lesson from it yourself || *cuento chino* or *tártaro* cock-and-bull story || *cuento de viejas* old wives' tale || *dejarse de cuentos* to come to the point || *¡déjate de cuentos!* stop beating about the bush, get to the point (no andar con rodeos), stop telling fibs!, don't tell tales! (un niño), get away with you!, come off it! (no mentir) || *es cuento largo* it's a long story || *es el cuento de nunca acabar* there's no end to it, it goes on and on || *eso es el cuento de la lechera* don't count your chickens before they're hatched || FIG *estar en el cuento* to be in the picture, to be well-informed || *esto parece cuento* it's unbelievable || *ir con el cuento a alguien* to go and tell s.o. || *nada de cuentos* no fuss (a un niño), don't come that with me (a una persona mayor) || *no venir a cuento* to be irrelevant, to have nothing to do with it (no ser pertinente) || *¡puro cuento!* a likely story! all lies! || *sin cuento* numberless, countless, innumerable || *tener mucho cuento* to be always having people on (engañar), to put on airs, to give o.s. airs (presumir), to make a lot of fuss, to exaggerate (exagerar) || *traer a cuento* to bring up (mencionar) || *¡váyase con el cuento a otra parte!* tell that to the marines! || *venir a cuento* to be opportune (ser oportuno), to be relevant (ser pertinente).

cuera *f* AMER legging (polaina) | smack, spank (azotaina) | leather jacket (chaqueta).

cuerazo *m* AMER lash (latigazo).

cuerda *f* rope; *cuerda de cáñamo* hemp rope || cord (de tamaño medio) || string (bramante) || measuring tape (en topografía) || ANAT chord; *cuerdas vocales* vocal chords || chain (del reloj antiguo) || spring (muelle) || chain gang (presos) || fuse (mecha) || DEP rails *pl* (de la pista de un hipódromo) | inside (de la pista de un estadio) || MAT chord || MÚS voice (voz) | range (extensión de la voz) | string (de la guitarra, del violín) || — FIG *acabársele a uno la cuerda* to be at the end of one's tether | *aflojar la cuerda* to ease up | *andar* or *bailar en la cuerda floja* to walk the tightrope | *apretar la cuerda* to clamp down, to tighten up || *cuerda de plomada* plumbline || *cuerda de tripas* catgut || *cuerda floja* tightrope || FIG *dar cuerda a algo* to prolong sth. | *dar cuerda a uno* to encourage s.o. [to speak], to start s.o. off [speaking] || *dar cuerda a un reloj* to wind (up) a clock || *estar con la cuerda al cuello* to have one's neck in a noose | *no ser de la misma cuerda* not to be of the same opinion (tener opiniones distintas) | *obrar bajo cuerda* to act in an underhand way | *parece que a éste le han dado cuerda* he's away, he's off, he's started | *siempre se rompe la cuerda por lo más delgado* the weakest goes to the wall | *tener cuerda para rato* to have still a long way to go | *tirar de la cuerda* to go too far (abusar) | *tocar la cuerda sensible* to touch s.o.'s soft spot.
◆ *pl* DEP ropes (del ring) || MÚS strings (instrumentos) | voices (voces).

cuerdamente *adv* prudently, wisely, sensibly.

cuerdo, da *adj* sane (sano de juicio) || wise, prudent, sensible (sensato).
◆ *m/f* sane *o* rational person (sano de juicio) || wise *o* prudent *o* sensible person (sensato) || *de cuerdo y loco todos tenemos un poco* every man has a fool up his sleeve.

cuereada *f* AMER beating, thrashing (paliza).

cuerear *vt* AMER to skin, to flay (desollar) || to prepare [hides] | to beat, to thrash (golpear) | to denigrate, to vilify (hablar mal de uno).

cueriza *f* AMER FAM beating, thrashing (paliza).

cuerna *f* horns *pl* (cornamenta) || antlers *pl* (del ciervo) || horn (recipiente) || hunting horn (trompa).

cuerno *m* horn (asta) || antler (del ciervo) || horn (materia); *peine de cuerno* horn comb || horn (del caracol) || feeler, antenna (de los insectos) || cusp (de la Luna) || ANAT cornu (de médula) || MÚS horn || — FIG *coger el toro por los cuernos* to take the bull by the horns || *cuerno de caza* hunting horn || *cuerno de la abundancia* horn of plenty, cornucopia || FIG & FAM *estar en los cuernos del toro* to be in the lion's mouth, to have the tiger by the tail | *irse al cuerno* to fall through (un proyecto) | *levantar* or *poner en los cuernos de la Luna* to praise to the skies | *mandar a uno al cuerno* to send s.o. packing, to send s.o. about his business | *no valer un cuerno* not to be worth a farthing | *poner a uno en los cuernos del toro* to put s.o. in a dangerous situation | *poner los cuernos a* to be unfaithful to, to cuckold (hacer cornudo) | *saber a cuerno quemado* to be distasteful, to make a disagreeable impression (desagradable), to be suspicious (sospechoso) | *¡váyase al cuerno!* go to the devil!, go to blazes!
◆ *interj* *¡cuerno!* golly!, gosh!, blimey! (con asombro, admiración), darn it!, dash it! (con enfado).

cuero *m* hide, skin (piel) || leather; *zapatos de cuero* leather shoes || wineskin (odre) || washer (del grifo) || AMER whip (látigo) || — AMER FAM *arrimar el cuero* or *dar* or *echar cuero a uno* to give s.o. a hiding *o* a beating || *cuero adobado* tanned skin || *cuero cabelludo* scalp || FAM *en cueros* naked, in one's birthday suit | *en cueros vivos* stark naked, starkers | *estar hecho un cuero* to be canned *o* sozzled | *quedarse en cueros* to be cleaned out (quedarse sin nada).

cuerpear *vi* AMER to dodge.

cuerpo *m* body; *el cuerpo humano* the human body || body, figure; *tiene un cuerpo fabuloso* she's got a fabulous figure || body (de un tejido, de un vino, de una salsa) || bodice, body (de un vestido) || body (cadáver) || section, part, piece; *armario de dos cuerpos* two-piece wardrobe, wardrobe in two sections *o* parts || stage; *nave espacial de un solo cuerpo* single-stage spaceship || volume (libro); *biblioteca de mil cuerpos* library with a thousand volumes || corps; *cuerpo diplomático* diplomatic corps; *cuerpo de sanidad* medical corps || body; *cuerpo legislativo* legislative body || body, staff (personal); *cuerpo docente* teaching body || ANAT corpus, body; *cuerpo amarillo* corpus luteum, yellow body || ASTR body; *cuerpo celeste* heavenly body || DEP length; *ganar por medio cuerpo* to win by half a length || ARQ main part *o* body [of a building] || JUR corpus, body (compilación) || IMPR body, size (de una letra) || MIL body, corps || QUÍM, FÍS & MAT body || FIG main part (parte principal) || — *a cuerpo, a cuerpo gentil* without a coat, not wearing a coat || *a cuerpo descubierto* exposed, unprotected (sin protección), defenceless, unarmed (sin armas), without *o* not wearing a coat *o* cloak || *a cuerpo limpio* defenceless, unarmed (sin armas) || *a medio cuerpo* up to the waist || *bañador de cuerpo entero* one-piece bathing costume || *bañador de medio cuerpo* bathing trunks *pl* || *cuerpo a cuerpo* hand-to-hand; *combate cuerpo a cuerpo* hand-to-hand combat, hand-to-hand fight; *un cuerpo a cuerpo encarnizado* a fierce hand-to-hand fight || *cuerpo a tierra* on one's stomach, flat on one's face || QUÍM *cuerpo compuesto* compound || TEATR *cuerpo de baile* corps de ballet || *cuerpo de bomberos* fire brigade || *cuerpo de casa* housework (limpieza), maid (criada) || *cuerpo de guardia* guard (soldados), guardhouse (edificio) || JUR *cuerpo del delito* corpus delicti || *cuerpo electoral* constituent body || MIL *cuerpo expedicionario* expeditionary force, task force || *cuerpo facultativo* medical profession, doctors *pl* || *cuerpo legislativo* legislative body || MAR *cuerpo muerto* mooring buoy || QUÍM *cuerpo simple* element || *dar con el cuerpo en tierra* to fall down || *dar cuerpo* to give body, to thicken (a un líquido) || *de cuerpo entero* full-length (retrato), real, true (auténtico) || *de cuerpo presente* in person (en persona), laid out (un cadáver), lying in state (un personaje importante) || *de medio cuerpo* half-length; *retrato de medio cuerpo* half-length portrait; up to the waist, up to one's waist; *entrar en el agua de medio cuerpo* to go into the water up to one's waist || FIG & FAM *en cuerpo y alma* heart and soul, totally | *estar a cuerpo de rey* to live like a king || *formar cuerpo con* to form one *o* a whole with || FAM *hacer de* or *del cuerpo* to empty the bowels || *hurtar el cuerpo* to dodge, to swerve (fintar) || FAM *me pide el cuerpo hacerlo* I'm dying to *o* longing to do it | *mi cuerpo serrano* yours truly | *no quedarse con nada en el cuerpo* to confess everything, to get it off one's chest || *no tener nada en el cuerpo* to have an empty stomach || FIG *pertenecer a alguien en cuerpo y alma* to belong to s.o. body and soul || FAM *sacarle a uno algo del cuerpo* to get sth. out of s.o., to make s.o. tell sth. | *saltar a cuerpo limpio* to clear, to jump over | *tener buen cuerpo* to have a good figure (una mujer) | *¡tengo un miedo en el cuerpo!* I'm scared stiff! | *tomar* or *cobrar cuerpo* to take shape (un proyecto), to thicken (una salsa) || FIG *tratar a uno a cuerpo de rey* to treat s.o. like a king.

cuervo *m* ZOOL crow | raven || — FIG *cría cuervos y te sacarán los ojos* a dog bites the hand that feeds it | *criar cuervos* to nourish a viper in one's bosom || — ZOOL *cuervo marino* cormorant (mergo) | *cuervo merendero* rook.

cuesco *m* stone (hueso de fruta) || POP fart (pedo).

cuesta *f* slope, hill (pendiente) || GEOGR cuesta, escarpment || — *a cuestas* on one's back; *llevar un bulto a cuestas* to carry a bundle on one's back; on one's shoulders (una responsabilidad) || *a la mitad de la cuesta* halfway up (the hill) || FIG *cuesta de enero* money problems, due to Christmas spending || *en cuesta* on a slope, sloping || FIG *este trabajo se me ha hecho cuesta arriba* I've found this work hard going || *ir cuesta abajo* to go downhill (bajar), to go downhill, to decline (decaer) || *ir cuesta arriba* to go uphill || FIG *tener a uno a cuestas* to have s.o. in one's charge *o* care.
— OBSERV The Spanish word *cuesta* is recognized in international geographical language as denoting an *escarpment*.

cuestación *f* collection.

cuestión *f* subject, topic, question (tema); *una cuestión interesante* an interesting topic; *poner una cuestión sobre el tapete* to bring up a subject [for discussion] || matter, question; *es cuestión de vida o muerte* it's a matter of life and death; *es cuestión de un cuarto de hora* it's a question of a quarter of an hour || dispute, quarrel (riña) || fuss, trouble, bother (dificultad, lío); *no quiero cuestiones con nadie* I want no fuss from *o* trouble with anyone || JUR question (tormento) || — *cuestión batallona* vexed *o* much-debated question, moot point || *cuestión candente* burning question || *cuestión previa* previous question || *en cuestión* in question (de que se trata), at issue; *la controversia en cuestión* the controversy at issue || *en cuestión de* as regards, in the matter of (en materia de), in a matter of; *en cuestión de quince días* in a matter of a fortnight || *eso es cuestión mía* that's my affair *o* business || *eso es otra cuestión* that's a different kettle of fish, that's another matter || *la cuestión es que...* the thing is that... || *la cuestión está en saber si...* the question is whether...

cuestionable *adj* debatable, questionable (discutible).

cuestionar *vt* (p us) to debate, to question, to discuss (discutir).
◆ *vi* to argue.

cuestionario *m* questionnaire (en una encuesta) || question paper, questions *pl* (en un examen).

cuestor *m* quaestor (magistrado) || collector (el que pide para una cuestación).

cuestura *f* quaestorship (oficio del cuestor).

cueto *m* fortified peak || high crag, rocky peak.

cueva *f* cave; *las cuevas de Altamira* the caves of Altamira || cellar (subterráneo, cabaret) || *cueva de ladrones* den of thieves.

cuévano *m* pannier (cesto grande).

cueza *f*; **cuezo** *m* trough (de albañil).

cúfico, ca *adj* kufic, cufic (escritura).

cuí *m* AMER guinea pig (conejillo de Indias).

cuica *f* AMER earthworm (lombriz).

cuicacoche *f* AMER kind of thrush.

cuico *m* AMER foreigner (extranjero) || AMER FAM copper, cop (agente de policía).

cuidado *m* care, caution (atención) || care, charge (dependencia) || affair, concern; *eso es cuidado tuyo* that's your affair; *correr al cuidado de uno* to be s.o.'s concern || care, worry (preocupación); *vivir libre de cuidados* to live free from worries || *al cuidado de* in *o* under the care of, in the charge *o* hands of (cargo) || *al cuidado del Sr. Pérez* care of Mr. Pérez (en cartas) || *andar* or *ir con cuidado* to be careful, to go carefully, to watch one's step || *bajo el cuidado de* in *o* under the care of || *¡cuidado!* look out!, watch out!, be careful!, careful! || *cuidado con* mind (atención); *¡cuidado con el coche!* mind the car!; *¡cuidado con la pintura* mind the paint!; beware of; *¡cuidado con el perro!* beware of the dog!; what (para censurar); *¡cuidado con el niño!* what a brat! || *¡cuidado con Juan, qué pesado es!* how tiresome that John is! || *de cuidado* seriously, gravely; *está enfermo de cuidado* he is seriously ill; shocking; *un catarro de cuidado* a shocking cold || *dejar a uno el cuidado de hacer algo* to leave it to s.o. to do sth. || *estar al cuidado de* to be in *o* under the care of (persona), to be in the charge *o* hands of (cargo) || *hombre de cuidado* dangerous man, man to be wary of || FAM *me tiene* or *me trae sin cuidado* I don't care, I don't give a damm, I couldn't care less || *no hay cuidado, pierda cuidado* don't worry || *poner cuidado en* to take care in, to be careful in || *poner fuera de cuidado a un enfermo* to pull a patient through || *salir de cuidado* to be delivered of a child (en un parto), to pull through (en una enfermedad) || *ser de cuidado* to be dangerous (peligroso), to be unreliable *o* untrustworthy (poco seguro), to be serious; *esta herida es de cuidado* this wound is serious || *sin cuidado* carelessly, without care || *¡ten cuidado!* be careful! || *tener cuidado con* to be careful of.
◆ *pl* care *sing*, attention *sing* (del médico).

cuidador, ra *adj* careful, cautions.
◆ *m* trainer (en rugby, fútbol, etc.), second (en boxeo).
◆ *f* AMER nurse (enfermera) | nursemaid, nanny (niñera).

cuidadosamente *adv* carefully, with care, pains-takingly (con aplicación) || cautiously, carefully, prudently, warily (con precaución).

cuidadoso, sa *adj* careful (aplicado) || concerned, anxious (atento); *cuidadoso del resultado* anxious about the outcome || cautious, wary, prudent (prudente) || particular, attentive; *cuidadoso de los detalles* particular about details, attentive to detail.

cuidar *vt* to look after, to care for, to nurse (asistir); *cuidar a un enfermo* to look after a sick person || to look after, to take care of; *en esta pensión me cuidan mucho* in this boardinghouse I am well looked after *o* well taken care of; *cuidar la casa* to look after the house; *cuidar su ropa* to take care of one's clothes || MED to attend | to nurse (una herida) || FIG to pay attention to; *cuidar los detalles* to pay attention to details.
◆ *vi* *cuidar de* to look after, to take care of; *cuidar de su salud, de los niños* to take care of one's health, to look after the children; to fuss over, to wait on (s.o.) hand and foot (asistir solícitamente) || *cuidar de que* to take care that, to see that || *cuidar de sus obligaciones* to fulfil one's obligations.
◆ *vpr* to take care of o.s., to look after o.s. (la salud) || — *cuidarse bien de hacer algo* to take good care not to do sth. || *cuidarse de* to take care of, to look after (la salud, etc.), to bother about, to worry about; *no se cuida del qué dirán* he does not worry about what people will say; to mind, to watch, to be careful of; *cuídate de lo que dices* mind what you say; to take care of, to look after (ocuparse de) || *cuidarse mucho* to take great care of s.o., to mollycoddle o.s. (*fam*) || *dejar de cuidarse* to let o.s. go.

cuido *m* care, minding.

cuija *f* AMER small lizard (lagartija) | FIG skinny woman (mujer flaca).

cuita *f* worry, trouble (preocupación) || sorrow, grief (pena) || AMER bird dropping, birdlime || *las cuitas del joven Werther* the sorrows of Werther (de Goethe).

cuitado, da *adj* worried, troubled (preocupado) || bashful, shy, timid (apocado).

cuja *f* (p us) bedstead (armazón de la cama) || lance *o* standard bucket (para la lanza *o* la bandera) || AMER bed (cama).

culada *f* fall on one's backside.

culantrillo *m* BOT maidenhair.

culantro *m* BOT coriander.

culata *f* cylinder head, head (de motor) || breech (del cañón) || butt (de escopeta) || FIG rear, back (parte posterior) || croup [of horse] (anca) || MIN collet (de la talla de un diamante).

culatazo *m*; **culatada** *f* blow with the butt [of a gun] (golpe) || kick, recoil (retroceso de un arma).

culazo *m* fall on one's backside.

culear *vi* FAM to wiggle.

culebra *f* ZOOL snake || worm (del alambique) || FIG & FAM disturbance, din (alboroto) || — ZOOL *culebra de cascabel* rattlesnake || FIG & FAM *saber más que las culebras* to be as sly *o* as cunning as a fox.

culebrear *vi* to slither (en el suelo) || to snake, to meander, to wind, to zigzag (un río, un camino) || to zigzag, to stagger (una persona).

culebreo *m* slither (de la serpiente) || winding, twisting, zigzag (de un río, de un camino) || zigzagging (una persona).

culebrilla *f* MED tetter (herpes) || young of a snake (cría de culebra) || BOT green dragon || crack (en un cañón) || *papel de culebrilla* tissue paper.

culebrina *f* culverin (cañón) || lightning (relámpago).

culera *f* stain left on a baby's nappy (mancha) || seat (de pantalón), patch (remiendo).

culero, ra *adj* lazy, sluggish, slothful.
◆ *m* baby's nappy [US diaper].

culi *m* coolie.

culibajo, ja *adj* FAM dumpy.

culiblanco *m* ZOOL wheatear.

culinario, ria *adj* culinary (de cocina).

culmen *m* summit, peak (cumbre).

culminación *f* ASTR culmination || FIG culmination, crowning *o* culminating point.

culminante *adj* culminating.

culminar *vi* to culminate || ASTR to culminate || FIG *su carrera culminó en la presidencia* his career culminated in his becoming president.

culo *m* FAM backside, bottom, arse (*pop*) [US ass] (asentaderas); *caer de culo* to fall on one's backside || FIG bottom (de algunos objetos); *el culo de una botella* the bottom of a bottle | end (extremo) || — IMPR *culo de lámpara* tailpiece, cul-de-lampe || FAM *culo* or *culillo de mal asiento* fidget, fidget breeches, fidgety *o* restless person || FIG & FAM *culo de pollo* pucker, ill-mended part in stockings or clothes || *culo de vaso* bottom of a glass (de una copa), imitation precious stone (piedra falsa) || FAM *dejar a alguien con el culo al aire* to leave s.o. in a mess | *ir de culo* to go downhill | *poner los labios de culo* or *de culito de pollo* to purse the lips | *vamos de culo* things are going very badly for us.

culombio *m* ELECTR coulomb.

culón, ona *adj* FAM broad-bottomed, big-bottomed, broad in the beam (persona).
◆ *m* (ant) disabled soldier (soldado).

culote *m* base (casquillo).

culpa *f* fault; *es culpa suya* it's his fault; *¿de quién es la culpa?* whose fault is it? || blame; *echar la culpa de algo a uno* to throw *o* to put the blame for sth. on s.o. || — *echar la culpa de* to blame for, to throw *o* to put the blame (on s.o.) for; *me ha echado la culpa de su fracaso* he has blamed me for his failure || *es culpa mía* I'm to blame, it's my fault || *la culpa es de David* it is David's fault, David is to blame, the fault lies with David || *no tengo la culpa* it's not my fault, I'm not to blame || *por culpa de* because of through; *por culpa de lo que dijiste* because of what you said || *por culpa tuya* because of *o* through you, thanks to you, through fault of yours || *tener la culpa de* to be to blame for, to be guilty of.
◆ *pl* sins; *pagar las culpas ajenas* to pay for s.o. else's sins.

culpabilidad *f* culpability || JUR guilt || — JUR *declaración de no culpabilidad* declaration of innocence | *solicitar la declaración de culpabilidad* to plead guilty.

culpable *adj* guilty, culpable, to blame, at fault || JUR guilty || — *declarar culpable* to find guilty || *declararse culpable* to plead guilty.
◆ *m/f* JUR culprit, guilty party, offender || culprit (persona responsable) || *él es el culpable de todo* he is to blame for everything.

culpado, da *adj* guilty || accused (acusado).
◆ *m/f* accused, culprit, guilty party, offender.

culpar *vt* to accuse (de un delito, etc.) || to accuse; *yo no culpo a nadie* I accuse no one || to

blame; *le culpo de nuestra derrota* I blame him for our defeat; *culpar al padre de los daños causados por su hijo* to blame the father for the damage caused by his son.
◆ *vpr* to blame o.s., to accuse o.s.

cultalatiniparla *f* FAM euphuistic language, preciosity | bluestocking (mujer pedante).

cultamente *adj* elegantly, in a refined manner (de modo culto) || FIG in an affected manner (con afectación).

culteranismo *m* Gongorism || affected style (afectación).

culterano, na *adj* euphuistic, euphuistical, affected.
◆ *m/f* euphuist, affected person.

cultiparlista *adj* euphuistic, euphuistical, affected (culterano).
◆ *m/f* euphuist, affected person.

cultismo *m* Gongorism (culteranismo) || learned word (palabra culta).

cultivable *adj* cultivable, cultivatable, arable.

cultivado, da *adj* cultured.

cultivador, ra *adj* farming.
◆ *m/f* farmer (agricultor) || cultivador, grower (de plantas).
◆ *f* cultivator (máquina).

cultivar *vt* AGR to cultivate, to farm, to till (la tierra) | to cultivate, to grow, to farm (las plantas) || FIG to cultivate (las bellas artes, la amistad, etc.) | to train, to develop (la memoria).

cultivo *m* AGR cultivation, farming; *cultivo extensivo, intensivo* extensive, intensive cultivation | growing, cultivation, farming (de plantas) | crop; *rotación de cultivos* rotation of crops || FIG cultivation; *el cultivo de las ciencias* the cultivation of the sciences || BIOL culture; *cultivo de tejidos* tissue culture || — *caldo de cultivo* culture fluid, culture medium || *cultivo de hortalizas* market gardening || *cultivo de regadío* irrigation farming || *cultivo de secano* dry farming || *cultivo en bancales* or *de terrazas* terrace cultivation || *cultivo frutícola* fruit growing || *cultivo migratorio* shifting cultivation || *poner en cultivo* to cultivate.

culto, ta *adj* AGR cultivated || FIG cultured, cultivated, educated (instruido) | learned; *palabra culta* learned word | euphuistic, affected (afectado).
◆ *m* REL worship (veneración); *culto a los santos* worship of the saints; *libertad de cultos* freedom of worship | cult (ritos) || cult (estimación extraordinaria) || — *culto a la personalidad* personality cult || *culto de hiperdulía* hyperdulia || *culto de latría* latria || *culto de los antepasados* ancestor worship || *rendir culto a* to worship (un santo, una persona), to pay homage *o* tribute to; *rendir culto a la valentía de una persona* to pay homage to a person's courage.

cultura *f* culture; *hombre de gran cultura* man of great culture; *cultura clásica, física* classical, physical culture.

cultural *adj* cultural.

culturismo *m* DEP body-building.

cumbarí *m* AMER chili (ají).

cumbre *f* summit, top (cima) || FIG height, zenith, pinnacle; *la cumbre de la gloria* the pinnacle of glory || *conferencia en la cumbre* summit conference.

cumbrera *f* ARQ ridge (de un tejado) | lintel (dintel) || AMER summit, top (cumbre).

cúmel *m* kummel (bebida).

cumpa *m* AMER FAM chum, pal.

cúmplase *m* official approval [enforcing a decree or nomination].

cumpleaños *m inv* birthday; *feliz cumpleaños* happy birthday.

cumplidamente *adv* duly (como es debido) || sufficiently, amply (ampliamente) || completely (completamente).

cumplido, da *adj* fulfilled; *una profecía cumplida* a fulfilled prophecy || full, complete; *pago cumplido* full payment || perfect (perfecto); *un cumplido caballero* a perfect gentleman; *un modelo cumplido de virtudes* a perfect model of virtue || accomplished; *un cumplido jinete* an accomplished horseman || complete, utter; *un cumplido bribón* an utter scoundrel || ample, large, big; *un abrigo demasiado cumplido* too large an overcoat || polite, courteous (bien educado); *persona muy cumplida* very polite person || — *soldado cumplido* soldier who has completed his service || *tener veinte años cumplidos* to have turned twenty, to be all of twenty.
◆ *m* compliment (alabanza); *basta de cumplidos* enough of your compliments || — *de cumplido* courtesy; *visita de cumplido* courtesy visit || *devolverle el cumplido a uno* to return s.o.'s compliment || *es una señora de mucho cumplido* she is a stickler for ceremony || *ir a algún sitio por cumplido* to go somewhere out of a sense of duty || *por cumplido* out of courtesy, out of pure politeness.
◆ *pl* politeness *sing*, courtesy *sing*, attentions; *deshacerse en cumplidos* to be profuse in (one's) attentions || — *andarse con* or *hacer cumplidos* to stand on ceremony || *sin cumplidos* informal; *cena sin cumplidos* informal dinner; informally; *recibir a alguien sin cumplidos* to receive s.o. informally.

cumplidor, ra *adj* dependable, reliable, trustworthy (de fiar); *un muchacho cumplidor* a dependable boy || who fulfils; *persona cumplidora de sus obligaciones* person who fulfils his obligations || *hombre cumplidor de sus promesas* man of his word.
◆ *m/f* reliable *o* dependable person.

cumplimentar *vt* to congratulate, to compliment (felicitar) || to pay a courtesy call to, to go and pay one's respects to (ir a saludar) || to execute, to carry out (órdenes) || *el ministro fue cumplimentado por el gobernador* the minister was paid a complimentary visit by the governor.

cumplimiento *m* execution, carrying out; *cumplimiento de una orden* execution of an order || enforcement, application; *el cumplimiento de un decreto* the application of a decree || observance (acatamiento); *cumplimiento de los requisitos legales* observance of statutory provisions || fulfilment [US fulfillment], honouring; *cumplimiento de los compromisos* fulfilment of one's commitments || fulfilment [US fulfillment] (de los deseos) || courtesy, politeness (cortesía) || ceremony (ceremonia) || FIG completion (de una obra) | expiry (vencimiento) || complement (complemento) || — *cumplimiento pascual* Easter duty || *dar cumplimiento a los nuevos estatutos* to put the new statutes into operation, to enforce the new statutes || *en cumplimiento de* in accordance with, in pursuance of, in compliance with || *por cumplimiento* out of courtesy, out of politeness.

cumplir *vt* to do (hacer); *cumplir su deber* to do one's duty; *cumplir el servicio militar* to do one's military service || to execute, to carry out (ejecutar); *cumplir una orden* to carry out an order || to keep, to carry out; *cumplir una promesa* to keep a promise || to fulfil, to fulfill; *cumplir un deseo* to fulfil a desire || to honour, to fulfil; *cumplir sus compromisos* to honour one's obligations || to turn; *ha cumplido veinte años* he has turned twenty || to be, to reach the age of; *hoy cumple cinco años* today he is five (years old), today he has reached the age of five; *cuando cumplas 21 años* when you are 21 || to observe, to abide by (una ley) || to comply with (lo estipulado) || — *cumplir condena* to serve one's time [in prison] || *hoy cumple años Pedro* it's Peter's birthday today.
◆ *vi* to keep *o* to fulfil one's word *o* one's promise || to do *o* to carry out *o* to perform one's duty (su deber), to honour *o* to fulfil one's obligations || to do, to carry out, to perform; *cumplir con su deber* to perform one's duty || to fulfil, to honour; *cumplir con sus obligaciones* to fulfil one's obligations || to observe, to abide by; *cumplir con los requisitos legales* to observe *o* to abide by the statutory provisions || to expire (un plazo) || to fall due (un pago); *el pagaré cumple mañana* the bill falls due tomorrow || MIL to finish one's military service (soldado) || — *cumple a Juan hacer esto* it is for John to do this, John should do this, John is supposed to do this, it behoves John to do this (ant) || *cumplir con la Iglesia* or *con Dios* or *con sus deberes religiosos* to fulfil one's religious obligations || *cumplir con los requisitos* to fulfil the requirements || *cumplir con su palabra* to keep one's word || *cumplir con todos* to fulfil one's duty to everyone, not to fail in one's duty to anyone || *para cumplir, por cumplir* as a mere formality.
◆ *vpr* to be fulfilled, to come true; *se cumplieron sus vaticinios* his prophecies were fulfilled || to expire (un plazo) || *este año se cumple el centenario de su nacimiento* this year is the centenary of his birth.

cúmquibus *m* FAM dough (dinero).

cumulativo, va *adj* cumulative.

cúmulo *m* accumulation, pile, heap (de cosas) || cumulus (nube) || FIG load, lot; *un cúmulo de disparates* a load of rubbish | concurrence, conjunction; *un cúmulo de circunstancias* a concurrence of circumstances.

cumulonimbo *m* cumulonimbus.

cumuloso, sa *adj* cumulous.

cuna *f* cradle (cama) || foundling hospital (inclusa) || FIG cradle; *Grecia, cuna de la civilización* Greece, the cradle of civilization | birth, origin, lineage (origen de una persona); *de ilustre cuna* of illustrious birth | birthplace (lugar de nacimiento) | early childhood (niñez) || cradle (del cañón) || space between the horns (de un toro) || rustic rope bridge (puente) || — *canción de cuna* lullaby, cradlesong || *casa cuna* foundling hospital || *criarse en buena cuna* to be born with a silver spoon in one's mouth || *cuna colgante* swing cot || *el juego de la cuna* cat's cradle.

cundir *vi* to spread, to become widespread; *cundió la noticia, el pánico* the news, the panic spread || to go a long way (rendir); *esa pierna de cordero cundió mucho* that leg of lamb went a very long way || to swell, to increase in volume; *el arroz cunde al cocer* rice swells when cooked || to progress (un trabajo) || to increase, to multiply (multiplicarse) || to spread; *las manchas de aceite cunden rápidamente* oil stains spread rapidly || — *cunde la voz que...* rumour has it that..., it is rumoured that... || *el tiempo no me cunde* time is too short, I haven't enough time || *le cunde el trabajo* he gets through a lot of work.

cunear *vt* to rock, to cradle (mecer).
◆ *vpr* to rock, to sway, to swing.

cuneco, ca *m/f* youngest son, daughter (hijo menor).

cuneiforme *adj* cuneiform; *escritura cuneiforme* cuneiform writing.

cuneo *m* rocking (mecedura).

cunero, ra *adj* foundling, abandoned (expósito) || unpedigreed (toro) || external *o* alien and patronized by the Government [deputy, candidate] || FAM of a little-known make *o*

brand (de una marca insignificante), bearing no trademark (sin marca); *una estilográfica cunera* a fountain pen bearing no trademark | second-class, second-rate (de poca categoría).
◆ *m/f* foundling (expósito).
◆ *m* unpedigreed bull (toro) | external *o* alien deputy *o* candidate patronized by the government.

cuneta *f* ditch (de una carretera) || hard shoulder (arcén) || gutter (de una calle) || cunette (fortificación).

cuña *f* wedge, chock (para detener una rueda) || wedge (para rajar la madera) || wedge heel, wedge [of shoe] (para un pie más corto que el otro) || wedge-shaped reinforcement for worn part of shoe (refuerzo) || IMPR quoin || FIG & FAM influence (apoyo) || ANAT cuneiform bone, tarsal bone || — *cuña de altas presiones* band of high pressure || MAT *cuña esférica* segment || *cuña publicitaria* (advertising) jingle || FIG *no hay peor cuña que la de la misma madera* a man's worst enemies are often those of his own house | *tener cuña* to have influential friends, to have friends at court.

cuñado, da *m/f* brother-in-law (hombre), sister-in-law (mujer).

cuño *m* die (para monedas) || stamp (huella que deja el cuño) || FIG mark, impression; *dejar el cuño de su personalidad* to leave the mark of one's personality || — FIG *de buen cuño* of the right stamp | *de nuevo cuño* new, modern.

cuota *f* quota, share (parte proporcional); *pagar su cuota* to pay one's share || fees *pl*, subscription; *ha subido la cuota del club* the club fees have gone up || contribution (contribución) || cost (gastos); *la cuota de instalación de teléfono* the cost of installing a telephone || AMER instalment, payment (de una compra a plazos) | tariff (tarifa) || — ECON *cuota de mercado* market share || AMER *venta por cuotas* hire-purchase [US installment plan].

cuotidiano, na *adj* (p us) daily.

cupé *m* coupé (coche).

cupido *m* FIG & FAM lady-killer, Casanova.

Cupido *npr m* Cupid.

cupla *f* AMER couple, pair (par).

cuplé *m* variety song, music-hall song (copla).

cupletista *m/f* variety singer, music-hall singer.

cupo *m* quota, share (cuota) || MIL contingent, quota (reclutas) || COM quota || AMER capacity, content (cabida).

cupón *m* coupon (de un título de renta) || ticket (de lotería) || reply coupon (para un concurso) || coupon, form; *cupón de pedido* order coupon || *cupón de cartilla de racionamiento* ration voucher, coupon.

cupresáceas *f pl* BOT cupressaceae.

cúprico, ca *adj* QUÍM cupric.

cuprífero, ra *adj* cupriferous.

cuprita *f* MIN cuprite.

cuproníquel *m* QUÍM cupronickel.

cuproso, sa *adj* QUÍM cuprous.

cúpula *f* ARQ cupola, dome (bóveda) || BOT cupule || MAR & MIL turret, cupola (blindaje).

cupulíferas *f pl* BOT cupuliferae.

cupulino *m* ARQ lantern (de una cúpula).

cuquillo *m* cuckoo (cuclillo).

cura *m* parish priest (sacerdote) || FAM [Roman Catholic] priest (sacerdote católico) | spray (de saliva) || AMER avocado, alligator pear (aguacate) || — *casa del cura* presbytery || *cura párroco* parish priest || FAM *este cura* yours truly (yo).

cura *f* care; *curas médicas* medical care || treatment (tratamiento) || cure; *hacer una cura de aguas* to undergo a water cure || dressing [of a wound] (apósito) || — *cura de almas* care of souls || *cura obrero* worker-priest || FAM *no tener cura* to be incorrigible || *ponerse en cura* to undergo treatment || *primera cura* first aid || *tener cura* to be curable.

curabilidad *f* curability.

curable *adj* MED curable.

curaca *f* AMER Indian chief, chief, headman (cacique).

curación *f* MED cure (cura) | recovery (restablecimiento) | healing (de una herida) | treatment (tratamiento) | dressing (apósito) || *curación milagrosa* miracle healing.

curado, da *adj* FIG hardened, inured, accustomed to hardship (persona) || cured; *jamón curado* cured ham || tanned (pieles) || AMER drunk, intoxicated (ebrio) || FIG *estoy curado de espanto* nothing can shock me any more, I've known worse.

curador, ra *adj* JUR guardian, tutor (tutor).
◆ *m/f* guardian, tutor (tutor).
◆ *m* quack healer, charlatan (curandero) || caretaker, curator (administrador).

curaduría *f* JUR guardianship, tutorage, tutorship (cargo de tutor).

curalotodo *m* cure-all.

curandería *f*; **curanderismo** *m* quackery, charlatanry, charlatanism.

curandero, ra *m/f* quack, quack doctor, charlatan (de enfermedades).

curar *vi* MED to heal (up) (una herida) | to get well, to recover (una persona) || FIG to be cured (de un mal moral).
◆ *vt* MED to cure (sanar) | to get rid of, to cure; *pastillas que curan la gripe* tablets which cure flu | to treat; *curar a un enfermo con antibióticos* to treat a patient with antibiotics | to dress; *curar una herida* to dress a wound || to cure (carne, pescado) || to tan (pieles) || to season (pipa) || to bleach (hilos, lienzos) || FIG to remedy || AMER *curar un mate* to season a maté.
◆ *vpr* to be treated; *esta enfermedad se cura con penicilina* this disease is treated with penicillin || to get well *o* better, to recover [one's health]; *si quieres curarte tienes que guardar cama* if you want to get well you must stay in bed; *se está curando* he's getting better || to heal up (una herida) || AMER FAM to get sozzled (emborracharse) || — *curarse de...* to take care of... || FIG *curarse en salud* to take precautions (precaverse).

curare *m* curare, curari (veneno).

curasao *m* curacao (licor).

curativo, va *adj* curative.

curato *m* office of a parish priest, priesthood (cargo) || parish (parroquia).

Curazao *n pr* GEOGR Curaçao (isla).

curco, ca; curcuncho, cha *adj* AMER hunchbacked, humpbacked.
◆ *m/f* hunchback, humpback.
◆ *f* hunch, hump (joroba).

curcusilla *f* rump (rabadilla de un ave).

curda *f* FAM drunkenness, intoxication (borrachera) || FAM *coger una curda* to get sozzled.
◆ *adj* FAM sozzled, sloshed, canned; *estoy curda* I'm sozzled.

curdo, da *adj* Kurdish (del Curdistán).
◆ *m/f* Kurd.

cureña *f* gun carriage (del cañón) || gunstock, stock (del mortero).

cureta *f* MED curette.

curia *f* HIST curia (de los romanos) || curia (de la Iglesia) || legal profession, bar (abogados, procuradores, funcionarios) || JUR Court of Litigation || — *Curia Romana* Curia Romana || *gente de curia* legal profession.

curial *adj* curial (de la curia).
◆ *m* HIST officer of the Curia Romana || court clerk (subalterno).

curialesco, ca *adj* legalistic.

curiana *f* cockroach, blackbeetle (*fam*) (cucaracha).

curie *f* FÍS curie (unidad de radioactividad).

curieterapia *f* MED curietherapy, radiotherapy.

curio *m* QUÍM curium (elemento).

curiosamente *adv* curiously (con curiosidad) || neatly, cleanly, tidily (con limpieza) || carefully, painstakingly (cuidadosamente).

curiosear *vi* FAM to poke one's nose into *o* to pry into other people's affairs (entremeterse) || to pry, to nose about *o* around, to ferret about; *está curioseando por toda la casa* he's prying all around the house || to browse; *curiosear por una librería* to browse around *o* through a bookshop.
◆ *vt* to poke one's nose into, to pry into, to nose into (fisgonear) || *los chicos curioseaban los cuartos de la casa* the children were ferreting *o* nosing about in the rooms of the house.

curiosidad *f* curiosity (deseo de conocer) || cleanliness, tidiness, neatness (limpieza) || inquisitiveness (indiscreción) || care, carefulness (cuidado, esmero) || curio, curiosity (cosa curiosa); *es aficionado a curiosidades* he is interested in curios || — *mirar con curiosidad* to look at curiously || *tener curiosidad por saber* to be curious to know.

curioso, sa *adj* curious (que tiene curiosidad); *ser curioso por naturaleza* to be curious by nature, to be naturally curious; *curioso por conocer la verdad* curious to know the truth || inquisitive (indiscreto) || clean, tidy, neat (limpio) || careful (cuidadoso) || curious, odd, peculiar, unusual, strange (raro) || *curioso de noticias* eager for news.
◆ *m/f* onlooker, spectator (mirón) || busybody, nosy person (persona indiscreta).

curista *m/f* person taking water cures (agüista).

curita *f* AMER sticking plaster (tirita).

curling *m* DEP curling.

currar; currelar *vi* FAM to toil, to slog away (trabajar).

curre *m* FAM job.

currículo *m* curriculum.

curriculum vitae *m* curriculum vitae (historial).

curruca *f* ZOOL whitethroat.

curruscante *adj* crunchy, crispy, crisp; *pan curruscante* crispy bread.

curruscar *vi* to crunch.

currutaco, ca *adj* dandyish, foppish [US dudish] (hombre) || over-fashionable (mujer).
◆ *m* dandy, fop [US dude] (petimetre) || nobody (hombre insignificante).
◆ *f* over-fashionable woman.

curry *m* curry.

cursar *vt* to study, to take (a course on), to follow a course on; *cursar literatura* to study literature || to deal with, to see to (una solicitud) || to transmit, to convey, to pass (órdenes) || to send (cartas) || *cursar estudios* to study, to take a course.

cursi; cursilón, ona *adj* FAM pretentious, showy; *un piso muy cursi* a very pretentious flat | affected (amanerado) | genteel (exageradamente refinado) || pretentious (presumido) || snobbish.

◆ *m/f* affected person (amanerado) || genteel person (exageradamente refinado) || pretentious person (presumido) || snob.
— OBSERV The correct plural is *cursis*, not *cursiles*.

cursilada; cursilería *f* FAM pretentiousness, showiness (presunción) | affectation (afectación) | vulgarity (vulgaridad) | gentility (refinamiento exagerado) | snobbishness, snobbery | pretentious *o* showy *o* flashy object.

cursilón, ona *adj/s* ⟶ **cursi.**

cursillista *m/f* student on a short course (estudiante) || trainee (de un período de prácticas) || *profesor cursillista* student teacher.

cursillo *m* short course (de corta duración) || course of lectures (conferencias) || — REL *cursillo de cristiandad* religious instruction || *cursillo de capacitación* training course || *cursillo intensivo* intensive course || *un cursillo de vuelo sin visibilidad* a course on blind flying.

cursivo, va *adj* cursive || *letra cursiva* italics *pl.*
◆ *f* italics *pl* (letra).

curso *m* course; *el curso de un río, de un astro, de la historia, de los acontecimientos* the course of a river, of a heavenly body, of history, of events || course (clase, tratado); *dar un curso de filosofía* to give a course on philosophy || school year (para la enseñanza primaria y media), academic year (para la enseñanza superior) || direction || COM tender; *este billete tiene curso legal* this note is legal tender || course; *en el curso de la semana* during the course of the week || course, progress (de una enfermedad) || — *apertura de curso* beginning of term || *curso acelerado, por correspondencia* crash, correspondence course || *curso de orientación universitaria* pre-university, secondary school course and qualification || *dar curso a* to give rein *o* vent to; *dar libre curso a su cólera* to give free rein to *o* full vent to one's anger; to deal with, to see to, to take appropriate action concerning (ocuparse de); *dar curso a una solicitud* to deal with a request || *dar libre curso a su fantasía* to give free rein *o* free play to one's imagination, to let one's imagination run wild || *en curso* under way, in process; *la construcción de esta casa está en curso* the building of this house is in process; under way; *este proyecto está en curso* this plan is under way; current; *el año en curso* the current year; in hand; *asuntos en curso* matters in hand; in circulation (monedas) || *en curso de realización* under construction (construyéndose), under way (un trabajo) || *tercer curso* third year (en enseñanza).

cursor *m* TECN slide [of mathematical instrument].

curtido, da *adj* FIG experienced; *militar curtido* experienced soldier; *una persona curtida en negocios* a person experienced in business | hardened; *estar curtido contra el frío* to be hardened to the cold | sunburnt, tanned (por el sol), weather-beaten (por el tiempo) || tanned (cuero).
◆ *m* tanning (del cuero) || *industria de curtidos* tanning industry.

curtidor *m* tanner (de cueros).

curtiduría *f* tannery.

curtiembre *f* AMER tannery.

curtimiento *m* tanning.

curtir *vt* to tan (el cuero) || FIG to tan (la piel) | to harden, to inure (acostumbrar a la vida dura).
◆ *vpr* to become tanned (por el sol), to become weather-beaten (por el tiempo) || to become hardened *o* inured (acostumbrarse a la vida dura) || to become experienced, to accustom o.s. (avezarse).

curul *adj* curule (magistrado y silla).

curva *f* curve (línea) || bend, curve; *curva peligrosa* dangerous bend; *curva cerrada* sharp bend; *curva muy cerrada* hairpin bend; *tomar la curva muy cerrada* to take the bend tightly; *sortear una curva* to take a bend || bend, turn (de un río) || FAM curve (del cuerpo) || — ECON *curva de costes* cost curve || *curva de natalidad* birthrate curve || *curva de nivel* contour line || *curva de temperatura* temperature curve.

curvar *vt* to curve, to bend.

curvatura *f* curvature (cualidad, estado) || bending (acción).

curvilíneo, a *adj* curvilinear, curvilineal || curvaceous, shapely (mujer).

curvímetro *m* curvometer.

curvo, va *adj* curved, bent || *línea curva* curved line.

cusca *f* FAM *hacer la cusca a* to bother (fastidiar).

cuscurrante *adj* crunchy, crispy, crisp.

cuscurrear *vi* to crunch.

cuscurro; cuscurrón *m* crust (de pan).

cuscús *m* couscous (alcuzcuz).

cusí cusí *adj* AMER so-so (así así).

cusma *f* AMER ⟶ **cuzma.**

cúspide *f* peak, summit (cima, cumbre) || ANAT & BOT cusp || MAT apex; *cúspide de la pirámide* apex of the pyramid || FIG zenith, pinnacle, height; *llegar a la cúspide de la gloria* to reach the height of glory.

custodia *f* custody, care, safekeeping (vigilancia); *bajo la custodia de* in the custody of || custodian, guardian (vigilante) || REL monstrance (vaso sagrado).

custodiar *vt* to guard, to take care of (conservar) || to guard, to watch over (vigilar) || to defend, to uphold (proteger).

custodio *adj/sm* guardian; *ángel custodio* guardian angel.
◆ *m* custodian, guardian.

cusumbe; cusumbo *m* AMER coati.

cususa *f* AMER tafia (ron).

cutáneo, a *adj* cutaneous || *enfermedad cutánea* skin disease.

cúter *m* MAR cutter.

cuti *f* MED skin test (cutirreacción).

cutí *m* ticking (tela).

cutícula *f* cuticle (epidermis).

cutirreacción *f* skin test; *ha sido sensible a la cutirreacción* his skin test has proved positive.

cutis *m inv* skin, complexion, cutis.

cutre *adj* mean, miserly, stingy (tacaño) || FAM grotty, seedy.
◆ *m/f* miser.

cuy *m* AMER guinea pig.

cuyo, ya *pron rel* whose, of which (de cosas); *la casa cuyo tejado es de tejas* the house whose roof *o* the roof of which *o* of which the roof is tiled; *el cuarto en cuyo fondo está la chimenea* the room at the back of which is the fireplace || whose, of whom (de personas); *el niño cuyos padres están en Madrid* the child whose parents *o* the parents of whom are in Madrid; *el amigo a cuya generosidad debo esto* the friend to whose generosity *o* to the generosity of whom I owe this || (p us) whose; *¿cuya es esta capa?* whose is this cape? || — *a cuyo efecto, con cuyo objeto, para cuyo fin* to which end, for which || *en cuyo caso* in which case || *por cuya causa* because of which.
◆ *m* FAM (p us) lover (enamorado).

¡cuz, cuz! *interj* here boy! (para llamar un perro).

cuzcuz *m* couscous (alcuzcuz).

cuzma; cusma *f* AMER long sleeveless shirt.

cuzquear *vt* AMER to court, to woo (galantear).

czar *m* czar, tsar (soberano).

czarda *f* czardas (danza).

czarevitz *m* czarevitch, tsarevitch.

czarina *f* czarina, tsarina.
— OBSERV In Spanish the more usual spellings of *czar, czarevitz* and *czarina* are *zar, zarevitz* and *zarina*.

CH

ch *f* ch.

— OBSERV *Ch* is a letter in its own right in Spanish and is completely independent of the letter *c*. It comes between the letters c and *d* in the alphabet. It is pronounced like *ch* in *church*.

chabacanada *f* ⟶ **chabacanería.**

chabacanear *vi* to behave in a coarse *o* vulgar *o* rude way.

chabacanería; chabacanada *f* coarse *o* vulgar *o* rude thing; *decir una chabacanería* to say sth. rude ‖ vulgarity, tastelessness (falta de gusto).

chabacano, na *adj* common, plain, ordinary; *una mujer chabacana* a common woman ‖ vulgar, coarse, common, uncouth; *tiene un aspecto chabacano* he looks uncouth ‖ rude, coarse, crude, vulgar; *un chiste chabacano* a crude joke.
◆ *m* AMER apricot (albaricoque).

chabola *f* hut, shack, shanty (choza) ‖ shed (caseta) ‖ *las chabolas* the shanty town (barrio de las latas).

chabolismo *m* shanty towns *pl*, slums *pl*; *hay que terminar con el chabolismo* we must clear the slums.

chacal *m* ZOOL jackal.

chacalín *m* AMER shrimp (camarón).

chácara *f* AMER farm (chacra) | bag (bolsa) | sore (llaga).

chacarero, ra *adj/s* AMER peasant, farmer.
◆ *f* peasant dance [in Argentina, Uruguay and Bolivia].

chacina *f* pork sausage meat (carne) ‖ pork sausages *pl* (conjunto de los embutidos).

chacinería *f* porkbutcher's shop (tienda).

chacó *m* shako (morrión).

chacolí *m* «chacoli» [a Basque wine].

chacolotear *vi* to clatter (la herradura).

chacoloteo *m* clatter, clattering.

chacona *f* MÚS chaconne.

chacota *f* joking, banter ‖ — FAM *echar* or *tomar a chacota, hacer chacota de* to make fun of (burlarse de) | *estar de chacota* to be in a joking mood | *tomar a chacota* to take as a joke (no tomar en serio).

chacotear *vi* to make fun [of everything] (burlarse) ‖ to mess about, to clown around (hacer *or* decir tonterías).
◆ *vpr* to make fun; *chacotearse de una persona* to make fun of s.o.

chacoteo *m* messing about, clowning, kidding, ragging, joking (regocijo) ‖ mockery (burla).

chacotero, ra *adj* FAM mocking, teasing, jesting, fun-loving.
◆ *m/f* joker, tease, wisecrack.

chacra *f* AMER farm.

chacuaco, ca *adj* AMER clumsy, careless (chapucero) | coarse, rough (grosero).
◆ *m* cigarette end *o* butt (colilla) ‖ badly-made cigar (puro malhecho) ‖ smelting furnace (horno).

chacha *f* FAM maid, nursemaid (niñera) | girl, lass (muchacha) | maid (criada).

cháchara *f* FAM small talk, chatter (charla) ‖ FAM *estar de cháchara* to chatter, to gossip, to chat.
◆ *pl* AMER trinkets, baubles (baratijas).

chacharear *vi* FAM to chatter, to gossip, to chat.

chacharero, ra *adj* FAM talkative.
◆ *m/f* FAM chatterbox, chatterer.

chacharón, ona *m/f* FAM chatterbox.

chachi *adj/adv* ⟶ **chanchi.**

chachito, ta *adj/s* AMER love (cielito).

chacho, cha *m/f* FAM boy, lad, kid (muchacho), girl, lass (muchacha); *¡ven acá, chacho!* come here, lad! ‖ AMER servant.

Chad *npr m* GEOGR Chad.

chafaldete *m* clew line.

chafalonía *f* scrap gold (oro) *o* silver (plata).

chafalote *adj* AMER uncouth, vulgar, coarse (grosero).
◆ *m* AMER kind of scimitar (alfanje).

chafallar *vt* FAM to botch, to make a mess of.

chafallo *m* FAM botched job, mess.

chafallón, ona *adj* FAM careless, slapdash, amateurish, shoddy (chapucero).
◆ *m/f* botcher, shoddy worker, careless worker.

chafar *vt* to flatten, to squash, to crush (aplastar) ‖ to crease, to crumple (arrugar) ‖ to flatten (el peinado) ‖ to dent (un coche) ‖ FIG to nonplus, to floor, to stump, to cut (s.o.) short (en una discusión) | to shatter (abatir) | to ruin; *la lluvia me ha chafado el plan* the rain has ruined my plans.
◆ *vpr* to be squashed, to be crushed (ser aplastado).

chafarote *m* kind of scimitar (alfanje).

chafarrinar *vt* to daub, to smear, to spot

chafarrinón *m* daub, smear, stain.

chafe *m* AMER FAM copper, cop, bobby (policía).

chaflán *m* bevel, chamfer (bisel) ‖ cant (de un edificio) ‖ *casa que hace chaflán* corner house.

chaflanar *vt* to bevel, to chamfer (abiselar).

chagarro *m* AMER little shop (tiendecita).

chagra *m* AMER peasant.
◆ *f* AMER farm (chacra).

chaguar *vt* to wring (out) (la ropa) ‖ AMER to milk (ordeñar).

chah *m* shah (soberano de Irán).

chahuistle *f* AMER mildew, rust, blight (roya).

chaina *f* AMER goldfinch (jilguero) | Mexican flute (flauta).

chaira; cheira *f* steel, sharpener (para afilar cuchillos) ‖ paring knife (de zapatero).

chajá *m* AMER chaja, crested screamer (ave).

chal *m* shawl (mantón).

chala *f* AMER husk, shuck (del maíz).

chalado, da *adj* FAM dotty, round the bend, touched | crazy, mad; *está chalado por Ana, por la música de jazz* he's crazy about Anna, about jazz.
◆ *m/f* FAM nut.

chaladura *f* FAM fancy *o* crazy idea; *le ha dado la chaladura de dejarse crecer la barba* he's got the fancy idea of growing a beard | craze (manía) | stupid thing (tontería) | crush (enamoramiento).

chalán *m* horse dealer (comerciante en caballos) ‖ sharp dealer (que engaña) ‖ AMER horse breaker, broncobuster (domador).

chalana *f* MAR barge, wherry, lighter (gabarra).

chalanear *vi* FAM to be a sharp dealer.
◆ *vt* AMER to train, to break (adiestrar).

chalaneo *m*; **chalanería** *f* sharp practice *o* dealing (en los negocios) ‖ AMER horsebreaking.

chalanesco, ca *adj* sharp, tricky, wily (del chalán).

charlar *vt* FAM to drive crazy, to drive round the bend (enloquecer).
◆ *vpr* to go mad (perder la cabeza) ‖ to get a crush, to be crazy; *chalarse por* to get a crush on, to be crazy about.

chalaza *f* chalaza.

chalcha *f* AMER double chin (papada).

chalchihuite *m* AMER kind of rough emerald | trinket (baratija).

chalé; chalet *m* (detached) house (casa con jardín) ‖ country house (en el campo) ‖ chalet (suizo) ‖ villa (casa lujosa) ‖ bungalow (en la playa).

— OBSERV *Chalé* is a more common form than *chalet*; it becomes *chalés* in the plural.

chaleco *m* waistcoat [US vest] ‖ — *chaleco antibalas* bullet-proof vest ‖ AMER *chaleco de fuerza* straightjacket ‖ *chaleco de punto* pullover ‖ *chaleco salvavidas* life jacket.

chalet *m* ⟶ **chalé** ‖ *chalet adosado* semi-detached house.

chalina *f* cravat (corbata).

chalón *m* AMER shawl.

chalote *m* BOT shallot (cebolla).

chaludo, da *adj* AMER FAM wealthy, well-to-do (que tiene mucho dinero).

chalupa *f* launch, shallop, boat (lancha) ‖ AMER maize tortilla [kind of pancake] | canoe (canoa).

challenger *m* challenger (candidato).

chamaco, ca *m/f* AMER boy, lad, kid (muchacho), girl, lass (muchacha).

chamada *f* brushwood (leña menuda) ‖ blaze (llama) ‖ FAM streak *o* run of bad luck (mala racha).

chamagoso, sa *adj* AMER greasy, grimy, dirty (mugriento) | common, vulgar (vulgar).

chamal *m* AMER blanket used by the Araucanian Indians as a cape.

chamanto *m* AMER kind of poncho.

chámara; chamarasca *f* brushwood (leña menuda) || blaze (llama).

chamarilear *vt* to swap, to barter, to exchange.

chamarileo *m* secondhand dealing, junk dealing.

chamarilero, ra *m/f* junk dealer, secondhand dealer.

chamariz *m* greenfinch (pájaro).

chamarra *f* sheepskin jacket (chaqueta).

chamarro *m* AMER serape [kind of shawl].

chamba *f* FAM fluke, lucky break (en el billar) || FIG & FAM fluke (casualidad); *he aprobado por chamba* it was a fluke that I passed, I passed by a fluke || AMER turf (césped) | job (trabajo) | deal (trato).

chambelán *m* chamberlain.

chambergo *adj m* *sombrero chambergo* soft hat with a wide brim upturned on one side.

chambón, ona *adj* FAM jammy, lucky (suertudo) | awkward, clumsy (torpe).
◆ *m/f* FAM jammy *o* lucky person (con suerte) | bungler (torpe).

chambonada *f* FAM awkwardness, clumsiness (torpeza) | fluke (suerte) | blunder (pifia).

chambra *f* camisole (prenda femenina).

chambrana *f* casing (de puerta, ventana, etc.) || AMER din, row, racket (jaleo).

chamelicos *m pl* AMER things, belongings (cachivaches).

chamicado, da *adj* AMER taciturn (taciturno) | tipsy, merry (achispado).

chamicera *f* patch of burnt land (monte quemado).

chamico *m* AMER stramonium, thorn apple (planta) || AMER FIG *dar chamico a uno* to bewitch s.o.

chamiza *f* chamiso [graminaceous plant whose stalk may be used for thatching] || brushwood (leña menuda) || → **chamizo.**

chamizo *m* thatched hut (choza) || hovel (casucha) || FAM gambling den, gambling joint (garito) | halfburned log *o* tree (tronco quemado).

chamorra *f* FAM shaved *o* shorn head.

chamorro, rra *adj* shaved, shorn (rapado) || *trigo chamorro* summer *o* beardless wheat.
◆ *m/f* person with a shaved *o* shorn head.

champa *f* AMER piece of turf, sod (hierba con tierra) | tangle (cosa enmarañada).

champán *m* champagne (vino) || sampan (embarcación).

champaña *m* champagne.

champiñón *m* mushroom.

champú *m* shampoo.
— OBSERV pl *champúes* or *champús.*

champurrar *vt* to mix (licores).

chamuchina *f* AMER rabble, riffraff (chusma).

chamullar *vt* FAM to speak, to talk (hablar) | to speak a little *o* a few words of, to have a smattering of; *yo chamullo el inglés* I speak a little English.

chamuscar *vt* to singe (el pelo, un pollo, etc.) || to scorch (papel, madera, etc.).

chamusquina *f* singeing (acción de chamuscar) || smell of burning (olor a quemado) || FIG & FAM fight (camorra) || FIG & FAM *esto huele a chamusquina* it smacks of heresy (una herejía), it looks like trouble (va a ocurrir algo grave), it smells fishy, it seems doubtful (esto es sospechoso).

chamuyo *m* AMER Argentinian slang.

chancaca *f* AMER loaf sugar (azúcar).

chancadora *f* mineral crusher (de minerales).

chancar *vt* AMER to crush (minerales) || to grind (triturar).

chance *m* chance (posibilidad) || good luck (suerte).

chancear *vi* to joke, to fool, to crack jokes.
◆ *vpr* to make fun; *chancearse de* to make fun of.

chancero, ra *adj* fond of a joke, jocose.

chanciller *m* chancellor (canciller).

chancillería *f* chancery.

chancla *f* old shoe (zapato viejo) || slipper (zapatilla); *en chanclas* in one's slippers.

chancleta *f* old shoe (zapato viejo) || slipper (zapatilla) || AMER FAM baby girl (niña).
◆ *m/f* AMER FIG & FAM good-for-nothing, nin-compoop (inepto).

chancletear *vi* to shuffle (about).

chanclo *m* clog (sandalia de madera) || galosh, over-shoe (de goma).

chancro *m* MED chancre || BOT canker.

chancha *f* AMER sow (cerda) || AMER FIG & FAM slovenly woman, filthy woman || AMER *hacer la chancha* to play truant [US to play hooky].

chanchada *f* AMER FAM dirty trick (cochinada).

cháncharras máncharras *f pl* beating about the bush *sing* || FAM *no andemos en cháncharras máncharras* let's not beat about the bush.

chanchería *f* AMER pork butcher's.

chanchero, ra *m/f* AMER pork butcher.

chanchi; chachi *adj/adv* FAM great, terrific, fantastic; *el plan nos ha salido chanchi* our plan turned out great; *el málaga es un vino chanchi* Malaga is a terrific wine.

chancho, cha *adj* AMER dirty, filthy (sucio).
◆ *m* AMER pig (cerdo) | boar (macho) || blocked pawn (en el ajedrez).
◆ *f* → **chancha.**

chanchullero, ra *adj* FAM fiddling, crooked.
◆ *m/f* FAM fiddler, crook, twister.

chanchullo *m* FAM wangle fiddle; *andar en chanchullos* to be on the fiddle.

chandal *m* DEP track suit.

chanelar *vi* FAM to understand, to get (comprender) | to understand, to be up on (saber); *yo chanelo de este asunto* I'm up on this subject.

chanfaina *f* offal stew.

changa *f* AMER joke (broma) | work of a porter.

changador *m* AMER porter.

changar *vi* AMER to do odd jobs.

chango *m* AMER monkey.

changuear *vi* AMER to joke (bromear).

changuero, ra *adj* AMER fond of a joke, jocose.
◆ *m/f* AMER one for a joke, joker.

changüí *m* FAM joke (broma) || trick, hoax (engaño) || *dar changüí a uno* to play a joke on s.o. (gastar una broma), to trick *o* to hoax s.o. (engañar).

chanquete *m* very small type of edible fish.

chantaje *m* blackmail || *hacer chantaje a uno* to blackmail s.o.

chantajista *m/f* blackmailer.

chantre *m* REL precentor.

chanza *f* joke; *gastar chanzas* to crack jokes || — *de chanza* jokingly, in fun || FIG *entre chanzas y veras* half jokingly, half in earnest.

chanzoneta *f* FAM joke (chanza).

¡chao! *interj* FAM bye-bye!, cheerio!, so long!, ciao!

chapa *f* plate, sheet (de metal) || AUT bodywork || panel (de madera), veneer (enchapado) || metal top, cap (de una botella) || iron; *chapa ondulada* corrugated iron || tray (del horno) || tag, tally, check (contraseña en un guardarropa) || plywood (contrachapado) || rouge (en las mejillas) || FIG & FAM common sense (seriedad) || AMER lock (cerradura) || *chapa de estarcir* stencil.
◆ *pl* game of tossing up coins (juego).

chapadanza *f* AMER joke (chanza).

chapado, da *adj* TECN veneered (cubierto con chapas de madera) || plated; *reloj chapado de oro* gold-plated watch || FIG *chapado a la antigua* old-fashioned.

chapalear *vi* to splash about (chapotear) || to clatter (chacolotear).

chapaleo *m* splashing about (chapoteo) || clatter (chacoloteo).

chapaleta *f* flap valve, clack valve (válvula).

chapaleteo *m* lap, lapping (del agua en la orilla) || pitter-patter, pattering (de la lluvia).

chapapote *m* AMER bitumen, asphalt.

chapar *vt* TECN to plate (metal) | to veneer (madera) | to tile (pared) || FIG to come out with, to let out (encajar).

chaparral *m* chaparral, thicket.

chaparrazo *m* AMER downpour, cloudburst (chaparrón).

chaparreras *f pl* AMER chaps (pantalones de piel).

chaparro *m* ilex, holm oak, holly oak (carrasca) || kermes oak (coscoja) || chaparro (planta malpigiácea) || chaparral (chaparral) || FIG tubby *o* chubby *o* plump person (rechoncho).

chaparrón *m* downpour, cloudburst; *cayó un chaparrón* there was a downpour || FIG & FAM shower (de preguntas, etc.) || *llover a chaparrones* to pour, to pour down, to rain cats and dogs.

chape *m* AMER plait (trenza).

chapeado, da *adj* plated (de metal) || veneered (de madera) || AMER rich (rico).
◆ *m* TECN plating (de metal) || veneering (de madera).

chapear *vt* TECN to plate (metal) | to veneer (madera) | to tile (pared) || AMER to clear (the land) (limpiar la tierra).
◆ *vi* to clatter (chacolotear).

chapeca *f*; **chapecán** *m* AMER plait (trenza).

chapecar *vt* AMER to plait (trenzar).

chapeleta *f* TECN valve (válvula).

chapeo *m* hat (sombrero).

chapería *f* TECN veneering (ebanistería).

chapeta *f* → **chapa** || FIG rosy cheek.

chapetón, ona *adj/s* AMER European recently settled in Latin America || novice (bisoño).
◆ *m* downpour, cloudburst (chaparrón).

chapetonada *f* «chapetonada» [illness which Europeans contracted on first arriving in Latin America] || AMER FIG blunder (novatada).

chapetonear *vi* AMER to make blunders through inexperience.

chapín *m* chopine (calzado) || coffer fish (pez) || AMER Guatemalan (guatemalteco).

chapino, na *adj* AMER which cuts itself as it walks (un caballo).

chápiro *m* hat (sombrero) ‖ FAM *¡por vida del chápiro* or *del chápiro verde!, ¡voto al chápiro!* confound it!, darn it!

chapista *m* sheet metal worker ‖ AUT panel beater ‖ *taller de chapista* body repair shop (para coches).

chapistería *f* sheet metal work ‖ AUT panel beating.

chapitel *m* ARQ spire (de torre) | capitel (de columna) ‖ cap (de brújula).

chapodar *vt* AGR to prune, to trim.

chapón *m* ink blot (borrón).

chapopote *m* AMER bitumen, asphalt.

chapotear *vt* to moisten, to sponge, to dampen, to damp [with a sponge] (mojar).
◆ *vi* FAM to splash about (en el agua) ‖ to squelch about (en el barro) ‖ *ir chapoteando* to paddle.

chapoteo *m* sponging, moistening (acción de mojar) ‖ splashing (en el agua) ‖ squelching (en el barro).

chapucear *vt* to botch, to make a mess of, to make a shoddy job of (hacer muy de prisa y mal) ‖ AMER to deceive (engañar).

chapucería *f* botched job, shoddy *o* amateurish piece of work (trabajo mal hecho) ‖ patching up (arreglo rápido) ‖ shoddiness (mala calidad).

chapucero, ra *adj* careless, slapdash, amateurish, shoddy; *un trabajo chapucero* a shoddy piece of work.
◆ *m/f* careless worker, shoddy worker, botcher (frangollón) ‖ liar (mentiroso).
◆ *m* blacksmith (herrero).

chapulín *m* AMER grasshopper (saltamontes).

chapurrar *vt* ⟶ **chapurrear.**

chapurrear *vt* to speak a little, to speak a few words of, to have a smattering of (hablar imperfectamente un idioma); *chapurrear el francés* to speak a little French, to have a smattering of French ‖ to mix (los licores).

chapurreo *m* jabbering.

chapuz *m*; **chapuza** *f* odd job (trabajo de poca importancia) ‖ botched job, shoddy *o* amateurish piece of work (trabajo mal hecho) ‖ patching up (arreglo rápido) ‖ spare-time job (trabajo hecho fuera de las horas de jornal) ‖ ducking (en el agua).

chapuzar *vt* to duck.
◆ *vi* to dive.
◆ *vpr* to dive (in) (tirarse de cabeza) ‖ to have a dip (bañarse).

chapuzón *m* dive (zambullida) ‖ dip, swim (baño corto) ‖ *darse un chapuzón* to have a dip (en el mar).

chaqué; chaquet *m* tailcoat morning coat.
— OBSERV *Chaqué* is the most common form of the word, and becomes *chaqués* in the plural.

chaquense; chaqueño, ña *adj* of *o* from El Chaco.
◆ *m/f* inhabitant *o* native of El Chaco.

chaqueta *f* jacket; *con chaqueta* wearing a jacket, with one's jacket on; *chaqueta de smoking* dinner jacket ‖ — FAM *cambiarse la chaqueta* to change sides, to turn one's coat (cambiar de opinión o de partido) | *ser más vago que la chaqueta de un guardia* to be bone idle ‖ *traje de chaqueta* (woman's) tailored suit.

chaquete *m* backgammon (juego).

chaquetear *vi* FIG to change sides, to be a turncoat (cambiar de opinión) | to back down, to go back on one's word (rajarse) | to flee (huir).

chaqueteo *m* FIG flight, running away (huida) ‖ change (cambio).

chaquetero, ra *m/f* turncoat.

chaquetilla *f* short jacket, bolero (de los toreros, camareros) ‖ bolero (para mujeres).

chaquetón *m* donkey jacket, pea jacket, threequarter coat (para hombres) ‖ three-quarter coat (para mujeres).

charada *f* charade (juego).

charal *m* small Mexican fish (pez) ‖ FIG & FAM *estar hecho un charal* to be as thin as a rake.

charamusca *f* AMER brushwood (leña menuda) | row, din (alboroto) | candy twist (dulce).

charanga *f* brass band (orquesta).

charango *m* AMER «charango» [small guitar].

charanguero *m* careless worker, shoddy worker, botcher (chapucero) ‖ pedlar, hawker, street salesman (buhonero) ‖ coaster (barco).

charca *f* pond, pool.

charco *m* puddle, pool ‖ FIG & FAM *cruzar* or *pasar el charco* to cross the water (cruzar el mar), to cross the herring pond (ir a América).

charcutería *f* pork butcher's.

charla *f* FAM chat, talk (conversación) ‖ talk (conferencia informal) ‖ ZOOL missel thrush, stormcock (cagaaceite).

charlador, ra *adj* FAM talkative, garrulous (hablador) | gossipy (murmurador).
◆ *m/f* FAM chatterbox (hablador) | gossip (murmurador).

charladuría *f* chatter, prattle, small talk (conversación) ‖ gossip (crítica).

charlar *vi* FAM to chat, to talk (hablar), | to chatter, to prattle (hablar demasiado) ‖ FAM *charlar por los codos* to be a real chatterbox.

charlatán, ana *adj* talkative, garrulous (que habla mucho) ‖ gossipy (chismoso).
◆ *m/f* chatterbox (que habla mucho) ‖ gossip, gossipmonger (chismoso) ‖ quack, charlatan (curandero) ‖ hawker, pedlar (vendedor callejero) ‖ trickster, swindler (engañador).

charlatanear *vi* to chatter, to prattle (hablar mucho) ‖ to gossip (hablar indiscretamente).

charlatanería *f* talkativeness, verbosity (cualidad de charlatán) ‖ gossip (chismorreo) ‖ spiel (del vendedor callejero, etc.).

charlatanesco, ca *adj* charlatanic.

charleston *m* charleston (baile).

charlista *m/f* lecturer.

charlotear *vi* FAM to chatter, to prattle.

charloteo *m* FAM chatter, prattle | chat (charla) ‖ FAM *gustarle mucho a uno el charloteo* to be a real chatterbox.

charnela; charneta *f* hinge (bisagra) ‖ ZOOL hinge (de algunos moluscos).

charol *m* varnish (barniz) ‖ patent leather (cuero barnizado); *zapatos de charol* patent leather shoes ‖ AMER tray (bandeja) ‖ FIG *darse charol* to boast, to brag, to blow one's trumpet.

charola *f* AMER tray (bandeja).
◆ *pl* AMER FAM big eyes.

charolado, da *adj* varnished, polished (barnizado) ‖ shiny, bright (lustroso).

charolar *vt* to varnish (recubrir con charol).

charpa *f* pistol belt (tahalí) ‖ MED sling (cabestrillo).

charque *m* AMER ⟶ **charqui.**

charqueada *f* AMER curing, jerking, drying.

charquear *vt* AMER to cure, to jerk, to dry, to make into charqui (la carne) ‖ to slice (rebanar) ‖ FIG to carve up, to wound badly.

charqueo *m* AMER curing, drying, jerking.

charqui; charque *m* AMER charqui, charque, jerked meat (tasajo) | dried fruit (fruta seca) | dried vegetables (legumbres).

charquicán *m* AMER stew made mainly from charqui.

charra *f* peasant woman ‖ AMER broad-brimmed hat.

charrada *f* boorishness, uncouthness (torpeza) ‖ «charro» dance (baile) ‖ FIG gaudy ornament (adorno tosco).

charrán *m* rascal, rogue, scoundrel (granuja).

charranada *f* FAM dirty trick, low-down trick (granujada).

charranería *f* FAM dirty trick, low-down trick (acción) | roguery, knavery (comportamiento).

charretera *f* MIL epaulette, epaulet.

charro, rra *adj* of the peasants of Salamanca ‖ FIG & FAM coarse, common, uncouth, ill-bred (rústico) | flashy, gaudy, jazzy, loud (llamativo).
◆ *m/f* Salamanca peasant.
◆ *m* AMER Charro, Mexican horseman sombrero, wide-brimmed hat (sombrero).
— OBSERV The *charro*, with his wide-brimmed sombrero, his superb horsemanship and his richly adorned outfit, represents the traditional Mexican.

charrúa *adj/s* AMER Uruguayan.

¡chas! *interj* pow!, wham!

chasca *f* brushwood (leña menuda) ‖ AMER mop of tangled hair (pelo).

chascar *vi* to click one's tongue (la lengua) ‖ to snap (los nudillos) ‖ to crack (madera, látigo) ‖ to crunch (un manjar duro).
◆ *vt* to click (la lengua) ‖ to crack (látigo, etc.) ‖ to crunch (un manjar duro) ‖ to snap (los nudillos).

chascarrillo *m* joke.

chascás *m* MIL schapska (casco).

chasco *m* joke (broma), trick (engaño); *dar un chasco a uno* to play a joke on s.o., to play a trick on s.o. ‖ disappointment (decepción) ‖ — *dar un chasco a uno* to pull s.o.'s leg (broma y engaño), to disappoint s.o., to let s.o. down (decepcionar) ‖ *llevarse un chasco* to be disappointed, to get a big disappointment (estar decepcionado).

chasis *m* AUT chassis ‖ FOT plate holder, frame ‖ FIG & FAM *quedarse en el chasis* to be all skin and bone.

chasponazo *m* bullet mark, graze (de proyectil).

chasquear *vt* to play a trick on (engaño) ‖ to play a joke on (broma) ‖ to disappoint, to let down (decepcionar) ‖ to crack (el látigo) ‖ to click (la lengua) ‖ to snap (los dedos) ‖ to crunch (un manjar duro) ‖ to break (promesa) ‖ *chasquear a alguien* to pull s.o.'s leg (burla y engaño).
◆ *vi* to crack (la madera, el látigo) ‖ to click one's tongue (con la lengua) ‖ to snap (con los dedos) ‖ to crunch (un manjar).
◆ *vpr* to be disappointed (sufrir un desengaño) ‖ to come to nothing (fracasar).

chasqui *m* AMER mail (correo) | messenger (mensajero).

chasquido *m* crack (de madera, látigo); *cuando se rompe una rama seca se oye un chasquido* when you break a dry branch you hear a crack ‖ click (de la lengua) ‖ snap (de los dedos) ‖ crunch (de un manjar duro) ‖ bang (de aviones y proyectiles).

chasquilla *f* AMER fringe (flequillo).

chata *f* barge (chalana) ‖ bedpan (orinal) ‖ truck (vagón).

chatarra *f* scrap iron, scrap (hierro viejo) ‖ FIG scrap | slag (escoria).
◆ *pl* FAM scrap metal *sing*, junk *sing*, medals (condecoraciones).

chatarrero *m* scrap-iron merchant, scrap-metal merchant, scrap merchant, scrap dealer.

chatear *vi* FAM to have a few (drinks).

chateo *m* FAM *ir de chateo* to go drinking *o* on a pub crawl [US to go barhopping].

chato, ta *adj* snub, flat; *nariz chata* snub nose ‖ snub-nosed, pug-nosed; *persona chata* snub-nosed person ‖ FIG shallow, flat (barco) | blunt, flattened (objeto) | low (torre, etc.) ‖ AMER poor (pobre) ‖ — FAM *chata mía* my dear, my darling | *dejar chato a uno* to stop s.o. short, to take the wind out of s.o.'s sails | *quedarse chato* to be dumbfounded *o* flabbergasted (pasmado), to fail (fracasar).
◆ *m* FAM (small) glass; *un chato de vino* a glass of wine.

chatre *adj* AMER smart, elegant, richly dressed.

chatungo, ga *adj* snub-nosed, pug-nosed.

¡chau! *interj* AMER FAM bye-bye!, cheerio!, so long!, ciao!

chaucha *adj inv* AMER insipid, dull (deslucido).
◆ *f* AMER coin [of small value] | French bean (judía verde) ‖ AMER *pelar la chaucha* to brandish a knife.

chauffeur *m* → **chófer.**

chauvinismo *m* chauvinism (patriotería).

chauvinista *adj* chauvinist, chauvinistic.
◆ *m/f* chauvinist.

chaval, la *m/f* FAM lad, boy, youngster, kid (muchacho), girl, youngster, lass (muchacha) ‖ FAM *estar hecho un chaval* to look very young (parecer), to feel very young (sentirse).

chavalería *f* FAM kids *pl*, kiddies *pl*, children *pl*.

chavea *m* FAM kid, lad, boy.

chaveta *f* TECN key, cotter (clavija) | cotter pin (clavo hendido) ‖ — FIG & FAM *estar chaveta* to be off one's rocker, to be round the bend, to have a screw loose | *perder la chaveta* to go off one's rocker, to go round the bend, to go mad | *perder la chaveta por* to be crazy about.

chavo *m* FAM brass, coin, farthing (ochavo) ‖ FAM *no tener un chavo* not to have a brass farthing [US not to have a red cent].

chavó *m* FAM kid, lad, boy (chaval).

chayotera *f* BOT chayote (planta).

che *f* name of the letter *ch*.
◆ *interj* AMER hey!

checar *vt* AMER → **chequear.**

checo, ca *adj/s* Czech, Czechoslovak, Czechoslovakian (checoslovaco).

checoslovaco, ca *adj/s* Czechoslovak, Czechoslovakian.

Checoslovaquia *npr f* GEOGR Czechoslovakia.

chécheres *m pl* AMER things, bits and pieces odds and ends, stuff *sing*, belongings.

cheira *f* → **chaira.**

chele *adj* AMER blonde, blond.
◆ *m* AMER rheum, sleep (legaña).

chelín *m* shilling (moneda).

chelo, la *adj/s* AMER blonde, blond (rubio).
◆ *m* MÚS cello (instrumento) | cellist (músico).

chepa *f* FAM hump (joroba).
◆ *m* hunchback (persona).

cheque *m* cheque [US check]; *extender un cheque de mil pesetas* to write a cheque *o* to make out a cheque for a thousand pesetas ‖ — *cheque al portador* bearer cheque, open cheque, cheque payable to bearer ‖ *cheque cruzado* crossed cheque ‖ *cheque de viaje* or *de viajero* traveller's cheque ‖ *cheque en blanco* blank cheque ‖ *cheque nominal* cheque to order, order cheque ‖ *cheque sin fondos* or *sin provisión* cheque without cover, dud cheque, N. S. F. cheque, worthless cheque, cheque that bounces (*fam*) ‖ *cobrar un cheque* to cash a cheque ‖ *talonario de cheques* chequebook [US checkbook].

chequear *vt* to check (averiguar) ‖ to compare (cotejar) ‖ to check (refrenar) ‖ MED to give a checkup to.

chequeo *m* MED checkup (examen médico) ‖ check (averiguación) ‖ comparison (comparación).

chequera *f* AMER chequebook [US checkbook].

chester *m* Cheshire cheese (queso).

cheurón; cheurrón *m* HERÁLD chevron.

cheuronado, da *adj* HERÁLD chevronny.

chévere *adj* AMER FAM brilliant (estupendo).

cheviot *m* cheviot (tejido).

chibalete *m* IMPR composing frame *o* stand.

chibcha *adj* chibchan.
◆ *m/f* chibcha.

chibola *f* AMER bump (chichón).

chibuquí *f* AMER chibouque, chibouk (pipa turca).

chic *adj inv* chic, elegant.
◆ *m* chic, stylishness, elegance.

chica *f* girl (muchacha) ‖ maid, servant (criada) ‖ *chica para todo* maid.

chicada *f* childish trick *o* prank.

chicana *f* AMER chicanery, quibbling.

chicanear *vt/vi* AMER to chicane.

chicanero, ra *adj* AMER crafty, tricky.
◆ *m/f* AMER chicaner.

chicano, na *adj* «chicano» (mexicano que ha emigrado a los Estados Unidos).

chicar *vt* to chew (mascar tabaco).

chicarrón, ona *m/f* FAM strapping lad, sturdy boy (hombre), strapping lass, sturdy girl (mujer).

chicle *m* chewing gum (goma de masticar) ‖ chicle (gomorresina) ‖ AMER dirt, filth (suciedad) ‖ *chicle de globo* bubble gum.

chiclear *vi* AMER to chew, to chew gum (mascar) | to extract gum (extraer el chicle).

chicler *m* jet (del carburador).

chico, ca *adj* small, little; *un libro chico* a small book ‖ — FIG & FAM *dejar a uno chico* to put s.o. in the shade, to make s.o. look small | *una perra chica* a five-cent piece.
◆ *m/f* boy (hombre), girl (mujer); *un buen chico* a good boy; *una chica guapa* a pretty girl ‖ son, boy (hijo), daughter, girl (hija).
◆ *f* FAM small coin [of little value] (moneda).
◆ *m* child, youngster; *dar la merienda a los chicos* to give the children their tea ‖ measure of capacity (medida) ‖ — *chico con grande* big and small alike, no matter what size; *a diez pesetas la docena, chico con grande* ten pesetas a dozen, big and small alike ‖ *chico de la calle* street urchin (golfillo) ‖ *chico de los recados* office boy (de oficina), errand boy (para cualquier establecimiento) ‖ *es buen chico* he's a good lad ‖ *¡oye, chico!* listen here, my old son; listen here, my friend ‖ FAM *tan feliz como un chico con zapatos nuevos* as happy as a sandboy.

chicolear *vi* FAM to say nice things, to pay compliments (decir frases amables) | to flirt (coquetear).
◆ *vpr* AMER FAM to enjoy o.s.

chicoleo *m* FAM compliment, flirtatious remark (requiebro) | flirting (coqueteo) ‖ AMER childish thing ‖ *decir chicoleos* to say nice things, to pay compliments (decir frases amables), to flirt.

chicoria *f* BOT chicory.

chicotazo *m* jet (chorro) ‖ AMER lash (latigazo).

chicote, ta *m/f* FAM fine *o* strapping lad (hombre), fine girl (mujer).
◆ *m* MAR end of cable, rope end (de cuerda) ‖ FIG & FAM cigar (stub) (puro) ‖ AMER whip (látigo).

chicotear *vt* AMER to whip (azotar).

chicozapote *m* BOT sapodilla, chicozapote (zapote).

chicuelo, la *adj* very small.
◆ *m/f* urchin, kid, youngster.

chicha *adj* MAR *calma chicha* dead *o* absolute calm.
◆ *f* chicha, maize liquor [US corn liquor] (bebida alcohólica) ‖ (fruit) liquor (hecha con fruta) ‖ juice (zumo) ‖ meat (in children's language) ‖ — FIG & FAM *de chicha y nabo* run-of-the-mill, nondescript, ordinary | *esas son economías de chicha y nabo* that is cheeseparing (economy) | *no ser ni chicha ni limonada* to be neither one thing nor the other, to be neither fish nor fowl | *sacarle la chicha a alguien* to make s.o. sweat | *tener pocas chichas* to be all skin and bone, to have no meat on one (flaco), to have no go (pocas fuerzas).

chícharo *m* pea (guisante) ‖ chick-pea (garbanzo).

chicharra *f* cicada (cigarra) ‖ FIG & FAM *hablar como una chicharra* to be a real chatterbox.

chicharrero *m* FAM oven, hothouse (sitio muy caluroso) | suffocating heat (calor sofocante).

chicharro *m* horse mackerel, caranx (pez).

chicharrón *m* piece of crackling (residuo muy frito de pella de cerdo) ‖ FIG *estar hecho un chicharrón* to be burnt to a cinder (carne), to be as brown as a berry (persona).
◆ *pl* crackling *sing*.

chiche *m* AMER FAM knick-knack (chuchería) | toy (juguete) | jewel (joya) | breast (pecho) | nurse, wet nurse (nodriza) | meat (carne).
◆ *adj* easy (fácil).

chichería *f* AMER chicha shop | tavern, bar.

chichi *f* AMER FAM breast (pecho) | nurse, wet nurse (nodriza).

chichimeca; chichimeco, ca *adj* Chichimecan.
◆ *m/f* Chichimec, Chichimeca, Chichimeco.

chichinabo (de) *loc adv* → **chicha.**

chichisbeo *m* gallant, suitor (hombre) ‖ flattery, gallantry (atenciones).

chicholo *m* AMER sweetmeat wrapped in maize leaf.

chichón *m* bump (en la cabeza o en la frente).

chichonear *vi* AMER to joke.

chichonera *f* helmet.

chifla *f* whistling (silbido) ‖ whistle (silbato, pito) ‖ skiver, parer, whitening knife (para adelgazar las pieles) ‖ hissing, catcalls *pl* (de protesta) ‖ *menuda chifla se llevó* he was booed *o* hissed by everyone.

chifladera *f* whistle (silbato).

chiflado, da *adj* FAM cracked, touched, daft, barmy (loco, tocado) ‖ — FAM *estar chiflado* to be round the bend, to be barmy | *estar chiflado por* or *con* to be mad on *o* about, to be

crazy on *o* about; *estar chiflado por la música* to be mad on music; to be head over heels in love with, to be mad *o* crazy about (enamorado); *estar chiflado por Juana* he's mad about Joan.
◆ *m/f* FAM nut, crackpot (loco).
◆ *m* FAM fan; *los chiflados del fútbol* football fans.

chifladura *f* whistle, whistling (silbido) ‖ FAM daftness, craziness (estado de loco) | craze (afición exagerada) | whim (capricho) | infatuation (amor exagerado).

chiflar *vi* to whistle (silbar).
◆ *vt* to skive, to pare (el cuero) ‖ to hiss, to boo, to give the bird to (a un actor) ‖ FAM to swig, to knock back, to down, to gulp down (vino, etc.) ‖ — *cazar es lo que le chifla* he's mad about hunting ‖ *ese chico me chifla* I am crazy about that boy ‖ *esto me chifla* I think this is great *o* fantastic, I love this.
◆ *vpr* to be crazy *o* mad about, to have a crush on (por una persona), to be mad on, to have a craze on *o* for (por una cosa); *chiflarse por una actriz* to be mad about a film star; *chiflarse por el cine* to be mad on films.

chiflato *m* whistle (silbato).

chifle *m* whistle (silbato) ‖ decoy (reclamo) ‖ powder horn (para la pólvora).

chiflete *m* whistle (silbato).

chiflido *m* whistle (ruido) ‖ whistling (acción).

chiflo *m* whistle (silbato).

chiflón *m* draught (corriente de aire) ‖ AMER waterfall (cascada) | drain (canal) | rockfall (derrumbe).

chigua *f* AMER hamper.

chigüín *m* AMER kid (chiquillo).

chihuahua *m* chihuahua (perro).

chiíta *m/f* Shiah, Shiite.

chilaba *f* jellaba, djellaba, jelab (de los árabes).

chilacayote *m* BOT chilacayote, chilicojote (planta cucurbitácea).

chilar *m* AMER chili field, chile field.

chile *m* chili, chile, chilli.

Chile *npr m* GEOGR Chile.

chilenismo *m* Chilean word *o* expression.

chilenizar *vt* to make Chilean.

chileno, na *adj/s* Chilean.

chilindrina *f* FAM trifle (cosa insignificante) | anecdote, story (anécdota) | joke (chiste).

chilindrinero, ra *adj* witty, funny, fond of joke.
◆ *m/f* joker, witty person.

chilindrón *m* Pope Joan (juego de baraja) ‖ CULIN *pollo al chilindrón* chicken garnished with tomatoes and peppers.

chilmole *m* AMER sauce made from peppers.

chilpayate, ta *m/f* kid (chiquillo).

chiltepe; chiltipiquín *m* AMER chili, chile, chilli (pimiento).

chilla *f* decoy (reclamo para la caza) ‖ lath (tabla) ‖ long thick fur (de animal) *o* hair (de hombre) ‖ down (de las plantas) ‖ AMER poverty (pobreza).

chillado *m* roof made from laths (techo de listones y tablas).

chillador, ra *adj* screaming, shrieking, yelling.
◆ *m/f* screamer.

chillante *adj* loud, gaudy, lurid (color) ‖ shrieking (voz).

chillar *vi* to scream, to shriek (gritar); *el niño no para de chillar* the child is always screaming ‖ to cry, to wail (llorar) ‖ to howl (gato) ‖ to squeak (ratón) ‖ to squawk, to screech (ave) ‖ to squeal (cerdo) ‖ to creak (chirriar); *la puerta chilla* the door creaks ‖ to blare (radio) ‖ to screech, to squeal (frenos) ‖ to call (la caza) ‖ FIG to be loud *o* gaudy (un color), to clash (detonar varios colores) ‖ AMER to protest, to complain (protestar) ‖ *fue chillado por el público* he was booed *o* hissed by the audience.
◆ *vpr* AMER to get angry *o* annoyed (enojarse).

chillería *f* screaming, yelling, shouting, howling (alboroto de gritos) ‖ dressing down, talking-to, scolding (regaño).

chillido *m* scream, yell, cry, howl (grito de persona) ‖ howl (de gato) ‖ squeak (de ratón) ‖ squawk, screech (de ave) ‖ creak, creaking; *el chillido de una puerta* the creaking of a door.

chillo *m* decoy (reclamo).

chillón, ona *adj* noisy, screaming; *un niño chillón* a noisy child ‖ FIG loud, gaudy, lurid (color) ‖ shrill, screechy, strident (sonido); *una voz chillona* a shrill voice.
◆ *m/f* noisy person ‖ TECN lath nail (clavo).

chimar *vt* AMER to annoy (fastidiar).
◆ *vpr* AMER to hurt o.s. (lastimarse).

chimba *f* AMER opposite bank (orilla) | ford (vado) | noncentral part of town.

chimbar *vt* AMER to ford (vadear).

chimenea *f* chimney (de casa, de fábrica) ‖ chimney [US smokestack] (de locomotora) ‖ funnel, stack (de barco) ‖ fireplace (hogar para calentarse) ‖ shaft (en una mina, etc.) ‖ nipple (de armas de fuego) ‖ — *chimenea de campana* canopy fireplace ‖ *chimenea de paracaídas* parachute vent ‖ *chimenea de tiro* chimney ‖ *chimenea de ventilación* air shaft, air well ‖ *chimenea estufa* closed stove ‖ *chimenea francesa* fireplace ‖ *chimenea volcánica* throat *o* vent *o* chimney of a volcano ‖ FIG *fumar como una chimenea* to smoke like a chimney.

chimiscolear *vi* AMER to wander about, to hang about (vagar) | to gossip (chismear).

chimó *m* AMER plug of tobacco and natron paste [as chewed by Indians].

chimpancé *m* ZOOL chimpanzee.

china *f* pebble (piedrecita) ‖ china (porcelana) ‖ china silk (tejido) ‖ FIG & FAM money (dinero) ‖ — *echar algo a chinas* to draw lost for sth. ‖ *jugar a las chinas* to play a guessing game ‖ FIG *poner chinas a uno* to put difficulties *o* obstacles in s.o.'s way | *tocarle a uno la china* to win the draw.

china *f* AMER ⟶ **chino** (2° artículo).

China *npr f* GEOGR China.

chinampa *f* «chinampa», floating garden [near Mexico City].

chinampero, ra *adj* grown in the «chinampa».
◆ *m* keeper of a «chinampa».

chinazo *m* stone (piedra) ‖ blow with a pebble (golpe).

chincaste *m* AMER brown sugar (azúcar).

chincol; chincolito *m* AMER brandy mixed with water, brandy and soda (agua con aguardiente).

chincual *m* AMER measles (sarampión).

chincha *f* AMER bug (chinche) | drawing pin [US thumbtack] | skunk (mofeta).

chinchal *m* AMER small shop (tenducho).

chinchar *vt* FAM to pester, to annoy, to bug (molestar) | to annoy; *me chincha tener que hacerlo* it annoys me to have to do it | to do in, to kill (matar).
◆ *vpr* FAM to get on with it; *tú lo querías, así que chínchate* you wanted it, so get on with it ‖ FAM *chínchate, para que te chinches* so there; *me lo dieron a mí, ¡para que te chinches!* they gave it to me, so there!

chincharrero *m* bug-infested place (nido de chinches) ‖ AMER small fishing boat (barco).

chinche *f* ZOOL bug ‖ drawing pin [US thumbtack] (clavito).
◆ *m/f* FIG & FAM nuisance, bore, pest (pesado) ‖ FIG & FAM *morir* or *caer como chinches* to die *o* to fall *o* to drop like flies.

chinchel *m* AMER bar, pub, eating house.

chincheta *f* drawing pin [US thumbtack] (clavito).

chinchibí *m* AMER ginger beer.

chinchilla *f* chinchilla (animal y piel).

chinchín *m* FAM blare, pom pom pom; *el chinchín de la banda* the pom pom pom of the band ‖ AMER drizzle (llovizna) | rattle (sonajero).

chinchona *f* BOT & MED quinine.

chinchorrera *f* FIG & FAM nuisance, annoyance (molestia) | hairsplitting, quibbling, overfussiness (minuciosidad exagerada) | gossip (chisme).

chinchorrero, ra *adj* fussy (difícil de contentar) ‖ gossipy (chismoso).
◆ *m/f* fussy person (difícil de contentar) ‖ gossip, scandalmonger (chismoso).

chinchorro *m* MAR seine, sweep net (red) | dinghy (bote).

chinchoso, sa *adj* FIG & FAM tiresome, annoying (cargante).
◆ *m/f* FIG & FAM nuisance, drag (*fam*).

chinchulines *m pl* AMER grilled tripe *sing*.

chiné *adj* chiné (de colores).
◆ *m* chiné (tejido).

chinear *vt* AMER to carry in one's arms (en los brazos), to carry on one's back (a cuestas) | to flirt with (requebrar) | to spoil (mimar).

chinela *f* slipper (zapatilla) ‖ clog (chanclo).

chinería *f*; **chinerío** *m* AMER riffraff, rabble.

chinero *m* dresser (mueble).

chinesco, ca *adj* Chinese ‖ *sombras chinescas* shadow theatre.
◆ *m* MÚS pavillon chinois, Chinese crescent, jingling Johnny.

chinga *f* AMER ZOOL skunk | FAM drunkenness (borrachera) | fag end (colilla de cigarro).

chingada; chingadura *f* FAM bother ‖ AMER failure, flop (fracaso).

chingado, da *adj* AMER nackered (jodido).

chingana *f* AMER drive, club (tabernucha) | festival with drinking and dancing (fiesta) | underground cave *o* passage.

chinganear *vi* AMER to go on a spree.

chingar *vt* FAM to down, to put away, to drink a lot of (beber mucho) | to annoy, to get on (s.o.'s) nerves (dar la lata) ‖ AMER to cut off the tail of (cortar el rabo) | to joke (bromear) | POP to fuck, to screw (tener relaciones sexuales con).
◆ *vpr* FAM to get annoyed (enfadarse) | to get sloshed *o* sozzled (emborracharse) ‖ AMER to fail (fracasar) | to fizzle out (fuego artificial).

chingaste *m* AMER sediment (poso).

chingo, ga *adj* AMER small (pequeño) | short (corto) | tailless (rabón) | flat (chato); *nariz chinga* flat nose.

chinguirito *m* AMER rum (aguardiente).

chinita *f* AMER ladybird [US ladybug] (mariquita).

chino, na *adj* Chinese (de China) ‖ *tinta china* Indian ink [US India ink].
◆ *m* Chinese, Chinaman (hombre) ‖ Chinese (idioma).

◆ *f* Chinese, Chinese woman (mujer) || — FAM *engañar a uno como a un chino* to take s.o. for a ride | *eso es chino para mí* that's Greek to me || *los chinos* the Chinese || FIG & FAM *trabajar como un chino* to work like a slave.

chino, na *adj/s* AMER Indian (indio) | half-breed, half-caste (mestizo) | mulatto (mulato) | darling, dear (calificativo cariñoso).
◆ *adj* AMER angry (airado) | curly (pelo) | yellowish (amarillento).
◆ *m* AMER kid, youngster (niño) | servant (criado) | curl (rizo).
◆ *f* AMER peasant girl (campesina) | maid (criada) | companion (compañera) | nursemaid (niñera) | girl friend (novia) | mistress (amante) | spinning top (peonza).

chipa *f* AMER fruit basket (cesto) | pad (rodete) || AMER FAM clink, prison (cárcel).

chipá *m* AMER manioc cake.

chipe; chipén; chipendi (de) *loc adv* FAM great, marvellous, super, smashing (de órdago) || — FAM *hemos comido de chipén* we've had a great *o* super *o* smashing meal | *la chipén* the truth.

chipichape *m* FAM fight (zipizape) | blow (golpe).

chipichipi *m* AMER drizzle (llovizna).

chipirón *m* squid (calamar); *chipirones fritos* fried squid.

Chipre *n pr* GEOGR Cyprus.

chipriota; chipriote *adj/s* Cypriot, Cypriote.

chiqueadores *m pl* AMER headache plasters.

chiquear *vt* AMER to pamper, to mollycoddle (mimar) | to flatter (adular).
◆ *vpr* AMER to swagger, to strut (contonearse).

chiqueo *m* AMER pampering, mollycoddling (mimo) | piece of flattery (adulación).

chiquero *m* pigsty (pocilga) || TAUR toril, bullpen (toril) || AMER cow shed (establo).

chiquichaque *m* sawyer (aserrador).

chiquilicuatro *m* FAM whippersnapper, runt (mequetrefe).

chiquilín *m* small boy.

chiquillada *f* childish prank *o* trick (niñería) || foolish *o* childish thing (acción poco sensata) || *hacer chiquilladas* to behave childishly.

chiquillería *f* kids *pl*, chindren *pl*.

chiquillo, lla *m/f* lad, boy, kid (muchacho), girl, kid (muchacha) || *los chiquillos* the kids.
◆ *adj* stupid, childish; *no seas chiquillo* don't be stupid.

chiquirritico, ca; chiquirritillo, lla; chiquirritito, ta; chiquitín, ina *adj* tiny, teeny (*fam*).

chiquitear *vi* FAM to have a few (drinks).

chiquiteo *m* pub, crawl, going drinking from bar to bar || *ir de chiquiteo* to go drinking *o* on a pub crawl [US to go barhopping].

chiquito, ta *adj* tiny, small.
◆ *m/f* kid, child, youngster (chico, chica) || FAM *no andarse con chiquitas* not to beat about the bush, not to mess about, not to hem and haw (no vacilar), to be generous (no escatimar nada).
◆ *m* FAM glass, glass of wine, wine (vaso de vino); *vamos a tomar unos chiquitos* let's have a few glasses of wine.

chiribita *f* spark (chispa).
◆ *pl* spots before the eyes (de la vista) || FIG & FAM *echar chiribitas* to fume, to blow one's top, to be furious.

chiribitil *m* garret, attic (desván) || small room, den, cubbyhole (cuchitril).

chirigota *f* FAM joke (chanza, broma) || FAM *a chirigota* as a joke, lightly; *tomar algo a chirigota* to take sth. as a joke.

chirigotero, ra *adj* fond of a joke, funny, jocose.
◆ *m/f* joker.

chirimbolo *m* FAM thing (chisme) | contraption (cosa de forma complicada).
◆ *pl* FAM things, gear *sing*, stuff *sing*, odds and ends (trastos) | tools, gear *sing*, things (utensilios).

chirimía *f* MUS chirimia, chirimilla, shawn.

chirimoya *f* cherimoya fruit, soursop (fruto).

chirimoyo *m* cherimoya (árbol).

chirinada *f* AMER failure (fracaso).

chiringuito *m* snack bar, stall.

chirinola *f* quarrel (gresca) || libely discussion (conversación) || skittles *pl* (juego) || FIG trifle (cosa insignificante) || *de chirinola* in a good mood.

chiripa *f* fluke (en el billar) || FIG & FAM fluke, stroke of luck (suerte) || — FIG & FAM *de* or *por chiripa, por pura chiripa* by a fluke, by sheer luck | *he aprobado por chiripa* it was a fluke that I passed, I passed by sheer luck *o* by a fluke.

chiripá *m* AMER chiripa [garment].

chiripear *vi* to win points by a fluke (en billar).

chiripero *m* lucky *o* fluky person.

chirivía *f* BOT parsnip (pastinaca) || wagtail (ave).

chirla *f* clam (almeja).

chirle *adj* FAM tasteless, wishy-washy, insipid (sin gracia).
◆ *m* droppings *pl*.

chirlo *m* gash, slash (herida) | scar (cicatriz) || AMER lash (latigazo).

chirola *f* AMER coin [of little value].

chirona *f* FAM clink, nick, prison; *meter en chirona* to put in clink || FAM *estar en chirona* to be inside, to be in clink *o* in the nick.

chirote *m* AMER FAM idiot, fool (tonto).

chirriador, ra; chirriante *adj* creaking (que rechina) || crackling, sizzling (al freírse una cosa) || cheeping (pájaro) || FIG shrill, piercing (voz).

chirriar *vi* to creak (gozne, eje de carro, etc.) || to sizzle, to crackle (al freír) || to cheep (los pájaros) || to chirp (el grillo) || to screech, to squeal (frenos) | to chirp (grillo) || FIG & FAM to sing out of tune, to sing badly (cantar mal) | to bawl, to yell (gritar) || AMER to go drinking, to go on a spree (ir de juerga) | to shiver (tiritar).

chirrido *m* chirp, chirping, cheeping (pájaros) || creak, creaking (ruido desagradable); *el chirrido de la puerta* the creaking of the door || screech, squeal (de los frenos) || crackling (del fuego) || sizzling (de una cosa al freírse) || FIG & FAM yell, shriek (grito) || *el chirrido del grillo* the chirping of the cricket.

chirrión *m* heavy cart (carro) || AMER leather whip (látigo) | chat (conversación).

chirumen *m* FAM common sense, intelligence.

chirusa; chiruza *f* AMER coarse *o* uncouth woman.

¡chis!; ¡chist!; ¡chit! *interj* ssh!, hush! (chitón).

chischás *m* clash (ruido de las espadas al entrechocarse).

chisgarabís *m* FAM whippersnapper, runt (mequetrefe) | busybody, meddler (entrometido).

chisguete *m* FAM drink, swig (trago); *echar un chisguete* to have a swig | jet, spurt, squirt (chorro) || AMER rubber tube (tubo).

chisguetear *vi* FAM to have a drink (beber).

chisme *m* piece of gossip (hablilla) || FAM knick-knack (objeto sin importancia) | thingumajig, thing (cosa); *¡qué chisme tan raro!* what a funny thing! | gadget (dispositivo).
◆ *pl* gossip *sing* (chismorreo) || things, stuff *sing*, odds and ends (trastos) || — *el cuarto de los chismes* the lumber room, the box room, the glory hole || *los vecinos andan siempre con chismes* the neighbours are always gossiping || *meter* or *traer chismes* to gossip, to tell tales.

chismear *vi* to gossip, to tell tales.

chismería *f* gossip, piece of gossip (chisme).

chismografía *f* FAM gossiping, gossip (habladuría).

chismorrear *vi* to gossip (chismear).

chismorreo *m* gossip, gossiping.

chismoso, sa *adj* fond of telling tales, gossipy, gossiping.
◆ *m/f* gossip, scandalmonger.

chispa *f* spark; *chispa eléctrica* electric spark; *echar chispas* to give off sparks || flash (relámpago) || sparkle, glitter (en una cosa brillante) || small diamond (diamante pequeño) || drop, small drop (de lluvia) || FIG crumb, scrap (pedazo de una cosa); *no sobró ni una chispa de pan* there wasn't a scrap of bread left | a little (un poquito); *una chispa, nada más* just a little | drop (gota) | spark, glimmer; *una chispa de inteligencia* a glimmer of intelligence | liveliness (viveza) | wit (gracia) || FAM drunkenness (borrachera) || AMER lie (mentira) || — *caen chispas* it's drizzling (llueve) || *de chispa* flint (escopeta) || FIG & FAM *echar chispas* to be hopping mad [US to spit fire] | *ni chispa* nothing (nada), at all; *no me gusta ni chispa* I don't like it at all | *no tiene ni chispa de gracia* it's not funny at all, it's not a bit funny | *ser una chispa* to be lively (ser muy vivo) | *tener chispa* to be witty *o* funny, to be a live wire (persona graciosa), to be funny (cosa graciosa), to be lively (ser muy vivo).
◆ *interj* goodness me!

chisparse *vpr* FAM to get drunk (emborracharse) || AMER to run away (escaparse).

chispazo *m* spark; *le saltó un chispazo a la cara* a spark flew into his face || burn (quemadura) || FIG spark; *los primeros chispazos de la guerra* the first sparks of the war || FAM piece of gossip (chisme) || FIG *chispazo de ingenio* flash of genius.

chispeante *adj* which gives off sparks (que echa chispas) || sparkling; *ojos chispeantes* sparkling eyes || FIG *tener un ingenio chispeante* to sparkle with wit.

chispear *vi* to give off sparks, to spark (echar chispas) || to spark (echar una chispa) || FIG to sparkle; *chispear de alegría* to sparkle with joy | to be brilliant; *su discurso chispeó* his speech was brilliant | to spit, to drizzle (lloviznar).

chispero *m* blacksmith (herrero) || FIG & FAM man from the lower classes of Madrid.

chispo, pa *adj* FAM merry, tipsy.
◆ *m* FAM swig, drink (trago).

chispoleto, ta *adj* bright, wide-awake, sharp (listo).

chisporroteante *adj* crackling (fuego).

chisporrotear *vi* to crackle; *el fuego chisporrotea* the fire is crackling || to spit, to sizzle (aceite) || RAD to crackle.

chisporroteo *m* crackling (de la leña) || spitting, sizzling (del aceite) | RAD crackling (ruido parásito).

chisquero *m* tinder lighter.

¡chist! *interj* ssh!, hush!

chistar *vi* to speak, to open one's mouth, to say a word; *no chistó mientras estuvimos allí* he didn't say a word whilst we were there || — *sin chistar* without saying a word, without opening one's mouth (sin decir nada), without turning a hair (sin protestar) || FAM *sin chistar ni mistar* without a word.

chiste *m* joke, funny story (cuento gracioso); *contar un chiste* to tell a joke || — *caer en el chiste* to get the joke, to get it || *con chiste* wittily, in a funny way || *chiste verde* dirty joke *o* story || *esto tiene chiste* that's not funny, some joke (irónico) || *es una cosa sin chiste* it's not funny || *hacer chiste de algo* to make a joke of sth., to take sth. as a joke || *hacer chiste de uno* to make fun of s.o. || *no le veo el chiste a lo que ha dicho* I don't see what's funny in what he said || *tener chiste* to be funny.

chistera *f* creel, angler's basket (cesta de pescador) || FIG & FAM top hat, topper (sombrero de copa) || basket (para jugar a la pelota).

chistoso, sa *adj* funny, witty, fond of a joke, jocose (persona) || funny; *una anécdota muy chistosa* a very funny anecdote || — *es chistoso que siempre me pida a mí que lo haga* it's getting beyond a joke that he always asks me to do it || *lo chistoso* the funny part (extraño o gracioso).
◆ *m/f* laugh, comic (persona graciosa).

chistu *m* Basque flute.

chistulari *m* Basque flute player.

¡chit! *interj* ssh!, hush!

chita *f* ANAT anklebone (hueso) || quoits *pl* (juego) || AMER net bag (bolsa de red) || — FIG & FAM *a la chita callando* on the quiet, on the sly; *le hizo una mala jugada a la chita callando* he played a dirty trick on him on the quiet | *me acerqué a él a la chita callando* I crept up on him, I approached him stealthily | *se marchó a la chita callando* he slipped away, he left quietly.

chiticalla *m/f* FAM discreet person, clam (*fam*).

chiticallando *adv* FAM —> **chita.**

chito *m* kind of quoits *pl* (juego).

¡chito!; ¡chitón! *interj* FAM ssh!, nush!

chiva *f* kid, young she-goat (cabrita) || AMER blanket (manta) | goatee (perilla) | drunkenness (borrachera) | rage (berrinche) | minx (mujer inmoral).

chivar *vt* FAM to annoy, to get on s.o.'s nerves.
◆ *vpr* FAM to tell, to split (entre niños); *chivarse de algo al maestro* to tell the teacher *o* to split to the teacher about sth.; *¡cuidado, que me voy a chivar!* look out or I'll tell! | to inform (soplonear); *me voy a chivar a la policía de las actividades de Juan* I'm going to inform the police about John's activities.

chivata *f* shepherd's stick.

chivatazo *m* FAM telling, informing (delación) || FAM *dar el chivatazo* to spill the beans, to split, to inform (delatar).

chivatear *vi* FAM to inform, to split, to tell tales (soplonear) || AMER to scream, to shout (gritar).

chivateo *m* FAM telling, splitting, informing.

chivato, ta *m/f* FAM informer (delator) | telltale (acusica).
◆ *m* kid, young goat (chivo) || AMER bigwig (persona importante).

chivo *m* kid, young goat (cría de la cabra) || *chivo emisario* or *expiatorio* scapegoat (entre los judíos).

chocante *adj* shocking, offensive; *unas costumbres chocantes* shocking habits || surprising, startling, striking (sorprendente) || unpleasant; *voz chocante* unpleasant voice || odd, strange (raro) || *lo chocante es que* the striking thing is that.

chocar *vi* to hit, to run (*con* into), to collide (*con* with); *el coche chocó con* or *contra la farola* the car ran into *o* collided with *o* hit the lamppost || to collide, to run into each other (dos) *o* one another (más de dos), to hit each other *o* one another; *chocaron dos trenes* two trains collided, two trains ran into each other || to hit; *la pelota chocó contra la pared* the ball hit the wall || FIG to clash (pelear); *los ejércitos chocaron en esta ciudad* the armies clashed in this town | to shock; *me chocó mucho su contestación* his reply really shocked me | to argue (reñir); *chocar con uno* to argue with s.o. | to be surprising (sorprender) || — *coches que chocan* dodgems [US bumper cars] || *chocar de frente* to hit head on.
◆ *vt* to clink (vasos) || to shake; *chocar la mano con* to shake hands with || to surprise (sorprender) || *¡chócala!* shake!, shake on it!

chocarrear *vi* to tell dirty *o* coarse *o* rude *o* crude jokes.

chocarrería *f* dirty *o* coarse *o* crude *o* rude joke.

chocarrero, ra *adj* dirty, coarse, crude, rude.
◆ *m/f* coarse comic, person who tells dirty jokes.

choclo *m* clog (chanclo) || AMER cob of tender corn (maíz) | food made mainly from tender corn (alimento) | FIG & FAM worry (preocupación), burden, responsability (carga) || AMER FAM *¡qué choclo!* what a nuisance!

choclón *m* AMER FAM crowd (muchedumbre).

choco, ca *adj* AMER one-legged (con una pierna) | one-eared (con una oreja) | one-eyed (con un ojo) | curly-haired (de pelo rizado).
◆ *m* small cuttlefish (jibia) || AMER water spaniel (perro de aguas) | stump (muñón).

chocolate *m* chocolate; *pastilla de chocolate* piece *o* square of chocolate; *tableta de chocolate* bar *o* slab *o* tablet of chocolate || drinking chocolate, cocoa; *jícara de chocolate* cup of drinking chocolate || — *chocolate a la taza, con leche* drinking chocolate, milk chocolate || *chocolate para crudo* plain *o* dark chocolate || FIG *ésas son economías del chocolate del loro* that is cheeseparing (economy) | *hacer economías del chocolate del loro* to count every penny, to overeconomize || FIG & FAM *las cosas claras y el chocolate espeso* let's get things clear || AMER *sacar chocolate* to make (s.o.'s) nose bleed (hacer sangrar las narices).
◆ *adj* chocolate-coloured (color).

chocolatera *f* chocolate pot || FAM old crock (coche viejo) | old tub, hulk (barco).

chocolatería *f* chocolate factory (fábrica) || chocolate shop (tienda).

chocolatero, ra *adj* chocolate-loving, fond of chocolate.
◆ *m/f* chocolate maker (fabricante) || chocolate seller (vendedor) || chocolate lover, chocolate eater (aficionado al chocolate).

chocolatín *m*; **chocolatina** *f* bar of chocolate (alargado), chocolate (redondo).

chocha; chochaperdiz *f* ZOOL woodcock (ave).

chochear *vi* to dodder, to be in one's dotage, to be senile (tener debilitadas las facultades mentales) || *el amor hace chochear con frecuencia a los hombres* love often makes men soft.

chochera; chochez *f* dotage, senility (cualidad de chocho) || FAM doting (admiración excesiva).

chocho *m* lupin seed (altramuz) || cinnamon sweet (confite) || sweet [US candy] (golosina).

chocho, cha *adj* doddering, doddery, senile (un anciano) || — *estar chocho por* to be soft on, to have a crush on || *viejo chocho* old dodderer.

chochocol *m* AMER pitcher, jug.

chófer; chauffeur *m* chauffeur (al servicio particular de alguien) || driver (conductor) || *chófer de camión* lorry driver [US truck driver, trucker].

chofes *m pl* lights, lungs (bofes).

chola *f* FAM —> **cholla.**

cholada *f*; **cholerío** *m* AMER group of half-breeds, group of mestizos.

cholo, la *adj* AMER half-breed, mestizo (mestizo).
◆ *m/f* AMER half-breed, mestizo | civilized Indian | one of the common people (plebeyo).

cholla *f* FAM nut, block, head (cabeza) | brains *pl* (inteligencia) || AMER wound, injury (llaga) | laziness (pereza) || FAM *no le queda un solo pelo en la cholla* he hasn't got a hair on his head.

chollar *vt* AMER to injure, to wound (herir).

chollo *m* FAM soft *o* cushy job, good number (trabajo fácil) | bargain (ganga) | luck (suerte).

chomba; chompa *f* AMER sweater, jumper (suéter).

chompipe *m* AMER turkey (pavo).

chonchón *m* AMER kind of kite (cometa) | bird of ill omen (ave fatídica) | undesirable person (persona despreciable).

chongo *m* AMER curl (rizo) | bun (moño) | milk and syrup sweet (dulce) | joke (broma) | blunt knife (cuchillo que no corta).

chonguear *vi* AMER to joke.

chonta *f* AMER palm tree (palmera) | black snake (serpiente).

chontal *adj* AMER coarse, rough, uneducated (inculto) | uncivilized (indio).

chopazo *m* AMER punch (puñetazo).

chope *m* AMER kind of hoe (azadón) | punch (puñetazo).

chopera *f* poplar grove.

chopo *m* BOT poplar (álamo) | black poplar (álamo negro) || FAM rifle, gun (fusil).

choque *m* shock; *amortiguar un choque* to absorb a shock || FIG shock; *la muerte de su hija fue un choque muy fuerte para ella* the death of her daughter was a great shock for her || impact, collision (colisión) || jolt (de un coche en movimiento) || crash, smash (coches, trenes) || ELECTR shock || FIG clash (de dos ejércitos, de dos personas, etc.) || MED shock; *choque operatorio* postoperative shock || clinking, clink (de vasos) || clatter (de platos) || — *choque de frente* head-on collision || *precio de choque* bargain price.

choquezuela *f* ANAT patella, kneecap (rótula).

chorear *vi* AMER FAM to grumble, to moan.

choricería *f* sausage shop (salchichería).

chorizo *m* sausage [seasoned with red peppers], «chorizo» || FAM thief (ladrón) || balancing pole (balancín) || AMER loin (lomo) | daub (para revocar) | idiot (mentecato).

chorlito *m* plover (pájaro) || FIG & FAM *cabeza de chorlito* scatterbrain.

choro *m* AMER mussel (mejillón).

chorote *m* AMER chocolate pot (chocolatera) | chocolate (chocolate).

choroy *m* AMER small parrot (pájaro).

chorra *f* FAM luck, jam (suerte) || FAM *tener mucha chorra* to be very lucky, to be jammy.

chorrada *f* extra measure (de líquido) || FAM stupid thing; *soltar chorradas* to say stupid things | unnecessary adornment (adorno superfluo).

chorreado, da *adj* striped (animal) || AMER dirty, stained (sucio).

chorreadura *f* dripping (chorreo) || stain [caused by dripping] (mancha).

chorrear *vi* to flow, to run; *líquido que chorrea* flowing liquid || to drip (gotear); *la ropa está chorreando* the washing is dripping || — FAM *estar chorreando* to be soaking, to be dripping wet || *estar chorreando de sudor* to be dripping with sweat.

◆ *vt* to pour; *chorrear agua por el suelo* to pour water on the floor || to drip with; *el cuerpo chorreando sudor* his body dripping with sweat || FIG & FAM to give in dribs and drabs (dar poco a poco).

◆ *vpr* AMER FAM to pinch (robar); *chorrearse algo* to pinch sth.

chorreo *m* dripping, trickle (en gotas), gush, gushing (en chorro); *el chorreo del agua* the dripping of water || FIG flow, flood; *un chorro de gente, de turistas* a flood of people, of tourist | constant drain (gasto).

chorreón *m* dripping (chorreadura) || squirt, dash; *echar un chorreón de aceite en la ensalada* to add a dash of oil to the salad || stain (mancha).

chorrera *f* channel (sitio) || mark left by dripping water (señal) || rapids *pl* (de un río) || frill, jabot (de camisa) || AMER string; *una chorrera de desatinos* a string of stupid things.

chorretada *f* spurt, gush, squirt, jet (chorro) || extra measure (chorrada).

chorrillo *m* spurt, squirt, small jet (de un líquido) || small jet (de gas) || dash, squirt; *un chorrillo de aceite* a dash of oil || FIG trickle (cantidad pequeña) || AGR *sembrar a chorrillo* to sow in a straight line.

chorro *m* jet, spurt, gush, squirt, spout (de un líquido) || jet (de gas) || jet, stream (de áridos) || trickle (caudal muy pequeño) || FIG shower, flood, stream; *un chorro de pesetas* a shower of pesetas | stream, torrent; *un chorro de palabras* a stream of words | flood; *un chorro de luz* a flood of light || AVIAC jet || — *a chorros* in plenty || *avión de chorro* jet plane || *beber a chorro* to pour drink into one's mouth [without touching the bottle or glass with the lips] || TECN *chorro de arena* sandblasting || *chorro de vapor* steam jet || *de propulsión a chorro* jet-propelled || FIG *hablar a chorros* to gabble, to jabber || *llover a chorros* to pour down || FIG *estar (limpio) como los chorros de oro* to be as clean as a whistle || *salir a chorros* to squirt out || FIG *soltar el chorro de la risa* to burst out laughing || *sudar a chorros* to drip with sweat.

chotacabras *f inv* nightjar (pájaro).

chote *m* AMER chayote (chayote).

chotearse *vpr* FAM to make fun (*de* of), to take the mickey (*de* out of) (burlarse).

choteo *m* FAM teasing (zumba) || FAM *tomárselo todo a choteo* to take everything as a joke.

chotis *m* schottische (danza).

choto, ta *m/f* kid, young goat (cabrito) || calf (ternero) || FAM *estar como una chota* to be round the bend, to be barmy.

chotuno, na *adj* of a kid, of a young goat || FAM *oler a chotuno* to stink to high heaven.

chova *f* chough (ave).

chovinismo *m* chauvinism.

chovinista *adj* chauvinistic.

◆ *m/f* chauvinist.

choza *f* hut; *choza de paja* straw hut || shack, shanty (cabaña).

chozo *m* small hut.

christmas *m inv* Christmas card.

chubasco *m* squall, heavy shower, downpour (aguacero); *chubasco de origen tormentoso* stormy shower || MAR squall (lluvia) || FIG setback, cloud, adversity (adversidad).

chubascoso, sa *adj* squally, stormy.

chubasquero *m* oilskins *pl* (de marinero) || oilskin raincoat (impermeable).

chubesqui *m* stove, heater (estufa).

chúcaro, ra *adj* AMER wild (animales) | shy (personas).

◆ *m/f* AMER wild mule.

chucero *m* pikeman (soldado).

chucha *f* FAM bitch (perra) | peseta || AMER maraca (maraca) | opossum (zarigüeya) || *¡chucha!* shoo!, scat!, go on!, go home! (dirigiéndose a un perro).

chuchear *vi* to whisper (cuchichear) || to hunt with traps (cazar con trampas) *o* decoys (con señuelos) || FAM to nibble sweet's.

chuchería *f* knick-knack, trinket (fruslería) || titbit, sweet [US piece of candy] (golosina) || hunting with traps (trampas) *o* decoys (señuelos).

chucho *m* hound, dog (perro) || AMER malaria (paludismo) | shiver (escalofrío).

◆ *interj* shoo!, scat!, go on!, go home! (al perro).

chuchoca *f* AMER roasted maize.

chuchurrido, da *adj* FAM faded; *flores chuchurridas* faded flowers | wrinkled (arrugado) | wizened; *una vieja chuchurrida* a wizened old woman.

chueca *f* ball (de un hueso) || stump (tocón) || game resembling hockey (juego) || FIG & FAM joke (chasco).

chueco, ca *adj* AMER *piernas chuecas* bow-legs, bandy legs.

chufa *f* BOT chufa, earth almond (planta) || *horchata de chufas* orgeat made from chufas.

chufar; chufear *vi* to mock, to make fun (*de* of).

chufla; chufleta *f* FAM joke (broma) || FAM *gastar chufletas a uno* to pull s.o.'s leg.

chuflarse; chuflearse *vpr* FAM to make fun (*de* of) || FAM *chuflearse de uno* to pull s.o.'s leg.

chuflay *m* AMER toddy, alcoholic drink.

chufletear *vi* FAM to joke, to jest (bromear).

chufletero, ra *adj* FAM fond of a joke (bromista) | fond of leg-pulling (burlón).

◆ *m/f* FAM joker, laugh, comic (bromista) | leg-puller, tease (burlón).

chulada *f* FAM lovely thing, pretty thing (cosa mona) | coarse *o* vulgar thing (cosa grosera) | funny thing (agudeza) | cheek, cheekiness, barefacedness, insolence (insolencia) | showing off, show-off (jactancia) || FAM *decir una chulada, hacer chuladas* to be cheeky (desfachatez), to brag, to show off (jactancia).

chulapo, pa; chulapón, ona *m/f* FAM dandy, spiv, beau (hombre), elegant young woman from the lower classes of Madrid (mujer).

◆ *adj* cheeky, cocky (chulo).

chulé *m* FAM five peseta piece.

chulear *vt* to get cocky with (ponerse chulo); *a mí no me chulea nadie* nobody gets cocky with me || to touch for; *me ha chuleado veinte duros* he's touched me for a hundred pesetas || AMER to flirt with (decir piropos).

◆ *vpr* to make fun (*de* of), to pull the leg of; *chulearse de uno* to pull s.o.'s leg || FAM to show off (presumir).

chulería *f* FAM cheek, cheekiness, barefacedness, insolence (insolencia) | showing off, show-off (jactancia) | saucy wit (donaire) || FAM *obrar con chulería* to be cheeky *o* cocksure.

chulesco, ca *adj* FAM cheeky, barefaced (descarado); *gesto chulesco* cheeky manner || flashy (propio del chulo madrileño).

chuleta *f* chop, cutlet (costilla); *chuleta empanada* chop fried in bradcrumbs; *chuleta de cerdo* pork chop || FIG & FAM slap (bofetada) | crib [US trot] (de los estudiantes).

◆ *m* FAM cheeky *o* barefaced individual.

chulo, la *adj* FAM cheeky, barefaced, cocky, impudent, saucy, insolent; *un gesto chulo* an insolent gesture; *si se pone usted chulo le expulsamos* if you get cheeky, we'll throw you out | flashy, natty (vistoso) || from the lower classes of Madrid, lower class Madrid; *la manera de hablar chula de Madrid* the lower class Madrid way of speaking || AMER nice, pretty (bonito) || FAM *ir muy chulo* to swagger along, to show off; *iba muy chulo con su traje nuevo* he was swaggering along with his new suit.

◆ *m* souteneur, pimp (rufián) || typical Madrilenian (equivalent to cockney) || FAM ruffian (de mala vida) | spiv, dandy, beau (petimetre) || TAUR bullfighter's assistant || FAM *chulo de putas* pimp, pander.

chulpa; chullpa *f* AMER stone tomb (tumba).

chullo *m* AMER «chullo», woollen cap.

chuma *f* AMER drunkenness (borrachera).

chumacera *f* TECN bearing || MAR strengthening plate [to receive rowlock].

chumarse *vpr* AMER to get drunk.

chumbe *m* AMER sash.

chumbera *f* BOT prickly pear.

chumbo, ba *adj* *higuera chumba* prickly pear || *higo chumbo* prickly pear.

◆ *m* AMER bullet (bala).

chuminada *f* POP bloody stupid thing.

chunga *f*; **chungueo** *m* FAM joke (broma) || — FAM *estar de chunga* to be in a joking mood | *por chunga* jokingly | *tomar a* or *en chunga* to take as a joke.

chungarse; chunguearse *vpr* FAM to joke (bromear) | to make fun (*de* of) (burlarse).

chungueo *m* —→ **chunga.**

chuño *m* AMER potato starch.

chupa *f* kind of tight-fitting waistcoat (prenda) || AMER drunkenness (borrachera) || FIG *poner a uno como chupa de dómine* to call s.o. all the names under the sun (insultar), to haul s.o. over the coals (reprender).

chupacirios *m/f inv* FAM sanctimonious man (hombre) *o* woman (mujer) (beato).

chupada *f* puff, drag (*fam*) (de cigarro); *dar una chupada al cigarro* to have a puff at the cigarette || suck (de una sustancia) || — *dar chupadas a un cigarro* to puff at a cigarette || *el niño dio una chupada al pirulí* the child sucked the lollipop.

chupado, da *adj* FAM skinny, thin (flaco) | tight; *falda chupada* tight skirt || AMER tight, drunk (borracho) || — FIG & FAM *con la cara chupada* hollow-cheeked | *está chupado* it's as easy as ABC, it's as easy as pie | *mejillas chupadas* hollow cheeks.

chupador, ra *adj* sucking (que chupa) || BOT sucker || ZOOL suctorial.

◆ *m* dummy [US pacifier] (chupete) || teat (de biberón) || BOT sucker root || ZOOL sucker, suctorial organ || AMER drinker (bebedor) smoker (fumador).

chupadura *f* suck, sucking.

chupaflor *m* AMER hummingbird (pájaro).

chupar *vt* to suck; *chupar un limón* to suck a lemon || to absorb, to take in, to suck up; *las raíces chupan la humedad del suelo* the roots absorb the humidity from the ground || to puff

at (cigarro) || to lick (lamer) || to sip (beber) || to suck (un caramelo) || ZOOL to suck || to suck, to feed from (mamar) || to soak up, to absorb (absorber); *el papel secante chupa la tinta* blotting paper soaks up ink || to lick, to moisten (un sello de correo) || FIG & FAM to bleed (dinero); *chuparle a uno el dinero* to bleed s.o. of his money || AMER to smoke (fumar) | to drink (beber) || — FIG *chuparle la sangre a uno* to bleed s.o. white *o* dry | *tanto trabajo le chupa la salud* all that work is undermining his health.
◆ *vi* to suck.
◆ *vpr* to lick (lamerse); *chuparse los dedos* to lick one's fingers || FIG & FAM to go thin, to lose weight (ir enflaqueciendo) | to spend; *chuparse seis meses de prisión* to spend six months in prison || AMER to drink (beber) || — FAM *¡chúpate esa!* put that in your pipe and smoke it || AMER *chuparse un insulto* to swallow an insult.

chupatintas *m/f inv* FAM pen-pusher.

chupe *m* FAM dummy [*US* pacifier] (chupete) || AMER stew (guiso).

chupendo *m* FAM strong suck.

chupeta *f* small tight-fitting waistcoat (chupa) || MAR roundhouse, cabin (en la popa) || AMER dummy [*US* pacifier] (chupete).

chupete *m* dummy [*US* pacifier] (para niños) || teat (de biberón) || AMER lollipop (pirulí).

chupetear *vi* to suck at, to suck away at.

chupeteo *m* sucking, sucking away at.

chupetón *m* strong suck.

chupinazo *m* loud bang; starting signal (fuegos artificiales) || FAM hard kick (en el balón).

chupo; chupón *m* AMER boil.

chupón, ona *adj* sucking (que chupa) || FIG & FAM parasitic, sponging (que vive de otros).
◆ *m/f* sucker (que chupa) || FIG parasite, sponger, leech (que vive de otros).
◆ *m* BOT sucker, shoot (brote) || puff (chupada) || strong suck (chupendo) || plunger (desatrancador neumático) || ZOOL live feather || TECN piston, sucker (de bomba) || lollipop (pirulí) || teat (de biberón) || dummy [*US* pacifier] (chupete) || AMER boil.

chupóptero *m* FAM parasite, sponger, leech.

churra *f* sandgrouse (ortega).

churrasco *m* AMER barbecued steak, «churrasco» (carne asada).

churrasquear *vi* AMER to have a barbecue (comer churrasco) | to barbecue, to roast (hacer un churrasco).

churrasquería *f* AMER steak house.

churre *m* TECN wool grease (de la lana) || FIG & FAM filth, grime, grease (suciedad).

churrear *vi* AMER to have diarrhoea.

churrería *f* «churro» shop, «churrería».

churrero, ra *m/f* «churro» seller.
◆ *f* utensil for shaping «churros».

churrete; churretón *m* mark, streak (en la cara) || AMER FAM poor bloke.

churretoso, sa *adj* dirty, filthy (sucio).

churri *adj* FAM worthless, useless.

churriento, ta *adj* dirty, filthy, grimy.

churrigueresco, ca *adj* ARQ churrigueresque (estilo) || FIG overelaboratore, florid (recargo).

— OBSERV The *churrigueresque* style (from the name of the architect José de Churriguera, 1665-1723) was a feature of Spanish architecture at the end of the 17th and the beginning of the 18th centuries. It is an exuberant baroque style approaching rococo.

churro, rra *adj* coarse (lana) || coarse-wooled (ganado).
◆ *m* cruller, twist of batter deep-fried, «churro» (masa frita) || FAM shoddy piece of work, amateurish job (chapuza) | dead loss, flop; *esta película es un churro* this picture is a flop || — FAM *salirle a uno un churro* to make a complete mess of; *me ha salido un churro* I've made a complete mess of it | *ser un churro* to be a fluke (chiripa); *este gol ha sido un churro* that goal was a fluke; to be useless, to be a dead loss (fracaso).

— OBSERV *Churros,* an extremely popular Spanish sweetmeat, are made from a type of stiff batter squeezed out into sticks or rings and deep-fried. They are sprinkled with sugar and eaten for breakfast or as a snack often accompanied by coffee or drinking chocolate.

churroso, sa *adj* AMER suffering from diarrhoea.

churruscarse *vpr* to burn (el pan, un guiso, etc.).

churrusco *m* piece of burnt toast.

churumbel *m* FAM kid, nipper.

churumbela *f* MÚS sort of hornpipe || AMER «bombilla», tube for drinking mate (bombilla).

chus ni mus (no decir) *loc* not to say a word.

chuscada *f* funny thing; *decir chuscadas* to say funny things.

chuscamente *adv* in a funny way, wittily, funnily.

chusco, ca *adj* funny (gracioso y sorprendente) || AMER mongrel (perro) | pretty (bonito).
◆ *m/f* joker, wit.
◆ *m* MIL ration bread (pan).

chusma *f* gang of galley slaves (de galeotes) || rabble, riffraff (gentuza).

chusmaje *m* AMER FAM rabble, riffraff (gentuza).

chuspa *f* AMER leather bag.

chusquero *m* FAM ranker (en el ejército).

chut *m* shot, kick (puntapié).

chutar *vi* to shoot (fútbol) || — FAM *este asunto va que chuta* things are going very well, things are coming along nicely | *¡y va que chuta!* and that's fine!

chute *m* fix of heroin (drogas).

chuza *f* AMER strike (boliche) | pike (lanza).

chuzo *m* metal-tipped stick (del sereno) || pike (arma) || AMER leather whip (látigo) || FIG *llover a chuzos, caer chuzos de punta* to pour down, to pour, to rain cats and dogs.

D

d *f* d (letra)

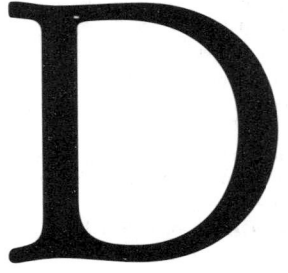

— OBSERV At the beginning of a breath group or when preceded by *l* or *n*, the Spanish *d* is pronounced in approximately the same way as the English *d*. When in a final or intervocalic position, it is similar to the voiced *th* in *the*, and sometimes it is barely pronounced at all, as the final *d* in *Madrid*.

D. *abrev de Don* courtesy title used before Christian name for a man.

D.ª *abrev de Doña* courtesy title used before Christian name for a woman.

daca (contraction of *da acá*) give me; *daca el dinero* give me the money ‖ *a toma y daca* on a give and take basis.

Dacca *n pr* GEOGR Dacca.

dacio, cia *adj/s* Dacian.

dación *f* JUR dation, giving (acción de dar).

dacrioadenitis *f inv* MED dacryoadenitis.

dacriocistitis *f inv* MED dacryocystitis.

dactilar *adj* finger, digital ‖ *huellas dactilares* fingerprints.

dáctilo *m* dactyl (verso).

dactilografía *f* typewriting, typing.

dactilógrafo, fa *m/f* typist.

dactiloscopia *f* fingerprint identification.

dadaísmo *m* dadaism.

dadaísta *adj/s* dadaist.

dádiva *f* donation (donación) ‖ present, gift (regalo).

dadivosidad *f* generosity.

dadivoso, sa *adj* generous.

dado *m* die; *echar los dados* to throw the dice ‖ ARQ dado, die (de un pedestal) ‖ TECN block ‖ — *cargar los dados* to load the dice ‖ FIG & FAM *correr el dado* to be in luck *o* lucky ‖ *echarlo a los dados* to throw (the dice) for it, to decide by throwing the dice.

— OBSERV El plural de *die* es *dice*.

dado, da *adj* given (véase DAR); *en un caso dado* in a given case ‖ addicted, given (inclinado); *dado a la bebida* given to drinking ‖ gone, past; *son las once dadas* it's past eleven o'clock ‖ — *dado* in view of; *dada su timidez* in view of his shyness ‖ *dado que* as, since ‖ FAM *ir dado* to be in for trouble; *¡vas dado con esos obreros!* you're in for trouble with those workmen! ‖ *ser dado a* to be given to, to be fond of; *es muy dado a criticar a sus amigos* he is very fond of criticizing his friends, he is much given to criticizing his friends.

dador, ra *m/f* giver.

◆ *m* bearer (el que entrega una carta) ‖ COM drawer (de una letra de cambio).

Dafne *npr f* Daphne.

Dafnis *npr m* Daphnis.

daga *f* dagger (puñal) ‖ AMER machete.

daguerrotipo *m* daguerreotype (aparato o imagen) ‖ daguerreotypy (arte).

Dahomey *npr m* GEOGR Dahomey.

dahomeyano, na *adj/s* Dahoman.

daifa *f* mistress.

Dakar *n pr* GEOGR Dakar.

dalai lama *m* REL Dalai Lama.

dalia *f* BOT dahlia.

Dalila *npr f* Delilah.

Dalmacia *npr f* GEOGR Dalmatia.

dálmata *adj/s* Dalmatian (de Dalmacia).

◆ *m* Dalmatian (perro).

dalmática *f* dalmatic (vestidura).

daltoniano, na *adj* MED daltonian, colour blind.

◆ *m/f* MED person who suffers from colour blindness, daltonian.

daltonismo *m* MED colour blindness [*US* color blindness], daltonism.

dalla *f*; **dalle** *m* scythe (guadaña).

dallar *vt* to scythe.

dama *f* lady (señora) ‖ lady-in-waiting (de cámara) ‖ (p us) mistress (manceba) ‖ king (del juego de damas); *hacer dama* to make a king ‖ queen [in chess] ‖ MAR rowlock, oarlock ‖ — *dama cortesana* courtesan (mujer liviana) ‖ *dama de honor* lady-in-waiting (de una reina), bridesmaid (en una boda) ‖ TEATR *dama joven* ingénue | *primera, segunda dama* leading lady, supporting role ‖ *ser una dama* to be a lady.

◆ *pl* draughts [*US* checkers] (juego) ‖ *¡damas y caballeros!* Ladies and Gentlemen! ‖ *tablero de damas* draughtboard [*US* checkerboard].

damaceno, na *adj* → **damasceno.**

damajuana *f* demijohn.

damán *m* ZOOL marmot (marmota).

damasana *f* AMER demijohn (damajuana).

damascado, da *adj* damasked, damask.

damasceno, na *adj/s* Damascene (de Damasco) ‖ *ciruela damascena* damson.

damasco *m* damask (tela).

Damasco *npr m* GEOGR Damascus ‖ REL *camino de Damasco* road to Damascus.

damasquillo *m* light fabric resembling damask ‖ apricot (albaricoque).

damasquina *f* BOT French marigold.

damasquinado *m* damascene [work].

damasquinar *vt* to damascene, to damask.

damasquino, na *adj* Damascene (de Damasco) ‖ damask (tela) ‖ *sable damasquino* Damascus blade.

damisela *f* young miss, young lady, damsel (irónico) ‖ courtesan (cortesana).

damnificado, da *adj* injured, harmed (persona) ‖ damaged (cosa).

◆ *m/f* victim; *los damnificados por la inundación* the victims of the flood.

damnificar *vt* to harm, to injure (persona) ‖ to damage (cosa).

Damocles *npr m* Damocles; *espada de Damocles* Damocles' sword.

Danaides *npr f* MIT Danaids.

dáncing *m* dance hall, ballroom.

dandi; dandy *m* dandy.

dandismo; dandysmo *m* dandysm.

danés, esa *adj* Danish.

◆ *m/f* Danishman (hombre), Danishwoman (mujer), Dane (hombre o mujer).

◆ *m* Great Dane (perro) ‖ Danish (idioma).

danta *f* ZOOL elk (anta) | tapir (tapir).

dante *adj* giving (que da).

◆ *m/f* giver (el que da).

dantellado, da *adj* HERÁLD dentelated.

dantesco, ca *adj* Dantesque, Dantean.

Danubio *npr m* GEOGR Danube.

danza *f* dance; *una danza ritual* a ritual dance ‖ FAM (shady) deal (negocio sucio); *¿por qué te metiste en tal danza?* why did you get mixed up in such a deal? | mess (lío) | deal; *¿cómo va la danza?* how's the deal getting on? | row (riña) ‖ — *danza de espadas* sword dance ‖ *danza de la muerte, danza macabra* dance of death, danse macabre.

danzante *adj* dancing; *procesión danzante* dancing procession.

◆ *m/f* dancer (en una procesión) ‖ FIG & FAM featherbrain (casquivano) | meddler, busybody (entrometido).

danzar *vt* to dance (bailar) ‖ FAM to poke *o* to stick one's nose (*en* into) (intervenir); *¿qué danza usted en este asunto?* what are you doing sticking your nose into this affair?

◆ *vi* to dance (bailar) ‖ FIG to wander, to roam; *va danzando por las bibliotecas* he wanders from library to library | to lie around; *no me gusta que mis libros estén danzando por ahí* I don't like to see my books lying around here | to shuttle; *ahora la tienen danzando de un servicio a otro* they keep shuttling her from one department to another.

danzarín, ina *m/f* dancer.

danzón *m* Cuban dance derived from the «habanera».

dañado, da *adj* spoiled (que empieza a pudrirse) ‖ damaged (fruta) ‖ damaged; *ciudades dañadas por la guerra* towns damaged by the war ‖ evil, wicked (malo); *hombre muy dañado* very wicked man.

dañar *vt* to damage, to spoil, to harm; *el granizo ha dañado las cosechas* hail has spoiled the harvest ‖ to injure, to harm, to hurt (a una persona) ‖ to damage (fruta) ‖ FIG to harm, to damage, to stain, to mar; *eso dañará su reputación* that will stain his reputation; *dañarle a uno en su honra* to mar s.o.'s good name | to condemn (condenar).

◆ *vpr* to spoil, to get damaged (estropearse) ‖ to go bad (fruta, comestibles).

dañino, na *adj* harmful, destructive ‖ *animales dañinos* pests, vermin *sing*.

daño *m* wrong, injury, harm; *reparar el daño que se ha hecho* to redress the wrong *o* harm that has been done, to redress the injury that has been caused ‖ damage; *el daño causado* or *los daños causados por el granizo* the damage caused by hail ‖ MED trouble (mal) ‖ — *daños materiales* material damage ‖ JUR *daños y perjuicios* damages ‖ *hacer daño* to hurt (doler); *me* *hace daño el pie* my foot hurts; to harm; *hará daño al país* it will harm the country; to be bad for; *el chocolate te hace daño* chocolate is bad for you || *hacerse daño* to hurt o.s.

— OBSERV La palabra *damage* se utiliza siempre en singular salvo en el sentido jurídico de *daños y perjuicios.*

dañoso, sa *adj* harmful (*para* to), injurious (*para* to).

dar* *vt* to give; *dar una propina, noticias, un consejo, batalla* to give a tip, some news, a piece of advice, battle || to deal (naipes) || to give; *dar una bofetada, un puntapié* to give a slap, a kick || to hit (pegar); *darle a uno en la cabeza* to hit s.o. on the head || to give (proporcionar); *dar trabajo a uno* to give s.o. work || to strike; *el reloj da las dos, la media* the clock strikes two, the half-hour || to produce, to bear, to yield (fruta) || to produce; *el rosal da rosas* the rosebush produces roses || to give, to cause, to produce (sentimiento) || to give; *la vaca da leche* the cow gives milk || to show (en el cine); *hoy dan una película de miedo* they are showing a horror film today || to put on, to perform (en el teatro) || to play (obra de música) || to give (grito, suspiro) || to say; *dar los buenos días, las buenas tardes* to say hello, good afternoon || to set (ejemplo) || to go for; *dar un paseo en coche* to go for a ride in a car || to take (paseo, paso) || to give, to hand, to pass; *¿me puede dar el pan, por favor?* could you pass me the bread, please? || to bear, to give; *su mujer le dio dos hijos* his wife bore him two children || to give off (desprender); *dar un olor* to give off a smell || to give, to grant (permiso, etc.) || to show (mostrar); *dar señales de* to show signs of || to yield, to bear (interés) || — FAM *ahí me las den todas* that's the least of my worries, I couldn't care less || *al dar las diez* on the stroke of ten || *da gusto* or *da gloria verlo* it is a joy to behold, it is a delight to see || *¡dale!* hit him! (pégalo), go on! (¡anda!), not again! (¡otra vez!) || *dale que dale, dale que te pego* not again! (¡otra vez!), on and on; *y siguió dale que te pego hablando de su familia* and he kept on and on talking about his family; *está todo el día dale que dale al piano* he goes on and on all day playing the piano || *da lo mismo, lo mismo da* it doesn't matter, it's all the same, it makes no difference || *dar algo por* to give anything for; *yo daría algo por tenerlo* I would give anything to have it || *dar a luz* to give birth to || *dar celos a uno* to make s.o. jealous || *dar clase* to teach (el profesor), to lecture (en la universidad) || *dar clase a alguien* to teach s.o., to give a lesson *o* lessons to s.o. (en general), to lecture s.o., to give lectures to s.o. (en la universidad) || *dar como* to consider; *dar como falso* to consider (to be) false || FIG *dar cuerda a algo* to prolong sth. | *dar cuerda a uno* to encourage s.o. (to speak), to start s.o. off [speaking] | *dar cuerda a un reloj* to wind (up) a clock || *dar de comer a* to feed (animales, personas hambrientas), to feed, to give a meal to (convidados) || *dar de lado* to discard (una cosa), to cold-shoulder, to desert (a una persona) || *dar gusto* to be nice *o* good *o* a joy; *da gusto ver cómo se divierten los niños* it is nice to see the children enjoying themselves || *dar la mano a alguien* to shake hands with s.o. || *dar las gracias por* to say thank you for *o* to thank for || *darle a uno calentura, un ataque* to have a temperature, an attack || *darle a uno un dolor en* to feel a pain in || FAM *darle el día a uno* not to give s.o. a minute's peace all day | *darle la noche a uno* not to give s.o. a minute's peace all night, not to let s.o. get a wink of sleep all night; *el niño me ha dado la noche* the child didn't give me a minute's peace all night, the child didn't let me get a wink of sleep all night || *dar muerte a* to kill || *dar por* to assume; *le dan por muerto* he is assumed dead; to consider (considerar); *dar por hecha* or *concluida una cosa* to consider sth. finished || *dar por perdida una cosa* to give sth. up as lost || *dar prestado* to lend || *dar que hablar* or *que decir* to give people sth. to talk about, to set tongues wagging; *están dando que hablar con sus reuniones* they are giving people sth. to talk about with their meetings || *dar que hacer* to make a lot of work for; *los niños te darán que hacer* the children will make a lot of work for you || *dar que pensar, dar en que pensar* to set thinking; *sus palabras me dieron que pensar* what he said set me thinking; to give food for thought; *lo que voy a decir les dará a todos que pensar* what I'm about to say will give you all food for thought || *dar recuerdos* to give regards *o* love; *da recuerdos a tu madre de mi parte* give my regards to your mother || *dar saltos* to jump up and down || FIG *dársela a alguien* to sake s.o. in, to fool s.o. || *dar testimonio de* to testify to, to bear witness to || *dar voces* to shout || FAM *donde las dan las toman* tit for tat || *me da no sé qué* it upsets me, it troubles me; *me da no sé qué ver al pobre mendigo* it upsets me to see the poor beggar; I don't like, I feel awkward; *me da no sé qué pedirle un favor* I don't like to ask a favour to him, I feel awkward about asking him a favour || *¿qué más da?* what does it matter?, what difference does it make?

◆ *vi* to hit; *dar a la pelota con un palo* to hit the ball with a stick; *le dio una bala perdida* he was hit by a stray bullet, a stray bullet hit him || to strike; *dan las tres* it is striking three || to press; *dar al botón* to press the button || to turn; *dar a la manilla* to turn the doorhandle || to start; *dar a la máquina* to start the machine || to shine; *el sol me daba en la cara* the sun was shining in my face || to blow; *el viento me daba en la cara* the wind was blowing in my face || to be in; *el sol y el viento me daban en la cara* the sun and wind were in my face || FIG *ahora le ha dado por ahí* that's his latest craze || *da igual* it doesn't matter, it's all the same, it makes no difference; *me da igual* it's all the same to me, it makes no difference to me || *dar a* to look (out) onto, to overlook; *la ventana da al patio* the window looks onto *o* overlooks the yard; to face; *la casa da al norte* the houses faces north || *dar a la luz* to put *o* to turn *o* to switch the light on || *dar con* to come across (una cosa), to find; *no conseguí dar con él en todo el día* I couldn't find him all day; to find, to hit on; *dar con la solución* to find the solution; to meet (encontrar a uno), to bump into, to run into (tropezar); *al salir di con él* I bumped into him as I went out; to knock with (llamar); *dar con la aldaba* to knock with the doorknocker; to bang, to bump, to hit; *dar con la cabeza contra la pared* to bang one's head against the wall || *dar con algo en el suelo* to drop sth. || *dar consigo en el suelo* to fall on the floor (dentro), to fall on the ground (fuera) || *dar consigo en una ciudad* to end up in a city (ir a parar) || FAM *dar con sus huesos* to end up; *dio con sus huesos en la cárcel* he ended up in prison || *dar de* to fall flat on; *dar de espaldas* to fall flat on one's back || *dar de barniz* or *de betún a* to varnish, to polish || *dar de cuchilladas, de patadas, de puñetazos a uno* to stab s.o., to kick s.o., to punch s.o. || *dar de sí* to stretch, to give (estirarse), to go a long way (el dinero, la comida, etc.) || *dar en* to get, to understand, to grasp; *dar en el chiste* to get the joke; to find, to hit on; *dar en la solución* to find the answer; to persist in; *ha dado en decir que no hay que ir* he persists in saying we shouldn't go; to hit, to strike; *dar en el blanco* to hit the target || *dar en creer que...* to get into one's head that... || *darle a algo* to work at sth. (trabajar); *darle fuerte a las matemáticas* to work hard at mathematics || *dar para* to be enough for (ser suficiente) || *dar para más* to get more from; *este negocio no da para más* you won't get any more from this business || *dar por* to take to; *a Juan le ha dado por el vino, por viajar* John has taken to drinking, to travelling; to (suddenly) decide; *de vez en cuando le da por no estudiar* every so often he decides that he won't do any work || *dar por tierra con algo* to floor, to ruin (proyectos, etc.), to refute, to prove wrong, to put an end to (teoría) || *este día no me ha dado de sí* I haven't been able to do *o* to get through all I wanted to today || *le dio un ataque* he had a fit || *le dio un resfriado, una pulmonía* he caught *o* got a cold, he caught *o* got pneumonia || *me va a dar algo* I'm going to go out of my mind, I'm going to have a fit || *tener para dar y tomar* to have (sth.) to spare; *tiene orgullo para dar y tomar* he has pride to spare.

◆ *vpr* to surrender, to give o.s. up, to give in (entregarse) || to give oneself over *o* up, to take to; *darse a la bebida* to give o.s. over to drink, to take to drinking || to devote o.s. to; *se da toda a sus hijos* she devotes herself entirely to her children || to bump; *darse con* or *contra un árbol* to bump into a tree || to matter; *¿y a mí qué se me da de todo esto?* what does all that matter to me? || AGR to grow (crecer); *se da bien el tabaco en esta provincia* tobacco grows well in this province || to be found, to grow (cultivarse); *el tabaco no se da aquí* tobacco is not found here, tobacco doesn't grow here || — *darse a* to make o.s., to become; *darse a conocer* to make o.s. known, to become known || *dársele bien, mal algo a uno* to be good, bad at; *la natación se me da muy bien* I am very good at swimming; *el latín se me da mejor que las matemáticas* I am better at Latin than at mathematics; to turn out well, bad; *se le ha dado muy bien la conferencia* his lecture turned out very well; to have a knack for, not to have the knack of; *se le da bien coser* she has a knack for sewing || *darse con la cabeza contra* to bang *o* to knock *o* to hit one's head against || FIG *dárselas de* to make (o.s.) out to be; *dárselas de valiente* to make o.s. out to be brave; to fancy o.s. as; *se las daba de duquesa* she fancied herself as a duchess || *darse por* to consider o.s.; *darse por contento* to consider o.s. lucky || FIG *darse por aludido* to take the hint (cuando es una indirecta), to feel as though one is being got at (*fam*), to take it personally | *no darse por aludido* to turn a deaf ear || *darse por ofendido* to take offence || *que darse pueda* that could be, imaginable; *es la persona más estúpida que darse pueda* he is the most stupid person that could be, he is the most stupid person imaginable || *si se diese el caso de que...* should it happen that...

Dardanelos *npr mpl* GEOGR Dardanelles.

dardo *m* spear (arma arrojadiza) || dart, arrow (flecha) || FIG dig, cutting remark (dicho satírico) || ZOOL sting (aguijón) | bleak, dace (pez).

dares y tomares *loc* FAM give and take || *andar en dares y tomares* to bicker, to quarrel.

Darío *npr m* Darius.

dársena *f* MAR dock, basin.

darvinismo *m* Darwinism.

darvinista *adj/s* Darwinist.

data *f* (p us) date (fecha) || COM item || regulated outlet (orificio).

datar *vt* to date, to put a date on (fechar) || COM to credit, to enter.

◆ *vi* to date; *este castillo data del siglo XV* this castle dates from the 15th century *o* dates back to the 15th century.

dátil *m* date (fruto) || date mussel, date shell (molusco).

◆ *pl* FAM fingers (dedos).

datilera *adj f* date; *palmera datilera* date palm.

◆ *f* date palm.

dativo, va *adj* GRAM dative || JUR dative; *tutor dativo* tutor dative.
◆ *m* GRAM dative; *en dativo* in the dative.

dato *m* fact, piece of information, datum (información).
◆ *pl* data, facts, information *sing; por falta de datos* through lack of data || INFORM data; *datos de entrada* entry data; *datos de salida* exit data || MAT information *sing,* data (de un problema) || — *datos estadísticos* statistic data || *datos personales* personal details *o* data || INFORM *llamar datos* to call data || *procesamiento* or *proceso de datos* data processing.

daza *f* BOT sorghum.

Dcha. *abrev de derecha* r/R, Right.

DDT *abrev de diclorodifeniltricloretano* DDt, dichlorodiphenyltrichloroethane (insecticida).

de *f* d (letra).

de *prep*

1. POSESIÓN Y PERTENENCIA **2.** ORIGEN, PROCEDENCIA **3.** COMPOSICIÓN **4.** CONTENIDO **5.** INTRODUCE EL AGENTE **6.** APOSICIÓN **7.** USO **8.** SUPOSICIÓN **9.** CAUSA **10.** INTRODUCE UN ADVERBIO DE LUGAR **11.** PRECIO, MEDIDA **12.** CON EL VERBO «SER» SEGUIDO POR UN NÚMERO **13.** CARACTERÍSTICA **14.** DESCRIPCIÓN **15.** INTRODUCE ORACIONES SUSTANTIVADAS **16.** MODO **17.** TIEMPO **18.** LOCUCIONES DIVERSAS.

1. POSESIÓN Y PERTENENCIA of; *el lomo del libro* the spine of the book || 's (genitivo sajón); *el lápiz de Juan* John's pencil; *los lápices de los alumnos* the pupil's pencils; *la casa es de Pablo* the house is Paul's || in; *los muebles del cuarto* the furniture in the room; *comprar acciones de una compañía* to buy shares in a company; *una subida de precios* a rise in prices.
2. ORIGEN, PROCEDENCIA from; *soy de Barcelona* I'm from *o* I come from Barcelona; *ir de Madrid a Londres* to go from Madrid to London || from; *este tren viene de Madrid* this train comes from Madrid; *el avión procedente de Londres* the plane arriving from London || of; *cinco de los nuestros* five of our men || of; *los descendientes de los Incas* the descendants of the Incas; *su carta de hace dos años* his letter of two years ago || from; *lo conozco de cuando estuvo aquí* I know him from when he was here; *de esto se deduce que...* from this one can deduce that... || as; *la conocí de pequeña* I knew her as a child || by; *tiene una hija de su primera mujer* or *de su primer matrimonio* he has a daughter by his first wife *o* by his first marriage.
3. COMPOSICIÓN (sin traducción); *una camisa de seda* a silk shirt; *una mesa de madera* a wooden table || in, made of (sin traducción o con el verbo «to be»); *esta mesa es de nogal* this table is walnut *o* made of walnut *o* in walnut || in (con los demás verbos); *lo compré de madera* I bought it in wood; *lo hicieron de cristal* they made it in glass.
4. CONTENIDO of; *una caja de naranjas* a box of oranges; *un vaso de vino* a glass of wine.
5. INTRODUCE EL AGENTE by; *acompañado de dos mujeres* accompanied by two women; *respetado de todos* respected by all; *un libro de Cervantes* a book by Cervantes.
6. APOSICIÓN of; *el mes de junio* the month of June; *la ciudad de Madrid* the city of Madrid || (sin traducción); *pobrecillo de mi hermano* my poor little brother; *¡pobre de mí!* poor old me!, woe is me! || for; *¿qué hay de postre?* what is there for dessert? || *la ciudad de Méjico* Mexico City.
7. USO (sin traducción); *máquina de coser* sewing machine; *salida de emergencia* emergency exit; *hoja de afeitar* razor blade.
8. SUPOSICIÓN if; *de haberlo sabido antes, no hubiera venido* if I had known earlier, I shoudn't have come.
9. CAUSA because; *lo sé de haberlo oído antes* I know because I have already heard it || because of; *del dolor que tenía no pude dormir* I couldn't sleep because of the pain || so; *de tanto frío como hacía, no pude salir* it was so cold that I couldn't go out || with; *llorar de alegría* to cry with joy || of; *morir de hambre, de miedo, de frío* to die of hunger, of fright, of cold || *no vino de la vergüenza que tenía* he was so ashamed that he did not come, he did not come out of shame, he was too ashamed to come.
10. INTRODUCE UN ADVERBIO DE LUGAR (sin traducción); *la casa de al lado del río* the house by the river; *el piso de arriba* the flat above; *los vecinos de al lado* the next-door neighbours.
11. PRECIO, MEDIDA (sin traducción); *un libro de a diez pesetas* a ten-peseta book; *manzanas de a dos pesetas el kilo* apples at two pesetas a kilo; *una moneda de (a) cinco pesetas* a five-peseta piece; *una botella de (a) litro* a litre bottle || *una carretera de veinte kilómetros* a road twenty kilometres long.
12. CON EL VERBO «SER» SEGUIDO POR UN NÚMERO (sin traducción); *la velocidad máxima del coche es de 120 kilómetros por hora* the maximum speed of the car is 120 kilometres an hour; *el número de lectores es de cinco millones* the number of electors is *o* totals five million.
13. CARACTERÍSTICA with; *la señora de las gafas* the lady with the glasses; *un hombre de tez morena* a man with a dark complexion || (sin traducción); *avión de reacción* jet plane; *nuestra profesora de búlgaro* our Bulgarian teacher; *barco de vapor* steamship || of; *una playa de arena fina* a beach of fine sand.
14. DESCRIPCIÓN in; *ciego de un ojo* blind in one eye; *mejor de salud* better in health; *cinco kilómetros de largo* five kilometres in length || by; *es médico de profesión* he's a doctor by profession || — *con cara de español* with a Spanish-looking face || *de piernas largas* long in the leg, long-legged || *de baja estatura* short || *era pequeño de cuerpo* he had a small body.
15. INTRODUCE ORACIONES SUSTANTIVADAS that (o *sin traducción*); *estoy seguro de que vendrá* I am sure (that) he will come; *es una prueba de que estaba* it is proof (that) he was here; *yo tenía miedo de que muriera* I was afraid (that) he would die.
16. MODO in; *de paisano* in civilian clothes; *vestido de blanco* dressed in white; *el oficial iba de gala* the officer was in dress uniform; *de luto* in mourning || in; *hacer algo de mala manera* to do sth. in a bad way; *de moda* in fashion; *de buen humor* in a good mood || (sin traducción); *ir de falda corta* to wear a short skirt || as; *me lo dieron de regalo* they gave it to me as a present || in; *de un trago* in one gulp || as; *trabajar de camarero* to work as a waiter || with; *de un golpe, de un salto* with one blow, with one bound || in, with; *cubierto de nieve* covered in snow.
17. TIEMPO in; *a las dos de la tarde, de la mañana* at two o'clock in the afternoon, in the morning || at; *a las diez de la noche* at ten o'clock at night.
18. LOCUCIONES DIVERSAS *coger a uno de la mano* to take s.o. by the hand, to take hold of s.o.'s hand, to hold s.o.'s hand || *compañero de clase* classmate || *de a caballo* mounted, on horseback; *tropas de a caballo* mounted troops, troops on horseback || *de a pie* foot; *soldados de a pie* foot soldiers || *de cabeza* headfirst; *tirarse de cabeza* to dive headfirst || *de cara a* facing; *estar de cara al sol* to be facing the sun || *de casa en casa* from house to house, from one house to the next || *de día, de noche* by day, in the daytime; by night, at night || *de dos en dos* two by two, in twos || *de él, de ella, de ellos, de ellas* his (persona), its (cosa), its (suyo); *el coche de él* his car; *este coche es de él* this car is his || *de hecho* in fact (en realidad) || *de madrugada* early in the morning (temprano), in the small hours (hasta las cuatro) || *de mal en peor* from bad to worse || *de no ser así* if it were not so, were it not so || *de puro cansancio* out of sheer tiredness || *de que, de quien* about which, about whom; *la mujer de quien te hablé* the woman about whom I spoke to you || *de usted a mí* between you and me || *de verdad, de veras* really, truly || *de vez en cuando* from time to time, occasionally || *el camino de Londres* the road to London, the London road || *el mejor del mundo* the best in the world || *el tiempo de siempre* the usual weather, the same old weather || *es de los que lucharon en la segunda guerra mundial* he is one of those who fought in the Second World War || *está de paseo* he has gone for a walk, he is taking a walk || *estar de* to work as; *está de conserje en el casino* he is working as a doorman in the casino || *fácil de hacer, de decir* easy to do, to say || *hablar de* to talk about || *hacer de* to act as; *yo hice de cobaya* I acted as guinea pig; to play, to take the part of; *ese actor hace de Otelo* that actor plays Othello || *hombre de treinta años (de edad)* man thirty years of age, man thirty years old, thirty-year-old man, man of thirty || *hora de comer* lunchtime || *más de* more than || *muy de las mujeres, de los niños* typical of women, of children || *pidió del pastel que estaba en la mesa* he asked for some of the cake which was on the table || *ser de día* to be light, to be daylight || *ser de noche* to be dark || *silencio de muerte* deathly silence || *un libro de geografía* a geography book || *uno de cada tres* on out of (every) three, one in three || *vamos a casa de Fernando* we are going to Fernando's.

— OBSERV In Spain, after her marriage, a woman keeps her maiden name and adds her husband's name, preceded by *de,* e. g. *Doña María López de Velasco.* In English she would be called Mrs. María Velasco, her maiden name being López. In conversation, the form *Señora de Velasco* Mrs. Velasco, is often used. *Señores de Velasco* is translated by Mr. and Mrs. Velasco.

— OBSERV The *de* and *del* in names such as *Miranda de Ebro* and *Francfort del Meno* are equivalent to the English use of *on* and *upon* (Upton-upon-Severn).

— OBSERV La mayor parte de los nombres geográficos compuestos como *Francfort del Meno* se suelen dejar en inglés en su ortografía original: *Frankfurt am Main.*

dé *pres del subj* → **dar.**

deambular *vi* to stroll, to saunter (andar, pasear).

deambulatorio *m* ARQ ambulatory.

deán *m* dean.

deanato; deanazgo *m* deanery.

debacle *f* disaster.
— OBSERV The word *debacle* is a Gallicism.

debajo *adv* underneath; *estar debajo* to be underneath || — *debajo de* under, underneath, beneath, below; *debajo de la mesa* under the table || *el, la de debajo* the one underneath, the one below; *mi libro es el de debajo* my book is the one underneath *o* below || *por debajo* underneath; *¡pasa por debajo!* go underneath || *por debajo de* below; *la producción anual está por debajo de lo normal* the annual production is below normal; *el equipo estuvo por debajo de sus posibilidades* the team was below form; under, underneath, beneath, below; *el avión pasó por debajo del puente* the plane flew under the bridge.

— OBSERV *Debajo de* expresses the concrete meanings of *under, beneath, etc.,* whilst *bajo* is usually reserved for the more abstract cases: *bajo la República* under the Republic.

debate *m* debate, discussion.

debatir *vt* to debate, to discuss || *hoy se debatió el proyecto de ley de reforma de la enseñanza* today there was a debate on the education reform bill.

debe *m* COM debit side; *una partida del debe* an entry on the debit side | debit; *el debe y el haber* the debit and credit.

debelar *vt* (p us) MIL to defeat (vencer).
— OBSERV This word is used mostly in Latin America.

deber *m* duty; *yo he cumplido con mi deber* I've carried out *o* done my duty || obligation (obligación) || — *creo mi deber permanecer aquí* I feel it (is) my duty to stay here || *cumplir (con) los deberes militares* to do one's National Service || *es mi deber decírselo* it is my duty to tell you.
◆ *pl* homework *sing.*

deber *vt/vi* to owe; *te debo cincuenta pesetas* I owe you fifty pesetas; *le debo carta* I owe him a letter; *¿a qué debo tan grata visita?* to what do I owe the pleasure of your visit? || must, to have to, to have got to (obligación presente y futura); *debo marcharme a las seis* I must go at six, I have to go at six, I have got to go at six; *debes hacerlo ahora* you must do it now || should, ought to (obligación pasada); *debía haberlo hecho ayer* you should have done it yesterday, you ought to have done it yesterday || must, should, ought to (obligación moral); *no debes fumar tanto* you shouldn't smoke so much || — FAM *deber a medio mundo* to owe money right and left || *deber de* must (probabilidad); *debe de ser rico* he must be rich; *no lo encuentro aquí, debe de estar en mi casa* I can't find it here, it must be at home; should; *el tren debe de llegar de un momento a otro* the train should arrive any time now; can, must (en frase negativa); *no debe estar porque no veo su coche* he can't be there because I can't see his car || *debería haber ido, debía haber ido, hubiera debido ir* I ought to have gone, I should have gone || *debería ir, debía ir* I ought to go, I should go || *debía ir* I was to go, I was meant to go (pensaba ir) || *debo de haberlo visto, he debido haberlo visto, he debido verlo* I must have seen it || FAM *quien debe y paga no debe nada* out of debt, out of danger || *ser debido a* to be due to; *el accidente fue debido al mal tiempo* the accident was due to the bad weather.
◆ *vt* to have a duty towards; *deberse a la patria* to have a duty towards one's country || to be due to; *esto se debe a su ignorancia* it is due to his ignorance || — *¿a qué se debe esto?* what's the reason for this?, why is this so? || *reclamar lo que se le debe a uno* to claim one's due from s.o.

debidamente *adv* properly; *portarse debidamente* to behave properly || duly (en debida forma).

debido, da *adj* due; *la suma debida* the sum due; *con el debido respeto* with due respect || proper, fitting; *comportamiento debido* proper behaviour || right; *pagar a su debido precio* to pay the right price for || — *a su debido tiempo* in due course, in due time || *como es debido* properly, as is proper; *habla como es debido* speak properly; good, proper, real; *vamos a hacer una fiesta como es debido* let's have a real party || *debido a* due to, because of, through; *debido a la lluvia no pude salir* due to the rain I couldn't go out || *debido a que* because; *no ha salido bien debido a que cuando lo hicimos ya era de noche* it didn't work because it was already dark when we did it || *en debida forma* in due form || *más de lo debido* too much.

débil *adj* weak; *está un poco débil todavía* he is still a little weak || feeble, weak; *un niño débil* a weak child; *una luz débil* a feeble light || weak (sin voluntad); *es muy débil con sus alumnos* he is very weak with his pupils || faint; *ruido débil* faint noise || weak (corriente eléctrica) || halfhearted, feeble, weak; *débil esfuerzo* halfhearted effort || weak (en fonética).
◆ *m/f* weak person || — *débil mental* mentally retarded *o* mentally deficient person || *los débiles* the weak.

debilidad *f* weakness, feebleness, debility; *la debilidad de un convaleciente* a convalescent's weakness || faintness (de un sonido) || weakness (de una corriente eléctrica) || FIG weakness; *la música de jazz es su debilidad* jazz is his weakness | soft spot, weakness; *tengo debilidad por mi hijo menor* I have a soft spot for my younger son || — *caerse de debilidad* to be dropping on one's feet, to be faint with weakness || MED *debilidad mental* mental deficiency.

debilitación *f*; **debilitamiento** *m* weakening, debilitation || weakening (en fonética) || falling (de las cotizaciones en la Bolsa).

debilitante *adj* weakening, debilitating (que debilita).

debilitar *vt* to weaken; *la enfermedad le ha debilitado* the illness has weakened him || MED to debilitate || to weaken (en fonética).
◆ *vpr* to weaken, to get *o* to become weak; *me he debilitado mucho con la enfermedad* I have become very weak from the illness || FIG to weaken; *su voluntad se ha debilitado* his willpower has weakened.

debilucho, cha *adj* weakly, delicate, frail (enclenque) || weak, feeble (excesivamente débil).
◆ *m/f* weakling.

debitar *vt* AMER to debit (cargar en cuenta).

débito *m* debit (debe) || debt (deuda).

debut *m* début (primera actuación).
— OBSERV This word, like *debutante* and *debutar*, is a Gallicism.

debutante *m/f* beginner, newcomer (principiante) || *el debutante Rafael Vargas tuvo una actuación lucida* Rafael Vargas, making his début *o* his first appearance, performed brilliantly.
◆ *f* débutante (en una fiesta de sociedad).

debutar *vi* to make one's début, to make one's first appearance.

década *f* decade (diez años) || period of ten days (diez días).

decadencia *f* decadence, decline, decay; *decadencia moral* moral decadence || — *caer en desgracia* to fall into decline *o* decay || *la decadencia del Imperio Romano* the decline of the Roman Empire.

decadente *adj* decadent.
◆ *m/f* decadent.
◆ *m pl* decadents (escritores y artistas de la escuela simbolista).

decaedro *m* MAT decahedron.

decaer*; **descaecer*** *vi* to declive (venir a menos) || COM to fall off, to decline, to dwindle; *el negocio decae* business is falling off || to fall off, to flag; *el interés no decayó* interest didn't flag || to weaken, to flag (fuerzas) || to drop; *el viento decae* the wind is dropping || to decay (costumbres) || to go down (fiebre) || to go down, to lose, to deteriorate; *ha decaído mucho, ya no es el hombre que era* he has gone down a lot, he is no longer the man he was || to become low-spirited; *antes era muy divertido, pero ha decaído mucho* he was very funny before, but now he has become very low-spirited || MAR to drift off course (separarse de su rumbo) || — *ha decaído en belleza, en inteligencia* she has lost her good looks, her intelligence || *su ánimo no decae a pesar de tantas dificultades* he doesn't lose heart in spite of so many difficulties.

decagonal *adj* decagonal.

decágono *m* decagon.

decagramo *m* decagram, decagramme.

decaído, da *adj* weak (débil) || depressed, discouraged, downhearted, crestfallen (sin ánimos) || COM slack (Bolsa, mercado).

decaimiento; **descaecimiento**; **descaimiento** *m* weakness, weakening (físico) || COM falling-off || decline, decay (decadencia) || dejection, low spirits *pl* (desaliento).

decalcificación *f* MED decalcification.

decalcificar *vtr* MED to decalcify.

decalitro *m* decalitre [*US* decaliter].

decálogo *m* decalogue [*US* decalog].

decámetro *m* decametre [*US* decameter].

decampar *vi* MIL to strike *o* to break camp, to decamp.

decanato *m* deanery, deanship (cargo) || deanery (despacho).

decano, na *m/f* dean (de universidad, etc.) || doyen, senior member (miembro más antiguo).

decantación *f* decantation, decanting || *depósito de decantación* sedimentation basin.

decantador *m* decanter.

decantar *vt* to decant, to pour off (un líquido) || to praise, to laud; *decantar las proezas de un héroe* to praise the prowess of a hero.

decapado *m* TECN scaling (de los metales).

decapante *adj* TECN scaling || *producto decapante* scaler.
◆ *m* TECN scaler (para los metales) | remover (para la pintura).

decapar *vt* to scale, to descale (desoxidar) || to remove (the paint) from, to strip (quitar la pintura).

decapitación *f* beheading, decapitation.

decapitar *vt* to behead, to decapitate.

decápodo *m* ZOOL decapod.

decasílabo, ba *adj/sm* decasyllabic, decasyllable.

decatlón *m* DEP decathlon.

deceleración *f* deceleration.

decelerar *vi* to decelerate.

decena *f* ten; *¿cuántas decenas tiene la centena?* how many tens are there in a hundred? || ten or so, about ten; *una decena de personas* ten or so people || — *decenas de miles* tens of thousands || *hace una decena de años* some ten years ago, about ten years ago || *por decenas* in tens.

decenal *adj* decennial || *período decenal* period of ten years.

decenario *m* decennary (diez años) || decade (de rosario).

decencia *f* honesty (honradez) || decency; *la decencia de un bañador, de una mujer* the decency of a bathing costume, of a woman || *con decencia* decently.

decenio *m* decade (diez años).

deceno, na *adj* tenth (décimo).

decentar* *vt* to start, to break into (empezar).
◆ *vpr* to become sore (la piel).

decente *adj* honest, honourable, upright (honrado) || decent; *un nivel de vida decente* a decent standard of living || decent, modest, seemly, proper; *un bañador decente* a decent bathing costume || decent, respectable, modest; *una mujer decente* a decent woman || decent, good; *este abrigo está todavía decente* this coat is still decent || clean, tidy (limpio).

decenvir; **decenviro** *m* decemvir (magistrado).

decepción *f* disappointment, disenchantment; *en su vida se llevó grandes decepciones* he suffered great disappointments in his life.

decepcionante *adj* disappointing.

decepcionar *vt* to disappoint; *el resultado me ha decepcionado* the result has disappointed me.

deceso *m* decease (muerte).

decibel; decibelio *m* FÍS decibel.

decible; decidero, ra *adj* which can be said, utterable, mentionable || *no es decible lo que me aburrí* there are no words to express how bored I was, I can't express how bored I was.

decididamente *adv* determinedly, resolutely, with determination; *lanzarse decididamente* to go at it with determination || definitely (realmente).

decidido, da *adj* determined, resolute; *adversario decidido* determined opponent; *entró con paso decidido* he went in with determined steps || — *apoyo decidido* solid support || *está decidido a hacerlo* he is determined *o* resolved to do it, he has made up his mind to do it.

decidir *vt* to settle, to decide (una cuestión, un asunto, etc.) || to decide, to convince, to persuade (incitar, convencer) || to decide; *decidieron salir* they decided to go out || to resolve (resolución categórica); *decidió quedarse* he resolved to stay.
◆ *vi* to decide, to choose; *decidir entre dos candidatos* to decide between two candidates || to decide; *decidir el futuro de la humanidad* to decide the future of humanity; *decidir en una cuestión* to decide on a question || *decidir sobre qué conviene más* to decide what is more suitable.
◆ *vpr* to make up one's mind; *hay que decidirse* we've got to make up our minds || to decide, to make up one's mind; *decidirse a hacer algo* to make up one's mind to do sth., to decide to do sth. || *decidirse por* to decide on, to choose; *decidirse por un sistema* to decide on a system, to choose a system.

decigramo *m* decigram, decigramme.

decilitro *m* decilitre [US deciliter].

décima *f* tenth, tenth part (una de las diez partes) || tithe (diezmo) || stanza of ten octosyllabic lines (composición poética) || FAM *tener décimas* to have a slight temperature.

decimal *adj/sm* decimal.

decimar *vt* (ant) to decimate (diezmar).

decímetro *m* decimetre [US decimeter].

décimo, ma *adj* tenth || the tenth; *Alfonso X* (décimo) Alfonso X [the tenth] || *en décimo lugar* tenthly, in the tenth place.
◆ *m/f* tenth.
◆ *m* tenth part [of a lottery ticket] (lotería) || small ten-cent silver coin of Colombia and Ecuador.

decimoctavo, va *adj/s* eighteenth.

decimocuarto, ta *adj/s* fourteenth.

decimonónico, ca *adj* nineteenth-century; *edificio decimonónico* nineteenth-century building.

decimonono, na; decimonoveno, na *adj/s* nineteenth.

decimoquinto, ta *adj/s* fifteenth.

decimoséptimo, ma *adj/s* seventeenth.

decimosexto, ta *adj/s* sixteenth.

decimotercero, ra; decimotercio, cia *adj/s* thirteenth.

decir *m* saying || short mediaeval poem || — *al decir de Juan* according to John, according to what John says || *al decir de todos* by all accounts || *es un decir* it's a manner of speaking || *los decires* rumours, hearsay *sing.*

decir* *vt/vi* to say (pronunciar palabras); *has dicho algo que no me gusta* you have said sth. I don't like; *dice que va a llover* he says that it's going to rain || to tell (contar); *dime lo que piensas de esto* tell me what you think of this; *decir mentiras, un secreto* to tell lies, a secret || to tell (revelar); *su expresión dice que no está contento* his expression tells you he isn't happy; *decirle a alguien la buena ventura* to tell s.o.'s fortune || to call (llamar); *le dicen Juan* they call him John || to speak, to tell (verdad) || to mention, to tell, to say; *no me habías dicho nada de esto* you hadn't mentioned anything of it to me, you hadn't told me anything about it, you hadn't said anything to me about it || to speak; *esto dice mal de la cortesía de los ingleses* this speaks poorly of English politeness || to think (opinar); *¿qué dice de este cuadro?* what do you think of this picture? || to tell (ordenar); *le dijo que hiciese el trabajo* he told him to do the job || to recite; *decir un poema* to recite a poem || to read, to say; *el texto dice lo siguiente* the text reads as follows *o* says the following || — *a decir verdad* to tell the truth || *al decir esto* with these words || *¿cómo diríamos?* how shall I put it? || *como quien dice, como si dijéramos* as it were, so to speak || *como quien no dice nada* nonchalantly, as if it were the most natural thing in the world || *con eso queda todo dicho* the rest goes without saying || *¿decía Vd.?, ¿decías?* you were saying? || *decir adiós a* to say goodbye to (una persona, una cosa) || *decir agudezas* to be witty || *decir bien* to be right || *decirle a uno cuatro frescas* to tell s.o. a few home truths || *decirle a uno cuatro verdades* or *las verdades del barquero* to give s.o. a piece of one's mind, to tell s.o. a few home truths || *decir lo que uno piensa* to say what one is thinking, to speak one's mind || FIG *decirlo todo* to speak volumes; *una mirada que lo dice todo* a look which speaks volumes || *decir mal* to be wrong, to be mistaken || *decir misa* to say Mass || *decir para sí* or *para su capote* or *para su coleto* or *para sus adentros* to say to o.s. || *decir que no, que sí* to say no, yes || *de paso diremos que...* let me say in passing that... || *dicho de otro modo* in other words || *dicho sea de paso* let it be said in passing || *dicho sea* or *sea dicho entre nosotros* between you and me || *dicho y hecho* no sooner said than done || *¿diga?, ¿dígame?* hello? (teléfono), yes? (¿qué desea?) || *¡dígamelo a mí!* you're telling me!, you can say that again! || *digamos* say, let's say || *digámoslo así* so to speak, as it were || *digan lo que digan, dígase lo que se diga* whatever they say || *¡digo!, ¡digo!* well now! || *digo yo* that's what I think || *dime con quién andas y te diré quién eres* a man is known by the company he keeps || *dirá Vd., querrá Vd. decir* you must mean || *el qué dirán* what people say *o* think || *es decir* that is to say || *es fácil decirlo* it is easy to say, it is easily said || *es mucho decir* that's saying a lot, that's going a bit far || *esto me dice algo* that rings a bell || *esto se dice pronto* it is easily said || *¡haberlo dicho!* you should have said so! || *he dicho lo que tenía que decir* I've had my say || *huelga decir que...* needless to say... || *lo dicho, dicho* what's said is said (no se puede negar lo dicho), a promise is a promise (hay que cumplir las promesas) || *lo dije sin querer* I didn't mean to say it || *lo que tú digas* whatever you say, it's up to you || *mandar decir a alguien que...* to send word to s.o. that... || *me permito decir que...* I submit that..., I venture to say that... || *ni qué decir tiene* it goes without saying, needless to say, doubtless, undoubtedly (como aprobación) || *no decir esa boca es mía, no decir ni pío* not to say a word, not to open one's mouth || *no hay más que decir* there's nothing more to be said, the rest goes without saying || *no he dicho nada* forget what I said (olvida lo dicho) || *no le dejaron decir una palabra* they wouldn't let him get a word in (edgeways) || *no lo digo por ti* I'm not referring to you || *¡no me diga!* go on!, you don't say!, get away! || *¡no se lo diré dos veces!* I shan't tell you again!, I shan't tell you twice! || *no te digo más* you know what I mean, need I say more?, you can see what I'm getting at || *o mejor dicho* or rather || *para decirlo con otras palabras* to put in other words || *para que no se diga* for the sake of appearances || *por decirlo así* so to speak, as it were || *por* or *según lo que se dice* according to what people say || *por más que diga* whatever he says, in spite of all he says || *que digamos* particularly, to speak of; *no es rico que digamos* he is not particularly rich || *¿qué me dice?* what did you say? || *¡que no te digo nada!, ¡ya me dirá usted!* marvellous, fantastic; *te traigo un pastel que no te digo nada* I've brought you a marvellous cake || *querer decir* to mean (significar) || *¿quién lo diría?* who would have thought so? || *se lo dije bien claro* I told you so || *te digo que no* I've told you, no; I said no || *usted dirá* it's up to you (para una decisión), go ahead, I'm listening (lo escucho), say when (al echar vino, comida, etc.) || *¡ya me dirás!* you bet! (¡ya lo creo!), you'll see, you'll find out (ya lo verás) || *¡y no digamos...!* not to mention || *¡y que lo digas!, ¡y usted que lo diga!* you bet!
◆ *vpr* to be said; *esto se dice mucho en inglés* that is said a lot in English; *se dice que es el asesino* he is said to be the murderer; *se dice que es hija ilegítima del Rey* it is said that she is the King's illegitimate daughter || — *¿cómo se dice esto en español?* how do you say this in Spanish?, what is the Spanish for this? || *fue lo que se dice un éxito clamoroso* it was what you would call *o* what you call a resounding success || *lo menos que puede decirse* the least one can say || *lo que se dice* what you would really call; *criminal, lo que se dice criminal, no es* he isn't what you would really call a criminal || *se dicen tantas cosas* people say so many things || *sé lo que me digo* I know what I'm saying, I know what I'm talking about || *se me ha dicho que...* I have been told that...

decisión *f* decision; *el Gobierno ha tomado una decisión* the Government has taken *o* made a decision || determination, resolution, decision; *mostrar decisión* to show determination || *con decisión* determinedly, resolutely.

decisivo, va *adj* decisive; *un acontecimiento decisivo en la historia* a decisive event in history || *tiene motivos decisivos para marcharse* he has reasons which force him to go.

declamación *f* declamation (arte) || recitation.

declamar *vt/vi* to declaim, to recite; *declamar versos* to declaim poetry.

declamatorio, ria *adj* declamatory, bombastic.

declaración *f* statement, declaration; *el Presidente ha hecho una declaración a la prensa* the President has made a statement to the Press || declaration (anuncio importante) || declaration, return; *declaración de impuestos* tax *o* Fiscal declaration; *declaración de renta* income tax declaration || declaring, declaration (en las aduanas) || JUR statement, evidence, deposition; *hacer una declaración* to make a statement *o* deposition, to give evidence | evidence, testimony; *prestar declaración* to give evidence *o* testimony || bid, call (en el bridge) || INFORM declaration || — *declaración de amor* declaration of love || *declaración de guerra* declaration of war || *declaración de no culpabilidad* veredict of not guilty || *declaración de quiebra* declaration of bankruptcy (por la autoridad competente), filing of petition in bankruptcy (por el quebrado) || *declaración de siniestro* claim (de seguros) || JUR *prestar declaración jurada* to testify under oath.
◆ *pl* statement *sing*, declaration *sing*; *hacer declaraciones* to make a statement || comment *sing*, statement *sing* (comentario); *se negó a hacer declaraciones* he refused to make any comment.

declaradamente *adv* openly, manifestly.

declarado, da *adj* open, professed.

declarante *adj* who declares || JUR who gives evidence, testifying.
◆ *m/f* declarer, declarant || JUR deponent, witness.

declarar *vt* to declare, to state (manifestar) || to declare; *el jurado le declaró vencedor* the jury declared him the winner; *declarar la guerra a un país* to declare war on a country; *les declaró lo que ganaba* he declared his earnings to them; *¿tiene algo que declarar?* have you anything to declare? || to bid, to declare, to call (en el bridge) || JUR to find; *declarar culpable* to find guilty.
◆ *vi* to declare || JUR to testify, to give evidence.
◆ *vpr* to declare o.s. || to break out (epidemia, fuego, etc.) || to come out, to start (una enfermedad) || to declare one's love (declarar su amor) || — *declararse a favor de* or *por un candidato* to declare o.s. in favour of a candidate, to come out on the side of a candidate || JUR *declararse culpable* to plead guilty || *declararse enfermo* to report sick || *declararse en huelga* to go on strike || *declararse en quiebra* to file one's petition.

declaratorio, ria *adj* declaratory.

declinable *adj* GRAM declinable.

declinación *f* ASTR declination || GRAM declension || FIG decline (decadencia) || *declinación magnética* declination, magnetic variation.

declinante *adj* declining; *poder declinante* declining power.

declinar *vi* to decline, to slope downwards (inclinarse) || to vary from the true meridian (una brújula) || FIG to decline, to diminish (las fuerzas) | to decay (decaer) | to diminish, to abate (fiebre) || to draw to a close; *está declinando el día, la batalla* the day, the battle is drawing to a close || to sink, to decline (el sol) || FIG to fade, to fail, to fall off, to decline, to be on the wane (belleza) | to get weaker (debilitarse); *ha declinado mucho desde la última vez que le vi* he has got a lot weaker since the last time I saw him | to depart; *declinar del camino derecho* to depart from the straight and narrow || ASTR to decline.
◆ *vt* to decline, to refuse (rechazar) || GRAM to decline.

declive *m* slope, incline, declivity (cuesta) || FIG decline (decadencia) || *en declive* sloping, on a slope (inclinado).

decocción *f* decoction || MED amputation.

decodificación *f* INFORM decoding.

decodificador *m* decoder.

decodificar *vt* INFORM to decode.

decolaje *m* AMER takeoff (despegue).

decolar *vi* AMER to take off (despegar).

decoloración *f* fading || bleaching (del pelo).

decolorante *m* bleaching agent.

decolorar *vt* to discolour, to fade (rebajar o quitar el color); *cortinas decoloradas por el sol* curtains faded by the sun || to bleach (dejar blanco); *pelo decolorado* bleached hair.
◆ *vpr* to fade, to become discoloured (perder el color) || to be bleached (quedar blanco).

decomisar *vt* to confiscate, to seize.

decomiso *m* confiscation, seizure (acción) || confiscated article (objeto confiscado).

decoración *f* decoration (acción) || decoration, décor (efecto); *la decoración de una habitación* the decoration of a room || TEATR scenery, set (decorado) || *decoración de escaparates* window dressing.

decorado *m* TEATR scenery, set || decoration (acción) || decoration, décor (efecto).

decorador, ra *adj* decorating || — *decorador de escaparates* window dresser || *pintor decorador* painter and decorator.
◆ *m/f* decorator || TEATR stage *o* set designer.

decorar *vt* to decorate, to adorn (adornar) || to decorate (una casa).

decorativo, va *adj* decorative, ornamental || fairly attractive (una chica) || — *artes decorativas* decorative arts || FIG & FAM *hacer de figura decorativa* to play a minor part, to be mere decoration.

decoro *m* dignity (dignidad) || decorum, propriety (honra) || respect (respeto); *guardar el decoro a uno* to show respect for s.o. || decorum, decency (decencia) || — *acabar con decoro* to finish off in splendour || *con decoro* decently; *con menos dinero no se puede vivir con decoro* you can't live decently on less money; decently, modestly (con pudor); *comportarse con decoro* to behave decently; decent, modest; *una mujer con decoro* a modest woman || *sin decoro* indecent *adj*, indecently *adv*.

decorosamente *adv* with dignity (con dignidad) || with decorum (como se debe) || decently (decentemente).

decoroso, sa *adj* proper, seemly, decorous (conveniente) || honourable; *una profesión decorosa* an honourable profession || decent (decente); *un sueldo decoroso* a decent wage || decent, modest, decorous (conforme al pudor); *una mujer decorosa* a decent woman || respectable (digno) || *tener un final muy decoroso* to finish off in splendour.

decrecer* *vi* to decrease || to diminish, to dwindle (disminuir) || to go down, to subside (aguas) || to get shorter, to draw in (días).

decreciente *adj* decreasing, decrescent.

decrepitar *vi* to decrepitate.

decrépito, ta *adj* decrepit; *anciano decrépito* decrepit old man.

decrepitud *f* decrepitude.

decrescendo *adj/adv/sm* MÚS decrescendo (de una melodía).

decretal *f* decretal (decisión del papa).

decretar *vt* to decree (por decreto) || to ordain, to order (ordenar).

decreto *m* decree, order || enactment (para poner en ejecución las leyes) || decree (del papa) || *decreto ley* decree-law, [equivalent of] order in council || *por real decreto* by Royal decree.

decúbito *m* MED decubitus; *decúbito supino, prono* dorsal *o* supine, prone decubitus.

decuplar; decuplicar *vt* to decuple, to increase tenfold.
◆ *vpr* to decuple, to increase tenfold.

décuplo, pla *adj* tenfold, decuple, ten times (as much as); *cuarenta es décuplo de cuatro* forty is decuple four, forty is tenfold four, forty is ten times four.
◆ *m* decuple.

decurrente *adj* BOT decurrent.

decurso *m* course; *el decurso de los años* the course of the years.

dechado *m* model (modelo) || sampler (en costura) || model, perfect example, paragon (arquetipo); *este libro es un dechado de armonía* this book is a model of harmony; *un dechado de virtudes* a paragon of virtue || *ser un dechado de perfecciones* to be perfect in every way, to be a model of perfection.

dedada *f* fingerful (cantidad que se coge con el dedo); *una dedada de mermelada* a fingerful of jam || fingermark (mancha) || FIG *dedada de miel* consolation.

dedal *m* thimble (para coser).

dedalera *f* BOT foxglove.

dédalo *m* labyrinth, maze (laberinto).

Dédalo *npr m* MIT Daedalus.

dedicación *f* dedication, consecration (de una iglesia) || devotion, dedication (entrega); *su dedicación al partido* his devotion to the party || devotion (de tiempo, de dinero, de esfuerzos, etc.) || — *de dedicación exclusiva, de plena dedicación* full-time; *empleo de dedicación exclusiva* full-time job || *le consagra una dedicación completa* he devotes all his time to it.

dedicado, da *adj* INFORM dedicated.

dedicar *vt* to dedicate, to consecrate (una iglesia, etc.) || to dedicate (un libro) || to inscribe, to dedicate (cada ejemplar de un libro, de una fotografía, etc.) || to devote (dinero, tiempo, esfuerzos, etc.); *cada día hay que dedicar una hora a los estudios* you must devote an hour every day to studying || to give over; *dedicó una parte de su tierra a pastos* he gave over part of his land to grazing || to address (palabras) || to have, to show; *le dedica mucha admiración* he has great admiration for him || *emisión dedicada a España* programme about Spain, programme devoted to Spain.
◆ *vpr* to devote o.s., to dedicate o.s.; *dedicarse al estudio* to devote o.s. to study || to dedicate one's life, to give up one's life; *dedicarse a los enfermos* to dedicate one's life to the sick || to spend one's time, to go in for (con el infinitivo); *se dedica a cazar* he spends him time hunting || *¿a qué se dedica usted?* what do you do (for a living)?, what is your line of business?

dedicatoria *f* dedication, inscription (de un libro, de un objeto de arte, etc.).

dedicatorio, ria *adj* dedicatory.

dedil *m* fingerstall; *dedil de goma* rubber fingerstall.

dedillo *m* *al dedillo* at one's fingertips; *hacer algo al dedillo* to have sth. at one's fingertips.

dedo *m* finger (de la mano) || toe (del pie) || finger, fingerbreadth, digit (medida) || — *beber un dedo de vino* to have a drop of wine || *contar con los dedos* to count on one's fingers || FIG *cogerse los dedos* to get caught || *chuparse el dedo* to suck one's thumb (un niño) || FIG *dale un dedo y se tomará hasta el codo* give him an inch and he'll take a mile || *dedo anular* third finger, ring finger || *dedo del pie* toe || *dedo gordo* thumb || *dedo gordo del pie* big toe || *dedo índice* forefinger, index, index finger || *dedo medio* or *del corazón* middle finger || *dedo meñique* or *pequeño* little finger || *dedo pulgar* thumb || FAM *es* or *está para chuparse los dedos* it's delicious (comida), it's great (cosa) || *escaparse de entre los dedos* to slip through one's fingers || FIG *estar a dos dedos de* to be on the point *o* on the verge of, to be inches away from | *meter los dedos a uno* to worm sth. out of s.o., to make s.o. talk || *meterse los dedos en la nariz* to pick one's nose, to put one's fingers up one's nose || FIG *morderse los dedos* to regret it, to kick o.s.; *decidió no irse de vacaciones y ahora se muerde los dedos* he decided not to go on holiday and now he regrets it *o* and now he could kick himself | *no chuparse* or *no mamarse el dedo* not to have been born yesterday | *nombrar a dedo* to handpick | *no mover un dedo de la mano* not to lift a finger | *no tener dos dedos de frente* to be as thick as two planks || *poner a uno los cinco dedos en la cara* to slap s.o. across the face, to give s.o. a slap across the face || MÚS *poner bien los dedos* to play an instrument well || FIG *poner el dedo en la llaga* to touch on a sore point || *señalar a uno con el dedo* to point at s.o. (dirigir el dedo hacia uno), to put the finger on s.o. (destacar) || *tocar algo con el dedo* to put one's finger on sth. || *yema* or *punta del dedo* fingertip.

deducción *f* deduction, inference || COM deduction (acción de descontar) || MÚS diatonic scale || *deducción del salario* deduction from one's salary || *deducción fiscal* tax deduction, tax.

deducible *adj* deducible, inferable || COM deductible.

deducir* *vt* to deduce, to infer; *deduzco de* or *por ello que no lo vas a hacer* from that I deduce that you are not going to do it || COM to deduct; *deducir los gastos de las ganancias* to deduct expenses from the earnings; *deducir algo del salario* to deduct sth. from one's salary || JUR to adduce, to present, to allege (pruebas, razones), to claim, to assert (derechos).
◆ *vpr* to follow.

defalcar *vt* to deduct (rebajar) || to embezzle, to misappropriate (robar).

defasado, da *adj* ELECTR out of phase.

defasaje *m* ELECTR phase shift, dephasing, phase difference || FIG difference, gap.

defasar *vt* ELECTR to dephase.

defecación *f* defecation, defaecation.

defecar *vt* to defaecate, to defecate.

defección *f* defection, desertion.

defectivo, va *adj* defective (defectuoso) || GRAM defective (verbo).
◆ *m* GRAM defective verb.

defecto *m* defect, fault (físico, de una máquina, etc.) || imperfection, flaw (de una joya) || fault, defect, shortcoming (moral); *esta persona tiene muchos defectos* this person has a lot of faults || flaw (en un argumento) || lack, absence (falta) || IMPR oddment, waste sheet || — *a defecto de* for want of || *defecto de pronunciación* speech defect, speech impediment || *defecto físico* physical defect.

defectuosidad *f* defectiveness, faultiness, unsoundness || defect, flaw, imperfection (defecto).

defectuoso, sa *adj* defective, faulty.

defender* *vt* to defend (*contra* against; *de* from); *defender la patria contra el enemigo* to defend one's country against the enemy || to protect (*contra* against; *de* from), to protect (proteger); *la montaña defiende la ciudad del viento norte* the mountain protects the town from the north wind || to defend, to uphold (argumento, ideas, etc.) || JUR to argue, to plead; *defender una causa* to argue a cause | to defend (al acusado).
◆ *vpr* to defend o.s. || FIG & FAM to get along, to manage, not to do badly (no dársele mal); *se defiende en ruso* he gets along in Russian.

defendido, da *adj* JUR defendant.
◆ *m/f* JUR defendant.

defenestración *f* defenestration.

defensa *f* defence [US defense]; *defensa de una ciudad, de una idea* defence of a town, of an idea || JUR defence; *conceder la palabra a la defensa* to call upon the defence to speak | speech for the defence (discurso) || MIL & MAR defence; *defensa pasiva* passive defence || leg guard (moto) || MAR fender (de barco) || DEP defence, defenders *pl* (jugadores) | pad (protección para las piernas) || — *en defensa de* in defence of || *en defensa mía* or *propia* in self-defence || *legítima defensa* self-defence [US self-defense] || *salir en defensa de alguien* to come out in defence of s.o.
◆ *pl* tusks (colmillos).

defensa *m* DEP back, fullback; *defensa izquierda, derecha, central* left, right, centre back | defender (cada jugador que no es delantero).

defensiva *f* defensive; *estar, ponerse a la defensiva* to be, to go on the defensive || DEP *jugar a la defensiva* to play a defensive game.

defensivo, va *adj* defensive; *táctica defensiva* defensive tactics.

defensor, ra *adj* defending, who defends || JUR *abogado defensor* counsel for the defence [US counsel for the defense].
◆ *m/f* defender || JUR counsel for the defence || *defensor de la fe* defender of the faith || *defensor del pueblo* ombudsman || *defensor del soldado* military ombudsman.

deferencia *f* deference, regard; *por* or *en deferencia a* in *o* out of deference to, out to regard for.

deferente *adj* deferential (atento) || ANAT *conducto deferente* deferent conduit.

deferir* *vi* to defer; *deferir al dictamen ajeno* to defer to s.o. else's judgment.
◆ *vt* JUR to refer, to transfer, to delegate; *deferir una causa a un tribunal* to transfer a case to a court.

deficiencia *f* insufficiency, lack (insuficiencia) || deficiency; *deficiencia de salud* health deficiency || defectiveness, faultiness (imperfección) || defect (defecto) || shortcoming; *las deficiencias de un equipo* the shortcomings of a team || MED *deficiencia mental* mental deficiency.

deficiente *adj* deficient; *salud deficiente* deficient health || insufficient, lacking (insuficiente) || defective, faulty (defectuoso) || poor; *alumno deficiente* poor pupil; *trabajo deficiente* poor piece of work.
◆ *m/f* MED *deficiente mental* mentally retarded person, mentally deficient person.

deficientemente *adv* insufficiently || poorly; *trabajo hecho deficientemente* work poorly done.

déficit *m* deficit; *déficit presupuestario* budget deficit || FIG shortage (carencia).
— OBSERV pl *déficits*.

deficitario, ria *adj* showing a deficit; *balance deficitario* balance showing a deficit.

definición *f* definition || TECN definition (telescopio, televisión) || *por definición* by definition; *el hombre es egoísta por definición* man is selfish by definition.

definido, da *adj* definite; *artículo definido* definite article || *bien definido* well-defined.

definir *vt* to define; *definir claramente una palabra* to define a word clearly || to determine (actitud, postura) || to put the finishing touches to (una pintura).

definitivamente *adv* finally; *las obras están definitivamente terminadas* the road works have finally been finished || for good, once and for all; *marcharse definitivamente* to go for good || decisively.

definitivo, va *adj* final, definitive; *el proyecto definitivo* the final plan || permanent; *poner un puente provisional mientras se construye el definitivo* to put up a temporary bridge while the permanent one is being built || *en definitiva* really; *no sé aún lo que voy a hacer en definitiva* I still don't really know what to do; all things considered (considerándolo todo); *en definitiva, esto no me interesa* all things considered, this doesn't interest me; in short (en resumen); *en definitiva, todo sigue igual* in short, everything is still the same.

deflación *f* deflation.

deflacionista *adj* deflationary.

deflagración *f* deflagration.

deflagrador *m* detonator, igniter (para barrenos).

deflagrar *vi* to deflagrate.

deflector *m* TECN deflector, baffle || quarter light (de coche).

defoliación *f* BOT defoliation.

deformación *f* deformation || FÍS deformation, strain || distortion (televisión) || TECN warping (alabeo) || *deformación profesional* occupational idiosincracy.

deformar *vt* to deform; *deformar un miembro* to deform a limb; *deformar el carácter de una persona* to deform a person's character || to put out of shape, to deform; *la lluvia ha deformado el sombrero* the rain has put the hat out of shape || to distort; *el flemón le ha deformado la cara* the gumboil has distorted his face; *deformar la verdad, una imagen* to distort the truth, a picture || to twist, to warp (la conciencia) || FÍS to strain || TECN to warp (alabear).
◆ *vpr* to be deformed (un miembro, etc.) || to go out of shape, to lose one's shape; *los zapatos se deforman con la lluvia* shoes lose their shape in the rain || to be distorted (cara, imagen, conciencia) || TECN to warp (alabearse).

deforme *adj* deformed (miembro) || distorted (cara, imagen) || misshapen, shapeless (cosa).

deformidad *f* deformity, malformation; *una deformidad física* a physical deformity || FIG moral shortcoming, perversion.

defraudación *f* FIG disappointment (decepción) || fraud (fraude) || swindle (estafa) || *defraudación fiscal* or *de impuestos* tax evasion.

defraudado, da *adj* FIG disappointed (decepcionado) | frustrated (esperanzas).

defraudador, ra *adj* disappointing (decepcionante) || deceiving, cheating (que engaña).
◆ *m/f* evader; *defraudador fiscal* tax evader || swindler (estafador).

defraudar *vt* to disappoint (decepcionar) || to frustrate, to dash (esperanzas) || to defraud, to cheat; *defraudar a sus acreedores* to defraud one's creditors || to swindle (estafar) || to evade; *defraudar al fisco* to evade taxes || *defraudar la confianza de alguien* to betray s.o.'s confidence.

defunción *f* decease, demise (fallecimiento) || death; *esquela de defunción* death announcement, notification of death; *partida de defunción* death certificate || *cerrado por defunción* closed due to bereavement.

degeneración *f* degeneration (de las células) || degeneracy, degeneration (moral).

degenerado, da *adj/s* degenerate.

degenerante *adj* degenerative, degenerating || ARQ flat (arco).

degenerar *vi* to degenerate (persona, animal, cosa) || FIG to degenerate; *partido de fútbol que degeneró en batalla campal* football match which degenerated into a pitched battle.

degenerativo, va *adj* degenerative.

deglución *f* deglutition, swallowing.

deglutir *vt/vi* to swallow.

degollación *f* throat cutting (degüello) || decapitation, beheading (decapitación) || *la degollación de los Inocentes* the Slaughter of the Innocents.

degolladero *m* throat, windpipe [of animals to be slaughtered] || slaughterhouse (matadero) || scaffold (cadalso) || FIG *llevar al degolladero* to lead to the slaughterhouse.

degolladura *f* cut (in the throat) (herida) || joint (entre ladrillos).

degollar* *vt* to cut the throat of (cortar la garganta) || to behead, to decapitate (decapitar) || FIG to ruin, to spoil (arruinar); *esto degüella todos mis proyectos* that ruins all my plans | to murder (representar mal una obra, etc.) || TAUR to kill badly, to butcher || MAR to slash (una vela).

degollina *f* FAM slaughter, massacre (matanza) || FAM *el profesor hizo una degollina en los exámenes* the teacher was very severe in his exam marking.

degradación *f* demotion, degradation (de un militar) || FIG degradation, debasement (envilecimiento) | depravity (depravación) || ARTES gradation.

degradador *m* FOT vignetter (desvanecedor).

degradante *adj* degrading; *conducta degradante* degrading conduct.

degradar *vt* to degrade || to demote, to degrade; *degradar a un militar* to demote a soldier || FIG to degrade, to debase; *el abuso del alcohol degrada al hombre* too much drink degrades a man || ARTES to degrade (el color) || FÍS to degrade.
◆ *vpr* to lower o.s., to degrade o.s.

degüello *m* throat cutting (acción de cortar el cuello) || beheading, decapitation (decapitación) || massacre, slaughter (matanza) || — MIL *entrar a degüello* to massacre, to slaughter, to put to the sword; *entraron a degüello en la ciudad* they massacred the city, they put the city to the sword || FIG *tirar a uno a degüello* to have one's knife in s.o., to be gunning for s.o.

degustación *f* tasting.

degustar *vt* to taste (probar, catar).

dehesa *f* pasture, meadow.

dehiscente *adj* BOT dehiscent.

deicida *adj* deicidal.
◆ *m/f* deicide.

deicidio *m* deicide.

deidad *f* deity, god (dios); *las deidades griegas* the Greek deities || deity (divinidad).

deificación *f* deification.

deificar *vt* to deify.

deísmo *m* deism.

deísta *adj* deistic.
◆ *m/f* deist.

dejación *f* surrender, relinquishment, cession, renunciation; *dejación de bienes* surrender of property.

dejada *f* surrender, relinquishment || DEP drop shot (en tenis).

dejadez *f* neglect, slovenliness (falta de cuidado) || negligence, carelessness, slackness (negligencia) || laziness (pereza).

dejado, da *adj* slovenly, untidy (descuidado) || negligent, slack, careless (negligente) || lazy (perezoso) || dejected, depressed, listless (desanimado) || *dejado de la mano de Dios* godforsaken.
◆ *m/f* sloven, slovenly person (descuidado).

dejamiento *m* neglect, slovenliness (falta de cuidado) || negligence, slackness, carelessness (negligencia) || laziness (pereza) || relinquishment (dejación) || dejection, despondency (decaimiento).

dejar *vt* to leave, to forget; *lo he dejado en casa* I've left it at home || to leave; *le ha dejado algo por* or *sin hacer* he has left you sth. to do; *déjalo tranquilo* leave him alone; *dejar a uno el cuidado de hacer algo* to leave it to s.o. to do sth.; *dejar improductivo un capital* to leave capital uninvested; *dejar para mañana* to leave till tomorrow || to leave, to bequeath (la herencia) || to drop, to put down, to leave (depositar); *el coche te dejará en la estación* the car will drop you at the station || to leave, to abandon, to forsake (abandonar); *dejar a su mujer* to leave one's wife || to give up, to leave (un empleo) || to stop, to finish; *dejo de trabajar a las seis* I finish work at six o'clock || to stop, to leave off; *dejó de escribirme* he stopped writing to me || to bring in, to make (dar); *este negocio deja mucho dinero* this business brings in a lot of money || to yield, to produce, to bring in (beneficios) || to lend (prestar); *déjame veinte duros* lend me a hundred pesetas || to forget, to leave out, to omit (omitir) || to drop; *dejemos esta discusión* let's drop this argument || to let, to allow (permitir); *no dejo salir a mi hija* or *que salga mi hija después de las diez* I don't let my daughter go out *o* allow my daughter to go out later than ten o'clock || to let (permitir); *déjalo trabajar en paz* let him work in peace; *si el chico quiere salir, déjalo* if the boy wants to go out, let him; *déjalo jugar* or *que juegue* let him play || to put down; *deje ese libro y coja otro* put that book down and get another || to leave alone; *deja eso y no lo toques* leave that alone and don't touch it || to make; *me ha dejado los zapatos como nuevos* he has made my shoes as good as new; *la ducha me ha dejado como nuevo* that shower has made a new man of me || to keep; *deja tus observaciones para cuando te las pidan* keep your remarks until you are asked for them || to wait (esperar); *deja que pase la tormenta* wait until the storm has passed || — REL *dejad que los niños se acerquen a mí* suffer the little children to come unto me || FAM *¡déjalo!* stop it (no hagas eso), forget it, don't worry (no te preocupes) || *¡déjame!, ¡déjame en paz!* leave me alone!, leave me in peace!, go away! || *dejando a salvo, si dejamos a salvo* with the exception of, except for || *dejar al descubierto* to expose (un ejército); *dejar al descubierto un flanco* to expose a flank || *dejar aparte* to leave aside || *dejar atrás* to leave behind, to outstrip, to outdistance || *dejar a un lado* or *de lado* to leave aside (apartar), to omit, to pass over (omitir) || FIG *dejar caer* to drop, to slip; *dejó caer en la conversación que quería irse a España* he slipped it into the conversation that he wanted to go to Spain; to drop (un objeto) | *dejar chiquito* to put in the shade (superar); *este nuevo modelo deja chiquito al anterior* this new model puts the former one in the shade || *dejar dicho* to say; *como dejo dicho* as I have said; to leave word; *he dejado dicho que no me despierten* I have left word that I don't want to be awakened || FAM *dejar en la estacada* to leave in the lurch || *dejar entrar* to let in || FAM *dejar fresco* to leave cold; *eso me deja fresco* that leaves me cold || *dejar mucho que desear* to leave a lot to be desired || *dejar (el) paso libre* to get out of the way of; *dejar el paso libre a los bomberos* to get out of the way of the firemen; to let pass; *los aduaneros dejaron paso libre al automovilista* the customs officers let the motorist pass; to keep the way clear (no obstruir el paso) || FAM *dejar a uno plantado* to stand s.o. up, not to turn up (no acudir a una cita), to leave s.o. standing there (dejar solo), to walk out on s.o. (abandonar), to finish with s.o. (entre novios), to let s.o. down (no prestar ayuda) || *dejarlo todo plantado* to drop everything, to leave everything where it is || *dejar por heredero a uno* to name *o* to leave s.o. as one's heir || *dejar por imposible* to give up as impossible || *dejar salir* to let out (alguien que está encerrado, animal), to allow out (persona) || *dejar tiempo al tiempo* to wait, to let things take their time || *dejar tirado a alguien* to leave s.o. in the lurch (dejar en la estacada), to leave s.o. miles behind (en una carrera) || *¡déjeme paso!* let me get past!, let me through! || *dejémoslo así* let's leave it there, let's leave it at that || FIG *no dejarle a uno un hueso sano* to break every bone in s.o.'s body, to make mincemeat of s.o. (pegándole), to pull *o* to pick s.o. to pieces (criticar mucho) || *no dejar piedra por mover* to leave no stone unturned || *no dejes para mañana lo que puedes hacer hoy* do not put off till tomorrow what you can do today.
◆ *vi* *dejar de* to stop; *no dejó de hablar* he didn't stop talking; to give up, to stop; *ha dejado de jugar al fútbol* he has given up playing football || *no dejar de* not to fail to, not to neglect to; *no dejes de venir* don't fail to come || *no deja de extrañarme su conducta* his behaviour never fails to surprise me || *no por eso deja de ser un disparate* it is still stupid || *no por eso dejaré de ir* that won't stop me going || *no puedo dejar de extrañarme* I cannot but be surprised, I can't help being surprised.
◆ *vpr* to make o.s.; *la influencia de la literatura moderna se deja sentir* the influence of modern literature is making itself felt || to let o.s., to allow o.s.; *no te dejes explotar* don't you let yourself be exploited || to let o.s. go, to neglect o.s. (abandonarse) || to leave, to forget (olvidar); *me he dejado el libro en casa* I've left my book at home || to forget; *te has dejado este ejercicio sin hacer* you have forgotten to do this exercise || to be; *se deja convencer fácilmente* he is easily convinced || — *consentir sin dejarse rogar* to consent readily || *dejarse abatir* to get depressed || *dejase caer* to drop, to fall, to flop; *se dejó caer en el sillón* he flopped into the armchair; to drop in, to pop in; *me dejé caer por su casa a las ocho* I dropped in to see him at eight o'clock || FIG & FAM *dejarse caer con* to come up *o* out with; *dejarse caer con una noticia sensacional* to come up with a sensational piece of news || *dejarse crecer la barba* to grow a beard || *dejarse de* to stop; *déjate de historias* stop beating about the bush; *déjese de llorar* stop crying || *dejarse de cuentos* or *de rodeos* not to beat around *o* about the bush, to get (straight) to the point || *dejarse ir* to let o.s. go || *dejarse llevar por* to be carried away with; *dejarse llevar por la cólera* to be carried away with anger; to be influenced by; *dejarse llevar por los demás* to be influenced by others || *dejarse oír* to be (able to be) heard, to make o.s. heard || *dejarse querer* to like attention || *dejarse rogar* to play hard to get || *¡déjate de bromas!* that's enough of your joking!, stop your clowning! || *déjate de tonterías* don't be silly || *este vinillo se deja beber* this is a very drinkable *o* nice little wine || *se deja sentir el frío* you can feel the cold.

— OBSERV *Dejar* followed by the past participle of a verb is equivalent to the same verb used in its finite form. The difference lies in the emphasis this construction gives to the verb: *dejar a uno asombrado* (asombrar) to amaze s.o.; *dejar desamparado* (desamparar) to forsake.

deje *m* (slight) accent, lilt (modo de hablar).

dejillo *m* (slight) accent, lilt (modo de hablar) | aftertaste (sabor) || *este vino tiene un dejillo amargo* this wine leaves a bitter taste in your mouth.

dejo *m* (slight) accent, lilt (modo de hablar) || aftertaste (sabor) || slackness (dejadez) || abandonment, surrender (abandono) || end, termination (fin) || *una victoria con un dejo amargo* a victory which leaves a nasty taste in one's mouth.

del *art* (contraction of *de* and *el*) of the, from the, etc. (véase en DE).

delación *f* denunciation, accusation.

delantal *m* apron (sin peto) || pinafore (con peto) || smock (babero).

delante *adv* in front, ahead (con movimiento); *ir delante* to walk in front || in front (sin movimiento); *lleva botones delante* the buttons are in front || — *de delante* in front; *el de delante* the one in front; *el coche de delante* the car in front; front; *la puerta de delante* the front door || *delante de* in front of, ahead of, before (con movimiento); *andaba delante de mí* he was walking in front of me; in front (sin movimiento); *hay un árbol delante de mi casa* there is a tree in front of my house; outside; *me estaba esperando delante del cine* he was waiting for me outside the cinema || *por delante* in front; *abierto por delante* open in front || FIG *se lleva todo por delante* he lets nothing stand in his way || *tenemos dos días por delante* we still have two days to go || *tenemos esa lista delante mientras trabajamos* we have that list in front of us while we work || FAM *tener algo delante* *de sus narices* to have sth. under one's nose || *tener mucho trabajo por delante* to have a lot of work in front of one, to have a lot of work ahead of one.

delantera *f* front, front part (de casa, de prenda de vestir, etc.) || front row (fila de teatro, etc.) || front row seat (asiento) || lead (ventaja); *tomar la delantera* to take the lead; *llevar la delantera* to be in the lead || forward line, forwards *pl*; *la delantera de un equipo de fútbol* the forward line of football team || — *coger* or *tomar a uno la delantera* to take the lead over s.o., to get ahead of s.o. (en una carrera), to get there before s.o., to beat s.o. to it (anticiparse); *fui a solicitar un trabajo pero me cogieron la delantera* I went for a job but s.o. beat me to it.

delantero, ra *adj* front; *parte, fila, rueda delantera* front part, row, wheel || DEP forward || *pata delantera* foreleg, front leg.
◆ *m* DEP forward; *delantero centro* centre forward || front (de un jersey, vestido, etc.).

delatar *vt* to denounce, to inform on; *delatar a los cómplices* to denounce one's accomplices || FIG to give away; *el ruido que hizo lo delató y lo cogieron* the noise he made gave him away and they caught him.

delator, ra *adj* who informs, who denounces.
◆ *m/f* informer, delator.

delco *m* AUT distributor.

dele; deleátur *m* IMPR dele.

delectación *f* delight, delectation.

delegación *f* delegation (acción de delegar) || office (cargo y oficina) || local office; *delegación de Hacienda* local tax office || branch; *la compañía tiene una delegación en Madrid* the company has a branch in Madrid || delegation (conjunto de delegados) || *delegación comercial* local office, branch || *delegación de Hacienda* local tax office || *delegación sindical* union delegation (conjunto de delegados), local union (office) (en España).

delegado, da *adj* delegated.
◆ *m/f* delegate || COM representative (de una sucursal) || *delegado de Hacienda* chief tax inspector || *delegado del gobierno* government representative || *delegado sindical* trade union representative.

delegar *vt* to delegate; *delegar sus poderes a* or *en una persona* to delegate one's powers to s.o.

deleitación *f*; **deleitamiento** *m* delight, pleasure, delectation.

deleitar *vt* to delight, to please; *la música deleita el oído* music delights the ear.
◆ *vpr* to delight, to take delight *o* great pleasure; *deleitarse en la lectura* to delight in reading, to take great pleasure in reading; *deleitarse con* or *en la contemplación de* to delight in the contemplation of.

deleite *m* delight, pleasure, joy; *leer con deleite* to read with delight || *el clima de Mallorca es un verdadero deleite* Majorca's climate is really delightful.

deletéreo, a *adj* noxious, poisonous, deleterious; *gas deletéreo* noxious gas.

deletrear *vt* to spell, to spell out; *deletree su apellido* spell your name || FIG to decipher; *deletrear jeroglíficos* to decipher hieroglyphics.

deletreo *m* spelling, spelling out (de palabras o de sílabas) || deciphering (desciframiento).

deleznable *adj* crumbly, friable; *arcilla deleznable* crumbly clay || slippery (resbaladizo) || FIG fragile, frail, ephemeral (que dura poco) | weak; *razones deleznables* weak reasons | unstable (inestable).

delfín *m* dolphin (cetáceo) || dauphin (príncipe).

delfina *f* dauphiness, dauphine (esposa del delfín de Francia).

Delfos *n pr* GEOGR Delphi.

delgadez *f* slimness, slenderness (esbeltez) || thinness (flacura); *la delgadez de un enfermo* the thinness of a sick person || *delgadez cadavérica* emaciation.

delgado, da *adj* thin; *una lámina de metal muy delgada* a very thin sheet of metal || slim, slender (esbelto); *una mujer delgada* a slim woman || thin (flaco); *este niño no come lo suficiente y se ha quedado muy delgado* this child doesn't eat enough and is very thin || FIG sharp (agudo, ingenioso) || poor (tierra de cultivo) || — FIG *hilar delgado* to split hairs || ANAT *intestino delgado* small intestine || *ponerse delgado* to lose weight, to get thin (ponerse flaco); *se ha puesto delgado durante el servicio militar* he has lost weight in the army; to lose weight, to slim (a propósito); *su hermana se ha puesto muy delgada* his sister has lost a lot of weight *o* has slimmed a lot.
◆ *m pl* flanks (de un animal).

delgaducho, cha *adj* FAM skinny, thin; *niño delgaducho* skinny child.

deliberación *f* deliberation.

deliberadamente *adv* deliberately, on purpose, intentionally.

deliberado, da *adj* deliberate, intentional.

deliberante *adj* deliberative; *asamblea deliberante* deliberative assembly.

deliberar *vi* to deliberate (*sobre* on).
◆ *vt* to decide.

deliberatorio, ria *adj* deliberative.

delicadeza *f* delicacy (de máquina, de situación, etc.) || delicacy, frailty (de salud) || squeamishness (remilgos) || hypersensivity (sensibilidad excesiva) || tactfulness (tacto) || delicacy, daintiness (de rasgos, etc.) || refinement (de modales) || exquisiteness (de un manjar) || — *con delicadeza* delicately, gently (suavemente), tactfully (con tacto) || *falta de delicadeza* lack of refinement (en los modales), tactlessness (falta de tacto) || *fue una delicadeza de su parte* it was a nice gesture on his part || *tener mil delicadezas con* to make a great fuss of, to devote all one's attention to || *tuvo la delicadeza de...* he was thoughtful enough to...

delicado, da *adj* delicate; *una máquina delicada* a delicate machine; *una situación delicada* a delicate situation; *un color delicado* a delicate colour || delicate, frail (enfermizo); *es delicado de salud* his health is delicate || very sensitive, hypersensitive (muy sensible) || fussy, particular, fastidious, hard to please (exigente) || squeamish (remilgado) || dainty, delicate, exquisite; *los rasgos delicados de un rostro* the dainty lines of a face || exquisite (un manjar) || refined, polite (cortés) || sharp, subtle (sutil) || tactful (que tiene tacto) || refined; *Eduardo tiene gustos muy delicados* Edward has very refined tastes || considerate, thoughtful (atento) || — *hacerse el delicado* to be overfussy || *manjar delicado* delicacy.

delicaducho, cha *adj* FAM delicate, frail, weakly, sickly.

delicia *f* delight; *Juanito es la delicia de sus padres* Johnny is his parent's delight || — *el jardín de las delicias* the Garden of Earthly Delights || *hacer las delicias de* to delight; *los columpios hacen las delicias de los niños* the swings delight the children || *no hay delicia comparable a...* there is nothing like... || *pensar con delicia en* to delight in the idea *o* in the thought of || *su casa es una delicia* his house is delightful, he has a delightful house.

delicioso, sa *adj* delightful (deleitable) || delicious (sabor, etc.) || charming, delightful (encantador); *es una mujer deliciosa* she is a charming woman || FAM funny (gracioso).

delictivo, va; delictuoso, sa *adj* criminal, punishable.

delicuescencia *f* deliquescence.

delimitación *f* delimitation.

delimitar *vt* to delimit, to delimitate, to mark the boundaries of || to define (atribuciones, etc.).

delincuencia *f* delinquency; *delincuencia juvenil* juvenile delinquency.

delincuente *m/f* delinquent, offender || — *delincuente habitual* habitual offender || *delincuente sin antecedentes penales* first offender || *delincuente juvenil, joven delincuente* juvenile delinquent.
◆ *adj* delinquent.

delineación *f* delineation, outlining.

delineante *m* draughtsman, draftsman || *delineante proyectista* designer (que idea los proyectos).

delinear *vt* to delineate, to sketch, to outline || *relieve bien delineado* well-defined relief.

delinquir *vi* to commit an offence, to break the law.

deliquio *m* faint, fainting fit (desmayo) || ecstasy (éxtasis).

delirante *adj* delirious || frenzied, delirious; *imaginación, ovaciones delirantes* delirious imagination, ovation.

delirar *vi* to be delirious || FIG to talk nonsense, to rave (desatinar) | to rave (*por* about, over), to rave (estar entusiasmado).

delirio *m* delirium (desvarío) || FIG ravings *pl* (ilusión) | stupid thing, nonsense (disparate) || — *con delirio* madly || *delirio de grandezas* delusions of grandeur || *delirio de persecución* persecution mania || FIG & FAM *¡el delirio!* it was great! || *estar en delirio* to be delirious || FIG & FAM *tener delirio por...* to be crazy about...

delirium tremens *m* MED delirium tremens.

delito *m* crime, offence [US offense] || — *cogido en flagrante delito* caught red-handed || *delito común* crime, offence [in common law] || *delito de lesa majestad* lese majesty, lèse majesté || *delito flagrante* flagrante delicto || *delito político* political crime *o* offence || *el cuerpo del delito* the corpus delicti.

delta *f* delta (letra griega) || DEP hang-gliding.
◆ *m* GEOGR delta.

deltaico, ca *adj* deltaic.

deltoideo, a *adj* ANAT deltoid, deltoidal.

deltoides *adj inv* ANAT deltoid, deltoidal.
◆ *m inv* ANAT deltoid.

demacración *f* emaciation (adelgazamiento).

demacrado, da *adj* emaciated; *rostro demacrado* emaciated face.

demacrarse *vpr* to waste away, to become emaciated.

demagogia *f* demagogy.

demagógico, ca *adj* demagogic, demagogical.

demagogo *m* demagogue [US demagog, demagogue].

demanda *f* JUR petition, claim (petición) | lawsuit, action (acción) || COM demand; *la ley de la oferta y la demanda* the law of supply and demand; *este artículo tiene mucha demanda* there is a large demand for this article || request, appeal (petición); *rechazar una demanda* to turn down a request || quest, search (busca) || — *en demanda de* asking for (pidiendo); *en demanda de ayuda* asking for help; in search of, seeking (buscando) || JUR *estimar una demanda* to allow a claim | *presentar una demanda contra uno* to bring an action against s.o., to sue s.o., to take legal proceedings against s.o.

— OBSERV The Spanish word *demanda* is used mostly as a legal term; *demand* is normally translated by *reclamación, exigencia*.

demandado, da *adj* JUR *parte demandada* defendant.
◆ *m/f* JUR defendant.

demandante *adj* JUR *parte demandante* plaintiff.
◆ *m/f* plaintiff.

demandar *vt* JUR to sue, to file a suit against, to bring an action against; *demandar a una persona* to sue s.o. || (p us) to request (pedir) || (p us) to desire (desear) || JUR *demandar a uno por daños y perjuicios* to sue s.o. for damages.

demaquillador *m* makeup remover.

demarcación *f* demarcation, demarkation || district (territorio) || *línea de demarcación* demarcation line, line of demarcation.

demarcador, ra *adj* demarcating, of demarcation.

demarcar *vt* to demarcate, to delimit, to mark out || MAR to take a ship's bearings.

demás *adj/pron indef* other, rest of the; *la demás gente* the rest of the people, the other people; *los demás invitados* the other guests, the rest of the guests; *poco importa lo que piensan los demás* it matters little what the others *o* the rest (of them) think || — *lo demás* the rest || *por lo demás* otherwise, apart from that; *es díscolo, pero por lo demás muy buen chico* he is mischievous, but otherwise a very good boy.
◆ *adv* besides, moreover (además) || — *por demás* no good, in vain; *está por demás que le escribas* it is no good your writing to him, you are writing to him in vain; too (con adjetivo), too much of a (con sustantivo); *es por demás cobarde* he is really too much of a coward || *y demás* etcetera, etc.; *visitamos el Tate Gallery, la torre de Londres y demás* we visited the Tate Gallery, the Tower of London, etc.

— OBSERV In the plural the adjective is not always preceded by the article: *Andrés y demás alumnos* Andrew and the other pupils.

demasía *f* surplus, excess (que sobra) || outrage, disregard (atropello, abuso) || insolence, audacity, lack of respect (falta de respeto) || — *cometer demasías* to commit outrages *o* excesses, to go too far || *en* or *con demasía* in excess, excessively.

demasiado, da *adj* too much *sing*, too many *pl*; *demasiada agua* too much water; *demasiados libros* too many books; *¿tienes bastantes revistas? tengo demasiadas* have you got enough magazines? I have got too many || excessive; *la demasiada confianza es perjudicial* excessive familiarity is dangerous.
◆ *adv* too; *es demasiado buena* she is too good || too much; *pides demasiado* you are asking too much || too much, excessively; *bebe demasiado* he drinks excessively || *sería demasiado* that would be too much.

demasiarse *vpr* to go too far.

demencia *f* madness, insanity, dementia || MED *demencia precoz* dementia praecox.

demente *adj* mad, insane, demented.
◆ *m/f* lunatic, mental patient (de hospital).

demérito *m* demerit.

demiurgo *m* FIL demiurge.

democracia *f* democracy.

demócrata *adj* democratic.
◆ *m/f* democrat.

democratacristiano, na; democristiano, na *adj* Christian Democratic.
◆ *m/f* Christian Democrat.

democrático, ca *adj* democratic.

democratización *f* democratization.

democratizar *vt* to democratize.
◆ *vpr* to democratize.

democristiano, na *adj/s* → **democratacristiano.**

Demócrito *npr m* Democritus.

demografía *f* demography.

demográfico, ca *adj* demographic || population; *explosión demográfica* population explosion; *crecimiento demográfico* population increase.

demógrafo *m* demographer.

demoledor, ra *adj* demolishing (herramienta) || FIG devastating; *crítica demoledora* devastating criticism.
◆ *m/f* housebreaker [*US* wrecker] (de edificios).

demoler* *vt* to demolish, to pull down || FIG to demolish (una organización, etc.).

demolición *f* demolition.

demoniaco, ca *adj* demoniac, demoniacal, demonic, possessed of the devil.
◆ *m/f* demoniac (endemoniado).

demonio *m* devil, demon || — FAM *a demonios* ghastly, horrible; *oler, saber a demonios* to smell, to taste ghastly | *¿cómo demonios...?* how the devil...? | *como el demonio* like hell | *darse a todos los demonios* to fly off the handle | *de mil demonios, de todos los demonios* a hell of a; *una casa, un resfriado de mil demonios* a hell of a house, a hell of a cold; devilish, hellish; *hacía un frío de todos los demonios* it was hellish cold | *¡demonio!, ¡demonios!* well, I'll be blowed! (sorpresa), hell!, damn! (disgusto) || *¡demonio de niño, estate quieto!* keep still, you little devil! || *ese demonio de hombre* that devil of man || *estar poseído por el demonio* to be possessed of the devil || FAM *¡ni qué demonios!* like hell!, my foot!; *¡qué abogado ni qué demonios!* like hell he's a lawyer!, a lawyer my foot! || *ponerse como un demonio* to go mad, to get mad, to fly off the handle || FAM *¡qué demonios!, ¡qué demonio!* damn it!; *si nadie va a trabajar, yo tampoco, ¡qué demonios!* if no one is going to work, then I'm not either, damn it! | *¿qué demonios?* what the hell?; *¿qué demonios estás haciendo?* what the hell are you doing? || *¡que me lleve el demonio si...!* I'll be hanged *o* blowed if..!, the devil take me if...!; *¡que me lleve el demonio si comprendo algo de esto!* I'll be blowed if I can understand any of this; cross my heart and hope to die; *¡que me lleve el demonio si es mentira!* it's true, cross my heart and hope to die || *¿quién demonios...?* who the devil...? || *ser el mismo demonio* to be a real devil (un niño), to be a sly *o* crafty devil (muy hábil) || *tener el demonio en el cuerpo* to have the devil in one, to be full of devilment, to be possessed of the devil, to be full of the devil.

demontre *m* FAM demon, devil || FAM *¡qué demontre!* damn it!; *si nadie va a trabajar, yo tampoco, ¡qué demontre!* if no one is going to work, then I'm not either, damn it!

demora *f* delay; *demora en la entrega de un pedido* delay in the delivery of an order || wait; *¿qué demora tiene una conferencia telefónica con Manchester?* how long is the wait for a call to Manchester? || *sin demora* without delay.

demorar *vt* to delay, to put off (retrasar); *tuve que demorar el viaje* I had to delay the journey || to delay, to hold up; *no quiero demorarte más* I don't want to delay you any longer || to hold up; *el barco fue demorado por el mal tiempo* the boat was held up by the bad weather.
◆ *vi* to stay on, to linger on (detenerse).
◆ *vpr* to take time, to be a long time, to take a long time; *perdóname, me he demorado un poco* forgive me, I've been rather a long time *o* I've taken rather a long time.

Demóstenes *npr m* Demosthenes.

demostrable *adj* demonstrable.

demostración *f* demonstration; *hacer una demostración de cómo funciona un aparato* to give a demonstration of how a piece of equipment works || show, display, demonstration; *demostración de fuerza, de cariño* show of strength, of affection || sign; *las lágrimas son una demostración de dolor* tears are a sign of grief || display; *una demostración gimnástica* a gymnastic display || MAT proof || demonstration, proof (de una proposición, etc.) || MIL demonstration || *hacer la demostración de* to demonstrate.

demostrar* *vt* to show, to prove; *lo mal que vive demuestra que no tiene mucho dinero* the poor way in which he lives shows he hasn't much money || to show; *demostrar su ignorancia en la materia* to show one's ignorance on the subject || to prove; *su respuesta demuestra su inteligencia* his answer proves his intelligence || to show; *demostrar interés* to show interest; *el prestidigitador nos demostró varios trucos* the conjurer showed us a few tricks || to demonstrate, to show (hacer una demostración) || MAT to prove || to prove (una teoría, etc.).

demostrativo, va *adj/sm* GRAM demonstrative.

demótico, ca *adj* demotic.

demudación *f*; **demudamiento** *m* paling (del color de la cara) || change (de la expresión).

demudar *vt* to turn pale (el color de la cara) || to change (la expresión) || *tenía el rostro demudado por la cólera* his face was distorted with anger.
◆ *vpr* to change (la expresión) || to pale (el color) || to be distorted (la cara).

denantes *adv* FAM before.

denario, ria *adv* denary (decimal).
◆ *m* denarius (moneda).

dendrita *f* MIN & BIOL dendrite.

denegación *f* refusal, rejection (rechazo) || denial (negación) || — JUR *denegación de demanda* dismissal | *denegación de paternidad* disowning of offspring.

denegar* *vt* to refuse, to reject (rehusar) || to deny (negar) || JUR to reject (un recurso) | to dismiss; *denegar una demanda a uno* to dismiss s.o.'s claim.

denervación *f* MED denervation.

dengoso, sa *adj* affected, finicky (melindroso).

dengue *m* affectation (melindre) || kind of shawl (mantón) || MED dengue [fever] (enfermedad tropical) || *no me vengas con dengues* don't act like a spoilt child, don't be silly, don't be so finicky.

denguear *vi* to put on airs, to be affected.

denier *m* TECN denier.

denigración *f* denigration, disparagement.

denigrante *adj* disparaging (insultante) || denigrating (deshonroso).
◆ *m/f* denigrator, disparager.

denigrar *vt* to denigrate, to run down, to disparage || to insult (injuriar).

denodadamente *adj* valiantly, bravely, boldly (valientemente) || stoutly, with determination (esforzadamente).

denodado, da *adj* valiant, brave, bold, intrepid, courageous (valiente) || determined, resolute; *un esfuerzo denodado* a determined effort.

denominación *f* denomination, naming (acción) || denomination, name (nombre) || *de-*

nominación de origen «appellation d'origine» (de los vinos).

denominado, da *adj* MAT *número denominado* compound number.

denominador, ra *adj* denominative.
◆ *m* MAT denominator; *el mínimo común denominador* the least *o* the lowest common denominator.

denominar *vt* to name, to denominate, to call.

denominativo, va *adj* denominative.

denostador, ra *adj* insulting.

denostar* *vt* to insult.

denotar *vt* to denote, to indicate, to reveal, to show; *su manera de hablar denota una baja cultura* the way he speaks denotes a low level of education || to mean (significar).

densidad *f* density; *densidad de población* population density || FÍS density || darkness, blackness (de la noche) || thickness, denseness (de la niebla, de un bosque) || INFORM *doble densidad* double density (de un disquete).

densificar *vt* to densify || to thicken (espesar).

densímetro *m* FÍS densimeter.

denso, sa *adj* FÍS dense || dense (población, multitud) || dense, thick; *humo denso* thick smoke; *bosque denso* dense wood || FIG black, dark; *noche densa* dark night | dense; *discurso denso* dense speech.

dentado, da *adj* toothed (que tiene dientes) || cogged, toothed (rueda) || serrated (cuchillo) || BOT dentate; *hoja dentada* dentate leaf || HERÁLD indented.
◆ *m* perforation; *el dentado de un sello* the perforation of a stamp.
◆ *f* AMER bite (dentellada).

dentadura *f* teeth *pl*, set of teeth; *tiene una dentadura muy bonita* he has a very nice teeth, he has a very nice set of teeth || *dentadura postiza* false teeth *pl*, denture, dentures *pl*.

dental *adj* dental; *prótesis dental* dental prothesis || *crema dental* toothpaste.
◆ *adj/sf* dental || *consonante dental* dental consonant.
◆ *m* AGR sole (del arado).

dentar* *vt* to provide with teeth *o* cogs (una rueda) || to provide with teeth (una sierra) || to serrate (un cuchillo) || to perforate (un sello).
◆ *vi* to teethe, to cut teeth (un niño).

dentario, ria *adj* dental.

dentelaria *f* BOT plumbago, leadwort.

dentellada *f* snap of the jaws (movimiento) || bite (mordisco) || toothmark (señal) || — *a dentelladas* with one's teeth || *dar dentelladas a algo* to bite sth. || *morder a dentelladas* to bite.

dentellado, da *adj* HERÁLD engrailed || ⟶ **dentado.**

dentellar *vi* *dentellaba de miedo* his teeth were chattering with fear.

dentellear *vt* to nibble, to nibble at (mordiscar).

dentellón *m* ARQ tooth (de la adaraja) | dentil, denticle (dentículo).

dentera *f* setting on edge (en los dientes) || FIG & FAM envy (envidia) || *dar dentera a uno* to make s.o. green with envy (dar envidia), to set s.o.'s teeth on edge; *ese ruido me da dentera* that noise sets my teeth on edge.

dentición *f* teething, cutting of the teeth, dentition (acción de dentar) || set of teeth, dentition (de los niños) || set of teeth (serie completa de dientes); *primera, segunda dentición* first, second set of teeth.

denticulado, da *adj* ARQ denticulate, denticulated.

dentículo *m* ARQ dentil, denticle.

dentífrico, ca *adj* tooth || *pasta dentífrica* toothpaste.
◆ *m* toothpaste, dentifrice (p us).

dentina *f* dentine [US dentin] (de los dientes).

dentista *m* dentist; *ir al dentista* to go to the dentist's.

dentistería *f* AMER dental clinic (consultorio de dentista).

dentística *f* AMER dentistry.

dentón, ona *adj/s* ⟶ **dentudo.**

dentro *adv* inside; *está dentro* he is inside || indoors, inside (en casa); *hace frío, vamos a jugar dentro* it's cold, let's play indoors || — *ahí dentro* in there (de una cosa), indoors, inside (de la casa) || *de* or *desde dentro* from inside || *dentro de* in, inside, within (p us); *dentro de la casa* in the house; in, inside; *meter algo dentro de una caja* to put sth. in a box; in, in... 's time (tiempo fijo); *venga a verme dentro de un día, dos semanas* come and see me in a day *o* in a day's time, in two weeks *o* in two week's time || *dentro de lo posible* as far as possible, as much as possible || *dentro de poco* soon, shorthy, within a short time || *está* or *entra dentro de lo posible* it is possible || *ir hacia dentro* or *para dentro* to go indoors *o* inside (en casa) || *llevo el patriotismo muy dentro* I feel patriotism deep down *o* deep inside || *meter hacia dentro* to push in (algo que sobresale), to pull in; *meter el estómago hacia dentro* to pull one's stomach in || *por dentro* inside, on the inside (en el interior), inwardly, inside; *sentirse muy triste por dentro* to feel very sad inwardly || *tener los pies hacia dentro* to be pigeon-toed.

dentudo, da; dentón, ona *adj* toothy, goofy.
◆ *m/f* toothy *o* goofy person.

denudación *f* GEOL denudation.

denudar *vt* GEOL to denude, to lay bare.

denuedo *m* bravery, courage.

denuesto *m* insult.

denuncia; denunciación *f* reporting (acción de denunciar un delito) || report (documento) || denunciation (delación) || accusation; *denuncia falsa* false accusation || denunciation, notice of termination (de un tratado) || denunciation, censure (crítica severa) || JUR *presentar una denuncia contra alguien* to lodge a complaint against s.o., to bring an action against s.o.

denunciar *vt* to report; *denunciar un robo a la policía* to report a theft to the police || to denounce; *el periódico denunció la invasión de anglicismos* the newspaper denounced the invasion of Anglicisms || to expose (exponer) || to indicate, to betray (indicar) || to denounce, to give notice of the termination of (un tratado) || to denounce (delatar) || *denunciar una mina* to apply for a mining concession, to register a claim to a mine.

denunciatorio, ria *adj* who reports [a crime] || denouncing (que delata o condena).

deontología *f* deontology.

deontológico, ca *adj* deontological.

deparar *vt* to give, to afford; *este libro me deparó una satisfacción enorme* this book afforded me a great deal of pleasure || to give, to provide with; *tu visita me ha deparado la oportunidad de explicarte una cosa* your visit has provided me with the opportunity of explaining sth. to you || to cause; *su enfermedad me deparó un gran disgusto* his illness caused me great grief || to bring; *veamos lo que nos depara el año nuevo* let us see what the new year brings || to provide (solución) || — *¡Dios te la depare buena!* and the best of luck to you!, the best of British luck (to you)! || *entré en el primer cine que me deparó la suerte* I went into the first cinema I chanced upon.

departamental *adj* departmental.

departamento *m* province, district, department, administrative district (división territorial) || department, section (división administrativa, de un almacén) || compartment (de un tren); *departamento de no fumadores* non-smoking compartment || compartment, section (de una caja, etc.).
— OBSERV Certain Latin American countries are divided into *departamentos* (Bolivia, Colombia, Perú, Uruguay, etc.).

departir *vi* to talk, to converse.

depauperación *f* impoverishment || MED weakening (debilitación).

depauperar *vt* to impoverish (empobrecer) || MED to weaken (debilitar).

dependencia *f* dependence, dependance, reliance; *la dependencia de una persona con respecto a otra* the dependence of one person on another || dependency (país) || department, section (sección de una oficina, etc.) || branch [office] (sucursal) || — *dependencia asistencial* small clinic [giving free medical aid] || *estar bajo la dependencia de* to be dependent on.
◆ *pl* outbuildings; *las dependencias de un castillo* the outbuildings of a castle.

depender *vi* to depend || — *depender de* to depend on; *lo que gasto depende de lo que gano* what I spend depends on what I earn; to be under (estar bajo la autoridad de uno); *veinte empleados dependen de él* twenty employees are under him; to be dependent on; *todavía el chico depende de sus padres* the boy is still dependent on his parents; to turn on, to depend on; *todo depende de su contestación* everything turns on his answer || *depende de ti* it rests with you, it is up to you || *en lo que de mí (de nosotros, etc.) depende* as far as I (we, etc.) am concerned || *eso depende* it depends.

dependienta *f* shop assistant, sales assistant, salesgirl, saleslady, saleswoman.

dependiente *adj* dependent (*de* on).
◆ *m* shop assistant, salesman [US clerk].

depilación *f* depilation.

depilar *vt* to depilate.
◆ *vpr* to pluck (las cejas); *las mujeres se depilan las cejas* women pluck their eyebrows || to depilate (las piernas, etc.).

depilatorio, ria *adj/sm* depilatory.

deplorable *adj* deplorable, lamentable, regrettable.

deplorar *vt* to deplore, to regret deeply; *deploramos su muerte* we regret his death deeply || to deplore, to lament (lamentar).

deponente *adj* JUR testifying, giving evidence || GRAM deponent (verbo).
◆ *m/f* JUR deponent, witness.
◆ *m* GRAM deponent, deponent verb.

deponer* *vt* to lay down; *deponer las armas* to lay down one's arms || to remove from office; *deponer a un cónsul de su cargo* to remove a consul from office || to depose (al rey) || JUR to give evidence of, to testify; *deponer algo ante el tribunal* to give evidence of sth. before the court || FIG to banish; *deponer el temor* to banish fear.
◆ *vi* JUR to give evidence || to defecate (defecar) || AMER to vomit.

deportación *f* deportation.

deportado, da *adj* deported.
◆ *m/f* deported person, deportee.

deportar *vt* to deport.

deporte *m* sport; *deportes de invierno* winter sports; *campo de deportes* sports ground; *hacer deporte* to practise sport || — *deporte de remo* rowing || *deporte de vela* yachting (con yate, en los juegos olímpicos), sailing (como recreo).

deportismo *m* sport, practice of sport (práctica) || enthusiasm for sport (afición).

deportista *adj* keen on sport, sporty.
◆ *m* sportsman (que practica deporte) || sports fan (aficionado).
◆ *f* sportswoman (que practica deporte) || sports fan (aficionada).

deportividad *f*; **deportivismo** *m* sportsmanship.

deportivo, va *adj* sports (relativo a los deportes); *periódico deportivo* sports paper; *club deportivo* sports club; *coche deportivo* sports car; *campo deportivo* sports ground; *chaqueta deportiva* sports jacket || sporty, sporting (aficionado a los deportes).

deposición *f* deposition, deposal (de un rey) || removal from office, deposition; *la deposición del cónsul* the removal of the consul from office || JUR testimony, evidence, deposition || excretion, defecation (evacuación del vientre).

depositador, ra *m/f* depositor.

depositante *adj* who deposits.
◆ *m/f* depositor.

depositar *vt* to deposit; *depositar fondos en el banco* to deposit money in the bank; *depositó los diamantes en la caja de caudales* he deposited the diamonds in the safe || to place, to deposit; *depositó los libros en el suelo* he placed the books on the floor || FIG to place; *la madre tiene depositada en él toda su esperanza* his mother has placed all her hope in him || to deposit, to leave; *el vino deposita heces* wine leaves a sediment || to deposit, to store; *depositar las mercancías en un almacén* to store goods in a warehouse || *depositar algo en manos de uno* to entrust s.o. with sth., to entrust sth. to s.o.
◆ *vpr* to settle (líquido, polvo, etc.).

depositaría *f* depository, depositary.

depositario, ria *m/f* depositary, depository, trustee (de dinero, etc.) || repository (de secreto, confianza, etc.) || *hacer de uno depositario de un secreto* to confide in s.o., to make s.o. the depository of a secret.
◆ *m* cashier (cajero) || treasurer (tesorero).

depósito *m* deposit (de una suma) || store, depot, warehouse (almacén) || dump, depot (de municiones) || tank; *depósito de gasolina* petrol tank || depot, yard; *depósito de madera, de carbón* timber, coal yard || tip, dump (de basuras) || scale (en una caldera, conducto, etc.) || deposit, sediment (sedimento) || — *casco en depósito* returnable bottle || ECON *depósito a plazo* term deposit || *depósito bancario* bank deposit || *depósito de aceite combustible* fuel tank || *depósito de agua* water tank, cistern || *depósito de cadáveres* morgue, mortuary || *depósito de decantación* sedimentation basin || *depósito de equipajes* left-luggage office [US checkroom] || *depósito de locomotoras* engine shed [US roundhouse] || *depósito de objetos perdidos* lost-property office || *depósito legal* copyright [of a book] || *en depósito* in bond; *mercancías en depósito* goods in bond.

depravación *f* depravity, depravation.

depravado, da *adj* depraved.
◆ *m/f* depraved person, degenerate.

depravar *vt* to deprave.
◆ *vpr* to become depraved.

deprecación *f* prayer, deprecation.

deprecar *vt* to beg, to implore.

depreciación *f* depreciation.

depreciador, ra *adj* depreciating, depreciatory.
◆ *m/f* depreciator.

depreciar *vt* to depreciate.
◆ *vpr* to depreciate.

depredación *f* pillaging, depredation (saqueo).

depredador, ra *adj* depredatory.
◆ *m/f* pillager, depredator.

depredar *vt* to pillage, to depredate.

depresión *f* depression, hollow (concavidad) || depression (del ánimo) || depression, slump (económica) || — *depresión atmosférica* atmospheric depression || *depresión nerviosa* nervous breakdown.

depresivo, va *adj* depressing (deprimente) || MED depressive.

depresor, ra *adj* depressing.
◆ *m* MED depressor (en general) | tongue depressor (para la lengua) || ANAT depressor (músculo).

deprimente *adj* depressing.

deprimir *vt* to depress || FIG to depress (quitar los ánimos) || *frente deprimida* receding forehead.
◆ *vpr* to get depressed.

deprisa *adv* ⟶ **prisa (de).**

de profundis *m inv* de profundis.

depuesto, ta *pp* ⟶ **deponer.**

depuración *f* purification, depuration (del agua) || cleansing (de la sangre) || FIG purge, purging.

depurador, ra *adj* purifying; *planta* or *estación depuradora* purifying plant.
◆ *m* depurative (sustancia) || purifier (aparato).

depurar *vt* to purify, to depurate; *depurar el agua* to purify the water || to cleanse (la sangre) || FIG to purify (refinar) | to purge (en política) || FIG *estilo depurado* pure *o* purified style.

depurativo, va *adj/sm* depurative.

deque *adv* FAM when, as soon as (en cuanto).

derby *m* DEP derby.

derecha *f* right hand (mano) || right (lado); *aquél de la derecha* that one on the right || — *a la derecha* on the right, on the right-hand side || *la derecha* the right wing, the right (en política) || *no hacer nada a derechas* not to do anything right, to do nothing right || *ser de derechas* to be right-wing || *torcer a la derecha* to turn right, to turn to the right.

derechamente *adv* straight, directly; *fue derechamente hacia él* he went straight to him; *ir derechamente al asunto* to go straight to the point || FIG properly; *obrar derechamente* to act properly.

derechazo *m* TAUR «muleta» pass with the right hand || right (boxeo).

derechismo *m* rightist policy.

derechista *adj* rightist, right-wing (política).
◆ *m/f* rightist, right-winger (en política).

derecho *m* JUR law; *derecho administrativo, canónico, civil, consuetudinario, fiscal, foral, internacional, laboral, natural, marítimo, mercantil, penal, político, procesal* administrative, canon, civil, consuetudinary *o* customary (en Inglaterra, common), fiscal *o* tax, statutory, international, labour, natural, maritime, commercial, criminal, constitutional, procedural law; *estudiar derecho* to read *o* to study law || right, claim; *su derecho al trono* his right to the throne || right; *los derechos civiles* civil rights; *los derechos de una persona* a person's rights || right side; *el derecho de una tela, de un calcetín* the right side of a material, of a sock || — *conforme al derecho* in accordance with the law || *con derecho a* with the right to || *con derecho, sin derecho* rightly, wrongly || *¿con qué derecho?* what right?; *¿con qué derecho has hecho eso?* what right did you have to do that? || *corresponder de derecho a uno* to be s.o.'s right; *le corresponde de derecho pedirlo* it is his right to ask for it || *dar derecho* to entitle, to give the right to; *billete que da derecho (a uno) a entrar* ticket which gives you the right to go in *o* which entitles you to go in || *de derecho* by right; *te corresponde de derecho* it is yours by right || *de pleno derecho* full; *miembro de pleno derecho* full member || *derecho al voto* the right to vote, the vote || *derecho del más fuerte* the rule of the survival of the fittest || *derecho de paso* right of way || *derecho divino* divine right || *derecho habiente* rightful claimant || *derecho sucesorio* death duty, death tax || *estar en su derecho* to be within one's rights, to be in the right || *hacer algo con todo* or *con pleno derecho* to have every right to do sth., to be within one's rights to do sth. || *no hay derecho* it's not fair || *por derecho propio* in one's own right || *reservado el derecho de admisión* the management reserves the right to refuse admission || *según derecho* in accordance with the law (ley), by rights (con razón) || *tener derecho* to have the right, to be entitled; *cada uno de los niños tiene derecho a una porción de pastel* each of the children is entitled to a piece of cake *o* has the right to a piece of cake; to be entitled, to have a *o* the right; *tengo derecho a quejarme* I have a right *o* the right to complain, I am entitled to complain || *usar de su derecho* to exercise one's right.
◆ *pl* fees (de un notario, etc.) || duties, taxes (impuestos) || *derechos aduaneros* or *arancelarios* or *de aduana* customs duties || *derechos de autor* royalties || *derechos de entrada* import duties || *derechos del hombre, derechos humanos* rights of man; *declaración de los derechos del hombre* declaration of the rights of man || *derechos de matrícula* enrolment *o* registration fees || *derechos de peaje* toll duties || *derechos de puerto* harbour dues [US harbor dues] || *reservados todos los derechos* copyright, all rights reserved.

derecho *adv* straight; *andar derecho* to walk straight; *fue derecho a su casa* he went straight home || *siga* or *vaya (todo) derecho* carry *o* go straight on.

derecho, cha *adj* right; *el brazo derecho* the right arm || straight, upright, erect; *aunque es viejo, todavía va muy derecho* although he is old, he is still very upright; *ponerse derecho* to stand up straight || upright; *un poste derecho* an upright pole || — *derecho como una vela* as straight as a die || *es un hombre hecho y derecho* he is a man in every sense of the word, he is a real man.

derechohabiente *m* rightful claimant.

derechura *f* straightness || uprightness (verticalmente) || *en derechura* straight.

deriva *f* MAR drift, leeway || — *a la deriva* drifting, adrift || MAR & FIG *ir a la deriva* to drift || AVIAC *plano de deriva* rudder.

derivable *adj* derivable.

derivación *f* derivation (de una palabra) || origin (origen) || change, deviation (cambio) || diversion (de un canal, etc.) || MAT derivation (de una derivada) || ELECTR shunt.

derivado, da *adj* derived, derivative (palabra).
◆ *m* derivative (palabra) || QUÍM derivative, byproduct.
◆ *f* MAT derivative [of a function].

derivar *vi* to incline, to drift, to derive, to tend; *desde pequeño su interés derivó hacia la pintura* from a child his interest inclined towards painting || to stem, to spring, to come, to arise; *de ahí deriva su amistad* that is where their friendship stems from || MAR to drift || to be derived, to derive; *«librero» deriva de «libro»* «librero» is derived from «libro».

◆ *vt* to direct, to divert; *no pude derivar la conversación hacia otro asunto más agradable* I couldn't divert the conversation to a pleasanter subject ‖ to divert, to tap; *derivar de un río un canal de riego* to tap a river for an irrigation channel, to divert an irrigation channel from a river ‖ to derive; *derivar una palabra del griego* to derive a word from the Greek ‖ MAT to calculate (función derivada) ‖ ELECTR to shunt.
◆ *vpr* to change, to drift (*hacia* to), to change, to drift (conversación, etc.) ‖ to come out of (salir) ‖ to be derived; *esta palabra se deriva del griego* this word is derived from the Greek ‖ to result, to stem, to arise (*de* from), to result, to stem, to arise (resultar).

derivativo, va *adj/m* derivative.

dermatitis *f inv* MED dermatitis.

dermatoesqueleto *m* exoskeleton, dermoskeleton.

dermatología *f* MED dermatology.

dermatólogo *m* MED dermatologist.

dermatomo; dermatotomo *m* MED dermatome (instrumento).

dermatosis *f inv* MED dermatosis.

dérmico, ca *adj* ANAT dermal, dermic, skin.

dermis *f inv* ANAT dermis, derm, cutis.

dermitis *f inv* MED dermatitis.

dermografía *f* MED dermography.

dermografismo *m* MED dermatographism.

dermoide *m* MED dermoid cyst.

dermopatía *f* MED dermatopathy.

dermorreacción *f* skin test.

derogable *adj* repealable, which can be annulled.

derogación *f* JUR repeal, repealing, derogation, abolition (de una ley).

derogar *vt* JUR to repeal, to derogate, to annul, to abolish (ley) ‖ to rescind, to cancel (contrato, etc.).

derogatorio, ria *adj* JUR abolishing, annulling, repealing.

derrama *f* assessment, distribution, apportionment, sharing out (de impuestos) ‖ special tax (contribución).

derramadero *m* spillway (de agua) ‖ tip, rubbish dump (de residuos).

derramamiento *m* spilling (involuntario) ‖ overflowing (rebosamiento) ‖ pouring out (de líquido) ‖ scattering (de una familia, de un pueblo) ‖ flowing (chorreo) ‖ spreading, spread (de una noticia) ‖ — *derramamiento de sangre* bloodshed, spilling of blood ‖ *revolución sin derramamiento de sangre* bloodless revolution ‖ *sin derramamiento de sangre* without bloodshed, without a drop of blood being spilt (función adverbial).

derramar *vt* to spill (involuntariamente); *derramar un vaso de agua* to spill a glass of water ‖ to pour, to pour out; *derramar arena al* or *en* or *por el suelo* to pour sand on *o* over the floor ‖ FIG to spread; *derramar una noticia* to spread a piece of news | to overflow with; *derramar ternura* to overflow with tenderness ‖ to share out, to distribute (los impuestos) ‖ — *derramar lágrimas* to shed tears ‖ *derramar sangre* to shed blood, to spill blood.
◆ *vpr* to spill (agua, etc.) ‖ to pour out, to spill out (arena, etc.) ‖ to scatter, to spread (esparcirse) ‖ to spread (una noticia) ‖ to be shed, to be spilt (sangre) ‖ to overflow (rebosar).

derrame *m* spilling (involuntario) ‖ pouring out (voluntario) ‖ shedding, spilling (de sangre) ‖ leakage, waste (pérdida) ‖ overflow (rebosamiento) ‖ MED discharge (externo) | extravasation, effusion (interno) ‖ fork, forking (de un valle) ‖ ARQ splay (de puertas y ventanas) ‖ slope, incline (declive) ‖ spreading, scattering (esparcimiento) ‖ MED *derrame cerebral* brain haemorrhage | *derrame sinovial* water on the knee.

derramo *m* ARQ splay (derrame).

derrapar *vi* AUT to skid (patinar).
— OBSERV This word is a Gallicism.

derredor *m* surroundings *pl*, surrounding part (que rodea) ‖ *al* or *en derredor* round, around (véase ALREDEDOR).

derrelicción *f* dereliction (abandono).

derrelicto, ta *adj/sm* derelict.

derrengadura *f* exhaustion (cansancio) ‖ sprained back (del espinazo).

derrengar *vt* to sprain the back of (lastimar el espinazo) ‖ to twist (torcer) ‖ FIG & FAM to exhaust, to wear out, to shatter (cansar); *estoy derrengado* I'm shattered, I'm worn out.
◆ *vpr* to sprain one's back ‖ FIG & FAM to wear o.s. out, to knock o.s. out, to exhaust o.s. (cansarse).

derretido, da *adj* melted (hielo, nieve, mantequilla, etc.) ‖ melted, molten; *sebo derretido* melted tallow; *plomo derretido* molten lead ‖ FIG madly in love, crazy; *está derretido por ella* he is madly in love with her, he is crazy about her.

derretimiento *m* melting, thawing (de nieve) ‖ melting (de hielo, de mantequilla, de metal, etc.) ‖ FIG squandering, wasting (de una fortuna) | passionate love (amor).

derretir* *vt* to melt (manteca, sebo, etc.) ‖ to thaw, to melt (hielo, nieve) ‖ to melt down (metales) ‖ FIG to waste, to squander (derrochar) | to exasperate (exasperar).
◆ *vpr* to melt (manteca, sebo, etc.); *la mantequilla se derrite con el calor* butter melts with the heat ‖ to melt, to become molten (metales) ‖ to thaw, to melt (hielo, nieve) ‖ FIG to be crazy (*por* about), to be crazy (estar enamorado) | to fall madly in love (*por* with) (enamorarse) | to burn (*de* with) (de amor, de impaciencia) | to fret, to worry, to be worried stiff (inquietarse).

derribador *m* feller (que derriba) ‖ FIG overthrower.

derribar *vt* to knock down, to pull down, to demolish; *derribar una muralla* to knock down a wall ‖ to batter down (una puerta) ‖ to knock over, to upset (una silla) ‖ to knock down; *el conductor derribó a un transeúnte* the driver knocked a pedestrian down ‖ to floor, to throw (en la lucha) ‖ to throw; *el caballo derribó al jinete* the horse threw its jockey ‖ to blow down (el viento) ‖ to shoot down, to bring down; *derribar un avión* to shoot a plane down ‖ to bring down, to knock down (al perseguir a alguien); *derribó al criminal* he brought the criminal down ‖ FIG to overthrow, to bring down (gobierno) | to remove *o* to oust from office, to topple (a un ministro, etc.) | to obtain the dimissal of (a un empleado).
◆ *vpr* to fall down, to throw o.s. to the ground (tirarse al suelo) ‖ to fall down (caer).

derribo *m* demolition, pulling down, knocking down (demolición) ‖ demolition site (lugar).
◆ *pl* rubble *sing* (materiales); *construir con derribos* to build with rubble ‖ *materiales de derribo* rubble *sing*.

derrocamiento *m* hurling down ‖ demolition (de un edificio) ‖ FIG overthrow (de un rey, de un gobierno) | removal from office, toppling (de un ministro, etc.).

derrocar *vt* to hurl down (despeñar) ‖ FIG to knock down, to pull down, to demolish (un edificio) | to overthrow, to bring down; *derrocar la monarquía, el gobierno* to overthrow the king, the government | to remove *o* to oust from office, to topple (a un ministro, etc.).

derrochador, ra; derrochón, ona *adj* spendthrift, wasteful, squandering.
◆ *m/f* spendthrif, wasteful person, squanderer.

derrochar *vt* to squander, to waste; *derrochar su fortuna* to squander one's fortune ‖ FIG to be brimming with *o* full of (salud, energía, simpatía).

derroche *m* waste, squandering (despilfarro) ‖ FIG profusion, abundance; *un derroche de luces* a profusion of lights | burst; *un derroche de energía* a burst of energy ‖ *hacer un derroche de energía en* to put a lot of energy into (hacer un gran esfuerzo), to waste energy in (despilfarrar).

derrochón, ona *adj/s* → **derrochador.**

derrota *f* defeat; *su derrota en las elecciones fue un golpe duro para el partido* his defeat in the elections was a hard blow to the party; *la derrota del equipo nacional* the defeat of the national team ‖ failure, setback; *las derrotas en la vida* life's setbacks ‖ MIL defeat, rout; *sufrir una derrota* to suffer a defeat | débâcle, debacle (en todos los frentes) ‖ path (camino) ‖ MAR course (rumbo).

derrotado, da *adj* defeated ‖ FIG ragged, in tatters (andrajoso) | shabby (persona, muebles).

derrotar *vt* to defeat; *en las elecciones el candidato de la oposición derrotó al del gobierno* the opposition candidate defeated the government candidate in the elections ‖ to beat, to defeat; *el equipo nacional derrotó a su oponente por 2 a 1* the national team beat their opponents 2-1 ‖ MIL to defeat | to rout, to put to flight (hacer huir) ‖ TAUR to butt, to gore; *toro que derrota por la izquierda* bull which butts to the left ‖ to squander (su fortuna) ‖ to ruin (salud).
◆ *vpr* MAR to drift off course.

derrote *m* TAUR butt (con los cuernos).

derrotero *m* MAR course (rumbo) | book of sailing directions, pilot book (libro) ‖ FIG course, plan of action (para llegar a un fin).

derrotismo *m* defeatism.

derrotista *adj/s* defeatist.

derrubiar *vt* to erode, to undermine, to wash away (las aguas corrientes); *el agua derrubia las orillas* water washes away the banks.

derrubio *m* erosion, undermining, washing away ‖ alluvium (tierra).

derruido, da *adj* in ruins (ruinoso).

derruir* *vt* to knock down, to pull down, to demolish (derribar).

derrumbadero; derrumbe *m* precipice, cliff (despeñadero) ‖ FIG pitfall, hazard, danger.

derrumbamiento; derrumbe *m* collapse, falling down (desplome) ‖ demolition, knocking down (demolición) ‖ caving-in, falling in (del techo) ‖ headlong fall (caída) ‖ FIG overthrow (derrocamiento) | collapse, fall; *el derrumbamiento del Imperio Romano* the collapse of the Roman Empire | collapse, sharp fall (de precios) ‖ MIN cave-in (en la mina) ‖ *derrumbamiento de tierra* landslide.

derrumbar *vt* to throw down, to hurl down (despeñar) ‖ to knock down, to pull down, to demolish; *derrumbar una casa* to pull a house down ‖ to knock over (volcar).
◆ *vpr* to collapse, to fall down; *la casa se derrumbó* the house collapsed ‖ to fall in, to cave in (techo) ‖ FIG to collapse | to flop, to fall, to collapse (en un asiento) ‖ FIG *se derrumbaron*

todas mis esperanzas all my hopes were shattered.

derrumbe *m* ⟶ **derrumbadero, derrumbamiento.**

derrumbo *m* precipice.

derviche *m* dervish.

desabastecer *vt* to leave short of supplies, to deprive of supplies || *desabastecido de carbón* short of *o* out of coal.

desabastecimiento *m* shortage.

desabollar *vt* to smooth out, to remove the dents from; *desabollar una cacerola* to remove the dents from a pan.

desabonarse *vpr* to withdraw one's subscription.

desabono *m* withdrawal of subscription || discredit (descrédito).

desaborido, da *adj* insipid, tasteless || FIG & FAM dull, wet; *una chica desaborida* a dull girl.
◆ *m/f* dull *o* wet person.
— OBSERV Often pronounced *esaborío* in Andalusia.

desabotonar *vt* to unbutton, to undo (ropa).
◆ *vi* to open out, to blossom (out), to bloom (las flores).
◆ *vpr* to unbutton one's clothes (desabrocharse) || to come undone (una prenda).

desabridamente *adv* insipidly || gruffly; *contestar desabridamente* to reply gruffly.

desabrido, da *adj* bad tasting (de mal sabor) || insipid, tasteless (soso) || unpleasant (tiempo) || surly; *tiene un carácter desabrido* he has a surly character || abrupt (estilo) || harsh, sharp, gruff (tono, frase) || bitter (discusión).

desabrigado, da *adj* uncovered (sin abrigo) || FIG unprotected, defenceless (sin amparo) || open, exposed to the wind (expuesto a los vientos) || *vas muy desabrigado con el frío que hace* you're not wrapped up well enough for this cold weather.

desabrigar *vt* to uncover (descubrir) || to take off some of the clothes of; *desabrigar a un niño* to take off some of a child's clothes || to leave without shelter (dejar sin refugio).
◆ *vpr* to take some *o* any clothes off, to take one's warm clothing off; *no debe uno desabrigarse cuando está sudando* you should not take any clothes off when you are sweating || to uncover o.s. || to throw off one's bedcovers (en la cama).

desabrigo *m* uncovering (acción) || lack of covering *o* shelter, exposure (falta de protección) || FIG desertion, destitution, abandonment (abandono).

desabrimiento *m* unpleasant taste (sabor desagradable) || insipidness, insipidity, tastelessness (insipidez) || unpleasantness (tiempo) || surliness (del carácter, etc.) || abruptness (del estilo) || harshness, sharpness, gruffness (del tono, etc.) || bitterness (de discusión) || grief (pena) || *contestar con desabrimiento* to reply gruffly.

desabrir *vt* to give an unpleasant taste to (dar mal sabor) || to make insipid *o* tasteless, to take the taste away from || FIG to distress (apenar) | to annoy (enfadar).
◆ *vpr* FIG to be annoyed (enfadarse).

desabrochar *vt* to undo, to unfasten; *desabrochar la camisa a un niño* to undo a child's shirt || to unfasten *o* to undo the clothes of; *desabrochó al niño* she undid the child's clothes || FIG to open (abrir).
◆ *vpr* to undo *o* to unfasten one's clothes; *los niños no saben desabrocharse* children don't know how to undo their clothes || to come undone, to come unfastened (una prenda) || FIG & FAM to unbosom o.s. (*con* to) || *desabrocharse la chaqueta* to undo *o* to unfasten one's coat.

desacalorarse *vpr* to cool down, to cool off (refrescarse) || FIG to calm down, to cool down (calmarse).

desacatador, ra *adj* insolent, impertinent, impudent (insolente) || disrespectful (falto de respeto).
◆ *m/f* insolent person || disrespectful person.

desacatamiento *m* ⟶ **desacato.**

desacatar *vt* to have *o* to show no respect for, to be disrespectful to; *desacatar a sus padres* to be disrespectful to one's parents || not to observe, not to respect, to disobey; *desacatar las órdenes* to disobey orders.

desacato; desacatamiento *m* lack of respect (*a* for), disrespect (*a* for) || JUR disrespect (*a* for), contempt (*a* of) (las leyes) || JUR *desacato a la autoridad* contempt.

desaceitado, da *adj* lacking oil.

desaceitar *vt* to remove the oil from || to scour (lana).

desacerar *vt* to take the steel off.

desacerbar *vt* to sweeten, to temper (templar).

desacertadamente *adv* wrongly, mistakenly (erróneamente) || unfortunately (inadecuadamente) || poorly, clumsily (torpemente) || tactlessly (sin tino).

desacertado, da *adj* ill-advised, unwise (poco recomendable) || unsuccessful (de mal resultado) || unfortunate (inadecuado); *respuesta desacertada* unfortunate reply || poorly chosen (mal elegido) || wrong mistaken (erróneo) || not fitting, unwise; *sería desacertado que fueses a verlo ahora* it would not be fitting *o* it would be unwise for you to go and see him now || poor, clumsy; *una jugada desacertada de la defensa* a poor piece of play by the defence || tactless (sin tacto); *observación desacertada* a tactless remark.

desacertar* *vi* to be wrong, to be mistaken (errar) || to lack tact, to be tactless (no tener tacto).

desacierto *m* mistake (error); *ha sido un desacierto comprar la casa* it was a mistake buying the house || lack of tact (falta de tacto) || unfortunate *o* tactless remark (al hablar) || bad *o* poor choice; *el título del libro fue un desacierto* the title of the book was a bad choice.

desaclimatado, da *adj* unacclimatized.

desacobardar *vt* to encourage, to reassure.

desacomodado, da *adj* badly off, poor (por falta de dinero) || unemployed, out of work (sin empleo) || uncomfortable (incómodo) || inconvenient (molesto) || AMER untidy (desordenado).

desacomodamiento *m* discomfort (incomodidad) || inconvenience (molestia).

desacomodar *vt* to inconvenience, to put out (molestar) || to discharge, to dismiss (despedir).
◆ *vpr* to lose one's job (quedarse sin empleo).

desacomodo *m* discomfort (incomodidad) || inconvenience (molestia) || discharge, dismissal (de un criado).

desacompañar *vt* to leave.

desaconsejable *adj* inadvisable.

desaconsejado, da *adj* unwise, not advisable; *está desaconsejado bañarse después de comer* it is unwise to go swimming after a meal || foolish (imprudente).
◆ *m/f* fool (imprudente).

desaconsejar *vt* to advise against, to dissuade; *quería marcharse a América pero se lo desaconsejé* he wanted to go to America but I advised him against it.

desacoplamiento *m* TECN uncoupling, disconnecting, disconnection || lack of coordination (de un equipo).

desacoplar *vt* TECN to remove; *desacoplar una rueda del eje* to remove a wheel from the axle | to uncouple, to disconnect (dos piezas de un mecanismo) || ELECTR to disconnect || to uncouple (un vagón del tren) || to upset the coordination of (un equipo) || to upset, to disrupt (trastornar).

desacordado, da *adj* MÚS out of tune || discordant, clashing (sin armonía).

desacordar* *vt* MÚS ⟶ **desafinar.**

desacorde *adj* discordant; *instrumentos desacordes* discordant instruments || FIG conflicting, discordant, clashing (opiniones) || clashing (colores).

desacostumbrado, da *adj* unusual, uncommon.

desacostumbrar *vt* to break of the habit of *o* from the habit of; *desacostumbrar a uno del tabaco* to break s.o. of the habit of smoking.
◆ *vpr* to break o.s. of the habit of, to give up; *me he desacostumbrado de la bebida* I have given up drinking || to get out of *o* to get rid of the habit of.

desacreditar *vt* to run down, to disparage, to discredit (denigrar) || to bring discredit on, to bring into discredit, to discredit, to disgrace; *este producto desacredita al fabricante* this product brings discredit on the manufacturer, this product brings the manufacturer into discredit.
◆ *vpr* to disgrace o.s., to let o.s. down, to discredit o.s. || to become discredited.

desacuerdo *m* disagreement, discord; *estar en desacuerdo* to be in disagreement || *estar en desacuerdo con* to be in disagreement with; *esta copia está en desacuerdo con el original* this copy is in disagreement with the original version; not to be in keeping with; *su conducta está en desacuerdo con lo que predica* his conduct is not in keeping with what he preaches; not to match (no hacer juego).

desadornar *vt* to strip of ornaments, to unadorn.

desadvertido, da *adj* inadvertent.

desadvertir* *vt* to fail to notice.

desafear *vt* to improve the looks of.

desafección *f* disaffection.

desafecto, ta *adj* opposed, disaffected || *las personas desafectas al gobierno* the people hostile to the government *o* opposed to the government.
◆ *m* lack of affection, coldness; *mostrar desafecto a uno* to show coldness *o* a lack of affection towards s.o.

desaferrar *vt* to let go, to release (soltar) || MAR to weight (las anclas) || FIG to dissuade, to bring round (disuadir).
◆ *vpr* to let go, to release one's grip (soltarse) || to change one's mind, to come around.

desafiador, ra *adj* ⟶ **desafiante.**
◆ *m/f* challenger.

desafiante; desafiador, ra *adj* challenging (que reta) || defiant; *actitud desafiante* defiant attitude.

desafiar *vt* to challenge (retar); *les desafiaron a un partido de fútbol* they challenged them to a game of football || to dare; *desafiar a alguien a hacer algo* to dare s.o. to do sth. || to challenge [to a duel] (por el honor) || to defy; *desafió la ira de su padre* he defied his father's anger || to brave, to defy, to face; *desafiar el peligro* to defy danger.

◆ *vpr* to challenge each other.

desafición *f* lack of affection, coldness.

desaficionar *vt* to make s.o. dislike, to turn s.o. against *o* off; *desaficionar a uno del tabaco* to make s.o. dislike smoking.
◆ *vpr* to come to dislike, to go off; *desaficionarse de algo* to come to dislike sth.

desafilar *vt* to blunt, to dull (el filo).
◆ *vpr* to lose its edge, to get blunt.

desafinación *f*; **desafinamiento** *m* MÚS dissonance, being out of tune (estado) | going out of tune | putting out of tune.

desafinadamente *adv* out of tune.

desafinado, da *adj* out of tune.

desafinar *vi* MÚS to be out of tune; *este piano desafina* this piano is out of tune | to go out of tune; *el violín desafinó hacia el final del concierto* the violin went out of tune towards the end of the concert | to play out of tune (tocar) | to sing out of tune (cantar) || FIG & FAM to ramble (desvariar) | to speak out of turn (decir algo inoportuno).
◆ *vt* MÚS to put out of tune.
◆ *vpr* MÚS to go out of tune.

desafío *m* challenge (reto) || duel (duelo) || defiance (provocación) || competition, rivalry (competencia).

desaforadamente *adv* in a disorderly fashion (atropelladamente) || outrageously (de una manera escandalosa) || excessively; *comer desaforadamente* to eat excessively || furiously (con furia) || *gritar desaforadamente* to shout one's head off.

desaforado, da *adj* unbounded, boundless; *ambición desaforada* unbounded ambition || huge, enormous (gigantesco) || terrible, terrifying, mighty; *dar voces desaforadas* to give terrible shouts || outrageous (escandaloso) || ardent; *partidario desaforado de una reforma* ardent supporter of a reform || illegal, lawless (contra fuero) || *gritar como un desaforado* to shout one's head off.

desaforar* *vt* to encroach on *o* upon the rights of (violar los fueros) || to deprive of one's privileges (abolir los fueros).
◆ *vpr* to go too far, to act outrageously || to get worked up (irritarse).

desafortunado, da *adj* unlucky, unfortunate (desgraciado) || unfortunate (desacertado).

desafuero *m* infringement of the laws, lawlessness (violación de las leyes) || infringement of *o* encroachment upon rights (violación de los fueros) || deprivation of a right (derecho) *o* privilege (privilegio) || FIG liberty, improper act (desacato) | outrage, excess (abuso) || *cometer un desafuero* to break *o* to infringe the law (violar la ley), to commit an outrage (cometer un abuso).

desagraciado, da *adj* ungraceful, graceless, lacking charm.

desagraciar *vt* to spoil, to spoil the beauty of.

desagradable *adj* unpleasant, disagreeable.

desagradar *vt* to displease || — *este libro me desagrada* I don't like this book || *me desagrada hacerlo* I don't like doing it, I dislike doing it || *que desagrada* unpleasant; *palabra que desagrada* unpleasant word.
◆ *vi* to be unpleasant.
— OBSERV El inglés suele emplear el verbo *not to like*, y el sujeto del verbo español viene a ser el complemento del verbo inglés: *esto me desagrada* I don't like this.

desagradecer* *vt* to be ungrateful for, to show ingratitude for || *desagradece todo el bien que se le ha hecho* he shows no gratitude for all the good that has been done for him.

desagradecido, da *adj* ungrateful; *desagradecido con* or *para su bienhechor* ungrateful towards one's benefactor || *mostrarse desagradecido* to be ungrateful *o* unappreciative, to show ingratitude.
◆ *m/f* ungrateful person, ingrate.

desagradecimiento *m* ingratitude, ungratefulness.

desagrado *m* displeasure; *mostrar desagrado* to show displeasure || — *con desagrado* reluctantly, against one's will; *lo hace, pero con desagrado* he does it, but reluctantly || *esta noticia me causó desagrado* I didn't welcome this news, I didn't like this news.

desagraviar *vt* to make amends to; *desagraviar a uno de una ofensa* to make amends to s.o. for an insult || to indemnify (indemnizar) || to apologize to (disculparse).

desagravio *m* amends *pl*, atonement, satisfaction (acción) || compensation, indemnification, satisfaction (indemnización) || — *acto de desagravio* act of atonement || *en desagravio de* to make amends for, in amends for || *exigir un desagravio* to demand satisfaction.

desagregación *f* disintegration.

desagregar *vt* to disintegrate, to break up || FIG to break up.
◆ *vpr* to disintegrate, to break up || FIG to break up.

desaguadero *m* drain (desagüe) || FIG drain.

desaguador *m* drain, drainpipe (conducto) || drain (canal).

desaguar *vt* to drain, to empty, to run off || FIG to dissipate, to squander.
◆ *vi* to drain, to drain away *o* off (un líquido) || to flow *o* to drain into; *el río desagua en el mar* the river flows into the sea || to drain (un depósito).
◆ *vpr* to drain || FIG to vomit (vomitar) | to relieve o.s. (orinar).

desagüe *m* drainage, draining (acción) || drain, outlet (orificio, canal) || — *conducto* or *tubo de desagüe* downspout, drainpipe (canalón), overflow pipe (para el agua sobrante) || *desagüe del radiador* radiator overflow pipe || *desagüe directo* direct-tosewer drainage.

desaguisado, da *adj* illegal, unlawful (contra la ley) || outrageous, unreasonable (hecho sin razón).
◆ *m* offence (delito) || insult (insulto) || outrage, injustice (atropello) || — *hacer desaguisados* to get up to mischief (niño) || *hacer desaguisados en* to damage || *ocurrió un desaguisado en* sth. went wrong in.

desahogadamente *adv* easily; *aquí caben desahogadamente dos coches* two cars can easily fit in here || comfortably, easily; *viven desahogadamente con su sueldo* they can live comfortably on his wage || freely, at ease (fácilmente) || impudently, brazenly (con insolencia).

desahogado, da *adj* spacious, roomy (espacioso); *habitación desahogada* spacious room || uncluttered (desembarazado) || wide (ancho) || comfortable, well-to-do, well-off (adinerado); *una familia desahogada* a comfortable family, a family which is well-off || well-paid, comfortable (situación) || loose, roomy (ropa) || FIG impudent, brazen, shameless, barefaced (descarado) || — *existencia desahogada* comfortable existence || *vida desahogada* easy life || *vivir desahogado* to live comfortably, to be comfortably off.

desahogar *vt* to relieve (aliviar) || to comfort, to console (consolar) || to ease (dolor) || FIG to vent; *desahogar su ira con uno* to vent one's anger on s.o. | to pour out, to open; *desahogar su corazón* to pour out one's heart | to take a weight *o* a load off; *las lágrimas desahogan el corazón* tears take a weight off your heart.
◆ *vpr* to make o.s. comfortable (ponerse cómodo) || to relax, to take it easy (esparcirse); *después de haber trabajado mucho hace falta desahogarse* one needs to relax after a hard day's work || to rid *o* to free o.s. [from obligations, work, debt, etc.] || FIG to unbosom o.s., to confide, to open one's heart (confiarse); *desahogarse con* or *a un amigo* to unbosom o.s. to a friend, to confide in a friend, to open one's heart to a friend | to get sth. off one's chest (descargarse de una preocupación) | to let off steam (desfogarse); *todo esto lo hace para desahogarse* he does all that just to let off steam.

desahogo *m* relief (alivio) || FIG comfort, ease (holgura económica) | space, room; *quitar un mueble para tener más desahogo* to take away a piece of furniture so as to have more space | outlet, vent (expansión) | relaxation (descanso) | impudence, barefacedness, brazenness (descaro) || liberty, freedom (libertad) || — *expresarse con desahogo* to speak one's mind, to say what one really thinks || *le sirve de desahogo* it helps him to let off steam || *vivir con desahogo* to be comfortably off, to live comfortably.

desahuciado, da *adj* evicted, ejected (de una casa) || hopeless (enfermo).

desahuciar *vt* to deprive of all hope (quitar toda esperanza) || to give up hope for (declarar sin esperanza); *han desahuciado al enfermo* they have given up hope for the patient || to evict, to eject (a un inquilino).

desahucio *m* eviction, ejection (de un inquilino).

desairadamente *adv* ungracefully (sin garbo) || rudely (descortésmente); *contestar desairadamente* to answer rudely.

desairado, da *adj* spurned; *pretendiente desairado* spurned suitor || unattractive, ungraceful (sin garbo) || humiliating (humillante) || awkward (molesto); *situación desairada* awkward situation || *hacer un papel desairado, quedar desairado* to be unsuccessful, to come off badly (quedar mal).

desairar *vt* to snub, to spurn (desdeñar) || to slight (ofender); *acepté su invitación para no desairarle* I accepted his invitation so as not to slight him || to rebuff, to reject (rechazar).

desaire *m* slight, snub, rebuff (desprecio) || ungracefulness, lack of charm (falta de gracia) || — *hacer el desaire a uno de rechazar una oferta* to snub s.o. by refusing an offer || *hacer un desaire a uno* to snub s.o., to slight s.o., to rebuff s.o. || *sufrir un desaire* to be snubbed, to suffer a rebuff.

desajustar *vt* to upset the adjustment of, to put out of order (una máquina) || to pull apart (dos piezas) || FIG to spoil, to upset; *esto desajusta mis planes* that upsets my plans || *me desajustó el tiro* he made me miss.
◆ *vpr* to go wrong, to break down, to get out of working order (una máquina) || to come apart (dos piezas) || to break (romper un contrato).

desajuste *m* breakdown (avería) || maladjustment (cuando está mal ajustada la máquina) || pulling apart (de dos piezas) || breaking (de un acuerdo) || FIG upsetting.

desalabear *vt* TECN to straighten *o* to flatten out, to upwarp (enderezar) | to surface (allanar).

desalabeo *m* TECN straightening out, flattening out, unwarping (enderezamiento) | surfacing (allanamiento).

desalación *f* desalination (del agua de mar).

desalado, da *adj* unsalted (sin sal) || wingless (sin alas) || anxious (ansioso) || — *correr de-*

salado a un sitio to hurry *o* to dash *o* to rush to a place || *ir desalado* to be in a hurry (tener prisa).

desalar *vt* to remove the salt from, to desalt, to unsalt (quitar la sal) || to desalinate (el agua de mar) || to clip *o* to remove the wings of (quitar las alas).
◆ *vpr* to hurry, to rush (apresurarse) || FIG to long to, to yearn to; *se desalaba por conseguir una buena colocación* he longed to obtain a good job.

desalazón *f* removal of salt, desalting.

desalbardar *vt* to remove the packsaddle from.

desalbardillar *vt* to remove the coping from (un muro).

desalentadamente *adv* dispiritedly, unenthusiastically.

desalentador, ra *adj* discouraging, disheartening; *una noticia desalentadora* a discouraging piece of news.

desalentar* *vt* to leave *o* to make breathless, to put out of breath || FIG to discourage, to dishearten (desanimar); *el fracaso le ha desalentado* the failure has discouraged him.
◆ *vpr* to get discouraged, to lose heart; *no debemos desalentarnos ante la adversidad* we must not lose heart in the face of adversity.

desalfombrar *vt* to remove *o* to take up the carpets of; *desalfombrar una casa* to take up the carpets of a house.

desalforjar *vt* to take from the saddlebag (sacar de las alforjas) || to remove the saddlebags from (quitar las alforjas).

desalhajar *vt* to empty, to strip, to remove the furnishings from (una habitación).

desaliento *m* discouragement, loss of heart.

desalinear *vt* to put out of line.
◆ *vpr* to fall out of line (salirse de la línea) || to go out of line.

desalinización *f* desalination.

desalinizar *vt* to desalinate.

desaliñadamente *adv* scruffily, untidily.

desaliñado, da *adj* scruffy, slovenly, dishevelled, untidy; *tiene un aspecto desaliñado* he looks scruffy || slovenly, down-at-heel (siempre descuidado); *es una persona desaliñada* he is a slovenly person || FIG slipshod, slovenly, careless (estilo).

desaliñar *vt* to disarrange (desarreglar) || to dirty (ensuciar) || to make untidy, to mess up (*fam*) || to crease (arrugar); *desaliñar un vestido* to crease a dress.

desaliño *m* scruffiness, slovenliness, untidiness (descuido) || carelessness (del estilo) || *ir vestido con desaliño* to be scruffily dressed.

desalmado, da *adj* wicked (malvado) || cruel, heartless (cruel).
◆ *m/f* wicked person, scoundrel (malvado) || heartless person (cruel).

desalmarse *vpr* to long, to crave (*por* for).

desalmenar *vt* to remove the battlements from.

desalmidonar *vt* to remove the starch from.

desalojado, da *adj* evicted (inquilino) || homeless (sin hogar).
◆ *m/f* homeless person (sin vivienda) || *los desalojados* the homeless.

desalojamiento; desalojo *m* eviction, ejection (expulsión) || MIL dislodging || removal, moving house (cambio de residencia) || evacuation, abandonment (abandono).

desalojar *vt* MIL to dislodge; *desalojar al enemigo del fortín* to dislodge the enemy from the fort | to evacuate, to abandon, to move out of (marcharse de); *desalojar un pueblo* to evacuate a town || to evict, to eject; *desalojar a una persona de su casa* to eject s.o. from his house || to vacate (marcharse); *desalojar una casa* to vacate a house || to clear, to evacuate (hacer salir a la gente); *desalojaron el bar* they cleared the bar || MAR to have a displacement of, to displace (desplazar); *el barco desaloja tantas toneladas* the boat has a displacement of so many tons.
◆ *vi* to move house, to move out (mudarse); *el vecino desaloja* our neighbour is moving house || FAM to clear off, to clear out (irse).

desalojo *m* ⟶ **desalojamiento.**

desalquilado, da *adj* vacant, unrented (un piso).

desalquilar *vt* to stop renting || to vacate (dejar libre).
◆ *vpr* to become vacant.

desalquitranar *vt* to remove the tar from (quitar el alquitrán de) || to clean the tar off (para limpiar).

desamarrar *vt* MAR to cast off, to unmoor (largar las amarras) || to untie (desatar).

desambientado, da *adj* out of place; *en un país extranjero uno se encuentra desambientado* in a foreign country one feels out of place || *esta sala de baile está muy desambientada* this ballroom really lacks atmosphere *o* is really lacking in atmosphere.

desamontonar *vt* to unpile.

desamor *m* coldness, indifference, lack of affection (frialdad); *su desamor a los padres* his coldness *o* indifference towards his parents, his lack of affection for his parents || lack of affection (falta de amor) || dislike (antipatía).

desamorado, da *adj* cold, indifferent.

desamortizable *adj* alienable, disentailable; *bienes desamortizables* alienable property.

desamortización *f* alienation, disentailment.

desamortizar *vt* to alienate, to disentail.

desamparadamente *adv* without protection.

desamparado, da *adj* forsaken, abandoned (abandonado) || helpless, unprotected (sin protección) || open, exposed to the wind (desabrigado) || lonely (solo, aislado) || *niño desamparado* waif.

desamparar *vt* to abandon, to forsake, to desert; *desamparar a un niño* to desert a child || to leave (un sitio) || JUR to renounce, to relinquish || MAR to dismantle.

desamparo *m* helplessness, lack of protection || desertion, abandonment (abandono) || distress (aflicción) || *en desamparo* helpless, forsaken, deserted, abandoned; *un anciano en desamparo* a forsaken old man.

desamueblado, da *adj* unfurnished; *piso desamueblado* unfurnished flat.

desamueblar *vt* to remove the furniture from, to strip *o* to clear of furniture.

desanclar; desancorar *vi* MAR to weigh anchor.

desandar* *vt* *desandar el camino* or *lo andado* to retrace one's steps, to go back.

desangelado, da *adj* insipid, dull, lacking in charm (persona) || insipid (cosa).

desangrado, da *adj* *está desangrado* he has lost blood || *morir desangrado* to bleed to death.

desangramiento *m* bleeding (pérdida de sangre) || draining (desagüe).

desangrar *vt* to bleed (sangrar) || to drain (un lago) || FIG to bleed white (empobrecer); *desangrar a los contribuyentes* to bleed the taxpayers white.
◆ *vpr* to bleed (perder la sangre) || to bleed to death (morir).

desangre *m* bleeding.

desanidar *vi* to leave the nest (las aves).
◆ *vt* FIG to oust, to dislodge (desalojar).

desanimado, da *adj* low-spirited, downhearted, dejected (sin ánimo) || lifeless, dull (fiesta).

desanimar *vt* to depress; *este tiempo me desanima* this weather depresses me || to discourage; *el fracaso le ha desanimado* the failure has discouraged him.
◆ *vpr* to be discouraged, to lose heart (desalentarse) || to get depressed (abatirse) || *¡no se desanime!* don't be discouraged!, don't lose heart.

desánimo *m* discouragement, despondency, dejection (desaliento) || depression (abatimiento) || dullness, lifelessness (falta de animación).

desanudar *vt* to untie, to undo, to unknot; *desanudar una corbata* to undo a tie || FIG to clear up, to straighten *o* to sort out (una situación confusa).

desapacibilidad *f* surliness, harshness, unpleasantness (del genio) || unsettled nature, unpleasantness, inclemency (del tiempo) || harshness, unpleasantness (de un sonido).

desapacible *adj* harsh, unpleasant, surly; *tono desapacible* harsh tone; *persona desapacible* surly person || unpleasant, unsettled (tiempo) || harsh, unpleasant (sonido) || bitter, heated (discusión).

desapadrinar *vt* (p us) FIG to disapprove of (desaprobar) || to withdraw one's support from (retirar el apoyo).

desapareado, da *adj* odd; *calcetín desapareado* odd sock.

desaparear *vt* to lose one of.

desaparecer* *vi* to disappear || to vanish, to disappear (de repente) || to wear off; *el efecto ha desaparecido* the effect has worn off || — FAM *desaparecer del mapa* to disappear completely, to vanish from the face of the earth || *hacer desaparecer* to hide (ocultar), to smooth out, to get rid of (una arruga), to remove, to make off with (llevarse).

desaparecido, da *adj* missing.
◆ *m/f* missing person.
◆ *pl* missing; *los desaparecidos* the missing; *hay veinte desaparecidos* there are twenty missing.

desaparejar *vt* to unharness (quitar los arreos) || MAR to unrig.

desaparición *f* disappearance.

desapasionadamente *adv* dispassionately, objectively, impartially.

desapasionado, da *adj* dispassionate, objective, impartial.

desapasionar *vt* to make (s.o.) lose interest in; *desapasionar a uno de algo* to make s.o. lose interest in sth.
◆ *vpr* to lose interest, to become indifferent; *desapasionarse por alguien* to lose interest in s.o., to become indifferent to s.o. || to lose interest *o* enthusiasm, to become indifferent; *desapasionarse del juego* to lose interest in gambling, to become indifferent to gambling || to overcome one's passion for (haciendo un esfuerzo).

desapegar *vt* FIG to estrange, to separate, to alienate (hacer perder el afecto).
◆ *vpr* FIG to lose interest in, to turn away from, to go off (desaficionarse, perder el cariño).

desapego *m* FIG coldness, indifference; *mostrar desapego a una persona* to show indifference towards a person | estrangement, separation (de dos personas) || lack of interest, indifference, dislike; *desapego a los estudios* lack of interest in *o* indifference towards one's studies, dislike for *o* of studying.

desapercibidamente *adv* without being seen (sin ser visto); *aproximarse desapercibidamente* to approach without being seen.

desapercibido, da *adj* unprepared, unready (no preparado) || unnoticed; *pasar desapercibido* to go unnoticed || — *coger desapercibido* to catch unawares, to take by surprise || *no me ha pasado desapercibido lo que ha dicho* I didn't miss what he said.

desapercibimiento *m* unpreparedness.

desapestar *vt* to disinfect.

desaplacible *adj* unpleasant, disagreeable.

desaplicación *f* lack of application, slackness, laziness (falta de aplicación).

desaplicadamente *adv* without application, lazily.

desaplicado, da *adj* slack, lazy; *alumno desaplicado* slack pupil.
◆ *m/f* lazybones, idler.

desapoderamiento *m* dispossession (privación) || deprivation of power (poder), authority (autoridad) || FIG rage, fury, wildness (desenfreno).

desapoderar *vt* to deprive of one's power (poder), *o* authority (autoridad) || to dispossess (quitar).

desapolillar *vt* to get rid of the moths from; *desapolillar la ropa* to get rid of the moths from one's clothes.
◆ *vpr* FIG & FAM to get rid of the cobwebs; *salió a desapolillarse* he went out to get rid of the cobwebs.

desaposentar *vt* to evict, to throw out (de una habitación) || FIG to cast aside.

desapoyar *vt* to withdraw one's support.

despreciar *vt* to underestimate (infraestimar).

desaprender *vt* to forget, to unlearn (olvidar).

desaprensar *vt* to free (soltar) || to take the gloss *o* finish off (una tela).

desaprensión *f* unscrupulousness, lack of scruples.

desaprensivo, va *adj* unscrupulous, inconsiderate.
◆ *m/f* unscrupulous person.

desapretar*, desapretarse *v tr y pr* to loosen.

desaprobación *f* disapproval.

desaprobador, ra; desaprobatorio, ria *adj* disapproving, of disapproval; *mirada desaprobadora* look of disapproval, disapproving look || unfavourable, adverse; *juicio desaprobador* adverse judgment.

desaprobar* *vt* to disapprove, to disapprove of, to frown on; *desaprueba mi conducta* he disapproves of my conduct || to reject (rechazar) || *desaprueba que yo vaya* he disapproves of my going, he does not think it right that I should go.

desaprobatorio, ria *adj* → **desaprobador.**

desapropiar to deprive (*de* of).
◆ *vpr* to give up, to surrender, to cede, to abandon; *desapropiarse de un bien* to give up a possession.

desaprovechado, da *adj* slack, who does not make the best use of his possibilities, who could do better; *alumno desaprovechado* pupil who does not make the best use of his possibilities || wasted (tiempo, dinero, comida, oportunidad) || FIG fruitless, unprofitable (infructuoso).

desaprovechamiento *m* wasting, waste, misuse (del tiempo, del dinero, etc.) || lack of progress (falta de progresos).

desaprovechar *vt* not to take advantage of, to waste, to fail to make the best use of; *desaprovechar el buen tiempo, sus dotes, una influencia* not to take advantage of the fine weather, one's talents, s.o.'s influence || to waste; *desaprovechar el tiempo, el dinero, la comida* to waste time, money, food || *desaprovechar una ocasión* to miss *o* to waste *o* to throw away an opportunity.

desapuntalar *vt* to remove the shores *o* props from.

desarboladura *f* MAR dismasting.

desarbolar *vt* MAR to dismast.
◆ *vpr* to lose her mast.

desarenar *vt* to remove sand from, to clear of sand.

desarmado, da *adj* → **desarmar** || in pieces (desmontado).

desarmador *m* trigger (de un arma) || *AMER* screwdriver (destornillador).

desarmadura *f*; **desarmamiento** *m* → **desarme.**

desarmar *vt* to disarm (un país, una bomba, una persona, etc.) || to dismantle, to take to pieces, to take apart, to strip down (un motor) || to dismantle, to take to pieces, to take apart; *desarmar un reloj* to dismantle a watch || to dismantle, to take down (una tienda de campaña) || MAR to lay up (un buque) || FIG to unarm, to disarm; *su respuesta me desarmó* his reply disarmed me | to calm, to appease; *desarmar la cólera de uno* to calm s.o.'s anger | to stump, to floor (confundir) || — *desarmar un arco* to unstring a bow || MIL *desarmar pabellones* to unpile arms.
◆ *vi/vpr* MIL to disarm || to come apart, to come to pieces (deshacerse).

desarme *m*; **desarmadura** *f*; **desarmamiento** *m* disarmament; *conferencia sobre* or *para el desarme* disarmament conference || dismantling, taking apart (de una máquina).

desarmonizar *vt* to disharmonize.

desarraigado, da *adj* uprooted (árbol) || FIG uprooted, rootless (persona) | eradicated, wiped out (vicio, etc.).

desarraigar *vt* to uproot, to deracinate; *desarraigar un árbol* to uproot a tree || FIG to uproot; *desarraigar un pueblo* to uproot a people | to wipe out, to eradicate; *desarraigar el vicio* to wipe out vice | to extirpate (extirpar).
◆ *vpr* *desarraigarse de su patria* to break all ties with one's country, to abandon one's country.

desarraigo *m* uprooting, rooting up (de un árbol) || FIG uprooting (de un pueblo, etc.) | eradication (de un vicio, etc.) | extirpation.

desarrapado, da *adj/s* → **desharrapado.**

desarregladamente *adv* unmethodically (sin método) || untidily (sin orden).

desarreglado, da *adj* untidy; *una habitación desarreglada* an untidy room || slovenly, untidy (aspecto); *una chica desarreglada* a slovenly girl || disorderly (desordenado); *una vida desarreglada* a disorderly life || out of order, faulty; *reloj desarreglado* clock which is out of order, faulty clock || upset (estómago).

desarreglar *vt* to mess up, to upset, to disturb, to make untidy, to disarrange; *desarreglar la casa, el peinado* to make the house untidy, to mess up one's hairdo || to spoil, to upset; *la lluvia ha desarreglado mis planes* the rain has spoilt my plans || to put out of order; *desarreglar un reloj* to put a clock out of order.

desarreglo *m* disorder, confusion, mess, chaos; *en el más completo desarreglo* in total confusion, in a terrible mess || faulty condition, trouble (de un mecanismo) || untidiness (de la ropa) || upset, disorder (del estómago).

desarrendar* *vt* to stop leasing (sin dejar de arrendar) || to stop renting (dejar de alquilar) || to unbridle (una caballería).

desarrimar *vt* to move away (apartar); *desarrimar el armario de la pared* to move the wardrobe away from the wall || FIG to dissuade (disuadir).

desarrollable *adj* developable, which can be developed (expresión, industria, teoría, etc.) || which can be spread out (superficie).

desarrollado, da *adj* developed || *país desarrollado* developed country.

desarrollar *vt* to unroll, to unfold; *desarrollar un mapa* to unroll a map || to develop; *la lluvia y el sol desarrollan la semilla* the rain and sun develop the seed || to develop; *desarrollar el cuerpo, la industria* to develop one's body, industry || to expound, to explain, to develop (una teoría) || to carry out (realizar) || MAT to expand, to develop (una expresión algebraica) || MÚS to develop || — *desarrollar actividades subversivas* to carry on subversive activities || *desarrollar una inteligencia enorme* to show great intelligence || *desarrollar una velocidad de* to develop a speed of.
◆ *vpr* to unroll, to unfold (un mapa) || to develop; *la industria de este país se ha desarrollado mucho* this country's industry has developed a lot || to develop fully (alcanzar la madurez); *esta planta se desarrolla en dos meses* this plant takes two months to develop fully || to take place (tener lugar) || to happen, to take place (suceder) || to go off; *la entrevista se desarrolló como previsto* the interview went off as planned.

desarrollo *m* development; *niño en pleno desarrollo* child at the most rapid stage of development; *el desarrollo de una planta, de la industria* the development of a plant, of industry || DEP run, course (de un partido, etc.) || MAT expansion (de una expresión algebraica) | development (geometría) || unrolling (de un papel) || FIG development, course, unfolding; *el desarrollo de los acontecimientos* the development of events || TECN distance covered by bicycle for each revolution of pedal || MÚS development || — *índice de desarrollo* growth rate || *industria en pleno desarrollo* rapidly developing industry || *niño que está en la edad del desarrollo* child going through puberty || *países en vías de desarrollo* developing countries || *plan de desarrollo* development plan.

desarropar *vt* to uncover (descubrir) || to uncover (en la cama) || to undress (desnudar) || to take some clothes off (quitar parte de la ropa).
◆ *vpr* to take some clothes off; *no te desarropes, que estás sudando* don't take any clothes off, you're perspiring || to get undressed (desnudarse) || to remove *o* to throw off the blankets (de la cama) || *hace demasiado frío para desarroparse* it is too cold to wear lighter clothing.

desarrugar *vt* to smooth, to smooth out (alisar) || to get the creases out of; *voy a colgar el traje para desarrugarlo* I'm going to hang up the dress to get the creases out || *desarrugar el entrecejo* to stop frowning.
◆ *vpr* to become smooth (quitarse las arrugas) || *voy a colgar el traje para que se desarrugue* I'm going to hang up the dress so that the creases will drop out *o* come out *o* to get the creases out.

desarrumar *vt* MAR to unstow.

desarticulación *f* putting out of joint, disarticulation, dislocation (de los huesos) || disconnection (de dos piezas) || FIG breaking up;

desarticulación de un partido breaking up of a party.

desarticulado, da *adj* disjointed.

desarticular *vt* to put out of joint, to disarticulate, to disjoint, to dislocate (huesos) ‖ to disconnect (dos piezas) ‖ to take apart, to take to pieces (dividir en partes) ‖ FIG to break up (un partido, un complot, etc.) | to spoil, to upset; *la lluvia ha desarticulado mis planes* the rain has spoilt my plans.

desartillar *vt* to deprive of artillery.

desarzonar *vt* to throw, to unseat, to unsaddle.

desasar *vt* to break the handle of.

desaseado, da *adj* untidy, dirty (sucio) ‖ slovenly, scruffy, untidy, unkempt (descuidado).
◆ *m/f* scruff, untidy person.

desasear *vt* to dirty, to soil (ensuciar) ‖ to mess up (desordenar).

desasentar* *vt* to move.

desaseo *m* dirtiness, uncleanliness (suciedad) ‖ untidiness, slovenliness, scruffiness (falta de aseo) ‖ mess (desorden).

desasimiento *m* release, releasing (acción de soltar) ‖ detachment (acción de desprender) ‖ relinquishment (acción de ceder) ‖ loosening (acción de soltarse) ‖ FIG disinterestedness, unselfishness (desinterés).

desasimilación *f* dissimilation.

desasimilar *vt* to dissimilate.

desasir* *vt* to release, to let go, to loose (soltar) ‖ to detach (desprender).
◆ *vpr* to come off (desprenderse) ‖ *desasirse de* to give up, to part with (ceder), to rid o.s. of, to get rid of (deshacerse de), to rid o.s. of, to free o.s. of (liberarse).

desasistencia *f* desertion, abandonment.

desasistir *vt* to desert, to abandon, to forsake (abandonar) ‖ *estar desasistido* to be neglected; *estaba muy desasistido en el hospital* he was rather neglected in hospital.

desasnar *vt* FIG & FAM to polish up, to teach civilized manners to, to refine.

desasociar *vt* to dissociate, to disassociate.

desasosegadamente *adv* uneasily, restlessly, anxiously.

desasosegado, da *adj* uneasy, restless, anxious.

desasosegar* *vt* to disturb, to make restless *o* uneasy, to disquiet.
◆ *vpr* to become uneasy *o* restless.

desasosiego *m* uneasiness, anxiety, disquiet, restlessness (inquietud) ‖ unrest (malestar).

desastradamente *adv* dirtily (suciamente) ‖ scruffily, untidily, slovenly (descuidadamente) ‖ in tatters (con andrajos).

desastrado, da *adj* dirty (sucio) ‖ scruffy, untidy, slovenly (descuidado) ‖ in tatters, ragged (harapiento); *traje desastrado* ragged dress, dress which is in tatters ‖ unfortunate (desgraciado) ‖ disorderly; *llevar una vida desastrada* to lead a disorderly life.
◆ *m/f* scruff, tramp.

desastre *m* disaster (catástrofe) ‖ MIL defeat (derrota) ‖ FIG disaster, complete failure; *el baile fue un desastre* the dance was a disaster | absolute mess; *esta falda es un desastre* this skirt is an absolute mess ‖ — *correr al desastre* to court disaster ‖ FIG *este niño es un verdadero desastre* this child is absolutely hopeless | *¡qué desastre!* what a calamity! | *un desastre de hombre* a dead loss, a disaster.

desastrosamente *adv* disastrously.

desastroso, sa *adj* disastrous, calamitous.

desatado, da *adj* undone ‖ FIG wild, mad (sin contención) | uncontrolled (pasiones, etc.) ‖ FIG *está desatado* there's no holding him (desenfrenado).

desatadura *f* undoing, unfastening, untying (acción de desatar) ‖ FIG clearing up, solving (aclaración) | outburst (desencadenamiento).

desatar *vt* to untie, to undo, to unfasten; *desatar un nudo* to undo a knot ‖ to untie, to undo; *desatar un paquete* to undo a parcel ‖ to unbutton (desabotonar) ‖ to unleash, to let go; *desatar el perro* to let the dog go ‖ FIG to loosen (la lengua) | to unleash, to let loose (las pasiones) | to unleash (represiones) | to spark off, to give rise to (provocar) | to clear up, to unravel, to untangle; *desatar una intriga* to clear up an intrigue ‖ REL *atar y desatar* to do and to undo.
◆ *vpr* to come undone, to come untied, to come unfastened (lo atado) ‖ to undo, to unfasten, to untie; *desatarse los zapatos* to undo one's shoes ‖ to get free (prisionero) ‖ to get loose, to break loose (perro) ‖ FIG to lose one's temper, to get worked up (encolerizarse) | to get carried away (hablar con exceso) | to get out (de un compromiso) | to get carried away, to go too far, to forget o.s., to lose one's head (perder los estribos) | to begin to rage; *los elementos se desataron* the elements began to rage | to break, to burst; *la tempestad se desató* the storm broke | to explode; *su cólera, odio, entusiasmo se desató* he exploded with anger, hatred, enthusiasm | to break out (revolución, motín) ‖ — FIG *desatarse en injurias* or *en improperios* to pour out a stream of insults | *se le desató la lengua* he began to talk.

desatascador *m* plunger (para tuberías).

desatascamiento *m* clearing, unblocking (de una tubería).

desatascar *vt* to pull out of the mud (sacar de un atascadero) ‖ to clear, to unblock (una cañería) ‖ FIG & FAM to get out of a jam *o* of a scrape (sacar de un apuro).

desatasco *m* clearing, unblocking (de una cañería).

desatavío *m* untidiness, disarray, scruffiness.

desatención *f* inattention, lack of attention (distracción) ‖ disrespect, discourtesy, impoliteness, rudeness (descortesía) ‖ neglect (negligencia).

desatender* *vt* to neglect; *desatender a sus huéspedes* to neglect one's guests ‖ not to pay attention to, to disregard, to ignore; *desatender lo que se dice* not to pay attention to what is being said ‖ to neglect; *desatender sus deberes, las órdenes* to neglect one's duties, orders ‖ to slight (ofender) ‖ *dejar una tienda desatendida* to leave a shop unattended.

desatentado, da *adj* foolish, wild, rash, reckless ‖ extreme, excessive, severe (riguroso).

desatentamente *adv* inattentively, without paying attention (sin prestar atención) ‖ impolitely, rudely (descortésmente).

desatento, ta *adj* inattentive; *un alumno desatento* an inattentive pupil ‖ careless (descuidado) ‖ impolite, discourteous, unmannerly (grosero) ‖ *está desatento en clase* he doesn't pay attention in class.

desatinadamente *adv* wildly, madly, rashly (insensatamente) ‖ foolishly, recklessly, rashly (de manera imprudente) ‖ clumsily, stupidly, awkwardly (torpemente).

desatinado, da *adj* foolish, silly (tonto) ‖ rash, unwise (imprudente) ‖ wild, reckless, rash (sin juicio).

desatinar *vt* to exasperate, to bewilder (exasperar) ‖ to make lose one's head (atolondrar).
◆ *vi* to talk nonsense, to rave (decir desatinos) ‖ to blunder, to make blunders (cometer desaciertos).

desatino *m* silly thing, absurdity (dislate) ‖ mistake, blunder (equivocación) ‖ lack of tact, tactlessness (falta de tacto) ‖ foolishness, silliness (falta de cordura) ‖ — *cometer un desatino* to do sth. silly, to do a silly thing (hacer una tontería).
◆ *pl* nonsense *sing*, silly things; *decir desatinos* to talk nonsense, to say silly things ‖ silly things; *cometer desatinos* to do silly things ‖ *discurso lleno de desatinos* speech full of absurdities *o* nonsense.

desatolondrarse *vpr* to come to one's senses, to gather one's wits.

desatollar *vt* to pull out of the mud.

desatontarse *vpr* to come to, to come to one's senses, to gather one's wits.

desatoramiento *m* clearing, unblocking.

desatorar *vt* to clear, to unblock (desatascar) ‖ MAR to unstow (la estiba) ‖ MIN to clear.

desatornillador *m* screwdriver.

desatornillar *vt* to unscrew (destornillar).

desatracar *vt* MAR to push off, to cast off, to unmoor (separar del atracadero).
◆ *vi* MAR to move away, to shove off.

desatraillamiento *m* unleashing (de un perro) ‖ uncoupling (de un conjunto de perros).

desatraillar *vt* to unleash (perro) ‖ to uncouple (conjunto de perros).

desatrancador *m* plunger.

desatrancar *vt* to unbar (una puerta) ‖ to clear, to unblock (una cañería) ‖ to clean out (pozo).

desatufarse *vpr* FIG to calm down, to cool off (calmarse) | to get some fresh air (tomar el fresco).

desaturdir *vt* to wake up, to bring to one's senses.
◆ *vpr* to wake up, to come round, to come to one's senses.

desautoridad *f* lack of authority.

desautorización *f* denial (mentís) ‖ disapproval (desaprobación) ‖ discredit (descrédito).

desautorizadamente *adv* without authorization.

desautorizado, da *adj* unauthorized ‖ denied (desmentido) ‖ forbidden (prohibido).

desautorizar *vt* to deny (desmentir); *el ministro desautorizó el rumor* the minister denied the rumour ‖ to forbid (prohibir) ‖ to declare unauthorized, to disallow (declarar que no se autoriza) ‖ to disapprove, to disapprove of (desaprobar) ‖ to discredit (desacreditar).

desavenencia *f* disagreement, discord (desacuerdo) ‖ row, quarrel (riña).

desavenido, da *adj* incompatible ‖ on bad terms, who have fallen out (reñidos); *familias desavenidas* families on bad terms, families who have fallen out ‖ contrary, opposing (opuesto) ‖ *países desavenidos* countries which are in disagreement.

desavenir* *vt* to cause a rift between, to cause to break up *o* to quarrel, to split; *desavenir a dos amigos* to cause two friends to quarrel.
◆ *vpr* to quarrel, to have a difference of opinion, to fall out (*fam*); *desavenirse con alguien* to have a difference of opinion with s.o.

desaventajado, da *adj* at a disadvantage (en situación desventajosa) ‖ disadvantageous, unfavourable, which has its drawbacks (poco ventajoso).

desaviar *vt* to put out, to inconvenience (molestar) ‖ to send the wrong way (desviar) ‖ to deprive of necessities (desproveer).

desavío *m* inconvenience; *hacer desavío* to cause inconvenience ‖ misleading (desvío).

desavisado, da *adj* reckless, foolish (incauto).

desayunado, da *adj* who has had breakfast; *estoy desayunado* I have had (my) breakfast.

desayunar *vi* to have breakfast, to breakfast; *esta mañana he desayunado muy temprano* this morning I had breakfast very early ‖ *desayunar con pan y café* to have bread and coffee for breakfast, to breakfast on bread and coffee.
◆ *vt* to breakfast on, to have for breakfast.
◆ *vpr* to have breakfast, to breakfast; *aún no me he desayunado* I haven't had breakfast yet ‖ — FIG *desayunarse de* to get the first news of (enterarse) | *ahora me desayuno* it's the first I hear *o* I've heard of it.

desayuno *m* breakfast.

desazogar *vt* to remove the mercury *o* quicksilver from.

desazón *f* tastelessness (insipidez) ‖ AGR poverty (falta de sazón) ‖ FIG uneasiness, anxiety, restlessness (desasosiego) | grief (pesadumbre) ‖ — FIG *le causa desazón no saber dónde va a trabajar* it worries him not knowing where he is going to work ‖ *sentir una desazón en el estómago* to have an upset stomach.

desazonado, da *adj* insipid, tasteless (soso) ‖ AGR poor (la tierra) ‖ FIG uneasy, restless, anxious (intranquilo).

desazonar *vt* to take away the taste of, to make tasteless *o* insipid (hacer insípido) ‖ FIG to upset, to annoy (disgustar) | to make uneasy, to worry, to disturb, to upset (inquietar).
◆ *vpr* FIG to get angry (enfadarse) | to worry (preocuparse) | to feel off-colour, not to feel well (sentirse mal de salud).

desbabar *vt* to clean, to remove the slime from (los caracoles).
◆ *vi/vpr* to slobber, to drivel, to dribble, to drool.

desbancar *vt* to take the bank from (en el juego) ‖ FIG to supplant, to replace (suplantar).
◆ *vi* to break the bank (en el juego).

desbandada *f* scattering ‖ MIL rout, stampede ‖ — *a la desbandada* in disorder, in confusion ‖ *hubo una desbandada general* everybody scattered.

desbandarse *vpr* MIL to flee in disorder, to disband, to disperse in confusion; *las tropas se desbandaron* the troops fled in disorder ‖ to disperse, to scatter (dispersarse) ‖ to remain aloof (apartarse).

desbarajustar *vt* to throw into confusion (causar confusión en) ‖ to upset (poner en desorden) ‖ *está todo desbarajustado* everything is in a mess *o* is upside down.

desbarajuste *m* confusion, disorder, chaos ‖ — *hay tal desbarajuste en la casa que no encuentro nada* the house is in such a mess that I can't find anything ‖ *¡qué desbarajuste!* what a mess!

desbaratado, da *adj* wrecked, ruined (estropeado) ‖ broken, ruined (roto) ‖ FIG & FAM dissipated, wild (disipado) ‖ MIL in confusion.

desbaratamiento *m* disorder, confusion (desorden) ‖ waste, squandering (derroche) ‖ wrecking, destruction ‖ spoiling, frustration (de proyectos, planes, etc.) ‖ raving (disparates) ‖ thwarting, foiling, frustration (de intriga) ‖ MIL rout.

desbaratar *vt* to spoil, to mess up; *el viento desbarató su peinado* the wind messed up her hairdo ‖ to wreck, to ruin (destrozar) ‖ to put out of order, to ruin, to break; *desbaratar un reloj* to ruin a watch ‖ to spoil, to thwart, to ruin; *desbaratar los planes de uno* to spoil s.o.'s plans ‖ to thwart, to foil, to frustrate (hacer fracasar); *desbaratar una intriga* to frustrate a plot ‖ to demolish (un razonamiento) ‖ to waste, to squander (derrochar); *desbaratar una fortuna* to squander a fortune ‖ MIL to put to flight, to rout, to throw into confusion; *desbaratar a los adversarios* to rout the enemy.
◆ *vi* to talk nonsense (disparatar).
◆ *vpr* to fall apart ‖ FIG to blow up, to go off the deep end (irritarse), to get carried away (pasarse de la raya).

desbarbado *m* TECN trimming, removal of the rough edges.

desbarbar *vt* to trim the rootlets off (quitar las raíces) ‖ to trim (papel) ‖ to trim, to remove the rough edges from (metal) ‖ FAM to shave (afeitar).
◆ *vpr* FAM to shave.

desbarbillar *vt* AGR to trim the rootlets off.

desbardar *vt* to remove the brambles from (a wall).

desbarrancadero *m* AMER precipice.

desbarrar *vi* to slip (resbalar) ‖ FIG to talk nonsense (decir disparates) | to do silly *o* stupid things (hacer tonterías).

desbarro *m* slip (resbalón) ‖ FIG silly thing, absurdity (disparate).

desbastador *m* TECN roughing chisel (herramienta) | roughing mill (laminador).

desbastadura *f* TECN → **desbaste.**

desbastar *vt* TECN to rough down, to rough-plane (madera) | to rough down (metal) | to roughhew, to scabble (piedra) ‖ to smooth down (suavizar) ‖ FIG to knock the rough corners off, to teach civilized manners to, to polish; *desbastar a un palurdo* to knock the rough corners off a yokel.
◆ *vpr* FIG to acquire some polish.

desbaste *m* TECN roughing-down, rough-planing (de madera) | roughing-down (de metal) | roughhewing, scabbling (de piedra) | bloom (pieza de acero) ‖ FIG polishing, refinement (de una persona) ‖ *en desbaste* roughly-worked, roughhewn.

desbautizar *vt* to take away the name of (quitar el nombre) ‖ to change the name of, to rename (poner otro nombre).
◆ *vpr* to lose one's temper (encolerizarse).

desbloquear *vt* COM to unfreeze, to unblock ‖ TECN to free ‖ MIL to raise the blockade on.

desbloqueo *m* COM unfreezing, unblocking ‖ MIL raising of the blockade ‖ TECN freeing.

desbocado, da *adj* runaway (caballo) ‖ FIG wild; *imaginación desbocada* wild imagination | uncontrollable, wild; *hoy los niños están desbocados* the children are uncontrollable today ‖ bell-mouthed, wide-mouthed (arma de fuego) ‖ with a chipped rim (vasija de boca mellada) ‖ with a broken rim (de boca rota) ‖ overflowing (río) ‖ FIG & FAM foulmouthed (malhablado) ‖ cheeky (descarado).
◆ *m/f* foulmouthed person (malhablado) ‖ cheeky person (descarado).

desbocamiento *m* bolting (de un caballo) ‖ FIG & FAM cheek, insolence (descaro) | coarse language (grosería) | insults *pl*, abuse.

desbocar *vt* to chip the rim of (mellar) ‖ to break the rim of (romper).
◆ *vi* → **desembocar.**
◆ *vpr* to bolt, to run away (caballo) ‖ FIG to blow up, to go off the deep end (irritarse) | to go too far, to get carried away (pasarse de la raya) | to let out a stream of abuse (insultar).

desbordamiento *m* overflowing; *el desbordamiento de un río* the overflowing of a river ‖ MIL outflanking, envelopment ‖ FIG excitement (exaltación) | explosion, outbreak, outburst (de cólera, etc.).

desbordante *adj* overflowing, bursting; *el cine estaba desbordante de gente* the cinema was overflowing with people; *persona desbordante de entusiasmo* person overflowing with enthusiasm ‖ unrestrained, boundless, unbounded; *alegría desbordante* unbounded joy.

desbordar *vi* to overflow, to brim over; *el cesto desbordaba de naranjas* the basket was overflowing with oranges ‖ to overflow, to flood; *el río desbordó por los campos* the river overflowed into the fields ‖ FIG to overflow, to bubble over; *su alegría desborda* he is overflowing with joy, he is bubbling over with joy | to burst with (entusiasmo) ‖ to project, to protrude, to jut out (sobresalir).
◆ *vt* to overflow; *el río desbordó su cauce* the river overflowed its banks ‖ FIG to burst through, to overwhelm; *desbordaron las líneas enemigas* they overwhelmed the enemy lines | to pass, to go beyond (superar) | to exceed, to surpass (exceder) ‖ — FIG *esto desborda mi capacidad de comprensión* that is beyond me | *esto desborda mi paciencia* that is more than I can stand.
◆ *vpr* to overflow its banks, to flood, to run over; *el río se desbordó* the river overflowed its banks ‖ to overflow; *la piscina se desborda* the pool is overflowing ‖ to spill over, to brim over, to overflow; *se desborda el agua del vaso* the glass is brimming over with water ‖ FIG to go wild, to get carried away (exaltarse) | to burst; *su corazón se desborda de alegría* his heart is bursting with joy.

desborde *m* AMER → **desbordamiento.**

desborrar *vt* to burl (limpiar el paño).

desbotonar *vt* to remove the buds from (plantas) ‖ to take the button off (un florete).

desbravar *vt* to tame, to train (animal) ‖ to break in (caballo).
◆ *vi/vpr* to become less wild (hacerse más sociable) ‖ to calm down, to become calm (calmarse); *el mar se desbrava* the sea is becoming calm ‖ to lose its strength (un licor).

desbravecer* *vi/vpr* → **desbravar.**

desbridamiento *m* MED debridement.

desbridar *vt* to unbridle (una caballería) ‖ MED to debride (los tejidos).

desbriznar *vt* to mince (la carne) ‖ to chop finely (las verduras, etc.) ‖ to remove the stamens from [the crocus] (el azafrán).

desbroce *m* → **desbrozo.**

desbrozar; desembrozar *vt* to clear of weeds (la hierba) ‖ to clear of undergrowth (matorrales) ‖ to clear, to grub (un terreno) ‖ FIG to clear (camino) | to do the spadework on (un tema).

desbrozo; desbroce *m* clearing of weeds (de la hierba) ‖ clearing of undergrowth (de matorrales) ‖ clearing, grubbing (del terreno) ‖ rubbish (desechos) ‖ prunings *pl* (ramas) ‖ FIG spadework.

desbulla *f* oyster shell (concha) ‖ shelling (acción de abrir una ostra).

desbullador *m* oyster fork (tenedor) ‖ oyster opener (cuchillo) ‖ oyster sheller (persona).

desbullar *vt* to shell (oysters).

descabal *adj* odd (no cabal) ‖ incomplete.

descabalado, da *adj* incomplete (incompleto) ‖ odd; *guante descabalado* odd glove.

descabalamiento *m* spoiling.

descabalar *vi* to spoil, to leave incomplete (dejar incompleto) ‖ to split, to separate (desemparejar).

descabalgar *vi* to dismount.

descabellado, da *adj* FIG wild, crazy; *ideas, teorías descabelladas* wild ideas, theories; *es descabellado hacer tal cosa* it's crazy to do such a thing.

descabellar *vt* to ruffle *o* to tousle the hair of (despeinar); *mujer descabellada* woman with ruffled hair ‖ TAUR to kill the bull with a «descabello».

descabello *m* TAUR «descabello» [a sharp stab with the sword between the first and second cervical vertebrae, designed to kill the bull after an unsuccessful «estocada»] | sword used for the «descabello».

descabezado, da *adj* decapitated, beheaded, headless (decapitado) ‖ headless (cosa desprovista de cabeza) ‖ FIG wild, crazy, reckless (insensato) | absurd, ridiculous (absurdo) | forgetful, absentminded (desmemoriado).

descabezamiento *m* decapitation, beheading (decapitación) ‖ pollarding, cutting the top off (árbol).

descabezar *vt* to behead, to decapitate (a una persona) ‖ to take the head off (una cosa); *descabezar un clavo* to take the head off a nail ‖ to cut the top off, to pollard, to lop (un árbol) ‖ to top (plantas) ‖ FIG to remove the head of; *descabezar una organización* to remove the head of an organization ‖ MIL to change the direction of (hacer cambiar de dirección) ‖ — FIG & FAM *descabezar una dificultad* to start to surmount *o* to get over a difficulty | *descabezar un sueño* to take forty winks, to have a nap.
◆ *vpr* to shed grain (las espigas) ‖ FIG to rack one's brains (persona).

descachalandrado, da *adj* AMER scruffy, untidy (desharrapado).

descacharrante *adj* FAM hilarious, killing (muy divertido).

descacharrar *vt* to break (romper) ‖ to ruin, to spoil, to mess up (estropear).

descaecer* *vi* ⟶ **decaer.**

descaecimiento *m* ⟶ **decaimiento.**

descafeinar *vt* to decaffeinate, to decaffeinize; *café descafeinado* decaffeinated coffee.

descaimiento *m* ⟶ **decaimiento.**

descalabazarse *vpr* FIG & FAM to rack one's brains.

descalabrado, da *adj* with a head injury, injured in the head (herido en la cabeza) ‖ FIG injured (herido) ‖ FIG *salir descalabrado de un negocio* to come out of a business the worse for wear.

descalabradura *f* head injury, head wound ‖ scar (cicatriz).

descalabrar; escalabrar *vt* to injure the head of, to injure in the head (herir en la cabeza); *descalabrar a uno* to injure s.o.'s head, to injure s.o. in the head ‖ to injure (herir) ‖ FIG to give a rough time to, to knock about (maltratar) | to harm (perjudicar) ‖ to defeat (al enemigo).
◆ *vpr* to injure one's head.

descalabro *m* setback, blow, misfortune; *sufrir muchos descalabros en la vida* to undergo many setbacks in one's life ‖ MIL defeat (derrota) ‖ disaster (desastre); *esta derrota fue un descalabro* this defeat was a disaster.

descalaminado *m* TECN removing of calamine.

descalaminar *vt* to remove the calamine from.

descalce *m* undermining (socava).

descalcificación *f* MED decalcification.

descalcificar *vt* MED to decalcify.
◆ *vpr* MED to become decalcified.

descalificación *f* disqualification; *descalificación de un equipo* a team's disqualification ‖ discredit (descrédito).

descalificar *vt* to disqualify; *descalificar a un equipo de fútbol* to disqualify a football team ‖ to bring discredit on (desacreditar).

descalzar *vt* to take off (s.o.'s) shoes (quitar el calzado) ‖ to remove the wedge *o* the chocks from (quitar el calzo) ‖ AGR to dig under, to undermine (socavar).
◆ *vpr* to take off one's shoes (quitarse los zapatos) ‖ to lose *o* to cast a shoe (caballo) ‖ to take off (los guantes, las gafas) ‖ FIG to become a discalced Carmelite (fraile).

descalzo, za *adj* barefoot, barefooted, shoeless; *ir descalzo* to go barefoot ‖ FIG badly shod (mal provisto de calzado) ‖ poor, destitute, down and out (pobre) ‖ discalced (fraile).

descamación *f* MED desquamation, peeling.

descamar *vt* MED to desquamate.
◆ *vpr* MED to desquamate, to scale off.

descambiar *vt* to change back (again).

descaminadamente *adv* *ir descaminadamente* to be on the wrong track, to go the wrong way.

descaminar; desencaminar *vt* to mislead, to misdirect, to send the wrong way, to put on the wrong road (hacer perder el camino) ‖ FIG to lead astray, to mislead, to lead off the straight and narrow; *las malas compañías lo descaminaron* bad company led him astray ‖ — FIG *andar* or *estar* or *ir descaminado* to be on the wrong road, to have the wrong idea, to be on the wrong track ‖ *ir descaminado* to be on the wrong road ‖ FIG *no andas muy descaminado* you're not far wrong.
◆ *vpr* to take the wrong road, to go the wrong way ‖ FIG to go astray, to go the wrong way, to go off straight and narrow.

descamino *m* losing one's way (desorientación) ‖ FIG error.

descamisado, da *adj* shirtless, without a shirt (sin camisa) ‖ FIG in rags, ragged (desharrapado) | wretched (muy pobre).
◆ *m* tramp (desharrapado) ‖ wretch (pobre).
◆ *pl* HIST descamisados (Spanish liberals who took part in the 1820 revolution. In Argentinian history, the name given to supporters of General Perón and his wife).

descamisar *vt* to take the shirt off ‖ AMER FIG to ruin (arruinar) | to rob (robar).

descampado, da *adj* open (un terreno).
◆ *m* open piece of ground, open field ‖ *al* or *en descampado* in the open country.

descampar *vi* to clear up, to stop raining (escampar).

descangallado, da *adj* AMER gawky, graceless (desgarbado).

descansadamente *adv* without effort, effortlessly, without tiring o.s. (out); *nadar descansadamente* to swim effortlessly ‖ in a leisurely manner (sin prisa).

descansadero *m* resting place.

descansado, da *adj* rested; *ya estoy descansado* I'm rested now ‖ relaxed (relajado) ‖ easy, carefree; *vida descansada* easy life ‖ effortless, easy; *trabajo descansado* easy job ‖ restful, peaceful, quiet (tranquilo) ‖ — *este trabajo es mucho más descansado que el otro* this job is much less tiring than the other ‖ *puede usted estar descansado que...* you can rest assured that... ‖ *tiene un negocio descansado* his is a cushy business.

descansapiés *m inv* footrest (reposapiés).

descansar *vi* to rest (reparar las fuerzas); *está descansando de su viaje* he is resting after his journey ‖ to sleep (dormir); *¡que descanse!* sleep well; *¿qué tal ha descansado usted?* did you sleep well? ‖ to lie down (echarse) ‖ to take a rest, to have a break (en el trabajo) ‖ to rest, to be supported; *la viga descansa en la pared* to beam rests upon the wall, the beam is supported by the wall ‖ to find relief (después de un dolor, de una pena) ‖ to be idle, to be out of work (holgar) ‖ to rest, to lie (muertos); *aquí descansa* here lies ‖ to be based on (basarse); *este razonamiento descansa sobre una base falsa* this argument is based on a false premise ‖ to abate (tempestad) ‖ to lie fallow, to rest (la tierra) ‖ to relax (relajarse) ‖ to rely on (contar con); *puede usted descansar en mí* you can rely on me ‖ — *no descanso en todo el día* I don't have a moment's rest all day, I never stop all day ‖ *que en paz descanse* may he rest in peace.
◆ *vt* to rest; *para descansar la vista* to rest your eyes; *descansar la cabeza en* or *sobre la almohada* to rest one's head on the pillow ‖ to rest, to lean (apoyar) ‖ to help, to give a hand to (ayudar) ‖ MIL to order; *descansar las armas* to order arms ‖ MIL *¡descansen armas!* order arms.
◆ *vpr* to rest, to relax ‖ to sleep (dormir) ‖ to rely, to count (contar con); *descansarse en alguien* to rely on *o* to count on s.o.

descansillo *m* landing (rellano).

descanso *m* rest; *tomar un rato de descanso* to take a moment's rest ‖ halt, stop (en la marcha) ‖ break; *en la oficina tenemos un descanso a las diez* we have a break in the office at ten o'clock ‖ leave; *descanso por enfermedad* sick leave ‖ landing (descansillo de escalera) ‖ half time, interval (en un partido de fútbol); *en el descanso* at half time, during the interval ‖ interval (cine, teatro) ‖ TECN support, seat ‖ FIG relief, comfort (alivio) ‖ AMER toilet (retrete) ‖ — *descanso de maternidad* maternity leave ‖ *descanso eterno* last sleep ‖ *descanso semanal* day off ‖ *día de descanso* day off (del trabajo), day of rest (domingo), rest day (en una competición, etc.), day on which there is no performance (en el teatro) ‖ *no dar el menor descanso* not to give a minute's peace ‖ *sin descanso* without a break.

descantillar; descantonar *vt* to chip (desportillar) ‖ FIG to deduct (rebajar).
◆ *vpr* to get chipped (desportillarse).

descañonar *vt* to pluck (desplumar) ‖ to shave close (afeitar) ‖ FIG & FAM to fleece (en el juego).

descaperuzar *vt* to unhood.

descapirotar *vt* to unhood.

descapotable *adj/sm* convertible (coche).

descapotar *vt* to put the (car's) hood down.

descapsulador *m* bottle opener.

descaradamente *adv* barefacedly, shamelessly.

descarado, da *adj* cheeky, impudent, insolent (insolente); *niño descarado* cheeky boy ‖ blatant, shameless, barefaced (falto de recato) ‖ *mentira descarada* barefaced lie.
◆ *m/f* scoundrel (granuja) ‖ cheeky devil (insolente).

descararse *vpr* to be cheeky *o* insolent *o* impudent (obrar con insolencia); *descararse con un anciano* to be cheeky to an old man ‖ to be barefaced (obrar con cinismo) ‖ *se descaró a pedir...* he had the nerve to ask for..., he was cheeky enough to ask for...

descarbonatar *vt* QUÍM to decarbonate (quitar el ácido carbónico).

descarburación *f* TECN decarbonization, decarburization, decarbonizing, decarburizing.

descarburar *vt* TECN to decarbonize, to decarburize.

descarga *f* unloading (acción de descargar); *descarga de un barco* unloading of a boat ‖ firing, discharge (de armas) ‖ salvo, volley (fuego simultáneo de armas) ‖ ELECTR discharge; *tubo de descarga* discharge tube ‖ ARQ relieving (aligeramiento) ‖ *descarga cerrada* volley, salvo (de armas de fuego).

descargadero *m* wharf, landing stage, unloading dock.

descargado, da *adj* flat (una batería).

descargador *m* docker, stevedore (que descarga barcos) ‖ unloader (en general) ‖ wormer, wad hook (de arma).

descargar *vt* to unload, to discharge; *descargar una barcaza* to unload a barge; *descargar el azúcar de un barco* to unload the sugar from a boat ‖ MIL to fire, to discharge, to shoot (disparar un arma) | to disarm, to unload (quitar la carga) ‖ ELECTR to discharge | to run down (una batería) ‖ to deal; *descargar golpes* to deal blows ‖ to evacuate (el vientre) ‖ FIG to give vent to, to vent; *descargar uno la ira en contra de alguien* to give vent to one's wrath on s.o., to vent one's anger on s.o. | to relieve, to free, to release (*de* from), to relieve, to free, to release (de una obligación, de una preocupación) | to free (de una deuda) | to clear, to absolve, to acquit (*de* of), to clear, to absolve, to acquit (de culpa) | to unburden (el corazón) | to ease, to relieve (aliviar) ‖ — *las nubes descargaron lluvia* the clouds burst, the rain came pouring down ‖ *descargar un golpe sobre* or *contra uno* to hit out at s.o., to let fly at s.o.
◆ *vi* to flow (*en* into), to flow (río) ‖ to break; *una tempestad descargó sobre Madrid* a storm broke over Madrid ‖ to burst (las nubes) ‖ ELECTR to discharge.
◆ *vpr* ELECTR to discharge ‖ to shift, to unload; *descargarse de sus obligaciones en* or *sobre un colega* to unload one's responsibilities onto a colleague ‖ to resign (dimitir) ‖ to unburden o.s. (de penas, etc.) ‖ to blow one's top, to blow up (desahogarse) ‖ JUR to clear o.s. (*de* of).

descargo *m* unloading (descarga) ‖ COM credit (abono en cuenta) | receipt, voucher (recibo) ‖ FIG relief (alivio) ‖ JUR acquittal, discharge (de acusación) ‖ release (de obligación) ‖ — *en descargo de conciencia* for conscience's sake ‖ JUR *en* or *para su descargo* in his defence | *pliego de descargo* evidence for the defence | *testigo de descargo* witness for the defence.
◆ *pl* excuse *sing* (disculpa) ‖ JUR plea *sing* (del acusado) | evidence *sing* (pruebas).

descargue *m* unloading (descarga).

descarnadamente *adv* frankly, plainly, to the point (sin rodeos).

descarnado, da *adj* lean, thin, scrawny; *cara descarnada* lean face ‖ clean (hueso) ‖ FIG plain, bare (escueto) | frank, straightforward, candid (sincero) ‖ straightforward, plain; *estilo descarnado* straightforward style.

descarnador *m* scraper (del dentista).

descarnadura *f* removal of flesh (acción de quitar carne) ‖ FIG emaciation.

descarnar *vt* to strip the flesh from (hueso) ‖ FIG to lay bare, to strip (descubrir) | to wear away; *rocas descarnadas por la acción de las olas* rocks worn away by the action of waves.
◆ *vpr* to lose flesh, to waste away.

descaro *m* cheek, impudence, insolence, nerve, impertinence (insolencia); *su descaro me asombra* his cheek amazes me ‖ effrontery, barefacedness (cinismo) ‖ — *¡qué descaro!* what cheek!, what a nerve! ‖ *tuvo el descaro de venir a mi casa* he had the cheek *o* the nerve to come to my house.

descarozar *vt* AMER to stone, to pit (fruta).

descarriamiento *m* ⟶ **descarrío.**

descarriar *vt* to send the wrong way, to misdirect, to put on the wrong road (descaminar) ‖ to separate from the herd (una res) ‖ FIG to lead astray ‖ FIG *oveja descarriada* lost sheep.
◆ *vpr* to get lost, to go the wrong way ‖ to stray, to wander, to stray from the herd (res) ‖ FIG to go astray, to go the wrong way, to go off the straight and narrow.

descarrilamiento *m* derailment; *no hubo heridos en el descarrilamiento del tren París-Roma* no one was injured in the derailment of the Paris-Rome train.

descarrilar *vi* to be derailed, to run off the rails (un tren) ‖ FIG to get off the track.

descarrío; descarriamiento *m* losing one's way ‖ FIG going astray | error.

descartar *vt* to discard, to put aside, to reject; *descartar un proyecto* to discard a plan ‖ to discard, to throw away, to throw down (los naipes) ‖ — *descartar una posibilidad* to eliminate *o* to dismiss *o* to rule out a possibility ‖ *quedar descartado* to be left out.
◆ *vpr* *descartarse de* to discard, to throw away, to throw down (naipes), to get out of (un compromiso).

descarte *m* discarding, throwing-away, discard (acción) ‖ discarded cards *pl*, discard (naipes descartados) ‖ discarding, ruling out (acción de desechar) ‖ rejection (acción de rechazar) ‖ FIG excuse (excusa).

descasar *vt* to annul *o* to dissolve the marriage of (anular un matrimonio) ‖ to estrange, to separate (separar) ‖ FIG to upset; *descasar los sellos de una colección* to upset the stamps in a collection | to separate (dos cosas).
◆ *vpr* to separate ‖ to get divorced (divorciarse).

descascar; descascarar *vt* to shell (nuez, grano de café, huevo duro, etc.) ‖ to peel (naranja, limón).

descascarillado *m* husking (acción de quitar la cascarilla) ‖ peeling off, flaking (de pintura, esmalte).

descascarillar *vt* to husk, to remove the husk from ‖ *arroz descascarillado* husked rice.
◆ *vpr* to peel off, to flake off.

descaspar *vt* to remove the dandruff *o* the scurf from (quitar la caspa).

descastado, da *adj* unaffectionate, cold (poco cariñoso).

descatolizar *vt* to dechristianize.

descebar *vt* to unprime (un arma).

descendencia *f* descent (*de* from) ‖ descendants *pl*, offspring (hijos); *su descendencia vive en Madrid* his descendants live in Madrid ‖ *morir sin descendencia* to die without issue.

descendente *adj* descending, downward; *curso descendente* downward course ‖ of descent; *línea descendente (del árbol genealógico)* line of descent ‖ diminishing (que disminuye) ‖ MAT & ASTR & MED descending ‖ outgoing (marea) ‖ MÚS falling (escala) ‖ *tren descendente* down train.

descender* *vi* to descend, to go down, to come down (bajar); *descender de una cima* to descend from a summit ‖ to go down; *ha descendido mucho en mi estima* he has gone down a lot in my esteem ‖ to go down, to fall, to drop (fiebre, temperatura, nivel, etc.); *el nivel del mercurio ha descendido* the mercury level has gone down ‖ to hang (las cortinas) ‖ — FIG *descender a* to lower o.s. to, to stoop to (rebajarse a) ‖ *descender de* to descend from, to be descended from, to issue from; *todos descendemos de Adán y Eva* we are all descended from Adam and Eve; to come from (proceder).
◆ *vt* to take down, to get down, to bring down, to lower ‖ to go down, to descend; *descender la escalera* to go down the stairs.

descendiente *adj* descending (que desciende) ‖ — *se cree descendiente de la pata del Cid* he thinks he's the cat's whiskers, he thinks he's the Lord God Almighty ‖ *ser descendiente de* to come from, to be a descendant of; *era descendiente de una familia linajuda* he came from a noble family, he was a descendant of a noble family.
◆ *m/f* descendant; *un descendiente de Newton* a descendant of Newton.
◆ *pl* issue *sing*, progeny *sing*, descendants.

descendimiento *m* ⟶ **descenso** ‖ descent; *descendimiento de la Cruz* descent from the Cross ‖ MED prolapse (de un órgano).

descenso; descendimiento *m* descent, going down, coming down (acción de descender) ‖ fall, drop (de fiebre, de temperatura) ‖ fall (de paracaídas) ‖ DEP downhill race (esquí) ‖ MED prelapse ‖ fall, subsidence; *descenso del nivel de un río* fall in the level of a river, subsidence of a river ‖ decline, drop, fall, falling-off (desnivel, disminución) ‖ fall (de los precios) ‖ demotion (degradación) ‖ slope (declive) ‖ way down; *el descenso hacia el río* the way down to the river ‖ FIG declive (decadencia) ‖ *descenso a segunda división* relegation to the second division (fútbol).

descentración *f* putting off centre (acción) ‖ eccentricity (resultado).

descentrado, da *adj* eccentric, off centre ‖ FIG all at sea, bewildered, lost; *me encuentro descentrado en esta ciudad* I feel lost in this town | unbalanced (desequilibrado) | out of focus (problema, etc.).
◆ *m* putting off centre (acción) ‖ eccentricity (resultado).

descentralización *f* decentralization.

descentralizado, da *adj* decentralized.

descentralizador, ra *adj* decentralizing.
◆ *m/f* decentralizer.

descentralizar *vt* to decentralize.

descentramiento *m* putting off centre (acción) ‖ eccentricity (resultado) ‖ FIG confusion, bewilderment (desorientación) | unbalanced state (desequilibrio).

descentrar *vt* to put off centre ‖ FIG to unbalance (desequilibrar).

desceñir* *vt* to loosen, to undo (soltar).
◆ *vpr* to come loose (aflojarse) ‖ to loosen (aflojar) ‖ to take off (quitarse).

descepar *vt* to uproot (planta) ‖ FIG to wip out, to eradicate (extirpar).

descercar *vt* to relieve (ciudad) ‖ to remove the wall from (quitar la muralla) ‖ to remove the fence from (quitar la cerca).

descerebración *f* MED decerebration.

descerebrar *vt* MED to decerebrate.

descerezar *vt* to pulp (el café).

descerrajado, da *adj* forced (cerradura) ‖ FIG licentious, loose, corrupt (de mal vivir).

descerrajadura *f* forcing (de una cerradura).

descerrajar *vt* to force, to break open (una cerradura, una puerta) ‖ FIG & FAM to fire, to let off; *descerrajar un tiro* to fire a shot ‖ to drop, to say (decir) | to ask (preguntar).

descifrable *adj* decipherable (signo con sentido oculto) | legible (letra).

descifrado *m* deciphering (de una escritura) || decoding (con clave) || MÚS sight reading.

descifrador, ra *adj* deciphering.
◆ *m/f* decipherer (de signo con sentido oculto) || decoder (de mensaje).

desciframiento *m* deciphering (de una escritura) || decoding (con clave).

descifrar *vt* to decipher (signo con sentido oculto) || to decode (conociendo la clave) || FIG to solve, to figure out (un misterio).

descifre *m* deciphering (de una escritura) || decoding (con clave).

descinchar *vt* to ungirth, to remove the girth from (quitar la cincha) || to slacken the girth of (aflojar la cincha).

desclavador *m* nail puller, nail wrench.

desclavar *vt* to unnail, to remove the nails from (algo sujeto con clavos) || to unstick (algo pegado).

descoagulante *adj* liquefying.

descoagular *vt* to liquefy, to dissolve.

descobajar *vt* to stem, to remove the stem from (los racimos de uvas).

descocado, da *adj* forward, brazen; *una mujer descocada* a brazen woman || cheeky, impudent (descarado).

descocamiento *m* brazennes, forwardness (atrevimiento) || cheek, impudence (descaro).

descocar *vt* AGR to remove the insects from.

descocarse *vpr* FAM to be brazen *o* forward (ser atrevido) | to be cheeky *o* impudent (descararse).

descoco *m* brazennes, forwardness (atrevimiento) || cheek, impudence (descaro).

descogotar *vt* to kill [with a blow on the back of the neck] (acogotar) || to cut off the antlers of (stag) (el venado).

descojonarse *vpr* POP to piss o.s. laughing.

descolgar *vt* to dock the tail of.

descolgadura *f*; **descolgamiento** *m* taking down (de un cuadro, etc.) || lowering, letting down (desde una posición alta) || lifting (del teléfono).

descolgar* *vt* to take down; *descolgar un cuadro* to take down a picture || to lift, to pick up (el teléfono) || to let down, to lower (desde una posición alta) || *dejar el teléfono descolgado* to leave the telephone off the hook.
◆ *vpr* to come down; *se ha descolgado el cuadro* the picture has come down || to lower o.s., to let o.s. down (bajar por una cuerda); *descolgarse de* or *por una pared* to lower o.s. down *o* to let o.s. down a wall || to slip, to slide (*por* down) (bajar escurriéndose) || to come down, to rush down (bajar rápidamente); *las tropas se descolgaron de las montañas* the troops rushed down the mountains || FIG & FAM to drop, to turn, to pop; *a veces se descuelga por casa a la hora de comer* he sometimes drops in *o* turns up *o* pops in at our house at lunchtime | to come up, to come out; *se descolgó con una noticia sensacional* he came up with a sensational piece of news | to surprise; *su tío se descolgó con mil pesetas* his uncle surprised him with a thousand pesetas | to descend, to turn up; *se descolgó pidiéndome dinero* he descended on me asking for money || FIG & FAM *descolgarse con* to come out with, to blurt out (decir, soltar).

descolocado, da *adj* unemployed, jobless, out of work.

descolonización *f* decolonization.

descolonizar *vt* to decolonize.

descoloración *f* bleaching (del cabello).

descolorado, da *adj* discoloured [*US* discolored] || faded (tela, color).

descolorar; descolorir *vt* to discolour [*US* to discolor] (hacer perder el color) || to fade (tela, color); *el sol descolora todos los vestidos* the sun fades all clothes || to bleach (el cabello).
◆ *vpr* to lose colour [*US* to lose color] (perder el color) || to fade (una tela, un color) || to be bleached (quedar blanco) || to bleach one's hair (una persona).

descolorido, da *adj* discoloured [*US* discolored] || faded (tela, color) || pale (pálido) || FIG dull, lifeless, colourless [*US* colorless] (estilo).
◆ *m* discolouration [*US* discoloration] || fading (de una tela, de un color) || bleaching (del pelo).

descolorimiento *m* → **descolorido.**

descolorir *vt* → **descolorar.**

descolladamente *adv* brilliantly, outstandingly; *siempre ha intervenido descolladamente en las sesiones del Parlamento* he has always spoken brilliantly in parliamentary debates.

descollamiento *m* superiority.

descollante *adj* outstanding.

descollar* *vi* to stand out, to excel; *este alumno descuella mucho entre los demás* this pupil stands out a great deal amongst the others || to stand out, to be outstanding; *no hay nada que descuelle en su vida* there is nothing which stands out in his life || to distinguish o.s., to excel; *ha descollado en la pintura de frescos* he has distinguished himself in fresco painting || to rise, to stand out (una montaña, etc.).

descombrar *vt* to clear (despejar).

descombro *m* clearing.

descomedidamente *adv* rudely, insolently (con insolencia); *hablar descomedidamente* to speak rudely || excessively, to excess, immoderately; *beber descomedidamente* to drink excessively.

descomedido, da *adj* rude, insolent (insolente) || excessive, immoderate (desmedido) || extreme (extremoso).

descomedimiento *m* rudeness, insolence (insolencia) || excess (exceso).

descomedirse* *vpr* to go too far (excederse) || to be rude *o* insolent (faltar al respeto).

descompaginar *vt* to upset, to disarrange (descomponer) || FIG to upset, to disrupt; *la huelga descompagina todos mis proyectos* the strike upsets all my plans.

descompás *m* disproportion, lack of proportion.

descompasadamente *adv* out of time (sin ritmo) || excessively, immoderately (con exceso) || rudely (con insolencia).

descompasado, da *adj* out of time (sin ritmo) || disproportionate, immoderate (desproporcionado) || rude (insolente).

descompasarse *vpr* to be rude *o* insolent (faltar al respeto) || to go too far (excederse).

descompensación *f* decompensation.

descomponer* *vt* to decompose, to rot, to decay; *descomponer un cuerpo* to decompose a body || QUÍM to decompose || FÍS to resolve (una fuerza) || MAT to split up (una fracción) || GRAM to split up (una frase) || to break down; *descomponer en partes una teoría* to break down a theory into parts || to break, to put out of order (un mecanismo); *descomponer un reloj* to break a watch; *descomponer un motor* to put an engine out of order || to disturb, to mess up, to upset (los proyectos) || to spoil; *me has descompuesto el peinado* you have spoiled my hairdo || to disarrange, to disrupt, to upset (el orden) || FIG to upset, to disturb; *me descompone ver tantas injusticias* it upsets me to see so much injustice | to annoy, to irritate, to put out (irritar) | to distort, to convulse; *el miedo descompuso sus rasgos* fear distorted his features || *descomponerle a uno el intestino* or *el vientre* to upset s.o.'s stomach.
◆ *vpr* to decompose, to decay, to rot; *el cadáver se ha descompuesto* the corpse has decomposed || QUÍM to decompose || FÍS to resolve (fuerzas) || GRAM & MAT to split up (una frase, una fracción) || to get out of order, to break down (mecanismo) || FIG to get angry *o* annoyed, to get worked up, to lose one's temper (irritarse) | to get upset; *me descompongo cuando veo todo lo que tengo que hacer* I get upset when I see all that I have to do | to be distorted (rasgos, cara, etc.) | to go to pieces (estropearse) || *se me descompuso el intestino* or *el vientre* I had an upset stomach, my stomach was upset.

descomposición *f* decay, rotting, decomposition (acción de pudrirse) || QUÍM decomposition || FÍS resolution (de fuerzas) || MAT factoring, factorizing (de un número) || GRAM construing (de una frase) || FIG decadence, decline; *la descomposición del Imperio Romano* the decadence of the Roman Empire | distortion, discomposure, convulsion (de la cara) | breakdown, failure (de un mecanismo) || *descomposición intestinal* or *del vientre* diarrhoea (diarrea).

descompostura *f* breaking (rotura) || breakdown (de un motor) || slovenliness, untidiness, carelessness (desaliño) || impudence, rudeness, brazenness (descaro) || lack of modesty (falta de pudor) || discomposure, distorsion (del rostro) || disorder (desorden).

descompresión *f* decompression.

descompresor *m* reducing valve (válvula) || AUT decompressor.

descomprimir *vt* to decompress || to depressurize.

descompuesto, ta *adj* decomposed, decayed, rotten (podrido) || QUÍM decomposed || broken; *reloj descompuesto* broken watch || broken down, out of order; *motor descompuesto* broken down engine || FIG upset (trastornado) | brazen, impudent (descarado) | distorted, convulsed; *rostro descompuesto* distorted face | angry; *gritos descompuestos* angry shouts || untidy (desordenado) || slovenly (desaliñado) || — *estar descompuesto* to have diarrhoea (tener diarrea) || FIG *tener el cuerpo descompuesto* not to feel well || *tener el vientre descompuesto* to have diarrhoea (tener diarrea), to have an upset stomach.

descomunal *adj* enormous, huge, colossal; *estatura descomunal* huge stature; *mentira descomunal* huge lie || FIG & FAM fantastic, magnificent; *una película descomunal* a fantastic film.

descomunalmente *adv* extremely, extraordinarily, tremendously || excessively, to excess, too much; *beber descomunalmente* to drink excessively || FAM magnificently, superbly, tremendously well (muy bien).

desconcentración *f* decentralization.

desconcentrar *vt* to decentralize, to break up

desconceptuar *vt* to misjudge (juzgar mal) || to discredit (desacreditar).

desconcertante *adj* disconcerting, upsetting.

desconcertar* *vt* FIG to disconcert, to upset, to put out (perturbar) | to confuse, to disconcert (desorientar); *lo hago para desconcertar al adversario* I do it to confuse my opponent; *mi pregunta lo ha desconcertado* my question has confused him || to dislocate (hueso).
◆ *vpr* FIG to be disconcerted *o* put out (turbarse) | to lose one's temper (enfadarse) | to be upset (el estómago) | to break down, not

to work (un mecanismo) | to be dislocated (huesos) || *yo no me desconcierto por cualquier cosa* I don't let anything upset me.

desconcierto *m* FIG disorder, confusion (desorden); *sembrar el desconcierto en el país* to cause disorder in the country | disagreement, discord (desavenencia) | confusion, perplexity, bewilderment (confusión).

desconchado *m*; **desconchadura** *f* peeling, flaking (de una pared) || bare patch (parte sin enlucido) || chipping (de la loza) || chip, nick (parte desconchada de la loza).

desconchar *vt* to make peel *o* flake, to peel off; *la humedad ha desconchado la pared* the damp has made the wall flake || to chip (la loza) || *pared desconchada* flaking *o* peeling wall.
◆ *vpr* to peel off, to flake off (una pared) || to get chipped, to chip (la loza).

desconchón *m* bare patch, patch of flaking paint; *la pared tiene desconchones* there are bare patches on the wall || chip (en la loza).

desconectar *vt* ELECTR to disconnect | to switch off, to turn off (la radio, etc.) | to take out, to pull out (el enchufe) | to unplug (desenchufar) || FIG *estar desconectado de* not to have contact with, not to be in contact with.
◆ *vpr* to become disconnected.

desconexión *f* ELECTR disconnexion, disconnection || FIG disconnection.

desconfiado, da *adj* distrustful; *una persona desconfiada* a distrustful person || unsure, suspicious (que tiene sospechas); *estar desconfiado* to be suspicious.
◆ *m/f* wary *o* distrustful person.

desconfianza *f* distrust, mistrust, wariness, suspicion (falta de confianza).

desconfiar *vi* to distrust, not to trust, to have no confidence; *desconfío de ese hombre* I do not trust that man, I have no confidence in that man || to be distrustful (ser desconfiado) || to doubt, not to be sure (no creer); *desconfío de que las ostras estén frescas* I doubt that oysters are fresh || to suspect (sospechar) || — *¡desconfíe!* beware! || *desconfíe de las imitaciones* beware of imitations.

desconforme *adj* ⟶ **disconforme.**

desconformidad *f* ⟶ **disconformidad.**

descongelación *f* unfreezing (de créditos) || defrosting (de la nevera) || thawing (del hielo, de la nieve).

descongelar *vt* to defrost (nevera) || to unfreeze; *descongelar créditos* to unfreeze credits.

descongestión *f* relieving of congestion, clearing.

descongestionar *vt* to relieve congestion in; *descongestionar la cabeza, una calle* to relieve congestion in the head, in a street || FIG to clear (despejar).

desconocer* *vt* not to know, not to be acquainted with; *desconozco a esta persona* I do not know this person || not to know, to be unaware of, to be ignorant of; *desconozco su punto de vista* I do not know his point of view || not to recognize; *tanto ha cambiado que lo desconocí* he has changed so much that I didn't recognize him || to deny (negar); *desconozco esas afirmaciones* I deny those statements || to disown; *desconoció a su hijo* he disowned his son || not to recognize; *desconoce los méritos de los demás* he does not recognize other people's merits.

desconocido, da *adj* unknown; *un pintor, un país desconocido* an unknown painter, country; *desconocido de* or *para todos* unknown to everyone || unrecognizable (que ha cambiado); *desde su enfermedad está desconocido* since his illness he is unrecognizable || unrecognized; *méritos desconocidos* unrecognized merits || strange, unfamiliar (que no se conoce) || ungrateful (desagradecido) || *vivir desconocido* to live unnoticed.
◆ *m/f* stranger, unknown person || newcomer (recién llegado) || — *lo desconocido* the unknown || *un ilustre desconocido* a nobody.

desconocimiento *m* ignorance (*de* of), disregard (*de* for), disregard (ignorancia) || repudiation (de los deberes) || ingratitude.

desconsideración *f* lack of consideration, thoughtlessness, inconsiderateness.

desconsideradamente *adv* inconsiderately, without consideration, thoughtlessly.

desconsiderado, da *adj* inconsiderate, thoughtless.

desconsiderar *vt* to be inconsiderate towards, to lack consideration for.

desconsoladamente *adv* sadly, disconsolately, sorrowfully.

desconsolado, da *adj* unconsoled (que no recibe consuelo) || disconsolate, distressed, grieved (afligido) || sad (triste) || dejected (desanimado).

desconsolador, ra *adj* distressing, heartbreaking, grievous.

desconsolar* *vt* to distress, to grieve.

desconsuelo *m* distress, grief, affliction (pena) || sadness, sorrow (tristeza).

descontado, da *adj* ⟶ **descontar.**

descontaminación *f* decontamination.

descontaminar *vt* to decontaminate.

descontar* *vt* to deduct; *descontar el diez por ciento* to deduct ten per cent || not to count; *descontando las vacaciones y los domingos quedan más de doscientos cincuenta días de trabajo* not counting holidays and Sundays there are more than two hundred and fifty working days left || FIG to discount, to disregard; *hay mucho que descontar en las alabanzas que le tributan* you must discount a lot in people's praises for him || to take for granted (considerar seguro) || COM to discount (un efecto a pagar) || — *dar por descontado* to take for granted; *doy por descontado su éxito* I am taking his success for granted || *descontarse años* to make out that one is younger than one is || *por descontado* of course.

descontentadizo, za *adj* hard to please, fastidious.

descontentar *vt* to displease, to make discontent.
◆ *vpr* to be displeased.

descontento, ta *adj* discontented, unhappy, displeased, dissatisfied; *descontento con su propia suerte, de sí mismo* unhappy with one's lot, with o.s.
◆ *m/f* discontented *o* dissatisfied person || *los descontentos declararon una huelga* the discontented *o* the dissatisfied declared a strike.
◆ *m* displeasure, dissatisfaction || discontent, unrest (de la población).

descontrolado, da *adj* uncontrolled.

desconvenir* *vi* not to agree, to disagree (en las opiniones) || not to go together, not to match (cosas).

descoordinación *f* lack of coordination.

descorazonador, ra *adj* discouraging, disheartening.

descorazonamiento *m* FIG disheartenment, discouragement, dejection.

descorazonar *vt* FIG to dishearten, to get down, to discourage (desanimar); *este tiempo me descorazona* this weather disheartens me || (p us) to tear out the heart of (arrancar el corazón de).
◆ *vpr* to lose heart, to get discouraged.

descorchador *m* bark stripper (of cork trees) (obrero) || corkscrew (sacacorchos).

descorchar *vt* to strip the bark from (cork trees) (los alcornoques) || to uncork (una botella) || FIG to force (abrir por la fuerza).

descorche *m* bark stripping (de los alcornoques) || uncorking (de una botella).

descordar* *vt* MÚS to remove the strings from [an instrument] || TAUR ⟶ **descabellar.**

descornar* *vt* to dehorn (arrancar los cuernos de).
◆ *vpr* FIG & FAM to rack one's brains (pensar) | to slog away (trabajar).

descoronar *vt* to discrown, to depose (a un rey).

descorrer *vt* to draw, to open; *descorrer las cortinas* to draw the curtains || to remove (un velo) || *descorrer el cerrojo* to unbolt the door.

descortés *adj* impolite, rude, discourteous.

descortesía *f* impoliteness, rudeness, discourtesy.

descortezadura *f* piece of bark (trozo de corteza) || bare patch (parte descortezada).

descortezamiento *m* bark stripping, decortication (de los árboles) || peeling (de la fruta).

descortezar *vt* to strip the bark from, to decorticate (árboles) || to cut the crust off (el pan) || to peel (la fruta) || FIG & FAM to knock the rough edges off *o* the corners off, to refine (desbastar).

descosedura *f* ⟶ **descosido.**

descoser *vt* to unpick, to unstitch (las costuras).
◆ *vpr* to come undone *o* unstitched.

descosido, da *adj* unpicked, unstitched (en costura) || undone, unstitched (estado accidental) || FIG disjointed, disconnected; *discurso descosido* disjointed speech | talkative, indiscreet (indiscreto).
◆ *m* open seam, seam which has come undone *o* unstitched (costura) || — FIG & FAM *beber como un descosido* to drink like a fish | *comer como un descosido* to eat like a horse | *correr como un descosido* to run like the devil | *hablar como un descosido* to talk nineteen to the dozen | *reír como un descosido* to laugh one's head off, to split one's sides laughing.

descostillarse *vpr* to fall flat on one's back (caerse).

descostrar *vt* to cut the crust off.

descotado, da *adj/sm* ⟶ **escotado.**

descotar *vt* ⟶ **escotar.**

descote *m* ⟶ **escote.**

descoyuntamiento *m* MED dislocation || dislocation (de cosas) || exhaustion, fatigue (malestar).

descoyuntar *vt* MED to dislocate || to dislocate (cosas) || FIG to twist, to force the sense of (desvirtuar) || FIG *estar descoyuntado* to be double-jointed (un artista de circo).
◆ *vpr* to dislocate; *descoyuntarse la cadera* to dislocate one's hip || to get dislocated; *se descoyuntó la articulación* his joint got dislocated || FIG & FAM *descoyuntarse de risa* to split one's sides laughing.

descrédito *m* disrepute, discredit; *caer en descrédito* to fall into disrepute || *ir en descrédito de* to be to the discredit of, to damage the reputation of.

descreído, da *adj* disbelieving, unbelieving.
◆ *m/f* disbeliever, unbeliever.

descreimiento *m* disbelief, unbelief.

descremado, da *adj* skimmed.

descremar *vt* to skim (la leche).

descrestar *vt* to cut off the crest of || FIG to deceive (engañar).

describible *adj* describable.

describir *vt* to trace, to describe (trazar); *describir una órbita* to trace an orbit || to describe; *describir un paisaje* to describe a landscape.

descripción *f* tracing, describing, description (acción de trazar) || description; *una hermosa descripción* a beautiful description.

descriptivo, va *adj* descriptive; *geometría, anatomía descriptiva* descriptive geometry, anatomy.

descrismar *vt* FAM to smash *o* to bash (s.o.'s) face in (pegar).
◆ *vpr* FAM to break one's neck (romperse la cara) || FIG & FAM to fly off the handle (encolerizarse) | to slog away, to work o.s. to death, to wear o.s. out (trabajar) | to rack one's brains (pensar).

descristianización *f* dechristianization.

descristianizar *vt* to turn away from Christianity, to dechristianize.

descrito, ta *adj* described, traced (trazado) || described (narrado).

descruzar *vt* to uncross; *descruzar los brazos* to uncross one's arms.

descuadernar *vt* to unbind, to remove the binding from (un libro) || FIG to confuse, to upset (turbar).
◆ *vpr* to come apart, to come unbound (un libro).

descuadrillado, da *adj* VET hipshot (caballo).
◆ *m* VET sprained haunch (del caballo).

descuajar *vt* to liquefy, to dissolve (poner líquido) || FIG & FAM to dishearten, to discourage (desanimar) || AGR to uproot (desarraigar) || FIG to wipe out, to eradicate (extirpar).
◆ *vpr* to liquefy, to dissolve.

descuajaringar *vt* FAM to take *o* to pull to pieces (descomponer) || FAM *estar descuajaringado* to be exhausted *o* worn out (de cansancio).

descuaje; descuajo *m* AGR uprooting.

descuartizamiento *m* quartering (suplicio) || cutting into joints, quartering, cutting up (de un animal).

descuartizar *vt* to quarter (en un suplicio) || to cut into joints, to quarter (the carcass of), to cut up; *descuartizar un ternero* to cut a calf into joints || FAM to pull to pieces, to tear apart.

descubierta *f* MIL scouting, reconnoitering, reconnaissance || MAR inspection of the rigging || — *a la descubierta* openly (sin disfraz), in the open (sin protección) || MIL *ir a la descubierta* to scout, to reconnoitre.

descubiertamente *adv* openly.

descubierto, ta *adj* discovered || uncovered (no cubierto) || clear; *el cielo estaba descubierto* the sky was clear || exposed, open (expuesto) || open (automóvil) || open, bare, treeless (terreno) || bareheaded, hatless, without a hat (persona) || bare (cabeza) || *iban descubiertos* they were not wearing hats.
◆ *m* COM deficit (de cuenta corriente) | bears *pl*, shorts *pl* (en Bolsa) | shortage (en el presupuesto) || open space (lugar) || REL exposition [of the Sacrament] || — *al descubierto* openly (sin disfraz), in the open (sin protección) || *en todo lo descubierto* in the whole world || *estar en descubierto* to be overdrawn, to be in the red (ser deudor), to be stuck for words (quedarse cortado) || *poner algo al descubierto* to bring sth. into the open || *quedar al descubierto* to come out into the open, to be exposed, to be revealed.

descubridor, ra *adj* discovering || MAR reconnaissance, scouting (embarcación).
◆ *m/f* discoverer.
◆ *m* MIL scout (batidor).

descubrimiento *m* discovery; *el descubrimiento de América* the discovery of America; *la época de los descubrimientos* the age of discovery || unveiling (de una estatua, de una lápida).

descubrir *vt* to uncover (quitar lo que cubre) || to take the lid off (una cacerola) || to discover; *descubrir un país* to discover a country; *descubrir un nuevo antibiótico* to discover a new antibiotic || to unveil; *descubrir una estatua* to unveil a statue || to find (un tesoro, minas de oro, etc.) || to reveal (revelar); *descubrir sus intenciones* to reveal one's intentions || to bring to light (un crimen) || to detect (un criminal, un fraude) || to discover, to find out (una conjuración) || to unmask (un impostor) || to be able to see, to make out (divisar); *desde la ventana descubríamos todo el valle* from the window we could see the whole valley || to bare (la cabeza) || to expose, to lay down (los naipes) || MAR to sight (la tierra) || MIL to expose (la retaguardia) || REL to expose [the Sacrament] || — FIG *descubrir América* or *el Mediterráneo* to force an open door || *descubrir su juego* to show one's hand *o* one's cards.
◆ *vpr* to be discovered || to take off one's hat (quitarse el sombrero) || to raise one's hat (para saludar) || to clear (el cielo) || to come into sight (verse) || FIG to come out, to come to light (un crimen, un secreto, la verdad) | to confide, to open one's heart; *descubrirse con alguien* to confide in *o* to open one's heart to s.o. || to reveal o.s., to show o.s. (mostrarse) || to lower one's guard (en esgrima, boxeo) || FAM *¡hay que descubrirse!* bravo!, well done!

descuento *m* deduction (acción de descontar) || COM discount; *con descuento* at a discount | discount, reduction; *conceder un descuento a un cliente* to give a discount *o* a reduction to a client || stoppage; *descuento del salario* ware stoppage || — *descuento por no declaración de siniestro* no-claims bonus || COM *descuento por pronto pago* cash discount || *descuento racional* or *matemático* true *o* arithmetical discount || *tipo de descuento* discount rate (privado), bank rate (de un estado).

descuerar *vt* to skin (reses) || AMER to pull to pieces, to criticize (criticar).

descuidadamente *adv* carelessly, negligently (sin cuidado) || in a slovenly way, untidily (con desaseo) || rashly, thoughtlessly, without thinking, carelessly (sin pensarlo) || nonchalantly, carefree, casually (sin preocupación).

descuidado, da *adj* careless, negligent, thoughtless (negligente) || untidy, slovenly (en su aseo personal) || casual, easygoing, carefree; *es muy descuidado, no se preocupa por nada* he's very casual, he doesn't worry about a thing || unprepared (desprevenido) || neglected; *libro, niño descuidado* neglected book, child || — *coger descuidado* to catch unawares *o* napping *o* off guard || *estar descuidado* to relax, not to worry, to rest assured (no preocuparse); *puedes estar descuidado* you can relax, you need not worry.

descuidar *vt* to neglect; *descuidar sus deberes* to neglect one's duties || to free, to release (de una obligación) || to distract (distraer).
◆ *vi* not to worry; *¡descuida!* don't worry || to forget (*de* to), to neglect (*de* to).
◆ *vpr* to neglect; *descuidarse de su trabajo* to neglect one's work || to be careless (no prestar atención) || to let o.s. go, to neglect o.s. (en el atavío) || not to be careful, not to watch out; *si te descuidas, te roban la cartera* if you are not careful, you will have your wallet stolen || not to bother, not to worry (no preocuparse); *siempre se descuida de todo* he never bothers about anything || to neglect one's health; *se ha descuidado y ahora tiene gripe* he has neglected his health and now he has influenza || — *en cuanto se descuida usted* if you are not careful, if you do not watch out || *me descuidé un momento y tropecé con un árbol* my attention wandered for a minute and I bumped into a tree || *si me descuido* if I am not careful (presente), if I hadn't been careful (pasado).

descuidero *m* sneak thief, pickpocket.

descuido *m* negligence, carelessness, neglect (negligencia); *el accidente ocurrió por un descuido del automovilista* the accident happened because of negligence on the part of the motorist || absentmindedness, inadvertence, inattention (falta de atención); *un momento de descuido* a moment's inadvertence || slip, mistake (error); *hay muchos descuidos en ese libro* there are many mistakes in that book || slovenliness, untidiness (en el arreglo personal) || — *al descuido* negligently, carelessly (sin cuidado), casually, nonchalantly (con descuido afectado) || *al menor descuido* if my (your, his, etc.) attention wanders (wandered, etc.) for a minute || *con descuido* without thinking || *en un descuido* when least expected || *por descuido* inadvertently.

descular *vt* to break the bottom of.

desde *adv* since (tiempo); *desde el año cero* since the year dot || from (lugar); *desde Madrid hasta Londres* from Madrid to London || — *desde abajo* from below || *desde ahora* from now on || *desde arriba* from above || *desde ayer acá* since yesterday || *¿desde cuándo?* since when? || *desde entonces* since then, from that time on; *no le volví a ver desde entonces* I haven't seen him again since then || *¿desde hace cuánto tiempo?* how long?; *¿desde hace cuánto tiempo está lloviendo?* how long has it been raining? || *desde hace poco* for a short time, not for long; *tiene un coche desde hace poco* he has had a car for a short time, he hasn't had a car for long || *desde hace tiempo* or *mucho tiempo* for a long time; *está allí desde hace mucho tiempo* he has been there for a long time || *desde hace (hacía) un mes* for a month, it is (was) a month since; *no le he visto desde hace un mes* I haven't seen him for a month, it is a month since I saw him; *no le había visto desde hacía un mes* I hadn't seen him for a month it was a month since I had seen him || *desde... hasta* from... to, from... until; *desde las ocho hasta las diez* from eight o'clock to ten || *desde lejos* from afar, from a long way off || *desde lo alto de* from the top of || *desde luego* of course, certainly || *desde mi punto de vista* as I see it, as far as I can see || *desde niño* since (you, he, etc.) was (were, etc.) a child, from childhood || *desde que* since || *desde siempre* for ever || AMER *desde ya* from now on (de ahora en adelante), right now (ahora mismo).

desdecir* *vi* to be unworthy of, to let down; *desdecir de su familia* to be unworthy of one's family, to let one's family down || not to go, not to match; *su corbata desdice de su traje* his tie does not go with his suit || to be inconsistent (*de* with) || — *desdecir de su pasado* to decline, to degenerate, to go downhill || *desdecir uno de otro* not to match (colores).
◆ *vpr* to take back what one has said (retractarse) || to go back, to retract, to withdraw; *desdecirse de su promesa* to go back on one's promise, to retract one's promise || to repudiate, to disown; *desdecirse de sus opiniones* to repudiate one's opinions || to contradict o.s. (contradecirse).

desdén *m* contempt, scorn, disdain (desprecio) || *al desdén* casually, nonchalantly.

desdentado, da *adj* toothless || ZOOL edentate.

◆ *m pl* ZOOL edentata.

desdentar* *vt* to remove the teeth of.

desdeñable *adj* insignificant, negligible (insignificante) || despicable, contemptible (despreciable) || *no desdeñable* far from negligible.

desdeñar *vt* to scorn, to disdain; *desdeña a sus compañeros* he scorns his companions || to turn one's nose up at, to scorn; *desdeña mis ofertas* he turns his nose up at my offers || to forget, to ignorer (ignorar).

◆ *vpr* not to deign; *desdeñarse de hablar* not to deign to speak.

desdeñoso, sa *adj* scornful, disdainful, contemptuous.

desdibujado, da *adj* blurred; *contornos desdibujados* blurred outlines.

desdibujarse *vpr* FIG to fade, to become faint *o* blurred (borrarse).

desdicha *f* misfortune (desgracia); *sufrir continuas desdichas* to suffer continuous misfortunes || unhappiness, wretchedness, misfortune, misery (infelicidad) || — *para colmo de desdichas* to top it all || *por desdicha* unfortunately.

desdichado, da *adj* unfortunate, poor, pitiful, unlucky (desgraciado) || unhappy (triste) || wretched, despicable (despreciable).

◆ *m/f* poor devil, poor wretch (pobre desgraciado) || wretch (persona despreciable) || *¡desdichado de mí, de ti* woe is me, woe is you.

desdoblamiento *m* straightening (de un alambre, etc.) || unfolding (de una sábana, etc.) || splitting (conversión en dos) || FIG explanation, elucidation (aclaración) || *desdoblamiento de la personalidad* split personality.

desdoblar *vt* to straighten (un alambre, etc.) || to unfold; *desdoblar un mapa* to unfold a map || to split (convertir en dos).

desdorar *vt* to remove the gilt from || FIG to tarnish (la reputación de uno).

desdoro *m* tarnishing || FIG stain, blot || *sin desdoro de* without tarnishing *o* harming; *puedes hacerlo sin desdoro de tu fama* you can do it without tarnishing your reputation.

deseable *adj* desirable || *poco deseable* undesirable.

deseado, da *adj* desired.

deseador, ra *adj* desirous.

desear *vt* to want (querer); *deseo que hable* I want you to speak; *¿qué desea de mí?* what do you want of me? || to desire, to long for, to wish for; *deseamos la libertad* we desire liberty || to wish; *desearía que me ayudases* I wish you would help me; *desearía ser* I wish I were || to wish, to desire, to want; *desear hacer algo* to wish to do sth. || to long for; *estoy deseando que llegue mi amigo* I am longing for my friend to arrive || to wish; *le deseo mucho éxito* I wish you every success || — *cuanto más se tiene más se desea* the more you have, the more you want || *dejar bastante que desear* to leave a lot to be desired || *desear con ansia* to long *o* to yearn for || *desearía tener amigos* I should like to have friends || *es de desear* it is to be hoped || *hacerse desear* to make o.s. wanted, to keep people waiting || *¿qué desea?* what would you like? (qué quiere), what can I do for you? (en qué puedo servirle).

desecación *f*; **desecamiento** *m*; **desecado** *m* drying, desiccation (de comestibles) || drying (natural) || withering (de plantas) || draining, drainage, reclaiming; *desecación de una marisma* draining of marsh.

desecado, da *adj* dried, desiccated.

◆ *m* ⟶ **desecación.**

desecador, ra *adj* drying || QUÍM desiccative, desiccating.

◆ *m* desiccator.

desecamiento *m* ⟶ **desecación.**

desecante *adj* drying || QUÍM desiccative, desicating, desiccant.

desecar *vt* to dry up; *el calor deseca la tierra* heat dries up the earth || to drain; *desecar un estanque* to drain a pond || QUÍM to desiccate.

◆ *vpr* to dry up.

desecativo, va *adj* drying || QUÍM desiccative, desiccating, desiccant.

desechable *adj* disposable, throw-away.

desechar *vt* to discard, to throw away *o* out (tirar); *desechar un traje viejo* to discard an old suit || to put aside, to get rid of, to cast aside; *debes desechar estos malos pensamientos* you should put aside these bad thoughts || to reject; *desechar un consejo, una proposición* to reject advice, a suggestion || to drop, to discard (una idea, un proyecto) || to refuse, to turn down (un empleo, una dignidad).

desecho *m* cast-off (prenda de vestir); *armario lleno de desechos* wardrobe full of cast-offs || piece of rubbish, throw-out (cosa tirada) || throw-out, reject (después de elegir lo bueno) || offal (de carnicero) || FIG contempt, scorn (desprecio) | scum, dregs *pl* (lo peor) | dead loss (persona inútil) || — *de desecho* cast-off (vestidos), scrap (máquina), waste (producto) || TAUR *desecho de tienta* bull that has not proved brave enough in the «tienta» [test] [it is either slaughtered for meat or used in a *becerrada* or a *novillada*].

◆ *pl* rubbish *sing*; *el desván está lleno de desechos* the attic is full of rubbish || cast - offs (vestidos) || waste *sing* (de una industria) || rejects, throw-outs (después de elegir lo bueno) || — *desechos de metal* scrap metal || *desechos radiactivos* radioactive waste.

deselectrizar *vt* ELECTR to discharge.

desellar *vt* to unseal.

desembalaje *m* unpacking.

desembalar *vt* to unpack; *desembalar una máquina* to unpack a machine.

desembaldosar *vt* to remove the tiles *o* flagstones from, to untile, to unpave.

desembanastar *vt* to take out of a basket || FIG to chatter about (hablar) || to draw (un arma).

desembarazado, da *adj* free, clear (libre) || free and easy (desenvuelto) || uncluttered, unencumbered (desahogado).

desembarazar *vt* to clear (un camino) || to empty, to clear (un piso).

◆ *vpr* to rid o.s. of, to get rid of; *desembarazarse de algo, de alguien* to rid o.s. of sth., of s.o.; to get rid of sth., of s.o.

desembarazo *m* clearing || self-confidence, ease (desenfado) || AMER childbirth (parto).

desembarcadero *m* landing stage, pier, wharf.

desembarcar *vt* to unload, to disembark; *desembarcar mercancías* to unload merchandise || to land, to put ashore (personas).

◆ *vi* to disembark, to land, to go ashore, to debark (p us); *desembarcamos en el puerto por la noche* we disembarked in the port at night || to disembark (de un avión) || FIG & FAM to lead (*en* to), to lead (una escalera) | to land (llegar).

desembarco *m* landing, disembarkation (de personas) || landing (de tropas); *el desembarco de Normandía* the Normandy landing || landing (de escalera).

desembargar *vt* to clear (desembarazar) || JUR to lift *o* to raise the embargo on (suprimir el embargo).

desembargo *m* JUR lifting *o* raising of an embargo.

desembarque *m* disembarkation, landing (de pasajeros) || unloading, disembarkation (de mercancías) || disembarkation (de un avión) || *tarjeta de desembarque* landing card.

desembarrancar *vt* to refloat (un barco).

desembarrar *vt* to clear the mud from, to clean the mud off (quitar el barro).

desembaular *vt* to take out (sacar) || to unpack (desembalar) || FIG & FAM to get (sth.) off one's chest (desahogarse).

desembelesarse *vpr* to recover, to come to one's senses (salir de su embeleso).

desembocadero *m* ⟶ **desembocadura.**

desembocadura *f*; **desembocadero** *m*; **desemboque** *m* mouth, outlet (de un río, de una cañería) || opening, end (de una calle).

desembocar; desbocar *vi* to flow, to run; *este río desemboca en el océano Atlántico* this river flows into the Atlantic Ocean || to meet, to join, to lead into; *esta avenida desemboca en la calle mayor* this avenue meets the main street || FIG to lead, to end; *disturbios que pueden desembocar en la guerra* disturbances which can lead to war *o* end in war; *razonamientos que no desembocan en nada* reasoning which leads to nothing *o* leads nowhere || *el río Mersey desemboca en Liverpool* the mouth of the river Mersey is in Liverpool, the river Mersey ends in Liverpool.

desembojar *vt* to remove (the silk cocoons) from the bushes.

desembolsado, da *adj* paid-up; *acciones desembolsadas* paid-up shares (en la Bolsa) || spent; *cantidad desembolsada* sum spent.

desembolsar *vt* to pay (pagar) || FIG to lay out (gastar).

desembolso *m* payment (pago) || payment, instalment [*US* installment] (cada uno de los pagos) || *desembolso inicial* down payment (al comprar a plazos), initial outlay (gastos iniciales).

◆ *pl* expenses, costs (gastos).

desemboque *m* ⟶ **desembocadura.**

desemborrachar *vt* to sober up.

desembotar *vt* FIG to sharpen (s.o.'s wits).

desembozar *vt* to uncover, to reveal, to unmask (quitar el embozo de) || FIG to uncover, to bring out into the open (descubrir).

desembragar *vt* to disengage, to disconnect || AUT to release (el embrague).

◆ *vi* AUT to declutch, to put the clutch out.

desembrague *m* disengaging, disconnecting || AUT declutching | clutch pedal (pedal).

desembravecer* *vt* to tame (animales) || FIG to calm.

◆ *vpr* to become tame (animales) || FIG to calm down.

desembriagar *vt* to sober up.

◆ *vpr* to sober up.

desembridar *vt* to unbridle.

desembrollar *vt* FAM to sort out, to clear up, to clarify (aclarar) || to unravel, to disentangle (una madeja, etc.).

desembrozar *vt* ⟶ **desbrozar.**

desembrujar *vt* to remove a spell from (s.o.), to free (s.o.) from a spell.

desembuchar *vt* to disgorge (los pájaros) || FIG & FAM to come out with, to let out (revelar).

◆ *vi* FIG & FAM to spill the beans (confesar) || *¡desembucha!* out with it!

desemejante *adj* dissimilar, different.

desemejanza *f* dissimilarity, difference.

desemejar *vi* not to be alike, to differ, to be dissimilar, to be unlike.

◆ *vt* to alter, to change (cambiar).

desempacar *vt* to unpack.

desempachar *vt* to relieve from indigestion.
◆ *vpr* to be relieved from indigestion (el estómago) || FIG to come out of one's shell (perder la timidez).

desempacho *m* relief from indisgestion (del estómago) || FIG self-confidence, ease (soltura).

desempalagar *vt* to restore one's appetite, to settle one's stomach.
◆ *vpr* to recover one's appetite, to feel better.

desempañar *vt* to take the nappy off (a un niño) || to clean, to polish (un cristal).

desempapelar *vt* to take the paper off, to unwrap (un paquete) || to strip the walls of; *desempapelar una habitación* to strip the walls of a room.

desempaque; desempaquetado *m* unpacking, unwrapping.

desempaquetar *vt* to unpack, to unwrap.

desemparejado, da *adj* odd; *tengo un calcetín desemparejado* I've got an odd sock || without a partner, odd (desparejado).

desemparejar *vt* to separate, to lose one of (un par de calcetines, etc.) || to leave without a partner (en un baile, etc.).

desempastar *vt* to remove the filling from.

desempaste *m* removal of a filling (de un diente).

desempatar *vt* to break the tie between; *desempatar los votos* to break the tie between the votes.
◆ *vi* DEP to take the lead (en un partido) | to play off, to play a deciding match (jugar un partido de desempate).

desempate *m* play-off (en fútbol) || — DEP *gol de desempate* deciding goal | *jugar un partido de desempate* to play off, to play a deciding match.

desempedrado *m* removal of paving.

desempedrar* *vt* to take up the paving of, to unpave.

desempeñar *vt* to take out of pawn, to redeem (de una casa de empeño); *desempeñar sus alhajas* to take one's jewels out of pawn || to free from debt, to pay the debts of (pagar las deudas); *desempeñó a Juan* he freed John from debt, he paid John's debts || to carry out, to fulfil; *desempeñar una misión peligrosa* to carry out a dangerous mission || to fill, to occupy, to hold (un cargo) || to discharge, to fulfil, to carry out (el deber) || TEATR & CINEM to play; *desempeñar el papel de Desdémona* to play the part of Desdemona; *desempeñar un papel muy importante* to play an important role || to get out of a fix *o* of difficulty (sacar de apuro).
◆ *vpr* to get out of debt, to free o.s. from debt || to get out of a fix *o* of difficulty (salir de apuro).

desempeño *m* redeeming, redemption (de una prenda empeñada) || discharge, carrying out, fulfilment (de un deber) || carrying out, fulfilment, performance (de un cargo, etc.) || freeing from *o* paying of debts (para otra persona) || paying (de sus propias deudas) || playing, acting, performance (de un papel).

desemperezar *vi* to make an effort, to shake o.s., to pull o.s. together.
◆ *vpr* to make an effort, to shake o.s., to pull o.s. together.

desempleado, da *adj* unemployed, out of work.
◆ *m/f* unemployed man, unemployed woman || *los desempleados* the unemployed.

desempleo *m* unemployment.

desemplumar *vt* to pluck.

desempolvadura *f* dusting.

desempolvar *vt* to dust (quitar el polvo) || FIG to revive, to unearth; *desempolvar viejos recuerdos* to revive old memories.

desemponzoñar *vt* to detoxicate, to detoxify (a una persona) || to remove the poison from (una cosa).

desempuñar *vt* to let go.

desencabestrar *vt* to untangle (a horse's) feet from the halter (el caballo).

desencadenamiento *m* unchaining, unleashing (de un perro) || FIG outbreak (de un ataque) | outburst (de protestas, de hilaridad).

desencadenar *vt* to unchain (quitar las cadenas) || to unleash (un perro) || FIG to start, to spark off; *desencadenar una guerra* to start a war | to unleash (las pasiones) | to give rise to; *desencadenar aplausos, protestas* to give rise to applause, to protests || FIG *desencadenar la hilaridad* to set everyone off laughing, to raise a storm of laughter.
◆ *vpr* FIG to break out (ovaciones, guerra); *los aplausos se desencadenaron* applause broke out | to burst, to break; *la tempestad se desencadenó* the storm broke | to break loose, to explode (la cólera) | to rage (viento, pasión) || to break loose (soltarse).

desencajado, da *adj* twisted, contorted, distorted (cara) || wild (ojos) || dislocated (huesos) || disconnected (desconectado).

desencajamiento *m* dislocation (de los huesos) || distortion (del rostro) || disconnection.

desencajar *vt* to dislocate (los huesos) || to disjoint (separar) || to disconnect, to disengage (desconectar) || to unwedge, to free, to unblock (liberar una pieza) || to distort (demudar).
◆ *vpr* to become distorted (el rostro) || to look wild (los ojos) || to come apart (deshacerse) || to come off (una pieza).

desencajonamiento *m* TAUR removal (of the bull) from the transport crate || unpacking.

desencajonar *vt* to unpack, to uncrate || ARQ to remove the coffering from (un pozo) | to remove the timbering from (una galería) || TAUR to remove (the bull) from the transport crate.

desencalladura *f*; **desencallamiento** *m* refloating.

desencallar *vt* to refloat.

desencaminar *vt* ⟶ **descaminar.**

desencanallar *vt* to put back on the straight and narrow.

desencantamiento *m* disenchantment.

desencantar *vt* to remove a spell from, to disenchant (quitar el hechizo) || to disillusion, to disappoint (decepcionar).
◆ *vpr* to be disappointed *o* disillusioned.

desencanto *m* disappointment, disillusionment (desengaño) || freeing from a spell, disenchantment (desencantamiento) || *sufrir un desencanto* to be disappointed.

desencapillar *vt* MAR to unrig.

desencapotar *vt* (p us) to uncloak, to take the cloak off || FIG to uncover, to uncloak (descubrir).
◆ *vpr* to take off one's cloak || to clear (el cielo) || FIG to brighten up.

desencaprichar *vt* to rid (s.o.) of a whim *o* fancy.

desencarcelar *vt* to release from prison, to free.

desencargar *vt* to cancel an order for.

desenclavar *vt* to unnail (desclavar).

desenclavijar *vt* to remove the pegs from.

desencofrado *m* removal of shuttering *o* formwork (del hormigón) || MIN removal of timbering.

desencofrar *vt* to remove the shuttering *o* formwork from (el hormigón) || to remove the timbering from (una galería).

desencoger *vt* to stretch out (extender) || to unfold (desdoblar).
◆ *vpr* FIG to come out of one's shell.

desencogimiento *m* self-confidence, ease.

desencoladura *f* ungluing, unsticking.

desencolar *vt* to unglue, to unstick.
◆ *vpr* to come unglued *o* unstuck.

desencolerizar *vt* to calm (down), to pacify.
◆ *vpr* to calm down, to cool down *o* off.

desenconar *vt* to relieve the inflammation of || FIG to calm, to soothe (la cólera).
◆ *vpr* to calm down, to cool off (calmarse) || to control one's temper (contenerse).

desencono *m* MED relief of inflammation || calming, pacification (acción de calmar) || calm (calma) || restraint, control (contención).

desencordar* *vt* to unstring (un instrumento).

desencordelar *vt* to untie (desatar).

desencorvar *vt* to straighten.

desencuadernar *vt* to unbind, to remove the binding from.
◆ *vpr* to come apart, to come unbound || *el libro se desencuadernó* the binding came off the book.

desenchufar *vt* to unplug, to disconnect.

desenchufe *m* unplugging.

desendemoniar; desendiablar *vt* to drive the evil spirits from, to exorcise.

desendiosar *vt* FIG to take down a peg or two (humillar) | to show up in one's true light, to show up for what one really is; *desendiosar a un gran personaje* to show a great man up in his true light.

desenfadadamente *adv* with ease *o* self-assurance, confidently.

desenfadaderas *f pl* resourcefulness *sing* || *tiene desenfadaderas* he is resourceful.

desenfadado, da *adj* self-confident, self-assured, confident (desenvuelto) || carefree, free and easy, easy, easygoing (despreocupado); *hablar con un tono desenfadado* to speak in a carefree tone.

desenfadar *vt* to calm down, to quieten.

desenfado *m* openness, frankness, ease (franqueza) || self-confidence, assurance (desenvoltura) || ease (facilidad) || freedom from care (despreocupación).

desenfilada *f* MIL defilade.

desenfilar *vt* MIL to defilade, to cover from enemy fire (poner a cubierto).

desenfocado, da *adj* out of focus.

desenfocar *vt* to put out of focus (fotografía) || FIG to approach from the wrong angle (un problema).

desenfoque *m* *el desenfoque es muy grande* it is right out of focus.

desenfrenado, da *adj* wild, frantic; *baile desenfrenado* wild dance || unbridled, uncontrolled, ravenous; *apetito desenfrenado* unbridled appetite || unrestrained, unbridled, wild, frantic (pasiones).

desenfrenamiento *m* ⟶ **desenfreno.**

desenfrenar *vt* to unbridle (el caballo).
◆ *vpr* FIG to be let *o* to break loose (pasiones) | to give o.s. over to vice (caer en el desenfreno) | to break, to burst (tempestad) | to rage (viento) | to run riot, to go wild (la multitud).

desenfreno; desenfrenamiento *m* wantonness, licentiousness (vicio) || unleashing, unbridling (de las pasiones).

desenfundar *vt* to remove from its case || to draw (un arma) || to uncover (un mueble).

desenfurecer* *vt* to calm *o* to quieten down, to pacify.

desenfurruñar *vt* to calm down, to pacify.

desengalgar *vt* to unchock (una rueda).

desenganchar *vt* to unhook || to take off; *desenganchar un abrigo de una percha* to take a coat off a coat hanger || to unhitch (caballerías) || to uncouple (vagones) || TECN to disengage (piezas).

desenganche *m* unhitching (de las caballerías) || uncoupling (de dos vagones) || unhooking.

desengañado, da *adj* disillusioned (desilusionado); *estar desengañado de* or *con* to be disillusioned by *o* with || disappointed (decepcionado) || AMER hideous, ugly (muy feo).

desengañador, ra *adj* disillusioning (que desilusiona) || disappointing (que decepciona).

desengañar *vt* to enlighten, to open the eyes of, to undeceive; *le creía inteligente pero sus profesores me han desengañado* I thought he was intelligent but his teachers have enlightened me *o* have opened my eyes || to disillusion (desilusionar) || to disappoint (decepcionar).

◆ *vpr* to realize the truth (ver la realidad) || to be disillusioned (desilusionarse) || to be disappointed (decepcionarse) || to realize; *¿te has desengañado de que no era verdad?* have you realized that it was not true? || — *¡desengáñate!* don't you believe it! || *desengañarse de sus ilusiones* to lose one's illusions.

desengaño *m* enlightenment || eye-opener (cosa que abre los ojos a uno) || disillusion, disillusionment (desilusión) || disappointment (decepción) || *llevarse* or *sufrir un desengaño* to be disillusioned, to be disappointed || *sufrir un desengaño amoroso* to have an unhappy love affair.

desengarzar *vt* to unthread (quitar el hilo) || to unstring (perlas) || to remove from its setting, to unset (joyas).

desengastar *vt* to remove from its setting, to unset (una piedra preciosa).

desengaste *m* unsetting, removal of a jewel from its setting.

desengomado *m*; **desengomadura** *f* ungluing || boiling off (de seda).

desengomar *vt* to unglue || to boil off (tejidos).

desengoznar *vt* to unhinge.

desengranar *vt* to disengage.

desengrasado *m* removal of the grease || scouring (de la lana).

desengrasador *m* cleaner.

desengrasadora *f* scourer (de la lana).

desengrasar; desgrasar *vt* to degrease, to remove the grease from (limpiar) || to scour (la lana).

◆ *vi* FAM to lose weight (adelgazar).

desengrase; desgrase *m* removal of grease || scouring (de la lana).

desengrosar* *vt* to make thin (enflaquecer) || to slim (adelgazar).

◆ *vi* to lose weight (perder peso) || to slim, to grow thin (adelgazar).

desenguantarse *vpr* to take off one's gloves.

desenhebrar *vt* to unthread (una aguja).

◆ *vpr* to come unthreaded.

desenhornamiento *m* taking out of the oven or of the kiln.

desenhornar *vt* to take out of the oven (horno pequeño) || to take out of the kiln (horno grande).

desenjaezar *vt* to unharness (quitar los jaeces).

desenjalmar *vt* to take the packsaddle off, to unsaddle.

desenjaular *vt* to let out of a cage, to release, to uncage.

desenlace *m* ending, denouement (de una obra literaria) || ending (final) || outcome, result (resultado).

desenladrillar *vt* to remove *o* to dig up *o* to take up the bricks from.

desenlatar *vt* to open, to take out (of a tin).

desenlazar *vt* to unfasten, to undo, to untie (desatar) || FIG to clear up, to unravel (un asunto) | to solve (un problema).

◆ *vpr* to come undone (desatarse) || *la obra se desenlaza muy mal* the work has a very poor ending *o* denouement.

desenlodar *vt* to clean the mud from.

desenlosar *vt* to take up the tiles from || to take up the paving stones from *o* the flags from (véase OBSERV en ENLOSAR).

desenlutar *vt* to bring out of mourning, to make (s.o.) give up mourning.

◆ *vpr* to give up mourning.

desenmarañar *vt* to untangle, to unravel, to disentangle || FIG to unravel, to clarify, to clear up, to sort out (un asunto).

desenmascarar *vt* to unmask (quitar la máscara) || FIG to unmask, to expose; *desenmascarar a un hipócrita* to unmask a hypocrite.

desenmohecer* *vt* to remove the rust from || to remove the mildew *o* the mould from.

desenmudecer* *vt* to loosen the tongue of (hacer hablar) || to cure from tongue-tie (devolver el sentido de la palabra).

◆ *vi* to recover from tongue-tie, to recover one's speech || FIG to break one's silence.

desenojar *vt* to calm down, to soothe (desenfadar).

◆ *vpr* to calm down || FIG to amuse o.s. (entretenerse).

desenredar *vt* to untangle, to unravel, to disentangle (desenmarañar) || FIG to clear up, to unravel, to disentangle (una intriga, etc.) | to straighten out, to sort out (arreglar).

◆ *vpr* FIG to extricate o.s. (salir de apuro).

desenredo *m* disentanglement, unravelling (de una madeja, etc.) || disentanglement, solution, clearing-up (de un problema) || way out (de un apuro) || ending, denouement (desenlace) || ending, outcome (de una situación crítica).

desenrollar *vt* to unroll || to unwind (hilo).

desenroscar *vt* to unscrew (destornillar) || to unwind, to uncoil (un hilo, etc.).

◆ *vpr* to unwind, to uncoil (serpiente, hilo, etc.).

desensamblar *vt* to take apart, to take to pieces (desmontar) || to separate (separar).

desensañar *vt* to calm down, to appease.

desensartar *vt* to unthread, to unstring (soltar cosas ensartadas); *desensartar un collar* to unstring a necklace || to unthread (desenhebrar); *desensartar una aguja* to unthread a needle.

desensibilización *f* desensitization.

desensibilizar *vt* to desensitize.

desensillar *vt* to unsaddle (un caballo).

desensoberbecer* *vt* to humble, to make less arrogant *o* conceited.

desensortijado, da *adj* straightened, straight (pelo).

desentarimar *vt* to take up the parquet flooring of (un suelo).

desentenderse* *vpr* to want nothing to do, to want no part; *me desentiendo por completo de ese negocio* I want absolutely nothing to do with that business, I want absolutely no part in that business || to pretend not to know (*de* about), to pretend not to know (afectar ignorancia).

desentendido, da *adj* (ant) ignorant || *hacerse el desentendido* to turn a deaf ear, to pretend not to hear *o* to notice.

desenterrado, da *adj* exhumed (un cadáver) || unearthed, disinterred, dug up (un objeto).

desenterramiento *m* exhuming, disinterment (de un cadáver) || unearthing, digging up, disinterment.

desenterrar* *vt* to exhume, to disinter (un cadáver) || to dig up, to unearth, to disinter (un objeto) || FIG to revive, to recall.

desentierramuertos *m/f inv* FIG & FAM scandalmonger, backbiter.

desentoldar *vt* to remove the awning *o* sunshade from (una calle, etc.) || to take the drapes down from (quitar los adornos).

desentonación *f* → **desentono.**

desentonadamente *adv* out of tune; *cantar desentonadamente* to sing out of tune.

desentonar *vi* to sing out of tune, to be out of tune (cantar falso) || to be out of tune (instrumento) || to be inharmonious (la música) || FIG not to match (colores) | to be out of place; *el chico desentonó en la reunión* the boy was out of place at the meeting | not to fit in, to clash; *modales que desentonan con su educación* manners which do not fit in with *o* which clash with his upbringing.

◆ *vpr* to be rude *o* insolent (*con, contra* with, to) || to raise one's voice (*contra* to) (alzar la voz).

desentono *m*; **desentonación** *f* poor intonation || dissonance (disonancia) || FIG rudeness, insolence.

desentorpecer* *vt* to take the numbness *o* the stiffness out of; *desentorpecer el brazo* to take the stiffness out of one's arm || FIG to smarten up, to knock the edges off (a un necio) || *desentorpecer las piernas* to stretch one's legs.

◆ *vpr* to come back to life (la pierna, etc.) || to smarten up, to brighten up (una persona).

desentrampar *vt* FAM to get out of debt.

◆ *vpr* FAM to get out of debt, to pay off one's debts.

desentrañar *vt* (p us) to disembowel, to eviscerate || FIG to figure out, to work out; *ha conseguido desentrañar el misterio* he has managed to figure out the mystery.

◆ *vpr* to give one's all.

desentrenado, da *adj* out of training.

desentrenamiento *m* lack of training.

desentrenarse *vpr* to get *o* to be out of training.

desentumecer*; desentumir *vt* to revive the feeling in, to take the numbness *o* the stiffness out of; *desentumecer el brazo* to revive the feeling in one's arm || DEP to loosen up || *desentumecer las piernas* to stretch one's legs.

desentumecimiento *m* recovery of feeling.

desentumir *vt* → **desentumecer.**

desenvainar *vt* to unsheathe, to draw; *desenvainar el sable* to draw one's sword || FIG to bare, to show (its claws) (un animal).

desenvergar *vt* MAR to unbend.

desenvoltura *f* ease, grace, naturalness (en los movimientos) || self-confidence, assurance (falta de timidez); *en la reunión habló con desenvoltura* at the meeting he spoke with assurance | rudeness, insolence, boldness, forwardness (descaro) || brazenness, shamelessness (de una mujer) || carefreeness (despreocupación).

desenvolver* *vt* to unwrap (un paquete) || to unwind (hilo) || to unroll (desenrollar) || FIG to develop, to expound (una idea, una teoría) | to disentangle, to clear up (aclarar) | to expand (un negocio).
◆ *vpr* to come unwrapped (un paquete) || to develop, to evolve (desarrollarse) || to expand (crecer) || to prosper (prosperar) || FIG to fend for o.s., to look after o.s.; *desenvolverse en la vida* to fend for o.s. in life | to manage (arreglárselas); *con ochenta libras al mes me desenvuelvo muy bien* I manage very well with eighty pounds a month | to go (off); *el partido se desenvolvió sin incidente* the game went (off) without incident.

desenvolvimiento *m* unwrapping (de un paquete) || development, expansion (desarrollo) || exposition, development (de una idea, etc.) || disentanglement, clearing up (aclaración).

desenvueltamente *adv* gracefully, naturally, with ease (en los movimientos) || confidently, naturally, with assurance (sin timidez) || rudely, insolently, boldly (descaradamente) || brazenly, shamelessly (una mujer) || openly (abiertamente).

desenvuelto, ta *adj* FIG graceful, natural, agile (en los movimientos) | eloquent (al hablar) | confident, assured, natural (sin timidez) | carefree, free and easy, easygoing (despreocupado) | brazen, forward (descarado) | resourceful (ingenioso).

desenzarzar *vt* to pull out of the brambles (sacar de las zarzas) || FIG & FAM to pull apart, to separate (a personas que riñen).

deseo *m* desire, want, wish; *satisfacer los deseos de alguien* to satisfy s.o.'s wishes || desire (cosa deseada) || wish, desire (aspiración); *según sus deseos* according to his wishes || wish; *deseos de felicidad* wishes for happiness || vow (voto); *formular un deseo* to make a vow || — *a medida de mi deseo* to my liking || *arder en deseos de* to burn with desire for, to long for, to yearn for || *buenos deseos* good intentions || *es nuestro mayor deseo* it is our dearest wish || *tener deseo de algo* to want sth. || *tener deseo de hacer algo* to want to do sth., to feel like doing sth.

deseoso, sa *adj* desirous, eager, anxious || longing, wishful; *mirada deseosa* longing look || — *estar deseoso de hacer algo* to be eager *o* anxious to do sth., to desire to do sth. || *estar deseoso de una cosa* to long for *o* to yearn for sth., to be eager *o* anxious for sth.

desequilibrado, da *adj* off balance, unbalanced || FIG unbalanced (persona, mente).
◆ *m/f* unbalanced person.

desequilibrar *vt* to put off *o* to throw off *o* to knock off balance, to unbalance || FIG to unbalance; *la guerra ha desequilibrado las mentes de muchos hombres* the war has unbalanced the minds of many men | to unbalance mentally (a una persona).
◆ *vpr* to lose one's balance (perder el equilibrio) || FIG to become mentally unbalanced.

desequilibrio *m* lack of balance || FIG unbalance (de la mente) | unbalanced mind (de una persona) | imbalance; *suprimir el desequilibrio entre las importaciones y las exportaciones* to correct the imbalance between imports and exports.

deserción *f* desertion (del ejército) || FIG abandoning, abandonment, desertion (abandono) || JUR dropping [of proceedings].

desertar *vi* to desert; *desertar del ejército* to desert from the army || FIG to abandon, to desert; *desertar de un círculo* to desert a circle | to neglect (los deberes) || JUR to drop [proceedings] || *desertar al campo contrario* to go over to the enemy.
◆ *vt* to desert.

desértico, ca *adj* desert, barren (como un desierto) || deserted (vacío) || GEOGR desert.

desertificación *f* desertification.

desertor *m* deserter.

desescalada *f* de-escalation.

desescalar *vt* to de-escalate.

desescombrar *vt* to clear up, to clear of rubbish.

deseslabonar *vt* to unlink (cadena).

desespaldar *vt* to break the back of.
◆ *vpr* to break one's back.

desespañolizar *vt* to take away the Spanish qualities *o* characteristics of.
◆ *vpr* to lose one's Spanish qualities.

desesperación *f* despair (desesperanza total) || desperation; *estar loco de desesperación* to be out of one's mind with desperation || exasperation (rabia) || — *con desesperación* desperately || *me da* or *me causa desesperación* it exasperates me || *ser la desesperación de* to be the despair of || *ser una desesperación* to be exasperating, to be unbearable.

desesperado, da *adj* desperate, despairing (sin esperanza) || exasperated (exasperado) || hopeless; *una situación desesperada* a hopeless situation || MED hopeless (caso) || furious (esfuerzo) || — *estar desesperado* to be desperate, to have lost hope, to despair || *me tiene desesperado* he exasperates me (irritar), he makes me despair (desanimar).
◆ *m/f* desperate person || — *a la desesperada* in desperation, as a last hope || *correr como un desesperado* to run like mad.

desesperante *adj* exasperating || hopeless (persona) || FIG discouraging (descorazonador).

desesperanza *f* hopelessness, despair, desperation.

desesperanzar *vt* to make despair, to drive to despair.
◆ *vpr* to despair, to lose hope.

desesperar *vt* to make despair, to drive to despair || to exasperate (irritar).
◆ *vi* to have lost hope, to despair; *desespero de que venga* I have lost hope that he will come, I despair of his coming; *desespero de verle un día* I have lost hope of ever seeing him.
◆ *vpr* to despair, to lose hope; *me desespero por no recibir noticias suyas* I despair at not hearing from him || to become desperate (no tener esperanza alguna) || to be exasperated (irritarse).

desespero *m* despair.

desesterar *vt* to take up the mats from.

desestero *m* removal of mats.

desestima *f* lack of respect *o* esteem, disrespect.

desestimación *f* lack of respect *o* esteem, disrespect || JUR refusal, rejection; *desestimación de una demanda* refusal of a claim.

desestimar *vt* to have no respect for, to have a low opinion of, to hold in low esteem (despreciar) || to underestimate (menospreciar) || JUR to reject, to refuse; *han desestimado mi demanda* they have rejected my claim.

desfacedor, ra *m/f* undoer || FAM *desfacedor de entuertos* righter *o* redresser of wrongs.

desfachatado, da *adj* FAM cheeky, insolent, brazen, barefaced.

desfachatez *f* FAM cheek, nerve; *tiene una desfachatez inmensa* he's got a fantastic cheek.

desfalcador, ra *m/f* embezzler, defaulter.

desfalcar *vt* to embezzle, to defalcate; *desfalcar fondos* to embezzle funds || to remove a part of (quitar una parte).

desfalco *m* embezzlement, defalcation (malversación).

desfallecer* *vi* to weaken (perder las fuerzas) || to faint (desmayarse) || to fail (la voz).
◆ *vt* to weaken (debilitar).

desfallecido, da *adj* faint (desmayado) || weak (débil).

desfallecimiento *m* weakening (debilidad) || faint (desmayo).

desfasado, da *adj* FIG behind the times (anticuado) | out of place (fuera de su ambiente) || TECN out of phase.

desfasaje *m* ELECTR phase shift, phase difference.

desfasar *vt* to phase out.

desfase *m* ELECTR phase shift, phase difference || FIG imbalance (desequilibrio) | gap (diferencia).

desfavorable *adj* unfavourable.

desfavorecer* *vt* to put at a disadvantage, to be disadvantageous to, to disadvantage (perjudicar) || to have a low opinion of (tener mala opinión de) || not to flatter, not to suit, not to do anything for; *este color te desfavorece* this colour does not flatter you.

desfibrado *m*; **desfibración** *f* TECN removal of fibres | shredding (fabricación del papel).

desfibradora *f* TECN shredder (máquina).

desfibrar *vt* TECN to shred (fabricación del papel) | to remove the fibre from (quitar las fibras).

desfibrilación *f* MED defibrillation.

desfiguración *f*; **desfiguramiento** *m* disfiguring, disfiguration (de una persona) || distortion (de los hechos) || defacement (de una estatua, etc.).

desfiguramiento *m* → **desfiguración.**

desfigurar *vt* to disfigure; *una cicatriz ancha le desfigura* a large scar disfigures him || to distort; *desfigurar la verdad, los hechos* to distort the truth, the facts || to deface (un monumento, etc.) || to blur (las formas) || FIG to disguise, to alter (la voz).
◆ *vpr* to be disfigured.

desfiladero *m* narrow pass, defile (paso estrecho).

desfilar *vi* MIL to march in files || to walk in file (andar en fila) || to march, to parade; *durante la manifestación desfilaron dos mil personas* two thousand people marched in the demonstration | to march past; *los soldados desfilaron ante el presidente* the soldiers marched past in front of the president || FAM to file by (pasar) | to file out (irse).

desfile *m* MIL march-past, parade; *desfile de la victoria* victory parade || procession, parade; *un desfile de carruajes* a procession of carriages || march (en una manifestación); *había un desfile para protestar contra las reformas* there was a march to protest against the reforms || *desfile de modelos* or *de modas* fashion show, fashion parade.

desflecadura *f* fraying, fringing.

desflecar *vt* to fray, to fringe.

desflemar *vi* MED to cough up phlegm.

desfloración *f*; **desfloramiento** *m* defloration, deflowering || fading, withering (ajamiento).

desflorar *vt* to strip the flowers from, to deflower (hacer caer la flor) || to deflower (a una mujer) || to spoil, to tarnish (estropear) || FIG to skim over, to touch lightly on (no profundizar).

desflorecer* *vi* to wither, to lose its bloom.

desflorecimiento *m* loss of bloom (de una planta).

desfogar *vt* to give vent, to vent; *desfogó su cólera en* or *con su hermano* he vented his anger on his brother || to slake (la cal).
◆ *vi* MAR to break, to burst (una tormenta).
◆ *vpr* to let off steam, to give vent to one's anger; *después de la bronca que le habían echado se desfogó con nosotros* after the telling off they gave him he let off steam on us || to let off steam; *de vez en cuando los niños necesitan desfogarse* children need to let off steam now and again.

desfogue *m* vent (del fuego) || outburst, venting, vent (de una pasión) || letting-off (of) steam (acción de desfogarse) || *AMER* outlet [of a pipe].

desfondamiento *m* ⟶ **desfonde.**

desfondar *vt* to go through *o* to break the bottom of (romper el fondo de) || AGR to plough deeply (la tierra) || to damage the bottom of, to bilge (un barco).
◆ *vpr* MAR to bilge || FIG to wear o.s. out (de cansancio) || *el sillón se ha desfondado* the bottom *o* the seat has come out of the armchair.

desfonde; desfondamiento *m* breaking of the bottom; *el desfonde de un tonel* the breaking of the bottom of a barrel || MAR bilging || FIG exhaustion (cansancio).

desformar *vt* to deform.

desfosforar *vt* TECN to dephosphorize.

desfruncir *vt* to take the gathers out of, to ungather || to unfold, to unfurl (desplegar).

desgaire *m* nonchalance (descuido) || slovenliness, carelessness (en el vestir) || scornful gesture (gesto de desprecio) || — *al desgaire* nonchalantly (con descuido afectado), carelessly, sloppily (con descuido) || *andar con desgaire* to walk nonchalantly || *vestir con desgaire* to dress untidily *o* scruffily.

desgajar *vt* to tear off, to break off; *desgajar las ramas de un árbol* to tear off the branches of a tree || to tear up (desarraigar) || to tear out; *desgajar la hoja de un cuaderno* to tear out a leaf of an exercise book || to break (romper) || to tear *o* to rip apart *o* to pieces (desgarrar) || FIG to uproot (personas).
◆ *vpr* to come off, to break off || FIG *desgajarse de su patria* to abandon one's country, to break all ties with one's country.

desgalichado, da *adj* FAM gawky, ungainly.

desgana *f* reluctance, unwillingness (disgusto) || lack of appetite (falta de apetito) || — *comer con desgana* to eat without appetite *o* reluctantly || *hacer una cosa a* or *con desgana* to do sth. reluctantly.

desganado, da *adj* without appetite (sin apetito) || halfhearted, unenthusiastic (sin entusiasmo) || reluctant (poco entusiasta) || — *el equipo jugó desganado* the team played halfheartedly *o* unenthusiastically || *estoy desganado* I have no appetite, I'm not hungry.

desganar *vt* to spoil the appetite of (cortar el apetito) || to turn (s.o.) off (quitar las ganas).
◆ *vpr* to lose one's appetite (el apetito) || to get bored (*de* with), to go off (cansarse).

desgañitarse *vpr* to shout one's head off || *gritar hasta desgañitarse* to shout o.s. hoarse.

desgarbado, da *adj* ungainly, ungraceful, gawky.

desgarbo *m* gawkiness, ungainliness, lack of grace.

desgargantarse *vpr* FAM to shout one's head off, to shout at the top of one's voice.

desgarrador, ra *adj* heartrending, heartbreaking; *oíanse gritos desgarradores* you could hear heartrending cries || bloodcurdling (que da mucho miedo).

desgarradura *f*; **desgarramiento** *m* rip, tear, rent (de una tela) || tear (de un músculo).

desgarrar *vt* to rip, to tear, to rend; *desgarrar un vestido* to rip a dress || FIG to break, to rend (afligir); *sus desgracias me desgarran el corazón* his misfortunes break my heart | to rend; *la tos le desgarraba el pecho* his cough rent his chest.
◆ *vpr* to rip, to tear || FIG *desgarrarse uno a otro* to make each other suffer.

desgarro *m* tear (muscular) || tear, rip, rent (de una tela, etc.) || grief (aflicción) || FIG rudeness, effrontery, insolence (descaro) | forwardness, shamelessness (de una mujer) | boasting, bragging (jactancia) || *AMER* spittle (escupitajo).

desgarrón *m* rip, tear || tatter (jirón) || tear (muscular).

desgastamiento *m* ⟶ **desgaste.**

desgastar *vt* to wear away (gastar progresivamente) || to wear out; *un niño que desgasta mucho la ropa* a child who wears out his clothes quickly || to erode (una roca) || to corrode (un metal) || to fray, to chafe, to wear (una cuerda, etc.) || FIG to weaken (debilitar).
◆ *vpr* to wear away (ropa, objeto) || FIG to weaken (debilitarse) | to wear o.s. out (agotarse).

desgaste; desgastamiento *m* wearing away, erosion; *el desgaste de una roca* the wearing away of a rock || wear (de un objeto, de un motor, de un vestido, etc.) || chafing, fraying (de una cuerda, etc.) || deterioration, damage, spoiling (deterioro) || corrosion (de un metal) || FIG weakening (debilitación) | waste (desperdicio) || *guerra de desgaste* war of attrition.

desglosar *vt* to detach (un escrito de otro) || CINEM to cut, to edit (una película) || to break down (gastos) || JUR to sever (dos causas).

desglose *m* CINEM cutting, editing || breakdown; *desglose de los gastos* breakdown of expenses || JUR severance || removal (de páginas, etc.) || *hacer el desglose de* to break down.

desgobernar* *vt* to upset (perturbar) || to misgovern, to misrule (gobernar mal) || to mismanage (llevar mal) || to dislocate (huesos) || MAR to steer badly (un barco).
◆ *vpr* to become dislocated (huesos).

desgobierno *m* mismanagement (de la casa) || misgovernment, misrule (en un país) || disorderliness (en la vida) || bad handling, mishandling (en los gastos).

desgolletar *vt* to break the neck of (botella).

desgomar *vt* to degum (una tela).

desgonzar; desgoznar *vt* to unhinge.

desgracia *f* misfortune; *ser* or *verse perseguido por la desgracia* to have nothing but misfortune; *labrarse la propia desgracia* to bring about one's own misfortune || blow; *el accidente ha sido una desgracia* the accident was a blow || mishap (contratiempo) || disfavour, disgrace (pérdida de favor) || bad luck (mala suerte) || lack of charm *o* grace, awkwardness (torpeza) || — *caer en desgracia* to lose favour, to fall into disgrace || *en la desgracia se conoce a los amigos* a friend in need is a friend indeed || *las desgracias nunca vienen solas* it never rains but it pours || *no ha habido que lamentar desgracias personales* there were no casualties, no one was hurt || *para colmo de desgracias, para mayor desgracia* to top everything || *por desgracia* unfortunately || *¡qué desgracia!* what a shame! || *ser la desgracia de la familia* to be the disgrace of one's family || *tener la desgracia de* to be unfortunate enough to.

desgraciadamente *adv* unfortunately.

desgraciado, da *adj* unfortunate, unlucky; *desgraciado en el juego* unlucky in gambling || unhappy (infeliz); *era desgraciada en el matrimonio* she was unhappy in her marriage || unfortunate; *un suceso desgraciado* an unfortunate event || poor (pobre) || unattractive, graceless (sin atractivo) || unpleasant (desagradable) || wretched (miserable); *una vida desgraciada* a wretched life; *¡qué desgraciado soy!* how wretched I am!
◆ *m/f* unlucky *o* unfortunate person (infortunado) || unhappy person (infeliz) || wretch (miserable) || rotter, scoundrel (mala persona) || — *¡desgraciado de ti si...!* woe betide you if...! || *los desgraciados* the poor (pobres) || *pobre desgraciado* poor devil, poor wretch, unlucky devil (infortunado), wretch (sentido despectivo).

desgraciar *vt* to spoil (estropear); *las arrugas desgracian su vestido* the creases spoil your dress || to damage (un mecanismo) || to maim (lisiar) || to deflower, to dishonour (a una mujer).
◆ *vpr* to be ruined (estropearse) || to turn out badly, to fail (malograrse) || to fall through, to collapse (un proyecto) || to quarrel, to fall out (desavenirse) || — *si no se desgracia* all being well; *si no se desgracia, la cosecha será buena* all being well the harvest will be good || *su niño se desgració antes de nacer* she had a miscarriage.

desgramar *vt* to remove the bermuda grass from.

desgranador, ra *adj* shelling || threshing, shelling.
◆ *m* sheller (de maíz, de guisantes, etc.) || thresher (de trigo, etc.).
◆ *f* sheller (de maíz) || threshing machine (de trigo).

desgranamiento; desgrane *m* shelling (de maíz, de guisantes, etc.) || threshing, shelling (de trigo) || picking of grapes (de un racimo de uvas).

desgranar *vt* AGR to shell (maíz, guisantes) | to thresh, to shell (trigo) || to pick the grapes off (un racimo de uvas) || to pick the seeds out of (una granada) || to tell; *desgranar las cuentas de un rosario* to tell one's beads || FIG to reel off (decir, soltar).
◆ *vpr* to lose its corn (maíz) || to lose its grain (trigo) || to lose its grapes (uva) || to come unstrung (cuentas) || *AMER* to separate (desbandarse).

desgrane *m* ⟶ **desgranamiento.**

desgranzar *vt* AGR to separate (grain) from the chaff || to carry out the first grinding on (colores).

desgrasar *vt* ⟶ **desengrasar.**

desgrase *m* ⟶ **desengrase.**

desgravación *f* reduction of taxes || reduction of duties (en las aduanas).

desgravar *vt* to reduce the tax on || to reduce the duties on (en las aduanas).

desgreñado, da *adj* dishevelled, tousled, ruffled || *tenía el pelo desgreñado* his hair was dishevelled *o* tousled *o* ruffled, he was dishevelled.

desgreñar *vt* to dishevel *o* to ruffle *o* to tousle the hair of (despeinar).

◆ *vpr* to get ruffled *o* dishevelled *o* tousled (el pelo) ‖ to ruffle *o* to dishevel *o* to tousle one's hair; *la niña se desgreñó* the girl ruffled her hair ‖ FIG to argue, to quarrel (reñir).

desguace *m* MAR breaking-up, shipbreaking (de un barco) ‖ roughhewing (de un madero) ‖ taking-down, pulling-down (de una estructura) ‖ car breaking (de automóviles).

desguarnecer* *vt* to take the trimmings off, to untrim (quitar los adornos de) ‖ to dismantle (una máquina, una plaza fuerte) ‖ to unharness (una caballería) ‖ to strip; *desguarnecer de cuerdas un violín* to strip a violin of its strings, to strip the strings off a violin.

desguazar *vt* to roughhew (un madero) ‖ to break up (un barco, un automóvil) ‖ to take *o* to pull down (una estructura).

desguince *m* ⟶ **esguince.**

desguindar *vt* MAR to haul down, to lower.
◆ *vpr* MAR to slide down; *desguindarse de un mastelero* to slide down a mast.

desguinzado *m* rag cutting.

desguinzadora *f* TECN rag-cutting machine.

desguinzar *vt* to cut (rags).

deshabillé *m* negligé [*US* negligee] (salto de cama).

deshabitado, da *adj* uninhabited, unoccupied; *una casa deshabitada* an uninhabited house.

deshabitar *vt* to leave, to vacate, to abandon (abandonar) ‖ to leave without inhabitants, to depopulate; *la guerra deshabitó la provincia* the war left the province without inhabitants.

deshabituación *f* loss of habit.

deshabituar *vt* to break (s.o.) from *o* of the habit.
◆ *vpr* to get out of the habit, to lose the habit.

deshacedor, ra *adj* (p us) undoing.
◆ *m deshacedor de agravios* or *de entuertos* righter *o* redresser of wrongs.

deshacer* *vt* to destroy (destruir) ‖ to damage (estropear) ‖ to undo, to unpick; *deshacer una costura* to undo a seam ‖ to take apart *o* to pieces (desmontar) ‖ to upset (desordenar) ‖ to retrace (pasos, camino) ‖ to melt (derretir); *el sol ha deshecho la nieve* the sun has melted the snow ‖ to wear down (metales) ‖ to dissolve (disolver) ‖ to ruin, to spoil; *deshacer los proyectos de uno* to ruin s.o.'s plans ‖ to spoil, to damage (la vista) ‖ to beat, to defeat (ganar) ‖ TECN to take to pieces (un motor) ‖ to undo, to unpack, to unwrap (un paquete) ‖ to unpack (una maleta) ‖ to undo, to unfasten, to untie; *deshacer un nudo* to undo a knot ‖ to unmake, to strip (la cama) ‖ to unknit, to ravel (un tejido de punto) ‖ to cancel, to annul (un contrato) ‖ to break (un tratado) ‖ to divide up (dividir) ‖ to break off (un casamiento) ‖ to frustrate, to thwart; *deshacer una intriga* to frustrate a plot ‖ to right (los males) ‖ to wear out; *el trabajo me ha deshecho* the work has worn me out ‖ to prove the undoing of, to ruin (arruinar); *la guerra ha deshecho el país* the war has ruined the nation ‖ MIL to rout, to put to flight (vencer) ‖ — *deshacer agravios* or *entuertos* to right *o* to redress wrongs ‖ *es él quien hace y deshace* he's the boss, he rules the roost.
◆ *vpr* to get rid, to rid o.s.; *deshacerse de algo* to get rid of sth. ‖ to break; *el vaso se deshizo al caer* the glass broke when it fell ‖ to come undone *o* untied *o* unfastened (nudo, etc.) ‖ to come unsewn (una costura) ‖ to come to pieces (un objeto) ‖ to melt (derretirse); *el hielo se ha deshecho* the ice has melted ‖ to dissolve; *el azúcar se deshace en el agua* sugar dissolves in water ‖ to break up (una reunión) ‖ to break *o* to rid o.s. of (de una costumbre) ‖ to disappear (desvanecerse) ‖ to go to pieces (moralmente); *cuando murió su mujer el pobre hombre se deshizo* the poor man went to pieces when his wife died ‖ to wear o.s. out, to tire o.s. out (agotarse); *deshacerse trabajando, en esfuerzos baldíos* to tire o.s. out working, with vain efforts ‖ to do one's utmost, to try one's hardest (hacer todo lo posible); *se deshizo por terminar pronto* he did his utmost to finish quickly ‖ to go out of one's way; *deshacerse por uno, por agradar a uno* to go out of one's way for s.o., to please s.o. ‖ to be mad; *se deshace por las antigüedades* he is mad about antiques ‖ — *deshacerse como el humo* to disappear *o* to vanish into thin air ‖ FIG *deshacerse en* to dissolve into ‖ *deshacerse en alabanzas* or *en cumplidos* to be full of praise *o* of compliments, to dissolve into praise *o* into compliments ‖ *deshacerse en atenciones con alguien* to lavish attention on s.o. ‖ *deshacerse en excusas* to apologize profusely ‖ *deshacerse en imprecaciones* to curse vehemently ‖ *deshacerse en lágrimas* to burst into tears ‖ *deshacerse en llanto* to sob one's heart out ‖ *deshacerse en suspiros* to heave deep sighs.

desharrapado, da; desarrapado, da *adj* tattered, ragged, shabby.
◆ *m/f* shabby person, tramp.

deshebillar *vt* to unbuckle.

deshebrar *vt* to ravel, to undo (una tela) ‖ to unthread (una aguja) ‖ to remove the strings from (judías verdes) ‖ to tear into shreds (deshacer en briznas).

deshechizar *vt* to remove the spell from, to break the spell on.

deshecho, cha *adj* destroyed (destruido) ‖ undone, untied, unfastened (nudo, lazos, etc.) ‖ unsewn (costura) ‖ melted (hielo, nieve) ‖ dissolved; *deshecho en agua* dissolved in water ‖ in pieces (desmontado) ‖ defeated, beaten (vencido) ‖ unpacked (maleta) ‖ open, unwrapped (paquete) ‖ ruined (arruinado, estropeado) ‖ dishevelled (los pelos) ‖ discomposed (rostro) ‖ worn-out, tired out, exhausted (rendido de cansancio) ‖ worn-out; *zapatos deshechos* worn-out shoes ‖ broken (salud) ‖ violent (tempestad) ‖ strong (lluvia) ‖ — *con los nervios deshechos* at one's wits' end ‖ *estar deshecho* to have gone to pieces; *desde la muerte de su mujer el pobre hombre está deshecho* since the death of his wife the poor man has gone to pieces; to be upset *o* troubled (consternado).

deshelador *m* deicer.

deshelar* *vt* to thaw out; *deshelar una cañería* to thaw out a pipe ‖ to deice (coche, avión) ‖ to defrost (una nevera) ‖ to melt, to thaw (derretir).
◆ *vpr* to thaw out (descongelarse) ‖ to melt, to thaw (río).

desherbaje *m* weeding.

desherbar* *vt* to weed.

desheredado, da *adj* disinherited ‖ FIG underprivileged; *gente desheredada* underprivileged people.
◆ *m/f* disinherited person ‖ FIG underprivileged person ‖ *ayudar a los desheredados* to help the underprivileged.

desheredamiento *m* disinheritance, disinheriting.

desheredar *vt* to disinherit.

desherencia *f* disinheritance, disinheriting.

deshermanado, da *adj* odd; *un calcetín deshermanado* an odd sock.

deshermanar *vt* to separate.
◆ *vpr* to forsake one's brother, to behave in an unbrotherly way ‖ to separate, to be split up.

desherradura *f* bruised hoof (de los caballos).

desherrar* *vt* to unshoe (a una caballería) ‖ to unchain, to unshackle (a un prisionero).
◆ *vpr* to throw a shoe (una caballería) ‖ to break free from one's chains *o* shackles (un prisionero).

desherrumbrar *vt* to remove the rust from.

deshidratación *f* dehydration.

deshidratado, da *adj* dehydrated.

deshidratar *vt* to dehydrate.
◆ *vpr* to become dehydrated.

deshidrogenación *f* dehydrogenation.

deshidrogenar *vt* to dehydrogenate, to dehydrogenize.

deshielo *m* thaw (del tiempo) ‖ deicing (de un coche, de un avión) ‖ defrosting (de una nevera) ‖ thawing (de un río) ‖ thawing-out (de una cañería, etc.) ‖ FIG thawing; *el deshielo de las relaciones internacionales* the thawing of international relations.

deshijar *vt* AMER to trim shoots off [plants] ‖ to take the young away from (animales).

deshilachado *m*; **deshilachadura** *f* ravelling ‖ fraying (acción de deshilacharse).

deshilachar *vt* to ravel.
◆ *vpr* to fray.

deshilado, da *adj* in single file (en fila india) ‖ frayed; *la solapa está deshilada* the lapel is frayed ‖ *a la deshilada* in single file.
◆ *m* openwork (bordado).

deshilar *vt* to ravel ‖ to draw threads from (para bordar) ‖ FIG to cut into thin pieces.
◆ *vpr* to fray (deshilacharse).

deshilvanado, da *adj* untacked (costura) ‖ FIG disjointed, disconnected; *estilo, discurso, juego deshilvanado* disjointed style, speech, play.

deshilvanar *vt* to take the tacking out of, to untack.

deshinchado, da *adj* flat (neumáticos) ‖ deflated (globo, balón, etc.) ‖ *tengo el brazo deshinchado* the swelling in my arm has gone down.

deshinchadura *f*; **deshinchamiento** *m*; **deshinchazón** *f* deflation, letting down; *deshinchadura de un neumático* deflation of a tyre ‖ reduction of swelling (de un miembro) ‖ going down (acción de deshincharse).

deshinchar *vt* to deflate, to let down; *deshinchar un globo, un neumático* to deflate a balloon, a tyre ‖ to reduce a swelling in, to make the swelling go down in (un miembro, etc.) ‖ FIG to give vent to, to vent (la cólera).
◆ *vpr* to go flat, to go down, to deflate (un neumático) ‖ to go down (la hinchazón); *se te ha deshinchado la pierna* the swelling in your leg has gone down ‖ FIG & FAM to get down from one's high horse (perder la presunción) ‖ to climb down (rajarse).

deshipnotizar *vt* to dehypnotize.

deshipotecar *vt* to free from mortgage, to pay off the mortgage on.

deshojado, da *adj* leafless (árbol) ‖ stripped of its petals (flor).

deshojadura *f*; **deshojamiento** *m* stripping of leaves, defoliation (de un árbol, etc.) ‖ stripping of petals (de una flor).

deshojar *vt* to strip of leaves, to defoliate (un árbol) ‖ to strip of petals (una flor) ‖ to tear the pages out of (un libro).
◆ *vpr* to lose its leaves (árbol) *o* its petals (flor).

deshoje *m* fall of leaves.

deshollejar *vt* to peel (la fruta, etc.).

deshollinadera *f* wall brush (escobón).

deshollinador, ra *adj* who sweeps chimneys (que deshollina) || FIG & FAM nosey, inquisitive.
◆ *m/f* FIG & FAM busybody, nosey parker (fisgón).
◆ *m* chimney sweep, sweep (persona) || chimney sweep's brush (cepillo) || wall brush (escobón).

deshollinar *vt* to sweep, to clean (chimeneas) || to clean [the walls and ceilings of] (la casa) || FIG & FAM to scrutinize, to examine closely.

deshonestidad *f* dishonesty (cualidad de no honesto) || indecency, immodesty, impropriety (indecencia).

deshonesto, ta *adj* dishonest (no honesto) || indecent, immodest, improper (obsceno).

deshonor *m* disgrace, dishonour [US dishonor] (pérdida del honor) || disgrace; *es el deshonor de su familia* he is the disgrace of his family; *vivir en el deshonor* to live in disgrace || insult (afrenta) || disgrace (cosa que deshonra); *ser pobre no es ningún deshonor* it's no disgrace to be poor.

deshonorar *vt* to disgrace, to dishonour [US to dishonor].

deshonra *f* disgrace, dishonour [US dishonor] (pérdida del honor) || disgrace (vergüenza) || *tener a deshonra* to find below one's dignity, to consider shameful.

deshonrar *vt* to disgrace, to dishonour [US to dishonor], to bring disgrace on; *deshonrar (a) la familia* to disgrace one's family || to dishonour [US to dishonor] (a una mujer) || to insult (afrentar).
◆ *vpr* to disgrace o.s.

deshonrosamente *adv* disgracefully, dishonourably.

deshonroso, sa *adj* disgraceful, shameful, dishonourable; *acto deshonroso* disgraceful act.

deshora *f* inconvenient time || *a deshora, a deshoras* at an untimely *o* inconvenient moment (a hora inoportuna), at an unusual time (a hora desacostumbrada), very late, at an unreasonable hour (muy tarde).

deshornar *vt* to take out of the oven (pequeño horno) || to take out of the kiln (horno grande).

deshuesado, da *adj* boned, off the bone (carne) || stoned, pitted (fruta).

deshuesadora *f* stoning *o* pitting machine (para fruta) || boning machine (para carne).

deshuesamiento *m* stoning, pitting (de fruta) || boning (de carne).

deshuesar *vt* to stone, to pit (fruta) || to bone (carne).

deshumanización *f* dehumanization.

deshumanizar *vt* to dehumanize.

deshumano, na *adj* inhuman.

deshumedecer* *vt* to dry up, to dehumidify.
◆ *vpr* to dry up.

desiderata *m pl* desiderata.

desiderativo, va *adj* desiderative (verbo).

desiderátum *m* desideratum.

desidia *f* negligence, slovenliness, laziness || slovenliness (al vestir).

desidioso, sa *adj* negligent, lazy, slovenly || slovenly (al vestir).

desierto, ta *adj* deserted, uninhabited (deshabitado) || desolate, bleak; *llanura desierta* desolate plain || GEOGR desert || void; *el premio Nobel ha sido declarado desierto* the Nobel prize has been declared void || FIG deserted; *calle desierta* deserted street || *isla desierta* desert island.
◆ *m* desert || FIG *predicar* or *clamar en el desierto* to preach in the wilderness.

designación *f* appointment, designation (para un empleo) || representation, indication, designation (representación) || designation, name (nombre).

designar *vt* to appoint, to designate, to assign (nombrar); *designar a alguien para un puesto* to appoint s.o. to a post || to point out (señalar) || to represent, to indicate, to designate (representar) || to appoint, to decide on, to fix; *designar la hora de una cita* to decide on the time of an appointment.

designio *m* intention; *con el designio de* with the intention of || design, project, plan (proyecto).

desigual *adj* unequal, uneven; *batalla desigual* unequal battle || different; *dos hermanas muy desiguales* two very different sisters || unfair, inequitable (tratamiento) || changeable (cambiadizo); *persona, tiempo desigual* changeable person, weather || uneven, rough, rugged (terreno) || uneven (escritura, estilo); *letra desigual* uneven writing || inconsistent; *un alumno desigual* an inconsistent pupil || FIG & FAM *salir desigual* to come out *o* to be different; *las dos figuras me salieron completamente desiguales* the two figures were completely different.

desigualar *vt* to make unequal (dos cosas) || to make different (una cosa de otra) || to make unequal *o* uneven; *desigualar una lucha* to make a fight unequal *o* uneven || to make uneven *o* rough (terreno).
◆ *vpr* to excel (aventajar) || to get ahead (adelantarse).

desigualdad *f* inequality; *desigualdades sociales* social inequalities || roughness, unevenness, ruggedness (del terreno) || changeableness (del tiempo, del carácter) || unevenness (de la letra, del estilo) || inconsistency (inconsistencia) || difference, inequality; *desigualdad entre los salarios agrícolas e industriales* difference between *o* inequality of agricultural and industrial wages || MAT inequality.

desigualmente *adv* unequally; *en ese país la renta está dividida desigualmente* the income is unequally divided in that country || unevenly; *la carretera está asfaltada desigualmente* the road is unevenly asphalted || inconsistently; *este futbolista juega muy desigualmente* this footballer plays very inconsistently || unevenly (letra, estilo).

desilusión *f* disappointment (decepción); *sufrir una desilusión* to suffer a disappointment || disillusion, disillusionment (pérdida de ilusiones).

desilusionado, da *adj* disappointed (decepcionado) || disillusioned (sin ilusiones).

desilusionante *adj* disappointing, disillusioning.

desilusionar *vt* to disappoint (decepcionar) || to disillusion (quitar las ilusiones).
◆ *vpr* to be disappointed || to get disillusioned.

desimanación *f* demagnetization.

desimanar *vt* to demagnetize.

desimantación *f* demagnetization.

desimantar *vt* to demagnetize.

desimpresionar *vt* to enlighten, to undeceive, to open the eyes of (desengañar).
◆ *vpr* to be enlightened, to have one's eyes opened.

desincrustación *f* descaling, unscaling.

desincrustante *adj* water-softening.
◆ *m* water softener.

desincrustar *vt* to descale, to unscale.

desinencia *f* GRAM ending, desinence (p us).

desinencial *adj* GRAM desinential.

desinfartar *vt* MED to cure of an infarct.

desinfección *f* disinfection.

desinfectante *adj/sm* disinfectant.

desinfectar; desinfestar *vt* to disinfect.

desinflacionista *adj* disinflationary, deflationary.

desinflado; desinflamiento *m* deflation, letting down (de un neumático).

desinflamación *f* reduction of inflammation.

desinflamar *vt* MED to reduce the inflammation in.
◆ *vpr* MED *se le ha desinflamado la herida* the inflammation in his wound has gone down, his wound has become less inflamed.

desinflar *vt* to deflate, to let down (un neumático).
◆ *vpr* to go flat, to go down, to deflate (un neumático) || FAM to climb down (rajarse) | to climb down from one's high horse (perder la presunción).

desinformación *f* disinformation.

desinsectación *f* fumigation, disinfection.

desinsectar *vt* to fumigate, to disinfect.

desintegración *f* disintegration (en fragmentos) || breaking up, disintegration; *la desintegración de un sindicato* the breaking up of a union || FÍS disintegration, fission, splitting; *desintegración atómica, nuclear* atomic disintegration, nuclear fission.

desintegrar *vt* to disintegrate; *desintegrar una roca* to disintegrate a rock || FIG to break up; *desintegrar un grupo de amigos* to break up a group of friends || FÍS to split (el átomo).
◆ *vpr* to disintegrate || FIG to break up || FÍS to split (el átomo).

desinterés *m* disinterestedness, impartiality (imparcialidad) || unselfishness, altruism, generosity (generosidad) || (p us) lack of interest (falta de interés).

desinteresadamente *adv* disinterestedly, impartially (imparcialmente) || unselfishly, altruistically, generously (generosamente).

desinteresado, da *adj* not interested || disinterested, unbiased, unprejudiced (consejo) || unselfish, altruistic (motivo) || unselfish, altruistic, disinterested (persona) || impartial (imparcial).

desinteresarse *vpr* to lose interest; *se ha desinteresado de la pintura* he has lost interest in painting || to take no interest; *se desinteresó completamente de las conversaciones* he took no interest in the talks.

desintoxicar *vt* MED to detoxicate, to detoxify.
◆ *vpr* FIG & FAM to get away from; *desintoxicarse de la rutina cotidiana* to get away from the routine of everyday life.

desistimiento *m* desistance, giving-up || JUR waiving [of a right].

desistir *vi* to give up, to desist; *desistió de su empresa* he gave up his undertaking, he desisted from the undertaking || to give up the idea; *he desistido de encontrarlo* I have given up the idea of finding it || JUR to waive [a right] || to stand down, to withdraw (candidato).

desjarretar *vt* to hamstring.

desjarrete *m* hamstringing.

desjuiciado, da *adj* senseless, unwise, injudicious.

desjuntar *vt* to separate, to divide.

deslabonamiento *m* unlinking (de una cadena).

deslabonar *vt* to unlink (una cadena).

desladrillar *vt* to remove the bricks from.

deslastrar *vt* to unballast, to remove the ballast from.

deslavado *m*; **deslavadura** *f* rinsing, rinse || washing out, fading (acción de desteñir).

deslavar *vt* to rinse through || to wash out, to fade (desteñir).

deslavazado, da *adj* faded, washed out (desteñido) || limp (lacio) || insipid (comida) || FIG disjointed, disconnected (estilo) | colourless (insípido).

deslavazar *vt* to fade, to wash out (desteñir) || to rinse through (aclarar) || to make limp (volver lacio) || to make insipid (una comida).

deslave *m* AMER erosion (acción) | alluvion (tierra).

desleal *adj* disloyal; *desleal con su hermano* disloyal to his brother || unfair (entre comerciantes).

deslealtad *f* disloyalty || unfairness (entre comerciantes).

desleidura *f*; **desleimiento** *m* dissolving (de un sólido en líquido) || dilution (de un líquido espeso).

desleír* *vt* to dissolve (un sólido) || to dilute (un líquido espeso) || to thin down (una salsa) || FIG to dilute.
◆ *vpr* to dissolve (un sólido) || to be diluted (un líquido espeso) || to thin out (una salsa).

deslendrar *vt* to clean the nits from.

deslenguado, da *adj* FIG cheeky, insolent, rude (insolente) | foulmouthed, coarse (grosero).

deslenguamiento *m* FIG & FAM cheek, insolence (insolencia) | foul *o* bad language (lenguaje grosero).

deslenguar *vt* to cut out the tongue of.
◆ *vpr* FIG & FAM to be cheeky *o* insolent *o* rude (con insolencia) | to swear, to curse, to use foul *o* bad language (hablar groseramente) | to talk too much (hablar mucho).

desliar *vt* to open (un paquete) || to unfasten, to undo, to untie (desatar) || to unwrap (desenvolver) || to separate lees from (mosto).
◆ *vpr* to come undone *o* unfastened *o* untied.

desligado, da *adj* loose, free.

desligadura *f*; **desligamiento** *m* untying, unfastening, unbinding || FIG freeing (de una obligación) | detachment (desapego) | separation (separación) | disentanglement, clearing-up (desenredo).

desligar *vt* to untie, to unfasten, to unbind (desatar) || FIG to free (liberar) | to excuse, to release; *desligar a alguien de una promesa* to release s.o. from a promise | to separate, to detach (separar) | to clear up, to sort out, to disentangle (desenredar) || MÚS to detach.
◆ *vpr* to break away, to separate; *se desligó de su familia* he broke away from his family || to free o.s., to excuse o.s., to release o.s.; *desligarse de un compromiso* to free o.s. from an obligation || to come undone *o* loose (desatarse).

deslindador *m* land surveyor.

deslindamiento; deslinde *m* marking of boundaries, delimitation, demarcation (de un terreno, etc.) || FIG defining, demarcation | explanation, definition (explicación).

deslindar *vt* to mark the boundaries of, to mark out, to fix the limits of, to demarcate, to delimitate, to delimit; *deslindar un jardín* to mark the boundaries of a garden || to mark the boundary between (dos cosas) || FIG to define the limits of, to demarcate; *deslindar las actividades de dos organizaciones* to define the limits of two organizations' activities | to outline (delimitar); *deslindar un problema* to outline a problem.

deslinde *m* → **deslindamiento.**

desliz *m* slipping, slip (de personas) || sliding (de cosas) || gliding (sobre agua) || FIG & FAM slip, mistake, error (equivocación) | lapse, slip, error (indiscreción) || *cometer* or *tener un desliz* to go wrong, to slip up, to make a slip.

deslizable *adj* slippery (que se desliza) || sliding (corredizo).

deslizadero *m* slippery spot || TECN slide, chute.

deslizamiento *m* slipping, slip (de personas) || sliding (de cosas) || *deslizamiento de tierra* landslide.

deslizante *adj* slippery, slippy || sliding (corredizo).

deslizar *vt* to slide; *deslizó la mano por el pasamanos* he slid his hand along the handrail || to slip; *deslizó un billete en su bolsillo* he slipped a ticket into his pocket; *deslizar unas críticas en un discurso* to slip a few criticisms into a speech || to let slip (un secreto).
◆ *vi* to slide, to slip.
◆ *vpr* to slide; *el trineo se deslizó sobre* or *en* or *por el hielo* the sledge slid over the ice || to slip (caerse uno) || to glide (sobre el agua) || to slither (una serpiente) || to run, to flow; *la arena se deslizó entre sus dedos* the sand ran through his fingers || to flow (una corriente líquida) || to slip by, to pass, to glide past (tiempo) || FIG to slip away, to slip off (escaparse); *deslizarse de un sitio* to slip away from a place | to slip; *se deslizó en la sala* he slipped into the room | to slip out (un secreto) | to slip in (una falta, un error) | to weave, to slip away; *deslizarse por entre la muchedumbre* to weave through *o* to slip away through the crowd | to go wrong, to make a slip, to slip up (cometer una falta) || *deslizarse entre las manos de uno* to slip through one's hands.

deslomado, da *adj* worn-out, exhausted.

deslomadura *f* exhaustion.

deslomar *vt* to exhaust, to wear out, to break s.o.'s back (derrengar) || to break s.o.'s back (romper la espalda) || *deslomar a uno a palos* to beat s.o. black and blue, to beat s.o. up.
◆ *vpr* FAM to wear o.s. out, to break one's back (trabajar demasiado) || to put one's back out, to hurt one's back.

deslucidamente *adv* unimpressively (sin brillo) || shabbily, dowdily; *vestir deslucidamente* to dress shabbily || ungracefully, gracelessly (sin gracia).

deslucido, da *adj* unimpressive, tarnished, uninspiring; *el torero tuvo una deslucida actuación* the bullfighter gave an unimpressive performance || shabby, dowdy; *sillón, vestido deslucido* shabby armchair, dress || dull, lacklustre (sin gracia) || undistinguished (poco distinguido) || lifeless, lacklustre (sin vida, sin brillo) || unsuccessful (fracasado).

deslucimiento *m* unimpressiveness, insignificance (falta de brillantez) || shabbiness, dowdiness (de vestidos, de muebles, etc.) || dullness (falta de gracia) || lifelessness (falta de vitalidad) || failure, unsuccessfulness (fracaso).

deslucir* *vt* to spoil, to ruin (estropear) || to tarnish (quitar el brillo a) || to tarnish (the reputation of), to discredit (desacreditar) || to dull (quitar brillantez).
◆ *vpr* FIG to fail, to be unsuccessful (fracasar) || to become tarnished *o* dull (perder el brillo) || to be discredited.

deslumbrador, ra; deslumbrante *adj* dazzling (luz, actuación, etc.) || overwhelming (que asombra).

deslumbramiento *m* dazzle, dazzling.

deslumbrar *vt* to dazzle || FIG to dazzle; *nos deslumbró con sus promesas, con su habilidad* he dazzled us with his promises, with his skill.

deslustrado, da *adj* dull, tarnished (sin lustre) || frosted, ground (vidrio) || unglazed (loza).
◆ *m* steaming (de los paños de lana) || → **deslustre.**

deslustrar *vt* to tarnish, to dull, to take the shine off (quitar el lustre) || to grind, to frost (el vidrio) || TECN to steam (los paños de lana) | to remove the finish from (los paños de algodón) | to unglaze (el papel, la loza) | to mat, to dull (oro, plata) || FIG to tarnish (the reputation of) (desacreditar) | to dull, to tarnish (la brillantez) | to disgrace (deshonrar).

deslustre; delustrado *m* dullness, lack of shine (falta de lustre) || steaming (del paño de lana) || removal of finish (del paño de algodón) || unglazing (del papel) || grinding, frosting (del vidrio) || matting, dulling (del oro, de la plata) || FIG stain, spot (mancha) | discredit (descrédito) | disgrace (deshonra).

desmadejado, da *adj* FIG weak, run-down, exhausted (sin energía) | lanky, gawky, ungainly (desgarbado).

desmadejamiento *m* FIG weakness, exhaustion (falta de energía) | lankiness, gawkiness, ungainliness (desgarbo).

desmadejar *vt* FIG to weaken, to exhaust (debilitar).

desmadrar *vt* to take (an animal) from its mother.

desmagnetización *f* TECN demagnetization.

desmagnetizar *vt* TECN to demagnetize.

desmajolar* *vt* to clear of young vines (un campo) || to unfasten, to untie (los zapatos).

desmalezar *vt* AMER to weed.

desmallar *vt* to ladder (una media) || to break the mesh of (una red) || to break the mail of (una cota de malla) || to unravel (un tejido de punto).
◆ *vpr* to ladder (una media).

desmán *m* outrage, abuse, excess (ultraje); *cometer desmanes* to commit outrages || misfortune, mishap (desdicha) || ZOOL desman, muskrat.

desmanarse *vpr* to stray from the flock (ovejas) || to stray from the herd (vaca, caballo).

desmanchar *vt* AMER to clean, to get the marks off.
◆ *vpr* AMER to go one's own way.

desmandado, da *adj* insubordinate, rebellious, out of hand (indómito) || uncontrollable (incontrolable) || unruly, unbridled (desenfrenado) || disobedient, unruly, intractable (desobediente) || runaway (caballo) || stray (otros animales) || *muchedumbre desmandada* crowd that has got out of hand *o* out of control.

desmandamiento *m* countermand, revoking (revocación de una orden) || insubordination, disobedience (desobediencia) || insolence, impudence, impertinence (falta de cortesía).

desmandar *vt* to countermand, to revoke.
◆ *vpr* to go too far, to forget o.s. (descomedirse) || to get out of hand *o* out of control; *el profesor debe cuidar que sus alumnos no se desmanden* the teacher must be careful that his pupils don't get out of hand || to rebel (rebelarse) || to behave badly (portarse mal) || to be disobedient (desobedecer); *como te desmandes te metemos en un internado* if you are disobedient we'll send you to a boarding school || to run wild, to get out of hand (animales) || to bolt (caballo) || FIG to go one's own way (separarse).

desmangado, da *adj* handleless, with no handle.

desmangar *vt* to take the handle off.

desmano (a) *loc adv* out of reach || *me coge a desmano* it's out of my way.

desmantecar *vt* to skim (la leche) || to remove the fat *o* grease from (quitar la grasa) || *leche desmantecada* skim milk.

desmantelado, da *adj* dismantled || MAR dismasted (desarbolado) | unrigged (desaparejado).

desmantelamiento *m* dismantling || MAR dismasting | unrigging.

desmantelar *vt* to dismantle (una fortificación) || to dismantle (una estructura) || MAR to dismast, to unmast (desarbolar) | to unrig (desaparejar) || to strip (down), to dismantle; *desmantelar una máquina* to strip a machine || to clear, to empty, to dismantle (un local, una casa) || FIG to disband; *desmantelar una organización* to disband an organization.

desmaña *f* clumsiness.

desmañado, da *adj* clumsy, bungling, hamfisted.
◆ *m/f* clumsy person, bungler.

desmaquillador *m* cleansing cream *o* milk, make-up remover.

desmarcaje; desmarque *m* DEP *esperar el desmarcaje de un compañero de equipo* to wait until a teammate is unmarked | *provocar el desmarcaje de un compañero* to allow a teammate to get into an unmarked position.
◆ *vpr* DEP to get into an unmarked position.

desmarcar *vt* to remove the marks from || DEP to allow to get into an unmarked position, to leave unmarked.
◆ *vpr* DEP to get into an unmarked position.

desmarque *m* ⟶ **desmarcaje.**

desmarrido, da *adj* downhearted, dejected, crestfallen (alicaído) || exhausted, weak (desmadejado).

desmaterialización *f* dematerialization.

desmayado, da *adj* unconscious, who has fainted (sin sentido) || dejected, dismayed, disheartened (desanimado) || exhausted, worn-out (agotado) || faint with hunger (hambriento) || dull, wan, washed-out (color).

desmayar *vt* to make faint; *la noticia le desmayó* the news made him faint.
◆ *vi* FIG to lose heart, to be dismayed.
◆ *vpr* to faint, to swoon (p us).

desmayo *m* faint, fainting fit, swoon (p us) || unconsciousness (estado) || BOT weeping willow (sauce llorón) || FIG depression, dismay, downheartedness (desánimo) | faltering, flagging (de la voz) || — *sin desmayo* unfaltering, without flinching; *siguió trabajando sin desmayo* he worked on unfaltering || *tener un desmayo* to faint.

desmedido, da *adj* excessive (excesivo) || immoderate, disproportionate (inmoderado) || unbounded, boundless, limitless; *ambición desmedida* unbounded ambition.

desmedirse* *vpr* to go too far, to forget o.s.

desmedrado, da *adj* puny, emaciated (enclenque).

desmedrar *vi* to fall off, to decline, to go down, to deteriorate; *este negocio ha desmedrado mucho* this business has greatly declined *o* deteriorated, this business has fallen off a lot *o* gone down a lot || MED to grow weak.
◆ *vt* to impair (perjudicar).
◆ *vpr* to fall off, to decline, to go down, to deteriorate (deteriorarse) || to waste away (de salud).

desmedro *m* decline, deterioration (decaimiento) || wasting away, puniness (de una persona) || impairment (perjuicio).

desmejora *f* ⟶ **desmejoramiento.**

desmejoramiento *m*; **desmejora** *f* deterioration, decline (de la salud) || deterioration, spoiling.

desmejorar *vt* to spoil, to impair, to damage, to deteriorate (menoscabar).
◆ *vi/vpr* to lose one's health, to deteriorate *o* to decline in health (una persona) || to deteriorate, to get worse; *la situación se ha desmejorado rápidamente* the situation has quickly deteriorated.

desmelenado, da *adj* dishevelled, tousled, with ruffled hair.

desmelenar *vt* to dishevel, to tousle the hair of, to ruffle the hair of.

desmembración *f*; **desmembramiento** *m* dismemberment || FIG division, dismemberment (división) | separation (separación).

desmembrar* *vt* to dismember || FIG to divide up, to break up; *desmembrar un imperio* to divide up an empire | to separate (separar).

desmemoriado, da *adj* forgetful, absent-minded || *ser desmemoriado* to have a bad memory, to be forgetful *o* absentminded.

desmemoriarse *vpr* to become forgetful, to lose one's memory.

desmentida *f*; **desmentido** *m* denial || contradiction (contradicción).

desmentidor, ra *adj* denying.

desmentir* *vt* to deny; *el ministro desmintió el rumor* the minister denied the rumour || to contradict, to give the lie to, to belie; *desmentir a alguien* to contradict s.o. || to prove wrong, to refute (teoría, sospecha, indicios) || to go against (una conducta, una palabra dada) || to belie (temores, promesas).
◆ *vpr* to contradict o.s. || to go back on one's word (desdecirse).

desmenuzamiento *m* crumbling.

desmenuzar *vt* to crumble (pan, etc.) || to chop up (carne) || to break into small pieces || FIG to examine minutely, to sift, to scrutinize.
◆ *vpr* to crumble.

desmerecedor, ra *adj* unworthy.

desmerecer* *vt* not to deserve, to be unworthy of.
◆ *vi* to be inferior, to compare unfavourably; *el cuadro desmerece de* or *al lado de los otros de la exposición* the painting is inferior to *o* compares unfavourably with the rest in the exhibition || to deteriorate, to decline, to get worse (decaer) || to lose; *este verde desmerece al ponerlo al lado del rojo* this green loses when it is put next to red || *no desmerecer* to compare favourably.

desmerecimiento *m* demerit.

desmesura *f* immoderacy, immoderation, lack of moderation || disproportion.

desmesuradamente *adv* uncommonly, extremely; *ojos desmesuradamente grandes* uncommonly large eyes || excessively, inordinately, extremely (excesivamente) || disproportionately, inordinately.

desmesurado, da *adj* excessive, inordinate, disproportionate (desmedido) || unbounded, boundless, inordinate, limitless; *ambición desmesurada* unbounded ambition || insolent, impudent, cheeky (descarado).

desmesurarse *vpr* to go too far, to forget o.s.

desmigajar; desmigar *vt* to crumble.
◆ *vpr* to crumble.

desmilitarización *f* demilitarization.

desmilitarizar *vt* to demilitarize.

desmineralización *f* demineralization.

desmirriado, da *adj* FAM weedy, puny.

desmochar *vt* to pollard, to lop (los árboles) || to blunt the horns of (una res) || FIG to cut (una obra, un texto).

desmoche *m* pollarding, lopping (de árboles) || blunting of the horns (de una res).

desmonetizar *vt* to demonetize.

desmontable *adj* that can be dismantled *o* taken to pieces, dismountable [US knock-down] (máquina) || collapsible; *armario desmontable* collapsible wardrobe || detachable (que se quita) || ARQ portable, sectional (construcción).
◆ *m* *desmontable para neumáticos* tyre lever.

desmontaje *m* removal (de una rueda, etc.) || TECN dismounting, disassembling (de una máquina) || uncocking (de un arma de fuego).

desmontar *vt* to remove, to take off; *desmontar una rueda* to remove a wheel || to dismantle, to take to pieces, to disassemble, to dismount (un mecanismo) || to strip (un motor) || to dismantle, to take down; *desmontar un andamio* to take down a scaffold || to unset, to unmount (un diamante, una piedra) || to unhinge (una puerta) || to unstitch (un traje) || MAR to unship (el timón) || MIL to dismount (un cañón) || to uncock (arma de fuego) || to dismount, to unhorse, to throw (el caballo al jinete) || to clear (cortar árboles) || to level (allanar).
◆ *vi* to dismount (apearse).
◆ *vpr* to come to pieces (deshacerse) || to dismount (apearse).

desmonte *m* clearing [of trees] (tala de árboles) || levelling (nivelación) || clearing (terreno sin árboles) || levelled ground (terreno allanado) || cutting (para ferrocarriles) || rubble, excavated soil (escombros).

desmoralización *f* demoralization || corruption.

desmoralizante *adj* demoralizing || corrupting (que corrompe).

desmoralizar *vt* to demoralize (desalentar) || to corrupt, to deprave (corromper).
◆ *vpr* to become demoralized || to become corrupt *o* depraved.

desmoronadizo, za *adj* crumbly.

desmoronamiento *m* decay, crumbling; *desmoronamiento de un muro* crumbling of a wall || FIG destruction (ruina) | crumbling, decaying, decline; *desmoronamiento de un régimen* crumbling of a régime.

desmoronar *vt* to wear away || FIG to corrode, to erode (arruinar lentamente).
◆ *vpr* to crumble, to decay, to fall to pieces; *esta casa se desmorona* this house is crumbling || FIG to crumble (imperio, proyectos) | to decline (decaer).

desmotadera *f* TECN cotton gin.

desmotador, ra *m/f* burler (de lana) || ginner (de algodón).
◆ *f* cotton gin.

desmotar *vt* to burl (lana) || to gin (algodón).

desmovilización *f* demobilization, demob (*fam*).

desmovilizar *vt* to demobilize, to demob (*fam*).

desmultiplicador *adj* TECN reducing, reduction; *engranaje desmultiplicador* reducing gear.

desmultiplicar *vt* TECN to gear down.

desnacionalización *f* denationalization.

desnacionalizar *vt* to denationalize.

desnarigado, da *adj* noseless (sin narices) || snub-nosed (chato).

desnarigar *vt* to cut off the nose of || to knock off the nose of (con un golpe).

desnatadora *f* cream separator, skimmer.

desnatar *vt* to skim, to separate the cream from (la leche) || FIG to take the cream of (tomar lo mejor) || *leche sin desnatar* whole milk.

desnaturalización *f* denaturalization || corruption, perversion (del carácter, de una persona) || misrepresentation, distortion, adulteration (de un hecho, de la verdad) || adulteration (de la leche).

desnaturalizado, da *adj* denaturalized (sin nacionalidad) || corrupt, perverted (corrompido) || misrepresented, distorted; adulterated (un hecho, la verdad, etc.) || adulterated (leche) || unnatural; *padre desnaturalizado* unnatural father || QUÍM denatured; *alcohol desnaturalizado* denatured alcohol.

desnaturalizar *vt* to denaturalize (quitar la naturalización) || to corrupt, to pervert (corromper) || to misrepresent, to distort, to adulterate; *desnaturalizar los hechos* to misrepresent the facts || to adulterate, to change the nature of (leche, alcohol, etc.) || QUÍM to denature.
◆ *vpr* to give up one's nationality, to become stateless.

desnicotinizar *vt* to denicotinize (tabaco).

desnitrar *vt* to denitrate.

desnitrificación *f* denitrification, denitration.

desnitrificar *vt* to denitrify.

desnivel *m* unevenness || slope (pendiente) || depression (depresión) || FIG difference, inconsistency, inequality; *desnivel cultural entre las regiones* cultural difference between the districts || *hay un desnivel entre estos puntos* these points are not level *o* not on a level.

desnivelado, da *adj* uneven; *terreno desnivelado* uneven ground || which are not on a level *o* not level; *puntos desnivelados* points which are not on a level || FIG uneven, unequal.

desnivelar *vt* to make uneven; *desnivelar un campo* to make a field uneven || to put on different levels; *desnivelar varias cosas* to put several things on different levels || FIG to unbalance, to throw out of balance (un presupuesto) || to tip (una balanza).

desnucar *vt* to break the neck of.
◆ *vpr* to break one's neck.

desnudamiento *m* stripping, undressing || FIG denudation.

desnudar *vt* to undress, to strip (quitar la ropa a) || to bare (un arma, una espada) || FIG to strip; *desnudar a alguien de sus bienes* to strip s.o. of his possessions; *el viento desnudó los árboles de sus hojas* the wind stripped the trees of their leaves | to lay bare (descubrir) | to ruin (arruinar) | to fleece, to clean out (*fam*) (en el juego).
◆ *vpr* to strip, to get undressed (quitarse la ropa); *desnudarse hasta la cintura* to strip to the waist || FIG to lose, to shed; *el árbol se está desnudando de hojas* the tree is losing its leaves | to rid o.s., to cast aside; *desnudarse de sus efectos* to rid o.s. of *o* to cast aside one's faults.

desnudez *f* nakedness, nudity.

desnudismo *m* nudism.

desnudista *adj/s* nudist.

desnudo, da *adj* undressed, naked, nude, bare (desvestido) || naked; *el hombre nace desnudo* man is born naked || FIG bare; *una pared desnuda* a bare wall | bare, naked, drawn (espada) | bare, naked; *los árboles están desnudos* the trees are bare | devoid (falto de); *desnudo de méritos* devoid of merits | clear, apparent (patente) | penniless, destitute (pobre) | ruined (arruinado) || — *con las piernas desnudas* bare-legged || *la verdad desnuda* the plain truth, the naked truth.
◆ *m* ARTES nude.

desnutrición *f* malnutrition, undernourishment.

desnutrido, da *adj* undernourished.

desnutrirse *vpr* to suffer from malnutrition, to be undernourished.

desobedecer* *vt* to disobey; *desobedecer la ley, a sus padres* to disobey the law, one's parents.

desobediencia *f* disobedience.

desobediente *adj* disobedient.
◆ *m/f* disobedient person.

desobligar *vt* to free [from an obligation] || to offend, to disoblige (causar disgusto a).

desobstrucción *f* removal of obstructions, clearing (de un camino) || unblocking (de un conducto, etc.).

desobstruir* *vt* to remove the obstructions from, to clear (un camino, etc.) || to unblock (un conducto).

desocupación *f* vacation (de una casa) || MIL evacuation || leisure, idleness (ocio) || unemployment (desempleo).

desocupado, da *adj* idle (ocioso) || unoccupied; *alquilar un piso desocupado* to rent an unoccupied flat || empty, vacant, unoccupied (terreno, asiento, etc.) || spare, free (tiempo) || unemployed, out of work (sin empleo) || *estar desocupado* to have nothing to do, to be idle, to be at a loose end (*fam*).
◆ *m/f* idler (ocioso) || unemployed person (sin empleo).

desocupar *vt* to vacate; *desocupar una casa* to vacate a house || MIL to evacuate || to clear (desobstruir) || to empty (vaciar).
◆ *vpr* to become empty (quedar vacío) || to free o.s., to get away (de una ocupación).

desodorante *adj/sm* deodorant.

desodorización *f* deodorization.

desodorizar *vt* to deodorize.

desoír* *vt* not to listen to, to ignore, to take no notice of; *desoí los consejos de mi padre* I didn't listen to *o* I took no notice of my father's advice || to take no notice of; *desoyó la prescripción médica* he took no notice of the doctor's orders.

desojar *vt* to break the eye of (una aguja).

desolación *f* desolation || FIG distress, grief.

desolado, da *adj* desolate (desierto) || desolated, devastated (devastado) || disconsolate, heartbroken, distressed (afligido).

desolador, ra *adj* desolating (que aflige) || devastating, ravaging, desolating; *una epidemia desoladora* a devastating epidemic.

desolar* *vt* to desolate, to distress, to grieve (afligir) || to devastate, to ravage, to lay waste, to desolate (devastar).
◆ *vpr* to be distressed *o* grieved.

desoldar* *vt* to unsolder.

desolidarizarse *vpr* to break away, to break with; *desolidarizarse de sus compañeros* to break away from *o* to break with one's companions.

desolladero *m* slaughterhouse (matadero).

desollado, da *adj* FAM insolent, impudent, cheeky (descarado) || FAM *salir desollado* to be pulled to pieces, to be slated (ser muy criticado).
◆ *m/f* insolent *o* impudent *o* cheeky person.

desollador *m* skinner (en el matadero) || FIG flayer (criticón) | fleecer (en el juego) || ZOOL butcher-bird (alcaudón).

desolladura *f* skinning, flaying (de las reses) || graze (arañazo).

desollar* *vt* to skin, to flay; *desollar un conejo* to skin a rabbit || to skin, to graze (arañar) || FIG & FAM to fleece (hacer pagar muy caro) | to flay, to slate (criticar) || — FIG *desollar a uno vivo* to make s.o. pay through the nose, to fleece s.o. (vender caro), to clean s.o. out (en el juego), to pull s.o. to pieces, to slate s.o., to flay s.o. (criticar) | *queda el rabo por desollar* the worst is yet to come.

desollón *m* FAM graze (arañazo).

desorbitado, da *adj* exhorbitant; *precios desorbitados* exhorbitant prices || exaggerated (exagerado) || *tener los ojos desorbitados* to be wide-eyed.

desorbitar *vt* to exaggerate; *un periódico que desorbita los hechos* a newspaper which exaggerates the facts.
◆ *vpr* to bulge (los ojos) || FIG to lose one's sense of proportion || to leave its orbit (satélite).

desorden *m* disorder, confusion; *reinaba gran desorden en la administración* complete disorder reigned in the administration || muddle, mess; *la habitación está en desorden* the room is in a mess || FIG disorderliness (de la conducta) || — *con el pelo en desorden* with untidy *o* ruffled *o* tousled hair || *poner en desorden* to upset, to muddle, to mix up, to disarrange.
◆ *pl* disturbances, riots, disorder *sing*; *desórdenes estudiantiles* student disturbances || disorders; *el alcohol puede ocasionar desórdenes en el estómago* alcohol can cause stomach disorders || excesses (excesos).

desordenadamente *adv* in disorder, in confusion; *huyeron desordenadamente* they fled in disorder || disjointedly, confusedly; *hablar desordenadamente* to speak disjointedly.

desordenado, da *adj* untidy (persona, habitación, trabajo) || muddled, jumbled, disordered (objetos) || FIG disorderly; *vida desordenada* disorderly life || unruly (revoltoso).

desordenar *vt* to upset, to disarrange; *desordenar un cajón* to upset a drawer || to make a mess in, to make untidy (una habitación) || to mix up, to jumble (mezclar) || to throw into confusion (causar confusión).
◆ *vpr* to become untidy (una habitación, etc.) || to get into a muddle, to get muddled up; *los papeles se desordenaron* the papers got muddled up || to get out of order *o* out of control.

desorejado, da *adj* without handles (vasija) || TAUR earless [after the bullfight].

desorejar *vt* to cut the ears off.

desorganización *f* disorganization, lack of organization.

desorganizadamente *adv* in a disorganized way.

desorganizar *vt* to disorganize, to disrupt; *desorganizar una fábrica* to disorganize a factory || to disband, to break up, to disperse (desagregar).

desorientación *f* disorientation, loss of one's bearings (acción de perderse) || FIG confusion.

desorientado, da *adj* lost || FIG confused.

desorientar *vt* to make lose one's bearings *o* one's way, to mislead, to disorientate; *el letrero me desorientó* the sign made me lose my bearings, the sign disorientated me || FIG to confuse, to throw; *mi pregunta lo desorientó* my question confused him.
◆ *vpr* to lose one's way, to get lost || to get confused *o* mixed up (confundirse).

desorillar *vt* to cut the selvedge off (una tela) || to cut the edge off (papel).

desornamentado, da *adj* plain, not decorated, bare.

desosar* *vt* to bone (pescado, carne) || to stone, to pit (fruta).

desovar *vi* to oviposit, to lay eggs (insectos) || to spawn (peces, anfibios).

desove *m* spawning (de los peces, los anfibios) || ovipositing, egg-laying (de los insectos) || spawning *o* egg-laying season (temporada).

desovillar *vt* to unwind, to unravel.

desoxidación *f* deoxidization || cleaning, removal of oxide (de un metal).

desoxidante *adj* deoxidizing.
◆ *m* deoxidizer.

desoxidar *vt* to deoxidize || to clean, to remove the oxide from (limpiar los metales).
◆ *vpr* to be deoxidized.

desoxigenar *vt* QUÍM to deoxygenate, to deoxidize.

desoxirribonucleico, ca *adj* QUÍM deoxyribonucleic, desoxyribonucleic.

despabiladeras *f pl* snuffers.

despabilado, da espabilado, da *adj* wide-awake (despierto) || FIG quick, alert, sharp, smart (despejado); *un niño muy despabilado* a very quick child || FIG *ser despabilado* to have one's wits about one.

despabilador *m* snuffer (en el teatro) || snuffers *pl* (despabiladeras).

despabilar; espabilar *vt* to snuff (una vela) || to trim (una mecha) || FIG & FAM to wake up (despertar) | to brighten *o* to smarten up, to wake up (avivar el ingenio de); *hay que despabilar a ese alumno* we shall have to brighten up that pupil | to eat up, to finish; *despabiló dos raciones de calamares fritos* he ate up two helpings of fried squid | to squander; *despabilar una fortuna* to squander a fortune | to rush off; *despabiló el trabajo* he rushed off the work | to pinch, to knock off, to steal (robar) | to kill, to do in (matar).
◆ *vpr* FIG to wake up (despertarse) | to liven up, to wake up, to pull o.s. together, to get a move on; *¡despabílate que nos tenemos que ir!* wake up, we've got to go! || AMER to leave, to go away (marcharse).

despacio *adv* slowly; *hable más despacio* speak more slowly, speak slower || quietly (silenciosamente) || gradually, slowly (poco a poco).
◆ *interj* take it easy!, easy does it!

despacito *adv* FAM slowly.
◆ *interj* FAM take it easy!, easy does it!

despachaderas *f pl* surliness *sing*, curtness *sing* (brusquedad) || cheek, insolence (insolencia) || resourcefulness *sing* (recursos) || FIG *tener buenas despachaderas* to be on the ball.

despachante *m* AMER customs officer (aduanero).

despachar *vt* to settle, to dispatch, to finish (terminar) || to deal with, to attend to; *despachar la correspondencia* to deal with the mail || to see to, to attend to, to serve; *me despachó este dependiente* this salesman served me || to sell (vender); *despachar localidades* to sell tickets || to send, to dispatch; *despachar un recadero* to send an errand boy || to send, to dispatch (cartas, paquetes) || to dismiss, to sack (despedir); *despachó a la criada* he dismissed the maid || to send off, to send packing; *vino pidiendo limosna y lo despaché* he came begging and I sent him packing || to settle (un negocio, un problema, un convenio) || FAM to polish off, to dispatch; *despachar un bocadillo, una botella de vino* to polish off a sandwich, a bottle of wine | to get through, to get out of the way; *el orador despachó su conferencia en media hora* the speaker got through his lecture *o* got his lecture out of the way in half an hour | to dispatch, to do in (matar) | to reel off (una historia).
◆ *vi* to hurry, to hurry up (apresurarse) || to attend to business; *el director despachará mañana* the manager will attend to business tomorrow || to do business; *no despachamos los días de fiesta* we don't do business on holidays || to serve (en una tienda).
◆ *vpr* to get rid, to rid o.s.; *despacharse de algo* to get rid of sth. || to finish (terminar); *suele despacharse a las seis* he usually finishes at six || to get out of the way; *quiso despacharse del asunto* he wanted to get the matter out of the way || to hurry, to hurry up (darse prisa) || — FIG & FAM *despacharse a su gusto* to let go, to go the whole way | *despacharse a su gusto con uno* to tell s.o. what one thinks of him, to give s.o. a piece of one's mind.

despacho *m* dispatch, sending (envío) || sale (venta) || store, shop (tienda); *despacho de vinos* wine store || office (oficina); *el despacho del jefe* the boss's office || study (en una casa) || settlement (de un negocio, de un convenio) || dispatch (de un asunto) || dispatch; *despacho diplomático* diplomatic dispatch || message; *un despacho telefónico* a telephone message || MIL commission (título de oficial) || office; *despacho de billetes, de localidades* ticket, box office || AMER grocery shop (tienda de comestibles) || *despacho telegráfico* telegram.

despachurramiento; despachurro *m* squashing.

despachurrar *vt* FAM to squash, to flatten.

despajar *vt* AGR to winnow || MIN to sieve, to sift, to riddle (la tierra).

despaldar *vt* to break the shoulder of.

despaldillar *vt* to break (romper) *o* to dislocate (dislocar) the shoulder of.

despalillar *vt* to strip (el tabaco) || to remove the stalks from (las uvas) || AMER to kill (matar).

despampanadura *f* AGR trimming, pruning.

despampanante *adj* FAM stunning.

despampanar *vt* AGR to trim, to prune || FIG & FAM to astonish, to stun (sorprender).
◆ *vpr* FIG & FAM to fall and hurt o.s.

despampanillar *vt* to trim, to prune (las vides).

despanchurrar; despanzurrar *vt* FAM to disembowel (romper la panza de) | to squash (aplastar) | to burst (reventar) | to tear apart; *casa despanzurrada por los obuses* house torn apart by shells.

desparejado, da *adj* odd; *un zapato desparejado* an odd shoe || without a partner, odd (en un baile).

desparejar *vt* to separate.

desparejo, ja *adj* odd; *los dos guantes son desparejos* the two gloves are odd.

desparpajado, da *adj* self-confident, sure of o.s. (desenvuelto) || cheeky, rude, impudent (descarado) || brisk, prompt, alert (rápido).

desparpajar *vt* to spoil, to ruin (estropear) || to mess up, to disarrange (desordenar) || to scatter, to spread (desparramar).
◆ *vi* to talk one's head off, to prattle away.

desparpajo *m* self-confidence, ease (desenvoltura) || cheek, impudence (descaro) || briskness, ease (soltura) || AMER FAM disorder, confusion.

desparramado, da *adj* scattered; *flores desparramadas por el suelo* flowers scattered over the floor || spilt (un líquido) || FIG scattered, sprawling (que se extiende mucho); *una ciudad muy desparramada* a very scattered town.

desparramamiento *m* scattering || sprinkling (de gotas) || spilling (de un líquido) || spreading (de una noticia) || FIG squandering (de dinero) | disorder (desorden).

desparramar *vt* to scatter; *desparramar flores en el suelo* to scatter flowers on the ground || to spread (una noticia) || to sprinkle (un líquido en gotas) || to spill, to splash; *desparramó la leche por la mesa* he spilled the milk all over the table || FIG to squander; *desparramó su fortuna* he squandered his fortune || FIG *desparramar la atención* to divide one's attention amongst too many things.
◆ *vpr* to scatter || to spread (una noticia) || to splash, to spill (un líquido) || FIG to let o.s. go, to let one's hair down, to enjoy o.s. (divertirse).

desparramo *m* AMER ⟶ **desparramamiento.**

desparvar *vt* AGR to pile up (cereals).

despatarrada *f* FAM splits *pl* (en algunas danzas).

despatarrar *vt* FAM to make (s.o.) open his legs wide || FIG to astonish, to astound, to flabbergast (asombrar) || FIG *dejar a uno despatarrado* to astonish *o* to astound *o* to flabbergast s.o.
◆ *vpr* to open one's legs wide (separar las piernas) || FIG to go sprawling (caerse) | to be astonished *o* astounded *o* flabbergasted.

despatillado *m* tenon (carpintería).

despatillar *vt* to tenon (en carpintería) || to shave off the sideboards *o* sideburns of (quitar las patillas a).

despavesaderas *f pl* AMER snuffers.

despavesar *vt* to snuff (una vela) || to trim (la mecha) || to blow the ashes off [embers].

despavonar *vt* TECN to remove the bluing from.

despavoridamente *adv* in terror.

despavorido, da *adj* terrified.

despavorirse* *vpr* to be terrified.

despeado, da *adj* footsore.

despearse *vpr* to be footsore, to have sore feet (al andar) || VET to bruise its hooves (el caballo) | to have foot rot (corderos).

despectivamente *adj* disparagingly, contemptuously, scornfully || GRAM pejoratively.

despectivo, va *adj* contemptuous, disparaging, derogatory, scornful; *hablar con tono despectivo* to speak in a disparaging tone || GRAM pejorative; *sentido despectivo* pejorative sense.

despechar *vt* FAM to wean (destetar) || to vex, to make resentful *o* indignant (causar despecho a).
◆ *vpr* to get angry (enfadarse) || to despair (estar desesperado).

despecho *m* spite || indignation || despair (desesperación) || FAM weaning (destete) || — *a despecho de* in spite of, despite || *a despecho suyo* in spite of o.s. || *por despecho* out of spite.

despechugado, da *adj* FAM bare breasted.

despechugar *vt* to cut the breast off (un ave).
◆ *vpr* FIG & FAM to bare one's breast (descubrir el pecho) | to open one's collar (abrir el cuello).

despedazamiento *m* tearing *o* pulling to pieces (por la fuerza) || falling to pieces (al deshacerse algo) || smashing, shattering (de una vasija, etc.).

despedazar *vt* to tear to pieces *o* to shreds; *el león despedazaba su presa* the lion was tearing its prey to pieces || to smash, to shatter (romper) || FIG to break; *despedazarle el corazón a uno* to break s.o.'s heart.
◆ *vpr* to fall to pieces (caerse) || to smash (una vasija, etc.).

despedida *f* good-bye, farewell; *una despedida conmovedora* a touching good-bye; *cena de* *despedida* farewell dinner || farewell, send-off (antes de un viaje) || closing formula (en una carta) || envoi, last verse (de un canto) || dismissal (de un trabajo) || *despedida de soltero* stag party [for bridegroom before the wedding].

despedir* *vt* to give off *o* out, to emit; *el sol despide rayos de luz* the sun gives off light rays || to eject, to throw out; *la fuerza del golpe le despidió de su asiento* the force of the blow threw him out of his seat || to throw (el caballo al jinete) || to send out, to eject; *despedir un chorro de agua* to send out a jet of water || to give out (jugo) || to shoot out; *en este juego el resorte despide la bola* in this game the spring shoots the ball out || to say good-bye to, to see off; *despedir a uno en la estación* to see s.o. off at the station || to see out; *por favor, despide tú a los invitados* could you see the guests out, please? || to dismiss, to sack (*fam*) (a un empleado) || to throw out (echar); *despedir a un invitado descortés* to throw out an impolite guest || to evict (a un inquilino) || to get rid of (librarse de) || to dismiss (una idea) || *salir despedido* to be thrown out; *salió despedido de su asiento* he was thrown out of his seat.
◆ *vpr* to say good-bye, to take one's leave; *se fue sin despedirse de su hermano* he went without saying good-bye to his brother || to see (s.o.) off (en la estación, terminal, etc.) || to leave; *despedirse de un empleo* to leave a job || FIG to say good-bye; *te puedes despedir del libro que le prestaste* you can say good-bye to the book you lent him || — FIG *despedirse a la francesa* to take French leave || *me despido de usted con un saludo afectuoso* yours sincerely (en una carta) || *se despide de usted su seguro servidor q. e. s. m.* yours faithfully (en una carta).

despegado, da *adj* unstuck || which has come unstuck; *un sello despegado* a stamp which has come unstuck || FIG detached, cold (poco afectuoso).

despegadura *f* unsticking || FIG detachedness, detachment, coldness.

despegamiento *m* detachment, coldness (despego).

despegar *vt* to unstick; *despegar dos cosas, un sobre* to unstick two things, an envelope || to take off, to detach; *despegar la etiqueta de una botella* to take the label off a bottle || to take out (descoser) || FIG *no despegar los labios* not to open one's mouth, not to say a word.
◆ *vi* AVIAC to take off; *el avión para Manchester despega en seguida* the plane for Manchester will take off immediately | to blast off (un cohete).
◆ *vpr* to come unstuck || FIG to break away, to separate; *despegarse de sus padres* to break away from one's parents | to become separated (por las circunstancias).

despego *m* detachment, alienation (separación) || indifference, coldness (falta de cariño) || indiference (indiferencia).

despegue *m* AVIAC takeoff | blast-off (de un cohete) || FIG launching || *pista de despegue* runway.

despeinado, da *adj* unkempt, dishevelled, tousled.

despeinar *vt* to dishevel, to tousle *o* to ruffle the hair of.

despejado, da *adj* confident, sure of o.s. (seguro de sí) || quick, clever, sharp, bright (listo) || clear (camino, vista) || open, clear; *un campo despejado* an open field || clear, cloudless (cielo) || broad (frente) || spacious, uncluttered; *una plaza despejada* a spacious square || wide-awake, awake (sin sueño).

despejar *vt* to clear; *la policía despejó el local, el camino* the police cleared the premises, the way; *despejar la calle de escombros* to clear the street of rubble || FIG to clear up, to clarify, to sort out (aclarar) | to explain, to clarify (explicar) | to get rid of; *despejar las dificultades* to get rid of the difficulties | to clear; *el portero despejó la pelota* the goalkeeper cleared the ball || MAT to find; *despejar la incógnita* to find the unknown quantity | to solve (resolver) || FIG *despejar el terreno* to clear the ground *o* the way.
◆ *vi* to clear the way, to move away; *¡despejen!* clear the way! || DEP to clear.
◆ *vpr* to clear up (el tiempo) || to clear (el cielo) || to abate (la fiebre) || to gain self-confidence (adquirir soltura) || to become clearer (un misterio) || to wake up, to brighten up (espabilarse) || to enjoy o.s., to let o.s. go (esparcirse) || to clear one's head, to wake o.s. up; *dar un paseo para despejarse* to go for a walk to clear one's head.

despeje *m* clearance (en el fútbol).

despejo *m* clearing.

despelotado, da *adj* FAM stark-naked.

despelotarse *vpr* FAM to strip naked | to take care of o.s., to fend for o.s. (arreglárselas).

despeluchar *vt* to ruffle the hair of.

despeluzar; despeluznar *vt* to ruffle the hair of (despeinar) || to make s.o.'s hair stand on end (erizar) || to terrify, to scare (aterrar) || AMER to clean out, to fleece (en el juego).
◆ *vpr* to ruffle one's hair, to mess one's hair up (el pelo) || to be scared (aterrarse).

despellejadura *f* skinning (desolladura).

despellejar *vt* to skin; *despellejar un conejo* to skin a rabbit || FIG to flay, to slate, to pull to pieces (criticar) | to ruin, to fleece (arruinar).

despenalización *f* legalization.

despenalizar *vt* to legalize.

despenar *vt* to console || FAM to kill (matar).

despensa *f* pantry, larder (para guardar las provisiones) || provisions *pl*, supplies *pl* (provisiones) || storeroom, pantry (de una nave) || post of steward *o* pantryman (oficio de despensero).

despensería *f* post of steward *o* pantryman.

despensero, ra *m/f* pantryman, steward (hombre), pantrywoman (mujer).

despeñadero, ra *adj* steep, precipitous (abrupto).
◆ *m* precipice, cliff || FIG risk, danger, hazard (riesgo).

despeñamiento; despeño *m* fall, headlong fall (caída) || MED diarrhoea.

despeñar *vt* to hurl, to throw; *despeñar a alguien por un precipicio* to hurl s.o. down from a cliff, to throw s.o. over a cliff.
◆ *vpr* to hurl *o* to throw o.s. (down); *despeñarse por una roca* to hurl o.s. (down) from a cliff || to fall (down), to fall headlong (involuntariamente).

despepitar *vt* to remove the pips from, to pit.
◆ *vpr* to bawl, to shout, to rant (gritar) || to be rash, to forget o.s. (hablar o actuar descomedidamente) || *despepitarse por algo* to be dying for sth. (desear mucho), to be mad about sth. (apreciar).

desperdiciado, da *adj* wasted, squandered, gone to waste.

desperdiciador, ra *adj* wasteful (con cosas) || spendthrift, wasteful (con dinero).
◆ *m/f* spendthrift, waster (persona).

desperdiciar *vt* to waste; *desperdiciar el tiempo, la comida* to waste time, food || to waste, to squander (dinero) || to miss, to throw away, to waste; *desperdiciar una ocasión* to miss an opportunity || *ha desperdiciado todos mis consejos* he has not taken any of my advice.

desperdicio *m* waste; *desperdicio de tiempo* waste of time || *este trozo no tiene desperdicio* there is no waste on this piece of meat || FIG & FAM *no tener desperdicio* to be faultless (una obra de arte), to be good in all that he *o* she does (una persona), to be good all the way through (un libro, una película).
◆ *pl* rubbish *sing* (basura) || waste *sing*; *desperdicios de comida, de papel* waste food, paper || — *desperdicios de cocina* kitchen scraps.

desperdigar *vt* to scatter, to disperse; *mis hermanos andan desperdigados por el mundo entero* my brothers are scattered all over the world || to divide, to dissipate (la atención, la actividad).
◆ *vpr* to scatter, to disperse || to become scattered *o* dispersed.

desperecer* *vi* to perish (perecer).
◆ *vpr* to be dying, to crave, to yearn (desear).

desperezarse *vpr* to stretch (estirarse).

desperezo *m* stretch.

desperfecto *m* flaw, blemish; *hay un desperfecto en la tela* there is a flaw in the cloth || damage (deterioro) || imperfection || *sufrir desperfectos* to be *o* to get damaged.

despernada *f* splits *pl* (en el baile).

despernado, da *adj* lame (animal) || FIG footsore, weary (cansado).

despernar* *vt* to lame.

despersonalizar *vt* to depersonalize.

despertador, ra *adj* awakening, arousing.
◆ *m* alarm clock (reloj).
◆ *m/f* knocker-up, waker-up (persona).

despertar* *vt* to wake up, to wake, to awaken, to awake; *el ruido me despertó* the noise woke me up || FIG to rouse, to stir up, to awake (deseo, pasión, sentimiento) | to arouse, to awaken (la esperanza, el apetito) | to revive, to recall (recordar); *esto despierta recuerdos de mi niñez* this revives memories of my childhood | to wake up, to brighten up (espabilar).
◆ *vi/vpr* to wake up, to wake, to awake, to awaken; *se despertó a las seis de la mañana* he woke up at six in the morning || FIG to wake up, to brighten up, to liven up (espabilarse).

despertar *m* awakening; *el despertar de un pueblo* the awakening of a people.

despestañar *vt* to pluck out the eyelashes of.
◆ *vpr* FIG to strain one's eyes.

despezuñarse *vpr* to damage its hooves (un animal) || AMER to rush (apresurarse).

despiadado, da *adj* pitiless, merciless, remorseless; *una crítica despiadada* pitiless criticism || heartless, inhuman, merciless (persona).

despicar *vt* to calm down, to appease.
◆ *vpr* to get one's own back, to take one's revenge, to get even.

despichar *vt* to dry (secar) || to exude, to give out (escurrir) || AMER to squash (aplastar).
◆ *vi* FAM to kick the bucket, to snuff it (morir).

despido *m* dismissal, discharge; *despido improcedente* unfair dismissal || *notificación previa de despido* notice.

despiertamente *adv* cleverly.

despierto, ta *adj* awake || FIG quick, sharp, bright; *una muchacha muy despierta* a very bright girl | lively (vivaz) | alert (alerto).

despilfarrado, da *adj* → **despilfarrador.**

despilfarrador, ra; despilfarrado, da *adj* spendthrift, wasteful (con dinero) || wasteful (con cosas, comida, etc.).

◆ *m/f* spendthrift, squanderer, waster (con dinero) || waster (con cosas).

despilfarrar *vt* to waste, to squander (dinero) || to waste (cosas, comida, etc.).
◆ *vpr* to waste *o* to squander one's money.

despilfarro *m* wasting, squandering (acción de despilfarrar); *el despilfarro de una fortuna* the wasting of a fortune || wastefulness, wasteful spending; *el despilfarro es la ruina de la economía de un país* wasteful spending is the ruin of a country's economy || extravagance; *no pienso pagar todos tus despilfarros* I don't intend to pay for all your extravagances || *hacer un despilfarro* to throw away one's money, to squander one's money.

despimpollar *vt* AGR to trim, to prune (la vid).

despinochar *vt* to remove the husk from (el maíz).

despintar *vt* to take the paint off (quitar pintura) || FIG to misrepresent, to change (un suceso).
◆ *vi* to be worse; *éste no despinta de los demás* this one is no worse than the rest.
◆ *vpr* to fade (lo teñido) || FIG to fade from the memory of; *despintarse a alguien* to fade from s.o.'s memory || *aquel hombre no se me despintará nunca* I shall never forget that man.

despiojar *vt* to delouse (quitar los piojos a) || FIG & FAM to pull out of the gutter (sacar de la miseria).

despiole *m* AMER FAM mess (revoltijo) | muddle (lío) | fuss (jaleo).

despique *m* revenge, satisfaction (desquite).

despistado, da *adj* absentminded (distraído) || unpractical (poco práctico) || lost (desorientado); *estoy despistado* I'm lost || confused, bewildered, muddled (confuso).
◆ *m/f* scatterbrain, absentminded person || *hacerse el despistado* to act dumb (hacerse el tonto), to pretend not to see s.o. (para no saludar).

despistar *vt* to throw off the scent; *la liebre despistó a los perros* the hare threw the dogs off the scent || to put off the track, to shake off (*fam*); *despistar a la policía* to put the police off the track || to mislead, to make lose one's way, to put on the wrong road; *el letrero mal puesto me despistó* the badly placed sign misled me || FIG to mislead; *lo que me dijiste me despistó* what you told me misled me.
◆ *vi* to be misleading; *el problema es tan fácil que despista* the problem is so easy that it is misleading.
◆ *vpr* to get lost, to lose one's way (extraviarse) || to put off the track, to shake off (*fam*); *el ladrón se ha despistado de la policía* the thief has put the police off the track || to leave the road *o* the track (un coche) || FIG *se despistó y cogió mi cartera en vez de la suya* he absentmindedly *o* unthinkingly picked up my briefcase instead of his own.

despiste *m* leaving the road (de un coche) || FIG absentmindedness (distracción) | confusion, bewilderment (confusión) | mistake, slip (error) || — *momento de despiste* moment's inattentiveness || *tener un despiste enorme* to be terribly absentminded, to have one's head in the clouds (ser despistado), to be terribly bewildered *o* muddled *o* confused (estar despistado) || *tiene tanto despiste que nunca sabe qué camino tomar* he has such a poor sense of direction that he never knows which way to go.

desplacer *m* displeasure.

desplacer* *vt* to displease (disgustar) || to grieve (afligir).

desplantación *f* AGR uprooting, taking up.

desplantador *m* trowel (utensilio).

desplantar *vt* AGR to uproot, to pull up, to take up; *desplantar tomates* to pull up tomatoes.

desplante *m* bad stance (en esgrima, danza) || act of defiance *o* insolence (acción descarada) || boast (jactancia) || TAUR defiant stance [assumed in front of the bull] (véase OBSERV en ADORNO) || *hacer un desplante a uno* to defy s.o.

desplatar *vt* TECN to desilverize, to desilver, to remove the silver from.

desplatear *vt* AMER to desilver, to desilverize (lo plateado) || AMER FAM to get money out of (sacar dinero a).

desplazado, da *adj* out of place; *me encuentro desplazado aquí* I feel out of place here.

desplazamiento *m* MAR & FÍS displacement || moving, removal (acción de trasladar) || travelling, journey (viaje); *gastos de desplazamiento* travelling expenses || shifting (cambio de sitio) || movement (de tropas) || transference, swing (de votos).

desplazar *vt* to move, to shift; *desplazar una mesa* to move a table || to remove (quitar) || TECN to displace, to move; *desplazar un eje tres milímetros* to displace an axle three millimetres || FÍS & MAR to displace; *este cuerpo desplaza una mayor cantidad de agua* this body displaces a larger quantity of water || to displace, to replace; *en aquella fábrica los jóvenes han desplazado a las personas mayores* in that factory young people have displaced the older people || to transfer, to move (tropas).
◆ *vpr* to move (una cosa) || to travel; *tiene que desplazarse seis kilómetros cada día* he has to travel six kilometres every day || to swing (votos, tendencias).

desplegable *m* folder, brochure, pamphlet.

desplegadura *f* unfolding, spreading out || unfurling.

desplegar* *vt* to unfold (lo plegado); *desplegar el mantel* to unfold the tablecloth || to unfold, to open out (un periódico) || to spread out, to open out; *desplegar un mapa* to spread out a map || to spread (las alas) || to stretch out (los brazos) || to unfurl (una bandera) || to spread, to unfurl (las velas) || FIG to display, to show; *desplegar inteligencia, celo* to show intelligence, zeal || to clarify, to elucidate (aclarar) || MIL to deploy (tropas).
◆ *vpr* to spread, to unfold (las alas) || to fly, to unfurl (bandera) || MIL to deploy, to spread out.

despliegue *m* MIL deployment; *despliegue de misiles* deployment of missiles || unfolding, opening (abertura) || unfurling (de una bandera) || display, show (ostentación).

desplomar *vt* to put off the vertical *o* out of plumb || AMER to scold, to reprimand (regañar).
◆ *vpr* to lean, to tilt (inclinarse) || to topple over, to fall down, to collapse (derrumbarse); *la torre se desplomó* the tower toppled over || to drop (una cosa pesada) || to collapse (una persona); *su madre se desplomó al oír la noticia* his mother collapsed when she heard the news || to tumble, to drop (precios).

desplome *m* collapse, fall (caída) || ARQ overhang (saledizo).

desplumadura *f* plucking.

desplumar *vt* to pluck; *desplumar un ganso* to pluck a goose || FIG to fleece, to clean out (sacar el dinero).
◆ *vpr* to moult [US to molt] (ave).

despoblación *f*; **despoblamiento** *m* depopulation || — *despoblación del campo* rural depopulation, drift from the land *o* to the cities || *despoblación de un río* unstocking || *despoblación forestal* deforestation, clearing.

despoblado, da *adj* depopulated (con pocos habitantes) || uninhabited (sin habitantes) || deserted (desierto) || — *despoblado de árboles* deforested || *frente despoblada* receding hairline.
◆ *m* wilderness, deserted place || *en despoblado* in the wilds.

despoblamiento *m* → **despoblación.**

despoblar* *vt* to depopulate; *la peste ha despoblado el país* the plague has depopulated the country || to clear (despojar); *despoblar un campo de hierbas* to clear a field of grass || FIG to lay waste, to ravage (devastar) || *despoblar de árboles* to deforest, to clear.
◆ *vpr* to become depopulated *o* deserted (un lugar).

despoetizar *vt* to take all poetry out of; *despoetizar la vida* to take all poetry out of life.

despojar *vt* to deprive, to strip, to despoil (p us), to divest; *despojar a uno de todo lo que posee, de sus derechos* to deprive s.o. of all he possesses, of his rights; *despojaron la iglesia de todas sus obras de arte* they stripped the church of all its works of art || to strip, to divest; *despojar a uno de sus vestidos* to strip s.o. of his clothes || to strip; *despojar un árbol de su corteza* to strip a tree of its bark || FAM to clean out, to fleece (quitarle todo el dinero) || JUR to dispossess.
◆ *vpr* to give up, to forsake; *despojarse de sus bienes* to give up one's wealth || to take off; *despojarse de su abrigo* to take off one's coat || BOT to shed (de hojas) || FIG to put aside; *despojarse de su orgullo* to put aside one's pride.

despojo *m* depriving, divestment, divestiture || stripping || dispossession (desposeimiento) || plundering, despoiling (robo) || booty, plunder, spoils *pl* (botín).
◆ *pl* offal *sing* (de animales) || leftovers (de comida) || remains (cadáver) || rubble *sing* (de un edificio) || *despojos mortales* mortal remains.

despolarización *f* FÍS depolarization.

despolarizador, ra *adj* FÍS depolarizing.
◆ *m* FÍS depolarizer.

despolarizar *vt* FÍS to depolarize.

despopularizar *vt* to make unpopular.
◆ *vpr* to lose popularity.

desportilladura *f*; **desportillamiento** *m* chipping (acción) || chip (en un jarro, etc.).

desportillar *vt* to chip (una vasija).

desposado, da *adj* newly married || handcuffed (preso).
◆ *m/f* newlywed (recién casado).

desposar *vt* to marry, to wed (casar).
◆ *vpr* to get engaged (contraer esponsales); *desposarse con* to get engaged to || to get married (*con* to), to marry (casarse).

desposeer *vt* to dispossess; *desposeer a un propietario de su casa* to dispossess an owner of his house || to oust (de un cargo) || to remove (de la autoridad).
◆ *vpr* to give up, to renounce.

desposeído, da *m/f* *los desposeídos* the have-nots.

desposeimiento *m* dispossession.

desposorios *m pl* engagement *sing*, betrothal *sing* (ant) (esponsales) || marriage *sing* (matrimonio) || wedding *sing*, marriage ceremony *sing* (boda).

déspota *m* despot; *Nerón fue un déspota cruel* Nero was a cruel despot; *el niño es un verdadero déspota* the child is a real despot.

despóticamente *adv* despotically.

despótico, ca *adj* despotic; *un gobierno, un marido despótico* a despotic government, husband.

despotismo *m* despotism; *el despotismo ilustrado* enlightened despotism.

despotizar *vt* AMER to tyrannize, to oppress.

despotricar *vi* FAM to rant on, to carry on (hablar sin reparo) || FIG *despotricar contra alguien* to run s.o. down.

despotrique *m* FAM carrying on, ranting on.

despreciable *adj* despicable, contemptible; *una persona despreciable* a despicable person || negligible (insignificante); *un error despreciable* a negligible error || worthless, paltry (de poca monta).

despreciador, ra *adj* scornful, contemptuous.

despreciar *vt* to despise, to scorn; *despreciar a un empleado* to despise an employee || to depreciate, to disparage, to belittle (menospreciar) || to neglect, to ignore (no hacer caso de); *no hay que despreciar esta posibilidad* we should not neglect this possibility || to ignore; *despreciar un peligro* to ignore a danger || to snub, to slight, to spurn (desairar).

despreciativo, va *adj* scornful, contemptuous; *un gesto despreciativo* a scornful gesture.

desprecio *m* scorn, contempt, disdain; *con desprecio de las convenciones* with contempt for convention || slight, snub (desaire) || *con desprecio de su propia vida* without a thought for his own life, with disregard for his own life.

desprender *vt* to remove, to detach; *desprender un sello del sobre* to remove a stamp from an envelope || to release, to loosen (soltar) || to take off; *desprender una manga de una chaqueta* to take a sleeve off a jacket || to give off; *esta flor desprende un olor agradable* this flower gives off a pleasant smell || to throw off (chispas) || to give off (gas).
◆ *vpr* to come off *o* away; *la etiqueta se ha desprendido de la botella* the label has come off the bottle || to come out *o* off; *la manga se desprendió de su vestido* the sleeve came out of her dress *o* came off her dress || to be given off, to emanate (olor) || MED to be detached (la retina) || to fly off, to fly out, to shoot out (chispas) || to be given off, to issue (el gas) || to shed (la piel) || FIG to part with, to forsake, to give up; *se tuvo que desprender de sus joyas* she had to part with her jewels | to get rid of, to do away with; *desprenderse de lo que no le interesa a uno* to get rid of everything that doesn't interest one | to get free (de estorbos) | to cast *o* to put aside; *desprenderse de sus escrúpulos* to cast aside one's scruples || to follow, to be implied (deducirse); *de todo aquello se desprenden dos conclusiones* two conclusions follow from all that, two conclusions are implied by all that || — *de aquí se desprende que...* it can be deduced from this that..., from this it follows that..., this implies that... || *por lo que se desprende de* judging by, going by.

desprendido, da *adj* loose, detached (una pieza) || generous, unselfish, altruistic (generoso) || disinterested (desinteresado).

desprendimiento *m* unselfishness, generosity (generosidad) || desinterestedness (desinterés) || unsticking (despegadura) || separation (de cápsula de cohete) || giving off, emission (de un olor, del gas) || shedding (de la piel) || ARTES deposition (de Cristo) || — MED *desprendimiento de la retina* detachment of the retina || *desprendimiento de tierras* landslide.

despreocupación *f* lack of care, unconcern (falta de preocupación) || carelessness, negligence (descuido) || impartiality, freedom from bias, open-mindedness (imparcialidad) || unconcernedness, indifference.

despreocupado, da *adj* carefree, unconcerned (sin preocupación) || unworried (sin inquietud) || careless, negligent (descuidado) || unconcerned, indifferent (indiferente) || impartial, unbiased (imparcial) || casual; *despreocupado en el vestir* casual in his dress.

despreocuparse *vpr* to be neglectful, not to bother (descuidarse) || to stop worrying (dejar de preocuparse) || to be unconcerned *o* indifferent (ser indiferente) || *despreocuparse de* to forget.

desprestigiar *vt* to discredit, to cause (s.o.) to lose prestige, to ruin (s.o.'s) reputation; *su comportamiento lo ha desprestigiado* his behaviour has ruined his reputation || to discredit, to disparage, to decry (criticar); *desprestigiar a sus colegas* to discredit one's colleagues; *una marca injustamente desprestigiada* an unjustly disparaged brand.
◆ *vpr* to lose prestige, to lose one's reputation, to fall into discredit; *el rey se desprestigió completamente* the king lost all prestige.

desprestigio *m* loss of reputation *o* prestige, discredit (descrédito).

despresurización *f* depressurization.

desprevenidamente *adv* without warning, unexpectedly (sin previo aviso) || unawares, by surprise (de improviso).

desprevenido, da *adj* improvident (imprevisor) || unawares, unprepared, off guard; *coger a una persona desprevenida* to catch a person unawares.

desproporción *f* disproportion, lack of proportion.

desproporcionado, da *adj* disproportionate, disproportional, disproportioned, out of proportion.

desproporcionar *vt* to disproportion.

despropósito *m* irrelevant remark, nonsense, rubbish; *decir muchos despropósitos* to make a lot of irrelevant remarks, to talk a lot of nonsense || blunder (metedura de pata) || *con despropósito* irrelevantly.

desprotección *f* lack of protection.

desprotegido, da *adj* unprotected.

desproveer *vt* to deprive.

desprovisto, ta *adj* lacking, without, devoid; *desprovisto de interés* lacking interest, devoid of interest || *estar desprovisto de* to lack, to be lacking.

despueble; despueblo *m* depopulation.

después *adv* afterwards, later; *no tengo tiempo ahora, después hablaremos* I haven't got time now, we'll have a talk afterwards; *varios días después* several days later || then, next, afterwards (a continuación); *después fuimos a la playa* then we went to the beach; *hay un pasillo y después una habitación grande* there is a corridor and then a large room || — *después de* after; *después de la guerra* after the war; *después de cenar* after supper; *mi nombre viene después del tuyo en la lista* my name comes after yours on the list; from, since; *después de esa fecha no la ha vuelto a ver* since that date he hasn't seen her; from, after; *después de hoy no habrá reuniones* from today there will be no meetings; después de (con participio pasado) once; *después de hecho* once done; *después de cerrada la ventana* once the window was *o* had been closed || *después de hacerlo, después de haberlo hecho* having done it, after doing it || *después de todo* after all || *después que* after; *llegó después que yo* he arrived after me; after, when; *después que saliste, lo hicimos* we did it when *o* after you (had) left; *después que llegue hablaremos de ello* we shall talk about it when he arrives *o* when *o* after he has arrived || (ant) *después que* since (desde que) || *el año después* the year after, the next year, the following year; *el día después* the day after, the next day, the following day || *poco después* shortly after, soon after.

despulmonarse *vpr* FAM to shout o.s. hoarse (desgañitarse).

despulpar *vt* to pulp || *máquina de despulpar* pulper.

despumar *vt* to skim (espumar).

despuntado, da *adj* blunt.

despuntador *m* AMER pick, pickaxe [of miner].

despuntar *vt* to blunt, to break off the point of (embotar) || MAR to round (pasar una punta, un cabo) || to cut away the empty combs of (a beehive).
◆ *vi* to bud (las flores), to sprout (las plantas) || FIG to break (la luz del día); *el alba despunta* the dawn breaks | to show intelligence *o* wit (manifestar inteligencia) | to excel, to stand out; *este niño despunta entre los demás* this child stands out amongst the rest; *despuntó por sus cualidades de orador* he excelled for his qualities as an orator || FIG *al despuntar el alba* at day-break.

despunte *m* blunting (embotadura) || AMER twig, sprig (rama).

desquebrajar *vt* to crack, to split (resquebrajar).

desquejar *vt* AGR to slip.

desqueje *m* AGR slipping.

desquiciado, da *adj* FIG unbalanced, unsettled, deranged; *una persona desquiciada* an unbalanced person | unsettled, topsy-turvy, mad; *vivimos en un mundo desquiciado* we live in an unsettled world.

desquiciador, ra *adj* distressing, disturbing (que turba) || unsettling (que trastorna).

desquiciamiento *m* FIG unsettling, perturbation (perturbación) | unsettled state, unsettledness (desequilibrio) | disturbance (trastorno).

desquiciar *vt* to unhinge (una puerta) || FIG to distress, to disturb (perturbar) | to upset (trastornar) | to unsettle, to unhinge; *la guerra ha desquiciado a muchos hombres* the war has unsettled many men | to unbalance, to unhinge, to derange (afectar profundamente).
◆ *vpr* to come off its hinges (una puerta) || to be disturbed (perturbarse).

desquicio *m* AMER ⟶ **desquiciamiento.**

desquijerar *vt* ARQ to tenon.

desquitar *vt* to compensate; *desquitar a uno por los estropicios producidos* to compensate s.o. for the damage caused.
◆ *vpr* to make good, to recoup; *desquitarse de una pérdida* to make good a loss || to make up for it; *hoy no he dormido mucho pero me desquitaré mañana* I haven't slept much today but I'll make up for it tomorrow || to take (one's) revenge, to get one's revenge, to get even; *el equipo se desquitó* the team got its revenge.

desquite *m* revenge; *tomar un desquite* to take revenge || compensation (compensación) || DEP return match || *en desquite* in return, in retaliation.

desramar *vt* to prune, to lop (podar).

desrame *m* pruning, lopping.

desratización *f* deratting, deratization.

desratizar *vt* to derat, to clear of rats.

desrazonable *adj* FAM unreasonable.

desrielar *vi* AMER to derail, to run off the rails.

desriñonar *vt* to break the back of, to cripple (derrengar).

desrizar *vt* to take the curls out of (el pelo).

desrodrigar *vt* AGR to remove the prop from.

destacado, da *adj* distinguished, prominent, outstanding (notable); *persona destacada* distinguished person || outstanding, remarkable; *un trabajo destacado* an outstanding piece of work || outstanding; *los hechos más destacados* the most outstanding events || choice; *ocupar un lugar destacado en la jerarquía eclesiástica* to occupy a choice position in the ecclesiastical hierarchy.

destacamento *m* MIL detachment, detail.

destacar *vt* MIL to detach, to detail (tropas); *destacar unos soldados para una expedición peligrosa* to detach some soldiers for a dangerous expedition || FIG to underline, to point out, to emphasize; *conviene destacar la importancia de esta decisión* it is appropriate to underline the importance of this decision | to make (sth.) stand out, to highlight, to bring out; *el pintor quiso destacar a sus personajes* the painter wished to make his characters stand out | to honour, to confer an honour upon; *destacar a una persona por los servicios prestados* to honour a person for services rendered.
◆ *vi/vpr* to stand out; *destaca por su inteligencia* he stands out for his intelligence.
◆ *vpr* to stand out, to be highlighted (cosas, colores); *la silueta de la torre se destacaba en el cielo* the silhouette of the tower stood out against the sky || to break away, to draw ahead (corredor) || to stand out (descollar).

destajador *m* TECN blacksmith's hammer.

destajar *vt* to settle the conditions for [a job] || to cut (naipes) || AMER to cut up (cortar).

destajero, ra; destajista *m/f* pieceworker.

destajo *m* piecework || — *a destajo* by the job, by the piece; *pagado a destajo* paid by the piece || FAM *hablar a destajo* to talk nineteen to the dozen || *precio a destajo* piecework price || *trabajar a destajo* to be on piecework (por piezas), to work hard (trabajar mucho) || *trabajo a destajo* piecework.

destalonar *vt* to wear down the heel of; *destalonar el calzado* to wear down the heels of one's shoes || to detach, to tear off [leaves from a stub book].

destapado *m*; **destapadura** *f* uncorking (tapón), opening, uncapping (chapa), removal of (the) lid (tapadera).

destapar *vt* to uncork (quitar el tapón) || to take the top *o* cap off, to uncap, to open (quitar la chapa) || to take the lid off, to open, to remove the lid from (quitar la tapa) || to open (abrir) || to uncover; *destapar al niño* to uncover the child || *destapar la cama* to pull the covers back.
◆ *vpr* to throw off one's bedclothes (en la cama) || to uncover o.s., to get uncovered (descubrirse) || FIG to unbosom o.s., to open one's heart; *se destapó con su amigo* he opened his heart to his friend | to reveal *o* to show one's real *o* true self (revelarse) | to turn up; *se destapó con un regalo estupendo* she turned up with a fantastic present.

destape *m* striptease || FIG liberalization.

destapiar *vt* to pull down the walls of.

destaponar *vt* to uncork (una botella) || to unplug, to unstop.

destarar *vt* to deduct the tare on (de un peso).

destartalado, da *adj* rambling, ramshackle; *una casa destartalada* a rambling house || rickety (coche).

destejar *vt* to untile the roof of; *destejar una casa* to untile the roof of a house || FIG to expose, to leave unprotected (descubrir).

·**destejer** *vt* to unweave, to undo, to unravel; *Penélope destejía por la noche la tela que tejía durante el día* Penelope unwove at night the cloth that she wove during the day || FIG to undo.

destellar *vi* to flash (con luz repentina) || to sparkle, to glitter (piedra preciosa, etc.) || to twinkle (estrellas).
◆ *vt* to flash, to give *o* to send off; *destellar rayos de luz* to flash rays of light.

destello *m* twinkling (de las estrellas) || flash, flash of light (luz repentina) || sparkle, glitter (de una piedra preciosa) || FIG scrap, bit (atisbo) | flash, glimmer, spark; *destello de genio* flash of wit.

destemplado, da *adj* harsh, angry, gruff (irritado); *con voz destemplada* in a harsh voice || bad-tempered, irritable (carácter) || unsettled, unpleasant (tiempo) || MÚS out-of-tune, out of tune, untuned; *una guitarra destemplada* an out-of-tune guitar; *la guitarra está destemplada* the guitar is out of tune | inharmonious, dissonant (voz, música) || MED feverish, a little feverish, off colour || ARTES inharmonious (cuadro) || TECN untempered, softened, weakened (acero).

destemplanza *f* unsettledness (del tiempo) || intemperance, lack of moderation (abuso) || FIG irascibility, irritability (impaciencia) | lack of moderation *o* restraint (falta de moderación) || MED slight fever || MÚS inharmoniousness (de voz, de música) | dissonance (de un instrumento).

destemplar *vt* MÚS to put out of tune, to untune || to unsettle (el tiempo) || to untemper (el acero) || MED to give a slight fever || to infuse (en infusión).
◆ *vpr* to become unsettled (el tiempo) || MÚS to go *o* to get out of tune (un instrumento) || MED to have a touch of fever || to become *o* to get angry (irritarse) || TECN to lose its temper (acero) || AMER to have one's teeth on edge (sentir dentera).

destemple *m* MÚS dissonance (de un instrumento) | inharmoniousness (de voz, de música) || TECN loss of temper, untempering (del acero u otros metales).

desteñir* *vt* to discolour [*US* to discolor], to fade; *el sol ha desteñido las cortinas* the sun has faded the curtains || to discolour; *la camisa roja ha desteñido la sábana* the red shirt has discoloured the sheet || *esta tela no destiñe* this fabric will not run.
◆ *vpr* to lose its colour [*US* to lose its color], to discolour [*US* to discolor], to fade; *desteñirse con el uso* to lose its colour with use.

desternillarse *vpr* *desternillarse de risa* to split one's sides laughing || *es cosa de desternillarse de risa* it's a scream, it's enough to make you die laughing.

desterrado, da *adj/s* exile.

desterrar* *vt* to banish, to exile (término político y jurídico) || to remove the earth from [roots of plants, minerals] (quitar la tierra) || FIG to banish, to expel; *desterrar la tristeza* to banish sadness | to abolish, to do away with (abolir).
◆ *vpr* to go into exile (exilarse), to leave one's country (abandonar su país).

desterronadora *f* AGR clod crusher (arado).

desterronar *vt* to break up *o* to crush the clods in.

desterronamiento *m* breaking-up *o* crushing of (the) clods.

destetar *vt* to wean.
◆ *vpr* to be weaned.

destete *m* weaning.

destiempo (a) *adv* inopportunely, at an inopportune moment, at the wrong moment; *lo hace todo a destiempo* he does everything at the wrong moment.

destierro *m* exile, banishment; *vivir en el destierro* to live in exile || place of exile (lugar).

destilación *f* distillation || secretion, exudence (de humores).

destiladera *f* still, alembic (alambique).

destilado *m* distillate (producto de la destilación).

destilador, ra *adj* distilling.
◆ *m* still, alembic (alambique) || filter (filtro) || distiller (persona).

destilar *vt* to distil, to distill; *destilar vino* to distil wine || to exude, to secrete; *destilar pus, veneno* to exude pus, venom || to filter, to filtrate (filtrar) || FIG to exude; *este libro destila una profunda amargura* this book exudes a profound bitterness.
◆ *vi* to trickle, to drip (gotear) || to ooze, to seep, to exude (rezumar).
◆ *vpr* to be distilled; *la gasolina se destila del petróleo* petrol is distilled off petroleum || to filter (filtrarse).

destilería *f* distillery.

destinación *f* destination.

destinar *vt* to destine; *destinar un buque al transporte de carbón* to destine a boat for the transportation of coal; *destinar a su hijo al foro* to destine one's son for the bar || to appoint, to assign; *lo han destinado al consulado de España* he has been appointed to the Spanish consulate || to send; *fue destinado a Madrid de cónsul* he was sent to Madrid as consul || to post, to station; *militar destinado en Burgos* soldier posted in Burgos || COM to allot, to earmark, to assign, to appropriate; *destinar una cantidad* to earmark a sum of money || to address; *un paquete destinado a ti* a parcel addressed to you.
◆ *vpr* to intend to take up, to intend to enter (pensar dedicarse).

destinatario, ria *m/f* addressee (de una carta) || consignee; *el destinatario de un paquete* the consignee of a parcel || payee (de un giro).

destino *m* destiny, fate, lot, fortune (hado); *un destino desgraciado* a hapless fate || function, use; *este edificio ha cambiado de destino* this building has changed function || destination; *el destino de un barco* the destination of a ship || post, station (de un militar) || position, post (colocación, empleo) || earmarking (de dinero) || — *con destino a* bound for, going to; *barco con destino a África* ship bound for Africa; to (tren), going to, for (viajeros), to, addressed to; *cartas con destino a Madrid* letters to Madrid || FIG *dar destino a* to find a home for, to put to use || *estación* or *lugar de destino* destination || *llegar a destino* to arrive at *o* to reach one's destination || *salir con destino a* to leave for.

destitución *f* dismissal, removal from office *o* from one's post, discharge; *destitución de un ministro* removal of a minister from office.

destituidor, ra *adj* who *o* which dismisses.

destituir* *vt* to dismiss, to remove from office *o* from one's post, to discharge; *destituir a un jefe de Estado* to remove a Head of State from office || to deprive (privar).

destocar *vt* (p us) to ruffle the hair of (despeinar).
◆ *vpr* to take off one's hat (one's scarf, etc.) (descubrirse).

destorcer* *vt* to untwist; *destorcer un cable* to untwist a cable || to straighten (out) (enderezar); *destorcer una varilla* to straighten a stick.
◆ *vpr* to become untwisted, to untwist || to straighten (out) || MAR to drift off course, to drift (salirse un barco de su ruta).

destornillado, da *adj* FAM screwy, nutty, dotty (atolondrado).

destornillador *m* screwdriver || FAM screwdriver (bebida).

destornillamiento *m* unscrewing.

destornillar *vt* to unscrew; *destornillar una bisagra* to unscrew a hinge.
◆ *vpr* to come unscrewed || FAM to go round the bend *o* round the twist *o* off one's rocker (perder el juicio).

destrabar *vt* to unfetter, to untie || to separate, to disconnect (cosas).
◆ *vpr* to get loose *o* free, to free o.s. (liberarse) || to come apart *o* away (separarse).

destral *m* hatchet, small axe.

destramar *vt* to unweave, to undo the weft of.

destrenzar *vt* to unbraid, to unplait.

destreza *f* skill (habilidad) || dexterity (agilidad) || (ant) fencing [sport] || — *este prestidigitador tiene mucha destreza* this magician is very skilful || *obrar con destreza* to act skilfully *o* deftly.

destripado; destripamiento *m* gutting (del pescado) || disembowelling.

destripador, ra *adj* ripper.

destripar *vt* to gut (el pescado) || to disembowel (un animal, una persona) || to rip open (una cosa); *destripar un colchón* to rip open a mattress || to crush, to squash (despachurrar) || FIG to ruin, to ruin the effect of [joke, etc.] || AGR *destripar los terrones* to crush *o* to break up (the) clods.

destripaterrones *m inv* FIG & FAM clodhopper.

destrísimo, ma *adj* very dextrous *o* skilful.

destronamiento *m* dethronement || FIG overthrow.

destronar *vt* to dethrone, to depose || FIG to overthrow (un gobierno), to supplant (a una persona).

destroncar *vt* to chop *o* to cut down, to fell (un árbol) || FIG to maim, to mutilate (lastimar) | to upset, to ruin, to spoil, to thwart (proyectos) | to clip [(s.o.'s) wings (a una persona) | to tire out, to wear out, to exhaust (cansar) | to interrupt (un discurso) | to mutilate, to retrench (a text) (cortar) || AMER to uproot (descuajar).

destroyer *m* MAR destroyer (destructor).

destrozar *vt* to break (into pieces), to smash, to shatter (romper) || to tear up, to tear to shreds; *destrozar un libro* to tear up a book || to ruin, to spoil, to smash, to dash (estropear) || MIL to wipe out, to smash, to crush (deshacer un ejército) | to rout (derrotar) || FIG to break; *destrozar el corazón de alguien* to break s.o.'s heart | to ruin, to mar; *destrozar la carrera, la salud de alguien* to ruin s.o.'s career, health | to ruin, to upset, to spoil; *su llegada ha destrozado mis planes* his arrival has ruined my plans | to dissipate (una fortuna) | to shatter, to tire out, to wear out, to exhaust; *estoy destrozado de tanto andar* I'm shattered from all this walking | to shatter; *la triste noticia lo ha destrozado* the sad news has shattered him.
◆ *vpr* to break (into pieces), to smash, to shatter.

destrozo *m* destruction || rout (derrota).
◆ *pl* damage *sing* (daño) || ruins, debris *sing* (pedazos).

destrozón, ona *adj* destructive (que lo rompe todo) || hard on one's clothes (que rompe la ropa).
◆ *m/f* destructive person.

destrucción *f* destruction.

destructible *adj* destructible.

destructividad *f* destructiveness.

destructivo, va *adj* destructive.

destructor, ra *adj* destructive.
◆ *m/f* destructive person.
◆ *m* MAR destroyer (buque).

destruible *adj* destructible.

destruir* *vt* to demolish, to destroy; *destruir una casa* to demolish a house || to destroy; *destruir un país, un ejército* to destroy a country, an army || FIG to destroy, to dash (esperanza) | to destroy, to ruin, to wreck (proyecto) | to demolish, to refute (argumento).
◆ *vpr* MAT to cancel (each other) out.

desuello *m* FIG effrontery, impudence (descaro) || skinning, flaying.

desuerar *vt* to drain the whey from (milk).

desuero *m* draining of the whey.

desuncir *vt* to unyoke [oxen].

desunidamente *adv* separately.

desunión *f* separation, disunion, disjunction || discord, disunity, dissension; *la desunión de los países, de una familia* the discord between countries, in a family.

desunir *vt* to separate, to disunite, to disjoin || to disunite, to bring about discord between; *la cuestión de la esclavitud desunió a los norteamericanos* the question of slavery disunited the Americans.

desusadamente *adv* behind the times, out of date (anticuadamente) || uncommonly.

desusado, da *adj* out of date, antiquated, old-fashioned (anticuado); *modos desusados* antiquated ways || obsolete, archaic (caído en desuso); *palabra desusada* obsolete word || uncommon, rare (poco usado) || unusual, strange (extraño); *hablar en tono desusado* to speak in a strange tone of voice.

desuso *m* disuse, obsolescence, desuetude (p us); *caer en desuso* to fall into disuse || *expresión caída en desuso* obsolete expression.

desvaído, da *adj* pale, dull, faded (descolorido) || vague, blurred (borroso) || FIG dull, spiritless (de poca personalidad) | lanky (desgarbado).

desvainadura *f* shelling [of peas, etc.].

desvainar *vt* to shell (legumbres).

desvalido, da *adj* destitute, needy.
◆ *m/f* destitute *o* needy person || *socorrer a los desvalidos* to help the needy *o* the destitute.

desvalijador, ra *m/f* robber, thief (ladrón) || burglar (saqueador).

desvalijamiento; desvalijo *m* theft, robbery.

desvalijar *vt* to rob (robar a alguien) || to steal (robar algo) || to burgle (saquear) || FIG to strip (bare); *cuando vienen sus nietos le desvalijan la despensa* when his grandchildren come they strip his larder bare.

desvalimiento *m* destitution, need.

desvalorar *vt* to devalue, to devaluate (moneda) || to depreciate (una cosa) || to discredit (desacreditar).

desvalorización *f* depreciation, fall in value (de una cosa) || devaluation (de la moneda).

desvalorizar *vt* to depreciate, to reduce the value of (una cosa) || to devalue, to devaluate (la moneda).

desván *m* attic, garret, loft.

desvanecedor *m* FOT vignetter, mask.

desvanecer* *vt* to dispel, to make disappear, to disperse, to dissipate; *el viento desvanece el humo* the wind dispels smoke || to tone down (colores) || to blur (los contornos) || FIG to dispel, to remove, to banish, to dismiss (temores, sospechas, etc.) || FOT to vignette, to mask || RAD to fade.
◆ *vpr* to disperse, to dissipate, to be dispelled (el humo, etc.) || FIG to disappear, to vanish (desaparecer) | to faint, to swoon (desmayarse) | to fade, to die (recuerdos) | to lose its flavours (perder el sabor) | to pride o.s. (enorgullecerse).

desvanecido, da *adj* vain, conceited (vanidoso) || smug, complacent, self-satisfied (presumido) || MED faint; *caí desvanecido* I fell in a faint.

desvanecimiento *m* dispersal, dissipation (del humo) || toning-down (de los colores) || dispelling, driving-away, removal (de sospechas, dudas, temores) || disappearance (desaparición) || MED fainting fit, faint, swoon (desmayo) || FIG smugness, complacency, self-satisfaction (presunción) | arrogance, haughtiness (altanería) || RAD fading (of signals).

desvarar *vt* MAR to refloat.
◆ *vi* to slide, to slip (resbalar).

desvariar *vi* to be delirious, to rave (enfermo o loco) || to talk nonsense (desatinar).

desvarío *m* delirium, raving (enfermo o loco) || FIG foolish remark, piece of nonsense (desatino) | wandering, raving; *los desvaríos de una imaginación enfermiza* the wanderings of an unhealthy imagination | act of folly *o* madness; *la compra de esta casa ha sido un desvarío* buying this house was an act of madness | vicissitude; *los desvaríos de la fortuna* the vicissitudes of fortune | whim (capricho).

desvelado, da *adj* awake, unable to sleep; *se quedó desvelado toda la noche* he stayed awake all night, he was unable to sleep all night.

desvelar *vt* to prevent (s.o.) *o* to stop (s.o.) from sleeping, to keep (s.o.) awake; *el café desvela* coffee keeps you awake; *las preocupaciones desvelan a todo el mundo* worries keep everyone awake.
◆ *vpr* to stay awake (no poder dormir) || FIG to devote o.s., to dedicate o.s.; *una madre que se desvela por sus hijos* a mother who devotes herself to her children || *desvelarse por que todo esté bien* to take great pains to see that everything is right.

desvelo *m* insomnia || trouble, pains *pl* (trabajo); *todos sus desvelos resultaron inútiles* all his trouble was *o* all his pains were of no avail || effort (esfuerzo); *merced a mis desvelos* thanks to my efforts || worry, care (preocupación) || devotion, dedication; *el desvelo por la causa común* dedication to the common cause.

desvenar *vt* to remove the veins from [meat] (de la carne) || MIN to extract (ore) from a vein || to strip, to remove the strings *o* veins from (el tabaco).

desvencijado, da *adj* insecure, unsteady, shaky; *una puerta desvencijada* an insecure door || ramshackle, tumbledown, dilapidated; *una casa desvencijada* a ramshackle house || rickety; *una silla desvencijada* a rickety chair || broken-down, ramshackle; *una máquina desvencijada* a broken-down machine.

desvencijar *vt* to put out of action (un mecanismo) || to break (romper) || to ruin (estropear) || to weaken (debilitar) || to dilapidate (una casa, etc.) || to exhaust (agotar).
◆ *vpr* to come *o* to fall apart, to come *o* to fall to pieces (puerta, silla, máquina) || to dilapidate, to fall apart, to go to ruin (una casa).

desvendar *vt* to remove a bandage from, to unbandage (quitar una venda).

desventaja *f* disadvantage; *en su desventaja* to his disadvantage || drawback, disadvantage; *las desventajas de una política* the drawbacks of a policy || handicap; *su peso es una desventaja* his weight is a handicap || — *estar en desventaja* to be at a disadvantage || *tener una desventaja de dos goles* to be two goals down, to be losing by two goals.

desventajoso, sa *adj* disadvantageous, unfavourable [*US* unfavorable] || disadvantageous, which has its drawbacks || unprofitable (no provechoso).

desventura *f* misfortune, (piece of) bad luck (desgracia) || misery, unhappiness (infortunio).

desventuradamente *adv* unfortunately.

desventurado, da *adj* unfortunate, wretched (desgraciado) || poor (pobre) || spiritless, timid (tímido) || ill-fated, disastrous; *un día desventurado* one ill-fated day || unlucky (de poca suerte).
◆ *m/f* poor wretch, poor devil || *socorrer a los desventurados* to help the unfortunate.

desvergonzadamente *adv* impudently, cheekily (descaradamente) || insolently, rudely (insolentemente).

desvergonzado, da *adj* impudent, cheeky (descarado) || insolent, shameless (sinvergüenza).
◆ *m/f* impudent *o* cheeky person || insolent *o* shameless person.

desvergonzarse* *vpr* to go to the bad, to get into bad ways, to go downhill (perder la vergüenza) || to swallow one's shame (vencer la vergüenza); *desvergonzarse a hacer algo* to swallow one's shame and do sth. || to be rude *o* insolent; *desvergonzarse con uno* to be rude to s.o.

desvergüenza *f* impudence, nerve, effrontery, cheek (descaro); *tuvo la desvergüenza de pedírmelo* he had the cheek to ask me for it || insolence (insolencia) || dissoluteness, wantonness, shamelessness (mala conducta) || rude thing, shameless remark; *decir desvergüenzas* to say rude things, to make shameless remarks.

desvestir* *vt* to strip, to lay bare (una cosa) || to unclothe, to undress, to strip (a una persona) || FIG *desvestir un santo para vestir otro* to rob Peter to pay Paul.
◆ *vpr* to undress, to take off one's clothes.

desviación; deviación *f* deviation, deflection; *desviación de la luz, de la aguja imantada* deviation of light, of a magnetic needle || curvature; *desviación de la columna vertebral* curvature of the vertebral column || diversion, detour; *hay una nueva desviación en la carretera* there is a new diversion in the road || departure, deviation (de principios) || deflection (de un golpe).

desviacionismo *m* deviationism.

desviacionista *adj/s* deviationist.

desviar *vt* to deviate, to deflect; *desviar una línea* to deflect a line || to deflect, to turn aside, to ward off; *desviar un golpe* to deflect a blow || to deflect (el balón) || to parry (en esgrima) || to divert (un río) || to divert (un avión, un barco, etc.); *desviar a uno de su ruta* to divert s.o. from his route || FIG to dissuade, to put off; *desviar a uno de un proyecto* to put s.o. off a plan, to dissuade s.o. from a plan | to keep *o* to steer clear of *o* away from; *desviar a uno de las malas compañías* to steer s.o. clear of bad company | to change, to turn; *desviar la conversación* to change the subject || *desviar la mirada* to look aside *o* away, to turn away.
◆ *vpr* to be deflected *o* deviated (una línea) || to be deflected *o* turned aside *o* warded off (un golpe) || to change *o* to alter (its) course (un barco, un avión) || to drift, to go *o* to sail off course (un barco) || to go *o* to fly off course (un avión) (a causa de una tempestad, etc.) || to take a detour; *se desviaron para evitar el tráfico* they took a detour to avoid the traffic || to go astray, to lose one's way (descaminarse) || to stray; *desviarse de su camino* to stray from one's route || FIG to stray, to wander, to get away from; *desviarse del tema* to stray from the point | to deviate (de los principios).

desvinculación *f* freeing, releasing, discharging (de un compromiso) || cutting-off, separation.

desvincular *vt* to free, to release, to discharge; *desvincular a uno de un compromiso* to free s.o. from a commitment || to cut off, to separate; *desvinculado de su familia* cut off from his family || *desvincularse con* to break one's links with, to lose contact with.

desvío *m* deviation, deflection (desviación) || diversion, detour (en una carretera) || coldness, indifference (frialdad).

desvirgar *vt* to deflower, to devirginate.

desvirtuar *vt* to impair, to spoil (estropear) || to adulterate, to spoil (adulterar) || FIG to detract from (quitar valor a); *tu argumento no desvirtúa mi razonamiento* your argument doesn't detract from my reasoning | to distort (viciar); *desvirtuar el sentido de una palabra* to distort the meaning of a word | to misrepresent, to distort; *desvirtuar los hechos* to misrepresent the facts.
◆ *vpr* to spoil, to go off (el vino, el café).

desvitalizar *vt* to devitalize.

desvitrificación *f* devitrification.

desvitrificar *vt* to devitrify.

desvivirse *vpr* to be dying, to long; *desvivirse por ir al teatro* to be dying to go to the theatre || to be madly in love, to be head over heels in love; *desvivirse por una chica* to be madly in love with a girl || to do one's utmost, to strive; *desvivirse por hacer el bien* to strive to do good || to devote o.s. to, to dedicate o.s. to, to live for; *una madre que se desvive por sus hijos* a mother who devotes herself to her children.

desyemar *vt* AGR to disbud.

desyerbar *vt* to weed.

detal; detall *m* *vender al detall* to retail, to sell retail.
— OBSERV *Al detall* is a Gallicism for *al por menor*.

detalladamente *adv* in detail.

detallar *vt* to relate in detail, to detail, to give the details of (contar con detalles) || COM to retail, to sell retail.

detalle *m* detail || kind thought, nice gesture *o* thought (cosa amable); *eso fue un detalle de su parte* that was a nice thought on his part || AMER retailing || — *ahí está el detalle* that's the secret || COM *al detalle* retail || *con todo el detalle* in full detail, in great detail || *no meterse en detalles* not to go into details || *no perder detalle* not to miss a thing, to miss nothing || *¡qué detalle!* how thoughtful!, how considerate! || *sin entrar en detalles* without going into details || *tener muchos detalles con una persona* to be very considerate towards s.o. *o* with s.o. || *tuvo el detalle de traerme flores* he was thoughtful enough to bring me flowers || *un mal detalle* a rotten thing to do.

detallista *m/f* retailer (comerciante).

detección *f* detection.

detectar *vt* to detect; *detectar aviones enemigos* to detect enemy aircraft.

detective *m* detective; *detective privado* private detective.

detector *m* detector; *detector de incendios* fire detector; *detector de mentiras* lie detector; *detector de minas* mine detector || scanner, monitor (de radar).
◆ *adj* detecting.

detención *f*; **detenimiento** *m* stopping, halting (acción de parar) || stoppage, standstill (estancamiento) || stop, halt (alto) || holdup, delay (retraso) || care, thoroughness (cuidado) || delay (dilación); *lo llamé y vino sin detención* I called him and he came without delay || JUR arrest (acción de detener) | detention, confinement (prisión) || DEP stoppage (en el juego) || *examinar con detención* to examine carefully *o* thoroughly.

detenedor, ra *adj* stopping (que para) || delaying (que retrasa) || detaining.

detener* *vt* to stop, to halt (parar); *detuvo el coche* he stopped the car || JUR to arrest; *detener a un asesino* to arrest a murderer | to detain (encarcelar) || to hold up, to delay (paralizar); *detener las negociaciones* to hold up (the) negotiations || to delay, to detain, to keep, to hold up (retrasar); *no quiero detenerle más* I don't want to keep you any longer || to keep, to retain (guardar) || *detener la mirada en* to settle one's gaze upon.
◆ *vpr* to stop; *detenerse mucho tiempo en un paraje* to stop for a long time in one place || to dwell; *detenerse en una idea* to dwell upon an idea || to stop off; *detenerse en casa de un amigo* to stop off at a friend's house || to stay, to linger (quedarse).

detenidamente *adv* carefully, closely; *mirar detenidamente algo* to look closely at sth. || carefully, in detail, thoroughly; *estudiar detenidamente un problema* to study a problem carefully.

detenido, da *adj* JUR detained, in custody (mantenido preso) | under arrest; *queda Vd. detenido* you are under arrest || careful, thorough, detailed (minucioso); *un estudio detenido* a detailed study.
◆ *m/f* prisoner (preso).

detenimiento *m* → **detención.**

detentación *f* JUR unlawful *o* illegal possession, detainer, deforcement (posesión ilegal).

detentador, ra *adj* JUR who is in unlawful possession, who holds unlawfully.
◆ *m/f* unlawful holder, deforciant || holder (de un récord).

detentar *vt* JUR to be in unlawful possession of, to hold unlawfully, to have illegal possession of (poseer) || to hold (un récord).

detente *m* HIST talisman, emblem representing the Sacred Heart of Jesus bearing the motto «*detente, bala*» (halt, bullet) worn for protection by Carlist soldiers.

detentor, ra *m/f* JUR unlawful holder || holder (de un récord).

detergente *adj/sm* detergent, detersive.

deterger *vt* to deterge (limpiar); *deterger una herida* to deterge a wound.

deterioración *f* → **deterioro.**

deteriorado, da *adj* damaged (mercancías, etc.).

deteriorar *vt* to damage, to impair, to spoil (estropear) || to wear out (desgastar).
◆ *vpr* to be damaged *o* impaired *o* spoilt (estropearse) || to wear out (desgastarse) || FIG to deteriorate.

deterioro *m*; **deterioración** *f* deterioration, damage, spoiling || wear and tear (con el uso) || FIG impairment, damage, harm (daño) | deterioration (empeoramiento).

determinable *adj* determinable.

determinación *f* fixing, settling; *la determinación de una fecha* the fixing of a date || decision, resolution; *tomar una determinación* to take a decision, to make a resolution || determination, resolution; *mostrar determinación* to show determination || *tener poca determinación* to be irresolute, to lack determination.

determinado, da *adj* resolute, determined, firm (resuelto) || definite (definido) || specific, particular (preciso) || appointed (día, etc.) || decided, determined; *disposiciones determinadas de antemano* measures determined beforehand || MAT determinate || GRAM definite (artículo).

determinante *adj* determining, decisive, determinant.

◆ *m* MAT determinant.

determinar *vt* to determine; *determinar las causas de un accidente* to determine the causes of an accident || to fix, to set, to appoint; *determinar la fecha* to fix the date || to decide, to make up one's mind, to determine, to resolve; *eso me determinó a hacerlo* that decided me to do it; *determinaron firmar la paz* they decided to sing a peace treaty || to stipulate, to lay down, to specify; *la ley determina que...* the law stipulates that... || to cause, to bring about (causar).
◆ *vpr* to decide, to determine, to make up one's mind, to resolve (decidir).

determinativo, va *adj/sm* GRAM determinative.

determinismo *m* FIL determinism.

determinista *adj/s* FIL determinist.

detersión *f* detersion, cleansing.

detersivo, va; detersorio, ria *adj/sm* detersive, detergent.

detestable *adj* detestable, hateful, loathsome; *una persona detestable* a detestable person || horrible, awful (tiempo, sabor, gusto).

detestación *f* detestation, hatred, horror.

detestar *vt* to detest, to hate, to loathe; *detestar a una persona, los viajes* to detest a person, travelling.

detonación *f* detonation, explosion.

detonador *m* detonator (fulminante).

detonante *adj* detonating, explosive; *mezcla detonante* explosive mixture.
◆ *m* explosive.

detonar *vi* to detonate, to explode.

detracción *f* denigration, defamation, disparagement (murmuración) || withdrawal (retiro).

detractar *vt* to denigrate, to defame, to disparage.

detractor, ra *adj* denigrating, defamatory, disparaging.
◆ *m/f* denigrator, defamer, disparager.

detraer* *vt* to denigrate, to defame, to disparage (desacreditar) || to withdraw (quitar).

detrás *adv* behind; *las chicas iban delante y los chicos detrás* the girls went in front and the boys behind || on the back; *la carpeta del disco trae la letra detrás* the record sleeve has the words on the back || after (después) || — *detrás de* behind; *detrás de la casa* behind the house; *dejó un buen recuerdo detrás de él* he left a good memory behind him; behind one's back (a espaldas) || *estar detrás de alguna cosa* to be after sth. || *por detrás* on the back (en la parte posterior), behind, round the back; *pasar por detrás* to go behind; from behind; *se acercaron a mí por detrás* they approached me from behind; behind one's back; *por detrás hablan mal de él* they speak ill of him behind his back || *por detrás de* behind.

detrimento *m* detriment; *en detrimento de* to the detriment of; *sin detrimento de* without detriment to || damage, harm, injury (daño).

detrito; detritus *m* GEOL detritus.

deuda *f* debt; *tener una deuda con uno, estar en deuda con uno* to be in debt to s.o.; *pagar una deuda* to pay (off) a debt || REL trespass; *perdónanos nuestras deudas* forgive us our trespasses || — *contraer deudas* to contract debts, to run into debt || *deuda a largo plazo* long-term debt || *deuda consolidada* funded *o* consolidated debt || *deuda exterior* external *o* foreign debt || *deuda flotante* floating debt || *deuda interior* internal debt || *deuda morosa* bad debt || *deuda pública* national *o* public debt || FIG *estar en deuda con uno* to be indebted to s.o., to be in s.o.'s debt || *lo prometido es deuda* a promise is a promise.

deudo, da *m/f* relative, relation.
◆ *m* relationship, kinship (parentesco).

deudor, ra *adj* indebted || — *saldo deudor* debit balance || FIG *ser deudor de una persona* to be indebted to a person.
◆ *m/f* debtor.

deuterio *m* QUÍM deuterium.

deuterón *m* FÍS deuteron.

Deuteronomio *npr m* Deuteronomy.

deuteropatía *f* MED deuteropathy.

devaluación *f* devaluation (moneda).

devaluar *vt* to devaluate, to devalue.

devanadera *f* reel, spool, bobbin (bobina) || winder, winding frame (utensilio para devanar).

devanado *m* ELECTR winding, coiling (del alambre).

devanador, ra *adj* winding.
◆ *m/f* winder.
◆ *m* reel, spool, bobbin (carrete) || AMER winder (devanadera).

devanamiento *m* reeling, winding (del hilo) || winding (de la lana) || winding, coiling (del alambre).

devanar *vt* to reel, to wind (un hilo) || to coil, to wind (un alambre) || FAM *devanarse los sesos* to rack one's brains.

devanear *vi* to be delirious, to rave, to talk nonsensically.

devaneo *m* flirtation (amorío) || delirium, raving, nonsensical utterings *pl* (delirio) || frivolity, timewasting pastime *o* action (fruslería).

devastación *f* devastation, destruction.

devastador, ra *adj* devastating, destructive.
◆ *m/f* devastator.

devastar *vt* to devastate, to ravage, to lay waste, to destroy (destruir); *casa devastada* devastated house || *regiones devastadas* devastated areas (después de la guerra).

devengado, da *adj* COM due, outstanding || *intereses devengados* outstanding *o* accrued interest.

devengar *vt* to be owed, to have due (tener que cobrar) || to yield, to bear, to bring in (intereses).

devengo *m* amount due.

devenir* *vi* (p us) to happen, to occur (suceder) || FIL to become (cambiarse en).

devenir *m* FIL flux.

deviación *f* —→ **desviación.**

devoción *f* devotion; *La Devoción de la Cruz* The Devotion to the Cross (obra de Calderón) || devotion, devoutness (piedad) || devotion, strong attachment (afición) || habit, custom (costumbre); *tengo por devoción pasear todos los días* I am in the habit of going *o* it is my custom to go for a walk every day || — *con devoción* devoutly || FIG *estar a la devoción de uno* to be at s.o.'s disposal | *Miguel no es santo de mi devoción, a Miguel no le tengo mucha devoción* I'm not exactly fond of Michael.
◆ *pl* devotions (oraciones, etc.).

devocionario *m* prayer book.

devolución *f* return, giving-back || refund, repayment; *devolución del importe de una entrada* refund of an entrance fee || COM returning, return (de una mercancía) || JUR devolution (de propiedades) || DEP return (de la pelota) || return (correo); *devolución al remitente* return to sender || — *no se admiten devoluciones* no goods returnable (recuperando el dinero), no goods exchanged (cambiando el artículo por otro) || *sin devolución* nonreturnable.

devolver* *vt* to return, to give back; *devolver un libro prestado* to return a borrowed book || to return, to send back (correo); *devolver una carta* to return a letter || to return, to put back; *devolver algo a su sitio* to put sth. back in its place, to return sth. to its place || to return, to take *o* to send back (una mercancía) || to repay, to refund; *devolver el importe de la entrada* to refund the entrance fee || FIG to give back, to restore; *la operación le devolvió la vista* the operation gave him back his sight *o* restored his sight || to restore; *devolver algo a su antiguo estado* to restore sth. to its former state || to return, to pay back (un favor, una visita, un cumplido) || DEP to return (la pelota) || to free from, to release from; *devolverle la palabra a uno* to free s.o. from his promise || FAM to bring up, to throw up (vomitar) || — *devolver (el) bien por (el) mal* to repay evil with good || *devolver la palabra* to give back the floor (a un orador) || FIG *devolver la pelota a uno* to give s.o. tit for tat || *devuélvase al remitente* return to sender (en el correo).
◆ *vpr* AMER to return, to go back (volver).

devoniano, na; devónico, ca *adj/sm* GEOL devonian.

devorador, ra; devorante *adj* devouring, consuming (fuego, pasión, etc.) || *hambre devoradora* ravenous hunger.

devorar *vt* to devour; *el lobo devoró al cordero* the wolf devoured the lamb || to devour, to wolf, to gobble (up) (comer ávidamente) || FIG to devour, to consume; *el fuego lo devoró todo* the fire devoured everything; *esta pasión que me devora* this passion which devours me | to destroy (destruir) | to squander, to dissipate (disipar su fortuna) | to devour, to swallow up; *el juego ha devorado toda mi fortuna* gambling has swallowed up all my fortune || to devour; *devorar una novela* to devour a novel; *devorar a uno con los ojos* to devour s.o. with one's eyes.

devoto, ta *adj* devout, pious (piadoso) || of devotion, devotional; *imagen devota* devotional image || devoted; *devoto de su amo* devoted to his master || *su muy devoto* your devoted servant.
◆ *m/f* devotee, devout *o* pious person || enthusiast, devotee (aficionado).

devuelto, ta *pp* —→ **devolver.**

dextrina *f* QUÍM dextrin.

dextrógiro, ra *adj* FÍS dextrorotatory [US dextrorotary].

dextrorso, sa *adj* dextrorse.

dextrosa *f* QUÍM dextrose.

dey *m* dey (príncipe musulmán).

deyección *f* MED defecation, defaecation.
◆ *pl* GEOL debris *sing* (de roca) | ejecta (de un volcán) || MED dejecta.

deyector *m* apparatus for preventing the formation of fur inside steam boilers.

día *m* day; *noche y día* night and day, day and night; *el día que llegues* the day you arrive; *un día hermoso, soleado* a lovely, sunny day || daytime (las horas de luz) || name day (día del santo) || birthday (día del cumpleaños) || weather, day; *hace buen día* it's a fine *o* nice weather, it's a fine *o* nice day || *a la luz del día* in daylight, in the daytime, in the light of day || *al día* up to date (sin retraso); *poner al día* to bring up to date; up to date (moderno), in the know, informed, up to date; *estar al día de lo que pasa* to be informed on what is happening; from hand to mouth (con estrechez); *vivir al día* to live from hand to mouth; daily, everyday, day-to-day (cotidiano); *la vida madrileña al día* daily life in Madrid; in fashion, fashionable (de moda), per day, a day; *dos litros al día* two litres per day; by the day; *alquilar una habitación al día* to rent a room by

the day || *al otro día, al día siguiente* on the next day, (the) next day, (on) the following day, the day after || *al romper* or *al despuntar* or *al rayar el día* at daybreak, at break of day || *cada día más* (seguido de un adjetivo) more and more, more... each day, more... every day (véase OBSERV); *es cada día más complicado* it gets more and more complicated, it gets more complicated every day *o* each day; (seguido de un sustantivo) more and more like, more like... each day, more like... every day; *es cada día más su padre* he is more like his father every day || *cada día menos* (seguido de un adjetivo o de un sustantivo en singular) less and less, less... each day, less... every day; (seguido de un sustantivo en plural) fewer and fewer, fewer... each day, fewer... every day, less and less; *hay cada día menos solicitudes* there are fewer applications each day || *cierto día* one fine day, one day || *como de la noche al día, como del día a la noche* as different as night and day || *cualquier día* any day; *ven cualquier día* come any day || *de cada día* daily, everyday, day-to-day || *de día* by day || *de día en día* from day to day || *dejar para el día del juicio final* to put off until judgment day || *del día* today's, fresh (fresco, reciente), latest (moda) || *de un día a* or *para otro* any day now || *día a día* day by day || *día civil* civil day || *día D* D day || *día de Año Nuevo* New Year's Day || *día de asueto* day off || *día de ayuno* fast day || *día de carne* meat day, meat-eating day || *día de descanso* day off (del trabajo), day of rest (domingo), rest day (en una competición, etc.), day on which there is no performance (en el teatro) || *día de fiesta* or *festivo* feast day, holiday || *día de la banderita* flag day || *día de la madre* mother's day || *día del Corpus* Corpus Christi || *día del juicio final* judgment day, doomsday || *día de paga* payday || COM *día de pago* payday || *día de recibo* at-home day || *día de Reyes* Epiphany || *día de trabajo* working day, workday || *día de vigilia* or *de viernes* or *de pescado* day of abstinence, fish day || *día entre semana* weekday || *día feriado* or *festivo* holiday || *día laborable* or *hábil* working day, workday || *día lectivo* school day, teaching day || *día libre* day off || *día tras día* day after day || *el día de hoy* today (hoy), nowadays (actualmente) || *el día de mañana* tomorrow (mañana), one day soon, in the near future (en tiempo venidero) || *el día de San Pablo* Saint Paul's day || *el día siete* (on) the seventh (del mes) || *el mejor día, el día menos pensado* any day, when least expected, some fine day, one of these days || *en pleno día* in broad daylight || *en su día* in due time *o* course, at the proper time || *es de día* it's daylight || *hacerse de día* to break (the day), to dawn; *se está haciendo de día* the day is breaking, it is dawning || *¡hasta otro día!* I'll be seeing you || *hoy día, hoy en día, en nuestros días* nowadays, these days, at the present time, today || *hoy, día 22 de febrero* today, the 22nd of February; today, February 22nd || *mañana será otro día* tomorrow is another day || *otro día* some other day, another day; *lo haremos otro día* we'll do it some other day || *¿qué día es hoy?* what's the date today? || *romper el día* to break (the day), to dawn || *si algún día* if ever; *si algún día le encuentras* if ever you meet him || FAM *todo el santo día* all day long, all the livelong day || *un buen día* one fine day || *un día de éstos* one of these days || *un día señalado* a great day, an important day, a red-letter day || *un día sí y otro no* every other day, every two days, on alternate days.
◆ *pl* days (vida); *hasta el fin de sus días* until the end of his days; *mis días de corredor* my days as a runner || — *a días* some days, at times || *a los pocos días* a few days later || *a los pocos días de* a few days after || *a tantos días vista* or *fecha* so many days after sight || *¡buenos días!* good morning!, good day! || *cada dos días* every other day, every two days || *cada tres días* every three days || *dar los buenos días* to say good morning || *dar los días a uno* to wish s.o. (a) birthday; to congratulate s.o. on his name day || *en los días de* in the days of, in the time of || *en mis días* in my time, in my day || *en sus mejores días* in his heyday || *tiene contados los días* his days are numbered || FAM *hay más días que longanizas* there's no hurry, there's no rush, there's all the time in the world || AMER *los otros días* the other day || *no todos los días son iguales* who knows what tomorrow holds || *ocho días* a week || *quince días* a fortnight || *tener días* to have one's good days and one's bad days, to have one's on days and one's off days || *todos los días* every day

— OBSERV Las formas *more and more, more each day* y *more every day* se sustituyen por el comparativo en *-er* cuando el adjetivo que sigue la expresión *cada día más* se traduce en inglés por una palabra corta: *es cada día más mona* she gets prettier and prettier, she gets prettier every day.

diabetes *f* MED diabetes.

diabético, ca *adj/s* MED diabetic.

diabla *f* FAM she-devil || two-wheeled carriage, cabriolet (coche) || FAM *a la diabla* any old how, any old way (de cualquier modo).

diablear *vi* FAM to get up to mischief, to get up to one's tricks, to play up (un niño).

diablejo *m* little devil, imp.

diablesa *f* she-devil.

diablillo *m* FIG & FAM little devil, little imp, mischief-maker (persona traviesa).

diablo *m* devil, demon || FIG devil, little devil, scamp; *este niño es un diablo* this child is a devil | rogue (canalla) | monster (monstruo) || AMER two-wheeled cart (carromato) || — *al diablo* to the devil || *anda el diablo en Cantillana* there's trouble afoot || *¿cómo diablos...?* how the devil...? || *cuando el diablo no tiene que hacer con el rabo mata moscas* the devil finds work for idle hands || *del diablo, de todos los diablos* the devil of a; *un problema de todos los diablos* the devil of a problem || *¡diablos!* by Jove!, golly! (admiración, sorpresa, etc.) || *el abogado del diablo* the devil's advocate || *el Diablo* the Devil, Satan || *el diablo cojuelo* The Devil on Two Sticks (título de una obra literaria) || *el diablo encarnado* or *hecho carne* a real devil (un niño), the devil himself, the devil in person (un hombre) || *el diablo que lo entienda* I'll be blowed *o* damned if I understand || *enviar al diablo* to send to the devil || *más sabe el diablo por viejo que por diablo* nothing like the old horse for the hard road || *no es tan feo el diablo como lo pintan* the devil is not so black as he is painted || *¿qué diablos...?* what the devil...?, what the deuce...?, what the blazes...? || *¡qué diablos!* damn it!, hang it! || *tener el diablo en el cuerpo, ser de la piel del diablo* to be a little devil (travieso) || *¡váyase al diablo!* go to the devil!, go to hell!, go to blazes!

diablura *f* mischief; *las diabluras de los niños* the children's mischief || practical joke, prank (travesura) || wonder, miracle; *este malabarista hace diabluras con sus aros* this juggler works wonders *o* performs miracles with his hoops || *hacer diabluras* to get up to mischief, to get up to one's tricks.

diabólico, ca *adj* diabolical, diabolic, devilish.

diábolo *m* diabolo (juguete).

diaconado *m* diaconate, deaconate, deaconship.

diaconal *adj* REL diaconal.

diaconato *m* diaconate, deaconate, deaconship.

diaconía *f* deaconry.

diaconisa *f* deaconess.

diácono *m* deacon; *ordenar de diácono* to ordain deacon.

diacrítico, ca *adj* GRAM diacritic, diacritical || MED diagnostic.

diadema *f* diadem (corona).

diafanidad *f* diaphaneity, diaphanousness, transparency.

diáfano, na *adj* diaphanous, filmy, transparent || FIG transparent.

diafragma *m* diaphragm.

diagnosis *f inv* MED diagnosis.

diagnosticar *vt* to diagnose.

diagnóstico, ca *adj* MED diagnostic.
◆ *m* MED diagnosis, diagnostic (calificación de una enfermedad) | diagnostic, diagnostics (ciencia).

diagonal *adj* diagonal.
◆ *f* diagonal || *en diagonal* diagonally.

diagrama *m* diagram.

dial *m* dial (de radio).

dialectal *adj* dialectal.

dialectalismo *m* dialectalism.

dialéctica *f* dialectics.

dialéctico, ca *adj* dialectic, dialectical.
◆ *m/f* dialectician.

dialecto *m* dialect.

dialectología *f* dialectology.

diálisis *f inv* QUÍM dialysis || MED dialysis; *diálisis peritoneal* peritoneal dialysis.

dializar *vt* QUÍM to dialyze.

dialogar *vi* to dialogue, to dialogize, to hold a dialogue || to talk (hablar) || INFORM to communicate (with), to talk (to).
◆ *vt* to write in dialogue form, to set down as a dialogue.

diálogo *m* dialogue [US dialogue, dialog].

dialoguista *m/f* dialogist, dialogue writer.

diamagnetismo *m* ELECTR diamagnetism.

diamantado, da *adj* diamond-like [like a diamond].

diamantar *vt* to diamond, to make sparkle.

diamante *m* diamond; *diamante en bruto* rough *o* uncut diamond || diamond (naipe) || — FIG *bodas de diamante* diamond wedding || *edición diamante* midget *o* miniature edition.

diamantífero, ra *adj* diamantiferous, diamond-bearing, diamond-yielding || *zona* or *región diamantífera* diamond field.

diamantino, na *adj* diamond-like || diamond (de diamante) || FIG & POÉT adamantine.

diamantista *m* diamond cutter (que labra diamantes) || diamond merchant (vendedor).

diametral *adj* diametral, diametric, diametrical.

diametralmente *adj* diametrically.

diámetro *m* MAT diameter || bore (de cilindro de motor).

diana *f* MIL reveille; *tocar diana* to sound the reveille || bull's-eye, bull (blanco); *hacer diana* to hit the bull's-eye *o* bull, to score a bull.

¡dianche!; ¡diantre! *interj* FAM hang it!, damn it! (enfado) | by Jove!, golly! (sorpresa, admiración).

diapasón *m* MÚS tuning fork, diapason (para afinar) | diapason, range (notas que abarca un instrumento) | fingerboard (del violín) || FIG *bajar, subir el diapasón* to lower, to raise one's tone [of voice].

diapositiva *f* FOT slide, transparency.

diariamente *adv* daily, every day.

diario, ria *adj* daily, everyday.
◆ *m* dayly newspaper, daily, paper (periódico) || diary (relación de acontecimientos) || COM journal, daybook || daily expenses *pl*

(gasto diario) ‖ — *a* or *de diario* daily, every day ‖ MAR *diario de a bordo* logbook ‖ INFORM *diario de bitácora* or *de servicio* log ‖ *diario de la mañana, diario matinal* morning paper, morning daily ‖ *diario de la noche, diario vespertino* evening paper ‖ *diario de sesiones* parliamentary report, report of proceedings in Parliament ‖ *diario hablado* news bulletin, news ‖ *traje de diario* everyday dress.

diarismo *m* AMER journalism (periodismo).

diarista *m/f* diarist (persona que escribe un diario) ‖ AMER journalist.

diarquía *f* diarchy, dyarchy.

diarrea *f* MED diarrhoea.

diastasa *f* BIOL diastase (fermento).

diástole *f* ANAT diastole (dilatación del corazón) ‖ GRAM diastole (cambio de una sílaba).

diastólico, ca *adj* diastolic.

diatermia *f* diathermy.

diátesis *f* diathesis.

diatómico, ca *adj* diatomic.

diatónico, ca *adj* MÚS diatonic.

diatriba *f* diatribe; *lanzar* or *dirigir una diatriba* to pronounce a diatribe.

diávolo *m* diabolo (juguete).

diazoico, ca *adj* diazo; *compuestos diazoicos* diazo compounds.

dibásico, ca *adj* QUÍM dibasic.

dibujante *adj* who draws *o* sketches, drawing, sketching.

◆ *m/f* sketcher, drawer ‖ designer (de moda) ‖ cartoonist (de dibujos animados, de caricaturas, etc.) ‖ TECN draughtsman, draftsman (de dibujo lineal).

dibujar *vt* to draw; *dibujar con* or *a pluma, con* or *a lápiz, a mano alzada, del natural* to draw in ink, in pencil, freehand, from nature ‖ to sketch (bosquejar) ‖ to design (diseñar) ‖ FIG to describe, to outline, to depict (describir) | to describe, to sketch (un carácter).

◆ *vpr* to stand out, to be outlined; *a lo lejos se dibuja una torre contra el cielo* in the distance a tower is outlined against the sky ‖ FIG to take shape, to materialize (concretarse) | to be written, to show; *en su cara se dibuja el dolor* pain is written across his face.

dibujo *m* drawing; *dibujo al carbón, a lápiz, a pluma, a mano alzada* charcoal, pencil, ink, freehand drawing ‖ drawing, sketching (arte) ‖ sketch (bosquejo) ‖ TECN design ‖ cartoon (en un periódico) ‖ pattern, design (de papel, de una tela) ‖ FIG outline (del paisaje, del rostro) | description, depiction (descripción) ‖ — *academia de dibujo* art school, school of art ‖ INFORM *dibujo asistido por ordenador* computer-assisted *o* computer-aided drafting ‖ *dibujo del natural* drawing from nature *o* life ‖ *dibujo lineal* draughtsmanship, draftsmanship, mechanical drawing ‖ *dibujos animados* cartoons.

dicción *f* diction (pronunciación) ‖ word (palabra).

diccionario *m* dictionary, lexicon; *diccionario bilingüe, de bolsillo, electrónico* bilingual, pocket, electronic dictionary.

diccionarista *m/f* lexicographer.

díceres *m pl* AMER gossip *sing*.

diciembre *m* December; *el 25 de diciembre* December 25 *o* 25th, the 25th of December.

dicotiledón; dicotiledóneo, a *adj* BOT dicotyledonous.

◆ *f* dicotyledon.

◆ *pl* dicotyledoneae.

dicotomía *f* dichotomy.

dicroísmo *m* FÍS dichroism (coloración doble).

dicromático, ca *adj* dichromatic.

dicromatismo *m* dichromatism.

dictado *m* dictation; *hacer un dictado* to do a dictation; *dictado musical* musical dictation; *escribir al dictado* to take dictation ‖ title, epithet (calificativo).

◆ *pl* FIG dictates; *los dictados de la conciencia* the dictates of conscience.

dictador *m* dictator.

dictadura *f* dictatorship ‖ *dictadura del proletariado* dictatorship of the proletariat.

dictáfono *m* dictaphone.

dictamen *m* opinion; *abundo en su dictamen* I wholeheartedly agree with your opinion; *dar un dictamen desfavorable* to give an unfavourable opinion ‖ advice (consejo) ‖ report (informe); *dictamen de las comisiones* commissions' report; *dictamen facultativo* medical report ‖ — *dictamen médico* diagnosis ‖ *dictamen pericial* expert advice.

dictaminar *vt* to consider, to hold the opinion, to be of the opinion; *el grafólogo dictamina que la letra es la de un tímido* the graphologist considers that the handwriting is that of a timid person ‖ to prescribe (un médico) ‖ JUR to report (en un juicio).

◆ *vt/vi* to advise, to give one's advice (dar consejo) ‖ to give *o* to express one's opinion; *han dictaminado sobre el proyecto de ley* they have given their opinion on the bill ‖ JUR to pass judgment.

díctamo *m* BOT dittany.

dictar *vt* to dictate; *dictar una carta* to dictate a letter ‖ to enact, to decree (leyes) ‖ to promulgate, to issue, to proclaim (decreto) ‖ to give, to issue (órdenes) ‖ to suggest, to say, to dictate, to advise (aconsejar) ‖ to give (clases) ‖ to deliver (conferencias) ‖ JUR to pronounce (sentencia) ‖ — *dictar condiciones* to dictate terms ‖ *dictar disposiciones* to take *o* to adopt measures ‖ *dictar la ley* to lay down the laws.

dictatorial *adj* dictatorial.

dicterio *m* insult.

dicha *f* happiness (felicidad) ‖ joy (alegría) ‖ good luck (buena suerte) ‖ — *nunca es tarde si la dicha es buena* better late than never ‖ *por dicha* happily, fortunately, luckily, by chance ‖ *ser un hombre de dicha* to be a lucky *o* a fortunate man.

dicharachero, ra *adj* witty, racy, spicy, funny (gracioso) ‖ talkative, chatty, loquacious (parlanchín).

◆ *m/f* joker, wag, tease, character (gracioso) ‖ chatterbox (parlanchín).

dicharacho *m* rude language (lenguaje inconveniente) ‖ racy remark *o* joke (observación).

dicho, cha *p p de decir/adj* ⟶ **decir** ‖ — *dicho de otro modo* in other words, to put it another way ‖ *dicho está* it's settled ‖ *dicho esto* this said ‖ *dicho sea de paso* let it be said in passing ‖ *dicho y hecho* no sooner said than done ‖ *mejor dicho* rather; *alto, o mejor dicho gigantesco* tall, or rather, gigantic.

◆ *adj dem* this, these *pl*, the said; *dicha ciudad* this city.

◆ *m* expression, saying; *un dicho de Cicerón* one of Cicero's sayings ‖ remark, statement; *un dicho desacertado* an unfortunate remark ‖ proverb, saying, adage (refrán) ‖ FAM insult (insulto) | rude expression (expresión desvergonzada) ‖ JUR statement, declaration (de un testigo) ‖ — FIG *del dicho al hecho hay mucho* or *un gran trecho* there's many a slip twixt the cup and the lip, saying and doing are different things ‖ *dicho de las gentes* rumour, gossip ‖ *dicho gracioso* witty remark, witticism ‖ *lo dicho* what has been said *o* decided, what said *o* decided; *lo dicho ayer vale todavía* what was said yesterday still goes ‖ *lo dicho dicho está* what was said *o* what has been said still stands.

◆ *pl* betrothal pledge *sing* (compromiso matrimonial) ‖ engagement *sing*, betrothal *sing* (esponsales) ‖ *tomarse los dichos* to become engaged *o* betrothed.

dichosamente *adv* happily, fortunately, luckily.

dichoso, sa *adj* happy, content; *dichoso con su suerte* content with his lot ‖ lucky, fortunate (afortunado) ‖ FIG & FAM tiresome, wearisome, boring; *¡dichosa visita!* what a tiresome visit! | cursed, damned, blessed, confounded, blasted; *ese dichoso individuo* that blasted fellow; *ese dichoso trabajo me impide salir* that cursed work stops me going out.

didáctico, ca *adj* didactic.

◆ *f* didactics *pl*.

diecinueve *adj* nineteen; *hay diecinueve personas* there are nineteen people ‖ nineteenth; *el siglo XIX (diecinueve)* the 19th [nineteenth] century.

◆ *m* nineteen; *juego siempre el diecinueve* I always play nineteen ‖ nineteenth; *hoy estamos a 19 de febrero* today is the 19th *o* nineteenth of February, today is February 19th *o* the nineteenth.

diecinueveavo, va *adj/s* nineteenth.

dieciochavo, va *adj/s* eighteenth ‖ *en dieciochavo, en 18.°* in eighteenmo, in 18.°, in eighteens (libro).

dieciochesco, ca *adj* eighteenth-century, 18th-century, of the eighteenth *o* 18th century; *pintura dieciochesca* eighteenth-century painting.

dieciocho *adj* eighteen ‖ eighteenth; *el siglo XVIII (dieciocho)* the 18th [eighteenth] century.

◆ *m* eighteen; *tres por seis, dieciocho* three times six makes eighteen ‖ eighteenth; *llegaron el 18 de enero* they arrived on the eighteenth of January.

dieciséis *adj* sixteen ‖ sixteenth; *el siglo XVI (dieciséis)* the 16th [sixteenth] century.

◆ *m* sixteen; *dieciséis es el cuadrado de cuatro* sixteen is the square of four ‖ sixteenth; *el 16 de julio* July 16th, the sixteenth of July.

dieciseisavo, va *adj/s* sixteenth ‖ *en dieciseisavo, en 16.°* in sixteenmo, in 16.°, in sixteens (libro).

diecisiete *adj* seventeen ‖ seventeenth; *el siglo XVII (diecisiete)* the 17th [seventeenth] century.

◆ *m* seventeen; *el diecisiete es un número primo* seventeen is a prime number ‖ seventeenth; *me voy el 17* I'm leaving on the 17th [seventeenth].

diecisieteavo, va *adj/s* seventeenth.

diedro *adj m* dihedral; *ángulo diedro* dihedral angle.

◆ *m* dihedron.

diego *m* BOT marvel of Peru, four o'clock flower.

Diego *npr m* James (Jaime).

dieléctrico, ca *adj/sm* dielectric.

diente *m* tooth; *dientes de leche* milk teeth; *diente picado* bad *o* decayed tooth ‖ tooth (de un peine, de una sierra) ‖ prong (de un bieldo, de un rastrillo, de un tenedor) ‖ ARQ toothing stone (adaraja) ‖ BOT tooth, serration (de una hoja) | clove (de ajo) ‖ TECN cog (de rueda dentada) ‖ FIG & FAM *aguzarse los dientes* to get one's hand in, to cut one's teeth | *alargársele a uno los dientes* to be filled with longing (desear) | *armado hasta los dientes* armed to the teeth ‖ *con todos sus dientes* greedily, hungrily (morder) ‖ FIG *crujirle* or *rechinarle a uno los dientes* to have one's teeth set on edge (por una sensación desagradable), to gnash *o* to grind one's teeth (de rabia) || *da diente con diente, le castañetean los dientes* his teeth are chattering || FIG *decir de dientes afuera* or *para fuera* to say insincerely || *diente canino* or *columelar* canine tooth (de personas), fang (de animales) || *diente de león* dandelion (planta) || TECN *diente de lobo* burnisher || *diente incisivo* incisor || FIG *diente por diente* a tooth for a tooth || *dientes postizos* false teeth || *echar los dientes, salirle a uno los dientes* to cut one's teeth, to teethe (un niño) || FIG *enseñar* or *mostrar los dientes* to bare *o* to show one's teeth | *hablar entre dientes* to mumble, to mutter (mascullar) || FIG & FAM *hincar el diente en* to get one's teeth into, to grapple with (emprender), to slate [US to cut down] (criticar), to put the bite on (sacar provecho) || AMER *pelar el diente* to smile falsely, to give a false smile || FIG & FAM *ponerle a uno los dientes largos* to make one's mouth water (un plato apetitoso), to make s.o. green with envy (darle envidia) | *reír de dientes afuera* to force a smile, to give a sickly smile | *tener a uno entre dientes* not to be able to stand *o* bear *o* stomach s.o. | *tener buen diente* to be a hearty eater | *tener los dientes largos* to have an itching palm.

diéresis *f* GRAM & MED diaeresis.

diesel *adj* diesel.
◆ *m* diesel engine, diesel (motor).

diesi *f* MÚS sharp (sostenido).

diestra *f* right hand.

diestramente *adv* cleverly, skilfully, deftly.

diestro, tra *adj* right; *la mano diestra* the right hand || clever, skilful [US skillful], deft; *diestro en hablar* a skilful speaker; *diestro en su oficio* skilful at his job || shrewd (astuto) || HERÁLD dexter || — *a diestro y siniestro* right and left (por todas partes), at random (sin método) || *golpear a diestro y siniestro* to hit out *o* to lash out left right and centre.
◆ *m* TAUR matador || bridle (correa), halter (rienda) || (ant) swordsman.

dieta *f* HIST diet (congreso) || MED diet; *poner a dieta* to put on a diet; *dieta láctea alta en calorías* calory-rich milk diet.
◆ *pl* emoluments [of a member of Parliament] (de diputados) || per diem allowance *sing*, per diem *sing* (de un empleado que está de viaje) || emoluments, fees (de un juez).

dietario *m* account book.

dietético, ca *adj* dietetic || *médico dietético* dietician, dietitian.
◆ *f* dietetics *pl*.

diez *adj num* ten; *diez pesetas* ten pesetas || tenth (ordinal); *el (día) 10 (diez) de mayo* the 10th [tenth] of May, May 10th [the tenth]; *el siglo X (diez)* the 10th [tenth] century.
◆ *m* ten || decade (del rosario) || paternoster [bead] (cuenta gruesa del rosario) || ten (naipes) || — FIG & FAM *estar en las diez de últimas* to be at death's door, to have one foot in the grave | *hacer las diez de últimas* to queer one's own pitch, to damage one's own cause || *las diez de últimas* ten points which go to the winner of the last trick (naipes) || *son las diez* it is 10 o'clock || *unos diez libros* about ten books.

— OBSERV The cardinal numbers from 16 to 19 can be written in two ways: *diez y seis* or *dieciséis, diez y siete* or *diecisiete, etc.*

diezmar *vt* to decimate.
◆ *vi* to pay the tithe (pagar el diezmo).

diezmilésimo, ma *adj/s* ten thousandth.

diezmilímetro *m* tenth of a millimetre.

diezmillonésimo, ma *adj/s* ten millionth.

diezmo *m* tithe (impuesto) || tenth (part).

difamación *f* defamation, slander (hablando) || defamation, libel (por escrito).

difamador, ra *m/f* defamer, slanderer (de palabra) || defamer, libeller [US libeler] (por escrito).
◆ *adj* → **difamatorio.**

difamante *adj* → **difamatorio.**

difamar *vt* to defame, to slander (hablando) || to defame, to libel (por escrito).

difamatorio, ria; difamador, ra; difamante *adj* defamatory, slanderous (de palabra) || defamatory, libellous [US libelous] (por escrito).

difásico, ca *adj* FÍS two-phase, diphase.

diferencia *f* difference; *la diferencia de edad* the difference in age, the age difference || difference (of opinion), disagreement, dispute; *arreglar una diferencia* to settle a dispute || — *a diferencia de* unlike, contrary to || *pagar la diferencia* to pay the difference || *partir la diferencia* to split the difference.

diferenciación *f* differentiation.

diferencial *adj* differential; *ecuación, cálculo diferencial* differential equation, calculus.
◆ *f* MAT differential.
◆ *m* TECN differential.

diferenciar *vt* to differentiate || to distinguish (distinguir) || MAT to differentiate.
◆ *vi* to differ (in opinion), to disagree, not to be of *o* not to hold the same opinion (de opinión); *en este punto diferenciamos* we disagree on this point.
◆ *vpr* to differ (in opinion), to disagree, to hold different *o* differing opinions; *en esta cuestión nos diferenciamos mucho* on this matter we differ greatly (in opinion), we hold vastly different *o* widely differing opinions on this matter || to differ, to be different (ser diferente) || to stand out, to distinguish o.s. (distinguirse); *esta chica se diferencia de sus compañeras* this girl stands out from her friends.

diferendo *m* AMER difference, quarrel, disagreement.

diferente *adj* different; *diferente a* or *de* different to *o* from || *diferentes veces* several times.

diferible *adj* deferable, deferrable.

diferido, da *adj* deferred, postponed, put off || *emisión diferida* recorded transmission.

diferir* *vt* to defer, to postpone, to put off (aplazar); *han diferido la reunión* they have postponed the meeting || JUR to reserve (un fallo).
◆ *vi* to differ, to be different (ser diferente).

difícil *adj* difficult, hard; *difícil de decir* hard to say; *cada vez más difícil* more and more difficult; *hacer difícil* to make *o* to render difficult || difficult (carácter) || hard; *difícil de contentar* hard to please || FIG unpleasant, odd, disagreeable (cara) || — *difícil de llevar* wayward, ungovernable; *un niño difícil de llevar* a wayward child; difficult to run *o* manage; *esta empresa es difícil de llevar* this firm is difficult to manage; difficult to keep (cuenta), difficult to wear; *este traje es difícil de llevar* this dress is difficult to wear; difficult to follow; *un compás difícil de llevar* a beat difficult to follow || *es difícil que venga* it is unlikely that he will come || *no es muy difícil que digamos* it's not exactly difficult.

difícilmente *adv* hardly; *difícilmente se puede creer* you'd hardly believe it || with difficulty.

dificultad *f* difficulty; *vencer dificultades* to surmount difficulties; *sin dificultad alguna* without the least difficulty || trouble (molestia) || obstacle (obstáculo) || problem, difficulty (problema) || inconvenience (inconveniente) || *tener dificultad para andar* to have difficulty in walking.
◆ *pl* difficulties; *poner dificultades a todo* to create difficulties in everything; *ponerle dificultades a uno* to present s.o. with difficulties || trouble, *sing*; *dificultades mecánicas* mechanical trouble || objections; *poner dificultades* to raise objections.

dificultador, ra *adj* difficult, fussy (dificultoso).

dificultar *vt* to make *o* to render difficult, to hinder, to obstruct, to hamper.

dificultosamente *adv* with difficulty.

dificultoso, sa *adj* difficult, hard; *trabajo dificultoso* difficult work || FIG & FAM unpleasant, disagreeable (rostro) || fussy, difficult (exigente).

difluir* *vi* to be diffused, to disperse, to spread out.

difracción *f* FÍS diffraction.

difractar *vt* FÍS to diffract.

difractivo, va; difrangente *adj* FÍS diffractive.

difteria *f* MED diphtheria.

diftérico, ca *adj* MED diphtheric, diphtheritic.

difuminación *f* stumping.

difuminar; difumar *vt* to stump.

difumino *m* stumping (acción) || stump (lápiz) || *dibujo al difumino* stump drawing.

difundir *vt* to spread; *las ratas difunden las epidemias* rats spread epidemics || to diffuse; *difundir la luz* to diffuse light || to disseminate (diseminar) || to broadcast, to transmit; *difundir una emisión radiofónica* to broadcast a radio transmission, to transmit a radio broadcast || to spread, to radiate; *difundir la felicidad* to spread happiness || to spread, to divulge; *difundir una noticia* to spread a piece of news || to disseminate, to propagate (una doctrina).
◆ *vpr* to diffuse, to be diffused; *la transpiración se difunde por los poros* perspiration diffuses through the pores || to (be) spread, to be propagated (una doctrina) || to spread (una noticia).

— OBSERV The verb *difundir* has two past participles: the regular, *difundido*, is used to form compound tenses, and the irregular, *difuso*, is used as an adjective.

difunto, ta *adj/s* deceased, defunct.
◆ *adj* late; *mi difunto padre* my late father.
◆ *m* casualty (víctima) || — *día de (los) Difuntos* All Souls' Day || FIG & FAM *oler a difunto* to smell fusty *o* musty (una habitación), to look as if one is not long for this world (antes de morir uno).

difusible *adj* diffusible.

difusión *f* spreading (de una epidemia, etc.) || diffusion (de luz, de calor, de agua) || RAD broadcasting, transmission (acción), broadcast (programa) || diffusion, spreading, dissemination, propagation (de una noticia).

difuso, sa *adj* diffuse, wordy (explicación, estilo) || wide (extenso).

difusor, ra *adj* propagating, disseminating, who *o* which propagates *o* disseminates (de una doctrina) || spreading (de una noticia) || diffusive, diffusing, who *o* which diffuses (del agua, de la luz) || RAD broadcasting, transmitting.
◆ *m/f* propagator, disseminator (de una doctrina).
◆ *m* TECN diffuser.
◆ *f* RAD broadcasting station.

digerible *adj* digestible.

digerir* *vt* to digest (la comida) || FIG to suffer, to endure, to stand, to bear (una ofensa) | to digest, to assimilate; *no ha digerido la lección* he has not digested the lesson || FAM *no poder digerir a uno* not to be able to stand *o* to bear s.o.
◆ *vpr* to digest.

digestibilidad *f* digestibility.

digestible *adj* digestible.

digestión *f* digestion.

digestivo, va *adj/sm* digestive.

digesto *m* JUR digest.

digestónico, ca *adj/sm* digestive.

digitación *f* MÚS fingering, digitation.

digitado, da *adj* BOT & ZOOL digitate.

digital *adj* digital || INFORM digital || finger (dactilar) || *huellas digitales* fingerprints.
◆ *f* BOT foxglove, digitalis || MED digitalis.

digitalina *f* digitalin (medicina).

digitalización *f* INFORM digitization.

digitalizador *m* INFORM digitizer.

digitalizar *vt* INFORM to digitize.

digitiforme *adj* digitiform.

digitígrado, da *adj/sm* ZOOL digitigrade.

dígito *m* MAT digit.

dignamente *adv* with dignity.

dignarse *vpr* to deign, to condescend; *no se dignó contestarme* he did not deign to answer me || — *dígnese usted hacer lo que le pido* (will you) be so good *o* kind as to do what I ask of you || *Señor, dígnate aceptar este sacrificio* Lord, accept this sacrifice (oración).

dignatario *m* dignitary.

dignidad *f* dignity || self-respect, dignity (de uno mismo) || office, post, rank (cargo).

dignificante *adj* dignifying (gracia).

dignificar *vt* to dignify.

digno, na *adj* worthy, deserving; *digno de admiración* worthy of admiration || fitting, appropriate; *el digno castigo* the fitting punishment || worthy, honourable, meritorious (que merece respeto); *hombre digno* honourable man; *conducta digna* worthy conduct || decent (decente, decoroso); *viviendas, condiciones de trabajo dignas* decent houses, working conditions || — *digno de compasión* pitiable, pitiful || *digno de encomio* praiseworthy || *digno de ser mencionado* worth mentioning || *digno de verse* worth seeing || *ejemplo digno de imitación* example worth emulating || *él, muy digno, rehusó* he, with great dignity, refused.

digresión *f* digression.

dije *m* trinket, locket, charm; *esta pulsera tiene muchos dijes* this bracelet has many trinkets || FIG & FAM treasure, jewel, gem; *esta criada es un dije* this maid is a treasure || AMER nice, lovely.
◆ *pl* FAM bragging *sing*, boasting *sing*, bravado *sing* (bravuconerías).

dilaceración *f* dilaceration, laceration || MED tearing (músculo).

dilacerar *vt* to dilacerate, to lacerate, to tear asunder || to tear (un músculo) || FIG to hurt, to harm, to wound (el orgullo, etc.).

dilación *f* delay, delaying (retraso) || delay (demora) || *sin dilación* without delay, immediately.

dilapidación *f* squandering, wasting, dissipation.

dilapidador, ra *adj* squandering, wasteful.
◆ *m/f* squanderer, waster.

dilapidar *vt* to squander, to waste, to dissipate.

dilatabilidad *f* FÍS expansibility, expandability || dilatability (de la pupila).

dilatación *f* FÍS expansion || dilation (de la pupila) || MED dilatation, dilation || protraction, prolongation (del tiempo).

dilatadamente *adv* extensively, widely (extensamente) || at length, diffusely, long-windedly; *hablar dilatadamente de algo* to speak at length on sth.

dilatado, da *adj* FÍS expanded || dilated (la pupila) || extensive, vast (extenso) || long; *un dilatado período de tiempo* a long period of time || FIG unlimited, wide; *horizontes dilatados* unlimited prospects, wide horizons.

dilatador, ra *adj* MED dilative, which dilates || FÍS which causes expansion, which expands, expanding.
◆ *m* MED dilator.

dilatar *vt* to expand; *el calor dilata los metales* heat expands metals || MED to dilate || FIG to postpone, to delay, to put off, to defer (retrasar); *dilató su regreso por un año* he postponed his return by a year | to enlarge, to widen (ampliar) | to prolong, to protract, to drag out (prolongar) || *dilatar un asunto* to drag out an affair.
◆ *vpr* to expand; *el agua se dilata al congelarse* water expands on freezing || MED to dilate || to dilate (la pupila) || FIG to be diffuse (al hablar) | to drag on (un relato) | to extend, to stretch; *la llanura se dilataba hasta el horizonte* the plain extended as far as the horizon || AMER to take *o* to be long *o* a long time, to be slow, to linger, to tarry, to delay (tardar); *no te dilates para salir* don't be slow leaving.

dilatorio, ria *adj* JUR dilatory, delaying.
◆ *f* delay || *andar* or *venir con dilatorias* to delay, to drag things out, to waste time.

dilección *f* love, affection.

dilecto, ta *adj* dearly beloved, beloved; *mi dilecto amigo* my dearly beloved friend.

dilema *m* dilemma.

diletante *m* dilettante (aficionado).

diletantismo *m* dilettantism.

diligencia *f* diligence, application, care (cuidado) || speed, rapidity (rapidez) || step, measure; *hacer diligencias para* to take steps to, to take the necessary steps *o* measures to || (piece of) business, job, affair (gestión) || diligence, stagecoach (coche) || JUR proceeding; *diligencias judiciales* judicial proceedings || — JUR *diligencias previas* inquiry || *tengo que ir a unas cuantas diligencias* I have a few things to see to, I have some business to see to.

diligenciar *vt* to take the necessary steps *o* measures to obtain, to go through the necessary procedures to obtain; *diligenciar un pasaporte* to take the necessary steps to obtain a passport.

diligente *adj* diligent || quick, speedy (rápido).

dilucidación *f* elucidation, explanation.

dilucidador, ra *adj* elucidatory, explanatory.
◆ *m/f* elucidator, explainer.

dilucidar *vt* to elucidate, to explain (aclarar) || to solve, to clear up (un misterio, etc.).

dilución *f* dissolution, dissolving (de un sólido en un líquido) || dilution (entre dos líquidos).

diluente *adj* diluting, solvent.

diluir* *vt* to dissolve (un sólido en un líquido) || to dilute (líquidos) || to thin (salsas) || FIG to water down.
◆ *vpr* to become diluted, to dilute.

diluvial *adj* diluvial.
◆ *m* diluvium.

diluviano, na *adj* diluvian; *lluvia diluviana* diluvian rain.

diluviar *vi* to pour with rain, to pour down, to teem (llover mucho).

diluvio *m* deluge, flood || FIG flood, storm, torrent; *un diluvio de protestas* a storm of protest; *un diluvio de injurias* a torrent of abuse || FIG *tras mí, el diluvio* I'm all right, Jack.

dimanar *vi* to flow, to run (el agua) || FIG to emanate, to issue, to derive, to originate; *el poder dimana del pueblo* power emanates *o* issues *o* derives from the people, power originates in the people || to arise, to follow, to result (resultar).

dimensión *f* dimension || magnitude, size (tamaño).
◆ *pl* dimensions, size *sing*; *de grandes dimensiones* of great size || — *dimensiones exteriores* overall *o* external dimensions || *tomar las dimensiones de* to measure out, to take the measures of.

dimensional *adj* dimensional.

dimes y diretes *loc* FAM bickering, quibbling, argument || *andar en dimes y diretes* to bicker, to quibble, to argue.

diminución *f* diminution, diminishing, reduction.

diminuendo *adj/sm* MÚS diminuendo.

diminuir *vt* to diminish, to reduce (disminuir).

diminutivo, va *adj/sm* diminutive.

— OBSERV Diminutives are much more commonly used in Spanish than in English. Besides implying the idea of smallness they are often used affectionately. They are formed as follows:
1.° With the suffix *-ito*, for polysyllables ending in *a*, *o* or a consonant other than *n* and *r* (*mesita, librito, españolito*);
2.° With the suffix *-cito*, for polysyllables ending in *e*, *n* or *r* (*pajecito, silloncito, lunarcito*);
3.° With the suffix *-ecito*, for monosyllables or for disyllables containing an accented diphthong or a final diphthong (*panecito, cuerpecito, indiecito*);
4.° The same rules apply for the suffixes *-illo, -cillo, -ecillo; -uelo, -zuelo, -ezuelo; -ico, -cico, -ecico* (*mesilla, libruelo, panecico*).

diminuto, ta *adj* tiny, minute, diminutive.

dimisión *f* resignation; *presentar su dimisión* to hand in *o* to tender one's resignation || *hacer dimisión de un cargo* to resign from *o* to resing a post.

dimisionario, ria; dimitente *adj* resigning, outgoing.
◆ *m/f* resigner.

dimisorias *f pl* dimissory letters.

dimitente *adj/s* → **dimisionario.**

dimitir *vt/vi* to resign, to resign from; *dimitir (de) un cargo* to resign a post.

dimorfo, fa *adj* dimorphous, dimorphic.

din *m* (p us) money, dough || FIG *poco importa el don sin el din* a lord without riches is a soldier without arms.

dina *f* FÍS dyne (unidad de fuerza).

Dinamarca *npr f* GEOGR Denmark.

dinamarqués, esa *adj* Danish.
◆ *m/f* Dane.

dinámico, ca *adj* dynamic.
◆ *f* FÍS dynamics.

dinamismo *m* dynamism.

dinamista *adj* dynamistic.
◆ *m/f* dynamist.

dinamita *f* dynamite || — *voladura con dinamita* dynamiting || *volar con dinamita* to dynamite.

dinamitar *vt* to dynamite.

dinamitazo *m* explosion, blast.

dinamitero, ra *m/f* dynamiter.

dinamo; dínamo *m* ELECTR dynamo.

dinamoeléctrico, ca *adj* dynamoelectric, dynamoelectrical.

dinamometría *f* dynamometry.

dinamómetro *m* dynamometer.

dinar *m* dinar (moneda).

dinastía *f* dynasty.

dinástico, ca *adj* dynastic, dynastical.

dinerada *f*; **dineral** *m* fortune, great deal *o* large sum of money; *costó un dineral* it cost a fortune.

dinerillo *m* FAM a little (money), a bit (of money) || pocket money (dinero para gastos menudos).

dinero *m* money; *dinero para gastos menudos* or *de bolsillo* pocket money; *andar escaso de dinero* to be short of money; *hacer algo por dinero* to do sth. for money || denarius (moneda antigua o denario); *Judas vendió a Jesucristo por treinta dineros* Judas betrayed Christ for thirty denarii || FIG & FAM money, wealth (riqueza) || — *de dinero* rich, wealthy, moneyed; *familia, hombre de dinero* wealthy family, man || *de dineros y bondad quita siempre la mitad, de dinero y calidad, la mitad de la mitad* believe only half of what you hear of a man's wealth and goodness || *dinero acuñado* minted money || *dinero contante y sonante* hard cash || *dinero de bolsillo* pocket money || *dinero de curso legal* legal tender || *dinero de San Pedro* Peter's pence || *dinero efectivo* or *en metálico* cash || *dinero falso* counterfeit money || *dinero líquido* ready money || *dinero negro* or *sucio* dirty money || *dinero suelto* change, loose change (moneda suelta); *no tengo dinero suelto* I have no change || *dineros son calidad* you're nobody without money || *(el) dinero llama (al) dinero* money makes money || *el dinero no tiene olor* money is welcome though it comes in a dirty clout || *estar mal de dinero* to be hard up, to be short of money || FIG & FAM *ganar dinero a espuertas* to make tons of money, to make a pile | *hacer dinero* to make money || *invertir dinero* to invest money || *poderoso caballero es don Dinero* money talks || *por dinero baila el perro* there is nothing money cannot buy (con dinero se consigue todo), you never get sth. for nothing || *sacar dinero de las piedras* to be a skinflint || *sacarle jugo al dinero* to make the most of one's money, to get one's money's worth, to get value for money || *tirar el dinero por la ventana* to throw money down the drain.

dingo *m* dingo (perro de Australia).

dinosaurio *m* dinosaur.

dintel *m* ARQ lintel (parte superior de las puertas) | overdoor (decoración) | threshold (umbral).

diñar *vt* POP to give (dar) || POP *diñarla* to kick the bucket.

diocesano, na *adj/s* diocesan.

diócesis; diócesi *f* diocese.

diodo *m* diode.

dionisiaco, ca; dionisíaco, ca *adj* Dionysiac, Dionysian.
◆ *f pl* Dionysia.

Dioniso; Dionisos *npr m* Dionysus, Dionysos.

dioptra *f* FÍS diopter, alidade.

dioptría *f* FÍS & MED diopter, dioptre.

dióptrico, ca *adj* FÍS dioptric, dioptrical.
◆ *f* dioptrics.

diorita *f* MIN diorite.

dios *m* REL God || — *¡a Dios!* good-bye, farewell, adieu (véase OBSERV en ADIÓS) || *¡a Dios gracias!, ¡gracias a Dios!* thank God!, thank heaven! || *a Dios rogando y con el mazo dando* God helps those who help themselves || *¡alabado sea Dios!* God be praised!, praise be to God! || *a la buena de Dios* in a slapdash way, any old how, at random || *¡anda* or *vete con Dios!* farewell!, God be with you!, God go with you!, adieu! || *armar la de Dios es Cristo* to raise hell || *¡ay Dios!* God!, my God! || *¡bendito sea Dios!* God be praised! || *clamar a Dios* to cry out to heaven || *como Dios le da a entender* as best one can, (in) one's (own) way; *hágalo como Dios le dé a entender* do it as best you can, do it your way || *como Dios manda* properly; *vestido como Dios manda* properly dressed; according to the rules; *jugar como Dios manda* to play according to the rules; as it should be (como se debe) || FAM *¡con Dios!* good-bye! || *dar gracias a Dios* to thank God, to give thanks to God, to thank one's lucky stars || *digan, que de Dios dijeron* say what you like, it doesn't worry me || *Dios aprieta pero no ahoga* God tempers the wind to the shorn lamb || *Dios da ciento por uno* God repays a hundredfold || *¡Dios dirá!* time will tell!, we shall see! || *Dios es testigo que...* God *o* heaven knows... || *Dios Hijo, Dios hecho Hombre* God the Son, God made Man || *¡Dios le ampare!* God protect you! || *¡Dios le asista* or *le ayude!* God help you! || *¡Dios le bendiga!* God bless (you)! || *Dios le ha dejado de su mano* God has forsaken him || *¡Dios lo quiera!, ¡quiera Dios!* let us hope so!, would to God! || *Dios los cría y ellos se juntan* birds of a feather flock together || *¡Dios me confunda!* damn! || *Dios mediante* God willing || *¡Dios me libre!* God *o* heaven forbid! || *¡Dios (mío)!* good heavens!, my God! || *Dios no le ha llamado por el camino de* he's not cut out for || *¡Dios proveerá!* God will provide! || *Dios sabe, sabe Dios* God *o* Heaven knows (con un complemento), God *o* Heaven only knows (al final) || *¡Dios santo!* good God!, my God!, good heavens! || *¡Dios se lo pague!* God bless you! || *Dios Todopoderoso* almighty God || *estaba de Dios* God (had) willed it, it was inevitable || *hay que dar a Dios lo que es de Dios y al César lo que es del César* render therefore unto Caesar the things which are Caesar's and unto God the things that are God's || FAM *no había ni Dios* there wasn't a soul (there) || *no (lo) quiera Dios* God *o* Heaven forbid || *no temer ni a Dios ni al diablo* to fear neither man nor beast || *pasar la de Dios es Cristo* to have a rough time of it, to suffer great hardship, to go through hell || *poner a Dios por testigo* to swear by Heaven above, to swear by almighty God || *¡por Dios!* for goodness' sake!, for God's sake! || *¡que Dios le guarde!* God protect you! || *que Dios le tenga en su (santa) gloria* may his soul rest in peace || *que Dios me perdone, pero* (may) God *o* Heaven forgive me, but || *que Dios nos asista* or *nos coja confesados* God *o* Lord help us || *quiera Dios que...* if only..., would to God that... || *sea lo que Dios quiera* God's will be done || *se va a armar la de Dios es Cristo* there's going to be a tidy row *o* a hell of a row, there's going to be real trouble || *si Dios quiere* God willing || *¡válgame Dios!* by Jove!, bless my soul! (sorpresa), Lord, give me strenght! || *¡vaya con Dios!* farewell!, God be with you!, God go with you! || *¡vaya por Dios!* good God!, my God! || *¡vive Dios!, ¡voto a Dios!* (ant) zounds!, gadzooks!
◆ *pl* gods; *los dioses del Olimpo* the gods of Olympus || *jurar por todos los dioses* to swear by all the gods.

diosa *f* goddess.

diplejía *f* MED diplegia.

diplodoco *m* diplodocus (fósil).

diploma *m* diploma.

diplomacia *f* diplomacy.

diplomado, da *adj* qualified, having a diploma, who holds a diploma.
◆ *m/f* diplomate, qualified person || graduate (en la universidad) || *diplomada en belleza* qualified beautician.

diplomar *vt* AMER to grant a diploma to.
◆ *vpr* to graduate (en la universidad).

diplomática *f* diplomatics.

diplomático, ca *adj* diplomatic; *cuerpo diplomático* diplomatic corps; *valija diplomática* diplomatic bag || FIG & FAM diplomatic, tactful (sagaz).
◆ *m* diplomat, diplomatist.

dipsomanía *f* dipsomania (sed violenta).

dipsómano, na *adj* dipsomaniacal, dipsomaniac.
◆ *m/f* dipsomaniac.

díptero, ra *adj* ARQ dipteral; *un templo díptero* a dipteral temple || ZOOL dipterous, dipteran.
◆ *m* ZOOL dipteran.
◆ *pl* ZOOL diptera.

díptico *m* diptych.

diptongación *f* GRAM diphthongization.

diptongar *vt* GRAM to diphthongize.
◆ *vpr* GRAM to diphthongize.

diptongo *m* GRAM diphthong.

diputación *f* deputation (delegación) || post of member of Parliament (en Gran Bretaña) || post of congressman (en Estados Unidos) || post of member of the Spanish Cortes (en España) || AMER town hall (ayuntamiento) || *diputación provincial* county council.

diputado *m* representative, delegate, deputy (delegado) || member of Parliament (en Gran Bretaña) || congressman (en Estados Unidos) || member of the Cortes *o* of the Spanish Parliament (en España) || *diputado provincial* county councillor.

diputar *vt* to deputize, to delegate.

dique *m* MAR dike, breakwater, mole, jetty (muro) | dry dock (en la dársena) | dike (en Holanda) || FIG check, rein (obstáculo); *poner un dique a las pasiones* to put a check *o* rein on passions || GEOL dike (filón volcánico vertical) || — *dique de carena* dry dock || *dique de contención* dam || *dique flotante* floating dock || *dique seco* dry dock || *entrar en dique* to dock || FIG *poner un dique a* to restrain, to curb, to check, to repress (contener).

diquelar *vt* FAM to look at (mirar) | to see, to get (entender).

dirección *f* direction; *le confiaron la dirección de la obra* they entrusted him with the direction of the work || direction, way; *vamos en la misma dirección* we're going in the same direction, we're going the same way || address (señas); *mi dirección es calle Mayor 13* my address is 13 calle Mayor || managership, directorship (función de director) || management, board of directors; *por orden de la dirección* by order of the management || TECN steering (de coche, de avión, etc.); *dirección asistida* servo-assisted steering || INFORM address; *dirección virtual* virtual address || leadership (de un partido) || headship (de una escuela) || editorship (de un periódico) || office (de la administración pública) || TEATR production || CINEM direction || MAR course, route (rumbo) || — *calle de dirección única* one-way street || *dirección escénica* production (teatro), direction (cine) || *dirección general* head office, headquarters *pl* || *dirección general de producción* executive direction (cine) || *dirección por radio* radio control || *dirección prohibida* no entry || *en dirección a* in the direction of, towards || *llevar la dirección de* to direct.

direccionales *m pl* AMER indicators (intermitentes del automóvil).

direccionamiento *m* INFORM addressing.

direccionar *vt* INFORM to address.

directamente *adv* directly || *fuimos allí directamente* we went straight there.

directivo, va *adj* directive || managerial, managing (de la dirección de una empresa) || guiding; *principio directivo* guiding principle || *junta directiva* board of directors, directors *pl*.
◆ *m* director, board member.

◆ *f* board [of directors] || guideline, directive, instruction; *no me dio ninguna directiva* he gave me no instructions.

directo, ta *adj* direct || direct, straight (línea) || lineal (herencia) || GRAM direct || — *emisión en directo* live transmission || *tren directo* through *o* direct train.

◆ *m* straight (boxeo); *directo de izquierda, de derecha* straight left, right.

◆ *f* top gear (coche); *poner la directa* to go into *o* to engage top gear.

director, ra *adj* governing, steering (junta, asamblea) || guiding, master (idea) || directive (función) || master (plan) || guiding (principio) || TECN controlling (fuerza).

◆ *m/f* director, head (hombre), directress, head (mujer) (administración) || director, manager (hombre), directress, manageress (mujer) (de sociedad) || headmaster (hombre), headmistress (mujer) (de un colegio) || president (de una academia) || governor, warden (de prisión) || editor (hombre), editress (mujer) (de periódico) || manager (hombre), manageress (mujer) (de hotel) || — *director de cine* film director || *director de emisión* producer || *director de escena* producer (teatro), director (cine) || *director de orquesta* conductor || *director de producción* director of production || *director espiritual* spiritual director || *director general* director general, managing director || *director gerente* managing director.

directoral *adj* directorial.

directorio, ria *adj* directive, directorial, directory.

◆ *m* directory (de direcciones, de normas) || governing body (asamblea directiva) || INFORM directory.

Directorio *m* HIST Directory (en Francia).

directriz *adj f* MAT dirigent, describing (línea).

◆ *f* MAT directrix.

◆ *f pl* instructions, guidelines; *les he dado directrices perfectamente claras* I have given them perfectly clear instructions.

dirigente *adj* directing, leading || — *clase dirigente* ruling class || *personal dirigente* executives *pl*.

◆ *m/f* leader || manager (director).

dirigible *adj/sm* AVIAC dirigible.

dirigir *vt* to direct, to point, to aim, to level (un arma); *dirigió la pistola hacia el ladrón* he pointed the pistol at the thief || to direct, to point, to aim; *dirigir un telescopio hacia la luna* to direct a telescope at the moon || to drive, to steer (un coche) || to steer, to pilot (un avión, un barco) || to address (una carta) || to direct, to address; *dirigir una observación* to address a remark || to direct; *me dirigió a la estación* he directed me to the station || to manage (una empresa) || to run (negocio, escuela) || to control (el tráfico) || to administer (los asuntos públicos) || to edit (un periódico) || to conduct, to lead (una orquesta) || to direct, to conduct (operaciones, negociaciones) || to lead. to head (una sublevación, una expedición) || to dedicate; *dirigió todos sus esfuerzos a terminar sus estudios* he dedicated all his efforts to finishing his studies || to level, to make (una acusación) || to bend (los pasos) || to turn (la mirada) || to guide (guiar) || to direct, to supervise; *dirigir un seminario* to supervise a seminary || to superintend (obras) || to direct, to guide; *dirigir espiritualmente a uno* to direct s.o. spiritually || TEATR to produce || CINEM to direct || — FIG *dirigir el baile* to rule the roost, to run the show || *dirigir la mirada* to direct *o* to turn one's gaze, to look || *dirigir por radio* to radio-control.

◆ *vpr* to make one's way, to go; *dirigirse a su casa* to make one's way homewards || to be managed (una empresa) || to address, to speak; *dirigirse a uno* to address s.o., to speak to s.o. || to write (escribir); *me dirijo a usted* I am writing to you || to apply (para solicitar algo) || to aim, to be aimed at (crítica, acusación, etc.) || to turn (la mirada).

dirigismo *m* state control.

dirimente *adj* JUR diriment, nullifying.

dirimir *vt* to settle (una contienda) || to annul, to dissolve, to declare void; *dirimir el matrimonio, un contrato* to annul the marriage, a contract.

discar *vt* AMER to dial (marcar).

discernible *adj* discernible.

discernimiento *m* discernment, perception || discernment, discrimination || discernment, judgment (criterio); *actuar con discernimiento* to act with discernment || JUR appointment (designación).

discernir* *vt* to discern, to distinguish; *discernir el bien del mal* to discern good from evil || JUR to appoint (s.o.) as guardian.

— OBSERV This verb is sometimes used with the meaning *to award*, which is better expressed by *conceder*.

disciplina *f* discipline (sometimiento a reglas) || doctrine (doctrina) || subject (asignatura) || scourge, whip, discipline (azote).

disciplinadamente *adv* with discipline.

disciplinado, da *adj* disciplined || FIG variegated, marbled (jaspeado).

disciplinante *m/f* flagellant, disciplinant (en Semana Santa).

disciplinar *vt* to discipline (un ejército, sus instintos) || to scourge, to whip, to discipline (azotar) || to teach, to instruct (instruir).

◆ *vpr* to discipline o.s.

disciplinario, ria *adj* disciplinary; *castigo, batallón disciplinario* disciplinary punishment, batallion.

discípulo, la *m/f* disciple (el que sigue a un maestro) || pupil, student [of a teacher] (escolar, alumno); *un discípulo aplicado* a studious pupil.

disc jockey *m* disc jockey.

disco *m* discus; *lanzamiento del disco* throwing the discus || disk, disc; *disco de Newton* Newton's disc || record, disc (de fonógrafo); *poner un disco* to play a record || light (en las calles); *disco rojo, verde* red, green light || signal (de ferrocarriles) || dial (del teléfono) || TECN disk, disc (del freno) | plate, disc (del embrague) || INFORM disk || MED disk, disc (de las vértebras) || FAM bore, drag (cosa pesada); *¡qué disco ir allí!* what a bore going there! | same old story *o* song, same string; *siempre estás con el mismo disco* you're always telling the same old story, you're always singing the same old song, you're always harping on the same string, it's the same old story *o* song || — FIG & FAM *cambiar el disco* to change the record || *disco compacto* compact disk || *disco de control* parking disc || *disco de larga duración* long-playing record || *disco de señales* (disc) signal (ferrocarril) || INFORM *disco duro* or *rígido* hard disk | *disco flexible* flopppy disk | *disco magnético* magnetic disk | *disco óptico* optical disk | *disco removible* removable disk || *disco selector* dial (teléfono) || *pasar con el disco cerrado, abierto* to go through a red light, to proceed on green.

discóbolo *m* discobolus, discus thrower.

discófilo, la *m/f* record fan, discophile.

discografía *f* discography.

discoidal; discoideo, a *adj* discoid, discoidal.

díscolo, la *adj* disobedient, ungovernable, wayward.

disconforme; desconforme *adj* not in agreement, in disagreement; *estoy disconforme contigo* I am not in agreement with you || differing, disagreeing (diferente).

disconformidad; desconformidad *f* disagreement (desacuerdo) || difference, nonconformity, divergence; *disconformidad de opiniones* difference of opinions.

discontinuación *f* discontinuation, discontinuance.

discontinuar *vt/vi* to discontinue, to cease.

discontinuidad *f* discontinuity, lack of continuity.

discontinuo, nua *adj* discontinuous || MAT *función discontinua* discontinuous function.

disconveniencia *f* incongruity.

disconvenir* *vi* not to agree, to disagree (en las opiniones) || not to go together, not to match (cosas).

discordancia *f* MÚS discordance, dissonance || clashing, incongruity (de colores) || difference, divergence, nonconformity (de opiniones) || disagreement, discordance, nonconformity; *discordancia entre los dichos y los hechos* disagreement between the statements and the facts || discord (discordia).

discordante *adj* MÚS discordant, dissonant || clashing, incongruous (colores) || differing, divergent, nonconforming (opiniones) || disagreeing, discordant, nonconforming (que no coinciden).

discordar* *vi* MÚS to be discordant *o* dissonant || to clash (colores) || to disagree, not to agree, to be in disagreement, to differ (in opinion) (no estar de acuerdo) || to differ; *discordamos en pareceres* we differ in opinion || not to tally *o* agree (no coincidir).

discorde *adj* MÚS discordant, dissonant || clashing (colores) || differing, diverging (opiniones) || in disagreement, not in agreement; *estamos discordes* we are not in agreement || disagreeing, discordant (que no coinciden).

discordia *f* discord, dissension; *sembrar la discordia* to sow discord || — *manzana de la discordia* apple of discord || *tercero en discordia* arbitrator.

discoteca *f* record collection (colección) || record library; *la discoteca de la B. B. C.* the record library of the B. B. C. || record rack (soporte) || discothèque (salón de baile).

discreción *f* discretion, prudence, tact, circumspection (prudencia, tacto) || discretion (no divulgación) || wit (ingenio) || — *a (la) discreción de* at the discretion of, at (s.o.'s) discretion || MIL *¡descanso a discreción!* stand easy! || *vino a discreción* as much wine as one wants, unlimited wine.

discrecional *adj* discretionary, discretional; *poder discrecional* discretionary power || optional (facultativo) || request; *parada discrecional* request stop || *servicio discrecional* private, special (autobuses).

discrecionalmente *adv* at one's discretion.

discrepancia *f* discrepancy; *discrepancia de ideas, de dos textos* discrepancy between ideas, between two texts || disagreement, difference of opinion (desacuerdo).

discrepante *adj* discrepant || disagreeing, differing.

discrepar *vi* to differ; *nuestras opiniones discrepan* our opinions differ || to disagree, to differ in opinion, to hold differing opinions (dos o más personas) || to disagree (no estar de acuerdo).

discretear *vi* to try to be witty (dárselas de ingenioso).

discreteo *m* show of wit (ingenio).

discreto, ta *adj* discreet (reservado) || unobtrusive, modest (poco visible) || discreet, prudent, cautious, tactful, circumspect (cuerdo) || witty (ingenioso) || moderate, reasonable, average; *una inteligencia discreta* an average intelligence || sober (traje) || subdued, sober (color) || MAT & MED discrete.
◆ *m/f* discreet person (reservado) || discreet *o* prudent *o* tactful *o* circumspect person (cuerdo) || witty person, wit (ingenioso) || superior's assistant and adviser (en una comunidad religiosa).

discriminación *f* discrimination; *discriminación racial* racial discrimination.

discriminante *m* MAT discriminant.

discriminar *vt* to discriminate (distinguir) || to discriminate against (por motivos raciales, etc.).

discriminatorio, ria *adj* discriminatory.

discromía *f* MED dyschroa, dyschroia.

disculpa *f* apology (por una ofensa) || excuse; *tiene disculpa por ser joven* he has the excuse of being young, his excuse is that he's young; *esta falta no tiene disculpa* there is no excuse for this mistake || — *dar disculpas* to make excuses || *pedir disculpas a alguien* to apologize to s.o., to offer one's apologies to s.o.

disculpable *adj* excusable, pardonable.

disculpar *vt* to excuse, to forgive; *disculpe mi retraso* forgive my delay || to excuse; *su inexperiencia le disculpa* his inexperience excuses him.
◆ *vpr* to apologize, to excuse o.s.; *disculparse por su retraso* to apologize for one's delay.

discurrir *vi* to think, to reflect, to ponder, to meditate (reflexionar); *discurrir en* to think about, to reflect on, to ponder, to meditate on || to speak, to discourse (hablar) || to roam, to walk (about) (andar) || to flow, to run (líquidos) || to pass (tiempo) || to go by (la vida) || to go on (una reunión).
◆ *vt* to invent, to think up, to devise (inventar).

discursar *vi* to discourse (*sobre* on), to speak (*sobre* about).

discursear *vi* FAM to spout, to make a speech.

discursista *m/f* windbag (parlanchín).

discursivo, va *adj* thoughtful, reflective, meditative || discursive; *método discursivo* discursive method.

discurso *m* speech; *pronunciar un discurso en el Parlamento* to deliver a speech in Parliament || ratiocination, reasoning (raciocinio) || discourse, dissertation (escrito) || course (del tiempo) || meditation (meditación).

discusión *f* discussion (normal) || argument, dispute (muy fuerte); *una discusión acalorada* a heated argument || — *en discusión* in debate (debatido), under discussion, pending, at issue (sin decidir) || *eso no admite discusión* there can be no argument about that.

discutible *adj* debatable, disputable || questionable, doubtful (dudoso).

discutido, da *adj* controversial.

discutir *vt* to discuss, to debate; *discutir el pro y el contra de una propuesta* to discuss the pros and cons of a proposal || to argue about *o* over (argumentar); *discutir el precio del coche* to argue over the price of the car || to question, to contest; *discutir las órdenes de alguien* to question s.o.'s orders || *un libro muy discutido* a much-discussed *o* much-talked-about book.
◆ *vi* to discuss, to talk about; *discutir de* or *sobre política* to discuss politics || to argue (argumentar) || *¡no discutas!* don't argue!

disecación *f* dissection || stuffing (de un animal muerto).

disecador, ra *m/f* dissector || taxidermist (el que conserva animales).

disecar *vt* to dissect (un cadáver, una planta) || to stuff (conservar un animal muerto) || FIG to dissect, to analyse (analizar).

disección *f* dissection || stuffing (de un animal muerto).

disecea *f* MED defective hearing.

disector *m* dissector || taxidermist (el que conserva animales).

diseminación *f* dissemination, spreading.

diseminar *vt* to disseminate, to scatter, to spread.
◆ *vpr* to spread.

disensión *f* dissidence, disagreement, dissent (disentimiento) || quarrel (riña).
◆ *pl* discord *sing*, strife *sing*, dissension *sing*.

disenso *m* dissidence, disagreement.

disentería *f* MED dysentery.

disentérico, ca *adj* MED dysenteric.
◆ *m/f* person suffering from dysentery.

disentimiento *m* dissidence, disagreement, dissent (desacuerdo).

disentir* *vi* to disagree, to differ; *disentimos en esto* we disagree on that || to dissent, to disagree; *disentir de la opinión general* to dissent from *o* to disagree with general opinion || to differ; *nuestras opiniones disienten* our opinions differ.

diseñador, ra *m/f* designer.

diseñar *vt* to design.

diseño *m* design, sketch || (brief) description, outline, sketch (por palabra) || INFORM *diseño asistido por ordenador* computer-aided *o* computer-assisted design.

disertación *f* dissertation, lecture, discourse (conferencia) || dissertation, disquisition (escrito).

disertador, ra; disertante *adj* dissertative.
◆ *m/f* lecturer, discourser (conferenciante).

disertar *vi* to discourse, to dissert, to lecture (hablar) || to discourse, to dissertate (escribir).

diserto, ta *adj* fluent, eloquent.

disestesia *f* MED dysaesthesia.

disfasia *f* dysphasia (dificultad en el habla).

disforme *adj* deformed (deformado) || shapeless (sin forma) || enormous (enorme) || disproportionate, out of proportion (desproporcionado).

disfraz *m* disguise || fancy dress (traje) || mask (máscara) || FIG disguisement, dissimulation (disimulación) | pretence, appearance (apariencia); *bajo el disfraz de* under the pretence of || — *baile de disfraces* fancy dress ball || *sin disfraz* plainly; *hablar sin disfraz* to speak plainly.

disfrazado, da *adj* *disfrazado de* disguised as.

disfrazar *vt* to disguise || FIG to disguise; *disfrazar la voz* to disguise one's voice | to conceal, to hide, to disguise (la verdad) | to dissemble (con malos designios) | to disguise, to dissimulate, to hide, to conceal (los sentimientos, etc.) || *asesinato disfrazado de suicidio* murder made to look like suicide.
◆ *vpr* to disguise o.s., to dress up; *disfrazarse de chino* to disguise o.s. as a Chinaman.

disfrutar *vt* to own, to possess, to enjoy (poseer) || to receive (una renta) || to enjoy (la salud) || to make the most of; *¡disfrútelo!* make the most of it!; *disfrutar sus vacaciones* to make the most of one's holidays.
◆ *vi* to enjoy, to have the benefit of (sacar provecho); *disfrutar de* or *con la renta de una finca* to enjoy the income from a property || to enjoy, to have, to possess (de salud, favor, herencia) || to enjoy o.s., to have a good time; *he disfrutado mucho en esta ciudad* I've enjoyed myself immensely *o* I've had a very good time in this city || to enjoy (gozar de); *madre que disfruta de la compañía de sus hijos* mother who enjoys the company of her children || *disfrutar con la música* to enjoy listening to music, to take pleasure in listening to music.

disfrute *m* enjoyment || benefit (provecho) || use (uso) || possession.

disfumar *vt* to stump (difumar).

disfumino *m* stump (difumino).

disfunción *f* MED dysfunction.

disgregación *f* disintegration (desintegración) || dispersion, breaking-up (dispersión).

disgregante *adj* disintegrating || dispersing.

disgregar *vt* to disintegrate; *rocas disgregadas por las heladas* rocks disintegrated by the frosts || to disperse, to break up; *disgregar la muchedumbre* to disperse the crowd.
◆ *vpr* to disintegrate || to disperse, to break up.

disgustado, da *adj* angry, annoyed, displeased; *disgustado con* or *de uno* angry with s.o.; *disgustado con* or *de una cosa* angry about sth. || disappointed (decepcionado); *disgustado con la actitud del ministro* disappointed by the minister's attitude || FAM *estoy disgustado con este coche* I'm not pleased with this car.

disgustar *vt* to displease; *tu carta me disgustó* your letter displeased me || to annoy (contrariar) || to anger, to make angry (enfadar) || *me disgusta este olor* I don't like this smell, I dislike this smell.
◆ *vpr* to get *o* to become angry; *disgustarse con uno por una tontería* to get angry with s.o. over a trifle || to fall out, to make each other angry (enfadarse dos personas) || to be annoyed; *se disgustará si no la invita* she'll be annoyed if you don't invite her || to be displeased (molestarse) || to have had enough, to be tired (hartarse).

disgusto *m* annoyance, anger (enfado); *no pudo ocultar su disgusto* he was unable to hide his annoyance || displeasure (desagrado) || misfortune, (piece of) bad luck (revés); *ha tenido muchos disgustos* he has suffered many misfortunes, he has had a lot of bad luck || trouble, difficulty (molestia) || sorrow, pain, grief, blow (pesadumbre); *la muerte de su madre le dio un gran disgusto* the death of his mother caused him great sorrow *o* grief, his mother's death was a great blow to him || repugnance, repulsion (tedio, repulsión) || quarrel, argument, row (desavenencia) || — *a disgusto* unwillingly, against one's will, reluctantly, with displeasure || *estar* or *hallarse a disgusto en* to be ill at ease in, to be unhappy in || *llevarse un gran disgusto* to be very upset || FIG & FAM *matar a disgustos a uno* to drive s.o. mad, to make s.o.'s life a misery, to worry s.o. to death || *tener disgustos con uno* to have trouble *o* difficulty with s.o.

disidencia *f* dissidence, disagreement || REL dissent.

disidente *adj* dissident, dissentient.
◆ *m/f* dissident (en política, etc.) || dissenter, nonconformist (en religión).

disidir *vi* to dissent.

disilábico, ca; disílabo, ba *adj* disyllabic, dissyllabic.
◆ *m* disyllable, dissyllable.

disimetría *f* dissymmetry.

disimétrico, ca *adj* dissymmetric, dissymmetrical.

disímil *adj* dissimilar.

disimilación *f* dissimilation.

disimilar *vt* to dissimilate.

disimilitud *f* dissimilitude, dissimilarity.

disimulable *adj* concealable (ocultable) || excusable, pardonable (disculpable).

disimulación *f* dissimulation, hiding, concealment, disguising (ocultación) || excusing, pardoning, pardon (disculpa).

disimuladamente *adv* furtively.

disimulado, da *adj* dissembling, who dissembles (hipócrita) || hidden (oculto) || — *a lo disimulado, a la disimulada* furtively || *hacerse el disimulado* to feign ignorance, to act dumb.

disimulador, ra *adj* dissimulating, dissembling.
◆ *m/f* dissimulator, dissembler.

disimular *vt* to hide, to conceal (ocultar) || to disguise, to dissimulate, to dissemble, to hide, to conceal; *disimular su alegría* to hide one's joy || to excuse, to pardon, to overlook (disculpar).
◆ *vi* to dissemble, to pretend.
◆ *vpr* to conceal o.s. || to be concealed.

disimulo *m* hiding, concealment (ocultación) || indulgence, leniency, tolerance || dissimulation, disguising (fingimiento) || — *con disimulo* furtively || *hablar sin disimulo* to speak plainly.

disipable *adj* dispersable (nubes) || easily dispelled (ilusiones) || easily squandered (una fortuna).

disipación *f* dissipation, squandering, wasting (del dinero) || dissipating, dispersion (de nubes) || dispelling (de ilusiones) || dissipation (libertinaje).

disipado, da *adj* dissipated || dissipated, dissolute (persona, vida) || restless, unruly (alumno) || wasteful (derrochador).

disipador, ra *adj* squandering, wasteful, prodigal.
◆ *m/f* spendthrift, squanderer.

disipar *vt* to dissipate, to disperse, to scatter, to dispel; *el sol disipó las nubes* the sun dissipated the clouds || to dispel (dudas, temores, ilusiones) || to destroy (las esperanzas) || to squander, to fritter away, to dissipate (una fortuna) || to waste (energía) || to clear up (un malentendido) || to allay (las sospechas).
◆ *vpr* to dissipate, to disperse, to be dispelled (nubes, etc.) || to clear up, to dissipate (una tormenta) || to vanish (el humo) || to be dispelled, to vanish (ilusiones, sospechas, dudas) || to be squandered, to be frittered away (fortuna) || to fail, to flag (energías).

dislate *m* blunder, bloomer (disparate) || absurdity (absurdo).

dislocación; dislocadura *f* dislocation (de huesos) || FIG dismembering, dismemberment (de un imperio, de un estado, etc.) || breaking-up (de una reunión, de un cortejo, etc.) || distortion, misrepresentation (de hechos) || GEOL slip, fault.

dislocar *vt* to dislocate, to put out of joint (los huesos) || FIG to dismember; *dislocar un imperio* to dismember an empire || to distort, to misrepresent (desfigurar) || FIG & FAM *estar dislocado de alegría* to be beside o.s. with joy.
◆ *vpr* to dislocate; *dislocarse el brazo* to dislocate one's arm || to be dislocated, to come out of joint (los huesos) || to break up (separarse).

disloque *m* FAM tops, top notch, first rate (muy bueno); *esta película es el disloque* this film is first rate *o* is the tops || last straw, end, limit (el colmo); *es el disloque* that's the end.

disminución *f* fall, drop, decrease (de temperatura) || decrease, reduction (de velocidad) || reduction, diminution (de las dimensiones) || decrease, fall (de población) || cutting down, diminution (de cargas financieras, de raciones) || decrease, diminution (de las fuerzas de uno) || reduction, drop, fall, lowering (de precios) || depreciation (del valor) || MED assuagement (del dolor) | abatement (de la fiebre) || *ir en disminución* to diminish (las fuerzas), to fall (la temperatura, los precios), to decrease (la velocidad, la población).

disminuido, da *m/f* disabled; *disminuido físico, psíquico* physically, mentally disabled.

disminuir* *vt* to lower, to cause to fall *o* drop (la temperatura) || to reduce, to decrease (la velocidad) || to reduce, to diminish (las dimensiones) || to decrease, to cause a decrease in (la población) || to cut down, to curtail, to reduce (las cargas financieras, las raciones) || to decrease, to diminish (las fuerzas de uno) || to reduce, to lower, to bring down (los precios) || to lower, to bring down (el valor) || to relieve, to assuage (el dolor) || to diminish, to weaken (la autoridad, el prestigio) || to lighten (la pena) || to damp, to diminish (el entusiasmo).
◆ *vi* to diminish (en altura, las raciones, las fuerzas) || to fall, to drop, to go down (la temperatura, los precios) || to slacken (la velocidad) || to decrease (la población) || to relax (el frío) || to grow shorter (el día) || to decline (la luz) || to fall off, to dwindle (el número, los beneficios) || to abate (la fiebre) || to decline (las fuerzas, la salud) || to fail (la memoria, la vista) || to wane (la fama).

disnea *f* MED dyspnoea [US dyspnea].

disociable *adj* dissociable.

disociación *f* dissociation.

disociar *vt* to dissociate.

disolubilidad *f* QUÍM solubility, dissolubility.

disoluble *adj* soluble, dissoluble.

disolución *f* dissolution (de un cuerpo, de un matrimonio, de una sociedad, del Parlamento) || breaking-up (de una manifestación, de una asociación, de una reunión) || AUT rubber solution (para un neumático) || FIG dissoluteness, profligacy (de las costumbres) || QUÍM solution, dissolution.

disoluto, ta *adj* dissolute, profligate.
◆ *m/f* dissolute person, debauchee.

disolvente *adj* dissolvent, solvent.
◆ *m* QUÍM dissolvent, solvent || thinner (para pinturas).

disolver* *vt* to dissolve (cuerpo, matrimonio, sociedad, Parlamento) || FIG to break up (manifestación, reunión) || to annul (contrato).
◆ *vpr* to dissolve || to be dissolved (una sociedad) || to break up (reunión).

disonancia *f* MÚS dissonance || FIG dissonance, lack of harmony, disharmony (falta de armonía) | discord, disagreement (desacuerdo).

disonante *adj* MÚS dissonant, discordant || FIG out of keeping, discordant.

disonar* *vi* MÚS to be dissonant *o* discordant, to be out of tune || FIG to lack harmony (no armonizar) | to disagree (no estar de acuerdo).

dispar *adj* unlike, different, disparate.

disparada *f* AMER flight (fuga) || — AMER FAM *a la disparada* full pelt, flat out, hell for leather (a todo correr) | *de una disparada* straight away, at once (inmediatamente) | *tomar la disparada* to take to one's heels.

disparadamente *adv* hurriedly, precipitously (rápidamente) || suddenly (de pronto) || foolishly (disparatadamente) || *salió disparadamente* he was off like a shot, he dashed *o* bolted out.

disparadero *m* trigger (en las armas) || FIG & FAM *poner* or *estar en el disparadero* to drive s.o. up the wall.

disparado, da *adj* —→ **disparar.**

disparador *m* firer (el que dispara) || trigger (en las armas) || shutter release (de cámara fotográfica) || escapement (de reloj) || FIG & FAM *poner a uno en el disparador* to push s.o. too far, to provoke s.o.

disparar *vt* to fire; *disparar un cañón, un tiro* to fire a cannon, a shot || to fire, to shoot (un arco, una flecha) || to fire *o* to shoot at; *disparar a alguien* to fire at s.o. || to hurl, to throw (arrojar una piedra, etc.) || DEP to shoot at goal (el balón) || — FIG & FAM *estar disparado* to be (all) on edge | *salir disparado* to go off like a shot (from a gun), to bolt *o* to fly *o* to dart *o* to dash off (salir corriendo), to fly, to be flung *o* hurled; *salir disparado de su asiento* to fly out of one's seat.
◆ *vi* to fire, to shoot; *disparar contra el enemigo* to fire at *o* on the enemy, to shoot at the enemy || FIG to talk nonsense (decir tonterías), to act foolishly, to blunder (hacer tonterías) || AMER to dash off, to bolt.
◆ *vpr* to go off (un arma de fuego) || to shoot *o* to rush *o* to dash off (arrojarse) || to bolt, to run away (un caballo) || to fly off, to shoot off (desprenderse violentamente) || to race (un motor) || FIG & FAM to fly off the handle (enfadarse).

disparatadamente *adv* foolishly, absurdly, senselessly.

disparatado, da *adj* foolish, absurd, senseless (absurdo) || FAM absurd, excessive (excesivo).

disparatar *vi* to talk nonsense (decir disparates) || to blunder, to act foolishly (hacer un disparate).

disparate *m* silly thing, foolish *o* senseless act, act of folly (acción irreflexiva) || blunder, mistake, bloomer (*fam*), boob (*fam*); *libro lleno de disparates* book full of blunders || silly thing, foolish remark; *soltar un disparate* to say sth. silly, to make a foolish remark || — *costar un disparate* to cost a bomb || *¡qué disparate!* how absurd!, how ridiculous! || FIG *un disparate* a heck of a lot (mucho).
◆ *pl* nonsense *sing*; *decir disparates* to talk nonsense.

disparejo, ja *adj* different, disparate, unlike (distinto) || uneven, unequal (desigual).

disparidad *f* disparity, difference, dissimilarity.

disparo *m* firing (acción de disparar un arma) || shot (tiro) || shot (en el fútbol) || FIG silly thing, foolish *o* senseless act (disparate) | attack; *los disparos de los periodistas se centraron en él* the newspapermen's attacks were directed against him || MAR *disparo de aviso* or *de advertencia* warning shot.

dispendio *m* waste, squandering.

dispendioso, sa *adj* expensive, costly (caro).

dispensa *f* exemption, dispensation (*de* from) || REL dispensation || *dispensa de edad* waiving of age limit.

dispensable *adj* exemptable || REL dispensable || pardonable, excusable (perdonable).

dispensación *f* dispensation, exemption.

dispensar *vt* to confer (honores) || to grant, to bestow (mercedes) || to show (interés) || to have (admiración) || to pay (atención) || to give (recibimiento, ayuda) || to dispense, to administer (justicia, asistencia médica) || to exempt, to excuse (eximir) || REL to dispense || to forgive, to excuse, to pardon; *dispénseme por llegar tan tarde* forgive me for arriving so late || — *dispensar a uno (de) algo* to excuse s.o. from sth. || *dispense usted* forgive me, excuse me, (I'm) sorry.

dispensaría *f* AMER clinic.

dispensario *m* clinic, dispensary (consultorio).

dispepsia *f* MED dyspepsia.

dispéptico, ca *adj/s* dyspeptic.

dispersar *vt* to disperse, to scatter (diseminar) || to disperse (rayos luminosos) || to break up, to disperse (una manifestación) || MIL to disperse, to scatter, to put to flight || FIG to divide (esfuerzos, atención, actividad, etc.).
◆ *vpr* to disperse, to scatter || to break up, to disperse (una muchedumbre) || MIL to spread out, to deploy (desplegarse).

dispersión *f* dispersion || FIG division (de la atención, de la actividad, etc.).

dispersivo, va *adj* dispersive.

disperso, sa *adj* dispersed, scattered || MIL *en orden disperso* in disorder, in disarray.

displacer* *vt* to displease.

displasia *f* MED dysplasia.

displicencia *f* indifference, coolness, coldness (en el trato) || indifference, lack of enthusiasm (desgana) || nonchalance (descuido) || despair, discouragement (desaliento) || *trabajar con displicencia* to work unenthusiastically *o* reluctantly.

displicente *adj* unpleasant, disagreeable; *tono displicente* unpleasant tone || indifferent, unenthusiastic (desganado).

disponer* *vt* to arrange, to dispose; *disponer las naves en orden de batalla* to arrange the ships in battle order || to set out, to lay out; *disponer los platos en la mesa* to set out the plates on the table || to prepare, to get ready (preparar) || to order (ordenar) || to provide, to stipulate; *la ley dispone que...* the law provides that... || MIL to form up, to line up || *disponer la mesa* to set *o* to lay the table.
◆ *vi* to have, to have at one's disposal, to have available; *no disponemos de mucho tiempo* we haven't a lot of time || to have the use, to have at one's disposal; *todavía no puede disponer de sus bienes* he cannot yet have the use of his goods || to dispose (vender, dar, etc.); *disponer de una finca* to dispose of an estate || to order; *disponer de la vida de uno* to order one's own life || — *disponer de dinero* to have money in hand *o* at one's command || *disponga de mí a su gusto* I am entirely at your disposal || *los medios de que dispone* the means available to him.
◆ *vpr* to prepare, to get ready; *disponerse a* or *para marcharse* to prepare to leave || MIL to form up.

disponibilidad *f* availability || *en disponibilidad* unattached, unassigned (empleado).
◆ *pl* COM resources, financial assets, available funds, cash *sing* on hand (dinero) | available stocks (mercancías).

disponible *adj* available, at (s.o.'s) disposal (utilizable) || unoccupied, unengaged, disengaged, free (libre) || spare, free (tiempo) || on hand, available (dinero) || available, vacant; *dos plazas disponibles* two available seats || vacant (puesto) || unattached, on call (militar, empleado).

disposición *f* arrangement, disposition, disposal (arreglo) || layout; *la disposición de los cuartos de un piso* the layout of the rooms of a flat || JUR ordinance, order, decree (ley) | provision (cláusula) || FIG natural aptitude, gift, talent, disposition (don); *tener disposición para la música* to have a gift for music | disposition, bent, inclination (propensión) | disposition (de ánimo) || disposal; *tener la libre disposición de sus bienes* to have one's goods entirely at one's disposal || MIL formation (de tropas) || — *a la disposición de* at the disposal of || *a su disposición* at your service, at your disposal || *a su libre disposición* (I am) entirely at your service *o* disposal || *disposición de ánimo* attitude, frame of mind, disposition || *disposición escénica* stage positioning [of actors] || *estar* or *hallarse en disposición de* to be ready to || *estoy a la disposición de usted* or *a su disposición* I am at your service *o* disposal || *salvo disposición contraria* unless otherwise provided || *tener la libre disposición de* to be free to dispose of || *última disposición* last will and testament.
◆ *pl* arrangements, preparations | steps (medidas) || — *disposiciones legales* statutory provisions || *disposiciones testamentarias* dispositions of a will || *tomar las disposiciones para* to make preparations *o* arrangements for (con sustantivo), to take steps to (con verbo).

dispositivo *m* device (de una máquina) || appliance, device, gadget (aparato) || — INFORM *dispositivo de alimentación* feeding device | *dispositivo de almacenamiento* storage device || *dispositivo de seguridad* safety device (de una máquina), security measures (en un acto oficial) || *dispositivo intrauterino* intrauterine device.

dispuesto, ta *adj* ready (listo); *dispuesto para la marcha* ready to leave || arranged, disposed (arreglado) || disposed, inclined, prepared, willing (inclinado) || helpful, who is always willing to help (servicial) || clever, go-ahead (vivo, hábil) || — *bien, mal dispuesto con uno* well-disposed, ill-disposed towards s.o. || *lo dispuesto* the provisions, what is stipulated; *en cumplimiento de lo dispuesto en el artículo* in accordance with the provisions of *o* with what is stipulated in the article || *poco dispuesto a* unwilling to, reluctant to.

disputa *f* dispute, argument (discusión) || dispute, controversy (controversia) || — *sin disputa* indubitably, indisputably, undoubtedly (indudablemente) || *tener una disputa* to quarrel, to have an argument.

disputar *vt* to contend *o* to compete for, to dispute; *disputar el primer puesto a uno* to contend with s.o. for the first place || DEP to play (jugar).
◆ *vi* to dispute, to argue; *disputar por* to dispute, to argue about *o* over.
◆ *vpr* to contend *o* to compete for, to dispute; *se disputan el premio* they are contending for the prize || to be debated, to be discussed (discutirse) || to be contested, to be disputed (ser disputado) || DEP to be played (jugarse).

disquete *m* INFORM floppy disk, diskette.

disquetera *f* INFORM disk drive.

disquinesia *f* MED dyskinesia.

disquisición *f* disquisition.
◆ *pl* digressions.

disruptor *m* ELECTR circuit breaker, spark breaker, cutout.

distancia *f* distance; *a dos kilómetros de distancia* at a distance of two kilometres || difference (diferencia); *hay* or *va mucha distancia de las promesas a los hechos* there's a lot of difference between promises and actions || FIG distance; *guardar las distancias* to keep one's distance || — *acortar las distancias* to cut down *o* to reduce the distance || *a distancia, a la distancia* at *o* from a distance || *a respetable* or *respetuosa distancia* at *o* from a respectable distance || *avión de larga distancia* long-haul *o* long distance aeroplane || AUT *distancia de seguridad* safety distance || *distancia focal* focal length || *mantener* or *tener a distancia* to keep at a distance.

distanciado, da *adj* remote (remoto) || distant (distante) || separated (separado) || isolated (aislado) || far apart (muy separados).

distanciamiento *m* spacing out (espaciamiento) || remoteness, isolation (aislamiento) || FIG distance.

distanciar *vt* to place farther apart *o* at a distance, to separate (separar, apartar) || to cause a rift between (reñir) || to leave behind, to outdistance (dejar atrás); *un corredor que distancia a su rival* a runner who leaves his rival behind || — *acompañarte a tu casa me distancia de mi camino* accompanying you to your house takes me out of my way || *estar distanciado de su familia* to be estranged from one's family, to no longer see one's family.
◆ *vpr* to become separated || to get ahead (de un seguidor) || to fall out (disgustarse) || to become estranged, to drift away, to no longer see; *se ha distanciado de sus amigos* he has become estranged from his friends, he has drifted away from his friends.

distante *adj* distant, far (espacio) || distant, remote, far-off (espacio y tiempo); *en época distante* in a distant epoch || FIG distant || *la ciudad está distante de cincuenta kilómetros* the town is fifty kilometres away *o* is fifty kilometres distant.

distar *vi* to be distant, to be away; *distar dos leguas* to be two leagues distant || to be after; *su llegada no distó de la mía más de cinco días* his arrival was no more than five days after mine || FIG to be far, to be a long way; *dista mucho de ser bueno* he's a long way from being a good man.

distender* *vt* to slacken, to loosen (aflojar) || MED to strain, to pull (músculo) | to distend (piel).
◆ *vpr* to distend, to be distended (hincharse) || to slacken (aflojarse) || to relax (relajarse) || to be strained (un músculo).

distensión *f* distension || strain (de un músculo) || slackening (aflojamiento) || *tener* or *sufrir una distensión* to pull a muscle.

dístico *m* POÉT distich.

distinción *f* distinction; *hacer distinción entre* to make a distinction between || distinction, honour [*US* honor] (honor) || distinction, refinement (refinamiento) || deference, consideration, respect, regard, esteem (miramiento); *tratar a un superior con distinción* to treat a superior with deference || — *a distinción de* unlike, in contrast to, as distinct from || *distinción honorífica* honour || *de gran distinción* highly distinguished || *sin distinción* without distinction || *sin distinción de edades* irrespective of age || *sin distinción de personas* without respect to persons || *sin distinción de raza* without any racial discrimination.

distingo *m* reservation, qualification (salvedad) || distinction.

distinguido, da *adj* distinguished; *un escritor distinguido* a distinguished writer || distinguished, refined (modales, persona) || gentlemanly (caballero).

distinguir *vt* to distinguish; *distinguir una cosa de otra* to distinguish one thing from another || to distinguish, to tell (reconocer) || to distinguish, to differenciate (diferenciar) || to mark out, to distinguish (singularizar) || to discern, to distinguish (discernir) || to pay honour *o* tribute to; *el general le distinguió ascendiéndole a coronel* the general paid honour to him by raising him to the rank of colonel || to honour; *me ha distinguido con su amistad* he has honoured me with his friendship || to show a preference for (preferir) || *saber distinguir* to be a good judge (of).
◆ *vi* to distinguish, to discriminate.
◆ *vpr* to be distinguished, to differ (diferenciarse) || to distinguish o.s.; *distinguirse por su valor* to distinguish o.s. for one's valour || to be noticeable, to stand out; *se distingue por*

su belleza she is noticeable for her beauty || to be audible (oírse) || to be visible (verse) || *a lo lejos se distinguía una torre* far off a tower could be distinguished.

distintivo, va *adj* distinguishing, distinctive, characteristic; *signo distintivo* distinguishing mark.
◆ *m* symbol; *el caduceo es el distintivo de la profesión médica* the caduceus is the symbol of the medical profession || badge, emblem (emblema) || distinctive *o* distinguishing feature *o* quality (cualidad) || distinguishing mark (aspecto).

distinto, ta *adj* distinct (claro) || different; *distinto a* or *de* different from; *quiero uno distinto* I want a different one.
◆ *pl* different, various, diverse, several (varios).

distocia *f* MED dystocia.

distorsión *f* distortion.

distracción *f* recreation, distraction, pastime; *mi distracción favorita es la pesca* my favourite recreation is fishing || form of amusement; *el cine es una distracción muy criticada* the cinema is a much-criticized form of amusement || amusement, diversion, entertainment; *hay muchas distracciones en esta ciudad* there are many amusements in this city || inattention, distraction, absentmindedness (descuido) || dissipation, debauchery (libertinaje).

distraer* *vt* to distract (apartar la atención) || to amuse, to entertain (entretener) || to take s.o.'s mind off (de una pena, de un dolor); *distraer a uno de su preocupación* to take s.o.'s mind off his worry || to take (s.o.) away from, to divert (de un trabajo) || to embezzle, to misappropriate (fondos) || MIL *distraer al enemigo* to distract the enemy.
◆ *vi* to be relaxing, to be entertaining.
◆ *vpr* to amuse *o* to enjoy o.s. (divertirse) || to enjoy; *distraerse con la lectura* to enjoy reading || to pass the time (pasar el tiempo); *mientras esperaba se distrajo leyendo una revista* while he waited he read a magazine to pass the time || to be inattentive, to let one's mind wander, not to pay attention (descuidarse).

distraído, da *adj* amusing, entertaining (divertido); *una película distraída* an amusing film || casual; *una mirada distraída* a casual glance || absentminded (persona) || inattentive, absentminded (desatento) || dissolute (disoluto) || AMER untidy, slovenly (desaseado).
◆ *m/f* absentminded person, scatterbrain || *hacerse el distraído* to pretend not to notice.

distribución *f* distribution || delivery (del correo, etc.); *distribución de la leche* milk delivery || giving out (de prospectos) || AUT & IMPR distribution || layout (plano de una casa) || service, supply (del agua, del gas) || sharing out (de dividendos, del trabajo) || *distribución de premios* prizegiving.

distribuidor, ra *adj* distributing, distributive.
◆ *m/f* distributor.
◆ *m* AUT distributor || dealer, agent (de un producto comercial) || *distribuidor automático* slot machine [US vending machine].

distribuir* *vt* to distribute (repartir); *distribuir dinero entre los pobres* to distribute money among the poor || to deliver; *distribuir el correo* to deliver the mail || to allot; *distribuir trabajo a los obreros* to allot work to the workers || to award, to give out (premios) || to design, to lay out (la disposición de una casa) || to give out (prospectos) || to deal out (golpes) || to supply (el agua, el gas).

distributor, ra; distribuyente *adj* distributing.
◆ *m/f* distributor.

distrito *m* district || *distrito electoral* constituency || *distrito postal, federal* postal, federal district.

distrofia *f* MED dystrophy.

disturbar *vt* to disturb.

disturbio *m* disturbance (alteración de la tranquilidad) || disturbance, trouble (desorden).

disuadir *vt* to dissuade (*de* from).

disuasión *f* dissuasion || MIL *fuerza* or *poder de disuasión* striking force (capacidad), deterrent (arma).

disuasivo, va; disuasorio, ria *adj* dissuasive || MIL *fuerza disuasiva, poder disuasivo* striking force (capacidad), deterrent (arma).

disuelto, ta *adj* dissolved.

disúrico, ca *adj* MED dysuric.

disyunción *f* disjunction.

disyuntiva *f* alternative || *no tengo otra disyuntiva* I have no other choice *o* alternative.

disyuntivo, va *adj* disjunctive.

disyuntor *m* ELECTR circuit breaker, cutout.

dita *f* surety, bond (garantía) || AMER debt (deuda) || *vender a dita* to sell on credit.

ditirámbico, ca *adj* dithyrambic.

ditirambo *m* dithyramb.

DIU *abrev de dispositivo intrauterino* IUD, intrauterine device.

diuresis *f* MED diuresis.

diurético, ca *adj/sm* MED diuretic.

diurno, na *adj* diurnal, daily.
◆ *m* REL diurnal (libro).

diuturnidad *f* diuturnity.

diva *f* POÉT goddess || MÚS diva, prima donna.

divagación *f* digression (al hablar).
◆ *pl* wanderings.

divagador, ra *adj* digressive || wandering.

divagar *vi* to wander, to roam || to digress, to ramble (al hablar).

diván *m* divan, couch (canapé) || diwan, divan (consejo y gobierno turco) || diwan, divan (poesía oriental).

divergencia *f* divergence.

divergente *adj* divergent || FIG divergent, differing.

divergir *vi* to diverge || FIG to diverge, to differ || to diverge, to fork (carreteras).

diversidad *f* diversity, variety.

diversificación *f* diversification || diversity (diversidad).

diversificar *vt* to diversify, to vary.
◆ *vpr* to be diversified || to vary (variar).

diversiforme *adj* diversiform.

diversión *f* recreation, distraction, pastime; *la caza es su diversión preferida* hunting is his favourite pastime || amusement, diversion, entertainment; *hay pocas diversiones en este pueblo* there are few amusements in this town || MIL diversion || *servir de diversión* to keep one amused, to be a pastime.

diverso, sa *adj* diverse || different (diferente).
◆ *pl* several, different, various; *en diversas oportunidades* on several occasions; *artículos de diversas categorías* articles of different kinds || varied (variado); *el orador habló sobre los temas más diversos* the orator spoke on the most varied themes || miscellaneous (extractos) || sundry (gastos) || several, various (razones) || *artículos diversos* sundries.

divertido, da *adj* amusing, entertaining, funny; *una película divertida* an entertaining film || funny (chiste) || funny, amusing (persona).

divertimento *m* MÚS divertissement.

divertimiento *m* (p us) diversion, amusement.

divertir* *vt* to amuse, to entertain; *ese cuento me divirtió muchísimo* that tale amused me immensely || to distract, to divert (distraer la atención); *una estratagema para divertir al enemigo* a stratagem to distract the enemy.
◆ *vpr* to amuse o.s. (distraerse); *divertirse pintando* to amuse o.s. painting || to enjoy o.s., to have a good time (pasarlo bien); *divertirse a costa de uno* to enjoy o.s. at s.o.'s expense || to be diverted *o* distracted (la atención, etc.).

dividendo *m* MAT & COM dividend || — COM *dividendo acumulado, provisional* accrued, interim dividend | *sin dividendos* ex-dividend.

dividir *vt* to divide; *dividir 60 por 6* to divide 60 by 6 || to divide, to separate; *los Pirineos dividen España de Francia* the Pyrenees separate Spain from France || to divide, to disunite || to split, to divide; *dividir un pastel en cuatro porciones* to divide a cake into four portions; *el asunto dividió el pueblo en dos bandos* the affair divided the population into two camps || to divide (out), to split, to share (out) (repartir); *dividir un pastel entre cuatro personas* to share a cake out between four people || *divide y vencerás* divide and conquer.

dividivi *m* BOT divi-divi.

divieso *m* boil, furuncle (furúnculo).

divinatorio, ria *adj* divinatory.

divinidad *f* divinity, deity (del paganismo) || God (Dios) || divinity, godhead (naturaleza) || — FIG *¡qué divinidad!* how divine! | *¡es una divinidad!* it's (she's, etc.) gorgeous *o* divine!

divinización *f* deification || glorification (ensalzamiento).

divinizar *vt* to deify || FIG to exalt, to glorify.

divino, na *adj* divine; *castigo divino* divine punishment || FIG divine, lovely, gorgeous (precioso).

divisa *f* emblem, ensign; *el águila es la divisa del país* the eagle is the country's emblem || COM currency; *el dólar es una divisa muy fuerte* the dollar is a very strong currency || HERÁLD motto (lema) | device (emblema) || TAUR owner's coloured rosette fixed to bull's neck.
◆ *pl* COM foreign exchange *o* currency; *control de divisas* foreign exchange control.

divisar *vt* to make out, to distinguish, to discern.

divisibilidad *f* divisibility.

divisible *f* divisible.

división *f* division || GRAM hyphen, dash (guión) || MIL division || FIG difference, division, divergence; *división de opiniones* divergence of opinion | discord; *sembrar la división en una familia* to sow discord within a family | split (de un partido) || DEP *división de honor* league of honour | *primera, segunda división* first, second division.

divisional; divisionario, ria *adj* divisional.

diviso, sa *adj* divided, split.

divisor, ra *adj* dividing.
◆ *m* divider || MAT divisor | factor; *máximo común divisor* highest common factor.

divisorio, ria *adj* dividing; *pared divisoria* dividing wall || *línea divisoria de las aguas* watershed [US divide].

divo, va *adj* POÉT divine.
◆ *m/f* FIG star (figura principal).
◆ *m* pagan god, deity (divinidad).
◆ *f* POÉT goddess || MÚS diva, prima donna.

divorciado, da *adj* divorced.
◆ *m/f* divorcee.

divorciar *vt* to divorce.
◆ *vpr* to get *o* to be divorced ‖ *divorciarse de uno* to divorce s.o., to get a divorce from s.o.

divorcio *m* divorce ‖ FIG disagreement.

divulgación *f* divulging, disclosure, divulgation (revelación) ‖ extension; *divulgación agrícola* agricultural extension ‖ popularizing, spreading (de una canción) ‖ spreading, circulation (propagación).

divulgador, ra *adj* divulging, revealing.
◆ *m/f* divulger, revealer.

divulgar *vt* to divulge, to disclose (revelar) ‖ to spread, to circulate (propagar); *divulgar una noticia* to spread a piece of news ‖ to disseminate, to spread, to popularize; *la radio ha divulgado la música clásica* radio has popularized classical music.
◆ *vpr* to come out.

divulsión *f* MED divulsion.

dizque *adv* AMER apparently, seemingly (al parecer).

DNI *abrev de Documento Nacional de Identidad* ID, Identity Card.

do *m* MÚS do, doh (de la solfa) | C (primera nota de la escala diatónica) ‖ — *do de pecho* high C ‖ FIG & FAM *dar el do de pecho* to surpass o.s.
◆ *adv* POÉT where (donde) | whence (de donde).

dobladillo *m* hem (costura) ‖ turnup [US cuff] (de los pantalones).

doblado, da *adj* doubled, double ‖ bent (encorvado) ‖ folded (plegado) ‖ FIG stocky, thickset (estatura) ‖ deceitful, two-faced (engañoso) ‖ FIG & FAM dead beat (agotado).

doblaje *m* CINEM dubbing.

doblar *vt* to fold; *doblar un papel en dos* to fold a piece of paper in two ‖ to turn up (los bajos de un pantalón) ‖ to double (duplicar); *doblar un sueldo* to double a salary ‖ to bend; *doblar la rodilla, el codo* to bend one's knee, one's elbow; *doblar una vara de hierro* to bend an iron bar ‖ to turn, to go round; *doblar una esquina* to turn a corner ‖ MAR to round; *doblar un cabo* to round a cape ‖ FIG to subdue, to reduce to submission (dominar) | to make (s.o.) change his mind, to bring (s.o.) round (hacer cambiar de parecer) ‖ to double (en el bridge) ‖ CINEM to dub (una película) | to double for; *en esta escena un jinete experto dobla a la estrella* in this scene an expert horseman doubles for the star ‖ FIG & FAM to wear out (cansar mucho) ‖ AMER to shoot down (matar) ‖ — FIG & FAM *doblar a uno a palos* or *a golpes* to beat s.o. up ‖ *doblar el pico de una página* to turn down the corner of a page ‖ *le doblo la edad* I'm twice as old as he is, I'm twice his age.
◆ *vi* to double (duplicarse); *sus fuerzas doblaron en dos meses* his strength doubled in two months ‖ to turn; *doblar a la derecha* to turn right; *en ese punto la carretera dobla hacia el río* at that point the road turns towards the river ‖ to toll (tocar a muerto); *las campanas están doblando por alguien* the bells are tolling for s.o. ‖ FIG to give in, to yield, to submit (ceder) | TAUR to collapse, to crumple up (el toro al morir) ‖ to double, to play two roles (un actor).
◆ *vpr* to fold (plegarse) ‖ to double (duplicarse) ‖ to bend, to give, to buckle; *las ramas se doblan bajo el peso del fruto* the branches give beneath the weight of the fruit ‖ to stoop, to bend down (persona) ‖ FIG to give in, to yield (ceder) ‖ FAM *doblarse por la cintura* to be in stitches (de risa).

doble *adj* double; *esta casa es doble de alta que ésa* this house is double the height of that one; *un doble error* a double error; *un geranio doble* a double geranium; *doble sentido* double meaning ‖ dual (mando, nacionalidad, etc.) ‖ stocky, thickset (rechoncho) ‖ thick (fuerte); *una tela muy doble* a very thick cloth ‖ FIG two-faced, deceitful (disimulado) ‖ — *con* or *de doble sentido* ambiguous ‖ COM *contabilidad por partida doble* double-entry book-keeping ‖ *de doble fondo* double-bottomed ‖ *en doble ejemplar* in duplicate.
◆ *m* double; *has pagado el doble de lo que vale* you payed double what it's worth ‖ duplicate; *el doble de un acta* the duplicate of a deed ‖ carbon copy (con papel carbón) ‖ fold, crease (pliegue) ‖ knell, toll (toque de campana) ‖ DEP doubles *pl*; *doble caballeros* or *masculino* men's doubles (tenis); *doble damas* ladies' doubles; *doble mixto* mixed doubles ‖ double (cantidad doble de whisky, cerveza) ‖ double (en los naipes) ‖ double (sosia) ‖ CINEM double, stand-in ‖ — *doble contra sencillo* two-to-one (apuesta) ‖ CINEM *doble especial* stunt man ‖ *doble o nada* double or quits (juego) ‖ *el doble* twice as much; *costar el doble* to cost twice as much ‖ *el doble de la distancia* twice *o* double the distance ‖ *el doble que* twice as much as; *come el doble que tú* he eats twice as much as you.
◆ *adv* double; *ver doble* to see double ‖ *al doble* twofold.

doblegable *adj* FIG pliable, pliant; *carácter muy doblegable* very pliable character.

doblegar *vt* to fold (doblar) ‖ to bend (curvar) ‖ to twist (torcer) ‖ to brandish (un arma) ‖ FIG to make (s.o.) give in (hacer ceder) | to humble.
◆ *vpr* to fold (doblarse) ‖ to bend (encorvarse) ‖ to twist (torcerse) ‖ FIG to yield, to give in (ceder).

doblemente *adv* doubly; *doblemente magnánimo* doubly magnanimous ‖ FIG deceitfully, two-facedly (con falsedad); *actuar doblemente* to act deceitfully.

doblete *adj* medium, medium-thick.
◆ *m* GRAM doublet ‖ doublet (piedra falsa).

doblez *m* fold (pliegue) ‖ hem (dobladillo).
◆ *f* deceitfulness, two-facedness, duplicity, double-dealing (falsedad).

doblón *m* doubloon (moneda antigua).

doce *adj* twelve; *los doce apóstoles* the twelve apostles ‖ twelfth; *Pío XII (doce)* Pius XII [the twelfth].
◆ *m* twelve; *en la lotería ha salido el doce* twelve has come up in the lottery ‖ twelfth; *el doce de agosto* the twelfth of August.
◆ *f pl* *las doce de la noche* midnight, twelve o'clock at night ‖ *son las doce (del día)* it's twelve o'clock, it's twelve noon, it's midday *o* noon.

doceavo, va *adj* twelfth.

docena *f* dozen; *una docena de ostras* a dozen oysters ‖ — *a docenas* by the dozen (venta), in dozens, by the dozen; *llegaban a docenas* they were arriving in dozens ‖ FIG *la docena del fraile* the baker's dozen ‖ *por docenas* by the dozen.

doceno, na *adj* twelfth (duodécimo).

docente *adj* teaching; *cuerpo, personal docente* teaching body, staff ‖ educational, teaching; *centro docente* educational centre.

dócil *adj* docile, meek, mild; *dócil de condición* of a docile nature ‖ obedient; *me gustan los niños dóciles* I like obedient children.

docilidad *f* docility, meekness, mildness ‖ obedience.

dócilmente *adv* docilely, meekly, mildly ‖ obediently.

dock *m* dock (dársena) ‖ warehouse (almacén).

dócker *m* docker (descargador).

doctamente *adv* learnedly.

docto, ta *adj* learned, erudite (sabio) ‖ *muy docto en historia* well versed in history.
◆ *m/f* scholar, learned person (erudito).

doctor, ra *m/f* doctor; *la señora de Jáuregui es doctora en filosofía* Mrs. Jáuregui is a doctor of philosophy; *la mujer del farmacéutico es doctora* the chemist's wife is a doctor ‖ — REL *doctor de la Iglesia* doctor of the Church ‖ *doctor honoris causa* honorary doctor ‖ *investir a alguien doctor honoris causa* to award s.o. an honorary degree.

doctorado *m* doctorate.

doctoral *adj* doctoral ‖ pompous, pedantic; *habla siempre en tono doctoral* he always speaks in a pompous tone.

doctorando *m* candidate for a doctor's degree.

doctorar *vt* to confer a doctor's degree on.
◆ *vpr* to take one's doctorate (hacer el doctorado) ‖ to receive one's doctorate (obtener el doctorado).

doctorear *vi* FAM to talk pompously.

doctrina *f* doctrine; *la doctrina aristotélica, budista* Aristotelian, Buddhist doctrine ‖ teaching (enseñanza) ‖ knowledge, learning (ciencia) ‖ catechism (catecismo).

doctrinal *adj* doctrinal.

doctrinar *vt* to teach (enseñar) ‖ FIG to indoctrinate (convencer).

doctrinario, ria *adj/s* doctrinaire.

doctrinarismo *m* doctrinairism.

doctrinero *m* catechist ‖ AMER parish priest.

doctrino *m* orphan, child raised in an orphanage.

documentación *f* documentation ‖ papers *pl* (de identidad) ‖ — *documentación del buque* ship's papers ‖ *documentación del coche* car licence and insurance papers of a car.

documental *adj* documentary; *prueba documental* documentary proof.
◆ *m* CINEM documentary.

documentalista *m/f* CINEM documentarist.

documentar *vt* to document; *una causa bien documentada* a well-documented case.
◆ *vpr* to gather documentary evidence ‖ — *documentarse para un libro* to gather material for a book ‖ *documentarse sobre un tema* to read up on *o* to do some research on a subject.

documento *m* document ‖ — *documento de identidad* proof of identity ‖ *documento justificativo* voucher, certificate ‖ *Documento Nacional de Identidad* national identity card.
◆ *pl* papers (de identidad).

dodecaedro *m* MAT dodecahedron.

dodecafónico, ca *adj* MÚS dodecaphonic.

dodecafonismo *m* MÚS dodecaphony.

dodecágono, na *adj* MAT dodecagonal.
◆ *m* dodecagon.

dodecasílabo, ba *adj* alexandrine, twelve-syllable, dodecasyllabic.
◆ *m* alexandrine, dodecasyllable.

dogal *m* halter (para atar un animal) ‖ noose, hangman's rope (para ahorcar) ‖ FIG & FAM *estar con el dogal al cuello* to be in a tight spot, to have one's neck in a noose.

dogaresa *f* dogaressa.

dogma *m* dogma.

dogmático, ca *adj* dogmatic.
◆ *m/f* dogmatist.
◆ *f* dogmatics.

dogmatismo *m* dogmatism ‖ dogma.

dogmatista *m* dogmatist.

dogmatizador, ra; dogmatizante *m/f* dogmatizer, dogmatist.

dogmatizar *vi* to dogmatize.

dogo *m* bulldog (perro).

doladera *f* TECN cooper's adze (herramienta).

doladura *f* hewing (desbastadura) || shaving (viruta).

dolaje *m* wine absorbed by the cask.

dólar *m* dollar.

dolencia *f* complaint, ailment (achaque) || ache, pain (dolor).

doler* *vi* to hurt; *me duele la cabeza* my head is hurting; *sus insultos me han dolido mucho* I was very hurt by his insults || to have a pain; *me duele el estómago* I have a pain in my stomach || to ache (producir un dolor continuo); *me duele la cabeza, el estómago* my head, my stomach aches || to grieve, to pain, to distress (afligir); *me duele ver tanta injusticia* it grieves me to see so much injustice || to hurt, to pain, to be sorry; *me duele tener que decirle esto* I am sorry to have to tell you this, it hurts me to have to tell you this || — FIG *ahí le duele* that's where the shoe pinches || *estar dolido* to be hurt (ofendido), to be grieved (afligido).
◆ *vpr* to feel the effects of; *dolerse del golpe* to feel the effects of the blow || to regret; *dolerse de haber dicho tales cosas* to regret having said such things || to sympathize with, to pity, to have pity on (compadecer) || to complain (quejarse); *se duele de lo mal que lo han tratado* he complains about how badly he has been treated || to grieve (*de* at, over; *por* for) (afligirse) || *dolerse de sus pecados* to repent of one's sins.

dolicocefalia *f* dolichocephalism, dolichocephaly.

dolicocéfalo, la *adj* dolichocephalic.
◆ *m/f* dolichocephal.

doliente *adj* sick, ailing, poorly (que tiene dolencia) || aching (que duele) || sad, sorrowful (triste).
◆ *m/f* mourner (en entierro) || MED sick person.

dolmán *m* dolman.

dolmen *m* dolmen.

dolo *m* JUR wilful misrepresentation (en contrato, trato) | fraud, dolus (fraude).

Dolomitas *npr fpl* GEOGR Dolomites.

dolor *m* pain; *sintió un dolor repentino en el brazo* he felt a sudden pain in his arm || ache; *tengo un dolor latente en la espalda* I have a nagging ache in my back || FIG sorrow, grief, regret (pena); *con harto dolor de mi parte* with great regret || — FIG *causar dolor* to pain, to grieve || *dolor de cabeza* headache || FIG *dolor de corazón* remorse || *dolor de costado* stitch, (ant) pneumonia || *dolor de estómago, de muelas, de oído, de tripas* , stomachache, toothache, earache, bellyache || *dolores del parto* labour pains || *dolor sordo* dull ache || *estar con los dolores* to be in labour (mujer).

— OBSERV *Ache* es un dolor que suele ser continuo e interno, y no causado por una herida. *Pain* es más general y puede ser continuo o repentino, interno o externo.

dolora *f* short poem on a philosophical theme of the type composed by Campoamor.

dolorido, da *adj* painful, aching, sore; *tengo la pierna dolorida del golpe de ayer* my leg is sore from the knock I received yesterday || FIG pained, grieved, grief-stricken (afligido) || sad, sorrowful (triste).

doloroso, sa *adj* painful; *una operación, una decisión dolorosa* a painful operation, decision || FIG painful, grievous, distressing (afligente) | pitiable, pitiful (que inspira compasión).
◆ *f* ARTES Madonna (representación de la Virgen) || FAM *tráigame la dolorosa, por favor* what's the damage? (al pedir la cuenta).

doloroso, sa *adj* dolose, fraudulent.

doma; domadura *f* taming (de fieras) || breaking in (de caballerías) || training (adiestramiento) || FIG taming, mastering, control (de las pasiones) || *La doma de la bravía* The Taming of the Shrew (de Shakespeare).

domador, ra *m/f* tamer (que amansa animales salvajes) || trainer (que los adiestra) || — *domador de caballos* horsebreaker, broncobuster || *domador de leones* lion tamer.

domadura *f* ⟶ **doma.**

domar *vt* to tame, to domesticate (fieras) || to break in (una caballería) || to train (adiestrar) || FIG to break in; *domar zapatos nuevos* to break in new shoes | to tame, to bring under control (a alguien) | to tame, to master, to control (las pasiones).

domeñable *adj* tamable || trainable (adiestrable) || FIG controllable, tamable (pasiones, persona).

domeñar *vt* to subdue, to reduce to obedience (a una persona) || to subdue, to control, to master (las pasiones) || *domeñar la resistencia de uno* to break down s.o.'s resistance.

domesticable *adj* domesticable, tamable (que se puede amansar) || trainable (que se puede adiestrar).

domesticación *f* domestication || taming (domadura) || training (adiestramiento).

domesticar *vt* to domesticate, to tame; *domesticar un ratón* to domesticate a mouse || to train (adiestrar); *domesticar un elefante, pulgas* to train an elephant, fleas || FIG to subdue, to reduce to submission (domar a alguien) | to educate (educar a alguien).
◆ *vpr* to become domesticated (un animal) || FIG to become sociable (una persona).

domesticidad *f* domesticity.

doméstico, ca *adj* domestic; *servicio, animal doméstico* domestic service, animal || domestic, home; *economía doméstica* domestic economy; *artes domésticas* domestic arts.
◆ *m/f* servant, domestic.

domiciliación *f* domiciliation || COM *domiciliación bancaria* payment by standing order.

domiciliado, da *adj* living, resident, domiciled (p us); *está domiciliado en el 4 de la calle de Alcalá* he is resident at n.° 4 calle de Alcalá.

domiciliar *vt* to domicile || *domiciliar una cuenta* to give the number of an account (for automatic payment).

domiciliario, ria *adj* domiciliary || house; *arresto domiciliario* house arrest.
◆ *m/f* inhabitant, resident, tenant.

domicilio *m* residence, home, domicile (p us), abode (p us); *elegir domicilio* to take up residence *o* one's domicile *o* one's abode, to make a home; *domicilio particular* private residence || — *a domicilio* home || ECON *domicilio fiscal* fiscal residence || *domicilio social* head office, registered office || *entrega a domicilio* home delivery service || *sin domicilio fijo* of no fixed abode.

dominación *f* domination || dominion, rule, power, control || MIL commanding position, high ground [dominating an area] || pull-up (en gimnasia).
◆ *pl* REL dominions, dominations (ángeles).

dominante *adj* dominating, dominant, ruling; *el poder dominante* the dominat power || dominant (altura) || commanding, dominant, dominating (posición, situación) || prevailing, predominating (viento, color, opinión) || governing, leading, master (idea) || predominant (interés) || domineering (despótico); *tiene una mujer muy dominante* he has a very domineering wife || MÚS dominant || *carácter dominante* domineering *o* dominant character.
◆ *f* dominant feature *o* characteristic || BIOL & MÚS dominant.

dominar *vt* to dominate, to rule, to control; *Napoleón quiso dominar Europa* Napoleon wanted to rule Europe || to control; *dominar un caballo, un barco, los nervios* to control a horse, a boat, one's nerves || to overpower (a un adversario) || to put down, to subdue (una revolución, rebelión) || to control, to contain, to check (una epidemia, un incendio) || to control, to master, to restrain (las pasiones) || to get over (una pena) || to have a good *o* sound knowledge of, to master (un tema); *dominar la química* to have a good knowledge of chemistry || to have a good command of, to master, to know well, to be fluent in (idioma) || to rise above (el ruido) || to dominate, to tower over; *el ayuntamiento domina la plaza* the city hall towers over the square || to command, to overlook; *la casa domina toda la bahía* the house commands the whole bay || — *desde ese pico se domina toda la ciudad* you can see the whole city from that peak || *dominar la situación* to master the situation, to have the situation under control || *te domina la envidia* you are ruled by envy.
◆ *vi* to dominate || to predominate || to stand out (un color, etc.).
◆ *vpr* to restrain o.s., to control o.s., to keep o.s. under control.

dominatriz *adj f* dominating || domineering (mujer).
◆ *f* domineeering woman.

dómine *m* latin teacher || FIG pedant.

domingo *m* Sunday; *vendré el domingo* I shall come on Sunday || — *domingo de Carnaval* Shrove Sunday || *domingo de Cuasimodo* Low Sunday || *Domingo de Ramos* Palm Sunday || *Domingo de Resurrección* Easter Sunday || *hacer domingo* to have a day off || *traje de los domingos* Sunday best.

Domingo *npr m* Dominic.

Domingo (Santo) *npr m* GEOGR Santo Domingo [Dominican Republic].

dominguejo *m* tumbler (juguete) || AMER non-entity (persona insignificante).

dominguillo *m* tumbler (juguete) || FIG & FAM *traer a uno como un dominguillo* to twist s.o. round one's little finger (manejar), to have s.o. running round at one's beck and call (mandar de un lado a otro).

Dominica *npr f* Dominique || GEOGR *La Dominica* Dominica (Antillas).

domínica *f* REL Sunday, the Sabbath | Sunday office (textos).

dominical *adj* Sunday, dominical || *la oración dominical* the Lord's Prayer.

dominicano, na *adj/s* Dominican (religioso y persona de la República Dominicana) || *República Dominicana* Dominican Republic.

dominico, ca *adj/s* Dominican (religioso).

dominio *m* authority, control (autoridad); *tener bajo su dominio* to have under one's authority; *un maestro que tiene dominio sobre sus alumnos* a teacher who has control over his pupils || dominion, power (soberanía) || domination (predominancia) || domain (territorio) || dominion (en el Commonwealth) || supremacy; *dominio del aire, de los mares* air, sea supremacy || FIG good knowledge, mastery; *tiene un gran dominio de las matemáticas* he has a very good knowledge of mathematics | good command (de un idioma) | control, restraint (de las pasiones) || JUR ownership, dominion (de bienes) || — *con pleno dominio de sus facultades* in full control of one's faculties || *dominio de sí mismo* self-control || *dominio público* public property || *recobrar el dominio de sí mismo* to pull o.s. together || *ser del dominio público* to be common knowledge.

dominó *m* dominoes *pl* (juego) || set of dominoes (conjunto de las fichas) || domino (disfraz).

domo *m* ARQ dome, cupola (cúpula).

don *m* gift, present (regalo) || donation (a una institución, etc.) || (natural) gift, talent (talento); *el don de lenguas* a gift for languages, a talent for languages || wish (en cuentos y leyendas); *el hada le concedió varios dones* the fairy granted him several wishes || — *don de acierto* knack for doing the right thing, savoir faire || *don de errar* knack for doing the wrong thing || *don de mando* qualities *pl* of a leader || *tener don de gentes* to have charm *o* magnetism, to get on well with people, to have a way with people || *tener el don de la palabra* to have a way with words, to have the gift of the gab (*fam*).

don *m* Mr; *Don Fulano de Tal* Mr So-and-So || — *Don Juan* don Juan (tenorio), womanizer, lady-killer, Casanova, don Juan (mujeriego) || *Señor Don (Sr. D., Sr. Dn.)* Esquire (Esq.); *Sr. Dn. Martín Rodríguez* Martín Rodríguez Esq (en un sobre).

— OBSERV *Don* is only used before the Christian name, which may or may not be followed by the surname.

— OBSERV Cuando *don* va seguido simplemente por el nombre de pila, no se traduce en inglés: *don Tomás* Thomas.

donación *f* donation (a una institución, etc.) || gift, present (regalo) || bequest (en testamento) || JUR *donación entre vivos* donation inter vivos.

donador, ra *adj/s* → **donante.**

donaire *m* grace, poise, elegance; *andar con mucho donaire* to walk with great poise || wit (en el hablar) || witticism, bon mot (agudeza).

donante; donador, ra *adj* donating.

◆ *m/f* donor || *donante de órgano, de sangre* organ, blood donor.

donar *vt* to donate, to give, to bestow.

donatario, ria *m/f* donee, donatory.

donativo *m* donation.

doncel *m* (ant) young nobleman *o* squire (joven noble) || king's pageboy, donzel (paje) || young nobleman in the king's army || chaste youth (muchacho virgen).

doncella *f* virgin, maid, maiden (virgen) || maiden, damsel (ant), girl (chica) || maid, housemaid (criada) || doncella, wrasse (pez) || *AMER* whitlow (panadizo) || *la Doncella de Orleáns* the Maid of Orleans (Juana de Arco).

doncellez; doncellería *f* virginity, maidenhood.

donde *adv* where; *¿dónde estás?* where are you?; *lo compré donde tú me dijiste* I bought it where you told me; *¿de dónde vienes?* where have you come from? || where, in which; *es un sitio donde abundan los peces* it is a spot where there are plenty of fish *o* in which there are plenty of fish || (ant) whence (de donde) || at *o* to the house of; *voy donde Juan* I am going to John's (house) || — *a donde* where; *¿a dónde vas?* where are you going? || *de* or *desde donde* where from, whence (ant) || *donde no* otherwise || *donde sea* anywhere || *el pueblo de donde viene* the village he comes from || *en donde* where, in which, wherein (ant); *la casa en donde nací* the house in which I was born || *estés donde estés* wherever you are || *hacia donde* towards which, where || *hasta donde* up to which || *¿hasta dónde?* how far? || FIG *¡mira por dónde!* fancy that! || *por donde* where; *el sitio por donde paseaba* the place where he was walking; through which; *la ciudad por donde pasé* the city which I passed through; whereupon, from which; *por donde se infiere que* whereupon *o* from which it follows that; by which, through which; *la ventana por donde entré* the window through which I got in || *¿por dónde?* why? (por qué), where?, whereabouts? (en qué sitio), which way? (por qué camino).

— OBSERV The interrogative adverb *dónde* always bears an accent.

dondequiera *adv* anywhere (en cualquier parte) || everywhere (en todas partes) || *dondequiera que* wherever, anywhere.

dondiego *m* BOT marvel-of-Peru, four o'clock || — *dondiego de día* morning glory || *dondiego de noche* marvel of Peru, four o'clock.

donjuán *m* BOT marvel of Peru, four o'clock.

donjuanesco *adj m* fond of women, donjuanesque.

donjuanismo *m* philandering, womanizing, donjuanism.

donosamente *adj* wittily; *habla muy donosamente* he speaks very wittily || gracefully, elegantly, with great poise.

donosidad *f* → **donosura.**

donoso, sa *adj* witty (divertido); *una observación donosa* a witty remark || light (estilo) || graceful, elegant, poised (elegante) || fine (con ironía); *¡donosa pregunta!* that's a fine thing to ask! || — *¡donosa ocurrencia!* what a bright idea! || *donosa cosa es que...* the best part of it is that...

donostiarra *adj* [of *o* from] San Sebastián.

◆ *m/f* native *o* inhabitant of San Sebastián.

donosura; donosidad *f* wit (gracia, humor) || witticism, bon mot (agudeza) || grace, poise, elegance (elegancia) || lightness (del estilo).

doña *f* Mrs, mistress (ant), madam (p us); *doña Dolores Valdés* Mrs Dolores Valdés || *Señora Doña (Sra. D.ª)* Mrs (en un sobre).

— OBSERV *Doña* indicates a married woman or a widow and is only used before the Christian name, which may be followed by the surname or not.

— OBSERV Cuando *doña* va seguido simplemente por el nombre de pila, no se traduce o se emplea la fórmula anticuada *mistress*: *doña María* Mary *o* mistress Mary.

dopaje *m* doping.

dopante *adj* doping.

dopar *vt* to drug, to dope (drogar con estimulante).

doping *m* doping, drugging.

doquier; doquiera *adv* anywhere || *por doquier* everywhere.

dorada *f* gilthead (pez).

doradilla *f* BOT scale fern || gilthead (dorada).

dorado, da *adj* golden (de color de oro) || gilt (cubierto de oro) || FIG golden; *edad, juventud dorada* golden age, golden years of youth; *el siglo dorado* the golden age || bay (caballo) || *libro de cantos dorados* gilt-edged book.

◆ *m* gilding (acción de dorar) || gilt (capa de oro) || dorado (pez).

Dorado (El) *npr m* El Dorado (país legendario).

doradura *f* gilding (acción de dorar).

dorar *vt* to gild, to cover with gold || to goldplate (un objeto de metal) || — FIG & FAM *dorar la píldora* to gild the pill || CULIN *hacer dorar* to brown.

◆ *vpr* to turn brown *o* golden.

dórico, ca *adj* Dorian (de los dorios) || ARQ Doric; *orden dórico* Doric order.

◆ *m* doric (dialecto griego).

Dórida; Dóride *npr f* GEOGR Doris.

dorífera; dorífora *f* ZOOL colorado beetle.

dorio, ria *adj/s* Dorian (de Dóride).

dormán *m* Dolman (chaqueta).

dormición *f* dormition (de la Virgen).

dormida *f* short, sleep, nap.

dormidero, ra *adj* soporific, sleep-inducing.

dormido, da *adj* asleep; *estar medio dormido* to be half asleep || sleepy (con sueño) || — *quedarse dormido* to fall asleep (dormirse), to oversleep (pegársele a uno las sábanas) || FIG *tengo la pierna dormida* my leg has gone dead *o* has gone to sleep.

dormilón, ona *adj* sleepy-headed, fond of one's bed *o* of sleeping, lazy.

◆ *m/f* sleepyhead.

◆ *f* earring (arete) || comfortable armchair [used for taking a nap].

dormir* *vi* to sleep || to spend *o* to pass the night (pernoctar); *dormimos en Madrid* we spent the night in Madrid || FIG to hang fire (un asunto) || — *¡a dormir!* to bed! || *dormir al raso* or *al sereno* or *con cortinas verdes* to sleep outdoors *o* in the open *o* under the stars || FIG *dormir como un lirón* or *como un tronco* or *a pierna suelta* or *como una marmota* to sleep like a log, to sleep soundly | *dormir con un ojo abierto* to sleep with one eye open || *dormir de un tirón* to sleep soundly all night || *dormir doce horas de un tirón* to sleep for twelve hours solid || *echarse a dormir* to go to bed || *ganas de dormir* sleepiness || *quien duerme cena* he who sleeps forgets his hunger || *ser de mal dormir* to sleep badly, to be a very light sleeper.

◆ *vt* to put *o* to send *o* to lull to sleep; *dormir a un niño* to put a child to sleep || to send to sleep; *esta música me duerme* this music sends me to sleep || to put *o* to send to sleep (anestesiar) || — *dormir el sueño de los justos* to sleep the sleep of the just || *dormir el último sueño* to be at rest || FAM *dormir la mona* to sleep it off || *dormir la siesta* to have a siesta *o* a nap.

◆ *vpr* to go to sleep, to fall asleep, to drop off (to sleep) || FIG to go to sleep, to go dead; *se me ha dormido la pierna* my leg has gone to sleep || MAR to heel *o* to list badly (inclinarse el barco) || *dormirse sobre los laureles* to rest on one's laurels.

dormitar *vi* to doze, to snooze.

dormitorio *m* bedroom (alcoba) || dormitory (en una escuela, etc.).

dornajo; dornillo *m* round bowl (artesa).

dorsal *adj* dorsal, back; *músculos dorsales* dorsal muscles || GRAM dorsal (consonante).

◆ *m* number (en la espalda de un atleta).

dorso *m* back (de un animal) || back; *el dorso de una carta* the back of a letter || *véase al dorso* see over, please turn over (P. T. O.).

dos *adj/sm* two; *dos y dos son cuatro* two and two are four; *el dos de bastos* the two of clubs || second (segundo); *el 2 (dos) de enero* 2nd [the second of] January || second, (number) two; *el tomo dos* the second volume, volume (number) two || — *a dos pasos de aquí* a few steps away, a short way away, nearby || *cada dos días* every other day, every two days || *cada dos por tres* every five minutes || *de dos en dos* in twos, two by two; *llegaban de dos en dos* they arrived in twos; into twos, into groups of two; *dividir de dos en dos* to divide into twos || *dos a dos* two by two, in twos; *los alumnos andaban dos a dos* the pupils were walking in twos || *dos por dos* two by two, two times two, two twos (multiplicación), in twos, two by two (dos a dos), in twos (en grupos de dos) || *dos tes* double t || *dos veces* twice || *ellos dos* or *entre los dos* between the two of them, both of them || FAM *en un dos por tres* in a jiffy, in a flash, before you can say Jack Robinson || *es para los dos* it's for both of you || *hacer un trabajo entre dos* to share a job || *las dos* two o'clock || *los dos* both; *vinieron los dos* they both came; *los dos chicos son estudiantes* both boys are students || *no hay dos sin tres* misfortune always comes in threes || *para nosotros dos* for us two || *una de dos* one of the two.

dosalbo, ba *adj* with two white feet (caballo).

doscientos, tas *adj/sm* two hundred; *dos mil doscientos* two thousand two hundred; *había doscientas personas en la sala* there were two hundred people in the room || two hundredth (ordinal) || *mil doscientos* one thousand two hundred, twelve hundred.

dosel *m* canopy, baldachin (p us), dais (ant) (sobre altar, trono, cama, etc.).

dosificación *f* dosage || QUÍM titration.

dosificador *m* dosimeter.

dosificar *vt* to dose (un medicamento) || QUÍM to titrate || FIG to measure out, to apportion.

dosis *f inv* MED dose; *a* or *en pequeña dosis* in a small dose, in small doses || QUÍM proportion || FIG dose (cantidad) | admixture (de un defecto) || — MED *dosis de recuerdo* booster (de una vacuna) || FIG *en pequeñas dosis* in small doses || *tener una buena dosis de* to have one's share of.

dossier *m* dossier (expediente).

dotación *f* endowment; *dan cien libras como dotación* to give an endowment of a hundred pounds || MAR crew, complement (tripulación) || personnel, staff (en oficina, etc.) || dowry (de una mujer).

dotado, da *adj* gifted || endowed (*de* with) || equipped, fitted (una máquina).

dotal *adj* dowry, dotal.

dotar* *vt* to give a dowry, to give as a dowry, to dower (p us); *dotó a su hija con medio millón* he gave his daughter a dowry of half a million *o* half a million as a dowry || to endow, to provide; *dotar a un pueblo de una escuela* to endow a town with a school; *la naturaleza le ha dotado de buena vista* nature endowed him with good eyesight || to provide funds for, to assign money to (subvencionar) || to equip (equipar) || to staff (oficina) || to man (tripular un barco).

dote *f* dowry, marriage portion || portion brought by a nun on entering a convent or by a monk on entering a monastery.
◆ *pl* talent *sing*, gift *sing*; *tiene dotes para la música* he has a talent for music || — *dotes de mando* qualities of a leader || *es un niño de excelentes dotes* he is a very gifted child.

dovela *f* ARQ voussoir (cuña de piedra) | soffit (superficie).

dovelar *vt* ARQ to hew (a stone) into a voussoir, to make wedge-shaped.

dozavo, va *adj/s* twelfth (duodécimo) || IMPR *en dozavo* in duodecimo *o* twelvemo.

dracma *f* drachma (moneda) || dram (peso).

draconiano, na *adj* draconian, drastic.

draga *f* dredge, dredging machine (para limpiar) || drag (para buscar) || dredger (barco).

dragado; dragaje *m* dredging (para limpiar o excavar) || dragging (para encontrar algo perdido).

dragador, ra *adj* dredging.
◆ *m* dredger (boat).

dragaje *m* → **dragado.**

dragaminas *m inv* MAR minesweeper.

dragar *vt* to dredge (limpiar o excavar) || to drag (para encontrar algo perdido) || to sweep (minas).

dragea *f* (ant) sugar-coated pill (píldora).

drago *m* BOT dragon tree.

dragomán *m* dragoman, interpreter (intérprete).

dragón *m* dragon (animal fabuloso) || MIL dragoon (soldado) || ZOOL flying dragon (reptil) | greater weever (pez) || BOT snapdragon || TECN mouth, throat (de un horno).

dragona *f* MIL epaulette (charretera) | sword knot (de la espada).

dragoncillo *m* BOT tarragon.

dragonear *vi* AMER to pose, to pass o.s. off; *dragonear de médico* to pose *o* to pass o.s. off as a doctor | to boast (jactarse).

drama *m* TEATR drama; *drama lírico* lyric drama | drama, play (obra de teatro) || FIG drama.

dramática *f* dramatic art, dramaturgy (arte de escribir) || drama (género teatral).

dramático, ca *adj* dramatic.
◆ *m* dramatist (autor).

dramatismo *m* dramatism, drama.

dramatizar *vt* to dramatize.

dramaturgia *f* dramatic art, dramaturgy.

dramaturgo, ga *m/f* playwright, dramatist, dramaturge (p us), dramaturgist (p us).

dramón *m* FAM melodrama.

drapeado *m* ARTES drapery.

drapear *vt* to drape.

drástico, ca *adj* MED drastic || drastic (acción, medidas, etc.).
◆ *m* MED drastic purgative.

drávida *m/f* Dravidian.

drenaje *m* drainage (de un campo, un absceso, etc.) || — *colector de drenaje* main drain || *tubo de drenaje* drain, drainpipe.

drenar *vt* to drain (un terreno, un absceso, etc.).

drepanocitosis *f inv* MED drepanocytosis, sickle-cell anaemia.

dríada; dríade *f* dryad.

driblar *vi* DEP to dribble (regatear en el fútbol).

drible *m* DEP dribble (regate).

dril *m* drill, duck (tela).

drive *m* DEP drive (tenis, golf).

driza *f* MAR halyard.

drizar *vt* to hoist.

droga *f* drug || FIG & FAM story, tale, fib (mentira) | trick (engaño) | practical joke (broma) || FAM bother, nuisance (lata) || AMER bad debt (deuda) || *droga blanda* soft drug || *droga dura* hard drug.

drogadicción *f* drug addiction.

drogadicto, ta *adj/s* drug addict.

drogado, da *adj* drugged, doped.
◆ *m/f* drug addict.
◆ *m* doping.

drogar *vt* to drug, to dope.
◆ *vpr* to drug o.s.

drogata; drogota *m/f* FAM junkie.

drogmán *m* dragoman, interpreter (intérprete).

drogodependencia *f* dependence on drugs.

droguería *f* drysaltery, chandler's (ant) [*US* drugstore].

droguero, ra *m/f* drysalter [*US* druggist] || *AMER* swindler.

droguista *m/f* drysalter [*US* druggist] || *AMER* swindler.

dromedario *m* ZOOL dromedary.

druida *m* druid.

drupa *f* BOT drupe.

drusa *f* MIN druse.

dual *adj* dual.
◆ *adj/m* GRAM dual.

dualidad *f* duality || MIN dimorphism || *AMER* tie, draw (empate).

dualismo *m* dualism.

dualista *adj* dualistic.
◆ *m/f* dualist.

dubitación *f* doubt.

dubitativo, va *adj* doubting, dubitative, doubtful (que expresa duda) || dubitative (conjunción).

Dublín *n pr* GEOGR Dublin.

ducado *m* duchy, dukedom (territorio) || dukedom (título) || ducat (moneda).

ducal *adj* ducal; *palacio ducal* ducal palace.

ducentésimo, ma *adj/s* two hundredth.

duco *m* thick paint, lacquer.

dúctil *adj* ductile (metal, arcilla, etc.) || FIG ductile, pliant, pliable (persona).

ductilidad *f* ductility.

ducha *f* shower; *tomar* or *darse una ducha* to take *o* to have a shower || douche (para una parte del cuerpo) || FIG & FAM *esto vino como una ducha de agua fría* this put the damper on everything.

duchar *vt* to give a shower || MED to douche || FAM to douse, to dowse (mojar).
◆ *vpr* to have *o* to take a shower || to douche.

ducho, cha *adj* expert, skilful, well up; *ducho en latín* expert *o* skilful at Latin, well up in *o* on Latin || *estar ducho en la materia* to be well up on the subject.

duda *f* doubt; *sin la menor duda* without the slightest doubt; *sin duda alguna* without any doubt; *sin sombra de duda* without the shadow of a doubt; *fuera de duda* beyond doubt || — *en duda* in question || *en la duda abstente* when in doubt, don't; when in doubt, abstain || *entrar en la duda* to begin to have doubts || *estar en la duda* to be doubtful, to be in doubt || *no cabe duda, no hay duda, sin lugar a dudas* there is no doubt || *no te quepa duda* make no mistake about it || *poner en duda* to question, to doubt || *sacar de dudas a uno* to dispel s.o.'s doubts || *salir de dudas* to shed one's doubts || *sin duda* no doubt, undoubtedly, without a doubt.

dudar *vi/vt* to doubt, to have doubts, to be in doubt; *estoy dudando* I'm having doubts || to doubt, to have doubts about; *lo dudo* I doubt it; *dudo haber dicho eso* I doubt having said that || — *dudar de* or *sobre* or *acerca de algo* to doubt sth., to be in doubt *o* to have doubts about *o* as to sth.; *dudo de su honradez* I have doubts about his honesty; to question (poner en tela de juicio), to suspect (sospechar); *la policía duda del cajero* the police suspect the cashier || *dudar en* to hesitate to; *dudo en salir por si acaso vienen* I hesitate to go out lest they should arrive || *dudar entre* (con infinitivo), to be not sure *o* not certain whether to (with infinitive); *dudo entre ir por avión o ir en tren* I am not sure whether to go by plane or train (con sustantivo), to be unable to decide *o* to make up one's mind between; *dudo entre los dos* I can't decide between the two || *dudar que* to doubt whether *o* if; *dudo que sea tan tacaño* I doubt whether he is such a skinflint; *dudo que pueda venir tan tarde* I doubt whether he can come *o* whether he will be able to come so late || *dudar si* to doubt whether *o* if; *dudo si llegaré a tiempo* I doubt if I will get there on time; to be not sure *o* not certain whether; *dudo si he cerrado bien la puerta* I am not certain whether I closed the door properly || *no dudo de ello* I don't doubt it, I have no doubt about it.

dudosamente *adv* doubtfully (sin certeza) || hesitantly (vacilando) || dubiously (sospechosamente).

dudoso, sa *adj* doubtful, uncertain; *la fecha de su llegada es dudosa* the date of his arrival is doubtful || hesitant, undecided (vacilante) || dubious (sospechoso); *un tipo dudoso* a dubious character || questionable (discutible).

duela *f* stave (de tonel).

duelista *m* duellist [US duelist].

duelo *m* duel (combate); *batirse en duelo* to fight a duel || sorrow, grief, affliction (dolor) || mourning (luto) || mourners *pl* (los dolientes) || funeral procession (cortejo) || *presidir el duelo* to lead the mourning, to be chief mourner.
◆ *pl* toils, labours, trials (trabajos) || — CULIN *duelos y quebrantos* fried dish made with eggs and brains, bacon, etc. || FAM *los duelos con pan son menos* money lessens the blow.

duende *m* goblin, elf, imp (espíritu) || FIG imp, mischievous child (niño travieso) | magic; *el duende de una persona* a person's magic || — *andar como un duende, parecer un duende* to be a will-o'-the-wisp, to be always popping up all over the place || *tener duende* to have sth. on one's mind (estar preocupado), to have a certain magic (persona, sitio, etc.).
◆ *pl* FIG magic *sing; los duendes del flamenco* the magic of flamenco.

dueña *f* owner (propietaria) || owner, mistress (de un perro, gato, etc.) || owner, proprietress (de un negocio) || landlady (de una pensión) || mistress, lady (de una casa) || matron, married woman (señora) || (ant) duenna, governess (dama de compañía) || FIG mistress (dominadora) || — *dueña de honor* lady-in-waiting || FIG & FAM *ponerle a uno cual digan dueñas* to abuse s.o. (insultarle), to drag s.o.'s name through the mud (insultarle a espaldas suyas).

dueño *m* owner (propietario) || owner, master (de un perro, gato, etc.) || owner, proprietor (de un negocio); *es dueño de un bar* he is the proprietor of a bar || landlord (de una taberna, una pensión) || master, head of the household (cabeza de familia) || FIG master; *ser dueño de la situación* to be the master of the situation || — *dueño y señor* lord and master || *hacerse dueño de* to take command of, to master (una situación, etc.), to take possession of || *ser dueño de sí mismo* to be one's own master, to be free to do as one pleases (ser libre), to be master of o.s., to have self-control (dominarse) || *ser dueño de sus pasiones* to be master of *o* in control of one's passions || *ser muy dueño de* to be entirely free *o* at liberty to; *es usted muy dueño de aceptar o rehusar* you are entirely free to accept or refuse.

Duero *npr m* GEOGR Douro, Duero.

duetista *m/f* duettist.

dueto *m* MÚS short duet.

dulce *adj* sweet; *el café está muy dulce* the coffee is very sweet; *la música dulce de la flauta* the sweet music of the flute; *el dulce placer de la vuelta al hogar* the sweet joy of a homecoming || mild, gentle (carácter, clima, voz) || soft (viento, brisa) || loving, soft (palabras) || gentle, tender (mirada) || fresh (agua) || soft (metal).
◆ *m* sweet [US candy] || preserved *o* candied fruit (fruta) || — FIG *a nadie le amarga un dulce* a gift is always welcome || *dulce de fruta* candied fruit || AMER *dulce de leche* custard cream || *dulce de membrillo* quince preserve || *en dulce* candied (confitado); *fruta en dulce* candied fruit; in syrup; *melocotón en dulce* peaches in syrup.
◆ *pl* sweetmeats, sweets, sweet things (golosinas) || *a mí me gustan los dulces* I am fond of sweet things, I have a sweet tooth.

dulcera *f* preserve dish, sweet dish.

dulcería *f* confectionery, confectioner's [US candy store].

dulcero, ra *adj* sweet-toothed (goloso) || *ser dulcero* to have a sweet tooth.
◆ *m/f* confectioner.

dulcificación *f* sweetening || FIG soothing.

dulcificante *adj* sweetening || FIG soothing.

dulcificar *vt* to sweeten || FIG to soften, to soothe.
◆ *vpr* to become milder (el tiempo).

Dulcinea *f* sweetheart, lady-love, Dulcinea.

dulia *f* REL dulia, veneration of angels and saints.

dulzaina *f* MÚS «Dulzaina», pipe [popular folk instrument similar to the «chirimia» and usually played to the accompaniment of the «tamboril»] || FAM sweet stuff, sweet things *pl* (palabras melosas).

dulzarrón, ona; dulzón, ona *adj* sickly, oversweet; *una pequeña tarta dulzarrona* a sickly little tart || FIG sickly (persona).

dulzor *m* sweetness (del azúcar, de una sonrisa, etc.) || gentleness, sweetness (del carácter).

dulzura *f* sweetness; *la dulzura de la miel, de su sonrisa* the sweetness of honey, of her smile || gentleness, sweetness (del carácter) || mildness (del clima).

duma *f* duma (asamblea en Rusia zarista).

dum-dum *f* dumdum (bala explosiva).

dumping *m* COM dumping.

duna *f* dune.

dundeco, ca *adj* AMER ⟶ **dundo.**

dundera *f* AMER silliness, stupidity, foolishness.

dundo, da *adj* AMER silly, stupid, foolish.
◆ *m/f* fool, dolt, ass.

dúo *m* MÚS duet, duo.

duodecimal *adj* duodecimal.

duodécimo, ma *adj/s* twelfth || *en duodécimo lugar* twelfth, in twelfth place.

duodenal *adj* MED duodenal.

duodenitis *f inv* MED duodenitis.

duodeno, na *adj* (p us) twelfth.
◆ *m* ANAT duodenum.

duodenotomía *f* MED duodenectomy.

dúplex *adj/sm* TECN duplex || duplex, duplex telegraphy; *enlace dúplex* duplex line *o* link || splitlevel flat, maisonette [US duplex] (piso).

dúplica *f* JUR rejoinder.

duplicación *f* duplication (de documentos, etc.) || doubling; *la duplicación de la producción* the doubling of output.

duplicado *m* duplicate, copy; *el duplicado de un acta* the copy of a deed || duplicate; *el duplicado de una llave* a duplicate key.
◆ *adj* in duplicate || double (doblado) || A; *calle Miracruz número 17 duplicado* nº 17A, Miracruz Street || *por duplicado* in duplicate.

duplicador, ra *adj* duplicating.
◆ *m* duplicator (máquina).

duplicar *vt* to duplicate (reproducir); *duplicar un documento* to duplicate a document || to double (multiplicar por dos); *duplicar la producción* to double production || JUR to answer [the plaintiff's reply].
◆ *vpr* to double; *la población se ha duplicado* the population has doubled.

duplicidad *f* duplicity, double-dealing, two-facedness.

duplo, pla *adj/sm* double || *ocho es el duplo de cuatro* eight is twice four, eight is double four.

duque *m* duke (título); *el señor duque* his Grace the Duke.

duquesa *f* duchess; *la señora duquesa* her Grace the Duchess.

durabilidad *f* durability.

durable *adj* durable, lasting.

duración *f* duration, length; *la duración de nuestra estancia en España* the length of our stay in Spain; *la duración del día, de la película* the length of the day, of the film || life (de un coche, una bombilla, una pila, etc.) || — *de corta o poca duración* short-lived; *moda, felicidad de poca duración* short-lived fashion, happiness; short; *una visita de poca duración* a short visit || *de larga duración* long-lasting, lengthy (enfermedad), long-life (pila, bombilla, etc.), long (estancia, vacaciones, etc.), lasting (éxito, placer), long-playing (disco) || *duración media de la vida* average life span, average life expectancy.

duraderamente *adv* durably.

duradero, ra *adj* durable, lasting || lasting; *paz duradera* lasting peace.

duraluminio *m* duralumin (aleación).

duramadre; duramáter *f* ANAT dura mater.

duramen *m* BOT duramen.

duramente *adv* hard; *trabajar duramente* to work hard || harshly, severely; *la vida le trató duramente* life treated him very harshly.

durante *prep* during; *durante las vacaciones* during the holidays || in; *durante el día* in the daytime || for; *vivió en España durante diez años* he lived in Spain for ten years.

durar *vi* to last, to continue, to go on for; *el mitin duró cuatro horas* the rally lasted four hours || to remain (permanecer) || to last, to wear (well) (ropa); *esos zapatos le durarán mucho* those shoes will last him a long time *o* will wear well || *¿cuánto duró su estancia en Buenos Aires?* how long was your stay in Buenos Aires?

duraznero *m* BOT peach tree (melocotonero).

duraznillo *m* BOT persicaria, lady's thumb.

durazno *m* BOT peach (fruto) | peach tree (árbol).

Durero *n pr* Dürer.

dureza *f* hardness (de agua, hierro, oído, etc.) || toughness (de alimentos) || stiffness (de un mecanismo) || hardheartedness, insensitivity (insensibilidad) || harshness, severity (severidad) || obstinacy, stubbornness (obstinación) || difficulty (dificultad) || harshness (luz, sonido) || toughness, strength (resistencia) || steeliness (de la mirada) || MED callosity, hard patch || *dureza de corazón* hardheartedness, hardness.

durita *f* (nombre registrado)AUT hose, radiator hose.

durmiente *adj* sleeping; *la Bella Durmiente del bosque* Sleeping Beauty.
◆ *m* ARQ sleeper (madero para sostener) || sleeper [US tie] (traviesa de ferrocarril).

duro, ra *adj* hard; *el acero es duro* steel is hard || tough (alimentos); *la carne está dura* the meat is tough || stale, old (pan) || hardhearted, insensitive (insensible) || harsh, severe, hard, tough; *un clima duro* a harsh climate; *una dura reprimenda* a severe reprimand; *un juez, un dictador duro* a severe judge, dictator || stony, stern (mirada) || stony, hard (corazón) || hard, difficult, tough; *una subida dura* a hard climb; *un problema duro* a tough problem || stiff (cerradura, puerta, mecanismo, palanca, cuello, etc.) || harsh; *luz dura, sonido duro* harsh light, sound || tough, strong (capaz de aguantar mucho); *un coche duro* a tough car || hardy, tough, strong (persona, raza, planta que aguanta) || stubborn, obstinate (terco) || DEP rough (juego) || rough, bumpy (aterrizaje) || — *agua dura* hard water || *de facciones duras* hard-featured || FIG *duro de corazón* hardhearted | | *duro de roer* or

de tragar hard to swallow | *estar a las duras y a las maduras* to take the rough with the smooth || *hacer algo a duras penas* to do sth. with great difficulty || *huevo duro* hard-boiled egg || FIG *más duro que una piedra* as hard as nails || *duro de cabeza* to be slow on the up-take, to be thick-headed | *ser duro de casco* to be obstinate *o* stubborn || FIG & FAM *ser duro de mollera* to be hardheaded *o* obstinate (obstinado), to be thick *o* dense (torpe) || *ser duro de oído* to be hard of hearing || FIG *ser duro de pelar* to be a hard nut || *sufrir dura prueba* to have a bad time of it, to suffer great hardships || FIG & FAM *tener ya dura la mollera* to be too old to change .
◆ *adv* hard; *pegar duro* to hit hard; *trabajar duro, darle duro al trabajo* to work hard.
◆ *m* five pesetas, five-peseta coin (dinero) || FAM tough guy (persona) || FAM *estar sin un duro* to be broke || *lo que faltaba para el duro* it's the last straw || *vale veinte duros* it costs a hundred pesetas.

Düsseldorf *n pr* GEOGR Düsseldorf.

duunvir; dunnviro *m* HIST duumvir.

duunvirato *m* HIST duumvirate.

dux *m* HIST doge.

duz *adj* sweet (dulce) || mild, gentle || — *caña duz* sugar cane || *palo duz* liquorice root.

E

e *f* e; *una e mayúscula* a capital e.
— OBSERV The pronunciation of the Spanish *e* is similar to that of the first *e* in the English word *element.*

e *conj* and.
— OBSERV The conjunction *e* replaces *y* before words beginning with *i* or *hi* (vocalic *i*): *Federico e Isabel* Frederick and Elizabeth; *madre e hija* mother and daughter. However, at the beginning of an interrogative or exclamatory sentence, or before a word beginning with *y* or *hi* followed by a vowel (consonantal *i*), the *y* is retained: *¿y Ignacio?* and Ignatius?; *vid y hiedra* vine and ivy; *tú y yo* you and I.

¡ea! *interj* come on! (para animar) || so what! (para terminar una discusión).

ebanista *m* cabinetmaker.

ebanistería *f* cabinetmaking (arte) || cabinetmaker's workshop (taller) || cabinetwork (muebles).

ébano *m* ebony (madera) || ebony (tree) (árbol) || FIG *ébano vivo* black ivory.

ebenáceas *f pl* BOT ebenaceae.

ebonita *f* ebonite (caucho endurecido).

ebriedad *f* drunkenness, intoxication, inebriation || *en estado de ebriedad* inebriated, intoxicated.

ebrio, a *adj* drunk, inebriated, intoxicated (embriagado) || FIG blind; *ebrio de ira* blind with anger | drunk; *ebrio de poder* power drunk | beside o.s.; *estaba ebrio de alegría* I was beside myself with happiness.
◆ *m/f* drunkard, drunk.

Ebro *npr m* GEOGR Ebro.

ebullición *f* boiling, ebullition (de un líquido) || FIG ebullience || — FIG *estar en ebullición* to be boiling over [with excitement] || *punto de ebullición* boiling point.

ebúrneo, a *adj* eburnean, ivory-like.

eccehomo; ecce homo *m* ecce homo || FIG *estar hecho un eccehomo* to cut a sorry figure.

eccema *m* MED eczema.

eccematoso, sa *adj* eczematous.

eclampsia *f* MED eclampsia.

eclecticismo *m* eclecticism.

ecléctico, ca *adj/s* eclectic.

eclesiastés *npr m* Ecclesiastes (libro de la Biblia).

eclesiástico, ca *adj* ecclesiastical, ecclesiastic.
◆ *m* ecclesiastic, clergyman (clérigo) || Ecclesiasticus (libro de la Biblia).

eclipsar *vt* ASTR to eclipse || FIG to eclipse, to outshine, to overshadow (deslucir).
◆ *vpr* to be eclipsed (desaparecer).

eclipse *m* ASTR eclipse; *eclipse de Luna* or *lunar, de Sol* or *solar* lunar, solar eclipse || FAM eclipse, disappearance.

eclipsis *f* GRAM ellipsis.

eclíptico, ca *adj/s f* ecliptic.

eclisa *f* TECN fishplate (vía).

eclosión *f* hatching (de un huevo) || opening, blooming (de una flor) || FIG appearance (aparición).

eco *m* echo (acústica) || distant sound, echo; *oía el eco de su voz* I could hear the distant sound of his voice || echo (del radar, en poesía) || FIG word; *no tenemos eco de lo ocurrido* we have no word of what has happened | rumour (noticia imprecisa) | echo (persona que repite o repetición servil) || — *ecos de sociedad* society news *sing*, society column *sing* || *hacerse eco de* to echo || *tener eco* to make news (tener difusión), to catch on (ser adoptado), to get a response (obtener una reacción).

ecospecie *f* BIOL ecospecies *npl.*

ecografía *f* echography.

ecología *f* BIOL ecology.

ecológico, ca *adj* ecological.

ecologista *adj* ecological.
◆ *m/f* ecologist.

ecólogo *m* ecologist.

economato *m* discount store, cooperative store.

econometría *f* econometrics || *especialista en econometría* econometrician.

economía *f* economics; *estudiar economía* to study economics || economy; *economía planificada* planned economy || economy (de esfuerzo, de palabras) || saving (ahorro); *hacer una economía de cien pesetas* to make a saving of one hundred pesetas; *una economía de quince minutos* a saving of fifteen minutes || economy, thrift (moderación en los gastos) || — *economía de libre mercado* free market economy || *economía de mercado* market economy || *economía doméstica* household economy || *economía mixta* mixed economy || *economía política* political economy || *economía sumergida* black *o* hidden economy.
◆ *pl* savings (ahorros) || — ECON *economías de escala* economies of scale || FAM *esas son economías de chicha y nabo* or *del chocolate del loro* that's cheeseparing (economy) || *hacer economías* to economize.

económico, ca *adj* economic; *Comunidad Económica Europea* European Economic Community || economic, financial; *crisis económica* financial crisis || economical, cheap, inexpensive; *restaurante económico* economical restaurant || economical, thrifty (persona) || — *año* or *ejercicio económico* financial *o* fiscal year || *cocina económica* wood-fired stove.

economista *m/f* economist.

economizar *vt* to save, to economize (dinero, esfuerzos, tiempo).
◆ *vi* to economize, to save; *economizar para las vacaciones* to save for the holidays.

ecónomo, ma *m/f* treasurer, bursar.

ectodermo *m* BIOL ectoderm.

ectoparásito, ta *adj* ectoparasitic.
◆ *m* ectoparasite.

ectoplasma *m* BIOL ectoplasm.

ecu *m* ecu (moneda).

ECU *abrev de European Unit Currency .*

ecuación *f* MAT equation; *ecuación de segundo grado* quadratic equation; *ecuación de primer grado* simple equation; *ecuación diferencial* differential equation || — *raíz de una ecuación* root of an equation || *sistema de ecuaciones con varias incógnitas* simultaneous equations.

ecuador *m* equator || — FAM *el paso del ecuador* halfway point [in a course of study] || *pasar el ecuador* to cross the line.

Ecuador (El) *npr m* GEOGR Ecuador.

ecuánime *adj* impartial, fair, unprejudiced (imparcial) || calm, composed, level-headed (equilibrado).

ecuanimidad *f* impartiality, fairness (justicia); *la ecuanimidad de un juez* the fairness of a judge || equanimity, composure (serenidad).

ecuatoreñismo *m* → **ecuatorianismo.**

ecuatorial *adj* equatorial.
◆ *m* ASTR equatorial.

ecuatorianismo; ecuatoreñismo *m* word or expression characteristic of the Spanish of Ecuador, Ecuadorianism.

ecuatoriano, na *adj/s* Ecuadorian, Ecuadoran, Ecuadorean.

ecuestre *adj* equestrian; *estatua ecuestre* equestrian statue.

ecumene *m* ecumene, oecumene.

ecuménico, ca *adj* ecumenical, oecumenical.

ecumenismo *m* ecumenicalism, ecumenism, oecumenicalism, oecumenism.

eczema *m* MED eczema.

echada *f* throw (lanzamiento) || length (en una carrera); *ganar por tres echadas* to win by three lengths || AMER boast (mentira).

echado, da *adj* lying down (tumbado) || FAM *un hombre echado para adelante* a bold *o* fearless man.

echador, ra *adj* throwing (que echa) || AMER boastful (fanfarrón).
◆ *m/f* thrower (que tira).
◆ *f echadora de buenaventura* or *de cartas* fortune-teller.

echar *vt/vi*

> **1.** TIRAR, ARROJAR **2.** DESPEDIR, EXPULSAR **3.** BROTAR, SALIR **4.** PONER, APLICAR **5.** DECIR **6.** OTROS SENTIDOS **7.** CON PREPOSICIÓN **8.** LOCUCIONES DIVERSAS **9.** VERBO PRONOMINAL.

1. TIRAR, ARROJAR to throw; *echar un hueso a un perro* to throw a bone to a dog; *echar por la borda* to throw overboard || to give off; *echar chispas* to give off sparks; *estas flores echan un olor agradable* these flowers give off a nice smell || to put (poner); *echar leña al fuego* to put wood on the fire || to pour; *echar agua en un vaso* to pour water into a glass || to serve, to give (comida) || to shed; *echar lágrimas* to shed tears || to post [US to mail]; *echar una carta* to post a letter || to add, to put in; *echar sal* to add

salt || to toss (una moneda) || to throw (los dados) || to deal (los naipes) || to cast (redes, ancla, anzuelo)
2. DESPEDIR, EXPULSAR to throw out, to turn out, to eject; *le echaron de la sala* he was thrown out of the room; *me han echado del piso* they have turned me out of my flat || to throw out, to sack; *le han echado de su trabajo* he has been thrown out of his job, he has been sacked from his job || to throw out, to expel (de una sociedad, club, etc.) || to bring on, to send on; *¡que echen el toro!* send on the bull! || to take off, to send (off); *echar el toro al corral* to send the bull to the pen.
3. BROTAR, SALIR to put out, to sprout (raíces, hojas) || to grow (pelo) || to cut (dientes); *el niño está echando los dientes* the baby is cutting his teeth.
4. PONER, APLICAR to put on, to apply; *echar un remiendo* to put on a patch || to spread (mantequilla) || to impose; *echar una multa* to impose a fine || to put on, to apply (el freno) || to put on, to bet, to wager (apostar) || to mate (aparear)
5. DECIR to tell; *echar la buenaventura a alguien* to tell s.o.'s fortune || to recite; *echar versos* to recite poetry || to hurl (blasfemias) || to give; *echar un sermón, una reprimenda* to give a sermon, a reprimand || to give, to make (un discurso)
6. OTROS SENTIDOS to do; *echar cálculos* to do calculations || to play, to have (jugar); *echar una partida de cartas* to play a game of cards || to have, to take; *echar una mirada a algo* to have a look at sth || to give, to throw; *me echó una mirada furibunda* he gave me a furious look || to have, to take (tener); *echar una siesta* to have a siesta || to give; *¿qué edad le echas?* what age would you give him? || to push, to move; *echó la silla hacia atrás* he pushed the chair backwards || to put on, to show; *echar una película* to put on a film || to add up (la cuenta) || to have, to smoke (un cigarrillo) || to lay (los cimientos) || to take; *echo una hora en ir de Madrid a Toledo* I take an hour *o* it takes me an hour to go from Madrid to Toledo || to turn (la llave) || to shoot (el cerrojo) || to slide (el pestillo) || to put to bed; *voy a echar al niño* I'm going to put the child to bed.
7. CON PREPOSICIÓN *echar a* (con infinitivo), *to begin, to start; echar a llorar* to begin crying, to begin to cry || *echar a volar* to take wing, to fly away *o* off (un pájaro) || *echar de comer, de beber* to feed, to water || *echar por* to take; *echar por la primera calle* to take the first street; to bear; *echar por la derecha* to bear right.
8. LOCUCIONES DIVERSAS *echando por largo* at the outside, at the very most || *echar abajo* or *por tierra* to pull down, to demolish (derribar), to ruin (reputación), to bring down, to overthrow (un gobierno), to break down (una puerta) || *echar a broma* to turn into a joke, to take as a joke || *echar a cara y cruz* to toss for || FIG *echar agua en el mar* to carry coals to Newcastle || *echar a la calle* to turn out, to chuck out (*fam*) || *echar a la lotería* to play the lottery || *echar a perder* to spoil, to ruin; *echar a perder un vestido* to ruin a dress; to waste (no aprovechar) || *echar a pique* to sink (un barco, un negocio), to ruin (los proyectos, una empresa) || *echar atrás* to set back || *echar barriga* or *vientre* to get a potbelly, to put on weight || *echar bolas* to tell fibs *o* lies (mentir) || *echar bravatas* to brag, to boast || *echar carnes* to put on weight || *echar de menos* to miss; *echo de menos (a) mi pueblo* I miss my home town || *echar de ver* to notice || *echar el cerrojo* to bolt the door, to lock the door (cerrar) || FIG & FAM *echar el guante a uno* to catch hold of s.o., to get hold of s.o. | *echar el resto* to put all one has into it, to give it all one has got (trabajar mucho), to stake everything one has got, to put one's shirt on it (naipes) | *echar en cara a alguien* to throw in s.o.'s face | *echar fuego por los ojos* to look daggers || *echar humo* to smoke, to give off smoke || *echar juramentos* to swear || *echar la bendición* to bless, to give one's blessing || FIG *echar la casa por la ventana* to spare no expense, to go overboard, to lash out (*fam*) || *echar las bases de* to lay the foundations for || *echar las bendiciones* to marry || *echar (las) cartas* to deal the cards (repartir), to tell fortunes by cards (adivinar) || *echar las cortinas* to draw *o* to pull the curtains || *echarle gracia a una cosa* or *echarle sal y pimienta* to add character to sth., to add that certain something to sth || FIG *echar leña al fuego* to add fuel to the fire || *echar los brazos al cuello de alguien* to fling one's arms round s.o.'s neck || FIG *echarlo todo a rodar* to ruin everything (estropear), to give up (abandonar) || *echar mano a* to reach for (alargar la mano), to go for (un arma), to get hold of, to lay one's hands on (agarrar) || *echar mano de* to make use of, to fall back on; *echar mano de las reservas* to fall back on the reserves; to turn to (persona) || FIG *echar pajas* to draw straws | *echar pestes de alguien* to heap abuse on s.o., to drag s.o. through the mud, to run s.o. down (criticar mucho) || *echar sangre* to bleed || FAM *echar sangre como un cochino* or *un toro* to bleed like a pig *o* profusely || *echar sangre por las narices* to have a nosebleed, to bleed from the nose || *echar suertes, echar a suertes* to draw lots; *echar algo a suertes* to draw lots for sth.; to toss (for sth.) (a cara o cruz) || FIG *echar tierra a un asunto* to hush up an affair | *echar una mano a alguien* to give *o* to lend s.o. a hand || FAM *echar un bocado, un trago* to have a bite *o* sth. to eat, to have sth. to drink || FIG *echar un capote a uno* to give s.o. a helping hand, to help s.o. out | *echar un párrafo* to have a chat | *no lo eche usted en saco roto* take good note of that | *¿qué (película) echan en el Astoria?* what's on at the Astoria?
9. (VERBO PRONOMINAL), to throw o.s. (arrojarse); *echarse en brazos de alguien* to throw o.s. into s.o.'s arms || to lie down (tumbarse); *échate en la cama* lie down on the bed || to sit, to brood (aves) || to die down, to drop (el viento) || to put (ponerse) || to get o.s. (una novia) || to have, to smoke (un cigarrillo) || to have (una siesta) || FIG to become addicted to, to take to; *echarse a la bebida* to take to drink | to treat o.s. to (regalarse); *se ha echado un abrigo de visón* she has treated herself to a mink coat || MAR to settle on her beam-ends || AMER to wear, to have on; *echarse zapatos* to have shoes on || — *echarse a dormir* to go to bed *o* to sleep || FAM *echarse algo al cuerpo* to have sth. (comer); *echarse al cuerpo una buena comida* to have a good feed | *echarse al monte* to take to the hills | *echarse a morir* or *a temblar* to be panic-stricken || *echarse a perder* to go bad (alimentos), to go to the dogs (personas), to be ruined *o* spoiled (estropearse) || *echarse atrás* to lean back (inclinarse hacia atrás), to throw o.s. back (para evitar algo), to back down (arrepentirse) || *echarse a un lado* to move aside || *echarse de ver* to be obvious || *echarse encima to throw o.s. onto o* at (atacar); *se echaron encima del enemigo* they threw themselves at the enemy; to bear down on; *se nos echó encima el camión* the lorry bore down on us; to overtake; *la noche se nos echó encima* nightfall overtook us; to take upon o.s., to undertake (encargarse de); *echarse encima un trabajo* to undertake a job; to shoulder (una responsabilidad), to set against o.s. (indisponer); *se echó encima a todos los críticos* he set all the critics against him || *echárselas de enfermo* to sham *o* to feign illness, to pretend to be ill || *echárselas de héroe* to play the hero.

echarpe *m* shawl (chal).

echón, ona *adj* AMER boastful, swaggering.

echona; echuna *f* AMER sickle (hoz).

edad *f* age; *diez años de edad* ten years of age; *a la edad de 10 años* at the age of 10; *no aparentar su edad* not to look one's age || age (época); *la Edad de Piedra* the Stone Age; *Edad de Oro* Golden Age; *Edad Moderna* Modern Age; *Edad de Bronce* Bronze Age || time, date, period; *por aquella edad* at that time || — *a mi edad* at my age || *de cierta edad* elderly || *de corta* or *poca edad* of tender years, young || *de edad, de edad avanzada* elderly; *persona de edad* elderly person || *de edad provecta* elderly || *de edad temprana* of tender years || *de más edad* older, elder || *de mediana edad* middle-aged || *de menor edad* younger || *edad crítica* puberty (adolescencia), change of life, menopause (de una mujer) || *edad de la razón* or *del juicio* age of reason || AMER *edad del chivateo* awkward age || *edad del retiro* retirement age || *edad del pavo* awkward age || *Edad Media* Middle Ages || *edad núbil* nubility || *en edad de* old enough to || *en edad escolar* of school age || *en su edad temprana* in his early years, in his childhood || *entrado en edad* elderly || *llegar a la mayoría de edad* to come of age || *menor edad* minority, nonage, infancy (minoría de edad) || *primera edad* infancy, childhood || *¿qué edad le das* or *le echas?* how old do you think he is?, what age would you give him? || *¿qué edad tienes?* how old are you? || *representar la edad que se tiene* to look one's age || *ser mayor de edad* to be of age || *ser menor de edad* to be under age, to be a minor || *tener edad para* to be old enough to || *un chico de diez años de edad* a ten-year-old boy || *un mayor de edad, un menor de edad* a major, a minor (personas).

edecán *m* aide-de-camp.

edelweiss *m* BOT edelweiss.

edema *f* MED edema, oedema.

Edén *m* Eden || FIG *aquello era un Edén* it was a garden of Eden.

edénico, ca *adj* Edenic.

edición *f* edition (de un libro); *primera edición* first edition; *edición en rústica* paperbound *o* paperback edition || edition, issue edition (de periódico, de revista) || INFORM editing || — *edición de bolsillo* pocket edition || *edición extraordinaria* special edition || *Ediciones Larousse* Larousse Publications || *edición pirata* pirated edition *o* copy || *edición príncipe* editio princeps.

edicto *m* edict, decree.

edificación *f* construction, building || FIG edification.

edificante *adj* edifying; *un ejemplo edificante* an edifying example.

edificar *vt* to build, to construct; *edificar en la arena* to build on sand || FIG to edify; *edificar con el ejemplo* to edify by one's example.
◆ *vpr* to be built (up); *las grandes fortunas se edifican con el trabajo* great fortunes are built (up) on hard work.

edificativo, va *adj* edifying.

edificio *m* building, edifice; *el Prado es un edificio hermoso* the Prado is a magnificent building || FIG structure, edifice; *el edificio social* the social structure.

edil *m* aedile, edile (magistrado romano) || municipal official, town councillor.

Edimburgo *n pr* GEOGR Edinburgh.

Edipo *npr m* Oedipus.

editar *vt* to publish; *editar un libro* to publish a book.

editor, ra *adj* publishing; *casa editora* publishing house.
◆ *m/f* publisher (persona).
◆ *f* publishing house (casa).
◆ *m* INFORM editor; *editor de fichero* file editor; *editor de textos* text editor.

editorial *adj* editorial || publishing.
◆ *m* editorial, leading article (artículo de fondo).
◆ *f* publishing house.

editorialista *m* editorialist, leader writer.

edredón *m* eiderdown.

eduardiano, na *adj* Edwardian.

Eduardo *npr m* Edward.

educable *adj* educable, teachable.

educación *f* education (enseñanza) || upbringing (crianza) || (good) manners *pl*, politeness, breeding (modales); *no tiene educación* he has no manners || — *educación ambiental* environmental education || *educación física* physical education *o* training || *educación sanitaria* health education || *educación sexual* sex education || *mala educación* bad manners || *Ministerio de Educación y Ciencia* Ministry of Education || *¡qué falta de educación!* how rude!, what bad manners!

educacionista *m/f* educationist, educationalist, educator.

educado, da *adj* educated || well-mannered, polite (formal) || — *bien educado* well-bred, well-mannered || *mal educado* ill-bred, bad-mannered, rude.

educador, ra *m/f* educator.
◆ *adj* educating.

educando, da *m/f* pupil, student.

educar *vt* to educate (dar instrucción) || to bring up; *educar con* or *en buenos principios* to bring up on good principles || to train, to educate (el oído, los miembros) || to educate, to develop (el gusto) || to bring up, to rear (criar).
◆ *vpr* to be brought up || to be educated.

educativo, va *adj* educative, educational (que sirve para educar) || educative, instructive.

educción *f* eduction.

edulcoración *f* sweetening.

edulcorar *vt* to edulcorate, to sweeten.

EE UU *abrev de Estados Unidos* USA, United States of America.

efe *f* f [name of the letter *f*].

efebo *m* ephebe.

efectismo *m* sensationalism, striving for effect (en arte y literatura) || trompe-l'oeil.

efectista *adj* sensationalist || trompe-l'oeil; *pintura efectista* trompe-l'oeil painting.

efectivamente *adv* really, in fact (en realidad) || indeed, exactly (por supuesto).

efectividad *f* effectiveness.

efectivo, va *adj* effective || real (verdadero) || permanent, regular (empleo) || — *dinero efectivo* cash, ready money || *hacer efectivo un cheque* to cash a cheque || *hacerse efectivo* to take effect, to come into effect || TECN *potencia efectiva* brake horsepower.
◆ *m* cash; *efectivo en caja* cash in hand; *pagar en efectivo* to pay (in) cash.
◆ *pl* MIL effective (force) *sing*, total strength *sing* (de un ejército).

efecto *m* effect, result (resultado); *la escasez de alimentos fue uno de los efectos de la guerra* the food shortage was one of the effects of the war || effect, impression, impact (impresión hecha en el ánimo); *la noticia le hizo un gran efecto* the news made a great impression on him || spin (picado); *dar efecto a la pelota* to put a spin on the ball || ARTES trompe-l'oeil || COM document | bill (letra de cambio) || — *a este* or *a tal efecto* for that purpose, to that end || *con efecto retroactivo* retroactive || *dar efecto* to implement (a unas disposiciones) || *efecto retardado* delayed action || *efecto útil* output || *en efecto* in fact, really, as a matter of fact, in effect (efectivamente), indeed (por supuesto) || *eso hace buen efecto* that looks well || *hacer* or *surtir efecto* to have an effect (medicina), to work, to have the desired effect (estratagema), to come into force, to take effect (ley) || FAM *hacer un efecto bárbaro* to have a great effect || *lanzar con efecto una pelota* to spin a ball || *llevar a efecto* to put into effect, to carry out || *ser de buen, de mal efecto* to create a good, bad effect *o* impression || FIG *ser de efecto retardado* to be slow on the uptake || *tener efecto* to take effect, to come *o* go into effect *o* operation (entrar en vigor); *el nuevo horario tendrá efecto a partir de mañana* the new timetable will go into effect tomorrow; to take place (celebrarse); *mañana tendrá efecto la inauguración del estadio* the opening of the stadium will take place tomorrow || *tener por efecto* to result in, to have as a result.
◆ *pl* goods (mercancías) || belongings, effects (cosas personales) || effects, property *sing*, possessions (bienes) || — *a efectos de* with the object of || *efectos de consumo* consumer goods || CINEM *efectos especiales* special effects || *efectos mobiliarios* chattels || *efectos secundarios* side effects || *efectos sonoros* sound effects (cine, teatro, radio) || *efectos visuales* visual effects.

efectuar *vt* to effect, to carry out, to do, to perform; *efectuar una multiplicación* to do a multiplication || to make; *efectuar una detención, una visita, un viaje* to make an arrest, a visit, a journey.
◆ *vpr* to take place (celebrarse).

efedrina *f* ephedrine.

efemérides *f pl* ASTR ephemerides (almanaque astronómico) || ephemeris *sing* (ant), diary *sing* (diario) || list of the day's anniversaries which appears in a newspaper (en un periódico).
— OBSERV This word is often used in the singular (una *efeméride* or una *efemérides*) although only the plural is accepted by the Academy.

eferente *adj* ANAT efferent.

efervescencia *f* effervescence, effervescency || FIG excitement, agitation, effervescence.

efervescente *adj* effervescent || fizzy (bebidas).

Éfeso *n pr* GEOGR Ephesus.

eficacia *f* efficacy, effectiveness (de cosas) || efficiency (de personas).

eficaz *adj* efficacious, efficient, effective (que produce el efecto deseado) || efficient (eficiente) || *con su eficaz ayuda* with your able assistance.
— OBSERV *Efficient, efficacious* y *effective* significan todos *que logra un efecto determinado; efficient* significa además *que anda bien* o, tratándose de una máquina, *que produce gran rendimiento.*

eficiencia *f* efficiency.

eficiente *adj* efficient.

efigie *f* effigy, image.

efímera *f* ZOOL ephemera, mayfly.

efímero, ra *adj* ephemeral.

eflorescencia *f* efflorescence.

eflorescente *adj* efflorescent.

efluvio *m* effluvium, exhalation || *los primeros efluvios de la primavera* the first breath of spring.

efracción *f* effraction.

efugio *m* subterfuge, evasion.

efusión *f* effusion || FIG effusion || — *con efusión* effusively || *efusión de sangre* bloodshed.

efusivo, va *adj* effusive || GEOL effusive, extrusive.

EGB *abrev de Enseñanza General Básica* general basic education up to school leaving age.

Egeo *npr m* GEOGR *mar Egeo* Aegean (Sea).

Egeria *npr f* Egeria.

égida; egida *f* aegis || *bajo la égida de* under the aegis *o* the auspices *o* the sponsorship of.

egipcio, cia *adj/s* Egyptian.

Egipto *npr m* GEOGR Egypt.

egiptología *f* Egyptology.

egiptólogo, ga *m/f* Egyptologist.

égira *f* hegira, hejira (hégira).

Egisto *npr m* Aegisthus.

eglantina *f* BOT eglantine.

égloga *f* eglogue, short pastoral poem.

ego *m* FIL ego.

egocéntrico, ca *adj* egocentric, egocentrical, self-centred [*US* self-centered].

egocentrismo *m* egocentrism, egocentricity, self-centredness [*US* self-centeredness].

egoísmo *m* selfishness, egoism, egotism || FIL egoism.

egoísta *adj* selfish, egoistic, egotistic, egoistical || FIL egoistic.
◆ *m/f* egoist, egotist, selfish person || FIL egoist.

ególatra *adj* self-worshipping.

egolatría *f* self-worship.

egotismo *m* egotism.

egotista *adj* egotistic, egotistical, egoistic.
◆ *m/f* egotist.

egregio, gia *adj* illustrious, eminent.

egresado, da *adj/s* graduate.

egresar *vi* *AMER* to pass out (de una academia militar) || to leave, to graduate (terminar sus estudios).

egreso *m* passing-out (de una academia militar) || graduation (de una universidad) || expenditure.

eh *interj* eh!, hey! (para llamar la atención) || O. K.?, understood?, all right?; *que no vuelva a ocurrir, ¿eh?* don't let it happen again, understood? || — *esto es muy malo, ¿eh?* this is very bad, isn't it? || *y ahora te vas a la cama, ¿eh?* and now you'll go to bed, won't you?

eider *m* eider (pato).

einstenio *m* QUÍM einstenium.

eirá *m* eyra (especie de puma).

Eire *npr m* GEOGR Eire.

eje *m* TECN axle (de una rueda); *eje trasero, delantero* rear, front axle | shaft (árbol) || axis; *eje del mundo* earth's axis || MAT & FÍS axis; *eje de revolución, de simetría* axis of rotation, of symmetry; *eje óptico* optical axis || FIG hub, core, crux (de un argumento) || — TECN *caja del eje* axle box | *chaveta del eje* axle pin | *eje de levas* camshaft || MAT *eje de ordenadas, de abscisas* y-axis, x-axis || *el Eje* (Berlín-Roma) the Axis || *el eje de una calle, de un río* the centre line of a street, of a river || *idea eje* central idea || TECN *manga del eje* axle arm, axle journal || FAM *¡me parte por el eje!* it's a big nuisance!

ejecución *f* execution, carrying-out; *la ejecución de un proyecto* the execution of a plan || execution (de un condenado) || MÚS & TEATR performance, interpretation || JUR distraint, distress (de un deudor) | seizure, attachment (embargo) || INFORM execution (de una instrucción, etc.) || — *pelotón de ejecución* firing squad || *poner en ejecución* to put into execution, to carry out.

ejecutante *m/f* executor [one who carries out a plan] || MÚS executant, performer.
◆ *m* JUR distrainor.

ejecutar *vt* to execute, to carry out (un proyecto, una orden, etc.) || to execute (a un condenado) || MÚS & TEATR to perform, to interpret || JUR to distrain upon (deudor) | to seize, to attach (embargar).

◆ *vi* to act || *usted manda y yo ejecuto* you give the orders and I carry them out.

ejecutivamente *adv* promptly, quickly || JUR by distraint.

ejecutivo, va *adj* executive (que ejecuta); *consejo ejecutivo* executive council; *el poder ejecutivo* the executive power || expeditious, prompt (rápido).
◆ *m* the executive (poder) || executive (director).

ejecutor, ra *m/f* executant, executor || — *ejecutor de la justicia* executioner || *ejecutoria testamentaria* executrix || *ejecutor testamentario* executor.

ejecutoria *f* letters *pl* patent of nobility || FIG record, accomplishments *pl* (historial) || JUR writ of execution (acto que confirma un juicio).

ejecutoría *f* executorship.

ejecutoriar *vt* to confirm (un juicio) || to verify (comprobar).

ejecutorio, ria *adj* JUR executory.

¡ejem! *interj* ahem!, hum!

ejemplar *adj* exemplary; *conducta ejemplar* exemplary behaviour; *castigo ejemplar* exemplary punishment.
◆ *m* copy (unidad); *una tirada de diez mil ejemplares* a run of ten thousand copies; *ejemplar gratuito* free copy || number, issue (de una revista) || specimen, example; *un ejemplar magnífico de mariposa* a magnificent example of a butterfly || FAM *¡menudo ejemplar!* sly bird!, wily bird!

ejemplaridad *f* exemplariness, exemplarity.

ejemplarizar *vt* to set an example to, to exemplify.

ejemplificación *f* exemplification, illustration.

ejemplificar *vt* to exemplify, to illustrate.

ejemplo *m* example; *un diccionario sin ejemplos es un esqueleto* a dictionary without examples is a mere skeleton || model, epitome; *es un ejemplo de generosidad* he is a model of generosity, he is the epitome of generosity || — *a ejemplo de* after the example of, after the manner of || *dar ejemplo* to set an example || *por ejemplo* for example, for instance || *predicar con el ejemplo* to set an example (actuando) || *servir de ejemplo* to serve as an example || FIG *sin ejemplo* unprecedented || *tomar ejemplo de alguien* to follow s.o.'s example, to take a leaf out of s.o.'s book || *tomar por ejemplo* or *como ejemplo* to take as an example.

ejercer *vi* to practise, to be in practice; *es abogado pero ya no ejerce* he is a lawyer but no longer practises *o* is no longer in practice.
◆ *vt* to exert (influencia, poder) || to exercise (ejercitar) || to exercise, to use; *ejercer el derecho de voto* to use one's right to vote || to exercise (autoridad) || to practise; *ejercer la medicina* to practise medicine || to perform (unas funciones).

ejercicio *m* practice; *el ejercicio de la medicina* the practice of medicine || exercise, use (de un derecho) || exertion (de una influencia, de un poder) || performance (de una función) || exercise; *ejercicios de latín* Latin exercises || homework (trabajos para hacer en casa) || test (examen o prueba); *ejercicio escrito, oral* written, oral test || exercise (esfuerzo corporal); *hacer ejercicios* to do exercises || MIL training, exercise, drill, practice || — *ejercicio económico* financial *o* fiscal year || *ejercicio fiscal* tax *o* fiscal year || REL *ejercicios espirituales* spiritual retreat || *en ejercicio* practising; *un abogado en ejercicio* a practising lawyer || *presidente en ejercicio* acting chairman (de una reunión).

ejercitación *f* practice (de una profesión) || exercise (de un derecho, de la autoridad).

ejercitado, da *adj* trained.

ejercitante *adj* training.
◆ *m/f* person in spiritual retreat.

ejercitar *vt* to exercise || to practise (una profesión) || to drill; *ejercitar a un alumno en latín* to drill a pupil in Latin || MIL to drill, to train.
◆ *vpr* to train, to practise; *ejercitarse en el tiro al arco* to practise archery, to train in archery.

ejército *m* army || — *Ejército del Aire* Air Force || *Ejército de Salvación* Salvation Army.

ejido *m* common (land) (de un pueblo).

ejote *m* AMER runner bean, green bean.

el *art def m sing* the; *el pozo* the well || the one; *el de Málaga está enfermo* the one from Málaga *o* the Málaga one is ill || — *el del abrigo negro* the one in the black coat, the one with the black coat || *el de las gafas* the one with spectacles || *el de usted* yours || *el que* he who, the one who (personas, sujeto); *el que vino ayer* the one who came yesterday; the one whom, the one that, the one (personas, complemento); *el que veré mañana* the one I'll see tomorrow; the one which, the one that, the one (cosas) || *¡el... que...!* what a...!; *¡el susto que me dio!* what a fright it gave me! || *el tuyo es mejor* yours is better || *en el año 1979* in 1979 || *no es mi libro sino el de tu padre* it is not my book but your father's || *ser... el que* to be the one that *o* the one which (cosas), to be the one who (personas); *es el avión del general el que está despegando* the one which *o* the one that is taking off is the general's plane; *soy yo el que ha de decidir* I'm the one who has to decide.

— OBSERV *El* debe traducirse a menudo por el adjetivo posesivo en inglés: *llevaba el sombrero puesto* he had his hat on; *extendió el brazo* he stretched out his arm. Cuando antecede un día de la semana, se traduce por *on*: *vino el lunes, me iré el viernes* he came on Monday, I shall leave on Friday, excepto en casos similares a los siguientes: *el lunes pasado, el lunes que viene* last Monday, next Monday; *el lunes es mal día* Monday is a bad day. Tampoco se suele usar el artículo en inglés delante de los nombres de países: *el Japón, el Perú* Japan, Peru, y en otros muchos casos: *me gusta el té* I like tea; *está en el hospital* he is in hospital; *en el Madrid actual* in present-day Madrid; *el capitán X* captain X.

— OBSERV In proper names like *El Greco, El Escorial* the article is never contracted to *al* or *del*: *un cuadro de El Greco, voy a El Escorial*.

— OBSERV *El* replaces the feminine article before a word beginning with accentuated *a* or *ha* (*el ala, el hacha*).

él *pron pers m sing* he (personas); *él viene* he is coming || he, him (enfático); *es él* it is he, it is him (véase OBSERV) || him (complemento, si se trata de personas); *hablo de él* I am talking about him; *trabajo con él* I work with him || it (cosas); *se me olvidó el pañuelo y no puedo prescindir de él* I forgot my handkerchief and I can't manage without it || — *de él* his (persona), its (cosa) (suyo); *el coche es de él* his car; *este coche es de él* this car is his || *él mismo* himself; *lo dijo él mismo* he said it himself.

— OBSERV *Él*, as the subject, is usually omitted before the verb: *(él) se marchó* he left. It is generally only included either to avoid ambiguity or to add emphasis; the latter may be conveyed in English by stressing *he*: *él se fue, yo me quedé* he left, I remained.

— OBSERV Cuando *él* se emplea con el verbo *ser* se traduce frecuentemente en inglés por el pronombre complemento *him* aunque sea incorrecto desde un punto de vista puramente gramatical.

elaboración *f* elaboration, processing (de una materia prima) || working (de metal, de madera) || production, manufacture (de un producto) || production; *la elaboración de la miel* honey production || elaboration, preparation, working-out; *la elaboración de una ley* the preparation of a law.

elaborar *vt* to elaborate, to process (materia prima) || to work (la madera, el metal) || to manufacture, to make, to produce (producto); *elaborar chocolate* to manufacture chocolate || to make, to produce; *la seda es elaborada por un gusano* silk is produced by a worm || to elaborate, to prepare, to work out; *elaborar un proyecto* to prepare a plan.

elan *m* FIL *el elan vital* the élan vital.

elástica *f* vest [*US* undershirt] (camiseta) || DEP singlet [*US* athletic jersey].

elasticidad *f* elasticity (en general) || stretch (de tejidos) || FIG flexibility, elasticity (de un horario, un reglamento, etc.) || ECON *elasticidad de la demanda* elasticity of demand | *elasticidad de la oferta* elasticity of supply.

elástico, ca *adj* elastic (en general) || stretch, elastic (tejidos) || FIG flexible, elastic; *un horario elástico* a flexible timetable.
◆ *m* elastic, elastic band (cinta) || welt (banda de punto extensible).
◆ *pl* braces [*US* suspenders] (tirantes).

elatérido, da *adj* ZOOL elaterid.

Elba *npr m* GEOGR Elbe (río).
◆ *f* Elba (isla).

Eldorado *npr m* Eldorado, El Dorado.

ele *f* l [name of the letter *l*].

eléboro *m* BOT hellebore.

elección *f* choice, choosing, selection; *la elección de una carrera* the choice of a career || choice, alternative (posibilidad de elegir) || election; *la elección del Presidente de la República* the election of the President of the Republic; *presentarse a una elección* to stand for an election || — *a elección de* at the choice of, to suit; *a elección del cliente* to suit the client || *tierra de elección* the country of one's choice.
◆ *pl* election *sing*; *elecciones generales* general election; *convocar a elecciones* to call *o* hold an election || — *elecciones autonómicas* elections in the autonomous regions [of Spain] || *elecciones municipales* municipal elections.

electivo, va *adj* elective.

electo, ta *adj* elect; *el presidente electo* the president-elect.

— OBSERV The adjective *electo* is the irregular past participle of the verb *elegir*. It is only applied to a successful candidate who has not yet taken up his post. The perfect sense of *elegir* is formed with the regular past participle: *elegido*.

elector, ra *adj* electing.
◆ *m/f* elector, voter (en elecciones, referéndum, etc.).
◆ *m* HIST elector (antiguo príncipe alemán).

electorado *m* electorate, electoral body, voters *pl* || HIST electorate; *el Electorado de Maguncia* the Electorate of Mainz.

electoral *adj* electoral; *censo electoral* electoral roll; *colegio electoral* electoral college.

electoralismo *m* electioneering.

electoralista *adj* electioneering.

Electra *npr f* Electra.

electricidad *f* electricity; *electricidad estática* static electricity.

electricista *adj* electrical; *ingeniero electricista* electrical engineer.
◆ *m/f* electrician.

eléctrico, ca *adj* electric, electrical || — *azul eléctrico* electric blue || *manta eléctrica* electric blanket || *silla eléctrica* electric chair.
◆ *m* FAM electrician (electricista).

— OBSERV *Electric* y *electrical* son sinónimos. Sin embargo *electric* es mucho más corriente y se aplica generalmente a los objetos que funcionan con electricidad: *electric lamp, elec-*

tric car, electric train. *Electrical* se utiliza sobre todo en términos de física o mecánica: *electrical conductivity, electrical drainage, electrical engineering.*

electrificación *f* electrification.

electrificar *vt* to electrify; *electrificar un ferrocarril* to electrify a railway (véase OBSERV en ELECTRIZAR).

electriz *f* electress.

electrizable *adj* electrifiable.

electrización *f* electrification.

electrizante *adj* electrifying.

electrizar *vt* to electrify (cargar de electricidad) ‖ FIG to electrify; *electrizar una asamblea* to electrify a meeting.

— OBSERV *Electrificar* and *electrizar* are not synonymous but are both rendered by the English *electrify*. *Electrificar* means to convert to electric power (e. g. a machine), *electrizar* means to produce an electric charge or current in.

electroacústica *f* FÍS electroacoustics.

electroanálisis *m* QUÍM electroanalysis.

electrobomba *f* electric pump.

electrocardiografía *f* electrocardiography.

electrocardiógrafo *m* electrocardiograph.

electrocardiograma *m* MED electrocardiogram.

electrocauterio *m* MED electrocautery.

electrocinética *f* electrokinetics.

electrocoagulación *f* MED electrocoagulation.

electrocución *f* electrocution.

electrocutar *vt* to electrocute.
◆ *vpr* to be electrocuted.

electrochoque; electroshock *m* MED electroshock.

electrodinámico, ca *adj* FÍS electrodynamic.

electrodinamómetro *m* electrodynamometer.

electrodo *m* FÍS electrode.

electrodoméstico, ca *adj* electrical household; *aparatos electrodomésticos* electrical household appliances.
◆ *m pl* electrical household appliances.

electroencefalografía *f* electroencephalography.

electroencefalográfico, ca *adj* MED electroencephalographic.

electroencefalógrafo *m* electroencephalograph.

electroencefalograma *m* electroencephalogram.

electrófono *m* record player.

electróforo *m* FÍS electrophorus.

electrógeno, na *adj* generating, generator; *grupo electrógeno* generator set.
◆ *m* electric generator.

electroimán *m* FÍS electromagnet.

electrólisis *f* QUÍM electrolysis.

electrolítico, ca *adj* QUÍM electrolytic.

electrólito *m* QUÍM electrolyte.

electrolización *f* QUÍM electrolysis.

electrolizar *vt* to electrolize.

electromagnético, ca *adj* FÍS electromagnetic; *onda electromagnética* electromagnetic wave.

electromagnetismo *m* FÍS electromagnetism.

electromecánico, ca *adj* electromechanical.
◆ *f* electromechanics (ciencia).

electrometalurgia *f* electrometallurgy.

electrometría *f* FÍS electrometry.

electrómetro *m* electrometer.

electromiografía *f* MED electromyography.

electromotor, ra *adj* FÍS electromotive.
◆ *m* electromotor, electric motor.

electromotriz *adj f* electromotive; *fuerza electromotriz* electromotive force.

electrón *m* FÍS electron.

electronegativo, va *adj* FÍS electronegative.

electrónico, ca *adj* electronic ‖ — *microscopio electrónico* electron microscope ‖ *tubo electrónico* thermionic valve, electron tube.
◆ *f* electronics.

electronvoltio *m* electron volt.

electropositivo, va *adj* FÍS electropositive.

electroquímico, ca *adj* QUÍM electrochemical.
◆ *f* electrochemistry.

electroscopio *m* FÍS electroscope.

electroshock *m* → **electrochoque.**

electrostático, ca *adj* FÍS electrostatic.
◆ *f* electrostatics.

electrotecnia *f* FÍS electrotechnics, electrical engineering.

electrotécnico, ca *adj* electrotechnical.

electroterapia *f* MED electrotherapy.

electrotermia *f* electrothermy.

electrotérmico, ca *adj* FÍS electrothermic.
◆ *f* electrothermy.

electuario *m* electuary.

elefancía *f* MED elephantiasis.

elefancíaco, ca; elefanciaco, ca *adj* elephantiasic.

elefanta *f* female elephant, cow elephant.

elefante *m* elephant ‖ *elefante marino* sea elephant, elephant seal.

elefantiásico, ca *adj* MED elephantiasic.

elefantiasis *f* MED elephantiasis.

elegancia *f* elegance, style.

elegante *adj* elegant, stylish, smart ‖ well-turned (frase).
◆ *m* man of fashion, dandy.
◆ *f* fashionable woman.

elegantemente *adv* elegantly, stylishly, smartly, fashionably.

elegantón, ona *adj* FAM smart; *el novio iba muy elegantón* the bridegroom looked very smart.

elegantoso, sa *adj* AMER elegant, smart.

elegía *f* elegy.

elegíaco, ca *adj* elegiac.

elegibilidad *f* eligibility.

elegible *adj* eligible.

elegido, da *adj* chosen, elected; *elegido por la mayoría* chosen by the majority ‖ favourite, preferred (predilecto) ‖ select, choice (selecto) ‖ *el presidente elegido* the president-elect.
◆ *m/f* elected person ‖ one chosen (escogido) ‖ one chosen by God, predestinate.
◆ *m pl* the elect.

elegir* *vt* to choose, to select (escoger) ‖ to elect (por voto) ‖ — *dos platos a elegir entre los siguientes* choice of two dishes from the following (en un menú) ‖ *te toca a ti elegir* the choice is yours.

elemental *adj* elementary; *eso es elemental* that's elementary ‖ basic, elementary; *una gramática elemental* a basic grammar ‖ elemental (de los elementos).

elemento *m* element (parte de una cosa) ‖ part, component (de una máquina) ‖ section, unit (muebles); *una biblioteca de siete elementos* a seven-section bookcase ‖ member; *los elementos de una junta* the members of a board; *un buen elemento del equipo* a good member of the team, a good team-member ‖ constituent, ingredient (ingrediente) ‖ FIG & FAM individual, type, character; *reunirse con elementos sospechosos* to join up with suspicious characters ‖ FIG factor; *elementos que contribuyen al desorden* factors which contribute to the confusion ‖ MAT element ‖ ELECTR cell (de una batería) ‖ QUÍM & BIOL element ‖ AMER fool, idiot (tonto) ‖ INFORM *elemento binario* binary element ‖ *el líquido elemento* the sea (mar), water (agua) ‖ FIG *estar en su elemento* to be in one's element ‖ *la furia de los elementos* the fury of the elements ‖ FAM *¡menudo elemento!* wily *o* sly bird!
◆ *pl* elements, basic principles; *elementos de geometría* basic principles of geometry ‖ means (medios) ‖ *elementos de juicio* facts to formulate an opinion; *no tengo bastantes elementos de juicio* I have insufficient facts to formulate an opinion.

Elena *npr f* Helen.

elenco *m* catalogue [US catalog], list ‖ CINEM & TEATR cast (reparto) | company, troupe.

elevación *f* raising, lifting (de un peso) ‖ erection (de un edificio) ‖ raising, rise, increase (de precios) ‖ raising (de la voz) ‖ elevation, height (de una montaña) ‖ rise in the ground, hill (eminencia) ‖ FIG raising (de protestas) | elevation; *su elevación a la nobleza* his elevation to the peerage | ascent (en una jerarquía) | loftiness, grandness, elevation (del estilo, etc.) | raising; *la elevación del tono en una discusión* the raising of voices in a discussion | ecstasy, rapture, transport (del alma) ‖ MAT raising (a una potencia) ‖ ARQ & ASTR & REL elevation.

elevadamente *adv* elevatedly, loftily.

elevado, da *adj* high; *un precio, un edificio elevado* a high price, building ‖ high, elevated (rango, etc.) ‖ elevated, lofty, grand (estilo) ‖ — MAT *elevado a* (raised) to the power of; *diez elevado a tres es mil* ten (raised) to the power of three is a thousand ‖ *elevado al cuadrado* squared; *dos elevado al cuadrado* two squared.

elevador, ra *adj* elevating ‖ ANAT *músculo elevador* elevator muscle.
◆ *m* lift, service lift, goods lift, hoist (montacargas) ‖ AMER lift [US elevator] (ascensor) ‖ ANAT elevator (músculo) ‖ ELECTR step-up transformer; *elevador-reductor* step-up-step-down transformer ‖ TECN jack; *elevador de rosca* or *de tornillo* screw jack | ramp; *elevador hidráulico* hydraulic ramp ‖ *elevador de voltaje* booster.

elevadorista *m/f* AMER lift attendant (ascensorista).

elevalunas *m* AUTOM window winder; *elevalunas eléctrico* electric window winder.

elevamiento *m* FIG ecstasy, rapture, transport.

elevar *vt* to raise, to lift (un peso) ‖ to erect, to put up (un monumento, un edificio) ‖ to raise, to increase, to put up (precios) ‖ to raise (la voz) ‖ FIG to promote, to raise; *elevar a alguien a un alto cargo* to promote s.o. to a high position | to raise, to elevate (a una dignidad) | to elevate, to raise (el tono) | to elevate (el estilo) ‖ MAT to raise; *elevar a la enésima potencia* to raise to the power of n ‖ *elevar al cuadrado, al cubo* to square, to cube ‖ FIG *elevar protestas* to make a protest, to raise a protest.
◆ *vpr* to rise (up), to ascend; *elevarse por los aires* to rise into the air; *elevarse en la jerarquía* to ascend in the hierarchy ‖ to go up, to increase, to rise (precio) ‖ FIG to raise o.s., to elevate o.s. ‖ to amount to; *el total se eleva a* the total amounts to ‖ to become vain *o* conceited (engreírse) ‖ to be transported, to be enrap-

tured (enajenarse) || — *el pico más alto se eleva a cinco mil metros* the highest peak rises to *o* reaches five thousand metres || *los edificios más grandes de la ciudad se elevan en esta calle* the city's largest buildings stand in this street.

elevón *m* AVIAC elevator, aileron.

elfo *m* elf.

elidir *vt* to weaken || GRAM to elide.
◆ *vpr* to elide, to be elided.

eliminación *f* elimination.

eliminador, ra *adj* eliminating, eliminative.
◆ *m/f* eliminator.

eliminar *vt* to eliminate; *eliminar a un concursante* to eliminate a competitor || to eliminate, to remove, to exclude; *le han eliminado del equipo* they have excluded him from the team || to get rid of, to cast aside, to expel; *tenemos que eliminar estos temores* we must cast aside these fears || MED to eliminate, to expel (cualquier sustancia nociva) || MAT *eliminar una incógnita* to eliminate an unknown quantity.

eliminatorio, ria *adj* eliminatory; *un examen eliminatorio* an eliminatory examination.
◆ *f* DEP heat, qualifying round (en atletismo) | preliminary round (en otros deportes).

elinvar *m* elinvar (aleación de níquel y cromo).

elipse *f* MAT ellipse.

elipsis *f inv* GRAM ellipsis.

elipsoidal *adj* MAT ellipsoidal.

elipsoide *m* MAT ellipsoid.

elíptico, ca *adj* elliptic, elliptical.

elisabetiano, na *adj* Elizabethan.

Elíseo *npr m* MIT Elysium.

elíseo, a *adj* MIT Elysian || MIT *Campos Elíseos* Elysian Fields.

elisión *f* GRAM elision.

élite *f* élite; *la élite de la nación* the nation's élite.
— OBSERV This word is a commonly used Gallicism.

élitro *m* ZOOL elytrum, elytron (de insecto).

elixir *m* elixir.

elocución *f* elocution (manera de hablar) || *tiene la elocución fácil* he has the gift of the gab.

elocuencia *f* eloquence.

elocuente *adj* eloquent || telling, significant; *un silencio elocuente* a telling silence.

elogiable *adj* praiseworthy, laudable.

elogiador, ra *adj* laudatory, eulogistic.
◆ *m/f* praiser, eulogist.

elogiar *vt* to praise, to laud, to eulogize || *discurso muy elogiado* highly praised speech.

elogio *m* eulogy, praise || — *deshacerse en elogios* to be lavish in one's praise || *digno de elogio* praiseworthy. || *está por encima de todo elogio* he is beyond praise || *hacer elogios de* to sing the praises of, to eulogize || *hacer un caluroso elogio de* to praise highly.

elogiosamente *adv* eulogistically, with great praise.

elogioso, sa *adj* eulogistic, laudatory; *habló de él en términos elogiosos* he spoke about him in laudatory terms || laudable (digno de elogio); *una acción elogiosa* a laudable act.

elongación *f* ASTR & MED elongation.

elote *m* AMER ear of green corn (mazorca de maíz).

elucidación *f* elucidation, explanation.

elucidar *vt* to elucidate, to explain (aclarar).

elucubración *f* lucubration.

elucubrar *vt* to lucubrate.
— OBSERV *Elucubración* and *elucubrar* are Gallicisms used for *lucubración* and *lucubrar*.

eludible *adj* avoidable, evadable, eludible.

eludir *vt* to avoid, to elude, to evade; *eludir una pregunta* to avoid a question || to avoid; *eludió mirarme a la cara* he avoided looking me in the face.

elzevir; elzevirio *m* elzevir (libro).

ella *pron pers f sing* she (sujeto, personas); *ella viene* she is coming || her, herself (enfático, personas); *es ella* it's her; *lo hizo ella* she did it (herself) || her (con preposición, personas); *hablo de ella* I am talking about her; *lo hice por ella* I did it for her || it (sujeto o con preposición, cosas) || — FAM *allí fue ella* then the trouble began || *de ella* hers (persona); *mi libro y el de ella* my book and hers; its (cosa) || *ella misma* (she) herself || FAM *mañana será ella* there will be trouble tomorrow.
— OBSERV The subject pronoun *ella* is only used in Spanish to avoid ambiguity or when emphasis is required; the latter may be conveyed in English by stressing *she*.

ellas *pron pers pl* ⟶ **ellos.**

elle *f* ll [name of the letter *ll*].

ello *pron pers neutro* it; *no pienses más en ello* don't think about it any more || — FAM *aquí* or *allí fue ello* then the trouble began || *ello es que...* the fact is that..., the thing is that... || *por ello me gusta* that's why I like it || *¡vamos a ello!* let's get on with it!

ellos, ellas *pron pers pl* they (sujeto) || them, themselves (complemento) || — *¡a ellos!, ¡a por ellos!* forward!, at them! (para atacar) || *de ellos, de ellas* theirs || *ellos mismos, ellas mismas* themselves; *ellos mismos lo han hecho* they have done it themselves.

emaciación *f* emaciation.

emaciado, da *adj* emaciated.

emanación *f* emanation.

emanar *vi* to emanate; *el olor que emana de la panadería* the smell emanating from the bakery || to emanate, to be sent out; *la orden emana del gerente* the order emanates from *o* is sent out by the manager || to arise, to result; *esta obligación emana del contrato* this obligation arises from the contract.

emancipación *f* emancipation.

emancipado, da *adj* emancipated.

emancipador, ra *adj* emancipatory.
◆ *m/f* emancipator.

emancipar *vt* to emancipate.
◆ *vpr* to become emancipated || to free o.s., to liberate o.s. (liberarse).

emarginado, da *adj* BOT emarginate.

emasculación *f* emasculation.

emascular *vt* to emasculate (mutilar).

embabiamiento *m* FAM absentmindedness.

embadurnar *vt* to daub, to smear; *embadurnar con* or *de pintura* to daub with paint.
◆ *vpr* to smear o.s., to plaster o.s.; *embadurnarse de grasa* to plaster o.s. with grease.

embaimiento *m* deception, trickery.

embaír* *vt* to deceive, to trick, to mislead.
— OBSERV This verb is defective, existing only in the forms whose endings begin with *i*.

embajada *f* embassy || ambassadorship (función del embajador) || FIG errand, job (encargo) | message (mensaje) || FAM *no me vengas ahora con esa embajada* don't come to me with these stories.

embajador, ra *m/f* ambassador (hombre), ambassadress (mujer); *embajador en* or *cerca de* ambassador in *o* to.

embalador, ra *m/f* packer, wrapper, packager.

embalaje; embalamiento *m* packing, packaging || *papel de embalaje* wrapping paper, brown paper.

embalar *vt* to pack, to package (muebles, etc.) || to rev (un motor).
◆ *vi* to race (un motor).
◆ *vpr* to race (un motor) || to sprint (correr) || to gabble (hablar de prisa) || to get worked up, to get excited (entusiasmarse).

embaldosado, da *adj* tiled.
◆ *m* tiled floor (suelo) || tiling.

embaldosar *vt* to tile (con baldosas).

embalsadero *m* bog, quagmire.

embalsamador, ra *adj* embalming.
◆ *m* embalmer.

embalsamamiento *m* embalmment, embalming || perfuming, scenting, embalming (perfume).

embalsamar *vt* to embalm (un cadáver) || to perfume, to scent, to embalm (perfumar).

embalsar *vt* to dam, to dam up (agua) || MAR to sling, to hoist (izar).
◆ *vpr* to be dammed up.

embalse *m* damming, damming-up (acción de embalsar) || dam (presa) || reservoir, dam (lago artificial) || collecting (de una cantidad de agua) || MAR slinging, hoisting.

emballenado, da *adj* boned, stiffened.
◆ *m* boning, stiffening.

emballenar *vt* to bone, to stiffen (con ballenas).

embanastar *vt* to put in a basket || FIG to pack, to crowd, to cram (a la gente).

embancarse *vpr* MAR to run aground (encallarse) || AMER to silt up, to block, to become blocked (río o lago) || AMER TECN to adhere to the furnace walls.

embanderar *vt* to adorn *o* to deck with flags *o* bunting.

embanquetado *m* AMER pavement [US sidewalk].

embanquetar *vt* AMER to build a pavement on.

embarazada *adj f* pregnant (mujer); *estar embarazada de seis meses* to be six months pregnant; *quedarse embarazada* to become pregnant; *dejar embarazada a una mujer* to get a woman pregnant || FIG embarrassed (confusa).
◆ *f* pregnant woman, expectant mother.

embarazado, da *adj* embarrassed (persona) || hampered, hindered (estorbado) || inconvenienced, troubled (molesto) || blocked, obstructed (obstruido).

embarazador, ra *adj* embarrassing (que pone en un apuro) || hampering, hindering, encumbering (que estorba) || obstructive (que obstruye).

embarazar *vt* to embarrass (hacer pasar un apuro) || to hinder, to hamper, to encumber; *su abrigo le embaraza* his overcoat hampers him; *esto embaraza sus movimientos* this hampers his movements || to inconvenience, to trouble (molestar) || to block, to obstruct; *embarazar el paso* to block the way || to make pregnant (a una mujer).
◆ *vpr* to get embarrassed (estar confuso) || to be hindered *o* hampered (molestarse) || to get blocked, to become obstructed (obstruirse) || to become pregnant (quedarse encinta).

embarazo *m* embarrassment (apuro) || hindrance, encumbrance (estorbo) || obstacle, obstruction (obstáculo) || pregnancy (de la mujer) || — *embarazo ectópico* or *extrauterino* ectopic *o* extrauterine pregnancy || *embarazo fantasma* phantom pregnancy || *embarazo múltiple* multiple pregnancy.

embarazoso, sa *adj* embarrassing; *una pregunta embarazosa* an embarrassing question || hampering, encumbering, hindering (molesto) || obstructive (que obstruye).

embarbillado *m* TECN rabbeting (acción) | rabbet (ensambladura).

embarbillar *vt* TECN to rabbet.

embarcación *f* boat, craft; *embarcación de pesca, de recreo* fishing, pleasure boat || embarkation, embarcation (embarco) || voyage (viaje) || *embarcación fueraborda* speedboat [with outboard motor].

embarcadero *m* MAR landing stage (plataforma) | quay, jetty, pier (muelle para viajeros) | dock, wharf (muelle para mercancías) || AMER goods station, loading platform (de ferrocarriles).

embarcar *vt* to embark (pasajeros) || to ship aboard (mercancías) || FAM to involve; *embarcar a alguien en un asunto* to involve s.o. in an affair.
◆ *vpr* to embark, to go aboard; *embarcarse en un vapor* to go aboard a steamer; *mañana me embarco a las nueve* I embark tomorrow at nine o'clock || FIG & FAM to embark upon, to launch into, to engage in (un negocio, un pleito, etc.).
◆ *vi/vpr* AMER to board (en un vehículo).

embarco *m* embarkation, embarcation (de personas).

embardar *vt* to top with spikes *o* barbed wire *o* broken glass (una pared).

embargar *vt* FIG to overcome (la emoción, el dolor) || JUR to seize, to distrain, to sequestrate || MAR to lay an embargo upon (un barco) || (p us) to hinder, to hamper (estorbar).

embargo *m* JUR seizure, sequestration, distraint || MAR embargo || MED indigestion || FIG access (de una emoción) || — JUR *ejecución de embargo* distress, execution | *embargo de bienes litigiosos* seizure under a prior claim | *embargo de la cosecha en pie* distraint by seizure of crops | *embargo de retención* attachment || *sin embargo* however, nevertheless.

embarnizamiento *m* varnishing.

embarnizar *vt* to varnish.

embarque *m* loading, shipment (de mercancías).

embarrada *f* AMER blunder (patochada).

embarrado, da *adj* muddy.

embarrancar *vi* MAR to go *o* to run aground (encallarse) || FIG to get bogged down.
◆ *vpr* MAR to go *o* to run aground || to get stuck, to get bogged down (atascarse).

embarrar *vt* to cover *o* to splash with mud (salpicar de barro) || to daub, to smear (embadurnar) || AMER FIG to sling mud at (envilecer) | to involve (a una persona en un asunto).
◆ *vpr* to get dirty, to get covered with mud || to take refuge in the trees (perdices).

embarrilado; embarrilamiento *m* casking, barrelling.

embarrilar *vt* to cask, to barrel.

embarullador, ra *adj* muddling || FAM slapdash, careless, bungling (chapucero).
◆ *m/f* muddler, muddlehead || FAM bungler, slapdash *o* careless person.

embarullar *vt* to muddle, to mix up || FAM to do in a careless *o* in a slapdash manner, to bungle (chapucear).

embasamiento *m* ARQ foundation.

embastar *vt* to baste, to tack (hilvanar) || to put in an embroidery frame (una tela) || to quilt (un colchón) || to put a packsaddle on, to load (las caballerías).

embaste *m* tacking, basting.

embastecer* *vi* to grow stout, to grow fat (engordar).
◆ *vpr* to become rude *o* coarse.

embate *m* MAR dashing, breaking (de olas) || sea breeze (viento) || FIG sudden attack (acometida).

embaucador, ra *adj* deceptive, deceiving (que engaña) || cajoling (engatusador).
◆ *m/f* trickster, swindler, cheater (timador) || cajoler (engatusador).

embaucamiento *m* deception, deceit, cheating (engaño) || cajolery (seducción).

embaucar *vt* to deceive, to cheat, to dupe (engañar); *embaucar a uno con promesas* to deceive s.o. with promises | to cajole, to wheedle (seducir).

embaulado, da *adj* FIG packed, crammed (apretado).

embaular *vt* to pack (in a trunk) || FIG & FAM to pack, to cram (personas o cosas) || to put away, to gorge, to guzzle (engullir).

embebecer* *vt* to delight, to fascinate (embelesar).
◆ *vpr* to be delighted, to be fascinated.

embebecimiento *m* delight, fascination.

embeber *vt* to absorb, to soak up; *la esponja embebe el agua* a sponge absorbs water || to soak, to saturate, to drench; *embeber algo en agua* to soak sth. in water || to fit in, to insert (encajar) || to take in (acortar) || to contain (contener).
◆ *vi* to shrink (encogerse) || to be absorbent (el lienzo pintado al óleo).
◆ *vpr* FIG to absorb o.s., to immerse o.s., to become absorbed; *embeberse en un libro* to become absorbed in a book | to soak o.s. (en alcohol, etc.).

embebimiento *m* shrinking.

embelecador, ra *adj* deceptive, deceiving (engañador) || cajoling, wheedling (engatusador).

embelecamiento *m* deception, deceit (engaño).

embelecar *vt* to deceive, to cheat, to dupe (engañar) || to cajole, to wheedle (seducir).

embeleco *m* deceit, deception (engaño).

embelesador, ra *adj* charming, enchanting (encantador) || bewitching (hechicero).

embelesamiento *m* → **embeleso.**

embelesar *vt* to delight, to charm, to enchant (encantar) || to fascinate, to enrapture, to enthrall (maravillar) || FIG to bewitch (embrujar).
◆ *vpr* to be delighted, to be fascinated; *embelesarse con un espectáculo* to be delighted by a show.

embeleso; embelesamiento *m* delight, enchantment (encanto) || fascination, rapture, enthrallment || FIG bewitchment (embrujo) || BOT plumbago, leadwort.

embellaquecerse* *vpr* to go to the bad, to become a rogue.

embellecedor *m* AUT hubcap (tapacubos).

embellecer* *vt* to embellish, to beautify, to adorn || FIG to idealize.
◆ *vi* to improve in looks (naturalmente).
◆ *vpr* to beautify o.s. (adomándose).

embellecimiento *m* embellishment.

embermejar; embermejecer* *vt* to make red, to redden || to make blush (sonrojar).
◆ *vi* to redden, to turn red || to blush (cara).
◆ *vpr* to blush.

emberrechinarse; emberrincharse *vpr* FAM to fly into a tantrum.

embestida; embestidura *f* attack, assault, onslaught || charge; *la embestida del toro* the bull's charge || FIG & FAM touch [for a loan].

embestidor, ra *adj* attacking || charging (toro).

embestidura *f* → **embestida.**

embestir* *vt* to attack, to assail, to assault (asaltar) || to charge; *el toro embistió al matador* the bull charged the matador || FIG & FAM to smash (un coche) || FIG & FAM *embestir a alguien* to go at s.o., to throw o.s. at s.o.
◆ *vi* to attack.

embetunar *vt* to black, to polish (zapatos) || to tar, to asphalt (asfaltar).

embicar *vt* MAR to luff (orzar) || AMER to insert (una cosa en otra).
◆ *vi* AMER to head straight for the coast.

embizcar *vi* to become cross-eyed.

emblandecer* *vt* to soften.
◆ *vpr* to soften, to grow soft || FIG to soften up, to relent.

emblanquecer* *vt* to bleach, to whiten.
◆ *vpr* to turn white, to bleach.

emblanquecimiento *m* bleaching, whitening.

emblema *m* emblem || badge (insignia).

emblemático, ca *adj* emblematic.

embobado, da *adj* agape, dumbfounded, flabbergasted (boquiabierto) || dazed, stupefied, bewildered (sin reacción).

embobamiento *m* fascination, amazement || stupefaction, bewilderment (estupefacción).

embobar *vt* to amaze, to dumbfound, to astound (atontar) || to stupefy, to bewilder (dejar sin reacción) || to fascinate.
◆ *vpr* to be amazed *o* astounded *o* stupefied *o* fascinated.

embobecer* *vt* to make *o* to turn silly *o* stupid.

embobecimiento *m* stupefaction.

embocado, da *adj* smooth (vino).

embocadura *f* mouth (de un río, de un canal) || taste (de vino) || bit (de freno de caballo) || TEATR proscenium arch || MÚS mouthpiece (boquilla).

embocar *vt* to put in the mouth || to enter; *el barco embocó el canal* the ship entered the canal || to insert || MÚS to put to one's lips (un instrumento) || to catch in the mouth (coger con la boca) || FIG & FAM to make believe *o* swallow (hacer creer) | to scoff, to guzzle, to bolt (engullir).
◆ *vpr* to squeeze in (meterse en un lugar estrecho).

embocinado, da *adj* trumpet-shaped.

embodegar *vt* to store (in the cellar) (vino, etc.).

embojar *vt* to put on branches to encourage the formation of cocoons (gusanos de seda).

embojo *m* branches *pl* [used for silkworms] || putting (silkworms) on branches (acción).

embolado *m* bull with protective wooden balls on the horns (toro) || TEATR minor role || FIG & FAM story, fib (engaño) | thankless task, irksome job (trabajo) || FAM *¡pues vaya un embolado!* what a job!

embolador *m* AMER bootblack (limpiabotas).

embolar *vt* TAUR to put protective wooden balls on (the horns of a bull) || AMER to black, to polish (shoes).
◆ *vpr* AMER to get drunk.

embolia *f* clot, embolism.

embolismar *vt* FAM to gossip about.

émbolo *m* TECN piston.

embolsar *vt* to pocket.

embonar *vt* AMER to manure (con abonos) || to suit (ir bien) || to join (juntar).

emboñigar *vt* to cover in cow dung.

emboquillado, da *adj* filter-tipped, tipped, filter (cigarrillos).

emboquillar *vt* to tip, to filter-tip (un cigarrillo) || MIN to open up, to make an entrance to (una galería, un túnel).

emborrachamiento *m* intoxication, drunkenness.

emborrachar *vt* to intoxicate, to make drunk (embriagar) || to get drunk; *emborrachar a alguien* to get s.o. drunk.
◆ *vpr* to get drunk, to become intoxicated; *emborracharse con* or *de coñac* to get drunk on brandy.

emborrascarse *vpr* to become stormy (el tiempo) || to fail, to go wrong (negocios, etc.) || to get angry *o* annoyed (irritarse) || AMER to become exhausted (una mina).

emborrizar *vt* to card (la lana) || to coat (en pan rallado, harina, azúcar, etc.); *emborrizar un pescado en harina* to coat a fish in *o* with flour.

emborronador, ra *m/f* *emborronador de cuartillas* or *de papel* hack, scribbler, second-rate author (escritor), scribbler (garrapateador).

emborronar *vt* to scribble (escribir mal) || to scribble on (llenar de garabatos) || to blot (con borrones).

emboscada *f* ambush; *tender una emboscada* to lay an ambush || FIG trap.

emboscado *m* MIL soldier under cover *o* in ambush.

emboscar *vt* MIL to place under cover *o* in ambush.
◆ *vpr* to lie in ambush, to ambush || FIG to get a cushy job.

embosquecer* *vi* to become wooded.

embotado, da *adj* dull, blunt.

embotadura *f*; **embotamiento** *m* blunting (acción) || bluntness, dullness (estado) || FIG dulling (de los sentidos).

embotar *vt* to blunt, to dull (una herramienta, etc.) || FIG to dull, to deaden (los sentidos) | to enervate (a una persona) || to pack in a jar (el tabaco).
◆ *vpr* to become blunt *o* dull || FIG to become enervated (persona) | to be dulled, to be deadened (sentidos) || FAM (p us) to put on one's boots.

embotellado, da *adj* bottled || FIG jammed, blocked (circulación) | stored in one's mind, learnt by heart (aprendido de memoria) | prepared in advance (discurso, conferencia) || MAR blocked, bottled up.
◆ *m* bottling.

embotellador *m* bottler.

embotelladora *f* bottling machine.

embotellamiento *m* bottling (en botellas) || jam (en la vía pública); *un embotellamiento de coches* a traffic jam.

embotellar *vt* to bottle (poner en botellas) || FIG to jam, to block (la circulación) | to learn by heart, to memorize (aprender) || MAR to block, to bottle up (no dejar salir un barco enemigo).
◆ *vpr* to learn by heart; *se embotelló todo el código civil* he learned all the civil code by heart.

embotijar *vt* to put in jugs.
◆ *vpr* FIG & FAM to swell (hincharse) | to become angry *o* annoyed (encolerizarse).

embovedar *vt* ARQ to arch, to vault (over).

embozar *vt* to cover (the lower part of the face), to muffle up (con la capa, etc.) || to muzzle (poner un bozal) || FIG to conceal, to cloak, to disguise (ocultar).
◆ *vpr* to wrap *o* to muffle o.s. up, to cover one's face; *embozarse en la capa* to cover one's face with one's cloak.

embozo *m* fold, flap (de una capa) || turnover, fold (de una sábana) || FIG disguise (disfraz), covering-up, concealment, dissimulation (disimulo) || — FIG & FAM *hablar con embozo* to talk equivocally *o* ambiguously | *quitarse el embozo* to take off one's mask, to reveal one's intentions.

embragar *vt* TECN to connect, to engage.
◆ *vi* TECN to engage the clutch, to let the clutch in.

embrague *m* TECN engaging of the clutch (acción de embragar) | clutch; *embrague automático, de disco, de fricción, magnético, hidráulico* automatic, disc, friction, magnetic, hydraulic clutch.

embravecer* *vt* to enrage, to infuriate, to incense.
◆ *vpr* to become furious *o* enraged (una persona) || to grow wild (el mar) || to flourish, to thrive (plantas).

embravecido, da *adj* furious, incensed (persona) || raging, wild, rough (el mar) || wild (el viento).

embravecimiento *m* fury, rage.

embrazadura *f* handle (de escudo).

embrazar *vt* to take up (a shield).

embreado *m*; **embreadura** *f* tarring.

embrear *vt* to tar.

embriagado, da *adj* intoxicated, drunk.

embriagador, ra; embriagante *adj* intoxicating.

embriagamiento *m* intoxication, inebriation.

embriagar *vt* to intoxicate, to inebriate (emborrachar) || FIG to enrapture (enajenar) | to elate, to intoxicate, to make drunk; *embriagado por el éxito* intoxicated with success.
◆ *vpr* to become intoxicated, to get drunk || FIG to become elated *o* intoxicated *o* drunk (*de* with).

embriaguez *f* drunkenness, intoxication, inebriation (borrachera) || FIG elation, intoxication | rapture (enajenación).

embridar *vt* DEP to bridle (poner la brida) | to make (a horse) carry its head well (con las riendas).

embriología *f* BIOL embryology.

embriólogo *m* embryologist.

embrión *m* BIOL embryo || FIG embryo (principio) || *en embrión* embryonic, in embryo.

embrionario, ria *adj* in embryo, embryonic.

embrocación *f* MED embrocation.

embrocar *vt* to decant (un líquido) || to turn upside down (poner boca abajo) || TECN to wind on to a bobbin (el hilo) | to nail on (la suela de un zapato) || TAUR to catch between the horns.

embrochalar *vt* ARQ to support with a header beam.

embrolladamente *adv* confusedly, in a confused fashion; *hablar embrolladamente* to talk confusedly.

embrollador, ra *adj* confusing, muddling.
◆ *m/f* troublemaker.

embrollar *vt* to muddle, to tangle up, to mix up (enmarañar) || to confuse, to mix up, to muddle (confundir) || to involve (en un asunto).
◆ *vpr* to get mixed up, to get tangled *o* muddled (enmarañarse) || to get confused, to get mixed up, to get in a muddle (confundirse) || to get involved (meterse en un asunto).

embrollo *m* tangle (enredo); *un embrollo de hilo* a tangle of thread || FIG jumble, muddle, mess (confusión) | mess; *¡en menudo embrollo se ha metido!* he's got himself into a fine mess! | trick, lie (embuste).

embrollón, ona *adj* confusing, muddling.
◆ *m/f* troublemaker.

embromado, da *adj* AMER *estar embromado* to be in a fix.

embromar *vt* to make fun of, to tease (burlarse de) || to hoax, to fool (engañar) || AMER to annoy (fastidiar) | to damage (perjudicar) | to delay (entretener, retrasar).

embroquelarse *vpr* ⟶ **abroquelarse.**

embroquetar *vt* to skewer (un ave para asarla).

embrujado, da *adj* bewitched (persona) || haunted (sitio).

embrujamiento *m* bewitchment.

embrujar *vt* to cast a spell on, to bewitch (persona) || to haunt (sitio) || FIG to enchant, to bewitch (encantar).

embrujo *m* bewitchment (embrujamiento) || curse, spell (maleficio) || FIG spell, charm (encanto).

embrutecedor, ra *adj* brutalizing.

embrutecer* *vt* to brutalize, to bestialize, to brutify (volver bruto) || to besot (por el alcohol) || to stupefy, to deaden, to dull (por la sorpresa).
◆ *vpr* to become brutalized | to grow stupid, to become dull (volverse tonto).

embrutecimiento *m* brutishness, sottishness || degradation.

embuchado *m* sausage (embutido) || FIG adlibbing (añadidura a un texto) | rigging of an election (fraude).

embuchar *vt* to cram, to force-feed (un ave) || to stuff [with sausage meat] (para hacer embutidos) || FAM to gulp down, to gobble (engullir).

embudar *vt* to put a funnel into || FIG to trick (engañar).

embudo *m* funnel (para trasegar líquidos) || FIG trick, deception (engaño) || crater (de bomba, meteorito, etc.).

embullo *m* AMER bustle, noise.

emburujar *vt* FAM to heap together (amontonar) | to jumble (mezclar) || AMER to mix up (confundir).
◆ *vpr* AMER to muffle up, to wrap o.s. up (arrebujarse).

embuste *m* lie; *una sarta de embustes* a string of lies || trick (engaño).

embustería *f* lying (mentiras) || deceit (engaño).

embustero, ra *adj* lying (mentiroso) || deceitful (engañoso).
◆ *m/f* liar.

embute *m* AMER bribe (soborno).

embutición *f* stamping, pressing.

embutidera *f* TECN nail set, cupping machine.

embutido *m* sausage || stuffing (acción de embutir) || inlay, marquetry (taracea) || TECN stamping, pressing (de las chapas) || AMER insertion (bordado).
— OBSERV *Embutido* is a generic term including all types of sausage.

embutir *vt* to stuff [with sausage meat] (para hacer embutidos) || to stuff, to pack (rellenar); *embutir lana en una almohadilla* to stuff a cushion with wool, to stuff wool into a cushion || to insert (introducir) || TECN to inlay (taracea) | to stamp, to press (metal) || FIG & FAM to drive in (meter en la cabeza) || FIG

& FAM *embutido en un abrigo* wrapped *o* muffled up in an overcoat.
◆ *vt/vpr* FAM to wolf down, to bolt down, to gulp down (engullir).

eme *f* m [name of the letter *m*].

emergencia *f* emergence (acción de emerger) || emergency; *en caso de emergencia* in case of emergency, in an emergency || — *estado de emergencia* state of emergency || *salida de emergencia* emergency exit || *solución de emergencia* emergency solution.

emergente *adj* emergent (que emerge) || FIG resulting, resultant (que resulta).

emerger *vi* to emerge (de un líquido) || to surface (submarino) || to come into view, to emerge, to appear (aparecer) || to project, to jut out; *la roca emerge en medio del río* the rock juts out in the middle of the river || FIG to result.

emérito, ta *adj* emeritus [retired].

emersión *f* ASTR emersion.

emético, ca *adj/sm* MED emetic.

emétrope *adj* emmetropic (de vista normal).
◆ *m/f* emmetrope.

emetropía *f* MED emmetropia.

emigración *f* emigration; *fomentar la emigración a Australia* to encourage emigration to Australia || migration (de un pueblo, de aves, etc.) || FIG *emigración de capitales* outflow *o* flight of capital.

emigrado, da *m/f* emigrant, political exile, émigré.

emigrante *adj/s* emigrant.

emigrar *vt* to emigrate; *emigrar a la Argentina* to emigrate to Argentina || to migrate (un pueblo, las aves, etc.).

emigratorio, ria *adj* emigratory, migratory.

eminencia *f* hill, height, eminence (elevación de terreno) || FIG eminent figure (persona) || — FIG *eminencia gris* grey eminence, éminence grise | *Su Eminencia* His Eminence (tratamiento eclesiástico).

eminente *adj* FIG eminent, outstanding, distinguished || high, eminent (alto).

eminentemente *adv* eminently.

eminentísimo *adj* most eminent.

emir *m* emir (jefe árabe).

emirato *m* emirate.

Emiratos Árabes Unidos *n pr* GEOGR The United Arab Emirates.

emisario, ria *m/f* emissary (enviado).

emisión *f* emission || RAD transmission, broadcasting (acción de emitir) | broadcast (programa); *la emisión de la tarde* the afternoon broadcast || issue (de papel moneda, de sellos, de valores, etc.) || RAD *director de emisión* producer || ECON *emisión de obligaciones* issue of debentures | *emisión de valores* issue of securities.

emisivo, va *adj* emissive.

emisor, ra *adj* issuing; *banco emisor* issuing bank || RAD *centro emisor, estación emisora* transmitter, broadcasting station.
◆ *m* issuer || RAD transmitter (aparato) | station (de radar) || *emisor receptor* walkie-talkie.
◆ *f* transmitter, radio station, broadcasting station; *emisora de onda corta* shortwave radio station.

emitir *vt* to emit; *emitir luz, sonidos* to emit light, sounds || to give off (olor) || to issue (poner en circulación) || FIG to express, to give; *emitir un juicio* to express an opinion || to give, to cast (un voto) || RAD to transmit, to broadcast; *emitir en onda corta* to transmit on short wave || *sufragios emitidos* votes cast.
◆ *vi* RAD to transmit.

emoción *f* emotion (sentimiento profundo) || excitement, thrill; *la emoción de la aventura* the excitement of adventure || *¡qué emoción!* how exciting!

emocionado, da *adj* moved, touched; *emocionado con sus lágrimas* moved by her tears || upset (perturbado).

emocional *adj* emotional.

emocionante *adj* moving, touching (conmovedor) || exciting, thrilling; *un libro, una película emocionante* an exciting book, film.

emocionar *vt* to move, to touch (conmover); *me emocionó su bondad* I was moved by his kindness || to excite, to thrill; *una excursión al mar siempre emociona a los niños* a trip to the coast always thrills the children || to upset (perturbar); *le emociona ver sangre* the sight of blood upsets him.
◆ *vpr* to be moved, to be touched || to be *o* to get excited *o* thrilled; *se emocionó tanto* he got so excited || to be *o* to get upset, to upset o.s.

emoliente *adj/sm* MED emollient.

emolumento *m* emolument.

emotividad *f* emotionality.

emotivo, va *adj* emotional; *una niña emotiva* an emotional little girl || emotive (que suscita emoción) || moving, touching (conmovedor).

empacador, ra *adj* packing.
◆ *m/f* packer, baler.
◆ *f* baler, baling machine, packing machine.

empacamiento *m* AMER packing | obstinacy.

empacar *vt* to pack (empaquetar) || to bale (el algodón, etc.).
◆ *vpr* AMER to get stubborn *o* obstinate (obstinarse) | to get confused (turbarse) | to stop dead, to balk (un animal) (plantarse).

empacón, ona *adj* AMER stubborn, obstinate | balky (caballo, etc.).

empachado, da *adj* clumsy, awkward (torpe) || *estar empachado* to have indigestion (del estómago), to be fed up, to be sick (estar harto).

empachar *vt* to surfeit, to satiate (saciar) || to give indigestion (a una persona) || to upset (el estómago) || FIG to hinder, to impede (estorbar) | to embarrass (hacer pasar un apuro) | to hide, to conceal (ocultar) | to sicken, to weary (fastidiar).
◆ *vpr* to have indigestion || FIG to get mixed up *o* confused (turbarse) | to be embarrassed *o* ashamed (avergonzarse) | to get fed up, to get sick (hartarse).

empacho *m* indigestion || (p us) hindrance, obstacle (estorbo) || FIG embarrassment (embarazo) | bashfulness, shame (vergüenza) | confusion || — *¡qué empacho de niño!* what a troublesome child! || FIG *tener un empacho de* to have had one's fill of.

empachoso, sa *adj* heavy, indigestible, cloying (alimento) || FIG sickly, sugary (empalagoso) | troublesome, annoying (pesado) | embarrassing, shameful (vergonzoso) | confusing.

empadrarse *vpr* to become excessively attached to one's father *o* to one's parents.

empadronador *m* keeper of the electoral roll || census taker.

empadronamiento *m* enrolment [in the register of electors] || census (censo).

empadronar *vt* to take a census of (la población) || to register in a census *o* on the electoral roll.
◆ *vpr* to have one's name registered on the electoral roll *o* in a census.

empajar *vt* to cover with straw (un semillero, etc.) || to stuff with straw (rellenar con paja) || to bottom with straw (un asiento) || AMER to thatch (techar con paja) | to mix with straw (el barro).
◆ *vpr* AMER to produce much straw and little fruit (cereales).

empalagamiento *m* ⟶ **empalago.**

empalagar *vt/vi* to cloy, to surfeit, to satiate (los alimentos) || FIG to annoy, to sicken, to weary (fastidiar).
◆ *vpr* FIG to get fed up, to get sick.

empalago; empalagamiento *m* sickness (malestar) || surfeit (exceso) || disgust, repugnance (asco) || FIG annoyance, boredom.

empalagoso, sa *adj* sickly, cloying (alimento) || FIG cloying, sickening, mawkish (zalamero) | sugary, sickly (película, novela, voz, etc.) | wearisome, trying (fastidioso).

empalamiento *m* impalement.

empalar *vt* to impale (atravesar con un palo).
◆ *vpr* AMER to be persistent *o* obstinate (obstinarse) | to become numb *o* stiff (envararse).

empalizada *f* MIL palisade, stockade (estacada) || fence (valla).

empalizar *vt* MIL to palisade, to stockade || to fence (vallar).

empalmadura *f* ⟶ **empalme.**

empalmar *vt* to connect, to join, to fit together (unir) || to butt join, to join (en carpintería) || to splice (cuerda, película) || DEP to kick on the volley (la pelota) || FIG to link up (ideas, planes).
◆ *vi* to fit (encajar) || to join, to meet, to connect (caminos, líneas de ferrocarril) || to connect (trenes, autocares) || *empalmar con* to follow, to succeed (seguir).

empalme *m*; **empalmadura** *f* joint, join, connection (conexión) || joint, butt joint (en carpintería) || splice (de cuerda, película cinematográfica) || junction (de líneas de ferrocarril) || intersection, junction (de carreteras) || connection (de trenes, autocares) || kick on the volley (en fútbol).

empalletado *m* MAR mat.

empamparse *vpr* AMER to get lost in the pampas | to lose one's way (extraviarse).

empampirolado, da *adj* FAM conceited, vain.

empanada *f* CULIN turnover, pie || FIG fraud || FIG & FAM *empanada mental* mental confusion, muddle..

empanadilla *f* CULIN turnover (de carne, de pescado, con dulce).

empanado, da *adj* CULIN covered in breadcrumbs, breaded.

empanar *vt* to coat in breadcrumbs, to bread.

empantanado, da *adj* flooded, swampy.

empantanar *vt* to flood, to swamp (inundar) || to bog down (meter en un barrizal) || FIG to bog down, to hold up (detener); *empantanar un asunto* to bog down an affair.
◆ *vpr* to be *o* to become flooded; *la carretera se empantanó* the highway was flooded || to get bogged down; *la carreta se empantanó* the cart got bogged down || FIG to be held up *o* bogged down; *se empantanó el plan* the plan was held up | to mark time (persona) | to make no headway; *asunto que se empantana* affair which makes no headway.

empañado, da *adj* misty, steamy (un cristal) || faint (voz) || tarnished, blemished (la honra).

empañar *vt* to put a nappy on [*US* to diaper], to swaddle (ant) (a un niño) || to steam up, to cloud, to mist; *el vapor empañó el cristal* the steam clouded the glass || to dull, to tarnish (quitar el brillo) || FIG to tarnish, to blemish, to sully (la reputación) || — FIG *empañar el honor de alguien* to cast a stain *o* a slur on s.o.'s honour | *voz empañada por la emoción* voice choked with emotion.
◆ *vpr* to get steamed up, to mist up (cristales) || to falter (la voz).

empapamiento *m* soaking, steeping (de la ropa al lavar) || soaking, saturation, drenching (por la lluvia, etc.) || absorption (absorción) || mopping-up (acción de enjugar).

empapar *vt* to soak, to steep (mojar completamente); *empapar sopas en vino* to soak crumbs in wine; *empapar la ropa sucia* to soak the dirty linen || to soak, to saturate, to drench; *la lluvia me empapó* the rain drenched me || to saturate, to soak; *empapar una esponja en agua* to saturate a sponge with water || to absorb, to soak up (absorber); *la tierra empapa la lluvia* the earth absorbs the rain || to sponge up, to mop up (enjugar); *empapar la leche vertida con un trapo* to mop the spilt milk up with a rag || FIG to soak || — *estar empapado* to be drenched *o* sodden *o* soaked || *estar empapado en sudor* to be drenched in sweat, to be dripping with perspiration *o* sweat.
◆ *vpr* to be soaked, to be steeped; *el pan se empapa en leche* the bread is steeped in milk || to be *o* to become *o* to get soaked *o* drenched *o* saturated; *me empapé con la lluvia* I got soaked in the rain || to be *o* to become saturated *o* soaked; *el papel secante se empapó de tinta* the blotting paper became saturated with ink || to be absorbed *o* soaked up; *la tinta se empapa en el papel secante* the ink is absorbed by the blotting paper || FIG to become imbued *o* pervaded *o* possessed with; *empaparse de ideas nuevas* to become imbued with new ideas || to soak o.s.; *se empapó de obras revolucionarias* he soaked himself in revolutionary literature | to get into one's head; *empápate bien esta regla* get this rule into your head || FIG & FAM to stuff o.s. (saciarse).

empapelado *m* wallpaper (papel para las paredes) || wallpapering, papering, paperhanging (colocación del papel) || lining (de un baúl, etc.).

empapelador *m* paperhanger (de paredes).

empapelar *vt* to paper, to wallpaper (las paredes) || to line with paper (un baúl, etc.) || to wrap in paper (envolver) || FIG & FAM to have up (formar causa criminal a uno).

empapirotarse *vpr* FAM to dress up, to put on one's Sunday best.

empaque *m* packing (acción de empaquetar) || packing (materiales empleados) || bearing, presence (de una persona) | gravity (solemnidad) | *AMER* cheek, impudence, effrontery (descaro) || *un caballo de mucho empaque* a good stepper.

empaquetado; empaquetamiento *m* packing.

empaquetador, ra *m/f* packer.

empaquetadura *f* packing.

empaquetar *vt* to package, to pack up, to make into a parcel, to parcel up (embalar) || to pack (colocar apretadamente) || FIG to pack *o* to cram together (a personas).

emparamarse *vpr* *AMER* to freeze to death.

emparedado, da *adj* walled in, immured || confined, imprisoned (prisionero) || in reclusion (ermitaño).
◆ *m/f* prisoner, captive (por castigo) || recluse, hermit (por propia voluntad).
◆ *m* sandwich.

emparedamiento *m* immurement || confinement (de un prisionero) || reclusion (de un ermitaño).

emparedar *vt* to immure, to wall in || to confine, to imprison (encerrar).

emparejadura *f*; **emparejamiento** *m* matching || levelling.

emparejar *vt* to match; *emparejar dos candelabros* to match two candelabra || to make level, to bring to the same level (poner una cosa a nivel con otra) || to level (off), to smooth, to flush, to make even (alisar) || to level (off) (tierra).
◆ *vi* to match; *su blusa empareja con su falda* her blouse matches her skirt || to catch up, to draw level; *el coche aceleró y emparejó con la moto* the car speeded up and drew level with the motorbike || to catch up; *emparejó con sus rivales* he caught up with his rivals.
◆ *vpr* to match (dos cosas) || to catch up, to draw level (ponerse juntos) || to pair off (dos personas).

emparentado, da *adj* related.

emparentar* *vi* to become related by marriage || to be related (ser pariente) || *emparentar con* to marry into (una familia).

emparrado *m* trained vine (parra) || arbour [*US* arbor], bower (bóveda de jardín) || trellis, trelliswork, latticework (armazón).

emparrandarse *vpr* *AMER* FAM to go on a spree *o* on a binge (ir de parranda).

emparrar *vt* to train (una planta).

emparrillado *m* grillage, grating.

emparrillar *vt* to grill (asar en la parrilla) || ARQ to reinforce with a grillage *o* a grating.

emparvar *vt* AGR to lay for threshing (la mies).

empastador *m* paste brush (pincel) || *AMER* book-binder (encuadernador).

empastado, da *adj* filled, stopped (muela) || clothbound (libro).

empastar *vt* to paste (cubrir de pasta) || to bind (encuadernar) || to fill, to put a filling in, to stop (un diente) || ARTES to impaste || *AMER* to turn into pasture, to pasture (un terreno).
◆ *vpr* to be filled *o* stopped (muelas) || *AMER* to suffer from meteorism (el ganado) | to become covered in weeds (un terreno).

empaste *m* filling (de un diente) || bookbinding (encuadernación) || ARTES impasto, impasting || *AMER* meteorism (del ganado).

empastelar *vt* FIG & FAM to find a way out of (a difficulty) (para salir del paso) || IMPR to pie (mezclar fundiciones distintas) | to transpose accidentally, to mix up (composición tipográfica).
◆ *vpr* IMPR to become pied | to become transposed, to get mixed up.

empatar *vi* to draw, to tie; *los dos candidatos empataron* the two candidates drew; *empatar a dos* to draw two all [*US* to tie two to two] || DEP to equalize; *Gómez empató en el minuto diecisiete* Gómez equalized in the seventeenth minute | to tie, to have a dead heat (en las carreras de caballos) || *AMER* to fit (empalmar) || — *empatados a dos* two all [*US* two to two] (fútbol) || *estar empatados* to be equal *o* tying || *salir* or *quedar empatados* to draw, to tie.

empate *m* draw, tie (en un partido, un concurso, una elección) || dead heat (en una carrera) || division (de opiniones) || *AMER* joint, connection || — *el gol de empate* the equalizing goal, the equalizer || *empate a dos* two all (tanteo), two all draw (resultado) [*US* tie two to two] || *empate a quince* fifteen all (tenis).

empavesado, da *adj* dressed (buque) || decked, decorated (calles) || veiled (monumento).
◆ *m* dressing, bunting (del buque).
◆ *f* MAR hammock cloth (para los coyes) || MIL pavis.

empavesar *vt* to dress (un buque) || to deck, to decorate (las calles) || to veil (un monumento).

empavonado; empavonamiento *m* TECN blueing (de un metal).

empavonar *vt* to blue (los metales) || *AMER* to grease.

empecatado, da *adj* incorrigible, wicked (malvado) || cursed, wretched (maldito); *ese empecatado crío me exaspera* that wretched brat is driving me round the bend || unlucky, ill-fated (desgraciado).

empecer* *vi* *lo que no empece* which does not prevent.

empecinado, da *adj* obstinate, stubborn (terco) || *el Empecinado* nickname of Martín Díaz [a hero of the Spanish War of Independence].

empecinamiento *m* obstinacy, stubbornness.

empecinarse *vpr* to be *o* to become obstinate *o* stubborn.

empedarse *vpr* *AMER* FAM to get drunk.

empedernido, da; encallecido, da *adj* FIG heavy, confirmed, inveterate (bebedor, fumador, jugador) | hardened, confirmed (criminal) || confirmed (solterón) || inveterate (mentiroso, odio) || callous, unfeeling, hard-hearted (insensible).

empedernir* *vt* to harden, to toughen (volver duro) || FIG to harden, to toughen up (curtir el cuerpo) | to make hardhearted *o* callous *o* unfeeling (insensibilizar).
◆ *vpr* to become hard, to harden || FIG to toughen o.s. up, to get fit (para los deportes, para un trabajo duro) | to become hardhearted *o* callous *o* unfeeling (insensibilizarse).
— OBSERV This verb is defective, and exists only in the forms whose endings begin with *i* (*empederní, empedernía, empederniera, etc.*).

empedrado, da *adj* paved (con adoquines) || cobbled (con guijarros) || dappled (color de caballerías) || pockmarked (cara).
◆ *m* paving (adoquinado) || cobbles *pl* (enguijarrado).

empedramiento *m* ⟶ **empedrado.**

empedrar* *vt* to pave (con adoquines) || to cobble (con guijarros) || FIG to sprinkle, to lard; *empedrar un discurso de galicismos, de citas* to lard a speech with Gallicisms, quotations.

empega *f* pitch (pez) || pitch mark made on sheep (señal).

empegado *m* tarpaulin.

empegar *vt* to pitch, to coat with pitch || to mark with pitch (el ganado lanar).

empeine *m* instep (del pie, de un zapato) || groin (parte baja del vientre) || MED impetigo (en la piel) || BOT hepatica, liverwort.

empelotarse *vpr* FAM to squabble, to row (reñir) || *AMER* FAM to strip, to undress (desnudarse) || *AMER* FAM *empelotarse por* to be *o* to become crazy *o* mad about (chiflarse).

empeltre *m* AGR shield graft (injerto de escudete).

empellada *f* push, shove.

empellar; empeller *vt* to push, to shove.

empellón *m* push, shove (empujón) || — *a empellones* roughly, violently (bruscamente), by force (a la fuerza), in *o* by fits and starts (con interrupciones) || *dar empellones* to shove, to jostle || *hablar a empellones* to gabble.

empenachar *vt* to plume, to adorn with plumes.

empenaje *m* AVIAC empennage, tail unit.

empeñado, da *adj* vehement, heated; *una discusión empeñada* a heated argument ‖ determined (decidido) ‖ insistent, persistent (porfiado) ‖ in debt; *empeñado hasta los ojos* up to one's neck in debt ‖ in pawn, pawned (en el Monte de Piedad).

empeñar *vt* to leave *o* to give as security, to pledge (dar como fianza) ‖ to pawn (en el monte de piedad) ‖ to plege, to plight; *empeñar su palabra, la fe* to pledge one's word, one's faith ‖ to bind, to commit (s.o. to sth.) (obligar a alguien a una cosa) ‖ to engage in, to begin (una lucha) ‖ to begin, to start (una discusión) ‖ to involve, to embroil; *empeñaron el país en una guerra sangrienta* they embroiled the country in a bloody war ‖ FAM *empeñar hasta la camisa* to stake one's shirt.
◆ *vpr* to commit *o* to bind o.s. (to) (obligarse a una cosa) ‖ to begin, to start (una discusión) ‖ to engage in (una lucha) ‖ to get involved *o* embroiled; *se han empeñado en una discusión sobre fútbol* they've got embroiled in an argument about football ‖ to persist, to insist; *empeñarse en hacer algo* to persist in doing sth., to insist on doing sth.; *puesto que te empeñas, te lo diré* since you insist, I'll tell you ‖ to be determined to (estar decidido a) ‖ to endeavour, to strive, to take pains (esforzarse); *me empeñaba en hacerlo lo mejor posible* I endeavoured to do it as well as possible ‖ to get into debt (endeudarse) ‖ *empeñarse por alguien* to intercede for s.o.

empeñero, ra *m/f* AMER pawnbroker.

empeño *m* pledging (acción de empeñar) ‖ pawning (en el Monte de Piedad) ‖ obligation (obligación) ‖ embroilment, involvement (participación) ‖ eagerness, zeal (afán) ‖ desire, aim (objetivo) ‖ determination; *su empeño en hacerlo* his determination to do it ‖ insistence, persistence (insistencia) ‖ backer, patron (apoyo, relación) ‖ — *casa de empeños* pawnshop ‖ *en empeño* in pawn ‖ *papeleta de empeño* pawn ticket ‖ *poner* or *tomar empeño en* to take pains to ‖ *tengo empeño en que este trabajo esté acabado hoy* I am determined that this work be finished today, I am eager for this work to be finished today.

empeñoso, sa *adj* AMER persevering.

empeoramiento *m* deterioration, worsening.

empeorar *vt* to worsen, to make worse, to deteriorate.
◆ *vi/vpr* to worsen, to get worse, to deteriorate; *la situación se ha empeorado rápidamente* the situation has rapidly deteriorated ‖ to get worse (un enfermo).

empequeñecer* *vt* to make smaller, to diminish, to reduce (hacer más pequeño) ‖ FIG to dwarf, to make look small; *el nuevo rascacielos empequeñece los demás edificios* the new skyscraper dwarfs the other buildings | to put in the shade, to overshadow; *nos empequeñece con todas sus hazañas* he puts us in the shade with all his achievements | to belittle, to disparage (desprestigiar).

empequeñecimiento *m* diminution, reduction (disminución) ‖ FIG belittling, disparagement (desprestigio).

emperador *m* emperor ‖ swordfish (pez espada).

emperatriz *f* empress.
— OBSERV The form *emperadora* is archaic.

emperejilarse; emperifollarse *vpr* FAM to doll o.s. up, to dress up.

empernar *vt* TECN to bolt (down or together).

empero *conj* (p us) but (pero) ‖ nevertheless, none the less (sin embargo).
— OBSERV The use of this conjunction is generally restricted to literary contexts.

emperramiento *m* FAM mulishness, stubbornness (obstinación) | insistence, determination | rage, anger (rabia).

emperrarse *vpr* FAM to be dead set (obstinarse); *se emperró en hacerlo como él quería* he was dead set on doing it his own way ‖ to insist, to be determined (estar decidido) ‖ to be obsessed *o* infatuated (*con* with) (encapricharse) ‖ to flare up, to lose one's temper (irritarse).

empezar* *vt* to begin, to start; *empezó su discurso hablando de la guerra* he began *o* he started his speech by talking about the war; *empezamos la semana con una discusión* we started the week with an argument ‖ to start; *¿has empezado la botella de coñac?* have you started the bottle of brandy? ‖ *empezar de nuevo* or *volver a empezar* to start again *o* afresh, to begin again.
◆ *vi* to begin, to start; *empezar a trabajar* to start working, to start to work; *empezaré por abrir todas las ventanas* I shall begin by opening all the windows; *todo empezó cuando cayó enfermo* everything started when he fell ill; *empezamos a las nueve* we begin at nine; *empezó a tiros* he started shooting; *empezó recordándome que...* he began by reminding me that... ‖ — *al empezar* at the beginning ‖ *empezar con* to open with, to start with ‖ *haber empezado con nada* to have started from nothing ‖ *para empezar* to begin with ‖ *todo es empezar* the first step is the hardest.

empicarse *vpr* to become infatuated (*por* with) ‖ *empicarse en el juego* to get the gambling itch.

empicotar *vt* to pillory, to put in the pillory.

empiece *m* FAM beginning, start.

empiezo *m* AMER beginning, start (comienzo).

empilar *vt* to pile, to pile up, to stack.

empinado, da *adj* erect, upright (erguido) ‖ steep; *camino empinado* steep path ‖ very high (alto) ‖ on tiptoe (persona) ‖ rearing (caballo) ‖ FIG haughty, stuck-up (orgulloso).

empinadura *f*; **empinamiento** *m* standing up, setting straight (enderezamiento) ‖ rearing (up) (del caballo) ‖ standing on tiptoe ‖ AVIAC zooming.

empinar *vt* to stand (up), to set straight (poner derecho o vertical) ‖ to raise, to tip up (una botella para beber) ‖ FAM *empinar el codo* to drink a lot, to tipple (beber mucho).
◆ *vpr* to rear (up) (caballo) ‖ to stand on tiptoe (ponerse de puntillas) ‖ to tower, to rise up (árbol, edificio, montaña, etc.) ‖ AVIAC to zoom.

empingorotado, da *adj* FIG upper-class, of high social standing ‖ haughty, stuck-up (orgulloso).

empingorotarse *vpr* to climb, to go up (subirse) ‖ FIG to become haughty *o* stuck-up (engreírse).

empiparse *vpr* FAM to stuff o.s. (*de* with),to gorge (*de* on) (atracarse).

empíreo, a *adj* empyreal.
◆ *m* empyrean (cielo).

empírico, ca *adj* empirical, empiric.
◆ *n* empiric, empiricist.

empirismo *m* empiricism.

empitonar *vt* TAUR to gore, to catch with the horns (cornear).

empizarrado, da *adj* covered with slates.
◆ *m* slate roof (tejado).

empizarrar *vt* to cover *o* to roof with slates, to slate.

emplasto *m* MED plaster ‖ FIG makeshift arrangement, unsatisfactory compromise (componenda) ‖ AMER bore (aburrido).

emplazado, da *adj* HIST *Fernando IV el Emplazado* Ferdinand IV the Summoned.

emplazamiento *m* JUR summons ‖ MIL positioning; *emplazamiento de una batería* positioning of a battery | emplacement (posición) ‖ location (situación) ‖ *emplazamiento arqueológico* archaeological site ‖ INFORM *emplazamiento de memoria* memory location.

emplazar *vt* JUR to summon ‖ to locate, to situate (colocar) ‖ MIL to position.

empleado, da *m/f* employee ‖ clerk (oficinista); *empleado de banco* bank clerk ‖ *empleados del Estado* civil servants.

empleador, ra *adj* employing.
◆ *m/f* employer.

emplear *vt* to use; *emplear un utensilio, una palabra* to use a tool, a word; *ha empleado toda su astucia para conseguir este puesto* he has used all his cunning to get this job ‖ to employ; *esta fábrica emplea a mil obreros* this factory employs a thousand workers ‖ to spend, to occupy, to employ (tiempo) ‖ to invest; *emplear su fortuna en fincas* to invest one's fortune in real estate ‖ — *bien empleado le está, lo tiene bien empleado* he deserves it, it serves him right ‖ *dar por bien empleado* to consider well spent (tiempo, dinero) ‖ *emplear mal* to misuse.
◆ *vpr* to be used; *esa palabra ya no se emplea* that word is no longer used ‖ to be employed ‖ *emplearse a fondo* to do one's utmost.

empleita *f* plaited esparto.

empleo *m* job, post; *tiene un buen empleo* he has a good job; *busco un empleo* I am looking for a job ‖ employment; *pleno empleo* full employment ‖ spending, use (del tiempo) ‖ use (uso); *modo de empleo* instructions for use; *el empleo de una palabra* the use of a word ‖ investment (del dinero) ‖ MIL rank ‖ — *empleo comunitario* community work ‖ *empleo juvenil* youth employment ‖ *sin empleo* unemployed ‖ *solicitud de empleo* application for a job ‖ *suspender a uno del empleo* to relieve s.o. of his duties.

empleomanía *f* FAM eagerness to hold public office.

emplomado *m* leading (de una ventana) ‖ lead covering, lead lining (revestimiento) ‖ lead roof (tejado) ‖ lead seal (sello).

emplomadura *f* AMER filling (de diente).

emplomar *vt* to cover with lead, to line with lead (revestir) ‖ to roof with lead (tejado) ‖ to lead, to join with lead (vidrieras) ‖ to seal with lead (precintar) ‖ AMER to fill (dientes).

emplumar *vt* to feather (una flecha) ‖ to put feathers on, to put a feather on, to plume ‖ AMER to deceive (engañar) ‖ AMER FAM *emplumarlas* to beat it, to skedaddle (huir).
◆ *vi* to grow feathers, to fledge (pájaro) ‖ AMER to beat it, to skedaddle (huir) ‖ *serpiente emplumada* plumed serpent.

emplumecer* *vi* to grow feathers, to fledge (pájaro).

empobrecer* *vi* to impoverish.
◆ *vi/vpr* to become poor *o* impoverished.

empobrecimiento *m* impoverishment.

empodrecer* *vi* to rot (pudrir).

empolvado, da *adj* dusty (cubierto de polvo) ‖ powdered (cubierto de polvos).
◆ *m* powdering.

empolvar; empolvorar; empolvorizar *vt* to cover with dust (ensuciar) ‖ to cover; *el viento empolva la ropa con arena* the wind covers the clothes in sand ‖ to powder (cara, pelo).
◆ *vpr* to become covered in dust, to get dusty (los muebles) ‖ to powder one's face (la cara).

empolvoramiento *m* covering with dust ‖ layer *o* deposit *o* accumulation of dust (capa de polvo).

empolvorar; empolvorizar *vt* → **empolvar.**

empollado, da *adj* FAM well up; *está empollado en matemáticas* he is well up on mathematics.
◆ *m/f* FAM brainbox.

empolladura *f* brood of bees.

empollar *vt* to brood (huevos) ‖ FAM to mug up, to swot up [*US* to bone up] (estudiar mucho); *empollar química* to mug up chemistry.
◆ *vi* to sit, to brood (aves) ‖ to breed (los insectos) ‖ FAM to mug up, to swot up [*US* to bone up] (estudiar).
◆ *vpr* FAM to mug up, to swot up [*US* to bone up] (una lección) ‖ *AMER* to get *o* to develop blisters (levantar ampollas).

empollón, ona *adj* FAM swot, grind.

emponchado, da *adj* *AMER* wearing a poncho, in a poncho | FIG suspicious.

emponcharse *vpr* *AMER* to put on a poncho.

emponzoñador, ra *adj* poisoning, poisonous ‖ FIG harmful (perjudicial).
◆ *m/f* poisoner.

emponzoñamiento *m* poisoning.

emponzoñar *vt* to poison (envenenar) ‖ FIG to poison; *país emponzoñado por el vicio* country poisoned by vice | to embitter (riña, discusión).

empopar *vi* MAR to sail before the wind | to be low in the stern (calar).

emporio *m* emporium, mart, market *o* trade centre (centro comercial) ‖ centre [*US* center]; *emporio de las artes* artistic centre ‖ *AMER* store, department store.

emporrado, da *adj* stoned (drogado).

empotrado, da *adj* built-in, fitted (alacena).

empotramiento *m* embedding, bedding (con cemento) ‖ building-in, fitting (de un armario, etc.).

empotrar *vt* to embed, to bed (fijar con cemento) ‖ to build in, to fit; *armario empotrado* built-in *o* fitted cupboard.

empotrerar *vt* *AMER* to pasture, to put out to pasture (el ganado).

empozar *vt* to put in a well (echar en un pozo) ‖ to ret (el lino o el cáñamo).
◆ *vi* *AMER* to stagnate (estancarse).
◆ *vpr* FIG to be shelved, to be forgotten (un asunto).

emprendedor, ra *adj* enterprising, go-ahead.

emprender *vt* to undertake (un trabajo, una tarea) ‖ to embark upon, to set out on (un viaje) ‖ to start (empezar) ‖ to attack (atacar) ‖ — *emprender el regreso* to go back, to turn back ‖ *emprender el vuelo* to take flight, to take off (aves), to clear off (marcharse) ‖ FAM *emprenderla con uno* to pick a quarrel *o* a fight with s.o. ‖ *emprender la retirada* to retreat.

empresa *f* enterprise, undertaking, venture; *la subida al Everest fue una empresa atrevida* the ascent of Everest was a daring venture ‖ enterprise; *empresa privada* private enterprise ‖ company, firm, concern (sociedad) ‖ management (dirección); *la empresa no es responsable de los objetos perdidos* the management accepts no responsibility for lost articles ‖ emblem, device (emblema) ‖ — *empresa de seguridad* security firm ‖ *empresa de venta por correo* mail-order firm ‖ *empresa filial* subsidiary company ‖ *empresa funeraria* undertaker's ‖ *libre empresa* free enterprise ‖ *empresa multinacional* multinational company ‖ *empresa pública* public corporation ‖ *jurado de empresa* works council.

empresariado *m* employers *pl.*

empresarial *adj* management, managerial (del empresariado); *dificultades empresariales* management difficulties ‖ *la clase empresarial* the employers.

empresario, ria *m/f* employer (empleador) ‖ operator (explotador) ‖ contractor; *empresario de obras públicas* public works contractor ‖ manager (director, gerente).
◆ *m* TEATR impresario ‖ DEP manager (de un equipo, de un boxeador, etc.) ‖ *empresario de pompas fúnebres* undertaker, funeral director ‖ *pequeño empresario* small businessman.

emprestar *vt* (p us) to lend (prestar) | to borrow (pedir prestado).

empréstito *m* loan; *un empréstito al 3 por ciento* a loan at 3 percent interest ‖ government *o* public loan (del Estado) ‖ *lanzar* or *hacer un empréstito* to float a loan.

empringar *vt* to grease, to cover *o* to smear with grease (untar) ‖ to stain *o* to spot with grease (ensuciar).

empujar *vt* to push, to shove (mover) ‖ TECN to thrust ‖ to press (el timbre, etc.) ‖ FIG to urge, to push (incitar).
◆ *vi* to push, to shove.

empuje *m* push, shove (empujón) ‖ pressure (presión) ‖ ARQ & AVIAC & FÍS thrust ‖ FIG energy, go, drive; *tiene mucho empuje* he has got a lot of go ‖ FIG *hombre de empuje* man of action.

empujón *m* push, shove; *dar un empujón a uno* to give s.o. a push ‖ — *abrirse paso a empujones* to push one's way through ‖ *a empujones* roughly, violently (bruscamente), by force (a la fuerza), in *o* by fits and starts (con interrupciones) ‖ *dar empujones* to push, to shove, to jostle ‖ FIG & FAM *dar un empujón a algo* to give sth. a push forward ‖ *entrar, salir, avanzar a empujones* to push one's way in, out, forward.

empulgadura *f* notching, nocking (de una ballesta).

empulgar *vt* to brace [a crossbow].

empulguera *f* nock, notch (de una ballesta).
◆ *pl* thumbscrew *sing* (suplicio).

empuñadura *f* hilt (de espada, etc.); *le clavó la daga hasta la empuñadura* he drove the dagger in him up to the hilt ‖ handle (de paraguas, etc.) ‖ grip, handle (de una herramienta).

empuñar *vt* to seize, to grasp, to take hold of (asir) ‖ to take up (la pluma, la espada, etc.) ‖ FIG to land (un empleo).

empuñidura *f* MAR earing.

EMT *abrev de Empresa Municipal de Transporte* Spanish municipal transport company.

emú *m* emu (ave).

emulación *f* emulation ‖ INFORM emulation.

emulador, ra *adj* emulative, emulating.
◆ *m/f* emulator, rival ‖ INFORM emulator.

— OBSERV *Emulador* suggests *jealousy* while *émulo* does not.

emular *vt* to emulate.

émulo, la *adj* emulous ‖ INFORM to emulate.
◆ *m/f* emulator, rival.

emulsión *f* QUÍM emulsion.

emulsionar *vt* to emulsify.

emulsivo, va *adj* emulsive.

en *prep*

1. LUGAR **2.** TIEMPO **3.** MODO **4.** LOCUCIONES DIVERSAS.

1. LUGAR in; *en Francia, en Madrid* in France, in Madrid; *en la Francia de hoy* in present-day France; *en el Perú* in Peru; *en la Plaza Mayor* in the main square; *en la jaula* in the cage; *estar en la cama* to be in bed; *sentarse en una butaca* to sit in an armchair ‖ in, into; *poner algo en una caja* to put sth. in *o* into a box ‖ on; *el libro está en la mesa, en el suelo* the book is on the table, on the floor; *sentarse en una silla, en la cama* to sit on a chair, on the bed; *en la carretera de Ávila* on the Ávila road; *en la página trece* on page thirteen; *hay un buen programa en el primer canal* there's a good programme on channel one ‖ into; *entrar en* to go into ‖ at; *estar en casa* to be at home; *en casa de Juan* at John's house; *en la estación* at the station ‖ *en donde* where; *¿en dónde nos hemos de reunir?* where are we to meet?.

2. TIEMPO in; *en 1980, en el año 1980* in 1980, in the year 1980; *en el 45* in 45; *en el siglo XX* in the 20th century; *en invierno, en septiembre* in winter, in September; *terminó la novela en dos semanas* he finished his novel in two weeks; *en mi juventud* in my youth; *en tiempos de* in the time of; *en mi tiempo, en mis tiempos* in my time; *en mi vida he visto tal cosa* I've never seen such a thing in my life ‖ on; *en el día 18* on the 18th; *sucedió en domingo* it happened on a Sunday; *en una tarde calurosa* on a hot afternoon; *en vísperas de* on the eve of ‖ at; *en esa época* at that time; *en ese momento* at that moment ‖ — *de hoy en ocho días* a week (from) today ‖ *el año en que te conocí* the year (in which) I met you ‖ *en cuanto* as soon as ‖ *en esto* thereupon ‖ *en llegando el general, disparó la artillería* upon the general's arrival, the artillery fired (véase OBSERV) ‖ *en tanto que* as long as, while, whilst (mientras que), until (hasta que) ‖ *no he dormido en toda la noche* I haven't slept a wink all night.

3. MODO in; *en voz alta* in a loud voice; *en mangas de camisa* in shirt sleeves; *escribir en verso* to write in verse ‖ by; *le conocí en el andar* I recognized him by his gait; *ir en bicicleta, en tren* to go by bicycle, by train; *aumentar en un diez por ciento* to increase by ten percent ‖ — *en broma* as a joke, jokingly; *lo dije en broma* I said it jokingly ‖ *en guerra* at war ‖ *en haciendo lo que te digo triunfarás* if you do what I tell you you'll succeed (véase OBSERV) ‖ *hábil en manejar las armas* skilful at handling arms ‖ *lento en obrar* slow to act, slow in acting ‖ *ponerse en círculo* to form a circle ‖ *vender en veinte pesetas* to sell for twenty pesetas.

4. LOCUCIONES DIVERSAS *convertir en* to turn into ‖ *de casa en casa* from house to house ‖ *doctor en ciencias, en medicina* doctor of science, of medicine ‖ *en cambio* on the other hand, however (al contrario), in return; *hazme este favor y en cambio te haré otro* do me this favour and in return I'll do you one ‖ *en cuanto a* as regards, regarding, with respect to ‖ *¿en qué quedamos?* what is it to be?, what shall we do? (¿qué hacemos?), so (entonces) ‖ *pensar en* to think of *o* about.

— OBSERV When *en* precedes the gerund this indicates that the action expressed by the gerund takes place immediately before the action expressed in the main clause: *en diciendo estas palabras, se marchó* upon saying these words, he left; or is a prerequisite: *en tomando tú el coche, te acompañaré* if you take the car, I'll go with you.

enaceitar *vt* to oil.
◆ *vpr* to go rancid (ponerse rancio) ‖ to become oily (ponerse aceitoso).

Enagas *abrev de Empresa Nacional del Gas* Spanish national gaz company.

enagua *f* petticoat, underskirt.
◆ *pl* petticoat *sing*, underskirt *sing*.

enaguachar *vt* to soak, to drench, to flood.

enaguar *vt* to soak, to drench, to flood.

enaguazar *vt* to soak, to flood (la tierra).

enaguillas *f pl* short petticoat *sing*, short underskirt *sing* || fustanella *sing* (del traje nacional griego).

enajenable *adj* alienable.

enajenación *f*; **enajenamiento** *m* alienation (cesión) || FIG panic (turbación) || rapture (éxtasis) | absentmindedness (distracción) || *enajenación mental* mental derangement, alienation, insanity.

enajenar *vt* to alienate, to transfer (bienes) || FIG to drive mad (volver loco); *el dolor le enajenaba* the pain was driving him mad | to drive to distraction (distraer) | to estrange, to alienate (una amistad) | to intoxicate, to make drunk (embriagar); *enajenado por el éxito* intoxicated with success | to enrapture (extasiar) || *enajenado por el furor, la alegría, la inquietud* beside o.s. with rage, joy, worry.
◆ *vpr* FIG to be driven mad (volverse loco) | to lose one's self-control (no poder dominarse) | to become drunk *o* intoxicated (por el poder, el éxito, etc.) | to go *o* to fall into rapture *o* ecstasy (extasiarse) || *enajenarse la amistad de uno* to lose s.o.'s friendship, to become estranged *o* alienated from s.o.

enalbardar *vt* to put a packsaddle on (poner la albarda) || CULIN to coat [in batter *o* in breadcrumbs] | to lard (un ave).

enaltecer* *vt* to ennoble, to do (s.o.) credit, to be a credit (to s.o.); *esta acción le enaltece* this action does him credit || to praise, to exalt, to extol, to glorify (alabar).

enaltecimiento *m* ennobling, ennoblement || praise, exaltation, extolling, glorification (alabanza).

enamoradizo, za *adj* who is always falling in love.

enamorado, da *adj* in love; *está perdidamente enamorado de ella* he is madly in love with her || amorous (amoroso).
◆ *m/f* sweetheart, lover || lover; *es un enamorado de Mozart* he is a lover of Mozart; *los enamorados de los deportes de invierno* winter sports lovers || *una pareja de enamorados* a courting couple.

enamoramiento *m* falling in love || love (amor).

enamorar *vt* to win the heart of || to court (cortejar).
◆ *vpr* to fall in love (*de* with).

enamoriscarse; enamoricarse *vpr* FAM to take a fancy (*de* to).

enanismo *m* nanism, dwarfism.

enanito, ta *m/f* dwarf.

enano, na *adj/s* dwarf || FAM *trabajar como un enano* to work like a Trojan.

enantes *adv* (ant) before, previously (antes).

enarbolar *vt* to hoist (una bandera) || to brandish (una espada) || MAR to fly; *enarbolar bandera argentina* to fly the Argentinian flag.

enarcar *vt* to arch (arquear) || to hoop (toneles) || to raise; *enarcar las cejas* to raise one's eyebrows.

enardecedor, ra *adj* exciting (excitante) || inflaming (que enfervoriza).

enardecer* *vt* to inflame (las pasiones, una discusión, etc.).
◆ *vpr* to become inflamed *o* excited (una persona) || to become inflamed (una parte del cuerpo).

enardecimiento *m* inflaming, excitation (acción de enardecer) || excitement (excitación) || inflammation (del cuerpo).

enarenamiento *m* sanding.

enarenar *vt* to sand, to cover with sand (cubrir de arena) || to cover with gravel (cubrir de gravas) || MIN to mix (ore) with sand.
◆ *vpr* MAR to run aground (encallar).

enastar *vt* to put a handle *o* shaft on (un arma, etc.).

encabalgadura *f* TECN overlap, overlapping.

encabalgamiento *m* TECN support of crossbeams || MIL gun carriage (cureña) || POÉT enjambment.

encabalgar *vi* TECN to rest, to lean (una viga en otra) || to mount a horse.
◆ *vt* to overlap || to provide with horses.

encaballado *m* IMPR pieing.

encaballadura *f* TECN overlap, overlapping.

encaballar *vt* TECN to overlap (tejas) || IMPR to pie, to mix up.
◆ *vi* TECN to rest, to lean (una viga).
◆ *vpr* IMPR to become pied, to get mixed up.

encabestramiento *m* entanglement in the halter.

encabestrar *vt* to put a halter on, to halter || TAUR to lead (a bull) with an ox.
◆ *vpr* to get tangled in the halter.

encabezamiento *m* headline, title, heading, caption (en un periódico) || form of adress (fórmula) || heading (al principio de una carta) || preamble (preámbulo) || epigraph (epígrafe) || registration in the census || census (padrón) || tax roll (impuestos).

encabezar *vt* to lead, to head (una rebelión, etc.) || to title, to head (un periódico) || to head (una carta) || to lead (una carrera) || to head (una lista) || to introduce; *encabezó su libro con la frase siguiente* he introduced his book with the following sentence || to open, to start off; *encabezar una suscripción* to open a subscription || to take a census of (empadronar) || to include in a census (registrar) || to fortify (el vino con alcohol) || TECN to join (tablones o vigas).

encabricarse *vpr* to rear || to nose up (un avión).

encabronar *vt* FAM to piss s.o. off.
◆ *vpr* to be pissed off.

encabuyar *vt* AMER to tie (atar) | to wrap (envolver).

encachado *m* TECN stone *o* concrete lining.

encachar *vt* TECN to line with stones *o* concrete (el cauce de un río).

encadenación *f* ⟶ **encadenamiento.**

encadenado *m* ARQ buttress, pier || CINEM dissolve.

encadenamiento; *m*; **encadenación** *f* chaining || FIG connection, linking, concatenation.

encadenar *vt* to chain, to shackle, to fetter (a un prisionero) || to chain up (a una persona, un perro, una cosa) || FIG to tie down, to chain down; *sus tareas domésticas la encadenan a la casa* her housework ties her down in the house | to connect, to link up (razonamientos, pruebas, ideas) || CINEM to fade in.

encajador *m* enchaser (persona) || enchasing tool (herramienta) || FAM boxer who can take punishment (boxeador).

encajadura *f* setting (de un hueso) || socket (hueco).

encajar *vt* to fit, to insert (ajustar); *encajar una pieza en otra* to fit one part into another || to join, to fit together (juntar) || to set (un hueso) || FIG to suffer, to bear; *encajar críticas* to suffer criticism | to stand, to take (soportar); *encajar un golpe* to take a blow | to pocket, to swallow (una afrenta) | to drop (una indirecta) | to hurl (un insulto) | to palm off on, to foist off on, to unload on, to pass off on; *le encajaron diez billetes falsos* they palmed off ten forged banknotes on him | to land, to strike; *le encajó un golpe* he landed him a blow || TECN to enchase | to join, to dovetail (dos maderos) || FIG *nos encajó un sermón* he made us listen to *o* sit through a sermon.
◆ *vi* to fit; *la puerta no encaja bien con la humedad* because of the damp, the door doesn't fit properly; *dos piezas que encajan perfectamente* two parts which fit perfectly || FIG to fit; *este ejemplo encaja con mi hipótesis* this example fits my hypothesis | to fit in; *Pedro no encaja en el grupo de amigos que tengo* Peter does not fit in with my circle of friends; *eso encaja en mis proyectos* that fits in with my plans | to correspond (to), to fit in (with), to tally (with); *su versión de lo que pasó no encaja con la del testigo ocular* his version of what happened does not tally with that of the eyewitness | to suit, to go with; *ese atavío no encaja con la solemnidad del acto* that getup doesn't go with the solemnity of the ceremony | to take punishment, to be able to stand a lot of punishment (un boxeador) || — FIG *encajar bien en un papel* to suit the part | *está ya encajado en su nuevo destino* he has now settled down in his new job || *la puerta no está bien encajada* the door is not properly shut.
◆ *vpr* to jam, to stick, to get stuck; *la rueda se encajó entre dos piedras* the wheel got stuck between two stones | to squeeze in (introducirse) || to slip on, to pull on; *encajarse un gabán* to slip on an overcoat || to put on (un sombrero) || FIG & FAM to go (ir) | to settle down (llevar una vida ordenada).

encaje *m* lace; *una blusa de encaje* a lace blouse || fitting, insertion (acción de encajar) || joining together (acción de juntar) || setting (de un hueso) || joint (empalme) || TECN socket (hueco de un hueso o en una pieza) | housing (caja) || AMER COM reserve || *encaje de blonda* blonde lace.

encajetar *vt* ⟶ **encajar.**

encajonado, da *adj* incised; *un río profundamente encajonado* a deeply incised river || hemmed in, boxed in; *una calle encajonada entre edificios altos* a street hemmed in by tall buildings || *estar encajonado* to run through a cutting (una carretera, un ferrocarril).
◆ *m* ARQ cofferdam (ataguía) | mud wall (tapia).

encajonamiento *m* narrowness (de un río, una carretera) || boxing, casing, crating, packing (acción de poner en un cajón) || ARQ coffering (de un pozo) | shuttering (de una galería) || TAUR crating (de un toro para transportarlo).

encajonar *vt* to box, to case, to crate, to pack (poner en un cajón) || to squeeze in (meter en un sitio estrecho) || ARQ to coffer (un pozo) | to put up shuttering for (una galería) || TAUR to crate (un toro).
◆ *vpr* to narrow.

encalabrinar *vt* to irritate, to exasperate (exasperar) | to go to one's head (olor, vino).
◆ *vpr* to become infatuated *o* obsessed (*con* with) (encapricharse) || to be *o* to become obstinate *o* stubborn (empeñarse).

encalado *m*; **encaladura** *f* whitewashing (de paredes) || whitening (de pieles) || AGR liming.

encalador *m* whitewasher.

encaladura *f* ⟶ **encalado.**

encalamocar *vt* AMER to stun.
◆ *vpr* AMER to be stunned.

encalar *vt* to whitewash (blanquear) || AGR to lime.

encalmarse *vpr* to become calm, to calm down (el mar) || to drop (el viento) || to calm down, to regain one's composure (una persona) || VET to be overheated || *mercado encalmado* slack *o* quiet market (en la Bolsa).

encalvecer* *vi* to go bald.

encalladero *m* MAR sandbank, shoal, reef.

encalladura *f*; **encallamiento** *m* MAR running aground, grounding, stranding.

encallar *vi* MAR to run aground || FIG to founder.
◆ *vpr* to harden (un alimento).

encallecer* *vi* to become callous *o* hard (la piel).
◆ *vpr* to become callous *o* hard (la piel) || to harden || FIG to become callous *o* hardhearted *o* unfeeling (insensibilizarse) | to become hardened (en un trabajo o vicio).

encallecido, da *adj* → **empedernido.**

encamarse *vpr* to confine o.s. to bed, to take to one's bed (un enfermo) || to hide, to couch (la caza) || AGR to bend over, to droop (las mieses).

encaminamiento *m* guiding, guidance, direction (dirección) || FIG guidance (orientación).

encaminar *vt* to direct, to put on the right road (poner en camino) || to direct, to guide (orientar) || to route (expedición) || — *asunto bien encaminado* affair that is going well || *encaminar sus esfuerzos a* (followed by infinitive) or *hacia* (followed by noun) to direct *o* to channel one's efforts towards, to concentrate one's efforts on (con sustantivo o gerundio) || *medidas encaminadas a reducir los gastos públicos* measures aimed at reducing public spending.
◆ *vpr* to make one's way, to head (*a, hacia* towards); *encaminarse a un pueblo* to head towards a town || to be aimed at (con sustantivo o gerundio), to be intended to (con infinitivo), to be intended to (tener como objetivo).

encamisar *vt* to put a shirt on || to cover up, to put a cover on (enfundar) || FIG to disguise.
◆ *vpr* to put one's shirt on.

encamotarse *vpr* *AMER* FAM to fall in love.

encampanado, da *adj* bell-shaped (acampanado).

encampanarse *vpr* to widen out at the mouth || to flare out, to be flared (una falda) || TAUR to stand defiantly with the head raised (el toro) || *AMER* to swagger, to strut (pavonearse).

encanallamiento *m* debasement, degradation.

encanallar *vt* to corrupt, to debase.
◆ *vpr* to go to the dogs, to degrade o.s., to become corrupted.

encanastar *vt* to put in a basket.

encandecer* *vt* to make white-hot.

encandelar *vi* to blossom with catkins.

encandilado, da *adj* FAM erect (erguido) || *mirar con ojos encandilados* to gaze starry-eyed at.

encandilar *vt* to dazzle || FIG to bewilder (dejar pasmado) | to stimulate (estimular) | to dazzle (deslumbrar) || FAM to stir, to poke (la lumbre).
◆ *vpr* to light up (los ojos, el rostro).

encanecer* *vi* to go grey (el cabello, una persona) || to grow old (envejecer); *encanecer en el oficio* to grow old in service *o* in the job.

encanijado, da *adj* puny, weak (canijo).

encanijamiento *m* puniness, weakness.

encanijarse *vpr* to grow *o* to become puny *o* weak.

encanillar *vt* to wind on [a spool or bobbin].

encantación *f* → **encantamiento.**

encantado, da *adj* enchanted, charmed, delighted || FIG & FAM absentminded (distraído) || haunted; *casa encantada* haunted house || *encantado (de conocerle)* pleased to meet you.

encantador, ra *adj* charming, delightful, enchanting; *una niña encantadora* a charming little girl || fascinating (belleza, mirada) || glamorous (noche) || bewitching (sonrisa) || lovely (lugar).
◆ *m/f* charmer, enchanter (hombre), enchantress (mujer) || — *encantador de serpientes* snake charmer || *Merlín el Encantador* Merlin, the Magician.

encantamiento *m*; **encantación** *f* (magia); *como por encantamiento* as if by magic || bewitchment, witchcraft (hechizo) || spell, charm, incantation (invocación mágica) || delight, enchantment.

encantar *vt* to bewitch, to cast a spell on (con magia) || to charm, to delight; *estoy encantado con tu regalo* I am delighted with your present || *me encanta su manera de cantar* I love the way she sings; *me encanta trasnochar* I love staying up late.

encante *m* auction (subasta); *vender muebles al encante* to sell furniture by auction || auction room, saleroom (lugar).

encanto *m* magic; *como por encanto* as if by magic || spell, charm, enchantment (invocación mágica) || delight, enchantment || charm (atractivo); *¡qué encanto tiene esta mujer!* what charm this woman has! || — *el niño es un encanto* the child is a treasure *o* a jewel || *el sitio es un encanto* the place is beautiful *o* delightful *o* lovely || *la casa es un encanto* the house is a dream || *¡ven aquí, encanto!* come here, darling!
◆ *pl* charms.

encañada *f* gorge, ravine (entre dos montes).

encañado *m* piping, tubing (canalización) || AGR trellis (para las plantas) | drainage pipe (tubo de desagüe) || drainage, draining (avenamiento) || TECN lathing, lathwork.

encañar *vt* to pipe (agua) || to channel (por conductos) || AGR to drain (un terreno húmedo) | to stake, to prop up (los tallos de algunas plantas) || to wind on [a bobbin or spool] (hilo, seda).

encañizada *f* crawl, weir made of reeds (para la pesca) || AGR trellis.

encañizado *m* wire netting, fence.

encañonado *m* goffering, crimping (planchado).

encañonar *vt* to pipe (agua) || to channel (encauzar) || to wind on a bobbin, to quill (enrollar) || to aim at, to point at (con un arma) || to goffer, to crimp (una pechera).
◆ *vi* to grow feathers, to fledge (los pájaros).

encaparazonar *vt* to caparison (un caballo).

encaperuzado, da *adj* hooded.

encapilladura *f* MAR top-rigging.

encapillar *vt* MAR to rig || MIN to enlarge [a gallery] || to hood (un ave) || to send to the prison chapel [a condemned man].
◆ *vpr* FAM to slip on over the head (un vestido).

encapirotar *vt* to hood (un halcón).

encapotado, da *adj* overcast, cloudy; *cielo, tiempo encapotado* cloudy sky, weather || cloaked (con capa o capucha).

encapotadura *f*; **encapotamiento** *m* frown (ceño) || clouding-over (acción de encapotarse el cielo) || cloudiness (nubosidad).

encapotar *vt* to cloak, to put a cloak on.
◆ *vpr* to put a cloak on || to cloud over, to become overcast *o* cloudy (el cielo) || to frown (mostrar descontento) || to hold its head too low (el caballo).

encaprichamiento *m* infatuation || whim, fancy (capricho).

encapricharse *vpr* to take it into one's head to, to set one's mind on; *el niño se ha encaprichado con ir al circo* the child has set his mind on going to the circus || FAM *encapricharse por* or *con* to become infatuated with *o* mad about (enamorarse), to take a fancy to (encariñarse).

encapuchar; encapuzar *vt* to hood, to put a hood on.
◆ *vpr* to put one's hood on.

encarado, da *adj* *bien encarado* good-looking, nice-looking, pleasant-looking || *mal encarado* nasty-looking, evil-looking.

encaramar *vt* to put high up (colocar muy alto) || FIG to elevate *o* to promote to a high position.
◆ *vpr* to climb (subir); *encaramarse a* or *en un árbol* to climb a tree || FIG to reach a high position (alcanzar un puesto elevado) || *AMER* to blush (avergonzarse).

encaramiento *m* encounter, confrontation (de personas) || facing (de una dificultad).

encarapitarse *vpr* *AMER* to climb.

encarar *vt* *AMER* to climb.

encarar *vt* to face (up to), to confront (una dificultad) || to aim (un arma).
◆ *vpr* to face (up to), to confront; *encararse con un peligro* to face a danger; *encararse con uno* to face up to s.o. || to be faced *o* confronted with; *nos encaramos con un problema muy grave* we are faced with a very serious problem.

encarcelación *f*; **encarcelamiento** *m* imprisonment, incarceration || *registro* or *asiento de encarcelamiento* prison register.

encarcelar *vt* to imprison, to jail, to put in prison, to incarcerate (p us) || TECN to embed *o* to set in mortar (asegurar con yeso) | to clamp (dos piezas de madera) || *estar encarcelado* to be in prison *o* in jail.

encarecer* *vt* to raise *o* to put up the price of (hacer más caro) || FIG to praise, to extol (elogiar) | to emphasize, to stress (the importance of); *encareció la importancia de llegar puntualmente* he emphasized the importance of arriving on time | to recommend earnestly, to urge; *le encareció que trabajase* he urged him to work, he earnestly recommended him to work || *se lo encarezco* I beg of you, please.
◆ *vi* to go up, to rise in price, to become dearer; *la vida ha encarecido* the cost of living has gone up.

encarecidamente *adv* earnestly; *se lo ruego encarecidamente* I earnestly beg of you || insistently (con insistencia) || *elogiar algo encarecidamente* to praise sth. warmly *o* highly.

encarecido, da *adj* highly recommended *o* praised (persona) || warm (elogio).

encarecimiento *m* rise *o* increase in the price, price increase, rise *o* increase in the cost; *el encarecimiento del pan* the rise in the price *o* in the cost of bread; *el encarecimiento de la vida* the rise in the cost of living || extolling (alabanza) || stressing, emphasis (acentuación) || recommendation (recomendación) || *con encarecimiento* earnestly; *se lo ruego encarecidamente* I earnestly beg of you || insistently (con insistencia).

encargado, da *m/f* person in charge || manager (de un negocio) || employee, clerk, attendant (empleado) || — *encargado de curso* course tutor || *encargado de mostrador* counter clerk || *encargado de negocios* chargé d'affaires || *encargado de relaciones públicas* public relations officer || *encargado de un surtidor de gasolina* pump

attendant ‖ *Pilar fue la encargada de la comida* Pilar was in charge of the meal.
◆ *adj* in charge.

encargar *vt* to entrust with, to put in charge of; *encargar un asunto a uno* to entrust s.o. with an affair; *encargar a alguien del teléfono* to put s.o. in charge of the telephone ‖ to instruct, to ask (pedir); *le encargué a usted que escribiera* I instructed you to write ‖ to order; *encargó un almuerzo para diez personas* he ordered lunch for ten ‖ to order, to have made (mandar hacer); *encargar un vestido* to have a dress made ‖ to advise, to recommend (aconsejar); *me encargó mucho que tratase de conseguirlo* he strongly advised me to try and get it.
◆ *vpr* to take charge of, to undertake responsibility for; *encargarse de la venta* or *de vender* to take charge of sales *o* of selling ‖ to look after, to attend to; *me encargo de la biblioteca* I look after the library ‖ to take care of, to see about; *yo me encargaré del vino* I'll take care of the wine ‖ to be in charge of (ser responsable de) ‖ to order, to have made; *encargarse un traje* to order a suit ‖ FAM to deal with, to see to, to attend to; *¡ya me encargaré yo de él!* I'll deal with him!

encargo *m* errand (recado); *hacer encargos* to run errands ‖ job, assignment, mission; *cumplir un encargo* to carry out a job, to fulfil an assignment ‖ responsability ‖ COM order; *hacer un encargo* to place an order ‖ — FIG *como hecho de encargo* as if made to measure ‖ *de encargo* to measure (a la medida), to order (a petición).

encariñado, da *adj* attached.

encariñar *vt* to endear, to arouse affection in.
◆ *vpr* to become fond of, to take a liking to, to get attached to, to take to; *me he encariñado mucho con él* I have become very fond of him, I have taken a strong liking to him.

encarna *f* fleshing of the hounds (caza).

encarnación *f* incarnation ‖ flesh colour ‖ FIG *es la encarnación de la bondad* he is the soul *o* the epitome of kindness, he is kindness itself *o* personified.

encarnado, da *adj* incarnate; *el diablo encarnado* the devil incarnate ‖ red, incarnadine (p us) (color) ‖ ruddy (complexión) ‖ ingrowing (uña).
◆ *m* red (rojo) ‖ flesh colour (color de carne).

encarnadura *f* wound (herida) ‖ fleshing (del perro de caza) ‖ — *buena encarnadura* skin with good healing qualities *o* which heals well ‖ *mala encarnadura* skin with poor healing qualities *o* which does not heal easily.

encarnamiento *m* MED healing, closing-up (de una herida).

encarnar *vi* to become incarnate (el Verbo Divino) ‖ MED to be ingrowing (una uña) | to heal (over), to close up (cicatrizarse) ‖ to penetrate the flesh (un arma).
◆ *vt* to personify, to embody; *personaje que encarna la justicia* character who personifies justice ‖ to flesh (los perros) ‖ to bait (colocar el cebo en el anzuelo) ‖ ARTES to give flesh colour to, to incarnadine ‖ TEATR to play (un papel).
◆ *vpr* to feed on the entrails of game (los perros de caza) ‖ FIG to join, to mix (mezclarse).

encarne *m* fleshing of the hounds.

encarnecer* *vi* to put on weight, to put on flesh, to get fat (engordar).

encarnizadamente *adv* brutally, cruelly, bitterly, fiercely, mercilessly (luchar).

encarnizado, da *adj* bloody, bitter, fierce, hardfought (batalla) ‖ furious, bitter (riña) ‖ bloodshot (ojos).

encarnizamiento *m* bitterness, fierceness, cruelty (en la lucha).

encarnizar *vt* to flesh (los perros de caza) ‖ to brutalize, to make brutal *o* cruel *o* savage; *la guerra encarniza a los hombres* war makes men brutal.
◆ *vpr* to become fierce *o* savage (una batalla) ‖ to treat cruelly (con su víctima) ‖ to turn nasty *o* savage (*con* with) (de palabra) ‖ *encarnizarse en la lucha* to fight bitterly.

encarpetar *vt* to put in a file *o* in a portfolio ‖ *AMER* FIG to shelve, to pigeonhole (dejar un asunto sin resolver).

encarrilamiento *m* FIG guidance, orientation.

encarrilar *vt* to put back on the rails (un vehículo descarrilado) ‖ FIG to direct, to guide (encaminar un carro, un coche, etc.) | to guide, to direct, to put on the right road (dar una buena orientación) | to orient, to orientate; *encarrilar su vida* to orientate one's life ‖ *hemos encarrilado mal el asunto* we got off to a bad start, we started off on the wrong track.
◆ *vpr* MAR to get fouled in the sheave (una cuerda).

encarroñar *vt* to rot.
◆ *vpr* to decay, to rot (pudrirse).

encarrujarse *vpr* to curl (rizarse).

encartar *vt* to proscribe, to outlaw (proscribir) ‖ to summon (emplazar) ‖ to register [for taxes] (incluir en un padrón) ‖ to insert; *encartar una página suplementaria en un libro* to insert an extra page in a book ‖ to involve, to implicate; *las personas encartadas en este asunto* the people involved in this affair ‖ to lead (naipes).
◆ *vi* FIG & FAM to be suitable, to do (ser conveniente); *eso no encarta* that won't do | to fit in, to go; *eso no encarta con mis proyectos* that doesn't fit in with my plans.
◆ *vpr* FIG & FAM *si se encarta* should the occasion arise.

encarte *m* lead (naipes) ‖ order of the cards (orden de los naipes) ‖ IMPR insert, inset.

encartonar *vt* to bind with cardboard (los libros) ‖ to cover with cardboard.

encascabelar *vt* to adorn with bells.

encasillado *m* grid, table, squares *pl* (cuadro con casillas) ‖ pigeonholes *pl* (casillero).

encasillar *vt* to set out in a table *o* grid, to tabulate (cifras, datos, etc.) ‖ to pigeonhole (distribuir en casillas) ‖ to class, to classify (clasificar); *en seguida le encasillé entre los comunistas* I immediately classed him with the communists *o* as a communist ‖ to typecast (a un actor) ‖ to designate as a government candidate (en las elecciones para diputados).
◆ *vpr* FIG to limit o.s.

encasquetar *vt* to put on, to pull down (el sombrero) ‖ FIG to get *o* to put into s.o.'s head (idea, opinión) ‖ FIG *nos encasquetó un discurso interminable* he made us listen to an endless speech, he forced us to sit through an endless speech.
◆ *vpr* to put on, to pull down (el sombrero) ‖ FIG *se le encasquetó la idea de estudiar ruso* he got the idea of studying Russian into his head.

encasquillador *m* *AMER* farrier, blacksmith.

encasquillamiento *m* jamming (de un arma).

encasquillar *vt* *AMER* to shoe (el caballo).
◆ *vpr* to jam (arma de fuego).

encastillado, da *adj* fortified (with castles) ‖ FIG osbtinate | haughty, lofty (soberbio).

encastillamiento *m* (p us) fortification ‖ FIG insolation, detachment (aislamiento) | obstinancy.

encastillar *vt* (p us) to fortify with castles (un lugar) ‖ to pile, to pile up (apilar) ‖ to provide with scaffolding, to erect scaffolding round (una obra).
◆ *vpr* to take refuge in a castle ‖ to take refuge [in the hills, etc.] ‖ FIG to stick to one's opinion *o* to one's guns, to persist obstinately in one's views (emperrarse) | to withdraw into one's shell, to become withdrawn (retirarse) ‖ *encastillarse en su dignidad* to wrap o.s. in one's dignity.

encastrar *vt* to imbed, to embed, to fit in, to set in ‖ TECN to mesh, to engage (endentar).

encauchar *vt* to rubberize.

encausar *vt* to prosecute.

encausticar *vt* to polish, to beeswax.

encáustico, ca *adj* encaustic.
◆ *m* polish, beeswax.

encausto *m* encaustic; *pintura al encausto* encaustic painting.

encauzamiento *m* channeling, canalization ‖ embanking (para que no se salga un río) ‖ FIG guidance, orientation.

encauzar *vt* to channel, to canalize ‖ to embank (poner dique) ‖ FIG to direct, to channel, to guide (un asunto, una discusión, investigaciones).

encebollado *m* CULIN stew flavoured with onions.

encebollar *vt* to flavour *o* to cook with onions.

encefalalgia *f* MED cephalalgia, headache.

encefálico, ca *adj* ANAT encephalic.

encefalitis *f* MED encephalitis.

encéfalo *m* ANAT encephalon.

encefalografía *f* MED encephalography.

encefalograma *m* MED encephalogram, encephalograph.

encefalomielitis *f* MED encephalomyelitis.

encelamiento *m* jealousy (celos).

encelar *vt* to make jealous.
◆ *vpr* to become jealous ‖ to rut, to be in rut *o* on heat (animales).

encella *f* cheese mould (molde).

encellar *vt* to mould (el queso).

encenagado, da *adj* muddy (lleno de lodo) ‖ silted up (puerto) ‖ bogged down, stuck in the mud (atascado) ‖ covered in mud (sucio) ‖ FIG wallowing (en el vicio).

encenagamiento *m* sticking *o* sinking in the mud (atascamiento) ‖ silting up (de un puerto) ‖ FIG wallowing (en el vicio).

encenagarse *vpr* to get stuck *o* bogged down (atascarse) ‖ to become boggy *o* muddy (un terreno) ‖ to get covered in mud, to get muddy (ensuciarse) ‖ to silt up (un puerto) ‖ to wallow in mud (revolcarse) ‖ FIG to wallow (envilecerse en el vicio, en la ignorancia).

encendajas *f pl* kindling *sing*.

encendedor *m* lighter; *encendedor de gas* gas lighter ‖ lamplighter (persona).

encender* *vt* to light; *encender una vela, un cigarrillo, el fuego* to light a candle, a cigarette, the fire ‖ to ignite; *encender una mezcla combustible* to ignite a combustible mixture ‖ to set on fire, to set fire to, to set alight (pegar fuego a); *encender el rastrojo, un montón de basura* to set fire to the stubble, to a pile of rubbish ‖ to turn on, to switch on, to put on (la radio, la luz eléctrica) ‖ to light, to put on (el gas) ‖ to strike, to light (una cerilla) ‖ FIG to inflame, to kindle (una discordia, un conflicto, las pasiones) | to arouse (el entusiasmo) |

to spark off (una guerra) | to awake (los celos, el odio, etc.) || — *la fiebre encendía sus mejillas* her cheeks were burning with fever || *me encendía el odio* hatred was burning me up.
◆ *vpr* to light; *esta vela, este cigarrillo, la cocina no quiere encenderse* this candle, this cigarette, the cooker will not light || to ignite, to catch fire; *sería muy peligroso si el gas que se ha escapado se encendiera* it would be very dangerous if the gas which has escaped were to ignite || to burn up, to flare up (una llama) || FIG to light up; *su cara se encendió* her face lit up | to get excited (inflamarse) | to blush, to get red (ruborizarse) | to break out (un conflicto) || *encenderse de ira* to flare up with rage.

encendidamente *adv* ardently, passionately || enthusiastically.

encendido, da *adj* lit (el fuego, un cigarrillo) || on, switched on; *la luz está encendida* the light is on || burning, on fire (incendiado) || FIG bright red (rojo) | fiery; *una mirada encendida* a fiery glance | flushed, red; *tener la cara encendida* to have a flushed face | crimson, purple; *tiene la cara encendida por la ira* his face is purple with rage || FIG *encendido como la grana* or *como un pavo* as red as a beetroot.
◆ *m* lighting; *el encendido de los faroles* the lithting of the lamps || AUT ignition; *avance en el encendido* ignition advance || firing (de un cohete) || *encendido de alta tensión* high-tension ignition.

encendimiento *m* burning || FIG redness | blushing (de la cara) | ardour (de una pasión).

encenizar *vt* to cover with ashes.

encentamiento *m* beginning, start.

encentar* *vt* to start, to begin (empezar).

encepar *vi* to take root (una planta).
◆ *vt* to pillory, to put it the stocks (a un prisionero) || to stock, to fit with a stock (un arma, un ancla) || TECN to join.

encepe *m* AGR rooting, taking root.

encerado *adj* waxed, polished (suelo, mueble) || wax-coloured.
◆ *m* waxing, polishing (del suelo, de un mueble) || wax (capa de cera) || blackboard (pizarra para escribir) || oilcloth (tela para proteger una mesa), oilskin (tela para las prendas) || MAR tarpaulin.

encerador, ra *adj* waxing, polishing.
◆ *m/f* floor polisher *o* waxer (persona).
◆ *f* floor polisher *o* waxer (aparato).

enceramiento *m* waxing, polishing.

encerar *vt* to wax, to polish (dar cera) || to spot, to soil with wax (las velas) || to thicken (la argamasa).
◆ *vi/vpr* to turn yellow (las mieses).

encerotar *vt* to wax.

encerradero *m* pen, fold (aprisco) || TAUR bullpen.

encerrar* *vt* to shut in, to shut up; *encerrar a alguien* to shut s.o. up; *encerrar un perro* to shut a dog up || to lock in, to lock up, to put under lock and key (con llave); *encerrar a un prisionero, un objeto precioso* to put a prisoner, a valuable object under lock and key || to put; *encerrar una frase entre comillas, en un paréntesis* to put a sentence in inverted commas, in brackets || FIG to contain, to include; *este libro encierra unas agudezas muy graciosas* this book includes some very amusing witticisms | to contain; *sus palabras encierran un profundo significado* his words contain deep significance; *el museo encierra unas magníficas obras de arte* the museum contains some magnificent works of art | to involve; *el proyecto encierra grandes dificultades* the project involves serious difficulties | to block (en el ajedrez) || *encerrar en la cárcel* to put in jail.
◆ *vpr* to shut o.s. in *o* up, to lock o.s. in || FIG to go into retreat *o* seclusion || FIG *encerrarse en una idea* to stick obstinately to an idea.

encerrona *f* FAM retreat, seclusion (retiro) || TAUR private bullfight || FIG trap || FIG & FAM *le prepararon una encerrona para que votase a su favor* they trapped him into voting for them.

encespedar *vt* to turf, to cover with turf.

encestar *vi* to score a basket [*US* to make a basket] (in basketball).

enceste *m* basket (en el baloncesto); *marcar un enceste* to score a basket.

encía *f* ANAT gum.

encíclico, ca *adj/s f* encyclical.

enciclopedia *f* encyclopedia, encyclopaedia || FIG *esa chica es una enciclopedia* or *una enciclopedia viviente* that girl is a walking encyclopedia.

enciclopédico, ca *adj* encyclopedic, encyclopaedic, encyclopedical, encyclopaedical.

enciclopedismo *m* encyclopedism, encyclopaedism.

enclopedista *adj/s* encyclopedist, encyclopaedist.

encierro *m* confinement (de una persona) || seclusion, retreat (retiro) || penning (del ganado vacuno), folding (del ganado lanar) || pen, fold (corral) || cell (calabozo) || TAUR driving of the bulls into the pen before a bullfight | bullpen (toril) | «encierro».
— OBSERV The *encierro* is part of the fiestas of San Fermín which begin on 7th July in Pamplona. In the *encierro* the bulls chase young men through the town to the bullring, where they are then shut in the *toriles*.

encima *adv* above; *encima hay un reloj colgado en la pared* above, there is a clock hanging on the wall || on top; *un edificio enorme con dos grúas encima* a huge building with two cranes on top; *llevaba un jersey y el abrigo encima* I was wearing a pullover and my overcoat on top; *queso con una lonja de jamón encima* cheese with a slice of ham on top || overhead, above; *teníamos encima la Estrella Polar* we had the Pole Star overhead || in addition, as well, on top of that (además); *le dio diez pesos y otros dos encima* he gave him ten pesos and another two as well || FAM on top of that; *le insultaron y encima le pegaron* they insulted him, and on top of that they hit him; *es caro y encima feo* it's expensive, and on top of that ugly || — *ahí encima* over there on (the) top || *aquí está su cama con la foto colgada encima* here is his bed with the picture above it || *de encima* on top, top; *quieres pasarme el libro de encima* will you pass me the top book *o* the book on top || *echarse encima* to throw o.s. onto *o* at (atacar); *se echaron encima del enemigo* they threw themselves at the enemy; to bear down on; *se nos echó encima el camión* the lorry bore down on us; to overtake; *la noche se nos echó encima* nightfall overtook us; to take upon o.s., to undertake (encargarse de); *echarse encima un trabajo* to undertake a job; to shoulder (una responsabilidad), to set against o.s. (indisponer); *se echó encima a todos los críticos* he set all the critics against him || *encima de* on, on top of (sobre); *encima de la mesa* on the table; above, over (más arriba); *la nariz está encima de la boca* the nose is above the mouth; in addition to (además de) || *encima de (que)* besides, as well as; *encima de ser* or *de que es perezoso, es mentiroso* as well as (his) being lazy he is a liar || *encima mío* or *de mí* above me || *llevar encima* to have on one; *no llevo dinero encima* I haven't any money on me || FIG *pasar por encima* to look *o* to glance through (un escrito), to overlook, to turn a blind eye to (hacer la vista gorda) || *por encima* on top (sobre), above, over, overhead (más arriba), quickly, superficially; *leer algo por encima* to read through sth. quickly || *por encima de* above; *está por encima de los demás alumnos* he is above the other pupils; *el jefe está por encima de todos los problemas menores de la empresa* the boss is above all the petty problems of the firm; beyond; *el problema está por encima de él, por encima de su inteligencia* the problem is beyond him, beyond his intelligence; over; *pasó por encima del arroyo* he stepped *o* strode over the stream; in spite of (a pesar de) || *por encima de todo* above all (sobre todo) || *puso el sombrero en la silla y luego se sentó encima* he put his hat on the chair and then sat on it || *quitarse de encima* to clear o.s. of (deudas), to get out of (un problema, dificultades), to get rid of (una cosa), to get rid of, to shake off (una persona); *creía que no podría nunca quitármelo de encima* I thought I would never be able to get rid of him || *ya están encima las vacaciones* the holidays are almost here.
— OBSERV *Encima* is used in preference to *sobre* when one object is placed on another at some distance from the ground (e. g. *encima del armario, del tejado*).

encimar *vt* to put on top || to add to (a stake) (en el juego del tresillo) || *AMER* to throw in (añadir algo más a lo estipulado).
◆ *vpr* to rise [above].

encimero, ra *adj* top, on (the) top; *la sábana encimera* the top sheet.
◆ *f* *AMER* leather saddle cover.

encina *f*; **encino** *m* BOT holm oak, ilex.

encinal; encinar *m* grove of holm oaks.

encinchar *vt* *AMER* to girth, to cinch (un caballo).

encino *m* ⟶ **encina**.

encinta *adj f* pregnant.

encintado *m* kerb [*US* curb] (de la acera).

encintar *vt* to beribbon, to adorn with ribbon || to put a kerb on, to kerb [*US* to curb] (una acera).

encizañar *vt/vi* to sow discord, to cause trouble (sembrar discordia) || *encizañar contra* to incite aginst.

enclaustrar *vt* to cloister, to shut up in a convent || FIG to cloister, to shut up.
◆ *vpr* FIG to shut o.s. up *o* in.

enclavar *vt* to enclave (territorio) || to situate, to locate, to place (situar) || to nail (clavar) | to pierce, to transfix (traspasar) || VET to prick.

enclave *m* enclave (territorio) || setting, situation (emplazamiento).

enclavijar *vt* to peg.

enclenque *adj* sickly (enfermizo) || skinny (delgaducho).
◆ *m/f* sickly person || skinny person.

enclítico, ca *adj/s f* enclitic.

enclocar* ; **encloquecer*** *vi* to become broody (la gallina).

encocorante *adj* FAM annoying.

encocorar *vt* FAM to get on s.o.'s nerves, to annoy.

encofrado *m* TECN formwork, shuttering (para el hormigón) | timbering (en una mina).

encofrar *vt* TECN to put up shuttering for (el hormigón) | to timber, to plank (galería de mina).

encoger *vt* to shrink (estrechar); *el lavado encoge ciertos tejidos* washing shrinks certain fabrics || to contract (contraer) || FIG to intimidate (dar miedo).
◆ *vi* to shrink (tela).
◆ *vpr* to shrink (tela) || to hunch up (el cuerpo) || FIG to feel small (achicarse) || — *encogerse de hombros* to shrung one's shoulders || *se le*

encogió el corazón his heart stood still (de miedo, sorpresa), his heart sank (de tristeza).

encogido, da *adj* shrunk, shrunken (tela) || hunched up (el cuerpo) || FIG timid, bashful, shy (tímido) | fainthearted (pusilánime) || — FIG *tenía el estómago encogido* his stomach was in knots | *tenía el corazón encogido* his heart was in his mouth (de miedo), he had a heavy heart (de tristeza).

encogimiento *m* shrinkage (de una tela) || hunching (del cuerpo) || FIG bashfulness, shyness, timidity (timidez) || *encogimiento de hombros* shrug (of the shoulders).

encolado, da *adj* AMER FIG stuck-up (vanidoso).

◆ *m* clarification (del vino) || gluing, gumming, sticking (con cola) || sizing (para pintar).

encoladora *f* TECN slasher (textiles) | splicer (cine).

encolamiento *m* gluing, gumming, sticking || sizing (para pintar) || clarification (del vino).

encolar *vt* to glue, to gum, to stick (pegar) || to size (antes de pintar) || to clarify (el vino).

encolerizar *vt* to anger, to infuriate, to exasperate.

◆ *vpr* to get angry, to lose one's temper.

encomendar* *vt* to commend, to entrust (confiar); *le encomiendo a usted mi hijo* I entrust *o* commend my child to you, I entrust you with my child; *le encomiendo esta misión* I entrust you with this mission || to commend; *encomendar algo a la memoria* to commend sth. to memory.

◆ *vpr* to commend o.s., to entrust o.s.; *encomendarse a la bondad de alguien* to commend o.s. to s.o.'s good graces || — *encomendarse a Dios* to commend one's soul to God || *en vuestras manos me encomiendo* I put myself in your hands || FIG *no saber a qué santo encomendarse* to be at one's wits' end, not to know where to turn.

encomendero *m* HIST «encomendero», master of an «encomienda».

encomiar *vt* to praise, to extol, to laud.

encomiasta *m* praiser, extoller, eulogist.

encomiástico, ca *adj* eulogistic, laudatory.

encomienda *f* assignment (encargo) || commandery (antigua dignidad) || HIST «encomienda» (véase OBSERV) || AMER packet, package, parcel; *encomienda postal* postal packet.

— OBSERV *Encomiendas* (concessions, holdings) were estates granted to Spanish settlers in Latin America in the colonial era. The Indians living on the land were put into the service of their *encomendero* or had to pay him taxes. For his part, the *encomendero* was supposed to look after the interests of the Indians in his territory and convert them to Christianity.

encomio *m* praise, eulogy.

encomioso, sa *adj* eulogistic, laudatory.

encompadrar *vi* FAM to become friends, to pal up.

enconado, da *adj* inflamed (inflamado) || infected (infectado) || passionate, ardent, eager; *bibliófilo enconado* passionate booklover; *partido enconado* ardent supporter || bitter, fierce; *adversario enconado* bitter opponent; *lucha enconada* fierce struggle || angry (enfadado).

enconadura *f*; **enconamiento** *m* inflammation (inflamación), infection (infección) || FIG rancour [*US* rancor], ill will (rencor) | bitterness, fierceness (en una lucha, una discusión).

enconar *vt* to inflame (inflamar), to infect (infectar) || FIG to inflame (una disensión, una lucha) | to anger (enfadar).

◆ *vpr* to become inflamed (inflamarse), to become infected (infectarse) || FIG to grow bitter (una lucha, una discusión) | to get angry (enfadarse).

encono *m* rancour [*US* rancor], ill will (rencor) || bitterness, fierceness (en una lucha, una discusión).

encontradizo, za *adj* *hacerse el encontradizo con alguien* to pretend to meet s.o. by chance.

encontrado, da *adj* opposing, contrary; *intereses encontrados* opposing interests.

encontrar *vt* to find; *encontrar una solución* to find a solution; *la encontré anegada en lágrimas* I found her crying her eyes out || to find, to come across; *encontré un libro muy interesante* I came across a very interesting book || to meet, to come across, to bump into (*fam*) (tropezar con); *acabo de encontrar a Rafael en la calle* I've just met Raphael in the street || to encounter, to come across, to find (dificultades) || to see; *no sé lo que encuentras en ella* I don't know what you see in her || to think of (parecer); *¿cómo encuentras mi anillo?* what do you think of my ring? || to find; *¿cómo has encontrado la película?* how did you find the film? || — FIG *encontrar la horma de su zapato* to find just what the doctor ordered (lo deseado), to find Mr. *o* Miss Right, to meet one's perfet match (a un novio o a una novia conveniente), to meet one's match (a alguien con quien medirse) || *no encuentro palabras para expresarle mi agradecimiento* I can't tell you how grateful I am.

◆ *vpr* to meet, to meet each other, to bump into (*fam*), to bump into each other (*fam*); *se encontraron en la plaza* they bumped into each other in the square; *me encontré con él en el bulevar* I met him in the boulevard || to collide (chocar) || to be (estar); *se encuentra en el Brasil* he is in Brazil || to meet (reunirse); *quedaron en encontrarse en el bar* they arranged to meet in the bar || FIG to be, to feel; *me encuentro mucho mejor* I feel much better | to clash (ser contrarias las opiniones, etc.) || — *encontrarse con* to meet (a alguien), to run into (tropezar con), to encounter, to run up against (problemas) || *encontrarse con ánimo para* to feel up to || FAM *no me encuentro entre gente tan presumida* I don't feel right among such pretentious people.

encontrón; encontronazo *m* collision, crash.

encopetado, da *adj* upper-crust, upper-class (de alto copete) || haughty, conceited (presumido).

encopetarse *vpr* to put on airs (engreírse).

encorajar *vt* to encourage.

◆ *vpr* to get angry.

encorajinar *vt* to provoke, to make angry.

◆ *vpr* to lose one's temper, to get angry, to see red (encolerizarse) || to pluck up courage (animarse).

encorchar *vt* to hive (abejas) || to cork (botella).

encorchetar *vt* to fit with a clasp *o* hook and eye (poner un corchete) || to fasten with a hook and eye *o* with a clasp (abrochar) || to cramp (piedras).

encordar* *vt* to string (un instrumento de música, una raqueta de tenis) || to tie with laces.

◆ *vpr* to rope up (alpinismo).

encordelar *vt* to tie up (atar).

encordonar *vt* to tie up (atar).

encornado, da *adj* horned || *toro bien encornado* bull with good horns.

encornadura *f* horns *pl* (de un toro) || antlers *pl* (del venado) || shape *o* position of the horns.

encornar *vt* to gore (cornear).

encorozar *vt* to put a cone-shaped cap a (a un condenado).

encorralar *vt* to pen (animales).

encorsetar *vt* to corset || FIG to straightjacket (paralizar).

◆ *vpr* to put on a corset.

encorvado, da *adj* curved, bent (en curva) || stooped, bent (por la edad) || bent over (agachado).

encorvadura *f*; **encorvamiento** *m* bending, curving (acción) || bend, curve (curva) || stoop (de una persona de edad).

encorvar *vt* to bend, to curve; *tiene la espalda encorvada por la edad* his back is bent with age.

◆ *vpr* to curve, to bend || to become stooped, to become bent (una persona) || to bend down, to bend over (agacharse) || to warp (madera) || to give, to bend, to buckle (bajo una carga) || to buck (caballo).

encostalar *vt* to put in sacks *o* bags, to bag (ensacar).

encostrar *vt* to cover with a crust || to put a crust on (un pastel).

◆ *vpr* to form a crust || to form a scab, to scab over (una herida).

encrasar *vt* to thicken (espesar) || AGR to fertilize, to manure (la tierra).

encrespado, da *adj* curly (el pelo) || choppy, rough (el mar).

encrespamiento *m* tight curling, frizzing (del pelo) || erection (del plumaje) || bristling (del pelo, por miedo) || roughness, choppiness (del mar) || FIG excitement (de las pasiones) | irritation, provocation (irritación) | entanglement (enredo).

encrespar *vt* to curl tightly, to frizz (rizar); *cabello encrespado* tightly curled hair || to set (one's hair) on end (erizar el pelo) || to erect (el plumaje) || to make rough *o* choppy (el agua) || FIG to work up, to excite (las pasiones) | to irritate, to provoke, to infuriate (irritar).

◆ *vpr* to become rough *o* choppy (el mar) || to curl up, to go frizzy (el cabello) || to stand on end, to bristle (erizarse) || FIG to boil, to become heated (las pasiones) | to become entangled *o* mixed up (enredarse) | to become irritated, to get cross (enfadarse).

encristalar *vt* to glaze.

encrucijada *f* crossroads, intersection || FIG crossroads; *la encrucijada de la vida* the crossroads of life; *París, encrucijada de Europa* Paris, crossroads of Europe | dilemma.

encrudecer* *vt* FIG to irritate.

◆ *vi/vpr* to grow worse *o* colder (el tiempo).

encruelecer* *vt* to make cruel.

◆ *vpr* to become cruel.

encuadernación *f* bookbinding (oficio) || binding (de un libro); *encuadernación en tela, en cuero* cloth, leather binding || *taller de encuadernación* bindery.

encuadernador, ra *m/f* bookbinder.

encuadernar *vt* to bind || — *libro encuadernado en rústica* paperback || *sin encuadernar* unbound.

encuadramiento *m* CINEM framing || FIG frame, framework (límite) || MIL officering (de tropas).

encuadrar *vt* to frame (encerrar en un marco) || to fit in, to insert (encajar) || FIG to surround (rodear) | to put in, to incorporate (en un grupo); *han encuadrado a los nuevos reclutas en el primer batallón* the new recruits have been incorporated into the first batallion || CINEM to frame (la imagen) || MIL to officer (proveer de oficiales).

encuadre *m* CINEM framing ‖ setting (situación) ‖ FIG frame, framework (límite) ‖ MIL officering (de tropas).

encuartelar *vt* *AMER* to quarter in barracks (acuartelar) | to confine to barracks (recluir).

encubamiento *m* vatting.

encubar *vt* to vat (el vino).

encubierta *f* fraud.

encubiertamente *adv* secretly, in secret ‖ fraudulently (fraudulentamente).

encubierto, ta *adj* hidden, concealed, secret (oculto) ‖ fraudulent, underhand (fraudulento) ‖ — FIG *hablar con palabras encubiertas* to talk cryptically *o* guardedly ‖ *paro encubierto* underemployment.

encubridor, ra *adj* hiding, concealing.
◆ *m/f* JUR receiver, fence (*fam*) (de mercancías robadas) | accessory after the fact (que encubre un delito o a un delincuente) | harbourer [*US* harborer] (de un criminal) ‖ procurer (hombre), procuress (mujer) (alcahuete).

encubrimiento *m* hiding, concealment (ocultación) ‖ JUR receiving (de lo robado) | harbouring [*US* harboring], concealment (de un criminal).

encubrir *vt* to hide, to conceal (ocultar) ‖ JUR to receive (mercancías robadas) | to harbour [*US* to harbor], to conceal (a un delincuente).

encuentro *m* meeting (reunión, entrevista); *un encuentro casual* a chance meeting ‖ rendezvous (cita); *el encuentro de los astronautas en el espacio* the astronauts' rendezvous in space ‖ discovery (descubrimiento) ‖ collision (colisión) ‖ meeting (coincidencia) ‖ DEP match (partido) | meeting, clash (entre dos personas, campeones) | meeting; *encuentro deportivo* sports meeting ‖ FIG find (hallazgo) | clash (de ideas, de intereses) ‖ ANAT armpit (axila) ‖ ARQ angle ‖ MIL skirmish, encounter, clash (lucha).
◆ *pl* wing joint *sing* (en las aves) ‖ withers (de una caballería) ‖ IMPR blanks, spaces [left for printing in another colour] ‖ — *ir al encuentro de* to go to meet ‖ *salir al encuentro de* to go to meet (ir a buscar), to contradict (contradecir), to oppose, to make a stand against (oponer), to anticipate (anticiparse), to face (afrontar una dificultad).

encuerado, da *adj* *AMER* naked, nude.

encuerar *vt* *AMER* to strip, to undress (desnudar) ‖ *AMER* FIG to fleece, to rob, to skin (en el juego).
◆ *vpr* to get undressed (desnudarse).

encuesta *f* poll, opinion poll, survey (sobre la opinión pública); *hacer una encuesta* to carry out an opinion poll ‖ inquiry, investigation (investigación).

encuestado, da *m/f* person asked in a poll or survey.

encuestador, ra *m/f* pollster.

encumbrado, da *adj* of high social standing, upperclass (socialmente) ‖ eminent, distinguished (eminente) ‖ high, lofty (alto).

encumbramiento *m* rise, raising, elevation ‖ exaltation, eminence (exaltación) ‖ praise, extolling (ensalzamiento) ‖ climbing (de un monte) ‖ height (altura).

encumbrar *vt* to raise, to elevate (levantar) ‖ FIG to honour, [*US* to honor], to exalt, to dignify (elevar) | to extol, to praise (ensalzar); *encumbrar hasta las nubes* to praise to the skies.
◆ *vpr* to rise ‖ FIG to rise to a high social position | to put on airs, to be haughty (envanecerse).

encunar *vt* to put in the cradle (poner en la cuna) ‖ TAUR to catch between its horns (el toro al torero).

encureñar *vt* to mount (un cañón).

encurtidos *m pl* pickles (pepinillos, cebollas, etc.).

encurtir *vt* to pickle (pepinillos, etc.) ‖ *AMER* to tan (curtir).

enchalecar *vt* POP to pocket (robar) ‖ *AMER* to put (s.o.) into a straightjacket.
◆ *vpr* POP to pocket (embolsarse).

enchancletar *vt* to put on (poner zapatillas) ‖ to drag (one's shoes) like slippers (arrastrar los zapatos).
◆ *vpr* to put slippers on.

enchapado *m* veneer (chapa de madera) ‖ veneering (acción) ‖ plating (de metal).

enchapar *vt* to veneer (con madera) ‖ to plate (con metal).

encharcado, da *adj* flooded, swamped.

encharcamiento *m* flooding, swamping (de un terreno).

encharcar *vt* to flood, to swamp (un terreno).
◆ *vpr* to be flooded (un terreno) ‖ to become bloated (el estómago).

enchastrar *vt* *AMER* to dirty, to make dirty.

enchicharse *vpr* *AMER* to get drunk (on corn liquor).

enchilada *f* *AMER* rolled corn omelette spiced with chili.

enchilado, da *adj* *AMER* spiced with chili ‖ red (rojo) ‖ *AMER* FIG hot-tempered.
◆ *m* *AMER* stew spiced with chili.

enchilar *vt* *AMER* to season with chili | FIG to annoy (molestar).
◆ *vpr* *AMER* FIG to become irritated *o* angry.

enchinar *vt* to pave with pebbles *o* cobbles ‖ *AMER* to curl (rizar).

enchiqueramiento *m* TAUR shutting in the bullpen ‖ FIG & FAM imprisonment (en la cárcel).

enchiquerar *vt* TAUR to shut in the bullpen ‖ FIG & FAM to put in clink *o* in the nick (encarcelar).

enchironar *vt* FAM to put in clink *o* in the nick.

enchufado, da *adj* FAM well in (recomendado) | who has sinecure *o* a cushy job ‖ FAM *estar enchufado* to have friends in the right places *o* useful contacts, to be well in (estar recomendado), to have a cushy job (tener una colocación buena).
◆ *m/f* FAM person who has succeeded through contacts, wirepuller | slacker (soldado).

enchufar *vt* ELECTR to plug in, to connect ‖ to fit together, to couple (tubos) ‖ FIG & FAM to pull wires for (ejercer influencia).
◆ *vpr* FAM to get a cushy job.

enchufe *m* ELECTR socket, plug, point (hembra); *enchufe para la luz relámpago* flash socket | plug (macho) ‖ joint, connection (de dos tubos) ‖ FIG & FAM wirepulling (influencia) | contacts *pl* (relaciones) | cushy job (puesto) ‖ — *enchufe flexible* adapter ‖ FIG & FAM *tener enchufe* to have a cushy job (tener una colocación buena), to have friends in the right places *o* useful contacts (tener relaciones).

enchufismo *m* FIG & FAM wirepulling.

ende *adv* (ant) there ‖ *por ende* therefore, hence.

endeble *adj* weak, frail, feeble (persona, argumento) ‖ puny, sickly (enclenque) ‖ flimsy, fragile (cosa).

endeblez *f* weakness, frailty, feebleness (de personas, argumentos) ‖ flimsiness, fragility (de cosas).

endecágono, na *adj* MAT hendecagonal.
◆ *m* hendecagon.

endecasílabo, ba *adj* hendecasyllabic.
◆ *m* hendecasyllable.

endecha *f* lament, dirge (lamento) ‖ POÉT quatrain with lines of six or seven syllables, usually assonant ‖ *endecha real* quatrain of three usually heptasyllabic lines followed by one hendecasyllable.

endeja *f* ARQ toothing (adaraja).

endemia *f* MED endemic disease, endemic.

endémico, ca *adj* MED endemic, endemical ‖ FIG chronic.

endemoniado, da *adj* possessed (of the devil) ‖ evil, wicked (malo) ‖ devilish, mischievous (travieso) ‖ diabolical, terrible; *un olor endemoniado* a diabolical smell ‖ furious, wild (irritado) ‖ damned, wretched, cursed (maldito); *ese endemoniado disco me vuelve loco* that wretched record drives me mad ‖ wild, frenzied; *un ritmo endemoniado* a frenzied rhythm.
◆ *m/f* person possessed ‖ FIG *chillar como un endemoniado* to shriek like a madman.

endemoniar *vt* to bedevil, to possess with an evil spirit *o* with the devil ‖ to anger, to infuriate (enojar).

endenantes *adv* FAM before (antes) | previously, formerly (en otro tiempo).

endentar* *vt* TECN to tooth (poner dientes a una rueda) | to mesh (ruedas dentadas) ‖ to interlock (encajar).

endentecer* *vi* to cut one's teeth, to teethe.

enderezado, da *adj* favourable, appropriate, suitable (propicio).

enderezador, ra *m/f* righter, redresser (de entuertos).

enderezamiento *m* straightening out or up (de algo torcido) ‖ reerection (de algo tendido) ‖ righting, redressing (de un entuerto, de una situación).

enderezar *vt* to straighten (out *o* up), to put straight (poner derecho) ‖ to reerect, to set upright again (algo que estaba tendido) ‖ to right (un barco) ‖ FIG to put right, to right, to redress (entuertos, una situación) | to direct (encaminar) | to reform (enmendar).
◆ *vi* to head, to make one's way (dirigirse).
◆ *vpr* to straighten (out or up) ‖ to be directed *o* aimed (*a*, at) (encaminarse) ‖ to stand up straight (una persona).

ENDESA *abrev de Empresa Nacional de Electricidad S.A.* Spanish national electricity company.

endeudarse *vpr* to get *o* to run *o* to fall into debt (entramparse) ‖ FIG to become indebted (*con*, to) (tener que estar agradecido).

endiabladamente *adv* evily, wickedly ‖ mischievously, devilishly (de modo travieso) ‖ furiously, angrily.

endiablado, da *adj* possessed (of the devil) ‖ evil, wicked (malo) ‖ mischievous, devilish (travieso) ‖ diabolical, terrible; *tiene un sabor endiablado* it tastes terrible, it has a terrible taste ‖ furious, wild (irritado) ‖ blessed, wretched, cursed (maldito) ‖ wild, frenzied; *un ritmo endiablado* a frenzied rhythm ‖ ugly, horrible (feísimo).

endiablar *vt* to bedevil, to possess with the devil *o* with an evil spirit (endemoniar).

endibia *f* BOT endive.

endilgar; indilgar *vt* FAM to palm off, to lumber; *no me endilgues ese trabajo* don't palm that job off on me, don't lumber that job on me | to land, to deal (una bofetada) | to send off, to dispatch (mandar) ‖ FAM *le endilgué todo mi poema* I made him listen to *o* sit through my whole poem.

endino, na *adj* FAM wicked.

endiñar *vt* POP to land, to deal (un golpe) | to fetch (un tortazo).

endiosado, da *adj* conceited, stuck-up (vanidoso) || deified (considerado como un dios).

endiosamiento *m* FIG pride, vanity, conceit.

endiosar *vt* to deify.
◆ *vpr* to become proud *o* stuck-up *o* conceited.

enditarse *vpr* AMER to run *o* to fall *o* to get into debt (endeudarse).

endocardiaco, ca *adj* ANAT endocardial.

endocardio *m* ANAT endocardium.

endocarditis *f* MED endocarditis.

endocarpio *m* BOT endocarp.

endocervitis *f* MED endocervitis.

endocráneo *m* ANAT endocranium.

endocrino, na *adj* BIOL endocrine, endocrinal, endocrinic, endocrinous || *glándula endocrina* endocrine gland.

endocrinología *f* MED endocrinology.

endocrinológico, ca *adj* MED endocrinological, endocrinologic.

endocrinólogo, ga *m/f* endocrinologist.

endocrinopatía *f* MED endocrinopathy.

endodermo *m* BIOL endoderm.

endodermis *f* BIOL endodermis.

endoesqueleto *m* ANAT endoskeleton.

endogamia *f* endogamy, inbreeding.

endogénesis *f* BIOL endogeny.

endógeno, na *adj* endogenous.

endometriosis *f* MED endometriosis.

endometritis *f* MED endometritis.

endomingado, da *adj* dressed up, in one's Sunday best.

endomingar *vt* to dress up in one's Sunday best.
◆ *vpr* to put on one's Sunday best.

endoparásito, ta *adj* endoparasitic.
◆ *m* endoparasite.

endoplasma *m* endoplasm.

endosador, ra; endosante *adj* COM endorsing.
◆ *m/f* endorser.

endosar *vt* COM to endorse || FIG to shoulder, to lumber (una responsabilidad, una carga) | to palm off, to foist (un trabajo a otro).

endosatario, ria *m/f* COM endorsee.

endoscopia *f* MED endoscopy.

endoscopio *m* MED endoscope.

endoselar *vt* to provide with a canopy.

endosmómetro *m* BIOL endosmometer.

endósmosis; endosmosis *f* QUÍM endosmosis.

endosmótico, ca *adj* endosmotic.

endoso *m* COM endorsement, endorsing.

endosperma *m* BOT endosperm.

endotelio *m* ANAT endothelium.

endotelioma *m* MED endothelioma.

endotérmico, ca *adj* QUÍM endothermic, endothermal.

endotoxina *f* BIOL endotoxin.

endovenoso, sa *adj* intravenous.

endrino, na *adj* blue-black.
◆ *m* BOT blackthorn, sloe (arbusto).
◆ *f* BOT sloe (fruto).

endrogarse *vpr* AMER to get into debt.

endulzar *vt* to sweeten; *endulzar con miel* to sweeten with honey || FIG to soften, to alleviate, to ease (el sufrimiento) | to brighten up; *las visitas de sus nietos endulzaron su vejez* her grandchildren's visits brightened up her old age || ARTES to tone down, to soften (las tintas y contornos).

endurecer* *vt* to harden, to make hard (poner duro) || FIG to harden, to toughen, to inure; *la vida militar endurece a los hombres* life in the army hardens men.
◆ *vpr* to harden, to become hard || FIG to become inured *o* hardened (volverse resistente) | to become hardhearted (volverse insensible).

endurecimiento *m* hardening (acción) || hardness (estado) || FIG hardening, inurement (del cuerpo, de las emociones) | hardheartedness (insensibilidad) | obstinacy.

ene *f* n [name of the letter *n*] || X; *hace ene años* X years ago.

enea *f* BOT —› **anea.**

Eneas *npr m* Aeneas.

enebro *m* BOT juniper (árbol).

Eneida *npr f* Aeneid.

eneldo *m* BOT anethum, dill.

enema *m* (ant) MED ointment (ungüento) | enema (ayuda).
— OBSERV In its second sense the word *enema* can be either masculine or feminine. The Academy prefers the feminine.

enemiga *f* ill will (antipatía); *tenerle enemiga a alguien* to bear s.o. ill will || enmity, hostility (enemistad).

enemigo, ga *adj* enemy, hostile; *el ejército enemigo* the enemy army || FIG *ser enemigo de* to dislike.
◆ *m/f* enemy, adversary, foe || MIL enemy || — FIG *al enemigo que huye puente de plata* let sleeping dogs lie | *enemigo malo* devil | *hacerse enemigos* to make enemies | *no hay enemigo pequeño* do not underrate your enemy || *pasarse al enemigo* to go over to the enemy.

enemistad *f* enmity.

enemistar *vt* to make enemies of, to set at odds; *enemistar a dos personas* to set two people at odds.
◆ *vpr* to become enemies || to fall out (enfadarse).

energético, ca *adj* energy.
◆ *f* energetics.
◆ *m pl* fuels.

energía *f* FÍS energy; *energía cinética, potencial, química* kinetic, potential, chemical energy || energy power; *energía nuclear, eléctrica* nuclear, electric power || energy, vitaly, vigour [US vigor] (fuerzas); *una persona de mucha energía* a person with lots of energy || spirit (ánimo) || — *energía atómica* atomic energy || *energía eólica* wind power || *energía hidráulica* waterpower, hydraulic power || *energía solar* solar energy *o* power.

enérgico, ca *adj* energetic, spirited, vigorous (carácter) || forceful (decisión, medida) || strenuous (esfuerzo) || vigorous, strong (ataque) || emphatic (negativa) || forcible, strong (palabras) || MED powerful, drastic (medicina).

energúmeno, na *m/f* madman (hombre), madwoman (mujer); *comportarse como un energúmeno* to behave like a madman || fanatic || energumen (persona poseída del demonio).

enero *m* January; el 5 de enero, the 5th of January, January 5th.

enervación *f*; **enervamiento** *m* enervation || effeminacy.

enervador, ra; enervante *adj* enervating.

enervar *vt* to enervate || FIG to weaken.

enésimo, ma *adj* MAT nth, n; *elevar a la enésima potencia* to raise to the nth power *o* to the power of n || *te lo digo por enésima vez* I'm telling you for the nth time *o* for the umpteenth time.

enfadar *vt* to annoy, to irritate, to get on s.o.'s nerves (disgustar) || to anger, to infuriate, to madden (enojar).
◆ *vpr* to be *o* to become irritated *o* annoyed || to get angry *o* mad, to lose one's temper; *se enfada por cualquier cosa* he gets mad about anything || *enfadarse con uno* to get angry *o* cross with s.o. (enojarse), to fall out with s.o. (enemistarse).

enfado *m* annoyance, irritation (descontento) || anger (enojo) || quarrel, tiff (disgusto) || *causar enfado* to annoy, to irritate, to get on s.o.'s nerves (disgustar), to anger, to infuriate, to madden (enojar).

enfadosamente *adv* annoyingly, irritatingly || unpleasantly (de manera desagradable) || unwillingly, begrudgingly (a regañadientes).

enfadoso, sa *adj* annoying, irritating, irksome (molesto) || unpleasant, disagreeable (desagradable).

enfangar *vt* to cover with mud.
◆ *vpr* to cover o.s. in mud, to get covered in mud (llenarse de fango) || FIG & FAM to dirty one's hands (en negocios vergonzosos) | to wallow in vice (en placeres) | to degrade o.s. (deshonrarse) || MAR to stick in the mud.

enfardadora *f* AGR baler, baling machine.

enfardar *vpr* to wrap up, to parcel up (empaquetar) || AGR to bale.

énfasis *m* emphasis, stress (insistencia) || emphasis (en retórica) || *dar énfasis a algo* to give sth. emphasis, to emphasize sth., to put *o* to lay stress on sth., to stress sth.

enfático, ca *adj* emphatic.

enfatizar *vt* to emphasize.

enfatuarse *vpr* to become conceited.

enfebrecido, da *adj* AMER febrile, feverish.

enfermar *vi* to fall ill, to be taken ill || *enfermar del pecho* to contract a chest complaint.
◆ *vt* to make ill || FIG to make sick, to make ill (irritar); *las injusticias me enferman* injustice makes me sick | to weaken (debilitar).

enfermedad *f* illness, disease (afección); *su enfermedad era muy grave* his illness was very serious || illness, ill health, sickness (indisposición); *a consecuencia de enfermedad* through illness *o* ill health || FIG malady || — *ausentarse por enfermedad* to be away ill *o* sick || *enfermedad adquirida* acquired disease || *enfermedad aguda* acute illness || *enfermedad azul, contagiosa, de Parkinson, profesional* blue, contagious, Parkinson's, occupational disease || *enfermedad carencial* deficiency disease || *enfermedad congénita* congenital disease || *enfermedad del hígado* liver complaint || *enfermedad del sueño* sleeping sickness || *enfermedad hereditaria* hereditary disease || *enfermedad infantil* child's complaint || *enfermedad infecciosa* infectious disease || *enfermedad mental* or *nerviosa* mental illness *o* disease || *enfermedad venérea* venereal disease || *salir de una enfermedad* to recover from an illness || *una enfermedad larga* a long illness.

enfermería *f* infirmary, sick bay (de un colegio, etc.) || hospital.

enfermero, ra *m/f* male nurse (hombre), nurse (mujer).

enfermizo, za *adj* sickly; *persona enfermiza* sickly person || unhealthy, morbid; *pasión enfermiza* unhealthy obsession || unhealthy (alimento, comarca).

enfermo, ma *adj* ill, sick; *ponerse* or *caer enfermo* to fall ill, be taken ill || — *enfermo de amor* lovesick || *enfermo de gravedad* seriously ill || *fingirse enfermo* to pretend to be ill, to malinger || FIG *poner enfermo a alguien* to make s.o. ill *o* sick, to give s.o. a pain in the neck; *su conversación me pone enfermo* his conversation makes me sick.

◆ *m/f* sick person, invalid || patient (en el hospital) || *enfermo de aprensión* hypochondriac.

enfermucho, cha *adj* ailing, sickly.

enfervorizar; fervorizar *vt* to encourage (animar) || to enthuse; *su discurso enfervorizó al público* his speech enthused the audience.

enfeudación *f*; **enfeudamiento** *m* HIST enfeoffment, infeudation.

enfeudar *vt* to enfeoff.

enfiebrecido, da *adj* febrile, feverish.

enfilada *f* MIL enfilade || MIL *tiro de enfilada* raking *o* enfilading fire.

enfilado *m* stringing, threading (de perlas).

enfilar *vt* to string, to thread (ensartar); *enfilar perlas* to string pearls || to align, to line up (colocar en fila) || to take, to go along (una calle) || to direct, to point, to train (apuntar); *enfilar un cañón* to point a gun || MIL to enfilade, to rake.

enfisema *m* MED emphysema.

enfisematoso, sa *adj* emphysematous.

enfistolarse *vpr* MED to turn into fistula.

enfiteusis *f* JUR long lease, emphyteusis.

enfiteuta *m/f* JUR emphyteuta.

enfitéutico, ca *adj* JUR emphyteutic.

enflaquecer* *vt* to make thin (adelgazar) || FIG to weaken (debilitar).

◆ *vi* to lose weight, to get thin (adelgazar) || FIG to lose heart (desanimarse).

enflaquecimiento *m* losing weight, slimming (acción de enflaquecer) || loss of weight (pérdida de peso) || FIG weakening (debilitación).

enflatarse *vpr* AMER to become sad.

enflautada *f* AMER absurdity.

enflautado, da *adj* FIG bombastic, highflown.

enflautar *vt* FAM to deceive, to cheat (engañar) | to inflate (hinchar) || AMER FAM to unload on.

enfocar *vt* to shine on; *le enfocó con su linterna* he shone his torch on him || to focus (una lente, cámara, etc.) || to point, to train (gemelos) || FIG to approach, to consider, to look at (una cuestión); *enfocar un asunto desde el punto de vista religioso* to consider a subject from the religious point of view || FIG *enfocar algo de distinta manera* to see sth. from a different point of view, to have a different view of sth.

◆ *vi/vpr* to focus.

enfoque *m* FOT focusing, focussing (acción de enfocar) | focus (resultado obtenido) || FIG point of view, approach (óptica).

enfrascamiento *m* FIG absorption.

enfrascar *vt* to put in a flask, to bottle (embotellar).

◆ *vpr* to enter into a thicket (en una maleza) || FIG to get involved *o* engrossed *o* absorbed (en una ocupación) || FIG *estaba enfrascado en la lectura* he was buried in a book.

enfrentar *vt* to face, to confront (un peligro, adversidades, etc.) || to bring face to face, to confront (poner frente a frente); *enfrentar a una persona con otra* to bring two people face to face, to confront two people, to confront one person with another.

◆ *vpr* to meet, to confront, to encounter; *nuestro ejército se enfrentó a* or *con el ejército enemigo* our army encountered the enemy army || to face up to, to face (arrostrar); *tendrás que enfrentarte con muchas dificultades* you will have to face up to many difficulties || to meet, to encounter, to come up against (encontrar); *al día siguiente se enfrentó con la primera dificultad* on the next day he met the first difficulty || to meet (equipos); *el equipo del Real Madrid se enfrentó con el del Manchester United* Real Madrid met Manchester United; *los dos equipos se enfrentaron en Madrid* the two teams met in Madrid || to stand up to, to face up to; *se enfrentó conmigo* he stood up to me || to antagonize; *se ha enfrentado con sus amigos* he has antagonized his friends || to meet (satisfacer); *enfrentarse con las necesidades de* to meet the needs of.

enfrente *adv* opposite, in front, facing; *enfrente de mi casa* opposite my house; *enfrente mía* opposite me || against; *incluso su propia madre se le puso enfrente* even his own mother sided against him || — *allí enfrente* over there, there in front of (me, you, him, etc.) || *en la página de enfrente* on the opposite *o* facing page || *tu casa y la suya están una enfrente de otra* your house and his are opposite each other.

enfriadera *f* cooler [for drinks].

enfriadero *m* cold room.

enfriador, ra *adj* cooling.

◆ *m* cooler (aparato) || cold room (fresquera).

enfriamiento *m* cooling (acción de enfriar) || MED cold, chill (catarro).

enfriar *vt* to cool, to cool down; *enfriar un líquido* to cool a liquid || FIG to cool down (una pasión, etc.) | to dampen; *enfriar el entusiasmo de uno* to dampen s.o.'s enthusiasm || AMER to kill (matar).

◆ *vi* to cool, to cool down, to cool off (ponerse frío) | to go *o* to get cold.

◆ *vpr* to cool, to cool down, to cool off (ponerse frío) || to go cold, to get cold; *se está enfriando el té* your tea is going cold || to catch a cold (acatarrarse) || FIG to cool off, to grow cold (pasiones, etc.); *se enfrió el entusiasmo* the enthusiasm cooled off.

enfundadura *f* casing || sheathing (de espada, puñal, etc.) || covering (de un mueble).

enfundar *vt* to put in its case; *enfundar una cosa* to put sth. in its case || to sheathe (envainar la espada, el puñal, etc.) || to holster (una pistola) || to cover (un mueble) || TECN to case, to sheathe.

enfurecer* *vt* to make mad, to infuriate, to enrage, to madden || *mar enfurecido* stormy *o* raging sea.

◆ *vpr* to lose one's temper, to fly into a rage, to become furious; *enfurecerse con* to lose one's temper with || to get rough, to start to rage (el mar).

enfurecimiento *m* fury, rage.

enfurruñamiento *m* FAM (slight) anger.

enfurruñarse *vpr* FAM to sulk (enfadarse) | to cloud over (el cielo).

enfurtido *m* fulling (del paño) || felting (del fieltro).

enfurtir *vt* to full (el paño) || to felt (el fieltro).

engafar *vt* MAR to hook.

engaitar *vt* FAM to take in, to trick (engañar) | to wheedle, to coax (engatusar).

engalanar *vt* to adorn, to dress up, to deck out (adornar); *engalanar con* to deck out with || to decorate (decorar) || to dress up, to deck out [in fine clothes]; *estar muy engalanada* to be really dressed up || MAR to dress, to deck out.

◆ *vpr* to be decked out, to be adorned, to be dressed up (adornarse) || to dress up, to deck o.s. out [in fine clothes].

engalgar *vt* to chock, to scotch (una rueda) || to set on the track of (un perro).

engallado, da *adj* FIG arrogant, haughty (presumido) | daring (envalentonado).

engalladura *f* cicatricule, tread (galladura).

engallamiento *m* FIG arrogance.

engallarse *vpr* FIG to put on airs and graces, to be arrogant (envalentonarse) || to hold up its head (el caballo).

enganchamiento *m* hooking || MIL enrolment, enlistment, recruitment.

enganchar *vt* to hook (coger con un gancho); *enganchar un pez* to hook a fish || to hang (up); *enganchar la gabardina en la percha* to hang up one's raincoat on the coat hanger || to harness, to hitch (las caballerías a un carruaje) || to hitch (un remolque) || to couple (dos vagones) || MIL to enlist, to recruit (reclutar) || TECN to engage (engranar) | to couple, to connect (empalmar) || FIG & FAM to get round, to wheedle, to persuade, to rope in (atraer a una persona) | to hook (un marido) | to catch; *la policía enganchó al ladrón* the police caught the thief || TAUR to catch (coger).

◆ *vpr* to get caught; *se le enganchó el pantalón en un clavo* his trousers got caught on a nail || to get hooked up (en un gancho) || MIL to enlist, to enrol, to sign on, to join up.

enganche *m* hook (gancho) || hooking (up) || coupling (de vagones) || hitching-up (de remolques) || harnessing (de las caballerías) || TECN engaging (trinquete) | connection (empalme) || MIL recruitment, enlistment, enrolment.

enganchón *m* snag (desgarrón en una prenda).

engañabobos *m inv* confidence trickster, swindler [US con man] (persona) || confidence trick, con (engaño) || ZOOL nightjar (chotacabras).

engañar *vt* to deceive, to trick; *engañar a un cliente* to deceive a customer || to take in, to fool, to dupe (ocultar la verdad); *a él nadie le engaña* there's no fooling him || to cheat, to swindle, to trick (estafar) || to be unfaithful to (adulterio) || to mislead; *me engañó con sus consejos falsos* he misled me with his false advice; *le engaña su buena voluntad* he is misled by his good will || FIG to deceive; *me engaña la vista* my eyes are deceiving me | to stave off, to stay, to ward off; *engañar el hambre* to stave off hunger | to kill, to while away; *engañar el tiempo* to while away the time, to kill time || FAM *¡a mí no me engañan!* they can't fool me!, I wasn't born yesterday!

◆ *vi* to be deceptive, to be misleading || *las apariencias engañan* appearances are deceptive, you can't judge by appearances.

◆ *vpr* to be mistaken, to be wrong (equivocarse); *se engaña Ud* you are mistaken || to make a mistake; *engañarse con uno* to make a mistake about s.o. || to deceive o.s., to delude o.s. (no querer admitir la verdad) || *si no me engaño* if I'm not mistaken.

engañifa *f* FAM deceit, deception | swindle, fraud (estafa).

engaño *m* mistake (equivocación); *salir del engaño* to realize one's mistake || deceit, deception, trickery (acción de engañar) || fraud, trick, swindle (timo) || deception, trick (lo que engaña) || TAUR muleta (muleta) | cape (capa) || bait (para pescar) || — *deshacer un engaño* to establish the truth || *llamarse a engaño* to claim that one has been deceived.

engañoso, sa *adj* deceptive; *apariencias engañosas* deceptive appearances || deceitful (con malicia); *palabras engañosas* deceitful words || misleading; *consejo engañoso* misleading piece of advice.

engarabatar *vt* to hook (con un garabato).

engarabitarse *vpr* to climb (trepar).

engaratusar *vt* AMER → **engatusar.**

engarce *m*; **engarzadura** *f* threading, stringing (acción de engarzar perlas) || string (hilo de un collar, etc.) || setting, mounting (de una piedra) || FIG linking, connection (de ideas, etc.).

engargantar *vt* to cram (las aves).
◆ *vi* to mesh, to engage (engranar).

engargolado *m* TECN groove-and-tongue joint (ensambladura) | groove (de una puerta de corredera).

engargolar *vt* TECN to fit with a groove-and-tongue joint.

engarzador, ra *adj* who threads *o* strings (de perlas) || mounting, setting (de piedras).

engarzadura *f* ⟶ **engarce.**

engarzar *vt* to thread, to string (las cuentas o las perlas de un collar) || to set, to mount (joyas) || to curl (rizar) || FIG to link, to connect (enlazar).
◆ *vpr* to get tangled (enredarse).

engastador, ra *adj* setting, mounting.
◆ *m* setter, mounter (de joyas).

engastadura *f* ⟶ **engaste.**

engastar *vt* to set, to mount, to enchase (piedras preciosas); *engastar un diamante en oro* to set a diamond in gold.

engaste *m*; **engastadura** *f* setting, mounting, enchasing (acción) || setting (cerco de metal que sujeta la piedra) || imperfect pearl (perla).

engatillar *vt* ARQ to clamp, to cramp.

engatusador, ra *adj* coaxing, wheedling.
◆ *m/f* coaxer, wheedler.

engatusamiento *m* coaxing, wheedling.

engatusar *vt* FAM to get round; *engatusó a sus acreedores* he got round his creditors | to coax, to wheedle; *engatusar a alguien para que haga algo* to coax *o* to wheedle s.o. into doing sth.

engavillar *vt* AGR to sheave, to bind into sheaves.

engendrador, ra *adj* begetting, engendering.

engendramiento *m* begetting, engendering.

engendrar *vt* to engender, to beget || FIG to give rise to, to engender; *engendrar la duda en una persona* to engender doubt in s.o.'s mind | to cause (provocar) | to produce; *engendrar una corriente eléctrica* to produce an electric current.

engendro *m* foetus (feto) || deformed child, stunted child (criatura informe) || freak, monster (monstruo) || FIG botched job, bad piece of work (algo mal hecho) | brainchild, wild plan (proyecto) || FIG & FAM *¡mal engendro!* little monster!

englobar *vt* to include (comprender) || to bracket, to lump together (incluir).

engolado, da *adj* FIG presumptuous, arrogant (persona) | high-flown, bombastic (estilo).

engolamiento *m* presumption, arrogance.

engolfar *vi* MAR to lose sight of land, to make for the open sea.
◆ *vpr* MAR to make for the open sea || FIG to become lost *o* absorbed *o* engrossed; *engolfarse en la meditación* to become lost in thought.

engolillado, da *adj* FIG & FAM straitlaced, old-fashioned.

engolosinador, ra *adj* tempting, enticing.

engolosinar *vt* to tempt, to entice.
◆ *vpr* to acquire *o* to develop a taste; *engolosinarse con algo* to develop a taste for sth.

engolletarse *vt* FAM to give o.s. airs.

engomado *m*; **engomadura** *f* gluing, gumming (acción de engomar) || gum, glue (pegamento) || sizing (de los tejidos).

engomar *vt* to glue, to gum (pegar) || to size (los tejidos) || *papel engomado* sticky *o* adhesive paper.

engorda *f* AMER fattening (ceba) | fattening animals *pl* (ganadero).

engordadero *m* fattening sty (sitio) || fattening period (tiempo) || fattening fodder (alimento).

engordar *vt* to make fat, to fatten (a una persona) || to fatten (up) (los animales).
◆ *vi* to get fatter, to put on weight; *has engordado mucho* you have got much fatter, you have put on a lot of weight || to be fattening; *el pan engorda* bread is fattening.

engorde *m* fattening [up] (de los animales).

engorro *m* nuisance, bother (molestia) || FAM snag, difficulty, catch (dificultad); *asunto lleno de engorros* matter full of snags.

engorroso, sa *adj* annoying, trying, bothersome (molesto); *asunto engorroso* annoying affair.

engoznar *vt* to hinge.

engranaje *m* TECN gear; *engranaje diferencial* differential gear; *engranaje de distribución* timing gear | cogs *pl*, gear teeth *pl* (conjunto de dientes) | gears *pl*, gearing (conjunto); *el engranaje de un máquina* the gearing of a machine | cogwheels *pl* (de un reloj) || engaging, meshing, gearing (transmisión) || FIG connection, linking || FIG *estar preso en el engranaje* to be caught up in the machinery.

engranar *vt/vi* TECN to engage, to mesh, to gear || FIG to connect, to link (enlazar).

engrandecer* *vt* to enlarge, to make bigger (hacer mayor) || FIG to enhance, to exalt (enaltecer) | to praise, to exalt (alabar) | to promote, to raise (elevar) | to widen, to broaden; *la lectura engrandece el espíritu* reading widens the mind | to magnify (exagerar).
◆ *vpr* FIG to rise, to be promoted.

engrandecimiento *m* enlargement (agrandamiento) || FIG enhancement, exaltation (enaltecimiento) | praise, exaltation (alabanza) | promotion | magnification (exageración).

engranujarse *vpr* to become pimply (llenarse de granos) || to become a rogue (hacerse granuja).

engrapado *m* ARQ cramping || stapling (de papeles).

engrapar *vt* ARQ to cramp (fijar con grapas) || to staple (papeles).

engrasado *m* greasing, lubrication.

engrasador, ra *adj* greasing.
◆ *m* grease gun.

engrasamiento *m* ⟶ **engrase.**

engrasar *vt* TECN to grease, to lubricate; *engrasar un coche* to grease a car | to oil (aceitar) || to oil up (las bujías) || to make greasy, to stain with grease (ensuciar) || AGR to manure, to fertilize (abonar).
◆ *vpr* TECN to get oiled up (una bujía de motor).

engrase; engrasamiento *m* greasing, lubrication (con grasa) || oiling, lubrication (con aceite) || oiling-up (de una bujía) || lubricant (materia lubricante).

engreído, da *adj* presumptuous, conceited, arrogant || AMER spoiled (mimado) || *engreído de sí mismo* fond of o.s., full of self-importance, blown-up.

engreimiento *m* presumptuousness, conceit, arrogance, self-importance.

engreír* *vt* to make conceited, to make presumptuous *o* arrogant || AMER to spoil (mimar).
◆ *vpr* to become conceited *o* presumptuous *o* arrogant (envanecerse) || AMER to become fond (encariñarse) | to get spoiled (con mimos).

engrescar *vt* to cause trouble between, to cause an argument between, to antagonize.
◆ *vpr* to quarrel, to argue (disputarse).

engrifarse *vpr* FAM to drug o.s., to take drugs.

engrillar *vt* to fetter, to shackle (poner grilletes).

engringarse *vpr* AMER to adopt foreing ways.

engrosamiento *m* fattening (de una persona) || increase, enlargement (de un cosa) || thickening (espesamiento).

engrosar* *vt* to increase (aumentar) || to enlarge (agrandar) || to swell (un río) || to thicken (espesar).
◆ *vi* to get fatter, to put on weight (una persona) || to swell (un río).
◆ *vpr* to increase || to enlarge.

engrudamiento *m* pasting (de papeles).

engrudar *vt* to paste (papeles).

engrudo *m* paste.

engruesar *vi* ⟶ **engrosar.**

engrumecerse* *vpr* to clot (la sangre) || to curdle (la leche) || to go lumpy (hacerse grumos).

enguachinar *vt* to soak, to flood (enaguazar).

engualdrapar *vt* to put a horsecloth on.

enguantado, da *adj* gloved; *una mano enguantada* a gloved hand || *iban todos enguantados* they all had gloves on, they were all wearing gloves.

enguantarse *vpr* to put on one's gloves.

enguatar *vt* to pad.

enguedejado, da *adj* long-haired (persona) || long (pelo).

enguijarrado *m* pebbling (acción) || cobbles, *pl* (pavimento).

enguijarrar *vt* to pebble, to cobble.

enguirnaldar *vt* to garland, to wreathe.

engullimiento *m* gobbling, gulping.

engullir* *vt* to gobble up, to gulp down.

engurruñar *vt* to crease, to wrinkle, to crumple.
◆ *vpr* FAM to get sad.

enhacinar *vt* to pile up, to heap up.

enharinar *vt* to flour (cubrir con harina) || to sprinkle with flour (echar harina) || to whiten [the face].

enhebrado; enhebramiento *m* threading.

enhebrar; enhilar *vt* to thread (una aguja) || to string, to thread (perlas) || FIG to link, to connect (ideas) || — FIG *enhebrar una mentira tras otra* to reel off a string of lies | *una cosa es enhebrar, otra es dar puntadas* it is easy to criticize.

enhiesto, ta *adj* erect, upright, straight.

enhilar *vt* ⟶ **enhebrar.**

enhorabuena *f* congratulations *pl* || — *dar a uno la enhorabuena* to congratule s.o. || *estar de enhorabuena* to be very happy || *mi más cordial enhorabuena* my very best wishes.
◆ *adv* thank heavens that, thank God; *¡que se vaya enhorabuena!* thank God he is going! || very good (de acuerdo) || *venga usted enhorabuena* you're welcome to come.

enhoramala *adv* inopportunely; *enhoramala habló* he spoke inopportunely || *haber nacido enhoramala* to be born under an unlucky star || *¡iros enhoramala!* good riddance!

enhornar *vt* to put into the oven.

enigma *m* riddle, enigma (dicho) || puzzle, mystery; *su comportamiento es un enigma para mí* his behaviour is a puzzle to me.

enigmático, ca *adj* enigmatic, puzzling, mysterious.

enilismo *m* alcoholism [produced by wine].

enjabonado *m*; **enjabonadura** *f* soaping.

enjabonar *vt* to soap || FIG & FAM to give (s.o.) a dressing down, to give (s.o.) a telling off (reprender) | to soft-soap, to butter up (adular).

enjaezamiento *m* harnessing.

enjaezar *vt* to harness.

enjalbegado *m* whitewashing (de una pared).

enjalbegador *m* whitewasher.

enjalbegadura *f* whitewashing.

enjalbegar *vt* to whitewash (blanquear) || FIG to paint (el rostro).

enjalma *f* packsaddle (albarda).

enjalmar *vt* to put a packsaddle on (albardar).

enjambrar *vt/vi* to swarm, to hive.

enjambrazón *m* swarming.

enjambre *m* swarm (de abejas) || FIG swarm, crowd, throng || ASTR cluster (de estrellas).

enjaquimar *vt* to halter, to put the halter on (una caballería).

enjarciar *vt* MAR to rig (un barco).

enjaretado *m* lattice screen, latticework.

enjaretar *vt* to thread through a hem (cordón, cinta) || FIG & FAM to reel off, to spill out; *nos enjaretó unos versos* he reeled some poetry off to us | to palm off, to lumber; *enjaretar a uno un trabajo molesto* to palm off an annoying job on s.o. | to rush through (hacer rápidamente).

enjaulamiento *m* caging.

enjaular *vt* to put into a cage, to cage (meter en una jaula) || FAM to put inside, to put in (the) clink, to lock up, to jail (encarcelar).

enjebe *m* alum (alumbre) || lye, bleach (lejía) || lying, bleaching (de los tejidos) || whitewashing (de las paredes).

enjoyar *vt* to decorate *o* to adorn with jewels (cosas) || to dress *o* to deck with jewels *o* jewellery (a una persona) || FIG to adorn, to beautify (embellecer) || TECN to set with precious stones (engastar).

enjuagadientes *m inv* mouthwash.

enjuagadura *f* rinsing (lavado) || rinsing water (líquido).

enjuagar *vt* to rinse (la ropa).
◆ *vpr* to rinse out (one's mouth).

enjuague *m* rinsing (lavado) || rinsing water (líquido) || finger bowl (lavafrutas) || mouthwash (enjuagadientes) || FIG plot, scheme (estratagema).

enjugador *m* clothes drier || TECN drier.

enjugamanos *m inv* AMER towel (toalla).

enjugar *vt* to dry (secar) || to wipe up, to mop up (un líquido) || to dry, to wipe; *enjugar los platos* to dry the dishes || to wipe away; *enjugar el llanto de alguien* to wipe away s.o.'s tears || to mop, to wipe (la frente) || FIG to cancel, to wipe out; *enjugar un déficit* to cancel a deficit.
◆ *vpr* to dry, to wipe.
— OBSERV This verb has two past participles, *enjugado* which is used to form compound tenses and *enjuto*, used as an adjective *(han enjugado la deuda: dama enjuta)*.

enjuiciamiento *m* JUR trial, prosecution (criminal) | lawsuit (civil) | procedure (procedimiento) || judgment (acción de juzgar).

enjuiciar *vt* JUR to sue (civil) | to prosecute (criminal) | to try (someter a juicio) || to judge, to examine (juzgar).

enjulio; enjullo *m* TECN beam, roller (de un telar).

enjundia *f* fat (grasa) || FIG substance; *un libro de mucha enjundia* a book with a lot of substance | force, vitality, strength (vigor) | character; *una persona de mucha enjundia* a person with a lot of character.

enjundioso, sa *adj* fatty (grasiento) || FIG substantial (sustancioso) | full of character (persona).

enjuta *f* ARQ spandrel || pendentive (de una cúpula).

enjutar *vt* ARQ to fill up.

enjuto, ta *adj* lean, skinny (flaco) (véase OBSERV en ENJUGAR).

enlace; enlazamiento *m* connection, connexion, relationship, link (relación); *hay un enlace entre las dos ideas* there is a link between the two ideas || marriage, union (casamiento) || linking (de dos familias) || liaison (en la pronunciación) || junction (de vías férreas) || connection (de tren, autobús) || meeting, rendezvous (encuentro) || MIL liaison || ELECTR linkage || QUÍM bond; *enlace covalente, iónico, metálico* covalent, ionic, metallic bond || — MIL *agente de enlace* liaison officer || *carretera de enlace* link road, connecting road || *enlace matrimonial* marriage || *enlace sindical* shop steward [*US* union delegate].

enladrillado *m* brick floor, brick paving.

enladrillar *vt* to pave with bricks.

enlardar *vt* to coat with grease, to baste, to lard.

enlatado, da *adj* canned, tinned (en lata).
◆ *m* canning, tinning.

enlatar *vt* to can, to tin (en botes de lata).

enlazamiento *m* → **enlace.**

enlazar *vt* to tie together, to bind (unir con lazos) || to tie, to fasten (atar) || FIG to connect, to relate, to link (trabar); *enlazar una idea con otra* to link one idea with another || to lasso (un animal) || to connect (dos ciudades, etc.).
◆ *vi* to connect (avión, tren, etc.).
◆ *vpr* to link (up), to be linked (unirse) || to get married, to marry (novios) || to become linked by marriage (dos familias) || to be connected *o* linked *o* related (dos ideas).

enlistonado *m* TECN laths *pl.*

enlodar; enlodazar *vt* to muddy, to cover with mud (cubrir de lodo) || to splash *o* to splatter with mud (manchar de lodo) || FIG to stain, to besmirch (la fama).
◆ *vpr* to get muddy.

enloquecedor, ra *adj* maddening.

enloquecer* *vt* to drive mad, to madden, to drive crazy (turbar) || to drive mad *o* insane (volver loco) || *me enloquece la pintura* I am mad about painting.
◆ *vi/vpr* to go mad *o* insane.

enloquecimiento *m* madness, insanity.

enlosado *m* tiling (de baldosas) || paving (de losas).

enlosar *vt* to tile (con baldosas) || to pave, to flag (con losas).
— OBSERV *To tile* se emplea para las baldosas que se ponen en las casas y *to pave* o *to flag* para las losas más grandes que se ven en las iglesias, los jardines, etc.

enlucido, da *adj* plastered (pared) || whitewashed (blanqueado) || polished (armas).
◆ *m* plaster, coat of plaster (de una pared).

enlucimiento *m* plastering (de las paredes) || polishing (de las armas).

enlucir* *vt* to plaster (una pared) || to polish (armas).

enlutado, da *adj* in mourning.

enlutar *vt* to dress in mourning (vestir de luto) || to cast into mourning, to bereave; *la catástrofe enlutó a numerosas familias* the disaster cast many families into mourning || FIG to sadden (entristecer) | to darken (oscurecer).
◆ *vpr* to wear mourning, to dress in mourning (vestirse de luto).

enllantado *m* TECN rimming (de una rueda).

enllantar *vt* to rim (poner llantas).

enmaderado; enmaderamiento *m* timbering, woodwork (obra de madera) || wooden panelling (revestimiento de madera) || floorboards *pl* (del suelo).

enmaderar *vt* to panel (revestir una pared) || to lay floorboards of (revestir el suelo) || to timber, to build the wooden framework of (construir el maderamen).

enmadrarse *vpr* to become excessively attached to one's mother (un niño).

enmalezarse *vt* to get overgrown with weeds.

enmaniguarse *vt* AMER to get overgrown with trees.

enmarañamiento *m* tangle, entanglement (de cosas) || FIG muddle, confusion (de un asunto).

enmarañar *vt* to tangle up, to entangle (enredar) || FIG to muddle up, to confuse, to make more involved (un asunto).
◆ *vpr* to get into a tangle, to get entangled, to get tangled || FIG to get muddled *o* confused, to get more involved (un asunto).

enmarcar *vt* to frame (en un marco) || to surround (rodear).

enmaridar, enmaridarse *vi/vpr* to get married, to marry [a woman].

enmarillecerse* *vpr* to turn yellow.

enmaromar *vt* to tie up (with a rope), to rope.

enmascarado, da *m/f* masked person.

enmascaramiento *m* MIL camouflage.

enmascarar *vt* to mask || MIL to camouflage.
◆ *vpr* to put on a mask, to mask o.s. (ponerse una careta) || to masquerade as (disfrazarse de).

enmasillar *vt* to putty (poner masilla).

enmendadura *f* correction.

enmendar* *vt* to correct, to reform (corregir); *enmendar un texto* to correct a text || JUR to amend (una ley) | to revise (un juicio) || to repare, to put right (un daño) || to correct, to rectify; *enmendar un defecto* to rectify a fault || to make amends for, to compensate for (compensar) || AGR to improve, to fertilize (la tierra) || MAR to alter, to change (el rumbo, el fondeadero).
◆ *vpr* to change *o* to mend one's ways, to reform; *era un criminal pero se ha enmendado* he was a criminal but he has changed his ways || to correct; *enmendarse de una equivocación* to correct one's mistake || TAUR to move; *dio cinco pases sin enmendarse* he made five passes without moving.

enmicado *m* AMER plastic covering.

enmicar *vt* AMER to coat with plastic (documentos, mapas, etc.).

enmienda *f* correction, amendment; *hacer muchas enmiendas en un texto* to make many corrections in a text || repair, indemnity, compensation (de un daño) || amendment (de textos oficiales, de un juicio, de una ley) || correction, rectification, amendment (de un defecto) || AGR fertilizer (fertilizante) | fertilizing, improvement (acción de abonar) || — *enmien-*

da de la vida mending *o* changing of one's ways || *no tener enmienda* to be incorrigible || *poner enmienda* to amend, to correct || *tener propósito de enmienda* to resolve to do better.

enmohecer* *vt* to rust (el metal) || to make mouldy (materia orgánica) || FIG to make rusty (embotar).

◆ *vi* FIG to get rusty, to rust up (embotarse).

◆ *vpr* to get rusty, to rust (el metal) || to get mouldy (materia orgánica) || FIG to get rusty, to rust up (embotarse).

enmohecimiento *m* rusting (acción), rustiness (estado), rustiness (metales) || mouldering (acción), mouldiness (estado) (materias orgánicas) || FIG rustiness (embotamiento).

enmudecer* *vt* to silence, to make quiet || FIG to dumbfound, to leave speechless (por el temor, etc.).

◆ *vi* to become dumb, to lose one's voice *o* speech (perder el habla) || FIG to be dumbfounded, to be speechless (por el miedo, la sorpresa, etc.) | to keep quiet, to be silent, to say nothing (callar).

ennegrecer* *vt* to blacken, to turn black (poner negro) || FIG to darken (oscurecer).

◆ *vi/vpr* to turn black, to go black || FIG to be dark, to darken.

ennegrecimiento *m* blackening.

ennoblecer* *vt* to ennoble (dar título de nobleza) || FIG to add an air of distinction to; *estas cortinas ennoblecen la habitación* these curtains add an air of distinction to the room | to do honour to, to be a credit to; *esas ideas le ennoblecen* those ideas do him honour, those ideas are a credit to him.

ennoblecimiento *m* ennobling, ennoblement || FIG distinction.

enojado, da *adj* angry; *estar enojado con uno* to be angry with s.o. || cross, angry (ligeramente enfadado).

enojar *vt* to make angry, to anger (enfadar) || to annoy, to irritate (molestar) || to offend.

◆ *vpr* to get angry; *enojarse con sus criados* to get angry with one's servants || to get irritated *o* annoyed (molestarse); *se enoja al ver todos los papeles en el suelo* he gets annoyed when he sees all the papers on the floor || to get cross *o* angry (enfadarse ligeramente); *enojarse con los niños* to get cross with the children || to get rough, to grow rough (el mar) || to get stronger (el viento).

enojo *m* anger (ira) || annoyance, irritation (molestia) || *causar enojo a* to anger, to make angry.

enojosamente *adv* angrily.

enojoso, sa *adj* annoying, irritating, troublesome.

enología *f* oenology (ciencia de los vinos).

enólogo, ga *m/f* oenologist.

enorgullecer* *vpr* to make proud, to fill with pride.

◆ *vpr* to be proud, to pride o.s.; *enorgullecerse de* or *con sus éxitos* to be proud of *o* to pride o.s. on one's successes.

enorgullecimiento *m* pride (orgullo) || filling with pride (acción de enorgullecer).

enorme *adj* enormous, massive, gigantic, huge; *una casa enorme* a massive house || enormous, great, huge; *la diferencia es enorme* the difference is enormous || FIG horrible, wicked (muy malo).

enormemente *adv* extremely, tremendously.

enormidad *f* enormity, hugeness || enormity, wickedness (de un pecado) || monstrous thing (monstruosidad) || ridiculous *o* gross mistake; *un libro lleno de enormidades* a book full of gross mistakes || stupidity (estupidez) || *— es una enormidad dejar a los niños solos en casa* it is a crime to leave children alone in the house || *me gusta una enormidad* I love it, I like it tremendously.

ENPETROL *abrev de Empresa Nacional de Petróleos* Spanish national oil company.

enquiciar *vt* to put (a door) on, to put (a window) in.

enquillotrarse *vpr* (p us) to become conceited (engreírse) || FAM to fall in love (enamorarse).

enquistado, da *adj* MED encysted.

enquistamiento *m* BIOL encystment.

enquistarse *vpr* MED to encyst || FIG to become embedded (una cosa) || FIG *estar enquistado en una familia* to impose on *o* to be an intruder in a family.

enrabiar *vt* to infuriate, to enrage.

◆ *vpr* to be furious, to rage, to get enraged.

enraizar *vi* to take root.

enramada *f* branches *pl* (conjunto de ramas) || bower, arbour [US arbor] (cobertizo) || decoration *o* garland made of branches (adorno).

enramado *m* MAR frames *pl.*

enramar *vt* to decorate with branches (adornar) || to put an arbour over (para sombra) || MAR to fit the frames to [a ship].

◆ *vi* to put out branches (un árbol).

enrarecer* *vt* to rarefy (aire, etc.) || to make scarce (hacer escaso).

◆ *vi/vpr* to rarefy (el aire) || to become scarce (escasear).

enrarecido, da *adj* rarefied.

enrarecimiento *m* rarefaction || scarcity (escasez).

enrasar *vt* to make flush *o* level; *enrasar una cosa con otra* to make a thing flush with another || to smooth (allanar) || to level up (un líquido).

◆ *vi* to be at the same level.

enrase *m* levelling [US leveling].

enredadera *adj f* climbing; *planta enredadera* climbing plant.

◆ *f* BOT bindweed || BOT *enredadera de campanillas* convolvulus.

enredador, ra *adj* mischievous; *un niño enredador* a mischievous child || troublemaking (que causa riñas) || gossipy (chismoso) || *es una mujer enredadora* she is a busybody (que se entromete).

enredar *vt* to tangle up, to entangle (enmarañar) || FIG to confuse, to complicate; *enredar un asunto* to confuse matters | to involve, to implicate, to mix up; *enredar a una persona en un negocio peligroso* to mix a person up in a dangerous business | to cause trouble, to sow discord; *enredar a dos personas* to cause trouble between two people; *enredó a su familia* he sowed discord in his family || to net, to catch in a net (coger con una red).

◆ *vi* to get into mischief, to play about; *este niño siempre está enredando en clase* this child is always getting into mischief at school | to mess about, to play about (desordenar); *no enredes con esos papeles* do not mess about with those papers.

◆ *vpr* to get into a tangle, to get entangled *o* tangled up (enmarañarse) || to catch on (engancharse) || FIG to become muddled *o* confused *o* complicated (un asunto) | to get involved *o* implicated *o* mixed up (en un mal negocio) || FAM to get involved, to have an affair (amancebarse).

enredijo *m* FAM tangle (enredo).

enredista *adj* AMER ⟶ **enredador.**

enredo *m* tangle (maraña); *un enredo de alambres* a tangle of wires || FIG muddle, confusion, complication (confusión) | mess, mix-up, muddle (situación inextricable); *¡qué enredo!* what a mix-up! | shady business (asunto poco claro); *no se meta en aquel enredo* do not get mixed up in that shady business | mischief (travesura) | deceit (engaño) | plot (de un libro) | affair, love affair (amancebamiento) || intrigue; *comedia de enredo* comedy of intrigue.

◆ *pl* stuff *sing,* things (trastos) || mischievous stories (mentiras).

enredoso, sa *adj* complicated, involved (complicado) || FIG mischievous (niño) | troublemaking (que provoca desavenencias).

enrejado *m* railings *pl* (rejas) || bars *pl* (de una jaula, una celda) || wire netting (alambrada) || trellis (de un jardín) || lattice, trellis (de ventana) || openwork (bordado) || grating, grille (para la ventilación).

enrejar *vt* to surround with railings, to rail off (cerrar con rejas) || to put bars on (una ventana) || to put wire netting on (con alambrada) || to fix a grating to (para la ventilación) || AGR to fit the share to (the plough) | to wound the feet of [with a ploughshare].

enrevesado, da *adj* intricate, complicated; *un nudo enrevesado* an intricate knot || difficult, complicated; *este crucigrama es muy enrevesado* this crossword is very difficult.

enriado; enriamiento *m* retting.

enriar *vt* to ret (el lino, el cáñamo).

enrielar *vt* to make into ingots (un metal) || to pour into an ingot mould (echar en la rielera) || AMER to put on the rails (encarrilar) | FIG to put on the right track (un negocio).

enripiar *vt* to fill with rubble.

Enrique *npr m* Henry.

enriquecer* *vt* to enrich, to make rich || FIG to enrich; *enriquecer la tierra* to enrich the land | to embellish (una cosa).

◆ *vi/vpr* to get rich || *enriquecerse a costa ajena* to get rich at other people's expense.

enriquecimiento *m* enrichment.

enriscar *vt* FIG to raise, to lift.

◆ *vpr* to take refuge *o* to hide among the rocks.

enristrar *vt* to string, to make a string of (ensartar) || to couch (la lanza).

enristre *m* couching (de la lanza).

enrocar *vt* to castle (en el ajedrez).

enrodrigar; enrodrigonar *vt* AGR to stake, to prop up.

enrojecer* *vt* to turn red, to redden (poner rojo) || FIG to turn red, to flush; *la cólera enrojecía su rostro* anger turned his face red || to head red-hot (el hierro).

◆ *vi/vpr* to turn red, to redden (ponerse rojo) || to turn red, to blush (persona) || to become red-hot (el hierro).

enrojecimiento *m* reddening, glowing (del metal) || blush (del rostro).

enrolamiento *m* signing-up, enrolment [US enrollment] (reclutamiento) || MIL enlistment.

enrolar *vt* to sign up, to enrol, to enroll (reclutar) || MIL to enlist.

enrollable *adj* roll-up.

enrollamiento *m* rolling up (de papel) || winding (del hilo) || coiling (de cables).

enrollar *vt* to roll up (papel) || to wind (hilo) || to coil (cables) || to wrap up (una persona en algo) || to cobble (empedrar).

◆ *vpr* to be wound, to be rolled (*en,* round) || to wrap o.s. (una persona) || FAM *enrollarse con uno* to get off with s.o..

enronquecer* *vt* to make hoarse *o* husky; *el frío le enronqueció* the cold made him hoarse.

◆ *vi/vpr* to go hoarse; *se ha enronquecido con tanto hablar* he has gone hoarse from talking so much.

enronquecido, da *adj* hoarse, husky.

enronquecimiento *m* hoarseness, huskiness.

enroque *m* castling (ajedrez).

enroscadura *f*; **enroscamiento** *m* coiling.

enroscar *vt* to coil, to wind (*en* round) (arrollar) || to screw in (atornillar).
◆ *vpr* to wind o.s., to coil o.s. (*en* round) (una serpiente, etc.).

enrostrar *vt* AMER to reproach (echar en cara).

enrular *vt* AMER to curl.

ensabanar *vt* to cover with a sheet.

ensacado *m* sacking, bagging, putting into sacks.

ensacador, ra *m/f* sacker, bagger.
◆ *f* sacking *o* bagging machine (máquina).

ensacar *vt* to sack, to put into sacks, to bag.

ensaimada *f* spiral pastry.

ensalada *f* salad || FIG mess, mix-up, muddle (lío); *armar una ensalada* to make a mess || MÚS medley, potpourri || — *ensalada de fruta* fruit salad || *ensalada rusa* Russian salad.

ensaladera *f* salad bowl.

ensaladilla *f* diced vegetable salad || FIG mess, mix-up, muddle (lío) || *ensaladilla rusa* Russian salad.

ensalivar *vt* to moisten with saliva.

ensalmador, ra *m/f* quack (curandero) || bonesetter (de los huesos).

ensalmar *vt* to set (los huesos) || to cure, to heal (un curandero).

ensalmo *m* quack remedy (de curandero) || incantation (conjuro) || *como por ensalmo* as if by magic.

ensalzamiento *m* exaltation (engrandecimiento) || praise exaltation (elogio).

ensalzar *vt* to exalt (enaltecer) || to praise, to exalt, to extol (alabar).
◆ *vpr* to boast.

ensamblado *m* joint.

ensamblador *m* joiner || INFORM assembler, linker.

ensambladura *f*; **ensamblaje** *m*; **ensamble** *m* joining (acción) || joint; *ensambladura de cola de milano* dovetail joint.

ensamblar *vt* to join || INFORM to assemble (un programa) | to link (módulos, etc.).

ensamble *m* → **ensambladura.**

ensanchador, ra *adj* widening.
◆ *m* glove stretcher.

ensanchamiento *m* widening, broadening || expansion, enlargement (de una ciudad).

ensanchar *vt* to widen, to broaden; *ensanchar una carretera* to widen a road || to enlarge, to expand; *ensanchar una ciudad* to enlarge a city || to widen, to make bigger; *ensanchar una abertura* to make an opening bigger || to stretch (la tela) || to let out (una prenda) || FIG to gladden, to cheer (alegrar).
◆ *vpr* to get wider || FIG to become conceited (envanecerse) || to stretch (dar de sí).

ensanche *m* widening, broadening; *ensanche de la acera* widening of the pavement || enlargement, expansion; *ensanche de una ciudad* enlargement of a city || new district, area of expansion, new development area, extension (barrio nuevo) || widening, extension, enlargement (de un edificio) || tuck (costura).

ensangrentado, da *adj* bloodstained.

ensangrentar* *vt* to stain with blood (manchar) || FIG to steep *o* to bathe in blood, to cause great bloodshed in; *la guerra ensangrentó el país* the war caused great bloodshed in the country.
◆ *vpr* to get stained with blood (mancharse) || FIG to fly into a temper (enfurecerse) || FIG *ensangrentarse con* or *contra* to treat brutally, to be merciless with.

ensañamiento *m* mercilessness, cruelty, brutality || rage fury (cólera).

ensañar *vt* to infuriate, to enrage.
◆ *vpr* to be merciless, to treat brutally; *ensañarse con su víctima* to be merciless with one's victim, to treat one's victim brutally.

ensartar *vt* to thread, to string; *ensartar perlas* to string pearls || to thread; *ensartar una aguja* to thread a needle || to run through (atravesar) || FIG to reel off, to rattle off; *ensartar una serie de disparates* to reel off a string of nonsense.

ensayador *m* assayer (de metales).

ensayar *vt* to test, to try out; *ensayar un prototipo* to test a prototype || to assay (metales) || to rehearse (un espectáculo) || to try out, to try; *ensayar un nuevo sistema* to try out a new system || to trait (un animal).
◆ *vi* TEATR to rehearse.
◆ *vpr* to practise [US to practice], to rehearse; *ensayarse a* or *para cantar* to practise singing.

ensaye *m* assay (de metales).

ensayista *m* essayist (autor de ensayos).

ensayo *m* test, testing, trial; *el ensayo de una máquina* the trial of a machine || trial; *ensayo de un nuevo método* trial of a new method || test; *vuelo de ensayo* test flight || essay (obra literaria) || try (rugby) || assay (de metales) || QUÍM test; *tubo de ensayo* test tube || FIG attempt (intento) || TEATR rehearsal; *ensayo general* dress rehearsal || *a modo de ensayo* as an experiment.

ensebar *vt* to grease.

enseguida; en seguida *adv* at once, immediately, straight away [US right away].

ensenada *f* GEOGR inlet, cove || AMER enclosure.

enseña *f* standard, emblem, ensign.

enseñado, da *adj bien, mal enseñado* well-bred, ill-bred || *perro enseñado* house-trained dog.

enseñanza *f* teaching; *dedicarse a la enseñanza* to devote o.s. to teaching || education; *enseñanza laboral* or *técnica* technical education || training (instrucción) || FIG lesson || — INFORM *enseñanza asistida por ordenador* computer-aided *o* computer-assisted instruction || *enseñanza estatal* or *pública* state education || *enseñanza general básica* general basic education up to school leaving age || *enseñanza privada* private education || *enseñanza superior* higher education || *enseñanza universitaria* university education || *escuela de primera enseñanza* primary school || *primera enseñanza, enseñanza primaria* primary education || *segunda enseñanza, enseñanza media* secondary education.

enseñar *vt* to teach; *enseñar a uno a hablar* to teach s.o. to speak; *enseñar latín en la universidad* to teach Latin in the university || to show (mostrar); *enseñar el camino* to show the way; *me enseñó cómo funcionaba* he showed me how it worked || *enseñar con el dedo* to point at.

enseñoramiento *m* taking over, taking possession.

enseñorearse *vpr* to take over, to take possession; *se enseñoreó de mi casa* he took over my house.

enseres *m pl* equipment *sing*, goods; *enseres domésticos* household equipment || tools (herramientas) || utensils (utensilios).

enseriarse *vpr* AMER to turn *o* to become serious.

ensilado; ensilaje; ensilamiento *m* AGR ensilage.

ensilar *vt* AGR to silo, to ensilage, to ensile, to store in a silo.

ensillado, da *adj* saddled || saddlebacked (caballo).

ensilladura *f* saddling (acción de ensillar) || back (lomo del caballo) || curvature (de la columna vertebral).

ensillar *vt* to saddle (el caballo).

ensimismado, da *adj* deep in thought, pensive (absorto) || *ensimismado en la lectura, en sus pensamientos* lost *o* engrossed *o* absorbed in a book, in his thoughts.

ensimismamiento *m* pensiveness, absorption, deep thought || AMER conceit.

ensimismarse *vpr* to become lost *o* absorbed *o* engrossed (en algo) || to become lost *o* absorbed *o* deep in thought (quedarse abstraído) || AMER to become conceited *o* full of conceit (envanecerse).

ensoberbecer* *vt* to make proud, to make conceited.
◆ *vpr* to become proud, to grow conceited || FIG to become rough (el mar).

ensombrecer* *vt* to darken || FIG to darken; *esta desgracia ensombreció su vida* this misfortune darkened his life | to overshadow (ocultar).
◆ *vpr* to darken (oscurecer) || FIG to turn gloomy (entristecerse).

ensombrerado, da *adj* FAM with a hat on, wearing a hat.

ensopar *vt* to dunk (empapar).

ensordecedor, ra *adj* deafening.

ensordecer* *vt* to deafen; *nos ensordecía con sus gritos* he deafened us with his shouts || to make deaf, to deafen (provocar sordera) || to deafen, to muffle (amortiguar); *ensordecer un sonido* to muffle a sound.
◆ *vi* to turn deaf, to go deaf (quedarse sordo) || FIG to pretend not to hear.

ensordecimiento *m* deafening (acción) || deadening, muffling (de un sonido) || deafness (sordera).

ensortijamiento *m* curling (de los cabellos) || curls *pl* (rizos) || coiling (de hilo).

ensortijar *vt* to curl (los cabellos) || to coil, to wind (enrollar).
◆ *vpr* to curl (los cabellos).

ensuciamiento *m* dirtying, soiling (acción) || dirtiness, dirt (suciedad).

ensuciar *vt* to dirty, to soil; *ensuciar algo con lodo* to dirty sth. with mud || to dirty, to make dirty; *el humo de la fábrica ensucia los cristales* the smoke from the factory dirties the windows || to get dirty, to dirty; *no te ensucies el vestido* don't get your dress dirty || to stain (manchar) || FIG to sully, to tarnish, to besmirch, to stain (el honor, la reputación, etc.).
◆ *vi* FAM to make a mess, to mess (necesidades corporales).
◆ *vpr* to get dirty || FAM to make a mess, to mess (necesidades corporales) || FIG to sully *o* to tarnish *o* to besmirch *o* to stain one's reputation || FIG *ensuciarse por dinero* to accept bribes.

ensueño *m* dream (durante el sueño) || FIG dream; *país de ensueño* dream country | dream, fantasy (ilusión) || *¡ni por ensueño!* never!, not likely!

ensullo *m* TECN beam, roller (de un telar).

entabicar *vt* to partition off.

entablado *m* TECN boarding, planking, planks *pl* (conjunto de tablas) || wooden floor (suelo) || floorboards, *pl* (tablas del suelo).

entabladura *f* boarding, planking, planks, *pl.*

entablamento *m* ARQ entablature.

entablar *vt* to begin, to start (empezar); *intentó entablar conversación* he tried to begin a conversation; *entablaron una discusión* they began a discussion || to begin, to engage (un combate) || to open, to begin, to enter into; *entablar negociaciones* to open negotiations || to start, to begin, to open; *entablar conversaciones* to begin talks || JUR to bring, to file; *entablar un pleito* to file a suit || to establish, to set up; *entablar relaciones* to establish relations || to place, to set out [the pieces] (en juegos) || to board up, to plank (poner tablas) || MED to put in a splint, to splint (entablillar) || *AMER* to train (livestock) to stay in a herd || — *entablar amistad* to become friends || *entablar amistad con* to strike up friendship with, to make friends with.
◆ *vi* *AMER* to draw (empatar) | to boast, to brag (fanfarronear).
◆ *vpr* to begin, to start (empezar) || *AMER* to settle (el viento) | to refuse to turn (el caballo).

entablerarse *vpr* TAUR to stay close to the barrier.

entablillar *vt* MED to put in a splint, to splint || *entablillar un brazo* to put an arm in a splint.

entalegar *vt* to put into a bag (meter en un saco) || FAM to hoard, to save (ahorrar dinero) | to pocket (embolsar).
◆ *vpr* FAM to make (ganar) | to pocket (embolsarse).

entalingadura *f* MAR clinch.

entalingar *vt* MAR to clinch.

entalla *f* notch.

entalladura *f;* **entallamiento** *m* notch (corte) || TECN mortising | mortise, notch (muesca) || sculpture (en mármol) || carving (en madera) || engraving (grabado).

entallamiento *m* ⟶ **entalladura || fitting, tailoring (de un vestido).**

entallar *vt* to notch (hacer un corte) || to tap (un árbol para sacar resina) || TECN to mortise, to mortice || to sculpture (el mármol) || to carve (la madera) || to engrave (grabar) || to tailor, to fit (un vestido).
◆ *vi* to be tailored, to fit; *este vestido entalla bien* this dress is well tailored *o* fits well.

entallecer* *vi* to sprout, to shoot, to grow shoots (las plantas).

entarimado *m* parquet, parquetry || parquet laying (acción) || *entarimado de espinapez* herringbone parquet.

entarimar *vt* to parquet.

entarquinar *vt* AGR to fertilize with silt || to splatter with mud (manchar).

entarugado *m* wooden paving.

entarugar *vt* to pave in wood.

éntasis *f* ARQ entasis (de una columna).

ente *m* being, entity (ser) || firm, company (comercial) || organization, body, institution (organismo) || FAM specimen (persona notable o ridícula) || *ente de razón* imaginary being.

enteco, ca *adj* puny.

entechar *vt* *AMER* to roof.

entejar *vt* *AMER* to roof with tiles, to tile (tejar).

entelequia *f* FIL entelechy.

entena *f* MAR lateen yard.

entendederas *f pl* FAM brains || FAM *ser duro de entendederas* to be slow on the uptake, to be slow.

entendedor, ra *adj* well-up; *es muy entendedor de esas cosas* he is very well-up on those things || intelligent, clever (listo).
◆ *m/f* expert || FIG *al buen entendedor con pocas palabras basta, al buen entendedor pocas palabras bastan* a word to the wise is enough.

entender* *vt* to understand (comprender); *entender un problema* to understand a problem; *no entiendo nada* I don't understand anything; *tengo que confesar que no te entiendo* I must confess that I don't understand you; *ahora entiendo por qué no vino* now I understand why he did not come; *entender el inglés* to understand English; *es difícil entender a los niños* it is difficult to understand children || to believe, to think (creer); *entiendo que sería mejor callarse* I believe it would be better to keep quiet || to mean, to intend, to want (querer); *entiendo que se me obedezca* I mean to be obeyed || to understand, to take it; *¿debo entender que quiere que me marche?* am I to take it that you want me to leave? || to mean; *¿qué entiende usted por esta palabra?* what do you mean by this word? || — *dar a entender* to hint, to insinuate (insinuar), to let it be known (manifestar), to mean (significar) || *entender a medias palabras* to read between the lines || *entender mal* to misunderstand || *hacer como quien lo entiende todo* to act as if one understands, to pretend to understand || *hacerse entender* to make o.s. understood || FAM *no entender ni jota* or *ni pizca* not to understand a thing || *¿qué debo entender por eso?* what is that supposed to mean?
◆ *vi* to understand, to know about; *usted entiende mucho de esto* you understand a lot about this, you know all about this; *entiendo poco de cocina* I know little about cooking || — *a mi, tu, su entender* to my, your, his mind || *entender en* to know about (conocer una materia determinada), to be in charge of, to deal with; *entender en un asunto* to deal with a matter || *ya entiendo* I see now, now I understand.
◆ *vpr* to make o.s. understood; *entenderse por señas* to make o.s. understood by signs || to be understood (comprenderse); *se entiende que será así* it is understood that it will be like that || to be meant (significar) || to understand each other (dos personas) || to agree, to come to an agreement (ponerse de acuerdo); *entenderse con sus socios* to agree with one's associates || to get on *o* along (llevarse bien); *no se entiende con su hermano* he does not get on with his brother || to get in touch (ponerse en relación); *te entenderás con él para este trabajo* you will get in touch with him about this work || to have an affair (relación amorosa) || — *allá se las entienda* let him work it out for himself || *yo me entiendo* I know what I am saying (lo que digo), doing (lo que hago).

entendido, da *adj* understood (comprendido) || agreed (de acuerdo) || well up, well informed; *es entendido en coches* he is well up on *o* he is well informed about cars || well up; *es muy entendido en matemáticas* he is very well up in mathematics || clever, skilled (hábil) || clever, intelligent (inteligente) || — *bien entendido que...* on the understanding that... || *no darse por entendido* to pretend not to have heard *o* understood, to turn a deaf ear || *según tenemos entendido* as far as we know || *tenemos entendido que...* we understand that..., we gather that...
◆ *m/f* expert, authority, connoisseur (enterado); *según los entendidos* according to the experts.
◆ *interj* all right!, agreed!, right!, O. K.! (de acuerdo), understood! (comprendido).

entendimiento *m* understanding (comprensión) || judgement, understanding, sense (juicio) || intelligence, understanding (inteligencia) || mind (mente) || — *ser corto de entendimiento, tener el entendimiento limitado* to be slow to understand, to be slow || *un hombre de entendimiento* a wise *o* judicious man.

entenebrecer* *vt* to darken.
◆ *vpr* to darken, to get dark (oscurecerse) || FIG to darken.

entente *f* entente; *entente cordial* entente cordiale.

enterado, da *adj* aware (que sabe) || well up, well informed; *enterado de asuntos comerciales* well up on *o* well informed about commercial matters || knowledgeable; *un profesor muy enterado* a very knowledgeable teacher || *AMER* haughty, arrogant (orgulloso) || — *darse por enterado de algo* to be well aware of sth. || *dese por enterado* don't make me tell you again || *estar enterado de una noticia* to be aware of *o* to know about *o* to have been informed about a piece of news || *no darse por enterado* to pretend not to have heard *o* understood, to turn a deaf ear.
◆ *m/f* expert, authority, connoisseur || FAM know-all [*US* know-it-all] (sabelotodo).

enteralgia *f* MED enteralgia.

enteramente *adv* completely, entirely, fully.

enterar *vt* to inform || *AMER* to pay (pagar) | to complete (completar).
◆ *vpr* to find out, to get to know; *enterarse de lo que ha pasado* to find out what has happened || to learn, to hear, to become aware; *me enteré de la muerte de tu tío* I heard about your uncle's death || to realize, to be aware (darse cuenta); *pasaba las páginas sin enterarme de lo que leía* I turned the pages without realizing what I was reading || to pay attention, to take note (prestar atención); *entérate de lo que te digo* take note of what I am telling you || FAM *¿te enteras?* have you got it?, do you understand?

entercarse *vpr* to persist, to insist.

entereza *f* integrity, uprightness (integridad) || FIG firmness (firmeza) | strength; *entereza de carácter* strength of character | force, energy (energía) | strictness (observancia perfecta).

enteritis *f* MED enteritis.

enternecedor, ra *adj* touching, moving.

enternecer* *vt* to soften (ablandar) || to make tender (la carne) || FIG to touch, to move (conmover).
◆ *vpr* FIG to be moved *o* touched (conmoverse) | to relent (ceder).

enternecidamente *adv* tenderly.

enternecimiento *m* tenderness (cariño) || pity (compasión).

entero, ra *adj* whole, in one piece (no roto) || entire, whole, complete; *leerse el libro entero* to read the whole book || full, whole; *un saco entero de naranjas* a whole sack of oranges || whole, entire; *viajar por el mundo entero* to travel the whole world over || complete; *a mi entera satisfacción* to my complete satisfaction || FIG firm (firme) | strong; *carácter entero* strong character | fair, just (justo) | upright (honrado) | robust, strong (fuerte) || strong, thick (telas) || entire, uncastrated (no castrado) || pure, virginal (virgen) || MAT whole (número) || *AMER* FAM identical (parecido) || — *darse por entero a* to give o.s. up to, to devote o.s. entirely to || *por entero* entirely, completely.
◆ *m* point (Bolsa); *estas acciones han perdido muchos enteros* these shares have lost many points || MAT whole number, integer (número) || *AMER* payment (remesa de dinero) | balance (saldo).

enterrador *m* gravedigger || ZOOL burying beetle.

enterramiento *m* burial, interment (entierro) || grave (tumba) || burying, burial (de una cosa).

enterrar* *vt* to bury, to inter (una persona) || to bury; *enterrar un tesoro* to bury a treasure || FIG to bury, to abandon, to give up, to forget (olvidar); *enterrar sus ilusiones* to give up one's dreams | to outlive, to bury (sobrevivir a); *nos enterrará a todos* he will outlive us all | to drive in, to sink (clavar).
◆ *vpr* FIG to bury o.s., to hide away; *enterrarse en un convento* to bury o.s. in a convent.

entesar* *vt* to tighten, to stretch (poner tieso) || to strengthen (reforzar).

entibación *f*; **entibado** *m* MIN timbering, shoring || timbering (de pozos).

entibador *m* timberman.

entibar *vt* MIN to timber, to shore || to timber (un pozo).

entibiar *vt* to make lukewarm (poner tibio) || FIG to cool down, to moderate, to temper (las pasiones).
◆ *vpr* to become lukewarm (un líquido) || FIG to cool down.

entibo *m* ARQ & MIN prop, shore || buttress (de una bóveda).

entidad *f* society, firm, concern; *entidad privada* private concern || company; *entidad de seguros* insurance company || organization, body (organización) || FIG significance, importance; *un asunto de poca entidad* a matter of little significance || FIL entity.

entierro *m* burial, interment (acción) || funeral (ceremonia); *asistí al entierro* I went to the funeral || grave (sepulcro) || FAM buried treasure || — FIG *¿quién te dio vela en este entierro?* who asked you to poke your nose in? | *ser más triste que un entierro de tercera* to be like death warmed-up (una persona), to be like (being at) a funeral (fiesta).

entintado *m* IMPR inking.

entintador, ra *adj* IMPR inking; *rodillo entintador* inking roller.

entintar *vt* IMPR to ink (aplicar tinta) || to stain with ink (manchar) || FIG to dye (teñir).

entoldado *m* awnings *pl.*

entoldamiento *m* covering with an awning.

entoldar *vt* to put an awning over; *entoldar una calle* to put an awning over a street.
◆ *vpr* to become overcast, to cloud over (el cielo).

entomófago, ga *adj* ZOOL entomophagous.

entomofilia *f* entomophily.

entomología *f* entomology.

entomológico, ca *adj* entomological, entomologic.

entomólogo *m* entomologist.

entonación *f* intonation (música, fonética) || FIG arrogance, haughtiness, presumption, conceit.

entonado, da *adj* arrogant, haughty, presumptuous, conceited (presumido) || in tune; *tiene la voz entonada* his voice is in tune || FIG on form (en forma) | brisk (Bolsa).

entonador *m* MÚS organ blower.

entonar *vt* MÚS to intone (cantar); *entonar un salmo* to intone a psalm | to work the bellows of (el órgano) | to give, to pitch (una nota) || FIG to put right, to tone up; *este ponche me ha entonado* this punch has put me right | to brighten up (alegrar) | to sound (alabanzas) | to match (colores) || FIG *entonar el yo pecador* to confess one's sins.
◆ *vi* MÚS to intone | to sing in tune || FIG to match, to be in tune; *este azul no entona con el rojo* this blue does not match the red | to be in tune, to harmonize (armonizar) | to put one right, to tone one up (animar).
◆ *vpr* to be arrogant *o* conceited (engreírse) || to recover (fortalecerse) || FIG to tone o.s. up.

entonces *adv* then; *llamó a la puerta y entonces entró* he knocked at the door and then he came in || at that time, then (en aquel tiempo) || so, then (en ese caso) || — *desde entonces* since then || *el entonces presidente* the then president || *en* or *por aquel entonces* at that time, then || *¿entonces?* so? || *entonces fue cuando entró* it was then that he came in || *hasta entonces* till *o* until then || *la gente de entonces* people of that time.

entonelado; entonelamiento *m* casking (en un barril), barrelling (en un tonel).

entonelar *vt* to cask (en un barril), to barrel (en un tonel).

entono *m* presumption, arrogance, conceit, haughtiness (engreimiento) || MÚS intonation.

entontecer* *vt* → **atontar.**

entontecimiento *m* → **atontamiento.**

entorchado *m* braid (para bordar) || MIL braid, braiding || FIG title (título); *consiguió el entorchado de internacional a los 25 años* he got the international title when he was twenty-five || MÚS bass string.

entorchar *vt* to twist (un hilo) || to braid (galones) || *columna entorchada* wreathed column.

entornado, da *adj* half-closed.

entornar *vt* to half-close, to leave ajar (puerta, ventana) || to half-close (ojos).
◆ *vpr* to half-close.

entorno *m* environment, surroundings *pl* || INFORM environment.

entorpecedor, ra *adj* numbing (que embota) || FIG hindering, hindersome (que molesta) | dulling, deadening, numbing (que adormece).

entorpecer* *vt* to numb; *el frío entorpece las manos* the cold numbs one's hands || FIG to hinder, to obstruct (estorbar) | to delay (retrasar) | to dull, to deaden, to numb (la imaginación, etc.).
◆ *vpr* to grow numb (los miembros) || FIG to be dulled *o* deadened *o* numbed || to be delayed || to get stuck (un mecanismo).

entorpecimiento *m* numbness (estado), numbing (acción) (de un miembro) || FIG dullness, numbness (estado), dulling, deadening, numbing (acción) (del entendimiento, etc.) | hindering, obstructing (acción), hinderance, obstruction (estado) (estorbo) | delay (retraso) || sticking (de un mecanismo).

entozoario *m* ZOOL entozoan.

entrada *f* entry, entrance; *entrada triunfal* triumphal entry || entrance, entry; *entrada principal* main entrance; *entrada a la ciudad* entry to the city || hall (vestíbulo) || entry, admittance; *se prohíbe la entrada al almacén* no entry into the store, no admittance into the store || way in, entrance (de parque) || entrance (de un cine, teatro, museo, etc.) || beginning; *la entrada del invierno* the beginning of winter || entrée (en una comida) || beginning (de una carrera, un libro, un discurso, etc.) || entrance (examen de ingreso) || admission (en una academia, un club, etc.) || entrance (salida a escena) || cue (de un actor de teatro) || influx (de turistas, etc.) || audience, house; *anoche hubo una gran entrada en el teatro* last night there was a large audience at the theater || crowd, spectators *pl* (público de un encuentro deportivo) || takings *pl*, receipts *pl* (lo recaudado en un espectáculo) || gate (lo recaudado en un partido de fútbol, etc.) || admission; *¿cuánto cuesta la entrada en este museo?* how much is the admission to this museum?; *derecho de entrada* right of admission; *entrada gratis* admission free || ticket; *fui a sacar las entradas gratis* admission free || ticket; *fui a sacar las entradas del cine* I went to get the tickets for the cinema; *entrada de favor* complimentary ticket || COM incomings *pl*; *las entradas y las salidas* incomings and outgoings | receipts *pl*; *entrada bruta* gross receipts | earnings *pl* (ingresos) || incoming (de cables del teléfono) || down payment; *al comprar este piso tuvo que pagar una entrada de doscientas libras* when I bought this flat I had to make a down payment of 200 pounds; *sin entrada* no down payment || inning (en béisbol) || tackle (en fútbol) || TECN intake, inlet (de aire) || INFORM entry, input || MIL invasion || admission, acceptance (de una palabra en un diccionario) || entry (artículo tratado en un diccionario) || — *dar entrada a* to lead into (conducir), to admit (admitir) || *de entrada* straight away, right away, from the outset || *de primera entrada* at first sight || INFORM *entrada de datos* data entry *o* input || *entrada en materia* introduction || *entrada general* standing room || *entrada prohibida* no admittance, no entry || INFORM *entrada vocal* voice input || *hacer su entrada* to make one's entry || *media entrada* half-price ticket (precio), half-capacity crowd (público) || *puerta de entrada* front door (de una casa), main door (de un edificio grande) || *se prohíbe la entrada* no admittance, no entry || FIG *tener entrada en una casa* to be always welcome in a house || *tiene entradas en la frente* his hair is receding.

entramado *m* lattice, trellis (de un tabique) || half-timbering, wooden framework (de un muro) || framework (de un puente).

entramar *vt* to make a lattice *o* a framework for.

entrambos, bas *adj/pron ind pl* both; *lo hicieron entrambos hermanos* both brothers did it; *entrambos vinieron* they both came || FIG *lo mío, mío, y lo tuyo de entrambos* what's yours is mine and what's mine is my own.

entrampar *vt* to trap, to snare (un animal) || FIG to trap, to catch out (engañar) | to muddle, to mess up (un negocio) || *estar entrampado* to be up to one's eyes in debt.
◆ *vpr* to fall into a trap || to fall *o* to get into debt (contraer deudas).

entrante *adj* incoming, entering (que entra) || coming, next; *el año entrante* the coming year, next year || incoming; *el presidente entrante* the incoming president || — MAT *ángulo entrante* re-entering *o* re-entrant angle || *guardia entrante* new *a* relieving *o* relief guard.
◆ *m/f* person who is entering, incomer, ingoer; *los entrantes y los salientes* the incomers and out-goers.
◆ *m* ARQ recess || inlet (ensenada).

entraña *f* ANAT entrails *pl*, bowels *pl* || FIG core, root (lo esencial).
◆ *pl* ANAT entrails, bowels || FIG bowels; *las entrañas de la Tierra* the bowels of the earth | feelings, heart *sing* (ternura); *no tener entrañas* to have no feelings | nature *sing* (índole) || — FIG & FAM *arrancársele a uno las entrañas* to break s.o.'s heart | *de malas entrañas* callous | *echar las entrañas* to spew, to puke, to be as sick as a dog (vomitar), to put all one has into it, to give it everything one has got (echar el resto) | *¡entrañas mías!*; *¡hijo de mis entrañas!* my little love! | *sacar las entrañas* to disembowel, to rip open | *ser de buenas entrañas* to be big-hearted.

entrañable *adj* dear; *amigo entrañable* dear friend || dearly loved, beloved; *Soria, lugar entrañable de Castilla* Soria, a dearly loved spot in Castile || deep, dear; *los más entrañables deseos* the deepest wishes.

entrañablemente *adv* deeply, dearly.

entrañar *vt* to involve (implicar) || to entail (acarrear) || to contain, to carry within (contener) || to bury deep (introducir).
◆ *vpr* to penetrate, to go deeply (penetrar) || FIG to become very fond *o* very attached (*con* to).

entrar *vi* to enter, to go in, to come in (véase OBSERV); *entrar por la puerta* to enter through the door, to go in through the door; *¡entre!* come in!; *entró llorando* he came in crying || to enter, to go, to come (*en* into) (véase OBSERV); *entramos en un bar* we went into a bar; *entramos en un periodo de crisis* we are entering a period of crisis; *entró sonriendo en la habitación* he came into the room smiling || to go in, to enter; *el estoque entró hasta la empuñadura* the sword went in up to the hilt || to fit, to go (caber, encajar); *este abrigo no entra en la maleta* this coat doesn't fit in the suitcase; *el anillo no le entra en el dedo* the ring doesn't fit on his finger; *esta pieza no entra en la otra* this piece doesn't fit in the other || to get, to fit; *no entro en su coche* I can't get in his car, I don't fit in his car || to fit; *esta sortija no me entra* this ring doesn't fit me (véase OBSERV) || to begin, to start; *ya ha entrado el invierno* winter has begun || to join; *entrar en el ejército, en el club* to join the army, a club || to take up; *entrar en una profesión* to take up a profession || to open, to begin; *la carta entra diciendo* the letter opens saying; *el libro entra tratando de* the book begins by dealing with || to take part (in) (participar) || FIG to get (into), to enter [into]; *entrar en malas costumbres* to get into bad habits || to enter, to come; *esto no entra en mis atribuciones* this does not enter into my duties; *esto no entra en mis planes* this does not enter into my plans | to come over; *le entró calentura, frío, sueño, miedo* fever, cold, sleep, fear came over him | to reach; *entrar en los sesenta* to reach sixty | to go; *en la paella entran arroz y carne* rice and meat go into paella || to flow into, to join (ríos) || AUT to engage; *no entra la tercera* third gear will not engage || MÚS to enter, to come in || TAUR to charge; *el toro no entra* the bull will not charge || to invade (invadir) || to be the bidder (en los juegos de cartas) || — *el año que entra* next year, the coming year | *entrado en años* elderly || *entrar en escena* to go off (stage) || *entrar a servir con uno* to start working for s.o., to enter s.o.'s service || FIG *entrar bien* to be appropriate (ser oportuno) | *entrar como un torbellino* to burst in | *entrar con buen pie* to start off on the right foot *o* footing || MIL *entrar de guardia* to come on watch || *entrar en años* to be getting on in years || MIL *entrar en campaña* to take the field, to begin a campaign || *entrar en contacto con uno* to get in touch with s.o., to contact s.o. || *entrar en cólera* to get angry || *entrar en conversaciones* to start *o* to begin talks || *entrar en detalles* to go into details || *entrar en el marco de* to be within the framework of || *entrar en las miras de* to have in view *o* in mind; *este proyecto entra en sus miras* he has this plan in view *o* in mind || *entrar en materia* to give an introduction || MIL *entrar en posición* to be brought into position (cañones) || *entrar en religión* to enter a religious order || *entrar en servicio* to go into service || FAM *entrar por los ojos a uno* to catch s.o.'s eye || *hacer entrar a uno en el despacho* to show s.o. into the office || *hacer entrar en razón a alguien* to make s.o. see sense || *hasta muy entrada la noche* until late at night || FAM *le entra la prisa (por hacer algo)* he gets the urge (to do sth.) | *me entra bien esa chica* I think that girl is nice, I quite like that girl || *me entran ganas de...* I feel like... || FAM *no entro ni salgo* I want nothing to do with it | *no me entra ese tío* I can't stand *o* I can't bear that bloke | *no me entra la comida* I can't eat | *no me entra la geometría* I can't get the hang of geometry | *por un oído me entra y por otro me sale* it goes in one ear and out of the other || *una vez bien entrado el mes de mayo* once we are well into May.
◆ *vt* to put; *entrar el coche en el garaje* to put the car in the garage || to bring in, to take in (véase OBSERV); *entrar el carbón para la calefacción* to bring coal in for the heating || to show in, to bring in (introducir a uno) || to smuggle (de contrabando) || to invade, to attack (invadir) || to take in (en costura) || MAR to overtake.
◆ *vpr* to get in (con una idea de esfuerzo).
— OBSERV El verbo *entrar* se traduce por *to go in, to take in* o *to come in, to bring in* según que la persona que habla se encuentre fuera o dentro del lugar considerado.
— OBSERV Cuando *entrar* significa *caber* se suele emplear el verbo auxiliar *will* antes de la traducción del verbo: *este abrigo no entra en la maleta* this coat will not fit in the suitcase.

entre *prep* between; *vacilar entre dos partidos* to hesitate between two parties; *llegaron entre las dos y las tres* they arrived between two and three || among, amongst; *entre mis amigos* amongst my friends; *entre (los) romanos* amongst the Romans || among, amongst, in the midst of; *entre la muchedumbre* amongst the crowd, in the midst of the crowd || in; *lo cogió entre sus manos* he took it in his hands; *entre paréntesis* in brackets || in; *tuvo que conducir entre la niebla* he had to drive in the fog || half... half; *entre dulce y amargo* half sweet half bitter; *una mirada entre cariñosa y hostil* a half affectionate half hostile look || — *de entre* out of, from among || *dividir algo entre dos personas, entre cuatro personas* to divide sth. between two people, between *o* amongst four people || *entre gris y negro* midway between grey and black, of some colour between grey and black || *entre el ruido y el frío no he dormido* what with the noise and the cold I haven't slept || *entre ellos se quieren mucho* they love each other a great deal || *entre esto y lo otro* what with one thing and another || *entre jóvenes y viejos serán unos veinte* counting the young people and the old people there will be about twenty || *entre los cuatro hicieron el trabajo* the four of them did the work together, they did the work between the four of them || *entre nosotros, dicho sea entre nosotros, entre tú y yo* between ourselves, between the two of us, between you and me || *entre otras cosas* amongst other things; namely (en particular) || *entre que* while, whilst || *entre tanto* in the meanwhile, meanwhile, in the meantime || *entre todos había 50 personas* there were 50 people in all || *entre unas cosas y otras* what with one thing and another || *estar entre la vida y la muerte* to be at death's door || *pensar entre sí* to think to o.s. || *por entre* amongst, among; through (a través de).

entreabierto, ta *adj* half-open || half-open, ajar (puerta, ventana).

entreabrir *vt* to half-open; *entreabrir los ojos* to half-open one's eyes || to half-open, to leave ajar (puerta).
◆ *vpr* to half-open, to be ajar.

entreacto *m* interval, entr'acte (intermedio).

entreayudarse *vpr* to help one another.

entrebarrera *f* TAUR passageway [for spectators].

entrecalle *f* ARQ quirk.

entrecanal *m* ARQ fillet (de columna).

entrecano, na *adj* greying; *pelo entrecano* greying hair || with greying hair, who is going grey (persona).

entrecejo *m* space between the eyebrows || — *fruncir* or *arrugar el entrecejo* to frown || *mirar a uno con entrecejo* to frown at s.o., to give s.o. a frown.

entrecerrar* *vt* AMER to half-close (entornar).

entreclaro, ra *adj* fairly light, fairly clear.

entrecomillar *vt* to put in inverted commas *o* in quotation marks.

entrecoro *m* chancel (de una iglesia).

entrecortado, da *adj* faltering, broken; *voz entrecortada* faltering voice || laboured, difficult; *respiración entrecortada* laboured breathing.

entrecortar *vt* to make a partial cut in, to cut partially || FIG to cut off, to interrupt; *los sollozos entrecortaban su discurso* his sobs interrupted his speech | to cause to falter (la voz).

entrecote *m* sirloin.

entrecruzamiento *m* interlacing, intertwining || intersection (de carreteras).

entrecruzar *vt* to interlace, to intertwine.
◆ *vpr* to intersect (carreteras).

entrecubierta *f* MAR between decks.

entredicho, cha *adj* interdicted, under interdict.
◆ *m* pr[illegible] oition || REL interdict (censura eclesiástica); *poner en entredicho a alguien* to lay s.o. under an interdict || — FIG *estar en entredicho* to be in question | *poner algo en entredicho* to question sth.

entredós *m* insertion (en costura) || dresser (mueble).

entrefilete *m* short article, paragraph (en un periódico).

entrefino, na *adj* medium quality.

entrega *f* handing over; *la entrega de las llaves* the handing over of the keys || delivery (de géneros, compras, periódico); *entrega contra reembolso* cash on delivery || fascicle, instalment (fascículo) || devotion; *entrega a una causa* devotion to a cause || surrender (rendición) || pass (en fútbol) || ARQ end of beam [embedded in wall] || — *entrega a domicilio* home delivery || *entrega de los premios* presentation of the prizes (a los galardonados), prizegiving (ceremonia) || *hacer entrega de* to hand over (dar), to deliver (cartas, paquetes, etc.), to present (premios) || *novela por entregas* serialized novel, novel by instalments.

entregar *vt* to deliver; *entregar un pedido* to deliver an order || to give (dar); *me entregó esta carta* he gave me this letter || to hand over; *entregar los poderes* to hand over the powers; *le entregó la carta en propia mano* he handed the letter over to him personally || to surrender (rendir) || to betray (por traición); *entregar una ciudad* to betray a city || to hand in, to give in [US to turn in]; *entregar al profesor los ejercicios* to hand in one's exercises to the teacher || FIG to surrender, to give over; *entregar a alguien a su suerte* to surrender s.o. to his fate || — *entregar a la voluntad de* to leave at the mercy of || *entregar el alma* to pass away, to breathe one's last, to give up the ghost || *para entregar* care of (carta); *señor Taylor para entregar a la señora Rodríguez* Mrs. Rodríguez, care of Mr. Taylor.
◆ *vpr* to surrender, to give o.s. up (rendirse) || FIG to devote o.s.; *entregarse al estudio* to devote o.s. to studying | to give o.s. over *o* up; *entregarse a la bebida* to give o.s. over to drink | to sink into; *entregarse al sueño* to sink into sleep | to give in, to give up (ceder) | to confide in people (confiarse) || *entregarse al lujo* to indulge in luxury.

entrehierro *m* ELECTR air gap.

entrejuntar *vt* to assemble.

entrelargo, ga *adj* medium length.

entrelazamiento *m* intertwining, interlacing.

entrelazar *vt* to intertwine, to interlace.

entrelínea *f* interlineation (añadido).

entrelinear *vt* to interline.

entrelistado, da *adj* striped, with coloured stripes.

entremedias *adv* in between, halfway (en medio) || in the meanwhile, meantime, meanwhile (mientras tanto) || *entremedias de* between.

entremés *m* CULIN hors d'oeuvre || TEATR interlude, short comedy.

entremeter; entrometer *vt* to mix (mezclar) || to insert, to put between (poner entre).
◆ *vpr* to interfere, to meddle; *no te entremetas en eso* do not interfere in that || to butt in (en una conversación).

entremetido, da; entrometido, da *adj* interfering, meddlesome; *una persona entremetida* an interfering person.
◆ *m/f* busybody, meddler, interferer.

entremetimiento; entrometimiento *m* interfering, meddling.

entremezclar *vt* to intermingle, to mix.

entrenador, ra *m/f* DEP trainer, coach.
◆ *m* AVIAC simulator.

entrenamiento *m* DEP training, coaching.

entrenar *vt* DEP to train, to coach || *estar entrenado* to be fit, to be in training.
◆ *vpr* to train.

entreoír* *vt* to hear vaguely, to half-hear.

entrepaño *m* ARQ bay (entre columnas o huecos) || panel (de puerta) || shelf (estante).

entrepierna *f* crotch, crutch, fork.
◆ *pl* crotch *sing*, crutch *sing*, fork *sing* (de cuerpo, pantalón).

entrepiso *m* MIN space between galleries || AMER mezzanine, entresol (entresuelo).

entrepuente *m* MAR between decks.

entrerrenglonadura *f* interlineation, writing between the lines.

entrerrenglonar *vt* to interline (escribir entre dos renglones).

entrerriano, na *adj* AMER of *o* from Entre Ríos [province of Argentina].
◆ *m/f* native *o* inhabitant of Entre Ríos.

entrerriel *m* gauge.

entresacar *vt* to pick out, to select (escoger) || to prune (un árbol) || to thin (el pelo, un bosque) || to thin out (plantas).

entresijo *m* ANAT mesentery (mesenterio) || FIG secret, mystery (misterio) || difficulty, snag (dificultad) || — FIG *conocer todos los entresijos* to know all the ins and outs | *tener muchos entresijos* to be very complicated, to be full of complications (una cosa), to be mysterious (una persona).

entresuelo *m* mezzanine, entresol [floor between first floor and ground floor].

entresurco *m* AGR space between furrows.

entretallar *vt* to carve in bas-relief || to do openwork on (hacer calados en) || FIG to stop.

entretanto *adv* meanwhile, meantime, in the meantime, in the meanwhile (mientras tanto) || *en el entretanto* in the meantime, in the meanwhile.

entretecho *m* AMER attic, loft (desván).

entretejedura *f* interweaving.

entretejer *vt* to interweave (hilos) || to intertwine, to interlace (entrecruzar) || to mix (mezclar) || FIG to weave into (un escrito).

entretejido *m* interweaving, intertwining, interlacing.

entretela *f* interlining (para reforzar) || buckram (tela gruesa) || IMPR surfacing.
◆ *pl* FAM heart *sing*.

entretención *f* AMER entertainment, recreational activity.

entretener* *vt* to entertain, to amuse (recrear) || to occupy, to keep occupied (distraer); *mientras uno le entretenía el otro le robó* while one kept him occupied the other robbed him || to keep; *no quiero entretenerle demasiado* I don't want to keep you too long || to keep busy *o* occupied; *estas gestiones me han entretenido toda la mañana* these transactions have kept me busy all morning || to put off, to delay, to hold up (dar largas); *están entreteniendo la resolución de la cuestión* they are putting off the solution of the question || FIG to stave off, to ward off; *entretener el hambre* to ward off hunger | to keep at bay, to delay; *entretener la muerte* to keep death at bay, to delay death | to relieve, to allay (el dolor) | to ward off, to divert (el enemigo) | to while away, to pass (el tiempo) | to keep alive; *entretener una esperanza* to keep a hope alive | to keep alive *o* going; *entretener el fuego* to keep the fire going | to put off, to deceive; *entretener con promesas* to put off with promises || to maintain (cuidar) || — FIG *entretener a alguien con esperanzas* to keep s.o. hoping, to keep s.o.'s hopes up | *entretener la soledad de una persona* to keep s.o. company.
◆ *vpr* to pass the time, to amuse s.o.; *entretenerse en leer* or *leyendo* to pass the time reading || FIG to waste one's time (perder el tiempo) | to linger, to loiter, to dally, to hang about (*fam*); *entretenerse en casa de alguien* to linger at s.o.'s house || *por entretenerse* for amusement, to amuse o.s.

entretenido, da *adj* entertaining, amusing (divertido) || demanding (que requiere mucho tiempo) || busy, occupied (ocupado).

entretenimiento *m* entertainment, amusement (recreo) || amusement; *en el jardín hay entretenimientos para los niños* in the garden there are amusements for children || pastime (pasatiempo) || maintenance, upkeep; *gastos de entretenimiento* maintenance costs || conversation, talk (conversación) || delaying, putting off (acción de dar largas) || diversion (del enemigo).

entretiempo *m* between-season [used in spring of autumn]; *traje de entretiempo* between-season suit.

entreventana *f* ARQ pier.

entrever* *vt* to be able to make out, to make out; *allá entreveía unos árboles* over there he could make out some trees || to foresee; *entreveo esa posibilidad* I can foresee that possibility || to guess (vislumbrar).

entreverado *m* AMER roasted offal (asadura) || *tocino entreverado* streaky bacon.

entreverar *vt* to intermingle, to mingle, to mix.

entrevero *m* AMER crowd (gentío) | muddle, confusion (mezcla) | hand-to-hand fight [between horse soldiers] (lucha).

entrevía *f* gauge.

entrevista *f* meeting (entre varias personas) || interview; *tuve una entrevista con el director* I had an interview with the director || interview (de periodista) || *hacer una entrevista a* to interview.

entrevistador, ra *m/f* interviewer (periodista) || pollster (encuestador).

entrevistar *vt* to interview.
◆ *vpr* to have a meeting *o* an interview; *el presidente se entrevistó con el ministro* the president had a meeting with the minister || to interview; *el periodista se entrevistó con el actor* the journalist interviewed the actor.

entripado, da *adj* intestinal.
◆ *m* stuffing (relleno de un asiento) || FIG bitterness, resentment (encono) || AMER concealed anger (enfado).

entristecedor, ra *adj* saddening.

entristecer* *vt* to sadden, to make sad, to grieve (contristar) || to sadden, to make sad (dar aspecto triste).
◆ *vpr* to be sad, to grieve; *entristecerse con* or *de* or *por algo* to be sad about sth., to grieve about *o* over sth. || FIG to cloud over (cielo, rostro).

entrojar *vt* to garner.

entrometer *vt* ⟶ **entremeter.**

entrometido, da *adj/s* ⟶ **entremetido.**

entrometimiento *m* ⟶ **entremetimiento.**

entromparse *vpr* POP to get sozzled *o* stewed *o* canned (emborracharse) || AMER to get angry (enfadarse).

entronar *vt* to enthrone.

entroncamiento; entronque *m* relationship (parentesco) || relationship by marriage (parentesco que se contrae) || FIG relationship || AMER junction (ferrocarril).

entroncar *vt* to establish a relationship between, to link, to connect.
◆ *vi* to be related; *mi familia entronca con la tuya* my family is related to yours || to become related by marriage (contraer parentesco); *sus familias entroncaron en el siglo XVIII* their families became related by marriage in the eighteenth century || to marry (emparentar); *entroncar con una familia* to marry into a family || AMER to join (railway lines).
◆ *vpr* AMER to join (railway lines).

entronización *f*; **entronizamiento** *m* enthroning, throning (acción) || enthronement (estado).

entronizar *vt* to throne, to enthrone, to put on the throne (colocar en el trono) || FIG to worship, to exalt (adorar).

entronque *m* ⟶ **entroncamiento.**

entruchada *f*; **entruchado** *m* FAM plot; *armar una entruchada* to hatch a plot | trick (trampa).

entruchar *vt* FAM to trick, to lure (engañar).

entubación *f* TECN piping, tubing || MED tubing.

entubado *m* TECN tubing, casing (de sondeo) || MED tubing.

entubar *vt* TECN to pipe, to tube (poner tubos) | to tube, to case (para sondear) || MED to tube.

entuerto *m* injury (daño) || offence, insult (agravio) || wrong; *deshacer* or *enderezar entuertos* to right wrongs.
◆ *pl* MED afterpains.

entullecer* *vi/vpr* to become paralyzed.

entumecer* *vt* to numb, to make numb; *el frío entumece los dedos* the cold numbs one's fingers.
◆ *vpr* to get *o* to go numb (por el frío) || FIG to surge (mar).

entumecido, da *adj* numb.

entumecimiento *m* numbness (adormecimiento) || swelling, swell (hinchazón).

entumirse *vpr* to go *o* to get numb (entumecerse).

enturbiar *vt* to make cloudy, to cloud; *enturbiar el agua con barro* to cloud the water with mud || FIG to cloud (estropear) | to mix up, to muddle up, to confuse (enredar) | to dampen (la alegría).

entusiasmar *vt* to inspire, to excite, to fire with enthusiasm || *le entusiasma la música* he is mad about *o* very keen on music, he loves music.
◆ *vpr* to be very keen *o* mad, to love; *se entusiasma con el teatro* he is very keen on *o* mad about the theatre, he loves the theatre || to get

enthusiastic, to get excited (tener entusiasmo); *se entusiasma con* or *por cualquier cosa* they get enthusiastic about anything || to be delighted (estar encantado).

entusiasmo *m* enthusiasm || excitement || *con entusiasmo* enthusiastically.

entusiasta *adj* enthusiastic; *un público muy entusiasta* a very enthusiastic audience.
◆ *m/f* enthusiast, fan (*fam*).

entusiástico, ca *adj* enthusiastic; *un recibimiento entusiástico* an enthusiastic welcome.

enucleación *f* MED enucleation; *la enucleación de un ojo, de un tumor* the enucleation of an eye, of a tumour.

enuclear *vt* MED to enucleate.

enumeración *f* enumeration || summary, summing-up (resumen) || JUR census (de población).

enumerar *vt* to enumerate.

enumerativo, va *adj* enumerative.

enunciación *f*; **enunciado** *m* enunciation || declaration, statement (de hechos) || wording (de ideas, de un problema).

enunciar *vt* to enounce, to enunciate (una teoría) || to declare, to state (una condición) || to explain (un problema) || to state, to express (una idea) || to word (fórmula).

enunciativo, va *adj* enunciative || GRAM declarative (oración).

envainador, ra *adj* BOT *hoja envainadora* sheath.

envainar *vt* to sheathe.

envalentonamiento *m* boldness, daring, courage (valor) || encouragement (estímulo).

envalentonar *vt* to make bold *o* daring *o* brave *o* courageous (dar valor) || to encourage (estimular).
◆ *vpr* to get brave *o* bold *o* daring, to pluck up courage || to be encouraged; *se envalentonó con aquellas palabras elogiosas* he was encouraged by those words of praise || to boast (presumir).

envanecer* *vt* to make conceited *o* vain, to fill with conceit *o* vanity (poner vanidoso) || to make proud, to fill with pride (causar orgullo legítimo a).
◆ *vpr* to be conceited *o* vain (ponerse vanidoso); *envanecerse con* or *de* or *por sus éxitos* to be conceited about one's successes || to be proud (con orgullo legítimo); *puede envanecerse de su hijo* he can be proud of his son.

envanecimiento *m* vanity, conceit (vanidad) || pride (orgullo).

envaramiento *m* numbness (entumecimiento) || stiffness (tiesura).

envarar *vt* to make numb, to numb (entumecer) || to stiffen, to make stiff (poner tieso) || to hinder *o* to restrict the movements of; *esta chaqueta le envara* this jacket hinders his movements.
◆ *vpr* to go numb (entumecerse) || to go stiff (ponerse tieso).

envasado, da *adj* tinned, canned (frutos, pescado, etc.) || bottled (líquidos) || in cylinders (butano) || in barrels (en toneles) || packed (empaquetado).
◆ *m* tinning, canning (en latas, etc.) || bottling (en botella) || putting in cylinders (de gas butano) || packing (empaquetado) || sacking (de granos).

envasador *m* tinner, canner (que pone en latas) || bottler (que pone en botella) || packer (empaquetador) || large funnel (embudo grande).

envasar *vt* to put into a container (poner en un recipiente) || to tin, to can (poner en latas) || to bottle (líquidos) || to barrel (poner en toneles) || to put in cylinders (gas butano) || to pack (empaquetar) || to put in sacks (poner en sacos).

envase *m* → **envasado** || container (recipiente); *envases desechables* disposable containers || tin, can (lata) || box (caja) || bottle (botella) || sack (saco) || packing, package (embalaje); *envase de materia plástica* plastic packing || cylinder (de gas butano) || *leche en envase de cartón* milk in a carton.

envejecer* *vi* to get old, to age; *ha envejecido mucho* he has got very old, he has aged a lot || to age (el vino) || FIG to become out-of-date.
◆ *vpr* to get old, to age (de modo natural) || to make o.s. look older (aparentar ser más viejo de lo que se es).

envejecido, da *adj* aged, old || FIG old-looking (aspecto) | out-of-date (pasado de moda) | obsolete (anticuado) | experienced.

envejecimiento *m* aging, ageing.

envenenador, ra *adj* poisonous.
◆ *m/f* poisoner.

envenenamiento *m* poisoning || pollution (contaminación); *el envenenamiento del aire* the pollution of the air || FIG poisoning.

envenenar *vt* to poison || to pollute (el aire) || FIG to embitter, to poison, to envenom; *la envidia ha envenenado su vida* envy has embittered his life | to misconstrue, to interpret wrongly; *envenenar las palabras de una persona* to misconstrue a person's words, to interpret a person's words wrongly | to turn sour, to embitter (relaciones, discusiones).
◆ *vpr* to poison o.s., to take poison || FIG to become envenomed, to grow bitter.

enverar *vi* to begin to ripen (las frutas).

envergadura *f* MAR breadth, spread [of a sail] || wingspan, span, spread (de las aves) || AVIAC wingspan, span || FIG importance | scope (de un programa) || reach (de un boxeador) || — *de mucha envergadura* very important, of great importance || *de poca envergadura* unimportant, of little importance.

envergar *vt* MAR to bend (una vela).

envergue *m* MAR roband.

envés *m* wrong side, back (de tela) || back, flat (de una espada) || verso, reverse, back (de una página) || BOT reverse || FAM back (espalda).

enviada *f* → **envío.**

enviado, da *adj* sent.
◆ *m/f* representative || envoy (de un gobierno); *enviado extraordinario* envoy extraordinary || messenger (mensajero) || *enviado especial* special correspondent (de un periódico).

enviar *vt* to send; *me envió un ramo de flores* he sent me a bouquet of flowers; *ha enviado a su hijo a España* he has sent his son to Spain || — FAM *enviar a uno al diablo* or *a paseo* to send s.o. packing || *enviar de* to send as; *le enviaron de embajador* they sent him as (an) ambassador || *le envió por unos libros* he sent him for some books.

enviciar *vt* to corrupt, to lead astray; *enviciar a un adolescente* to corrupt an adolescent, to lead an adolescent astray.
◆ *vi* to be addictive, to be habit-forming (un vicio) || to produce too much foliage (un árbol) || *está enviciado en el juego, en los deportes, en la droga* he is addicted to gambling, to sports, to drugs.
◆ *vpr* to be corrupted, to acquire bad habits, to go astray; *se ha enviciado con el contacto de las malas compañías* he has been corrupted by bad company || to become *o* to get addicted; *enviciarse en la bebida* to become addicted to drink.

envidada *f* raise [in cards].

envidar *vi* to raise the wager [in cards] || *envidar en falso* to bluff.

envidia *f* envy; *la envidia es uno de los siete pecados capitales* envy is one of the seven deadly sins; *con una mirada de envidia* with a look of envy || jealousy (celos) || emulation, rivalry (emulación) || — *dar envidia* to make jealous *o* envious || *muerto de envidia* green with envy || *se lo comía la envidia* he was eaten up with envy || *tener envidia a uno* to envy s.o. || *te tengo envidia de haber hecho este viaje* I envy you that journey you made.

envidiable *adj* enviable; *una posición envidiable* an enviable position.

envidiar *vt* to envy, to be envious of; *envidiar a uno* to envy s.o., to be envious of s.o.; *envidia tu tranquilidad* he envies your tranquillity, he is envious of your tranquility || to envy; *envidiar el cargo a uno, envidiar a uno por su cargo* to envy s.o. his post || *más vale ser envidiado que envidioso* better to be envied than envious.

envidioso, sa *adj* envious; *envidioso de la felicidad ajena, de su hermano* envious of other people's happiness, of his brother || jealous (celoso); *envidioso de su amigo* jealous of his friend.
◆ *m/f* envious *o* jealous man, envious *o* jealous woman.

envido *m* raise [in cards].

envigado *m* ARQ beams *pl*, rafters *pl*.

envigar *vt* to put the beams *o* the rafters in.

envilecer* *vt* to degrade, to debase (hacer vil) || to devalue, to depreciate (despreciar).
◆ *vpr* to degrade o.s., to debase o.s.

envilecimiento *m* degradation, debasement.

envinado, da *adj* AMER wine-coloured (color).

envinagrar *vt* to put vinegar on.

envinar *vt* to pour wine into (water).
◆ *vpr* AMER to get drunk (emborracharse).

envío *m*; **enviada** *f* sending, dispatch (acción de enviar) || shipment (expedición de mercancías) || consignment (remesa) || remittance (de dinero) || letter (carta) || package, parcel (paquete) || — *envío contra reembolso* cash on delivery || *gastos de envío* post and packing.

enviscar *vt* to smear with birdlime, to birdlime (untar con liga) || to tease [dogs] (azuzar).
◆ *vpr* to get stuck in birdlime.

envite *m* raise [in cards] || FIG push, shove (empujón) | offer (ofrecimiento) || — *aceptar el envite* to see (cards) || *al primer envite* right away, from the outset, at the beginning, in the first place.

enviudar *vi* to become a widow, to be widowed (mujer) || to become a widower (hombre).

envoltijo; envoltorio *m* wrapper, wrapping (envoltura de papel) || cover (cubierta) || bundle (lío, fardo).

envoltura *f* wrapping (acción) || wrapper, wrapping (de papel) || cover (cubierta) || coating (de medicamentos) || BIOL & BOT envelope.
◆ *pl* swaddling clothes (pañales).

envolvente *adj* MIL encircling, outflanking; *movimiento envolvente* encircling movement || MAT enveloping; *línea envolvente* enveloping line.
◆ *f* MAT envelope.

envolver* *vt* to wrap, to wrap up; *envolver algo en un papel* to wrap sth. *o* to wrap sth. up in a piece of paper || to wrap, to muffle up; *envuelto en una capa* wrapped in a cloak || to wind; *envolver hilo en un carrete* to wind thread

onto a spool || to cover, to coat; *envolver una avellana en chocolate* to coat a hazelnut with chocolate || to coat (medicamentos) || to wrap, to swathe, to swaddle (a los niños) || to envelop, to enshroud; *la niebla envuelve la casa* the fog envelops the house || FIG to envelop, to shroud; *el misterio que envuelve el asunto* the mystery which shrouds the matter | to involve, to get involved, to implicate, to mix up; *le han envuelto en el proceso* they have involved him in *o* they have got him involved in the trial, they have mixed him up in the trial | to imply; *sus palabras envuelven una crítica* his words imply criticism | to stump, to floor (liar en una discusión) || MIL to encircle, to surround || *papel de envolver* brown paper, wrapping paper.
◆ *vpr* to wrap up, to wrap o.s. up; *envolverse en* or *con una manta* to wrap up in a blanket || to be wrapped; *el chocolate suele envolverse en papel de estaño* chocolate is usually wrapped in silver paper || FIG to get involved *o* mixed up *o* implicated | to wrap o.s. up; *envolverse en su dignidad* to wrap o.s. up in one's dignity.

envolvimiento *m* wrapping || winding (enrollamiento) || coating (de medicamentos) || MIL encircling, encirclement, surrounding.

envuelto, ta *adj* wrapped, wrapped up; *envuelto en papel* wrapped in paper || wound (en un carrete) || coated (medicamentos) || FIG envelopped, shrouded; *envuelto en misterio* shrouded in mystery | involved, mixed up, implicated; *envuelto en una serie de robos* involved in a series of robberies.
◆ *m* AMER rolled tortilla (tortilla).

enyerbarse *vpr* AMER to get *o* to become overgrown with grass | to poison o.s. (envenenarse).

enyesado *m*; **enyesadura** *f* plastering || MED plaster, plaster cast (escayolado).

enyesar *vt* to plaster; *enyesar una pared* to plaster a wall || MED to put in plaster *o* in a plaster cast; *enyesar una pierna rota* to put a broken leg in plaster.

enyugar; enyuntar *vt* to yoke.

enzarzar *vt* to cover with brambles (una tapia) || FIG to cause trouble among (engrescar).
◆ *vpr* to get caught (in brambles) || FIG to get mixed up, to get involved (enredarse en un asunto) | to get involved (en una discusión).

enzima *f* BIOL enzyme.

enzootia *f* enzootic (enfermedad de animales).

enzunchar *vt* TECN to bind with hoops *o* rings.

eñe *f* name of the letter *ñ*.

eoceno *adj/sm* GEOL Eocene.

eólico, ca; eolio, lia *adj* Aeolian.

eolito *m* eolith.

Eolo *npr m* MIT Aeolus.

¡epa! *interj* AMER hello! (¡hola!) | come on! (¡ea!).

eparca *m* eparch.

epazote *m* AMER BOT wormseed, Mexican tea.

epeira *f* epeira (araña).

epéntesis *f* GRAM epenthesis.

eperlano *m* ZOOL sparling (pez).

epiblasto *m* BIOL epiblast.

épica *f* epic poetry.

epicarpio *m* BOT epicarp.

epiceno *adj m* GRAM epicene.

epicéntrico, ca *adj* epicentral.

epicentro *m* GEOL epicentre [*US* epicenter].

epicíclico, ca *adj* epicyclic.

epiciclo *m* ASTR epicycle.

epicicloidal *adj* epicycloidal.

epicicloide *f* MAT epicycloid.

épico, ca *adj* epic; *poema épico* epic poem.

epicureísmo *m* FIL Epicureanism, epicurism.

epicúreo, a *adj* epicurean.
◆ *m/f* epicurean.

Epicuro *npr m* Epicurus.

epidemia *f* epidemic || FIG plague, wave, epidemic (oleada).

epidémico, ca *adj* epidemic, epidemical.

epidérmico, ca *adj* epidermic, epidermal.

epidermis *f* ANAT epidermis || FIG & FAM *tener la epidermis fina* to be thin-skinned.

epidermólisis *f* MED epidermolysis.

epididimitis *f* MED epididymitis.

epidídimo *m* ANAT epididymis.

Epifanía *f* REL Epiphany.

epifenomenismo *m* epiphenomenalism.

epifenómeno *m* epiphenomenon.

epífisis *f* ANAT epiphysis.

epifito, ta *adj* BOT epiphysis.

epifito, ta *adj* BOT epiphytic, epiphytical.
◆ *m* BOT epiphyte.

epigástrico, ca *adj* epigastric.

epigastrio *m* ANAT epigastrium.

epigénesis *f* BIOL epigenesis.

epigenético, ca *adj* epigenetic.

epigeo, a *adj* BOT epigeal, epigean, epigeous.

epiglotis *f* ANAT epiglottis.

epígono *m* epigone.

epígrafe *m* epigraph.

epigrafía *f* epigraphy.

epigráfico, ca *adj* epigraphic, epigraphical.

epigrafista *m/f* epigraphist.

epigrama *f* epigram (pieza satírica).

epigramático, ca *adj* epigrammatic, epigrammatical.

epigramatista; epigramista *m* epigrammatist.

epilepsia *f* MED epilepsy.

epiléptico, ca *adj/s* MED epileptic.

epilogación *f* epilogue (epílogo).

epilogal *adj* compendious, summary.

epilogar *vt* to summarize, to sum up (resumir) || to round off, to round out (terminar).

epílogo *m* epilogue (conclusión) || summary (compendio).

episcopado *m* REL episcopate, episcopacy, bishopric (dignidad) | episcopacy, episcopate (obispos).

episcopal *adj* episcopal.

episcopalismo *m* REL episcopalism.

episcopalista *adj/s* REL episcopalian.

episiotomía *f* MED episiotomy.

episódico, ca *adj* episodic, episodical.

episodio *m* episode.

episternón *m* ANAT episternum.

epístola *f* epistle.

epistolar *adj* epistolary.

epistolario *m* collection of letters || epistolary (libro litúrgico).

epitafio *m* epitaph.

epitalámico, ca *adj* epithalamic, epithalamial.

epitalamio *m* epithalamium, epithalamion (canto).

epitelial *adj* epithelial; *tejidos epiteliales* epithelial tissues.

epitelio *m* ANAT epithelium.

epitelioma *m* MED epithelioma (tumor maligno).

epitelitis *f* MED epithelitis.

epítesis *f* MED epithesis.

epíteto *m* epithet.

epítome *m* epitome, summary.

epizootia *f* VET epizootic.

época *f* epoch, age, era, time; *en la época del cine mudo* in the epoch of silent films || time (temporada); *época de siembra* sowing time || period; *la época entre fines del siglo XV y principios del XVII* the period between the end of the 15th century and the beginning of the 17th || — *de los que hacen época* to beat all; *un gol de los que hacen época* a goal to beat all goals; epoch-making (de mucha resonancia) || *en esta época* at this time || *en la época de Felipe II* at the time of Philip II || *en mi época* in my day || *hacer época* to make history, to mark an era *o* epoch || *muebles de época* period furniture || *ser de su época* to be up to date, to be with the times.

epodo *m* epode.

epónimo, ma *adj* eponymous, eponymic.
◆ *m* eponym.

epopeya *f* epic poem, epopee (poema) || epic poetry, epopee (poesía) || FIG epic.

épsilon *f* epsilon.

eptágono, na *adj* MAT heptagonal.
◆ *m* MAT heptagon.

equiángulo, la *adj* MAT equiangular.

equidad *f* equity, fairness (justicia).

equidistancia *f* equal distance, equidistance.

equidistante *adj* equidistant.

equidistar *vi* MAT to be equidistant.

équido, da *adj/sm* equine.

equilátero, ra *adj/sm* MAT equilateral; *triángulos equiláteros* equilateral triangles.

equilibrado, da *adj* balanced || FIG sensible (sensato); *una persona equilibrada* a sensible person | balanced; *espíritu equilibrado* balanced mind.

equilibrar *vt* to balance; *equilibrar la carga de un camión* to balance a lorry's load || to equilibrate, to counterbalance; *equilibrar un peso con otro* to equilibrate one weight with another || to balance (un presupuesto, la mente, etc.).
◆ *vpr* to balance (objetos) || to equilibrate, to counterbalance (fuerzas) || FIG to recover one's balance (mente).

equilibrio *m* FÍS equilibrium || balance; *perder el equilibrio* to lose one's balance || counterbalance, counterpoise (contrapeso) || FIG poise, calmness, composture (serenidad) | balance, harmony (armonía) || — FIG *equilibrio de poderes* or *político* balance of power || *equilibrio ecológico* ecological balance, balance of nature || FIG *hacer equilibrios* to perform miracles (con el dinero) || *mantener el equilibrio* to keep one's balance; *mantuvo el equilibrio sobre la cuerda* he kept his balance on the rope; to maintain the balance; *mantener el equilibrio entre la demanda y la oferta* to maintain the balance between supply and demand || *mantener en equilibrio* to balance; *mantener algo en equilibrio sobre la cabeza* to balance sth. on one's head || *mantenerse en equilibrio* to keep one's balance.

equilibrista *m/f* acrobat, equilibrist || ropewalker, tightrope walker, equilibrist (funámbulo).

equimolecular *adj* QUÍM equimolecular.

equimosis *f* MED ecchymosis.

equino, na *adj* equine, horse (relativo al caballo) || FIG equine.
◆ *m* sea urchin, echinus (erizo de mar) || ARQ echinus (moldura).

equinoccial *adj* equinoctial.
◆ *f* equinoctial line.

equinoccio *m* ASTR equinox.

equinodermo *m* ZOOL echinoderm.

equinoideo *m* echinoid.

equipaje *m* luggage, baggage; *viajar con mucho equipaje* to travel with a lot of luggage || MAR crew (tripulación) || — *equipaje de mano* hand luggage || *exceso de equipaje* excess baggage.

equipar *vt* to equip; *equipar el ejército de* or *con armamento moderno* to equip the army with modern arms || to fit out (de ropa) || MAR to fit out (un barco).

equiparable *adj* comparable (*con* to).

equiparación *f* comparison.

equiparar *vt* to compare, to put on the same level; *equiparar Alejandro a* or *con César* to compare Alexander with Caesar.

equipo *m* team; *equipo de colaboradores* team of collaborators; *equipo de fútbol* football team || shift (de trabajadores) || equipment, kit, gear; *el equipo de un alpinista, de un soldado* a mountaineer's, a soldier's equipment || instruments *pl* || equipment; *equipo eléctrico* electrical equipment || outfit (de colegial) || trousseau (de novia) || — *bienes de equipo* capital goods || *compañero, compañera de equipo* team member (jugador), team mate (en relación uno con otro) || DEP *equipo ascensor* team which can move up into a higher division || *equipo de oficina* office equipment || *equipo de rescate* rescue team || INFORM *equipo lógico* software || *equipo quirúrgico* surgical instruments *pl* (colección de instrumentos), surgical unit (en un hospital).

equiponderar *vi* to be equal in weight.

equis *f* x [name of the letter *x*] || MAT x [any number].

equitación *f* horse riding, riding, equitation (p us) (acción); *al niño le gusta la equitación* the child likes riding || horsemanship, equitation (p us) (arte).

equitativo, va *adj* equitable, fair (justo).

equivalencia *f* equivalence, equivalency.

equivalente *adj/sm* equivalent.

equivaler* *vi* to be equivalent, to be equal, to be the equivalent; *tres duros equivalen a quince pesetas* three «duros» are equal to *o* are equivalent to *o* are the equivalent of fifteen pesetas || to mean; *eso equivaldría a un fracaso* that would mean failure || *eso equivale a decir que* that amounts to saying that, that means that; *eso equivale a decir que no quiere ir* that amounts to saying that he does not want to go.

equivocación *f* mistake, error; *cometer* or *tener una equivocación* to make a mistake || misunderstanding (malentendido) || *por equivocación* by mistake, in error.

equivocadamente *adv* by mistake, mistakenly.

equivocado, da *adj* wrong, mistaken; *un juicio equivocado* a wrong judgment; *estar equivocado* to be wrong, to be mistaken.

equívocamente *adv* ambiguously, equivocally.

equivocar *vt* to get wrong, to mistake; *equivoqué la fecha* I got the date wrong, I mistook the date || to get mixed up; *equivocar los abrigos de los niños* to get the children's coats mixed up || to confuse, to get mixed up; *si hablas mientras estoy contando me equivocas* if you talk while I'm counting, you get me mixed up || to mislead; *su respuesta me equivocó* his answer misled me.
◆ *vpr* to be mistaken, to make a mistake, to mistake, to get wrong; *equivocarse de fecha* to be mistaken about *o* to make a mistake about the date, to mistake the date, to get the date wrong || to make a mistake, to be mistaken, to be wrong (no tener razón); *reconozco que me equivoqué* I admit that I was mistaken || to make a mistake; *equivocarse en un cálculo* to make a mistake in a calculation || to be mistaken (juzgar mal); *me equivoqué con ese chico* I was mistaken about that boy || — *equivocarse de casa* to go to the wrong house || *equivocarse de camino* to take the wrong road || *si no me equivoco* if I'm not mistaken.

equívoco, ca *adj* ambiguous, equivocal; *frase equívoca* ambiguous sentence || misleading (engañoso) || strange, queer (persona).
◆ *m* ambiguity, ambiguous *o* equivocal expression *o* word; *discurso lleno de equívocos* speech full of ambiguities || misunderstanding, mistake (malentendido) || *andar con equívocos* to play on words.

era *f* era; *la era cristiana* the Christian era || FIG age, era; *la era atómica* the atomic age || AGR threshing floor; *trillar en la era* to thresh grain on the threshing floor | patch (para hortalizas) | bed (para flores) || MIN pithead.

eral *m* bullock [less than two years old].

erario *m* treasury, funds *pl* || *erario público* treasury, publics funds *pl*, exchequer.

erasmismo *m* Erasmianism.

erasmista *adj/s* Erasmian.

Erasmo *npr m* Erasmus.

erbio *m* erbium (metal).

ere *f* r [name of the Spanish single *r*].

erección *f* erection, raising (de un monumento) || FIG setting-up, establishment (de una institución) || erection (en fisiología).

eréctil *adj* erectile.

erecto, ta *adj* erect.

eremita *m* hermit, eremite (ermitaño).

eremítico, ca *adj* hermitical, eremitic; *vida eremítica* hermitical life.

eretismo *m* MED erethism.

erg; ergio *m* FÍS erg.

ergosterol *m* MED ergosterol.

ergotismo *m* MED ergotism || sophistry.

ergotizar *vi* to argufy, to quibble (*fam*).

erguimiento *m* raising, lifting-up.

erguir* *vt* to raise, to lift up; *erguir la cabeza* to raise one's head.
◆ *vpr* to rise; *la montaña se yergue a lo lejos* the mountain rises in the distance || to straighten up (enderezarse) || FIG to swell with pride (envanecerse).

erial *adj* uncultivated, untilled (tierra).
◆ *m* uncultivated *o* untilled land.

erigir *vt* to erect, to raise, to set up (un monumento) || to build, to construct (un edificio) || FIG to establish, to set up, to found (una institución).
◆ *vpr* to set o.s. up; *erigirse en juez* to set o.s. up as judge.

Erín *npr f* (ant) Erin (irlanda).

erisipela *f* MED erysipelas.

eritema *m* MED erythema (inflamación).

Eritrea *npr f* GEOGR Eritrea.

eritroblasto *m* erythroblast (célula).

eritrocito *m* BIOL erythrocyte (glóbulo rojo).

erizado, da *adj* bristly, prickly; *erizado de espinas* bristly with thorns || FIG *problema erizado de dificultades* thorny *o* prickly problem, problem bristling with difficulties.

erizar *vt* to bristle (un animal) || FIG *el miedo le erizó el pelo* fear made his hair stand on end.
◆ *vpr* to stand on end; *se me erizó el pelo* my hair stood on end || to bristle; *se le erizó el pelo al perro* the dog's fur bristled.

erizo *m* hedgehog (animal) || bur, burr (envoltura de la castaña) || FIG & FAM surly person, prickly customer (persona arisca) || row of spikes (defensa de púas en un muro) || BOT burr, prickly plant || globefish (pez) || *erizo de mar* sea urchin.

ermita *f* hermitage.

ermitaño *m* hermit (hombre) || ZOOL hermit crab.

erogación *f* distribution || AMER expenditure (gasto) | payment (pago) | contribution.

erogar *vt* to distribute (distribuir) || AMER to pay (pagar) | to spend (gastar) | to contribute (contribuir).

erógeno, na *adj* erogenous.

Eros *npr m* Eros.

erosión *f* erosion; *erosión eólica, glacial, pluvial* wind, glacial, pluvial erosion || MED graze.

erosionar *vt* to erode.

erótico, ca *adj* erotic.

erotismo *m* erotism, eroticism.

erotomanía *f* MED erotomania.

erotómano, na *adj* erotic.
◆ *m/f* erotomaniac.

errabundo, da *adj* wandering, roving.

erradicación *f* eradication.

erradicar *vt* to uproot (un árbol, una planta) || FIG to eradicate, to uproot; *erradicar un vicio* to eradicate a vice.

errado, da *adj* wrong, mistaken (equivocado); *estar errado* to be mistaken || wide of the mark (tiro) || *golpe, tiro errado* miss.

erraj *m* fuel made from crushed olive stones.

errante *adj* wandering, roaming, roving || nomadic (nómada) || MED erratic || stray (animal) || *estrella errante* planet.

errar* *vi* to wander, to rove, to roam (vagar) || to make a mistake, to be mistaken, to be wrong (equivocarse) || to err, to go astray; *errar es humano* to err is human || FIG to wander (la imaginación).
◆ *vt* to miss; *errar el blanco* to miss the target || FIG to miss || — *errar el camino* to take the wrong road (en un viaje), to miss one's vocation *o* one's calling (en la vida) || *errar el golpe* to miss || FIG *errar el tiro* to miss the mark, to fail || *errar la respuesta* to give the wrong answer, to get the answer wrong.

errata *f* erratum || *fe de erratas* errata.

errático, ca *adj* wandering || GEOL & MED erratic.

erre *f* r [name of the Spanish *rr* and the initial *r*] || — FAM *erre que erre* stubbornly | *tropieza en las erres* his speech is slurred (un borracho).

erróneamente *adv* mistakenly, erroneously.

erróneo, a *adj* erroneous, incorrect, mistaken (falso) || *identificación errónea* mistaken identity.

error *m* mistake, error (engaño, equivocación); *cometer un error, incurrir en un error* to make a mistake || mistake, fault; *un texto lleno de errores* a text full of mistakes || mistake; *ha sido un error obrar de esta manera* it was a mistake to do that || MAT mistake, fault || INFORM error, mistake, bug || — *caer en un error* to fall into error, to make a mistake || *error de imprenta* misprint || *error de máquina* or *tipográfico* typing mistake *o* error || JUR *error judicial* miscarriage of justice || *estar en un error* to be mistaken, to be wrong || *por error* by mistake || *salvo error u omisión* errors and omissions excepted.

eructar *vi* to belch, to eructate, to burp (*fam*).

eructo *m* belch, eructation, burp (*fam*).

erudición *f* learning, erudition, scholarship | knowledge (conocimientos).

erudito, ta *adj* scholarly, erudite, knowledgeable, learned; *un hombre muy erudito* a very scholarly man.
◆ *m/f* scholar, erudite || — FAM *erudito a la violeta* pseudo-intellectual || *erudito en* widely read in, well up in || *los eruditos en la materia* those who are expert in this subject.

erupción *f* eruption (volcánica) || MED rash, eruption (cutánea) | eruption (de los dientes) || FIG eruption, outbreak || — *entrar en erupción* to erupt || *estar en erupción* to be erupting.

eruptivo, va *adj* eruptive.

esa *adj dem* ⟶ **ese.**

ésa *pron dem* ⟶ **ése.**

esbeltez *f* slenderness, litheness, svelteness.

esbelto, ta *adj* slender, lithe, svelte.

esbirro *m* bailiff (alguacil) || FIG henchman (ayudante).

esbozar *vt* to sketch; *esbozar un dibujo a lápiz* to sketch a drawing in pencil || to rough out, to outline (un proyecto) || *esbozar una sonrisa* to give a faint smile.

esbozo *m* sketch, outline.

escabechado, da *adj* in a marinade, pickled, soused; *atún escabechado* tuna in a marinade.
◆ *m* preservation in a marinade.

escabechar *vt* to marinate, to preserve in a marinade, to pickle, to souse (conservar) || FIG & FAM to bump off, to kill (matar) | to fail, to plough (en un examen).

escabeche *m* marinade, pickle, souse; *atún en escabeche* tuna in a marinade || pickled fish, fish in a marinade (pescado escabechado).

escabechina *f* FIG & FAM massacre, slaughter (matanza); *la batalla fue una escabechina* the battle was a massacre | trail of destruction, wholesale destruction (de cosas) || FIG & FAM *el profesor ha hecho una escabechina en los exámenes* the teacher has failed a lot of students in the exams.

escabel *m* footstool (para los pies) || stool (asiento).

escabiosa *f* BOT scabious.

escabioso, sa *adj* MED scabious.

escabro *m* VET scab, mange (de las ovejas).

escabrosamente *adv* crudely.

escabrosidad *f* roughness, unevenness, ruggedness (del terreno) || FIG difficulty, toughness, thorniness (dificultad) | crudeness, scabrous nature, dirtiness (inmoralidad) | harshness (del carácter).

escabroso, sa *adj* rough, uneven, rugged (terreno) || FIG difficult, tough, thorny (difícil) | crude, dirty, scabrous; *historia escabrosa* crude story | harsh (carácter).

escabullirse* *vpr* to slip away || *escabullirse por* to slip through.

escacharrar *vt* FAM to break, to bust (romper) | to spoil, to ruin (estropear).
◆ *vpr* FAM to break, to bust (romperse) | to be spoilt *o* ruined (estropearse).

escafandra *f*; **escafandro** *m* diving suit || *escafandra autónoma* scuba.

escafoides *adj/sm* ANAT scaphoid.

escala *f* scale (graduación, proporción); *la escala de un mapa, de un termómetro* the scale of a map, of a thermometer || ladder (escalera de mano) || intermediate stop, stopover (de avión) || port of call (de barco) || MIL promotion roster *o* list || MÚS scale; *escala mayor, menor, cromática* major, minor, cromatic scale || range (gama) || — *a escala* to scale; *dibujar algo a escala* to draw sth. to scale || *a escala internacional* on an international scale || *a gran, a pequeña escala* large-scale, small-scale; *mapa a gran escala* large-scale map || *en gran, en pequeña escala* on a large, on a small scale || *escala de cuerda* rope ladder || MIL *escala de reserva* inactive list, reserve of officers || *escala móvil* sliding scale; *escala móvil salarial* sliding wage scale || MAR *escala real* accommodation ladder || *hacer escala en* to call in at, to stop in || *vuelo sin escala* non-stop flight.

escalabrar *vt* ⟶ **descalabrar.**

escalada *f* climbing (de una montaña) || scaling (de una pared, un acantilado) || escalade (con una escalera) || break-in (de una casa) || MIL escalation || escalade (de la guerra, de precios, etc.).

escalador, ra *m/f* climber, mountaineer (montañero) || climber (ciclista) || burglar, housebreaker (ladrón).

escalafón *m* promotion, list, promotion roster, roll (de empleados, de soldados, etc.) || table, list (cuadro) || *seguir el escalafón* to work one's way up.

escalamiento *m* scaling (de una pared, un acantilado) || escalade (con una escalera) || climbing (de una montaña) || break-in (de una casa) || MIL escalation.

escálamo *m* MAR thole, tholepin.

escalar *vt* to scale (una pared, un acantilado) || to escalade (con una escalera) || to climb (una montaña) || to break into, to burgle (una casa) || to lift [a sluice gate].
◆ *vi* to climb || to escalate (en la guerra, los precios, etc.).

escalar *adj* MAT & FÍS scalar.

Escalda *npr m* GEOGR Scheldt.

escaldado, da *adj* scalded || FIG wary, cautious (receloso).
◆ *m* scalding.

escaldadura *f* scald (quemadura) || scalding (acción) || FIG lesson.

escaldar *vt* to scald (con agua caliente) || to make red hot (poner al rojo) || FIG to teach a lesson; *aquella experiencia te escaldó* that experience taught you a lesson.
◆ *vpr* to scald o.s., to get scalded.

escaleno *adj/sm* MAT scalene.

escalera *f* staircase, stairway; *escalera de caracol* spiral staircase; *escalera excusada* or *falsa* private staircase || stairs *pl*; *subir, bajar la escalera* to go up, to go down the stairs || straight (en el póker), sequence (naipes) || — *escalera abajo* downstairs, down the stairs; *cayó escalera abajo* he fell downstairs || *escalera de color, real* straight, royal flush || *escalera de gancho* scaling ladder || *escalera de incendios* fire escape || *escalera de mano* ladder || *escalera de servicio* service stairs, backstairs || *escalera de tijera* stepladder, steps *pl* || *escalera mecánica* or *automática* escalator || FIG *gente de escaleras abajo* servants *pl*.

escalerilla *f* sequence of three cards (tres naipes seguidos) || small staircase (escalera) || small ladder (escala) || MAR gangway (de barco) || steps *pl* (de avión) || VET metal instrument for keeping horse's mouth open.

escalfado, da *adj* poached (huevo) || blistered (pared).

escalfador *m* hot-water container (de barbero) || chafing dish (para calentar) || poacher (para los huevos).

escalfar *vt* to poach (los huevos).

escalinata *f* flight of steps.

escalo *m* scaling (acción de escalar) || *robo con escalo* burglary, housebreaking.

escalofriante *adj* bloodcurdling.

escalofrío *m* chill, shiver (de fiebre) || shiver (de frío) || FIG shiver (de miedo, etc.) || *tener escalofríos* to shiver.

escalón *m* step, stair (de escalera) || rung (de escala) || FIG step (en una jerarquía) | stepping stone (para progresar) || MIL echelon || *cortar el pelo en escalones* to cut hair unevenly.

escalonado, da *adj* spread out, spaced out || graded (en serie ascendente o descendente) || staggered (huelga, vacaciones) || in stages (por etapas); *aprendizaje escalonado* apprenticeship in stages.

escalonamiento *m* spreading out, spacing out || staggering; *escalonamiento de las vacaciones* staggering of holidays.

escalonar *vt* to spread out, to space out; *escalonar soldados* to space out soldiers || to grade; *escalonar la dosis* to grade the doses || to stagger (huelga, producción, vacaciones) || to do *o* to carry out in stages (hacer por etapas) || to terrace (land).

escalonia; escaloña *f* BOT shallot (chalote).

escalope *m* veal cutlet, escalope.

escalpar *vt* to scalp.

escalpe; escalpo *m* scalp.

escalpelo *m* MED scalpel.

escama *f* scale (de pez, de serpiente) || MED flake, scale (de la piel) || BOT scale || FIG suspicion, mistrust, wariness (desconfianza) || *jabón en escamas* soap flakes.

escamado, da *adj* FAM suspicious, wary.

escamar *vt* to scale (quitar las escamas) || FIG & FAM to make suspicious *o* wary; *la experiencia le ha escamado* the experience has made him wary || FIG & FAM *esto me ha escamado siempre* I have always been suspicious about this, I have always been wary about this.
◆ *vpr* FIG & FAM to become wary *o* suspicious.

escamón, ona *adj* suspicious, wary.

escamonda *f* pruning.

escamondadura *f* pruned branches *pl*.

escamondar *vt* AGR to prune (podar) || FIG to prune, to cut down (lo superfluo) | to clean (limpiar) | to wash (lavar).

escamoso, sa *adj* scaly (que tiene escamas) || flaky, scaly (piel) || FIG suspicious, wary.

escamoteador, ra *m/f* conjuror, conjurer (prestidigitador) || FIG & FAM thief, swindler (ladrón).

escamotear *vt* to make disappear, to make vanish; *el prestidigitador escamoteó las cartas* the magician made several cards vanish || FIG & FAM to pinch, to lift, to take (robar) | to skip (una dificultad).

escamoteo *m* sleight of hand, conjuring (de un prestidigitador) || vanishing, disappearing (desaparición) || FIG & FAM lifting, pinching (robo) | skipping (de una dificultad) || AVIAC retraction (de las ruedas).

escampada *f* clear spell (de la lluvia).

escampar *v impers* to stop raining, to clear up; *espera que escampe* wait till is stops raining.

escampavía *f* MAR scout (barco que acompaña a otro) | coastguard vessel, revenue cutter [US coastguard cutter] (para vigilar las costas).

escanciador *m* wine waiter || HIST cupbearer (de los reyes).

escanciar *vt* to serve, to pour (vino).
◆ *vi* to drink wine.

escandalera *f* FAM → **escándalo.**

escandalizar *vt* to shock, to scandalize; *su conducta me escandaliza* his conduct shocks me.
◆ *vi* to make a fuss (armar un escándalo).
◆ *vpr* to be shocked *o* scandalized; *se escandalizó de tu conducta* he was shocked by your conduct ‖ to protest, to be scandalized (protestar).

escándalo *m* scandal; *este crimen fue el mayor escándalo del año* this crime was the biggest scandal of the year ‖ row, racket, uproar, din (alboroto) ‖ JUR disturbance of the peace ‖ — *armar un escándalo* to make a row *o* a racket *o* a din, to cause an uproar (hacer ruido), to make a scene (hacer una escena), to cause a scandal (provocar indignación) ‖ *armar* or *formar un escándalo a uno* to give s.o. a dressing down *o* a telling off ‖ *causar escándalo* to cause a scandal ‖ *con gran* or *con el consiguiente escándalo de* to the indignation of ‖ *piedra de escándalo* cause of the scandal ‖ *ser un escándalo* to be scandalous *o* disgusting *o* shocking; *es un escándalo cómo suben los precios* it is scandalous the way prices are rising.

escandalosa *f* MAR gaff, topsail (vela) ‖ FIG & FAM *echar la escandalosa a uno* to give s.o. a telling off *o* a piece of one's mind.

escandalosamente *adv* scandalously, shockingly ‖ noisily (ruidosamente) ‖ flagrantly (claramente).

escandaloso, sa *adj* scandalous, outrageous, shocking (que causa escándalo); *injusticia escandalosa* scandalous injustice ‖ rowdy, noisy (que mete jaleo) ‖ scandalous, notorious; *una vida escandalosa* a notorious life ‖ flagrant (a la vista de todos); *crimen escandaloso* flagrant crime ‖ uproarious (risa) ‖ loud (colores chillones).
◆ *m/f* *mi vecina es una escandalosa* my neighbour is always kicking up a fuss.
◆ *f* MAR gaff, topsail (vela) ‖ FIG & FAM *echar la escandalosa a uno* to give s.o. a telling off *o* a piece of one's mind.

escandallar *vt* MAR to sound ‖ COM to fix the price of (determinar el precio) | to sample (para comprobar la calidad).

escandallo *m* MAR sounding lead ‖ COM price fixing, pricing (de mercancías) | sampling (prueba).

Escandinavia *npr f* GEOGR Scandinavia.

escandinavo, va *adj/s* Scandinavian.

escandio *m* QUÍM scandium.

escandir *vt* to scan (versos).

escáner *m* scanner.

escantillón *m* TECN template, templet, pattern.

escaño *m* bench (banco) ‖ seat (de diputado).

escapada *f* escape, flight (acción de escapar) ‖ escapade (travesura) ‖ breakaway (de un ciclista) ‖ quick trip (excursión) ‖ *hacer una escapada al campo* to escape to the country, to slip away to the country, to make a quick trip to the country.

escapado, da *adj* *irse, volver escapado* to rush off, to rush back.

escapamiento *m* escape, flight.

escapar *vi* to escape; *escapar de un peligro, de una enfermedad* to escape a danger, an illness; *escapar del naufragio* to escape from the shipwreck ‖ to escape; *escapar de la cárcel, de la jaula* to escape from prison, from the cage ‖ to escape, to run away, to flee (huir) ‖ to break away (un ciclista, etc.) ‖ — *¡de buena hemos escapado!* we had a narrow escape! ‖ *dejar escapar* to let out; *dejó escapar un suspiro* he let out a sigh; to let go; *dejar escapar una oportunidad* to let an opportunity go ‖ *escapar bien* to get off lightly ‖ *escapar con vida de un accidente* to survive an accident ‖ *eso escapó a mi vista* I missed that, than escaped my notice.
◆ *vt* to run *o* ride hard (un caballo).
◆ *vpr* to escape, to get out; *el canario se ha escapado de la jaula* the canary has escaped from the cage *o* got out of the cage ‖ to escape, to run away, to flee (huir) ‖ to slip away (irse discretamente) ‖ to leak, to escape (gas, líquido) ‖ to escape (no llegar a comprenderse); *este sentido se te escapa* this meaning escapes you ‖ to break away (en deportes) ‖ — *escapársele de las manos a alguien* to slip out of s.o.'s hands; *el plato se le escapó de las manos* the plate slipped out of his hands ‖ *escaparse por un pelo* or *por tablas* to have a narrow escape *o* a close shave, to escape by the skin of one's teeth ‖ *se le escapó la mano* he let fly ‖ *se le escapó un suspiro* he let out a sigh ‖ *se me escapó la lengua* I couldn't keep my mouth shut ‖ *se me escapó la palabra* the word slipped out, I let the word slip out ‖ *su cumpleaños se me ha escapado* his birthday slipped my mind.

escaparate *m* window; *¿quiere enseñarme la corbata que está en el escaparate?* will you show me the tie that is in the window? ‖ shop window; *los escaparates están todos iluminados* the shop windows are all lit up ‖ showcase, display cabinet (vitrina) ‖ AMER wardrobe (armario) ‖ *decorador, decoradora de escaparates* window dresser.

escaparatista *m/f* window dresser.

escapatoria *f* way out (salida); *es la única escapatoria* it is the only way out ‖ loophole, means of evasion (para eludir una obligación, etc.) ‖ excuse, subterfuge (excusa) ‖ trip (escapada) ‖ escape, flight (huida) ‖ *no me venga usted con escapatorias* don't try to worm your way out of it, don't try to put me off with excuses.

escape *m* escape (huida) ‖ leak, escape (de gas) ‖ FIG way out (salida) ‖ TECN exhaust (de motor); *tubo de escape* exhaust pipe | exhaust valve (válvula) | escapement (de reloj) ‖ — *a escape* at full speed; *correr a escape* to run at full speed ‖ FIG *puerta de escape* way out.

escápula *f* ANAT scapula, shoulder blade.

escapular *adj* scapular (del hombro).

escapulario *m* REL scapular, scapulary.

escaque *m* square (del tablero de ajedrez) ‖ HERÁLD square.
◆ *pl* chess *sing* (ajedrez).

escaqueado, da *adj* checked, checkered.

escaquearse *vpr* FAM to skive off, to dodge (de un trabajo u obligación).

escara *f* MED eschar, scab.

escarabajear *vi* FIG to mill around (moverse) ‖ FAM to worry, to bother (preocupar); *este problema me escarabajea* this problem bothers me ‖ FIG to scrawl, to scribble (escribir mal).

escarabajeo *m* FAM worry, bother ‖ FIG scrawling, scribbling (garabateo).

escarabajo *m* beetle (insecto coleóptero) ‖ FIG & FAM dwarf, stunted person (persona de mal aspecto) ‖ TECN flaw (en un tejido) ‖ fault in the bore (de un cañón).
◆ *pl* FIG scrawl *sing*, scribble *sing* (al escribir).

escaramucear *vi* to skirmish.

escaramujo *m* BOT dog rose (rosal silvestre) | hip (fruto) ‖ ZOOL barnacle (crustáceo).

escaramuza *f* MIL skirmish ‖ FIG brush (fricción).

escaramuzar *vi* to skirmish.

escarapela *f* rosette, cockade (insignia) ‖ FIG quarrel (riña).

escarbadientes *m inv* toothpick (mondadientes).

escarbaorejas *m inv* earpick.

escarbar *vt/vi* to scratch; *las gallinas escarban la tierra* hens scratch the ground ‖ to pick (dientes, oídos) ‖ to poke (la lumbre) ‖ FIG to forage in, to rummage in; *escarbar (en) los archivos* to forage in the archives | to delve; *escarbar (en) un asunto* to delve into a matter ‖ AGR to scrape.

escarbo *m* scratching.

escarcear *vi* AMER to prance, to caracole.

escarcela *f* pouch (bolsa de cazador) ‖ purse (para el dinero) ‖ cap (cofia) ‖ cuisse (de armadura).

escarceo *m* MAR ripple.
◆ *pl* prances, caracoles, prancing *sing* (del caballo) ‖ FIG wanderings, ramblings (rodeos) ‖ — FIG *escarceos amorosos* flirtation *sing* ‖ *hacer escarceos* to prance, to caracole (el caballo).

escarcha *f* frost (rocío congelado) ‖ frost, hoarfrost (niebla condensada).

escarchado, da *adj* frost-covered, frosty, frosted; *árbol escarchado* frost-covered tree ‖ candied, crystallized; *fruta escarchada* candied fruit ‖ frosted, iced; *pastel escarchado* frosted cake ‖ *aguardiente escarchado* brandy containing crystallized anise branch.
◆ *m* silver embroidery (de plata), gold embroidery (de oro) ‖ crystallizing, candying (de frutas).

escarchar *v impers* to freeze; *anoche ha escarchado* it froze last night ‖ *escarcha* it's frosty.
◆ *vt* to crystallize, to candy (frutas) ‖ to ice, to frost (pasteles) ‖ to crystallize an anise branch in (brandy) (el aguardiente).
◆ *vi* to become frosty *o* covered with frost.

escarda *f* AGR weeding hoe (instrumento) | weeding (acción) | weeding time (época).

escardadera *f* AGR weeding hoe.

escardador, ra *m/f* weeder (persona).
◆ *m* weeding hoe (instrumento).

escardadura *f* AGR weeding.

escardar *vt* AGR to weed (out) ‖ FIG to weed out ‖ FIG & FAM *mandar a uno a escardar cebollinos* to send s.o. packing, to tell s.o. to jump in the lake.

escardilla *f* AGR weeding hoe.

escardillar *vt* to weed (out) (escardar).

escardillo *m* weeding hoe (herramienta).

escariado *m* TECN reaming.

escariador *m* TECN reamer.

escariar *vt* TECN to ream (un agujero).

escarificación *f* MED scarification.

escarificador *m* scarifier.

escarificar *vt* AGR & MED to scarify.

escarlata *f* scarlet (color y tela) ‖ MED scarlet fever.
◆ *adj* scarlet.

escarlatina *f* MED scarlet fever.

escarmenar *vt* → **carmenar.**

escarmentado, da *adj* *estar escarmentado* to have learnt one's lesson, to have learnt from experience.
◆ *m/f* *de los escarmentados salen los avisados* once bitten, twice shy.

escarmentar* *vt* to teach a lesson; *escarmentar a un niño* to teach a child a lesson.
◆ *vi* to learn one's lesson; *no escarmienta nunca* he never learns his lesson ‖ — *¡así escarmentarás!* that'll teach you! ‖ *escarmentar en cabeza ajena* to learn from s.o. else's mistakes ‖ *hacer escarmentar a uno* to teach s.o. lesson ‖

nadie escarmienta en cabeza ajena one only learns by one's own mistakes.

escarmiento *m* lesson (lección) || punishment (castigo) || *servirle de escarmiento a uno* to be a lesson *o* a warning to s.o.

escarnecer* *vt* to jeer at, to scoff at, to mock.

escarnecimiento; escarnio *m* mockery, scoffing, jeering, jeers *pl* (burla) || derision, ridicule (ridículo) || shame (vergüenza); *para mayor escarnio mío* to my great shame.

escarola *f* endive (verdura) || (ant) ruff (cuello alechugado).

escarpa *f* steep slope, escarpment, scarp (cuesta empinada) || escarpment, scarp (de fortificación).

escarpado, da *adj* steep, sheer, precipitous; *orillas escarpadas* steep banks || craggy, cragged (montaña, peñón) || sheer, steep (pendiente).

escarpadura *f* steep slope, escarpment, scarp.

escarpar *vt* to escarp (subir) || TECN to rasp.

escarpia *f* hook (alcayata).

escarpidor *m* large-toothed comb (peine).

escarpín *m* pump (zapato) || slipper (calzado interior).

escarzano *adj m* ARQ segmental (arco).

escasamente *adv* scarcely, barely, hardly; *trabajó escasamente una hora* he worked scarcely an hour || only just (por muy poco); *los liberales ganaron escasamente* the liberals only just won || — *cielo escasamente nublado* sky with scattered clouds || *vivir escasamente* to make ends meet.

escasear *vt* to be sparing with, to be mean with (escatimar) || TECN to bevel.
◆ *vi* to be scarce (ser poco abundante); *escasea el arroz* rice is scarce.

escasez *f* shortage, scarcity; *escasez de agua, de mano de obra* shortage of water, of manpower || lack, shortage; *escasez de dinero* lack of money || want, need (pobreza) || scantiness; *la escasez de sus recursos* the scantiness of his resources || stinginess, meanness (tacañería) || — *año de escasez* lean year || *con escasez* hardly, scarcely, barely (apenas), stingily, meanly (con mezquindad), in need, on a shoestring (*fam*); *vivir con escasez* to live in need.

escaso, sa *adj* scarce (poco abundante) || very little; *escaso tiempo* very little time || poor, meagre; *escasa recompensa* poor recompense || poor, low; *escaso salario* poor wage; *escasa visibilidad* poor visibility || only just, hardly, barely, scarcely; *dos días escasos* hardly two days; *una hora escasa* only just an hour || low; *los víveres son escasos* provisions are low || thin, sparse (cosecha) || low; *escasas lluvias* low rainfall || scant, scanty, very little; *escasa vegetación* scant vegetation || scanty, scant, meagre; *una comida escasa* a scanty meal || scanty, very limited; *recursos escasos* scanty resources || few (pocos); *escasos visitantes* few visitors || small (reducido); *un público escaso* a small audience || slight, slim, slender (alguna); *una escasa posibilidad* a slight possibility || only a few; *desplazamiento de escasos milímetros* displacement of only a few millimetres || miserly, mean, stingy (tacaño) || — *andar escaso de* to be short of || *andar escaso de dinero* to be short of money || *la comida va a resultar escasa* there won't be enough food || *ser escaso de inteligencia* to have a low intelligence.

escatimar *vt* to be mean *o* stingy with, to skimp on (ser poco generoso con); *escatimar la comida* to be mean with the food, to skimp on the food || to be sparing with; *escatima hasta las sonrisas* he is sparing even with his smiles; *hay que escatimar el azúcar porque ya no queda mucho* we'll have to be sparing with the sugar because there is not much left || to stint; *no escatimaba sus elogios* he did not stint his praise || to save; *escatimar sus energías* to save one's strenght || *no escatimar esfuerzos, gastos* to spare no effort, no expense.

escatología *f* scatology || FIL eschatology.

escatológico, ca *adj* scatological (excrementicio) || FIL eschatological.

escayola *f* plaster of paris (yeso) || stucco (estuco) || MED plaster.

escayolado, da *adj* MED in a plaster cast, in plaster (miembro).
◆ *m* plastering.

escayolar *vt* MED to put in a plaster cast *o* in plaster; *escayolar un brazo* to put an arm in a plaster cast.

escena *f* TEATR scene (subdivisión de un acto) | stage (escenario); *salir a escena* to go on stage | scene (lugar de la acción) | theatre [*US* theater] (arte dramático) || FIG scene; *una escena conmovedora* a moving scene || — *director de escena* producer (teatro) || *escena retrospectiva* flashback (en cine) || FIG *hacer una escena* to make a scene || *poner en* or *llevar a escena* to stage || *puesta en escena* staging || *su vocación es la escena* his vocation is the stage || *volver a la escena* to make one's comeback.

escenario *m* TEATR stage; *estar en el escenario* to be on stage; *nunca volvió a pisar un escenario* he never set foot on a stage again || set (plató de cine) || FIG scene, setting; *ese lugar fue el escenario de una batalla* that place was the setting of a battle | surroundings *pl* (ambiente).

escénico, ca *adj* scenic.

escenificación *f* dramatizing, adaptation for the stage (de una obra literaria) || staging (presentación).

escenificar *vt* to dramatize, to adapt for the stage; *escenificar una novela* to dramatize a novel, to adapt a novel for the stage || to stage (poner en escena).

escenografía *f* scenography (arte) || scenery (conjunto de decorados).

escenográfico, ca *adj* scenographical, scenographic.

escenógrafo, fa *m/f* producer.

escepticismo *m* scepticism [*US* skepticism].

escéptico, ca *adj/s* sceptic [*US* skeptic].

Escila *n pr* GEOGR Scylla || FIG *estar entre Escila y Caribdis* to be between Scylla and Charybdis | *librarse de Caribdis y caer en Escila* to jump out of the frying pan into the fire.

escinco *m* skink (lagarto).

escindible *adj* divisible || FÍS fissionable.

escindir *vt* to divide, to split || FÍS to split (the atom).
◆ *vpr* to split.

Escipión *npr m* Scipio; *Escipión el Africano* Scipio Africanus.

escisión *f* splitting, scission (acción) || split, division; *la escisión de un partido político* the split in a political party || FÍS fission (on the atom); *escisión nuclear* nuclear fission || MED excision.

Escitia *npr f* GEOGR scythia.

esclarecer* *vt* FIG to throw light on, to clarify, to elucidate (una cosa dudosa) | to enlighten (explicar) | to ennoble (ennoblecer) | to make illustrious.
◆ *vi ya esclarece* the day is breaking, it is getting light.

esclarecidamente *adv* illustriously.

esclarecido, da *adj* illustrious, distinguished, outstanding.

esclarecimiento *m* elucidation, elucidating (acción de esclarecer) || enlightenment (información) || FIG illustriousness (celebridad) | ennoblement (ennoblecimiento).

esclava *f* → **esclavo.**

esclavina *f* short cape (capa) || large collar (de capa).

esclavista *adj* pro-slavery.
◆ *m/f* slavery supporter.

esclavitud *f* slavery; *vivir en la esclavitud* to live in slavery || FIG slavery; *este trabajo es una esclavitud* this job is pure slavery.

esclavizar *vt* to enslave || FIG to overwork, to slave-drive (hacer trabajar mucho); *el jefe esclaviza a todos los empleados* the boss slave-drives all the employees | to dominate (dominar).

esclavo, va *m/f* slave || FIG slave; *un esclavo de la bebida, del trabajo* a slave to drink, to work.
◆ *f* bracelet, bangle (pulsera).
◆ *adj* enslaved || FIG tied; *ser esclavo de la casa, del despacho* to be tied to the house, to the office | devoted (entregado); *ser esclavo de sus amigos* to be devoted to one's friends | addicted; *es esclavo de la bebida* he is addicted to drink || — *esclavo de su palabra* faithful to one's word || *ser esclavo de su deber* to be a slave to one's duties.

esclerosis *f* MED sclerosis (endurecimiento) || *esclerosis múltiple* multiple sclerosis || FIG paralysis (de una industria, etc.).

escleroso, sa *adj* MED sclerotic, sclerosed.

esclerótica *f* ANAT sclerotic, sclera.

esclusa *f* lock, sluice (de un canal) || floodgate (compuerta) || *esclusa de aire* airlock.

esclusero, ra *m/f* lockkeeper.

escoba *f* broom (utensilio) || broomstick (de bruja) || BOT broom || — DEP *camión escoba* support vehicle || *pasar la escoba* to sweep up.

escobajo *m* old broom || stalk (del racimo de uvas).

escobazo; escobonazo *m* blow with a broom || — *le dio un escobazo en la cabeza* she hit him on the head with the broom || FIG & FAM *lo echaron a escobazos* they botted him out.

escobén *m* MAR hawsehole.

escobilla *f* brush (cepillo) || small broom (escoba pequeña) || TECN brush (de dinamo) || BOT teasel (cardencha) | heather (brezo).

escobillar; escobillear *vt* to brush.
◆ *vi AMER* to do shuffing steps (baile).

escobillón *m* MIL swab.

escobina *f* filings *pl* (de un metal) | sawdust (de la madera).

escobón *m* large broom || wall brush (de mango largo) || short broom (de mango corto) || chimney-sweeping brush (deshollinador).

escobonazo *m* → **escobazo.**

escocedor, ra *adj* painful, hurtful.

escocedura *f*; **escocimiento** ; **escozor** *m* sore (en la piel) || sting, smarting, soreness (de una herida) || FIG hurt feelings *pl* (en el sentimiento).

escocer* *vi* to smart, to sting (irritar); *me escuece la herida* my wound stings || FIG to hurt the feelings of, to hurt; *su falta de respeto me escoció* his lack of respect hurt me *o* hurt my feelings.
◆ *vt* to chafe; *tengo la piel escocida* my skin is chafed.
◆ *vpr* to get sore (la piel, etc.) || — *el niño se ha escocido* or *está escocido* the baby is all sore || FIG *se escoció por lo que le dije* he was hurt *o* his feelings were hurt by what I said to him.

escocés, esa *adj* Scottish, Scots (persona) || Scotch (comida, whisky) || *tela escocesa* tartan, plaid.
◆ *m/f* Scotsman, Scot (hombre), Scotswoman, Scot (mujer).
◆ *m* Scottish, Scots (lengua).

Escocia *npr f* GEOGR Scotland || *Nueva Escocia* Nova Scotia.

escocimiento *m* → **escocedura.**

escoda *f* TECN stonecutter's hammer, bushhammer.

escodar *vt* TECN to cut (with a hammer) || to rub (el ciervo).

escofia; escofieta *f* cap, coif (cofia).

escofina *f* TECN rasp; *escofina de mediacaña* half-round rasp.

escofinar *vt* TECN to rasp.

escoger *vt* to choose, to pick, to select; *escoger una manzana de una cesta* to choose an apple from a basket || to choose; *escoge entre estos dos colores* choose between these two colours; *escoger entre muchas cosas* to choose from many things || — *a escoger* to choose from; *hay cinco platos a escoger* there are five plates to choose from || *escoger a bulto* or *al buen tuntún* to choose at random || *escoger como* or *para* or *por mujer* to choose as one's wife || *muchos son los llamados y pocos los escogidos* many are called but few are chosen || *tener de sobra donde escoger* to have more than enough to choose from || *tener donde escoger* to have a good choice *o* selection.

escogidamente *adv* discerningly (con discernimiento) || perfectly (muy bien).

escogido, da *adj* chosen, selected || selected; *obras escogidas* selected works || choice, select (de calidad); *mercancías escogidas* choice goods || MIL *tropas escogidas* crack troops.

escogimiento *m* choice, selection.

escolanía *f* choir school (escuela) || choirboys *pl* (escolanos).

escolano *m* choirboy, chorister.

escolapio *m* monk who teaches in a charity school (religioso) || charity school pupil (alumno).

escolar *adj* school, scholastic; *edad escolar* school age; *curso escolar* school year || — *comportamiento escolar* conduct in school || *libro escolar* school book (para estudiar), report book (para consignar las notas).
◆ *m/f* schoolboy, pupil (muchacho), schoolgirl, pupil (muchacha).

escolaridad *f* schooling; *se exige un mínimo de escolaridad* a minimum of schooling is required; *escolaridad obligatoria* compulsory schooling || *prolongar la escolaridad hasta los dieciséis años* to raise the school-leaving age to sixteen.

escolarización *f* schooling.

escolástica *f*; **escolasticismo** *m* scholasticism.

escolástico, ca *adj* scholastic; *doctrina escolástica* scholastic doctrine.
◆ *m/f* scholastic.

escolio *m* scholium (nota) || MAT scholium.

escoliosis *f* MED scoliosis.

escolopendra *f* ZOOL scolopendrid, scolopendra, centipede (ciempiés) || BOT scolopendrium, hart's-tongue (lengua de ciervo).

escolta *f* escort || MAR escort (barco) || *dar escolta a* to escort.

escoltar *vt* to escort.

escollar *vi* AMER to run aground (encallarse) | FIG to fail (malograrse).

escollera *f* breakwater (rompeolas).

escollo *m* reef (arrecife) || FIG difficulty, stumbling block; *tropezar con un escollo* to come up against a difficulty | danger (peligro).

escombrar *vt* to clear (quitar los escombros de).

escombrera *f* rubbish dump, tip || tip (de mina de carbón) || slag heap (de escoria).

escombro *m* mackerel (pez).

escombros *m pl* debris *sing*, rubble *sing* (de un edificio, etc.) || slag *sing* (escoria).

esconce *m* recess (ángulo entrante) || corner, angle (ángulo saliente).

escondedero *m* hiding place (escondrijo).

esconder *m* hide-and-seek (escondite).

esconder *vt* to hide; *el niño escondió la muñeca en el cajón* the child hid the doll in the drawer || to hide, to conceal; *su sonrisa esconde su tristeza* his smile conceals his sadness.
◆ *vpr* to hide; *esconderse de uno* to hide from s.o. || to hide o.s., to hide; *se escondió en el armario* he hid himself in the cupboard || to lurk, to hide, to be concealed *o* hidden; *en su alma se esconde la tristeza* sadness lurks in his soul.

escondidamente *adv* secretly, on the sly.

escondidas *f pl* AMER hide-and-seek (juego).
◆ *adv* *a escondidas* secretly || *hacer algo a escondidas de alguien* to do sth. without s.o.'s knowledge.

escondido *m* AMER hide-and-seek (escondite).

escondite *m* hiding place (escondrijo) || hide-and-seek (juego de niños); *jugar al escondite* to play (at) hide-and-seek.

escondrijo *m* hiding place.

escopeta *f* shotgun, rifle; *escopeta de dos cañones* double-barrelled shotgun || — FIG & FAM *aquí te quiero ver, escopeta* let's see what you can do, show us what you can do || *escopeta de aire comprimido* air gun, air rifle.

escopetazo *m* (shotgun) shot, gunshot (disparo) || shotgun wound (herida) || FIG piece of bad news, blow.

escopetear *vt* to shoot at with a shotgun *o* rifle.
◆ *vi* to fire a shotgun.
◆ *vpr* FIG to shower each other with compliments *o* with flattery (lisonjearse) | to shower each other with insults (con insultos) | to fire questions at each other (con preguntas).

escopeteo *m* (shotgun) shooting || FIG & FAM *un escopeteo de insultos, de cortesías, de preguntas* a shower of insults, of politeness, of questions.

escopetería *f* MIL gunshots *pl* || men *pl* armed with shotguns *o* rifles, riflemen *pl* (hombres).

escopetero *m* soldier armed with a shotgun, rifleman (soldado) || man armed with a shotgun (hombre) || gunsmith (fabricante) || ZOOL bombardier beetle.

escopladura; escopleadura *f* TECN cut made with a chisel (corte) | chiselling (acción).

escoplear *vt* to chisel.

escoplo *m* TECN chisel.

escora *f* MAR level line (línea del fuerte) | stanchion, prop (puntal) | list (inclinación del barco).

escorar *vt* MAR to stanchion, to prop (apuntalar).
◆ *vi* MAR to list (un barco); *escora a estribor* she is listing to starboard.

escorbútico, ca *adj* MED scorbutic.

escorbuto *m* MED scurvy.

escoria *f* slag (de mina) || slag, dross, scoria (de alto horno) || scoria (de volcán) || FIG scum, dregs *pl*; *la escoria de la sociedad* the scum of society.

escoriáceo, a *adj* scoriaceous.

escoriación *f* chafing, excoriation (p us).

escorial *m* slag heap.

Escorial (El) *npr m* El Escorial.

escoriar *vt* to chafe, to excoriate (p us).
◆ *vpr* to chafe.

escorificación *f* slagging, scorification.

escorificar *vt* to slag, to scorify.

Escorpio; Escorpión *m* ASTR Scorpio.

escorpión *m* scorpion || FIG *lengua de escorpión* evil tongue.

escorzado *m* → **escorzo.**

escorzar *vt* ARTES to foreshorten.

escorzo; escorzado *m* ARTES foreshortening (acción y efecto) | foreshortened figure (figura).

escorzonera *f* BOT viper's grass, scorzonera.

escota *f* MAR sheet.

escotado, da; descotado, da *adj* low-necked, low-cut (vestido) || wearing a low-necked *o* a low-cut dress (persona) || *iba muy escotada* she was wearing a very low-necked dress.
◆ *m* (low) neck, (low) neckline (escotadura).

escotadura *f* scooping-out (corte) || (low) neck, (low) neckline (abertura del cuello) || armhole (de una manga) || TEATR large trapdoor.

escotar; descotar *vt* to scoop out *o* to cut out the armhole in (para la manga) || to scoop out *o* to cut out the neckline in (para el cuello) || to lower the neckline of (para ensanchar) || to cut to fit (para ajustar) || to divert water from (a river) || to contribute; *todos escotaron su parte* everybody contributed his share.
◆ *vi/vpr* to chip in, to pay one's share *o* way (pagar su cuota) || to go Dutch (una pareja) || to club together, to chip in; *vamos a escotarnos para comprarle un regalo* let's club together to buy him a present.

escote; descote *m* neck, neckline (corte del cuello) || low neck, low neckline, décolleté, décolletage (abertura grande alrededor del cuello) || armhole (para la manga) || lace frill (adorno) || neck (parte del cuerpo descubierta) || share, contribution (cuota) || — *comprar algo a escote* to club together to buy sth. || *pagar a escote* to go Dutch (una pareja) || *pagar algo a escote* to chip in to pay for sth. (entre varias personas) || *pagar su escote* to pay one's share *o* one's way, to chip in, to make one's contribution, to contribute; *cada chico pagó su escote* each boy paid his share, each boy made his contribution *o* contributed.

escotilla *f* MAR hatchway.

escotillón *m* MAR & TEATR trapdoor.

escozor *m* → **escocedura.**

escriba *m* scribe.

escribanía *f* portable writing case (caja portátil) || writing desk (mueble) || writing materials *pl* (recado de escribir) || notary's position (oficio de notario) || notary's office (despacho del notario) || clerkship (oficio de secretario judicial) || clerk's office (despacho del secretario judicial).

escribano *m* clerk, secretary (escribiente) || clerk of the court (secretario judicial) || notary (notario) || ZOOL whirligig beetle.

escribido, da *adj* FAM *ser muy leído y escribido* to be well read, to be very knowledgeable (presumir de sabio).

escribidor *m* FAM hack writer.

escribiente *m/f* clerk.

escribir *vt* to write; *escribe cuentos para niños* he writes children's stories || to write, to compose (música) || to spell (ortografiar); *no sabe escribir esta palabra* he cannot spell this word || to write to tell; *me ha escrito que vendrá mañana* he has written to tell me that he is coming tomorrow || — *escribir algo a mano* to write by hand || *escribir algo a máquina* to type sth. || *escribir algo de su puño y letra* to write sth. by hand, to do sth. in one's own handwriting || *máquina de escribir* typewriter || *papel de escribir* writing paper, notepaper.
◆ *vi* to write; *me escribe cada mes* he writes to me every month.
◆ *vpr* to be spelt, to spell; *¿cómo se escribe la palabra?* how is the word spelt?, how do you spell the word? || *se escriben cada semana* they write to each other every week.

escriño *m* straw basket (cesta) || coffer (cofrecito).

escrito, ta *adj* written; *examen escrito* written examination; *avaricia escrita en su cara* greed written on his face || — *escrito a mano* handwritten || *escrito a máquina* typewritten, typed; *una carta escrita a máquina* a typewritten letter || FIG *estaba escrito* it was inevitable || *lo arriba escrito* what has been said above, the above | FIG *lo escrito, escrito está* it's down in writing, it's down in black and white.
◆ *m* writing, work; *los escritos de Ortega* the works of Ortega || letter; *le mandó un escrito* he sent him a letter || document (documento) || written exam (examen) || writing; *había un escrito en la pared* there was some writing on the wall || JUR writ || *poner por escrito* to put down *o* to put in writing, to write down.

escritor, ra *m/f* writer.

escritorio *m* bureau [US secretary] (mueble) || office (despacho) || — *gastos de escritorio* stationery expenses || *objetos de escritorio* stationery *sing*, writing materials.

escritorzuelo, la *m/f* third-rate writer, hack writer.

escritura *f* writing; *la escritura de una carta* the writing of a letter; *la escritura griega* Greek writing || script; *escritura fonética* phonetic script || writing, handwriting (letra) || document (documento) || JUR deed; *escritura de propiedad* title deed; *escritura notarial* notarial deed | bill; *escritura de venta* bill of sale || *la Sagrada Escritura* the Holy Scripture.

escriturar *vt* to legalize with a written document, to execute by deed, to notarize || to book, to engage (a un artista).

escriturario, ria *adj* notarial.
◆ *m* bible scholar, scripturalist.

escrófula *f* MED scrofula.

escrofuloso, sa *adj* MED scrofulous.

escroto *m* ANAT scrotum.

escrúpulo *m* scruple; *tener escrúpulos* to have scruples || scrupulousness, conscientiousness, extreme care (escrupulosidad); *hacer algo con escrúpulo* to do sth. with extreme care || stone [in one's shoe] (piedrecilla) || — *escrúpulos de conciencia* qualms of conscience || *me da escrúpulo beber en el vaso de otro* I have qualms about drinking from another person's glass || *un hombre de negocios sin escrúpulos* an unscrupulous businessman.

escrupulosidad *f* scrupulousness, extreme care.

escrupuloso, sa *adj* scrupulous (que tiene escrúpulos de conciencia) || scrupulous, concientious (concienzudo) || scrupulous, meticulous; *con escrupulosa atención* with meticulous care || fussy, particular; *no me gusta invitar a esa gente porque es demasiado escrupulosa* I don't like inviting those people because they are too fussy.

escrutador, ra *adj* scrutinizing, examining || searching; *mirada escrutadora* searching look.
◆ *m/f* teller (en una asamblea) || scrutineer (que comprueba la validez de los votos).

escrutar *vt* to scrutinize, to examine || to count (votos).

escrutinio *m* count, counting of the votes (recuento) || examination, scrutiny (averiguación); *hacer el escrutinio de una cosa* to carry out an examination on sth. || *efectuar* or *hacer el escrutinio* to count the votes.

escuadra *f* square (instrumento) || angle iron (pieza para consolidar) || MIL squad | rank of corporal (cargo de cabo) || FIG gang (de obreros) || MAR squadron, fleet || DEP angle (fútbol) || — *a escuadra* at right angles || *corte a escuadra* squaring || *escuadra de agrimensor* surveyor's cross || *falsa escuadra, escuadra móvil* bevel square || *fuera de escuadra* on the bevel || *labrar a escuadra* to square.

escuadrar *vt* to square.

escuadreo *m* squaring (medición por áreas).

escuadrilla *f* MAR & AVIAC squadron.

escuadrón *m* MIL squadron || *escuadrón de la muerte* death squad.

escuálido, da *adj* skinny, thin (delgado) || filthy, squalid (sucio).

escualo *m* ZOOL shark (pez).

escucha *f* listening (acción de escuchar) || nun acting as a chaperon (monja) || listening-in (de comunicaciones) || — *estación de escucha* listening-in station || *estar a la escucha* to be listening || *ponerse a la escucha* to listen.
◆ *m* MIL scout (centinela) || monitor (sistema de detección) || listener (radioyente).

escuchar *vt* to listen to; *escuchar música* to listen to music || to hear (oír) || to listen to, to pay attention to (un consejo).
◆ *vi* to listen; *escuchar detrás de las puertas* to listen at doors.
◆ *vpr* to like to hear o.s. talk.

escuchimizado, da *adj* thin, puny.

escudar *vt* to shield, to protect with a shield || FIG to shield, to protect (proteger).
◆ *vpr* to shield o.s., to protect o.s. with a shield || FIG to hide, to use as an excuse; *siempre se escuda con el trabajo para no ayudarme* he always hides behind his work *o* he always uses his work as an excuse so that he doesn't have to help me.

escudería *f* squiredom, position as squire || AUT stable (de coches).

escudero *m* squire (paje) || nobleman (hidalgo) || lady's page (servidor de señora) || shield maker (fabricante).

escudete *m* small shield (escudo pequeño) || gusset (costura) || escutcheon (de una cerradura) || AGR shield; *injerto de escudete* shield grafting || BOT water lily.

escudilla *f* bowl (recipiente) || bowlful (contenido) || AMER large cup (tazón).

escudo *m* shield (arma defensiva) || escudo (moneda) || HERÁLD coat of arms || escutcheon (de una cerradura) || gun shield (del cañón) || MAR escutcheon (espejo de popa) || AGR shield || FIG shield, protection (defensa, protección) || shoulder (del jabalí) || *escudo de armas* coat of arms.

escudriñamiento *m* investigation, inquiry, examination (investigación) || search, scanning (del horizonte, etc.) || scrutinizing, examination (acción de mirar cuidadosamente).

escudriñar *vt* to investigate, to inquire into, to examine (examinar); *escudriñar la vida de alguien* to investigate *o* to inquire into s.o.'s life || to search, to scan; *escudriñar el horizonte* to scan the horizon || to scrutinize, to examine; *escudriñar un mapa para encontrar una pequeña calle* to examine a map to find a small street.

escuela *f* school; *escuela de párvulos* infant school; *escuela de equitación* riding school; *escuela de Bellas Artes* Art School || training (instrucción); *tiene buena disposición para el clarinete, pero le falta escuela* he's well suited for the clarinet, but he needs training || teaching (métodos de enseñanza) || FIG school; *escuela racionalista, holandesa* rationalist, Dutch school || — *alta escuela* higher horsemanship (equitación) || *escuela de artes y oficios* technical school || *escuela de comercio* business school || *escuela de ingenieros agrónomos* agricultural college || *escuela de negocios* business school || *escuela de primera enseñanza, de enseñanza secundaria* or *media* primary, secondary school || *escuela nocturna* night school || *escuela normal* teachers' training college [US Normal School] || *escuela privada* private school || *escuela pública* state school || *escuela universitaria* school attached to a university || *formar escuela* to found a school || *ser de la vieja escuela* to be of the old school || *tener buena escuela* to be well trained.

escuerzo *m* toad (sapo) || FIG rake, bean pole (persona flaca).

escueto, ta *adj* concise (conciso); *un informe muy escueto* a very concise report || simple, unadorned; *lenguaje, estilo escueto* simple language, style || plain; *la verdad escueta* the plain truth.

escuincle, cla *m/f* AMER kid (chiquillo, muchacho).

Esculapio *npr m* Aesculapius.

esculpir *vt* to sculpture; *esculpir una estatua en piedra* to sculpture a statue in stone || to engrave (grabar) || to carve (madera).

escultor, ra *m/f* sculptor (hombre), sculptress (mujer); *escultor en mármol* sculptor of marble.

escultura *f* sculpture || carving (de madera) || engraving (grabado).

escultural *adj* sculptural || FIG statuesque (cuerpo de una mujer).

escupida *f* AMER spit (salivajo).

escupidera *f* spittoon, cuspidor (para escupir) || chamber pot (orinal).

escupidura *f* spit, spittle (esputo) || phlegm (flema) || cracking [of the lips] (en los labios).

escupir *vi* to spit; *se prohibe escupir* no spitting || FIG to blot, to make blots (una pluma) || FAM to cough up (pagar) || — FAM *escupir a uno* to spit in s.o.'s face | *es su padre escupido* he is the spit and image of his father, he is the spitting image of his father | *si escupes al cielo, en la cara te caerá* chickens and curses come home to roost.
◆ *vt* to spit, to spit out; *escupir sangre* to spit blood || FIG to belch out; *el volcán escupía lava* the volcano was belching out lava | to throw out; *escupir metralla* to throw out shrapnel | to spit out (injurias, etc.) || FAM to fork out, to cough up (dinero) || *esta pluma escupe tinta* this fountain pen blots *o* makes blots.

escupitajo *m*; **escupitina** *f*; **escupitinajo** *m*; **escupo** *m* spit, spittle.

escurialense *adj* of *o* from El Escorial.

escurrebotellas *m inv* draining rack [for bottles].

escurreplatos *m inv* plate rack, dish rack.

escurridero *m* draining rack (de botellas) || plate rack, dish rack (de vajilla) || draining board (del fregadero).

escurridizo, za *adj* slippy, slippery (resbaladizo) || FIG elusive; *idea escurridiza* elusive idea | slippery; *problema escurridizo* slippery problem; *persona escurridiza* slippery person || FAM *hacerse el escurridizo* to slip off *o* away, to sneak off *o* away.

escurrido, da *adj* narrow-hipped, slim-hipped (de caderas) || wearing a tight skirt (una mujer) || *AMER* ashamed (avergonzado).

escurridor *m* dish rack, plate rack (escurreplatos) || draining board (del fregadero) || colander (colador) || wringer (para la ropa).

escurriduras *f pl* dregs (de un vaso o botella) || drips; *escurriduras de pintura* paint drips.

escurrimiento *m* draining (de platos, manjares) || dripping (de la ropa) || FIG slip (desliz).

escurrir *vt* to drain || to wring (la ropa) || FAM *escurrir el bulto* to get out of it, to dodge it.
◆ *vi* to drip (líquidos, ropa) || to be slippery (ser resbaladizo); *este suelo escurre* this floor is slippery.
◆ *vpr* to slip; *escurrirse en el hielo* to slip on the ice; *escurrirse de* or *entre las manos de alguien* to slip out of s.o.'s hands || to drip (líquidos, ropa) || FIG & FAM to slip off *o* away, to sneak off *o* away (escabullirse) | to give o.s. away (en la conversación) | to make a slip (equivocarse).

esdrujulizar *vt* to accentuate the antepenultimate syllabe of.

esdrújulo, la *adj* proparoxytone, accented on the antepenultimate syllabe.
◆ *m* proparoxytone, word accented on the antepenultimate syllabe.

ese *f* s [name of the letter *s*] || zigzag; *las eses de la carretera* the zigzags in the road || s-hook (gancho) || sound hole (de violín, etc.) || — *andar haciendo eses* to stagger (dando traspiés), to zigzag (zigzaguear) || *hundir el puñal hasta la ese* to push a dagger in up to the hilt || *la carretera hace eses* the road twists and turns.

ese, esa; esos, esas *adj dem* that; those; *esa mujer* that woman; *esos libros son tuyos* those books are yours.
— OBSERV *Ese* denotes proximity to the person spoken to (see *aquel* and *este*). When placed after the noun, *ese* often has a pejorative meaning: *¡qué pesado es el niño ese!* what a nuisance that child is!

ése, ésa; ésos, ésas *pron dem* that one; those; *me gusta más esta casa que ésa* I like this house more than that one; *ésos son tus poderes* those are your powers || the former (el último) || he, she, that one; they, those, those ones (véase OBSERV); *ése lo sabe* he knows; *ésos se quedan* they stay || him, her, that one; them, those, those ones (véase OBSERV); *se lo he dado a ése* I've given it to him || — FIG & FAM *¡conque ésas tenemos!* so that's it! | *¡choque usted ésa!* shake on it! || *en una de ésas* one of these days || *ése que* that one who; *ése que vino ayer* that one who came yesterday || *llegaré a ésa mañana* I shall arrive in your town tomorrow || FAM *ni por ésas* even so; *ni por ésas lo consiguió* even so he didn't get it | *¡no me vengas con ésas!* don't come to me with that story.
— OBSERV According to the Spanish Academy the accents on the pronouns *ése, ésa, ésos, ésas* are optional. The accent on the pronouns was originally intended to distinguish them from adjectives. Now it may be omitted in all cases where no confusion is possible.
— OBSERV Cabe señalar que los pronombres *ése, ésa, ésos* se traducen por *he, she, it, they* cuando tienen la función de sujeto, y por *him, her, it, them* cuando tienen la función de complemento directo o indirecto. Cuando *ése* y *ésa* tienen un sentido despectivo equivalen a *that one* (véase OBSERV en ESE).

esecilla *f* TECN small S-hook (alacrán).

esencia *f* essence; *esencia del liberalismo* essence of liberalism || essence, entity (entidad) || essence (extracto concentrado); *esencia de café* coffee essence || perfume; *un frasco de esencia* a bottle of perfume || QUÍM essence, essential oil || FIG heart, core, essence (de un problema) || — FIG *contar algo en esencia* to give a brief outline of sth. | *en esencia* essentially, in essence (esencialmente) || *quinta esencia* quintessence.

esencial *adj* essential; *la aplicación es esencial en los estudios* application is essential in studying; *aceite esencial* essential oil || — *en lo esencial* in the main || *lo esencial* the main *o* the essential thing; *lo esencial es ser honrado* the main thing is to be honest || *no esencial* nonessential, inessential.

esfenoidal *adj* ANAT sphenoidal.

esfenoideo, a *adj* ANAT sphenoidal.

esfenoides *adj/sm* ANAT sphenoid.

esfera *f* sphere; *esfera armilar* armillary sphere; *esfera celeste* celestial sphere || dial, face (de reloj) || TENC dial || circle, sphere (ambiente); *salirse de su esfera* to leave one's circle || field, sphere; *esfera de actividad* field of action || — *esfera terrestre* (terrestrial) globe || *las altas esferas* high circles; *se dice en las altas esferas que...* it is being said in high circles that...

esfericidad *f* sphericity.

esférico, ca *adj* MAT spherical.
◆ *m* FAM ball (balón).

esferoidal *adj* MAT spheroidal.

esferoide *m* MAT spheroid.

esferómetro *m* spherometer.

esfigmografía *f* MED sohygmography.

esfigmómetro *m* MED sphygmometer.

esfinge *f* sphinx || ZOOL hawkmoth (mariposa nocturna) || FIG sphinx.

esfínter *m* ANAT sphincter.

esforzado, da *adj* courageous, valiant (valiente) || vigorous, energetic (vigoroso).

esforzar* *vt* (p us) to encourage.
◆ *vpr* to make an effort, to exert o.s. (hacer un esfuerzo físico); *el niño tuvo que esforzarse para levantar la silla* the child had to make an effort *o* the child had to exert himself to lift the chair || to strive; *se esfuerza en* or *por llevar una vida moral* he strives to lead a moral life || to try hard, to make an effort (intentar); *esfuérzate por* or *para aprenderlo* try hard to learn it || to do one's best (hacer todo lo posible); *me esforzaré en* or *por darle satisfacción* I'll do my best to please you || MED to strain o.s.

esfuerzo *m* effort; *redoblar los esfuerzos* to double one's efforts || effort, endeavour, attempt (intento) || TECN stress (en mecánica) || — *aplicar la ley del mínimo esfuerzo* to make the least effort possible || *hacer esfuerzos* or *un esfuerzo* to make an effort, to exert o.s. (hacer un esfuerzo físico), to try hard, to make an effort (intentar), to do one's best (hacer todo lo posible) || *sin esfuerzo* effortlessly.

esfumación *f* stumping, toning down.

esfumar *vt* to stump, to tone down.
◆ *vpr* to fade away, to disappear.

esfuminar *vt* to stump.

esfumino *m* stump (lápiz) || stump drawing (dibujo).

esgrima *f* fencing; *maestro de esgrima* fencing master || *practicar la esgrima* to fence.

esgrimir *vt* to brandish; *esgrimir un palo* to brandish a stick || to wield (una espada) || FIG to use [as a weapon]; *esgrimir un argumento* to use an argument.
◆ *vi* to fence.

esgrimista *m/f* *AMER* fencer.

esguince; desguince *m* MED sprain, twist (torcedura) || swerve, dodge (del cuerpo) || (p us) frown (gesto de desagrado) || *el accidente le produjo un esguince en el tobillo* he sprained his ankle in the accident.

eslabón *m* link (de cadena) || steel (para sacar chispas) || steel (para afilar) || ZOOL scorpion (alacrán) || FIG link || VET splint || MAR *eslabón giratorio* swivel.

eslabonamiento *m* linking.

eslabonar *vt* to link together || FIG to link, to interlink, to connect.
◆ *vpr* FIG to be linked.

eslavizar *vt* to slavicize.

eslavo, va *adj* Slav, Slavonic.
◆ *m/f* Slav (persona).
◆ *m* Slavonic (lengua).

eslinga *f* MAR sling (cabo).

eslogan *m* slogan.

eslora *f* MAR length (de un barco); *eslora total* overall length.
◆ *pl* MAR binding strakes (brazolas).

esmaltado *m* enamelling.

esmaltador, ra *m/f* enameller.

esmaltar *vt* to enamel || to varnish, to paint (las uñas) || FIG to be scattered over; *flores de varios colores esmaltan el prado* flowers of several colours are scattered over the meadow | to adorn, to sprinkle; *esmaltar una conversación con* or *de citas latinas* to adorn a conversation with Latin quotations.

esmalte *m* enamel; *esmalte campeado* champlevé enamel || enamel (de los dientes) || enamelling (decoración, arte) || enamelled object (objeto esmaltado) || smalt (color) || HERÁLD tincture || *esmalte de* or *para uñas* nail varnish, nail enamel, nail polish.

esmeradamente *adv* carefully, with great care (con cuidado) || elegantly (con elegancia).

esmerado, da *adj* carefully done, neat (bien hecho); *un ejercicio esmerado* a carefully done exercise || careful, painstaking; *una criada esmerada* a careful maid || elegant.

esmeralda *f* emerald.

esmerar *vt* to tidy up, to clean up (limpiar).
◆ *vpr* to take pains, to take care (esforzarse); *esmerarse en el trabajo* to take pains over one's work || to do one's best (hacer todo lo posible).

esmeril *m* emery (piedra) || *papel de esmeril* emery paper.

esmerilado, da *adj* TECN ground (vidrio) | polished with emery (pulido) || *papel esmerilado* emery paper.
◆ *m* TECN grinding | polishing (acción de pulir).

esmerilar *vt* TECN to grind; *esmerilar una válvula, vidrio* to grind a valve, glass | to polish with emery (pulir).

esmero *m* care; *trabajar, escribir con esmero* to work, to write with care || neatness (aseo) || — *estar vestido con esmero* to be neatly dressed || *poner esmero en* to take pains over, to take care over; *puso mucho esmero en esta carta* he took great pains over this letter.

Esmirna *npr f* GEOGR Smyrna, Izmir.

esmirriado, da *adj* puny, thin (escuchimizado) || FIG scraggy; *árbol esmirriado* scraggy tree.

esmoquin *m* dinner jacket [*US* tuxedo].

esmorecerse *vpr* to faint.

esnifada *f* sniff, snort (de droga).

esnifar *vtr* to sniff, to snort (droga).

esnob *adj* snobbish.
◆ *m/f* snob.

esnobismo *m* snobbery, snobbishness.

esnórquel *m* MAR snorkel.

eso *pron dem neutro* that; *eso no me gusta* I don't like that; *antes, después de eso* before, after that || — *a eso de* at about; *a eso de las nueve* at about nine o'clock || *a pesar de eso* in spite of that || *en eso* at that moment, at that point || *¡eso!, ¡eso es!* that's it || *eso de no tener salud es muy fastidioso* (the fact of) being unhealthy is very annoying || *eso de tu accidente no es más que...* all that about your accident is just... || *eso mismo* just that, exactly || *¡eso no!* certainly not!; *¿vienes? ¡eso no!* are you coming? certainly not! || *eso que me contaste ayer* that story you told me yesterday || *eso que me dijiste me parece excelente* what you told me sounds excellent || *¡eso sí!* of course! certainly! || *¡eso sí que es...!* that certainly is...!; *¡eso sí que es una buena acción!* that certainly is a good deed! || *¡eso sí que no!* certainly not! || *hace diez años de eso* it's ten years since then (diez años han transcurrido), ten years before that (diez años antes de ese acontecimiento) || *¡nada de eso!* none of that! || *¿no es eso?* isn't that right?, isn't that so? || *no es eso ni mucho menos* it's not that at all, it's nothing like that || *por eso* that's why; *por eso lo hice* that's why I did it; therefore (por consiguiente) || *¿qué es eso?* what's that? || *y eso que* although, in spite of the fact that; *habla mal el inglés, y eso que ha vivido en Londres* he speaks English badly although he has lived in London.

esos, esas *adj dem pl* → **ese.**

ésos, ésas *pron dem* → **ése.**

esófago *m* ANAT Oesophagus [*US* esophagus].

Esopo *npr m* Aesop.

esotérico, ca *adj* esoteric (oculto, secreto).

esoterismo *m* esoterism, esotericism.

esotro, tra, esotros, tras *adj dem* (contraction of «ese» and «otro» that other, those others.

◆ *pron* that other one, those other ones.
— OBSERV Like *ese, esotro* can have a pejorative meaning.

espabiladeras *f pl* snuffers.

espabilado, da *adj* → **despabilado.**

espabilar *vt* → **despabilar.**

espaciador *m* space bar, spacer (en una máquina de escribir).

espacial *adj* space; *vuelo espacial* space flight; *encuentro espacial* space rendezvous || — *nave espacial* spaceship || *vehículos espaciales* spacecraft.

espaciamiento *m* spacing (distancia) || staggering (escalonamiento).

espaciar *vt* to space out, to spread out (poner espacio entre) || to stagger, to space out; *espaciar los pagos* to stagger payments || IMPR to space; *espaciar los renglones* to space lines of type | to spread (divulgar).

◆ *vpr* to spread (divulgarse) || FIG to expatiate; *espaciarse en una carta* to expatiate in a letter | to enjoy o.s. (distraerse).

espacio *m* space; *espacio entre dos cosas* space between two things; *viaje por el espacio* space journey || room, space; *este armario ocupa mucho espacio* this wardrobe takes up a lot of room || space, period (de tiempo) || distance (distancia) || IMPR & MÚS space || FIG slowness (tardanza) || programme [*US* program] (en televisión) || — *a doble espacio* double-spacing || *doble espacio* double spacing || *espacio aéreo* air space || INFORM *espacio de dirección* address space || IMPR *espacio interlineal* line spacing || *espacio publicitario* advertising spot (en televisión), advertising slot (en la prensa) || *espacio-tiempo* space-time || *espacio vital* living space || *espacios verdes* green open space, open space || *por espacio de* during, for.

espacioso, sa *adj* spacious, roomy (amplio); *un cuarto espacioso* a spacious room || slow (lento).

espachurrar *vt* FAM to squash.

espada *f* sword; *traer la espada al cinto* to be wearing one's sword || FIG swordsman (persona); *ser buena espada* to be a good swordsman | authority, important figure; *es una de las primeras espadas en su profesión* he is one of the biggest authorities *o* he is one of the most important figures in his profession || — *cruzar la espada con alguien* to cross swords with s.o. || *de capa y espada* cloak and dagger || *desenvainar* or *desnudar la espada* to unsheathe *o* to draw one's sword || FIG & FAM *echar su cuarto a espadas* to butt in, to put one's oar in || *envainar la espada* to sheathe one's sword || *espada de dos filos* two-edged sword (espada), double-edged argument (argumento) || FIG *estar entre la espada y la pared* to be between the devil and the deep blue sea || *meter la espada hasta la guarnición* to plunge one's sword in up to the hilt || *pez espada* swordfish || FIG *quienes matan con la espada por la espada morirán* he who lives by the sword will die by the sword.

◆ *pl* «espadas» [corresponds to spades in the English pack of cards].

espada *m* TAUR matador.

espadachín *m* good swordsman (buen esgrimidor) || bully (bravucón).

espadaña *f* BOT bulrush || ARQ bell gable.

espadín *m* ceremonial sword || sprat (pez).

espaguetis *m pl* spaghetti *sing*.

espalda *f* back || DEP backstroke; *200 metros espalda* 200 metres backstroke || MIL rearguard || FIG *cubrir las espaldas* to cover o.s. || — *dar* or *volver la espalda a uno* to turn one's back on s.o. || FAM *echarse entre pecho y espalda* to put away, to tuck away (comida, bebida) || *en la espalda* in one's back || *espalda con espalda* back to back || *herir a uno por la espalda* to injure s.o. in the back (con un arma), to stab s.o. in the back (con una mala acción) || *nadar de espalda* to swim backstroke, to swim on one's back || *por la espalda* from behind || FIG *tener muchos años a la espalda* to have a lot of years behind one || *volver la espalda* to turn round (volverse) || *volver la espalda a uno* to turn one's back on s.o. (sentido propio), to give s.o. the cold shoulder, to turn one's back on s.o. (sentido figurado).

◆ *pl* back *sing* (de persona, de cosa) || — *a espaldas de alguien* behind s.o.'s back || *a las espaldas* in one's back; *con el sol a las espaldas* with the sun in one's back || *anchura de espaldas* width of shoulders || *caer* or *caerse* or *dar de espaldas* to fall (flat) on one's back || *cargado de espaldas* round-shouldered; *este joven es cargado de espaldas* this young man is round-shouldered || *de espaldas* from behind; *sólo le vi de espaldas* I only saw him from behind || FAM *echarse algo a las espaldas* to forget about sth. | *echarse una cosa sobre las espaldas* to take sth. on, to take sth. upon o.s. | *esta noticia me tiró de espaldas* this news knocked me flat || *estar de espaldas* to have one's back turned || *estar tendido de espaldas* to be lying on one's back || FIG *guardar las espaldas* to keep sth. in reserve || *guardar las espaldas de alguien* to back s.o. || FIG & FAM *hablar por las espaldas* to talk behind people's backs || FIG *medirle a uno las espaldas* to give s.o. a beating, to beat s.o. up || *poner de espaldas* to pin (en la lucha) || *ser ancho de espaldas* to be broad-shouldered || FIG *tener buenas espaldas* or *anchas espaldas* to be easygoing | *tener guardadas las espaldas* to be well backed.

espaldar *m* back plate (de coraza) || back (de un asiento, del cuerpo) || AGR espalier.

espaldarazo *m* accolade [of a knight]; *dar el espaldarazo a* to give the accolade || FIG backing (apoyo).

espaldera *f* AGR espalier.

◆ *pl* DEP wall bars.

espaldilla *f* shoulder blade (omóplato) || shoulder (de reses).

espantada *f* bolt (del caballo) || running away (huida) || stampede (de un grupo) || sudden scare, sudden fear (miedo) || *dar una* or *la espantada* to run away, to take to one's heels (huir), to bolt (el caballo), to stampede (un grupo), to get cold feet, to get scared (desistir).

espantado, da *adj* frightened, scared, terrified.

espantajo *m* scarecrow (espantapájaros) || FIG sight (persona fea) | bogeyman (coco) | deterrent (cosa que infunde miedo); *este argumento sirve de espantajo* this argument is a deterrent.

espantalobos *m inv* BOT bladder senna.

espantamoscas *m inv* fly whisk, flyswatter.

espantapájaros *m inv* scarecrow.

espantar *vt* to frighten, to scare (dar miedo a) || to frighten away *o* off, to scare away (ahuyentar); *espantar a un caballo, a un ladrón* to frighten off a horse, a robber || to drive away, to shoo away; *espantar las moscas* to drive away the flies || FIG to ward off (miedo, sueño, etc.) | to terrify, to frighten; *me espantan los exámenes* examinations terrify me | to horrify, to disgust (horrorizar).

◆ *vpr* to be frightened away *o* off, to be scared away (ahuyentarse); *el caballo se espantó con el tiro* the horse was frightened away by the shot || to be frightened *o* scared (asustarse); *espantarse de* or *por algo* to be frightened about sth; *los caballos se espantan fácilmente* horses are easily frightened *o* scared || to be astonished *o* amazed (admirarse).

espanto *m* fright, terror; *causar espanto* to be a source of fright; *llenar de espanto* to fill with fright || threat (amenaza) || astonishment (asombro) || horror, disgust (horror) || ghost (fantasma) || — *de espanto* frightening, terrifying (que da miedo), horrible, terrible (feo) || FAM *estoy curado de espanto* nothing can shock me any more, I have known worse | *ser un espanto* to be frightening *o* appalling *o* dreadful; *es un espanto lo cara que está la carne ahora* it's frightening how expensive meat is now.

espantoso, sa *adj* frightening, terrifying (que causa espanto) || frightening, appalling, dreadful; *un aumento de precios espantoso* a dreadful rise in prices || terrible, dreadful; *un ruido espantoso* a terrible noise || horrible, disgusting (horroroso) || incredible (pasmoso).

España *npr f* GEOGR Spain || *la España de pandereta* the tourist's Spain, typical Spain.

español, la *adj* Spanish || *a la española* in the Spanish way.

◆ *m/f* Spaniard.

◆ *m* Spanish (lengua).

◆ *pl* Spanish, Spaniards (gente, pueblo).

españolado, da *adj* Spanish-like.

◆ *f* exaggerated portrait of Spain (espectáculo) || typically Spanish idea *o* mannerism *o* action.

españolismo *m* Spanish nature, Spanishness (carácter español) || love of Spain (amor a lo español) || hispanicism (hispanismo).

españolizar *vt* to make Spanish, to hispanicize.

◆ *vpr* to adopt Spanish ways.

esparadrapo *m* MED sticking plaster.

esparaván *m* sparrow hawk (gavilán) || VET spavin.

esparavel *m* casting net (red) || TECN mortarboard (de albañil).

esparceta *f* BOT sainfoin (pipirigallo).

esparciata *adj/s* Spartan (de Esparta).

esparcido, da *adj* scattered; *flores esparcidas por el campo* flowers scattered over the field || FIG widespread; *una noticia muy esparcida* a very widespread piece of news || gay, merry (alegre).

esparcidora *f* spreader.

esparcimiento *m* spreading (de un líquido) || scattering (dispersión) || AGR spreading (de abonos) || FIG spreading (de una noticia, etc.) | merriness, gaiety (alegría) | relaxation; *tomarse unas horas de esparcimiento* to take a few hours relaxation | amusement, diversion (recreo).

esparcir *vt* to scatter; *esparcir flores por el camino* to scatter flowers over the road || to spread (derramar) || AGR to spread (abono) || FIG to spread (una noticia).

◆ *vpr* to scatter, to be scattered (desparramarse) || to spread (derramarse) || FIG to spread; *la noticia se esparció como una mancha de aceite* the news spread like wildfire | to relax, to take is easy (descansar) | to amuse o.s. (recrearse).

espárrago *m* BOT asparagus; *espárrago triguero* wild asparagus || post (palo) || peg ladder (escalera) || TECN stud || FAM lanky person (flacucho) || — FAM *estar hecho un espárrago* to be as thin as a rake | *mandar a uno a freír espárragos* to send s.o. packing || CULIN *puntas de espárragos* asparagus tips || FAM *¡vete a freír espárragos!* go jump in the lake!

esparraguera *f* asparagus [plant] (planta) || asparagus patch (plantación) || asparagus dish (plato).

esparraguina *f* MIN apatite.

esparrancado, da *adj* straddling, with one's legs wide apart (persona) || too wide apart (cosas).

esparrancarse *vpr* FAM to open *o* to spread one's legs.

Esparta *n pr* GEOGR & HIST Sparta.

espartano, na *adj/s* Spartan (de Esparta).

espartería *f* esparto workshop (taller) || esparto work (oficio).

espartero, ra *m/f* esparto worker.

esparto *m* BOT esparto (planta).

espasmo *m* spasm.

espasmódico, ca *adj* spasmodic; *tos espasmódica* spasmodic cough.

espata *f* BOT spathe.

espatarrarse *vpr* to open one's legs wide.

espático, ca *adj* MIN spathic.

espato MIN spar; *espato de Islandia* Iceland spar || *espato de flúor* fluorspar, fluorite.

espátula *f* spatula (paleta) || palette knife (de pintor) || spoonbill (ave) || *espátula de modelar*, drove.

espatulado, da *adj* spatular || BOT spatulate.

especería *f* → **especiería**.

especia *f* spice.

especiado, da *adj* spiced, spicy.

especial *adj* special || *en especial* especially.

especialidad *f* speciality, specialty || *especialidad de la casa* speciality of the house || *especialidad farmacéutica* patent medicine.

especialista *adj/s* specialist; *un especialista en neurología* a neurology specialist || *médico especialista* specialist.

especialización *f* specialization.

especializado, da *adj* specialized; *obrero especializado* specialized worker.

especializar *vt* to specialize.

◆ *vpr* to specialize; *especializarse en historia romana* to specialize in Roman history.

especie *f* species; *especie humana* human species; *la propagación de la especie* the propagation of the species || kind, sort, type (género, clase) || matter, affair (asunto) || piece of news (noticia); *propagar una especie falsa* to spread a false piece of news || — *en especie* in kind; *pagar en especie* to pay in kind || REL *especies sacramentales* species.

especiería; especería *f* grocer's shop [US grocery store] (tienda) || spices *pl*, spicery (especias).

especificación *f* specification.

específicamente *adv* specifically.

especificar *vt* to specify.

específico, ca *adj* specific; *peso específico* specific gravity.

◆ *m* MED specific (medicamento para tratar una enfermedad determinada) | patent medicine.

espécimen *m* specimen.

— OBSERV pl *especímenes*.

especioso, sa *adj* specious (engañoso) || (p us) beautiful.

espectacular *adj* spectacular.

espectáculo *m* entertainment (diversión); *el circo es un espectáculo que gusta a los niños* circus is a popular entertainment among children || show; *espectáculo de variedades* variety show || performance; *ver el espectáculo de la tarde* to see the afternoon performance || spectacle, sight; *el espectáculo grandioso de las cataratas del Niágara* the imposing spectacle of Niagara falls || *dar el espectáculo en la calle* to make a scene *o* to cause a scandal in the street.

◆ *pl* entertainments; *guía de espectáculos* entertainments guide; *durante el festival dieron buenos espectáculos* during the festival they provided some goods entertainments || *sala de espectáculos* theatre [US theater] (teatro), cinema (cine).

espectador, ra *m/f* spectator (en teatro, cine, deportes) || onlooker; *miraba como espectador* he was an onlooker.

◆ *pl* audience *sing* (público) || spectators (en deportes) || *sala que tiene cabida para dos mil espectadores* theatre with seating for two thousand *o* that seats two thousand.

espectral *adj* ghostly; *luz espectral* ghostly light || FÍS spectral; *análisis espectral* spectral analysis.

espectro *m* spectre [US specter] ghost || FÍS spectrum || FIG spectre; *el espectro de la guerra* the spectre of war | ghost (persona cadavérica).

espectrografía *f* FÍS spectrography.

espectrógrafo *m* FÍS spectrograph.

espectrograma *f* FÍS spectrogram.

espectroscopia *f* FÍS spectroscopy.

espectroscópico, ca *adj* FÍS spectroscopic.

espectroscopio *m* FÍS spectroscope.

especulación *f* speculation; *especulación en la Bolsa* speculation on the Stock Exchange || speculation, contemplation, meditation (meditación) || conjecture, speculation (conjetura).

especulador, ra *adj* speculating.

◆ *m/f* speculator.

especular *vi* to speculate; *especular en la Bolsa, en cereales* to speculate on the Stock Exchange, in cereals; *especula con la concesión de los permisos* he speculates with the granting of licences.

especulativo, va *adj* speculative.

◆ *f* intellect, understanding (facultad del espíritu).

espéculo *m* MED speculum.

espejear *vi* to shine, to gleam.

espejeo *m* gleaming shining (brillo) || mirage (espejismo).

espejería *f* mirror shop.

espejismo *m* mirage (fenómeno de óptica) || FIG illusion, mirage (ilusión engañosa).

espejo *m* mirror, looking glass (ant); *mirarse en el espejo* to look at o.s. in the mirror; *el espejo de las aguas* the mirror of the waters || FIG reflection; *el teatro es el espejo de la vida* the theatre is the reflection of life | model (dechado) || — *espejo de cuerpo entero* full-length mirror || *espejo retrovisor* driving mirror, rear-view mirror || FÍS *espejo ustorio* burning glass || FIG *mirarse en uno como en un espejo* to model o.s. on s.o. (imitar), to be very fond of s.o. (querer) | *mírate en este espejo* let this be an example to you.

espejuelo *m* MIN selenite (yeso cristalizado) | flake of talc (hoja de talco) || lark mirror (para cazar) || FIG bait (atractivo) || crystallized citron (confitura) || VET chestnut (excrecencia córnea de los caballos).

◆ *pl* spectacle lenses (cristales) || glasses, spectacles (anteojos).

espeleología *f* speleology, potholing.

espeleológico, ca *adj* speleological.

espeleólogo *m* speleologist.

espeluznante *adj* FAM hair-raising, horrifying.

espeluznar *vt* to make (s.o.'s) hair stand on end; *la idea de la muerte me espeluzna* the thought of death makes my hair stand on end.

espeluzno *m* shiver, shudder.

espeque *m* MAR handspike || prop (puntal).

espera *f* wait; *la espera fue muy larga* the wait was very long || waiting; *sala de espera* waiting room || JUR respite, stay (plazo) || patience (paciencia) || — *cazar a espera* to lie in wait for game || *compás de espera* bar rest (música), time lag, delay (pausa) || *en espera de* while waiting for; *en espera de tu llegada se puso a leer una novela* while waiting for you to arrive he started reading a novel; awaiting; *en espera de su respuesta* awaiting your reply || *estar a la espera* to be waiting.

esperantista *adj/s* Esperantist.

esperanto *m* Esperanto (lengua).

esperanza *f* hope (virtud); *la esperanza consuela a los infelices* hope consoles unhappy people || hope (confianza); *la esperanza en el éxito* hope of *o* for success || hope, prospect (perspectiva); *ahora hay esperanzas de paz* there are now hopes of peace || faith (fe); *esperanza en Dios, en uno* faith in God, in s.o. || expectation; *defraudar las esperanzas de alguien* to disappoint s.o.'s expectations; *esperanza de vida* life expectation || — *abrigar esperanzas* to foster hopes || *alimentarse de esperanzas* to live on hope *o* on hopes || *como última esperanza* as a last hope || *con la esperanza de* or *de que* in the hope of *o* that || *dar esperanzas de* or *de que* to give hope for *o* that || *esperanza de vida* life expectancy || *la esperanza es lo último que se pierde* one should never lose hope, we must hope against hope || *llenar la esperanza de uno* to fulfil s.o.'s hopes *o* expectations || *mientras hay vida, hay esperanza* whilst there is life, there is hope || *no hay esperanza* there is no hope || *tener esperanza* to have a hope; *tiene esperanza de obtener el premio* he has a hope of winning the prize; to have hopes; *tengo la esperanza de que venga mañana* I have hopes that he will come tomorrow || *tener muchas esperanzas* to have high hopes || *tener pocas esperanzas* to have little hope || *vivir de esperanzas* to live on hope.

esperanzador, ra *adj* encouraging; *resultados esperanzadores* encouraging results.

esperanzar *vt* to give hope to || *estar esperanzado* to be hopeful.

esperar *vt* to wait for (aguardar); *te esperaré hasta las ocho* I shall wait for you until eight o'clock; *estaba esperando que le recibieran* he was waiting for them to see him || to hope (desear); *espero que vendrás* I hope (that) you will come; *espero sacar un premio en la lotería* I hope to win a prize in the lottery || to hope for; *esperemos días mejores* let us hope for better days || to expect (contar con la llegada de); *esperamos a muchos espectadores para el partido* we expect a lot of spectators for the match; *estar esperando una llamada* to be expecting a call || to expect (creer); *¡yo que esperaba que hiciera buen tiempo!* and I expected the weather to be fine! || to await, to be in store for; *mal día nos espera* a bad day is in store for us *o* awaits us || to be expecting (un bebé) || — *ahí lo espero* I'll get him there || *esperar como agua de mayo* or *como el santo advenimiento* to be longing for || *estar esperando familia* to be expecting a baby || FAM *espéreme sentado* don't hold your breath! || FIG & FAM *te espero fuera* I'll deal with you later, I'll see you outside.
◆ *vi* to wait; *esperaré a que vengas para comer* I will wait until you come to eat || — *esperar en Dios* to put one's faith in God, to trust in God || *esperar en Dios que...* to hope to God that... || *esperar en uno* to trust in s.o. || *espero que sí, que no* I hope so, I hope not || *hacer esperar a uno* to keep s.o. waiting, to make s.o. wait || *hacerse esperar* to keep people waiting || *nada se pierde con esperar* we shall lose nothing by waiting || *quien espera desespera* a watched pot never boils.
◆ *vpr* to expect; *no me esperaba tantos éxitos* I didn't expect so many successes || to wait; *¡espérate un momento!* wait a minute! || — *cuando menos se lo esperaban* when least expected || FAM *¡espérate sentado!* you could wait for ever!, don't hold your breath! || *la producción no fue tan alta como se esperaba* production was not so high as expected || *se espera que...* it is hoped that...

esperma *f* sperm || AMER candle || *esperma de ballena* spermaceti, sperm oil.

espermaceti *m* spermaceti, sperm oil.

espermático, ca *adj* spermatic.

espermatocito *m* spermatocyte.

espermatofita *f* BOT spermatophyte.

espermatogénesis *f* spermatogenesis.

espermatógeno, na *adj* spermatogenetic.

espermatozoide *m* spermatozoid.

espermatozoo *m* spermatozoon.

esperpento *m* FAM fright, sight (persona o cosa fea); *¡qué esperpento!* what a fright! | nonsense, absurdity (disparate).

espesado; espesamiento *m* thickening.

espesar *m* thicket (espesura).

espesar *vt* to thicken; *espesar una salsa* to thicken a sauce || to weave tighter (un tejido) || to press together (apretar).
◆ *vpr* to thicken (chocolate, salsa) || to thicken, to get thicker (hierba) || to get thicker *o* bushier (árbol) || to get denser *o* thicker (bosque).

espeso, sa *adj* thick; *tejido, caldo espeso* thick material, soup || dense, thick; *bosque espeso* dense wood || stiff; *pasta espesa* stiff dough || bushy, thick (árbol) || dirty (sucio) || FAM *estar espeso* to be filthy (una persona).

espesor *m* thickness || — *de mucho espesor* very thick || *espesor de nieve* depth of snow.

espesura *f* thickness (de un tejido, un caldo, una salsa, etc.) || stiffness (de la pasta) || denseness, thickness (de un bosque) || bushiness, thickness (de un árbol) || thicket (matorral) || dirtiness (suciedad).

espetar *vt* to spit (con un asador largo) || to skewer (con una broqueta) || FIG to run through, to skewer (traspasar) || FIG & FAM to make sit through, to make listen to (encajar); *nos espetó un discurso aburrido* he made us sit through a boring speech | to spring, to pop (con brusquedad); *nos espetó una pregunta* he sprang a question on us | to rap out (una orden).

espeto *m* spit (asador) || skewer (broqueta).

espetón *m* spit (asador) || skewer (broqueta).

espía *m/f* spy || *espía doble* double agent.
◆ *f* MAR warping (acción de espiar) | warp (cabo).

espiar *vt* to keep watch on (observar, acechar); *espiar las acciones de los demás* to keep watch on other people's movements || to spy on; *espiar el ejército enemigo* to spy on the enemy army.
◆ *vi* to spy || MAR to warp (remolcar).

espícula *f* spicule.

espichar *vt* to prick || FAM *espicharla* to kick the bucket (morir).
◆ *vi* FAM to kick the bucket (morir) || AMER to make a speech (hacer un discurso).
◆ *vpr* AMER to lose weight (adelgazar) | to be ashamed (avergonzarse).

espiche *m* peg, plug (para caños, toneles, etc.) || MAR plug || AMER speech.

espiga *f* BOT ear, spike || herringbone (dibujo en un tejido) || tang (de espada) || tenon (de un madero) || pin, peg (clavija) || MAR masthead.

espigadera *f* gleaner.

espigado, da *adj* which has gone to seed (planta) || FIG tall and graceful, slender; *una muchacha espigada* a tall and graceful girl.

espigadora *f* gleaner (espigadera).

espigar *vt* AGR to glean || FIG to collect, to glean (en libros) || TECN to tenon.
◆ *vi* to ear, to produce ears *o* spikes (cereales) || AGR to glean || FIG to glean *o* to collect data (en libros) | to shoot up (personas).
◆ *vpr* to shoot up (personas); *esta muchacha se ha espigado mucho este año* this girl has shot up a lot this year || to run to seed (hortalizas).

espigón *m* point (punta) || jetty, pier, breakwater (dique) || ear [of corn] (mazorca) || peak (cerro).

espigueo *m* gleaning.

espiguilla *f* herringbone (dibujo); *tela de espiguillas* herringbone material || BOT spikelet.

espín *m* porcupine (puerco espín) || FÍS spin (momento cinético del electrón).

espina *f* thorn (de vegetal); *clavarse una espina en el dedo* to get a thorn in one's finger || splinter (astilla) || bone [of a fish] (de los peces) || ANAT spine, backbone (espinazo) || FIG difficulty (dificultad) || — FIG & FAM *eso me da mala espina* I don't like the look of that || BOT *espina blanca* cotton thistle || *espina dorsal* spine, backbone || BOT *Espina Santa* Christ's-thorn || FIG *problema lleno de espinas* thorny problem | *sacarse la espina* to remove the thorn from one's side (salir del apuro), to get even (desquitarse) | *tener clavada una espina en el corazón* to have a thorn in one's side.

espinaca *f* BOT spinach.
◆ *pl* CULIN spinach *sing*.

espinal *adj* spinal; *médula espinal* spinal marrow.

espinapez *m* *entarimado de espinapez* herringbone parquet *o* flooring.

espinar *m* hawthorn bushes *pl* (espinos) || thorny thicket (matorral) || FIG jam, thorny situation (enredo) | difficulty.

espinar *vt* to prick (herir) || AGR to protect with thorn branches (los árboles) || FIG to hurt, to offend (zaherir).

espinazo *m* ANAT spine, backbone || CULIN chine || ARQ keystone (clave) || — FIG & FAM *doblar el espinazo* to bow down | *romperse el espinazo* to break one's back (cayendo, trabajando).

espinela *f* stanza with ten octosyllabic lines [named after the Spanish poet Espinela].

espineta *f* MÚS spinet (clavicordio).

espingarda *f* small cannon (cañón) || Arab shotgun (escopeta de los moros) || FIG beanpole (mujer).

espinilla *f* ANAT shinbone (tibia) || blackhead, spot (en la piel).

espinillera *f* greave (de la armadura) || DEP shinpad, shin guard.

espino *m* BOT hawthorn || — BOT *espino albar* or *blanco* (English) hawthorn || *espino artificial* barbed wire || BOT *espino cerval* purging buckthorn (arbusto) | *espino majoleto* (English) hawthorn | *espino negro* blackthorn.

espinoso, sa *adj* thorny (planta) || bony (pescado) || FIG thorny (difícil).

espionaje *m* espionage, spying || *novela de espionaje* spy story.

espira *f* ARQ surbase (de columna) || MAT spire (de una espiral) | spiral (espiral) || ZOOL spire, whorl || ELECTR turn.

Espira *n pr* GEOGR Speyer.

espiración *f* breathing out, expiration, exhalation.

espirador *adj m* ANAT expiratory; *músculo espirador* expiratory muscle.

espiral *adj* spiral; *escalera espiral* spiral staircase || *muelle espiral* hairspring (de reloj).
◆ *f* hairspring (de reloj) || MAT spiral || spiral (de humo) || *en espiral* corkscrew; *rabo en espiral* corkscrew tail; spiral; *muelle, escalera en espiral* spiral spring, staircase.

espirar *vt* to breathe out, to exhale, to expire (el aire) || to give off (un olor).
◆ *vi* to breathe out, to exhale, to expire || FIG to blow gently (el viento).

espiritado, da *adj* possessed (of the Devil) || FIG & FAM thin, skinny (flaco).

espiritismo *m* spiritualism, spiritism.

espiritista *adj* spiritualistic, spiritualist.
◆ *m/f* spiritualist.

espiritoso, sa *adj* spirited (vivo) || spirituous (vino).

espíritu *m* spirit, soul (alma) || spirit (ser); *los ángeles son espíritus* angels are spirits || spirit, ghost (aparecido); *creer en los espíritus* to believe in ghosts; *comunicación de los espíritus* spirit rapping || spirit (energía); *espíritu de lucha* fighting spirit || spirit (disposición); *espíritu de justicia, de trabajo* spirit of justice, of work || spirit (adhesión); *espíritu de clase, de partido* class, party spirit || mind (mente, persona); *tener el espíritu vivo* to have a lively mind; *un gran espíritu de nuestra época* a great mind of our time || spirit (sentido); *espíritu de una ley, de un siglo* spirit of a law, of a century || wit (vivacidad del ingenio) || breathing (signo gráfico griego) || — *dar* or *exhalar* or *entregar* or *rendir el espíritu* to give up the ghost || *espíritu de contradicción* contrariness || *espíritu de cuerpo* esprit de corps, corporate feeling || *espíritu de equipo* team spirit || *espíritu de profecía* gift of prophecy (don sobrenatural) || QUÍM *espíritu de sal* spirits of salt || *espíritu de vino* spirit *o* spirits of wine || *espíritu maligno* evil spirit || REL *Espíritu Santo* Holy Ghost, Holy Spirit || *firmeza de espíritu* firmness || *grandeza de espíritu* noble heartedness || *levantar el espíritu* to cheer up || *levantar el espíritu a alguien* to raise s.o.'s spir-

its, to cheer s.o. up ‖ *pobre de espíritu* poor in spirit ‖ *tener espíritu de contradicción* to be contrary.
◆ *pl* demons (demonios).

espiritual *adj* spiritual; *pasto, vida espiritual* spiritual food, life ‖ witty (ingenioso) ‖ *patria espiritual* spiritual home.

espiritualidad *f* spirituality; *la espiritualidad del alma* the spirituality of the soul ‖ wittiness (ingenio).

espiritualismo *m* spiritualism.

espiritualizar *vt* to spiritualize.

espiritualmente *adv* spiritually (con el espíritu) ‖ wittily (ingeniosamente).

espirituoso, sa *adj* witty, funny (ingenioso) ‖ spirituous (bebida).

espiroidal; espiroideo, a *adj* spiral, spiroid.

espirómetro *m* MED spirometer.

espiroqueta *f* ZOOL spirochaete [*US* spirochete].

espita *f* faucet, spigot (de tonel) ‖ FIG & FAM drunkard, boozer (borracho).

esplender *vi* to shine.

esplendidez *f* splendour [*US* splendor], magnificence (magnificencia) ‖ beauty (belleza) ‖ generosity, lavishness (generosidad).

espléndido, da *adj* splendid, magnificent (magnífico) ‖ beautiful (bello) ‖ generous, lavish (generoso) ‖ resplendent (resplandeciente).

esplendor *m* splendour [*US* splendor], magnificence; *el esplendor del día* the splendour of the day ‖ splendour, magnificence, lavishness; *el esplendor de la ceremonia* the lavishness of the ceremony ‖ grandeur, glory, splendour (apogeo, nobleza); *una época de esplendor* an age of splendour ‖ resplendence, shining (resplandor).

esplendorosamente *adv* resplendently (con resplandor) ‖ splendidly, magnificently, lavishly.

esplendoroso, sa *adj* resplendent (resplandeciente) ‖ splendid, magnificent, lavish (magnífico).

esplénico, ca *adj* splenic, splenetic.

esplenio *m* ANAT splenius (músculo).

espliego *m* BOT lavender.

esplín *m* melancholy, spleen (tedio).

espolada *f*; **espolazo** *m* prod with a spur.

espoleadura *f* spur wound.

espolear *vt* to spur (el caballo) ‖ FIG to spur on, to stimulate (estimular); *espolear a uno para que haga algo* to spur s.o. on to do sth.

espoleo *m* spurring.

espoleta *f* fuse (de proyectil); *espoleta de percusión* percussion fuse ‖ wishbone (clavícula del ave) ‖ *quitar la espoleta de* to defuse, to disarm.

espolio *m* effects *pl* [of a dead bishop].

espolique *m* footman.

espolón *m* spur (de ave) ‖ fetlock (de caballo) ‖ cutwater (de puente, de barco) ‖ spur (de montaña) ‖ levee (de río) ‖ sea wall (malecón) ‖ promenade (paseo a orillas del mar) ‖ ARQ buttress (contrafuerte) ‖ ram (de barco antiguo) ‖ FAM chilblain (sabañón) ‖ MAR *embestir con el espolón* to ram.

espolonazo *m* blow with the spur (de gallo) ‖ ramming (de barco).

espolvoreadora *f* AGR sprayer.

espolvorear *vt* to sprinkle (esparcir algo hecho polvo) ‖ to dust (quitar el polvo de).

espondaico, ca *adj* spondaic.

espondeo *m* spondee.

espongiarios *m pl* ZOOL spongiae.

esponja *f* sponge; *esponja sintética, de platino* synthetic, platinum sponge ‖ towelling (tejido) ‖ FIG & FAM sponger (gorrón) ‖ — FIG & FAM *beber como una esponja* to drink like a fish | *pasemos la esponja por eso* let us say no more about it, let bygones be bygones | *ser una esponja* to be a heavy drinker, to drink like a fish (beber mucho), to be able to hold *o* to take one's drink (aguantar) | *tirar* or *arrojar la esponja* to throw in the towel *o* the sponge.

esponjado, da *adj* spongy ‖ fluffy (lana, pelo).
◆ *m* sugar bar (azucarillo).

esponjadura *f* fluffiness (de la lana) ‖ sponginess (esponjosidad).

esponjar *vt* to make spongy ‖ to soften (la tierra) ‖ to fluff up, to make fluffy (la lana).
◆ *vpr* to become spongy ‖ to become fluffy, to fluff up (la lana) ‖ FIG to become puffed up with pride, to assume a pompous air (engreírse) | to glow with health (rebosar de salud).

esponjera *f* sponge holder, sponge rack.

esponjosidad *f* sponginess ‖ fluffiness (de la lana).

esponjoso, sa *adj* spongy.

esponsales *m pl* engagement *sing*, betrothal *sing* (ant) (desposorios) ‖ *contraer esponsales* to get engaged, to become betrothed (ant).

espontanearse *vpr* to open up one's heart, to unbosom o.s. (franquearse).

espontaneidad *f* spontaneity.

espontáneo, a *adj* spontaneous; *generación, combustión espontánea* spontaneous generation, combustion ‖ spontaneous, unbidden; *ayuda espontánea* spontaneous help ‖ wild, spontaneous (plantas) ‖ spontaneous, natural; *es una persona muy espontánea* he is a very natural person.
◆ *m* TAUR «espontáneo» [spectator who tries to join in a bullfight].

espora *f* BOT & BIOL spore.

esporadicidad *f* sporadicalness.

esporádico, ca *adj* sporadic ‖ MED isolated.

esporangio *m* BOT sporangium, spore case.

esporidio *m* BOT sporidium.

esporozoario; esporozoo *m* ZOOL sporozoan.
— OBSERV El plural de *sporozoan* es *sporozoa*.

esportada *f* basketful, frailful (cantidad que cabe en una espuerta) ‖ FIG & FAM *a esportadas* in abundance, by the ton.

esportear *vt* to carry *o* to transport in frails *o* baskets.

esportilla *f* small basket, small frail.

esportillero *m* street porter.

esportillo *m* esparto basket.

esportón *m* large basket ‖ FIG & FAM *a esportones* in abundance, by the ton.

esporulación *f* BOT sporulation.

esposa *f* wife, spouse (ant) (mujer) ‖ *AMER* Episcopal ring.
◆ *pl* handcuffs (de un preso); *poner las esposas a uno* to put handcuffs on s.o.

esposado, da *adj* newly married (recién casado) ‖ handcuffed (un preso).
◆ *m/f* newlywed.

esposar *vt* to handcuff, to put handcuffs on.

esposo *m* husband, spouse (ant) ‖ *los esposos* the husband and wife, the couple.

esprint *m* DEP sprint.

esprintar *vi* to sprint.

esprinter *m/f* sprinter.

espuela *f* spur (del jinete) ‖ FIG spur, incentive, stimulus (estímulo) ‖ *AMER* spur (del gallo) ‖ — FIG *aguijoneado por la espuela del deseo* spurred on by desire | *echar* or *tomar la espuela* to have one for the road (tomar la última copa) | *el miedo pone espuelas* fear gives wings to the feet ‖ *picar (con las dos) espuelas, dar espuelas a* to spur, to put the spurs to (a horse) ‖ FIG *poner espuelas* to spur on (estimular).

espuerta *f* (two-handled) basket, frail ‖ FIG & FAM *tener dinero a espuertas* to have bags *o* loads *o* lots *o* tons of money.

espulgar *vt* to delouse, to rid of fleas *o* lice (quitar las pulgas) ‖ FIG to examine closely, to scrutinize.

espulgo *m* delousing, ridding of lice *o* fleas (de pulgas) ‖ FIG close examination, scrutiny (examen).

espuma *f* foam (en el mar) ‖ froth (en las bebidas) ‖ head (en un vaso de cerveza) ‖ lather (de jabón) ‖ scum (espuma acompañada de impurezas) ‖ foam (tejido) ‖ FIG & FAM cream (lo mejor) ‖ MAR spray (en el aire) ‖ — FIG *crecer como la espuma* to shoot up, to grow like wildfire ‖ *espuma de caucho* foam rubber ‖ MIN *espuma de mar* meerschaum ‖ *hacer espuma* to foam (las olas), to froth (las bebidas), to lather (el jabón).

espumadera *f* skimmer (para quitar la espuma) ‖ slice (paleta).

espumado *m* skimming.

espumajear; espumajar *vi* to foam *o* to froth at the mouth ‖ FIG *espumajear de ira* to foam with rage, to foam at the mouth.

espumajo *m* ⟶ **espumarajo.**

espumar *vt* to skim (quitar la espuma).
◆ *vi* to foam (el mar) ‖ to froth (la cerveza) ‖ to lather (el jabón) ‖ to sparkle (el vino).

espumarajo; espumajo *m* scum (en el agua) ‖ foam, froth (arrojado por la boca) ‖ FIG & FAM *echar espumarajos por la boca* to foam with rage, to foam at the mouth.

espumosidad *f* foaminess, frothiness ‖ sparkles *pl* (del champán, etc.).

espumoso, sa *adj* foamy, frothy; *una ola espumosa* a foamy wave ‖ sparkling (vino) ‖ lathery (jabón).

espúreo, a; espurio, ria *adj* illegitimate, bastard (bastardo); *hijo espúreo* illegitimate child ‖ spurious, false (falso) ‖ adulterated (adulterado).
— OBSERV The form *espúreo* is a barbarism but is more common than the original form *espurio*.

espurrear; espurriar *vt* to spray, to sprinkle (por la boca).

esputar *vt* to spit, to expectorate.

esputo *m* spit, spittle (saliva) ‖ MED sputum.

esqueje *m* AGR cutting, slip.

esquela *f* note, short letter (carta breve) ‖ invitation (para invitar) ‖ notice, announcement (para avisar) ‖ — *esquela amorosa* love letter ‖ *esquela mortuoria* or *de defunción* obituary notice.

esquelético, ca *adj* skeletal, of the skeleton (del esqueleto) ‖ FIG very thin, bony, like a skeleton.

esqueleto *m* ANAT skeleton ‖ FIG outline, sketch, skeleton (de una novela, discurso, etc.) | framework (armazón) ‖ *AMER* preliminary plan | form (formulario) ‖ FIG & FAM *estar hecho un esqueleto* to be like a skeleton | *menear* or *mover el esqueleto* to move one's body (bailar).

esquema *f* outline, sketch (bosquejo) ‖ diagram (diagrama) ‖ outline, plan, sketch (de un proyecto, un discurso, etc.) ‖ REL & FIL schema.

esquemático, ca *adj* schematic, diagrammatic.

esquematización *f* schematization.

esquematizar *vt* to schematize ‖ to outline, to sketch (esbozar).

esquí *m* ski; *un esquí metálico* a metal ski ‖ skiing (deporte); *esquí náutico* or *acuático* water-skiing; *esquí alpino* Alpine skiing; *esquí nórdico* or *de fondo* Nordic *o* cross-country skiing.
— OBSERV pl *esquíes* o *esquís*.

esquiador, ra *m/f* skier.

esquiar *vi* to ski.

esquife *m* skiff (barco).

esquila *f* bell, cowbell (cencerro) ‖ handbell, small bell (campanilla) ‖ shearing, clipping, sheepshearing (esquileo) ‖ BOT squill (cebolla albarrana) ‖ ZOOL squill, squilla, mantis prawn (camarón).

esquilador, ra *m/f* sheepshearer (persona).
◆ *f* sheepshearer (tijeras).

esquilar *vt* to shear, to clip.

esquileo *m* shearing, clipping, sheepshearing (acción) ‖ shearing time (época).

esquilmar *vt* AGR to harvest (cosechar) | to exhaust (el suelo) ‖ FIG to impoverish (empobrecer) ‖ FIG & FAM to fleece (despojar).

Esquilo *npr m* Aeschylus.

esquilón *m* large bell ‖ large cowbell.

esquimal *adj/s* eskimo.

esquina *f* corner; *doblar la esquina* to turn the corner; *calle Velázquez, esquina Goya* on the corner of the «calle Velázquez» and the «calle Goya» ‖ — FIG *a la vuelta de la esquina* just round the corner (muy cerca) | *encontrarse a la vuelta de la esquina* to be two a penny [US to be a dime a dozen] ‖ *hacer esquina* to be on the corner, to be on a corner (un edificio), to join, to meet (dos calles) ‖ *las cuatro esquinas* puss in the corner (juego).
— OBSERV The word *esquina* is used to indicate a projecting corner such as between two streets. *Rincón* is the word for a recessed corner such as in a room.

esquinado, da *adj* angular (anguloso) ‖ on the corner, on a corner (que forma esquina) ‖ FIG badtempered, prickly, difficult to get on with (persona), prickly, unpleasant (carácter).

esquinar *vt* to put in the *o* in a corner (poner en la esquina) ‖ to form a corner with (formar esquina) ‖ FIG to set against, to estrange (enemistar); *esquinar a dos personas* to set two people against each other ‖ TECN to square (un madero).
◆ *vi* to be on the corner (*con* of) (estar en la esquina) ‖ to form a corner, to join, to meet (formar esquina).
◆ *vpr* to sulk (enfurruñarse), to fall out (enfadarse).

esquinazo *m* FAM corner ‖ AMER serenade ‖ — FAM *dar esquinazo a alguien* to stand s.o. up (no acudir a una cita), to walk out on s.o. (dejar plantado), to shake s.o. off, to give s.o. the slip (deshacerse de alguien).

Esquines *npr m* Aeshines.

esquinzar *vt* TECN to cut (trapos).

esquirla *f* splinter (astilla).

esquirol *m* FAM blackleg, scab, strikebreaker.

esquisto *m* MIN schist ‖ — *aceite de esquisto* shale oil ‖ *esquisto bituminoso* bituminous shale.

esquistoso, sa *adj* MIN schistose.

esquivar *vt* to avoid, to evade (evitar) ‖ to dodge, to avoid; *esquivar un golpe* to dodge a blow.
◆ *vpr* to make o.s. scarce (irse) ‖ to dodge (de un golpe) ‖ to back out (para no cumplir algo).

esquivo, va *adj* aloof, cold, disdainful (desdeñoso) ‖ shy, bashful (huraño) ‖ unsociable (carácter).

esquizofrenia *f* MED schizophrenia.

esquizoide *adj/s* MED schizoid.

esta *adj dem* —> **este.**

ésta *pron dem* —> **éste.**

estabilidad *f* stability ‖ balance, equilibrium; *recuperó su estabilidad* he regained his balance.

estabilización *f* stabilization ‖ balancing (equilibrio) ‖ *estabilización económica* economic stabilization ‖ AVIAC *planos de estabilización* stabilizers.

estabilizador, ra *adj* stabilizing.
◆ *m* stabilizer ‖ AVIAC *estabilizador giroscópico* gyrostabilizer.

estabilizar *vt* to stabilize (barco, avión, precios).
◆ *vpr* to become stable, to becom stabilized.

estable *adj* stable; *un edificio, una situación estable* a stable building, situation ‖ balanced (equilibrado).

establecer* *vt* to establish, to set up, to found (una monarquía, una sucursal, una universidad, una fundación) ‖ to settle (colonos) ‖ to take up, to establish (el domicilio) ‖ to take (un censo) ‖ to make (investigaciones) ‖ to establish (la verdad, una relación, un precedente) ‖ to prepare, to draw up (planos) ‖ to set up (un récord) ‖ to lay down (una regla) ‖ *establecer un campamento* to pitch camp, to set up camp.
◆ *vpr* to settle down, to set up (instalarse); *se ha establecido en Roma* he has settled down in Rome ‖ to set (o.s.) up, to set up on one's own; *se ha establecido de abogado* he has set himself up as a lawyer ‖ to set up (in business) on one's own; *estaba antes de dependiente en una tienda pero ahora se ha establecido* he was a shop assistant before, but now he has set up on his own.

establecido, da *adj* established ‖ customary (habitual) ‖ — *conforme a lo establecido en el artículo 43* according to the provisions of article 43 ‖ *dejar establecido* to establish.

establecimiento *m* establishment, setting up, foundation (de una sucursal, monarquía, etc.) ‖ establishment (de la verdad, de una relación) ‖ preparation, drawing up (de planos, etc.) ‖ establishment (local); *establecimiento comercial* commercial establishment ‖ settlement (colonia).

establo *m* cowshed, stall ‖ MIT *establos de Augias* Augean stables.

estabulación *f* stabling.

estabular *vt* to stable.

estaca *f* stake, post (que se clava en el suelo) ‖ stick, cudgel (para apalear) ‖ AGR cutting (rama) ‖ TECN spike (clavo de hierro) ‖ AMER mineral concession | spur (espolón).

estacada *f* palisade, fence, picket fence (valla) ‖ palisade, stockade (fortificación) ‖ MAR breakwater, pier ‖ — FIG & FAM *dejar a uno en la estacada* to leave s.o. in the lurch | *quedarse en la estacada* to be left dead on the field (morir), to be beaten (ser vencido), to be floored (en una disputa), to be left in the lurch (en una situación apurada), to fail miserably (fracasar).

estacado *m* duelling ground.

estacar *vt* to stake out (señalar los límites) ‖ to fence with stakes (vallar) ‖ MIL to stockade, to palisade ‖ to picket, to stake (un animal) ‖ AMER to stake out on the ground (pieles).
◆ *vpr* FIG to freeze to the spot (quedarse inmóvil) ‖ AMER to get a splinter (clavarse una astilla) | to balk (un caballo).

estacazo *m* blow with a stick *o* a stake ‖ FIG blow.

estación *f* season (del año); *las cuatro estaciones* the four seasons ‖ season (temporada); *la estación de las lluvias* the rainy season ‖ station (de ferrocarril, de metro) ‖ (research) station; *una estación agronómica* an agricultural research station ‖ station; *estación de radio, repetidora* radio, relay station ‖ REL station; *estaciones del Via Crucis* stations of the Cross ‖ time (época); *en la estación actual* at the present time ‖ resort; *estación veraniega* summer resort ‖ position (estado); *estación vertical* vertical position ‖ — *estación balnearia* spa, watering place (medicinal), seaside resort (en el mar) ‖ *estación clarificadora* filter plant *o* station ‖ *estación climática* or *termal* thermal spa ‖ *estación de apartado* or *de clasificación* marshalling yard ‖ *estación de empalme* junction ‖ *estación de esquí* ski resort ‖ *estación de gasolina* petrol *o* filling station ‖ *estación de mercancías* goods station ‖ *estación depuradora* purifying plant ‖ *estación de seguimiento* tracking station (espacial) ‖ *estación de servicio* service station ‖ INFORM *estación de trabajo* work station ‖ RAD *estación emisora* broadcasting station, transmitter ‖ *estación espacial* space station ‖ *estación meteorológica* weather station.

estacional *adj* seasonal ‖ ASTR stationary.

estacionamiento *m* parking (acción de aparcar); *prohibido el estacionamiento* no parking; *estacionamiento el línea* parking nose to tail ‖ parking place *o* space (lugar) ‖ stationing (de tropas).

estacionar *vt* to station ‖ to park (un coche).
◆ *vpr* to remain stationary (permanecer estacionario) ‖ to come to a standstill (dejar de progresar) ‖ to park (coche) ‖ to loiter (personas).

estacionario, ria *adj* stationary (inmóvil) ‖ COM slack ‖ *mar estacionario* slack sea.

estada *f* stay (estancia).

estadía *f* stay (estancia) ‖ sitting (ante un pintor, etc.) ‖ stadia (rod) (topografía) ‖ MAR lay day (plazo) | demurrage (indemnización).

estadio *m* stadium; *estadio olímpico* olympic stadium ‖ stadium (medida antigua) ‖ stage, phase (periodo).
— OBSERV El plural de *stadium* (medida antigua) es *stadia*.

estadista *m* statesman (hombre de Estado) ‖ statistician (estadístico) ‖ FAM *los estadistas de café* armchair politicians.

estadística *f* statistics (ciencia) ‖ statistic (dato).

estadístico, ca *adj* statistical; *estudio estadístico* statistical survey.
◆ *m/f* statistician.

estado *m* state, condition (condición); *estado físico* physical condition ‖ state; *estado sólido* solid state; *estado gaseoso* gasesous state ‖ order, condition; *una bicicleta en buen, en mal estado* a bicycle in good, in bad condition; *en estado de funcionamiento* in working order ‖ State (gobierno, nación); *secretos de Estado* State secrets; *razón de Estado* reason of State ‖ status; *estado civil* marital *o* civil status ‖ HIST estate (clase en la Europa medieval) ‖ statement; *estado de cuenta* statement of account ‖ — *estado de alma* or *de ánimo* state of mind, mood ‖ *estado de bienestar* welfare state ‖ *estado de cosas* state of affairs ‖ *estado de emergencia* or *de excepción, de sitio* state of emergency, state of siege ‖ REL *estado de gracia* state of grace ‖ *estado de guerra* state of war ‖ *estado de*

la nieve snow report || *estado de salud* health || *estado de soltero* celibacy, bachelorhood || *estado de viuda, de viudo* widowhood, widowerhood || *estado llano* or *común* third estate, commons || MIL *estado mayor* staff || *estar en buen, en mal estado* to be in good, in bad condition || *estar en estado de merecer* to be eligible *o* marriegeable || *estar en estado (interesante)* to be expecting *o* pregnant || *hombre de Estado* Statesman || (ant); *Ministerio de Estado* Foreign Office (en Gran Bretaña), State Department (en Estados Unidos) || *tomar estado* to marry (casarse), to take holy orders (entrar en religión).
◆ *pl* lands, states (de un señor).

Estados Unidos *npr mpl* GEOGR United States *sing.*
— OBSERV The abbreviation for *Estados Unidos* is *EE.UU.*

estadounidense *adj* American, United States.
◆ *m/f* American, United States citizen.

estafa *f* swindle || racket (fraude organizado).

estafador, ra *m/f* swindler || racketeer.

estafar *vt* to swindle, to cheat; *estafar dinero a alguien* to swindle s.o. out of money.

estafermo *m* HIST quintain (muñeco) || FAM simpleton, dumbbell (necio).

estafeta *f* courier (correo) || sub-post office [*US* branch post office] (de correos) || diplomatic bag (correo diplomático) || *estafeta móvil* mobile post office.

estafilococo *m* MED staphylococcus.

estagnación *f* AMER ⟶ **estancamiento.**

estalactita *f* stalactite.

estalagmita *f* stalagmite.

estalinismo *m* Stalinism.

estalinista *adj* Stalinist.

estallar *vi* to explode, to blow up; *la mina, el avión estalló* the mine, the plane blew up || to burst (un neumático) || to shatter (el cristal) || to crack (el látigo) || to break (una ola) || to crash (el trueno) || FIG to break (un escándalo) | to break out (la guerra, una revolución, una epidemia, un incendio) | to split (un vestido) | to blow up (with rage), to fly off the handle; *estas palabras le hicieron estallar* these words made him blow up || — FIG *estallar de alegría, de risa, en aplausos* to leap with joy, to burst out laughing, to burst into applause | *estallar en llanto* to burst into tears || *hacer estallar* to explode (una mina), to burst (un neumático), to shatter (un cristal), to split (un vestido), to spark off, to trigger off (una rebelión).

estallido *m* explosion (de una bomba, un polvorín, etc.) || bursting (de neumático) || crack (de látigo) || clap (de trueno) || splitting (de madera, etc.) || shattering (de cristal) || outbreak (de la guerra, revolución, etc.) || outburst, burst (de ira, de risa, de alegría, de aplausos) || *dar un estallido* to burst (neumático).

estambre *m* long-fibred wool (mechón) || worsted yarn (hilo) || worsted (tela) || warp (urdimbre) || BOT stamen.

Estambul *n pr* GEOGR Istanbul.

estamento *m* each of the four estates in the «Cortes» of Aragon || either of the two legislative bodies in nineteenth-century Spain || class, stratum (clase) || state (estado).

estameña *f* serge, worsted, estamene (tela).

estaminífero, ra *adj* BOT staminiferous, staminate.

estampa *f* IMPR print (imagen) | plate (en un libro) | lithograph (litografía) | engraving (grabado) | printing (imprenta) || picture; *a los niños les gustan los libros con estampas* children like books with pictures in || FIG look, appearance; *tiene estampa de malvado* he has the look of a villain | hallmark, mark; *la estampa del genio* the hallmark of genius | image; *es la viva estampa de su padre* he is the very image of his father || — *dar a la estampa* to print (imprimir), to publish (publicar) || FIG & FAM *¡maldita sea su estampa!* damn him!, blast him! | *romper la estampa a uno* to do s.o. in || *sección de estampas* print room (de una biblioteca) || FAM *tener estampa de* to look (like); *tiene estampa de torero* he looks a bullfighter | *una persona de buena, mala estampa* a decent-looking, shady-looking person | *un toro de buena, de mala estampa* a fine-looking, poor-looking bull.

estampación *f*; **estampado** *m* stamping || printing (impresión) || engraving (grabado) || embossing (del cuero, etc.) || corrugating (del papel) || punching *o* stamping out (recortado) || tooling (de la encuadernación).

estampado *m* stamped || printed (impreso) || engraved (grabado) || embossed (cuero) || corrugated (papel) || stamped *o* punched out (recortado) || printed; *tela estampada* printed material || print, printed (traje) || tooled (encuadernación).
◆ *m* ⟶ **estampación** || **cotton print (tela).**

estampador *m* stamper || embosser (de cuero).

estampar *vt* to stamp (sacar relieve) || to emboss (el cuero) || to stamp out, to punch out (recortar); *estampar arandelas* to punch out washers || to print engravings, cloth || to tool (la encuadernación) || to engrave (grabar) || to stamp; *estampar el pie en la arena* to stamp one's foot in the sand || FIG to imprint, to stamp (inculcar) || FIG & FAM to fling, to hurl; *estampó la botella contra la pared* he hurled the bottle against the wall | to deal, to give (una bofetada) | to plant (un beso).

estampía (de) *loc adv* *entrar en estampía* to burst *o* to rush in || *salir en estampía* to go *o* to be off like a shot *o* like a rocket.

estampida *f* explosion, bang (estampido) || AMER stampede.

estampido *m* explosion, bang || *dar un estampido* to bang.

estampilla *f* rubber stamp (sello de goma) || seal (precinto) || AMER stamp (sello de correos) | revenue stamp (sello fiscal).

estampillado *m* rubber-stamping (con sello de goma) || sealing (con precinto).

estampillar *vt* to rubber-stamp (con sello de goma) || to seal (con precinto).

estampita *f* print.

estancación *f*; **estancamiento** *m* checking of the flow (de la sangre) || damming (up) (embalse) || stagnation, stagnancy (del agua) || FIG stagnation (de un asunto) | standstill (de negociaciones) || State monopolization, State monopoly (de mercancías) || ECON *estancamiento económico* economic stagnation.

estancado, da *adj* stagnant (agua) || FIG bogged down, stagnant (asunto) | at a standstill, bogged down (negociaciones).

estancar *vt* to check *o* to stem *o* to stop the flow of (la sangre) || to dam (up); *estancar un río* to dam up a river || to turn into a State monopoly (monopolizar) || FIG to block, to delay, to hold up; *estancar una transacción* to hold up a deal | to bring to a standstill (negociaciones).
◆ *vpr* to stagnate, to become stagnant (líquidos) || FIG to stagnate, to get bogged down, to make no headway (un asunto, un negocio) | to come to a standstill, to get bogged down (negociaciones).

estancia *f* stay; *después de diez días de estancia en Madrid, se marchó* after ten days' stay *o* after a ten-day stay in Madrid, he left || day (spent in a hospital) || abode, dwelling (morada) || room (habitación) || POÉT stanza || AMER «estancia», farm, ranch (hacienda).

estanciera *f* AMER pickup (camioneta).

estanciero *m* AMER farmer, rancher.

estanco, ca *adj* watertight; *compartimientos estancos* watertight compartments.
◆ *m* state tobacco shop, tobacconist's [*US* cigar store] (tienda donde se venden tabaco y sellos) || State monopoly; *el estanco del tabaco* the State tobacco monopoly || (ant) archives *pl.*

estandard; estándar *m* ⟶ **standard.**

estandardización; estandarización *f* ⟶ **standardización.**

estandardizar; estandarizar *vt* ⟶ **standardizar.**

estandarte *m* standard, banner.

estannato *m* QUÍM stannate.

estánnico, ca *adj* QUÍM stannic (de estaño).

estannífero, ra *adj* stanniferous, tin-bearing.

estanque *m* (ornamental) lake (en jardines) || reservoir (para el riego) || pond, pool (pequeño) || AMER tank (de gasolina) || *estanque de sedimentación* sedimentation tank.

estanqueidad *f* watertightness.

estanquero, ra *m/f* tobacconist.

estanquidad *f* watertightness.

estante *m* shelf (anaquel) || bookcase (para libros) || stand (soporte para máquina, etc.) || AMER stay, prop (puntal).
— OBSERV El plural de *shelf* es *shelves.*

estantería *f* shelving, shelves *pl* (anaquel) || bookcase (para libros).

estantigua *f* ghost, phantom (fantasma) || FIG & FAM scarecrow (persona desgarbada y mal vestida).

estañado *m* tin-plating (acción y efecto de estañar) || soldering (acción y efecto de soldar).

estañador *m* tinsmith.

estañadura *f* tin-plating (acción y efecto de estañar) || soldering (acción y efecto de soldar).

estañar *vt* to tin, to tin-plate || to solder (soldar).

estañero *m* tinsmith.

estaño *m* tin (metal) || ARTES pewter.

estaqueada *f* AMER beating, thrashing (paliza).

estaquear *vt* AMER to stake out on the ground.

estaquilla *f* peg, pin (de madera) || brad (de metal) || spike (clavo largo).

estar* *vi*

1. POSICIÓN ESPACIAL O TEMPORAL **2.** ESTADO TRANSITORIO **3.** PASIVO **4.** FORMA REFLEXIVA **5.** CON GERUNDIO **6.** SEGUIDO DE UNA PREPOSICIÓN **7.** LOCUCIONES DIVERSAS.

1. POSICIÓN ESPACIAL O TEMPORAL to be; *está en Sevilla, en casa* he is in Seville, at home; *la señora de la casa, el libro no está* the landlady is not in *o* at home, the book is not here; *si no estoy* if I'm not there (sin indicación del lugar hay que añadir un adverbio); *estamos en verano* it is summer || to be, to stay; *estuve seis días en Córdoba* I was *o* stayed in Cordoba for six days.

2. ESTADO TRANSITORIO to be; *el suelo está húmedo* the ground is damp; *mi tío está enfermo* my uncle is ill; *¿cómo estás?* how are you?; *estar bien, malo, mejor* to be well, ill, better (de salud) || to look; *estás muy favorecida hoy* you look very nice today.
3. PASIVO to be (describing the state resulting from an action); *la puerta está cerrada* the door is closed; *estos libros están bien impresos* these books are well printed.
4. FORMA REFLEXIVA) to remain, to stay; *os podéis estar con nosotros unos días* you can stay with us a few days; *ahí se estuvo hasta la vuelta de su hermana* there he remained until his sister came back || to keep; *¡estaos quietos!* keep still!
5. CON GERUNDIO to be; *está escribiendo una novela* he is writing a novel; *estaba muriéndose, se estaba muriendo* he was dying || *le estuve esperando dos horas* I waited for him two hours, I spent two hours waiting for him.
6. SEGUIDO DE UNA PREPOSICIÓN a) *estar a* to be, to cost; *las patatas están a cinco pesetas* potatoes are five pesetas || — *¿a cuánto* or *cuántos estamos?* what is the date? || *estamos a 22 (veintidós) de febrero* it is 22nd [the twenty-second of] February.| b) *estar de* to be (más gerundio); *estar de paso, de caza, de mudanza, de vacaciones* to be passing through, hunting, moving house, on holiday || to be; *estar de buen humor* to be in a good mood || to be (working as); *está de camarero en un hotel* he is working as a waiter in a hotel || to be (dressed) in; *estar de uniforme, de paisano, de etiqueta* to be in uniform, in civilian clothes, in formal dress || *estar de rodillas* to be on one's knees. | c) *estar en* to understand (entender); *estoy en lo que usted dice* I understand what you say || to know (saber, estar enterado de); *tú no estás en nada* you don't know anything || to think, to believe (creer); *estoy en que vendrá Juanita* I think Jean will come || to intend to (tener la intención de hacer algo); *está en venir cuanto antes* he intends to come as soon as possible || to agree to (estar conforme con) || to be up to (depender de); *está en ti hacerlo* it is up to you to do it || to stand at; *el récord está en 10 segundos* the record stands at 10 seconds || — *el problema está en la fecha* the problem lies in the date || *todo está en que él pueda venir para entonces* everything depends on *o* hangs on whether he can make it then. | d) *estar para* to be about to; *el Presidente está para llegar de un momento a otro* the President is about to arrive any minute || to be in the mood for, to feel like; *no estoy para frivolidades* I am in no mood for frivolities || to be in a state *o* condition for; *no estoy para emprender largos viajes* I am in no state for making long journeys || *estamos para servirles* we are at your service, we are here to serve you. | e) *estar por* to remain to be, to have yet to be; *la historia de esa época está por escribir* the history of that period remains to be written *o* has yet to be written; *eso está por ver* that remains to be seen || to be about to (estar a punto de) || to be tempted to (estar tentado de hacer algo); *estoy por venir contigo* I'm tempted to come with you || to be in favour of, to favour, to be for; *todos están por él* everyone is for him; *yo estoy por hacerlo así* I'm in favour of doing it like this. | f) *estar sin* to be without || *la casa está sin vender* the house is unsold *o* has not been sold.
7. LOCUCIONES DIVERSAS *aquí estoy y aquí me quedo* here I am and here I'll stay || FIG *como estamos aquí tú y yo* as sure as I'm standing here || *déjame estar* let me be, leave me alone || *está bien* it's all right (bien hecho), all right (de acuerdo) || FIG & FAM *está hasta en la sopa* there's no getting away from him (al estar harto de alguien), I am tired of hearing about him (harto de oír hablar de alguien) || *¿estamos?* right? (comprender), right?, ready? (estar listo) || *estamos todavía a tiempo de* we are still in time to || *estar (a) bien, (a) mal con uno* to be on good, on bad terms with s.o. || *estar a la que salga* to be always ready to seize an opportunity || *estar al caer* to be about to strike; *están al caer las diez* ten is about to strike; to be imminent; *la guerra está al caer* war is imminent || *estar al corriente* or *al tanto de, to be aware of, to know about;* to be up to date (estar al día); *estoy al tanto de las noticias* I am up to date on the news; to be in the alert (estar a la expectativa) || *estar a matar* to be at loggerheads *o* at daggers drawn || *estar a oscuras* to be in the dark (sin luz o no enterado) || *estar a pan y agua* to be on bread and water || *estar a punto de* or *a pique de* to be about to, to be on the point of || *estar bueno* to be edible *o* eatable *o* all right (comestible), to be nice *o* tasty (sabroso), to be well (de salud) || *estar con gripe* to have flu || FIG *estar con uno* to be (in agreement) with s.o. (estar de acuerdo) || *estar de más* or *de sobra* to be unnecessary *o* superfluous (superfluo), to be unwanted *o* in the way (importuno) || *estar en todo* to look after everything, to keep an eye on everything (ocuparse), to think of everything (pensar), to have a finger in every pie (meterse) || *estar fuera* to be away from home, to be away (de viaje), to be out (haber salido), to be abroad *o* out of the country (en otro país), to be out (en deporte) || *estar fuera de sí (de ira, etc.)* to be beside o.s. (with rage, etc.) (estar muy enojado) || *estar hecho* to be, to have turned into, to have become; *el caballo está hecho una ruina* the horse is a wreck || *estarle* (followed by an adjective) *a uno (una prenda de vestir),* to be too (más adjetivo), for s.o.; *este sombrero me está ancho* this hat is too big for me || *estarle bien a uno* to suit (ropa) || *estar para todo* to take care of *o* to look after everything || *estar siempre sobre uno* to be always hovering over s.o. (vigilar) || FAM *estoy que me subo por las paredes* I'm going up the wall || *estoy que no puedo ni moverme* I'm in such a state I can't even move || *si estuviese en tu lugar* if I were you, if I were in your place *o* in your shoes || *ya está* that's it || *¡ya está bien!* that'll do!, that's enough! (¡basta!) || *ya que estamos* while we're here, while we're at it.

estarcido *m* stencil (dibujo).

estarcir *vt* to stencil.

estasis *f* MED stasis.

estatal *adj* state.

estático, ca *adj* static || FIG dumbfounded (pasmado).
◆ *f* TECN statics.

estatificar *vt* to nationalize (nacionalizar).

estatismo *m* statism, State control || immobility.

estator *m* TECN stator.

estatorreactor *m* AVIAC ramjet.

estatoscopio *m* FÍS statoscope.

estatua *f* statue; *estatua yacente, ecuestre* recumbent, equestrian statue || FIG *quedarse hecho una estatua* to be dumbfounded (pasmado), transfixed (con admiración), petrified (con miedo).

estatuario, ria *adj* statuary; *arte, mármol estatuario* statuary art, marble || TAUR *pase estatuario* statuesque pass [made without moving the body].
◆ *m* statuary, sculptor.
◆ *f* statuary (arte).

estatuilla *f* statuette.

estatuir* *vt* to enact, to decree || to provide (disponer) || to establish (establecer).

estatura *f* stature, height (de una persona).

estatuto *m* statute || *estatuto formal* protocol.

estay *m* MAR stay || *estay mayor* mainstay.

este *m* east || east wind, easterly (viento) || — *del este* eastern; *las provincias del este* the eastern provinces; east; *Alemania del Este* East Germany; east, easterly; *viento del este* easterly wind || MAR *este cuarta al nordeste, al sudeste* east by north, by south.
◆ *adj* east; *el ala este de la casa* the east wing of the house || easterly; *rumbo este* easterly direction || easterly, east (wind).

este, esta, estos, estas *adj dem* this, these; *no conozco a esta mujer* I am not acquainted with this woman.

éste, ésta, éstos, éstas *pron dem* this, this one; *me gusta más esa casa que ésta* I prefer that house to this one || he, she, they (véase OBSERV en ÉSE); *nadie me lo dijo, aunque éste lo sabía* nobody told me, although she knew || him, her, them (véase OBSERV en ÉSE); *se lo he dado a éste* I've given it to him || the latter; *Juan y Carlos estaban sentados; éste se levantó y aquél se quedó* John and Charles were seated; the latter got up and the former remained seated || *ésta* the place in which a document or letter is signed; *hecho en ésta (Madrid) a 10 de octubre* Madrid, 10th October || FAM *ésta y nunca* or *no más* never again (nunca más), this is the very last time (por última vez).
— OBSERV The written accent may be omitted where no confusion with the adjectives *este, esta, etc.* is possible.

estearato *m* QUÍM stearate.

esteárico, ca *adj* QUÍM stearic.

estearina *f* stearin || AMER candle.

esteatita *f* MIN steatite, soapstone.

esteba *f* MAR steeve (pértiga para apretar la carga).

estela *f* wake (de un barco) || trail (de un avión, un cohete) || trail (de una estrella fugaz) || stele (monumento) || FIG wake; *dejar una estela de descontento* to leave a wake of discontent || BOT stele || *estela de condensación* contrail, vapour trail.

estelar *adj* ASTR stellar || FIG star; *combate estelar* star bout (boxeo).

estelaridad *f* AMER popularity.

estelión *m* ZOOL gecko (salamanquesa) || toadstone (piedra fabulosa).

estelionato *m* stellionate, fraud in real estate deals.

estenio *m* sthene (unidad de fuerza).

estenocardia *f* MED stenocardia, angina pectoris.

estenografía *f* stenography, shorthand.

estenografiar *vt* to take down in shorthand, to write in shorthand, to stenograph.

estenográfico, ca *adj* stenographic, stenographical, in shorthand (escritura).

estenógrafo, fa *m/f* stenographer, shorthand writer.
— OBSERV *Taquígrafo, taquígrafa* are more common.

estenordeste *m* east-northeast.

estenotipia *f* stenotypy (arte) || stenotype (máquina).

estenotipista *m/f* stenotypist.

estenotipo *m* stenotype.

estentóreo, a *adj* stentorian; *voz estentórea* stentorian voice.

estepa *f* steppe (llanura) || BOT rockrose (jara).

estepario, ria *adj* steppe.

éster *m* QUÍM ester.

estera *f* matting (tejido); *estera de juncos* rush matting || mat (alfombra) || doormat (felpudo) || *darle a uno más palos que a una estera* to give s.o. a good beating *o* thrashing.

esterar *vt* to cover with mats *o* matting.

estercoladura *f*; **estercolamiento** *m* AGR manuring.

estercolar *vt* to manure (la tierra).
◆ *vi* to dung (los animales).

estercolero *m* dunghill, manure heap || FIG pigsty (sitio muy sucio).

estéreo *m* stere, cubic metre (medida para madera).
◆ *adj* stereo; *un disco estéreo* a stereo record.

estereóbato *m* ARQ stereobate.

estereofonía *f* stereophony, stereo.

estereofónico, ca *adj* stereophonic, stereo.

estereografía *f* stereography.

estereograma *m* stereogram, stereograph.

estereometría *f* stereometry.

estereómetro *m* stereometer.

estereoquímica *f* stereochemistry.

estereoscopia *f* stereoscopy.

estereoscópico, ca *adj* stereoscopic, stereoscopical.

estereoscopio *m* stereoscope.

estereotipado *m* stereotyping.

estereotipado, da *adj* stereotyped || FIG stereotyped; *sonrisa, actitud estereotipada* stereotyped smile, attitude | hackneyed, stereotyped; *expresión estereotipada* hackneyed phrase.

estereotipar *vt* to stereotype.

estereotipia *f* stereotypy (proceso) || stereotype (máquina) || MED stereotypy (repetición).

estereotipo *m* stereotype.

estereotomía *f* stereotomy.

esterería *f* mat shop (tienda) || mat workshop (taller).

esterero *m* mat layer (colocador) || mat maker (fabricante) || mat dealer (comerciante).

esterificación *f* QUÍM esterification.

esterificar *vt* QUÍM to esterify.

estéril *adj* sterile, barren, infertile (terreno) || sterile, infertile (mujer) || sterile (hombre) || barren (animal) || sterile (aséptico) || FIG futile, unfruitful, fruitless; *conversaciones estériles* futile talks.

esterilidad *f* sterility, barrenness, infertility (de un terreno) || sterility, infertility (de una mujer) || sterility (de un hombre) || barrenness (de un animal) || sterility (asepsia) || FIG futility, unfruitfulness, fruitlessness.

esterilización *f* sterilization.

esterilizador, ra *adj* sterilizing.
◆ *m* sterilizer (aparato).

esterilizar *vt* to sterilize.

esterilla *f* small mat (alfombrilla) || rush matting (de juncos) || gold *o* silver braid (trencilla) || *esterilla de baño* bath mat.

esterlina *adj f* sterling; *libra esterlina* pound sterling.

esternón *m* ANAT sternum, breastbone.

estero *m* mat laying (colocación de esteras) || estuary (de un río) || AMER bog, swamp (pantano).

esterol *m* QUÍM sterol.

estertor *m* death rattle (al morir) || MED stertor || *estar en los últimos estertores* to be at the point of death, to be in the article of death.

estesudeste *m* east-southeast.

esteta *m/f* aesthete.

esteticismo *m* aestheticism.

estético, ca *adj* aesthetic, esthetic; *desde el punto de vista estético* from the aesthetic point of view || artistic, beautiful (bello) || *cirugía estética* cosmetic *o* plastic surgery.
◆ *m* aesthetician.
◆ *f* aesthetics.

estetoscopia *f* MED stethoscopy.

estetoscopio *m* MED stethoscope.

esteva *f* plough handle [*US* plow handle].

estevado, da *adj* bowlegged, bandy-legged.
◆ *m/f* bowlegged person.

estiaje *m* low water (de un río).

estiba *f* MAR stowing, stowage (colocación de la carga) | trimming (distribución de los pesos) || place for packing wool in bags.

estibador *m* MAR stevedore.

estibar *vt* to pack tight, to compress (apretar) || MAR to stow (colocar la carga) | to trim (equilibrar la carga).

estiércol *m* dung, manure || *jugo de estiércol* liquid manure.

estigio, gia *adj* Stygian || MIT *laguna Estigia* Styx.

estigma *m* BOT ZOOL & MED stigma || FIG stigma, disgrace; *el estigma de la quiebra* the stigma attached to bankruptcy | stigma, brand (señal).
◆ *pl* REL stigmata (en el cuerpo de algunos santos).

estigmatismo *m* stigmatism (óptica).

estigmatización *f* branding (de un animal, un esclavo, etc.) || FIG branding, stigmatization || REL stigmatization, marking with stigmata.

estigmatizar *vt* to brand (con hierro candente) || FIG to brand, to stigmatize || REL to stigmatize, to mark with stigmata.

estilar *vt* JUR to draw up (in due form) (un documento) || to be in the habit of (acostumbrar).
◆ *vi/vpr* to be used, to be in use (emplearse); *esta palabra no se estila aquí* this word is not used here || to be in fashion *o* fashionable, to be worn (estar de moda); *los botines ya no se estilan* spats are no longer fashionable || to be normal *o* customary *o* usual (ser corriente); *no se estila llevar sombrero de paja en invierno* it is not customary to wear a straw hat in winter || to be the done thing; *son costumbres sociales que ya no se estilan* these social customs are no longer the done thing.

estilete *m* style (para escribir, de un aparato grabador) || stiletto (puñal) || MED stylet, probe.

estilismo *m* stylism (en el arte, en la literatura).

estilista *m/f* stylist (escritor) || stylist, designer; *estilista de coches* car designer.

estilístico, ca *adj* stylistic.
◆ *f* stylistics.

estilización *f* stylizing, stylization.

estilizado, da *adj* stylized || streamlined (aerodinámico) || slender (esbelto).

estilizar *vt* to stylize.

estilo *m* style, stylus (para escribir) || style (en arte, en literatura) || style, manner (manera) || style, fashion (moda); *es el último estilo* it's the latest style || FIG style; *tiene mucho estilo* he has a lot of style || BOT style || DEP stroke; *estilo mariposa* butterfly stroke || type; *vino espumoso estilo champán* sparkling wine, champagne type || gnomon, style (de reloj de sol) || — *a* or *al estilo de* in the style of, in the... style; *al estilo de España, de su país* in the Spanish style, in the style of his country || *carrera de 400 metros estilos* 400-metres medley race (natación) || *de buen, mal estilo* in good, bad taste; *una broma de mal estilo* a joke in bad taste; the done thing, not the done thing; *es de buen estilo ir a ese restorán* it is the done thing to go to that restaurant || *estilo de vida* way of life || GRAM *estilo directo* direct speech || *estilo libre* freestyle (natación) || *por el estilo* of the kind, of that sort || *todo está por el estilo* it's all very much the same.

estilográfico, ca *adj* stylographic || *pluma estilográfica* fountain pen.
◆ *f* fountain pen, pen.

estima *f* esteem, respect; *le tengo poca estima* I have little respect for him; *tener en gran estima a uno* to hold s.o. in high *o* great esteem || MAR dead reckoning.

estimabilidad *f* estimableness.

estimabilísimo, ma *adj* highly estimable.

estimable *adj* estimable || FIG considerable (grande).

estimación *f* estimation, valuation (evaluación comercial) || estimate; *estimación presupuestaria* budget estimate || esteem, respect (estima) || — JUR *estimación de una demanda* admittance of a claim || *estimación propia* self-esteem, self-respect || *según estimación común* according to general opinion.

estimado, da *adj* esteemed, respected || dear; *Estimado señor* Dear Sir.

estimar *vt* to esteem, to respect, to hold in esteem, to have respect for; *estimar (en) mucho a uno* to hold s.o. in great esteem, to have great respect for s.o., to respect s.o. highly || to value; *estimaron la sortija en mil libras* they valued the ring at a thousand pounds || to consider, to think, to deem, to esteem (juzgar); *no lo estimo necesario* I don't think it necessary || FAM to like, to be fond of; *le estimo, pero no le quiero* I am fond of him but I am not in love with him || JUR *estimar una demanda* to admit a claim.
◆ *vpr* to hold each other in esteem, to respect each other (dos personas) || to have a high opinion of o.s. (uno mismo) || to be valued (un objeto) || — *ninguna persona que se estime haría eso* no self-respecting person would do that || *se estima que la temperatura es hoy de cinco grados* today's temperature is estimated at five degrees.

estimativa *f* judgment (juicio) || instinct (instinto).

estimatorio, ria *adj* estimative.

estimulación *f* stimulation.

estimulante *adj* encouraging, stimulating; *una noticia estimulante* an encouraging piece of news || stimulative; *remedio estimulante* stimulative drug.
◆ *m* MED stimulant || FIG stimulus, incentive.

estimular *vt* to encourage; *estimula a su hijo a estudiar* he encourages his son to study || to promote, to encourage; *el gobierno quiere estimular la industria y las artes en esta región* the government wishes to encourage industry and the arts in this area || to stimulate (el apetito) || to incite, to stir, to urge; *los agitadores estimularon a los estudiantes a sublevarse* the agitators incited the students to rebel.

estímulo *m* stimulant, stimulus (estimulante); *sus palabras fueron un estímulo para mí* his words acted as a stimulus for me || encouragement, stimulation; *un poco de estímulo de parte de la dirección no estaría de más* a little encouragement from the management would not be amiss || incentive (incentivo) || BIOL stimulus.

estinco *m* skink (reptil).

estío *m* summer (verano).
— OBSERV The use of *estío* is restricted to literary contexts.

estipendiar *vt* to pay a stipend to, to remunerate.

estipendio *m* remuneration, pay, stipend (salario).

estípite *m* ARQ pedestal [in the form of an inverted pyramid] || BOT stipe, stalk (de palmera, etc.).

estíptico, ca *adj/sm* styptic.

estipulación *f* stipulation.

estipular *vt* to stipulate.

estiradamente *adv* scarcely *o* hardly *o* barely enough; *tener estiradamente para vivir* to have barely enough to live on.

estirado, da *adj* stretched || FIG dressed to kill (acicalado) | lofty, haughty (presumido) | stiff, starchy (tieso) || FIG & FAM stingy, miserly, tight-fisted (avaro) || *andar estirado* to walk stiffly.
◆ *f* dive (en fútbol) || *hacer una estirada* to dive.
◆ *m* straightening (del pelo) || TECN drawing (del metal, de fibras) || facelift (de la piel).

estirador, ra *adj* TECN *máquina estiradora* wire drawer (para el metal), drawing frame (para tejidos).

estiraje *m* TECN drawing (de metales o de fibras).

estiramiento *m* stretching.

estirar *vt* to stretch (alargar) || to tauten, to draw tight (poner tenso) || to stretch out; *estirar el brazo* to stretch out one's arm || to pull up (las medias) || to pull down (la falda) || TECN to draw (el metal, las fibras) || FIG to stretch out, to spin out (un ensayo, un discurso, etc.) | to stretch, to eke out (el dinero) || MAR to run out (un cable) || AMER FAM to bump off (matar) ||— *estirar con la plancha* to run an iron over (la ropa) || FIG & FAM *estirar la pata* to kick the bucket, to snuff it (morir) | *estirar las piernas* to stretch one's legs.
◆ *vpr* to stretch || to stretch out (tumbarse).

estireno; estiroleno *m* QUÍM styrene.

estirón *m* pull, tug, jerk (tirón) || sudden rapid growth (crecimiento rápido) || FIG & FAM *dar un estirón* to shoot up (crecer rápidamente).

estirpe *f* stock (origen de una familia); *es de buena estirpe* he comes of a sound stock || lineage, ancestry (descendencia) || FIG *no niega su estirpe* he takes after his parents.

estival *adj* summer, estival (p us); *calor, ropa estival* summer heat, clothing; *solsticio estival* summer solstice.

esto *pron dem neutro* this; *yo quiero esto* I want this; *esto es verdad* this is true ||— *en esto* at that point, then (entonces), thereupon (inmediatamente después) || *esto...* er... (cuando se vacila) || *esto es* right (de acuerdo), that is (to say) (o sea) || *no hay como esto para darte ánimo* there's nothing like this to cheer you up || *y en esto* when (cuando); *estaba nadando tranquilamente y en esto apareció un tiburón* I was happily swimming when a shark appeared; whereupon (y luego); *me enfadé y en esto él se marchó* I got angry, whereupon he left.

estocada *f* thrust, lunge, stab (acción) || stab, stab wound (herida) || TAUR (sword) thrust, «estocada»; *una estocada en lo alto* a well-placed «estocada».

estocafís *f* stockfish (pescado).

Estocolmo *n pr* GEOGR Stockholm.

estofa *f* brocade (tela) || quality (de una cosa) || type, class; *no queremos nada con gente de su estofa* we don't want anything to do with (people of) his type || *de baja estofa* low-class (personas), low quality (cosas).

estofado, da *adj* CULIN stewed || quilted (acolchado).
◆ *m* CULIN stew; *estofado de vaca* beef stew.

estofar *vt* to stew (guisar) || to quilt (acolchar).

estoicismo *m* Stoicism (escuela) || FIG stoicism.

estoico, ca *adj* Stoic, stoical; *la doctrina estoica* the Stoic doctrine || FIG stoic, stoical; *estoico ante la desgracia* stoic in the face of misfortune.
◆ *m/f* stoic; *Séneca fue un estoico* Seneca was a Stoic || FIG stoic; *es un verdadero estoico* he's a real stoic.

estola *f* stole.

estolidez *f* stupidity.

estólido, da *adj* stupid.

estolón *m* BOT stolon, sucker, runner || large stole (de sacerdote).

estoma *m* BOT & ZOOL stoma.

estomacal *adj/sm* stomachic || *trastorno estomacal* stomach upset.

estomagante *adj* indigestible || FIG sickening.

estomagar *vt* to give indigestion (empachar) || FIG to sicken.

estómago *m* stomach; *con el estómago vacío* on an empty stomach ||— *boca del estómago* pit of the stomach || *dolor de estómago* stomachache || FIG *hacerse el estómago a algo, a alguien* to get used to sth., to s.o. | *revolver el estómago a uno* to turn s.o.'s stomach (causar repugnancia) | *tener a uno cogido por el estómago* to have s.o. where one wants him | *tener a uno sentado en el estómago* or *en la boca del estómago* to be unable to stomach s.o. | *tener el estómago en los pies, tener el estómago pegado al espinazo* to be faint with hunger, to be starving | *tener estómago* or *mucho* or *buen estómago* to be able to stand a lot, to be tough (aguantar mucho), to have guts (tener valor), not to be overscrupulous (ser poco escrupuloso) | *tener los ojos más grandes que el estómago* to have eyes bigger than one's belly | *tener un estómago de piedra* to have a cast-iron stomach | *tener un vacío en el estómago* or *el estómago vacío* to have an empty stomach, to feel empty *o* hungry.

estomatitis *f* MED stomatitis.

estomatología *f* MED stomatology.

estomatólogo, ga *m/f* MED stomatologist.

Estonia *n pr* GEOGR Estonia.

estopa *f* tow (fibra) || burlap (tela) || MAR oakum || *estopa de acero* steel wool.

estopilla *f* cheesecloth, lawn (tela).

estopor *m* MAR stopper (del ancla).

estoque *m* rapier, tuck (ant) [espada] || TAUR matador's sword, «estoque» || BOT gladiolus.

estoqueador *m* TAUR matador.

estoquear *vt* TAUR to stab (with the sword).

estoraque *m* styrax, storax (árbol) || storax (resina).

estorbar *vt* to hinder, to hamper, to impede, to get in the way of; *el abrigo me estorba para correr* the overcoat gets in my way when I run || to thwart, to frustrate (frustrar); *la lluvia estorbó nuestros planes* the rain thwarted our plans || to annoy, to bother, to trouble (molestar) || to block, to obstruct; *estorbar el paso* to block the way; *estorbar el tráfico* to block the traffic || to hold up (negociaciones, etc.).
◆ *vi* to be in the way.

estorbo *m* hindrance, encumbrance (molestia); *este paquete es un estorbo* this parcel is a hindrance || obstacle (obstáculo) || obstruction || nuisance (molestia).

estornino *m* starling (ave).

estornudar *vi* to sneeze.

estornudo *m* sneeze.

estos, estas *adj dem* these—> **este.**

éstos, éstas *pron dem* these —> **éste.**

estovar *vt* CULIN to cook in butter or oil on a low flame.

estrábico, ca *adj* strabismal, strabismic, strabismical.

estrabismo *m* MED strabismus, squint.

estradivario *m* stradivarius (violín).

estrada *f* road, highway.

estrado *m* stage, platform (tarima) || (ant) drawing room (sala) || (ant) drawing-room furniture (mobiliario).
◆ *pl* JUR court rooms.

estrafalariamente *adv* outlandishly, eccentrically, bizarrely (de modo extraño) || in a slovenly fashion (desaliñadamente).

estrafalario, ria *adj* outlandish, eccentric, bizarre (extraño) || slovenly (desaliñado).
◆ *m/f* eccentric.

estragamiento *m* devastation, ravage.

estragar *vt* to devastate, to ruin, to ravage (causar estragos) || to corrupt, to deprave (corromper) || to spoil (estropear); *estragar el apetito* to spoil one's appetite || *tener el gusto* or *el paladar estragado* to have a jaded palate.

estrago *m* destruction, devastation, ruin (destrucción) || damage; *el terremoto ha causado muchos estragos* the earthquake has caused a lot of damage || corruption, perversion (en las costumbres) || FIG ravage; *los estragos de los años* the ravages of time || *causar* or *hacer estragos* to work havoc; *el torbellino, la epidemia ha causado estragos en todo el país* the whirlwind, epidemic has wrought havoc throughout the whole country.

estragón *m* BOT & CULIN tarragon.

estrambote *m* extra verses *pl* [added to a poem].

estrambóticamente *adv* outlandishly, bizarrely.

estrambótico, ca *adj* outlandish, bizarre, weird.

estramonio *m* BOT thorn apple, stramonium.

estrangulación *f* strangulation, strangling || MED strangulation.

estrangulado, da *adj* strangled || MED strangulated; *hernia estrangulada* strangulated hernia.

estrangulador, ra *adj* strangling || MED strangulating.
◆ *m/f* strangler (persona).
◆ *m* AUT choke.

estrangulamiento *m* strangling || MED strangulation || FIG bottleneck (en la carretera).

estrangular *vt* to strangle (ahogar) || MED to strangulate || AUT to choke || TECN to throttle.
◆ *vpr* to strangle o.s. (matarse).

estrapada *f* strappado (suplicio).

estraperlear *vi* FAM to deal in black-market goods.

estraperleo *m* FAM blackmarketing.

estraperlista *m/f* FAM blackmarketeer.
◆ *adj* black-market.

estraperlo *m* FAM black market; *vender de estraperlo* to sell on the black market.

estrás *m* strass (vidrio).

estratagema *f* stratagem.

estratega *m* MIL strategist || FAM *los estrategas de café* armchair strategist.

estrategia *f* strategy.

estratégicamente *adv* strategically.

estratégico, ca *adj* strategic.
◆ *m/f* strategist.

estratificación *f* stratification.

estratificar *vt* to stratify.
◆ *vpr* to stratify, to be stratified.

estrato *m* GEOL & BIOL stratum ‖ stratus (nube) ‖ FIG stratum; *estratos sociales* social strata.

estratocumulo *m* stratocumulus.

estratosfera *f* stratosphere.

estratosférico, ca *adj* stratospheric.

estrave *m* MAR stem.

estraza *f* rag, shred ‖ *papel de estraza* brown paper.

estrechamente *adv* narrowly ‖ tightly (con poco espacio) ‖ FIG closely; *estrechamente vinculados* closely linked ‖ — FIG *estrechamente unidos* very close (personas) | *vivir estrechamente* to live poorly *o* meagrely (con poco dinero), to live in cramped conditions (con poco espacio).

estrechamiento *m* taking-in (de la ropa) ‖ narrowing (acción de estrecharse un valle, una carretera, etc.) ‖ narrow point, narrow part (punto estrecho) ‖ FIG tightening; *estrechamiento de los lazos económicos entre ambos países* tightening of the economic links between the two countries ‖ — *estrechamiento de carretera* road narrows (señal de tráfico) ‖ *estrechamiento de manos* handshake.

estrechar *vt* to take in, to make smaller; *estrechar un vestido* to take in a dress ‖ to make narrower, to narrow; *están estrechando la carretera* they are making the road narrower ‖ to squeezer (apretar) ‖ FIG to bring closer together; *la desgracia estrecha a la familias* misfortune brings families closer together | to tighten; *estrechar los lazos de amistad* to tighten the bonds of friendship ‖ FIG to compel, to oblige (obligar, forzar) | to harass (acosar) ‖ — *estrechar a uno entre los brazos* to embrace s.o., to hug s.o. ‖ *estrechar la mano a uno* to shake s.o.'s hand, to shake hands with s.o. ‖ MIL *estrechar las filas* to close the ranks.
◆ *vpr* to become narrower, to narrow; *en el valle la carretera se estrecha* in the valley the road becomes narrower ‖ to squeeze together *o* up; *estrechaos un poco para que yo entre* squeeze up a bit so as I can get in ‖ FIG to grow tighter (lazos económicos, etc.) | to make economies, to cut down, to tighten one's belt (reducir los gastos) | to become close *o* closer (intimar) ‖ to shake (las manos).

estrechez *f* narrowness (anchura) ‖ tightness (poco espacio) ‖ FIG tight spot (apuro) ‖ poverty, want, need (falta de dinero); *vivir con mucha estrechez* to live in great poverty ‖ closeness, intimacy (intimidad) ‖ strictness, rigidity (lo estricto) ‖ austerity (austeridad) ‖ MED stricture ‖ — *estrechez de espíritu* or *de conciencia* or *de miras* narrow-mindedness ‖ *pasar estrecheces* to be harp up ‖ *vivir con estrechez* to live poorly *o* meagrely (con poco dinero), to live in cramped conditions (en poco espacio).

estrecho, cha *adj* narrow; *calle estrecha* narrow street ‖ tight (demasiado pequeño); *zapato estrecho* tight shoe ‖ cramped, small; *una habitación estrecha* a cramped room ‖ tight, short (de dinero) ‖ packed; *íbamos los seis muy estrechos en el coche* there were six of us tightly packed in the car ‖ FIG close; *amistad, relación estrecha* close friendship, relationship; *estrechos vínculos* close links | narrow; *espíritu estrecho* narrow mind | strict, rigid; *una moral estrecha* strict morals | stingy, miserly, tight (avaro) ‖ *de espíritu estrecho, de miras estrechas* narrow-minded.
◆ *m* GEOGR straits *pl*, strait; *el estrecho de Gibraltar* the Straits of Gibraltar ‖ FIG tight spot (apuro).

estregadera *f* scrubbing brush (cepillo) ‖ footscraper (para los zapatos).

estregar* *vt* to rub (frotar con la mano, un trapo, etc.) ‖ to scrub (con un cepillo) ‖ to scour (con abrasivo).
◆ *vpr* to rub o.s.

estregón *m* hard rubbing.

estrella *f* ASTR star; *estrella fugaz* shooting star ‖ star, blaze, white mark (de caballo) ‖ IMPR asterisk, star ‖ MIL star, pip (en el uniforme) ‖ FIG fate, destiny; *lo quiso mi estrella* fate willed it | star; *es una estrella de cine* he's a movie star; *estrella invitada* guest star ‖ — *dormir bajo las estrellas* to sleep under the stars ‖ ZOOL *estrella de mar* starfish ‖ *estrella errante* planet ‖ *estrella matutina* or *del alba* morning star ‖ *estrella polar* pole star ‖ *estrella vespertina* evening star ‖ FIG & FAM *haber nacido con buena estrella* to be born under a lucky star | *levantarse con las estrellas* to get up before daybreak | *poner por* or *sobre las estrellas* to praise to the skies | *tener mala estrella* to be unlucky | *ver las estrellas* to see stars.

estrellado, da *adj* starry, star-spangled (cielo) ‖ star-shaped, stellate (en forma de estrella) ‖ with a star *o* a blaze *o* a white mark on its forehead (caballo) ‖ CULIN fried (huevos) ‖ FIG smashed, shattered (con un porrazo).

estrellamar *m* ZOOL starfish ‖ BOT plantain.

estrellar *adj* stellar.

estrellar *vt* to smash, to dash, to shatter (romper); *estrelló un vaso contra la pared* he smashed a glass against the wall ‖ CULIN to fry (huevos) ‖ to stud *o* to spangle *o* to cover with stars.
◆ *vpr* to smash, to shatter (romperse) ‖ to crash; *el coche se estrelló contra el parapeto* the car crashed into *o* against the parapet ‖ to dash; *las olas se estrellaban contra el rompeolas* the waves dashed against the breakwater ‖ FIG to fail (fracasar) ‖ — FIG *estrellarse con una dificultad* to run into a difficulty | *estrellarse con uno* to run into s.o., to come up against s.o.

estrellato *m* stardom; *ese disco le lanzó al estrellato* that record launched him into stardom.

estrellón *m* star-shaped firework ‖ AMER crash.

estremecedor, ra *adj* startling (que asusta) ‖ bloodcurdling (espeluznante) ‖ violent (violento).

estremecer* *vt* to shake (sacudir); *el terremoto estremeció la casa* the earthquake shook the house ‖ to startle, to make (s.o.) jump (asustar); *el escopetazo me estremeció* the rifle shot startled me ‖ FIG to shake; *nuevas ideas que estremecen los cimientos de la sociedad* new ideas which shake the foundations of society | to make (s.o.) shudder (el miedo, etc.).
◆ *vpr* to shake, to shudder; *las ventanas se estremecen cuando truena* the windows shake when it thunders ‖ to jump, to start (sobrecogerse) ‖ to tremble, to shake, to quiver (*de* with) (emoción, miedo) ‖ to tremble (de ilusión, de alegría) ‖ to tremble, to shiver (de frío) ‖ FIG to shudder; *se estremece uno al pensar en la posibilidad de una epidemia* one shudders at the thought of a possible epidemic | to come into question; *se estremece la moral tradicional* traditional morals are coming into question ‖ *se estremeció al oír un ruido* a noise made him start *o* jump.

estremecimiento *m* shaking, shuddering (acción de sacudir) ‖ shake, shudder (sacudida) ‖ start, jump (sobresalto) ‖ trembling, shaking, quivering (acción), tremble, shake, quiver (hecho) (de emoción) ‖ shivering (acción), shiver (hecho) (de frío).

estrenar *vt* to use for the first time; *estrenar un nuevo bolígrafo* to use a new ball-point for the first time ‖ to wear for the first time (un traje, zapatos, etc.) ‖ TEATR to perform for the first time (una comedia) ‖ CINEM to show for the first time, to release, to put on release (una película) ‖ *estrenar un piso* to give a housewarming party.
◆ *vpr* to make one's début; *estrenarse como futbolista* to make one's début as a footballer ‖ TEATR to open ‖ CINEM to have its première ‖ COM to make one's first sale of the day (un vendedor).

estreno *m* first use ‖ first time on (ropa) ‖ début; *su estreno como vendedor fue un desastre* his début as a salesman was a disaster ‖ TEATR & CINEM premiere, first night; *estreno mundial* world premiere | new play (comedia), new release, new film (película) | début, first appearance (de un actor) ‖ *cine de estreno* first-run cinema.

estreñido, da *adj* MED constipated, costive ‖ FIG mean, stingy (avaro).

estreñimiento *m* MED constipation.

estreñir* *vt* MED to constipate.
◆ *vpr* MED to become constipated.

estrépito *m* din, racket (ruido fuerte) ‖ clatter, crash (ruido brusco) ‖ FIG flourish, fuss, ostentation; *lo hace todo con mucho estrépito* he does everything with lots of flourish.

estrepitosamente *adv* noisily, with a din *o* racket.

estrepitoso, sa *adj* noisy, deafening, clamorous; *una pita estrepitosa* deafening jeers ‖ noisy, rowdy (persona) ‖ FIG resounding; *un fracaso, un éxito estrepitoso* a resounding failure, success.

estreptococia *f* MED streptococcosis.

estreptococo *m* BIOL streptococcus.

estreptomicina *f* streptomycin (antibiótico).

estría *f* groove (ranura) ‖ ARQ flute, fluting ‖ rifling (de arma de fuego) ‖ GEOL stria, striation.

estriación; estriado *m* grooving ‖ ARQ fluting ‖ rifling (de arma de fuego) ‖ GEOL striation.

estriar *vt* to groove (hacer ranuras) ‖ ARQ to flute (una columna) ‖ to rifle (el cañón de un arma de fuego) ‖ GEOL to striate.

estribación *f* GEOGR spur.
◆ *pl* foothills.

estribadero *m* support.

estribar *vi* to rest; *el depósito estriba en cuatro pilares* the tank rests on four pillars ‖ FIG to lie; *la belleza de la sala estriba en su altura* the beauty of the room lies in its height; *su éxito estriba en su poder de persuasión* his success lies in his power of persuasion | to be based on (fundarse).

estribillo *m* refrain (en poesía) ‖ chorus (en canciones) ‖ catchphrase, pet word *o* phrase (muletilla).

estribo *m* stirrup ‖ step (de carruaje) ‖ running board (de coche) ‖ ANAT stirrup bone, stapes ‖ ARQ buttress (contrafuerte) | abutment (de un puente) ‖ GEOGR spur ‖ FIG foundation, basis (fundamento) ‖ — FIG *con el pie en el estribo* about to *o* ready to leave ‖ *hacer estribo con las manos a uno* to give s.o. a leg up ‖ FIG *perder los estribos* to lose one's temper, to fly off the handle (perder el control), to lose one's head (perder la serenidad).

estribor *m* MAR starboard.

estricnina *f* strychnine.

estricto, ta *adj* strict.

estridencia *f* stridency, stridence, shrillness.

estridente *adj* strident, shrill, grating (ruido).

estridor *m* stridor, strident sound (ruido estridente) || stridulation, chirring, chirping (de los insectos) || MED stridor.

estridulación *f* stridulation, chirring, chirping (de saltamontes, etc.).

estridular *vi* to stridulate, to chirr, to chirp.

estro *m* inspiration; *estro poético* poetic inspiration || ZOOL oestrus, heat, rut (celo) | botfly (insecto).

estroboscopio *m* stroboscope.

estrofa *f* verse, stanza, strophe.

estrógeno, na *adj* BIOL oestrogenic [*US* estrogenic].
◆ *m* BIOL oestrogen [*US* estrogen].

estroncio *m* QUÍM strontium (metal).

estropajo *m* scourer (para fregar) || loofah [*US* luffa] (planta y esponja vegetal) || FIG useless person, dead loss (persona) | useless thing, piece of rubbish (cosa) || *estropajo de aluminio* scouring pad.

estropajoso, sa *adj* tough, leathery (alimentos) || ragged (andrajoso) || slovenly (desaseado) || stammering (que pronuncia mal) || *tener la lengua estropajosa* to have a pasty tongue.

estropear *vt* to damage, to ruin, to spoil (poner en mal estado o volver inservible); *las heladas han estropeado la cosecha* the frosts have ruined the harvest; *he estropeado mi traje al caer* I ruined my suit when I fell over || to break, to damage, to ruin (un mecanismo); *los niños han estropeado la máquina de escribir, el ascensor* the children have damaged the typewriter, the lift || to spoil, to ruin (proyectos) || to hurt, to injure (lastimar) || to maim, to cripple (lisiar) || to age (envejecer) || to mix, to wet (el mortero) || — *estar estropeado* to be broken down *o* out of action *o* out of order (no funcionar), to be ruined (deteriorado) || *tengo el estómago estropeado* my stomach is out of order, I have an upset stomach.
◆ *vpr* to be *o* to get damaged *o* ruined *o* spoilt || to break down; *el coche se ha estropeado* the car has broken down || to spoil, to go bad (la fruta, etc.) | to go wrong, to fail (proyectos).

estropicio *m* clatter, crash (rotura estrepitosa); *se armó un gran estropicio en la cocina* there was a loud crash in the kitchen || damage (destrozo) || mess (desorden); *hacer un estropicio en la mesa* to make a mess on the table || rumpus (jaleo).

estructura *f* structure; *estructura social, celular, de hormigón* social, cellular, concrete structure || framework, frame (armazón).

estructuración *f* structuring, organization, construction.

estructural *adj* structural.

estructuralismo *m* structuralism.

estructurar *vt* to organize, to construct, to structure.

estruendo *m* roar, din; *el estruendo de las cataratas, de los motores* the roar of the waterfall, of engines || din, racket (ruido fuerte) || clatter, crash (ruido brusco) || tumult, uproar (de una muchedumbre) || show, pomp, ostentation (fausto).

estruendoso, sa *adj* thunderous, deafening (muy fuerte); *aplausos estruendosos, voz estruendosa* thunderous applause, voice || noisy (ruidoso).

estrujadora *f* squeezer, lemon squeezer.

estrujadura *f*; **estrujamiento** *m* squeezing (de limón) || pressing (de uva).

estrujar *vt* to squeeze (exprimir); *estrujar un limón* to squeeze a lemon || to press (uva) || to screw up, to crumple up; *estrujó la carta con ira* he screwed the letter up with rage || to wring (la ropa, el cuello) || FIG to bleed dry; *el gobierno está estrujando al pueblo con impuestos* the government is bleeding the country dry with taxation | to exploit (explotar) | to get everything one can out of (sacar el mejor rendimiento).
◆ *vpr* to crowd, to press, to throng; *los aficionados se estrujaban a la puerta del estadio* the fans were crowding at the gates of the stadium || FIG & FAM *estrujarse los sesos* to rack one's brains.

estrujón *m* squeezing || pressing.

Estuardo *n pr* Stuart.

estuario *m* estuary.

estucado *m* stucco, stuccowork.

estucador *m* stucco plasterer, stucco worker.

estucar *vt* to stucco.

estuco *m* stucco.

estuche *m* case; *estuche de gafas, de violín, de peine* glasses case, violin case, comb case || set (conjunto); *estuche de instrumentos* set of instruments || sheath (vaina) || casket (cofrecito) || — *estuche de joyas* jewel case, jewel box || *estuche de tocador* makeup case || FIG *ser un estuche* to be a jack-of-all-trades.

estuchista *m* case *o* box maker.

estudiado, da *adj* studied, elaborate; *una indiferencia estudiada, un gesto estudiado* studied indifference, a studied gesture || mannered (amanerado) || — *precio estudiado* rock-bottom price || *vehículo bien estudiado* carefully designed vehicle.

estudiantado *m* students *pl*, student body.

estudiante *m/f* student; *estudiante de Derecho* law student; *estudiante de medicina* medical student.

— OBSERV *Estudianta* is sometimes used in spoken language instead of the correct feminine form *estudiante*.

estudiantil *adj* student.

estudiantina *f* student band.

estudiar *vt/vi* to study; *estudiar filosofía, español, un proyecto* to study philosophy, Spanish, a plan || to read, to study (en la universidad); *estudia geografía en Cambridge* he's reading geography at Cambridge || to work, to study; *ayer me quedé toda la noche estudiando* I stayed up all last night working || to think about, to consider (una proposición) || — *estudiar de memoria* to learn by heart || *estudiar para cura, para maestro* to study to be a priest, to be a schoolteacher.

estudio *m* study; *aplicarse en los estudios* to work hard at one's studies; *un estudio sobre la desnutrición* a study on malnutrition || survey, research (encuesta); *un estudio del mercado* a market survey || investigation (investigación) || MÚS étude, study || ARTES study (dibujo) || study (despacho) || studio; *estudio cinematográfico, de artista, de fotógrafo* film, artist's, photographer's studio || bed-sitter, bed-sitting-room (piso) || — *cursar* or *hacer estudios* to study || *dar estudios a uno* to pay for s.o.'s studies, to finance s.o.'s schooling || *estar en estudio* to be under consideration || ECON *estudio del mercado* marketing, market research || *estudios empresariales* business *o* management studies || *estudios mayores* advanced studies || *hacer estudios* to study || *tener estudios* to be well educated.

estudioso, sa *adj* studious.
◆ *m* scholar, specialist.

estufa *f* stove, heater (para la calefacción) || fire (de gas, de electricidad) || hothouse, greenhouse (invernadero de plantas) || steam room (para baños de vapor) || heat cabinet (para secar, evaporar, etc.) || small brasier, foot warmer (estufilla) || — FIG *criar en estufa* to mollycoddle | *esta habitación es una estufa* this room is like an oven, it's like an oven in this room || *estufa de desinfección* sterilizer.

estufilla *f* small brasier, foot warmer (brasero) || muff (manguito).

estulticia *f* stupidity, foolishness (necedad).

estulto, ta *adj* stupid, foolish.

estupefacción *f* astonishment, stupefaction, amazement.

estupa *m* FAM drug squad.
◆ *m/f* policeman, policewoman of the drug squad.

estupefaciente *adj* astonishing, amazing, stupefying (que produce estupefacción) || narcotic (sustancia).
◆ *m* MED drug, narcotic.

estupefacto, ta *adj* astonished, amazed, stupefied, flabbergasted; *estupefacto con la noticia* astonished at *o* by the news || *dejar estupefacto* to astonish, to amaze, to stupefy, to flabbergast.

estupendamente *adv* wonderfully, marvellously, fantastically; *el coche funciona estupendamente* the car runs marvellously.

estupendo, da *adj* marvellous, wonderful, fantastic, stupendous (bueno) || beautiful (hermoso) || — FAM *¡estupendo!* great! | *un tío estupendo* a great chap.

estupidez *f* stupidity, silliness || — *cometer una estupidez* to do sth. stupid || *eso es una estupidez* that's a stupid thing to do (haciendo), that's a stupid thing to say (hablando).

estúpido, da *adj* stupid, silly.
◆ *m/f* idiot.

estupor *m* astonishment, amazement, stupefaction (asombro) || stupor.

estuprar *vt* to rape.

estupro *m* rape (violación).

estuque *m* stucco (estuco).

estuquista *m* stucco plasterer, stucco worker.

esturión *m* sturgeon (pez).

esvástica *f* swastika.

esviaje *m* ARQ skew, obliqueness (oblicuidad).

eta *f* eta (letra griega).

etalaje *m* bosh (de alto horno).

etano *m* QUÍM ethane.

etapa *f* stage; *hacer un viaje en dos etapas* to make a journey in two stages; *una etapa de cuarenta kilómetros* a stage of forty kilometres || leg, stage (en una carrera) || stop, stage; *nuestra primera etapa fue Londres* our first stop was London || FIG stage, phase (fase) || stage (cuerpo de cohete) || MIL halt, stop (lugar de parada) || — *por etapas* in stages || FIG *quemar etapas* to get on in leaps and bounds.

etcétera *f* et cetera, etc. || — *etcétera etcétera* and so on and so forth, et cetera et cetera || *y un largo etcétera* and many more besides.

éter *m* ether, aether || POÉT sky, heavens *pl*.

etéreo, a *adj* ethereal (del éter) || POÉT *la bóveda etérea* the ethereal vault.

eterificar *vt* QUÍM to etherify.

eterismo *m* MED etherism.

eterizar *vt* MED to etherize.

eternidad *f* eternity; *por* or *para toda la eternidad* for all eternity.

eternizar *vt* to eternalize, to eternize, to make eternal || FIG to make everlasting (hacer durar) | to immortalize.
◆ *vpr* to be endless, to drag on (*fam*); *la discusión se eternizaba* the discussion was endless || to stay for ages; *me eternizaría aquí* I could stay here for ages || to take ages; *esta chica se*

eterniza arreglándose this girl takes ages to get ready.

eterno, na *adj* eternal; *la vida eterna* eternal life || FIG endless, everlasting; *amistad eterna* endless friendship || *Padre Eterno* Eternal Father.

eterómano, na *adj* addicted to ether.
◆ *m/f* ether addict.

ético, ca *adj* ethical (moral) || FIG skinny (muy flaco) || MED consumptive.
◆ *m* moralist.
◆ *f* ethics (conjunto de principios); *ética profesional* professional ethics || ethics (parte de la filosofía).

etileno *m* QUÍM ethylene.

etílico, ca *adj* ethylic || *alcohol etílico* ethyl alcohol.

etilismo *m* MED alcoholism.

etilo *m* QUÍM ethyl.

etimología *f* etymology.

etimológico, ca *adj* etymological.

etimologista *m/f* etymologist.

etimologizar *vi* to etymologize.

etimólogo, ga *m/f* etymologist.

etiología *f* aetiology, etiology.

etiológico, ca *adj* aetiological, etiological.

etíope; etiope *adj/s* Ethiopian.

Etiopía *npr f* GEOGR Ethiopia.

etiqueta *f* ceremonial, ceremony, etiquette; *la etiqueta de la Corte* the Court ceremonial || pomp, ceremony; *recibir a uno con mucha etiqueta* to entertain s.o. with great ceremony || label (marbete, rótulo) || tag (inscripción atada a un paquete) || INFORM label, tag || — *de etiqueta* formal; *baile de etiqueta* formal ball || *se ruega* or *se suplica etiqueta* formal dress || *traje de etiqueta* formal dress || *vestirse de etiqueta* to wear formal dress.

etiquetado *m* labelling.

etiquetadora *f* labelling machine.

etiquetar *vt* to label.

etiquetero, ra *adj* ceremonious, formal.

etmoidal *adj* ethmoidal.

etmoides *adj/sm* ethmoid (hueso del cráneo).

etnarca *m* ethnarch.

etnarquía *f* ethnarchy.

etnia *f* ethnos.

étnico, ca *adj* ethnic.

etnografía *f* ethnography.

etnográfico, ca *adj* ethnographic, ethnographical.

etnógrafo *m* ethnographer.

etnología *f* ethnology.

etnólogo *m* ethnologist.

etrusco, ca *adj/s* Etruscan.

eucalipto *m* BOT eucalyptus.

eucaliptol *m* eucalyptol.

Eucaristía *f* Eucharist.

eucarístico, ca *adj* Eucharistic, Eucharistical; *congreso eucarístico* Eucharistic congress.

Euclides *npr m* Euclid; *postulado de Euclides* Euclid's postulate.

euclidiano, na *adj* Euclidean (de Euclides).

eucrasia *f* MED eucrasia.

eufemismo *m* euphemism.

eufemístico, ca *adj* euphemistic.

eufonía *f* euphony.

eufónico, ca *adj* euphonic, euphonious.

euforbio *m* BOT euphorbia (planta) || euphorbium (resina).

euforia *f* euphoria.

eufórico, ca *adj* euphoric.

Éufrates *npr m* GEOGR the River Euphrates.

eufuismo *m* euphuism.

eufuista *adj/s* euphuist.

eufuístico, ca *adj* euphuistic.

eugenesia *f* BIOL eugenics.

eugenésico, ca *adj* eugenic.

eulogia *f* eulogia.

eunuco *m* eunuch.

eupatorio *m* BOT eupatorium.

eupepsia *f* MED eupepsia, eupepsy.

eupéptico, ca *adj* MED eupeptic.

Eurasia *npr f* GEOGR Eurasia.

eurasiático, ca *adj/s* Eurasian.

¡eureka! *interj* eureka!

Eurípides *npr m* Euripides.

euritmia *f* eurythmy (movimiento armonioso) || eurythmics (rítmica).

eurítmico, ca *adj* eurythmic, eurythmical.

eurocomunismo *m* Eurocommunism.

eurocomunista *adj/s* Eurocommunist.

eurodiputado, da *m/f* MEP, Member of the European Parliament.

eurodivisa *f* Eurocurrency.

Europa *npr f* GEOGR Europe.

europeísmo *m* Europeanism.

europeísta *adj* pro-European, in favour of Europeanism.
◆ *m/f* pro-European, supporter of Europeanism *o* of European unity.

europeización *f* Europeanization.

europeizante *adj/s* pro-European.

europeizar *vt* to Europeanize.
◆ *vpr* to become Europeanized.

europeo, a *adj/s* European.

europio *m* QUÍM europium.

Eurovisión *npr f* Eurovision.

éuscaro, ra *adj/s* Euskarian, Basque.

euskera *m* Basque language.

eusquera *adj* pertaining to the Basque language.

Eustaquio *npr m* Eustachius || ANAT *trompa, válvula de Eustaquio* Eustachian tube, valve.

eutanasia *f* euthanasia.

eutrapelia *f* (p us) moderation [in one's pastimes] (moderación) || innocent pastime (distracción) || lighthearted joke (broma).

Eva *npr f* Eve.

evacuación *f* evacuation.

evacuado, da *m/f* evacuee.

evacuar *vt* to evacuate; *la policía evacuó el local* the police evacuated the premises; *los habitantes evacuaron la ciudad* the inhabitants evacuated the town || to evacuate (expeler del cuerpo) || to carry out (llevar a cabo).

evadido, da *adj* escaped.
◆ *m/f* escapee, fugitive.

evadir *vt* to avoid, to evade; *evadir una dificultad* to avoid a difficulty; *evadió hablar del asunto* he avoided talking about the matter || to escape, to avoid, to evade (peligro) || to shirk (responsabilidad).
◆ *vpr* to escape; *el preso se evadió* the prisoner escaped.

evaluación *f* evaluation.

evaluar *vt* to evaluate, to assess; *evaluar algo en cien libras* to evaluate sth. at a hundred pounds.

evanescente *adj* evanescent.

evangeliario *m* Gospel book.

evangélico, ca *adj* evangelical, evangelic.

evangelio *m* REL Gospel; *el evangelio según San Juan* the Gospel according to Saint John || FIG Gospel truth (verdad); *esto es el evangelio* this is the Gospel truth.

evangelismo *m* evangelism.

evangelista *adj/s* evangelist || AMER letter writer (memorialista) || *San Juan Evangelista* Saint John the Evangelist.

evangelización *f* evangelization, evangelizing.

evangelizador, ra *adj* evangelizing.
◆ *m/f* evangelist.

evangelizar *vt* to evangelize, to preach the Gospel to.

evaporación *f* evaporation.

evaporar *vt* to evaporate.
◆ *vpr* to evaporate || FIG to disappear, to vanish, to evaporate.

evaporizar *vt/vi* to vaporize.
◆ *vpr* to vaporize.

evasión *f* escape (fuga) || excuse, dodge, evasion (evasiva) || flight; *evasión de capitales, de divisas* capital flight || evasion; *evasión fiscal* tax evasion.

evasiva *f* excuse || *andarse con evasivas* to hedge.

evasivo, va *adj* evasive.

evección *f* ASTR evection.

evento *m* event (acontecimiento) || *a todo evento* at all events.

eventual *adj* possible (posible); *un viaje eventual* a possible journey || temporary, casual, provisional (provisional) || fortuitous (casual) || incidental (gastos).

eventualidad *f* eventuality, possibility.

eventualmente *adv* by chance (por casualidad) || possibly (probablemente).

Everest *npr m* GEOGR Everest.

evicción *f* JUR eviction.

evidencia *f* obviousness, clearness (cualidad de evidente) || certainty (certidumbre) || JUR evidence, proof || — *con toda evidencia* obviously || *poner en evidencia* to show, to make obvious *o* evident, to demonstrate; *el experimento puso en evidencia la verdad de la teoría* the experiment showed *o* demonstrated the truth of the theory, the experiment made the truth of the theory obvious; to show up (persona); *le puso en evidencia delante de su mujer* he showed him up in front of his wife || *ponerse en evidencia* to become clear *o* obvious (cosas, hechos), to show o.s. up, to reveal o.s. (personas).

evidenciar *vt* to show, to demonstrate, to make obvious *o* evident; *esto evidencia su inteligencia* this shows his intelligence.
◆ *vpr* to be obvious *o* evident; *se evidencia la necesidad de ensanchar esa calle* it is obvious that that street needs widening || to stand out, to be evident; *su talento se evidencia en sus obras* his talent stands out in his works.

evidente *adj* obvious, clear, evident.

evidentemente *adv* obviously, clearly, evidently.

evitable *adj* avoidable || that can be prevented *o* avoided (que se puede impedir).

evitar *vt* to avoid (eludir); *evitó hablar conmigo* he avoided speaking to me || to escape, to avoid, to evade; *evitar un peligro* to escape a danger || to save, to spare (ahorrar); *no pude evitarle este sufrimiento* I couldn't spare him this suffering || to avoid, to prevent (impedir); *no pudo evitar el accidente* he couldn't avoid the accident || to shun (las tentaciones).

evocable *adj* evocable.

evocación *f* evocation, recalling, conjuring up (acción) || evocation, recollection (descripción); *evocación de su niñez* evocation of his childhood.

evocador, ra *adj* evocative, evocatory.

evocar *vt* to evoke, to recall, to call forth, to conjure up; *evocar recuerdos* to recall memories || to evoke; *una casa que evoca las del siglo XVIII* a house which evokes those of the 18th century || to invoke (a los espíritus).

evocativo, va *adj* evocative.

evocatorio, ria *adj* evocatory.

evolución *f* evolution || development, evolution (de ideas, del pensamiento) || MIL evolution, manoeuvre || evolution, turn (vuelta).

evolucionado, da *adj* fully-developed; *pueblo evolucionado* fully-developed nation.

evolucionar *vi* to evolve || to evolve, to change, to develop (ideas, pensamiento, etc.) || MIL to manoeuvre, to carry out evolutions || to turn (dar vueltas).

evolucionismo *m* evolutionism.

evolucionista *adj/s* evolutionist.

evoluta *f* evolute (curva).

evolutivo, va *adj* evolutionary, evolutional.

evolvente *f* MAT involute.

ex *pref* ex-, former; *ex ministro* ex-minister, former minister || — *el Congo ex belga* the former Belgian Congo || *ex alumno* old boy (chico), old girl (chica) (de un colegio) || former student (de la universidad) || *los ex combatientes* the ex-servicemen [US the veterans].

— OBSERV En inglés siempre hay un guión entre *ex* y el nombre.

ex abrupto *adv* abruptly, sharply.

exabrupto *m* FAM abrupt *o* sharp remark.

exacción *f* exaction; *exacción de tributos* exaction of taxes || extortion, exaction (abuso).

exacerbación *f*; **exacerbamiento** *m* exasperation || exacerbation, aggravation (de enfermedad, de dolor) || exacerbation (de sentimientos).

exacerbante *adj* irritating, exasperating.

exacerbar *vt* to exasperate, to irritate (irritar) || to exacerbate, to aggravate (enfermedad, dolor, etc.) || to exacerbate (los sentimientos).

exactitud *f* exactness || accuracy (de copia, cálculo, versión, etc.) || precision || correctness, truth (verdad).

exacto, ta *adj* exact; *la hora exacta* the exact time || faithful, exact, accurate; *una copia exacta* a faithful copy || accurate, correct; *cálculo exacto* accurate calculation; *versión exacta del accidente* correct version of the accident || correct, true, right (verdadero) || punctual (puntual) || — *en cumplimiento exacto de sus órdenes* assiduously carrying out his orders || *es un exacto cumplidor de* he carries out assiduously *o* scrupulously || *tres metros exactos* exactly three metres.

◆ *adv* exactly.

exageración *f* exaggeration || *eso es una exageración* that's going too far, that's overdoing it, that's exaggerating.

exageradamente *adv* exaggeratedly || exceedingly, extremely; *es un hombre exageradamente amable* he is an exceedingly kind man.

exagerado, da *adj* exaggerated, farfetched; *relato exagerado* exaggerated story || excessive (excesivo); *severidad exagerada* excessive severity || exorbitant, outrageous (precio) || overdemonstrative (persona) || — *confianza exagerada* overconfidence || *ser exagerado* to overdo it, to go too far, to exaggerate.

exagerar *vt* to exaggerate; *exagerar lo ocurrido* to exaggerate what happened || to overdo, to go too far with; *no exageres el entrenamiento* don't overdo your training.

◆ *vi* to overdo, to go too far with; *exagerar con los baños de sol* to overdo one's sunbathing || to overdo it, to go too far, to exaggerate; *tú exageras* you are overdoing it, you are going too far.

exaltación *f* extolling, exalting, praising; *exaltación de la virtud* extolling of virtue || elation, exaltation (alegría) || exaltation, overexcitement (por una pasión) || exaltation, promotion; *exaltación al grado de general* exaltation to the rank of general || extremism (politics) || *exaltación de la Santa Cruz* exaltation of the Holy Cross.

exaltado, da *adj* exalted, extolled, praised (alabado) || extreme (político) || excitable, hotheaded; *un chico muy exaltado* a very excitable boy || worked up, overexcited; *hoy está exaltado* he's worked up today.

◆ *m/f* hothead || extremist (político).

exaltador, ra; exaltante *adj* exalting.

exaltar *vt* to extol, to exalt, to praise (enaltecer) || to work up, to overexcite (excitar) || to elate (con alegría) || to exacerbate, to increase (pasión) || to exalt, to raise (elevar).

◆ *vpr* to be extolled *o* exalted *o* praised (enaltecerse) || to get worked up *o* overexcited *o* carried away (excitarse); *¡no te exaltes tanto!* don't get so worked up! || to increase, to run high (pasión) || to get heated (en una pelea) || to be exalted *o* raised (elevarse).

exalumno, na *m/f* old boy (chico), old girl (chica) (de un colegio) || former student (de la universidad).

examen *m* examination, exam; *tener un examen* to sit *o* to take *o* to do an examination; *aprobar un examen* to pass an exam || examination, consideration, study (de un problema, de una situación) || survey (indagación) || — *examen de conciencia* self-examination || *examen de conducir* driving test || *examen de ingreso* entrance examination || JUR *examen de testigos* interrogation *o* examination of witnesses || *examen eliminatorio* qualifying examination || *examen final* final examination || *examen médico* medical examination *o* checkup || *examen oral* oral *o* viva examination || *examen parcial* partial examination || *libre examen* personal interpretation [of the Bible] || *presentarse a un examen* to take *o* to sit an exam || *someter a examen* to examine || *sufrir un examen* to take *o* to sit *o* to do an exam.

examinador, ra *adj* examining.

◆ *m/f* examiner.

examinado, da *m/f* candidate, examination candidate, examinee.

examinante *adj* examining.

examinar *vt* to examine || to consider, to study, to examine; *examinar un documento* to consider a document || to examine (a un candidato, a un enfermo).

◆ *vpr* to take *o* to sit *o* to do an examination; *examinarse de historia* to take a history examination *o* an examination in history.

exangüe *m* bloodless, exsanguine (falto de sangre) || FIG exhausted, worn-out (sin fuerzas) | dead (muerto).

exánime *adj* dead (muerto) || lifeless, inanimate (inanimado) || exhausted, worn-out (sin fuerzas), .

exantema *m* MED exanthema, exanthem (erupción).

exarca *m* exarch.

exarcado *m* exarchate.

exasperación *f* exasperation.

exasperador, ra *adj* exasperating (irritante).

exasperante *adj* exasperating.

exasperar *vt* to exasperate.

◆ *vpr* to get exasperated.

excarcelación *f* release (from prison) (liberación).

excarcelar *vt* to release (from prison) (liberar).

ex cátedra *adj/adv* ex cathedra.

excavación *f* excavation, digging; *excavación de zanjas* digging of ditches || excavation; *hacer excavaciones en Egipto* to carry out excavations in Egypt.

excavador, ra *adj* excavating, digging.

◆ *m/f* excavator (persona).

◆ *f* digger, excavator || — *excavadora de mandíbulas* grab || *excavadora mecánica* mechanical digger, shovel.

excavar *vt* to dig, to excavate; *excavar una zanja* to dig a ditch || to excavate, to dig up; *excavar el suelo* to excavate the ground || to excavate (en arqueología) || AGR to clear the soil around (plants).

excedencia *f* leave (de funcionario, de militar); *pedir la excedencia por un año* to ask for a year's leave || leave pay (sueldo) || sabbatical leave (de profesor) || *excedencia por un año* sabbatical year (de profesor).

excedente *adj* excess, surplus (que sobra) || excessive (excesivo) || on leave (funcionario, soldado) || on sabbatical leave (profesor).

◆ *m* surplus; *el excedente de productos en un país* a country's surplus products || what is left (sobra); *quédate con el excedente* keep what is left || MIL *excedente de cupo* young man exempt from military service after lottery || *excedentes agrícolas* agricultural surplus.

exceder *vi* to exceed, to surpass, to be more than; *los ingresos exceden a los gastos en cien libras* income exceeds *o* surpasses expenditure by a hundred pounds, income is a hundred pounds more than expenditure || to surpass, to excel; *mi coche excede al tuyo en velocidad* my car surpasses yours in speed || to be beyond; *el trabajo excede a su capacidad* the work is beyond his capacity.

◆ *vpr* to exceed; *se excedió en sus funciones* he exceeded his duty || to overdo, to go too far *o* to the extreme (exagerar); *se han excedido en el castigo* they have overdone the punishment, they have gone to the extreme *o* too far with the punishment || to be extremely kind (friendly, generous, etc.); *se excedieron conmigo* they were extremely kind to me || — *excederse a sí mismo* to excel o.s. || *no se han excedido conmigo* they weren't overkind to me, they weren't exactly kind to me.

excelencia *f* excellence || excellency (tratamiento honorífico) || — *por excelencia* par excellence || *Su Excelencia* His Excellency.

excelente *adj* excellent.

excelentísimo, ma *adj* most excellent.

excelsitud *f* sublimity, sublimeness, loftiness.

excelso, sa *adj* sublime, lofty.

◆ *m* *el Excelso* the Most High.

excentricidad *f* MAT eccentricity; *la excentricidad de una elipse* the eccentricity of an ellipse || FIG oddity, eccentricity, peculiarity (cosa rara, extravagancia) | eccentricity (de una persona).

excéntrico, ca *adj* MAT eccentric || FIG eccentric, odd.

◆ *m/f* eccentric.

◆ *f* TECN eccentric.

excepción *f* exception; *ser una excepción a la regla* to be an exception to the rule || — *a* or *con excepción de* except for, with the exception of; *me gustan todos los vestidos a excepción del rojo* I like all the dresses with the exception of the red one || *estado de excepción* state of emergency || *hacer excepción de* not to include || *hacer una excepción* to make an exception || *la excepción confirma la regla* the exception proves the rule || *si se hace excepción de* except for, apart from, with the exception of; *si se hace excepción de dos o tres, todos vienen* apart from *o* with the exception of *o* except for two or three, they are all coming.

excepcional *adj* exceptional (extraordinario); *un libro excepcional* an exceptional book || unusual, exceptional (raro); *una coincidencia excepcional* an unusual coincidence.

excepto *prep* except for, excepting, apart from; *excepto eso, todo va bien* except for that, everything is going well || except, except for, apart from; *vienen todos, excepto Pedro* they are all coming, except Peter; *salgo todos los días, excepto cuando llueve* I go out every day, except when it rains.

exceptuar *vt* to except, to exclude, not to include, to leave out; *exceptuaron a los niños de esta regla* they excepted children from this rule || JUR to exempt || *exceptuando a los niños* children excepted, except for children.
◆ *vpr* to be excepted *o* excluded, not to be included || *se vacunará a todos los niños, pero se exceptúa a los de menos de un año* all children will be vaccinated, except *o* except for *o* apart from those under one year of age.

excesivo, va *adj* excessive; *una carga excesiva* an excessive load.

exceso *m* excess || excess, surplus (excedente) || surfeit (de comida) || FIG excess; *pagar los excesos de su juventud* to pay for the excesses of one's youth || — *cometer excesos en la bebida* to drink too much, to drink to excess || *cometer excesos en la comida* to overeat, to eat to excess || *con exceso* too much; *fumar con exceso* to smoke too much || *el exceso de ejercicio es malo* too much *o* excessive exercise is bad || *en exceso* excessively, in excess || *exceso de comida, de peso* overeating, overweight || *exceso de equipaje* excess baggage || *exceso de velocidad* speeding.

excipiente *m* MED excipient.

excisión *f* MED excision.

excitabilidad *f* excitability.

excitable *adj* excitable, easily worked up || temperamental (nervioso) || excitable (en fisiología).

excitación *f* rousing, stirring up, inciting, exciting (incitación) || rousing, stirring up, stimulation (de una pasión) || restlessness, uneasiness, agitation (agitación) || excitement (de alegría, de entusiasmo) || activation (activación) || stimulation (del apetito, etc.) || ELECTR excitation.

excitador *m* FÍS & ELECTR exciter.

excitante *adj* exciting || stimulating, excitant; *una bebida excitante* a stimulating drink.
◆ *m* stimulant, excitant.

excitar *vt* to rouse, to incite, to stir up, to excite; *excitar a un pueblo a la rebelión* to rouse a nation to rebellion || to arouse, to stir up, to excite, to stimulate; *excitar la ira, el deseo* to arouse anger, desire || to get worked up, to put on edge, to make restless *o* uneasy (poner en estado de nerviosismo o impaciencia) || to excite, to get worked up (con alegría, con entusiasmo) || to activate (activar) || to stimulate (el apetito, la circulación de la sangre) || ELECTR to excite; *excitar una dinamo* to excite a dynamo || *excitarle los nervios a alguien* to put s.o.'s nerves on edge.
◆ *vpr* to get excited || to get worked up *o* carried away *o* excited (por alegría, entusiasmo) || to get worked up *o* restless *o* uneasy (por nerviosismo, impaciencia) || to be roused *o* incited *o* stirred up *o* excited (a la rebelión, etc.).

exclamación *f* exclamation || cry (grito) || exclamation mark (signo de admiración).

exclamar *vt/vi* to exclaim.

exclamativo, va; exclamatorio, ria *adj* exclamatory, exclamative (ant).

exclaustración *f* secularization.

exclaustrado, da *m/f* secularized monk (monje), secularized nun (monja).

exclaustrar *vt* to secularize (mandar abandonar el claustro a un religioso).

excluir* *vt* to exclude (no incluir) || to exclude, to shut out (de un círculo, etc.) || to throw out (expulsar) || to reject (rechazar).

exclusión *f* exclusion || *con exclusion de* excluding, to the exclusion of.

exclusiva *f* exclusive *o* sole right (privilegio); *dar la exclusiva a un editor* to give the sole right to a publisher || exclusive (en un periódico) || — *en exclusiva* exclusively || *tener la exclusiva* to have the exclusive rights, to have a monopoly || *venta en exclusiva* exclusive sale.

exclusive *adv* exclusively (únicamente) || exclusive; *desde el dos hasta el diez de abril exclusive* from the second to the tenth of April exclusive.

exclusividad *f* exclusiveness (cualidad de exclusivo) || exclusive *o* sole right (exclusiva).

exclusivismo *m* exclusivism.

exclusivista *adj/s* exclusivist.

exclusivo, va *adj* exclusive, sole; *agente exclusivo* sole agent.

excogitar *vt* to excogitate.

excombatiente *m* ex-serviceman [US veteran].

excomulgado, da *adj* excommunicate, excommunicated.
◆ *m/f* excommunicant, excommunicated person.

excomulgar *vt* to excommunicate; *excomulgar a un hereje* to excommunicate a heretic || FIG to ban.

excomunión *f* excommunication || excommunication order (decreto); *fulminar una excomunión* to fulminate an excommunication order.

excoriación *f* chafing, rubbing, excoriation || graze (desolladura).

excoriar *vt* to chafe, to rub, to excoriate (la piel) || to graze (desollar).
◆ *vpr* to be chafed.

excrecencia *f* excrescence.

excreción *f* excretion.

excrementar *vi* to excrete, to defecate, to defaecate.

excremento *m* excrement.

excrescencia *f* excrescence.

excretar *vt* to excrete.

excretor, ra; excretorio, ria *adj* ANAT excretory; *conducto excretor* excretory duct.

exculpación *f* exculpation, exoneration || JUR acquittal.

exculpar *vt* to exculpate, to exonerate (descargar de culpa) || JUR to acquit (absolver).

excursión *f* trip, excursion, outing; *ir de excursión, hacer una excursión* to go on a trip, to go on an excursion.

excursionismo *m* outings *pl*, excursions *pl* || hiking (a pie).

excursionista *m/f* excursionist, tripper || hiker (a pie).

excusa *f* excuse (pretexto); *¡nada de excusas!* no excuses! || apology, excuse (disculpa) || — *dar excusas* to make excuses || *deshacerse en excusas* to apologize profusely || *presentar sus excusas a* to apologize to, to give one's apologies to, to excuse o.s. to, to make one's excuses to.

excusable *adj* excusable, pardonable.

excusado, da *adj* excused, pardoned (perdonado) || unnecessary, superfluous, needless (inútil) || exempt (exento); *excusado de ir* exempt from going || concealed; *puerta excusada* concealed door || private, reserved (reservado) || *excusado es decir que* needless to say that.
◆ *m* toilet (retrete).

excusar *vt* to excuse, to pardon (disculpar) || to avoid, to prevent (impedir); *excusar disturbios* to avoid disturbances || to save, to spare; *esto te excusa venir* this saves your coming || to have no need; *excusas venir* you have no need to come || to exempt (eximir) || to dodge, to shirk; *excusar responsabilidades* to dodge responsibilities || — *excúsame con tu madre* apologize to your mother for me, give my apologies to your mother.
◆ *vpr* to excuse o.s. || to apologize; *excusarse con uno* to apologize to s.o.; *excusarse de* or *por haber hecho algo* to apologize for having done sth. || *el que se excusa, se acusa* to excuse o.s. is to accuse o.s.

exeat *m inv* discharge, exeat (permiso de salida).

execrable *adj* abominable, loathsome, execrable.

execración *f* execration || curse; *proferir execraciones* to utter curses.

execrar *vt* to loathe, to detest, to execrate (odiar) || to execrate, to curse (maldecir).

exégesis *f* exegesis.

exegeta *m* exegete.

exegético, ca *adj* exegetic, exegetical.

exención *f* exemption.

exentar *vt* (p us) to exempt.

exento, ta *adj* exempt || free; *exento de toda obligación* free from any obligation || open (descubierto) || — *exento de aduanas* duty-free; *productos exentos de aduanas* duty-free goods || *no exento de riesgos* not without dangers.

exequátur *m inv* exequatur.

exequias *f pl* funeral rites, funeral ceremony *sing*, obsequies, exequies.

exergo *m* exergue (de una medalla).

exfoliación *f* exfoliation.

exfoliador *m* AMER tear-off calendar (calendario de taco).

exfoliar *vt* to exfoliate.

exfoliativo, va *adj* exfoliative.

exhalación *f* exhalation, giving off (acción de exhalar) || exhalation, effluvium (efluvio) || vapour, exhalation (vapor) || shooting star (estrella fugaz) || flash of lightning (rayo) || — FIG *irse como una exhalación* to be gone in a flash | *pasar como una exhalación* to flash past.

exhalar *vt* to exhale, to give off *o* out; *exhalar un olor* to give off a smell || FIG to breathe, to heave; *exhalar suspiros* to heave sighs | to utter (quejas) || *exhalar el último suspiro* to heave one's last sigh, to breathe one's last.
◆ *vpr* to run quickly.

exhaustivo, va *adj* exhaustive (completo) || *tratar un tema de modo exhaustivo* to deal exhaustively with a subject.

exhausto, ta *adj* exhausted, worn-out (muy cansado) || exhausted (agotado).

exheredar *vt* to disinherit.

exhibición *f* exhibition, show (demostración, exposición) || presentation, show, exhibition (de modelos de alta costura) || showing (en un cine) || *exhibición de fieras* menagery.

exhibicionismo *m* exhibitionism.

exhibicionista *m/f* exhibitionist.

exhibidor, ra *adj* showing.
◆ *m* CINEM cinema owner [US exhibitor].

exhibir *vt* to put on show (mostrar) || to exhibit (cuadros, etc.) || to show; *exhibió su pasaporte* he showed his passport || to present, to show (modelos de alta costura) || to show (en un cine) || FIG to show off (mostrar con orgullo) | to let show (hacer alarde) || AMER to pay (pagar).
◆ *vpr* to make an exhibition of o.s., to show o.s. (mostrarse en público).

exhortación *f* exhortation.

exhortador, ra *adj* exhorting.

exhortar *vt* to exhort.

exhortativo, va *adj* exhortative.

exhortatorio, ria *adj* exhortatory.

exhorto *m* JUR letters rogatory *pl.*

exhumación *f* exhumation.

exhumar *vt* to exhume || FIG to dig up; *exhumar el pasado* to dig up the past.

exigencia *f* exigency, demand || requirement (lo necesario) || — *él tiene muchas exigencias* he is very demanding || *según las exigencias del caso* as the situation requires.

exigente *adj* demanding, exacting, exigent || *es muy exigente conmigo* he asks a lot of me, he is very demanding with me.

exigibilidad *f* liability to be demanded.

exigible *adj* demandable, exactable, exigible || payable on demand (una deuda).

exigir *vt* to demand, to exact; *exigir un pago* to demand a payment || to insist upon, to ask for, to demand; *exigir ropa de buena calidad* to insist upon good quality clothing || to require, to call for; *medidas exigidas por las circunstancias* measures required by the circumstances || to demand, to call for; *crimen que exige venganza* crime which calls for revenge || *exiges demasiado* you are very demanding.

exigüidad *f* smallness; *la exigüidad de un cuarto* the smallness of a room || meagerness, scantiness, exiguity; *la exigüidad de sus recursos* the meagerness of his resources.

exiguo, gua *adj* small, tiny, exiguous (casa, etc.) | meager, exiguous, scanty (cantidad, recursos, etc.).

exilado, da; exiliado, da *adj* exiled, in exile.
◆ *m/f* exile.

exilar; exiliar *vt* to exile.
◆ *vpr* to go into exile.

exilio *m* exile (destierro); *enviar al exilio* to send into exile; *gobierno en el exilio* government in exile.

eximente *adj* JUR absolving, absolutory.

eximio, mia *adj* renowned, distinguished, eminent; *el eximio poeta* the distinguished poet.

eximir *vt* to exempt (de impuestos, de servicio militar) || to free (liberar); *esto le exime de cualquier obligación conmigo* this frees him from any obligation to me.
◆ *vpr* to free o.s. (liberarse).

existencia *f* existence.
◆ *pl* COM stock *sing*, stocks; *liquidación de existencias* clearance sale of stock; *las existencias de un género* the stock of an article || COM *renovar las existencias* to restock.

existencial *adj* existential.

existencialismo *m* existentialism.

existencialista *adj/s* existentialist.

existente *adj* existent, existing || existing, in stock (reservas).

existir *vi* to exist (ser) || — *aún existe uno* there is still one left || *existe desde hace cien años* it has existed *o* has been in existence for a hundred years.

éxito *m* success; *esta película ha sido un éxito clamoroso* this film was an overwhelming success || success, hit (canción, novela, obra de teatro, etc.) || outcome, result (resultado) || — *con éxito* successfully || *éxito de taquilla* box-office success || *no tener éxito* to fail, not to succeed || *novela de gran éxito editorial* best seller || *tener éxito* to succeed; *tener éxito en la vida* to succeed in life; to be successful; *este actor tiene mucho éxito* this actor is very successful; to be popular (tener muchos admiradores); *esta chica tiene mucho éxito* this girl is very popular.

exitosamente *adv* AMER successfully.

exitoso, sa *adj* AMER successful.

ex libris *m* ex libris, bookplate.

exocrino, na *adj* exocrine.

éxodo *m* exodus; *éxodo rural* rural exodus.

exoftalmía *f* MED exophthalmus, exophthalmos.

exogamia *f* exogamy.

exógamo, ma *adj* exogamic, exogamous.

exógeno, na *adj* exogenous.

exoneración *f* freeing, exoneration || *exoneración de base* basic (tax) abatement (en un impuesto).

exonerar *vt* to free, to exonerate (de una obligación) || to exempt (de impuestos) || to dismiss (de un cargo) || *exonerar el vientre* to relieve o.s.

exónfalo *m* MED exomphalos.

exorbitancia *f* exorbitance, exorbitancy.

exorbitante *adj* exorbitant.

exorcismo *m* exorcism.

exorcista *m* exorcist, exorciser, exorcizer.

exorcizar *vt* to exorcize, to exorcise.

exordio *m* exordium, introduction, preamble (preámbulo) || FAM beginning.

exornar *vt* to adorn, to embellish.

exósmosis *f* exosmosis.

exotérico, ca *adj* exoteric.

exotérmico, ca *adj* exothermic.

exótico, ca *adj* exotic.

exotismo *m* exoticism.

expandir *vt* to expand (desarrollar, dilatar) || to spread (propagar).
◆ *vpr* to expand (extenderse) || to spread; *la noticia se ha expandido por todo el país* the news has spread throughout the country.

expansibilidad *f* FÍS expansibility, expandability || FIG expansiveness.

expansible *adj* expansible, expandable.

expansión *f* expansion (dilatación) || spreading (de una idea, de un uso, de una noticia) || relaxation (recreo) || expansion; *expansión industrial, colonial* industrial, colonial expansion || expansion, increase (aumento) || FIG openness, frankness, expansiveness (franqueza) || — INFORM *expansión de memoria* memory expansion || *expansión económica* economic expansion.

expansionar *vt* to expand.
◆ *vpr* to expand (dilatarse) || to open one's heart; *expansionarse con uno* to open one's heart to s.o. || to relax (recrearse).

expansionismo *m* expansionism.

expansionista *adj/s* expansionist.

expansivo, va *adj* open, frank, expansive (franco) || expansible, expandable (expansible).

expatriación *f* expatriation (exilio) || emigration.

expatriado, da *adj/s* expatriate.

expatriar *vt* to banish, to expatriate.
◆ *vpr* to leave one's country, to go into exile (exiliarse) || to emigrate (emigrar).

expectación *f* expectation, expectancy, anticipation; *había gran expectación en la ciudad ante la llegada de la reina* the queen's arrival caused great expectation in the city || excitement (emoción) || waiting (espera).

expectante *adj* expectant.

expectativa *f* expectation, expectancy || prospect (perspectiva) || hope (esperanza) || — *estar a la expectativa de algo* to be on the lookout for sth., to be on the watch for sth. || *expectativa de vida* life expectancy.

expectoración *f* MED expectoration | sputum (esputo).

expectorante *adj/sm* MED expectorant.

expectorar *vt/vi* MED to expectorate.

expedición *f* expedition (excursión) || party, expedition; *expedición de salvamento* search party, rescue expedition || dispatch, shipping, sending (envío de mercancías) || shipment (mercancías enviadas) || sending (de un paquete) || dispatch (de un asunto).

expedicionario, ria *adj* sending, dispatching (que envía) || expeditionary; *cuerpo expedicionario* expeditionary force.
◆ *m/f* sender (expedidor) || member of an expedition (que participa en una expedición).

expedidor, ra *adj* sending, dispatching, shipping, forwarding (de mercancías) || sending (de un paquete, etc.).
◆ *m/f* sender, dispatcher, shipper, forwarding agent (de mercancías) || sender (de un paquete, etc.).

expedientado, da *adj* under enquiry.

expedientar *vt* to place under enquiry || to make a file on (la policía).

expediente *adj* expedient.
◆ *m* expedient, means (medio); *un hábil expediente* a clever expedient || JUR case, proceedings *pl*; *instruir un expediente* to open a case *o* proceedings || file, dossier (documentos); *tiene un expediente cargado en la policía* the police have a full file on him || enquiry; *formar* or *instruir expediente a un funcionario* to open an enquiry on a civil servant || record; *expediente académico, profesional* academic, professional record || — FIG *cubrir el expediente* to do one's duty || *dar expediente a un asunto* to dispose of *o* to expedite a matter || ECON *expediente de regulación de empleo* job adjustment plan || *tener recurso al expediente de* to resort to (the device of).
◆ *pl* proceedings (trámites).

expedienteo *m* red tape (papeleo).

expedir* *vt* to send, to dispatch, to forward, to ship (enviar mercancías) || to send (un paquete, etc.) || JUR to draw up; *expedir un contrato* to draw up a contract || to issue; *pasaporte expedido en París* passport issued in Paris || to deal with (un asunto) || FIG to dispose of, to dispatch (hacer rápidamente).

expeditar *vt* AMER to solve (un asunto).

expeditivo, va *adj* expeditious.

expedito, ta *adj* clear, free; *la vía quedó expedita* the road was clear || expeditious, speedy, quick, prompt; *expedito para obrar* expeditious to act.

expelente *adj* expelling || *bomba expelente* force pump.

expeler *vt* to expel (a uno) || to give out, to throw out, to eject; *el volcán expele rocas* the volcano throws out rocks || MED to spit out (mucosidades) | to eliminate (cálculo).

expendedor, ra *adj* spending.
◆ *m/f* dealer, retailer (vendedor al detalle) || ticket agent (de localidades) || tobacconist [US dealer in tobacco] (de tabaco) || person who spreads counterfeit money (de moneda falsa) || *expendedor automático* vending machine.

expendeduría *f* retail store (tienda) || retailing (venta) || ticket office (de localidades para espectáculos) || ticket office (de lotería) || *expendeduría de tabaco* tobacconist's [US cigar store].

expender *vt* to retail (vender al por menor) || to spend (gastar) || to circulate, to pass [counterfeit money] (moneda falsa).

expendio *m* AMER → **expendeduría.**

expensar *vt* AMER to pay the expenses of.

expensas *f pl* expenses (gastos) || JUR costs || *a expensas de* at the expense of.

experiencia *f* experience; *tener experiencia* to have experience || FÍS & QUÍM experiment (experimento) || — *por experiencia* from experience || *saber por propia experiencia* to know from one's own experience.

experimentación *f* testing, experimenting, experimentation; *la experimentación de un nuevo procedimiento de televisión* the testing of a new television process || experiment (experimento).

experimentado, da *adj* experienced (persona) || tested, tried (método, etc.).

experimentador, ra *adj* experimenting.
◆ *m/f* experimenter.

experimental *adj* experimental.

experimentar *vt* to carry out experiments on, to test, to try out (científicamente) || to test; *experimentar un nuevo método* to test a new method || to experience (probar) || to have, to experience (dificultades) || to have, to experience, to feel (sentir); *experimentar una sensación desagradable* to experience an unpleasant sensation || to feel (una emoción) || to show (un aumento) || to suffer (sufrir) || to suffer, to sustain; *experimentar una derrota* to suffer a defeat || to undergo, to experience; *experimentar una renovación completa* to undergo a complete renovation.

experimento *m* experiment; *un experimento de química* a chemistry experiment || experimenting, experimentation (acción de experimentar).

expertamente *adv* expertly, skilfully.

experto, ta *adj/s* expert || *ser experto en la materia* to be an expert in the matter *o* on the subject.

expiable *adj* expiable.

expiación *f* expiation, atonement.

expiar *vt* to expiate, to atone for (un pecado) || to serve (una pena).

expiativo, va; expiatorio, ria *adj* expiatory.

expiración *f* expiration.

expirante *adj* expiring.

expirar *vi* to die, to expire, to breathe one's last (morir) || JUR to expire (contrato, etc.) || FIG to expire; *su pena ha expirado ya* his sentence has now expired.

explanación *f* levelling (de un terreno) || FIG explanation, elucidation (aclaración).

explanada *f* esplanade || glacis, esplanade (fortificación).

explanar *vt* to level (un terreno) || FIG to explain, to elucidate, to clear up (aclarar).

explayar *vt* to spread out, to extend.
◆ *vpr* to be long-winded, to speak at length, to expatiate; *explayarse en un discurso* to be longwinded in a speech || to open one's heart, to confide (confiarse); *se explayaba en sus cartas a sus amigos* in his letters he opened his heart to his friends, in his letters he confided in his friends || *explayarse al gusto de uno* to talk one's head off.

expletivo, va *adj* expletive.

explicable *adj* explicable, explainable || justifiable.

explicación *f* explanation || reason, explanation; *sin dar ninguna clase de explicaciones* without giving any reason at all || excuse, explanation (excusa) || *tener una explicación con alguien* to come to an explanation with s.o., to have it out with s.o.

explicaderas *f pl* FAM way *sing* of explaining || FAM *tener buenas explicaderas* to have a way of explaining things.

explicar *vt* to explain; *explícame cómo ha ocurrido* explain to me how it happened || to lecture in, to teach (enseñar) || to expound, to explain, to explicate; *explicar una teoría* to expound a theory || to explain, to comment upon (un texto) || to justify (justificar); *explicó su intervención* he justified his intervention || *explicar algo con pelos y señales* to explain sth. in the minutest detail.
◆ *vpr* to explain o.s. || to understand, to make out, to be able to understand; *no me explico cómo he podido perderlo* I can't understand how I could have lost it || to express o.s. (expresarse) || to explain o.s. (justificarse) || *eso se explica difícilmente* this is difficult to explain.

explicativo, va *adj* explanatory, explicative.

explícito, ta *adj* explicit.

exploración *f* exploration (de un territorio, de una herida) || prospecting (de minas) || scanning (radar, televisión); *línea de exploración* scanning line || MIL reconnaissance, scouting || INFORM scanning || — *exploración del espacio* space exploration || *exploración submarina* underwater exploration (investigaciones), skin diving (deporte).

explorador, ra *adj* exploring, exploratory || TECN scanning (en televisión, radar); *haz explorador* scanning beam || MIL scouting; *barco explorador* scouting vessel.
◆ *m/f* explorer.
◆ *m* MIL scout || boy scout (niño) || TECN scanner (radar, televisión) || MED probe.
◆ *f* girl guide [US girl scout] (niña).

explorar *vt* to explore; *explorar la costa africana* to explore the African coast || to prospect (minas) || TECN to scan (con un haz electrónico) || MED to explore, to probe || MIL to scout, to reconnoitre || FIG to explore, to examine || — *explorar con la vista* to scan || FIG *explorar el terreno* to see how the land lies.

exploratorio, ria *adj* exploratory; *conversaciones exploratorias* exploratory talks || MED exploratory, probing.

explosión *f* explosion, blowing up; *la explosión de una bomba* the explosion of a bomb || bursting (de un balón) || outburst, blast (detonación) || FIG outburst; *explosión de entusiasmo, de ira* outburst of enthusiasm, of anger || — *explosión demográfica* population explosion || *hacer explosión* to explode || *motor de explosión* internal combustion engine.

explosionar *vt* to explode.
◆ *vi* to explode, to blow up.

explosivo, va *adj/sm* explosive.
◆ *adj/sf* GRAM plosive, explosive (consonante).

explotable *adj* workable, exploitable (mina) || which can be cultivated *o* farmed (terreno).

explotación *f* working, exploitation (de una mina); *explotación a cielo abierto* opencast working || cultivation, farming (de un terreno) || tapping, exploitation; *la explotación de los recursos naturales* tapping of natural resources || commercial use, exploitation, working (de un bosque, etc.) || operating, running, operation (de una fábrica, de una línea de comunicaciones, etc.) || management (de un negocio) || plant (conjunto de instalaciones); *explotación industrial* industrial plant || exploitation (abuso); *la explotación de los obreros* the exploitation of the workers || — *explotación agrícola* farm (granja), farming (organización agrícola) || *explotación forestal* timber farm, timber industry || *explotación minera* mine (mina), mining (industria) || *gastos de explotación* operating costs.

explotador, ra *adj* operating; *compañía explotadora* operating company || AGR working, farming || exploiting (que abusa).
◆ *m/f* operator (el que explota) || AGR exploiter, farmer, cultivator (cultivador) || worker (de una mina) || exploiter (el que abusa).

explotar *vt* to work, to exploit (una mina) || to cultivate, to farm (terreno) || to tap, to exploit (recursos) || to manage (un negocio) || to put to commercial use, to exploit (comercializar) || to operate, to run (una fábrica, una línea de trenes, autobuses, etc.) || to exploit (abusar); *explota su bondad* he exploits his kindness || to exploit (a los obreros) || to explode (una bomba).
◆ *vi* to explode, to blow up (una bomba, etc.).

expoliación *f* despoiling, spoliation.

expoliador, ra *adj* despoiling (persona) || spoliatory (medida).
◆ *m/f* despoiler, spoliator.

expoliar *vt* to despoil, to spoliate (despojar).

exponenciación *f* MAT exponentiation.

exponencial *adj* MAT exponential.

exponente *adj* exponent, expounding (que expone).
◆ *m* MAT exponent, index || exponent (representante); *Cervantes es el máximo exponente de la literatura española* Cervantes is the greatest exponent of Spanish literature || proof, example (prueba); *nuestras exportaciones son un magnífico exponente de la vitalidad de la industria nacional* our exports are a magnificent proof of the vitality of the national industry.

exponer* *vt* to expound; *exponer una teoría* to expound a theory || to put forward; *exponer una propuesta* to put forward a proposal || to set out, to state, to set forth (hechos) || to explain (explicar); *exponer su pensamiento* to explain one's thought || to show, to exhibit, to put on show; *exponer un cuadro* to put a painting on show || to display; *el comerciante expone su mercancía en el escaparate* the dealer displays his goods in the window || to expose (al aire, al sol, al viento) || to risk, to expose (arriesgar) || FOT to expose || REL to expose (el Santísimo Sacramento) || to abandon (un niño) || *exponer mucho* to take great risks *o* a lot of risks, to run a lot of risks.
◆ *vpr* to expose o.s. || to run the risk, to take the risk; *exponerse a un fracaso, a que se enfade* to run the risk of a failure, of his getting angry.

exportable *adj* exportable.

exportación *f* exportation, exporting (acción de exportar) || export; *las exportaciones han aumentado* exports have increased; *comercio de exportación* export trade; *artículo de exportación* export item; *exportaciones de naranjas* orange exports.

exportador, ra *adj* exporting; *país exportador* exporting country.
◆ *m/f* exporter.

exportar *vt* to export; *exportar naranjas de España* to export oranges from Spain ‖ INFORM to transfer (ficheros, archivos, documentos).

exposición *f* exhibition (de cuadros, etc.) ‖ show; *exposición del automóvil* motor show ‖ display (de mercancías) ‖ exposition (de una teoría) ‖ putting forward (de una propuesta) ‖ exposition, disclosure (de ideas) ‖ exposition, statement (declaración) ‖ explanation, exposé; *este periódico hace una exposición clara de los hechos* this paper gives a clear explanation of the facts ‖ exposition (en literatura y música) ‖ exposing (al aire, al sol, al viento) ‖ exposition (de una casa) ‖ risk, danger (riesgo) ‖ FOT exposure ‖ REL exposition ‖ — FOT *exceso de exposición* overexposure ‖ JUR *exposición de motivos* motivation ‖ *Exposición Universal* Universal Exhibition, World Fair ‖ FOT *falta de exposición* underexposure ‖ *sala de exposición* showroom ‖ FOT *tiempo de exposición* exposure time.

expositivo, va *adj* explanatory, expositive, expository.

expósito, ta *adj* abandoned.
◆ *m/f* foundling; *casa de expósitos* home for foundlings.

expositor, ra *adj/s* exponent.
◆ *m/f* exhibitor (en una exposición).

exprés *m* express (tren) ‖ espresso (café).

expresado, da *adj* expressed (expreso) ‖ mentioned, above-mentioned (mencionado).

expresamente *adv* specifically, expressly, especially (concretamente) ‖ purposely, on purpose (a propósito) ‖ explicitly (explícitamente).

expresar *vt* to express; *expresar una idea* to express an idea ‖ to show, to express (un sentimiento); *expresar alegría* to show happiness ‖ to convey (comunicar).
◆ *vpr* to express o.s.; *no me expreso bien* I don't express myself well ‖ to be expressed (cosa, sentimiento, idea) ‖ to state; *como se expresa más adelante* as is stated below.
— OBSERV *Expresar* has two past participles. One regular, *expresado*, which is used with *haber* and *tener*, and one irregular, *expreso*, which is used only as an adjective.

expresión *f* expression ‖ — *perdone* or *válgame la expresión* pardon the expression ‖ *reducir a la mínima expresión* to reduce to the simplest expression, to reduce to the lowest terms (una fórmula), to reduce to almost nothing, to make as small as possible (un objeto).
◆ *pl* regards, greetings (recuerdos); *dale expresiones de mi parte* give him my regards.

expresionismo *m* expressionism.

expresionista *adj/s* expressionist.

expresivamente *adv* expressively ‖ affectionately, warmly (con cariño).

expresivo, va *adj* expressive; *un gesto muy expresivo* a very expressive gesture ‖ significant; *silencio expresivo* significant silence ‖ sincere; *mi más expresivo agradecimiento* my sincerest thanks ‖ affectionate, warm (cariñoso).

expreso, sa *adj* expressed (dicho) ‖ express (especificado); *por orden expresa de la autoridad* by express order of the authority ‖ express; *tren expreso* express train.
◆ *m* express (tren) ‖ express messenger (mensajero).

exprimelimones *m inv* lemon squeezer.

exprimidera *f*; **exprimidero** *m* → **exprimidor.**

exprimidor *m* squeezer, lemon squeezer.

exprimir *vt* to squeeze (extraer el jugo de) ‖ FIG to exploit, to get the most out of (explotar); *su patrón trata de exprimirle al máximo* his boss is trying to exploit him as much as he can *o* to get the most he can out of him ‖ to bleed dry (sacar dinero) ‖ FIG *exprimirse el cerebro* to rack one's brains.

ex profeso *adv* specifically, especially, purposely.

expropiación *f* expropriation.

expropiador, ra *adj* expropriating.
◆ *m/f* expropriator.

expropiar *vt* to expropriate.

expuesto, ta *adj* on display, on show, displayed; *las prendas estaban expuestas en el escaparate* the garments were on display in the window ‖ exhibited, on show; *los cuadros expuestos* the exhibited pictures, the pictures on show ‖ exposed; *una casa expuesta al viento* a house exposed to the wind ‖ dangerous (peligroso) ‖ expounded (teoría) ‖ explained, shown (explicado) ‖ *estar expuesto a* to be exposed to, to be open to (una persona); *estar expuesto a las críticas* to be open to criticism.

expugnar *vt* MIL to take by storm.

expulsar *vt* to eject, to throw out, to expel (echar) ‖ to expel (de un colegio, de un instituto, etc.) ‖ to send down [US to expel] (de la universidad) ‖ to expel, to eject (del cuerpo) ‖ MED to bring up, to spit out ‖ DEP to send off (fútbol).

expulsión *f* ejection, expulsion ‖ expulsion (de un colegio, de un instituto, etc.) ‖ sending down [US expulsion] (de la universidad) ‖ expulsion, ejection (del cuerpo) ‖ MED bringing-up, spitting-out ‖ DEP sending-off ‖ AVIAC ejection (eyección).

expulsivo, va *adj* expulsive ‖ MED expellant.

expulsor *m* ejector (de armas).

expurgación *f* expurgation (de un libro, de un texto, etc.) ‖ FIG purging, purgation, purge.

expurgar *vt* to expurgate; *expurgar una novela* to expurgate a novel ‖ FIG to purge.

expurgatorio, ria *adj* expurgatory ‖ FIG purging.

expurgo *m* expurgation (de un libro, etc.) ‖ purge.

exquisitamente *adv* exquisitely.

exquisitez *f* exquisiteness ‖ refinement, exquisiteness (delicadeza).

exquisito, ta *adj* exquisite; *belleza exquisita* exquisite beauty ‖ exquisite, delicious (sabor) ‖ delightful, exquisite (lugar) ‖ refined, exquisite; *gusto, hombre exquisito* refined taste, man.

extasiar *vt* to enrapture, to send into raptures.
◆ *vpr* to go into raptures *o* ecstasies; *extasiarse con algo* to go into raptures over sth.

éxtasis *f inv* ecstasy, rapture (de alegría, de admiración, etc.) ‖ REL ecstasy ‖ *estar sumido en éxtasis* to be in ecstasy *o* raptures.

extático, ca *adj* ecstatic, enraptured.

extemporal; extemporáneo, a *adj* unseasonable; *lluvia extemporal* unseasonable rain ‖ ill-timed, untimely, inappropriate; *respuesta extemporánea* ill-timed reply.

extender* *vt* to spread; *el ave extendió las alas* the bird spread its wings; *extender el mantel sobre la mesa* to spread the tablecloth over the table ‖ to spread out; *extender un mapa* to spread out a map; *extender una manta en el suelo* to spread a blanket out on the ground ‖ to spread out (esparcir) ‖ to spread (mantequilla, pintura) ‖ to spread (una noticia, etc.) ‖ to extend; *extender su influencia* to extend one's influence; *extender una red de autopistas* to extend a network of motorways ‖ to extend (ampliar); *extendieron la ley a otros casos* they extended the law to other cases ‖ to draw up (documento, contrato) ‖ to issue (un certificado) ‖ to make out (cheque, recibo).
◆ *vpr* to spread; *la epidemia se ha extendido* the epidemic has spread; *la mancha de tinta se ha extendido* the ink stain has spread ‖ to go, to range, to extend; *hasta ahí no se extienden mis conocimientos* my knowledge does not extend that far ‖ to enlarge; *extenderse sobre un tema* to enlarge on a subject ‖ to expatiate ‖ to stretch, to extend (ocupar espacio); *el campo se extendía hasta el horizonte* the countryside stretched to the horizon; *el bosque se extiende desde el río hasta la ciudad* the wood stretches from the river to the city ‖ to stretch out, to lie; *la llanura se extendía delante del ejército* the plain lay before the army ‖ to extend, to last (durar); *su reinado se extendió desde el año 1533 hasta el año 1603* her reign extended from 1533 to 1603 ‖ to stretch out (echarse); *extenderse en el suelo* to stretch out on the ground ‖ — *el fuego se extendió al tejado* the fire spread to *o* reached the roof ‖ *extenderse en consideraciones sobre algo* to expound sth. at length.

extendidamente *adv* → **extensamente.**

extendido, da *adj* spread out, extended ‖ widespread; *una costumbre muy extendida* a very widespread custom ‖ outstretched; *con los brazos extendidos* with arms outstretched.

extensamente; extendidamente *adv* at length; *trató el tema extensamente* he dealt with the subject at length ‖ widely (ampliamente).

extensibilidad *f* extensibility.

extensible *adj* extensible, extendible, extensile ‖ *mesa extensible* extending table.

extensión *f* extension (acción de ampliar) ‖ spreading (de las alas) ‖ spreading out (de un mapa, de una manta, etc.) ‖ area (superficie); *la extensión de un país* the area of a country ‖ size (tamaño) ‖ length, duration; *la extensión de un discurso, de la vida* the length of a speech, of life ‖ length (de una carta, de un escrito, etc.) ‖ extent; *la extensión de mis conocimientos* the extent of my knowledge ‖ expanse (del mar) ‖ range (de una voz, de un instrumento) ‖ MAT extension ‖ GRAM extension; *por extensión* by extension ‖ application, extension; *el término «fruta» tiene más extensión que «manzana»* the term «fruit» has a wider application than «apple» ‖ extension (del teléfono) ‖ *en toda la extensión de la palabra* in every sense of the word.

extensivo, va *adj* extendable, extendible; *la ley es extensiva a otros casos* the law is extendable to other cases ‖ — AGR *cultivo extensivo* extensive cultivation ‖ *hacer extensivo algo a alguien* to extend sth. to s.o. ‖ *ser extensivo a* to extend to, to apply to.

extenso, sa *adj* extensive, vast (amplio); *un extenso país* an extensive country ‖ large, sizeable (grande); *una sala extensa* a large room ‖ widespread (conocimientos) ‖ long (largo); *viaje, discurso extenso* long journey, speech ‖ full, extensive (reportaje) ‖ *por extenso* at length, in detail, in full.

extensor *adj* extending ‖ ANAT *músculo extensor* extensor muscle.
◆ *m* DEP chest expander.

extenuación *f* exhaustion (agotamiento) ‖ weakening (debilitación) ‖ emaciation (enflaquecimiento).

extenuado, da *adj* exhausted (agotado) ‖ weak (débil) ‖ emaciated (delgado).

extenuante *adj* exhausting.

extenuar *vt* to exhaust (agotar) ‖ to weaken (debilitar).
◆ *vpr* to exhaust o.s.

exterior *adj* outer, external, exterior; *la parte exterior de un mueble* the outer part of a piece of furniture ‖ outward, external; *aspecto exterior* outward appearance ‖ outside; *ventana, habitación exterior* outside window, room ‖ foreign; *asuntos exteriores* foreign affairs; *comercio exterior* foreign trade ‖ *dimensiones exteriores* overall *o* external dimensions.
◆ *m* outside, exterior; *el exterior de un edificio* the outside of a building ‖ appearance (apariencia) ‖ — *al exterior* out, outside ‖ *noticias del exterior* overseas news, news from abroad.
◆ *pl* CINEM exteriors.

exterioridad *f* outward *o* external appearance.

exteriorización *f* showing, manifestation, externalization, revelation.

exteriorizar *vt* to show, to manifest, to externalize, to reveal.

exteriormente *adv* externally, outwardly.

exterminación *f* extermination, wiping out (supresión) ‖ destruction.

exterminador, ra *adj* exterminating.
◆ *m/f* exterminator.

exterminar *vt* to exterminate, to wipe out (suprimir) ‖ to destroy.

exterminio *m* extermination, wiping out (supresión) ‖ destruction.

externado *m* day school.

externamente *adv* outwardly, externally.

externo, na *adj* external; *medicamento de uso externo* medicine for external use ‖ outward; *signos externos de riqueza* outward signs of richness ‖ external, outer; *parte externa* outer part ‖ exterior; *ángulo externo* exterior angle ‖ day; *alumno externo* day pupil ‖ *en la parte externa* on the outside.
◆ *m/f* day pupil (alumno), day student (estudiante).

extinción *f* extinction (del fuego) ‖ wiping out, obliteration (de una epidemia) ‖ extinction, dying out (de la raza).

extinguido, da *adj* → **extinto.**

extinguir *vt* to extinguish, to put out (fuego, luz) ‖ to wipe out, to obliterate, to make extinct (una raza) ‖ to wipe out, to obliterate (una epidemia) ‖ to put down (rebelión) ‖ to wipe out (deuda).
◆ *vpr* to die out, to go out (fuego) ‖ to go out (luz) ‖ to die away; *su amor se extinguió* his love died away ‖ to become extinct, to die out (una raza) ‖ to die (morirse).

extinto, ta; extinguido, da *adj* extinguished, out (fuego, luz) ‖ extinct; *raza extinta* extinct race; *volcán extinto* extinct volcano ‖ wiped out, obliterated (epidemia) ‖ *AMER* dead (muerto).

extintor, ra *adj* extinguishing.
◆ *m/f* extinguisher.
◆ *m* extinguisher; *extintor de espuma* foam extinguisher; *extintor de incendios* fire extinguisher.

extirpable *adj* extirpable (tumor) ‖ FIG eradicable.

extirpación *f* uprooting (de plantas) ‖ extraction, pulling (de un diente) ‖ extirpation, excision, removal (de un tumor) ‖ FIG eradication, stamping out, wiping out.

extirpador, ra *adj* extirpating.
◆ *m* AGR cultivator.

extirpar *vt* to uproot (planta, árbol) ‖ to extract, to pull out (diente) ‖ to extirpate, to excise, to remove (tumor) ‖ FIG to eradicate, to stamp out, to wipe out; *extirpar los vicios* to eradicate vices.

extorsión *f* extortion, exaction (despojo) ‖ FIG inconvenience; *causarle mucha extorsión a uno* to cause great inconvenience to s.o.

extorsionar *vt* to extort, to exact (despojar) ‖ FIG to inconvenience.

extorsionista *m/f* extortionist.

extra *adj* FAM extra | best-quality; *vino extra* best-quality wine ‖ *horas extras* overtime.
◆ *m* FAM extra ‖ CINEM & TEATR extra.

extracción *f* extraction; *la extracción de un diente* the extraction of a tooth; *extracción de una raíz cuadrada* extraction of a square root; *la extracción del carbón* the extraction of coal ‖ FIG extraction, descent; *de humilde extracción* of humble descent ‖ INFORM *extracción de datos* data retrieval.

extracorriente *f* ELECTR self-induced current.

extractar *vt* to summarize (compendiar).

extractivo, va *adj* extractive.

extracto *m* extract, excerpt (trozo de una obra) ‖ summary (resumen) ‖ extract (de una sustancia) ‖ *extracto de cuentas* statement (of account).

extractor *m* extractor.

extradición *f* extradition ‖ *aplicar la extradición a* to extradite.

extradós *m* ARQ extrados.

extraer* *vt* to extract (sacar); *extraer una muela* to extract a molar ‖ MAT to extract (una raíz) ‖ QUÍM to extract (algo de una sustancia) ‖ to take out (líquido de un recipiente) ‖ to excerpt (trozos de una obra).

extraescolar *adj* out-of-school.

extrafino, na *adj* superfine, best-quality, best.

extraíble *adj* extractable, extractible.

extrajudicial *adj* extrajudicial.

extralegal *adj* extralegal.

extralimitación *f* abuse.

extralimitarse *vpr* to overdo, to overstep, to go too far; *come bien sin extralimitarse en nada* he eats well without overdoing it *o* overstepping the mark *o* going too far ‖ to take liberties, to go too far (ir demasiado lejos) ‖ to abuse (en sus atribuciones).

extramuros *adv* outside the city.

extranjería *f* alienage, alienism (condición).

extranjerismo *m* foreign expression, foreignism.

extranjerizante *adj* fond of foreign things.

extranjerizar *vt* to introduce foreign customs into (un país).

extranjero, ra *adj* foreign, alien (de otro país).
◆ *m/f* foreigner (sentido general); *le gusta hablar con extranjeros* he likes talking to foreigners ‖ alien, foreigner (término oficial y jurídico); *los extranjeros tienen los mismos derechos que los naturales del país* aliens have the same rights as nationals.
◆ *m* foreign countries *pl* ‖ — *del extranjero* from abroad ‖ *en* or *por el extranjero* abroad ‖ *ir al extranjero* to go abroad.

extranjis *adv* FAM *de extranjis* secretly, on the sly (de tapadillo).

extrañación *f* banishment.

extrañamente *adv* strangely.

extrañamiento *m* banishment ‖ astonishment, surprise (asombro).

extrañar *vt* to surprise (sorprender); *le extrañó que no se lo hubiese dicho* he was surprised that you should not have told him ‖ not to be used to, to find strange (sentir la novedad de); *extraña la cama en el hotel* he is not used to the hotel bed, he finds the hotel bed strange ‖ to be shy; *el niño extraña a los desconocidos* the child is shy with strangers ‖ to banish (de una comunidad, de un país) ‖ *AMER* to miss (echar de menos) ‖ — *eso me extraña* I'm surprised at that, that's surprise to me, that surprises me ‖ *me extraña que haya venido* I'm surprised *o* it surprises me that he has come ‖ *me extraña tu presencia* I am surprised at your being here ‖ *me extraña verte aquí* I'm surprised *o* it surprises me to see you here ‖ *me extraña verte con ese peinado* it's funny to see you with that hairstyle ‖ *no es de extrañar que* it is not surprising that, no wonder that.
◆ *vi* to be strange *o* funny (ser extraño); *extraña oírle cantar* it is strange to hear him singing ‖ to be surprising (ser sorprendente); *extraña ver a tanta gente aquí* it is surprising to see so many people here.
◆ *vpr* to leave one's country, to go into exile (de un país) ‖ to leave (de una comunidad, de un grupo) ‖ to be surprised; *extrañarse de algo, de que no esté* to be surprised at sth., that he is not in.

extrañeza *f* strangeness (cualidad de extraño) ‖ surprise (asombro) ‖ *causar extrañeza a* to surprise.

extraño, ña *adj* strange, odd, peculiar (raro) ‖ foreign; *cuerpo extraño* foreign body ‖ extraneous, outside; *influencias extrañas* extraneous influences ‖ — *el nuevo sistema me es extraño* I am not used to the new system ‖ *hace extraño verte sin gafas* it's funny *o* strange to see you without glasses ‖ *no es extraño que...* no wonder that..., it is not surprising that... ‖ *ser extraño a* to have nothing to do with; *soy extraño a esta discusión* I have nothing to do with this argument ‖ *una persona extraña* a stranger.
◆ *m/f* stranger; *es un extraño en su familia* he is a stranger in his family.
◆ *m* shying (del caballo) ‖ *hacer un extraño* to shy (el caballo).

extraoficial *adj* unofficial, nonofficial.

extraordinariamente *adv* extremely, extraordinarily ‖ extremely well (muy bien).

extraordinario, ria *adj* extraordinary; *un suceso extraordinario* an extraordinary event; *embajador extraordinario* ambassador extraordinary ‖ uncommon, unusual, rare (poco común) ‖ queer, odd, singular (raro) ‖ surprising (sorprendente) ‖ wonderful (maravilloso) ‖ additional (añadido); *gastos extraordinarios* additional expenses ‖ bonus; *pagas extraordinarias* bonus payments ‖ special (edición) ‖ *horas extraordinarias* overtime.
◆ *m* special delivery (correo especial) ‖ extra dish (plato suplementario) ‖ special issue (de periódico).

extraplano, na *adj* slimline (reloj, maleta, etc.).

extrapolación *f* MAT extrapolation.

extrapolar *vt/vi* to extrapolate.

extrarradio *m* suburbs *pl*, outskirts *pl*.

extrasensible *adj* extrasensory.

extraterreno, na; extraterrestre *adj* extramundane, extraterrestrial.

extraterritorial *adj* extraterritorial.

extrauterino, na *adj* extrauterine.

extravagancia *f* extravagance, eccentricity, oddness (cualidad de extravagante) ‖ eccentricity, oddity (cosa, costumbre, etc.) ‖ *decir, hacer extravagancias* to say, to do odd *o* eccentric things.

extravagante *adj* eccentric, odd (raro) ‖ extravagant; *lenguaje extravagante* extravagant language.
◆ *m/f* eccentric.

extravasar *vt* to extravasate.
◆ *vpr* MED to extravasate.

extravenarse *vpr* MED to extravasate (sangre).

extraversión *f* extraversion, extroversion.

extravertido, da; extrovertido, da *adj* extraverted, extroverted.
◆ *m/f* extravert, extrovert.

extraviado, da *adj* lost, mislaid (perdido); *departamento de objetos extraviados* lost property department || stray, lost, missing; *niño, perro extraviado* lost child, dog || out of the way, isolated (lugar) || vacant; *ojos extraviados* vacant eyes || FIG & FAM touched (algo loco); *está algo extraviado* he's slightly touched || — *estar extraviado* to have gone astray, to be lost, to have lost one's way (haber perdido el camino) || *un hombre extraviado* a man who has gone astray (de mala vida).

extraviar *vt* to make lose one's way, to make get lost (desorientar); *el mapa era tan malo que me extravió* the map was so bad that it made me lose my way || to mislead; *su falso argumento me extravió* his false argument misled me || to misplace, to mislay, to lose; *he extraviado las tijeras* I have misplaced the scissors || to lead astray (pervertir).
◆ *vpr* to get lost; *me extravié en el bosque* I got lost in the wood || to be missing, to get mislaid; *se han extraviado dos libros* two books are missing, two books have got mislaid || FIG to go astray (llevar mala vida) | to wander (la mirada) | to be mistaken (equivocarse) | to go slightly weak in the head (volverse un poco loco) || *se me han extraviado los papeles* I have misplaced *o* mislaid the papers.

extravío *m* misplacing, mislaying, loss (de una cosa) || misleading (de una persona) || losing one's way, getting lost (acción de perderse una persona) || FIG leading astray (acción de pervertir) | going astray (acción de pervertirse) | mistake (error) | error; *los extravíos de la juventud* the errors of youth | misconduct (mala conducta).

extremadamente *adv* extremely.

extremado, da *adj* extreme.

Extremadura *npr f* GEOGR Estremadura.

extremar *vt* to carry to an extreme, to go to an extreme with, to overdo; *extremar las precauciones* to carry precautions to an extreme.
◆ *vpr* to take great pains, to do one's utmost.

extremaunción *f* REL extreme unction.

extremeño, ña *adj* [of *o* from] Estremadura.
◆ *m/f* native *o* inhabitant of Estremadura.

extremidad *f* end, extremity (extremo).
◆ *pl* extremities.

extremismo *m* extremism.

extremista *adj/s* extremist.

extremo, ma *adj* extreme; *frío extremo* extreme cold; *extrema derecha en política* extreme right wing in politics || furthest (más alejado) || extreme, utmost; *amabilidad extrema* utmost kindness || dire, utmost; *necesidad extrema* dire necessity || last (último) || — *el Extremo Oriente* the Far East || *el punto extremo de una península* the tip of a peninsula || *en caso extremo* as a last resort.
◆ *m* end; *el extremo de un palo* the end of a stick || point, pitch (situación extremada); *llegó a tal extremo que quiso matarse* he got to such a point that he wanted to kill himself || extreme, extent (colmo); *está preocupado hasta el extremo de no comer* he is worried to the extreme that he doesn't eat || MAT extreme || point, question, item; *sobre ese y otros extremos no se pusieron de acuerdo* on this and several other points no agreement was reached || wing, winger (en fútbol) || — *con* or *en extremo* in the extreme, extremely || *de extremo a extremo* from one end to the other, from end to end || *en último extremo* as a last resort || DEP *extremo derecha, izquierda* outside-right, outside-left (fútbol), right wing, left wing (hockey) || FIG *los extremos se tocan* extremes meet | *pasar de un extremo a otro* to go from one extreme to the other.

extremoso, sa *adj* demonstrative, effusive || extreme, excessive (excesivo).

extrínseco, ca *adj* extrinsic.

extrofia *f* MED extrophia.

extrorso, sa *adj* BOT extrorse.

extroversión *f* extroversion.

extrovertido, da *adj/s* → **extravertido.**

extrusión *f* TECN extrusion.

exuberancia *f* exuberance, abundance (abundancia) || exuberance (carácter demostrativo).

exuberante *adj* exuberant, abundant (abundante) || exuberant (demostrativo).

exudación *f* exudation.

exudado *m* exudate.

exudar *vt/vi* to exude (transpirar).

exulceración *f* MED exulceration.

exultación *f* exultation.

exultar *vi* to exult, to rejoice.

exvoto *m* REL ex-voto, votive offering.

eyaculación *f* ejaculation; *eyaculación retardada* delayed ejaculation.

eyacular *vt* to ejaculate.

eyección *f* ejection.

eyectable *adj* ejectable || *asiento eyectable* ejector *o* ejection seat.

eyectar *vt* to eject.

eyector *m* ejector.

Ezequías *npr m* Hezekiah.

F

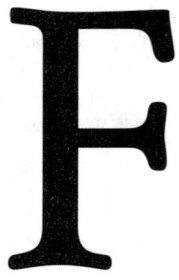

f *f* (letra); *una f mayúscula* a capital f.

fa *m* MÚS F; *clave de fa* F clef | fa (en la escala de do).

fabada *f* Asturian dish made of beans, pork sausage and bacon.

fabla *f* imitation of old Spanish.

fabordón *m* MÚS faux-bourdon.

fábrica *f* factory; *trabaja en una fábrica* he works in a factory || factory, works *pl*; *fábrica siderúrgica, de jabón* iron and steel, soap factory || mill (de textiles, papel, aceite, azúcar) || manufacture (fabricación) || plant (instalación) || building (edificio) || fabric (estructura) || ARQ masonry || fabric (bienes de una iglesia) || — *de fábrica* stonework; *construcción de fábrica* stonework construction || *fábrica de cerveza* brewery || *fábrica de conservas* canning plant || *fábrica de harina* flour mill || *fábrica de hilados* spinning mill || *fábrica de montaje* assembly plant || *fábrica de muebles* furniture factory || *marca de fábrica* trademark || *precio de fábrica* factory price, exworks price.

fabricación *f* manufacture; *fabricación de bicicletas* bicycle manufacture || manufacture, making, fabrication; *fabricación defectuosa* faulty manufacture || — *de fabricación casera* home-made || *estar en fabricación* to be in production || *fabricación en serie* mass production.

fabricante *m/f* manufacturer, maker.

fabricar *vt* to manufacture, to make; *fabricar automóviles* to manufacture cars || to build, to construct (edificar) || FIG to fabricate, to invent; *fabricar una mentira* to fabricate a lie | to make (hacer); *fabricó solo su fortuna* he made his fortune by himself || — *fabricado en España* made in Spain || *fabricar cerveza* to brew beer || *fabricar en serie* to mass-produce.

fabril *adj* manufacturing; *industria fabril* manufacturing industry.

fabriquero *m* REL churchwarden.

fábula *f* fable; *las fábulas de La Fontaine* the fables of La Fontaine || FIG fable, invention (mentira); *esta historia es una fábula* this story is an invention | laughingstock (hazmerreír) | piece of gossip (habladuría) | plot (argumento) || FIG *es algo de fábula* it's fabulous.

fabulario *m* collection of fables.

fabulista *m* fabulist, fable writer, writer of fables.

fabuloso, sa *adj* fabulous, fabled (de las fábulas) || FIG fabled, fictitious (inventado) | incredible (inverosímil) | fabulous (enorme); *una fortuna fabulosa* a fabulous fortune.

faca *f* large knife [with curved blade].

facción *f* faction; *una facción autonomista* an autonomist faction || band, gang (bando) || MIL *estar en facción* to be on guard [duty].

◆ *pl* features (rasgos de la cara); *hermosas facciones* beautiful features.

faccioso, sa *adj* factious, rebellious, seditious (rebelde).

◆ *m/f* factious person, rebel (rebelde) || troublemaker, agitator (revoltoso).

faceta *f* facet; *las facetas de un diamante* the facets of a diamond || FIG facet, side; *una faceta desconocida de España* an unknown facet of Spain; *otra faceta del asunto* another side of the affair || *tallar* or *labrar en facetas* to facet.

facial *adj* facial; *nervio, ángulo facial* facial nerve, angle || — *técnica facial* beauty treatment || *técnico facial* beautician.

facies *f inv* MED facies; *facies hipocrática* Hippocratic facies.

fácil *adj* easy; *problema fácil* easy problem; *criticar es fácil* it is easy to criticize; *una vida muy fácil* a very easy life; *fácil de hacer* easy to do || simple, easy (sencillo) || likely, probable; *es fácil que venga hoy* it is likely that he will come today || easygoing, compliant; *este hombre es muy fácil, se entiende con todos* this man is very easygoing, he gets on with everyone || good, well-behaved, easy to bring up (niño) || loose, of easy virtue (mujer) || — *de puro fácil* so easy; *de puro fácil que es, no hay que explicarlo* it is so easy that there is no need to explain it || *fácil de creer* easy to believe, easily believed || *fácil de digerir* easy to digest, easily digested || *soy fácil de contentar* I am easy to please || *soy fácil de hacer reír* it is easy to make me laugh.

◆ *adv* easily.

facilidad *f* easiness, facility; *la facilidad de su trabajo* the easiness of his work || ease; *hacer algo con la mayor facilidad* to do sth. with the greatest of ease || simplicity (sencillez) || complaisance, docility, easygoing nature (docilidad) || wantonness, looseness (de una mujer) || fluency; *facilidad de palabra* fluency in speech || gift, aptitude, talent; *tener facilidad para el estudio, para los idiomas* to have a gift for studying, for languages || facility; *aquí no hay facilidades para practicar deportes* there are no facilities here for practising sport || facility (condición favorable); *facilidades de crédito* credit facilities || — *facilidades de pago* easy terms || *tener facilidad para acatarrarse* to catch a cold easily || *tener facilidad para olvidar* to be forgetful.

facilillo, lla *adj* FAM as easy as winking *o* as pie.

facilitación *f* facilitation || provision (acción de proporcionar).

facilitar *vt* to facilitate, to make easy (hacer fácil) || to make easier, to facilitate (hacer más fácil) || to get; *la agencia le facilitó el piso* the agency got him the flat || to provide (proporcionar); *facilitar informaciones a uno* to provide s.o. with information || to arrange; *facilitar una entrevista* to arrange an interview.

fácilmente *adv* easily; *lo hizo fácilmente* he did it easily; *tendrá fácilmente cincuenta años* he is easily fifty years old.

facilón, ona *adj* FAM dead easy, rather simple; *un problema facilón* a dead easy problem.

facineroso, sa *adj* criminal || wicked (malévolo).

◆ *m/f* criminal || robber (ladrón) || wicked person, villain (persona malévola).

facistol *m* lectern (atril).

facón *m* AMER dagger, large knife [used by «gauchos»] || AMER *pelar el facón* to unsheathe one's knife.

factible *adj* feasible, possible (posible) || workable (realizable).

factor *m* factor (elemento); *el factor humano* the human factor || BIOL factor; *factor Rhesus* Rhesus factor || MAT factor || luggage and goods clerk (de ferrocarril) || agent, factor (de comercio).

factoría *f* trading post (establecimiento de comercio) || factorage, position of agent *o* factor (cargo de factor) || agency (agencia) || factory (fábrica).

factorial *f* MAT factorial.

factótum *m* factotum.

factura *f* COM bill; *me dio la factura de la reparación* he gave me the repair bill | invoice (de géneros vendidos); *factura pro forma* pro forma invoice || manufacture (hechura) || — *extender una factura* to make out a bill *o* an invoice || *según factura* as per invoice.

facturación *f* COM invoicing (de géneros vendidos) | bill; *facturación por mil pesetas* bill for a thousand pesetas | turnover (volumen de negocios) || registration (en ferrocarril).

facturar *vt* COM to invoice (géneros vendidos) | to charge for; *facturarle a uno el transporte* to charge s.o. for the transport || to register [*US* to check] (en ferrocarril).

fácula *f* ASTR facula (del sol).

facultad *f* faculty (poder); *facultad de hablar, de sentir* faculty of speech, of feeling || faculty, school (en la universidad); *facultad de Derecho* faculty of Law; *facultad de Filosofía y Letras* faculty of Arts || MED strength, resistance || ability (capacidad) || FIG power (derecho); *tener facultad para* to have the power to || *tener facultad para* to be authorized to.

◆ *pl* faculties, powers; *en pleno uso de sus facultades* in possession of his faculties; *facultades mentales* mental powers || *en la plenitud de sus facultades* at one's peak.

facultar *vt* to authorize, to empower, to give the power to; *facultar a alguien para* to authorize s.o. to, to give s.o. the power to.

facultativo, va *adj* optional, facultative (no obligatorio) || medical; *cuadro facultativo* medical staff; *parte facultativo* medical bulletin || faculty (de una facultad universitaria) || professional || MED *el cuerpo facultativo* the doctors, the Faculty.

◆ *m* doctor (médico) || surgeon (cirujano).

facundia *f* gift for talking, gift of the gab (*fam*) (verbosidad); *tener facundia* to have a gift for talking, to have the gift of the gab || eloquence.

facundo, da *adj* talkative (parlanchín) || eloquent.

facha *adj/s* FAM fascist.

◆ *f* FAM appearance, look, looks *pl*; *me gusta la facha de este chico* I like the look of this boy | mess, sight; *estar hecho una facha* to look a

mess || — MAR *estar en facha* to heave to || FAM *tener buena facha* to be good-looking.
◆ *m* mess, sight (adefesio).

fachada *f* ARQ façade, front | frontage (dimensión) || FIG show, façade, front; *la prosperidad del país era pura fachada* the country's prosperity was nothing but show *o* nothing but a façade || title page (de un libro) || — *con fachada a* facing; *una casa con fachada al mar* a house facing the sea || *hacer fachada con* to be opposite to, to face.

fachear *vi* MAR to heave to.

fachenda *f* FAM swanking, bragging, showing off (presunción).
◆ *m* FAM show-off, swank (fachendoso).

fachendear *vi* FAM to swank, to show off.

fachendista; fachendón, ona; fachendoso, sa *adj* FAM swanky, snooty.
◆ *m/f* show-off, swank.

fachinal *m* AMER marsh (pantano).

fachoso, sa; fachudo, da *adj* odd-looking (extraño) || AMER FAM swanky, snooty (fachendoso).

fading *m* RAD fading (de las ondas).

faena *f* task, job; *las faenas diarias* the daily tasks | work; *tengo mucha faena* I've got a lot of work || TAUR «faena» [series of passes with the muleta] || MIL fatigue || MAR fishing || FIG & FAM dirty trick; *hacer una faena a alguien* to play a dirty trick on s.o. || — *estar en plena faena* to be hard at work || *las faenas de la casa* or *domésticas* the household chores, the housework || *las faenas del campo* agricultural work || MIL *uniforme de faena* fatigue dress || FAM *¡vaya faena!, ¡qué faena!* that was a dirty trick!

faenar *vi* MAR to fish.

faenero *m* AMER agricultural labourer, farmhand.

faetón *m* phaeton (coche).

fafarachero, ra *m/f* AMER boaster, braggart.
◆ *adj* boastful.

fagocítico, ca *adj* phagocytic.

fagocito *m* BIOL phagocyte.

fagocitosis *f* BIOL phagocytosis.

fagot *m* MÚS bassoon (instrumento) | bassoonist (músico).

fagotista *m* MÚS bassoonist.

fahrenheit *adj inv* Fahrenheit.

faisán *m* pheasant (ave).

faisana *f* hen pheasant (ave).

faja *f* strip, belt; *faja de terreno* strip of land || girdle, corset (de mujer); *faja de embarazo* maternity girdle || MED belt; *faja abdominal* body belt || bandage (para niños) || sash, cummerbund (de vestido, de traje) || wrapper (de periódico) || band (de puro, de un libro) || sash (insignia) || ARQ fascia (moldura) || FÍS band || HERÁLD fesse, fess || *faja braga* pantie girdle.

fajada *f* AMER attack.

fajado, da *adj* bandaged (con venda) || swaddled (niño) || TAUR with a light coloured band round its body.
◆ *m* MIN prop (madero).

fajadura *f*; **fajamiento** *m* swaddling (de un niño) || bandaging (con vendas) || MAR tarred outer covering [for underwater cables].

fajar *vt* to gird, to put a sash on (ceñir con una faja) || to wrap (envolver) || to bandage (con venda) || to swaddle (a un niño) || to swathe (un miembro) || to put a wrapper on, to wrap up (un periódico) || AMER to give; *fajar una bofetada* to give a slap | to beat (golpear) || AMER *fajar con uno* to attack s.o.
◆ *vpr* to put one's sash on || to fight (luchar).

fajilla *f* AMER wrapper (de periódico).

fajín *m* sash (de militar).

fajina *f* AGR shock || bundle of firewood *o* of faggots *o* of kindling (hacecillo) || job, task, chore (faena) || MIL fascine (haz de ramas) | mess call (toque) || FAM *meter fajina* to ramble on.

fajo *m* bundle (haz) || wad; *un fajo de billetes de banco* a wad of bank notes.
◆ *pl* swaddling clothes (de un niño).

fakir *m* fakir (faquir).

falacia *f* deceit (engaño) || deceitfulness, falseness || fallacy (cosa falsa).

falange *f* ANAT phalanx, phalange | HIST phalanx || Falange (en la política española).

falangero *m* ZOOL phalanger.

falangeta *f* ANAT third phalanx.

falangina *f* ANAT second phalanx.

falangio *m* ZOOL haverstman, harvest spider, daddy longlegs.

falangista *adj/s* Falangist.

falangismo *m* Falangism.

falaz *adj* fallacious, false (engañoso) || deceitful; *una persona falaz* a deceitful person.

falda *f* skirt; *falda acampanada, tubo* bell, straight skirt || side (de una montaña) || skirt (de la armadura) || skirt, cover (de una mesa camilla) || brim (de un sombrero) || lap, knees *pl*; *tener un niño en la falda* to have a child on one's lap || brisket (de las reses) || *falda pantalón* culotte skirt, divided skirt || *falda de colina* or *de monte* hillside || *falda escocesa* kilt.
◆ *pl* skirt *sing* (faldillas) || — FIG & FAM *andar siempre entre faldas* to be always with the girls | *es un asunto de faldas* there are women mixed up in it | *estar pegado* or *cosido a las faldas de su madre* to be tied to one's mother's apron strings || FIG & FAM *le gustan mucho las faldas* he is a one for the girls *o* ladies, he is very fond of the girls.

faldear *vt* to skirt (un monte, etc.).

faldellín *m* short skirt (falda corta) || AMER christening gown (de bautizo).

faldero, ra *adj* skirt (de la falda) || — FIG *hombre faldero* one for the girls *o* ladies || *niño faldero* mother's child || *perro faldero* lapdog.

faldicorto, ta *adj* short-skirted, wearing a short skirt.

faldillas *f pl* skirt *sing* (que cuelgan de un vestido).

faldón *m* skirt (faldillas) || tail (de un frac, de una camisa) || ARQ gable (de un tejado) | mantelpiece (de chimenea) || *estar colgado de* or *agarrado a los faldones de uno* to be always at s.o.'s heels.

falena *f* ZOOL phalaena, moth.

falibilidad *f* fallibility.

fálico, ca *adj* phallic.

falo *m* phallus.

falocracia *f* male chauvinism (machismo) || male supremacy (dominio).

falócrata *adj/s* male chauvinist.

falsario, ria *adj* → **falseador.**

falsarregla *f* bevel square (falsa escuadra) || underlines *pl* (falsilla).

falseador, ra *adj* falsifying (que adultera) || forging, counterfeiting (que fabrica algo falso) || lying (embustero).
◆ *m/f* falsifier || forger, counterfeiter || liar (embustero).

falseamiento *m* falsification.

falsear *vt* to falsify (adulterar) | to distort; *han falseado mis declaraciones* they have distorted my statements | to forge, to counterfeit (fabricar algo falso) || to bevel (un madero, una piedra).
◆ *vi* ARQ to sag (viga) || to buckle (pared) || MÚS to be out of tune.

falsedad *f* falseness, hypocrisy (hipocresía) || falseness, falsity (carácter de falso) || falsehood, lie (mentira) || JUR forgery (falsificación).

falseo *m* ARQ bevel, bevelling.

falseta *f* MÚS flourish [on the guitar].

falsete *m* bung (de tonel) || joining door (puerta) || MÚS falsetto; *voz de falsete* falsetto voice.

falsía *f* falseness, hypocrisy (falsedad).

falsificación *f* forgery, forging, counterfeiting (acción); *falsificación de moneda* money counterfeiting || forgery, forging, faking (de una firma) || falsification (adulteración) || forgery, counterfeit (objeto falsificado); *falsificación de escritura pública* forgery of a public document.

falsificado, da *adj* forged, counterfeit || fake (falso).

falsificador, ra *adj* forging, counterfeiting (que fabrica algo falso) | falsifying (que adultera).
◆ *m/f* forger, counterfeiter (el que fabrica algo falso) || falsifier (el que adultera) || faker.

falsificar *vt* to forge, to counterfeit (moneda, documento) || to forge, to fake (una firma) || to falsify (adulterar) || to adulterate (un líquido) || to fake (un objeto antiguo).

falsilla *f* underlines *pl*.

falso, sa *adj* false; *noticia falsa* false piece of news || false, deceitful, untrustworthy; *una persona falsa* a false person || untrue, not true, false; *esto es falso* this is untrue || unfounded, false (sin fundamento) || unsound (argumento) || wrong, incorrect, inexact; *una medida falsa* an incorrect measurement || false, counterfeit (moneda) || fake, imitation (piedra preciosa) || false (nota de música) || false (forzado) || BOT false; *acacia falsa* false acacia || vicious (caballo) || — *este Renoir es falso* this Renoir is a fake || *falsa alarma* false alarm || *falsa puerta* concealed door || *más falso que Judas* false to the core || *monedero falso* counterfeiter.
◆ *m* reinforcement (de tela) || lining (forro de un vestido) || — *dar un golpe en falso* to miss one's mark || *dar un paso en falso* to stumble, to trip (fallar al andar), to make a wrong move (cometer un error) || *envidar en falso* to bluff || *estar en falso* to be overhanging, to be out of plumb || *jurar en falso* to commit perjury || *lo falso* falsehood; *distinguir lo falso de lo verdadero* to distinguish truth from falsehood || *tachar algo de falso* to indict sth. as false, to deny sth.

falta *f* lack (privación); *falta de dinero* lack of money || shortage (escasez); *falta de obreros* shortage of workmen || absence (ausencia) || need (necesidad) || fault, defect (defecto de una cosa) || fault, shortcoming, failing (defecto de una persona) || lack; *falta de respeto, de tacto* lack of respect, of tact || mistake (error); *falta de ortografía* spelling mistake; *tiene cinco faltas* he has made five mistakes || fault (culpa); *fue falta tuya* it was your fault || DEP foul | fault (en tenis) || diminution of weight (de las monedas) || misdeed (mala acción) || JUR misdemeanour [US misdemeanor] (infracción) || — *a falta de, por falta de* for want of, for lack of; *a falta de otra cosa* for want *o* for lack of sth. better || *a falta de pan buenas son tortas* half a loaf is better than none || *coger a uno en falta* to catch s.o. at fault || *cometer una falta* to make a mistake || *echar en falta* to miss; *echa en falta a su hija* he misses his daughter || *falta de delicadeza* lack of tact || *falta de educación* bad manners *pl*, lack of education || *falta de imprenta* misprint || *falta de pago* nonpayment || DEP *falta máxima* penalty || *hace falta tener mucha paciencia* you need (to have) a lot of patience, one must have a lot of patience || *hace falta que vengas ahora* you must come now || *hace falta una* *cuerda* we need a rope, a rope is necessary || *hace falta una lámpara aquí* a lamp is wanting *o* is needed here || *incurrir en falta* to commit a foul (deportes), to make a mistake (cometer un error) || *me hace falta tu presencia* I need you || *me hacen falta diez libras* I need ten pounds || *no hay falta sin perdón* everything can be forgiven || *notar la falta de* to miss; *notó mucho la falta de su coche cuando estaba estropeado* he missed his car a lot when it was broken down || *poner falta a* to mark absent || *sacar faltas a alguien* to point out s.o.'s defects || *sacar* or *poner faltas* to find fault; *a todo le pone faltas* he finds fault with everything || DEP *sacar una falta* to take a free kick (fútbol), to take a free hit (hockey) || *ser una falta* to be bad manners, to be impolite; *fue una falta no contestarle* it was bad manners not to answer him || *si hace falta* if necessary || *sin falta* without fail || *si no fui, no fue por falta de ganas* if I didn't go, it was not because I didn't want to.

faltar *vi* to be missing; *faltan dos libros en la biblioteca* two books are missing from the library || to be lacking, to be wanting, to be needed, not to be enough; *aquí falta luz* light is lacking here, there is not enough light here || to lack (véase OBSERV); *la chica es muy guapa, pero le falta carácter* the girl is very pretty but she lacks character || to need (véase OBSERV) ; *me falta un cuchillo para cortarlo* I need a knife to cut it; *me faltan diez pesetas más* I need ten more pesetas || to miss, not to go (no ir); *faltó a clase* he missed school || to stay away, not to go; *faltó a la oficina* he didn't go to the office, he stayed away from the office || to be missing *o* absent (estar ausente) || to fail (no cumplir); *faltar a un deber, a sus compromisos* to fail in a duty, in one's obligations || to fail (arma, mecanismo) || to be direspectful (desmandarse); *le faltó a su padre* he was disrespectful to his father || to be unfaithful (mujer) || to betray; *ha faltado a nuestra confianza, a nuestra amistad* he has betrayed our confidence, our friendship || — *el jersey está casi terminado, sólo falta una manga* the jumper is almost finished, there is only one sleeve to do || *falta mucho para Navidad* Christmas is a long way off || *faltan tres días para mi cumpleaños* my birthday is three days off, there are three days to go to my birthday || *faltan veinte segundos para las tres* it is twenty seconds to three o'clock || *falta por* there is still... to be; *falta por coser una manga* there is still a sleeve to be sewn || *falta por hacer* it remains to be done, it has yet to be done || *falta por ver si él aceptará* whether he will accept remains to be seen || *falta que lo pruebes* you still have to prove it || *faltar a la verdad* to lie, not to tell the truth || *faltar al honor* to forfeit one's hònour || *faltar al respeto a uno* to lack respect for s.o. || *faltar a su palabra, a una promesa* to break one's word, one's promise; not to keep one's word, one's promise || *faltar a una cita* to miss an appointment, to fail to keep an appointment || *faltar de palabra a uno* to insult *o* to offend s.o. || *falta y pasa* manque and passe (en la ruleta) || *me falta tiempo para hacerlo* I haven't time to do it, I am short of time to do it || *mucho falta* far from it || *nada* or *poco faltó para que* almost, nearly; *poco faltó para que se cayera* he almost fell || *¡no faltaba más!, ¡lo que faltaba!, ¡sólo faltaba eso!* that's all we needed!, that tops it all!, that crowns it all! || *¡no faltaría más!, ¡no faltaba más!* of course (naturalmente), don't mention it (no hay de qué).

— OBSERV In these cases the subject of the Spanish verb becomes the object of the English verb and vice versa.

falto, ta *adj* lacking, wanting (*de* in); *falto de cortesía* lacking in politeness; *espíritu falto de ideas* mind lacking in ideas || without (sin); *falto de recursos* without resources || short; *estaba falto de dinero* I was short of money || (p us) short; *una libra falta* a short pound.

faltón, ona *adj* AMER disrespectful (irrespetuoso) || FAM unreliable (que no es de fiar).

faltoso, sa *adj* lacking, wanting (necesitado) || incomplete (incompleto) || quarrelsome (peleón).

faltriquera *f* pocket (bolsillo) || purse (monedero) || fob (de chaleco) || small box (palco) || FAM *rascarse la faltriquera* to dig into one's pocket.

falúa *f* MAR launch.

falucho *m* felucca (embarcación).

falla *f* faille (tela) || GEOL fault (grieta) || defect, fault (defecto) || AMER bonnet (gorrito) || «falla» [in Valencia, grotesque and humorous scenes made up of cardboard figures].
◆ *pl* «fallas» [celebrations in Valencia on the feast of St. Joseph].

fallar *vt* to ruff (naipes) || JUR to pronounce; *fallar una sentencia* to pronounce sentence || — *fallar el golpe* to miss (al disparar, etc.), to miss one's target (no alcanzar el objetivo) || *fallar un premio literario* to award a literary prize.
◆ *vi* to fail; *le falló el corazón* his heart failed him; *me falló la memoria* my memory failed me || to give way; *la viga ha fallado* the beam has given way; *le fallaron las piernas* his legs gave way || to fail, to let down; *mi amigo me ha fallado* my friend has let me down || to fail (fracasar); *ha fallado su proyecto* his plan has failed || to miss (un golpe, un tiro) || to miss (un motor) || to fail (frenos, arma) || not to work properly, to have sth. wrong with it (mecanismo) || to prove wrong, to be wrong; *sus pronósticos fallaron* his forecasts proved wrong || JUR to pass judgment, to pronounce sentence || *sin fallar* without fail.

falleba *f* espagnolette, hasp (dispositivo) || handle [of an espagnolette] (manivela).

fallecer* *vi* to die; *falleció a los ochenta años* he died at the age of eighty.

fallecido, da *adj* deceased, late.
◆ *m/f* deceased.

fallecimiento *m* death, demise, decease.

fallero, ra *adj* of the «fallas» [en Valencia].
◆ *m/f* «falla» maker (fabricante), «fallas» organizer (el que organiza) || — *fallera mayor* queen of the «fallas» || *fallero mayor* king of the «fallas».

fallido, da *adj* vain, frustrated; *esfuerzos fallidos* vain efforts; *esperanzas fallidas* vain hopes || unsuccessful; *resultó fallido su proyecto* his plan turned out unsuccessful || bad, unsuccessful (tiro) || bad, poor; *cosecha fallida* bad harvest || COM bankrupt (que ha quebrado) | irrecoverable (incobrable) | bad (deuda).
◆ *m* bankrupt (comerciante).

fallo, lla *adj* void (en naipes); *estoy fallo de corazones* I am void in hearts.
◆ *m* JUR judgment, sentence; *emitir un fallo* to pass judgment, to pronounce sentence || ruff (en naipes) || miss (de un golpe, de un tiro) || awarding (de un premio) || failure (del corazón, de las fuerzas) || giving way (de una viga, etc.) || FIG decision (decisión) | failure (fracaso) | shortcoming, fault; *es un buen sistema, sin embargo tiene muchos fallos* it is a good system, however it has many shortcomings | fault (falta) || TECN failure (de los frenos) || — TECN *fallo del motor* engine failure *o* trouble || *tener fallo a espadas* to be void in spades (en naipes) || *tiene fallos de memoria* he has lapses of memory.

fallutería *f* AMER hypocrisy (hipocresía) || untrustworthiness (falta de fiabilidad).

falluto, ta *adj* AMER failed (fracasado) | hypocrite (hipócrita) | untrustworthy (poco fiable).

fama *f* fame, renown (celebridad) || reputation; *tener buena fama, mala fama* to have a good reputation, a bad reputation || — *buena fama* good name *o* reputation || *cobra* or *cría buena fama y échate a dormir* build yourself a good reputation and you can sit back and relax || *conquistar fama* to become famous || *dar fama a* to make famous || *de buena fama* of good repute || *de fama* well-known, famous, renowned (afamado) || *de mala fama* of ill repute, ill-famed || *es fama que* it is rumoured that, they say that || *mala fama* bad name *o* reputation || *tener fama de* to have a reputation for; to have the reputation of being; *ese hombre tiene fama de cruel* that man has a reputation for cruelty || *tener mucha fama* to be very well-known *o* very famous.

famélico, ca *adj* starving, famished.

familia *f* family; *de buena familia* of a good family || BOT & ZOOL family || GRAM family (de palabras, etc.) || children *pl*, family; *tiene mucha familia* he has a lot of children *o* a big family; *tiene poca familia* he has not many children, he has a small family; *tener familia* to have children *o* a family || servants *pl*, domestic staff (servidumbre) || household (los que viven en la casa) || — *en familia* with one's family || FIG & FAM *estábamos en familia* there was hardly anybody there || JUR *familia numerosa* large family || *la familia política* the in-laws || REL *la Sagrada Familia* the Holy Family || *Pedro debe ser su hermano porque tiene un parecido de familia* Peter must be his brother because there's a family likeness *o* resemblance about him || *ser como de la familia* to be one of the family || *venir de familia* to run in the family.

familiar *adj* family (relativo a la familia); *lazos familiares* family ties; *parecido familiar* family resemblance *o* likeness; *subsidio familiar* family allowance || colloquial, familiar; *expresión familiar* colloquial expression || informal; *estilo familiar* informal style || familiar (conocido); *su cara me es familiar* his face is familiar to me || familiar; *sus respuestas son a veces demasiado familiares* at times his answers are too familiar || — *demonio familiar* familiar spirit || *el inglés le es muy familiar* he is very familiar with English.
◆ *m* relative, relation (pariente) || intimate *o* good friend (amigo) || (p us) servant (criado) || familiar (eclesiástico) || *familiar del Santo Oficio* Inquisition officer.
◆ *pl* suite *sing*, attendants, entourage *sing*; *los familiares del rey* the king's suite.

familiaridad *f* familiarity || *tomar familiaridades con* to get familiar with.

familiarizar *vt* to familiarize.
◆ *vpr* to familiarize o.s., to make o.s. familiar.

familión *m* FIG large family.

famoso, sa *adj* famous; *un artista famoso* a famous artist || FAM fantastic, great, famous, fabulous.

fámula *f* FAM maid, servant.

fámulo *m* FAM manservant, servant.

fan *m/f* fan.

fanal *m* MAR lantern, lamp (farol) || bell glass (para proteger del polvo) || glass shade [for lamp or lantern].
◆ *pl* big eyes (ojos).

fanático, ca *adj* fanatic, fanatical.
◆ *m/f* fanatic.

fanatismo *m* fanaticism.

fanatizar *vt* to make a fanatic.

fandango *m* MÚS fandango (baile) || FAM row, rumpus (jaleo).

fandanguero, ra *m/f* reveller.

fandanguillo *m* dance similar to the fandango.

fané *adj* AMER FAM shabby, tired.

fanega *f* fanega [unit of capacity which varies between 22.5 litres and 55.5 litres according to the district] || *fanega de tierra* fanega [unit of area approximately equal to 6.6 square metres].

fanerógamo, ma *adj* BOT phanerogam, phanerogamous.
◆ *f* phanerogam.

fanfarrear *vi* ⟶ **fanfarronear.**

fanfarria *f* ⟶ **fanfarronada** || MÚS fanfare (de trompetas).

fanfarrón, ona *adj* swanky, boastful.
◆ *m* show-off, swank, braggart, swaggerer.

fanfarronada; fanfarronería *f* showing-off, swanking, bragging, boasting, swaggering (acción) || brag, boast (dicho) || swankiness, boastfulness (cualidad de fanfarrón).

fanfarronear; fanfarrear *vi* to show off, to swank, to brag, to boast, to swagger (presumir).

fanfarronería *f* ⟶ **fanfarronada.**

fangal; fangar *m* bog, mudpit, mudhole (lodazal).

fango *m* mud (barro) || FIG degradation (deshonor) | dirt, grime, slime (suciedad).

fangoso, sa *adj* muddy.

fantasear *vi* to daydream, to dream (soñar) || to romance (imaginar).

fantaseo *m* AMER dreaming, daydreaming, imagining.

fantasía *f* imagination, fantasy, fancy (imaginación); *un relato lleno de fantasía* a story full of imagination || fantasy, fancy, dream; *estos viajes son fantasías suyas* these journeys are only his fantasies || fantasy, fancy; *esto es pura fantasía* this is pure fantasy || FAM vanity, conceit (presunción) || whim, fancy (capricho) || MÚS fantasia || *de fantasía* fancy; *artículos, chaleco de fantasía* fancy goods, waistcoat; imitation, fancy; *una joya de fantasía* a piece of imitation jewellery.

fantasioso, sa *adj* stuck-up (*fam*), conceited (presumido) || imaginative (fantaseador).
◆ *m/f* show-off, swank, braggart (presumido) || imaginative person (fantaseador).

fantasista *m* variety artist.

fantasma *m* ghost, phantom (espectro) || ghost, phantasm (aparecido) || FIG & FAM show-off, conceited person (vanidoso).
◆ *adj* ghost, phantom; *buque fantasma* ghost ship.

fantasmagórico, ca *adj* phantasmagoric.

fantasmal *adj* ghostly, phantasmal (irreal) || phantasmal (de los fantasmas).

fantasmón, ona *adj* FAM stuck-up, conceited.

fantástico, ca *adj* fantastic, fanciful (quimérico); *un relato fantástico* a fantastic story || fantastic, great, fabulous, terrific; *una casa, una memoria fantástica* a terrific house, memory || phantasmal, ghostly (fantasmal).

fantochada *f* FIG invention, bright idea; *es otra fantochada del alcalde* it's another invention of the mayor's.

fantoche *m* puppet, marionette (títere) || FIG puppet (persona manejable) | storyteller (cuentista) | popinjay, swank, show-off, braggart, swaggerer (presumido) || nincompoop (persona inútil).

FAO *abrev de Organización para la Agricultura y la Alimentación* FAO, Food and Agriculture Organization.

faquir *m* fakir.

farad *m* ELECTR farad.

faraday *m* ELECTR & QUÍM faraday.

farádico, ca *adj* faradic.

faradio *m* ELECTR farad.

faradización *f* faradism, faradization.

faralá *m* flounce, frill (de un vestido).
◆ *pl* FAM frills, flounces (adornos de mal gusto) || *traje de faralaes* frilly dress (vestido andaluz).
— OBSERV pl The plural form of *faralá* is *faralaes*.

farallón *m* rock [jutting out of the sea].

faramalla *f* FAM patter, claptrap (charla) | piece of trumpery (cosa sin valor) || AMER bragging, swanking, swaggering (fanfarronada).
◆ *m/f* bamboozler, trickster.

faramallear *vi* AMER to brag, to show off, to swank, to swagger (farolear).

faramallero, ra; faramallón, ona *adj* bamboozling, cajoling (engatusador) || AMER swankly, boastful (fanfarrón).
◆ *m/f* bamboozler, trickster.

farándula *f* theatre [US theater], acting, stage (trabajo de los cómicos) || troupe of strolling players (compañía) || FIG & FAM patter, claptrap (charla).

farandulero, ra *m/f* strolling player (farsante) || FAM swindler, trickster, bamboozler (estafador).

faraón *m* pharaoh.

faraónico, ca *adj* pharaonic.

faraute *m* messenger, herald (mensajero) || FIG & FAM busybody (entrometido).

farda *f* bundle (lío pequeño) || bale (bala) || parcel (paquete) || TECN mortise (en carpintería).

fardar *vt* to dress, to outfit.
◆ *vi* FAM to be classy; *tener un coche deportivo farda mucho* it's very classy to have a sports car | to show off, to swank (presumir).

fardo *m* bundle (lío pequeño) || bale (bala) || parcel (paquete).

fardón, ona *adj* FAM classy, flashy (cosa) | boastful, conceited (persona).
◆ *m/f* FAM show-off, swank (presumido).

farfalá *f* flounce, frill (faralá).

farfallón, ona *adj* ⟶ **farfullero.**

fárfara *f* inner shell membrane (binza del huevo) || *en fárfara* without shell (huevo), unfinished, incomplete (incompleto).

farfolla *f* husk (del maíz) || FIG baubie, piece of trumpery (oropel).

farfulla *f* FAM jabbering, spluttering.
◆ *m/f* jabberer, gabbler.
◆ *adj* jabbering, gabbling, spluttering (persona).

farfullar *vt* to jabber, to gabble, to splutter (hablar mal) || FIG & FAM to scamp, to botch (trabajo).
◆ *vi* to jabber, to gabble, to splutter.

farfullero, ra *adj* FAM jabbering, gabbling, spluttering (que habla mal) || FIG & FAM careless, slapdash, shoddy (chapucero) || *ser muy farfullero* to jabber *o* to gabble a lot (hablar muy mal).
◆ *m/f* FAM jabberer, gabbler (que habla mal) || slapdash *o* shoddy *o* careless worker (chapucero).

farináceo, a *adj* farinaceous.

faringe *f* ANAT pharynx.

faríngeo, a *adj* ANAT pharyngeal, pharyngal.

faringitis *f* MED pharyngitis.

fariña *f* AMER coarse manioc flour (harina).

fario *m* FAM *traer mal fario* to be a jinx.

farisaico, ca *adj* Pharisaic, Pharisaical.

farisaísmo; fariseísmo *m* pharisaism, phariseeism.

fariseo *m* Pharisee || FIG hypocrite, pharisee.

farmacéutico, ca *adj* pharmaceutical, pharmaceutic.
◆ *m/f* pharmacist (título universitario) || chemist [US druggist, pharmacist] (en una tienda) || pharmacist (en un laboratorio).

farmacia *f* pharmacy (estudios) || chemist's, chemist's shop [US drugstore, pharmacy] (tienda) || pharmacy (de un hospital, de una empresa, etc.).

fármaco *m* medicine (medicamento).

farmacología *f* pharmacology.

farmacológico, ca *adj* pharmacological.

farmacólogo, ga *m/f* pharmacologist, pharmacist.

farmacopea *f* pharmacopoeia.

faro *m* lighthouse (torre) || beacon (señal luminosa) || light, lantern (farol) || AUT headlight, headlamp || FIG guiding light.

farol *m* lantern (luz) || streetlamp, gas lamp (en las calles) || light (de locomotora) || FIG & FAM bluff (en el juego) | swank, show-off (farolero) | showing off, swanking (faroleo) || TAUR «farol» [pass which the bullfighter ends with a flourish of the cape above his head] || AMER balcony (balcón) || — FAM *¡adelante con los faroles!* carry on!, keep it up!, come on then! || *farol a la veneciana* Chinese lantern || MAR *farol de popa, de proa* stern, bow light || FAM *tirarse* or *marcarse* or *echarse un farol* to spin a yarn, to swank, to show off.

farola *f* streetlamp (del alumbrado público) || gas lamp (de gas) || lantern, lamp (fanal) || FAM lighthouse, beacon (de la costa).

farolear *vi* FAM to brag, to boast, to swank, to show off | to bluff (en los naipes).

faroleo *m* FAM boasting, showing off.

farolero, ra *adj* FIG & FAM swanky, boastful (presumido) | bluffing (en el juego).
◆ *m/f* FIG & FAM swank, show-off (presumido) | bluffer (en el juego).
◆ *m* lantern maker (el que hace faroles) || lamplighter (el que enciende las farolas).

farolillo; farolito *m* Chinese lantern (de papel) || BOT Canterbury bell (campánula) || FIG *el farolillo rojo* the last one (en una carrera, una clasificación).

farra *f* ZOOL lavaret (pez) || FAM *ir de farra* to go on a binge *o* a spree.

fárrago *m* jumble, hotchpotch, mess.

farragoso, sa *adj* involved, confused (discurso, escrito) || fussy (decoración).

farrear *vi* AMER to go on a binge *o* a spree.

farrista *m/f* AMER fun lover, reveller [US reveler].
◆ *adj* fun-loving.

farruco, ca *m/f* Galician *o* Asturian emigrant.
◆ *adj* FAM defiant, bold (desafiante) | cocky (muy seguro de sí mismo) | proud, pleased with o.s.; *iba muy farruco con su traje nuevo* he was very pleased with himself in his new suit, he looked very proud of his new suit.

farruto, ta *adj* AMER puny, weak, sickly (enclenque).

farsa *f* farce (comedia) || theatre [US theater], stage (teatro) || FIG sham, make-believe (simulación, engaño) | farce; *este sistema parlamentario es una farsa* this parliamentary system is a farce.

farsante *m* actor || FIG humbug, charlatan, sham.

farsear *vi* AMER to joke.

fas o por nefas (por) *loc adv* FAM rightly or wrongly, by hook or by crook.

fascículo *m* fascicle.

fascinación *f* fascination.

fascinador, ra; fascinante *adj* fascinating.

fascinar *vt* to fascinate; *los juguetes fascinan a los niños* toys fascinate children.

fascismo *m* fascism.

fascista *adj/s* fascist.

fase *f* phase, stage (etapa); *las fases de una enfermedad* the phases of an illness ‖ ASTR phase; *las fases de la luna* the moon's phases ‖ ELECTR phase ‖ TECN stage; *la primera fase de un cohete* the first stage of a rocket ‖ stage (de una obra); *entrega de la primera fase en 1980* handing over of the first stage in 1980.

fastidiar *vt* to spoil s.o.'s plans, to upset s.o.'s plans; *me fastidió la lluvia* the rain spoiled my plans ‖ to upset, to spoil, to mess up; *esto fastidia todos los proyectos* this spoils all the plans ‖ to annoy, to be a nuisance for, to bother; *me fastidia tener que ir a pie* it annoys me having to walk, it's a nuisance for me to have to walk; *deja de fastidiarme* stop bothering me, stop being a nuisance ‖ to get on the nerves of, to annoy; *me fastidia este niño con sus gritos* this child gets on my nerves with his shouting ‖ to disgust (causar asco) ‖ to damage, to ruin, to spoil (poner en mal estado o volver inservible); *el granizo ha fastidiado la cosecha* the hail has ruined the harvest; *he fastidiado mi traje al caer* I spoilt my suit when I fell over ‖ to break, to damage, to ruin (un mecanismo) ‖ to injure, to hurt (una parte del cuerpo) ‖ — *estar fastidiado* to be broken down *o* out of action (no funcionar), to be damaged (funcionar mal), to be spoilt (estar deteriorado) ‖ *me fastidia esa chica* I can't stand that girl ‖ FAM *¡no fastidies!* you're kidding! ‖ *tengo el estómago fastidiado* I have an upset stomach, my stomach is out of order.
◆ *vpr* to get bored, to get fed up (*fam*); *fastidiarse con la charla de uno* to get bored with s.o.'s chatter ‖ to put up with (aguantarse); *para que tú te vayas él tiene que fastidiarse* he has to put up with staying here so that you can go; *si habéis tenido mala suerte esta vez, os fastidiáis* if you have been unlucky this time you will just have to put up with it ‖ to be damaged *o* ruined *o* spoilt; *se ha fastidiado la cosecha con el granizo* the harvest has been ruined by the hail; *el traje se fastidió con la lluvia* the suit was ruined in the rain ‖ to break down, to be damaged, to be ruined (un mecanismo) ‖ to hurt, to injure (una parte del cuerpo) ‖ — FAM *¡fastídiate!* that's your hard luck! | *¡para que te fastidies!* so there! | *¡que se fastidie!* that's his hard luck!

fastidio *m* nuisance, bother (molestia); *es un fastidio tener que quedarnos aquí* it's a nuisance having to stay here ‖ nuisance; *es un fastidio que llueva ahora* it's a nuisance that it's raining now ‖ annoyance (enfado de poca importancia) ‖ boredom (aburrimiento) ‖ — *este olor me causa fastidio* this smell makes me feel sick ‖ *¡qué fastidio!* what a nuisance!, how annoying *o* tiresome!

fastidioso, sa *adj* troublesome, trying, annoying; *un niño fastidioso* a troublesome child ‖ annoying, irksome; *acontecimiento fastidioso* annoying event ‖ tedious, boring, irksome; *trabajo fastidioso* tedious work.

fasto, ta *adj* fortunate, happy, auspicious, lucky; *día fasto* fortunate day.
◆ *m* pomp, display, splendour (fausto).
◆ *pl* annals, archives (anales).

fastuosidad *f* splendour, pomp, lavishness.

fastuoso, sa *adj* splendid, pompous, lavish (ceremonia) ‖ lavish, ostentatious (persona).

fatal *adj* inevitable, fateful ‖ fatal; *fatales circunstancias* fatal circumstances; *una caída fatal* a fatal fall ‖ FIG horrible, terrible, lousy, rotten (pésimo); *una película fatal* a lousy film ‖ — FAM *estar fatal* to feel terrible *o* awful; *estoy fatal* I feel terrible; to be seriously ill; *el enfermo está fatal* the patient is seriously ill ‖ *mujer fatal* vamp, femme fatale ‖ FAM *tener una suerte fatal* to have rotten luck.
◆ *adv* very badly; *esquía fatal* he skis very badly.

fatalidad *f* fate, fatality (destino) ‖ misfortune (desgracia).

fatalismo *m* fatalism.

fatalista *adj* fatalistic.
◆ *m/f* fatalist.

fatalmente *adv* inevitably; *había de suceder aquello fatalmente* that inevitably had to happen ‖ unfortunately (desafortunadamente) ‖ very badly (mal).

fatídico, ca *adj* ominous, fateful; *signo fatídico* ominous sign ‖ fatidical; *número fatídico* fatidical number ‖ fatal; *momento fatídico* fatal moment.

fatiga *f* fatigue, tiredness, weariness (cansancio) ‖ laboured breathing (respiración dificultosa) ‖ fatigue (de metales) ‖ FAM *me da fatiga pedirle dinero prestado* I feel ashamed to borrow *o* I don't like to borrow money from him.
◆ *pl* troubles, difficulties (dificultades) ‖ troubles (penas) ‖ nausea *sing*, sickness *sing* (náusea).

fatigar *vt* to tire, to weary (cansar) ‖ to tire; *fatigar un caballo* to tire a horse ‖ to make breathless, to take away the breath of; *la altitud me fatiga* altitude makes me breathless *o* takes my breath away ‖ to annoy (molestar).
◆ *vpr* to tire, to get tired; *fatigarse corriendo* to get tired running.

fatigosamente *adv* with difficulty, painfully.

fatigoso, sa *adj* tiring, fatiguing (que cansa) ‖ painful (trabajoso) ‖ tiresome (fastidioso) ‖ laboured (respiración) ‖ breathing heavily, wheezing (jadeante).

fatuidad *f* fatuity, fatuousness.

fatuo, tua *adj* fatuous (necio) ‖ vain, conceited, fatuous (engreído) ‖ *fuego fatuo* will-o'-the wisp, Jack-o'-lantern.

fauces *f pl* ANAT fauces ‖ mouth (de un animal).

fauna *f* fauna.

fauno *m* MIT faun.

Fausto *npr m* Faust.

fausto, ta *adj* fortunate, happy, lucky, auspicious.
◆ *m* pomp, display, splendour (esplendor).

fautor, ra *m/f* accomplice, abettor, abetter (cómplice) ‖ instigator (autor).

fauvismo *m* ARTES fauvism.

favo *m* MED favus.

favor *m* favour [US favor], good turn; *prestar* or *hacer un favor a uno* to do s.o. a favour ‖ favour; *solicitar un favor a alguien* to ask a favour of s.o. ‖ favour, grace; *buscar el favor del rey* to seek the favour of the king ‖ favour (cinta) ‖ favour (de una mujer) ‖ — *a favor de* in favour of; *testamento a favor de su hijo* will in favour of one's son; with the aid of, thanks to (gracias a), in favour of; *estar a favor de la pena de muerte* to be in favour of capital punishment ‖ *de favor* complimentary (billete) ‖ *en favor de* in favour of (a beneficio de) ‖ *ganarse el favor de alguien* to come into favour with s.o. ‖ *gozar del favor de alguien* to be in s.o.'s favour *o* in favour with s.o. ‖ *haber perdido el favor de alguien* to be out of favour with s.o. ‖ *hacer el favor de* to be so kind as to; *haga el favor de salir ahora* would you be so kind as to go out now?; to do the pleasure *o* favour; *hágame el favor de cenar conmigo* do me the pleasure of dining with me ‖ *hacer favor a uno* to be kind to s.o. ‖ *haga el favor de esperar* please wait ‖ *pedir algo por favor a uno* to ask s.o. for sth. politely (cortésmente), to beg sth. of s.o. (suplicar) ‖ *por favor* please; *¿qué hora es, por favor?* what time is it please? ‖ *tener algo, tener a alguien a* or *en su favor* to have sth., to have s.o. in one's favour.

favorable *adj* favourable [US favorable], suitable; *condiciones favorables para* suitable conditions for ‖ favourable (propicio); *viento favorable* favourable wind ‖ optimistic; *diagnóstico favorable* optimistic diagnosis ‖ *mostrarse favorable a algo* to be in favour of sth., to favour sth.

favorecedor, ra *adj* favouring [US favoring], favourable [US favorable] ‖ flattering; *un retrato favorecedor* a flattering portrait ‖ becoming; *un peinado favorecedor* a becoming hairdo.
◆ *m/f* client, customer (cliente).

favorecer* *vt* to favour [US to favor]; *esta reforma favorece las injusticias* this reform favours injustice; *la fortuna favorece a los audaces* fortune favours the brave ‖ to be in the favour of; *las circunstancias me han favorecido* circumstances were in my favour ‖ to help (ayudar) ‖ to flatter, to favour; *esta foto, este vestido te favorece* this photo, this dress flatters you ‖ *ser favorecido con* to win, to be awarded; *ha sido favorecido con el premio gordo* he has won the first prize.
◆ *vpr* *favorecerse de* to avail o.s. of, to fall back on (valerse de).

favorecido, da *adj* favoured [US favored] ‖ *cláusula del país más favorecido* most-favoured nation clause.
◆ *f* AMER letter (carta).

favoritismo *m* favouritism [US favoritism].

favorito, ta *adj* favourite [US favorite]; *mi deporte favorito* my favourite sport.
◆ *m/f* favourite.

fax *m* fax.

faya *f* faille (tela).

fayuquero *m* AMER seller of smuggled goods (vendedor de contrabando).

faz *f* face; *la faz de la tierra* the face of the earth ‖ obverse, head (de una moneda) ‖ — *a la faz de* in front of ‖ *faz a faz* face to face ‖ *la Sacra* or *Santa Faz* the Holy Face.

FBI *abrev de Buró Federal de Investigación norteamericano* FBI, Federal Bureau of Investigation.

fe *f* faith; *la fe cristiana* the Christian faith; *tener fe en el porvenir* to have faith in the future ‖ certificate (documento); *fe de bautismo, de matrimonio* baptism, marriage certificate ‖ faithfulness (fidelidad); *fe conyugal* faithfulness between husband and wife ‖ — *a fe de* on the word of; *a fe de caballero* on the word of a gentleman ‖ *a fe mía, por mi fe* on my honour, upon my faith ‖ *buena, mala fe* honesty, dishonesty ‖ *dar fe de* to attest, to certify ‖ *de buena fe* with good intentions, in good faith ‖ *de mala fe* in bad faith ‖ *en fe de lo cual* in witness whereof ‖ *fe de erratas* list of errata ‖ *fe de vida* document to prove that a person is still alive ‖ *hacer fe* to certify, to attest ‖ *la fe mueve montañas* faith moves mountains ‖ *prestar fe a* to believe in, to have faith in ‖ *profesión de fe* profession of faith ‖ *tener buena, mala fe* the be honest, dishonest ‖ *tener una fe ciega en* to have blind faith in.

fealdad *f* ugliness || FIG unseemliness; *la fealdad de su conducta* the unseemliness of his behaviour.

feamente *adv* in an ugly manner || FIG unseemingly, indecorously || *mató al toro feamente* he killed the bull very badly.

Febo *npr m* Phoebus (el sol).

febrero *m* February; *ocurrió el 27 de febrero* it happened on the 27th of February.

febrífugo, ga *adj/sm* febrifuge; *la quinina es un febrífugo* quinine is a febrifuge.

febril *adj* feverish.

febrilidad *f* feverishness.

fecal *adj* faecal [*US* fecal].

fécula *f* starch.

feculencia *f* starchiness || feculence (impureza).

fecundación *f* fertilization, fecundation; *fecundación in vitro* in vitro fertilization || *fecundación artificial* artificial insemination (de la mujer).

fecundador, ra; fecundante *adj* fertilizing, fecundating.

fecundar *vt* to fertilize, to fecundate || to make fertile (un terreno).

fecundidad *f* fertility, fecundity || FIG productivity, fruitfulness (productividad).

fecundizar *vt* to fertilize, to fecundate || to make fertile (un terreno).

fecundo, da *adj* fertile, fecund || FIG prolific (prolífico) | fruitful (fructífero) | productive (productivo) | fertile, rich (imaginación) | full; *fecundo en consecuencias* full of consequence.

fecha *f* date; *¿cuál es la fecha de hoy?* what is the date today?, what is today's date? || day; *mi carta tardó tres fechas* my letter took three days || — *a estas fechas* now, by now || *a fecha fija* on a fixed date || *a partir de esta fecha* from today || *a tres días fecha* three days after sight || *con fecha del 10* dated the 10th || *de fecha de* dated; *una carta de fecha 3* a letter dated the 3rd || *de fecha reciente* recent || COM *de larga fecha* long-dated || *en fecha próxima* at an early date, in the near future || *fecha de caducidad* sell-by date || *fecha tope* final *o* closing date || *hasta la fecha* so far || *poner la fecha en una carta* to put the date on a letter, to date a letter || *por estas fechas* this time; *el año pasado por estas fechas hubo un terremoto* this time last year there was an earthquake || *señalar fecha* to fix a date || *sin fecha* undated.

fechador *m* date stamp (matasellos).

fechar *vt* to date, to put the date on.

fecho, cha *adj* (ant) ⟶ **hecho.**

fechoría *f* misdeed, misdemeanour [*US* misdemeanor]; *cometer fechorías* to commit misdeeds || mischief; *los niños hicieron fechorías* the children got up to mischief || *le han hecho una fechoría con el traje* they have ruined his suit.

FEDER *abrev de Fondo Europeo de Desarrollo Regional* ERDF, European Regional Development Fund.

federación *f* federation.

federado, da *adj* federate, federated.
◆ *m* federate.

federal *adj/sm* federal.

federalismo *m* federalism.

federalista *adj/s* federalist.

federalizar *vt* to federate.

federar *vt* to federate.
◆ *vpr* to federate.

federativo, va *adj* federative.

Federico *npr m* Frederick.

féferes *m pl* AMER things, bits and pieces, paraphernalia (trastos).

fehaciente *adj* authentic, reliable (documento) || irrefutable; *prueba fehaciente* irrefutable proof.

feldespato *m* MIN feldspar, feldspath.

feldmariscal *m* field marshall (mariscal de campo).

felice *adj* POÉT happy.

felicidad *f* happiness, felicity (p us) || prosperity, success (prosperidad) || — FAM *deseos de felicidad* best wishes | *la curva de la felicidad* potbelly, paunch (tripa) || *felicidades, muchas felicidades* congratulations (acontecimiento feliz), best wishes, Happy New Year (Año Nuevo), many happy returns, happy birthday (cumpleaños), best wishes (santo) || FIG *hicieron el viaje con toda felicidad* their journey went off without a hitch, their journey went off very smoothly || *os deseo toda clase de felicidades* I wish you every happiness.

felicitación *f* congratulation; *mis mejores felicitaciones por su éxito* my sincere congratulations on your success || compliment; *mis felicitaciones por tu peinado* my compliments on your hairdo || greeting, wish (escrito, expresión); *ha recibido muchas felicitaciones* he has received a lot of greetings.

felicitar *vt* to congratulate; *le felicité por el nacimiento de su hijo* I congratulated him on the birth of his son || to congratulate; *te felicito por el gusto con que te peinas* I congratulate you on your taste in hairstyles || to compliment, to congratulate; *todo el mundo la felicitó por su cocina* everyone complimented her on her cooking || — *felicitar a uno* to wish s.o. a Happy New Year (Año Nuevo) || *felicitarle a uno (por) su santo, (por) su cumpleaños, (por) las Navidades o las Pascuas, (por) el Año Nuevo* to wish s.o. a happy name day, a happy birthday, a Happy Christmas, a Happy New Year || *¡te felicito!* congratulations!
◆ *vpr* to be happy *o* glad; *me felicito de que haya tenido éxito* I am glad that he has been successful || to congratulate o.s.

félido *m* ZOOL felid.
◆ *pl* ZOOL felidae.

feligrés, esa *m/f* parishioner.

feligresía *f* parish (parroquia) || parishioners *pl*, parish (feligreses).

felino, na *adj/sm* ZOOL feline.

Felipe *npr m* Philip (nombre actual) || Philippe (nombre de los reyes de Francia) || FIG *se lo ponen como a Felipe II (segundo)* he gets everything handed to him on a plate.

feliz *adj* happy; *feliz con su suerte* happy with one's lot; *existencia feliz* happy existence || clever (acertado); *una decisión feliz* a clever decision || fortunate, lucky (afortunado) || felicitous, happy (expresión) || good; *fue un viaje muy feliz* it was a very good journey || successful (que tiene éxito) || — *desearle a uno un feliz Año Nuevo* to wish s.o. a Happy New Year || *¡Felices Pascuas!* the season's greetings!, compliments of the season! || *¡Feliz Año Nuevo!* Happy New Year! || *feliz con saber algo* happy to know sth. || *feliz desenlace* happy ending || *¡feliz viaje!* have a good journey!, bon voyage! || *más feliz que nadie* as happy as the day is long *o* as a king || *no me hace feliz tener que viajar de noche* I'm not happy about having to travel by night.

felizmente *adv* fortunately (por fortuna); *felizmente la tempestad fue de poca duración* fortunately the storm was short || uneventfully, smoothly, without a hitch (sin ninguna pega); *la fiesta terminó felizmente* the celebrations finished uneventfully || happily; *vivieron muchos años felizmente* they lived happily for many years || successfully (con éxito).

felón, ona *adj* treacherous, villainous, perfidious.
◆ *m/f* traitor, villain.

felonía *f* treachery, perfidy, betrayal (traición).

felpa *f* plush (tela parecida al terciopelo) || towelling, terry cloth (tela para toallas, manoplas, etc.) || FIG & FAM beating, hiding (paliza) || dressing down, telling off (reprensión severa); *darle* or *echarle una felpa a uno* to give s.o. a telling off || *oso de felpa* teddy bear.

felpar *vt* to cover with plush.
◆ *vpr* FIG to be carpeted *o* covered (*de* with).

felpilla *f* chenille (cordón felpudo).

felpudo, da *adj* plushy, plush-like, velvety.
◆ *m* doormat (esterilla).

femenil *adj* feminine, womanly.

femenino, na *adj* feminine; *gracia femenina* feminine grace; *terminación femenina* feminine ending || BIOL & BOT female; *sexo femenino* female sex || *equipo femenino* women's team.
◆ *m* GRAM feminine.

fementido, da *adj* false, treacherous, perfidious.

feminidad *f* femininity (de una mujer) || effeminacy (afeminación).

feminismo *m* feminism.

feminista *adj/s* feminist.

feminización *f* feminization.

femoral *adj* femoral.
◆ *f* femoral artery.

fémur *m* ANAT femur.

fenecer* *vi* to die, to pass away (morir) || to perish (perecer) || to come to an end (terminarse).
◆ *vt* to settle, to finalize, to finish.

fenecimiento *m* passing away, death, decease (muerte) || close, end (de un plazo) || end, finish (final).

fenestración *f* MED fenestration.

fenestrado, da *adj* fenestrate.

feniano *m* HIST fenian.

Fenicia *npr f* GEOGR Phoenicia, Phenicia.

fenicio, cia *adj/s* Phoenician, Phenician.

fenilo *m* phenyl.

fénix *m inv* phoenix, phenix.

fenol *m* QUÍM phenol.

fenomenal *adj* phenomenal || FIG extraordinary, phenomenal; *un talento fenomenal* an extraordinary talent | fantastic, wonderful (magnífico) | huge, colossal (enorme).

fenomenalismo; fenomenismo *m* phenomenalism.

fenómeno *m* phenomenon; *los fenómenos de la naturaleza* the phenomena of nature || FIG freak; *enseñan fenómenos en el circo* they are showing freaks in the circus | phenomenon (suceso, cosa).
◆ *adj* FAM fantastic, great, terrific; *este chico es fenómeno* this boy is great || FAM *pasarlo fenómeno* to have a terrific *o* a great time.
◆ *interj* FAM great!, fantastic!, terrific!

fenomenología *f* phenomenology.

fenomenólogo *m* phenomenologist.

feo, a *adj* ugly; *una persona fea* an ugly person || awful, terrible; *una película fea* an awful film || not nice; *es feo mentir* it is not nice to lie || unbecoming, unseemly (poco decoroso); *es feo fumar en la calle* it is unbecoming to smoke in the street || unsightly (repugnante) || dirty, nasty; *una acción fea* a dirty action || foul, nasty; *hace un tiempo feo* the weather is nasty || serious, nasty (situación) || — *la cosa se está poniendo fea* things are taking a nasty turn || *más feo que Picio, de un feo que asusta* as ugly as sin

|| FIG *tocarle a uno bailar con la más fea* to get the short end of the stick.
◆ *m* insult, slight, affront (afrenta) || ugliness (fealdad) || *hacer un feo a alguien* to offend s.o., to slight s.o.
◆ *adv* AMER nasty, awful; *saber, oler feo* to taste, to smell nasty.

feracidad *f* fertility, fecundity.

feral *adj* (p us) fierce, feral.

feraz *adj* fertile (fértil).

féretro *m* coffin (ataúd) || bier (andas).

feria *f* fair; *feria del campo, de ganado* agricultural, livestock fair || fair, carnival (verbena) || REL feria (día de la semana) || holiday, day of rest (día de descanso) || AMER tip (propina) || — FIG *cada uno habla de la feria según le va en ella* everyone sees things in his own way || *feria de muestras* trade fair, trade exhibition.
◆ *pl* gifts (regalos).

feriado *adj m* *día feriado* holiday.

ferial *adj* fair (de la feria) || REL ferial (de los días).
◆ *m* fairground (de una feria).

feriante *m/f* fairgoer (el que va a la feria) || exhibitor (en una feria de muestras).

feriar *vt* to buy at the fair (comprar) || to trade (comprar o vender).
◆ *vi* to be on holiday (no trabajar).

ferino, na *adj* ferine, feral || MED *tos ferina* whooping cough, hooping cough.

fermentación *f* fermentation.

fermentar *vt/vi* to ferment.

fermento *m* ferment.

fermio *m* QUÍM fermium.

Fernando; Fernán *npr m* Ferdinand.

ferocidad *f* ferocity, fierceness, ferociousness.

ferodo *m* brake lining (forro de freno).

feromona *f* QUÍM pheromone.

feróstico, ca *adj* FAM unruly, wild (rebelde) | irritable (irritable) | ugly (feo).

feroz *adj* ferocious, fierce (animal) || fierce, savage (persona) || fierce, raging (tempestad, viento) || fierce, ferocious; *feroz resistencia* fierce resistance || terrible (tremendo) || — *el lobo feroz* the big bad wolf || *tener un hambre feroz* to be ravenous.

ferrar *vt* to cover with iron (cubrir) || to trim with iron (guarnecer).

ferrato *m* QUÍM ferrate.

férreo, a *adj* ferreous, ferrous [of or like iron] || FIG of iron, iron; *voluntad férrea* iron will, will of iron || *vía férrea* railway [US railroad].

ferrería *f* forge (forja) || ironworks (fábrica).

ferrete *m* copper sulfate || iron punch (punzón).

ferretería *f* ironmonger's shop, ironmongery, hardware shop (tienda) || ironmongery, hardware (profesión).

ferretero *m* ironmonger, hardware dealer.

ferricianuro *m* QUÍM ferricyanide.

férrico, ca *adj* QUÍM ferric.

ferrífero, ra *adj* QUÍM ferriferous.

ferrita *f* MIN ferrite.

ferrito *m* QUÍM ferrite (sal).

ferrobús *m* railcar, monorail car.

ferrocarril *m* railway [US railroad]; *ferrocarril de cremallera* rack railway || *por ferrocarril* by rail, by train.

ferrocianuro *m* QUÍM ferrocyanide.

ferromagnético, ca *adj* ferromagnetic.

ferromagnetismo *m* ferromagnetism.

ferromanganeso *m* ferromanganese.

ferroníquel *m* ferronickel.

ferroprusiato *m* ferroprussiate.

ferroso, sa *adj* QUÍM ferrous.

ferroviario, ria *adj* railway, rail [US railroad]; *red ferroviaria* rail network.
◆ *m* railwayman, railway worker, railway employee (empleado) || *huelga de ferroviarios* rail strike.

ferry boat; ferry *m* ferryboat, train ferry (transbordador).

fértil *adj* fertile || FIG fertile; *imaginación fértil* fertile imagination | rich; *año fértil en* or *de acontecimientos* year rich in events.

fertilidad *f* fertility, fecundity.

fertilización *f* fertilization.

fertilizante *adj* fertilizing.
◆ *m* fertilizer; *fertilizantes nitrogenados* nitrate fertilizers.

fertilizar *vt* to fertilize.

férula *f* BOT ferula || cane, ferule (del maestro) || FIG *estar bajo la férula de uno* to be under s.o.'s thumb *o* under s.o.'s rule.

férvido, da *adj* fervent, fervid, ardent; *defensor férvido* fervent defender.

ferviente *adj* fervent, ardent.

fervor *m* fervour [US fervor].

fervorín *m* short prayer.

fervorizar *vt* → **enfervorizar.**

fervoroso, sa *adj* fervent, fervid, ardent.

festejar *vt* to celebrate; *festejar un aniversario* to celebrate an anniversary || to wine and dine, to feast, to entertain; *festejar a un huésped* to wine and dine a guest || to court (cortejar) || AMER to beat, to thrash (azotar).

festejo *m* entertainment, feast (de un huésped) || celebration || courting, wooing (cortejo).
◆ *pl* festivities, rejoicings (regocijos, fiestas).

festín *m* banquet, feast.

festival *adj* festive, feast (festivo).
◆ *m* festival; *festival de cine* film festival.

festivamente *adv* wittily (chistosamente).

festividad *f* festivity, celebration (fiesta alegre) || ceremony (acto solemne) || feast day (fiesta) || festivity, gaiety (alegría) || wit, humour (agudeza).

festivo, va *adj* feast, festive; *día festivo* feast day || festive, joyful (alegre); *estar de un humor festivo* to be in a festive mood || witty, humorous (chistoso).

festón *m* festoon, garland (guirnalda) || scallop (adorno).

festoneado *m* festoonry.

festonear *vt* to festoon || to scallop (en costura).

fetal *adj* foetal [US fetal]; *vida fetal* foetal life.

fetén *adj* FAM fantastic, great, terrific (formidable) | hundred per cent, genuine, through and through; *un madrileño fetén* a hundred per cent *o* a genuine Madrilenian, a Madrilenian through and through.

feticidio *m* foeticide [US feticide].

fetiche *m* fetish.

fetichismo *m* fetishism.

fetichista *adj* fetishistic, fetishist.
◆ *m/f* fetishist.

fetidez *f* foetidness [US fetidness], foetidity [US fetidity], foulness, stench.

fétido, da *adj* foetid [US fetid], foul-smelling, stinking || *bomba fétida* stink bomb.

feto *m* foetus [US fetus] || FIG & FAM monster (persona contrahecha).

feúco, ca; feúcho, cha *adj* FAM plain.

feudal *adj* feudal; *señor feudal* feudal lord.

feudalidad *f* feudality.

feudalismo *m* feudalism.

feudatario, ria *adj/s* feudatory.

feudo *m* fief, feud (territorio) || vassalage (vasallaje) || — *dar en feudo* to enfeoff || *feudo alodial* alodium.

fez *m* fez.

fi *f* phi (letra griega).

fiabilidad *f* reliability.

fiable *adj* trustworthy, reliable (seguro) || solvent.

fiado, da *adj* trusting (confiado) || on credit; *comprar fiado* to buy on credit || *al fiado* on credit.

fiador, ra *m/f* JUR guarantor, surety.
◆ *m* snap fastener, press stud (presilla de capa) || sword knot (del sable) || TECN safety catch (de la escopeta) | tumbler (cerrojo) | pin, clip (garfio) | bracket (de los canalones) || FAM buttocks *pl* (nalgas) || AMER chin strap (barboquejo) || JUR *salir* or *ser fiador de* to go bail for, to stand surety for (pagar fianza), to vouch for (garantizar).

fiambre *adj* cold (alimentos) || FIG & FAM stale, old; *una noticia fiambre* stale news.
◆ *m* cold meat [US cold cuts] (alimento frío) || FAM stiff (cadáver) || AMER funeral, boring party (reunión desanimada) || — FAM *dejar fiambre* to kill, to do in (matar) | *está (hecho) fiambre* he has kicked the bucket (ha muerto) || *fiambres variados* assorted cold meats [US assorted cold cuts].

fiambrera *f* lunch box [US dinner pail *o* bucket] (para llevar los alimentos) || AMER meat safe, food safe (fresquera).

fiambrería *f* AMER coldmeat store, sausage store.

fianza *f* deposit (dinero); *dejar como fianza* to leave as a deposit || surety, security (objeto) || guarantor, surety (fiador) || — JUR *contrato de fianza* security || *dar fianza* to pay a deposit (dinero) || *fianza de arraigo* mortgage || *libertad bajo fianza* release on bail.

fiar *vt* to guarantee (garantizar) || JUR to go bail for, to stand surety for (salir fiador por) || to confide; *fiarle a uno un secreto* to confide a secret to s.o. || to sell on credit (vender) || *cuán largo me lo fiáis* I've got a long time to think about that.
◆ *vi* to trust; *fiar en una cosa* to trust sth., to trust in sth. || *no es persona de fiar* he's not a person to be trusted, he's not a trustworthy *o* a reliable person.
◆ *vpr* to trust; *fiarse de* or *en uno, de* or *en algo* to trust s.o., to trust in s.o.; to trust sth., to trust in sth. || — *fiarse de las apariencias* to trust appearances || *no se fía* no credit given (letrero colocado en ciertas tiendas).

fiasco *m* fiasco, failure (fracaso); *ser un fiasco* to be a fiasco.

fiat *m* fiat, blessing; *dar el fiat* to give one's blessing.

fibra *f* fibre [US fiber]; *fibra textil* textile fibre || grain (de madera) || FIG push, go, energy, vigour (vigor) || — *fibra de vidrio* fibreglass [US fiberglass] || *fibra óptica* optical fibre || *fibras artificiales* artificial *o* man-made fibres.

fibrana *f* staple fibre [US staple fiber].

fibrilación *f* MED fibrillation.

fibrilla *adj* ANAT fibril, fibrilla

fibrina *f* BIOL & QUÍM fibrin.

fibrinógeno *m* fibrinogen.

fibrocemento *m* fibrocement.

fibroma *m* MED fibroma.

fibrosis *f* MED fibrosis.

fibroso, sa *adj* fibroid, fibrous.

fíbula *f* fibula (broche, peroné).

fibular *adj* fibular.

ficción *f* fiction ‖ — JUR *ficción de derecho* or *legal* legal fiction ‖ *la realidad y la ficción* fact and fiction.

ficomiceto *m* BOT phycomycete.

ficticio, cia *adj* fictious; *nombre ficticio* fictious name ‖ false; *amabilidad ficticia* false kindness.

ficha *f* index card, file *o* filing card (tarjeta) ‖ counter (en los juegos) ‖ chip (en los juegos de naipes) ‖ piece, man (de ajedrez) ‖ domino ‖ token (para el teléfono) ‖ registration form (en los hoteles) ‖ record; *ficha policiaca* police record ‖ FIG rogue, villain (pillo) ‖ — INFORM *ficha perforada* punched card ‖ CINEM *ficha técnica* credit titles *pl*, credits *pl* ‖ *sacar fichas* to make file cards.

fichaje *m* signing-up [of a player with a team].

fichar *vt* to put on an index card (apuntar en una ficha) ‖ to file, to index (clasificar) ‖ to draw up a dossier on, to put in the files (hacer la ficha antropométrica) ‖ to sign on, to sign up (un futbolista) ‖ FIG to size up, to tape; *le tengo fichado* I've got him sized up *o* taped ‖ — *estar fichado por la policía* to be in the police records *o* files, to have a criminal record ‖ FIG *estar fichado por un jefe* to be on a boss's black list.

◆ *vi* to sign up, to sign on; *fichar por un equipo* to sign up with a team ‖ to clock in (en una empresa).

fichero *m* file, filing cabinet (mueble) ‖ card index (fichas) ‖ records *pl* (de la policía) ‖ INFORM file; *fichero principal* main *o* master file.

fichú *m* fichu, headscarf (toquilla).

fidedigno, na *adj* reliable, trustworthy; *fuentes fidedignas* reliable sources.

fideicomiso *m* JUR trusteeship; *en* or *bajo fideicomiso* in trusteeship.

fidelidad *f* faithfulness, fidelity ‖ accuracy (exactitud) ‖ RAD *alta fidelidad* high fidelity.

fideo *m* noodle ‖ FAM skinny person (persona flaca) ‖ FAM *estar como un fideo* to be as thin as a rake [*US* as thin as a rail].

Fidji *npr f* GEOGR Fiji.

fiduciario, ria *adj* fiduciary; *moneda fiduciaria* fiduciary money.

◆ *m* fiduciary, trustee.

fiebre *f* MED fever; *fiebre álgida, amarilla, intermitente, tifoidea* algid, yellow, intermittent, typhoid fever ‖ FIG fever; *fiebre electoral* election fever ‖ — *fiebre de Malta* or *mediterránea* Malta fever ‖ *fiebre láctea* milk fever ‖ *fiebre palúdica* malaria ‖ *fiebre recurrente* recurrent fever ‖ *tener fiebre* to have a temperature *o* a fever ‖ *tener mucha fiebre* to run a very high temperature *o* a high fever.

fiel *adj* faithful, loyal; *fiel a su juramento* faithful to one's oath; *fiel a* or *con* or *para sus amigos* faithful to one's friends; *fiel al rey* loyal to the king ‖ reliable; *memoria fiel* reliable memory ‖ faithful, accurate, exact; *un relato fiel de los sucesos* a faithful report of the events ‖ honest (honrado).

◆ *m* faithful person (cristiano) ‖ inspector, supervisor (verificador) ‖ needle, pointer (de balanza) ‖ screw (de las tijeras) ‖ — FIG *inclinar el fiel de la balanza* to tip the balance *o* the scales ‖ *los fieles* the faithful.

fielato *m* tollhouse.

fieltro *m* felt (tejido) ‖ felt hat (sombrero) ‖ *ponerse como el fieltro* to felt (una prenda de lana).

fiemo *m* manure (estiércol).

fiera *f* wild animal ‖ TAUR bull ‖ FIG beast, brute (hombre cruel) | dragon, vixen (mujer cruel e irritable) | bad-tempered devil (hombre irritable) ‖ — *casa de fieras* menagerie ‖ FIG *estar hecho una fiera* to be wild, to be in a rage | *luchar como una fiera* to fight like a tiger | *ser una fiera para...* to be a fiend for...

fierabrás *m* FIG rebel (rebelde) | little devil, imp (niño travieso).

fierecilla *f* *La fierecilla domada* The Taming of the Shrew (obra de Shakespeare).

fiereza *f* fierceness, ferocity (ferocidad) ‖ cruelty (crueldad) ‖ wildness (cualidad de no domesticado).

fiero, ra *adj* fierce, ferocious (feroz) ‖ cruel (cruel) ‖ wild (no domesticado) ‖ FIG terrible, frightful (horrible) | ugly (feo) | huge, enormous (enorme).

◆ *m pl* boasting *sing*, swanking *sing*, bragging *sing* (fanfarroneo) ‖ *echar fieros* to boast, to brag, to swank.

fierro *m* iron (hierro) ‖ *AMER* knife (navaja).

fiesta *f* party (en una casa particular); *dar una fiesta* to give a party ‖ party, celebration; *hicieron una fiesta con motivo del bautizo de su hijo* they held a celebration *o* they gave a party for their son's baptism ‖ REL holy day, feast ‖ holiday; *el dos de mayo es fiesta* May 2nd is a holiday ‖ ceremony (acto solemne) ‖ FIG treat; *tu carta fue una fiesta para mí* your letter was a treat for me ‖ — FIG *aguar la fiesta* to be a wet blanket *o* a killjoy, to spoil the fun | *estar de fiesta* to be in a festive mood (alegre), to be celebrating (celebrando), to be on holiday (no trabajar) ‖ REL *fiesta de guardar* or *de precepto* day of obligation ‖ *fiesta de la banderita* flag day ‖ *fiesta de la raza* Columbus day ‖ *fiesta del trabajo* Labour Day ‖ *fiesta fija* immovable *o* fixed feast ‖ *fiesta movible* or *móvil* movable feast ‖ *fiesta nacional* bank holiday (en Inglaterra), national *o* public holiday (en los demás países) ‖ *guardar* or *hacer fiesta* to take a day off ‖ *la fiesta brava* or *nacional* bullfighting ‖ *tengamos la fiesta en paz* let's have less of that, cut that out | *y como fin de fiesta* to round everything off.

◆ *pl* celebrations, festivities; *las fiestas de Valencia* the festivities in Valencia ‖ holidays; *las fiestas de Navidad* the Christmas holidays ‖ soothing words, flattering words (palabras cariñosas) ‖ — *hacer fiestas* to play about (bromear) ‖ *hacer fiestas a uno* to make a fuss of s.o. ‖ FIG *no estar para fiestas* to be in no mood for jokes.

fiestero, ra *adj* FAM party-loving, fun-loving (a quien le gustan las fiestas) | gay (alegre).

FIFA *abrev de Federación Internacional de Fútbol Asociación* FIFA, Fédération Internationale de Football Association.

fifí *m* *AMER* dandy, fop (señorito).

fifiriche *m* *AMER* fop, dandy (elegantón) | puny person, weakling (enclenque).

fígaro *m* barber (barbero) ‖ bolero (chaquetilla).

figón *m* eating house, cheap restaurant (tasca).

figonero, ra *m/f* keeper of an eating house *o* of a cheap restaurant.

figulino, na *adj* earthenware, fictile (de arcilla).

figura *f* shape, form (forma); *¿qué figura tiene?* what shape is it? ‖ figure (de persona); *en el cuadro hay una figura de mujer* on the picture there is a figure of a woman ‖ shape; *figuras de madera* wooden shapes ‖ (ant) face (rostro) ‖ figure (tipo); *tener buena figura* to have a good figure ‖ FIG personality, figure (personaje); *ser una gran figura* to be an important figure | character (de una obra teatral) ‖ GRAM figure; *figura retórica* or *de construcción* figure of speech ‖ MÚS note ‖ chessman (de ajedrez) ‖ court card, face card (naipe) ‖ figure (de una danza) ‖ MAT figure ‖ — *figura central* central figure (en un drama) ‖ *figura de bulto* statue, figure ‖ *hacer figuras* to pull faces ‖ *ser la figura de la fiesta* to be the central figure at a party (el más importante), to be the life and soul of the party (ser el alma de la fiesta).

figuración *f* imagination (acción de figurarse) ‖ *eso son figuraciones tuyas* these are figments of your imagination.

figuradamente *adv* figuratively, with a figurative meaning.

figurado, da *adj* figurative ‖ *en sentido figurado* figuratively, with a figurative meaning.

figurante *m/f* TEATR extra, supernumerary, walker-on.

figurar *vt* to simulate, to feign (fingir) ‖ to represent, to depict; *esta esfera figura la Tierra* this sphere represents the Earth ‖ to outline (delinear).

◆ *vi* to act, to figure; *figurar como* or *de profesor* to act as the teacher ‖ to appear, to figure, to be; *su nombre figura en la lista* his name appears on the list ‖ to be important (ser importante); *es la persona que más figura en la alta sociedad* he is the most important person in high society ‖ to show off (presumir).

◆ *vpr* to imagine, to think; *se figuraba que era el único en su caso* he imagined he was the only one in his condition ‖ — *figúrate, figúrese* just imagine ‖ *¿qué te has figurado?* what do you think this is? ‖ *ya me lo figuraba* I thought as much.

figurativo, va *adj* figurative; *arte figurativo* figurative art.

figurín *m* sketch, design (dibujo) ‖ fashion magazine (revista) ‖ FIG & FAM fop, dandy (elegantón).

figurinista *m/f* costume designer.

figurón *m* FIG & FAM show-off, swank, swaggerer (presumido) ‖ character actor (actor) ‖ — MAR *figurón de proa* figurehead ‖ *comedia de figurón* comedy of character.

fijacarteles *m inv* billposter.

fijación *f* setting, fixing; *fijación de una fecha* fixing of a date ‖ fastening, fixing; *la fijación del lienzo en el bastidor* the fixing of the canvas to the frame ‖ sticking (de un sello) ‖ posting, putting up (de un cartel) ‖ securing (acción de asegurar) ‖ FOT fixing; *baño de fijación* fixing bath ‖ QUÍM fixation ‖ *la fijación del impuesto* tax assessment.

fijado *m* FOT fixing.

fijador, ra *adj* fixative.

◆ *m* fixative (para el pelo) ‖ pointer (en albañilería) ‖ ARTES fixative ‖ FOT fixer, fixative.

fijamente *adv* fixedly.

fijapelo *m* fixative.

fijar *vt* to fix, to fasten; *fijar un lienzo en el bastidor* to fasten a canvas to the frame ‖ to stick; *fijar un sello en un sobre* to stick a stamp on an envelope ‖ to post, to put up (un cartel) ‖ to fix; *fijar un poste en tierra* to fix a post in the ground ‖ to secure (asegurar) ‖ to fix, to set; *fijar un precio* to fix a price; *fijar la fecha de un viaje* to fix the date of a journey ‖ to determine; *fijar un reglamento* to determine regulations ‖ to draw up; *fijar un plan* to draw up a plan ‖ to install (puerta, ventana) ‖ to point (ladrillos) ‖ FOT & QUÍM to fix ‖ — *fijar domicilio en* to take up residence in ‖ *fijar la atención* or *el pensamiento en* to fix one's attention on, to concentrate on ‖ *fijar la mirada* or *los ojos en* to fix one's eyes on, to stare at ‖ *prohibido fijar carteles* or *anuncios* post *o* stick no bills.

◆ *vpr* to settle (establecerse); *el dolor se ha fijado en el brazo* the pain has settled in his arm ‖ FIG to take notice; *fíjate en todo lo que vas a ver para contármelo luego* take notice of everything you see so that you can tell me about it later | to notice; *¿no te has fijado en mi vestido nuevo?* haven't you noticed my new dress? | to look; *fíjate como ha crecido el niño* look how the child has grown | to pay attention, to be careful; *fíjate en lo que dices* pay attention to what you are saying, be careful what you are saying ‖ — *¡con que fíjate!* just imagine!, just think! ‖ *¡fíjate!* look! (¡mira!), imagine!, just think! (¡te das cuenta!) ‖ *se ha estado fijando en ella toda la noche* he has had his eyes on her all night.

fijativo, va *adj* fixative.
◆ *m* ARTES fixative ‖ FOT fixer, fixative.

fijeza *f* fixity, firmness (estabilidad) ‖ fastness (de colores) ‖ certainty (seguridad) ‖ — *mirar algo con fijeza* to stare at sth. ‖ *saber algo con fijeza* to know sth. for certain.

fijo, ja *adj* fastened, fixed (sujeto) ‖ steady, stable, firm, secure; *no subas porque la escalera no está bien fija* don't go up because the ladder is not very steady ‖ settled; *estoy fijo en París* I am settled in Paris ‖ fixed; *fiesta fija* fixed feast ‖ definite; *ya saben el día fijo de la boda* now they know the definite date of the wedding ‖ fixed; *una renta fija* a fixed income ‖ permanent; *un empleo fijo* a permanent job ‖ fast (color) ‖ stationary (inmóvil) ‖ QUÍM fixed; *un ácido fijo* a fixed acid ‖ — *con la mirada fija en algo* staring at sth. ‖ *de fijo* for certain, for sure ‖ *mirada fija* fixed gaze, stare ‖ *sueldo fijo* fixed salary.
◆ *adv* *mirar fijo* to stare at.
◆ *m* fixed salary (sueldo).

fila *f* file; *en fila india, en fila de a uno* in single *o* Indian file ‖ row (teatro, cine); *en primera fila* in the front row ‖ line, queue (de gente esperando) ‖ MIL rank ‖ — MIL *alistarse en filas* to sign up | *alistarse en las filas de* to sign up for | *cerrar* or *estrechar las filas* to close the ranks | *estar en filas* to be in the army *o* in the ranks *o* on active service | *llamar a filas* to call up ‖ *ponerse en fila* to line up ‖ MIL *¡rompan filas!* fall out!, dismiss! | *romper filas* to break ranks ‖ FAM *tenerle fila a uno* to have sth. against s.o.

Filadelfia *n pr* GEOGR Philadelphia.

filamento *m* filament.

filamentoso, sa *adj* filamentous.

filantropía *f* philanthropy.

filantrópico, ca *adj* philanthropic, philanthropical.

filántropo, pa *adj* philanthropic, philanthropical.
◆ *m/f* philanthropist.

filaria *f* MED filaria (parásito).

filariasis; filariosis *f* MED filariasis, filariosis.

filarmonía *f* love of music.

filarmónico, ca *adj* MÚS philharmonic.

filatelia *f* philately, stamp collecting.

filatélico, ca *adj* philatelic.

filatelista *m/f* philatelist, stamp collector.

filete *m* sirloin (solomillo) ‖ fillet (trozo de carne, de pescado) ‖ fillet (moldura) ‖ edging (ribete de la ropa) ‖ snaffle bit, snaffle (embocadura del caballo) ‖ IMPR fillet (adorno) ‖ TECN thread (de un tornillo).

fileteado *m* TECN thread (rosca de un tornillo).

filetear *vt* to fillet, to decorate with fillets (adornar) ‖ to thread (un tornillo).

filfa *f* FAM hoax (engaño); *¡eso es pura filfa!* this is all a hoax | fib, lie (mentira).

filhelénico, ca *adj* philhellenic.

filhelenismo *m* philhellenism (amor a los griegos).

filheleno, na *adj* philhellenic.
◆ *m/f* philhellene, philhellenist.

filiación *f* particulars *pl* (datos personales) ‖ description (señas personales) ‖ filiation (procedencia) ‖ affiliation (afiliación) ‖ MIL record card.

filial *adj* filial; *amor filial* filial love, filial piety ‖ COM subsidiary, affiliated.
◆ *f* COM branch (sucursal); *establecer una filial en Londres* to set up a branch in London | subsidiary (empresa dirigida por otra).

filiar *vt* to take the particulars of.
◆ *vpr* MIL to sign up, to enlist (engancharse) ‖ to affiliate (*a* with).

filibusterismo *m* filibustering.

filibustero *m* filibuster, freebooter (pirata).

filiforme *adj* filiform ‖ FIG skinny (persona) | thread-like (cosa).

filigrana *f* filigree (obra de orfebrería) ‖ watermark (en el papel) ‖ delicately worked object (objeto).

Filipenses *npr mpl* Philippians; *Epístola a los Filipenses* Epistle to the Philippians.

filípica *f* philippic.

filipino, na *adj/s* Philippine, Filipino ‖ FAM *es un punto filipino* he is a scoundrel *o* a rogue.

Filipinas *npr fpl* GEOGR Philippines ‖ *las islas Filipinas* the Philippine Islands.

Filipo *npr m* HIST Philip (rey de Macedonia).

filisteo, a *adj/s* HIST Philistine.
◆ *m* FIG & FAM colossus, Goliath, giant (hombre corpulento) | Philistine (inculto).

film; filme *m* film, picture [*US* movie] (película).

filmación *f* filming, shooting (rodaje).

filmadora *f* movie camera.

filmar *vt* to film, to shoot (rodar).

filme *m* ⟶ **film.**

fílmico, ca *adj* film.

filmología *f* study of the influence of cinema on social and moral matters.

filmoteca *f* film library.

filo *m* edge, cutting edge; *el filo de la navaja* the edge of a razor ‖ BIOL phylum ‖ *AMER* hunger (hambre) ‖ — *al filo de la medianoche* on the stroke of midnight ‖ *al filo del mediodía* on the stroke of twelve, at midday ‖ FIG *arma de dos filos* double-edged argument, argument which cuts both ways ‖ *dar* or *sacar filo a* to sharpen ‖ FIG *dormir hasta en el filo de una navaja* to be able to sleep anywhere ‖ MAR *filo del viento* direction of the wind ‖ *pasar al filo de la espada* to put to the sword.

filocomunista *adj* with Communist sympathies, pro-Communist.

filodendrón *m* BOT philodendron.

filogenia *f* BIOL phylogeny.

filología *f* philology.

filológico, ca *adj* philological, philologic.

filólogo *m* philologist.

filón *m* MIN vein, seam ‖ FIG & FAM cushy job (ganga) | gold mine (fuente de riquezas).

filoso, sa *adj* *AMER* sharp (afilado).

filosofador, ra *m/f* philosophizer.

filosofal *adj* philosopher's, philosophers'; *piedra filosofal* philosopher's stone.

filosofar *vi* to philosophize.

filosofastro *m* philosophaster.

filosofía *f* philosophy ‖ FIG *tomar algo con filosofía* to be philosophical about sth., to accept sth. philosophically.

filosófico, ca *adj* philosophic, philosophical.

filosofismo *m* philosophism.

filósofo, fa *adj* philosophic, philosophical.
◆ *m/f* philosopher.

filoxera *f* BOT phylloxera.

filtración *f* filtration ‖ FIG misappropriation (malversación) | leak (indiscreción) ‖ FIG *la decisión se conoció por una filtración* the decision leaked out.

filtrado, da *adj* filtered ‖ QUÍM *líquido filtrado* filtrate.

filtrar *vt/vi* to filter.
◆ *vpr* to filter; *filtrarse a través de* or *por un papel* to filter through a paper ‖ FIG to disappear (dinero, bienes) | to leak out; *los secretos se han filtrado* the secrets have leaked out | to filtrate; *elementos revolucionarios se han filtrado en el país* revolutionary elements have filtrated into the country.

filtro *m* filter ‖ philtre [*US* philter], love potion (bebida mágica) ‖ FOT filter ‖ — *cigarrillo con filtro* filter cigarette, filter-tip cigarette, tipped cigarette ‖ AUT *filtro de aceite, de gasolina* oil, petrol filter | *filtro de aire* air filter, air cleaner.

filudo, da *adj* *AMER* sharp (afilado).

fimo *m* manure (estiércol).

fimosis *f* MED phimosis.

fin *m* end; *el fin del mundo* the end of the world; *el fin del carrete* the end of the reel ‖ objective, aim, end, purpose (objetivo); *conseguir sus fines* to achieve one's aims ‖ finish (acabado) ‖ — *a fin de* in order to, so as to; *a fin de terminarlo* in order to finish it ‖ *a fin de que* so that, in order that; *date prisa a fin de que podamos salir* hurry up so that we can go out ‖ *a fines de* at the end of ‖ *al fin* at last, finally ‖ *al fin y al cabo* after all, when all is said and done ‖ *con buen fin* with good intentions; *lo hizo con buen fin* he did it with good intentions ‖ *con el fin de* with the purpose *o* the aim of ‖ *con el solo* or *el único fin de* with the sole object of *o* purpose of, merely for the purpose of ‖ *con este fin, para este fin* to this end, with this aim ‖ *dar* or *poner fin a* to put an end to, to end ‖ *el fin justifica los medios* the end justifies the means ‖ *en fin* in short (en resumen), well (bueno) ‖ *en fin de cuentas* after all, when all is said and done ‖ *fin de semana* weekend ‖ *llegar* or *tocar a su fin* to come to an end, to reach its end ‖ *noche de fin de año* New Year's Eve ‖ *por fin* finally ‖ *¡por fin!* at last! ‖ *sin fin* endless; *correa, tornillo sin fin* endless belt, screw ‖ *tener fin* to end ‖ *un sin fin de cosas* no end of things, piles *o* loads of things.

finado, da *m/f* deceased, defunct.
◆ *adj* late, deceased.

final *adj* final, last; *la letra final de una palabra* the last letter of a word ‖ final; *decisión final* final decision ‖ GRAM final; *conjunción final* final conjunction ‖ *el Juicio Final* the Last Judgment.
◆ *m* end; *hasta el final* until the end ‖ end (muerte); *un trágico final* a tragic end ‖ ending; *película con final feliz* film with a happy ending ‖ conclusion ‖ MÚS finale ‖ — *al final* in the end ‖ *al final del año* at the end of the year.
◆ *f* final; *la final de copa* the cup final; *cuartos de final* quarter finals ‖ *final de línea* terminus, terminal (transportes).

finalidad *f* FIG objective, aim, purpose, object (propósito) ‖ FIL finality.

finalista *adj* in the final; *el equipo finalista* the team in the final.
◆ *m/f* finalist.

finalización *f* termination, conclusion.

finalizar *vt/vi* to conclude, to finish, to end ‖ *finalizaba el invierno* winter was drawing to a close.

finalmente *adv* finally.

finamente *adv* finely; *escribir finamente* to write finely || in a refined manner; *hablar finamente* to speak in a refined manner || acutely, shrewdly (con agudeza) || delicately (delicadamente).

finamiento *m* demise, death (fallecimiento).

financiación *f*; **financiamiento** *m* financing.

financiar *vt* to finance || AMER to buy on credit.

financiero, ra *adj* financial || *compañía financiera* finance company.
◆ *m* financier.

financista *m* AMER financier.

finanzas *f pl* finance *sing* (hacienda).

finar *vi* to die, to pass away.
◆ *vpr* to long, to yearn (*por* for).

finca *f* property, real estate (propiedad) || estate (tierras); *una finca rústica* or *de campo* a country *o* rural estate || farm (granja) || *finca urbana* building.

fincar *vi* to buy property *o* real estate (comprar fincas) || AMER to lie, to rest (la dificultad).

finés, esa *adj* Finnic (del pueblo antiguo o de la subfamilia de lenguas finesas) || Finnish (finlandés).
◆ *m/f* Finn (persona).
◆ *m* Finnic (subfamilia de lenguas) || Finnish (lengua actual de Finlandia).

fineza *f* fineness (cualidad de fino) || refinement, courtesy, politeness (refinamiento, cortesía) || kindness (amabilidad) || nice thing (cosa agradable) || gift (obsequio).

fingido, da *adj* false, feigned, sham || *nombre fingido* false *o* assumed name.

fingidor, ra *adj* false, fake.
◆ *m/f* fake, sham.

fingimiento *m* feigning, pretence [US pretense], simulation.

fingir *vt/vi* to feign, to simulate; *fingir sorpresa, alegría* to feign surprise, happiness || to simulate, to represent; *con luces rojas finge el fuego* he simulates fire with red lights || to pretend; *finge que duerme* he is pretending to be asleep, he is pretending he is asleep; *fingir creer algo* to pretend to believe sth., to pretend one believes sth.
◆ *vpr* to pretend to be, to sham; *fingirse amigos* to pretend to be friends, to sham friendliness; *fingirse muerto* to pretend to be dead, to sham death.

finiquitar *vt* COM to close, to settle (una cuenta) || FIG & FAM to bump off (matar).

finiquito *m* COM settlement, closing (de una cuenta) | final discharge (documento) || *dar finiquito a una cuenta* to settle *o* to close an account.

finito, ta *adj* finite || *lo finito y lo infinito* the finite and the infinite.

finlandés, esa *adj* Finnish.
◆ *m/f* Finn.
◆ *m* Finnish (idioma).

Finlandia *npr f* GEOGR Finland.

fino, na *adj* fine (papel, hilo, lluvia, piel) || delicate (facciones) || slender; *talle fino* slender waist || fine, sharp (punta) || keen, sharp, acute; *olfato, oído fino* keen sense of smell, keen hearing || thin; *un lonja fina* a thin slice || refined, polite (cortés, bien educado) || shrewd, acute (inteligencia) || subtle (ironía, humor) || elegant || choice (alimentos); *vino fino* choice wine || pure, fine (oro) || fine (gusto, tela) || select (tabaco) || — *bailar por lo fino* to do ballroom dancing || *jerez fino* dry sherry || *piedra fina* semi-precious stone.

finolis *adj* FAM genteel, affected (afectado).

finta *f* feint (boxeo, esgrima, etc.).

fintar *vi* to feint.

finura *f* fineness || slenderness (del talle, etc.) || sharpness, keenness (del oído, del olfato) || sharpness (de una punta) || delicacy (delicadeza) || politeness, refinement (cortesía) || acuteness, shrewdness (agudeza) || subtlety (sutileza) || elegance || excellence, high quality (de alimentos) || *bailó con gran finura* she danced very gracefully.

fiord; fiordo *m* fiord, fjord.

fique *m* AMER agave fibre.

firma *f* signature; *firma en blanco* blank signature || signing (acto) || firm (empresa) || — *estampar su firma* to sign || FIG *llevar la firma de* to represent, to act for.

firmamento *m* firmament.

firmante *adj* signatory; *los países firmantes* the signatory countries.
◆ *m/f* signatory; *los firmantes de un acuerdo* the signatories to an agreement || — *el abajo firmante* the undersigned, I the undersigned || *los abajo firmantes* the undersigned.

firmar *vt/vi* to sign; *firmar un cheque (en blanco)* to sign a (blank) cheque.

firme *adj* firm, secure, steady, stable (estable) || solid (sólido) || rigid (rígido) || hard (duro) || straight, erect (erguido); *mantenerse firme* to keep straight || fast (color) || settled (tiempo) || COM steady, strong (mercado) | steady, firm (precios), | firm; *oferta firme* firm offer || FIG firm; *amistad, idea, creencia firme* firm friendship, idea, belief | firm, unswerving, steadfast; *firme en sus ideas* steadfast in one's ideas || — *andar con paso firme* to walk with a determined step || *andar con pie firme, tener el pie firme* to walk steadily || *a pie firme* with a firm step, steadfastly || *esperar a pie firme* to wait resolutely || MIL *estar firmes* to stand at attention | *¡firmes!* attention! || FIG *mantenerse firme* to stand fast, to hold one's ground || MIL *ponerse firme* to come to attention || JUR *sentencia firme* final judgment || *tierra firme* terra firma.
◆ *m* solid *o* firm ground || foundation (de edificio) || roadbed, foundation (cimientos de carretera) || surface (pavimento de carretera); *firme deslizante* slippery surface.
◆ *adv* hard; *trabajar, estudiar, pegar firme* to work, to study, to hit hard || — *de firme* hard; *trabajar de firme* to work hard; *llueve de firme* it is raining hard || COM *vender en firme* to make a firm sale.

firmemente *adv* firmly, solidly; *clavado firmemente en hormigón* firmly set in concrete || firmly, strongly; *lo creo firmemente* I strongly believe it || FIG firmly, steadfastly (resueltamente).

firmeza *f* firmness, stability, steadiness (estabilidad) || solidity (solidez) || rigidity (rigidez) || FIG firmness; *firmeza de creencias, de convicciones, de carácter* firmness in one's beliefs, in one's convictions, of character | firmness, steadfastness (resolución) || COM steadiness || AMER old Argentinian folk dance (baile).

firuletes *m pl* AMER adornments, ornaments.

fiscal *adj* fiscal, treasury (del fisco) || financial (financiero) || tax (de los impuestos).
◆ *m* JUR public prosecutor [US district attorney] || treasury official (empleado del fisco) || FIG & FAM snooper (entremetido).

fiscalía *f* JUR public prosecutor's office [US district attorney's office] || *fiscalía de tasas* rationing department.

fiscalización *f* supervision (vigilancia) || inspection (inspección) || FIG prying, snooping.

fiscalizador *adj* FIG prying, snooping.
◆ *m/f* FIG snooper.

fiscalizar *vt* to supervise (controlar) || FIG to pry into (curiosear) | to keep an eye on, to inspect, to check up on (vigilar); *siempre está fiscalizando nuestro trabajo* he is always checking up on our work | to criticize (criticar).

fisco *m* treasury, exchequer.

fisga *f* banter, raillery, chaff (mofa).

fisgar *vt* to pry into (un asunto) || to spy on (una persona) || to harpoon (pescar con arpón).
◆ *vi* to pry, to snoop.
◆ *vpr* to mock, to scoff, to make fun; *fisgarse de uno* to make fun of *o* to scoff at *o* to mock s.o.

fisgonear *vt* to pry into (un asunto) || to spy on (un vecino, etc.).
◆ *vi* to snoop, to pry.

fisgoneo *m* snooping, prying.

fisible *adj* fissile.

física *f* physics; *física nuclear* nuclear physics.

físicamente *adv* physically.

físico, ca *adj* physical; *un cambio físico en una sustancia* a physical change in a substance; *geografía, imposibilidad física* physical geography, impossibility || AMER affected, finicky (remilgado).
◆ *m* physique (forma del cuerpo) || face, features *pl* (cara) || appearance, looks *pl* (aspecto) || (ant) physician (médico) || *tener un físico agradable* to be pleasant-looking.
◆ *m/f* physicist (científico).

fisicoquímico, ca *adj* physicochemical.
◆ *f* physical chemistry.

físil *adj* fissile.

fisiócrata *m/f* physiocrat.

fisiografía *f* physiography.

fisiógrafo *m* physiographer.

fisiología *f* physiology.

fisiológico, ca *adj* physiological, physiologic.

fisiólogo, ga *m/f* physiologist.

fisión *f* FÍS & BIOL fission.

fisionomía *f* ⟶ **fisonomía.**

fisioterapeuta *m/f* physiotherapist.

fisioterapia *f* physiotherapy.

fisonomía; fisionomía *f* physiognomy, face, features *pl* (cara) || aspect, appearance (aspecto).

fisonómico, ca *adj* physiognomical, physiognomic.

fisonomista; fisónomo, ma *m/f* physiognomist || *ser buen, mal fisonomista* to be good, no good at remembering faces.

fisotórax *m* MED physothorax.

fístula *f* MED fistula; *fístula lagrimal* lachrymal fistula || pipe, tube (conducto) || MÚS fistula.

fistular *adj* fistular, fistulous.

fistulización *f* MED fistulization.

fisura *f* MED & MIN fissure.

fitófago, ga *adj* phytophagous, plant-eating.

fitografía *f* phytography [descriptive botany].

fitología *f* phytology [botany].

fitozoario *m* ZOOL phytozoon.
◆ *pl* ZOOL phytozoa.

flabelo *m* flabellum.

flacidez; flaccidez *f* flabbiness, limpness, flaccidity.

flácido, da; fláccido, da *adj* flabby, limp, flaccid; *músculos fláccidos* flabby muscles.

flaco, ca *adj* thin, lean, skinny (muy delgado) || weak, feeble (sin fuerzas) || FIG weak, weak-willed (poco resistente a las tentaciones); *la carne es flaca* the flesh is weak | bad, short (memoria) || — *argumento flaco* weak argument || *punto flaco* weak point, weak spot; *la ortografía es su punto flaco* spelling is his weak point; *la conclusión ofrece varios puntos flacos* the conclusion has several weak points; *su punto flaco es la afición a la bebida* his weak point is drink.
◆ *m* weak point, weak spot (punto flaco); *conozco su flaco* I know his weak point.

flacucho, cha *adj* FAM very thin, skinny.

flacura *f* thinness, leanness, skinniness (delgadez) || weakness, feebleness (debilidad).

flagelación *f* whipping, scourging, flagellation.

flagelado, da *adj* flagellate.
◆ *m pl* ZOOL flagellatae.

flagelador, ra *adj* whipping, scourging, flagellant.
◆ *m/f* flagellant, scourger, flagellator.

flagelar *vt* to whip, to lash, to scourge, to flagellate || FIG to revile, to flay (censurar).

flagelo *m* whip, scourge, lash (azote) || FIG scourge (calamidad) || BIOL flagellum (filamento).

flagrancia *f* flagrancy.

flagrante *adj* flagrant || *en flagrante delito* in the act, red-handed (in fraganti).

flamante *adj* (ant) blazing, flaming (llameante) || FIG splendid, magnificent (brillante) | brand-new (nuevo); *un coche flamante* a brand-new car.

flameado, da *adj* CULIN flambé; *plátanos flameados* flambé bananas.
◆ *m* flaming.

flamear *vi* to flame, to blaze, to burn (llamear) || to flutter (bandera, etc.) || MAR to flap (vela).
◆ *vt* to flame, to sterilize (esterilizar) || CULIN to flame.

flamenco, ca *adj* Flemish (de Flandes) || flamenco; *guitarra flamenca* flamenco guitar; *cante flamenco* flamenco singing || Andalusian Gypsy (gitano) || *AMER* thin, lean (flaco) || FIG & FAM *ponerse flamenco* to get cocky (chulo).
◆ *m/f* Fleming (persona de Flandes).
◆ *m* Flemish (lengua) || flamenco (cante y baile) || ZOOL flamingo (ave) || *AMER* dagger (facón).

flamenquería *f* cheekiness, cockiness (chulería).

flamenquismo *m* cheekiness, cockiness (chulería) || love of flamenco (afición al flamenco).

flamígero, ra *adj* POÉT flaming, blazing || ARQ flamboyant.

flámula *f* pennant, streamer (gallardete).

flan *m* CULIN caramel custard (crema) || baked custard (pastel) || *flan de arena* sand pie.

flanco *m* flank, side (de persona) || MIL flank; *atacaron por el flanco derecho* they attacked on the right flank.

Flandes *npr m* GEOGR Flanders || FAM *ser de mantequilla de Flandes* to be a weakling.

flanero *m* custard mould [*US* custard mold].

flanqueado, da *adj* flanked; *flanqueado por montañas* flanked by mountains.

flanquear *vt* to flank.

flanqueo *m* flanking.

flap *m* AVIAC flap (alerón).

flaquear *vi* to weaken, to flag; *me flaquean las fuerzas* my strength is flagging; *su resistencia, su entusiasmo flaqueaba* his resistance, his enthusiasm was weakening || to fail, to flag (el valor) || to slacken, to flag (esfuerzos) || to flag, to become tired (cansarse) || to fail (salud, vista, memoria) || to lose heart (abatirse) || to give way (viga, contrafuerte, piernas, etc.); *me flaquearon las piernas* my legs gave way.

flaqueza *f* thinness, leanness (delgadez) || weakness (debilidad) || FIG weakness (punto flaco); *la afición al alcohol es una de sus flaquezas* one of his weaknesses is drink | frailty; *la flaqueza humana* human frailty.

flash *m* FOT flash, flashlight || RAD flash, newsflash (boletín corto).

flato *m* wind, flatus (gas intestinal) || *AMER* melancholy, sadness || (ant) wind (viento) || *echar flatos* to have wind, to burp (niño).

flatulencia *f* flatulence.

flatulento, ta *adj* flatulent.

flatuosidad *f* flatulence, wind (*fam*).

flauta *f* MÚS flute; *flauta travesera* transverse *o* German flute || — FIG *cuando pitos, flautas, cuando flautas, pitos* if it's not one thing it's another | *entre pitos y flautas* what with one thing and another || *flauta de Pan* pipes *pl* of Pan || *AMER* FAM *¡la gran flauta!* good Lord!, good heavens! || FAM *y sonó la flauta por casualidad* how lucky can you get!
◆ *m* flautist (flautista).

flautado, da *adj* flute-like.
◆ *m* MÚS flute (de órgano).

flautero *m* flute maker.

flautín *m* MÚS piccolo.

flautista *m* MÚS flautist, flutist.

flebectomía *f* MED phlebectomy.

flebitis *f* MED phlebitis.

flebografía *f* MED phlebography.

flebolito *m* MED phlebolith, phlebolithe.

flebopatía *f* MED phlebopathy.

flebotomía *f* MED phlebotomy.

flebotrombosis *f* MED phlebothrombosis.

fleco *m* fringe (adorno) || fringe, bang [*US* bangs *pl*] (flequillo) || frayed edge, fraying (borde desgastado).

flecha *f* arrow (de arco), dart (más pequeña) || bolt (de ballesta) || AUT direction indicator, trafficator (indicador de dirección) || MAT sagitta || ARQ rise (de arco) | spire, fleche (en una torre, etc.) || — FIG *correr como una flecha* to run like the wind || *salir como una flecha* to fly *o* to shoot out.

flechador *m* archer, bowman.

flechar *vt* to draw (the bow) (estirar la cuerda) || to shoot with an arrow (asaetear) || FIG & FAM to inspire love at first sight in, to make a hit with (enamorar a alguien) || — FAM *ir flechado* to fly, to rush, to hurry, to dart | *voy flechado a por tabaco* I'm going to nip out for some cigarettes.
◆ *vpr* FAM to fall in love at first sight (enamorarse).

flechaste *m* MAR ratline.

flechazo *m* arrow shot || arrow wound (herida) || FIG & FAM love at first sight.

flechilla *f* dart, small arrow.

flegma *f* —→ **flema.**

flegmático, ca *adj* (ant) —→ **flemático.**

flegmón *m* (ant) —→ **flemón.**

fleje *m* TECN metal strip *o* band (para ceñir) | hoop (de tonel).

flema; flegma *f* phlegm (humor, mucosidad) || FIG phlegm, calm, coolness, imperturbability (imperturbabilidad) | sluggishness (torpeza).

flemático, ca *adj* phlegmatic, stolid, stoic, imperturbable.

fleme *m* VET fleam (lanceta).

flemón *m* MED phlegmon, abscess | gumboil (en las encías).

flequillo *m* fringe, bang [*US* bangs *pl*] (de pelo).

fletador *m* MAR & AVIAC charterer, freighter, shipper || hirer.

fletamento; fletamiento *m* MAR & AVIAC chartering (acción de fletar) | charter party (contrato).

fletante *m* *AMER* shipowner | person who has animals of burden for hire.

fletar *vt* MAR & AVIAC to charter (alquilar) | to freight, to load (embarcar mercancías) || *AMER* FAM to hire (un vehículo, un animal de carga, etc.) || *vuelo fletado* charter flight.
◆ *vpr* *AMER* FAM to skedaddle, to beat it (largarse).

flete *m* MAR & AVIAC freight, cargo (carga) | freightage (precio) || *AMER* load (carga en cualquier vehículo) | haulage, transportation charge (precio) | packhorse (caballo) || *contrato de flete* charter party.

fletero, ra *adj* *AMER* for hire.
◆ *m/f* owner of vehicles for hire.

flexibilidad *f* flexibility || FIG adaptability, pliability (de persona) | flexibility (de reglamento, etc.).

flexible *adj* flexible || soft (sombrero) || FIG adaptable, pliable; *carácter flexible* adaptable character | flexible (reglamento, etc.) | compliant (persona).
◆ *m* ELECTR flex, wire [*US* electric cord] || soft hat (sombrero).

flexión *f* flexion || GRAM inflection, inflexion.

flexor *m* ANAT flexor (músculo) || *músculo flexor* flexor, flexor muscle.

flint-glass; flintglas *m* TECN flint glass.

flipar *vt* POP to send *o* to drive s.o. wild.
◆ *vpr* POP to get stoned (drogarse).

flirt *m* flirtation, flirting (galanteo) || flirtation (amorío) || boyfriend (hombre), girlfriend (mujer) || *es un antiguo flirt suyo* she's an old flame of his.

flirtear *vi* to flirt.

flirteo *m* flirting, flirtation (galanteo) || flirtation (amorío).

flit *m* FAM insecticide spray.

floculación *f* QUÍM flocculation.

flocular *vi* QUÍM to flocculate.

floculento, ta *adj* flocculent.

flóculo *m* QUÍM floc, floccule || ASTR flocculus.

flogisto *m* HIST phlogiston.

flojear *vi* to ease up, to let up, to slacken; *el calor, el viento empieza a flojear* the heat, the wind is beginning to ease up || to fall off, to go down (disminuir); *la producción ha flojeado* production has fallen off || to grow weak, to weaken (debilitarse) || to slack (no trabajar como es debido).

flojedad *f* slackness, looseness (de nudo, cuerda, etc.) || flabbiness, limpness, flaccidity (flaccidez) || weakness (debilidad) || slackness (del mercado) || lightness, slackness (del viento) || slackness, laziness (pereza) || carelessness (descuido) || *flojedad de voluntad* spinelessness, lack of spirit.

flojel *m* down (vello de las aves) || fluff (que se desprende del paño) || *pato de flojel* eider.

flojera *f* FAM laziness, slackness (pereza) | weakness (debilidad).

flojo, ja *adj* slack, loose; *nudo, cable flojo* slack knot, cable || flabby, limp, flaccid (fláccido) || weak; *tela, cerveza floja* weak material, beer || weak, poor; *excusa floja* weak excuse; *estilo flojo* poor style; *película floja* poor film;

flojo en matemáticas weak at mathematics || light, slack (viento) || poor, meagre (escaso); *producción floja* meagre output || weak, feeble (débil) || slack (inactivo); *la Bolsa estaba floja* things were slack at the Stock Exchange || slack, lazy, idle, indolent (holgazán); *estudiante, obrero flojo* slack student, workman || CULIN low (horno) || *AMER* cowardly || *flojo de voluntad* spineless, spiritless.

flor *f* BOT flower; *cultiva flores* to grow flowers | flower, bloom; *planta en flor* plant in flower *o* in bloom | blossom (de árbol frutal); *flor de azahar* orange blossom; *en flor* in blossom | bloom (capa en las uvas, ciruelas, etc.) || flowers *pl* (del vino) || QUÍM flowers *pl*; *flor de azufre* flowers of sulphur || grain side (de pieles curtidas) || FAM compliment; *decirle* or *echarle flores a una chica* to pay a girl compliments || FIG flower (lo más selecto) || *AMER* white spot (de la uña) || — *a flor de* at... level; *a flor de tierra* at ground level || *a flor de agua* awash (submarino, roca) || *a flor de piel* skin-deep || TECN *ajustado a flor* flush (a nivel) || FIG *en la flor de la edad* or *de la vida* in the prime of life | *en la flor de la juventud* in the flower of youth || *flor artificial* artificial flower || *flor de harina, harina de flor* wheatmeal, pure wheaten flour || *flor de la Pasión* passionflower || BOT *flor de la Trinidad* pansy || *flor de lis* fleur-de-lis, fleur-delys (emblema heráldico), amaryllis (planta) || FIG *la flor y nata* the cream, the pick, the best, the flower; *la flor y nata de la sociedad londinense* the cream of London society || *no se admiten flores ni coronas* no flowers, by request (en un entierro) || *tienda de flores* florist's (shop).

flora *f* flora.

floración *f* flowering, blooming (planta), blossoming (árbol frutal) || flowering time, blooming time, blossoming time (época).

floral *adj* floral.

florar *vi* to flower, to bloom || to blossom (árbol frutal).

floreado, da *adj* flowered, flowery, decorated with flowers; *cortinas floreadas* flowered curtains || FIG flowery, florid (estilo) || *pan floreado* fine wheaten bread.

florear *vt* to decorate with flowers (adornar con flores) || to sift out the finest flour from (la harina).
◆ *vi* to brandish a sword (con la espada) || MÚS to play in arpeggio (la guitarra) || FAM to pay compliments (echar flores) || FIG to elaborate; *florear sobre un tema* to eleborate on a theme.

florecer* *vi* to flower, to bloom (una planta) || to blossom (un árbol frutal) || to flourish, to thrive, to prosper (prosperar); *las ciencias florecían en esa época* the sciences flourished during that period || to flourish; *Dryden floreció en el siglo XVII* Dryden flourished in the 17th century.
◆ *vpr* to mildew, to go mouldy [*US* to go moldy] (cubrirse de moho).

floreciente *adj* BOT flowering, blooming || FIG flourishing, prosperous.

florecimiento *m* flowering, blooming (de una planta) || blossoming (de un árbol frutal) || FIG flourishing, prospering, thriving || moulding [*US* molding], mildewing (enmohecimiento).

Florencia *n pr* GEOGR Florence.

florentino, na *adj/s* Florentine.

floreo *m* idle wordplay (conversación de pasatiempo) || witty remark (dicho frívolo) || flourish (en esgrima, música, escritura) || caper (en el baile) || FIG *andarse con floreos* to beat about the bush.

florería *f* florist's, florist's shop.

florero, ra *m/f* florist (vendedor).
◆ *m* (flower) vase.

florescencia *f* BOT florescence || QUÍM efflorescence.

floresta *f* wood, thicket, grove (bosque) || glade (lugar frondoso y agradable) || FIG anthology (florilegio).

florete *m* foil (espadín) || fencing with the foil (esgrima).
◆ *adj* superfine (muy fino).

floretista *m* foilsman, fencer.

floricultor, ra *m/f* flower grower, floriculturist.

floricultura *f* flower growing, floriculture.

floridez *f* floweriness; *la floridez de la primavera* the floweriness of spring || FIG floridity, floweriness.

florido, da *adj* flowery, full of flowers; *un jardín florido* a flowery garden || FIG select (selecto) | flowery, florid (lenguaje, estilo) || — *gótico florido* flamboyant Gothic || FIG *lo más florido* the cream || *Pascua florida* Easter.

florilegio *m* anthology, florilegium (antología).

florín *m* florin (moneda).

floripondio *m* BOT datura || FIG gaudy flower (flor grande de mal gusto); *cortinas salpicadas de enormes floripondios rojos* curtains bespattered with huge gaudy red flowers.

florista *m/f* florist (que tiene una tienda de flores) || flower maker (que fabrica flores artificiales) || *florista callejera* flower seller.

floristería *f* florist's shop.

florón *m* large flower || ARQ rosette, fleuron (en el techo) || HERÁLD fleuron || IMPR tailpiece.

flósculo *m* BOT floret.

flota *f* fleet; *flota pesquera, aérea* fishing, air fleet || *flota mercante* merchant navy [*US* merchant marine].

flotabilidad *f* buoyancy, floatability (capacidad de flotar) || floatability (de una vía fluvial).

flotación *f* floating, floatation, flotation (acción de flotar) || fluttering, flapping (de una bandera) || MIN floatation, flotation || floating (de la moneda).

flotador, ra *adj* floating.
◆ *m* float (de caña de pescar, carburador, hidroavión, etc.) || water wings *pl* (para nadar) || ball (en depósitos) || *flotador de alarma* boiler float.

flotante *adj* floating; *costillas, riñones flotantes* floating ribs, kidneys; *ancla, dique, eje flotante* floating anchor, dock, axle; *moneda, deuda flotante* floating currency, debt || loose (capa) || flowing (cabellos, etc.).

flotar *vi* to float || to flutter, to float, to wave (bandera, gallardete, etc.) || to stream; *su cabellera flotaba al viento* her hair streamed in the wind || to float (la moneda).

flote *m* floating, floatation, flotation (flotación) || — *a flote* afloat; *estar a flote* to be afloat; on one's feet (fuera de apuro); *ponerse a flote* to get back on one's feet || *poner a flote* to set afloat, to float (una embarcación) || *sacar a flote* to refloat, to set afloat (un barco), to put on its feet (un negocio) || *salir a flote* to get back on one's feet, to get out of difficulty (después de un apuro), to become solvent again, to get out of the red (*fam*) (después de una crisis financiera).

flotilla *f* flotilla, fleet of small ships.

fluctuación *f* fluctuation; *fluctuaciones del mercado* market fluctuations || FIG vacillation, irresolution, hesitation, wavering (vacilación).

fluctuar *vi* to fluctuate; *el precio fluctúa entre nueve y diez libras* the price fluctuates between nine and ten pounds || FIG to oscillate; *su humor fluctúa entre el abatimiento y la exaltación* his mood oscillates between dejection and exaltation | to vacillate, to waver, to hesitate (entre dos soluciones) || to bob (up and down) (sobre el agua).

fluente *adj* fluid (fluido) || flowing (que fluye).

fluidez *f* fluidity || FIG fluency.

fluidificar *vt* to fluidify || FIG *fluidificar el tráfico* to make the traffic flow.

fluido, da *adj* fluid || FIG fluent (lenguaje, manera de expresarse) | flowing, fluent (estilo).
◆ *m* FÍS fluid || ELECTR current || *mecánica de los fluidos* fluid mechanics.

fluir* *vi* to flow, to run.

flujo *m* flow, stream; *flujo de sangre, de palabras* flow of blood, of words || MAR flow, rising tide || MED discharge (de un humor) || QUÍM & FÍS flux || INFORM flow, flux; *flujo de datos, de información* data, information flow || — MED *flujo blanco* leucorrhoea, whites *pl* (*fam*) || ECON *flujo de caja* cash flow || MED *flujo de vientre* diarrhoea || *flujo magnético* magnetic flux || *flujo y reflujo* ebb and flow.

fluminense *adj* [of *o* from] Rio de Janeiro.
◆ *m/f* native *o* inhabitant of Rio de Janeiro.

flúor *m* QUÍM fluorine || *espato flúor* fluorspar.

fluoración *f* fluoridation.

fluorescencia *f* fluorescence.

fluorescente *adj* fluorescent.

fluorhidrato *m* QUÍM hydrofluoride.

fluorhídrico, ca *adj* QUÍM hydrofluoric.

fluorita *f* MIN fluorite.

fluoruro *m* QUÍM fluoride.

fluvial *adj* fluvial, river; *tráfico fluvial* river traffic; *residuos fluviales* fluvial deposits || *vía fluvial* waterway.

flux *m inv* flush (en los naipes) || *AMER* suit (traje) || FIG & FAM *hacer flux* to blow *o* to squander one's money.

fluxión *f* MED congestion (de la nariz) | fluxion.

FMI *abrev de Fondo Monetario Internacional* IMF, International Monetary Fund.

fobia *f* phobia.

foca *f* ZOOL seal || sealskin (piel).

focal *adj* focal; *distancia focal* focal lenght.

focalización *f* FÍS focalization.

focalizar *vt* FÍS to focalize.

focense *adj/s* phocian.

foco *m* FÍS & MAT focus || FIG focus, focal point, centre [*US* center]; *el foco de la civilización griega* the focus of Greek civilization | seat (de un incendio) || spotlight, floodlight (lámpara potente) || MED focus, seat (de un trastorno) | centre; *foco de infección* centre of infection || — FOT *foco fijo* fixed focus | *fuera de foco* out of focus (desenfocado) | *profundidad de foco* depth of focus.

fofo, fa *adj* spongy, soft (esponjoso, poco denso) || flabby; *carne fofa* flabby flesh.

fogarada *f* bonfire (hoguera) || blaze (llamarada).

fogata *f* bonfire (hoguera) || blaze (llamarada) || small land mine (explosivo) || *fogata de San Juan* Midsummer Day bonfire.

fogón *m* hearth (hogar) || kitchen range (cocina de carbón) || cooker, stove; *fogón de gas* gas cooker || firebox (de caldera) || vent (de arma de fuego).

fogonadura *f* MAR mast hole.

fogonazo *m* flash ‖ FOT flash.

fogonero *m* stoker, fireman (de máquina de vapor).

fogosidad *f* fire, ardour [US ardor], spirit (ardor) ‖ dash (ímpetu) ‖ fieriness (de un caballo).

fogoso, sa *adj* fiery, spirited (lleno de ardor); *corcel fogoso* fiery steed.

fogueado, da *adj* experienced, hardened.

foguear *vt* to harden *o* to accustom (men, horses) to war ‖ to inure, to harden, to accustom (a una cosa desagradable) ‖ to train (formar para un trabajo) ‖ TAUR to place «banderillas de fuego» in (the bull) ‖ VET to cauterize.
◆ *vpr* to become hardened *o* inured.

fogueo *m* training (de caballos para la guerra) ‖ — *cartucho de fogueo* blank cartridge ‖ *tiro de fogueo* firing with blank cartridges.

foja *f* coot (ave) ‖ AMER JUR leaf, page (página de documento, de libro), sheet (hoja suelta).

folía *f* (ant) madness | «folia» [dance of Portugese origin, song of the Canary Isles].

foliáceo, a *adj* BOT foliaceous.

foliación *f* foliation ‖ IMPR foliation, page numbering.

foliado, da *adj* foliated, numbered (páginas) ‖ BOT foliate.

foliar *adj* BOT foliar.

foliar *vt* to foliate, to number (paginar).

foliatura *f* foliation.

folicular *adj* follicular.

foliculario *m* pamphleteer.

foliculina *f* folliculin.

foliculitis *f* MED folliculitis.

folículo *m* BOT & ZOOL follicle.

folio *m* leaf (hoja) ‖ IMPR folio (hoja, número) | running head, running title (encabezamiento) ‖ — FIG *de a folio* enormous (disparate, tontería) ‖ IMPR *en folio* folio, in folio; *edición en folio* folio edition, edition in folio | *folio atlántico* atlas size | *folio explicativo* running head, running title.

folíolo *m* BOT foliole.

folklore *m* folklore.

folklórico, ca *adj* folk, popular, folkloric (p us); *baile folklórico* folk dance.

folklorista *m/f* floklorist.

follada *f* small puff pastry pie ‖ POP *tener mala follada* to be a damned nuisance (ser un pesado), to be unlucky (tener mala suerte).

follaje *m* foliage, leaves *pl* (fronda) ‖ FIG adornments *pl*, ornamentation, decoration (adornos) | verbiage, verbosity (palabrería).

follar* *vt* to blow with bellows (soplar).
◆ *vt/vi* POP to fuck (practicar el coito).
◆ *vpr* POP to drop a silent one (ventosear).

folletín *m* newspaper serial (novela por entregas en un periódico) ‖ FIG melodrama.

folletinesco, ca *adj* melodramatic ‖ unlikely (inverosímil).

folletinista *m/f* serial writer.

folletista *m/f* pamphleteer.

folleto *m* pamphlet, brochure; *folleto turístico* tourists' brochure ‖ folder, leaflet (desplegable) ‖ handout (de publicidad) ‖ *folleto explicativo* instruction booklet.

follón, ona *adj* (p us) lazy, indolent, slothful (vago) ‖ arrogant (arrogante) ‖ blustering (fanfarrón) ‖ cowardly (cobarde)
◆ *m/f* good-for-nothing, loafer (vago) ‖ arrogant person, blusterer (arrogante) ‖ coward, poltroon (ant) (cobarde).
◆ *m* silent rocket (cohete) ‖ FAM row, shindy, rumpus (alboroto); *armaron un follón en la calle* they kicked up a rumpus in the street | chaos (situación confusa); *fue un follón cuando las luces fallaron* it was chaos when the lights failed | jumble (montón desordenado); *un follón de libros en la mesa* a jumble of books on the table | mess (situación enmarañada); *está metido en un follón* he has got himself into a mess, he is in a mess | bore, drag (persona o cosa pesada) ‖ POP silent fart (ventosidad).

fomentar *vt* to warm (calentar suavemente) ‖ to incubate, to brood (huevos) ‖ MED to foment, to put a poultice on (en un tumor, etc.) ‖ FIG to encourage, to promote, to foster; *fomentar el comercio entre dos países* to encourage trade between two countries | to foment (la rebelión, el odio, etc.).

fomento *m* warmth (calor) ‖ warming (acción de calentar) ‖ incubation (de huevos) ‖ MED fomentation | poultice (compresa caliente) ‖ FIG promotion, encouragement, fostering; *fomento de las ventas* sales promotion ‖ fomentation (de una rebelión, etc.) ‖ — *banco de fomento* development bank [promoting the development of industry, agriculture, etc.] ‖ (ant) *Ministerio de Fomento* Ministry of Public Works and the Economy.

fon *m* FÍS phon (unidad de potencia sonora).

fonación *f* phonation.

fonda *f* tavern (ant), inn (ant), small restaurant (restaurante barato) ‖ boarding house (hospedería) ‖ buffet (en las estaciones).

fondeadero *m* MAR anchorage.

fondeado, da *adj* anchored, at anchor ‖ AMER rich, wealthy (rico).

fondear *vt* to anchor (un barco) ‖ to sound, to take soundings in (sondear) ‖ to search (registrar una embarcación) ‖ FIG to get to the bottom of (una cuestión) | to sound out (una persona).
◆ *vi* MAR to anchor, to cast *o* to drop anchor.
◆ *vpr* AMER to get rich.

fondeo *m* MAR search, searching (del cargamento) | anchoring.

fondero *m* AMER ⟶ **fondista.**

fondillos *m pl* seat *sing* (de pantalones).

fondista *m pl* innkeeper (ant), restaurant owner (de restaurante) ‖ boarding house keeper (de pensión).

fondo *m* bottom (parte más baja); *el fondo de un valle, de una taza, de un saco* the bottom of a valley, of a cup, of a sack ‖ bottom, end (parte más lejana); *el fondo de un pasillo, de una calle* the bottom of a corridor, of a street ‖ back; *en el fondo del salón, del escenario* at the back of the lounge, of the stage ‖ bottom, bed, floor; *fondo del mar* bottom of the sea, sea bed, sea floor ‖ background; *el fondo de un cuadro* the background of a painting; *una tela con fondo azul* a fabric with a blue blackground; *música de fondo* background music ‖ depth (profundidad); *la piscina tiene cinco metros de fondo* the depth of the swimming pool is five metres; *la casa tiene poca fachada pero veinte metros de fondo* the house has a short frontage but a depth of twenty metres ‖ fund; *Fondo Monetario Internacional* International Monetary Fund; *fondo de amortización* sinking fund; *fondo para la construcción* building fund ‖ money, resources *pl* (dinero) ‖ collection (de una librería, de una biblioteca) ‖ FIG substance (de un libro, de un discurso, etc.); *forma y fondo* form and substance | bottom; *vayamos al fondo del asunto* let's get to the bottom of the matter; *el fondo de un problema* the bottom of a problem | stock, fund (caudal); *tener un fondo de sabiduría* to possess a stock of knowledge *o* a fund of wisdom | stamina (resistencia) ‖ head, bottom (de tonel) ‖ lunge (en la esgrima) ‖ — *a fondo* thoroughly; *estudiar un asunto a fondo* to study a question thoroughly; thorough; *una limpieza a fondo* a thorough cleaning ‖ *al fondo de* at the bottom of ‖ *artículo de fondo* leading article, leader ‖ MAR *dar fondo* to drop *o* to cast anchor, to anchor ‖ *de bajo fondo* shallow ‖ *de cuatro en fondo* in column of fours (término militar), four abreast (término normal) ‖ *de fondo* long-distance; *corredor, carrera de fondo* long-distance runner, race ‖ *de medio fondo* middle-distance ‖ *doble fondo* false bottom (fondo falso), ballast tank (de un barco) ‖ *echar a fondo* to sink, to send to the bottom (un barco) ‖ FIG *en el fondo* deep down, at heart; *parece un poco tacaño pero en el fondo es muy generoso* he seems a bit of a skinflint but deep down he is very generous; really, basically; *en el fondo tiene usted razón* basically you are right ‖ ECON *Fondo de Garantía de Depósitos* Spanish deposit guarantee fund | *fondo de inversión* investment fund | *fondo de operaciones* working capital | *fondo de pensiones* pension fund | *fondo de rotación* revolving fund | *fondo perdido* life annuity | *fondo de reserva* reserve fund | *Fondo Social Europeo* European Social Fund ‖ MAR *irse a fondo* to sink, to go down ‖ *maquillaje de fondo* foundation ‖ *mar de fondo* ground swell (marejada), undercurrent of tension (tensión latente) ‖ FIG *tener buen fondo* to be good-natured ‖ *tirarse a fondo* to lunge (esgrimidor).
◆ *pl* funds; *fondos disponibles* available funds; *estar en fondos* to be in funds ‖ *bajos fondos* scum, dregs (de la sociedad) ‖ *cheque sin fondos* cheque without cover, dud cheque, N. S. F. cheque, worthless cheque, cheque that bounces (*fam*) ‖ COM *fondos bloqueados* frozen assets ‖ *fondos públicos* public funds, government stock *sing* ‖ *reunir* or *recoger fondos* to raise funds.

fondón, ona *adj* FAM big-bottomed.

fonducho *n* cheap eating house, cheap restaurant.

fonema *m* phoneme.

fonémico, ca *adj* phonemic.
◆ *f* phonemics.

fonendoscopio *m* stethoscope.

fonético, ca *adj* phonetic.
◆ *f* phonetics.

fonetista *m/f* phonetician, phonetist.

foniatra *m* MED phoniatrician.

foniatría *f* MED phoniatrics.

fónico, ca *adj* phonic.

fonio; fono *m* FÍS phon (fon).

fono *m* AMER earpiece (auricular) | telephone number (número de teléfono).

fonocaptor *m* TECN pickup.

fonocardiografía *f* MED phonocardiography.

fonográfico, ca *adj* phonographic.

fonógrafo *m* phonograph.

fonograma *m* phonogram.

fonolita *f* MIN phonolite.

fonolocalización *f* sound ranging.

fonología *f* phonology.

fonólogo, ga *m/f* phonologist.

fonometría *f* phonometry.

fonómetro *f* phonometer.

fonoteca *f* record library.

fontana *f* POÉT spring, fountain.

fontanal *adj* spring; *aguas fontanales* spring water.

fontanal; fontanar *m* spring.

fontanela *f* ANAT fontanel, fontanelle.

fontanería *f* plumbing.

fontanero *m* plumber.

foque *m* MAR jib (vela); *foque volante* flying jib.

forajido, da *adj* outlawed.
◆ *m/f* outlaw.

foral *adj* relative to the «fueros» or privileges, statutory.

foralmente *adv* according to the «fueros» or privileges.

foráneo, a *adj* strange (extraño) ‖ foreign, alien (extranjero).
◆ *m/f* stranger (forastero) ‖ foreigner, alien (extranjero).

forastero, ra *adj* strange (extraño) ‖ foreign, alien (extranjero) ‖ outside (de fuera).
◆ *m/f* stranger (desconocido) ‖ outsider (persona que viene de fuera); *muchos forasteros vinieron para la feria del pueblo* a lot of outsiders came to the village fair.

forcejar; forcejear *vi* to struggle, to wrestle (para deshacerse de una sujeción) ‖ to struggle (luchar) ‖ to strive (afanarse).

forcejeo *m* struggle, struggling.

fórceps *m inv* MED forceps.

forense *adj* forensic; *medicina forense* forensic medicine ‖ strange (forastero).
◆ *m* MED forensic surgeon ‖ stranger (forastero).

forero, ra *adj* relative to a «fuero» or privilege, statutory.

forestación *f* AMER reafforestation [US reforestation].

forestal *adj* forest ‖ — *guarda forestal* forester [US forest ranger] ‖ *patrimonio forestal del Estado* State forests *pl* ‖ *repoblación forestal* reafforestation [US reforestation].

forja *f* forge (fragua) ‖ ironworks, foundry (ferrería) ‖ forging (acción y arte de forjar) ‖ mortar (argamasa).

forjado, da *adj* wrought (hierro) ‖ FIG made-up, invented (inventado) | made (hecho) ‖ built-up (ilusiones, etc.).

forjador *m* forger.

forjar *vt* to forge; *forjar en frío* to forge cold ‖ to forge, to make, to form (formar) ‖ FIG to fabricate, to make up (mentiras, una excusa) ‖ to make (un proyecto) | to hatch (un complot) | to build up, to create (sueños, ilusiones, etc.) ‖ — *forjar palabras nuevas* to coin new words ‖ *hierro forjado* wrought iron.
◆ *vpr* to forget o.s.; *forjarse una buena reputación, un porvenir* to forge o.s. a good reputation, a future ‖ *forjarse ilusiones* to build up false hopes.

forma *f* shape; *la forma de un coche, de un edificio* the shape of a car, of a building; *tiene forma redonda* it has a round shape ‖ form; *se publicó en forma de libros* it was published in book form; *forma y fondo* form and substance; *su discurso tomó la forma de una charla amistosa* his speech took the form of a friendly chat ‖ form, manner, method; *forma de pago* form of payment ‖ way; *hay varias formas de decirlo* there are several ways of saying it ‖ way, means (modo); *no hay forma de hacerlo* there is no means of doing it ‖ GRAM & FIL form ‖ JUR form (de un acto o de una sentencia) ‖ mould [US mold], form (horma) ‖ block (de sombrero) ‖ last (de zapatero) ‖ IMPR format (formato) ‖ form (molde) ‖ DEP form ‖ — *dar forma a* to shape (un objeto), to put into shape (una idea), to formulate, to express (expresar) ‖ *de esta forma* in this way ‖ *de forma que* so, so that; *había huelga, de forma que tuvimos que ir a pie* there was a strike, so we had to walk ‖ *de todas formas* anyway, at any rate, in any case ‖ *en debida forma* in due form ‖ *en forma de* -shaped; *en forma de hongo* mushroom-shaped ‖ *es pura forma* it's just for form's sake, it's a mere matter of form ‖ *estar en baja forma, no estar en forma* to be off form ‖ *estar en forma* to be in good form ‖ *estar en plena forma* to be on the top of one's form ‖ *no veo la forma de evitarlo* I see no way of avoiding it ‖ *ponerse en forma* to get fit ‖ REL *sagrada forma* host, consecrated wafer.
◆ *pl* conventions (reglas sociales) ‖ manners (modales); *buenas formas* good manners ‖ figure *sing* (silueta) ‖ *guardar las formas* to keep up appearances.

formación *f* formation; *formación geológica* geological formation ‖ MIL formation; *formación en orden cerrado* close-order formation; *formación de a tres* formation in threes ‖ upbringing (educación) ‖ education (enseñanza); *se recibe una buena formación en ese colegio* they give you a good education at that school; *formación universitaria* university education ‖ training; *formación profesional* vocational training; *centro de formación obrera* workers' training centre.

formal *adj* formal; *requisito, petición formal* formal requisite, request ‖ formal, express (promesa) ‖ FIG reliable, dependable, responsible (persona de fiar) ‖ serious, serious-minded (persona seria); *es una chica muy formal* she is a very serious-minded girl ‖ correct (correcto) ‖ *ser formal* to behave o.s. (niños).

formaldehído *m* QUÍM formaldehyde.

formalidad *f* formality (requisito); *hay que pasar por muchas formalidades para entrar* one must go through a lot of formalities to get in ‖ FIG reliability (confianza, fiabilidad) ‖ seriousness (seriedad) | good behaviour (de los niños) ‖ *hablemos con formalidad* let's talk seriously.

formalina *f* QUÍM formalin, formaline.

formalismo *m* formalism.

formalista *adj* formalistic.
◆ *m/f* formalist.

formalizar *vt* to formalize (hacer formal); *formalizar un noviazgo* to formalize an engagement ‖ to put into proper form, to legalize (dar forma legal); *formalizar un contrato* to put a contract into proper form ‖ to put in order (regularizar una situación, etc.).
◆ *vpr* to become serious ‖ to take offence (ofenderse).

formalote *adj* serious, formal.

formar *vt* to form; *formar un equipo, un círculo* to form a team, a circle ‖ to make; *formar una bola de nieve* to make a snowball ‖ to fashion, to shape; *formar una escultura con barro* to fashion a sculpture out of clay ‖ to form; *formar una frase* to form a sentence ‖ to constitute, to form, to make up; *tres hombres forman el comité de acción* three men make up the action committee; *las ocho provincias que forman Andalucía* the eight provinces forming Andalusia ‖ to build up (reservas) ‖ to make up, to lay (un proyecto) ‖ FIG to bring up (educar) | to educate (enseñar) | to train (entrenar); *formar a los nuevos reclutas* to train the new recruits ‖ to form, to shape (el carácter) ‖ MIL to muster (tropas) ‖ — *formar filas* to fall into line *o* into rank, to fall in (militares), to line up (personas) ‖ *formar parte de* to be *o* to form a part of (algo), to be a member of (ser miembro), to be attached to (depender) ‖ *una mujer bien formada* a well-formed woman.
◆ *vi* MIL to form up, to fall in; *el escuadrón formó en el patio del cuartel* the troop formed up on the parade ground ‖ MIL *¡a formar!* fall in!
◆ *vpr* to form, to be formed; *se formó un círculo, un comité* a circle, a committee was formed ‖ to be trained, to be educated (educarse) ‖ to form; *nubes empezaban a formarse* clouds began to form ‖ to take shape (tomar forma) ‖ to develop; *su estilo se está formando* his style is developing ‖ to form (una opinión) ‖ DEP to line up ‖ MIL to form up, to fall in ‖ — *formarse una idea falsa de* to get the wrong idea about ‖ FAM *¡menudo lío se formó!* it was a right mess!

formateado *m* INFORM formatting.

formatear *vt* INFORM to format.

formativo, va *adj* formative; *los años formativos de la vida* the formative years of life ‖ educational; *una película formativa* an educational film ‖ GRAM formative (sufijo, etc.).

formato *m* IMPR & INFORM format ‖ size (tamaño).

formero *m* ARQ supporting arch (de una bóveda).

formicación *f* MED formication.

fórmico *adj m* QUÍM formic ‖ *aldehído fórmico* formaldehyde, formic aldehyde.

formidable *adj* formidable; *una tarea formidable* a formidable task ‖ enormous, huge, tremendous (muy grande) ‖ marvellous, terrific, wonderful, fantastic (muy bueno) ‖ *¡formidable!* great!

formol *m* QUÍM formol.

formón *m* TECN firmer chisel (herramienta).

Formosa *npr f* GEOGR Formosa.

fórmula *f* formula; *fórmula de cortesía* courtesy formula; *la fórmula para una medicina* the formula for a medicine ‖ method (método) ‖ solution ‖ MAT & QUÍM formula ‖ CULIN recipe ‖ MED prescription (receta) ‖ AUT formula; *coche de fórmula uno* formula one car ‖ — ECON *fórmula de revisión de precios* price review formula ‖ *por fórmula* as a matter of form, for form's sake.

formulación *f* formulation.

formular *vt* to formulate; *formular una teoría* to formulate a theory ‖ to make; *formular quejas, una petición* to make complaints, a request ‖ to express; *formular críticas* to express criticism; *formular un deseo* to express a wish ‖ to ask (una pregunta) ‖ — *formular una reclamación* to make a claim, to put in a claim ‖ *formular votos por* to express one's sincere wishes for.

formulario *m* formulary (reunión de fórmulas) ‖ form; *formulario de inscripción* application form; *llenar un formulario* to fill in a form.

formulismo *m* formulism.

fornicación *f* fornication.

fornicador, ra *m/f* fornicator.

fornicar *vi* to fornicate.

fornido, da *adj* strong, robust, hefty.

fornituras *f pl* MIL cartridge belt *sing*.

foro *m* HIST forum ‖ court of justice, lawcourt (tribunal) ‖ bar (ejercicio de la abogacía) ‖ TEATR back (del escenario) ‖ — *desaparecer por el foro* to disappear into the background.

forofo, fa *m/f* FAM fan, supporter.

forraje *m* fodder, forage; *forraje verde, mixto* green, mixed fodder; *carro de forraje* forage wagon ‖ foraging (acción de forrajear) ‖ FIG & FAM hodgepodge (fárrago).

forrajeador *m* MIL forager.

forrajear *vt/vi* to forage.

forrajero, ra *adj* fodder; *plantas forrajeras* fodder crops.
◆ *f* forage rope *o* net (cuerda o red) ‖ braid (cordón del uniforme).

forrar *vt* to line (interiormente); *forrar un abrigo, un cajón, cortinas con* or *de seda* to line a coat, a drawer, curtains with silk ‖ to cover (exteriormente); *forrar una puerta con* or *de chapas de acero* to cover a door with steel sheets; *forrar un sillón* to cover an armchair ‖ to sheathe (el casco de un barco) ‖ to back [a book] (para protección) ‖ TECN to line, to co-

ver (revestir) || FIG *estar forrado de oro, estar bien forrado* to be rolling in money.
◆ *vpr* FAM to stuff o.s. (with food) (comer mucho) | to feather one's nest (enriquecerse), to line one's pockets (por medios deshonestos).

forro *m* lining; *forro de un vestido, de un armario, de un canal* lining of a dress, of a cupboard, of a canal || cover (funda); *forro de sillón* chair cover || cover (de un libro) || MAR sheathing (del casco) | plating (conjunto de chapas de metal) | planking (conjunto de tablones) || TECN liner (de cilindro, etc.) | lining (revestimiento); *forros de freno* brake linings || — FAM *ni por el forro* not in the slightest, not at all | *no conoce la medicina ni por el forro* he doesn't know the slightest thing about medicine | *no conoce el latín ni por el forro* he doesn't know a word of Latin.

forsythia *f* BOT forsythia.

fortachón, ona *adj* FAM strong, hefty, tough.

fortalecedor, ra *adj* fortifying.

fortalecer* *vt* to fortify, to strengthen (una persona, un lugar) || to give strength, to fortify (dar fortaleza espiritual).
◆ *vpr* to fortify o.s. || to become stronger (una creencia).

fortalecimiento *m* fortification, fortifying (fortificación) || strengthening; *el fortalecimiento de la economía* the strengthening of the economy.

fortaleza *f* strength, vigour [*US* vigor] (de una persona) || fortitude (fuerza moral) || MIL fortress, stronghold (recinto fortificado) || AVIAC *fortaleza volante* flying fortress.

forte *adv m* MÚS forte.
◆ *interj* MAR avast!

fortificación *f* fortification, fortifying (de la salud, un lugar, una posición, etc.) || strengthening (de una construcción).
◆ *pl* fortifications.

fortificante *adj* fortifying.
◆ *m* fortifier, tonic.

fortificar *vt* to fortify; *fortificar la salud, una ciudad* to fortify the health, a town || to strengthen, to fortify (una construcción) || *plaza fortificada* stronghold, fortified town *o* place.
◆ *vpr* to gain strength (fortaleza moral) || to build up one's strength (fortaleza física) | to build fortifications (para defenderse).

fortín *m* MIL small fort | blockhouse, pillbox (emplazamiento para armas) | bunker (refugio).

fortiori (a) *loc adv* a fortiori, all the more.

fortísimo, ma *adj* very strong, extremely strong || MÚS fortissimo.
◆ *adv* MÚS fortissimo.

fortran *m* INFORM FORTRAN [formula translation].

fortuito, ta *adj* fortuitous, chance; *un encuentro fortuito* a chance meeting || *caso fortuito* accidental case, accident (imprevisto), act of God (jurídico).

fortuna *f* fortune, fate, destiny (destino); *la rueda de la fortuna* the wheel of fortune || luck, fortune (suerte); *buena fortuna* good luck; *golpe de fortuna* stroke of luck || fortune (bienes); *fue a América del Sur para hacer fortuna* he went to South America to make his fortune || storm, squall (borrasca) || — MAR *correr fortuna* to weather a storm || *mala fortuna* misfortune || *por fortuna* fortunately, luckily || *probar fortuna* to try one's luck || *tener la fortuna de* to have the good fortune to.

fortunón *m* FAM immense fortune | stroke of luck (suerte).

forúnculo *m* MED boil, furuncle.

forzadamente *adv* forcibly, by force (por fuerza) || forcedly, in a forced way (no naturalmente) || with difficulty (con dificultad) || *sonreír forzadamente* to force a smile.

forzado, da *adj* hard; *trabajos forzados* hard labour || forced; *sonrisa forzada* forced smile || farfetched, contrived (rebuscado); *un chiste forzado* a contrived joke | compulsory (obligatorio) || — MIL *a marcha forzada* by forced march || FIG *a marchas forzadas* in double quick time (acabar algo), at a rapid pace, against the clock (trabajar).
◆ *m* HIST galley slave (galeote).

forzamiento *m* forcing.

forzar* *vt* to force; *forzar una llave* to force a key; *forzar una sonrisa* to force a smile || to force, to oblige, to compel; *forzar a alguien a hacer algo* or *a que haga algo* to force s.o. to do sth. || to force, to pick, to break open (una cerradura, un cajón, etc.) || to break into, to force one's way into (una casa, un edificio) || to break down, to break open, to force (una puerta) || to rape, to ravish (violar a una mujer) || AGR to force || MIL to take by force || — *forzar el paso* to force *o* to quicken one's pace || *forzar la mano a uno* to force s.o.'s hand.
◆ *vpr* to force o.s.

forzosamente *adv* unavoidably, inevitably, inescapably (inevitablemente) || necessarily (necesariamente) || compulsorily (obligatoriamente).

forzoso, sa *adj* unavoidable, inevitable, inescapable (inevitable); *consecuencia forzosa* inevitable consequence || obligatory, compulsory; *la asistencia es forzosa* attendance is obligatory || necessary (necesario) || — *aterrizaje forzoso* forced landing || *es forzoso que* it is inevitable that || *forzoso es reconocer que* one must admit that || *heredero forzoso* heir apparent || *trabajos forzosos* hard labour [*US* hard labor].

forzudo, da *adj* strong, tough.
◆ *m* strong man, tough guy (*fam*).

fosa *f* grave; *fosa común* common grave || pit (hoyo) || ANAT fossa; *fosas nasales* nasal fossae || — *fosa oceánica* ocean deep || *fosa séptica* septic tank.

fosca *f* haze, mist (calina).

fosco, ca *adj* sullen, surly, gruff (hosco) || dark (oscuro).

fosfatado, da *adj* phosphatized.
◆ *m* AGR fertilizing with phosphates, phosphatizing.

fosfatar *vt* to add phosphate to, to phosphatize || AGR to fertilize with phosphates, to phosphatize.

fosfático, ca *adj* QUÍM phosphatic.

fosfato *m* QUÍM phosphate; *fosfato de cal* phosphate of lime, calcium phosphate.

fosfeno *m* phosphene.

fosfito *m* QUÍM phosphite.

fosforado, da *adj* phosphoretted, phosphuretted [*US* phosphoreted, phosphureted].

fosforar *vt* to phosphorate.

fosforecer* ; **fosforescer*** *vi* to phosphoresce.

fosforera *f* matchbox || matchbox holder (estuche) || match factory (fábrica).

fosforero, ra *adj* match-manufacturing, match; *industria fosforera* match industry.
◆ *m/f* match seller (vendedor).
◆ *f* matchbox (caja de cerillas).

fosforescencia *f* phosphorescence.

fosforescente *adj* phosphorescent.

fosfórico, ca *adj* QUÍM phosphoric.

fosforismo *m* MED phosphorism.

fósforo *m* QUÍM phosphorus || match (cerilla).

fosforoso, sa *adj* phosphorous.

fosgeno *m* QUÍM phosgene.

fósil *adj/sm* fossil || FIG & FAM fossil (persona).

fosilización *f* fossilization.

fosilizarse *vpr* to fossilize, to become fossilized.

foso *m* ditch, trench (zanja) || hole, pit (hoyo) || fosse, moat (en fortificaciones) || inspection pit (en un garaje) || TEATR pit, below-stage (del escenario) | pit; *foso de orquesta* orchestra pit || DEP pit (de arena) | dugout (emplazamiento del entrenador) || AGR ditch, trench.

fot *m* FÍS phot (unidad de iluminación).

foto *f* photo, photograph; *sacar fotos* to take photos || FÍS phot (fot).

fotocalco *m* photoprint.

fotocoagulación *f* MED photocoagulation.

fotocomponedora *f* phototypesetter, photocomposer.

fotocomponer *vt* to phototypeset, to photocompose.

fotocomposición *f* phototypesetting.

fotoconductor, ra *adj* photoconductive.

fotocontrol *m* photocontrol.

fotocopia *f* photocopy.

fotocopiadora *f* photocopier.

fotocopiar *vt* to photocopy.

fotocromía *f* photochromy (procedimiento), photochrome (prueba).

fotodermatosis *f* MED photodermatosis.

fotoelasticidad *f* FÍS photoelasticity.

fotoelectricidad *f* FÍS photoelectricity.

fotoeléctrico, ca *adj* FÍS photoelectric || — *célula fotoeléctrica* photoelectric cell, photocell || *corriente fotoeléctrica* photocurrent || *tubo fotoeléctrico* phototube.

fotoelectrón *m* FÍS photoelectron.

fotoemisión *f* FÍS photoemission.

fotoforesis *f* FÍS photophoresis.

fotóforo *m* photophore.

fotogénico, ca *adj* photogenic.

fotógeno, na *adj* photogenic.

fotograbado *m* photogravure, photoengraving.

fotograbador *m* photoengraver.

fotograbar *vt* to photoengrave.

fotografía *f* photography; *fotografía aérea* aerial photography || photograph; *sacar una fotografía* to take a photograph || — *fotografía instantánea* snapshot, snap || *sacarse una fotografía* to have one's photograph taken || *sale mal en las fotografías* he doesn't photograph well.

fotografiar *vt* to photograph, to take a photograph of || *máquina de fotografiar* camera.

fotográfico, ca *adj* photographic || *máquina fotográfica* camera.

fotógrafo, fa *m/f* photographer; *fotógrafo callejero* street photographer.

fotograma *m* photogram || CINEM still.

fotogrametría *f* photogrammetry.

fotólisis *f* photolysis.

fotolito *m* photolith, photolitho.

fotolitografía *f* photolithography (procedimiento) || photolitograph (prueba).

fotolitografiar *vt* to photolithograph.

fotolitográfico, ca *adj* photolithographic.

fotoluminescencia *f* FÍS & QUÍM photoluminescence.

fotomatón *m* photographic booth.

fotomecánico, ca *adj* IMPR photomechanical.

◆ *f* process engraving.

fotometría *f* FÍS photometry.

fotométrico, ca *adj* photometric, photometrical.

fotómetro *m* photometer, exposure meter.

fotomicrografía *f* photomicrography (procedimiento), photomicrograph (prueba).

fotomodelo *m* photographic model.

fotomontaje *m* photomontage.

fotón *m* FÍS photon.

fotonovela *f* photo romance.

fotoquímica *f* photochemistry.

fotorrobot *f* Identikit, Photofit picture.

fotosensible *adj* photosensitive.

fotosfera *f* photosphere.

fotosíntesis *f* photosynthesis.

fotostático, ca *adj* photostatic.

fotostato *m* FOT photostat.

fototeca *f* photograh library.

fototerapia *f* MED phototherapy.

fototipia *f* IMPR phototypy.

fototipo, *m* IMPR phototype.

fototipografía *f* IMPR phototypography.

fototropismo *m* BOT phototropism.

fotuto *m* AMER horn, hooter (bocina).

foul *m* DEP foul.

fox terrier *m* fox terrier (perro raposero).

fox trot *m* fox-trot (baile).

foyer *m* TEATR foyer.

frac; fraque *m* dress coat, tails *pl.*
— OBSERV pl *fraques* or *fracs.*

fracasado, da *adj* unsuccessful.
◆ *m/f* failure.

fracasar *vi* to fail, to be unsuccessful; *el ataque fracasó* the attack failed; *las negociaciones fracasaron* the negotiations were unsuccessful || to fall through, to fail (proyectos).

fracaso *m* failure; *el fracaso del experimento* the failure of the experiment; *la obra fue un fracaso* the play was a failure; *sufrir un fracaso* to meet with failure; *como médico es un fracaso* as a doctor he is a failure || — *fracaso amoroso* disappointment in love || *ir a un fracaso* to court failure *o* disaster.

fracción *f* breaking (into pieces), fraction (ant); *la fracción del pan* the breaking of the bread, the fraction of the bread || part, portion, fraction (parte) || faction, group (dentro de un partido) || MAT fraction (quebrado); *fracción continua, decimal, impropia, propia* continued, decimal, improper, proper fraction || QUÍM fraction.

fraccionamiento *m* breaking-up, division || TECN cracking (del petróleo) || QUÍM fractionation.

fraccionar *vt* to break up, to break into pieces, to divide || to fraction, to fractionize (dividir en fracciones) || TECN to crack (petróleo) || QUÍM to fractionate || FIG to divide, to split; *el asunto fraccionó la opinión pública* the affair divided public opinion || QUÍM *destilación fraccionada* fractional distillation.

fraccionario, ria *adj* MAT fractional || *se ruega moneda fraccionaria* please tender the exact fare (rótulo en transportes públicos) || *moneda fraccionaria* small change.

fractura *f* break, fracture (rotura) || GEOL & MED fracture; *fractura concoidea* conchoidal fracture; *fractura complicada, conminuta, en tallo verde* compound, comminuted, greenstick fracture || JUR *robo con fractura* burglary, housebreaking.

fracturar *vt* to fracture, to break; *fracturar el cráneo a uno* to fracture s.o.'s skull || to force (una cerradura).
◆ *vpr* to fracture, to break; *fracturarse la pierna* to break one's leg.

fraga *f* rough ground covered in brambles || BOT raspberry bush (frambueso).

fragancia *f* fragrance.

fragante *adj* fragrant, sweet-smelling || flagrant (flagrante) || *en fragante* in the act, red-handed (en flagrante delito).

fraganti (in) *adv* in the act, red-handed.

fragata *f* MAR frigate || frigate bird (ave).

frágil *adj* fragile, delicate; *un vaso, un mecanismo frágil* a fragile glass, mechanism || FIG delicate, frail, fragile (salud, persona) | weak (memoria) | weak (con poca fortaleza moral).

fragilidad *f* fragility, delicacy (de una cosa) || FIG frailty (de la salud, de una persona) | weakness (debilidad).

fragmentación *f* fragmentation || fragmentation, division (de terrenos).

fragmentar *vt* to fragment || to fragment, to divide up (terrenos).

fragmentario, ria *adj* fragmentary.

fragmento *m* fragment || passage, excerpt (de un discurso) || snatch (de conversación, de canción).

fragor *m* din (estrépito); *en el fragor de la batalla* amid the din of battle || rumble (del trueno) || roar (de la tempestad).

fragoroso, sa *adj* deafening, thunderous.

fragosidad *f* rough ground covered in brambles (terreno lleno de malezas) || roughness, unevenness (del terreno) || thickness, denseness (de la selva).

fragoso, sa *adj* rough, uneven (terreno), brambly (con malezas) || dense (selva) || deafening, thunderous (ruidoso).

fragua *f* forge.

fraguado *m* setting (del cemento).

fraguador, ra *m/f* schemer || — *fraguador de líos* troublemaker || *fraguador de mentiras* liar, story-teller.

fraguar *vt* to forge (hierro) || FIG to fabricate, to concoct (mentiras) | to hatch (complot) | to make, to cause; *fraguar un lío* to cause trouble || *fraguar quimeras* to daydream.
◆ *vi* to set, to harden (cemento).

fraile *m* friar, monk || IMPR friar || — FIG *fraile de misa y olla* ignorant friar || *meterse a fraile* to become a friar.

frailecillo *m* puffin (ave).

frailengo, ga; fraileño, ña *adj* FAM monkish, monk-like.

frailería *f* FAM friars *pl*, monks *pl* | priests *pl* (curas).

frailero, ra; frailesco, ca *adj* FAM monkish, monk-like.

frailuno, na *adj* FAM monkish, monk-like.

framboyán *m* BOT royal poinciana, flamboyant.

frambuesa *f* BOT raspberry.

frambueso *m* BOT raspberry bush.

francachela *f* FAM spread, feast (comilona) | good time, spree, binge (juerga); *estar de francachela* to be on a binge *o* on a spree, to be having a good time.

francés, esa *adj* French || — *a la francesa* in the French way *o* style, French-style || *de habla francesa* French-speaking || FIG & FAM *despedirse a la francesa* to take French leave || *tortilla a la francesa* plain *o* French omelette.
◆ *m* French (idioma); *francés antiguo* old French || Frenchman (hombre) || *los franceses* the French.
◆ *f* Frenchwoman (mujer).

francesada *f* Napoleonic invasion of Spain || typically French turn of phrase *o* action, etc.

francesilla *f* BOT buttercup.

Francia *npr f* GEOGR France.

francio *m* QUÍM francium (elemento).

francisca *f* HIST frankish battle-axe (segur).

Francisca *npr f* Frances.

franciscano, na; francisco, ca *adj/s* Franciscan.

Francisco *npr m* Francis, Frank.

francmasón *m* freemason (masón).

francmasonería *f* freemasonry (masonería).

franco, ca *adj* frank, candid (sincero); *mirada franca* frank looks || open (abierto); *franco con* or *para todos* open with everybody || clear, obvious (patente) || exempt, free (exento); *franco de impuestos* free from taxation, tax-free || free; *puerto franco* free port; *entrada franca* free entry || HIST Frankish || Franco (prefijo que significa *francés*); *franco-belga* Franco-Belgian || — *franco de aduana* duty-free || *franco de gastos* free of expenses || *tener mesa franca* to keep open house.
◆ *m/f* HIST frank.
◆ *m* Frankish (idioma de los francos) || franc (unidad monetaria); *franco belga* Belgian franc.
◆ *adv* free; *franco a bordo* free on board, f. o. b. || — *franco de porte* carriage-paid (transporte), post-paid, postfree (correos) || *franco de porte y embalaje* post and package free.

francoespañol, la *adj* Franco-Spanish.

francófilo, la *adj/s* Francophile.

francófobo, ba *adj/s* francophobe.

francofonía *f* French-speaking countries *pl.*

francófono, na *adj* French-speaking.
◆ *m/f* French-speaking person.

francote, ta *adj* FAM extremely frank *o* open, outspoken, forthright.

francotirador *m* sniper (guerrillero).

franchute, ta *m/f* FAM frog, froggy, Frenchy.

franela *f* flannel (tela).

frangollar *vt* FIG & FAM to hurry over, to scamp, to botch, to bungle, to do carelessly (un trabajo).

frangollo *m* porridge, boiled cereal (trigo cocido) || FIG & FAM scamping, bungling, botching (de un trabajo) | botch, mess, sloppy piece of work (trabajo mal hecho) || AMER sweet made from green bananas (dulce de las Antillas) | swill (comida mal hecha) | hodgepodge, jumble (revoltijo).

frangollón, ona *adj* slapdash, bungling.
◆ *m/f* slapdash *o* careless *o* sloppy worker, bungler.

franja *f* trimming, border (adorno) || fringe (de flecos) || band, stripe (banda) || strip (de tierra) || fringe (de árboles) || FÍS *franja de interferencia* interference fringe.

franjar; franjear *vt* to trim, to border (poner una franja), to fringe (poner flecos).

franqueable *adj* which can be crossed *o* passed, passable, crossable || breachable (barrera) || fordable (río) || surmountable (obstáculo).

franqueadora *adj f* *máquina franqueadora* franking machine.

franqueamiento *m* crossing (de un río, etc.) || surmounting (de obstáculos) || franking, stamping (de carta) || enfranchisement, freeing (de esclavo).

franquear *vt* to free, to clear (desembarazar); *franquear el pasillo, el paso* to clear the corridor, the way || to exempt, to free; *fran-*

quear a uno de un tributo to exempt s.o. from a tax ‖ to cross, to pass *o* to go through *o* across *o* over, to clear; *franquear un puerto, el umbral* to go over a pass, to cross the threshold ‖ to overcome, to surmount (un obstáculo) ‖ to frank, to stamp (una carta) ‖ to free, to enfranchise, to liberate (un esclavo) ‖ to grant (conceder) ‖ — *franquear un río a nado* to swim across a river ‖ *máquina de franquear* franking machine.
◆ *vpr* to unbosom o.s., to open one's heart; *franquearse con un amigo* to unbosom o.s. to a friend.

franqueo *m* franking, stamping (acción de franquear una carta) ‖ postage (cantidad que se paga) ‖ *franqueo concertado* postage paid.

franqueza *f* frankness, candidness (sinceridad); *dispense mi franqueza* pardon my frankness ‖ openness (carácter abierto) ‖ familiarity, intimacy (confianza) ‖ generosity (generosidad) ‖ — *con franqueza* frankly ‖ *tiene bastante franqueza con él para decirle la verdad* he is on intimate enough terms with him to tell him the truth.

franquía *f* MAR searoom ‖ FIG *estar en franquía* to be in the clear.

franquicia *f* exemption (exención); *franquicia aduanera, postal* exemption from customs duty *o* from postal charges.

franquismo *m* Franco's regime, doctrine.

franquista *adj/s* francoist.

fraque *m* → **frac.**

frasco *m* small bottle; *un frasco de agua de Colonia* a small bottle of eau de Cologne ‖ flask (para licor, de laboratorio) ‖ MIL powder flask (para la pólvora) ‖ FAM *¡toma del frasco!* put that in your pipe and smoke it!

frase *f* sentence (oración); *la estructura de la frase* the structure of the sentence ‖ phrase, expression (expresión) ‖ MÚS phrase ‖ — *frase hecha* or *acuñada* set phrase *o* expression ‖ *frase proverbial* proverbial phrase, proverb, saying ‖ FAM *gastar frases* to speak in flowery *o* pretentious language.

frasear *vt/vi* to phrase.

fraseo *m* MÚS phrasing.

fraseología *f* phraseology.

frasquera *f* flask *o* bottle carrier.

fratás *m* trowel (utensilio de albañilería).

fraterna *f* dressing down, lecture (reprensión).

fraternal *adj* fraternal, brotherly.

fraternidad *f* fraternity, brotherhood.

fraternización *f* fraternization.

fraternizar *vi* to fraternize.

fraterno, na *adj* fraternal, brotherly.

fratría *f* HIST phratry.

fratricida *adj* fratricidal.
◆ *m/f* fratricide (persona).

fratricidio *m* fratricide (acto).

fraude *m* fraud; *fraude fiscal* tax fraud ‖ cheating, dishonesty; *ha habido fraude en los exámenes* there has been cheating in the examinations.

fraudulencia *f* fraudulence.

fraudulentamente *adv* fraudulently, by fraud.

fraudulento, ta *adj* fraudulent; *quiebra fraudulenta* fraudulent bankruptcy.

fraustina *f* dummy head (cabeza de madera).

fray *m* brother, friar [only used before names].

frazada *f* blanket (manta).

freático, ca *adj* phreatic ‖ *capa freática* water table, groundwater table.

frecuencia *f* frequency; *la frecuencia de sus visitas* the frequency of his visits ‖ RAD frequency; *baja, alta frecuencia* low, high frequency; *emisora de frecuencia modulada* frequency modulation transmitter ‖ — *con frecuencia* frequently ‖ *con mucha frecuencia* very frequently.

frecuencímetro *m* frequency meter.

frecuentación *f* frequentation, frequenting.

frecuentar *vt* to frequent, to visit frequently ‖ REL *frecuentar los sacramentos* to frequent the sacraments.

frecuentativo, va *adj/sm* GRAM frequentative.

frecuente *adj* frequent ‖ common (corriente).

frecuentemente *adv* frequently, often.

fregadero *m* sink (en la cocina).

fregado *m* washing (del suelo, de los cristales, etc.) ‖ washing up (de la vajilla) ‖ scouring (de las cacerolas) ‖ FIG & FAM rumpus, racket, shindy (alboroto); *¡menudo fregado armaron!* they kicked up a right shindy! | mess (lío); *meterse en un fregado* to get into a mess ‖ — FIG & FAM *lo mismo sirve para un fregado que para un barrido* he is a jack-of-all-trades | *tener un fregado con alguien* to have a row with s.o.
◆ *adj* AMER obstinate, stubborn (obstinado) | annoying (molesto).

fregador, ra *m/f* dishwasher.
◆ *m* sink (fregadero) ‖ dishcloth (estropajo), scouring pad (de aluminio).

fragamiento *m* AMER rub, rubbing (fricción).

fregar* *vt* to rub (frotar) ‖ to scrub (limpiar con cepillo), to scour (con abrasivo, con estropajo metálico); *fregar las cacerolas* to scour the saucepans ‖ to wash up (platos) ‖ to mop, to scrub (el suelo) ‖ AMER to annoy, to bother (fastidiar) ‖ — *agua de fregar* dishwater ‖ *fregar la loza* or *los platos* to do the washing up, to wash the dishes, to wash up.

fregona *f* dishwasher (fregadora) ‖ skivvy (sirvienta) ‖ mop (utensilio).

fregotear *vt* to give a quick wipe.

fregoteo *m* quick wipe.

freidora *f* fryer.

freidura *f* frying.

freiduría *f* fish shop.

freír* *vt* CULIN to fry ‖ FIG & FAM to bother, to exasperate ‖ — FIG *al freír será el reír* he who laughs last laughs longest ‖ FAM *freír a preguntas* to bombard *o* to plague with questions.
◆ *vpr* CULIN to fry ‖ FIG *freírse de calor* to be boiling hot *o* baking hot.
— OBSERV *Freír* has two past participles, the regular (*freído*), and the more common (*frito*) (véase FRITO).

fréjol *m* bean, kidney bean (judía).

frenado; frenaje *m* braking.

frenar *vt* to brake, to apply the brake to ‖ FIG to check, to restrain; *frenar la producción* to check production | to stop, to restrain; *su marido le frena para que no coma demasiado* her husband stops her from eating too much.

frenazo *m* sudden braking ‖ *dar un frenazo* to brake hard, to jam on *o* to slam on the brakes.

frenesí *m* frenzy.

frenético, ca *adj* frenetic, frenzied, frantic ‖ mad, furious, wild (colérico); *ponerse frenético* to go mad.

frenetismo *m* frenzy.

frénico, ca *adj* ANAT phrenic.

frenillo *m* ANAT frenum ‖ — *no tener frenillo en la lengua* to speak one's mind, not to mince one's words ‖ *tener frenillo* to lisp, to be tongue-tied.

freno *m* bit (de caballería) ‖ brake (de coche, etc.); *freno de pedal* foot brake; *freno de tambor, de disco, asistido* drum, disc, power brake; *freno delantero, trasero* front, back brake ‖ FIG check, curb ‖ AMER hunger (hambre) ‖ — *echar los frenos* to brake, to put the brakes on ‖ *freno de mano* handbrake ‖ *poner el freno* to put the brake on ‖ FIG *poner freno a* to curb, to check, to bridle; *este contratiempo puso freno a sus ambiciones* this setback curbed his ambitions ‖ *potencia de freno* brake horsepower ‖ *soltar el freno* to release the brake ‖ FIG & FAM *tascar el freno* to champ at the bit.

frenogástrico, ca *adj* MED phrenogastric.

frenógrafo *m* MED phrenograph.

frenología *f* phrenology.

frenólogo *m* phrenologist.

frente *f* ANAT forehead, brow ‖ FIG head; *con la frente alta* with one's head held high ‖ *frente a frente* face to face ‖ *frente calzada* low forehead.
◆ *m* front (parte delantera de una cosa) ‖ façade, front (fachada de un edificio) ‖ MIL front; *frente de batalla* battle front ‖ MIN face; *frente de corte* working face ‖ front (agrupación política); *frente popular* popular front ‖ GEOGR front (entre dos zonas atmosféricas); *frente frío, cálido* cold, warm front ‖ top, head (de una página); *al frente* at the top ‖ — *al frente* at the head; *al frente de su compañía iba el capitán* the captain was riding at the head of his company; forward; *dos pasos al frente* two steps forward ‖ *atacar de frente* to make a frontal attack | *de frente* forward (no oblicuamente); *entrar de frente y no de lado* to go in forward and not sideways; abreast (uno al lado del otro), head on (en un choque); *los coches chocaron de frente* the cars hit each other head on; resolutely (con determinación) ‖ MIL *¡de frente!, ¡ar!* forward, march! | *de frente en columna de a tres* forward in threes ‖ *en frente* opposite (enfrente) ‖ *en frente de* opposite, facing, in front of ‖ *frente a* as opposed to (en comparación con) ‖ *frente a, frente de* opposite, opposite to, facing (enfrente de), faced with, confronted with (un problema) ‖ *frente por frente* opposite ‖ *hacer frente a* to face, to stand up to ‖ *hacer frente común* to make common cause ‖ *mirar a uno frente a frente* to look s.o. straight in the face ‖ FIG & FAM *no tener dos dedos de frente* to be as thick as two planks ‖ *poner frente a frente* to confront.

fresa *f* BOT strawberry plant, strawberry (planta); *fresa silvestre* wild *o* wood strawberry | strawberry (fruto) ‖ TECN milling cutter (herramienta) | drill (de dentista).

fresado *m* TECN milling.

fresador, ra *m/f* miller, milling-machine operator.
◆ *f* TECN milling machine.

fresal *m* strawberry patch, strawberry field.

fresar *vt* TECN to mill.

fresca *f* fresh *o* cool air; *tomar la fresca* to get some fresh air ‖ cool [of the day, of the evening]; *pasear con la fresca de la tarde* to stroll in the cool of the evening ‖ FIG & FAM home truth (verdad); *decirle cuatro frescas a uno* to tell s.o. a few home truths | cheeky *o* impertinent remark *o* comment (impertinencia); *soltar frescas* to make cheeky remarks | cheeky girl *o* woman (mujer descarada) | brazen *o* shameless woman (mujer liviana).

frescachón, ona *adj* FAM healthy, robust (robusto) | buxom (mujer) | cheeky (descarado) ‖ MAR *viento frescachón* brisk wind.

frescales *m/f inv* FAM cheeky devil *o* monkey.

frescamente *adv* freshly, newly, recently (recientemente) || FIG cheekily, impertinently (descaradamente).

fresco, ca *adj* cool, fresh; *viento fresco* cool wind || fresh; *pescado fresco* fresh fish || newlaid, fresh (huevos) || fresh, new (pan) || cold (agua) || cool (ropa, bebida) || FIG fresh, new (reciente); *noticias frescas* fresh news | fresh; *tez fresca* fresh complexion; *después de una noche de viaje llegó tan fresco* after travelling all night he arrived as fresh as a daisy || FIG & FAM calm, cool, unruffled (sereno); *se quedó tan fresco con la noticia* he was quite unruffled by the news, he remained calm on hearing the news | cheeky, impudent, saucy, fresh (descarado) | shameless (desvergonzado) | thin, light (telas) || — FIG & FAM *está fresco si cree que se lo voy a hacer* he'll be lucky *o* he's got a hope if he thinks I'll do it for him, if he thinks I'll do it for him he's got another think coming | *¡estamos frescos!* we're in a fine pickle *o* in a fine mess! || *hacer fresco* to be chilly *o* cool || *ponerse fresco* to put on light clothes (vestirse ligeramente) || FAM *¡qué fresco!* what a nerve! || FIG *sentirse fresco como una rosa* to feel as fresh as a daisy.
◆ *m* fresh air, cool air; *tomar el fresco* to get some fresh air || cool; *con el fresco de la tarde muchos salen a pasear* a lot of people go out for a stroll in the cool of the evening || ARTES fresco; *pintura al fresco* painting in fresco || FIG fresco; *un vasto fresco histórico* a vast historical fresco || FIG & FAM cheeky *o* impudent person, shameless person || *AMER* cool drink (refresco) || — *al fresco* in the cool, out of the heat; *pon las bebidas al fresco* put the drinks in the cool; in the open air; *comimos al fresco en la terraza* we ate in the open air on the terrace || FIG & FAM *mandar a tomar el fresco* to send packing.

frescor *m* coolness, freshness || ARTES pinkness, freshness (de la carne).

frescote, ta *adj* FIG & FAM healthy, ruddy, radiant with health (saludable) | buxom (mujer) | cheeky (descarado).

frescura *f* coolness, freshness (temperatura); *la frescura del agua* the coolness of the water || freshness (del pan, de los huevos, del rostro, etc.) || FIG & FAM cheek, nerve, sauce; *con mucha frescura me pidió dinero* he had the nerve to ask me for money; *¡qué frescura!* what a nerve!; *¡vaya una frescura que tiene usted!* you've got a cheek! | cheeky *o* impertinent remark *o* comment (impertinencia); *soltar frescuras* to come out with impertinent comments | calmness, calm, coolness (serenidad) || — *con la mayor frescura* with the greatest unconcern || FAM *tomar las cosas con frescura* to take things calmly *o* without batting an eyelid.

fresneda *f* ash grove (bosque de fresnos).

fresnillo *m* BOT fraxinella.

fresno *m* BOT ash, ash tree.

fresón *m* BOT strawberry.

fresquera *f* meat safe, food safe.

fresquería *f* *AMER* refreshment bar.

fresquero, ra *m/f* fresh-fish seller, fishmonger.

fresquete; fresquito, ta *adj* chilly.

freudiano, na *adj/s* Freudian.

freza *f* dung (estiércol) || spawn (huevos de los peces) || spawning (desove) || spawning season (período del desove) || hole made by an animal.

frezar *vi* to dung (evacuar excrementos los animales) || to spawn (los peces) || to root (hozar).

friabilidad *f* friability.

friable *adj* friable.

frialdad *f* coldness (de la temperatura) || FIG indifference, coldness (indiferencia); *la frialdad del público* the indifference of the audience | coldness; *la frialdad de su estilo, de su tono* the coldness of his style, of his tone | coldness, coolness (desapego) || MED frigidity (sexual) || FIG *recibir a alguien con frialdad* to receive s.o. coldly *o* cooly, to give s.o. a cool reception.

fríamente *adv* coldly, cooly || *recibir a uno fríamente* to receive s.o. coldly *o* cooly, to gibe s.o. a cool reception.

Friburgo *n pr* GEOGR Freiburg.

fricandó *m* CULIN fricandeau.

fricativo, va *adj/s f* GRAM fricative.

fricción *f* rub, rubbing (friega) || massage (masaje); *darse una fricción en el cuero cabelludo* to give o.s. a scalp massage || TECN friction (roce) || FIG friction, trouble, discord; *fricción entre varios grupos étnicos* friction between different ethnic groups.

friccionar *vt* to rub (frotar) || to massage (dar masajes).

friega *f* rub, rubbing || MED massage || *AMER* beating, thrashing (zurra) || *dar friegas* to massage.

friegaplatos *m/f inv* dishwasher.

Frigia *npr f* GEOGR Phrygia.

frigider; friyider *m* *AMER* fridge (nevera).

frigidez *f* coldness, frigidity || MED frigidity.

frígido, da *adj* cold, frigid || MED frigid.

frigio, gia *adj/s* Phrygian; *gorro frigio* cap of liberty, Phrygian cap.

frigoría *f* FÍS kilocalorie.

frigorificación *f* refrigeration.

frigorífico, ca *adj* refrigerating; *mezcla, máquina frigorífica* refrigerating mixture, machine || refrigerator; *vagón, camión frigorífico* refrigerator car, lorry || — *armario frigorífico* refrigerator || *cámara frigorífica* cold-storage room.
◆ *m* refrigerator, fridge (*fam*) (doméstico) || cold-storage room (cámara) || cold-storage plant (establecimiento industrial).

frigorista *m* refrigerating engineer.

frigorizar *vt* to refrigerate.

fríjol; frijol *m* *AMER* bean, kidney bean.
◆ *pl* *AMER* boasting *sing*, bragging *sing* (fanfarronería).

frijón *m* bean, kidney bean.

frío, a *adj* cold; *una comida fría* a cold meal; *un día frío* a cold day || FIG cold (carente de sensibilidad) | cold, cool, unfriendly; *un recibimiento frío* a cold reception | indifferent, cold (falto de entusiasmo) | cold, detached, objective (desapasionado) | cold (sereno) | cold (lejos de la cosa buscada) | cold (muerto) | frigid (poco amoroso) || ARTES cold (colores) || — FIG *dejar frío* to leave cold (dejar indiferente), to dumbfound (dejar pasmado) || *guerra fría* cold war || FIG *más frío que el hielo* as cold as ice | *quedarse frío como el mármol* to be left cold (indiferente), to be dumbfounded (pasmado).
◆ *n* cold || — *coger frío* to catch cold || *en frío* cold, when cold; dispassionately (desapasionadamente) || FIG *esto no me da ni frío ni calor* it's all the same to me, it leaves me quite cold *o* indifferent || *hace mucho frío* it is very cold || FAM *hace un frío que pela* or *un frío de perros* it is freezing cold, it is icy || *¡qué frío!* isn't it cold! || *pasar* or *tener frío* to be cold || *tener mucho frío* to be very cold.

friolera *f* trifle, trinket, bauble (cosa de poco valor) || *la moto le costó la friolera de mil libras* the motorbike cost him a mere thousand pounds (irónico).

friolero, ra *adj* sensitive to the cold, chilly.

frisa *f* frieze (tela) || fraise (en fortificaciones).

frisadora *f* friezing machine.

frisar *vt* to frieze, to frizz (los tejidos) || to seal, to pack (las junturas).
◆ *vt/vi* to be getting on for, to be close on; *frisa (en) los ochenta años* he is getting on for eighty.

Frisia *npr f* GEOGR Friesland.

frisio, sia *adj/s* Frisian (de Frisia) || *islas Frisias* Frisian Islands.

friso *m* ARQ frieze.

frita *f* TECN frit.

fritada *f* fried dish, fry || *fritada de tomates* fried tomatoes.

fritado; fritaje *m* TECN fritting.

fritanga *f* fried dish, fry (fritura) || greasy mess (fritura mala).

fritar *vt* TECN to frit (sinterizar).

frito, ta *adj* fried; *huevos fritos* fried eggs || — FAM *estar frito* to be exasperated (exasperado), to be fed up (harto), to be done for (perdido) | *estar frito de calor* to be baking hot *o* boiling hot | *estar frito por hacer algo* to be dying to do sth. | *me tiene* or *me trae frito con sus preguntas* I'm sick to death of *o* sick and tired of him and his questions || *patatas fritas* chips [*US* French fries] || FAM *quedarse frito* to fall asleep, to nod off (dormirse).
◆ *m* fried dish, fry (fritura).

fritura *f* fried dish, fry || RAD crackling (ruido) || *fritura de sesos* fried brains.

frivolidad *f* frivolity.

frívolo, la *adj* frivolous.

friyider *m* *AMER* ⟶ **frigider.**

fronda *f* frond (hoja), foliage, leaves *pl* (follaje).
◆ *pl* foliage *sing*, leaves (follaje).

Fronda *npr f* HIST Fronde.

frondosidad *f* leafiness (cualidad de frondoso) || luxuriance (de la vegetación) || foliage, leaves *pl* (follaje).

frondoso, sa *adj* leafy (árbol) || luxuriant (vegetación) || close, thick (bosque).

frontal *adj* ANAT frontal.
◆ *m* frontal (de altar) || ANAT frontal bone || *AMER* browband, headband (del caballo).

frontalera *f* browband, headband (del caballo) || yoke pad (de los bueyes).

frontalero, ra *adj* frontier (fronterizo).

frontera *f* frontier, border (de un Estado) || FIG limit, bounds *pl*; *no hay frontera para su generosidad* there is no limit to his generosity, his generosity knows no bounds | borderland (área sin límites precisos) || *sus ademanes están en la frontera de lo ridículo* his gestures border on the ridiculous.

fronterizo, za *adj* frontier, border; *ciudad fronteriza* frontier town || opposite (colocado enfrente) || *España y Portugal son fronterizos* Portugal borders on Spain, Portugal has a common border with Spain.

frontero, ra *adj* opposite, facing; *casa frontera a la mía* house facing mine.
◆ *adv* opposite; *frontero a la iglesia* opposite the church.

frontis *m* ⟶ **frontispicio.**

frontispicio *m* ARQ façade, ornamental front (fachada) | pediment, frontispiece (frontón) || frontispiece (de libro).

frontón *m* ARQ pediment, fronton ‖ DEP pelota court | wall of a pelota court (pared) ‖ cliff (en la costa).

frotación *f* rubbing, rub ‖ TECN friction.

frotar *vt* to rub ‖ to strike (una cerilla).
◆ *vpr* to rub ‖ *frotarse las manos* to rub one's hands.

frote *m* rub, rubbing.

fructífero, ra *adj* BOT fructiferous, fruit-bearing ‖ FIG fruitful; *un viaje fructífero* a fruitful trip.

fructificación *f* fructification.

fructificar *vi* to fructify, to bear fruit ‖ FIG to be productive *o* fruitful.

fructosa *f* QUÍM fructose.

fructuoso, sa *adj* fruitful (fructífero).

frufrú *m* frou-frou.

frugal *adj* frugal; *una comida, una vida frugal* a frugal meal, life.

frugalidad *f* frugality.

frugívoro, ra *adj* frugivorous, fructivorous, fruit-eating; *animales frugívoros* frugivorous animals.

fruición *f* enjoyment, pleasure, delight ‖ *hacer algo con fruición* to enjoy doing sth. (disfrutar), to do sth. with great pleasure (hacerlo con gusto).

frumentario, ria; frumenticio, cia *adj* frumentaceous.

frunce *m* gather, shirr (pliegue) ‖ gathers *pl*, gathering (arrugas en la tela) ‖ *con frunces* gathered, shirred.

fruncido, da *adj* gathered, shirred; *una falda fruncida* a gathered skirt ‖ wrinkled (arrugado) ‖ *con el ceño fruncido* frowning.
◆ *m* gathers *pl*, gathering, shirrs *pl*, shirring (de una tela) ‖ wrinkling (del entrecejo) ‖ pursing, puckering (de los labios).

fruncimiento *m* gathering, shirring (de vestidos) ‖ pursing, puckering (de los labios) ‖ *fruncimiento del entrecejo* frown.

fruncir *vt* to gather, to shirr; *fruncir una tela* to gather a fabric ‖ to purse, to pucker (los labios) ‖ *fruncir el entrecejo* or *el ceño* to frown, to knit one's brow.

fruslería *f* trifle, trinket (chuchería) ‖ titbit, sweet [*US* piece of candy] (golosina) ‖ triviality, silly thing (tontería) ‖ mere nothing (nadería).

frustración *f* frustration.

frustrado, da *adj* frustrated, thwarted; *frustradas sus esperanzas* his hopes frustrated ‖ unsuccessful; *un golpe de estado frustrado* an unsuccessful coup d'état ‖ — *es un escritor frustrado* as a writer he is a failure ‖ *sentirse frustrado* to feel frustrated (insatisfecho), to be disappointed (defraudado).

frustrar *vt* to frustrate, to thwart ‖ to disappoint (defraudar); *quedar frustrado* to be disappointed.
◆ *vpr* to fail, to come to nothing (fracasar); *su intento se ha frustrado* his attempt has failed ‖ to be frustrated; *sus esperanzas se frustraron* his hopes were frustrated.

fruta *f* fruit; *la pera es una fruta sabrosa* the pear is a delicious fruit; *no como nunca fruta* I never eat fruit ‖ FIG fruit ‖ *AMER* apricot (albaricoque) ‖ — *fruta bomba* papaya, papaw (papaya) ‖ *fruta de la pasión* passion-fruit ‖ *fruta del tiempo* fresh fruit, fruit in season (fruta de la temporada), seasonal feature (cosa propia de una época) ‖ *fruta de sartén* fritter ‖ *fruta escarchada* candied fruit ‖ FIG *fruta prohibida* forbidden fruit ‖ *frutas confitadas* comfits [*US* preserved fruit] ‖ *fruta seca* dried fruit ‖ *fruta temprana* early fruit.

— OBSERV The word *fruta* is used for the edible fruits such as pears, cherries, strawberries, etc. In the singular form it can signify fruit in general: *a mí me gusta la fruta* I like fruit, I am fond of fruit.

— OBSERV La palabra *fruit* se puede aplicar al conjunto de las frutas.

frutal *adj* fruit; *árboles frutales* fruit trees.
◆ *m* fruit tree (árbol).

frutería *f* fruiterer's.

frutero, ra *adj* fruit; *industria frutera* fruit industry ‖ *plato frutero* fruit dish, fruit bowl.
◆ *m/f* fruiterer (vendedor de fruta).
◆ *m* fruit dish, fruit bowl (recipiente).

frutilla *f* *AMER* strawberry (fresa).

frutillar *m* *AMER* strawberry patch, strawberry field.

fruto *m* fruit; *frutos carnosos, secos* fleshy, dry fruits ‖ FIG fruit; *los frutos del trabajo, de una mala educación* the fruits of one's work, of a bad upbringing | fruit, produce *inv*; *el fruto de la tierra* the fruit of the land | offspring, child (hijo) | profit, benefit (beneficio); *sacar fruto de* to derive benefit from | result; *el trabajo no ha dado ningún fruto* the work hasn't given any result ‖ — *dar fruto* to bear fruit, to fruit (plantas), to bear fruit, to be fruitful (ser provechoso) ‖ REL *el fruto de tu vientre* the fruit of thy womb | *fruto prohibido* forbidden fruit ‖ JUR *frutos civiles* unearned income ‖ *frutos industriales* earnings ‖ FIG *no dar fruto* to be fruitless | *por el fruto se conoce el árbol* the tree is known by its fruit | *sacar fruto de algo* to derive benefit from sth., to profit from sth. | *sin fruto* fruitless; *trabajo sin fruto* fruitless work; fruitlessly; *trabajar sin fruto* to work fruitlessly | *trabajar con fruto* to work successfully *o* profitably.

— OBSERV *Fruto* is a botanical term referring to the large reproductive body of a seed plant.

FSLN *abrev de Frente Sandinista de Liberación Nacional* FSLN, Nicaraguan Liberation Front.

ftaleína *f* QUÍM phthalein.

fu *m* hiss [noise made by an angry cat] ‖ — *¡fu!* ugh! (repugnancia), huh!, phooey! (desprecio) ‖ *hacer fu a* to snub, to give the cold shoulder to (a personas), to pooh-pooh (a cosas) ‖ *ni fu ni fa* so-so.

fucilar *vi* POÉT to fulgurate, to flash (fulgurar).

fucilazo *m* POÉT flash of sheet lightning.

fuco *m* BOT fucus.

fucsia *f* BOT fuchsia (arbusto).

fucsina *f* QUÍM fuchsine, fuchsin.

fuego *m* fire; *encender un fuego de leña* to light a wood fire; *apagar el fuego* to put out the fire; *atizó el fuego* he poked the fire ‖ fire (incendio); *hay fuego en el pueblo* there is a fire in the town ‖ light (lumbre); *¿tiene usted fuego, por favor?* have you got a light, please? ‖ burner, ring (de cocina de gas) ‖ home (hogar); *una aldea de diez fuegos* a village with ten homes ‖ MIL fire (de arma de fuego); *abrir fuego contra* to open fire on; *estar bajo el fuego* to be under fire ‖ MAR beacon ‖ MED rash (erupción) ‖ FIG ardour, zeal; *trabajar con fuego* to work with zeal | fire, passion (pasión) | heat; *en el fuego de la discusión* in the heat of the discussion ‖ — *a fuego lento* on a low flame (en cocina), slowly (lentamente) ‖ *a fuego y sangre* mercilessly ‖ *¡alto el fuego!* cease fire!, cease firing! ‖ MIL *apagar los fuegos* to silence the enemy guns ‖ *arma de fuego* firearm ‖ FIG *atizar el fuego de la discordia* to stir up discord ‖ CULIN *cocer a fuego lento* to cook on a low flame, to cook slowly *o* gently (gas, electricidad) | *cocer a fuego vivo* to cook quickly (electricidad), to cook on a high flame (gas) ‖ FIG *echaba fuego por los ojos* he was looking daggers, his eyes glared | *echar leña al fuego* to add fuel to the fire | *estar entre dos fuegos* to be between two fires, to be caught in a cross fire ‖ *¡fuego!* fire! ‖ *fuego a discreción* fire at will ‖ *fuego cruzado* cross fire ‖ *fuego de campamento* campfire ‖ *fuego de San Telmo* Saint Elmo's fire, corposant ‖ *fuego fatuo* will-o'-the-wisp, Jack-o'-lantern ‖ MIL *fuego graneado* running fire ‖ *fuego griego* Greek fire ‖ MIL *fuego nutrido* heavy fire | *fuego por descarga* volley ‖ *fuegos artificiales* fireworks ‖ MIL *hacer fuego* to fire (*sobre* at, on) ‖ CULIN *hervir a fuego lento* to simmer ‖ FIG *jugar con fuego* to play with fire | *mantener el fuego sagrado* to keep enthusiasm alive ‖ *marcar a fuego* to brand (reses) ‖ FIG *matar a fuego lento* to torture to death | *meter fuego* to add spice (animar) ‖ *meter* or *pegar* or *prender fuego a* to set on fire, to set fire to ‖ FIG *poner las manos en el fuego por* to stake one's life on ‖ *prueba del fuego* trial by fire ‖ MIL *romper fuego* to open fire ‖ *tocar a fuego* to ring the fire alarm.

fueguero *m* *AMER* pyrotechnist.

fueguino, na *adj/s* Fuegian [of Tierra del Fuego].

fuel; fuel-oil *m* fuel oil ‖ *calefacción por fuel-oil* oil-fired central heating.

fuelle *m* bellows *pl* (de órgano, para el fuego, de máquina fotográfica, de acordeón, etc.) ‖ accordion pleats *pl* (en la ropa, un bolso, una cartera) ‖ folding hood, folding top (de carruaje) ‖ bag (de gaita) ‖ connecting corridor (de tren) ‖ FIG & FAM telltale (soplón) ‖ FIG *tener mucho fuelle* to have good wind.

fuente *f* fountain; *una fuente monumental* a monumental fountain ‖ drinking fountain (para beber) ‖ spring (manantial); *una fuente cristalina* a clear spring ‖ dish, serving dish [*US* platter] (plato grande y su contenido); *una fuente de verduras* a dish of vegetables ‖ source (de un río) ‖ FIG source; *fuente de divisas, de suministro, de infección* source of foreign currency, supply, infection | origin ‖ MED exutory (exutorio) ‖ — FIG *beber en buenas fuentes* to have a reliable source of information, to be well-informed | *de fuente desconocida* from an unknown source | *de fuentes bien informadas* or *fidedignas* from reliable sources ‖ *fuente bautismal* baptismal font ‖ *fuente de horno* ovenproof *o* fireproof dish [*US* ovenproof platter].
◆ *adj/sf* INFORM source.

fuer *m* ⟶ **fuero** ‖ *a fuer de* as a; *a fuer de hombre honrado* as an honest man.

fuera *adv* out; *echar fuera a alguien* to throw s.o. out; *cenar fuera* to dine out ‖ outside; *la calma reina en el país pero no fuera* calmness reigns in our country but not outside ‖ abroad (en el extranjero) ‖ — *aquí fuera, allí fuera* out here, out there ‖ *con la lengua fuera* with one's tongue hanging out ‖ *de fuera* outside, outer ‖ *desde fuera* from (the) outside (desde el exterior), from abroad (desde el extranjero) ‖ DEP *el equipo de fuera* the away team ‖ *estar fuera* to be away from home, to be away (de viaje), to be out (haber salido), to be abroad *o* out of the country (en otro país), to be out (en deporte) ‖ DEP *estar fuera de juego* to be offside (persona), to be out (of the court) (pelota), to be out of play (el balón en fútbol, en rugby) ‖ *estar fuera de sí* to be beside o.s. ‖ *esto está fuera de la cuestión* this is irrelevant ‖ *esto está fuera de lo común* or *de lo corriente* this is unusual *o* out of the ordinary ‖ *esto está fuera de su competencia* that does not come within his province, that is outside his scope ‖ *¡fuera!* out!, get out!, go away! ‖ *fuera de* outside of, outside; *vivo fuera de la ciudad* I live outside the city; out of; *fuera del contexto* out of context; except for, besides, apart from (exceptuando); *fuera de ti, no conozco a nadie aquí* except for you I don't know anybody here;

besides, as well as (además de) || *fuera de alcance* out of reach, beyond one's reach || *¡fuera de aquí!* get out of here!, out of here!, away from here! || *fuera de casa* away from home || JUR *fuera de causa* irrelevant || *fuera de combate* out of action; knocked out (en boxeo) || *fuera de concurso* not competing || *fuera de duda* beyond doubt || *fuera de esto* besides this, in addition to this || *fuera de lo normal* out of the ordinary, unusual || *fuera de lugar* out of place, inappropriate; *su observación está fuera de lugar* his comment is out of place || *fuera de moda* out of fashion || *fuera de peligro* out of danger || *fuera de propósito* irrelevant, beside the point || *fuera de que* besides the fact that, apart from the fact that || *fuera de serie* out of the ordinary, unusual || *ir fuera* to go out || *jugar fuera* to play away (un equipo) || *lámina fuera de texto* plate || *persona fuera de la ley* outlaw || *por fuera* outside (exteriormente), on the outside (en apariencia) || FIG *poner fuera de sí* to drive crazy.

fuera borda; fuera bordo *m inv* MAR outboard (motor, canoa).

fuero *m* JUR law [special law in a certain region, city] | «fuero», code of laws (compilación de leyes) | privilege (privilegio) | jurisdiction || — *a fuero* according to regional law and custom || *en mi, tu, su fuero interno* or *interior* in my, your, his heart of hearts; deep down.
◆ *pl* FAM arrogance *sing*, conceit *sing* || — *fueros municipales* municipal code of laws || *no tenga tantos fueros* don't put on such airs.

fuerte *adj* strong; *un hombre fuerte* a strong man || strong (olor, viento, bebida) || loud (voz, ruido) || strong, resistant; *una tela muy fuerte* a very strong fabric || intense (calor, frío, color) || heavy (abundante); *una fuerte nevada* a heavy snowfall || strong; *una nación fuerte* a strong nation || heavy; *un golpe fuerte* a heavy blow || strong (moneda) || high (fiebre) || severe; *un fuerte resfriado* a severe chill || great (dolor) || strong; *nudo fuerte* strong knot || hard (duro) || great, large; *una fuerte cantidad de dinero* a great sum of money || heavy, big (comida) || important (importante) || FIG good, well up; *estar fuerte en latín* to be good at *o* well up in Latin | strong (palabras) | risqué (chiste) || — *fuerte como un roble* or *un toro* as strong as an ox || *hacerse fuerte en* to entrench o.s. on *o* in (fortificarse), to remain firm in (mantener su actitud) || *plato fuerte* main course (manjar), main attraction (atracción principal) || *plaza fuerte* stronghold || *precio fuerte* full price.
◆ *m* strong; *proteger al débil contra el fuerte* to protect the weak from the strong || MIL fort, fortress, stronghold || FIG strong point, forte; *la música es su fuerte* music is his forte.
◆ *adv* hard; *jugar, trabajar, pegar, apretar fuerte* to play, to work, to hit, to squeeze hard || heavily; *beber fuerte* to drink heavily || loudly; *hablar fuerte* to speak loudly || — *comer fuerte* to eat a lot, to eat too much || *¡más fuerte!* speak up, louder (a un orador).

fuertemente *adv* strongly || loudly; *hablar fuertemente* to speak loudly.

fuerza *f* strength; *la fuerza de un atleta* the strength of an athlete || force; *recurrir a la fuerza* to resort to force || power; *la fuerza de una máquina* the power of a machine || strength; *la fuerza de un ácido* the strength of an acid || resistance (resistencia) || FÍS force; *fuerza centrífuga, electromotriz* centrifugal, electromotive force; *fuerza de gravedad, de inercia* force of gravity, of inertia | power; *fuerza motriz* motive power; *fuerza hidráulica* water power | energy (energía) | power (electricidad) || FIG force, strength; *la fuerza de un argumento* the force of an argument | strength, force (de carácter) || — FAM *a éste se le va la fuerza por la boca* he is all words and no action || *a fuerza de* by dint of, by force of; *ha llegado a fuerza de trabajo* he has arrived by dint of hard work; by means of; *hace sus traducciones a fuerza de diccionarios* he does his translations by means of dictionaries || *a la fuerza* of necessity, perforce (por necesidad); *tiene que pasar por aquí a la fuerza* he has to pass here of necessity; by force, forcibly; *tuvieron que hacerle entrar en la cárcel a la fuerza* they had to get him into prison by force; compulsively (por obligación) || FIG *a la fuerza ahorcan* I (*o* you *o* he, etc.) have no choice *o* alternative || *a viva fuerza* by main *o* sheer force || JUR *caso de fuerza mayor* case of dire necessity (necesidad) || *con todas sus fuerzas* with all of one's energy, with all one's might || *de grado o por fuerza* willy-nilly || *es fuerza confesarlo* one must admit *o* confess || *es fuerza hacerlo* it's necessary to do it || *fuerza bruta* brute force || *fuerza de disuasión* or *disuasoria* deterrent || *fuerza de la costumbre* force of habit || *fuerza de sustentación* lift (de un avión) || JUR *fuerza mayor* force majeure, act of God || *fuerza pública* police force || *hacer fuerza sobre* or *a uno para que* to put pressure on s.o. to || *la fuerza de la edad* the prime of life || *la fuerza de la sangre* the call of blood || *por fuerza* by force, forcibly (usando la fuerza), of necessity, perforce (necesariamente).
◆ *pl* MIL forces; *las fuerzas españolas* the Spanish forces || strength *sing* (de una persona); *recobrar fuerzas* to regain *o* to recover strength || *fuerzas aéreas* Air Force *sing* || *fuerzas armadas* armed forces || *fuerzas terrestres* land forces || *las fuerzas del orden* the forces of law and order || *restar fuerzas a* to weaken || *sacar fuerzas de flaqueza* to muster up one's courage, to take one's courage in both hands || *sacar fuerzas para* to find the energy to || *sentirse con fuerzas para* to feel up to || *tener fuerzas para* to have the strength to, to be strong enough to.

fuete *m* AMER whip (látigo).

fuga *f* flight; *poner en fuga* to put to flight; *darse a la fuga* to take (to) flight || escape (evasión) || elopement (de un hombre y una mujer) || leak (de gas, etc.) || MÚS fugue || FIG flight; *fuga de capitales* flight of capital | ardour (impetuosidad) || — FIG *fuga de cerebros* brain drain || *ponerse en fuga* to flee, to take (to) flight.

fugacidad *f* fugacity.

fugarse *vpr* to escape, to flee; *fugarse de la cárcel* to escape from jail || to run away; *fugarse de casa* to run away from home || to elope (un hombre y una mujer).

fugaz *adj* fleeting, brief, transient, fugacious (p us) || *estrella fugaz* shooting star.

fugitivo, va *adj* fugitive, fleeing (que se fuga) || fleeting, brief, transient, fugacious (p us) fleeting, brief, transient, fugacious (fugaz) || fugitive (efímero).
◆ *m/f* fugitive, runaway.

fuguillas *m/f inv* FAM fidget.

fuina *f* ZOOL stone *o* beech marten (garduña).

ful *adj* FAM bogus, sham, phony (cosa) | phony (persona) | phony, sham (fiesta, recepción).

fulano, na *m/f* so-and-so, what's his name; *he visto a Fulano* I have seen what's his name || — *Don Fulano de Tal* John Smith, Mr. So-and-So, Mr. what's his name || *ese fulano* that fellow || *Fulano, Mengano y Zutano* Tom, Dick and Harry || *una fulana* a whore, a tart (prostituta) || *un fulano* a fellow.

fular *m* foulard (tela y pañuelo para el cuello).

fulastre; fulastrón, ona *adj* FAM rotten (malo) | bungling (chapucero) | slapdash, shoddy (mal hecho) | poor-quality, shoddy (de poca calidad).
◆ *m/f* bungler.

fulcro *m* TECN fulcrum (de la palanca).

fulero *adj* bungling.
◆ *m/f* bungler.

fulgente; fúlgido, da *adj* brilliant, resplendent.

fulgir *vi* to shine, to glow (brillar) || to glitter, to sparkle (centellear).

fulgor *m* brilliance, shine, glow (brillo) || glitter, sparkle (centelleo) || FIG splendour.

fulguración *f* brilliance, flash || fulguration (p us).

fulgurante *adj* flashing, shining, fulgurant, brilliant (luz) || withering (mirada).

fulgurar *vi* to flash (intermitentemente) || to shine, to glow (brillar) || to glitter, to sparkle (centellear).

fúlica *f* coot (ave).

fulmicotón *m* guncotton (algodón pólvora).

fulminación *f* fulmination (explosión) || lightning stroke (por el rayo).

fulminado, da *adj* struck by lightning.

fulminante *adj* fulminating; *pólvora fulminante* fulminating powder || MED fulminant; *apoplejía fulminante* fulminant apoplexy || FIG stagg ring (éxito) || FIG *mirada fulminante* withering look.
◆ *m* fuse, detonator (mecha) || cap (cápsula).

fulminar *vt* to strike by lightning (matar por el rayo) || to hurl (bomba) || FIG to thunder forth, to fulminate (excomuniones, amenazas) | to strike down; *fulminado por la enfermedad* struck down by illness || — FIG *fulminar con la mirada* to cast a withering look at, to look daggers at || *morir fulminado* to be struck by lightning.
◆ *vi* to explode, to fulminate.

full *m* full house (en el póker).

fullear *vi* to cheat (en los naipes).

fullerear *vi* AMER to gabble (farfullar) || to swank (presumir).

fullería *f* cardsharping, cheating (naipes) || trick (trampa) || guile (astucia) || *hacer fullerías* to cheat.

fullero, ra *adj* cheating, crooked.
◆ *m/f* cardsharper [*US* cardsharp], cheat.

fumable *adj* smokable || FIG & FAM acceptable.

fumada *f* puff (de humo).

fumadero *m* smoking room || smoking den (de opio, etc.).

fumador, ra *adj* smoking.
◆ *m/f* smoker; *fumador pasivo* passive smoker.

fumante *adj* QUÍM fuming.

fumar *vt/vi* to smoke; *fumar en pipa* to smoke a pipe || — FAM *fumar como una chimenea* to smoke like a chimney || *papel de fumar* cigarette paper || *se prohíbe fumar* no smoking.
◆ *vpr* to smoke; *fumarse un pitillo* to smoke a cigarette || FAM to squander (gastar); *fumarse la paga del mes* to squander one's monthly salary | *fumarse una clase* to skip a class (escuela), to skip a lecture (universidad).

fumarada *f* puff of smoke (de humo) || pipeful, pipe (de tabaco).

fumarola *f* fumarole.

fumigación *f* fumigation.

fumigador *m* fumigator.

fumigar *vt* to fumigate.

fumigatorio, ria *adj* fumigatory.
◆ *m* perfume brazier.

fumígeno, na *adj* smoking, smoke-producing.

fumista *m* stove *o* heater repairman ‖ AMER joker (bromista).

fumistería *f* stove *o* heater shop (tienda) ‖ stove *o* heater repairing (oficio).

funambulesco, ca *adj* relating to ropedancing.

funámbulo, la *m/f* tightrope walker, ropewalker, ropedancer, funambulist.

función *f* function; *la función de la fuerza pública* the function of the police force ‖ duty, function; *desempeñar las funciones de secretario* to carry out secretarial duties ‖ ANAT function; *funciones del corazón* functions of the heart ‖ TEATR performance, show (espectáculo) ‖ REL religious ceremony, function ‖ party (fiesta) ‖ MAT & QUÍM & GRAM function ‖ FAM scene; *armar una función* to make a scene ‖ — *en función de* in terms of ‖ *entrar en funciones* to take office, to take up one's duties ‖ *estar en funciones* to be in office ‖ *función benéfica* charity performance ‖ *función de gala* or *de etiqueta* gala performance ‖ *función de la tarde* matinée ‖ *función de noche* late performance ‖ *no hay función* no performance (teatro, espectáculos, etc.) ‖ *presidente en funciones* acting president.

funcional *adj* functional.

funcionamiento *m* functioning ‖ TECN operation, working, running (de motor, de máquina) | performance (cualidades técnicas) ‖ — *mal funcionamiento* malfunction ‖ *poner en funcionamiento* to put into operation.

funcionar *vi* to operate, to run, to work, to function; *esta máquina funciona bien* this machine operates well ‖ — *hacer funcionar* to operate, to work, to run | *no funciona* out of order (teléfono, ascensor, etc.).

funcionario, ria *m/f* civil servant, official, functionary; *funcionario público* public official.

funda *f* cover (de tela, de plástico) ‖ case, slip (de almohadón, etc.) ‖ case (de violín, gafas, fusil) ‖ sheath (de puñal, espada, cable) ‖ cover (de un paraguas) ‖ — *funda de almohada* pillowcase, pillowslip ‖ *funda de arzón* (saddle) holster.

fundación *f* foundation.

fundacional *adj* constituent; *acta fundacional* constituent act.

fundadamente *adv* with good reason.

fundado, da *adj* founded, well-founded, justified.

fundador, ra *m/f* founder ‖ *miembro fundador* foundation member [US charter member].

fundamentación *f* foundation.

fundamental *adj* fundamental.

fundamentalmente *adv* fundamentally, basically.

fundamentar *vt* to found, to establish (establecer) ‖ to lay the foundations of (sentar las bases de) ‖ to base, to found (*en* on).
◆ *vpr* to be based, to be founded; *esto se fundamenta en principios sólidos* this is based on sound principles.

fundamento *m* foundation (de un edificio) ‖ FIG foundation, basis, grounds *pl* (base) | reason (razón) | reliability (confianza) | seriousness (seriedad) ‖ *sin fundamento* unfounded, groundless.

fundar *vt* to found (edificar) ‖ to set up, to establish (crear) ‖ FIG to found, to base; *fundar sus sospechas en* to base one's suspicions on.
◆ *vpr* to be based, to rest (estribar); *el arco se funda en los pilares* the arch rests on the pillars ‖ FIG to be based, to be founded (fundamentarse) | to base one's opinion; *¿en qué te fundas para decir esto?* what do you base your opinion on?

fundente *adj* melting.
◆ *m* flux.

fundición *f* melting (acción de fundir) ‖ smelting, casting (de los metales) ‖ cast iron (hierro colado) ‖ foundry, smelting works (lugar donde se funde) ‖ IMPR fount, font (de letras) ‖ TECN *fundición de acero* steelworks.

fundido *m* CINEM fade-in; fade-out.

fundidor *m* founder, smelter, caster (obrero).

fundir *vt* to found, to cast (campana, cañón) ‖ to smelt; *fundir hierro* to smelt iron ‖ to melt (plomo, nieve) ‖ to cast (vaciar una estatua) ‖ to blend (colores) ‖ to merge, to amalgamate (fusionar) ‖ to unite, to join (unir) ‖ ELECTR to fuse (una bombilla, etc.).
◆ *vpr* to melt (volverse líquido) ‖ to merge, to amalgamate (unirse) ‖ to seize up (una biela) ‖ to go, to burn out (bombilla) ‖ to blow, to burn out (fusible) ‖ to blend (colores) ‖ AMER FAM to be ruined, to ruin o.s. (arruinarse).

fundo *m* JUR piece of real estate, country estate (finca rústica).

fúnebre *adj* funeral; *canto fúnebre* funeral chant ‖ FIG mournful, gloomy, funereal (triste) ‖ — *coche fúnebre* hearse ‖ *pompas fúnebres* funeral (ceremonia), undertaker's, funeral director's (funeraria).

funeral *adj* funeral.
◆ *m* memorial service (en el aniversario) ‖ funeral (entierro).
◆ *pl* funeral *sing* (exequias).

funerala (a la) *loc adv* with reversed arms, with arms inverted (fusiles) ‖ FAM *ojo a la funerala* black eye, shiner.

funerario, ria *adj* funerary.
◆ *f* undertaker's [US funeral parlor].
◆ *m* undertaker [US mortician].

funesto, ta *adj* fatal, ill-fated; *un día funesto* a fatal day ‖ fatal, unfortunate; *una batalla funesta* a fatal battle ‖ disastrous, fatal; *consejo funesto* disastrous advice ‖ baneful; *influencia funesta* baneful influence.

fungible *adj* JUR fungible.

fungicida *adj* fungicidal.
◆ *m* fungicide.

fungir *vi* AMER to act.

fungo *m* MED fungus.

fungosidad *f* fungosity.

fungoso, sa *adj* fungous.

funicular *adj/sm* funicular (tren) ‖ *funicular aéreo* cable car (teleférico).

furcia *f* POP tart, whore (prostituta).

furgón *m* van, wagon ‖ luggage van, goods wagon [US boxcar] (de tren) ‖ *furgón de cola* guard's van.

furgoneta *f* van ‖ *furgoneta familiar* station wagon, estate car.

furia *f* fury, rage; *hablar con furia* to speak with fury ‖ violence (violencia) ‖ frenzy (frenesí) ‖ fury; *la furia del mar* the fury of the sea ‖ FIG fury (mujer enfadada) ‖ — AMER *a toda furia* like fury ‖ *estar hecho una furia* to be in a fury *o* rage ‖ *ponerse hecho una furia* to become furious, to fly into a rage.

Furias *npr fpl* MIT Furies.

furibundo, da *adj* furious, enraged; *miradas furibundas* furious looks ‖ *batalla furibunda* furious battle, raging battle.

furiosamente *adv* furiously.

furioso, sa *adj* furious ‖ FIG furious, raging; *viento furioso* furious wind | tremendous, enormous; *un gasto furioso* a tremendous expense ‖ *ponerse furioso* to become *o* to get furious *o* livid.

furor *m* fury, rage; *gritar con furor* to scream with rage ‖ FIG furor, ardour [US ardor]; *el furor de la juventud* the furor of youth | fever; *el furor del juego* gambling fever ‖ — *con furor* madly, ardently ‖ *furor uterino* nymphomania ‖ FIG *hacer furor* to be all the rage.

furriel *m* quartermaster.

furtivo, va *adj* furtive, sly, stealthy; *mirada furtiva* furtive look ‖ — *caza* or *pesca furtiva* poaching ‖ *cazador* or *pescador furtivo* poacher.

furúnculo *m* MED furuncle, boil.

furunculosis *f* MED furunculosis.

fusa *f* MÚS demisemiquaver.

fuselaje *m* AVIAC fuselage.

fusibilidad *f* fusibility.

fusible *adj* fusible.
◆ *m* fuse (electricidad).

fusil *m* gun, rifle ‖ — *echarse el fusil a la cara, encararse el fusil* to aim one's rifle, to put one's rifle to one's shoulder ‖ *fusil ametrallador* automatic rifle ‖ *fusil con alza automática* rifle with automatic sight ‖ *fusil de aguja, de chispa* needle gun, flintlock ‖ *fusil de repetición* repeater, magazine rifle.

fusilamiento *m* execution, shooting ‖ FIG plagiarism (plagio) ‖ *fusilamiento en masa* mass execution.

fusilar *vt* to execute (by shooting), to shoot ‖ FAM to plagiarize (plagiar).

fusilería *f* rifles *pl* (fusiles) ‖ fusiliers *pl* (fusileros) ‖ *descarga* or *fuego de fusilería* fusillade.

fusilero *m* fusilier, fusileer, rifleman.

fusión *f* fusion, melting (de los metales) ‖ melting, thawing (de la nieve) ‖ merger, amalgamation (de sociedades); *fusión por absorción* take-over merger.

fusionamiento *m* merger, amalgamation.

fusionar *vt* to fuse (unir) ‖ COM to merge, to amalgamate (varias sociedades).
◆ *vpr* to fuse ‖ COM to merge, to amalgamate; *los bancos se han fusionado* the banks have merged.

fusta *f* brushwood, twigs *pl* (varas) ‖ riding whip (látigo).

fustán *m* fustian (tela) ‖ AMER white petticoat (enaguas blancas).

fuste *m* shaft (de lanza) ‖ saddletree (de la silla de montar) ‖ ARQ shaft ‖ wood, timber (madera) ‖ FIG importance, consequence; *negocio de poco fuste* business of little importance | substance, essence (fundamento) ‖ *gente de fuste* important people, people of consequence.

fustigación *f* whipping, lashing ‖ FIG sharp reprimand, censure (censura).

fustigar *vt* to whip, to lash ‖ FIG to reprimand sharply, to censure.

fútbol *m* DEP football, soccer ‖ — *fútbol americano* American football ‖ *fútbol sala* indoor *o* five-a-side football.

futbolín *m* table football (juego de mesa).

futbolista *m* footballer, football *o* soccer player.

futbolístico, ca *adj* football; *un torneo futbolístico* a football tournament.

futesa *f* FAM trifle.

fútil *adj* futile, trivial, pointless, trifling; *hablar de cosas fútiles* to talk about futile things.

futileza *f* ⟶ **futilidad**.

futilidad *f* futility, triviality (falta de sustancia); *la futilidad de una conversación* the futility of a conversation ‖ frivolity (de una persona) ‖ worthlessness (inutilidad); *la futilidad del argumento* the worthlessness of the argument ‖ triviality, trifle (cosa insustancial) ‖ *hablar de futilidades* to talk trivia, to talk piffle.

futre *m* AMER FAM dandy, toff, fop.

futura *f* FAM bride-to-be, intended, fiancée (novia).

futurismo *m* futurism.

futurista *adj* futuristic.
◆ *m/f* futurist.

futuro, ra *adj* future ‖ — *en lo futuro* in (the) future ‖ *en los años futuros* in the years to come ‖ *la vida futura* the life to come.
◆ *m* future ‖ FAM intended, fiancé (novio) ‖ — *en un futuro próximo* in the (very) near future ‖ GRAM *futuro imperfecto* future | *futuro perfecto* or *anterior* future perfect.
◆ *pl* COM futures (entregas a plazo).

G

g *f* g; *una g minúscula* a small g.
— OBSERV Followed by *e* or *i*, the *g* is pronounced as the Spanish *j*. Followed by a consonant or *a, o, u* it is similar in sound to the hard English *g*, as in *gun*.

gabacho, cha *adj/s* (French) Pyrenean (montañés de los Pirineos franceses) || FAM frog, froggy, Frenchy.
◆ *adj* feather-legged (paloma).
◆ *m* FAM Frenchified Spanish [language].

gabán *m* overcoat, topcoat.

gabardina *f* gabardine (tela) || gabardine raincoat (impermeable hecho con esta tela) || mac, mackintosh, raincoat (impermeable en general).

gabarra *f* barge, lighter (embarcación).

gabarrero *m* bargee, lighterman [*US* bargeman].

gabarro *m* flaw (defecto de un tejido) || nodule (nódulo) || VET tumour [*US* tumor] (del caballo) | pip (pepita de las gallinas) || FIG error, mistake.

gabazo *m* husks *pl*.

gabela *f* tax, duty (impuesto) || FIG burden || *AMER* advantage (ventaja).

gabinete *m* study (para recibir visitas) || room (sala); *gabinete de lectura* reading room || section (conjunto de salas); *gabinete de historia natural* natural history section || museum (museo) || laboratory (laboratorio) || consulting room (de médico) || boudoir (de una señora) || cabinet (de ministros) || — FIG *estrategas de gabinete* armchair strategists || *gabinete de consulta* consulting room || *gabinete de crisis* emergency cabinet.

gablete *m* ARQ gable.

Gabón *npr m* GEOGR Gabon.

Gabriel, ela *npr m/f* Gabriel, Gabriella.

gabrieles *m pl* FAM chick-peas (garbanzos).

gacela *f* ZOOL gazelle.

gaceta *f* gazette (periódico) || (ant) official gazette [in Spain] || FIG gossip, gossipmonger (correveidile) || TECN sagger || FIG & FAM *mentir más que la gaceta* to lie one's head off (una persona), to be a pack of lies; *este libro miente más que la gaceta* this book is a pack of lies.

gacetero *m* gazette writer, newspaper writer, journalist (periodista).

gacetilla *f* gossip column (noticias sobre personas conocidas) || section of short news items (noticias breves) || FIG gossip, gossipmonger (correveidile).

gacetillero *m* writer of short news items, gossip columnist (escritor de gacetillas) || newshound (reportero).

gacetista *m* FAM avid gazette reader.

gacha *f* porridge, pap (papilla) || FIG paste, mush (masa blanda) || *AMER* bowl, basin.
◆ *pl* porridge *sing*, pap *sing* (papilla) || FAM cajolery *sing*, blandishments || FIG & FAM *hacerse unas gachas* to get mushy.

gaché; gachó *m* name given by Gypsies to Andalusians || FAM bloke, guy, fellow; *un gachó poco recomendable* not a very recommendable bloke.

gacheta *f* TECN spring catch (de cerradura).

gachí *f* FAM bird, chick (mujer, muchacha).
— OBSERV pl *gachís*.

gacho, cha *adj* bowed (la cabeza) || drooping (orejas de un animal); *el cócker tiene las orejas gachas* the cocker spaniel has drooping ears || downturned (cuerno) || with downturned horns (buey o vaca) || which tends to hold its head too low (caballo) || — *a gachas* on all fours || *sombrero gacho* slouch hat || FIG & FAM *volver con las orejas gachas* to return with one's tail between one's legs.

gachó *m* → **gaché.**

gachón, ona *adj* FAM sweet, charming, nice (atractivo) | spoilt, spoiled (mimado).
◆ *f* FAM bird, chick (mujer).
◆ *m pl* blokes, guys, fellows (gachós).

gachumbo *m* *AMER* shell (cáscara del coco).

gachupín *m* *AMER* Spanish immigrant [living in South America] | Spaniard (español).

gádido, da *adj/sm* gadid, gadoid.

gaditano, na *adj* Gaditan, of *o* from Cádiz.
◆ *m/f* Gaditan, native *o* inhabitant of Cádiz.

gadolinio *m* gadolinium (metal).

gaélico, ca *adj* Gaelic (céltico).
◆ *m/f* Gael.
◆ *m* Gaelic (lengua).

gafa *f* MAR hook (garfio) || clamp (grapa).
◆ *pl* glasses, spectacles (anteojos); *llevar gafas de oro* to wear gold-framed spectacles; *calarse las gafas* to put on one's glasses || goggles (submarinas, de motorista) || — *gafas bifocales* bifocals, bifocal spectacles || *gafas de sol* sunglasses.

gafar *vt* to hook, to seize with a hook (con un gancho), to grasp with the nails (con las uñas), to grasp with the claws (un animal) || MAR to hook || FAM to bring (s.o.) bad luck, to bring bad luck upon, to jinx (a una persona) | to bring bad luck upon, to jinx; *gafar las cartas a alguien* to jinx s.o.'s cards.

gafe *m* FAM jinx || FAM *ser gafe* to be a jinx, to bring *o* to be bad luck (para otras personas), to be jinxed, to have bad luck (para sí mismo).

gafedad *f* claw hand || leprosy causing claw hand (lepra).

gafete *m* hook and eye.

gafo, fa *adj* claw-handed || leprous (leproso) || *AMER* footsore (caballerías).

gag *m* comic situation, gag (situación cómica).

gaita *f* MÚS bagpipes *pl*, bagpipe (gallega), Breton bagpipes *pl*, Breton pipes *pl* (en Bretaña) | flageolet [type of chirimía] (flauta) | hurdy-gurdy (zanfonía) || FIG & FAM neck (pescuezo); *estirar la gaita* to crane one's neck | nuisance, drag, bother; *es una gaita tener que escribir esta carta* it's a nuisance having to write this letter | job, right game; *aparcar allí es una gaita* it's a right game parking there || — *alegre como una gaita* as happy as a lark, chirpy as a cricket || FAM *no me vengas con gaitas* don't bother me with all that | *templar gaitas* to pour oil on troubled waters, to smooth things out.

gaitero, ra *adj* FAM gaudy, loud, flashy (vestido) | buffoonish, clownish (bufo).
◆ *m/f* buffoon, clown (bufo) || MÚS bagpiper, piper.

gajes *m pl* emoluments, remuneration *sing* (salario) || FAM *los gajes del oficio* the occupational hazards.

gajo *m* branch, broken-off branch (rama) || small bunch *o* cluster (de frutas) || segment (de naranja, de limón) || prong, tine (de horcas, de bieldos, etc.).

gal *m* FÍS gal (unidad de aceleración).

gala *f* best clothes *pl*, Sunday best (vestido) || elegance, grace, poise, gracefulness (garbo) || flower, jewel, pride; *la gala del pueblo* the flower of the village || cream, flower; *la gala de la sociedad* the cream of society || *AMER* tip (propina) || — MIL *con traje* or *uniforme de gala* in full-dress uniform, in dress uniform, in ceremonial dress, in full regimentals || *estar en traje de gala* to be in full dress || *función, baile de gala* gala performance, gala ball || *hacer gala de* to glory in, to take pride in (gloriarse), to make a show of, to show off; *hacer gala de sus riquezas* to make a show of one's wealth; to show, to display; *hacer gala de una gran habilidad* to show great skill || *la ciudad está de gala* the town is bedecked (adornada) || *tener a gala* to pride o.s. on; *tiene a gala hacerlo todo por sí mismo* he prides himself on doing it all by himself.
◆ *pl* finery *sing*, regalia (vestidos), jewellery *sing* (joyas), decorations, regalia (condecoraciones) || wedding presents (regalos de boda) || *galas de novia* bridal attire.

galáctico, ca *adj* ASTR galactic.

galactómetro *m* lactometer.

galactosa *f* QUÍM galactose.

galatita *f* galalith.

galaico, ca *adj* Galician (gallego).

galán *m* gallant, beau (galante), lover (enamorado) || suitor (pretendiente) || handsome man, handsome young man (apuesto, bien parecido) || TEATR leading man, lead || — BOT *galán de día, de noche* day, night jasmine || TEATR *galán joven* juvenile lead [*US* juvenile] | *segundo galán* second lead.

galancete *m* handsome young man || TEATR juvenile lead [*US* juvenile].

galanía *f* elegance (galanura).

galano, na *adj* smartly-dressed, smart, spruce (bien vestido) || elegant, nicely-turned (frase), elegant, polished (estilo) || good-looking (de hermoso aspecto) || *AMER* mottled (una vaca).

galante *adj* gallant [attentive to women] || polite (cortés) || flirtatious, fond of male attention (que gusta de galanteos), loose, licentious (de costumbres licenciosas).

galantear *vt* to pay compliments to, to say flattering *o* nice things to (requebrar) || to flirt with (coquetear) || to court, to woo (cortejar).

galanteo *m* flattery (requiebro) || flirting, flirtation (coqueteo) || courting, wooing (cortejo).

galantería *f* gallantry (caballerosidad) || politeness (cortesía) || gallantry, compliment (expresión obsequiosa), gallant deed, act of gallantry (hecho) || elegance (elegancia) || generosity (generosidad).

galantina *f* CULIN galantine.

galanura *f* elegance (de estilo, de concepto) || gracefulness, elegance (al andar) || *vestir con galanura* to dress elegantly.

galapagar *m* place full of turtles.

galápago *m* turtle (tortuga) || MIL testudo, tortoise || slade, sole (del arado) || TECN ingot, pig (lingote) | tile mould (para tejas) || MED bandage (vendaje) || light saddle (silla de montar) || VET grease *o* greasy heel (úlcera del caballo) || MAR cleat.

Galápagos (islas) *f pl* GEOGR Galápagos Islands.

galardón *m* reward.

galardonado, da *adj* (who has been) rewarded || prizewinning, who has won a prize.
◆ *m/f* prizewinner.

galardonar *vt* to reward (recompensar) || to award a prize to; *ha sido galardonado por su novela* he has been awarded a prize for his novel || *galardonar con una medalla* to award a medal to.

galaxia *f* ASTR galaxy.

galbana *f* FAM laziness, sloth, slackness (pereza).

galdosiano, na *adj* of Pérez Galdós.

galeaza *f* MAR galleass, galliass.

galena *f* MIN galena, lead sulphide [*US* lead sulfide].

galeno, na *adj* MAR gentle, soft (viento).
◆ *m* FAM quack [*US* medic] (médico).

galeón *m* MAR galleon (barco).

galeota *f* galliot (barco).

galeote *m* galley slave (forzado).

galeoto *m* pimp, procurer (alcahuete).
— OBSERV This word, taken from a play by Echegaray, *El Gran Galeoto,* has no connection with *galeote.*

galera *f* MAR galley || four-wheeled covered wagon (carro) || ward (crujía de hospital) || women's prison (cárcel) || MAT two perpendicular lines separating divisor from dividend in a division || IMPR galley | galley, galley proof (prueba) || MIN crucible furnace || ZOOL squilla || *AMER* top hat (sombrero) | shed (cobertizo).
◆ *pl* galleys (condena); *condenar a galeras* to condemn to the galleys.

galerada *f* wagonload (carga) || IMPR galley, galley proof (prueba).

galería *f* gallery (en una casa, de pinturas, de mina, militar) || TEATR gallery (localidades, público) || MAR stern gallery (de popa) || pelmet, valance (para cortinajes) || FIG gallery; *para la galería* to the gallery || — *galería comercial* shopping arcade, shopping center || *galería de tiro* shooting gallery.

galerín *m* IMPR small galley.

galerna *f* MAR strong north-west wind (viento).

galerón *m* *AMER* shed (cobertizo) | popular song and dance [in Venezuela].

Gales *n pr* GEOGR Wales || *el País de Gales* Wales.

galés, esa *adj* Welsh.
◆ *m/f* Welshman (hombre), Welshwoman (mujer).
◆ *m* Welsh (lengua) || *los galeses* the Welsh.

galga *f* boulder (piedra) || strap (cinta del zapato) || millstone (del molino) || MED rash (erupción cutánea) || TECN hub brake [which presses on waggon axle] (freno) | gauge (calibrador).

galgo, ga *m/f* ZOOL greyhound (perro) || — FIG *correr como un galgo* to run like a hare | *de casta le viene al galgo el ser rabilargo* like father, like son || FAM *¡échale un galgo!* some hopes!
◆ *adj* *AMER* sweet-toothed (goloso).

Galia *npr f* HIST Gaul.

galibar *vt* MAR to trace (using a template).

gálibo *m* TECN gauge (galga) || MAR template, templet, pattern || ARQ perfect proportion.

galicado, da *adj* full of Gallicisms, gallicized.

galicanismo *m* Gallicanism.

galicano, na *adj* Gallic (de los galos) || Gallican (adepto al galicanismo).

Galicia *npr f* GEOGR Galicia [Spain].

galicismo *m* Gallicism.

galicista *adj* fond of using Gallicisms.
◆ *m/f* lover of Gallicisms, person fond of using Gallicisms.

gálico, ca *adj* Gallic (de los galos) || QUÍM gallic.
◆ *m* MED syphilis.

Galilea *npr f* GEOGR Galilee.

galileo, a *adj/s* Galilean (de Galilea).

galillo *m* ANAT uvula.

galimatías *m* FAM gibberish, nonsense.

galio *m* gallium (metal).

galiparla *f* language full of Gallicisms.

galiparlista *m/f* person who uses many Gallicisms.

galipote *m* MAR galipot, gallipot.

Galitzia *npr f* GEOGR Galicia (Polonia).

galo, la *adj* HIST Gallic.
◆ *m/f* Gaul.

galocha *f* wooden *o* iron clog (calzado).

galón *m* braid (cinta) || MIL stripe || gallon (medida).

galonear *vt* to trim with braid, to braid.

galonista *m* outstanding pupil in a military academy.

galop *m* galop (baile) || *bailar el galop* to galop.

galopada *f* gallop.

galopante *adj* galloping || MED galloping.

galopar *vi* to gallop.

galope *m* gallop; *galope sostenido, medio galope* hand gallop || — *a* or *de galope* at a gallop (un caballo), quickly, speedily, in a rush (muy rápidamente) || *a galope tendido* at full gallop (un caballo), at full speed, with utmost haste (muy rápidamente) || *ir a* or *de galope* to gallop.

galopear *vi* to gallop (galopar).

galopín *m* ragamuffin, urchin (niño) || rogue (bribón) || MAR ship's boy, cabin boy.

galorromano, na *adj* Gallo-Roman.

galpón *m* *AMER* shed (cobertizo) | (ant) slaves' quarters *pl* on a «hacienda».

galucha *f* *AMER* gallop (galope).

galuchar *vi* *AMER* to gallop (galopar).

galvánico, ca *adj* FÍS galvanic.

galvanismo *m* FÍS galvanism.

galvanización *f* FÍS galvanization.

galvanizar *vt* FÍS to galvanize || FIG to galvanize.

galvano *m* electrotype.

galvanocauterio *m* MED galvanocautery.

galvanómetro *m* FÍS galvanometer.

galvanoplastia *f* galvanoplasty, galvanoplastics.

galvanoplástico, ca *adj* galvanoplastic.

galvanotipar *vt* to electrotype.

galvanotipia *f* electrotyping.

galladura *f* cicatricle (del huevo).

gallarda *f* galliard (danza) || IMPR brevier (carácter).

gallardamente *adv* elegantly, gracefully (airosamente) || gallantly, valiantly, bravely (con valentía) || nobly (con nobleza).

gallardear *vi* to strut (pavonearse).

gallardete *m* pennant.

gallardía *f* elegance, poise, gracefulness (bizarría) || gallantry, valour, bravery (valor) || nobleness (nobleza).

gallardo, da *adj* elegant, charming, debonair (airoso) || gallant, valiant, brave (valeroso) || noble (noble) || FIG excellent (excelente).

gallareta *f* ZOOL coot.

gallarón *m* ZOOL little bustard (sisón).

gallear *vt* to tread (el gallo).
◆ *vi* FIG & FAM to show off (presumir) | to brag (fanfarronear) | to strut (pavonearse) || TECN to flaw [on cooling] (metales).

gallegada *f* word *o* phrase *o* action typical of a Galician || Galician dance (baile).

gallego, ga *adj/s* Galician (de Galicia).
◆ *m* Galician (lengua) || *AMER* Dago (español).

galleguismo *m* Galician word *o* expression *o* idiom.

galleo *m* TECN flaw (de un metal fundido) || TAUR swerve [of the body to avoid the bull's horns] || FIG showing off (presunción) | bragging (jactancia).

gallera; gallería *f* *AMER* cockpit, cockfight arena.

galleta *f* CULIN biscuit (bizcocho) | ship's biscuit, hardtack (de marinero) || FAM slap (bofetada) || nuts *pl* (carbón) || *AMER* recipient for drinking maté | brown bread (pan) || *AMER* FAM *colgar la galleta* to sack, to fire (despedir).

gallina *f* hen, chicken (ave) || — FIG *acostarse con las gallinas* to go to bed early || *caldo de gallina* chicken broth || FIG *dar con la gallina que pone los huevos de oro* to find the goose that lays the golden eggs | *en casa de Gonzalo más puede la gallina que el gallo* the wife wears the trousers in that house | *estar como gallina en corral ajeno* to be like a fish out of water | *gallina ciega* blindman's buff (juego) || *gallina clueca* broody hen || *gallina de agua* coot (foja), moorhen (polla de agua) || *gallina de Guinea* Guinea fowl || *gallina de río* coot || *gallina ponedora* layer, laying hen || *gallina sorda* woodcock || FIG *gallina vieja da buen caldo* there's many a good tune played on an old fiddle | *matar la gallina de los huevos de oro* to kill the goose that lays the golden eggs.
◆ *m/f* FIG & FAM coward, chicken || *es un gallina* he wouldn't say boo to a goose.

gallináceo, a *adj* ZOOL gallinaceous.
◆ *f* gallinacean.
◆ *pl* gallinaceae.

gallinaza *f* turkey buzzard (gallinazo) || hen droppings *pl* (estiércol).

gallinazo *m* turkey buzzard (buitre de América).

gallinería *f* hens *pl* (conjunto de gallinas) || poultry shop (tienda) || FIG cowardice (cobardía).

gallinero *m* henhouse, henroost, coop (recinto para aves de corral) ‖ poulterer, poultry dealer (vendedor de gallinas) ‖ hen basket, poultry basket (cesto para transportar) ‖ TEATR gods *pl* ‖ FIG madhouse (sitio ruidoso) ‖— FIG & FAM *dejar a uno como palo de gallinero* to drag s.o. through the mud | *estar más sucio que el palo de un gallinero* to be filthy *o* dirty.

gallineta *f* ZOOL coot (fúlica) | woodcock (chocha) ‖ *AMER* Guinea fowl (pintada).

gallito *m* ZOOL cockerel, young cock ‖ *AMER* cock of the rock (gallito de roca) | dart (rehilete) ‖— FIG *gallito del pueblo* cock of the walk ‖ *gallito del rey* wrasse (budión).

gallo *m* ZOOL cock, rooster (ave) | John dory, dory (pez) ‖ FIG & FAM squawk (nota falsa); *soltar un gallo* to let out a squawk | boss (el que manda) | cock of the walk (persona mandona) | cocky person (presumido, bravucón) ‖ POP spit, phlegm (esputo) ‖— FAM *alzar el gallo* to get on one's high horse | *en menos que canta un gallo* in a flash, before you can say Jack Robinson ‖ *entre gallos y media noche* at an unearthly time ‖ *gallo de monte, gallo silvestre* cock of the wood, capercaillie (urogallo) ‖ FIG *gallo de pueblo* cock of the walk ‖ *gallo de riña* or *de pelea* gamecock, fighting cock ‖ *gallo de roca* cock of the rock ‖ *misa del gallo* midnight mass ‖ FIG *otro gallo cantara* it would have been quite different ‖ DEP *peso gallo* bantamweight (boxeo) ‖ FAM *ser engreído como gallo de cortijo* to be too big for one's boots ‖ *AMER ser muy gallo* to be very courageous.

gallofero, ra; gallofo, fa *m/f* beggar (pordiosero) ‖ vagabond, tramp (vagabundo).

gallón *m* clod (terrón), piece of turf (de césped) ‖ ARQ ovolo (ornamento).

gallup *m* Gallup poll (sondeo de la opinión pública).

gama *f* ZOOL doe (hembra del gamo) ‖ MÚS scale (escala); *hacer gamas en el piano* to play scales on the piano ‖ FIG range, scale, gamut (serie) ‖ ECON *gama de artículos* range of goods.

gamada *adj f* *cruz gamada* swastika, gammadion, gammation, fylfot.

gamarra *f* martingale (correa).

gamba *f* variety of prawn.

gamberrada *f* act of hooliganism, piece of loutish behaviour ‖ act of vandalism (vandalismo).

gamberrear *vi* to act like a hooligan, to behave loutishly.

gamberrismo *m* hooliganism, vandalism; *ola de gamberrismo* wave of vandalism ‖ libertinism, dissolution (libertinaje).

gamberro, rra *adj* loutish (mal educado, grosero) ‖ vandalistic (vandálico) ‖ rakish, dissolute (libertino).
◆ *m/f* hooligan, lout (golfo) ‖ vandal (vándalo) ‖ libertine (libertino).
◆ *f* tart, whore (ramera).

gambeta *f* cross step (en la danza) ‖ curvet (corveta) ‖ DEP dribble ‖ *AMER* dodge (esguince) | excuse (excusa).

gambetear *vi* to cross-step (en la danza) ‖ to curvet (caballo) ‖ DEP to dribble.

gambeteo *m* DEP dribbling.

Gambia *n pr* GEOGR Gambia.

gambito *m* gambit (en el ajedrez).

gamella *f* half of the yoke [on each ox's neck] ‖ feeding trough (artesa).

gameto *m* BIOL gamete.

gamezno *m* ZOOL fawn (cría del gamo).

gamín *m* *AMER* kid (chiquillo).

gamma *m* gamma (letra griega) ‖ FÍS *rayos gamma* gamma rays.

gamo *m* ZOOL fallow deer, buck ‖ FIG *correr como un gamo* to run like a hare.

gamón *m* BOT asphodel.

gamonal *m* asphodel field ‖ *AMER* cacique, chief.

gamonalismo *m* *AMER* caciquism.

gamopétalo, la *adj* BOT gamopetalous.

gamosépalo, la *adj* BOT gamosepalous.

gamusino *m* imaginary animal [invented by hunters to hoax novices].

gamuza *f* Pyrenean chamois, izard (animal) ‖ chamois (piel) ‖ duster (trapo).

gana *f* desire, wish (deseo); *la gana* or *las ganas de bañarse en el mar* the desire to go for a swim in the sea ‖ longing (vivo deseo) ‖— *como te dé la gana* just as you wish ‖ *de buena gana* with pleasure, willingly (con gusto), willingly (con buena voluntad) ‖ *de buena o mala gana* like it or not ‖ *de mala gana* reluctantly, unwillingly ‖ *AMER es gana* it's impossible, there's no chance ‖ *hace lo que le da la gana* he does just what he likes ‖ *hacer algo con poca gana* to do sth. reluctantly ‖ FAM *lo haré cuando me dé la real gana* I'll do it when I feel like it *o* when I want to ‖ *no me da la gana* I don't feel like it, I don't want to.
◆ *pl* appetite *sing*, hunger *sing* (hambre) ‖— *abrir las ganas a* to give an appetite to, to make hungry ‖ *comer con ganas* to eat heartily ‖ *comer sin ganas* to pick at one's food, to eat without appetite ‖ *darle ganas a uno de* to like to, to feel like; *me dan ganas de bailar* I feel like dancing, I'd like to dance ‖ *ganas locas* wild desire, mad urge ‖ *le dieron ganas de saltar* he felt like leaping about, he could have leaped about ‖ *me dejaron* or *me quedé con las ganas* I had to go without *o* to do without, I just had to forget the idea, I didn't get what I wanted ‖ *morirse de ganas de* to be dying to ‖ *quitar las ganas* to stop (s.o.'s) wanting, to make (s.o.) stop wanting; *el accidente me ha quitado las ganas de comprar un coche* the accident has stopped my wanting to buy a car; to take away *o* to spoil the appetite (quitar el hambre) ‖ *tener ganas de* to be longing to, to want (anhelar, desear); *tengo ganas de verte* I'm longing to see you; to feel like, to fancy (apetecer); *tengo ganas de comer un pastel* I feel like eating a cake; to have a mind to; *tengo ganas de decirle lo que pienso de él* I have a mind to tell him what I think of him ‖ FIG *tenerle ganas a uno* to bear a grudge against s.o. ‖ *tener muchas ganas* or *unas ganas locas de* to really fancy, to really feel like; *tengo unas ganas locas de ir al teatro* I really fancy going to the theatre ‖ *tener pocas ganas de* not to really want to (con infinitivo), not to really feel like (con gerundio).

ganadería *f* cattle raising, stockbreeding (cría del ganado) ‖ stock farm, cattle farm (sitio donde se cría) ‖ strain, breed (raza); *ganadería de toros de lidia* strain of fighting bulls ‖ cattle, livestock (ganado).

ganadero, ra *adj* cattle, cattle-raising, stockbreeding; *región ganadera* cattle-raising region ‖ cattle, livestock (del ganado).
◆ *m/f* cattle raiser, stockbreeder, stock farmer.

ganado *m* cattle, livestock, stock (en general); *ganado en pie* cattle on the hoof; *cabeza de ganado* head of cattle ‖ hive, hiveful (de abejas) ‖ FIG & FAM crowd, people (gente) ‖ — *ganado caballar* horses *pl* ‖ *ganado cabrío* goats *pl* ‖ *ganado de cerda* or *moreno* or *porcino* pigs *pl* ‖ *ganado de engorde* fattening livestock ‖ FIG *ganado humano* (human) chattels (esclavos) ‖ *ganado lanar* sheep ‖ *ganado mayor* bovine cattle, horses and mules ‖ *ganado menor* sheep, goats and pigs ‖ *ganado ovino* sheep ‖ *ganado vacuno* cattle, bovine cattle.

ganador, ra *adj* winning.
◆ *m/f* winner ‖ *jugar a ganador* to bet (on a horse) to win.

ganancia *f* gain, profit (beneficio); *obtener ganancia* to make a profit ‖ *AMER* bonus, extra (adehala) ‖ FAM *no le arriendo la ganancia* I wouldn't like to be in his shoes, rather him than me, I don't envy him.
◆ *pl* earnings; *compré un coche con las ganancias del año pasado* I bought a car on last year's earnings ‖ winnings (en el juego, etc.) ‖ COM *pérdidas y ganancias* profit and loss.

ganancial *adj* JUR *bienes gananciales* acquest, property acquired in married life.

ganapán *m* casual odd-jobber, casual odd-jobman ‖ porter (que lleva cargas) ‖ messenger (recadero).

ganapierde *m* giveaway (juego de damas).

ganar *vt* to earn, to make, to get; *ganar con que vivir* to earn enough to live on; *gana mucho dinero* he earns a lot of money ‖ to win (una apuesta, una batalla, una carrera, un pleito, un premio) ‖ to win, to gain (la estima, la fama) ‖ to beat, to defeat (vencer); *ganar a uno al ajedrez* to beat s.o. at chess ‖ to surpass (superar); *ganar a uno en inteligencia* to surpass s.o. in intelligence ‖ to outstrip (aventajar, adelantar) ‖ to reach, to arrive at (alcanzar); *ganar la meta en segundo lugar* to reach the finish in second position ‖ MIL to take, to capture; *ganar a los romanos la ciudad* to take the city from the Romans ‖ to win over; *ganar a uno para la causa* to win s.o. over to the cause ‖ to get, to obtain, to win; *ganar el apoyo del gobierno* to obtain the support of the government ‖ to reclaim (tierras) ‖— FIG & FAM *¡a idiota no hay quien te gane!* you're a prize idiot! ‖ *ganar el premio gordo* to win the first prize ‖ FIG *ganar la partida a uno, ganarle a uno por la mano* to beat s.o. to it ‖ *ganarle a uno en fuerza* to be stronger than s.o. ‖ *ganar terreno* to gain ground; *con la campaña publicitaria hemos ganado mucho terreno* we have gained a lot of ground with the advertising campaign; to gain, to gain ground; *el corredor ganó terreno a su rival* the runner gained on his rival ‖ *ganar tiempo* to gain time ‖ *le gané cinco libras al póker* I won five pounds from him at poker ‖ *no hay quien le gane a Pedro al ajedrez* Peter has no equal at chess, there's no one to touch Peter at chess ‖ *nunca me dejo ganar por el pesimismo* I never let pessimism get the better of me ‖ *Pedro le gana a Juan estudiando* Peter is a better student than John.
◆ *vi* to improve (mejorar); *ganar en salud* to improve in health ‖ to win (vencer); *ganar por un largo* to win by length ‖ to earn; *ganar bien* to earn well ‖— *gana con el trato* he's quite nice once you get to know him ‖ *ganar en peso* to put on *o* to gain weight ‖ DEP *ir ganando* to lead, to be winning; *ir ganando por tres a uno* to lead *o* to be leading *o* winning three-one ‖ FIG *llevar las de ganar* to hold all the winning cards, to look like a winner | *salir ganando* to come out better off, to come out ahead.
◆ *vpr* to earn; *ganarse la vida* to earn one's living *o* one's livelihood ‖ to earn o.s., to earn; *me gané mil pesetas* I earned myself a thousand pesetas ‖ to deserve (merecer); *se lo ha ganado* he deserved it ‖ to win, to gain, to earn; *ganarse el respeto de todos* to gain everyone's respect ‖ to bring upon o.s., to incur; *ganarse el desprecio general, un castigo* to bring general disdain upon o.s., to incur a punishment ‖— FIG & FAM *ganarse una bofetada* or *una torta* to get a slap in the face ‖ FAM *hay que ganarse el puchero* a man must earn a living | *¡la que se va a ganar!* he's going to cop it! ‖ *¡se lo ha ganado a pulso!* he's earned it!

ganchero *m* raftsman (el que guía los maderos).

ganchete *m* AMER *a medio ganchete* half | *de ganchete* arm in arm | *de medio ganchete* about *o* ready to fall (a punto de caer).

ganchillo *m* crochet hook (aguja de gancho para labores) || crochet, crochet work (labor) || hairpin (horquilla) || — *hacer ganchillo* to crochet.

gancho *m* hook, crook (instrumento corvo) || hook, hanger (para colgar) || hook (de carnicero) || crochet, crochet work (crochet) || crook (cayado) || snag (de una rama que se rompe), stub (rama cortada) || DEP hook (boxeo) || FIG & FAM enticer, coaxer (el que convence a otro) | decoy (asistente de charlatán) | pimp, procurer (alcahuete) | sex appeal, attractiveness; *mujer que tiene gancho* woman who has sex appeal || AMER hairpin (horquilla) | lady's saddle (silla de montar) | help, aid (auxilio) || — FAM *echar el gancho a* to hook | *mujer de gancho* club hostess.

ganchoso, sa; ganchudo, da *adj* hooked.

gándara *f* low wasteland.

gandinga *f* MIN fine washed ore.

gandul, la *adj* FAM good-for-nothing (inútil) | idle, lazy (perezoso).
◆ *m/f* FAM good-for-nothing (inútil) | lazybones (perezoso).

gandulear *vi* to idle, to loaf.

gandulería *f* idleness, laziness.

gandumbas *m inv* FAM lazybones.

gang *m* gang (banda).

ganga *f* ZOOL sandgrouse || FIG & FAM bargain, gift (cosa buena y barata) | cushy *o* soft job (buena situación) || MIN gangue (del mineral) || — *andar a caza de gangas* to go bargain hunting | *aprovechar una ganga* to snap up a bargain (en las rebajas) || *¡menuda ganga!, ¡vaya una ganga!* what a bargain!, it's a giveaway! (cosa buena y barata), what a cushy job! (buena situación) || *precio de ganga* bargain price, giveaway price.

Ganges *npr m* GEOGR Ganges.

ganglio *m* ANAT & MED ganglion.

gangosear *vi* → **ganguear.**

gangoso, sa *adj* nasal (voz) || *hablar gangoso* to speak through one's nose *o* with a twang.

gangrena *f* MED gangrene.

gangrenarse *vpr* MED to gangrene.

gángster *m* gangster (atracador).

gangsterismo *m* gangsterism.

ganguear; gangosear *vi* to speak through one's nose *o* with a twang.

gangueo *m* nasal intonation, nasal accent, twang.

gánguil *m* MAR hopper (draga) | fishing barge (barco de pesca) | sweep net (red).

gansada *f* FAM silly *o* daft thing (hecho y dicho).

gansarón *m* goose (ganso).

gansear *vi* to do *o* to say daft things.

gansería *f* silly *o* daft thing (gansada).

ganso, sa *m/f* goose (hembra), gander (macho) || FIG & FAM goose, simpleton, dope (persona poco inteligente) || — *hablar por boca de ganso* to speak from hearsay || *hacer el ganso* to act the goat || *los gansos del Capitolio* the geese of the Capitol || MIL *paso de ganso* goose step || *ser muy ganso* to be a silly goose, to be as daft as a brush.

Gante *npr m* GEOGR Ghent.

gantés, esa *adj* Ghent, of *o* from Ghent.
◆ *m/f* native *o* inhabitant of Ghent.

ganzúa *f* picklock (garfio) || FIG & FAM picklock, thief (ladrón) | inquisitive person, prying sort (sonsacador) || — *abrir con ganzúa* to pick || *ladrón de ganzúa* picklock, housebreaker.

gañán *m* farmhand (en una hacienda) || FIG & FAM big brute (hombre fuerte y tosco).

gañanía *f* farmhands *pl* (gañanes) || farmhands' quarters *pl* (local).

gañido *m* yelp, yelping (de perro) || caw, cawing, croak, croaking (de aves) || FIG & FAM scream, shriek (chillido) | wheeze (voz ronca).

gañir* *vi* to yelp (aullar) || to caw, to croak (aves) || FIG & FAM to scream, to shriek (chillar) | to croak, to wheeze (con voz ronca).

gañote *m* FAM gullet, throat (garganta) || FAM *de gañote* free, gratis.

garabatear *vi* to sling a hook *o* hooks (para asir con un garabato) || to scribble, to scrawl (garrapatear) || FIG & FAM to beat about the bush (andar con rodeos).
◆ *vt* to scribble, to scrawl (palabras), to scribble on, to scrawl over (hojas, cuartillas, etc.).

garabateo *m* scribbling (acción), scribble, scrawl (escritura) || FIG beating about the bush.

garabato *m* hook (gancho) || meat hook, butcher's hook (de carnicero) || scribble (garrapato, dibujo mal hecho), scrawl, scribble (mala letra) || FIG & FAM attractiveness, sex appeal (en la mujer).
◆ *pl* exaggerated gestures *o* finger movements (ademanes) || scrawl *sing*, scribble *sing* (mala letra).

garaje *m* garage.

garajista *m* garage owner (propietario), garage attendant (encargado).

garambaina *f* frippery (adorno).
◆ *pl* FAM ridiculous grimaces (muecas) | scribble *sing*, scrawl *sing* (garabateo).

garandumba *f* AMER barge, large raft (embarcación) || FIG & FAM big woman (mujer corpulenta).

garante *adj* acting as guarantor, responsible.
◆ *m/f* guarantor, guarantee (fiador).

garantía *f* guarantee, warranty (de la calidad de un objeto) || JUR security, guarantee (fianza) | pledge (de cumplimiento de un contrato) || assurance, guarantee; *la autoridad ha dado garantías de que el orden público no será alterado* the authorities have given their assurance that the peace will not be disturbed || — *certificado de garantía* guarantee, certificate of guarantee || ECON *garantía bancaria* bank guarantee || *garantías constitucionales* constitutional rights.

garantir* *vt* → **garantizar.**

garantizado, da *adj* guaranteed, under guarantee; *garantizado por un año* guaranteed for a year, under a year's guarantee || warranted; *oro de 18 quilates garantizado* warranted 18-carat gold.

garantizar; garantir* *vt* to guarantee, to warrant; *garantizar un reloj por un año* to guarantee a clock for a year || to assure, to guarantee; *le garantizo que es la pura verdad* I assure you it is the honest truth || to act as guarantor for, to vouch for (avalar).

garañón *m* stud jackass (asno) || AMER stallion (semental).

garapiña *f* frozen state (de un líquido) || browning in boiling sugar (de las almendras) | braid (galón) || AMER pineapple-skin drink (bebida).

garapiñado, da *adj* frozen (helado) || *almendra garapiñada* praline.

garapiñar *vt* to freeze (helar) || to brown in boiling sugar (las almendras).

garapullo *m* dart (rehilete) || TAUR banderilla.

garba *f* AGR sheaf (haz de mieses).

garbancero, ra *adj* chick-pea (relativo al garbanzo), suitable for chick-pea growing (terreno, tiempo).

garbanzal *m* chick-pea field.

garbanzo *m* BOT chick-pea || — FIG & FAM *en toda tierra de garbanzos* everywhere, all over the world | *garbanzo negro* black sheep.
◆ *pl* FIG & FAM bread and butter *sing*, daily bread *sing* || FIG & FAM *contar los garbanzos* to count every penny.

garbear *vi* to strut (al andar).
◆ *vpr* FAM to take a stroll, to go for a stroll; *voy a garbearme por el parque* I'm going to go for a stroll in the park | to fend for o.s., to manage, to get along, to get by (componérselas).

garbeo *m* FAM stroll (vuelta); *darse un garbeo* to go for a stroll, to take a stroll | tour, trip (viaje); *me voy a dar un garbeo por España* I'm going to go on a tour of Spain *o* a trip round Spain.

garbillar *vt* to sieve (granos) || to riddle, to screen (minerales).

garbillo *m* esparto sieve (para granos) || riddle, screen (para minerales).

garbo *m* gracefulness, poise, graceful deportment, fine bearing (al andar) || gracefulness and ease, poise, grace (airosidad) || attractiveness (atractivo) || elegance (del estilo) || FIG generosity || *andar con garbo* to walk gracefully.

garbosamente *adv* gracefully (con gracia) || proudly and gracefully (airosamente) || elegantly (con elegancia) || FIG generously (con generosidad).

garboso, sa *adj* graceful (andar), elegant, graceful (persona) || attractive (atractivo) || elegant (estilo) || FIG generous.

garceta *f* ZOOL egret (ave) || antler (mogote del venado) || sidelock (pelo).

gardenal *m* gardenal.

gardenia *f* BOT gardenia.

garden-party *f* garden party.

garduña *f* ZOOL stone marten, beech marten.

garduño *m* FAM sneak thief, pickpocket (ratero).

garete (irse al) *loc* MAR to drift, to go adrift.

garfear *vi* to throw a hook *o* hooks.

garfio *m* hook (gancho) || grapnel, grapple (con varias puntas).

gargajear *vi* to spit [phlegm] (escupir) || to hawk (carraspear).

gargajeo *m* spitting.

gargajo *m* FAM spit, gob.

garganta *f* ANAT throat (exterior), throat, gullet (interior) || FIG instep (del pie) || ARQ neck || GEOGR gorge || groove (de polea) || — *agarrar por la garganta* to seize by the throat || *dolerle a uno la garganta* to have a sore throat || FIG & FAM *lo tengo atravesado en la garganta* he *o* it sticks in my throat *o* in my gullet || FIG *tener* or *atravesársele a uno un nudo en la garganta* to have *o* to feel a lump in one's throat | *tener buena garganta* to have a good voice.

gargantear *vi* to warble [in singing].

garganteo *m* warbling.

gargantilla *f* short necklace (collar).

Gargantúa *npr m* Gargantua.

gárgara *f* gargling, gargle || — *hacer gárgaras* to gargle || FIG & FAM *mandar a uno a hacer gárgaras* to send s.o. packing.

gargarismo *m* gargling, gargle (tratamiento) || gargle (líquido).

gargarizar *vi* to gargle.

gárgol *m* groove.

gárgola *f* ARQ gargoyle || boll [of flax] (baga).

garguero; gargüero *m* throat, gullet, windpipe.

garita *f* box (caseta) || sentry box (de centinela) || porter's lodge (de portero) || watchtower, lookout turret (en un castillo) || lavatory (retrete).

garitero *m* gambling-house keeper (amo) || gambler, frequenter of gambling houses (jugador).

garito *m* gambling den, gambling house, gaming house (casa de juego) || gambling profits *pl*, winnings *pl* (ganancia sacada del juego).

garitón *m* AMER city gate (puerta de la ciudad).

garla *f* FAM chatter, gossip.

garlar *vi* FAM to chatter, to gossip.

garlito *m* fish trap (red de pescar) || FIG & FAM trap (trampa); *caer en el garlito* to fall into the trap.

garlopa *f* TECN jack plane.

garlopín *m* TECN trying plane.

garnacha *f* gown, robe (de magistrado) || judge (juez) || purplish grape (uva roja amoratada), «garnacha» wine (vino) || AMER meat turnover || *gente de garnacha* gentlemen *pl* of the robe.

Garona *npr m* GEOGR Garonne.

garra *f* claw (uña de animal) || talon (de las aves de rapiña) || FIG & FAM claw, paw, hand (de una persona) || MAR hook || AMER hard, wrinkled piece of leather (pedazo de cuero) || — FIG & FAM *caer en las garras de uno* to fall into s.o.'s clutches | *echar la garra a uno* to lay one's hands on s.o.
◆ *pl* rags, tatters (harapos).

garrafa *f* carafe, decanter || demijohn (damajuana).

garrafal *adj* producing large, tasty cherries (cerezo) || FIG & FAM enormous, huge (error), whopping (mentira) || — *cereza garrafal* bigarreau cherry | *una falta garrafal* an enormous blunder.

garrafón *m* large carafe || demijohn (damajuana).

garrapata *f* tick (insecto) || FAM hack, crock (mal caballo).

garrapateador, ra *m/f* scribbler, scrawler.

garrapatear *vi* to scribble, to scrawl.

garrapato *m* scribble, scribbling.
◆ *pl* scrawl *sing*, scribble *sing* (escarabajos).

garrar *vi* MAR to drag, to drag anchor.

garrear *vi* MAR to drag, to drag anchor || AMER to live at s.o. else's expense.
◆ *vt* AMER to steal (robar).

garrete *m* AMER back of the knee (del hombre) | hock (del caballo).

garrido, da *adj* good-looking (mozo), pretty (moza).

garrocha *f* barbed lance, pike (vara) || goad (aguijada) || TAUR pike, lance (en las tientas) || AMER pole; *salto con garrocha* pole vault.

garrochazo *m* TAUR thrust with the lance (golpe) | lance wound (herida).

garrochear *vt* TAUR to weaken (the bull) with the lance.

garrochista *m* TAUR picador || herdsman armed with a goad (en las fincas).

garrotazo *m* cudgel blow, blow with a club *o* stick.

garrote *m* club, cudgel, stick (palo) || garotte, garrotte [US garrote] (ejecución e instrumento), garotting, garrotting [US garroting] (acción de dar garrote) || MED tourniquet || bulge, bulging (pandeo de una pared) || AMER brake (freno) || *dar garrote a* to garotte, to garrotte [US to garrote].

garrotear *vt* AMER to club, to cudgel (apalear).

garrotillo *m* MED croup.

garrotín *m* popular late 19th century Spanish dance.

garrucha *f* pulley (polea).

garrulería *f* garrulity, loquacity (garrulidad) || prattle, chatter (charla).

gárrulo, la *adj* twittering, chirping (aves) || FIG garrulous, talkative, loquacious (hablador) || POÉT babbling, purling (agua); *un arroyo gárrulo* a babbling brook | sighing (viento).

garúa *f* AMER drizzle (llovizna).

garuar *v impers* AMER to drizzle (lloviznar).

garufa *f* AMER FAM spree, binge (juerga).

garujo *m* concrete (hormigón).

garulla *f* loose grapes (uva desgranada) || rascal, scoundrel (granuja, pillo) || FIG & FAM mob, rabble, disorderly crowd (muchedumbre).

garza *f* ZOOL heron (ave) || — *garza imperial* purple heron || *garza real* grey heron [US gray heron].

garzo, za *adj* blue; *ojos garzos* blue eyes || blue-eyed (persona).

garzota *f* ZOOL tufted heron (ave) || aigrette, plume (adorno).

gas *m* FÍS & QUÍM gas; *gas de alumbrado* illuminating *o* coal gas; *gas hilarante, lacrimógeno* laughing, tear gas || AMER petrol [US gas] (gasolina) || — *asfixiar con gas* to gas || *a todo gas* flat out, at full speed; *correr a todo gas* to run flat out || *cámara de gas* gas chamber || *cocina, estufa, hornillo de gas* gas cooker, fire, ring || *contador de gas* gas meter || *gas de agua* water gas || *gas de combate* or *asfixiante* asphyxiating *o* lethal *o* poison gas || *gas de los pantanos* marsh gas || *gas pobre* producer gas || *mechero de gas* gas lighter (encendedor), gas burner (de laboratorio) || FIG *pérdida de gas* loss of speed.
◆ *pl* exhaust *sing*, exhaust fumes (de escape).

gasa *f* gauze (tela) || MED gauze || crêpe, crepe, crape (de luto).

gascón, ona *adj/s* Gascon.

Gascuña *npr f* GEOGR Gascony.

gaseoso, sa *adj* gaseous || aerated, carbonated; *agua gaseosa* aerated water || fizzy (espumoso).
◆ *f* lemonade (bebida).

gasfitería *f* AMER gas fitter's workshop (tienda del gasista) | plumber's workshop (fontanería).

gasfitero *m* AMER gas fitter, gasman (gasista) | plumber (fontanero).

gasificación *f* gasification.

gasificar *vt* to gasify.

gasista *m* gas fitter, gasman (empleado del gas).

gasoducto *m* gas pipeline.

gasógeno *m* gasogene, gazogene (en vehículos).

gas-oil; gasóleo *m* gas oil || diesel oil (para motores diesel).

gasolina *f* QUÍM & AUT petrol [US gas, gasoline, gasolene] || — *gasolina-plomo* high-grade petrol [US high-octane gasoline] || *surtidor de gasolina* petrol pump [US gasoline *o* gas pump], petrol station [US gas station].

gasolinera *f* motorboat (lancha) || petrol station [US gas station] (estación de gasolina).

gasómetro *m* TECN gasometer [US gasholder].

gastado, da *adj* worn (away); *piedras gastadas por las olas* stones worn away by the waves || worn-out, worn-away (neumáticos, telas, madera, metales), worn-out (zapatos, vestidos); *zapatillas gastadas* worn-out slippers || worn-out, broken, weary (personas) || spent; *dinero bien gastado* money well spent || FIG hackneyed, trite (tema) || FIG *gastado por los placeres* pleasure-worn.

gastador, ra *adj* spendthrift, wasteful.
◆ *m/f* spendthrift.
◆ *m* MIL pioneer || convict (en los presidios).

gastamiento *m* wearing away (de piedras), wearing out, wearing away (de neumáticos, madera, telas, metales, etc.), wearing out (de zapatos, de vestidos).

gastar *vt* to spend (dinero) || to expend, to lay out (invertir dinero) || to use, to consume (consumir); *mi coche gasta mucha gasolina* my car uses a lot of petrol || to spend; *gastar el tiempo, las fuerzas* to spend time, effort || to waste (emplear mal o en vano); *gastar palabras* to waste words || to use up (agotar) || to wear away (piedras) || to wear out *o* away (neumáticos, telas, madera, metales, etc.) || to wear out (zapatos, vestidos); *gastó sus pantalones en el tobogán* he wore out his trousers on the helter-skelter || to wear, to have; *gastar bigote, gafas, sombrero* to wear a moustache, glasses, a hat || to have, to run (coche) || — *gastar bromas* to play practical jokes || FAM *gastarlas* to behave, to act; *así las gastas tú* so that's how you behave || *gastar mal humor* to be bad-tempered, to have a bad temper || *gastar saliva* to waste one's breath || *hacer gastar mucha tinta* to cause much ink to flow || *no gastar ni medio* not to spend a penny || FIG & FAM *ya sé cómo las gasta usted* I know what you're like | *ya verá cómo las gasto* you'll see what stuff I'm made of.
◆ *vi* to spend; *a mi mujer le gusta gastar* my wife likes to spend.
◆ *vpr* to wear out (deteriorarse las telas, los zapatos, etc.), to wear away (piedras), to wear out *o* away (neumáticos, madera, metales, etc.) || to run out (agotarse) || to wear o.s. out (arruinarse la salud) || FAM to be worn; *esa clase de peinado ya no se gasta* that kind of hairstyle isn't worn any more.

gasterópodos *m pl* ZOOL gasteropods.

gasto *m* expense, expenditure, expenses *pl*, outlay (cantidad de dinero que se gasta); *el gasto diario* daily expenses || spending, expenditure (acción de gastar); *gasto de dinero, de energía* spending of money, of energy || FÍS output, volume of flow (de agua, electricidad, gas, etc.) || consumption (consumo); *elevado gasto de gasolina* high petrol consumption || — *con poco gasto* at little cost *o* expense || ECON *gasto público* public spending *o* expenditure || *hacer el gasto de la conversación* to do all the talking.
◆ *pl* expenses, costs, cost *sing*; *gastos de mantenimiento* maintenance costs || — *cubrir gastos* to cover costs *o* expenses || *dinero para gastos menudos* pocket money, petty cash || *gastos accesorios* incidental expenses, contingencies || *gastos corrientes* running expenses || *gastos deducibles* deductible expenses, allowable expenses || *gastos de escritorio* stationery expenses || *gastos de representación* entertainment allowance || *gastos e ingresos* outgoings and incomings, expenditure and income || *gastos fijos* fixed costs, standing charges || *gastos generales* overheads, overhead expenses || *meterse en gastos* to go to expense.

gastoso, sa *adj* spendthrift, wasteful, extravagant.

gastralgia *f* MED gastralgia.

gástrico, ca *adj* gastric; *jugo gástrico* gastric juice.

gastrina *f* MED gastrin.

gastritis *f* MED gastritis.

gastrocele *m* MED gastrocele.

gastroenteritis *f* MED gastroenteritis.

gastroenterología *f* MED gastroenterology.

gastronomía *f* gastronomy.

gastronómico, ca *adj* gastronomic, gastronomical.

gastrónomo, ma *m/f* gastronome, gastronomist.

gastropatía *f* MED gastropathy.

gastrópodo *m* ZOOL gastropod.

gastroscopia *f* MED gastroscopy.

gata *f* cat, tabby, she-cat (animal) || hill cloud (nubecilla) || FAM Madrilenian girl *o* woman || *AMER* maid, servant (sirvienta) | crank (manubrio).

gatas (a) *loc adv* on all fours || *AMER* scarcely, hardly (apenas) || — *andar a gatas* to go on all fours, to crawl (cualquier persona), to crawl (un niño) || FAM *salir a gatas de un apuro* to squeeze out of a scrape | *ser más viejo que andar a gatas* to be as old as the hills | *¡y lo que anduvo a gatas!* and the rest! [to s.o. who says he is younger than he really is].

gatazo *m* large tomcat (gato) || FAM swindle (engaño) || FAM *dar gatazo a* to swindle.

gatear *vi* to clamber, to climb (trepar) || FAM to go on all fours, to crawl (andar a gatas) || *AMER* to go womanizing.
◆ *vt* to scratch (arañar) || FAM to pinch, to swipe (robar) || *AMER* to flirt with, to make advances to (requebrar).

gatera *f* cathole (para un gato) || MAR cathole (escobén) || FAM young pickpocket (ratero) | urchin (golfillo) || *AMER* market stallholder (vendedora).

gatero, ra *adj* frequented by cats (lugar) || catloving (aficionado a los gatos).
◆ *m/f* catlover (aficionado a los gatos) || cat dealer (vendedor).

gatillazo *m* click of the trigger [when gun is fired].

gatillero *m* *AMER* hired killer (pistolero a sueldo).

gatillo *m* trigger (de un arma de fuego); *con el dedo en el gatillo* with one's finger on the trigger || forceps (de dentista) || part of the neck between the nape and the withers (de ciertos animales) || TECN clamp (de carpintero) | jack (para levantar cargas).

gatito *m* small cat, kitten.

gato *m* cat, tomcat; *gato callejero* alley cat, stray cat || FIG hoard (dinero que se guarda), money bag (bolso o talego) || TECN jack (para levantar cargas) | clamp (de carpintero) || FAM Madrilenian (madrileño) | pickpocket (ratero) | fox (hombre astuto) || *AMER* fleshy part of the arm (del brazo) | popular dance (baile) | open-air market (mercado) | servant (criado) || — FIG & FAM *buscarle tres pies al gato* to split hairs (hilar muy fino), to make life more difficult than it is, to complicate matters (complicarse la vida) | *caer de pie como los gatos* to fall on one's feet | *cuando el gato no está los ratones bailan* when the cat's away the mice will play | *cuatro gatos* hardly a soul, hardly anybody | *dar gato por liebre a uno* to take s.o. in, to sell s.o. a pig in a poke (engañar) | *defenderse como gato panza arriba* to defend o.s. like a demon *o* like demons || *el gato con botas* Puss in Boots || FIG & FAM *eso lo sabe hasta el gato* everyone knows that || ZOOL *gato cerval* lynx || FIG *gato con guantes no caza ratones* a cat in mittens catches no mice || ZOOL *gato de algalia* civet cat | *gato de Angora* Angora cat || FIG & FAM *gato escaldado del agua fría huye* once bitten twice shy || *gato montés* wildcat || *gato romano* tabby || *gato siamés* Siamese cat || FIG & FAM *hay gato encerrado* I smell a rat, there's a nigger in the woodpile | *llevarse como el perro y el gato* to fight like cat and dog | *llevarse el gato al agua* to bring it off | *no hay ni un gato* there isn't a soul | *no hay perro ni gato que no lo sepa* it's common knowledge.

GATT *abrev de Acuerdo General sobre Aranceles Aduaneros y Comerciales* GATT, General Agreement on Tariffs and Trade.

gatuno, na *adj* catlike, feline.

gatuña *f* BOT cammock, restharrow.

gatuperio *m* hotchpotch, hodgepodge (mezcla) || imbroglio (embrollo) || intrigue (intriga) || deceit (engaño) || dirty business (negocio sucio).

gauchada *f* typical gaucho act || *AMER* favour; *hacer una gauchada a uno* to do s.o. a favour.

gauchaje *m* group of gauchos, gauchos *pl.*

gauchear *vi* to live like a gaucho.

gauchesco, ca *adj* gaucho (relativo al gaucho); *vida gauchesca* gaucho life || gaucho-like, like a gaucho (parecido al gaucho) || *poema gauchesco* poem about gauchos and the pampas.

gauchismo *m* «gauchismo» [Argentinian literary movement of the second half of the 19th century. Its authors, notably H. Ascasubi, Estanislao del Campo and J. Hernández, described gaucho life on the pampas].

gaucho, cha *adj* gaucho; *un payador gaucho* a gaucho minstrel || *AMER* pleasant, nice (bonito) | rough, boorish (grosero) | cunning, crafty (astuto) | good, expert (jinete).
◆ *m* gaucho || *AMER* wide-brimmed straw hat.

gaudeamus *m* FAM beano (festín) || FAM *andar de gaudeamus* to whoop it up.

gauderio *m* (ant) *AMER* gaucho | lazy (holgazán).

gauss *m* FÍS gauss.

gavanza *f* BOT dog rose [flower].

gavanzo *m* BOT dog rose [plant].

gaveta *f* drawer (cajón).

gavia *f* ditch (zanja) || (p us) padded cell (para locos furiosos) || MAR topsail (vela) | top (cofa) || ZOOL seagull (ave).
◆ *pl* mental asylum *sing* (manicomio).

gavial *m* ZOOL gavial (cocodrilo).

gaviero *m* MAR topman.

gavieta *m* MAR mizen crow's nest (sobre la mesana), bowsprit crow's nest (sobre el bauprés).

gavilán *m* sparrow hawk (ave) || FIG hawk (persona) || quillon (de la espada) || flourish, stroke [at the end of a letter] (de una letra) || nib (división de la plumilla) || BOT thistle flower || MAR boathook || *AMER* ingrowing nail (uñero).

gavilla *f* sheaf (de cereales) || bundle (de sarmientos, etc.) || FIG gang, band; *gavilla de ladrones* band of thieves || *la gente de gavilla* the underworld.

gavión *m* MIL gabion || FAM large hat (sombrero).

gaviota *f* ZOOL seagull, gull (ave).

gavota *f* gavotte (baile y música).

gaya *f* coloured stripe [*US* colored stripe] (lista) || Victor's sash (insignia) || (p us) magpie (urraca).

gayadura *f* coloured stripes *pl* (del vestido).

gayar *vt* to adorn with coloured stripes.

gayo, ya *adj* gay, merry (alegre) || showy (vistoso) || *gaya ciencia* gay science, poetry.

gayola *f* cage (jaula) || FIG & FAM clink, jail (cárcel).

gaza *f* MAR eye splice, loop, bight.

gazapa *f* FAM fib, lie.

gazapo *m* young rabbit (conejillo) || FIG & FAM sly customer, fox (hombre astuto) | slip (lapso) | bloomer (enlace vicioso en la pronunciación de dos letras) | blunder, bloomer (disparate) | IMPR printing error, misprint (error en un impreso).

gazmoñada; gazmoñería *f* prudery, priggishness (modestia afectada) || sanctimoniousness, religious hypocrisy (santurronería).

gazmoño, ña *adj* prudish, priggish (de virtud fingida) || sanctimonious (devoto fingido).
◆ *m/f* prude, prig || sanctimonious person.

gaznápiro, ra *adj* FAM dense, stupid (palurdo).
◆ *m/f* FAM blockhead, simpleton.

gaznate *m* throat, gullet, windpipe (garguero) || *AMER* sweet of pineapple and coconut || FAM *refrescarse el gaznate* to wet one's whistle.

gazpacho *m* CULIN «gazpacho», cold soup of bread, tomatoes, garlic, salt, vinegar and oil.

gazpachuelo *m* egg soup seasoned with vinegar or lemon.

gazuza *f* FAM ravenous hunger (hambre) || *tener gazuza* to be starving *o* famished *o* ravenous.

ge *f* g [name of the letter *g*].

gehena *f* gehenna, hell (infierno).

géiser *m* GEOGR geyser.

geisha *f* geisha.

gel *m* QUÍM gel.

gelatina *f* QUÍM gelatine, gelatin || jelly (de carne).

gelatinoso, sa *adj* gelatinous.

gélido, da *adj* POÉT gelid, icy.

gelificarse *vpr* QUÍM to gel.

gelignita *f* QUÍM gelignite.

gema *f* MIN gem, precious stone || BOT bud, gemma || *sal gema* rock salt.

gemación *f* gemmation.

gemelo, la *adj/s* twin || — *alma gemela* kindred spirit || *hermanos gemelos* twin brothers || ANAT *músculos gemelos* gemelli.
◆ *m pl* binoculars (anteojos) || cufflinks (de camisa) || ASTR Gemini, the Twins (Géminis) || *gemelos de campaña, de teatro* field, opera glasses.

gemido *m* groan, moan || wail (lamento).

geminado, da *adj* geminate.

Géminis *npr mpl* ASTR Gemini, the Twins.

gémino, na *adj* geminate.

gemiquear *vi* *AMER* to whimper, to snivel.

gemir* *vi* to moan, to groan || to wail (lamentarse) || to whine (animales) || to howl, to moan (el viento).

gemonías *f pl* humiliating punishment *sing.*

Gemonías *f pl* HIST Gemonies (en Roma).

gen *m* BIOL gene.

genciana *f* BOT gentian.

gendarme *m* gendarme (en Francia).

gendarmería *f* gendarmerie, gendarmery.

gene *m* BIOL gene.

genealogía *f* genealogy.

genealógico, ca *adj* genealogical || *árbol genealógico* family tree, genealogical tree (de una persona), pedigree (de un animal).

genealogista *m/f* genealogist.

generación *f* generation ‖ (p us) descent (descendencia) ‖ — INFORM *generación de máquinas* generation (edad de una tecnología) ‖ *generación espontánea* spontaneous generation, abiogenesis.

generador, ra *adj* generating.
◆ *m* TECN generator.

general *adj* general; *parálisis general* general paralysis; *la opinión general* the general opinion ‖ common (común, corriente) ‖ — *en general* in general ‖ *por lo general* generally.
◆ *m* MIL general ‖ REL general ‖ — MIL *general de división, de brigada* major general, brigadier [*US* brigadier general] ‖ *general en jefe* supreme commander.

generala *f* general's wife ‖ MIL *tocar generala* to call to arms.

generalato *f* generalship, office of general.

generalidad *f* generality; *limitarse a generalidades* to confine o.s. to generalities ‖ majority (mayoría) ‖ «Generalitat» [autonomous government of Catalonia] ‖ *con generalidad* in broad outline; *tratar una cosa con generalidad* to treat sth. in broad outline.

generalísimo *m* generalissimo, supreme commander.

generalización *f* generalization ‖ widening, escalation (de un conflicto).

generalizado, da *adj* generalized ‖ widespread; *la opinión más generalizada* the most widespread opinion.

generalizador, ra *adj* generalizing.

generalizar *vt/vi* to generalize.
◆ *vpr* to become general ‖ to widen, to escalate (un conflicto).

generalmente *adv* generally.

generar *vt* to generate; *generar una corriente eléctrica* to generate an electric current ‖ (ant) to generate, to procreate (procrear) ‖ FIG to engender (tener como resultado).

generativo, va *adj* generative.

generatriz *f* MAT generatrix.

genérico, ca *adj* generic.

género *m* race (raza) ‖ sort, type, kind (clase); *los distintos géneros de automóviles* the different kinds of motorcars ‖ style, manner, way (manera) ‖ ARTES genre; *pintor de género* genre painter ‖ BIOL genus (grupo taxonómico) ‖ article, piece of merchandise (mercancía) ‖ material, fabric, cloth (tela) ‖ GRAM gender; *género masculino, femenino, neutro* masculine, feminine, neuter gender ‖ — *género chico* genre comprising one-act comedies and «zarzuelas» [at the end of 19th century] ‖ *genero humano* human race, mankind.
◆ *pl* goods, merchandise *sing*, articles ‖ *géneros de punto* knitted goods, knitwear *sing* ‖ *vendedor, fabricante de géneros de punto* dealer in knitted garments, knitwear manufacturer.

generosidad *f* generosity ‖ *no peca de generosidad* he's not overgenerous.

generoso, sa *adj* generous (propenso a dar) ‖ magnanimous, noble (magnánimo) ‖ generous, noble (acciones, palabras) ‖ noble (estirpe) ‖ generous, liberal (liberal) ‖ fertile (fértil) ‖ valiant, courageous (valiente) ‖ generous, full-bodied (vino) ‖ excellent (excelente).

genésico, ca *adj* genetic.

génesis *f* genesis (origen).

Génesis *npr m* Genesis (libro de la Biblia).

genética *f* genetics.

genético, ca *adj* BIOL genetic.

genetista; geneticista *m/f* geneticist.

genial *adj* full of genius, inspired, brilliant (dotado de genio creador) ‖ outstanding, brilliant, of genius; *una obra genial* a brilliant work ‖ brilliant (idea) ‖ witty (gracioso, ocurrente) ‖ genial, pleasant (agradable) ‖ characteristic (característico).

genialidad *f* genius (genio) ‖ stroke of genius, brilliant idea; *eso fue una genialidad* that was a stroke of genius ‖ genial *o* brilliant work (obra) ‖ eccentricity (excentricidad) ‖ originality.

geniazo *m* FAM foul *o* violent temper; *tener un geniazo horrible* to have a horribly violent temper.

genio *m* nature, disposition (carácter) ‖ temper, mood; *estar de mal genio* to be in a bad temper ‖ bad temper (mal carácter) ‖ genius (facultad creadora) ‖ genius (persona dotada de dicha facultad); *Shakespeare fue un genio* Shakespeare was a genius ‖ genius (espíritu de un país, de una época, etc.); *el genio de la lengua* the genius of the language ‖ genie, jinn (ser sobrenatural) ‖ spirit (espíritu) ‖ — *corto de genio* spiritless, timid ‖ *de mal genio* bad-tempered ‖ *genio del mal* evil spirit ‖ *genio y figura hasta la sepultura* the leopard cannot change its spots ‖ *genio vivo* quick temper ‖ *pronto* or *vivo de genio* quick-tempered ‖ *tener el genio atravesado* to have a foul temper ‖ *tener mal genio* to be bad-tempered *o* ill-natured.

genioso, sa *adj* AMER *mal genioso* ill-natured, bad-tempered.

genital *adj* genital.
◆ *m pl* genitals, genitalia.

genitivo *m* GRAM genitive.

genitor *adj m* generating, begetting.
◆ *m* begetter.

genitourinario, ria *adj* ANAT genitourinary.

genízaro *m* janizary, janissary (soldado turco).

genocidio *m* genocide.

genol *m* MAR futtock.

genopatía *f* MED genopathy.

genotipo *m* BIOL genotype.

Génova *n pr* GEOGR Genoa.
— OBSERV Do not confuse *Geneva* (Ginebra) with *Genoa* (Génova).

genovés, esa *adj/s* Genoese (de Génova).

gente *f* people *pl*; *había mucha gente en la calle* there were a lot of people in the street; *¡había una de gente!* there were no end of people there!; *gente joven* young people; *la gente del campo* (the) country people; *¿qué dirá la gente?* what will people say? ‖ people, nation (nación) ‖ FAM folks *pl*, relatives *pl*; *¿cómo está tu gente?* how are your folks? ‖ retinue (seguidores de un soberano) ‖ tribe; *la gente alada* the feathered tribe ‖ MIL men of a unit ‖ AMER upper-class people ‖ followers (seguidores, partidarios) ‖ — *de gente en gente* from generation to generation ‖ *gente armada* or *de guerra* men *pl* in arms, armed troops *pl* ‖ *gente baja* low-class people ‖ *gente bien* the best people (de la alta sociedad), nice people (respetable) ‖ *gente copetuda* or *de alto copete* upper-crust *o* high-class people *pl* ‖ *gente de baja estofa* low-class people, people of low degree ‖ *gente de bien* honest people, decent folk ‖ *gente de capa parda* countryfolk *pl*, rustics *pl* ‖ *gente de color* coloured people ‖ *gente de cuidado* or *de mala vida* or *de mal vivir* or *maleante* bad people, shady characters *pl* ‖ *gente de Iglesia* clergy ‖ *gente de la ciudad* townspeople *pl* ‖ *gente de mar* seamen *pl* ‖ *gente de medio pelo* or *de poco más o menos* people of no account ‖ *gente de negocios* businessmen *pl*, business people *pl* ‖ *gente de paz* friend, friends; *¿quién va? ¡gente de paz!* who goes there? friend! ‖ *gente gorda* people of influence *o* standing, bigwigs *pl* ‖ *gente de pluma* writers *pl* (escritores), clerks *pl*, penpushers *pl* (escribanos) ‖ *gente de vida airada* libertines *pl* ‖ *gente humilde* or *modesta* humble people ‖ *gente menuda* children *pl*, little ones *pl* (niños), people of small means (plebe) ‖ *hacer gente* to make a crowd ‖ *la gente en general* people at large ‖ *la mayoría de la gente* most people ‖ *ser gente* to be somebody (ser importante).
◆ *pl* gentiles; *el apóstol de las gentes* the Apostle of the gentiles ‖ JUR *derecho de gentes* law of nations.

gentecilla; gentezuela *f* FAM rabble, riffraff.

gentil *adj* heathen, pagan (pagano) ‖ gentile (que no es judío) ‖ attractive (atractivo) ‖ pleasant (agradable) ‖ charming; *una gentil doncella* a charming young girl ‖ graceful, elegant; *de gentil porte* of graceful deportment ‖ FAM huge (enorme).
◆ *m* heathen, pagan (pagano) ‖ gentile (no judío).

gentileza *f* gracefulness, elegance, poise (garbo) ‖ charm (encanto) ‖ kindness, goodness (amabilidad); *tuvo la gentileza de prestarme cien libras* he had the kindness to lend me a hundred pounds ‖ politeness, courtesy (cortesía) ‖ *¿tendría usted la gentileza de...?* would you be so kind as to...?

gentilhombre *m* gentleman; *gentilhombre de cámara* gentleman in waiting ‖ (p us) handsome young man (buen mozo).
— OBSERV pl *gentileshombres*.

gentilicio, cia *adj* gentilic, gentile (de una nación); *nombre, adjetivo gentilicio* gentilic noun, adjective.
◆ *m* gentilic, name of an inhabitant *o* of inhabitants of a country, region or city.

gentilidad *f*; **gentilismo** *m* gentilism, heathenism, paganism (religión de los gentiles) ‖ heathendom, gentiles *pl* (conjunto de gentiles).

gentilmente *adv* gracefully, elegantly (con gracia); *bailar gentilmente* to dance gracefully ‖ kindly (amablemente).

gentío *m* crowd, throng, mob (multitud) ‖ *¡qué gentío!* what a lot of people!

gentleman *m* gentleman.
— OBSERV pl *gentlemen* in both languages.

gentualla; gentuza *f* rabble, riffraff (populacho).

genuflexión *f* genuflexion, genuflection.

genuino, na *adj* genuine, true; *un genuino representante del pueblo* a genuine representative of the people ‖ pure; *en genuino inglés* in pure English ‖ genuine, real, authentic; *un caso genuino de esquizofrenia* a genuine case of schizophrenia.

geocéntrico, ca *adj* ASTR geocentric.

geoda *f* GEOL geode.

geodesia *f* geodesy.

geodésico, ca *adj* geodetic, geodesic.
◆ *f* geodetics, geodesy.

geofísico, ca *adj* geophysical.
◆ *m* geophysicist.
◆ *f* geophysics.

geografía *f* geography.

geográfico, ca *adj* geographical; *latitud geográfica* geographical latitude ‖ geographic; *milla geográfica* geographic mile.

geógrafo *m* geographer.

geoide *m* GEOGR geoid.

geología *f* geology.

geológico, ca *adj* geological, geologic.

geólogo *m* geologist.

geomagnético, ca *adj* geomagnetic.

geómetra *m* geometer, geometrician.

geometral *adj* geometric, geometrical.

geometría *f* geometry; *geometría plana, descriptiva, del espacio* plane, descriptive, solid geometry.

geométrico, ca *adj* geometric; *progresión geométrica* geometric progression || geometrical; *construcción geométrica* geometrical construction.

geomorfología *f* geomorphology.

geopolítica *f* geopolitics.

Georgia *npr f* GEOGR Georgia.

georgiano, na *adj/s* Georgian.

geórgico, ca *adj* georgic (agrícola).
◆ *f pl* Georgics (de Virgilio).

geosinclinal *adj* GEOL geosynclinal.
◆ *m* geosyncline, geosynclinal.

geranio *m* BOT geranium.

Gerardo *npr m* Gerard, Gerald.

gerbo *m* ZOOL gerbil, gerbille (roedor).

gerencia *f* management (gestión) || manager's office (oficina) || managership (cargo).

gerente *m* manager, director; *gerente de publicidad* advertising manager *o* director || *gerente de una tienda* shop manager.

geriatra *m/f* MED geriatrician.

geriatría *f* MED geriatrics.

gerifalte *m* ZOOL gerfalcon (ave) || FIG & FAM bigwig, big shot (personaje importante).

germanesco, ca *adj* slang || HIST relative to the «germanías».

Germania *npr f* HIST Germania (antigua región).

germanía *f* thieves' slang, cant (jerga) || HIST «germanía» [revolutionary movement in Valencia at the beginning of the 16th century] || (p us) concubinage (amancebamiento).

germánico, ca *adj/sm* Germanic.

germanio *m* QUÍM germanium (elemento metálico).

germanismo *m* Germanism.

germanista *m/f* Germanist, German scholar.

germano, na *adj* German, Germanic, Teutonic.
◆ *m/f* German, Teuton.

germanófilo, la *adj/s* Germanophile.

germanófobo, ba *adj/s* Germanophobe.

germen *m* BIOL germ || FIG origin, germ.

germicida *adj* germicidal.
◆ *m* germicide.

germinación *f* germination.

germinal *adj* BOT germinal.

germinar *vi* to germinate.

gerontocracia *f* gerontocracy.

gerontología *f* MED gerontology.

gerontólogo, ga *m/f* gerontologist.

gerundense *adj* [of *o* from] Girona.
◆ *m/f* native *o* inhabitant of Girona.

gerundio *m* GRAM gerund (en español, en latín) | present participle (en inglés).

gesta *f* heroic deed, exploit || *cantar de gesta* chanson de geste.

gestación *f* BIOL gestation.

Gestapo *f* Gestapo.

gestar *vt* to gestate.

gestatorio, ria *adj* gestatorial; *silla gestatoria* gestatorial chair.

gestear *vi* → **gesticular.**

gesticulación *f* grimace, face (mueca) || gesticulation (ademán).

gesticulador, ra *adj* given to grimacing *o* pulling faces (que hace muecas) || gesticulative, given to gesticulating (que hace ademanes).

gesticular; gestear *vi* to grimace, to pull faces *o* a face (hacer muecas) || to gesticulate (hacer ademanes).

gestión *f* step, measure (trámite); *hacer gestiones* to take steps || management, conduct (administración) || INFORM *gestión de ficheros* file management.
◆ *pl* business *sing* (asunto).

gestionar *vt* (to take steps) to acquire *o* to procure; *gestionar un pasaporte, un permiso* to take steps to acquire a passport, a permit || to negotiate; *gestionar una transacción, una venta, un empréstito* to negotiate a deal, a sale, a loan || to manage, to conduct; *su agente gestiona sus asuntos durante su ausencia* his agent manages his affairs while he is away.

gesto *m* expression (expresión del rostro); *un gesto de alegría* an expression of joy || face (rostro); *torcer el gesto de dolor* to twist one's face with pain || grimace, face, wry face (mueca) || gesture, gesticulation (con las manos) || FIG gesture; *su donación al asilo fue un gesto generoso* his donation to the home was a generous gesture || — *estar de buen, de mal gesto* to be in a good, in a bad mood || *fruncir el gesto* to frown, to scowl || *hacer gestos* to pull *o* to make faces (cara), to gesticulate (manos) || *me hizo un gesto para que me callase* he gestured to me to be silent || *poner mal gesto, torcer el gesto* to pull a face (hacer una mueca), to scowl (estar enfadado) || *poner un gesto de enfado* to scowl.

gestor, ra *m/f* agent (que gestiona) || manager, administrator (administrador) || manager (gerente de una empresa).
◆ *adj* managing || negotiating.

gestoría *f* agency.

Getsemaní *n pr* Gethsemane.

geyser *m* GEOGR geyser.

Ghana *n pr* GEOGR Ghana.

ghanés, esa *adj/s* Ghanaian.

ghetto *m* ghetto.

giba *f* hump (del camello) || hump, hunch, humpback, hunchback (de una persona) || FIG & FAM nuisance, bore, bother (molestia).

gibado, da; giboso, sa *adj* humpbacked, hunchbacked, gibbous (p us) (corcovado).
◆ *m/f* humpback, hunchback.

gibar *vt* to curve, to bend, to arch || FIG & FAM to annoy, to bother, to give the hump (fastidiar).

gíbaro, ra *adj/s* → **jíbaro.**

gibón *m* ZOOL gibbon (mono).

gibosidad *f* hump, gibbosity (giba).

giboso, sa *adj/s* → **gibado.**

Gibraltar *n pr* Gibraltar; *el peñón, el estrecho de Gibraltar* the Rock, the Straits of Gibraltar.

gibraltareño, ña *adj* [of *o* from] Gibraltar.
◆ *m/f* Gibraltarian.

giga *f* jig (danza y música).

giganta *f* giantess || BOT sunflower (girasol).

gigante *adj* giant, gigantic.
◆ *m* giant.

gigantesco, ca *adj* gigantic, giant.

gigantez *f* gigantic size.

gigantismo *m* gigantism, giantism.

gigantón, ona *m/f* giant [in a procession].
◆ *m* AMER sunflower (girasol).

gigolo *m* gigolo.

gigote; jigote *m* minced meat stew.

gijonense; gijonés, esa *adj* [of *o* from] Gijón.
◆ *m/f* native *o* inhabitant of Gijón.

gil, gila *m/f* AMER FAM fool (tonto).

gilí *adj/s* FAM → **jilí.**

gilipolla *m/f* POP → **jilipolla.**

gilipollada *f* POP → **jilipollada.**

gilipollez *f* POP → **jilipollez.**

gimnasia *f* gymnastics || physical training (educación física) || FAM *confundir la gimnasia con la magnesia* not to know one's left hand from one's right || — *gimnasia correctiva, médica* or *terapéutica* corrective gymnastics, remedial gymnastics || *gimnasia deportiva* gymnastics || *gimnasia rítmica* eurhythmics || *gimnasia sueca* Swedish gymnastics.

gimnasio *m* gymnasium (para hacer gimnasia) || gymnasium, grammar school [*US* high school] (colegio en Alemania).

gimnasta *m/f* gymnast.

gimnástico, ca *adj* gymnastic.
◆ *f* gymnastics (gimnasia).

gimnosperma *f* BOT gymnosperm.

gimoteador, ra *adj* whining, snivelling, whimpering.
◆ *m/f* whiner, sniveller, whimperer.

gimotear *vi* to whimper, to whine, to snivel.

gimoteo *m* whimpering, whining, snivelling.

gindama *f* FAM jitters; *tener gindama* to have the jitters.

ginebra *f* gin (licor) || MÚS xylophone (xilófono) || FIG confusion (confusión) | hubbub (ruido).

Ginebra *n pr* GEOGR Geneva.

ginebrés, esa; ginebrino, na *adj/s* Genevan, Genevese.

gineceo *m* HIST gynaeceum || BOT gynoecium [*US* gynecium].

ginecología *f* MED gynaecology [*US* gynecology].

ginecológico, ca *adj* MED gynaecological [*US* gynecological].

ginecólogo, ga *m/f* MED gynaecologist [*US* gynecologist].

gineta *f* ZOOL genet (jineta).

gingival *adj* ANAT gingival.

gingivitis *f* MED gingivitis.

Gioconda (La) *npr f* The Mona Lisa, the Gioconda.

gira *f* picnic, outing, excursion (excursión); *ir de gira* to go on an outing *o* an excursion, to go for a picnic || tour (viaje por varios sitios) || tour (de un artista).

girado, da *m/f* COM drawee.

girador, ra *m/f* COM drawer.

giralda *f* weather vane, weathercock (veleta).

giraldilla *f* weather vane, weathercock (veleta) || popular Asturian dance (baile) || TAUR type of pass with the «muleta».

girándula *f* girandole.

girar *vi* to rotate, to revolve, to go round; *las ruedas giran* the wheels go round || to rotate, to revolve, to gyrate (alrededor de un eje) || to spin (un trompo, etc.) || to revolve; *la Tierra gira alrededor del Sol* the Earth revolves around the Sun || FIG to turn on, to center on; *la conversación giraba alrededor de la eutanasia* the conversation turned on euthanasia || to turn; *la carretera gira a la izquierda* the road turns to the left || to swing, to turn; *la puerta gira en sus goznes* the door swings on its hinges || COM to do business; *girar bajo la razón social de* to do business under the name of || TECN to rotate || — AUT *coche que gira bien* car with a good *o* a small turning circle, car with a good lock || FIG *girar alrededor de* to be approximately *o* around *o* in the region of; *el número de víctimas gira alrededor de cien mil* the number of victims

is in the region of a hundred thousand || *hacer girar la llave en la cerradura* to turn the key in the lock.
◆ *vt* to spin; *girar un trompo* to spin a top || to turn; *girar el volante* to turn the steering wheel || COM to draw (una letra de cambio) | to transfer (enviar por giro postal) || *girar una visita oficial* to make an official visit.

girasol *m* BOT sunflower || MIN girasol, girasole || sycophant (adulador).

giratorio, ria *adj* gyratory; *un movimiento giratorio* a gyratory movement || revolving; *puerta giratoria* revolving door || — *placa giratoria* turntable (ferrocarriles) || *puente giratorio* swing bridge || *silla giratoria* swivel chair.

giro *m* turn, turning, spinning (acción de girar) || turn (vuelta) || rotation, revolution (revolución) || FÍS gyration || FIG course (curso) | turn; *su carrera ha tomado un nuevo giro* his career has taken a new turn || turn of phrase (locución); *un giro arcaico* an archaic turn of phrase || COM draft | bill of exchange (letra de cambio) | transfer (de una persona a otra) || — AUT *ángulo de giro* steering lock || *giro postal* money order, postal order || *giro telegráfico* telegraphic money order || AUT *radio de giro* turning circle.

giro, ra *adj* AMER yellow (gallo).

girocompás *m* gyrocompass.

girola *f* ARQ apse aisle, ambulatory.

Gironda *npr m* GEOGR Gironde.

girondino, na *adj/s* HIST Girondist (partido de la revolución francesa).

giropiloto *m* AVIAC gyropilot.

giroscópico, ca *adj* gyroscopic || *estabilizador giroscópico* gyrostabilizer.

giroscopio *m* gyroscope.

giróstato *m* gyrostat.

gis *m* AMER chalk (tiza).

gitanada *m* Gipsy-like action, Gipsy-like trick || FIG cajolery, wheedling (zalamería).

gitanear *vi* to cajole to wheedle.

gitanería *f* Gipsy-like action, Gipsy-like trick (gitanada) || wheedling, cajolery (zalamería) || band of Gipsies (grupo de gitanos).

gitanismo *m* Gipsy way of life, Gipsy customs *pl* || Gipsy expression *o* phrase *o* word (giro, palabra).

gitano, na *adj* Gipsy, Gypsy || FIG cajoling, wheedling.
◆ *m/f* Gipsy, Gypsy; *una familia de gitanos* a family of Gipsies.

glabro, bra *adj* glabrous (lampiño).

glaciación *f* GEOL glaciation.

glacial *adj* glacial; *zonas glaciales* glacial zones; *período glacial* glacial period || FIG icy; *recibimiento, viento glacial* icy reception, wind.

glaciar *m* GEOL glacier.
◆ *adj* glacial; *depósitos glaciares* glacial deposits.

glaciología *f* glaciology.

glacis *m* glacis (en fortificaciones).

gladiador *m* HIST gladiator.

gladio; gladiolo; gladíolo *m* BOT gladiolus.

glande *m* ANAT glans penis.

glándula *f* gland; *glándula lagrimal* lachrymal gland; *glándula de secreción interna* ductless gland.

glandular *adj* glandular.

glaseado, da *adj* glazed, glossy.
◆ *m* glazing (de cuero, papel, tela, repostería, etc.).

glasear *vt* to glaze.

glasto *m* BOT woad.

glauco, ca *adj* glaucous.

glaucoma *m* MED glaucoma.

gleba *f* clod [of earth turned over by the plough] || HIST *siervo de la gleba* serf.

glena *f* ANAT glenoid cavity.

glenoideo, a *adj* ANAT glenoid.

glicemia *f* MED glucemia.

glicérido *m* QUÍM glyceride.

glicerina *f* QUÍM glycerin, glycerine, glycerol.

glicerofosfato *m* QUÍM glycerophosphate.

glicerol *m* QUÍM glycerol.

glicina *f* BOT wistaria.

glicógeno *m* QUÍM glycogen (glucógeno).

glicol *m* QUÍM glycol.

glifo *m* ARQ glyph.

glíptica *f* ARTES glyptic.

gliptodonte *m* ZOOL glyptodon, glyptodont.

gliptografía *f* ARTES glyptography.

global *adj* global; *vista global* global view; *método global* global method || overall (de conjunto) || comprehensive; *un estudio global* a comprehensive study || total, aggregate (cantidad) || lump (suma).

globalmente *adv* as a whole, all in all.

globo *m* globe, sphere (esfera) || spherical lampshade (de lámpara) || balloon (aeróstato); *montar en globo* to go in a balloon || balloon (juguete) || — DEP *dar un globo* to lob the ball (en tenis) || *en globo* as a whole, all in all (en conjunto) || *globo aerostático* balloon, aerostat || *globo cautivo* captive balloon || MIL *globo de barrera* barrage balloon || *globo dirigible* dirigible || ANAT *globo ocular* eyeball || *globo sonda* sounding balloon || *globo terráqueo* or *terrestre* globe, earth.

globular *adj* globular.

globulina *f* BIOL globulin.

glóbulo *m* globule || ANAT corpuscle; *glóbulos rojos, blancos* red, white corpuscles.

gloria *f* glory (fama alcanzada); *cubrirse de gloria* to cover o.s. in glory *o* with glory || glory (que causa honor); *Cervantes es una de las glorias de España* Cervantes is one of the glories of Spain || glory (majestad, magnificencia); *la gloria de Dios* the glory of God || ARTES glory, aureole, gloria (aureola) | gloria (representación del cielo) || delight (cosa que produce gran placer); *es una gloria* or *da gloria ver a los niños tan felices* it is a delight to see the children so happy || REL heaven, paradise, glory (cielo) || CULIN custard tart || — *a gloria* heavenly, divine; *oler, saber a gloria* to smell, to taste divine *o* heavenly || *Dios le tenga en su gloria* God rest his soul || FIG *estar en la gloria* to be in seventh heaven *o* in one's glory || *ganarse la Gloria* to go to Heaven || *¡que Santa Gloria goce!* God rest his soul || *una vieja gloria* a has-been.
◆ *m* REL gloria (cántico o rezo).

gloriarse *vpr* to glory; *gloriarse de sus hazañas* to glory in one's achievements || to boast (vanagloriarse).

glorieta *f* arbour [US arbor], bower (cenador) || roundabout (encrucijada) || square (plaza ajardinada).

glorificación *f* glorification.

glorificar *vt* to glorify, to praise.
◆ *vpr* to glory (gloriarse); *glorificarse de haber hecho algo* to glory in having done sth. || to boast (*de, en* of) (vanagloriarse).

glorioso, sa *adj* glorious || blessed; *la gloriosa Virgen María* the blessed Virgin Mary || vainglorious (vanidoso).
◆ *f* the blessed Virgin Mary || HIST Spanish revolution of 1868.

glosa *f* gloss, marginal note (comentario, explicación de un texto) || FIG comment, note || gloss (composición poética) || MÚS variation.

glosador, ra *m/f* glossarist, glossator.

glosar *vt* to gloss (un texto) || FIG to comment on (comentar) | to put an unfavourable interpretation on, to gloss (interpretar en mala parte).

glosario *m* glossary.

glose *m* glossing (acción de glosar).

glosopeda *f* VET foot-and-mouth disease.

glótico, ca *adj* ANAT glottal, glottic.

glotis *f inv* ANAT glottis.

glotón, ona *adj* gluttonous, greedy.
◆ *m/f* glutton.
◆ *m* ZOOL glutton.

glotonear *vi* to guzzle, to devour, to eat greedily (comer con avidez).

glotonería *f* gluttony, greed, greediness.

glucemia *f* MED glucemia.

glúcido *m* QUÍM glucide.

glucinio *m* QUÍM glucinium, glucinum.

glucógeno *m* ANAT glycogen.

glucómetro *m* glucometer.

glucosa *f* QUÍM glucose.

glucósido *m* QUÍM glucoside.

gluglú *m* gurgle (del agua) || gobble (del pavo) || *hacer gluglú* to gurgle (agua), to gobble (pavo).

gluglutear *vi* to gobble (el pavo).

gluten *m* gluten.

glúteo, a *adj* ANAT gluteal.
◆ *m* gluteus (músculo).

glutinoso, sa *adj* glutinous, viscous.

gneis *m* GEOL gneiss.

gnomo *m* gnome (duende).

gnomon *m* gnomon (instrumento astronómico o índice de reloj de sol).

gnosis *f* FIL gnosis.

gnosticismo *m* FIL gnosticism.

gnóstico, ca *adj/s* FIL gnostic.

gnu *m* ZOOL gnu.

gobernable *adj* governable (país) || manageable (negocio) || steerable (barco).

gobernación *f* government.

gobernador, ra *adj* governing; *junta gobernadora* governing board.
◆ *m* governor; *gobernador del Banco de España* governor of the Bank of Spain || — *gobernador civil* provincial governor || *gobernador general* governor-general.
◆ *f* governor's wife.

gobernalle *m* MAR rudder, helm (timón).

gobernante *adj* governing, ruling.
◆ *m/f* ruler, governor (dirigente).
◆ *m* FAM self-appointed head.

gobernar* *vt* to govern (un país) || to run, to manage, to control, to direct, to conduct, to handle (dirigir) || to lead (una procesión, la danza, etc.) || MAR to steer.
◆ *vi* to govern || MAR to steer.

Gobi (desierto de) *npr m* GEOGR the Gobi Desert.

gobierno *m* government (de un país); *gobierno federal, totalitario* federal, totalitarian government || governorship (cargo de gobernador y duración) || running, management, direction (administración); *el gobierno de un negocio* the running of a business || guidance; *se lo digo a usted para su buen gobierno* I am telling you for your own guidance || MAR rudder, helm (timón) | steering (docilidad al timón) || — *gobierno autónomo* autonomous government || *gobierno central* central government ||

gobierno civil provincial government (institución), civil governorship (cargo), government office *o* house (edificio) || *gobierno de la casa* housekeeping || *gobierno de transición* caretaker government || *gobierno interino* caretaker government || *gobierno militar* military government || *gobierno parlamentario* parliamentary government || *gobierno presidencialista* presidential government || *servir de gobierno* to be a guide.

gobio *m* ZOOL gudgeon (pez de agua dulce).

goce *m* enjoyment (disfrute); *el goce de un privilegio* the enjoyment of a privilege || pleasure; *goces materiales, sensuales* material, sensual pleasures.

godo, da *adj* Gothic.
◆ *m* HIST Goth || (ant) FIG noble || *AMER* Dago, Spaniard (used contemptuously).

gofo, fa *adj* coarse, rough, uncouth.

gofrado *m* TECN embossing (del cuero) | corrugating (del papel) | goffering (de la tela).

gofradora *f* TECN embosser (para el cuero) | goffer (para la tela).

gofrar *vt* TECN to emboss (el cuero) | to corrugate (el papel) | to goffer, to gauffer (la tela).

gol *m* DEP goal (tanto); *marcar* or *meter un gol* to score a goal || — DEP *área de gol* goal area | *gol average* goal average | *tiro a gol* shot.

gola *f* FAM gullet (garganta) || MIL gorget (pieza de armadura) || ruff (cuello alechugado) || ARQ cyma, ogee || MAR channel, narrows *pl* (paso).

goleada *f* DEP very high score || FAM *ganar por una goleada* to walk away with the match.

goleador *m* DEP goal scorer.

golear *vt* DEP to score a series of goals against.
◆ *vi* DEP to score.

goleta *f* MAR schooner.

golf *m* golf (juego) || — *jugador de golf* golfer || *palo de golf* golf club || *terreno de golf* golf course, golf links *pl*.

golfa *f* FAM little hussy, shameless hussy (mala) | tart (prostituta).

golfear *vi* to live like a ragamuffin, to roam the streets (un pilluelo) || to behave like a scoundrel, to get up to no good (un granuja) || to loiter *o* to loaf about (vagabundear).

golfería *f* gang of urchins *o* scoundrels (conjunto de golfos) || mischief, mischievous *o* naughty trick (acción de un pilluelo) || (piece of) roguery (de un granuja) || vandalism, hooliganism (gamberrismo).

golfillo *m* street urchin.

golfista *m/f* golfer, golf player.

golfo *m* GEOGR gulf; *el golfo de México* the Gulf of Mexico; *el golfo Pérsico* the Persian Gulf | bay; *el golfo de Vizcaya* the Bay of Biscay || urchin, ragamuffin (pilluelo) || scoundrel, rogue (granuja) || loafer (holgazán).

Gólgota *npr m* GEOGR Golgotha.

goliardo, da *adj* debauched, immoderate.
◆ *m* HIST goliard (clérigo o estudiante vagabundo).

Goliat *npr m* Goliath (gigante).

golilla *f* ruff (gola) || starched white collar (de magistrado) || ruff (of poultry) || TECN collar, flange (empalme) || *AMER* (peasant's) scarf *o* neckerchief.
◆ *m* FIG & FAM lawyer.
◆ *pl* FIG & FAM legal fraternity *sing*.

golondrina *f* ZOOL swallow (ave) || MAR motorboat (lancha) || — *golondrina de mar* tern (ave), swallow fish (pez) || FIG *una golondrina no hace verano* one swallow does not make a summer || FIG & FAM *voló la golondrina* the bird has flown.

golondrino *m* ZOOL young swallow (pollo de la golondrina) | swallow fish (pez) || (p us) FIG rolling stone (vagabundo) | deserter (soldado desertor) || MED FAM boil *o* tumour in the armpit || FIG & FAM *voló el golondrino* the bird has flown.

golosear *vi* to nibble at *o* to eat sweets.

golosina *f* titbit, delicacy (manjar delicado) || sweet (dulce) || FIG desire, longing (vivo deseo) | greed, greediness (gula).

golosinar; golosinear *vi* → **golosear.**

goloso, sa *adj* sweet-toothed, fond of sweets *o* of delicacies || greedy (que come mucho) || appetizing, inviting (apetitoso) || FIG attractive, inviting (atractivo) || *ser goloso* to have a sweet tooth.
◆ *m/f* gourmand || *tener muchos golosos* to arouse envy.

golpazo *m* heavy *o* violent blow (golpe fuerte) || violent impact (choque violento) || *cerrar la puerta de un golpazo* to slam the door.

golpe *m* blow, knock; *recibió un golpe en la cabeza* he received a blow on the head || bump, collision (choque); *los coches chocaron con un golpe fuerte* the cars collided with a violent bump, the cars hit each other in a violent collision || jolt (sacudida) || gust (de viento) || beat (latido) || DEP shot, stroke (con un palo, con una raqueta) | kick, shot (en el fútbol) | punch, blow (en el boxeo); *golpe bajo* low punch | stroke (con un remo) || crowd, throng (gran cantidad de gente) || FIG blow; *sufrió un golpe duro con la muerte de su madre* he suffered a severe blow when his mother died | shock (sorpresa) | witty remark, stroke of wit, flash of wit (agudeza) | coup (acción astuta y afortunada); *dar un buen golpe* to pull off a successful coup | job (acción realizada por malhechores) | fit, attack, access; *un golpe de risa, de tos* a fit of laughter, of coughing || TECN spring lock (de cerradura) | stroke (de émbolo) || flap (cartera de bolsillo) || AGR hole for planting (hoyo) || — *abrir de golpe* to fling open || *abrirse de golpe* to fly open || *acusar el golpe* to feel the blow || *a golpe de* by means of || *a golpes* by force (con golpes), intermittently, in fits and starts (intermitentemente) || *a golpe seguro* surely (sin duda), without any risk (sin riesgo) || *¡buen golpe!* well done! || *cerrar de golpe* to slam (una puerta) || FIG & FAM *dar el golpe* to cause a sensation, to be a hit; *con ese sombrero vas a dar el golpe* you'll cause a sensation with that hat on || *dar golpes en* to beat (on), to hammer (on), to knock (on) || *dar* or *asestar un golpe a alguien* to deal *o* to strike s.o. a blow || *darse golpes de pecho* to beat one's chest || *darse un golpe en el brazo* to bang *o* to knock *o* to hit one's arm || *de golpe* suddenly, all of a sudden || FAM *de golpe y porrazo* suddenly (de repente), very hurriedly (precipitadamente) || *de un golpe* at one go, at one fell swoop (de una vez) || *errar el golpe* to miss || *golpe bien dado* hit || *golpe de efecto* coup de théâtre || *golpe de Estado* coup d'état || *golpe de fortuna* stroke of luck *o* of fortune || *golpe de gracia* coup de grâce, death blow || ARTES *golpe de luz* highlight || MIL *golpe de mano* raid, sudden attack || *golpe de mar* huge wave || FIG *golpe de pecho* confession (of one's sins), mea culpa || *golpe de suerte* stroke of luck || *golpe de vista* glance; *al primer golpe de vista* at first glance || *golpe doble* double hit (esgrima) || DEP *golpe franco* free kick || *golpe maestro* master stroke || *más fue el susto que el golpe* I (you, he, etc.) was more frightened than hurt || FAM *no dar (ni) golpe* not to do a stroke || *tener buenos golpes* or *cada golpe* to be very witty, to be always coming out with witty remarks.

golpeador, ra *adj* beating, knocking.
◆ *m/f* beater, knocker.
◆ *m* door knocker.

golpear *vt* to hit, to strike, to knock (dar un golpe) || to beat, to pound, to hammer (dar varios golpes) || to punch (dar con el puño) || to bang (dar golpes fuertes) || to tap (golpetear) || to beat against; *la lluvia golpeaba los cristales* the rain beat against the windowpanes.
◆ *vi* to knock.

golpetazo *m* violent blow (golpe violento) || violent collision (choque fuerte) || *cerrar la puerta de un golpetazo* to slam the door.

golpete *m* door *o* window catch [to keep the door or the window open].

golpetear *vt/vi* to pound, to beat, to hammer (dar repetidos golpes) || to tap, to beat lightly, to drum (dar pequeños golpes) || to pitter-patter (la lluvia) || to rattle, to bang; *el postigo estuvo golpeteando toda la noche* the shutter banged *o* rattled all night.

golpeteo *m* tapping, drumming, beating || pitter-patter (de la lluvia) || rattling (de un postigo, de una puerta, etc.) || knocking, knock (de un motor).

golpiza *f* *AMER* beating (paliza).

gollería *f* delicacy, titbit (golosina) || FIG nicety, dainty *o* fancy thing (delicadeza) || FIG *pedir gollerías* to ask for the moon and stars.

golletazo *m* blow on the neck of a bottle [in order to break it] || TAUR sword thrust into the neck of the bull which pierces the animal's lungs || FIG *dar un golletazo a un asunto* to cut a matter short, to put an end to a matter.

gollete *m* throat, neck (cuello) || neck (de botella) || FIG & FAM *estar hasta el gollete* to be fed up, to have had enough (estar harto), to be full (up) (haber comido mucho).

goma *f* gum, glue (para pegar) || rubber (caucho); *suelas de goma* rubber soles || rubber band (para sujetar objetos) || elastic (en costura) || MED gumma || POP rubber (condón) || — *borrar con goma* to rub out, to erase || *AMER* FAM *estar de goma* to have a hangover (tener resaca) || *goma adragante* tragacanth || *goma arábiga* gum arabic || *goma de borrar* rubber, eraser || *goma de mascar* chewing gum || *goma de pegar* glue || *goma espuma* foam rubber || *goma guta* gamboge || *goma laca* shellac.

gomal *m* *AMER* rubber plantation.

gomero, ra *adj* rubber || gum.
◆ *m* *AMER* rubber plantation worker (obrero) | rubber planter (plantador) | gum tree, rubber tree (árbol).

gomespuma *f* foam rubber.

gomina *f* hair dressing, hair cream.

gomita *f* rubber band.

Gomorra *n pr* HIST Gomorrah.

gomorresina *f* gum resin.

gomosidad *f* gumminess, viscosity.

gomoso, sa *adj* gummy, viscous || MED gummatous.
◆ *m* FAM dandy, fop (pisaverde).

gónada *f* ANAT gonad.

góndola *f* gondola (embarcación) || gondola (de aeronave, de globo) || *AMER* omnibus | wagon (coche).

gondolero *m* gondolier.

gonfalón *m* gonfalon, banner, standard (bandera).

gonfalonero *m* gonfalonier, standard bearer.

gong *m* gong.

gongorismo *m* gongorism, euphuism (culteranismo).

goniometría *f* goniometry.

goniómetro *m* goniometer.

gonococo *m* MED gonococcus.

gonorrea *f* MED gonorrhoea [*US* gonorrhea].

gordal *adj* big, fat, large.

gordana *f* animal fat.

gordiano *adj* gordian.

gordiflón, ona; gordinflón, ona *adj* FAM chubby, podgy.
◆ *m/f* FAM chubby person, fatty.

gordito, ta; gordo, da *m/f* AMER love (cariño, mi vida).

gordo, da *adj* fat (persona); *un hombre gordo* a fat man ‖ big (cosa); *una manzana muy gorda* a very big apple ‖ thick; *hilo gordo* thick thread ‖ thick, coarse (tela) ‖ thick; *una rama gorda* a thick branch ‖ fat, fatty; *tocino gordo* fatty bacon ‖ FIG & FAM huge (enorme) | important, big (acontecimiento) ‖ — *agua gorda* hard water ‖ FAM *algo gordo ha ocurrido* sth. really big has happened ‖ *dedo gordo del pie* big toe ‖ FAM *de los gordos, de las gordas* enormous, huge; *es una equivocación de las gordas* it is an enormous error ‖ FIG *hacer la vista gorda* to turn a blind eye, to close one's eyes ‖ *lengua gorda* furry tongue ‖ FAM *me cae gordo* he gets on my nerves, I can't stand him ‖ FIG & FAM *peces gordos, gente gorda* bigwigs, big shots, V. I. P.'s | *premio gordo* first prize, grand prize (lotería) ‖ FIG & FAM *reventar de gordo* to be as fat as a pig | *vacas gordas* years of plenty | *ya vendrán las vacas gordas* my (*o* our, etc.), ship will come in.
◆ *m* fat; *no me gusta la carne con gordo* I don't like meat with fat on ‖ FAM first prize, grand prize; *le ha caído* or *tocado el gordo* he has won the grand prize.
◆ *f* FAM ten-cent piece (moneda) ‖ — FAM *armar la gorda* to cause a rumpus *o* a ruckus | *estoy sin una gorda* I don't have a penny to my name | *se va a armar la gorda* there is going to be (big) trouble.
◆ *m/f* AMER ⟶ **gordito.**

gordolobo *m* BOT mullein (verbasco).

gordura *f* fat (grasa) ‖ corpulence ‖ AMER cream.

gorgojarse; gorgojearse *vpr* AGR to be infested with weevils (semillas).

gorgojo *m* weevil (insecto) ‖ FIG & FAM midget, dwarf, small person.

Gorgona *npr f* MIT Gorgon.

gorgoritos *m pl* MÚS roulades, warble *sing* ‖ quaver *sing*, warble *sing* (de la voz al hablar).

gorgotear *vi* to gurgle.

gorgoteo *m* gurgle.

gorguera *f* ruff (cuello) ‖ gorget (armadura) ‖ BOT involucre.

gori *m* FAM row, racket, ruckus; *armar gori* to make a racket, to kick up a row.

gorigori *m* FAM dirge, funeral chant.

gorila *m* ZOOL gorilla.

gorjal *f* bands *pl* (de la ropa sacerdotal) ‖ gorget (de armadura).

gorjeador, ra; gorjeante *adj* warbling, chirping, twittering.

gorjear *vi* to chirp, to warble, to twitter (los pájaros) ‖ MÚS to sing roulades, to warble.
◆ *vpr* to gurgle (los niños).

gorjeo *m* warbling, chirping, twittering (de los pájaros) ‖ roulade, warble (canto) ‖ gurgle (balbuceo de los niños).

gorra *f* peaked cap, cap with visor ‖ bonnet (de niños) ‖ cap (de jockey) ‖ MIL bearskin, busby (de granaderos) ‖ *gorra de plato* peaked cap.
◆ *m* FIG & FAM sponger, scrounger, cadger (gorrón) ‖ — FAM *comer de gorra* to have a buckshee meal | *de gorra* free (gratis) | *pasar la gorra* to pass the hat | *vivir de gorra* to sponge, to cadge, to scrounge.

gorrear *vi* AMER to sponge, to cadge, to scrounge.

gorrero, ra *m/f* maker *o* seller of caps.
◆ *m* FAM sponger, scrounger, cadger (gorrón).

gorrinada; gorrinería *f* piggishness (porquería) ‖ dirty trick (mala jugada).

gorrino, na *m/f* sucking pig (cerdo de menos de cuatro meses), piglet, pigling (cerdo pequeño) ‖ pig, hog (cerdo) ‖ FAM pig (sucio).

gorrión *m* ZOOL sparrow (pájaro) ‖ AMER colibri, hummingbird.

gorriona *f* female sparrow.

gorrista *adj* FAM sponging, cadging.
◆ *m/f* FAM sponger, scrounger, cadger (gorrón).

gorro *m* cap; *gorro militar, de baño* military, swimming *o* bathing cap ‖ bonnet (de niños) ‖ hat (de cocinero) ‖ — FAM *estar hasta el gorro de algo* to be fed up with sth. ‖ *gorro de dormir* nightcap ‖ *gorro frigio* cap of liberty, Phrygian cap ‖ FAM *poner el gorro a uno* to embarrass s.o. (molestar), to deceive (ser infiel).

gorrón *m* pebble (guijarro) ‖ silkworm that does not complete its cocoon (gusano de seda) ‖ TECN pivot, gudgeon.

gorrón, ona *adj* sponging, cadging ‖ *pasa gorrona* big raisin.
◆ *m/f* sponger, scrounger, cadger.

gorronear *vi* to sponge, to scrounge, to cadge.

gorronería *f* sponging, cadging.

gota *f* drop (de líquido) ‖ ARQ gutta ‖ MED gout ‖ FIG drop (pequeña cantidad); *una gota de vino* a drop of wine ‖ — *caer cuatro gotas* to spit with rain ‖ *caer gota a gota* to drip ‖ *gota a gota* drop by drop ‖ MED *gota coral* epilepsy ‖ *gota militar* gleet ‖ FIG *la última gota hace rebasar la copa* it's the last straw that breaks the camel's back | *no ver ni gota* to be as blind as a bat (estar medio ciego), not to be able to see one's hand in front of one's face (a causa de la oscuridad) | *parecerse como dos gotas de agua* to be as like as two peas in a pod | *sudar la gota gorda* to be dripping with sweat (transpirar), to sweat blood (para hacer un trabajo) ‖ *transfusión gota a gota* drip transfusion.

gotear *vi* to drip, to dribble (caer gota a gota); *el agua gotea del tejado* the water drips from the roof ‖ to leak (salirse un líquido) ‖ to gutter (las velas).

goteo *m* dripping.

gotera *f* gutter (canalón) ‖ leak, leakage (en un techo) ‖ stain resulting from dripping water (mancha) ‖ valance (de cama).
◆ *pl* FIG aches and pains (achaques) ‖ AMER outskirts, environs (afueras).

gotero *m* AMER dropper (cuentagotas).

goterón *m* ARQ throat ‖ big raindrop (de lluvia).

gótico, ca *adj* Gothic; *lengua, letra gótica* Gothic language, type ‖ FIG noble ‖ FAM *niño gótico* show-off.
◆ *m* Gothic; *gótico flamígero* flamboyant Gothic.

gotita *f* droplet ‖ FIG drop, little drop (pequeña cantidad).

gotoso, sa *adj* MED gouty.
◆ *m/f* person with gout.

goyesco, ca *adj* characteristic *o* in the style of Goya.

gozar *vi* to enjoy ‖ to be delighted (alegrarse); *gozo con su visita* I am delighted by your visit ‖ *gozar del beneficio de la duda* to have *o* to enjoy the benefit of the doubt.
◆ *vt* to enjoy; *gozar de buena salud* to enjoy good health ‖ FAM *gozarla* to have a good time, to enjoy o.s. (divertirse).
◆ *vpr* to enjoy, to rejoice in; *gozarse en hacer daño* to enjoy doing harm.

gozne *m* hinge.

gozo *m* joy (alegría); *saltar de gozo* to jump for joy ‖ pleasure, enjoyment (placer) ‖ delight (regocijo) ‖ — *mi gozo en un pozo* that's just my luck ‖ *no caber en sí de gozo* to be beside o.s. with joy.
◆ *pl* poem *sing* in honour of the Virgin.

gozoso, sa *adj* joyful, delighted (alegre).

gozque; gozquejo *m* little yapping dog.

grabación *f* recording (discos, etc.) ‖ INFORM recording ‖ *grabación en una cinta magnetofónica* tape recording.

grabado *m* engraving; *grabado punteado* stipple engraving ‖ picture, illustration (estampa); *un libro con muchos grabados* a book with many pictures ‖ recording (discos, cinta magnetofónica, etc.) ‖ — *grabado al agua fuerte* etching ‖ *grabado en cobre* or *en dulce* copperplate ‖ *grabado en hueco* intaglio ‖ *grabado en madera* woodcut.

grabador, ra *adj* recording.
◆ *m/f* engraver.
◆ *f* AMER recorder; *grabadora de cinta* tape recorder ‖ — *grabador al agua fuerte* etcher ‖ *grabador de cinta* tape recorder.

grabadura *f* engraving.

grabar *vt* to engrave; *grabar al buril* to engrave with a burin ‖ to carve, to engrave (madera) ‖ to record (discos, cintas magnetofonicas) ‖ FIG to engrave, to imprint; *grabar en la memoria* to engrave on one's mind *o* on one's memory ‖ — *grabar al agua fuerte* to etch ‖ *grabar en relieve* to emboss.

gracejo *m* wit, humour (humor) ‖ bantering manner (modo de decir festivo).

gracia *f* grace (divina) ‖ favour; *conceder una gracia* to concede *o* to grant a favour ‖ pardon, mercy (indulto) ‖ grace, gracefulness (atractivo, donaire) ‖ charm (atractivo); *no es guapa pero tiene cierta gracia* she isn't pretty but she has a certain charm ‖ grace (título) ‖ joke (broma), witty remark (dicho chistoso); *siempre está diciendo gracias* he is always telling jokes, he is always making witty remarks ‖ wit, humour (humor) ‖ FAM favour, dirty trick (mala pasada); *me hizo una gracia que me ha costado cien mil pesetas* he did me a favour *o* he played a dirty trick on me that has cost me a hundred thousand pesetas ‖ name (nombre de pila) ‖ — *ahí está la gracia* that's what's funny about it, that's where the humour is ‖ *caer en gracia a uno* to make a hit with s.o. ‖ *de gracia* free (gratis) ‖ REL *en estado de gracia* in a state of grace ‖ *en gracia a* because of (a causa de) ‖ *estar en gracia cerca de alguien* to be in s.o.'s good graces ‖ *hacer gracia* to like (gustar); *este hombre no me hace gracia* I don't like this fellow; to strike as funny, to amuse; *este chiste no me hace gracia* this joke doesn't strike me as funny ‖ *hacer gracia de* to spare; *le hago gracia de todos los detalles* I shall spare you all the details ‖ *¡maldita la gracia que tiene esto!, ¡menuda gracia tiene!, ¡tiene muy poca gracia!* it's not a bit funny! ‖ *más vale caer en gracia que ser gracioso* charm can do more than merit ‖ *me hace poca gracia hacerlo ahora* I'm not keen on doing it now, I don't exactly feel like doing it now ‖ *no le veo la gracia* I don't see what's funny ‖ *no tener ni pizca de gracia* not to be a bit funny ‖ *por la gracia de Dios* by the grace of God ‖ FIG *por obra y gracia del Espíritu Santo* as if by magic ‖ *¡qué gracia tiene!* how funny! ‖ *sin gracia* graceless; *facciones sin gracia* graceless features ‖ *tener gracia* to be funny; *tiene mucha gracia* it is very funny ‖ *tener toda la gracia* to be really funny ‖ COM *un día de gracia* a day's grace.
◆ *pl* thanks (agradecimiento); *miles de gracias* a thousand thanks ‖ MIT Graces; *las tres Gracias* the three Graces ‖ REL *acción de gracias*

thanksgiving || *dar gracias al cielo* or *a Dios* to give thanks to God || *dar las gracias a* to thank, to say thank you to, to give thanks to || *¡gracias!* thank you, thanks! (*fam*) || *gracias a* thanks to || *¡gracias a Dios!, ¡a Dios gracias!* thank God!, thank Heaven! || *gracias a que* thanks to the fact that || *gracias por* thank you for, thanks for; *gracias por haber venido* thanks for coming, thanks for having come || *¡muchas gracias!* thank you very much!, thanks very much!, many thanks!, thanks a lot! (*fam*) || *no estar para gracias* not to be in the mood for jokes || *y gracias si* and be thankful if.

grácil *adj* gracile, slender, slim (delgado) || slender; *árboles gráciles* slender trees || delicate (delicado).

gracilidad *f* slenderness, slimness.

graciosamente *adv* gracefully, graciously (con garbo) || amusingly, funnily (divertidamente) || gratuitously, free (gratis).

gracioso, sa *adj* funny, amusing (divertido); *un chico muy gracioso* a very funny boy || witty (agudo) || comical (cómico) || charming, graceful, gracious (encantador) || gratuitous, free (gratuito) || *Su Graciosa Majestad* His *o* Her Gracious Majesty.
◆ *m* TEATR «gracioso», comic character [buffoon in Spanish comedy] || — FAM *hacerse el gracioso* to clown around || *lo gracioso de la cosa, lo gracioso del caso* the funny thing about it.
◆ *f* TEATR soubrette.

grada *f* step, stair (peldaño) || row (línea de asientos) || tier (de anfiteatro, de estadio) || step (al pie del altar) || grille, grill (celosía, verja de locutorio) || AGR harrow || MAR slip, slipway (para construir un barco).
◆ *pl* flight *sing* of steps (escalinata).

gradación *f* gradation || climax (figura retórica).

gradar *vt* AGR to harrow.

gradería *f*; **graderío** *m* steps *pl*, flight of steps || rows *pl* (teatro) || tiers *pl* (anfiteatro, estadio) || *gradería cubierta* grandstand (tribuna).

gradiente *m* FÍS gradient || *AMER* gradient (declive).

gradilla *f* small stepladder (escalerilla) || TECN brick mould [*US* brick mold] (molde para ladrillos).

grado *m* degree; *la temperatura es de diez grados bajo cero* the temperature is ten degrees below zero || degree (parentesco) || degree, grade (jerarquía) || degree (porcentaje); *grado de humedad* degree of humidity || content (contenido) || degree (nivel); *grado de invalidez* degree of disablement || stage, step (fase); *los diferentes grados de la evolución de las especies* the different stages of the evolution of the species || MIL rank || degree (título universitario) || year, form [*US* grade]; *alumno del segundo grado* second year student || GRAM & MAT & FÍS degree || step (peldaño) || willingness (voluntad) || — *de grado, de buen grado* willingly || *de grado o por fuerza, de buen o mal grado* willy-nilly || *de mal grado* unwillingly || MAT *ecuación de segundo grado* quadratic equation, equation of the second degree || *en sumo* or *en último* or *en alto grado, en grado superlativo* in the extreme, extremely || *mal de mi, de tu, de su grado* against my, your, his *o* her will, unwillingly || *primo en tercer grado* third cousin, cousin three times removed || *vino que tiene once grados* wine which is eleven degrees proof.

graduable *adj* adjustable; *tirantes graduables* adjustable braces || that can be graduated.

graduación *f* graduation || QUÍM strength (porcentaje de alcohol) || determination of the strength (evaluación del porcentaje de alcohol) || MIL rank || FIG progression.

graduado, da *adj* graduated; *escala graduada* graduated scale || graduate; *graduado en la universidad de París* graduate of the university of Paris || *vaso graduado* graduate flask.
◆ *m/f* graduate || *graduado escolar* certificate showing a student has passed EGB [elementary school studies in Spain].

graduador *m* TECN gauge, graduator (utensilio) | adjusting screw (tornillo).

gradual *adj* gradual.
◆ *m* REL gradual.

graduando, da *m/f* undergraduate.

graduar *vt* to graduate (termómetro) || to regulate, to set, to adjust; *graduar la temperatura* to regulate the temperature || to measure *o* to determine the strength of (alcohol, vino) || to measure (medir) || to calibrate (calibrar) || to test (la vista) || to confer the rank of, to commission as; *graduar de capitán a uno* to confer the rank of captain on s.o. || to confer a degree on; *graduar a un estudiante de doctor* to confer a doctor's degree on a student || to grade (escalonar).
◆ *vpr* MIL to take a commission, to receive the rank of; *graduarse de capitán* to take a commission as captain || to graduate (*de* as), to receive the degree (*de* of); *graduarse de doctor en filosofía* to graduate as a doctor of philosophy.

grafía *f* sign or signs representing the sound of a word || spelling (ortografía).

gráfica *f* —> **gráfico.**

gráfico, ca *adj* graphic || FIG graphic, vivid; *me hizo una descripción muy gráfica* he gave me a very graphic description || *artes gráficas* graphic arts.
◆ *m/f* MAT graph || chart (de la temperatura) || diagram (esquema).

gráfila *f* milled edge (de una moneda).

grafilar *vt* to mill, to knurl.

grafismo *m* writing.

grafito *m* MIN graphite, black lead.

grafología *f* graphology.

grafólogo *m* graphologist.

gragea *f* sugar-coated pill (medicamento) || sugar almond [*US* Jordan almond].

graja *f* ZOOL rook, crow.

grajo *m* ZOOL rook, crow (graja) || *AMER* body odour [*US* body odor] (mal olor).

grama *f* BOT Bermuda grass.

gramática *f* grammar; *gramática comparada, histórica* comparative, historical grammar || FAM *gramática parda* gumption.

gramatical *adj* grammatical; *análisis gramatical* grammatical analysis.

gramático, ca *adj* grammatical.
◆ *m/f* grammarian.

gramil *m* gauge, marking gauge (herramienta).

gramilla *m* brake (agramadera) || BOT brake (agramadera).

gramíneo, a *adj* BOT gramineous, graminaceous.
◆ *f pl* BOT gramineae, graminaceae.

gramo *m* gramme, gram.

gramófono *m* gramophone [*US* phonograph].

gramola *f* gramophone [*US* phonograph].

grampa *f* *AMER* staple (grapa).

gran *adj* —> **grande.**

grana *f* seeding (acción de granar) || seeding time (época) || seed (semilla) || ZOOL cochineal (cochinilla) || kermes (quermes) || scarlet (color) || scarlet cloth (tela) || — *dar grana* to go to seed (las plantas) || *ponerse rojo como la grana* to turn as red as a lobster *o* as a beetroot.
◆ *adj* scarlet (color).

granada *f* BOT pomegranate || MIL grenade; *granada de mano* hand grenade | shell (de cañón); *granada de mortero* mortar shell.

Granada *n pr* GEOGR Granada.

granadero *m* MIL grenadier (soldado).

granadilla *f* passionflower, granadilla, grenadilla.

granadino, na *adj* [of *o* from] Granada.
◆ *m/f* inhabitant *o* native of Granada.
◆ *f* grenadine (jarabe) || beverage made with grenadine syrup (bebida) || flamenco song from Granada.

granado *m* BOT pomegranate tree (arbusto).

granado, da *adj* grainy (espiga) || ripe (trigo) || FIG notable, distinguished (notable) | select (escogido) | mature (maduro) | tall (alto) || FIG *lo más granado* the most select, the pick.

granalla *f* granular metal.

granar *vi* BOT to seed || FIG to mature (los jóvenes).

granate *m* MIN garnet || *granate almandino* almandine, almandite.
◆ *adj* garnet (color).

granazón *f* seeding || FIG maturity (de las personas).

Gran Bretaña *npr f* GEOGR Great Britain.

Gran Cañón *npr m* GEOGR the Grand Canyon.

grande; gran *adj* big, large; *una casa muy grande* a very big house || big, tall (alto); *es un chico muy grande* he is a very big boy || great, big; *oímos un gran ruido* we heard a great noise || great, high (elevado); *el avión vuela a gran altura* the aeroplane flies at great altitude; *gran velocidad* high speed || great, large; *un gran número de gente* a large number of people || FIG great; *un gran hombre* a great man | grand, great; *ha dado una gran fiesta* he gave a grand party | eminent (eminente) || *AMER* middle-aged (de cierta edad) || — *a lo grande* on a grand scale, in a big way; *vivir a lo grande* to live on a grand scale || *en grande* as a whole (en conjunto) || *le queda grande este vestido* this dress is too big *o* too large for you || GEOGR *los Grandes Lagos* the Great Lakes || FIG & FAM *¡mira que esto es grande!* that's the limit!, that's the last straw! | *pasarlo en grande* to have a whale of a time, to have a fabulous time (divertirse mucho) | *¡sería una gran cosa!* that would be great! || *venir grande* to be too big || FIG *ver las cosas en grande* to see things on a grand scale *o* in a big way.
◆ *m* grandee; *grande de España* Spanish grandee || eldest (niño mayor) || *los Cuatro Grandes* the Big Four.
— OBSERV The apocopated form of *grande, gran,* is used before singular nouns of both genders.

grandeza *f* greatness, magnitude; *la grandeza de un proyecto* the greatness of a project || size (tamaño) || grandeur, splendour [*US* splendor], magnificence (esplendor) || greatness, grandeur, nobleness (nobleza de sentimientos) || status of grandee (dignidad de grande de España) || grandees *pl* (conjunto de los grandes).

grandilocuencia *f* grandiloquence.

grandilocuente; grandílocuo, cua *adj* grandilocuent.

grandiosidad *f* grandeur, magnificence, splendour [*US* splendor]; *la grandiosidad del espectáculo* the grandeur of the spectacle.

grandioso, sa *adj* magnificent, grand || grandiose (más ostentoso).

grandor *m* size (tamaño) || magnitude.

grandote, ta *adj* FAM very big.

grandullón, ona *adj* FAM very big, oversized.

graneado, da *adj* granulated (granulado) ‖ MIL *fuego graneado* running fire.
◆ *m* grain (del cuero, del tejido).

granear *vt* to sow (sembrar el grano) ‖ TECN to stipple (para el grabado al humo) | to grain (piedra litográfica).

granel (a) *loc adv* in bulk; *cereales, colonia a granel* cereals, cologne in bulk ‖ loose; *naranjas a granel* loose oranges ‖ FIG in abundance, galore (en abundacia).

granero *m* granary, barn.

granillo *m* (small) pimple (en la piel) ‖ small tumour (de los pájaros).

granítico, ca *adj* granitic, granite.

granito *m* MIN granite ‖ MED granule (en la piel) | pimple (acné) ‖ small grain (grano pequeño) ‖ FIG *echar su granito de sal en la conversación* to put a word in (the conversation).

granívoro, ra *adj* granivorous, grain-eating.

granizada *f* hailstorm, hail (tormenta de granizo) ‖ FIG hail; *una granizada de golpes* a hail of blows ‖ iced drink (bebida).

granizado *m* iced drink ‖ *granizado de limón* iced lemon.

granizar *vi* to hail.

granizo *m* hail ‖ hail, hailstones *pl* (granos de la granizada).

granja *f* farm; *granja modelo* model farm; *granja avícola* poultry farm.

granjear *vi* (p us) to trade, to deal ‖ MAR to gain, to fetch; *granjear a barlovento* to gain the wind, to fetch to windward.
◆ *vt* AMER to steal (robar).
◆ *vpr* to gain, to win, to earn (conquistar); *granjearse la confianza de* to gain the confidence of; *se granjeó su afecto* he won his affection ‖ to earn (una reputación).

granjería *f* profits *pl*, gains *pl* (ganancia).

granjero, ra *m/f* farmer.

grano *m* grain (de los cereales) ‖ seed (semilla) ‖ grape (de uva) ‖ bean (de café) ‖ grain (partícula); *grano de arena, de sal* grain of sand, of salt ‖ MED pimple, spot (tumorcillo) ‖ grain (estructura); *madera de grano grueso* coarse-grained wood, wood with a coarse grain ‖ FOT grain ‖ — FIG *apartar el grano de la paja* to separate the wheat from the tares ‖ *grano de pimienta* peppercorn ‖ FAM *ir al grano* to get to the point, to go straight to the point | *no es grano de anís* it is no trifle, it is no small matter ‖ FIG *un grano no hace granero pero ayuda al compañero* many a mickle makes a muckle, every little bit helps.
◆ *pl* grain *sing*, cereals.

granoso, sa *adj* granular ‖ grainy; *cuero granoso* grainy leather.

granuja *f* loose grapes *pl* (uva) ‖ pips *pl*, seeds *pl* (semillas) ‖ FAM gang (banda de granujas).
◆ *m* rogue, scoundrel, knave, rascal (canalla) ‖ ragamuffin, urchin (pilluelo).

granujada; granujería *f* gang of rogues *o* of urchins (conjunto de granujas) ‖ FIG roguish *o* knavish trick, piece of roguery *o* of knavery.

granujiento, ta *adj* pimply.

granujilla *m* rascal.

granulado, da *adj* granulated.
◆ *m* granulation.

granular *adj* granular ‖ pimply (granujiento).

granular *vt* to granulate.
◆ *vpr* to granulate ‖ to break out in pimples (cubrirse de granos).

gránulo *m* granule ‖ MED small pill.

granuloma *m* MED granuloma.

granuloso, sa *adj* granular.

granza *f* BOT madder (rubia).
◆ *pl* chaff *sing* (de las semillas) ‖ dross *sing*, slag *sing* (del metal).

grao *m* beach, shore (playa) ‖ *el Grao* the port of Valencia (España).

grapa *f* staple ‖ cramp, clamp (para la madera) ‖ ARQ cramp (para sujetar) | keystone (adorno) ‖ MED stitch ‖ — *coser con grapas* to staple ‖ *sujeción con grapas* stapling.
◆ *pl* VET grapes.

grasa *f* fat (cuerpo graso); *grasa vegetal* vegetable fat ‖ grease (sustancia grasienta) ‖ grease (mugre, suciedad) ‖ grease, lubricating oil (lubricante) ‖ FAM *criar grasa* to get fat.
◆ *pl* MIN slag *sing* (de metal).

grasera *f* container for grease *o* fat *o* drippings (para conservar la grasa) ‖ dripping pan (para recoger la grasa).

grasiento, ta *adj* greasy, oily ‖ grimy, filthy (sucio) ‖ greasy (resbaladizo).

graso, sa *adj* fatty ‖ *cuerpo graso* fatty body.

grasoso, sa *adj* fatty (graso) ‖ greasy, oily (grasiento).

gratar *vt* TECN to burnish (la plata o el oro).

gratén *m* CULIN gratin; *lenguado al gratén* sole au gratin.

gratificación *f* reward (recompensa) ‖ gratuity, tip (propina) ‖ bonus (sobresueldo) ‖ bounty (subvención) ‖ gratification (agrado, satisfacción).

gratificante *adj* gratifying.

gratificar *vt* to reward (recompensar) ‖ to tip, to give a gratuity to (dar una propina) ‖ to give a bonus to (dar sobresueldo) ‖ to gratify (satisfacer).

grátil; gratil *m* MAR foreleech, head (de la vela).

gratín *m* CULIN gratin.

gratis *adv* gratis, free, for nothing.

gratitud *f* gratitude.

grato, ta *adj* pleasing, agreeable; *grato al paladar* pleasing to the taste ‖ pleasant, pleasing, agreeable; *grato de oír* pleasant to hear; *recuerdo grato* pleasing memory ‖ welcome, appreciated (apreciado) ‖ AMER grateful (agradecido) ‖ — *en espera de sus gratas noticias* hoping to hear from you soon ‖ *me es grato anunciar que* I am pleased to announce that.

gratuidad *f* gratuitousness ‖ FIG gratuitousness, lack of foundation ‖ *la gratuidad de las clases* the fact that the classes are free.

gratuitamente *adv* free, for nothing (gratis) ‖ FIG gratuitously, unfoundedly.

gratuito, ta *adj* free; *entrada gratuita* free entrance ‖ FIG uncalled-for, unwarranted, gratuitous; *afirmación gratuita* gratuitous remark.

grava *f* gravel.

gravamen *m* obligation (obligación) ‖ tax (impuesto) ‖ burden (carga, peso) ‖ encumbrance (estorbo) ‖ inconvenience (molestia).

gravar *vt* to tax (imponer contribución); *gravar las importaciones* to tax the imports ‖ to levy, to impose (un impuesto) ‖ to burden, to encumber (imponer gravamen); *gravar un país con impuestos* to burden a country with taxes ‖ to burden; *tener un coche grava mucho un pequeño presupuesto* having a car heavily burdens a small budget.

grave *adj* serious, grave; *enfermedad, situación grave* grave illness, situation ‖ grave; *una persona grave* a grave person ‖ grave, serious (mistake) ‖ serious (herida) ‖ low, deep; *una voz grave* a low voice ‖ solemn, serious; *estilo grave* solemn style ‖ MÚS low, deep ‖ FÍS heavy, weighty (atraído por la tierra) ‖ GRAM paroxytone (palabra) | grave; *acento grave* grave accent ‖ *estar grave* to be seriously ill.
◆ *m* FÍS heavy body ‖ MÚS bass.

gravedad *f* gravity, seriousness (de una enfermedad, una falta, un accidente) ‖ solemnity, seriousness; *la gravedad de sus palabras* the solemnity of his words ‖ seriousness, gravity (de un personaje) ‖ FÍS gravity; *leyes de la gravedad* laws of gravity; *centro de gravedad* centre of gravity ‖ MÚS depth ‖ — *enfermo de gravedad* seriously *o* gravely ill ‖ *herido de gravedad* seriously *o* badly hurt *o* wounded.

gravidez *f* pregnancy.

grávido, da *adj* gravid, pregnant.

gravilla *f* (fine) gravel ‖ *cubrir una carretera con gravilla* to gravel a road.

gravimetría *f* gravimetry.

gravitación *f* FÍS gravitation; *gravitación universal* universal gravitation.

gravitar *vi* FÍS to gravitate ‖ FIG *gravitar sobre* to rest on (apoyarse), to rest upon, to lie upon (recaer), to weigh on, to burden down (pesar); *gravitaba sobre él toda la responsabilidad* all the responsibility weighed on him *o* burdened him down; to hang over (una amenaza).

gravoso, sa *adj* costly (costoso) ‖ onerous (oneroso) ‖ burdensome, heavy (pesado) ‖ boring, tiresome (molesto).

graznador, ra *adj* cawing (cuervo) ‖ squawking (aves en general) ‖ quacking (pato), cackling, gaggling (ganso).

graznar *vi* to caw (cuervo) ‖ to quack (pato) ‖ to squawk (aves en general) ‖ to cackle, to gaggle (ganso).

graznido *m* caw, cawing (cuervo) ‖ quack, quacking (pato) ‖ squawk, squawking (aves en general) ‖ cackle (ganso).

greba *f* greave (armadura).

greca *f* ARQ fret.

Grecia *npr f* GEOGR Greece.

greco, ca *adj* (ant) Greek, Grecian.
◆ *m/f* (ant) Greek (griego).

grecolatino, na *adj* Greco-Latin.

grecorromano, na *adj* Greco-Roman.

greda *f* MIN fuller's earth, clay.

gredal *m* clay pit.

gredoso, sa *adj* clayey.

gregario, ria *adj* gregarious ‖ *instinto gregario* herd instinct.
◆ *m* FAM teammate who helps the team leader during a race (en ciclismo).

gregoriano, na *adj* Gregorian; *canto, calendario gregoriano* Gregorian chant, calendar.

Gregorio *npr m* Gregory.

greguería *f* hubbub, uproar (algarabía) ‖ «greguería» [a type of aphorism created by the Spanish writer Ramón Gómez de la Serna].

gregüescos *m pl* breeches (calzones).

grelos *m pl* turnip tops.

gremial *adj* HIST guild ‖ union (de una asociación).
◆ *m* HIST guildsman ‖ union member ‖ REL gremial (paño del obispo).

gremio *m* HIST guild (individuos de igual oficio) ‖ association, society, union (asociación); *gremio de panaderos* association of bakers ‖ brotherhood, fraternity (fraternidad).

greña *f* mop *o* shock *o* mat of hair (cabellera descuidada) ‖ tangle, entanglement (maraña) ‖ FAM *andar a la greña* to tear each other's hair, to fight (pelear), to squabble, to argue (discutir).

greñudo, da *adj* dishevelled, unkempt (mal peinado).

gres *m* GEOL sandstone || potter's clay (mezcla para hacer cerámica) || stoneware; *vasija de gres* stoneware pot || — *gres cerámico* stoneware || *gres flameado* glazed earthenware.

gresca *f* hubbub, uproar (ruido); *armar* or *meter gresca* to create an uproar || row (jaleo) || quarrel, row, fight (riña); *andar a la gresca* to look for a fight.

grey *f* flock, herd (rebaño) || FIG group (individuos de igual raza o nación) | congregation, flock (fieles).

grial *m* grail (vaso místico) || *el Santo Grial* the Holy Grail.

griego, ga *adj* Greek, Grecian.
◆ *m/f* Greek.
◆ *m* Greek (idioma); *griego antiguo* Ancient Greek || — FAM *esto es griego para mí* that's Greek to me, that's double Dutch to me | *hablar en griego* to speak gibberish, to talk double Dutch.

grieta *f* crack, fissure, crevice (en el suelo) || crack, crevice (en el hielo de un glaciar) || crack, chink, cranny (en una pared) || MED chap (en la piel).

grieteado, da *adj* cracked.
◆ *m* TECN crackle.

grietearse *vpr* to crack || to crackle (cerámica) | to get chapped (la piel).

grifa *f* AMER claw (garra) || FAM marijuana.

grifería *f* plumbing (grifos y accesorios) || manufacture of plumbing materials (fabricación).

grifero, ra *m/f* AMER petrol-pump attendant.

grifo, fa *adj* dishevelled (desgreñado), curly (rizado), kinky (crespo).
◆ *m* griffin, griffon (animal fabuloso) || tap [US faucet] (llave o caño) || spigot (de barril) || AMER petrol pump [US gas pump] (surtidor de gasolina).

grifón *m* griffon (perro).

grill *m* grill.

grilla *f* ZOOL female cricket || AMER row (riña).

grillera *f* cricket hole (agujero) || cricket cage (jaula) || FIG & FAM bedlam.

grillete *m* MAR shackle, fetter.
◆ *pl* shackles, fetters (cadena de los presos).

grillo *m* ZOOL cricket || BOT shoot, sprout || ZOOL *grillo cebollero* or *real* mole cricket.
◆ *pl* shackles, fetters (grilletes) || FIG shackles.

grima *f* annoyance, displeasure (disgusto) || disgust (repulsión) || horror (horror) || *dar grima a uno* to get on one's nerves (irritar); *me da grima verle* it gets on my nerves to see him; to give one the shivers (horrorizar).

grímpola *f* pennant (gallardete).

gringada *f* action typical of a «gringo».

gringo, ga *adj* foreign.
◆ *m/f* foreigner || AMER Yankee (norteamericano) || AMER *hablar en gringo* to speak gibberish, to speak double Dutch.
— OBSERV The word *gringo* is used contemptuously and applies primarily to North Americans.

griñón *m* wimple (de monjas) || BOT nectarine.

gripa *f* AMER MED influenza, flu.

gripal *adj* MED flu, grippy.

gripe *f* MED influenza, flu; *coger la gripe* to catch the flu; *estar con gripe* to have the flu.

griposo, sa *adj* MED *estar griposo* to have the flu.

gris *adj* grey [US gray] (color) || FIG dull, gloomy (triste).
◆ *m* grey [US gray] (color) || ZOOL miniver (ardilla) || FAM cop (policía) || cold wind; *hace gris* there's a cold wind || *gris marengo* charcoal grey || *gris perla* pearl grey [US pearl gray].

grisáceo, a *adj* greyish [US grayish].

grisalla *f* grisaille.

grisgris *m* amulet (amuleto).

grisú *m* firedamp; *explosión de grisú* firedamp explosion.

grita *f* shouting, screaming, uproar, clamour (gritería) || booing, hooting (reprobación general).

gritar *vi* to shout, to yell; *gritar desaforadamente* to shout like mad *o* at the top of one's lungs || to scream, to cry out (con voz estridente) || *gritar a voz en cuello* to shout at the top of one's voice.
◆ *vt* to shout at; *gritar a alguien* to shout at s.o. || to boo, to jeer at, to hoot (silbar); *gritar a un actor* to boo an actor.

gritería *f*; **griterío** *m* shouting, uproar, din, screaming || outcry (protesta) || booing, hooting (en el teatro).

grito *m* shout, yell (de dolor, de sorpresa, etc.) || shriek, scream, cry (más agudo) || shout (de aclamación) || boo, hoot (de desaprobación) || cry (de guerra) || cry (de los animales) || — *a grito herido* or *pelado* or *limpio, a voz en grito* at the top of one's voice, at the top of one's lungs (en muy alta voz) || *alzar el grito* to raise one's voice (gritar) || *andar a gritos* to be always arguing (reñir) || *asparse a gritos* to shout o.s. hoarse (desgañitarse) || *cantar a voz en grito* to sing at the top of one's voice || *dar gritos* to shout || FIG *el último grito* the latest thing *o* craze || *estar en un grito* not to be able to take any more [from constant pain] || *pedir a gritos* to clamour for || FAM *pegarle a uno cuatro gritos* to haul s.o. over the coals || *poner el grito en el cielo* to raise the roof, to raise an outcry, to kick up a fuss.

gritón, ona *adj* FAM shouting, screaming (que grita) | noisy (ruidoso).
◆ *m/f* shouter, screamer.

groenlandés, esa *adj* Greenlandic.
◆ *m/f* Greenlander.

Groenlandia *npr f* GEOGR Greenland.

grog *m* grog, rum punch (bebida).

groggy *adj* groggy (boxeador) || FIG groggy.

groom *m* page boy [US bellboy, bellhop] (botones).

grosella *f* BOT currant (fruto) || — *grosella espinosa* gooseberry || *grosella negra* black currant || *grosella roja* redcurrant.

grosellero *m* BOT currant bush (planta) || — *grosellero espinoso* gooseberry bush || *grosellero negro* blackcurrant bush.

grosería *f* coarseness, rudeness, crudeness, vulgarity (falta de educación, acción inconveniente) || coarse thing, rude thing, crude thing, vulgar thing (palabra inconveniente) || roughness, coarseness (tosquedad) || stupidity (ignorancia) || *decir una grosería* to say sth. rude.

grosero, ra *adj* coarse, rude, crude, vulgar; *¡qué tipo más grosero!* what a crude fellow! || rude, ill-bred, ill-mannered (descortés) || coarse, rough (basto) || gross; *error grosero* gross error.

grosor *m* thickness.

grosso modo *loc adv* roughly.

grosura *f* fat (grasa), suet (sebo) || *comer grosura* to eat meat.

grotesco, ca *adj* ARTES grotesque || bizarre, absurd, grotesque (ridículo).
◆ *m* ARTES grotesque (grutesco).

grúa *f* crane; *grúa de pórtico, de puente* gantry, bridge crane || derrick.

grueso, sa *adj* thick, heavy; *hilo grueso* heavy thread || thick (espeso) || fat, stout, big; *una mujer gruesa* a fat woman || heavy, thick, big; *un palo grueso* a heavy stick || thick; *cristales gruesos* thick glasses || heavy; *líneas gruesas* heavy lines || coarse; *tela gruesa* coarse fabric || MAR heavy; *mar gruesa* heavy sea || FIG dense, dull (poco agudo) || *intestino grueso* large intestine.
◆ *m* thickness (volumen, espesor) || main body; *el grueso del ejército* the main body of the army || downstroke (de una letra) || heaviness, thickness (grosor); *el grueso de un alambre, del papel* the heaviness of a wire, of paper || depth (en geometría).
◆ *f* gross (doce docenas) || MAR *préstamo a la gruesa* bottomry loan.
◆ *adv* big; *escribir grueso* to write big || *en grueso* in bulk, in gross.

gruir* *vi* to cry (las grullas).

gruísta *m* crane driver *o* operator.

grujidor *m* TECN glass cutter.

grujir *vt* to trim [glass] (el vidrio).

grulla *f* ZOOL crane (ave).

grullo, lla *adj* AMER dark grey (caballo).
◆ *m* AMER dark grey horse (caballo) | peso (dinero).

grumete *m* cabin boy (marinero).

grumo *m* curd (leche coagulada) || clot, grume (sangre) || lump, clot (líquido) || cluster, bunch (de cosas apiñadas) || wing tip (del ave).

grumoso, sa *adj* curdled, clotted (sangre) || lumpy, clotted (líquido).

gruñido *m* grunt (cerdo), growl, snarl (perro, etc.) || FIG grumble, grunt (refunfuño).

gruñidor, ra *adj* grunting (cerdo), growling, snarling (perro, etc.) || FIG grumbling, grouchy, grumpy.
◆ *m/f* grumbler, grouch (refunfuñador).

gruñir* *vi* to grunt (cerdo) || to growl, to snarl (perro, etc.) || FIG to grumble (refunfuñar) | to creak (una puerta).

gruñón, ona *adj* FAM grumpy, grouchy, grumbling.
◆ *m/f* FAM grumbler, grouch.

grupa *f* hindquarters *pl*, croup, rump (parte trasera del caballo) || crupper; *llevar a la grupa* to take on the crupper || — *montar a la grupa* to ride pillion [US to ride on the pillion pad] || FIG *volver grupas* to turn back (volverse atrás).

grupera *f* pillion (de la silla de montar) || crupper (baticola).

grupo *m* group || cluster, clump (de árboles) || TECN unit, set; *grupo electrógeno* generator set || — ECON *grupo de empresas* group of companies, consortium | *Grupo de los Siete* the Group of Seven, the Big Seven || *grupo de presión* pressure group || *grupo de trabajo* working party, working team || *grupo rockero* rock group || *grupo sanguíneo* blood group [US blood type].

gruta *f* grotto, cavern, cave (cueva).

grutesco, ca *adj/sm* grotesque.

gruyere *m* gruyère (queso).

¡gua! *interj* AMER oh!

guaca; huaca *f* AMER Indian tomb (sepultura) | buried treasure (tesoro) | money box (hucha).

guacal; huacal *m* AMER wooden crate *o* hamper (cesta) || calabash tree (árbol) || calabash, gourd (fruto y vasija).

guacamaya *f*; **guacamayo** *m* macaw (ave).

guacamol; guacamole *m* AMER guacamole [salad of chopped avocado, tomato, onion and spices].

guacamote *m* AMER yucca.

guacarnaco, ca *adj* AMER fool.

guaco *m* BOT guaco ‖ ZOOL curassow (ave) ‖ AMER pre-Columbian pottery.
◆ *adj* AMER harelipped (labihendido) | twin (mellizo).

guachacai *m* AMER very bad quality liquor.

guachada *f* AMER FAM dirty *o* rotten trick (canallada).

guachafita *f* AMER FAM racket, din (alboroto).

guachalomo *m* AMER sirloin (solomillo).

guachapear *vt* to splash with the feet (el agua) ‖ FIG & FAM to botch, to gungle (chapucear) ‖ AMER to steal, to rob.
◆ *vi* to rattle, to clatter, to clank.

guachimán *m* AMER watchman (vigilante).

guachinango *m* AMER porgy (pez).

guacho, cha *adj* AMER orphaned (huérfano) | odd (descabalado).
◆ *m* fledgling (pollo de pájaro) ‖ AMER furrow (surco).

guadal *m* AMER swamp, bog.

guadalajarense *adj* [of *o* from] Guadalajara.
◆ *m/f* native *o* inhabitant of Guadalajara (México).

guadalajareño *adj* [of *o* from] Guadalajara.
◆ *m/f* native *o* inhabitant of Guadalajara (España).

guadaloso, sa *adj* AMER swampy, boggy.

Guadalquivir *npr m* GEOGR the Guadalquivir.

Guadalupe *npr f* GEOGR Guadeloupe (isla).

guadamací; guadamecí *m* embossed leather.

guadaña *f* scythe.

guadañador, ra *m/f* mower.
◆ *f* mowing machine, mower (máquina).

guadañar *vt* to mow, to scythe.

guadañero; guadañil *m* mower.

guadarnés *m* harness room (lugar) ‖ harness keeper (guardia) ‖ armory (armería).

Guadiana *npr m* GEOGR the Guadiana.

guagua *f* trifle (cosa baladí) ‖ AMER baby | bus (autobús) ‖ — FAM *de guagua* free, gratis | *¡qué guagua!* what a bargain!

guaica *f* AMER glass bead (abalorio) | rosary bead (cuenta de rosario).

guaico; huaico *m* AMER basin, hollow (hondonada) | rubbish dump [US garbage dump] (vertedero).

guaira *f* AMER smelting furnace (hornillo) ‖ MAR triangular sail ‖ AMER Indian panpipe.

guajá *f* AMER heron.

guaje *adj/s* AMER fool (tonto).
◆ *m* AMER calabash, gourd (calabaza) | trinket (baratija).

guajiro, ra *m/f* AMER Cuban peasant.
◆ *f* Cuban peasant song.

guajolote *m* AMER turkey (pavo) | FAM jackass, fool (bobo).

gualda *f* BOT dyer's weed, weld.

gualdado, da *adj* yellow.

gualdera *f* cheek (del cañón).

gualdo, da *adj* yellow (amarillo); *la bandera roja y gualda* the red and yellow flag.

gualdrapa *f* housing, trappings *pl*, caparison (manta para el caballo) ‖ FAM tatter, rag (harapo).

gualdrapazo *m* flap [of sail against the mast].

gualdrapear *vi* to flap (las velas).

gualicho; gualichú *m* AMER devil, evil spirit [to «gauchos»] | talisman.

guama *f* BOT guama tree (árbol), guama fruit (fruta) ‖ AMER lie (mentira).

guamo *m* BOT guama tree (árbol).

guampa *f* AMER horn (cuerno de vacuno).

guanábana *f* soursop (fruto).

guanábano *m* BOT soursop (árbol) ‖ AMER fool (tonto).

guanaco *m* ZOOL guanaco.

guanajo, ja *adj* foolish (tonto).
◆ *m/f* fool.
◆ *m* AMER turkey (pavo).

guanche *adj/s* guanche [first inhabitants of the Canary Islands].

guanear *vt* AMER to fertilize with guano.

guanero, ra *adj* guano.

guano *m* guano [fertilizer] ‖ AMER FAM dough (dinero) ‖ FAM *¡vete al guano!* go to hell!

guantada *f*; **guantazo** *m* FAM slap.

guante *m* glove; *guantes de boxeo* boxing gloves ‖ FIG & FAM bribe (gratificación) ‖ — FIG *arrojar el guante a uno* to throw down the gauntlet (desafiar) | *dar un guante a uno* to bribe s.o., to grease s.o.'s palm (untar la mano) | *de guante blanco* formal (reunión) | *echar el guante a alguien* to seize *o* to get hold of s.o. | *echar el guante a una cosa* to seize sth., to grab sth. | *estar* or *ponerse más suave que un guante* to be *o* to become as meek as a lamb | *recoger el guante* to take up the gauntlet, to take up the challenge | *sentar como un guante* to fit like a glove.

guantear *vt* to slap.

guantelete *m* gauntlet (manopla).

guantería *f* glove factory (taller), glove shop (tienda).

guantero, ra *m/f* glover.
◆ *f* glove box, glove compartment (en el coche).

guapear *vi* FAM to show bravery *o* courage (ser valiente) | to dress showily (hacer alarde de gusto) ‖ AMER to brag, to boast (fanfarronear).

guaperas *adj/m inv* FAM smoothie.

guapetón, ona *adj* FAM very good-looking, handsome (guapo) | dashing (garboso) | flashy (ostentoso).

guapeza *f* FAM boldness, bravery, dash (ánimo) | showiness, flashiness (en el vestir) ‖ handsomeness, good looks *pl* (de un hombre guapo) ‖ prettiness, attractiveness (de una mujer guapa).

guapo, pa *adj* good-looking, handsome (hombre) ‖ pretty, attractive, good-looking (mujer); *una muchacha guapa* a pretty girl ‖ smart (elegante) ‖ flashy, showy (ostentoso) ‖ bold, brave, dashing (valiente).
◆ *m* braggart, boaster (fanfarrón) ‖ bully (pendenciero) ‖ FAM lover, gallant (galán) ‖ good-looking young man (joven apuesto) ‖ *echárselas* or *dárselas de guapo* to brag, to boast (fanfarronear), to boast of being a lover *o* a Don Juan (presumir).
◆ *interj* love; *¡ven aquí, guapa!* come over here, love!

guapote, ta *adj* FAM good-looking, handsome (hombre) | good-looking, pretty (mujer) ‖ good-natured (de buen carácter).

guapura *f* FAM good looks *pl.*

guaraca *f* AMER sling.

guaracha *f* AMER Antillean song and dance.

guarache; huarache *m* AMER Indian sandal.

guaragua *f* AMER swinging (contoneo) | roundabout way, beating about the bush (al hablar).
◆ *pl* AMER trinkets, baubles (perifollos).

guarangada *f* AMER rudeness, crudeness, coarseness (cualidad) | rude, crude, coarse thing (dicho o hecho).

guarango, ga *adj* AMER coarse, rude, crude (grosero).

guaraní *adj/s* Guarani.

guarapo *m* sugar-cane juice (zumo de la caña de azúcar) ‖ sugar-cane liquor (bebida).

guarda *m/f* guard (vigilante) ‖ keeper (en un jardín zoológico, parque, museo) ‖ custodian (de edificio público, de monumento histórico) ‖ AMER tram conductor (cobrador) ‖ — *Ángel de la Guarda* guardian angel ‖ *guarda de caza* gamekeeper [US game warden] ‖ *guarda de noche* or *nocturno* night watchman ‖ *guarda de pesca* water bailiff [US fish warden] ‖ *guarda de ribera* river police ‖ *guarda forestal* forester [US forest ranger] ‖ *guarda jurado* rural policeman.
◆ *f* custody (custodia) ‖ protection, safekeeping (protección); *la guarda de sus derechos* the protection of his rights ‖ observance (de una ley) ‖ guard (de la espada) ‖ endpaper flyleaf (de un libro).
◆ *pl* wards (de una cerradura) ‖ outer ribs (de un abanico).

guardabarrera *m/f* crossing keeper.

guardabarros *m inv* mudguard [US fender].

guardabosque *m* forester [US forest ranger], gamekeeper [US game warden].

guardabrisa *f* lantern shade (fanal) ‖ windscreen [US windshield] (parabrisas).

guardacabo *m* MAR thimble.

guardacabras *m/f inv* goatherd.

guardacadena *m* chain guard.

guardacantón *m* spur stone, corner post.

guardacoches *m inv* parking attendant.

guardacostas *m inv* MAR coastguard vessel, revenue cutter [US coastguard cutter].

guardador, ra *adj* careful, provident (que guarda bien sus posesiones) ‖ observant (que observa una ley, una orden) ‖ stingy, miserly (tacaño).
◆ *m/f* keeper ‖ observer (de una ley) ‖ miser (avaro) ‖ careful person.

guardaespaldas *m inv* bodyguard.

guardafrenos *m inv* brakeman (de ferrocarril).

guardagujas *m inv* switchman (de ferrocarril).

guardainfante *m* farthingale.

guardalmacén *m* warehouseman, storekeeper.

guardalodos *m inv* mudguard [US fender].

guardamalleta *f* valance (para ventanas).

guardamano *m* guard (de espada).

guardameta *m* DEP goalkeeper.

guardamonte *m* trigger guard (de arma de fuego) ‖ gamekeeper [US game warden] (guarda de caza) ‖ AMER chaps *pl* (de jinete).

guardamuebles *m inv* furniture warehouse, furniture repository.

guardapelo *m* locket (medallón).

guardapiés *m inv* skirt (falda) ‖ petticoat (refajo).

guardapolvo *m* dustcoat (prenda de vestir) ‖ overall (de niño, de dependiente) ‖ housecoat [US duster] (bata de ama de casa) ‖ dust cover, dust sheet (funda contra el polvo) ‖ small roof (tejadillo) ‖ inner lid (de un reloj).

guardar *vt* to keep; *guardar algo con* or *bajo llave* to keep sth. under lock and key; *guardar un secreto* to keep a secret ‖ to guard, to keep; *guardar las puertas de la ciudad* to keep the gates of the city ‖ to protect (proteger) ‖ to take care of (cuidar) ‖ to tend, to guard; *guardar un rebaño de ovejas* to tend a flock of sheep ‖ to guard, to watch over (los presos) ‖ to put aside, to save, to keep; *guardó la copia de su artículo* he saved the copy of his article ‖ to put away; *guarda el dinero en tu bolso* put the money away in your handbag ‖ to put by, to lay by (poner de lado) ‖ to save, to keep; *guárdame sitio en la cola* save me a place in the queue ‖ to have; *guarda un buen recuerdo de su estancia en Londres* he has pleasant memories of his stay in London ‖ to observe (una ley, etc.) ‖ to keep (mandamientos) ‖ to show, to have (respeto, atenciones, etc.) ‖ to keep (conservar); *te guardaré la cena caliente* I'll keep the dinner warm for you ‖ — *¡Dios guarde la Reina!* God save the Queen! ‖ *fiesta de guardar* day of obligation ‖ *¡guarda!* look out!, watch out!, be careful! ‖ *guardar cama* to be confined to bed ‖ *guardar con siete llaves* to keep under lock and key ‖ *guardar la derecha* to keep right, to keep to the right ‖ *guardar las distancias* to keep one's distance ‖ *guardar silencio* to keep *o* to be quiet, to keep *o* to be silent ‖ *guardar su palabra* to keep one's word ‖ *no me guardes rencor* don't resent me ‖ *si Dios le guarda* God willing.
◆ *vpr* to look out for o.s., to be on one's guard (preservarse) ‖ to avoid, to refrain from, to guard against (con gerundio), to be careful not to (con infinitivo); *guárdate de hacer tal cosa* avoid doing such a thing, be careful not to do such a thing ‖ to keep; *guardarse un libro prestado* to keep a borrowed book ‖ FAM *guardársela a uno* to have it in for s.o., to bear a grudge against s.o.

guardarropa *m/f* cloakroom attendant (persona encargada de la ropa), wardrobe (en la casa real) ‖ TEATR wardrobe keeper.
◆ *m* wardrobe (armario y ropa) ‖ cloakroom [*US* checkroom] (en establecimientos públicos).

guardarropía *f* TEATR wardrobe (para la ropa), props *pl* (para los accesorios) ‖ FIG *de guardarropía* fake, sham, make-believe.

guardarruedas *m inv* spur stone, corner post.

guardasellos *m inv* (ant) Keeper of the Seals.

guardasilla *f* chair rail.

guardatimón *m* MAR stern chaser (cañón).

guardavallas *m inv* AMER DEP goalkeeper.

guardavela *m* AMER furling line.

guardavía *m* linesman [*US* trackman].

guardería *f* guard ‖ *guardería infantil* day nursery.

guardia *f* guard (cuerpo de tropa) ‖ custody, care (custodia) ‖ MAR watch; *estar de guardia* to keep watch, to be on watch ‖ guard (boxeo, esgrima) ‖ — *aflojar* or *bajar la guardia* to lower one's guard ‖ *cuerpo de guardia* guardroom, guardhouse ‖ *entrar de guardia* to go on guard ‖ *estar de guardia* to be on duty, to be on guard ‖ FIG *estar en guardia* to be on one's guard ‖ *guardia baja* low guard (boxeo) ‖ *guardia civil* civil guard ‖ *guardia entrante, saliente* new *o* relieving guard, outgoing guard ‖ *guardia municipal* or *urbana* municipal police ‖ MIL *hacer guardia, montar guardia* to mount guard ‖ *la vieja guardia* the old guard ‖ *poner en guardia a uno* to put s.o. on his guard ‖ *ponerse en guardia* to put o.s. on guard ‖ *relevar la guardia* to change the guard ‖ *salir de guardia* to come off guard.
◆ *pl* wards (de la cerradura).
◆ *m* MIL guard, guardsman ‖ policeman (del tráfico, del orden público) ‖ — *guardia civil* Spanish civil guard (policía), dragon, bossy woman (mujer autoritaria) ‖ *guardia de corps* bodyguard ‖ *guardia marina* midshipman ‖ *guardia de tráfico* traffic policeman ‖ *jugar a guardias y ladrones* to play cops and robbers ‖ FAM *ser más vago que la chaqueta de un guardia* to be bone idle.

guardiamarina *m* midshipman.

guardián, ana *m/f* guardian, keeper ‖ keeper (de jardín zoológico, de parque) ‖ caretaker (de un edificio) ‖ watchman (encargado de vigilar) ‖ warder (de prisiones).
◆ *m* MAR hawser (cable) ‖ REL guardian (de convento franciscano).

guardilla *f* attic, garret (buhardilla).

guardín *m* MAR tiller rope (del timón).

guarecer* *vt* to protect (proteger) ‖ to shelter, to take in, to give shelter to (abrigar) ‖ to nurse, to treat (a un enfermo).
◆ *vpr* to take shelter *o* refuge (refugiarse) ‖ to take refuge, to protect o.s., to shelter, to take shelter; *guarecerse de la lluvia* to take refuge from the rain.

guarida *f* den, lair (de los animales) ‖ FIG haunt, hideout (de ladrones), hangout, haunt (de amigos), refuge, shelter (refugio).

guarismo *m* number, figure (número).

guarnecer* *vt* to equip, to provide; *guarnecer un barco de velas* to equip a boat with sails ‖ to adorn, to decorate, to embellish; *guarnecer una ventana con cortinas* to decorate a window with curtains ‖ to trim (un vestido) ‖ MIL to be garrisoned in; *el regimiento de Covadonga guarnece Alcalá* the Covadonga regiment is garrisoned in Alcalá | to garrison (establecer una guarnición) ‖ to plaster, to stucco (revocar) ‖ CULIN to garnish ‖ TECN to line (frenos) | to set; *guarnecer una sortija de* or *con diamantes* to set a ring with diamonds.

guarnecido *m* stucco, plaster ‖ plastering, stuccoing.

guarnés *m* harness room (guadarnés).

guarnición *f* adornment (adorno) ‖ trimming, binding (de un traje) ‖ guard (de espada) ‖ provision, equipment (avío) ‖ MIL garrison ‖ CULIN garnish ‖ harness (arreos) ‖ TECN lining (del freno) | setting (para piedras preciosas) | stuccoing, plastering (revoque) ‖ *estar de guarnición en una ciudad* to be garrisoned *o* in garrison in a city.

guarnicionar *vt* MIL to garrison.

guarnicionería *f* harness shop.

guarnicionero *m* harness maker.

guarnir *vt* MAR to rig.

guarrada *f* ⟶ **guarrería.**

guarrazo *m* FAM fall ‖ FAM *darse un guarrazo* to fall, to come a cropper.

guarrería; guarrada *f* FAM dirtiness, filthiness (cualidad de sucio) | filth, muck (suciedad) | mess; *¡qué guarrería está haciendo este niño!* what a mess this child is making! | obscenity (indecencia) | dirty trick, foul trick, lousy trick (mala pasada) ‖ — FAM *decir guarrerías* to use foul language, to have a foul tongue *o* a foul mouth | *este libro es una guarrería* this book is obscene *o* disgusting.

guarro, rra *m* pig, hog (macho), sow (hembra) ‖ FAM pig, dirty pig.
◆ *adj* dirty, filthy (muy sucio).

guarura *m* AMER FAM bodyguard (guardaespaldas).

guasa *f* joke (broma) ‖ joking (acción de bromear) ‖ teasing (burla) ‖ irony, banter, sarcasm (ironía); *la guasa andaluza* Andalusian sarcasm ‖ dullness (sosería) ‖ — *con* or *en* or *de guasa* in fun, for fun, jokingly ‖ *estar siempre de guasa* to be always joking ‖ FIG *es una guasa hacer esto* it's a pain in the neck *o* it's a nuisance doing this ‖ *hablar en guasa* to speak jokingly ‖ *sin guasa* without joking, seriously, joking aside ‖ *tomar a guasa* to take as a joke, not to take seriously.

guasada *f* AMER crudeness.

guasca *f* AMER strap, thong (correa) | whip (látigo) ‖ AMER *dar guasca* to whip.

guascazo *m* AMER lash.

guasearse *vpr* FAM to joke, to tease, to kid (bromear) | to make fun, to scoff; *se guasea de todo* he makes fun of everything, he scoffs at everything.

guaseo *m* leg-pull (mofa) ‖ FAM *traerse un guaseo con uno* to pull s.o.'s leg.

guasería *f* AMER crudeness, rudeness.

guasipongo *m* ⟶ **huasipongo.**

guaso, sa *adj* AMER coarse, crude, rude.
◆ *m/f* AMER Chilean peasant.

guasón, ona *adj* jocular, humorous, fond of joking (bromista) ‖ sarcastic (sarcástico).
◆ *m/f* joker, banterer, wag.

guasquear *vt* AMER to whip.

guata *f* raw cotton (algodón en rama) ‖ padding (para acolchados) ‖ AMER belly, paunch (vientre) | bulging, warping (pandeo).

guate *m* AMER maize plantation [for fodder].

guatear *vt* to pad, to quilt.

Guatemala *npr f* GEOGR Guatemala.

guatemalteco, ca *adj/s* Guatemalan.

Guatepeor *n pr* FAM *salir de Guatemala y meterse* or *entrar en Guatepeor* to jump *o* to fall out of the frying pan into the fire.

guateque *m* party (fiesta).

guatón, ona *adj* AMER fat-bellied (barrigón).
◆ *m/f* AMER person with a fat belly.

guatusa *f* AMER agouti.

guau *m* bow-wow (del perro).

guay *adj* FAM great, fabulous.
◆ *interj* alas!, woe! ‖ — *¡guay de los vencidos!* woe betide the conquered! ‖ *¡guay de mí!* woe is me!

guaya *f* complaint, lament.

guayaba *f* BOT guava (fruto) ‖ guava jelly (dulce) ‖ pretty young girl (jovencita) ‖ AMER fib, lie (mentira) | hoax (embuste).

guayabal *m* guava grove.

guayabero, ra *adj* AMER lying.
◆ *f* lightweight jacket.

guayabo *m* BOT guava.

guayaca *f* AMER tobacco pouch (para tabaco) | amulet (amuleto).

guayacán; guayaco *m* BOT guaiacum.

guayacol *m* guaiacol.

Guayana *npr f* GEOGR Guiana.

guayaquileño, ña *adj* [of *o* from] Guayaquil (Ecuador).
◆ *m/f* native *o* inhabitant of Guayaquil.

guayín *m* AMER van (furgoneta).

gubernamental *adj* governmental.
◆ *m/f* loyalist.

gubernativo, va *adj* governmental.

gubernista *adj* AMER governmental.

gubia *f* TECN gouge.

gudari *m* Basque soldier.

guedeja *f* long hair ‖ mane (del león).

guedejón, ona; guedejoso, sa; guedejudo, da *adj* long-haired.

güegüecho, cha *adj* AMER goitrous (con bocio) | stupid, silly, foolish (tonto).
◆ *m* AMER goitre [*US* goiter] (bocio).

Güeldres *npr f* GEOGR Gelderland, Guelders.

Guernesey *n pr* GEOGR Guernsey.

güero, ra *adj* AMER blond, fair.

guerra *f* war (conflicto); *guerra civil* civil war; *guerra fría, de nervios, nuclear* cold war, war of nerves, nuclear war; *consejo de guerra* war council ‖ warfare (sistema, método); *guerra bacteriológica, atómica, nuclear, química, de guerrillas, de trincheras* germ, atomic, nuclear, chemical, guerrilla, trench warfare ‖ hostility (hostilidad) ‖ — FAM *dar mucha guerra* to be a nuisance to, to annoy ‖ *declarar la guerra a* to declare war on ‖ FAM *esta paella está pidiendo guerra* this paella is just crying out to be eaten ‖ *estar en guerra* to be at war ‖ *guerra a muerte* war *o* fight to the death ‖ *guerra de las galaxias* Star Wars ‖ ECON *guerra de precios* price war ‖ *guerra mundial* world war ‖ *guerra relámpago* lightning war ‖ *guerra sin cuartel* merciless war *o* fight ‖ *hacer la guerra a* to wage war on, to make war on ‖ *tenerle declarada la guerra a uno* to be openly at war with s.o.

guerrear *vi* to war, to wage war, to fight ‖ FIG to resist.

guerrero, ra *adj* warring ‖ warlike, martial ‖ fighting (belicoso) ‖ FIG & FAM mischievous, troublesome (travieso) ‖ *danza guerrera* war dance.
◆ *m/f* warrior, soldier.
◆ *f* tunic (del uniforme militar).

guerrilla *f* MIL guerrilla band (partida) | guerrilla warfare (tipo de guerra) | line of riflemen (línea de tiradores) ‖ beggar-my-neighbour (juego de naipes) ‖ MIL *marchar en guerrilla* to march in skirmishing *o* extended order.

guerrillear *vi* to wage guerrilla warfare, to skirmish.

guerrillero *m* guerrilla, guerrilla fighter, partisan.

gueto *m* ghetto.

güevón *m* AMER POP stupid fool [US jerk] (gilipollas).

guía *m/f* guide (de museo, de montaña, etc.) ‖ courier, guide (de un grupo de turistas).
◆ *m* MIL guide ‖ FIG guide, adviser (que da consejos).
◆ *f* guidance (orientación) ‖ handlebar (de bicicleta) ‖ (telephone) directory (de teléfono) ‖ timetable (de ferrocarriles) ‖ street guide (de calles) ‖ guidebook (libro); *guía turística* tourist guidebook ‖ BOT main stem ‖ COM waybill (hoja de ruta) ‖ MIN leader (vetilla) ‖ MAR fairleader ‖ TECN guide | curtain rail (de cortina) ‖ leader (caballo).
◆ *pl* reins (riendas) ‖ ends (del bigote).

guiadera *f* TECN guide.

guiahílos *m inv* thread guide (de máquina de coser).

guiar *vt* to guide; *guiar a unos turistas* to guide some tourists ‖ to lead (llevar); *las huellas les guiaron hasta la cueva* the tracks led them to the cave ‖ to drive (conducir); *guiar un coche* to drive a car ‖ MAR to steer ‖ AVIAC to pilot ‖ to train (una planta) ‖ FIG to guide, to drive, to move, to motivate; *le guía sólo el interés* he is driven only by personal interest | to advise, to direct, to guide (aconsejar); *guiar a uno en sus estudios* to direct s.o. in his studies.
◆ *vpr* to be guided *o* ruled by, to go by; *se guiaba por su instinto* he was guided by his instinct; *me guiaré por sus consejos* I will go by your advice.

Guido *npr m* Guy.

guija *f* pebble, small stone (china) ‖ BOT vetch.

guijarral *m* stony place.

guijarreño, ña *adj* ⟶ **guijarroso.**

guijarro *m* pebble, stone (piedra) ‖ cobblestone, cobble (para carreteras).
◆ *pl* shingle *sing*, pebbles (en una playa).

guijarroso, sa; guijarreño, ña *adj* stony, plebbly (terreno) ‖ shingly, pebbly (playa).

guijo *m* gravel ‖ AMER shaft (eje).

guilda *f* guild.

guillado, da *adj* FAM nutty, crazy.

guilladura *f* FAM madness, craziness.

guillame *m* TECN rabbet plane (de carpintero).

guillarse *vpr* FAM to become crazy *o* nutty (*por* about), to become crazy *o* nutty (chiflarse por) ‖ FAM *guillárselas* to beat it, to run away (largarse).

Guillermo *npr m* William.

guillotina *f* guillotine (para decapitar) ‖ paper cutter, guillotine (para papel) ‖ *ventana de guillotina* sash window.

guillotinar *vt* to guillotine ‖ to cut, to guillotine (papel).

guimbalete *m* TECN pump handle (de la bomba).

guimbarda *f* TECN router plane, grooving plane (cepillo de carpintero).

guinchar *vt* to goad, to prod, to prick.

güinche *m* AMER crane, derrick (grúa) | winch (cabrestante).

guinda *f* sour cherry, morello cherry (fruta) ‖ maraschino cherry (en pastelería) ‖ MAR height (de la arboladura).

guindaleta *f* MAR hemp rope.

guindaleza *f* MAR hawser.

guindar *vt* to hoist, to hang up high ‖ FAM to swipe; *guindar un empleo a uno* to swipe a job from s.o.; *guindarle la novia a uno* to swipe s.o.'s girlfriend | to hang (ahorcar).

guindaste *m* MAR windlass (cabria).

guindilla *f* BOT red pepper.
◆ *m* FAM cop (guardia).

guindo *m* BOT sour cherry tree, morello cherry tree.

guindola *f* MAR boatswain's chair (andamio para limpiar el casco) | life buoy (boya) | log chip (de la corredera).

guinea *f* guinea (antigua moneda inglesa).

Guinea *npr f* GEOGR Guinea.

Guinea-Bissau *n pr* GEOGR Guinea-Bissau.

Guinea Ecuatorial *n pr* GEOGR Equatorial Guinea.

guineo, a *adj/s* Guinean.

guiñada *f* wink (del ojo) ‖ MAR yaw.

guiñapo *m* rag, tatter (harapo) ‖ FIG reprobate (persona despreciable) ‖ — FIG *estar hecho un guiñapo* to feel as limp as a rag (estar muy débil), to have no backbone (no tener voluntad) | *poner a uno como un guiñapo* to haul s.o. over the coals, to give s.o. a dressing down (reprender), to call s.o. all the names under the sun (insultar).

guiñaposo, sa *adj* ragged, tattered (haraposo).

guiñar *vt* to wink at; *le guiñó* he winked at her ‖ *guiñar el ojo* to wink.
◆ *vi* to wink ‖ MAR to yaw.
◆ *vpr* to wink at each other.

guiño *m* wink ‖ *hacer guiños a uno* to wink at s.o. (hacer señas con los ojos), to make eyes at s.o. (para conquistar a una persona).

guiñol *m* puppet show.

guión *m* MIL guidon (estandarte) ‖ REL processional cross, processional banner ‖ royal standard (estandarte) ‖ outline (esquema) ‖ CINEM script, scenario (de una película) ‖ hyphen (raya en las palabras compuestas o cortadas) ‖ dash (raya en el diálogo o como paréntesis) ‖ leader (el que dirige).

guionista *m* CINEM scriptwriter, scenarist.

guipar *vt* FAM to see (mirar) | to get (understand).

guipur *m* guipure (encaje).

guipuzcoano, na *adj* [of *o* from] Guipúzcoa.
◆ *m/f* native *o* inhabitant of Guipúzcoa.

güira *f* BOT calabash (árbol y fruto) ‖ AMER FAM nut (cabeza).

guiri *m/f* POP foreigner, tourist.

guirigay *m* FAM hubbub, hullabaloo, fuss, commotion (jaleo) | gibberish (lenguaje inintelígible).
— OBSERV pl *guirigays, guirigayes.*

guirlache *m* almond brittle.

guirlanda; guirnalda *f* garland ‖ wreath (de forma redonda) ‖ chaplet, wreath (en la cabeza) ‖ BOT globe amaranth.

güiro *m* AMER calabash (árbol), calabash, gourd (fruto) | musical instrument made from a gourd (instrumento de música) | stalk of unripe maize (tallo de maíz).

guisa *f* manner, way; *obrar a su guisa* to work in one's own way ‖ — *a guisa de* as, for (a manera de) ‖ *de tal guisa, en tal guisa* in such a manner, in such a way.

guisado *m* stew; *guisado de cordero* lamb stew.

guisante *m* BOT pea (planta y legumbre) ‖ — *guisante de olor* sweet pea ‖ *guisante mollar* sugar pea.

guisar *vi* to cook.
◆ *vt* to cook (cocinar), to stew (un estofado) ‖ FIG to prepare, to arrange (preparar) ‖ — *ellos se lo guisan y ellos se lo comen* as you make your bed so you must lie on it ‖ *la comida está guisada* lunch *o* dinner is ready, lunch *o* dinner is served.

guiso *m* CULIN (cooked) dish; *echar a perder un guiso* to spoil a dish ‖ stew; *guiso de patatas* potato stew.
◆ *pl* dishes, cooking *sing*; *me gustan los guisos españoles* I like Spanish cooking.

guisote *m* FAM poorly made stew.

guisotear *vt* to cook, to prepare, to make.
◆ *vi* to cook.

güisqui *m* whisky.

guita *f* twine (cuerda) ‖ FAM dough (dinero).

guitarra *f* MÚS guitar; *guitarra eléctrica* electric guitar ‖ TECN beater (del yesero) ‖ FIG & FAM *chafar la guitarra a uno* to mess sth. up for s.o. ‖ *tener bien, mal templada la guitarra* to be in a good, in a bad mood.

guitarrear *vi* to play the guitar.

guitarreo *m* strumming on the guitar.

guitarrero *m* guitar maker *o* seller ‖ guitarist.

guitarrillo *m* small four-string guitar.

guitarrista *m/f* guitarist.

guitarrón *m* large guitar ‖ FAM sly rascal (tunante).

güito *m* FAM hat (sombrero).

gula *f* gluttony; *pecado de gula* sin of gluttony.

gules *m pl* HERÁLD gules.

gulusmear *vi* to sniff and taste what is cooking ‖ to nibble titbits (comer golosinas) ‖ to snoop around (curiosear).

gumía *f* moorish dagger.

gurí *m*; **gurisa** *f* AMER kid (chiquillo).

guripa *m* FAM soldier, private (soldado raso) | rogue, scoundrel (golfo).

gurriato; gurripato *m* ZOOL young sparrow ‖ FAM youngster, kid (niño).

gurrumino, na *adj* FAM mean (ruin) | weak, puny, sickly (enclenque).
◆ *m* FAM uxorious man (que idolatra a su mujer) | henpecked husband, henpeck (que se deja dominar).
◆ *m/f* FAM youngster, kid.
◆ *f* FAM uxoriousness (idolatría).

gurú *m* guru.

gusanear *vi* to swarm, to teem (hormiguear).

gusanera *f* worms *pl* (conjunto de gusanos) || breeding ground for worms (sitio donde se crían) || FIG great passion.

gusanillo *m* small worm || FIG & FAM bug (afición); *le entró el gusanillo de la afición a los toros* he got the bullfight bug || — FIG & FAM *gusanillo de la conciencia* remorse, nagging conscience | *matar el gusanillo* to take a nip first thing in the morning (beber aguardiente por la mañana).

gusano *m* ZOOL worm | earthworm (lombriz) | maggot (larva de mosca doméstica) | caterpillar (oruga) || FIG worm (persona despreciable) || — FIG & FAM *criar gusanos* to be pushing up daisies || *gusano blanco* grub (larva de abejorro) || FIG & FAM *gusano de la conciencia* nagging conscience, remorse || *gusano de luz* glowworm || *gusano de seda* silkworm.

gusarapo *m* small worm (gusanillo) || little creature, tiny animal (animalillo).

gustación *f* tasting, sampling, gustation (p us).

gustar *vt* to taste, to try, to sample (probar).
◆ *vi* to please, to be pleasing || to like; *me gusta mucho este escritor* I like this author very much; *a Juan no le gusta leer novelas policíacas* John doesn't like reading detective novels; *no me gusta su hermano* I don't like his brother || — *¡así me gusta!* that's what I like || *como le guste* as you like, as you wish || *cuando le guste* whenever you wish, whenever you like || *gustar de* to like, to enjoy; *gusto de leer* I like to read, I enjoy reading; *no gusto de su compañía* I don't like *o* I don't enjoy your company || *una novela que gusta* a novel which is popular *o* that people like || *¿usted gusta?* would you like some?

— OBSERV The intransitive verb *gustar* is construed like the English verb *to please: eso me gusta* that pleases me. However the verb *to like* is more commonly used, in which case the subject of *gustar* becomes the object of *like: eso me gusta* I like that; *a María no le gustan los pasteles* Mary does not like pastries.

gustativo, va *adj* gustative.

gustazo *m* FAM great pleasure, immense pleasure; *me ha dado un gustazo ver lo que le ocurría* it gave me great pleasure to see what happened to him || — FAM *darse el gustazo de* to treat o.s. to; *me di el gustazo de ir al teatro* I treated myself to the theatre; to allow o.s. the great pleasure of; *me di el gustazo de decirle cuatro verdades* I allowed myself the great pleasure of giving him a piece of my mind || *un gustazo por un trancazo* a great pleasure is worth any price.

gustillo *m* aftertaste (regusto) || tang, slight taste; *esta sopa tiene un gustillo extraño* this soup has a strange tang *o* a slightly strange taste || slight pleasure (placer).

gusto *m* taste, flavour (sabor) || taste (sentido) || taste; *hombre de buen gusto* man of good taste; *una cosa de buen gusto* a thing in good taste || pleasure; *tengo el gusto de acogerle aquí* I have the pleasure of welcoming you here || fancy, whim (capricho) || liking (afición) || style, fashion (estilo) || — *a gusto* at ease, comfortable; *estoy muy a gusto con estas personas* I feel very comfortable with these people, I am very much at ease with these people; comfortable; *estoy a gusto en este sillón* I am comfortable in this armchair; happily, with pleasure; *lo haría muy a gusto* I would do it happily; easily; *pesa muy a gusto sus cien kilos* he very easily weighs one hundred kilos || *a gusto de* to the liking of, to the taste of; *a gusto de todos* to everybody's liking || *al gusto del consumidor* according to the client's taste || *canta que da gusto* he sings magnificently, his singing is a delight || *coger* or *tomar el gusto a algo* to take a liking to, to acquire *o* to develop a taste for || *con gusto* with pleasure; *con mucho gusto* with great pleasure; *con sumo gusto* with the greatest pleasure; willingly; *estudia con gusto* he studies willingly; heartily; *come con gusto* he eats heartily || *dar gusto a* to please, to give pleasure to || *darse el gusto de* to allow o.s. the pleasure of, to treat o.s. to || *despacharse a su gusto* to let go, to go the whole way || *despacharse a su gusto con uno* to tell s.o. what one thinks of him, to give s.o. a piece of one's mind || *el gusto es mío* the pleasure is mine || *encontrar algo al gusto de uno* to find sth. to one's taste || *encontrar gusto en* to find pleasure in, to enjoy || *en la variedad está el gusto* variety is the spice of life || *hay gustos que merecen palos* some people have no taste, there is no accounting for tastes || *hay para todos los gustos* there is sth. for everyone *o* sth. to suit every taste || *mal a gusto* uncomfortable, ill at ease || *mucho gusto* or *tanto gusto en conocerle* how do you do?, pleased to meet you || *no hay gusto sin disgusto* there is no rose without a thorn || *no tener gusto para nada* not to feel like anything (no querer comer), not to feel like doing anything, not to be in the mood for anything (no querer hacer nada) || *por gusto* for the pleasure of it, for the sake of it, because one likes to || *que da gusto* marvellously, beautifully (adverbe), lovely, wonderful (adjectif) || *se está más a gusto aquí* we are better here, we are more comfortable here || *sobre* or *de gustos no hay nada escrito* everyone to his own taste, there's no accounting for tastes || *tener gusto a* to taste of, to taste; *tiene gusto a naranja* it tastes of orange, it tastes orangy || *tener mucho gusto en* to be very pleased to *o* glad to || *tomar gusto a* to take a liking to, to develop a taste for || *tonto que da gusto* prize idiot (tonto de remate).

gustosamente *adv* with pleasure, gladly (con placer) || tastefully.

gustoso, sa *adj* tasty, savoury [*US* savory]; *fruta gustosa* tasty fruit || pleasant, delightful, agreeable || — *gustoso le escribo a usted* I have the pleasure of writing to you || *hacer una cosa muy gustoso* to do sth. with great pleasure || *lo haré gustoso* I'll do it with pleasure, I'll do it gladly.

gutapercha *f* gutta-percha.

gutiámbar *f* gamboge.

gutural *adj/s f* guttural.

Guyana *npr f* GEOGR Guyana.

Guyana francesa *npr f* GEOGR French Guiana.

gymkhana *f* gymkhana.

H

h *f* h ‖ — *la hora H* zero hour ‖ *por H o por B* for one reason or another.

— OBSERV This letter is not usually sounded. However in popular Andalusian speech it is sometimes pronounced rather like the Spanish *j*.

¡ha! *interj* aha!, ah!

haba *f* BOT broad bean | bean (de cacao, de café) ‖ voting ball (para votar) ‖ MED bruise (cardenal) | swelling (bulto) ‖ MIN nodule (nódulo) ‖ VET tumour on a horse's palate (tumor) ‖ — *echar las habas a* to cast a spell on ‖ *en todas partes cuecen habas* it's the same the whole world over ‖ *esas son habas contadas* it's a certainty, it's a sure thing ‖ *haba de las Indias* sweet pea (guisante de olor) ‖ *haba panosa* or *menor* horsebean ‖ *haba tonca* tonka bean.

Habana (La) *n pr* GEOGR Havana.

habanera *f* habanera [Afro-Cuban dance or music].

habanero, ra *adj/s* Havanan (de La Habana).

habano, na *adj* Havanan, Havana, of Havana.
◆ *adj/s* Havanan (habitante).
◆ *m* Havana [cigar].

habar *m* bean field.

hábeas corpus *m* JUR habeas corpus.

haber *m* COM assets *pl*, credit (side); *debe y haber* liabilities and assets, debit and credit.
◆ *pl* assets, property *sing*, estate *sing* (bienes) ‖ income *sing*, salary *sing* (retribución) ‖ — FIG *tener en su haber* to be to one's credit; *tiene en su haber una gran generosidad* his great generosity is to his credit ‖ *tengo miles de pesetas en mi haber* I have thousands of pesetas in my account *o* to my credit.

haber* *vt* to have (tener) (véase OBSERV) ‖ to catch (detener); *hubieron al ladrón* they caught the thief.
◆ *v aux* to have; *he dicho* I have said; *lo hubieras encontrado* you would have found it; *de haberlo hecho yo* if I had done it.
◆ *v impers* to be; *ayer hubo fiesta en el pueblo* yesterday there was a celebration in the village; *las había muy hermosas antes* there were very lovely ones before ‖ — FAM *¡allá te las hayas!* that's your problem! ‖ *¡bien haya quien!* blessed be he who ‖ *¿cuánto hay de aquí a León?* how far is it from here to León? ‖ *era el más valiente si los hay* if anyone, he was the bravest ‖ *es de lo que no hay* there are few like him ‖ FIG *esto es lo que hay* that's all there is ‖ *es un cobarde como hay pocos* there are few as cowardly as he, he is a coward the likes of which I've rarely seen before ‖ *haber de* to have to; *han de salir mañana* they have to leave tomorrow; *no sabía que habías de salir* I didn't know that you had to leave; must (presente); *se han de pronunciar bien todas las letras* one must pronounce all the letters well; might (pasado); *hubo que pensar que* he might have thought that; will; *he de decírselo mañana* I will tell him tomorrow; to be to; *¿cómo había de saberlo?* how was I to know?; can; *¿cómo había de ser de otro modo?* how could it be otherwise? ‖ *haber que* to be necessary to, to have to, must; *hay que comer para vivir* one must eat *o* one has to eat to live, it's necessary to eat to live ‖ *habérselas con uno* to have it out with s.o., to deal with s.o. (tener que discutir con), to be up against s.o. (estar opuesto) ‖ *¡había que verlo!* you should have seen it! ‖ *habidos y por haber* past, present and future ‖ *habrá quince días que ha llegado* it must be fifteen days since he arrived, it must have been fifteen days ago that he arrived, he must have arrived about fifteen days ago ‖ *¡habráse visto!* have you ever seen such a thing? ‖ *hay* there is *sing*, there are *pl*; *hay poca gente aquí* there are few people here ‖ *¿hay manzanas?* have you any apples?, are there any apples? ‖ *lo que hay es que* the fact is that ‖ *los hay que* there are some who, there are those who ‖ *no hay de qué* don't mention it, not at all [US you're welcome] ‖ *no hay más que hablar* there is nothing more to be said ‖ *no hay más que pedir* one couldn't expect more *o* ask for more ‖ *no hay nada como el té para quitar la sed* there's nothing like tea for quenching one's thirst ‖ *no hay para* there is no reason to ‖ *no hay tal cosa* there is no such thing ‖ *poco tiempo ha* a short time ago ‖ *¿qué hay?* how are you?, what's new? (¿qué tal?), what's up?, what's the matter? (¿qué pasa?) ‖ *¿qué hay de nuevo?* what's new? ‖ *¿qué le he de hacer?* what can I do? ‖ *Simón, que Dios haya en su gloria* Simon, God rest his soul ‖ *ya no hay más* there's nothing more, there's no more.

— OBSERV *Haber* retains the antiquated transitive meaning in expressions such as: *los hijos habidos de ese matrimonio* the children from that marriage; *¡mal haya quien!* woe betide he who; *haber menester de* to need, to have need of.

— OBSERV *Haber de* is sometimes, in the present and imperfect, a substitute for the future and conditional: *¿ha de venir mañana?* will he come tomorrow?; *¿quién había de decirme que iba a ser millonario?* who could have told me that he was going to be a millionaire?

habichuela *f* bean (judía) ‖ *habichuelas verdes* French beans, green beans.

habiente *adj* having ‖ JUR *habiente, habiente derecho, derecho habiente* rightful claimant *o* owner, beneficiary, interested party.

hábil *adj* skilful [US skillful]; *un cirujano hábil* a skilful surgeon ‖ proficient, expert, good (perito) ‖ capable (capaz) ‖ clever, skilful; *una maniobra hábil* a clever manoeuvre ‖ good, suitable, adequate (adecuado); *una sala hábil para conferencias* a good room for meetings ‖ JUR competent, qualified; *hábil para testar* competent to make a will ‖ — *días hábiles* working days ‖ *en tiempo hábil* duly, at the proper time ‖ *hábil para un empleo* fit for *o* qualified for a job ‖ *ser hábil en* to be good at.

habilidad *f* skill, ability, expertise, dexterity (destreza); *tener mucha habilidad* to have a great deal of skill; *la habilidad de un político* the skill of a politician ‖ expertise, expertness (pericia) ‖ JUR capacity, competency, competence; *habilidad para suceder* capacity to succeed ‖ feat, trick; *hace muchas habilidades en el trampolín* he does a lot of feats on the trampoline ‖ talent; *la niña tuvo que lucir todas sus habilidades delante de la familia* the girl had to display all of her talents before the family ‖ DEP *prueba de habilidad* slalom (esquí).

habilidoso, sa *adj* skilfull, clever, capable, able.

habilitación *f* JUR qualification (acción de habilitar) ‖ authorization ‖ paymastership (cargo de habilitado) ‖ paymaster's office (oficina) ‖ financing (financiación) ‖ fitting out (de una casa).

habilitado *m* paymaster.

habilitar *vt* JUR to qualify, to entitle; *habilitar a uno para suceder* to qualify s.o. to succeed | to enable (permitir) | to empower (dar poderes) ‖ COM to provide; *habilitar con fondos* to provide with funds | to finance ‖ to set up, to fit out; *habilitar una casa* to set up a house ‖ *local habilitado para establecimiento comercial* suitable premises for a commercial establishment.

habiloso, sa *adj* AMER shrewd, astute (hábil, astuto).

habitabilidad *f* habitability.

habitable *adj* habitable, inhabitable.

habitación *f* dwelling, habitation (morada) ‖ habitation, residence (hecho de vivir en un sitio) ‖ room; *piso con cinco habitaciones* apartment with five rooms; *habitación de invitados* guest room; *habitación individual* single room; *habitación doble* double room ‖ bedroom (cuarto de dormir) ‖ habitat (de vegetales o de animales).

habitáculo *m* POÉT dwelling ‖ cabin (de astronave).

habitante *m/f* inhabitant; *ciudad de un millón de habitantes* city of a million inhabitants.

habitar *vt* to live in, to inhabit, to dwell in (un país, una ciudad) ‖ to live in, to reside in, to occupy (una casa).
◆ *vi* to live.

habitat; hábitat *m* habitat.

hábito *m* habit (vestidura de los religiosos) ‖ habit (costumbre); *tener malos hábitos* to have bad habits ‖ — FIG & FAM *ahorcar* or *colgar los hábitos* to give up the cloth ‖ FIG *el hábito no hace al monje* it is not the cowl that makes the monk, clothes don't make the man ‖ *tomar el hábito* to take holy orders, to take the habit, to take vows (un hombre), to take the veil, to become a nun (una mujer).

habituación *f* habituation.

habituado, da *m/f* habitué, regular [customer].

— OBSERV This word is a Gallicism used in place of *aficionado* or *parroquiano*.

habitual *adj* habitual, customary (acostumbrado) || usual, normal (usual) || regular; *un cliente habitual* a regular customer.

habitualmente *adv* habitually.

habituar *vt* to habituate, to accustom (*a* to).
◆ *vpr habituarse a* to become accustomed to, to get used to.

habitud *f* relation, connection [between two things] || habit (costumbre).

habla *f* speech (facultad de hablar) || language (lengua, idioma); *el habla española* the Spanish language || dialect, speech; *la gente de esta región tiene un habla especial* the people in this region have a special dialect || talk; *el habla de los niños* baby talk || speech, discourse, address (discurso) || — MAR *al habla* within hail || *¡al habla Miguel!* Michael speaking! (al teléfono) || *de habla española* Spanish-speaking; *países de habla española* Spanish-speaking countries || *estar al habla* or *en habla con* to be in contact with, to be in touch with || *negarle el habla a uno* not to be on speaking terms with s.o. || *perder el habla* to become speechless || *ponerse al habla con* to get in touch with (entrar en contacto), to speak to (al teléfono) || *prensa de habla francesa* French-language newspapers *pl*.

habladas *f pl* AMER boasting *sing*, bragging *sing*.

hablado, da *adj* spoken; *una lengua mal hablada* a poorly-spoken language || — *bien hablado* well-spoken || *cine hablado* talking cinema, talkies *pl* (*fam*) || *mal hablado* rude, foulmouthed.

hablador, ra *adj* talkative (que habla mucho) || gossipy (chismoso).
◆ *m/f* chatterbox, talker (parlanchín) || gossip (chismoso).

habladuría *f* rumour [*US* rumor], piece of gossip (chisme).
◆ *pl* gossip *sing* (cotilleo).

hablanchín, ina *adj* FAM talkative.
◆ *m/f* FAM talker, chatterbox.

hablante *adj* speaking.
◆ *m/f* speaker.

hablar *vi* to speak, to talk; *hablar con el vecino* to speak with the neighbour *o* to the neighbour; *estuvo hablando de ti ayer* he was speaking of you yesterday, he talked about you yesterday || FIG to go out; *habló dos años con Carmen* he went out with Carmen for two years || — *¿con quién se cree usted que está hablando?* who do you think you are talking to? || *dar mucho que hablar* to cause a lot of talk || *dejar hablar a uno* to let s.o. speak || *el hablar bien no cuesta dinero* good words cost nothing but are worth much || *eso es hablar* now you're talking || *estar hablando* to be almost alive (un retrato, una estatua) || *hablando del rey de Roma por la puerta asoma* talk of the devil (and he will appear) || *hablar al alma* to touch one's heart || *hablar alto, hablar bajo* to speak up *o* loudly, to speak softly *o* in a low voice || *hablar a medias palabras* to speak cryptically || *hablar a solas* to speak to o.s. || *hablar a tontas y a locas* to talk without rhyme or reason || *hablar bien, mal de uno* to speak well, ill *o* badly of s.o. || *hablar clara y llanamente* to speak plainly and frankly || *hablar como los indios* to speak pidgin Spanish (English, etc.), to speak broken Spanish (English, etc.) || *hablar como quien habla a la pared* or *como si lo hiciese a la pared* to be like talking to a brick wall; *estoy hablando como quien habla a la pared* it is like talking to a brick wall || *hablar como una verdulera* to speak like a fishwife || *hablar como un carretero* to swear like a trooper || *hablar como un libro* to speak like a book || *hablar con el corazón en la mano* to speak from the heart, to speak sincerely || *hablar con la nariz* to speak through one's nose || *hablar con soltura* to speak fluently *o* with fluency || *hablar de negocios, de política* to talk (about) business, (about) politics || *hablar de todo un poco* to talk about this, that and the other || *hablar de trapos* to talk about clothes || *hablar de tú, de usted a alguien* to address as «tú» *o* to address familiarly *o* to be on friendly terms with s.o. (ser amigos); to address as «usted» *o* to use the polite form of address with s.o. || *hablar en broma* to be joking || *hablar en crudo* to speak one's mind, to speak straight from the shoulder || *hablar en plata* to put it plainly || *hablar entre dientes* to mumble, to mutter || *hablar en voz alta* to speak up *o* loudly || *hablar en voz baja* or *queda* to speak in a low voice || *hablar largo y tendido de algo* to talk sth. over || *hablar más que siete* or *más que un papagayo* to talk nineteen to the dozen, to be a real chatterbox, to talk the hind leg off a donkey || *hablar para su coleto* or *para el cuello de su camisa* or *para sí* or *solo* to talk to o.s. || *hablar por boca de ganso* to speak from hearsay || *hablar por hablar* to talk for the sake of talking || *hablar por los codos* to be a real chatterbox || FIG *hablar por sí mismo* to speak volumes || *hablar por uno mismo* to speak for o.s. || *hablar sin rodeos* not to mince one's words || *hablar sin ton ni son* to talk without rhyme or reason || *hablemos poco y bien* let's get straight to the point, let's be brief || *habló el buey y dijo mu* what can you expect from a pig but a grunt? || *miente más que habla* he lies like a thief || FAM *¡ni hablar!* out of the question! || *no hay más que hablar* there's nothing more to be said || *¡puede hablar!* you're through! (al teléfono) || *¿quién habla?* who's speaking? (al teléfono) || *quien mucho habla mucho yerra* leats said soonest mended, the less said the better || *sin hablar de* without mentioning, not to mention || *sólo le falta hablar* it almost speaks, it seems almost alive (retrato), it does everything but talk (animal).
◆ *vt* to speak; *hablar (el) francés* to speak French || talk (decir); *hablar disparates* to talk nonsense || *sin hablar palabra* without saying a word, without a word.
◆ *vpr* to converse, to speak, to talk || to be spoken; *en México se habla español* Spanish is spoken in Mexico || — FIG *Pedro ya no se habla con Juana* Peter does not speak to Jane, Peter is not on speaking terms with Jane || *se está hablando de una reforma* there's some talk about a reform || *se habla español* Spanish spoken (en un letrero).

hablilla *f* rumour [*US* rumor], piece of gossip.
◆ *pl* gossip *sing* (cotilleo).

hablista *m/f* purist [of language].

Habsburgo *n pr* Hapsburg, Habsburg.

hacecillo *m* BOT fascicle || small bunch *o* bundle *o* sheaf (de mieses).

hacedero, ra *adj* feasible, practicable.

hacedor, ra *m/f* creator, maker || *el Sumo* or *el Supremo Hacedor* the Creator, the Maker.

hacendado, da *adj* landed, property-owning; *un hombre hacendado* a landed man.
◆ *m/f* landowner (terrateniente) || AMER farmer [*US* rancher] (ganadero).

hacendar* *vt* to make over *o* to give property to.
◆ *vpr* to settle; *hacendarse en Argentina* to settle in Argentina.

hacendero, ra *adj* industrious, hard-working.

hacendista *m* economist, financial expert.

hacendoso, sa *adj* industrious, hard-working || *hacendoso como una hormiga* as busy as a bee.

hacer*

> **1.** FABRICAR, EJECUTAR, COMPONER **2.** CAUSAR **3.** ACOSTUMBRAR **4.** OTROS SENTIDOS **5.** PARA SUSTITUIR OTRO VERBO **6.** LOCUCIONES DIVERSAS **7.** CONVENIR, CONCORDAR **8.** HACER DE **9.** HACER PARA, POR, COMO **10.** HACER, CON INFINITIVO **11.** IMPERSONAL **12.** VERBO PRONOMINAL

1. FABRICAR, EJECUTAR, COMPONER *vt* to make; *hacer muebles, un pastel, la cama* to make furniture, a cake, one's bed; *hacer una lista* to make a list; *hacer planes* to make plans || to do; *hacer sus deberes* to do one's homework; *haz lo que te dijeron* do as they told you || to make, to create (crear) || to write, to compose, to make up; *hacer un poema* to write a poem || to write (un libro) || to work, to do; *hacer un milagro, maravillas* to work a miracle, wonders || to draw up; *hacer un contrato* to draw up a contract || to make, to build (una casa) || to pack (la maleta) || to make, to deliver (un discurso) || to pay (una visita) || to wage (la guerra) || to make (un error)
2. CAUSAR *vt* to make; *hacer humo* to make smoke; *el retraso hizo que perdiésemos el tren* the delay made us miss the train || to give, to cast; *hacer sombra* to give shade, to cast a shadow.
3. ACOSTUMBRAR *vt* to accustom; *hacer su cuerpo a la fatiga* to accustom one's body to fatigue.
4. OTROS SENTIDOS *vt* to hold, to contain; *esta botella hace un litro* this bottle holds a litre || to make (nombrar); *le hicieron presidente* they made him (their) president; *hacerle a alguien heredero* to make s.o. one's heir || to think, to believe, to suppose (pensar); *yo te hacía en Montevideo* I thought you were in Montevideo; *le hacía estudiando* I thought he was studying || to do (la barba, el pelo) || to cut (las uñas) || to do, to make (guisar) || to make (obligar); *hizo que la señora se sentara* he made the lady sit down || to make (volver); *esto lo hace más fácil* this makes it easier || to make (sumar); *esto hace veinte* this makes twenty || TEATR to act, to play the part of (representar un papel)
5. PARA SUSTITUIR OTRO VERBO *vt* to do; *salió y los demás hicieron lo mismo* he went out and the others did the same.
6. LOCUCIONES DIVERSAS *vt a lo hecho pecho* it is no use crying over spilt milk, what is done is done || *¡buena la has hecho!* you've done it now! || *dar que hacer* to give a lot to do, to give trouble || *el que la hace la paga* one must face the music, one must face the consequences || *hacer bien* to do the right thing || AUT & AVIAC *hacer cien kilómetros por hora* to do *o* to go a hundred kilometres per hour || FOT *hacer una copia* to make a print || *hacer daño* to hurt, to harm || *hacer de su hijo un médico* to make one's son a doctor || *hacer el amor* to court (cortejar), to make love || *hacer el bobo* to act the clown || *hacer el papel de* to play, to play the part of || *hacer las veces de* to act as, to serve as || FAM *hacerle la pascua* or *hacerle un pie agua a uno* to mess things up for s.o. (fastidiar) || *hacerle la vida imposible a uno* to make life impossible for s.o. || *hacer otro tanto* to do the same thing || *hacer pedazos* to tear to pieces (desgarrar), to smash to pieces, to break to pieces (romper) || *hacer presente* to let know, to notify, to inform, to tell (avisar), to state (declarar) || *hacer recados* to run errands || FAM *hacer sus necesidades* to answer nature's call, to relieve o.s. || *hacer tiempo* to kill time || *hacer todo lo posible para* to do everything possible to, to do one's best to || *hacer una apuesta* to lay a bet || *hacer una cosa arrastrando* to do sth. against one's will *o* unwillingly || *hacer una cosa con los pies* to botch *o* to bungle sth., to do sth. in a slapdash way (hacerla muy mal) || *hacer una de las*

suyas to be up to one's (old) tricks || *hacer una objeción* to make *o* to raise an objection || *hacer una pregunta a* to ask a question, to put a question to || COM *hacer una rebaja* to give a reduction || *hacer un favor a alguien* to do s.o. a favour || *hacer uso de la palabra* to take the floor, to speak (en una conferencia, etc.) || *hacer vida ascética* to lead an ascetic life || *haga lo que quiera* do as you please || *haz bien y no mires a quien* do well and dread no shame || *mandar hacer un vestido* to have a dress made || *más hace el que quiere que el que puede* where there's a will there's a way || *no tener nada que hacer* not to have anything to do || *por más que haga, haga lo que haga* whatever he does || *¿qué hemos de hacer?* what can we do? || *¿qué le vamos a hacer?* what are we going to do? || *¿qué quiere que haga?* what do you want me to do? || *¿qué tiempo hace?* what is the weather like? || FIG *ser el que hace y deshace* to rule the roost, to be the boss | *¡ya la hizo!* now you've done it!
7. CONVENIR, CONCORDAR *vi* to go; *esto hace con aquello* this goes with that || to be suitable, to be fitting (convenir) || — *eso no le hace* that has no importance, that doesn't matter || *mil dólares más o menos no le hace* a few thousand dollars don't matter to him || *no hace al caso* it has nothing to do with it.
8. HACER DE to work as; *hace de portero* he works as a caretaker || to act as, to serve as; *hacer de madre para alguien* to act as a mother to s.o. || to act; *hacer de tonto* to act the fool || to act, to pretend to be (simular); *hacer de valiente* he acts brave || to do; *hacer de todo un poco* to do a little of everything || TEATR to act as, to play the part of, to do; *hace de Hamlet* he plays the part of Hamlet.
9. HACER PARA, POR, COMO to do one's best to (hacer todo lo posible); *hizo para venir* he did his best to come || to try to (intentar) || — *hacer como que* or *si* to pretend (that), to act as if; *hace como que no sabe nada* he acts as if he knows nothing || FIG & FAM *hacer por la vida* to eat.
10. HACER, CON INFINITIVO to make; *hacer reír, llorar a alguien* to make s.o. laugh, cry || to make (obligar); *la hizo venir* he made her come || — JUR *hacer comparecer* to summon to appear || *hacer entrar, subir a uno* to bring *o* to send *o* to ask s.o. in, up || *hacerle esperar a uno* to keep s.o. waiting || *hacer saber* to inform, to let know, to tell || *hacer saltar las lágrimas a uno* to make s.o. cry, to bring tears to s.o.'s eyes || FAM *hacer sudar a alguien* to give s.o. a lot of trouble || *no hice más que* or *sino decírselo* I only told him, all I did was tell him.
11. IMPERSONAL to be; *hace calor, frío, mucho calor, mucho frío* it is hot, cold, very hot, very cold || ago (tiempo); *hace tres días* three days ago; *hace mucho tiempo* a long time ago; *¿cuánto tiempo hace?* how long ago? || — *¿cuánto tiempo hace que?* how long has it been since?, how long is it since? || *desde hace dos años* for two years; *no le veo desde hace dos años* I haven't seen him for two years || FAM *¿hace?* OK?, is it a deal?
12. VERBO PRONOMINAL *a)* volverse to become; *hacerse sacerdote* to become a priest; *el Verbo se hizo carne* the Word became flesh; *hacerse un atleta* to become an athlete; *el ruido se hizo demasiado fuerte* the noise became too loud; *hacerse rico* to become wealthy *o* rich || to become, to change into; *el vino se hizo vinagre* the wine changed into vinegar || to get, to become, to grow; *hacerse tarde* to get late; *hacerse viejo* to grow old || to mature, to ripen; *el vino se hace* wine matures; *b)* acostumbrarse to become accustomed, to get used; *hacerse al calor* to become accustomed to the heat; *no me hice a vivir solo* I couldn't get used to living alone; *c)* estar hecho to be made; *el pan se hace con harina* bread is made with flour; *d)* locuciones diversas *hacerse a la mar* to put to sea || *hacerse a la vela* to set sail || *hacerse a sí mismo* to be a self-made man || *hacerse atrás* to move back || *hacerse a un lado, echarse a un lado* to step *o* to stand aside, to make way, to move over (una persona), to draw *o* to pull to one side (un vehículo) || *hacerse cortar el pelo* to have one's hair cut || *hacerse de* or *con* to get (conseguir), to get hold of (tomar), to make off with (apropiarse); *se ha hecho con mi libro* he has made off with my book; to get hold of (en deporte); *se hizo con el balón* he got hold of the ball || *hacerse de nuevo con* to regain; *hacerse de nuevo con el poder* to regain power || *hacerse de rogar* to take a lot of asking, to play hard to get, to have to be coaxed || *hacerse el* or *la* to act like, to pretend to be (fingir, blasonar) || FAM *hacerse el remolón* to shirk, to slack (eludir el trabajo), to refuse to budge (no moverse) || *hacerse fuerte en* to entrench o.s. on *o* in (fortificarse), to remain firm in (mantener una actitud) || *hacerse indispensable* to make o.s. indispensable || *hacerse el olvidadizo* to pretend to be forgetful || *hacerse pasar por* to pass o.s. off as || *hacerse tres mil dólares al mes* to make three thousand dollars a month || *se me hace que va a llover* it seems to me that it is going to rain, I think that it is going to rain.

haces *m pl* —> **haz.**

hacia *prep* towards, toward; *hacia la derecha* towards the right || near (cerca de) || at about; *hacia las dos* at about two o'clock || towards (para con) || — *hacia abajo* down, downwards || *hacia acá* this way, here, over here || *hacia adelante* forwards || *hacia arriba* up, upwards || *hacia atrás* backwards || *hacia casa* homeward, towards home, home || *hacia donde* where, wither || *vamos hacia allá* let's start making our way there, let's go over there.

hacienda *f* country property (propiedad rural) || hacienda, ranch (en América del Sur) || property, fortune, possessions *pl* (bienes) || AMER livestock, cattle (ganado) || — *hacienda pública* public treasury || *Ministerio de Hacienda* Exchequer (en Gran Bretaña), Treasury (en Estados Unidos), Ministry of Finance (en los demás países) || *Ministro de Hacienda* Chancellor of the Exchequer (en Gran Bretaña), Secretary of the Treasury (en Estados Unidos), Minister of Finance (en los demás países).

hacina *f* stack, rick (conjunto de haces) || FIG heap, pile.

hacinamiento *m* stacking, piling, heaping.

hacinar *vt* to stack (colocar en hacinas) || FIG to stack (up), to pile (up) (amontonar); *hacinar las pruebas contra un culpable* to stack up proof against a guilty person.
◆ *vpr* to be crowded, to be piled, to be huddled; *la familia se hacinaba en una choza* the family was crowded into a hut.

hacha *f* torch (antorcha) || large candle (de cera).

hacha *f* axe [*US* ax]; *un hacha de armas* a battle-axe || hatchet (más pequeña) || FIG & FAM ace [*US* whiz]; *ser un hacha en matemáticas* to be an ace at mathematics; *es un hacha del volante* he is an ace driver, he is an ace at the wheel.

hachazo *m* axe blow, stroke with an axe, hack || lunge (de un toro).

hache *f* aitch (nombre de la letra h) || — FIG & FAM *llámele usted hache* call it what you like, it's all the same.

hachear *vt/vi* to chop, to hew.

hachero *m* torch stand (candelero) || candlestick (para vela) || woodcutter, lumberjack (leñador).

hachís *m* hashish.

hacho *m* torch (antorcha) || beacon, beacon hill *o* head (altozano).

hachón *m* —> **hacha.**

hachuela *f* hatchet.

hada *f* fairy || *cuento de hadas* fairy tale.

Hades *npr m* MIT Hades (Plutón).

hado *m* fate, destiny.

hagiografía *f* hagiography (vida de los santos).

hagiográfico, ca *adj* hagiographic.

hagiógrafo *m* hagiographer.

hagiología *m* hagiology.

haiga *m* FAM superluxurious limousine.

Haití *npr m* GEOGR Haiti.

haitiano, na *adj/s* Haitian (de Haití).

¡hala! *interj* come on!, go on!

halagador, ra *adj* flattering.

halagar *vt* to flatter || to please, to gratify; *me halaga tu propuesta* your proposal pleases me || to cajole (adular).

halago *m* flattery (lisonja) || cajolery (adulación) || *palabras de halago* flattering words.

halagüeño, ña *adj* flattering (lisonjero) || promising (alentador); *perspectivas halagüeñas* promising prospects || pleasing, gratifying (agradable) || attractive (atractivo).

halar *vt* MAR to haul, to pull, to heave (un cabo) | to tow (una gabarra).

halcón *m* falcon, hawk (ave) || FIG hawk || AMER FAM government-paid thug (matón a sueldo del Gobierno) || — *halcón campestre* domesticated falcon || *halcón niego* eyas || *halcón palumbario* goshawk || *halcón peregrino* peregrine falcon || *halcón zahareño* haggard hawk.

halconería *f* falconry, hawking (caza con halcón).

halconero *m* falconer.

¡hale! *interj* get going!, come on!, go on!

haleche *m* anchovy (boquerón).

halibut *m* ZOOL halibut.

haliéutico, ca *adj* halieutic.
◆ *f* halieutics.

hálito *m* breath (aliento) || POÉT breath of wind, zephyr, gentle breeze.

halo *m* halo.

halógeno, na *adj* QUÍM halogenous.
◆ *m* QUÍM halogen.

haloideo, a *adj* QUÍM haloid.
◆ *m* QUÍM haloid.

haltera *f* DEP dumbbell.

halterofilia *f* DEP weight-lifting, weightlifting.

halterófilo, la *adj* weight-lifting, weighlifting.
◆ *m/f* weight-lifter.

hall *m* hall [*US* entrance hall].

hallado, da *adj* found, discovered || — FIG *bien hallado* at ease, in one's element | *mal hallado* uneasy, ill at ease, out of one's element.

hallar *vt* to find (encontrar); *quien busca halla* seek and ye shall find || to discover (descubrir) || to come across, to run across (topar) || to find, to locate (una persona).
◆ *vpr* to be (encontrarse); *hallarse en Madrid* to be in Madrid || to be; *hallarse muy enfermo* to be very sick || — *hallarse con una cosa* to find sth. || *hallarse en todo* to have a hand in everything || *no hallarse* to feel out of place, to feel like a fish out of water.

hallazgo *m* discovery, finding (descubrimiento) || find, finding (cosa descubierta) || find; *esta expresión es un hallazgo* this expression is a find.

hamaca *f* hammock (cama) || deck chair [US canvas lawn chair] (tumbona) || palanquin (vehículo) || AMER swing (columpio).

hamadría *f*; **hamadriada** *f* MIT hamadryad.

hámago *m* propolis, bee glue (de las abejas).

hamaquear *vt* AMER to rock, to swing (mecer).

hambre *f* hunger; *aplacar el hambre* to satisfy one's hunger || famine || starvation (escasez); *salario de hambre* starvation salary || FIG & FAM hunger, longing, desire (deseo) || — *a buen hambre no hay pan duro* hunger is the best sauce || *confundir el hambre con las ganas de comer* to confuse the chaff with the grain || *el hambre aguza el ingenio* hunger sharpens the wit || FIG *el hambre es mala consejera* hunger is a poor adviser || *engañar el hambre* to stave off hunger || *huelga del hambre* hunger strike || FIG & FAM *juntarse el hambre con las ganas de comer* to combine (two circumstances) || *matar a uno de hambre* to starve s.o. to death || *matar el hambre* to stave off hunger || *morir* or *morirse de hambre* to starve to death, to die from starvation (morir), to starve (estar hambriento) || *pasar hambre* to be hungry, to go hungry || FIG & FAM *ser más listo que el hambre* to be (as) sharp as a needle || *tener hambre* to be hungry (de comida), to hunger; *tiene hambre de riquezas* he hungers for riches || FAM *tengo un hambre que no veo* or *un hambre canina* I am hungry enough to eat a horse, I am starving, I am as hungry as a wolf, I am ravenously hungry.

— OBSERV The word *hambre*, although feminine, is preceded by the masculine article *el* to avoid hiatus.

hambreador, ra *adj* AMER exploiting (que abusa).

◆ *m/f* AMER exploiter (el que abusa).

hambriento, ta *adj* hungry, starving, famished || FIG *hambriento de* longing for, hungry for.

◆ *m/f* starving person.

◆ *m pl* the hungry, the starving, starving people.

hambrina; **hambruna** *f* AMER ravenous hunger.

hambrón, ona *adj* FAM famished, starving.

◆ *m/f* glutton [never satisfied] || starving person (persona hambrienta).

Hamburgo *n pr* GEOGR Hamburg.

hamburgués, esa *adj* Hamburg.

◆ *m/f* native *o* inhabitant of Hamburg.

◆ *f* hamburger, hamburg steak, hamburger steak.

hamburguesería *f* fast food.

hampa *f* underworld; *el hampa de Chicago* the Chicago underworld.

hampesco, ca *adj* underworld, of the underworld.

hampón, ona *adj* bullying, rowdy (pendenciero) || roguish, shady (bribón).

◆ *m* thug, tough.

hámster *m* ZOOL hamster (roedor).

handicap *m* DEP handicap; *sufrir un handicap* to have a handicap.

hangar *m* AVIAC hangar (cobertizo).

Hanoi *n pr* GEOGR Hanoi.

hansa *f* hanse.

hanseático, ca *adj* hanseatic.

haragán, ana *adj* idle, lazy.

◆ *m/f* idler, lazybones.

haraganear *vi* to idle, to loaf around, to lounge.

haraganería *f* idleness, laziness.

harakiri; **haraquiri** *m* hara-kiri.

harapiento, ta *adj* ragged, tattered, in rags.

harapo *m* rag, tatter (andrajo) || weak *o* low grade alcohol (aguardiente) || *andar hecho un harapo* to be in rags.

haraposo, sa *adj* ragged, tattered, in rags.

haraquiri *m* → **harakiri.**

Harare *n pr* GEOGR Harare [Salisbury].

harca; **jarca** *f* Morrocan military expedition || band of Morrocan rebels.

— OBSERV The initial *h* is aspirate.

hardware *m* hardware (de una computadora).

harem; **harén** *m* harem.

harina *f* flour; *el pan se hace con harina* bread is made with flour || meal, flour; *harina de pescado* fish meal || powder (polvo menudo) || — *almacén de harina* granary || FAM *donde no hay harina, todo es mohína* when poverty comes in the door love flies out of the window | *eso es harina de otro costal* that's another kettle of fish || *fábrica de harina* flour mill || *harina de avena* oatmeal || *harina de flor* wheatmeal || *harina de maíz* cornflour || *harina lacteada* malted milk || *metido en harina* doughy, heavy (pan), engrossed, absorbed (absorto), busy (ocupado), stout, fat (gordo).

harinero, ra *adj* flour || *molino harinero* flour mill.

harinoso, sa *adj* floury; *pan harinoso* floury bread || farinaceous (farináceo).

harmonía *f* (y sus derivados) → **armonía.**

harnero *m* sifter, sieve (criba).

harpa *f* MÚS harp.

harpía *f* → **arpía.**

harpillera *f* sacking, sackcloth (tela).

hartada *f* → **hartazgo.**

hartar *vt* to satiate, to satisfy (calmar el hambre) || FIG to satisfy (un deseo) | to weary, to bore, to tire (cansar) | to annoy (fastidiar) || *hartar de palos* to shower blows on.

◆ *vpr* to eat one's fill (comer bastante) || to gorge o.s., to stuff o.s. (comer demasiado); *hartarse de pasteles* to stuff o.s. with cakes, to gorge o.s. on cakes || FIG to get tired (*de* of), to get fed up (*de* with); *hartarse de esperar* to get tired of waiting || — FAM *hartarse de* dormir to have one's fill of sleep || *hasta hartarse* one's fill; *comer hasta hartarse* to eat one's fill; until one has had enough, until one is fed up.

hartazgo *m*; **hartada** *f* bellyful (*fam*), (exceso, demasía) || — *darse un hartazgo* to eat one's fill (comer bastante), to overeat, to eat too much, to get indigestion (comer demasiado), to have one's fill of; *nos dimos un hartazgo de música anoche* we had our fill of music last night; to have a bellyful (*fam*); *me he dado un hartazgo de cine* I've had a bellyful of the pictures.

harto, ta *adj* full, satiated (de comer) || FIG tired, fed up (cansado) || — FIG & FAM *estar harto de* to be fed up with, to be sick of; *estoy harto de oír tus quejas* I am fed up with listening to your complaints.

◆ *adv* enough (bastante) || very, quite (muy).

hartón *m* FAM bellyful (hartazgo) || AMER glutton.

hartura *f* satiety (de comer) || abundance || FIG fulfilment [US fulfillment], satisfaction (de un deseo) || — FIG & FAM *me entró tal hartura que...* I got so fed up that... | *¡qué hartura!* what a drag!, what a bore! || *tener una hartura de* to be fed up with, to have had one's fill of; *tengo una hartura de cine* I am fed up with the cinema, I have had my fill of the pictures.

hasta *prep* up to, as far as; *hasta allí* as far as there; *hasta aquí* up to here || to; *desde París hasta Madrid* from Paris to Madrid || until, till; *no vendrá hasta mañana* he won't come until tomorrow; *no se levantó hasta terminar su lectura* he didn't get up until he had finished reading || — *es malo hasta más no poder* he is as evil as can be || *hasta ahora, hasta la fecha* until now, up to now, so far, to date || *¡hasta ahora!* see you later!, see you! || *¿hasta cuándo?* until when?, how long? || *¿hasta dónde?* how far?, up to where? || *hasta el punto que* to such a point that || *hasta entonces* until then, until that time, up to then || *¡hasta la vista!* see you!, good-bye! || *¡hasta luego!, ¡hasta después!, ¡hasta pronto!* see you later!, see you!, see you soon [US so long!] || *¡hasta mañana!* see you tomorrow || *hasta más no poder* as much (hard, fast, etc.) as one can, as much as can be *o* as possible; *correr hasta más no poder* to run as fast as one can || *hasta que* until, till || *hasta tal punto que* to such a point that || *¡hasta más ver!* I'll be seing you! [US so long!].

◆ *adv* even; *hasta los niños saben esto* even children know this; *hasta dice que* he even says that; *hasta se burla de nosotros* he even mocks us.

hastiado, da *adj* disgusted (*de* with), (asqueado) || tired (*de* of), (cansado).

hastial *m* gable end || FIG lout (hombre tosco) || MIN lateral wall of an excavation.

— OBSERV When *hastial* means *lout* the *h* is aspirate.

hastiar *vt* to disgust, to sicken (asquear) || to annoy (fastidiar) || to bore, to weary (aburrir).

◆ *vpr* to get fed up (*de* with), to get tired (*de* of).

hastío *m* disgust (asco) || weariness, boredom (tedio) || — *causar hastío* to bore (aburrir), to sicken, to disgust (dar asco) || *sentir hastío de un trabajo* to be fed up with a job, to be sick of a job.

hatajo *m* small herd *o* flock (rebaño) || FIG & FAM heap, bunch, lot; *un hatajo de disparates* a lot of nonsense.

hatijo *m* cover of beehive entrance.

hatillo *m* small flock *o* herd (rebaño) || bundle [of belongings] (paquetito) || FAM *tomar* or *coger su hatillo* to pack one's bags.

hato *m* flock, herd (rebaño) || provisions *pl* (víveres) || belongings *pl* things, *pl* (efectos) || FIG band, gang; *hato de pícaros* band of rogues | lot, heap, bunch (de cosas) || AMER cattle ranch (hacienda) || — FAM *andar con el hato a cuestas* to be a rover, to roam about | *liar el hato* to do a bunk, to hop it (irse), to kick the bucket (morir).

Hawai *n pr* GEOGR Hawaii.

hawaiano, na *adj/s* Hawaiian.

haya *f* BOT beech, beech tree.

Haya (La) *n pr* GEOGR The Hague.

hayaca *f* AMER turnover made of corn and filled with meat or fish then wrapped in a banana leaf.

hayal; **hayedo** *m* beech grove.

hayo *m* BOT coca || coca leaves [chewed by Indians].

hayucal *m* beech grove.

hayuco *m* beechnut (fruto del haya).

haz *m* bundle, bunch (de cosas) || FÍS beam (de rayos luminosos); *haz de electrones* electron beam || sheaf (de trigo) || truss (de paja) faggot, bundle (de leña) || bundle (fajo).

◆ *f* face (rostro) || right side (lado opuesto al envés) || surface, face; *la* or *el haz de la Tierra* the face of the earth.

◆ *pl* fasces *pl* (de los lictores).

haza *f* plot of arable land.

hazaña *f* exploit, feat, deed; *las hazañas del Cid* the feats of El Cid.

hazañería *f* fuss.

hazmerreír *m* laughingstock; *ser el hazmerreír del pueblo* to be the laughingstock of the village.

HB *abrev de Herri Batasuna* Basque independence party.

¡he! *interj* hey!

he *adv dem* (used with the adverbs *«aquí»* or *«allí»* and with the pronouns *«me», «te», «le», «la», «lo»* etc.) *he aquí* here is, here are; *he allí* there is; *heme aquí* here I am; *hete aquí* here you are; *hele aquí* here he is; *he aquí las consecuencias de su comportamiento* these are the consequences of your behaviour.

hebdomadario, ria *adj* weekly.

hebén *adj* type of large, white grape (uva).

hebijón *m* tongue *o* pin of a buckle (de una hebilla).

hebilla *f* buckle, clasp; *hebilla de cinturón* belt buckle.

hebra *f* thread (hilo) || lenght of thread (trozo de hilo) || fibre [US fiber], string (de verduras) || sinew (de carne) || filament (filamento) || grain (de madera) || thread (de araña, gusano de seda) || FIG thread (del discurso) || MIN vein || — AMER *de una hebra* all at once, in one breath || FAM *pegar la hebra* to start a conversation (entablar una conversación), to chat (estar charlando).
◆ *pl* POÉT hair.

hebraico, ca *adj* Hebraic.

hebraísmo *m* Hebraism.

hebraísta; hebraizante *m/f* Hebraist.

hebreo, a *adj/s* Hebrew.

Hébridas *npr fpl* GEOGR Hebrides.

hecatombe *f* hecatomb || FIG hecatomb, slaughter (matanza) | disaster (desastre).

heces *f pl* faeces (excrementos).

hectárea *f* hectare (medida).

héctico, ca *adj* MED hectic, consumptive.

hectogramo *m* hectogramme [US hectogram].

hectolitro *m* hectolitre [US hetoliter].

hectómetro *m* hectometre [US hectometer].

hectovatio *m* ELECTR hectowatt.

hecha *f* date (fecha) || *de esta, aquella hecha* from now, then on.

hechicería *f* witchcraft, sorcery || FIG enchantment, charm, spell (seducción).

hechicero, ra *adj* magic, bewitching, enchanting || FIG charming, enchanting, bewitching; *mujer, mirada hechicera* bewitching woman, look.
◆ *m* sorcerer, wizard (brujo) || charmer, enchanter || witch doctor (en África, etc.).
◆ *f* witch, sorceress (bruja).

hechizar *vt* to cast a spell on, to bewitch || FIG to bewitch, to enchant, to fascinate.

hechizo *m* magic, sorcery, witchcraft (hechicería) || charm, spell (sortilegio) || FIG enchantment, fascination, spell, charm (encanto) | charmer (persona que hechiza).

hecho, cha *p p* de «hacer» || — *bien hecho* well made, well done (cosa), well-proportioned, shapely (mujer), well-built (hombre) || *¡bien hecho!* well done! || *dicho y hecho* no sooner said than done || FIG *está hecho un monstruo* he is a monster | *estar hecho* to be like (parecer), to have become (haberse vuelto) || *¡hecho!* agreed!, done!, all right! || *hecho a la medida* made to measure [US custom-made]; *pantalón hecho a la medida* trousers made to measure [US custom-made trousers] || *hecho a mano* hand-made || *hecho a máquina* machine-made || *lo hecho hecho está* what is done is done || *mal hecho* badly made, badly done (cosa), oddly-shaped (persona) || *ropa hecha* ready-made clothes, ready-to-wear clothes.
◆ *adj* mature; *hombre hecho* mature man || finished (terminado) || — *hecho y derecho* real, in every sense of the word; *un hombre hecho y derecho* a real man || *muy hecho* overdone (carne) || *poco hecho* underdone (carne).
◆ *m* act, deed (acción) || feat; *hecho de armas* feat of arms || fact; *debido al hecho de que...* due to the fact that... || matter (cuestión) || event (suceso) || — *de hecho* in fact, as a matter of fact, actually (en realidad), de facto (sentido jurídico) || *del dicho al hecho hay mucho* or *gran trecho* there's many a slip twixt the cup and the lip, saying and doing are different things || *el hecho es que...* the fact is that... || *es un hecho que...* it's a fact that... || *hecho consumado* fait accompli, accomplished fact || JUR *hecho jurídico* juridical event || REL *Hechos de los Apóstoles* Acts of the Apostles || *hechos y milagros* doings, exploits || *no hay que tomar las palabras por hechos* one should not take words at their face value || *vías de hecho* acts of violence, assault and battery || *volvamos al hecho* let's get back to the matter in hand.

hechura *f* making (fabricación) || making-up, confection (confección de un traje) || cut (forma de la ropa) || form, shape (forma de un objeto) || workmanship (calidad de la fabricación) || build, form, shape (del cuerpo) || FIG creation, doing (obra) || creature; *somos hechuras de Dios* we are creatures of God || FIG *entre sastres no se pagan hechuras* what's a favour between friends?

heder* *vi* to stink, to reek (oler mal).

hediente; hediento, ta *adj* stinking, reeking, fetid.

hediondez *f* stench, stink, reek, fetidness (hedor).

hediondo, da *adj* stinking, foul-smelling, smelly, fetid (pestilente) || FIG repulsive, revolting.

hedonismo *m* hedonism.

hedonista *adj* FIL hedonistic, hedonic.
◆ *m/f* hedonist.

hedor *m* stench, stink, reek, fetidness.

hegelianismo *m* FIL Hegelianism.

hegeliano, na *adj/s* Hegelian.

hegemonía *f* hegemony.

hégira; héjira *f* hegira, hejira (era mahometana).

helada *f* freeze (fenómeno atmosférico) || frost (escarcha) || *helada blanca* hoarfrost.

heladera *f* (ice-cream) freezer (para hacer helados) || AMER refrigerator.

heladería *f* ice-cream stall *o* parlour *o* shop.

heladero *m* ice-cream man.

helado, da *adj* frozen, icy || freezing cold, icy (muy frío) || frozen, as cold as ice, freezing; *tengo los pies helados* my feet are frozen || iced (café) || — *estoy helado* I am chilled to the bone, I am freezing (cold) || FIG *quedarse helado* to be dumb-founded *o* flabbergasted (sorpresa), to be scared stiff (miedo).
◆ *m* ice cream; *un helado de vainilla* a vanilla ice cream || *helado de corte* wafer.

heladora *f* (ice-cream) freezer (para hacer helados) || refrigerator, icebox (nevera).

heladura *f* crack.

helamiento *m* freezing.

helar* *vt* to freeze; *el frío hiela el agua de los ríos* the cold freezes the water in the rivers || to harden, to set, to congeal (aceite, grasa) || to ice, to chill (enfriar mucho) || FIG to dumbfound (dejar pasmado) | to daunt, to discourage (desanimar) || *hace un frío que hiela las piedras* it's freezing cold.
◆ *vpr* to freeze, to congeal (líquidos) || to harden, to set, to congeal (aceite, grasa) || to become frozen, to freeze over (un estanque, etc.) || to freeze (motor) || to ice up (alas, carriles) || to be frost-bitten (plantas) || FIG to freeze to death; *en invierno se hiela uno* in winter one freezes to death || FIG *se me heló la sangre* my blood curdled *o* ran cold.
◆ *v impers* to freeze; *ayer heló* it froze yesterday.

helechal *m* fern-covered ground.

helecho *m* BOT fern.

Helena *npr f* Helen.

helénico, ca *adj* Hellenic, Greek (griego).

helenio *m* BOT elecampane.

helenismo *m* Hellenism.

helenista *adj* Hellenistic.
◆ *m/f* Hellenist.

helenístico, ca *adj* Hellenistic.

helenización *f* Hellenization.

helenizar *vt* to hellenize.

heleno, na *adj* Hellenic, Greek.
◆ *m/f* Hellene, Greek (griego).

helera *f* AMER refrigerator.

helero *m* glacier (ventisquero) || snow cap (capa de nieve) || ice sheet (masa de hielo).

helgadura *f* gap (entre los dientes).

heliaco, ca *adj* ASTR heliacal.

hélice *m* propeller, airscrew (de avión) || propeller, screw (de barco) || ANAT helix (de la oreja) || MAT helix || ZOOL helix (caracol) || spiral (espiral).

helicoidal *adj* helicoidal.

helicoide *m* MAT helicoid.

helicón *m* MÚS helicon.

helicóptero *m* AVIAC helicopter.

heliocéntrico, ca *adj* ASTR heliocentric.

heliogábalo *m* glutton || *comer como un heliogábalo* to eat like a horse.

Heliogábalo *npr m* Heliogabalus.

heliograbado *m* IMPR heliogravure, photoengraving.

heliograbador *m* IMPR photoengraver.

heliografía *f* heliography.

heliógrafo *m* heliograph.

helión *m* FÍS helium nucleus.

helioscopio *m* helioscope.

heliosis *f* MED heliosis.

helioterapia MED heliotherapy.

heliotipia *f* heliotype.

heliotropina *f* QUÍM heliotropin.

heliotropismo *m* BOT heliotropism.

heliotropo *m* BOT & MIN heliotrope.

helipuerto *m* heliport.

helmintiasis *f* MED helminthiasis.

helminto *m* ZOOL helminth.

Helsinki *n pr* GEOGR Helsinki.

Helvecia *npr f* GEOGR Helvetia [Switzerland].

helvecio, cia *adj/s* Helvetian, Swiss.

helvético, ca *adj* Helvetic, Helvetian.
◆ *m/f* Helvetian.

hemático, ca *adj* haematic [US hematic].

hematíe *m* ANAT red corpuscle (glóbulo rojo).

hematina *f* haematin [US hematin, hematine].

hematites *f* MIN haematite [US hematite].

hematocito *m* haematocyte, haemocyte [US hematocyte, hemocyte].

hematología *f* MED haematology [*US* hematology].

hematológico, ca *adj* MED haematological, haematologic.

hematólogo *m* MED haematologist [*US* hematologist].

hematoma *m* MED hematoma.

hematosis *f* BIOL haematosis [*US* hematosis].

hematozoario *m* ZOOL haematozoan, haematozoon [*US* hematozoan, hematozoon].

hematuria *f* MED haematuria [*US* hematuria].

hembra *f* female, she (de los animales); *la yegua es la hembra del caballo* the mare is the female horse *o* the she-horse || female, hen (de las aves) || FAM girl; *tiene tres hijos, dos hembras y un varón* he has three children, two girls and one boy | woman; *una buena hembra* a good-looking woman || TECN female | clasp (de broche) | eye (de corchete) | socket (de enchufe) | nut (de tornillo).
◆ *adj* female || feminine (femenino) || *una mujer muy hembra* a real woman.

hembraje *m* AMER female stock.

hembrilla *f* TECN female (de ciertas piezas) | eyebolt (armella).

hembruno, na *adj* female.

hemeroteca *f* newspaper library.

hemiciclo *m* hemicycle || floor (del Parlamento).

hemicránea *f* MED hemicrania.

hemiedro, dra *adj* hemihedral.

hemiplejía *f* MED hemiplegia.

hemipléjico, ca *adj/s* MED hemiplegic.

hemíptero, ra *adj* ZOOL hemipterous.
◆ *m* ZOOL hemipteran [*US* hemipteron].
◆ *pl* ZOOL hemiptera.

hemisférico, ca *adj* hemispheric, hemispherical.

hemisferio *m* hemisphere.

hemistiquio *m* hemistich (en poesía).

hemofilia *f* MED haemophilia [*US* hemophilia].

hemofílico, ca *adj* haemophilic [*US* hemophilic].
◆ *m/f* haemophiliac [*US* hemophiliac].

hemoglobina *f* BIOL haemoglobin [*US* hemoglobin].

hemograma *m* MED haemogram.

hemólisis *f* MED haemolysis [*US* hemolysis].

hemoptisis *f* MED haemoptysis [*US* hemoptysis].

hemorragia *f* MED haemorrhage, hemorrhage || FIG drain || *hemorragia nasal* nosebleed.

hemorrágico, ca *adj* MED haemorrhagic [*US* hemorrhagic].

hemorroidal *adj* MED haemorrhoidal [*US* hemorrhoidal].

hemorroides *f pl* MED haemorrhoids [*US* hemorrhoids], piles (almorranas).

hemostático, ca *adj/sm* MED haemostatic [*US* hemostatic].

henal *m* AGR hayloft.

henar *m* hayfield (prado) || hayloft (henil).

henchidura *f*; **henchimiento** *m* filling, stuffing.

henchir* *vt* to fill (up), to stuff, to cram (llenar) || to fill; *henchir de aire los pulmones* to fill one's lungs with air.
◆ *vpr* to stuff o.s. (de comida) || FIG *henchirse de orgullo* to swell with pride.

hendedura *f* ⟶ **hendidura.**

hender* *vt* to cleave, to split (cortar) || to crack, to split (partir) || FIG to cleave (el aire, el agua) | to make one's way through, to elbow one's way through (abrirse paso).
◆ *vpr* to split, to crack.

hendible *adj* cleavable.

hendido, da *adj* cloven; *pie hendido* cloven hoof.

hendidura; hendedura *f* split, cleft (corte) || crack, fissure (grieta) || crevice (ancha grieta) || slot (ranura) || groove (de una polea) || GEOL fissure, rift.

hendimiento *m* splitting, cleaving, cracking.

hendir* *vt* (p us) ⟶ **hender.**

henequén *m* AMER henequen (pita).

henificación *f* AGR haymaking.

henificar *vt* to ted, to toss (el heno).

henil *m* AGR hayloft.

heno *m* hay (hierba cortada y seca); *segar el heno* to reap hay.

henrio *m* FÍS henry (unidad).

hepático, ca *adj* hepatic, liver.
◆ *f* BOT liverwort, hepatica (flor).

hepatitis *f* MED hepatitis.

hepatólogo, ga *m/f* MED hepatologist.

heptaedro *m* MAT heptahedron.

heptagonal *adj* MAT heptagonal.

heptágono, na *adj* MAT heptagonal.
◆ *m* heptagon.

heptámetro *m* heptameter (verso).

heptarquía *f* heptarchy (forma de gobierno).

heptasílabo, ba *adj* heptasyllabic.
◆ *m* heptasyllable.

Heracles *npr m* Heracles (Hércules).

heráldico, ca *adj* heraldic (relativo al blasón).
◆ *m* heraldist (heraldista).
◆ *f* heraldry.

heraldista *m* heraldist.

heraldo *m* herald.

herbáceo, a *adj* BOT herbaceous.

herbajar *vt* to put out to pasture, to graze.

herbaje *m* herbage, grass, pasture (conjunto de hierbas) || grazing fee, herbage (derecho de pastoreo).

herbario, ria *adj* herbal.
◆ *m* herbarium (colección de plantas) || herbal (libro) || herbalist (persona que colecciona plantas) || botanist (botánico) || rumen (de un rumiante).

herbazal *m* grassland.

herbecer* *vi* to become green (with grass) (los campos), to begin to grow, to come up (la hierba).

herbero *m* rumen (de los rumiantes).

Herberto *npr m* Herbert.

herbicida *adj/sm* weed killer, herbicide.

herbívoro, ra *adj* herbivorous, grass-eating.
◆ *m/f* herbivore.
◆ *m pl* herbivora.

herbolario *m* herbalist, herborist || herbalist's shop (tienda).

herboristería *f* herbalist's shop.

herborización *f* herborization.

herborizar *vi* to gather herbs || to herborize, to botanize (un herbolario).

herboso, sa *adj* grassy.

herciniano, na *adj* GEOL Hercynian.

hercio *m* FÍS hertz.

hercúleo, a *adj* Herculean.

hércules *m* FAM Hercules (hombre fuerte).

Hércules *npr m* Hercules.

heredable *adj* inheritable.

heredad *f* country estate *o* farm *o* property.

heredado, da *adj* landed, property-owning.

heredar *vi* to inherit; *heredar a* or *de un tío* to inherit from an uncle.
◆ *vt* to inherit; *heredar una fortuna* to inherit a fortune; *heredar una casa de su padre* to inherit a house from one's father || FIG *heredar las virtudes de sus padres* to inherit the virtues of one's parents.

heredero, ra *adj* inheriting.
◆ *m* heir (*de* to), inheritor (*de* of) || — *heredero forzoso* heir apparent || *heredero universal* general devisee, general legatee || *instituir heredero* or *por heredero a uno* to appoint s.o. as one's heir || *presunto heredero* heir presumptive || *príncipe heredero* crown prince.
◆ *f* heiress, inheritor, inheritress.

hereditario, ria *adj* hereditary; *enfermedad hereditaria* hereditary disease.

hereje *m/f* heretic || FIG rascal (sinvergüenza).

herejía *f* heresy || FIG heresy; *herejía científica* scientific heresy | insult | dirty trick (mala jugada).

herencia *f* inheritance; *recibir una herencia* to receive an inheritance || legacy (legado) || FIG heritage || BIOL heredity || — JUR *adición de la herencia* acceptance of an inheritance || *herencia yacente* unclaimed estate, estate in abeyance || FAM *lo tiene de herencia* it runs in the family.

heresiarca *m* heresiarch.

herético, ca *adj* heretical.

herida *f* injury || wound (de soldado, combatiente, etc.) || wound (llaga) || FIG insult, outrage (ofensa) | injury, wound (del alma, etc.) || — *herida contusa* contusion || FIG *hurgar en la herida* to turn the knife in the wound | *renovar la herida* to open up an old wound | *tocar en la herida* to put one's finger on the sore spot.

herido, da *adj* wounded, injured, hurt; *herido de gravedad, mal herido* seriously *o* badly wounded; *herido de muerte* mortally wounded || FIG hurt, wounded (ofendido).
◆ *m* injured person, wounded person || MIL *los heridos* the wounded.

herir* *vt* to hurt, to injure; *herir a uno en el brazo* to injure s.o.'s arm, to injure s.o. in the arm || to wound; *herir a uno con la espada* to wound s.o. with a sword || to fall on, to strike, to hit (los rayos de sol) || to beat down on (el sol) || MÚS to play, to pluck (pulsar, tocar) || FIG to hurt, to offend (ofender) | to hurt; *este ruido hiere mi oído* this noise is hurting my ears | to hurt, to wound; *herir a alguien en su amor propio* to hurt s.o.'s pride | to offend; *esta palabra hiere mi oído* this word offends my ears || — *herir a alguien por la espalda* to knife *o* to shoot s.o. in the back || *herir de muerte* to mortally wound || *herir el aire con sus gritos* to rend the air with one's screams || FIG *herir en carne viva* to touch *o* to cut to the quick (ofender), to rub salt in a wound (volver a herir) || *herir en lo vivo* to touch *o* to cut *o* to hurt to the quick || *herir la vista* to hurt one's eyes.
◆ *vpr* to injure o.s., to hurt o.s.

hermafrodita *adj* hermaphroditic, hermaphrodite, hermaphroditical.
◆ *m/f* hermaphrodite.

hermafroditismo *m* hermaphroditism.

hermana *f* sister; *hermana mayor* eldest sister, big sister || REL sister; *hermana de la Caridad* Sister of Charity || FIG other half (de un par) || — *hermana gemela* twin sister || *hermana* *política* sister-in-law ‖ *media hermana* half sister ‖ *prima hermana* first cousin.

hermanado, da *adj* FIG similar; *conceptos hermanados* similar ideas ‖ matched (que hace juego) ‖ twin (ciudad).

hermanal *adj* brotherly, fraternal.

hermanamiento *m* fraternal *o* brotherly union ‖ twinning [of towns] (de ciudades).

hermanar *vt* to match (reunir las cosas parecidas) ‖ to join (unir) ‖ to combine (combinar) ‖ to twin; *han hermanado a León con San Francisco* they twinned León and San Francisco.

◆ *vpr* to match (dos o varias cosas) ‖ to become brothers in spirit (dos o varias personas).

hermanastra *f* stepsister ‖ half sister (media hermana).

hermanastro *m* stepbrother ‖ half brother (medio hermano).

hermandad *f* fraternity, brotherhood (entre hermanos), fraternity, sisterhood (entre hermanas) ‖ brotherhood (cofradía) ‖ association, league (asociación); *hermandad de ganaderos* association of cattlemen ‖ FIG similarity, likeness (semejanza) ‖ HIST Spanish militia formed about the XIIth century to maintain public order ‖ *convenio de hermandad* twin city agreement.

hermano, na *adj* similar (semejante) ‖ brother; *pueblos hermanos* brother peoples ‖ sister (lengua).

◆ *m* brother; *el hermano mayor* the eldest brother; *tengo dos hermanos mayores y uno menor* I have two older brothers and a younger one ‖ REL brother; *hermano lego* lay brother ‖ — *hermano carnal* full brother ‖ *hermano de leche* foster brother ‖ *hermano de trabajo* porter (ganapán) ‖ *hermano de madre* or *uterino* half brother on the mother's side ‖ *hermano de padre* half brother on the father's side ‖ *hermano gemelo* twin brother ‖ *hermano político* brother-in-law (cuñado) ‖ REL *¡hermanos!* brothers!, brethren! ‖ *hermanos siameses* Siamese twins ‖ *medio hermano* half brother ‖ *primo hermano* first cousin.

hermenéutico, ca *adj* hermeneutic, hermeneutical.

Hermés *npr m* Hermes (Mercurio).

herméticamente *adv* hermetically.

hermeticidad *f* airtightness, watertightness ‖ FIG impenetrability | watertightness (de una teoría).

hermético, ca *adj* hermetic, airtight, watertight ‖ FIG impenetrable (impenetrable) | watertight; *razonamiento hermético* watertight reasoning.

hermetismo *m* hermeticism, hermetism ‖ FIG impenetrability | watertightness (de un razonamiento) | secrecy, secretiveness (carácter reservado).

hermosamente *adv* beautifully, handsomely ‖ FIG admirably, perfectly.

hermosear *vt* to beautify, to embellish (embellecer) ‖ to adorn (adornar).

hermoso, sa *adj* beautiful, lovely; *una mujer hermosa* a beautiful woman ‖ handsome (hombre) ‖ bonny (niño) ‖ beautiful (cosa); *un hermoso edificio* a beautiful building ‖ splendid (espléndido) ‖ — *¡hermoso día!* fine *o* lovely *o* beautiful day! ‖ *más hermoso que un sol* as pretty as a picture, divine (chica, niño), fine-looking, handsome (adolescente).

hermosura *f* beauty; *la hermosura del paisaje* the beauty of the landscape ‖ beauty, loveliness (de una mujer) ‖ handsomeness (de un hombre) ‖ — *este coche es una hermosura* this car is a beauty ‖ *¡qué hermosura!* what a beauty!

hernia *f* MED hernia, rupture ‖ MED *hernia estrangulada* strangulated hernia.

herniado, da *adj* ruptured ‖ suffering from a hernia *o* rupture.

◆ *m/f* person suffering from a hernia.

herniario, ria *adj* MED hernial.

herniarse *vpr* to rupture o.s. ‖ FIG & FAM to bust a gut.

Herodes *npr m* Herod ‖ *andar* or *ir de Herodes a Pilatos* to fall out of the frying pan into the fire.

Herodoto; Heródoto *npr m* Herodotus.

héroe *m* hero.

heroicamente *adv* heroically.

heroicidad *f* heroism (heroísmo) ‖ heroic deed, exploit (hazaña).

heroico, ca *adj* heroic ‖ FIG heroic; *medicamento heroico* heroic remedy ‖ *verso heroico* heroic verse.

heroicocómico, ca *adj* heroicomic, mock-heroic.

heroína *f* heroine ‖ MED heroin (alcaloide).

heroinómano, na *m/f* heroin addict.

heroísmo *m* heroism ‖ *acto de heroísmo* heroic deed.

herpe *m/f* MED herpes.
— OBSERV This word is often used in the plural form.

herpético, ca *adj* MED herpetic.

herpetismo *m* MED herpetism.

herpetología *f* herpetology.

herrada *f* bucket.

herradero *m* branding (acción de marcar el ganado) ‖ branding place (sitio) ‖ branding time (temporada).

herrador *m* blacksmith, farrier [who shoes horses].

herradura *f* horseshoe ‖ — ARQ *arco de herradura* horseshoe arch, Moorish arch ‖ *camino de herradura* bridle path ‖ *mostrar las herraduras* to kick (dar coces), to show a clean pair of heels, to take to one's heels (huir).

herraj *m* charcoal fuel made from the stones of pressed olives (erraj).

herraje *m* metal *o* iron fittings *pl*, ironwork ‖ AMER horseshoe (herradura).

herramental *m* tools *pl*, set of tools, tool kit (herramientas) ‖ toolbox (caja) ‖ toolbag (bolsa) ‖ tool rack (de un carpintero).

herramienta *f* tool ‖ tools *pl*, tool kit, set of tools (conjunto de herramientas) ‖ FIG & FAM horns *pl* (de un toro) | weapon (arma) | teeth *pl* (dentadura) ‖ *bolsa de herramientas* toolbag.

herrar* *vt* to shoe (una caballería) ‖ to brand (el ganado) ‖ to trim with iron.

herrería *f* blacksmithing (oficio) ‖ smithy, forge, blacksmith's workshop (taller) ‖ ironworks *pl* (fábrica siderúrgica) ‖ FIG uproar, racket (ruido).

herrerillo *m* ZOOL great tit (ave).

herrero *m* blacksmith.

herreruelo *m* ZOOL coal tit, coletit.

herrete *m* metal tip, tag (de cordones, cintas, etc.).

herretear *vt* to put a metal tip on, to tip (poner herretes) ‖ (ant) to brand (marcar con hierro).

herrín *m* rust (herrumbre).

herrumbrar *vt* to rust (aherrumbrar).

herrumbre *f* rust (orín) ‖ iron taste (sabor a hierro).

herrumbroso, sa *adj* rusty.

hertz; hertzio *m* FÍS hertz.

hertziano, na *adj* FÍS hertzian; *onda hertziana* hertzian wave.

hervidero *m* boiling, bubbling, seething (de un líquido) ‖ bubbling spring (manantial) ‖ FIG swarm, throng (de gente) | hotbed; *un hervidero de intrigas* a hotbed of intrigue.

hervidor *m* kettle, pot, pan (para hervir líquidos) ‖ TECN heater (de caldera).

hervir* *vt/vi* to boil; *el agua hierve a 100 grados* water boils at 100 degrees ‖ to bubble, to seethe (borbotear) ‖ to seethe, to surge (el mar) ‖ FIG to boil (la sangre, de enfado) | to swarm, to teem, to seethe; *la plaza hierve de gente* the square is swarming with people ‖ — *hervir a fuego lento* to simmer ‖ FIG *hervir en cólera* to boil *o* to seethe with anger | *hervir en deseos de* to be consumed with desire to, to have a burning desire to.

hervor *m* boiling, seething (acción de hervir) ‖ bubbling, seething, bubble (burbujeo) ‖ FIG ardour, fire (fogosidad).

hervoroso, sa *adj* impetuous, fiery, ardent (ardoroso) ‖ boiling, seething (hirviente).

hesitar *vi* (p us) to hesitate (dudar).

Hespérides *npr fpl* MIT Hesperides.

hetaira; hetera *f* hetaera, hetaira (cortesana).

heteróclito, ta *adj* heteroclite.

heterodino, na *adj/sm* ELECTR heterodyne.

heterodoxia *f* heterodoxy.

heterodoxo, xa *adj* heterodox, unorthodox.

heterogamia *f* BIOL & BOT hetorogamy.

heterógamo, ma *adj* heterogamous.

heterogeneidad *f* heterogeneity.

heterogéneo, a *adj* heterogeneous.

heterogenia *f* heterogenesis.

heteronomía *f* heteronomy.

heterónomo, ma *adj* heteronomous.

heterosexual *adj/s* heterosexual.

heterosexualidad *f* heterosexuality.

hético, ca *adj* MED consumptive, hectic (tísico) ‖ emaciated (flaco).

hetiquez *f* MED consumption, tuberculosis.

heurístico, ca *adj* heuristic.

hevea *m* BOT hevea.

hexacordo *m* MÚS hexachord.

hexadecimal *adj* hexadecimal.

hexaédrico, ca *adj* hexahedral, six-sided.

hexaedro *m* hexahedron.

hexagonal *adj* hexagonal, six-sided.

hexágono *m* hexagon.

hexámetro, tra *adj* hexametrical (verso).

◆ *m* hexameter.

hez *f* sediment, dregs *pl*, lees *pl* ‖ FIG dregs, *pl*, scum.

◆ *pl* excrement *sing*, faeces (excrementos) ‖ *heces fecales* faeces.

hi *m/f* son (hijo).
— OBSERV Only employed in the composition of the word *hidalgo* and its derivatives, and in certain insulting expressions such as *hi de perro* son of a bitch.

hialino, na *adj/s f* MIN hyaline.

hialita *f* MIN hyalite.

hiato *m* GRAM hiatus.

hibernación *f* hibernation.

hibernal *adj* winter (frío, etc.) ‖ wintry (tiempo) ‖ hibernal (que tiene lugar durante el invierno).

hibernar *vi* to hibernate.

hibisco *m* BOT hibiscus.

hibridación *f* hybridization.

hibridismo *m* hybridism, hybridity.

hibridizar *vt* to hybridize.

híbrido, da *adj/sm* hybrid.

hico *m* AMER clew.

hicotea *f* AMER hicatee, hicotee.

hidalgo *m* hidalgo, nobleman, noble [Spanish noble] || — *hidalgo de bragueta* noble who acquired his title by siring seven male children in succession || *hidalgo de cuatro costados* noble descended from four noble grandparents || *hidalgo de ejecutoria* noble who has documentary proof of his noble ancestry || *hidalgo de gotera* noble of little account whose title was only valid in his home town || *hidalgo de privilegio* noble who purchased his title.
◆ *adj* noble || FIG noble, generous | gentlemanly (caballeroso).
— OBSERV In the plural, the noun *hidalgo* becomes *hijosdalgo* and the adjective becomes *hidalgos*.

hidalguez; hidalguía *f* nobility || FIG nobleness, generosity | gentlemanliness, chivalry (caballerosidad).

hidátide *f* MED hydatid.

hidra *f* MIT & ZOOL hydra.

hidrácido *m* QUÍM hydracid.

hidrargirismo *m* MED hydrargyriasis, hydrargyrism.

hidrargiro *m* QUÍM hydrargyrum.

hidrartrosis *f* MED hydrarthrosis.

hidratación *f* QUÍM hydration.

hidratante *adj* moisturizing; *crema hidratante* moisturizing cream.

hidratar *vt* QUÍM to hydrate.

hidrato *m* QUÍM hydrate || *hidrato de carbono* carbohydrate.

hidráulico, ca *adj* hydraulic; *prensa hidráulica* hydraulic press; *freno hidráulico* hydraulic brake; *cemento hidráulico* hydraulic cement || — *fuerza hidráulica* hydraulic power, waterpower || *rueda hidráulica* waterwheel.
◆ *f* hydraulics (ciencia).

hídrico, ca *adj* hydric.

hidroavión *m* seaplane, flying boat.

hidrocarbonato *m* QUÍM hydrocarbonate.

hidrocarburo *m* QUÍM hydrocarbon.

hidrocefalia *f* MED hydrocephalus.

hidrocéfalo, la *adj/s* MED hydrocephalic.

hidrocele *f* MED hydrocele.

hidrocloruro *m* QUÍM hydrogen chloride.

hidrodinámico, ca *adj* FÍS hydrodynamic.
◆ *f* hydrodynamics.

hidroeléctrico, ca *adj* ELECTR hydroelectric.

hidroelectricidad *f* hydroelectricity.

hidrófilo, la *adj* hydrophilic || absorbent; *algodón hidrófilo* absorbent cotton.
◆ *m* ZOOL water beetle.

hidrofobia *f* hydrophobia (horror al agua) || rabies (rabia).

hidrófobo, ba *adj* hydrophobic.
◆ *m/f* hydrophobic person, hydrophobe.

hidrófugo, ga *adj* waterproof, water-repellent, damp-proof || *hacer hidrófugo* to waterproof.

hidrogel *m* QUÍM hydrogel.

hidrogenación *f* hydrogenation.

hidrogenado, da *adj* hydrogenated, hydrogenized, hydrogenous.

hidrogenar *vt* to hydrogenate, to hydrogenize.

hidrógeno *m* hydrogen || *hidrógeno pesado* heavy hydrogen, deuterium.

hidrografía *f* hydrography.

hidrográfico, ca *adj* hydrographic.

hidrógrafo, fa *m/f* hydrographer.

hidrólisis *f* QUÍM hydrolysis.

hidrolizable *adj* QUÍM hydrolysable.

hidrolizar *vt* QUÍM to hydrolyze, to hydrolyse.

hidrología *f* hydrology.

hidrológico, ca *adj* hydrologic, hydrological.

hidrólogo *m* hydrologist.

hidromasaje *m* hydromassage.

hidromecánico, ca *adj* hydromechanical.
◆ *f* hydromechanics.

hidromel *m* hydromel (aguamiel).

hidrometría *f* hydrometry.

hidrométrico, ca *adj* hydrometric, hydrometrical.

hidrómetro *m* hydrometer.

hidroneumático, ca *adj* hydropneumatic.

hidropedal *m* paddle boat, pedal boat (embarcación de recreo).

hidropesía *f* MED dropsy, hydrops, hydropsy.

hidrópico, ca *adj* MED hydropic, dropsical.
◆ *m/f* person suffering from dropsy.

hidroplano *m* MAR hydroplane || seaplane, flying boat (hidroavión).

hidroscopio *m* hydroscope.

hidrosfera *f* GEOL hydrosphere.

hidrosilicato *m* QUÍM hydrosilicate.

hidrostático, ca *adj* FÍS hydrostatic.
◆ *f* hydrostatics.

hidroterapia *f* MED hydrotherapy.

hidroterápico, ca *adj* MED hydrotherapeutic, hydrotherapeutical.

hidróxido *m* QUÍM hydroxide.

hidroxilo *m* QUÍM hydroxyl.

hidrozoario *m* hydrozoan.

hidruro *m* QUÍM hydride.

hiedra *f* BOT ivy.

hiel *f* ANAT bile, gall || FIG bitterness, gall (amargura) || — FIG & FAM *echar* or *sudar la hiel* to sweat blood | *no hay miel sin hiel* no rose without a thorn.
◆ *pl* sorrows, troubles.

hielo *m* ice; *hielo en barras* blocks of ice || frost (escarcha) || FIG coldness, indifference (frialdad) || — *estar cubierto de hielo* to be icy (un camino) || FIG & FAM *estar hecho un hielo* to be frozen, to be freezing cold || FIG *romper el hielo* to break the ice | *ser más frío que el hielo* or *como un pedazo de hielo* to be as cold as ice.

hiemal *adj* wintry.

hiena *f* ZOOL hyena, hyaena || FIG brute (persona cruel).

hierático, ca *adj* hieratic.

hieratismo *m* hieratic attitude.

hierba *f* grass || herb; *hierbas medicinales* medicinal herbs || flaw (defecto en la esmeralda) || — *en hierba* green; *cebada en hierba* green oats || BOT *hierba buena* mint (hierbabuena) | *hierba del Paraguay, hierba mate* maté, Paraguay tea || *hockey sobre hierba* field hockey || *mala hierba* weed (planta dañina), evil people, bad lot (mala gente) || FIG *mala hierba nunca muere* ill weeds grow apace | *pañuelo de hierba* chequered handkerchief | *sentir crecer la hierba* to be a deep one | *y otras hierbas* and others, and so forth.
◆ *pl* grass *sing*, pastureland *sing* (pasto) || poison *sing* [from herbs] || years (de los animales); *este toro tiene tres hierbas* this bull is three years old || CULIN *finas hierbas* herbs for seasoning.

hierbabuena *f* BOT mint.

hierbajo *m* weed.

hierbal *m* AMER grassland.

hierbecilla *f* FAM grass.

hierofanta; hierofante *m* hierophant.

hieroglífico, ca *adj* hieroglyphic.
◆ *m pl* hieroglyphics.

hierra *f* AMER branding.

hierro *m* iron (metal); *hierro forjado, candente* wrought, red-hot iron || branding iron (para marcar el ganado, etc.) || brand (marca) || head, point (de una lanza, etc.) || FIG steel, weapon, blade (arma) | iron (resistencia) || — *a hierro y fuego* to fire and sword || FIG & FAM *al hierro candente batir de repente* strike while the iron is hot | *comer* or *mascar hierro* to court an Andalusian girl through the grille of her window | *de hierro* (of) iron, cast iron; *voluntad de hierro* will of iron, iron will || *hierro albo* white-hot iron || *hierro colado* or *fundido* cast iron || *hierro comercial* merchant iron || *hierro cuadradillo* or *cuadrado* square iron bar || *hierro de doble T* I bar || *hierro dulce* soft iron || *hierro en lingotes* pig iron || *hierro palanquilla* billet || *hierro redondo* round iron || *hierro viejo* old iron, scrap iron || FIG *machacar en hierro frío* to bang one's head against a brick wall | *quien a hierro mata a hierro muere* he who lives by the sword dies by the sword.
◆ *pl* irons, chains (grillos, esposas, etc.).

higa *f* (fist-shaped) amulet || FIG scorn, contempt (desprecio) | derison, mockery (burla) || (ant) nose-thumbing, fig (ant) (gesto de burla) || — FIG *dar una higa, dar higas, hacer la higa* to thumb one's nose, to fig (ant) to cock a snook (burlarse) | *no daría dos higas por* I wouldn't give tuppence [US two cents] for | *no me importa una higa* I don't give a fig *o* a damm *o* a hang.

higadilla *f*; **higadillo** *m* liver [of small animals, birds] || — FIG & FAM *comerse los higadillos* to pull each other to pieces, to quarrel | *echar los higadillos* to work one's fingers to the bone | *sacar hasta los higadillos a uno* to bleed s.o. white.

hígado *m* ANAT liver.
◆ *pl* FIG & FAM guts (valentía); *¡qué hígados tiene!* what guts he has! || — FIG & FAM *echar los hígados* to work one's fingers to the bone | *hay que tener muchos hígados para trabajar con él* you need a lot of guts *o* a strong stomach to work with him.

higiene *f* hygiene.

higiénico, ca *adj* hygienic || sanitary; *paños higiénicos* sanitary towels || *papel higiénico* toilet paper *o* tissue.

higienista *m* hygienist.

higienizar *vt* to make sth. hygienic.

higo *m* BOT fig; *higo seco* dried fig || FIG & FAM *de higos a brevas* once in a blue moon, once in a while | *hecho un higo* wizened (muy arrugado) || BOT *higo chumbo* or *de tuna* or *de pala* prickly pear || FAM *más seco que un higo* as dry as a bone (no húmedo), completely wizened (flaco) || *no dársele a uno un higo de algo* not to care a fig *o* a rap about sth. | *no valer un higo* not to be worth a brass farthing [US two cents].

higroma *m* MED hygroma.

higrometría *f* hygrometry.

higrométrico, ca *adj* hygrometric, hygrometrical.

higrómetro *m* hygrometer.

higroscopia *f* hygrometry.

higroscópico, ca *adj* hygroscopic.

higroscopio *m* hygroscope.

higuera *f* BOT fig tree || — FIG *caer de la higuera* to come back to earth || BOT *higuera chumba or de Indias* or *de pala* prickly pear || FIG *estar en la higuera* to be in the clouds, to be in another world.

hija *f* daughter; *tiene un hijo y dos hijas* he has a son and two daughters || child || — *¡hija mía!* my dear, my child, my daughter || *hija política* daughter-in-law.

hijastro, tra *m/f* stepchild (hijo o hija) || stepson (hijo) || stepdaughter (hija).

hijo *m* son; *hijo mayor* eldest son; *hijo menor* youngest son || child; *tiene tres hijos* he has three children; *hijos crecidos* grown children || son, native son; *los hijos de España* the sons of Spain || — FAM *cualquier* or *todo hijo de vecino* everyone, anyone, every mother's son || *el hijo del Hombre* or *de Dios* the Son of Man *o* of God || *es hijo de su padre* he's a chip off the old block, he's a son who takes after his father || *hacerle a una un hijo* to get s.o. pregnant || *hijo adoptivo* adopted son *o* child || *hijo bastardo* or *espurio* bastard (child) || *hijo de bendición* or *legítimo* legitimate child || *hijo de buena familia* boy from a very good family || *hijo de ganancia* or *natural* bastard, illegitimate *o* natural child || AMER *hijo de la chingada* bastard, son of a bitch || *hijo del diablo* child of the devil || *hijo de leche* foster child || *hijo de papá* daddy's boy || POP *hijo de puta* bastard, son of a bitch || *hijo ilegítimo* illegitimate child || *hijo incestuoso* child of an incestuous relationship || *hijo mío* son, my boy (a un chico), old chap, old boy (a un hombre) || *hijo político* son-in-law || *hijo predilecto* favourite child *o* son (de una familia), favourite son (de una comunidad) || *hijo pródigo* prodigal son || *hijo único* only child || *José García, hijo* José García junior || *nombrar hijo predilecto de la ciudad* to give the freedom of the city.
◆ *pl* children, sons and daughters || descendants, offspring *sing* (descendientes).

hijodalgo *m* hidalgo, nobleman.
— OBSERV pl *hijosdalgo.*

hijuela *f* piece of material added to enlarge a garment (añadido) || branch (dependencia) || small mattress (colchoneta) || small irrigation ditch (acequia) || secondary path (camino) || JUR portion (of an inheritance) (de una herencia) | document stating the inheritance of one of several inheritors (documento) || BOT palm seed (semilla) || REL pall || AMER small inherited portion of a farm.

hijuelo *m* BOT shoot (retoño).

hila *f* row, line (hilera) || thin gut (tripa delgada) || spinning (acción de hilar) || *a la hila* in a line, in file, in a row.
◆ *pl* lint *sing* [for dressing wounds] (para vendar heridas).

hilacha *f*; **hilacho** *m* ravelled thread (hilo que se desprende) || shred, thread (brizna de hilo).
◆ *m pl* rags, tatters (andrajos).

hilada *f* row, line (hilera) || ARQ course (hilera horizontal de piedras).

hiladillo *m* ferret, floss silk (hilo de seda) || band, braid (cinta).

hilado *m* spinning (acción de hilar) || thread, yarn (materia textil hilada) || *fábrica de hilados* spinning mill.

hilador, ra *m/f* spinner (persona que hila).
◆ *f* spinning machine (máquina).

hilandería *f* spinning (trabajo de artesanía) || spinning mill (fábrica).

hilandero, ra *m/f* spinner (persona que hila).

hilar *vt* to spin (hilo) || FIG to reflect on, to think about (cavilar) | to infer (deducir) | to hatch, to weave (tramar); *hilar una intriga* to hatch a plot || — FIG & FAM *hilar delgado* or *muy fino* to split hairs || *máquina de hilar* spinning machine.

hilarante *adj* hilarious || *gas hilarante* laughing gas.

hilaridad *f* hilarity, laughter, mirth; *causar la hilaridad* to cause laughter.

hilatura *f* spinning || spinning mill (fábrica).

hilaza *f* yarn, thread (hilado) || coarse thread *o* yarn (hilo grueso) || thread (de una tela) || FIG & FAM *descubrir la hilaza* to show one's true colours *o* one's true nature | *se le ve la hilaza* he is showing his true colours.

hilera *f* row, line; *una hilera de árboles, de espectadores* a row of trees, of spectators || fine thread (hilo fino) || TECN drawplate || ARQ ridgepole, ridgepiece || MIL rank, file || *en hilera* in line.

hilo *m* thread, yarn; *hilo de coser* sewing thread; *hilo de hilvanar* basting thread || linen (tejido); *sábanas de hilo* linen sheets || ELECTR & TECN wire | thin beam (de luz) || trickle (de agua) || thin column *o* line (de humo) || string (de un collar) || thread (de araña) || BOT fibre [US fiber], string || FIG course; *el hilo de la vida* the course of life | thread; *el hilo de la narración* the thread of the story; *cortar el hilo del discurso* to break the thread of the speech | train (de pensamiento) || — *al hilo* on the straight, on the grain (tela), on the grain (madera) || FIG *el hilo siempre se rompe por lo más delgado* a chain is only as strong as its weakest link | *estar con el alma en un hilo* to be worried stiff, to be on tenterhooks (estar inquieto), to be scared stiff, to have one's heart in one's mouth (de miedo) | *estar cosido con hilo gordo* to be obvious, to be transparent | *estar hecho un hilo* to be as thin as a rake | *estar pendiente de un hilo* to be hanging by a thread || *hilo de bramante* twine || FIG *hilo de voz* thin *o* tiny voice || *hilo musical* piped music, Muzak | FIG *írsele a uno el hilo* to lose the thread | *mover los hilos* to pull the strings | *por el hilo se saca el ovillo* it is just a question of putting two and two together || *telegrafía sin hilos* wireless telegraphy.

hilván *m* tacking, basting || tacking *o* basting stitch (punto) || AMER hem (dobladillo).

hilvanado, da *adj* tacked, basted.
◆ *m* tacking, basting || tacking *o* basting stitch (punto).

hilvanar *vt* to tack, to baste || FIG to outline (bosquejar) || FIG & FAM to throw together (hacer muy de prisa).

Himalaya *npr m* GEOGR Himalayas *pl.*

himen *m* ANAT hymen, maidenhead.

himeneo *m* wedding, marriage || epithalamium.

himenóptero, ra *adj* ZOOL hymenopterus.
◆ *m* hymenopteran [US hymenopteron].
◆ *pl* ZOOL hymenoptera.

himnario *m* hymnbook, hymnal.

himno *m* anthem; *el himno nacional* the national anthem || hymn (cántico).

himplar *vi* to roar, to growl (pantera, onza).

hincada *f* AMER sinking, driving, thrusting (hincadura) | genuflection (genuflexión).

hincadura *f* driving, thrusting, sinking.

hincapié *m* firm footing || *hacer hincapié en* to insist on, to stress, to emphasize; *hacer hincapié en la necesidad de una reforma* to insist on the necessity of a reform.

hincar *vt* to drive (in), to sink (clavar); *hincar un clavo* to sink a nail || to sink (los dientes) || to drive, to thrust, to push, to plunge; *hincar un puñal en el corazón de alguien* to plunge a dagger into s.o.'s heart || to set firmly (el pie) || — FIG *hincar el diente en* to get one's teeth into, to grapple with (emprender), to slate [US to cut down] (criticar), to put the bite on (sacar provecho) || FAM *hincar el pico* to kick the bucket, to peg out (morir), to throw in the sponge, to give in (darse por vencido) || *hincar la rodilla* to kneel [on one knee].
◆ *vpr* to sink (*en* into) || *hincarse de rodillas* to kneel (down).

hincha *f* FAM grudge (odio) || FAM *tener hincha a alguien* to have it in for s.o., to bear a grudge against s.o.
◆ *m* fan, supporter [US rooter] (de un club deportivo); *los hinchas del fútbol* football fans.

hinchada *f* AMER FAM fans *pl*, supporters *pl* [US rooters].

hinchado, da *adj* blown up, inflated; *globo hinchado de gas* balloon blown up with gas || swollen (up), puffed up (la piel), swollen, distended (el vientre) || FIG swollen, puffed up (orgulloso) | pompous, high-flown, bombastic (estilo).

hinchamiento *m* swelling.

hinchar *vt* to blow up (con la boca), to inflate (con la boca o una bomba), to pump up (con una bomba); *hinchar un globo* to blow up a balloon || to swell, to distend (el vientre) || to swell up, to puff up (la piel, el cuerpo) || FIG to inflate, to exaggerate; *hinchar un acontecimiento* to exaggerate an event | to make pompous *o* high-flown *o* bombastic (el estilo) || FAM *hincharle a uno la cabeza con* to stuff s.o. with.
◆ *vpr* to swell (up), to puff up (el cuerpo y la piel) || MED to swell (up); *se le había hinchado la rodilla* his knee had swollen || to swell; *el río se hincha con las lluvias* the river swells with the rains || FIG to become *o* to get bigheaded *o* conceited *o* puffed up; *hincharse con sus éxitos* to get conceited about one's success | to have one's fill, to be satiated (hartarse) || FAM to line one's pockets (ganar mucho dinero) || — FIG & FAM *hincharse, hincharse de comer* to gorge *o* to stuff o.s. with food | *hincharse como un pavo* to be as proud as a peacock | *hincharse de correr, de reír* to run, to laugh a lot | *se le hinchan las narices* he flares up [US he gets his dander up].

hinchazón *f* swelling; *hinchazón de la cara* swelling of the face || lump, bumb (protuberancia) || distension, swelling (del vientre) || swelling, puffiness (de las carnes, de carácter morboso) || FIG vanity, conceit (vanidad) | pomposity, bombast (del estilo).

hindi *m* Hindi (idioma).

hindú *adj/s* Indian (de la India) || Hindu (que practica el hinduismo).

hinduismo *m* REL Hinduism.

hiniesta *f* BOT broom, genista (retama).

hinojal *m* fennel bed, fennel field.

hinojo *m* BOT fennel || *hinojo marino* sea fennel, samphire.
◆ *pl* knees (rodillas) || — *de hinojos* on one's knees, kneeling || FAM *¡hinojos!* oh my goodness! || *ponerse de hinojos* to kneel (down).

hioideo, a *adj* hyoid.

hioides *adj/sm inv* ANAT hyoid.

hipar *vi* to hiccup, to hiccough (tener hipo) || to pant (los perros que corren) || to whimper, to whine (gimotear) || FIG *hipar por* to long to, to yearn to; *está hipando por ir al teatro* he is longing to go to the theatre; to long for, to yearn for (algo).
— OBSERV The initial *h* of *hipar* is aspirate when the meaning is *to whimper, to whine.*

Hiparco *npr m* Hipparchus.

hiperacidez *f* MED hyperacidity.

hipérbaton *m* GRAM hyperbaton.
— OBSERV The Spanish word has two plurals: *hiperbatones* o *hipérbatos.*

hipérbola *f* MAT hyperbola.

hipérbole *f* GRAM hyperbole (exageración).

hiperbólico, ca *adj* hyperbolic, hyperbolical.
hiperboloide *m* MAT hyperboloid.
hiperbóreo, a; hiperboreal *adj* hyperborean.
hipercalórico, ca *adj* high-calorie.
hiperclorhidria *f* MED hyperchlorhydria.
hipercolesterinemia; hipercolesterolemia *f* MED hypercholesterolaemia.
hipercrisis *f* MED grave crisis.
hipercrítico, ca *adj* hypercritical.
hiperdulía *f* REL hyperdulia.
hiperfocal *adj* hyperfocal [distance].
hiperglucemia *f* MED hyperglycaemia.
hipermercado *m* hypermarket.
hipermétrope *adj* MED hypermetropic, longsighted.
hipermetropía *f* hypermetropia, longsightedness.
hipermnesia *f* MED hypermnesia.
hipernervioso, sa *adj* hypernervous.
hipersecreción *f* MED hypersecretion.
hipersensibilidad *f* hypersensitivity.
hipersensibilización *f* MED hypersensitiveness.
hipersensible *adj* hypersensitive.
hipertensión *f* MED hypertension, high blood pressure.
hipertenso, sa *adj* suffering from high blood pressure, hypertensive.
hipertermia *f* hyperthermia.
hipertiroidismo *m* MED hyperthyroidism.
hipertonía *f* MED hypertonicity.
hipertónico, ca *adj* hypertonic.
hipertrofia *f* MED hypertrophy.
◆ *vpr* to hypertrophy.
hipertrofiar *vt* MED to hypertrophy.
◆ *vpr* to hypertrophy.
hipertrófico, ca *adj* MED hypertrophic.
hipervitaminosis *f* MED hypervitaminosis.
hipiátrico, ca *adj* veterinary.
◆ *f* veterinary (veterinaria).
hípico, ca *adj* horse; *concurso hípico* horse show ‖ equine ‖ *club hípico* riding club.
hipido *m* whimper, sob, whine (gimoteo).
— OBSERV The initial *h* of *hipido* is aspirate.
hipismo *m* horse racing.
hipnosis *f* MED hypnosis.
hipnótico, ca *adj/sm* MED hypnotic.
hipnotismo *m* MED hypnotism.
hipnotización *f* hypnotisation.
hipnotizador, ra *adj* hypnotizing.
◆ *m/f* hypnotist, hypnotizer.
hipnotizar *vt* to hypnotize.
hipo *m* hiccup, hiccough; *tener hijo* to have (the) hiccups ‖ FIG longing, yearning (deseo muy vivo) | grudge (animadversión) ‖ FAM *quitar el hipo* to take one's breath away (dejar estupefacto).
hipocampo *m* sea horse (caballo marino).
hipocausto *m* hypocaust.
hipocentro *m* hypocentre [*US* hypocenter].
hipoclorhidria *f* MED hypochlorhydria.
hipoclorito *m* QUÍM hypochlorite.
hipocloroso, sa *adj* hypochlorous.
hipocondría *f* MED hypochondria.
hipocondríaco, ca *adj/s* hypochondriac.
hipocondrio *m* ANAT hypochondrium.
hipocorístico, ca *adj* *nombre hipocorístico* pet name (nombre cariñoso), diminutive.
Hipócrates *npr m* Hippocrates.
hipocrático, ca *adj* Hippocratic.
hipocratismo *m* Hippocratism.
hipocresía *f* hypocrisy.
hipócrita *adj* hypocritical.
◆ *m/f* hypocrite.
hipodérmico, ca *adj* hypodermic; *inyección hipodérmica* hypodermic injection.
hipodermis *f* ANAT hypodermis.
hipódromo *m* racetrack (para carreras de caballos) ‖ HIST hippodrome.
hipofagia *f* hippophagy.
hipofágico, ca *adj* hippophagous, hippophagistical ‖ *carnicería hipofágica* horsemeat butcher's shop.
hipófago, ga *adj* hippophagous.
hipófisis *f* ANAT hypophysis.
hipogástrico, ca *adj* ANAT hypogastric.
hipogastrio *m* ANAT hypogastrium.
hipogeo *m* hypogeum, hypogaeum (subterráneo).
hipogrifo *m* MIT hippogriff, hippogryph.
hipomóvil *adj* horse-drawn.
hipopótamo *m* ZOOL hippopotamus.
hipóstilo, la *adj* ARQ hypostyle.
hiposulfito *m* QUÍM hyposulphite, thiosulphate.
hipotálamo *m* ANAT hypothalamus.
hipoteca *f* mortgage; *levantar una hipoteca* to raise a mortgage.
hipotecable *adj* mortgageable.
hipotecar *vt* to mortgage ‖ FIG to risk, to endanger.
hipotecario, ria *adj* mortgage; *contrato hipotecario* mortgage deed.
hipotensión *f* hypotension, low blood pressure.
hipotenso, sa *adj* hypotensive.
hipotensor *m* MED hypotensive.
hipotenusa *f* MAT hypotenuse.
hipotermia *f* MED hypothermia.
hipotérmico, ca *adj* MED hypothermic.
hipótesis *f inv* MAT hypothesis ‖ hypothesis, supposition (supuesto).
hipotético, ca *adj* hypothetical, hypothetic.
hipotiroidismo *m* MED hypothyroidism.
hipotonía *f* MED hypotonicity.
hipotónico, ca *adj* MED hypotonic.
hipovitaminosis *f* MED hypovitaminosis, vitamin deficiency.
hippy; hippie *m/f* hippy, hippie.
hipsometría *f* hypsometry (medida de las alturas).
hipsómetro *m* FÍS hypsometer.
hirco *m* wild goat.
hiriente *adj* offensive (arma, objeto) ‖ FIG offensive, wounding, cutting (palabras).
hirsutismo *m* MED hirsutism.
hirsuto, ta *adj* shaggy, hirsute ‖ bristly (erizado) ‖ FIG surly, brusque, rough (persona, carácter).
hirviente *adj* boiling, seething.
hisopada; hisopadura *f* aspersion.
hisopar; hisopear *vt* to sprinkle (with holy water).
hisopazo *m* aspersion.
hisopo *m* BOT hyssop ‖ REL aspergillum, sprinkler (para el agua bendita) ‖ *AMER* paintbrush (para pintar) | shaving brush (para afeitarse).
hispalense *adj/s* Sevillan, Sevillian (de Sevilla).
Híspalis *n pr* HIST Hispalis [Roman name of Seville].
Hispania *npr f* HIST Hispania [Roman name for Iberian Peninsula].
hispánico, ca *adj* Hispanic, Spanish.
hispanidad *f* Spanishness (cualidad de español) ‖ Spanish *o* Hispanic world (conjunto de los pueblos hispanos) ‖ *Día de la Hispanidad* Columbus Day.
hispanismo *m* love of Spain (afición a España) ‖ Hispanicism (giro español).
hispanista *m/f* Hispanicist, Hispanist (que estudia la cultura española) ‖ lover of Spain (aficionado a España).
hispanizar *vt* to hispanicize, to hispanize.
hispano, na *adj* Spanish.
◆ *m/f* Spaniard.
Hispanoamérica *npr f* GEOGR Spanish America, Hispano-America.
— OBSERV *Hispanoamérica* refers to those countries of North, Central, and South America where Spanish is spoken. It therefore excludes Brazil. The English expression *Latin America* (i. e. including Brazil) may be rendered by *Iberoamérica, América Latina* or even simply *América*.
hispanoamericanismo *m* Spanish Americanism, Hispano-Americanism.
hispanoamericanista *m/f* Spanish Americanist, Hispano-Americanist.
hispanoamericano, na *adj/s* Spanish American, Hispano-American.
hispanoárabe *adj* Hispano-Arabic.
◆ *m/f* Spanish Arab.
hispanofilia *f* love of Spain, fondness for Spanish things.
hispanófilo, la *adj* fond of Spain.
◆ *m/f* hispanophile, lover of Spain.
hispanofobia *f* hispanophobia.
hispanófobo, ba *adj* hispanophobic.
◆ *m/f* hispanophobe.
hispanófono, na *adj* Spanish-speaking.
◆ *m pl* Spanish-speaking people.
— OBSERV Esta palabra no figura en el DRAE.
hispanohablante *adj* Spanish-speaking.
◆ *m pl* Spanish-speaking people.
hispanojudío, a *adj* Hispano-Jewish.
◆ *m/f* Spanish Jew.
híspido, da *adj* hispid.
histamina *f* BIOL histamine.
histerectomía *f* MED hysterectomy.
histéresis *f* FÍS hysteresis.
histeria *f* MED hysteria ‖ hysterics.
histérico, ca *adj* hysteric, hysterical.
histerismo *m* hysteria ‖ FIG hysterics.
histograma *m* histogram.
histología *f* BIOL histology.
histológico, ca *adj* BIOL histological.
histólogo, ga *m/f* histologist.
historia *f* history; *las lecciones de historia* the lessons of history; *la historia de la literatura, de la aviación* the history of literature, of aviation ‖ story, tale (relato); *contar la historia de su vida* to tell the story of one's life ‖ past, history (de una persona); *una mujer con historia* a woman with a past ‖ FAM story, tale, fib (cosa inventada); *no me vengas con historias* don't come telling stories to me | gossip, tale (chisme) | trouble (lío, problema) ‖ — FAM *armar historias* to make trouble ‖ *¡así se escribe la historia!* that's the way history is written! ‖ FAM *dejarse de historias* to get to the point ‖ *historia antigua* ancient history ‖ *historia del arte* history of art,

art history || *historia natural* natural history || REL *Historia Sacra* or *Sagrada* sacred history, Bible history, Holy Scripture || *historia universal* world history || FIG *la historia de siempre* the same old story, the same old song || *pasar a la historia* to go down in history.

historiado, da *adj* historiated; *letra historiada* historiated letter || storied (friso, tapiz, etc.) || FIG overornate (recargado).

historiador, ra *m/f* historian.

historial *m* historical record, account (reseña) || curriculum vitae (profesional) || background (pasado) || DEP record.

historiar *vt* to tell the history *o* the story of || to depict (representar).

historicidad *f* historical authenticity, historicity.

histórico, ca *adj* historical (relativo a la historia o sucedido realmente); *una novela, una figura histórica* a historical novel, figure; *exactitud histórica* historical accuracy || historic (de gran importancia o que figura en la historia); *un acontecimiento histórico* a historic event; *una fecha histórica* a historic date; *fue un momento histórico en su vida* this was a historic moment in his life || GRAM *presente histórico* historical present.

historieta *f* anecdote, short story, tale || strip cartoon, comic strip (ilustrada con dibujos).

historiografía *f* historiography.

histrión *m* histrion, actor || FIG buffoon, clown.

histriónico, ca *adj* histrionic.

histrionismo *m* histrionics *pl*, theatrical behaviour || acting world, theatre [*US* theater] (mundo de los actores).

hita *f* TECN small headless nail || boundary stone, milestone ⟶ **hito.**

hitita *adj/s* HIST Hittite.

hito *m* boundary stone (para marcar un límite), milestone (para indicar distancias) || bull's eye (del blanco) || FIG target, aim, goal (objetivo) | milestone, landmark; *acontecimiento que será un hito en la historia* event which will be a milestone in history || quoits *pl* (juego) || — FIG *dar en el hito* to hit the mark, to hit the nail on the head | *mirar de hito en hito* to stare at.

hobby *m* hobby (entretenimiento).

hocicada *f* ⟶ **hocicazo.**

hocicar *vt* to root among *o* in.
◆ *vi* FAM to fall on one's face (caerse) | to hit one's face; *hocicar con* or *en la pared* to hit one's face against the wall || FIG to come up against, to run into (con un obstáculo, una dificultad) | to bow one's head, to bow down (ceder, humillarse) || MAR to pitch (hundirse la proa) || FAM to smooch, to kiss (besarse).

hocicazo *m*; **hocicada** *f* FAM fall on one's face (caída) || FAM *darse un hocicazo con el suelo, con la puerta* to fall flat on one's face, to hit one's face against the door.

hocico *m* snout (de porcinos, etc.) || muzzle (de perro, de lobo, de oso) || FIG & FAM blubber lips *pl* (labios abultados) | snout (cara de persona) | pout (mueca) || — FAM *caer* or *darse de hocicos con el suelo, con la puerta* to fall flat on one's face, to hit one's face against the door | *¡cierra el hocico!* shup up! | *dar con la puerta en los hocicos de uno* to slam the door in s.o.'s face | *dar de hocicos contra* to bump into | *estar de* or *hacer* or *poner hocico* to pout | *meter el hocico en todo* to poke one's nose into everything | *romperle a uno los hocicos* to smash s.o.'s face in.

hocicón, ona; hocicudo, da *adj* big-snouted (animal) || FIG & FAM thick-lipped, blubber-lipped (con labios abultados) | big-nosed (de nariz saliente).

hocino *m* billhook (para cortar) || trowel (herramienta para transplantar) || narrows *pl* (angostura de un río) || valley shoulder (entre río y montaña).

hociquear *vi* ⟶ **hocicar.**

hociquera *f* AMER muzzle (de la cabezada).

hockey *m* DEP hockey; *hockey sobre hielo* ice hockey; *hockey sobre ruedas* or *patines* hockey on skates; *hockey sobre hierba* field hockey.

hodierno, na *adj* modern.

hogaño *adv* nowadays (hoy en día) || (p us) this year.

hogar *m* hearth, fireplace (de la chimenea), firebox (de cocina, de locomotora) || TECN furnace (de caldera) | hearth (de horno) || FIG home; *sin casa ni hogar* without house or home; *fundar un hogar* to establish a home || — *hogar del soldado* soldier's home *o* institute || *la vida del hogar* home *o* family life || *sin hogar* homeless.
◆ *pl* home *sing*; *volver a sus hogares* to return home.

hogareño, ña *adj* home, family; *vida hogareña* home life || home-loving, stay-at-home (persona).

hogaza *f* large loaf (of bread).

hoguera *f* bonfire; *encender una hoguera* to light a bonfire || FIG blaze || — *hoguera de San Juan* midsummer bonfire [lit on 24th June] || FIG *la casa era una verdadera hoguera* the house was a blazing inferno || *morir en la hoguera* to die at the stake.

hoja *f* BOT leaf; *hoja aovada, caduca* ciliate, deciduous leaf; *hoja seca* dead leaf | petal (pétalo de flor) || sheet (de metal, madera) || sheet, leaf (de papel) || leaf (de un libro); *hoja suelta* or *volante* loose *o* mobile leaf || handout, leaflet (prospecto) || blade (de espada, cuchillo, patines, etc.); *hoja de afeitar* razor blade || POÉT blade, sword, steel (espada) || leaf (puerta, ventana, biombo, tríptico) || flap, leaf (de mesa) || piece (of armour) (de la armadura) || AGR fallow land (barbecho) || newspaper (periódico) || form, sheet (formulario) || side, flitch (de tocino) || TECN leaf (de un muelle) || — *de hoja caduca* deciduous || *de hoja perenne* evergreen || INFORM *hoja de cálculo* or *electrónica* spreadsheet || *hoja de lata* tinplate, tin || MIL *hoja de movilización* call-up papers *pl* [*US* draft card] || *hoja de paga* payroll, pay sheet || *hoja de parra* fig leaf || COM *hoja de ruta* waybill || *hoja de servicios* service record (de los militares), record (de los deportistas) || *hoja suelta* leaflet (prospecto) || FIG *no tiene vuelta de hoja* there's no doubt about it (está claro), there is no alternative (no hay otra solución) | *temblar como una hoja* to shake like a leaf | *tener hoja* to ring false (una moneda) | *volver la hoja* to change the subject (cambiar de conversación), to turn over a new leaf (cambiar de vida).
— OBSERV El plural de la palabra inglesa *leaf* es *leaves*.

hojalata *f* tinplate, tin || *un bote de hojalata* a tin can.

hojalatería *f* tinsmith's workshop (taller), tinsmith's shop (tienda) || tinware (objetos) || tinwork (oficio).

hojalatero *m* tinsmith.

hojaldrado, da *adj* CULIN puff, flaky; *pasta hojaldrada* puff pastry || *pastel hojaldrado* puff.
◆ *m* rolling out to make puff pastry.

hojaldrar *vt* CULIN to make into puff pastry, to roll out into flaky pastry (pasta).

hojaldre *m* CULIN puff pastry (pasta) || *pastel de hojaldre* puff.

hojarasca *f* dead *o* fallen leaves *pl* || excessive foliage (de las plantas) || FIG verbiage, wordiness (palabrería) | rubbish (cosas inútiles) || FIG *tus promesas son hojarasca* your promises are just a lot of wind.

hojear *vt* to turn the pages of, to leaf through (pasar las hojas de un libro) || to glance through (leer superficialmente).

hojudo, da *adj* leafy.

hojuela *f* BOT leaflet, small leaf (hoja pequeña) | leaflet, foliole (de una hoja compuesta) || CULIN pancake (tortita) || pressed olive skins *pl* (de las aceitunas) || foil (de oro, plata, etc.) || FAM *miel sobre hojuelas* so much the better, better still.

¡hola! *interj* FAM hello!, hallo!, hullo! (expresión de saludo o de sorpresa) || AMER hello!, hallo!, hullo! (teléfono).

Holanda *npr f* GEOGR Holland (provincia), the Netherlands, Holland (país).
— OBSERV El nombre oficial del país es *The Netherlands* pero en el lenguaje corriente se emplea más *Holland*.

holandés, esa *adj* Dutch || *a la holandesa* quarterbound (encuadernación).
◆ *m* Dutchman || Dutch (idioma).
◆ *f* Dutchwoman || sheet of paper 21 × 27 cm.
◆ *m pl* Dutch (habitantes).

holding *m* COM holding company.

holgadamente *adv* easily (con holgura); *caben cinco personas holgadamente* five people fit in easily || comfortably (cómodamente) || *vivir holgadamente* to be well-off.

holgado, da *adj* loose, full; *una chaqueta holgada* a loose jacket || baggy (demasiado ancho) || big (demasiado grande); *esos zapatos me están un poco holgados* those shoes are rather big for me || roomy (espacioso) || FIG comfortable; *vida holgada* comfortable life | comfortably-off, well-off; *familia holgada* well-off family | idle (desocupado) || — FIG *estar holgado de tiempo* to have time to spare || *estar muy holgado en un sitio* to have plenty of room to spare in a place.

holganza *f* idleness (ociosidad) || rest (descanso) || leisure (ocio) || enjoyment, pleasure, fun, entertainment (diversión).

holgar* *vi* to rest (descansar) || not to work, to have a day off; *huelgo los jueves* I don't work on Thursdays || to be idle (estar ocioso) || to be out of use (estar sin uso) || to be unnecessary (estar de más) || (ant) to enjoy o.s. (divertirse) || — *huelga añadir que...* there is no need to add that... || *huelga decir que...* needless to say (that)... || *¡huelgan los comentarios!* no comment!
◆ *vpr* to amuse o.s., to enjoy o.s. (divertirse) || to be pleased (alegrarse); *me huelgo de* or *con su visita* I am pleased by your visit.

holgazán, ana *adj* lazy, idle.
◆ *m/f* loafer, lazybones, idler.

holgazanear *vi* to loaf, to laze, to idle.

holgazanería *f* laziness, idleness.

holgorio *m* FAM ⟶ **jolgorio.**

holgura *f* looseness, fullness; *la holgura de un abrigo* the looseness of a coat || bagginess (amplitud excesiva) || roominess (espacio) || FIG affluence (bienestar económico) || (ant) enjoyment (diversión) || (ant) merriment (regocijo) || TECN play || — *cabemos los tres con holgura* the three of us fit in with ease *o* with room to spare || FIG *vivir con holgura* to live comfortably, to be well-off.

holmio *m* QUÍM holmium.

holocausto *m* HIST holocaust, burnt sacrifice *o* offering || FIG sacrifice || *ofrecerse en holocausto* to sacrifice o.s.

holoédrico, ca *adj* holohedral.

holoturia *f* ZOOL holothurian (cohombro de mar).

holladura *f* treading (acción de pisar) ‖ trampling (acción de pisotear) ‖ FIG trampling ‖ (ant) toll levied for the passing of livestock.

hollar* *vt* to tread on, to tread (pisar); *hollar la alfombra* to tread on the carpet ‖ to trample down (pisotear) ‖ to tread; *hollar regiones desconocidas* to tread unknown regions ‖ FIG to trample on *o* underfoot; *hollar los derechos de uno, la memoria de uno* to trample on s.o.'s rights, on s.o.'s memory | to humiliate (humillar).

hollejo; hollejuelo *m* skin, peel (de uva, etc.).

hollín *m* soot (tizne) ‖ FAM row, set-to (disputa).

hombrada *f* manly action.

hombradía *f* manliness, virility.

hombre *m* man; *los hombres y las mujeres* men and women; *el sistema digestivo en el hombre* man's digestive system ‖ mankind, man (la especie humana) ‖ FAM man (marido, amante) ‖ — *buen hombre* good fellow ‖ *como un hombre* like a man ‖ *como un solo hombre* as one man ‖ *de hombre a hombre* man-to-man ‖ *el abominable hombre de las nieves* the abominable snowman ‖ *el hombre de la calle* the man in the street ‖ *el hombre del día* the man of the moment *o* of the day ‖ *el hombre fuerte* the strong man ‖ *el hombre medio* the average man ‖ *el hombre propone y Dios dispone* Man proposes, God disposes ‖ *es el hombre para el caso* he's the man for the job, he's our man ‖ *está ya hecho un hombre* he's quite a young man already (un niño) ‖ *gran hombre* great man ‖ *hacer un hombre* to make a man of; *el ejército le hará un hombre* the army will make a man of him ‖ *hombre anuncio* sandwich man ‖ FAM *hombre de agallas* man with guts ‖ *hombre de armas* man-at-arms ‖ *hombre de bien* honest man ‖ *hombre de Estado* statesman ‖ *hombre de las cavernas* caveman ‖ *hombre de letras* man of letters ‖ *hombre del saco* bogeyman ‖ *hombre del tiempo* weatherman ‖ *hombre de mar* seafaring man, seaman ‖ *hombre de mundo* man of the world ‖ *hombre de negocios* businessman ‖ *hombre de paja* man of straw ‖ *hombre de palabra* man of his word ‖ FAM *hombre de pelo en pecho* real man ‖ FIG *hombre de peso* man of influence ‖ *hombre de pro* upright man, honest man ‖ *hombre de puños* strong man ‖ *hombre lobo* werewolf ‖ *hombre máquina* automaton ‖ *hombre orquesta* one-man band ‖ *hombre prevenido vale por dos* forewarned is forearmed ‖ *hombre público* politician ‖ *hombre rana* frogman ‖ *hombre serpiente* or *de goma* contortionist ‖ *nuestro hombre* our hero (en un cuento) ‖ *pobre hombre* nobody (don nadie), poor devil (hombre desgraciado) ‖ *poco hombre* not much of a man ‖ *portarse como un hombre* to act like a man ‖ *ser hombre para* to be man enough to *o* for ‖ *ser muy hombre* to be a real man ‖ *ser otro hombre* to be a different *o* changed man.
◆ *interj* my boy!, man! (al dirigirse a una persona) ‖ my dear fellow! (expresión de cariño); *¡hombre! ¡no sabía que estuvieras aquí!* my dear fellow! I didn't know you were here! ‖ good heavens!, I never! (sorpresa) ‖ you bet! (confirmación); *¿te hace ilusión ir al teatro? —¡hombre!* are you excited about going to the theatre? you bet (I am)! ‖ well (pues); *hombre, tal vez* well, perhaps ‖ dear me! (compasión) ‖ come now! (protesta) ‖ — *¡hombre al agua* or *a la mar!* man overboard! ‖ *¡pero hombre!* but my dear fellow!, but really!; heavens, man! (enfado).
— OBSERV The exclamation *¡hombre!* is very common in conversation and may express many different shades of meaning. It may also be used when addressing a woman.

hombrear *vi* to play *o* to act the man (dárselas de hombre) ‖ to push with the shoulders (empujar) ‖ AMER to behave like a man (una mujer) ‖ *hombrear con* to try to keep up with.

hombrera *f* epaulet, epaulette (tira de tela en el hombro) ‖ shoulder plate, épaulière (de armadura) ‖ shoulder pad (almohadilla) ‖ shoulder strap (tirante).

hombretón *m* well-built fellow.

hombría *f* manliness, virility ‖ *hombría de bien* integrity, honesty.

hombro *m* shoulder; *hombros caídos* drooping shoulders ‖ — *a* or *en hombros* on the shoulders; shouldered (arma) ‖ MIL *¡arma al hombro!* shoulder *o* slope arms! ‖ FIG *arrimar* or *meter el hombro* to put one's shoulder to the wheel (trabajar mucho), to lend a hand (ayudar) | *echarse al hombro algo* to shoulder sth., to take sth. upon o.s. (encargarse de algo) ‖ *encogerse de hombros* to shrug one's shoulders ‖ *estar hombro a hombro* or *hombro contra hombro* or *hombro con hombro* to be shoulder to shoulder ‖ FIG *estar hombro a hombro con alguien* to rub shoulders with s.o. | *hurtar el hombro* to shirk [work, a responsibility, etc.] ‖ *llevar a hombros* to carry on one's shoulders (transportar), to carry shoulder-high (en triunfo) ‖ *mirar por encima del hombro* to look down on, to look down one's nose at ‖ *sacar a hombros a uno* to carry s.o. shoulder-high (a un torero, etc.) ‖ *salir a hombros* to be carried out shoulder-high ‖ FIG *tener la cabeza sobre los hombros* to have one's head squarely on one's shoulders.

hombruno, na *adj* mannish, masculine (una mujer).

homenaje *m* JUR homage; *rendir homenaje al rey* to pay homage to the king | allegiance (juramento de fidelidad) ‖ FIG tribute; *rendir homenaje a* to pay a tribute to ‖ — *banquete en homenaje al presidente* banquet in honour of *o* in homage to the president ‖ *torre del homenaje* keep.

homeópata *adj* MED homeopathic.
◆ *m* homeopath.

homeopatía *f* MED homeopathy.

homeopático, ca *adj* MED homeopathic.

homérico, ca *adj* Homeric.

Homero *npr m* Homer.

homicida *adj* homicidal ‖ murderous, murder; *arma homicida* murder weapon.
◆ *m* homicide, murderer (asesino).
◆ *f* homicide, murderess (asesina).

homicidio *m* JUR homicide, murder (voluntario) | manslaughter (involuntario).

homilía *f* homily (sermón).

homocentro *m* MAT homocentre.

homofonía *f* homophony.

homófono, na *adj* homophonous, homophonic.
◆ *m* homophone.

homogeneidad *f* homogeneity.

homogeneización *f* homogenization.

homogeneizar *vt* to homogenize.

homogéneo, a *adj* homogeneous.

homografía *f* homography.

homógrafo, fa *adj* GRAM homographic.
◆ *m* homograph.

homologación *f* homologation, confirmation.

homologar *vt* to confirm.

homología *f* homology.

homólogo, ga *adj* QUÍM & MAT homologous.

homonimia *f* homonymy.

homónimo, ma *adj* homonymous.
◆ *m* homonym.

homosexual *adj/s* homosexual.

homosexualidad *f* homosexuality.

homotecia *f* MAT similarity.

homotético, ca *adj* MAT homothetic.

homúnculo *m* homunculus ‖ FIG runt, squirt.

honcejo *m* billhook (hocino).

honda *f* sling (arma).

hondear *vt* to sound (sondar) ‖ to unload (descargar una embarcación).
— OBSERV Do not confuse with *ondear* (to wave).

hondero *m* slinger.

hondo, da *adj* deep; *un recipiente hondo* a deep vessel; *raíces hondas* deep roots ‖ low, low-lying (terreno) ‖ FIG profound, deep, intense (sentimientos) ‖ — *cante hondo* «cante hondo», flamenco song ‖ *en lo hondo de su alma* in the depths of his heart ‖ *plato hondo* soup plate *o* dish.
◆ *m* bottom ‖ depth (profundidad) ‖ *tiene unos cinco metros de hondo* it is about five metres deep.

hondonada *f* depression, hollow, dip (depresión en el terreno) ‖ ravine (valle encajonado).

hondura *f* depth ‖ FIG *meterse en honduras* to get out of one's depth, to get into deep water.

Honduras *npr f* GEOGR Honduras.

hondureñismo *m* word or turn of phrase characteristic of Honduras.

hondureño, ña *adj/s* Honduran.

honestamente *adv* in an upright *o* an honourable way, honestly ‖ decently, decorously (decorosamente) ‖ modestly (con pudor) ‖ fairly (con justicia).

honestidad *f* uprightness, honourableness, honesty (honradez) ‖ decency, decorum (decoro) ‖ modesty (pudor) ‖ fairness (justicia).

honesto, ta *adj* upright, honourable, honest (honrado) ‖ decent, decorous (decoroso) ‖ reasonable fair (justo) ‖ modest (púdico) ‖ *estado honesto* celibacy (de una mujer).

hongo *m* BOT fungus | mushroom (comestible) | toadstool (venenoso) ‖ bowler hat [US derby] (sombrero) ‖ — FIG *crecer como hongos* to spring up *o* to grow like mushrooms, to mushroom | *hongo atómico* mushroom cloud ‖ *hongo yesquero* tinder fungus.

Honolulu *n pr* GEOGR Honolulu.

honor *m* honour [US honor]; *hombre de honor* man of honour; *su honor está en juego* his honour is at stake; *su visita ha sido un gran honor para mí* his visit has been a great honour for me ‖ reputation, good name, honour (reputación); *una mancha en el honor* a stain on one's reputation ‖ virtue, honour, purity (de una mujer) ‖ — *a gran señor gran honor* honour where honour is due ‖ *campo de honor* field of honour ‖ *dama de honor* lady-in-waiting (de una reina), bridesmaid (en una boda) ‖ *en honor a la verdad* for truth's sake ‖ *en honor de* in honour of ‖ *hacer honor a* to honour ‖ *jurar por su honor* to swear on one's honour ‖ *lance de honor* challenge ‖ *Legión de Honor* Legion of Honour ‖ *palabra de honor* word of honour ‖ *¡palabra de honor!* on my honour! ‖ *tener el honor de* to have the honour to.
◆ *pl* honours; *aspirar a los honores* to aspire to honours; *honeres de guerra* war honours; *con todos los honores militares* with full military honours ‖ honorary titles *o* positions ‖ *hacer los honores de la casa* to do the honours ‖ *hicimos los honores al almuerzo* we did justice to the lunch ‖ *rendir honores a* to do *o* to pay honour to ‖ *tener honores de bibliotecario* to be an honorary librarian.

honorabilidad *f* honourableness [US honorableness], honour [US honor].

honorable *adj* honourable [US honorable], honest.

honorar *vt* to honour [US to honor] (honrar).

honorario, ria *adj* honorary; *miembro honorario* honorary member.
◆ *m pl* fees, fee *sing*, honorarium, *sing*, emoluments.

honorífico, ca *adj* honorific || *mención honorífica* honourable mention.

honra *f* honour [US honor]; *luchó en defensa de su honra* he fought to defend his honour || dignity (dignidad) || reputation, good name, honour (buena fama) || honour, virtue (de una mujer) || honour; *ser la honra de su país* to be an honour to one's country || — *tener a honra hacer algo* to be proud to do sth., to deem *o* to regard it an honour to do sth. || *tener una cosa a mucha honra* to be proud of sth. || *¡y a mucha honra!* and (I'm) proud of it!
◆ *pl* last honours (por un difunto).

honradez *f* honesty, integrity, uprightness.

honrado, da *adj* honest (que es de fiar) || honourable [US honorable] (que cumple con sus deberes) || upright (recto).

honrar *vt* to honour [US to honor], to do honour to; *honrar a una persona con su amistad, con su presencia* to honour s.o. with one's friendship, with one's presence; *honrar a su país* to do honour to one's country || to honour (premiar) || COM to honour (una deuda, etc.) || to honour (venerar); *honrar a Dios* to honour God; *honrar padre y madre* to honour one's father and mother || to do credit; *su comportamiento le honra* his behaviour does him credit || *muy honrado con* or *por su visita* I am highly honoured by your visit.
◆ *vpr* to be honoured; *me honro con su amistad* I am honoured by his friendship.

honrilla *f* concern for one's reputation || *por la negra honrilla* out of concern for one's reputation.

honroso, sa *adj* honourable [US honorable].

hontanar *m* springs *pl*, place with springs.

hopear *vi* to wag the tail (menear la cola) || to run about (corretear).

hopo *m* shock of hair (mechón) || bushy tail, brush (rabo).
◆ *interj* out!, hop it!, scram!
— OBSERV When *hopo* means *tail*, the *h* is aspirate.

hora *f* hour; *una hora tiene sesenta minutos* there are sixty minutes in an hour; *hace tres horas* three hours ago; *una hora y media* an hour and a half || time; *¿a qué hora?* at what time?; *¿qué hora es?* what time is it?, what is the time?; *la hora de comer* dinner time || hour; *la hora fatal* the fateful hour; *horas de visita* visiting hours || time (momento de la muerte); *le llegó su hora* his time came || league (medida de distancia) || — *¡a buena hora!* about time! (al llegar ya tarde algo o alguien) || *¡a buena hora me lo dices!* now you tell me! || FAM *¡a buena hora mangas verdes!* too late!, it's no good shutting the stable door after the horse has bolted! || *a cualquier hora* at any hour, at any time of the day || *a la hora* punctually, on time (puntualmente), hourly, per hour; *cien pesetas a la hora* a hundred pesetas per hour || *a la hora de ahora* at this time of day || *a la hora en punto* right on time, on the hour || *a primera hora* first thing in the morning || *a última hora* at the end; *ven a última hora de la tarde* come at the end of the afternoon; at the last minute *o* moment; *llegó a última hora* he arrived at the last minute; last thing at night (muy tarde por la noche) || *dar hora* to fix a time, to make an appointment (concertar cita), to give an appointment; *el médico me dio hora para las tres* the doctor gave me an appointment for three || *dar la hora* to strike the hour (reloj) || *de hora en hora* hour by hour || *de última hora* last-minute || *en buena hora* at the right time (en el momento oportuno), fortunately (afortunadamente) || *en mala hora* at the wrong time (inoportunamente), unluckily (desafortunadamente) || *es hora de* it's time to; *es hora de que me vaya* it's time for me to go || *¡es la hora!* time's up! || *ésta es la hora en que no sé si voy a ir de excursión o no* I still don't know *o* I don't yet know whether I am going picnicking or not || FIG *ha llegado su hora* his time has come || *hora de almorzar* lunchtime || *hora de comer* mealtime || *hora de Greenwich* Greenwich Mean Time || *hora de la verdad* moment *o* hour of truth || *hora de mayor afluencia* or *de mayor aglomeración, hora punta* rush hour, peak hour (transportes) || *hora de mayor consumo* peak hour (electricidad, gas) || *hora de verano* summer time || *hora H* zero hour || *hora legal* or *oficial* civil *o* standard *o* official time || *hora suprema* supreme moment || *la hora de irse a la cama* bedtime || *media hora* half an hour, half hour; *dentro de media hora* within a half hour, within half an hour || FAM *no da ni la hora* he wouldn't even give you the time of day (tacaño) || *no tener una hora libre* to have no time to o.s. || *noticias de última hora* stop press *sing* (en periódico), latest news (televisión, etc.) || FIG *no ver la hora de* to look forward to || *pedir hora* to request an appointment, to make an appointment (*a* with) || *poner en hora* to set (un reloj) || *por hora* per hour, an hour; *cien kilómetros por hora* a hundred kilometres per hour; hourly, per hour; *salario por hora* hourly wage, wage per hour; *dos libras por hora* two pounds per hour, two pounds hourly || FIG *suena la hora de que lo haga* the time has come for him to do it || *tener hora* to have an appointment (cita) || *¿tiene usted hora?* have you got the time? || *una hora escasa* scarcely *o* barely an hour || *una hora larga* a good hour || *¡ya era hora!* and about time too! || *ya es hora de que* it's high time (that); *ya es hora de que aprendas la lección* it's high time you learnt the lesson.
◆ *pl* REL hours || *horas de insolación* hours of sunshine || *a estas horas* now, by now; *a estas horas debe de haber recibido la carta* he must have received the letter by now || *altas horas de la noche* or *de la madrugada* small hours || *a todas horas* all the time, at all hours (incesantemente) || *entre horas* between meals; *comer entre horas* to eat between meals || *ganar horas* or *ganar las horas* to save time || *horas de menor consumo* or *de menor afluencia* off-peak hours || *horas de oficina* office *o* business hours || *horas de trabajo* working hours || *horas de vuelo* flying hours || *horas enteras* hours on end || *horas extraordinarias* overtime *sing* || *horas libres* free time *sing*, spare time *sing* || *horas muertas* wasted time *sing*, wasted hours || *horas y horas* hours and hours || *pasar las horas en blanco* to have a sleepless night (no dormir), to waste one's time, to spend one's time doing nothing (no hacer nada) || *por horas* by the hour; *trabajar por horas* to work by the hour; *estoy pagado por horas* I am paid by the hour || *¿qué horas son éstas para llegar?* what sort of time do you think this is to arrive? || FIG *sus horas están contadas* his days are numbered || *tener muchas horas de vuelo* to be all there || *una jornada de ocho horas* an eight-hour day || *¡vaya unas horas para salir!* what a fine time to go out!.
◆ *adv* (p us) now (ahora).

Horacio *npr m* Horace.

horadación *f* boring, drilling, piercing.

horadador, ra *adj* boring, drilling, piercing.
◆ *m* drill (máquina) || driller (persona).

horadar *vt* to bore (through), to drill (taladrar) || to pierce, to perforate (perforar) || *horadar un túnel en* to tunnel through, to open a tunnel in.

horario, ria *adj* hour; *ángulo horario* hour angle || time; *huso horario* time zone || hourly (cada hora) || *círculo horario* hour circle, meridian.
◆ *m* timetable (de clases, trenes, aviones, etc.); *horario de verano* summer timetable || hour hand (de reloj) || hours *pl* (horas de trabajo) || — *horario comercial* business hours (empresa), opening hours (tienda) || *horario laboral* working hours.

horca *f* gallows, gibbet (para ahorcar a los condenados) || gibbet (para los ajusticiados) || AGR fork | winnowing fork (herramienta para aventar) | pitchfork (para amontonar paja, etc.) | forked prop (horquilla) | yoke (para cerdos, perros, etc.) || string (de ajos, cebollas) || AMER gift, present (regalo) || — *merecer la horca* to deserve to be hanged || *pasar por las horcas caudinas* to pass under the yoke || *señor de horca y cuchillo* feudal lord invested with civil and criminal jurisdiction (sentido propio), Grand Panjandrum (sentido irónico) (déspota).

horcadura *f* fork (de árbol).

horcajadas (a) *loc adv* astride, astraddle.

horcajadura *f* ANAT crotch, fork.

horcajo *m* yoke (de mula) || GEOGR fork (de dos ríos) | gully (entre dos vertientes).

horchata *f* orgeat, cold drink made of almonds or chufas || FIG *tener sangre de horchata* to have water in one's veins, to have no blood in one's veins.

horchatería *f* milk bar, orgeat shop.

horchatero, ra *m/f* orgeat seller *o* maker.

horda *f* horde.

horizontal *adj/s f* horizontal.

horizontalidad *f* horizontality.

horizonte *m* horizon; *en el horizonte* on the horizon || FIG horizon, outlook; *ampliar los horizontes* to broaden one's horizons *o* outlook; *tiene horizontes muy estrechos* he has very narrow horizons || *línea del horizonte* skyline.

horma *f* form (molde) || last (para fabricar zapatos) || shoe tree, boot tree (para conservar la forma) || hat block (para sombreros) || drystone wall (muro) || FIG *encontrar la horma de su zapato* to find just what the doctor ordered (lo deseado), to find Mr *o* Miss Right, to meet one's perfect match (a un novio o una novia conveniente), to meet one's match (a alguien con quien medirse).

hormiga *f* ZOOL ant || MED formication (enfermedad) || — *hormiga blanca* white ant || *hormiga león* ant lion || FIG & FAM *ser una hormiga* to be industrious and thrifty.

hormigón *m* concrete; *hormigón armado, pretensado* or *precomprimido* reinforced, prestressed concrete.

hormigonado *m* concreting.

hormigonera *f* cement mixer, concrete mixer.

hormigueamiento *m* ⟶ **hormigueo.**

hormiguear *vi* to swarm, to teem (bullir) || *me hormiguea la pierna* I have got pins and needles in my leg, my leg is tingling.

hormigueo; hormigueamiento *m* swarming, teeming || pins and needles *pl*, tingling sensation (sensación cutánea); *sentir hormigueo en la pierna* to have pins and needles in one's leg || FIG anxiety (desasosiego).

hormiguero *m* ant's nest (donde viven las hormigas) || anthill (montoncito) || FIG swarm [of people] | anthill, place swarming with people || — *la salida del estadio era un hormiguero* the exit of the stadium was swarming with people || *oso hormiguero* anteater.

hormiguilla *f* pins and needles *pl*, tingling sensation (cosquilleo) || FIG nagging conscience || FIG *ser una hormiguilla* to be industrious and thrifty.

hormiguillo *m* pins and needles *pl*, tingling sensation (hormigueo) || chain (para pasar algo de mano en mano) || VET founder (enfermedad del casco) || FIG & FAM *parece que tiene hormiguillo* he's got ants in his pants.

hormiguita *f* FIG *ser una hormiguita* to be industrious and thrifty.

hormona *f* BIOL hormone.

hormonal *adj* BIOL hormonal.

hornablenda *f* MIN hornblende.

hornacina *f* ARQ niche.

hornacho *m* MIN excavation.

hornada *f* batch; *hornada de pan* batch of bread.

hornaguera *f* coal.

hornaza *f* TECN silversmith's crucible (horno pequeño) | light yellow glazing (para vidriar).

hornear *vt/vi* to bake.

hornería *f* baking.

hornero, ra *m/f* baker.
◆ *f* oven floor (suelo de un horno).
◆ *m* AMER ovenbird (ave).

hornija *f* firewood [for heating the oven].

hornilla *f*; **hornillo** *m* cooker, stove; *hornillo de gas* gas stove || ring (con una sola placa); *hornillo portátil de gas* portable gas ring || ring, burner (de cocina de gas), hotplate, ring (de cocina eléctrica); *cocina con cuatro hornillos* cooker with four rings || MIN blast hole || MIL land mine || bowl (de pipa) || *hornillo de atanor* athanor (horno de alquimista).

horno *m* oven; *horno de panadero* baker's oven; *horno eléctrico* electric oven; *horno microondas* or *de microondas* microwave oven || TECN kiln (para ladrillos, cerámica, etc.); *horno de esmalte* enamel kiln | furnace (para la fundición); *alto horno* blast furnace; *horno de hogar abierto* open-hearth furnace; *horno de reverbero* reverberatory furnace; *horno de arco* arc furnace || — *fuente de horno* ovenproof *o* fireproof dish [US ovenproof platter] || *horno crematorio* crematory, crematorium || FIG & FAM *no está el horno para bollos* or *para tortas* this is not the right time, the time is not right.

Hornos (cabo de) *n pr* GEOGR Cape Horn.

horóscopo *m* horoscope; *hacer un horóscopo* to cast a horoscope || astrologer (adivino).

horqueta *f* AGR pitchfork, winnowing fork (horca) || fork (de árbol) || AMER bend (de río).

horquilla *f* AGR fork, pitchfork, winnowing fork (horca) || fork (bifurcación) || forked prop (palo bifurcado para sostener árboles, etc.) || hairpin (para sujetar el moño), hair clip (para sujetar el peinado) || wishbone (de ave) || MED split ends *pl* (enfermedad del pelo) || forks *pl* (de bicicleta).

horrendo, da *adj* → **horroroso.**

hórreo *m* granary (granero).

horrible *adj* horrible, dreadful, awful.

hórrido, da *adj* → **horroroso.**

horrificar *vt* to horrify.

horrífico, ca *adj* horrific.

horripilación *f* horripilation (estremecimiento) || horror, dread, terror (miedo).

horripilante *adj* hair-raising, terrifying.

horripilar *vt* to make one's hair stand on end, to terrify, to horrify, to give the creeps (*fam*); *es un cuento que horripila* it is a tale which makes your hair stand on end.

horrísono *adj* dreadful, terrible, blood-curdling (ruido).

horro, ra *adj* enfranchised (esclavo) || free, exempt (exento) || lacking (carente); *horro de vigor* lacking in energy || sterile (estéril).

horror *m* horror, dread, terror (miedo intenso); *pálido de horror* pale with horror || horror (que causa miedo); *los horrores de la guerra* the horrors of war || atrocity (atrocidad) || horrible thing; *dice horrores de los franceses* he says horrible things about the French || — *da horror verle tan flaco* it is horrible *o* it horrifies me to see him so thin || *divertirse horrores* to have a whale of a time, to have a jolly good time || *me gusta horrores* I like it very much, I love it || *¡qué horror!* how horrible!, how awful! || *querer horrores a uno* to be madly in love with s.o. (estar enamorado) || *tener horror a la mentira* to hate *o* to detest lies, to have a horror of lies || *un horror de gente* masses *pl* of people.

horrorizar *vt* to horrify, to terrify || *estar horrorizado* to be horrified, to be aghast, to be horror-stricken.
◆ *vpr* to be horrified *o* horror-stricken, to be aghast.

horrorosamente *adv* horribly; *horrorosamente desfigurado* horribly disfigured || FAM awfully, dreadfully, terribly, frightfully; *es horrorosamente difícil* it's frightfully difficult.

horroroso, sa *adj* horrible, horrifying, frightful, horrid (que da horror) || hideous, horrible, terribly ugly (muy feo) || horrible, terrible, awful (muy malo); *hace un tiempo horroroso* the weather is awful || *tengo un hambre horrorosa* I'm terribly *o* awfully hungry.

hortaliza *f* vegetable; *hortalizas tempranas* early vegetables.

hortelano, na *adj* market-gardening; *una región hortelana* a market-gardening region.
◆ *m/f* gardener (jardinero) || market gardener (que cultiva para la venta).
◆ *m* ortolan (ave).

hortense *adj* market-garden, vegetable; *producción hortense* vegetable production.

hortensia *f* BOT hydrangea.

hortera *f* wooden bowl.
◆ *m* FAM shop assistant (dependiente de comercio) | flashy type (hombre atildado).

hortícola *adj* horticultural.

horticultor *m* horticulturist.

horticultura *f* horticulture.

hosanna *m* REL hosanna.

hosco, ca *adj* surly, sullen; *tenía una expresión hosca* he looked surly || dark, gloomy; *el cielo cobró un aspecto hosco* the sky began to look gloomy || dark, dark-skinned, swarthy (muy moreno).

hospedaje; hospedamiento *m* lodging (acción de alojar) || rent (alquiler); *pagar poco hospedaje* to pay a low rent || lodgings *pl*; *mi hospedaje está lejos de aquí* my lodgings are a long way from here || *tomar hospedaje en un hotel* to lodge in a hotel, to put up at a hotel.

hospedar *vt/vi* to put up, to lodge; *hospedar a un invitado* to put a guest up.
◆ *vpr* to lodge, to stay, to put up; *hospedarse en casa de un amigo* to lodge at a friend's house.

hospedera *f* innkeeper, landlady (de un establecimiento) || landlady (de casa de huéspedes).

hospedería *f* hostelry, inn (establecimiento) || guest room (habitación) || REL hospice || lodging (hospedaje).

hospiciano, na *m/f* inmate of an orphanage or a poorhouse.

hospiciante *m/f* AMER → **hospiciano.**

hospicio *m* REL hospice (para peregrinos, viajeros) || poorhouse (para los pobres) || orphanage (para huérfanos).

hospital *m* hospital || (ant) hospice || — *buque hospital* hospital ship || MIL *hospital de sangre* field hospital || *tren hospital* hospital train.

hospitalario, ria *adj* hospitable (acogedor) || hospital; *instalaciones hospitalarias* hospital facilities || *Caballero Hospitalario* Knight Hospitaller [US Knight Hospitaler].
◆ *m* REL hospitaller [US hospitaler].

hospitalidad *f* hospitality; *dar hospitalidad a una persona* to show s.o. hospitality.

hospitalización *f* hospitalization.

hospitalizar *vt* to hospitalize, to send *o* to take to hospital.
◆ *vpr* to go into hospital.

hosquedad *f* surliness, sullenness (del rostro) || gloominess, darkness (de un lugar, del cielo, etc.) || darkness, swarthiness (de la piel).

hostal *m* hostelry, inn.

hostelero, ra *m/f* innkeeper.

hostería *f* inn, hostelry.

hostelería *f* hotel-keeping, hotel management; *escuela de hostelería* school of hotel management || hotel business *o* trade; *la hostelería española está en pleno desarrollo* the Spanish hotel trade is developing fast.

hostia *f* REL (communion) wafer, host || POP blow, bash (golpe) | pain in the neck (pesado) || POP *pegarle una hostia a alguien* to give s.o. a belting.
◆ *interj* POP damn it!, hell! (de enfado) | christ! (de sorpresa, admiración).

hostiario *m* wafer box.

hostigador, ra *adj* annoying, tiresome (molesto) || harassing (fastidioso) || urging (incitador).

hostigamiento *m* whipping (del caballo) || FIG harassment, pestering, plaguing (acción de molestar) | encouragement, urging (incitación).

hostigar *vt* to whip (fustigar) || FIG to urge; *le hostigué para que trabajase más de prisa* I urged him to work faster | to plague, to harass, to pester (fastidiar) || MIL to harass (al enemigo).

hostigoso, sa *adj* AMER cloying, sickening (empalagoso) | annoying, tiresome, bothersome (molesto).

hostil *adj* hostile.

hostilidad *f* hostility; *romper, reanudar las hostilidades* to begin, to renew hostilities.

hostilizar *vt* to antagonize || MIL to harass.

hotel *m* hotel; *alojarse en un hotel* to put up at a hotel || villa, house (casa particular).

hotelero, ra *adj* hotel; *industria hotelera* hotel trade, hotel industry.
◆ *m/f* hotelkeeper.

hotelito *m* villa, house (casa particular).

hotentote, ta *adj/s* Hottentot.

hoy *adv* today; *hoy estamos a viernes* today is Friday || now, nowadays, today (en la actualidad) || — *de hoy a mañana* at any moment || *de hoy en adelante* from now on, henceforth, as of today || *de hoy en quince días* today fortnight, a fortnight today || *desde hoy* from now on, as of today || *en el día de hoy* today || *hoy día, hoy en día* nowadays || *hoy por hoy* for the time being (de momento), nowadays (actualmente) || *hoy por la mañana, por la tarde* this morning, this afternoon || *hoy por mí y mañana por ti* today me, tomorrow thee || *no dejes para mañana lo que puedes hacer hoy* do not put off till tomorrow what you can do today.

hoya *f* pit, ditch, hole || grave (sepultura) || GEOGR valley, dale || AGR seedbed (semillero) || — AGR *plantar a hoya* to plant in holes || FIG *tener un pie en la hoya* to have one foot in the grave.

hoyada *f* depression, hollow, dip (hondonada).

hoyar *vt* AMER to dig *o* to make holes in.

hoyo *m* hole ‖ pockmark (de las viruelas) ‖ grave (fosa) ‖ dimple (hoyuelo) ‖ DEP hole (golf) ‖ FAM *el muerto al hoyo, el vivo al bollo* let the dead bury the dead.

hoyuelo *m* dimple (en la barbilla y las mejillas).

hoz *f* AGR sickle, scythe ‖ gorge, ravine (valle) ‖ FIG *meter la hoz en mies ajena* to poach on s.o.'s preserves.

hozada *f* stroke of the sickle.

hozadero *m* rooting place.

hozar *vt* to root (up).

huaca *f* AMER ⟶ **guaca.**

huacal *m* AMER ⟶ **guacal.**

huaco *m* AMER ⟶ **guaco.**

huachafería *f* AMER FAM middle-class snobbery, pretentiousness (cursilería).

huachafo, fa *m/f* AMER FAM snobbish, pretentious person (cursi).

huacho, cha *m/f* AMER illegitimate child (hijo natural).

huahua *m/f* AMER ⟶ **guagua.**

huaico *m* AMER ⟶ **guaico.**

huarache *m* AMER ⟶ **guarache.**

huarapón *m* AMER wide-brimmed hat.

huaro *m* AMER tafia, rum (aguardiente de caña).

huasca *f* AMER strap (correa) | whip (látigo) ‖ AMER *dar huasca a uno* to whip s.o.

huascazo *m* AMER whipping, flogging.

huasipongo; huasipungo; guasipongo *m* AMER land given to Ecuadorian workers in addition to their salaries.

huaso, sa *m/f* AMER Chilean peasant.

huasquear *vt* AMER to whip.

huata *f* AMER ⟶ **guata.**

huatón, ona *adj* AMER potbellied.

hucha *f* moneybox, piggy bank (alcancía) ‖ chest (arca) ‖ FIG savings *pl*, nest egg (*fam*) (ahorros).

huebra *f* AGR day's ploughing [US day's plowing] (tierra labrada en un día) | pair of mules and driver [hired by the day] | fallow land (barbecho).

hueca *f* spiral groove in a spindle.

hueco, ca *adj* hollow; *árbol hueco* hollow tree ‖ concave (cóncavo) ‖ empty (vacío) ‖ deep; *voz hueca* deep voice ‖ hollow; *sonido hueco* hollow sound ‖ FIG empty; *estilo hueco* empty style | vain, conceited (presumido) ‖ spongy (esponjoso) ‖ fluffy (mullido) ‖ loose; *tierra hueca* loose earth.

◆ *m* hollow; *algo que cabe en el hueco de la mano* sth. that fits in the hollow of one's hand ‖ hole (agujero) ‖ spare time (tiempo libre) ‖ interval, lapse (intervalo) ‖ empty space (sitio libre) ‖ ARQ opening ‖ FIG & FAM vacancy (empleo vacante) | gap; *su jubilación dejó un hueco en el equipo* his retirement left a gap in the team ‖ — *el hueco de la escalera* the stairwell, the stair well ‖ *el hueco del ascensor* the lift *o* elevator shaft ‖ *el hueco de una puerta* the doorway ‖ *grabado en hueco* intaglio ‖ FIG *hacer su hueco* to make o.s. a place | *sonar a hueco* to sound hollow.

huecograbado *m* photogravure.

huecú *m* AMER grass-covered swamp *o* bog.

huélfago *m* VET heaves *pl* (de los caballos).

huelga *f* strike; *declararse en huelga, declarar la huelga* to declare o.s. on strike, to go on strike; *estar en huelga* to be on strike ‖ good time, amusement, enjoyment (recreo) ‖ — *huelga a la japonesa* work-in ‖ *huelga de brazos caídos* or *de brazos cruzados* down tools, sit-down strike ‖ *huelga de celo* work-to-rule ‖ *huelga del hambre* hunger strike ‖ *huelga escalonada* or *alternativa* or *por turno* staggered strike ‖ *huelga general* general strike (en todo el país), all-out strike (de todos los empleados) ‖ *huelga indefinida* indefinite strike ‖ *huelga intermitente* go-slow [US slow-down] ‖ *huelga por solidaridad* sympathetic strike ‖ *huelga salvaje* wildcat strike ‖ *subsidio de huelga* strike pay.

huelgo *m* breath (aliento) ‖ TECN play (juego).

huelguista *m/f* striker.

huelguístico, ca *adj* strike ‖ *movimiento huelguístico en las minas* wave of strikes in the mines.

huella *f* footprint, footstep, track (del pie, de una persona); *se ven huellas en la nieve* footprints can be seen in the snow ‖ track (de animales, de vehículos) ‖ trace, mark (señal); *el tiempo ha dejado huellas en su rostro* time has left its mark on his face ‖ tread (de un escalón) ‖ — *dejar huellas* to leave one's mark; *hecho que dejará sus huellas en la historia* event that will leave its mark on history ‖ *huella digital* or *dactilar* fingerprint ‖ *no encontrar huellas de* not to find a trace of ‖ *seguir las huellas de alguien* to follow s.o.'s tracks *o* trail, to trail s.o. (seguir el rastro), to follow in s.o.'s footsteps (hacer lo mismo).

huello *m* step, pace (de un caballo) ‖ sole (del casco del caballo) ‖ surface (superficie) ‖ path, track (camino).

huérfano, na *adj* orphaned, orphan ‖ *huérfano de* devoid of, without, lacking.

◆ *m/f* orphan ‖ — *asilo de huérfanos* orphanage ‖ *huérfano de guerra* war orphan ‖ *huérfano de madre* motherless child ‖ *huérfano de padre* fatherless child.

huero, ra *adj* FIG empty; *un discurso huero* an empty speech ‖ rotten (podrido) ‖ AMER blond, blonde (rubio) ‖ FIG *salir huero* to be a failure.

huerta *f* large kitchen garden, large vegetable garden (para cultivo de hortalizas) ‖ «Huerta», irrigated and cultivated plain (tierra de regadío, especialmente en Valencia y Murcia) ‖ orchard (de árboles frutales) ‖ market garden [US truck garden] (de cultivo para la venta) ‖ *productos de la huerta* market-garden produce.

— OBSERV *La huerta* is generally much larger than *el huerto* and more vegetables than fruits are grown there.

huertano, na *adj* pertaining to an inhabitant of the «Huerta» ‖ market-garden (de la huerta).

◆ *m/f* inhabitant of the «Huerta».

huertero, ra *m/f* AMER gardener.

huerto *m* orchand (de árboles frutales) ‖ vegetable garden, kitchen garden (de hortalizas) ‖ market garden [US truck garden] (de cultivo para la venta).

huesa *f* grave; *tener un pie en la huesa* to have one foot in the grave.

huesillo *m* AMER sun-dried peach.

hueso *m* ANAT bone; *los huesos del pie* the bones of the foot ‖ stone [US pit] (de una fruta) ‖ bone (sustancia); *botones de hueso* buttons made of bone ‖ FIG & FAM hard work, drudgery; *el latín para mí es un hueso* Latin is hard work *o* a drudgery for me | pain in the neck; *¡este tío es un hueso!* that fellow is a pain in the neck! | snag (dificultad) ‖ AMER FIG government job ‖ — FIG *¡a otro perro con ese hueso!* pull the other one!, don't give me that, tell it to the Marines! (no me lo creo), no chance, you'll be lucky!, come off it! (para rechazar una proposición desagradable) ‖ FAM *dar en (un) hueso* or *tropezar con un hueso* to hit a snag | *darle a la sin hueso* to tongue-wag | *en carne y hueso* in the flesh | *este profesor es un hueso* or *un rato hueso* or *muy hueso* this teacher is a stickler ‖ *hueso de la alegría* or *de la suegra* funny bone ‖ *hueso sacro* sacrum ‖ FIG & FAM *la sin hueso* the tongue | *no dejarle a uno un hueso sano* to break every bone in s.o.'s body, to make mincemeat of s.o. (pegándole), to pull *o* to pick s.o. to pieces (criticar mucho) | *ser un hueso duro de roer* to be a hard nut to crack.

◆ *pl* bones (restos de una persona) ‖ — *calado hasta los huesos* soaked to the skin, wet through, drenched ‖ *acabar con sus huesos (en la cárcel, etc.)* to end one's days (in prison, etc.) ‖ FAM *¡choca esos huesos!* it's a deal!, put it there! | *dar con los huesos en el suelo* to come a cropper, to fall flat | *dar con los huesos* to end up; *dio con sus huesos en la cárcel* he ended up in jail | *estar* or *quedarse en los huesos* to be nothing but skin and bone, to be a bag of bones | *estoy por sus huesos* I'm head-over-heels in love with him ‖ FIG & FAM *no llegará a hacer huesos viejos* he won't make old bones, he will not live long | *no poder uno con sus huesos* to be done in, to be all in | *romperle a uno los huesos* or *un hueso* to beat s.o. to a pulp | *tener los huesos duros* to be too old [for certain types of work] (ser demasiado viejo), to be as hard as nails (aguantar mucho) | *tener los huesos molidos* to be all in *o* bushed *o* shattered.

huésped, da *m/f* host (hombre que invita), hostess (mujer que invita) ‖ guest (invitado); *estar de huésped en casa de* to be a guest in the house of ‖ innkeeper (mesonero) ‖ BIOL & BOT host ‖ — *casa de huéspedes* boardinghouse ‖ *cuarto de huéspedes* guest room ‖ FIG *hacérsele a uno los dedos huéspedes* to imagine things (imaginarse cosas), to count one's chickens (crearse ilusiones) ‖ *huésped de una pensión* boarder, lodger ‖ FIG & FAM *no contar con la huéspeda* to reckon without one's host.

hueste *f* (ant) host, army (ejército) ‖ followers *pl* (partidarios).

huesudo, da *adj* big-boned, bony (persona) ‖ bony; *manos huesudas* bony hands.

hueva *f* roe, fish eggs *pl*, spawn.

huevada *f* POP AMER bloody stupid thing.

huevar *vi* to begin to lay (las aves).

huevear *vi* AMER FAM to mess about (hacer tonterías).

huevería *f* egg shop *o* store.

huevero, ra *m/f* egg dealer.

◆ *f* eggcup (para comer los huevos) ‖ egg stand (para servir los huevos) ‖ ANAT oviduct (de las aves).

huevo *m* egg (de ave, etc.); *poner un huevo* to lay an egg ‖ darning egg (para zurcir) ‖ POP ball (testículo) ‖ — FIG & FAM *andar* or *ir pisando huevos* to walk carefully ‖ POP *costar un huevo* to cost the earth, to cost a fortune ‖ AMER *huevo a la copa* boiled egg ‖ *huevo de Colón* sth. that seems at first to be difficult but has a simple solution ‖ *huevo de Pascuas* Easter egg ‖ *huevo duro* hard-boiled egg ‖ *huevo escalfado* poached egg ‖ *huevo estrellado* or *frito* or *al plato* fried egg ‖ *huevo fresco* new-laid egg ‖ *huevo huero* wind egg ‖ *huevo pasado por agua* boiled *o* soft-boiled egg ‖ *huevos batidos a punto de nieve* egg whites beaten stiff ‖ *huevos moles* dessert of egg-yolk and sugar ‖ *huevos revueltos* scrambled eggs ‖ AMER *huevo tibio* boiled *o* soft-boiled egg ‖ FIG *no es tanto por el huevo sino por el fuero* it's a matter of principle | *parecerse como un huevo a otro huevo* to be as like as two peas in a pod | *parecerse como un huevo a una castaña* to be as different as chalk and cheese ‖ POP *se lo puse a huevo* I handed it to him on a plate [US I gave it to him on a silver platter] | *tener huevos* to have guts.

huevón *m* AMER POP stupid fool [US jerk].

Hugo *npr m* Hugh, Hugo.

hugonote, ta *adj/s* Huguenot.

huida *f* flight, escape (acción de huir) || EQUIT shy.

huidero, ra *adj* fleeting.
◆ *m* cover, shelter (de los animales).

huidizo, za *adj* shy (tímido) || elusive (esquivo) || fleeting (fugaz) || shy (animal).

huido, da *adj* fugitive || shy of people, withdrawn.

huilón, ona *adj* AMER inclined to flee (que huye) | cowardly (cobarde).

huincha *f* AMER ribbon (cinta) | tape measure (para medir).

huinche *m* AMER winch.

huipil *m* AMER woman's tunic.

huir* *vi/vt* to flee, to escape; *huir de la cárcel* to flee from jail || to flee, to run away; *huir del vicio* to flee from vice || to run away; *huir a* or *de una persona* to run away from s.o. || to fly; *¡cómo huyen las horas!* how time files! || *huir de* (con el infinitivo), to avoid, to shun; *huir de ir a hacer visitas* to avoid making visits.

huiro *m* AMER seaweed (alga).

hule *m* oilcloth (para mesa, etc.) || oilskin (para ropa) || rubber sheet (para recién nacidos) || AMER rubber (caucho) || — FIG *ayer hubo hule en la corrida de toros* there was an accident in yesterday's bullfight | *ayer hubo hule en la calle* there was fighting *o* trouble in the street yesterday.

hulería *f* AMER plantation of rubber trees.

hulero *m* AMER rubber worker.

hulla *f* coal || — *hulla blanca* water power, white coal || *mina de hulla* coal mine, colliery.

hullero, ra *adj* coal; *cuenca hullera* coal bed.

humanamente *adv* humanly; *hacer lo humanamente posible* to do what is humanly possible || humanely (tratar, etc.).

humanar *vt* to humanize (humanizar).
◆ *vpr* to become more human || to become man (Dios) || AMER to condescend (condescender).

humanidad *f* mankind, humanity (género humano) || FIG humanity, humaneness || FAM corpulence || FIG & FAM *este cuarto huele a humanidad* this room smells stuffy.
◆ *pl* humanities; *estudiar humanidades* to study humanities.

humanismo *m* humanism.

humanista *m/f* humanist.

humanístico, ca *adj* humanistic.

humanitario, ria *adj* humane (humano).
◆ *adj/s* humanitarian.

humanitarismo *m* humanitarianism.

humanización *f* humanization.

humanizar *vt* to humanize.
◆ *vpr* to become more human.

humano, na *adj* human; *el cuerpo humano* the human body || humane; *tiene un trato muy humano con sus empleados* he has a very humane relationship with his employees || *todo cabe en lo humano* anything is possible.
◆ *m* human, human being.

humarada; humareda *f* cloud of smoke.

humarazo *m* dense smoke.

humazo *m* dense smoke || fumigation.

humeada *f* AMER puff of smoke.

humeante *adj* smoking, smoky (cenizas, etc.) || steaming; *sopa humeante* steaming soup.

humear *vi* to smoke; *carbón, chimenea que humea* coal, chimney that smokes || to be steaming hot; *sopa que humea* soup that is steaming hot || FIG not to be completely settled (riña) | to be conceited (presumir).
◆ *vt* AMER to fumigate (fumigar).

humectante *adj* moistening.

humectar *vt* —→ **humedecer.**

humedad *f* humidity, dampness, damp, moisture || FÍS humidity; *humedad relativa* relative humidity.

humedecedor *m* humidifier.

humedecer*; humectar *vt* to moisten, to dampen, to humidify.
◆ *vpr* to become moist *o* wet *o* damp || *se le humedecieron los ojos* his eyes became watery, tears filled his eyes.

humedecimiento *m* moistening, dampening, humidification.

húmedo, da *adj* humid, moist, damp (clima) || damp; *ropa húmeda* damp clothes; *suelo húmedo* damp ground || wet (mojado).

humera *f* FAM drunkenness (borrachera).
— OBSERV The «*h*» is aspirate.

humeral *adj* ANAT humeral.
◆ *m* REL humeral (veil).

humero *m* chimney, smokestack.

húmero *m* ANAT humerus.

humidificador, ra *adj* humidifying.
◆ *m* humidifier.

humidificar *vt* to humidify.

húmido, da *adj* POET humid, moist.

humildad *f* humility; *con toda humildad* with all humility || humbleness, lowliness (de nacimiento).

humilde *adj/s* humble; *la gente humilde* the humble people || FIG humble, lowly; *de humilde cuna* of humble birth || — *a mi humilde parecer* in my humble opinion || *favorecer a los humildes* to favour the humble.

humillación *f* humiliation.

humilladero *m* calvary (cruz al entrar en un pueblo).

humillante *adj* humiliating.

humillar *vt* to humiliate; *humillar a un hombre* to humiliate a man || to humble; *humillar a los enemigos* to humble the enemy || to bow (bajar); *humillar la frente* to bow one's head || to bend (la rodilla) || TAUR *humillar la cabeza* to lower its head (el toro).
◆ *vi* to lower its head (el toro).
◆ *vpr* to humble o.s.

humillo *m* FIG conceit, airs *pl*, vanity (vanidad) || VET disease of sucking pigs.

humo *m* smoke || steam, vapour [US vapor] (vapor) || fumes *pl* (gas nocivo) || — FIG & FAM *a humo de pajas* thoughtlessly || *cortina de humo* smoke screen || *curar al humo* to smoke [ham, fish, etc.] || *echar* or *hacer humo* to smoke; *la chimenea echa humo* the chimney smokes || FIG *hacer humo a uno* to ignore s.o. || AMER *hacerse humo* to vanish into thin air (desaparecer) || *irse todo en humo* to go up in smoke || FIG *quedar en humo de pajas* to come to nothing.
◆ *pl* hearths, homes || FIG conceit *sing*, airs (orgullo) || — FIG & FAM *bajarle los humos a uno* to take s.o. down a peg, to put s.o. in his place || FIG & FAM *¡cuántos humos tiene!* how presumptuous he is! || FIG *se le bajaron los humos* he was put in his place | *se le subieron los humos a la cabeza* he got on his high horse, he became conceited | *tener muchos humos* to put on airs, to think a lot of o.s.

humor *m* mood, temper, humour [US humor]; *buen, mal humor* good, bad mood || character, nature, temper (índole) || ANAT humour; *humor ácueo, vítreo* aqueous, vitreous humour || FIG wit, humour (agudeza) || humour (gracia); *tiene sentido del humor* he has a sense of humour; *humor negro* sick *o* black humour || — *estar de buen, mal humor* to be in a good, bad mood, to be in a good, bad temper || FAM *humor de todos los diablos* very bad temper || *no estoy de* or *no tengo humor para bromas* I'm in no mood for jokes || *remover los humores* to disturb || *seguirle el humor a uno* to go along with s.o., to humour s.o. || *si estás de humor* if you like, if you feel like it.

humorada *f* joke (broma) || fancy, caprice, whim (capricho) || gall, nerve; *tuvo la humorada de decirme esto* he had the gall to tell me that.

humorado, da *adj* *bien humorado* good-humoured [US good-humored], good-tempered || *mal humorado* bad-humoured, bad-tempered.

humoral *adj* ANAT humoral.

humorismo *m* humour [US humor], humorousness.

humorista *adj* humorous, humoristic.
◆ *m/f* humorist.

humorístico, ca *adj* humoristic, humorous.

humoso, sa *adj* smoky.

humus *m* AGR humus (mantillo).

hundido, da *adj* sunken; *barco hundido* sunken boat || hollow, sunken (mejillas) || deep-set, sunken; *ojos hundidos* deep-set eyes || *hundido en sus pensamientos* sunk in thought.

hundimiento *m* sinking (acción de hundir) || cave-in (del terreno, socavón) || collapse (de una casa) || depression (de la moral) || collapse, fall, downfall (de un imperio) || crash (de la Bolsa) || slump (de los precios, cotizaciones) || sinking (de un barco).

hundir *vt* to sink; *hundir un barco* to sink a ship || to cause to sink *o* to subside; *la lluvia hunde el suelo* the rain causes the ground to sink || to plunge, to immerse (sumergir) || to drive, to thrust (un puñal) || to drive, to sink (una estaca) || FIG to confound (confundir) | to depress (deprimir) | to overwhelm (abrumar) | to ruin (arruinar) | to squander (una fortuna).
◆ *vpr* to fall down, to tumble down, to collapse (un edificio) || to subside, to cave in (el terreno) || to sink (irse al fondo) || to fall, to collapse (un imperio) || to sink, to flag (la moral) || to collapse (la economía) || to crash (la Bolsa) || to slump (los precios, cotizaciones) || to come to nothing (proyectos) || to become hollow *o* sunken (las mejillas, los ojos) || MAR to sink (un barco, un avión); *el avión se hundió en el mar* the plane sank into the sea.

húngaro, ra *adj/s* Hungarian.

Hungría *npr f* GEOGR Hungary.

huno *m* HIST Hun.

huracán *m* hurricane.

huracanado, da *adj* hurricane, tempestuous; *viento huracanado* hurricane wind.

huraño, ña *adj* unsociable (insociable), surly (arisco), shy (tímido).

hurgador *m* poker (persona, utensilio).

hurgar *vt* to poke, to stir (el fuego) || to rummage in, to poke around in (en un bolso, papeles) || FIG to incite, to stir up (incitar) || — FIG *hurgar en la herida* to turn the knife in the wound || FAM *peor es hurgarlo* better leave it alone.
◆ *vpr* FAM to pick; *hurgarse las narices, los dientes* to pick one's nose, one's teeth.

hurgón *m* poker (persona, utensilio).

hurgonada *f* poking.

hurgonazo *m* thrust *o* jab with a poker.

hurgonear *vt* to poke, to stir (el fuego).

hurgonero *m* poker (utensilio).

hurguillas *m/f inv* busybody (bullebulle).

hurí *f* houri.

hurón *m* ZOOL ferret (animal) || FIG & FAM prier, snooper, busybody (persona entrometida) | unsociable person (persona huraña).

hurón, ona *adj/s* Huron (indio de América del Norte).
◆ *adj* shy, reserved (tímido) || unsociable (poco sociable).

Hurón *npr m* GEOGR Lake Huron.

hurona *f* female ferret.

huronear *vi* to ferret, to hunt with a ferret (cazar) || FIG & FAM to pry, to ferret, to snoop (escudriñar).

huronera *f* ferret hole || FIG & FAM hinding place, hideout (escondrijo) | den, hideout (para maleantes).

huronero *m* ferreter, ferret keeper.

¡hurra! *interj* hurrah!

hurraca *f* magpie (urraca).

hurtadillas (a) *loc adv* stealthily, on the sly.

hurtar *vt* to steal (robar) || to cheat, to give short measure (engañar en el peso) || FIG to wash *o* to wear *o* to eat away (tierras) | to plagiarize, to lift (plagiar) || *hurtar el cuerpo* to dodge.
◆ *vpr* FIG to hide; *hurtarse a los ojos de uno* to hide from s.o. | to shirk, to evade; *hurtarse a las responsabilidades* to evade responsabilities.

hurto *m* petty theft *o* larceny (robo) || loot, stolen object (cosa robada).

husada *f* spindleful (de hilo).

húsar *m* MIL hussar.

husillo *m* screw, worm [of a press] (de molino) || drain (conducto) || small spindle (huso) || TECN spindle.

husita *adj/s* HIST Hussite.

husma *f* snooping, prying || FAM *andar a la husma* to go snooping around.

husmeador, ra *adj* FAM prying, snooping.
◆ *m/f* prier, snooper.

husmear *vt* to scent, to smell out || FIG & FAM to pry into, to snoop into (indagar) | to smell (presentir); *husmear el peligro* to smell danger.
◆ *vi* to smell bad *o* off (las carnes) || to snoop around (curiosear).

husmeo *m* scenting || FIG snooping, prying.

husmo *m* bad *o* rotten smell (olor).

huso *m* spindle (para hilar) || fuselage (de los aviones) || spindle (de torno) || HERÁLD lozenge || — MAT *huso esférico* lune || *huso horario* time zone || FIG & FAM *ser más derecho* or *tieso que un huso* to be as straight *o* as stiff as a poker.

¡huy! *interj* ouch! (dolor) || well! (sorpresa).

I

i *f* i; *una i mayúscula* a capital i ‖ FIG *poner los puntos sobre las íes* to dot the i's and cross the t's.

iatrogenia *f* MED iatrogeny.

Iberia *npr f* GEOGR Iberia.

ibérico, ca; iberio, ria *adj/s* Iberian; *la Península Ibérica* the Iberian Peninsula.

ibero, ra; íbero, ra *adj/s* Iberian.

Iberoamérica *npr f* GEOGR Latin America.

iberoamericano, na *adj/s* Latin-American.
— OBSERV *Iberoamericano* and *hispanoamericano* are the terms used in Spain. Latin Americans do more commonly use the term *latinoamericano*.

íbice *m* ZOOL ibex (cabra montés).

ibicenco, ca *adj/s* Ibizan (de Ibiza).

ibídem *adv lat* ibidem (en el mismo lugar).
— OBSERV Abreviación: *ibid* or *ib.* en ambos idiomas.

ibis *m* ibis (ave).

Ibiza *n pr* GEOGR Ibiza.

icaco *m* BOT icaco, coco plum, cocoa plum.

icáreo, a; icario, ria *adj* Icarian.

Ícaro *npr m* MIT Icarus.

iceberg *m* iceberg.

icefield *m* icefield.

ICI *abrev de Instituto de Cooperación Iberoamericana* institute for Latin-American co-operation.

ICONA *abrev de Instituto Nacional para la Conservación de la Naturaleza* national conservancy council.

icono *m* icon.

iconoclasia *f* iconoclasm.

iconoclasta *adj* iconoclastic.
◆ *m/f* iconoclast.

iconolatría *f* iconolatry, image worship.

iconología *f* iconology.

iconoscopio *m* RAD iconoscope.

icor *m* MED ichor.

icosaedro *m* MAT icosahedron.

ictericia *f* MED icterus, jaundice.

ictérico, ca *adj* MED icteric, suffering from jaundice.
◆ *m/f* MED person suffering from jaundice.

icterógeno, na *adj* MED icterogenic.

icterohepatitis *f inv* MED icterohepatitis.

ictiocola *f* ichthyocolla, fish glue, isinglass.

ictiofagia *f* ichthyophagy.

ictiófago, ga *adj* ichthyophagous.
◆ *m/f* ichthyophagist.

ictiol *m* QUÍM ichthyol.

ictiología *f* ichthyology.

ictiólogo *m* ichthyologist.

ictiosauro *m* ichthyosaur.

ictus *m* MED ictus ‖ ictus (acento).

ida *f* going, outward journey; *me gusta la ida, pero no la vuelta* I like the going, but not the coming back ‖ departure (salida); *¿a qué hora es la ida?* what time is the departure? ‖ FIG impulsive action, impetuous action (ímpetu) ‖ attack (esgrima) ‖ track, trail (caza) ‖ — *billete de ida y vuelta,* AMER *billete de ida y llamada* return ticket [US round-trip ticket] ‖ *idas y venidas* comings and goings ‖ *perdimos una hora en la ida* we lost an hour going, we lost an hour on the outward journey ‖ *viaje de ida* outward journey ‖ *viaje de ida y vuelta* round trip, return trip *o* journey.

idea *f* idea; *idea preconcebida* preconceived idea; *tengo una idea* I've (got) an idea ‖ memory, thought (recuerdo); *no puedo borrar su idea de la mente* I cannot erase his memory *o* the thought of him from my mind ‖ intention (intención); *lo hizo con buena idea, pero* his intentions were good *o* he did it with good intention, but ‖ concept, idea (concepto) ‖ opinion, impression; *tener buena idea de uno* to have a good opinion of s.o. ‖ idea, belief (creencia); *una idea muy extendida por el mundo* an idea widely spread throughout the world ‖ idea, outline (esquema) ‖ idea (habilidad); *no tiene mucha idea para pintar* he hasn't much idea of *o* about painting ‖ — *cambiar* or *mudar de idea* to change one's mind ‖ *dar idea de* to give an idea of ‖ *darle* or *ocurrírsele a uno la idea de* to get the idea of, to take it into one's head to; *le dio súbitamente la idea de escalar el Mont Blanc* he suddenly took it into his head to climb Mont Blanc ‖ *formarse una idea* to form *o* to get an idea ‖ *hacer algo con mala idea* to do sth. with ill intentions ‖ *hacerse a la idea de que...* to get used to the idea that... ‖ *hacerse una idea de* to get an idea of ‖ *idea eje* central idea ‖ *idea fija* obsession, fixed idea, idée fixe ‖ *idea general* or *de conjunto* general idea, general outline ‖ *idea genial* or *luminosa* brilliant idea, brain wave [US brain storm] ‖ *idea vacía* empty idea ‖ *llevar* or *tener idea de* to intend to, to have the intention of ‖ *metérsele a uno una idea en la cabeza* to get an idea into one's head ‖ *¡ni idea!* no idea! ‖ FIG *no tener idea buena* to be always up to no good ‖ *no tengo ni la más ligera* or *remota idea* I haven't a clue, I haven't the slightest *o* the remotest idea ‖ *¿qué idea tienes del director?* what impression do you have of the director? ‖ *tener idea* to have an idea *o* the idea; *se ve que tiene idea* he has obviously got an idea ‖ *tener mala idea* to be malicious *o* ill-intentioned ‖ FIG *tener una idea en la cabeza* to be up to sth., to have sth. up one's sleeve.

ideal *adj* ideal (de la idea o de las ideas) ‖ imaginary, hypothetical, ideal (imaginado, supuesto) ‖ ideal; *sueña con un mundo ideal* he dreams of an ideal world ‖ gorgeous, lovely (muy bonito); *lleva un traje ideal* she is wearing a gorgeous dress.
◆ *m* ideal; *hombre de ideales* man of ideals ‖ *lo ideal* the ideal thing.

idealismo *m* idealism.

idealista *adj* idealistic.
◆ *m/f* idealist.

idealización *f* idealization.

idealizar *vt* to idealize.

idear *vt* to think up, to conceive (concebir) ‖ to invent, to devise, to contrive; *un aparato ideado por un ingeniero* an appliance devised by an engineer ‖ to design; *ha sido ideado para ir a quinientos por hora* it is designed to do five hundred miles per hour.

ideario *m* ideology.

ideático, ca *adj* AMER eccentric (venático) ‖ ingenious (ingenioso).

ídem *adv* idem, ditto ‖ *Carlos es un vago y un embustero y su padre ídem de ídem* Charles is an idler and a liar, and his father is the same *o* and the same goes for his father.

idéntico, ca *adj* identical.

identidad *f* identity; *tarjeta* or *documento* or *carnet de identidad* identity card ‖ FIG identity (semejanza); *identidad de pareceres* identity of opinions.

identificable *adj* identifiable.

identificación *f* identification.

identificar *vt* to identify.
◆ *vpr* to identify o.s., to identify (*con* with) ‖ *identificarse plenamente con su papel* to identify with one's role, to really live the part.

ideograma *m* ideograph, ideogram.

ideología *f* ideology.

ideológico, ca *adj* ideological, ideologic.

ideólogo *m* ideologist.

idílico, ca *adj* idyllic.

idilio *m* idyll, idyl ‖ amorous talk (coloquio amoroso) ‖ amorous relationship, romance (relaciones).

idiocia *f* MED idiocy.

idioma *m* language, tongue; *el idioma inglés* the English language ‖ parlance, idiom, language; *idioma de la corte* language of the Court, Court parlance *o* idiom ‖ FIG *no hablamos el mismo idioma* we just don't speak the same language, we're not on the same wavelength.

idiomático, ca *adj* idiomatic ‖ *expresión idiomática* idiom, idiomatic expression.

idiopatía *f* idiopathy.

idiosincrasia *f* idiosyncrasy.

idiosincrático, ca *adj* idiosyncratic.

idiota *adj* idiotic, stupid, foolish.
◆ *m/f* idiot, fool ‖ *¡idiota!* you idiot!

idiotez *f* idiocy, foolishness (cualidad) ‖ idiotic thing (hecho, dicho) ‖ — *decir idioteces* to talk nonsense ‖ *hacer idioteces* to fool about, to be silly.

idiotismo *m* GRAM idiom ‖ ignorance (falta de instrucción).

idiotizar *vt* to idiotize.

ido, da *adj* FAM miles away (distraído); *perdóname, estaba ido* I'm sorry, I was miles away ‖ touched, cracked (chiflado).

idólatra *adj* idolatrous.
◆ *m/f* idolater (hombre), idolatress (mujer).

idolatrar *vt* to worship ‖ FIG to idolize; *idolatrar a sus padres* to idolize one's parents.

idolatría *f* idolatry.

idolátrico, ca *adj* idolatrous; *culto idolátrico* idolatrous cult || FIG idolatrous.

ídolo *m* idol || FIG idol; *hacerse el ídolo de* to become the idol of.

idoneidad *f* suitability, fitness (conveniencia) || ability, capability (capacidad).

idóneo, a *adj* suitable, fit (*para* for) (conveniente) || capable, competent, able (capaz).

idos; idus *m pl* ides.

íes *f pl* FIG *poner los puntos sobre las íes* to dot the i's and cross the t's.

iglesia *f* church (edificio) || church; *Iglesia militante, purgante, triunfante* Church militant, suffering, triumphant || (ant) sanctuary (inmunidad) || — *acogerse a la Iglesia, entrar en la Iglesia* to enter the Church, to take holy orders || FIG & FAM *casarse por detrás de la iglesia* to live together [as a married couple] || *casarse por la Iglesia* to get married in church || FIG *¡con la Iglesia hemos topado!* now we are really up against it! || *cumplir con la Iglesia* to fulfil one's religious duties *o* obligations || *el seno de la Iglesia* the bosom of the Church || *Iglesia Anglicana* Church of England, Anglican Church || *iglesia parroquial* parish church || *llevar a la Iglesia a una mujer* to lead a woman to the altar || *los Padres de la Iglesia* the Fathers of the Christian Church || *Santa Madre Iglesia* Mother Church.

iglú *m* igloo.

Ignacio *npr m* Ignatius.

ignaro, ra *adj* ignorant.
◆ *m/f* ignoramus.

ígneo, a *adj* igneous.

ignición *f* ignition || combustion, burning.

ignifugación *f* fireproofing.

ignífugo, ga *adj* fireproof, fire-resisting.

ignominia *f* ignominy, disgrace (deshonra) || humiliation, degradation (humillación) || injustice (injusticia) || crime, shame; *sería una ignominia cortarle sus hermosos rizos* it would be a crime to cut off her beautiful curls.

ignominioso, sa *adj* ignominious.

ignorancia *f* ignorance; *ignorancia crasa* or *supina* crass ignorance || *la ignorancia de la ley no exime su cumplimiento* ignorance of the law is no excuse.

ignorante *adj* ignorant (que carece de instrucción) || uninformed, unaware (que no ha sido informado).
◆ *m/f* ignoramus (que carece de instrucción) || dunce, ignoramus (estúpido).

ignorantismo *m* ignorantism, obscurantism.

ignorantista *m/f* obscurantist.

ignorantón, ona *adj* FAM very ignorant.
◆ *m/f* FAM ignoramus, dunce.

ignorar *vt* not to know, to be unaware *o* ignorant of; *ignoraban su presencia* they were unaware of his presence || to ignore (no tener en cuenta, no prestar atención) || *no ignorar que...* to be fully aware that...

igual *adj* even, level, smooth; *terreno, borde igual* even ground, edge || steady, even, smooth; *la marcha igual del tren* the steady motion of the train || alike, similar; *los dos hermanos son iguales* the two brothers are alike || equal; *dos cantidades iguales* two equal quantities || the same; *nuestros pareceres son prácticamente iguales* our opinions are practically the same; *tengo uno igual que el tuyo* I have one the same as yours; *¿cómo está el enfermo? =m igual* how is the patient? =m still the same || constant, even; *temperatura igual* constant temperature || equable; *clima igual* equable climate || even, equable (carácter) || the same (indiferente); *todo le es* or *le da igual* it is all the same to him || — *es igual* it makes no difference, it doesn't matter || *nunca he visto cosa igual* I've never seen the like of it *o* anything like it || *su coche es igual que el mío* his car is like mine *o* is the same as mine || MAT *X igual a Y* X equals Y.
◆ *adv* easily; *igual podías haberte matado* you could easily have killed yourself || *igual han tenido algún problema con el coche* they might (well) have had trouble with the car.
◆ *m* equal; *es su igual* he is your equal || MAT equal sign || — *al igual que* (just) like, the same as, just as || *de igual a igual* as (to) an equal, as (to) one's equal, as (to) one's equals, as equals; *hablar a uno, tratar a uno de igual a igual* to speak to s.o. as to one's equal, to treat s.o. as an equal || *el sin igual cantante X* the incomparable singer X || *igual ocurre con Y* the same with Y, the same holds good of Y, so it is with Y || *igual que* (the same) as; *igual que antes* as before; *igual que yo* the same as me || *no tiene (otro) igual* he has no equal, there isn't another like him || *por igual* evenly, equally (uniformemente) || *sin igual* unequalled, unparalelled, unique, without equal.
◆ *pl* lottery ticket [on behalf of the «Organización Nacional de Ciegos» in Spain] || — *ir iguales* to be level, to be even (en una carrera) || DEP *quince iguales, iguales a quince* fifteen all.

iguala *f* equalization (igualación) || agreed fee (cuota pagada al médico, veterinario, etc.) || agreement, contract (ajuste) || FAM friendly society (igualatorio) || rule (de albañil) || TECN smoothing.

igualación *f* equalization, equalizing || levelling (del terreno) || planing, smoothing (de madera) || smoothing (de cuero, metal) || FIG agreement, contract (convenio) || MAT equating.

igualado, da *adj* smooth (césped) || similar, alike (semejante) || level (en situación muy semejante); *todos los caballos entraron en la meta muy igualados* all the horses came home very level || even; *un partido muy igualado* a very even game.

igualador, ra *adj* equalizing, who *o* which makes equal (que iguala).

igualamiento *m* equalization, equalizing (igualación) || agreement, contract (convenio).

igualar *vt* to equal (ser igual); *nada iguala la belleza de este paisaje* there is nothing to equal the beauty of this scenery || to make equal, to equalize (volver igual) || to consider equal, to place on an equal footing (a dos o más personas) || to even out, to adjust (ajustar) || to level off *o* out, to level (el terreno) || to trim (el césped) || TECN to plane, to smooth (madera) | to smooth off (cuero, metal) || MAT to equate || to match (la pintura) || to conclude (por un contrato); *igualar una venta* to conclude a sale.
◆ *vi* to be equal (ser igual) || to match (colores) || DEP to equalize || *igualar a 2* to bring the score to 2-2, to make it 2-2 (durante un partido), to draw 2-2 (al final de un partido).
◆ *vpr* to be equal, to equal each other *o* one another; *se igualan en fuerza* they are equal in strength || to become equal *o* the same (en magnitud) || to become level (nivelarse) || *igualarse con uno* to place o.s. on an equal footing with s.o.

igualatorio *m* friendly society (asociación) || medical centre (centro médico).

igualdad *f* equality; *igualdad de oportunidades* equality of opportunity || sameness; *igualdad de opiniones* sameness of opinions || similarity (semejanza) || smoothness (de la madera) || evenness, levelness (del terreno) || evenness, equableness (del carácter) || — DEP *a igualdad de tanteo* in the event of a tie || *en igualdad de condiciones* on equal terms || *en un pie de igualdad* on an equal footing || *igualdad de salario* equal pay.

igualitario, ria *adj/s* equalitarian.

igualmente *adv* equally || the same, in the same way; *las dos van igualmente vestidas* they both dress the same || likewise, also (además, también) || *¡que te diviertas mucho! =m igualmente* have a good time! =m the same to you!

iguana *f* ZOOL iguana.

iguanodonte *m* ZOOL iguanodon.

Iguazú (cataratas del) *n pr* GEOGR the Iguaçu Falls.

ijada *f* flank (de un animal) || loin (del hombre).

ijar *m* flank (de un animal) || loin (del hombre).

ikastola *f* school where classes are taught in Basque.

ikurriña *f* official Basque flag.

ilación *f* illation, deduction (deducción) || connection (enlace de las ideas) || cohesion (de un discurso).

ilativo, va *adj* illative || GRAM illative (conjunción).

ilegal *adj* illegal.

ilegalidad *f* illegality.

ilegibilidad *f* illegibility.

ilegible *adj* illegible; *firma ilegible* illegible signature.

ilegitimar *vt* to illegitimate.

ilegitimidad *f* illegitimacy.

ilegítimo, ma *adj* illegitimate; *hijo ilegítimo* illegitimate son || illegitimate, ilegal, illicit (ilícito).

íleo *m* MED ileus (cólico).

ileocecal *m* ANAT ileocecal.

ileostomía *f* MED ileostomy.

ilerdense *adj* [of *o* from] Lérida.
◆ *m/f* native *o* inhabitant of Lérida.

ilergete *adj* of *o* from a region that comprised part of the provinces of Huesca, Zaragoza and Lérida.

ileso, sa *adj* unhurt, unscathed, unharmed, uninjured; *el conductor resultó* or *salió ileso* the driver was unhurt; *salir ileso de un accidente* to come out of an accident unscathed.

iletrado, da *adj/s* illiterate (analfabeto).

iliaco, ca; ilíaco, ca *adj* ANAT iliac; *hueso iliaco* iliac bone.

Ilíada *npr f* Iliad (de Homero).

ilicitano, na *adj* [of *o* from] Elche [formerly «Ilici»].
◆ *m/f* native *o* inhabitant of Elche.

ilícito, ta *adj* illicit (ilegal).

ilicitud *f* illicitness.

ilimitado, da *adj* unlimited, limitless, illimited.

iliterato, ta *adj* illiterate.

ilógico, ca *adj* illogical.

ilogismo *m* illogicality, illogicalness.

ilota *m* helot (esclavo en Esparta).

ilotismo *m* helotism.

iluminación *f* illumination (acción de iluminar) || lighting (alumbrado); *iluminación artificial, indirecta* artificial, indirect lighting || floodlighting (de un estadio) || illumination (de estampas, letras, libro) || FIG enlightenment || FÍS illumination, illuminance.
◆ *pl* illuminations.

iluminado, da *adj* illuminated || FIG enlightened || *la casa está iluminada* the house is lit up.
◆ *m/f* illuminist (visionario).

◆ *m pl* illuminati.

iluminador, ra *m/f* illuminator (de estampas).

iluminancia *f* FÍS illuminance, illumination.

iluminar *vt* to illuminate, to light up (alumbrar); *iluminar un monumento* to illuminate a monument || to light, to illuminate; *cuarto iluminado por cuatro velas* room lit by four candles || to illuminate (adornar con luces) || to floodlight (un estadio) || to colour, to illuminate (estampas, letras, etc.) || to illuminate (un libro, una página, etc.) || to provide (prints, engravings, etc.) with a coloured background (con fondo de color) || FIG to illuminate, to light up; *una amplia sonrisa iluminó su rostro* a broad smile illuminated her face | to illuminate, to enlighten (ilustrar el entendimiento) | to illuminate, to throw light upon, to enlighten (un asunto, un problema, etc.) || to illuminate (teología).
◆ *vpr* to light up; *su cara se iluminó* his face lit up.

iluminarias *f pl* lights, illuminations.

iluminismo *m* illuminism.

ilusamente *adv* mistakenly, erroneously; *creía ilusamente en las buenas intenciones de su amigo* he mistakenly believed in his friend's good intentions.

ilusión *f* illusion; *ilusión óptica* optical illusion || dream; *su ilusión era ir a París* his dream was to go to Paris; *vivir de ilusiones* to live on dreams || FIG thrill, pleasure, joy (alegría) | hopefulness, hopeful anticipation (esperanza); *esperar el resultado con cierta ilusión* to await the outcome with a certain hopefulness || illusion, illusory hope *o* belief, delusion (esperanza vana) || — *con ilusión* hopefully || *forjarse* or *hacerse ilusiones* to build up one's hopes (*de* of), to cherish hopes (*de* of), to indulge in wishful thinking || *hacerse la ilusión de que...* to imagine that... || *me hace mucha ilusión ir a Acapulco* I'm so looking forward *o* I'm really looking forward to going to Acapulco || *¡qué ilusión ir esta noche al teatro!* how thrilling to be going to the theatre tonight! || *tener ilusión por* to be looking forward to || *trabajar con ilusión* to work with a will || *tu visita me hizo mucha ilusión* I was thrilled by your visit.

ilusionar *vt* to build up (s.o.'s) hopes, to deceive (hacer concebir esperanzas) || — *estar ilusionado con* to be thrilled with (presente), to be thrilled *o* excited about (futuro) || *me ilusiona el viaje* I'm looking forward to the journey, I'm thrilled about the journey.
◆ *vpr* to have hopes for; *los padres se ilusionan mucho con el primer hijo* the parents have great hopes for their first son || to be *o* to become thrilled *o* excited; *se ilusionó cuando le hablé del viaje* he was thrilled when I spoke to him about the journey || to have unfounded hopes (tener esperanzas infundadas) || *no te ilusiones mucho* don't build your hopes too high.

ilusionismo *m* illusionism.

ilusionista *m/f* illusionist, conjurer (prestidigitador).

iluso, sa *adj* dreamy, who indulges in flights of fancy (soñador) || easily deceived *o* duped (inocentón).
◆ *m/f* dreamer (soñador) || dupe (inocentón).

ilusorio, ria *adj* illusory (hopes) || imaginary (imaginario) || false, empty (promesas).

ilustración *f* erudition, learning (instrucción) || illustration, picture (grabado) || illustration (conjunto de grabados) || illustrated magazine (publicación) || HIST *la Ilustración* the Enlightenment.

ilustrado, da *adj* erudite, cultured, learned (docto) || illustrated (con dibujos, citas, etc.) || enlightened; *el despotismo ilustrado* the enlightened despotism.

ilustrador, ra *adj* illustrative.
◆ *m/f* illustrator (dibujante).

ilustrar *vt* to explain, to make clear, to enlighten; *eso me ilustró sobre sus intenciones* that explained his intentions to me, that made his intentions clear to me || to illustrate; *ilustrar con dibujos, con citas* to illustrate with drawings, by means of quotations || to make illustrious, to make famous (hacer ilustre) || to enlighten (el entendimiento).
◆ *vpr* to acquire knowledge (*sobre* of) || to learn (*sobre* about) || to become famous (personas).

ilustrativo, va *adj* illustrative.

ilustre *adj* illustrious, famous (célebre, famoso) || distinguished.

ilustrísimo, ma *adj* most illustrious || *Su Ilustrísima* His Lordship, His Grace.

imagen *f* image: *imagen religiosa* religious image || statue, image (p us): *una imagen de bronce* a bronze statue || picture (en televisión) || image (símbolo, metáfora) || FÍS image: *imagen invertida, real, virtual* inverted, real, virtual image || mental picture (en la mente) || — *Dios creó al hombre a su imagen y semejanza* God created man after His own image and likeness || FIG & FAM *quedarse para vestir imágenes* to be left on the shelf, to remain an old maid || FIG *ser la imagen viva de* to be a picture of: *es la imagen viva de la desesperación* she is a picture of despair | *ser la viva imagen de alguien* to be the living image *o* the spitting image of s.o.

imaginable *adj* imaginable.

imaginación *f* imagination (facultad) || FIG fancy (fantasía) || — *eso no es verdad, son imaginaciones tuyas* that's not true, you're imagining things *o* it's all in your imagination || *no se le pasó por la imaginación* it never occurred to him || *¡no te dejes llevar por la imaginación!, don't let your imagination run away with you!*

imaginar *vt* to imagine || to think up (idear).
◆ *vpr* to imagine: *me imagino lo que te habrá costado* I can imagine what it must have cost you || to picture, to imagine (representarse) || — *imagínate lo que ha pasado hoy* guess what happened today || *me imagino que sí* I suppose so, I imagine so || *me lo imagino* I can just imagine.

imaginaria *f* MIL reserve guard.

imaginario, ria *adj* imaginary || *lo imaginario* the imaginary.

imaginativo, va *adj* imaginative: *facultad imaginativa* imaginative power.
◆ *f* imagination, imaginativeness (facultad de imaginar) || common sense (sentido común).

imaginería *f* REL religious imagery || embroidery (bordado).

imaginero *m* (religious) image maker.

imán *m* magnet (hierro imantado): *imán artificial* artificial magnet || FIG magnetism, charm (atractivo) || imam, imaum (sacerdote mahometano) || *imán de herradura* horseshoe magnet.

imanación *f* magnetization.

imanar *vt* to magnetize.
◆ *vpr* to become magnetized.

imanato *m* imanate (dignidad del imán).

imantación *f* magnetization.

imantar *vt* to magnetize.
◆ *vpr* to become magnetized.

imbatible *adj* unbeatable, invincible.

imbatido, da *adj* unbeaten.

imbebible *adj* undrinkable.

imbécil *adj* MED imbecile || stupid, silly (tonto).
◆ *m/f* MED imbecile || idiot, imbecile (tonto) || *¡imbécil!,* you idiot!, you imbecile!

imbecilidad *f* imbecility (falta de inteligencia) || stupidity, silliness (tontería) || *decir imbecilidades* to talk nonsense.

imberbe *adj* beardless.

imbibición *f* absorption, soaking-up, imbibing.

imbornal *m* MAR scupper.

imborrable *adj* indelible, ineffaceable (indeleble) || indelible, unforgettable: *recuerdo imborrable* indelible memory.

imbricación *f* imbrication, overlapping.

imbricado, da *adj* imbricate, imbricated, overlapping.

imbricar *vt* to imbricate, to overlap.

imbuido, da *adj* imbued, steeped: *imbuido de su importancia* imbued with *o* steeped in one's own importance.

imbuir* *vt* to imbue, to inculcate, to instil (infundir): *imbuir a uno ideas falsas* to imbue s.o. with false ideas, to inculcate *o* to instil false ideas into s.o.
◆ *vpr* to become imbued *o* inculcated (*de* with).

imitable *adj* imitable.

imitación *f* imitation || pastiche (en literatura) || TEATR imitation, impersonation || — *a imitación de* in imitation of || *bolso imitación cocodrilo* imitation crocodile bag || *imitación fraudulenta* forgery (de billetes de banco, etc.), fraudulent imitation (de cualquier cosa) || *joyas de imitación* imitation jewelry.

imitador, ra *adj* imitating, imitative.
◆ *m/f* imitator || writer of pastiches (escritor).

imitamonos *m inv* FIG copycat.

imitar *vt* to imitate.

imitativo, va *adj* imitative: *armonía imitativa* imitative harmony; *artes imitativas* imitative arts.

impacción *f* MED impaction.

impaciencia *f* impatience.

impacientar *vt* to make (s.o.) lose patience, to exasperate, to make (s.o.) impatient.
◆ *vpr* to grow impatient: *impacientarse por no recibir noticias* to grow impatient at the lack of news || to lose one's patience, to get impatient (con alguien).

impaciente *adj* impatient: *impaciente por salir* impatient to go out || anxious, restless (intranquilo) || *impaciente con* or *por la tardanza* impatient at *o* made impatient by the delay.

impacto *m* impact: *punto de impacto* point of impact || impact mark (huella) || MIL hit (en el blanco) || FIG impact: *causar un impacto* to cause *o* to have an impact | incidence (repercusión).

impagable *adj* unpayable (no pagable) || FIG invaluable (inestimable).

impagado, da *adj* unpaid.

impago, ga *adj* AMER unpaid.

impalpabilidad *f* impalpability.

impalpable *adj* impalpable.

impar *adj* odd, uneven: *número impar* odd number || unpaired: *órgano impar* unpaired organ.

imparable *adj* unstoppable (en deporte).

imparcial *adj* impartial (justo): *un juez imparcial* an impartial judge || unbiased (objetivo).

imparcialidad *f* impartiality.

impartir *vt* to impart (otorgar) ‖ — JUR *impartir auxilio* to demand assistance ‖ *impartir su bendición* to give one's blessing.

impás o **impase** *m* finesse (bridge).

impasibilidad *f* impassiveness, impassivity, impassibility.

impasible *adj* impassive, impassible (insensible).

impavidez *f* fearlessness, dauntlessness, courage (arrojo) ‖ impassiveness, imperturbability (impasibilidad) ‖ *AMER* barefacedness, cheek (descaro).

impávido, da *adj* fearless, dauntless, courageous (atrevido) ‖ impassive (impasible) ‖ *AMER* barefaced, insolent, cheeky (descarado) ‖ *recibió impávido la noticia* he remained impassive at the news, he was unmoved by the news.

impecabilidad *f* impeccability.

impecable *adj* impeccable.

impedancia *f* ELECTR impedance.

impedido, da *adj* disabled, crippled (tullido) ‖ *impedido de las dos piernas* disabled in both legs, without the use of both legs.
◆ *m/f* disabled person, cripple.

impedimenta *f* MIL impedimenta *pl.*

impedimento *m* prevention: *en caso de impedimento* in case of prevention ‖ hindrance, impediment, obstacle (traba) ‖ JUR *impedimento dirimente* diriment impediment.

impedir* *vt* to prevent, to stop: *la lluvia le impidió que saliera* the rain prevented him from going out ‖ to impede, to hinder (el movimiento) ‖ to obstruct, to block (el paso) ‖ — *eso no impide que...* that does not alter the fact that... ‖ *me veo impedido para venir* it is impossible for me to come, I'm afraid I cannot come.

impelente *adj* impellent, impelling, propelling, driving: *fuerza impelente* impelling force ‖ *bomba impelente* force pump.

impeler *vt* to propel, to drive forward, to impel: *el viento impelió la barca* the wind drove the boat forward ‖ TECN to drive, to propel ‖ FIG to drive, to impel: *impelido a la venganza* driven to vengeance ‖ *los cruzados, impelidos por su fe...* the crusaders, driven up by their faith...

impenetrabilidad *f* impenetrability.

impenetrable *adj* impenetrable: *coraza impenetrable* impenetrable armour ‖ unfathomable, impenetrable (misterio, enigma, etc.).

impenitencia *f* impenitence.

impenitente *adj* impenitent, unrepentant ‖ FIG inveterate, confirmed (bebedor, jugador) ‖ confirmed (criminal) ‖ inveterate (mentiroso).

impensable *adj* unthinkable.

impensadamente *adv* unexpectedly (llegar) ‖ without thinking, inadvertently, unintentionally (decir una cosa).

impensado, da *adj* unexpected (imprevisto) ‖ spontaneous (respuesta).

impepinable *adj* FAM certain, sure, undeniable, beyond doubt ‖ FAM *eso es impepinable* there's no doubt about that, that's for sure.

imperante *adj* ruling (dinastía) ‖ prevailing (viento, tendencia).

imperar *vi* to reign, to rule (un emperador) ‖ FIG to reign: *impera una atmósfera de pesimismo* there reigns an atmosphere of pessimism | to prevail, to predominate: *impera el viento norte* the north wind prevails | to be current (precios).

imperativo, va *adj* imperious (persona) ‖ imperative (tono) ‖ imperative, imperious (urgente) ‖ GRAM imperative: *modo imperativo* imperative mood.
◆ *m* GRAM imperative ‖ FIG imperative (necesidad absoluta) | consideration, imperative: *imperativos económicos* economic considerations ‖ JUR *por imperativo legal* by legal imperative.

imperceptibilidad *f* imperceptibility.

imperceptible *adj* imperceptible: *sonido, diferencia imperceptible* imperceptible sound, difference.

imperdible *adj* unlosable, that cannot be lost.
◆ *m* safety pin (alfiler).

imperdonable *adj* unpardonable, unforgivable.

imperecedero, ra *adj* imperfect ‖ defective, faulty (defectuoso) ‖ GRAM *pretérito imperfecto* imperfect.

imperforación *f* MED imperforation.

imperial *adj* imperial (del emperador, del imperio); *corona imperial* imperial crown.
◆ *f* top deck, upper deck, imperial (de un carruaje).

imperialismo *m* imperialism ‖ *imperialismo económico* economic imperialism.

imperialista *adj* imperialistic.
◆ *m/f* imperialist.

impericia *f* unskilfulness (inhabilidad) ‖ inexperience (falta de experiencia).

imperio *m* empire; *el Sacro Imperio* the Holy Roman Empire ‖ emperorship (cargo, dignidad del emperador) ‖ FIG domination, authority, power (poder) | pride, haughtiness (orgullo) ‖ MIL mess.
◆ *adj* empire; *estilo Imperio* Empire style.

imperioso, sa *adj* imperious, overbearing (persona) ‖ imperative, imperious; *necesidad, orden imperiosa* imperative need, command.

imperito, ta *adj* inexpert, unskilled.

impermeabilidad *f* impermeability ‖ TECN imperviousness | watertightness (estanqueidad).

impermeabilización *f* waterproofing.

impermeabilizar *vt* to waterproof, to make waterproof.

impermeable *adj* impermeable, impervious ‖ waterproof; *una tela impermeable* a waterproof fabric.
◆ *m* raincoat, mackintosh, mac.

impermutable *adj* unexchangeable.

impersonal *adj* impersonal.

impersonalidad *f* impersonality.

impersonalizar *vt* to use (a verb) impersonally.

impertérrito, ta *adj* imperturbable (de carácter) ‖ impassive, unmoved (en un momento dado).

impertinencia *f* impertinence (cualidad) ‖ impertinent remark (dicho) ‖ *con impertinencia* impertinently.

impertinente *adj* impertinent (insolente) ‖ impertinent, irrelevant (no pertinente).
◆ *m/f* impertinent fellow (hombre), impertinent woman (mujer).
◆ *m pl* lorgnette *sing.*

imperturbabilidad *f* imperturbability.

imperturbable *adj* imperturbable.

impétigo *m* MED impetigo.

impetración *f* impetration, entreaty, beseeching (petición) ‖ impetration, obtaining by entreaty (consecución).

impetrar *vt* to ask for, to entreat, to beseech, to impetrate (solicitar); *impetrar la protección divina* to impetrate divine protection ‖ to impetrate, to obtain by entreaty (obtener).

ímpetu *m* violence (de las olas, de los ataques, etc.) ‖ energy (brío, energía) ‖ impetuosity (fogosidad) ‖ impetus, momentum, impulse (impulso).

impetuosidad *f* violence; *la impetuosidad de un ataque* the violence of an attack ‖ impetuosity, impulsiveness (fogosidad).

impetuoso, sa *adj* violent (olas, viento, ataques, etc.) ‖ impetuous, impulsive (fogoso) ‖ *torrente impetuoso* rushing torrent.

impiedad *f* impiety.

impío, a *adj* impious, irreligious, godless (falto de fe religiosa) ‖ irreligious, irreverent (irreverente).
◆ *m/f* infidel.

implacabilidad *f* implacability, relentlessness (del odio, de un enemigo, etc.) ‖ inexorability (de un juez, de un adversario, etc.).

implacable *adj* implacable, relentless; *enemigo, odio implacable* implacable enemy, hatred; *la furia implacable del mar* the sea's relentless fury ‖ inexorable; *un juez implacable* an inexorable judge.

implantación *f* implantation (de costumbres, ideas) ‖ introduction (de una moda, de reformas) ‖ MED implantation.

implantar *vt* to implant (costumbres, ideas) ‖ to introduce (una moda, reformas) ‖ MED to implant.
◆ *vpr* to be *o* to become implanted (costumbres, ideas) ‖ to be introduced (moda, reformas).

implemento *m* implement.

implicación *f* implication ‖ contradiction.

implicancia *f* *AMER* legal impediment | incompatibility (incompatibilidad).

implicar *vt* to implicate, to involve (envolver); *está implicado en un delito* he is implicated in a crime ‖ to imply (llevar en sí) ‖ to mean (entrañar); *la derrota del equipo implicaría el descenso inmediato* the team's defeat would mean instant relegation.

implicatorio, ria *adj* implicative, implicatory.

implícitamente *adv* implicitly.

implícito, ta *adj* implicit, implied.

imploración *f* supplication, entreaty.

implorante *adj* imploring, entreating.

implorar *vt* to implore, to beseech, to beg, to entreat; *implorar perdón* to implore forgiveness.

implosivo, va *adj* GRAM implosive.

implume *adj* featherless.

impoluto, ta *adj* unpolluted.

imponderabilidad *f* imponderability.

imponderable *adj* imponderable ‖ FIG invaluable (inapreciable).
◆ *m* imponderable.

imponente *adj* imposing; *persona imponente* imposing person ‖ FAM sensational, terrific; *una chica, un coche imponente* a sensational girl, car ‖ tremendous (enorme) ‖ *hace un frío imponente* it's freezing cold.

imponer* *vt* to impose (disciplina, multa, obligación, tributo, silencio, voluntad) ‖ to set (una tarea) ‖ to exact, to demand (requerir) ‖ to lay down, to impose (una condición) ‖ FIG to inspire (el temor) | to command (el respeto, la obediencia) | to impute [falsely] (atribuir falsamente) ‖ to impose, to lay; *imponer las manos sobre* to impose one's hands on ‖ to deposit; *imponer dinero en un banco* to deposit money in a bank ‖ to give; *imponer un nombre a* to give a name to ‖ to award; *imponer una condecoración a un militar* to award a soldier a medal ‖ to instruct (enseñar); *imponer a uno en contabilidad* to instruct s.o. in bookkeeping ‖ to acquaint, to inform; *imponer a alguien de los*

hechos to acquaint s.o. with the facts, to inform s.o. of the facts || IMPR to impose [type].
◆ *vi* to command *o* to inspire respect (respeto) || to inspire admiration (admiración) || to inspire fear (miedo) || to be impressive *o* imposing (edificios).
◆ *vpr* to be imposed || to be imperative *o* necessary (ser necesario) || to show authority (*a* over), to assert o.s. (*a* over), to impose one's authority (*a* on) (hacerse obedecer) || to command respect (*a* from) (hacerse respetar) || to show one's superiority (*a* over) (mostrar su superioridad) || to take on (comprometerse a hacer) || to get on (situarse); *imponerse por su mérito* to get on through one's own merit || to acquaint o.s. (*de* with), to find out (*de* about) (instruirse) || to dominate; *imponerse a las circunstancias* to dominate the circumstances || to prevail (prevalecer).

imponible *adj* taxable; *riqueza imponible* taxable wealth || — *base imponible* taxable income || *no imponible* tax-free.

impopular *adj* unpopular.

impopularidad *f* unpopularity.

importable *adj* importable.

importación *f* importation, importing (acción) || — *bienes de importación* imported goods || *licencia de importación* import licence.
◆ *pl* imports (cosas importadas).

importador, ra *adj* importing; *país importador* importing country.
◆ *m/f* importer.

importancia *f* importance; *conceder* or *dar importancia a* to attach *o* to give importance to || size, magnitude || — *darse uno importancia* to give o.s. airs, to put on airs || *de importancia* important, of importance || *de gran* or *mucha importancia* of great importance, very important *o* significant || *herido de importancia* seriously wounded || *no tiene la menor importancia* it's not important, it has not the slightest importance, it doesn't matter in the least || *sin importancia* unimportant, insignificant.

importante *adj* important; *modificaciones importantes* important modifications || considerable, sizeable; *una suma importante de dinero* a considerable sum of money || — *dárselas* or *echárselas de importante* to be full of self-importance, to think too much of o.s. || *lo importante* what is important, the important *o* main thing || *poco importante* unimportant.

importar *vt* to import (de un país extranjero); *importar arroz* to import rice || to cost (valer); *el libro importa cien pesetas* the book costs a hundred pesetas || to come to, to amount to; *la cuenta importa cien pesetas* the bill comes to one hundred pesetas || FIG to mean, to bring about, to cause (acarrear) | to entail (llevar consigo) | to involve, to imply (implicar).
◆ *vi/v imp* to be important, to be of importance; *importa hacerlo* it is important that it be done *o* for it to be done || to matter; *no importa lo que digas* it doesn't matter what you say || to interest; *lo que más me importaba de él era su erudición* what interested me most about him was his erudition || to concern (afectar) || — *a Juan nada le importa* John does not care about anything || *¿le importaría traerme ese libro?* would you mind bringing me that book? || FIG & FAM *me importa un comino* or *tres pepinos* or *un bledo* or *un pito* or *un adarme* I don't give a damn *o* a hang, I couldn't care less || *no importa* it doesn't matter, never mind || *¿qué importa?* what does it matter?, what difference does it make? || *¿y a ti qué te importa?* what's it to you?, what's it got to do with you?, what concern is it of yours?

importe *m* price, cost (valor) || total amount, total (total); *hasta el importe de cien pesetas* up to a total of a hundred pesetas || amount; *el importe de una factura* the amount of a bill || *por importe de* for the sum of.

importunamente *adv* inopportunely (de manera inoportuna) || in a bothersome *o* tiresome way (de manera importuna).

importunar *vt* to importune, to bother, to pester.

importunidad *f* importunity, importuning, pestering (molestia) || bothersomeness, troublesomeness (pesadez) || nuisance, bother, importunity (cosa importuna).

importuno, na *adj* inopportune, ill-timed (que no es oportuno) || bothersome, troublesome, tiresome, trying, annoying (fastidioso) || importunate, importune (que molesta con peticiones).

imposibilidad *f* impossibility || inability (de una persona).

imposibilitado, da *adj* disabled, crippled (inválido); *tras el accidente se quedó imposibilitado para toda la vida* the accident left him crippled for life || prevented, unable; *estuvo imposibilitado de salir* he was prevented from going out, he was unable to go out.

imposibilitar *vt* to make impossible; *la lluvia imposibilitó el ataque* the rain made attack impossible || to prevent, to stop (impedir); *la lluvia me imposibilitó salir* the rain prevented my going out || to disable (físicamente).
◆ *vpr* to be *o* to be left disabled *o* crippled.

imposible *adj* impossible; *nada es imposible en la vida* nothing in life is impossible; *se ha puesto imposible* he has become impossible || FIG terrible, awful (muy malo); *hacía un tiempo imposible* the weather was terrible || filthy, dirty (sucio).
◆ *m* impossible; *pedir un imposible* to ask the impossible || — *Dios no pide imposibles* you cannot expect s.o. to do the impossible || *hacer lo imposible* to perform *o* to do the impossible (hacer algo que no parecía posible), to do one's utmost (hacer todo lo posible) || *¡me parece imposible que estés aquí!* I can hardly believe you're here! || *¡parece imposible!* I don't *o* I can hardly believe it!

imposición *f* REL imposition, laying on (de manos) || imposition (de una condición, una disciplina, una multa, una obligación, un tributo, un silencio, una voluntad) || setting (de una tarea) || deposit (cantidad en depósito); *imposición a plazo* time *o* term deposit || tax, imposition (impuesto) || IMPR imposition || *imposición de condecoraciones* investiture.

impositivo, va *adj* tax, of taxes || *sistema impositivo* taxation, tax system.

impositor *m* IMPR typesetter.

imposta *f* ARQ impost.

impostergable *adj* unpostponable, that cannot be put off *o* delayed.

impostor, ra *m/f* impostor (suplantador) || slanderer (calumniador).

impostura *f* imposture || slander, slur (calumnia).

impotencia *f* powerlessness, impotence, helplessness; *la impotencia del gobierno contra la rebelión* the government's powerlessness in the face of the rebellion || inability (incapacidad) || MED impotence.

impotente *adj* powerless, impotent, helpless (sin fuerza suficiente) || unable (incapaz) || MED impotent.

impracticabilidad *f* impracticability.

impracticable *adj* impracticable, unfeasible; *proyecto impracticable* impracticable plan || impassable (carretera).

imprecación *f* imprecation, curse.

imprecar *vt* to imprecate, to curse.

imprecatorio, ria *adj* imprecatory.

imprecisión *f* lack of precision, vagueness, imprecision (falta de precisión).

impreciso, sa *adj* imprecise, vague.

impregnación *f* impregnation.

impregnar *vt* to impregnate; *impregnar en* or *de* to impregnate with || FIG to cover; *cara impregnada de tristeza* face covered in sadness.
◆ *vpr* to become impregnated.

impremeditación *f* unpremeditation.

impremeditadamente *adv* unpremeditatedly.

impremeditado, da *adj* unpremeditated.

imprenta *f* printing (arte y actividad) || printing house (taller) || FIG press; *libertad de imprenta* freedom of the press || printed matter (cosas impresas) || — *dar a la imprenta* to send to press, to submit for printing || *escribir en letras de imprenta* to print.

imprescindible *adj* essential, indispensable.

imprescriptibilidad *f* imprescriptibility.

impresentable *adj* unpresentable, not presentable.

impresión *f* impression, impressing, imprinting (de una marca en un sitio) || impression, imprint (huella, marca) || IMPR printing | printing, print; *una impresión deficiente hace desagradable la lectura* faulty print *o* a faulty printing makes for unpleasant reading || edition; *una impresión de veinte ejemplares* an edition of twenty copies || FOT print || impression; *hacerle buena, mala impresión a alguien* to make a good, a bad impression on s.o. || recording (en disco o en cintas magnetofónicas) || — *cambiar impresiones con* to exchange views with || *causar impresión en* to make an impression on || *causar la impresión de que...* to give the impression that... || *impresión dactilar* or *digital* fingerprint || *la primera impresión es la que vale* it is the first impression that counts || *me da la impresión de que...* I get the impression that... || *tener la impresión de que...* to have the impression that...

impresionabilidad *f* impressionability.

impresionable *adj* impressionable.

impresionante *adj* impressive (que causa impresión) || amazing (sorprendente).

impresionar *vt* to impress, to make an impression on (causar impresión) || to move, to touch (conmover); *me impresiona su generosidad* I am touched by his generosity || to record (los sonidos) || to cut (un disco) || FOT to expose || — *quedarse bien, mal impresionado* to have *o* to be left with a good, a bad impression || FOT *rollo sin impresionar* unexposed film.
◆ *vi* to impress.
◆ *vpr* to be impressed || to be moved *o* touched (conmovido).

impresionismo *m* impressionism.

impresionista *m* impressionist.

impreso, sa *adj* printed.
◆ *m* printed sheet *o* paper (papel) || printed book (libro) || form (formulario); *impreso de solicitud* application form.
◆ *pl* printed matter *sing.*

impresor, ra *m/f* printer || INFORM printer; *impresora de margarita* daisywheel printer; *impresora láser* laser printer; *impresora matricial* dot-matrix printer; *impresora por chorros de tinta* ink-jet printer.

imprevisible *adj* unforeseeable, unpredictable.

imprevisión *f* lack of foresight.

imprevisor, ra *adj* unforeseeing, lacking in foresight.

imprevisto, ta *adj* unforeseen, unexpected (que no se ha previsto); *suceso imprevisto* unexpected event || — *lance imprevisto* coup de théâtre || *lo imprevisto* the unforeseen, the unexpected || *si ocurre algo imprevisto* if anything unexpected turns up *o* happens.
◆ *m pl* incidental expenses.

imprimación *f* ARTES priming (acción de imprimar).
— OBSERV Do not confuse with *impresión*.

imprimar *vt* to prime (lienzos).

imprimátur *m* imprimatur.

imprimir *vt* to impress, to imprint, to stamp (una marca) || IMPR to print (un libro, etc.) || FIG to impart, to transmit (comunicar); *imprimir un movimiento a un cuerpo* to impart motion to a body | to impress, to imprint (en la mente) | to write; *la desesperación estaba impresa en su rostro* despair was written across his face.
— OBSERV The past participle of *imprimir* is irregular: *impreso. Imprimido* is archaic.

improbabilidad *f* improbability, unlikelyhood.

improbable *adj* improbable, unlikely.

improbidad *f* improbity, dishonesty, lack of integrity.

ímprobo, ba *adj* dishonest, lacking integrity (sin probidad) || very hard, laborious (muy duro); *labor ímproba* very hard work || strenuous (esfuerzo).

improcedencia *f* unseemliness (inconveniencia) || inappropriateness, unsuitability (inadecuación) || JUR irrelevancy | inadmissibility.

improcedente *adj* improper, unseemly (inconveniente) || inappropriate, unsuitable (inadecuado) || JUR irrelevant | inadmissible (protesta, etc.).

improductividad *f* unproductiveness.

improductivo, va *adj* unproductive (esfuerzo, terreno) || unproductive, unprofitable (negocio).

impromptu *m* impromptu.

impronta *f* (relief) impression (reproducción) || FIG impression, mark, stamp (huella).

impronunciable *adj* unpronounceable.

improperio *m* insult, abusive remark.
◆ *pl* REL reproaches || *llenar a uno de improperios* to shower s.o. with abuse.

impropiedad *f* unsuitability (inadecuación) || impropriety (de comportamiento, lenguaje, etc.) || impropriety, incorrectness (inexactitud).

impropio, pia *adj* unsuited, unsuitable, inappropriate, improper (inadecuado); *es un sitio impropio para el cuadro* it's an unsuitable *o* inappropriate *o* improper place for the picture, it's a place unsuited to the picture || unbecoming, unfitting, improper; *comportamiento impropio de su edad* unbecoming behaviour for (a man of) his age || improper, incorrect (no exacto); *uso impropio de una palabra* improper use of a word || MAT improper (fracción).

improrrogable *adj* that cannot be prolonged *o* extended *o* protracted.

impróvido, da *adj* unprepared, improvident.

improvisación *f* improvisation.

improvisadamente *adj* unexpectedly, without warning, suddenly.

improvisado, da *adj* improvised, impromptu; *discurso improvisado* improvised speech || rough-and-ready, makeshift; *una reparación improvisada* a makeshift repair || MÚS extempore, impromptu.

improvisador, ra *m/f* improviser.

improvisar *vt* to improvise || to get ready, to knock up; *improvisó una cena en un cuarto de hora* she got some dinner ready in a quarter of an hour || MÚS to extemporize.

improviso, sa *adj* unforeseen, unexpected || — *al* or *de improviso* unexpectedly, suddenly, without warning || *coger de improviso* to catch unawares.

improvisto, ta *adj* unforeseen, unexpected || — *a la improvista* unexpectedly, suddenly, without warning || *de improvisto* unexpectedly, suddenly.

imprudencia *f* imprudence || indiscretion (indiscreción) || JUR *imprudencia temeraria* negligence.

imprudente *adj* imprudent, unwise (poco juicioso) || rash (atrevido, peligroso) || careless (conductor, etc.) || indiscreet (indiscreto).

impúber; impúbero, ra *adj* impubic, under the age of puberty.
◆ *m/f* child under the age of puberty.

impublicable *adj* unpublishable, unprintable.

impudencia *f* impudence (al hablar) || shamelessness, immodesty, impudence (desvergüenza).

impudente *adj* impudent (en el habla) || shameless, immodest, impudent (desvergonzado).

impudicia; impudicicia *f* impudicity, immodesty (falta de pudor) || shamelessness (desvergüenza).

impúdico, ca *adj* immodest || shameless (desvergonzado).

impudor *m* impudicity, immodesty (falta de pudor) || shamelessness (desvergüenza).

impuesto, ta *adj* imposed || FIG *estar impuesto de* or *en* to be acquainted with *o* informed of.
◆ *m* tax (tributo); *impuesto de utilidades* or *sobre la renta* income tax; *impuesto territorial* land tax; *exento de impuesto* free of tax, tax-exempt || rate, tax (sobre una propiedad) || duty (derecho); *impuesto del timbre* stamp duty || — *gravar con un impuesto* to levy a tax on, to impose a tax on || *impuesto concertado* composition tax || *impuesto de circulación* Road (Fund) tax || *impuesto degresivo* degressive taxation || *impuesto de lujo* luxury tax || *impuesto de plusvalía* capital gains tax || *impuesto directo* direct tax || *impuesto indirecto* indirect *o* excise tax || *impuestos municipales* municipal taxes *o* rates || *impuesto sobre los espectáculos públicos* entertainment tax || *impuesto sobre sucesiones* death tax *o* duty.

impugnable *adj* impugnable, refutable (refutable) || challengeable, contestable, impugnable (que puede combatirse) || JUR challengeable, contestable.

impugnación *f* impugnment, impugnation, refutation (refutación) || challenge, contestation, impugnment || JUR challenge, challenging, contestation.

impugnador, ra *adj* impugning, refuting (refutador) || challenging, contesting, opposing, impugning || JUR challenging.
◆ *m/f* refuter.

impugnar *vt* to challenge, to contest, to oppose (combatir) || to refute, to impugn; *impugnar un argumento* to refute an argument || JUR to challenge, to contest (una sucesión, un jurado).

impugnativo, va *adj* impugning, challenging || refuting.

impulsar *vt* to impel, to drive forward (empujar) || FIG to impel, to drive (incitar) | to promote, to give an impuls to; *impulsar el comercio* to promote trade.

impulsión *f* impulsion || TECN drive (empuje) || momentum, impetus (fuerza existente) | impulse; *impulsión específica* specific impulse | impulse (corriente) || FIG impulse (impulso).

impulsividad *f* impulsiveness, impulsivity.

impulsivo, va *adj* impulsive.

impulso *m* impulse, impulsion, thrust, push, drive; *el impulso del émbolo se transmite a las ruedas de la locomotora por medio de las bielas* the piston thrust is transmitted to the wheels of the locomotive through the connecting rods || momentum, impetus; *el gran impulso del coche hizo que no pudiera detenerse a tiempo* the car's momentum prevented it from stopping in time || FIG impulse, prompting; *impulsos del corazón* promptings of the heart || impulse (en fisiología) || RAD pulse || ELECTR impulse || — *a impulsos de* driven by, prompted by || *en el impulso del momento* on the spur of the moment || *hacer una cosa llevado por un impulso* to do sth. on impulse || *por propio impulso* on one's own initiative || DEP *tomar impulso* to (take a) run up.

impulsor, ra *adj* TECN impelling, driving || instigating.
◆ *m* instigator.

impune *adj* unpunished; *el crimen quedó impune* the crime went unpunished.

impunemente *adv* with impunity.

impunidad *f* impunity.

impureza *f* impurity || FIG immorality, impurity.

impurificar *vt* to adulterate, to make impure.

impuro, ra *adj* impure || FIG immoral, impure.

imputabilidad *f* imputability.

imputable *adj* imputable, chargeable.

imputación *f* imputation, charge.

imputar *vt* to impute, to charge with (acusar) || to impute, to attribute (atribuir) || COM to allocate, to assign (asignar).

imputrescibilidad *f* imputrescibility (de la carne, de la fruta) || rot resistance (de la madera).

inabarcable *adj* too wide, too large; *un programa inabarcable* too wide a programme.

inabordable *adj* unapproachable, inaccessible.

inacabable *adj* interminable, endless.

inaccesibilidad *f* inaccessibility || unapproachability, inaccessibility (de una persona).

inaccesible *adj* inaccessible || unapproachable, inaccessible (persona) || FIG prohibitive, inaccessible (precio).

inacción *f* inaction, inactivity.

inacentuado, da *adj* unaccented, unaccentuated, unstressed.

inaceptable *adj* unacceptable.

inacostumbrado, da *adj* unaccustomed.

inactividad *f* inactivity.

inactivo, va *adj* inactive.

inadaptable *adj* inadaptable, unadaptable.

inadaptación *f* maladjustment || failure to adjust.

inadaptado, da *adj* maladjusted.
◆ *m/f* misfit.

inadecuación *f* inadequacy (insuficiencia) || unsuitability (impropiedad).

inadecuado, da *adj* unsuitable, inappropriate (inapropiado) || inadequate (insuficiente).

inadmisibilidad *f* inadmissibility || intolerability || incredibility (incredibilidad) || JUR irreceivability.

inadmisible *adj* inadmissible || intolerable (intolerable) || incredible (increíble) || JUR irreceivable (demanda).

inadoptable *adj* unadoptable.

inadvertencia *f* inadvertence, inadvertency, inattention || inadvertence, oversight (error) || *por inadvertencia* inadvertently.

inadvertidamente *adv* inadvertently.

inadvertido, da *adj* unnoticed, unobserved, unseen (no visto) || inadvertent, inattentive (distraído) || *pasar inadvertido* to escape notice, to pass unnoticed.

inagotable *adj* inexhaustible (bondad, fuente, mina, paciencia, etc.) || endless (conversación) || tireless, indefatigable; *un atleta inagotable* a tireless athlete.

inaguantable *adj* unbearable, intolerable.

inalámbrico, ca *adj* wireless (telégrafo).

in albis *adv* FAM *quedarse in albis* not to have a clue, not to understand a thing, to be completely flummoxed, to be left in the dark.

inalcanzable *adj* unreachable, unattainable || beyond (s.o.'s) understanding *o* grasp *o* reach; *concepto inalcanzable por el hombre medio* concept beyond the grasp of the average man.

inalienabilidad *f* inalienability.

inalienable *adj* inalienable.

inalterabilidad *f* inalterability, unalterability || unchangingness, immutability (de un paisaje, un régimen político) || fastness (de un color) || FIG impassivity (de una persona, un rostro, etc.) | immutability (de la serenidad, etc.) | constancy (de una amistad) | imperishability (de alimentos).

inalterable *adj* inalterable, unalterable || unchanging, immutable (paisaje, régimen político) | permanent, fast (color) || FIG impassive (persona, rostro, etc.) | immutable (serenidad) | undying (amistad) | imperishable (alimentos).

inalterado, da *adj* unaltered || unchanged (paisaje, régimen político) || FIG impassive, unmoved (persona, rostro, etc.) | unaffected; *alimentos inalterados por el calor* foodstuffs unaffected by the heat.

inamovible *adj* irremovable.

inamovilidad *f* irremovability.

inane *adj* inane, empty, insubstantial.

inanición *f* MED inanition || starvation; *morir de inanición* to die of starvation.

inanidad *f* inanity, emptiness, insubstantiality.

inanimado, da *adj* inanimate.

inánime *adj* lifeless; *cuerpo inánime* lifeless body.

inapelable *adj* without appeal, unappealable.

inapercibido, da *adj* unperceived, unnoticed.

— OBSERV This word is a Gallicism for *inadvertido*.

inapetencia *f* inappetence, lack of appetite.

inapetente *adj* inappetent, having no appetite.

inaplazable *adj* unpostponable, undeferable || urgent, pressing; *necesidad inaplazable* pressing need.

inaplicable *adj* inapplicable.

inaplicación *f* lack of application.

inaplicado, da *adj* slack (desaplicado).

inapolillable *adj* mothproof (tejido).

inapreciable *adj* inappreciable, imperceptible; *diferencia inapreciable* imperceptible difference || inestimable, invaluable (inestimable).

inapropiado, da *adj* inappropriate.

inaprovechado, da *adj* unused || undeveloped (tierras).

inaptitud *f* incapability, inaptitude (incapacidad) || unsuitability (inadecuación).

inapto, ta *adj* incapable (incapaz) || unsuitable (*para* for), unsuited (*para* to) (inadecuado).

inarmonía *f* inharmony.

inarmónico, ca *adj* inharmonic, inharmonious.

inarrugable *adj* crease-resistant (ropa).

inarticulado, da *adj* inarticulate.

in artículo mortis *adv* in articulo mortis.

inasimilable *adj* unassimilable.

inasistencia *f* absence.

inastillable *adj* shatterproof (cristal).

inatención *f* inattention || discourtesy (descortesía).

inaudible *adj* inaudible.

inaudito, ta *adj* unheard-of (nunca oído) || unprecedented, extraordinary (extraordinario) || outrageous (ultrajante).

inauguración *f* inauguration || unveiling (de una estatua) || opening (de una reunión) || — *inauguración de una casa particular* housewarming || *inauguración de una exposición de arte* varnishing day, vernissage.

inaugural *adj* inaugural, opening; *discurso inaugural* inaugural speech || MAR maiden (viaje).

inaugurar *vt* to inaugurate, to open; *inaugurar una escuela* to inaugurate a school || to open (una exposición) || to unveil (una estatua) || *inaugurar una casa particular* to have a housewarming.

inca *adj/s* Inca.

◆ *m* (ant) inca [Peruvian gold coin].

incaico, ca; incásico, ca *adj* Inca, Incan.

incalculable *adj* incalculable.

incalificable *f* unqualifiable || indescribable, unspeakable (crimen).

incandescencia *f* incandescence || *lámpara de incandescencia* incandescent lamp.

incandescente *adj* incandescent.

incansable *adj* tireless, indefatigable, untiring.

incansablemente *adj* tirelessly, indefatigably.

incantable *adj* unsingable.

incapacidad *f* incapacity, incapability || incapacity, unfitness; *incapacidad para gobernar* incapacity to govern || incapacity, inefficiency, inability, incompetence (incompetencia) || disability (física) || FIG dullness, stupitidy (rudeza) || — *incapacidad laboral* incapacity to work || JUR *incapacidad legal* legal incapacity, disabitity.

incapacitado, da *adj* JUR incapacitated | disqualified (sujeto a interdicción).

incapacitar *vt* to incapacitate, to make unfit, to disqualify; *su edad le incapacita para la guerra* his age incapacitates him for war || to incapacitate, to disable; *incapacitado por la enfermedad* incapacitated by illness || JUR to incapacitate, to declare incapable.

incapaz *adj* incapable; *incapaz de matar una mosca* incapable of harming a fly || incapable, unfit; *incapaz de gobernar* incapable of *o* unfit for governing, unfit to govern || incapable, inefficient, incompetent (incompetente) || JUR incompetent, incapable || AMER unbearable, insufferable (fastidioso).

◆ *m/f* *es un incapaz* he's good for nothing.

incasable *adj* unmarriable, unmarriageable.

incásico, ca *adj* ⟶ **incaico.**

incautación *f* JUR seizure, confiscation.

incautamente *adv* incautiously, unwarily.

incautarse *vpr* JUR to seize, to confiscate; *la policía se incautó de todos los ejemplares del libro* the police seized all copies of the book.

incauto, ta *adj* incautious, unwary (imprudente) || gullible (fácil de engañar).

incendajas *f pl* kindling *sing* (para prender fuego).

incendiado, da *adj* which is on fire, burning (que arde) || burnt-out (destruido por un incendio).

incendiar *vt* to set on fire, to set fire to, to set alight.

◆ *vpr* to catch fire.

incendiario, ria *adj* incendiary (bomba, persona) || FIG incendiary, inflammatory; *discurso incendiario* incendiary speech || *mirada incendiaria* fiery glance (con enfado).

◆ *m/f* incendiary.

incendio *m* fire; *provocar un incendio* to start a fire || FIG fire (de las pasiones) || — *incendio premeditado* arson, fire-raising || *los damnificados por un incendio* the fire victims.

incensar* *vt* REL to cense, to incense || FIG to flatter (lisonjear).

incensario *m* censer, thurible, incensory || FAM *romperle a uno el incensario en las narices* to shower flattery *o* praise upon s.o., to butter s.o. up.

incentivación *f* incentives.

incentivo *m* incentive (estímulo); *el interés es un incentivo potente* interest is a powerful incentive || attraction (atractivo) || *el incentivo de la ganancia* the lure *o* incentive of gain.

incertidumbre *f* uncertainty, incertitude.

incesable; incesante *adj* incessant, unceasing, uninterrupted.

incesantemente *adv* incessantly, unceasingly.

incesto *m* incest.

incestuoso, sa *adj* incestuous.

incidencia *f* incident (incidente) || FÍS incidence; *ángulo de incidencia* angle of incidence || FIG repercussion, implication, consequence (consecuencia) || *por incidencia* by chance, accidentally.

incidental *adj* incidental; *observación incidental* incidental remark || GRAM parenthetic (oración).

◆ *f* GRAM parenthetic clause.

incidentalmente *adv* incidentally, in passing.

incidente *adj* FÍS & JUR incident || incidental.

◆ *m* incident; *un incidente diplomático* a diplomatic incident || *una vida llena de incidentes* a life full of incident.

incidentemente *adv* incidentally, in passing.

incidir *vi* to fall (*en* into) (una falta, un error) || FÍS to fall, to strike; *el rayo incide en la superficie con un ángulo de 45 grados* the ray falls upon *o* strikes the surface at an angle of 45 degrees || to affect; *el impuesto incide más en nosotros* the tax affects us worst || to influence (influir) || MED to make an incision, to incise.

incienso *m* incense || frankincense (término bíblico) || FIG flattery, incense (lisonja) || FIG *echar incienso a* to flatter.

inciertamente *adv* uncertainly.

incierto, ta *adj* uncertain, doubtful (dudoso) || unsteady; *con mano incierta* with (an) unsteady hand || hesitant (paso) || unsettled (tiempo) || indistinct (perfil) || unknown (desconocido).

incineración *f* incineration || cremation (de cadáveres).

incinerador *m* incinerator.

incinerar *vt* to incinerate || to cremate (cadáveres).

incipiente *adj* dawning; *el día incipiente* the dawning day || budding; *un poeta incipiente* a budding poet || incipient; *parálisis incipiente* incipient paralysis.

incircunciso, sa *adj* uncircumcised.

incircunscrito, ta *adj* uncircumscribed.

incisión *f* incision || caesura (en un verso).

incisivo, va *adj* incisive (diente) || incisive, incisory (instrumento) || FIG incisive, biting, trenchant.
◆ *m* incisor (diente).

inciso, sa *adj* jerky (estilo).
◆ *m* GRAM incidental clause (frase corta) | comma (coma) | sub-subparagraph || *a modo de inciso* in passing, incidentally.

incisura *f* MED incision.

incitación *f* incitation, incitement; *incitación al crimen* incitement to crime.

incitador, ra *adj* inciting.
◆ *m/f* inciter.

incitamento; incitamiento *m* incitement.

incitante *adj* inciting || provocative (provocativo).

incitar *vt* to incite, to stir (estimular); *incitar al pueblo a la rebelión* to incite the people to rebellion || FIG to incite, to urge; *incitar al gasto* to urge to spend | to encourage (animar).

incitativo, va *adj* inciting.

incivil *adj* rude, uncivil (grosero).

incivilidad *f* incivility, rudeness.

incivilizado, da *adj* uncivilized.

inclasificable *adj* unclassifiable, nondescript.

inclaustración *f* entry into a convent *o* monastery.

inclemencia *f* inclemency.

inclemente *adj* inclement.

inclinación *f* inclination, inclining, slanting, sloping, tilting (acción) || inclination, slant, slope (posición oblicua) || inclination, bow (saludo con la cabeza) || nod (señal de asentimiento) || pitch, slant, slope (de un tejado) || list (de un barco) || ASTR inclination || gradient, incline, slope, inclination (ferrocarriles, carretera) || GEOL dip || FÍS dip, inclination; *inclinación magnética* magnetic dip || FIG inclination, propensity, tendency (propensión) | inclination, penchant, liking (afición); *tener inclinación hacia la música* to have an inclination towards *o* a penchant for music || FIG *de malas inclinaciones* evilly inclined.

inclinar *vt* to incline, to slant, to slope, to tilt (ladear) || to bow, to bend; *árbol inclinado por el viento* tree bowed by the wind || to incline, to bow (saludar con la cabeza) || to nod (asentar con la cabeza) || FIG to incline, to induce, to dispose; *razones que me inclinan a aceptar* reasons which incline me to accept || *plano inclinado* inclined plane (en un dibujo), incline (pendiente).
◆ *vi* to lean, to slope; *inclinar a* or *hacia la derecha* to lean to the right.
◆ *vpr* to lean, to slope, to slant, to incline; *inclinarse hacia adelante* to lean forward || to stoop down, to bend down (para coger algo del suelo) || to bow (al saludar) || MAR to list || — *inclinarse a* to be inclined to; *me inclino a creerle* I'm inclined to believe him; to be similar to, to resemble (parecerse) || FIG *inclinarse ante* to bow to.

ínclito, ta *adj* illustrious.

incluido, da *adj* included; *todo está incluido* everything is included || enclosed (en cartas) || — *precio todo incluido* inclusive *o* all-in price || *todo incluido* all *o* everything included, all in.

incluir* *vt* to include (en precios, en una lista, etc.) || to enclose (en cartas) || to insert (introducir) || to contain (contener) || to comprise (comprender) || *sin incluir* not including, not included.

inclusa *f* foundling home.

inclusero, ra *adj* *niño inclusero* foundling.
◆ *m/f* foundling.

inclusión *f* inclusion || (p us) friendship (amistad) || *con inclusión de* including.

inclusivamente; inclusive *adv* inclusive; *de domingo a sábado inclusive* Sunday to Saturday inclusive || — *hasta el lunes inclusive* up to and including Monday || *los niños inclusive* including the children, the children included.

inclusivo, va *adj* inclusive.

incluso, sa *adj* included (en precios, una lista, etc.) || enclosed; *la carta inclusa* the enclosed letter.
◆ *adv* including, included; *todos vinieron incluso los niños* everyone came, including the children *o* the children included || even; *incluso le hablé* I even talked to him.

incoación *f* inchoation, commencement, inception.

incoado, da *adj* JUR inchoate.

incoagulable *adj* incoagulable.

incoar *vt* to commence, to initiate, to begin (empezar) || to initiate, to institute; *incoar expediente contra* to initiate proceedings against.

incoativo, va *adj* inchoate, inchoative, incipient, inceptive, initial (que empieza) || inchoative (verbo).

incobrable *adj* irrecoverable.

incoercibilidad *f* incoercibility.

incoercible *adj* incoercible.

incógnita *f* MAT unknown, unknown quantity; *despejar la incógnita* to find the unknown quantity || FIG mystery (cosa misteriosa) | hidden motive (razón oculta).

incógnito, ta *adj* unknown; *regiones incógnitas* unknown regions.
◆ *m* incognito; *guardar el incógnito* to preserve one's incognito || *de incógnito* incognito; *viajar de incógnito* to travel incognito.

incognoscible *adj* not knowable, unknowable.

incoherencia *f* incoherence, incoherency.

incoherente *adj* incoherent.

íncola *m* inhabitant.

incoloro, ra *adj* colourless [US colorless] || FIG colourless [US colorless], dull, insipid.

incólume *adj* unharmed, unhurt, safe (and sound).

incombustibilidad *f* incombustibility.

incombustible *adj* incombustible.

incomestible *adj* inedible, uneatable.

incomible *adj* uneatable, inedible.

incomodar *vt* to inconvenience, to incommode (causar incomodidad) || to annoy, to vex, to anger (disgustar) || to bother, to annoy, to trouble, to pester, to incommode (fastidiar).
◆ *vpr* to get angry *o* vexed *o* annoyed (enfadarse) || to bother, to put o.s. out, to trouble o.s.; *no te incomodes, que lo haré yo* don't bother, I'll do it.

incomodidad *f* discomfort, uncomfortableness (falta de comodidad) || inconvenience, annoyance, bother, nuisance (molestia) || discontent, displeasure (disgusto) || unrest, uneasiness (malestar) || vexation (desazón) || inconvenience, discomfort (inconveniente); *una casa con muchas incomodidades* a house with many inconveniences.

incómodo, da *adj* uncomfortable; *calor incómodo* uncomfortable heat; *postura incómoda* uncomfortable position; *silla incómoda* uncomfortable chair; *encontrarse incómodo en una silla* to feel uncomfortable in a chair || uncomfortable, awkward, ill at ease; *me siento incómodo en su compañía* I feel uncomfortable in his company || awkward, cumbersome (que abulta mucho) || bothersome (molesto).

incomparable *adj* incomparable (sin puntos comunes) || incomparable, matchless, beyond compare (sin par).

incomparecencia *f* JUR default, nonappearance (ausencia) || DEP walk over.

incompartible *adj* unsharable, unshareable.

incompasivo, va *adj* incompassionate, unsympathetic (sin compasión) || incompassionate, merciless, pitiless (cruel).

incompatibilidad *f* incompatibility; *incompatibilidad de caracteres* incompatibility of character.

incompatible *adj* incompatible || INFORM incompatible, inconsistent.

incompetencia *f* incompetence.

incompetente *adj/s* incompetent.

incompleto, ta *adj* incomplete || unfinished; *la Sinfonía Incompleta* the Unfinished Symphony.

incomprehensible *adj* incomprehensible.

incomprendido, da *adj* misunderstood || unappreciated (no apreciado).
◆ *m/f* misunderstood person || *el poeta era un gran incomprendido* the poet was grossly misunderstood.

incomprensibilidad *f* incomprehensibility.

incomprensible *adj* incomprehensible.

incomprensión *f* incomprehension.

incomprensivo, va *adj* incomprehensive.

incompresibilidad *f* incompressibility.

incompresible; incomprimible *adj* incompressible.

incomprobable *adj* unverifiable.

incomunicabilidad *f* incommunicability.

incomunicación *f* JUR solitary confinement || lack of communication (falta de comunicación) || isolation (aislamiento).

incomunicado, da *adj* incommunicado, in solitary confinement (preso) || isolated, cut off, without means of communication (aislado); *varios pueblos quedaron incomunicados después del terremoto* several towns remained cut off after the earthquake.

incomunicar *vt* to place in solitary confinement (a un preso) || to cut off, to deprive of (means of) communication, to isolate (aislar) || to shut off (una habitación).
◆ *vpr* to cut *o* to shut o.s. off, to isolate o.s.

inconcluso, sa *adj* unfinished.

inconcuso, sa *adj* indubitable, unquestionable, undeniable, incontrovertible.

incondicional *adj* unconditional || absolute, unfailing (amistad, obediencia, etc.) || staunch (adepto, amigo) || unquestioning, total (fe) || wholehearted (apoyo).
◆ *m/f* staunch follower *o* supporter.

inconexión *f* disconnection (falta de conexión) || incoherence.

inconexo, xa *adj* disconnected, unconnected (sin conexión) || incoherent.

inconfesable *adj* unconfessable, shameful, disgraceful, unspeakable (vergonzoso).

inconfeso, sa *adj* unconfessed (reo).

inconformista *m/f* nonconformist.

inconfortable *adj* uncomfortable.

inconfundible *adj* unmistakable || unique (único).

incongelable *adj* uncongealable, unfreezable.

incongruencia *f* incongruence, incongruity, incongruousness (cualidad de incongruente) || incongruity (cosa incongruente).

incongruente *adj* incongruent, incongruous; *respuesta incongruente* incongruous reply.

incongruidad *f* incongruity.

incongruo, grua *adj* incongruous, incongruent (incongruente) || REL inadequate [emolument] | who does not receive an adequate emolument [priest].

incomensurabilidad *f* incommensurability.

inconmensurable *adj* incommensurable || MAT incommensurate || FAM immense, vast, enormous (inmenso) | fantastic, marvellous, great (fantástico).

inconmovible *adj* firm, solid (cimientos) || firm (amistad, principios) || inexorable (ante súplicas) || unshakable, unyielding (ante amenazas).

inconmutabilidad *f* immutability | incommutability.

inconmutable *adj* immutable (inmutable) || incommutable (no conmutable).

inconquistable *adj* unconquerable, invincible || impregnable (fuerte, castillo, etc.) || FIG incorruptible | unyielding (que no se deja convencer).

inconsciencia *f* unconsciousness (de un acto) || unconsciousness (pérdida del conocimiento) || unawareness, unconsciousness; *inconsciencia del riesgo* unawareness of the risk | thoughtlessness, irresponsibility (irreflexión).

inconsciente *adj* unconscious || unconscious; *dejar inconsciente a uno* to knock s.o. unconscious || unconscious, unaware; *inconsciente del peligro* unaware of the danger || thoughtless, irresponsible (irreflexivo) || subconscious (subconsciente).

inconsecuencia *f* inconsistency (falta de concordancia); *inconsecuencia entre los principios y la conducta* inconsistency between principles and conduct || inconsequence, inconsistency (falta de lógica) || inconsistency (acción inconsecuente).

inconsecuente *adj* inconsistent; *inconsecuente en sus ideas políticas* inconsistent in one's political ideas || inconsequent, inconsequential (sin lógica).
◆ *m/f* inconsistent person.

inconsideración *f* inconsiderateness, thoughtlessness (cualidad) || inconsiderate act (acción).

inconsiderado, da *adj* inconsiderate, thoughtless (irreflexivo) || hasty, rash (precipitado).
◆ *m/f* inconsiderate person.

inconsistencia *f* inconsistency (de una sustancia) || FIG insubstantiality; *la inconsistencia de un argumento* the insubstantiality of an argument.

inconsistente *adj* inconsistent (sustancia) || FIG insubstantial; *argumento inconsistente* insubstantial argument.

inconsolable *adj* unconsolable, inconsolable.

inconstancia *f* inconstancy || inconstancy, fickleness (de una persona).

inconstante *adj* inconstant || inconstant, fickle (que cambia de opinión, etc.) || changeable, variable (tiempo).
◆ *m/f* fickle person.

inconstitucional *adj* unconstitutional.

inconstitucionalidad *f* unconstitutionality.

inconsulto, ta *adj* AMER inconsiderate.

inconsútil *adj* seamless.

incontable *adj* countless, innumerable (muy numeroso); *incontables granos de arena* countless grains of sand || untellable (que no puede ser narrado).

incontaminado, da *adj* uncontaminated, unpolluted.

incontenible *adj* unrestrainable, uncontrollable, irrepressible (cólera, risa) || uncheckable, unrestrainable, uncontrollable (ímpetu) || uncontrollable (llanto) || uncontainable (alegría, entusiasmo).

incontestabilidad *f* incontestability, indisputability.

incontestable *adj* incontestable, indisputable, unquestionable (indiscutible) || undeniable (innegable).

incontestado, da *adj* uncontested, unquestioned, undisputed || undenied (no negado) || unanswered (pregunta).

incontinencia *f* incontinence || incontinence, unchastity (falta de castidad) || MED *incontinencia de orina* incontinence of urine.

incontinente *adj* incontinent || incontinent, unchaste (falto de castidad) || MED incontinent.
◆ *adv* instantly, immediately.

incontinenti *adv* instantly, immediately, forthwith.

incontrastable *adj* indisputable, undeniable, unquestionable (indiscutible) || invincible, unconquerable (invencible) || unshakable, unyielding (que no cede).

incontrito, ta *adj* uncontrite.

incontrolable *adj* uncontrollable.

incontrovertible *adj* incontrovertible, uncontrovertible, indisputable.

incontrovertido, da *adj* undisputed, uncontroverted.

inconveniencia *f* inconvenience, disadvantage; *ésas son las inconveniencias de tener tantos hijos* those are the inconveniences of having so many children || unsuitability, inappropriateness (inoportunidad) || inadvisability (imprudencia) || impropriety, unseemliness, indecorousness (indecoro) || crude *o* coarse remark (grosería) || insolent remark, insolence (insolencia).

inconveniente *adj* inconvenient; *llegó a una hora inconveniente* he arrived at an inconvenient time || unsuitable, inappropriate (inapropiado) || inadvisable (imprudente) || improper, unseemly, indecorous (poco decoroso); *conducta inconveniente* improper behaviour || impolite, uncivil (descortés) || coarse, crude (grosero).
◆ *m* objection; *no tengo inconveniente en que usted salga* I've no objection to your going out || drawback, disadvantage (desventaja) || obstacle (dificultad) || trouble, difficulty; *el inconveniente es que sea tan tarde* the trouble is that it is too late || *¿tienes algún inconveniente en venir?* do you mind coming?

inconvertible *adj* inconvertible.

incoordinación *f* incoordination.

incordiar *vt* FAM to bother, to pester || *¡no incordies!* behave yourself!, don't be such a nuisance! (¡no seas molesto!).

incordio *m* MED bubo || FIG & FAM nuisance, bother (molestia, persona molesta).

incorporable *adj* incorporable.

incorporación *f* incorporation (acción de incorporar) || sitting-up (en la cama) || MIL induction.

incorporado, da *adj* incorporated || sitting up (en la cama) || TECN built-in.

incorporal *adj* incorporeal || impalpable (al tacto).

incorporar *vt* to incorporate; *incorporar Saboya a Francia* to incorporate Savoy with France; *incorporar artículos en una lista* to incorporate items in *o* into a list || to mix (ingredientes) || MIL to induct || *incorporar a uno* to help s.o. to sit up (en la cama).
◆ *vpr* to incorporate || to join (una sociedad, un regimiento, etc.) || to sit up (cuando se está acostado); *se incorporó en la cama* he sat up in his bed || — MIL *incorporarse a filas* to join the ranks || *incorporarse a su cargo* to start one's job (por primera vez), to go back to one's job (volver).

incorporeidad *f* incorporeity.

incorpóreo, a *adj* incorporeal.

incorrección *f* incorrectness, inaccuracy (inexactitud) || impropriety, unseemliness; *la incorrección de su conducta* the impropriety of his behaviour || discourtesy (descortesía) || impropriety (acción) || *cometiste una grave incorrección* that was very rude of you, that was a very improper thing for you to do.

incorrecto, ta *adj* incorrect, inaccurate (inexacto) || improper, indecorous, incorrect (conducta) || impolite, discourteous (descortés).

incorregibilidad *f* incorrigibility.

incorregible *adj* incorrigible; *pereza incorregible* incorrigible laziness.

incorruptibilidad *f* incorruptibility.

incorruptible *adj* incorruptible.

incorrupto, ta *adj* uncorrupted, incorrupt (no podrido); *el cuerpo incorrupto del santo* the uncorrupted body of the saint || FIG uncorrupted, incorrupt (moralmente) | pure, chaste (mujer).

incredibilidad *f* incredibility.

incredulidad *f* incredulity || REL unbelief.

incrédulo, la *adj* incredulous || REL unbelieving.
◆ *m/f* unbeliever.

increíble *adj* incredible, unbelievable.

incrementar *vt* to increase; *incrementar una renta, las exportaciones* to increase an income, exports || to promote; *incrementar las relaciones económicas* to promote economic relations || INFORM to increment.

incremento *m* increase; *el incremento de una renta* the increase of an income || growth; *el incremento de un negocio* the growth of a business || MAT & INFORM increment || *incremento térmico* rise in temperature.

increpación *f* rebuke.

increpador, ra *adj* scolding, rebuking.

increpar *vt* to scold, to rebuke (reñir) || to insult (insultar).

incriminable *adj* chargeable, accusable.

incriminación *f* incrimination || charge, accusation (acusación).

incriminar *vt* to incriminate, to accuse; *su prueba incriminó al médico* his evidence incriminated the doctor.

incrustación *f* incrustation, inlay || incrustation (con una costra) || scale (depósito en una caldera).

incrustar *vt* to incrust, to inlay; *incrustado con piedras preciosas* incrusted with gems || to incrust (cubrir con una costra) || FIG to engra-

ve; *incrustado en la mente* engraved upon the mind.
◆ *vpr* to embed itself; *la bala se le incrustó en el cerebro* the bullet embedded itself in his brain || to scale (en una caldera) || FIG to dig o.s. in || FIG *incrustarse algo en la cabeza* to get sth. into one's head.

incubación *f* incubation; *período de incubación* incubation period.

incubador, ra *adj* incubative.
◆ *f* incubator.

incubar *vt* to incubate (los huevos) || MED to be getting, to be sickening for, to incubate; *estoy incubando las paperas* I'm getting the mumps || FIG to hatch (tramar).
◆ *vi* to incubate.

incuestionable *adj* unquestionable, indisputable.

inculcación *f* inculcation.

inculcador, ra *m/f* inculcator.

inculcar *vt* to inculcate, to instil [*US* to instill] || IMPR to compose (type) too close together.

inculpabilidad *f* inculpability, guiltlessness, blamelessness || JUR *veredicto de inculpabilidad* verdict of not guilty.

inculpación *f* inculpation (acción de inculpar) || accusation, charge (cosa de que se acusa a alguien).

inculpado, da *adj/s* accused.

inculpar *vt* to accuse (*de* of), to charge (*de* with), to charge (acusar) || to inculpate, to incriminate, to accuse (incriminar).

incultivable *adj* uncultivable, uncultivatable.

inculto, ta *adj* uncultured, uneducated (sin cultura) || uncouth, coarse (tosco) || unrefined (poco refinado) || uncultivated, untilled (terreno).
◆ *m/f* ignoramus.

incultura *f* lack of culture, ignorance (falta de cultura) || uncouthness (tosquedad).

incumbencia *f* line, province, field; *la crítica teatral no es de mi incumbencia* theatre criticism is not in my line *o* is not my province || incumbency, obligation, duty (obligación) || JUR jurisdiction.

incumbir *vt* to be incumbent on *o* upon, to be the duty *o* the obligation of; *te incumbe a ti* it is incumbent on you, it is your duty || JUR to be within the jurisdiction (*a* of).

incumplido, da *adj* unfulfilled.

incumplimiento *m* nonfulfilment (de un deber) || failure to keep; *incumplimiento de la palabra dada* failure to keep one's word || nonexecution (de una orden) || nonobservance (de un reglamento) || breach (de un contrato, de una promesa).

incumplir *vt* not to fulfill, to fail to fulfill || to break (contrato, compromiso); *incumplir una promesa* to break a promise || to fail to observe (una regla), to fail to carry out (una orden).

incunable *adj* incunabular.
◆ *m* incunable, incunabulum.
◆ *pl* incunabula.

incurabilidad *f* incurability.

incurable *adj* incurable || FIG irremediable, hopeless, incurable.
◆ *m/f* incurable; *hospital de incurables* home for incurables.

incuria *f* carelessness, negligence.

incurrir *vi* to incur; *incurrir en la desgracia del rey, en castigo, en odio* to incur the king's disfavour, punishment, hatred || to fall; *incurrir en falta, en delito* to commit a fault, a crime || *incurrir en olvido* to forget.

— OBSERV The verb *incurrir* has an irregular past participle: *incurso*.

incursión *f* incursion, raid || *incursión aérea* air raid.

incurso, sa *adj* guilty, culpable.

indagación *f* investigation, inquiry || JUR inquiry, inquest.

indagador, ra *adj* investigating, inquiring.
◆ *m/f* investigator.

indagar *vt* to investigate, to inquire into (investigar); *indagar las causas de la explosión* to investigate the causes of the explosion.

indagatorio, ria *adj* JUR investigatory || *comisión indagatoria* board of inquiry.
◆ *f* JUR unsworn statement.

indebidamente *adv* unduly || wrongly (injustamente) || improperly, unduly (desconsideradamente) || unlawfully, illegally (ilegalmente).

indebido, da *adj* undue || improper, undue (desconsiderado); *una respuesta indebida* an improper answer || unlawful, illegal, undue (ant) (ilegal).

indecencia *f* indecency || obscenity (obscenidad) || *su vestido es una indecencia* her dress is indecent.

indecente *adj* indecent, obscene; *vestido indecente* indecent dress; *película, lenguaje indecente* obscene film, language || FIG foul, wretched (muy malo); *fue una comida indecente* it was a foul meal | miserable; *tiene un salario indecente* he has a miserable wage | squalid, wretched (miserable); *viven en un cuartucho indecente* they live in a squalid little room || — *es una persona indecente* he is a wretched sort || *la casa está indecente de polvo* the house is terribly dusty.

indecible *adj* unspeakable, inexpressible, indescribable || *he sufrido lo indecible* I can't tell you how I've suffered.

indecisión *f* indecision, irresolution, hesitancy.

indeciso, sa *adj* undecided, not yet determined; *los resultados de la elección son todavía indecisos* the election results are still undecided || indecisive; *batalla indecisa* indecisive battle || indecisive, irresolute, hesitant (que vacila); *hombre indeciso* irresolute man || indistinct, vague (contorno).

indeclinable *adj* GRAM indeclinable, undeclinable || that cannot be declined *o* refused, unavoidable (que no se puede rechazar).

indecoro *m* indecorum, indecorousness, unseemliness || indecency, immodesty (indecencia).

indecoroso, sa *adj* indecorous, unseemly || indecent, immodest; *vestido indecoroso* indecent dress.

indefectibilidad *f* indefectibility.

indefectible *adj* indefectible, unfailing.

indefectiblemente *adv* indefectibly, unfailingly || *y llevará indefectiblemente el traje azul oscuro* and he'll be wearing the inevitable dark blue suit.

indefendible; indefensible *adj* indefensible.

indefenso, sa *adj* defenceless [*US* defenseless] || helpless (desamparado).

indefinible *adj* indefinable, undefinable.

indefinido, da *adj* indefinite; *límite, período de tiempo indefinido* indefinite boundary, period of time || GRAM indefinite; *artículo, adjetivo, pronombre indefinido* indefinite article, adjective, pronoun.

indeformable *adj* that keeps its shape.

indehiscente *adj* BOT indehiscent.

indelebilidad *f* indelibility.

indeleble *adj* indelible.

indeliberación *f* indeliberation.

indeliberado, da *adj* unintentional, indeliberate (no intencionado) || irreflexive (irreflexionado).

indelicadeza *f* indelicacy.

indelicado, da *adj* indelicate; *fue un acto muy indelicado invitarnos y no invitaros a vosotros* it was very indelicate of them to invite us and not you || unscrupulous (falto de escrúpulo).

indemne *adj* unhurt, unharmed, uninjured (persona) || undamaged (cosa).

indemnidad *f* indemnity, insurance (seguridad) || indemnity, immunity (inmunidad).

indemnizable *adj* that can be indemnified.

indemnización *f* indemnification (acción de indemnizar) || indemnity, compensation (compensación) || *indemnización por despido* severance pay.

indemnizado, da *adj* indemnified, compensated.

indemnizar *vt* to indemnify, to compensate.

indemorable *adj* that cannot be deferred (pago) *o* postponed (mitin, viaje, etc.).

indemostrable *adj* indemonstrable, undemonstrable.

independencia *f* independence || — *con independencia de* independently of || *conseguir la independencia* to gain independence.

independiente *adj/s* independent.

independientemente *adv* independently || irrespectively, regardless (aparte de, además de).

independista *adj/s* independent.

independentista *adj* pro-independence [movement].
◆ *m/f* advocate of independence.

independizar *vt* to make independent, to free.
◆ *vpr* to become independent.

indescifrable *adj* indecipherable || FIG impenetrable.

indescriptible *adj* indescribable.

indeseable *adj/s* undesirable.

indestructibilidad *f* indestructibility.

indestructible *adj* indestructible.

indeterminable *adj* indeterminable, undeterminable.

indeterminación *f* indetermination.

indeterminado, da *adj* indeterminate (indefinido) || imprecise, vague; *contornos indeterminados* vague outlines || indeterminate, irresolute (persona) || GRAM indefinite (artículo, pronombre).

indeterminismo *m* indeterminism.

indeterminista *adj/s* indeterminist.

índex *m* index, index finger, forefinger (dedo índice).

indexación *f* INFORM indexing.

India *npr f* GEOGR India.

indiada *f* AMER crowd *o* group of Indians | typically Indian saying (dicho) *o* action (acto).

indiana *f* printed calico (tela).

indianismo *m* indianism.

indianista *m/f* indianist.

indiano, na *adj/s* Latin American (natural de América) || West Indian (antillano).
◆ *m* Spanish emigrant returned from Latin America || FIG Spanish emigrant who returns to Spain after having made a fortune in Latin America.

— OBSERV *Indiano* is better replaced by *indio* when meaning a native of Latin America.

Indias *npr fpl* GEOGR Indies; *Indias Occidentales, Orientales* West, East Indies.

— OBSERV At the time of the colonization *Indias* was the term used to designate America. The name is still to be found in the denomination of such institutions as *los Archivos de Indias, el Consejo de Indias, etc.*

indicación *f* indication, sign (señal) || suggestion; *fui a ese dentista por indicación de tu padre* I went to that dentist at your father's suggestion || hint (clave) || directions *pl*; *le pregunté el camino del museo pero me dio una falsa indicación* I asked him the way to the museum but he gave me the wrong directions || note; *una indicación al margen* a note in the margin || direction, instruction; *indicaciones sobre el manejo de una máquina* directions for the use of a machine || remark, observation (observación).

indicado, da *adj* suitable, good (adecuado); *la persona más indicada para la tarea* the best *o* the most suitable person for the job; *el día más indicado* the best *o* the most suitable day || recommended, advised (aconsejado) || — *en el momento menos indicado* at the worst possible moment || *tú eres el menos indicado para protestar* you are the last person who should complain || *un comentario poco indicado* an inopportune comment || *un sitio muy indicado para descansar* a very good place *o* an ideal place to go for a rest || *un traje indicado para la ocasión* a dress suited to *o* suitable for the occasion.

indicador, ra *adj* indicating, indicatory || *lámpara indicadora* warning light.
◆ *m* indicator || store guide (en un almacén) || — AUT *indicador de carretera* road sign | *indicador de dirección* indicator (en general), trafficator (mecánico), indicator, flasher, blinker, winker (intermitente) || *indicador de escape de gas* (gas-) leak detector || *indicador de fichero* file divider (para clasificar) || *indicador de horarios* timetable (de trenes) || AUT *indicador del nivel de aceite, del nivel de gasolina* (oil) dipstick, petrol gauge [US fuel gauge] | *indicador de presión del aceite* oil-pressure gauge | *indicador de velocidad* speedometer.

indicar *vt* to point out, to show; *indicar el camino a uno* to show s.o. the way || to indicate, to tell; *indíqueme lo que piensa de esto* tell me what you think about this || to indicate, to denote, to betoken (revelar); *un gesto que indica impaciencia* a gesture that indicates impatience || to advise (aconsejar) || to indicate, to suggest, to intimate; *les indicó que su presencia no era grata* he indicated that their presence was undesirable || to show, to read (un termómetro) || TECN to indicate, to register, to show (un indicador) || — *a la hora indicada* at the scheduled *o* specified time || *indicar con el dedo* to point out || *indicar el día* to name the day.

indicativo, va *adj/sm* indicative.

indicción *f* indicción || convocation.

índice *m* indication, sign, index (indicio) || index, table (tabla) || table of contents, index (de un libro) || catalogue, index (de una biblioteca) || index finger, index, forefinger (dedo de la mano) || pointer, needle, hand (de un cuadrante), index, gnomon (de un reloj de sol) || FÍS & MAT index; *índice de refracción* refractive index || percentage; *índice de alcohol* percentage of alcohol || rate (coeficiente); *índice de natalidad* birth rate; *índice de incremento* rate of increase || index; *índice del coste de vida* cost-of-living index; *índice de precios* price index || REL Index; *meter* or *poner en el Índice* to put on the Index || — *índice de compresión* compression ratio || AUT *índice de octano* octane number.
◆ *adj* index (dedo).

indiciar *vt* to indicate (indicar) || to suspect (sospechar).

indicio *m* indication, sign; *es indicio de mala educación* it is a sign of bad manners || trace; *descubrir indicios de albúmina* to discover traces of albumin || trace, sign; *no hay el menor indicio del libro* there is no sign of the book || JUR piece of evidence *sing.*
◆ *pl* JUR evidence *sing.*

indicioso, sa *adj* suspicious.

índico, ca *adj* Indian; *océano Índico* Indian Ocean.

indiferencia *f* indifference.

indiferente *adj* indifferent; *dejar indiferente* to leave indifferent || indifferent, apathetic (apático) || *me es indiferente el color que escojas* the colour you choose is indifferent to me, it makes no difference to me *o* it's all the same to me *o* it's immaterial to me what colour you choose.

indiferentismo *m* indifferentism.

indígena *adj* indigenous (*de* to), native (*de* of).
◆ *m/f* native.

indigencia *f* poverty, destitution, need, indigence; *estar en la indigencia más completa* to be in direst poverty.

indigenismo *m* indianism [Latin-American politico-literary movement in favour of the Indians].

indigenista *adj/s* indigenist.

indigente *adj* destitute, poverty-stricken, needy, poor, indigent.
◆ *m/f* *los indigentes* the needy, the poor.

indigestarse *vpr* to cause *o* to give indigestion (producir indigestión) || to get indigestion (tener indigestión) || — *la comida se me indigestó* the meal gave me indigestion || FIG & FAM *se me indigesta ese tío* I can't stomach that fellow.

indigestibilidad *f* indigestibility.

indigestión *f* indigestion.

indigesto, ta *adj* undigested (no digerido) || indigestible (difícil de digerir) || FIG unbearable (persona) || *estar* or *sentirse indigesto* to have indigestion.

indignación *f* indignation, anger.

indignado, da *adj* indignant, angry.

indignante *adj* infuriating, outrageous (que indigna).

indignar *vt* to infuriate, to anger, to make angry *o* indignant, to rouse to indignation.
◆ *vpr* to be *o* to get indignant, to feel indignation; *indignarse por algo, con alguien* to get indignant at *o* about sth., with s.o. || *¡es para indignarse!* it's infuriating!, it's maddening!

indignidad *f* unworthiness (cualidad de indigno) || indignity (afrenta) || dirty trick (canallada).

indigno, na *adj* unworthy (*de* of) || contemptible, despicable (merecedor de desprecio).

índigo *m* indigo (color, planta).

indilgar *vt* → **endilgar.**

indino, na *adj* FAM mischievous, naughty (travieso) | bad (malo).

indio, dia *adj/s* Indian (de la India, de América) || — FIG *en fila india* in single file, in Indian file || FAM *hablar como los indios* to speak pidgin Spanish (English, etc.), to speak broken Spanish (English, etc.) | *hacer el indio* to act the fool (hacer el tonto).
◆ *m* indium (metal).

indiófilo, la *adj* who admires the Indians and their customs.

indirecta *f* allusion, insinuation, hint; *tirar* or *soltar una indirecta* to drop a hint || — FAM *indirecta del padre Cobos* broad hint || *lanzaron* or *tiraron indirectas sobre la infidelidad de su esposa* they alluded to *o* insinuated *o* hinted at his wife's infidelity.

indirecto, ta *adj* indirect.

indiscernible *adj* indiscernible, imperceptible.

indisciplina *f* indiscipline, lack of discipline.

indisciplinado, da *adj* undisciplined, unruly.

indisciplinarse *vpr* to become undisciplined *o* unruly.

indiscreción *f* indiscretion (acto) || tactless remark (dicho) || — *cometer la indiscreción de* to be so tactless as to || *si no es indiscreción* without being indiscreet.

indiscreto, ta *adj* indiscreet, tactless.
◆ *m/f* indiscreet person.

indisculpable *adj* inexcusable, unpardonable, unforgivable.

indiscutible *adj* indisputable, unquestionable, incontrovertible; *prueba indiscutible* incontrovertible proof || undisputed; *jefe, verdad indiscutible* undisputed leader, truth.

indisolubilidad *f* indissolubility.

indisoluble *adj* indissoluble.

indispensable *adj* indispensable, essential.

indisponer* *vt* to indispose, to make unwell, to upset (hacer enfermar) || FIG *indisponer a una persona con otra* to set a person against another.
◆ *vpr* to become indisposed, to fall ill (ponerse enfermo) || FIG *indisponerse con uno* to fall out with s.o.

indisponibilidad *f* unavailability.

indisposición *f* indisposition.

indispuesto, ta *adj* indisposed, slightly ill, unwell (ligeramente enfermo) || *está indispuesto con su hermano* he has fallen out with his brother, he is on bad terms with his brother.

indisputable *adj* indisputable, unquestionable.

indistinguible *adj* indistinguishable, undistinguishable.

indistintamente *adv* indistinctly (poco claramente) || indifferently (indiferentemente).

indistinto, ta *adj* indistinct.

individuación *f* individuation.

individual *adj* individual || single; *habitación individual* single room.
◆ *m* singles *pl* (tenis); *individual caballeros* men's singles.

individualidad *f* individuality.

individualismo *m* individualism.

individualista *adj* individualistic.
◆ *m/f* individualist.

individualización *f* individualization.

individualizar *vt* to individualize.

individuar *vt* to individuate.

individuo, dua *adj* individual.
◆ *m* individual (ser, vegetal o animal) || member (de una corporación, de una academia) || member, fellow (de una sociedad) || FAM individual, fellow, person (hombre indeterminado) || *cuidar bien de su individuo* to take good care of o.s.

indivisibilidad *f* indivisibility.

indivisible *adj* indivisible.

indivisión *f* indivision || JUR co-ownership, joint ownership.

indiviso, sa *adj* JUR undivided, joint; *bienes indivisos* joint estate.

Indo *npr m* GEOGR Indus.

indo, da *adj/s* Hindu (cuya religión es el hinduismo) || Indian (indio).

indócil *adj* indocile, headstrong, unruly (difícil de educar) || disobedient (desobediente).

indocilidad *f* indocility, unruliness.

indocto, ta *adj* unlearned, uneducated, ignorant.

indocumentado, da *adj* without (identification) papers.
◆ *m/f* person without identification papers || FAM *es un indocumentado* he's a duffer.

Indochina *npr f* GEOGR Indochina.

indochino, na *adj/s* Indochinese, Indo-Chinese.

indoeuropeo, a *adj/s* Indo-European.

indofenol *m* QUÍM indophenol.

indogermánico, ca *adj/s* Indo-Germanic.

índole *f* nature, disposition; *de índole perezosa* of a lazy disposition || kind, sort; *regalos de toda índole* gifts of all kinds || nature; *dada la índole de nuestra revista* given the nature of our magazine || *personas de la misma índole* people of the same stamp, birds of a feather (*fam*).

indolencia *f* indolence.

indolente *adj* indolent.
◆ *m/f* idler.

indoloro, ra *adj* indolent, painless.

indomable *adj* untamable (animal) || unbreakable (caballo) || ungovernable, unsubmissive, unruly (pueblo) || ungovernable, unmanageable, uncontrollable, unruly (niño) || uncontrollable, indomitable (pasión) || indomitable (orgullo, valor).

indomado, da *adj* untamed, wild (animal) || unbroken (caballo) || uncontrolled (pasión).

indomeñable *adj* untamable (animal) || ungovernable, unruly (pueblo) || uncontrollable, indomitable (pasión).

indomesticable *adj* untamable.

indómito, ta *adj* untamed (no domado) || untamable (indomesticable) || unsubmissive, unruly (persona).

Indonesia *npr f* GEOGR Indonesia.

indonesio, sia *adj/s* Indonesian.

Indostán *npr m* GEOGR Hindustan || India.

indostanés, esa; indostano, na *adj/s* Hindustani.

indostaní *m* Hindustani (lengua).

indostánico, ca *adj* (p us) Hindustani.

indubitable *adj* indubitable, doubtless, certain.

indubitado, da *adj* certain, doubtless.

inducción *f* induction || MED induction || ELECTR *bobina* or *carrete de inducción* induction coil.

inducido, da *adj* ELECTR induced.
◆ *m* armature.

inducimiento *m* inducement.

inducir* *vt* to lead; *inducir a error* to lead into error || to induce, to lead (mover a); *condiciones que habían inducido a mucha gente a emigrar* conditions which had induced many people to emigrate || to induce, to infer (inferir) || ELECTR to induce.

inductancia *f* ELECTR inductance.

indúctil *adj* FÍS inductile.

inductivo, va *adj* inductive.

inductor, ra *adj* inducing || ELECTR inductive.
◆ *m/f* inducer.
◆ *m* ELECTR & QUÍM inductor.

indudable *adj* indubitable, doubtless, certain || *es indudable que...* there is no doubt that...

indulgencia *f* indulgence, leniency || REL indulgence; *indulgencia plenaria* plenary indulgence.

indulgente *adj* indulgent, lenient; *indulgente con* or *hacia* indulgent towards, lenient with.

indultar *vt* to pardon (de una pena) || to excuse, to exempt (de una obligación, de un pago).

indulto *m* mercy (compasión) || reprieve, pardon (de un reo) || exemption (de un pago) || indult (concedido por el Papa).

indumentaria *f* clothing, clothes *pl*, garments *pl* (ropa) || historical study of costume (estudio) || *lleva la indumentaria más extravagante que te puedas imaginar* he dresses up in the most extravagant garb *o* apparel imaginable.

indumento *m* clothing, clothes *pl*, garments *pl*.

induración *f* MED induration.

indurar *vt* to indurate.

industria *f* industry; *industria clave* key industry; *industria pesada* heavy industry; *industria siderúrgica* iron and steel industry.

industrial *adj* industrial.
◆ *m* industrialist, industrial.

industrialismo *m* industrialism.

industrialización *f* industrialization.

industrializar *vt* to industrialize.
◆ *vpr* to become industrialized.

industriar *vt* to instruct, to train.
◆ *vpr* to find means *o* a way; *industriarse para conseguir algo* to find means *o* a way of obtaining sth., to find a way to obtain sth. || to manage, to get along *o* by (arreglárselas).

industrioso, sa *adj* industrious (trabajador, diligente) || ingenious, skilful [US skillful] (ingenioso).

inecuación *f* MAT inequation, inequality.

inédito, ta *adj* unpublished || FIG unknown (desconocido).

ineducación *f* impoliteness, unmannerliness, ill-breeding (malos modales) || lack of education (falta de educación).

ineducado, da *adj* impolite, unmannerly, ill-bred (mal educado) || uneducated (sin educar).

inefabilidad *f* ineffability, inexpressibility.

inefable *adj* ineffable, inexpressible, indescribable.

ineficacia *f* inefficacy, ineffectiveness.

ineficaz *adj* inefficacious, inefficient, ineffective, ineffectual.

ineficiencia *f* inefficiency.

ineficiente *adj* inefficient.

inejecución *f* inexecution, non-execution.

inelegancia *f* inelegance, inelegancy.

inelegibilidad *f* inelegibility.

inelegible *adj* ineligible.

ineluctable *adj* ineluctable, inevitable, inescapable.

ineludible *adj* ineludible, inescapable.

Inem *abrev de Instituto Nacional de Empleo* national employment agency.

inembargable *adj* JUR not attachable *o* distrainable *o* seizable.

inenarrable *adj* indescribable, inexpressible.

inencogible *adj* nonshrink.

inepcia; ineptitud *f* inability (incapacidad) || ineptitude, inaptitude, incompetence (incompetencia) || ineptitude, foolishness (necedad).

inepto, ta *adj* incapable (incapaz) || inept, inapt, incompetent (incompetente) || unsuitable, inapt (inadecuado) || inept, foolish, preposterous (necio).
◆ *m/f* incompetent, dead loss (*fam*).

inequívoco, ca *adj* unequivocal, unmistakable; *inequívocas señales de embriaguez* unmistakable signs of inebriation.

inercia *f* TECN inertia || inertia, lifelessness (falta de vivacidad) || *fuerza de inercia* inertial force.

inerme *adj* BOT & ZOOL without prickles or spines || unarmed (sin armas) || defenceless (sin defensa).

inerte *adj* inert || inert, lifeless (falto de energía o vivacidad) || inert (gas).

inervación *f* innervation.

inervar *vt* to innervate.

Inés *npr f* Agnes.

inescrutabilidad *f* inscrutability.

inescrutable; inescudriñable *adj* inscrutable (insondable); *los caminos del Señor son inescrutables* the ways of the Lord are inscrutable.

inesperadamente *adv* unexpectedly.

inesperado, da *adj* unexpected, unforeseen.

inestabilidad *f* instability.

inestable *adj* unstable, instable, unsteady.

inestimable *adj* inestimable, invaluable || *de inestimable valor* priceless.

inestimado, da *adj* unestimated, unappraised (no tasado) || underestimated (subestimado).

inevitabilidad *f* inevitability.

inevitable *adj* inevitable, unavoidable.

inexactitud *f* inexactitude, inexactness, inaccuracy (falta de precisión) || inexactitude, incorrectness (falsedad).

inexacto, ta *adj* inexact, inaccurate (impreciso) || inexact, incorrect (erróneo) || untrue (falso).

inexcusable *adj* inexcusable, unforgivable (imperdonable) || inevitable, unavoidable (inevitable).

inexcusabilidad *f* inexcusability.

inexigibilidad *f* nonexigibility.

inexigible *adj* inexigible.

inexistencia *f* inexistence, nonexistence.

inexistente *adj* nonexistent, inexistent.

inexorabilidad *f* inexorability.

inexorable *adj* inexorable.

inexperiencia *f* inexperience (falta de experiencia) || unskilfulness, inexpertness (falta de habilidad).

inexperimentado, da *adj* inexperienced.

inexperto, ta *adj* inexperienced (falto de experiencia) || inexpert (falto de habilidad).

inexpiado, da *adj* unexpiated.

inexplicable *adj* inexplicable.

inexplicado, da *adj* unexplained.

inexplorable *adj* unexplorable.

inexplorado, da *adj* unexplored || uncharted (indicación en un mapa).

inexplotable *adj* unexploitable.

inexplotado, da *adj* unexploited.

inexpresable *adj* inexpressible.

inexpresivo, va *adj* inexpressive.

inexpugnable *adj* inexpugnable, impregnable.

in extenso *loc adv* in extenso, at full length.

inextingible *adj* inextinguishable || unquenchable (sed) || eternal (amor).

inextirpable *adj* inextirpable, ineradicable.

in extremis *loc adv* in extremis.

inextricable *adj* insolvable, inextricable (problema) || inextricable (laberinto) || impenetrable.

infalibilidad *f* infallibility; *infalibilidad pontificia* papal infallibility.

infalible *adj* infallible || certain, sure, inevitable; *éxito infalible* certain success.

infaliblemente *adv* infallibly || certainly, surely (seguramente).

infalsificable *adj* unfalsifiable || unforgeable (moneda).

infamador, ra *adj* defamatory, slanderous.
◆ *m/f* slanderer, defamer (difamador) || discreditor, detractor (el que desacredita).

infamante *adj* shameful (castigo).

infamar *vt* to defame, to slander, to infame (ant) (difamar, ofender) || to discredit, to dishonour [*US* to dishonor] (desacreditar).

infamatorio, ria *adj* defamatory, slanderous (que difama) || discrediting (que desacredita).

infame *adj* infamous, odious, wicked, vile (vil) || infamous (de mala fama) || FIG vile, foul, odious; *tiempo infame* vile weather || thankless, odious (tarea).
◆ *m/f* infamous *o* wicked person.

infamia *f* infamy.

infancia *f* infancy, childhood || children *pl* (niños) || FIG infancy (principio); *en la infancia del mundo* in the world's infancy || — *en la primera infancia* in one's early childhood || *ha vuelto a la infancia* he is in his second childhood || FIG *no estás en la primera infancia* you're not a child any more.

infanta *f* infanta, princess (hija del rey o esposa de un infante) || infant, little girl (niña).

infantado *m* appanage, apanage, territory assigned to an infante *o* to an infanta.

infante *m* infante, prince (hijo del rey) || infant, little boy (niño) || infantryman (soldado).

infantería *f* MIL infantry; *infantería motorizada* motorized infantry || MIL *la infantería de marina* the marines *pl*.

infanticida *adj* infanticidal.
◆ *m/f* infanticide, child killer.

infanticidio *m* infanticide (asesinato).

infantil *adj* infantile; *enfermedad infantil* infantile disease || child's; *tamaño infantil* child's size || infantile, childish (aniñado); *comportamiento infantil* infantile behaviour || childlike; *una cara infantil* a childlike face || — *literatura infantil* children's literature || DEP *prueba para infantiles* infants' *o* children's event.

infantilidad *f* childishness (niñería).

infantilismo *m* infantilism (anormalidad).

infanzón, ona *m/f* nobleman *o* noblewoman [member of the lowest rank of the nobility].

infarto *m* MED infarct; *infarto de miocardio, pulmonar* infarct of the myocardium, of the lungs; *infarto mesentérico* mesenteric infarct | engorgement (hinchazón).

infatigable *adj* indefatigable, tireless, untiring.

infatuación *f* conceit, vanity, pride (engreimiento).

infatuar *vt* to make conceited.
◆ *vpr* to become conceited; *infatuarse con un éxito* to become conceited about one's success.

infausto, ta *adj* unfortunate, unlucky, unhappy.

infección *f* infection.

infeccionar *vt* to infect (inficionar).

infeccioso, sa *adj* infectious; *una enfermedad infecciosa* an infectious disease.

infectar *vt* to infect; *herida infectada* infected wound.
◆ *vpr* to become infected.

infecto, ta *adj* infected, contaminated || foul (repugnante).

infecundidad *f* infecundity, sterility (esterilidad).

infecundo, da *adj* infertile, infecund, barren, sterile (suelo) || infecund, sterile (mujeres).

infelice *adj* POÉT unfortunate, unhappy (infeliz).

infelicidad *f* unhappiness, misfortune, infelicity.

infeliz *adj* unhappy, unfortunate (desgraciado) || miserable, wretched (miserable) || FAM good-natured, kind-hearted (bondadoso) | gullible (inocente).
◆ *m/f* poor devil || FAM good-natured fellow | simpleton (inocentón).

infelizote *m* good-natured fellow (buena persona) || simpleton (inocentón).

inferencia *f* inference.

inferior *adj* lower; *la mandíbula inferior* the lower jaw; *la parte inferior* the lower part || inferior; *este libro es inferior al otro* this book is inferior to the other; *de calidad inferior* of inferior quality; *no ser inferior a nadie* to be inferior to none || less; *veinte es inferior a treinta* twenty is less than thirty || — *el lado inferior* the underside, the underneath || *una cantidad inferior* a lesser *o* smaller quantity || *un número inferior a treinta* a number under thirty *o* less than thirty.
◆ *m* inferior.

inferioridad *f* inferiority; *complejo de inferioridad* inferiority complex.

inferir* *vt* to infer, to deduce (sacar una conclusión); *de ello infiero que...* from this I infer that... || to cause; *inferir daños* to cause damage || to inflict (una herida).

infernáculo *m* hopscotch (juego).

infernal *adj* infernal || FIG devilish, infernal; *niño infernal* devilish child; *un ruido infernal* an infernal din *o* racket || — *fuego infernal* hellfire || *máquina infernal* infernal machine.

infernillo *m* stove.

infestar *vt* to infest (causar estragos) || to overrun, to swamp, to invade (llenar) || to infect (corromper).

infeudar *vt* to enfeoff (enfeudar).

inficionar *vt* to infect (infectar) || to contaminate (contaminar) || FIG to corrupt; *inficionar a la juventud con malos ejemplos* to corrupt youth by bad examples.

infidelidad *f* infidelity, unfaithfulness; *infidelidad conyugal* infidelity in marriage || REL unbelief | infidels *pl*, unbelievers *pl* (los infieles).

infiel *adj* unfaithful; *marido infiel* unfaithful husband; *persona infiel con* or *a* or *para con sus promesas* person unfaithful to his promises || disloyal, faithless; *un amigo infiel* a disloyal friend || inaccurate, inexact; *nos dio una versión infiel de lo que pasó* he gave us an inaccurate version of what happened || REL infidel, unbelieving || FIG *la memoria me fue infiel* my memory failed me.
◆ *m/f* REL infiel, unbeliever.

infiernillo *m* stove; *infiernillo de alcohol* spirit stove.

infierno *m* hell; *ir al infierno* to go to hell || FIG & FAM hell || TECN tank [in olive production] || — FAM *¡anda* or *vete al infierno!* go to hell! || FIG *el camino del infierno está empedrado de buenas intenciones* the road to hell is paved with good intentions || FAM *en el quinto infierno, en los quintos infiernos* miles from anywhere, in the middle of nowhere, at the back of beyond.
◆ *pl* MIT Hades.

infijo *m* GRAM infix.

infiltración *f* infiltration.

infiltrado *m* MED infiltrate.

infiltrar *vt* to infiltrate.
◆ *vpr* to infiltrate (*en* into) || FIG to infiltrate.

ínfimo, ma *adj* lowest (muy bajo) || worst, poorest (peor) || ridiculously low (precios).

infinidad *f* infinity; *la infinidad del universo* the infinity of the universe || — *en infinidad de ocasiones* on countless *o* innumerable occasions, time and again || *había infinidad de gente* there were countless people *o* an awful lot of people there || *me tuvo allí una infinidad de tiempo* he kept me there for ages || *te lo he dicho infinidad de veces* I've told you time and again o over and over o I don't know many times || *tengo infinidad de cosas que hacer* I've got a million things to do *o* countless things to do || *una infinidad de* countless, innumerable, an infinity of.

infinitesimal *adj* infinitesimal.

infinitésimo, ma *adj* infinitesimal.

infinito, ta *adj* infinite || *a lo infinito* ad infinitum.
◆ *m* infinite || MAT & FÍS infinity.
◆ *adv* infinitely, extremely; *se lo agradezco infinito* I am infinitely grateful.

infinitud *f* infinitude, infinity.

infirmación *f* invalidation.

infirmar *vt* JUR to invalidate.

inflación *f* inflation; *inflación monetaria* monetary inflation; *inflación galopante* runaway inflation || FIG conceit, vanity || swelling (hinchamiento).

inflacionario, ria *adj* inflationary.

inflacionismo *m* inflationism, inflation.

inflacionista *adj* inflationary.
◆ *m/f* inflationist.

inflado *m* inflation.

inflamabilidad *f* inflammability.

inflamable *adj* inflammable.

inflamación *f* inflammation || MED inflammation.

inflamar *vt* to set on fire, to inflame || FIG to inflame, to arouse.
◆ *vpr* to catch fire || FIG to become inflamed || MED to become inflamed.

inflamatorio, ria *adj* inflammatory.

inflamiento *m* swelling, inflation.

inflar *vt* to inflate, to swell, to fill out; *el viento infla las velas* the wind swells the sails || to inflate, to blow up; *inflar un globo, un neumático* to inflate a balloon, a tyre || to puff out (los carrillos) || FIG to exaggerate, to blow up (exagerar); *inflar un suceso* to exaggerate an event | to swell up, to make conceited (envanecer).
◆ *vpr* to fill out, to swell (las velas de un barco) || to inflate (un globo, un neumático, etc.) || to puff out (los carrillos) || FIG to get conceited; *inflarse con un éxito* to get conceited about a success || FIG *inflarse de orgullo* to swell with pride.

inflexibilidad *f* inflexibility.

inflexible *adj* inflexible || FIG inelastic, inflexible (reglas) | unyielding, inflexible, unbending (que no cede) | strict, inflexible (severo).

inflexión *f* inflection, inflexion.

infligir *vt* to inflict; *infligir un castigo a uno* to inflict punishment upon s.o.; *infligir una derrota a* to inflict defeat on *o* upon.

influencia *f* influence ‖ — *ejercer una influencia sobre uno* to have an influence upon *o* over s.o., to influence s.o. ‖ *persona de mucha influencia* very influential person ‖ *valerse de sus influencias* to use one's influence.

influenciable *adj* easily influenced, impressionable.

influenciar *vt* to influence (influir).

influenza *f* MED influenza, flu (*fam*).

influir* *vi* to influence, to have an influence; *el clima influye en* or *sobre la vegetación* the climate influences the vegetation, the climate has an influence on the vegetation ‖ to bear (*en* upon); *influyó en un amigo suyo para que me diera el puesto* he bore upon a friend of his to give me the post.
◆ *vt* to influence.

influjo *m* influence (influencia) ‖ rising tide (flujo de la marea) ‖ impulse; *influjo nervioso* nerve impulse.

influyente *adj* influential.

infolio *m inv* folio (libro).

información *f* information ‖ JUR inquiry (investigación) | report, account (informe) ‖ MIL intelligence ‖ section, news (en un periódico); *información deportiva* sports news; *información financiera* financial section *o* news ‖ data *pl*; *tratamiento de la información* data processing ‖ directory inquiries (teléfono) ‖ references (de un empleado) ‖ — *a título de información* by way of information ‖ *información secreta* classified *o* top-secret information ‖ JUR *información sumaria* summary proceedings ‖ *para su información* for your information ‖ MIL *servicio de información* intelligence service ‖ *una información* a piece of news, some news.
◆ *pl* news *sing* (en radio, televisión).

informado, da *adj* informed; *fuentes bien informadas* well-informed sources ‖ with references; *se necesita un empleado bien informado* an employee with references is needed.

informador, ra *adj* informing.
◆ *m/f* informant.
◆ *m* AMER rapporteur (ponente).

informal *adj* unmannerly, incorrect (conducta) ‖ unreliable, untrustworthy (poco de fiar); *persona informal* unreliable person ‖ irregular (no normal) ‖ bad-mannered (mal educado).

informalidad *f* unmannerliness, incorrectness (de la conducta) ‖ unreliability, untrustworthiness (de una persona) ‖ irregularity (irregularidad) ‖ bad manners *pl* (incorrección).

informante *adj* informing.
◆ *m* informant (que informa) ‖ rapporteur (de una comisión).

informar *vt* to inform, to tell, to make known to ‖ to report; *los cosmonautas informaron que todo iba bien* the astronauts reported that all was well.
◆ *vi* JUR to enquire (investigar); *informar sobre algo* to enquire into sth. | to plead (un abogado) | to inform (denunciar) | to report; *informar de las decisiones de una comisión* to report on the decisions of a commission.
◆ *vpr* to enquire, to inquire; *infórmense en nuestras oficinas* enquire in our offices; *informarse sobre algo* to enquire into sth.; *informarse sobre un empleado* to enquire about an employee ‖ to find out (*de* about) (enterarse) ‖ *informarse sobre un asunto* to look into a matter.

informático, ca *adj* computer, computing.
◆ *m/f* INFORM computer expert *o* specialist.

informática *f* computer science, data processing ‖ *informática distribuida* distributed data processing ‖ *informática gráfica* graphic data processing.

informativo, va *adj* informative ‖ information; *servicios informativos* information services.

informatizar *vt* to computerize.

informe *adj* formless, shapeless.
◆ *m* report (de policía, de una sociedad, etc.); *el informe de la comisión* the commission's report; *informe anual* annual report ‖ piece of information (información) ‖ JUR pleading (exposición) | dossier (expediente).
◆ *pl* references; *se necesita cocinero con buenos informes* cook with good references needed ‖ information *sing*; *pedir informes sobre* or *de* to request information about; *tomar informes* to get information.

infortunado, da *adj* unfortunate.
◆ *m/f* unfortunate person, unfortunate (p us).

infortunio *m* misfortune.

infosura *f* VET founder.

infracción *f* infraction, infringement ‖ AUT offence.

infractor, ra *m/f* offender, infractor.

infradotado, da *adj* MED handicapped (físicamente) | subnormal (mentalmente).

infraestructura *f* infrastructure.

in fraganti *loc adv* in the act, red-handed; *coger a uno in fraganti* to catch s.o. red-handed.

infranqueable *adj* impassable ‖ FIG insurmountable.

infraoctava *f* REL octave.

infraorbitario, ria *adj* MED infraorbital.

infrarrojo, ja *adj* FÍS infrared.
◆ *m* infrared radiation, infrared.

infrascripto, ta; infrascrito, ta *adj/s* undersigned; *Yo, el infrascrito* I the undersigned ‖ here-inafter mentioned (mencionado más adelante).

infrasonido *m* FÍS infrasonic wave.

infravalorar *vt* to undervalue, to underestimate.

infrecuente *adj* infrequent.

infringir *vt* to infringe, to transgress, to break.

infructífero, ra *adj* unproductive; *campo infructífero* unproductive field ‖ FIG fruitless, unfruitful.

infructuosidad *f* unfruitfulness, fruitlessness.

infructuoso, sa *adj* unfruitful, fruitless, vain, useless; *esfuerzo infructuoso* unfruitful effort.

ínfulas *f pl* infulae (antiguo ornamento sacerdotal, cintas de la mitra episcopal) ‖ FIG pretension *sing*, conceit *sing* ‖ FIG *darse* or *tener muchas ínfulas* to put on airs.

infumable *adj* not smokable, unsmokable ‖ FAM unbearable (insoportable).

infundado, da *adj* unfounded, groundless.

infundio *m* FAM lie, story, tale; *circulan infundios sobre ti* people are spreading lies about you.

infundioso, sa *adj* false, untrue.

infundir *vt* to instil, to infuse, to inspire; *infundir terror, respeto, ánimo, ideas* to instil fear, respect, courage, ideas ‖ to cause; *infundir sospechas, dudas* to cause suspicion, doubt ‖ to inject; *infundir un espíritu nuevo a una empresa* to inject new life into a firm.

infusión *f* infusion.

infuso, sa *adj* inspired; *ciencia infusa* inspired knowledge ‖ FAM *tener la ciencia infusa* to be a born genius.

infusorios *m pl* ZOOL infusoria.

ingeniar *vt* to invent, to conceive, to devise, to think up.
◆ *vpr* to manage to; *ingeniarse para vivir decentemente* to manage to live decently ‖ *ingeniárselas* to manage; *siempre se las ingenia para no trabajar* he always manages to get out of work.

ingeniería *f* engineering (ciencia) ‖ *ingeniería civil* civil engineering ‖ *ingeniería genética* genetic engineering.

ingeniero *m* engineer ‖ — *ingeniero agrónomo* agriculturist ‖ *ingeniero civil* civil engineer ‖ *ingeniero consultor* consulting engineer ‖ *ingeniero de Caminos, Canales y Puertos* civil engineer ‖ *ingeniero de minas* mining engineer ‖ *ingeniero de montes* forestry expert ‖ INFORM *ingeniero de sistemas* systems engineer ‖ *ingeniero de sonido* sound technician *o* engineer ‖ *ingeniero industrial* industrial engineer ‖ *ingeniero militar* army engineer ‖ *ingeniero naval* naval architect ‖ *ingeniero químico* chemical engineer ‖ *ingeniero de telecomunicaciones* electronic engineer.

ingenio *m* ingenuity, ingeniousness, genius (talento) ‖ inventiveness, creativeness (inventiva) ‖ wit, humour (agudeza) ‖ genius (persona) ‖ appliance, machine (aparato o máquina) ‖ device (militar) ‖ TECN cutter (máquina de encuadernación) ‖ — *aguzar el ingenio* to sharpen one's wits ‖ *ingenio de azúcar* sugar mill ‖ *ingenio espacial* space missile ‖ *tener ingenio* to be witty.

ingeniosidad *f* ingenuity, ingeniousness; *la ingeniosidad de un mecanismo, de un razonamiento* the ingenuity of a mechanism, of a reasoning ‖ FIG bright idea (genialidad).

ingenioso, sa *adj* ingenious (máquina, idea, etc.) ‖ ingenious, resourceful (persona) ‖ witty (agudo) ‖ *echárselas de ingenioso* to try to be witty.

ingénito, ta *adj* innate, inborn (innato) ‖ unbegotten (no engendrado).

ingente *adj* enormous, huge.

ingenuidad *f* ingenuousness, naïveté.

ingenuo, nua *adj* naïve, ingenuous.
◆ *m/f* naïve person.
◆ *f* TEATR ingénue.

ingerencia *f* interference.

ingerir* *vt* to ingest, to take (in), to consume, to eat; *ingerir alimentos* to ingest food ‖ to take (in), to consume, to drink (beber) ‖ to insert, to introduce (introducir).
◆ *vpr* to interfere; *ingerirse en los asuntos ajenos* to interfere in other people's affairs.

ingestión *f* ingestion.

Inglaterra *npr f* GEOGR England.

ingle *f* ANAT groin.

inglés, esa *adj* English ‖ *patatas fritas a la inglesa* crisps [*US* potato chips].
◆ *m* Englishman ‖ English (language) (idioma); *hablar inglés* to speak English.
◆ *f* Englishwoman ‖ English (letra).
— OBSERV *Inglés* is often used by Spanish speakers to mean *British*.

inglesismo *m* Anglicism.

inglete *m* forty-five degree angle (ángulo) ‖ mitre joint [*US* miter joint] (en la escuadra) ‖ TECN *caja de ingletes* mitre box [*US* miter box].

ingobernable *adj* ungovernable (en política) ‖ uncontrollable.

ingratitud *f* ingratitude, ungratefulness ‖ *mostrar ingratitud* to be ungrateful.

ingrato, ta *adj* ungrateful, ingrate (ant); *ingrato con* or *para con* ungrateful to *o* towards ‖ disagreeable, unpleasant (desagradable); *tiempo ingrato* disagreeable weather ‖ unrewarding, thankless; *una labor ingrata* an unrewarding task ‖ unproductive; *un terreno*

ingrato an unproductive field || *hijo ingrato* ungrateful child.
◆ *m/f* ungrateful person, ingrate (ant) || *de ingratos está lleno el mundo* the world is full of ungrateful people, one can't trust anybody.

ingravidez *f* weightlessness, lightness (carencia de peso) || absence *o* lack of gravity (falta de gravedad).

ingrávido, da *adj* weightless, light (sin peso) || lacking gravity (sin gravedad).

ingrediente *m* ingredient.

ingresado, da *adj* deposited (dinero) || entrant (persona).

ingresar *vi* to come in, to enter (dinero, fondos); *hoy han ingresado cinco millones de pesetas en el banco* five million pesetas have come into the bank today || to enrol, to register, to enter (en una escuela, una universidad, etc.) || to be admitted; *falleció a poco de ingresar en el hospital* he died shortly after being admitted to the hospital; *ingresar en la Academia* to be admitted to the Academy || to join, to become a member of (en una sociedad, un club) || MIL to enlist, to join; *ingresar en el ejército* to enlist in the army, to join the army.
◆ *vt* to deposit, to pay; *ingresar dinero en el banco* to deposit money in the bank; *ingresar una cantidad en cuenta* to pay an amount into one's account.
◆ *vpr* AMER to enlist (alistarse).

ingreso *m* entrance (entrada) || admission (en una academia, una escuela, un hospital) || COM receipt, entry (de dinero) | deposit (depósito) || *examen de ingreso* entrance examination.
◆ *pl* income *sing*; *los ingresos de un abogado* the income of a lawyer || revenue *sing* (del Estado) || *ingresos brutos* gross income.

inguinal; inguinario, ria *adj* inguinal.

ingurgitación *f* MED ingurgitation.

ingurgitar *vt* to ingurgitate (engullir).

inhábil *adj* unskilful [US unskillful]; *costurera inhábil* unskilful seamstress || incompetent (incompetente) || JUR incompetent; *abogado inhábil* incompetent lawyer; *inhábil para testificar* incompetent to testify || — *día inhábil* holiday || *hora inhábil* closing time || *inhábil para el trabajo* or *para trabajar* unfit for work *o* to work.

inhabilidad *f* unskilfulness [US unskillfulness] || incompetence (falta de competencia) || JUR incompetence.

inhabilitación *f* incapacitation, disablement, disqualification.

inhabilitar *vt* to disable, to incapacite, to disqualify.

inhabitable *adj* uninhabitable.

inhabitado, da *adj* uninhabitated (deshabitado).

inhabitual *adj* unusual.

inhacedero, ra *adj* unfeasible.

inhalación *f* inhalation.

inhalador, ra *adj* inhalant.
◆ *m* inhaler.

inhalar *vt* to inhale.

inherencia *f* inherence.

inherente *adj* inherent; *responsabilidad inherente a un cargo* inherent responsibility of a job, responsibility inherent in a job.

inhibición *f* inhibition (fisiológica o psíquica).

inhibidor *m* QUÍM inhibitor.

inhibir *vt* to inhibit (un proceso fisiológico o psicológico) || JUR to inhibit.
◆ *vpr* to be inhibited (fisiológica o psicológicamente) || to keep out; *inhibirse en un asunto* to keep out of a matter.

inhibitorio, ria *adj* inhibitory.

inhospitalario, ria *adj* inhospitable.

inhospitalidad *f* inhospitality.

inhóspito, ta *adj* inhospitable.

inhumación *f* inhumation, burial.

inhumanidad *f* inhumanity.

inhumano, na *adj* inhuman.

inhumar *vt* to inhume, to bury.

INI *abrev de Instituto Nacional de Industria* national industry institute.

iniciación *f* introduction; *iniciación a la filosofía* introduction to philosophy || initiation; *iniciación religiosa* religious initiation; *ceremonia de iniciación* initiation ceremony || beginning (principio).

iniciado, da *adj* initiated.
◆ *m/f* initiale.

iniciador, ra *adj* initiatory.
◆ *m/f* initiator || FIG pioneer (pionero).

inicial *adj* initial; *la velocidad inicial de un proyectil* the initial velocity of a missile.
◆ *f* initial (letra).

inicialización *f* INFORM initialization.

inicializar *vt* INFORM to initialize, to set up.

iniciar *vt* to initiate; *iniciar a uno en la masonería* to initiate s.o. into freemasonry || to begin, to start; *iniciar las negociaciones* to begin negotiations.
◆ *vpr* to learn by o.s. *iniciarse en el arte de tocar la guitarra* to learn to play the guitar by o.s. || to begin; *se inició el debate el lunes* the debate began on Monday.

iniciativa *f* initiative; *tomar la iniciativa* to take the initiative; *persona de mucha iniciativa* person with a lot of initiative; *obrar por propia iniciativa* to act upon one's own initiative || — *Iniciativa de Defensa Estratégica* Strategic Defence Initiative [SDI, also known as «star wars»] || *iniciativa privada* private enterprise.

iniciativo, va *adj* initiative.

inicio *m* beginning.

inicuo, cua *adj* iniquitous, wicked.

inigualado, da *adj* unequalled, unequaled.

in illo témpore *adv* formerly.

inimaginable *adj* unimaginable.

inimitable *adj* inimitable.

ininflamable *adj* uninflammable.

ininteligente *adj* unintelligent.

ininteligible *adj* unintelligible.

ininterrupción *f* uninterruption.

ininterrumpido, da *adj* uninterrupted.

iniquidad *f* iniquity, wickedness.

injerencia *f* interference.

injeridura *f* graft.

injerir *vt* to insert, to introduce (introducir una cosa en otra) || AGR to graft.
◆ *vpr* to interfere; *injerirse en los asuntos ajenos* to interfere in other people's affairs.

injertable *adj* that can be grafted.

injertador *m* grafter.

injertar *vt* AGR & MED to graft.

injerto *m* AGR graft; *injerto de corona* crown graft | graft, scion (yema implantada) || MED graft; *un injerto de piel* a skin graft || — AGR *injerto de aproximación* inarching | *injerto de escudete* shield grafting.

injuria *f* insult (insulto) || offence [US offense] (ofensa) || MED injury || FIG ravage; *las injurias del tiempo* the ravages of time || — *delito de injurias al jefe del Estado* crime of slander against the Head of State || *injurias y actos de violencia* slander and acts of violence.

injuriador, ra *adj* offensive.
◆ *m/f* offender.

injuriante *adj* offensive.

injuriar *vt* to offend, to insult, to abuse (ofender) || to injure, to harm (producir un daño material).

injurioso, sa *adj* offensive.

injusticia *f* injustice || unfairness (falta de equidad) || *con injusticia* unjustly.

injustificable *adj* unjustifiable.

injustificado, da *adj* unjustified.

injusto, ta *adj* unjust || unfair (*para, con* to, with) (sin equidad).

INLE *abrev de Instituto Nacional del Libro Español* national book institute.

inmaculado, da *adj* immaculate.
◆ *f* *la Inmaculada* the Immaculate Conception.

inmadurez *f* immaturity.

inmaduro, ra; inmaturo, ra *adj* unripe || FIG immature, unripe.

inmanejable *adj* unmanageable || AMER undriveable (automóvil).

inmanencia *f* immanence.

inmanente *adj* immanent.

inmanentismo *m* immanentism.

inmarcesible; inmarchitable *adj* unwithering, unfading; *la gloria inmarcesible* unfading glory.

inmaterial *adj* immaterial.

inmaterialidad *f* immateriality.

inmaterialismo *m* immaterialism.

inmaturo, ra *adj* ⟶ **inmaduro.**

inmediación *f* immediacy (carácter de lo inmediato).
◆ *pl* environs, neighbourhood *sing*; *Alcalá de Henares está en las inmediaciones de Madrid* Alcalá de Henares is in the environs of Madrid.

inmediatamente *adv* immediately, at once || *inmediatamente después de cenar, inmediatamente que cenemos* immediately after dinner.

inmediato, ta *adj* near, close to (cercano); *un pueblo inmediato a Londres* a town near London || next (contiguo); *en el cuarto inmediato al mío* in the next room to mine, in the room next to mine || immediate; *una medicina de efecto inmediato* a medicine with immediate effect || AMER *de inmediato* immediately, at once.

inmejorable *adj* unsurpassable, unimprovable || excellent (excelente) || unbeatable (precios).

inmemorial *adj* immemorial; *desde tiempo inmemorial* from time immemorial.

inmensidad *f* immensity, vastness.

inmenso, sa *adj* immense, huge, vast; *llanura inmensa* immense plain; *fortuna inmensa* immense fortune || FIG & FAM fabulous (magnífico) || — *me dio una pena inmensa* I was terribly upset || FIG & FAM *pasarlo inmenso* to have a fabulous time, to have a ball.

inmensurable *adj* immeasurable, unmeasurable.

inmerecidamente *adv* undeservingly.

inmerecido, da *adj* unmerited, undeserved.

inmergir *vt* to immerse (sumergir).

inmersión *f* immersion || dive (de un hombre rana).

inmerso, sa *adj* immersed (sumergido).

inmigración *f* immigration.

inmigrado, da *adj/s* immigrant.

inmigrante *adj/s* immigrant.

inmigrar *vi* to immigrate.

inmigratorio, ria *adj* immigratory.

inminencia *f* imminence, imminency.

inminente *adj* imminent (a punto de ocurrir) ‖ impending (amenaza, peligro).

inmiscuir *vt* (p us) to mix.
◆ *vpr* to interfere, to meddle; *inmiscuirse en un asunto* to interfere in a matter.

inmobiliario, ria *adj* real estate, property ‖ — *agente inmobiliario* estate agent [US real estate broker] ‖ *sociedad inmobiliaria* real estate company.
◆ *f* real estate company.

inmoble; inmovible *adj* motionless (que no se mueve) ‖ unmovable (que no se puede mover) ‖ FÍS firm.

inmoderado, da *adj* immoderate.

inmodestia *f* immodesty.

inmodesto, ta *adj* immodest.

inmolación *f* immolation, sacrifice.

inmolador *m* immolator.

inmolar *vt* to immolate, to sacrifice.
◆ *vpr* to immolate o.s., to sacrifice o.s.

inmoral *adj* immoral.

inmoralidad *f* immorality.

inmoralismo *m* immoralism.

inmoralista *m/f* immoralist.

inmortal *adj/s* immortal.

inmortalidad *f* immortality.

inmortalizar *vt* to immortalize.

inmotivadamente *adv* for no reason.

inmotivado, da *adj* unmotivated ‖ groundless (infundado).

inmovible *adj* → **inmoble.**

inmóvil *adj* motionless, still, immobile; *permanecer inmóvil* to remain motionless.

inmovilidad *f* immobility.

inmovilismo *m* opposition to progress, ultra-conservatism.

inmovilización *f* immobilization ‖ COM tying up (del capital).

inmovilizar *vt* to immobilize ‖ to paralyse, to bring to a standstill (una fábrica, la industria, un país) ‖ COM to tie up (el capital).

inmudable *adj* immutable.

inmueble *adj* JUR *bienes inmuebles* real estate *sing*, immovables.
◆ *m* building (edificio).

inmundicia *f* dirtiness, squalor (suciedad) ‖ FIG filth.
◆ *pl* rubbish *sing*, refuse *sing* (basura).

inmundo, da *adj* dirty, filthy, squalid ‖ unclean (impuro) ‖ FIG foul (language) ‖ *el espíritu inmundo* the spirit of evil (el demonio).

inmune *adj* MED immune; *estar inmune al cólera* to be immune to cholera.

inmunidad *f* immunity; *inmunidad contra una enfermedad* immunity to a disease; *inmunidad diplomática* diplomatic immunity; *inmunidad parlamentaria* parliamentary immunity.

inmunitario, ria *adj* MED immune.

inmunización *f* immunization.

inmunizador, ra *adj* immunogenic, immunizing.

inmunizar *vt* to immunize.

inmunodeficiencia *f* MED immunodeficiency.

inmunodepresor *m* MED immunodepressant.

inmunodiagnosis *f inv* MED immunodiagnosis.

inmunogenética *f* MED immunogenetics.

inmunoglobulina *f* MED immunoglobulin.

inmunología *f* MED immunology.

inmunológico, ca *adj* MED immunological, immunologic.

inmunólogo, ga *m/f* MED immunologist.

inmunoproteína *f* MED immunoprotein.

inmunoterapia *f* MED immunotherapy.

inmunotoxina *f* MED immunotoxin.

inmutabilidad *f* immutability.

inmutable *adj* immutable.

inmutación *f* alteration, change.

inmutar *vt* to alter, to change.
◆ *vpr* to change ‖ — *no inmutarse* to be unperturbed, not to flinch, not to bat an eyelid (*fam*) ‖ *se inmutó al leer la carta* his face fell upon reading the letter.

innato, ta *adj* innate, inborn.

innavegable *adj* unnavigable (río, mar) ‖ unseaworthy (barco).

innecesario, ria *adj* unnecessary.

innegable *adj* undeniable.

innoble *adj* ignoble.

innominable *adj* unnamable, unnameable.

innominado, da *adj* unnamed, nameless, innominate ‖ *hueso innominado* innominate bone.

innovación *f* innovation ‖ novelty, new thing (novedad).

innovador, ra *adj* innovative, innovatory.
◆ *m/f* innovator.

innovar *vt/vi* to innovate.

innumerabilidad *f* innumerability.

innumerable *adj* innumerable, countless.

inobediencia *f* disobedience.

inobediente *adj* disobedient.

inobservable *adj* unobservable.

inobservado, da *adj* unobserved.

inobservancia *f* inobservance, inobservancy.

inobservante *adj* inobservant, unobservant.

inocencia *f* innocence; *con toda inocencia* in all innocence.

Inocencio *npr m* Innocent.

inocentada *f* FAM practical joke (broma); *dar una inocentada a uno* to play a practical joke on s.o. | naïve remark (dicho ingenuo) | April Fool's joke (el día de los Inocentes).
— OBSERV In Spain these practical jokes take place on the 28th of December, Innocent's day, and not on the 1st of April as in England and the United States.

inocente *adj* innocent; *alma inocente* innocent soul; *broma inocente* innocent joke ‖ innocent, naïve (ingenuo).
◆ *m/f* innocent, innocent person (no culpable) ‖ simpleton (bobo) ‖ — *hacerse el inocente* to play innocent ‖ *los Santos Inocentes* the Holy Innocents.

inocentón, ona *adj* credulous, gullible, naïve.
◆ *m/f* simpleton.

inocuidad *f* innocuousness, harmlessness.

inoculación *f* inoculation.

inocular *vt* to inoculate; *inocular un virus a uno* to inoculate s.o. with a virus ‖ FIG to infect, to inoculate (ideas nocivas, etc.).

inocultable *adj* inconcealable.

inocuo, cua *adj* innocuous, harmless; *una droga inocua* an innocuous drug.

inodoro, ra *adj* odourless, inodorous.
◆ *m* AMER toilet, lavatory.

inofensivo, va *adj* inoffensive.

inoficioso, sa *adj* JUR inofficious.

inolvidable *adj* unforgettable.

inoperable *adj* inoperable; *tumor inoperable* inoperable tumour.

inoperante *adj* inoperative.

inopia *f* poverty, impecuniousness ‖ FIG *estar en la inopia* to be in the clouds (estar distraído).

inopinado, da *adj* unexpected.

inoportunidad *f* inopportuneness, untimeliness ‖ inconvenience (molestia).

inoportuno, na *adj* inopportune, untimely, ill-timed ‖ inconvenient (molesto).

inorgánico, ca *adj* inorganic.

inoxidable *adj* inoxidizable, rustless ‖ *acero inoxidable* stainless steel.

in péctore *loc adv* in petto.

in promptu *loc adv* impromptu.

inquebrantable *adj* unbreakable (irrompible) ‖ FIG unyielding; *fe inquebrantable* unyielding faith.

inquietante *adj* disturbing, alarming, worrying.

inquietar *vt* to disturb, to worry, to trouble ‖ MIL to harass.
◆ *vpr* to worry; *inquietarse por* to worry about.

inquieto, ta *adj* restless (agitado); *niño, mar inquieto* restless child, sea ‖ worried, anxious; *su madre está inquieta* his mother is worried.

inquietud *f* anxiety, worry, uneasiness (preocupación) ‖ restlessness (desasosiego).

inquilinaje *m* AMER tenants *pl* (inquilinos).

inquilinato *m* lease (arrendamiento) ‖ *impuesto de inquilinato* rates *pl*.

inquilino, na *m/f* tenant ‖ ZOOL inquiline.

inquina *f* FAM ill will, dislike, grudge; *tenerle inquina a alguien* to bear ill will towards s.o., to have a dislike for *o* a grudge against s.o. ‖ *tomarle inquina a alguien* to take a dislike to s.o.

inquiridor, ra *adj* inquiring, enquiring, investigating.
◆ *m/f* inquirer, enquirer, investigator.

inquirir* *vt/vi* to inquire *o* to enquire (into), to investigate; *la policía inquirió (sobre) la muerte del joyero* the police enquired into the jeweller's death.

inquisición *f* HIST Inquisition (antiguo tribunal eclesiástico) ‖ inquiry, enquiry, investigation (averiguación).

inquisidor, ra *adj* inquiring, inquisitive; *mirada inquisidora* inquiring glance.
◆ *m* inquisitor (juez de la Inquisición).

inquisitivo, va *adj* inquisitive; *le lanzó una mirada inquisitiva* he gave her an inquisitive glance.

inquisitorial *adj* inquisitorial, inquisitional.

inquisitorio, ria *adj* inquisitive.

inri *m* inri (en la Cruz) ‖ FIG insult (afrenta) ‖ — FIG *ponerle el inri a uno* to insult s.o. | *y para mayor inri* and to make it worse.

insaciabilidad *f* insatiability.

insaciable *adj* insatiable.

insalivación *f* BIOL insalivation.

insalivar *vt* BIOL to insalivate.

insalubre *adj* insalubrious, unhealthy.

insalubridad *f* insalubrity, unhealthiness.

Insalud *abrev de Instituto Nacional de la Salud* national health institute.

insalvable *adj* insurmountable (invencible).

insanable *adj* incurable.

insania *f* insanity (locura).

insano, na *adj* insane (loco) ‖ unhealthy (insalubre).

insatisfacción *f* dissatisfaction.

insatisfecho, cha *adj* unsatisfied, dissatisfied || unsatisfied; *venganza insatisfecha* unsatisfied revenge.

inscribir *vt* to inscribe (grabar) || to register, to enroll; *inscribir a alguien en un registro* to enroll s.o. in a register || to enter; *inscribir a alguien en una lista* to enter s.o.'s name on a list || to write down (escribir) || to register; *inscribir una declaración en las actas de una conferencia* to register a declaration in a conference record || to include, to place; *inscribir en el orden del día* to include in *o* to place on the agenda || MAT to inscribe.
◆ *vpr* to register, to enroll, to enter (one's name); *me he inscrito en el concurso* I have entered for the competition || to write one's name (apuntar su nombre).

inscripción *f* enrolment, registration || inscription; *había una inscripción sobre la tumba* there was an inscription over the grave.

inscrito, ta *adj* registered, enrolled, entered; *inscrito en un registro* entered *o* enrolled in a register || inscribed (grabado) || MAT inscribed; *polígono inscrito* inscribed polygon.

insecticida *adj* insecticidal, insecticide.
◆ *m* insecticide.

insectívoro, ra *adj* ZOOL insectivorous.
◆ *m* insectivore.
◆ *pl* insectivora.

insecto *m* insect.

inseguridad *f* insecurity (sentimiento) || uncertainty (duda) || unsafety (peligro); *inseguridad ciudadana* unsafety in the streets || unsteadiness, instability (inestabilidad).

inseguro, ra *adj* insecure (sentimiento, condición) || unsafe (peligroso) || uncertain (dudoso) || unsteady, unstable, insecure (inestable).

inseminación *f* insemination; *inseminación artificial* artificial insemination.

inseminar *vt* to inseminate.

insensatez *f* foolishness, stupidity, folly || FIG folly (tontería); *es una insensatez ir a verle a estas horas de la noche* it's folly to go to see him at this time of night | foolish remark (dicho estúpido).

insensato, ta *adj* foolish, stupid, senseless.
◆ *m/f* senseless person, fool.

insensibilidad *f* MED insensibility || insensitiveness, insensitivity (ante las emociones).

insensibilización *f* anaesthetization, anesthetization.

insensibilizador, ra *adj/sm* MED anaesthetic, anesthetic || *un agente insensibilizador* an anaesthetizing agent.

insensibilizar *vt* MED to anaesthetize, to anesthetize || FIG to make insensitive.

insensible *adj* MED insensible || insensitive, unfeeling (a las emociones) || imperceptible (imperceptible).

inseparabilidad *f* inseparability.

inseparable *adj* inseparable.

insepulto, ta *adj* unburied.

inserción *f* insertion.

insertable *adj* insertable.

insertar *vt* to insert; *insertar una cláusula en un tratado* to insert a clause in a treaty || to include (incluir).
◆ *vpr* BOT & ANAT to be inserted *o* attached.

inserto, ta *adj* inserted.

inservible *adj* unserviceable, useless.

insidia *f* trap, snare (trampa) || maliciousness (mala intención).

insidioso, sa *adj* insidious, treacherous || FIG insidious; *enfermedad insidiosa* insidious disease.
◆ *m/f* insidious person.

insigne *adj* famous, renowned, distinguished.

insignemente *adv* notably.

insignia *f* badge; *el policía lleva una insignia blanca* the policeman wears a white badge || banner; *el teniente llevaba la insignia del regimiento* the lieutenant carried the banner of the regiment || MAR pennant || *buque insignia* flagship.
◆ *pl* insignia.

insignificancia *f* insignificance || trifle; *el regalo que me hizo era una insignificancia* the gift that he gave me was a trifle; *el reloj me costó una insignificancia* my watch cost me a trifle.

insignificante *adj* insignificant, unimportant || trifling; *una cantidad insignificante de dinero* a trifling amount of money || insignificant, unimportant; *una persona insignificante* an insignificant person.

insinceridad *f* insincerity.

insincero, ra *adj* insincere.

insinuación *f* insinuation, hint; *es una insinuación inadmisible* it is an inadmissible insinuation || suggestion (sugerencia).

insinuante *adj* insinuating, suggestive.

insinuar *vt* to insinuate, to hint at; *¿qué es lo que insinúas?* what are you insinuating? || to insinuate, to hint; *insinuó que conocía el culpable* he insinuated he knew who the culprit was || to suggest (proponer); *insinúo que vayamos al campo* I suggest that we go to the country.
◆ *vpr* to make advances; *insinuarse a una mujer* to make advances to a woman || to gradually work one's way into (infiltrarse en).

insinuativo, va *adj* insinuating, insinuative.

insipidez *f* insipidity, insipidness.

insípido, da *adj* insipid, tasteless; *un alimento insípido* a tasteless food || FIG dull, insipid; *una comedia insípida* an insipid play.

insistencia *f* insistence; *la miró con insistencia* he looked at her with insistence || persistence; *la insistencia de la lluvia* the persistence of the rain.

insistente *adj* insistent (persona) || persistent (lluvia, quejas, etc.).

insistentemente *adv* insistently, with insistence || persistently.

insistir *vi* to insist; *insistir en* or *sobre un punto* to insist on *o* upon a point; *insistir en hablar* to insist on *o* upon talking; *insiste en que los inquilinos abandonen la casa* he insists that the tenants leave the house; *insisto en que tienes la culpa* I insist that you are at fault || to stress, to emphasize (hacer hincapié); *insistió en la importancia de* he stressed the importance of || to persist.

insobornable *adj* incorruptible.

insociabilidad *f* unsociability.

insociable *adj* unsociable.

insocial *adj* unsociable.

insolación *f* sunstroke, insolation (p us); *coger una insolación* to get sunstroke || insolation (en meteorología).

insolar *vt* to insolate, to expose to the sun's rays.
◆ *vpr* to get sunstroke.

insolencia *f* insolence || *decir insolencias* to be insolent.

insolentar *vt* to make insolent.
◆ *vpr* to be *o* to become insolent.

insolente *adj* insolent (descarado) || haughty, contemptuous (arrogante).
◆ *m/f* insolent person || haughty *o* contemptuous person.

insolidaridad *f* lack of solidarity, unsupportiveness.

insolidario, ria *adj* unsupportive.

insólito, ta *adj* unusual, unaccustomed.

insolubilidad *f* insolubility.

insoluble *adj* insoluble (no soluble) || unsolvable (imposible de resolver).

insolvencia *f* insolvency; *certificación de insolvencia* report of insolvency.

insolvente *adj/s* insolvent.

insomne *adj* insomnious, sleepless.
◆ *m/f* insomniac.

insondable *adj* unsoundable, unfathomable (muy profundo) || FIG unfathomable, inscrutable.

insonoridad *f* soundlessness.

insonorización *f* soundproofing.

insonorizado, da *adj* soundproof.

insonorizar *vt* to soundproof.

insonoro, ra *adj* insonorous, soundless.

insoportable *adj* unbearable, intolerable.

insoslayable *adj* inevitable, unavoidable (inevitable).

insospechable *adj* unexpected (sorprendente) || beyond suspicion (que no puede ser sospechado).

insospechado, da *adj* unsuspected.

insostenible *adj* unsustainable || untenable, indefensible, unmaintainable; *posición insostenible* untenable position.

inspección *f* inspection, examination || control || — *inspección ocular* visual inspection *o* examination || *inspección sanitaria* hygiene inspection.

inspeccionar *vt* to inspect, to examine.

inspector, ra *adj* inspecting.
◆ *m/f* inspector; *inspector de Hacienda* tax inspector.

inspectoría *f* AMER central police station.

inspiración *f* inspiration || inhalation, inspiration, breathing in (del aire).

inspirado, da *adj* inspired.

inspirador, ra *adj* inspirational, inspiring (que inspira) || inspiratory; *músculos inspiradores* inspiratory muscles.
◆ *m/f* inspirer.

inspirar *vt* to inspire || to inhale, to inspire, to breathe in (aire).
◆ *vpr* to be inspired; *el escritor se inspiró en la obra de Cervantes* the writer was inspired by Cervantes' works.

inspirómetro *m* MED inspirometer.

instabilidad *f* instability.

instable *adj* unstable.

instalación *f* installation, instalment (acción) || installation; *instalación frigorífica* refrigerator installation || plant (fábrica) || equipment (equipo) || laying; *instalación de la primera piedra* laying of the foundation stone || *instalación sanitaria* plumbing.

instalador *m* fitter.

instalar *vt* to install; *instalar la electricidad, el gas* to install electricity, gas || to fit out (proveer del equipo necesario) || to install, to settle; *han instalado a cien familias pobres en el barrio* they have installed a hundred poor families in the neighbourhood || to set up (tienda de campaña).
◆ *vpr* to settle, to install o.s.

instancia *f* request, petition (petición); *presentar una instancia* to present a request; *ceder a las instancias de uno* to give in to *o* to concede s.o.'s request || JUR instance; *tribunal de primera* *instancia* court of first instance || application form (solicitud) || — JUR *a instancia de* at the petition of || *a instancias de* at the request of || FIG *de primera instancia* first of all (en primer lugar) | *en última instancia* as a last resort || JUR *fallo en primera instancia* appealable judgment.

instantáneamente *adv* instantaneously.

instantaneidad *f* instantaneity.

instantáneo, a *adj* instantaneous || instant; *café instantáneo* instant coffee.
◆ *f* FOT snapshot, snap; *sacar instantáneas* to take snapshots.

instante *adj* insistent.
◆ *m* instant, moment; *en el mismo instante* in the same instant || — *a cada instante* all the time, constantly || *al instante* immediately, right away, at once || *dentro de un instante* in a moment, in an instant || *desde el instante en que...* from the moment that... *o* when... || *en este (mismo) instante* at this (very) moment || *por instantes* incessantly, all the time; *la multitud crecía por instantes* the crowd grew larger all the time || *por un instante te confundí con tu hermano* for an instant *o* for one moment I took you for your brother.

instar *vt* to urge, to press; *le instó a que se decidiese* he urged him to decide || (ant) to refute (impugnar).
◆ *vi* to be urgent *o* pressing; *insta que vayas a verla* it is urgent that you go to see her.

instauración *f* establishment.

instaurador, ra *adj* establishing.
◆ *m/f* establisher.

instaurar *vt* to establish, to set up (establecer).

instigación *f* instigation || *a instigación de* at *o* on the instigation of.

instigador, ra *adj* instigative, instigating.
◆ *m/f* instigator.

instigar *vt* to instigate, to incite (incitar).

instilar *vt* to instil [US to instill] (líquidos) || to instil [US to instill], to infuse; *instilar ideas en la mente de alguien* to instil ideas into s.o.'s head.

instintivo, va *adj* instinctive.

instinto *m* instinct; *hombre de malos instintos* man of evil instincts; *instinto de conservación* self-preservation instinct; *instinto materno* maternal instinct || urge, desire; *instinto sexual* sexual urge || *por instinto* by instinct, instinctively.

institución *f* institution, establishment (acción de instituir) || institution (organismo, entidad); *institución benéfica* charitable *o* welfare institution; *institución pública* public institution || — JUR *institución de heredero* appointment of an heir || FIG & FAM *Pedro es una institución en su pueblo* Peter is an institution in his town.
◆ *pl* institutions; *es un hombre que no respeta las instituciones* he is a man who does not respect institutions.

institucional *adj* institutional, institutionary.

institucionalización *f* institutionalization.

institucionalizar *vt* to institutionalize.

instituido, da *adj* instituted.

instituidor, ra *adj* founding.
◆ *m/f* institutor, founder.

instituir* *vt* to institute, to establish (entidad, principios, etc.) || to found, to institute (un premio) || to appoint; *instituir un heredero* to appoint an heir.

instituta *f pl* institutes [Roman civil law].

instituto *m* institute (institución); *instituto geográfico* geographical institute || grammar school [US high school], secondary school (de segunda enseñanza) || rule, principle (regla) || — *Instituto de Bachillerato* or *Enseñanza Media* State secondary school || *instituto de belleza* beauty salon, beauty parlour [US beauty parlor] || *Instituto de la Vivienda* housing office || *Instituto de Moneda Extranjera* foreign money exchange || *Instituto Laboral* technical school.

institutor, ra *adj* instituting, institutive, founding.
◆ *m/f* institutor, founder || AMER schoolmaster.

institutriz *f* governess.

instituyente *adj* instituting, institutive, founding.

instrucción *f* instruction (acción de instruir) || education; *instrucción primaria, pública* primary, public education || knowledge (ciencia) || MIL drill, training; *instrucción de las tropas* training of troops || JUR preliminary investigation || DEP training, coaching || INFORM instruction, order, command || *juez de instrucción* examining magistrate.
◆ *pl* instructions; *dar a uno instrucciones sobre algo* to give s.o. instructions on *o* about sth. || — *instrucciones para el uso* instructions, directions || *recibir instrucciones antes de llevar a cabo una misión* to be briefed before a mission.

instructivo, va *adj* instructive; *libro instructivo* instructive book || educational (película, viaje, etc.).

instructor, ra *adj* instructing || *juez instructor* examining magistrate.
◆ *m* instructor (en el cuartel).
◆ *m/f* DEP coach, trainer.

instruido, da *adj* educated, well-educated.

instruir* *vt* to educate, to teach (enseñar) || to instruct; *instruir a uno en el manejo de un arma* to instruct s.o. in the use of an arm || MIL to train, to drill || DEP to coach, to train || to inform; *me instruyó de* or *sobre lo ocurrido* he informed me of *o* about what had happened || JUR *instruir una causa* to investigate a case.
◆ *vpr* to teach o.s.

instrumentación *f* MÚS instrumentation, orchestration.

instrumental *adj* instrumental; *música instrumental* instrumental music || JUR documentary; *prueba instrumental* documentary evidence || *testigo instrumental* witness to a deed.
◆ *m* instruments *pl.*

instrumentalismo *m* instrumentalism.

instrumentar *vt* to orchestrate, to instrument || MED to lay out the instruments for an operation.

instrumentista *m/f* instrumentalist (músico) || instrument maker (fabricante) || operating theatre technician, nurse.

instrumento *m* instrument; *instrumento músico* musical instrument; *tocar un instrumento* to play an instrument || instrument, tool (herramienta); *instrumentos de precisión* precision instruments || instrument (documento) || FIG instrument, tool; *servir de instrumento a la venganza de uno* to serve as an instrument of s.o.'s revenge || — MÚS *instrumento de cuerda, de metal, de percusión, de viento* string, brass, percussion, wind instrument || AVIAC *instrumentos de mando* controls.

insubordinación *f* insubordination.

insubordinado, da *adj* insubordinate.
◆ *m* rebel.

insubordinar *vt* to stir up, to make unruly *o* rebellious, to incite to rebellion.
◆ *vpr* to become insubordinate, to rebel.

insubstancial; insustancial *adj* insubstantial || FIG empty, shallow, trite (conversación, etc.) | shallow, superficial (persona).

insubstancialidad; insustancialidad *f* insubstantiality || FIG emptiness, shallowness, triteness (de una conversación, etc.) | shallowness, superficiality (de una persona).

insubstancialmente *adv* insubstantially.

insubstituible *adj* irreplaceable.

insuficiencia *f* insufficiency, inadequacy, scarcity, shortage (escasez) || incompetency, inability, insufficiency (p us); *la insuficiencia de un empleado* the incompetency of an employee || MED insufficiency; *insuficiencia mitral* mitral insufficiency | failure; *insuficiencia cardiaca, renal* heart, kidney failure.

insuficiente *adj* insufficient, inadequate (escaso) || incompetent.

insuflación *f* insufflation.

insuflador *m* insufflator.

insuflar *vt* to insufflate.

insufrible *adj* insufferable, unbearable, intolerable (inaguantable).

ínsula *f* island (isla).

insular *adj* insular, island; *provincias insulares* island provinces || MED insular.
◆ *m/f* islander.

insularidad *f* insularity.

insulina *f* insulin.

Insulindia *n pr* GEOGR Indian Archipelago.

insulinoterapia *f* treatment by insulin.

insulsez *f* insipidity, tastelessness (falta de sabor) || FIG dullness, insipidness (falta de gracia) | insipid *o* flat remark (dicho sin gracia).

insulso, sa *adj* insipid, tasteless (comida, guiso, etc.) || FIG dull, insipid (conversación, tema).

insultador, ra *adj* insulting.
◆ *m/f* insulter.

insultante *adj* insulting, offensive.

insultar *vt* to insult.

insulto *m* insult.

insumergible *adj* insubmersible, insubmergible.

insumisión *f* insubordination.

insumiso, sa *adj* unsubmissive, insubordinate.

insumo *m* COM input.

insuperable *adj* unsurpassable (calidad, hazaña, trabajo, etc.) || insurmountable; *una dificultad insuperable* an insurmountable difficulty || *precios insuperables* unbeatable prices.

insurgente *adj* insurgent.
◆ *m/f* insurrectionist, insurgent, rebel.

insurrección *f* insurrection, revolt, rebellion.

insurreccional *adj* insurrectional, insurrectionary.

insurreccionar *vt* to incite to rebellion.
◆ *vpr* to rebel, to rise in revolt.

insurrecto, ta *adj* insurgent.
◆ *m/f* insurrectionist, insurgent, rebel.

insustancial *adj* → **insubstancial.**

insustancialidad *f* → **insubstancialidad.**

insustituible *adj* irreplaceable.

intacto, ta *adj* untouched (no tocado) || whole (entero) || intact, undamaged; *la casa salió intacta del bombardeo* the house remained undamaged after the bombing || FIG intact, undamaged (reputación, etc.) || *un tema que ha quedado intacto* a subject which has not been touched upon.

intachable *adj* irreproachable, blameless.

intangibilidad *f* intangibility.

intangible *adj* intangible.

integrable *adj* MAT integrable.

integración *f* integration || *integraciones bancarias* bank mergers.

integracionista *m/f* integrationist.

integrador, ra *adj* integrative.
◆ *m* integrator.

integral *adj* integral || — *cálculo integral* integral calculus || *pan integral* wholemeal bread.
◆ *f* MAT integral.

integralmente *adv* wholly, entirely, completely.

integrante *adj* integral, integrant.

integrar *vt* to compose, to make up; *varios estados integran la federación* several states make up the federation || to integrate; *integrar a los pobres en la sociedad* to integrate the poor into society || to complete, to make whole (completar) || to repay, to reimburse (reintegrar) || MAT to integrate || *AMER* to pay (pagar) || *la Asamblea General estará integrada por todos los miembros de la organización* the General Assembly shall be composed of all the members of the organization.

integridad *f* integrity || whole; *la integridad de su sueldo* the whole of his salary || integrity, uprightness (rectitud) || virginity (virginidad).

integrismo *m* late nineteenth century Spanish political party which advocated the preservation of national traditions.

íntegro, gra *adj* whole, entire, complete || FIG upright (honrado) || *en versión íntegra* in an unabridged version.

intelecto *m* intellect.

intelectual *adj/s* intellectual.

intelectualidad *f* intellectuality || intellectuals *pl*, intelligentsia.

intelectualismo *m* intellectualism.

intelectualista *adj* intellectualist, intellectualistic.
◆ *m/f* intellectualist.

intelectualizar *vt* to intellectualize.

inteligencia *f* intelligence; *dar pruebas de inteligencia* to show signs of intelligence || knowledge (conocimiento) || comprehension || — *en la inteligencia de que...* on the understanding that... || INFORM *inteligencia artificial* artificial intelligence || *los ladrones del expreso estaban en inteligencia con el guardafrenos* the robbers of the express were in league with the brakeman || *tener inteligencia para los negocios* to have a good head for business || *vivir en buena inteligencia con alguien* to live in harmony with s.o.

inteligenciado, da *adj* informed.

inteligente *adj* intelligent (dotado de inteligencia) || intelligent, clever (de mucha inteligencia); *un chico inteligente* a clever boy.
◆ *m/f* intelligent person.

inteligibilidad *f* intelligibility.

inteligible *adj* intelligible, understandable (comprensible) || audible.

intelligentsia *f* intelligentsia.

intemerata *f* FAM boldness (atrevimiento) || — FAM *formar la intemerata* to cause a rumpus | *saber la intemerata* to know a hell of a lot.

intemperancia *f* intemperance || immoderation; *el director no pudo soportar más las intemperancias de la actriz* the producer could no longer tolerate the immoderations of the actress.

intemperante *adj* intemperate, immoderate.

intemperie *f* inclemency (del tiempo) || — *dormir a la intemperie* to sleep out of doors *o* in the open || *estar a la intemperie* to be out in the open (estar fuera), to be at the mercy of the elements (sin protección de la lluvia, etc.).

intempestivamente *adv* inopportunely.

intempestivo, va *adj* inopportune, untimely.

intemporal *adj* intemporal.

intemporalidad *f* non-temporality.

intención *f* intention; *con la intención de* with the intention of || plan, intention (proyecto); *éstas son mis intenciones* these are my plans || will, testament; *las últimas intenciones del moribundo* the last testament of the dying man || JUR intent; *intención delictiva* criminal intent || MED intention; *cura de* or *por primera intención* healing by first intention || — *buena intención* good will, benevolence, good intention || *con intención* intentionally, on purpose, deliberately || MED *curar de primera intención a* to administer first aid to || *de intención* bad-tempered (animal) || *de primera intención* straightaway, right away || *mala intención* ill will, malevolence, ill intention || FIG *primera intención* frankness, candour; *obrar con primera intención* to act with frankness || *segunda intención* underhandedness, duplicity, deceitfulness || *tener (la) intención de* to intend to || *tener malas intenciones* to bear ill will, to be ill-intentioned || *tener una segunda intención* to have an ulterior motive.

intencionadamente *adv* intentionally, on purpose, deliberately.

intencionado, da *adj* intentioned, deliberate (intencional) || *bien intencionado* well-meaning, well-intentioned || *mal intencionado* ill-intentioned, malevolent.

intencional *adj* intentional, deliberate.

intencionalidad *f* intentionality.

intendencia *f* intendance, intendancy (funciones de intendente) || Service Corps [*US* Quartermaster Corps] (en el ejército).

intendenta *f* intendant's wife.

intendente *m* intendant (de un servicio administrativo del Estado) || MIL Quartermaster general.

intensidad *f* intensity || ELECTR strength || FÍS intensity.

intensificación *f* intensification.

intensificar *vt* to intensify.
◆ *vpr* to intensify, to strengthen (relaciones, etc.) || to intensify, to increase (comercio, etc.).

intensivista *m/f* intensive care specialist.

intensivo, va *adj* intensive; *curso intensivo* intensive course || GRAM intensive || AGR *cultivo intensivo* intensive cultivation *o* farming.

intenso, sa *adj* intense || acute (dolor) || ELECTR strong (light, current).

intentar *vt* to try, to attempt; *intentar salir de un mal paso* to try to get out of a tight spot || JUR to institute (proceedings) | to bring (an action) || *con intentarlo no se pierde nada* nothing is lost by trying.

intento *m* intent || intention (intención) || attempt; *al primer intento* at the first attempt || — *como de intento* as if intentionally || *de intento* intentionally, on purpose || *intento de suicidio* attempted suicide | *no pasar del intento* to fail in one's attempt || *tener intento de* to intend to.

intentona *f* FAM rash *o* foolhardy attempt.

interacción *f* interaction, interplay || INFORM interaction.

interactivo, va *adj* INFORM interactive.

interaliado, da *adj* interallied.

interamericano, na *adj* interamerican.

interandino, na *adj* interandean.

intercadencia *f* intercadence (del pulso).

intercadente *adj* intercadent (pulso).

intercalación *f* intercalation, insertion.

intercalar *adj* intercalary; *día intercalar* intercalary day.

intercalar *vt* to intercalate, to insert.

intercambiable *adj* interchangeable.

intercambiar *vt* to interchange, to exchange || to swap (trocar) || COM to exchange.

intercambio *m* exchange, interchange; *intercambio de cartas* exchange of letters || exchange; *intercambio cultural* cultural exchange || *intercambios comerciales* international trade *sing*.

interceder *vi* to intercede; *interceder con* or *cerca de alguien por otro* to intercede with s.o. on behalf of another.

intercelular *adj* intercellular.

intercepción *f* interception.

interceptación *f* interception || blockage (del tráfico, de la carretera, etc.).

interceptador *m* interceptor (avión).

interceptar *vt* to intercept || to block; *carretera interceptada* blocked road || to hold up, to block, to interrupt (la circulación); *continúa interceptada la circulación* the traffic is still held up.

intercesión *f* intercession.

intercesor, ra *adj* intercessory, interceding.
◆ *m/f* intercessor.

intercesoriamente *adv* intercessorily, by intercession.

intercolumnio; intercolunio *m* ARQ intercolumniation.

intercomunicación *f* intercommunication.

intercomunicador *m* intercommunication system, intercom (*fam*).

intercomunicarse *vpr* to intercommunicate.

interconectar *vt* ELECTR to interconnect || INFORM to interconnect, to hook up (to).

interconexión *f* interconnection.

intercontinental *adj* intercontinental.

intercostal *adj* ANAT intercostal; *músculos intercostales* intercostal muscles.

interdecir *vt* to prohibit, to forbid.

interdental *adj* interdental.

interdepartamental *adj* interdepartmental.

interdependencia *f* interdependence.

interdependiente *adj* interdependent.

interdicción *f* interdiction, prohibition || — JUR *interdicción civil* judicial restraint, civil interdiction (por locura o imbecilidad), suspension of civil rights (pena accesoria) || *interdicción de residencia* or *de lugar* prohibition from entering a specified area.

interdicto *m* interdiction, prohibition || REL interdict.

interdigital *adj* interdigital (músculo, membrana, espacio).

interés *m* interest; *este libro no tiene interés alguno* this book has no interest whatsoever; *en interés de* in the interest of || self-interest; *dejarse guiar por el interés* to allow o.s. to be guided by self-interest || FIG interest (inclinación); *despertar el interés de alguien* to arouse s.o.'s interest || COM interest (rédito); *interés compuesto, simple* compound, simple interest; *colocar dinero a interés* to invest money at interest; *un interés del diez por ciento* or *de un diez por ciento* a ten per cent interest, an interest of ten per cent || — COM *interés interbancario* interbank deposit rate || *merecer interés* to be interesting || *mostrar interés en* or *por* to show an interest in || *poner interés en* to take an interest in || *prestar con interés* to lend at interest || *prestar especial interés a* to show special interest in || *ser de gran interés* to be of great interest, to be very in-

teresting ‖ *tener interés en* or *por* to be interested in (interesarse), to be anxious for *o* that (desear); *tengo interés en que vengan* I am anxious for them to come *o* that they should come; to be in one's interest; *tienes interés en llevarte bien con el director* it is in your interest to keep on the right side of the manager ‖ *tomarse interés por algo, por uno* to take an interest in sth., in s.o. ‖ *un tema de interés* a topic of interest.
◆ *pl* COM interests (capital invertido en una industria) | interests (propiedades, bienes de fortuna) ‖ COM *intereses creados* vested interests | *devengar intereses* to bear interest | *tener intereses en* to hold shares in.

interesado, da *adj* interested; *interesado en un negocio* interested in a business ‖ biassed, prejudiced (parcial) ‖ selfish, self-interested (egoísta) ‖ *obrar de una manera interesada* to act out of self-interest.
◆ *m/f* interested (person); *los interesados se servirán pasar por nuestras oficinas* those (persons) interested please call in at our offices ‖ applicant (en una solicitud) ‖ *los interesados* those concerned, those interested.

interesante *adj* interesting ‖ *hacerse el interesante* to try to attract attention.

interesar *vt* to interest; *interesar a uno en una empresa* to interest s.o. in an enterprise ‖ to concern, to be of interest to; *es un caso que nos interesa a todos* it's a case which concerns us all ‖ MED to affect ‖ to take into, to give an interest in; *interesar a uno en un negocio* to take s.o. into a business ‖ — *este libro me interesa mucho* this book interests me a great deal ‖ *¿le interesa el deporte?* are you interested in sport?
◆ *vi* to be of interest; *interesa saber si...* it is of interest to know whether... ‖ *mi propuesta no interesó* no one was interested in *o* by my proposal, my proposal interested no one.
◆ *vpr* to be interested, to take an interest; *interesarse por* or *en* to be interested *o* to take a interest in.

interestelar *adj* interstellar.

interface *m*; **interfaz** *f* INFORM interface.

interfecto, ta *adj* JUR murdered.
◆ *m/f* JUR murder victim ‖ FAM person in question.

interferencia *f* FÍS interference (en radio, televisión); *franjas de interferencia* interference fringes *o* rings | jamming (para impedir la escucha, etc.) ‖ FIG interference, intervention.

interferir* *vi* to interfere (*en, con* in, with).
◆ *vt* RAD to interfere with; *interferir una emisión* to interfere with a broadcast | to jam (para impedir la escucha, etc.).

interfono *m* intercom (en oficinas, etc.).

interglacial *adj* interglacial.

intergubernamental *adj* intergovernmental.

ínterin *m* interim, meantime; *en el ínterin* in the meantime.
◆ *adv* meanwhile, in the meantime (mientras tanto) ‖ *por ínterin* temporarily.

interinamente *adv* meanwhile, in the meantime, in the interim (mientras tanto) ‖ temporarily (temporalmente).

interinar *vt* to occupy temporarily (un cargo) ‖ *interinar el cargo de presidente* to be acting president *o* acting chairman.

interinato *m* AMER interim (tiempo) ‖ temporary post (cargo).

interinidad *f* temporariness ‖ temporary employment.

interino, na *adj* interim ‖ provisional, interim, temporary (provisional); *una solución interina* a provisional solution ‖ acting; *presidente interino* acting president *o* chairman.
◆ *m/f* person who executes a duty in the absence of another ‖ acting president, acting chairman (presidente) ‖ deputy, stand-in (sustituto).
◆ *f* charwoman (asistenta).

interior *adj* interior, inside; *patio interior* inside patio ‖ inner (más cerca del centro); *la parte interior de una rueda* the inner part of a wheel ‖ inner (pensamientos) ‖ domestic, internal; *política interior* domestic policy ‖ GEOGR inland ‖ — *en la parte interior* on the inside, inside ‖ *ropa interior* underclothing, underclothes *pl*.
◆ *m* inside, interior ‖ GEOGR interior ‖ DEP inside forward (fútbol) ‖ local (en un sobre) ‖ — *dijo para su interior* he said to himself ‖ DEP *interior derecha* inside right | *interior izquierda* inside left.
◆ *pl* insides, entrails (entrañas) ‖ AMER underpants, briefs (calzoncillos).

interioridad *f* interiority, inwardness.
◆ *pl* personal affairs; *meterse en las interioridades de los demás* to interfere in other people's personal affairs ‖ FIG interior *o* inside aspects (de un asunto, etc.) | ins and outs (pormenores).

interiormente *adv* inwardly, inside.

interjección *f* GRAM interjection.

interjectivo, va *adj* interjectional.

interlínea *f* space between lines (espacio) ‖ IMPR lead (regleta).

interlineación *f*; **interlineado** *m* interlineation, interlining.

interlineal *adj* interlinear.

interlinear *vt* to interline.

interlocución *f* interlocution (conversación).

interlocutor, ra *m/f* interlocutor ‖ *su interlocutor* the person he was speaking to (persona a quien se habla), the person who spoke to him (persona que habla a otra) ‖ ECON *interlocutores sociales* unions and management.

interlocutorio, ria *adj* JUR interlocutory; *formar auto interlocutorio* to award an interlocutory decree.

intérlope *adj* interloping (fraudulento).

interludio *m* interlude.

intermaxilar *adj* ANAT intermaxillary.

intermediar *vi* to intermediate, to mediate.

intermediario, ria *adj* intermediary.
◆ *m/f* mediator, intermediary, go-between ‖ COM middleman ‖ *intermediario financiero* (stock) jobber.

intermedio, dia *adj* intermediate, medium ‖ intervening; *los años intermedios* the intervening years ‖ *precio intermedio* moderate price.
◆ *m* interval (intervalo) ‖ recess (Parlamento) ‖ interlude (televisión) ‖ intermission (cine) ‖ interval (teatro) ‖ — *en el intermedio* in the meantime ‖ *por intermedio de* through, by means of.

intermezzo *m* MÚS intermezzo.

interminable *adj* interminable, endless.

interministerial *adj* interministerial; *reunión interministerial* interministerial meeting.

intermisión *f* intermission.

intermitencia *f* intermittence, intermittency ‖ — *con* or *por intermitencia* intermittently ‖ MED *intermitencia de la fiebre* intermittence of fever.

intermitente *adj* intermittent; *luz intermitente* intermittent light.
◆ *m* AUT indicator, blinker, winker.

intermolecular *adj* intermolecular.

intermuscular *adj* intermuscular.

internación *f* internment (en una cárcel) ‖ confinement (en un hospital) ‖ penetration (en un país).

internacional *adj* international.
◆ *m/f* international (deportista).
◆ *f* international (asociación) ‖ internationale (himno).

internacionalidad *f* internationality.

internacionalismo *m* internationalism.

internacionalista *adj/s* internationalist.

internacionalización *f* internationalization.

internacionalizar *vt* to internationalize.

internado, da *adj* interned; *los prisioneros internados en el campo de concentración* prisoners interned in the concentration camp ‖ confined (en un hospital) ‖ *los ancianos internados en el asilo* the old people in the home.
◆ *m* boarding school (colegio) ‖ boarders *pl* [living in a boarding school] ‖ MIL internee.
◆ *f* DEP breakthrough.

internamente *adv* internally, inside.

internamiento *m* internment.

internar *vt* to intern (un prisionero) ‖ to commit (*en* to) (en un manicomio) ‖ to confine (en un hospital) ‖ to put in a home (a un anciano).
◆ *vpr* to penetrate (por la fuerza); *los moros se internaron en España* the Moors penetrated into Spain ‖ FIG to go deeply (*en* into) (profundizar) | to intrude (en la intimidad de uno) ‖ DEP to break through; *el extremo se internó por la izquierda* the winger broke through on the left | *internarse en* to go into the interior of (un país), to go into (un bosque).

internista *adj* *médico internista* internist.
◆ *m/f* internist.

interno, na *adj* internal, interior ‖ domestic, internal (del país) ‖ boarding (estudiante) ‖ *por vía interna* internally.
◆ *m/f* intern (de un hospital) ‖ boarder, boarding student (en un colegio) ‖ *poner* or *meter a un niño interno* to put *o* to place a child in a boarding school.

inter nos *loc adv lat* FAM between ourselves, between you and me.

internuncio *m* REL internuncio ‖ interlocutor ‖ spokesman (portavoz).

interoceánico, ca *adj* interoceanic.

interoceptivo, va *adj* MED interoceptive.

interpaginar *vt* to interpage.

interparietal *adj* ANAT interparietal.

interparlamentario, ria *adj* interparliamentary.

interpelación *f* interpellation ‖ appeal, plea (ruego).

interpelador, ra; interpelante *adj* interpellant.
◆ *m/f* interpellator, interpellant.

interpelar *vt* to interpellate (en el Parlamento) ‖ to appeal to, to implore, to beseech (rogar).

interpenetración *f* interpenetration.

interplanetario, ria *adj* interplanetary.

interpolación *f* interpolation.

interpolador, ra *adj* interpolating.
◆ *m/f* interpolator.

interpolar *vt* to interpolate (intercalar).

interponer* *vt* to interpose ‖ JUR *interponer recurso de apelación* to give notice of appeal.
◆ *vpr* to intervene.

interposición *f* interposition ‖ intervention ‖ JUR lodging of an appeal.

interpósita persona (por) *loc adv* by an intermediary.

interpretable *adj* interpretable.

interpretación *f* interpretation ‖ interpreting (profesión) ‖ MÚS & TEATR performance, interpretation ‖ *mala interpretación* misinterpretation.

interpretador, ra *adj* interpreting.
◆ *m/f* interpreter.

interpretar *vtr* to interpret ‖ to sing, to perform (una canción) ‖ TEATR to play, to act, to interpret (un papel) | to perform (una obra) ‖ to perform, to interpret (una obra de música).

interpretariado *m* interpreting.

interpretativo, va *adj* interpretative.

intérprete *m/f* interpreter; *intérprete de conferencia* conference interpreter; *intérprete jurado* sworn interpreter ‖ exponent, interpreter (de música) ‖ performer, artist (de una obra de teatro) ‖ singer (de una canción).

interprofesional *adj* interprofessional.

interpuesto, ta *adj* interposed.

interregno *m* interregnum.

interrogación *f* question, interrogation (pregunta) ‖ questioning, interrogation (acción de preguntar) ‖ GRAM *signo de interrogación* question *o* interrogation mark.

interrogador, ra *adj* interrogating ‖ inquisitive; *una mirada interrogadora* an inquisitive look.
◆ *m/f* interrogator, questioner.

interrogante *adj* interrogating, questioning ‖ *punto interrogante* question *o* interrogation mark.
◆ *m* question (pregunta) ‖ FIG question mark; *quedan muchos interrogantes todavía* there are still a lot of question marks.

interrogar *vt* to interrogate, to question; *interrogar a alguien acerca de* to interrogate s.o. about; *interrogaron al testigo* they interrogated the witness.

interrogativo, va *adj* interrogative.

interrogatorio *m* interrogation.

interrumpir *vt* to interrupt; *interrumpir a uno con una pregunta* to interrupt s.o. with a question ‖ to block, to obstruct, to interrupt; *el coche averiado interrumpía el tráfico* the broken-down car blocked the traffic ‖ to stop temporarily (parar provisionalmente) ‖ to cut off (el abastecimiento, etc.); *interrumpieron la corriente para reparar la avería* they cut off the current in order to repair the fault ‖ to cut short, to interrupt, to curtail; *tuvieron que interrumpir sus vacaciones* they had to cut their holiday short.

interrupción *f* interruption; *sin interrupción* without interruption ‖ interruption, break (para descansar).

interruptor, ra *adj* interrupting.
◆ *m* ELECTR switch ‖ *interruptor eléctrico automático* automatic time switch ‖ *interruptor general* main switch.

intersecarse *vpr* to intersect.

intersección *f* intersection.

intersexual *adj* intersexual.

intersideral *adj* ASTR interstellar.

intersindical *adj* inter-trade-union.

intersticial *adj* interstitial; *tejido intersticial* interstitial tissue.

intersticio *m* interstice (espacio) ‖ interval (intervalo).

intertrigo *m* MED intertrigo.

intertropical *adj* intertropical.

interurbano, na *adj* interurban ‖ — *central interurbana, teléfono interurbano* interurban telephone exchange ‖ *poner una conferencia interurbana* to make a long distance call *o* a trunk call.

intervalo *m* interval (tiempo) ‖ gap (espacio) ‖ MÚS interval ‖ *a intervalos* at intervals.

intervención *f* intervention ‖ tapping (del teléfono) ‖ auditing, audit (de cuentas) ‖ participation (en una conversación) ‖ control (de los precios) ‖ — MED *intervención quirúrgica* operation ‖ *política de no intervención* nonintervention policy.

intervencionismo *m* interventionism.

intervencionista *adj* interventionist.
◆ *m/f* interventionist.

intervenir* *vi* to intervene; *el ejército intervino en la batalla* the army intervened in the battle ‖ to intervene, to intercede (interceder) ‖ to interfere (entrometerse); *intervenir en un asunto familiar* to interfere in a family matter ‖ to participate, to take part (tomar parte); *¿en cuántas películas has intervenido?* in how many films have you taken part? ‖ to happen, to occur (acontecer).
◆ *vt* to control (precios) ‖ to audit (cuentas) ‖ to tap (teléfono) ‖ MED to operate on, to perform an operation on.

interventor *m* supervisor, inspector (inspector) ‖ controller (verificador) ‖ *interventor de cuentas* auditor.

intervertebral *adj* MED intervertebral.

interviú *f* interview ‖ *hacer una interviú a uno* to interview s.o.

interviuvar *vt* to interview (entrevistar).

interyacente *adj* interjacent.

intestado, da *adj/s* intestate.

intestinal *adj* intestinal; *lombrices intestinales* intestinal worms.

intestino, na *adj* internal, intestine; *luchas intestinas* internal conflicts.
◆ *m* ANAT intestine ‖ — ANAT *intestino ciego* caecum | *intestino delgado* small intestine | *intestino grueso* large intestine.

intimación *f* notification (mandato) ‖ JUR *intimación judicial* judicial notice.

intimar *vt* to notify, to summon; *le intiman a que pague la multa* they notify him to pay the fine ‖ to order (mandar).
◆ *vi* to become intimate *o* very friendly; *intimar con uno* to become intimate with s.o.

intimatorio, ria *adj* intimating, notifying.

intimidación *f* intimidation.

intimidad *f* intimacy (con alguien) ‖ privacy, private life (vida privada) ‖ — *en la intimidad* privately, in private ‖ *una persona de su intimidad* one of his circle.

intimidar *vt* to intimidate; *intimidar a uno con amenazas* to intimidate s.o. with threats ‖ to scare (asustar).

intimista *adj/s* intimist.

íntimo, ma *adj* intimate ‖ private (vida, boda, etc.) ‖ close, intimate (amistad, relaciones) ‖ innermost (pensamientos).
◆ *m* close friend, bosom friend; *un íntimo de la casa* a close friend of the family.

intitular *vt* to entitle.
◆ *vpr* to be entitled.

intocable *adj/s* untouchable.

intolerable *adj* intolerable.

intolerancia *f* intolerance.

intolerante *adj/s* intolerant.

intonso, sa *adj* with uncut hair, long-haired ‖ uncut (libro) ‖ FIG ignorant.

intoxicación *f* intoxication, poisoning ‖ food poisoning (debida a la comida).

intoxicado, da *adj* intoxicated, poisoned (envenenado) ‖ intoxicated, drunk (borracho).
◆ *m/f* intoxicated person.

intoxicar *vt* to intoxicate, to poison (envenenar).
◆ *vpr* to be intoxicated *o* poisoned.

intracelular *adj* intracellular.

intradérmico, ca *adj* intradermic.

intradermorreacción *f* MED intradermal reaction.

intradós *m* ARQ intrados.

intraducible *adj* untranslatable.

intramuros *adv* within the city, intramurally.

intramuscular *adj* intramuscular; *inyección intramuscular* intramuscular injection.

intranquilidad *f* restlessness, uneasiness, worry.

intranquilizador, ra *adj* disquieting, worrying.

intranquilizar *vt* to disquiet, to worry.

intranquilo, la *adj* restless, uneasy, worried.

intranscendencia *f* insignificance, unimportance.

intranscendente *adj* insignificant, unimportant.

intransferible *adj* untransferable, not transferable, nontransferable.

intransigencia *f* intransigence.

intransigente *adj* intransigent, uncompromising.

intransitable *adj* impassable.

intransitivo, va *adj/sm* GRAM intransitive.

intransmisible *adj* intransmissible.

intransportable *adj* not transportable, untransportable.

intranuclear *adj* intranuclear.

intrascendencia *adj* insignificance, unimportance.

intrascendente *adj* insignificant, unimportant.

intrasmisible *adj* intransmissible.

intratable *adj* intractable, unmanageable (difícil de tratar) ‖ unsociable (poco sociable).

intrauterino, na *adj* MED intrauterine.

intravenoso, sa *adj* intravenous; *inyección intravenosa* intravenous injection.

intrepidez *f* intrepidity, boldness, daring, fearlessness.

intrépido, da *adj* intrepid, bold, daring, fearless.

intriga *f* intrigue; *intrigas palaciegas* court intrigues ‖ *tramar* or *urdir intrigas* to plot, to intrigue, to scheme.

intrigante *adj* intriguing.
◆ *m* intriguer, intrigant.
◆ *f* intriguer, intrigante.

intrigar *vi* to intrigue, to plot, to scheme.
◆ *vt* to intrigue, to puzzle (dejar perplejo); *su conducta me intriga* his conduct intrigues me ‖ to intrigue, to fascinate (suscitar interés).

intrincación *f* intricacy.

intrincado, da *adj* intricate, involved, complicated (problema, asunto) ‖ dense (bosque).

intrincamiento *m* intricacy.

intrincar *vt* to complicate, to confuse.

intríngulis *m inv* FAM ulterior *o* hidden motive (razón oculta) | snag, difficulty; *ahí está el intríngulis* there's the snag | enigma, mystery; *el intríngulis de un asunto* the enigma of a matter.

intrínseco, ca *adj* intrinsic, intrinsical.

introducción *f* introduction.

introducir* *vt* to insert, to introduce; *introducir el dedo en un agujero* to insert one's finger into a hole ‖ to introduce; *introducir a uno en la*

alta sociedad to introduce s.o. into high society ‖ to introduce, to bring in; *introducir una nueva moda* to introduce a new fashion ‖ to show into; *la criada nos introdujo en el salón* the maid showed us into the living room ‖ to cause, to create, to bring on (provocar); *introducir el desorden, la discordia* to bring on disorder, discord.
◆ *vpr* to get into (meterse) ‖ to interfere (entremeterse).

introductor, ra *adj* introductory.
◆ *m introductor de embajadores* head of the Protocol Section of the Foreign Affairs department.

introductorio, ria *adj* introductory, introductive.

introito *m* REL introit (oración) ‖ prologue (principio, prólogo).

intromisión *f* meddling, interfering (entrometimiento) ‖ JUR intromission.

introspección *f* introspection.

introspectivo, va *adj* introspective.

introversión *f* introversion.

introverso, sa *adj* introversive.

introvertido, da *adj* introverted, introvert.
◆ *m/f* introvert.

intrusión *f* intrusion.

intruso, sa *adj* intrusive, intruding.
◆ *m/f* intruder.

intubación *f* MED intubation.

intubar *vt* MED to intubate.

intuición *f* intuition.

intuicionismo *m* intuitionism.

intuir* *vt* to sense; *avanza hacia el pueblo que intuye cercano* he moves towards the town which he senses to be near ‖ to feel; *se intuye la palpitación del campo en su poesía* one feels the palpitation of the country in his poetry ‖ to have a sense of, to have a feeling for; *este niño intuye la música* this child has a feeling for music ‖ to intuit; *intuir el porvenir* to intuit the future.

intuitivo, va *adj* intuitive.

intumescencia *f* intumescence, swelling.

intumescente *adj* intumescent.

inundación *f* inundation, flooding (acción) ‖ flood (efecto) ‖ FIG flood.

inundar *vt* to flood ‖ FIG to flood, to swamp, to inundate; *inundar el mercado de productos extranjeros* to flood the market with foreign products.

inurbano, na *adj* inurbane, discourteous.

inusitado, da *adj* unusual, uncommon.

inútil *adj* useless (inservible); *¿por qué guardas tantas cosas inútiles?* why do you keep so many useless things? ‖ unnecessary, needless; *es inútil decirlo* it's unnecessary to say it ‖ vain, fruitless (esfuerzo) ‖ unfit; *inútil para el servicio militar* unfit for military service ‖ good-for-nothing (incapaz) ‖ *es inútil que grites* it's no good your shouting, it's useless for you to shout.
◆ *m/f* FAM *un, una inútil* a good-for-nothing.

inutilidad *f* uselessness, unusefulness ‖ incompetence (de una persona) ‖ fruitlessness (de unos esfuerzos).

inutilizar *vt* to make unusable, to put out of action; *el niño ha inutilizado la máquina de escribir* the child has made the typewriter unusable ‖ to disable, to put out of action; *los aviones inutilizaron uno de los barcos* the planes disabled one of the ships ‖ to cancel (sello) ‖ to spoil, to ruin (estropear, echar a perder).

invadir *vt* to invade ‖ FIG to encroach upon (los derechos ajenos) ‖ to overcome; *le invadió una gran tristeza* he was overcome by deep sadness.

invaginación *f* MED invagination.

invaginar *vt* MED to invaginate.

invalidable *adj* that may be invalidated.

invalidación *f* invalidation.

invalidar *vt* to invalidate ‖ JUR to invalidate, to nullify, to annul (anular).

invalidez *f* invalidity ‖ *invalidez permanente* permanent disability.

inválido, da *adj* MED invalid, disabled ‖ JUR invalid, void, null.
◆ *m/f* MED invalid ‖ MIL disabled soldier.

invar *m* invar (metal).

invariabilidad *f* invariability.

invariable *adj* invariable.

invariadamente *adv* invariably.

invariado, da *adj* unvaried, unchanged.

invasión *f* invasion.

invasor, ra *adj* invading.
◆ *m* invader.

invectiva *f* invective; *fulminar invectivas contra uno* to thunder invectives against s.o. ‖ *lanzar invectivas contra* to inveigh against.

invencibilidad *f* invincibility.

invencible *adj* invincible ‖ unsurmountable (obstáculos) ‖ *la Armada Invencible* the Spanish Armada.

invención *f* invention ‖ — *de su propia invención* of his own invention ‖ REL *la invención de la Santa Cruz* the finding of the true Cross ‖ *patente de invención* patent.

invendible *adj* unsalable, unmarketable, unsellable.

invendido, da *adj* unsold.

inventar *vt* to invent ‖ to make up (mentiras, etc.) ‖ to invent, to think up (imaginar).

inventariar *vt* to inventory, to make an inventory of, to take stock of.

inventario *m* inventory; *hacer un inventario* to make an inventory ‖ inventory, stocktaking (acción).

inventivo, va *adj* inventive, creative (capaz de crear) ‖ resourceful (ingenioso).
◆ *f* inventiveness, creativeness (capacidad para crear) ‖ resourcefulness (ingeniosidad).

invento *m* invention.

inventor, ra *m/f* inventor.

invernación *f* hibernation.
— OBSERV This word is a barbarism used for *hibernación*.

invernáculo *m* greenhouse, hothouse.

invernada *f* wintertime, winter (invierno) ‖ AMER winter pasture.

invernadero *m* greenhouse, hothouse (para las plantas) ‖ winter quarters *pl* (refugio de invierno) ‖ winter pasture (pasto).

invernal *adj* wintry, wintery.
◆ *m* winter shed, winter stable.

invernar* *vi* to winter, to hibernate (pasar al invierno) ‖ ZOOL to hibernate.

inverosímil *adj* improbable, unlikely, implausible; *un relato inverosímil* an improbable story.

inverosimilitud *f* improbability, unlikelihood.

inversión *f* inversion ‖ COM investment.

inversionista *m* COM investor.

inverso, sa *adj* inverted; *la imagen inversa de un objeto* the inverted image of an object ‖ inverse, reverse; *en orden inverso* in inverse order ‖ opposite; *venía en sentido inverso* he was coming in the opposite direction ‖ — *a* or *por la inversa* the other way round (inversamente), on the contrary (al contrario) ‖ *a la inversa de* unlike (a diferencia de) ‖ *y a la inversa* and vice versa.

inversor *m* FÍS reversing device.

invertebrado, da *adj/sm* ZOOL invertebrate.
◆ *pl* invertebrata.

invertido, da *adj* inverted, reversed ‖ *azúcar invertido* invert sugar.
◆ *m/f* homosexual, invert.

invertir* *vt* to invert, to change, to reverse (cambiar); *invertir los papeles* to change roles ‖ to put upside down, to put the other way round (poner al revés) ‖ to invert (sistemáticamente); *invertir la imagen de un objeto* to invert the image of an object ‖ to reverse; *invertir el sentido de una corriente* to reverse the direction of a current ‖ to spend; *invirtieron 30 minutos en el recorrido* they spent 30 minutes on the journey ‖ COM to invest (capitales) ‖ MAT to invert.

investidura *f* investiture.

investigación *f* investigation, inquiry (policíaca, fiscal) ‖ research; *investigación científica* scientific research ‖ — *Consejo Superior de Investigaciones Científicas* Council for Scientific Research ‖ *investigación de mercados* market research, marketing ‖ *investigación de la paternidad* affiliation suit.

investigador, ra *adj* investigating ‖ inquiring, inquisitive; *mirada investigadora* inquiring look.
◆ *m/f* investigator ‖ researcher, research worker (científico).

investigar *vi* to investigate (la policía, etc.) ‖ to do research (científicos).
◆ *vt* to investigate, to inquire into, to look into; *investigar los móviles de un crimen* to inquire into the causes of a crime ‖ to find out; *tengo que investigar quién ha dicho esto* I have to find out who said this ‖ to do research on (los científicos).

investir* *vt* to invest (conferir una dignidad).

inveterado, da *adj* inveterate.

invicto, ta *adj* unconquered, unbeaten.

invierno *m* winter (estación); *en lo más crudo del invierno* in the dead of winter ‖ winter, wintertime (período) ‖ AMER rainy season (en las regiones ecuatoriales).

inviolabilidad *f* inviolability ‖ *inviolabilidad parlamentaria* parliamentary privilege.

inviolable *adj* inviolable.

inviolado, da *adj* inviolate.

invisibilidad *f* invisibility.

invisible *adj* invisible.

invitación *f* invitation.

invitado, da *adj* invited.
◆ *m/f* guest; *mañana tenemos invitados* we are expecting guests tomorrow.

invitante *adj* inviting.
◆ *m/f* host (hombre), hostess (mujer).

invitar *vt* to invite; *invitar a uno a una cena* to invite s.o. to dinner ‖ to call on; *invitar a alguien a hablar* to call on s.o. to speak ‖ FIG to tempt, to invite (impulsar) ‖ — *el tiempo invita a ir de excursión* it is tempting *o* inviting weather to go on an excursion ‖ *invitar a una copa* to buy a drink, to stand a drink.

invitatorio *m* REL invitatory.

invocación *f* invocation.

invocador, ra *adj* invoking.
◆ *m/f* invoker.

invocar *vt* to invoke (a Dios, etc.) ‖ to invoke, to beg for; *invocar la piedad de* to invoke the mercy of, to beg for mercy ‖ to invoke, to refer to (alegar).

invocatorio, ria *adj* invocatory.

involución *f* involution.

involucrado, da *adj* involucrate.

involucrar *vt* to introduce, to bring in (introducir) || to involve (entrañar, implicar).

involuntario, ria *adj* involuntary || unintentional (no intencionado).

involuta *f* MAT involute.

invulnerabilidad *f* invulnerability.

invulnerable *adj* invulnerable.

inyección *f* injection; *poner una inyección a* to give an injection to || injection; *motor de inyección* injection engine.

inyectable *adj* injectable.
◆ *m* injectable substance, injection.

inyectado, da *adj* injected || *ojos inyectados en sangre* bloodshot eyes.

inyectar *vt* to inject; *inyectar agua* to inject water; *inyectar algo a alguien* to inject s.o. with sth.

inyector *m* injector || TECN *inyector de aire* jet blower (de alto horno).

ion *m* FÍS & QUÍM ion.

iónico, ca *adj* FÍS & QUÍM ionic.

ionización *f* FÍS & QUÍM ionization.

ionizar, ionizarse *v tr y pr* FÍS & QUÍM to ionize.

ionosfera *f* ionosphere.

iontoforesis *f inv* MED iontophoresis.

iota *f* iota (letra griega).

ipecacuana *f* BOT ipecac, ipecacuanha.

iperita *f* yperite, mustard gas (gas).

ípsilon *f* upsilon (letra griega).

ipso facto *loc lat* ipso facto (por ese mismo hecho) || immediately (en el acto).

ir*

> **1.** SENTIDOS GENERALES DEL VERBO INTRANSITIVO **2.** IR, CON EL GERUNDIO **3.** IR, CON EL PARTICIPIO PASIVO **4.** IR, SEGUIDO DE PREPOSICIONES **5.** LOCUCIONES **6.** VERBO PRONOMINAL.

1. SENTIDOS GENERALES to go; *ir al campo* to go to the country; *el tren va de Madrid a Barcelona* the train goes from Madrid to Barcelona; *esta calle va del bulevar a la avenida* this street goes from the boulevard to the avenue; *vaya donde vaya no se escapará* he will not escape, wherever he goes *o* go where he may || to be becoming, to suit; *no te va muy bien este sombrero* this hat does not suit you very well *o* is not very becoming || to fit (por el tamaño) || to be coming along, to get along *o* on; *¿cómo te va en el nuevo trabajo?* how is your new job coming along?, how are you getting on in your new job? || to be; *no sabe por dónde va en su trabajo* he does not know where he is with his work || to be, to be getting along; *¿cómo va el enfermo hoy?* how is the patient (getting along) today? || to be; *va bien vestido* he is well dressed || to bet (apostar); *¿cuánto va a que yo llego primero?* how much do you bet that I arrive first? || to go, to lead (en juegos de cartas)
2. IR, CON EL GERUNDIO (indicates that the action is being realized or is just beginning); *vamos andando* we are walking; *su salud iba empeorando* his health was deteriorating; *va haciendo calor* it's getting hotter; *iba anocheciendo* it was beginning to get dark || *¡vamos andando!* let's walk!
3. IR, CON EL PARTICIPIO PASIVO (indicates the result of an action); *van escritas siete cartas* I have written seven letters, seven letters have been written; *ya van vendidos diez cuadros* ten paintings have already been sold.
4. IR, SEGUIDO DE PREPOSICIONES *ir a* to go to; *voy a Madrid* I am going to Madrid; *voy al médico* I am going to the doctor's; *voy a hacerlo mañana* I'm going to do it tomorrow; to be about to, to be just going to (estar a punto de); *iba a decir lo mismo* I was about to say the same thing || — *ir a caballo* to ride || *ir a dar a* to end at, to lead to; *camino que va a dar a la carretera* road that ends at the highway || *ir a la ruina* to go to wrack and ruin || *ir a parar* to get at; *¿dónde quiere usted ir a parar?* what are you getting at?; to get to, to be; *¿dónde ha ido a parar este libro?* where is that book?, where has that book got to?; to end up, to land up; *el hombre fue a parar a la cárcel* the man ended up in jail || *ir a lo suyo* to go one's own way (ser independiente), to take care of one's own interests, to look after number one (preocuparse por uno mismo) || *ir a pie* to walk, to go on foot || FIG *no irle a uno a la zaga* to be every bit as good a s.o. | *no ir a la zaga* not to be left behind, not to be outdone | *si vamos a eso* for that matter || — *ir con* to go with; *ir con su madre al cine* to go to the cinema with one's mother; *el azul va bien con el blanco* blue goes well with white; to be; *ir con cuidado, con miedo* to be careful, afraid || — *ir contra* to go against; *va contra sus principios, su dignidad* it goes against his principles, his dignity || — *ir de* to go for; *ir de paseo* to go for a walk; to go on; *ir de viaje* to go on a trip; to go; *ir de caza, de pesca* to go hunting, fishing; *ir de compras* to go shopping; *ir de juerga* to go and have a good time [US to go have a blast]; to be (dressed) in, to be wearing; *ir de uniforme* to be in uniform || — *esto va de veras* this is serious, this is no joke || *ir del brazo* to go arm in arm || *las noticias iban de boca en boca* the news spread *o* went from mouth to mouth || — *ir en* to go by (viajar); *ir en coche, en avión, en tren* to go by car, by plane, by train; to be at stake (estar en el juego); *en eso le va la salud* his health is at stake here; *te va en ello el honor* your honour is at stake || — *ir en bicicleta* to cycle || *¿qué le va en ello?* what does it matter to you? || *va mucho en ello* a lot is at stake, a lot depends on it || — *ir para* to be almost, to be getting on for, to be pushing (*fam*); *va para doce años* he is almost twelve years old; *va para los cincuenta* he's getting on for fifty, he's pushing fifty || — *ir para largo* to drag on || *ir para viejo* to be getting old || *va para médico* he's going to be a doctor || — *ir por* to go for, to go and fetch; *ir por vino a la bodega* to go to the cellar for wine; *ir por el médico* to go for the doctor; to be about; *María iba por los quince años* Mary was about fifteen years old || — *eso no va por usted* I wasn't referring to you || *¡vaya por...!* here's to... (brindis) || — *ir tras* to run after (correr), to pursue, to chase (perseguir), to be behind (estar detrás), to follow (seguir), to chase after (una chica).
5. LOCUCIONES FAM *a eso voy* or *vamos* I'm coming to that || *ahí van cien pesetas* here are *o* here you have a hundred pesetas || *¡allá va!* catch! || *¿cómo le va?, ¿cómo va eso?* how are you?, how's it going? || *con éste van veinte* that makes twenty || *de diez a quince van cinco* ten from fifteen leaves five || *en lo que va de año* so far this year || FAM *estar ido* to be crazy (chiflado), to be daydreaming (distraído) | *esto no me va ni me viene* that doesn't interest me (no me interesa), it's all the same to me (me da igual) | *esto no va contigo* this doesn't concern you || FIG *ir adelante* to make progress || *ir bien* to go well, to do well, to get on well; *los negocios van bien* business is going well || *ir de mal en peor* to go from bad to worse || *ir descalzo* to go barefoot || *ir descaminado* to be on the wrong road || FIG *no andas muy descaminado* you're not far wrong || FIG *ir lejos* to go far, to go a long way || *ir sin sombrero* to go hatless, to go bareheaded || FIG *ir sobre ruedas* to run *o* to go smoothly | *ir tirando* or *viviendo* to manage, to get along, to get by | *ir zumbando* to be streaking *o* whizzing *o* zooming along (un coche, etc.) | *¡lo que va de ayer a hoy!* how times have changed! | *¡lo que va del padre al hijo!* what a difference there is between father and son! | *no vaya a ser que* so as not to, in order not to, in case; *ponte el abrigo, no vaya a ser que te enfríes* put on your coat in case you catch a cold | *¡qué va!* nonsense!, rubbish!, nothing of the sort! || *¿quién va?, ¿quién va allá?* who goes there?, who is there? || *vamos* well (vacilación); *es guapa, vamos no es fea* she's pretty, well, she isn't ugly || *¡vamos, anda!* come on, hurry up! (date prisa), come on, do something! (haz algo), come now! go on!, come off it! (incredulidad) || *vamos a ver* let's see || FAM *¡vamos despacio!* slowly does it! | *¡vamos, una sonrisita!* come on, just a little smile! | *¡vaya!, ¡vamos!* fancy that!, you don't say!, come on now! (incredulidad), fancy that!, well, well! (indignación, sorpresa), let's go!, come on! (impaciencia), in short, when you come right down to it (al final de una frase); *es buen chico, ¡vaya!* when you come right down to it, he's a good lad | *¡vaya calor!* this heat! | *¡vaya equipo!* what a team! | *¡vaya susto que me has dado!* what a fright you gave me!, good grief, you scared me! || *voy y vengo* I'll be right back || *¡ya voy!* I'm coming!
6. VERBO PRONOMINAL to go away, to leave; *se fue ayer* he left yesterday; *¡idos!* go away!; *¡vete!* go away! || FIG to pass away, to die (morirse) || to lose, to slip; *se le fueron los pies* his feet slipped, he lost his footing || to leak (un recipiente, un líquido, un gas) || to go, to disappear (gastarse); *¡cómo se va el dinero!* how money goes! || to drop (un punto); *se le fue un punto* she dropped a stitch || to fade (un color, la luz) || to go away (un dolor, una mancha, etc.) || to wear out, to fall apart (desgarrarse, destrozarse) || POP to let off, to fart [US to cut one] (ventosear) || — FIG & FAM *¡allá se van los dos!* those two make a pretty pair!, those two are tarred with the same brush | *¡anda y vete por ahí!* push off!, clear off! || FIG *irse abajo* to collapse || *irse al otro mundo* to pass away || *irse a pique* to sink (un barco), to fail (fracasar), to be ruined (arruinarse, frustrarse) || *irse como se había venido* to leave the same way one came (in) || *irse de* to discard (en el juego de naipes) || *irse de la lengua, írsele a uno la lengua* to blab, to talk too much (de costumbre), to spill the beans (en una ocasión) || *irse de la memoria* to slip one's mind, to escape one; *su nombre se me ha ido de la memoria* his name has slipped my mind || FIG *írsele a uno de la mano* to slip through s.o.'s fingers || *írsele a uno de las manos* to slip out of one's hands; *el plato se le fue de las manos* the plate slipped out of her hands; to slip from one's hands *o* grasp, to slip through one's fingers; *su autoridad se le va de las manos* his authority is slipping from his grasp || FIG *írsele a uno la mano* to lose control, to let fly || *írsele la mano en* to go heavy on, to add too much (ingredientes), to go too far with (pasarse de la raya) || *por aquí se va a mi casa* this is the way to my house || *¿por dónde se va?* which is the way?, which way is it? || *¡vámonos!* let's go! || FAM *¡váyase lo uno por lo otro!* one thing compensates the other | *¡vete (iros) a paseo!, ¡vete (iros) al diablo!* go to blazes!, go to the devil! | *¡vete a saber!* who knows?, goodness knows.

— OBSERV The construction *ir y* followed by a verb occurs frequently in everyday language to express a sense of determination. It may sometimes be rendered in English by *to up and* or *to go and*: *cuando me insultó, fui y le di una torta* when he insulted me, I upped and slapped him; *fue y se tiró al río* he went and jumped in the river.

ira *f* wrath, anger, ire (ant); *la ira es mala consejera* wrath is a bad advisor; *en un arrebato de ira* in a fit of anger ‖ FIG fury, wrath (de los elementos) ‖ *— descargar la ira en uno* to vent one's wrath *o* spleen on s.o. ‖ FAM *¡ira de Dios!* by thunder!

iracundia *f* irascibility ‖ ire, wrath (ira).

iracundo, da *adj* irascible ‖ irate (enfadado) ‖ FIG & POÉT raging, wrathful (los elementos).

Irak; Iraq *npr m* GEOGR Iraq.

Irán *npr m* GEOGR Iran.

iraní *adj/s* Iranian.
— OBSERV The plural of the word *iraní* is *iraníes*.

iraqués, esa; iraquí *adj/s* Iraqi, Iraqian.
— OBSERV The plural of the word *iraquí* is *iraquíes*.

irascibilidad *f* irascibility.

irascible *adj* irascible, choleric, irritable.

Irene *npr f* Irene.

iribú *m* AMER urubu, black vulture (aura).

iridáceas *f pl* BOT iridaceae.

iridio *m* iridium (metal).

iridiscencia *f* iridescence.

iridiscente *adj* iridescent.

iris *m* rainbow (meteoro) ‖ ANAT iris (del ojo) ‖ MIN noble opal (ópalo) ‖ *arco iris* rainbow.

irisación *f* iridescence.

irisado, da *adj* rainbow-hued, iridescent.

irisar *vi* to iridesce, to be iridescent.
◆ *vt* to make iridescent.

Irlanda *npr f* GEOGR Ireland ‖ *— de Irlanda* Irish, of Ireland ‖ *Irlanda del Norte* Northern Ireland.

irlandés, esa *adj* Irish.
◆ *m* Irishman (hombre) ‖ Irish (idioma) ‖ *los irlandeses* the Irish.
◆ *f* Irishwoman (mujer).

ironía *f* irony.

irónicamente *adv* ironically.

irónico, ca *adj* ironic.

ironista *m/f* ironist (persona irónica).

ironizar *vt* to ridiculize, to treat ironically.

IRPF *abrev de Impuesto sobre la Renta de las Personas Físicas* income tax.

irracional *adj* unreasoning, irrational (carente de razón) ‖ irrational (contrario a la razón) ‖ MAT irrational.

irracionalidad *f* irrationality.

irracionalismo *m* irrationalism.

irracionalista *adj/s* irrationalist.

irradiación *f* irradiation.

irradiar *vt/vi* to irradiate, to radiate ‖ FIG to radiate (cultura).

irrazonable *adj* unreasonable.

irreal *adj* unreal.

irrealidad *f* unreality.

irrealismo *m* unrealism.

irrealizable *adj* unrealizable ‖ unattainable (imposible de conseguir o de alcanzar).

irrebatible *adj* irrefutable.

irreconciliable *adj* irreconcilable.

irreconocible *adj* irrecognizable, unrecognizable.

irrecuperable *adj* irrecoverable, irretrievable ‖ unrecoverable, irrecoverable (crédito, etc.).

irrecusable *adj* unchallengeable, unimpeachable.

irredentismo *m* irredentism.

irredentista *adj/s* irredentist.

irredento, ta *adj* unredeemed (territorio).

irredimible *adj* irredeemable.

irreducible *adj* irreducible; *fractura irreducible* irreducible fracture.

irreductibilidad *f* irreductibility.

irreductible *adj* irreducible; *fracción irreductible* irreducible fraction ‖ incompatible; *dos tendencias irreductibles* two incompatible tendencies ‖ unyielding (inflexible).

irreembolsable *adj* nonreturnable (sin reembolso).

irreemplazable *adj* irreplaceable.

irreflexión *f* irreflection, rashness, impetuosity.

irreflexivamente *adv* thoughtlessly, rashly.

irreflexivo, va *adj* thoughtless, unreflecting, rash.

irrefragable *adj* irrefragable, undeniable, irrefutable.

irrefrenable *adj* irrepressible, uncontrollable.

irrefutable *adj* irrefutable, indisputable; *argumento irrefutable* irrefutable argument.

irregular *adj* irregular; *polígono, pulso, verbo irregular* irregular polygon, pulse, verb ‖ abnormal (anormal) ‖ FIG dissolute; *una vida irregular* a dissolute life.

irregularidad *f* irregularity ‖ FIG disorder.

irreligión *f* irreligion, impiety.

irreligioso, sa *adj* irreligious, impious.
◆ *m/f* irreligious *o* impious person.

irremediable *adj* irremediable ‖ incurable (que no se puede curar).

irremisible *adj* irremissible, unpardonable, unforgivable.

irreparable *adj* irreparable.

irreprensible *adj* irreprehensible, irreproachable.

irrepresentable *adj* unpresentable.

irreprimible *adj* irrepressible.

irreprochable *adj* irreproachable.

irresistible *adj* irresistible.

irresoluble *adj* unsolvable (que no se puede resolver).

irresolución *f* irresolution.

irresoluto, ta *adj* irresolute, indecisive (persona) ‖ unresolved (problema).
◆ *m/f* indecisive *o* irresolute person.

irrespetuoso, sa *adj* disrespectful.

irrespirable *adj* irrespirable, unbreathable.

irresponsabilidad *f* irresponsibility.

irresponsable *adj* irresponsible.

irresuelto, ta *adj* irresolute (persona).

irretroactividad *f* nonretroactive character.

irreverencia *f* irreverence, disrespect.

irreverenciar *vt* to treat irreverently ‖ to profane (profanar).

irreverente *adj* irreverent, disrespectful.

irreversibilidad *f* irreversibility.

irreversible *adj* irreversible, nonreversible.

irrevocabilidad *f* irrevocability.

irrevocable *adj* irrevocable.

irrigable *adj* irrigable.

irrigación *f* irrigation ‖ MED irrigation.

irrigador *m* MED irrigator.

irrigar *vt* to irrigate ‖ MED to irrigate.

irrisible *adj* laughable, ludicrous, absurd, ridiculous.

irrisión *f* derision, ridicule ‖ laughingstock (objeto de burla); *ser la irrisión del pueblo* to be the laughingstock of the town ‖ *hacer irrisión de uno* to hold s.o. up to ridicule.

irrisorio, ria *adj* ridiculous, derisory, derisive; *oferta irrisoria* ridiculous offer ‖ giveaway (precio).

irritabilidad *f* irritability.

irritable *adj* irritable (persona) ‖ JUR which can be annulled.

irritación *f* irritation (enfado) ‖ MED irritation ‖ JUR invalidation, annulment.

irritado, da *adj* irritated ‖ POÉT *el mar irritado* the angry *o* turbulent sea.

irritante *adj* irritating ‖ MED irritant, irritating ‖ *agente irritante* irritant.

irritar *vt* to irritate, to anger, to exasperate (enfadar) ‖ FIG to excite (las pasiones) ‖ MED to irritate ‖ JUR to annul, to void.
◆ *vpr* to get angry, to lose one's temper; *irritarse con* or *por algo, con* or *contra alguien* to get angry about *o* at sth., with s.o.

írrito, ta *adj* JUR null and void, null, void, invalid.

irrogar *vt* to cause, to occasion (harm or damages).

irrompible *adj* unbreakable.

irrumpir *vi* *irrumpir en* to burst into.

irrupción *f* irruption.

Isaac *npr m* Isaac.

Isabel *npr f* Isabel, Elizabeth ‖ Elizabeth (refiriéndose a las reinas de Inglaterra).

isabelino, na *adj* Elizabethan (relativo a Isabel I de Inglaterra) ‖ stamped with the bust of Isabella II [coin] ‖ pearl-coloured, whitish-yellow (color).
◆ *adj/s* Isabelline (en España).

Isaías *npr m* Isaiah.

isba *f* isba (casa rusa de madera).

isidoriano, na *adj* Isidorian.
◆ *m* person of the order of Saint Isidore.

Isidoro; Isidro *npr m* Isidore.

isidro, dra *m/f* country bumpkin [*US* hick].
— OBSERV This word is employed exclusively in Madrid to designate a person from the provinces who comes to the capital for special occasions.

Isis *npr f* MIT Isis.

isla *f* island, isle ‖ block [of houses] (de casas) ‖ island (en una calle) ‖ AMER grove (bosquecillo) | flood plain (cerca de un río) ‖ *— islas Anglonormandas* Channel Islands ‖ *islas Baleares* Balearic Islands ‖ *islas Británicas* British Isles ‖ *islas Canarias* Canary Islands ‖ *islas Filipinas* Philippine Islands.

islam *m* Islam.

Islamabad *n pr* GEOGR Islamabad.

islámico, ca *adj* Islamic.

islamismo *m* Islamism, Mohammedanism (religión) ‖ Moslem world (pueblos musulmanes).

islamita *adj/s* Islamite.

islamización *f* Islamization.

islamizar *vt* to islamize.

islandés, esa *adj* Icelandic.
◆ *m/f* Icelander.
◆ *m* Icelandic (lengua).

Islandia *npr f* GEOGR Iceland.

isleño, ña *adj* island.
◆ *m/f* islander.

isleta *f* islet, small island ‖ island (en la calle).

islote *m* islet, small island.

Ismael *npr m* Ishmael.

ismaelita *adj/s* Ishmaelite.

ismo *m* ism.

isobara *f* isobar (línea isobárica).

isobárico, ca *adj* isobaric; *líneas isobáricas* isobaric lines.

isoclinal; isoclino *adj* GEOL isoclinal.
isocromático, ca *adj* isochromatic.
isócrono, na *adj* isochronous.
isogamia *f* BIOL isogamy.
isógamo, ma *adj* BIOL isogamous.
isoglosa *f* isogloss.
isógono *adj* isogonic, isogonal.
isomería *f* QUÍM isomerism.
isómero, ra *adj* isomeric, isomerous.
◆ *m* isomer.
isométrico, ca *adj* isometric, isometrical.
isomorfismo *m* isomorphism.
isomorfo, fa *adj* isomorphic, isomorphous.
isópodo, da *adj/sm* ZOOL isopod.
isósceles *adj* isosceles; *triángulo isósceles* isosceles triangle.
isotérmico, ca *adj* isothermic, isothermal; *vagón isotérmico* isothermic wagon.
isotermo, ma *adj* isothermal.
◆ *f* isotherm.
isotonía *f* FÍS isotonicity.
isotónico, ca; isótono, na *adj* FÍS isotonic.
isotopía *f* QUÍM isotopy.
isotópico, ca *adj* QUÍM isotopic.
isótopo *m* QUÍM isotope.
isotropía *f* BIOL & FÍS isotropy.
isótropo, pa *adj* BIOL & FÍS isotropous, isotropic.
◆ *m* isotropous body.
isquemia *f* MED ischemia.
isquion *m* ANAT ischium (hueso).
Israel *npr m* GEOGR Israel.
israelí *adj/s* Israeli (del Estado de Israel).
— OBSERV The plural of *israelí* is *israelíes*.
israelita *adj/s* Israelite.
istmeño, ña *adj* isthmian (en general) || Panamanian (de Panamá).
ístmico, ca *adj* isthmic, isthmian; *juegos ístmicos* isthmic games.
istmo *m* isthmus; *istmo de Panamá* Isthmus of Panama || ANAT isthmus.
Italia *npr f* GEOGR Italy.
italianismo *m* Italianism.
italianista *m/f* Italianist.
italianización *f* Italianization.
italianizar *vt* to italianize.
◆ *vpr* to italianize.
italiano, na *adj/s* Italian || *a la italiana* Italian style.
itálico, ca *adj* italic.
ítalo, la *adj/s* POÉT Italian.
itapá *f* AMER raft (balsa).
ítem *adv lat* item, likewise (además).
◆ *m* article, item (artículo).
iteración *f* (p us) iteration, repetition || INFORM iteration, iterative process.
iterar *vt* to iterate, to repeat.
iterativo, va *adj* iterative, repetitive.
iterbio *m* ytterbium (metal).
itinerante *adj* itinerant, roving, travelling; *embajador itinerante* itinerant ambassador || itinerant, floating; *campamento itinerante* floating camp.
itinerario, ria *adj/sm* itinerary.
itria *f* MIN yttria.
itrio *m* MIN yttrium.
IVA *abrev de Impuesto sobre el Valor Añadido* VAT, value added tax.
izar *vt* to hoist, to haul up, to heave.
izquierda *f* left hand (mano) || left (lado, dirección) || left wing (política) || — *a la izquierda* left, to the left (con movimiento), on the left (sin movimiento) || *de izquierdas* left-wing || MIL *¡izquierda, ar!* left face || *mantenerse a la izquierda* keep left, keep to the left (aviso) || FIG & FAM *ser un cero a la izquierda* to be a nobody || *un hombre de izquierda* a leftist, a man of the left, a left winger.
izquierdismo *m* leftism.
izquierdista *adj* leftist, left-wing.
◆ *m/f* leftist, left winger.
izquierdo, da *adj* left; *mano izquierda* left hand || knock-kneed (caballo) || left-handed (zurdo).
◆ *m/f* left-hander, southpaw (*fam*) (zurdo) || → **izquierda.**
izquierdoso, sa *adj* FAM leftish.

J

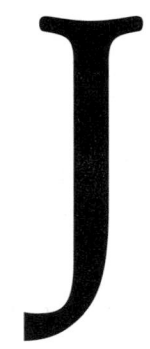

j *f* j; *una j mayúscula* a capital j.
— OBSERV The *jota* sound is similar to the Scottish *ch* [as in *loch*].

jabado, da *adj* AMER parti-coloured (gallo).

jabalcón *m* ARQ brace, strut (puntal).

jabalconar *vt* ARQ to brace, to strut (apuntalar).

jabalí *m* ZOOL wild boar, boar; *jabalí alunado* long-tusked boar.
— OBSERV pl *jabalíes*.

jabalina *f* wild sow, female wild boar (hembra del jabalí) || javelin (en deportes, arma); *lanzamiento de la jabalina* throwing the javelin.

jabato *m* young wild boar || FIG *¡es un jabato!* he's as bold as a lion! (valiente).

jábega *f* sweep net, dragnet (red) || fishing boat (embarcación).

jabegote *m* sweep-net fisherman.

jabeguero, ra *adj* sweep-net (pesca).
◆ *m/f* sweep-net fisherman.

jabeque *m* xebec (embarcación) || FIG & FAM wound, gash (herida).

jabí *m* AMER quebracho (árbol).

jabirú *m* ZOOL jabiru (pájaro).

jable *m* TECN croze (de los toneles).

jabón *m* soap; *pompa de jabón* soap bubble; *jabón de afeitar, de tocador* or *de olor* shaving, toilet soap || bar of soap (pastilla de jabón) || FIG & FAM dressing down, ticking off (reprensión); *dar* or *echar un jabón a alguien* to give s.o. a dressing down | soft soap, flattery (lisonja) || AMER fright, scare (susto) || — FIG & FAM *dar jabón a uno* to soft-soap s.o. (lisonjear) || *jabón blando* soft soap || *jabón de Marsella* household soap || *jabón de piedra* hard soap || *jabón de sastre* soapstone, steatite, French chalk || *jabón en escamas* soap flakes || *jabón en polvo* soap powder, washing powder.

jabonado *m* soaping (jabonadura) || washing, wash, laundry (ropa que se lava) || FAM dressing down, ticking off (reprensión).

jabonadura *f* soaping || FAM ticking off (reprensión) || *dar una jabonadura a alguien* to give s.o. a ticking off.
◆ *pl* soapy water *sing* || lather *sing*, soapsuds (espuma).

jabonar *vt* to soap, to wash (la ropa) || to lather (la barba) || FIG & FAM to give (s.o.) a dressing down *o* a ticking off, to tell (s.o.) off (reprender).

jaboncillo *m* bar of toilet soap (para lavarse) || BOT soapberry (árbol) || AMER soap powder (jabón en polvo), liquid soap (líquido) || *jaboncillo de sastre* soapstone, steatite, French chalk.

jabonera *f* soapdish (caja) || BOT soapwort.

jabonero, ra *adj* soap || off-white (toro).
◆ *m/f* soap manufacturer, soap maker (fabricante), soap dealer (vendedor).

jabonoso, sa *adj* soapy.

jaborandi *m* BOT jaborandi.

jabotí *m* AMER large tortoise.

jaca *f* pony, small horse (caballito) || horse (en general) || AMER small mare (yegua) | fighting cock (gallo de pelea).

jacal *m* AMER hut (cabaña).

jacamar *m*; **jacamara** *f* AMER jacamar (ave).

jácara *f* picaresque ballad (romance) || Spanish popular dance and its music (danza y música) || band of night revellers (juerguistas) || FIG & FAM bother, annoyance (molestia) | tale, fib (embuste); *contar jácaras* to tell tales || — *estar de jácara* to be very merry (alegre), to be living it up (de juerga) || *no estoy para jácaras* I'm not in the mood for jokes.

jacarandá *m* BOT jacaranda.

jacarandoso, sa *adj* FAM jolly, sprightly, lively, gay (alegre) || vain (presumido).

jacaré *m* AMER alligator.

jacarear *vi* to go singing through the streets || to sing picaresque ballads.

jacarero; jacarista *m* merrymaker, reveller.
◆ *adj* merry.

jácena *f* ARQ summer (viga maestra).

jacinto *m* BOT hyacinth || hyacinth, jacinth (piedra preciosa) || — *jacinto de Ceilán* zircon || *jacinto occidental* topaz || *jacinto oriental* ruby.

Jacinto *npr m* Hyacinth.

jaco *m* hack, nag (caballo malo) || young horse (caballo joven) || short-sleeved coat of mail (cota).

Jacob *npr m* Jacob.

jacobeo, a *adj* of Saint James || *peregrinación jacobea* pilgrimage to Santiago de Compostela.

jacobinismo *m* Jacobinism.

jacobino, na *adj/s* Jacobin.

jacobita *adj* Jacobitical, Jacobite.
◆ *m* Jacobite.

Jacobo *npr m* James.

jactación *f* MED jactation, jactitation.

jactancia *f* boastfulness (cualidad) || boasting, bragging (acción).

jactanciosamente *adv* boastfully.

jactancioso, sa *adj* boastful.
◆ *m/f* boaster, braggart.

jactarse *vpr* to boast, to brag (vanagloriarse); *jactarse de su fuerza* to boast of one's strength.

jaculatorio, ria *adj* ejaculatory, brief and fervent.
◆ *f* ejaculation (oración breve).

jade *m* jade (piedra).

jadeante *adj* panting, gasping.

jadear *vi* to pant, to gasp, to puff (and blow) || *llegar jadeando* to arrive out of breath.

jadeo *m* panting, gasping, breathlessness.

jaenés, esa *adj/s* → **jiennense.**

jaez *m* harness (del caballo) || FIG character, nature (carácter) | mood; *estar de mal jaez* to be in a bad mood | kind, sort (índole) | sort (despectivo); *no se mezcle con gente de ese jaez* don't get mixed up with that sort of people.
◆ *pl* trappings (del caballo).

jaguar *m* ZOOL jaguar.

jagüel; jagüey *m* AMER pool, pond (charco).

jai alai *m* «jai alai», pelota (pelota vasca) || pelota court (frontón).

jaiba *f* AMER crab (cangrejo).

jaibol *m* AMER highball (cóctel).

Jaime *npr m* James.

jaique *m* haik, haick (almalafa).

¡ja, ja, ja! *interj* ha, ha, ha!

Jakarta *n pr* GEOGR Jakarta.

jalapa *f* BOT jalap.

jalapeño, ña *adj* Jalapa, Jalapan [Guatemala and Mexico].
◆ *m/f* Jalapan.

jalar *vt* FAM → **jamar.**

jalbegar *vt* to whitewash (enjalbegar).

jalea *f* jelly || — FIG & FAM *hacerse* or *volverse una jalea* to turn *o* to go sweet || *jalea de cidra* citron jelly || *jalea real* royal jelly.

jaleador, ra *adj* noisy, rowdy (que hace ruido) || encouraging, cheering (que anima).

jalear *vt* to urge on (dogs) (caza) || to encourage [by clapping and shouting], to cheer on; *el público jaleó a la bailarina* the audience cheered on the dancer || AMER to pester (fastidiar).

jaleo *m* shouting [to urge on dogs] (en la caza) || cheering and clapping (para bailarines, cantantes, etc.) || popular Andalusian dance || FAM binge, good time (juerga) | row, din, racket (alboroto); *armar jaleo* to kick up a racket | jumble; *un jaleo de cifras y letras* a jumble of figures and letters | row (riña); *armar un jaleo con* to start a row with | fuss, to-do, commotion (escándalo); *se armó* or *hubo un jaleo enorme* there was a right to-do.

jaleoso, sa *adj* noisy, rowdy.

jalifa *f* supreme authority representing the sultan in the former Spanish protectorate of Morocco.

jalifato *m* dignity and jurisdiction of the «jalifa».

jalisco *adj m* AMER drunk.

jalma *f* packsaddle (enjalma).

jalón *m* range pole (estaca) || FIG milestone; *el viaje del escritor a Inglaterra constituyó un jalón en su vida* the writer's trip to England was a milestone in his life | stage (etapa) || AMER pull (tirón) | stretch, distance (distancia); *nos falta todavía un gran jalón* we still have a long stretch ahead of us || *jalón de mira* target levelling rod, level rod.

jalonamiento *m* staking *o* marking *o* laying out.

jalonar *vt* to stake out, to mark out, to lay out || FIG to mark, to dot; *estar jalonado de* to be dotted with.

Jamaica *npr f* GEOGR Jamaica.

jamaicano, na *adj/s* Jamaican.

jamancia *f* FAM grub, nosh (comida).

jamar *vt* FAM to stuff o.s. with, to tuck in to, to nosh [*US* to chow] (comer).
◆ *vi* FAM to nosh, to tuck in (comer).

jamás *adv* never; *jamás lo haré de nuevo* I shall never do it again, never shall I do it again; *jamás lo he visto, no lo he visto jamás* I've never seen it ‖ ever; *¿has visto jamás una cosa parecida?* have you ever seen such a thing? ‖ — *la mejor película que jamás se haya hecho* the best film that has ever been made, the best film ever made ‖ *jamás de los jamases* never ever, never on your life ‖ *nunca jamás* never ever; *nunca jamás lo haré de nuevo* I shall never ever do it again ‖ *para siempre jamás* for ever and ever.

jamba *f* ARQ jamb ‖ TECN post, jamb; *jamba de puerta* doorpost, doorjamb.

jambaje *m* ARQ doorframe (de puerta) ‖ windowframe (de ventana).

jámbico, ca *adj* iambic (verso).

jamboree *m* jamboree (de exploradores).

jamelgo *m* hack, jade, nag (caballo malo).

jamón *m* ham; *jamón ahumado* smoked ham; *huevos con jamón* ham and eggs ‖ — *codillo de jamón* knuckle of ham ‖ *jamón en dulce* ham boiled in white wine ‖ *jamón serrano* or *del país* cured ham ‖ *manga de jamón* leg-of-mutton sleeve ‖ *ser una mujer jamón* to be a knockout ‖ FAM *¡y un jamón!* or *¡y un jamón con chorreras!* not on your life!, you've got a hope!, nothing doing!

jamona *adj/f* FAM meaty, buxom.

jamúas *f*; **jamuga** *f*; **jamugas** *f pl* side-saddle.

jangada *f* MAR raft, float (balsa) ‖ *AMER* jangada [brazilian boat] | timber raft (armadía) | FAM daft thing, silly remark (tontería) | mean *o* dirty trick (trastada).

jansenismo *m* Jansenism.

jansenista *adj* Jansenistic, Jansenist.
◆ *m/f* Jansenist.

Japón *npr m* GEOGR Japan.

japonés, esa *adj/s* Japanese; *los japoneses* the Japanese.

japuta *f* pomfret (pez).

jaque *m* check (ajedrez) ‖ FAM bully (valentón) ‖ — *dar jaque* to check ‖ *dar jaque y mate* to checkmate ‖ *estar en jaque* to be in check ‖ *jaque al rey* cheeck ‖ *jaque mate* checkmate ‖ *jaque perpetuo* perpetual check ‖ FIG *tener* or *traer en jaque* to hold a threat over (sujetar bajo una amenaza), to harass, to worry (hostigar).

jaquear *vt* to check (en ajedrez) ‖ FIG to harass (hostigar) | to hold a threat over (amenazar).

jaqueca *f* migraine (dolor de cabeza) ‖ FIG & FAM bother, nuisance, pain in the neck; *¡qué jaqueca tener que hacer esto!* what a bother having to do this! ‖ — FIG & FAM *dar jaqueca a* to bother, to pester | *¡que tío jaqueca!* what a pest!

jaquecoso, sa *adj* suffering from migraine (con jaqueca) ‖ FIG bothersome (fastidioso).

jáquima *m* headstall (de caballos) ‖ *AMER* FAM *coger una jáquima* to get sozzled (emborracharse).

jaquimón *m* *AMER* headstall (jáquima).

jara *f* BOT rockrose ‖ spear (arma).

jarabe *m* syrup; *jarabe para la tos* cough syrup ‖ popular Mexican dance (baile) ‖ — FIG & FAM *dar jarabe a uno* to butter s.o. up, to soft-soap s.o. | *dar a uno jarabe de palo* to give s.o. a hiding | *estar hecho un jarabe* to go sweet | *jarabe de pico* blarney, mere words *pl*; *éso es todo jarabe de pico* that is a lot of blarney; gift of the gab; *tiene mucho jarabe de pico* he has really got the gift of the gab.

jaral *m* place full of rockroses.

jaramago *m* BOT hedge mustard (sisimbrio).

jarana *f* FAM spree, binge (juerga); *ir de jarana* to go on a spree | rumpus, racket, din (alboroto); *armar jarana* to kick up a rumpus | trick (trampa) | deceit, trickery (engaño) ‖ *AMER* joke (chanza) | debt (deuda) | small guitar (guitarra) | dance (baile).

jaranear *vi* to go on a binge *o* on a spree (ir de juerga) ‖ to make merry, to amuse o.s., to have a good time (divertirse).
◆ *vpr* to go on a binge *o* on a spree (irse de juerga) ‖ to laugh (*de* at) (reírse, no tomar en serio).

jaranero, ra *adj* fun-loving (a quien le gusta divertirse) ‖ rowdy, noisy (ruidoso) ‖ *AMER* tricky, deceitful, cheating (tramposo).
◆ *m/f* reveller.

jaranista *adj* *AMER* ⟶ **jaranero.**

jarca *f* ⟶ **harca.**

jarcia *f* MAR rigging, ropes *pl* (cabos y aparejos) | fishing tackle (para pescar) ‖ FIG jumble, mess (mescolanza) ‖ MAR *jarcia muerta* standing rigging.
◆ *pl* MAR rigging *sing.*

jarciar *vt* MAR to rig [a ship].

jardín *m* garden; *jardín colgante* hanging garden ‖ MAR latrine, head (*fam*) (retrete de un navío) ‖ TECN flaw (mancha en una esmeralda) ‖ — *jardín botánico* botanical garden ‖ *jardín de la infancia* kindergarten.

jardinaje *m* gardening.

jardinera *f* (woman) gardener ‖ jardinière, flower stand (para tiestos de flores) ‖ window box (en una ventana) ‖ open carriage (coche) ‖ open tramcar (coche de tranvía).

jardinería *f* gardening.

jardinero *m* gardener ‖ *jardinero paisajista* landscape gardener.

jareta *f* hem (dobladillo) ‖ MAR cable, rope (cabo) | netting (empalletado) ‖ FAM chatter (charla) ‖ FAM *dar jareta* to (have a) chat.

jaretón *m* wide hem.

jarillo *m* BOT arum (aro).

jarocho, cha *adj* uncouth, rude (tosco).
◆ *m/f* uncouth *o* rude person ‖ peasant from Veracruz.

jarope *m* syrup (jarabe).

jarra *f* jug, pitcher ‖ churn (de leche) ‖ beer mug, tankard (de cerveza) ‖ ancient Aragonese order of chivalry (orden antigua en Aragón) ‖ *de jarras, en jarra, en jarras* hands on hips, arms akimbo.

jarrete *m* back of the knee (del hombre) ‖ hock (corvejón de una res, de un caballo).

jarretera *f* garter (liga) ‖ Order of the Garter.

jarro *m* jug, jar, pitcher (recipiente) ‖ jar, jug, jarful, jugful (contenido) ‖ beer mug, tankard (para cerveza) ‖ — FIG & FAM *a jarros* buckets, cats and dogs (llover) | *echar un jarro de agua fría a* to pour cold water on.

jarrón *m* ARQ (ornamental) vase *o* urn ‖ vase (para flores).

jartar *vt/vi* FAM ⟶ **hartar.**

Jartum *n pr* GEOGR Khartoum.

jaspe *m* jasper (piedra) ‖ veined marble (mármol).

jaspeado, da *adj* marbled, mottled, streaked, veined ‖ variegated (hojas).
◆ *m* marbling, mottling ‖ marbling (de un libro).

jaspear *vt* to marble, to mottle, to vein, to streak.

Jauja *n pr* FIG promised land, paradise ‖ — *¡esto es Jauja!* this is the life! ‖ *tierra de Jauja* land of milk and honey, land of plenty, Never-Never land.
— OBSERV The Spanish noun *Jauja* is used in allusion to the Peruvian town and province of *Jauja*, noted for its wealth and the clemency of its climate.

jaula *f* cage (para animales) ‖ padded cell (para locos) ‖ crate (embalaje) ‖ lockup (en un garaje) ‖ playpen (para niños) ‖ MIN cage ‖ cage, car (de un ascensor) ‖ ELECTR *jaula de ardilla* squirrel cage.

jauría *f* pack [of hounds] (perros de caza) ‖ FIG pack; *jauría de acreedores* pack of creditors.

java *n pr* GEOGR Java.

javanés, esa *adj/s* Javanese.

Javier *npr m* Xavier.

jazmín *m* BOT Jasmine; *jazmín de España* or *real* Spanish *o* Catalonian jasmine.

jazz *m* jazz (música).

jazz-band *m* jazz band.

jazzístico, ca *adj* jazzy.

jazzman *m* jazzman, jazz musician.
— OBSERV *pl* jazzmen.

jebe *m* alum (alambre) ‖ *AMER* rubber (caucho).

jedive *m* khedive.

jeep *m* jeep (coche todo terreno).

jefa *f* boss ‖ head (de un departamento) ‖ (Lady) president (presidenta) ‖ manageress (directora) ‖ leader (de partido, etc.).

jefatura *f* leadership; *bajo la jefatura de* under the leadership of ‖ managership, management (dirección) ‖ position of head (de un departamento, de una familia) ‖ chieftaincy (de una tribu) ‖ *jefatura de policía* police headquarters.

jefe *m* boss (de un empleado, etc.); *mi jefe* my boss ‖ manager (director) ‖ leader (de un partido, de un sindicato, de una banda, etc.) ‖ head (de un departamento, de familia) ‖ chief, chieftain, headman (de una tribu) ‖ MIL officer in command ‖ scoutmaster (de exploradores) ‖ foreman (de un jurado) ‖ HERÁLD chief ‖ — *comandante en jefe* commander-in-chief ‖ *jefe de camareros* head waiter ‖ *jefe de cocina* chef, head cook ‖ *jefe de comedor* head waiter, maître d'hôtel ‖ *jefe de cordada* leader, first on the rope, head of the rope ‖ *jefe de escuadra* squadron commander ‖ *jefe de estación* stationmaster ‖ *jefe de Estado* head of State ‖ *jefe de Estado Mayor* Chief of Staff ‖ *jefe de estudios* year head ‖ *jefe de gobierno* head of (the) government ‖ *jefe de negociado* chief clerk, departmental head ‖ *jefe de redacción* editor-in-chief ‖ *jefe de taller* foreman ‖ *jefe de ventas* sales manager ‖ *jefe supremo* commander-in-chief ‖ *redactor jefe* editor-in-chief ‖ FIG *ser el jefe* to be the boss.

Jehová *m* Jehovah (Dios).

¡je, je, je! *interj* ha, ha, ha!, tee, hee, hee!

jején *m* *AMER* gnat (mosquito) | FIG lot, great number.

jemiquear *vi* to snivel, to whimper.

jengibre *m* BOT ginger.

jeniquén *m* henequen (henequén).

jenízaro, ra *adj* FIG mixed, hybrid (mezclado) ‖ *AMER* born of mixed parentage (de padres de distinta nacionalidad) | born of half-bred father and Chinese mother or vice versa.
◆ *m* janizary, janissary (soldado).

jenneriano, na *adj* jennerian.

Jenofonte *npr m* Xenophon.

jeque *m* sheikh, sheik (jefe árabe).

jerarca *m* hierarch (de una sociedad) || REL hierarch, dignitary || chief, leader (jefe) || important person.

jerarquía *f* hierarchy; *jerarquía administrativa, angélica, social* administrative, angelic, social hierarchy || scale; *jerarquía de valores* scale of values || hierarch, dignitary; *el arzobispo y otras jerarquías eclesiásticas* the archbishop and other ecclesiastical hierarchs || *elevarse en la jerarquía* to rise *o* to ascend in the hierarchy.

jerárquico, ca *adj* hierarchic, hierarchical.

jerarquización *f* hierarchization.

jerarquizar *vt* to hierarchize.

jerbo *m* ZOOL jerboa.

jeremiada *f* Jeremiad.

jeremías *m/f inv* whiner, whimperer.

Jeremías *npr m* Jeremy || Jeremiah (en la Biblia).

jeremiquear *vi* to snivel, to whimper.

jeremiqueo *m* snivelling, whimpering.

jerez *m* sherry (vino); *jerez fino* dry sherry.

jerezano, na *adj* [of *o* from] Jerez.
◆ *m/f* native *o* inhabitant of Jerez.

jerga *f* coarse woollen cloth, sackcloth (tela) || straw mattress (colchón) || jargon, slang, cant (lenguaje); *la jerga estudiantil* student jargon || gibberish, double Dutch (galimatías) || MIN jargon, jargoon (gema) || *hablar en jerga* to talk gibberish, to talk double Dutch.

jergal *adj* jargonistic, slangy.

jergón *m* straw mattress (colchón).

jergueta *f* coarse cloth (tela).

jerguilla *f* serge-like cloth (tela).

jeribeque *m* face, grimace (mueca) || blink (guiño).

Jericó *n pr* GEOGR Jericho.

jerifato; jerifazgo *m* dignity of *o* territory under a sherif.

jerife *m* sherif (jefe árabe).

jerifiano, na *adj* sherifian.

jerigonza *f* jargon, slang (jerga) || gibberish, double Dutch (galimatías).

jeringa *f* syringe (para inyecciones) || gun (para aceite) || FAM annoyance, bother (aburrimiento).

jeringador, ra *adj* FAM annoying, bothersome.
◆ *m/f* FAM pest, nuisance (latoso).

jeringar *vt* to inject, to syringe (inyectar) || to syringe (para limpiar) || FIG & FAM to bother, to annoy, to pester (molestar).

jeringazo *m* squirt [from a syringe] || syringe, syringeful (contenido).

jeringuilla *f* BOT mock orange || small syringe (para inyecciones) || *jeringuilla hipodérmica* hypodermic syringe.

Jerjes *npr m* HIST Xerxes.

jeroglífico, ca *adj* hieroglyphic.
◆ *m* hieroglyphic, hieroglyph || rebus, picture puzzle (juego).
◆ *pl* hieroglyphics.

jerónimo, ma *adj/s* hieronymite.

Jerónimo *npr m* Jerome, Hieronymus.

jersey *m* jersey, pullover, sweater.
— OBSERV pl *jerseys* or *jerseis.*

Jerusalén *n pr* GEOGR Jerusalem.

Jesucristo *m* Jesus Christ.

jesuita *adj/s* Jesuit.

jesuítico, ca *adj* Jesuitic, Jesuitical || FIG Jesuitical.

jesuitismo *m* Jesuitism.

Jesús *m* Jesus; *Jesús Nazareno* Jesus of Nazareth || — *el Niño Jesús* the Infant Jesus (Jesús niño), the Bambino (imagen) || FIG & FAM *en un decir Jesús, en un Jesús* in the twinkling of an eye, before you can *o* could say Jack Robinson, in a jiffy || FIG *sin decir Jesús* very suddenly (morir).
◆ *interj* Good heavens!, gracious! || *¡Jesús!, ¡Jesús, María y José!* bless you! (al estornudar).
— OBSERV *Jesús* is a common Spanish Christian name.

jeta *f* snout (hocico de cerdo) || thick lips *pl* (labios abultados) || FAM mug, face (cara) || — AMER FAM *estirar la jeta* to kick the bucket (morir) || FAM *le voy a romper la jeta* I'm going to smash his face in | *poner jeta* to pull a face.

jet-set *f* jet set.

jetudo, da *adj* thick-lipped.

jíbaro, ra; gíbaro, ra *adj* AMER country, rural, rustic (campesino) | Jivaroan (jívaro).
◆ *m/f* AMER rustic, peasant (campesino) | Jivaro (indio).

jibia *f* ZOOL cuttlefish, sepia (molusco) || cuttlebone (jibión).

jibión *m* cuttlebone.

Jibuti *n pr* GEOGR Djibouti.

jícara *f* cup; *una jícara de chocolate* a cup of chocolate || AMER calabash, gourd.

jicote *m* AMER hornet, big wasp (abejorro).

jicotera *f* AMER wasp's nest (nido).

jiennense; jaenés, sa *adj* [of *o* from] Jaén.
◆ *m/f* native *o* inhabitant of Jaén.

jifero *m* cleaver (cuchillo de carnicero) || slaughterer (el que mata las reses).

jigote *m* —> **gigote.**

¡ji, ji, ji! *interj* hee, hee, hee! tee, hee! (risa).

jijona *f* variety of large-grained yellowish wheat.
◆ *m* almond sweetmeat [made in Jijona].

jilguero *m* goldfinch (ave).

jilí; gilí *m* FAM cretin, idiot, imbecile.

jilipolla; jilipollas; gilipolla *m* POP twit, berk, cretin, idiot.

jilipollada; gilipollada *f* POP stupid thing to do (acción) | stupid thing to say (dicho).

jilipollez; gilipollez *f* POP stupid thing to do (acción) | stupid thing to say (dicho) || — POP *eso son jilipolleces* that's a load of old cobblers, that's a load of (old) rot | *¡qué jilipollez!* how stupid can you get!

jilote *m* AMER spike of maize [US spike of corn].

jimelga *f* MAR fish (refuerzo de madera).

jimia *f* she-ape.

jimio *m* ape, simian.

jinda; jindama *f* FAM fear, funk (miedo) || fright (susto).

jineta *f* horsewoman, rider (mujer que monta a caballo) || short lance [former insignia of infantry captains] (lanza corta) || (sergeant's) epaulette (hombrera) || ZOOL genet || *a la jineta* with short stirrups and knees bent.

jinete *m* horseman, rider (caballista) || MIL cavalryman || saddle horse (caballo) || thoroughbred horse (caballo de pura sangre) || *venía jinete en un caballo negro* he approached riding a black horse.

jinetear *vi* to ride around (on horseback) (pasearse a caballo) || to show off one's horsemanship (presumir).
◆ *vt* AMER to break in (horses).

jingoísmo *m* jingoism.

jingoísta *adj* jingoistic, jingo.
◆ *m/f* jingoist, jingo.

jínjol *m* BOT jujube [berry] (azufaifa).

jinjolero *m* jujube [tree] (azufaifo).

jiote *m* AMER impetigo (empeine).

jipar *vi* to hiccough, to hiccup (hipar) || to heave, to pant (jadear).

jipi *m* FAM Panama hat, straw hat (sombrero).

jipido *m* FAM hiccough, hiccup (hipo).

jipijapa *f* jipijapa (planta) || fine strip of straw [from jipijapa leaf].
◆ *m* Panama hat, straw hat (sombrero).
— OBSERV *Jipijapa* is a town in Ecuador where the so-called Panama hat actually originated.

jiquilete *m* indigo plant (añil).

jira *f* strip (of cloth) (tira) || shred of cloth (jirón) || picnic (merienda campestre) || excursion || tour; *hacer una jira por España* to go on a tour of Spain, to make a tour of Spain.

jirafa *f* giraffe (animal) || boom (de micrófono).

jirafista *m* boom operator.

jirón *m* shred, tatter (pedazo); *hacer jirones* to tear to shreds || FIG scrap, bit, piece (porción pequeña) || facing (de una falda) || HERÁLD gyron || AMER avenue, wide street || *hecho jirones* in rags, in tatters, in shreds.

jitomate *m* AMER tomato.

jiu-jitsu *m* jujitsu, jujutsu.

jívaro, ra *adj* Jivaroan (indio).
◆ *m/f* Jivaro.

Joaquín *npr m* Joachim.

Job *npr m* Job || *tener más paciencia que (el santo) Job* to have the patience of Job.

jockey *m* jockey.

jocosamente *adv* jocularly, humorously.

jocosidad *f* humour [US humor], humorousness (gracia) || jocularity, humour [US humor] (de una persona) || pleasantry, joke (chiste).

jocoso, sa *adj* humorous, amusing, funny, comical, jocular (cómico); *libro jocoso* humorous book.

jocundidad *f* jocundity, cheerfulness, gaiety.

jocundo, da *adj* jocund, cheerful, gay.

joder *vt/vi* POP to fuck (tener relaciones íntimas con) || FIG & POP to pester (importunar) | to get on (s.o.'s) nerves, to annoy (fastidiar, molestar); *ese maldito ruido me está jodiendo* that bloody noise is getting on my nerves | to be a drag *o* a bind (ser una pesadez); *jode mucho tener que levantarse tan temprano* it's a drag having to get up so early | to bugger up, to mess up, to ruin (estropear) || — FIG & POP *¡la jodiste!* you've made a right mess of things!, you've ruined everything! | *¡no me jodas!* stop pestering me! (no me des la lata), come off it! (no me digas).
◆ *vpr* FIG & POP to be a flop (fracasar) | to be ruined *o* spoilt *o* messed up; *la excursión se jodió con la lluvia* the trip was ruined by rain || — FIG & POP *¡hay que joderse!* to hell with it all! | *¡que se joda!* to hell with him! (her, it, etc.) | *¡que te jodas!* go to hell!

joder *interj* shit!, hell!, damn!

jodido, da *adj* FIG & POP shagged, shattered (rendido); *estoy jodido* I'm shagged | bloody (maldito); *este jodido coche* this bloody car | bloody awful (malísimo); *un trabajo jodido* a bloody awful job | ruined (estropeado, fastidiado) || — FIG & POP *esta radio está jodida* this radio has had it | *todo está jodido* everything's gone to pot, everything's ruined.

jofaina *f* washbasin.

joggin *m* jogging.

jolgorio; holgorio *m* FAM rave, spree, binge, merrymaking (fiesta) || fun, merriment, gaiety (alegría) || — *ir de jolgorio* to go on a binge *o* a spree || *¡qué jolgorio!* what fun!

¡jolín!; ¡jolines! *interj* damn!, hell!

jollín; hollín *m* FAM row, set-to (disputa).

Jonás *npr m* Jonah.

Jonatán; Jonatás *npr m* Jonathan.

Jonia *npr f* GEOGR Ionia.

jónico, ca *adj* Ionic, Ionian || ARQ Ionic; *orden jónico* Ionic order.
◆ *m/f* Ionian.
◆ *m* Ionic (en poesía).

jonio, nia *adj/s* Ionian.

jopo *m* tail (rabo).

¡jopo! *interj* FAM hop it!, scram!, beat it!, scat!

jordán *m* FIG fountain of Youth || FIG & FAM *ir al jordán* to be rejuvenated, to rejuvenate (remozarse), to convalesce, to pick up (convalecer).

Jordán *npr m* GEOGR Jordan [river].

Jordania *npr f* GEOGR Jordan [kingdom].

jordano, na *adj/s* Jordan, Jordanian.

Jorge *npr m* George.

jornada *f* working day (día de trabajo); *una jornada de ocho horas* an eight-hour working day || journey (viaje) || day's journey (camino recorrido en un día) || stage (etapa); *hice el viaje en tres jornadas* I did the journey in three stages || FIG lifetime || MIL day, battle (batalla) | expedition (expedición) || TEATR act [in Spanish classical plays] || CINEM part, episode; *película en tres jornadas* film in three parts || royal journey (viaje de la familia real) || royal visit (estancia) || IMPR sheets *pl* printed in a day || *jornada de reflexión* day prior to an election on which there is no political campaigning || *trabajo de media jornada, de jornada entera* part-time, full-time work.

jornal *m* daily *o* day's wage, daily *o* day's wages *pl* (retribución); *jornal mínimo* minimum daily wage || day's work (día de trabajo) || land measure (medida agraria) || — *a jornal* by the day; *trabajar a jornal* to work *o* to be paid by the day || *gana un buen jornal* he earns a good wage.

jornalero, ra *m/f* day labourer [*US* day laborer].

joroba *f* hump, hunch, hunched back (giba) || FIG & FAM bind, drag (molestia).

jorobado, da *adj* hunchbacked, humpbacked.
◆ *m/f* hunchback, humpback.

jorobadura *f* FAM bind, drag (molestia).

jorobar *vt* FIG & FAM to get on one's nerves (poner nervioso); *este calor me está jorobando* this heat is getting on my nerves | to bother (fastidiar) || — FIG & FAM *está jorobado* he's got the hump (de mal humor) | *¡no me jorobes!* get away with you!
◆ *vpr* FAM to get fed up (hartarse) || *¡hay que jorobarse!* damn it all!

jorobeta *m* FAM hunchback, humpback.

jorongo *m* (Mexican) poncho.

joropo *m* AMER popular dance of the Colombian and Venezuelan lowlanders.

jorrar *vt* to drag, to haul [a net].

Josafat *n pr* GEOGR Jehoshaphat; *el Valle de Josafat* the Valley of Jehoshaphat.

José *npr m* Joseph.

Josefa; Josefina *npr f* Josephine.

josefino, na *adj* HIST supporting Joseph Bonaparte || AMER belonging to the Chilean clerical party (clerical) | [of *o* from] San José (Costa Rica y Uruguay).
◆ *m/f* HIST partisan of Joseph Bonaparte || AMER member of the Chilean clerical party | native *o* inhabitant of San José.

Josué *npr m* Joshua.

jota *f* j (nombre de la letra *j*) || jota [popular Aragonese, Valencian and Navarrese dance and its music] || jack, knave (en la baraja inglesa) || FIG iota, jot, bit, scrap (cosa mínima) || vegetable soup (potaje) || AMER sandal (ojota) || — FIG & FAM *no decir ni jota* not to say a word | *no entiendo ni jota* I don't understand a word of it *o* a thing | *no falta una jota* not an iota *o* not one iota is wanting | *no sabe ni jota* or *no sabe jota de pintura* he doesn't know the first thing about painting | *no se ve una jota* you can't see a thing | *sin faltar una jota* without missing a single detail.

joto *m* AMER FAM pansy, queer [*US* fag].

joven *adj* young; *de muy joven se fue a Madrid* he went to Madrid when still very young; *un país joven* a young country; *todavía la noche es joven* the night is still young; *es dos años más joven que yo* he is two years younger than I || youthful, young; *rostro joven* youthful face || *de aspecto joven* young-looking, youthful in appearance.
◆ *m* young man, youth (hombre) || *los jóvenes* young people, youth.
◆ *f* young woman, girl (mujer).

jovencito, ta; jovenzuelo, la *adj* rather young, quite young, youngish (bastante joven), very young (muy joven).
◆ *m/f* youngster, young boy (hombre), young girl (mujer).

jovial *adj* jovial, jolly, cheerful (alegre) || Jovian (relativo a Júpiter).

jovialidad *f* joviality, jollity, cheerfulness.

jovialmente *adv* cheerfully, jovially.

joviano, na *adj* Jovian (relativo a Júpiter).

joya *f* jewel (alhaja) || piece of jewellery (objeto de adorno) || jewelled brooch (brocamantón) || gift, present (regalo) || FIG jewel, gem, treasure (cosa o persona); *la niña es una joya* the child is a jewel | treasure (persona valiosa); *el nuevo empleado es una joya* the new clerk is a treasure || ARQ astragal || *joya de familia* family heirloom.
◆ *pl* trousseau *sing* (de la novia) || jewellery *sing* [*US* jewelry], jewels; *joyas de imitación* or *de fantasía* imitation jewellery.

joyel *m* small jewel.

joyería *f* jewellery [*US* jewelry trade *o* business] (comercio) || jeweller's [*US* jeweler's], jeweller's shop, jewellery shop (tienda).

joyero *m* jeweller [*US* jeweler] (fabricante o comerciante) || jewel box, jewel case (estuche).

Juan *npr m* John; *Juan Bautista* John the Baptist || — FAM *Juan Lanas* simpleton (tonto), good sort (bonachón) || *yo soy Juan Palomo, yo me lo guiso y yo me lo como* I'm all right, Jack.
◆ *m* AMER FAM private, footslogger (soldado de línea).

Juana *npr f* Jean, Joan, Jane || *Juana de Arco* Joan of Arc.

juanete *m* prominent cheekbone (pómulo abultado) || bunion (callosidad) || MAR topgallant [sail]; *juanete mayor, de proa* main, fore topgallant.

juanetero *m* MAR topgallantman.

juanetudo, da *adj* with prominent cheekbones (pómulo) || suffering from bunions (que tiene callos).

juarista *adj* supporting Juárez [in Mexico].
◆ *m/f* partisan of Juárez.

jubete *m* coat of mail.

jubilación *f* retirement, pensioning-off (acción de jubilar) || retirement (acción de jubilarse, retiro); *jubilación anticipada* early retirement || pension (renta) || jubilation (alegría).

jubilado, da *m/f* pensioner, retired person.

jubilar *adj* jubilee (relativo al jubileo).

jubilar *vt* to retire, to pension off (a un trabajador) || FIG & FAM to scrap, to ditch, to get rid of (una cosa) | to ditch, to get rid of (una persona).
◆ *vi* to jubilate, to be jubilant, to rejoice (alegrarse).
◆ *vpr* to retire, to go into retirement (un trabajador) || to jubilate, to be jubilant, to rejoice (regocijarse) || AMER to become skilled, to acquire practice (instruirse).

jubileo *m* REL jubilee || FIG comings and goings *pl* (idas y venidas).

júbilo *m* jubilation || joy; *no caber en sí de júbilo* to be beside o.s. with joy || — *con júbilo* with jubilation, joyfully, jubilantly || *mostrar júbilo* to jubilate, to be jubilant.

jubiloso, sa *adj* jubilant, joyful.

jubón *m* jerkin, doublet (vestidura) || bodice (de mujer) || sleeved vest (de niño).

Judá *npr m* Judah.

judaico, ca *adj* Jewish, Judaic.

judaísmo *m* Judaism.

judaizante *adj* Judaizing.
◆ *m/f* Judaizer, Judaist.

judaizar *vi* to judaize.

judas *m* FIG Judas (traidor) | effigy of Judas burnt during Holy Week (muñeco).

Judas *npr m* Judas; *Judas Iscariote* Judas Iscariot || FIG & FAM *estar hecho* or *parecer un Judas* to be dressed in rags..

Judea *npr f* GEOGR Judaea, Judea.

judeoalemán *m* Yiddish, Judaeo-German (lengua).

judeocristiano, na *adj/s* Judaeo-Christian.

judeoespañol *adj/s* Judaeo-Spanish.

judería *f* Jewish quarter, Jewry (barrio judío) || Jewry (conjunto de judíos) || ancient tax (impuesto).

judía *f* BOT bean || — *judía blanca* haricot bean || *judía escarlata* runner bean || *judía verde* French bean, green bean.

judiada *f* FAM dirty trick (mala jugada) | extortion (lucro).

judicatura *f* judicature (cargo) || term of office of a judge, judgeship (mandato) || judicature, judiciary (conjunto de jueces).

judicial *adj* judicial, juridical || — *partido judicial* judicial district (de una provincia) || *recurrir a la vía judicial* to have recourse to the law.

judiciario, ria *adj* judicial.
◆ *m* astrologer (astrólogo).

judío, a *adj* Jewish.
◆ *m/f* Jew.

Judit *npr f* Judith.

judo *m* judo (lucha).

judoka *m* judoka (luchador).

juego *m* game (recreo) || sport (deporte) || game (en tenis) || court (terreno donde se juega) || game; *juegos de azar* games of chance; *juego de cartas* or *de naipes* card game || gambling; *ha perdido mucho dinero en el juego* he has lost a lot of money gambling; *casa de juego* gambling house || rubber (en bridge) || play; *juego limpio* fair play; *juego sucio* foul play || FIG game; *sé muy bien su juego* I know what his game is | play; *el juego de luces en el espejo* the play of light on the mirror || set; *juego de cepillos, de útiles* set of brushes, of tools || service, set; *juego de café, de té* coffee, tea service || set (de botones, de chimenea, de diamantes, de neumáticos) || suite (de muebles); *juego de comedor* dining-room suite || TECN play (holgura, movimiento); *hay juego entre estas dos pie-*

zas there is play between these two parts ‖ — *abrir el juego* to start the game ‖ *afortunado en el juego, desgraciado en amores* lucky at cards, unlucky in love ‖ *a juego* matching; *corbata y pañuelo a juego* matching tie and handkerchief ‖ FIG *dar juego* to make work; *el escándalo dio mucho juego a los periodistas* the scandal made a lot of work for the newspapermen | *entrar en el juego* or *hacer el juego a alguien* to play into s.o.'s hands (inconscientemente), to play s.o.'s game (conscientemente) | *entrar en juego* to be at work (intervenir) | *entre bobos anda el juego* they are as thick as thieves ‖ *estar en juego* to be in play (un balón), to be at stake (fortuna, intereses) ‖ *estar fuera de juego* to be offside (persona), to be out [of the court] (pelota), to be out of play (el balón en el fútbol, rugby, etc.) ‖ FIG *hacer doble juego* to be two-faced, to play a double game, to run with the hare and hunt with the hounds ‖ *hacer juego* to match; *estos dos candelabros hacen juego* the two candelabras match ‖ *¡hagan juego!* place your bets! ‖ *juego de Bolsa* speculation ‖ INFORM *juego de caracteres* set of characters ‖ *juego de damas* (game of) draughts [US checkers] ‖ *juego doble* double-dealing ‖ *juego de envite* gambling game ‖ *juego de la oca* snakes and ladders ‖ *juego de las canicas* marbles ‖ *juego de manos* sleight of hand ‖ *juego de palabras* pun, play on words ‖ DEP *juego de piernas* footwork (de un boxeador, etc.) ‖ *juego de prendas* game of forfeits ‖ FIG *no ser cosa de juego* to be no laughing matter ‖ *poner en juego* to bring into play, to put at stake; *poner en juego su posición* to put one's position at stake; to make use of (influencias, relaciones) ‖ *por juego* for fun ‖ *queda poco tiempo de juego* there is little time left to play ‖ FIG *seguirle el juego a alguien* to play along with s.o. | *ser juego de niños* to be child's play ‖ *tener buen juego* to have a good hand (naipes) ‖ FIG *verle a uno el juego* to be on to s.o., to see through s.o.

◆ *pl* Games; *Juegos Olímpicos* Olympic Games ‖ — *hacer juegos de ojos* to roll one's eyes ‖ *hacer juegos malabares* to juggle (en el circo) ‖ *juegos atléticos* sports, athletic sports ‖ *juegos florales* poetry competition ‖ *juegos malabares* juggling.

juerga *f* FAM binge, spree, good time [US blast] ‖ — FAM *estar de juerga* to be living it up *o* whooping it up | *irse de juerga* to go on a spree, to go and have a good time [US to go have a blast] | *llevar una vida de juerga* to lead a wild life | *tener ganas de juerga* to feel like a bit of fun | *¡vaya juerga que nos corrimos!* what a time we had!, what a laugh!

juerguearse *vpr* FAM to live it up, to have a good time, to enjoy o.s. (divertirse) | not to take (sth.) seriously (no tomar en serio) | to make fun (*de* of) (burlarse).

juerguista *adj* FAM fun-loving.
◆ *m/f* FAM reveller.

jueves *m* thursday; *el jueves que viene, el jueves pasado* next Thursday, last Thursday ‖ — *Jueves Santo* Maundy Thursday, Holy Thursday ‖ FAM *no es cosa* or *nada del otro jueves* there's nothing to it (no es difícil), it's nothing to write home about, it's nothing to make a fuss about (no es ninguna maravilla) | *parece que lo has aprendido en jueves* don't you know how to say anything else?

juez *m* judge ‖ — REL *el Juez Supremo* the Divine Judge ‖ *juez de instrucción* examining magistrate ‖ DEP *juez de línea* or *de banda* linesman ‖ *juez de menores* judge sitting in juvenile court ‖ FAM *juez de palo* or *lego* incompetent judge ‖ *juez de paz* justice of the peace ‖ *juez de primera instancia* country court judge, judge of the court of first instance ‖ AMER DEP *juez de raya* finish line judge (en las carreras de caballos) ‖ DEP *juez de salida* starter (carreras) | *juez de silla* umpire (tenis).
◆ *pl* judges, bench *sing.*

jugada *f* throw (flechas, dados, bolos) ‖ stroke (golf, tenis) ‖ move (ajedrez, damas) ‖ shot, stroke (billar, croquet) ‖ piece of play, play (en general) ‖ FIG dirty trick; *me hizo una jugada* he played a dirty trick on me ‖ — *jugada de Bolsa* piece of speculation ‖ FIG *mala jugada* dirty trick ‖ *una buena jugada* a good move (buena táctica), a nice piece of play, a nice move (en deportes), a dirty trick (jugarreta).

jugador, ra *m/f* player ‖ gambler (de casa de juego) ‖ — *jugador de Bolsa* speculator on the Stock Exchange ‖ *jugador de fútbol* footballer, football player ‖ *jugador de manos* magician, conjurer ‖ *jugador de ventaja* cardsharp (fullero).

jugar* *vi* to play; *los niños juegan a los indios en el patio* the children are playing (at) cowboys and Indians in the courtyard; *nuestro equipo jugará mañana* our team will play tomorrow; *jugar al tenis* to play tennis ‖ to play; *jugar a la Bolsa* to play the Stock Exchange ‖ to bet (apostar) ‖ TECN to play, to have play (moverse) ‖ — *eso no es jugar limpio* that isn't fair play, that isn't cricket ‖ *jugar a cartas vistas* to play with the cards on the table ‖ *jugar a ganador, a colocado* to bet (on a horse) to win, to bet (on a horse) to place ‖ *jugar al alza, a la baja* to bull, to bear the market ‖ *jugar algo a cara o cruz* to toss for sth. ‖ *jugar a la pídola* to play leapfrog ‖ FIG *jugar con dos barajas* to doubledeal | *jugar con fuego* to play with fire | *jugar con su salud* to play with one's health | *jugar con uno* to play with s.o., to use s.o. ‖ *jugar fuerte* or *grueso* to play *o* to bet heavy ‖ *jugar limpio* to play fair *o* fairly ‖ *jugar sucio* to play dirty, to play foul ‖ *¿quién juega?* whose go is it, whose turn is it? ‖ FIG *solamente está jugando con ella* he is just trifling *o* playing with her.
◆ *vt* to play; *jugar un partido, una partida, una carta* to play a match, a game, a card ‖ to stake (dinero) ‖ to wield; *jugar la espada* to wield one's sword ‖ — *jugar doble contra sencillo* to bet two to one ‖ *jugar una mala pasada* or *partida a uno* to play a dirty trick on s.o.
◆ *vpr* to risk (arriesgar); *jugarse la vida, el honor* to risk one's life *o* neck, one's honour ‖ to bet, to stake; *jugarse mil pesetas en* to stake a thousand pesetas on ‖ — FIG *el país se juega su futuro en las próximas elecciones* the forthcoming elections put the future of the country in the balance | *jugarse el pellejo* to risk one's neck *o* one's skin | *jugarse hasta la camisa, el alma* to stake one's shirt | *jugársela a alguien* to play a dirty trick on s.o. | *jugárselo todo a una carta, jugarse el todo por el todo* to stake everything one has (apostar), to go the whole hog, to take the plunge (tomar una acción drástica) | *me juego la cabeza a que...* I'd stake my life that... | *se juega su felicidad en eso* his happiness is at stake.

jugarreta *f* FAM bad move, bad play ‖ FIG & FAM dirty trick (trastada); *le hizo una jugarreta* he played a dirty trick on him.

juglar *m* minstrel (trovador) ‖ juggler (malabarista).

juglaresco, ca *adj* pertaining to minstrels ‖ *poesía juglaresca* poetry of the minstrels, minstrel poetry.

juglaría; juglería *f* minstrelsy.

jugo *m* juice; *jugo de limón* lemon juice; *jugo de carne* juice of the meat; *jugo gástrico, pancreático* gastric, pancreatic juice ‖ CULIN gravy ‖ FIG essence, substance, pith (lo esencial) ‖ — FIG & FAM *sacar el jugo de un libro* to get the pith and marrow out of a book | *sacarle el jugo a alguien* to bleed s.o. white, to bleed s.o. dry | *sacarle jugo al dinero* to make the most of one's money, to get one's money's worth, to get value for money.

jugosidad *f* juiciness, succulence ‖ FIG substance.

jugoso, sa *adj* juicy; *una fruta jugosa* a juicy fruit ‖ FIG lucrative, profitable (provechoso) | substantial, meaty, worthwhile, pithy (sustancioso) | rich (colores).

juguete *m* toy ‖ TEATR skit ‖ — FIG *ser el juguete de alguien* to be s.o.'s plaything ‖ *un coche de juguete* a toy car.

juguetear *vi* to play (jugar) ‖ to play, to toy; *está jugueteando con su pulsera* she is toying with her bracelet ‖ to romp, to frolic (retozar).

jugueteo *m* playing (diversión) ‖ romping, frolicking.

juguetería *f* toyshop (tienda) ‖ toy trade, toy business (comercio).

juguetón, ona *adj* playful; *niño, perro juguetón* playful child, dog ‖ frolicsome, frisky (retozón).

juicio *m* judgment, judgement; *tener el juicio recto* to have sound judgment ‖ mind, reason, sanity, senses *pl*; *perder el juicio* to lose one's mind ‖ common sense (sentido común); *tiene poco juicio* he lacks common sense ‖ good sense, sensibleness (sensatez) ‖ judgment; *emitir un juicio sobre alguien* to make a judgment about s.o. ‖ JUR trial (pleito) ‖ — *a juicio de* in the opinion of ‖ *a juicio de peritos* according to expert opinion ‖ *a mi juicio* in my opinion ‖ *asentar el juicio* to come to one's senses ‖ *dejar algo a juicio de uno* to leave sth. to s.o.'s discretion ‖ *estar en su juicio* or *en su cabal juicio* to be in one's right mind ‖ *estar fuera* or *falto de juicio* to be out of one's mind ‖ REL *juicio de Dios* trial by ordeal ‖ JUR *juicio definitivo* or *sin apelación* decree absolute | *juicio en rebeldía* judgment in contumacy, judgment by default ‖ REL *Juicio Final* Last Judgment ‖ *la edad del juicio* the age of reason ‖ *muela del juicio* wisdom tooth ‖ *no estar en su sano juicio* not to be in one's right mind ‖ *poner en tela de juicio* to question, to put in doubt ‖ *quitar el juicio a alguien* to drive s.o. out of his mind ‖ *someter a juicio pericial* to submit to expert opinion ‖ *volver en su juicio* to come to one's senses, to regain consciousness.

juicioso, sa *adj* judicious, wise (sensato) ‖ FIG appropriate, sensible (atinado).

jujeño, ña *adj* [of *o* from] Jujuy (Argentina).
◆ *m/f* native *o* inhabitant of Jujuy.

julepe *m* MED julep (poción) ‖ sort of card game (juego de naipes) ‖ FIG & FAM dressing down, scolding (reprimenda) ‖ AMER scare, fright (miedo) ‖ — *dar julepe a alguien* to leave s.o. without a trick (naipes) ‖ FIG & FAM *darse un julepe* to work like a dog *o* like the devil (trabajar mucho) ‖ AMER *dar un julepe a uno* to scare s.o., to give s.o. a fright.

julepear *vt* AMER to scare (asustar) | to hurry up (dar prisa) | to tire (fatigar).

Julián *npr m* Julian.

juliana *f* BOT rocket, damewort, dame's violet ‖ CULIN julienne soup (sopa).

Juliana *npr f* Juliana.

juliano, na *adj* Julian; *calendario juliano* Julian calendar; *era juliana* Julian era.

Julieta *npr f* Juliet.

julio *m* July (mes); *el 5 de julio* the 5th of July ‖ FÍS joule (unidad de trabajo).

Julio *npr m* Jules.

jumá; juma *f* FAM ⟶ **jumera.**

jumado, da *adj* FAM drunk, canned.

jumarse *vpr* FAM to get drunk *o* canned.

jumento, ta *m/f* ass, donkey.

jumera; jumá; juma *f* FAM *agarrar una jumera* to get drunk *o* canned.

juncáceas *f pl* BOT juncaceae.

juncal *adj* willowy (esbelto) || shapely (talle).

juncal; juncar *m* BOT rush bed, rushes *pl.*

juncia *f* BOT sedge.

junco *m* BOT rush || cane, stick (bastón) || MAR junk (embarcación china) || — BOT *junco de Indias* rattan | *junco florido* flowering rush | *junco oloroso* camel grass.

jungla *f* jungle.

juniense *adj* [of *o* from] Junín (Perú).
◆ *m/f* native *o* inhabitant of Junín.

junino, na *adj* [of *o* from] Junín (Argentina).
◆ *m/f* native *o* inhabitant of Junín.

junio *m* June (mes); *el 24 de junio* the 24th of June.

júnior *m* REL novice (monje) || junior (el más joven, deportista).

junípero BOT juniper (enebro).

junquera *f* BOT rush (junco) | rush bed (juncal).

junqueral *m* rush bed, rushes *pl.*

junquillo *m* BOT jonquil | rattan (junco de Indias) || Rattan [walking stick] (bastón) || strip of wood (varilla) || ARQ beading (moldura).

junta *f* meeting, assembly; *junta de accionistas* shareholders' meeting; *junta general* general meeting; *junta de gobierno* cabinet meeting || session, sitting (sesión) || board, council; *junta administrativa* administrative board || council; *junta de empresa* works council || board; *junta de beneficencia* charity board; *junta directiva* board of directors; *ser miembro de una junta* to serve on a board || junta (en los países ibéricos); *junta militar* military junta || ARQ jointing seam || MAR seam (entre tablones) || TECN joint; *junta estanca* watertight joint || — *celebrar junta* to hold a meeting, to sit || TECN *junta de culata* gasket | *junta universal* universal joint, cardan joint.
◆ *pl* AMER junction *sing* (de dos ríos).

juntamente *adv* together, jointly (conjuntamente) || at the same time, together (al mismo tiempo).

juntar *vt* to unite, to join; *juntar dos tablas* to join two boards || to put together, to assemble (varias piezas) || to unite; *la amistad les junta* friendship unites them || to joint, to put together (poner juntos) || to gather together; *juntar amigos en su casa* to gather friends together in one's home || to collect, to raise (dinero) || to collect, to gather (sellos, documentos, etc.).
◆ *vpr* to join (up with), to meet; *me juntaré al grupo en Madrid* I will join the group in Madrid || to join (dos ríos) || to meet, to assemble, to gather (together) (congregarse) || to join (forces with); *Pedro se ha juntado con Antonio para fundar una empresa* Peter has joined Anthony to start a business || to join together, to join forces (aunar sus fuerzas) || to live with (vivir con) || to live together (vivir juntos) || *Dios los cría y ellos se juntan* birds of a feather flock together.

juntillas (a pie); juntillo (a pie) → **pie.**

junto, ta *adj* joined, united; *dos tablas juntas* two joined boards || side by side (uno al lado de otro) || together; *vivían juntos* they were living together; *las niñas jugaban juntas* the girls were playing together; *todo junto, todos juntos* all together || put together; *un territorio tan extenso como seis provincias juntas* a territory as large as six provinces put together || — *demasiado juntos* too close || *muy juntos* very close together.
◆ *adv* *aquí junto* near by, close by || *demasiado junto* too close || *en junto, por junto* in all, in total, all together || *junto a* close to, near, next to (cerca de), next to (al lado de), against (contra) || *junto con* together with || *muy junto* very close, very near.

juntura *f* junction, join || ANAT joint || TECN joint, coupling || ANAT *juntura serrátil* serrated suture (articulación fija).

Júpiter *npr m* MIT Jupiter, Jove.

jupiteriano, na *adj* Jovian, relative to Jupiter.

jura *f* oath (acción) || swearing in (ceremonia) || *jura de (la) bandera* pledge of allegiance to the flag.

jurado, da *adj* sworn || sworn, sworn-in (que ha prestado juramento) || FIG *enemigo jurado* sworn enemy.
◆ *m* jury (tribunal) || juryman (miembro del tribunal) || panel of judges, jury (en un concurso) || — *jurado de cuentas* chartered accountant [US certified public accountant] || *jurado de empresa* works council.

juramentado, da *adj* sworn, sworn-in; *traductor juramentado* sworn-in translator.

juramentar *vt* to swear in, to put on oath.
◆ *vpr* to take an oath, to be sworn in.

juramento *m* oath; *prestar juramento* to take the oath || oath, curse, blasphemy (blasfemia) || — *bajo juramento* on *o* under oath || *juramento asertorio* assertory oath || *juramento falso* perjury || *juramento promisorio* promissory oath || *soltar juramentos* to curse, to blaspheme || *tomar juramento a alguien* to put s.o. on oath, to swear s.o. in.

jurar *vt/vi* to swear, to take an oath; *jurar sobre el Evangelio* to swear on the Gospel || to swear; *te juro que te he dicho la verdad* I swear that I have told you the truth || to swear, to curse (blasfemar) || — *jurar el cargo* to take the oath of office || *jurar en falso* to commit perjury, to bear false witness || *jurar (la) bandera* to pledge allegiance to the flag || *jurar por Dios que* to swear to God that... || *jurar por la salud de uno...* to swear on one's mother's grave || *jurar por lo más sagrado* or *por todos los dioses* to swear by all that is sacred *o* to swear by all the gods || *lo juraría* I would swear to it || *no jurar el santo nombre de Dios en vano* thou shalt not take the name of the Lord thy God in vain (mandamiento) || *te lo juro* I swear it.
◆ *vpr* *jurársela a uno* to swear to get even with s.o., to swear vengeance on s.o.

jurásico, ca *adj/sm* GEOL Jurassic (del Jura).

jurel *m* ZOOL horse mackerel, jack mackerel, scad, jurel, saurel (pez).

jurídico, ca *adj* legal, juridical; *problemas jurídicos* juridical problems || *persona jurídica* artificial person, body corporate, legal entity.

jurisconsulto *m* jurisconsult, legal expert.

jurisdicción *f* jurisdiction || FIG *caer bajo la jurisdicción de uno* to fall *o* to come under s.o.'s jurisdiction.

jurisdiccional *adj* jurisdictional || *aguas jurisdiccionales* territorial waters.

jurispericia *f* jurisprudence.

jurisperito *m* jurist, legal expert, jurisprudent.

jurisprudencia *f* jurisprudence || Case law (precedentes) || *sentar jurisprudencia* to be a test case.

jurisprudencial *adj* jurisprudential.

jurista m jurist, lawyer.

juro *m* right of perpetual ownership || pension (renta).

justa *f* joust, tilt (combate) || FIG contest, competition (certamen) || *justa poética* poetry contest.

justamente *adv* precisely, exactly; *es justamente lo que quería* it is exactly what I wanted || just enough; *tiene justamente para vivir* he has just enough to live on || justly, fairly (con justicia) || — *eso es, justamente* that's just it || *¡justamente!* precisely!

justicia *f* justice; *la justicia está cumplida* justice has been done || justice, fairness; *no hay justicia en el mundo* there is no justice in the world || execution (de un condenado a muerte) || — *administrar (la) justicia* to administer justice || *de justicia* justly, deservedly, duly || *ejecutor de la justicia* executioner || *es de justicia que...* it is just that..., it is right that... || *hacer justicia* to do justice || *ir por justicia* to go to law, to bring an action || *justicia distributiva* distributive justice || *justicia social* social justice || *justicias y ladrones* cops and robbers (juego) || *Ministerio de Justicia* Lord High Chancellor's Office [US Department of Justice] || *pedir en justicia* to go to court || *pedir justicia* to demand justice || *tomarse la justicia por su mano* to take the law into one's own hands.
◆ *m* *justicia mayor* supreme magistrate [in Aragon].

justiciar *vt* AMER to execute (ajusticiar) | to condemn (condenar).

justiciero, ra *adj* just, fair || *espíritu justiciero* sense of justice.
◆ *m/f* just *o* fair person.

justificable *adj* justifiable.

justificación *f* justification || IMPR justification || INFORM *justificación automática* automatic justification.

justificante *adj* justifying.
◆ *m* voucher, voucher copy (comercio) || JUR document in proof, relevant paper.

justificar *vt* to justify || IMPR to justify || *sin razón que lo justifique* without justifiable reason.
◆ *vpr* to clear o.s., to justify o. s; *justificarse con alguien* to justify o.s. with s.o.

justificativo, va *adj* justifying, justificatory.

justillo *m* jerkin (prenda de vestir).

Justiniano *npr m* Justinian.

justipreciar *vt* to appraise, to evaluate, to estimate (apreciar).

justiprecio *m* appraisal, estimate, evaluation.

justo, ta *adj* just, fair, right || tight (apretado); *me está muy justo* it's very tight || exact, right, correct (exacto) || sufficient, just enough (suficiente) || deserved, condign (castigo) || legitimate (cólera) || fair (trato) || right (cálculo, hora) || right, accurate, exact (palabra, dicho) || sound (razonamiento) || — *justo es que...* it is just that..., it is right that... || *llegamos al lugar justo del incidente* we arrived at the very place of the incident || *más de lo justo* more than enough || *mil pesetas justas* exactly one thousand pesetas.
◆ *m* righteous person || — *lo justo y lo injusto* right and wrong || *los justos* the righteous || *pagan justos por pecadores* the innocent must often pay for the guilty.
◆ *adv* just, exactly || — *llegar justo* to arrive just in (the nick of) time (a tiempo), to arrive just; *llegó justo cuando me iba* he arrived just as I was leaving || *tener justo para vivir* to have just enough to live on || *vivir muy justo* to scrape a bare living.

jutía *f* AMER hutia (mamífero).

Jutlandia *npr f* GEOGR Jutland.

juvenil *adj* young, youthful, juvenile; *aspecto juvenil* youthful appearance || youthful, young; *un traje juvenil* a youthful suit || *en los años juveniles* in one's youth.
◆ *m/f* DEP junior.

juventud *f* youth (edad) || youthfulness; *ha conservado su juventud* she has conserved her youthfulness || youth, young people (gente joven).

juzgado, da *adj* judged.
◆ *m* court, tribunal || judicature (judicatura) || — *juzgado municipal* magistrate's court || *ser una cosa de juzgado de guardia* to be a hanging matter.

juzgar *vt* to judge; *juzgar a un reo* to judge a criminal || to judge, to consider, to deem, to think; *yo no juzgo oportuno hacer esto* I don't think it fitting *o* right to do this || — *a juzgar por* judging by, judging from; *a juzgar por su apariencia* judging from his appearance || *juzgar mal* to misjudge || *juzgar por las apariencias* or *a la vista* to judge by appearances || *no se puede juzgar por las apariencias* one can't judge a book by its cover || *¡y juzgue mi sorpresa cuando le vi!* and just imagine my surprise when I saw him!

K

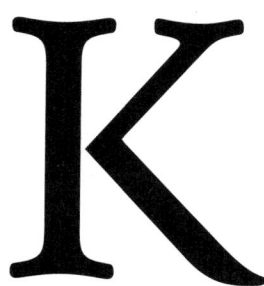

k *f* k; *una k mayúscula, minúscula* a capital, a small k.
— OBSERV The Spanish *k* is pronounced like the English *k* as in *kite*.

ka *f* k [name of the letter *k*].

kabila *adj/s* kabyle (cabila).

Kabul *n pr* GEOGR Kabul.

kainita *f* QUÍM kainite (sal).

káiser *m* Kaiser.

kakatoes *m* ZOOL cockatoo.

kaki; kaqui *adj* khaki (color).
◆ *m* kaki, Japanese persimmon (árbol y fruto) || khaki (color) || FAM khakies *pl* (uniforme militar).

Kalaharí *n pr* GEOGR the Kalahari Desert.

kaleidoscopio *m* kaleidoscope (caleidoscopio).

kamikaze *m* kamikaze (avión suicida) || FIG daredevil, madcap.

Kampala *n pr* GEOGR Kampala.

kan *m* khan (príncipe) || caravanserai (caravasar y mercado público).

kanato *m* khanate.

kantiano, na *adj/s* Kantian.

kantismo *m* Kantianism.

kapoc *m* kapok.

kappa *f* kappa (letra griega).

kaqui *adj/sm* ⟶ **kaki.**

karakul *m* ZOOL karakul, caracul (caracul).

karate *m* DEP karate.

karateka *m/f* karate expert.

kart *m* go-kart (vehículo).

karting *m* karting [*US* go-kart racing].

Katmandú *n pr* GEOGR Katmandu.

kayac *m* kayak (embarcación).

kéfir *m* kefir (bebida).

kelvin *m* kelvin.

Kenia *n pr* GEOGR Kenya.

keniano, na *adj/s* Kenyan.
— OBSERV El gentilicio es *keniano* y no *keniata*.

kenotrón *m* kenotron (tubo).

kepí; kepis *m* kepi (quepis).

kermes *m* kermes (quermes).

kermesse *f* charity fair.

kerosén *m* ⟶ **queroseno.**

ketchup *m* ketchup.

khedive *m* khedive.

kibutz *m* kibbutz.
◆ *pl* kibbutzim.
— OBSERV The plural of *kibutz* is *kibutzim*.

kieselgur *m* kieselguhr, kieselgur (silíceo).

kieserita *f* MIN kieserite.

kif *m* kif (polvo de cáñamo).

Kilimanjaro *npr m* GEOGR Mount Kilimanjaro.

kilo *m* kilo, kilogram, kilogramme (kilogramo).

kilocaloría *f* FÍS kilocalorie.

kilociclo *m* kilocycle.

kilogramo *m* kilogramme, kilogram.

kilojulio *m* kilojoule.

kilometraje *m* distance in kilometres || mileage (de un coche).
— OBSERV La palabra *mileage* se refiere a la distancia recorrida en millas.

kilometrar *vt* to measure in kilometres.

kilométrico, ca *adj* kilometric || FIG & FAM endless, interminable; *un pasillo kilométrico* an endless corridor || *mojón kilométrico* milestone [indicating distance in kilometres].
— OBSERV For long train journeys in Spain, one can obtain *un billete kilométrico*, in coupon form. Each coupon is valid for a certain distance in kilometres. There is a reduction in proportion to the number of kilometres travelled.

kilómetro *m* kilometre [*US* kilometer]; *kilómetro cuadrado* square kilometre.

kilotón *m* kiloton.

kilovatio *m* kilowatt.

kilovatio-hora *m* kilowatt-hour.

kilovoltio *m* kilovolt.

kilt *m* kilt (falda escocesa).

kimono *m* kimono.

kindergarten *m* kindergarten.

kinesiterapeuta *m/f* masseur (hombre), masseuse (mujer) (masajista).

kinesiterapia *f* massage, kinesitherapy, massage (curación por medio de masajes).

Kinshasa *n pr* GEOGR Kinshasa.

kiosco *m* kiosk || bandstand (de música) || *kiosko de periódicos* newsstand, newspaper stall.
— OBSERV The Spanish spelling *quiosco* is preferred.

kirie *m* kyrie || FIG & FAM *llorar los kiries* to cry one's eyes out.

kirieleisón *m* kyrie eleison || FAM funeral chant, dirge || FIG & FAM *cantar el kirieleisón* to beg for mercy.

kirsch *m* kirsch (aguardiente de cereza).

kit *m* kit.

kitsch *adj* kitschy.
◆ *m* kitsch.

kiwi *m* ZOOL kiwi (ave) || kiwi fruit (fruto).

klaxon *m* horn, hooter (bocina) || *tocar el klaxon* to sound *o* to honk the horn.

knock-out *m inv* knockout || *dejar* or *poner a alguien knock-out* to knock s.o. out.

knut *m* knout (látigo).

koala *m* ZOOL koala.

kola *f* kola *o* cola nut.

koljoz *m* kolkhoz (en Rusia).

kopek *m* copeck, kopeck, kopek (moneda rusa).

kraft *m* kraft (papel).

krausismo *m* philosophy of Krause.
— OBSERV *Krausismo* had a great influence on Spain in the nineteenth century.

krausista *adj* Krause; *doctrina krausista* Krause doctrine.
◆ *m/f* follower of Krause.

kremlin *m* kremlin.

kriptón *m* krypton (gas).

kronprinz *m* crown prince (de prusia).

kulak *m* kulak (campesino).

kumis *m* koumiss, kumiss (bebida).

kummel *m* kümmel (licor).

Kurdistán *npr m* GEOGR Kurdistan.

kurdo, da *adj* Kurdish, Kurd.
◆ *m/f* Kurd.

Kuwait *n pr* GEOGR Kuwait (país) || Kuwait city (capital).

L

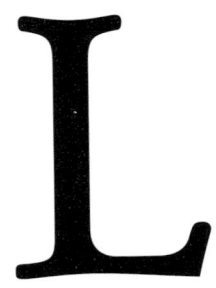

l *f* l (letra); *una l mayúscula* a capital l.
— OBSERV Pronounced like the English *l*.

la *m* MÚS la (nota de la escala vocal) | A (de la escala instrumental); *la sostenido* A sharp || *dar el la* to give the tuning A (a una orquesta).

la *art f sing* the; *la cabeza* the head.
— OBSERV When feminine nouns begin with a stressed *a* or *ha*, for euphonic reasons *la* is replaced by *el*: *el agua, el alma, el hambre*.
— OBSERV El artículo *la* debe traducirse en inglés por el adjetivo posesivo cuando se refiere a una parte del cuerpo: *dame la mano* give me your hand. Se omite delante de los nombres de países: *la Argentina* Argentina; excepto si se trata de una República: *la República Argentina* the Republic of Argentina. El uso popular de *la* delante del nombre existe en español pero no en inglés: *la María me lo dijo* Mary told me.

la *pron pers* her (persona); *yo la saludo* I greet her || you (cuando corresponde a «usted»); *la vi a usted ayer* I saw you yesterday || it (cosa); *la leo* I read it || the one; *la del tercer piso* the one on the third floor || — FAM *la de* the quantity of, the amount of; *si vieras la de vino que bebimos* you should have seen the quantity of wine we drank; the number of; *si vieras la de platos que pedimos* you should have seen the number of dishes we ordered || *la del abrigo negro* the one in the black coat, the one with the black coat || *la de Martínez* Mrs. Martínez || *la de Miguel es más grande* Michael's one *o* Michael's is bigger || *la de usted* yours || *la que* the one who, she who, she that (persona, sujeto); *la que vino ayer* the one who came yesterday; the one whom, the one that, the one (*persona, complemento*); *la que veré mañana* the one I'll see tomorrow; the one which, the one that, the one (cosas); *la que quiero* the one I want || *son... las que* it is... that; *son las de arriba las que están rotas* it is the upper ones that are broken; it is... who; *son María y Carola las que vienen* it is Mary and Carol who are coming.
— OBSERV *La* should not be used instead of *le* in the dative: *le hablé dos palabras, le di la mano*, not *la hablé dos palabras, la di la mano*. This improper use of *la* is called *laísmo*.

label *m* label (etiqueta de garantía).

laberíntico, ca *adj* labyrinthine, labyrinthian.

laberinto *m* labyrinth, maze || FIG tangle, maze (asunto embrollado).

labia *f* FAM glibness || *tener mucha labia* to have the gift of the gab.

labiado, da *adj* BOT labiate.
◆ *f* BOT labiate.

labial *adj/s f* labial.

labialización *f* labialization.

labializar *vt* to labialize.

labihendido, da *adj* harelipped.

labio *m* ANAT lip; *labio superior abultado* heavy upper lip | labium, lip (de vulva) || edge, rim, lip (reborde) || BOT lip, labrum, labium (lóbulo) || *labio belfo* thick lower lip || MED *labio leporino* harelip.
◆ *pl* FIG lips; *nunca le ofendieron mis labios* my lips have never uttered a word against him || lips (de una llaga) || — *apretar los labios* to clench *o* to screw up one's lips || FIG *cerrar* or *sellar los labios* to keep one's lips sealed, to keep one's mouth shut | *estar pendiente de los labios de alguien* to hang on to s.o.'s every word | *hablar con el corazón en los labios* to speak frankly *o* with an open heart *lamerse los labios* to lick one's lips | *morderse los labios* to bite one's lip | *no despegar* or *no descoser los labios* not to open one's mouth, not to say a word | *no morderse los labios* to speak one's mind, to be outspoken | *sellarle a uno los labios* to seal s.o.'s lips, to silence s.o.

labiodental *adj/s f* GRAM labiodental.

labiovelar *adj/s f* labiovelar.

labor *f* job, work, piece of work; *una labor productiva* a profitable piece of work || labour [US labor], work (tarea) || thousand tiles *o* bricks (tejas o ladrillos) || manufactured tobacco || MIN excavation, workings *pl* || — *caballo de labor* workhorse || *cesta de labores* sewing basket (de costura), knitting bag (de punto) || *dar dos labores a un campo* to plough a field twice || *labor de equipo* teamwork || *labores de aguja* needlework, sewing, embroidery || *labores de ganchillo* crochet || *labores de la casa* housework || *labores del campo* farm work (en general), tilling, ploughing [US plowing] (labranza) || *labores de punto* knitting || *sus labores* unemployed (solteras), housewife (casadas) || *tierra de labor* arable land.
— OBSERV The phrase *sus labores*, abbreviated *S. L.* represents the full expression *que hace sus labores en casa* and applies to all woman who do not work except in their own homes.

laborable *adj* working, work; *día laborable* working day || AGR arable, tillable, workable.

laboral *adj* labour [US labor]; *conflictos laborales* labour disputes || — *accidente laboral* industrial accident || *enseñanza laboral* technical education || *instituto laboral* technical college.

laborar *vt* to work, to till, to plough (la tierra).
◆ *vi* to work; *labora por el bien de su país* he is working for the good of his country.

laboratorio *m* laboratory || *ayudante de laboratorio* laboratory *o* lab assistant *o* technician.

laborear *vt* to work || AGR to work, to till, to plough || MIN to work [a mine].
◆ *vi* MAR to reeve.

laboreo *m* AGR tilling, ploughing [US plowing] (arado) | cultivation, working (de la tierra) || exploitation, working (de minas) || MAR reeving.

laboriosidad *f* laboriousness, industry.

laborioso, sa *adj* laborious, hard-working, industrious; *estudiante laborioso* hard-working student || laborious, difficult; *parto laborioso, digestión laboriosa* laborious delivery, difficult digestion || arduous, laborious (tarea).

laborismo *m* Labour Party (partido político) || Labour movement (movimiento).

laborista *adj* labour [US labor]; *partido laborista* Labour Party.
◆ *m/f* Labour Party member, Labour member *o* supporter || *los laboristas* Labour (partido).

labra *f* cutting, carving (de piedra, madera).

labrado, da *adj* worked (trabajado) || worked, ploughed [US plowed] (tierras) || cut, carved (piedra) || carved (madera) || wrought (metales) || worked (artesanía) || embroidered (tejido).
◆ *m* cutting, carving (de piedra) || carving (de madera) || working (de metales) || embroidery (de tejidos).
◆ *pl* cultivated fields.

labrador, ra *adj* farming, farm; *población labradora* farming population.
◆ *m/f* peasant (campesino).
◆ *m* farmer (dueño) || farm labourer, farm worker [US farmhand] (obrero agrícola) || ploughman [US plowman] (que ara) || *sindicato de labradores* farm worker's union.

labradorita *f* MIN labradorite.

labrantío, a *adj* arable, tillable.
◆ *m* arable *o* tillable land.

labranza *f* farming, cultivation (de la tierra) || farmland (campo) || work (trabajo) || *aperos* or *instrumentos de labranza* farming tools *o* implements.

labrar *vt* to work (trabajar) || to carve (madera) || to cut, to carve (piedra) || to work (los metales) || to plough [US to plow], to work, to till (arar) || to cultivate (cultivar) || to build (edificar) || to cut (piedras preciosas) || to embroider (bordar) || FIG to work for, to forge; *labrar la felicidad de uno* to work for s.o.'s happiness; *labraremos la grandeza del país* we shall forge the greatness of our country | to cause, to bring about (causar); *labrar su propia ruina* to cause one's own ruin || — *labrar chocolate* to manufacture *o* to produce chocolate || *labrar moneda* to coin money.
◆ *vi* to work; *labrar en madera, en mármol* to work in wood, in marble.
◆ *vpr* to make, to build, to forge; *labrarse un porvenir* to build one's future.

labriego, ga *m/f* peasant (campesino) || farm labourer *o* worker [US farmhand] (obrero agrícola) || farmer (dueño).

labro *m* labrum (en los insectos) || wrasse (pez).

laca *f* lac (resina) || lacquer (mueble) || lacquer, shellac (barniz) || lacquer, hair spray (para el pelo) || — *barnizar con laca* to varnish with shellac || *dar laca, pintar con laca* to lacquer || *goma laca* shellac || *laca para uñas* nail varnish *o* polish || *poner laca en, echar laca a* to lacquer, to spray [with hair spray] (el pelo).

lacayo *m* lackey, lacquey (criado), footman (de a pie), groom (de a caballo) || FIG lackey, flunkey, toady (persona servil).

laceador *m* AMER lassoer.

lacear *vt* to trim *o* to adorn with bows (adornar con cintas) || to lasso (coger con lazo) || to snare (la caza menor) || to drive (game) into range (disponer la caza).

Lacedemonia *npr f* GEOGR Lacedaemon.

laceración *f* laceration.

lacerado, da *adj* unhappy, unfortunate, unlucky (infeliz) || wounded (herido) || lacerated (desgarrado) || leprous (leproso).
◆ *m/f* leper (leproso) || (ant) miser.

lacerante *adj* wounding (palabras) || sharp (dolor) || heart-rending, harrowing (grito).

lacerar *vt* to lacerate, to tear (desgarrar) || FIG to damage, to harm, to injure (la reputación) | to rend, to lacerate (el corazón).

laceria *f* misery, poverty, want.

lacería *f* bows *pl*, ornamental bows *pl* (bordados) || ARQ interlacing arches.

lacero *m* lassoer (para toros, etc.) || poacher [using snares] (cazador furtivo) || dogcatcher (empleado municipal).

Lacio *npr m* GEOGR Latium.

lacio, cia *adj* withered, faded (marchito) || lank, straight; *con los cabellos lacios* with lank hair || FIG limp, languid (flojo).

lacolito *m* GEOL laccolith, laccolite.

lacón *m* shoulder of pork.

Laconia *npr f* GEOGR Laconia.

lacónico, ca *adj* laconic, terse (conciso).

laconismo *m* laconicism, terseness (concisión).

lacra *f* mark, scar [left by illness] || FIG blemish, stain, blot (de la reputación) | defect, flaw, fault (defecto) | scourge, blight, bane; *la miseria es una lacra que traspasa las fronteras* poverty is a scourge which knows no frontiers || *AMER* sore, wound (llaga) | scab (postilla).

lacrado *m* sealing (with wax) (de una carta).

lacrar *vt* to seal (with wax) (cerrar con lacre) || to strike (afligir a uno una enfermedad) || to contaminate (contagiar).

lacre *m* sealing wax || — *barra de lacre* stick of sealing wax || *cerrar con lacre* to seal with wax.
◆ *adj* red (rojo).

lácrima christi *m* lachryma *o* lacrima christi (vino).

lacrimal *adj* lachrymal, lacrimal, tear; *conductos lacrimales* tear ducts.

lacrimatorio, ria *adj/sm* lachrymatory, lacrimatory (vaso).

lacrimógeno, na *adj* tear-producing || FIG sentimental, tearful (comedia) || *gas lacrimógeno* tear gas.

lacrimoso, sa *adj* tearful, weeping || watering (ojos) || *una voz lacrimosa* a tearful voice.

lactancia *f* lactation, nursing, suckling.

lactante *adj* nursing, suckling (niño, madre).
◆ *m* suckling, unweaned baby (niño).

lactar *vt* to nurse, to breast-feed, to suckle (amamantar) || to bottle nurse, to bottle feed.
◆ *vi* to feed on milk, to nurse, to suckle.

lactasa *f* QUÍM lactase.

lactato *m* QUÍM lactate.

lacteado, da *adj* mixed with milk || *harina lacteada* malted milk.

lácteo, a *adj* milky, lacteous || milk; *dieta láctea* milk diet || — *productos lácteos* milk products, dairy products || *vasos lácteos* lacteal vessels || ASTR *Vía Láctea* Milky Way.

lactescente *adj* lactescent.

láctico, ca *adj* QUÍM lactic (ácido).

lactífero, ra *adj* ANAT lactiferous.

lactona *f* QUÍM lactone.

lactosa *f* QUÍM lactose, milk sugar.

lacunario *m* ARQ lacunar (artesonado).

lacustre *adj* lake, lacustrine; *vivienda lacustre* lake dwelling; *aldea lacustre* lake village.

lacha *f* anchovy (boquerón) || — *me da lacha* I feel *o* I am ashamed || *tener poca lacha* to be shameless.

ladear *vt* to lean, to tilt, to slant, to incline, to tip (inclinar) || to tilt, to incline to one side (la cabeza) || to bend (doblar); *ladear un clavo* to bend a nail || FIG to avoid (evitar) | to avoid, to evade, to get round (una dificultad) || — *el cuadro está ladeado* the picture is lopsided || *ladear una montaña* to go round *o* to skirt a mountain.
◆ *vi* to lean, to tilt, to slant, to incline || AVIAC to bank || FIG to go off the straight and narrow (salir del camino recto).
◆ *vpr* to lean, to incline [to one side] (una persona, un árbol, un edificio) || to bend (doblarse) || AVIAC to bank || to swerve (echarse a un lado) || FIG to be equal (*con* to) (igualarse) || *AMER* to fall in love (enamorarse).

ladeo *m* leaning, inclination, tilt (acción de inclinar o inclinarse) || bending (acción de doblarse) || AVIAC banking || FIG inclination.

ladera *f* slope, side, hillside (de una colina), slope, side, mountainside (de una montaña).

ladi *f* lady.

ladilla *f* crab louse (insecto) || variety of barley (especie de cebada) || FIG & FAM *pegarse como una ladilla* to cling *o* to stick like a leech.

ladillo *m* door panel (de coche) || IMPR marginal note.

ladino, na *adj* astute, shrewd, cunning, wily (astuto) || multilingual, poliglot || Rhaeto-Romanic (rético) || *AMER* Spanish-speaking [Indian] | of Spanish-Indian descent, half-breed || *lengua ladina* Spanish language [as opposed to Arabic].
◆ *m* Ladin, Rhaeto-Romanic (retorromano) || Ladino, Judeo-Spanish, Sephardic.

lado *m* side; *el lado izquierdo* the left side, the left-hand side || side; *pariente mío por el lado paterno* a relation on my father's side || room (sitio); *déjame un lado* make room for me || MAT side; *un triángulo tiene tres lados* a triangle has three sides || side (del cuerpo) || edge, side (en el perímetro de una cosa) || MIL flank || DEP end; *cambiar de lado* to change ends || FIG hand; *por un lado* on the one hand | way (camino); *me fui por otro lado* I went off by another way | side, aspect; *un lado nuevo del asunto* a new side to *o* a new aspect of the matter | patronage, protection (favor, protección) | side (opinión, punto de vista); *yo estoy de su lado* I am on his side || — *al lado* close by, nearby, near || *al lado de* at *o* by the side of, beside, next to (posición), next door to; *vivo al lado de tu casa* I live next door to your house *o* to you; compared to *o* with, next to (comparación) || *al otro lado de* on the other side of, over || *a mi lado, al lado mío* at *o* by my side, beside me, next to me || *cada uno por su lado* in different directions || FIG *cada uno tira* or *va por su lado* each goes his own way | *dar de lado* to cold-shoulder, to desert (a alguien), to discard (algo) || *de al lado* next door; *la casa de al lado* the house next door || *dejar de lado, dejar a un lado* to leave *o* to put *o* to set aside, to leave *o* to put *o* to set to one side (colocar), to omit, to pass over (descartar) || *de lado* aslant, to one side; *llevar el sombrero de lado* to wear one's hat aslant; sideways, sidewards, to one side; *volverse de lado* to turn sideways; crosswise, from the side; *el viento sopla de lado* the wind is blowing crosswise || *del lado de* on the side of (en una lucha), near (cerca de) || *de un lado para otro* up and down; *andar de un lado para otro en una habitación* to walk up and down a room; to and fro (por todas partes); *vagar de un lado para otro* to wander to and fro || *de uno y otro lado* on *o* from both sides || *echar a un lado* to cast aside || FIG *el lado bueno* the right side || *hacer lado* to leave *o* to make room || *hacerse* or *echarse a un lado* to step *o* to stand aside, to make way, to move over (una persona), to draw *o* to pull to one side (un vehículo) || *ir lado a lado* to go side by side (ir juntos), to go hand in hand, to go together (estar unidos) || *irse* or *tirar* or *echar por otro lado* to go off another way (ir por otro camino), to try another way, to try sth. else (utilizar otro medio) || *lado débil* or *flaco* weak point, weak spot || FIG *mirar de lado* or *de medio lado* to look down on (con desprecio), to look at out of the corner of one's eye, to look askance at (con disimulo) || FIG *poner a un lado* to put aside *o* on one side || *ponerse del lado de* to side with, to take sides with || *por el lado de* in the direction of || *por un lado..., por otro (lado)...* on the one hand..., on the other (hand)... || *ver el lado bueno de las cosas* to look on the bright side.
◆ *pl* aids, helpers, assistants (ayudantes), protectors, patrons (protectores), advisers (consejeros), set *sing* (íntimos) || — *por todos lados* on all sides || *una figura de tres lados* a three-sided figure .

ladrador, ra *adj* barking.

ladrar *vi* to bark (el perro) || to yap (perro pequeño) || FIG & FAM to growl, to bark || — FIG & FAM *hoy está que ladra* he's in a nasty mood today | *ladrar a la Luna* to bay (at) the moon | *me ladra el estómago* my stomach is rumbling.
◆ *vt* FIG to bark (out) (órdenes, etc.).

ladrería *f* lazaretto (para leprosos).

ladrido *m* bark || yap (agudo) || FIG & FAM growl (respuesta áspera, etc.).

ladrillado *m* brick floor || tiled floor (de azulejos).

ladrillal; ladrillar *m* brickworks, brickyard.

ladrillar *vt* to brick, to pave with bricks || to tile (con azulejos).

ladrillazo *m* blow with a brick || FIG *caer como un ladrillazo* to be heavy on the stomach (un alimento).

ladrillera *f* brick mould (molde) || brickworks (fábrica).

ladrillero, ra *adj* brickmaking; *industria ladrillera* brickmaking industry.
◆ *m/f* brickmaker (que hace ladrillos) || brick dealer (que vende ladrillos).

ladrillo *m* brick; *ladrillo hueco, macizo* hollow, solid brick || tile (azulejo) || FIG block (de chocolate) | check (en las telas) || — FAM *caer como un ladrillo* to be heavy on the stomach (la comida) || *color ladrillo* brick red, brick || FIG & FAM *es un ladrillo* he *o* it is deadly dull *o* deadly boring || *fábrica de ladrillos* brickworks || *horno de ladrillos* brick kiln || *ladrillo azulejo* tile || *ladrillo refractario* or *de fuego* firebrick || *ladrillo visto* mock brick.

ladrón, ona *adj* thieving, light-fingered.
◆ *m/f* thief, robber.
◆ *m* sluice gate (portillo para el agua) || ELECTR multiple socket || thief (de vela) || — *¡al ladrón!, ¡ladrones!* stop thief! || *cueva de ladrones* den of thieves || *el buen, el mal ladrón* the penitent, the impenitent thief (del Evangelio) || FIG *ladrón de corazones* ladykiller | *la ocasión hace al ladrón* opportunity makes the thief | *piensa el ladrón que todos son de su condición* we all judge others by our own standards.

ladronear *vi* to thieve, to steal.

ladronera *f* den of thieves (guarida).

ladronería *f* thieving, robbery, theft.

ladronesco, ca *adj* thievish.
◆ *f* FAM gang of thieves.

ladronzuelo, la *m/f* small-time *o* petty thief.

lady *f* lady.

lagaña *f* sleep, rheum (en los ojos).

lagar *m* press house (local) || wine *o* apple *o* olive press (prensa).

lagarejo *m* small press house || small wine *o* apple *o* olive press || *hacerse lagarejo* to be bruised *o* squashed (la uva).

lagarta *f* ZOOL female lizard | gipsy moth (mariposa) || FIG & FAM sly minx (mujer astuta y mal intencionada) || POP tart (prostituta).

lagartear *vt* AMER to pinion, to hold by the arms.

lagarterano, na *adj* [of *o* from] Lagartera [in the province of Toledo] || *manteles lagarteranos* Lagartera-embroidered tablecloths.
◆ *m/f* native *o* inhabitant of Lagartera.

lagartija *f* (small) lizard || FIG *moverse más que el rabo de una lagartija* to have ants in one's pants, to be fidgety.

lagartijero, ra *adj* lizard-hunting (animal) || TAUR *media lagartijera* short but effective sword thrust.

lagarto *m* ZOOL lizard (reptil) || ANAT biceps (músculo) || FIG & FAM sly devil, crafty fellow (hombre astuto) || red sword of the order of Santiago (insignia) || AMER alligator || *lagarto de Indias* alligator.
◆ *interj* touch wood! [superstitions exclamation].

lagartón, ona *adj* FIG & FAM sly, wily, crafty.
◆ *m* sly devil.
◆ *f* sly minx.

lago *m* lake; *lago de agua salada* saltwater lake || FIG sea; *lago de sangre* sea of blood.

Lagos *n pr* GEOGR Lagos.

Lago Superior *npr m* GEOGR Lake Superior.

lágrima *f* tear; *bañado en lágrimas* bathed in tears; *le corrían las lágrimas* tears streamed down his face || drop of sap [exuding from vine or tree] || drop (caramelo redondeado) || FAM drop (pequeña cantidad) || — *beberse las lágrimas* to hold back one's tears || *con lágrimas en los ojos* with tears in his eyes || *derramar lágrimas* to shed tears || *enjugarse las lágrimas* to dry one's eyes *o* one's tears || FIG & FAM *estar hecho un mar de lágrimas* to cry a sea of tears (persona), to be bathed in tears (cara) || *hacer saltar las lágrimas* to bring tears to one's eyes, to make one cry || *lágrimas de cocodrilo* crocodile tears || *lo que no va en lágrimas va en suspiros* she does nothing but weep and sigh || *llorar a lágrima viva* to sob one's heart out, to cry one's eyes out || FIG *llorar lágrimas de sangre* to weep tears of blood || *se me saltaron las lágrimas a los ojos* tears came to my eyes || FIG *ser el paño de lágrimas de alguien* to give s.o. a shoulder to cry on, to be s.o.'s consoler.

lagrimal *adj* lachrymal.
◆ *m* ANAT corner of the eye.

lagrimar *vi* to weep, to cry.

lagrimear *vi* to water (los ojos) || to weep, to shed tears (una persona).

lagrimeo *m* watering (de los ojos) || weeping, tears *pl* (de persona).

lagrimón, ona *adj* tearful.
◆ *m* big tear.

lagrimoso, sa *adj* watery (ojos) || tearful, lachrymose (persona).

laguna *f* small lake (lago pequeño), tarn (en el monte) || lagoon (de un atolón) || FIG gap, lacuna; *las lagunas de mi educación* the gaps in my education | gap, hiatus, lacuna (en un texto) || *laguna legal* legal loophole.

lagunar *m* ARQ coffer, lacunar (de techo).

lagunoso, sa *adj* full of lagoons.

laicado *m* laity.

laical *adj* lay, laical.

laicalización *f* AMER laicization.

laicalizar *vt* AMER to laicize.

laicidad *f* secularity, laicism.

laicismo *m* laicism.

laicización *f* laicization.

laicizar *vt* to laicize.

laico, ca *adj* lay, secular, laical; *escuela laica* secular school.

laísmo *m* use of *la* and *las* as indirect objects instead of *le* and *les*; *la dijeron* they told her (instead of *le dijeron*); *las sucedió* it happened to them (instead of *les sucedió*).

laísta *adj* who uses *la* and *las* as indirect objects.
◆ *m/f* person who uses *la* and *las* as indirect objects.

laja *f* flat stone, stone slab || MAR shoal.

lakismo *m* Lake School (escuela poética inglesa).

lakista *m/f* Lake poet.

lama *f* slime, mud silt (cieno).
◆ *m* REL lama.

lamaísmo *m* REL Lamaism.

lamaísta *adj/s* REL Lamaist.

lamasería *f* REL lamasery.

lambada *f* lambada (baile).

lambda *f* lambda (letra griega).

lambdacismo *m* lambdacism.

lambel *m* HERÁLD label.

lamber *vt* AMER FAM to lick (lamer).

lamé *m* lamé (tejido).

lameculos *m/f inv* POP bootlicker (cobista).

lamedor *adj* licking (que lame).
◆ *m* syrup (jarabe) || FIG flattery, cajolery (halago).

lamedura *f* licking, lick.

lamelibranquio *m* ZOOL lamellibranch.
◆ *pl* ZOOL lamellibranchia (clase de moluscos).

lamelicornio *adj/sm* ZOOL lamellicorn.
◆ *pl* ZOOL lamellicornia.

lamelirrostros *m pl* lamellirostres (aves).

lamentable *adj* lamentable, deplorable, pitiful; *en un estado lamentable* in a deplorable state || regrettable.

lamentación *f* lamentation, lament, lamenting.

lamentar *vt* to be sorry, to regret; *lamento que no hayas podido venir* I am sorry you could not come || to be sorry about; *lamento este accidente* I am sorry about this accident || to lament, to mourn; *tuvimos que lamentar muchas pérdidas* we had to mourn many losses || to lament, to grieve (sentir un dolor profundo) || *es de lamentar que...* it is to be regretted that..., it is regrettable that...
◆ *vpr* to complain (*de* about); *siempre te estás lamentando* you are always complaining || to lament, to bewail; *lamentarse de las desgracias de su familia* to lament the misfortunes of one's family.

lamento *m* lament, lamentation (por un dolor moral) || wail, moan (por un dolor físico).

lamentoso, sa *adj* plaintive, mournful (quejumbroso) || lamentable, deplorable, pitiful (lamentable).

lamer *vt* to lick || to lap; *el agua lame la orilla* the water is lapping the bank.

lametada *f*; **lametazo** *m*; **lametón** *m* lick || lap (de ola, etc.).

lameteo *m* FAM licking (acción de lamer).

lamido, da *adj* licked || FIG thin, scrawny (flaco) | dandified, done up (relamido) | spick and span, spruce (aseado) | finical, finicky (estilo, pintura) | (p us) worn-out (desgastado).
◆ *m* licking.

lámina *f* sheet, plate, lamina (de metal) || sheet (de madera, de vidrio, de mármol) || FOT & IMPR plate || ANAT & BOT lamina || FIG appearance (de caballo, etc.).

laminación *f* rolling (del acero, etc.) || splitting, lamination (división en hojas) || lamination (revestimiento con láminas) || TECN *tren de laminación* rolling mill.

laminado, da *adj* laminated, laminate || rolled (metal); *laminado en caliente* hot-rolled || *acero laminado* sheet steel, rolled steel.
◆ *m* rolling (de metal); *laminado en frío* cold rolling || laminate (producto para revestir).

laminador *m* rolling mill (laminadora) || roller, rolling mill operator (obrero).
◆ *adj* rolling; *cilindros laminadores* rolling mills.

laminadora *f* rolling mill (máquina).

laminar *adj* laminar; *estructura laminar* laminar structure; *corriente laminar* laminar flow.

laminar *vt* to roll [into sheets], to roll out (metal, etc.) || to split [into sheets], to laminate (dividiendo) || to laminate, to surface (cubrir con láminas); *laminar una mesa con plástico* to laminate a table with plastic.

laminilla *f* thin sheet || BOT & ANAT lamella.

laminoso, sa *adj* laminose, laminous, lamellar.

lampacear *vt* MAR to swab, to mop.

lampalagua *f* ZOOL anaconda.

lampante *adj* lamp; *aceite lampante* lamp oil.

lampar *vi* to long, to crave, to yearn; *lampar por algo, por hacer algo* to long for sth., to do sth.
◆ *vpr* to long, to crave, to yearn.

lámpara *f* lamp, light; *lámpara eléctrica, de gas* electric, gas lamp || bulb, lamp (bombilla) || RAD valve || FAM oil *o* grease stain (mancha) || — *lámpara colgante* hanging lamp || *lámpara de aceite* oil lamp || *lámpara de alcohol* spirit lamp || *lámpara de arco* arc lamp || *lámpara de incandescencia* or *incandescente* incandescent lamp || *lámpara de minero* or *de seguridad* miner's *o* safety lamp || *lámpara de pie* standard lamp || *lámpara de rayos infrarrojos, de rayos ultravioletas* infrared, ultraviolet lamp || AUT *lámpara de techo* interior light || *lámpara de vapor de mercurio* mercury vapour lamp || *lámpara indicadora* pilot *o* warning light || *lámpara para la mesilla de noche* reading lamp || FOT *lámpara relámpago* flash || *lámpara solar* sunray lamp.

lamparería; lampistería *f* lamp works (taller) || lamp shop (tienda).

lamparero; lamparista *m* lamp maker (que hace lámparas) || lamp dealer (que las vende).

lamparilla *f* small lamp || nightlight (mariposa).

lamparista *m* → **lamparero.**

lamparón *m* large lamp || FAM large grease stain (mancha en la ropa) || MED scrofula (escrófula).

lampazo *m* BOT burdock || MAR swab || AMER FAM lash (latigazo).

lampiño, ña *adj* beardless (sin barba) || hairless (con poco pelo o vello) || BOT glabrous (sin vello) | awnless (trigo).

lampista *m* lampmaker (que hace lámparas) || lamp dealer (que las vende).

lampistería *f* → **lamparería.**

lampo *m* POÉT refulgence, fulguration, effulgence.

lamprea *f* lamprey (pez).

lamprear *vt* to cook (meat) with wine, spices and honey or sugar.

lampreazo *m* FAM lash (latigazo).

lamprehuela; lampreílla *f* river lamprey (pez).

lana *f* wool || fleece, wool (del carnero vivo) || AMER FAM dough (dinero) || — *batir la lana* to shear the sheep || FIG & FAM *cardarle a uno la lana* to give s.o. a good telling off || *de lana* wool, woolen; *tejido de lana* woolen fabric || FIG *ir por lana y volver trasquilado* to go for wool and come home shorn || *lana de esquileo* shorn wool || *lana de vidrio* glass wool.
◆ *pl* FAM hair *sing*, mop *sing*; *voy a que me esquilen las lanas* I'm going to get my mop cut.

lanada *f* sponge, cleaning rod (para los cañones).

lanado, da *adj* BOT lanate.

lanar *adj* wool-bearing || *ganado lanar* sheep.

Lancaster *n pr* Lancashire (condado) || Lancaster (ciudad y dinastía).

lance *m* throw, cast (lanzamiento) || cast, casting (de la red de pesca) || catch (pesca que se saca) || episode, incident, event (suceso) || critical moment *o* juncture (trance crítico) || move, stroke (jugada) || TAUR pass with the cape || — *de lance* secondhand; *libros de lance* secondhand books || *lance apretado* tight spot, jam (*fam*) || *lance de amor* amorous adventure || *lance de fortuna* stroke of fortune || *lance de honor* question of honour; challenge (desafío).

lancear *vt* to spear, to lance || TAUR to play (the bull) using simple passes with the cape.

Lancelote *npr m* Lancelot, Launcelot.

lanceolado, da *adj* BOT lanceolate, lanceolar || ARQ lancet (arco).

lancero *m* lancer.
◆ *pl* lancers (baile).

lanceta *f* MED lancet || AMER sting (aguijón).

lancetada *f*; **lancetazo** *m* MED lancing.

lancetero *m* lancet case.

lanciforme *m* lanciform, lance-shaped.

lancinante *adj* stabbing, piercing (dolor).

lancinar *vi* to pierce, to stab (un dolor).

lancha *f* MAR boat (barco) | motor launch, motorboat (con motor) | pinnace (barca dependiente de un buque o de servicio portuario) || lighter, barge (barcaza) || flat stone, stone slab (piedra) || partridge trap (para coger perdices) || — MAR *lancha bombardera* or *cañonera* or *obusera* gunboat | *lancha de desembarco* landing craft | *lancha de socorro* or *de auxilio* lifeboat | *lancha motora* or *rápida* motorboat, speedboat | *lancha neumática* rubber dinghy | *lancha salvavidas* lifeboat (que lleva un barco) | *lancha torpedera* torpedo boat.

lanchada *f* boatful, boatload.

lanchaje *m* MAR lighterage (transporte, coste).

lanchar *m* quarry (cantera).

lanchero *m* boatman || lighterman, bargee (de la barcaza).

lanchón *m* lighter, barge.

landa *f* moor, moorland, heathland.

landgrave *m* HIST landgrave.

landgraviato *m* HIST landgraviate.

landó *m* landau (coche).

landrecilla *f* small fleshy lump.

lanería *f* wool shop.

lanero, ra *adj* wool; *industria lanera* wool industry
◆ *m/f* wool dealer, wool seller (persona).
◆ *m* wool warehouse (almacén).

langor *m* (ant) ⟶ **languidez.**

langosta *f* ZOOL locust (insecto) | (spiny) lobster (crustáceo) || FIG scourge (plaga).

langostero *m* lobster boat || lobster fisherman.

langostino *m* prawn (crustáceo).

langostón *m* grasshopper (insecto).

langucia *f* AMER hunger.

languidecer* *vi* to languish.

languidez *f* languor, languidness || lassitude, listlessness (falta de energía).

lánguido, da *adj* languid, languorous; *una mirada lánguida* a languid look || listless (sin energía).

lanífero, ra *adj* POÉT laniferous, woolly, lanigerous.

lanificación *f*; **lanificio** *m* woolwork, woollen manufacture || woollen goods *pl* [US woolen goods *pl*] (cosas hechas de lana).

lanilla *f* nap (pelillo en tejidos de lana) || flannel (tela fina de lana) || MAR bunting.

lanolina *f* lanolin, lanoline.

lanosidad *f* down (pelusa).

lanoso, sa *adj* ⟶ **lanudo.**

lansquenete *m* HIST lansquenet (soldado).

lantano *m* QUÍM lanthanum (metal).

lanudo, da; lanoso, sa *adj* woolly, fleecy (que tiene mucha lana) || downy, furry (que tiene vello) || AMER FAM coarse, uncouth (tosco).

lanuginoso, sa *adj* lanuginous, downy.

lanza *f* lance, spear (arma) || shaft, thill (de carruaje) || nozzle (de una manga de riego) || lancer (soldado) || — *correr lanzas* to joust || *estar con la lanza en ristre* to have one's lance at the ready (afianzada en el ristre), to be ready for action (preparado) || FIG *medir lanzas con alguien* to cross swords with s.o. | *no romper lanzas con nadie* not to argue with anybody | *romper una lanza en defensa de* to fight for, to defend.

lanzable *adj* *asiento lanzable* ejector seat.

lanzabombas *adj inv* MIL *dispositivo lanzabombas* bomb release gear (de avión).
◆ *m* MIL bomb release gear (de avión, etc.) | mortar (de trinchera).

lanzacabos *adj inv* MAR *cañón lanzacabos* lifesaving gun | *cohete lanzacabos* life-saving rocket.

lanzacohetes *m inv* MIL rocket launcher.

lanzada *f*; **lanzazo** *m* lance thrust, spear thrust (golpe) || lance wound, spear wound (herida).

lanzadera *f* shuttle (del telar) || marquise (anillo).

lanzado, da *adj* determined (decidido) || *ir lanzado* to speed *o* to tear along; *la moto iba lanzada* the motorbike was tearing along.
◆ *m* *pesca al lanzado* spinning, casting.

lanzador, ra *adj* throwing.
◆ *m/f* thrower || DEP bowler (en el cricket) | pitcher (béisbol) | thrower (de jabalina, disco) || promoter (promotor).

lanzafuego *m* (ant) MIL linstock (botafuego).

lanzagranadas *m inv* MIL grenade launcher.

lanzallamas *m inv* flamethrower.

lanzamiento *m* throw, fling, hurl; *con su primer lanzamiento batió el récord* with his first throw he beat the record || throwing, flinging, hurling; *el lanzamiento de almohadillas está prohibido* the throwing of cushions is forbidden || DEP put (del peso) | ball (en el cricket) | pitch (béisbol) | throw (del disco, de la jabalina) || firing; *lanzamiento de un proyectil, de un torpedo* firing of a missile, of a torpedo || launching; *lanzamiento de un barco* launching of a ship; *lanzamiento de una sonda lunar* launching of a moon probe || dropping (de una bomba) || drop (de paracaidistas) || jump (salto de un paracaidista) || release (de un ave) || COM launching (de una campaña, etc.) || FIG launching (de un ataque, etc.).

lanzaminas *m inv* MIN minelayer.

lanzaplatos *m inv* DEP trap (del tiro al plato).

lanzar *vt* to throw; *lanzar una pelota* to throw a ball || to fling, to hurl (con violencia) || to fire (una flecha, un proyectil, un torpedo, etc.); *lanzar un cohete de un avión* to fire a rocket from an aircraft || to launch (un satélite, etc.); *lanzar un cohete de la plataforma de lanzamiento* to launch a rocket from the launching pad || to drop, to release (una bomba) || to drop (paracaidistas) || to release (un ave) || DEP to throw (el disco, la jabalina) | to put (el peso) | to bowl (en cricket) | to pitch (béisbol) || MAR to launch (botar) || JUR to dispossess (de of) || FIG to launch; *lanzar un libro, un producto, una nueva línea, un ataque* to launch a book, a product, a new line, an attack | to utter (un grito, un gemido) | to hurl (un insulto, una maldición) | to heave (un suspiro) | to cast, to give (una mirada) | to make (una acusación) | to throw down, to throw out (un desafío) | to bring up (vomitar).
◆ *vpr* to rush, to hurl o.s., to fling o.s., to throw o.s.; *lanzarse contra alguien* to rush at s.o., to hurl o.s. at s.o.; *lanzarse contra la pared* to hurl o.s. against the wall || to rush, to hurtle; *lanzarse al ataque* to rush into the attack || to jump; *se lanzó al vacío desde el décimo piso* he jumped into the void from the tenth floor; *lanzarse al agua* to jump into the water || to dive (tirarse de cabeza) || AVIAC to jump (paracaidista), to bale out (en caso de emergencia) || FIG to launch o.s.; *lanzarse a los negocios* to launch o.s. in *o* into business | to embark upon (emprender) || *lanzarse en persecución de una persona* to dash off in pursuit of s.o.

Lanzarote *npr m* Lancelot, Launcelot.

lanzatorpedos *adj/sm inv* *(tubo) lanzatorpedos* torpedo tube.

lanzazo *m* ⟶ **lanzada.**

laña *f* clamp (grapa) || green coconut (coco verde).

lañador *m* clamper.

lañar *vt* to clamp (sujetar con lañas) || to clean [for salting] (el pescado).

Laodicea *npr f* GEOGR Laodicea.

Laos *npr m* GEOGR Laos.

laosiano, na *adj/s* Laotian.

lapa *f* ZOOL limpet (molusco) || vegetal film [on the surface of liquids] || BOT burdock || FAM hanger-on (persona pegajosa) || FIG & FAM *pegarse como una lapa* to stick like glue *o* like a leech.

La Paz *npr f* GEOGR La Paz.

lapicera *f* AMER penholder (palillero).

lapicero *m* propelling pencil (instrumento en que se pone la mina) || pen (pluma), pencil (lápiz de mina), crayon (de color) || AMER penholder (palillero).

lápida *f* memorial tablet *o* stone || — *lápida conmemorativa* memorial *o* commemorative stone *o* tablet || *lápida sepulcral* or *mortuoria* gravestone, tombstone.

lapidación *f* stoning (to death), lapidation.

lapidar *vt* to stone (to death), to lapidate || AMER to cut (piedras preciosas).

lapidario, ria *adj* lapidary; *estilo lapidario* lapidary style.
◆ *m* lapidary (de piedras preciosas) || monumental mason (de lápidas).

lapidificación *f* petrification, lapidification.

lapidificar *vt* to petrify, to lapidify.
◆ *vpr* to lapidify.

lapilli *m pl* GEOL lapilli.

lapislázuli *m* MIN lapis lazuli.

lápiz *m* lead, graphite (grafito) ‖ pencil; *escribir a lápiz* or *con lápiz* to write in pencil; *lápiz estilográfico* or *de mina* propelling pencil ‖ — *dibujo a lápiz* pencil drawing ‖ *lápiz de color* coloured pencil, crayon ‖ *lápiz de labios* lipstick ‖ *lápiz de ojos* eyebrow pencil ‖ *lápiz plomo* or *de plomo* graphite pencil, lead pencil.

lapizar *m* graphite mine.

lapo *m* lash (latigazo) ‖ blow (golpe) ‖ swig, swallow (trago) ‖ FAM spit (escupitajo) ‖ *AMER* slap (bofetada) | mug [*US* sucker] (inocentón).

lapón, ona *adj* Lapp.
◆ *m/f* Lapp, Laplander (persona).
◆ *m* Lapp (lengua).

Laponia *npr f* GEOGR Lapland.

lapso *m* lapse, space (de tiempo) ‖ slip, lapse (lapsus).

lapso, sa *adj* REL lapsed.

lapsus *m* slip, lapse ‖ *lapsus cálami, linguae* slip of the pen, of the tongue.

laque *m* *AMER* bola (tipo de lazo).

laquear *vt* to lacquer ‖ *AMER* to lasso with the bola.

lar *m* lar (divinidad de la casa); *los dioses lares* the lares ‖ hearth (fogón) ‖ FIG home (hogar); *el lar paterno* the family home.
◆ *pl* FIG home *sing* (hogar).
— OBSERV The plural form of this word in both languages is *lares*.

lardar; lardear *vt* to baste, to lard (la carne).

lardero *adj m* *jueves lardero* the Thursday before Lent.

lardo *m* bacon fat, pork fat (tocino) ‖ animal fat (grasa).

larense *adj* [of *o* from] Lara (en Venezuela).
◆ *m/f* native *o* inhabitant of Lara.

larga *f* lengthening piece joined to the last (en la elaboración de zapatos) ‖ longest billiard cue (billar) ‖ flourish with the cape [to draw the bull away from the picador] ‖ *a la larga* in the end, in the long run (al final).
◆ *pl* delay *sing* (dilación) ‖ *dar largas a un asunto* to put off a matter, to delay a matter.

largamente *adv* at length, for a long time; *hablar largamente de una cuestión* to talk about a matter at length ‖ generously (con generosidad).

largar *vt* to let go, to release (soltar) ‖ to slacken, to loosen, to ease off (ir soltando poco a poco) ‖ to unfurl (una bandera) ‖ FAM to land, to deal, to give (una bofetada, un golpe) | to give; *le largué una buena propina* I gave him a good tip | to utter (una exclamación, una palabrota, un suspiro, una imprecación, etc.) | to throw out, to see off (echar); *largó a la criada* he threw the maid out; *le largaron del hotel* he was thrown out of the hotel, he was seen off from the hotel | to drive out (expulsar); *largar los demonios* to drive out evil spirits | to get rid of, to unload (deshacerse de); *largó el perro al vecino* he got rid of the dog *o* he unloaded the dog on his neighbour | to give, to make (s.o.) sit through; *les largó un discurso interminable* he made them sit through an endless speech | to throw (arrojar) ‖ MAR to let out (las amarras) | to unfurl, to spread (velas) | to launch (una barca) | to discharge (lastre).
◆ *vpr* FAM to push off, to beat it, to hop it, to clear off (marcharse) ‖ MAR to put to sea (zarpar), to bear off (apartarse de otra embarcación) ‖ *AMER* to begin (*a* to) (comenzar) ‖ FAM *¡lárgate con viento fresco!* clear off!

largavistas *m pl* *AMER* binoculars (gemelos).

larghetto *adv/sm* MÚS larghetto.

largo, ga *adj* long, lengthy; *una carretera larga* a long road; *un viaje, un libro largo* a long journey, book ‖ long; *largo tiempo* a long time ‖ prolonged, long, lengthy; *retraso largo* prolonged delay; *visita larga* prolonged visit ‖ tall (persona alta) ‖ too long; *esta falda te está larga* this skirt is too long for you ‖ GRAM long (vocal, sílaba) ‖ good; *una hora larga* a good hour; *catorce millones largos de turistas* a good fourteen million tourists ‖ good, long; *dos largas millas* two long miles ‖ FIG quick-witted, sharp (astuto) | generous, liberal (generoso) ‖ MAR slack, loose ‖ RAD long (onda) ‖ — *a la larga* in the long run, in the end ‖ *a largo plazo* long-term; *previsiones a largo plazo* long-term forecasts ‖ *a lo largo* lengthwise, lengthways (longitudinalmente); *partir un tablón a lo largo* to split a plank lenghtwise; in the distance (a lo lejos) ‖ *a lo largo de* along; *anduvimos a lo largo del andén* we walked along the platform; all... long, throughout, all through; *a lo largo del día, del año* all day long, all year long; throughout (por dentro) ‖ *a lo largo y a lo ancho* up and down, to and fro ‖ *a lo largo y a lo ancho de* all over; *hay ríos trucheros a lo largo y a lo ancho de toda la región* there are trout rivers all over the area ‖ *a lo más largo* at the most, at the outside ‖ *caer cuan largo es uno* to fall full length ‖ *de largo a largo* from one end to the other ‖ *es largo de contar* it's a long story ‖ *hacerse largo* to drag ‖ *ir para largo* to drag on ‖ *largos años* many years, many a long year ‖ FIG *más largo que un día sin pan* very long ‖ *pasar de largo* to go straight past, to pass by (sin pararse), to pass over (un detalle) ‖ *poner cara larga* to pull a face *o* a long face ‖ *ponerse* or *vestirse de largo* to wear a long dress (para salir de noche), to come out, to make one's début in society (sentido figurado) ‖ FIG *poner* or *vestir de largo a su hija* to launch one's daughter into society, to give one's daughter her début | *puesta de largo* coming out, début (de una chica en la sociedad) ‖ *tener una cara larga* or *así de larga* to have a long face ‖ FIG *tirar largo* or *de largo* to spend lavishly (dinero), to use (etc.) freely; *si tiras de largo la pintura* if you put the paint on freely; to estimate high (calcular).
◆ *m* length (longitud); *el largo de un vestido* the length of a dress ‖ length; *hace falta tres largos de tela* three lengths of cloth are needed ‖ DEP length; *diez largos de la piscina* ten lengths of the pool; *ganar por un largo* to win by a length ‖ MÚS largo ‖ *tiene un metro de largo* it is one metre long.
◆ *adv* far (lejos); *muy largo de aquí* very far from here ‖ at length; *hablar largo de un asunto* to talk about a matter at length ‖ abundantly (abundantemente) ‖ — *hablar largo y tendido de algo* to talk sth. over ‖ *¡largo!, ¡largo de aquí!, ¡largo de ahí!* get away!, get out!, get out of my sight!

larguero *m* TECN longitudinal beam *o* girder ‖ jamb (de puerta) ‖ side (de cama) ‖ bolster (travesaño) ‖ DEP crossbar (barra horizontal), goal post (barra vertical) ‖ extension leaf (de una mesa) ‖ AVIAC spar (del ala), longeron (del fuselaje) ‖ AUT side member ‖ *mesa con largueros* extending table, draw-leaf table.

largueza *f* generosity ‖ length (longitud).

larguirucho, cha *adj* FAM gangling, lanky (alto).

largura *f* length (longitud).

laringe *f* ANAT larynx.

laringectomía *f* MED laryngectomy.

laríngeo, a *adj* laryngeal.

laringitis *f* MED laryngitis.

laringología *f* MED laryngology.

laringólogo *m* MED laryngologist.

laringoscopia *f* MED laryngoscopy.

laringoscopio *m* MED laryngoscope.

laringotomía *f* MED laryngotomy.

La Rioja *npr f* GEOGR La Rioja.

larva *f* MIT & ZOOL larva.
◆ *pl* larvae.

larvado, da *adj* MED larval, larvate.

larval *adj* larval.

larvícola *adj* larvicolous.

las *art def f pl* the; *ir a las islas Británicas* to go to the British Isles ‖ not translated; *le gustan mucho las patatas* he is very fond of potatoes; *todas las mujeres tienen cierta intuición* all women have a certain amount of intuition ‖ — *las García* the García girls, the García women, the Garcías ‖ *son las diez* it is ten o'clock.
◆ *pron pers f pl* them; *las vi* I saw them ‖ those, the ones; *las de Madrid son las mejores* the ones *o* those from Madrid are best; *las que he comprado* the ones (which) I have bought, those (which) I have bought ‖ not translated, some (con «haber» impersonal); *¿hay cartas? = m las hay* are there any letters? = m there are (some) ‖ — *las de usted* yours ‖ *las de Víctor son viejas* Victor's are old ‖ *¿las hay?* are there any? ‖ *las hay que...* there are those who..., there are some who... (personas), there are those that... (cosas); *las hay que siempre están hablando* there are those who are always talking ‖ *las que...* those who..., the ones who... (personas, sujeto), those whom..., the ones that... (personas, complemento), those (which), the ones (which), the ones (that)... (cosas) ‖ *son ellas las que lo dijeron* it is they who said it, they are the ones who said it ‖ *son mis hermanas las que vienen* it is my sisters that are coming, my sisters are the ones who are coming ‖ *una canción de las de los años 1930* a song typical of the 1930's.
— OBSERV The dative form of *las* is *les*: *les dije* I said to them. «Laísmo» (*las dije*) should be avoided.
— OBSERV *Las* is often translated by the possessive adjective; *tienes las manos sucias* your hands are dirty.

lasca *f* chip (of stone) ‖ slice (loncha).

lascar *vt* MAR to slacken (aflojar) ‖ *AMER* to chip (desconchar) | to scrape, to scratch (lastimar).

lascivia *f* lasciviousness, lechery, lewdness.

lascivo, va *adj* lascivious, lecherous, lewd ‖ playful, frisky (juguetón, alegre).

laser *m* TECN laser; *rayo laser* laser beam.

lasitud *f* (p us) lassitude (cansancio).

laso, sa *adj* tired, weary (cansado) ‖ weak (débil) ‖ languid (lánguido) ‖ TECN floss (seda).

Las Palmas de Gran Canaria *npr f* GEOGR Las Palmas.

lástex *m* lastex (nombre registrado).

lástima *f* pity, compassion, sympathy (compasión); *siento lástima por él* I feel pity for him ‖ complaint, lamentation, tale of woe; *déjame de lástimas* I've had enough of your tales of woe ‖ pity, shame; *¡qué lástima que no puedas venir!* what a shame you cannot come!; *es una lástima que se haya roto el disco* it is a pity the record got broken ‖ — *dar lástima* to be pitiful; *da lástima verle así* it is pitiful to see him like that ‖ *él me da lástima* I feel sorry for him ‖ *es digno de lástima por su mala suerte* he is to be pitied for his bad luck ‖ *estar hecho una lástima* to be in a pitiful state, to be a sorry sight ‖ *llorar lástimas* to moan and groan, to feel sorry for o.s. ‖ *que da lástima* pitifully; *es tan tonto que da lástima* he is pitifully stupid ‖ *¡qué lástima!* what a pity!, what a shame! ‖ *tener lástima de* to feel sorry for.

lastimado, da *adj* hurt (por un golpe, un insulto).

lastimadura *f* injury (acción y efecto de hacer daño).

lastimar *vt* to hurt, to injure (herir); *le lastimaron en el brazo* they hurt his arm ‖ to hurt (hacer daño); *estos zapatos me lastiman* these shoes hurt ‖ FIG to hurt, to offend; *le lastimó en su amor propio* it hurt his pride; *me lastimó su falta de consideración* I was hurt by his lack of consideration ‖ to pity, to feel sorry for, to sympathize with (compadecer) ‖ — FIG *lastimar el oído* or *los oídos* to hurt one's ears | *un color que lastima* a harsh *o* glaring colour.
◆ *vpr* to hurt o.s., to injure o.s. ‖ — *lastimarse de* to pity, to feel sorry for, to sympathize with (compadecer), to complain about (quejarse) ‖ *lastimarse la mano* to hurt one's hand.

lastimero, ra *adj* plaintive, doleful (palabras, etc.) ‖ injurious (que hace daño).

lastimoso, sa *adj* pitiful, piteous (digno de lástima); *el estado de la casa es lastimoso* the house is in a pitiful state; *una situación lastimosa* a pitiful situation; *una pérdida lastimosa de tiempo* a pitiful waste of time ‖ lamentable; *un accidente lastimoso* a lamentable accident.

lastra *f* flat stone, stone slab, flagstone (piedra).

lastrado *m* MAR ballasting.

lastrar *vt* MAR to ballast ‖ to weigh down.

lastre *m* MAR ballast; *en lastre* in ballast; *largar* or *echar* or *soltar lastre* to discharge ballast ‖ FIG steadiness (equilibrio) | nuisance (estorbo) | ballast, dead weight (cosa inútil).

lata *f* tinplate (hojalata) ‖ tin, can (envase); *una lata de melocotones* a tin of peaches ‖ lath (de madera) ‖ FIG & FAM drag, nuisance, bore, bind (cosa pesada); *es una lata tener que salir ahora* it's a drag having to go out now | bore, pest, drag, nuisance (persona pesada) ‖ — *barrio de las latas* shanty town ‖ FIG & FAM *dar la lata* to be a nuisance (persona), to be a drag *o* a bore (cosa) ‖ *en lata* tinned, canned ‖ AMER *estar en la lata, no tener ni una lata* to be broke *o* penniless | *¡qué lata!, ¡vaya una lata!* what a drag *o* a nuisance *o* a bore *o* a bind! ‖ *sonar a lata* to sound tinny (un ruido).

latazo *m* blow with a tin *o* a can ‖ FIG & FAM drag, nuisance, bore, bind (lata).

latente *adj* latent; *calor latente* latent heat; *en estado latente* in a latent state.

lateral *adj* side, lateral; *calle lateral* side street; *nave lateral* side aisle ‖ lateral (en fonética).
◆ *m* side ‖ side, wing (del escenario).

lateranense *adj* Lateran; *concilio lateranense* Lateran Council.

latero, ra *adj* annoying, boring, tiresome.
◆ *m* tinsmith (hojalatero).

látex *m* BOT latex.

latido *m* beating (acción de latir el corazón, etc.), beat (cada sonido o movimiento) ‖ throbbing (de una herida) ‖ yelping (del perro), yelp (cada ladrido).

latiente *adj* beating (pulso) ‖ throbbing (herida) ‖ yapping, yelping (perro).

latifundio *m* latifundium, large landed estate.
— OBSERV The plural of *latifundio* is *latifundios.*

latifundismo *m* latifundium system, ownership of latifundia.

latifundista *m/f* owner of a large estate.

latigazo *m* lash [with a whip] ‖ crack of a whip (chasquido) ‖ FIG verbal lashing, tongue lashing, harsh reprimand (reprimenda) ‖ FAM drink, swig (trago); *darse un latigazo* to have a drink ‖ *dar latigazos a* to whip, to lash.

látigo *m* whip; *hacer restallar el látigo* to crack the whip ‖ riding whip (de jinete) ‖ whip (en parque de atracciones) ‖ cord (cuerda) ‖ strap (correa) ‖ AMER lash (latigazo).

latiguear *vi* to crack one's whip ‖ AMER to lash, to whip.

latigueo *m* crack of a whip.

latiguillo *m* small whip ‖ BOT runner (estolón) ‖ overacting, hamming (de un actor) ‖ platitude, empty phrase; *un discurso lleno de latiguillos* a speech full of platitudes.

latín *m* Latin; *aprender latín* to learn Latin ‖ Latin word *o* phrase, Latinism; *echar latines* to come out with Latin phrases ‖ — *bajo latín* Low Latin ‖ FAM *latín de cocina* or *macarrónico* dog Latin ‖ *latín rústico* or *vulgar* Vulgar Latin ‖ FIG & FAM *sabe latín* or *mucho latín* he is nobody's fool, there are no flies on him.

latinajo *m* FAM dog Latin | Latin word *o* phrase, Latinism; *echar latinajos* to come out with Latin words.

latinar *vi* to speak, to write in Latin.

latinear *vi* to speak, to write in Latin ‖ to use Latinisms, to Latinize.

latinidad *f* latinity ‖ Latin countries *pl* ‖ Latin (latín).

latiniparla *f* Latinized language, language larded with Latinisms.

latinismo *m* Latinism.

latinista *m/f* Latinist.

latinización *f* Latinization.

latinizar *vt/vi* to latinize.

latino, na *adj/s* Latin.
◆ *adj* MAR lateen; *vela latina* lateen sail ‖ *cruz latina* Latin cross ‖ *la Iglesia latina* the Latin *o* Western Church.

Latinoamérica *npr f* GEOGR Latin America.

latinoamericano, na *adj/s* Latin-American.

latir *vi* to beat (el corazón, el pulso) ‖ to throb (una herida) ‖ to yelp (el perro).

latitud *f* width, breadth (anchura) ‖ extent, area (extensión) ‖ ASTR & GEOGR latitude; *a 40° de latitud* at latitude 40° ‖ FIG latitude, freedom (libertad); *las reglas me permiten cierta latitud para obrar* the rules allow me a certain degree of latitude within which to act.

latitudinario, ria *adj/s* latitudinarian.

lato, ta *adj* broad, wide (ancho) ‖ extensive, ample (extenso) ‖ FIG *en el sentido lato de la palabra* in the broad sense of the word.

latón *m* brass.

Latona *npr f* MIT Latona.

latonería *f* brassworks (taller) ‖ brassware shop.

latonero *m* brassworker, brazier.

latoso, sa *adj* annoying, boring, tiresome.
◆ *m/f* bore, drag, nuisance (persona pesada).

latría *f* REL latria.

latrocinar *vi* to rob, to steal.

latrocinio *m* robbery, theft.

laucha *f* AMER mouse (ratón) | nonentity, nobody (persona insignificante).

laúd *m* MÚS lute ‖ MAR catboat ‖ ZOOL leatherback (tortuga) ‖ *tañedor de laúd* lutanist, lutenist.

laudable *adj* laudable, praiseworthy.

láudano *m* laudanum (medicamento).

laudar *vt* JUR to pronounce sentence on, to render a decision on.

laudatoria *f*; **laudatorio** *m* panegyric, eulogy.

laudatorio, ria *adj* laudatory, eulogistic.

laude *f* engraved tombstone.
◆ *pl* REL lauds.

laudo *m* JUR decision, finding.

laureado, da *adj* prizewinning, award-winning (premiado) ‖ honoured [*US* honored] (honrado) ‖ decorated with the Cross of Saint Ferdinand (un militar) ‖ *poeta laureado* poet laureate.
◆ *m/f* laureate, recipient of an honour *o* of an award ‖ holder of the Cross of Saint Ferdinand.
◆ *f* Cross of Saint Ferdinand [the highest decoration in Spain].

laurear *vt* to crown with laurels ‖ to decorate with the Cross of Saint Ferdinand (a un militar) ‖ FIG to honour, to reward.

laurel *m* BOT laurel ‖ BOT *laurel cereza* or *real* cherry laurel | *laurel rosa* rosebay, oleander.
◆ *pl* FIG laurels (recompensa) ‖ — FIG *cargado de laureles* laden with laurels | *cosechar* or *conquistar laureles* to win *o* to reap laurels | *dormirse en los laureles* to rest on one's laurels | *mancillar sus laureles* to cast a stain in one's laurels.

laurencio *m* QUÍM lawrencium.

láureo, a *adj* laurel.

lauro *m* (p us) ⟶ **laurel.**

lauroceraso *m* cherry laurel (arbusto).

lava *f* lava (del volcán) ‖ MIN washing (de los metales).

lavable *adj* washable.

lavabo *m* washbasin (lavamanos) ‖ washstand (con soporte) ‖ washroom (cuarto de aseo) ‖ toilet, lavatory (retrete) ‖ REL lavabo (lavatorio).

lavacoches *m inv* car washer (persona).

lavacristales *m inv* window cleaner.

lavada *f* washing, wash (lavado).

lavadero *m* washing place (público, al aire libre) ‖ wash house (edificio) ‖ laundry (en una casa) ‖ MIN place where gold-bearing sands are panned.

lavadientes *m inv* (p us) mouthwash (enjuague).

lavado *m* washing, wash (de ropa, coche, persona, metales) ‖ washing out (del estómago) ‖ wash (dibujo) ‖ shampoo (de cabeza) ‖ MED lavage ‖ — FIG & FAM *dar un buen lavado a uno* to give s.o. a good talking-to ‖ FAM *lavado de cerebro* brainwashing ‖ *lavado en seco* dry cleaning.

lavador, ra *adj* washing ‖ *oso lavador* racoon.
◆ *m* washer ‖ AMER great anteater (oso hormiguero) ‖ *lavador de oro* gold washer.
◆ *f* washing machine, washer (para la ropa).

lavadura *f* washing (lavado) ‖ dirty water (agua sucia).

lavafrutas *m inv* finger bowl.

lavaje *m* washing (de la lana).

La Valeta *npr f* GEOGR Valetta.

lavamanos *m inv* washbasin, washstand.

lavamiento *m* enema ‖ washing (lavado).

lavanco *m* wild duck.

lavanda *f* BOT lavender (espliego).

lavandería *f* laundry ‖ launderette [*US* laundromat] (automática).

lavandero, ra *m/f* laundryman, launderer (hombre), laundress, washerwoman (mujer).

lavándula *f* lavender (espliego).

lavaojos *m inv* eyebath [*US* eyecup].

lavaparabrisas *m inv* AUT windscreen washer [*US* windshield washer].

lavaplatos *m/f inv* dishwasher, washer-up ‖ *máquina lavaplatos* dishwashing machine, dish washer.
◆ *m* sink (fregadero).

lavar *vt* to wash; *lavar la ropa* to wash clothes ‖ to paint in water colour (dibujo) ‖ to clean (pescado, etc.) ‖ — *lavar en seco* to dry-clean ‖ FIG *lavar la ofensa con sangre* to avenge an insult with blood ‖ *lavar y marcar* to shampoo and set (en la peluquería) ‖ *máquina de lavar* washing machine, washer (para la ropa), dishwasher (para los platos).
◆ *vpr* to wash (o.s.), to have a wash ‖ to wash; *lavarse la cabeza* to wash one's hair ‖ FIG *¡de eso me lavo las manos!* I wash my hands of that.

lavaseco *m* AMER dry cleaner's (tintorería).

lavativa *f* MED enema ‖ FIG & FAM nuisance, bind, bore (molestia).

lavatorio *m* washing (lavado) ‖ REL maundy (ceremonia religiosa) | lavabo (de la misa) ‖ MED lotion ‖ AMER washbasin (lavamanos).

lavavajillas *m inv* dishwasher.

lavazas *f pl* dishwater *sing*, dirty water *sing*.

lavotear *vt* to wash quickly and badly.
◆ *vpr* to have a quick wash.

lavoteo *m* quick *o* hurried wash.

laxación *f*; **laxamiento** *m* laxation, loosening, slackening ‖ laxity (laxitud).

laxante *adj/sm* laxative.

laxar *vt* to loosen, to slacken (aflojar) ‖ to loosen (the bowels) (vientre).

laxativo, va *adj/sm* laxative.

laxidad *f* laxity.

laxismo *m* laxism.

laxitud *f* laxity ‖ slackness (de una cuerda).

laxo, xa *adj* slack, loose, lax (no tenso) ‖ FIG lax, loose (moral, costumbres).

lay *m* lay (poema).

laya *f* sort, kind; *ser de la misma laya* to be of the same sort ‖ quality (calidad) ‖ AGR spade ‖ *laya de dientes* fork.

layar *vt* to dig with a spade.

lazada *f* bow, knot.

lazar *vt* to lasso, to rope (un animal).

lazareto *m* lazaretto, lazaret.

lazarillo *m* blind man's guide.
— OBSERV This word comes from the picaresque hero in Spanish literature, «Lazarillo de Tormes».

lazarino, na *adj* leprous.
◆ *m/f* leper.

lazarista *m* lazarist.

Lázaro *npr m* Lazarus.

lázaro *m* ragged beggar ‖ leper (leproso).

lazo *m* knot (nudo); *atar un lazo* to tie a knot ‖ bow (con una cinta) ‖ snare, trap (para cazar); *coger con lazo* to catch in a snare ‖ lasso (para sujetar caballos, etc.) ‖ loop, bend (de un camino) ‖ rope (cordel) ‖ FIG tie, bond (vínculo); *los lazos de la amistad* the bonds of friendship | link; *España sirve de lazo entre Europa y América del Sur* Spain serves as a link between Europe and South America | trap (trampa) ‖ ARQ interlaced design (ornamento) ‖ figure (en el baile) ‖ — FIG & FAM *caer en el lazo* to fall into the trap ‖ *lazo cerrado* loop (en el ferrocarril) ‖ INFORM *lazo de iteración* iteration loop | *lazo de programa* programme loop ‖ *lazo corredizo* slipknot ‖ *lazo de zapato* shoelace ‖ FIG *tender un lazo* to set a trap.

lazulita *f* MIN lazulite (lapislázuli).

le *pron* him, to him, her, to her (personas), it, to it (cosas) (dativo); *le dije, le doy* I said to him, I give (to) him ‖ him, her (acusativo); *le veo* I (can) see him (véase OBSERV) ‖ you, to you (cuando corresponde a «usted»); *le vi ayer pero no le pude hablar* I saw you yesterday, but I could not speak to you ‖ (for) him, (for) her, (for) it, (for) you (para él, para ella, etc.); *cómprale éste* buy him this one, buy this one for him ‖ from him, from her, from it, from you (de él, etc.); *le tomó el dinero* he took the money from him ‖ *le pregunté a mi hermano si...* I asked my brother if...
— OBSERV The Spanish Academy acknowledges the use of *le* instead of *lo* in the accusative case of the third person masculine singular but esteems it preferable to reserve this pronoun for the dative case. This use of *le* is far more common in Spain than in South America.

leal *adj* loyal; *un corazón leal* a loyal heart; *sentimientos leales* loyal sentiments ‖ faithful, loyal (partidario del gobierno) ‖ faithful, trustworthy, loyal (criado) ‖ faithful (animal).
◆ *m* loyalist.

leala *f* FAM peseta.

lealtad *f* loyalty ‖ loyalty, faithfulness, trustworthiness (de criado) ‖ faithfulness (de animal).

leandra *f* FAM peseta.

lebrada *f* hare stew.

lebrato *f* leveret.

lebrel *m* greyhound ‖ *perro lebrel* greyhound.

lebrero, ra *adj* harehunting.
◆ *m* greyhound (lebrel).

lebrillo *m* glazed earthenware bowl (gran recipiente) ‖ earthenware pot (pequeño recipiente).

lección *f* lesson ‖ reading (lectura) ‖ lesson, class (clase) ‖ lecture (en la Universidad) ‖ REL lesson, lection, reading (de la Biblia) ‖ — FIG *dar a uno una lección* to teach s.o. a lesson ‖ *dar la lección* to recite a lesson (discípulo) ‖ *dar lección* to give a lesson (el profesor) ‖ *dar lecciones* to teach, to give lessons (enseñar) ‖ *servir de lección* to serve as *o* to be a lesson; *esto le servirá de lección por haberse fiado de la gente* let this be a lesson to you for having trusted people ‖ *tomarle la lección a un niño* to make a child say his lesson.

lectivo, va *adj* school; *año lectivo* school year.

lector, ra *m/f* reader (que lee) ‖ assistant (profesor) ‖ INFORM *lectora de discos* diskette drive.
◆ *m* REL lector ‖ INFORM reader; *lector de cintas* or *de bandas* tape reader.

lectorado *m* assistantship ‖ REL lectorate.

lectoría *f* assistantship in a university.

lectura *f* reading ‖ reading matter (texto) ‖ culture, knowledge (conocimiento) ‖ IMPR pica, twelve-point type (carácter) ‖ INFORM reading ‖ — *dar lectura a* to read ‖ *una persona de mucha lectura* a well-read person.

lecha *f* milt, roe (de los peces).

lechada *f* whitewash (albañilería) ‖ TECN paste | pulp (de papel) ‖ milk-like *o* milky liquid (líquido blanco) ‖ *lechada de cal* milk of lime.

lechal *adj* sucking (animal); *cordero lechal* sucking lamb ‖ BOT lactiferous, milky (planta).
◆ *m* milky sap (de árboles) ‖ suckling (cordero).

lechaza *f* milt, roe (de los peces).

leche *f* milk; *leche cuajada, sin desnatar, desnatada, en polvo, condensada, homogeneizada* curdled, unskimmed, skim *o* skimmed, powdered, condensed, homogenized milk; *la leche se ha cortado* the milk has turned *o* curdled *o* gone sour ‖ BOT milky sap (látex) ‖ POP spunk, semen ‖ — *ama de leche* wet nurse ‖ *café con leche* (white) coffee ‖ *cochinillo de leche* sucking pig, young pig, piglet ‖ FIG *como una leche* like jelly ‖ *dientes de leche* milk teeth ‖ FIG & FAM *estar con* or *traer* or *tener la leche en los labios* to be still wet behind the ears ‖ POP *estar de mala leche* to be in a stinking *o* in a foul mood ‖ *gota de leche* centre where milk is given free ‖ POP *hacer algo con mala leche* to do sth. for the hell of it ‖ *hermano, hermana de leche* foster brother, foster sister [two people nursed by the same wet nurse] ‖ FIG & FAM *mamar una cosa en la leche* to have been brought up with sth. ‖ POP *¡leche!* hell! | *tener mala leche* to be spiteful *o* twisted, to be a nasty piece of work ‖ *ternera de leche* calf ‖ *vaca de leche* milch cow, milk cow.

lechecillas *f pl* sweetbreads (molleja) ‖ offal *sing* (asadura).

lechera *f* dairymaid, milkmaid (vendedora) ‖ milk churn [US milk can] (recipiente grande), milk can (recipiente pequeño de metal) ‖ milk jug (jarro) ‖ AMER milk cow, milch cow (vaca de leche).

lechería *f* dairy, creamery (tienda).

lechero, ra *adj* milk, dairy (industria); *industria lechera* milk industry ‖ FIG & FAM stingy, tight-fisted ‖ — *central lechera* dairy centre (cooperativa) ‖ *vaca lechera* milk cow, milch cow.
◆ *m* milkman (que reparte) ‖ dairyman (en una granja).
◆ *f* milkmaid (que ordeña) ‖ dairywoman (en una granja).

lechigada *f* brood (de aves) ‖ litter (de animales).

lecho *m* bed (cama); *estar en un lecho de rosas* to be on a bed of roses ‖ bed (de un río) ‖ bottom (fondo) ‖ ARQ base (de una piedra o de una columna) ‖ GEOL layer (estrato) ‖ — *abandonar el lecho* to get up, to get out of bed ‖ *en el lecho de la muerte* on one's deathbed ‖ TECN *lecho de colada* pig bed ‖ *lecho de roca* bedrock ‖ *lecho mortuorio* deathbed.
— OBSERV *Cama* is the usual word for *bed*, the word *lecho* being more literary.

lechón *m* sucking pig (cochinillo) ‖ hog, swine (puerco).

lechona *f* young sow (cerda) ‖ FIG & FAM pig, filthy woman (mujer sucia).
◆ *adj f* FIG & FAM filthy (sucia).

lechoncillo *m* sucking pig.

lechoso, sa *adj* milky.

lechuga *f* lettuce (planta); *ensalada de lechuga* lettuce salad ‖ ruff (cuello) ‖ pleat, flute, crimp (pliegue en una tela) ‖ — FIG & FAM *como una lechuga* as fresh as a daisy ‖ *lechuga romana* coslettuce [US romaine lettuce] ‖ FIG & FAM *ser más fresco que una lechuga* to be as cool as a cucumber.

lechuguilla *f* ruff (cuello) ‖ wild lettuce (lechuga silvestre).

lechuguina *f* FIG & FAM elegant young woman.

lechuguino *m* young lettuce (lechuga) ‖ plot of small lettuce (plantío) ‖ FIG & FAM dandy, beau (elegante).

lechuza *f* owl (ave) ‖ FIG & FAM hag (mujer fea).

lechuzo *m* FIG & FAM owl (hombre muy feo).

leer *vt/vi* to read; *leer en voz alta* to read aloud *o* out loud; *leer en voz baja* to read quietly; *leer música* to read music ‖ to teach, to lecture (enseñar un profesor) ‖ INFORM to read ‖ — MÚS *leer a primera vista* to read at sight, to sight-read ‖ *leer de corrido* to read fluently ‖ *leer de un tirón* to read straight through *o* in one go ‖ FIG *leer en los ojos* or *en la mirada de alguien* to read in s.o.'s eyes | *leer entre líneas* to read between the lines ‖ *leerle la mano a uno* to read s.o.'s palm.

lega *f* lay sister.

legacía *f* legateship (dignidad de legado).

legación *f* legation.

legado *m* legacy (manda testamentaria) || legate (del papa, de los romanos) || FIG legacy, bequest.

legajo *m* bundle of papers || dossier, file (carpeta).

legal *adj* legal (establecido por la ley); *procedimientos legales* legal procedures || lawful, legal; *contrato legal* lawful contract || scrupulous, honest, fair (en el ejercicio de sus poderes).

legalidad *f* legality, lawfulness (conformidad con la ley) || *salirse de la legalidad* to break the law.

legalismo *m* legalism.

legalista *adj* legalistic.
◆ *m/f* legalist.

legalizable *adj* legalizable.

legalización *f* legalization || authentication (de documentos).

legalizar *vt* to legalize || to authenticate (documentos) || *copia legalizada* certified copy.

legalmente *adv* legally, lawfully (conforme con la ley) || loyally (lealmente).

légamo *m* slime, ooze (cieno) || loam (arcilla).

legamoso, sa *adj* slimy, oozy (cenagoso) || loamy (arcilloso).

Leganés *n pr* GEOGR Leganes [a town near Madrid where there was a well known psychiatric hospital] || FAM *bueno para ir a Leganés* ready for the madhouse (loco).

legaña *f* sleep, rheum (en los ojos).

legañoso, sa *adj* rheumy, bleary.

legar *vt* to bequeath, to legate (hacer donación por testamento) || to delegate (enviar en legación) || FIG to bequeath (lengua, cultura).

legatario, ria *m/f* JUR legatee, heir; *legatario universal* general legatee.

legendario, ria *adj* legendary.
◆ *m* collection *o* book of legends.

leghorn *f* leghorn (raza de gallinas).

legibilidad *f* legibility.

legible *adj* legible.

legión *f* legion || — *Legión de Honor* Legion of Honour || *Legión Extranjera* Foreign Legion.

legionario, ria *adj* legionary; *fuerzas legionarias* legionary forces.
◆ *m* legionary.

legislación *f* legislation.

legislador, ra *adj* legislative.
◆ *m* legislator.

legislar *vi* to legislate.

legislativo, va *adj* legislative; *asamblea legislativa* legislative assembly.

legislatura *f* legislature.

legisperito *m* legal expert, jurist.

legista *m* legist (experto en leyes) || law student || *médico legista* forensic expert.

legitimación *f* legitimation, legitimization.

legitimador, ra *adj* legitimating.

legitimar *vt* to legitimize, to legitimate.

legitimidad *f* legitimacy || authenticity (de un producto).

legitimismo *m* legitimism.

legitimista *adj/s* legitimist.

legítimo, ma *adj* legitimate; *hijo legítimo* legitimate child || authentic, genuine, real; *champán legítimo* authentic champagne; *cuero legítimo* real leather || pure; *oro legítimo* pure gold || right (justo).

lego, ga *adj* lay, laic, secular (seglar) || lay; *hermano lego* lay brother || FIG ignorant (sin instrucción) | uninformed || FIG & FAM *ser lego en la materia* to know nothing about the subject.
◆ *m* layman || REL lay brother.

legra *f* MED raspatory (instrumento) | curette (de ginecólogo).

legración *f*; **legrado** *m*; **legradura** *f* MED scraping, scrape (de un hueso) | scraping, scrape, curetting (de la matriz).

legrar *vt* MED to scrape (huesos) | to scrape, to curette (la matriz).

legua *f* league (medida itineraria de 5572 m) || — FIG *a la legua* far away, miles away || *cómico de la legua* strolling player || *legua cuadrada* square league || *legua de posta* unit of distance of four kilometres || *legua marítima* marine league (5555 m) || FIG *se ve a la legua* it stands out a mile, you can see it a mile away.

legui *m* legging (polaina).

leguleyo *m* pettifogger [*US* shyster (*fam*)].

legumbre *f* BOT legume, pod vegetable; *legumbres secas* dried legumes || vegetable (verdura); *legumbres verdes* green vegetables.

leguminoso, sa *adj* leguminous.
◆ *f* pulse, leguminous plant.

leíble *adj* legible, readable (legible).

leída *f* reading; *de una leída* in one reading.

leído, da *adj* well-read (persona) || read; *una obra muy leída* a widely read work || — *leído y conforme* read and approved || FAM *ser muy leído y escribido* to be well read, to be very knowledgeable (presumir de sabio).

leísmo *m* use of the pronoun *le* in the masculine singular accusative case instead of the pronoun *lo* (*este lápiz no te le doy* instead of *no te lo doy*).

leísta *adj* who uses *le* as direct object.
◆ *m/f* person who uses *le* as direct object.

leitmotiv *m* leitmotiv, leitmotif (tema).

— OBSERV *Leitmotiv* is a Germanism which can be replaced by *tema central* (of a film, an opera, a novel, etc.).

lejanía *f* distance; *sonido debilitado por la lejanía* sound weakened by the distance || distant *o* remote place (paraje lejano) || *en la lejanía* in the distance.

lejano, na *adj* distant, remote, far-off; *el Japón es un país lejano* Japan is a distant country || distant; *pariente lejano* distant relative || — *Lejano Oriente* Far East || *un lugar lejano de mi casa* a place far from my home *o* a long way from my home.

lejía *f* lye (agua alcalina) || bleach (hipoclorito de sosa) || FIG & FAM dressing down (reprimenda) | scolding (bronca); *dar a uno una buena lejía* to give s.o. a good scolding.

lejío *m* dyers' lye.

lejísimos *adv* very far.

— OBSERV The incorrect form *lejísimo* should be avoided.

lejos *adv* far, far away; *¿estaba lejos?* was it far? || — *a lo lejos* in the distance; *ver a lo lejos* to see in the distance || *de lejos* from afar, from a distance; *la iglesia se ve de lejos* the church can be seen from afar; from a distance; *de lejos no veo nada* from a distance I can't see anything; by far; *es de lejos el mejor* he's by far the best || *desde lejos* from afar, from a long way off || FIG *ir* or *llegar lejos* to go far, to go a long way || *lejos de* a long way from, far from; *lejos de Madrid* a long way from Madrid; far from; *estaba lejos de saber lo que iba a sucederme* I was far from knowing what was to happen to me; instead of, far from; *lejos de asustarse, el niño se puso a acariciar al león* instead of getting frightened the boy began to pat the lion || FIG *llevar demasiado lejos* to carry too far; *llevó el asunto demasiado lejos* he carried the matter too far || *más lejos* further, further away || FIG *ni de lejos* far from it | *para no ir más lejos* to take an obvious example || *veo muy lejos la terminación del proyecto* I can't envisage an early completion of the plan.
◆ *m* appearance from a distance (aspecto) || background (pintura) || *tener buen lejos* to look good from a distance.

lelo, la *adj* silly, stupid, foolish (tonto) || — FAM *dejar a uno lelo* to leave s.o. stupefied, to stun s.o. | *estar lelo por* to be crazy about | *quedarse lelo* to be stunned *o* stupefied; *al ver el accidente me quedé lelo* I was stunned by the sight of the accident.
◆ *m* ninny, simpleton, fool.

lema *m* motto (en un escudo, en un monumento) || epigraph (en un libro) || lemma (en lógica) || theme, subject (tema) || assumed name (concurso) || MAT lemma || slogan (de un partido, etc.) || watchword (contraseña).

lemming *m* lemming (ratón campestre).

lemnáceas *f pl* lemnaceae.

lempira *f* lempira (moneda de Honduras).

lémur *m* ZOOL lemur.
◆ *pl* MIT lemures (almas de los muertos) || FIG phantoms, ghosts.

lencería *f* linen (ropa blanca) || underwear (ropa interior) || linen goods *pl* (géneros de lienzo) || linen shop, draper's (tienda de ropa blanca) || linen room (en un hospital).

lendrera *f* toothcomb [*US* fine-tooth comb] [for removing nits or lice].

lengua *f* ANAT tongue || language, tongue (p us) language, tongue (idioma); *lengua española, inglesa* Spanish, English language || clapper, tongue (badajo) || neck, spit, tongue (de tierra) || CULIN tongue || — FIG & FAM *andar en lenguas* to be the talk of the town | *atar la lengua a uno* to silence s.o. | *buscarle la lengua a uno* to ask for it, to provoke s.o., to pick a quarrel with s.o. (buscar pelea o discusión), to provoke s.o. to speak (incitar a hablar) | *calentársele a uno la lengua* to get worked up *o* steamed up | *con la lengua fuera* or *de un palmo* planting, puffing and panting | *darle a la lengua* to chatter | *de lengua en lengua* from mouth to mouth || *dominar una lengua* to master a language || FIG & FAM *estar con la lengua fuera* to be dead beat (de cansancio) | *hacerse lenguas de* to rave about | *hay que darle siete vueltas a la lengua antes de hablar* one must think twice before speaking | *írsele a uno la lengua, irse de la lengua* to blab, to talk too much (de costumbre), to spill the beans (en una ocasión) || *lengua aglutinante* agglutinative language || BOT *lengua de buey* oxtongue || FIG *lengua de estropajo* or *de trapo* stammerer, stutterer, mumbler (persona) | *lengua de fuego* tongue of fire | *lengua de gato* finger biscuit || *lengua de oc, de oïl* langue d'oc, d'oïl || FIG *lengua de víbora, lengua viperina* poisonous tongue || *lengua larga* gossip || *lengua madre* parent language [of other languages] || *lengua materna* or *nativa* mother *o* native tongue, native language || *lengua muerta* dead language || *lengua pastosa* or *gorda* coated tongue, furry tongue || *lenguas hermanas* sister tongues || *lengua viva* living language || FIG *ligero de lengua* loose-tongued | *mala lengua* evil tongue | *media lengua* childish talk *o* language | *morderse la lengua* to hold one's tongue | *no hay que prestar atención a las malas lenguas* one should not worry about what people say | *no morderse la lengua* not to mince one's words, to speak one's mind | *no tener pelos* or *pelillos en la lengua* not to mince one's words, to be outspoken | *pegársele a uno la lengua al paladar* to be unable to speak | *sacar la lengua* to stick out *o* to put out one's tongue (*a* at) (hacer burla) | *se me vino algo a la lengua* sth. came to my mind | *tener la lengua gorda* to be drunk (borracho), to have a furry tongue (lengua pastosa) | *tener uno mala lengua* to have a vicious tongue | *tener uno mucha lengua, tener la lengua suelta* to be outspoken | *tenía el nombre en la punta de la lengua* the name was on the tip of his tongue | *tenía la lengua fuera* his tongue was hanging out | *tirarle a uno de la lengua* to draw s.o. out, to make s.o. talk | *tomar lengua* or *lenguas* to find out, to inquire | *trabarse la lengua* to get tongue-tied; *se me trabó la lengua* I got tongue-tied | *traer en lenguas a uno* to criticize s.o. | *tragarse la lengua* to bite one's lip | *venírsele a uno a la lengua una cosa* to get an idea.

lenguado *m* sole; *lenguado a la parrilla* grilled sole.

lenguaje *m* language; *lenguaje culto, grosero, cifrado* cultured, foul, code language || idiom (de un autor) || speech (facultad de hablar) || FIG language; *el lenguaje de las flores* the language of flowers || style; *lenguaje literario* literary style || INFORM *lenguaje BASIC* BASIC [Beginners All-purpose Symbolic Instruction Code] | *lenguaje COBOL* COBOL [Common Business-Oriented Language] | *lenguaje de alto nivel* high-level language | *lenguaje de ordenador* computer language | *lenguaje de programación* programming language | *lenguaje FORTRAN* FORTRAN [Formula translation] | *lenguaje orientado al procedimiento* procedure-oriented language, procedural language.

lenguaraz *adj* talkative (hablador) || FIG slanderous, scurrilous (maldiciente) || polyglot, multilingual.
◆ *m/f* talkative person || slanderer (maldiciente) || polyglot.

lengüeta *f* pointer (de la balanza) || flap, tongue (de cartera, de bolso, etc.) || tongue (del calzado) || ANAT epiglottis || MÚS reed (de una flauta) || tenon, tongue (en carpintería) || barb (de una flecha) || barb (de anzuelo) || bit (barrena) || — *ensambladura de ranura y lengüeta* tongue-and-groove joint || *poner lengüetas* to reed (un órgano), to barb (una flecha).

lengüetada *f*; **lengüetazo** *m* lick.

lengüetear *vi* to lick || AMER to chatter.

lengüetería *f* reed stops *pl* (de un órgano).

lengüicorto, ta *adj* FAM timid, shy, quiet.

lengüilargo, ga *adj* FAM talkative (parlanchín) | foul-mouthed (deslenguado).

lengüón, ona *adj* AMER talkative (parlanchín) | gossipy (chismoso).
◆ *m/f* AMER chatterbox | gossip (chismoso).

lenidad *f* leniency, lenience (indulgencia).

lenificación *f* softening.

lenificar *vt* to soothe, to alleviate (el dolor) || to alleviate (otro sufrimiento).

lenificativo, va *adj* soothing, alleviating.

leninismo *m* Leninism.

leninista *adj/s* Leninist.

lenitivo, va *adj* soothing, lenitive.
◆ *m* MED lenitive || FIG lenitive, palliative.

lenocinio *m* pimping, procuring || *casa de lenocinio* brothel.

lente *m/f* lens (óptica); *lente de aumento* magnifying lens || magnifying glass (lupa); *mirar con lente* to look at through a magnifying glass || lens, glass (de gafas) || monocle (monóculo).
◆ *pl* glasses, spectacles (gafas) || pince-nez *sing*, eyeglasses (quevedos) || *lentes de contacto* contact lenses..
— OBSERV The ambiguous gender of this word sometimes causes difficulties, but it is usually masculine when meaning *spectacles* (*los lentes*) and feminine when it applies to *refractive lenses.*

lenteja *f* BOT lentil.

lentejar *m* lentil field.

lentejuela *f* sequin, spangle.

lenticular *adj* lenticular.

lentilla *f* contact lens.

lentiscal *m* grove of mastic trees.

lentisco *m* BOT lentiscus, lentisk, mastic tree.

lentitud *f* slowness, sluggishness.

lento, ta *adj* slow; *lento en actuar* slow to act; *lento en el trabajo* slow worker || slow, sluggish (persona) || MED viscous, viscid || *a cámara lenta* slow-motion (cine), in slow motion (rodar).

leña *f* firewood || FIG & FAM rough play; *hubo mucha leña durante el partido de fútbol* there was a lot of rough play during the football match || — FIG & FAM *añadir* or *echar* or *poner leña al fuego* to add fuel to the fire | *dar* or *repartir leña* to play rough (deportes), to lash out (pegar) | *dar leña a alguien* to give s.o. a beating || *leña menuda* kindling (wood) || *leña seca* deadwood || FIG *llevar leña al monte* to carry coals to Newcastle.

leñador, ra *m/f* woodcutter.

leñazo *m* FAM blow with a stick (garrotazo) | blow (golpe) || — FAM *me dieron un leñazo* they hit *o* walloped me | *me di un leñazo con el coche* I crashed my car.

¡leñe! *interj* POP Jesus!, Christ!

leñera *f* woodshed (sitio) || woodpile (montón).

leñero *m* wood seller || woodshed (leñera).
◆ *adj m* FAM rough; *equipo leñero* rough team.

leño *m* log (trozo de árbol) || firewood (leña) || FIG & POÉT vessel (embarcación) || FIG & FAM blockhead, thickhead (persona) || FAM *dormir como un leño* to sleep like a log.

leñoso, sa *adj* ligneous.

Leo *npr m* ASTR Leo.

león *m* ZOOL lion || ant lion (hormiga león) || FIG lion; *valiente como un león* as brave as a lion || HERÁLD lion || AMER puma || — *cachorro del león* lion cub || FIG *la parte del león* the lion's share || *león marino* sea lion (foca) || AMER *león miquero* puma || FIG *no es tan fiero* or *bravo el león como lo pintan* he is not as fierce *o* brave as he's made out to be (una persona), it is not as difficult as they make out (una cosa) | *ponerse como un león* to get furious.

leona *f* lioness.

leonado, da *adj* fulvous, tawny.

leonera *f* lion's den (foso) || lion's cage (jaula) || FIG & FAM *este cuarto es* or *está hecho una leonera* this room is a mess.

leonero *m* lion keeper.

leonino, na *adj* leonine || — *contrato leonino* one-side contract || *hacer un reparto leonino* to make an unfair distribution, to share sth. out unfairly.

Leonor *npr f* Eleanor.

leontina *f* watch chain (de reloj).

leopardo *m* ZOOL leopard.

leotardo *m* leotard (traje para gimnastas).
◆ *pl* tights (medias).

Lepanto *n pr* GEOGR Lepanto.

Lepe *n pr* *sabe más que Lepe (Lepijo y su hijo)*, he's got no flies on him, he's nobody's fool.

lépero, ra *adj* AMER coarse, vulgar (grosero).

lepidóptero, ra *adj* ZOOL lepidopterous, lepidopteran.
◆ *m* ZOOL lepidopteron, lepidopteran.
◆ *pl* lepidoptera.

leporino, na *adj* leporine || *labio leporino* harelip.

lepra *f* MED leprosy.

leprosaria *m* AMER leprosarium, lazaretto.

leprosería *f* leprosarium, lazaretto.

leproso, sa *adj* leprous.
◆ *m/f* leper.

lerdo, da *adj* dull, slow, dim (lento) || sluggish, lumbering, clumsy (torpe).
◆ *m* dullard, sluggard.

Lerna *n pr* MIT Lerna || *hidra de Lerna* Lernaean hydra.

les *pron pers m/f pl* to them, them (a ellos, a ellas), you, to you (a ustedes); *les presto (a ellas) mis joyas* I lend them my jewels, I lend my jewels to them || for them, them (para ellos), for you, you (para ustedes); *les traigo un regalo (a ustedes)* I have brought you a present *o* brought a present for you || for them (de ellos), from you (de ustedes); *les compré un coche* I bought a car from them.

lesa *adj* ⟶ **leso.**

lesbianismo *m* lesbianism.

lesbiano, na; lesbio, bia *adj/s* lesbian.

Lesbos *n pr* GEOGR Lesbos.

lesera *f* AMER nonsense, rubbish (tontería).

lesión *f* injury, wound, lesion; *lesión interna* internal injury; *lesión en la pierna* wound in the leg || damage (daño) || JUR injury (perjuicio).
◆ *pl* JUR assault and battery.

lesionado, da *adj* injured, wounded || damaged (dañado).
◆ *m/f* injured person.

lesionar *vt* to damage (dañar) || to wound, to injure (herir).
◆ *vpr* to get hurt, to be injured, to injure *o* to hurt o.s.

lesivo, va *adj* injurious, harmful.

lesna *f* awl.

leso, sa *adj* injured, wronged || FIG disturbed, warped (trastornado) || AMER stupid (tonto) || JUR *crimen de lesa majestad* high treason, lese majesty.

letal *adj* lethal, deadly (mortífero).

letanía *f* REL litany || supplicatory procession (procesión) || FIG & FAM string, long list (sarta).

letárgico, ca *adj* MED lethargic.

letargo *m* MED lethargy; *caer en estado de letargo* to fall into a state of lethargy || FIG lethargy, drowsiness (modorra).

letífero, ra *adj* lethal, deadly (letal).

letón, ona *adj* Latvian, Lettish.
◆ *m/f* Latvian, Lett (habitante).
◆ *m* Latvian, Lettish (idioma).

Letonia *npr f* GEOGR Latvia.

letra *f* letter; *la letra a* the letter a || character, letter (en imprenta) || handwriting, writing, hand; *tener buena letra* to have good handwriting || lyrics *pl*, words *pl* (de una canción) || inscription, motto (lema) || rondeau (poesía) || COM bill of exchange (letra de cambio) || FIG & FAM astuteness, cunning, artfulness (astucia) || — *a la letra, al pie de la letra* to the letter; *cumplió mis instrucciones al pie de la letra* he carried out my instructions to the letter; literally; *tomó al pie de la letra lo que dije y se enfadó* he took what I said literally and got angry; word for word; *copió el artículo al pie de la letra* he copied the article word for word || *atenerse a la letra, atarse a la letra* to stick to the literal meaning || *de su puño y letra* by his own hand || FIG & FAM *la letra con sangre entra* spare the rod and spoil the child || *letra abierta* letter of credit [for an unlimited amount] || COM *letra a la vista* sight draft || *letra bastardilla* italic letters, italics || *letra corrida* or *cursiva* cursive writing || *letra de cambio* bill of exchange || *letra de imprenta* or *de molde* print || COM *letra domiciliada* domiciliated bill || *letra dominical* dominical letter || *letra florida* ornamental capital, head letter || *letra gótica* Gothic lettering *o* script || *letra mayúscula, minúscula* capital, small letter || FIG *letra muerta* dead letter || *letra negrilla* bold type, boldface || *letra por letra* word for word || *letra redonda* or *redondilla* round hand || *letra versalita* small capital (letter) || COM *protestar una letra* to protest a bill || FIG *tener letra menuda* to be artful *o* cunning.

◆ *pl* letters (literatura) || arts; *licenciado en Letras* arts graduate; *facultad de Letras* Faculty of Arts || line *sing*, lines; *te pondré unas letras* I'll drop you a line, I'll write you a few lines || — *bellas* or *buenas letras* literature, belles lettres || *Ciencias y Letras* Arts and Sciences || *con todas sus letras* written out in full || *escribir en letras de molde* to print | *hombre, mujer de letras* man, woman of letters || *letras divinas* or *sagradas* the Bible, the Scriptures || *letras humanas* Humanities || FIG *ponerle a uno cuatro letras* to drop s.o. a line | *primeras letras* three R's.

letrado, da *adj* lettered, learned (instruido) || FAM pedantic (presumido).

◆ *m* lawyer (abogado).

Letrán *npr m* Lateran (palacio romano).

letrero *m* notice (anuncio) || sign (señal) || poster (cartel) || label (etiqueta) || inscription (inscripción) || *letrero luminoso* neon sign.

letrilla *f* rondeau (composición poética).

letrina *f* latrine.

leucemia *f* MED leucaemia [*US* leucemia], leukaemia [*US* leukemia].

leucémico, ca *adj* leucaemic [*US* leucemic], leukaemic [*US* leukemic].

◆ *m/f* leukaemic person || *es un leucémico* he suffers from leukaemia.

leucito *m* BOT leucite.

leucoblasto *m* BIOL leucoblast [*US* leukoblast].

leucocito *m* BIOL leucocyte [*US* leukocyte].

leucocitosis *f* MED leucocytosis [*US* leukocytosis].

leucoma *m* MED leucoma [*US* leukoma].

leucoplasto *m* BOT leucoplast [*US* leukoplast].

leucorrea *f* MED leucorrhoea [*US* leukorrhea].

leucosis *f* leucosis [*US* leukosis].

leudar *vt* to leaven.

◆ *vpr* to rise (la masa del pan).

leude *m* HIST leud.

leudo, da *adj* leavened (el pan).

leva *f* MAR weighing anchor (de un barco) || levy (reclutamiento) || TECN cam | vane (álabe) | lever (palanca) || *AMER* trick (engaño) || TECN *árbol de levas* camshaft.

levadizo *adj m* *puente levadizo* drawbridge.

levador *m* TECN vane (álabe).

levadura *f* leaven (para el pan) || yeast (de la cerveza, etc.) || FIG seed (germen) || — *levadura en polvo* baking powder || *pan sin levadura* unleavened bread.

levantada *f* getting up, rising (de la cama) || lift (halterofilia).

levantado, da *adj* lifted up || FIG lofty, elevated, high (elevado) || *votar por levantados y sentados* to vote by sitting and standing.

levantamiento *m* raising, lifting (acción de levantar) || erection (de una estatua) || construction (de un edificio) || elevation || insurrection, uprising (sedición) || TECN hoisting, lifting || GEOL upheaval || drawing up (de planos) || — *levantamiento de la veda* opening of the hunting *o* of the fishing season || *levantamiento de cadáver* removal of the corpse || *levantamiento de pesos* weight-lifting || *levantamiento topográfico* survey, land survey.

levantar *vt* to raise, to put up; *levantar la mano* to raise one's hand || to lift, to lift up; *no puedo levantar este paquete* I can't lift this parcel || to set *o* to put up; *levantar una escala* to set up a ladder || to throw up (en el aire) || to raise, to lift (alzar); *levantar los ojos* to raise one's eyes || to erect, to raise, to construct; *levantar un templo* to erect a temple || to set up; *levantar una fábrica* to set up a factory || to lift up, to pick up (recoger); *levanta la silla* pick up the chair || to cut (en los naipes) || to remove (quitar); *levantar el mantel* to remove the tablecloth || to draw up (un plano) || to do (un dibujo) || to put up; *levantar obstáculos* to put up obstacles || JUR to draw up (acta); *levantar un atestado* to draw up a report || to weigh; *levantar el ancla* to weigh anchor || to lift, to raise (el telón) || to raise (un chichón) || FIG to turn (trastornar); *levantar el estómago* to turn one's stomach | to turn (enemistar); *levantar a un hijo contra su padre* to turn a son against his father | to stir up; *levantar al pueblo* to stir up the people | to lift (el pensamiento, el corazón); *levantar el corazón a Dios* to lift one's heart to God | to raise; *levantar el nivel de vida* to raise the standard of living | to put on its feet; *levantar al país, la economía nacional* to put the country, the national economy on its feet | to cause, to give rise to, to entail; *la ejecución de un programa político levanta grandes dificultades* the carrying out of a political programme gives rise to great difficulties | to found, to institute (fundar) | to bear; *levantar falso testimonio* to bear false witness | to raise, to lift (una prohibición) | to adjourn (una sesión) | to take (un censo) | to suspend, to raise (una prohibición); *levantar la excomunión* to suspend the excommunication | to raise (la voz) || MIL to levy, to raise, to recruit (tropas) | to raise (un sitio) || DEP to rear (el caballo) | to lift (un peso) || to flush out (en la caza) || — FIG *levantar cabeza* to get better (estar mejor) || *levantar del suelo* to lift off the ground || *levantar el ánimo* to cheer *o* to buck s.o. up, to lift *o* to raise s.o.'s spirits || *levantar el cadáver* to remove the corpse || *levantar el campo* to strike *o* to break camp (sentido propio), to leave (largarse), to give up (abandonar el campo) || *levantar en alto* to lift up into the air || *levantar la baza* to win the trick (en los naipes) || *levantar la casa* to move house || *levantar la mano a uno* to raise one's hand to s.o. || *levantar la veda* to open the hunting *o* fishing season || FAM *levantarle a uno la tapa de los sesos* to blow s.o.'s brains out || *levantar polvo* to raise dust || JUR *levantar un proceso* to institute proceedings || *sin levantar la vista* without looking up, without raising *o* lifting one's eyes.

◆ *vpr* to get up; *levantarse temprano* to get up early || to stand up, to rise (ponerse de pie) || to stand out, to rise (erguirse) || to come out ahead (salir ganador) || to rise, to come up (el viento) || to lift (la niebla) || FIG to break out (escándalo, riña) | to rise up, to rise (sublevarse) | to rise, to be adjourned (una sesión) || — *al levantarse el telón* when the curtain rose *o* rises || *al levantarse la sesión* when the meeting rose *o* adjourned || FIG *levantarse con* to make off with (llevarse) || FAM *levantarse con el pie izquierdo* to get up on the wrong side of the bed || *levantarse de la cama* to get out of bed || *levantarse de la mesa, de la silla* to get up from the table, off *o* from the chair || *levantarse del suelo* to get up off the ground || *levantarse en armas* to rise up in arms || *levantarse pronto* to get up early || *se me levantó el estómago al ver la sangre* the sight of blood made my stomach turn.

levante *m* East, Orient || East wind, levanter (viento).

Levante *npr m* GEOGR Levante [a region in eastern Spain made up of Valencia and Murcia] || Levant (países al Este del Mediterráneo).

levantino, na *adj* of *o* from «Levante» || Levantine [of the Levant].

◆ *m/f* native *o* inhabitant of «Levante» (de España) || Levantine.

levantisco, ca *adj* turbulent, restless.

levar *vt* MAR to weigh (el ancla).

◆ *vpr* MAR to set sail, to weigh anchor.

leve *adj* light || FIG slight; *una herida leve* a slight wound | slight, trivial, unimportant (error, etc.).

levedad *f* lightness (ligereza) || FIG slightness, triviality, unimportance; *la levedad de una ofensa* the slightness of an offence.

levemente *adv* lightly || FIG slightly.

Leviatán *npr m* Leviathan.

levigación *f* levigation.

levita *m* Levite (de la tribu de Levi).

◆ *f* frock coat (chaqueta) || FIG & FAM *tirar de la levita* to butter up, to flatter (adular).

levitación *f* levitation.

levítico, ca *adj* Levitical || FIG clerical; *ambiente levítico* clerical atmosphere.

Levítico *npr m* Leviticus (libro de Moisés).

léxico, ca *adj* lexical.

◆ *m* lexicon, dictionary || vocabulary.

lexicografía *f* lexicography.

lexicográfico, ca *adj* lexicographic, lexicographical.

lexicógrafo, fa *m/f* lexicographer.

lexicología *f* lexicology.

lexicológico, ca *adj* lexicologic, lexicological.

lexicólogo, ga *m/f* lexicologist.

lexicón *m* lexicon, dictionary || vocabulary.

ley *f* JUR law; *respetar la ley* to respect the law; *ley vigente* law in force; *ley marcial* martial law || bill, act (en las Cortes); *aprobar una ley* to pass a bill || law; *la ley de la oferta y la demanda* the law of supply and demand; *leyes de la física* laws of physics || rule, law; *las leyes del juego* the rules of the game || religion; *la ley de los mahometanos* the religion of the Mahometans || quality (calidad), weight (peso), dimension (medida) || sterling (de la plata) || purity (de un metal) || statute (de una asamblea) || regulations *pl* (de un concurso) || liking (cariño) (*with the verbs cobrar, tener* and *tomar*) *tomar ley a alguien* to take a liking to s.o. || *al margen de la ley, fuera de la ley* outside the law || *bajar de ley* to lower the sterling content of, to lessen the purity of (un metal) || *bajo de ley* below sterling standard, base (plata) || *con todas las de la ley* fully-fledged, real; *ser un médico con todas las de la ley* to be a fully-fledged doctor; according to the rules (según las reglas), in due form (en debida forma) || *contra la ley* against the law || *de buena ley* sterling (en sentido propio y figurado) || *dictar la ley* to lay down the law || FIG *en buena ley* rightly, justly || *hecha la ley, hecha la trampa* laws are made to be broken || *la costumbre hace ley* or *tiene fuerza de ley* custom has the force of law || *la ignorancia de la ley no excusa su cumplimiento* ignorance of the law is no excuse || REL *la Ley* the Law || FIG *la ley del embudo* one law for oneself and one for everyone else || *ley de extranjería* law on aliens || *ley de incompatibilidades* law against holding multiple posts || *ley natural* natural law || *ley sálica* salic law || *ley seca* prohibition law [*US* dry law] || INFORM *ley sobre informática y libertades* Data Protection Act || *oro de ley* pure gold, standard gold || *plata*

de ley pure silver, sterling silver || *representante de la ley* officer of the law || *según la ley* according to the law, by law || *tener fuerza de ley* to have force of law || *venir contra la ley* to break the law.
◆ *pl* law *sing; estudiar leyes* to study law || — *allá van leyes do* or *donde quieren reyes* the strong man is a law unto himself || *dictar sus propias leyes* to be a law unto o.s.

Leyden *n pr* GEOGR Leyden || *botella de Leyden* Leyden jar.

leyenda *f* legend (vida de santos) || legend (cuento) || inscription, legend (de una moneda) || *leyenda negra* black legend.

lezna *f* awl (de zapatero).

liana *f* BOT liana (bejuco).

liar *vt* to tie, to bind; *liar un paquete con una cuerda* to tie a parcel with string || to tie up, to do up; *no puedo liar este paquete* I can't tie up this parcel || to wrap (up); *liar algo en una manta* to wrap sth. (up) in a blanket || to roll; *liar un cigarrillo* to roll a cigarette || FIG & FAM to coax (engatusar) | to take (s.o.) in (engañar) | to mix up, to involve; *no me líes en este asunto* don't mix me up in this matter | to muddle up (confundir); *trató de liarme con sus razonamientos* he tried to muddle me up with his reasoning | to complicate (volver más complicado) || — FAM *liar el hato, liarlas* to do a bunk, to hop it (irse), to kick the bucket (morir) | *liar los bártulos* to pack one's bags.
◆ *vpr* to wrap o.s. (up); *liarse en una manta* to wrap o.s. (up) in a blanket || FIG & FAM to get muddled up, to get confused (enredarse) | to become complicated; *el asunto se lió más de lo previsto* the matter became more complicated than was anticipated | to get *o* to become involved (meterse) | to interfere (intervenir) || FIG & POP to become lovers (dos personas), to become the lover (con of), (amancebarse) || FIG & FAM *liárselas* to do a bunk, to hop it (irse), to kick the bucket (morir).

lías; liásico *m* GEOL Lias.

liásico, ca *adj* GEOL Liassic.

libación *f* libation.

libanés, esa *adj/s* Lebanese.

Líbano *npr m* GEOGR Lebanon.

libar *vt* to suck (chupar).

libelar *vt* JUR to word (un documento) | to petition (demandar).

libelista *m/f* lampoonist (de escritos satíricos) || JUR libellist [*US* libelist].

libelo *m* lampoon (escrito satírico) || JUR libel.

libélula *f* dragonfly, libellula (insecto).

líber *m* BOT inner bark.

liberación *f* liberation (de un país, de la servidumbre) || release, freeing (de presos) || receipt (recibo) || remission (perdón, remisión) || exemption (de una obligación) || AMER delivery (parto) || *acto de liberación* order of release.

liberado, da *adj* liberated, freed; *país liberado* liberated country || exempted (de una obligación) || COM paid-up (pagado).

liberador, ra *adj* liberating.
◆ *m/f* liberator.

liberal *adj/s* liberal; *liberal con uno* liberal with s.o. || — *artes liberales* liberal arts || *los liberales* the liberals (en política) || *partido liberal* liberal party || *profesión liberal* (liberal) profession.

liberalidad *f* liberality.

liberalismo *m* liberalism.

liberalización *f* liberalization.

liberalizar *vt* to liberalize.
◆ *vpr* to become liberal.

liberalmente *adv* liberally, freely (con desprendimiento) || AMER rapidly, quickly (rápidamente).

liberar *vt* to liberate, to free || to free; *liberar un dedo cogido en el engranaje* to free a finger caught in the gears || FIG to free, to release; *liberar a uno de su promesa* to free s.o. from his promise | to exempt (de una obligación).

liberatorio, ria *adj* liberatory.

Liberia *npr f* GEOGR Liberia.

liberiano, na *adj/s* Liberian (de Liberia).

libérrimo, ma *adj* entirely free, completely free, very free || *por su libérrima voluntad* entirely of his own free will.

libertad *f* freedom (palabra general) || liberty, freedom; *hipotecar su libertad* to pledge one's liberty || familiarity (en el trato) || ease, freedom (desembarazo) || — *con entera* or *con toda libertad* with absolute *o* complete liberty || *en libertad para hacer algo* free to *o* at liberty to do sth || *estar en libertad* to be free, to be at large || *libertad bajo fianza* bail || *libertad bajo palabra* parole || *libertad condicional* probation || ECON *libertad de circulación de capitales* free movement of capital | *libertad de circulación de trabajadores* free movement of workers || *libertad de comercio* free trade || *libertad de conciencia, de cultos, de imprenta* or *de prensa, de palabra* or *de expresión* freedom of conscience, of worship, of the press, of speech || *libertad de reunión* freedom of assembly || *libertad individual* freedom of the individual || *libertad provisional* bail (bajo fianza), parole (bajo palabra) || *libertad vigilada* probation || *poner en libertad* to set free, to release || *tener plena libertad de* or *para* to be free to *o* at liberty to, to have complete liberty to || *tomarse la libertad de* to take the liberty of (con gerundio) || *una tarde de libertad* a free afternoon, an afternoon off.
◆ *pl* liberties; *tomarse libertades* to take liberties || liberties, privileges (prerrogativas).

libertador, ra *adj* liberating.
◆ *m/f* liberator || AMER *el Libertador* Simón Bolívar.

libertar *vt* to liberate, to free, to set free || to exempt, to release (de una deuda, de una obligación) || to emancipate (de la esclavitud) || to save, to deliver (preservar).

libertario, ria *adj/s* libertarian.

libertinaje *m* libertinism, licentiousness.

libertino, na *adj/s* libertine, profligate.
◆ *m/f* son or daughter of an emancipated slave (hijo de liberto).

liberto, ta *adj* emancipated.
◆ *m/f* freedman (hombre), freedwoman (mujer).

Libia *npr f* GEOGR Libya.

libídine *f* lewdness, libido.

libidinosidad *f* lasciviousness, lewdness, lustfulness.

libidinoso, sa *adj* libidinous, lewd, lustful.

libido *f* libido.

libio, bia *adj/s* Libyan.

libra *f* pound (peso, moneda) || AMER leaf of top quality tobacco || — FIG & FAM *de estos entran pocos en libra* these are rare, there are few like these, these are few and far between | *es un amigo de los que entran pocos en libra* he is an exceptionally good friend || *libra carnicera* kilogramme || *libra esterlina* pound sterling.

Libra *npr f* ASTR Libra (signo del zodíaco).

libraco *m* FAM worthless book (libro).

librador, ra *adj* liberating (que libra).
◆ *m/f* liberator, deliverer || COM drawer.
◆ *m* scoop [used in a grocery shop] (cogedor).

libramiento *m* liberation (acción de libertar) || deliverance (de un peligro) || exemption (de un cargo, de un trabajo) || order of payment (orden de pago).

librancista *m* bearer (de una letra de cambio).

librante *m* drawer (de una letra de cambio).

libranza *f* order of payment (orden de pago).

librar *vt* to save, to rescue (de un peligro) || to free, to liberate, to deliver; *librar de la tiranía* to free from tyranny || to relieve; *librar a uno de una preocupación* to relieve s.o. of a worry || to exempt, to free, to release (de un cargo o de un trabajo) || to place, to put (la confianza) || to join in, to engage (una batalla, dos ejércitos) || to join, to give; *librar combate por* to join battle for || to wage (la guerra) || to draw (letras de cambio, cheques, etc.); *librar un cheque contra alguien* to draw a cheque on s.o. || to pronounce, to pass (una sentencia) || to issue, to promulgate (un decreto) || — *¡Dios me libre!, ¡líbreme Dios!* Heaven forbid! || *librar su esperanza en Dios* to place one's hopes in God || *salir bien librado* to come out unscathed *o* well, to get off lightly || *salir mal librado* to come out the worse for wear, to suffer.
◆ *vi* to go out to receive visitors (una monja) || to give birth, to be delivered of a child (una mujer) || FAM to have one's day off (los obreros).
◆ *vpr* to avoid; *librarse de un golpe* to avoid a blow || to escape; *librarse de un peligro* to escape (from) danger || to get out (de of) (una cosa molesta) || to free o.s. (de of) (una obligación, un perjuicio) || to get rid of; *librarse de una persona molesta* to get rid of a bothersome person || — FAM *librarse de una buena* to have a narrow escape *o* a close call | *librarse por los pelos* to have a narrow escape, to escape by the skin of one's teeth, to have a close shave.

libre *adj* free; *es usted muy libre de ir* you are completely free to go; *amor, sociedad libre* free love, society || free (que no está preso) || open; *el aire libre* the open air || FIG free, clear (sitio desembarazado) | vacant (no ocupado) | bold, forward (atrevido) | familiar | outspoken (franco) | loose, licentious (licencioso) | independent (independiente) | free, out; *libre de deudas* free of debt | free, unattached (sin compromiso, suelto) || QUÍM free; *oxígeno libre* free oxygen || DEP freestyle; *los 100 metros libres* the 100 metres freestyle || — *entrada libre* admission free || *es libre en su lenguaje* he is one for plain speaking || *estar libre de alguien* to be rid of s.o. || *estudiar por libre* to be an external student || *libre albedrío* free will || *libre bajo palabra* on parole || *libre de* free from; *libre de penas* free from worries || *libre de cuidado* out of danger || *libre de derechos de aduana* duty-free, free of duty || *libre de impuestos* tax-free, free of tax, free from tax || FIG *más libre que un pájaro* as free as a bird || *oyente libre* auditor (en un curso) || *tener entrada libre en casa de alguien* to always have the door open to one || *traducción libre* free translation || *zona de libre cambio* or *de libre comercio* free trade area.

librea *f* livery (de un mayordomo) || coat (de los venados).

librecambio *m* free trade.

librecambismo *m* free trade.

librecambista *adj* free-trade; *política librecambista* free-trade policy.
◆ *m/f* free trader.

librepensador, ra *adj* freethinking.
◆ *m/f* freethinker.

librería *f* bookshop [*US* bookstore] (tienda); *librería de ocasión* or *de lance* secondhand bookshop || library (colección de libros) ||

bookcase, bookshelf (mueble) || book trade (industria).

librero, ra *m/f* bookseller.
◆ *m* *AMER* bookcase, bookshelf (mueble).

libresco, ca *adj* acquired from books, book || *conocimientos librescos* book learning.

libreta *f* notebook (cuaderno) || savings book (de caja de ahorros) || memorandum, agenda (agenda) || one-pound loaf (pan).

libretista *m/f* MÚS librettist.

libreto *m* MÚS libretto || *AMER* script (guión).

Libreville *n pr* GEOGR Libreville.

librillo *m* small book, booklet (libro) || ZOOL third stomach, omasum (de los rumiantes) || *librillo de papel de fumar* packet of cigarette papers.

libro *m* book (para leer); *libro de cabecera* bedside book || register, record book (para recoger datos) || notebook (cuaderno) || book; *libro de señas* or *de direcciones* address book || libretto (teatro) || ZOOL third stomach, omasum (de los rumiantes) || — FIG & FAM *ahorcar los libros* to burn one's books, to throw one's books away (dejar los estudios) || *hablar como un libro* to talk like a book || *libro amarillo, azul, blanco, rojo, etc.* yellow, blue, white, red, etc. paper (en diplomacia) || *libro antifonario* antiphonal, antiphonary || *libro borrador* daybook || COM *libro copiador* letter book || MAR *libro de a bordo* ship's log, ship's register, logbook || *libro de actas* minute book || *libro de asiento* or *de contabilidad* account book || *libro de bolsillo* paperback [US pocket book] (en rústica), pocket edition (edición de bolsillo) || *libro de caballerías* book of knight-errantry || COM *libro de caja* cashbook || *libro de cocina* cookery book [US cookbook] || *libro de consulta* reference book || *libro de cuentos* storybook || *libro de familia* booklet delivered by the priest to a married couple for the registration of births and deaths in the family || *libro de horas* Book of Hours || COM *libro de inventario* inventory (book) || *libro de lectura* reader || *libro de mano* manuscript || *libro de memoria* memorandum, memo (book) || *libro de misa* prayer book || *libro de música* music book || *libro de reclamaciones* complaints book || *libro de texto* textbook || COM *libro diario* diary || *libro empastado* or *encuadernado* bound book, hardback || *libro en rústica* paperback || *libro escolar* school report || *libro mayor* ledger || *libro talonario* counterfoil book [US stub book].
◆ *pl* books (contabilidad) || — *libros sagrados* sacred books || FIG *meterse en libros de caballerías* to poke one's nose into s.o. else's business || COM *llevar los libros* to keep the accounts, to keep the books || *tenedor de libros* book-keeper || *teneduría de libros* bookkeeping.

licántropo *m* MED lycanthrope.

licencia *f* permission, leave, licence [US license]; *con licencia de sus jefes* with his bosses' permission || bachelor's degree; *licencia en derecho, en filosofía y letras* bachelor's degree in law, in arts || permit, licence; *licencia de exportación, de importación* export, import licence || licence (libertad absoluta) || licence, permit; *licencia de caza, de pesca* hunting licence, fishing licence || licence (en poesía) || (ant) MIL leave (temporal) | discharge (definitiva) || leave; *licencia por enfermedad* sick leave || — MIL *licencia absoluta* discharge || *licencia de obras* planning permission || ECON *licencia fiscal* licence tax.

licenciado, da *adj* graduated (estudiante) || dismissed, discharged (despedido) || MIL discharged || priggish (presumido).
◆ *m/f* graduate, Bachelor [of Arts, Science, etc.].
◆ *m* lawyer (abogado) || discharged soldier (soldado) || FAM *licenciado Vidriera* timorous person.

licenciamiento *m* dismissal (de empleados) || graduation (de estudiantes) || MIL discharge of soldiers.

licenciar *vt* to dismiss (echar) || to confer a bachelor's degree upon (a un estudiante) || to licence [US to license], to authorize, to give permission (dar permiso) || to discharge, to demobilize, to demob (un soldado).
◆ *vpr* to graduate; *licenciarse en derecho, en filosofía y letras* to graduate in law, in arts || to become dissolute *o* lewd (volverse licencioso).

licenciatura *f* bachelor's degree (título); *licenciatura de derecho, de ciencias, de filosofía y letras* bachelor's degree in law, in science, in arts || degree (course) (estudios).

licencioso, sa *adj* licentious, dissolute.

liceo *m* literary society || grammar school, high school, secondary school (escuela) || lyceum (en Atenas) || *el Liceo* the Opera theatre in Barcelona.
— OBSERV Grammar school and secondary school in Spanish are more frequently called *instituto* (*de segunda enseñanza*) except in America where *liceo* is commonly used.

licitación *f* bidding [at an auction] (acción de licitar) || bid (cada oferta) || *sacar a licitación* to put up for auction (un objeto), to put out to tender, to invite tenders for (un trabajo).

licitador *m* bidder.

licitar *vt* to bid for (pujar un objeto) || to tender for (un trabajo).

lícito, ta *adj* JUR lawful, legal, licit || permissible, allowed.

licitud *f* JUR lawfulness, legality, licitness.

licor *m* liquid || liqueur (alcohólico); *beber un licor después de cenar* to drink a liqueur after dinner || — QUÍM *licor de Fehling* Fehling's solution | *licor de Schweitzer* Schweitzer's reagent.

licorera *f* cocktail cabinet [US liquor cabinet].

lictor *m* HIST lictor.

licuación *f* liquefaction || TECN liquation.

licuador *m*; **licuadora** *f* *AMER* mixer.

licuante *adj* liquefying || TECN liquating.

licuar *vt* to liquefy (volver líquido) || TECN to liquate.

licuefacción *f* liquefaction.

licuefacer *vt* to liquefy (licuar).

licuefactivo, va *adj* liquefactive, liquefacient.

licuescente *adj* liquescent.

lid *f* combat, fight (pelea) || FIG dispute (disputa) || — FIG *en buena lid* by fair means | *un hombre avezado a estas lides* an old hand, a man who knows how to handle these matters.

líder *m* leader (jefe de un partido).
— OBSERV pl *líderes*.

liderato; liderazgo *m* leadership.

lidia *f* fight, battle || TAUR bullfight || *toros de lidia* fighting bulls.

lidiador, ra *m/f* fighter || FIG arguer.
◆ *m* TAUR bullfighter.

lidiar *vt* TAUR to fight (bulls) || FIG to deal with (saber convencer); *sabe lidiar a la gente* he knows how to deal with people || FIG & FAM *harto de lidiar* for the sake of peace and quiet.
◆ *vi* to fight, to combat || FIG to put up (*con* with) (soportar); *he tenido que lidiar con* or *contra él* I have had to put up with him | to contend (*con* with) (contender).

liebre *f* hare (animal) || FIG & FAM coward, mouse, chicken (cobarde) || ASTR Hare (constelación) || *AMER* minibus (microbús) || — FIG & FAM *agarrar* or *coger una liebre* to come a cropper | *correr como una liebre* to run like a hare | *donde menos* or *cuando menos se piensa, salta la liebre* things always happen when you least expect them to | *levantar la liebre* to let the cat out of the bag, to spill the beans.

Liechtenstein *n pr* GEOGR Liechtenstein.

lied *m* MÚS lied.
— OBSERV pl *lieder* en ambos idiomas.

liendre *f* nit (huevo de piojo) || — FIG & FAM *cascarle* or *machacarle a uno las liendres* to beat s.o. up (aporrear), to give s.o. a telling off (reprender) | *sacar a uno hasta las liendres* to bleed s.o. white.

lienzo *m* fabric, material, cloth (tela en general) || linen (por oposición a la lana, etc.) || piece of cloth *o* of material (porción de tela) || handkerchief (pañuelo) || canvas (tela de un cuadro) || painting, canvas (cuadro) || ARQ façade, front [of a building] | stretch [of a wall] (de pared) || curtain (fortificación).

liga *f* garter (de mujeres y de hombres) || league (confederación) || DEP league || alloy (aleación) || mixture (mezcla) || BOT mistletoe (muérdago) || birdlime (materia pegajosa) || — *hacer buena, mala liga con uno* to get on *o* along well, badly with s.o. || *Liga Hanseática* Hanseatic League.

ligación *f* ligation, binding (acción) || bond, tie (ligadura) || mixture (mezcla) || link (enlace).

ligado *m* ligature (de dos letras) || MÚS ligature.

ligadura *f* ligature, tie, bond || soluble mixture (mezcla) || FIG bond, tie (vínculo) || tourniquet (para dar garrote) || ligature (de una arteria) || MÚS ligature || MAR lashing.

ligamen *m* undissolved marriage which prevents a second marriage.

ligamento *m* ANAT ligament || bond, tie (atadura) || weave (textiles).

ligamentoso, sa *adj* ligamentous.

ligamiento *m* tying, attaching (acción de ligar o atar) || FIG harmony.

ligar *vt* to tie, to bind, to fasten (atar) || to relate; *ligar una cosa con otra* to relate one thing to another || to alloy (los metales) || FIG to join, to unite; *sólo el interés nos liga* only interest unites us | to tie, to bind; *estoy ligado por esta promesa* I am bound by this promise || to league (en una liga) || to mix (bebidas) || MED to ligature (una arteria) || MÚS to slur [notes] || CULIN to thicken (una salsa) || *AMER* to pinch, to pilfer (sisar).
◆ *vi* to combine cards of the same suit || FAM to get on *o* along well (entenderse) | to pick up, to get off with, to flirt with (galantear); *ligar con una chica* to pick a girl up, to get off with a girl.
◆ *vpr* to bind o.s., to commit o.s.; *ligarse con* or *por una promesa* to commit o.s. by a promise || to unite, to combine (unirse).

ligazón *f* bond, tie, union (enlace) || MAR futtock.

ligeramente *adv* lightly (tocar, rozar, etc.) || slightly (un poco).

ligereza *f* lightness (de peso) || agility (agilidad) || swiftness (rapidez) || flippancy (falta de sensatez) || inconstancy, fickleness (de carácter) || *obrar con ligereza* to act rashly *o* without thinking.

ligero, ra *adj* light; *sueño, metal ligero* light sleep, metal; *comida ligera* light meal || light, nimble; *paso ligero* nimble step || swift (rápido) || agile, nimble (ágil) || weak (bebida) || FIG inconstant, fickle (inconstante) | flippant (poco serio) | unimportant, superficial (sin importancia) | slight; *tiene unos conocimientos muy ligeros del chino* he has a very slight knowledge of Chinese || — *ligero de manos* light-fingered ||

ligero de pies fleet-footed || *ligero de ropa* lightly clad || *ligero de tono* frivolous (conversación) || *ligero en su conducta* frivolous || *mujer ligera* loose woman || *peso ligero* lightweight (boxeo) || FIG & FAM *ser ligero de cascos* to be featherbrained, to be scatterbrained.
◆ *adv* fast, rapidly, quickly (de prisa); *hazlo ligero* do it fast || — *a la ligera* lightly, superficially; *tomar algo a la ligera* to take sth. lightly; superficially; *hacer algo a la ligera* to do sth. superficially || *de ligero* thoughtlessly, rashly (sin reflexión) || *juzgar a la ligera* to judge hastily.

ligio *adj m* liege (feudo).

lignificación *f* BOT lignification.

lignificarse *vpr* to lignify.

lignito *m* lignite (carbón).

lignum crucis *m* holy relic [consisting of a piece of wood from the cross of Christ].

ligón, ona *adj* lucky [at cards] || FAM *es una mujer muy ligona* she is good at picking up men (que liga), she is a flirt (que le gusta ligar).
◆ *m* FAM wolf, womanizer (con las mujeres).

liguero *m* suspender [*US* garter].
◆ *adj m* *campeonato liguero* league championship.

liguilla *f* narrow garter, narrow ribbon || championship in which only a few teams take part (deportes).

ligur *adj/s* Ligurian.

ligures *m pl* HIST Ligures.

Liguria *npr f* GEOGR Liguria.

lija *f* dogfish (pez) || sandpaper (papel esmerilado) || *papel de lija* sandpaper.

lijadora *f* sandpapering machine, sander (pulidor).

lijar *vt* to sand, to sandpaper (pulir).

lila *f* lilac (arbusto y flor) || wool (tela).
◆ *m* lilac (color) || FAM fool, simpleton (tonto).
◆ *adj* FAM foolish.

liliáceo, a *adj* BOT liliaceous.
◆ *f pl* liliaceae.

Liliput *n pr* Lilliput.

liliputiense *adj/s* Lilliputian.

lima *f* file (herramienta); *lima para uñas* nail file || filing (pulido) || BOT lime (fruta) | lime (tree) (árbol) || ARQ rafter (madero), hip (ángulo saliente) || FIG polish, polishing (enmienda) || — FIG *comer como una lima* to eat like a horse || ARQ *lima hoya* valley | *lima tesa* hip, arris || *lima sorda* dead-smooth file.

Lima *n pr* GEOGR Lima.

limado, da *adj* filed.
◆ *m* filing (acción de limar).

limadura *f* filing (acción de limar).
◆ *pl* filings (trocitos de metal).

limalla *f* filings *pl.*

limar *vt* to file, to file down || FIG to polish (retocar) || FIG *limar asperezas* to smooth things over.

limaza *f* slug (babosa).

limazo *m* sliminess, slime.

limbo *m* limb (de hoja, de astro) || MAT limb || hem, edge (de vestidura) || limbo (de las almas) || FIG & FAM *estar uno en el limbo* to be in the clouds, to be miles away (distraído).

limeño, ña *adj* [of *o* from] Lima.
◆ *m/f* native *o* inhabitant of Lima.

limero, ra *m/f* lime seller.
◆ *m* lime tree (árbol).
◆ *f* MAR rudder hole.

liminal *adj* liminal.

liminar *adj* liminary, introductory || *advertencia liminar* foreward.

limitación *f* limitation || limit (límite) || restriction (restricción) || *limitación de velocidad* speed limit.

limitado, da *adj* limited || dull-witted (poco inteligente) || *sociedad limitada* private company.

limitador, ra *adj* limitative, restrictive (restrictivo).

limitar *vt* to limit || FIG to limit, to cut down, to reduce; *hay que limitar sus prerrogativas* his prerogatives must be limited.
◆ *vi* *limitar con* to border on, to be bounded by.
◆ *vpr* to confine o.s., to limit o.s.; *limitarse a copiar* to limit o.s. to copying.

limitativo, va *adj* limitative, restrictive.

límite *m* limit || ceiling (tope); *el límite presupuestario* the budget ceiling || — *velocidad límite* speed limit.
◆ *pl* boundaries, borders (fronteras) || — *todo tiene sus límites* everything has its limits.

limítrofe *adj* bordering, neighbouring; *Francia y países limítrofes* France and its bordering countries.

limnología *f* limnology (estudio de lagos).

limo *m* mud, slime (légamo) || AMER lime tree (limero).

limón *m* lemon (fruto) || lemon tree (árbol) || shaft (de un coche) || ARQ string (de una escalera) || — FIG *estrujar a uno como un limón* to bleed s.o. white, to bleed s.o. dry || *limón natural, refresco de limón* lemonade.
◆ *adj inv* *amarillo limón* lemon, lemon-yellow.

limonada *f* lemonade (bebida) || FAM *ni chicha ni limonada* neither fish nor fowl, neither one thing nor the other.
— OBSERV En Inglaterra la palabra *lemonade* corresponde también a la *gaseosa* española.

limonado, da *adj* lemon, lemon-yellow.

limonar *m* lemon grove || AMER lemon tree (árbol).

limoncillo *m* AMER small lemon *o* lime.

limonera *f* shaft (de un coche).

limonero, ra *adj* shaft (caballo).
◆ *m/f* lemon dealer || shaft horse.
◆ *m* lemon tree (árbol).

limonita *f* limonite, marsh ore (mineral).

limosidad *f* muddiness, sliminess || tartar (sarro).

limosna *f* alms *pl*; *dar limosna* to give alms || — *pedir limosna* to beg || *vivo de limosna* I live on charity.

limosnear *vi* to beg.

limosneó *m* begging.

limosnera *f* alms bag *o* box.

limosnero, ra *adj* charitable, almsgiving (p us) || AMER beggarly (pordiosero).
◆ *m* person who collects alms (recolector de limosna) || AMER beggar (mendigo).

limoso, sa *adj* muddy, slimy.

limpia *f* cleaning, cleansing (limpieza) || FIG clean-up (purga).
◆ *m* FAM bootblack (limpiabotas).

limpiabarros *m inv* boot scraper.

limpiabotas *m inv* bootblack.

limpiacristales *m inv* window cleaner.

limpiachimeneas *m inv* chimney sweep (deshollinador).

limpiada *f*; **limpiado** *m* clean, clean-out, clean-up (limpieza).

limpiador, ra *adj* cleaning, cleansing.
◆ *m/f* cleaner (persona); *limpiador de cristales* window cleaner.

limpiamente *adv* cleanly, neatly || FIG skilfully, with ease (con destreza) | sincerely (con sinceridad) | honestly (honestamente) | fairly (jugando limpio).

limpiaparabrisas *m inv* AUT windscreen wiper [*US* windshield wiper].

limpiapipas *m inv* pipe cleaner.

limpiar *vt* to clean; *limpiar una habitación* to clean a room; *limpiar un vestido* to clean a dress || to wipe, to wipe off; *limpiar el sudor de la frente* to wipe the sweat from one's forehead || to wipe (las narices) || to sweep (la chimenea) || to shine (los zapatos) || FIG to take out (desembarazar) | to clear (la vía pública) | to prune (podar) | to cleanse; *limpiado de culpas* cleansed of faults || FIG & FAM to pinch, to nick (robar); *me limpiaron el reloj* they pinched my watch | to clean out (quitar todo el dinero) | to groom, to rub down (un caballo) || MIL to mop up || AMER to whip (castigar) | to kill (matar) | to beat (azotar) || — *limpiar el polvo* to dust || *limpiar en seco* to dry-clean.
◆ *vi* to clean.
◆ *vpr* to clean o.s. || *limpiarse las narices* to wipe one's nose.

limpiaúñas *m inv* nail cleaner.

limpidez *f* limpidity.

límpido, da *adj* limpid, crystal-clear.

limpieza *f* cleanness, cleanliness; *la limpieza de un cuarto* the cleanness of a room || cleaning; *limpieza en seco* dry cleaning || clearing (de la vía pública) || cleaning; *hacer la limpieza* to do the cleaning || shining (de zapatos) || FIG purity, chastity (pureza) | honesty, integrity (honradez) | fair play (juego limpio) | skill (destreza) | clean-up, clean-out (de maleantes, etc.) || — *artículos de limpieza* cleaning products || *ejecutar un trabajo con toda limpieza* to do a good, clean job || *hacer la limpieza del comedor, de la habitación* to clean up *o* to straighten up the dining room, the bedroom || FIG & FAM *hacer una limpieza general* to have a good clean-out (tirar lo innecesario), to purge (hacer una purga) || MIL *hacer una operación de limpieza* to mop up || FIG *limpieza de corazón* integrity, honesty || *limpieza de sangre* purity of blood || MIL *operación de limpieza* mopping-up operation.

limpio, pia *adj* clean; *platos limpios* clean plates; *un niño muy limpio* a very clean little boy || clean, tidy, neat (aseado) || pure (sangre) || clean (agua) || pure (puro); *el alma limpia de los niños* the pure souls of children || REL clean (alimentos, personas) || clear, net (sin cargas); *beneficio limpio* clear profit || free, clear; *limpio de toda sospecha* free of all suspicion || clear (foto) || DEP clean; *salto limpio* clean jump | fair, clean (jugador) || FIG & FAM clean, broke, penniless; *dejar limpio a uno* to leave s.o. broke; *estar limpio* to be clean || — FIG & FAM *a puñetazo limpio* with bare fists | *estaba limpio cuando fui al examen* I went to the exam completely unprepared *o* without knowing a single thing [*US* I went to the exam cold] || FIG *es un asunto poco limpio* it is a dirty affair || *intenciones poco limpias* dishonourable intentions || FIG *limpio como una patena* or *como un espejo* or *como los chorros del oro* as clean as a whistle *o* as a new pin | *limpio de polvo y paja* clear, net (precio y sueldo) | *llamar a grito limpio* to call at the top of one's voice.
◆ *adv* fairly; *jugar limpio* to play fairly || — *en limpio* net, clear; *ganar un millón en limpio* to win a million net || *pasar a limpio, poner en limpio* to make a clean *o* a fair copy of (un escrito) || *quedar en limpio que* to be clear that || *sacar algo en limpio de* to get sth. out of; *no he*

sacado nada en limpio I have not got anything out of it.

limusina *f* limousine (coche).

lináceo, a *adj* BOT linaceous.
◆ *f pl* linaceae.

linaje *m* lineage, line (alcurnia) ‖ FIG kind, category, type, genre; *este libro y los de su linaje* this book and those of its kind ‖ *el linaje humano* the human race, mankind.
◆ *pl* nobility *sing*.

linajudo, da *adj* highborn.

linaza *f* linseed, flax seed (simiente) ‖ *aceite de linaza* linseed oil.

lince *m* lynx (animal) ‖ FIG & FAM sharp-eyed person (persona muy perspicaz) ‖ *ojos de lince* sharp eyes.

linchamiento *m* lynching.

linchar *vt* to lynch.

lindamente *adv* prettily, neatly, elegantly ‖ FIG & FAM *se quedó lindamente sin la cena* he was simply left without dinner.

lindante *adj* bordering, adjoining, adjacent; *lindante con el jardín* bordering on *o* adjacent to *o* adjoining the garden.

lindar *vi* to border (con on), to adjoin, to be adjacent (con to), to adjoin, to be adjacent (estar contiguo); *tu jardín linda con el mío* your garden adjoins mine ‖ to border, to be bounded; *Francia linda con España* France borders on Spain, France is bounded by Spain ‖ FIG to border; *lindar en la locura* to border on madness.

linde *f* boundary, limit ‖ edge; *la linde del bosque* the edge of the forest.
— OBSERV According to the Spanish Academy, *linde* may be either masculine or feminine. It is usually now considered feminine.

lindera; lindería *f* boundary, limit.

lindero, ra *adj* bordering, adjoining, adjacent (lindante); *lindero con* bordering on, adjoining, adjacent to.
◆ *m* edge (de un bosque) ‖ edge, border (de un campo o de un huerto).

lindeza *f* beauty (belleza) ‖ niceness, graciousness (amabilidad) ‖ witticism (dicho gracioso).
◆ *pl* FIG & FAM insults, improprieties (insultos).

lindo, da *adj* pretty, lovely (hermoso); *linda casa* pretty house ‖ pretty, nice, charming (bonito) ‖ delicate (primoroso) ‖ first-rate (de primera categoría) ‖ FIG fine (irónico); *¡lindo amigo!* a fine friend! ‖ — FAM *¡lindas cosas me han dicho de ti!* I've heard some fine *o* pretty tales about you! | *¡sería demasiado lindo!* that would be too good to be true!
◆ *m* FIG & FAM coxcomb, dandy [*US* dude] ‖ *lindo Don Diego* fop, dandy.
◆ *adv* AMER prettily, nicely ‖ — *de lo lindo* a lot, a great deal (mucho), perfectly, marvellously, wonderfully (muy bien) ‖ *lo pasamos de lo lindo* we had a great *o* fantastic time.
— OBSERV The adjective *lindo* is used more frequently in America than in Spain, where *bonito, mono, precioso, hermoso* are more common.

línea *f* line; *línea recta, quebrada* straight, broken line ‖ line (renglón) ‖ class, order (clase) ‖ lineage, line, family (parentesco) ‖ line, cable (comunicaciones); *línea telegráfica, telefónica* telegraph, telephone line; *línea de alta tensión* high-tension cable ‖ line (de conducta, de un partido) ‖ MAR line (ruta) ‖ MIL line; *línea de fuego* firing line | line; *línea Maginot* Maginot line ‖ line (para pescar) ‖ figure (esbeltez) ‖ line (de coche, etc.) ‖ INFORM line, row ‖ — *cruzar la línea* to cross the line, to cross the equator ‖ *en líneas generales* in broad outline (sin detalle), approximately, roughly (aproximadamente) ‖ *en toda la línea* all along the line ‖ *final de línea* terminus ‖ *guardar la línea* to keep *o* to watch one's figure ‖ DEP *juez de línea* linesman ‖ FIG *leer entre líneas* to read between the lines ‖ AVIAC *línea aérea* airline ‖ *línea de abastecimiento* supply line ‖ MAR *línea de agua* waterline ‖ DEP *línea de banda* touchline, sideline ‖ *línea de batalla* battle line ‖ *línea de carga* load line ‖ *línea de conducta* line of behaviour (comportamiento), policy (norma) ‖ *línea de demarcación* line of demarcation, demarcation line ‖ TECN *línea de exploración* scanning line ‖ *línea de flotación* waterline ‖ DEP *línea de fondo* base line (en tenis) | *línea de gol, de puerta* goal line (fútbol) | *línea delantera* or *de ataque* forward line (fútbol) ‖ *línea de la vida* life line ‖ MAR *línea del viento* wind's line, direction of the wind | *línea de máxima carga* Plimsoll line, deep load line ‖ *línea de mira* line of sight ‖ *línea de montaje* assembly line ‖ ASTR *línea de nodos* line of nodes ‖ *línea derivada* extension (teléfonos) ‖ DEP *línea de saque* service line (tenis) ‖ *línea divisoria* dividing line ‖ *línea divisoria de las aguas* or *de cresta* watershed [*US* divide], crest line ‖ *línea férrea* railway line ‖ ASTR *línea meridiana* meridional line ‖ *línea punteada* or *de puntos* dotted line ‖ *línea saliente* arris ‖ FIG *poner unas líneas a uno* to drop s.o. a line ‖ MIL *primera línea* front line.
◆ *pl* lines (de la mano).

lineal *adj* lineal, linear ‖ *dibujo lineal* draughtsmanship, draftsmanship, mechanical drawing.

lineamento; lineamiento *m* lineament.

linear *vt* to draw lines on ‖ to sketch, to outline (bosquejar).

linfa *f* ANAT lymph.

linfangitis *f* MED lymphangitis.

linfático, ca *adj* lymphatic.

linfatismo *m* MED lymphatism.

linfocito *m* ANAT lymphocyte (leucocito).

linfocitosis *f* MED lymphocytosis.

linfoide *adj* lymphoid.

lingote *m* ingot (barra de metal) ‖ pig (fundición) ‖ IMPR slug ‖ — *lingote de primera fusión* or *de arrabio* pig iron ‖ *lingotes de oro* gold bullion *sing*, gold bars.

lingotera *f* ingot mould (molde).

lingual *adj/sf* lingual.

lingüista *m/f* linguist.

lingüístico, ca *adj* linguistic.
◆ *f* linguistics.

linimento *m* liniment.

lino *m* flax (planta y textil) ‖ linen (tela) ‖ FIG canvas (de barco) ‖ AMER linseed, flax seed (linaza).

linóleo; linóleum *m* linoleum, lino.

linotipia *f* IMPR linotype.

linotipista *m/f* linotypist, linotyper.

lintel *m* ARQ lintel (dintel).

linterna *f* lantern; *linterna mágica, sorda* magic, dark lantern ‖ torch (de bolsillo) ‖ ARQ lantern (torrecilla) ‖ TECN lantern pinion (piñón).

linternón *m* large lantern ‖ MAR poop lantern.

lío *m* bundle, parcel (paquete) ‖ FIG & FAM muddle, mess (embrollo) | problem; *Pedro tiene líos con su familia* Peter has problems with his family | trouble; *andar siempre metido en líos* to be always getting into trouble | trouble, jam; *meterse en un lío* to get into a jam, to get into trouble | mess, clutter (desorden) | headache; *este problema es un lío* this problem is a headache | jumble, hodgepodge (mezcla) | tale (chisme); *no me vengas con líos* don't come telling tales to me | affair (amancebamiento) ‖ — FIG & FAM *armar un lío* to make a fuss, to kick up a rumpus (dar un escándalo), to cause confusion (confundir) | *estar hecho un lío* to be completely mixed up | *formar un lío* to cause a scandal | *hacerse un lío* to get into a muddle *o* a mess.

liofilizar *vt* to lyophilize.

Liorna *n pr* GEOGR Leghorn.

lioso, sa *adj* FAM troublemaking, scheming (persona) | tangled, involved (cosa).
◆ *m/f* troublemaker ‖ *lo lioso* the hard part, the difficult part, the troublesome part.

lipasa *f* lipase.

lipemanía *f* MED melancholia.

lípido *m* QUÍM lipid, lipide (grasa).

lipoide *m* lipoid.

lipoideo, a *adj* lipoid.

lipoma *m* MED lipoma.

liquefacción *f* liquefaction.
— OBSERV Es barbarismo por *licuefacción*.

liquelique; liquilique *m* AMER blouse.

liquen *m* BOT lichen.

liquidable *adj* liquefiable (que se puede licuar) ‖ liquidatable (que puede ser liquidado).

liquidación *f* COM liquidation | clearance sale (en una tienda) | settlement (de una cuenta) ‖ liquefaction (acción de licuefacer) ‖ FIG liquidation (eliminación) ‖ — JUR *liquidación judicial* liquidation by decision of Court ‖ *vender en liquidación* to sell up.

liquidado, da *adj* COM liquidated ‖ liquefied (licuado).

liquidador, ra *adj* COM liquidating.
◆ *m/f* liquidator.

liquidámbar *m* liquidambar (bálsamo).

liquidar *vt* to liquefy (convertir en líquido) ‖ COM to liquidate, to wind up (un negocio) ‖ to sell up, to sell off, to clear; *hay que liquidar todas las mercancías* all the stock must be sold up ‖ to settle, to pay off, to clear, to discharge (pagar) ‖ to settle (una cuenta) ‖ to resolve, to clear up, to end (poner fin); *liquidar una situación difícil* to resolve a difficult situation ‖ FIG to liquidate (eliminar) ‖ FAM to murder, to kill off (matar).

liquidez *f* liquidity.

líquido, da *adj/sm* liquid; *medidas para líquidos* liquid measures ‖ GRAM liquid ‖ COM net ‖ — *dinero líquido* ready money, cash ‖ *el líquido elemento* (the) water ‖ *líquido amniótico* amniotic fluid ‖ *líquido imponible* taxable income.

lira *f* MÚS lyre ‖ lira (moneda italiana) ‖ stanza of five or six lines each of seven or eleven syllables (en poesía) ‖ lyrebird (ave).

Lira *n pr* ASTR Lyra.

lírica *f* lyric *o* lyrical poetry.

lírico, ca *adj* lyric, lyrical ‖ AMER fantastic, utopian (proyecto) | dreamy (persona).
◆ *m* lyric poet, lyrist ‖ AMER visionary, utopian.

lirio *m* BOT iris ‖ — BOT *lirio blanco* white lily (azucena) | *lirio cárdeno* purple iris | *lirio de agua* calla lily | *lirio de los valles* lily of the valley.

lirismo *m* lyricism ‖ FIG effusiveness.

lirón *m* ZOOL dormouse ‖ BOT water plantain ‖ FIG & FAM sleepyhead (dormilón) ‖ — FIG & FAM *dormir como un lirón* to sleep like a log *o* soundly ‖ *lirón gris* garden dormouse.

lirondo, da *adj* FIG & FAM *mondo y lirondo* pure and simple.

lis *f* BOT lily | iris ‖ HERÁLD fleur-de-lis.

lisa *f* ZOOL spiny loach (pez) | grey mullet, striped mullet (mújol).

lisamente *adv* frankly, plainly ‖ *lisa y llanamente* purely and simply (simplemente).

Lisboa *n pr* GEOGR Lisbon.

lisboeta; lisbonense; lisbonés, esa *adj* [of *o* from] Lisbon.
◆ *m/f* native *o* inhabitant of Lisbon.

lisiado, da *adj* disabled, maimed, crippled (tullido) ‖ injured (herido) ‖ FAM dead tired (cansado).
◆ *m/f* disabled *o* maimed person, cripple.

lisiadura *f* injury.

lisiar *vt* to disable, to cripple, to maim (tullir) ‖ to injure (herir).

Lisístrata *npr f* Lysistrata.

liso, sa *adj* flat (llano); *carrera de cien metros lisos* one hundred metre flat race ‖ flat (pecho) ‖ smooth, even (sin asperezas) ‖ plain (tela); *camisa lisa* plain shirt ‖ straight (pelo) ‖ calm (el mar) ‖ AMER shameless, brazen ‖ *pana lisa* velvet.
◆ *m* MIN smooth face [of a rock].

lisonja *f* flattery, piece of flattery (alabanza) ‖ HERÁLD lozenge (losange).
◆ *pl* flattery *sing.*

lisonjeador, ra *adj* flattering ‖ pleasing (agradable).
◆ *m/f* flatterer.

lisonjear *vt* to flatter (adular) ‖ to delight, to please (deleitar).

lisonjero, ra *adj* flattering ‖ gratifying; *un resultado lisonjero* a gratifying result ‖ pleasing, agreeable (agradable).
◆ *m/f* flatterer.

lista *f* stripe, band (raya) ‖ bill of fare, menu (restaurante) ‖ list (enumeración); *borrar de la lista* to strike off *o* to take off the list ‖ catalogue (catálogo) ‖ roll (recuento); *pasar lista* to call the roll ‖ register, roll (en un colegio) ‖ INFORM list ‖ — *lista de bajas* casualty list ‖ *lista de correos* poste restante [US general delivery] ‖ *lista de espera* waiting list ‖ *lista de precios* price list ‖ *lista de premios* prize list, honours list (en el colegio) ‖ *lista electoral* register (of voters) ‖ *lista negra* blacklist ‖ *pasar lista a los alumnos* to take *o* to call the register.

listado, da *adj* striped.
◆ *m* INFORM listing.

listar *vt* to list (alistar) ‖ to stripe (una tela).

listear *vt* to stripe.

listel *m* ARQ fillet, listel (moldura).

listero *m* roll taker ‖ timekeeper (en una fábrica).

listeza *f* cleverness (inteligencia) ‖ alertness, quickness (de entendimiento) ‖ shrewdness, cunningness (astucia).

listín *m* short list ‖ telephone directory *o* book ‖ AMER newspaper.

listo, ta *adj* clever (inteligente) ‖ alert, quick-witted (agudo) ‖ shrewd, cunning (astuto) ‖ ready, prepared (preparado); *estoy listo* I'm ready; *¿listo?* ready? ‖ — FIG & FAM *echárselas* or *dárselas de listo* to try to be clever | *¡estamos listos!* we're in a fine fix! | *listo como una ardilla* as cunning as a fox | *pasarse de listo* to be too clever by half.

listón *m* lath, strip (carpintería) ‖ ribbon (cinta) ‖ listel, fillet (moldura) ‖ DEP bar (para saltar).
◆ *adj m* with a white stripe down its back [bull].

listonado *m* lathing, lathwork.

listonar *vt* to lath.

lisura *f* smoothness (ausencia de asperezas) ‖ evenness (ausencia de elevaciones) ‖ plane surface (superficie plana) ‖ straightness (del pelo) ‖ FIG frankness, sincerity (sinceridad) ‖ AMER shamelessness, brazenness (desvergüenza).

lite *f* JUR lawsuit (pleito).

litera *f* litter (vehículo) ‖ berth, bunk (en barco, en tren) ‖ bunk bed, bunk (en un cuarto).

literal *adj* literal; *traducción literal* literal translation ‖ — AMER paragraph.

literalmente *adv* literally, to the letter ‖ *traducir literalmente* to translate literally *o* word for word.

literario, ria *adj* literary ‖ *la república literaria* the republic of letters.

literato, ta *adj* lettered.
◆ *m* writer, man of letters.
◆ *f* woman of letters.

literatura *f* literature; *la literatura española* Spanish literature ‖ FIG culture (instrucción general).

lítico, ca *adj* lithic.

litigación *f* litigation, lawsuit (pleito) ‖ pleading (alegato).

litigante *adj/s* litigant; *las partes litigantes* the litigant parties.

litigar; litigiar *vi* JUR to litigate ‖ to contend, to dispute ‖ *litigar por pobre* to file an appeal in forma pauperis.

litigio *m* lawsuit, litigation (pleito) ‖ dispute (contienda) ‖ *en litigio* in dispute, at stake.

litigioso, sa *adj* litigious.

litio *m* lithium (metal).

litisconsorte *m/f* JUR associate in a lawsuit, joint litigant (cointeresado).

litisexpensas *f pl* JUR costs [of a lawsuit].

litispendencia *f* JUR pendency [of a case].

litófago, ga *adj* ZOOL lithophagous.

litófito *m* BOT lithophyte.

litografía *f* lithography (arte) ‖ lithograph (reproducción).

litografiar *vt* to lithograph.

litográfico, ca *adj* lithographic.

litógrafo *m* lithographer.

litoral *adj* littoral, coastal, seaboard.
◆ *m* littoral, coast, seaboard.

litosfera *f* GEOL lithosphere.

lítote *f* litotes (atenuación).

litotipografía *f* lithotypography.

litri *adj* FAM dandified.

litro *m* litre [US liter] (medida).

Lituania *npr f* GEOGR Lithuania.

lituano, na *adj/s* Lithuanian.

liturgia *f* liturgy.

litúrgico, ca *adj* liturgical.

livianamente *adv* lightly (sin fundamento) ‖ FIG superficially ‖ licentiously, lewdly (lascivamente).

liviandad *f* lightness ‖ frivolity, triviality ‖ lewdness (lascivia).

liviano, na *adj* light (ligero) ‖ slight (pequeño, sin importancia) ‖ FIG inconstant, fickle (superficial, inconstante) | frivolous, trivial (frívolo) | loose; *una mujer liviana* a loose woman.
◆ *m* lights *pl* (bofe, pulmón) ‖ leading donkey.
◆ *f* popular Andalusian song.

lividecer *vi* to become livid.

lividez *f* lividity, lividness.

lívido, da *adj* livid.

living *m* living room.

lixiviar *vt* to lixiviate, to leach.

liza *f* lists (campo para la lid); *entrar en liza* to enter the lists ‖ contest (lid) ‖ mullet (pez).

lizo *m* heddle, headle (de un telar); *lizo bajo* low heddle ‖ warp (de un tejido).

lo *pron pers neutro* it; *yo lo creo* I believe it; *no lo es tampoco* that isn't it either.
◆ *pron pers m* him; *lo miro* I look at him (*véase* OBSERV).
◆ *art def neutro* (*followed by a qualifying adjective*) the... part, the... thing; *lo mejor* the best part; *lo triste del caso* the sad thing about it; the; *lo contrario* the opposite; what is; *lo útil y lo agradable* what is useful and agreeable; what; *según lo previsto por la ley* according to what has been provided in the law ‖ (*followed by a possessive pronoun*) mine, yours, his, etc. (lo que pertenece); *esto es lo tuyo* this is yours; what is mine, yours, etc.; *lo mío es tuyo* what is mine is yours; what concerns (lo que se refiere); *sólo me ocupo de lo mío* I only look after what concerns me ‖ — *a lo* like; *a lo loco* like a fool; style; *vestir a lo español* to dress Spanish style ‖ *a lo sumo* at (the) most ‖ *de lo más* most; *traje de lo más elegante que hay* a most elegant suit ‖ *de lo mejor que hay* the best there is ‖ *de lo que* what; *de lo que se trata aquí es* what one is dealing with here is ‖ *en lo, por lo* (*followed by an agreeing adjective*) because of; *por lo arrugada parecía muy vieja* because of her wrinkles she seemed very old; *por lo cerrado de su acento me pareció andaluz* because of his marked accent, I took him to be Andalusian ‖ *en lo alto* in *o* at the highest part ‖ *en lo alto de la casa, de la montaña* at the top of the house, of the mountain ‖ *hacer todo lo posible* to do everything within one's power *o* everything possible to, to do one's best *o* one's utmost to ‖ *lo caro no siempre es bueno* expensive things are not always good, what is expensive is not necessarily good ‖ *lo cual* which (*sujeto*); *lo cual quiere decir* which means; which (*complemento*); *lo cual dijo sin intención* which he said unintentionally ‖ *lo de* (*con sustantivo*), the affair *o* business of, the affair *o* business about; *lo del testamento fue muy desagradable* the business about the will was very unpleasant; *después de lo de la quiebra, desapareció* after the affair of the bankruptcy *o* the bankruptcy affair he disappeared; what about?, how about? (*en pregunta*); *¿y lo de tu viaje a Francia?* and what about your trip to France? ‖ *lo de* (*con infinitivo*), idea, project, business; *lo de vender la casa resulta difícil* the project of selling the house has created problems; *lo de irse de viaje no le gusta nada* he doesn't like the idea of going away on a trip ‖ *lo más... posible* as... as possible ‖ *lo mismo* the same (thing) ‖ *lo mucho que* how much (cuanto), the amount (la cantidad) ‖ *lo que* what (*sujeto, complemento*); *lo que ha de pasar* what is going to happen; *lo que pienso* what I think; *si tuviera lo que usted* if I had what you have; how much (cuanto); *sabes lo que te aprecio* you know how much I think of you; the same as, like (lo mismo); *hago lo que todos* I do the same as everyone else, I do like everyone does ‖ *lo... que* how; *no sabes lo cansada que estoy* you don't know how tired I am ‖ *¡lo que cuesta aprender un idioma!* isn't it difficult to learn a language! ‖ *lo que sea* anything (at all) (cualquier cosa), nothing, not... anything (nada) ‖ *lo sumo* the most ‖ *más... de lo que* more... than; *es más inteligente de lo que pensaba* he is more intelligent than I thought ‖ *todo lo... que* as... as; *no ha sido todo lo agradable que hubiera querido* it hasn't been as pleasant as I would have liked ‖ *todo lo que* everything which *o* that (*sujeto*), everything (*complemento*).

— OBSERV In South America the tendency to use *lo* as the personal pronoun for the 3rd person singular in the accusative case is far more widespread than in Spain, where the pronoun *le* is often used.

loa *f* praise; *cantar loa a, hacer loa de* to sing the praises of ‖ TEATR prologue (prólogo) |

short play presented at the beginning of a performance || elegy, eulogy, poem in honour of s.o. (poema).

loable *adj* laudable, praiseworthy.

loar *vt* to praise (alabar).

lob *m* lob (en tenis).

loba *f* she-wolf.

lobagante *m* lobster (bogavante).

lobanillo *m* cyst, wen (tumor) || BOT gall.

lobato *m* wolf cub (cachorro del lobo).

lobectomía *f* MED lobectomy.

lobera *f* wolf's lair (guarida del lobo).

lobero, ra *adj* wolf, wolfish.
◆ *m* wolf hunter.

lobezno *m* wolf cub (cachorro del lobo).

lobo *m* wolf (animal) || loach (pez) || lobe (lóbulo) || iron instrument for scaling walls || FIG & FAM drunkenness (borrachera) || FAM thief (ladrón) || AMER fox (zorro), coyote || — *caza de lobos* wolf hunt || *cazador de lobos* wolf hunter || *el lobo feroz* the big bad wolf || FIG *está como boca de lobo* it's pitch-dark || *ir a paso de lobo* to creep along || AMER *lobo acuático* otter || *lobo cerval* kind of lynx (lince), shark, profiteer (estafador) || FIG & FAM *lobo de mar* old salt, sea dog || *lobo marino* seal (foca), sea dog (marino experimentado) || FIG & FAM *meter el lobo en el redil* to let the cat among the pigeons || FIG *meterse en la boca del lobo* to put one's head into the lion's mouth || FIG & FAM *ser un lobo con piel de oveja* to be a wolf in sheep's clothing | *son lobos de la misma camada* they're tarred with the same brush, they are birds of a feather | *un lobo a otro no se muerden* there is honour among thieves.

Lobo *n pr* ASTR Wolf.

lobo, ba *adj/s* AMER half-breed (mestizo).

lobotomía *f* MED lobotomy.

lóbrego, ga *adj* gloomy dark, murky || FIG gloomy, sad.

lobreguecer* *vt* to darken, to make dark.
◆ *vi* to grow dark (anochecer).

lobreguez *f* gloom, gloominess, darkness, murkiness || FIG gloom, gloominess.

lobulado, da; lobular *adj* BOT & ZOOL lobulate, lobed, lobular.

lóbulo *m* lobe.

lobuno, na *adj* wolfish, wolf.

locación *f* JUR lease.

local *adj* local; *color local* local colour; *costumbres locales* local customs.
◆ *m* premises *pl* (edificios) || headquarters *pl* (domicilio social); *el local de la Cámara de Comercio* the headquarters of the Chamber of Commerce || site, place (lugar, sitio).

localidad *f* locality (pueblo) || place (lugar) || seat, ticket (de un espectáculo); *reservar una localidad* to book a seat; *sacar una localidad* to get a ticket || — *no hay más localidades* sold out, house full (teatro) || *reserva de localidades* booking, advanced booking || *venta de localidades* sale of tickets (acción de vender billetes), box office (taquilla).

localismo *m* regionalism, localism (exclusivismo) || localism, provincialism (palabra, expresión).

localista *adj* regional, local, of local interest; *problemas localistas* regional problems || parochial; *asuntos localistas* parochial affairs || limited, restricted (visión).

localizable *adj* localizable.

localización *f* localization || location (sitio) || location (encuentro) || placing, siting (situación).

localizar *vt* to find, to locate; *localizar un libro* to locate a book || to situate (situar) || to locate; *localizar un avión* to locate an aeroplane || to track down, to find; *no pude localizarte en todo el día* I couldn't track you down all day || to localize; *localizar una epidemia, un fuego* to localize an epidemic, a fire.

locatis *m/f* FAM madcap, nutcase.

locativo, va *adj* renting, letting, leasing || GRAM locative.
◆ *m* GRAM locative.

locería *f* crockery, china (cacharrería).

loción *f* lotion, wash || — *loción capilar* hair lotion || *loción facial* face lotion.

lockout *m* lockout (cierre patronal).

loco, ca *adj* insane, mad (alienado) || FAM mad, crazy; *empresa loca* crazy venture; *amor loco* mad love | tremendous, fantastic (tremendo) | huge, enormous (enorme) || ridiculous (excesivo, extraordinario); *precio loco* ridiculous price || wild; *avena loca* wild oats || TECN loose (polea, etc.) | mad (brújula) || — FIG & FAM *a locas, a tontas y a locas* without rhyme or reason | *a lo loco* wildly; *estaban bailando a lo loco* they were dancing wildly; without thinking, lightly; *decisión tomada a lo loco* decision taken lightly; helter-skelter, any old how; *hacer un trabajo a lo loco* to do a job helter-skelter | *anda loco con su trabajo* his job is driving him crazy | *andar* or *estar como loco* to act crazily | *como loco* like mad (correr, etc.) | *es para volverse loco* it is enough to drive you mad | *estar loco de* or *por* or *con* to be crazy *o* mad *o* wild about; *está loca por él* she is crazy about him; to be mad keen; *estar loco por hacer una cosa* to be mad keen on doing sth. | *estar loco de alegría* to be overjoyed *o* beside o.s. with joy, to be thrilled to bits | *estar loco de contento* to be blissfully happy | *loco de atar* or *de remate* or *rematado* or *como una cabra* as mad as a March hare *o* as a hatter, as mad as they come || *loco perdido* or *furioso* raving mad, stark mad || *risa loca* hysterical laughter || FIG *tener una suerte loca* to be ever so lucky | *traer* or *volver* or *tener loco a uno* to drive s.o. crazy *o* mad || *volverse loco, estar loco* to go crazy *o* mad, to be crazy *o* mad.
◆ *m/f* madman (hombre), madwoman (mujer) || lunatic (enfermo mental) || — FIG *cada loco con su tema* everyone has his hobbyhorse || *casa de locos* madhouse || FIG *correr como un loco* to run like mad | *gritar como un loco* to shout like mad *o* like a madman | *hacer el loco* to act the fool | *hacerse el loco* to play dumb || FIG & FAM *la loca de la casa* the imagination.

locomoción *f* locomotion.

locomotiva *f* AMER locomotive, engine.
— OBSERV Es galicismo por *locomotora*.

locomotor, ra *adj* locomotive, locomotor.
◆ *f* locomotive, engine (de un tren).

locomotriz *adj f* locomotor; *ataxia locomotriz* locomotor ataxy.

locomovible; locomóvil *adj* locomobile.

locro *m* AMER maize and meat stew.

locuacidad *f* loquacity, talkativeness.

locuaz *adj* loquacious, talkative.

locución *f* phrase, turn of phrase, locution, expression || GRAM phrase; *locución adverbial, prepositiva* adverbial, prepositional phrase.

locuelo, la *adj* FAM madcap, daft.
◆ *m/f* FAM madcap.

locura *f* madness, insanity, lunacy || act of madness *o* folly, mad *o* crazy thing (acción) || mad passion (cariño, afecto), wild enthusiasm (entusiasmo) || — *acceso* or *ataque de locura* fit of madness || *con locura* madly || *fue una locura hacer esto* it was madness *o* folly to do this || FIG *gastar una locura* to spend a fortune || *hacer* or *cometer locuras* to do foolish things || *la quiere con locura* he is crazy about her || *¡qué locura!* it's madness!

locutor, ra *m/f* announcer (que presenta) || commentator (que comenta).

locutorio *m* locutory, parlour, visiting room (de un convento), visiting room (de una cárcel) || telephone box *o* booth (de teléfono).

locha *f* loach (pez).

lodachar; lodazal; lodazar *m* mire, quagmire, muddy place.

loden *m* loden (tejido).

lodo *m* mud (fango); *baños de lodo* mud baths || MIN sludge || — FIG *arrastrar por el lodo* to drag through the mud || *poner de lodo a uno* to fling *o* to sling *o* to throw mud at s.o.

lodoso, sa *adj* muddy (cenagoso).

loess *m* GEOL loess, löss.

logarítmico, ca *adj* logarithmic.

logaritmo *m* MAT logarithm || *tabla de logaritmos* logarithm table.

loggia *f* ARQ loggia (galería).

logia *f* lodge (de masones).

logicial *m* software (en informática).

lógico, ca *adj* logical || — *como es lógico* naturally, of course || *ser lógico* to be logical, to stand to reason.
◆ *m/f* logician.
◆ *f* logic.

logístico, ca *adj* logistic.
◆ *f* MIL logistics.
◆ *m* MIL logistician.

logógrafo *m* logographer.

logogrifo *m* logogriph (enigma).

logomaquia *f* logomachy.

logos *m* FIL logos.

logrado, da *adj* successful.

lograr *vt* to get, to obtain (obtener) || to win, to achieve, to gain (victoria) || to achieve (éxito) || to win, to gain (premio) || to succeed in, to manage to; *logró escaparse* he succeeded in escaping, he managed to escape || to realize, to realise, to achieve (ambiciones) || to satisfy, to fulfil (deseos) || *eso lo puedes dar por logrado* you can take that for granted, you can bank on that.
◆ *vpr* to succeed, to be successful, to turn out well *o* successfully; *el plan de desarrollo se ha logrado* the development plan has been successful.

logrería *f* usury || profiteering.

logrero, ra *m/f* usurer, moneylender || profiteer (aprovechón).

logro *m* winning, achievement (de victoria) || achievement, attainment (de éxito) || winning (de un premio) || success (éxito); *su mayor logro* his greatest success || achievement, accomplishment; *los logros técnicos del siglo XX* the technical achievements of the 20th century || realization (de unas ambiciones) || satisfaction, fulfilment (de deseos) || gain, profit (lucro) || usury (usura) || *prestar* or *dar a logro* to lend at a high interest rate.

loísmo *m* GRAM exclusive use of *lo* instead of *le* in the dative of the personal pronoun *él*; *lo doy* instead of *le doy* I give (to) him || exclusive use of *lo* instead of *le* in the accusative; *lo miro* and not *le miro* I look at him.

loísta *adj* GRAM who uses *lo* instead of *le* in the acusative and dative of the masculine pronoun *él*.
◆ *m/f* person who uses *lo* and not *le*.

loma *f* hillock, hill, rise.

lombarda *f* red cabbage (col) || lombard (cañón).

Lombardía *npr f* GEOGR Lombardy.

lombriguera *f* earthworm *o* worm hole.

lombriz *f* earthworm, worm ‖ worm; *lombriz intestinal* intestinal worm ‖ *lombriz solitaria* tapeworm.

Lomé *n pr* GEOGR Lomé.

lomera *f* backband (de la guarnición del caballo) ‖ back, backband (de un libro) ‖ ridge (caballete de un tejado).

lomo *m* back (de un animal, de un cuchillo) ‖ spine, back (de un libro) ‖ fold, crease (doblez) ‖ ANAT loin (del hombre) ‖ chine (carne de cerdo) ‖ loin (de una colina) ‖ AGR ridge [between furrows] (caballón) ‖ — *a lomo de* on the back of (a mule, donkey, etc.) ‖ *arquear el lomo* to arch its back (el gato) ‖ FIG *de tomo y lomo* out-and-out, utter, first rate; *es un sinvergüenza de tomo y lomo* he's an out-and-out cad ‖ FIG & FAM *pasar la mano por el lomo, sobar el lomo* to soft-soap, to butter up | *sacudir el lomo a alguien* to give s.o. a hiding, to tan s.o.'s hide.
◆ *pl* ribs (costillas).

lona *f* MAR sailcloth (tela) | sail (vela) ‖ canvas; *zapatos de lona* canvas shoes ‖ canvas cover, canvas (para cubrir) ‖ big top (de circo) ‖ — *ciudad de lona* canvas town ‖ *hacer besar la lona a alguien* to floor s.o. (boxeo), to bring s.o. down (humillar).

loncha *f* slice; *una loncha de jamón* a slice of ham ‖ slab (de piedra).

londinense *adj* [of *o* from London].
◆ *m/f* Londoner (persona).

Londres *n pr* GEOGR London.

longanimidad *f* forbearance, magnanimity, longanimity.

longánimo, ma *adj* forbearing, magnanimous.

longaniza *f* sausage ‖ — FIG & FAM *allí no atan los perros con longanizas* money does not grow on trees there ‖ FAM *hay más días que longanizas* there's no hurry, there's no rush, there's all the time in the world.

longevidad *f* longevity.

longevo, va *adj* long-lived, longevous.

longitud *f* length; *su longitud es de seis metros* its length is six metres ‖ ASTR & GEOGR longitude ‖ — *longitud de onda* wavelength ‖ DEP *salto de longitud* long jump ‖ *tener seis metros de longitud* to be six metres long ‖ *35 ° longitud Oeste* 35 ° West.

longitudinal *adj* longitudinal.

longui *adj/s* FAM *hacerse el longui* to act dumb.

lonja *f* slice; *una lonja de jamón* a slice of ham ‖ rasher, slice (de tocino) ‖ commodity exchange (bolsa de comercio) ‖ wool warehouse (almacén) ‖ grocer's shop (tienda) ‖ ARQ porch, vestibule [of a church] ‖ leather strap (correa).

lonjear *vt* AMER to cut into strips (cortar en lonjas) | to remove the hair from (skins) | FAM to whip (azotar) ‖ (ant) to warehouse, to store (almacenar).

lontananza *f* ARTES background ‖ *en lontananza* in the distance, far off, far away.

looping *m* looping the loop (ejercicio), loop (rizo).

loor *m* praise (alabanza); *en loor de* in praise of ‖ *decir loores de* to praise, to sing the praises of, to speak in praise of.

López *n pr* FIG & FAM *esos son otros López* that's a different kettle of fish.

loquear *vi* to act *o* to play the fool (hacer), to talk nonsense (decir) ‖ FIG to make merry (retozar).

loquera *f* padded cell (jaula de locos).

loquería *f* AMER madhouse, lunatic asylum.

loquero *m* lunatic asylum nurse ‖ AMER hustle and bustle (bullicio).

lora *f* hen parrot, female parrot ‖ AMER parrot (loro).

loran *m* MAR & AVIAC loran (ayuda para la navegación a gran distancia).

lord *m* lord; *primer lord del Almirantazgo* First Lord of the Admiralty ‖ — *cámara de los Lores* House of Lords ‖ *lord mayor* Lord Mayor (de Londres).

lordosis *f* MED lordosis.

Lorenzo *m* Laurence, Lawrence.

loriga *f* lorica, coat of mail, suit of armour [*US* suit of armor] (de soldado) ‖ horse armour (de caballo) ‖ TECN band [reinforcing axlebox] (del buje de una rueda).

loro, ra *adj* dark brown (color).
◆ *m* parrot (papagayo) ‖ cherry laurel (lauroceraso) ‖ FAM hag (mujer fea) ‖ FAM *más viejo que un loro* as old as Methuselah.

lorquiano, na *adj* of García Lorca.

los *art def mpl* the; *los invitados han llegado* the guests have arrived; *los Smith* the Smiths ‖ (*not translated*); *los hombres no son inmortales* men are not immortal; *todos los hombres* all men.
◆ *pron pers mpl* them; *los he visto* I've seen them ‖ those, the ones; *los que he comprado* those (which) I have bought; *los de mi padre* those of my father, my father's ones ‖ (*not translated or translated by «some») (con haber,* impersonal); *¿hay libros? los hay* are there any books? there are (some) ‖ — *los de usted* yours ‖ *los de Víctor son viejos* Victor's are old ‖ *los hay que* there are those who, there are some who (personas), there are those that (cosas); *los hay que no saben nada* there are those who know nothing ‖ *los que* those who, the ones who (*personas, sujeto*), those whom, the ones that (*personas, complemento*), those which, the ones which, the ones that (cosas) ‖ *los que estáis aquí* those of you who are here ‖ *los que trabajamos* those of *o* among us who work ‖ *son... los que* it is... who (*personas, sujeto*), it is... whom (*personas, complemento directo*), they are... that *o* which (cosas); *son mis libros los que has cogido* they are my books that you have taken ‖ *un traje de los de 1930* a suit typical of the 1930's.

— OBSERV The dative form of *los* is *les: les hablo* I speak to them. *Loísmo* (see this word) should be avoided.

— OBSERV *Los* is often translated by the possessive adjective: *tiene los oídos tapados* his ears are blocked.

losa *f* stone slab ‖ paving stone, flagstone, flag (para pavimentar) ‖ tile (para cocina, etc.) ‖ — FIG *echar* or *poner una losa encima* to keep it under one's hat | *estar bajo la losa* to be six feet under ‖ *losa sepulcral* tombstone ‖ FIG *yo soy una losa* my lips are sealed.

losado *m* flagstones *pl*, flagging.

losange *m* HERÁLD lozenge.

loseta *f* small stone slab ‖ small paving stone *o* flagstone, small flag (para pavimentar) ‖ floor tile (baldosa) ‖ trap (trampa).

lota *f* burbot (pez).

lote *m* share, portion (parte) ‖ share (de herencia) ‖ COM lot (subasta) ‖ tombola prize (premio) ‖ FIG & FAM *darse un lote de comer higos* to stuff o.s. with figs.

lotería *f* lottery; *jugar a la lotería* to play on the lottery ‖ lotto (juego de niños) ‖ *caerle* or *tocarle a uno la lotería* to win a prize in the lottery (ganar), to strike it lucky (tener suerte).

lotero, ra *m/f* lottery-ticket seller.

loto *m* BOT lotus.
◆ *f* lottery.

Lovaina *n pr* GEOGR Louvain.

loza *f* (glazed) earthenware, pottery ‖ crockery (del ajuar doméstico) ‖ *fregar la loza* to wash up, to wash the dishes, to do the washing-up.

lozanía *f* luxuriance, lushness (de la vegetación, de las plantas), freshness (de una flor) ‖ vigour (vigor) ‖ robustness (aspecto saludable) ‖ freshness; *la lozanía de la tez* the freshness of the complexion ‖ sprightliness (de una persona mayor).

lozano, na *adj* luxuriant, lush (vegetación), fresh (verduras, flores) ‖ robust; *una campesina lozana* a robust country girl ‖ robust, vigorous, lusty (hombre) ‖ fresh (tez) ‖ sprightly (persona mayor).

Luanda *n pr* GEOGR Luanda.

lubina *f* (sea) bass (róbalo).

lubricación *f* lubrication.

lubricante *adj* lubricant, lubricating.
◆ *m* lubricant.

lubricar *vt* to lubricate.

lubricativo, va *adj* lubricant.

lubricidad *f* lubricity, lewdness, lasciviousness (lujuria) ‖ (p us) slipperiness, lubricity.

lúbrico, ca *adj* lubricous, lewd, lascivious (lujurioso) ‖ (p us) slippery, lubricous.

lubrificación *f* lubrication.

lubrificante *adj* lubricant, lubricating.
◆ *m* lubricant.

lubrificar *vt* to lubricate.

Lucas *npr m* Luke.

Lucayas *npr fpl* GEOGR Bahamas.

lucense *adj* [of *o* from] Lugo [Spanish town and province].
◆ *m/f* native *o* inhabitant of Lugo.

lucerna *f* chandelier (araña) ‖ skylight (lumbrera) ‖ glowworm (luciérnaga).

lucero *m* bright star (estrella) ‖ evening *o* morning star, Venus (planeta) ‖ window shutter (postigo) ‖ star (lunar en la frente del caballo) ‖ FIG lustre, brilliance (lustre) ‖ *el lucero del alba* or *de la mañana, de la tarde* the morning, the evening star (Venus).
◆ *pl* eyes (ojos).

luces *f pl* ⟶ **luz.**

lucidez *f* lucidity, clarity.

lucido, da *adj* brilliant; *un discurso lucido* a brilliant speech ‖ successful (que tiene éxito) ‖ elegant; *un vestido muy lucido* a very elegant dress ‖ generous (liberal) ‖ splendid, magnificent; *un papel lucido* a splendid role ‖ bonny (saludable); *tienen dos niños muy lucidos* they have two very bonny children ‖ — *¡estamos lucidos!* we're in a fine mess! ‖ *estás lucido si...* you've got another think coming if... ‖ *las fiestas del pueblo resultaron muy lucidas* the town festivities were a great success.

lúcido, da *adj* lucid, clear (claro) ‖ MED *intervalo lúcido* lucid interval.

luciérnaga *f* glowworm (insecto).

lucifer *m* Lucifer, Venus (lucero) ‖ FIG demon.

Lucifer *npr m* Lucifer.

luciferino, na *adj* satanic.

lucífero, ra *adj* POÉT luciferous.
◆ *m* Lucifer, Venus (lucero del alba).

lucimiento *m* lucidity, brilliance (brillo) ‖ triumph, success (éxito) ‖ — FIG *hacer algo con lucimiento* to do sth. brilliantly | *quedar con lucimiento* to come through (an enterprise) brilliantly *o* with flying colours.

lucio *m* luce, pike (pez).

lucio, cia *adj* shining, bright ‖ glossy; *el pelaje lucio del caballo* the horse's glossy coat.

lucir* *vi* to shine; *el sol lucía con resplandor* the sun shone brightly || to give off light; *una lámpara que luce poco* a lamp that gives off little light || to glitter, to sparkle (joyas) || FIG to shine (sobresalir) | to look nice (un vestido) | to be of benefit, to turn out to advantage (ser de provecho) || FIG *no le luce lo que come* the food he eats isn't doing him any good || AMER to look, to seem (parecer).
◆ *vt* to illuminate, to light up (iluminar) || FIG to show off, to make a show of, to display; *lucir su valor* to display one's bravery | to show off; *luciendo las piernas* showing off her legs || to sport; *lucía una magnífica corbata verde* he was sporting a splendid green tie || to plaster (enlucir).
◆ *vpr* to dress up, to deck o.s. out (engalanarse) || FIG to come out brilliantly *o* with flying colours (quedar bien) | to shine, to excel (o.s.), to distinguish o.s. (sobresalir); *Juan se ha lucido en una empresa tan difícil* John has excelled in such a difficult undertaking || FAM to make a fool of o.s. || — *lucirse en una prueba* to pass a test with flying colours || FIG & FAM *¡pues sí que nos hemos lucido!* we've really gone and done it now!

lucrar *vt* to gain, to obtain, to win.
◆ *vpr* to profit; *lucrarse a costa ajena* to profit at other people's expense.

lucrativo, va *adj* lucrative, profitmaking.

Lucrecia *npr f* Lucretia.

Lucrecio *npr m* Lucretius.

lucro *m* gain, profit (ganancia) || benefit, profit (beneficio) || — JUR *lucro cesante* lucrum cessans || *lucros y daños* profit and loss.

luctuoso, sa *adj* sorrowful, sad, mournful.

lucubración *f* lucubration.

lucubrar *vt* to lucubrate.

lucha *f* fight, struggle || conflict (conflicto); *en reñida lucha* in bitter conflict || FIG dispute (disputa) | war, struggle; *lucha de clases* class war || DEP wrestling; *lucha libre, grecorromana* freestyle, Graeco-Roman wrestling || *lucha por la existencia* fight *o* struggle for survival.

luchador, ra *m/f* fighter || DEP wrestler.

luchar *vi* to fight, to struggle (combatir) || FIG to quarrel, to argue, to fight, to dispute (pelearse) | to fight, to struggle; *luchar por la existencia* to struggle to survive, to fight for survival || DEP to wrestle || *luchar cuerpo a cuerpo* to fight hand to hand.

ludibrio *m* shame (vergüenza) || derision, mockery (mofa) || contempt, scorn (desprecio) || laughingstock (irrisión); *ser el ludibrio del pueblo* to be the laughingstock of the village || *para mayor ludibrio suyo* to his greater shame.

ludir *vt* to rub.

luego *adv* then, afterwards (después); *iré luego al cine* then I'll go to the cinema || then, next (después de otra cosa) || later, later on, afterwards (más tarde) || soon (pronto) || at once, straight away, immediately (sin dilación); *vuelvo luego* I'm coming back at once || AMER FAM *luego luego* right away (en seguida).
◆ *conj* therefore; *pienso, luego existo* I think, therefore I am || AMER sometimes, at times, from time to time (algunas veces) | near, close by (cerca) || — *desde luego* of course, certainly || *hasta luego* see you later [US so long] || *luego como* or *que* as soon as, the moment; *luego que llegues avísame* let me know the moment you arrive || *luego de* (*with the infinitive*) after, when; *luego de comer se fue* after eating *o* after he had eaten *o* when he had eaten, he left || *luego después* straight after, immediately (afterwards) || AMER *tan luego* as well, moreover | *tan luego como* as soon as.

lueguito *adv* AMER ⟶ **luego.**

luengo, ga *adj* long (largo) || *hace luengos años* many a long year ago.

lúe *f* syphilis.

lugar *m* place (paraje); *el lugar a donde voy de vacaciones* the place where I go for my holidays || spot, place; *hemos encontrado un lugar precioso* we found a lovely spot || place (sitio de una persona o de una cosa); *el libro no está en su lugar habitual* the book is not in its usual place || room (espacio); *hacer lugar* to make room || village (pueblo); *en un lugar de la Mancha de cuyo nombre no quiero acordarme* in a village of La Mancha whose name I do not wish to recall || locality, place, spot (localidad) || part; *en un lugar de la casa* in one part of the house || passage (de un libro); *lo encontrarás en un lugar de tu libro de texto* you'll find it in a passage in your textbook || position, post, office; *ocupa un buen lugar en la empresa* he holds a good post in the company || time, moment (tiempo, oportunidad); *no es el lugar de decirlo* now is no time to mention it, this is not the (right) moment to mention it || time; *no hay lugar para hacer tantas cosas* there is no time to do so many things || cause, reason, motive (motivo) || MAT locus || DEP place (posición); *en primer lugar* in first place || — *consérvese en lugar fresco* keep cool, keep in a cool place (alimentos) || *dar lugar a* to give rise to; *esta reforma dio lugar al descontento* this reform gave rise to unrest; to provoke, to give rise to; *su comportamiento dio lugar a que le criticasen* his behaviour provoked their criticism || *dejar en mal lugar a alguien* to let s.o. down || *en cualquier lugar* anywhere, any place (en cualquier sitio), everywhere, in all places (en todos los sitios) || *en lugar de* instead of, in place of || *en lugar seguro* in a safe place || *en primer lugar* in the first place *o* instance, first, firstly || MIL *en su lugar, ¡descanso!* stand at ease!, stand easy! || *en tiempo y lugar oportunos* at the right time, in the right place, in due course || *en último lugar* finally, last of all, lastly || *fuera de lugar* out of place (palabras) || JUR *ir al lugar del suceso* to go to the scene of the crime || *lugar arqueológico* archaeological site || *lugar común* commonplace, cliché (tópico) || *lugar de perdición* den of iniquity || *lugar de señorío* seignorial fief || *lugar destacado* prominent place; *ocupar un lugar destacado en la historia* to occupy a prominent place in history || *lugar preferente* choice *o* first-class position || *los Santos Lugares* the Holy Places || FIG *poner a alguien en su lugar* to put s.o. in his place | *poner las cosas en su lugar* to put things straight | *ponerse uno en lugar de otro* to put o.s. in s.o. else's place || JUR *providencia de no ha lugar* nonsuit, nolle prosequi || *sin dejar lugar a dudas* without any doubt || *tener lugar* to take place (suceder), to have room (tener cabida), to have (the) time (tener tiempo) || TEATR *unidad de lugar* unity of place || *yo, en tu lugar* if I were you, if I were in your place.

lugarejo *m* small village, hole (poblacho).

lugareño, ña *adj* village || country, rural (rural).
◆ *m/f* villager || countryman, countrywoman (campesino).

lugartenencia *f* lieutenancy.

lugarteniente *m* lieutenant, deputy.

lugre *m* MAR lugger (embarcación).

lúgubre *adj* lugubrious, dismal.

luis *m* louis (moneda).

Luis *npr m* Louis, Lewis.

Luisa *npr f* Louise.

Luisiana *npr f* GEOGR Louisiana.

lujo *m* luxury || — *con lujo de* with great (con abundancia de) || *de lujo* de luxe; *modelo de lujo* de luxe model; luxury; *artículos de lujo* luxury goods || *impuesto de lujo* luxury tax || *no poder permitirse el lujo de* to be unable to afford the luxury of || *vivir en un lujo asiático* to live in the lap of luxury.

lujoso, sa *adj* luxurious.

lujuria *f* lust, lechery, lewdness || FIG excess (demasía) | profusion, abundance (abundancia).

lujuriante *adj* luxurious, lush (vegetación) || lustful, lecherous, lewd (lascivo).

lujuriar *vi* to lust, to be lustful *o* lecherous || to copulate (los animales).

lujurioso, sa *adj* lustful, lecherous, lewd.
◆ *m/f* lecher.

lulú *m* Pomeranian (perro).

lumbago *m* MED lumbago.

lumbar *adj* ANAT lumbar; *región lumbar* lumbar region.

lumbrada; lumbrarada *f* big fire, blaze.

lumbre *f* fire (de la chimenea, etc.); *cerca de la lumbre* by the fire || glow, light (luz del fuego) || light (luz del sol, de candelero, de la vela, etc.) || light; *¿tienes lumbre?* have you got a light? || luminary, light (luminaria) || ARQ light (en una ventana) || toe (de la herradura) || battery (de un arma de fuego) || FIG brilliance, brightness (lucimiento) | radiance, splendour (esplendor) | surface (superficie del agua) || — *al amor de la lumbre* by the fireside, by the fire || *dar lumbre a uno* to give s.o. a light (dar fuego) || *encender la lumbre* to light the fire || *pedir lumbre* to ask for a light || FIG *ser la lumbre de los ojos de alguien* to be the apple of s.o.'s eye.
◆ *pl* tinderbox *sing* || sparks (chispas).

lumbrera *f* luminary, light (luminaria, cuerpo luminoso) || skylight (de un buque, abertura en un techo) || mouth [of plane] (de cepillo) || TECN port, vent; *lumbrera de escape* exhaust port || FIG luminary, leading light (persona muy sabia) || AMER box (en la plaza de toros).
◆ *pl* FIG eyes (ojos).

lumen *m* FÍS lumen (unidad de flujo luminoso).
— OBSERV The plural of the Spanish word should be *lúmenes* although *lumen* is also widely used.

luminar *m* luminary.

luminaria *f* light, lantern [for illuminations] || altar light, altar lamp [kept burning before the Holy Sacrament] (en las iglesias).
◆ *pl* illuminations.

luminescencia; luminiscencia *f* luminescence.

luminescente; luminiscente *adj* luminescent.

luminosidad *f* luminosity, brightness.

luminoso, sa *adj* luminous; *cuerpo luminoso* luminous body || bright (bombilla) || illuminating; *potencia luminosa* illuminating power || illuminated, luminous (p us); *fuente luminosa* illuminated fountain || FIG bright, brilliant; *idea luminosa* bright idea | luminous, crystal-clear (muy claro).

luminotecnia *f* lighting *o* illuminating engineering.

luminotécnico *m* lighting *o* illuminating engineer.

luna *f* moon (astro, satélite) || moonlight, moon (luz de la Luna) || moon (tiempo); *hace muchas lunas* many moons ago || mirror, glass (espejo) || window, window pane (de un escaparate) || lens, glass (cristal de gafas) || FIG wanderings *pl* of a madman, fit of lunacy | whim, passing fancy (capricho) || — AMER FIG & FAM *a la luna de Paita* or *de Payta* in the lurch || *armario de luna* wardrobe with a mirror || *claro de luna* moonlight || *estar de buena, de mala luna* to be in a good, in a bad mood || FIG *estar en* *la Luna* to be miles away | *ladrar a la Luna* to bay (at) the moon || *luna creciente* first quarter, waxing moon, crescent moon || *luna de abril* April moon || FIG *luna de miel* honeymoon || *luna llena* full moon || *luna menguante* last quarter, waning moon || *luna nueva* new moon || *media luna* half-moon (la mitad), crescent (del astro), Crescent, Turkish Empire (el Imperio turco), demilune (fortificación), butcher's curved knife (cuchilla), crescent-shaped jewel (joya) || FIG *pedir la Luna* to ask the earth, to ask for the moon || *pez luna* sunfish, moonfish || FIG *quedarse a la luna de Valencia* to be left in the lurch | *tener lunas* to be capricious *o* whimsical | *vivir en la Luna* to have one's head in the clouds.

lunación *f* lunation.

lunado, da *adj* lunate, crescent-shaped.

lunar *adj* lunar; *año lunar* lunar year.
◆ *m* mole, beauty spot (en la piel humana) || spot (en la piel de los animales, en los tejidos) || FIG stain (mancha) | flaw, blemish (defecto pequeño) || — *lunar postizo* beauty spot || *vestido de lunares* spotted dress, polka dot dress.

lunático, ca *adj* lunatic (loco) || whimsical (caprichoso).
◆ *m/f* lunatic (loco) || whimsical *o* fickle person (caprichoso).

lunch *m* buffet, buffet luncheon.

lunes *m* Monday; *vendré el lunes por la mañana* I shall come (on) Monday morning; *viene los lunes* or *cada lunes* he comes on Mondays *o* every Monday || — FIG *cada lunes y cada martes* every day of the week || *el lunes pasado* last Monday; *el lunes que viene* next Monday || AMER *hacer lunes* or *lunes porteño* to take Monday off || FIG & FAM *tener lunes* to have that Monday morning feeling, to be down in the dumps.

luneta *f* lens, glass (de gafas) || crescent-shaped ornament (adorno) || TEATR stall, orchestra seat (butaca) || backrest (de un torno) || lunette (fortificación) || ARQ front tile (bocateja) | lunette (bovedilla) || AUT rear window (cristal trasero).

luneto *m* ARQ lunette (bovedilla).

lunfardismo *m* Argentinian slang word *o* expression.

lunfardo *m* thief (ladrón) || Buenos Aires slang (jerga).
◆ *adj* slang [in Argentina].

lúnula *f* MAT lunule, lunula, lune || half-moon, lunule (de la uña).

lupa *f* magnifying glass, lens; *mirar algo con lupa* to look at sth. with *o* through a magnifying glass.

lupanar *m* brothel.

lupercales *f pl* lupercalia (fiestas romanas).

lupino, na *adj* lupine, wolf.
◆ *m* BOT lupin [US lupine] (altramuz).

lúpulo *m* BOT hop, hops.

Lusaka *n pr* GEOGR Lusaka.

Lusiadas (Los) *npr mpl* (The) Lusiads.

Lusitania *npr f* GEOGR Lusitania.

lusitanismo *m* Portuguese word *o* expression.

lusitano, na; luso, sa *adj/s* Lusitanian.

lustrabotas *m inv* AMER bootblack (limpiabotas).

lustración *f* lustration (purificación).

lustrado *m* shine (de los zapatos) || sheen (de tela).

lustrador *m* AMER bootblack (limpiabotas).

lustrar *vt* to polish, to shine (limpiar) || to lustrate (purificar).

lustre *m* lustre [US luster], shine, gloss, polish (brillo) || sheen, gloss (de telas) || shoe polish, polish (betún) || FIG splendour, distinction, glory (esplendor, distinción) | splendour; *el lustre de las fiestas* the splendour of the festivities || — *dar* or *sacar lustre a* to polish, to shine, to put a shine on || FIG *para su mayor lustre* to his greater glory.

lustrín *m* AMER bootblack's shoe-cleaning box (cajón de limpiabotas).

lustrina *f* lustring (tela) || lamé (tela de oro y de plata) || AMER shoe polish, polish (betún).

lustro *m* lustre [US luster], lustrum (espacio de cinco años) || hanging lamp (lámpara), lustre, chandelier (araña).

lustroso, sa *adj* shiny, glossy (brillante) || radiant (rostro) || healthy looking (animal).

Lutecia *npr f* HIST Lutetia (París).

lutecio *m* QUÍM lutetium.

luteína *f* BIOL lutein.

lúteo, a *adj* (of) mud (de lodo) || luteous, light yellow (color).

luteranismo *m* Lutheranism.

luterano, na *adj/s* Lutheran.

Lutero *npr m* Luther.

luto *m* mourning; *vestirse* or *ponerse de luto* to go into mourning; *vestir de luto* to be in mourning || grief, sorrow (dolor) || — *aliviar el luto* to go into half mourning || *de luto* in mourning; *estar de luto* to be in mourning || *luto riguroso* deep mourning || *llevar luto por* to be in mourning for || *medio luto* half mourning.

lutria *f* otter (nutria).

lux *m* FÍS lux (unidad de luz).

luxación *f* MED luxation, dislocation.

Luxemburgo *npr m* GEOGR Luxembourg, Luxemburg.

luxemburgués, esa *adj* Luxembourgian, Luxemburgian.
◆ *m/f* Luxembourger, Luxemburger.

Luxor *n pr* GEOGR Luxor.

luz *f* light || light (lámpara); *tráeme una luz* bring me a light || light, daylight (que se recibe en una casa) || light, daylight, daytime, day (día) || lighting (iluminación) || electricity; *en su casa no hay luz* there is no electricity in their house; *cortar la luz* to cut off the electricity || electricity bill; *pagar la luz* to pay the electricity bill || AUT light || ARQ window, light (ventana) | aperture, opening, light (abertura) | span (de un puente) || FIG light, luminary, guiding light (sabio) | news, information (noticia) || sparkle (destello de un diamante) || ARTES light || — FIG *a buena luz* in all awareness, aware of *o* in possession of all the facts | *a la luz de* by the light of (gracias a la luz de), in the light of (juzgando por) || TEATR *a la luz de las candilejas* in the foolights || *a la luz del día* in daylight, in the daytime, in the light of day || *año de luz* light year || *apagar la luz* to switch off *o* to put off *o* to turn off the light || *a primera luz* at daybreak, at first light || FIG *arrojar* or *echar luz sobre* to shed *o* to throw *o* to cast light on | *claro como la luz del día* as clear as daylight || *dar a luz* to give birth to (parir), to publish, to bring out (publicar) || *dar (a) la luz* to turn on *o* to put on *o* to switch on the light || *dar luz* to give (out) light; *una lámpara que da buena luz* a lamp that gives a good light; to shed *o* to throw light (*sobre* on), to shed *o* to throw light (dar aclaraciones) || *encender la luz* to switch on *o* to put on *o* to turn on the light || FIG *en plena luz* in broad daylight* || *gusano de luz* glowworm || FIG *hacer la luz sobre* to shed *o* to throw light on || *¡hágase la luz!* let there be light! || FIG *la luz de sus ojos* the apple of his eye || ASTR *luz cenicienta* earthlight, earthshine || *luz cenital* skylight (en una habitación), interior light (en un coche) || *luz de Bengala* Bengal light || AUT *luz de ciudad* or *de población* or *de posición* sidelight; *poner luces de población* to switch on the sidelights | *luz de estacionamiento* parking light || *luz de la Luna* moonlight || *luz del Sol* sunlight || FIG *luz de mis ojos* my sweet, my angel || MAR *luz de situación* riding light, position light || *luz eléctrica* electric light (lámpara), electricity (electricidad) || *luz intermitente* indicator, flasher [US winker] || AUT *luz larga* headlights on full beam || AMER *luz mala* will-o'-the-wisp, Jack-o'-lantern (fuego fatuo) || *luz negra* black light || AUT *luz posterior* rear light, tail light || *luz primaria* direct light || *luz refleja* or *secundaria* reflection, reflected light || *luz relámpago* flashlight || *luz roja* red light || *luz y sombra* light and shade || *luz y sonido* son et lumière || *media luz* half-light || *quitarle la luz a alguien* to stand in s.o.'s. light; *sacar a luz* to bring out, to publish (libro), to bring to light (descubrir) || *salir a luz* to come out, to appear, to be published (un libro), to come to light (hacerse patente) || FIG *ver la luz* to see the light of day, to draw one's first breath (nacer).
◆ *pl* lights; *las luces de la ciudad* the city lights || culture *sing* (cultura) || Enlightenment *sing*; *el Siglo de las Luces* the Age of Enlightenment || intelligence *sing* (inteligencia) || lights (de un coche) || — *a todas luces* obviously, evidently, clearly; *su proyecto es a todas luces irrealizable* your plan is obviously impracticable || *corto de luces* dim, stupid || *ingeniero de luces* lighting engineer || FIG *a dos luces* ambiguously | *de pocas luces* dim, stupid | *entre dos luces* at the break of day, at daybreak, at first light (al amanecer), in the dusk of the evening, at dusk, at twilight, in the twilight (en el crepúsculo), fuddled, tipsy, half-drunk (medio borracho) || *hombre de luces* educated *o* cultured man | *hombre de pocas luces* dim-witted man, man of limited intelligence || *luces de carretera, de cruce* headlights on full beam, dipped headlights (coche) || *luces de tráfico* traffic lights || *tener pocas luces* to be dim-witted, not to be very bright || TAUR *traje de luces* bullfighter's costume.

LL

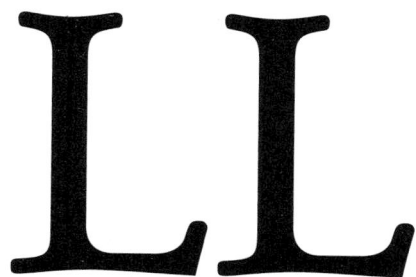

ll *f* ll; *una ll mayúscula* a capital ll.
— OBSERV *Ll* is pronounced like the *li* in the English *battalion*. In many parts of Spain, including Andalusia and Madrid, and in South America, *ll* often approximates to the Spanish *y*, so that, for instance, *pollo* and *poyo* are indistinguishable. This *«yeísmo»* is considered colloquial and is avoided in educated language.

llaga *f* ulcer, sore (úlcera) ‖ wound (herida) ‖ FIG wound; *renovar la llaga* to reopen the wound ‖ TECN joint (entre ladrillos) ‖ FIG *poner el dedo en la llaga* to touch on a sore point.

llagar *vt* to wound, to injure, to hurt.

llama *f* flame; *estallar en llamas* to burst into flames ‖ FIG flame, burning passion (sentimiento ardiente) ‖ marsh, swamp (terreno pantanoso) ‖ ZOOL llama (animal) ‖ — *en llamas* in flames, ablaze, burning ‖ *llama auxiliar* pilot light.

llamada *f* call; *hacer una llamada telefónica* to make a telephone call; *la llamada de la selva* the call of the wild; *llamada al orden* call to order ‖ knock, ring (en la puerta) ‖ reference mark (en un libro) ‖ sign, gesture (ademán) ‖ invitation to emigrate ‖ MIL fall-in; *tocar llamada* to sound the fall-in ‖ — AMER *billete de ida y llamada* return ticket [US round-trip ticket] ‖ *carta de llamada* letters *pl* of recall (de embajador) ‖ *da la señal de llamada* it is ringing (teléfono) ‖ TEATR *llamada a escena* curtain call ‖ *llamada a larga distancia* long-distance call ‖ INFORM *llamada a programa* programme call ‖ MAR *llamada de socorro* SOS, distress signal ‖ *llamada urbana* local call ‖ MIL *toque de llamada* fall-in.

llamadera *f* goad (aguijada).

llamado, da *adj* known as; *Enrique I llamado el Pajarero* Henry I, known as the Fowler ‖ so-called (supuesto); *los llamados juegos de suerte* the so-called games of chance ‖ so-called (que se nombra); *los llamados Picos de Europa* the so-called «Picos de Europa» ‖ — *Constantinopla, así llamada porque fue fundada por Constantino* Constantinople, so called because it was founded by Constantine ‖ *estar llamado a* to be destined to.
◆ *m* AMER call (llamada) ‖ *muchos son los llamados, pocos los escogidos* many are called but few are chosen.

llamador, ra *m/f* caller.
◆ *m* doorknocker (aldaba) ‖ doorbell (campana, timbre) ‖ push-button (botón).

llamamiento *m* call, appeal; *un llamamiento a todos los médicos de la población para que prestasen ayuda* an appeal for help sent out to all the town's doctors ‖ invitation to emigrate ‖ calling (de Dios) ‖ JUR nomination [of heir, trustee, etc.].

llamar *vt* to call (nombrar); *¿cómo le llamaremos?* what shall we call him? ‖ to nickname, to call (dar un apodo); *en el colegio le llaman Enano* at school they call him Tiny ‖ to call; *me llamó desde la cocina* he called me from the kitchen ‖ to ask for; *¿quién me llama?* who is asking for me? ‖ to summon, to call (convocar); *llamar a la criada* to call the maid ‖ to call for, to call in; *llamar al médico* to call for the doctor ‖ to beckon (con un ademán); *llamar a uno con la mano, con la cabeza* to beckon s.o. with one's hand, with a nod ‖ to call; *fue llamado al sacerdocio* he was called to the priesthood ‖ to appeal (hacer una petición); *llamar a la O. N. U.* to appeal to the U. N. ‖ to call, to ring up (por teléfono) ‖ to attract (atraer); *Norteamérica llama a muchos científicos europeos* many European scientists are attracted to North America; *llamar la atención* to attract attention ‖ to call (considerar); *lo llamo una estafa* I call it a swindle ‖ — FAM *llamar a alguien de todo* to call s.o. names ‖ TEATR *llamar a escena* to call back on, to give a curtain call ‖ *llamar a filas* to call up (para el ejército) ‖ *llamar al orden* to call to order ‖ *llamar a uno con un silbido* to whistle (to) s.o. ‖ *llamar a voces a uno* to shout for s.o., to call *o* to shout to s.o. ‖ *llamar de tú* to address as «tú», to address familiarly ‖ *llamar la atención a alguien* to attract s.o.'s attention (llamar), to tell s.o. off, to tick s.o. off (reprender), to catch s.o.'s eye, to attract s.o.'s attention (despertar la curiosidad) ‖ *llamar por señas* to signal to ‖ *llamar por teléfono* to telephone, to call (up), to phone, to ring (up) ‖ *no meterse donde no le llaman* to mind one's own business ‖ *que me llamen a las 3* get them to *o* have them call me at 3.
◆ *vi* to call (dar voces, por teléfono) ‖ to knock, to ring (en la puerta) ‖ *¿quién llama?* who is it?, who is there?
◆ *vpr* to be called; *se llama Carlos* he is called Charles ‖ MAR to haul, to shift (el viento) ‖ — *¿cómo se llama?* what is his name? ‖ *¡eso sí que se llama bailar!* now that's what I call dancing! ‖ *me llamo Juan* my name is John.

llamarada *f* flare-up, sudden blaze (llama rápida) ‖ FIG flush (de rubor) | outburst, flare-up (de entusiasmo, ira, pasión, etc.).

llamativo, va *adj* loud, gaudy, flashy (de color chillón); *una corbata llamativa* a loud tie ‖ ostentatious, flashy, showy (que llama la atención); *llevaba una indumentaria muy llamativa* he was wearing a very ostentatious outfit ‖ *un título llamativo* an impressive title.

llameante *adj* blazing, flaming; *un bosque, un horizonte llameante* a blazing wood, horizon.

llamear *vi* to blaze, to flame; *la casa llameaba todavía* the house was still blazing; *sus ojos llameaban con ira* her eyes were blazing with anger.

llamingo *m* AMER ZOOL llama (llama).

llampo *m* · AMER ore (mineral).

llana *f* TECN float, trowel (de albañil) ‖ page [of writing] (plana) ‖ plain (llanura).

llanada *f* flat ground, plain.

llanamente *adv* FIG naturally, plainly; *comportarse llanamente* to behave naturally ‖ plainly, straightforwardly, frankly (con franqueza) ‖ *lisa y llanamente* purely and simply.

llanca *f* AMER copper ore (mineral) | jewellery made from pebbles | earthworm (gusano).

llaneador *m* DEP rider who is good on the flat (ciclista).

llanear *vi* DEP to ride on the flat (ciclista).

llanero, ra *m/f* AMER plaindweller, lowlander, plainsman (hombre), plainswoman (mujer).

llaneza *f* simplicity, naturalness, plainness (de una persona) ‖ plainness, straightforwardness, frankness (franqueza) | informality (falta de ceremonias).

llanito, ta *m/f* FAM Gibraltarian (gibraltareño).

llano, na *adj* flat, level, even, smooth; *superficie, tierra llana* flat surface, land ‖ FIG natural, simple, unaffected; *gente llana* simple people; *modales llanos* simple manners | frank, straightforward, open, plain (al hablar) | simple, informal (sin ceremonias) ‖ GRAM paroxytone [with the penultimate syllable accentuated] ‖ HIST plebeian (pechero) ‖ — FAM *a la llana* simply ‖ *a la pata la llana* without ceremony, simply ‖ *canto llano* Gregorian chant, plain song ‖ FIG *de llano* plainly | *en lenguaje llano* in plain language | *estado llano* or *común* third estate, commons | *número llano* Roman numeral | *pueblo llano* common people.
◆ *m* plain (llanura) ‖ flatness, smoothness, evenness (lo llano).

llanote, ta *adj* FIG plain-spoken (al hablar) | uncomplicated (sencillo).

llanta *f* iron hoop (de rueda de carro) ‖ rim (de rueda de automóvil, de bicicleta) ‖ AMER tyre [US tire]; *llanta de goma* rubber tyre ‖ BOT type of cabbage (col) ‖ AMER sunshade (quitasol).

llantén *m* BOT plantain ‖ — *llantén de agua* water plantain ‖ *llantén menor* ribwort (plantain).

llantera; llantina *f* FAM blubber ‖ FAM *coger una llantera* to start blubbering, to burst into tears.

llantería *f*; **llanterío** *m* AMER weeping.

llantina *f* FAM ⟶ **llantera.**

llanto *m* weeping, crying (acción de llorar); *crisis de llanto* crying fit ‖ tears *pl*; *enjugar el llanto de alguien* to wipe s.o.'s tears ‖ AMER plaintive song, lament ‖ — *anegarse en llanto* to fill with tears (los ojos), to be bathed in tears (el rostro), to dissolve into tears (una persona) ‖ *deshacerse en llanto* to sob one's heart out ‖ *prorrumpir* or *romper en llanto* to burst into tears.

llanura *f* plain; *la llanura de Flandes* the plain of Flanders ‖ flatness, evenness (cualidad de llano).

llapa; napa *f* AMER MIN mercury [added to silver ore to aid extraction] ‖ AMER extra, bonus (adehala) | tip (propina) | thick end (del lazo).

llapango, ga *adj* barefoot (descalzo).

llapar *vi* AMER MIN to add mercury [to produce silver amalgam].
◆ *vt* to offer as a bonus *o* an extra.

llar *m* hearth (fogón).
◆ *f pl* pothanger *sing*, pothook *sing*.

llave *f* key; *llave maestra* skeleton *o* master key ‖ spanner [US wrench] (para las tuercas); *llave de tubo* box spanner [US socket wrench] ‖ tap [US faucet] (de grifo) ‖ ELECTR switch (interruptor) ‖ winder (de reloj) ‖ MÚS clef (signo); *llave de fa, de sol* bass clef, treble clef | stop (de órgano) | valve; *trombón de llaves* valve trombone | key (de clarinete, etc.) ‖ lock (de arma de fuego) ‖ IMPR square bracket (corchete), brace (para abarcar en cuadro sinóptico, etc.) ‖ FIG key (de una cifra) | key; *la llave del éxito* the key of success ‖ MED dentist's forceps *pl* ‖ wedge (cuña) ‖ DEP hold, lock (en lucha) ‖ — *ama de llaves* housekeeper ‖ *bajo llave* under lock and key ‖ *bajo siete llaves* safely under lock and key ‖ *cerrar con llave* to lock ‖ *cerrar con siete llaves* to lock and doublelock ‖ *echar la llave* to lock up ‖ *llave de contacto* ignition key ‖ *llave de paso* stopcock (espita) ‖ *llave inglesa* (monkey) wrench, adjustable spanner.

llavero, ra *m/f* keeper of the keys ‖ jailer, turnkey (ant) (de cárcel).
◆ *m* key ring (para poner las llaves).

llavín *m* latchkey (llave pequeña).

lleco, ca *adj* uncultivated, virgin (tierra).

llegada *f* arrival ‖ *a mi llegada a París* upon my arrival in Paris, when I arrived in Paris, on arriving in Paris.

llegado, da *adj* arrived; *recién llegado* newly arrived.
◆ *m/f* *los recién llegados* the newcomers, the new arrivals.

llegar *vi* to arrive; *llegaré a Londres mañana* I shall arrive in London tomorrow; *cuando llegó el buen tiempo* when the good weather arrived ‖ to come; *llegará un día en que se arrepienta* the day will come when he will be sorry; *llegará la paz* peace will come; *llegó su vez* his turn came ‖ to reach; *la escalera, la cuerda no llega* the ladder, the rope won't reach ‖ to suffice, to be enough *o* sufficient; *el dinero no llega para repartirlo entre todos* the money is not sufficient *o* there is not enough money to go round ‖ to be big enough (ser bastante grande) ‖ to come about, to happen (suceder); *llegó que* it came about that ‖ — FIG *¿adónde quiere llegar?* what's he getting at?, what's he driving at? | *aquello fue llegar y besar el santo* it was as easy as pie, it was a piece of cake, it was like taking candy from a baby | *hacer llegar el dinero* to make one's money last, to eke out one's money ‖ *llegar a* (con infinitivo) to succeed in, to manage to (conseguir); *llegué a ver al ministro* I succeeded in seeing *o* I managed to see the minister; to get to, to end up; *llegué a dudar si vendrías* I got to wondering *o* I ended up wondering if you were coming; *llegó a conocer todas las capitales del mundo* he got to know *o* he ended up knowing all the capitals of the world; to end up; *llegó a suicidarse* he ended up committing suicide; to be able to, to have time to; *no llegará a aburrise porque estará allí poco tiempo* he will not have time to get bored because he will not be there long ‖ *llegar a* (con sustantivo) to reach; *el niño no llegará al tirador de la puerta* the child can't reach the door handle; to reach, to arrive in *o* at, to get to; *llegar a Madrid, a la estación, a la cima* to arrive in Madrid, at the station, at the summit; to reach, to arrive at, to come to; *llegar a un acuerdo, a una conclusión* to reach an agreement, a conclusion; to attain; *llegar a la mayoría de edad, a la fama* to attain one's majority, to attain fame; to come to, to amount to; *su salario semanal no llega a dos mil pesetas* his weekly wage comes to less than two thousand pesetas; *los espectadores llegaban al millar* the spectators amounted to about a thousand; to become (llegar a ser); *llegó a presidente* he became president; to last out until (durar); *el nuevo régimen no llegará al año que viene* the new régime will not last out until next year ‖ *llegar a conocer a uno* to get to know s.o. ‖ *llegar a la vejez* to reach old age ‖ *llegar al extremo de* to go as far as to ‖ *llegar al poder* to come to power ‖ *llegar a saber* to find out ‖ *llegar a ser* to become ‖ FIG *no llegarle a uno a la suela del zapato* or *a la punta de la bota* not to hold a candle to s.o. ‖ *no me llega el dinero* I have not got enough money, I do not have enough money ‖ *si llego a saberlo* if I had known.
◆ *vt* to gather up (reunir) ‖ to draw up, to bring over (acercar).
◆ *vpr* to go (round), to come (round); *llégate a casa de tu hermano* go round to your brother's house ‖ to approach, to come near (acercarse).

llenado *m* filling.

llenar *vt* to fill, to fill up; *llenar de vino un tonel* to fill a barrel with wine; *las bicicletas llenan las calles de la población* the streets of the town are filled with bicycles ‖ to fill, to fill up, to satisfy (hartar de comida) ‖ to fill in [US to fill out] (rellenar); *llenar un cuestionario* to fill in a questionnaire ‖ to fill in (rellenar); *llenar un hoyo* to fill in a hole ‖ FIG to fill (colmar); *llenar a uno de ira, de confusión* to fill s.o. with rage, with confusion | to shower, to overwhelm; *me llenó de elogios, de favores, de injurias* he showered me with praise, with favours, with insults ‖ to fulfil, to satisfy (cumplir, satisfacer); *su viaje llena su mayor ambición* his trip fulfils his greatest ambition | to fulfil, to carry out (un cometido) ‖ FIG & FAM to satisfy, to convince; *el razonamiento de Alberto no me llena* Albert's reasoning does not convince me ‖ — *llenar ciertas condiciones* to meet certain requirements, to fulfil *o* to satisfy certain conditions ‖ FIG & FAM *llenar el ojo antes que la barriga* or *la tripa* to have eyes bigger than one's belly | *no me llena su nueva película* I'm not mad about his new film ‖ *vuelva a llenar (las copas)* the same again.
◆ *vi* to be full (la Luna) ‖ to be filling (la comida).
◆ *vpr* to be *o* to become filled *o* full; *llenarse de humo, de orgullo, de indignación* to become filled with *o* full of smoke, pride, indignation ‖ to fill up; *la tina se llenó de agua* the butt filled up with water ‖ to fill o.s. up (*de* with), to eat one's fill (*de* of), to eat one's fill (de alimento) ‖ to cover; *llenarse los dedos de tinta* to cover one's fingers with ink ‖ to get covered with (de polvo, etc.) ‖ *llenarse completamente* or *hasta los topes* to be filled to overflowing.

lleno, na *adj* full, filled; *vaso lleno de vino* glass full of wine; *lleno de enojo, de alegría* filled with anger, with happiness ‖ full, full up (teatro, cine) ‖ full (preñada) ‖ covered; *lleno de manchas* covered with stains; *estar lleno de polvo* to be covered in dust ‖ full, full up (de comida) ‖ FIG full, plump (un poco gordo); *tener una cara muy llena* to be very full in the face ‖ HERÁLD pale ‖ — *dar de lleno en* to flood (el sol) ‖ *dar de lleno en la cara* to hit squarely *o* right in the face ‖ *de lleno, de lleno en lleno* completely ‖ *es luna llena* there is a full moon ‖ *lleno de peligro* fraught with danger ‖ *lleno hasta los topes* full to the brim *o* to overflowing ‖ *voz llena* good *o* strong voice.
◆ *m* full moon (plenilunio) ‖ full house, sellout (en el teatro) ‖ FAM abundance (abundancia) ‖ FIG completion (último complemento de algo).
◆ *pl* MAR rounded hull *sing*.

lleudar *vt* to leaven.

llevadero, ra *adj* bearable, tolerable; *un calor llevadero* a bearable heat ‖ wearable (ropa).

llevar *vt* to carry; *llevar a un niño en brazos* to carry a child in one's arms; *llevar en la cabeza* to carry on one's head ‖ to carry, to transport; *el tren lleva carbón* the train is transporting coal; *el coche llevaba cuatro personas* the car was carrying four people ‖ to carry away (una cosa a lo lejos); *el viento lo llevó todo* the wind carried it all away ‖ to get, to win, to take; *este número lleva premio* this number gets a prize ‖ to take; *llévame a mi casa* take me home; *me llevaron al cine* they took me to the pictures ‖ to lead (inducir); *esto me lleva a pensar que* this leads me to think that ‖ to bring (traer); *voy a llevar a un amigo a casa* I'm going to bring a friend home; *el paro llevó el hambre a muchas familias* unemployment brought hunger to many families ‖ to have; *el cuadro lleva demasiadas flores* the painting has too many flowers in it; *su vestido no lleva cinturón* her dress does not have a belt; *el vino lleva muchas heces* the wine has a lot of lees; *llevar ventaja a* to have an advantage over ‖ to wear, to have on; *lleva un sombrero negro* he has a black hat on, he wears a black hat ‖ to have (on o.s.) (dinero); *llevo dos libras* I have two pounds (on me) ‖ to bear; *llevar una enfermedad con paciencia* to bear an illness with patience ‖ to take; *me llevará un día escribir el artículo* the article will take me a day to write ‖ to have been; *lleva un mes en la cama* he has been in bed (for) a month; *lleva cinco años de coronel* he has been a colonel (for) five years; *el restaurante llevaba abierto diez años* the restaurant had been open (for) ten years ‖ to bear (un nombre, un título) ‖ to charge; *no me ha llevado muy caro el sastre* the tailor has not charged me a great deal ‖ to take care of, to look after (ocuparse de); *el jefe lleva el asunto* the boss is looking after the matter ‖ to run, to manage; *lleva bien su negocio* he runs his business well; *me lleva la finca* he runs my property ‖ to manage, to control (un coche, un caballo) ‖ to lead; *llevar una vida muy ajetreada* to lead a very hectic life ‖ to offer, to present (dificultades, problemas) ‖ to keep (las cuentas, los libros) ‖ to lead, to take; *esta calle te lleva al ayuntamiento* this street leads you to the town hall ‖ to get, to lead (conducir); *¿adónde nos lleva la guerra?* where does war get us?; *¿adónde nos lleva esta discusión?* where is this discussion getting us? ‖ to have; *llevar estudiado* to have studied; *llevo el trabajo hecho* I have the work finished ‖ COM to keep (la contabilidad) ‖ MAT to carry (un número); *veintitrés, pongo tres y llevo dos* twenty-three, three down and carry two ‖ COM to bear, to carry (un interés) ‖ to be... older, taller, etc., than (exceder en años, en altura, etc.); *su hijo me lleva dos años, tres centímetros* his son is two years older than I, three centimetres taller than I ‖ to lead by, to be ahead of; *su coche me lleva diez kilómetros (de ventaja* or *de delantera)* his car is ten kilometres ahead of mine *o* leading mine by ten kilometres; *me lleva diez minutos (de ventaja* or *de delantera)* he is ten minutes ahead of me, he is leading me by ten minutes ‖ to follow (seguir); *¿qué dirección lleva el ladrón?* what direction is the thief following? ‖ to bear; *este árbol lleva manzanas* this tree bears apples ‖ — *¿cuánto tiempo llevas aquí?* how long have you been here? ‖ *dejarse llevar (por)* to be carried away with, to be influenced by; *dejarse llevar por los demás* to be influenced by others ‖ *llevar a cabo* to carry out (ejecutar, efectuar), to conclude (concluir) ‖ *llevar a cuestas* to carry on one's back (un bulto, a una persona), to give a piggyback (a un niño) ‖ *llevar adelante* to go ahead with, to carry out; *el general insiste en llevar adelante la ofensiva* the general insists on going ahead with the attack; to keep going, to maintain

(una familia), to carry on (un negocio) || *llevar a los tribunales* to take to court || *llevar a uno a aceptar su punto de vista* to bring s.o. round to one's point of view, to talk s.o. round || *llevar camino de ser un buen ingeniero, un buen médico* to look as if one will make a good engineer, a good doctor || *llevar consigo* to entail, to involve (dificultades, problemas, etc.) || *llevar de la mano a uno* to lead s.o. by the hand || *llevar el compás* to beat time (con la mano), to keep time (bailando) || *llevar el nombre de* to bear the name of || *llevar en peso algo* to hold sth. at arm's length || *llevar idea de* to intend to || *llevar la batuta* to direct *o* to conduct the orchestra (una orquesta), to be the boss, to rule the roost (dirigir un asunto) || *llevar la cabeza alta* to carry *o* to hold one's head high || *llevar la casa* to run the house || *llevar la contraria a uno* to oppose s.o., to get in s.o.'s way (poner obstáculo), to contradict s.o. (contradecir) || *llevar las de ganar* to hold all the winning cards, to look like a winner || *llevar las de perder* to be fighting a losing battle, to look like losing || FIG *llevar la voz cantante* to rule the roost | *llevar los pantalones* to wear the trousers (una mujer) || *llevar luto* to be in mourning || *llevar mala, buena conducta* to behave badly, well || *llevar puesto* to be wearing, to have on (ropa) || FIG *llevar su cruz* to bear one's cross || *llevar trazas de durar mucho* to look as if it will last a long time || *llevar ventaja a uno* to have the advantage over s.o. *o* the edge on s.o. || FAM *no llevarlas todas consigo* to have the wind up | *difícil de llevar* wayward, ungovernable; *un niño difícil de llevar* a wayward child; difficult to run *o* manage (empresa), difficult to follow (compás).
◆ *vi* to lead, to go (conducir); *todos los caminos llevan a Roma* all roads lead to Rome || *llevar y traer* to go around gossiping.
◆ *vpr* to take (away), to carry off, to make *o* to run off with; *alguien se ha llevado mi paraguas equivocadamente* s.o. has taken my umbrella by mistake; *el ratero se llevó mi cartera* the pickpocket made off with my wallet || to sweep away (con violencia); *el viento, el agua se llevó todos los detritos* the wind, the water swept away all the debris || to carry off, to win, to take (conseguir); *se han llevado el premio* they have taken the prize || to get; *se ha llevado el castigo que merece* he got the punishment he deserved || to take; *llévate a tu hermano al cine* take your brother to the pictures || to be popular, to be fashionable *o* in fashion; *esos sombreros ya no se llevan, esa actitud ya no se lleva* that type of hat, that attitude is no longer fashionable || MAT to carry (en aritmética) || to have, to get (sufrir); *llevarse un susto* to have a fright || to receive, to get; *llevarse una patada* to get a kick || — *llevarse bien, mal con alguien* to get on *o* along with s.o., not to get on *o* along with s.o. || *llevarse como el perro y el gato* to fight like cat and dog || FIG & FAM *llevarse la palma* to carry off the palm (triunfar), to take the cake (en sentido irónico) || *llevarse un chasco* to be disappointed, to get a big disappointment (estar decepcionado) || FAM *no tener qué llevarse a la boca* not to have a bite to eat | *¡que se lo lleve el diablo!* go to hell! (dirigiéndose a una persona), to hell with it *o* him! (hablando de una cosa o de otra persona) || *se lleva todo por delante* he lets nothing stand in his way.

lliclla *f* AMER shawl.

llorado, da *adj* late; *el llorado García Lorca* the late García Lorca.

lloraduelos *m/f inv* FIG & FAM moaner, whiner.

llorar *vi* to cry, to weep; *no lloréis por mí* don't cry on my account || to water, to run (los ojos) || — FIG *el que no llora no mama* he who doesn't ask doesn't get, you don't get anything unless you ask for it || *llorar a lágrima viva* or *a mares* or *a moco tendido* to cry bitterly, to cry one's eyes out, to sob one's heart out, to weep buckets || *romper a llorar* to begin to cry, to burst into tears.
◆ *vt* to shed, to weep (lágrimas) || to be sorry for, to regret; *en el futuro llorará su pereza* he will be sorry for his laziness in the future || to mourn, to weep for (la muerte de alguien) || to bemoan; *llorar sus desgracias* to bemoan one's misfortunes.

llorera *f* FAM (fit of) crying *o* weeping, blubbering.

llorica; lloricón, ona *adj* FAM blubbering.
◆ *m/f* FAM crybaby, blubberer.

lloriquear; llorisquear *vi* to whimper, to snivel, to whine.

lloriqueo *m* whimpering, whining, snivelling.

llorisquear *vi* → **lloriquear.**

lloro *m* crying, weeping, tears *pl.*

llorón, ona *adj* given to weeping *o* to crying || blubbering || BOT *sauce llorón* weeping willow.
◆ *m/f* crybaby (niño) || tearful person, blubberer (el que llora mucho).
◆ *m* plume (adorno de sombrero).
◆ *f* hired mourner (plañidera) || AMER spur (espuela).

lloroso, sa *adj* tearful, weeping.

llovedera; llovedero *m* AMER persistent rain.

llover* *v impers* to rain; *está lloviendo* it is raining || — FIG *como llovido, como llovido del cielo* out of the blue, heaven-sent | *es como quien oye llover* it's like talking to a brick wall | *habrá llovido para entonces* a lot of water will have passed under the bridge by then || *llover a cántaros* or *a chorros* or *a chuzos* or *a mares* to rain cats and dogs, to rain buckets, to pour (down) || FIG *llueve sobre mojado* it never rains but it pours, it's just one thing on top of another | *nunca llueve a gusto de todos* you can't please everybody.
◆ *vi* to shower; *en este negocio el dinero te lloverá* you will be showered with money in this business.
◆ *vpr* to leak (un tejado).

llovida *f* AMER rain.

llovizna *f* drizzle.

lloviznar *v impers* to drizzle.

llueca *adj f* broody (gallina).
◆ *f* brooder, broody hen.

lluvia *f* rain (agua que llueve); *salir bajo la lluvia* to go out in the rain; *el barómetro indica lluvia* the barometer shows rain || rainfall; *una región de poca lluvia* a region of limited rainfall || FIG shower; *lluvia de regalos, de piedras, de insultos, de desgracias* shower of gifts, of stones, of insults, of misfortunes | pile, heap (gran cantidad de dinero) || — *agua de lluvia* rainwater || *día de lluvia* rainy day || *lluvia ácida* acid rain || *lluvia atómica* atomic fallout || FIG *lluvia de estrellas* shower of shooting stars | *lluvia radiactiva* radioactive fallout || *lluvia torrencial* torrential rain.

lluvioso, sa *adj* rainy, wet.

M

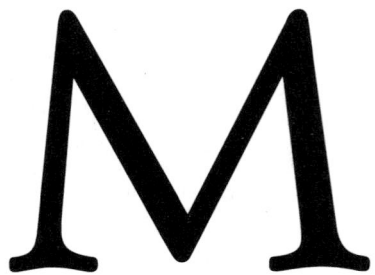

m *f* m (letra); *una m mayúscula* a capital m.
— OBSERV The pronunciation of the Spanish *m* is similar to that of the English *m*.

maca *f* bruise (en una fruta) || stain, spot (de prendas de lana) || FIG defect, flaw (defecto) | trick (engaño).

Macabeo *npr m* Maccabee.

macabro, ra *adj* macabre; *danza macabra* macabre dance.

macaco, ca *adj* AMER ugly, misshapen (feo) | foolish, idiotic (necio).
◆ *m* ZOOL macaque (mono) || FIG & FAM ugly man (hombre feo) | runt, squirt (hombre pequeño) || AMER bogeyman (coco) || *es un macaco* he is as ugly as sin.
◆ *f* AMER FAM binge, drinking spree [US drunk] (borrachera).

macadam; macadán *m* macadam.

macana *f* macana, Indian club, tool (arma) || heavy club (porra) || FIG & FAM piece of soiled stock (cosa deteriorada) | old rubbish (antigualla) || AMER blunder, faux pas (despropósito) | lie, fib (mentira) | bad job (trabajo malo) | joke (broma) | daft remark (tontería).
◆ *interj* AMER FAM that's a pack of lies! || *¡que se deje de macanas!* enough of your stories!

macanada *f* AMER foolishness, stupidity (estupidez) | nonsense, absurdity (disparate).

macanazo *m* blow with a club || AMER FAM nonsense, absurdity (disparate) | nuisance (aburrimiento).

macaneador, ra *adj* AMER fond of joking (bromista) | deceitful (engañoso) | unreliable (poco de fiar).
◆ *m/f* charlatan, storyteller.

macanear *vi* AMER to boast, to exaggerate (exagerar) | to joke (bromear) | to talk nonsense (disparatar) | to tell tall stories, to fib (contar cuentos) | to work hard (trabajar).

macanudo, da *adj* FAM terrific, great, fabulous, extraordinary (extraordinario).

macaón *m* swallow-tail butterfly (mariposa).

macaquear *vi* AMER to act like a monkey, to make faces (gesticular).

macarra *m* pimp (chulo) || lout, thug (pendenciero).

macarrón *m* macaroon (pastel).
◆ *pl* macaroni (pastas) || MAR stanchions.

macarronea *f* macaronic verse, macaronics *pl* [burlesque composition, generally in verse, in which Latin words are mixed with others to which Latin endings are added].

macarrónico, ca *adj* FAM macaronic || *latín macarrónico* pig Latin.

macarse *vpr* to start to rot *o* to go off, to get bruised (las frutas).

macear *vt* to hammer, to pound.
◆ *vi* to go on (insistir).

macedonia *f* CULIN salad, macedoine; *macedonia de frutas, de legumbres* fruit, vegetable salad.

Macedonia *npr f* GEOGR Macedonia.

macedónico, ca; macedonio, nia *adj/s* Macedonian.

macegual *m* AMER Indian peasant.

maceo *m* hammering, pounding.

maceración *f* maceration || FIG mortification.

macerador *m* macerator.

maceramiento *m* maceration.

macerar *vt/vi* to macerate || FIG to mortify.
◆ *vpr* to macerate || FIG to mortify o.s.

macero *m* mace-bearer, macer, mace.

maceta *f* flowerpot (tiesto) || mallet, small hammer (mazo pequeño) || stone hammer (martillo de escultor).

macetero *m* flowerpot stand || AMER flowerpot.

macetón *m* large flowerpot, tub (tiesto).

macilento, ta *adj* wan, lean; *rostro macilento* wan face || wan (luz).

macillo *m* hammer (del piano).

macizo, za *adj* solid; *de oro macizo* of solid gold || FIG solid; *argumento macizo* solid argument.
◆ *m* mass (masa) || massif, mountain mass (de montañas) || bed (de plantas) || clump (de árboles) || ARQ chimney breast | group (de edificios).

macla *f* HERÁLD mascle || MIN macle.

macolla *f* bunch, cluster (de planta).

macollo *m* AMER BOT bunch, cluster.

macramé *m* macramé.

macrobiótico, ca *adj* macrobiotic.
◆ *f* macrobiotics.

macrocardia *f* MED macrocardia.

macrocefalia *f* MED macrocephaly.

macrocéfalo, la *adj* MED macrocephalic, macrocephalous.

macrocito *m* BIOL macrocyte.

macrocosmo *m* macrocosm.

macrodactilia *f* MED macrodactyly.

macrodáctilo, la *adj* macrodactyl.

macroeconomía *f* ECON macroeconomics.

macroestructura *f* macrostructure.

macrófago, ga *adj* macrophagic.
◆ *m* macrophage.

macrofotografía *f* macrophotography.

macrogameto *m* BIOL macrogamete.

macromolécula *f* macromolecule.

macromolecular *adj* macromolecular.

macrópodo *adjm/sm* macropodid.

macrorrinia *f* MED macrorhinia.

macroscópico, ca *adj* macroscopic.

macrospora *f* BOT macrospore.

macrosporangio *m* BOT macrosporange.

macruro, ra *adj* macrural, macruran.
◆ *m* macruran.

macuache *m* AMER ignorant *o* illiterate Indian.

macuco, ca *adj* AMER terrific, marvellous (notable) | cunning, clever, crafty (taimado) | big, strong (grandullón).

mácula *f* spot, stain (mancha) || macula lutea (del ojo) || IMPR mackle || ASTR macula || FIG deception, trick.

macular *vt* to spot, to stain || IMPR to mackle.

maculatura *f* IMPR blurred sheet, mackle.

macuquero *m* illegal worker of an abandoned mine.

macuquino, na *adj* edgeless, cut down (moneda).

macurca *f* AMER cramp, ache.

macuto *m* MIL knapsack, haversack || AMER alms basket (para limosnas).

Mach *m* FÍS Mach.

macha *f* AMER tellina (molusco) || drunkenness (borrachera) | mannish woman, virago (marimacho).

machacador, ra *adj/s* crushing, pounding (que machaca) || grinding, crushing (que muele) || beating (que bate).
◆ *f* crushing *o* grinding machine.

machacante *m* FAM five peseta coin (moneda) || MIL sergeant's orderly *o* aid (soldado).

machacar; machaquear *vt* to pound, to crush (en un mortero) || to grind, to crush (moler) || MIL to bombard, to shell (bombardear) | to crush (al enemigo) || FIG & FAM to harp on, to go on about, to repeat (repetir) | to crush, to flatten (en una discusión) | to slash (los precios) || — FIG *hay que machacar el hierro mientras que está caliente* (one must) strike while the iron is hot | *machacando se aprende el oficio* practice makes perfect | *machacar en hierro frío* to bang one's head against a brick wall | *machacar los oídos* to say (the same thing) over and over again.
◆ *vi* FIG & FAM to be boring, to be a bore *o* a nuisance (aburrir) | to harp on a subject (repetir) | to swot, to cram, to grind (estudiar con ahínco).
◆ *vpr* FAM to spend (dinero, tiempo).

machacón, ona *adj* FAM repetitious, insistent (que repite) | boring, tiring (pesado) | hard-working, studious (muy estudioso) || *con machacona frecuencia* all the time, constantly, forever.
◆ *m/f* FAM bore, pest, nuisance (pesado) | swot, crammer (muy estudioso).

machaconería *f* FAM tiresomeness (pesadez) | insistence (insistencia) | harping (sobre un tema).

machada *f* flock of billy goats || FIG & FAM stupidity (necedad) | manly action (hombrada).

machamartillo (a) *loc adv* thoroughly, attentively (concienzudamente) || FIG obstinately || — *creo a machamartillo* I firmly believe || *cristiano a machamartillo* confirmed Christian, Christian through and through || *cumplir a machamartillo* to carry out (a task) to the letter || *hacer entrar una cosa a machamartillo* to drive sth. in *o* home || *repetir a machamartillo* to repeat time and again.

machaquear *vt* ⟶ **machacar.**

machaqueo *m* pounding, crushing (trituración) || grinding (molido) || FIG bombardment, pounding (bombardeo intenso) || FIG & FAM insistence, stubbornness (insistencia) | harping (sobre un tema).

machaquería *f* ⟶ **machaconería.**

macharse *vpr* AMER to get drunk (emborracharse).

machear *vi* to beget more males than females || FAM to play the tough guy (dárselas de hombre).

machetazo *m* blow with a machete (golpe) || wound from a machete (herida).

machete *m* machete (espada corta) || hunting knife (cuchillo).

machetear *vt* to slash *o* to strike *o* to wound with a machete (espada corta) *o* hunting knife (cuchillo de monte) || to cut down with a machete (la caña de azúcar, etc.).
◆ *vi* to drive stakes (clavar estacas) || AMER to persist, to insist | to work (trabajar) | to cram, to swot hard (empollar).

machetero *m* path clearer, trailblazer, person who clears a way with a machete (que desmonta) || cane cutter (que corta la caña) || AMER unskilled labourer (peón) | swot, crammer (empollón).

machi; machí *m* AMER medicine man (curandero).

machiega *adj f* *abeja machiega* queen bee.

machihembrado *m* tongue and groove [joint].

machihembrar *vt* to join with a tongue and groove (carpintería).

machismo *m* machismo, virility *o* masculinity cult || virility, manliness, masculinity (virilidad).

macho *adj m* male; *gorrión macho* male sparrow || FIG strong (fuerte); *vino macho* strong wine | manly, virile (varonil) || TECN male || AMER great, terrific (formidable).
◆ *m* male || he-mule (mulo) || hook (de un corchete) || tassel (borla) || FIG numbskull, fool (necio) || ARQ pilaster, buttress (pilar) || TECN male piece *o* part (pieza que penetra en otra) | plug (de un enchufe) | tenon (espiga) | sledgehammer (maza) | anvil block (banco de yunque) | square anvil (yunque) || FAM he-man, tough guy (hombre varonil) || — *macho cabrío* he-goat, billy-goat || TECN *macho de aterrajar* or *de roscar* screw tap.

machón *m* ARQ pilaster, buttress (pilar).

machorra *f* sterile *o* barren woman || FAM virago, mannish woman (marimacho).

machota *f* hammer, mallet (mazo) || brave woman *o* girl (valiente) || FAM mannish woman, virago (marimacho).

machote *adj m* virile, masculine || courageous (valiente).
◆ *m* mallet (mazo) || FAM he-man, tough guy (hombre varonil) || AMER rough draft (borrador) | model, pattern (modelo) | boundary stone (mojón).

machucado *m*; **machucadura** *f*; **machucamiento** *m* bruising, bruise (de una fruta) || bump (de un objeto) || contusion, bruise (herida).

machucar *vt* to crush (aplastar) || to bruise (una fruta) || to dent, to deform (abollar).

machucón *m* AMER ⟶ **machucado.**

Madagascar *n pr* GEOGR Madagascar.

madeja *f* hank, skein (de lana) || FIG tuft *o* mass *o* mop of hair (de pelo) || FIG & FAM layabout, loafer (hombre sin vigor) || — FIG *enredarse la madeja* to get complicated | *madeja de nervios* bundle of nerves.

madera *f* wood; *madera seca* dry wood || timber (de construcción) || horn *o* rind of horse's hoof (del casco de las caballerías) || DEP wood (en el golf) || FIG stuff (de una persona); *tiene madera de santo* his is the stuff *o* he is of the stuff saints are made of || — *a media madera* scarf (empalme) || *de madera* wooden, wood || *madera anegadiza* non-floating wood || *madera aserradiza, de construcción* sawn *o* hewn timber, construction timber || *madera blanca* deal || *madera contrachapada* plywood || *madera del aire* horn (de animal) || *madera en rollo* rough timber || *madera fósil* lignite || *madera plástica* plastic wood || *maderas preciosas* or *exóticas* fancy woods || FIG *tener buena madera para pintor* to have what it takes to be a painter, to have it in one to be a painter, to have the makings of a painter | *tocar madera* to touch wood [*US* to knock on wood].
◆ *m* Madeira (vino).

Madera *npr f* GEOGR Madeira (isla).

maderable *adj* timber-yielding.

maderada *f* raft.

maderaje; maderamen *m* wood, timber (madera) || framework (armazón) || timberwork, woodwork, timbering (enmaderamiento).

maderero, ra *adj* timber, lumber.
◆ *m* timber *o* lumber dealer.

madero *m* log, piece of wood || piece of timber, log (de construcción) || POP cop || FIG ship, vessel (buque) || FIG & FAM numbskull, blockhead, dolt (necio).

Madianitas *m pl* Midianites (antiguo pueblo de Arabia).

madona *f* REL Madonna.

madrás *m* madras (tejido).

madrastra *f* stepmother || FIG callous *o* cruel mother (madre cruel) | plague (cosa molesta).

madraza *f* FAM doting mother, mother hen.

madrazo *m* AMER blow (golpe fuerte).

madre *f* mother; *madre de familia* mother of a family; *futura madre* expectant mother || mother (de los animales); *una leona madre* a mother lioness || matron (de un hospital) || REL mother; *madre superiora* mother superior || FAM old mother (mujer vieja); *la madre Juana* old mother Jane || FIG mother, origin, cradle (origen); *Grecia, madre de las artes* Greece, mother of the arts | root; *la ociosidad es la madre de todos los vicios* idleness is the root of all evil || matrix, womb (matriz) || main sewer (cloaca maestra) || bed (de un río) || main irrigation ditch (acequia) || lees *pl*, dregs *pl* (del vino) || mother (del vinagre) || grounds *pl*, dregs *pl* (del café) || TECN main piece, spindle || — FIG *ahí está* or *ésa es la madre del cordero* that is the crux of the matter (lo esencial), there's the rub (dificultad), that is the key to it (causa) || FAM *como su madre lo echó al mundo* or *lo parió* stark naked, in one's birthday suit || *día de la madre* Mother's Day || *la Santa Madre Iglesia* Mother Church || *lengua madre de otras lenguas* mother language of other languages || *madre adoptiva* foster mother || *madre de alquiler* surrogate mother || *¡Madre de Dios!* good heavens! || *madre de leche* wet nurse || *¡madre mía!* good heavens || *madre patria* mother country || *madre política* mother-in-law || *madre soltera* unwed *o* unmarried mother || *Reina madre* Queen Mother || FIG & FAM *sacar de madre a uno* to make s.o. lose his patience || *salirse de madre* to overflow, to flood its banks, to run over (un río), to lose one's self-control (excederse) || *su señora madre* your mother.

madreperla *f* pearl oyster (ostra) || mother-of-pearl (nácar).

madrépora *f* ZOOL madrepore, white coral.

madreporarios *m pl* ZOOL madreporaria.

madreporita *f* madreporita.

madrero, ra *adj* FAM *ser muy madrero* or *demasiado madrero* to be tied to one's mother's apron strings, to be a mother's boy (hombre), *o* girl (mujer).

madreselva *f* BOT honeysuckle.

Madrid *n pr* GEOGR Madrid.

madrigal *m* POÉT madrigal.

madrigalesco, ca *adj* madrigalian || FIG delicate, elegant.

madriguera *f* burrow, hole (de conejos, etc.) || earth, lair, den (de zorros, de tejones) || FIG den [of thieves] (guarida).

madrileño, ña *adj/s* Madrilenian.

Madriles (Los) *npr mpl* FAM Madrid.

madrina *f* godmother (de un niño) || bridesmaid (de boda) (véase OBSERV) || FIG protectress (protectora) | sponsor (de un candidato) || post, pole (poste) || strap which connects the bits of two horses (correa) || AGR lead mare || MAR stanchion || AMER herd of tame animals used to lead a wild herd || *madrina de guerra* girl *o* woman who sends letters, gifts, etc. to a soldier during a war.

— OBSERV In Spain the *madrina* is the woman, generally the mother of the groom, who accompanies the groom into the church and is one of the witnesses to the wedding.

madrinazgo *m* role of godmother || sponsorship.

madroñal *m*; **madroñera** *f* patch of strawberry trees *o* madrona trees.

madroño *m* BOT strawberry tree, madrona (tree) (árbol) || small strawberry (fruta) || berry-shaped tassel (borlita).

madrugada *f* dawn (alba) || (early) morning; *a las dos de la madrugada* at two o'clock in the morning || early rising (acción de madrugar) || — *de madrugada* at daybreak || *levantarse de madrugada* to get up very early.

madrugador, ra *adj* early rising, who gets up early || *ser madrugador* to be an early riser.
◆ *m/f* early riser.

madrugar *vi* to get up early || — FIG *a quien madruga, Dios le ayuda* the early bird catches the worm || *no por mucho madrugar amanece más temprano* time must take its course.

madrugón, ona *adj* early rising.
◆ *m* very early riser || *darse un madrugón* to get up very early.

maduración *f* maturation, ripening.

maduradero *m* place for ripening fruit.

maduramiento *m* maturing, ripening, maturation.

madurar *vt* AGR to mature, to ripen || MED to ripen || FIG to think out, to mature (un plan); *madurar un problema* to think out a problem | to mature (una persona).
◆ *vi* to ripen, to mature (fruta, etc.) || FIG to mature || MED to ripen.
◆ *vpr* to ripen || FIG to mature.

madurez *f* ripeness, maturity || FIG maturity | wisdom, prudence (sabiduría).

maduro, ra *adj* ripe, mature (fruta) || FIG mature; *juicio maduro* mature judgment; *edad madura* mature age || MED ripe (absceso) || — *pera muy madura* mellow pear || *poco maduro* unripe, green (fruta), immature (persona).

maelstrom *m* maelstrom.

maesa *f* queen bee.

maese *m* (ant) master (maestro); *maese Pedro* master Peter || FAM *maese Zorro* Reynard the Fox.

maestoso *adv* MÚS maestoso.

maestra *f* school teacher, schoolmistress (de escuela) ‖ teacher's wife, wife of a teacher (esposa del maestro) ‖ teacher, instructor; *maestra de piano* piano teacher ‖ girl's school (escuela); *ir a la maestra* to go to a girl's school ‖ queen bee (abeja maestra) ‖ FIG teacher; *la desgracia es la mejor maestra del hombre* misfortune is the best teacher (of man) ‖ TECN guide line (listón que sirve de guía) ‖ *maestra de escuela* or *de primeras letras* teacher, schoolteacher, schoolmistress.

maestrante *m* member of a riding club.

maestranza *f* equestrian society of Spanish noblemen (sociedad de equitación) ‖ MAR petty officers *pl* ‖ MIL arsenal (talleres) | men who work in an arsenal (operarios).

maestrazgo *m* dignity of the grand master of a military order ‖ territory under jurisdiction of the grand master of a military order.

maestre *m* master [of a military order]; *el maestre de Santiago* the master of Santiago; *gran maestre* grand master.

maestresala *m* headwaiter, maître d'hôtel.

maestrescuela *m* cathedral dignitary who teaches divinity ‖ chancellor (en las universidades).

maestría *f* master's degree ‖ mastery, skill, talent; *pintar con maestría* to paint with skill.

maestril *m* queen cell (apicultura).

maestrillo *m* insignificant, schoolmaster ‖ FIG *cada maestrillo tiene su librillo* each person has his own way of thinking.

maestro, tra *adj* main, principal; *viga maestra* main beam ‖ skilled, expert (hábil) ‖ basic, governing (idea) ‖ trained (adiestrado); *perro maestro* trained dog ‖ — *abeja maestra* queen bee ‖ *clavija maestra* kingpin, kingbolt ‖ *con* or *de mano maestra* masterfully ‖ AVIAC & MAR *cuaderna maestra* midship frame ‖ *golpe maestro* masterstroke ‖ *llave maestra* key, skeleton key ‖ *obra maestra* masterpiece ‖ MAR *palo maestro* mainmast.
◆ *m* master (de un arte); *maestro de armas* or *de esgrima* fencing master ‖ teacher, schoolmaster, schoolteacher (profesor) ‖ master (práctico); *maestro sastre* master tailor ‖ master; *inspirarse en los maestros* to take one's inspiration from the masters ‖ MAR mainmast ‖ MÚS maestro ‖ — *gran maestro* grand master ‖ *maestro de baile* dancing master ‖ *maestro de capilla* chapel master, choirmaster ‖ *maestro de ceremonias* master of ceremonies ‖ *maestro de cocina* chef, master cook (cocinero) ‖ *maestro de escuela* schoolmaster ‖ *maestro de obras* master builder ‖ *ser maestro* or *maestro consumado en el arte de* to be a master at, to be a master in the art of.

maffia; mafia *f* Maffia, mafia.

mafioso, sa *adj* of the Maffia.
◆ *m/f* member of the Maffia, mafioso.

Magallanes *n pr* HIST Magellan ‖ GEOGR *estrecho de Magallanes* Magellan Straits.

magancear *vi* AMER to loaf about, to laze about, to lead an idle life.

maganza *f* AMER FAM laziness.

maganzón, ona *adj* AMER FAM lazy.
◆ *m/f* AMER FAM loafer, lazybones.

magdalena *f* madeleine, small sponge cake (pastel) ‖ FIG Magdalene, repentant woman.

Magdalena *npr f* Magdalene, Magdalen ‖ FIG & FAM *estar hecho una Magdalena, llorar como una Magdalena* to weep one's heart out.

magenta *adj* magenta ‖ *azul magenta* magenta.

magia *f* magic; *magia blanca, negra* white, black magic ‖ FIG magic, charm, spell (encanto) ‖ *por arte de magia* as if by magic, by magic.

magiar *adj/s* Magyar.

mágico, ca *adj* magic, magical; *poder mágico* magic power ‖ FIG wonderful, marvellous ‖ *varita mágica* magic wand.
◆ *m/f* magician (mago).
◆ *f* magic (magia).

magín *m* FAM imagination (imaginación) | mind (mente) | good sense (sentido común) ‖ — FAM *duro de magín* dense, as thick as a plank, as daft as a brush | *idea de su magín* figment of one's imagination | *se lo ha sacado de su magín* it is a figment of his imagination.

magister *m* FAM schoolmaster.

magisterial *adj* magisterial, teaching.

magisterio *m* teaching (enseñanza); *se dedicó al magisterio* he took up teaching ‖ teaching staff *o* body, teachers *pl* (conjunto de maestros) ‖ teaching profession (empleo) ‖ FIG affected solemnity.

magistrado *m* magistrate ‖ AMER *primer magistrado* president (presidente), prime minister (primer ministro).

magistral *adj* magistral, magisterial; *en tono magistral* with a magisterial tone ‖ masterful (excelente).

magistratura *f* magistracy, magistrature ‖ *Magistratura del Trabajo* conciliation board in industrial disputes.

magma *m* magma.

magnanimidad *f* magnanimity.

magnánimo, ma *adj* magnanimous.

magnate *m* magnate.

magnesia *f* QUÍM magnesia.

magnesiano, na *adj* QUÍM magnesian

magnésico, ca *adj* magnesic.

magnesífero, ra *adj* magnesiferous.

magnesio *m* QUÍM magnesium (metal) ‖ flashlight (de los fotógrafos).

magnesita *f* MIN magnesite.

magnético, ca *adj* magnetic; *campo, ecuador, polo magnético* magnetic field, equator, pole; *aguja, inducción, mina, tempestad magnética* magnetic needle, induction, mine, storm ‖ *grabación magnética* tape recording, magnetic recording.

magnetismo *m* magnetism ‖ magnetics (ciencia) ‖ *magnetismo animal* animal magnetism (hipnotismo).

magnetita *f* MIN magnetite.

magnetización *f* magnetization.

magnetizar *vt* to magnetize ‖ to hypnotize ‖ FIG to fascinate, to mesmerize, to magnetize.

magneto *f* magneto.

magnetoeléctrico, ca *adj* magnetoelectric.

magnetofón; magnetófono *m* tape recorder, magnetophone.

magnetofónico, ca *adj* magnetic ‖ *cinta magnetofónica* magnetic tape, recording tape.

magnetómetro *m* magnetometer.

magnetoscopio *m* magnetoscope.

magnetoterapia *f* MED magnetotherapy.

magnetrón *m* TECN magnetron.

magnicida *m* assassin, murderer.

magnicidio *m* assassination of an important person.

magnificar *vt* to magnify.

magnificat *f* magnificat (himno).

magnificencia *f* magnificence, grandeur ‖ generosity.

magnificente *adj* magnificent.

magnífico, ca *adj* magnificent ‖ generous (generoso) ‖ *el Rector Magnífico* the Rector.

magnitud *f* magnitude ‖ size (tamaño) ‖ greatness (grandeza) ‖ FIG order; *potencia nuclear de primera magnitud* nuclear power of the first order | magnitude; *un proyecto de gran magnitud* a project of great magnitude ‖ ASTR magnitude.

magno, na *adj* great, grand ‖ — *Alejandro Magno* Alexander the Great ‖ *aula magna* main amphitheatre ‖ *Carta Magna* Magna Carta, Magna Charta ‖ *Magna Grecia* Magna Graecia.

magnolia *f* BOT magnolia (árbol, flor).

magnoliáceas *f pl* BOT magnoliaceae.

magnolio *m* BOT magnolia (árbol).

mago, ga *adj* magian ‖ *los tres Reyes Magos* the tree Magi, the three Wise Men of the East, the Three Kings.
◆ *m* magician, wizard (que ejerce la magia) ‖ magus, sage (sacerdote de la religión de Zoroastro) ‖ *Simón Mago* Simon Magus.

magra *f* slice of ham.

magrear *vt* POP to pet, to paw.

Magreb *npr m* GEOGR Maghreb.

magro, gra *adj* meagre [*US* meager] (pobre) ‖ lean, thin, gaunt (persona) ‖ lean (carne).
◆ *m* lean meat (carne sin grasa).

maguer; magüer *conj* although (aunque).
— OBSERV *Magüer* is a barbarism.

maguey; magüey *m* BOT maguey (pita).
— OBSERV *Magüey* is a barbarism.

magulladura *f*; **magullamiento** *m* bruise, contusion.

magullar *vt* to bruise, to contuse (una persona) ‖ to bruise (una fruta).

magullón *m* AMER bruise.

Maguncia *n pr* GEOGR Mainz.

magyar *adj/s* Magyar.

maharajá *m* maharaja, maharajah.

maharaní *f* maharanee, maharani.

mahatma *m* mahatma.

Mahoma *npr m* Mohammed, Mahomet.

mahometano, na *adj/s* Mohammedan, Mahometan, Muslim.

mahometismo *m* Mohammedanism, Islam.

mahón *m* nankeen (tela).

mahonesa *f* mayonnaise (salsa).

maicena *f* cornflour [*US* cornstarch].

maicero *m* AMER maize dealer [*US* corn dealer].
◆ *adj* maize [*US* corn].

mail-coach *m* four-in-hand (berlina inglesa).

maillechort *m* nickel silver, German silver (metal).

maillot *m* maillot, bathing suit (traje de baño) ‖ DEP cyclist's jersey.

mainel *m* ARQ mullion (montante vertical), transom (montante horizontal).

maitinada *f* dawn (madrugada) ‖ aubade, dawn song *o* serenade (serenata).

maitines *m pl* REL matins; *llamar* or *tocar a maitines* to call *o* to ring to matins.

maíz *m* BOT maize [*US* corn]; *maíz tostado* toasted maize ‖ *roseta de maíz* popcorn.

maizal *m* maize field [*US* cornfield].

maja *f* elegant young girl (mujer) ‖ pestle (del mortero) ‖ → **majo**.

majada *f* sheepfold (aprisco) ‖ animal manure, dung (estiércol) ‖ AMER flock of sheep (rebaño).

majadal *m* pasture land for sheep (pastizal) ‖ sheepfold (majada).

majadería *f* nonsense, absurdity (necedad) || *decir majaderías* to talk nonsense, to make stupid remarks.

majadero, ra *adj* stupid, foolish (necio).
◆ *m/f* fool, clown, idiot (necio).
◆ *m* pestle (maza) || lace bobbin (del huso).

majado *m* crushing, pounding, grinding.

majadura *f* crushing, pounding, grinding (machacadura).

majagranzas *m inv* FAM bore (pesado) | clumsy, oaf, clod (torpe).

majamiento *m* crushing, pounding, grinding.

majar *vt* to crush, to pound, to grind; *majar algo en un mortero* to crush sth. in a mortar || FIG & FAM to bother, to pester, to get on [s.o.'s] nerves (molestar) | to wallop (pegar) | to wipe out, to annihilate; *majar un ejército* to wipe out an army || FIG *majar a uno a palos* to beat s.o. up.

majara; majareta *adj* FAM cracked, nuts, nutty, touched (loco).
◆ *m/f* FAM nut.

majestad *f* majesty || stateliness, grandeur (grandeza) || — *Su Divina Majestad* the Divine Majesty (Dios) || *Su Graciosa Majestad* His Majesty the King, Her Majesty the Queen (de Inglaterra) || *Su Majestad* Your Majesty, your Highness (dirigiéndose a un soberano), His *o* Her Majesty (hablando de un soberano) || *Su Majestad Católica* His Catholic Majesty [King of France] || *Su Majestad Cristianísima* His Christian Majesty [King of Spain].

majestuosidad *f* majesty, stateliness; *la majestuosidad de su porte* the majesty of his bearing.

majestuoso, sa *adj* majestic, stately, imposing.

majo, ja *adj* toffish (dicho de gentes del pueblo) (véase OBSERV) || FAM smart, well dressed (compuesto); *ir muy majo* to be very smart *o* very well dressed | nice, sweet, cute (mono) | pretty, beautiful (hermoso) | nice (simpático) | corky (bravucón) | showy, flashy (vistoso).
◆ *m/f* toff, dandy || *¡maja!, ¡majo!* love! [US honey]; *¡anda, majo!* come on, love!

— OBSERV *Majo* was applied chiefly to the young men of the 16th century from the lower classes who adopted the elegance and the carefree style of the nobles. They have been frequently represented by Goya in his paintings. Nowadays the usual meaning of the word is *pretty* or *nice*.

majolar *m* grove of hawthorns.

majoleto *m* BOT hawthorn (majuelo).

majuelo *m* BOT hawthorn (espino) | young gravepine (viña joven).

maki *m* ZOOL maki.

mal *adj* (apocopated form of *malo* used before a masculine sing noun) bad; *mal humor* bad humour || *tener mal color* to look off colour *o* poorly (tener mala cara).
◆ *m* evil; *los males de la guerra* the evils of war || evil, wrong, wrongdoing; *el bien y el mal* good and evil, right and wrong || harm, hurt, damage, wrong (daño, perjuicio); *para reparar el mal* to undo the harm, to right the wrong, to repair the damage || disease, illness (enfermedad) || misfortune (desgracia) || harm, ill; *no le deseo ningún mal* I don't wish him any harm || — *acogerse al mal menor* to choose the lesser of two evils || *a grandes males grandes remedios* desperate ills call for desperate measures || *caer en el mal* to fall into evil ways || *combatir el mal* to fight (against) evil || *del mal el menos* the lesser of two evils; of two evils one must choose the lesser || *el mal consiste en que* the trouble is || *estar a mal con alguien* to be on bad terms with s.o. || *hacer mucho mal* to do a lot of harm *o* evil (hacer daño) || *llevar a mal una cosa* to take sth. amiss, to be offended by sth. || *mal caduco* epilepsy || *mal de la tierra* homesickness || *mal de montaña* mountain sickness || *mal de muchos, consuelo de tontos* it's a fool's consolation to think everyone is in the same boat || *mal de ojo* evil eye || *mal de piedra* urinary calculi *pl* || *mal de San Vito* St Vitus's dance || *mal francés* syphilis || *¡mal haya...! mal haya quien mal piense* evil be to him who evil thinks || *¡mal haya sea!* damn it! || *mal menor* lesser evil || *no hay mal que dure cien años* everything will turn out all right in the end || *no hay mal que por bien no venga* every cloud has a silver lining || *ser un mal a medias* to be only half bad || *tomar a mal* to take badly; *tomó a mal mi broma* he took my joke badly.

mal *adv* badly, poorly; *escribir mal* to write badly || wrongly, badly; *escoger mal* to choose wrongly || bad; *oler mal* to smell bad || hardly, scarcely; *mal puede ayudarme* he can hardly help me || — *caer(le) bien, mal a alguien* to suit, not to suit s.o. (ropa); *no le cae bien esta chaqueta* this jacket does not suit him; to like, not to like ; *lo que dijo Juan me cayó mal* I did not like what John said || *caerle mal uno a alguien* to get on badly with s.o. || *decir* or *hablar mal de uno* to speak badly of s.o., to speak ill of s.o. || *encontrarse mal* to feel bad, to feel faint (en un momento) || *encontrarse mal de salud* not to feel well, to feel unwell || *estar mal de dinero* to be hard up, to be short of money || *estar mal de salud* to be ill, not to be well || *hacer mal* to do (sth.) badly; *hacer mal su trabajo* to do one's work badly; to be wrong; *hiciste mal obrando así* you were wrong to act like that; *hace mal en reír* he is wrong to laugh || *ir de mal en peor* to go from bad to worse || *mal de mi grado* against my will || *mal que bien* somehow (de un modo u otro) || *mal que le pese* like it or not || *¡menos mal!* what a relief!, thank heavens! || *menos mal que* it's a good job that [US it's a good thing that]; *menos mal que has venido* it's a good job that you came || *no está (nada) mal* it's not bad (at all) || *no estaría mal que viniese* it wouldn't be bad if he came, it would be a good thing if he came || *no hice mal en discutirlo con ella* it was rather a good idea to discuss it with her, I am glad I discussed it with her || *oír mal* not to hear very well || *por mal que le vaya* at the worst || *salir mal* not to do very well, to do badly, to come unstuck (una persona); *me salió mal el examen* I did badly in the exam; not to work, to go wrong, to misfire; *la estratagema le salió mal* his stratagem did not work; not to be very good, not to come out very well (fotografía, dibujo, retrato, etc.), to come out badly (de un mal paso), to be a failure (ser un fracaso) || *ser un mal pensado* to be evil-minded || *si mal no recuerdo* if I remember rightly *o* correctly || *venirle mal a uno* not to suit s.o., not to fit s.o. (traje), to be inconvenient for s.o., to be a nuisance for s.o. (no convenir); *me viene mal ir esta tarde* it is inconvenient for me to go this afternoon.

mala *f* trunk (baúl) || mailbag (correo).

malabar *adj/s* malabar || — *hacer juegos malabares* to juggle (en el circo) || FIG *hacer juegos malabares con las palabras* to make plays on words, to pun || *juegos malabares* juggling.

malabarismo *m* juggling || FIG jugglery || FIG *hacer malabarismos con los números* to juggle with numbers.

malabarista *m/f* juggler || AMER sly thief.

Malabo *n pr* GEOGR Malabo.

Malaca *n pr* GEOGR Malacca.

malacate *m* whim, winch (cabrestante) || AMER spindle (huso).

malacitano, na *adj* [of *o* from] Malaga.
◆ *m/f* native *o* inhabitant of Malaga.

malaconsejado, da *adj* ill-advised.

malacopterigio, gia *adj/sm* malacopterygian (peces).

malacostumbrado, da *adj* who has bad habits || ill-bred, ill-mannered (mal criado) || spoiled (mimado).

malacostumbrar *vt* to make s.o. get into bad habits || to spoil.
◆ *vpr* to get into bad habits.

malacrianza *f* bad breeding, lack of breeding, bad manners *pl*.

málaga *m* Malaga wine, Malaga (vino).

Málaga *n pr* GEOGR Málaga || FIG & FAM *salir de Málaga para entrar en Malagón* to jump out of the frying pan into the fire.

malage *m* insipidness, dullness, lack of wit *o* charm || — *cantó con malage* he sang without spirit || *es un malage* he is a bore, there is no life in him.

— OBSERV This word is an Andalusian deformation of *mal ángel*.

malagradecido, da *adj* ungrateful.

malagueña *f* malaguena [song].

malagueño, ña *adj* [of *o* from] Malaga.
◆ *m/f* native *o* inhabitant of Malaga.

malaleche *m/f* FIG & POP ill-intentioned person.

malamente *adv* FAM badly; *lo hice malamente* I did it badly.

malandante *adj* unfortunate (desafortunado) || unhappy (infeliz).

malandanza *f* misfortune.

malandrín, ina *adj* malign, perverse.
◆ *m* scoundrel.

malapata *m/f* FAM jinx (gafe).
◆ *f* bad luck (mala suerte).

malaquita *f* MIN malachite.

malar *adj/sm* ANAT malar.

malaria *f* MED malaria.

malasangre *adj* evil-minded.
◆ *m/f* evil-minded person || FIG & FAM *hacerse malasangre* to get worked up about sth.

Malasia *npr f* GEOGR Malaysia.

malasio, sia *adj/s* Malaysian.

malasombra *m/f* FAM bore, pest (persona sosa o molesta).
◆ *f* FAM bad luck (mala suerte) || lack of charm *o* wit, dullness, insipidness (falta de gracia) || FAM *¡qué malasombra tiene!* what a drag he is!

malatería *f* leprosery, leprosarium, lazaretto.

malatía *f* leprosy (lepra).

malaúva *f* spitefulness, malevolence.

malavenido, da *adj* incompatible (dos personas).

malaventura; malaventuranza *f* misfortune (desventura).

malaventurado, da *adj* unfortunate, poor.
◆ *m/f* poor soul.

malaxación *f* malaxation (de una sustancia) || massage (masaje).

malaxar *vt* to malaxate (amasar) || to massage (dar masajes).

malayo, ya *adj/s* Malay, Malayan.

Malaysia *n pr* GEOGR Malaysia.

malbaratador, ra *adj* squandering.
◆ *m/f* squanderer, spendthrift.

malbaratar *vt* to squander (malgastar) || to undersell (malvender).

malcarado, da *adj* grim-faced.

malcasado, da *adj* unfaithful (infiel) || married to s.o. below one's station (con persona de condición inferior).

◆ *m/f* unfaithful person (infiel) || person married to s.o. below his *o* her station.

malcasar *vt* to mismatch, to mismate.
◆ *vpr* to make a bad marriage || to marry beneath o.s. *o* below one's station.

malcomer *vi* to eat poorly.

malcomido, da *adj* underfed, undernourished.

malconsiderado, da *adj* inconsiderate, thoughtless.

malcontento, ta *adj* malcontent (contra las autoridades) || discontented, displeased, unhappy; *malcontento con su suerte* discontented with his lot.
◆ *m* malcontent.

malcriadez *f* AMER ⟶ **malacrianza.**

malcriado, da *adj* ill-bred, bad mannered.
◆ *m/f* ill-bred *o* bad mannered person.

malcriar *vt* to raise (a person) badly || to spoil (mimar).

maldad *f* badness, evil, wickedness (carácter de malo) || bad thing, evil thing, wicked thing || *cometer maldades* to do evil *o* wrong.

maldecido, da *adj* wicked, evil (malo) || damned (maldito).
◆ *m/f* wicked *o* evil person (persona mala).

maldecir* *vt* to curse (echar una maldición); *maldijo a su hijo* he cursed his son || to curse (renegar de); *maldecir su suerte* to curse one's luck.
◆ *vi* to backbite (murmurar) || to swear, to curse (blasfemar) || *maldecir de algo, alguien* to speak ill of sth., s.o. (hablar mal de); to curse sth., s.o. (echar maldiciones).

maldiciente; malediciente *adj* backbiting (que calumnia) || foulmouthed (que blasfema).
◆ *m/f* backbiter, evil-tongued person.

maldición *f* curse, malediction; *una maldición parecía haber caído sobre el pueblo* it seemed as if a curse had fallen upon the town || imprecation (imprecación) || blasphemy, curse, oath (blasfemia).
◆ *interj* damn it!, curse it!, damnation!

maldispuesto, ta *adj* indisposed (de salud) || ill-disposed, reluctant (sin ganas).

maldita *f* FAM tongue.

maldito, ta *adj* cursed, damned (condenado) || damned, confounded, bloody (*pop*), cursed; *¡maldito embustero!* damned liar! || lousy (*fam*), rotten (*fam*); *no tengo ni una maldita peseta* I haven't even got one lousy peseta || — *maldita la gana que tengo* I don't feel like it at all || *¡maldita sea!* damn it! || *maldito lo que le importa* he doesn't care a damn || *no le hago maldito caso* I don't take a blind bit of notice || *no sé maldita la cosa de eso* I know damn all about it || *no tiene maldita la gracia* I don't find it the least bit amusing.
◆ *m* devil (diablo) || TEATR extra.

Maldivas *npr fpl* *islas Maldivas* Maldive Islands.

maleabilidad *f* malleability.

maleabilizar *vt* to make malleable.

maleable *adj* malleable.

maleado, da *adj* corrupted, perverted.

maleamiento *m* corruption.

maleante *adj* corrupting (que corrompe) || perverse (perverso) || malicious, wicked (maligno) || shady (poco de fiar).
◆ *m* evildoer, crook, malefactor (malhechor) || vagrant (vagabundo).

malear *vt* to spoil, to ruin (estropear) || FIG to corrupt, to pervert (pervertir).
◆ *vpr* to go bad, to be corrupted *o* perverted (pervertirse) || to be spoilt *o* ruined (estropearse).

malecón *m* dike, mole, jetty (dique).

maledicencia *f* evil talk, slander.

malediciente *adj/s* ⟶ **maldiciente.**

maleducado, da *adj* ill-bred, bad-mannered.
◆ *m/f* boor, ill-bred *o* bad mannered person.

maleficencia *f* maleficence, wrongdoing.

maleficiado, da *adj* bewitched, under a spell.

maleficiar *vt* to harm, to injure (a uno) || to damage (algo) || to curse, to cast a spell on, to bewitch (embrujar).

maleficiente *adj* maleficent.

maleficio *m* evil spell, curse.

maléfico, ca *adj* maleficent, evil, harmful (dañino); *un poder maléfico* an evil power || malefic (en astrología).
◆ *m/f* sorcerer (que hace maleficios).

malencarado, da *adj* insolent, bad-mannered.

malentender *vt* to misunderstand.

malentendido *m* misunderstanding.

maléolo *m* ANAT maleolus.

malespín *m* AMER jargon used by street urchins.

malestar *m* malaise, indisposition; *sentir malestar* to feel malaise || FIG uneasiness (inquietud) | unrest (del pueblo por causas políticas, etc.).

maleta *f* suitcase, case (de ropa) || boot [US trunk] (de coche) || AMER bundle (lío de ropa) | saddlebag (de bicicleta, de una montura) || *hacer la maleta* to pack one's bags *o* one's suitcase.
◆ *m* bungler [said especially of bullfighters] || despicable person (hombre despreciable).

maletera *f* AMER trunk (baúl) | bundle (lío de ropa) | saddlebag (de bicicleta, de una montura).

maletero *m* suitcase maker (que hace maletas) || boot [US trunk] (de coche) || porter, station porter (mozo de estación).

maletilla *m* FAM novice, youth who aspires to become a bullfighter.

maletín *m* small suitcase, valise (maleta pequeña) || medical bag (de médico, de veterinario) || briefcase, attaché case (para documentos) || MIL *maletín de grupa* saddlebag.

maletón *m* big suitcase (maleta grande).

malevaje *m* AMER banditry.

malevo, va *adj* malevolent (malévolo).
◆ *m/f* AMER malefactor, evildoer.

malevolencia *f* malevolence, ill will.

malévolo, la *adj* malevolent.

maleza *f* weeds *pl* (hierbas) || undergrowth, underbrush, scrub (arbustos) || brambles *pl* (zarzas) || AMER pus.

malformación *f* malformation.

malgache *adj/s* Madagascan, Malagasy || *República Malgache* Malagasy Republic.

malgastador, ra *adj* wasteful, squandering.
◆ *m/f* squanderer, spendthrift.

malgastar *vt* to squander, to waste (bienes) || to ruin, to run down (salud) || to waste (tiempo).

malgeniado, da *adj* AMER irritable, bad-tempered.

malhablado, da *adj* foulmouthed.
◆ *m/f* foulmouthed person.

malhadado, da *adj* unfortunate, unlucky, ill-fated.

malhaya *adj* FAM damned, cursed || — *malhaya sea quien mal piense* evil be to him who evil thinks || *¡malhaya sea!* damn it!

malhecho, cha *adj* malformed, deformed, misshapen.
◆ *m* misdeed, malefaction.

malhechor, ra *adj* wicked, malefactory.
◆ *m/f* malefactor, wrongdoer, evildoer.

malherir* *vt* to wound *o* to injure badly.

malhumor *m* bad temper, ill-humour.

malhumorado, da *adj* bad-tempered, ill-humoured || *responder con tono malhumorado* to reply gruffly.

malhumorar *vt* to put in a bad mood, to annoy, to upset.

malicia *f* malice, maliciousness, wickedness (perversidad) || evil intention (maldad) || slyness, cunning, trickiness (astucia, sutileza) || mischievousness, mischief (de los niños) || roguishness, naughtiness (de la mirada, de un dicho) || viciousness (de un animal) || FIG & FAM *tener la malicia de que* to suspect that, to have a suspicion that (tener recelo); *tengo la malicia de que no ocurrió así* I suspect that it didn't happen like that.

maliciable *adj* suspicious (sospechoso) || corruptible.

maliciarse *vpr* to go bad (malearse) || to have one's suspicions about sth. *o* s.o. (sospechar) || *algo me malicio en ese lío* there is sth. fishy about this mess, I smell a rat in this mess.

malicioso, sa *adj* malicious, evil, wicked (malo) || shrewd, sly, cunning (astuto) || ill-intentioned (malintencionado) || roguish, naughty (mirada, chiste).

málico *adj m* QUÍM malic (ácido).

malignidad *f* malignity, malignancy.

malignizarse *vpr* MED to become malignant.

maligno, na *adj* malignant; *fiebre maligna* malignant fever; *tumor maligno* malignant tumour || malicious, malignant, perverse; *intención maligna* malicious intentions || wicked, evil (malo).

malilla *f* manille (en juegos de cartas).

malinas *f* Mechlin lace *sing* (encaje).

Malinas *n pr* GEOGR Malines, Mechlin.

malintencionado, da *adj* ill-intentioned, evil-intentioned.

malmandado, da *adj* disobedient.
◆ *m/f* disobedient person.

malmaridada *adj f* unfaithful.
◆ *f* unfaithful wife.

malmirado, da *adj* ill-considered || inconsiderate, discourteous (descortés).

malnacido, da *adj* malicious.

malnutrición *f* malnutrition.

malo, la *adj* bad (que no es bueno); *este vino es malo* this wine is bad; *una acción mala* a bad act *o* deed || evil, wicked, bad (perverso); *malos pensamientos* evil thoughts; *tu amigo es malo* your friend is wicked || mean, nasty; *es malo con* or *para con sus hermanos* he is mean to his brothers || naughty, mischievous (aplicado especialmente a los niños) || bad, nasty (sabor, olor) || sick, ill (enfermo); *estar malo* to be sick || unpleasant, disagreeable obnoxious (desagradable) || hard, difficult (dificultoso); *este perro es malo de enseñar* this dog is hard to train || bad, poor (insuficiente); *una mala cosecha* a bad crop || FAM no good (sin habilidad, que no sirve); *soy malo para las matemáticas* I'm no good at mathematics; *vamos a tirar todo lo que esté malo* let's throw away everything which is no good || — FIG *andar a malas* to be on bad terms || *dar mala vida a alguien* to make s.o.'s life a misery || *en mala hora* at the wrong time || FIG *estar de malas* to be down on one's luck (tener mala suerte), to be in a bad mood (de mal humor) | *estar de malas con la justicia* to be

on the wrong side of the law || *los ángeles malos* the fallen angels || *mala jugada* dirty trick || *¡mala suerte!* bad luck! || *mala temporada* wrong season *o* time of year || *más vale malo conocido que bueno por conocer* better the devil you know than the one you don't know || FIG *ponerse de malas con alguien* to fall out with s.o. || *ponerse malo* to get *o* to fall ill || *ponerse malo de risa* to die laughing, to split one's sides laughing || *por las buenas o por las malas* willy-nilly || *por las malas* by force || *tener mala cara* to look off-colour *o* under the weather *o* unwell || *tener mala suerte* to be unlucky, to have bad luck || FIG *venir de malas* to be in a bad mood.
◆ *m el Malo* the Devil (el diablo), the villain, the bad guy (*fam*), the villain, the bad guy (en una narración, en una película) || *lo malo es que* the trouble is that.
◆ *interj* that's bad! (un asunto) || naughty! (a un niño, etc.) || boo! (en un espectáculo).
— OBSERV One should not confuse *ser malo* to be bad *o* evil, with *estar malo* to be sick.
— OBSERV *Malo* is apocopated to *mal* before a masculine singular noun.

maloca *f* AMER attack on Indian territory | raid (correría).

malogrado, da *adj* ill-fated, unfortunate [applied to a person who died before reaching the climax of his career] (artista, etc.); *el malogrado poeta García Lorca* the ill-fated poet García Lorca || abortive (proyecto, etc.) || wasted (esfuerzo).

malograr *vt* to waste, to lose, to miss (no aprovecharse de); *malograr una oportunidad* to waste an opportunity || to spoil, to ruin (estropear) || *malograr la vida* to be a failure.
◆ *vpr* to fail, to fall through, to come to nothing (fracasar); *se malograron sus esperanzas* his hopes fell through || not to come up to s.o.'s expectations (autor, hijo, etc.) || to be wasted, to be lost *o* missed (oportunidad) || to be cut off in one's prime (morir prematuramente) || AGR to fail (la cosecha).

malogro *m* failure (fracaso) || untimely end (fin) || AGR failure.

maloliente *adj* smelly, foul-smelling, malodorous.

malón *m* AMER surprise attack by Indians, Indian raid.

maloquear *vi* AMER to make a surprise attack, to raid.

malparar *vt* to damage, to harm (estropear) || to hurt (maltratar) || — *dejar algo, a alguien malparado* to leave sth. *o* s.o. in a sorry state; *Francisco dejó malparado a Juan* Frank left John in a sorry state; *la enfermedad le ha dejado malparado* his illness has left him in a sorry state || *salir malparado de un negocio* to come off badly in a business deal.

malparida *f* woman who has miscarried.

malparir *vi* to miscarry, to have a miscarriage.

malparto *m* miscarriage (aborto).

malpensado, da *adj* nasty-minded, evil-minded, malicious.
◆ *m/f* nasty-minded person || — *es un malpensado* he is nasty-minded || *no seas malpensado* don't be nasty.

malquerencia *f* malevolence, ill will (malevolencia) || antipathy, dislike (antipatía).

malquerer* *vt* to dislike.

malquerido, da *adj* disliked, unpopular.

malquistar *vt* to set at loggerheads, to alienate, to estrange.
◆ *vpr* to fall out (enfadarse).

malquisto, ta *adj* estranged, alienated (enfadado) || disliked, unpopular (mal considerado).

malsano, na *adj* unhealthy (malo para la salud) || sick, morbid (mentalidad, pensamiento).

malsonante *adj* ill-sounding (que suena mal) || obnoxious, offensive, nasty (palabra).

malsufrido, da *adj* weak (débil) || impatient.

malta *f* malt (cebada) || AMER top quality beer (cerveza) || *fábrica de malta* malthouse.

Malta *n pr* GEOGR Malta; *caballero de Malta* Knight of Malta || *cruz de Malta* Maltese cross.

maltaje *m* TECN malting.

maltasa *f* maltase.

maltear *vt* TECN to malt.

malteado *m* TECN malting.

maltería *f* malthouse (fábrica).

maltés, esa *adj/s* Maltese.

maltosa *f* QUÍM maltose.

maltraer* *vt* to maltreat, to ill-treat, to treat badly (tratar mal) || FIG *llevar* or *traer a maltraer* to give s.o. a hard time.

maltraído, da *adj* AMER shabby, badly dressed, untidy, dishevelled (desaseado).

maltratamiento *m* maltreatment, ill-treatment, abuse.

maltratar *vt* to maltreat, to ill-treat, to treat badly, to mistreat (tratar mal); *no se debe maltratar a los animales* one should not ill-treat animals || to spoil, to damage (echar a perder).

maltrato *m* maltreatment, ill-treatment.

maltrecho, cha *adj* battered, wrecked, damaged || *dejar algo, a alguien maltrecho* to leave sth., s.o. in a sorry state; *dejar maltrecho al enemigo* to leave the enemy in a sorry state.

maltusianismo *m* Malthusianism.

maltusiano, na *adj/s* Malthusian.

malucho, cha *adj* FAM sickly, out of sorts (algo enfermo); *hoy está malucho* he is sickly today | rather bad (tirando a malo).

malva *f* BOT mallow || — FAM *estar criando malvas* to be pushing up the daisies || BOT *malva loca, real* or *rósea* rose mallow, hollyhock || FIG *ser como una malva* to be as meek as a lamb.
◆ *adj inv/sm* mauve (color).

malváceas *f pl* BOT malvaceae.

malvadamente *adv* spitefully, nastily (con maldad).

malvado, da *adj* evil, wicked, villainous.
◆ *m/f* evildoer, villain, wicked person.

malvaloca; malvarrosa *f* BOT rose mallow, hollyhock.

malvasía *f* malmsey (vino) || malvasia (uva).

malvavisco *m* BOT marshmallow.

malvender *vt* to sell at a loss, to sell off cheap, to sacrifice.

malversación *f* malversation, embezzlement, misappropriation.

malversador, ra *adj* embezzling.
◆ *m/f* embezzler.

malversar *vt* to embezzle, to misappropriate.

Malvinas *npr fpl* GEOGR *islas Malvinas* Falkland Islands.

malvinero, ra *adj* Falkland Island.
◆ *m/f* native *o* inhabitant of the Falkland Islands.

malvís *m* redwing, song thrush (ave).

malvivir *vi* to live badly.

malvón *m* AMER geranium.

malla *f* mesh (de una red) || net, network, mesh (red de hilo) || mail (de metal); *cota de mallas* coat of mail || AMER bathing costume, swimsuit (bañador) | tights *pl* (de deportista) | leggings (leotardo) || AMER *hacer malla* to knit.
◆ *pl* DEP net *sing* (de portería).

mallar *vi* to make meshing *o* netting *o* network.

mallo *m* mallet, maul (mazo) || mall, pall mall (juego y terreno).

Mallorca *n pr* GEOGR Majorca.

mallorquín, ina *adj/s* Majorcan.

mama *f* ANAT mamma, mammary gland (teta) | breast (pecho) || FAM mamma, mama, mommy, mom, mummy, mum (madre).

mamá *f* FAM mummy, mum, mamma, mama, mommy, mom (madre) || AMER *mamá señora* grandmother.

mamacallos *m inv* FIG & FAM fool, simpleton, dolt.

mamacita *f* AMER mommy, mummy.

mamacona *f* AMER Incan priestess.

mamada *f* nursing, sucking (acción) || feeding time [time a child nurses] (tiempo) || AMER FAM windfall (ganga) | booze-up, drinking spree [US drunk] (borrachera) || FAM *coger una mamada* to get drunk.

mamadera *f* breast pump || AMER teat [US nipple] (del biberón) | feeding bottle [US nursing bottle] (biberón).

mamado, da *adj* POP drunk, plastered, sloshed, canned, stoned (borracho) || AMER foolish (tonto) || POP *esto está mamado* this is a cinch, this is a piece of cake.

mamagrande *f* AMER grandmother.

mamaíta; mamita *f* FAM mummy, mommy.

mamancona *f* AMER fat old woman.

mamandurria *f* AMER sinecure (ganga).

mamar *vt* to suck, to nurse (el niño) || FIG & FAM to be suckled on, to grow up in *o* with *o* amidst; *mamar la honradez* to be suckled on honour | to learn from childhood, to grow up with; *haber mamado un idioma* to have learned a language from childhood | to swallow (engullir).
◆ *vi* to suck || *dar de mamar* to suckle, to give suck, to nurse.
◆ *vpr* FAM to get drunk *o* stoned *o* canned *o* sloshed *o* plastered (emborracharse) | to wangle, to fiddle, to get (ventajas, etc.) || FAM to stick, to swallow; *mamarse dos años de cárcel* to stick two years in prison || — AMER *mamarse a uno* to get the better of s.o. (aventajar), to cheat s.o., to take s.o. in (engañar), to do s.o. in, to do away with s.o. (matar) || FIG & FAM *no se mama el dedo* there are no flies on him, he wasn't born yesterday.

mamario, ria *adj* ANAT mammary.

mamarrachada *f* FAM daub, bad painting (cuadro malo) | washout, dead loss (libro, película) | nonsense, tomfoolery (idiotez).

mamarrachista *m/f* FAM botcher, dauber (pintor).

mamarracho *m* FAM ninny, clown, nincompoop (tonto) | puppet (fantoche) | horror, sight, hag (fealdad) | daub, bad painting (cuadro malo) | washout, dead loss (libro, película malos) || *iba hecho un mamarracho* he was dressed like a tramp *o* like a scarecrow.

mambí; mambís, isa *adj* rebellious, separatist [in Cuba in 1868].
◆ *m/f* rebel, separatist.

Mambrú *npr m* Marlborough.

mamela *f* FAM bribe (comisión extra).

mamelón *m* dug, teat (de animales) || knoll, hill (colina).

mameluco *m* mameluke || FIG & FAM dolt, simpleton (necio) || AMER overalls *pl* (prenda para obreros) | child's sleepsuit, rompers *pl* (para niños) | Brazilian mestizo, mameluco.

mamífero, ra *adj* mammalian, mammiferous.
◆ *m* mammal.
◆ *pl* mammalia, mammals.

mamila *f* ZOOL udder, teat (de la hembra) || ANAT nipple (del hombre).

mamilar *adj* ANAT mammillary.

mamografía *f* mammography.

mamola *f* chuck (under the chin) || FIG & FAM *hacer a uno la mamola* to make fun of s.o. (burlarse).

mamón, ona *adj* unweaned, nursing (que mama todavía) || *diente mamón* milk tooth.
◆ *m/f* unweaned child, suckling (que mama todavía).
◆ *m* BOT shoot, sucker (chupón) | genip (árbol) | AMER papaw, pawpaw, papaya (árbol y fruta) | sponge cake (bizcocho) || POP runt, squirt (persona despreciable) | swine (persona mala).

mamotreto *m* notebook, memo book || FIG & FAM big book (libraco) | monstrosity (armatoste).

mampara *f* screen (biombo) || padded door (puerta).

mamparo *m* MAR bulkhead; *mamparo estanco* watertight bulkhead.

mamporro *m* FAM blow, clout, punch (golpe).

mampostear *vt* ARQ to make *o* to build of rubble.

mampostería *f* rubblework.

mampostero *m* stonemason, roughsetter (albañil) || tithe collector (recaudador).

mamut *m* ZOOL mammoth.
— OBSERV pl *mamutes*.

mana *f* AMER manna | source, spring (manantial).

maná *f* manna (del cielo, de los árboles) || FIG manna, godsend; *esperar el maná* to wait for a godsend.

manada *f* flock, herd, drove (rebaño) || pack (bandada); *manada de lobos* pack of wolves || pride (de leones) || FIG & FAM crowd, mob (de personas) || handful (de hierbas) || FAM *a manadas* in droves, in crowds, in throngs (en tropel).

management *m* COM management.

manager *m* manager (de boxeador, de empresa).

Managua *n pr* GEOGR Managua.

managüense *adj* [of *o* from] Managua (Nicaragua).
◆ *m/f* native *o* inhabitant of Managua.

manantial *adj* spring || *agua manantial* spring water, running water.
◆ *m* source, spring || FIG source, origin (origen).

manar *vi* to flow, to run; *mana sangre de la herida* blood is flowing from the wound || FIG to abound (abundar).
◆ *vt* *la herida manaba sangre* blood flowed from the wound.

manatí *m* manatee, sea cow (mamífero).

manaza *f* FAM large hand || FAM *ser un manazas* to be clumsy.

mancar *vt* to cripple s.o.'s arms (las manos) || to maim, to cripple (cualquier miembro) || AMER to miss (fallar el tiro).

manceba *f* concubine.

mancebía *f* brothel.

mancebo *m* young man (joven) || bachelor (soltero) || clerk (dependiente) || pharmacist's assistant, dispenser (de farmacia).
◆ *pl* young men (mozos).

mancera *f* plough handle, ploughtail (del arado).

mancilla *f* FIG spot, stain, blemish.

mancillar *vt* to spot, to stain, to sully.

manco, ca *adj* one-handed (de una mano), with both hands missing (de las dos manos) || one-armed (de un brazo), armless (de los dos brazos) || FIG halting; *verso manco* halting verse || MAR without oars (barco) || FAM bad; *estas fiestas tampoco son mancas* these parties aren't bad either || — *manco de la izquierda* maimed in the left arm || FAM *no es manco* he's no fool, he knows what he is doing (es hábil) || FIG & FAM *no ser cojo ni manco* to be all there, to have one's head screwed on right.
◆ *m/f* one-armed person (del brazo) || one-handed person (de la mano).
◆ *m* nag (caballo malo) || *el manco de Lepanto* Cervantes [who injured an arm in battle there].

mancomún (de) *loc adv*; **mancomunadamente** *adv* in agreement, jointly, together, in common.

mancomunar *vt* to combine, to join, to unite (personas) || to pool (recursos) || to combine (intereses) || JUR to make (two or more parties) jointly liable.
◆ *vpr* to become associated; *mancomunarse con otro* to become associated with s.o. || to unite.

mancomunidad *f* union, association || commonwealth (de provincias, etc.) || pool (de recursos) || community (de intereses) || co-property, joint ownership (de una casa).

mancornas *fpl* AMER cuff links (gemelos).

mancuerna *f* pair (of oxen) tied together by the horns (pareja) || strap, thong (correa).
◆ *pl* AMER cuff links.

mancha *f* stain, spot; *quitar una mancha* to remove *o* to take out a stain || blot (de tinta) || bruise (en una fruta) || flaw, blemish (en una piedra preciosa) || patch (de vegetación) || FIG stain, blemish, stigma, blot (infamia); *hacer una mancha en su honor* to cast a stain on one's honour || ANAT spot; *mancha amarilla* yellow spot || ARTES rough sketch (boceto) || ASTR spot || AMER anthrax (tumor) || — FIG *extenderse como mancha de aceite* to spread like wildfire || *la mancha ha salido* the stain has come out (ha desaparecido) || *la mancha ha vuelto a salir* the stain has come up *o* out again (ha vuelto a aparecer) || *mancha solar* sunspot || *sin mancha* unblemished.

Mancha (La) *npr f* GEOGR La Mancha [region of Spain] || La Manche (departamento de Francia) || the English Channel (canal de la Mancha).

manchado, da *adj* spotted (la piel de un animal) || spotty (la piel) || stained, dirty (sucio) || smudged (una página, etc.).

manchar *vt* to spot, to stain (hacer una mancha); *manchar con* or *de tinta* to stain with ink || to dirty, to soil (ensuciar) || FIG to stain, to blemish, to tarnish (la reputación).
◆ *vpr* to get dirty || to stain *o* to spot one's clothing (hacerse una mancha) || to dirty *o* to soil one's hands *o* one's clothing (ensuciarse) || FIG to stain one's reputation.

manchego, ga *adj* [of *o* from] La Mancha [region of Spain].
◆ *m/f* native *o* inhabitant of La Mancha.
◆ *m* cheese from La Mancha (queso).

manchón *m* large spot *o* stain || patch of thick vegetation (de vegetación) || patch of pastureland (pasto).

manchú, úa *adj/s* Manchurian, Manchu.

manda *f* legacy, bequest (legado testamentario).

mandadero, ra *m/f* messenger, errand boy *o* girl (recadero).
◆ *m* office boy (botones).

mandado *m* errand (recado); *hacer los mandados* to do *o* to run errands || order (orden) || mandate (encargo, delegación) || — AMER *a su mandado* at your service || *bien mandado* obedient, well-behaved || *mal mandado* disobedient, badly-behaved.

mandamás *m* FAM big shot, bigwig; *es el mandamás del pueblo* he's the big shot of the town | leader, kingpin; *el mandamás de una rebelión* the leader of a rebellion.

mandamiento *m* command, order (orden) || REL commandment; *los diez mandamientos* the Ten Commandments || JUR writ, mandate | warrant; *mandamiento de arresto* or *de detención* warrant for arrest.
◆ *pl* FIG & FAM five fingers of the hand.

mandanga *f* FAM calmness (flema), sluggishness (lentitud) | dope, cocaine (droga).

mandar *vt* to order (ordenar); *me mandó que lo limpiase todo* he ordered me to clean it all || to command, to lead; *mandar un ejército* to command an army || to send, to mail (enviar por correo); *mandar una carta* to mail a letter || to send (enviar); *mandar a uno a la farmacia* to send s.o. to the chemist's; *mandar recuerdos* to send one's regards; *mandar buscar* to send for || to bequeath, to will, to leave (por testamento) || TECN to control (un mecanismo) || DEP to control, to manage [a horse] || — *bien, mal mandado* obedient, disobedient || *lo que usted mande, ¡mande!* at your service (criados) || FAM *mandar a alguien a freír espárragos* or *a freír monas* to send s.o. packing || POP *mandar a alguien a la mierda* to tell s.o. to go to hell || FAM *mandar a alguien al infierno* to tell s.o. to go to blazes *o* to the devil | *mandar a alguien a hacer gárgaras* or *a hacer puñetas* or *a la porra* or *al cuerno* or *a paseo* or *a tomar viento fresco* or *con viento fresco* to send s.o. packing, to tell s.o. to go to blazes, to tell s.o. to go (and) take a running jump, to tell s.o. to go (and) take a long jump off a short pier, to tell s.o. to go (and) jump in the lake || *mandar decir que* to send word that || *mandar hacer algo* to have something done || FAM *mandarlo todo a paseo* to chuck it all in, to give up || *mandar por* to send for; *mandar por el periódico* to send for the newspaper || AMER *mandar una bofetada a alguien* to land s.o. a clout, to clobber s.o. (*fam*).
◆ *vi* to be in command; *mandar en jefe* to be chief in command || TECN to be in control (un mecanismo) || — *aquí mando yo* I give the orders here, I'm the boss here || *como Dios manda* properly; *vestido como Dios manda* properly dressed; according to the rules; as it should be (como se debe) || AMER *¿mande?* pardon?, sorry? (*¿cómo?*).
◆ *vpr* to move about *o* to get around on one's own (un enfermo) || to communicate, to connect (dos habitaciones) || AMER to please (servirse); *mándese pasar* please enter | to go away (irse), to sneak away (solapadamente) || AMER *mandarse cambiar* or *mudar* to make o.s. scarce, to buzz off (*fam*).

mandarín *m* mandarin.

mandarina *f* mandarin, mandarine (fruta).

mandarino; mandarinero *m* BOT mandarin (árbol).

mandarino, na *adj* mandarin.

mandatario *m* mandatory || chief executive, president (gobernante).

mandato *m* order, command (orden) || mandate, term of office (de un diputado) || mandate (procuración, encargo, misión) || mandate (soberanía) || maundy (ceremonia religiosa) || — JUR *mandato judicial* writ, warrant, summons | *territorio bajo mandato* mandated territory.

mandíbula *f* ANAT & ZOOL mandible || jawbone; *mandíbula desencajada* dislocated jawbone || mandibula (de pájaros) || maxilla (de insectos y de crustáceos) || TECN jaw || FAM *reír* or *reírse a mandíbula batiente* to laugh till one's sides ache, to laugh one's head off, to laugh until one's jaws ache.

mandil *m* apron (delantal) || fine-meshed fishing net (red) || grooming cloth (para limpiar el caballo).

mandilete *m* tampion, tompion (de un cañón) || gauntlet (de una armadura).

mandinga *adj* AMER negro (de la raza negra) | Mandingo (raza africana) | effeminate (afeminado) | mischievous (travieso).
◆ *m/f* AMER Mandingo (raza africana) | negro.
◆ *m* AMER devil (el diablo) | imp, goblin (duende) | imp, little rogue (niño travieso) | sorcery (brujería).

mandingo *m/f* mandingo.

mandioca *f* manioc (planta) || tapioca (fécula).

mando *m* command, control; *el mando del ejército* command of the army || term of office (de un gobernante) || high-ranking officer; *los mandos de un regimiento* the high-ranking officers of a regiment || lead (en una carrera) || TECN control, drive (órgano de transmisión) || — *alto mando* high command || *ejercer el mando* to be in command || *entregar el mando* to hand over command || *estar bajo el mando de* or *al mando de un superior* to be under the command *o* the orders of a superior || *mando a distancia* remote control || *mando doble* dual drive *o* control || *palanca de mando* control lever (de una máquina), control stick, joy stick (de un avión) || *tener el mando de, estar al mando de* to be in command of || FIG *tener el mando y el palo* or *la estaca* to rule the roost || *tomar el mando* to take command.
◆ *pl* governing body *sing*, authorities; *los mandos del país* the governing body of the country || steering *sing*, steerage *sing* (de un barco) || controls (de un avión, de una radio, etc.) || *tablero de mandos* instrument panel (de un avión), dashboard, fascia (de un coche) || *torre de mandos* control tower (aeropuerto).

mandoble *m* two-handed blow with a sword || FAM large sword (espada grande) || FIG & FAM tonguelashing, piece of one's mind (reprimenda) | blow (golpe).

mandolina *f* MÚS mandolin, mandoline.

mandón, ona *adj* bossy, domineering.
◆ *m/f* bossy *o* domineering person.
◆ *m* boss, big shot (mandamás) || AMER foreman, boss [of a mine] (de una mina) | starter (en las carreras de caballos).

mandora *f* MÚS mandola.

mandrágora *f* mandragora, mandrake.

mandria *adj* worthless (inútil) || cowardly (cobarde).
◆ *m/f* idiot, fool (necio) || coward (cobarde).

mandril *m* ZOOL mandrill (mono) || TECN mandrel, mandril [of a lathe] (que asegura la pieza labrada) | chuck (que asegura la herramienta) || TECN *mandril del embrague* splined shaft.

mandrilado *m* TECN drifting, broaching, boring (calibrado).

mandriladora *f* TECN boring *o* broaching *o* drifting machine (máquina de calibrar).

mandrilar *vt* TECN to bore, to broach, to drift.

mandubí *m* AMER peanut.

manduca *f* FAM grub, chow (comida).

manducación *f* FAM eating.

manducar *vt/vi* FAM to eat, to nosh (comer).

manducatoria *f* FAM grub, chow (comida).

manea *f* shackle, fetter, hobble (maniota).

manecilla *f* hand (de un reloj) || clasp, book clasp (de un libro) || handle, hand lever (palanca) || IMPR index (signo tipográfico) || BOT tendril.

manejabilidad *f* manageability.

manejable *adj* manageable || handy, easy to use (de fácil uso) || manœuvrable (un coche, un avión, etc.).

manejador, ra *m/f* AMER driver (de un coche).

manejar *vt/vi* to handle, to wield; *manejar una espada* to handle a sword || to use (utilizar) || to handle (los caballos) || FIG to manage, to operate, to run (dirigir) | to administer, to administrate (administrar) | to handle (ocuparse de dinero, de negocios) | to handle, to manage (dirigir a una persona) || AMER to drive (un automóvil) || — FIG *manejar a uno a su antojo* to lead s.o. by the nose | *manejar el tinglado* to pull the strings | *manejar los cuartos* to hold the purse strings.
◆ *vi* AMER to drive (un coche).
◆ *vpr* to move about *o* to get around on one's own (un enfermo); *ya se maneja un poco* he is already moving about a bit on his own || to behave (portarse) || to behave o.s. (portarse bien) || to manage *o* to get on on one's own (arreglárselas).

manejo *m* handling (de un arma, de herramientas, de personas, de un caballo, de fondos) || running, working, operation (de una máquina) || FIG administration, management (de un negocio) | tricks *pl*, tactics *pl* (intriga); *conozco su manejo* I know his tricks | use (de la lengua) | handling (de muchos negocios) || AMER driving (de un automóvil) || — *de fácil manejo* easy-to-use || *instrucciones de manejo* directions, instructions || INFORM *manejo de ficheros* file management.

maneota *f* hobble (maniota).

manera *f* manner, way; *no me gusta su manera de hablar* I don't like his manner of speaking *o* the way he speaks || kind, sort (clase, forma) || ARTES manner, style || — *a la manera de* like, in the manner of || *a manera de* by way of; *a manera de prólogo* by way of a prologue || *a su manera* in one's own way, as one likes || *a su manera de ver* as he sees it, in his view, according to him || *cada cual a su manera* each to his own, each in his own way || *de cualquier manera* any old way (fácilmente), anyway (inevitablemente) || *de esta manera* this way, like this || *de la misma manera* in the same way, similarly || *de mala manera* badly; *conduce de mala manera* he drives badly; rudely, discourteously; *me contestó de mala manera* he answered me rudely || *de manera que* so that, so (así que) || *de ninguna manera* not at all, by no means, in no way || *de otra manera* otherwise || *de tal manera que* in such a way that || *de todas maneras* anyway, at any rate || *de una manera o de otra* one way or another, somehow or other || *en cierta manera* up to a point, to a certain extent || *en gran manera* a lot, a great deal, in great measure, very much; *contribuyó en gran manera al desarrollo* he contributed a great deal to the development || *la manera como* the way, how; *no entiendo la manera como sucedió* I don't understand how it happened || *manera de obrar* way of going about things, line of conduct, way of doing things || *manera de ser* the way one is; *es su manera de ser* that's the way he is || *manera de ver* outlook, point of view || *no hay manera* there's nothing one can do, there is no way || *¡qué manera de...!* what a way to...! || *sobre manera* exceedingly.
◆ *pl* manners (modales); *maneras distinguidas* distinguished manners.

Manes *m pl* Manes (almas de los muertos).

Manes; Maniqueo *npr m* Mani.

manezuela *f* small hand | handle (manija) || small lever (palanquilla) || clasp, buckle (de un broche).

manflor; manflora; manflorita *m* AMER pansy, fairy, effeminate man (afeminado).

manga *f* sleeve (del vestido); *manga de jamón* or *afarolada* leg-of-mutton sleeve || hose (de una bomba); *manga de riego* garden *o* watering hose (para regar), fire hose (de bombero) || waterspout (tromba) || arm [of an axletree] (de un carruaje) || portmanteau (bolso de viaje) || banner (estandarte) || cast net, casting net (esparavel) || net (red); *manga de mariposas* butterfly net || cloth strainer (para filtrar) || conical strainer (colador) || MAR airshaft, ventilation shaft (de ventilación) | breadth (ancho del buque) || DEP game (juego) || MIL detachment (destacamento) || BOT mango (fruta y árbol) || AMER cattle chute (paso) | mob, crowd (multitud) | poncho (abrigo) || *de manga corta, larga* short-sleeved, long-sleeved || — *manga acuchillada* slashed sleeve || *manga de agua* waterspout || *manga de aire, manga veleta* wind sock || *manga de ventilación* air vent (de un edificio), ventilation shaft (de una mina) || *manga de viento* whirlwind (torbellino) || *manga ranglán* ranglan sleeve || FIG & FAM *sacarse algo de la manga* to pull sth. out of one's hat | *ser de manga ancha, tener la manga ancha* to be broadminded || FIG & FAM *traer algo en la manga* to have sth. up one's sleeve.
◆ *pl* profits, gains (utilidades) || — FIG & FAM *¡a buena hora mangas verdes!* too late!, it's no good shutting the stable door after the horse has bolted! || FIG & FAM *ésas son otras mangas* that's a horse of a different colour, that is quite a different kettle of fish || *estar en mangas de camisa* to be in shirtsleeves || FIG & FAM *hacer mangas y capirotes de* to completely ignore, to pay no attention to (no hacer caso) || *sin mangas* sleeveless.

manganato *m* QUÍM manganate.

manganesa; manganesia *f* QUÍM manganese dioxide, pyrolusite.

manganésico, ca *adj* QUÍM manganous, manganesian.

manganeso *m* QUÍM manganese.

mangánico *adj* QUÍM manganic (ácido).

manganita *f* manganite.

mangante *adj* FAM pilfering (que roba) | cadging [*US* mooching] (pedigüeño).
◆ *m/f* FAM pilferer (ladrón) | cadger, sponger [*US* moodrer] (pedigüeño).

mangar *vt* FAM to pinch, to knock off, to pilfer (robar) | to sponge, to cadge [*US* to mooch] (pedir).

manglar *m* mangrove swamp.

mangle *m* BOT mangrove (árbol).

mango *m* handle (de un instrumento, de la sartén, de un cuchillo) || crop (de la fusta) || stock (del látigo) || helve (del hacha) || handle, stick (del paraguas) || BOT mango (árbol y fruta) || — *mango de cuchillo* razor clam (molusco) || *mango de escoba* broomstick.

mangoneador, ra *adj* bossy, domineering.

mangonear *vi* FAM to run things, to organize, to attend to *o* to see to everything (dirigir) | to boss people about (mandar) | to meddle, to pry (entremeterse) || AMER to use public office for personal gain.

mangoneo *m* FAM meddling, prying (entremetimiento) | running (mando) || *AMER* FAM graft.

mangosta *f* mongoose (animal).

mangostán *m* BOT mangosteen (árbol y fruto).

manguear *vt* *AMER* to beat, to flush (la caza) | to pen [*US* to corral] (el ganado) || FIG & FAM to coax.

manguera *f* hose, garden *o* watering hose (manga de riego) || MAR pump hose (de bomba) || air duct, ventilation shaft (ventilador) || waterspout (tromba) || *AMER* corral.

manguero *m* hoseman.

mangueta *f* enema (para lavados intestinales) || ARQ tie, beam (tirante) | strut, prop (jabalcón) || TECN lever (palanca) | steering knuckle spindle (de coche) | U-tube (de los retretes).

mangui *m / f* POP thief.

manguito *m* muff (de piel) || glove (manopla) || oversleeve (para proteger las mangas) || TECN bushing (anillo de acero) | sleeve, joint; *manguito de acoplamiento* coupling sleeve | mantle (incandescente) || *manguito roscado* threaded sleeve.

maní *m* peanut (fruto y planta).

manía *f* mania || mania, fad (obsesión, capricho) || craze; *la manía de coleccionar sellos* the stamp collecting craze || idiosyncrasy; *tener manías* to have idiosyncrasies || oddity, eccentricity (rareza) || FIG habit; *tiene la mala manía de conducir de prisa* he has the bad habit of driving fast || — *manía de grandezas* megalomania || *manía depresiva* manic-depressive psychosis || *manía persecutoria* persecution mania *o* complex || FAM *tenerle manía a uno* not to like s.o.

maniaco, ca *adj* maniacal, maniac, mad.
◆ *m/f* maniac; *maniaco sexual* sex maniac.

maniacodepresivo, va *adj* manic-depressive.

maniatar *vt* to tie (s.o.'s) hands, to handcuff || FIG to tie hand and foot.

maniático, ca *adj* fussy, finical || strange (extraño).
◆ *m/f* fussy *o* finical person || strange person.

manicero, ra *m/f* *AMER* peanut seller.

manicomio *m* mental hospital, mental asylum.

manicorto, ta *adj* FIG & FAM stingy, tight-fisted (avaro).
◆ *m/f* FIG & FAM skinfling (avaro).

manicuro, ra *m/f* manicurist.
◆ *f* manicure; *hacerle a uno la manicura* to give s.o. a manicure; *hacerse la manicura* to give o.s. a manicure (uno mismo), to get a manicure (por otra persona).

manido, da *adj* high (carne) || FIG trite, hackneyed (trillado, sobado); *un tema manido* a trite theme.

manierismo *m* mannerism (arte).

manierista *adj* manneristic (arte).
◆ *m/f* mannerist.

manifestación *f* manifestation || declaration (declaración) || demonstration, expression, show; *manifestaciones de amistad* demonstrations of friendship || (public) demonstration; *asistir a una manifestación* to attend a public demonstration || political meeting, mass meeting (reunión pública) || *hacer una manifestación* to demonstrate.

manifestante *m/f* demonstrator.

manifestar* *vt* to manifest; *manifestar su parecer* to manifest one's opinion || to demonstrate, to show (demostrar); *manifestar interés por alguien* to demonstrate an interest in s.o. || to make known, to declare, to state; *el ministro manifestó* the minister declared that || to express; *no sé cómo manifestarle mi agradecimiento* I don't know how to express my thanks to him || REL to expose (el Santísimo Sacramento).
◆ *vi* to demonstrate, to take part in a public demonstration.
◆ *vpr* to show, to be manifest || to appear, to come out (mostrarse) || to declare o.s. (declararse) || to make one's opinions known (exteriorizar sus opiniones) || to demonstrate (en una manifestación).

manifiesto, ta *adj* manifest, evident, clear (patente) || obvious, evident (error) || manifest (verdad) || *poner de manifiesto* to show, to reveal; *el balance pone de manifiesto un beneficio* the balance shows a profit; to make (sth.) clear (decir claramente).
◆ *m* manifesto (de carácter político) || MAR manifest || REL exposition (del Santísimo Sacramento).

manigua *f*; **manigual** *m* *AMER* brushland (monte bajo) | forest (selva) || *AMER echarse a la manigua* to take to the hills.

manija *f* handle (de un instrumento) || hobble (de un animal) || lever (palanca) || collar coupling (abrazadera de hierro) || AGR workman's glove || *AMER* strap [for fastening a whip to one's wrist].

manila *f* Manila, cigar (puro).

Manila *n pr* GEOGR Manila.

manilargo, ga *adj* long-handed || FIG generous, liberal, openhanded (generoso) | light-fingered (ladrón); *es muy manilargo* he is very light-fingered.

manilense; manileño, ña *adj* [of *o* from] Manila.
◆ *m/f* native *o* inhabitant of Manila.

manilla *f* hand (de reloj) || handle (de puerta o de ventana) || bracelet (pulsera) || manacle (de los presos).

manillar *m* handlebar, handlebars *pl* (de bicicleta).

maniobra *f* manœuvring [*US* maneuvering], handling, managing || TECN operation (de una máquina) | driving (de una grúa, etc.) || MAR manœuvring, handling || MIL manœuvre [*US* maneuver] || shunting (de ferrocarriles) || FIG move (movimiento) | manœuvre, move, stratagem (estratagema).
◆ *pl* MIL & MAR manœuvres || — MIL & MAR *estar de maniobras* to be on manœuvres || *hacer maniobras* to manœuvre [*US* to maneuver].

maniobrabilidad *f* manœuvrability [*US* maneuverability].

maniobrable *adj* manœuvrable [*US* maneuverable] || easy to handle (de fácil manejo).

maniobrar *vt* to work, to operate (una máquina) || to drive (una grúa, etc.) || MAR to manœuvre, to handle (un barco) | to work, to handle (las velas) || to shunt (ferrocarriles) || FIG to manœuvre [*US* to maneuver] (a una persona).
◆ *vi* to manœuvre [*US* to maneuver].

maniobrero, ra *adj* MIL manœuvring [*US* maneuvering].

maniobrista *adj* FAM good at manœuvring.
◆ *m/f* FAM good strategist || MIL skilled tactician.

maniota *f* hobble (de un animal).

manipulación *f* manipulation || handling (de mercancías).

manipulado *m* handling (de mercancías).

manipulador, ra *adj* manipulating || handling (de mercancías).
◆ *m/f* manipulator.
◆ *m* ELECTR telegraph key, tapper.

manipulante *adj* manipulating.
◆ *m/f* manipulator.

manipular *vt* to manipulate || to handle (mercancías) || to operate (en telégrafos) || FIG to manipulate (a una persona).

manípulo *m* maniple.

maniqueísmo *m* Manichaeism, Manicheism.

maniqueo, a *adj/s* Manichaean, Manichean.

maniquí *m* mannequin, dummy (de sastre, etc.) || FIG puppet (persona sin carácter).
◆ *f* mannequin, model (mujer que presenta).

manir* *vt* to hang (carne) || FIG to handle (manosear).

manirroto, ta *adj* lavish, spendthrift, wasteful.
◆ *m/f* spendthrift, waster; *es una manirrota* she is a spendthrift.

manís *m* *AMER* friend, brother (amigo).

manisero, ra *m/f* *AMER* peanut seller.

manitas *m inv* skilful person, handyman.

manito, ta *m/f* *AMER* brother (hermano), sister (hermana) | mate (amigote).
◆ *f* hand, small hand || — *hacer manitas* to hold hands || *manitas de plata* or *de oro* clever hands.
◆ *m* mild laxative || *AMER* mate (amigo).
— OBSERV The correct diminutive form of *mano* is *manecita*.

manitú *m* manitou.

manivela *f* crank (manubrio).

manjar *m* dish (alimento exquisito) || food (comestible) || FIG recreation, entertainment (deleite) || — CULIN *manjar blanco* blancmange || *manjar de (los) dioses* tasty dish.

mano *f* hand; *la mano derecha* the right hand || hand (de mono) || forefoot, front foot, front hoof (de caballo, cerdo, vaca, etc.) || front paw, forepaw (de gato, de perro, etc.) || trotter, foot (de los animales de carnicería); *mano de cerdo* pig's trotter || foot (del ave) || talon, claw (del ave de rapiña) || trunk (del elefante) || hand (manecilla de un reloj) || pestle (de almirez) || bunch, hand (de plátanos) || mano, handstone [for cocoa, maize, etc.] (rodillo de piedra) || quire (de papel) || coat (capa de color); *darle una segunda mano de pintura a la pared* to give the wall a second coat of paint || hand (grupo de cartas), hand, round (jugada), game (partido, conjunto de jugadas); *echar una mano de naipes* to play a game of cards || lead, leading hand (jugador que juega el primero); *tú eres mano* it's your lead || FIG series; *una mano de golpes* a series of blows | reprimand (reprensión) | side (lado) | hand (ayuda); *echarle una mano a uno* to lend *o* to give s.o. a hand | authority (autoridad) | influence (influencia) | labourer, hand, worker (persona que trabaja); *faltan manos en la agricultura* there is a shortage of labourers in agriculture | hand (persona que ejecuta una cosa); *dos retratos por la misma mano* two portraits by the same hand | hand (destreza); *tener buena mano para la pintura* to have a good hand for painting || DEP handball (falta en fútbol) || round (ronda); *una mano de vino* a round of wine | priority, right of way (en la carretera) || MÚS scale || *AMER* group of four similar objects | batch of thirty-four (panecillos) | brother (hermano) | mate (amigo) || FIG *abrir la mano* to become more lenient *o* tolerant (tolerante), to ease up on restrictions (atenuar las restricciones), to give generously (dar), to spend lavishly (gastar), to accept presents (admitir regalos) || *alzarle* or *levantarle la mano a uno* to raise one's hand to *o* against s.o. || *a mano* all square, quits (iguales), by hand; *hecho a mano* made by hand, hand-made; *escrito a mano* written by hand, hand-written; in handwriting, in longhand; *escribir algo a mano* to do sth. in handwriting, to write sth. in longhand; at hand, to hand, handy (cerca); *tener algo a mano* to have sth. at hand; on the way *o* route; *la tienda me coge a mano* the shop is on my way ‖ *a mano airada* violently ‖ *a mano alzada* freehand (dibujo) ‖ *a mano armada* armed; *ataque a mano armada* armed attack ‖ *a mano derecha, izquierda* on the right, on the right-hand side; on the left, on the left-hand side ‖ *a manos de* at the hands of; *murió a manos de su marido* she died at the hands of her husband ‖ FIG *a manos llenas, a mano abierta* liberally, generously ‖ *apretar la mano a* to shake hands with (para saludar), to clamp down on, to tighten up on (apretar las clavijas) ‖ FIG *a quien le dan el pie se toma la mano* give s.o. an inch and he'll take a mile ‖ *¡arriba las manos!, ¡manos arriba!* hands up! ‖ FIG *atar a uno de manos* or *las manos* to tie s.o.'s hands; *llevo las manos atadas* my hands are tied | *bajo mano* underhandedly, secretly, in secret | *buena mano* luck (suerte) | *caerse de las manos* to weary, to try one's patience (ser pesado) | *cambiar de manos* to change hands | *cargar la mano* to insist, to lay stress (*de* on), (insistir), to put one's foot down, to crack down (tener rigor), to be too strict (ser demasiado severo), to overcharge (*en* on), (en los precios), to add too much, to go heavy on [a certain ingredient to a stew, etc.] (con un ingrediente, etc.) | *cerrar la mano* to tighten one's belt (restringir los gastos), to be tightfisted (ser mezquino) | *coger con las manos en la masa* to catch red-handed ‖ *cogidos de la mano* holding hands, hand in hand ‖ FIG & FAM *comerse las manos* to be famished, to be starving ‖ FIG *con el corazón en la mano* with open heart, from the heart ‖ *con las manos, con ambas manos* with two hands, with both hands ‖ *con las manos en los bolsillos* hands in pockets, with one's hands in one's pockets ‖ *con las manos juntas* hands together ‖ *con las manos vacías* empty-handed; *volver con las manos vacías* to go *o* to come back empty-handed ‖ *con mano dura* with a hard *o* heavy hand ‖ *con* or *de mano maestra* masterfully ‖ *conocer algo como la palma de la mano* to know sth. like the back of one's hand ‖ FIG *con una mano atrás y otra delante* empty-handed | *dar de mano* to stop working, to knock off (*fam*), to stop working, to knock off (en el trabajo), to plaster (enlucir), to abandon (dejar) ‖ *daría mi mano derecha por* I would give my right arm to *o* for ‖ *dar la mano a* to shake hands with (saludo), to take by the hand; *dar la mano a un niño* to take a child by the hand; to give *o* to lend a hand (ayudar) ‖ FIG *dar la última mano a* to put the finishing touches to, to finish off | *darle una mano de azotes a uno* to give s.o. a beating *o* a flogging | *darse buena mano en una cosa* to do sth. skilfully | *darse la mano* to shake hands (estrecharse la mano) | *darse la mano con* to go hand in hand with (tener relación con) | *darse las manos* to join hands (coligarse), to bury the hatchet, to shake hands (reconciliarse) | *dar su mano* to give one's hand [in marriage] | *dar una mano de jabón a* to soap, to give a soaping | *dejar de la mano una cosa* to abandon sth., to drop sth. (abandonarla), to neglect sth. (descuidarla), to put sth. down (un libro, etc.) ‖ *de la mano* by the hand; *llevar de la mano* to hold by the hand; hand in hand, holding hands (cogidos de la mano), under the guidance *o* tutelage (*de* of) ‖ FIG & FAM *de la mano a la boca se pierde la sopa* there's many a slip 'twixt the cup and the lip ‖ *de mano* hand; *equipaje de mano* hand luggage; *granada de mano* hand grenade ‖ *de mano a mano* directly ‖ *de mano derecha, izquierda* right-hand, left-hand (puerta) ‖ *de mano en mano* from hand to hand ‖ FIG *de manos a boca* suddenly, unexpectedly | *de primera mano* firsthand; *informe de primera mano* firsthand account; *sé de primera mano que* I have it firsthand that | *de segunda mano* secondhand (ventas), at second hand (informaciones) | *echar mano a* to reach for (alargar la mano), to go for (un arma), to get hold of, to lay one's hands on (agarrar) ‖ *echar mano de* to make use of, to fall back on; *echar mano de las reservas* to fall back on the reserves; to turn to (persona) | *en buenas, malas manos* in good, bad hands ‖ *en mano* by hand; *entregar algo en mano* to deliver sth. by hand ‖ *en manos de* into the hands of; *caer en manos de* to fall into the hands of; in the hands of (al cuidado de) ‖ *en propias manos* in person, personally (a la persona misma); *se lo entregué en propias manos* I gave it to him in person *o* personally ‖ FIG *ensangrentarse las manos* to stain one's hands with blood | *ensuciarse las manos* to soil *o* to dirty one's hands ‖ FIG & FAM *estar con una mano atrás y otra delante* to be stony-broke ‖ FIG *estar dejado de la mano de Dios* to be godforsaken *o* unfortunate (desgraciado), to be a total failure (ser una calamidad) | *estar de mano, ser mano, tener la mano* to have the lead (en el juego) | *estar en la mano de todo el mundo* to be within the reach of everyone (fácil) | *estar en mano de uno* to lie with s.o., to be up to s.o.; *está en tu mano aceptarlo* it is up to you to accept ‖ *estar mano sobre mano* to sit twiddling one's thumbs, to sit idle, not to do a hand's turn ‖ *estrecharle la mano a uno* to shake s.o.'s hand, to shake hands with s.o. ‖ FIG *forzar la mano a uno* to force s.o.'s hand | *ganar a uno por la mano* to beat s.o. to it ‖ MIL *golpe de mano* raid ‖ *hablar con* or *por las manos* to use sign language, to talk with one's hands ‖ *hacer lo que está en su mano* to do all within one's power ‖ FIG *írsele a uno de la mano* to slip through s.o.'s fingers ‖ *írsele a uno de las manos* to slip out of one's hands; *el plato se le fue de las manos* the plate slipped out of her hands; to slip from one's hands *o* grasp, to slip through one's fingers; *su autoridad se le va de las manos* his authority is slipping from his grasp ‖ FIG *írsele* or *escapársele a uno la mano* to lose control, to let fly ‖ *írsele la mano en* to go heavy on, to add too much (ingredientes), to go too far with (pasarse de la raya) ‖ *juego de manos* sleight of hand ‖ FAM *juegos de manos, juegos de villanos* let's have no horseplay | *¡las manos quietas!* keep your hands to yourself!, hands off! ‖ FIG *lavarse las manos del asunto* to wash one's hands of the affair ‖ *¡levante la mano!* hands up!, raise your hands! ‖ *listo de manos* lightfingered ‖ *llegar* or *venir a las manos* to arrive, to reach; *tu carta llegó a mis manos ayer* your letter reached me yesterday *o* arrived yesterday; to come to blows (pegarse) ‖ *llevar de la mano a uno* to hold *o* to lead s.o. by the hand, to hold s.o.'s hand ‖ *llevarse* or *echarse las manos a la cabeza, ponerse las manos en la cabeza* to throw one's hands to one's head [in surprise, alarm] ‖ *mano a mano* together (juntos), on an equal footing, on equal terms (sin ventaja), competition (entre dos rivales), bullfight in which only two matadors take part [instead of three] (corrida), tête-à-tête (entrevista) ‖ FIG *mano de hierro en guante de seda* iron hand in a velvet glove ‖ *mano de obra* labour [US labor], manpower; *mano de obra especializada* skilled labour ‖ FIG *mano derecha* right-hand man; *ser la mano derecha de uno* to be s.o.'s right-hand man ‖ FAM *mano de santo* miraculous cure ‖ FIG *mano negra* occult powers ‖ *¡manos a la obra!* let's get down to work ‖ JUR *manos muertas* mortmain ‖ *me muerdo (me mordía) las manos por haber perdido la oportunidad* I could kick (could have kicked) myself for missing the chance ‖ FIG *meter las manos en* to have a hand in (tomar parte), to set one's hands to (emprender) | *meter mano a* to lay one's hands on, to seize (coger), to take action against (una persona), to touch (tocar), to touch up (*fam*), (indecentemente a una persona) | *no mover ni pie ni mano* not to lift a finger | *no saber uno lo que se trae entre manos* not to know what one is doing *o* what one is about | *no se veía la mano* you could not see your hand in front of you (in the darkness) ‖ FIG & FAM *nos quitan de las manos nuestras nuevas camisas* there is a rush on our new shirts, our new shirts are selling like hot cakes | *pasar la mano por el lomo a alguien* to butter s.o. up, to soft-soap s.o. | *pedir la mano de* to ask for the hand of | *poner en manos de* to place in the hands of, to entrust to | *poner la mano en el fuego por* to stake one's life on | *ponerle a uno la mano encima* to lay hands on s.o. ‖ *ponerse de manos* to sit up and beg (un oso, un perro, etc.), to rear (un caballo) ‖ FIG *ponerse en manos de uno* to place o.s. in s.o.'s hands | *poniéndose la mano en el pecho* hand on heart ‖ *por su propia mano* by one's own hand; *herido por su propia mano* wounded by his own hand; into one's own hands; *tomarse la justicia por su propia mano* to take the law into one's own hands ‖ *¡que Dios nos tenga en su santa mano!* God protect us! ‖ FIG *se me fue la mano* my hand slipped | *sentar la mano a uno* to give s.o. a good hiding (golpear), to fleece, to overcharge (cobrar demasiado) ‖ FIG *si a mano viene* should the occasion arise | *sin levantar mano* without letting up, without respite | *soltarse la mano en* to get one's hand in at ‖ *tender la mano* to offer one's hand (apoyo, saludo, reconciliación), to hold out a (helping) hand (*a* to), hand (ayudar) ‖ FIG *tener al alcance de la mano* to have within one's grasp | *tener buena mano para hacer algo* to be good at doing sth. | *tener en sus manos* to be in the hands of; *tienes la decisión, tu porvenir en tus manos* the decision, your future is in your hands; to have within one's grasp (al alcance de la mano) ‖ *tener entre manos* to have in hand | *tener las manos largas, ser largo de manos* to be free with one's fists (para pegar), to be free with one's hands (con las mujeres), to be light-fingered (para robar) | *tener mano con uno* to have an influence over s.o. | *tener mano izquierda* to have one's wits about one, to know what is what | *tener manos de trapo* to be a butterfingers | *tener manos de santo* to work miracles | *tener mucha mano* to be very influential | *tocar con la mano* to have within one's grasp | *tomar en sus manos* to take in hand ‖ *tradiciones que han llegado de mano en mano hasta nosotros* traditions which have been handed down to us ‖ FIG *traer a la mano* to bring back (caza) | *traerse* or *traer* or *llevar* or *tener entre manos* to plan (planear), to plot, to scheme (tramar), to have in hand *o* on one's hands, to be engaged in (estar ocupándose en), to be up to; *¿qué te traes entre manos?* what are you up to? ‖ FIG & FAM *untarle la mano a uno* to grease s.o.'s palm ‖ FIG *vivir de sus manos* to fend for o.s., to make one's living ‖ *votación a mano alzada* vote by show of hands.

mano *m* AMER FAM chum, pal (amigo) ‖ *¡eh, mano!* hey, old pal!

manodescompresor *m* TECN pressure-control valve [on butane cylinders, etc.].

manojo *m* bunch (haz); *manojo de llaves, de espárragos* bunch of keys, of asparagus ‖ bundle; *un manojo de estacas* a bundle of stakes ‖ FIG handful (puñado) | heap, pile (montón) | bunch (grupo) ‖ — FIG *a manojos* in abundance | *estar hecho un manojo de nervios* to be a bundle of nerves.

manoletina *f* TAUR a pass of the *muleta* invented by Manolete, the famous Spanish bullfighter.

manolo, la *m/f* typical Madrilenian of the popular quarters.

Manolo *npr m* (diminutive of Manuel), Emmanuel.

manómetro *m* FÍS manometer, pressure gauge.

manopla *f* gauntlet (de la armadura) ‖ mitten (guante) ‖ washing mitten, flannel [US facecloth] (para lavarse) ‖ working glove (guante de obreros) ‖ postilion's whip (látigo) ‖ AMER knuckleduster (arma).

manoseador, ra *m/f* person fond of handling *o* fingering *o* touching.

manosear *vt* to handle, to finger, to touch (tocar) ‖ FAM to paw ‖ FIG *tema manoseado* well-worn subject.

manoseo *m* handling, fingering, touching.

manotada *f*; **manotazo** *m* cuff, slap ‖ *quitarle a uno un libro de un manotazo* to knock a book out of s.o.'s hands.

manotear *vt* to slap, to cuff (golpear) ‖ AMER to steal (robar).
◆ *vi* to gesticulate.

manoteo *m* gesticulation.

manquedad; manquera *f* lack of one *o* both hands (las manos), lack of one *o* both arms (los brazos) ‖ FIG defect, imperfection.

mansalva (a) *loc adv* without taking any risk.

mansarda *f* attic.
— OBSERV *Mansarda* is a Gallicism for *buhardilla*.

mansedumbre *f* gentleness (de una persona) ‖ tameness (de un animal) ‖ mildness (del clima).

mansión *f* mansion (casa suntuosa) ‖ *mansión señorial* stately home.

manso, sa *adj* gentle; *manso como un cordero* as gentle as a lamb ‖ peaceful (apacible) ‖ tame (animal domesticado) ‖ calm, gentle, tranquil (cosas); *aguas mansas* calm waters ‖ AMER huge (enorme).
◆ *m* bellwether (de un rebaño) ‖ TAUR OX used to lead bulls.

mansurrón, ona *adj* very gentle ‖ very tame (animales).

manta *f* blanket (de cama, para las caballerías) ‖ travelling rug [US car blanket] (de viaje) ‖ poncho (abrigo) ‖ FIG & FAM beating (paliza) ‖ MIL mantelet (mantelete) ‖ AMER bag of agave for carrying ore (costal) | popular dance (baile) | cotton cloth (tela de algodón) ‖ — *a manta, a manta de Dios* a great deal; *ha llovido a manta* it has rained a great deal ‖ FIG *liarse uno la manta a la cabeza* to take the plunge ‖ *manta eléctrica* electric blanket ‖ *manta sudadera* numnah, saddle blanket ‖ FIG *tirar de la manta* to let the cat out of the bag, to spill the beans.

manteamiento *m* tossing (in a blanket).

mantear *vt* to toss (in a blanket).

manteca *f* grease, fat (grasa) ‖ lard (del cerdo) ‖ butter (mantequilla) ‖ cream (de leche) ‖ cocoa butter (de cacao) ‖ pulp (de fruta) ‖ FAM fat, blubber (gordura) | dough [US green stuff] (dinero) ‖ FIG cream (lo mejor) ‖ — FIG *derretirse como manteca* to melt like butter | *eso no se le ocurre ni al que asó la manteca* only a fool would think of doing that ‖ *manteca de cacahuete* peanut butter ‖ *manteca de vaca* butter ‖ *manteca requemada* browned butter ‖ FIG *ser como manteca* to be as meek as a lamb | *tener buenas mantecas* to be fat (gordo) ‖ *untar manteca en* to butter.

mantecada *f* slice of bread and butter ‖ butter bun (bollo).

mantecado *m* bun (bollo) ‖ dairy *o* vanilla ice cream (helado).

mantecón *adj m* FAM soft, fond of comfort (delicado) | fat (gordo).
◆ *m* FAM soft person, mollycoddle (delicado) | fatty (gordo).

mantecoso, sa *adj* creamy (la leche) ‖ buttery (como la manteca); *bizcocho mantecoso* buttery sponge.

mantel *f* tablecloth (de la mesa de comer) ‖ altar cloth (del altar) ‖ *mantel individual* table mat [US place mat].

mantelería *f* table linen.

manteleta *f* mantelet, shawl (prenda de mujer).

mantelete *m* mantelet, mantlet (fortificación).

mantenedor *m* president (en un torneo, juegos florales, etc.) ‖ *mantenedor de familia* breadwinner.

mantener* *vt* to feed, to sustain (alimentar); *mantener a uno con pan y agua* to feed s.o. on bread and water ‖ to maintain, to support; *mantener a una familia* to support a family ‖ to keep (a una mujer) ‖ to hold up, to support (sostener); *el muro mantiene el techo* the wall holds up the ceiling ‖ to keep; *mantener algo en equilibrio* to keep sth. balanced ‖ to keep in, to keep going (el fuego) ‖ FIG to support, to back (up), to stand up for, to stand by (apoyar a una persona, una idea) | to hold, to keep to, to maintain; *mantengo mi opinión* I maintain my opinion | to maintain, to affirm; *ella mantiene que...* she maintains that... | to keep up, to maintain (usos, reglas, amistades, etc.) | to keep; *mantener la ley, la paz* to keep the law, the peace ‖ to maintain, to keep (sth.) up (conservar en buen estado) ‖ to maintain, to defend, to uphold, to sustain; *mantener sus derechos* to maintain one's rights ‖ to hold (celebrar) ‖ to keep (conservar); *mantener la carne fresca* to keep the meat fresh; *mantener su rango social* to keep one's social status ‖ — *mantener a distancia* to keep at a distance ‖ *mantener al día* to keep up to date ‖ *mantener caliente* to keep (sth.) hot ‖ *mantener correspondencia con* to correspond with s.o., to be in correspondance with s.o. ‖ *mantener despierto a uno* to keep s.o. awake ‖ *mantener la neutralidad* to stay *o* to remain neutral ‖ *mantener los ojos cerrados* to keep one's eyes shut ‖ FIG *mantener una conversación* to hold a conversation, to keep up a conversation; *incapaz de mantener una conversación* incapable of keeping up a conversation; to hold an interview (celebrar una entrevista) | *mantener un cambio de impresiones, una entrevista* to have an exchange of ideas, an interview.
◆ *vpr* to feed o.s. (alimentarse) ‖ to live, to support o.s.; *se mantiene con su trabajo* he lives by his work ‖ to remain firm (en una posición, en una opinión, etc.) ‖ to hold o.s.; *mantenerse derecho* to hold o.s. straight ‖ to remain, to keep; *mantenerse tranquilo* to keep calm ‖ to remain the same *o* unchanged, to still hold *o* stand; *nuestro trato se mantendrá* our agreement will still stand ‖ — *mantenerse a distancia* to keep one's distance ‖ *mantenerse en contacto con* to keep in touch with, to keep in contact with ‖ *mantenerse en su puesto* to keep one's job (un trabajo), to know *o* to remember one's place (comportarse según su rango) ‖ *mantenerse en su sitio* to know *o* to remember one's place ‖ FIG & FAM *mantenerse en sus trece* to stick to one's guns, to stand one's ground ‖ *mantenerse firme* to stand firm, to hold one's ground ‖ *mantenerse serio* to keep *o* to remain serious.

mantenido, da *adj* kept (una persona).
◆ *f* kept woman.

mantenimiento *m* maintenance (subsistencia) ‖ sustenance (alimento) ‖ maintenance, upkeep; *el mantenimiento de una carretera, de una familia* the upkeep of a road, of a family ‖ maintenance, keeping; *el mantenimiento del orden* maintenance of order.

manteo *m* tossing (in a blanket) (manteamiento) ‖ long cloak *o* mantle (capa).

mantequera *f* dairywoman (persona) ‖ butter churn (máquina) ‖ butter dish (recipiente).

mantequería *f* creamery, dairy (tienda) ‖ dairy (fábrica) ‖ butter making (fabricación de la mantequilla).

mantequero, ra *adj* butter; *la industria mantequera* the butter industry.
◆ *m* dairyman (persona).

mantequilla *f* butter (manteca de vaca); *mantequilla fresca, salada* fresh, salted butter; *mantequilla derretida, requemada* melted, browned butter.

mantequillera *f* AMER → **mantequera.**

mantequillero *m* AMER dairyman (vendedor) | butter dish (recipiente).

mantilla *f* mantilla (de mujer) ‖ shawl (para los niños) ‖ trappings *pl*, caparison (del caballo) ‖ IMPR blanket.
◆ *pl* shawl *sing* ‖ — FIG *estar en mantillas* to be in one's infancy, to be in nappies [US to be in diapers] (un niño), to be in its infancy (empezar), to be in the dark, not to know anything (ignorar) ‖ FIG & FAM *ya he salido de mantillas* I wasn't born yesterday.

mantillo *m* vegetable mould, humus (capa del suelo) ‖ manure (estiércol).

mantisa *f* MAT mantissa.

manto *m* cloak, mantle (de mujer) ‖ shawl (chal) ‖ ceremonial robe (capa de ceremonia) ‖ mantel (de chimenea) ‖ MIN stratum (capa) ‖ ZOOL mantle (de los moluscos) ‖ FIG cover, cloak, mantle (lo que encubre); *bajo el manto de la indiferencia* under the cover of indifference ‖ FIG *tapar con un manto* to cover up.

mantón *m* shawl ‖ *mantón de Manila* embroidered silk shawl.

manual *adj* manual; *trabajo manual* manual labour *o* work ‖ manageable (manejable).
◆ *m* manual (libro) ‖ COM daybook (libro).

manubrio *m* crank (manivela) ‖ handle (mango) ‖ *piano de manubrio* street piano, hurdy-gurdy.

Manuel *npr m* Emmanuel.

manuela *f* open carriage.

manuelino *adj m* *estilo manuelino* architectural style prevalent in Portugal during the reign of Manuel I (1469-1521).

manufactura *f* factory, manufactory (fábrica) ‖ manufacture (fabricación) ‖ manufactured article.

manufacturado, da *adj* manufactured; *productos manufacturados* manufactured goods.

manufacturar *vt* to manufacture (fabricar).

manufacturero, ra *adj* manufacturing; *industria manufacturera* manufacturing industry.

manumisión *f* JUR manumission (del esclavo).

manumitir *vt* JUR to manumit, to emancipate.

manuscribir *vt* to write by hand.

manuscrito, ta *adj/sm* manuscript.

manutención *f* maintenance (mantenimiento); *la manutención de una familia* the maintenance of a family ‖ maintenance, upkeep (conservación).

manzana *f* apple (fruto) ‖ block (grupo de casas) ‖ pommel [of a sword] (de la espada) ‖ knob (adorno) ‖ AMER Adam's apple (nuez) ‖ — FIG & FAM *estar sano como una manzana, más sano que una manzana* to be as fit as a fiddle |

manzana de la discordia apple of discord | *manzana podrida* bad egg.

manzanar *m* apple orchard.

manzanilla *f* manzanilla (vino) || BOT manchineel berry (fruto) || chamomile, camomile (planta) || camomile tea (infusión) || manzanilla (aceituna) || pad, cushion (del pie de algunos mamíferos) || knob (adorno) || point of the chin (barba).

manzanillo *m* BOT manchineel (árbol) | manzanilla-olive tree (olivo).

manzano *m* BOT apple tree (árbol).

maña *f* skill, ability, know-how (habilidad) | cunning, astuteness (astucia) || bad habit (mala costumbre) || bunch (manojo) || — *darse maña para* to manage to, to contrive to || *más vale maña que fuerza* brain is better than brawn || *tener maña para* or *en hacer algo* to have the knack of doing sth., to be good at doing sth.

mañana *f* morning; *esta mañana* this morning; *a la mañana siguiente* the following morning; *estudio por la mañana* I study in the morning || — *a las tres de la mañana* at three o'clock in the morning, at three a. m. || *ayer mañana, ayer por la mañana* yesterday morning || *de la mañana a la noche* from morning to night || *de la noche a la mañana* overnight; *de la noche a la mañana ha cambiado* he has changed overnight; all night long, through the night; *leer de la noche a la mañana* to read all night long || *mañana por la mañana, por la noche* tomorrow morning, night || *tomar la mañana* to take a nip first thing in the morning (con aguardiente).
◆ *m* tomorrow, the future (futuro); *no pensar en el mañana* not to think about tomorrow.
◆ *adv* tomorrow; *mañana será domingo* tomorrow will be Sunday, it is Sunday tomorrow; *saldrá usted mañana mismo* you will leave tomorrow without fail || — *a partir de mañana* starting tomorrow, as from tomorrow || *de mañana* early (temprano), in the morning (por la mañana) || *de mañana en ocho días* a week tomorrow, tomorrow week || *el mundo de mañana* the world of tomorrow || *hasta mañana* see you tomorrow (fórmula de despedida) || *mañana será otro día* tomorrow is another day || *mañana, tarde y noche* morning, noon and night || *muy de mañana* very early || *no dejes para mañana lo que puedes hacer hoy* do not put off till tomorrow what you can do today || *pasado mañana* the day after tomorrow.
◆ *interj* we'll see!

mañanear *vi* to rise *o* to get up early.

mañanero, ra *adj* early-rising (madrugador).

mañanita *f* FAM daybreak, early morning || bed jacket (prenda de vestir).
◆ *pl* popular Mexican songs sung in honour of s.o. or sth.

maño, ña *m/f* FAM Aragonese.
◆ *m* AMER old man, old chap, my friend (expresión de cariño) | brother (hermano).
◆ *f* AMER my dear (expresión de cariño) | sister (hermana).

mañoco *m* tapioca || AMER Indian corn meal.
— OBSERV The Spanish for *manioc* is *mandioca*.

mañosamente *adv* skilfully, cleverly (con habilidad) || craftily (con astucia).

mañoso, sa *adj* skilful [US skillful], clever; *es un hombre muy mañoso* he is a very skilful man || clever, crafty, cunning (astuto) || AMER false, deceitful (falso) | balky, shy (que tiene resabios).

maoísmo *m* Maoism.

maoísta *m/f* Maoist.

maorí *adj/s* Maori.

mapa *m* map; *el mapa de España* the map of Spain; *mapa mudo* skeleton *o* blank map; *levantar un mapa* to draw up a map || — FIG & FAM *desaparecer del mapa* to disappear completely, to vanish from the face of the Earth | *esto no está en el mapa* this is way out *o* far out, I've never seen anything like this before | *hacer desaparecer una ciudad del mapa* to wipe a town off the map || *mapa físico* physical map || *mapa político* political map.
◆ *f* FAM best || FAM *llevarse la mapa* to top the lot, to be tops.

mapache; mapachín *m* ZOOL racoon (mamífero).

mapamundi *m* world map, map of the world || FAM backside, bottom, rear (nalgas).

Maputo *n pr* GEOGR Maputo.

maquear *vt* to lacquer || to varnish (barnizar) || FIG & FAM *estar bien maqueado* to be dressed up.
◆ *vpr* FAM to dress up (engalanarse).

maqueta *f* scale model, mock-up, maquette (boceto) || IMPR dummy (book).

maquetista *m/f* maquette maker.

maquiavélico, ca *adj* Machiavellian.

maquiavelismo *m* Machiavellianism, Machiavellism.

Maquiavelo *npr m* Machiavelli.

maquila *f* multure (tributo) || corn measure (para maquilar).

maquilar; maquilear *vt* to collect multure on.

maquilero *m* multurer.

maquillador, ra *m/f* makeup assistant.
◆ *f* makeup girl.

maquillaje *m* makeup (productos y arte de maquillarse) || making-up (acción) || *maquillaje de fondo* foundation.

maquillar *vt* to make up || FIG to falsify, to cover up (encubrir, falsificar).
◆ *vpr* to make o.s. up, to put one's makeup on (pintarse) || *no le gusta que me maquille* he doesn't like me to wear makeup.

máquina *f* machine; *máquina de sumar* adding machine || TEATR stage machinery (tramoya) || engine, locomotive (locomotora) || engine (motor) || bicycle, machine, bike (bicicleta) || car, automobile (coche) || camera (de fotografías) || INFORM machine; *lenguaje de máquina* machine language || FIG machine; *la máquina del Estado* the State machine | project, idea (proyecto) || — *a toda máquina* at full speed || MAR *cuarto* or *sala de máquinas* engine room || *entrar en máquina* to go to press [a newspaper]; *al entrar en máquina esta edición* as this edition goes to press || *escribir a máquina* to type || *escrito a máquina* typewritten || *forzar la máquina* to overwork the engine (motor), to overwork o.s. (una persona) || *hecho a máquina* machine-made || *máquina contabilizadora* or *contable* accounting machine || *máquina de afeitar eléctrica* electric razor || *máquina de calcular* calculator, calculating machine || *máquina de coser, de lavar, de volar* sewing, washing, flying machine || *máquina de escribir* typewriter || *máquina de vapor* steam engine || *máquina fotográfica* or *de fotografiar* or *de retratar* camera || *máquina herramienta* machine tool || *máquina herramienta de control numérico* numerically controlled machine tool || *máquina infernal* infernal machine || *máquina neumática* air pump || *máquina registradora* cash register || AMER FAM *máquina traganíqueles* slot machine, fruit machine || *máquina tragaperras* slot machine, fruit machine, one-armed bandit (de juego), slot machine, vending machine (expendedora automática).

maquinación *f* machination.

maquinador, ra *adj* machinating.
◆ *m/f* machinator || schemer, plotter (intrigante).

maquinal *adj* mechanical; *movimientos maquinales* mechanical movements.

maquinar *vt* to machinate, to plot.

maquinaria *f* machinery; *maquinaria agrícola* agricultural machinery || machinery, machines *pl* (conjunto de máquinas) || mechanism, workings *pl*; *conoce bien la maquinaria de este coche* he knows the mechanism of this car well || FIG machinery; *la maquinaria burocrática, administrativa* bureaucratic, administrative machinery.

maquinilla *f* small machine *o* device || MAR winch (chigre) || — *café de maquinilla* drip coffee || *maquinilla de afeitar* safety razor || *maquinilla eléctrica* electric shaver || *maquinilla para cortar el pelo* hair clippers *pl*.

maquinismo *m* mechanization.

maquinista *m* machinist, mechanic || engine driver, engineer (del tren) || TEATR stagehand.
◆ *f* machinist (costurera).

maquinizar *vt* to mechanize.

mar *m/f* sea; *mar interior* inland *o* landlocked sea; *mar Mediterráneo* Mediterranean Sea || swell (marejada) || — *al otro lado del mar* overseas || *alta mar* high seas, open sea; *en alta mar* on the high seas || FIG & FAM *arar en el mar* to plough the sands | *correr a mares* to stream, to flow; *el sudor corría a mares por su cara* the sweat streamed down his face; to flow freely; *el vino corría a mares* the wine flowed freely || *de alta mar* seagoing (barco), deep-water (pesca) || FIG & FAM *echar pelillos a la mar* to let bygones be bygones, to say no more about it, to bury the hatchet | *estamos la mar de bien aquí* it's great [US swell] here | *estar hecho un brazo de mar* to be dressed up to the nines, to be dressed to kill | *estar hecho un mar de lágrimas* to cry a sea of tears (persona), to be bathed in tears (cara) | *estar la mar de bien* to feel great (de salud), to look great (de aspecto), to be great (una película, un libro, etc.) || *golpe de mar* huge wave || FIG & FAM *hablar de la mar* to ask for the moon and stars || MAR *hacerse a la mar* to put to sea | *irse* or *hacerse mar adentro* to stand out to sea, to put to sea || FIG & FAM *la mar* loads, lots, hoards, swarms; *había la mar de niños* there were loads of children; loads, lots, stacks, no end; *la mar de trabajo* stacks of work; extremely, ever so, very; *es la mar de guapa* she is extremely pretty; very much, a lot, a hell of a lot; *me gusta la mar* I like it a lot | *la mar de bien* very well, awfully well, ever so well; *canta la mar de bien* he sings ever so well | *le sienta la mar de bien este vestido* this dress suits her to a tee *o* suits her down to the ground *o* looks great on her | *llover a mares* to rain cats and dogs, to rain buckets || *mar adentro* offshore, out to sea || *mar agitado* rough sea || *mar de arena* vast expanse *o* ocean of sand || *mar de fondo* ground swell (marejada), undercurrent of tension (tensión latente) || FIG *mar de sangre* bloodbath || *mar en bonanza* or *en calma* calm sea || *mar enfurecido* angry *o* raging *o* stormy sea || *mar gruesa* heavy sea || *mar picado, rizado* choppy sea || *por mar* by sea, by boat || FIG *quien no se arriesga no pasa la mar* nothing ventured, nothing gained.
— OBSERV The word *mar* is usually masculine in current speech (*the Red Sea* el mar Rojo) but feminine when used by fishermen and seamen and in expressions such as *la alta mar, la mar de cosas*, etc.

marabú *m* marabou, marabout (ave, plumas).

marabunta *f* plague of ants (plaga de hormigas) || FIG crowd (muchedumbre).

maraca *f* MÚS maraca.

maracucho, cha *adj* [of *o* from] Maracay.
◆ *m/f* native *o* inhabitant of Maracay.

maracure *m* vine from which curare is extracted.

maragatería *f* group of muleteers.

maragato, ta *adj/s* Maragaterian, from Maragateria [in the North of Spain].
◆ *m* muleteer (arriero).

maraña *f* thicket, brush (maleza) || BOT holm oak (encina) || FIG tangle, mess (confusión) | tangle (asunto intrincado) || — *¡qué maraña!* what a mess! || *una maraña de mentiras* a pack of lies || *una maraña de pelo* a mop of hair, a tangle of hair.

marasmo *m* MED marasmus || FIG apathy (apatía) | decline (disminución) | stagnation (estancamiento).

maratón *m* marathon (carrera).

maravedí *m* maravedi [coin].

maravilla *f* marvel; *éste es una maravilla* this one is a marvel || astonishment, amazement (asombro) || BOT marigold (flor anaranjada) | morning glory (flor azul) | marvel-of-Peru || — *a las mil maravillas, de maravilla* marvellously [US marvelously], wonderfully; *hablar a las mil maravillas* to speak wonderfully; *todo va de maravilla* everything is going marvellously || *contar* or *decir maravillas de* to speak wonderfully about (de personas o de cosas) || *hacer maravillas* to do *o* to work wonders; *hace maravillas con la guitarra, en el trapecio* he does wonders with a guitar, on the trapeze || *las siete maravillas del mundo* the seven wonders of the world || *¡qué maravilla!* marvellous! || *venirle a uno de maravilla* to be just what the doctor ordered.

maravillar *vt* to astonish, to amaze, to surprise (sorprender); *me maravilla su fracaso* his failure amazes me || to fill with admiration; *este cuadro maravilla a todos* this painting fills everyone with admiration || *quedarse maravillado* to marvel (*ante* at), to be amazed *o* astonished (*ante* at, by).
◆ *vpr* to marvel (*con* at), to wonder (*con* at), to be amazed (*con* at, by); *me maravillo con su paciencia* I marvel at his patience.

maravilloso, sa *adj* marvellous [US marvelous], wonderful (admirable).

marbete *m* label (etiqueta) || border, edge (borde) || FIG label, tag.

marca *f* mark, sign (señal) || trademark; *marca registrada* or *patentada* registered *o* patented trademark || make, brand; *¿qué marca compra Ud.?* what brand do you buy? || make; *¿de qué marca es su coche?* what make of car has he got? || scar, mark (cicatriz) || brand (con hierro candente) || branding (acción); *la marca del ganado* the branding of cattle || measuring stick (talla) || DEP record; *batir* or *mejorar una marca* to break *o* to beat a record | score (resultado) || march (provincia fronteriza) || MAR landmark || — *de marca* outstanding; *producto, personaje de marca* outstanding product, person || FIG & FAM *de marca mayor* first-class (excelente), huge, voluminous (muy grande o voluminoso), first-class; *un imbécil de marca mayor* a first-class idiot; enormous; *una tontería de marca mayor* an enormous blunder || *marca de fábrica* trademark || *papel de marca* foolscap paper.

Marca *npr f* GEOGR Marche.

marcadamente *adv* markedly, noticeably || *habla con un acento marcadamente español* he speaks with a marked *o* a noticeable Spanish accent.

marcado, da *adj* marked.
◆ *m* marking || setting (del cabello).

marcador, ra *adj* marking || branding (del ganado).
◆ *m* IMPR feeder || inspector (contraste de pesos y medidas) || scoreboard (deportes); *marcador simultáneo* simultaneous scoreboard || brander (del ganado) || marker (lápiz) || — DEP *abrir* or *hacer funcionar* or *inaugurar el marcador* to open the scoring | *adelantarse* or *ponerse por delante en el marcador* to go ahead in the scoring || *ir por delante en el marcador* to be ahead in the scoring || *marcador de votos* vote counter.

marcaje *m* marking (deportes).

marcar *vt* to mark; *marcar la ropa* to mark the clothes || to brand (el ganado); *marcar con hierro* or *a fuego* to brand with an iron || DEP to mark; *marcar a un contrario* to mark an opposing player | to score; *marcar un gol* or *un tanto* to score a goal (fútbol); *marcar una canasta* to score a basket (baloncesto) || to dial (un número de teléfono) || MAR to take (bearings) || to underline, to mark (subrayar, destacar) || to indicate, to show, to mark, to point to; *las agujas del reloj marcan las tres* the hands of the clock indicate three o'clock || to score (un punto en una discusión) || to show, to register, to record (el termómetro, el barómetro, etc.) || to mark out *o* off (delimitar un terreno) || to mark; *la Revolución Francesa marcó el comienzo de una nueva época* the French Revolution marked the beginning of a new era || to assign, to set; *el maestro marcó la lección para el día siguiente* the teacher assigned the lesson for the following day || to single out (destacar) || to mark (poner el precio) || to bid (los naipes) || to set (el pelo) || IMPR to feed || — *marcar el compás* to mark the rhythm, to beat time (con la mano o la batuta), to keep time (bailando, cantando) || MIL *marcar el paso* to mark time || *marcar el pelo* or *las ondas* to have one's hair set || *marcar las cartas* to mark the cards.
◆ *vi* to make a mark || DEP to score (un tanto) | to mark || to dial (en el teléfono).
◆ *vpr* to score (apuntarse un tanto) || — *marcarse un detalle* to make a nice gesture.

marcasita *f* MIN marcasite (pirita).

marceño, ña *adj* march.

marcial *adj* martial; *ley marcial* martial law || military; *porte marcial* military air || martial, chalybeate (que contiene hierro); *medicamento marcial* chalybeate medicine.

marcialidad *f* military air.

marciano, na *adj/s* Martian (de Marte).

marco *m* frame (de un cuadro, de una puerta o de una ventana) || FIG framework; *dentro del marco de* within the framework of | setting (lugar); *celebrar algo en un marco adecuado* to celebrate sth. in an appropriate setting || standard (patrón) || mark (moneda alemana) || mark (moneda de oro) || mark (medida antigua de peso) || goalpost (en deportes).

Marco *npr m* Marcus, Mark || — *Marco Antonio* Mark Antony || *Marco Aurelio* Marcus Aurelius.

Marcos *npr m* Mark.

marcha *f* march; *organizar una marcha de protesta* to organize a protest march; *en marcha* on the march (soldados) || MÚS march; *marcha fúnebre, nupcial* funeral, wedding march || departure (salida); *¿a qué hora es la marcha?* what time is the departure? || march, course (paso); *la marcha de los acontecimientos* the course of events || progress (progreso) || running; *la buena marcha de un negocio* the smooth running of a business || walking (deportes); *marcha atlética* walking race || functioning, working, operation, running (de una máquina) || speed (velocidad) || AUT gear (cambio de velocidades); *marcha directa, atrás* top, reverse gear || — *abrir la marcha* to be first || *a marchas forzadas* at a rapid pace, against the clock; *trabajar a marchas forzadas* to work against the clock || *a toda marcha* at full speed || *avanzar a buena marcha* to advance rapidly || *cerrar la marcha* to bring up the rear || *coger la marcha* to get the hang of it, to get into the swing of things || *dar marcha atrás* to reverse (un coche), to change one's mind (volverse atrás); *a última hora ha dado marcha atrás* at the last moment he changed his mind || *¡en marcha!* let's go (vamos), forward march! (militar) || *estar en marcha* to be underway (barco), to be on the move (progresar), to be running, to be working (funcionar) || MAR & TECN *la marcha de un motor* the running of a motor || *marcha atrás* reverse (gear); *meter la marcha atrás* to change *o* to go into reverse || *marcha forzada* forced march || *marcha moderada* slow down (señal de tráfico) || *Marcha Real* national anthem in Spain || *poner en marcha* to start (up) (un motor, un mecanismo) || *ponerse en marcha* to start (off) || *sobre la marcha* on the way, as one goes along.

marchador, ra *adj/m* DEP walker.

marchamar *vt* to mark, to stamp (en las aduanas).

marchamo *m* stamp, mark, seal (señal de las aduanas) || FIG mark; *un marchamo de elegancia* a mark of elegance || AMER duty charged for each head of cattle killed in the slaughterhouse || *un disparo con marchamo de gol* a shot which looked like a goal all the way.

marchante, ta *m/f* merchant, dealer || customer (parroquiano).

marchapié *m* MAR footrope.

marchar *vi* to go, to walk (andar) || to move (moverse) || MIL to march || to go, to work (funcionar); *el reloj no marcha* the clock isn't going || FIG to operate; *un negocio que marcha bien* a business that is operating well | to go (ir); *todo marcha bien* everything is going well || — FIG *marchar sobre ruedas* or *rieles* to run like clockwork || MIL *¡marchen!* forward march!
◆ *vpr* to go away, to leave; *¿se marchan?* are you leaving?; *se marchó a otro lugar* he went somewhere else, he left for another place || *marcharse por las buenas* to disappear (desaparecer), to leave for good (para no volver más).

marchitamiento *m* withering, wilting, fading.

marchitar *vt* to wither, to wilt, to shrivel, to fade (las flores, la hermosura).
◆ *vpr* to wither, to wilt, to shrivel, to fade.

marchitez *f* wilted *o* withered state *o* condition.

marchito, ta *adj* withered, wilted, faded.

marea *f* tide; *marea creciente, menguante* rising, ebb tide || sea breeze (viento) || dew (rocío) || drizzle (llovizna) || FIG flood (gran cantidad); *una marea humana* a flood of people | tide || — FIG *contra viento y marea* through *o* come hell and high water, against all odds || *está alta, baja la marea* it is high, low tide || *marea alta, baja* high, low tide *o* water || *marea entrante* or *ascendente* incoming *o* rising tide || *marea negra* oil slick || *marea saliente* or *descendente* outgoing tide, ebb tide || *marea viva* spring tide *o* water.

mareado, da *adj* sick (malo); *estoy mareado* I feel sick || seasick (en el mar) || drunk (bebido) || dizzy (aturdido).

mareaje *m* navigation, seamanship || course (rumbo del navío).

mareante *adj* nauseating, sickening (que marea) || sailing (navegante) || FIG & FAM boring; *una conversación mareante* a boring conversation | bothersome (molesto).
◆ *m* navigator.

marear *vt* MAR to navigate || to make feel sick, to upset one's stomach; *ese perfume me marea* that perfume makes me feel sick || to

make sick, to make feel seasick; *el movimiento del barco me marea* the movement of the ship makes me sick || FIG & FAM to annoy, to bother (molestar, fastidiar) | to make (s.o.) dizzy; *me mareas con tantas preguntas* you make me dizzy with so many questions || CULIN to cook over a fire in butter or oil (rehogar) || *aguja de marear* compass (brújula).
◆ *vpr* to be *o* to feel sick (tener náuseas) || to be *o* to get seasick (en un barco) || to get *o* to become dizzy (estar aturdido) || FAM to get a bit drunk (emborracharse un poco) || *me mareo con tanto ruido* all this noise makes me dizzy.

marejada *f* swell (del mar) || FIG excitement, agitation (agitación) | wave (oleada) | rumour (rumor) | undercurrent (de descontento).

maremagno; mare mágnum *m* FIG & FAM crowd, multitude (de personas) | ocean, sea (cosas).

maremoto *m* seaquake.

marengo *adj/s* dark grey (color) || CULIN *a la marengo* fricassee (en pepitoria).

mareo *m* sickness, nausea || seasickness (en un barco) || dizziness, vertigo || FIG & FAM bother, annoyance, nuisance (molestia).

mareógrafo *m* marigraph, mareograph.

mareomotor, triz *adj* tidal || *central mareomotriz* tidal power plant.

marfil *m* ivory || — *marfil vegetal* ivory nut || *negro de marfil* ivory black || FIG *torre de marfil* ivory tower.

marfileño, ña *adj* ivory || [of *o* from] the Ivory Coast.

marga *f* MIN marl, loam.

margal *m* marlpit.

margar *vt* AGR to marl.

margarina *f* margarine.

margarita *f* daisy (flor), marguerite (con flores grandes) || margarite pearl (perla) || ZOOL mollusc (molusco) | shellfish (concha cualquiera) || — FIG *deshojar la margarita* to play «she loves me, she loves me not» || FIG & FAM *echar margaritas a los cerdos* or *puercos* to cast pearls before swine.

Margarita *npr f* Margaret.

margen *m/f* margin (de una página); *dejar margen* to leave a margin || border, edge (borde) || marginal note (apostilla) || bank, side (de un río), margin, verge, side (de un camino), edge, border (de un campo) || FIG margin; *margen de error, de seguridad* margin of error, safety margin | margin, latitude (libertad); *dejarle margen a uno* to allow s.o. some margin | opportunity (oportunidad) | pretext, motive, cause, occasion (pretexto) || COM margin, mark-up; *margen de ganancias* profit margin, margin of profit || — *al margen* in the margin; *firmar al margen* to sign in the margin; on the fringe; *vivir al margen de la sociedad* to live on the fringe of society || FIG *dar margen para* to give occasion for (ocasión) | *dejar al margen a uno* to leave s.o. out | *mantenerse al margen* to keep out, to stand aside, to remain on the sidelines | *por un escaso margen* by a narrow margin, narrowly.

— OBSERV The gender of *margen* varies according to its meaning, it is generally masculine when denoting the space around the text of a page, and feminine when it means the bank of a river, etc.

marginación *f* exclusion; *marginación social* social exclusion.

marginado, da *adj* on the fringe.
◆ *m/f* dropout.

marginador *m* IMPR marginal stop.

marginal *adj* marginal; *tecla marginal* marginal stop.

marginalismo *m* marginalism.

marginar *vt* to margin, to leave a margin *o* margins on || to margin, to write notes in the margin *o* margins of (anotar al margen).

margoso, sa *adj* marly, loamy.

margrave *m* margrave || *mujer del margrave* margravine.

margraviato *m* margraviate.

marguera *f* marlpit (cantera), marl deposit (depósito).

María *npr f* Mary, Maria || AMER FAM Indian woman in the City of Mexico.

mariache; mariachi *m* AMER «mariachi» [popular music characteristic of the state of Jalisco, in Mexico, and the band that plays it].

marial *adj* Marian, containing canticles to the Virgin Mary (libro).

Mariana *npr f* Marian, Marianne, Marion.

Marianas *npr fpl* GEOGR *islas Marianas* Mariana Islands.

marianista *adj/s* marianist.

mariano, na *adj* Marian, of the Virgin Mary.

marica *f* magpie (urraca).
◆ *m* FIG & FAM pansy, fairy (homosexual).

Maricastaña *npr f* *en tiempos de Maricastaña* in the days of good Queen Bess, in days of yore || *del tiempo de Maricastaña* as old as the hills.

maricón *m* POP queer, puff (sodomita).

mariconada *f* POP sissy thing to do (tontería) || dirty trick (jugarreta).

mariconera *f* man's handbag.

mariconería *f* POP homosexualism.

maridaje *m* married life || FIG harmony, close relationship (armonía) | close understanding (entre personas) | unnatural alliance (contubernio).

maridar *vi* to marry (casarse) || to live together as husband and wife, to cohabit (sin estar casados).
◆ *vt* FIG to marry (unir, armonizar).

marido *m* husband.

mariguana; marihuana; marijuana *f* marijuana.

marimacho *m* FAM mannish woman.

marimandona *f* domineering woman, termagant, battle-axe (*fam*).

marimba *f* sort of drum (tambor) || AMER marimba (xilofón) | kettledrum (tímpano) | trashing, drubbing (paliza) | cowardly cock (gallo).

marimoños *f inv* FAM flirt, coquette.

marimorena *f* FAM row, squabble || FAM *armar la marimorena* to kick up a hell of a row.

marina *f* seacoast (costa) || seascape, seapiece, marine (cuadro) || navy, marine; *marina mercante* merchant navy || seamanship (arte de navegar) || — *de marina* nautical || *Infantería de Marina* marines *pl* || *Marina de guerra* Navy || *Ministerio de Marina* Admiralty [US Department of the Navy] || *Ministro de Marina* First Lord of the Admiralty [US Secretary of the Navy] || *oficial de Marina* naval officer || *servir en la marina* to serve in the Navy.

marinar *vt* to marinate, to marinade (escabechar) || MAR to man (tripular).

marinear *vi* to be a sailor.

marinera *f* —→ **marinero.**

marinería *f* crew (tripulación de un barco) || seamen *pl*, sailors *pl* (marineros) || sailoring (profesión).

marinero, ra *adj* seaworthy; *barco marinero* seaworthy ship || seaboard; *pueblo marinero* seaboard town || (of the) sea; *cuentos marineros* tales of the sea || sailor's, sailors'; *traje marinero* sailor's costume.
◆ *m* sailor, seaman, mariner || argonaut (molusco) || — FIG *marinero de agua dulce* landlubber, poor sailor || *traje de marinero* sailor's costume.
◆ *f* middy blouse (blusa de niño) || midly blouse, sailor blouse (de mujer) || AMER marinera [popular dance] || — *a la marinera* sailor-fashion (como los marineros) || *salsa, pescado a la marinera* matelote.

marinismo *m* marinism (preciosismo).

marinista *adj* seascape, marine.
◆ *m/f* seascapist.

marino, na *adj* marine; *vegetación marina* marine vegetation || sea; *brisa marina* sea breeze || *azul marino* navy blue.
◆ *m* sailor, seaman; *marino mercante* merchant seaman || nautics expert (experto en náutica).

marioneta *f* marionette, puppet (títere).
◆ *pl* puppet show *sing* (pantomima).

mariposa *f* butterfly (insecto) || variety of finch (ave) || TECN butterfly *o* wing nut (tuerca) || lamp (lamparilla) || AMER blindman's buff (juego) || — *braza mariposa* butterfly (natación) || *mariposa nocturna* moth.

mariposeador, ra *adj* inconsistent, fickle, always chopping and changing (inconstante) || flirtatious (galanteador) || always hovering around (que está dando vueltas).
◆ *m/f* chopper and changer || flirt (galanteador).

mariposear *vi* FIG to chop and change (ser inconstante) | to flirt (galantear) | to hover around (dar vueltas).

mariposón *m* FAM Romeo, flirt (galanteador) | pansy (marica).

mariquita *f* ladybird [US ladybug] (coleóptero) || bug (hemíptero) || parakeet (perico) || AMER popular dance (danza).
◆ *m* FAM sissy, cissy, pansy (afeminado) || FAM *mariquita azúcar* sissy.

marisabidilla *f* FAM bluestocking.

mariscal *m* MIL marshal || *mariscal de campo* field marshal.

mariscala *f* marshal's wife.

mariscalato *m*; **mariscalía** *f* marshalship.

mariscador *m* shellfisherman.

mariscar *vt* to fish for (shellfish).

marisco *m* shellfish, seafood.

marisma *f* salt marsh.
◆ *pl* *Las Marismas* marshy region at the mouth of the Guadalquivir.

marismeño, ña *adj* marsh.

marisquería *f* shellfish bar *o* restaurant.

marisquero, ra *m/f* shellfisherman, shellfisherwoman || shellfish seller (vendedor).

marista *adj/s* Marist (religioso).

marital *adj* marital || husband's; *autorización marital* husband's authorization || *vida marital* married life.

marítimo, ma *adj* maritime, sea; *navegación marítima* maritime navigation || seaboard (pueblo, etc.) || shipping, seaborne (comercio) || harbour (estación) || — *arsenal marítimo* naval dockyard || *seguro marítimo* marine insurance.

maritornes *f* FIG & FAM sluttish servant.

marjal *m* marsh, bog.

marjoleta *f* hawthorn berry, haw.

marjoleto *m* hawthorn.

marketing *m* marketing.

marmita *f* (cooking) pot (olla) || pressure cooker (para guisar a presión).

marmitón *m* kitchen hand, cook's help, scullion (ant) (pinche de cocina).

mármol *m* marble; *esculpido en mármol* sculpted in marble || marble (escultura) || — *cantera de mármol* marble quarry || FIG *de mármol* stony-hearted, as cold as marble.

marmolería *f* marbles *pl*, marblework (conjunto de mármoles) || marble (obra) || marble-cutter's workshop (taller).

marmolillo *m* spur stone (guardacantón) || FIG idiot, dolt (idiota) || TAUR indolent bull.

marmolista *m* marble cutter (el que labra) || marble dealer (vendedor).

marmóreo, a *adj* marmoreal.

marmota *f* ZOOL marmot (mamífero) || worsted cap (gorro) || FIG & FAM sleepyhead (dormilón) | charwoman, maid (criada) || *dormir como una marmota* to sleep like a log *o* soundly.

maro *m* BOT cap thyme, marum.

maroma *f* (thick) rope || MAR cable || *AMER* tightrope walking.

maromear *vi* *AMER* to perform on the tightrope || FIG to sit on the fence.

maromo *m* FAM man friend.

maronita *adj/s* Maronite.

marplatense *adj/s* [of *o* from] Mar del Plata [Republic of Argentina].

◆ *m/f* native *o* inhabitant of Mar del Plata.

marqués *m* marquis, marquess (título) || *los marqueses* the marquis and marquise.

marquesa *f* marquise, marchioness (título) || easy chair (sillón) || — *dárselas de marquesa* to put on airs || *marquesa de vidrio* glass canopy [*US* marquee].

marquesado *m* marquisate, marquessate.

marquesina *f* canopy (cobertizo) || *marquesina de cristales* glass canopy [*US* marquee].

marquesita *f* MIN marcasite (marcasita).

marquetería *f* marquetry, marqueterie, inlaid work || *especialista en marquetería* specialist in marquetry, inlayer.

marquista *m* proprietor of one or more brands of wine.

marra *f* gap, space (espacio) || lack (falta) || stone hammer (almádena).

marrajo, ja *adj* mean, vicious (toro) || FIG shrewd, cunning (malicioso).

◆ *m* shark (tiburón).

marrana *f* sow (hembra del cerdo) || FIG & FAM slut, trollop, slattern (sucia, indecente) || TECN axle (de una noria).

marranada; marranería *f* FIG & FAM dirty *o* filthy *o* foul *o* rotten trick (cochinada) || filthy *o* mucky *o* grubby thing (cosa suciamente hecha) || *este cuarto está hecho una marranada* this room is like a pigsty.

marrano, na *adj* filthy, dirty.

◆ *m* hog (cerdo) || FIG & FAM swine (mala persona) | pig, slob (sucio) || piece securing drum to axle (de noria) || pressure-distributing board [in oil mills] (de una prensa) || timber supporting the bottom part of a well (de pozo) || HIST «Marrano» [converted Jew] (judío).

marrar *vi* to miss (errar) || to turn out badly, to fail (fallar); *ha marrado el proyecto* the project has failed || FIG to deviate, to branch off (desviarse) || *marrar el tiro* to miss; *marrar el tiro a una liebre* to miss a hare.

marras (de) *loc adv* FAM long ago (de antes) || in question; *el asunto, el individuo de marras* the matter, the individual in question || *el cuento de marras* the same old story.

marrasquino *m* maraschino (licor).

marrón *adj* brown (color) || pseudo-amateur, sham amateur (deportista).

◆ *m* brown (color).

marroquí *adj/s* Moroccan.

◆ *m* Morocco leather (tafilete).

— OBSERV pl *marroquíes*.

marroquín *m* Morocco leather (tafilete).

marroquinería *f* Morocco-leather dressing (preparación) || Morocco-leather tannery (taller) || leather goods *pl* (artículos de cuero) || leather goods store (tienda) || leather goods industry (industria).

marroquinero *m* Morocco-leather dresser (tafiletero).

marrubio *m* BOT marrubium (p us) hore-hound.

Marruecos *npr m* GEOGR Morocco.

marrullería *f* cajolery.

marrullero, ra *adj* cajoling, artful.

◆ *m/f* cajoler.

Marsella *n pr* GEOGR Marseilles.

marsopa; marsopla *f* porpoise (cetáceo).

marsupial *adj/sm* marsupial.

marta *f* ZOOL marten (mamífero) || sable (piel) || *marta cebellina* sable.

Marte *npr m* Mars (planeta) || Mars (dios).

martelo *m* jealousy (celos) | love, passion (amor).

martes *m inv* Tuesday (día); *vendrá el martes* he will come on Tuesday; *viene el martes, cada martes* he comes on Tuesday, every Tuesday || — *el martes pasado, que viene* last, next Tuesday || FIG *el martes ni te cases ni te embarques* never undertake anything on a Tuesday [an unlucky day like Friday in England] || *martes de Carnaval* Shrove Tuesday.

martiano, na; martiniano, na *adj* of José Martí [Cuban writer and hero].

martillada *f* hammer blow.

martillador *m* hammersmith, hammerer.

martillar *vt* to hammer || FIG to torment || — FIG *martillar en hierro frío* to bang one's head against a brick wall | *martillar los oídos* to hammer *o* to pound on one's ears.

martillazo *m* blow with a hammer || *a martillazos* with a hammer.

martillear *vt* to hammer || FIG *martillear los oídos* to hammer *o* to pound on one's ears.

◆ *vi* to knock (un motor).

martilleo *m* hammering || hammering (bombardeo intenso) || FIG pounding (ruido).

martillero *m* *AMER* auctioneer.

martillo *m* hammer (herramienta) || tuning hammer (templador) || hammer, striker (reloj) || ANAT malleus, hammer (del oído interno) || DEP hammer || ZOOL hammer-head shark (tiburón) || gavel (de presidente de sesión) || FIG one armed cross of the Order of St. John || auction room (para subastas) || *a martillo* with a hammer, by hammering || *martillo de fragua* blacksmith's hammer || *martillo de herrador* shoeing hammer || *martillo de picapedrero* stone hammer, braying hammer || *martillo de remachar* riveting hammer || *martillo neumático* air hammer, pneumatic drill || *martillo pilón* drop *o* steam hammer.

Martín *npr m* Martin || *día de San Martín* Martinmas.

martín del río *m* ZOOL heron.

martín pescador *m* ZOOL kingfisher.

martinete *m* ZOOL heron (ave) | heron plumes *pl* (penacho) || hammer (de piano) || TECN drop hammer (martillo pilón) | pile driver (para clavar estacas) || Andalusian song (cante).

martingala *f* martingale (en el juego) || FIG trick (artimaña).

◆ *pl* breeches worn under armour.

martiniano, na *adj* → **martiano.**

Martinica (La) *npr f* GEOGR Martinique.

mártir *m/f* martyr || — *capilla de mártires* martyry, shrine || FIG *dárselas de mártir* to make a martyr of o.s.

martirio *m* martyrdom.

martirizador, ra *adj* martyring, persecuting.

◆ *m* tormentor, torturer, persecutor.

martirizar *vt* to martyr, to martyrize (hacer sufrir martirio) || FIG to torture, to torment, to martyrize (hacer padecer).

martirologio *m* martyrology (lista de mártires).

marusiño, ña *adj/s* Galician.

marxismo *m* Marxism (doctrina); *marxismo-leninismo* Marxism-Leninism.

marxista *adj/s* Marxist.

marzo *m* March; *el 17 de marzo de 1915* 17th March 1915.

mas *conj* but (pero).

◆ *m* farm.

— OBSERV The conjunction *mas* bears no written accent.

más *adv* more; *no te digo más* I shall say no more; *tengo más trabajo que él* I have more work to do than he; *escribe más rápidamente que su hermana* he writes more quickly than his sister; *¿quieres más sopa?* do you want more soup *o* any more soup?; *este coche es más caro que ése* this car is more expensive than that one; *nos trajeron más armas* they brought us more arms (véase OBSERV I) || most (superlativo); *el chico más listo de la clase* the most intelligent boy in the class (véase OBSERV II) || over, more than (con un número); *tengo más de cien libras* I have over a hundred pounds *o* more than a hundred pounds || MAT plus, and; *dos más dos son cuatro* two plus two are *o* make four || after, past (con la hora); *son más de las nueve* it is after nine, it is past nine || more of a (con sustantivo); *es más coche* it is more of a car; *más hombre* more of a man || another, more (después de un sustantivo); *un kilómetro más* another kilometre, one more kilometre; *deme dos botellas más* give me two more bottles *o* another two bottles || longer; *quédate un poco más* stay a little longer; *durar más* to last longer || FAM so; *¡estaba más contento!* he was so happy!; *¡es más buena!* she is so kind! || as (tan); *es más pobre que las ratas* he is as poor as a church mouse; *más blanco que la nieve* as white as snow || (not translated); *¡qué manera más extraña de comer!* what a strange way to eat! || *a lo más* at the most, at most || *a más, a más de* besides, in addition || *a más correr* at full speed || *a más no poder* as much (fast, hard, etc.) as possible *o* as can be *o* as one can; *están trabajando a más no poder* they are working as hard as can be; *correr a más no poder* to run as fast as possible; *es tonto a más no poder* he is as silly as can be; *comimos a más no poder* we ate as much as we could || *a más tardar* at the latest || *a más y mejor* a lot, a great deal (mucho) || *cada vez más* more and more || *como el que más* as well as anyone, as well as the next man || *cuando más* at the most || *cuanto más... más* the more... the more || *cuanto más... menos* the more... the less || *de más* extra, spare (que sobra); *traje uno de más por si acaso* I brought an extra one just in case; too much, too many (demasiado); *me has dado veinte de más* you have given me twenty too many; unnecessary, superfluous (superfluo), out of place (poco apto) || *de más en más* more and more || *el más allá* the beyond || *el que más y el que menos* or *cual más cual menos* or *quien más quien menos sabe algo de matemáticas, tiene sus debilidades* we all have some knowledge of mathematics, our weaknesses || *en lo más mínimo* in the least, in the slightest, at all || *es más* mo-

reover, furthermore || — *estaban gritando a cuál más* they were trying to outshout each other || *estar de más* to be in the way (estorbar), not to be needed (innecesario) || *gustar más* to prefer, to like better; *me gusta más el pavo que el pollo* I prefer turkey to chicken || *las más de las veces* usually, most times, more often than not || *lo más* at the most, at most (a lo más) || *lo más posible* as much as possible || *lo más tarde* at the latest || *más adelante* further on || *más allá de* beyond, past, further than || *más aún* still more, even more || *más bien* rather || *más de, más de lo que* more than || *más de la cuenta* too much || *más de lo regular* more than usual || FAM *¡más lo eres tú!* you too!, the same to you! || *más o menos* more or less || *más que nunca* more than ever || *más tarde o más temprano* sooner or later || *más vale tarde que nunca* better late than never || *más y más* more and more || *mientras más... más* the more... the more || *mucho más* much more, a lot more || *nadie más* nobody else || *ni más ni menos* no more, no less (exactamente), quite simply (simplemente) || *no más* only; *me dio dos pesetas no más* he only gave me two pesetas; *ayer no más* only yesterday; as soon as, no sooner, just; *no más hubo llegado que* as soon as he arrived..., no sooner had he arrived than..., he had just arrived when; no more, that is enough (basta); *¡no más gritos!* no more shouting!; quite simply; *le dijo no más que era un negado* he quite simply told him he was useless; please, do (en América); *sírvese no más* please help yourself; *siéntese no más* do sit down || *no... más* no more, not any more; *no quiero más* I want no more, I don't want any more || *no más de* no more than || *no... más que* only, all, no more than; *no quiero más que veinte libras por semana* I only want twenty pounds a week, all I want is twenty pounds a week, I want no more than twenty pounds a week || *no veo más solución que* I see no other solution than || *poco más o menos* more or less || *poder más* to be stronger than, to prevail, to triumph; *el amor pudo más que el odio* love triumphed over hate || *por más* (con sustantivo), whatever, no matter what; *por más esfuerzos que hagas* whatever efforts you may make || *por más* (con adjetivo o adverbio), however, no matter how; *por más robusto que sea* no matter how strong he may be || *por más que* (con verbo), no matter how much, however much; *por más que trabajase, nunca saldría de pobre* no matter how much he were to work, he would never escape poverty; however fast, (hard, etc.); *por más que corra* however fast he runs || *¿qué más?* what else? || *¿qué más da?* what difference does it make? || *sin más, sin más ni más* without more ado, without further ado || *tanto más* the more, all the more || *tanto más... cuanto que* all the more... since o because || *todo lo más* at (the) most (como mucho), at the latest (como muy tarde) || *una vez más* one more time, once more, once again || *valer más* to be better; *más vale hacerlo enseguida* it is better to do it straight away || *y lo que es más* and furthermore || *¿y qué más?* and then what?
◆ *m* MAT plus (signo) || — *hubo sus más y sus menos* there was a clash of opinion (en una discusión) || *los más* most people || *los más de, las más de* the majority of, most; *las más de las mujeres* the majority of women, most women || *tener sus más y sus menos* to have one's *o* its difficulties (tener sus dificultades).

— OBSERV La mayoría de los adjetivos ingleses toman una forma comparativa: *este coche es más caro que ése* this car is dearer than that one; *mi casa es más bonita que la tuya* my house is nicer than yours.

— OBSERV La mayoría de los adjetivos ingleses toman una forma superlativa: *el chico más listo de la clase* the cleverest boy in the class; *el vino más seco que conozco* the driest wine I know.

masa *f* dough (del pan) || mortar, plaster (argamasa) || FÍS mass; *el gramo es una unidad de masa* the gram is a unit of mass || mass (cantidad, conjunto); *una masa de nieve, de nubes* a mass of snow, of clouds; *una masa gaseosa* a gaseous mass || masses *pl* (gente); *el control del país está en manos de la masa* or *de las masas* control of the country is in the hands of the masses || total; *la masa de bienes* the total fortune | ELECTR earth [US ground] || AMER cake, bun (pastelito) || — *de masas* mass; *medios de comunicación de masas* mass media || *llevar en la masa de la sangre* to have in one's blood (algo), to have got in one's blood (alguien) || *en masa* en masse; *llegaron en masa* they arrived en masse; mass; *manifestación en masa* mass demonstration || *masa coral* choir, chorale || FÍS *masa crítica* critical mass || *producción en masa* mass production.

masacre *m* massacre.

— OBSERV This word is a Gallicism used for *matanza*.

masada *f* farm.

masaje *m* massage || — *dar masajes a* to massage || *hacerse dar masajes* to have o.s. massaged.

masajista *m/f* masseur (hombre), masseuse (mujer).

mascabado, da *adj* muscovado, unrefined (azúcar).
◆ *m* muscovado.

mascada *f* AMER quid (de tabaco) | silk neckerchief (pañuelo) | chewing (mascadura).

mascadura *f* chewing, mastication.

mascar *vt* to chew, to masticate (masticar) || FIG & FAM to mumble (mascullar) || — FIG & FAM *dárselo todo mascado a uno* to hand it to s.o. on a spoon | *estar mascando tierra* to be pushing up daisies.
◆ *vi* to chew.

máscara *f* mask; *máscara antigás* gas mask || INFORM mask || FIG mask, pretence || masked figure, mask, masker (persona disfrazada con una máscara) || — INFORM *máscara de pantalla* screen form *o* format || *quitar la máscara a* to unmask || *quitarse la máscara* to unmask o.s., to take off one's mask, to reveal o.s. || *traje de máscara* fancy dress.
◆ *pl* masquerade *sing*, masked ball *sing* (fiesta).

mascarada *f* masquerade, masked ball, masque || FIG masquerade.

mascarilla *f* half mask || death mask (que se saca de un cadáver) || face mask (de cirujano) || face pack (de belleza) || mask (de oxígeno).

mascarita *f* small mask || FIG *te conozco mascarita aunque vengas disfrazada* it's easy to see what your little game is.

mascarón *m* large mask || ARQ mascaron, grotesque mask (adorno) || MAR *mascarón de proa* figurehead.

Mascate *n pr* GEOGR Muscat.

mascota *f* mascot.

mascujar *vt* → **mascullar.**

masculillo *m* bumping (juego de chicos) || FIG & FAM thwack, blow (porrazo).

masculinidad *f* masculinity, manliness.

masculinizar *vt* GRAM to make masculine || to make mannish (a una mujer).

masculino, na *adj* male; *un individuo del sexo masculino* a person of the male sex; *los órganos masculinos de una flor* the male organs of a flower || masculine, manly (propio de los hombres); *una característica masculina* a manly characteristic; *un color masculino* a masculine colour || mannish, masculine (mujer) || *ropa masculina* men's clothing.
◆ *adj/sm* GRAM masculine.

mascullar; mascujar *vt* to chew with difficulty, to chew badly (mascar mal) || to mumble, to mutter (pronunciar indistintamente).

maser *m* FÍS maser.

masera *f* trough (artesa) || type of crab (cangrejo).

masetero *m* ANAT masseter (músculo).

masía *f* farm (granja).

masilla *f* putty || *fijar con masilla* to putty.

masita *f* MIL uniform money.

masivo, va *adj* massive; *dosis masiva* massive dose || *manifestación masiva* mass *o* massive demonstration.

maslo *m* dock (tronco de la cola de un animal) || stem (de una planta).

masón *m* Mason, Freemason.

masonería *f* Masonry, Freemasonry.

masónico, ca *adj* Masonic; *logia masónica* Masonic lodge.

masoquismo *m* masochism.

masoquista *adj* masochistic.
◆ *m/f* masochist.

massé *m* massé (billar).

mastaba *f* mastaba (tumba).

mastalgia *f* MED mastalgia.

mastectomía *f* MED mastectomy.

mastelerillo *m* MAR topgallant mast || — *mastelerillo de juanete de proa* fore-topgallant mast | *mastelerillo de juanete mayor* or *de popa* main-topgallant mast.

mastelero *m* topmast || — *mastelero de gavia* or *mayor* main-topmast || *mastelero de perico* mizzen-topgallant mast || *mastelero de sobremesana* mizzen-topmast || *mastelero de velacho* fore-topmast.

masticación *f* chewing, mastication.

masticador *adj* chewing || ZOOL masticatory (aparato, animal).
◆ *m* salivant bit (del caballo) || masticator (aparato para triturar) || ZOOL masticator.

masticar *vt* to chew, to masticate || FIG to chew over, to ponder over, to ruminate.

masticatorio, ria *adj* masticatory.
◆ *m* masticatories *pl*.

mástil *m* MAR mast, spar | topmast (mastelero) || mast, pole (para sostener una antena, una bandera, etc.) || bedpost (de cama) || MÚS neck (de la guitarra, etc.) || stem (de planta) || barrel, quill (de una pluma) || stanchion (sostén).

mastín *m* ZOOL mastiff (perro) || *mastín danés* Great Dane.

mastitis *f* MED mastitis.

mastodonte *m* mastodon.

mastodóntico, ca *adj* FIG elephantine.

mastoideo, a *adj* ANAT mastoid.

mastoides *adj/sf* mastoid || ANAT mastoid.

mastoiditis *f* MED mastoiditis.

mastología *f* MED mastology.

mastólogo, ga *f / m* MED mastologist.

mastopatía *f* MED mastopathy.

mastuerzo *m* BOT cress || FIG & FAM dolt (necio).

masturbación *f* masturbation.

masturbar *vt* to masturbate.
◆ *vpr* to masturbate.

mata *f* plantation, grove (de árboles) || orchard (de árboles frutales) || shrub, bush (arbusto) || mastic tree (lentisco) || sprig, twig, tuft (trozo arrancado de una planta) || head of hair (pelo) || TECN matte (sulfuro múltiple) || — FIG & FAM *a salto de mata* from hand to mouth, from one day to the next (vivir al día), like a shot (con mucha velocidad), as it bolts from cover (liebre), haphazardly (de cualquier manera) || BOT *mata de la seda* milkweed || FIG & FAM *ser más tonto que una mata de habas* to be as daft as a brush, to be as mad as a hatter.

matacán *m* ARQ machicolation.

matadero *m* slaughterhouse, abattoir (de reses) || FIG & FAM backbreaking job, bind (trabajo) || *AMER* FIG & FAM bachelor's flat || FIG *llevar a uno al matadero* to lead s.o. to the slaughter.

matador, ra *adj* killing, murderous || FIG & FAM killing, backbreaking; *el trabajo es matador* the work is killing | deadly (pesado) | ridiculous, absurd.
◆ *m* killer, murderer (asesino) || TAUR matador, bullfighter || trump card [in the game of ombre].
◆ *f* killer, murderess (asesina).

matadura *f* harness sore.

matafuego *m* fire extinguisher (extintor) || fireman (bombero).

mátalas callando *m/f inv* FAM wolf in sheep's clothing.

matalotaje *m* MAR ship's stores *pl* (víveres) || FIG & FAM jumble, mess (desorden).

matalote *m* worn-out nag || ship; *matalote de proa, de popa* next ship ahead, astern.

matambre *m* *AMER* slice of meat.

matamoros *adj inv* blustering, arrogant, swashbuckling.
◆ *m inv* swashbuckler, braggart.

matamoscas *adj inv* *papel, bomba matamoscas* fly paper, fly spray || *pala matamoscas* fly swatter.
◆ *m inv* fly killer.

matanza *f* slaughter, slaughtering (de animales) || massacre, slaughter, butchery, killing (de muchas personas) || slaughtering season (época de la matanza) || pork products *pl* (productos del cerdo) || *hacer una matanza de mil personas* to slaughter *o* to butcher *o* to massacre a thousand people.

mataperrada *f* *AMER* mischievous prank.

mataperrear *vi* *AMER* to get up to mischief.

matapolillas *m inv* moth killer.

mataquintos *m inv* FAM bad tobacco.

matar *vt* to kill || to slaughter, to kill (reses) || FIG to kill; *los excesos le matarán* his excesses will kill him | to tire out (de trabajo) | to slake (la cal, el yeso) | to put out (un fuego) | to round, to bevel (una arista) | to lay (el polvo) | to kill, to stave off (el hambre) | to kill (el tiempo, la sed) | to kill, to tone down (apagar un color vivo) | to cancel, to obliterate (sello) || DEP to kill (la pelota) || — FIG *así me maten* for the life of me || TAUR *entrar a matar* to go in to kill *o* for the kill || FIG *estar a matar con uno* to be at loggerheads *o* at daggers drawn with s.o. | *matar a disgustos* to drive s.o. mad, to make one's life a misery | *matar a fuego lento* to torture to death | *matar a preguntas* to plague *o* to bombard with questions | *matar de aburrimiento* to bore to death *o* to tears || *matar de hambre* to starve to death | *matar el gusanillo* to take a nip first thing in the morning (beber aguardiente por la mañana) | *matarlas callando* to be a wolf in sheep's clothing | *¡que me maten si...!* I'll be damned if...!
◆ *vi* to kill || to mate (en ajedrez).
◆ *vpr* to kill o.s. (suicidarse) || to be *o* to get killed (en un accidente) || FIG to kill o.s., to wear o.s. out (en el trabajo); *matarse trabajando* to kill o.s. working; *matarse por conseguir algo* to kill o.s. getting sth.

matarife *m* butcher, slaughterer.

matarratas *m inv* rat killer || FIG rotgut, firewater (aguardiente malo).

matasanos *m inv* FAM quack (médico).

matasellar *vt* to cancel, to postmark, to obliterate.

matasellos *m inv* canceller (instrumento de correos) || postmark (marca).

matasiete *m* FAM braggart, blusterer, bully, boaster.

matasuegras *m inv* paper serpent (juguete).

matatías *m inv* FAM moneylender.

matazón *f* *AMER* massacre.

match *m* match (encuentro deportivo).

mate *adj* matt, dull (sin brillo) || dull (sonido).
◆ *m* checkmate, mate (ajedrez) || *AMER* maté, Paraguayan tea (bebida) || maté (calabaza seca) | maté (arbusto) | FIG & FAM nut (cabeza) || — *AMER cebar mate* to prepare maté || *dar jaque mate* to checkmate || *AMER hierba mate* maté || *jaque mate* checkmate || *AMER mate amargo, mate cimarrón* unsweetened maté, bitter maté.

matear *vi* to grow thickly (el trigo) || to search the undergrowth (caza) || *AMER* to have a drink of maté.

matemático, ca *adj* mathematical; *lógica matemática* mathematical logic.
◆ *m/f* mathematician.
◆ *f* mathematics, maths (*fam*).
◆ *pl* mathematics, maths (*fam*); *las matemáticas puras, aplicadas* pure, applied mathematics.

Mateo *npr m* Matthew; *evangelio según San Mateo* gospel according to Saint Matthew || FIG & FAM *estar como Mateo con la guitarra* to be as pleased as Punch *o* as pie.

materia *f* matter; *no se puede destruir la materia* matter cannot be destroyed; *el espíritu y la materia* mind and matter || material, substance (material) || matter, question, subject (cuestión); *eso es otra materia* that is another question || subject (asignatura); *estudia ocho materias* he studies eight subjects || MED matter, pus || — *en materia de* in the matter of, as regards || *entrar en materia* to get down to business || *índice de materias* table of contents || *materia colorante* dye stuff, colouring matter || *materia de Estado* affair *o* matter of State || *materia gris* grey matter || *materia prima* raw material.

material *adj* material; *necesidades materiales* material necessities || physical; *presencia, dolor, daño, goce material* physical presence, pain, damage, pleasure || materialistic; *un espíritu demasiado material* an over-materialistic mind || real; *el autor material de un hecho* the real instigator of a deed || — FIG *el tiempo material para algo, para hacer algo* just enough time for sth., to do sth. | *error material* clerical error.
◆ *m* material; *el vaso es de material plástico* the glass is made of a plastic material; *materiales de construcción* building materials || equipment; *material deportivo* sports equipment; *material de oficina* office equipment || AGR implements *pl* (de una granja) || TECN plant, equipment (maquinaria) || leather (de calzado) || — *material bélico* or *de guerra* war material || *material de desecho* waste material || *material escolar* teaching materials *pl*, school equipment || *materiales de derribo* rubble *sing* || *material móvil* or *rodante* rolling stock (ferrocarriles) || *material publicitario* advertising material || TECN *material refractario* heatproof material.

materialidad *f* materiality, material nature || — *no me importa la materialidad del dinero, sino que se lo llevase ese sinvergüenza* it is not the money itself which bothers me, but the fact that it was that scoundrel who took it || *no oye más que la materialidad de las palabras* he is incapable of taking what you say at anything other than its face value.

materialismo *m* materialism; *materialismo histórico* historical materialism.

materialista *adj* materialistic, materialist.
◆ *m/f* materialism.

materialización *f* materialization.

materializar *vt* to materialize.
◆ *vpr* to materialize.

materialmente *adv* materially || physically, utterly, absolutely.

maternal *adj* maternal, motherly.

maternidad *f* maternity, motherhood || maternity hospital *o* home (casa de maternidad).

materno, na *adj* motherly, maternal; *amor materno* motherly love || mother, native (lengua) || maternal; *abuela materna* maternal grandmother.

matero, ra *adj* fond of maté || of maté.
◆ *m/f* maté drinker.

matete *m* *AMER* mixture (mejunje) | dispute, row (riña) | confusion, mess (confusión).

matidez *f* dullness (de una superficie, de un sonido).

matinal *adj* morning, matinal.

matinée *f* TEATR matinée.

matiz *m* shade, hue, tint, nuance (de color) || FIG shade, nuance (de sentido) | touch (con ironía).

matización *f* harmonization, matching (de varios colores) || tingeing, shading, colouring (con un matiz de otra cosa) || nuances *pl*, shades *pl* (matices).

matizar *vt* to harmonize, to match (casar varios colores) || to tinge (un color de otro) || FIG to vary (introducir variedad); *matizar el tono de voz* to vary one's tone of voice | to tinge; *doctrinas matizadas de socialismo* doctrines tinged with socialism.

matojo *m* BOT bush, shrub (mata) | saltwort (planta quenopodiácea).

matón *m* FAM tough gúy, bully.

matonear *vi* FAM to play the tough guy.

matonería *f*; **matonismo** *m* bullying, terrorizing, loutishness.

matorral *m* brushwood, scrub || thicket (conjunto de matas).

matraca *f* rattle (instrumento) || — FIG & FAM *dar la matraca a uno* to get on s.o.'s nerves, to pester s.o. (dar la lata), to make fun of s.o., to scoff at s.o. (burlarse) | *ser una matraca* to be a pest *o* a nuisance.

matraquear *vi* to rattle, to make a noise with the rattle || FIG & FAM *dar la matraca a uno* to get on s.o.'s nerves, to pester s.o. (dar la lata), to make fun of s.o., to scoff at s.o. (burlarse).

matraqueo *m* rattling, rattle, noise made with the rattle || FIG & FAM pestering (molestia) | banter, scoffing (burla) | wearisome insistence (insistencia).

matraz *m* QUÍM matrass, glass vessel.

matrero, ra *adj* cunning, shrewd, astute (astuto) || *AMER* suspicious, distrustful (desconfiado).
◆ *m* *AMER* bandit, brigand (bandido).

matriarca *f* matriarch.

matriarcado *m* matriarchy.

matriarcal *adj* matriarchal.

matricaria *f* BOT feverfew.

matricida *adj* matricidal.
◆ *m/f* matricide (persona).

matricidio *m* matricide (acto).

matrícula *f* register, list, roll (lista) || registration, enrolment, matriculation (acto de matricularse en una universidad, etc.); *derechos de matrícula* registration fee || roll (número de alumnos o de estudiantes) || MAR register (lista de hombres o de embarcaciones) || AUT registration number (número), number plate [US license plate] (placa) || — *matrícula de honor* prize (universidad) || MAR *puerto de matrícula* port of registry.

matriculación *f* registration (de coche, barco, persona) || registration, enrolment, matriculation (en un centro de enseñanza).

matriculado, da *adj* registered, enrolled (en la universidad) || registered (coche, barco).
◆ *m/f* registered student.

matricular *vt* to register (un coche, una embarcación, a una persona) || to enrol, to register, to matriculate (a uno en la universidad, etc.).
◆ *vpr* to enrol, to matriculate, to register; *matricularse de física en la universidad de Granada* to matriculate in physics at the university of Granada || to register; *matricularse como médico* to register as a doctor.

matrimonial *adj* matrimonial, marital || — *capitulaciones matrimoniales* marriage settlement *sing o* contract *sing* || *vida matrimonial* married life, conjugal life.

matrimoniar *vi* to marry, to get married.

matrimonio *m* marriage, matrimony || married couple; *un joven matrimonio* a young married couple || married state (estado de casado) || marriage (casamiento, boda); *matrimonio civil* civil marriage || — *cama de matrimonio* double bed || *contraer matrimonio con* to take in marriage, to contract marriage with, to marry || *dar palabra de matrimonio* to plight one's troth (ant), to promise to marry || *fuera del matrimonio* out of wedlock || *matrimonio de conveniencia* or *de interés* marriage of convenience || *matrimonio no consumado* unconsummated marriage || FAM *matrimonio por detrás de la iglesia* marriage over the broomstick, companionate marriage || *matrimonio por poderes* marriage by proxy || *matrimonio rato* nonconsummated marriage || *partida de matrimonio* wedding certificate, certificate of marriage.

matritense *adj* [of *o* from] Madrid, Madrilenian.
◆ *m/f* native *o* inhabitant of Madrid, Madrilenian.

matriz *f* ANAT uterus, womb (de la mujer) || TECN die (troquel) | nut (tuerca) || IMPR type mould, matrix || stub, counterfoil (de talonario) || mother record [US master record] (de un disco) || master copy, original (original de un documento) || MAT & MIN matrix || TECN *matriz de terraja* extruder.
◆ *adj f* *casa matriz* motherhouse (de origen religioso), headquarters *pl*, head office (de una empresa).

matrona *f* matron (madre de familia de cierta edad) || midwife (partera, comadre) || matron (en una cárcel) || searcher (en la aduana).

Matusalén *npr m* Methuselah; *más viejo que Matusalén* as old as Methuselah.

matute *m* smuggling, contraband || smuggled goods *pl*, contraband.

matutear *vi* to smuggle.

matutero, ra *m/f* smuggler.

matutino, na *adj* morning, matutinal || — *estrella matutina* morning star || *persona matutina* early riser, early bird.

maula *f* piece of junk, useless thing (cosa inútil) || remnant (retal) || ruse, trick (engaño).
◆ *m/f* FIG & FAM dead loss, good-for-nothing (persona inútil) || bad payer (mal pagador) || *un buen maula* a tricky customer.

maulería *f* remnant shop (tienda de retales) || trickery, cunning (engaño).

maulero, ra *m/f* remnant seller (vendedor de retales) || trickster (tramposo).

maullar *vi* to miaow, to mew.

maullido *m* miaowing, mewing (acción) || miaow, mew (ruido) || *dar maullidos* to miaow, to mew.

Mauricio *npr m* Maurice, Morris || GEOGR Mauritius (isla).

Mauritania *npr f* GEOGR Mauritania.

mauritano, na *adj/s* Mauritanian.

máuser *m* mauser (fusil).

mausoleo *m* mausoleum; *los mausoleos* the mausoleums, the mausolea.

maxifalda *f* maxiskirt.

maxilar *adj* ANAT maxillary.
◆ *m* jaw, jawbone || *maxilar superior* maxilla.

maxilofacial *adj* MED maxillofacial.

máxima *f* maxim (aforismo) || maximum temperature; *las máximas del año* the year's maximum temperatures.
◆ *adj* → **máximo.**

máxime *adv* (all) the more, especially; *estaba muy contento, máxime porque había llegado su hija* he was very happy (all) the more as his daughter had come.

máximo, ma *adj* maximum, greatest, highest; *la máxima recompensa* the highest reward; *el punto máximo* the highest point; *el máximo esfuerzo* the greatest effort; *temperatura máxima* maximum temperature || greatest; *uno de los pintores máximos del mundo* one of the world's greatest painters || MAT *máximo común divisor* highest common factor.
◆ *m* maximum; *ley de los máximos* law of maxima; *la producción llegó al máximo* production reached a maximum || — *al máximo* to the maximum, to the utmost || *como máximo* at the most; *hay sitio para cuatro personas como máximo* there is room for four people at the most; at the latest; *saldremos como máximo a las siete* we shall leave at seven at the latest || *hacer el máximo* to do one's utmost.
— OBSERV El plural de *maximum* es *maxima* o *maximums*.

máximum *m* maximum.

maxisingle *m* MÚS twelve-inch single, maxi-single.

maxvelio; maxwell *m* FÍS maxwell (unidad de fluido magnético).

maya *f* BOT daisy (margarita).

maya *adj* Mayan.
◆ *m/f* Maya, Mayan.

mayar *vi* to miaow, to mew (maullar).

mayestático, ca *adj* majestic || GRAM *el tratamiento mayestático* the Royal «we».

mayéutica *f* FIL maieutics.

mayo *m* May (mes); *el primero de mayo* the first of May || maypole (palo) || FIG *hasta el cuarenta de mayo no te quites el sayo* ne'er cast a clout till May is out.

mayólica *f* majolica (loza esmaltada).

mayonesa *f* CULIN mayonnaise (salsa).

mayor *adj* bigger, larger (más grande) (comparativo); *mi casa es mayor que la suya* my house is bigger than his || biggest, largest (superlativo); *la mayor ciudad del país* the biggest city in the country || greater (superior) (comparativo); *su inteligencia es mayor que la mía* he is of greater intelligence than I || greatest (superlativo); *la mayor falta que ha cometido* the greatest mistake he has made; *su mayor enemigo* his greatest enemy || older, elder (de más edad) (comparativo); *mi amigo es mayor que yo* my friend is older than I; *mis dos hermanas mayores* my two elder sisters || oldest, eldest (superlativo); *mi hermano mayor* my eldest brother || elderly (de edad); *una señora mayor* an elderly lady || grown-up (adulto); *tiene dos hijas que ya son mayores* he has two grown-up daughters || major, main (principal) || main (plaza, calle, mástil) || high; *calle, misa mayor* high street, mass; *altar mayor* high altar || MÚS major || FIL major (término); *premisa mayor* major premise || REL major (orden) || — *al por mayor* wholesale (comercio) || *caballerizo mayor* Master of the Horse || *caza mayor* large game (jabalíes, ciervos, etc.), big game (leones, tigres, etc.) || *colegio mayor* hall of residence (residencia de estudiantes) || *en su mayor parte* mainly, for the most part || *estado mayor* staff; *jefe de estado mayor* chief of staff || *ganado mayor* bovine cattle, horses and mules || *hacerse mayor* to grow up, to come of age || GEOGR *Lago Mayor* Lake Maggiore || *la mayor parte* most, the majority || *libro mayor* ledger || *mayor de edad* elderly (entrado en años), of age (de 18 años o más) || *mayor edad* majority (mayoría) || *montero mayor* master of the hounds || MAR *palo mayor* mainmast.
◆ *m* head, chief (jefe) || FAM grown-up (persona adulta) || ledger (libro grande empleado en la contabilidad).
◆ *f* major [premise] (en lógica).
◆ *m/f* older, oldest, elder, eldest || — *mayor de edad* major, adult, person legally of age.
◆ *pl* ancestors, elders (antecesores) || — *por mayores razones* for imperative reasons || *respetar a los mayores* to show respect for one's elders.
— OBSERV Se emplea la forma comparativa en inglés cuando se trata de dos personas o cosas: *el mayor de los dos* the elder of the two; *el mayor de los dos coches* the bigger of the two cars. Si el número pasa de dos, se utiliza la forma superlativa: *el mayor de los tres coches* the biggest of the three cars.

mayoral *m* head shepherd (pastor) || AGR foreman, overseer (capataz) | farm manager (de una ganadería) || coachman (cochero) || AMER conductor (de tranvía).

mayorazgo *m* primogeniture || entailed estate [inherited by primogeniture] || heir to an entailed estate (heredero) || (p us) eldest son, first-born son (hijo mayor).

mayordomía *f* catering (de los aviones) || stewardship (de casa).

mayordomo *m* butler (de una casa) || steward (de una finca) || churchwarden (de iglesia) || HIST *mayordomo de palacio* mayor of the palace.

mayoreo *m* AMER COM wholesale.

mayoría *f* majority; *tres votos de mayoría* a majority of three; *mayoría abrumadora* overwhelming majority; *la mayoría está contenta* the majority are happy || majority, full legal age (de edad) || majority, most; *la mayoría de los participantes* most of the participants || MIL sergeant-major's office || — *en la mayoría de los casos* in most cases || *en su mayoría* in the main || *la inmensa mayoría* the great majority || *la mayoría de las veces* most times, usually || *llegar a la mayoría* to come of age, to reach one's majority || *mayoría absoluta, relativa* absolute, relative majority || *mayoría de edad* majority, adult age, full legal age.

mayoridad *f* majority (mayoría).

mayorista *m* wholesaler (comerciante).
◆ *adj* wholesale (comercio).

mayoritario, ria *adj* majority; *decisión mayoritaria* majority decision.

mayormente *adv* especially.

mayúsculo, la *adj/sf* capital (letra) || *amistad con mayúscula* friendship with a capital F.
◆ *adj* FAM monumental, enormous; *disparate mayúsculo* monumental boob || FAM *un susto mayúsculo* a terrible fright.

maza *f* mace (arma antigua, insignia del macero) || TECN pounder (utensilio para machacar, apisonar) | drop hammer (martinete) | pile driver (para clavar pilotes) | monkey (cabeza de martinete) | brake (para machacar el cáñamo) || butt (del taco de billar) || MÚS drumstick (del bombo) || FIG & FAM bore, pest (persona pesada) || AMER hub, nave (de rueda).

mazacote *m* soda (sosa) || concrete (hormigón) || FIG & FAM monstrosity, eye-sore (obra artística fea); *el nuevo monumento es un mazacote* the new memorial is a monstrosity | stodgy mess (plato mal hecho) | bore, pest (persona pesada) || AMER mess, mixture (mezcla).

Mazalquivir *n pr* GEOGR Mers-el-Kebir.

mazamorra *f* AMER boiled maze (gachas) || MAR broken biscuit (restos de galleta) || FIG crumbs *pl* (cosa desmenuzada).

mazapán *m* CULIN marzipan.

mazazo *m* blow with a mace *o* with a club.

mazdeísmo *m* REL Mazdaism.

mazmorra *f* dungeon (calabozo).

mazo *m* mallet (martillo de madera) || mallet (de croquet) || club, bat (en otros deportes) || bunch (manojo); *mazo de llaves, de plumas* bunch of keys, of feathers || wad (de papeles, de billetes de banco) || FIG & FAM bore, pest (pelma) || MÚS drumstick (maza) || FIG *a Dios rogando y con el mazo dando* God helps those who help themselves.

mazorca *f* AGR ear, spike, cob (de maíz) | cacao pod (del cacao) || spindle (husada de lino, etc.) || AMER despots *pl*, gang of despots || *maíz de* or *en la mazorca* corn on the cob.

mazorquero, ra *adj* AMER despotic.
◆ *m* despot.

mazurca *f* mazurka (danza, música).

mazut *m* fuel oil.

me *pron pers* me (acusativo); *me está usted fastidiando* you are annoying me; *llévame* take me || me, to me (dativo); *¡dámelo!* give me it!, give it to me!; *me dijo eso* he said that to me, he told me that || myself (reflexivo); *me corté afeitándome* I cut myself shaving; *me divierto* I enjoy myself || for me (para mí) || from me; *me lo quitó* he took it from me.

mea culpa *m inv* mea culpa || *decir su mea culpa* to confess one's error.

meada *f* POP piss; *echar una meada* to have a piss | urine stain (mancha).

meadero *m* POP loo (*fam*), urinal.

meados *m pl* POP piss *sing*.

meandro *m* meander (de río, de camino) || ARQ meander (adorno).
◆ *pl* FIG meanders.

mear *vi* FAM to pee, to piss.
◆ *vt* FAM to piss on.
◆ *vpr* FAM to wet o.s. || POP *mearse de risa* to piss o.s. laughing.

meato *m* ANAT & BOT meatus.

MEC *abrev de Ministerio de Educación y Ciencia* Ministry of Education and Science.

Meca (La) *npr f* GEOGR Mecca.

¡mecachis! *interj* confound it!, darn it!

mecánica *f* mechanics; *mecánica ondulatoria* wave mechanics || mechanism, works *pl*; *la mecánica de un aparato* the mechanism of an apparatus.

mecanicista *m/f* mechanist.

mecánico, ca *adj* mechanical (relativo a la mecánica) || machine-made (hecho con máquina) || FIG mechanical.
◆ *m* mechanic || driver (chófer).

mecanismo *m* mechanism || FIL mechanicalism || MÚS technique || FIG mechanism, machinery || — *mecanismo administrativo* administrative machine || *mecanismo de disparo, de expulsión* firing mechanism, ejector mechanism.

mecanización *f* mechanization || *mecanización contable* mechanized accounting.

mecanizado *m* TECN machining (de una pieza) || mechanization (de una fábrica, etc.).

mecanizar *vt* to mechanize; *mecanizar una fábrica* to mechanize a factory; *contabilidad mecanizada* mechanized accountancy || TECN to machine (una pieza).

mecano, na *adj/s* Meccan (de la Meca).
◆ *m* Meccano (juego).

mecanografía *f* typing, typewriting.

mecanografiado, da *adj* typewritten, typed.

mecanografiar *vt* to type, to typewrite.

mecanográfico, ca *adj* typewriting, typing.

mecanógrafo, fa *m/f* typist.

mecanograma *m* MED mechanogram.

mecanoterapia *f* MED mechanotherapy.

mecapal *m* AMER porter's leather strap.

mecapalero *m* AMER porter.

mecatazo *m* AMER whiplash (latigazo) | draught, gulp, swig (*fam*) (trago).

mecate *m* AMER pita cord *o* string.

mecatear *vt* AMER to whip (zurrar).

mecedero *m* TECN stirrer (mecedor).

mecedor, ra *adj* swinging || rocking.
◆ *m* swing (columpio) || stirrer [for wine in vats, soap in tubs, etc.].
◆ *f* rocking chair, rocker (silla).

Mecenas *m* Maecenas.

mecenazgo *m* patronage, maecenatism.

mecer *vt* to rock (a un niño, la cuna) || to swing (en un columpio) || to shake (un líquido, un recipiente) || to sway, to move to and fro (balancear).
◆ *vpr* to rock || to swing (en el columpio) || to sway, to move to and fro (balancearse).

mecografía *f* MED mecography.

mecómetro *m* MED mecometer.

mecha *f* wick (de lámpara) || fuse (de mina) || match (de arma de fuego) || pledget, tent (quirúrgica) || CULIN lardoon, lardon (tocino) || lock (de cabellos) || MAR spindle (pieza central de un palo), heel (parte inferior) || — FIG & FAM *aguantar mecha* to grin and bear it || FAM *a toda mecha* at full speed || *mecha de seguridad* or *lenta* safety fuse.

mechar *vt* CULIN to lard (la carne).

mechera *f* CULIN larding needle || FAM shoplifter (ladrona) || *aguja mechera* larding needle.

mechero *m* lighter, cigarette lighter, cigar lighter (encendedor) || burner (de gas); *mechero Bunsen* Bunsen burner || burner, jet (boquilla de lámpara) || wick holder (canutillo que contiene la mecha) || socket (de candelero) || FAM shoplifter (ladrón).

mechón *m* large wick (de lámpara) || lock, tuft (de cabellos) || tuft (de lana).

medalla *f* medal; *conceder una medalla a uno, premiar con una medalla a uno* to award s.o. a medal || pendant, medallion (colgada del cuello), medal (religiosa) || medallion, plaque (placa grande) || FIG *el reverso de la medalla* the other side of the coin (el aspecto opuesto), the complete opposite (la antítesis).

medallista *m* medallist [US medalist].

medallón *m* medallion (medalla grande) || locket (relicario) || ARQ (medallion) || CULIN pat.

médano; medano; mégano *m* (sand) dune (duna) || sandbank (banco de arena).

media *f* stocking (para las piernas); *media* or *medias de punto* net stocking; *ponerse las medias* to put on one's stockings || mean; *media aritmética* arithmetic mean || average (promedio) || half-back line (deportes) || AMER sock (calcetín) || — *hacer media* to knit || *hacer 60 km de media* to do 60 km on (an) average, to do an average of 60 km || *media geométrica* geometric mean || *media proporcional* mean proportional, geometric mean || *son las tres y media* it is half past three || *tocar la media* to strike half past, to strike the half hour.

Media *npr f* HIST Media.

mediacaña *f* ARQ gorge, cavetto (tipo de moldura) | listel, fillet (listón) || TECN gouge (gubia) | halfround file (lima) || curling tongs *pl* (tenacillas).

mediación *f* mediation || *por mediación de* through, through the instrumentality *o* agency of.

mediado, da *adj* half full, half empty; *está el jarro mediado* the jug is half full || halfway through; *llevo mediado el diccionario* I am halfway through the dictionary || — *a mediados de* in *o* about the middle of, in mid-; *a mediados de agosto* in mid-August || *mediada la noche* in the middle of the night, in the dead of night || *mediada la tarde* half-way through the afternoon.

mediador, ra *adj* mediating, mediative || intermediary, mediating (intermediario).
◆ *m/f* mediator || intermediary, mediator.

medialuna *f* croissant.

mediana *f* MAT median.

medianamente *adv* fairly, moderately.

medianería *f* party wall (pared) || party fence *o* hedge, fence *o* hedge common to two properties (seto) || joint ownership of party wall *o* dividing fence, adjacency (condición).

medianero, ra *adj* party, dividing (pared, valla, etc.) || mediating, interceding (mediador).
◆ *m/f* mediator (mediador) || neighbour [US neighbor], owner of an adjacent house *o* field (vecino) || métayer, tenant farmer (aparcero).

medianía *f* moderate means *pl*, moderate circumstances *pl*; *vivir en la medianía* to live on moderate means *o* in moderate circumstances || mean, average (término medio) || FIG mediocre person, mediocrity.

mediano, na *adj* middling, medium, average; *inteligencia mediana* average intelligence; *mediano de cuerpo* of medium build || mediocre, middling, fair (ni bueno ni malo); *cerveza mediana* mediocre beer || mediocre, middling (malo); *un trabajo muy mediano* a very middling piece of work || median; *línea mediana* median line || *de tamaño mediano* medium-sized.

medianoche *f* midnight; *a medianoche* at midnight || FIG ham sandwich.

mediante *prep* by means of, using, with, with the help of; *abrió la caja fuerte mediante una palanca* he opened the safe by means of a crowbar || through, thanks to; *mediante su ayuda* through his help; *mediante él* thanks to him || — *Dios mediante* God willing || *mediante presentación de la tarjeta* on presentation of the card.

mediar *vi* to be between (two things); *entre las dos casas media un jardín* between the two houses there is a garden || to be in the middle (*en* of), to get halfway (*en* through), to get halfway (estar en la mitad de) || to pass, to elapse (transcurrir); *entre las dos guerras mediaron veinte años* twenty years passed between the two wars || to intervene (ocurrir en el curso de otra cosa) || to mediate; *mediar entre dos enemigos* to mediate between two enemies; *mediar en un asunto* to mediate in an affair || to exist (existir) || to intercede, to plead (rogar); *mediar por* or *en favor de uno* to intercede for *o* on behalf of || — *mediado el mes* in the middle of the month, halfway through the month || *media el hecho de que* the fact is that, the fact remains that || *media un abismo entre* there is a wide gap between || *¿qué diferencia media entre tú y yo?* what difference is there between you and me?

mediatinta *f* halftone, middletone.

mediatizar *vt* to mediatize.

mediato, ta *adj* mediate.

mediatriz *f* MAT perpendicular bisector.

médica *f* woman *o* lady doctor, doctor.

medicación *f* medication, medical treatment (acción de medicar) || medications *pl*, medicaments *pl*, medicines *pl* (medicamentos).

medical *adj* medical.

medicamentar *vt* → **medicinar.**

medicamento *m* medicament, medicine.

medicar *vt* to medicate.

medicastro *m* medicaster, quack (médico malo).

medicina *f* medicine (arte); *estudiar medicina* to study medicine; *doctor en medicina* doctor of medicine || medicine, medicament (medicamento) || — *estudiante de medicina* medical student || *medicina alternativa* alternative medicine || *medicina legal* or *forense* forensic medicine || *medicina preventiva* preventive medicine.

medicinal *adj* medicinal || DEP *balón medicinal* medicine ball.

medicinar; medicamentar *vt* to treat, to give medicine to, to prescribe medicine for.
◆ *vpr* to take medicine, to dose o.s.

medición *f* measurement (medida).

médico, ca *adj* medical; *reconocimiento* or *examen médico* medical examination || HIST Median (de los medos) || — *cuadro médico* medical staff || *receta médica* medical prescription.
◆ *m* doctor, physician || — *consejero médico* medical adviser || *médico consultor* or *de apelación* or *de consulta* medical consultant, consultant doctor || *médico de cabecera* or *de familia* family doctor || *médico forense* forensic surgeon || *médico general* general practitioner || MIL *médico militar* or *castrense* army medical officer || *médico rural* country doctor.
◆ *f* woman *o* lady doctor, doctor.

medicolegal *adj* medico-legal, forensic.

medicucho *m* quack.

medida *f* measuring, measurement (acción de medir); *la medida del tiempo* the measurement of time || measurement (magnitud); *tomarle a uno las medidas* to take s.o.'s measurements (en costura); *tomar las medidas de la habitación* to take the measurements of the room || measure; *medida de capacidad, de superficie, de volumen* liquid *o* dry, square, cubic measure || measure (unidad); *pesas y medidas* weights and measures || measure (cosa medida); *tres medidas de vino* three measures of wine || extent, proportion, measure, degree; *en cierta medida* to some *o* to a certain extent || FIG moderation, restraint, measure (prudencia) || measure, step (disposición); *medida disciplinaria* disciplinary measure; *medida represiva* represive measure; *adoptar medidas enérgicas* to adopt strong measures; *tomar todas las medidas necesarias* to take all necessary steps || metre [US meter], measure (de un verso) || — *a la medida* to measure, to order [US custom-made]; *pantalón hecho a la medida* trousers made to measure [US custom-made trousers] || *a la medida de* in proportion to, as (proporcionado a) || *a medida de* in accordance with, according to; *a medida de tus deseos* in accordance with your wishes || *a medida que* as, with, at the same time as || *colmar* or *llenar la medida* to be the limit, to be the last straw || *en gran medida* to a great extent, largely || *en* or *hasta cierta medida* to a certain extent, up to a point || *en la medida de lo posible* as far as possible, insofar as it is possible || *en la medida en que* insofar as; *en la medida en que sea posible* insofar as it is possible; in that, insofar as (ya que), according to, in accordance with (proporcionalmente con) || *en menor medida* to a lesser extent, on a smaller scale || *eso pasa de la medida* that is the limit, that is the last straw, that is carrying things too far || *medida común* common measure || *medida del cuello* neck size || *sin medida* unbounded.

medidor, ra *adj* measuring.
◆ *m* measure, measurer (instrumento) || measurer (persona) || AMER meter (contador) || *fiel medidor* inspector of weights and measures.

mediero, ra *m/f* stocking maker (que hace medias), hosier, stocking seller (que vende medias) || métayer, tenant farmer (aparcero).

medieval *adj* medieval, mediaeval.

medievalismo *m* medievalism, mediaevalism.

medievalista *m/f* medievalist, mediaevalist.

medievo *m* Middle Ages *pl*.

medio *m* middle (centro); *está en medio* it is in the middle || half (mitad) || means *pl* (procedimiento); *el fin justifica los medios* the end justifies the means || means *pl*, way (manera) || means *pl*, way, possibility (posibilidad) || means *pl*, power (capacidad) || measure (medida); *tomar los medios necesarios* to take the necessary measures || means (recursos, elementos); *medios de producción, de transporte* means of production, of transport || class, set, circle (clase social) || medium, environment, surroundings *pl* (ambiente) || society (sociedad) || circle (círculo); *en los medios bien informados* in well-informed circles || middle finger (dedo) || DEP halfback, half; *medio derecho, izquierdo* right, left half || medium (médium) || BIOL medium || — *de medio a medio* completely (enteramente) || *de por medio* in the middle, in between (en medio), in the way (constituyendo un obstáculo) || *el coche de en medio* the middle car, the car in the middle, the car in between || *el justo medio* the happy medium, the golden mean || *en medio de* in the middle of; *en medio de la calle* in the middle of the street; among; *estar en medio de mucha gente* to be among a lot of people; in the face of, in the midst of; *en medio de todos esos inconvenientes* in the midst of all those drawbacks; *debatirse en medio de muchas dificultades* to struggle in the face of many difficulties; in spite of (a pesar de); *en medio de todo* in spite of everything || *en su medio* in one's element || *estar de por medio* to intervene (intervenir), to be involved (estar en juego) || *justo en medio* right in the middle || *medio ambiente* environment || *medio de cultivo* culture medium || *meterse* or *ponerse de por medio* to intervene (en una pelea), to interfere (entremeterse) || *no hay medio* there is no way || *poner tierra por medio* to make o.s. scarce || *por en medio* in the way || *por medio* in *o* down the middle; *cortar el pan por medio* to cut the loaf down the middle || *por medio de* through (the middle of); *el río pasa por medio del pueblo* the river passes through the middle of the town; by means of, with the help of (mediante), through (por el intermedio de) || *quitar de en medio* to get *o* to take out of the way (una cosa), to get rid of (a una persona) || *quitarse de en medio* to get out of the way (cambiar de sitio); *¡quítate de en medio!* get out of the way!; to disappear, to make o.s. scarse (irse) || *vivir pared por medio* to be neighbours.
◆ *pl* means (fortuna); *su padre es hombre de pocos medios* his father is a man of small means || TAUR centre *sing* of the ring || — *en los medios allegados a* in the entourage of || *estar corto de medios* to be short of funds || *medios de comunicación* media || *no ahorrar medios* to spare no expense (gastar dinero), to spare no effort (hacer esfuerzos) || *por sus propios medios* of one's own resources || *por todos los medios* by all manner of means, by all possible means

medio, dia *adj* half; *dos horas y media* two and a half hours; *saldré dentro de media hora* I shall go out in half an hour; *media botella de coñac* half a bottle of brandy, a half-bottle of brandy (véase OBSERV) || half; *fue a recibirle medio Madrid, media ciudad* half Madrid, half the city went to greet him || middle; *clase media* middle class; *corredor de medio fondo* middle-distance runner || mean, average; *temperatura media* mean temperature || average; *el español medio* the average Spaniard || central, centre, dividing; *línea media* centre line || — *a media cuesta* halfway up || *a media luz* in the half-light || *a media mañana* in mid-morning, in the middle of the morning || *a media pierna* up to the middle of the calf || *a media voz* in a low voice || *a medio camino* halfway, halfway there || *a medio cuerpo* up to the waist, waist-high || *de medio cuerpo* half-length (pintura), up to the *o* one's waist; *entrar en el agua de medio cuerpo* to go into the water up to one's waist || *de medio pelo* of no account, common (gente), mediocre, average, passable (cosa) || *Edad Media* Middle Ages *pl* || *media lengua* childish talk *o* language || *medio billete* half, half fare (en el autobús, etc.) || *medio hermano* half brother || *medio pariente* distant relation || DEP *medio tiempo* half time || *no hay término medio* there is no middle course || *Oriente Medio* Middle East || *por término medio* on the average || MAT *término medio* average.
◆ *adv* half; *medio muerta de frío* half frozen to death; *una botella medio llena* a half-full bottle, a bottle half full || — *a medias* half; *dormido, satisfecho a medias* half asleep, satisfied; half-; *medidas, verdad a medias* half-measures, half-truth; halves, fifty-fifty; *ir a medias en un negocio* to go halves in a business; *compramos el coche a medias* we went halves on the car; half and half, half each (cada uno la mitad) || *a medio* (con verbo en infinitivo), half (con participio pasivo); *a medio terminar* half finished || *es un escritor a medias* he is a writer of sorts || *medio loco* half crazy || *solución a medias* partial solution.

— OBSERV El inglés suele emplear el artículo indefinido con el adjetivo que equivale a *medio*. Lo coloca sea entre el adjetivo y el sustantivo sea antes del adjetivo: *esperó media hora* he waited half an hour; *compré medio kilo de garbanzos* I bought a half kilo of chickpeas.

mediocre *adj* mediocre.

mediocridad *f* mediocrity.

mediodía *m* midday, noon; *llegó a mediodía* he arrived at midday || South (sur); *se va al mediodía de Francia* he is going to the South of France.

medioeval *adj* mediaeval, medieval.

medioevo *m* Middle Ages *pl*.

mediopensionista *m/f* day pupil, day student, student who has lunch at school.

medir* *vt* to measure; *medir por litros, con cinta métrica* to measure in litres, with a tape measure || to measure out; *medir trigo* to measure out wheat || to scan (los versos) || to measure, to be (tener cierta longitud) || FIG to gauge (las fuerzas, las consecuencias, etc.) || to weigh; *medir las palabras* to weigh one's words || — *¿cuánto mides?* how tall are you? || *medir con la vista* to size up || FIG *medir de arriba*

abajo to look up and down, to give the once-over (con la mirada) | *medir el suelo* to fall full-length (caerse) | *medir las costillas a uno* to give s.o. a good hiding *o* a beating | *medir sus pasos* to watch one's step.
◆ *vpr* to measure o.s. || FIG to measure o.s., to pit o.s.; *medirse con uno* to measure o.s. against s.o. | to act with moderation, to be moderate (moderarse) || FIG *medirse consigo mismo* to test one's strength.

meditabundo, da *adj* pensive, thoughtful.

meditación *f* meditation.

meditar *vi* to meditate, to ponder, to think; *meditar en* or *sobre el pasado* to meditate on *o* upon the past.
◆ *vt* to think about, to meditate on, to meditate, to ponder || to prepare, to plan, to meditate (un proyecto, etc.).

meditativo, va *adj* meditative.

mediterráneo, a *adj* Mediterranean; *el clima mediterráneo* the Mediterranean climate || *el (mar) Mediterráneo* the Mediterranean [Sea].

médium *m* medium.

medo, da *adj* Median (de Media).
◆ *m/f* Mede.

medra *f*; **medro** *m* growth, increase (aumento) || improvement (mejora) || prosperity || progress.

medrar *vi* to grow, to thrive (plantas, animales) || FIG to prosper, to thrive | to improve (mejorar) | to increase, to grow (aumentar), || FAM *¡medrados estamos!* a lot of good that's done us!

medro *m* —> **medra.**

medroso, sa *adj* fearful (miedoso) || timorous, timid (tímido) || afraid, frightened (asustado) || fearsome, frightening (que causa miedo).

médula; medula *f* ANAT medulla, marrow; *médula oblonga* medulla oblongata || BOT medulla, pith, marrow (pulpa); *médula de saúco* elder medulla || FIG medulla, pith, marrow, essence || — FIG *hasta la médula* to the core || *médula espinal* spinal cord || *médula ósea* bone marrow || FAM *me sacarán hasta la médula* they'll bleed me white, they'll suck me dry.

medular *adj* medullary.

meduloso, sa *adj* ANAT marrowy || BOT pithy, marrowy.

medusa *f* ZOOL jellyfish.

Medusa *npr f* MIT Medusa.

Mefistófeles *npr m* Mephistopheles.

mefistofélico, ca *adj* Mephistophelian.

mefítico, ca *adj* mephitic.

megacéfalo, la *adj* megacephalic.

megaciclo *m* megacycle (unidad de frecuencia).

megafonía *f* public-address system.

megáfono *m* megaphone.

megajulio *m* million joules (unidad de trabajo).

megalítico, ca *adj* megalithic.

megalito *m* megalith.

megalocardia *f* MED megalocardia.

megalocefalia *f* MED megalocephaly.

megalocito *m* MED megalocyte.

megalocitosis *f inv* MED megalocytosis.

megalomanía *f* megalomania.

megalómano, na *adj/s* megalomaniac.

mégano *m* —> **médano.**

megaterio *m* megathere (mamífero fósil).

megatón *m* FÍS megaton.

megavatio *m* FÍS megawatt.

megavoltio *m* FÍS megavolt.

megohmio *m* FÍS megohm (unidad de resistencia).

meharista *m* meharist, mehariste.

meiosis *f* BIOL meiosis.

mejicanismo *m* Mexicanism.

mejicano, na *adj/s* Mexican.

Méjico *npr m* GEOGR Mexico (país) || Mexico City (la capital) (véase OBSERV en MÉXICO).

mejido *adj m* beaten (huevo).

mejilla *f* cheek.

mejillón *m* mussel (molusco) || *criadero de mejillones* mussel bed.

mejor *adj* better (comparativo); *este libro es mejor que el otro* this book is better than the other || best (superlativo); *es mi mejor amigo* he is my best friend || highest (bid, bidder) (puja, postor) || — *a falta de otra cosa mejor* for want of sth. better || *encontrar algo mejor* to find something better || *en las mejores condiciones* in the best condition (*para* for) || *es lo mejor que hay* it is the best there is || *hace mejor tiempo* the weather is better || *hago lo mejor que puedo* I do my best, I do the best I can || *lo mejor* the best (thing); *lo mejor que podemos hacer* the best thing we can do || *lo mejor del caso es que* the best (part) of it is that || *lo mejor del mundo* the best in the world || *lo mejor de lo mejor* superlative, the tops (*fam*) (óptimo), the pick of the bunch (la crema) || *lo mejor es enemigo de lo bueno* leave well enough alone || *lo mejor posible* as well as possible (de la mejor manera), as well as one can (todo lo que se puede); *lo hice lo mejor posible* I did it as well as I could || *llevarse lo mejor* to get the best of it || *nunca he visto cosa mejor* I have never seen anything better || *y lo que es mejor* better still.
◆ *adv* better (comparativo); *trabajas mejor que él* you work better than he || best (superlativo de bien); *es el libro mejor escrito de este autor* it is this author's best-written book || rather, sooner; *escogería mejor este abrigo* I should rather choose this overcoat || so much the better; *nos vamos en seguida, ¡mejor!* we're going at once, so much the better! || — *a lo mejor* perhaps, maybe, may; *a lo mejor no vendrá* perhaps *o* maybe he will not come, he might not come || *cada vez mejor* better and better || *estar mejor* to be better || *hubiera sido mejor no decir nada* you would have done better *o* it would have been better to say nothing || *ir mejor* to feel *o* to be better || *las dos trabajan a cuál mejor* the two work equally well, it is hard to say which of the two works better || *mejor dicho* rather || *mejor que mejor* so much the better || *mucho mejor* much better || *nada mejor* nothing better || *querer mejor* to prefer, to like better || *tanto mejor* so much the better, all the better.
◆ *m/f* better (de dos) || best (de más de dos); *es la mejor de las mujeres* she is the best of women || *en el mejor de los casos* at best.

mejora *f* improvement; *no hay mejora en su situación* there is no improvement in his situation; *la mejora del suelo* the improvement of the soil || improvement, betterment, progress (adelanto); *las mejoras producidas por la tecnología* the improvements brought about by technology || increase, raise (del sueldo) || higher bid (puja) || JUR improvement *o* betterment of an estate (hecha por un arrendatario) | additional portion of an inheritance set aside for one of the coheirs (en una herencia).

mejorable *adj* improvable.

mejoramiento *m* improvement.

mejorana *f* BOT sweet marjoram.

mejorar *vt* to improve, to better, to ameliorate (volver mejor); *mejorar su situación* to improve one's situation || to make better, to bring about an improvement in (a un enfermo); *la cura le ha mejorado mucho* the cure has made him a lot better *o* has brought about a great improvement in him || to increase, to raise (un sueldo) || to improve the lot of; *la nueva ley mejora a los funcionarios* the new law improves the lot of civil servants || to do better than, to better (superar) || to better (una oferta) || to raise (una puja) || JUR to will an additional bequest to (en un testamento) || DEP to beat, to break (un récord) || *mejorando lo presente* present company excepted.
◆ *vi* to improve, to get better (ponerse mejor, progresar) || to clear up (el tiempo) || — *mejorar de salud* to improve, to get better || *mejorar de situación* to improve one's situation || *¡que te mejores!* I hope you get better!, get well soon!

mejorcito, ta *adj* (diminutivo de *mejor*) FAM a little better, slightly improved; *el niño se encuentra mejorcito* the child is a little better | best; *Juana es la mejorcita de la clase* Joan is the best in the class || FAM *lo mejorcito* the very best.

mejoría *f* improvement.

mejunje; menjunje; menjurje *m* mixture (mezcla) || FIG brew (bebida) | fraud, fiddle (superchería).

melancolía *f* melancholy, despondency, gloom; *caer en un estado de melancolía* to sink into a state of melancholy || MED melancholia, melancholy.

melancólico, ca *adj* melancholic, melancholy, despondent, gloomy || MED melancholiac, melancholic.
◆ *m/f* melancholy person, melancholic (ant) || MED melancholiac, melancholic.

Melanesia *npr f* GEOGR Melanesia.

melanesio, sia *adj/s* Melanesian.

melar *adj* honey-sweet.

melaza *f* molasses, treacle.

Melbourne *n pr* GEOGR Melbourne.

melcocha *f* taffy.

Melchor *npr m* Melchior.

melée *f* scrum, scrummage (rugby); *medio de melée* scrum half.

melena *f* hair (pelo) || mane (del león).
◆ *pl* mop *sing*, dishevelled hair *sing* (greñas).

melenudo, da *adj* long-haired, shaggy (*fam*).

melífero, ra *adj* melliferous.

melificación *f* honey-making.

melificar *vi* to make honey (las abejas).

melífico, ca *adj* melliferous, honey-producing.

melifluo, flua *adj* mellifluous, honeyed; *palabras melifluas* mellifluous words.

Melilla *n pr* GEOGR Melilla.

melillense *adj/s* Melillan (de Melilla).

melindre *m*; **melindrería** *f* honey fritter (fruta de sartén) || sugared marzipan cake (de mazapán) || narrow ribbon (cinta estrecha) || FIG affectation (afectación), simpering (por coquetería), fussiness, finickiness (remilgo, delicadeza), priggishness (moral) || *andarse con melindres, hacer melindres, gastar melindres* to simper (por coquetería), to affect reluctance (hacerse de rogar), to be finicky (ser remilgado), to be priggish (moralmente).

melindrear *vi* *andarse con melindres, hacer melindres, gastar melindres* to simper (por coquetería), to affect reluctance (hacerse de rogar), to be finicky (ser remilgado), to be priggish (moralmente).

melindrería *f* —> **melindre.**

melindrosamente *adv* affectedly (con afectación), simperingly (por coquetería), fussily (con remilgo), priggishly (moral).

melindroso, sa *adj* affected (afectado), simpering (por coquetería), fussy, finicky (remilgado), prudish, priggish (moral).

melocotón *m* BOT peach (fruto) | peach, peach tree (árbol).

melocotonar *m* peach orchard.

melocotonero *m* BOT peach tree (árbol).

melodía *f* melody, tune ‖ melody, melodiousness (calidad).

melódico, ca *adj* melodic.

melodioso, sa *adj* melodious, tuneful.

melodista *m* melodist, melody writer.

melodrama *m* melodrama.

melodramáticamente *adv* melodramatically.

melodramático, ca *adj* melodramatic.

melodramatizar *vt* to melodramatize.

melomanía *f* melomania.

melómano, na *adj* melomane.
◆ *m/f* melomaniac.

melón *m* melon (fruta) ‖ FIG & FAM nut (cabeza) | noodle (imbécil) ‖ *melón de agua* watermelon.

melonada *f* FAM silly *o* daft thing (bobada).

melonar *m* melon patch.

meloncillo *m* small melon ‖ ZOOL [North African] mongoose.

melonero, ra *m/f* melon grower (que siembra) ‖ melon dealer (que vende).

melopea *f* MÚS melopoeia ‖ FAM *coger* or *agarrar* or *tener una melopea* to get *o* to be canned (emborracharse).

melopeya *f* MÚS melopoeia.

melosidad *f* sweetness (suavidad) ‖ FIG sweetness | sugariness (cualidad de almibarado).

meloso, sa *adj* honeyed, sweet ‖ FIG sweet, gentle, mellow | sugary (almibarado).

mella; melladura *f* notch, nick (rotura, hendedura) ‖ chip (en un plato) ‖ gap, hole (hueco) ‖ gap (en la dentadura) ‖ FIG harm, damage, injury (menoscabo) ‖ — FIG & FAM *hacer mella* to make an impression, to have an effect (impresionar); *las críticas no hacen la menor mella en él* criticism does not have the slightest effect on him; to cast a slur, to damage, to harm (menoscabar); *hacer mella en la reputación de alguien* to cast a slur on s.o.'s reputation; to make a hole *o* a dent; *hacer mella en la fortuna de alguien* to make a hole in s.o.'s fortune ‖ *tener dos mellas en la dentadura* to have two teeth missing.

mellado, da *adj* notched, nicked (desportillado) ‖ chipped (plato) ‖ gap-toothed (falto de algún diente); *una vieja mellada* a gap-toothed old woman.

melladura *f* ⟶ **mella.**

mellar *vt* to notch, to nick ‖ to chip (un plato) ‖ FIG *hacer mella* to make an impression, to have an effect (impresionar); to cast a slur, to damage, to harm (menoscabar); to make a hole *o* a dent.
◆ *vpr* to lose one's teeth ‖ to get chipped (un plato) ‖ FIG to be harmed *o* injured.

mellizo, za *adj/s* twin.
◆ *m pl* FIG & FAM pair of cops (policías).

memada *f* silly *o* daft thing.

membrana *f* membrane; *membrana mucosa* mucous membrane ‖ web, membrane (de los palmípedos).

membranoso, sa *adj* membranous.

membrete *m* letterhead, (letter) heading (del remitente) ‖ addressee's name and address (del destinatario) ‖ note (anotación).

membrillar *m* quince plantation.

membrillero *m* BOT quince, quince tree.

membrillo *m* BOT quince, quince tree (árbol) | quince (fruto); *carne* or *dulce de membrillo* quince preserve *o* jelly ‖ FIG *veranillo del membrillo* Indian summer.

membrudo, da *adj* burly, hefty, brawny (robusto).

memento *m* REL memento.

memez *f* silly *o* stupid thing (simpleza).

memo, ma *adj* silly, stupid.
◆ *m/f* fool, dolt, simpleton.

memorable *adj* memorable.

memorándum; memorando *m* memorandum (nota) ‖ notebook (carnet).

memorar *vt* (p us) to remember, to recall.

memoria *f* memory (facultad); *tener buena memoria* to have a good memory; *perder la memoria* to lose one's memory ‖ memory, recollection (recuerdo); *guardar memoria de* to retain the memory of ‖ statement, report, account (informe) ‖ memorandum (nota diplomática) ‖ essay, report, paper (estudio escrito) ‖ thesis, dissertation (tesis) ‖ account (factura) ‖ memorial, monument (monumento) ‖ legacy [bequeathed to a foundation perpetuating the legator's memory] (fundación) ‖ codicil (complemento a un testamento) ‖ INFORM memory, storage; *memoria central* central memory; *memoria de regeneración* or *de refrescamiento* refresh memory; *memoria estática* static memory, static storage; *memoria expandida* expanded memory; *memoria extendida* extended memory; *memoria intermedia* buffer; *memoria magnética* magnetic memory; *memoria masiva* mass memory; *memoria muerta* or *ROM* ROM, Read-Only Memory; *memoria programable* programmable memory; *memoria RAM* or *de acceso aleatorio* RAM, Random Access Memory; *memoria scratch* or *a corto plazo* or *auxiliar* scratch (pad) memory, auxiliar store; *memoria virtual* virtual storage, virtual memory ‖ — FIG *borrar de la memoria* to erase *o* to banish from memory | *borrarse de la memoria* to be forgotten (un recuerdo) ‖ *conservar la memoria de* to remember ‖ *de memoria* by heart; *aprender, saberse de memoria* to learn, to know by heart; from memory; *hablar de memoria* to speak from memory ‖ *en memoria de* in memory of, to the memory of ‖ *falta de memoria* forgetfulness ‖ *flaco de memoria* forgetful ‖ FIG *hacer memoria de* to remember, to recall | *irse de la memoria* to slip one's mind, to escape; *el nombre se me ha ido de la memoria* the name has slipped my mind, the name escapes me | *refrescar la memoria* to refresh one's memory ‖ *ser flaco de memoria* to have a short memory, to be forgetful ‖ *si la memoria no me falla, si tengo buena memoria* if my memory serves me well, if I am not mistaken ‖ FAM *tener una memoria como un colador* to have a head like a sieve ‖ *traer a la memoria* to recall, to bring to mind ‖ *venir a la memoria* to come to mind, to come back to one, to remember; *me vino a la memoria que* it came back to me that..., it came to my mind that..., I remembered that.
◆ *pl* memoirs (documento) ‖ regards; *dele usted memorias a su hermano* give my regards to your brother.

memorial *m* memorandum book (libro) ‖ memorial (petición) ‖ bulletin (publicación).

memorialista *m* memorialist.

memorión *m* good memory (memoria grande) ‖ *ser un memorión* to have a good memory.

memorístico, ca *adj* acquired by memory.

memorización *f* memorizing, memorization.

memorizar *vt* to memorize ‖ INFORM to store.

mena *f* MIN ore ‖ MAR size, thickness [of a cable].

ménade *f* MIT maenad (bacante).

menaje *m* furnishings *pl* (de una casa) ‖ furniture, fittings *pl* (de escuela) ‖ housekeeping (gobierno de la casa) ‖ kitchen utensils *pl*, kitchen equipment (de cocina).

menalgia *f* MED menalgia.

menarquía *f* MED menarche.

mención *f* mention; *mención honorífica* honourable mention ‖ *digno de mención* worth mentioning ‖ *hacer mención de* to make mention of, to mention.

mencionado, da *adj* mentioned, named (personas); *las anteriormente mencionadas* the above-mentioned ‖ this, that, in question; *la mencionada batalla* this battle, the battle in question ‖ *anteriormente mencionado* aforementioned, above-mentioned.

mencionar *vt* to mention, to name (nombrar) ‖ to point out, to call *o* to draw attention to (señalar) ‖ *sin mencionar a* not to mention.

menchevique *adj/s* Menshevik.

menda (mi) *loc* FAM yours truly.

mendacidad *f* mendacity (hábito de mentir) ‖ untruth, big lie (mentira).

mendaz *adj* lying, untruthful, mendacious.
◆ *m/f* liar.

mendelevio *m* QUÍM mendelevium.

mendelismo *m* Mendelism, Mendelianism.

mendicación *f* begging, mendicancy.

mendicante *adj/s* mendicant; *las órdenes mendicantes* the mendicant orders.

mendicidad *f* mendicity, mendicancy, begging (acción) ‖ mendicity, mendicancy, beggary (condición).

mendigante *m* beggar, mendicant.

mendigar *vt* to beg, to beg for ‖ FIG to beg; *mendigar una comida* to beg a meal.
◆ *vi* to beg.

mendigo, ga *m/f* beggar.

mendocino, na *adj* [of *o* from] Mendoza [Argentina].
◆ *m/f* native *o* inhabitant of Mendoza.

mendrugo *m/f* FIG & FAM chump (tonto).
◆ *m* crust, chunk (of hard bread) ‖ FIG *por un mendrugo (de pan)* for a crust of bread, for a bite to eat.

meneallo *mejor es no meneallo, peor es meneallo* the least said the better.

menear *vt* to move, to shake (la cabeza, la mano, etc.) ‖ to stir (un líquido) ‖ to wag (el rabo) ‖ to wiggle (las caderas) ‖ to waggle (las orejas) ‖ FIG to handle, to run (un negocio) ‖ — FIG & FAM *de no te menees* a hell of; *una bofetada, una fiesta de no te menees* a hell of a slap, of a party | *mejor es no meneallo, peor es meneallo* the least said the better.
◆ *vpr* to move, to shake (un miembro) ‖ to sway, to swing (contonearse) ‖ to move about, to fidget; *el niño se menea mucho* the child is fidgeting a lot ‖ to toss and turn (en la cama) ‖ to budge, to stir; *no te menees de aquí* don't budge from here ‖ FAM to be on the go, to bustle about (no parar) ‖ *¡menéate!* stir yourself!, get a move on!

menegilda *f* FAM housemaid, maidservant.

meneo *m* movement, shake, shaking (de la cabeza, de la mano, etc.) ‖ stir, stirring (de un líquido) ‖ wag, wagging (del rabo) ‖ wiggle, wiggling (de las caderas) ‖ waggle, waggling (de las orejas) ‖ jerk (sacudida) ‖ FIG & FAM hiding (vapuleo) ‖ — FIG & FAM *darle un meneo a* to have a go at; *le dio tal meneo a la botella que*

casi se la bebió he had such a go at the bottle that he almost drank it all || FAM *dar un meneo a uno* to give s.o. a hiding (vapulear), to boo s.o., to hiss s.o. (en un teatro, etc.), to jolt s.o. (sacudir).
◆ *pl* ups and downs, vicissitude *sing*; *los meneos de la vida* the ups and downs of life.

menester *m* need, necessity, want (necesidad) || occupation, work (ocupación) || work, duty, job (trabajo) || — *haber* or *tener menester de* to have need of, to need (una cosa), to need to (con un verbo) || *no ser menester* not to be necessary, not to have to; *no es menester que vayas ahí* it is not necessary for you to go there, you do not have to go there || *ser menester* to be necessary, to have to, must; *es menester comer para vivir* it is necessary to *o* one has to *o* one must eat to live.
◆ *pl* bodily needs (necesidades corporales) || FAM gear *sing*, tackle *sing*, tools (instrumentos de trabajo) || FIG *hacer sus menesteres* to do one's business.

menesteroso, sa *adj* needy, in want.
◆ *m/f* needy person || *los menesterosos* the needy.

menestra *f* kind of stew (con carne) || mixed vegetables *pl*, vegetable hotchpotch (de verdura).
◆ *pl* dried vegetables.

menestral *m* artisan, craftsman (artesano) || manual worker (trabajador manual).

menestralía *f* artisans *pl*, craftsmen *pl* (artesanos) || manual workers *pl* (trabajadores manuales).

menfita *adj/s* memphite.

mengano, na *m/f* what's-his-name (hombre), what's-her-name (mujer), so-and-so (hombre o mujer); *Fulano y Mengano* so-and-so and what's-his-name.
— OBSERV The noun *mengano* is only used after the word *fulano* to designate a person whose name is not known.

mengua *f* diminution, decrease, lessening, dwindling (en general) || wane, waning (de la luna) || lack, want (falta) || poverty (pobreza) || FIG discredit, disgrace (descrédito) | sinking, failing (falta de energía) | decline (intelectual, moral) || *en mengua de* to the detriment of; *lo hizo en mengua de su honra* he did it to the detriment of his honour.

menguado, da *adj* decreased, diminished (disminuido) || spineless, cowardly (cobarde) || miserable, wretched (desgraciado) || silly (tonto) || mean, stingy (avaro) || paltry, mean (reducido); *ha obtenido tan menguados éxitos* he has gained such paltry successes || *jersey menguado* fully-fashioned jersey.
◆ *m/f* coward (cobarde) || wretch (desgraciado) || miser (avaro).
◆ *m* decreased stitch (punto).

menguante *adj* diminishing, decreasing, dwindling, lessening (que mengua) || waning, on the wane (la luna) || ebb (marea) || *cuarto menguante* last quarter (de la luna).
◆ *f* fall, falling, subsidence, going-down (de las aguas de un río) || ebb tide (del mar) || waning (de la luna) || FIG decline, decadence.

menguar *vi* to diminish, to decrease, to dwindle, to lessen; *el número de estudiantes en la universidad mengua cada año* the number of students in the university decreases each year || to go down (la marea, etc.) || to wane (la luna) || FIG to sink, to fail (físicamente), to decline, to go downhill (*fam*), to decline, to go downhill (intelectual o moralmente) | to decrease (en las labores de punto) | to wane, to dwindle, to decrease (fama, gloria, etc.).
◆ *vt* to diminish, to decrease, to lessen (en general) || to reduce (la velocidad) || FIG to diminish, to lessen (la responsabilidad, etc.) | to detract from; *esto no mengua en nada su fama* this in no way detracts from his reputation.

menhir *m* menhir.

menina *f* maid of honour [*US* maid of honor].

meninge *f* ANAT meninx; *las meninges* the meninges.

meníngeo, a *adj* meningeal.

meningitis *f* MED meningitis.

meningococo *m* MED meningococcus (microbio).

meningoencefalitis *f inv* MED meningoencephalitis.

menipeo, a *adj* Menippean; *sátira menipea* Menippean satire.

menisco *m* FÍS & ANAT meniscus.

menjuí *m* BOT benzoin.

menjunje; menjurje *m* ⟶ **mejunje.**

Meno *npr m* GEOGR Main; *Francfort del Meno* Frankfurt-am-Main.

menonita *m* Mennonite.

menopausia *f* MED menopause.

menor *adj* smaller (más pequeño) (comparativo); *el número de niños en la clase es menor que el de niñas* the number of boys in the class is smaller than that of girls || smallest (superlativo); *la menor habitación de la casa* the smallest room in the house || lesser (más mínimo) (comparativo); *es un mal menor* it is a lesser evil || least (superlativo); *el menor ruido le asusta* the least noise frightens him || younger (de menos edad) (comparativo); *mis dos hermanas menores* my two younger sisters || youngest (superlativo); *mi hermano menor* my youngest brother || shorter (de menos duración) (comparativo); *el mes de febrero es menor que los demás* the month of February is shorter than the rest || shortest (superlativo); *el menor mes del año* the shortest month in the year || minor (de poca importancia); *los profetas menores* the minor prophets || minor; *órdenes menores* minor orders || MÚS minor; *en la menor* in A minor || — *al por menor* retail || *el menor, la menor* the smallest (one) (superlativo de pequeño); *deme la menor que hay* give me the smallest there is || *hermano, hermana menor* younger brother, sister (de dos), youngest brother, sister (de tres o más) || *menor de edad* under age || *menor edad* minority || MAT *menor que* less than || *no tengo la menor idea* I haven't the faintest idea, I haven't the slightest idea || *por menor* in detail, minutely (por extenso), retail (venta) || *rama menor* younger branch.
◆ *m/f* minor (menor de edad) || young person (niño) || — *juez de menores* juvenile court judge || *menor de edad* minor || *no apta para menores* adults only, persons under 18 not admitted, X-certificate (película) || *tribunal de menores* juvenile court.
◆ *m* minorite, Franciscan friar (monje).
◆ *f* minor premise (segunda proposición del silogismo).
◆ *pl* juniors (en el colegio) || elementary grammar class *sing* (clase) || GEOGR *Las Antillas Menores* the Lesser Antilles.
— OBSERV Se emplea la forma comparativa en inglés cuando se trata de dos personas o cosas: *el menor de los dos* the younger of the two; *el menor de los dos coches* the smaller of the two cars. Si el número pasa de dos, se utiliza la forma superlativa: *el menor de los tres coches*, the smallest of the three cars.

Menorca *n pr* GEOGR Minorca.

menorista *m* AMER retailer, retail dealer (minorista).

menorquín, ina *adj/s* Minorcan (de Menorca).

menorragia *f* MED menorrhagia.

menorrea *f* MED menorrhoea.

menos *adv* less; *menos caro* less expensive; *menos generoso* less generous || not so; *menos lejos* not so far || less (delante de un sustantivo y con idea de cantidad); *menos viento* less wind || fewer, less (con idea de número); *menos soldados* fewer soldiers || less (después de un sustantivo); *un litro menos* one litre less || less of a; *es menos coche* it is less of a car || least (superlativo de poco); *el alumno menos inteligente de la clase* the least intelligent pupil in the class || — *al menos, a lo menos, por lo menos* at least || *a menos de* for less than; *a menos de treinta pesetas el kilo* for less than thirty pesetas a kilo; less than, within; *a menos de diez kilómetros de aquí* less than ten kilometres from here; unless; *a menos de estar loco* unless he is mad || *a menos que* unless || *cada vez menos* less and less; *le veo cada vez menos* I see less and less of him || *cuando menos* at least || *cuanto menos... menos (más)* the less... the less (the more) || *de menos* short; *me han dado cien gramos de menos* they have given me a hundred grammes short; missing, short; *hay tres lápices de menos* there are three pencils missing || *dos de menos* two down (bridge) || *echar de menos* to miss; *echo de menos a mi país* I miss my country || *en menos* less, less highly; *valoro en menos su belleza que su encanto* I value her beauty less than her charm || *en menos de* by less than; *la producción ha bajado en menos de un dos por ciento* production has dropped by less than two per cent; in less than; *lo hizo en menos de una hora* he did it in less than an hour || *en menos de nada* in (less than) no time || *es lo menos que puede hacerse* it is the least that can be done || *eso es lo de menos* that's the least of it || *ir a menos* to lose status *o* social standing, to come down || *(la cosa) no es para menos* little wonder || *lo de menos es el ruido* it is not so much the noise || *lo menos* at least; *lo menos había mil personas* there were at least a thousand people there || *menos de, menos de lo que, menos que* less than || *mientras menos... menos* the less... the less; *mientras menos se habla, menos se equivoca uno* the less you speak, the less you are wrong || *nada menos que* no less than; *ha heredado nada menos que diez millones de pesetas* he has inherited no less than ten million pesetas || *ni mucho menos* far from it || *no menos de* no less than || *no pude menos de preguntarle si* I could not help asking him if || *poco menos* a little less; *poco menos de un litro* a little less than a litre; little less; *es poco menos que tonto* he is little less than stupid || *por menos de* for less than; *no trabajo por menos de cien libras* I won't work for less than a hundred pounds || *por menos de nada* at the slightest thing, for no reason at all; *por menos de nada se enfada* he gets angry at the slightest thing || *por no ser menos* not to be outdone || *¿qué menos?* it's the least one could expect || *ser lo de menos* to be the least important (thing) (lo menos importante), to be of no importance (no importar) || *si al menos* or *por lo menos* if only || *son menos de las diez* it is before ten o'clock || *tanto menos* so much the less, all the less || *tener a menos trabajar* to consider it beneath o.s. to work || *tener en menos* to look down on || *tener menos años que* to be younger than || *una familia venida a menos* a family which has seen better days *o* which has come down in the world || *venir a menos* to lose status, to come down in the world (personas), to go downhill (una empresa).
◆ *prep* but; *cualquier cosa menos eso* anything but that || except, but; *todos lo hicieron menos él* everyone did it except him; *todo incluido menos el transporte* everything included but the transport || save (ant); *todo está perdido menos el honor* all is lost save honour || MAT minus, less; *cuatro menos uno son tres* four minus one

is three || *son las tres menos diez* it is ten to three.

◆ *m* MAT minus (signo) || *los menos de, las menos de* the minority of.

menoscabar *vt* to diminish, to reduce, to lessen (disminuir); *una ley que menoscaba los derechos del propietario* a law which diminishes the rights of the landlord || FIG to impair, to spoil; *menoscabar la belleza, la reputación de uno* to impair s.o.'s beauty, reputation.

menoscabo *m* reduction, diminishing, lessening (mengua) || damage (daño) || FIG impairment (perjuicio) | discredit (descrédito) || — *con menoscabo de* to the detriment of || *sin menoscabo* unimpaired, unscathed || *sufrir menoscabo en su fortuna* to suffer heavy losses, to see one's fortune dwindle.

menospreciar *vt* to despise, to scorn (despreciar) || to ignore, to spurn, to shun (ignorar) || to underestimate, to underrate, to minimize; *menospreciar la importancia de un acontecimiento* to underestimate the importance of an event.

menospreciativo, va *adj* contemptuous, disdainful, scornful.

menosprecio *m* contempt, scorn; *con menosprecio de* in contempt of || underestimation, underrating (subestimación) || disrespect (falta de respeto) || *hacer menosprecio de* to make light of, to scoff at.

menostasia *f* MED menostasis.

mensaje *m* message || *mensaje de la Corona* King's *o* Queen's speech.

mensajería *f* transport service (transporte) || transport office (empresa) || *mensajería marítima* sea transport (transporte), shipping line (empresa).

mensajero, ra *adj* messenger, message-carrying || *paloma mensajera* carrier pigeon, homing pigeon, homer.

◆ *m/f* messenger || — *mensajera de la primavera* harbinger of spring (golondrina) || *mensajero de malas noticias* bearer of bad news.

menstruación *f* menstruation.

menstrual *adj* menstrual.

menstruar *vi* to menstruate.

menstruo *m* menses *pl*, menstruation.

mensual *adj* monthly || a month; *500 pesetas mensuales* 500 pesetas a month.

mensualidad *f* monthly *o* month's wage (salario); *cobrar su mensualidad* to draw one's monthly wage || monthly payment *o* instalment [*US* monthly installment] (renta); *pagar en doce mensualidades* to pay in twelve monthly instalments.

mensualización *f* payment by the month.

mensualizar *vt* to pay by the month.

ménsula *f* ARQ console || support, bracket (soporte).

mensura *f* *AMER* measure | measurement.

mensurable *adj* mensurable, measurable.

mensuración *f* mensuration, measurement.

mensurar *vt* to measure.

menta *f* BOT mint || peppermint (licor) || *con sabor a menta* mint-flavoured.

mentado, da *adj* aforementioned, in question (mencionado) || famous, renowned, well-known (famoso).

mental *adj* mental; *cálculo mental* mental calculation || *ser un atrasado mental* to be mentally retarded.

mentalidad *f* mentality || mind; *tener mentalidad abierta* to have an open mind.

mentalmente *adv* mentally || *hacer una multiplicación mentalmente* to do a multiplication in one's head *o* mentally.

mentar* *vt* to mention, to name.

mente *f* mind, intellect, intelligence (inteligencia) || mind (pensamiento); *tener en la mente* to have in mind || mind, intention (propósito); *no estaba en mi mente hacer eso* I had no mind to do that, it was not my intention to do that || — *irse de la mente* to slip one's mind || *traer a la mente* to call *o* to bring to mind; *esto me trae a la mente tristes recuerdos* this calls to mind sad memories || *venir a la mente* to cross one's mind; *la sospecha no me vino a la mente* the suspicion did not cross my mind; to come to mind; *me vienen a la mente tristes pensamientos* sad thoughts come to my mind.

mentecatada; mentecatería; mentecatez *f* half-wittedness, stupidity (falta de sensatez) || foolishness (necedad) || foolish *o* silly thing (acción) || stupid remark (palabras).

mentecato, ta *adj* half-witted, stupid (falto de sensatez) || foolish (necio).

◆ *m/f* simpleton, idiot, fool.

mentidero *m* FAM gossip corner, gossip shop.

mentir* *vi* to lie || to lie, to deceive, to be misleading *o* deceptive (equivocar); *las apariencias mienten* appearances lie || — *mentir sin necesidad* or *por costumbre* to lie for lying's sake || FAM *miente como un sacamuelas* or *más que habla* he is an arrant liar, he lies through his teeth, he lies like a thief || *¡miento!* I tell a lie!

mentira *f* lie (embuste); *mentira piadosa* white lie; *me cogió en una mentira* he caught me in a lie || lie, story, tale; *siempre está contando mentiras* he is always telling stories || story (cosa inventada) || FIG & FAM white spot [on fingernail] || mistake, error (errata) || — *aunque parezca mentira* strange as it may seem || *decir mentira por* or *para sacar la verdad* to angle for the truth with a lie, to try to draw s.o. out || *de luengas tierras, luengas mentiras* travellers from afar can lie with impunity || *¡eso es mentira!, ¡mentira!* that's a lie!, that's not true! || *parece mentira* it is unbelievable, it hardly seems possible || FAM *una mentira como una casa* a whopper, a whopping lie.

mentirijillas (de); de mentirillas *loc adv* as a joke, for fun, in jest, for a laugh.

mentiroso, sa *adj* lying (que miente) || full of misprints *o* errors (libro) || FIG deceitful, false, deceptive (engañoso); *proposiciones mentirosas* deceitful propositions.

◆ *m/f* liar.

mentís *m* denial || *dar un mentís a* to give the lie to.

mentol *m* menthol.

mentolado, da *adj* mentholated || *cigarrillos mentolados* menthol *o* mentholated cigarettes.

mentón *m* ANAT chin.

mentor *m* mentor.

menú *m* menu, bill of fare (minuta) || INFORM menu; *menú desenvolvente* drop-down menu.

— OBSERV pl *menús*.

menudear *vt* to do *o* to repeat frequently || to recount in detail (contar) || *AMER* to retail, to sell retail (vender al por menor).

◆ *vi* to happen frequently, to be frequent (ocurrir frecuentemente) || FIG to rain, to fall incessantly; *menudean los castigos sobre los malos* punishments rain upon the wicked || to go into detail (contar las cosas detalladamente) || to talk about trivialities (contar menudencias).

menudencia *f* trifle (cosa sin importancia) || minuteness, meticulousness (esmero) || minuteness (pequeñez) || detail (detalle) || pettiness (insignificancia).

◆ *pl* offal *sing* (de las reses), giblets (de las aves).

menudeo *m* retail trade || *venta al menudeo* retailing.

menudillo *m* fetlock joint (del pie de los cuadrúpedos).

◆ *pl* giblets (de las aves).

menudo, da *adj* small, tiny, minute (pequeño) || fine (lluvia) || slight (delgado) || small, trifling, petty (insignificante) || meticulous, scrupulous (exacto) || — *a menudo* often, frequently || *¡en menudo estado estaba!* he was in a fine state! || *la gente menuda* children *pl*, little ones *pl* (niños), people of small means (plebe) || FAM *¡menuda profesión!* what a job! | *¡menudo cuento!* a likely story! | *¡menudo jaleo!* a tidy old rumpus! | *¡menudo porrazo!* what a wallop! | *¡menudo precio!* it's daylight robbery!, it's no giveaway! (es muy caro) || *moneda menuda* small change || *por menudo* minutely, in minute detail (detalladamente), retail (al por menor).

◆ *m pl* offal *sing* (de las reses), giblets (de las aves) || small change *sing* (monedas).

meñique *adj* tiny, very small, minute (pequeño) || *dedo meñique* little finger.

◆ *m* little finger (dedo auricular).

meollada *f* brains *pl* (de una res).

meollar *m* MAR spun yarn.

meollo *m* brain, brains *pl* (seso) || marrow (médula) || crumb (miga del pan) || FIG pith, marrow, core, essence (lo principal) | brains *pl* intelligence (inteligencia) || FIG *entrar en el meollo del asunto* to come to the heart of the matter.

meón, ona *adj* FAM who is forever weeing.

◆ *m/f* FAM person who is forever weeing || FIG baby (niño).

mequetrefe *m* FAM whippersnapper.

Mequínez *n pr* GEOGR Meknès.

meralgia *f* MED meralgia.

meramente *adv* merely, purely, solely.

mercachifle *m* hawker, pedlar (buhonero) || FAM small tradesman (comerciante) | shark, profiteer (negociante rapaz).

mercadear *vi* to trade, to deal.

mercadeo *m* trade, trading (comercio) || marketing (estudio de mercados).

mercader *m* merchant, trader, dealer || — *el Mercader de Venecia* the Merchant of Venice || FIG *hacer oídos de mercader* to turn a deaf ear.

mercadería *f* commodity, article (mercancía).

◆ *pl* goods, merchandise *sing*.

mercadillo *m* small market, bazaar.

mercado *m* market; *mercado de pescado* fish market; *lanzar un nuevo producto al mercado* to launch a new product on to the market; *inundar el mercado de* to flood the market with; *sacar al mercado* to put on the market || — *acaparar el mercado de* to corner the market in || *el domingo hay mercado* Sunday is market day || *hay mucho* or *un gran mercado para* there is a good market for || *investigación* or *estudio de mercados* market research, marketing || *ir al mercado* to go to market || *mercado a tanto alzado* fixed-price market || *Mercado Común* Common Market || *mercado de cambios* foreign exchange market || *mercado de valores* stock market || *mercado exterior, interior* or *nacional* overseas, home market || *mercado libre, negro, paralelo* open, black, unofficial market || *mercado sostenido, encalmado* steady, quiet market.

mercancía *f* article, commodity.

◆ *pl* merchandise *sing* goods || *tren de mercancías* goods train, freight train.

mercante *adj* merchant; *marina mercante* merchant navy, merchant marine || *barco mer-*

cante merchant ship, merchantman, merchant boat.
◆ *m* merchantman, merchant ship (barco).

mercantil *adj* mercantile, commercial; *operaciones mercantiles* mercantile operations, commercial transactions ‖ mercantile, mercenary, money-grabbing (codicioso); *espíritu mercantil* mercantile mentality ‖ — *derecho mercantil* commercial *o* mercantile law ‖ *sociedad mercantil* trading company.

mercantilismo *m* mercantilism.

mercantilista *adj/s* mercantilist ‖ expert in commercial law (experto en derecho mercantil).

mercantilización *f* commercialization.

mercantilizar *vt* to consider in terms of money (valorar todo en dinero) ‖ to commercialize (comercializar).

mercar *vt* to buy (comprar).

Mercasa *abrev de Mercados Centrales de Abastecimientos, S.A.* central supply markets.

merced *f* grace, favour (gracia) ‖ (ant) grace, favour; *hágame la merced de* do me the grace of ‖ recompense, reward (recompensa) ‖ — *a (la) merced de* at the mercy of ‖ *la Merced* Our Lady of Mercy [order] ‖ *merced a* thanks to, by the grace of ‖ *muchas mercedes* many thanks ‖ *su* or *vuestra merced* your grace, your honour (título) ‖ *tenga la merced de* please be so kind as to.
— OBSERV *Vuestra merced* is today contracted to *usted* itself abbreviated to *Ud* or *Vd* usted.

mercedario, ria *adj* of the order of Our Lady of Mercy.
◆ *m/f* Mercedarian.
◆ *pl* Mercedarians (orden).

mercenario, ria *adj* mercenary; *soldado mercenario* mercenary soldier ‖ *mercenary* (ant) done solely for gain (un trabajo) ‖ mercenary, money-grabbing (codicioso).
◆ *m/f* mercenary ‖ day worker (jornalero) ‖ mercedarian (mercedario) ‖ ghost writer (escritor que hace el trabajo de otro).

mercería *f* haberdashery [US notions trade] (comercio) ‖ haberdasher's, haberdashery [US notions store] (tienda).

mercerizar *vt* to mercerize.

mercero, ra *m/f* haberdasher [US notions dealer].

mercurial *adj* mercurial.

mercúrico, ca *adj* QUÍM mercuric.

mercurio *m* QUÍM mercury (metal) ‖ *lámpara de vapor de mercurio* mercury-vapour lamp.

Mercurio *npr m* MIT & ASTR Mercury.

mercurioso *adj m* QUÍM mercurous (óxido).

merdellón *m* FAM status-seeking fop, coxcomb (p us) (hortera) | grubby servant *o* maid (criado o criada sucios).

merecedor, ra *adj* deserving, worthy ‖ — *hacerse merecedor de* to become worthy of ‖ *merecedor de confianza* trustworthy ‖ *ser merecedor de* to be worthy of, to deserve.

merecer* *vt* to deserve, to merit, to be worthy of; *merecer un premio* to merit a prize ‖ to deserve, to be worth, to merit; *el castillo merece una visita* the castle deserves a visit ‖ to deserve, to be worth (con infinitivo); *el cuento merece ser contado* the tale deserves to be told *o* is worth telling ‖ to need (tener necesidad); *esta noticia merece ser comprobada* this piece of news needs to be verified ‖ to earn, to get (valer); *su insolencia le mereció una bofetada* his insolence earned him a slap ‖ — *lo tiene bien merecido* he has well deserved it (un premio, etc.), it serves him right (un castigo, etc.) ‖ *merecer la pena* to be worth while, to be worth it; *merece la pena* it is worth it; to be worth, to be worth the trouble; *merece la pena visitar la catedral* the cathedral is worth visiting *o* worth a visit, it is worth the trouble to pay a visit to the cathedral ‖ *tener lo que uno se merece* to get what one deserves.
◆ *vi* to be deserving, to be worthy ‖ *mereció bien de la patria* he served his country well.
◆ *vpr* to deserve.

merecidamente *adv* deservedly, rightly.

merecido *m* deserts *pl*, due, deserved punishment ‖ — *a cada uno su merecido* give the devil his due ‖ FIG *dar su merecido* to settle one's account ‖ *llevar* or *tener su merecido* to get one's deserts *o* one's due, to get what is coming to one.

merecimiento *m* merit, worth.

merendar* *vi* to have *o* to take an afternoon snack, to have (a light) tea (tomar la merienda) ‖ to picnic (en el campo).
◆ *vt* to have as an afternoon snack, to have for tea; *merendar café y galletas* to have coffee and biscuits for tea.
◆ *vpr* FIG & FAM *merendarse una cosa* to land, to get hold of (conseguir) | *merendarse a* to get the better of (dominar), to lick, to trounce (derrotar), to rush off (hacer rápidamente), to throw down the drain (una fortuna).

merendero *m* refreshment room, teahouse, snack bar (donde se merienda) ‖ picnic spot (en el campo).

merendona *f* FIG spread (merienda abundante) | picnic (merienda campestre).

merengue *m* meringue (dulce) ‖ FIG weakling (débil) ‖ FIG & FAM *durará menos que un merengue en la puerta de una escuela* it will not last five minutes.

meretriz *f* harlot, prostitute, meretrix.

mergánsar; mergo *m* ZOOL cormorant, merganser.

Mérida *n pr* GEOGR Mérida.

meridano, na *adj* [of *o* from] Mérida [town in Mexico].
◆ *m/f* native *o* inhabitant of Mérida.

merideño, ña *adj* [of *o* from] Mérida [town in Extremadura (Spain), state of Venezuela].
◆ *m/f* native *o* inhabitant of Mérida.

meridiano, na *adj* meridian, midday, noon (de mediodía) ‖ meridian; *altitud, línea meridiana* meridian altitude, line ‖ dazzling, brilliant (luz) ‖ — FIG *con claridad meridiana* with striking clarity, very clearly | *ser de una claridad meridiana* to be as clear as day *o* as clear as crystal *o* crystal clear.
◆ *m* ASTR & GEOGR meridian; *primer meridiano* prime meridian.
◆ *f* couch (cama) | siesta, afternoon nap (siesta).

meridional *adj* meridional (del sur de Europa) ‖ Southern, South (en general); *América meridional* South America; *Europa meridional* Southern Europe.
◆ *m/f* meridional (del sur de Europa) ‖ Southerner (en general).

merienda *f* afternoon snack, tea (por la tarde) ‖ lunch, midday meal (del mediodía) ‖ picnic (campestre) ‖ packed lunch (provisiones para una excursión), picnic (para una merienda campestre) ‖ — *ir de merienda* to go for a picnic ‖ FIG & FAM *juntar meriendas* to join forces ‖ *merienda cena* high tea ‖ FIG & FAM *merienda de negros* free-for-all, bedlam.

merino, na *adj/s* merino (carnero, lana, tela).

mérito *m* merit; *obra de poco mérito* work of little merit ‖ worth (valor); *cosa de poco mérito* thing of little worth ‖ desert; *ser recompensado según sus méritos* to meet with one's deserts ‖ — *atribuirse el mérito de* to take the glory for ‖ *de mérito* of merit; *autor de gran mérito* author of great merit ‖ FIG *hacer méritos para* to strive to make o.s. deserving of ‖ *méritos de guerra* mention in dispatches ‖ *quitar méritos a* to detract from.

meritorio, ria *adj* meritorious, praiseworthy (cosa) ‖ of merit, deserving, worthy (persona).
◆ *m* improver, unpaid trainee (empleado).

Merlín *npr m* Merlin ‖ FIG *sabe más que Merlín* he knows everything.

merlo *m* black wrasse (pez) ‖ AMER idiot, ass (tonto).

merluza *f* hake (pez) ‖ FIG & FAM ass, idiot (tonto) ‖ FIG & FAM *coger, tener una merluza* to get *o* to be canned *o* sloshed (emborracharse).

merma *f* decrease, reduction (disminución) ‖ loss, wastage (pérdida).

mermar *vt* to decrease, to reduce, to cut down (la paga, las raciones, etc.) ‖ to deplete, to reduce; *capital mermado* depleted capital ‖ FIG to cast a slur on; *mermarle a uno la reputación* to cast a slur on s.o.'s reputation ‖ to cause to go down (un líquido).
◆ *vi* to decrease, to diminish, to lessen ‖ to go down (un líquido).

mermelada *f* jam, preserves *pl* (frutas cortadas y cocidas con azúcar); *mermelada de fresa* strawberry jam ‖ *mermelada de naranjas amargas* marmalade.

mero *m* grouper (pez).

mero, ra *adj* mere, pure, simple; *por el mero hecho de* through the mere fact of; *una mera casualidad* a pure coincidence ‖ AMER real (verdadero); *es el mero amo* he is the real boss ‖ — AMER *llegó a la mera hora* he arrived right on time (en el momento preciso) | *ser el mero malo* to be wickedness itself | *uno mero, una mera* only one | *yo mero* I myself.
◆ *adv* AMER really (verdaderamente) | exactly; *son mero las dos* it is exactly two o'clock (en punto).

merodeador, ra *adj* MIL marauding ‖ prowling.
◆ *m/f* MIL marauder ‖ prowler.

merodear *vi* MIL to maraud ‖ to prowl, to roam ‖ *merodear por* to scout *o* to snoop around (explorar, curiosear).

merodeo *m* MIL marauding ‖ prowling.

Meroveo *npr m* Meroveous, Merovaeous.

merovingio, gia *adj/s* HIST Merovingian.

mes *m* month; *en el mes de mayo* in the month of May; *dentro de un mes* within a month, in a month's time; *el mes pasado, que viene* last, next month; *cobra cien libras al* or *por mes* he is paid a hundred pounds a month ‖ monthly *o* month's pay *o* wage *o* salary, wage for the month (salario); *cobrar el mes* to draw one's monthly wage *o* one's wage for the month ‖ menses *pl* menstruation (menstruo) ‖ — *alquilar una habitación al* or *por mes* to rent a room by the month ‖ *el mes corriente* the current month ‖ *mes civil* calendar month ‖ *mes lunar* lunar month ‖ *pagar por meses* to pay by the month.

mesa *f* table; *en la mesa* on the table (encima), at the table (alrededor) ‖ bureau, desk, writing desk, writing table (escritorio de oficina) ‖ board, bureau, general committee (de una asamblea) ‖ GEOGR tableland, plateau, meseta (meseta) ‖ landing (de escalera) ‖ table (de una piedra preciosa) ‖ flat (de una hoja) ‖ revenue, income (renta eclesiástica) ‖ FIG table (comida); *en casa de mi tía siempre hay buena mesa* my aunt always keeps a good table ‖ game (partida de billar) ‖ — *¡a la mesa!* lunch (dinner, etc.) is ready! ‖ *alzar* or *quitar* or *levantar la mesa* to clear the table ‖ *a mesa puesta* with all one's needs provided for ‖ *bendecir la mesa* to say grace ‖ *de mesa* table; *vino de mesa* table wine || *estar a mesa y mantel en casa de uno* to receive free board from s.o. || *levantarse de la mesa* to leave the table || *mesa camilla* round table under which a brazier is placed || *mesa con largueros* draw-leaf *o* extension table || *mesa de alas* table with flaps || *mesa de altar* altar || MÚS *mesa de armonía* soundboard (de piano), belly (de violín) || *mesa de batalla* sorting table (correos) || *mesa de billar* billiard table || *mesa de juego* gambling *o* gaming table || *mesa de noche* bedside table || MED *mesa de operaciones* operating table || *mesa de tijera* or *plegable* folding table || *mesa electoral* electoral college || *mesa extensible* extension table || *mesa redonda* common table (de huéspedes mezclados), table d'hôte (en los restaurantes), round table, round-table discussion *o* conference (reunión) || FIG *mesa revuelta* hotchpotch, medley (batiburrillo), miscellany pages (de periódico) || *mesa y cama* bed and board || *poner la mesa* to lay *o* to set the table || *sentarse a la mesa* to sit down at the *o* to table, to sit down to lunch (dinner, etc.) || *servir la mesa* to wait at table || *tener a uno a mesa y mantel* to give s.o. free board || *tener mesa franca* to keep open house || *tener mesa franca en casa de uno* to be assured of a place at s.o.'s table.

mesadura *f* tearing [of the hair *o* beard].

Mesalina *npr f* Messalina.

mesana *f* MAR mizen, mizzen, mizzenmast, mizzenmast (mástil) | mizzensail, mizzensail (vela).

mesar *vt* to tear (at) (one's hair *o* beard).
◆ *vpr* to tear (at) (one's hair *o* beard).

mescal *m* AMER mescal.

mescolanza *f* FAM ⟶ **mezcolanza.**

mesencéfalo *m* MED mesencephalon.

mesenterio *m* ANAT mesentery.

mesera *f* AMER waitress (camarera).

mesero *m* AMER waiter (camarero).

meseta *f* plateau, tableland, meseta (llanura); *la meseta de Castilla* the plateau of Castile || landing (de escalera).

mesiánico, ca *adj* Messianic.

mesianismo *m* Messianism.

Mesías *m* Messiah.

mesilla *f* small table (mesa pequeña) || landing (de escalera) || ledge, sill (de ventana) || mantelpiece (de chimenea) || rail, coping (de balaustrada) || — *mesilla de noche* bedside table || *mesilla de ruedas* trolley.

mesmedad *f* FAM *por su propia mesmedad* by itself.

mesmo, ma *adj* (ant) FAM ⟶ **mismo.**

mesnada *f* armed retinue || FIG band, group, company (compañía).
◆ *pl* FIG followers (partidarios).

mesnadero *m* man-at-arms, member of an armed retinue.

mesocardia *f* MED mesocardia.

mesocarpio; mesocarpo *m* BOT mesocarp.

mesocéfalo, la *adj* mesocephalic, mesencephalic.

mesodermo *m* ANAT mesoderm.

mesolítico, ca *adj/sm* Mesolithic.

mesón *m* inn, tavern, hostelry (posada en tiempos antiguos) || old-style tavern (establecimiento moderno) || FÍS meson.

mesonero, ra *m/f* innkeeper (hombre o mujer), landlord (hombre), landlady (mujer).
◆ *adj* inn, tavern.

Mesopotamia *npr f* GEOGR Mesopotamia.

mesopotámico, ca *adj/s* Mesopotamian.

mesosfera *f* mesosphere.

mesotelio *m* mesothelium.

mesoterapia *f* MED mesotherapy.

mesotórax *m* mesothorax.

mesotrón *m* FÍS mesotron.

mesozoico, ca *adj* GEOL Mesozoic.

mesta *f* «mesta» [medieval association of cattle farmers].
◆ *pl* confluence [of streams] (confluente).

mester *m* (ant) trade, craft (oficio) || verse; *mester de clerecía, de juglaría* clerical, minstrel verse.

mestizaje *m* mestization, crossbreeding.

mestizar *vt* to crossbreed (cruzar razas).

mestizo, za *adj* half-bred, half-caste (persona) || crossbred, half-blooded (animal) || mongrel (perro) || hybrid (vegetal).
◆ *m/f* mestizo (hombre), mestiza (mujer), half-caste, half-breed (hombre o mujer) || crossbreed, half-blood (animal) || mongrel (perro) || hybrid (vegetal).

mesura *f* moderation, restraint, measure (moderación) || gravity, composure (compostura) || respect, civility (respeto) || (ant) temperance (templanza).

mesuradamente *adv* with moderation *o* restraint.

mesurado, da *adj* moderate, restrained (moderado) || circumspect (circunspecto) || temperate (templado) || grave, composed (sereno).

mesurar *vt* to moderate, to restrain (moderar) || to consider, to think over (considerar) || *mesurar sus palabras* to weigh one's words.
◆ *vpr* to moderate *o* to restrain o.s., to act with moderation *o* restraint || *mesurarse en sus palabras* to weigh one's words.

meta *f* goal, aim, objective (finalidad); *conseguir su meta* to reach one's goal; *fijarse una meta* to set oneself a goal || DEP goal (portería) | finish (en las carreras ciclistas, de automóviles), finish line, tape (en atletismo), winning post (de caballos).
◆ *m* goalkeeper (guardameta).

metabólico, ca *adj* BIOL metabolic.

metabolismo *m* BIOL metabolism.

metacarpiano, na *adj* ANAT metacarpal.

metacarpo *m* ANAT metacarpus.

metadona *f* methadone.

metafase *f* BIOL metaphase.

metafísico, ca *adj* metaphysical.
◆ *m/f* metaphysician.
◆ *f* metaphysics.

metáfora *f* metaphor.

metafórico, ca *adj* metaphorical, metaphoric.

metaforizar *vt* to metaphorize, to express metaphorically.

metagoge *f* personification, prosopopoeia.

metal *m* metal || brass (latón) || FIG timbre, ring (de la voz) | quality, condition (calidad) || HERÁLD metal (oro o plata) || — FAM *el vil metal* filthy lucre || MÚS *instrumentos de metal* brass (instruments) || *metal blanco* white metal, nickel *o* German silver || *metal de imprenta* type metal || *metal precioso* precious metal.

metaldehído *m* QUÍM metaldehyde.

metálico, ca *adj* metallic.
◆ *m* (hard) cash, specie (monedas y billetes); *pagar en metálico* to pay (in) cash || coin, specie (monedas).

metalífero, ra *adj* metalliferous, metal-bearing.

metalistería *f* metalwork.

metalización *f* metallization [US metalization].

metalizar *vt* to metallize [US to metalize].
◆ *vpr* to become metallized [US to become metalized] || FIG to go money-mad.

metaloide *m* QUÍM metalloid.

metalurgia *f* metallurgy.

metalúrgico, ca *adj* metallurgical, metallurgic.
◆ *m* metallurgist.

metamórfico, ca *adj* GEOL metamorphic.

metamorfismo *m* GEOL metamorphism.

metamorfosear *vt* to metamorphose, to change.
◆ *vpr* to be metamorphosed, to change completely.

metamorfosis; metamórfosis *f inv* metamorphosis, transformation; *sufrir una metamorfosis* to undergo metamorphosis.

metano *m* QUÍM methane.

metanol *m* QUÍM methanol.

metaplasmo *m* GRAM metaplasm.

metapsíquico, ca *adj* metapsychic, metapsychical.
◆ *f* metapsychology.

metástasis *f* MED metastasis.

metatarsiano *adj/sm* metatarsal.

metatarso *m* ANAT metatarsus.

metate *m* stone [for grinding cacao and maize].

metátesis *f* GRAM metathesis.

metatórax *m* metathorax (de insectos).

metazoario, ria *adj* ZOOL metazoan.
◆ *m* metazoan.
◆ *pl* metazoa.

metazoo *m* ZOOL metazoan.

meteco *m* foreigner, alien (extranjero).

metedor *m* napkin [US diaper] (de los niños) || smuggler, contrabandist (contrabandista) || IMPR imposing stone, imposing table.

metedura *f* FAM putting || FAM *metedura de pata* blunder, bloomer.

metempsicosis *f* metempsychosis.

meteórico, ca *adj* meteoric.

meteorismo *m* VET bloat || MED meteorism.

meteorito *m* meteorite.

meteorizar *vt* VET to produce bloat in || MED to produce meteorism in.
◆ *vpr* VET to get bloat || MED to become affected with meteorism || AGR to be affected by atmospheric agents (la Tierra).

meteoro *m* meteor.

meteorología *f* meteorology.

meteorológico, ca *adj* meteorological, meteorologic || *parte meteorológico* weather report.

meteorólogo, ga *m/f* meteorologist.

meter *vt*

> 1. INTRODUCIR 2. CAUSAR 3. OTROS SENTIDOS 4. LOCUCIONES 5. VERBO PRONOMINAL

1. INTRODUCIR to put; *meter la mano en el bolsillo* to put one's hand in *o* into one's pocket; *meter en la cama, en la cárcel* to put to bed, in prison || to put, to introduce, to insert; *meter un tubo en la tráquea de un enfermo* to introduce a tube into a patient's windpipe || to place, to put (colocar) || to squeeze in (en un sitio estrecho) || to smuggle in (en fraude); *meter tabaco* to smuggle in tobacco || FIG to get, to drive; *intenté meterle en la cabeza que* I tried to get it into his head that || to get *o* to find a job (poner a trabajar); *le han metido de carnicero* they have found him a job as a butcher || to take, to bring; *meter a su hijo en el negocio fa-*

miliar to bring one's son into the family business ‖ to send (*en* to), to put (*en* in), to put (a un niño en un colegio) ‖ FIG & FAM to get; *¡en menudo lío me has metido!* a fine mess you've got me into! | to involve, to get mixed up, to get involved (enredar); *no quiero que me metas en tus asuntos* I don't want you getting me mixed up in your affairs ‖ DEP to pocket (a ball) (en el billar), to hole (en golf), to basket (en baloncesto), to put in (en fútbol) ‖ *meter a uno a trabajar* to put s.o. to work, to set s.o. working.

2. CAUSAR to make; *meter ruido* to make a noise ‖ to make, to kick up (*fam*); *meter jaleo* to kick up a row ‖ to cause; *meter enredos* to cause confusion ‖ — *meterle a uno un susto* to give s.o. a fright ‖ *meterle miedo a uno* to frighten *o* to scare s.o. ‖ *meter un lío* to make a mess.

3. OTROS SENTIDOS to take up (acortar una prenda) ‖ to take in (estrechar una prenda) ‖ to compress, to squeeze *o* to cram together (apretar); *meter los renglones de una plana* to compress the lines on a page ‖ to present, to hand in (una solicitud) ‖ to stake, to bet, to put (en el juego, en la lotería) ‖ to put, to invest, to tie up (invertir) ‖ to pay in, to place (en un banco, en una caja de ahorros, etc.) ‖ DEP to score (un gol) ‖ FAM to give (un golpe, una paliza) | to tell (enbustes) | to spread, to start (chismes) | to give; *nos va a meter el rollo de siempre* he is going to give us his usual speech ‖ MAR to take in [the sails].

4. LOCUCIONES FAM *anda siempre metido con los golfillos de la calle* he is always knocking around with the little street urchins | *a todo meter* at full speed ‖ FIG *estar muy metido en política* to be deeply involved in politics | *meter baza en* to poke one's nose into, to interfere in (un asunto), to butt into, to intervene in, to interrupt (la conversación) | *meter cizaña* to sow discord, to cause *o* to make trouble | *meter en cintura* or *en vereda* to make s.o. behave, to bring s.o. into line *o* to heel ‖ FIG & FAM *meter la nariz* or *las narices en todo* to poke *o* to stick one's nose in everywhere, to be a busybody | *meter la pata* to put one's foot in it ‖ AUT *meter la primera (segunda, etc.)* to change into first (second, etc.) ‖ *meterle al público un producto por los ojos* to shove a product down the public's throat (elogiar) ‖ *meter prisa* to hurry (up), to make haste (uno mismo), to hurry, to rush (a otro) ‖ FIG *tener a uno metido en un puño* to have s.o. in the palm of one's hand.

5. VERBO PRONOMINAL to get; *meterse en la cama* to get into bed; *se me ha metido una carbonilla en el ojo* some soot has got in my eye ‖ FIG to get; *¿dónde te has metido?* where did you get to? | to go, to enter, to take; *se metió en una bocacalle* he went into a side street | to become; *meterse monja* to become a nun | to turn (soldado) | to jut out; *la costa se mete en el mar* the coast juts out into the sea ‖ — *¿dónde se habrá metido mi libro?* where can my book have got to? ‖ FIG *meterse a* to become (con sustantivo); *meterse a fraile* to become a monk; to start, to begin (con infinitivo); *meterse a escribir* to start writing *o* to write | *meterse con* to bother, to annoy (jorobar), to tease (embromar); *meterse con alguien (en plan de broma)* to tease s. o; to pick a quarrel with (buscar pelea), to pick on; *deja de meterte con tu hermanito* stop picking on your little brother; to attack; *todos los críticos se meten con él* all the critics attack him | *meterse en* to get into (aventuras, vicios, etc.), to go into (negocio), to get involved in, to get mixed up in; *se ha metido en un asunto poco claro* he has got involved in some shady deal; to meddle, to interfere; *siempre se mete donde no le llaman* he always meddles in things that do not concern him; *meterse en todo* to interfere in everything; to get into; *meterse en dificultades* to get into difficulties; to enter; *meterse en una discusión* to enter a discussion; *meterse en unas explicaciones inútiles* to enter into futile explanations; to go into, to enter; *se metió en una tienda* he went into *o* he entered a shop; to go; *esta pieza se mete aquí dentro* this piece goes in here | *meterse en gastos* to go to expense | *meterse en sí mismo* to withdraw into o.s., to go into one's shell | *metérsele a uno en la cabeza hacer algo* to take it into one's head to do sth. (ocurrírsele); *se le metió en la cabeza ir solo* he took it into his head to go alone; to set one's mind on doing sth. (empeñarse) | *métete en lo tuyo* or *en tus cosas* or *en lo que te importa* mind your own business | *¿por qué te metes?* what's it to you?, what business is it of yours?

meterete; metete *adj* AMER meddlesome, interfering.
◆ *m/f* AMER meddler, interferer.

metiche *adj* AMER meddlesome, interfering.
◆ *m/f* AMER meddler, interferer.

meticulosidad *f* meticulousness, meticulosity.

meticuloso, sa *adj* meticulous ‖ finicky (exageradamente cuidadoso) ‖ fearful, meticulous (ant) fearful, meticulous (miedoso).

metidito, ta *adj* FAM *metidita en carnes* plump, fleshy | *metidito en años* getting on, a little long in the tooth.

metido, da *adj* ⟶ **meter** ‖ — *metido en carnes* plump ‖ *metido en años* advanced in years ‖ *pan metido en harina* bread rich in flour.
◆ *m* punch (golpe) ‖ shove (empujón); *darle a uno un metido en la espalda* to give s.o. a shove in the back ‖ material let in, seam (al estrechar), material turned up, hem (al acortar) [en costura] ‖ napkin [*US* diaper] (metedor) ‖ FIG & FAM dressing down (reprensión); *darle a uno un metido* to give s.o. a dressing down.

metileno *m* QUÍM methylene ‖ *azul de metileno* methylene blue.

metílico, ca *adj* QUÍM methylic.

metilo *m* QUÍM methyl.

metódico, ca *adj* methodical.

metodismo *m* REL methodism.

metodista *adj/s* REL methodist.

metodizar *vt* to methodize.

método *m* method ‖ method, course; *método de lectura* reading method ‖ — *con método* methodically ‖ *método de piano* piano tutor.

metodología *f* methodology.

metomentodo *m/f* FAM meddler, busybody.

metonimia *f* metonymy.

metonímico, ca *adj* metonymical.

metopa *f* ARQ metope.

metraje *m* CINEM footage, length (of film) ‖ — *un corto metraje* a short film ‖ *un largo metraje* a full-length film, a feature film.

metralla *f* shrapnel (al estallar un proyectil) ‖ grapeshot (carga) ‖ *granada de metralla* frangible shell.

metralleta *f* tommy gun, submachine gum (arma).

métrica *f* POÉT metrics.

métrico, ca *adj* metric; *sistema métrico* metric system ‖ metrical (del verso, de la métrica) ‖ *cinta métrica* tape measure.

metrificación *f* metrification, versification.

metrificar *vi* to versify.
◆ *vt* to metrify, to versify.

metritis *f* MED metritis.

metro *m* metre [*US* meter] (medida); *metro cuadrado, cúbico* square, cubic metre ‖ metre [*US* meter] (verso) ‖ ruler (regla) ‖ tape measure (cinta) ‖ *medir por metros* to measure in metres *o* by the metre.

— OBSERV Como el *metro* no se emplea en los países anglosajones, en algunos casos se puede utilizar como equivalente la *yard*, que mide casi un metro: *¿cuántos metros le hacen falta?* how many yards do you need? (de una tela).

metro *m* underground, tube [*US* subway] (transporte) ‖ *metro aéreo* or *a cielo abierto* overhead railway.

metrología *f* metrology.

metrónomo *m* MÚS metronome.

metrópoli *f* metropolis ‖ metropolis, mother country (nación).

metropolitano, na *adj* metropolitan.
◆ *m* REL metropolitan ‖ underground, tube [*US* subway] (transporte).

mexicano, na *adj/s* Mexican.

México *npr m* GEOGR Mexico (país) | Mexico City (ciudad).

— OBSERV Although *México* (with an *x* instead of a *j*) is the only spelling accepted in Mexico, the pronunciation of the word is not affected.

mezcal *m* AMER mescal (pita, aguardiente).

mezcalina *f* mescaline.

mezcla *f* mixing, mixture, blending (acción de mezclar) ‖ mixture (resultado); *una mezcla de varios ingredientes* a mixture of several ingredients ‖ mixture, blend, combination; *mezcla de buenas y malas cualidades* blend of good and bad qualities ‖ mortar (argamasa) ‖ CINEM & RAD mixing ‖ AUT mixture ‖ mixture, fabric woven with different sorts of thread (tela).

mezclador, ra *m/f* mixer ‖ CINEM *mezclador de imagen, de sonido* image, sound mixer.
◆ *f* mixing machine, mixer (máquina).

mezcladura *f*; **mezclamiento** *m* mixture.

mezclar *vt* to mix; *mezclar una cosa con otra* to mix one thing with another ‖ to mix, to blend; *mezclar colores* to mix colours; *mezclar dos vinos* to blend two wines ‖ to mix up (desordenar) ‖ to mix, to mingle (reunir); *mezclar en la misma clase niños de distintas edades* to mix children of different ages in the same class ‖ FIG to mix, to mingle, to combine; *mezclar la amabilidad con la severidad* to combine kindness with severity ‖ to shuffle (los naipes).
◆ *vpr* to mix; *el aceite y el agua no se mezclan* oil and water do not mix ‖ to mingle; *mezclarse con la multitud* to mingle with the crowd ‖ FIG to mix; *no le gusta a su padre la gente con quien se mezcla* her father does not like the people she mixes with | to take part (tomar parte) | to meddle, to interfere; *no te mezcles en mis asuntos* don't meddle in my affairs | to get mixed up, to get involved (en negocios sucios).

mezclilla *f* mixture, light cloth woven with different sorts of thread (tela).

mezcolanza *f* mixture (mezcla) ‖ FAM hotchpotch, jumble [of ideas, etc.] (batiburrillo).

mezquindad *f* meanness, niggardliness, stinginess (tacañería) ‖ mean thing (acción tacaña) ‖ paltriness, scantiness (escasez) ‖ paltry thing (cosa insignificante).

mezquino, na *adj* mean, niggardly, stingy (tacaño) ‖ wretched, small (pequeño) ‖ paltry, scanty (escaso); *un salario mezquino* a paltry wage ‖ poor, wretched (pobre) ‖ petty, narrow, small (mentalidad).
◆ *m/f* mean person.

mezquita *f* mosque.

mi *m* MÚS Mi, me, E (nota).

mi, mis *adj poses de la 1ª pers* my; *mi libro, mi madre, mis zapatos* my book, my mother, my shoes.

mí *pron pers de la 1ª pers del sing* me (used with a preposition); *lo trajo para mí* he brought it for me; *nos acompañó a mi hermano y a mí* he accompanied my brother and me || — *¡a mí!* help! (socorro) || *¡a mí con ésas!* come off it! || *a mí me toca* or *me corresponde hacerlo* it is for me to do it || *en cuanto a mí respecta, para mí* or *por lo que a mí respecta* as for me, as far as I am concerned || *por mí mismo* by myself, on my own || FAM *¿(y) a mí qué?* what's it to me?, so what?.

— OBSERV *Mí* is not translated in constructions such as: *a mí no me importa* it's all the same to me; *a mí me gusta el jazz* I like jazz, etc.

miaja *f* crumb (migaja) || FAM bit; *ha heredado una miaja de dinero* he has come into a bit of money; *espérate una miaja* hang on a bit | scrap; *no tiene una miaja de inteligencia* he hasn't a scrap of intelligence.

mialgia *f* MED myalgia.

miasma *m* miasma.

— OBSERV The use of *miasma* as a feminine noun is incorrect.

— OBSERV El plural en inglés es *miasmas* o *miasmata*.

miau *m* miaow, mew, meow (del gato).

mica *f* MIN mica.

mica *f* female long-tailed monkey (mona) || AMER *agarrar una mica* to get sloshed (emborracharse).

micáceo, a *adj* MIN micaceous.

micado *m* mikado (emperador del Japón).

micción *f* micturition.

micela *f* micelle (partícula).

micelio *m* BOT mycelium.

Micenas *n pr* GEOGR Mycenae.

micer *m* messire, sir (título antiguo) || master (dicho de los abogados).

micifuz *m* FAM puss, pussy, kitty (gato).

mico *m* ZOOL monkey (mono) | long-tailed monkey (mono de cola larga) || FIG & FAM monkey face, ape (persona fea) | lecher (lujurioso) | little monkey [affectionate insult to a child] (niño) | conceited puppy (persona presumida) | runt (hombre pequeño) || — FIG & FAM *dar* or *hacer un mico a uno* to stand s.o. up (faltar a una cita) | *dar el mico* to disappoint | *dejar a uno hecho un mico* to make a monkey out of s.o., to put s.o. to shame | *quedarse hecho un mico* to be shown up *o* ridiculed, to be made a monkey of | *ser el último mico* not to count, to be the lowest of the low, to be the pip-squeak | *volverse mico* to strive hard, to take pains.

micosis *f* MED mycosis.

micra *f* micron (micrón).

micrero, ra *m/f* AMER minibus driver (conductor de microbús).

micro *m* FAM mike, microphone (micrófono) || AMER bus (autobús).

microanálisis *m* microanalysis.

microbiano, na *adj* microbic, microbial.

microbicida *m* microbicide.

microbio *m* microbe.

microbiología *f* microbiology.

microbús *m* minibus (pequeño autobús).

microcefalia *f* microcephaly.

microcéfalo, la *adj* microcephalic, microcephalous.

microcirugía *f* microsurgery.

microclimatología *f* microclimatology.

microclima *m* microclimate.

microcomputador, ra *m/f* INFORM microcomputer.

microcosmo *m* microcosm.

microcósmico, ca *adj* microcosmic.

microchip *m* INFORM microchip.

microeconomía *f* microeconomics.

microedición *f* INFORM desktop publishing.

microelectrónica *f* microelectronics.

microfaradio *m* FÍS microfarad.

microfilm; microfilme *m* microfilm.

— OBSERV The plural in Spanish is *microfilmes*.

microfilmar *vt* to microfilm.

microfísica *f* microphysics.

micrófono *m* microphone; *hablar por el micrófono* to speak through *o* over the microphone.

microfotografía *f* microphotography (arte) || microphotograph (fotografía).

micrografía *f* micrography.

microhmio; microhm *m* ELECTR microhm.

microinformática *f* INFORM microcomputing.

microlentillas *f pl* contact lenses.

micrométrico, ca *adj* micrometrical, micrometric.

micrómetro *m* micrometer.

micrón *m* micron (micra).

Micronesia *npr f* GEOGR Micronesia.

micronesio, sia *adj/s* Micronesian.

microonda *f* microwave.

microómnibus *m* minibus.

microordenador *m* INFORM microcomputer.

microorganismo *m* microorganism.

microprocesador *m* INFORM microprocessor.

microprograma *m* INFORM microprogram.

microprogramación *f* INFORM microprogramming.

microscopia *f* microscopy.

microscópico, ca *adj* microscopic, microscopical.

microscopio *m* microscope; *microscopio electrónico* electron microscope.

microsegundo *m* microsecond.

microsurco *adj m* microgroove (disco).
◆ *m* microgroove.

microtaxi *m* minicab.

microteléfono *m* handset [combined hand microphone and receiver].

michelín *m* FAM spare tyre (en la cintura).

micho, cha *m/f* FAM puss, pussy, kitty (gato).

midriasis *f* MED mydriasis.

MIE *abrev de Ministerio de Industria y Energía* Spanish Ministry of Industry and Energy.

mieditis *f* FAM jitters *pl*, funk (miedo) || — FAM *pasar mieditis* to have the jitters, to have the wind up | *tener mieditis* to be jittery *o* windy (permanentemente), to have the jitters, to have the wind up (temporalmente).

miedo *m* fear || — *dar miedo* to be frightening || *dar miedo a alguien* to frighten *o* to scare s.o. || FAM *de miedo* terrific, fantastic (formidable), awful, ghastly (horroroso), terribly well, marvellously (bien) || POP *estar cagado de miedo* to be scared stiff || *fue mayor el miedo que el daño, tuvimos más miedo que otra cosa* we were more frightened than hurt, we were more frightened than anything else || *meterle miedo a uno* to frighten *o* to scare s.o. || *morirse de miedo* to die of fright (sentido real), to be frightened *o* scared to death *o* out of one's wits (asustarse) || *pasar mucho miedo* to be very scared *o* frightened, to be terrified || *película de miedo* horror film || *por miedo a* for fear of || *por miedo a* or *de que* for fear that || *que da* or *que mete miedo* fearsome, frightful (adj), frighteningly, fearsomely, frightfully, dreadfully (adv); *de un feo que mete miedo* dreadfully ugly || *sin miedo y sin tacha* fearless and faultless, fearless and without reproach || *temblar de miedo* to tremble with fear, to quake in one's shoes || *tener más miedo que vergüenza o que once viejas* to be scared out of one's wits, to be in a blue funk (*fam*) (pasar miedo), to be cowardly (ser miedoso) || *tener miedo a* or *de* to be afraid *o* scared of, to fear; *tener miedo a la oscuridad* to be afraid of the dark || *tener miedo (de) que* to be afraid that; *tengo miedo que haga una tontería* I am afraid that he will do sth. stupid || *tener miedo hasta de la sombra de sí mismo* to be afraid of one's own shadow || *tener un miedo cerval* to be scared stiff.

miedoso, sa *adj* fearful, timorous || cowardly (cobarde).

miel *f* honey; *dulce como la miel* as sweet as honey || — FIG *dejar a uno con la miel en los labios* to leave s.o. unsatisfied, to cut short s.o.'s enjoyment | *hacerse de miel* to be too kind || *luna de miel* honeymoon || *miel de caña* molasses || FAM *miel sobre hojuelas* better still, so much the better || FIG *no hay miel sin hiel* no rose without a thorn | *palabras de miel* honeyed words || *panal de miel* honeycomb || FIG *ser todo miel* to be all (sugar and) honey.

mielga *f* BOT lucerne [US alfalfa].

mielgo, ga *adj* twin.

mielina *f* ANAT myelin, myeline.

mielitis *f* MED myelitis.

miembro *m* ANAT member, limb (brazo, pierna, etc.) | member (miembro viril) || MAT member (de una ecuación) || FIG member (de una comunidad); *miembro vitalicio* life member; *miembro con plenos poderes* fully-fledged member || ANAT *miembro viril* virile *o* male member.
◆ *adj* member; *estado miembro* member State.

miente *f* (ant) mind, thought || — *caer en* or *en las mientes* to come to mind || *ni por mientes* never || *parar* or *poner mientes en* to think of, to consider || *traer a las mientes* to recall, to bring to mind (recordar) || *venirse a las mientes* to occur to, to come to (s.o.'s) mind.

mientras *adv/conj* while, whilst; *mientras yo trabajo, él juega* while I work, he plays || (for) as long as, so long as; *mientras viva, pensaré en usted* I shall think of you as long as I live || meanwhile (mientras tanto) || — *mientras más* the more; *mientras más tiene, más desea* the more he has, the more he wants || *mientras que* whereas (oposición); *él lo confesó, mientras que tú no dijiste nada* he owned up to it, whereas you said nothing || *mientras no se pruebe lo contrario* until proven otherwise || *mientras tanto* meanwhile, in the meantime.

miera *f* juniper oil.

miércoles *m* Wednesday; *el miércoles pasado, que viene* last, next Wednesday; *vendré el miércoles* I shall come on Wednesday; *viene los miércoles, cada miércoles* he comes on Wednesday, every Wednesday || — *miércoles de ceniza* Ash Wednesday || *Miércoles Santo* Holy Wednesday [of Holy Week].

mierda *f* POP shit || FAM muck, filth (suciedad) || — POP *es una mierda* it is crap || *es un Don Mierda* he's a nobody | *¡váyase a la mierda!* go to hell!

mies *f* corn [US grain] (cereales ya maduros); *segar la mies* to reap the corn || harvest time (tiempo de la siega).

◆ *pl* corn, *sing; las mieses están a punto para ser segadas* the corn is ready for reaping ‖ cornfields (campos).

miga *f* crumb (migaja, parte interior del pan) ‖ bit, crumb (pedacito en general) ‖ FIG & FAM substance, marrow, pith, core (meollo) | snag (dificultad) ‖ (ant) pap (papilla) ‖ — FIG *tener mucha miga* to be marrowy *o* full of substance (tener sustancia), to be full of interest (ser interesante), to give sth. to think about, to be no straighforward matter (ser complicado) ‖ *tierra de miga* heavy *o* clayey soil.
◆ *pl* CULIN fried breadcrumbs ‖ — FIG & FAM *hacer buenas migas* to get on well (*con* with), to hit it off (*con* with) | *hacer malas migas* to get on badly (*con* with), not to hit it off, not to get on (*con* with) ‖ *hacer migas* to crumb (el pan), to smash to bits *o* pieces (hacer trizas), to shatter (cansar), to ruin (proyectos, etc.), to get (s.o.) down (fastidiar a una persona), to make mincemeat of (dejar muy maltrecho), to floor (confundir, derrotar en una discusión), to make (s.o.) go to pieces (deshacer moralmente) ‖ *hacerse migas* to be smashed to pieces ‖ *migas ilustradas* breadcrumbs fried with pieces of larding bacon.

migaja *f* crumb (de pan) ‖ bit, crumb, scrap (pedacito) ‖ FIG scrap, bit (de ciencia, etc.) ‖ *migaja de pan* breadcrumb.
◆ *pl* leftovers, leavings, scraps (sobras).

migajón *m* crumb ‖ FIG & FAM marrow, pith, substance.

migala *f* mygale (araña).

migar *vt* to crumble (partir en trozos) ‖ to put lumps of bread in [a liquid]; *migar la leche* to put lumps of bread in milk.

migración *f* migration.

migraña *f* migraine.

migratorio, ria *adj* migratory, migrating (las aves) ‖ migratory; *movimiento migratorio* migratory movement ‖ *cultivo migratorio* shifting cultivation.

Miguel *npr m* Michael (nombre de pila) ‖ *Miguel Ángel* Michelangelo.

mihrab *m* mihrab (de una mezquita).

mijo *m* BOT millet.

mil *adj* a thousand, one thousand; *mil hombres, mil años* one thousand men, a thousand years ‖ thousandth (milésimo) ‖ — *el año mil* the year one thousand ‖ *el año mil novecientos setenta y cinco* the year nineteen (hundred and) seventy-five ‖ *las Mil y Una Noches* the Thousand and One Nights ‖ *mil millones* one *o* a milliard, a thousand million [US a *o* one billion]; *cinco mil millones de pesetas* five milliard pesetas ‖ FIG *mil veces* thousands of times, a thousand times.
◆ *m* (one or a) thousand (número) ‖ — FIG *a las mil y quinientas* at an unearthly hour.
◆ *pl* thousands; *muchos miles de libras* many thousands of pounds ‖ *miles de veces* thousands of times ‖ *miles y miles* thousands and thousands.

milady *f* milady.

milagrería *f* fantastic tale, tale of miracles (narración) ‖ superstitious belief in miracles (tendencia a creer en milagros).

milagrero, ra *adj* FAM (who is) always imagining miracles (que imagina milagros) | miracle-working, miraculous (milagroso).

milagro *m* miracle ‖ wonder; *los milagros de la naturaleza* the wonders of nature ‖ miracle, wonder; *es un milagro que hayas salido vivo del accidente* it is a miracle you came out of the accident alive ‖ TEATR miracle play (en la Edad Media) ‖ votive offering (exvoto) ‖ — *cuéntenos su vida y milagros* tell us all about yourself, tell us your life history ‖ *de* or *por milagro* miraculously, by a miracle ‖ FIG *hacer milagros* to work wonders | *vive de milagro* it is a miracle he is still alive (persona enferma), it is amazing how he manages (persona pobre).

milagroso, sa *adj* miraculous ‖ miraculous, wonderful, extraordinary (maravilloso).

milamores *m* BOT red valerian.

Milán *n pr* GEOGR Milan.

milanés, esa *adj/s* Milanese.

Milanesado *npr m* GEOGR Milanese.

milano *m* kite (ave) ‖ flying gurnard (pez) ‖ TECN *cola de milano* dovetail (joint).

mildeu; mildiu *m* AGR mildew.

milenario, ria *adj* millenary, millennial.
◆ *m* millennium (período, aniversario).

milenio *m* millennium [one thousand years].

milenrama *f* BOT milfoil, yarrow.

milésimo, ma *adj* thousandth, millesimal.
◆ *m/f* thousandth.
◆ *f* AMER thousandth (de peso).

milhojas *f* BOT milfoil, yarrow.
◆ *m* millefeuille, flaky pastry (pastel).

mili *f* FAM military service ‖ *estar en la mili* to be in the army ‖ *hacer la mili* to do one's military service.

miliamperímetro *m* milliammeter.

miliamperio *m* ELECTR milliampere.

miliar *adj* milliary (columna) ‖ MED miliary; *fiebre miliar* miliary fever.

milibar *m* FÍS millibar.

milicia *f* militia (tropa); *milicias concejiles* municipal militia ‖ military service (servicio militar) ‖ soldiery, soldiering (profesión de soldado) ‖ art of war (arte de hacer la guerra) ‖ choir (de ángeles) ‖ *milicias universitarias* students' military service, *sing.*

miliciano, na *adj* (of the) militia, military.
◆ *m* militiaman.
— OBSERV El plural de *militiaman* es *militiamen.*

milicurie *m* FÍS millicurie.

miligramo *m* milligram, milligramme.

mililitro *m* millilitre [US milliliter].

milimétrico, ca *adj* millimetric.

milímetro *m* millimetre [US millimeter].

milimicra *f* millimicron.

militante *adj/s* militant.

militar *adj* military; *academia militar* military academy ‖ militia (de la milicia) ‖ — *arte militar* art of war ‖ *cartilla militar* military record ‖ *código militar* military law ‖ *gobierno militar* military government ‖ *tribunal militar* court-martial.
◆ *m* soldier, military man ‖ — *los militares* the military ‖ *militar de infantería* infantryman, foot-soldier.

militar *vi* to serve in the army, to soldier (en el ejército) ‖ to fight in the war, to militate (ant) (en la guerra) ‖ FIG to militate; *militan muchas pruebas en su favor* much evidence militates in his favour ‖ — *milita en el partido comunista* he is a militant Communist-party member ‖ *militar a favor de* or *en defensa de* to plead for, to speak for (defender).

militarismo *m* militarism.

militarista *adj* militarist, militaristic.
◆ *m/f* militarist.

militarización *f* militarization.

militarizar *vt* to militarize.

militarote *m* FAM military man, soldier.

milivoltio *m* FÍS millivolt.

milmillonésimo, ma *adj/s* thousand-millionth [US billionth].

milocha *f* kite (cometa).

milonga *f* AMER popular Argentinian song and dance ‖ Andalusian song.

milonguero, ra *m/f* singer *o* dancer of «milongas».

milord *m* My Lord (tratamiento), lord (nombre) ‖ light barouche (carruaje).
— OBSERV pl *milores.*

milpa *f* AMER maize field [US cornfield].

milpear *vi* AMER to till (labrar) | to sprout (el maíz).

milpiés *m* ZOOL wood louse (cochinilla) | millipede (miriápodo).

milrayas *m inv* striped cloth (tejido).

milla *f* nautical *o* geographical mile, mile (medida marina) ‖ mile (medida inglesa).

millar *m* thousand; *un millar de libras* a thousand pounds.
◆ *pl* thousands (gran cantidad); *millares y millares de personas* thousands and thousands of people ‖ *a millares* by the thousand, in thousands.
— OBSERV *A milliard* [US billion] in Spanish is *mil millones.*

millarada *f* about a thousand; *gastó una millarada de pesos* he spent about a thousand pesos ‖ thousands *pl* (muchos).

millón *m* million; *un millón de personas* a million people; *millones de habitantes* millions of inhabitants ‖ — *a millones* by the million, in millions ‖ *mil millones* one *o* a milliard, a thousand million [US one *o* a billion] ‖ *se lo he dicho millones de veces* I've told him thousands of times *o* time and time again ‖ *un millón de gracias* thanks a million.

millonada *f* about a million ‖ FIG small fortune, packet; *su traje costó una millonada* his suit cost a small fortune.

millonario, ria *adj/s* millionaire.

millonésimo, ma *adj/s* millionth.

mimar *vt* to pet, to coddle (acariciar) ‖ to pamper (tratar con muchas atenciones) ‖ to spoil, to overindulge (a los niños); *niño mimado* spoilt child ‖ to flatter (halagar) ‖ to mime (teatro).

mimbral *m* osiery, osier bed.

mimbre *m/f* osier (arbusto) ‖ wicker, withe (varita) ‖ *cesta de mimbre* osier *o* wicker basket.

mimbrear *vi* to sway (moverse).
◆ *vpr* to sway.

mimbreño, ña *adj* osier-like, willowy.

mimbrera *f* osier (arbusto) ‖ osier bed, osiery (mimbreral) ‖ willow (sauce).

mimbreral *m* osiery, osier bed.

mimbroso, sa *adj* osier, wicker (cosa) ‖ full of *o* covered in osiers (sitio).

mimeografía *f* AMER mimeographing.

mimeografiar *f* AMER to mimeograph.

mimeógrafo *m* AMER mimeograph.

mimético, ca *adj* mimetic.

mimetismo *m* mimicry.

mímico, ca *adj* mimic.
◆ *f* mimic art, mimicry.

mimo *m* mime (teatro, actor) ‖ coddling, petting (caricias, cariño) ‖ pampering (atenciones) ‖ spoiling, overindulgence (con los niños) ‖ *hacerle mimos a uno* to coddle *o* to pamper s.o., to make a fuss of s.o.

mimógrafo *m* mimographer, writer of mimes.

mimosa *f* mimosa (flor).

mimoso, sa *adj* finicky, fussy (melindroso) ‖ coddling, petting (muy afectuoso) ‖ pampering, full of attentions (excesivamente atento) ‖ spoilt, spoiled, pampered (mimado) ‖ flattering (halagador) ‖ delicate (delicado).

mina *f* mine (yacimiento, excavación); *mina de plata* silver mine ‖ underground conduit (para conducir aguas, etc.), underground passage, tunnel (comunicación) ‖ MIL mine (galería, explosivo); *mina anticarro, de acción retardada, contra personal, flotante, submarina* antitank, delayed-action, antipersonnel, floating, submarine mine ‖ lead; *mina de lápiz* pencil lead ‖ FIG mine, storehouse; *mina de información* mine of information ‖ sinecure, cushy *o* soft job (*fam*), sinecure, cushy *o* soft job (empleo) ‖ mina (moneda griega) ‖ — *cámara* or *hornillo de mina* mine chamber, blasthole ‖ *campo de minas* minefield ‖ *Escuela de Ingenieros de Minas* mining college *o* school ‖ *fondear minas* to lay mines ‖ *mina de carbón* coal mine ‖ FIG *mina de oro* gold mine ‖ *rastrear minas* to sweep mines.

minado *m* mining, mine-laying (colocación de minas).

minador, ra *adj* mining.
◆ *m* sapper (que abre minas), miner (que las instala), miner (soldado) ‖ mining engineer (ingeniero) ‖ MAR minelayer (buque).

minar *vt* to mine, to bore *o* to tunnel through; *minar una montaña* to mine a mountain ‖ MIL to mine (colocar minas); *minar un puerto* to mine a harbour ‖ to undermine, to wear away (cavar lentamente); *acantilados minados por las olas* cliffs undermined by the waves ‖ FIG to undermine (la autoridad, la salud, etc.) ‖ — FIG *las drogas le han minado* drugs have undermined his health ‖ *minarle a uno el terreno* to cut the ground from under s.o.'s feet.

minarete *m* minaret.
— OBSERV *Minarete* is a Gallicism for *alminar*.

mineral *adj* mineral; *reino mineral* mineral kingdom; *aguas minerales* mineral waters.
◆ *m* mineral ‖ ore; *mineral de hierro* iron ore ‖ fountainhead (origen).

mineralización *f* mineralization.

mineralizador, ra *adj* mineralizing.

mineralizar *vt* to mineralize.

mineralogía *f* mineralogy.

mineralógico, ca *adj* mineralogical.

mineralogista *m* mineralogist.

minería *f* mining (laboreo, trabajo) ‖ mining industry (industria) ‖ mines *pl* (minas de un país o de una comarca) ‖ miners *pl* (los mineros).

minero, ra *adj* mining; *zona minera* mining zone.
◆ *m* miner (obrero) ‖ mineowner (propietario), mineoperator (explotador) ‖ AMER mouse (ratón).

Minerva *npr f* Minerva.

minestrone *f* CULIN minestrone.

mingitorio *m* urinal.

mingo *m* (red) object ball (bola de billar) ‖ FAM *poner el mingo* to excel (sobresalir), to attract attention (llamar la atención), to cause a scandal (ser escandaloso).

miniar *vt* to paint in miniature.

miniatura *f* miniature; *en miniatura* in miniature ‖ *coche miniatura* miniature car.

miniaturista *m/f* miniaturist, miniature painter.

miniaturización *f* miniaturization.

miniaturizar *vt* to miniaturize.

minicadena *f* MÚS mini *o* compact hi-fi.

minifalda *f* miniskirt.

minifundio *m* small propertry *o* farm.

minigolf *m* pitch-and-putt.

mínima *f* MÚS minim [US half note] (nota) ‖ minimum temperature (temperatura) ‖ FIG smallest *o* slightest thing (cosa muy pequeña).

minimizar *vt* to minimize (quitar importancia a).

mínimo, ma *adj* minute, tiny (pequeño) ‖ minute, detailed (minucioso) ‖ minimum, lowest; *temperatura mínima* minimum temperature ‖ minimum, smallest, least; *la mínima cantidad* the smallest amount ‖ — *con el mínimo esfuerzo* with the minimum amount of effort ‖ *en lo más mínimo* in the least, in the slightest, at all ‖ *mínimo común múltiplo* lowest common multiple ‖ *sin hacer el más mínimo esfuerzo* without the slightest effort.
◆ *m* minim (religioso) ‖ minimum; *gana un mínimo de* he earns a minimum of ‖ — *al mínimo, a lo más mínimo* to a minimum ‖ *como mínimo* at least, at the very least.

mínimum *m* minimum.

minino, na *m/f* FAM puss, pussy, kitty (gato) ‖ child (niño).

minio *m* minium, red lead oxide.

ministerial *adj* ministerial.

ministerio *m* ministry ‖ — *Ministerio de Comercio* Board of Trade [US Department of Commerce] ‖ *Ministerio de Comunicaciones* G. P. O., General Post Office [US Post Office Department] ‖ *Ministerio de Educación Nacional* or *de Instrucción Pública* Ministry of Education [US Department of Education] (en España ahora ministerio de educación y ciencia) ‖ *Ministerio de Estado* (ant) or *de Asuntos Exteriores* or *de Relaciones Exteriores* Foreign Office [US State Department] ‖ *Ministerio de Gobernación* Ministry of the Interior [in Spain] ‖ *Ministerio de Hacienda* Exchequer (en Gran Bretaña), Treasury (en Estados Unidos), Ministry of Finance (en los demás países) ‖ *Ministerio de Información y Turismo* Ministry [US Department] of Information and Tourism ‖ *Ministerio de la Vivienda* Ministry [US Department] of Housing ‖ *Ministerio del Ejército* or *de la Guerra* War Office [US Defense Department] ‖ *Ministerio del Interior* Ministry of the Interior ‖ *Ministerio de Marina* Admiralty [US Department of the Navy] ‖ *Ministerio de Obras Públicas* Ministry [US Department] of Public Works ‖ *Ministerio de Trabajo* Ministry of Labour [US Department of Labor] ‖ *Ministerio público* or *fiscal* Department of the Public Prosecutor.

ministra *f* woman minister ‖ minister's wife (esposa de un ministro).

ministrable *adj* FAM likely to become a Minister of State.

ministro *m* minister; *ministro sin cartera* minister without portfolio; *ministro de la Iglesia* minister of Religion ‖ — *ministro de Comunicaciones* Postmaster General ‖ *ministro de Educación* Minister of Education [US Secretary of Education] ‖ *ministro de Estado* (ant) or *de Asuntos Exteriores* or *de Relaciones Exteriores* Secretary of State for Foreign Affairs, Foreign Secretary [US Secretary of State] ‖ *ministro de Gobernación* or *del Interior (véase* OBSERV en GOBERNACIÓN) ‖ *ministro de Hacienda* Chancellor of the Exchequer (en Gran Bretaña), Secretary of the Treasury (en Estados Unidos), Minister of Finance (en los demás países) ‖ *ministro de Trabajo* Minister of Labour [US Secretary of Labor] ‖ *ministro plenipotenciario* minister plenipotentiary ‖ *primer Ministro* Prime Minister, Premier (jefe del gobierno).

minnesinger *m* minnesinger, minnesänger (juglar alemán).

minoración *f* diminution, lessening, reduction.

minorar *vt* to diminish, to lessen, to reduce.

minoría *f* minority ‖ *minoría de edad* minority, infancy, nonage.

minoridad *f* (p us) minority, nonage, infancy.

minorista *m* retailer, retail dealer (comerciante al por menor) ‖ REL clergyman holding minor orders.
◆ *adj* retail (comercio).

minoritario, ria *adj* minority.

Minotauro *npr m* MIT Minotaur.

minucia *f* trifle (menudencia).
◆ *pl* (ant) tithe *sing* on fruit (diezmo) ‖ minutiae, minor details.

minuciosidad *f* meticulousness, thoroughness (de persona) ‖ minuteness (de inspección, de estudio, etc.).

minucioso, sa *adj* meticulous, thorough, scrupulous (persona) ‖ minute, detailed, thorough (inspección, estudio, etc.).

minué *m* minuet (baile).

minuendo *m* MAT minuend.

minúsculo, la *adj* minuscule, minute, diminutive (diminuto) ‖ minuscule, petty (insignificante) ‖ small (letra).
◆ *f* small letter.

minuta *f* menu (comida) ‖ draft (borrador) ‖ minute, memorandum (apunte) ‖ list of employees, payroll (lista) ‖ (lawyer's) bill (cuenta de un abogado).

minutar *vt* to draft [a contract].

minutario *m* minute book.

minutería *f* automatic time switch (interruptor).

minutero *m* minute hand (del reloj).

minuto *m* minute (tiempo); *vuelvo dentro de un minuto* I shall be back in a minute ‖ minute (de círculo) ‖ — *al minuto* a moment later; *y al minuto estaba de vuelta* and a moment later he was back; this very minute, at once; *tráigamelo al minuto* bring it to me this very minute ‖ *minuto a minuto* minute by minute.

Miño *npr m* GEOGR Minho (río).

miñona *f* IMPR minion.

mío, mía *adj pron pos de la 1ª pers* mine; *este libro es el mío* this book is mine; *esto es mío* this is mine ‖ of mine, my (después del sustantivo); *un amigo mío* a friend of mine, one of my friends; *amigo mío* my friend; *queridos hijos míos* my dear children ‖ FIG my dear (cariño); *padre mío* my dear father ‖ — *¡Dios mío!* my God!, good heavens! ‖ *en derredor mío* around me ‖ FIG & FAM *ésta es la mía* this is the moment I've been waiting for ‖ *esto es cosa mía* this is my affair *o* business ‖ FAM *hijo mío* my son (dicho por un cura), son, young fellow (en general) ‖ *lo mío* my affairs, what belongs to *o* concerns me; *no se meta en lo mío* don't interfere in my affairs ‖ *lo mío, mío y lo tuyo de entrambos* what's yours is mine and what's mine is my own ‖ *los míos* my folks, my people (familia).
— OBSERV The construction of the type *la casa mía* is frequent in Spanish and reinforces the idea of possession.

miocardio *m* ANAT myocardium; *infarto del miocardio* infarct of the myocardium.

miocarditis *f* MED myocarditis.

mioceno *adj/sm* GEOL Miocene.

miógrafo *m* myograph.

mioma *m* MED myoma.

miope *adj* myopic, shortsighted, nearsighted.
◆ *m/f* shortsighted *o* nearsighted person.

miopía *f* MED myopia, shortsightedness, nearsightedness.

miosota *f*; **miosotis** *m* BOT German madwort, forget-me-not.

mir *m* mir (comunidad agrícola en la Rusia zarista).

mira *f* sight (de un instrumento, de un arma) || levelling rod *o* staff (topografía) || watchtower (torre) || FIG intention, design (intención); *con miras poco honradas* with dishonourable intentions | objective, goal, aim (objetivo) || — *línea de mira* line of sight || *mira raquimétrica* stadia rod || FIG *poner la mira* or *las miras en* to cast one's eyes upon (mirar), to aspire to, to aim at (tener como objetivo); *poner la mira en el ascenso* to aim at promotion; to fix one's sights on, to have one's eyes on (echar el ojo a) || *punto de mira* front sight (de una escopeta), target (blanco).
◆ *pl* MAR prow guns || — *amplitud de miras* broad-mindedness || *con miras a* with a view to || *de miras estrechas* narrow-minded || *estar a la mira de* to be on the lookout for, to be watching out for || *estrechez de miras* narrow-mindedness || FIG *tener sus miras en* to have one's sights fixed on, to have designs on (codiciar).

mirabel *m* mock cypress, summer cypress || sunflower (girasol) || — *ciruela mirabel* mirabelle (plum) (fruto) || *ciruelo mirabel* mirabelle (plum tree) (árbol).

mirada *f* look; *una mirada severa* a stern look || eyes, *pl* look; *leer en la mirada* to read in s.o.'s eyes, to tell by s.o.'s look || glance (ojeada); *abarcar con una sola mirada* to take in with a single glance || gaze, stare, regard (p us) (prolongada) || look, expression (expresión); *una mirada melancólica* a melancholy look || knowing look (guiño) || — *apartar la mirada de* to look away from || *clavar* or *fijar la mirada en* to fix one's eyes on, to stare at || *detuvo la mirada en* his eyes fell upon || *echar una mirada a* to glance at, to run one's eye over (mirar), to keep an eye on (cuidar, vigilar) || *fulminar con la mirada* to look daggers at || *huir de las miradas de uno* to avoid looking s.o. in the eye (no mirar en los ojos), to avoid being seen by s.o., to hide from s.o.'s sight (evitar ser visto) || *lanzar una mirada a* to glance at || *levantar la mirada* to raise one's eyes, to look up || *mirada de soslayo* sidelong glance || *mirada fija* stare || *seguir con la mirada* to follow with one's eyes (algo, alguien que se mueve), to watch (sth. or s.o.) move *o* go away (algo, alguien que se aleja) || *ser el blanco de las miradas* to be the centre of attention || *tener la mirada perdida* to have a faraway *o* distant look in one's eyes || *volver la mirada* or *los ojos a* to look round at, to turn one's eyes towards.

miradero *m* centre of attention *o* attraction, cynosure (punto de mira) || vantage point, lookout, observatory (lugar de observación).

miradita *f* knowing look (guiño) || peek, quick glance (mirada).

mirado, da *adj* cautious, circumspect (receloso) || looked upon *o* on, thought of; *bien* or *mal mirado* well *o* badly looked on || considerate (considerado) || careful (cuidadoso); *es muy mirado con sus cosas personales* he is very careful with his personal belongings || *bien mirado, el asunto no tiene importancia* all things considered *o* all in all, the matter is of no importance.

mirador *m* mirador, windowed balcony, bay window (balcón) || mirador, observatory, vantage point, lookout (lugar de observación).

miraguano *m* BOT silver thatch, thatch palm.

miramiento *m* look, looking (acción de mirar) || caution, circumspection, prudence, care (circunspección) || considerateness, consideration, regard (comedimiento) || misgiving (timidez).
◆ *pl* respect *sing*, regard *sing*, consideration *sing*; *tener miramientos con las personas de edad* to show respect towards elderly people || — *andar con miramientos* to go *o* to tread carefully || *sin miramientos* inconsiderately, disrespectfully, without consideration, without regard (sin respeto), without ceremony (sin cumplidos).

mirar *vt/vi* to look || to look at; *mirar un cuadro* to look at a painting || to look in; *mirar un escaparate* to look in a shopwindow || to watch; *mirar un espectáculo* to watch a show || FIG to think (about), to consider (pensar); *sin mirar las consecuencias* without considering the consequences || to watch, to be careful, to mind, to look (to) (tener cuidado); *mire usted dónde pone los pies* watch where you're putting your feet || to go and see, to go and look, to see (informarse); *mira si ha llegado una carta* go and see if a letter has arrived || to see, to make sure (cuidar); *mire que no le falte nada* see that you're not short of anything || to keep an eye on, to watch (vigilar) || FIG to look to, to take account of, to tend to (tender, cuidar); *mirar por sus intereses* to look to one's interests || to look at *o* in, to search, to examine (registrar) || to look up to, to look highly upon (mostrar estimación a) || — *bien mirado todo, mirándolo bien, si se mira bien* all in all, upon reflexion, all things considered || FAM *de mírame y no me toques* very fragile (cosa frágil), unapproachable, like a bear with a sore head (de carácter áspero) || *¡mira!* look! (llamando la atención), look here! (protestando), why!, well I never! (sorpresa), listen! (¡oye!), look out! (cuidado) || *¡mira a quién se lo cuentas* or *se lo vas a contar!* you're telling me!, you can say that again!, you don't say! || *¡mira lo que haces!* watch what you're doing || *¡mira qué casa más hermosa!, ¡mira qué hermosa es!* what a beautiful house!, how beautiful it is! || *¡mira que no tiene suerte!* he really is unlucky! || *¡mira que si...!* imagine if...!, just think if...!; *¡mira que si no hubiera venido!* imagine if he hadn't come! || *¡mira que si es verdad!* if ever it is true! || *¡mira quien habla!* look *o* hark who's talking!, you can talk! || *mirar a* to look to, to think about; *sólo mira su provecho* he only looks to his own gain; to watch, to look at, to gaze at; *mirar a la gente que pasa* to watch the people go by; to overlook, to look out on, to look on to, to open on to; *mi ventana mira a la calle* my window overlooks the street; to face, to look towards; *la casa mira al sur* the house faces the south; to look in; *mirar a la cara* to look in the face *o* eye || *mirar al trasluz* to hold up to the light (por transparencia), to candle (un huevo) || *mirar atrás* to look back || FIG *mirar bien, mal a uno* to like, to dislike s.o. | *mirar con buenos, con malos ojos* to look round at, to turn one's eyes towards || *mirar con los ojos abiertos como platos* to look at goggle-eyed *o* wide-eyed, to goggle at || *mirar con mala cara* to scowl at || *mirar de arriba abajo* to look up and down, to eye from head to foot || *mirar de hito en hito* to stare at || *mirar de reojo* or *de soslayo* or *con el rabillo del ojo* to look at out of the corner of one's eye || *mirar de través* to look sideways at || *mirar fijamente a uno* to stare at s.o. || *mirar frente a frente* or *cara a cara* to look straight in the face *o* in the eye || *mirar por* to look out of; *mirar por la ventana* to look out of the window; to look through; *mirar por un agujero* to look through a hole; *mirar algo por el microscopio* to look at sth. through a microscope; to look to, to look after, to take care of, to tend to; *mirar por su salud* to look to one's health; *mirar por los niños* to look after the children; to think of; *mira por tu reputación* think of your reputation || *mirar por encima* to glance briefly at, to glance over, to skim || FIG & FAM *mirar por encima del hombro* to look down on, to look down one's nose at | *mirar por los cuatro costados* to eye up *o* over, to eye from head to foot (una persona), to look at from every angle (un problema) || *no se dignó mirarme* he would not *o* he did not deign to look at me || *se mire como se mire* or *por donde se mire* whichever way you look at it || *sin mirar en gastos* regardless of expense.
◆ *vpr* to look at o.s.; *mirarse al* or *en el espejo* to look at o.s. in the mirror || to look at one another *o* each other (dos o más personas) || to think carefully, to think twice; *se mirará muy bien de* or *antes de vender su casa* you had better think twice about *o* before selling your house || to look to one's dignity *o* decorum (comportarse con decoro), to look to one's modesty *o* decency (comportarse con recato) || FIG *mirarse en alguno* to be completely wrapped up in s.o. (querer mucho), to model o.s. upon (tomar como ejemplo).

mirasol *m* sunflower (girasol).

miríada *f* myriad || *miríadas de estrellas* myriads of stars, a myriad of stars.

miriagramo *m* myriagramme, myriagram.

miriámetro *m* myriametre [US myriameter].

miriápodo *adj/sm* ZOOL myriapod, myriopod.

mirífico, ca *adj* wonderful, marvellous.

mirilla *f* peephole, spyhole (para observar) || target, sight (para dirigir visuales) || MIL vision slit (de carros de combate).

miriñaque *m* crinoline (de falda) || trinket, bauble (alhaja) || AMER pilot, rail guard, cowcatcher (de locomotora).

mirlo *m* blackbird (ave) || FIG & FAM affected gravity *o* solemnity || — *buscar un mirlo blanco* to look for the impossible || FIG *un mirlo blanco* a rare bird, one in a million.

mirmidón *m* dwarf, very small man.

mirón, ona *adj* nosey [US nosy], inquisitive (curioso) || onlooking (mientras trabajan otros, etc.).
◆ *m/f* nosey-parker (curioso) || onlooker, spectator (espectador) || kibitzer (jugando a las cartas) || *estar de mirón* to stand by (quedarse sin hacer nada).

mirra *f* BOT myrrh.

mirtáceas *f pl* BOT myrtaceae.

mirtillo *m* BOT bilberry (arándano).

mirto *m* BOT myrtle (arrayán).

misa *f* Mass || — *ayudar a misa* to serve at Mass || *cantar misa* to sing *o* to say one's first Mass [a newly-ordained priest] || *decir misa* to say Mass || FIG *eso va a misa* you can take it from me, you can take it as read | *estar como en misa* to be deathly silent, to be as quiet as a mouse (una persona), *o* as mice (varias personas) (*fam*) || *ir a misa* to go to Mass, to attend Mass || *misa cantada* sung Mass || *misa de campaña* outdoor Mass || *misa de cuerpo presente* requiem *o* funeral Mass || *misa de difuntos* Mass for the dead, requiem || *misa del alba* morning Mass || *misa del gallo* midnight Mass [on Christmas Eve] || *misa mayor* high Mass || *misa negra* black Mass || *misa pontifical* pontifical Mass || *misa rezada* low Mass || FAM *no saber de la misa la media* not to know what one is talking about || *oír misa* to hear Mass || FAM *ser de misa y olla* to be ignorant || *tocar a misa* to ring for mass.

misacantano *m* priest saying his first Mass (por primera vez) || fully ordained priest [entitled to say Mass] (que puede celebrar misa).

misal *m* missal (libro).

misantropía *f* misanthropy.

misantrópico, ca *adj* misanthropic.

misántropo *adj m* misanthropic.
◆ *m* misanthrope, misanthropist.

miscelánea *f* miscellany, medley (mezcla) ‖ miscellany, miscellanea *pl* (colección); *miscelánea literaria* literary miscellany.

misceláneo, a *adj* miscellaneous.

miserable; mísero, ra *adj* wretched (muy pobre); *una habitación, una familia miserable* a wretched room, family ‖ miserable (ínfimo, escaso, lastimoso); *un sueldo miserable* a miserable wage; *estaba en un estado miserable* he was in a miserable condition ‖ shameful, despicable, contemptible, vile (malvado); *conducta miserable* shameful conduct ‖ miserly, mean, stingy (tacaño) ‖ *¡miserable de mí!* woe is me!
◆ *m/f* scoundrel, wretch (canalla) ‖ miser, skinflint (tacaño).

miserere *m* miserere ‖ MED *cólico miserere* ileus.

miseria *f* wretchedness, misery (de condiciones) ‖ misery, destitution, extreme poverty; *vivir en la miseria* to live in misery ‖ misery, misfortune, calamity (desgracia) ‖ miserliness, meanness, stinginess (avaricia) ‖ lice *pl* vermin *pl* (piojos) ‖ FIG & FAM pittance, next to nothing; *trabajar por una miseria* to work for a pittance *o* for next to nothing ‖ — *estar en la miseria* to be poverty-striken *o* down-and-out ‖ *miseria negra* dire poverty.

misericordia *f* mercy, compassion; *pedir misericordia* to beg for mercy ‖ misericord, misericorde (puñal, pieza en los coros de las iglesias).

misericordioso, sa *adj* merciful, compassionate; *misericordioso con los desvalidos* merciful to the destitute.

misero, ra *adj* FAM churchy, who attends Mass frequently ‖ who receives a stipend only for saying Mass (sacerdote).

mísero, ra *adj/s* → **miserable.**

misérrimo, ma *adj* very wretched (muy pobre) ‖ very miserly (tacaño).

misia; misiá *f* AMER FAM missus, missis (señora).

misil *m* missile (cohete).

misión *f* mission (cometido) ‖ REL mission.

misionero, ra *adj/s* missionary.

misionero, ra *adj* [of *o* from] Misiones (en Argentina y Paraguay).
◆ *m/f* native *o* inhabitant of Misiones.

Misisipí *npr m* GEOGR Mississippi.

misiva *f* missive (carta).

mismamente *adv* FAM just, precisely, exactly.

mismísimo, ma *adj* FAM himself, herself, themselves; *vi al mismísimo presidente* I saw the president himself ‖ very same, selfsame; *en ese mismísimo momento* at that very same moment ‖ — *en el mismísimo centro* in the very centre, right in the centre ‖ *es el mismísimo demonio* he is the devil himself *o* the devil in person.

mismo, ma *adj* same (antes del sustantivo); *del mismo color* of the same colour; *en la misma época* at the same time ‖ myself, yourself, himself, herself, ourselves, yourselves, themselves, etc. (después de pronombres personales); *yo mismo* I myself; *él mismo* he himself; *ellos mismos* they themselves ‖ itself themselves; *ocurrió en la ciudad misma* it happened in the city itself; *es la vanidad misma* he is vanity itself ‖ himself, herself, themselves (para corroborar la identidad de la persona); *el mismo presidente se levantó* the president himself stood up ‖ own, very, even (hasta); *sus mismos hermanos le odiaban* his own *o* very brothers hated him, even his brothers hated him ‖ just (igual); *esto mismo decías tú* that's just what you said ‖ right (después de los adverbios de lugar); *aquí mismo* right here ‖ — *ahora mismo* right now, right away ‖ *al mismo tiempo, a un mismo tiempo* at the same time ‖ *así mismo* likewise, in the same way (de la misma manera), also (también), that's it, that's right (así es) ‖ *ayer mismo* just yesterday, only yesterday ‖ *del mismo modo* in the same way (de la misma manera), likewise, also (también) ‖ FIG *el mismo que viste y calza* the very same, none other ‖ *en el mismo suelo* on the bare floor ‖ *en sí mismo* in itself ‖ *es lo mismo* it's all the same, it's the same thing, it makes no difference ‖ *eso viene a ser lo mismo* that amounts to *o* comes to the same thing ‖ *estar en las mismas* to be back where one started ‖ *este chico y el que vi ayer son el mismo* this boy and the one I saw yesterday are one and the same ‖ *hoy mismo* today, this very day ‖ *lo mismo* the same (thing) ‖ *lo mismo con* just like, the same goes for ‖ *lo mismo da* it doesn't matter, it's all the same, it makes no difference ‖ *lo mismo que* the same as, just like ‖ *lo mismo si... que si* it makes no difference whether... or whether ‖ *lo mismo uno que otro* both of them ‖ *mañana mismo* (as early as) tomorrow; *saldré mañana mismo* I shall leave (as early as) tomorrow ‖ *por lo mismo* for that reason, that is why ‖ *por lo mismo que* for the very reason that ‖ *por sí mismo* (by) o.s. ‖ *quedar en las mismas* to be back where one started ‖ *volver a las mismas* to get back to where one started.

misogamia *f* misogamy.

misoginia *f* misogyny.

misógino, na *adj* misogynous.
◆ *m* misogynist.

miss *f* miss.

mistar *vt* FAM *no mistar* to keep quiet *o* hush.

misterio *m* mystery ‖ TEATR mystery (auto) ‖ — *andar con misterios, hacer misterios* to act in a mysterious manner ‖ *hablar con misterio* to speak mysteriously ‖ *hacer algo con misterio* to do sth. secretly *o* in secret.

misterioso, sa *adj* mysterious.

mística *f* mystical theology ‖ mysticism.

misticismo *m* mysticism.

místico, ca *adj* mystical.
◆ *m/f* mystic.

mistificación; mixtificación *f* falsification ‖ trick (engaño).

mistificar; mixtificar *vt* to falsify (falsificar) ‖ to trick, to deceive (engañar).

mistral *m* mistral (viento).

Misuri *npr m* GEOGR Missouri.

mita *f* AMER mita | ancient tribute | cattle shipped by train.
— OBSERV La *mita* was an institution of indigenous origin which, adopted by the Spanish colonists, regulated the work of the Indians. The latter were contracted by drawing lots to work in the mines and on public works.

mitaca *f* AMER harvest (cosecha).

mitad *f* half; *a mitad de precio* at half price ‖ middle (centro); *en la mitad de la novela* in the middle of the novel | FAM half (esposa); *mi cara mitad* my better half ‖ — *en* or *a la mitad del camino* halfway, halfway there (yendo a un sitio) ‖ *en mitad de* in the middle of ‖ *mitad y mitad* half and half ‖ FAM *partir a uno por la mitad* to ruin s.o.'s plans ‖ *partir por la mitad* to cut in half, to cut into two (cortar).
◆ *adv* half; *mitad hombre, mitad animal* half man, half beast.

mitayo *m* Indian employed in the mines and on public works (véase OBSERV en MITA).

mítico, ca *adj* mythical.

mitigación *f* mitigation.

mitigador, ra *adj* mitigating, mitigative, mitigatory.
◆ *m/f* mitigator.

mitigante *adj* mitigating, mitigative, mitigatory.

mitigar *vt* to mitigate; *mitigar una pena* to mitigate a penalty ‖ to alleviate, to relieve (un dolor, la soledad) ‖ to quench (la sed) ‖ to satisfy (el hambre) ‖ to relieve; *mitigar el paro* to relieve unemployment ‖ to palliate (paliar) ‖ to allay (preocupaciones) ‖ to reduce (el calor).

mitin *m* meeting rally.
— OBSERV pl *mítines*.

mito *m* myth.

mitología *f* mythology.

mitológico, ca *adj* mythological.

mitólogo *m* mythologist.

mitomanía *f* mythomania.

mitómano, na *adj/s* mythomaniac.

mitón *m* mitt (guante).

mitosis *f* BIOL mitosis.

mitote *m* AMER dance of the Aztec Indians (baile) | FAM racket, din (alboroto).

mitra *f* mitre [US miter]; *recibir la mitra* to receive the mitre.

mitrado, da *adj* mitred [US mitered]; *abad mitrado* mitred abbot.
◆ *m* archbishop (arzobispo), bishop (obispo), prelate (prelado).

Mitrídates *n pr* HIST Mithridates.

mitridatismo *m* mithridatism.

miura *m* fierce breed of fighting bull (toro) ‖ FIG wild one (indomable) | devil (malintencionado).

mixomatosis *f* VET myxomatosis.

mixomicetos *m pl* BOT myxomycetes.

mixtificación *f* → **mistificación.**

mixtificar *vt* → **mistificar.**
— OBSERV This verb and its substantive, although in current use, are not admitted by the Academy.

mixto, ta *adj* mixed; *escuela mixta* mixed school; *comisión mixta* mixed committee ‖ half-bred (mestizo) ‖ — *tren mixto* passenger and goods train ‖ *tribunal mixto* mixed tribunal.
◆ *m* match (fósforo) ‖ inflammable compound (sustancia inflamable).

mixtura *f* mixture (mezcla) ‖ compound (medicamento) ‖ AMER flowers *pl* given as a gift (flores).

mixturar *vt* to mix.

mízcalo *m* edible milk mushroom (hongo).

mnemónico, ca *adj* mnemonic.
◆ *m/f* mnemonic person.

mnemotecnia; mnemotécnica *f* mnemonics.

mnemotécnico, ca *adj* mnemonic.

moabita *adj/s* Moabite.

moaré *m* moire (tela).

mobiliario *m* forniture ‖ JUR [household] furniture.

moblaje *m* furnishings *pl*, furniture.

moblar* *vt* to furnish.

moca *m* mocha.

mocar *vt* to blow *o* to wipe (s.o.'s) nose.
◆ *vpr* to blow *o* to wipe one's nose.

mocarrera *f* runny nose; *tener mocarrera* to have a runny nose.

mocarro *m* FAM snot [which runs from the nose].

mocasín *m* moccasin (calzado).

mocear *vi* FAM to sow one's wild oats (correr aventuras) | to act like a youngster (comportarse como un mozo).

mocedad *f* youth (juventud) || prank (travesura).
◆ *pl* youth *sing; en mis mocedades* in my youth.

mocerío *m* (group of) young people.

mocetón, ona *m/f* strapping lad (chico), strapping *o* buxom lass (chica).

moción *f* motion (proposición); *moción de censura* censure motion; *adoptar una moción* to carry a motion; *votar una moción* to vote on a motion; *presentar una moción* to bring forward *o* to table a motion; *se rechaza la moción* the motion is rejected *o* lost; *queda aprobada la moción por veinte votos a favor, siete en contra y dos abstenciones* the motion is carried by 20 votes to 7 with 2 abstentions; *apoyar una moción* to second a motion; *declarar una moción admisible* to declare a motion receivable; *aplazar una moción sine die* to table a motion; *¿se puede aceptar esta moción?* would this motion be in order? || motion, movement (movimiento) || inclination (inclinación) || divine inspiration.

mocito, ta *adj* very young.
◆ *m/f* youngster, lad (chico), young girl, youngster, lass (chica).

moco *m* mucus, mocusity (término científico), snot (*fam*) || snuff (cabo de la mecha) || drippings *pl* (de una vela) || caruncle (del pavo) || red-hot scoria *o* slag (del hierro) || MAR martingale || — FIG & FAM *caérsele el moco* to be a dunce || *limpiar los mocos a alguien* to wipe *o* to blow s.o.'s nose || *limpiarse los mocos* to blow one's nose || FIG & FAM *llorar a moco tendido* to cry bitterly, to cry one's eyes out, to sob one's heart out, to weep buckets | *no es moco de pavo* it's no trifle; *este trabajo no es moco de pavo* this job is no trifle || *seis mil dólares no son moco de pavo* six thousand dollars are not to be sniffed at || *se me caen los mocos* my nose is running.

mocoso, sa *adj* snotty-nosed || bad mannered (maleducado).
◆ *m/f* snotty-nosed child || FIG & FAM brat (niño mal educado).

mocosuena *adv* FAM *traducir «mocosuena, mocosuene»* to translate word for word.

mochales *adj inv* FAM *estar mochales* to be crazy *o* cracked (loco) | *estar mochales por* to be crazy about, to be head over heels in love with (enamorado).

moche *m a troche y moche* helter-skelter, pell-mell (rápida y confusamente), haphazardly (al azar).

mochila *f* pack (del soldado) || rucksack, pack, knapsack (de excursionista, etc.) || provisions *pl* (víveres).

mocho, cha *adj* blunt (sin punta) || hornless, dehorned (sin cuernos) || pruned (mondado de ramas) || topped (mondado de copa) || FIG & FAM shorn (pelado) || AMER mutilated (mutilado) | conservative (conservador) | reactionary (reaccionario) || *escopeta mocha* hammerless rifle.
◆ *m* handle (de un instrumento) || stock, butt (culata).

mochuelo *m* ZOOL little owl (ave) || FIG & FAM bore, burdensome task || IMPR omission (omisión) || — FIG *cada mochuelo a su olivo* everyone about his own business, everyone to his own home || FAM *cargar con el mochuelo* to get stuck *o* lumbered with the worst job (hacer el trabajo más fastidioso), to be left holding the baby [US to carry the can] (cargar con la responsabilidad).

moda *f* fashion, style; *la moda del año 1975* the 1975 fashion, the fashion in 1975 || — *a la moda* fashionable, in fashion, in (*fam*) (adjetivo), fashionably, in fashion (adverbio); *vestir a la moda* to dress fashionably || *a la moda de París* in the Paris fashion, in the Paris style || *de moda* in fashion, fashionable, in (*fam*); *estar de moda* to be in fashion, to be fashionable || *estar muy de moda* to be highly fashionable, to be all the rage (*fam*) || *fuera de moda* out of fashion || *pasado de moda* old-fashioned, out of date || *pasarse de moda* to go out of fashion || *ponerse de moda* to come into fashion, to become fashionable || *revista de modas* fashion magazine || *seguir la moda* to follow fashion || *ser la última moda* to be the latest fashion *o* the latest style || *tienda de modas* fashion shop.

modal *adj* modal.
◆ *m pl* manners; *modales distinguidos* distinguished manners; *modales finos* refined manners || — *con buenos modales* politely, courteously || *tener buenos, malos modales* to be well-mannered, ill-mannered || FAM *¡vaya modales!* what manners!

modalidad *f* modality || form, kind, type (clase) || category (categoría) || way, manner (modo) || *modalidad de pago* mode of payment.

modelado *m* modelling [US modeling]; *el modelado de una escultura* the modelling of a sculpture || shape (forma).

modelador, ra *adj* modelling [US modeling].
◆ *m* modeller [US modeler].

modelar *vt* to model || FIG to model, to pattern; *modelar su conducta según* to model one's behaviour on | to form, to shape; *modelar el alma de alguien* to form s.o.'s mind.

modelista *m/f* modeller [US modeler] (modelador) || dress designer (de costura).

modelo *adj inv* model; *es una niña modelo* she is a model child; *empresa modelo* model company.
◆ *m* model (patrón); *tomar por modelo* to take as a model || FIG model || *modelo reducido* scale model.
◆ *f* model, fashion model (de modas) || *desfile de modelos* fashion show, fashion parade.

módem *m* INFORM modem.

moderación *f* moderation; *obrar con moderación* to act in *o* with moderation.

moderado, da *adj/s* moderate.
◆ *adv* MÚS mezzo forte, moderato.

moderador, ra *adj* moderating.
◆ *m/f* moderator.
◆ *m* FÍS moderator.

moderar *vt* to moderate; *moderar sus deseos* to moderate one's desires || to control, to restrain (restringir) || to reduce (la velocidad).
◆ *vpr* to control o.s. || *moderarse en las palabras* to be careful what one says, to measure one's words (hablar con comedimiento).

modernamente *adv* recently (recientemente) || at the present (time), at the moment, nowadays (actualmente).

modernidad *f* modernity.

modernismo *m* modernism.

modernista *adj/s* modernist.

modernización *f* modernization.

modernizar *vt* to modernize.
◆ *vpr* to be modernized.

moderno, na *adj* modern; *la edad moderna* the modern age || *a la moderna* in the modern way.
◆ *m/f* modern (persona) || *lo moderno* modern things (cosas modernas), the modern thing.

modestia *f* modesty || *vestido con modestia* simply dressed (con sencillez), modestly dressed (con decoro).

modesto, ta *adj* modest.
◆ *m/f* modest person.

modicidad *f* moderateness, reasonableness.

módico, ca *adj* moderate, reasonable; *pagar una suma módica* to pay a moderate amount.

modificación *f* modification.

modificar *vt* to modify (transformar).

modificativo, va *adj* modifying.

modillón *m* ARQ modillion.

modismo *m* GRAM idiom.

modista *m/f* dressmaker, couturier, modiste.

modistería *f* AMER fashion shop.

modistilla *f* dressmaker's assistant (aprendiza) || dressmaker (modista importante).

modisto *m* dressmaker, couturier, modiste.
— OBSERV This word is a barbarism often used in place of *modista*.

modo *m* manner, way, mode (manera); *a su modo* in one's own way; *modo de pensar* way of thinking || GRAM mood || MÚS mode || — *adverbio de modo* adverb of manner || *modo adverbial* adverbial phrase || *modo de empleo* instructions *pl* for use || *modo subjuntivo* subjunctive mood.
◆ *pl* manners (modales); *buenos, malos modos* good, bad manners.
— OBSERV *Modo* and *manera* are often interchangeable. For the expressions in which *modo* is used see *manera*, which can be substituted by *modo*.

modorro, rra *adj* drowsy, heavy (adormecido) || infected by staggers (el ganado) || overripe, soft (una fruta) || FIG ignorant (ignorante).
◆ *m/f* ignorant person.
◆ *m* miner poisoned by mercury (minero).
◆ *f* drowsiness, heaviness (sueño pesado) || dullness, torpor (sopor) || VET staggers *pl* (del ganado lanar).

modosidad *f* quietness, good behaviour [US good behavior].

modoso, sa *adj* quiet, well-behaved || modest, demure (recatado).

modulación *f* modulation || *modulación de frecuencia* frequency modulation.

modulador, ra *adj* modulating.
◆ *m/f* modulator.

modular *vt/vi* to modulate.

módulo *m* MAT & FÍS modulus || module (en arquitectura) || anthropometric measurement (antropometría) || MÚS modulation || module (lunar).

modus vivendi *m* modus vivendi.

mofa *f* mockery (burla) || *hacer mofa de* to mock, to make fun of, to scoff at, to jeer at.

mofadura *f* mockery, scoffing.

mofar *vi* to mock, to scoff.
◆ *vpr* to mock, to make fun of, to scoff at.

mofeta *f* ZOOL skunk (mamífero) || mofette, moffette (fisura, gas) || firedamp (grisú).

moflete *m* FAM chubby cheek.

mofletudo, da *adj* chubby-cheeked || *una chica mofletuda* a girl with chubby cheeks.

Mogadischo *n pr* GEOGR Mogadishu, Mogadiscio.

mogol, la *adj/s* Mongolian, Mongol || *el Gran Mogol* the Great Mogul.

mogolismo *m* mongolism.

mogollón *m* meddling (entremetimiento) || FAM sponger (gorrón) || FAM *de mogollón* for nothing, free (gratis), without paying (sin pagar), effortlessly, without effort (sin esfuerzo), by chance, by accident (por casualidad) | *un mogollón de* a mass of, stacks of, piles of.

mogón, ona *adj* one-horned, broken-horned (res).

mogote *m* knoll, mound (montículo) ‖ stack (hacina) ‖ antler (del ciervo).

mohair *m* mohair.

moharra *f* spear head.

mohicano, na *adj/s* Mohican (indio).

mohín *m* grimace, face; *hacer un mohín* to make a face.

mohíno, na *adj* sulky (melancólico) ‖ gloomy, sad (abatido) ‖ annoyed (disgustado) ‖ black (caballo negro) ‖ *mulo mohíno* hinny (burdégano).
◆ *f* annoyance, anger (enojo).

moho *m* mould [US mold], mildew (hongos) ‖ rust (del hierro) ‖ verdigris (del cobre) ‖ mould (en peras y manzanas) ‖ — *criar moho* to go *o* to become mouldy (cubrirse de moho), to stagnate, to turn into a cabbage (vegetar) ‖ FIG *no criar moho* to be always on the go ‖ *oler a moho* to smell mouldy ‖ *saber a moho* to taste mouldy.

mohoso, sa *adj* mouldy [US moldy] (cosa orgánica) ‖ rusty (hierro) ‖ *ponerse mohoso* to go *o* to become mouldy (cosa orgánica), to rust (hierro).

moisés *m* cradle (cuna) ‖ carrycot (para transportar al niño).

Moisés *npr m* Moses.

mojado, da *adj* wet, damp, moist (una cosa) ‖ wet (mejillas, labios, ojos) ‖ FIG *llueve sobre mojado* it never rains but it pours, it's just one thing on top of another.

mojama *f* salted tuna.

mojar *vt* to wet, to damp, to moisten (humedecer) ‖ to dip; *mojar la pluma en el tintero, el pan en el chocolate* to dip one's pen in the inkwell, one's bread in one's chocolate ‖ to soak (la lluvia, etc.) ‖ to dampen (la ropa para lavar) ‖ to sprinkle (rociar) ‖ to palatalize (en fonética) ‖ FIG & FAM to celebrate; *mojar una victoria* to celebrate a victory | POP *mojar el gaznate* to wet one's whistle.
◆ *vi* FIG to get involved (*en* in) (en un negocio).
◆ *vpr* to get wet (por la lluvia, etc.).

mojicón *m* FAM blow (golpe); *pegarle un mojicón a uno* to give s.o. a blow (in the face) ‖ punch (puñetazo) ‖ sponge cake (bizcocho) ‖ bun (bollo).

mojiganga *f* masquerade, masked ball (fiesta de máscaras) ‖ farce (en teatro) ‖ FIG mockery.

mojigatería *f* hypocrisy ‖ prudishness (pudor exagerado) ‖ sanctimoniousness, religious bigotry (beatería).

mojigato, ta *adj* hypocritical (hipócrita) ‖ prudish (excesivamente púdico) ‖ sanctimonious (santurrón).
◆ *m/f* hypocrite (hipócrita) ‖ religious bigot, sanctimonious person (beato) ‖ prude.

mojinete *m* coping of a wall (caballete) ‖ crest (del tejado) ‖ AMER fronton (de fachada).

mojón *m* landmark (en el camino) ‖ pile (montón) ‖ dung (excremento) ‖ *mojón kilométrico* milestone.

moka *m* mocha (café).

mol *m* QUÍM mole.

molar *adj* ANAT molar.
◆ *m* molar, molar tooth.

molcajete *m* AMER mortar (mortero).

molde *m* TECN mould [US mold], cast ‖ knitting needle (para hacer punto) ‖ CULIN mould ‖ FIG model, pattern (modelo) ‖ IMPR form ‖ — *letras de molde* printed letters ‖ *pan de molde* soft, thin-crusted bread ‖ FIG *romper el molde* to break the mould ‖ *venirle a uno de molde* to be just what one needs, to be just right for one.

moldeable *adj* mouldable [US moldable] ‖ manageable (persona).

moldeado *m* moulding [US molding], casting (acción) ‖ cast (resultado).

moldeador, ra *adj* moulding [US molding].
◆ *m/f* moulder [US molder], caster.

moldear *vt* to cast (vaciar en yeso) ‖ to make a casting (en un molde) ‖ to mould [US to mold], to shape (dar forma) ‖ FIG to shape, to mould, to form; *la vida moldea a los hombres* life shapes men.

moldura *f* moulding [US molding] ‖ — *moldura cromada* chromium strip ‖ ARQ *moldura ovalada* gadroon.

moldurar *vt* to put a moulding on.

mole *adj* soft (muelle) ‖ *huevos moles* dessert of egg-yolk and sugar.
◆ *m* AMER fricassee of meat with chili sauce.
◆ *f* mass, bulk (cosa voluminosa).

molécula *f* FÍS molecule ‖ *molécula gramo* gram molecule.

molecular *adj* FÍS molecular.

moledor, ra *adj* grinding, crushing (que muele) ‖ FAM exhausting, tiring, wearisome (agotador) | boring, wearisome (aburrido).
◆ *m/f* FIG & FAM bore (persona).
◆ *m* grinder, crusher (de caña de azúcar).

moledura *f* grinding, milling (del trigo) ‖ FIG fatigue, exhaustion, weariness (cansancio).

moler* *vt* to grind (en general) ‖ to grind, to mill; *moler trigo* to grind wheat ‖ to pound (machacar) ‖ to pulverize (pulverizar) ‖ to press (aceituna) ‖ FIG to tire out, to wear out (cansar) | to bore (fastidiar) ‖ AMER to press, to express [sugar cane] ‖ FAM *moler a golpes* or *a palos* to beat up, to beat black and blue.

moleskín; molesquín *m* moleskin.

molestar *vt* to annoy (enfadar, irritar); *me molesta su falta de educación* his bad manners annoy me ‖ to get on s.o.'s nerves, to annoy (poner nervioso); *me molestan esos martillazos* that hammering is getting on my nerves *o* gets on my nerves ‖ to bother (incomodar); *¿le molesta el humo?* does the smoke bother you? ‖ to mind (importarle a uno); *no me molesta esperar* I don't mind waiting; *¿le molesta venir?* do you mind coming?; *¿le molestaría prestarme cien libras?* would you mind lending me a hundred pounds? ‖ to inconvenience, to mind (causar inconveniente); *¿le molestaría dejarlo para el viernes?* would it inconvenience you to leave it until Friday?, would you mind leaving it until Friday? ‖ to disturb, to bother, to trouble (importunar, interrumpir); *perdone que le moleste* I'm sorry to bother you; *que no me moleste nadie* I don't want to be disturbed, don't let anybody disturb me ‖ to worry (preocupar) ‖ to pester (importunar insistentemente); *siempre me molestan con la misma queja* they are always pestering me with the same complaint; *¡deja de molestarme ya!* stop pestering me! ‖ to hate, not to like (no gustarle a uno); *me molestaría llegar tarde* I should hate to arrive late, I shouldn't like to arrive late; *me molesta tener que repetirlo* I hate to *o* I don't like to have to repeat it ‖ to offend, to hurt (herir) ‖ to hurt (hacer daño); *estos zapatos me molestan* these shoes hurt me ‖ to trouble, to bother (un dolor) ‖ — *este asunto empieza a molestarme* this business is beginning to get on my nerves; I am beginning to get tired of this business ‖ *me molestaría verlo otra vez* I should hate to *o* I shouldn't like to meet him again, it would be awkward for me to meet him again.
◆ *vi* to be a nuisance (ser fastidioso) ‖ to be unpleasant (ser desagradable).
◆ *vpr* to worry, to bother (preocuparse); *no se moleste por mí* don't worry about me ‖ to take the trouble, to bother; *no se molestó en ayudarme* he didn't take the trouble to help me ‖ to take offence (ofenderse); *molestarse por* to take offence at ‖ to get angry *o* annoyed *o* cross (enfadarse) ‖ *no se moleste* don't bother.

molestia *f* annoyance, bother, trouble; *esto le acarreó muchas molestias* this caused him a lot of bother ‖ nuisance (fastidio); *dar* or *causar molestia a uno* to be a nuisance to s.o. ‖ inconvenience (inconveniente) ‖ discomfort (incomodidad) ‖ unpleasantness (cosa desagradable) ‖ FIG trouble (trabajo); *se tomó la molestia de ir* he took the trouble to go ‖ indisposition (de la salud) ‖ — *acusar* or *tener molestia en una pierna* to have a pain in the leg ‖ *¡qué molestia!* what a nuisance! ‖ *ser una molestia* to be a nuisance; *es una molestia ir a ese sitio ahora* it's a nuisance to go to this place now ‖ *si no es molestia, si no le sirve de molestia* if it's not too much trouble for you, if it doesn't bother *o* trouble you.

molesto, ta *adj* boring, tiresome (aburrido); *¡qué molesto es hacer cada día la misma cosa!* how boring it is doing the same thing every day! ‖ annoying, troublesome (fastidioso); *las faldas largas son molestas* long skirts are troublesome ‖ inconvenient; *ser molesto para uno* to be inconvenient for s.o. ‖ trying (pesado); *es un hombre muy molesto* he is a very trying man ‖ uncomfortable (incómodo); *viaje molesto* uncomfortable trip; *estar molesto en un sillón* to be uncomfortable in an armchair ‖ awkward (que estorba); *un paquete molesto* an awkward parcel ‖ unpleasant, nasty (sabor, olor) ‖ embarrassing, awkward; *una pregunta molesta* an embarrassing question ‖ irritating (irritante) ‖ embarrassed (confuso) ‖ cross (enfadado) ‖ offended (ofendido) ‖ discontented (descontento) ‖ — *lo molesto* the trouble; *lo molesto es tener que subir a pie* the trouble is having to go up on foot ‖ *si no es molesto para ti* if it is no trouble for you.

molestoso, sa *adj* AMER → **molesto.**

moleta *f* muller (piedra para moler) ‖ glass polisher (para pulir el vidrio).

molibdeno *m* molybdenum (metal).

molicie *f* softness ‖ fondness for luxury ‖ *vivir en la molicie* to have an easy *o* a soft life.

molido, da; molturado, da *adj* ground (en general) ‖ ground, milled; *trigo molido* milled wheat ‖ pulverized, powdered (triturado) ‖ granulated (azúcar) ‖ FIG & FAM beat, worn-out, all in (cansado).

molienda; molturación *f* grinding (en general) ‖ grinding, milling (del trigo) ‖ pulverizing, crushing (trituración) ‖ pressing, crushing (de las aceitunas) ‖ processing season (aceitunas, trigo, etc.) ‖ batch being ground (cantidad) ‖ FIG & FAM exhaustion (cansancio) | tiresome task (tarea pesada) | nuisance (cosa molesta).

moliente *adj* grinding, milling ‖ *corriente y moliente* common or garden, run-of-the-mill, ordinary.

molinera *f* miller's wife (mujer del molinero) ‖ miller (que se ocupa de un molino).

molinería *f* milling industry (industria) ‖ mills *pl* (molinos).

molinero, ra *adj* milling.
◆ *m* miller.

molinete *m* ventilator (de ventana) ‖ whirligig, windmill [US pinwheel] (juguete) ‖

circular swing *o* sweep (movimiento) ‖ MAR windlass ‖ *AMER* catherine wheel, girandole (de cohete).

molinillo *m* grinder, mill; *molinillo de café, de pimienta* coffee, pepper grinder ‖ mincer (de carne) ‖ whisk (de chocolatera) ‖ whirligig, windmill [*US* pinwheel] (juguete).

molino *m* mill; *molino de agua* water mill; *molino de papel* paper mill ‖ FIG tornado (persona bulliciosa) | nuisance, pest (persona molesta) ‖ — FIG *luchar contra los molinos de viento* to tilt at windmills ‖ *molino de sangre* animal-driven mill (de animales), hand-operated mill (de mano) ‖ *molino de viento* windmill ‖ FIG *molinos de viento* imaginary enemies.

molturación *f* ⟶ **molienda.**

molturado, da *adj* ⟶ **molido.**

molturar *vt* to grind, to mill.

molusco *m* ZOOL mollusc.

molla *f* lean [meat] (de la carne) ‖ crumb (miga).
◆ *pl* FAM flab *sing* (gordura de una persona).

mollar *adj* tender, soft (blando) ‖ FIG cushy, easy and lucrative ‖ — *carne mollar* boneless lean meat ‖ *tierra mollar* soft ground.

mollate *m* FAM red wine (vino).

molleja *f* gizzard (de las aves) ‖ sweetbread (de ternera, de cordero) ‖ ANAT thymus gland (timo).

mollera *f* ANAT crown of the head | fontanel, fontanelle (fontanela) ‖ FIG brains *pl*, common sense (seso) ‖ — FAM *cerrado de mollera* thick, dim, dense ‖ FIG & FAM *ser duro de mollera* to be hardheaded *o* obstinate (obstinado), to be thick *o* dense (torpe) | *tener ya dura la mollera* to be too old to change.

mollete *m* fleshy part, flab (del brazo) ‖ chubby cheek (moflete) ‖ roll (panecillo).

mollina; mollizna *f* drizzle, fine rain.

molliznar; molliznear *v impers* to drizzle.

momentáneamente *adv* momentarily (durante un momento) ‖ right now, at the moment (ahora mismo).

momentáneo, a *adj* momentary (breve).

momento *m* moment (tiempo muy corto); *lo haré dentro de un momento* I'll do it in a moment ‖ moment (ocasión); *escoger el momento favorable* to choose a favourable moment; *momento oportuno* opportune moment ‖ time; *ha llegado el momento de irse* the time has come to leave ‖ instant (instante) ‖ FIG moment (importancia) ‖ FÍS moment; *momento de inercia* moment of inertia | momentum (producto de la masa y la velocidad) ‖ — *a cada momento* all the time ‖ *a cualquier momento* at any moment *o* time ‖ *al momento* at once, immediately ‖ *del momento* of the day, current (actual); *la moda del momento* the fashion of the day, the current fashion ‖ *de momento* at the moment, at present (ahora), at first (primeramente) ‖ *dentro de un momento* in a moment ‖ *desde el momento en que* from the moment when, from the time when ‖ *desde ese momento, a partir de ese momento* from that moment ‖ *de un momento a otro* at any moment *o* time ‖ *en aquel momento* at that moment ‖ *en buen momento* at a good time, at the right time ‖ *en el mejor momento* at the best time ‖ *en el momento actual* at the present time ‖ *en el momento (en) que* at the very moment when, just when ‖ *en el momento menos pensado* when least expected ‖ *en el primer momento* in the beginning, at the start ‖ *en este momento* just now, at this moment ‖ *en estos momentos* at the moment, at present, at the present time *o* moment ‖ *en los momentos actuales* at present, at the present time ‖ *en mal momento* at a bad time ‖ *en todo momento* at any moment *o* time ‖ *hace un momento* not a moment ago ‖ *ha pasado su momento* he's had his day ‖ *momento crucial* crucial moment ‖ *momento fatídico* fatal moment ‖ *momento psicológico* psychological moment ‖ *momentos después* a few moments later, moments later ‖ *no tener un momento libre* not to have a minute free ‖ *por el momento* for the moment ‖ *por momentos* every moment, fast ‖ *ser el hombre del momento* to be the man of the moment ‖ *tener buenos momentos* to have one's (good) moments ‖ *últimos momentos* last minutes, last moments ‖ *¡un momento!* just a minute!, just a moment!

momia *f* mummy ‖ FIG *estar hecho una momia* to be all skin and bones.

momificación *f* mummification.

momificar *vt* to mummify.
◆ *vpr* to become mummified, to mummify.

momio, mia *adj* lean (carne) ‖ *AMER* FAM fuddy-duddy (carroza).
◆ *m* bargain (ganga) ‖ cushy job (trabajo fácil y rentable) ‖ extra, bonus (suplemento) ‖ FAM *de momio* free, for nothing (de balde).

mona *f* female monkey (hembra del mono) ‖ FAM copycat, ape (persona que imita) | drunkenness [*US* drunk] (borrachera) ‖ old maid (juego de cartas) ‖ TAUR metal leg guard ‖ *AMER* mannequin (maniquí) ‖ — FAM *aunque la mona se vista de seda, mona se queda* you can't make a silk purse out of a sow's ear | *coger* or *pillar una mona* to get sozzled *o* sloshed *o* stoned *o* plastered | *corrido como una mona, hecho una mona* ashamed | *dormir la mona* to sleep it off | *estar mona* to be stoned | *mandar a freír monas* to tell (s.o.) to jump in the lake | *quedarse corrido como una mona* or *hecho una mona* not to know where to put o.s., to be so embarrassed.

monacal *adj* monastic.

monacato *m* monkhood, monasticism.

monacillo *m* ⟶ **monaguillo.**

Mónaco *n pr* GEOGR Monaco.

monada; monería *f* kindness (amabilidad) ‖ pretty thing, lovely thing; *en esta tienda hay verdaderas monadas* in this shop there are some really pretty things ‖ pretty girl (chica bonita) ‖ flattery (halago) ‖ caress (carantoña) ‖ charming little way (acción graciosa de un niño) ‖ silliness (tontería) ‖ nasty trick, dirty trick (mala jugada) ‖ — FIG *¡qué hay monada!* hullo, beautiful! | *¡qué monada!* isn't it lovely?, how lovely! | *¡qué monada de pulsera!* what a lovely *o* a pretty bracelet! | *ser una monada* to be pretty, to be lovely; *esta niña es una verdadera monada* this girl is really pretty.
◆ *pl* simpering ways (melindres) ‖ grimaces, faces (gestos).

mónada *m* FIL monad.

monadismo *m* FIL monadism.

monago *m*; **monaguillo** *m*; **monacillo** *m* acolyte, altar boy, child who assists the priest.

monarca *m* monarch.

monarquía *f* monarchy; *monarquía absoluta* absolute monarchy.

monárquico, ca *adj* monarchical, monarchic.
◆ *m/f* monarchist.

monarquismo *m* monarchism.

monasterio *m* monastery.

monástico, ca *adj* monastic.

monda; mondadura *f* pruning, trimming (de los árboles) ‖ cleaning (limpieza) ‖ cleaning out (de los pozos) ‖ exhumation (de los restos humanos) ‖ — FAM *es la monda* it's great, it's terrific (magnífico), it's sheer hell (muy malo), it's killing, it's hilarious (es muy divertido) | *este tipo es la monda* this fellow is the limit *o* takes the cake (es el colmo), this chap is hilarious (muy gracioso), this fellow is great (estupendo).
◆ *pl* peelings (desperdicios); *mondas de patatas* potato peelings.

mondadientes *m inv* toothpick.

mondador, ra *m/f* pruner (de árboles) | peeler (de frutas y legumbres) ‖ cleaner (que limpia).

mondadura *f* ⟶ **monda.**

mondante *adj* FAM hilarious, killing.

mondaoídos *m inv* earpick.

mondar *vt* to clean (quitar lo inútil) ‖ to hull; *cebada mondada* hulled barley ‖ to trim, to prune (podar) ‖ to strip (el tronco de un árbol) ‖ to peel, to skin (patatas, tomates, fruta) ‖ to shell (guisantes, nueces, etc.) ‖ to dredge, to clean out (un río) ‖ to cut, to clip (cortar) ‖ FIG & FAM to clean out, to fleece (en el juego) ‖ — FAM *¡anda y que te monden!* get away! | *mondar a palos* to give a thrashing, to thrash.
◆ *vpr* FAM *mondarse de risa* to split one's sides laughing, to laugh one's head off ‖ *mondarse los dientes* to pick one's teeth.

mondo, da *adj* pure, clean ‖ plain; *el hecho mondo es* the plain fact is ‖ bare; *mi sueldo mondo es* my bare salary is ‖ — FIG & FAM *mondo y lirondo* pure and simple ‖ *es la verdad monda y lironda* it's the plain truth.

mondongo *m* innards *pl* (tripas) ‖ tripe (guiso) ‖ FAM intestines *pl* (intestinos) ‖ *AMER* FIG ridiculous get-up (adefesio).

mondonguería *f* tripe shop ‖ pork butcher's (shop) (charcutería).

mondonguero, ra *m/f* tripe shopkeeper ‖ pork butcher (charcutero).

moneda *f* money, currency; *la moneda española* the Spanish currency; *moneda extranjera* foreign currency ‖ coin (pieza) ‖ — *acuñar* or *labrar* or *batir moneda* to mint money ‖ *casa de la Moneda* mint ‖ *moneda contante y sonante* hard cash ‖ *moneda de cuenta* money of account ‖ *moneda de papel* paper money ‖ *moneda falsa* counterfeit money ‖ *moneda fiduciaria* fiduciary money ‖ *moneda fuerte* strong currency ‖ *moneda imaginaria* money of account ‖ *moneda suelta* or *fraccionaria* small change ‖ FIG *pagar a uno en* or *con la misma moneda* to give s.o. a taste of his own medicine, to pay s.o. back in his own coin ‖ *papel moneda* paper money ‖ FIG *ser moneda corriente* to be everyday stuff *o* run-of-the-mill stuff ‖ *se ruega moneda fraccionaria* please tender the exact fare (rótulo en transportes públicos).

monedero *m* minter (que hace moneda) ‖ purse (portamonedas) ‖ *monedero falso* counterfeiter.

monegasco, ca *adj/s* Monegasque, Monacan.

monería *f* ⟶ **monada.**

monetario, ria *adj* monetary.
◆ *m* collection of coins and medals.

monetización *f* monetization.

monetizar *vt* to monetize ‖ to mint (acuñar).

mongol, la; mongólico, ca *adj* Mongol, Mongolian, Mongolic (de Mongolia) ‖ Mongolic (idioma).
◆ *m/f* Mongol, Mongolian (persona de Mongolia).
◆ *m* Mongolic (idioma).

Mongolia *npr f* Mongolia; *Mongolia Interior, Exterior* Inner, Outer Mongolia.

mongólico, ca *adj/s* ⟶ **mongol** ‖ MED mongol, mongolian.

mongolismo *m* MED mongolism.

moni *m* FAM dough (dinero).

monicaco *m* FAM shrimp (hombrecillo).

monigote *m* lay brother (de un convento) || rag doll, paper doll (muñeco ridículo) || ridiculous figure [painted usually by children] (dibujo mal hecho) || FIG & FAM puppet (persona sin personalidad) || humorous sketch (dibujo humorístico) || bad painting (pintura mal hecha) || *monigote de nieve* snowman.

monín, ina; monino, na *adj* FAM → **mono.**

monipodio *m* unlawful meeting (conciliábulo) || *el patio de Monipodio* a den of thieves.

monís *f* trinket.

monises *m pl* FAM dough *sing*, money *sing* (dinero); *tener monises* to have dough.

monísimo, ma *adj* very pretty, very lovely, etc. || mono.

monismo *m* FIL monism.

monitor, ra *m/f* monitor.
◆ *m* INFORM monitor; *monitor en color* colour monitor.

monja *f* nun || *meterse a monja* to become a nun, to take the veil.

monje *m* monk (fraile) || anchorite (anacoreta) || coal tit (ave).

monjil *adj* nun's, of nuns (de monjas) || FIG excessively demure (excesivamente recatado).
◆ *m* nun's habit || mourning dress (traje de luto).

mono, na *adj* FAM pretty, good-looking (bonito); *¡qué chica más mona!* what a pretty girl! | lovely, nice (amable) | cute, lovely, pretty, nice; *¡qué abrigo más mono!* what a cute coat! | darling (gracioso); *un niño muy mono* a darling child.
◆ *m* monkey, ape (animal) || joker (en los naipes) || FIG & FAM withdrawal symptoms [US cold turkey] (droga) || FIG ape (burlón) | silhouette, drawing (de animal u hombre) | ridiculous figure (monigote); *pintar monos en la pared* to draw ridiculous figures on the wall | ape (hombre muy feo) | pansy (afeminado) || overalls *pl*, dungarees *pl* (traje de una sola pieza) || rompers *pl* (de niño) || — FIG *el último mono* the least important, the pip-squeak, the lowest of the low | *estar de monos* to be cross *o* angry || *mono aullador* howler monkey || *mono capuchino* capuchin monkey || FIG *mono de imitación* ape, copycat, imitator, mimic || *mono sabio* trained ape (en el circo), «monosabio», bullring attendant (en tauromaquia) || FIG & FAM *¿que me miras?, ¿tengo monos en la cara?* what are you looking at?, do you want a signed photograph?

monoácido, da *adj/sm* QUÍM monoacid.

monobásico, ca *adj* QUÍM monobasic.

monobloque *adj* monobloc.

monocamerismo *m* unicameralism.

monocarril *adj/sm* monorail.

monocasco *adj* monocoque (barco, avión).

monocilíndrico, ca *adj* single-cylinder.

monocorde *adj* MÚS single-string (instrumento) || monotonous (monótono).

monocordio *m* MÚS monochord.

monocotiledóneo, a *adj* BOT monocotyledonous.
◆ *f* monocotyledon.

monocromático, ca *adj* monochromatic.

monocromía *f* monochromy.

monocromo, ma *adj/sm* monochrome.

monóculo, la *adj* monocular.
◆ *m* monocle (lente) || eye patch (vendaje).

monocultivo *m* monoculture.

monodia *f* MÚS monody.

monofásico, ca *adj* monophase, single-phase.

monofisismo *m* monophysitism (herejía).

monofisita *adj* monophysitic.
◆ *m* monophysite (hereje).

monogamia *f* monogamy.

monógamo, ma *adj* monogamous.
◆ *m/f* monogamist.

monografía *f* monograph.

monográfico, ca *adj* monographic.

monograma *m* monogram.

monokini *m* monokini [topless bathing suit].

monolingüe *adj* monolingual.

monolítico, ca *adj* monolithic.

monolito *m* monolith.

monologar *vi* to soliloquize.

monólogo *m* monologue.

monomanía *f* monomania, fixed idea.

monomaniaco, ca; monomaníaco, ca; monomaniático, ca *adj* monomaniacal.
◆ *m/f* monomaniac.

monometalismo *m* monometallism.

monometalista *adj* monometallic.
◆ *m/f* monometallist.

monomio *m* MAT monomial.

monomotor *adj* AVIAC single-engine.
◆ *m* single-engine aeroplane.

mononuclear *adj* mononuclear.

mononucleosis *f* MED mononucleosis.

monopatín *m* skateboard.

monoplano *adj/sm* monoplane.

monoplaza *adj/sm* single-seater.

monopolio *m* monopoly.

monopolización *f* monopolization.

monopolizador, ra *adj* monopolizing, monopolistic.
◆ *m/f* monopolizer.

monopolizar *vt* to monopolize.

monorrail; monorriel *adj/sm* monorail.

monosabio *m* TAUR «monosabio», bullring attendant.

monosacárido *m* QUÍM monosaccharide.

monosilábico, ca *adj* GRAM monosyllabic; *lengua monosilábica* monosyllabic language.

monosílabo, ba *adj* GRAM monosyllabic.
◆ *m* monosyllable.

monotarea *f* INFORM single task.

monoteísmo *m* REL monotheism.

monoteísta *adj* REL monotheistic.
◆ *m/f* monotheist.

monotipia *f* IMPR monotype (procedimiento).

monotipo *m* IMPR monotype (máquina).

monotonía *f* monotony.

monótono, na *adj* monotonous.

monotremas *m pl* ZOOL monotremata.

monovalente *adj/sm* monovalent.

monseñor *m* Monseigneur || Monsignor (prelado italiano).

monserga *f* FAM boring *o* tiresome speech; *nos colocó la monserga de siempre* he gave us the same old boring speech | lectura, sermon; *no me vengas con monsergas* don't give me a lecture | story, tale, lie; *todo eso no son más que monsergas* it is all one big story || — FAM *dar la monserga a uno* to annoy *o* to pester s.o. | *¡qué monserga!* what a nuisance!

monstruo *adj inv* fantastic; *una cena monstruo* a fantastic dinner.
◆ *m* monster.

monstruosidad *f* monstrosity.

monstruoso, sa *adj* monstrous.

monta *f* mount (acción de montar) || mating season (apareamiento de caballo y yegua) || sum, total (suma) || value, account, importance; *negocio de poca monta* business of little importance; *libro, persona de poca monta* book, person of little value.

montacargas *m inv* hoist, goods lift, service lift [US freight elevator].

montado, da *adj* mounted (soldado, artillería) || saddled (caballo) || riding; *montado en un autobús, en bicicleta, en un asno* riding in a bus, riding a bicycle, riding an ass || organized, set up (organizado) || TECN set (diamante, etc.) | assembled (máquina) || TEATR staged (una obra) || *un hombre montado a caballo* a man on horseback.
◆ *m* mounted soldier (soldado).

montador, ra *m/f* fitter (el que monta) || assembler (operario) || setter (joyero) || TEATR stager, producer || mounter (fotógrafo) || CINEM film cutter.
◆ *m* horse block, mounting block (para montar a caballo) || *montador mecánico electricista* electrical assembler.

montaje *m* assembly, setting up, assembling, mounting (de una máquina) || fitting out (de un taller) || putting together, assembling, mounting (de un reloj) || setup, staging (en el teatro) || cutting, editing, mounting (de una película) || setting (de una joya) || building, putting together (de un aparato de radio) || *cadena* or *línea de montaje* assembly line.

montanera *f* acorn pasture [for hogs].

montanero *m* forest ranger.

montante *m* upright (de una armazón) || leg (de una máquina) || prop, post (de una mina) || stanchion (soporte) || total sum, amount (importe, total) || ARQ mullion (de una ventana) | post (de una puerta) | small window over a door (ventana) || espadon, two-handed sword (arma) || DEP goal post (de una portería).
◆ *f* high tide (marea).

montaña *f* mountain; *cadena de montañas* chain of mountains, mountain chain || FIG mountain; *una montaña de libros* a mountain of books || AMER undergrowth (monte bajo), brush, scrub (maleza) || — FIG *hacer de todo una montaña* to make a mountain out of a molehill || *La Montaña* region of Santander [Spain] || *montaña rusa* switchback, scenic railway [US roller coaster] (de un parque de atracciones).

Montañas Rocosas *npr f* GEOGR the Rocky Mountains.

montañero, ra *m/f* mountaineer, climber || *escuela de montañeros* mountaineering school.

montañés, esa *adj* mountain, highland || of «La Montaña» [region of Santander].
◆ *m/f* mountain dweller, highlander || inhabitant of «La Montaña».

montañismo *m* mountaineering, climbing || *escuela de montañismo* mountaineering school.

montañoso, sa *adj* mountainous.

montaplatos *m inv* food lift, service lift [US dumbwaiter].

montar *vi* to ride; *montar a caballo, en bicicleta, en burro, en coche* to ride a horse, a bicycle, on a donkey, in a car | to mount, to get on (subir); *montar a caballo* or *en un caballo* to mount one's horse || to go up; *no me gusta montar en avión, en globo* I don't like going up in an aeroplane, in a balloon || to get on, to board (pasajeros); *montar en un avión, en un tren, en un barco* to get on an aeroplane, on a train, on a boat || to get into; *montar en un coche* to get into a car || to be of importance; *este negocio monta poco* this business is of little importance || to amount to, to come to; *la cuenta montó a cien pesetas* the bill amounted to a hundred pesetas || — *montar a* or *en la grupa* to ride pil-

lion [*US* to ride on the pillion pad] || *montar a pelo* to ride bareback || FIG *montar en cólera* to flare up, to fly into a temper || *silla de montar* saddle || FIG *tanto monta* it's all the same || *tanto monta, monta tanto Isabel como Fernando* the motto of the Spanish Catholics rulers, Isabel and Fernando, indicating equal division of authority between the two.
◆ *vt* to mount, to get on (subirse a un caballo) || to ride (conducir) || to lift (subir) || to fit out (organizar) || to set up (una fábrica) || to mount, to set (una joya) || to assemble, to put together, to set up (una máquina) || to hang (una puerta) || to make (un vestido) || AUT to fit (un neumático) || to furnish, to set up (amueblar una casa) || to wind (un muelle) || to mount (la guardia) || to beat, to whip (los huevos) || to overlap (una cosa sobre otra) || to cover (a la hembra) || to cock (un arma) || TEATR to set, to mount (un decorado) | to stage (una obra dramática) || CINEM to edit, to mount (una película) || MIL to mount (una ofensiva).

montaraz *adj* savage, wild (animales) || rough, coarse (de modales toscos) || unsociable (arisco, insociable) || mountain, highland (de la sierra).

montazgo *m* tribute paid for the passage of cattle.

monte *m* mountain (montaña); *montes altos* high mountains; *Montes Cantábricos* Cantabrian Mountains || mount (aislado o con nombre propio); *Monte de los Olivos* Mount of Olives || forest, woodland (bosque); *monte espeso* thick forest || stack, pile (naipes que quedan por robar) || monte (juego) || *AMER* country (campo) || FIG & FAM mop (cabellera) || — *administración de montes* Forestry Commission [*US* Department of Forestry] || *conejo de monte* wild rabbit || *echarse* or *hacerse al monte* to take to the hills || *escuela de montes* forestry school || *monte alto* forest, trees *pl* || *monte bajo* scrub, underbrush, undergrowth || *monte de piedad* pawnshop || ANAT *monte de Venus* mons veneris (pubis), Mount of Venus (de la mano) || FIG *no todo el monte es orégano* it is not all plain sailing, life is not just a bowl of cherries.

montepío *m* assistance fund || *AMER* pawnshop (monte de piedad) | widow's pension fund (viudedad).

montera *f* cloth cap (para la cabeza) || bullfighter's hat (de los toreros) || huntress, hunter (que caza) || skylight, glass roofing (cubierta de cristales) || cover (de alambique) || MAR triangular sail (vela) || FAM *ponerse el mundo por montera* not to care what people think *o* what people say.

montería *f* venery (arte de cazar) || hunting (caza mayor).

monterilla *f* MAR triangular sail.
◆ *m* mayor [of a town] (alcalde).

montero *m* huntsman, hunter (cazador) || beater (ojeador) || *montero mayor* master of the hounds.

montés, esa *adj* wild || *gato montés* wildcat.

Montescos *npr mpl* Montagues.

montevideano, na *adj/s* Montevidean.

Montevideo *n pr* GEOGR Montevideo.

montículo *m* hillock, monticule.

montilla *m* montilla (vino).

monto *m* total, sum (total).

montón *m* heap, pile || FIG & FAM heap, pile, heaps *pl*, piles *pl*; *un montón de cosas* a heap of things; *un montón de papeles* a pile of papers | good many; *un montón de años, de días* a good many years, days | piles *pl*, bags *pl*, stacks *pl*; *tener montones de dinero* to have bags of money || — FIG *a montones* lots of (mucho); *pasteles a montones* lots of cakes | *del montón* ordinary, commonplace, average; *ser del montón* to be ordinary | *salirse del montón* to stand out from the crowd | *un montón de gente* lots *pl* of people.

montonera *f* *AMER* group of mounted rebels (de rebeldes) | stack, pile (almiar).

montonero *m* *AMER* guerrilla, fighter (guerrillero).

montuno, na *adj* mountain || *AMER* country, rustic (rústico) | wild (montaraz).

montuoso, sa *adj* mountainous (montañoso) || wooded (con bosque).

montura *f* mount (cabalgadura) || saddle (silla) || setting (de una joya) || frame (de gafas) || assembly, mounting (de una máquina).

monumental *adj* monumental || FIG & FAM well built (una mujer) | terrible, horrible, awful; *tener un catarro monumental* to have a terrible cold | enormous, huge (enorme) | terrific (estupendo).

monumento *m* monument, memorial; *monumento a los Caídos* war memorial || monument, building; *monumentos históricos* ancient monuments || temporary altar (el Jueves Santo) || FIG monument; *un monumento de erudición* a monument of learning || FIG & FAM *esta chica es un monumento* this girl is a beauty.

monzón *m/f* monsoon (viento).

moña *f* hair ribbon (lazo) || chignon, oun (moño) || TAUR coloured ribbons *pl* [worn by the bull for identification] | ornament of ribbons worn on the back of the head of the bullfighter || doll (muñeca) || FAM booze-up (borrachera).

moño *m* chignon, bun (de pelo) || bow [of ribbons] (lazo de cintas) || tuft, crest (de algunos pájaros) || — FIG & FAM *agarrarse del moño* to tear each other's hair out, to pull each other's hair | *estar hasta el moño* to be fed up | *ponerse moños* to brag, to boast (jactarse), to put on airs (presumir).

moñudo, da *adj* tufted, crested (ave).

MOPU *abrev de Ministerio de Obras Públicas y Urbanismo* Spanish Ministry of Public Works and Town Planning.

moquear *vi* to run [the nose].

moqueo *m* FAM runny nose.

moquero *m* handkerchief (pañuelo).

moqueta *f* moquette (alfombra).

moquete *m* FAM punch on the nose *o* in the face.

moquetear *vt* FAM to punch on the nose *o* in the face.
◆ *vi* to run (the nose).

moquillo *m* distemper (catarro de los perros) || pip (de las aves) || FAM *pasar el moquillo* to have a rough time of it.

moquita *f* mucus (moco fluido).

mor de (por) *loc adv* because of.

mora *f* BOT mulberry (fruto) || blackberry (zarzamora) || JUR delay, mora (demora) || Moorish woman (mujer árabe).

morabito *m* marabout.

morada *f* house, abode, dwelling (place) (casa o habitación) || stay, sojourn (estancia) || *la última morada* the last resting place.

morado, da *adj* purple, violet || — FIG & FAM *estar morado* to be sozzled *o* sloshed (borracho) | *pasarlas moradas* to have a rough time, to go through hell *o* murder | *ponerse morado* to stuff o.s.; *me puse morado de comer, de higos* I stuffed myself with food, with figs | *se puso morado de vino* he drank gallons of wine.

morador, ra *adj* dwelling, living, residing.
◆ *m/f* inhabitant, dweller, resident.

moral *adj* moral; *principios morales* moral principles.
◆ *m* mulberry tree (árbol).
◆ *f* morals *pl* (ética) || morale (ánimo); *la moral de las tropas, de un equipo* the morale of the troops, of a team; *levantar* or *elevar la moral* to raise the morale || *tener la moral baja, estar bajo de moral* to be in poor spirits, to be low spirited.

moraleja *f* moral (de una fábula).

moralidad *f* morality, morals *pl*.

moralismo *m* moralism.

moralista *adj* moralistic.
◆ *m/f* moralist.

moralización *f* moralization.

moralizador, ra *adj* moralizing.
◆ *m/f* moralizer, moralist.

moralizar *vt/vi* to moralize.

morapio *m* FAM red wine, plonk (vino).

morar *vi* to reside, to dwell.

moratoria *f* JUR moratorium.

moratorio, ria *adj* moratory.

morbididad *f* → **morbilidad.**

mórbido, da *adj* morbid (no sano); *estado mórbido* morbid state; *literatura mórbida* morbid literature || delicate, soft, tender (delicado).

morbilidad; morbididad *f* MED morbidity, sick rate (estadística).

morbo *f* disease, illness (enfermedad).

morbosidad *f* morbidity.

morboso, sa *adj* morbid, unhealthy (no sano) || morbific (que causa enfermedad) || sick, diseased (enfermo).

morcilla *f* CULIN black pudding, blood sausage || poisoned sausage [for killing dogs] || TEATR ad lib, improvised part (del actor) || FAM *¡que te den morcilla!* go to hell!, get lost!

morcillero, ra *m/f* pork butcher || ad-libber, improviser, extemporizer (actor).

mordacidad *f* mordacity, pungency, sting.

mordaga *f* FAM booze-up [*US* drunk] (borrachera) || FAM *coger una mordaga* to get sozzled *o* canned.

mordaz *adj* corrosive, mordant (corrosivo) || stinging, biting, pungent (al paladar) || FIG biting, caustic, pungent, burning; *críticas mordaces* biting criticism.

mordaza *f* gag (en la boca) || MAR compressor (del ancla) || VET pincers *pl* (para castrar) || TECN clamps *pl*, jaws *pl* (del torno) | fishplate (de carriles).

mordazmente *adv* bitingly, sarcastically, acrimoniously.

mordedura *f* bite.

morder* *vt* to bite; *le ha mordido una serpiente* a snake has bitten him || FIG to gossip about, to run down (murmurar) | to nibble away at, to wear down (quitar por porciones) || IMPR to etch (una plancha) || TECN to bite (la lima) || FIG *morder el polvo* to bite the dust.
◆ *vi* to bite || to catch (un engranaje) || FIG *está que muerde* he is in a nasty temper.
◆ *vpr* to bite; *morderse las uñas* to bite one's nails || FIG *morderse la lengua* to hold one's tongue | *morderse los labios* to bite one's lip (para no hablar o no reírse) | *morderse los puños* to kick o.s. | *no morderse la lengua* not to mince one's words, to speak one's mind.

mordicar *vt* to sting.

mordido, da *adj* bitten.
◆ *f* bite (en la pesca) || *AMER* bribe (soborno).

mordiente *adj* mordant, biting (que corroe).
◆ *m* mordant (sustancia corrosiva) || FIG bite, punch; *la delantera falta de mordiente* the forwardline lacks bite.

mordiscar; mordisquear *vt* to nibble (at).

mordisco *m* bite || — *dar* or *pegar* or *tirar un mordisco* to bite, to bite at, to take a bite at || *el perro me tiró un mordisco* the dog went for me.

mordisqueo *m* nibbling.

morena *f* muraena, moray (pez) || sheaf, bundle (de cereal segado) || moraine (de un glaciar).

moreno, na *adj* brown || tanned, brown (por el sol) || dark, black (pelo) || dark, swarthy, dark-skinned (de piel oscura) || AMER coloured, negro (de raza negra).
◆ *m/f* FIG & FAM negro (hombre), negress (mujer) (de raza negra) || AMER mulatto || dark man (hombre), brunette (chica) || — *pan moreno* brown bread || *ponerse moreno* to get tanned, to get a suntan.

morera *f* BOT white mulberry (árbol).

moreral *m* white mulberry field.

morería *f* Moorish district *o* neighbourhood (barrio) || Moorish country (país).

moretón *m* FAM bruise (equimosis).

morfema *m* GRAM morpheme.

Morfeo *npr m* MIT Morpheus.

morfina *f* morphine, morphia.

morfinismo *m* morphinism.

morfinomanía *f* addiction to morphine.

morfinómano, na *adj* morphine.
◆ *m/f* morphine addict, morphinomaniac.

morfología *f* morphology.

morfológico, ca *adj* morphologic, morphological.

morfosis *f* morphosis.

morganático, ca *adj* morganatic.

morgue *f* morgue.
— OBSERV Gallicism for *depósito de cadáveres.*

moribundo, da *adj/s* moribund.

morigeración *f* moderation, temperance.

morigerado, da *adj* well-mannered (de buenos modales) || moderate temperate (moderado).

morigerar *vt* to moderate (templar).

morilla *f* BOT morel (cagarria).

morillo *m* andiron, firedog.

morir* *vi* to die; *morir muy joven* to die very young; *morir de vejez* to die of old age || to end (una línea de transporte, etc.) || to die, to go out (el fuego) || to come out (una calle) || to fade, to droop (una flor) || to die out *o* away (un sonido) || FIG to die, to end; *mi amor por ella murió aquel mismo día* my love for her died that very day || — FIG & FAM *¡así se muera!* good riddance to him! || *haber muerto* to be dead || *moría la tarde* the afternoon was coming to a close *o* was almost over || *morir ahogado* to drown || *morir ahorcado* to be hanged || *morir al pie del cañón* to die with one's boots on, to die in harness || *morirás antes de que muera el día* you will die before the day is out *o* before the end of the day || *morir con las botas puestas* or *vestido* to die with one's boots on || *morir de frío* or *helado* to freeze to death || *morir de muerte natural* to die a natural death || *morir de repente* to die suddenly || *morir fusilado* to be shot || *¡muera el dictador!* down with *o* death to the dictator! || *muerto a tiros* shot [dead].
◆ *vt* to kill (matar).
◆ *vpr* to die; *morirse de cáncer* to die of cancer; *¡me muero!* I'm dying || — FIG *es para morirse de risa* it's absolutely killing *o* hilarious | *morirse de aburrimiento* to be bored stiff *o* bored to death | *morirse de envidia* to be green with envy | *morirse de frío* to freeze to death | *morirse de ganas de* to be dying to | *morirse de hambre* to starve to death, to die of starvation (sentido propio), to starve (sentido figurado) || FIG *morirse de inquietud* to be worried to death *o* worried sick | *morirse de miedo* to die of fright (sentido real), to be frightened *o* scared to death *o* out of one's wits (asustarse) | *morirse de risa* to die laughing, to be tickled to death || FIG & FAM *morirse por el cine, por una chica, por el fútbol* to be crazy about the cinema, about a girl, about football (gustarle a uno muchísimo) | *morirse por ir al cine, por salir con ella* to be dying to go to the cinema, to go out with her | *morirse sin decir Jesús* to die very suddenly | *¡que me muera si...!* may I be struck down if...

morisco, ca *adj* Moorish.
◆ *m/f* Morisco (moro bautizado).
— OBSERV The term *morisco* is applied to the Spanish Moors who, during the Reconquest (711 to 1492), accepted Christianity.

morisma *f* Moors *pl* || multitude of Moors.

morisqueta *f* grimace (mueca) || dirty trick (engaño).

morlaco, ca *adj* sly, cunning (taimado).
◆ *m/f* sly fox (*fam*), cunning person.
◆ *m* FAM bull (toro) || AMER peso (peso) | money (dinero).

mormón, ona *m/f* Mormon.

mormónico, ca *adj* Mormon.

mormonismo *m* Mormonism (doctrina religiosa).

moro, ra *adj* Moorish || Mohammedan (mahometano) || unbaptized (no bautizado) || white-stockinged (caballo).
◆ *m/f* Moor (árabe) || Mohammedan (mahometano) || Moro [Mohammedan native of Mindanao and other Malaysian islands] || — FIG & FAM *hay moros en la costa* the coast is not clear, watch out | *hubo moros y cristianos* there was trouble *o* a big brawl | *prometer el oro y el moro* to promise the earth, to promise the moon and stars.

morocho, cha *adj* FIG & FAM AMER robust, strong (fuerte) | swarthy, dark-skinned (moreno de piel) | dark, brunette (de pelo).
◆ *m* AMER type of maize (maíz).
◆ *pl* AMER twins (gemelos).

morosamente *adj* slowly (con lentitud) || late (con dilación).

morosidad *f* slowness, dilatoriness (lentitud) || lateness, delay (tardanza) || inactivity (falta de actividad) || JUR arrears *pl* of payment.

moroso, sa *adj* dilatory; *deudor moroso* dilatory debtor || slow, unhurried (lento) || lazy, sluggish (perezoso) || late, tardy (que se detiene) || *declaración morosa* morose declaration.
◆ *m/f* slow payer, defaulter (retrasado en el pago).

morrada *f* butt (golpe) || slap (guantada).

morral *m* gamebag (del cazador) || MIL knapsack, pack.

morralla *f* rubbish, trash (cosas sin valor) || small fish (pescadillos) || FIG rabble (gente despreciable) || AMER loose change (dinero suelto).

morrena *f* GEOGR moraine (de glaciar).

morrillo *m* fleshy part of the neck (de animal) || TAUR muscular protrusion on the bull's neck || FAM thick neck || pebble, round stone (canto rodado) || rubblework (mampostería).

morriña *f* homesickness, nostalgia (nostalgia) || sadness, despondency, gloom (tristeza) || VET dropsy.

morrión *m* morion (casco antiguo) || shako (gorro militar).

morro *m* snout, nose (hocico de animal) || FAM thick lips, *pl* (labios abultados) || FIG & FAM lips, *pl* (labios) || knoll, hill (monte) || pebble (guijarro) || MAR pier, jetty (malecón) || butt, grip (de pistola) || nose (de un avión) || nose cone (de un cohete) || nose, hood (de un coche) || head (la parte redonda) || — *beber a morro* to drink from the bottle, to drink straight from the bottle, to swig || *caer de morros* to nose-dive || FIG & FAM *estar de morros* to be in a bad mood (estar enfadado) | *estar de morros con* to be cross with || FAM *poner morros* to purse one's lips, to look cross | *¡qué morro!* what a nerve! | *romperle a alguien los morros* to punch s.o. in the nose.

morrocotudo, da *adj* FAM tremendous, terrible (imponente); *un susto, un batacazo morrocotudo* a tremendous scare, fall | huge, enormous (enorme) || magnificent, terrific (magnífico).

morrón *m* FAM blow, bang (golpe).

morrongo, ga *m/f* FAM cat (gato).

morsa *f* ZOOL walrus (mamífero).

morse *m* Morse (alfabeto).

mortadela *f* mortadella, bologna sausage.

mortaja *f* shroud (sudario) || TECN mortise (muesca) || AMER cigarette paper.

mortal *adj* mortal; *los seres mortales* mortal beings || mortal, fatal; *herida mortal* mortal wound || lethal, deadly; *una dosis mortal* a lethal dose || FIG mortal; *pecado mortal* mortal sin | mortal, deadly; *odio, dolor mortal* mortal hatred, pain | dreadful, awful; *aburrimiento, trabajo mortal* dreadful boredom, work | unbearable, unending (espera) || — *restos mortales* mortal remains || *salto mortal* somersault.
◆ *m/f* mortal; *un mortal feliz* a happy mortal.

mortalidad *f* mortality (condición de mortal) || mortality; *la mortalidad infantil* infant mortality || death rate, mortality (índice).

mortalmente *adv* mortally, fatally; *mortalmente herido* mortally wounded || FIG mortally; *odiar a uno mortalmente* to hate s.o. mortally | dreadfully, deadly, deathly; *una película, una fiesta mortalmente aburrida* a dreadfully boring film, party || — FIG *aburrirse mortalmente* to be bored stiff *o* to death || *pecar mortalmente* to commit a mortal sin.

mortandad *f* mortality, loss of life; *el bombardeo, la epidemia produjo* or *causó gran mortandad* the bombing, the epidemic caused heavy mortality || death toll (número de muertos).

mortecino, na *adj* dying, fading (que se apaga); *la luz mortecina del crepúsculo* the fading glow of twilight || dim, pale (débil); *la luz mortecina de una vela* the dim light of a candle || dull, faded (color) || moribund (moribundo).

morterada *f* MIL shot from a mortar || FIG volley (andanada).

morterete *m* small mortar (artillería) || gun for firing salutes (para salvas) || lampion (de iluminación) || brick (ladrillo).

mortero *m* mortar (almirez, argamasa) || MIL mortar (cañón).

mortífero, ra *adj* deadly, fatal; *una epidemia mortífera* a deadly epidemic || deadly, lethal; *un arma mortífera* a lethal weapon.

mortificación *f* mortification (privación) || torment.

mortificante *adj* mortifying || wounding, cutting (hiriente).

mortificar *vt* to mortify (dañar, humillar); *mortificar la carne* to mortify the flesh || to torment, to plague (atormentar) || to wound, to cut, to hurt (herir) | to mortify, to deaden (una parte del cuerpo).

mortinatalidad *f* infant mortality.

mortinato, ta *adj* stillborn.
◆ *m/f* stillborn child.

mortuorio, ria *adj* mortuary || of mourning, of the deceased; *casa mortuoria* house of mourning *o* of the deceased || — *lecho mortuorio* deathbed || *paño mortuorio* funeral pall.

morueco *m* ram (carnero).

moruno, na *adj* Moorish (moro).

morusa *f* FAM dough, money (dinero).

Mosa *npr m* GEOGR Meuse (río).

mosaico *m* mosaic (azulejo).

mosaico, ca *adj* Mosaic, of Moses (de Moisés).

mosaísmo *m* Mosaism.

mosca *f* fly (insecto) || fly (cebo para pescar); *caña de mosca* fly rod || tuft of hair (en la barbilla) || FIG & FAM dough, cash (dinero) | pest, nuisance (persona molesta) | nuisance, annoyance, bother (molestia) || — FIG & FAM *aflojar* or *soltar la mosca* to fork out, to cough up, to pay up | *caer como moscas* to drop *o* to fall like flies | *cazar* or *papar moscas* to gape, to catch flies, to daydream | *es incapaz de matar* or *hacer daño a una mosca* he wouldn't *o* he couldn't harm *o* hurt a fly | *estar mosca* to be suspicious | *más moscas se cogen con miel que con hiel* you catch more flies with honey than with vinegar | *mosca muerta* hypocrite | *no se oía ni una mosca* you could have heard a pin drop || *peso mosca* flyweight (boxeo) || FIG & FAM *por si las moscas* just in case | *¿qué mosca le ha picado?* what's eating you? | *tener la mosca* or *estar con la mosca detrás de* or *en la oreja* to be suspicious *o* uneasy.
◆ *pl* sparks (chispas) || spots before the eyes (en los ojos).

moscada *adj/f* *nuez moscada* nutmeg.

moscarda *f* blowfly, meat fly, bluebottle (moscón) || eggs *pl* (de las abejas).

moscardear *vi* to lay [eggs] (las abejas) || to rise (los peces) || FIG & FAM to nose around, to stick *o* to poke one's nose into everything.

moscardón *m* ZOOL botfly (parásito) | blowfly (moscón) | hornet (abejón) || FIG & FAM bore, nuisance, pest (persona pesada).

moscareta *f* flycatcher (pájaro).

moscarrón *m* botfly (insecto).

moscatel *adj* muscat (uva).
◆ *m* muscatel, muscadel (vino).
◆ *f* muscat (uva).

moscón *m* blowfly, meat fly, bluebottle (insecto) || FIG & FAM bore, nuisance, pest (persona pesada).

mosconear *vt* to annoy, to bother, to pester (molestar).
◆ *vi* to be a nuisance, to make a nuisance of o.s. (molestar) || to buzz (zumbar).

mosconeo *m* buzz, buzzing (zumbido) || FIG pestering (insistencia).

Moscovia *npr f* GEOGR Muscovy.

moscovita *adj/s* Muscovite.

Moscú *n pr* GEOGR Moscow.

mosén *m* sir (título antiguo).
— OBSERV Today this title is reserved for priests in certain regions of Spain (Catalonia, Aragon).

mosquear *vt* to shoo away (espantar las moscas) || to swat (matar las moscas) || FIG & FAM to smell fishy; *este asunto me mosquea* this business smells fishy to me.
◆ *vpr* to shoo flies away || FIG to get annoyed *o* irritated (picarse) | to take offence (ofenderse) | to become suspicious (sospechar algo).

mosqueo *m* shooing *o* swatting of flies || FIG resentment (pique) | suspicion (sospecha).

mosquetazo *m* musket shot (tiro) || musket wound (herida).

mosquete *m* musket (arma).

mosquetería *f* troop of musketeers, musketry || TEATR groundlings *pl* [spectators who stood at back of the theatre].

mosquetero *m* musketeer || TEATR groundling.

mosquetón *m* musketoon (arma).

mosquita *f* warble (ave) || — FIG & FAM *hacerse la mosquita muerta* to look as if butter would not melt in one's mouth | *mosquita muerta* hypocrite.

mosquitero *m* mosquito net.

mosquito *m* mosquito (insecto) || gnat, midge (mosca pequeña).

mostacilla *f* mustard-seed shot, dust shot (perdigón) || glass bead (abalorio).

mostacho *m* moustache, mustache (bigote) || FIG & FAM spot on the face (mancha) || MAR bowsprit.

mostachón *m* macaroon (bollo).

mostaza *f* mustard || mustard seed (semilla) || mustard-seed shot, dust shot (perdigones de caza).

mostense *adj/s* Premonstratensian (religioso).

mosto *m* must.

mostrador, ra *adj* demonstrating, showing.
◆ *m/f* demonstrator, exhibitor.
◆ *m* counter (en una tienda) || bar (en un café) || face (de reloj).

mostrar* *vt* to show (enseñar) || to show, to indicate (indicar) || to display, to exhibit, to show, to manifest (manifestar); *mostrar interés* to show interest || to demonstrate, to show (dar muestras de); *mostrar gran paciencia* to demonstrate great patience || to point out, to show (señalar) || FIG *mostrar las uñas* to show one's claws, to bare one's teeth.
◆ *vpr* to show o.s. || to appear; *mostrarse en público* to appear in public || to be; *se mostró muy amable conmigo* he was very kind to me || to prove, to make; *se mostró un excelente jefe* he made *o* he proved an excellent leader.

mostrenco, ca *adj* JUR ownerless (sin propietario); *bienes mostrencos* ownerless property || FAM homeless (sin casa) | stray (animal) | coarse (rudo) | dense, slow (ignorante) | fat, heavy (pesado, gordo).

mota *f* spot, speck, mote (mancha pequeña) || FIG slight flaw (defecto insignificante) || speck (en el ojo) || burl, knot (en el paño) || hillock (elevación del terreno).

mote *m* nickname (apodo); *poner mote* to give a nickname || device, motto (divisa) || *le pusieron como mote* they nicknamed him.

moteado *m* speckling, flecking (de un tejido).

motear *vt* to fleck, to speckle, to dapple.

motejar *vt* to tag, to label, to call; *le han motejado de avaro* they have labeled him a miser.

motel *m* motel (hotel).

motete *m* MÚS motet.

motilón, ona *adj* hairless (pelón).
◆ *m* FAM lay brother (lego).

motín *m* riot, uprising, insurrection (del pueblo) || mutiny (de tropas).

motivación *f* motivation.

motivar *vt* to motivate, to cause (causar) || to justify (justificar) || to explain (explicar).

motivo *m* motive, reason, cause; *motivo de disputa* cause of dispute || grounds *pl*; *motivos de divorcio* grounds for divorce || motif (en música, en pintura, etc.) || — *bajo ningún motivo* under no circumstances, on no account || *con este motivo* for this reason || *con mayor* or *con más motivo* even more so || *con motivo de* because of, owing to (debido a), on the occasion of || *dar motivo a* to give rise to, to provoke || *darle a uno motivo* or *motivos para* to give s.o. reason to (con verbo) *o* for (con sustantivo) || *de mi, tu, su motivo propio* on my, your, his (her) own initiative || *exposición de motivos* motivation || *motivo decorativo* or *ornamental* decorative *o* ornamental motif || *no ser motivo para* to be no reason to *o* for || *por cuyo motivo* on account of which || *por motivos de salud* for reason of health, for health reasons, on health grounds || *sin motivo alguno* without any reason, for no reason at all.

moto *f* motor bike, motorcycle.

motoarado *m* AGR motor tractor.

motobomba *f* motor pump.

motocarro *m* three-wheeler.

motocicleta *f* motorbike, motorcycle; *montar en motocicleta* to ride a motorcycle.

motociclismo *m* motorcycling.

motociclista *m/f* motorcyclist.

motocompresor *m* compressor.

motocross *m* moto-cross, cross-country motorcycle racing.

motocultivo *m* mechanized agriculture.

motoguadañadora *f* AGR motor scythe.

motón *m* MAR block, pulley; *motón de rabiza* tail block.

motonave *f* motorboat, motor ship.

motonería *f* MAR set of blocks or pulleys.

motoneta *f* AMER moped, scooter.

motoniveladora *f* leveller, bulldozer.

motopropulsor *m* motor propellor.

motor, ra *adj* motor; *músculos motores* motor muscles || moving (moviente) || *lancha motora* motorboat.
◆ *m* engine, motor; *motor de explosión, de reacción* internal combustion engine, jet engine || — *motor de arranque* starting motor || *motor de gasolina* petrol engine || *motor diesel* diesel engine || *motor eléctrico* electric motor || *motor fuera borda* outboard motor.

motora *f* motorboat.

motorismo *m* motorcycling (motociclismo).

motorista *m/f* motorcyclist || AMER driver (conductor).

motorización *f* motorization.

motorizado, da *adj* motorized; *división motorizada* motorized division.

motorizar *vt* to motorize.

motorreactor *m* jet engine.

motosegadora *f* AGR motor scythe.

mototractor *m* AGR (motor) tractor.

motovelero *m* motor sailer.

motovolquete *m* TECN mechanical tipping device.

motricidad *f* motivity.

motriz *adj f* motive, driving; *fuerza motriz* motive force.

movedizo, za *adj* moving, shifting (no firme) || loose (fácil de mover) || FIG inconsistent, fickle (persona) | unsettled, changeable (situación) || *arenas movedizas* quicksand *sing*.

mover* *vt* to move; *mover el brazo* to move one's arm || to shake (la cabeza para negar) || to nod (la cabeza para asentir) || to stir; *mover el café* to stir one's coffee || to wag (el rabo) || FIG to incite (incitar); *mover a la rebelión* to incite to rebellion | to stir up (a las masas) | to drive, to move; *movido por la curiosidad* driven by curiosity | to provoke, to cause (provocar); *mover discordia* to cause discord | to move, to stir (conmover) || to move (las piezas del ajedrez) || TECN to drive (impulsar) | to power (impeler) | to work (hacer funcionar) | to pull (arrastrar) || — FIG *mover a* to move to; *mover a compasión* to move to pity | *mover a uno a risa*

to make s.o. laugh | *mover cielo y tierra* to move heaven and earth || *mover la cabeza de arriba abajo* to nod || *mover la cabeza de un lado a otro* to shake one's head || FIG *mover la curiosidad* to arouse s.o.'s curiosity | *mover los hilos* to pull (the) strings | *ser movido por el interés* to be motivated by personal gain.
◆ *vi* ARQ to spring (un arco).
◆ *vpr* to move; *¡no se mueva!* don't move!; *moverse alrededor del Sol* to move round the sun; *se mueve con dificultad* he moves with difficulty || to wriggle, to fidget; *este niño no deja de moverse* this child never stops wriggling || FIG to move around; *para conseguir una buena colocación hay que moverse* in order to get a good job you have to move around | to make a move, to act (obrar) || to be rough (el mar) || FIG & FAM to get a move on; *¡muévete!* get a move on! || FIG & FAM *moverse más que el rabo de una lagartija* or *que un saco de ratones* to be fidgety, to have ants in one's pants.

movible *adj* movable, moveable.

movido, da *adj* moved; *movido de* or *por la piedad* moved by pity || blurred, fuzzy (fotografía) || motivated; *movido por el interés* motivated by personal gain || FIG active (persona) | lively (animado) || restless (que no deja de moverse) || AMER thin, skinny, rachitic (delgaducho) | rough, choppy (mar).

móvil *adj* movable, moveable; *fiesta móvil* movable feast || FIG unstable, changeable (inestable) || — TECN *material móvil* rolling stock (ferrocarril) || *timbre móvil* fiscal *o* revenue stamp.
◆ *m* motive; *el móvil de un crimen* the motive of a crime || FÍS moving body (cuerpo en movimiento) || ARTES mobile.

movilidad *f* mobility.

movilización *f* mobilization.

movilizar *vt* to mobilize.

movimiento *m* movement, motion; *el movimiento de las olas* the movement of the waves || FÍS motion; *movimiento perpetuo* perpetual motion || upheaval, uprising (revuelta) || movement; *movimiento revolucionario* revolutionary movement || shake (de cabeza, de un lado a otro), nod (de cabeza, de arriba abajo) || movement, activity (actividad) || traffic (de automóviles) || action (de un libro) || COM fluctuations *pl* (del mercado) | trend (de los precios) | change, movement (cambio) || FIG stir, change, evolution, movement (de ideas) | fit, outburst (de celos, de risa, etc.) || move (en los juegos) || GEOL tremor; *movimiento sísmico* earth tremor || MIL movement, move || ASTR movement || MÚS & MED movement || — *dar movimiento a, poner en movimiento* to put *o* to set in motion || *el movimiento del péndulo* the swing *o* the swinging of the pendulum || FIG *el movimiento se demuestra andando* one should always set a good example || *estar en movimiento* to be in motion, to be moving || COM *movimiento de existencias* rotation of stock || *movimiento de tierras* earthwork || MAR *movimiento de un puerto* shipping entries and clearances || MIL *movimiento envolvente* outflanking movement || *movimiento obrero* workers' movement || *tienda* or *comercio de mucho movimiento* busy shop.

moxte ⟶ **oxte.**

moyuelo *m* grits *pl* (salvado) || bran (afrecho).

moza *f* girl, young girl, lass (muchacha joven) || bachelor girl (soltera) || servant, maid (criada) || washerwoman's paddle (de las lavanderas) || last hand (última mano en los juegos) || — *buena moza* good-looking woman (mujer), good-looking girl (muchacha) || *es una real moza* she is a pretty girl *o* a good looker || *moza de fortuna* or *del partido* daughter of pleasure, prostitute.

mozalbete *m* young lad, young fellow.

Mozambique *n pr* GEOGR Mozambique.

mozambiqueño, ña *adj/s* Mozambican.

mozárabe; almozárabe *adj* Mozarabic.
◆ *m/f* Mozarab.
— OBSERV The term *Mozarab* applies to the Spanish Christians living in Moslem Spain, and their art and literature which flourished especially in the kingdom of León in the 10th and early 11th centuries.

mozarrón, ona *m/f* hearty lad (muchacho), hearty lass (muchacha).

mozo, za *adj* young (joven) || single, unmarried (soltero) || *en sus años mozos* when he was young, in his youth.
◆ *m/f* young boy, lad (muchacho), young girl, lass (muchacha) || bachelor (soltero), bachelor girl (soltera).
◆ *m* waiter (camarero) || servant (criado) || porter [US porter, redcap] (de estación) || conscript (soldado) || coat hanger, clothes hanger (percha) || — *mozo de caballos, de cuadra* stableboy, groom || *mozo de café* waiter || *mozo de carnicero* butcher's boy || *mozo de comedor* waiter || *mozo de cordel* or *de cuerda* porter || *mozo de espuelas* footman || *mozo de estación* porter || TAUR *mozo de estoques* sword boy, bullfighter's aid || *mozo de habitación* valet (en un hotel) || *mozo de labranza* farmhand || *ser un buen mozo* to be a fine figure of a man.

mozuelo, la *m/f* youngster.

muaré *m* moiré (tela).

mucamo, ma *m/f* AMER servant (hombre o mujer), maid (mujer).

muceta *f* mozetta, mozzetta (vestidura eclesiástica) || hood (en la universidad).

mucílago *m* BOT mucilage.

mucosidad *f* mucosity, mucus.

mucoso, sa *adj* mucous.
◆ *f* mucosa, mucous membrane.

múcura; mucura *f* AMER pitcher, earthenware jar (vasija).

mucus *m* mucus.

muchachada; muchachería *f* kids *pl*, boys and girls *pl*, group of kids (pandilla) || prank (acción propia de niño).

muchachear *vi* to act childishly.

muchachería *f* ⟶ **muchachada.**

muchacho, cha *m/f* youngster, youth (joven).
◆ *m* servant (criado) || lad, boy, youth (chico).
◆ *f* maid (criada) || young girl, lass (chica).

muchachuelo, la *m/f* kid.

muchedumbre *f* crowd, flock (de gente) || flock (de pájaros).

muchísimo, ma *adj* very much, a lot of.
◆ *adv* a great deal, a lot.

mucho, cha *adj* a lot of (gran cantidad); *mucha agua* a lot of water || many, a lot of (numerosos); *muchos niños* many children, a lot of children || many (*con «los», «sus», etc.*); *a causa de sus muchas tareas no puede salir* because of his many tasks he can't go out || much, a lot of; *¿tienes mucho trabajo?* have you much work?; *no tengo mucho trabajo* I have not much work || great, very great (grande); *es mucha tu responsabilidad en este asunto* your responsability in this matter is very great || — *aquí hay mucho estudiante* there are lots of students here || *¡es mucha mujer!* what a woman she is! || *éste es mucho coche para ustedes* this car is far too big for you || *hace mucho calor, frío* it is very hot *o* warm, cold || *muchas gracias* thank you very much || *muchas veces* very often, many times || FIG *mucho ruido y pocas nueces* much ado about nothing || *muchos pocos hacen un mucho* every little (bit) helps, many a little makes a mickle || *mucho tiempo* a long time.
◆ *pron* many (people), a lot (of people); *muchos piensan que...* many people think that..., a lot of people think that... || many, a lot; *muchos de mis amigos son extranjeros* many of my friends are foreigners || a lot; *me queda mucho por hacer* I still have a lot to do || much, a lot; *¿te queda mucho todavía?* do you still have much left? || — *los muchos que...* everyone who..., all those who... || *son muchos los que...* or *muchas las que...* there are many (people) who...
◆ *adv* much; *mucho más joven que...* much younger than... || a lot; *ha viajado mucho* he has travelled a lot || a lot, very much; *¿te has divertido? =m —sí, mucho* have you enjoyed yourself?, did you enjoy yourself? =m —yes, very much || a long time; *hace mucho que no le veo* I have not seen him for a long time || — *como mucho* at the most, at the outside; *ganarás como mucho diez mil pesetas* you will earn ten thousand pesetas at the most || *con mucho* by far, far and away, easily; *es con mucho el más simpático* he is by far the nicest | *correr mucho* to run fast || *ir mucho* to go often || *me alegro mucho* I am very glad || *mucho antes* a long time before, long before || *mucho después* a long time after, long after || *mucho más* much more, a lot more || *mucho mejor* much better, a lot better || *mucho menos* much less, a lot less || *mucho peor* much worse, a lot worse || *muy mucho* very much || *ni con mucho* not nearly, nothing like; *no es con mucho tan simpático como su hermano* he is not nearly as nice as his brother || *ni mucho menos* not by any means, by no means; *no es tonto, ni mucho menos* he is by no means stupid, he is not stupid by any means || *no es para mucho* it's not up to much || *pesar mucho* to be heavy, to weigh a lot || *por mucho que* no matter how much, however much; *por mucho que trabaje, no consigue nada* no matter how much he works, he never gets anywhere; *por mucho que insistas, no lo haré* however much you insist, I shall not do it; however fast, however hard, etc.; *por mucho que corra* however fast it goes; *por mucho que trabaje* however hard he works || *quedarse mucho* to stay long *o* a long time || *ser mucho para* to mean a lot to || *si no es mucho pedir* if it's not asking too much || *tener en mucho* to think a lot of, to think highly of, to hold in high esteem (apreciar mucho) || *trabajar mucho* to work hard.
◆ *interj* quite, quite right.
— OBSERV Aunque *much* corresponda a *mucho* conviene señalar que no se suele usar en frases afirmativas. Por otra parte es preciso subrayar que *much* sólo puede ir acompañado de una palabra singular y *many* de un término en plural.

muda *f* change of underwear (ropa) || moult, moulting [US molt, molting] (cambio de la piel en los animales) || moulting season [US molting season] (estación en que se realiza) || slough (de las serpientes) || breaking (de la voz) || moving house, move, removal (traslado de domicilio).

mudable *adj* changeable (cambiable) || inconstant, fickle (cambiadizo).

mudada *f* AMER change of underwear.

mudanza *f* change (cambio) || removal, move (de domicilio) | moving into a house (instalación de una casa) || figure, movement (de baile) || MÚS shift | — *camión de mudanzas* removal van || *estar de mudanza* to be moving || *hacer la mudanza* to move house, to move || *hacer la mudanza de los muebles* to have one's furniture removed.

mudar *vt/vi* to change (cambiar); *mudar el agua en vino* to change water into wine; *han mudado de oficina* they have changed office; *mudar de ropa* to change one's clothes ‖ to change (a un niño) ‖ to moult [US to molt] (un animal) ‖ to break (la voz); *el chico está mudando la voz* the boy's voice is breaking ‖ to move (cambiar de destino); *le han mudado de oficina* they have moved him to another office ‖ to move (instalarse); *mudar el piso* to move to a new flat; *mudar de casa* to move house ‖ FIG to change (variar); *mudar de idea* or *de parecer* to change one's mind; *mudar de color* to change colour ‖ — FIG *muda el lobo los dientes mas no las mientes* a leopard cannot change its spots ‖ *mudar de piel* to shed its skin, to moult [US to molt] ‖ *mudar de pluma* to moult [US to molt].

◆ *vpr* to change, to get changed (cambiarse de ropa) ‖ *mudarse de falda* to change one's skirt ‖ to move house, to move (cambiar de domicilio) ‖ *se te está mudando la voz* your voice is breaking.

mudéjar *adj/s* Mudejar.

— OBSERV The word applies to those Moslems who remained in Castile after the Reconquest and to their art, which dates from the 12th to the 16th century and is characterized by Islamic influence (minarets, multicoloured decorations, etc.).

mudez *f* dumbness, muteness ‖ silence (silencio).

mudo, da *adj* dumb; *es mudo de nacimiento* he was born dumb ‖ FIG mute, silent (callado); *se quedó mudo durante toda la reunión* he remained silent throughout the whole meeting | speechless, dumb (sin poder hablar) ‖ silent, mute (letra) ‖ GEOGR blank, skeleton (mapa) ‖ — *cine mudo, película muda* silent cinema *o* films, silent film ‖ FIG & FAM *mudo como un muerto* or *como una tumba* as close as a clam ‖ *mudo de admiración* speechless with admiration ‖ *quedarse mudo de asombro* to be dumbfounded *o* awestruck.

◆ *m/f* dumb *o* mute person ‖ deaf-mute (sordomudo) ‖ *los mudos* the dumb, the mute.

mueble *m* piece of furniture ‖ cabinet (armario) ‖ — *mueble bar* cocktail cabinet ‖ *mueble cama* foldaway bed unit.

◆ *pl* furniture *sing* ‖ — *con muebles* furnished ‖ *tienda de muebles* furniture shop.

◆ *adj* *bienes muebles* personal property *sing*, personalty *sing* movables.

mueblería *f* furniture shop.

mueblista *m* furniture maker (que fabrica) ‖ furniture dealer (que vende).

mueca *f* face (burlesca) ‖ grimace (de dolor, de disgusto) ‖ *hacer muecas a* to make faces at, to pull faces at.

muecín *m* muezzin (almuédano).

muela *f* millstone (de molino) ‖ grindstone, whetstone (de afilar) ‖ molar (diente molar) ‖ tooth (diente); *el niño está echando las muelas* the baby is cutting his teeth; *empastar una muela* to fill a tooth ‖ hillock (cerro) ‖ BOT vetch (planta) ‖ — *dolor de muelas* toothache ‖ *muela cordal* or *del juicio* wisdom tooth ‖ *muela picada* decayed tooth ‖ *muela postiza* false tooth ‖ FIG & FAM *no hay ni para una muela* there is not enough to feed a sparrow.

muellaje *m* MAR dockage, wharfage.

muelle *adj* soft (blando) ‖ luxurious, soft, easy; *llevar una vida muelle* to lead a luxurious life.

◆ *m* MAR wharf, dock (de un puerto) ‖ pier (malecón) ‖ embankment (a lo largo de un río) ‖ freight platform (de ferrocarril) ‖ spring (de un mecanismo); *colchón de muelles* spring mattress ‖ — TECN *muelle antagonista* or *de retorno* pullback spring ‖ *muelle en espiral* coil spring, spiral spring.

muera *f* salt (sal).

muérdago *m* BOT mistletoe.

muermo *m* glanders *pl* (del caballo) ‖ drag, bore, pain (pesadez) ‖ FIG blues (malestar, depresión).

muerte *f* death; *condenado a muerte* condemned to death; *fiel hasta la muerte* faithful unto death ‖ murder (homicidio) ‖ FIG death (desaparición) ‖ TAUR the kill ‖ — *a muerte* to the death; *luchar a muerte* to fight to the death ‖ *a vida o muerte* life-and-death, life-or-death; *una operación a vida o muerte* a life-and-death operation ‖ FIG *con la muerte en el alma* sick at heart ‖ *dar muerte a* to kill, to put to death ‖ FIG & FAM *de mala muerte* crummy, lousy, rotten; *un coche de mala muerte* a lousy car; *una película de mala muerte* a crummy film; *pueblo de mala muerte* dump, hole [US hick town] ‖ *de muerte* big, enormous; *un susto de muerte* a big fright ‖ *encontrar la muerte* to meet one's death ‖ *en el artículo de la muerte* in the article of death, at the point of death ‖ *estar a dos pasos de la muerte* to be at death's door ‖ *estar a la muerte* to be dying ‖ *estar a las puertas de la muerte* to be at death's door ‖ *estar en su lecho de muerte* to be on one's deathbed ‖ *guerra a muerte* war to the knife, war to the bitter end ‖ *hasta la muerte* to the death ‖ *morir de muerte natural* to die a natural death ‖ JUR *muerte civil* civil death, attainder ‖ FIG & FAM *muerte chiquita* nervous shudder ‖ *muerte repentina* sudden death ‖ DEP *muerte súbita* sudden death play-off [tie break] ‖ *odiar a muerte* to loathe ‖ *pasar de vida a muerte* to pass away ‖ *retar a muerte* to challenger to a fight to the death ‖ FIG *ser la muerte* to be deadly | *sufrir mil muertes* to die a thousand deaths.

muerto, ta *adj* dead ‖ FAM killed (matado); *muerto en la guerra* killed in the war, killed in action | dead (muy cansado) ‖ FIG dead, flat, dull (colores) | dead, lifeless (sin actividad) ‖ DEP dead ‖ JUR dead (letra) ‖ — *caer muerto* to drop down dead ‖ *cal muerta* slaked lime ‖ *dar por muerto a uno* to assume s.o. dead ‖ FIG *estar más que muerto* to be dead and buried | *estar muerto de cansancio* to be dead tired | *estar muerto de frío* to be freezing *o* frozen to death | *estar muerto de hambre* to be starving to death | *estar muerto de miedo* to be scared to death ‖ *horas muertas* dead hours ‖ *lengua muerta* dead language ‖ *más muerto que vivo* more dead than alive, half-dead ‖ *medio muerto* half-dead ‖ FIG & FAM *muerto el perro se acabó la rabia* dead dogs don't bite ‖ *nacido muerto* stillborn ‖ ARTES *naturaleza muerta* still life (bodegón) ‖ FIG & FAM *no tener dónde caerse muerto* not to have a penny to one's name ‖ MAR *obra muerta* upperworks *pl* ‖ *punto muerto* neutral (en un coche), dead centre (en mecánica), stalemate, deadlock, impasse (en negociaciones, etc.) ‖ *se busca vivo o muerto* wanted dead or alive ‖ FIG & FAM *ser letra muerta* to become a dead letter.

◆ *m/f* dead person, dead man (hombre), dead woman (mujer) ‖ corpse, body (cadáver).

◆ *m* dummy (en los naipes) ‖ — FIG *caer como un muerto* to fall in a heap | *callarse como un muerto* to keep quiet, not to say a word | *cargar con el muerto* to be left holding the baby *o* the bag [US to carry the can] ‖ *doblar* or *tocar a muerto* to toll, to toll the knell ‖ FIG & FAM *echarle a uno el muerto* to pass the buck to s.o. | *hacer el muerto* to float on one's back (natación) | *hacerse el muerto* to play possum *o* dead | *más pálido que un muerto* as pale as death, as white as a sheet ‖ *ser un muerto de hambre* to be a starveling.

◆ *pl* casualties; *en ese accidente hubo diez muertos* there were ten casualties in that accident ‖ dead; *los vivos y los muertos* the quick and the dead; *resucitar de entre los muertos* to rise from the dead.

— OBSERV *Muerto* is the past participle of *morir*.

muesca *f* notch, nick (corte) ‖ TECN mortise, mortice (entalladura) | mortising, morticing (operación) ‖ earmark, nick in the ear (en el ganado) ‖ TECN *hacer muesca en* to mortise, to mortice.

muestra *f* sample (de una tela o mercancía) ‖ show, display (exposición de mercancías) ‖ specimen (de un libro) ‖ sign, signboard (de una tienda) ‖ model (modelo) ‖ face, dial (esfera de reloj) ‖ sample (en estadística) ‖ MIL review (revista) ‖ turnup (naipes) ‖ FIG sample; *nos dio una muestra de su saber* he gave us a sample of his knowledge | proof (prueba); *esto es muestra de que no me quiere* this is proof that he does not love me; *ser buena muestra de algo* to be good proof of sth. | sign; *muestra de cansancio* sign of fatigue | show, token; *muestra de aprecio* token of esteem ‖ — *botón de muestra* sample ‖ *como botón de muestra* as a sample ‖ *dar muestras de* to show signs of ‖ *feria de muestras* trade fair ‖ *hacer muestras de* to show, to display ‖ TECN *muestra de perforación* core sample (en un pozo de petróleo) ‖ *muestra gratuita* free sample ‖ FIG *para muestra basta un botón* one example is enough ‖ *perro de muestra* pointer ‖ FIG *por la muestra se conoce el paño* you can judge a man by his work ‖ *vivienda* or *piso de muestra* model home *o* apartment.

muestrario *m* collection of samples.

Muface *abrev de Mutualidad General de Funcionarios Civiles del Estado* Spanish State health service for Civil servants.

muestreo *m* sampling (estadística).

mufla *f* TECN muffle (hornillo).

muftí *m* mufti (jurisconsulto musulmán).

mugido *m* moo, mooing, low, lowing (de la vaca) ‖ bellow, bellowing (del toro) ‖ FIG howl, moan (del viento).

mugir *vi* to low, to moo (las vacas) ‖ to bellow (el toro) ‖ FIG to bellow, to roar (de ira) | to moan, to howl (el viento).

mugre *f* filth, dirt, grime (suciedad).

mugriento, ta *adj* filthy, grimy, dirty.

mugrón *m* AGR layer (tallo de la vid) | sucker, shoot, sprig (brote de una planta).

muguete *m* BOT lily of the valley (planta) ‖ MED thrush (enfermedad).

mujer *f* woman; *diez mujeres* ten women ‖ wife (esposa); *le presento a mi mujer* may I introduce you to my wife ‖ — FAM *es una mujer de bandera* or *de tronío* she is a knockout *o* a bombshell *o* an eye-opener ‖ *mi futura mujer* my bride-to-be ‖ *¡mujer!* woman; *¡mujer, no llores tanto!* don't cry so, woman! ‖ *mujer de gobierno* housekeeper ‖ *mujer de la limpieza* charwoman, cleaning lady ‖ *mujer de su casa* housewife, homemaker ‖ *mujer de vida airada, de mal vivir, mundana* or *perdida* loose *o* scarlet woman ‖ *mujer fatal* femme fatale, vamp ‖ *mujer pública* prostitute, street-walker ‖ *ser mujer* to be a grown woman ‖ *ser muy mujer* to be very feminine ‖ *tomar mujer* to take a wife, to marry ‖ *tomar por mujer* to take to wife *o* for one's wife.

mujercilla *f* little *o* small woman ‖ worthless woman, woman of no account (mujer poco estimable) ‖ strumpet, tart (prostituta).

mujerero *adj m* AMER fond of the girls, woman-izing (mujeriego).

mujeriego, ga *adj* feminine, womanly (propio de mujeres) || — *montar a la mujeriega* or *a mujeriegas* to ride sidesaddle || *ser mujeriego* to be fond of the girls, to be a woman chaser, to be one for the girls.
◆ *m* wolf, womanizer, woman chaser.

mujeril *adj* feminine, womanly, woman's (propio de mujeres) || womanish, effeminate (afeminado).

mujerío *m* (crowd of) women.

mujerona *f* big *o* strapping woman.

mujeruca *f* old woman.

mujerzuela *f* small *o* little woman (mujer chiquita) || loose woman, hussy, prostitute (prostituta) || fishwife (maleducada).

mujic *m* moujik (campesino ruso).

mújol *m* ZOOL mullet (pez).

mula *f* ZOOL mule, she-mule (animal) || mule, slipper (calzado) || shoe worn by the Pope (calzado del Papa) || FIG mule; *testarudo como una mula* as stubborn as a mule | brute, animal, beast (bruto) | ass, idiot (idiota) || *AMER* shoulder pad (de los cargadores).

mulada *f* drove of mules (recua) || FIG & FAM stupid *o* foolish thing (tontería).

muladar *m* rubbish dump, tip, shoot (vertedero de basuras) || dungheap (estiércol) || FIG dump (sitio sucio o corrompido).

muladí *adj/s* renegade [Spaniard who accepted Mohammedanism during the Reconquest].

mular *adj* mule, of a mule *o* mules || *ganado mular* mules.

mulato, ta *adj* mulatto || FIG dark, dark-skinned, dark-complexioned (moreno) || *AMER* dark silver ore.
◆ *m/f* mulatto (hombre), mulattress (mujer).

mulé (dar) *loc* FAM to bump off (matar).

mulero, ra *adj* mule (mular) || mule-breeding (relativo a la producción).
◆ *m* muleteer (mozo).

muleta *f* crutch (para andar) || TAUR «muleta»; *torear de muleta* to fight (the bull) with the «muleta» || support, prop (sostén).

muletear *vt* TAUR to fight (the bull) with the «muleta».

muletero *m* muleteer || TAUR bullfighter who uses the «muleta» matador.

muletilla *f* TAUR «muleta» || button (botón) || cross-handle cane (bastón) || FIG pet word *o* phrase (estribillo) | padding, fill-in (palabra inútil).

muletón *m* melton (tela) || undertablecloth (mantel).

mulillas *f pl* TAUR mules that drag the dead bull from the ring.

mulo *m* mule || FIG & FAM ass, idiot (idiota) | mule (testarudo) | brute, animal, beast (bruto) || — FIG *estar hecho un mulo* to be as strong as an ox (muy fuerte) | *hacer el mulo* to be a brute | *trabajar como un mulo* to work like a dog *o* a horse.

multa *f* fine || ticket (por estar mal aparcado, etc.) || — *imponer* or *poner* or *echar una multa a uno* to fine s.o., to impose a fine on s.o. (en general), to give s.o. a ticket (por estar mal aparcado) || *me pusieron una multa de mil pesetas* I was fined a thousand pesetas.

multar *vt* to fine; *multar a uno en mil pesetas* to fine s.o. one thousand pesetas.

multicanal *adj* multichannel (en televisión).

multicelular *adj* multicellular.

multicolor *adj* multicoloured [*US* multicolored].

multicopia *f* duplicating.

multicopiar *vt* to duplicate.

multicopista *f* duplicator, mimeograph, duplicating machine || *tirar* or *hacer con multicopista* to duplicate.

multiforme *adj* multiform.

multilateral *adj* multilateral.

multimedia *adj* INFORM multimedia.
◆ *m pl* mass media.

multimillonario, ria *adj/s* multimillionaire.

multinacional *adj* multinational.

multíparo, ra *adj* multiparous (mujer o animal).
◆ *f* multipara.

multiplano m AVIAC multiplane.

múltiple *adj* multiple; *sistema múltiple* multiple system || many, manifold (numerosos).
◆ *m* manifold.

múltiplex *adj* multiplex (telégrafo).

multiplexor *m* multiplexer.

multiplicable *adj* multipliable.

multiplicación *f* multiplication.

multiplicado, da *adj* multiplied || TECN *directa multiplicada* overgeared fourth, overdrive.

multiplicador, ra *adj* multiplying.
◆ *m* multiplier.

multiplicando *m* MAT multiplicand.

multiplicar *vt* to multiply || TECN to gear up || FIG to multiply, to increase || *tabla de multiplicar* multiplication table.
◆ *vpr* to multiply || FIG to go out of one's way, to exert o.s. to the utmost, to be everywhere (hacer el máximo); *se multiplicaba para hacernos la estancia más agradable* she went out of her way to make our stay more enjoyable || *creced y multiplicaos* go forth and multiply.

multiplicidad *f* multiplicity.

múltiplo, pla *adj* MAT multiple.
◆ *m* MAT multiple.

multiprocesador *m* INFORM multiprocessor.

multiprogramación *f* INFORM multiprogramming.

multipuesto *adj* INFORM multistation.
◆ *m* INFORM multi-terminal system.

multisecular *adj* centuries-old.

multitarea *adj* INFORM multi-tasking.
◆ *f* INFORM multitasking.

multitud *f* multitude; *una multitud de detalles* a multitude of details || multitude, crowd (muchedumbre) || *tener multitud de ocupaciones* to have lots of things to do.

multitudinario, ria *adj* multitudinous.

multiuso *adj* all-purpose, multipurpose.

multiusuario *m* INFORM multi-user system.
◆ *adj* INFORM multiuser.

mullido, da *adj* fluffy, soft, downy (blando y cómodo); *cama mullida* soft bed.
◆ *m* flock, stuffing (para rellenar).

mullir* *vt* to beat, to soften (la lana) || to fluff up (un colchón) || to loosen, to break up, to hoe (la tierra).

muncho, cha *adj/adv* (ant) FAM ⟶ **mucho.**

mundanal *adj* worldly, of the world, mundane (p us) || *huir del mundanal ruido* to flee the hubbub of worldly life.

mundanalidad *f* worldliness.

mundanear *vi* to be wordly-minded.

mundanería *f* worldliness, wordly-mindedness (apego a lo terrestre) || social-mindedness (afición a la vida social) || worldly behaviour (acción mundana).

mundano, na *adj* worldly, of the world, earthly, mundane (p us); *placeres mundanos* worldly pleasures || social-minded; *persona mundana* social-minded person || society; *reunión mundana* society gathering || — *la vida mundana* social life || *llevar una vida muy mundana* to lead a very active social life || *mujer mundana* loose *o* light *o* scarlet woman (prostituta).
◆ *m/f* worldly person, socialite.

mundial *adj* world; *la primera guerra mundial* the First World War; *a escala mundial* on a world scale || worldwide, universal; *una organización mundial* a worldwide organization.
◆ *m* world championship.

mundillo *m* world, circles *pl*; *el mundillo financiero* the financial world; *el mundillo literario* the literary world || clotheshorse (secadero) || pillow for making lace (para hacer encaje) || bedwarmer (calentador para la cama) || BOT snowball.

mundo *m* world; *dar la vuelta al mundo* to go around the world || FIG world, realm; *el mundo de los negocios* the business world; *el mundo literario* the literary world | world of difference; *hay un mundo entre las dos versiones* there is a world of difference between the two versions | experience || saratoga trunk (baúl) || REL world, secular life || BOT snowball || — FIG *al fin del mundo* at the back of beyond (sitio), at the end of time (tiempo) | *anda* or *está el mundo al revés* it's a topsy-turvy world | *así va el mundo* so it goes, that's the way it goes | *aunque se hunda el mundo* come what may | *como todo el mundo* like everyone else, like other people || *conocido por* or *en el mundo entero* known the world over, world-famous || FIG *correr mundo* to roam the world over, to travel far and wide, to see the world | *dar un mundo por* to give the world for | *de mundo* of the world; *hombre de mundo* man of the world; *mujer de mundo* woman of the world | *desde que el mundo es mundo* since the world began, from *o* since the beginning of time | *echar al mundo* to bring into the world, to give birth to, to bring forth | *echarse al mundo* to become a prostitute | *el gran mundo* high society, high life | *el mundo es de los audaces* fortune helps those who help themselves | *el mundo es un pañuelo, ¡qué pequeño es el mundo!* it's a small world | *el mundo no se hundirá por eso* it's not the end of the world || *el Nuevo, el Antiguo* or *Viejo Mundo* the New, the Old World || *en el mundo entero* all over the world, the world over, throughout the whole world || FIG *en el otro mundo* in the next World, in the hereafter | *en este mundo de Dios, en este bajo mundo* here below | *en todo el mundo* everywhere | *entrar en el mundo* to come out, to make one's début in society | *estar todavía en el mundo de los vivos* to be still living, to be in land of the living | *hacerse un mundo de algo* to make a big thing of sth. | *hasta el fin del mundo* to the edges of the earth | *irse al otro mundo* to pass away | *mandar* or *enviar al otro mundo* to bump s.o. off, to do s.o. in | *medio mundo* loads of people, no end of people | *no es cosa* or *nada del otro mundo* it's nothing to write home about, it's nothing to make a fuss about (no es ninguna maravilla), there's nothing to it (no es difícil) | *no ser de este mundo* to live in a world of one's own | *ponerse el mundo por montera* not to care what people think *o* what people say | *por esos mundos de Dios* here and there (en varios sitios), God Knows where (no se sabe dónde) | *por nada del mundo, por todo el oro del mundo* not for all the world, not for (anything in) the world, not for all the tea in China, not for all the money in the world | *prometer este mundo y el otro* to promise the earth, to promise the moon and stars | *recorrer* or *rodar mundo* to roam the world over, to see the world | *salir de* or *dejar este mundo* to depart this world, to pass away (morir) | *se le hundió el mundo* his world tumbled down around him, his world caved in | *tener mundo* to have savoir vivre, to be a man of the world, to know how to act in society, to know one's way around | *todo el mundo* everyone, everybody | *traer al mundo* to bring into the world | *valer un mundo* to be worth one's weight in gold, to be worth one's salt (persona), to be worth its weight in gold (cosa) | *venir al mundo* to come into the world | *ver mundo* to see the world, to see things, to see life | *vivir en el otro mundo* to live at the back of beyond (vivir muy lejos) | *vivir en otro mundo* to live in another world.

mundología *f* worldliness, worldly wisdom (experiencia) || savoir vivre (reglas mundanas).

mundonuevo *m* peep show (cosmorama).

mundovisión *m* transoceanic television, broadcasting, broadcasting by satellite (televisión).

munición *f* MIL ammunition, munition || shot (perdigones); *munición menuda* small shot || load, charge (carga) || — *disparar con munición de fogueo* to fire blanks || *municiones de boca* provisions, rations || *pan de munición* ration bread.

municionero, ra *m/f* supply officer.

municipal *adj* municipal.
◆ *m* policeman.

municipalidad *f* municipality.

municipalización *f* municipalization.

municipalizar *vt* to municipalize.

munícipe *m* inhabitant of a district.

municipio *m* municipality (término municipal) || district (conjunto de vecinos) || town council (concejo) || town hall (alcaldía).

Munich *n pr* GEOGR Munich.

munificencia *f* munificence.

munífico, ca *adj* munificent.

muniqués, esa *adj* [of *o* from] Munich.
◆ *m/f* native *o* inhabitant of Munich.

muñeca *f* writs (del brazo) || doll (juguete); *muñeca de trapo* rag doll || dummy, mannequin (maniquí) || polishing bag, pouncing bag, pad (para barnizar o estarcir) || FIG & FAM doll (muchacha guapa) || *AMER* dummy (maqueta de un libro).

muñeco *m* boy doll (juguete) || puppet (marioneta) || funny figure (figura tosca, dibujo, etc.) || FIG & FAM puppet, pawn (persona dominada por otra) | popinjay (jovenzuelo presumido) || *muñeco de nieve* snowman.

muñeira *f* popular Galician dance.

muñequera *f* wristlet, wristband (de los gimnastas) || (p us) watch strap, watchband (de reloj de pulsera).

muñequilla *f* polishing bag, pad (para barnizar) || *AMER* small ear of maize [*US* of corn] || *dar con la muñequilla* to French-polish (un mueble).

muñidor *m* beadle (de una cofradía).

muñón *m* stump (en una amputación) || trunnion, gudgeon (del cañón).

muñonera *f* MIL trunnion hole, gudgeon socket.

murajes *m* BOT pimpernel.

mural *adj* mural; *pintura mural* mural painting || wall; *mapa mural* wall map.
◆ *m* mural, fresco (fresco).

muralla *f* wall, rampart (muro muy grueso); *las murallas de Ávila* the ramparts of Ávila || wall; *la Gran Muralla de China* the Great Wall of China.

murar *vt* to wall, to surround with a wall.

Murcia *npr f* GEOGR Murcia.

murciélago *m* ZOOL bat.

murena *f* ZOOL moray, muraena (pez).

múrex *m* ZOOL murex.

murga *f* band of street, musicians (compañía de músicos) || foul-smelling liquid which runs from piled-up olives (alpechín) || — FIG & FAM *dar la murga, ser una murga* to be a drag *o* a bind *o* a bore | *¡qué murga!* what a drag *o* a bind *o* a bore!
◆ *m* FAM drag, bind, bore (lata, pesadez).

murguista *m* street musician.

múrice *m* ZOOL murex || POÉT murex, purple.

murmullo *m* murmur, murmuring (ruido sordo) || murmur, whispering (de las voces) || babbling, rippling, murmuring (de un arroyo) || sigh, sighing, murmur, whisper (del viento) || buzzing (zumbido).

murmuración *f* gossip, backbiting.

murmurador, ra *adj* murmuring (ruido sordo) || gossiping (maldiciente).
◆ *m/f* gossip.

murmurar *vt/vi* to murmur; *el viento murmura* the wind murmurs || to whisper (hablar en voz baja) || FIG to mutter; *¿qué está usted murmurando?* what are you muttering about? | to mutter, to grumble (con hostilidad) || to gossip (criticar); *murmurar de alguien* to gossip about s.o.

muro *m* wall; *muro de contención* retaining wall || rampart (muralla) || *muro del sonido* sound barrier.

murria *f* FAM sadness, blues *pl* (tristeza) || FAM *tener murria* to have the blues, to be down in the dumps, to feel low.

murrio, rria *adj* FAM sad, blue.

mus *m* card game.

musa *f* muse.

musaraña *f* shrew, shrewmouse (ratón del campo) || FIG small creature (animalejo) || FIG & FAM *mirar a las musarañas, pensar en las musarañas* to be in the clouds, to be miles away, to be day-dreaming.

muscular *adj* muscular.

musculatura *f* musculature (conjunto de los músculos) || muscularity (grado de fortaleza) || *tener musculatura* to have muscles, to be muscular.

músculo *m* muscle || — *hombre de músculos* muscleman || *tener músculos* to have muscles.

musculoso, sa *adj* muscular (que tiene músculos) || brawny, beefy (robusto).

muselina *f* muslin (tela).

museo *m* museum; *museo de historia natural* natural history museum || — *museo de (figuras de) cera* waxworks, wax museum || *museo de pintura* art gallery.

muserola *f* noseband (correa).

musgaño *m* shrew.

musgo *m* BOT moss || *cubierto de musgo* mossy, moss-grown, moss-covered.

música *f* music; *música de cámara, instrumental, sacra, vocal* chamber, instrumental, sacred, vocal music; *poner música a un poema* to set a poem to music || band (banda) || — *caja de música* musical box [*US* music box] || *escuela de música sacra* choir school || FIG & FAM *irse con la música a otra parte* to clear out, to sling one's hook, to buzz off | *mandar con la música a otra parte* to send s.o. packing *o* to blazes | *música celestial* drivel, hot air || *música de fondo* background music || *música ligera* light music || *música y letra* words and music, music and lyrics || FIG & FAM *música ratonera* caterwauling | *venir con músicas* to talk bunkum *o* baloney.

musical *adj* musical; *comedia musical* musical comedy.

musicalidad *f* musicality, musicalness.

músico, ca *adj* musical.
◆ *m/f* musician.

musicógrafo, fa *m/f* musicographer.

musicología *f* musicology.

musicólogo, ga *m/f* musicologist.

musicómano, na *m/f* melomane.

musiquilla *f* FAM cheap *o* paltry music.

musitar *vi* to whisper (susurrar) || to mumble, to mutter (hablar entre dientes).

muslo *m* ANAT thigh || drumstick, leg (de pollo).

musmón *m* ZOOL mouflon.

mustang; mustango *m* mustang (caballo).

mustela *f* ZOOL dogfish (pez) | weasel (comadreja).

musteriense *adj* mousterian.
◆ *m* mousterian period (prehistoria).

mustiarse *vpr* to wither, to wilt.

mustio, tia *adj* withered, wilted (planta) || gloomy, sad (persona).

musulmán, ana *adj/s* Moslem, Mussulman, Muslim.

mutabilidad *f* mutability, changeableness.

mutable *adj* mutable.

mutación *f* change, mutation (cambio) || BIOL mutation || TEATR change of scene, scene change || change of weather (del tiempo).

mutante *adj/s* BIOL mutant.

mutilación *f* mutilation || disablement.

mutilado, da *adj* crippled, disabled (persona) || mutilated.
◆ *m/f* cripple, disabled person.

mutilador, ra *adj* mutilating || crippling, maiming.
◆ *m/f* mutilator.

mutilar *vt* to mutilate, to mangle (destrozar) || to cripple, to maim (dejar inválido) || to deface (una estatua) || FIG to mutilate (un texto).

mutis *m* TEATR exit || *hacer mutis* to keep quiet, to say nothing (callarse), to go away (irse), to exit (en teatro).

mutismo *m* silence, mutism (p us).

mutual *adj* mutual (mutuo).
◆ *f* mutual benefit society.

mutualidad *f* mutuality || mutual benefit society (asociación).

mutualismo *m* mutualism.

mutualista *adj* mutualistic || mutual-benefit-society (de la asociación).
◆ *m/f* mutualist || member of a mutual benefit society.

mutuamente *adv* mutually.

mútulo *m* ARQ mutule.

mutuo, tua *adj* mutual, joint; *por mutuo consentimiento* by mutual consent || reciprocal, mutual; *odio mutuo* mutual hatred || *seguro mutuo* mutual insurance (seguro), mutual insurance agency (agencia de seguros).
◆ *f* mutual benefit society (mutualidad) || *mutua de seguros* mutual insurance company.

muy *adv* very, quite; *muy inteligente* very intelligent; *muy lejos* very far; *eso es muy inglés* that's very English; *se fue muy satisfecho* he left quite happy || very, extremely (más ponderativo); *estoy muy satisfecho* I'm extremely satisfied || very, quite (con adverbio de manera); *iba muy despacito* he went very slowly || too (demasiado) || much; *muy estimado* much esteemed || widely, much; *muy leído* widely read || — FAM *el muy mentiroso de Juan* that great liar of a John || *fue muy de lamentar* it was much to be regretted || *la realidad es muy otra* it's very different in reality, the truth is quite different || *muy conocido* very well-known || *muy de noche* very late at night || *muy de nuestro tiempo* very much a part of our times || *muy hombre* very much of a man, a real man || FAM *muy mucho* very much || *Muy señor mío* Dear Sir [beginning of a letter] || *por muy... que* however..., no matter how; *por muy idiota que sea* however stupid he may be; *por muy de prisa que vayas* it doesn't matter how fast you go || *ser muy de* to be just like, to be very (much) like; *eso es muy de él* that is just like him || *tener muy en cuenta* to bear very much in mind.

my *f* mu (letra griega).

N

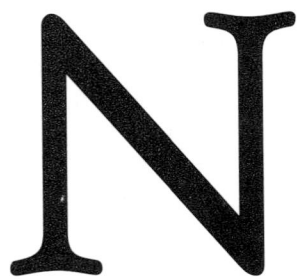

n *f* n (letra del alfabeto) ‖ MAT n (potencia); *diez a la potencia n* ten to the power of n ‖ X (fulano); *la condesa N* Countess X.

— OBSERV The Spanish *n* is pronounced like the English *n*.

nabab *m* nabob.

nabo *m* BOT turnip (planta) | root vegetable (raíz cualquiera) ‖ dock (de la cola de un animal) ‖ ARQ central pillar (eje) | newel (de escalera de caracol) ‖ MAR mast (palo) ‖ FIG *cada cosa en su tiempo y los nabos en adviento* there is a time and place for everything, all in good time.

naborí *m* AMER Indian freeman who worked as a servant.

naboría *f* AMER distribution of Indians to serve under the conquistadores.

Nabucodonosor *npr m* Nabuchadnezzar.

nácar *m* nacre, mother-of-pearl.

nacarado, da *adj* nacreous, pearly.

nacarar *vt* to give a pearly lustre to.

nacarino, na *adj* mother-of-pearl, nacreous (de nácar o que lo parece).

nacela *f* ARQ scotia (moldura cóncava).

nacencia *f* MED growth.

nacer* *vi* to be born (hombre o animal); *le nació un hijo* a son was born to her; *cuando nazca mi primer hijo* when my first baby is born ‖ to hatch (de un huevo) ‖ to begin to grow, to sprout (vegetal) ‖ to rise (el sol, la luna) ‖ to start, to begin (carreteras) ‖ to break, to dawn (el día) ‖ to rise, to have its source (río) ‖ to spring up (agua) ‖ FIG to be born *o* conceived (ideas) | to form (una sospecha) | to originate (originarse) | to stem, to spring (surgir) ‖ — *al nacer* at birth ‖ *entre ellos ha nacido el odio* hatred has grown between them ‖ *nacer el amor* to awaken to love ‖ *nacer con buena estrella* to be born under a lucky star ‖ FIG & FAM *nacer de pie* to be born under a lucky star ‖ *nacer para* to be born to (con verbo); *nació para sufrir* she was born to suffer; to be a born (con sustantivo); *nació para soldado* he is a born soldier ‖ *nadie nace enseñado* we all have to learn ‖ FIG & FAM *no nací ayer* I wasn't born yesterday | *volver a nacer* to have a narrow escape *o* a close shave (salvarse).

◆ *vpr* to split (abrirse la tela).

— OBSERV The verb *nacer* has two past participles, one regular, *nacido*, and the other irregular, *nato*.

nacido, da *adj* born; *nacido de padres humildes* born of humble parents ‖ né, née; *la señora de Thomas, nacida Johnson* Mrs. Thomas, née Johnson ‖ — *bien nacido* of noble birth (linaje), well-bred (bien educado) ‖ *mal nacido* mean (vil), ill-bred (mal educado) ‖ *recién nacido* newborn.

◆ *m* *los nacidos* human beings (seres humanos) ‖ *los nacidos en España* those born in Spain ‖ *ningún nacido* nobody ‖ *todos los nacidos* everybody ‖ *un recién nacido* a newborn baby.

naciente *adj* nascent ‖ rising; *el Sol naciente* the rising sun ‖ dawning; *el día naciente* the dawning day ‖ growing; *el naciente interés por la política* the growing interest in politics ‖ FIG new (reciente) | budding, nascent (amor, amistad) ‖ HERÁLD issuant.

◆ *m* east (oriente).

nacimiento *m* birth; *partida de nacimiento* birth certificate; *de nacimiento noble* of noble birth ‖ hatching (de huevos) ‖ source (de un río) ‖ spring (agua) ‖ REL nativity scene, crib ‖ FIG birth; *nacimiento de una nación* birth of a nation | source, origin, root (origen) | beginning, start (principio) ‖ — FIG *dar nacimiento a* to give rise to ‖ *de nacimiento* born, from birth; *es ciego de nacimiento* he was born blind, he has been blind from birth; by birth; *español de nacimiento* Spanish by birth ‖ *lugar de nacimiento* place of birth, birthplace ‖ *regulación de nacimientos* birth control.

nación *f* nation; *las Naciones Unidas* the United Nations ‖ country, state (país, estado) ‖ people (pueblo) ‖ — FAM *ser español de nación* to be Spanish by birth | *un inglés de nación* a native Englishman, an Englishman by birth.

nacional *adj* national; *la prensa nacional* the national press; *himno nacional* national anthem; *renta nacional* national income; *producto nacional bruto* gross national product ‖ domestic; *vuelo, mercado nacional* domestic flight, market ‖ *carretera nacional* A road, arterial road [*US* arterial highway].

◆ *m* national.

◆ *pl* national militia *sing* [in the Spanish Civil War].

nacionalidad *f* nationality ‖ *doble nacionalidad* dual nationality *o* citizenship.

nacionalismo *m* nationalism.

nacionalista *adj* nationalist, nationalistic.

◆ *m/f* nationalist.

nacionalización *f* nationalization ‖ naturalization (de una persona).

nacionalizar *vt* to nationalize (industria, ferrocarriles, etc.) ‖ to naturalize (naturalizar).

◆ *vpr* to become naturalized (naturalizarse).

nacionalsindicalismo *m* National Syndicalism.

nacionalsindicalista *adj/s* National Syndicalist.

nacionalsocialismo *m* National Socialism.

nacionalsocialista *adj/s* National Socialist.

nada *f* nothingness (el no ser) ‖ nothing; *hombre salido de la nada* man risen from nothing.

◆ *m* the slightest thing, anything at all (la menor cosa); *un nada le asusta* the slightest thing frightens him.

◆ *pron* nothing, not... anything; *no ha hecho nada nuevo* he has done nothing new, he has not done anything new ‖ anything (algo); *¿has visto nada igual?* have you ever seen anything like it?

◆ *adv* not at all; *no es nada guapa* she is not at all pretty; *no nos ayudó nada* he did not help us at all.

◆ *interj* not at all, you're welcome (de nada, no es nada) ‖ no! (¡no!); *¡nada, nada!* no, no! ‖ nothing much (poca cosa); *¿qué hay de nuevo? —nada; fuimos a...* what's new? —nothing much, we went to... ‖ well (pues); *nada, que fuimos al cine y...* well, we went to the cinema and... ‖ AMER *a cada nada* continually, every five minutes ‖ *¡ahí es nada!* just fancy! ‖ *antes de nada* first of all ‖ *casi nada* hardly; *no habla casi nada* he hardly speaks; hardly... any; *no hace falta casi nada de dinero* you hardly need any money; next to nothing, hardly... anything; *no me costó casi nada* it cost me next to nothing, it hardly cost me anything ‖ *como si nada* as though it were nothing at all ‖ *con intentarlo no se pierde nada* there's no harm in trying ‖ *con nada se caerá este cuadro, está muy poco seguro* it will not take much to make this picture fall, it is very unsafe ‖ *de nada* don't mention it, you're welcome ‖ *dentro de nada* in a moment ‖ *en nada estuvo que cayera* he very nearly fell ‖ *hace nada* just a moment ago ‖ *lo haré en nada de tiempo* I'll do it in no time at all ‖ *nada* right; *nada, hay que proseguir* right, let's go on ‖ *nada de* no; *nada de excusas* no excuses; *nada de jugar aquí* no playing here; nothing (con adjetivo); *nada de extraordinario* nothing unusual; no... at all (con sustantivo); *no tiene nada de paciencia* he has no patience at all ‖ *nada de eso* nothing of the sort ‖ *nada de nada* nothing at all; *no sabe nada de nada* he knows nothing at all; not at all (de ningún modo) ‖ *nada de salir ahora* (you can) forget about going out now ‖ *nada más* that's all (eso es todo), no sooner (en cuanto); *nada más verla corrió a saludarla* no sooner did he see her than he ran to meet her; nothing more; *(no hay) nada más difícil que...* (there is) nothing more difficult than... ‖ *nada más y nada menos* no more, no less ‖ *nada más y nada menos que* no more, no less; *me pidió nada más y nada menos que mil pesetas* he asked me for a thousand pesetas, no more, no less ‖ *nada menos* no less; *es el alcalde, nada menos* he is the mayor, no less ‖ *nada menos que* no less than; *ha heredado nada menos que diez millones de pesetas* he has inherited no less than ten million pesetas ‖ FAM *ni nada* or anything; *no quiere estudiar ni nada* he won't study or anything ‖ *no es nada* it's nothing ‖ *no hace nada que salió* he left just a moment ago ‖ *(no hay) nada como un vaso de buen vino* (there's) nothing like a glass of good wine ‖ *no hay nada de eso, de eso nada* nothing of the sort ‖ *no los nombró para nada* he never mentioned them at all ‖ *no me dice nada* I don't think much of it ‖ *no reparar en nada* to stop at nothing ‖ *no ser nada* to be a nobody (personas), to be nothing (accidentes, heridas, etc.) ‖ *no servir para nada* to be of no use at all, to be completely useless ‖ *no tener nada que ver con* to have nothing to do with ‖ *no tiene nada de particular* there is nothing special about it (es corriente), there is not much in it (no es complicado) ‖ *no tocarle nada a uno* to be no relation of s.o., not to be related at all to s.o.; *esta chica no me toca nada* this girl is no relation of mine ‖ *peor es nada* it's better than nothing ‖ *por menos de* *nada* at the slightest thing, for no reason at all; *por menos de nada se enfada* he gets angry at the slightest thing || *por nada* for no reason (por la menor razón), for next to nothing; *lo compré por nada* I got it for next to nothing || *por nada del mundo* not for anything (in the world), not for all the tea in China; *por nada del mundo haría eso* I wouldn't do that for anything *o* for all the tea in China || *pues nada* right (then), O. K (then) || *quedarse en nada* to come to nothing || *tener en nada* to think very little of, to take no notice of (no hacer caso a).

nadador, ra *m/f* swimmer.
◆ *adj* swimming.

nadar *vi* to swim; *nadar de espalda* to swim backstroke *o* on one's back || FIG to be rolling, to wallow; *nadar en dinero* to be rolling in money | to swim (en un vestido demasiado amplio) || — FIG & FAM *nadar en sudor* to be bathed *o* soaked in sweat | *nadar entre dos aguas* to run with the hare and hunt with the hounds | *nadar y guardar la ropa* to have the best of both worlds.
◆ *vt* to swim, to do; *nadar el crawl* to do the crawl.

nadería *f* mere trifle, mere nothing.

nadie *pron indef* nobody, no-one, no one, not anybody; *no había nadie* there was nobody; *no lo sabe nadie* no one knows || — *a nadie se le ocurre hacer tal cosa* nobody would think of doing such a thing || *nadie es profeta en su tierra* a prophet is without honour in his own country || *nadie más* nobody else || *no he hablado con nadie* I haven't spoken to anybody.
◆ *m* FIG nobody, insignificant person || — *no ser nadie* to be a nobody (no ser importante), to be not just anybody (ser alguien) || *no somos nadie* how insignificant we all are || *un don nadie* a nobody || *usted no es nadie para decirme eso* you have no right to say that to me, who are you to say that?.
— OBSERV When *nadie* procedes the verb, the negative particle *no* is omitted.

nadir *m* ASTR nadir.

nado (a) *adv* *cruzaremos el río a nado* we shall swim across the river || *se salvó a nado* he swam to safety.

nafta *f* naphtha || *AMER* petrol [*US* gasoline].

naftalina *f* naphthalene.

nafteno *m* QUÍM naphthene.

naftol *m* QUÍM naphthol.

nailon *m* nylon.

naipe *m* card, playing card; *barajar los naipes* to shuffle the cards; *una baraja de naipes* a pack of cards || — FIG *castillo de naipes* house of cards || *tener buen* or *mal naipe* to be lucky *o* unlucky (en el juego).

Nairobi *n pr* GEOGR Nairobi.

naja *f* ZOOL naja (serpiente) || POP *salir de naja* or *de najas* to push off, to get out of it (irse).

najarse *vpr* POP to push off, to get out of it, to clear off (irse).

nalga *f* buttock.
◆ *pl* bottom *sing*, buttocks (trasero).

nana *f* FAM gran, granny, grandma, nan, nanna, nanny (abuela) | lullaby (canción de cuna) || *AMER* nanny (niñera) | wet nurse (nodriza) || FAM *en el año de la nana* in the year dot.

¡nanay! *interj* POP nothing doing! (¡ni hablar!).

nanita; nanaya *f* *AMER* grandmother (abuela) | lullaby (canción de cuna).

nano, na *m/f* imp (insulto cariñoso).

nanosegundo *m* nanosecond.

nanquín *m* nankeen (tela).

nao *f* ship, vessel (barco).

naonato, ta *adj* born at sea.

napa *m* glacé lamb (piel).

napalm *m* napalm; *bomba de napalm* napalm bomb.

napias *f pl* POP conk *sing*, snout *sing* (narices).

napoleón *m* Napoleon [former French gold coin] || *AMER* pliers (alicates).

Napoleón *npr m* Napoleon.

napoleónico, ca *adj* Napoleonic.

Nápoles *n pr* GEOGR Naples.

napolitano, na *adj/s* Neapolitan.

naranja *f* orange (fruto); *zumo de naranja* orange juice || — FIG *media naranja* dome, cupola (cúpula), better *o* other half (esposa o marido) || *naranja navel* navel orange || POP *¡naranjas!, ¡naranjas de la China!* nothing doing! (¡ni hablar!) || *naranja sanguina* blood orange || *naranja tangerina* tangerine.
◆ *adv inv/sm* orange; *un vestido naranja* an orange dress; *naranja claro* light orange.

naranjada *f* orangeade.

naranjado, da *adj* orange, orange-coloured (naranja) || orangish (tirando a naranja).

naranjal *m* orange grove.

naranjero, ra *adj* orange, of oranges || having a diameter of eight to ten centimetres (cañón, tubo).
◆ *m/f* orange seller (vendedor) || orange grower (cultivador).
◆ *m* blunderbuss (trabuco).

naranjo *m* orange tree.

narcisismo *m* narcissism.

narcisista *m/f* narcissist.
◆ *adj* narcissistic.

narciso *m* BOT narcissus (flor) || FIG narcissus, narcissist (hombre enamorado de sí mismo).

Narciso *npr m* Narcissus.

narcoanálisis *m* MED narcoanalysis.

narcosis *f* MED narcosis.

narcótico, ca *adj/sm* MED narcotic; *el opio es un narcótico* opium is a narcotic.

narcotina *f* QUÍM narcotine.

narcotismo *m* MED narcotism, narcosis.

narcotizante *adj/sm* MED narcotic.

narcotizar *vt* to narcotize.

narcotraficante *m/f* drug trafficker, drug dealer.

narcotráfico *m* drug trafficking, drug dealing.

nardo *m* BOT nard, spikenard.

narguile *m* narghile, hookah (pipa turca).

narigón, ona *adj* long-nosed, big-nosed.
◆ *m/f* long-nosed person.
◆ *m* long *o* big nose.

narigudo, da *adj* long-nosed, big-nosed.

nariguera *f* nose ring.

nariz *f* nose; *nariz aguileña* or *aquilina* aquiline nose || nostril (orificio nasal) || FIG sense of smell, nose (olfato) | bouquet (del vino) || TECN nose (de una herramienta) | nozzle (de un tubo) | catch (del picaporte) || — FIG & FAM *darle a uno en la nariz* to have a feeling; *me da en la nariz que no vendrá* to have a feeling he will not come || FIG *hablar con* or *por la nariz* to speak through one's nose || *nariz chata* snub nose || *nariz perfilada* perfect *o* regular *o* well-shaped nose || *nariz respingada* or *respingona* or *remangada* turned-up nose.
◆ *pl* nose *sing* || — FIG & FAM *caerse de narices* to nose-dive (un avión), to fall flat on one's face (una persona) | *darle a uno con la puerta en las narices, cerrar la puerta en las narices de alguien* to shut *o* to slam the door in s.o.'s face || *darle a uno en las narices* to show s.o. what for; *el actor bordó su papel para darles en las narices a sus detractores* the actor gave a brilliant perfomance to show his critics what for || FIG & FAM *darse de narices con* to bump into | *darse de narices en* to come up against (un obstáculo) | *dejarle a uno con un palmo* or *con dos palmos de narices* to let s.o. down || FIG *en mis mismas narices* right under my very nose || FIG & FAM *estar hasta las narices de* to be fed up to teeth with *o* of, to have had enough of | *hacer algo por narices* to do something because one feels like it | *hinchársele las narices a uno* to flare up || *limpiarse las narices* to wipe one's nose || FIG & FAM *meter la nariz* or *las narices en todo* to poke *o* to stick one's nose in everywhere, to be a busybody || FAM *¡narices!* rubbish!, rot! || FIG & FAM *¡ni narices!* or anything; *¡ni postre ni narices!* no sweet or anything! | *no ver más allá de sus narices* not to be able to see further than the end of one's nose | *quedarse con un palmo de narices* to be out of luck | *¡qué narices!* my foot!, my eye! | *refregar* or *refrotar algo a alguien por las narices* to rub sth. in | *romperse las narices, darse de narices* to fall flat on one's face || *sangrar* or *echar sangre por las narices* to have a nose-bleed, to bleed from the nose || FIG *sólo hace lo que le sale de las narices* he only does what he feels like doing || *sonarse las narices* to blow one's nose || FIG & FAM *tener a alguien agarrado por las narices* to lead s.o. by the nose | *tener a alguien montado en las narices* not to be able to stand *o* to stomach s.o.; *la tengo montada en las narices* I can't stand her || *tienes el libro delante de tus narices* the book is right under your nose.

narizón, ona *adj* FAM big-nosed, long-nosed.

narizota *f* FAM big nose, conk.
◆ *m/f pl* FAM long-nosed man, woman.

narración *f* narrating, narration (acto de narrar) || narrative, narration, account (relato) || narrative (parte de un discurso).

narrador, ra *adj* narrative.
◆ *m/f* narrator.

narrar *vt* to relate, to tell, to narrate.

narrativa *f* narrative, account (relato) || narrative (arte de narrar).

narrativo, va *adj* narrative.

narria *f* trolley, dolly (vehículo).

nártex *m* ARQ narthex.

narval *m* narwhal, narwal, narwhale (pez).

nasa *f* fish trap (para el pescado) || basket (cesta) || bin (para el pan).

nasal *adj/sf* nasal || — *consonante nasal* nasal consonant || ANAT *fosas nasales* nasal fossae.

nasalidad *f* nasality.

nasalización *f* nasalization; *nasalización de un sonido* nasalization of a sound || speaking through one's nose (gangueo).

nasalizar *vt* to nasalize.
◆ *vi* to speak through one's nose (defecto).

nasofaríngeo, a *adj* MED nasopharyngeal.

nasofaringitis *f inv* MED nasopharyngitis.

Nassau *n pr* GEOGR Nassau.

nata *f* fresh cream, cream (de la leche) || skin (encima de la leche cocida) || FIG cream, pick, best (lo mejor) || *AMER* slag (escoria) || — FIG *la flor y nata* the cream, the pick, the best, the flower; *la flor y nata de la sociedad londinense* the cream of London society || *nata batida* whipped cream.

natación *f* swimming.

natal *adj* natal (relativo al nacimiento) || native; *mi país natal* my native country || home; *mi ciudad natal* my home town.
◆ *m* birth (nacimiento) || birthday (cumpleaños).

natalicio, cia *adj* birthday.
◆ *m* birth (nacimiento) || birthday (cumpleaños).
◆ *pl* births column *sing* (en un periódico).

natalidad *f* natality, birthrate || *índice de natalidad* birthrate, natality.

natatorio, ria *adj* swimming, natatorial, natatory || *vejiga natatoria* air *o* swimming bladder.

natillas *f pl* custard *sing* (dulce).

natividad *f* nativity.

Natividad *f* Christmas (Navidad).

nativismo *m* nativism.

nativista *adj/s* nativist.

nativo, va *adj* native (natural); *oro nativo* native gold; *profesor nativo* native teacher || natural, innate, inborn, native (innato) || — *lengua nativa* native language, mother tongue || *suelo nativo* native soil, homeland, motherland.
◆ *m/f* native; *los nativos* the natives || *inglés por nativos* English classes given by native teachers.

nato, ta *adj* born; *enemigo nato* born enemy; *es un artista nato* he is a born artist.

natrón *m* MIN natron.

natura *f* nature (naturaleza) || *contra natura* unnatural.

natural *adj* natural; *recursos naturales* natural resources; *gas natural* natural gas || native (de un país) || fresh (fruta) || straight, neat (whisky, etc.) || natural (sencillo, sin afectación); *una persona muy natural* a very natural person || MÚS natural || — *agua natural* tapwater || *ciencias naturales* natural sciences || *de tamaño natural* life-sized; *retrato de tamaño natural* life-sized portrait || *es muy natural que...* it is perfectly natural that... || *hijo natural* illegitimate *o* natural child || *historia natural* natural history, nature study || *ley natural* natural law || MAT *logaritmo natural* natural logarithm || *muerte natural* natural death || *ser natural de* to come from; *es natural de Sevilla* he comes from Seville.
◆ *adv* naturally, of course (por supuesto).
◆ *m* nature (carácter); *de un natural celoso* of a jealous nature || native; *los naturales de un país* the natives of a country || TAUR natural pass [made with the muleta in the left hand] || — *al natural* natural, in its own juice (productos de conserva), realistic (descripción) || *de buen, mal natural* good-natured, bad-natured || *parecer muy natural* to seem quite natural || *pintar del natural* to paint from nature || *ser guapa al natural* to be pretty without make-up on || *ser lo más natural del mundo* to be the most natural thing in the world.

naturaleza *f* nature; *la Madre Naturaleza* Mother Nature; *amante de la naturaleza* nature lover || nature (natural, clase) || nationality (nacionalidad) || naturalization; *carta de naturaleza* naturalization papers || — *ciencias de la naturaleza* natural sciences || *contra la naturaleza* against nature, unnatural || *dejar obrar a la naturaleza* to let nature take its course || *las leyes de la naturaleza* the laws of nature || *naturaleza divina, humana* divine, human nature || ARTES *naturaleza muerta* still life || *por naturaleza* by nature, naturally; *los jóvenes son generosos por naturaleza* the young are generous by nature *o* naturally generous || *vuelta a la naturaleza* return to nature.

naturalidad *f* naturalness, native ease || citizenship, nationality (pertenencia a un pueblo) || — *aquí te roban con la mayor naturalidad* they rob you here and think nothing of it || *con la mayor naturalidad* as if it were the most natural thing in the world || *díselo con toda naturalidad* tell him quite simply *o* frankly *o* straightforwardly || *leyó la noticia con toda naturalidad* he read the news in a natural voice || *oyó la noticia con la mayor naturalidad* he took the news quite calmly.

naturalismo *m* naturalism (doctrina, literatura).

naturalista *adj* naturalistic.
◆ *m/f* naturalist.

naturalización *f* naturalization.

naturalizado, da *adj* naturalized.
◆ *m/f* naturalized person.

naturalizar *vt* to naturalize.
◆ *vpr* to become naturalized.

naturismo *m* naturism.

naturista *adj* naturistic.
◆ *m/f* naturist.

naufragar *vi* to sink, to be wrecked (barcos) || to be shipwrecked (personas) || FIG to fall through, to fail (un negocio).

naufragio *m* shipwreck wreck (barco) || FIG failure, disaster.

náufrago, ga *adj* shipwrecked (personas).
◆ *m/f* shipwreck, wreck (barco) || shipwrecked person, castaway (persona).
◆ *m* shark (tiburón) || *sociedad de salvamento de náufragos* lifeboat institution.

náusea *f* nausea, sickness (ganas de vomitar) || seasickness (en un barco) || FIG disgust, repulsion (asco) || — *dar náuseas a uno* to make s.o. sick, to sicken s.o., to nauseate s.o. || *sentir* or *tener náuseas* to feel sick.

nauseabundo, da *adj* sickening, nauseating, nauseous.

nauta *m* POÉT mariner.

náutico, ca *adj* nautical || — *club náutico* yacht club || *deportes náuticos* water *o* aquatic sports || *rosa náutica* compass card.
◆ *f* navigation, seamanship.

nautilo *m* nautilus (molusco).

navaja *f* penknife, pocketknife (de bolsillo) || razor (de afeitar) || razor clam (molusco) || tusk (de un jabalí) || sting (de insecto) || — *navaja barbera* cutthroat razor [*US* straight razor] || *navaja de injertar* grafting knife || *navaja de muelle* flickknife [*US* switchblade knife].

navajada *f*; **navajazo** *m* stab (profunda) || gash (superficial) || slash, stab (golpe).

naval *adj* naval; *agregado naval* naval attaché || — *base naval* naval base || *combate naval* naval *o* sea battle || *Escuela Naval* Naval College.

Navarra *npr f* GEOGR Navarre.

navarro, rra *adj/s* Navarrese.

nave *f* ship, vessel (barco) || nave (de una iglesia) || shop (parte de una fábrica) || — REL *la Nave de San Pedro* the Roman Catholic Church || *nave lateral* aisle (de iglesia) || FIG *quemar las naves* to burn one's boats [*US* to burn one's bridges] || *se alquila nave industrial* industrial premises *o* factory to let.

navecilla *f* censer (para incienso).

navegabilidad *f* navigability (de río, etc.) || seaworthiness (de barco) || airworthiness (de avión).

navegable *adj* navigable (río, etc.) || seaworthy (barco) || airworthy (avión).

navegación *f* navigation; *navegación submarina, aérea* submarine, aerial navigation || shipping; *abierto a la navegación* open to shipping || — *certificado de navegación* seaworthiness certificate || *líneas de navegación* shipping lines || *navegación a vela* yachting || *navegación costera* or *de cabotaje* coastal navigation || *navegación de altura* ocean navigation || *navegación fluvial* river navigation.

navegante *adj* sailing, navigating.
◆ *m* MAR & AVIAC navigator.

navegar *vi* to navigate, to sail (barcos) || to navigate, to fly (aviones) || — *navegar a la vela* to sail || *navegar en conserva* to sail in convoy *o* together || FIG *saber navegar* to know what one is doing.
◆ *vt* to sail, to navigate (barcos); *navegar los mares* to sail the seas.

naveta *f* small ship (barco) || censer (para el incienso) || drawer (gaveta) || ARQ prehistoric tomb in the Balearic Islands.

navicert *m* navicert, navigation certificate (licencia de navegación en tiempo de guerra).

Navidad *f* REL Nativity (nacimiento de Jesucristo) || Christmas (fiesta cristiana) || — *árbol de Navidad* Christmas tree || *canción de Navidad* Christmas carol (villancico) || *Pascua de Navidad* Christmas || *por Navidad* at Christmas || *tarjeta de felicitación de Navidad* Christmas card.
◆ *pl* Christmas *sing*; *en Navidades* at Christmas; *felices Navidades* merry *o* happy Christmas; *felicitar las Navidades* to wish s.o. a happy Christmas.

navideño, ña *adj* Christmas.

naviero, ra *adj* shipping.
◆ *m* shipowner (armador).
◆ *f* shipping company (compañía).

navío *m* ship, vessel (barco) || *capitán de navío* sea captain.

náyade *f* MIT naiad, water nymph || BOT naiad.

nazareno, na *adj/s* Nazarene.
◆ *m* penitent [in Holy Week processions] || *el Nazareno* Jesus of Nazareth, The Nazarene.

Nazaret *n pr* GEOGR Nazareth.

nazi *adj/s* Nazi (nacionalsocialista).

nazismo *m* Nazism (nacionalsocialismo).

nebladura *f* smut (tizón del trigo).

neblina *f* mist (niebla).

nebulosidad *f* nebulosity, cloudiness (cualidad de nebuloso) || obscurity, haziness (de ideas, etc.).

nebuloso, sa *adj* nebulous || cloudy, hazy, misty (cielo) || FIG hazy, vague, obscure (ideas).
◆ *f* nebula.

necear *vi* to talk nonsense (decir tonterías) || to play the fool (hacer tonterías).

necedad *f* foolishness, silliness, stupidity, nonsense (tontería) || — *decir necedades* to talk nonsense || *hacer una necedad* to do sth. stupid || *soltar una necedad* to say sth. stupid, to come out with a silly remark.

necesariamente *adv* necessarily, of necessity || really; *tenemos que ir necesariamente* we really must go.

necesario, ria *adj* necessary; *cumple las condiciones necesarias* he has the necessary qualifications, he fulfils the necessary requirements || — *no ser necesario* not to be necessary, there to be no need, not to have to, not to need to; *no es necesario que vengas si no quieres* it is not necessary for you to come *o* there is no need for you to come if you do not want to, you need not come *o* you do not need to come *o* you do not have to come if you do not want to || *ser necesario* must, to have to (obligación); *es necesario que abonen este terreno* you must fertilize *o* you have to fertilize this land; must, to have to, to need to (necesidad); *es necesario que lleguemos a las siete para coger el tren* we must arrive *o* we have to arrive *o* we need to arrive at seven o'clock to catch the train; to need, to be needed (con sustantivo); *es necesario un millón de pesetas para llevarlo a cabo* we need a million pesetas to complete it, a million pesetas are

needed to complete it || *si es necesario* if necessary, if need be.
◆ *m* *lo necesario* what is necessary || *lo estrictamente necesario* the bare necessities; *sólo he comprado lo estrictamente necesario* I only bought the bare necessities; what is *o* was strictly necessary; *sólo le he dicho lo estrictamente necesario* I only told him what was strictly necessary.

neceser *m* toilet case (bolsa de aseo) || kit (estuche con utensilios); *neceser de afeitar* shaving kit || *neceser de costura* workbox, sewing box.

necesidad *f* necessity; *hoy en día el coche es una necesidad* these days a car is a necessity || need; *la necesidad de una reforma agraria* the need for agricultural reform || need, want, poverty, necessity, straits *pl* (pobreza); *al morir su padre quedaron en la mayor necesidad* when their father died they were left in dire need || starvation, hunger (hambre); *morir de necesidad* to die of starvation *o* hunger || — *artículos de primera necesidad* basic necessities || *de necesidad* of necessity, necessarily || *en caso de necesidad* if necessary, if need be, in case of need || *hacer de necesidad virtud* to make a virtue of necessity || *la necesidad aguza el ingenio* necessity is the mother of invention || *la necesidad carece de ley* necessity knows no law || FIG *obedecer a la necesidad* to act out of necessity || *por necesidad* out of necessity || *tener necesidad de* to need || *verse en la necesidad de* to feel it necessary to, to feel obliged to.
◆ *pl* needs; *gana bastante para satisfacer sus necesidades* he earns enough to satisfy his needs || FAM needs; *necesidades corporales* bodily needs || hardships (dificultades); *pasar necesidades* to suffer hardships || FAM *hacer sus necesidades* to answer nature's call, to relieve o.s.

necesitado, da *adj* in need; *estoy necesitado de consejo* I am in need of advice || needy (pobre); *es una familia muy necesitada* they are a very needy family || — *andar necesitado de, estar necesitado de* to need || *andar un poco necesitado de dinero* to be a little short of money || *verse necesitado a* to feel it necessary to, to feel the need to, to feel obliged to (con verbo) || *verse necesitado de* to need (con sustantivo).
◆ *m/f* needy *o* poor person (pobre).
◆ *pl* *los necesitados* the needy, the poor.

necesitar *vt* to need, to require, to necessitate (exigir) || to need; *necesito tu ayuda, dinero* I need your help, money *o* some money || to want; *se necesita mecanógrafa* typist wanted || must, to need to, to have to (ser preciso); *necesito hablarte mañana* I must speak to you tomorrow.
◆ *vi* to need; *necesito de usted* I need you.
◆ *vpr* to be needed, to be wanted.

necio, cia *adj* silly, foolish.
◆ *m/f* fool, idiot (idiota).

necrófago, ga *adj* necrophagous.

necrofilia *f* necrophilia.

necrofobia *f* necrophobia.

necróforo *m* burying beetle (insecto).

necrología *f* necrology || obituary column (en un periódico).

necrológico, ca *adj* necrological || *nota necrológica* obituary notice.

necrólogo *m* necrologist.

necromancia *f* necromancy.

necrópolis *f* necropolis.

necropsia *f* necropsy, autopsy.

necrosis *f* MED necrosis.

néctar *m* nectar.

nectáreo, a *adj* nectareous, nectarous.

neerlandés, esa *adj* Dutch, [of *o* from the] Netherlands.
◆ *m/f* Dutchman (hombre), Dutchwoman (mujer), Netherlander (persona).
◆ *m* Dutch (lengua).
◆ *pl* *los neerlandeses* the Dutch.

nefando, da *adj* abominable, hateful, odious || *un crimen nefando* a heinous crime.

nefasto, ta *adj* unlucky, ill-fated, fateful.

nefelión *m* MED nubecula.

nefralgia *f* MED nephralgia.

nefrítico, ca *adj* nephritic, renal.

nefritis *f* MED nephritis.

nefrología *f* MED nephrology.

nefrológico, ca *adj* MED nephrological.

nefrólogo, ga *m/f* MED nephrologist.

nefroma *m* MED nephroma.

negación *f* negation, denial (de un hecho) || refusal (negativa) || GRAM negative || — *dos negaciones equivalen a una afirmación* two negatives make an affirmative *o* a positive || FIG *es la negación de la belleza* she is anything but beautiful.

negado, da *adj* FIG incapable, incompetent (incapaz) || FIG & FAM useless; *alguien negado para las matemáticas* s.o. useless at mathematics.
◆ *m/f* FIG & FAM dead loss (nulidad).

negar* *vt* to deny; *negar un hecho* to deny a fact; *no niego que sea cierto* I do not deny that it might be true || to refuse, to reject, to deny (rechazar); *negar una acusación* to deny a charge || to refuse (rehusar); *negar un permiso* to refuse permission; *negar la mano a uno* to refuse to shake hands with s.o.; *le negaron la entrada* they refused him entry || to disclaim (responsabilidad) || to deny (a Cristo).
◆ *vpr* to refuse; *se niega a pagar* he refuses to pay || to decline (una invitación) || *negarse a una visita* to refuse to see a visitor.

negativa *f* negative; *contestar con la negativa* to reply in the negative || denial (de un hecho) || refusal; *su negativa le trajo muchas dificultades* his refusal caused him a lot of difficulties; *negativa rotunda* flat refusal.

negativamente *adv* negatively || *responder negativamente* to answer in the negative.

negativismo *m* negativism.

negativo, va *adj* negative || MAT minus; *signo negativo* minus sign.
◆ *m* FOT negative.

negatón *m* FÍS negatron, negaton.

negligé *m* néglige, negligee (bata).

negligencia *f* neglect (abandono, dejadez) || negligence, carelessness (en el vestir, la conducta, etc.).

negligente *adj* negligent, neglectful; *negligente en* or *para sus deberes* negligent in carrying out his duties, neglectful of his duties || careless; *es un conductor negligente* he is a careless driver.
◆ *m/f* careless person.

negociable *adj* negotiable.

negociación *f* negotiation; *en negociación* under negotiation; *entablar negociaciones* to enter into *o* to open negotiations || clearance (de un cheque) || *negociación colectiva* collective bargaining || *negociación sindical* trade union talks.

negociado *m* section, department (en una oficina) || *jefe de negociado* head of department.

negociador, ra *adj* negotiating.
◆ *m/f* negotiator.

negociante *m/f* merchant; *negociante al por mayor* wholesale merchant || dealer; *negociante en coches* car dealer.

◆ *m* businessman (hombre de negocios).

negociar *vt/vi* to negotiate; *negociar un tratado de paz* to negotiate a peace treaty || to negotiate, to trade (comerciar); *negociar con Francia* to negotiate *o* to trade with France || to trade, to deal; *negociar en cereales* to trade in cereals || *negociar al por mayor, al por menor* to trade wholesale, retail.

negocio *m* business; *dedicarse a los negocios* to be in business || business, trade (comercio); *el negocio de los vinos* the wine trade || business, concern (empresa); *tiene un negocio de vinos* he has a wine business || affair, concern, business (asunto); *eso no es negocio suyo* that is not his affair || deal, transaction (transacción comercial) || bargain (compra ventajosa) || shop, store (tienda) || — *hacer negocio* to do good business || *hacer un buen, mal negocio* to make a good, bad deal || FIG & FAM *¡mal negocio!* it looks bad!, nasty business! | *¡menudo negocio has hecho!* you've done well for yourself, haven't you? || *negocio redondo* profitable deal (transacción), profitable business (comercio) || *negocio sucio* or *turbio* dirty business, shady deal || *poner un negocio* to set up *o* to start up a business || *traspasar un negocio* to transfer a business.
◆ *pl* business *sing* || — *encargado de negocios* chargé d'affaires (diplomático) || FIG *hablar de negocios* to talk shop || *hombre de negocios* businessman.

negra *f* —> **negro.**

negrada; negrería *f* AMER black slaves *pl* (esclavos negros) | negroes *pl* (conjunto de negros).

negrear *vi* to look black (parecer negro) || to darken, to blacken (ponerse oscuro).

negrería *f* AMER —> **negrada.**

negrero, ra *adj* black slave; *barco negrero* black slave ship.
◆ *m/f* slave trader (persona que se dedica al comercio de esclavos) || FIG slave driver (jefe exigente) | tyrant (tirano).

negrilla *f* IMPR boldface.

negrillo *m* elm (olmo) || AMER silver ore (mineral).

negrita *f* IMPR boldface (negrilla).

negrito, ta *m/f* little negro boy (chico), little negro girl (chica), piccaninny [US pickaninny] || Negrillo (pigmeo de África) || Negrito (pigmeo de Asia y Oceanía).

negro, gra *adj* black; *un coche negro* a black car; *tus manos están negras* your hands are black || dark, black (oscuro); *pelo negro, ojos negros* dark *o* black hair, dark *o* black eyes; *tabaco negro* black tobacco || negro (de raza negra); *tribu, raza negra* negro tribe, race || coloured, black (de color) || FIG black, gloomy (sombrío); *¡qué perspectiva más negra!* what a gloomy outlook! | FIG & FAM furious, hopping mad (enfadado) || — HIST *camisa negra* blackshirt || *cerveza negra* brown ale; stout || DEP *cinturón negro* black belt || FIG & FAM *estar negro con* to be livid with *o* mad at (una persona), to be desperate about (una cosa) | *estar negro de envidia* to be green with envy || *lista negra* black list || *magia negra* black magic, black art || *mercado negro* black market || *misa negra* black mass || *negro como el azabache* jetblack (pelo) || *negro como el carbón* or *como un tizón* as black as coal, as black as soot || *negro como la pez* pitch-black, as black as pitch, pitch-dark || *negro como la boca del lobo* as black as pitch, like the black hole of Calcutta (sin luz) || FIG *oveja negra, garbanzo negro* black sheep || *pan negro* brown bread || FIG & FAM *pasarlas negras* to have a rough time || *peste negra* black death || *pimienta negra* black pepper || FIG & FAM *poner a uno negro* to make s.o. mad (enfadar), to beat s.o. black and blue (de golpes) | *ponerse negro* to get mad, to lose one's temper (ponerse furio-

so), to get a suntan (broncearse), to look bad (un asunto) || HIST *Príncipe Negro* Black Prince || *Selva Negra* Black Forest || FIG & FAM *suerte negra* tough *o* rotten luck | *tener ideas negras* to be down in the dumps | *verlo todo negro* to be very pessimistic | *verse negro para, vérselas negras para* to have a lot of trouble to || MED *vómito negro* black vomit.
◆ *m/f* negro (hombre), negress (mujer) || FIG & FAM *trabajar como un negro* to work like a black *o* like a slave.
◆ *m* black (color) || tan (bronceado) || black *o* dark tobacco (tabaco); *no me gusta el negro* I don't like black tobacco || — FOT *en blanco y negro* in black and white || QUÍM *negro animal* animal charcoal || *negro de humo, de marfil* lampblack, ivory black.
◆ *f* MÚS crotchet [US quarter note] || buttonned foil (espada) || bad luck (mala suerte) || FIG & FAM *hacer pasar las negras a alguien* to give s.o. a rough time.

negroide *adj* Negroid.

negror *m*; **negrura** *f* blackness, darkness.

negruzco, ca *adj* blackish, darkish.

neguilla *f* BOT corn cockle (planta abundante en los sembrados) | nigella (arañuela).

negus *m* negus.

nematelmintos *m pl* ZOOL nemathelminthes.

nematodos *m pl* ZOOL nematodes.

nemoroso, sa *adj* POÉT sylvan.

nemotecnia *f* mnemonics, mnemotechny.

nemotécnico, ca *adj* mnemotechnic.

nene, na *m/f* baby (niño pequeño).
◆ *f* love, dear, darling (expresión cariñosa).

nenúfar *m* BOT water lily.

neocaledonio, nia *adj/s* New Caledonian.

neocapitalismo *m* ECON neocapitalism.

neocatolicismo *m* Neo-Catholicism.

neocatólico, ca *adj* Neo-Catholic.

neocelandés, esa; neozelandés, esa *adj* [of *o* from] New Zealand.
◆ *m/f* New Zealander.

neoclasicismo *m* neoclassicism.

neoclásico, ca *adj* neoclassic, neoclassical.
◆ *m/f* neoclassicist.

neocolonialismo *m* neocolonialism.

neocolonialista *adj/s* neocolonialist.

neocristianismo *m* Neo-Christianity.

neocristiano, na *adj/s* Neo-Christian.

neoescolástico, ca *adj* Neo-Scholastic.
◆ *f* Neo-Scholasticism.

neofascismo *m* neofascism.

neófito, ta *m/f* neophyte, novice.

neógeno *m* GEOL neocene.

neogótico, ca *adj* Neo-Gothic.

neogriego, ga *adj* Neo-Greek.

neoimpresionismo *m* Neo-Impressionism.

neolatino, na *adj* Neo-Latin || *lenguas neolatinas* Romance languages.

neolítico, ca *adj* Neolithic.
◆ *m* Neolith.

neologismo *m* neologism.

neólogo, ga *m/f* neologist.

neomaltusianismo *m* Neo-Malthusianism.

neón *m* neon (gas); *alumbrado de neón* neon lighting.

neoplatonismo; neoplatonicismo *m* neoplatonism.

neoplatónico, ca *adj* neoplatonic.
◆ *m/f* neoplatonist.

neopositivismo *m* neopositivism.

neorrealismo *m* neorealism.

neorrealista *adj/s* neorealist.

neorromanticismo *m* neoromanticism.

neorromántico, ca *adj/s* neoromantic.

neotomismo *m* Neo-Thomism.

neoyorquino, na *adj* [of *o* from] New York.
◆ *m/f* New Yorker.

neozelandés, esa *adj/s* → **neocelandés.**

neozoico, ca *adj* GEOL Neozoic.

Nepal *npr m* Nepal.

nepalés, esa *adj/s* Nepalese.

neperiano, na *adj* MAT Napierian.

nepote *m* nepote.

nepotismo *m* nepotism.

neptúneo, a; neptúnico, ca *adj* Neptunian.

neptunio *m* QUÍM neptunium.

Neptuno *npr m* MIT Neptune.

nequáquam *adv* FAM certainly not.

nereida *f* MIT Nereid, sea nymph || ZOOL Nereid.

Nerón *npr m* Nero || FIG tyrant (tirano).

neroniano, na *adj* Neronian.

nervadura *f* ARQ ribs *pl* || BOT venation, nervation || ZOOL veins *pl* (de insectos).

nerviado, da *adj* BOT nervate.

nervio *m* ANAT nerve; *nervio óptico* optic nerve || rib, vein, nerve (de una hoja) || sinew (de la carne) || ARQ rib, nerve || MÚS string || TECN band (de un libro) || ZOOL vein (en insectos) || FIG sinews *pl*; *el nervio de la guerra* the sinews of war | nerve (valor) | energy, strength, vigour, mettle (energía) || — *ataque de nervios* fit of hysterics, hysterics; *hizo que le diera un ataque de nervios* he sent her into hysterics || *crisparle los nervios a uno* to get on s.o.'s nerves || *estar enfermo de los nervios* to suffer from a nervous complaint || FIG *estar hecho un manojo de nervios* to be a bundle of nerves || *guerra de nervios* war of nerves || *nervio de buey* bull's pizzle || *nervios de acero* nerves of steel || *poner los nervios de punta* to set one's nerves on edge, to get on s.o.'s nerves || *tener los nervios de punta* to be (all) on edge || *tener los nervios bien templados* to have steady nerves || *tener nervio* to have nerve.

nerviosidad *f*; **nerviosismo** *m* nervousness, nerves *pl* || irritability, excitability (excitación) || agitation (agitación) || impatience (impaciencia) || *quitar a uno el nerviosismo* or *la nerviosidad* to soothe s.o.'s nerves.

nervioso, sa *adj* nervous; *sistema nervioso* nervous system; *depresión nerviosa* nervous breakdown || nerve (célula, centro) || sinewy, wiry (cuerpo, miembro) || AUT responsive, lively (motor) || BOT nervate (hoja) || FIG fidgety, nervy (impaciente) | excitable, highly-strung (impresionable) | irritable || — *¡no te pongas nervioso!* don't get excited!, take it easy!, calm down! || *poner nervioso a alguien* to get on s.o.'s nerves || *ponerse nervioso* to get excited, to get worked up || *tiene una depresión nerviosa* he has had a nervous breakdown.

nervudo, da *adj* vigorous, strong (fuerte) || FAM sinewy, wiry (miembro).

nervura *f* ribbing (de un libro).

nesga *f* bias (en un vestido) || gore (pieza triangular).

nesgado, da *adj* cut on the bias.

nesgar *vt* to cut on the bias (cortar al bies) || to gore (poner una pieza triangular).

nestorianismo *m* Nestorianism.

nestoriano, na *adj/s* Nestorian.

neto, ta *adj* pure, simple (una verdad) || clear (ideas, estilo, conciencia) || net; *peso, precio, beneficio neto* net weight, price, profit.

neuma *m* MÚS neume.

neumático, ca *adj* pneumatic.
◆ *m* tyre [US tire] || — *juego de neumáticos* set of tyres || *neumáticos contra pinchazos, sin cámara de aire* puncture-proof, tubeless tyres.

neumococo *m* pneumococcus.

neumogástrico *adj/sm* pneumogastric (nervio).

neumonía *f* MED pneumonia.

neumónico, ca *adj* pneumonic.

neumotórax *m* MED pneumothorax.

neuralgia *f* MED neuralgia.

neurálgico, ca *adj* MED neuralgic || FIG *punto neurálgico* weak spot, weakness.

neurastenia *f* MED neurasthenia.

neurasténico, ca *adj* MED neurasthenic.

neurisma *m* MED aneurism.

neurítico, ca *adj* MED neuritic.

neuritis *f* MED neuritis.

neuroblasto *m* BIOL neuroblast.

neurocirugía *f* MED neurosurgery.

neurocirujano, na *m/f* neurosurgeon.

neuroesqueleto *m* ZOOL neuroskeleton.

neurología *f* MED neurology.

neurológico, ca *adj* MED neurological.

neurólogo *m* MED neurologist.

neuroma *m* MED neuroma.

neurona *f* ANAT neuron.

neurópata *m/f* MED neuropath.

neuropatía *f* MED neuropathy.

neuropatología *f* MED neuropathology.

neuróptero *adj m/sm* ZOOL neuropteran.
◆ *m pl* neuroptera.

neurosis *f* MED neurosis.

neurótico, ca *adj/s* MED neurotic.

neurotomía *f* MED neurotomy.

neurovegetativo, va *adj* ANAT neurovegetative.

neutoniano, na *adj* FÍS → **newtoniano.**

neutonio *m* FÍS → **newton.**

neutral *adj/s* neutral.

neutralidad *f* neutrality || *mantener la neutralidad* to remain neutral.

neutralismo *m* neutralism.

neutralista *adj/s* neutralist.

neutralización *f* neutralization.

neutralizador, ra; neutralizante *adj* QUÍM neutralizing.
◆ *m* neutralizer, neutralizing agent.

neutralizar *vt* to neutralize.

neutrino *m* FÍS neutrino.

neutro, tra *adj* GRAM neuter || JUR, ELECTR, MIL & QUÍM neutral || BIOL sexless, neuter.
◆ *m* GRAM neuter.

neutrón *m* FÍS neutron.

nevada *f* snowfall; *fuerte nevada* heavy snowfall.

nevadilla *f* BOT whitlowwort (planta).

nevado, da *adj* snow-covered; *montañas nevadas* snow-covered mountains || covered with snow; *la carretera está nevada* the road is covered with snow || POÉT & FIG snowy, snow-white (blanco).
◆ *m* AMER snow-capped mountain, mountain with perpetual snow || AMER *el nevado de Sajama* Mount Sajama.

nevar* *v impers* to snow; *nevar mucho* to snow heavily.

◆ *vt* to cover with snow (cubrir de nieve) ‖ FIG to whiten (poner blanco).

nevasca *f* snowfall (nevada) ‖ blizzard (ventisca).

nevatilla *f* wagtail (ave).

nevera *f* refrigerator, fridge *(fam)*, (refrigerador) ‖ FIG icebox (sitio muy frío); *esta habitación es una nevera* this room is like an icebox.

nevero *m* perennial snowcap *o* snowfield.

nevisca *f* light snowfall.

neviscar *v impers* to snow lightly *o* a little.

nevo *m* naevus, birthmark (mancha en la piel) ‖ mole (lunar).

nevoso, sa *adj* snowy.

newton; neutonio *m* FÍS Newton.

newtoniano, na; neutoniano, na *adj* FÍS Newtonian.

nexo *m* link, bond, tie, nexus (vínculo) ‖ connection (relación) ‖ *palabras sin nexo* unrelated *o* unconnected words.

ni *conj* neither, nor; *él no lo hizo, ni ella* he did not do it, neither did she ‖ not even (ni siquiera); *ni lo dijo a sus amigos* he did not even tell his friends; *no tenía ni donde pasar la noche* he did not even have anywhere to spend the night; *ni que fueras su padre* not even if you were his father ‖ — *ni más ni menos* no more, no less ‖ *ni nada* or anything, nor anything; *no sabe leer ni nada* he cannot read or anything, he can neither read nor anything; *no le gusta ni el arroz, ni la carne, ni el pescado, ni nada* he does not like rice, or meat, or fish, or anything *o* he likes neither rice, nor meat, nor fish, nor anything ‖ *ni... ni* neither... nor; *ni tú ni yo le podemos ayudar ahora* neither you nor I can help him now; *no tengo ni té ni café* I have neither tea nor coffee; *no tiene ni bolígrafo ni lápiz* he has neither a pen nor a pencil; *ni come ni duerme* he neither eats nor sleeps ‖ *ni que fuesen niños, ni que fueses un niño* they are worse than children, you are worse than a child ‖ *ni que fuera suyo* anyone would think it were yours *o* his *o* hers ‖ *ni que fuera tonto* what do you take me (*o* him *o* her) for? ‖ *ni siquiera* not even; *no quedó ni siquiera una silla vacía* there was not even one free seat left; *ni siquiera me lo dijo* he did not even tell me ‖ *ni un, ni una* not... a...; *no me quedaré ni un minuto más aquí* I shall not stay here a minute more ‖ *ni uno, ni una* not one; *ni uno se quedó* not one remained ‖ *ni uno ni otro* neither, neither the one nor the other (sujeto); *ni uno ni otro nos parece bien* neither seems right to us; not... either (of them) (complemento); *no pienso comprar ni uno ni otro* I do not intend to buy either (of them) ‖ *ni unos ni otros* none of them (sujeto); *no vinieron ni unos ni otros* none of them came; not... any of them (complemento); *no compres ni unos ni otros* do not buy any (of them) ‖ *no... ni* not... or, neither... nor; *no come ni duerme* he does not eat or sleep, he neither eats nor sleeps ‖ *no... ni... ni* not... either... or; *no quiero ni agua ni vino* I do not want either water or wine ‖ *sin... ni* without... or; *salió sin beber ni comer* he went out without drinking or eating.

Niágara *npr m* GEOGR Niagara; *las cataratas del Niágara* Niagara Falls.

Niamey *n pr* GEOGR Niamey.

nibelungos *m pl* MIT Nibelungen.

nicaragua *f* BOT balsam apple.

Nicaragua *npr f* GEOGR Nicaragua.

nicaragüense *adj/s* Nicaraguan.

Nicosia *n pr* GEOGR Nicosia.

nicotina *f* QUÍM nicotine.

nicotínico, ca *adj* nicotinic.

nicotinismo; nicotismo *m* MED nicotinism, nicotine poisoning.

nictación *f* nictation (parpadeo).

nictalopía *f* MED day blindness (visión mejor de noche) ‖ nyctalopia (visión mejor de día).

nictitante *adj* ZOOL nictitating.

nicho *m* niche, recess (hornacina).

nidación *f* MED nidation.

nidada *f* brood (de pollos) ‖ clutch (de huevos).

nidal *m* nest (ponedero de las gallinas) ‖ nest egg (huevo) ‖ FIG haunt, hangout (lugar frecuentado por una persona) | hiding place (escondrijo).

nidificación *f* nidification, nest building.

nidificar *vi* to nest, to nidify, to build a nest.

nido *m* nest ‖ FIG den, nest; *nido de bandidos* den of thieves | hiding place (escondrijo) | nest (hogar) | hotbed (criadero) | source (fuente, origen) ‖ — FIG *caer del nido* to come down to earth with a bump ‖ *camas de nido* pullout beds ‖ FIG *encontrar el pájaro en el nido* to find the person for whom one was searching | *en los nidos de antaño, no hay pájaros hogaño* where are the snows of yesteryear? ‖ *mesas de nido* nest of tables ‖ *nido de abejas* smocking (costura), honeycomb (de un radiador, etc.) ‖ MIL *nido de ametralladoras* machine gun nest | *nido de urraca* outwork (trinchera) ‖ FIG *nido de víboras* nest of vipers | *parece que se ha caído del nido* he is still wet behind the ears.

niebla *f* fog (densa) ‖ mist (neblina) ‖ BOT mildew (hongo parásito) ‖ MED nubecula (en el ojo, en la orina) ‖ FIG mental confusion, fogginess (confusión) ‖ — *hay niebla* it is foggy ‖ FAM *niebla meona* drizzle ‖ *tarde de niebla* foggy afternoon.

niel *m* TECN niello (del metal).

nielado *m* TECN niello (procedimiento).

nieto, ta *m/f* grandson (chico), granddaughter (chica).

◆ *m pl* grandchildren.

nieve *f* snow; *blanco como la nieve* as white as snow ‖ — CULIN *a punto de nieve* stiff; *claras batidas a punto de nieve* egg whites beaten till stiff ‖ *copo de nieve* snowflake.

◆ *pl* snow *sing*, snows; *son las primeras nieves* it is the first snow.

nife *m* GEOL core [of the Earth].

Níger *npr m* GEOGR Niger ‖ the (River) Niger.

Nigeria *npr f* Nigeria.

nigeriano, na *adj/s* Nigerian.

nigromancia *f* necromancy.

nigromante; nigromántico, ca *m/f* necromancer.

◆ *adj* necromantic.

nigua *f* ZOOL chigoe (parásito).

nihilismo *m* nihilism.

nihilista *adj* nihilistic.

◆ *m/f* nihilist.

níkel *m* nickel (metal).

Nilo *npr m* GEOGR Nile; *Alto Nilo* Upper Nile.

nilón *m* nylon (textil).

nimbar *vt* to encircle with a halo.

nimbo *m* nimbus (nube) ‖ halo (en la cabeza, etc.).

nimboestrato *m* nimbostratus (nube).

nimiedad *f* triviality (pequeñez) ‖ trifle (fruslería) ‖ excess (demasía) ‖ verbosity (prolijidad) ‖ meticulousness (meticulosidad).

nimio, mia *adj* insignificant, petty, unimportant, minor, trivial (de poca importancia); *detalles nimios* petty details ‖ overmeticulous (muy meticuloso) ‖ excessive (excesivo) ‖ verbose (prolijo) ‖ stingy (mezquino) ‖ *de nimia importancia* quite unimportant, minor.

ninfa *f* MIT & ZOOL nymph ‖ ANAT nympha ‖ FIG *ninfa Egeria* Egeria.

ninfea *m* BOT nymphaea, water lily (nenúfar).

ninfómana; ninfomaníaca *f* nymphomaniac.

ninfomanía *f* MED nymphomania.

ningún *adj indef* ⟶ **ninguno.**

— OBSERV *Ningún* is the apocopated form of *ninguno*. It is used before a masculine singular noun.

ninguno, na *adj indef* no; *ninguna casa me conviene* no house suits me ‖ no, not any (con negación); *no voy a ninguna escuela* I do not go to any school, I go to no school; *no tiene valor ninguno* it has no value, it hasn't any value ‖ — *de ninguna manera, de ningún modo* not at all, by no means, in no way ‖ *en ninguna parte* nowhere ‖ *ninguna cosa* nothing ‖ *no es ningún imbécil* he is no fool.

◆ *pron indef* none, not one, not any; *ninguno entre ellos* none of them ‖ neither, not... either (de dos); *no tomo ninguno de estos dos libros* I will take neither of these two books, I will not take either of these two books ‖ no one, nobody (nadie); *ninguno lo sabrá* no one will know ‖ *como ninguno* like no one else (does *o* did).

— OBSERV When *ninguno* precedes the verb, the adverb *no* disappears: *ninguno sabe* but *no sabe ninguno* nobody knows.

niña *f* girl, little girl; *una niña encantadora* a charming girl ‖ ANAT pupil (del ojo) ‖ FAM dear, my dear (término de cariño) ‖ FIG *es la niña de mis ojos, le quiero como a la niña de mis ojos* she is my pride and joy *o* the apple of my eye.

niñada *f* childishness, childish thing.

niñear *vi* to act like a child, to act childishly.

niñería *f* childish act *o* thing, childishness (acción propia de niño) ‖ FIG trifle, trifling matter, triviality (cosa sin importancia).

niñero, ra *adj* fond of children (aficionado a los niños).

◆ *f* nursemaid, nanny.

niñez *f* childhood, infancy ‖ FIG infancy ‖ *volver a la niñez* to be in one's second childhood.

◆ *pl* childishness *sing* (niñerías).

niño, ña *adj* young, small; *es aún muy niña para ir de compras* she is still very young to go shopping ‖ childish (infantil) ‖ FIG immature, inexperienced (sin experiencia).

◆ *m* boy; *un niño muy simpático* a very nice boy ‖ baby; *voy a tener un niño* I am expecting a baby ‖ FAM dear, my dear (voz de cariño) ‖ — *de niño* as a child ‖ *desde niño* from childhood ‖ *es el niño mimado de su madre* he is his mother's pet *o* his mother's blue-eyed boy ‖ FIG & FAM *estar como un niño con zapatos nuevos* to be like a dog with two tails ‖ *hacer un niño a una chica* to get a girl in the family way, to get a girl pregnant ‖ *niño bitongo* young upstart (repipi) ‖ *niño bonito* pet (persona preferida), show-off (presumido) ‖ *niño de la Bola* Baby Jesus ‖ *niño de pecho* or *de teta* babe-in-arms ‖ *niño expósito* or *de la piedra* foundling ‖ *niño gótico* show-off ‖ *niño Jesús* Baby Jesus ‖ *niño mimado* spoilt child ‖ *niño probeta* test-tube baby ‖ *niño prodigio* child prodigy ‖ *niño zangolotino* big baby ‖ *¡no seas niño!* don't be such a baby! ‖ FIG & FAM *¡qué poeta ni qué niño muerto!* he is about as much a poet as I am.

◆ *f* ⟶ **niña.**

◆ *pl* children; *tengo dos niños, un hijo y una hija* I have two children, a boy and a girl.

niobio *m* QUÍM niobium.

nipón, ona *adj/s* Japanese, Nipponese.

níquel *m* nickel (metal).

niquelado *m*; **niqueladura** *f* nickel-plating, nickelling.

niquelar *vt* to nickel-plate, to nickel.

niqui *m* tee-shirt (camisa).

Nirvana *m* REL Nirvana.

níspero *m* BOT medlar (árbol y fruto).

nitidez *f* brightness, clarity, clearness (brillo) ‖ clearness, clarity; *la nitidez del agua* the clearness of the water ‖ sharpness, clarity, clearness (de una foto) ‖ FIG unblemished nature, purity.

nítido, da *adj* clear, sharp; *foto nítida* sharp photograph ‖ bright, clean (limpio) ‖ clear (agua).

nitración *f* QUÍM nitration.

nitrado, da *adj* nitrated.

nitral *m* nitre *o* saltpetre works *o* bed [*US* niter *o* saltpeter works *o* bed].

nitratar *vt* QUÍM to nitrate.

nitrato *m* QUÍM nitrate; *nitrato sódico* sodium nitrate ‖ *nitrato de Chile* Chile saltpetre [*US* Chile saltpeter].

nitrería *f* nitre bed [*US* niter bed].

nítrico, ca *adj* QUÍM nitric.

nitrificación *f* nitrification.

nitrificar *vt* QUÍM to nitrify.

nitrilo *m* QUÍM nitrile.

nitrito *m* QUÍM nitrite.

nitro *m* QUÍM nitre [*US* niter], saltpetre [*US* saltpeter].

nitrobenceno *m* QUÍM nitrobenzene.

nitrocelulosa *f* QUÍM nitrocellulose.

nitrogenado, da *adj* QUÍM nitrogenous.

nitrógeno *m* QUÍM nitrogen (gas).

nitroglicerina *f* QUÍM nitroglycerine.

nitroso, sa *adj* QUÍM nitrous.

nitrotolueno *m* QUÍM nitrotoluene.

nitruración *f* TECN nitrogenation, nitriding.

nitruro *m* QUÍM nitride.

nivel *m* level ‖ level, height (altura) ‖ FIG level; *al nivel nacional, ministerial* at a national, ministerial level; *nivel económico* economic level | standard; *esta universidad tiene un nivel más alto que la otra* the standard in this university is higher than in the other one ‖ TECN level (instrumento); *nivel de burbuja* spirit level ‖ MIN level (en minas) ‖ — *al mismo nivel* at the same level, level ‖ *al nivel de* at the same level as, on a level with, level with ‖ *al nivel del mar* at sea level ‖ *a nivel* level ‖ *conferencia de alto nivel* top-level *o* high-level conference ‖ *estar al nivel de las circunstancias* to rise to the occasion ‖ *la ciudad está a 500 metros sobre el nivel del mar* the city is 500 metres above sea level ‖ *nivel de agua* water level ‖ *nivel de vida* standard of living ‖ *paso a nivel* level crossing [*US* railroad *o* grade crossing].

nivelación *f* levelling [*US* leveling].

nivelador, ra *adj* levelling [*US* leveling].
◆ *m/f* leveller [*US* leveler].

nivelamiento *m* FIG levelling [*US* leveling].

nivelar *vt* to level (poner al mismo nivel) ‖ to level, to make even (allanar el terreno) | to survey (en topografía) ‖ FIG to even out, to make even *o* equal (igualar) | to balance; *nivelar el presupuesto* to balance the budget.
◆ *vpr* to become level, to level out.

níveo, a *adj* POÉT niveous, snowy.

nivoso, sa *adj* snowy.

no *adv* no (en respuestas); *no, señor* no, Sir ‖ not (delante de un verbo); *no deberías* you should not, you shouldn't; *no vinieron* they did not come, they didn't come; *no lo hagas* do not do it, don't do it; *no comer* not to eat ‖ not any, no (ningún); *no tiene dinero* he has not any money, he has no money ‖ not (en frases sin verbo); *todavía no* not yet; *¿por qué no?* why not?; *¡yo no!* not I ‖ — *¡a que no!* I bet you don't! ‖ *¿a que no?* do you want to bet? ‖ *¡Carlos no, Felipe sí!* Charles out, Philip in!, down with Charles, up with Philip! ‖ *¡cómo no!* of course ‖ *¡cómo que no!* no?, what do you mean, no? ‖ *creo que no* I don't think so ‖ *cuidado que no se escape* be careful (that) he does not escape ‖ *decir que no* to say no ‖ *Ernesto vino ayer, ¿no?* Ernest came yesterday, didn't he? ‖ *es inglés, ¿no?* he is English, isn't he? ‖ *¡eso sí que no!* certainly not!, of course not! ‖ *no aceptación* nonacceptance ‖ *no agresión* nonaggression; *firmar un pacto de no agresión* to sign a nonaggression pact ‖ *no alineación* nonalignement ‖ *no alineado* nonaligned ‖ *no beligerancia* nonbelligerancy ‖ *no bien* no sooner; *no bien llegué, me llamaron* I had no sooner arrived than they called me ‖ *no... casi* hardly; *no habla casi* he hardly speaks ‖ *no combatiente* noncombatant ‖ *no comprometido* noncommittal ‖ *no conformidad, no conformismo* nonconformity ‖ *no cooperación* noncooperation ‖ *no digo que no* I won't say no ‖ *no es que...* it is not that... ‖ *no existencia* nonexistence ‖ *no existente* nonexistent ‖ *no ferroso* nonferrous ‖ *no hay de qué* don't mention it, not at all, you are welcome ‖ *no hay para qué* or *por qué* there is no reason to ‖ *no intervención* nonintervention ‖ *no menos de* no less than ‖ *no mucho* not much ‖ *no... nada* not at all; *no te entiendo nada* I do not understand you at all ‖ *no negociable* nonnegotiable ‖ *no por cierto* certainly not, indeed not ‖ *no sea que* in case ‖ *no sectario* nonsectarian ‖ *no... sino* not... but; *no es militar sino abogado* he is not a soldier but a lawyer; nothing but; *no hace sino criticar* he does nothing but criticize; just, only (sólo) ‖ *no sólo... sino también* or *sino que* not only... but also ‖ *no tal* no such thing ‖ *no violencia* nonviolence ‖ *no ya* not only ‖ FIL *no yo* nonego ‖ *¡que no!* no!, certainly not! ‖ *ya no* no longer, not... any more; *ya no leo* I no longer read, I do not read any more.
◆ *m* no; *contestó con un no categórico* he replied with a definit no.

— OBSERV In Latin America, *no más* occurs in a number of idioms, such as: *aquí no más* right here; *así no más* middling; *ayer no más* only *o* just yesterday; *tome no más* do take it.

— OBSERV Las contracciones *don't, can't, won't, etc.* son ligeramente familiares. Por lo tanto es preferible evitarlas en la lengua escrita.

nobelio *m* QUÍM nobelium.

nobiliario, ria *adj* nobiliary, noble.

nobilísimo, ma *adj* very noble, most noble.

noble *adj* noble (aristócrata) ‖ noble, honest, upright (honrado) ‖ *noble en su porte* distinguished looking.
◆ *m* noble, nobleman (aristócrata).
◆ *pl* nobles, nobility *sing*.

nobleza *f* nobility, aristocracy (nobles, aristocracia) ‖ nobility (cualidad de noble) ‖ honesty, uprightness, nobleness (honradez) ‖ — *nobleza obliga* «noblesse oblige» ‖ *tener sus títulos de nobleza* to be of the nobility.

noción *f* notion, idea; *no tiene noción de francés* he has no idea of French.
◆ *pl* slight knowledge *sing*; *tiene nociones de matemáticas* he has a slight knowledge of mathematics ‖ smattering *sing*; *tener nociones de inglés* to have a smattering of English.

nocividad *f* noxiousness, harmfulness.

nocivo, va *adj* noxious; *gas nocivo* noxious gas ‖ harmful, injurious; *nocivo a* or *para la salud* harmful to the health.

noctambulismo *m* noctivagation, noctambulism.

noctámbulo, la *adj* noctivagant, noctambulant.
◆ *m/f* noctivagant, noctambule.

noctívago, ga *adj* POÉT noctivagant.

nocturnidad *f* JUR nocturnal character [of a crime] ‖ JUR *con nocturnidad y alevosía* undercover of night and with ill-intent.

nocturno, na *adj* nocturnal; *aparición nocturna* nocturnal apparition ‖ evening; *clases nocturnas* evening classes ‖ night; *avión, tren, vuelo nocturno* night plane, train, flight; *vida nocturna* night life ‖ BOT & ZOOL nocturnal, night; *aves nocturnas* night birds.
◆ *m* MÚS nocturne.

noche *f* night; *la noche anterior* the previous night, the night before; *ayer por la noche* last night ‖ late evening, night; *ven por la noche después de cenar* come round late in the evening, come round at night after dinner ‖ nighttime, night; *cuando vino la noche* when nighttime came, when night fell ‖ FIG dark (oscuridad); *le asusta la noche* he is scared of the dark | night; *las noches oscuras del alma* the dark nights of the soul ‖ — *a boca de noche* at dusk, at twilight ‖ *al caer la noche* at nightfall ‖ *buenas noches* good evening (al atardecer), good night (al despedirse); *dar las buenas noches* to say good evening *o* good night ‖ *cerrada la noche, ya entrada la noche* after nightfall ‖ *de la noche a la mañana* overnight; *de la noche a la mañana ha cambiado* he has changed overnight; all night, through the night; *leer de la noche a la mañana* to read all night long ‖ *de noche* at night ‖ FIG *de noche todos los gatos son pardos* everything looks the same in the dark ‖ *durante la noche* in the night ‖ *en las altas horas de la noche* in the small hours, late at night ‖ *es de noche* it is dark *o* nighttime ‖ *esta noche* tonight ‖ *función de noche* late performance ‖ *hacer de la noche día* to turn night into day ‖ *hacer noche* to spend the night (pasar la noche) ‖ *hacerse de noche* to grow dark (anochecer) ‖ *¡hasta la noche!* see you tonight ‖ *hasta muy entrada la noche* until late at night ‖ *la noche de San Bartolomé* St. Bartholomew's massacre ‖ *las mil y una noches* the Arabian Nights ‖ *mañana por la noche* tomorrow night ‖ *media noche* midnight ‖ *Noche Buena* Christmas Eve ‖ *noche cerrada* dark night ‖ *noche de bodas* wedding night ‖ *noche de estreno* first night ‖ *noche en claro* or *en blanco* or *en vela* or *toledana* sleepless night ‖ *Noche Vieja* New Year's Eve ‖ *noche y día* night and day ‖ *pasar la noche de juerga* to make a night of it ‖ *por la noche* at night, at nighttime, by night, in the night ‖ *se está haciendo de noche* night is falling *o* coming on, it is growing dark ‖ FIG *ser la noche y el día* to be as different as night and day ‖ *toda la noche* all night, the whole night ‖ *trabajar de noche* or *por la noche* to work at night (cualquier persona), to work nights (un trabajador) ‖ *traje de noche* evening dress, evening gown.

Nochebuena *f* Christmas Eve.

nochero *m* AMER night watchman (guarda) | bedside table (mesilla de noche).

Nochevieja *f* New Year's Eve ‖ — *cena de Nochevieja* New Year's Eve dinner ‖ *día de Nochevieja* New Year's Eve.

nodal *adj* nodal; *punto nodal* nodal point.

nodo *m* node.

No-Do *m* CINEM newsreel.

— OBSERV *No-Do* was the abbreviation of *noticiario documental* in Spain.

nodriza *f* wet nurse (ama de cría) ‖ nanny (niñera) ‖ TECN vacuum tank (depósito) ‖ *avión, buque nodriza* mother aircraft, ship.

nodular *adj* nodular (relativo a los nódulos) ‖ nodulose, nodulous (que tiene nódulos).

nódulo *m* nodule, node.

Noé *npr m* Noah || *el arca de Noé* Noah's ark.

nogal *m* walnut (árbol, madera).

nogalina *f* walnut stain.

noguera *f* BOT walnut tree.

nogueral *m* walnut grove, wood of walnut trees.

nómada *adj* nomadic.
◆ *m/f* nomad.

nomadismo *m* nomadism.

nombradía *f* renown, fame (fama).

nombrado, da *adj* famous, renowned, well-known (célebre) || aforementioned (susodicho) || *nombrado más adelante* hereinafter mentioned.

nombramiento *m* appointment (designación para un cargo) || confirmation of appointment (título).

nombrar *vt* to appoint; *nombrar a alguien para un cargo* to appoint s.o. to a post; *nombrar a alguien alcalde* to appoint s.o. (as) mayor || to name, to mention (mencionar) || JUR to name, to appoint (un heredero) || MIL to commission.

nombre *m* GRAM noun (sustantivo); *nombre común, propio* common, proper noun || name, Christian name, first name (nombre de pila) || name (apellido y nombre de pila); *su nombre es John Smith* his name is John Smith || FIG name (fama); *hacerse un nombre* to make a name for o.s. || — *caer en el nombre de una persona* to remember s.o.'s name || *dar un nombre a* to give a name to, to call || *decir el nombre de* to name, to say the name of; *decir el nombre de sus cómplices* to name one's accomplices || *de nombre* in name only; *rey de nombre* king in name only; called, named; *un chico, Pedro de nombre* a boy called Peter; by name; *le conozco sólo de nombre* I know him only by name || *en nombre de* in the name of; *en nombre de la ley* in the name of the law; on behalf of; *dar las gracias en nombre del presidente* to give thanks on behalf of the president || *en nombre mío, tuyo, etc.* in my name, in your name, etc. || *le pusieron el nombre de su padre* they named him after his father || *llamar a las cosas por su nombre* to call a spade a spade || *nombre artístico, comercial* stage, trade name || *nombre de pila* Christian *o* first name || *nombre gentilicio* gentilic name || *nombre postizo* assumed name || *nombre y apellidos* full name, name in full || FIG *no tener nombre* to be unspeakable (ser incalificable) || *poner de nombre* to call; *mis padres me pusieron de nombre Úrsula* my parents called me Ursula || *por el nombre* by name; *llamar a alguien por el nombre* to call s.o. by name || *responder al nombre de* to answer to the name of || *sin nombre* unspeakable, nameless (incalificable).

nomenclador; nomenclátor *m* catalogue of names || *nomenclátor de calles* list of streets, street index.

nomenclatura *f* nomenclature.

nomeolvides *m inv* BOT forget-me-not (planta).

nómina *f* list (lista) || COM payroll (lista de personal) || — *cobrar la nómina* to be paid || *estar en nómina* to be on the staff || *nómina de salarios* payroll.

nominación *f* appointment, nomination.

nominal *adj* nominal; *valor nominal* nominal value || nominal, in name only; *el jefe nominal* the nominal leader || GRAM nominal, substantival.

nominalismo *m* FIL nominalism.

nominalista *adj* nominalist, nominalistic.
◆ *m/f* nominalist.

nominar *vt* to name, to call (nombrar).

nominativo, va *adj* GRAM nominative || COM nominal (título) | bearing a person's name (cheque).
◆ *m* GRAM nominative; *nominativo absoluto* nominative absolute.

nominilla *f* pay warrant, voucher.

non *adj* (p us) odd, uneven (impar).
◆ *m pl* odds; *jugar a pares y nones* to play odds and evens || — FIG & FAM *decir nones* to refuse point blank | *quedar de non* to be odd man out, to be left out, to be left without a partner.

nona *f* nones *pl* (hora canónica) || nones *pl* (del calendario romano).

nonada *f* trifle, trifling *o* unimportant thing.

nonagenario, ria *adj/s* nonagenarian, ninety-year-old.

nonagésimo, ma *adj/s* ninetieth || *nonagésimo primero, segundo* ninety-first, ninety-second.

nonato, ta *adj* born by Caesarian section || FIG unborn, nonexistant (que aún no existe).

noningentésimo, ma *adj/s* ninehundredth.

nonio *m* TECN nonius, vernier.

nono, na *adj* ninth || *décimo nono* nineteenth.

non plus ultra *loc lat* nec plus ultra.

nopal *m* BOT nopal, prickly pear.

noquear *vt* DEP to knock out (boxeo).

noray; norai *m* MAR bollard.

nordeste *adj* northeast, northeastern (parte) || northeasterly (dirección, viento).
◆ *m* northeast || northeasterly (viento) || — *nordeste cuarta al este* northeast by east || *nordeste cuarta al norte* northeast by north.

nórdico, ca *adj* Northern (del Norte) || Nordic (escandinavo, etc.).
◆ *m/f* Northerner || Nordic (escandinavo, etc.).
◆ *m* Norse (idioma).

nordista *adj* Northern, unionist.
◆ *m/f* Northerner, Unionist (en la guerra de Secesión norteamericana).

noreste *m* ⟶ **nordeste.**

noria *f* noria, waterwheel (para sacar agua) || big wheel [US ferris wheel] (en una feria).

norirlandés, esa *adj* Northern Irish.
◆ *m/f* citizen of Northern Ireland.

norma *f* rule, norm, standard; *hay que respetar ciertas normas de conducta* certain norms of behaviour must be observed || principle, norm, rule (principio) || *normas de ortografía* spelling rules.

normal *adj* normal; *estado normal* normal state; *es normal que se disculpe* it is normal that he should apologize || QUÍM & MAT normal || — *Escuela Normal* Teacher's Training College [US Normal School] || *lo normal* the normal thing || *superior a lo normal* above normal, above average.
◆ *f* MAT normal (perpendicular) || Teacher's Training College [US Normal School] (escuela).

normalidad *f* normality || — *con normalidad* normally || *con toda normalidad* quite normally || *la situación en el país ha vuelto a la normalidad* the situation in the country has returned to normal, calm has been completely restored in the country.

normalización *f* normalization || standardization (en la industria).

normalizar *vt* to normalize, to restore to normal || to standardize (en la industria).
◆ *vpr* to return to normal.

Normandía *npr f* GEOGR Normandy.

normando, da *adj/s* Norman.
◆ *m* Norman French (lengua) || HIST Norseman (vikingo).

normativo, va *adj* normative.

nornordeste *adj/sm* north-northeast.

nornoroeste; nornorueste *adj/adv/sm* northnorthwest.

noroeste; norueste *adj* northwest, northwesterly, northwestern || — *noroeste cuarta al norte* northwest by north || *noroeste cuarta al oeste* northwest by west || *viento noroeste* northwest *o* northwesterly wind.
◆ *m* northwest.

norte *m* north || north wind, northerly wind (viento) || FIG aim, goal (objetivo); *la prosperidad del país debe ser nuestro norte* the prosperity of the country must be our aim | guide (orientación, guía) || — *del norte* northern; *las provincias del norte* the northern provinces; north; *África del Norte* North Africa; north, northerly; *viento del norte* northerly wind || MAR *norte cuarta al nordeste, al noroeste* north by northeast, by northwest | *norte de brújula* magnetic north || FIG *perder el norte* to lose one's bearings.
◆ *adj* north, northern; *el ala norte de la casa* the north wing of the house || northerly; *rumbo norte* northerly direction || north, northerly (viento).

norteafricano, na *adj/s* North African.

Norteamérica *npr f* GEOGR North America.

norteamericano, na *adj/s* American, North American (estadounidense).

nortear *vi* MAR to sail northwards (el buque) || to veer towards the north (el viento).

norteño, ña *adj* northern.
◆ *m/f* Northerner.

nórtico, ca *adj* nordic || northern.

Noruega *npr f* GEOGR Norway.

noruego, ga *adj/s* Norwegian.

norueste *adj/sm* ⟶ **noroeste.**

norvietnamita *m/f* North Vietnamese.

nos *pron pers de 1ª pers del pl m/f* us (complemento directo); *nos están llamando* they are calling us || us, to us (complemento indirecto); *nos dio caramelos* he gave us sweets, he gave sweets to us || us (forma reflexiva en imperativo); *sentémonos* let us sit down || ourselves (forma reflexiva en los demás tiempos); *nos estamos lavando* we are washing ourselves || [to] one another, [to] each other (forma pronominal); *nos queremos mucho* we love each other dearly; *nos escribimos a menudo durante el verano* we wrote to one another often during the summer || We (forma mayestática); *Nos, Carlos de Inglaterra* We, Charles of England || — *nos acostamos a las diez* we go to bed at ten || *nos lo compró* he bought it from us (de nosotros), he bought it for us (para nosotros) || *ruega por nos* pray for us || *venga a nos en tu reino* thy kingdom come (en el padrenuestro).

nosocomio *m* hospital.

nosotros, tras *pron pers de 1ª pers del pl m/f* we (sujeto); *nosotros somos ingleses* we are English || us (complemento); *vino con nosotros* he came with us || — *entre nosotros* between ourselves, between the two of us, between you and me (confidencialmente) || *para nosotros* for us; *lo hizo para nosotros* he did it for us; ourselves (reflexivo); *no compramos nada para nosotros* we didn't buy anything for ourselves || *somos nosotros* or *nosotras* it is we, it is us || *somos nosotros* or *nosotras quienes* or *los que* or *las que* we are the ones who, it is we who.
— OBSERV Since in Spanish the verb can be used without a subject pronoun (*iremos* we shall go), the use of *nosotros* as the subject implies a certain emphasis.

nostalgia *f* nostalgia.

nostálgico, ca *adj* nostalgic.

nóstico, ca *adj/s* Gnostic.

nota *f* note (anotación) ‖ footnote (al pie de una página) ‖ marginal note (al margen) ‖ note (apunte); *tomar notas* to take notes ‖ mark (en un ejercicio); *dar, sacar una mala nota* to give, to get a bad mark ‖ grade (en el bachillerato) ‖ class (en licenciatura) ‖ remark (observación) ‖ note (comunicación escrita); *nota diplomática* diplomatic note ‖ notice (reseña) ‖ MÚS note; *nota falsa* wrong note ‖ FIG note, touch; *dar una nota de elegancia* to add a touch of elegance ‖ — FIG & FAM *dar la nota* to make o.s. conspicuous (singularizarse), to lead the way, to set the fashion (dar el tono) ‖ FIG *de mala nota* of ill repute, with a bad reputation | *de nota* famous (célebre) ‖ FIG & FAM *forzar la nota* to go too far, to exaggerate ‖ FAM *ir para nota* to aim for a good pass mark ‖ *nota de gastos* expense account ‖ *nota de prensa* press release ‖ *notas de sociedad* society column ‖ *tomar nota de un pedido* to note down an order, to make a note of an order.

nota bene *f* note, nota bene, N. B.

notabilidad *f* noteworthiness, remarkableness ‖ notable (persona).

notabilísimo, ma *adj* very notable.

notable *adj* notable, remarkable, noteworthy; *una obra notable* a notable piece of work; *un abogado notable* a remarkable lawyer ‖ notable, appreciable (apreciable) ‖ considerable.
◆ *m* notable, worthy; *asamblea de notables* assembly of notables ‖ merit (en exámenes); *sacó un notable* he passed with merit.

notación *f* MAT & MÚS notation (signos) ‖ annotation (nota).

notar *vt* to notice, to note; *notar algo a primera vista* to notice sth. at first sight; *notar la diferencia* to note the difference; *notar una falta* to note a mistake ‖ to indicate, to point out (señalar) ‖ to mark (un escrito); *notar los errores al margen* to mark the mistakes in the margin ‖ to jot down, to take down (apuntar) ‖ to find; *te noto muy cambiado* I find you have changed a lot ‖ to feel; *noto que hay algo que no funciona bien* I feel that there is sth. wrong ‖ to criticize (criticar) ‖ — *hacer notar* to point out ‖ *hacerse notar* to stand out, to draw attention to o.s.
◆ *vpr* to feel; *me noto un poco extraño* I feel rather strange ‖ to show; *no se nota la mancha* the stain does not show ‖ to be apparent, to be able to be seen; *se nota cierto progreso económico* a certain amount of economic progress can be seen ‖ *no se nota* it does not show, you cannot tell, you would never know.

notaría *f* notarial profession ‖ notary's office (oficina).

notariado, da *adj* authenticated by a notary [US notarized].
◆ *m* body of notaries (corporación).

notarial *adj* notarial; *actas notariales* notarial deeds.

notario *m* commissioner for oaths (en Inglaterra); *ante notario* before a commissioner for oaths ‖ notary, solicitor (en los demás países excepto en Estados Unidos) ‖ notary public (en Estados Unidos) ‖ — *notario de diligencias* process server ‖ *pasante de notario* notary's clerk.

noticia *f* news, piece of news; *una mala noticia* bad news ‖ news item (en un periódico) ‖ — *circula la noticia de que...* it is rumoured that..., rumour has it that... ‖ *dar una noticia a alguien* to give s.o. some news *o* a piece of news (cualquier noticia), to break the news to s.o. (noticia importante) ‖ *es la primera noticia que tengo* it is the first I have heard of it ‖ FIG *¡esto es noticia!* there's a turnup for the books ‖ FIG *no tener noticia de* to have had no news from *o* of, not to have heard anything of, not to know anything about | *no tengo noticia* I've heard nothing about it, I have no idea ‖ FAM *noticia bomba* big news, sensational news ‖ *noticia necrológica* obituary (notice) ‖ *noticia remota* vague memory.
◆ *pl* news *sing*; *traer noticias* to bring news ‖ news *sing* (en la radio y la televisión) ‖ information *sing*; *según nuestras noticias* according to our information ‖ — *enviar a alguien a buscar noticias* to send s.o. for news ‖ *estar atrasado de noticias* to be out of date ‖ *las malas noticias llegan las primeras* no news is good news ‖ *tener noticias de uno* to hear from s.o.; *no tengo noticias suyas desde hace cinco años* I haven't heard from his for five years ‖ *últimas noticias* latest news.

noticiar *vt* to inform of, to notify.

noticiario *m* newscast, news bulletin (radio, televisión) ‖ newsreel (cine).

noticiero, ra *adj* news (periódico).
◆ *m/f* journalist, reporter (reportero).
◆ *m* newspaper (periódico).

notición *m* FAM sensational news, big news.

noticioso, sa *adj* well-informed ‖ learned (erudito) ‖ *noticioso de ello, corrió a contárselo a su padre* on hearing that *o* when he found out about that he ran to tell his father.

notificación *f* notification.

notificar *vt* to notify, to inform of.

notoriamente *adv* plainly, evidently (evidentemente).

notoriedad *f* fame (fama) ‖ notoriety (mala reputación).

notorio, ria *adj* famous, well-known (conocido) ‖ notorious; *un criminal notorio* a notorious criminal ‖ obvious (claro) ‖ — *notorio a todos* known by everyone ‖ *ser público y notorio* to be common knowledge.

noumeno *m* FIL noumenon.

nova *f* ASTR nova.

novación *f* JUR novation.

novar *vt* JUR to novate.

novatada *f* rough joke, ragging [US hazing] (broma pesada) ‖ beginner's blunder (acción de un novato) ‖ — *dar una novatada* to rag [US to haze] ‖ *pagar la novatada* to make a beginner's blunder.

novato, ta *adj* new, inexperienced; *novato en los negocios* new to *o* inexperienced in business.
◆ *m/f* novice, beginner.
◆ *m* recruit (en el ejército) ‖ fresher [US freshman] (en los colegios).

novecientos, tas *adj/s* nine hundred ‖ *mil novecientos* one thousand nine hundred, nineteen hundred (cifra), nineteen hundred (año).

novedad *f* newness, novelty; *la novedad de un producto* the newness of a product ‖ news (noticia) ‖ change (cambio); *sigue sin novedad* there is no change ‖ — *¿hay novedad?* have you heard anything?, anything new?, any news? ‖ *no es ninguna novedad* that is nothing new ‖ *sin novedad* no change, no news, nothing new (nada nuevo), safely, without incident; *aterrizó sin novedad* he landed without incident; nothing to report (militar); *sin novedad en el frente* nothing to report from the front ‖ FIG & FAM *tener novedad* to be expecting a happy event (una mujer) ‖ *tengo novedad* I have some news.
◆ *pl* latest fashions; *sólo vendemos novedades* we sell only the latest fashions.

novedoso, sa *adj* AMER novel.

novel *adj* new (nuevo).
◆ *m* beginner, novice, newcomer.

novela *f* novel; *novela por entregas* serialized novel ‖ FIG story (mentira) ‖ — *novela corta* short story ‖ *novela de capa y espada* cloak-and-dagger novel ‖ *novela de tesis* novel with a message ‖ *novela policiaca* detective story ‖ *novela radiofónica* radio serial ‖ *novela rosa* romance.

novelar *vt* to convert into novel form, to novelize.
◆ *vi* to write novels ‖ FIG to tell stories *o* fibs (mentir).

novelear *vi* FIG & FAM to exaggerate, to dramatize.

novelería *f* liking for all that is new (afición a novedades) ‖ liking for novels (afición a las novelas) ‖ romantic ideas.

novelero, ra *adj* curious about all that is new (amigo de novedades) ‖ fond of reading novels (aficionado a las novelas) ‖ highly imaginative (que tiene mucha imaginación).

novelesco, ca *adj* fictional (de la ficción) ‖ novelistic (referente a las novelas) ‖ novelesque; *situación novelesca* novelesque situation ‖ *género novelesco* fiction.

novelista *m/f* novelist.

novelística *f* fiction (género novelesco) ‖ art of writing novels ‖ novel (conjunto de novelas) ‖ treatise on the novel (tratado).

novelístico, ca *adj* fictional (de la ficción) ‖ novelistic (de la novela).

novelizar *vt* to novelize, to convert into novel form.

novelón *m* saga.

novena *f* novena.

novenario *m* first nine days of mourning (tiempo de luto) ‖ funeral service celebrated on the ninth day after a person's death ‖ novena, novenary (novena).

noveno, na *adj/s* ninth ‖ *la novena parte* a ninth.

noventa *adj/sm* ninety ‖ ninetieth (nonagésimo).

noventavo, va *adj/s* ninetieth (nonagésimo).

noventayochista *adj* of *o* relating to the generation of 1898 (de la generación del 98).
— OBSERV The *generación del 98* was a group of Spanish writers which formed after the loss of Cuba, Puerto Rico and the Philippines. *1898* marked the end of Spanish colonial power, and the writers were conscious of the isolation of their country, the failure of its policies and, at the same time, of its social, economic and artistic problems. The forerunners of the movement were Darra, Ganivet, Joaquín Costa and Macías Picavea and the most important figures in the *generación del 98* proper Unamuno, Azorín, Valle Inclán, Baroja, Antonio Machado, Ramiro de Maeztu and Benavente.

noventón, ona *adj* ninety-year-old, in one's nineties.
◆ *m/f* ninety-year-old, person in his (her) nineties.

novia *f* girlfriend (amiga) ‖ fiancée (prometida) ‖ bride (en el día de la boda) ‖ — *pedir a la novia* to ask for a girl's hand (in marriage) ‖ *traje de novia* wedding dress.

noviar *vi* AMER to be going out together, to be going out with s.o. (estar de novios).

noviazgo *m* courtship, engagement ‖ *han tenido un noviazgo de siete años* they have been going out together for seven years.

noviciado, da *m* REL noviciate ‖ FIG apprenticeship (aprendizaje).

novicio, cia *adj* FIG new; *novicio en los negocios* new to business.
◆ *m/f* REL novice ‖ FIG novice, apprentice, beginner (principiante).

noviembre *m* November; *el 11 de noviembre de 1918* the eleventh of November, 1918.

novilunio *m* new moon.

novilla *f* heifer.

novillada *f* TAUR bullfight with young bulls || herd of young bulls (rebaño).
— OBSERV In the *novillada* only young bulls and those unsuitable for the real *corridas* are used.

novillero *m* herdsman who cares for young bulls (vaquero) || TAUR apprentice matador [one who has not yet received the «alternativa» || FAM truant.

novillo *m* young bull, bullock (animal) || FIG & FAM *hacer novillos* to play truant [US to play hooky] (no ir a clase).

novio *m* boyfriend (amigo) || fiancé (prometido) || groom, bridegroom (en el día de la boda) || — *los novios* the newlyweds (recién casados), the bride and groom (antes de la ceremonia) || FIG *quedarse compuesta y sin novio* to be left in the lurch *o* high and dry (quedarse sin algo después de tenerlo preparado), to be jilted (los novios) || *ser novios formales* to be engaged || *viaje de novios* honeymoon.
— OBSERV La palabra *fiancé* se aplica solamente cuando existe un compromiso matrimonial.

novísimo, ma *adj* very new, brand new || latest (último) || *Novísima Recopilación* revised code of Spanish law, completed in 1845.
◆ *m pl* REL end *sing* of one's life [death, judgment, hell, heaven].

novocaína *f* QUÍM novocaine.

nubada; nubarrada *f* sudden shower, downpour (chaparrón) || FIG crowd, abundance (multitud).

nubarrado, da *adj* watered, moiré (tela); *seda nubarrada* watered silk.

nubarrón *m* large storm cloud.

nube *f* cloud || cloud (de polvo, de humo, etc.) || FIG swarm, cloud; *nube de langostas* cloud of locusts | swarm, crowd; *una nube de chiquillos* a swarm of little boys | cloud; *no hay una nube en mi felicidad* there is not a single cloud on my horizon || cloud (en una piedra preciosa) || MED cloud, film (en la córnea de los ojos) || — FIG *caer de las nubes* to wake up | *como caído de las nubes* out of the blue | *descargar la nube* to rain (llover), to hail (granizar), to explode with anger (desahogar la cólera) | *estar en las nubes* to be daydreaming | *estar por las nubes* to be sky-high (precios) | *nube de verano* passing cloud (disgusto pasajero) | *pasar como una nube de verano* to be short-lived | *poner en* or *por las nubes* to praise to the skies (ensalzar), to make (prices) soar *o* rocket (los precios) | *ponerse por las nubes* to praise o.s. to the skies (ensalzarse), to soar, to rocket (los precios).

núbil *adj* nubile.

nubilidad *f* nubility.

nublado, da *adj* cloudy (con algunas nubes); *un cielo nublado* a cloudy sky || overcast (cubierto de nubes).
◆ *m* cloud || FIG menace, threat (amenaza) | crowd (multitud) | anger (enfado).

nublar *vt* to cloud || FIG to cloud, to mar; *la discusión nubló la alegría reinante* the argument marred everyone's happiness.
◆ *vpr* to cloud over (el cielo) || FIG to cloud over; *se me ha nublado la vista* my eyes have clouded over.

nubloso, sa *adj* cloudy (nublado) || FIG unlucky.

nubosidad *f* cloudiness.

nuboso, sa *adj* cloudy.

nuca *f* nape || *golpe en la nuca* rabbit punch.

nuclear *adj* nuclear; *armas nucleares* nuclear weapons.

nucleico, ca *adj* nucleic; *ácido nucleico* nucleic acid.

nucleína *f* nuclein.

núcleo *m* kernel, stone [US pit] (hueso de una fruta) || FÍS nucleus; *núcleo atómico* atomic nucleus || ASTR, BIOL & QUÍM nucleus || ELECTR core (de una bobina) || FIG nucleus, hard core (elemento central) | central point (punto central) || — *núcleo de población* centre of population || INFORM *núcleo magnético* magnetic core || *núcleo residencial* residential area, housing estate.

nucléolo *m* BIOL nucleolus.

nucleón *m* FÍS nucleon.

nucleónico, ca *adj* FÍS nucleonic.
◆ *f* FÍS nucleonics.

nucleoplasma *m* BIOL nucleoplasm.

nucleoproteína *f* BIOL nucleoprotein.

nudillo *m* knuckle (articulación de los dedos) || TECN plug || FIG *comerse* or *morderse los nudillos* to bite one's nails [with impatience, etc.].

nudismo *m* nudism.

nudista *adj/s* nudist.

nudo, da *adj* JUR *nuda propiedad* ownership without usufruct, bare ownership | *nudo propietario* owner without usufruct, bare owner.

nudo *m* knot (de cuerda, de corbata, de árbol) || french knot (costura) || centre; *nudo de comunicaciones* communications centre || junction; *nudo ferroviario* railway junction || FIG bond, tie, link (vínculo) | crux; *el nudo de la cuestión* the crux of the problem; *el nudo de la novela* the crux of the novel || ANAT knot || MAR knot (unidad de velocidad); *navegar a quince nudos* to sail at fifteen knots || — *nudo corredizo* slipknot || *nudo de carreteras* intersection || *nudo gordiano* Gordian knot || *nudo plano* or *llano* reef knot || *tener un nudo en la garganta* to have a lump in one's throat.

nudosidad *f* MED nodosity.

nudoso, sa *adj* knotted, knotty (madera) || gnarled (tronco, bastón) || gnarled (mano).

nuera *f* daughter-in-law.

nuestro, tra *adj pos m/f* our; *nuestro país* our country; *nuestra casa* our house; *nuestros amigos* our friends || of ours, our; *un coche nuestro* a car of ours, one of our cars || — *en nuestro país, en nuestra casa* in our country, at home || *Nuestra Señora* Our Lady || *Padre nuestro que estás en los cielos* our Father which art in Heaven (en el padrenuestro) || *¡ya es nuestro!* we have got him *o* it.
◆ *pron pos* ours; *vuestra casa es mayor que la nuestra* your house is bigger than ours; *esta casa es nuestra* this house is ours.
◆ *m* *lo nuestro* (what is) ours || *pondremos de lo nuestro* we shall do our best, we shall put our best foot forward || *vayamos a lo nuestro* let us get back to the point *o* to the matter in hand.
◆ *pl* *los nuestros* our side, our friends, ours (nuestros amigos); *¿es usted de los nuestros?* are you one of our friends?, are you one of ours?, are you on our side?; our family, our people (nuestra familia).

nueva *f* piece of news || *la Buena Nueva* the Good News.
◆ *pl* news *sing*, tidings (noticias) || FIG *hacerse de nuevas* to feign surprise.

Nueva Delhi *npr f* GEOGR New Delhi.

nuevamente *adv* newly, recently (recientemente) || again, anew (de nuevo).

Nueva Escocia *npr f* GEOGR Nova Scotia.

Nueva York *n pr* GEOGR New York.

nueve *adj/sm* nine; *en este cuarto hay nueve personas* there are nine people in this room || ninth; *el nueve de agosto* the ninth of August || — *a las nueve* at nine o'clock || *son las nueve de la noche* it is nine p. m.

nuevo, va *adj* new; *casa nueva* new house; *luna nueva* new moon; *alumno nuevo* new pupil || — *Año Nuevo* New Year || *de nuevo* again (otra vez), new; *estar vestido de nuevo* to be wearing new clothes; *¿qué hay de nuevo?* what's new? || *el coche está nuevo* the car is as good as new || *¿es nueva esta técnica para ti?* are you new to this technique? || *no hay nada nuevo bajo el Sol* there's nothing new under the sun || *Nueva Caledonia, Guinea, Inglaterra, Orleáns, Zelanda* New Caledonia, Guinea, England, Orleans, Zealand || *ser nuevo en el oficio* to be new to the job.
◆ *m* *lo nuevo* new things *pl*; *lo nuevo gusta siempre* people always like new things; the new; *tirar lo viejo y quedarse con lo nuevo* to throw out the old and keep the new.

nuez *f* walnut (del nogal) || nut (en general); *cascar nueces* to crack nuts; *nuez de corojo* corozo nut || ANAT Adam's apple (en la garganta) || MÚS nut (de violín) || sear (de ballesta, de fusil) || — FAM *apretar a uno la nuez* to wring s.o.'s neck | *mucho ruido y pocas nueces* much ado about nothing || *nuez moscada* nutmeg || *nuez vómica* nux vomica.

nulamente *adv* in vain, with no effect, to no avail.

nulidad *f* JUR nullity || incompetence, incapacity || FAM *ser una nulidad* to be a nonentity, to be useless (ser un incapaz).

nulípara *adj* MED nulliparous.
◆ *f* MED nullipara.

nulo, la *adj* useless; *hombre nulo* useless man || void, null and void (sin valor) || zero, nonexistent (no existente) || — DEP *combate nulo* draw (boxeo, lucha) || JUR *nulo y sin valor* null and void.
◆ *pl* misère *sing* (en bridge).

numantino, na *adj/s* Numantian.

numen *m* divinity, numen (dios) || inspiration, muse; *numen poético* poetic inspiration.

numeración *f* numeration || numbering (acción de poner números) || numbers *pl*; *han cambiado la numeración de la calle* the house numbers have been changed || numerals *pl* (sistema); *numeración arábiga, romana* Arabic, Roman numerals || IMPR pagination.

numerador *m* MAT numerator || TECN numbering machine (aparato).

numeral *adj* numeral.

numerar *vt* to count (contar) || to number (poner un número) || IMPR to paginate.

numerario, ria *adj* numerary.
◆ *m* hard cash, cash, money (dinero).

numérico, ca *adj* numerical || INFORM digital, numeric.

número *m* number (cantidad); *un número crecido de alumnos* an increased number of pupils; *número de votos* number of votes || figure, numeral (cifra); *número romano* Roman numeral || number (en una serie); *número premiado* winning number || number, copy, issue (ejemplar de una publicación); *número atrasado* back number || TEATR number, act; *hacer un número cómico* to do a comedy act || FIG piece of outrageous behaviour, thing done to attract attention || size (medida de los zapatos, cuellos, guantes, etc.) || GRAM number; *número singular, plural* singular, plural number || — *académico de número* member of the Academy || *áureo número* golden number || *de número* regular, titular || *el mayor número de* the majority of, the greatest number of || ECON *estar en números rojos* to be in the red || *en gran número* in large numbers || *en números redondos* in round numbers *o* figures || *hacer número* to make up the number || FAM *hacer números* to reckon up || FIG *hacer un número* to do sth. outrageous [to attract attention] || *ley de los grandes números* law of large numbers || *libro de los Números* Book of Numbers (del Pentateuco) || FIG & FAM *montar el número* to kick up a fuss, to make a scene, to throw a fit || FÍS *número atómico* atomic number || *número cardinal, ordinal* cardinal, ordinal number || *número complementario* complementary number [lottery] || *número de matrícula* registration number (de un coche) || *número de referencia* reference number || GRAM *número dual* dual number || *número entero* whole number || *número extraordinario* special edition (de una publicación) || *número impar* odd number || *número mixto* fraction || *número par* even number || *número primo* prime number || *número quebrado* or *fraccionario* fraction || *número redondo* round number *o* figure || *número suelto* number, edition (periódico) || FIG *número uno* the best, (the) number one (el mejor) | *sin número* countless || FAM *¡vaya número!* what a carry on!

numerosidad *f* numerosity.

numeroso, sa *adj* numerous, many; *hay numerosos pueblos por el estilo* there are numerous villages like that || *familia numerosa* large family.

numismático, ca *adj* numismatic.
◆ *m/f* numismatist (perito en numismática).
◆ *f* numismatics.

numulita *f* nummulite (fósil).

nunca *adv* never; *no volveré nunca, nunca volveré* I shall never come back || ever; *¿has conocido nunca a tal hombre?* have you ever known such a man? || — *casi nunca* hardly ever || *¡hasta nunca!* farewell for ever! || *más que nunca* more than ever || *nunca jamás* never ever, never (emphatic form of «nunca») || *nunca más* never again, no more, nevermore.

nunciatura *f* nunciature.

nuncio *m* nuncio; *nuncio apostólico* papal nuncio || FIG omen, portent, forerunner (presagio); *este viento es nuncio de lluvia* this wind is an omen of rain || bearer; *ha sido el nuncio de la buena nueva* he was the bearer of the good tidings || — FAM *¡cuéntaselo al nuncio!* tell that to the marines! | *¡que te lo diga el nuncio!* don't ask me! || *que te lo haga el nuncio* don't ask me to do it.

nupcial *adj* nuptial, wedding || — *banquete nupcial* wedding breakfast || *galas nupciales* wedding dress *sing* || *marcha nupcial* wedding march.

nupcialidad *f* marriage rate.

nupcias *f pl* nuptials, wedding *sing* || — *contraer segundas nupcias* to remarry, to marry for the second time || *hijos de segundas nupcias* children of a second marriage.

nurse *f* nurse (niñera).

nutación *f* ASTR & BOT nutation.

nutria; nutra *f* ZOOL otter (mamífero).

nutricio, cia *adj* nutritious || foster (padre).

nutrición *f* nutrition.

nutrido, da *adj* nourished, fed (alimentado) || FIG large, abundant; *nutrida asistencia* large attendance | loud; *aplausos nutridos* loud applause || — MIL *fuego nutrido* heavy fire (graneado) || *mal nutrido* undernourished || FIG *nutrido de* full of.

nutrimento; nutrimiento *m* nourishment, nutriment.

nutrir *vt* to nourish, to feed || FIG to feed; *los recuerdos nutren su odio* his memories feed his hatred.
◆ *vpr* to feed, to live; *nutrirse de* to live on.

nutritivo, va *adj* nutritious || *el valor nutritivo de un alimento* a food's nutritional value, the food value of a product.

ny *f* nu (letra griega).

nylon *m* nylon (tejido); *camisa de nylon* nylon shirt.

Ñ

ñ *f* ñ (esta letra no existe en el alfabeto inglés).
— OBSERV The sound is that of the *ni* in onion.

ña *f* FAM *AMER* ⟶ **doña.**

ñacanina *f* *AMER* large poisonous snake.

ñaco *m* *AMER* porridge (gachas).

ñacurutú *m* *AMER* owl (lechuza).

ñame *m* BOT yam (planta) ‖ *AMER* FIG & FAM hoof, foot (pie).

ñandú *m* ZOOL rhea, nandu.

ñandubay *m* *AMER* nandubay.

ñandutí *m* *AMER* nanduti [lace made mainly in Paraguay].

ñango, ga *adj* *AMER* ungraceful, ungainly | weak (débil).

ñaña *f* *AMER* elder sister | nursemaid (niñera).

ñapa *f* *AMER* ⟶ **llapa.**

ñapango, ga *adj* mulatto.
◆ *m/f* mulatto, mestizo.

ñapindá *m* BOT mimosa.

ñato, ta *adj* *AMER* snub-nosed (chato) ‖ *AMER* FIG ugly (feo).

ñeque *adj* *AMER* strong, vigorous.
◆ *m* strength, vigour ‖ *hombre de ñeque* brave man.

ñiquiñaque *m* FAM piece of junk (cosa) | good-for-nothing (persona).

ñisñil *m* *AMER* BOT cattail (anea).

ño *m* *AMER* FAM mister (señor).

ñoclo *m* CULIN macaroon.

ñoñería; ñoñez *f* insipidity (sosería) ‖ prudery (mojigatería) ‖ fussiness, whining (melindrería).

ñoño, ña *adj* insipid (soso) ‖ prudish, straight-laced (mojigato) ‖ finnicky, fussy, whining (melindroso).
◆ *m/f* whiner, drip (*fam*), insipid character.

ñoqui *m* CULIN gnocchi.

ñorbo *m* *AMER* BOT passionflower.

ñu *m* ZOOL gnu (antílope).

ñudo *m* (ant) knot (nudo) ‖ *AMER al ñudo* in vain (en vano).

O

o *f* o (letra); *una o mayúscula, minúscula* a capital, small o ‖ *no saber hacer la o con un canuto* not to know a thing.

— OBSERV The Spanish *o* is pronounced like the *o* in the English word *hot.*

o *conj* or ‖ — *o... o* either... or; *iremos al teatro o al cine* we shall go either to the theatre or to the cinema ‖ *o sea* in other words, that is to say, that is ‖ *o sea que* in other words, so, that is to say (en conclusión).

— OBSERV When used between two numbers, *o* takes a written accent in order to avoid any possible confusion with zero: *10 ó 12* ten or twelve. *U* is used in place of *o* when the word following begins with *o* or *ho*: *siete u ocho* seven or eight; *uno u otro* one or the other; *ayer u hoy* yesterday or today.

oasis *m inv* oasis.

obcecación *f* blindness.

obcecado, da *adj* blinded; *obcecado por la pasión* blinded by passion ‖ obstinate.

obcecar *vt* to blind (ofuscar).
◆ *vpr* to be blinded.

obedecer* *vt* to obey; *obedecer las órdenes* to obey (the) orders; *obedecer al superior* to obey one's superior; *obedecer las leyes* to obey the law.
◆ *vi* to do as one is told, to obey; *calla y obedece* be quiet and do as you are told ‖ to respond; *la enfermedad obedeció a los medicamentos* the illness responded to the medicine ‖ — *esta reunión obedece a varias razones* this meeting has been called for a number of reasons ‖ *hacerse obedecer* to obtain *o* to command obedience ‖ *mi visita obedece a una razón* there is a reason for my visit ‖ *obedecer al hecho de que* to be due to.

obediencia *f* obedience.

obediente *adj* obedient.

obelisco *m* obelisk ‖ IMPR dagger, obelisk.

obencadura *f* MAR shrouds *pl*, set of shrouds.

obenque *m* MAR shroud.

obertura *f* MÚS overture.

obesidad *f* obesity.

obeso, sa *adj* obese.
◆ *m/f* obese person.

óbice *m* obstacle, impediment ‖ *eso no fue óbice para que siguiese mi camino* that did not prevent me from continuing on my way.

obispado *m* bishopric.

obispal *adj* episcopal.

obispalía *f* bishopric (obispado) ‖ episcopal palace.

obispo *m* bishop ‖ — *obispo auxiliar* auxiliary bishop ‖ FAM *trabajar para el obispo* to work for nothing.

óbito *m* decease, demise.

obituario *m* obituary (en un periódico).

objeción *f* objection; *levantar* or *poner una objeción* to raise an objection.

objetar *vt/vi* to object; *le objeté que no lo podríamos hacer* I objected that we should not be able to do it ‖ to object to (oponerse a) ‖ *no tengo nada que objetar* I have no objection *o* no objections.

objetivación *f* objectification.

objetivar *vt* to objectify.

objetividad *f* objectivity ‖ *con objetividad* objectively, with objectivity.

objetivismo *m* objectivism.

objetivo, va *adj* objective.
◆ *m* objective, aim, goal, end (finalidad); *perseguir un objetivo* to pursue a goal ‖ MIL target, objective ‖ FÍS objective ‖ FOT lens; *objetivo gran angular* wide-angle lens; *objetivo zoom* zoom lens.

objeto *m* object; *un objeto voluminoso* a large *o* cumbersome object ‖ object, aim, purpose, end (finalidad) ‖ theme, subject (tema) ‖ GRAM object ‖ INFORM object ‖ — *carecer de* or *no tener objeto* to be useless *o* of no purpose ‖ *con* or *al objeto de* in order to, to, with the aim of ‖ *¿con qué objeto?* to what end?, for what purpose? ‖ *con* or *a tal objeto* to this end, for this purpose ‖ *depósito de objetos perdidos* lost property office [US lost and found office] ‖ *hacerle a alguien objeto de* to make s.o. the object of ‖ *objetos de escritorio* writing materials ‖ *objetos de regalo* gifts, presents ‖ *ser objeto de* to be the object of ‖ *sin objeto* uselessly, pointlessly (adverbio), useless, pointless (adjetivo) ‖ *tiene por objeto* his aim is (persona), its purpose is, its aim is (cosa).

objetor *m* objector; *objetor de conciencia* conscientious objector.

oblación *f* oblation.

oblato, ta *adj/s* REL oblate.
◆ *f* REL oblation.

oblea *f* CULIN & REL wafer ‖ MED capsule (sello).

oblicuángulo, la *adj* oblique-angled.

oblicuar *vi* to slant ‖ MIL to incline (*hacia* to).
◆ *vt* to slant, to put into an oblique position.

oblicuidad *f* obliquity.

oblicuo, cua *adj* oblique, slanting ‖ MAT oblique ‖ *mirada oblicua* sidelong glance.
◆ *m* ANAT oblique (músculo).
◆ *f* MAT oblique (línea).

obligación *f* obligation (deber) ‖ duty, obligation; *conocer sus obligaciones* to know one's duties; *cumplir con sus obligaciones* to fulfil one's obligations ‖ obligation; *obligaciones matrimoniales* marital obligations ‖ constraint, obligation; *obligaciones sociales* social constraints ‖ COM bond; *obligación del Estado* Treasury bond ‖ — *antes es la obligación que la devoción* business before pleasure ‖ *faltar a sus obligaciones* to fail in one's duty ‖ *tener obligación de* to have to, to be under an obligation to.

obligacionista *m/f* COM bondholder.

obligado, da *adj* obliged; *estar* or *verse obligado a trabajar* to be obliged to work ‖ compulsory, obligatory (obligatorio); *la asistencia no es obligada* attendance is not obligatory ‖ — *es obligado decir* it is necessary to say ‖ *estar obligado a alguien* to be obliged to s.o.
◆ *m* supplier (abastecedor).

obligar *vt* to oblige, to compel, to force; *obligar a alguien a entregarse* to oblige s.o. to give himself up ‖ to force (empujar); *hay que obligarlo para que entre* one must force it to get it in.
◆ *vpr* to put o.s. under an obligation, to bind o.s. (comprometerse).

obligatoriedad *f* obligatoriness, compulsoriness.

obligatorio, ria *adj* obligatory, compulsory.

obliteración *f* MED obliteration.

obliterador, ra *adj* MED obliterating.

obliterar *vt* MED to obliterate (obstruir).

oblito *m* MED foreign body [left in patient after operation].

oblongo, ga *adj* oblong.

obnubilación *f* obnubilation.

oboe *m* MÚS oboe (instrumento) | oboist (oboísta).

oboísta *m/f* MÚS oboist (músico).

óbolo *m* mite; *dar su óbolo* to give one's mite.

obra *f* work (trabajo); *poner manos a la obra* to get down to work ‖ piece of work; *la mesa que ha hecho es una obra preciosa* the table he has made is a beautiful piece of work ‖ work (libro, pieza musical, cuadro, etc.); *una obra de Calderón* a work by Calderón ‖ works *pl*, œuvre (producción total); *su obra es muy extensa* he has a very large œuvre, he has written many works ‖ work (buena acción); *obras de beneficencia* charitable works; *buenas obras* good works ‖ work (poder); *por obra de la Divina Providencia* by work of Divine Providence ‖ act (acto) ‖ workmanship (ejecución); *en esta pulsera tiene más valor la obra que los materiales* the value of this bracelet lies more in the workmanship than in the materials used ‖ work; *obra de mampostería* masonry work ‖ work; *obras públicas* public works ‖ building site, construction site; *hay una obra frente a mi casa* there is a building site opposite my house ‖ TECN hearth [of a kiln furnace] ‖ — *al pie de la obra* delivered on site ‖ *atención, obras* danger, men at work (construcción de un edificio), roadworks ahead (en la carretera) ‖ *cerrado por obras* closed for repairs ‖ *contratista de obras* building contractor ‖ *contratista de obras públicas* public works contractor ‖ *de obra* in deed; *maltratar de obra* to mistreat in deed ‖ *estar de obras* to have workmen in; *los vecinos están de obras* the neighbours have got workmen in ‖ *estar en obras* to be under construction (en construcción), to be undergoing modifications (renovación), to be under repair (reparación) ‖ *maestro de obras* master builder ‖ *¡manos a la obra!* let's get down to work! ‖ *meterse en obras* to undertake a job ‖ *Ministerio de Obras Públicas* Ministry [US Department] of Public Works ‖ *obra de arte* work of art ‖ *obra de caridad* charitable deed *o* work ‖ *obra de construcción* construction *o* building site ‖ *obra de encargo* commissioned work ‖ *obra de hierro* ironwork ‖ FIG *obra de romanos* Herculean task ‖ *obra de teatro* (stage) play ‖ *obra exterior* outwork (fortificación) ‖ *obra maestra* masterpiece ‖ MAR *obra muerta* upperworks ‖ *obra pía* religious foundation (fundación religiosa), charity, charitable institution (institución de beneficencia) ‖ *obras completas* complete works, collected works ‖ *obras pías* charity ‖ *obras son amores, que no buenas razones* actions speak louder than words ‖ MAR *obra viva* quickwork ‖ *poner algo en* or *por obra* to carry out sth. ‖ *por obra de* thanks to ‖ *por obra y gracia del Espíritu Santo* by the grace of God.

obrador, ra *adj* working (que obra).
◆ *m* workshop (taller).

obrar *vt* to do (hacer); *obrar el bien* to do good ‖ to work (la madera) ‖ to have an effect on (una medicina) ‖ to build, to construct (construir) ‖ to work, to bring about (milagros, etc.).
◆ *vi* to act (actuar); *obrar libremente* to act freely; *obrar como una persona honrada* to act honourably ‖ to behave (comportarse) ‖ to act, to do; *obrar bien, mal* to act well, badly ‖ to proceed; *obré según lo previsto* I proceeded as planned ‖ to work, to have an effect; *el remedio comienza a obrar* the remedy is beginning to have an effect ‖ FAM to do one's duty (exonerar el vientre) ‖ to be; *el papel obra en sus manos* the paper is in his hands ‖ *obra en mi poder su atenta carta del 19* I acknowledge receipt of *o* I have received your letter of the 19th.

obrerada *f* FAM workmen *pl*, workers *pl*.

obrería *f* funds *pl* [for the upkeep of a church].

obrerismo *m* labour movement [US labor movement] (movimiento obrero) ‖ workmen *pl*, workers *pl* (conjunto de obreros).

obrero, ra *adj* working; *clase obrera* working class ‖ labour [US labor]; *sindicato obrero* labour union ‖ worker (insecto).
◆ *m/f* worker (en una fábrica).
◆ *m* workman, labourer [US laborer] (fuera de una fábrica) ‖ labourer [US laborer] (en el campo) ‖ churchwarden (de iglesia).
◆ *f* ZOOL worker (abeja, etc.) ‖ — *obrero especializado* skilled workman ‖ *obrero estacional* or *temporero* seasonal *o* temporary worker ‖ *obrero portuario* dock worker, docker.

obscenidad *f* obscenity.

obsceno, na *adj* obscene.

obscuramente *adv* → **oscuramente.**

obscurantismo *m* → **oscurantismo.**

obscurantista *adj/s* → **oscurantista.**

obscurecer *vt* → **oscurecer.**

obscurecimiento *m* → **oscurecimiento.**

obscuridad *f* → **oscuridad.**

obscuro, ra *adj* → **oscuro.**

obseder *vt* to obsess.

obsequiado, da *adj* who receives a gift ‖ in whose honour a reception is held.
◆ *m/f* receiver of a gift ‖ guest of honour.

obsequiador, ra; obsequiante *adj* attentive, obliging (obsequioso) ‖ who gives (que regala).
◆ *m/f* host ‖ giver (que regala).

obsequiar *vt* to give, to offer, to bestow upon; *obsequiar a un amigo con libros* to give books to *o* to bestow books upon a friend ‖ to offer; *obsequiar con una copa de vino español* to offer a glass of Spanish wine to ‖ to hold (sth.) in s.o.'s honour; *obsequiar a alguien con un banquete* to hold a banquet in s.o.'s honour ‖ to lavish attention on (agasajar) ‖ to court (galantear).

obsequio *m* gift, present (regalo) ‖ honour; *en obsequio del artista* in honour of the artist ‖ attention, kindness (agasajo) ‖ — *deshacerse en obsequios con uno* to lavish attention on s.o. ‖ *obsequio del autor* complimentary copy.

obsequiosamente *adv* obligingly ‖ obsequiously (con exceso).

obsequiosidad *f* obligingness ‖ obsequiousness (cumplidos excesivos).

obsequioso, sa *adj* obliging, attentive; *obsequioso con las damas* obliging with *o* attentive to the ladies ‖ obsequious (excesivamente atento).

observación *f* observation (de un fenómeno) ‖ observation, remark, comment (indicación) ‖ note, observation (nota aclaratoria) ‖ objection ‖ — *enfermo en observación* patient under observation ‖ *hacer una observación* to make a remark.

observador, ra *adj* observant.
◆ *m/f* observer.

observancia *f* observance (de las reglas) ‖ *regular observancia* strict observance.

observante *adj* observing (que observa) ‖ observant (que cumple preceptos).
◆ *m/f* observer.
◆ *m* observant (de la orden de San Francisco).

observar *vt* to observe (mirar) ‖ to observe (cumplir) ‖ to notice, to observe; *he observado que ha cambiado mucho últimamente* I have noticed that he has changed a lot lately ‖ to observe, to remark (comentar).
◆ *vpr* to be noted.

observatorio *m* observatory.

obsesión *m* obsession ‖ *tener la obsesión de la muerte* to be obsessed with death.

obsesionante *adj* obsessive.

obsesionar *vt* to obsess; *obsesionado por los recuerdos* obsessed with *o* by memories.

obsesivo, va *adj* obsessive (que obsesiona) ‖ obsessional; *psicosis obsesiva* obsessional psychosis.

obseso, sa *adj* obsessed.
◆ *m/f* obsessed person.

obsidiana *f* MIN obsidian.

obsoleto, ta *adj* obsolete (anticuado).

obstaculizar *vt* to hinder, to hamper; *obstaculizar el movimiento* to hinder (s.o.'s) movement ‖ to obstruct, to block; *obstaculizar el paso* to obstruct the way.

obstáculo *m* obstacle; *superar* or *vencer un obstáculo* to overcome an obstacle ‖ — DEP *carrera de obstáculos* obstacle race (atletas), steeplechase (caballos) | *carrera sin obstáculos* flat race | *poner obstáculos a* to obstruct, to hinder, to put obstacles in the way of.

obstante (no) *adv* nevertheless, however, notwithstanding (sin embargo) ‖ all the same (de todos modos).
◆ *prep* in spite of, despite (a pesar de); *no obstante mis consejos hace lo que le da la gana* in spite of my advice he does as he pleases.

obstar *vi* to hinder, to obstruct (estorbar) ‖ to prevent (impedir); *eso no obsta para que continúe* that does not prevent my continuing.

obstetricia *f* MED obstetrics.

obstétrico, ca *adj* MED obstetric, obstetrical (relativo a la obstetricia).

obstinación *f* obstinacy, stubbornness (terquedad) ‖ steadfastness (tenacidad).

obstinado, da *adj* obstinate, stubborn (terco) ‖ steadfast (tenaz).

obstinarse *vpr* to become obstinate ‖ to persist; *se obstina en negarlo* he persists in denying it ‖ to stick to; *obstinarse en una decisión* to stick to a decision.

obstrucción *f* obstruction ‖ *tácticas de obstrucción* obstruction tactics.

obstruccionismo *m* obstructionism.

obstruccionista *adj/s* obstructionist.

obstructor *adj* MED obstruent.
◆ *m/f* obstructor.

obstruir* *vt* to obstruct, to block (cerrar) ‖ FIG to obstruct, to hinder, to impede, to interfere with (estorbar).
◆ *vpr* to get blocked (up) *se obstruyó el lavabo* the washbasin got blocked up.

obtemperar *vt* to obey, to comply with; *obtemperar una orden* to obey an order.

obtención *f* obtaining, obtention.

obtener* *vt* to obtain, to get; *obtener buenos resultados* to obtain good results.

obturación *f* obturation, plugging (de un conducto) ‖ closing, sealing off (de una cavidad) ‖ filling (de una muela) ‖ FOT *velocidad de obturación* shutter speed.

obturador, ra *adj* obturating, closing.
◆ *m* plug, stopper (para tapar) ‖ FOT shutter; *obturador de cortina* roller-blind shutter ‖ ANAT & TECN obturator.

obturar *vt* to obturate, to plug ‖ to close (una cavidad) ‖ to fill (una muela).

obtusángulo *adj m* MAT obtuse-angled; *triángulo obtusángulo* obtuse-angled triangle.

obtuso, sa *adj* MAT obtuse ‖ FIG dull, obtuse ‖ *obtuso de entendimiento* dense, slow, obtuse.

obús *m* shell, obus (proyectil) ‖ howitzer (cañón corto).

obviar *vt* to obviate, to remove; *obviar un inconveniente* to obviate a drawback ‖ to impede, to hinder (impedir).

obvio, via *adj* clear, evident, obvious (evidente) ‖ *obvio es decir* needless to say, obviously.

oc *m* *lengua de oc* langue d'oc.

oca *f* goose (ánsar) ‖ *juego de la oca* snakes and ladders.

ocarina *f* MÚS ocarina.

ocasión *f* occasion, time; *en aquella ocasión estaba lloviendo* it was raining that time *o* on that occasion ‖ opportunity, chance; *se nos presentó la ocasión de ganar mucho dinero* we had the opportunity to make a lot of money; *perder una ocasión* to miss a chance; *aprovechar una ocasión* to take an opportunity, to make the most of an opportunity; *esta reunión me da la ocasión de saludarle* this meeting gives me an opportunity to greet you ‖ bargain (mercancía de lance) ‖ reason, cause, occasion, motive; *no dar ocasión de quejarse* not to give cause for complaint ‖ (ant) hazardous situation ‖ — *a la ocasión la pintan calva* make hay while the sun shines, strike while the iron is hot ‖ *asir* or *coger* or *agarrar la ocasión por los cabellos* or *por los pelos* to seize the opportunity by the scruff of the neck ‖ *con ocasión de* on the occasion of ‖ *dar ocasión a* to give rise to ‖ *dejar escapar una ocasión* to miss one's chance, to let an opportunity go by ‖ *de ocasión* secondhand (de segunda mano), bargain (de precio reducido), reduced [in price] (de precio rebajado) ‖ *en cierta ocasión* on a certain occasion ‖ *en la primera ocasión* at the first opportunity ‖ *en ocasiones* at times, sometimes ‖ *en varias ocasiones* on several occasions ‖ *la ocasión hace al ladrón* opportunity makes the thief.

ocasional *adj* occasional (que ocurre de vez en cuando) ‖ chance, accidental (fortuito); *un encuentro ocasional* a chance meeting.

ocasionalismo *m* occasionalism.

ocasionalista *adj* occasionalistic.
◆ *m/f* occasionalist.

ocasionalmente *adv* by chance, accidentally (por casualidad) || occasionally (de vez en cuando).

ocasionar *vt* to occasion, to cause (causar) || (p us) to jeopardize, to endanger (poner en peligro).

ocaso *m* sunset (momento del día) || setting (de un astro); *el ocaso del Sol* the setting of the sun || occident, west (occidente) || FIG decline (decadencia); *el ocaso de un imperio* the decline of an empire | end; *su ocaso se acerca* his end is nigh || FIG *en el ocaso de la vida* in the twilight of life, in one's later years.

occidental *adj* western; *el mundo occidental* the western world || west; *Berlín Occidental* West Berlin.
◆ *m/f* westerner, person from the West.
◆ *pl* people of the western world, the western world *sing*.

occidentalismo *m* Westernism, Occidentalism.

occidentalista *m/f* Occidentalist.

occidentalización *f* Westernization, Occidentalization.

occidentalizar *vt* to westernize, to occidentalize.

occidente *m* west, occident; *al occidente* towards the west || *el Occidente* the West.

occipital *adj/sm* ANAT occipital (hueso).

occipucio *m* ANAT occiput.

occisión *f* violent death, murder.

occiso, sa *adj* murdered.
◆ *m/f* deceased, murder victim, victim (persona matada violentamente).

OCDE *abrev de Organización para la Cooperación y el Desarrollo Económico* OECD, Organization for Economic Cooperation and Development.

Oceanía *npr f* GEOGR Oceania.

oceánico, ca *adj* oceanic (del océano) || Oceanian, Oceanic (de Oceanía).

oceanicultura *f* cultivation of produce from the sea.

Oceánida *f* Oceanid (ninfa).

océano *m* ocean; *el Océano Índico* the Indian Ocean || FIG Ocean, sea; *un océano de amargura* a sea of bitterness.

oceanografía *f* oceanography.

oceanográfico, ca *adj* oceanographic, oceanographical.

oceanógrafo, fa *m/f* oceanographer.

ocelo *m* ocellus (mancha, ojo).

ocelote *m* ocelot (mamífero).

ocio *m* idleness (inactividad) || leisure time, leisure, spare time (tiempo libre); *la ocupación del ocio* the occupation of leisure time || pastime (diversión) || *ratos de ocio* leisure, spare *o* leisure time.

ociosamente *adv* idly.

ociosear *vi* AMER to idle (holgazanear).

ociosidad *f* idleness || *la ociosidad es madre de todos los vicios* idleness is the root of all evil.

ocioso, sa *adj* idle; *vida ociosa* idle life; *palabras ociosas* idle words || lazy (holgazán) || pointless, useless (inútil).
◆ *m/f* idler.

ocluir *vt* to occlude.
◆ *vpr* to become occluded.

oclusión *f* occlusion || stop (en fonética) || MED *oclusión coronaria* coronary occlusion.

oclusivo, va *adj/sf* occlusive; *consonante oclusiva* occlusive consonant.

ocre *m* ochre [US ocher]; *ocre amarillo* yellow ochre; *ocre rojo* red ochre.
◆ *adj inv* ochreous.

octaédrico, ca *adj* MAT octahedral.

octaedro *m* MAT octahedron.

octagonal; octogonal *adj* MAT octagonal.

octágono, na *adj* MAT octagonal.
◆ *m* octagon.

octanaje *m* octane rating *o* number.

octano *m* QUÍM octane || *índice de octano* octane number.

octante *m* MAR & MAT octant.

octava *f* REL & POÉT & MÚS octave.

octaviano, na *adj* HIST Octavian; *paz octaviana* Octavian peace.

octavilla *f* octavo (octava parte de un pliego de papel) || pamphlet, leaflet (hoja de propaganda) || octet (estrofa).

Octavio *npr m* Octavian.

octavo, va *adj/s* eighth || — *en octavo* octavo (libro) || *Enrique VIII (octavo)* Henry VIII [the eighth] || *la octava parte* an eighth || DEP *octavos de final* fourth round [round preceding quarter-finals].

octeto *m* MÚS octet.

octingentésimo, ma *adj/s* eight hundredth || *octingentésimo aniversario* octigentenary.

octogenario, ria *adj/s* octogenarian, eighty-year-old.

octogésimo, ma *adj/s* eightieth || *octogésimo primero, segundo* eighty-first, eighty-second.

octogonal *adj* MAT ⟶ **octagonal.**

octógono, na *adj* MAT octagonal.
◆ *m* octagon.

octópodo, da *adj/sm* ZOOL octopod, octopodan.

octosilábico, ca *adj* octosyllabic.

octosílabo, ba *adj* octosyllabic.
◆ *m* octosyllable.

octubre *m* October; *Madrid, 6* or *a 6 de octubre de 1972* Madrid, 6th October, 1972.

ocular *adj* ocular || *testigo ocular* eyewitness.
◆ *m* eyepiece, ocular.

oculista *adj* *médico oculista* oculist.
◆ *m/f* oculist.

ocultación *f* dissimulation || ASTR occultation || concealment (encubrimiento) || JUR *ocultación de parto* concealment of a child.

ocultador, ra *adj* concealing.
◆ *m/f* concealer.
◆ *m* FOT mask.

ocultamente *adv* occultly (misteriosamente) || stealthily (a hurtadillas) || secretly (secretamente).

ocultar *vt* to hide, to conceal; *ocultar un objeto* to hide an object; *ocultar su juego* to conceal one's game || ASTR to occult || to conceal (encubrir) || *ocultar a* or *de la vista de alguien* to hide *o* to conceal from s.o., to put out of s.o.'s sight.
◆ *vpr* to hide; *ocultarse de sus padres* to hide from one's parents || ASTR to occult.

ocultis (de) *loc* FAM on the sly (a hurtadillas).

ocultismo *m* occultism.

ocultista *adj/s* occultist.

oculto, ta *adj* secret (secreto); *influencia oculta* secret influence || hidden, concealed (escondido) || ulterior; *motivo oculto* ulterior motive || — *ciencias ocultas* occult sciences *o* arts || *de oculto* stealthily.

ocume *m* okoume, okume (árbol).

ocupación *f* occupation, profession (empleo) || occupation (de un lugar) || MIL occupation; *la ocupación de una ciudad* the occupation of a city || *tener muchas ocupaciones* to have many activities.

ocupado, da *adj* occupied (casa, ciudad, etc.) || taken; *¿está ocupado el asiento?* is this seat taken? || busy (que tiene mucho que hacer) || engaged (el retrete).

ocupante *m/f* occupant, occupier || occupant (de un vehículo) || MIL occupier.

ocupar *vt* to take up, to occupy; *la lectura ocupa mis ratos de ocio* reading takes up my spare time || to keep (s.o.) occupied *o* busy, to give (s.o.) sth. to do (dar que hacer) || to occupy (un país, una fábrica, un piso) || to employ (emplear obreros) || to take over (apoderarse de) || to occupy, to hold (un puesto) || — *el armario ocupa demasiado espacio* the wardrobe takes up too much space || *ocupar la presidencia* to occupy the chair (en una reunión).
◆ *vpr* to look after (cuidar); *ocuparse de un niño* to look after a child || to do (hacer); *¿de qué se ocupa este señor?* what does this man do? || to be in charge of; *se ocupa de la seguridad* he is in charge of security || to deal with, to do sth. about, to see to; *tenemos que ocuparnos de esta cuestión* we have to deal with this question || to engage; *ocuparse en obras útiles* to engage in useful works || to see to, to attend to (atender); *ocuparse de un cliente, de un enfermo* to see to a client, to a patient || to pay attention to (hacer caso) || *¡ocúpate de tus cosas!* mind your own business!

ocurrencia *f* occurrence, event (acontecimiento) || FIG witticism (chiste) || idea; *¡tienes cada ocurrencia!* what funny ideas you get!; *¡vaya ocurrencia!* what a funny idea! || *tener ocurrencia* to be witty.

ocurrente *adj* FIG witty (chistoso, gracioso) | imaginative, full of ideas.

ocurrir *vi* to occur, to happen (acontecer); *eso ocurre todos los años* that occurs every year || — *ocurra lo que ocurra* happen what may || *¿qué ocurre?* what's the matter?, what's going on? || *¿qué ocurrió?* what happened? || *¿qué te ocurre?* what's the matter (with you)?
◆ *vpr* to occur, to come; *la idea se me ocurrió ayer* the idea occurred to me yesterday; *es lo único que se me ocurre* it is the only thing that occurs to me || to take it into one's head to; *de repente se le ocurrió irse* all of a sudden he took it into his head to go || — *a nadie se le ocurre hacer esto* nobody would think of doing this || *que no se te ocurra repetirlo* don't let it happen again || *¡se le ocurre cada cosa!* he gets some odd ideas || *se me ocurre que...* it occurs to me that...

ochavo *m* brass coin, farthing (moneda) || — *no tener ni un ochavo* not to have a brass farthing [US not to have a red cent] || *no valer un ochavo* not to be worth a brass farthing *o* a damn.

ochavón, ona *adj/s* octoroon.

ochenta *adj/s* eighty || eightieth (octogésimo).

ochentavo, va *adj/s* eightieth.

ochentón, ona *adj* FAM eighty-year-old, in one's eighties.
◆ *m/f* FAM eighty-year-old, person in his (her) eighties.

ocho *adj* eight; *ocho personas* eight people || eighth (octavo); *en el año ocho de su reinado* in the eighth year of his reign || eighthly (en el octavo lugar) || — *a las ocho* at eight o'clock, at eight || *aplazar para dentro de ocho días* to put off for a week || *unos ocho niños* some eight children, eight or so children, about eight children || *volver a los ocho días* to return in a week *o* in a week's time *o* after a week.
◆ *m* eight || FIG *más chulo que un ocho* as proud as a peacock.

ochocientos, tas *adj/sm* eight hundred; *cuatro mil ochocientos* four thousand eight hundred ‖ *mil ochocientos* eighteen hundred.

oda *f* ode.

odalisca *f* odalisque.

Odense *n pr* GEOGR Odense.

odeón *m* odeon, odeum.

odiar *vt* to hate, to detest, to loathe; *te odio* I hate you; *odio las multitudes* I hate crowds.

odio *m* hatred, hate ‖ — *mirada de odio* look of hate *o* of hatred, hateful look ‖ *por odio a* out of hatred for ‖ *tener odio a uno* to hate s.o., to feel hatred towards s.o. ‖ *tomar* or *cobrar odio a* to take an extreme dislike to, to begin to hate.

odiosidad *f* hatefulness, odiousness ‖ disgracefulness, shamefulness (carácter vergonzoso).

odioso, sa *adj* hateful, odious, detestable ‖ *hacerse odioso* to become objectionable.

Odisea *npr f* Odyssey.

odontología *f* MED dentistry, odontology ‖ *escuela de odontología* school of dentistry.

odontólogo *m* dentist, odontologist, dental surgeon.

odorante *adj* odorous.

odorífero, ra; odorífico, ca *adj* odoriferous, odorous.

odre *m* wineskin (pellejo) ‖ FIG & FAM drunkard, boozer, old soak (borracho).

OEA *abrev de Organización de Estados Americanos* OAS, Organization of American States.

oersted; oerstedio *m* FÍS oersted (unidad).

oesnoroeste; oesnorueste *m* west-northwest.

oessudoeste; oessudueste *m* west-southwest.

oeste *m* west ‖ — *del oeste* western; *las regiones del oeste* the western regions; west, westerly; *viento del oeste* west wind ‖ *una película del Oeste* a western.

◆ *adj* west; *el ala oeste de la casa* the west wing of the house ‖ west, westerly; *viento oeste* west wind ‖ westerly; *rumbo oeste* westerly direction.

Ofelia *npr f* Ophelia.

ofender *vt* to offend, to insult.

◆ *vpr* to take offence [US to take offense]; *ofenderse por todo* to take offence at anything ‖ to fall out (reñir); *ofenderse con un amigo* to fall out with a friend.

ofendido, da *adj* offended ‖ *darse por ofendido* to take offence [US to take offense].

◆ *m/f*. offended person.

ofensa *f* offence [US offense].

ofensivo, va *adj* offensive, rude, nasty (persona, palabras) ‖ offensive, nasty, bad (molesto) ‖ MIL offensive.

◆ *f* offensive; *pasar a la ofensiva* to take the offensive; *estar a la ofensiva* to be on the offensive.

ofensor, ra *adj* offending.

◆ *m/f* offender.

oferta *f* offer (propuesta); *oferta en firme* firm offer ‖ tender (para realizar una obra); *hacer una oferta* to put in a tender ‖ bid, offer (para comprar algo); *me han hecho una oferta de un millón de pesetas por la casa* I have been made an offer of a million pesetas for the house ‖ gift, present (regalo) ‖ COM special offer; *oferta del día* today's special offer ‖ COM *ley de la oferta y la demanda* law of supply and demand ‖ ECON *oferta pública de adquisición* take-over bid ‖ *oferta pública de adquisición hostil* hostile take-over bid.

ofertorio *m* offertory (parte de la misa) ‖ humeral (humeral).

off (en) *loc adv* offstage.

office *m* pantry (antecocina).

offset *m* IMPR offset.

oficial *adj* official; *documento, hora oficial* official document, time.

◆ *m* skilled workman (en una fábrica) ‖ skilled labourer (en albañilería) ‖ office worker, employee, clerk (oficinista) ‖ civil servant (funcionario) ‖ official (juez eclesiástico) ‖ MIL officer; *oficial retirado, de complemento* retired, reserve officer; *oficial de la escala activa* officer on the active list ‖ — *oficial de peluquería* barber's assistant ‖ MAR *oficial de guardia* officer of the watch ‖ *oficial de sanidad* sanitary officer ‖ MIL *oficial de semana* orderly officer ‖ MIL *oficial subalterno* subaltern ‖ *primer oficial* head clerk (de un notario), mate (de la marina).

oficiala *f* (female) worker (obrera) ‖ female office worker *o* employee *o* clerk (de oficina) ‖ officer (del Ejército de Salvación) ‖ *oficiala de modistería* dressmaker's assistant.

oficialidad *f* MIL officers *pl* ‖ officiality (carácter oficial).

oficialismo *m* AMER the government party.

oficialización *f* officialization.

oficializar *vt* to make official.

oficiante *adj* REL officiant.

oficiar *vt* to celebrate (misa) ‖ to communicate officialy (una noticia).

◆ *vi* to officiate (el sacerdote) ‖ FIG *oficiar de* to act as, to officiate as.

oficina *f* office (despacho) ‖ agency; *oficina de colocación* employment agency ‖ laboratory (de farmacia) ‖ — *horas de oficina* business hours, office hours ‖ *oficina central* central office ‖ *oficina de empleo* hiring hall, body shop ‖ *oficina de objetos perdidos* lost property office [US lost and found office] ‖ *oficina de turismo* tourist information office ‖ *Oficina Internacional del Trabajo* International Labour Office.

oficinal *adj* MED officinal; *planta oficinal* officinal plant.

oficinista *m/f* office worker, clerk.

◆ *pl* white-collar workers.

oficio *m* occupation, profession (profesión) ‖ job (trabajo) ‖ post, position, office (puesto) ‖ trade; *aprender un oficio* to learn a trade; *hacer su oficio* to go about one's trade ‖ role, function (función) ‖ communiqué, official note (comunicación) ‖ pantry (antecocina) ‖ REL service | mass (misa) ‖ — *artes y oficios* arts and crafts ‖ *buenos oficios* good offices ‖ *de oficio* ex officio; *miembro de oficio* ex officio member; by trade; *ser albañil de oficio* to be a mason by trade; officially (oficialmente), automatically (automáticamente) ‖ FIG *esos son los gajes del oficio* those are the occupational hazards *o* the drawbacks ‖ *no hay oficio malo* no job is too menial ‖ *no tener oficio ni beneficio* to have no job, to be out of a job ‖ REL *oficio de difuntos* office for the dead | *oficio divino* or *mayor* Divine Service ‖ *oficio manual* handicraft ‖ *saber su oficio* to know one's job ‖ *Santo Oficio* Holy Office ‖ *ser del oficio* to be in the trade ‖ *tener mucho oficio* to be very skilful.

oficiosamente *adv* diligently (con diligencia) ‖ obligingly (con complacencia) ‖ officiously (con entrometimiento) ‖ unofficially (no oficialmente) ‖ semiofficially (semioficialmente) ‖ *decir algo oficiosamente* to say sth. off the record.

oficiosidad *f* diligence, industriousness (laboriosidad) ‖ complaisance, obligingness (solicitud) ‖ officiousness (importunidad) ‖ officiousness (no oficialidad).

oficioso, sa *adj* diligent, industrious (diligente) ‖ obliging (solícito) ‖ officious, meddlesome (importuno) ‖ unofficial (no oficial) ‖ semiofficial (semioficial) ‖ *de fuente oficiosa* unofficially, from an unofficial source.

ofidio, dia *adj/sm* ZOOL ophidian.

ofimática *f* INFORM office automation.

ofrecer* *vt* to offer; *ofrecer a uno un cigarrillo* to offer s.o. a cigarette; *le ofrecí mi amistad, mi ayuda* I offered him my friendship, my help ‖ to give (regalar) ‖ to give, to hold, to throw (un banquete, una fiesta) ‖ to bid, to offer; *ofreció cien libras por el cuadro* he bid a hundred pounds for the picture ‖ to offer (up) (un sacrificio) ‖ to present, to offer, to have; *ofrece muchas ventajas* it offers many advantages; *ofrecer un aspecto lúgubre* to present a dismal aspect; *ofrecer pocas posibilidades de éxito* to have little chance of success ‖ to offer, to give; *ofreció poca resistencia* it offered little resistance ‖ *ofrecer el brazo* to offer one's arm.

◆ *vpr* to offer o.s.; *ofrecerse en sacrificio* to offer o.s. in sacrifice ‖ to offer one's service as, to offer to be; *ofrecerse de ayudante* to offer one's services as an assistant, to offer to be an assistant ‖ to offer; *ofrecerse para hacer un trabajo* to offer to do a job; *se ofreció para llevarnos a la sierra* he offered to take us to the mountains ‖ FIG to occur to s.o., to come to s.o.'s mind (pensar) ‖ — *ofrecerse a la vista de alguien* to appear before s.o.'s eyes ‖ *¿qué se le ofrece a usted?* what can I do for you?, may I help you?

ofrecimiento *m* offer (oferta) ‖ offering (de un sacrificio).

ofrenda *f* offering.

ofrendar *vt* to offer, to make an offering of; *ofrendar su alma a Dios* to offer one's soul to God ‖ to offer, to give; *ofrendó su vida por su patria* he gave his life for his country.

oftalmía *f* MED ophthalmia.

oftálmico, ca *adj* MED ophthalmic; *arteria oftálmica* ophthalmic artery.

oftalmología *f* MED ophthalmology.

oftalmológico, ca *adj* MED ophthalmologic, ophthalmological.

oftalmólogo *m* ophthalmologist.

oftalmoscopia *f* MED ophthalmoscopy.

oftalmoscopio *m* ophthalmoscope.

ofuscación *f*; **ofuscamiento** *m* blindness (ceguera) ‖ blinding, dazzling (acción de cegar) ‖ confusion (mental).

ofuscar *vt* to blind, to dazzle; *el sol me ofuscó* the sun blinded me ‖ FIG to dazzle (deslumbrar) | to blind; *ofuscado por la pasión* blinded by passion | to confuse (confundir).

◆ *vpr* to be blinded *o* dazzled (por la luz) ‖ FIG to be dazzled; *no te dejes ofuscar por las apariencias* don't let yourself be dazzled by appearances | to be blinded | to be confused.

ogresa *f* ogress.

ogro *m* ogre.

oh! *interj* oh!

ohm; ohmio *m* ELECTR ohm.

óhmico, ca *adj* ELECTR ohmic.

oída *f* hearing ‖ *de* or *por oídas* by hearsay.

oídio *m* BOT oidium.

oído *m* ear (órgano); *taparse los oídos* to cover one's ears; *oído interno* inner ear ‖ hearing (sentido); *tener el oído fino* to have sharp hearing ‖ vent (de un arma de fuego) ‖ — FIG *abrir los oídos* to open one's ears | *aguzar el oído* to prick up one's ears ‖ *al oído* in one's ear; *hablar al oído* to whisper in s.o.'s ear; by ear (oyendo), to *o* on the ear; *agradable al oído* pleasant on the ear ‖ *a pregunta necia, oídos sordos* or *de mercader* ask a silly question, (and you will) get a silly answer || *caer en oídos sordos* to fall on deaf ears || *dar oídos a* to lend an ear to (prestar atención), to give credit to (creer) || MÚS *de oído* by ear || *dolerle a uno los oídos* to have earache || *duro de oído* hard of hearing || FIG *entrar por un oído y salir por el otro* to go in one ear and out the other || *estar mal del oído* to be hard of hearing || FIG *hacer oídos de mercader* or *oídos sordos* to turn a deaf ear || *ha llegado a mis oídos* it has come to my notice *o* attention || FIG *lastimar el oído* or *los oídos* to hurt *o* to split one's ears | *le estarán zumbando los oídos* his ears must be burning | *machacar los oídos* to say (the same thing) over and over again | *no dar crédito a sus oídos* not to (be able to) believe one's ears || FAM *¡oído al parche!* be careful!, look out!, watch your step! || *pegarse al oído* to be catchy (música, etc.) || *prestar oído* or *oídos a* to lend an ear to || FIG *regalarle el oído a uno* to flatter s.o. || *ser todo oídos* to be all ears || *tener (buen) oído* to have a good ear.

OIEA *abrev de Organismo Internacional para la Energía Atómica* IAEA, International Atomic Energy Agency.

oíl *m* oil; *lengua de oíl* langue d'oil.

oír* *vt* to hear; *oír un ruido* to hear a noise || to listen to, to hear (out) (atender, escuchar); *oír un ruego* to listen to a request || JUR to hear (un caso) || — *al oírle hablar así* to listen to him || *aquí donde usted me oye* as sure as I'm standing here || *como lo oyes* just as I've said || *dejarse oír* to be heard || *¡Dios le oiga!* may your prayers be answered || *Dios oyó mi ruego* God answered my prayer || FAM *es como quien oye llover* it's like talking to a brick wall | *estar harto de oír* to be sick of hearing || *he oído decir que...* I have heard that... || FIG *las paredes oyen* walls have ears || *lo oí caer* I heard it fall || FAM *¡lo que hay que oír!* what next! || FIG *ni visto ni oído* in a flash | *no hay peor sordo que el que no quiere oír* none so deaf as those who don't want to hear || *¡oiga!* I say!, hey! (para llamar la atención), hello! (teléfono) || *oír hablar de* to hear of; *en mi vida he oído hablar de eso* I have never heard of that in my life || *oír al revés* to misunderstand || *oír mal* to be hard of hearing, to be a little deaf (algo sordo), to misunderstand (entender mal) || *oír misa* to hear Mass || *oír, ver y callar* to keep one's lips sealed || FAM *¡oye!* hey!; *oye, ¿qué te has creído?* hey! what do you think this is?; now look here! (como reprensión) || FIG *usted ha oído campanas (y no sabe dónde)* you don't really know what you are talking about.

◆ *vpr* to be heard; *se oyó un grito estremecedor a lo lejos* a frightful cry was heard in the distance.

OIT *abrev de Organización Internacional del Trabajo* ILO, International Labour Organization.

ojal *m* buttonhole (para abrochar un botón); *con una flor en el ojal* with a flower in one's buttonhole || eye (agujero) || FAM hole, wound (herida); *abrirle uno un ojal* to make a hole in s.o.

¡ojalá! *interj* I hope so!, let's hope so!, I wish it were true!, if only he (it, they, etc.) would (could, did, etc.)!, would to God! (p us); *puede ser verdad... ¡ojalá!* it may be true... I hope so! || I (only) hope *o* wish (that), let's hope (that), would to God that (p us); *¡ojalá apruebe!* I hope he passes!, would to God that he pass! || if only; *¡ojalá viviera aún!* if only he were still alive!

ojeada *f* glance || FIG brief survey, glance; *echaron una ojeada a la situación actual* they made a brief survey of *o* they cast a glance at the present situation || — *echar* or *dar una ojeada a* to glance at, to run one's eye over, to take a quick look at || *echa una ojeada al niño* have a look at the baby.

ojeador *m* beater (en la caza).

ojear *vt* to eye (mirar) || to stare at (mirar fijamente) || to beat up [game] (en la caza) || FIG to scare off *o* away (espantar) | to cast the evil eye on (aojar).

ojén *m* anisette (bebida).

ojeo *m* beating (en la caza).

ojera *f* ring (de los ojos) || eyebath (lavaojos) || *tener ojeras* to have rings under one's eyes.

ojeriza *f* spite, ill will, grudge, dislike || — *tenerle ojeriza a uno* to have *o* to bear a grudge against s.o. || *tomarle ojeriza a uno* to take a dislike to s.o.

ojeroso, sa *adj* with rings under one's eyes (persona) || *estar ojeroso* to have rings under one's eyes.

ojete *m* eyelet, grummet (para pasar un cordón) || POP arse (ano).

ojímetro (a) *loc fam* FAM by eye, at a rough guess.

ojiva *f* ARQ ogive || MIL warhead (de proyectil) || nose cone (de un cohete espacial).

ojival *adj* ogival || *estilo ojival* Ogival *o* Gothic style.

ojo *m* eye; *tener ante los ojos* to have before one's eyes; *saltarle un ojo a alguien* to put out s.o. eye || hole (agujero) || opening (abertura) || speck of oil *o* of fat (en el caldo) || eye, hole (de pan, queso) || eye (de aguja) || bow (de llave) || keyhole (de cerradura) || span (de puente) || spring (manantial) || eye (de la cola del pavo) || soaping, lathering (jabonadura) || mesh (de red) || eye (de huracán) || IMPR face (de una letra) || TECN eye, helve ring (de una herramienta) || POP hole (ano) || FIG perspicacity | care, caution (cuidado) || — FIG *abrir el ojo* to keep one's eyes open || *andar ojo alerta* to keep one's eyes open || *a ojo* by eye || *a ojo (de buen cubero)* by guesswork, by rule of thumb (sin medir), in a rough and ready way (sin precisión) || *a ojo de buen cubero debe de pesar diez kilos* at a rough estimate it must weigh about ten kilos || FIG *costar* or *valer un ojo de la cara* to cost *o* to be worth a fortune | *daría un ojo de la cara por* I'd give my right arm *o* anything for | *dar un ojo a* to soap (la ropa) | *donde pone el ojo pone la bala* or *la piedra* he is a dead shot | *echar el ojo a* to set one's eye on, to have one's eyes on | *el ojo del amo engorda al caballo* the master's eye makes the mill go | *estar ojo avizor* to keep a sharp lookout || *guiñar el ojo* to wink || FIG *hacer ojo* to lather (el jabón) | *ir con mucho ojo* to tread very carefully | *llena antes el ojo que la barriga* or *la tripa* his eyes are bigger than his belly | *llorar con un ojo* to cry crocodile tears | *meterse por el ojo de una aguja* to have a finger in every pie | *mirar con el rabillo del ojo* to look out of the corner of one's eye (at) | *no pegar el ojo* or *ojo* not to sleep a wink, not to get a wink of sleep (no poder dormir) | *no quitar ojo a* not to take one's eyes off, to keep watching (no dejar de mirar), not to let out of one's sight, to keep an *o* one's eye on (vigilar) || *¡ojo!* look out!, careful!, watch out!, watch it! || FIG & FAM *ojo a la funerala* black eye, shiner || *ojo con* watch, be careful about *o* of *o* with, beware of || *ojo de besugo* bulging eye || *ojo de buey* bull's-eye window (ventana), porthole (en un barco) || *ojo de cristal* glass eye || *ojo de gallo* corn [on the foot] (callo) || *ojo de gato* cat's eye, tigereye (ágata) || *ojo de la escalera* hollow newel || *ojo de la llave* keyhole || FOT *ojo de pez* fisheye lens || *ojo eléctrico* electric eye || FAM *ojo en compota* black eye || RAD *ojo mágico* magic eye || FIG *ojo por ojo, diente por diente* an eye for an eye, a tooth for a tooth || FAM *ponerle a uno un ojo a la funerala* to give s.o. a black eye, to black s.o.'s eye || FIG *ser el ojo* or *el ojito derecho de alguien* to be s.o.'s [little] blue-eyed boy *o* girl | *tener buen ojo* or *ojo clínico para* to have a good *o* sure eye for | *tener mal de ojo* to be jinxed | *tener muy buen ojo para* to have a very good eye *o* a real flair for (ser perspicaz) | *tener ojo de buen cubero* to have a sure *o* an accurate eye || FAM *tener un ojo aquí y el otro en Pekín* to be cross-eyed (ser bizco).

◆ *pl* bows, rings (de tijeras) || — FIG *abrirle los ojos a uno* to open s.o.'s eyes | *abrir los ojos* to keep one's eyes open (vigilante), to open one's eyes (*ante* to) (percatarse de algo) | *alegrársele a uno los ojos* to shine *o* to sparkle with joy [the eyes]; *se le alegraron los ojos* his eyes shone with joy || *a (los) ojos de* in the eyes of (según) || *alzar los ojos al cielo* to raise *o* to lift one's eyes to heaven || FIG *andar con cien ojos* to keep one's eyes open, to be on one's guard || *a ojos cerrados* with one's eyes closed, blindfold || *a ojos vistas* visibly (claramente); *crecer a ojos vistas* to become visibly larger || FIG *bailarle a uno los ojos de alegría* to sparkle *o* to dance with joy [the eyes]; *le bailaban los ojos de alegría* his eyes sparkled with joy | *cerrar los ojos* to close one's eyes, to go to sleep (dormirse), to pass away (morir) | *cerrar los ojos a* to close *o* to shut one's eyes to | *comerse con los ojos* to gloat over, to look greedily at (codiciar), to devour with one's eyes (con amor), to look daggers at (con ira) | *como los ojos de la cara* like the apple of one's eye | *con los ojos cerrados* blindly, with one's eyes closed (sin reflexionar), with one's eyes shut, with complete confidence (con completa confianza) | *cuatro ojos* four-eyes (que lleva gafas) | *cuatro ojos ven más que dos* two heads are better than one || *dar en los ojos a uno* to be *o* to get in one's eyes (el sol) || FIG *delante de los ojos* right before one's eyes, before one's very eyes, under one's very nose || *¡dichosos los ojos que te ven!* how glad I am to see you!, you're a sight for sore eyes! || FIG *dormir con los ojos abiertos* or *con un ojo abierto como las liebres* to sleep with one eye open | *entrar por los ojos a uno* to catch s.o.'s eye, to take s.o.'s fancy | *en un abrir y cerrar de ojos* in the twinkling of an eye, in a wink | *hacer caer la venda de los ojos* to open s.o.'s eyes | *hasta los ojos* up to the eyes, up to one's neck | *írsele a uno los ojos por* or *tras una cosa* to eye sth. greedily (desear), to goggle at sth. (mirar) | *meterle al público un producto por los ojos* to shove a product down the public's throat (elogiar) || *mirar a* or *en los ojos* to look into s.o.'s eyes, to look s.o. in the eye || FIG *mirar con buenos ojos* to look favourably upon | *mirar con malos ojos* to frown on | *mirar con ojos de carnero degollado* to make sheep's eyes at | *mirar con ojos terribles* to look sternly at, to stare fiercely at, to glare at | *mirar con otros ojos* to see in a different light | *no dar crédito a sus ojos* not to believe one's eyes | *no quitar los ojos de encima* not to take one's eyes off, to keep watching (no dejar de mirar), not to let out of one's sight, to keep an *o* one's eye on (vigilar) | *no tener a quien volver los ojos* to have no one to look to *o* to turn to | *no tener a dónde volver los ojos* not to know which way to turn | *no tener ojos más que para...* to have eyes only for... | *no tener telarañas en los ojos* not to be blind, to have one's eyes about one || *ojos achinados* almond eyes || *ojos hundidos* sunken eyes || *ojos oblicuos* slant eyes || *ojos pícaros* saucy eyes || FIG *ojos que no ven, corazón que no siente* out of sight, out of mind || *ojos rasgados* almond eyes || *ojos saltones* bulging eyes || *ojos tiernos* tender eyes || *pasar a los ojos de uno como un tonto* to look a fool in s.o.'s eyes || *pasar los ojos por* to run one's eye over || FIG *poner los ojos* or *el ojo en* to set one's eye on, to fix one's sights on | *poner los ojos en blanco* to swoon (*delante de* over), (mostrar una admiración exagerada por) | *por sus lindos ojos* for nothing, gratis || *revolver los ojos* to roll one's eyes || FIG *sacar los ojos a uno* to bleed s.o. white (pedir mucho dinero) | *salta a los ojos* it is obvious, it is as plain as a pikestaff || *se le arrasaron los ojos* *en lágrimas* his eyes filled with tears || *se le humedecieron los ojos* tears came to his eyes || FIG *ser todo ojos* to be all eyes || FIG & FAM *tener cuatro ojos* to be a four-eyes (llevar gafas) | *tener entre ojos a uno* to have a grudge against s.o., to have it in for s.o. || FIG *tener los ojos puestos en* to have set one's heart on | *tener los ojos vendados, tener una venda en los ojos* to go around blindfolded *o* with one's eyes closed, to be blind | *tener ojos de lince* to have eyes like a hawk *o* sharp eyes || *torcer los ojos* to squint || FIG *traer entre ojos* to keep one's eye on | *ver con buenos ojos* to look favourably upon | *ver con malos ojos* to look unfavourably upon, to frown on | *ver algo con los mismos ojos* to see eye to eye over sth.

ojota *f* AMER sandal (sandalia).

okapí *m* ZOOL okapi (mamífero).

okumé *m* BOT okoume, okume (árbol africano).

okupa *m/f* FAM squatter.

ola *f* MAR wave || FIG wave; *la ola inflacionista, de protestas* wave of inflation, of protest || — FIG *la nueva ola* the new wave || *ola de calor, de frío* heat wave, cold spell.

¡ole!; ¡olé! *interj* bravo!, well done!

oleáceas *f pl* BOT oleaceae.

oleada *f* large wave, surge, billow (ola) || FIG surge, wave (de gente) | wave; *oleada de suicidios* wave of suicides.

oleaginoso, sa *adj* oleaginous || *semilla oleaginosa* oliseed.
◆ *m* oilseed.

oleaje *m* swell (marejada) || surf (olas espumosas).

olecráneo; olécranon *m* ANAT olecranon.

oleícola *adj* olive-growing (del cultivo del olivo) || of the olive oil industry, olive oil.

oleicultor *m* olive grower (cultivador) || olive oil manufacturer (productor).

oleicultura *f* olive growing (cultivo del olivo) || olive oil industry (producción de aceite).

oleífero, ra *adj* oleiferous, oil-producing; *planta oleífera* oleiferous plant.

oleína *f* QUÍM olein.

óleo *m* oil, olive oil (aceite de oliva) || REL chrism, oil || oil (pintura) || — *los Santos Oleos* Holy Oil || *pintar al óleo* to paint in oils || *pintura al óleo* oil painting.

oleoducto *m* pipeline.

oleografía *f* oleography.

oleómetro *m* oleometer.

oleosidad *f* oiliness.

oleoso, sa *adj* oily.

óleum *m* QUÍM oleum.

oler* *vt* to smell || FIG to smell, to scent (sospechar) | to nose into, to pry into (curiosear) | to smell out, to sniff out (descubrir).
◆ *vi* to smell; *oler a tabaco* to smell of tobacco; *oler bien, mal* to smell good *o* nice, bad *o* nasty || FIG to smell, to smack; *sus palabras huelen a traición* his talk smacks of treason | to sound; *huele a mentira, a traducción* it sounds like a lie, like a translation || — FIG *ese señor huele a policía* that gentleman has got policeman written all over him | *este asunto no me huele bien* this business smells fishy to me || FIG & FAM *oler a chamusquina* to smack of heresy (una herejía), to look like trouble (va a ocurrir algo grave), to smell fishy, to seem doubtful (ser sospechoso) || *oler a difunto* to smell fusty *o* musty (una habitación), to look as if one is not long for this world (antes de morir uno).
◆ *vpr* FIG to feel, to sense; *me huelo que va a llover* I feel that it is going to rain | to smell, to sense, to scent; *olerse un peligro, una intriga* to smell danger, a plot || — FIG *me lo olía* I sensed it, I thought as much | *olerse la tortilla* to see it coming.

olfatear *vt* to sniff, to smell || FIG & FAM to smell, to scent (sospechar) | to smell out, to sniff out (descubrir) | to nose into, to pry into (curiosear) | to smell *o* to nose out, to scent out [game] (los perros).

olfateo *m* sniffing, smelling || FIG snooping (curioseo).

olfato *m* smell, sense of smell || FIG intuition, instinct, flair (instinto) || FIG *tener olfato para los negocios* to have a flair *o* a nose for business.

olíbano *m* olibanum, frankincense.

oliente *adj* smelling, odorous || — *bien oliente* pleasant-smelling || *mal oliente* bad-smelling, malodorous.

oligarca *m* oligarch.

oligarquía *f* oligarchy.

oligárquico, ca *adj* oligarchic, oligarchical.

oligisto *adj/sm* MIN oligist || *oligisto rojo* haematite, hematite, red iron ore.

oligoceno, na *adj/sm* GEOL oligocene.

oligoelemento *m* trace element.

oligofrenia *f* oligophrenia.

Olimpia *npr f* HIST Olympia.

olimpiada; olimpíada *f* Olimpic games *pl*, Olympics *pl* (juegos) || Olympiad (período).

olímpicamente *adv* Olympianly, loftily; *despreciar olímpicamente* to despise Olympianly.

olímpico, ca *adj* Olympian (del Olimpo); *Júpiter olímpico* Olympian Jupiter || Olympic (de Olimpia); *juegos olímpicos* Olympic games || FIG Olympian, haughty, lofty (altivo); *desdén olímpico* Olympian contempt || *ciudad olímpica* Olympic village.

Olimpo *npr m* MIT Olympus; *Monte Olimpo* Mount Olympus.

oliscar; olisquear *vt* FAM to sniff, to smell (oler) || FIG to nose *o* to pry into (curiosear).
◆ *vi* to smell [bad].

oliva *f* olive (aceituna); *aceite de oliva* olive oil || olive, olive tree (olivo) || ZOOL owl (lechuza) || ANAT olivary body || *color verde oliva* olive, olive-green.

oliváceo, a *adj* olive, olive-green.

olivar *m* olive plantation, olive grove.

olivar *vt* AGR to cut off the lower branches of.

olivarero, ra *adj* olive-growing; *región olivarera* olive-growing region || olive; *industria olivarera* olive industry.

Oliveto (monte) *npr m* Mount of Olives.

olivícola *adj* olive-growing.

olivicultor *m* olive grower.

olivicultura *f* olive growing.

olivífero, ra *adj* covered with olive trees, oliviferous, rich in olives.

olivina *f*; **olivino** *m* MIN olivine.

olivo *m* olive tree, olive (árbol) || — *Huerto de los Olivos* Garden of Olives || *Monte de los Olivos* Mount of Olives || FIG *olivo y aceituno todo es uno* it's much of a muchness, it's as broad as it is long || FIG *tomar el olivo* to take shelter behind the barrier (el torero), to take to one's heels (huir).

olmeda *f*; **olmedo** *m* elm grove.

olmo *m* BOT elm, elm tree.

ológrafo, fa *adj/sm* holograph.

olor *m* smell, odour [US odor]; *un olor a rosa* a smell of roses || scent (de la caza) || scent, fragrance, perfume (buen olor) || FIG smell, smack || — *agua de olor* toilet water || *morir en olor de santidad* to die in the odour of sanctity || *olor corporal* BO [body odour] || *tener olor a* to smell of, to have a smell of.

oloroso, sa *adj* odorous, sweet-smelling, fragrant.

OLP *abrev de Organización para la Liberación de Palestina* PLO, Palestine Liberation Organization.

olvidable *adj* forgettable.

olvidadizo, za *adj* forgetful || FIG ungrateful, with a short memory (desagradecido) || *hacerse el olvidadizo* to pretend to forget, to pretend not to remember.

olvidado, da *adj* forgotten || forgetful (olvidadizo) || FIG ungrateful (desagradecido).
◆ *m/f* forgetful person (olvidadizo) || FIG ungrateful person.

olvidar *vt* to forget; *olvidar una fecha, la hora* to forget a date, the time; *olvidemos el pasado* let us forget the past || to leave behind, to forget; *olvidar el bolso* to leave one's bag behind || to forget, to omit, to leave out (omitir); *olvidar un nombre en una lista* to omit a name from a list.
◆ *vpr* to be forgotten (estar olvidado); *un favor no debe olvidarse* a good turn should not be forgotten || to forget; *no se te olvide* don't forget; *se me olvidó decírtelo, me olvidé de decírtelo* I forgot to tell you; *se le olvidaron todas nuestras atenciones* he forgot all the attention we lavished on him || FIG *olvidarse de sí mismo* not to think of o.s., to have no thought for o.s.

olvido *m* forgetting (acción de olvidar) || forgetfulness (descuido); *en un momento de olvido* in a moment's forgetfulness || omission, oversight (omisión) || oblivion (estado de lo olvidado); *caer en el olvido* to fall *o* to sink into oblivion || — *dar* or *echar al* or *en el olvido* to cast into oblivion, to forget || *dejar en el olvido* to leave in oblivion || *enterrar en el olvido* to cast into oblivion || *estar en el olvido* to lie in oblivion || *sacar del olvido* to rescue from oblivion.

olla *f* pot (vasija) || kettle (para hervir agua) || stew, hotpot (guisado) || eddy, whirlpool (remolino) || FIG hotchpotch || — FIG *olla de grillos* madhouse, bedlam, bear garden || *olla de presión, olla exprés* pressure cooker || *olla podrida* highly-seasoned hotpot.

ollar *m* nostril (de las caballerías).

ollero, ra *m/f* potter || FIG *cada ollero alaba su puchero* each of us blows his own trumpet at some time or other.

Omán *n pr* GEOGR Oman.

ombligo *m* ANAT navel, umbilicus || FIG centre || — FIG & FAM *encogérsele a uno el ombligo* to get cold feet || BOT *ombligo de Venus* Venus's-navelwort.

ombú *m* ombu (árbol de América).

ombudsman *m* ombudsman.

omega *f* omega (letra griega).

omento *m* ANAT & ZOOL omentum (redaño).

Omeyas *m pl* HIST Ommiads, Ommiad dynasty.

ómicron *f* omicron (letra griega).

ominoso, sa *adj* abominable, execrable (abominable) || ominous, foreboding (de mal agüero).

omisión *f* omission (abstención); *pecado de omisión* sin of omission || omission, neglect (descuido) || forgetfulness (olvido) || oversight (distracción).

omiso, sa *adj* neglectful, careless (descuidado) || *hacer caso omiso de* to take no notice of, to pay no attention to, to ignore.

omitir *vt* to omit, to neglect; *omitió decírmelo* he omitted to tell me || to omit, to leave out, to miss out (excluir) || to omit, to pass over, to skip (pasar en silencio).

ómnibus *m* omnibus, bus (carruaje público) || *tren ómnibus* slow *o* stopping train.

omnidireccional *adj* RAD omnidirectional, all direction.

omnímodamente *adv* absolutely, totally.

omnímodo, da *adj* all-embracing, absolute, total.

omnipotencia *f* omnipotence.

omnipotente *adj* omnipotent, almighty, all-powerful.

omnipresencia *f* omnipresence.

omnipresente *adj* omnipresent.

omnisapiente *adj* omniscient, all-knowing.

omnisciencia *f* omniscience.

omnisciente *adj* omniscient, all-knowing.

ómnium *m* COM general trading company || open race (carrera).

omnívoro, ra *adj* ZOOL omnivorous.
◆ *m/f* ZOOL omnivore.

omóplato; omoplato *m* ANAT shoulder blade, scapula.

OMS *abrev de Organización Mundial de la Salud* WHO, World Health Organization.

onagro *m* onager (asno salvaje).

onanismo *m* onanism.

onanista *adj* onanist.

once *adj* eleven; *once personas* eleven people || eleventh (undécimo); *el siglo XI* (once) the eleventh century; *Pío XI* (once) Pius XI [the eleventh].
◆ *m* eleven (equipo de fútbol) || eleven (número) || eleventh (fechas); *el once de mayo* the eleventh of May, May (the) eleventh || — *a las once* at eleven o'clock || *las once* elevenses (refrigerio) || *son las once de la noche* it is eleven p. m.

ONCE *abrev de Organización Nacional de Ciegos Españoles* Spanish national organization for the blind.

onceno, na *adj/s* eleventh.

oncogénico, ca *adj* oncogenic.

oncológico, ca *adj* oncologic, oncological.

oncólogo, ga *m/f* oncologist.

onda *f* wave (en el agua) || FÍS wave; *ondas acústicas, hertzianas, amortiguadas, portadoras* sound, Hertzian, damped, carrier waves || wave (en el pelo) || scallop (costura) || FIG flicker (de la llama) || — RAD *de onda corta* shortwave || FIG & FAM *estar en la onda* to be with it || RAD *longitud de onda* wavelength | *onda corta* short wave || *onda de choque, onda expansiva* shock wave (explosión) || RAD *onda extracorta* ultrashort wave | *onda larga* long wave | *onda media* medium wave || *onda supersónica* supersonic wave.

ondeado, da *adj* waving, undulating, waved, wavy || wavy, waved (pelo).

ondeante *adj* undulating || fluttering, waving, flapping (bandera).

ondear *vi* to undulate, to rise and fall in waves (mar) || to ripple (el agua) || to wave, to stream; *sus cabellos ondeaban al viento* her hair streamed in the wind || to flutter, to wave (una bandera) || to flicker, to waver (una llama) || to scallop (costura).
◆ *vpr* to swing, to sway.

ondeo *m* undulation, rippling (del agua) || waving (del pelo) || fluttering, waving, flapping (de una bandera) || flickering, waving (de una llama).

ondina *f* MIT undine.

ondulación *f* undulation || wave (del pelo) || wave, ripple (del agua) || winding (sinuosidad) || *ondulación permanente* permanent wave.

ondulado, da *adj* rolling (paisaje) || undulating (superficie) || uneven (carretera) || wavy (pelo) || corrugated (hierro, cartón).
◆ *m* wave (del pelo).

ondulante *adj* undulating || wavy (pelo) || rippling, undulating (agua) || flickering, waving (llama).

ondular *vt/vi* to wave (pelo) || to undulate, to wave, to ripple (trigo) || to slither (culebra) || to corrugate (hierro).

ondulatorio, ria *adj* undulatory || — *mecánica ondulatoria* wave mechanics || *movimiento ondulatorio* wave motion, undulatory movement.

oneroso, sa *adj* onerous.

ónice *m/f* MIN onyx (ágata).

onírico, ca *adj* oneiric (de los sueños).

ónix *m* MIN onyx (ágata).

onomástico, ca *adj* onomastic || — *día onomástico* saint's day || *índice onomástico* index of names.
◆ *f* onomastics || saint's day (día del santo).

onomatopeya *f* onomatopoeia.

onomatopéyico, ca *adj* onomatopoeic.

Ontario *npr m* GEOGR Ontario || *el lago Ontario* Lake Ontario.

ontología *f* FIL ontology.

ontológico, ca *adj* FIL ontological.

ontólogo *m* FIL ontologist.

ONU *abrev de Organización de las Naciones Unidas* UN, United Nations.

onubense *adj* [of *o* from] Huelva [formerly «Ónuba»]
◆ *m/f* native *o* inhabitant of Huelva.

onza *f* ounce (medida de peso) || ZOOL ounce.

onzavo, va *adj/s* eleventh.

oosfera *f* oosphere.

oospora *f* BOT oospore (huevo).

opa *adj* AMER stupid, idiotic (idiota) || *¡opa!* hullo!

opacidad *f* opacity, opaqueness.

opaco, ca *adj* opaque || dull, dim (ruido, luz) || FIG gloomy (triste).

opalescencia *f* opalescence.

opalescente *adj* opalescent.

opalino, na *adj* opal (del ópalo) || opaline (color).
◆ *f* opaline.

ópalo *m* MIN opal || *color de ópalo* opal.

opción *f* option, choice || right (derecho) || COM option; *opción de compra* call option; *opción de venta* put option.

open *m* DEP open.

ópera *f* opera || opera, opera house (edificio) || — *ópera bufa* opéra bouffe, comic opera || *ópera cómica* opéra comique.

operabilidad *f* INFORM operability.

operable *adj* operable.

operación *f* operation; *operación aritmética, quirúrgica* arithmetical, surgical operation || MIL operation || COM transaction, deal || — COM *fondo de operaciones* working capital || *operación cesárea* Caesarian *o* Caesarean section || MIL *operación de limpieza* mopping-up operation || INFORM *operaciones de bloque* block operation.

operacional *adj* operational.

operado, da *adj* who has been operated on.
◆ *m/f* surgical patient.

operador, ra *m/f* operator || surgeon (cirujano) || CINEM cameraman (de rodaje) || projectionist (de proyección) || INFORM *operador de consola* console operator || *operador turístico* tour operator.
◆ *m* MAT operator || INFORM *operador aritmético lógico* arithmetic logical operator.

operando *m* INFORM operand.

operante *adj* operating, working, operative || effective (que produce el efecto deseado).

operar *vt* to operate on *o* upon; *operar a uno de una pierna, de apendicitis* to operate on s.o.'s leg, on s.o. for appendicitis || to work (un milagro) || to bring about (una transformación, cierto efecto, etc.) || to effect, to bring about (una curación).
◆ *vi* to operate (actuar, obrar) || to operate, to work, to take effect; *la medicina empieza a operar* the medicine is beginning to work || COM to do business, to deal.
◆ *vpr* to occur, to come about (efectuarse) || MED to have an operation.

operario, ria *m/f* operative, worker, operator || — *operario de máquina* machinist, machine operator || *operario electricista* electrician.
◆ *m* monk who tends and confesses the sick (religioso).

operativo, va *adj* operative.

operatorio, ria *adj* operative || *choque operatorio* postoperative shock.

opérculo *m* operculum.

opereta *f* operetta.

operístico, ca *adj* operatic.

opimo, ma *adj* rich (rico) || abundant, plentiful (abundante).

opinar *vi* to think; *¿qué opinas de esto?* what do you think of this? || to express *o* to give one's opinion; *opinar de* or *sobre política* to express one's opinion of politics || to have an opinion, to think; *opinar bien de uno* to have a good opinion of s.o., to think well of s.o.

opinión *f* opinion; *la opinión pública* public opinion; *dar su opinión* to give one's opinion || view, opinion; *tenemos las mismas opiniones* we have the same views || — *andar en opiniones* to be talked about, to make tongues wag || *cambiar de opinión* to change one's mind || FIG *casarse uno con su opinión* to stick to one's opinion || *compartir la opinión de, abundar en la opinión de* to share the same opinion as || *en mi opinión* in my opinion || *es cuestión de opinión* that is a matter of opinion || *ese muchacho no me merece buena opinión* I have a poor opinion of that boy || *salvo mejor opinión* failing a better idea *o* suggestion || *según opinión de* in the opinion of || *ser de opinión que...* to be of the opinion that... || *sondeo de la opinión pública* public opinion poll.

opio *m* opium.

opiomanía *f* opium addiction.

opiómano, na *adj* addicted to opium, opium-addicted.
◆ *m/f* opium addict.

opíparamente *adv* in splendid style, sumptuously, lavishly.

opíparo, ra *adj* sumptuous, splendid, lavish; *banquete opíparo* sumptuous feast.

oponente *adj* opposing || ANAT opponent (músculo).
◆ *m/f* opponent.

oponer *vt* to oppose; *oponer una fuerza militar a otra* to oppose one military force against another; *oponer dos equipos* to oppose two teams || to offer, to put up (resistencia) || to raise (objeción) || to use (armas).
◆ *vpr* to oppose each other (dos personas) || to oppose, to be opposed to, to be against; *oponerse a un proyecto* to oppose a plan || to ob-

ject to (poner reparos a) ‖ to oppose, to go against, to be in opposition to, to contradict (contradecir) ‖ to resist (resistir) ‖ to be opposite, to face (estar enfrente) ‖ *oponerse a una moción* to oppose a motion.

oponible *adj* opposable.

oporto *m* port, port wine.

Oporto *n pr* GEOGR Oporto.

oportunidad *f* opportunity, chance; *tuve la oportunidad de ir a Australia* I had the opportunity of going to *o* to go to Australia; *en la primera oportunidad* at the first opportunity ‖ opportuneness, timeliness; *la oportunidad de su llegada* the timeliness of his arrival ‖ appropriateness, suitability, advisability (de una medida, etc.) ‖ — *aprovechar, no aprovechar una oportunidad* to seize, to miss an opportunity ‖ *no dejar escapar la oportunidad* not to let the opportunity slip by.

oportunismo *m* opportunism.

oportunista *adj* opportunist, opportunistic.
◆ *m/f* opportunist.

oportuno, na *adj* suitable, appropriate; *tomar las medidas oportunas* to take the appropriate measures ‖ opportune, timely, seasonable; *una llegada oportuna* a timely arrival ‖ suitable, fitting, apposite; *respuesta oportuna* suitable reply ‖ advisable (aconsejable) ‖ witty (persona) ‖ — *en el momento oportuno* at the right moment ‖ *oportuno en las réplicas* quick at repartee.

oposición *f* opposition; *se mantuvo firme en su oposición* he did not let up in his opposition ‖ competitive examination, competition (examen); *hacer una oposición a la cátedra de estudios hispánicos* to sit a competitive examination for the chair of Hispanic studies ‖ opposition (en política); *el líder de la oposición* the leader of the opposition ‖ ASTR opposition ‖ — *catedrático por oposición* professor selected by means of a competitive examination ‖ *en oposición con* in opposition to, opposed to ‖ *ganar las oposiciones a una cátedra* to win a chair in a competitive examination.

opositar *vi* to sit a competitive examination.

opositor, ra *m/f* opponent (adversario) ‖ candidate (candidato).

oposum *m* ZOOL opossum.

opresión *f* oppression (de un pueblo) ‖ *opresión en el* or *de pecho* tightness of the chest, difficulty in breathing.

opresivo, va *adj* oppressive; *ley opresiva* oppressive law; *clima opresivo* oppressive climate.

opreso, sa *adj* oppressed.

opresor, ra *adj* oppressing, oppressive.
◆ *m/f* oppressor.

oprimente *adj* oppressing, oppressive.

oprimido, da *adj* oppressed; *los pueblos oprimidos* oppressed peoples ‖ *tener el corazón oprimido* to be sick at heart.
◆ *m/f* oppressed person ‖ *los oprimidos* the oppressed.

oprimir *vt* to press; *oprimir un botón* to press a button ‖ to squeeze, to press (apretar) ‖ to be too tight; *me oprimen los zapatos* my shoes are too tight for me ‖ to compress (gas) ‖ to grasp (picaporte) ‖ FIG to oppress (tiranizar) | to weigh down (agobiar) | to seize, to overcome (afligir); *la emoción oprimía a los espectadores* the spectators were seized with emotion | to wring; *oprimir el corazón* to wring one's heart.

oprobiar *vt* to defame, to revile, to disgrace.

oprobio *m* opprobrium, ignominy, disgrace, shame; *cubrir de oprobio* to cover with opprobrium ‖ *ser el oprobio de su familia* to be a disgrace to one's family ‖ *y para mayor oprobio* and to my (your, his, etc.) great shame.

oprobioso, sa *adj* opprobrious, ignominious, shameful, disgraceful.

optar *vi* to opt, to choose; *optar por una línea de conducta* to opt for *o* to choose a line of conduct; *optó por quedarse* he opted *o* he chose to stay ‖ to choose; *optar entre dos candidatos* to choose between two candidates ‖ to apply (*a* for) (un puesto).

optativo, va *adj* GRAM optative ‖ optional (facultativo).
◆ *m* GRAM optative.

óptico, ca *adj* optic, optical (del ojo, de la visión); *nervio, ángulo óptico* optic nerve, angle ‖ optical (de la luz, de los lentes, etc.); *instrumentos ópticos* optical instruments ‖ — *ilusión óptica* optical illusion ‖ *telégrafo óptico* signal *o* optical telegraph.
◆ *f* FÍS optics ‖ optical system, optics [of camera, etc.] (aparato) ‖ FIG viewpoint, approach (enfoque) ‖ optician's shop (tienda).
◆ *m* optician (comerciante)

óptimamente *adv* in the best possible way, perfectly.

optimar *vt* to optimize.

optimismo *m* optimism.

optimista *adj* optimistic.
◆ *m/f* optimist.

optimizar *vt* to optimize.

óptimo, ma *adj* optimum, very best, most favourable ‖ *porvenir óptimo* brilliant future.
◆ *m* optimum.
◆ *interj* capital!, first rate!

opuestamente *adv* contrarily.

opuesto, ta *adj* opposed; *opuesto a una medida* opposed to a measure ‖ opposed, opposite, conflicting, contrary; *dos versiones opuestas* two opposed versions ‖ opposite; *en sentido opuesto* in the opposite direction ‖ conflicting (intereses) ‖ BOT & MAT opposite ‖ DEP opposing (equipo).

opugnar *vt* (p us) to oppose, to oppugn (oponerse) ‖ to oppugn, to controvert, to oppose (impugnar) ‖ to attack, to assail, to oppugn (asaltar).

opulencia *f* opulence.

opulento, ta *adj* opulent.

opus *m* MÚS opus.

opúsculo *m* opuscule, booklet (folleto).

oquedad *f* hole (hoyo) ‖ cavity, hollow (cavidad).

oquedal *m* wood [without undergrowth].

ora *conj* now; *ora sabio ora ignorante* now wise, now ignorant ‖ whether; *ora de día, ora de noche* whether by day, whether by night.

oración *f* REL prayer, orison (p us); *estar en oración* to be at prayer ‖ oration, speech (discurso) ‖ sentence (frase) ‖ GRAM speech; *parte de la oración* part of speech | clause; *oración relativa, condicional* relative, conditional clause ‖ — FIG *oración de ciego* monotonous drone, singsong ‖ *oración dominical* Lord's Prayer ‖ *oración fúnebre* funeral oration ‖ *oración mental, vocal* mental, vocal prayer.
◆ *pl* first part *sing* of the catechism, prayers ‖ angelus *sing* (toque de campanas) ‖ *rezar sus oraciones* to say one's prayers.

oracional *adj* GRAM sentential.
◆ *m* prayer book.

oráculo *m* oracle.

orador, ra *m/f* speaker, orator (que habla en público) ‖ *orador sagrado* preacher.
◆ *m* preacher (predicador).

oral *adj* oral; *aprobar los exámenes orales* to pass the oral exams.
◆ *m* oral, viva voce (examen)

Orange *n pr* HIST Orange.

orangután *m* ZOOL orangutan, orangoutang.

orante *adj* praying, in prayer ‖ *estatua orante* orant, statue in the posture of prayer.

orar *vi* to pray (*a* to; *por* for) (hacer oración); *orar por los difuntos* to pray for the dead ‖ to make a speech, to speak (hablar).

orate *m/f* madman (hombre), madwoman (mujer), lunatic ‖ *casa de orates* lunatic asylum.

oratoriano *m* oratorian (religioso).

oratorio, ria *adj* oratorical.
◆ *m* oratory, chapel (capilla) ‖ MÚS oratorio.
◆ *f* oratory, oratorical art.

orbe *m* orb, circle (círculo) ‖ orb, sphere (esfera) ‖ FIG world (mundo); *en todo el orbe* throughout the world ‖ ASTR orb.

orbícola *adj* found all over the world, worldwide.

órbita *f* ASTR orbit ‖ ANAT orbit, eye socket ‖ FIG sphere, field [of activity] ‖ — ASTR *en órbita* in orbit | *poner en órbita* to put into orbit | *puesta en órbita* putting into orbit.

orbital *adj* orbital; *vuelo orbital* orbital flight.

orbitario, ria *adj* orbital.

orca *f* ZOOL orc, grampus, killer whale (cetáceo).

Orcadas *npr fpl* GEOGR Orkneys, Orkney Islands (islas).

órdago *m* staking of all one's money (en juegos) ‖ — FAM *de órdago* great, fantastic [US swell]; *una película de órdago* a fantastic film; tidy, right old, terrific, hell of a [US helluva]; *un jaleo de órdago* a right old racket; complete, prize; *un idiota de órdago* a prize idiot; hell of a; *una tontería de órdago* a hell of a daft thing to do.

ordalías *f pl* ordeal *sing* (en la Edad Media).

orden *m/f* order, command; *obedecer una orden* to obey an order; *dar la orden de hacer algo* to give the order to do sth. ‖ order (disposición metódica, armoniosa); *por orden cronológico* in chronological order; *por orden de antigüedad* in order of seniority; *la habitación está en orden* the room is in order ‖ nature, character, order (categoría); *éstos son problemas de orden financiero* these are problems of a financial nature ‖ field (sector); *en el orden económico se plantean ciertos problemas* certain problems arise in the economic field ‖ ARQ & BOT & ZOOL order; *orden dórico, corintio, jónico* Doric, Corinthian, Ionic order; *orden de los coleópteros* order of coleoptera ‖ order; *una orden de caballería* an order of knighthood ‖ JUR writ (mandato) | warrant; *una orden de detención* or *de arresto, de embargo, de registro* a warrant for arrest, for attachment, search warrant | order, decision, decree (decisión) | order (paz); *restablecer el orden* to restore order ‖ MIL order; *orden cerrado, de batalla* close, battle order ‖ REL order ‖ COM order ‖ — *a la orden de* to the order of (cheque) ‖ *alterar el orden público* to disturb the peace ‖ *a sus órdenes* at your service ‖ MIL *¡a sus órdenes!, ¡a la orden!* Sir! | *citar en el orden del día* to mention in despatches ‖ *del orden de* of the order of ‖ *de orden de* by order of, on the orders of ‖ *de primer orden* first-class, first-rate ‖ *en el orden natural de las cosas* in the nature of things ‖ *en orden a* with regard to (en relación con), for (para) ‖ *en otro orden de cosas* going on to sth. else ‖ *fuerzas del orden* forces of law and order ‖ *hasta nueva orden* until further orders *o* notice ‖ *llamada al orden* call *o* calling to order ‖ *llamar al orden* to call to order ‖ *mantener el orden* to keep order ‖ MIL *marchar en orden disperso* to march in extended order ‖ *orden de antigüedad* seniority, length of service ‖ MIL *orden de combate* combat order ‖ JUR *orden de comparecencia* summons ‖ *orden de* *compra* purchase order || *orden de expedición* delivery order || *orden del día* agenda (reunión, asamblea, etc.), order of the day (militar) || *orden de sucesión* order of succession || COM *orden de pago* order of payment (libramiento) || REL *órdenes mayores, menores, mendicantes* major, minor, mendicant orders || *órdenes sagradas* holy orders || JUR *orden formal* or *terminante* injunction || *orden público* law and order, public order || *¡orden y compostura!* behave yourself! || COM *páguese a la orden de* pay to the order of || *poner en orden* to put in order || *por orden de* on the orders of, by order of || *por orden de aparición* or *de salida a escena* in order of appearance || *por su orden* in its turn, in its proper order || *Real orden* Order in Council || *sin orden ni concierto* without rhyme or reason; *hablar sin orden ni concierto* to talk without rhyme or reason; any old how (desordenado).

— OBSERV The word *orden* is feminine when it means *command* and in its military and ecclesiastic senses.

ordenación *f* order, arrangement (disposición) || ordering, arranging (acto de disponer) || row (en el punto) || ARQ arrangement [of rooms, etc.] || grouping, arrangement (de las figuras en un cuadro) || REL ordination (de un sacerdote) || development; *ordenación rural* rural development || INFORM sort, sorting || — *ordenación de los recursos de un país* regional planning || *ordenación de pagos* controller's office [in certain ministries].

ordenada *f* MAT ordinate.

ordenadamente *adv* in an orderly way, neatly.

ordenado, da *adj* ordered, in order, tidy (cosas) || orderly, tidy (persona) || REL ordained, in holy orders.

ordenador, ra *adj* ordering || REL ordaining.
◆ *m* REL ordainer || INFORM computer; *ordenador analógico* analog *o* analogue computer; *ordenador central* central computer, host computer; *ordenador digital* digital computer; *ordenador frontal* front-end computer; *ordenador personal* personal computer || *ordenador de pagos* controller, payments officer [in certain ministries].

ordenamiento *m* ordinance (ordenanza) || ordering, putting in order (de papeles, asuntos, etc.) || tidying up; *el ordenamiento de una biblioteca* the tidying up of a bookcase.

ordenancista *adj* strict, rigourous.
◆ *m/f* disciplinarian, martinet.

ordenanza *f* ordinance (disposición) || order, method (orden, método) || order, command (mandato) || *ordenanzas municipales* bylaws, byelaws.
◆ *m* MIL orderly (asistente) || office boy (en oficinas).

ordenar *vt* to order (mandar) || to put in order, to set in order; *ordenar unos papeles, sus asuntos* to put some papers, one's affairs in order || to tidy up, to set in order; *ordenar un armario* to tidy up a cupboard || to direct (encaminar); *ordenar los esfuerzos a* to direct one's efforts towards || REL to ordain, to confer holy orders on || — *ordenar de diácono* to ordain deacon || *ordenar en filas* to line up, to marshal.
◆ *vpr* REL to be *o* to become ordained, to take *o* to enter holy orders, to receive ordination.

ordeñador *m* milker.

ordeñadora *f* milkmaid (mujer) || milking machine, milker (máquina).

ordeñar *vt* to milk; *ordeñar una vaca* to milk a cow || to pick (las aceitunas).

ordeño *m* milking (de las vacas) || picking [of olives].

¡órdiga! *interj* FAM *¡anda la órdiga!* blimey! [*US* well, I'll be damned!].

ordinal *adj* ordinal; *adjetivos numerales ordinales* ordinal numeral adjectives.
◆ *m* ordinal (number) || REL ordinal.

ordinariamente *adv* ordinarily, usually, as a rule (normalmente) || rudely, coarsely (groseramente).

ordinariez *f* coarseness, vulgarity, rudeness (cualidad de grosero, vulgar) || coarse *o* vulgar *o* rude thing (dicho grosero) || — *decir ordinarieces* to be rude || *es una ordinariez* he (she) is awfully coarse || *¡qué ordinariez!* how vulgar!

ordinario, ria *adj* ordinary, usual, common, normal (corriente) || ordinary, mediocre (mediocre); *un trabajo muy ordinario* a very ordinary piece of work || daily (diario) || coarse, rude, vulgar (grosero); *una mujer ordinaria* a coarse woman; *un chiste ordinario* a coarse joke.
◆ *m* daily household expenses *pl* (gastos de casa) || messenger (recadero) || ordinary (obispo) || FIG coarse *o* uncouth *o* vulgar person || — *de ordinario* usually, ordinarily || *ordinario de misa* ordinary of the mass.

ordinariote, ta *adj* FAM very common.

oréada; oréade *f* MIT oread (ninfa).

orear *vt* to air; *orear una camisa, un cuarto* to air a shirt, a room.
◆ *vpr* to air, to be aired || FIG to get a breath of fresh air (airearse).

orégano *m* BOT origan, oregano, marjoram || FIG *no todo el monte es orégano* it is not all plain sailing, life is not just a bowl of cherries.

oreja *f* ear; *tener grandes orejas* to have big ears; *orejas tiesas, gachas* erect, drooping ears || flap (de zapato) || tab (para meter una bota) || handle (de vasija) || wing (de sillón) || palm, fluke (de ancla) || mouldboard [*US* moldboard] (del arado) || claw (de martillo) || TECN lug || — *aguzar las orejas* to prick up its ears (animal), to prick up one's ears (persona) || FIG & FAM *apearse* or *salir por las orejas* to be thrown over the horse's head || FIG *asomar* or *enseñar* or *descubrir la oreja* to show one's true colours | *calentarle a uno las orejas* to get on s.o.'s nerves (fastidiar), to box s.o.'s ears (pegar), to send s.o. away with a flea in his ear (reprender) || FIG *con las orejas gachas* crestfallen || TAUR *cortar una oreja, dos orejas* to win *o* to be awarded an ear, two ears [as a reward for a good performance] || FIG *estar* or *tener la mosca* or *la pulga detrás de la oreja* to be suspicions *o* uneasy | *haberle visto las orejas al lobo* to have had a narrow escape *o* a close shave | *hacer orejas de mercader* to turn a deaf ear | *mojarle a uno la oreja* to pick a quarrel with s.o., to provoke s.o. || *oreja de abad* pancake (tortita), Venus's navelwort (planta) || ZOOL *oreja marina* or *de mar* sea ear, abalone || FIG *ponerle a uno la mosca* or *la pulga detrás de la oreja* to arouse s.o.'s suspicious, to make s.o. suspicious | *tirar de la oreja a Jorge* to gamble || *tirar de las orejas a uno* to pull s.o.'s ears || FIG & FAM *untar la oreja con saliva a uno* to pick a quarrel with s.o. | *verle a uno la oreja* to see through s.o., to see s.o.'s true colours.

orejera *f* earflap (de gorra) || earpiece, cheek piece (de casco de guerra) || mouldboard [*US* moldboard] (de arado) || wing (de sillón) || disc worn in the ear by certains Indians.

orejón *m* dried peach *o* apricot (melocotón o albaricoque) || HIST Inca nobleman || FAM bigears (persona) || *darle a uno un orejón* to pull s.o.'s ear.

orejudo, da *adj* long-eared, lop-eared (animal) || big-eared (persona).
◆ *m* ZOOL long-eared bat (murciélago).

orejuela *f* handle (asa).

oreo *m* breeze, breath of wind (aire) || airing (ventilación).

orfanato *m* orphanage (asilo de huérfanos).

orfandad *f* orphanhood, orphanage (estado de huérfano) || orphan's allowance (pensión) || FIG forlornness, isolation.

orfebre *m* goldsmith, silversmith.

orfebrería *f* goldsmithery, silversmithing.

orfelinato *m* orphanage (orfanato).
— OBSERV This is a Gallicism for *orfanato*.

Orfeo *npr m* Orpheus.

orfeón *m* MÚS choral society.

orfeonista *m* member of a choral society.

órfico, ca *adj* Orphean, Orphic (de orfeo) || Orphic (poesías, dogmas, etc.).
◆ *f pl* Orphic festivities.

organdí *m* organdie [*US* organdy] (tela).
— OBSERV The Spanish word *organdí* has two plural forms, *organdís* and *organdíes*.

orgánico, ca *adj* organic.

organigrama *m* chart || INFORM flowchart.

organillero *m* organ-grinder.

organillo *m* barrel organ, hurdy-gurdy.

organismo *m* organism; *el organismo humano* the human organism || organization (organización) || body (institución) || *los organismos especializados de la ONU* the specialized agencies of the UN.

organista *m/f* MÚS organist.

organización *f* organization || *Organización de las Naciones Unidas (ONU)* United Nations Organization [UNO, UN].

organizado, da *adj* organized.

organizador, ra *adj* organizing.
◆ *m* BIOL organizer.

organizar *vt* to organize.
◆ *vpr* to be organized; *se organizó una fiesta* a party was organized || to get organized (arreglarse) || — FIG *menudo escándalo se organizó* there was a tidy rumpus | *se organizó una pelea* a fight broke out.

órgano *m* organ; *los órganos de la digestión* the digestive organs || body; *órgano legislativo* legislative body || MÚS organ (instrumento) || TECN part, member; *órgano de transmisión* driving part; *órgano motor* driving member || FIG organ (medio o agente) || *órgano de manubrio* barrel organ.

organum *m* MÚS organum.

orgasmo *m* orgasm.

orgía *f* orgy.

orgiástico, ca *adj* orgiastic.

orgullo *m* conceit, arrogance, haughtiness (arrogancia) || pride (sentimiento legítimo) || FIG pride; *es el orgullo de la familia* he is the pride of the family || *no caber en sí de orgullo, reventar de orgullo* to be bursting with pride.

orgulloso, sa *adj* proud, arrogant, haughty; *orgulloso de* or *por su riqueza* proud of *o* arrogant *o* haughty about one's wealth || conceited (engreído) || proud (legítimamente satisfecho); *estar orgulloso de su padre* to be proud of one's father || FIG *más orgulloso que don Rodrigo en la horca* as proud as a peacock.

orientable *adj* turning (que gira) || adjustable.

orientación *f* aspect, prospect, exposure (de un edificio) || orientation, guidance, direction (dirección); *orientación por las estrellas* orientation by the stars || pointing (de una aguja magnética, veleta, etc.) || positioning (de un cañón, una antena, etc.) || FIG tendency (tendencia) || MAR trimming (acción), trim (efecto) [of sails] || — *con orientación al mediodía* facing south, with a southern aspect || *no me gusta la orientación que están tomando las cosas* I don't like the way things are going || *orientación profesional* vocational guidance.

orientador, ra *m/f* adviser, counsellor (consejero) || careers adviser (orientación profesional).

oriental *adj* oriental, eastern.
◆ *m/f* oriental.

orientalismo *m* orientalism.

orientalista *adj/s* orientalist.

orientalizar *vt* to orientalize.
◆ *vpr* to orientalize.

orientar *vt* to orient, to orientate (un edificio) || to guide, to give directions to (a una persona) || to direct (dirigir) || to position; *orientar una antena, un cañón* to position an aerial, a cannon || FIG to guide (guiar) || MAR to trim [sails] || *casa orientada al sur* house facing *o* looking south.
◆ *vpr* to orient o.s., to get *o* to find one's bearings; *orientarse con una brújula* to orient o.s. with a compass || to point; *la aguja de la brújula se orienta hacia el norte* the compass needle points north || to head, to make (*hacia* for) (hacia un lugar) || *se orienta hacia la contabilidad* he is going in for accountancy.

oriente *m* east (punto cardinal) || east, orient (países asiáticos) || east wind (viento) || orient (de una perla) || FIG origin (origen) || — *Cercano* or *Próximo Oriente* Near East || *Extremo* or *Lejano Oriente* Far East || *Gran Oriente* Grand Lodge (de la masonería) || *Oriente Medio* Middle East.

orificación *f* MED filling (of a tooth) with gold, aurification.

orificar *vt* MED to fill (a tooth) with gold.

orífice *m* goldsmith.

orificio *m* orifice || TECN orifice, hole, opening || — TECN *orificio de admisión* inlet | *orificio de colada* taphole, tapping hole, draw hole | *orificio de salida* outlet.

oriflama *f* HIST oriflamme || banner, standard, banderole (bandera).

origen *m* origin, beginning, start (principio) || origin (procedencia); *una canción de origen español* a song of Spanish origin || origin, extraction, birth (familia); *de humilde origen* of humble origin || origin, cause, starting point (causa); *el origen de una disputa* the origin of a dispute || origin, source, derivation (de una palabra, una costumbre, etc.) || — *dar origen a* to give rise to || *desde su origen* from the beginning || *en su origen* originally, in the beginning || *tener su origen en* to originate in *o* with *o* from.

original *adj* original (cuadro, texto, etc.) || original, inventive, creative (escritor, etc.) || original, novel (argumento de un libro, idea, etc.) || odd, queer, singular (extraño) || of origin; *país original* country of origin || — *pecado original* original sin || CINEM *versión original* original version.
◆ *m/f* odd *o* singular character; *es un original* he's an odd character.
◆ *m* original (texto, modelo, cuadro); *leer a Shakespeare en el original* to read Shakespeare in the original || IMPR manuscript.

originalidad *f* originality || oddness, strangeness, singularity (carácter excéntrico).

originalmente *adv* originally, from the beginning (originariamente) || originally, with originality (de modo original) || oddly, strangely, singularly (extrañamente).

originar *vt* to originate, to give rise to, to cause, to start (causar).
◆ *vpr* to originate, to have its origin *o* source, to spring (proceder).

originariamente *adv* originally.

originario, ria *adj* original || originating, coming, native (que tiene su origen) || — *la costumbre es originaria de Escocia* the custom originated in Scotland || *soy originario de Gales* I come from Wales.

orilla *f* shore (del mar) || bank (de un río); *en las orillas del Támesis* on the banks of the Thames || side, edge, shore (de un lago) || edge, side (de un camino, un bosque, un campo) || rim (de un vaso) || edge (de una mesa, etc.) || selvedge, selvage, list (de una tela) || fresh breeze (vientecillo) || — *a orillas de* beside (al lado de) || *a orillas del mar* at the seaside (lugar de veraneo), on the seashore *o* coast; *el faro está a orillas del mar* the lighthouse is on the coast || *la casita está a orillas del lago* the little lakeside house, the little house by the lake || *Zaragoza está situado a orillas del Ebro* Saragossa is on the Ebro.

orillar *vt* to edge, to trim; *orillar con galón* to edge with braid || to selvedge (formar orillo en la tela) || to skirt, to go round (un bosque, un lago, etc.) || FIG to get round, to surmount (una dificultad) | to wind up, to settle (un asunto) | to settle; *orillar una diferencia* to settle a difference.
◆ *vi/vpr* to reach the bank (de un río) *o* the shore (del mar).

orillo *m* selvedge, selvage, list [of cloth].

orín *m* rust.
◆ *pl* urine *sing.*

orina *f* urine.

orinal *m* chamber pot || bedpan (para enfermos).

orinar *vt/vi* to urinate.
◆ *vpr* to wet o.s.

Orinoco *npr m* GEOGR Orinoco.

Orión *m* ASTR Orion.

oriundez *f* origin.

oriundo, da *adj* native, indigenous; *una planta oriunda de México* a plant native to Mexico, a plant indigenous in Mexico || from, native, originating; *persona oriunda de Escocia* person from Scotland, person native of *o* originating from Scotland.
◆ *m/f* native.

orla *f* border, edging, fringe (de una tela) || ornamental border (de una página) || HERÁLD orle.

orladura *f* border, edging, fringe (de la tela) || ornamental border (de una página).

orlar *vt* to border, to edge, to trim || to frame with an ornamental border (una página) || HERÁLD to provide with an orle || *orlar con* or *de árboles* to line with trees.

orlón *m* orlon (tela).

ornamentación *f* ornamentation, adornment.

ornamental *adj* ornamental.

ornamentar *vt* to adorn, to ornament.

ornamento *m* ornament, adornment, embellishment (adorno) || ARQ ornament, ornamentation (conjunto de adornos) || FIG moral qualities *pl.*
◆ *pl* REL ornaments.

ornar *vt* to adorn, to embellish, to ornament || *ornado en sus más bellas galas* decked out in all one's finery.

ornato *m* ARQ ornament || ornamentation (arte *o* manera de adornar) || adornment (adorno).

ornitología *f* ornithology.

ornitológico, ca *adj* ornithological.

ornitólogo *m* ornithologist.

ornitorrinco *m* ZOOL ornithorhynchus, duckbill, platypus.

oro *m* gold; *un reloj de oro* a gold watch; *dólar oro* gold dollar || — FIG *apalear oro* to be rolling in money | *comprar algo a peso de oro* to pay a fortune for sth., to pay the earth for sth. | *corazón de oro* heart of gold || *chapado en oro* gold-plated || *de oro* gold, golden || *fiebre del oro* gold rush, gold fever || FIG *guardar como oro en paño* to treasure | *hacerse de oro* to make a fortune || *la Edad de Oro* the Golden Age || *lavado del oro* gold washing || *libro de oro* visitor's book || *lingote de oro* gold ingot *o* bar || *mina de oro* gold mine || FIG *no es oro todo lo que reluce* all that glitters is not gold || *oro batido* beaten gold || *oro blanco* white gold || *oro de ley* fine gold || *oro en barras* gold bars, bullion || *oro en hojas* or *en panes* gold leaf || *oro en polvo* gold dust || *oro molido* ground gold || FIG *oro negro* black gold || *pan de oro* gold leaf || FIG *pedir el oro y el moro* to ask the earth | *por todo el oro del mundo* for all the money in the world | *prometer el oro y el moro* to promise the earth, to promise the moon and stars || *regla de oro* golden rule || *reserva de oro* gold reserve || FIG *ser una mina de oro* to be a gold mine | *tener voz de oro* to have a beautiful voice || *vajilla de oro* gold plate | *valer su peso en oro* or *tanto oro como pesa* to be worth it's *o* one's weight in gold.
◆ *pl* Spanish card suit bearing a representation of one or more gold coins [equivalent to diamonds] || FIG *oros son triunfos* it's money that counts.

orogénesis *f* GEOL orogenesis.

orogenia *f* GEOL orogeny.

orogénico, ca *adj* GEOL orogenic.

orografía *f* orography.

orográfico, ca *adj* orographic, orographical.

orometría *f* orometry.

orondo, da *adj* rounded (vasija) || FIG & FAM puffed up with pride, self-satisfied (orgulloso) | potbellied (gordo).

oropel *m* tinsel || FIG tinsel, frippery (falsa apariencia) || *de oropel* flashy.

oropéndola *f* oriole (ave).

oroya *f* AMER cable basket.

orozuz *m* liquorice, licorice.

orquesta *f* MÚS orchestra; *orquesta de cámara, sinfónica* chamber, symphony orchestra | band; *orquesta de baile* dance band || *director de orquesta* conductor.

orquestación *f* MÚS orchestration, scoring || FIG orchestration.

orquestal *adj* MÚS orchestral.

orquestar *vt* to orchestrate, to score; *orquestar una composición* to orchestrate a composition || FIG to orchestrate.

orquidáceas *f pl* BOT orchidaceae.

orquídeo, a *adj* BOT orchidaceous.
◆ *f* BOT orchid.

ortega *f* sandgrouse (ave).

ortiga *f* nettle (planta).

ortigal *m* nettle patch *o* field.

orto *m* rising [of sun or star].

ortocentro *m* MAT orthocentre [*US* orthocenter].

ortocromático, ca *adj* orthocromatic.

ortodoxia *f* orthodoxy.

ortodoxo, xa *adj/s* orthodox.

ortogénesis *f* BIOL orthogenesis.

ortogenético, ca *adj* BIOL orthogenetic.

ortognatismo *m* orthognatism.

ortogonal *adj* MAT orthogonal.

ortografía *f* spelling, orthography; *cometer una falta de ortografía* to make a spelling mistake || ARQ orthography, orthographic projection.

ortografiar *vt* to spell; *no saber ortografiar una palabra* not to know how to spell a word.

ortográfico, ca *adj* spelling, orthographic, orthographical.

ortología *f* orthoepy.

ortopedia *f* MED orthopaedics, orthopedics.

ortopédico, ca *adj* orthopaedic, orthopedic.
◆ *m/f* orthopaedist, orthopedist.

ortopedista *m/f* orthopaedist, orthopedist.

ortóptero, ra *adj* ZOOL orthopterous.
◆ *m* ZOOL orthopteran, orthopteron.
◆ *pl* ZOOL orthoptera.

ortótropo, pa *adj* BOT orthotropic, orthotropous.

oruga *f* ZOOL caterpillar ‖ BOT rocket (jaramago) ‖ TECN caterpillar (de vehículo) ‖ *auto oruga* caterpillar tractor, tracked vehicle.

orujo *m* marc [of grapes or olives].

orvallar *v impers* to drizzle.

orvallo *m* drizzle (llovizna).

orza *f* glazed earthenware jar (vasija) ‖ MAR luffing (acción de orzar) | centreboard [*US* centerboard], sliding keel (pieza).

orzar *vi* MAR to luff.

orzuelo *m* MED stye, sty ‖ trap (trampa).

os *pron pers 2.ª pers pl* you, to you (dativo); *os digo* I tell you, I say to you ‖ you (acusativo); *os vi ayer* I saw you yesterday ‖ yourselves, to yourselves (reflexivo); *vosotros os vestís* you dress yourselves ‖ each other, to each other (recíproco); *vosotros os escribís* you write to each other ‖ *os lo compré* I bought it for you (para vosotros), I bought it from you (de vosotros).

— OBSERV The enclitic use of this pronoun in the imperative causes the verb's final *d* to be dropped (*deteneos* stop) except with the verb *ir* (*idos* go away, leave).

osa *f* she-bear ‖ — FAM *¡anda la osa!* what a carry on! ‖ ASTR *Osa Mayor* Great Bear, Ursa Major | *Osa Menor* Little Bear, Ursa Minor.

osadía *f* daring, boldness, fearlessness ‖ boldness, audacity, impudence, shamelessness (descaro).

osado, da *adj* daring, bold, fearless (valeroso) ‖ bold, impudent, shameless (atrevido, descarado).

osamenta *f* skeleton (esqueleto) ‖ bones *pl* (conjunto de huesos).

osar *vi* to dare, to venture (atreverse).

osario *m* ossuary.

Oscar *m* Oscar (premio).

oscense *adj/s* Huescan [Huesca, town in Spain, formerly «Osca»].

oscilación *f* oscillation ‖ swinging (de péndulo) ‖ fluctuation (de precios) ‖ FIG hesitation, wavering (vacilación).

oscilador *m* FÍS oscillator.

oscilante *adj* oscillating.

oscilar *vi* to oscillate ‖ to swing (el péndulo) ‖ FIG to oscillate, to fluctuate, to vary; *los precios oscilan* prices fluctuate ‖ to oscillate, to waver, to hesitate (vacilar).

oscilatorio, ria *adj* oscillatory.

oscilógrafo *m* FÍS oscillograph.

oscilograma *m* oscillogram.

osciloscopio *m* FÍS oscilloscope.

ósculo *m* kiss; *ósculo de paz* kiss of peace ‖ osculum (en una esponja).

oscuramente; obscuramente *adv* obscurely.

oscurantismo; obscurantismo *m* obscurantism.

oscurantista; obscurantista *adj* obscurantist.
◆ *m/f* obscurantist, obscurant.

oscurecer*; obscurecer *vt* to darken, to obscure, to dim ‖ to darken, to deepen (un color) ‖ FIG to obscure, to fog, to cloud, to obfuscate (volver poco inteligible) | to confuse (la mente) | to put in the shade, to overshadow (deslucir); *él oscurece a sus hermanos* he puts his brothers in the shade | to obscure, to conceal; *oscurecer la verdad* to obscure the truth ‖ to tarnish (la reputación) ‖ ARTES to shade.
◆ *vi* to get dark, to grow dark.
◆ *vpr* to darken, to grow dark, to cloud over (el cielo) ‖ to grow dim (la vista) ‖ FIG to wane (la gloria, etc.).

oscurecimiento; obscurecimiento *m* darkening, clouding (del cielo) ‖ darkening, deepening (de un color) ‖ dimming (de la vista, la luz).

oscuridad; obscuridad *f* darkness (del cielo, de la noche) ‖ FIG obscurity, lack of clarity (falta de claridad) | obscurity; *vivir en la oscuridad* to live in obscurity ‖ *tener miedo a la oscuridad* to be afraid of the dark.

oscuro, ra; obscuro, ra *adj* dark; *cueva oscura* dark cave ‖ dark (color); *llevar un traje oscuro* to wear a dark suit; *gris oscuro* dark grey [*US* dark gray] ‖ dark, gloomy, overcast (nublado) ‖ obscure, inconspicuous (poco conocido) ‖ obscure; *de origen oscuro* of obscure origin ‖ FIG obscure, abstruse (difícil de comprender) | gloomy, black; *el porvenir es muy oscuro* the future is very gloomy | shady (sospechoso); *un asunto oscuro* a shady business ‖ — *a oscuras* in the dark ‖ FIG *llevar una vida oscura* to be *o* to keep in the background | *oscuro como boca de lobo* pitch-dark | *quedarse a oscuras* to be left in the dark.

oseína *f* ANAT ossein.

óseo, a *adj* osseous, bony; *tejido óseo* osseous tissue ‖ bone, of the bone (del hueso).

osera *f* bear's den.

osezno *m* ZOOL bear cub.

osificación *f* ossification.

osificar *vt* to ossify.
◆ *vpr* to ossify, to become ossified.

Osiris *npr m* MIT Osiris.

Oslo *n pr* GEOGR Oslo.

osmanlí *adj/s* Osmanli.

ósmico, ca *adj* QUÍM osmic.

osmio *m* osmium (metal).

osmómetro *m* FÍS osmometer.

ósmosis; osmosis *f* FÍS osmosis.

osmótico, ca *adj* osmotic.

oso *m* ZOOL bear; *oso blanco* or *polar, negro, pardo* polar, black, brown bear ‖ FIG ape, gorilla (hombre peludo o feo) | lone wolf (persona insociable) ‖ — FAM *hacer el oso* to act the goat (hacer reír), to court (cortejar) ‖ *oso de felpa* or *de peluche* teddy bear (muñeco) ‖ *oso gris* grizzly, grizzly bear ‖ *oso hormiguero* anteater ‖ *oso lavador* racoon [*US* raccoon] ‖ *oso marino* fur seal ‖ *oso marsupial* koala, koala bear.

ossobuco *m* CULIN osso bucco.

¡oste! *interj* —> **oxte.**

osteína *f* QUÍM ostein, ossein.

osteítis *f* MED osteitis.

ostensible *adj* obvious, patent, ostensible.

ostensivo, va *adj* ostensive, evident.

ostentación *f* ostentation, show, (vain) display ‖ — *con ostentación* ostentatiously ‖ *hacer ostentación de* to show off, to parade, to flaunt, to air; *hacer ostentación de sus riquezas* to show off one's wealth; *hacer ostentación de su antimilitarismo* to flaunt one's antimilitarism.

ostentador, ra *adj* ostentatious.
◆ *m/f* ostentatious person, show-off.

ostentar *vt* to show (mostrar) ‖ to show off, to parade, to flaunt, to air; *ostentar sus riquezas, sus ideas revolucionarias* to flaunt one's riches, one's revolutionary ideas ‖ to sport; *ostentar un sombrero nuevo* to sport a new hat ‖ to show; *ostenta un gran talento de escritor* he shows a great talent for writing ‖ to have, to hold (poseer); *ostentar un título de licenciado en ciencias* to have a Bachelor of Science degree.

ostentativo, va *adj* ostentatious.

ostentoso, sa *adj* ostentatious.

osteoartritis *f* MED osteoarthritis.

osteoblasto *m* osteoblast.

osteología *f* osteology.

osteológico, ca *adj* osteologic, osteological.

osteólogo, ga *m/f* osteologist.

osteoma *m* MED osteoma (tumor).

osteomielitis *f* MED osteomyelitis.

osteópata *m/f* osteopath.

osteopatía *f* osteopathy.

osteopático, ca *adj* osteopathic.

osteoplastia *f* MED osteoplasty.

osteotomía *f* MED osteotomy.

ostiario *m* ostiary, doorkeeper (clérigo).

ostión *m* large oyster (ostrón).

ostra *f* oyster (molusco).

ostracismo *m* ostracism ‖ *condenar al ostracismo* to ostracize.

ostral *m* oyster bed.

ostrero, ra *adj* oyster.
◆ *m/f* oyster seller (vendedor).
◆ *m* oyster bed (ostral) ‖ oyster catcher (ave).

ostrícola *adj* (of) oyster culture ‖ *la industria ostrícola* the oyster industry.

ostricultor *m* oyster producer.

ostricultura *f* oyster culture, ostreiculture.

ostrogodo, da *adj* Ostrogothic.
◆ *m/f* Ostrogoth.

ostrón *m* large oyster.

osuno, na *adj* bear-like.

otalgia *f* MED otalgia, earache.

otálgico, ca *adj* otalgic.

OTAN *abrev de Organización del Tratado del Atlántico Norte* NATO, North Atlantic Treaty Organization.

otaria *f* ZOOL otary.

otario, ria *adj* AMER silly, stupid, foolish (tonto).

oteador, ra *m/f* lookout, watcher.

otear *vt* to scan, to search; *otear el horizonte* to scan the horizon ‖ to survey, to observe; *desde este monte oteo toda la llanura* from this hill I can survey the whole plain ‖ to watch, to observe, to scrutinize (escudriñar).

Otelo *npr m* Othello.

otero *m* hillock, knoll (collado).

otitis *f* MED otitis, inflammation of the ear.

otolaringología *f* MED otolaryngology.

otología *f* MED otology.

otólogo *m* otologist.

otomano, na *adj/s* Ottoman.
◆ *f* ottoman (sofá).

otoñada *f* autumn.

otoñal *adj* autumnal, autumn, of autumn [*US* fall, of the fall, in the fall]; *la temporada otoñal* the autumnal season; *una mañana otoñal* one autumn morning.

otoñar *vi* to spend the autumn ‖ to grow in autumn (la hierba).

otoño *m* autumn [US fall]; *en el otoño* in autumn, in the fall || autumn aftermath (hierba) || FIG autumn; *en el otoño de la vida* in the autumn of one's life.

otorgamiento *m* granting, concession; *el otorgamiento de un privilegio* the granting of a privilege || authorization, consent, permission (permiso) || awarding (de un premio) || conferring (de poderes) || JUR deed of agreement, agreement, contract [drawn up before and authenticated by a notary].

otorgante *adj* granting (de privilegios, etc.) || awarding (de un premio) || conferring (de poderes).

otorgar *vt* to grant, to give; *otorgar un indulto, la mano de su hija* to grant pardon, one's daughter's hand || to award (un premio) || to confer (poderes, honores, etc.) || JUR to execute, to draw up [a deed in the presence of a notary] | to make, to draw up [a will] || — *nos ha otorgado su ayuda* he has graced us with his assistance || *quien calla otorga* silence gives consent.

otorragia *f* MED haemorrhage of the ear.

otorrinolaringología *f* MED otorhinolaryngology.

otorrinolaringólogo *m* MED otorhinolaryngologist.

otoscopio *m* otoscope.

otro, tra *adj* other; *¿leíste la otra novela?* did you read the other novel?; *¿no comiste los otros pasteles?* haven't you eaten the other cakes? || another; *tengo otra hermana* I have another sister; *lo haremos otro día* we shall do it another day || — *al otro día* (the *o* on the) next day, the following day, the day after || *con otras palabras* in other words || *del otro lado de la calle* on the other side of the street, across the street || *el otro día* the other day || *de otro modo, de otra manera* (in) another way; otherwise || *en otra época* in former times, in a bygone era || *en otra ocasión* on another occasion || *en otra parte* somewhere else, elsewhere || *en otro tiempo* in former times, formerly || *¿en qué otro sitio?* where else? || *entre otras cosas* among *o* amongst other things || *es otro yo* he is a second self *o* my alter ego || *esperamos tener una vida mejor en el otro mundo* we hope that we will live better in the next world || FIG *eso es otro cantar* that's a different kettle of fish!, that's different! || *los tiempos son otros* times have changed || *ninguna otra cosa* nothing else || *ninguna otra persona* nobody else || *no ha podido ir a otro sitio* he could not go to any other place *o* anywhere else || *nos dieron otras dos mil pesetas* they gave us another two thousand pesetas || *otra cosa* something else (algo diferente), another thing (algo más) || *otra persona* somebody else || *otra vez* again; *vendrá otra vez* he will come again; *¡otra vez usted!* you again! || *¡otra vez!* encore! (espectáculos) || *otros tantos* just as many, as many more || *por otra parte, por otro lado* on the other hand || *vinieron otras muchas mujeres* many other women came.
◆ *pron* another (one); *ésta es otra de mis hermanas* this is another of my sisters; *ayer vino otro* another one came yesterday; *hay uno para mí y otro para ti* there is one for me and another for you || someone else, somebody else; *que lo haga otro* let someone else do it || *algún otro* somebody else || *cualquier otro que* anyone (else) but; *cualquier otro que tú lo hubiese aceptado* anyone but you would have accepted it || FAM *¡cuénteselo a otro!* come off it!, pull the other leg!, tell it to the marines! || *el otro, la otra* the other (one); *este libro y el otro* this book and the other || *es una idea como otra cualquiera* it is an idea || *hablar de esto y de lo otro* to talk about this, that and the other; to talk about this and that || *¡hasta otra!* see you again!, see you soon!, so long! || *lo otro* the other thing (cosa distinta), the rest (lo demás); *lo otro me da igual* I don't care about the rest || *los otros, las otras* the others, the other ones || *ningún otro* nobody else || *no fue otro que el director* it was none other than the headmaster || *¡otra!* encore! (espectáculos) || *otro más* one more, another one || *otro que tal* another one || *otro tanto* the same (lo mismo), as much again (el doble) || *uno a otro, unos a otros* (to, at, etc.) each other, one another (reciprocidad); *mirarse uno a otro* to look at one another || *uno con otro* taking one thing with another, all things considered, all in all || *uno y otro* both; *uno y otro son muy simpáticos* they are both very nice.
◆ *pl* others; *unos no sabían, otros no querían* some did not know, others did not want to || — *algunos otros* some others, a few others || *entre otras* among *o* amongst other things || *otros dos* another two, two more, two others || *otros muchos* many others || *otros pocos* a few others || *otros tantos* just as many, as many more; *se marcharon veinte y otros tantos llegaron* twenty left and just as many arrived.

otrora *adv* formerly.

otrosí *adv* furthermore.
◆ *m* JUR petition [made after the principal petition] (apartado de una exposición).

Ottawa *n pr* GEOGR Ottawa.

ova *f* alga.

ovación *f* ovation.

ovacionar *vt* to give (s.o.) an ovation, to acclaim.

oval; ovalado, da *adj* oval, egg-shaped, oviform.

ovalar *vt* to make oval, to oval.

ovalización *f* ovalization.

ovalizar *vt* to ovalize, to oval, to make oval.

óvalo *m* oval.

ovar *vi* to lay, to lay eggs (las aves).

ovárico, ca *adj* ovarian.

ovariectomía *f* MED ovariectomy.

ovario *m* ANAT & BOT ovary || ARQ moulding decorated with ova.

ovariotomía *f* MED ovariotomy.

ovas *f pl* spawn *sing*, roe *sing*, fish eggs (hueva).

oveja *f* ewe (hembra del carnero) || sheep (carnero); *un rebaño de ovejas* a flock of sheep || AMER llama || — FIG *cada oveja con su pareja* every Jack has his Jill || — FIG *oveja descarriada* lost sheep | *oveja negra* black sheep | *contar ovejas* to count sheep (para dormirse) | *encomendar las ovejas al lobo* to set the cat among the pigeons .
◆ *pl* FIG sheep.

ovejero, ra *m/f* shepherd, shepherdess.
◆ *adj* *perro ovejero* sheepdog.

ovejuno, na *adj* sheep, sheep's || *ganado ovejuno* sheep.

overbooking *m* overbooking.

overo, ra *adj* peach-coloured (caballo).

overtura *f* MÚS overture.

ovetense *adj* [of *o* from] Oviedo [town in Asturias].
◆ *m/f* inhabitant *o* native of Oviedo.

Ovidio *npr m* Ovid.

óvidos *m pl* ZOOL ovidae.

oviducto *m* ZOOL oviduct.

oviforme *adj* oviform.

ovillar *vt* to roll *o* to wind into a ball.
◆ *vpr* to roll up into a ball, to curl up.

ovillejo *m* small ball (ovillo).

ovillo *m* ball (de hilo, de lana) || pile, heap (montón) || — *hacerse un ovillo* to crouch down, to curl up (acurrucarse), to get all tangled up *o* muddled up (confundirse) || *por el hilo se saca el ovillo* by putting two and two together (one gets four).

ovino, na *adj* ovine || *ganado ovino* sheep.
◆ *m* sheep.

oviparidad *f* oviparity.

ovíparo, ra *adj* ZOOL oviparous.

oviscapto *m* ZOOL ovipositor.

ovni *m* UFO, unidentified flying object.

ovo *m* ARQ ovum.

ovocito *m* BIOL oocyte.

ovoide *adj/sm* ovoid.

óvolo *m* ARQ ovolo.

ovovivíparo *adj* ZOOL ovoviviparous.

ovulación *f* ovulation.

ovular *adj* ovular.

ovular *vi* to ovulate.

óvulo *m* BOT & BIOL ovule.

oxácido *m* QUÍM oxyacid.

oxálico, ca *adj* QUÍM oxalic.

oxalidáceas *f pl* BOT oxalidaceae.

oxear *vt* to shoo away.

oxford *f* oxford (tejido).

oxhídrico, ca *adj* QUÍM oxyhydrogen; *soplete oxhídrico* oxyhydrogen torch.

oxhidrilo *m* QUÍM hydroxyl.

oxiacetilénico, ca *adj* oxyacetylene; *soplete oxiacetilénico* oxyacetylene torch.

oxidación *f* oxidation || rusting (moho).

oxidado, da *adj* rusty (mohoso) || oxidized.

oxidante *adj* oxidizing.
◆ *m* oxidizing agent, oxidant, oxidizer.

oxidar *vt* to oxidize || to rust (enmohecer).
◆ *vpr* to become oxidized, to oxidize || to rust, to get rusty; *el cerrojo se ha oxidado* the bolt has rusted.

óxido *m* QUÍM oxide || rust (orín).

oxigenación *f* QUÍM oxygenation.

oxigenado, da *adj* oxygenated || bleached, peroxided; *pelo oxigenado* bleached hair || *agua oxigenada* hydrogen peroxide, oxygenated water.

oxigenar *vt* QUÍM to oxigenate.
◆ *vpr* FAM to get a breath of fresh air.

oxígeno *m* oxygen; *cámara de oxígeno* oxigen tent.

oxigenoterapia *f* MED oxygen treatment.

oxihemoglobina *f* BIOL oxyhemoglobin, oxyhaemoglobin.

oxítono, na *adj/sm* GRAM oxytone.

oxiuro *m* oxyuris (lombriz).

oxoniense *adj* Oxford, Oxonian, Oxfordian.
◆ *m/f* Oxonian, Oxfordian.

¡oxte!; ¡oste! *interj* clear off!, shoo!, scat! || *sin decir oxte ni moxte* without (saying) a word.

oyente *adj* listening.
◆ *m/f* hearer, listener || auditor (estudiante).
◆ *pl* listeners (radio) || audience *sing* (público).

ozonador; ozonizador *m* ozonizer, ozonator.

ozonar; ozonificar; ozonizar *vt* to ozonize, to ozonate.

ozonización; ozonificación *f* ozonization, ozonation.

ozonizado, da *adj* ozonic.

ozono *m* QUÍM ozone.

ozonómetro *m* QUÍM ozonometer.

ozonosfera *f* ozonosphere.

ozonoterapia *f* MED ozonotherapy.

P

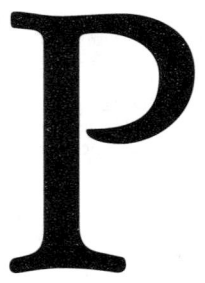

p *f* p; *una p minúscula* a small p.
— OBSERV The Spanish *p* is pronounced like the English *p*.

pabellón *m* pavilion (edificio); *el pabellón español en la feria de X* the Spanish pavilion in the X fair || summerhouse (en el jardín) || block [*US* pavilion] (de un hospital, etc.) || bell tent (tienda de campaña) || flag, banner (bandera); *izar el pabellón nacional* to hoist the national flag || MAR flag, nationality || canopy (cortina de cama) || hangings *pl*, drapings *pl* (de trono, de altar, etc.) || MÚS bell (de un instrumento) || horn (de fonógrafo) || HERÁLD pavilion || MIL stack (de fusiles) || ANAT external ear, outer ear, pavilion (de la oreja) || pavilion (de una piedra preciosa) || — *arriar pabellón* to lower the flag || *pabellón de caza* shooting box.

pabilo *m* wick (de vela).

Pablo *npr m* Paul.

pábulo *m* pabulum, food || — FIG *dar pábulo a* to encourage, to feed | *dar pábulo a las críticas* to lay o.s. open to criticism, to expose o.s. to criticism.

PAC *abrev de Política Agrícola Común* CAP, Common Agricultural Policy.

paca *f* ZOOL paca (roedor) || bale (fardo); *una paca de algodón* a bale of cotton.

pacana *f* pecan (árbol, fruto).

pacatería *f* prudery, prudishness (ñoñería) || calmness, quietness (tranquilidad).

pacato, ta *adj* gentle, calm, quiet (tranquilo) | prudish (ñoño).

pacay *m* AMER pacay tree (árbol).
— OBSERV pl *pacayes* or *pacaes*.

pacayar *m* AMER plantation of pacay trees.

pacense *adj* [of *o* from] Béja [Portugal] || [of *o* from] Badajoz [Spain].
◆ *m/f* inhabitant *o* native of Béja *o* of Badajoz.

paceño, ña *adj* [of *o* from] La Paz [Bolivia, Honduras and Salvador].
◆ *m/f* inhabitant *o* native of La Paz.

pacer* *vi* to pasture, to graze.
◆ *vt* to pasture, to graze (apacentar) || to eat (comer) || to gnaw (roer).

paces *f pl* peace *sing* || → **paz.**

paciencia *f* patience; *armarse de paciencia* to muster one's patience; *todo se alcanza con paciencia* everything is possible with (a little) patience || slowness (lentitud) || almond cake (bollo) || — *acabarle* or *consumirle a uno la paciencia* to make s.o. lose patience, to try one's patience || *acabársele* or *agotársele a uno la paciencia* to lose patience || *con paciencia se gana el cielo* all things come to him who waits, slow and steady wins the race || *esperar con paciencia* to wait patiently || *llevar* or *tomar algo con paciencia* to take sth. calmly || *perder la paciencia* to lose patience, to lose one's temper || *probarle a alguien la paciencia* to try s.o.'s patience || *tener paciencia* to have patience, to be patient (ser paciente), to wait patiently, to be patient (esperar) || *tener perdida la paciencia, habérsele agotado a uno la paciencia* to be at the end of one's tether.

paciente *adj/s* patient.

pacientemente *adv* patiently.

pacienzudo, da *adj* very patient.

pacificación *f* pacification || FIG appeasement, pacification (apaciguamiento).

pacificador, ra *adj* pacifying.
◆ *m/f* peacemaker.

pacificar *vt* to pacify (un país) || FIG to pacify, to calm (los ánimos) || to reconcile (las personas).
◆ *vpr* FIG to calm down, to grow calm (calmarse).

pacífico, ca *adj* calm, peaceful || peaceful; *coexistencia pacífica* peaceful coexistence || peaceable, peaceful, pacific (carácter).

Pacífico *npr m* Pacific || *el océano Pacífico* the Pacific Ocean.

pacifismo *m* pacifism.

pacifista *adj/s* pacifist.

pack *m* ice floe (banco de hielo) || pack (rugby).

paco *m* ZOOL alpaca, paco || sniper (guerrillero en Marruecos) || AMER paco (mineral de plata) | policeman (policía).

pacotilla *f* shoddy goods *pl*, trash (de poca calidad) || goods *pl* carried by seamen free of freight charges || *de pacotilla* shoddy, gimcrack, shoddily made (de poca calidad), gimcrack (joyas).

pacotillero *m* seller of shoddy goods || AMER hawker, pedlar [*US* peddler] (buhonero).

pactar *vi* to make a pact, to come to an agreement || FIG *pactar con el diablo* to sell one's soul to the devil, to make a pact with the devil.
◆ *vt* to agree upon *o* on *o* to.

pacto *m* pact, agreement; *pacto de no agresión* nonaggresion pact.

pactolo *m* FIG gold mine (fuente de riquezas).

pachá *m* pasha (bajá) || FIG *vivir como un pachá* to live like a king.
— OBSERV This word is a widely used Gallicism.

pachamama *f* AMER earth.

pachamanca *f* AMER meat roasted between hot stones | FIG disorder.

pachanga *f* AMER rowdy celebration (fiesta) | Mexican dance (baile).

pacholí *m* patchouli (planta y perfume).

pachón, ona *adj* basset (perro) || AMER hairy (peludo), woolly (lanudo).
◆ *m/f* basset hound (perro).
◆ *m* FAM phlegmatic fellow.

pachorra *f* FAM sluggishness, indolence, slowness (indolencia) | calmness (tranquilidad).

pachorrudo, da *adj* FAM sluggish, slow, indolent (indolente) | phlegmatic, calm (tranquilo).

pachucho, cha *adj* overripe (fruta) || FIG weak (débil) | unwell, sickly, shaky (malucho) || FIG *estar pachucho* to feel unwell, to be unwell.

pachulí *m* patchouli (planta y perfume).

paddock *m* paddock.

padecer* *vt* to suffer, to suffer from; *padecer dolores de estómago* to suffer from stomachache; *padecer hambre, frío* to suffer from hunger, from cold; *los males que padecen* the evils which they suffer || to endure (aguantar); *padecer privaciones* to endure privations || to have, to suffer from (enfermedades); *padecer viruela* to have smallpox || FIG to bear (soportar); *padecer castigo* to bear a punishment; *padecer las impertinencias de uno* to bear s.o.'s impertinence | to suffer, to know (pasar); *padecer grandes desgracias* to know great troubles | to suffer (agravios o insultos) || *padecer error* to be mistaken, to be a victim of error.
◆ *vi* to suffer; *padecimos mucho durante la epidemia* we suffered greatly during the epidemic || FIG to suffer, to be hurt; *padecer en la honra* to suffer in one's dignity || — *padecer de* to suffer from; *padecer de los nervios* to suffer from nerves || *padecer del corazón* to suffer from heart trouble, to suffer with one's heart, to have a heart condition.

padecido, da *adj* suffered.

padecimiento *m* suffering (sufrimiento) || ailment (enfermedad).

padrastro *m* stepfather (marido de la madre) || FIG & FAM harsh father (padre severo) || FIG obstacle, impediment (estorbo) || MED hangnail (en las uñas).

padrazo *m* FAM indulgent *o* easygoing father.

padre *m* father; *de padre a hijo* from father to son || priest (sacerdote) || father (religioso); *el padre Bartolomé de las Casas* Father Bartolomé de las Casas; *sí, Padre* yes, Father || male (macho) || FIG origin, mother | father, creator || — FIG *a padre ganador, hijo gastador* a miserly father makes a lavish son || FIG & FAM *darle a uno una paliza de padre y muy señor mío* to give s.o. a hell of a beating (pegarle fuerte) || *Dios Padre* God the Father || *el Padre Santo, el Santo Padre* the Holy Father, the Pope || *los Santos Padres, los Padres de la Iglesia* the Fathers of the Christian Church || FIG & FAM *no lo entiende ni su padre* it is absolutely incomprehensible || *padre conscripto* conscript father (senador de Roma) || *padre de almas* priest || *padre de familia* father || *padre de la patria* Father of his country, founding father || *padre espiritual* spiritual father || *Padre Eterno* Heavenly Father || *Padre Nuestro* Our Father, Lord's Prayer (oración) || *padre nutricio* foster father || *padre político* father-in-law || FIG & FAM *¡que lo haga su padre!* get someone else to do it! | *saber algo como el Padre Nuestro* to know sth. backwards *o* by heart *o* backwards and forwards | *ser un padre para* to be a father to.
◆ *pl* parents, father and mother; *sus padres son muy simpáticos* his parents are very nice.

◆ *adj* FAM terrific, huge, tremendous || FIG & FAM *llevarse un susto padre* to be frightened out of one's wits, to get the fright of one's life | *pegarse* or *darse la vida padre* to live like a king, to live it up | *tener un éxito padre* to be a big hit.

padrenuestro *m* Lord's Prayer, Our Father (oración) || FIG & FAM *en un padrenuestro* in a wink of an eye, in no time at all.

padrinazgo *m* godfathership || FIG protection, patronage, sponsorship.

padrino *m* godfather (de un niño) || second (en un desafío) || sponsor (que patrocina) || *padrino de boda* best man.
◆ *pl* godparents || FIG *el que no tiene padrinos, no se bautiza* you cannot get anywhere without connections.

padrísimo *adj* AMER splendid, fantastic (estupendo).

padrón *m* census (censo); *hacer el padrón* to take a census || model, pattern (dechado) || memorial, memorial pillar (columna conmemorativa) || FIG infamy, dishonour [US dishonor] || FAM indulgent *o* easy-going father (padrazo) || AMER stallion (semental).

padrote *m* AMER FAM pimp (alcahuete).

paella *f* paella [dish made with rice, meat, seafood and several vegetables].

paellera *f* paella pan.

paflón *m* ARQ soffit (sofita).

paga *f* pay, wages *pl* (sueldo); *cobrar la paga* to receive one's wages; *hoja de paga* pay slip || payment (pago) || payer (pagador) || — *día de paga* payday || *paga extraordinaria* extra pay.

pagadero, ra *adj* payable; *pagadero a la vista, a plazos, al portador* payable on *o* at sight, in instalments, to bearer.

pagado, da *adj* paid; *pagado por adelantado* paid in advance || returned (sentimiento) || — *asesino pagado* hired assassin || FIG *estamos pagados* we are quits || *pagado de sí mismo* self-satisfied.

pagador, ra *adj* paying.
◆ *m/f* payer.

pagaduría *f* pay office || *depositaría-pagaduría* disbursement office.

pagamiento *m* payment.

paganismo *m* paganism, heathenism.

paganizar *vt* to paganize.
◆ *vi* to become a pagan.

pagano, na *adj/s* pagan, heathen.
◆ *m* FAM scapegoat, victim (víctima) | payer (pagador) | one who pays; *siempre soy yo el pagano* I'm always the one who pays.

pagar *vt* to pay (una cantidad); *pagar al contado, por meses, a plazos, por adelantado* to pay cash, monthly, in instalments, in advance || to pay for; *¿cuánto pagaste tu vestido?* how much did you pay for your dress? || FIG to pay; *pagar las consecuencias* to pay the consequences | to pay for; *pagar cara una victoria* to pay dearly for a victory; *pagar un crimen* to pay for a crime | to return (afecto); *pagar a uno su cariño* to return s.o.'s affection | to repay; *pagar con ingratitud* to repay with ingratitude || — *a pagar a la recepción* cash on delivery || *¡Dios se lo pague!* God bless you! || FIG & FAM *el que la hace la paga* one must face the music, one must face the consequences || *pagar a toca teja* to pay cash down *o* cash || *pagar con su vida* to pay with one's life || FIG *pagar el daño* or *el pato* or *los vidrios rotos* to carry the can || *pagar en especie* to pay in kind || FIG *pagar en* or *con la misma moneda* to pay s.o. back in his own coin, to give s.o. a taste of his own medicine || *pagar en metálico* or *en efectivo* to pay (in) cash || *pagar las culpas ajenas* to pay for the sins of others || *un amor mal pagado* unrequited love || FAM *¡ya me las pagará!, ¡me las han de pagar!* you shall pay for it!
◆ *vi* to pay; *¿has pagado ya?* have you paid yet?
◆ *vpr* to be paid || to cost (costar); *la leche se paga a once pesetas el litro* milk costs eleven pesetas a litre || — FIG *pagarse de* to be proud of (ufanarse) | *pagarse de sí mismo* to be full of o.s., to be conceited.

pagaré *m* promissory note IOU || *pagaré del Tesoro* Treasury bill.

pagaya *f* paddle (remo).

pagel *m* red sea bream (pez).

página *f* page; *en la página anterior* on the previous page.

paginación *f* pagination, paging.

paginar *vt* to page, to paginate.

pago *m* payment; *pago al contado* cash payment; *hacer* or *efectuar un pago* to make a payment || estate, property, lands *pl* (finca) || FIG retribution; *recibir el pago de sus malas acciones* to receive retribution for ones evil deeds | return, payment; *en pago de* in return for | price; *el pago de la gloria* the price of fame || AMER country (país), village (pueblo), area, region (zona) || — *en pago* in payment (para pagar), in return (como recompensa) || *mediante el pago de mil pesetas* on payment of one thousands pesetas || *pago a cuenta* payment on account || *pago adelantado* or *anticipado* payment in advance, advance payment || *pago a plazos* payment in instalments, deferred payment || *pago contra entrega* cash on delivery || *pago de viñas* region of vineyards || AMER *pago en cuotas* payment in instalments, deferred payment || *pago en especie* payment in kind || *pago en metálico* payment in (hard) cash || *pago inicial* down payment.

pagoda *f* pagoda.

pagro *m* porgy (pez).

paguro *m* hermit crab (crustáceo) || sea spider (araña de mar).

paila *f* frying pan (sartén) || fried eggs (huevos fritos).

paipai *m* fan (abanico).

pairar *vi* MAR to lie to.

pairo *m* MAR *estar al pairo* to be lying to.

país *m* country (nación); *país satélite* satellite country || land, country; *país natal* native land || cloth *o* paper backing (del abanico) || FIG *en el país de los ciegos, el tuerto es rey* in the land of the blind the one-eyed man is king || ECON *país en vías de desarrollo* developing country | *países desarrollados* developed countries.

paisaje *m* countryside, landscape || cloth *o* paper backing (de abanico).

paisajista *adj/s* landscape painter.

paisana *f* country dance || —> **paisano.**

paisanada *f* AMER country people *o* folk *pl*, peasants *pl*.

paisanaje *m* civilians *pl*, civil population (población civil) || state of being a compatriot *o* a fellow citizen.

paisano, na *adj* of the same region *o* country.
◆ *m/f* compatriot, fellow countryman (hombre), fellow countrywoman (mujer) (del mismo país); *un paisano mío* a compatriot of mine || AMER countryman (hombre), countrywoman (mujer), peasant (campesino) || *es un paisano mío* he is from my home *o* from my region (de la misma región).
◆ *m* civilian (por oposición a militar) || — *ir de paisano* to be wearing civilian clothes || *traje de paisano* civilian clothes *pl*.

Países Bajos *npr mpl* GEOGR Netherlands (Holanda).
— OBSERV The name *Países Bajos* was given to the territories which were under Spain's dominion in the «Siglo de Oro» (Holland, Belgium and part of northern France). Nowadays it is the official Spanish name for the Netherlands.

País Vasco *npr m* GEOGR the Basque country.

paja *f* straw; *paja centenaza* rye straw || FIG rubbish, trash (nadería) | padding, waffle (en un artículo) || POP masturbation || AMER tap (grifo) || — FIG & FAM *a humo de pajas* thoughtlessly || *choza de paja* straw hut || *echar pajas* to draw straws (juego) || FIG *en un quítame allá esas pajas* in the wink of an eye, in a jiffy || POP *hacerse una paja* to masturbate || FIG *hombre de paja* man of straw | *meter paja* to fill out, to pad (en un artículo) || *patatas paja* potato straws || FIG *por un quítame allá esas pajas* for nothing, for no reason at all || *techo de paja* thatched roof || FIG *ver la paja en el ojo ajeno y no la viga en el propio* to see the mote in another's eye and not the beam in one's own.

pajar *m* straw loft.

pájara *f* (p us) hen bird (pájaro) || kite (cometa) || paper bird (de papel) || FIG sly woman (mujer astuta) | wicked woman (mujer mala) || FAM *pájara nocturna* tart (ramera).

pajarera *f* bird cage, aviary (jaula).

pajarería *f* bird shop (tienda) || flock of birds (bandada).

pajarero, ra *adj* bird, of *o* pertaining to birds || FAM chirpy, merry, gay, happy (alegre) || gaudy (telas) || loud, gaudy (colores) || shy, skittish (caballo).
◆ *m* bird dealer (vendedor de pájaros) || bird catcher *o* hunter, fowler (cazador) || *Enrique I el Pajarero* Henry I the Fowler.

pajarilla *f* small bird || kite (cometa) || — FAM *abrasársele a uno las pajarillas* to be boiling hot | *alegrársele a uno las pajarillas* to be overjoyed.

pajarita *f* paper bird (de papel) || kite (cometa) || — *corbata de pajarita* dickie bow, bow tie || *pajarita de las nieves* wagtail (aguzanieves).

pajarito *m* small bird, nestling (ave) || — FIG & FAM *comer como un pajarito* not to eat enough to feed a sparrow | *me lo ha dicho un pajarito verde, me lo dijo un pajarito* a little bird told me | *quedarse muerto como un pajarito* to die peacefully.

pájaro *m* bird; *coger pájaros* to catch birds || FIG sly old fox, cunning bird, crafty devil (astuto) || — FIG *a vista de pájaro* from a bird's eye view || FIG *el pájaro voló* the bird has flown | *más vale pájaro en mano que ciento volando* a bird in the hand is worth two in the bush | *matar dos pájaros de un tiro* to kill two birds with one stone || *pájaro bobo* penguin (pingüino) || *pájaro carpintero* woodpecker || FIG & FAM *pájaro de cuenta* or *de cuidado* nasty customer, nasty piece of work || FIG *pájaro de mal agüero* bird of ill omen || FAM *pájaro gordo* bigwig, big shot (pez gordo) || *pájaro mosca* hummingbird || FIG *tener pájaros en la cabeza, tener la cabeza llena de pájaros, tener la cabeza a pájaros* to have bats in the belfry (ser tonto), to be a scatterbrain (distraído).
— OBSERV The word *pájaro* is applied to small birds; for larger birds the word *ave* is used.

pajarraco *m* FAM ugly bird (pájaro grande y feo) || FIG & FAM rogue, villain (persona).

pajaza *f* leftover straw.

paje *m* page || MAR ship's boy, deck boy, cabin boy (grumete).

pajillero, ra *m/f* POP masturbator.

pajizo, za *adj* straw-coloured (color de paja) || straw, of straw (de paja).

pajolero, ra *adj* FAM damn, blasted, bloody (pop), damned; *estoy harto de esta pajolera casa* I'm fed up with this damn house | punctilious, fastidious (puntilloso).

pajón *m* coarse straw.

pajuela *f* sulphur match (para encender).

Pakistán *npr m* GEOGR Pakistan.

pakistaní *adj/s* Pakistani.

pala *f* shovel (instrumento) || shovelful (contenido de la pala) || bat [*US* paddle] (del juego del ping-pong) || bat (pelota y béisbol) || racket (tenis) || blade (de remo, de hélice, de la azada, etc.) || paddle (de la noria, para lavar, etc.) || slice (de cocina) || setting (de una sortija) || spade (de jardinero, de niño) || fleshing knife (de curtidores) || vamp (del calzado) || point (del cuello de una camisa) || BOT leaf (de chumbera) || flat surface [of a tooth] (de un diente) || incisor (incisivo del caballo) || straight part [of epaulette] (de charretera) || (hinge) blade (de bisagra) || — FAM *a punta de pala, a punta pala* in large quantity, a lot || *pala cargadora* mechanical digger || *pala de zapador* short-handled shovel || *pala mecánica* power shovel.

palabra *f* word (vocablo); *una palabra española* a Spanish word; *no decir palabra* not to say a word || word; *me repitieron sus palabras* they repeated his words to me || word (promesa); *hombre de palabra* man of his word; *tener palabra, cumplir su palabra* to keep one's word || speech, faculty of speech (don de hablar) || right to speak (derecho de hablar en una asamblea) || word (teología) || — *ahorrar palabras* not to waste words || *a buen entendedor, pocas palabras bastan* a word to the wise in enough || *al decir, al oír estas palabras* with *o* saying these words, (on) hearing these words || *a palabras necias, oídos sordos* I'll treat that remark with the contempt it deserves || *bajo palabra* on one's honour || *cogerle a uno la palabra* to take s.o. at his word || *comerse las palabras* to swallow one's words, not to articulate (articular mal), to eat one's words (retirar lo dicho) || FIG *comprender* or *entender a medias palabras* to read between the lines || *conceder la palabra a, dar la palabra a* to call upon, to give the floor to (en una asamblea) || *con medias palabras* cryptically; *decir con medias palabras* to say cryptically || *cortar la palabra* to interrupt || *cumplir con su palabra* to keep one's word || *dar palabra* to give one's word || *decir la última palabra* to have the last word || *decirle a uno cuatro palabras bien dichas* to tell s.o. a thing or two || *decir una palabra al oído* to whisper in s.o.'s ear || *dejar a uno con la palabra en la boca* not to let s.o. speak || *de palabra* by word of mouth, orally || *dichas estas palabras, con estas palabras* with these words || *dirigir la palabra a* to address, to speak to || *el delegado español tiene la palabra* the Spanish delegate has the floor || *empeñar la palabra* to give one's word || *en cuatro palabras* in (a) few words || *en otras palabras* in other words || *en pocas palabras* in brief (en un discurso) || *en toda la acepción* or *extensión de la palabra* in every sense of the word || *entretener con buenas palabras* to keep s.o.'s hopes up || *en una palabra* in a word, in short || *estar pendiente de las palabras de uno* to be hanging on s.o.'s every word || *faltar a su palabra* to break one's word, to go back on one's word || *gastar palabras* to waste words || *gastar pocas palabras* to speak concisely (ser conciso), not to be very talkative (ser poco hablador) || *hablar a medias palabras* to speak cryptically || *hacer uso de la palabra* to speak, to take the floor, to address the meeting || *juego de palabras* play on words, pun || *las palabras se las lleva el viento* words are not binding [it is better to have a promise in writing] || *llevar la palabra* to be the spokesman (ser el portavoz), to bear the word (de Cristo) || *mantener uno su palabra* to keep one's word || *me basta con su palabra* your word is good enough for me || *medir* or *sopesar las palabras* to weigh one's words || *ni una palabra* not a word || *ni una palabra más* not another word || *no entender palabra* not to understand a single word || *no saber ni una palabra de* to know nothing whatsoever about (un asunto), not to know a single word of (un idioma) || *no tener palabra* to be unreliable || *palabra clave* key word || *palabra de doble sentido* word with a double meaning || *palabra de honor* word of honour || *palabra de matrimonio* promise of marriage || *palabra por palabra* word for word || *palabras al aire* or *al viento* hot air || *palabras altisonantes* or *rimbombantes* pompous *o* high-flown words || *palabras cruzadas* crossword (crucigrama) || FIG *palabras del Evangelio* Grospel truth | *palabras encubiertas* cryptic words (medias palabras) || *palabras históricas* historical words || *palabras mayores* strong words || *pedir la palabra* to ask for the floor, to ask to speak || *pocas palabras pero buenas* let us be brief but to the point || *quitarle a uno la palabra de la boca* to take the words right out of s.o.'s mouth || *retiro mi palabra* I withdraw what I said || *según las palabras de Cristo* according to Christ's words || *ser de pocas palabras* not to be very talkative || *sin decir una palabra* without a word || *tener la palabra* to speak (hablar), to have the floor (en una conferencia) || *tener la última palabra* to have the last word || FIG *tener unas palabras con alguien* to have a few words with s.o. || *tomar la palabra* to take the floor, to address the meeting || *tomarle a uno la palabra* to take s.o. at his word || *tratar mal de palabra a uno* to insult s.o.
◆ *interj* on my honour!, I give you my word! (se lo aseguro), my word! (sorpresa).

palabrear *vi* FAM to chat.

palabreja *f* strange word.

palabreo *m* chatter.

palabrería *f*; **palabrerío** *m* FAM wordiness || *es pura palabrería* it's just words.

palabrita *f* pointed word || *le dije cuatro palabritas* I told him a thing or two.

palabrota *f* FAM swearword || *decir palabrotas* to swear.

palacete *m* mansion, manor (casa particular) || small palace.

palaciego, ga *adj* court; *vida palaciega* court life || palatial (magnífico).
◆ *m/f* courtier.

palacio *m* palace; *Palacio Real* Royal Palace; *palacio episcopal* episcopal palace || large mansion, palace (casa suntuosa) || — *el Palacio de Justicia* the Law Courts || FIG *las cosas de palacio van despacio* it all takes time || *palacio de congresos* conference centre || FIG *palacio encantado* enchanted castle.

palada *f* shovelful || stroke of an oar (golpe de remo).

paladar *m* ANAT palate || taste (sabor) || FIG palate, taste (gusto) || FIG *tener el paladar delicado* to have a delicate palate.

paladear *vt* to taste, to relish, to savour.

paladeo *m* tasting, relishing, savouring (saboreo).

paladial *adj/s/f* palatal.

paladín *m* paladin || FIG champion (defensor); *ser el paladín de la libertad* to be the champion of freedom.

paladinamente *adv* openly, clearly.

paladino, na *adj* clear, obvious.

paladio *m* palladium (metal).

paladión *m* palladium (estatua de Palas) || FIG palladium (salvaguardia).

palafito *m* palafitte, lake dwelling.

palafrén *m* palfrey || servant's horse.

palafrenero *m* groom (mozo de caballos) || equerry (de la casa real).

palanca *f* lever, crowbar || TECN lever || handle (manecilla) || hand brake (del freno) || stockade (fortificación) || springboard (trampolín) || FIG pull, influence (influencia) || — *palanca de cambio* gear stick, gear change [*US* gearshift] || *palanca de mando* control lever, control column || *palanca de mando del timón* rudder bar || *salto de palanca* high diving (deporte), high dive (cada salto).

palangana *f* washbasin (jofaina).
◆ *m* AMER FAM show-off, braggart (fanfarrón) | cheeky devil (descarado).

palanganada *f* AMER FAM bragging (fanfarronada).

palanganear *f* AMER FAM to brag (fanfarronear).

palanganero *m* washstand.

palangre *m* MAR boulter.

palanquear *vt* AMER to lever.

palanquera *f* stockade (empalizada).

palanqueta *f* crowbar, small lever (palanca pequeña) || jemmy [*US* jimmy], crowbar (para forzar puertas) || MAR bar shot.

Palas *npr f* Pallas.

palastro *m* sheet iron (chapa de hierro) || steel plate (de acero) || plate (de cerradura).

palatal *adj/s/f* GRAM palatal.

palatalización *f* GRAM palatalization.

palatalizar *vt* GRAM to palatalize.

Palatinado *npr m* GEOGR Palatinate.

palatino, na *adj* court (de palacio) || Palatine (del Palatinado) || ANAT of the palate, palatal, palatine || ANAT *bóveda palatina* roof of the mouth, palate.
◆ *m/f* palatine.

palco *m* box (espectáculo); *palco principal* first-tier box || — TEATR *palco de platea* ground-floor box | *palco de proscenio* stage *o* proscenium box.

palear *vt* to shovel.

palenque *m* arena (recinto) || palisade, fence (empalizada) || AMER hitching post (para atar animales) || — FIG *palenque político* political arena | *salir al palenque* to enter the arena *o* the fray.

paleo *m* shovelling.

paleogeografía *f* paleogeography.

paleografía *f* paleography.

paleográfico, ca *adj* paleographic.

paleógrafo *m* paleographer.

paleolítico, ca *adj* Paleolithic.

paleólogo *m* paleologist.

Paleólogo *n pr* Paleologus.

paleontología *f* paleontology.

paleontológico, ca *adj* paleontologic.

paleontólogo *m* paleontologist.

paleozoico, ca *adj/sm* Paleozoic.

palermitano, na *adj/s* Palermitan.

Palermo *n pr* GEOGR Palermo.

Palestina *npr f* GEOGR Palestine.

palestino, na *adj/s* Palestinian.

palestra *f* FIG arena; *la palestra parlamentaria* the parliamentary arena || FIG *salir* or *saltar a la palestra* to enter the fray *o* the arena.

paleta *f* small shovel || pastry slice (para dulces) || palette (de pintor) || trowel (palustre) || front tooth (diente) || slice (de cocina) || bat (de criquet) || pallet (de reloj) || paddle (de noria) || blade (de ventilador, de hélice, etc.) || blade (de remo) || coal shovel (badila) || ANAT shoulder blade || bat [*US* paddle] (de ping-pong) ||

MAR blade || TECN pallet (de carretilla) || FIG scale of colours, palette || INFORM *paleta gráfica* Paintbox.

paletada *f* shovelful (contenido de la pala) || trowelful (contenido de la llana) || blow with a shovel *o* a trowel (golpe) || FAM blunder (necedad) || — FIG & FAM *a paletadas* heaps of, loads of; *había pasteles a paletadas* there were heaps of cakes | *en dos paletadas* in a wink of an eye, in two ticks, in a thrice.

paletazo *m* glancing blow (del toro); *el toro le dio un paletazo* the bull's horn caught him a glancing blow.

paletear *vi* to thrash about with the oars, to row ineffectively.

paleteo *m* thrashing of the oars.

paletilla *f* ANAT shoulder blade (omoplato) | sternum cartilage || shoulder (en carnicería); *paletilla de cordero* shoulder of mutton || shoulder blade (del ganado) || candlestick (palmatoria).

paleto, ta *adj* FAM peasant, boorish.
◆ *m/f* FAM country bumpkin, peasant, yokel.

paletó *m* (p us) coat, greatcoat.

paletón *m* bit (de llave) || front tooth (diente).

paliación *f* palliation.

paliadamente *adv* secretly, in secret.

paliar *vt* to palliate.

paliativo, va *adj/sm* palliative.

palidecer* *vi* to turn pale, to pale; *hacer palidecer a alguien* to cause s.o. to turn pale || to fade, to grow pale (colores) || to wane (el día) || to grow dim (la luz) || FIG to be on the wane; *la fama de este artista está palideciendo* this artist's fame is on the wane.
◆ *vt* to make pale.

palidez *f* paleness, pallidness (de una persona) || paleness, pallor (de la tez) || wanness (de la luna).

pálido, da *adj* pale; *ponerse muy pálido* to turn very pale || pale, light (color) || — *estilo pálido* colourless style || FIG *rostro pálido* paleface.

paliducho, cha *adj* FAM palish, pale.

palier *m* TECN bearing.

palillero *m* penholder (portaplumas).

palillo *m* small stick || toothpick (mondadientes) || spindle (de encajera) || needle holder (para las agujas) || drumstick (de tambor) || thin loaf (de pan) || stem (de tabaco) || stalk (de uva) || spoon tool (de los escultores) || FAM *estar hecho un palillo* to be as thin as a rake.
◆ *pl* chopsticks; *los chinos comen con palillos* the Chinese eat with chopsticks || pins (del billar) || FAM banderillas || castanets (castañuelas) || — *tocar todos los palillos* to try all possible avenues || FAM *unas piernas como palillos* legs like matchsticks.

palimpsesto *m* palimpsest.

palíndromo, ma *adj* palindromic.
◆ *m* palindrome.

palingenesia *f* palingenesis.

palinodia *f* palinode || FIG & FAM *cantar la palinodia* to recant, to retract.

palio *m* pallium (manto griego) || pallium (pontifical) || canopy, baldachin (dosel) || HERÁLD pall (perla) || — *bajo palio* under a canopy || FIG *recibir con palio* or *bajo palio* to receive with great pomp.

palique *m* FAM chat || — FAM *dar palique a* to chat to *o* with | *estar de palique* to be chatting.

paliquear *vi* FAM to chat.

palisandro *m* rosewood (árbol, madera).

palista *m* pelota player (pelota vasca).

palito *m* small stick || AMER FAM *pisar el palito* to fall into the trap || CULIN *palitos de pescado* fish fingers.

palitoque; palitroque *m* stick (palo) || banderilla (de toros) || stroke (escritura).

paliza *f* beating, hiding, thrashing; *darle a uno una paliza* to give s.o. a hiding || — FIG & FAM *la excursión fue una paliza* the trip was exhausting | *le espera una paliza en casa* he's for it when he gets home | *les pegamos una paliza* we thrashed them, we beat them hollow (un equipo a otro).

palizada *f* palisade, fence (valla) || enclosure (sitio cercado).

palma *f* palm tree, palm (árbol) || palm leaf (hoja) || date palm, date tree (datilera) || palm (de la mano) || sole (de la pata del caballo) || palm [piece] (de un guante) || FIG palm (símbolo de triunfo) || — *conocer como la palma de la mano* to know like the back *o* the palm of one's hand || FIG & FAM *llevarse la palma* to carry off the palm (triunfar), to take the cake (en sentido irónico) || *palma datilera* date palm, date tree || *palma de abanico* palmyra || *palma indiana* coconut palm || FIG & FAM *ser liso como la palma de la mano* to be as flat as a pankake.
◆ *pl* applause *sing* (aplausos), clapping *sing* (para marcar el ritmo), slow handclapping *sing* (como desaprobación) || — *batir* or *dar palmas* to clap (one's hands), to applaud || *palmas de tango* rhythmic clapping || *traer en palmas a uno* to pamper s.o.

palmada *f* slap (golpe con la palma de la mano) || clapping (para llamar) || *darse una palmada en la frente* to tap one's forehead.
◆ *pl* applause *sing* (aplauso), clapping *sing* (para marcar el ritmo) || — *dar palmadas* to clap (one's hands).

Palma de Mallorca *n pr* GEOGR Palma de Majorca.

palmadita *f* tap || *dar una palmadita en el hombro* to tap on the shoulder.

palmar *adj* ANAT palmar; *músculo palmar* palmar muscle || FIG obvious, clear, evident (evidente) || one span long (longitud).
◆ *m* palm grove (sitio) || TECN card, teasel (cardencha) || FAM *más viejo que un palmar* as old as Methuselah, as old as the hills.

palmar *vi* FAM to kick the bucket, to snuff it (morir).

palmarés *m* service record (historial).

palmario, ria *adj* obvious; *error palmario* obvious mistake.

palmatoria *f* cane, palmer (de maestro) || candlestick (de una vela).

palmeado, da *adj* palmate, palm shaped (de forma de palma) || palmate, webbed (ligado por una membrana) || *pata palmeada* webfoot, webbed foot.

palmear *vi* to applaud, to clap (one's hands).

palmeo *m* measuring by palms *o* spans.

palmer *m* micrometer calliper *o* caliper.

palmera *f* palm tree (árbol) || palm leaf (hoja) || date palm, date tree (datilera) || palm cake (galleta) || *palmera datilera* date palm, date tree.

palmeral *m* palm grove.

palmero *m* AMER palm tree (árbol).

palmeta *f* cane (de los maestros) || caning (castigo).

palmetazo *m* caning (golpe con la palmeta) || slap (bofetada).

palmiche; palmicho *m* royal palm (árbol) || fruit of the royal palm (fruto).

palmípedo, da *adj* palmiped, web-footed.
◆ *m* palmiped, web-footed animal.

palmista *f* AMER palmist (quiromántica).

palmita *f* palm marrow (médula) || FIG *llevar* or *traer* or *tener en palmitas a alguien* to pamper s.o., to wait on s.o. hand and foot.

palmito *m* BOT palmetto (árbol) || palm heart (tallo comestible) || FIG & FAM little face (cara); *buen palmito* pretty little face | good looks *pl* (aspecto) || FIG & FAM *tener un buen palmito* to be good-looking.

palmo *m* span, palm (medida) || — FIG & FAM *con un palmo de lengua (fuera)* panting || FIG *conocer palmo a palmo* to know like the back of one's hand | *Cristóbal crece a palmos* you can almost see Christopher growing | *dejar con un palmo de narices* to let s.o. down | *hacer un palmo de narices* to thumb one's nose, to cock a snook || *palmo a palmo* step by step, inch by inch || FIG *palmo de tierra* small plot of land (espacio pequeño) | *quedarse con un palmo* or *dos palmos de narices* to be out of luck.

palmotear *vi* to clap (one's hands), to applaud (aplaudir).

palmoteo *m* applause, clapping (aplauso).

palo *m* stick; *esgrimía un palo* he was brandishing a stick || stick (trozo de madera) || staff, pole (grande, para andar o defenderse) || wood (madera) || blow with a stick (golpe) || handle (mango); *palo de una escoba* handle of a broom || FAM banderilla (toros) || MAR mast (mástil) || pole (vara) || pin (para jugar al billar) || shot (jugada en el billar) || gallows *pl* (suplicio) || suit [in cards]; *jugar del mismo palo* to follow suit || stroke (de una letra) || HERÁLD pale || stalk (del fruto) || perch (en un gallinero) || club (para jugar al golf) || stake (estaca) || AMER tree (árbol) | gulp (trago) || — AMER *a medio palo* half-finished || FIG *andar a palos* to be always quarrelling || *a palos* with a stick (con un palo) || FIG *a palo seco* under bare poles (barco), simply, on its own, just, nothing else (sin acompañamiento); *comimos pan a palo seco* we ate bread on its own, we just ate bread | *caérsele a uno los palos del sombrajo* to be discouraged | *dar (de) palos* to beat | *dar palos de ciego* to lash out wildly (golpear sin cuidado), to grope about in the dark (tantear) || FIG & FAM *dar un palo* to pull to pieces, to slate (criticar), to charge the earth; *en este restaurante te dan un palo* in this restaurant they charge the earth; to be a blow to; *esta reforma ha dado un palo a la agricultura* this reform has been a blow to agriculture || *de palo* wooden; *pierna de palo* wooden leg; *cuchara de palo* wooden spoon || FIG *de tal palo tal astilla* like father, like son | *estar hecho un palo* to be as thin as a rake || FIG & FAM *moler a palos* to beat black and blue, to beat up || FIG *no hay peor astilla que la del mismo palo* former friends can be dangerous enemies || *palo brasil* brazilwood || *palo campeche* camwood || AMER *palo de agua* downpour (chaparrón) || *palo de escoba* broomstick, broom handle || *palo de jabón* quillai, soapbark || MAR *palo de mesana* mizzenmast || *palo de Pernambuco* Pernambuco wood || *palo de rosa* rosewood || MAR *palo de trinquete* foremast || *palo dulce* liquorice root || AMER *palo ensebado* greasy pole (cucaña) || MAR *palo mayor* mainmast || *palo santo* lignum vitae || FIG & FAM *ser más tieso que un palo de una escoba* to be as stiff as a board || AMER FIG *ser un palo* to be remarkable.

— OBSERV *Palo santo* es barbarismo en el sentido de *palisandro*.

paloduz *m* liquorice root.

paloma *f* pigeon, dove || dove; *la paloma de la paz* the dove of peace || FIG lamb (persona bondadosa) | pure woman (mujer pura) || FAM anisette with water (bebida) || MAR sling of a yard || — *paloma buchona* pouter || *paloma casera* domestic pigeon || *paloma de moño* crested pigeon || *paloma mensajera* carrier pigeon, homing pigeon, homer || *paloma silvestre* wild

pigeon || *paloma torcaz* ringdove, wood pigeon || *paloma zurita* rock pigeon, rock dove (de color apizarrado), ringdove, wood pigeon (torcaz).
◆ *pl* whitecaps, white horses (olas pequeñas).

palomar *m* dovecote, pigeon house, pigeon loft.

palometa *f* butterfly nut, wing nut (tuerca).

palomilla *f* grain moth (polilla) || small butterfly (mariposa) || ZOOL nymph, chrysalis || back (del caballo) || wing nut, butterfly nut (tuerca) || *AMER* FAM rabble, mob (gente).
◆ *pl* whitecaps, white horses (del mar).

palomino *m* young pigeon *o* dove (pájaro) || stain on a shirttail (mancha) || *AMER* white horse (caballo) || FIG *un palomino atontado* a silly fool.

palomita *f* popcorn (roseta) || anisette and water (anís con agua) || *AMER* darling, love (amor) || *cuello de palomita* wing collar.

palomo *m* (cock) pigeon || FAM fool, idiot (necio).

palotazo *m* TAUR glancing blow (paletazo).

palote *m* small stick || pothook (para aprender a escribir) || *AMER* rolling pin (de cocina).

palpabilidad *f* palpability.

palpable *adj* palpable.

palpablemente *adv* palpably; *la producción ha aumentado palpablemente* production has increased palpably.

palpación *f* palpation, touching, feeling.

palpador *m* TECN testing spike.

palpadura *f*; **palpamiento** *m* palpation, touching, feeling.

palpar *vt* to palpate, to feel, to touch (tocar) || FIG to feel, to appreciate; *ahora palpa los efectos de su pereza* he is now feeling the effects of his laziness.
◆ *vpr* to grope (a oscuras) || FIG to be felt (percibirse); *se palpaba el malestar en toda la oficina* unease was felt throughout the office.

palpitación *f* palpitation, throbbing, throb (del corazón); *tener palpitaciones* to suffer from palpitations.

palpitante *adj* throbbing, palpitating; *con el corazón palpitante* with a throbbing heart || FIG trembling; *palpitante de júbilo* trembling with joy | burning (candente).

palpitar *vi* to palpitate, to throb || to palpitate, to beat (latir).

pálpito *m* *AMER* presentiment, hunch, feeling, foreboding (corazonada).

palta *f* *AMER* avocado pear (aguacate).

palto *m* *AMER* avocado (árbol).

palúdico, ca *adj* MED malarial || marshy, swampy (pantanoso) || *fiebre palúdica* malaria.
◆ *m/f* person suffering from malaria.

paludismo *m* MED malaria.

palurdo, da *adj* FAM boorish, peasant.
◆ *m/f* FAM boor, peasant, yokel, country bumpkin.

palustre *m* trowel (llana de albañil).
◆ *adj* boggy, marshy (de un pantano).

pallador *m* *AMER* ⟶ **payador.**

pallar *m* *AMER* haricot bean (judía).

pallar *vt* MIN to sort [ore].

pamela *f* broad-brimmed hat (sombrero).

pamema *f* FAM fuss (aspaviento) | rubbish, nonsense (tontería) | trifle (cosa insignificante) | flattery (halago) || FAM *déjate de pamemas* stop your fussing.

pampa *f* pampas *pl* (llanura).
◆ *m/f* pampean Indian (indio).
◆ *adj* *AMER* of *o* from the pampas, pampean; *indio pampa* Indian from the pampas | with a white head (animal) | dishonest (negocio) || — *AMER* *a la pampa* in the open air, under the stars | *estar en sus pampas* to be at one's ease | *quedar en pampa* to be disappointed.

pámpana *f* vine leaf (hoja de viña).

pámpano *m* tendril, vine shoot (zarcillo de la vid) || vine leaf (pámpana) || salp (pez).

pampeano, na *adj* *AMER* of *o* from the pampas, pampean.
◆ *m/f* inhabitant *o* native of the pampas, pampean.

pampear *vi* *AMER* to travel across *o* through the pampas.

pamperada *f* *AMER* season when the west wind blows.

pampero, ra *adj* of *o* from the pampas, pampean.
◆ *m/f* inhabitant *o* native of the pampas, pampean.
◆ *m* strong west wind blowing across the pampas.

pampino, na *adj* *AMER* ⟶ **pampero.**

pampirolada *f* sauce made from bread and garlic || FIG & FAM nonsense, rubbish (necedad).

pamplina *f* chickweed (planta) || FIG & FAM rubbish, nonsense, piffle (necedad); *déjeme de pamplinas* stop talking nonsense; *¡basta de pamplinas!* that's enough rubbish! | triffle (cosa sin importancia) || *pamplina de agua* brookweed.

pamplinada; pamplinería *f* FAM rubbish, nonsense.

pamplinero, ra; pamplinoso, sa *adj* stupid, foolish, silly.

Pamplona *n pr* GEOGR Pamplona (Navarra).

pamplonés, esa; pamplonica *adj* [of *o* from] Pamplona.
◆ *m/f* inhabitant *o* native of Pamplona.

pamporcino *m* BOT cyclamen, sowbread.

pan *m* bread; *pedazo de pan* piece of bread; *pan con mantequilla* bread and butter || loaf [of bread] (barra) || bar, cake (de jabón, de sal) || dough (para empanadas) || FIG wheat [*US* corn] (trigo) || loaf (masa); *pan de higo* fig loaf || leaf [of hammered gold or silver] || FIG living, bread; *ganarse el pan* to earn one's living || — FIG *a falta de pan buenas son tortas* half a loaf is better than none || *árbol del pan* breadfruit tree || FIG *cara de pan mascado* wan *o* pasty face || FAM *con su pan se lo coma* good luck to him || FIG *contigo pan y cebolla* we can *o* we shall live on love || *el pan nuestro de cada día* our daily bread || FIG *es pan comido* it's as easy as pie *o* as A B C, it's a piece of cake (es muy fácil) | *estar a pan y agua* to be on bread and water | *llamar al pan pan y al vino vino* to call a spade a spade | *no sólo de pan vive el hombre* man does not live on bread alone || *pan ácimo* unleavened bread || *pan bazo* or *moreno* brown bread || *pan bendito* Communion bread || *pan blanco* or *candeal* white bread || *pan casero* homemade bread || *pan de azúcar* sugar loaf || *pan de centeno* rye bread || *pan de flor* fine wheaten bread || *pan de molde* soft, thin-crusted bread || *pan de munición* ration bread || *pan de Viena* milk bread || *pan duro* stale bread || *AMER* FIG *pan francés* uproar, hubbub [made by discontented audience] (espectáculo) || *pan genovés* Genoese cake || *pan integral* wholemeal bread || *pan rallado* breadcrumbs || *pan tierno* fresh bread || *pan toast* rusk || *pan tostado* toast || FIG *por un mendrugo de pan* for a bite to eat, for a crust of bread | *quitarle a uno el pan de la boca* to take the bread out of somebody's mouth | *repartirse como pan bendito* to be distributed in driblets *o* sparingly | *ser un pan, ser bueno como un pedazo de pan* or *ser más bueno que el pan* to be kindness itself || *sopa de pan* soup in which bread is dunked || *tierra de pan llevar* wheatland || FIG *venderse como pan bendito* to sell like hot cakes (venderse en grandes cantidades).

PAN *abrev de Partido de Acción Nacional* Mexican political party.

Pan *npr m* MIT Pan.

pana *f* corduroy, cord (tela) || *AMER* breakdown (avería) || *pana lisa* velvet (terciopelo).

panacea *f* panacea (remedio).

panadería *f* baker's, bakery, bread shop || bread-making, baking (oficio del panadero).

panadero, ra *m/f* baker.

panadizo *m* MED felon, whitlow.

panafricanismo *m* Pan-Africanism.

panafricano, na *adj* Pan-African.

panal *m* honeycomb (de colmena) || honeycomb (dulce) || *en forma de panal* honeycombed.

panamá *m* panama [hat] (jipijapa).

Panamá *npr m* GEOGR Panama.

panameño, ña *adj/s* Panamanian.

panamericanismo *m* Pan-Americanism.

panamericanista *adj/s* Pan-Americanist.

panamericano, na *adj* Pan-American || *carretera panamericana* Pan-American Highway.

panarabismo *m* Pan-Arabism.

panarizo *m* felon, whitlow (panadizo).

pancarta *f* poster, placard.
— OBSERV This word is a Gallicism for *cartel.*

páncreas *m* ANAT pancreas.

pancreático, ca *adj* pancreatic; *jugo pancreático* pancreatic juice.

pancromático, ca *adj* panchromatic.

pancho, cha *adj* FAM *quedarse tan pancho* to be *o* to remain unmoved.

panda *m* panda (mamífero del Himalaya).
◆ *f* gallery of a cloister || FAM band, gang (pandilla).

pandear *vi/vpr* to warp, to bend (la madera) || to bulge, to sag (una pared).

pandectas *f pl* JUR pandect *sing* (código) || HIST the Pandects (de Justiniano) || index book *sing* (cuaderno).

pandemia *f* MED pandemic.

pandémico, ca *adj* MED pandemic.

pandemonio; pandemónium *m* pandemonium.

pandeo *m* warping (acción de combarse la madera) || warp, buckle (efecto) || bulging, sagging (de las paredes) || bulge (forma combada).

pandereta *f* tambourine || — *la España de pandereta* the tourist's Spain, typical Spain || FIG & FAM *zumbar la pandereta a uno* to thrash s.o.

panderete *m* *tabique de panderete* brick partition.

panderetero, ra *m/f* tambourine player || tambourine maker, tambourine seller.

pandero *m* MÚS tambourine || kite (cometa) || FIG & FAM bum, backside.

pandilla *f* band, gang; *una pandilla de niños* a gang of children || team; *¡vaya pandilla!* what a team! || clique, coterie (camarilla).

pandino, na *adj* [of *o* from] Pando [town in Bolivia].
◆ *m/f* native *o* inhabitant of Pando.

pandit *m* pandit (brahmán).

pando, da *adj* curved, bulging, sagging (pared) || warped, curved, bent (madera) || slow,

slow-moving (lento) || FIG slow, deliberate, unhurried (pausado).
◆ *m* plateau (entre montañas).

Pandora *npr f* MIT Pandora; *caja de Pandora* Pandora's box.

panear *vi* AMER to boast, to brag (fanfarronear).

panecillo *m* (bread) roll || FIG *venderse como panecillos* to sell like hot cakes.

panegírico, ca *adj* panegyrical.
◆ *m* panegyric.

panegirista *m* panegyrist.

panegirizar *vt* to panegyrize, to eulogize.

panel *m* panel (de una puerta) || AUT *panel de instrumentos* dashboard.
◆ *pl* ARQ panelling.

panera *f* breadbasket (cesta del pan).

panero *m* breadbasket.

paneslavismo *m* Pan-Slavism.

paneslavista *adj/s* Pan-Slavist.

paneuropeo, a *adj/s* Pan-European.

panfilismo *m* extreme kindness.

pánfilo, la *adj* FAM sluggish, slow (desidioso) | indolent (remolón) | stupid, foolish (tonto).

panfletista *m* pamphleteer, lampoonist.

panfleto *m* pamphlet, lampoon.
— OBSERV *Panfleto* and *panfletista* are Gallicisms for *libelo* and *libelista*.

pangermanismo *m* Pan-Germanism.

pangermanista *adj/s* Pan-Germanist.

pangolín *m* pangolin (mamífero).

panhelenismo *m* Panhellenism.

paniaguado *m* (p us) servant || FAM protégé; *los paniaguados del ministro* the minister's protégés.

pánico, ca *adj/sm* panic; *sembrar el pánico* to cause panic || *de pánico* wonderful, marvellous (magnífico), awful, ghatsly (horroroso).

paniego, ga *adj* wheat; *tierra paniega* wheatland || who eats a lot of bread, bread-loving (persona).

panificación *f* bread making, baking.

panificadora *f* industrial bakery.

panificar *vt* to make bread with (harina).

panislamismo *m* Pan-Islamism.

panizo *m* BOT millet (planta) | maize [*US* corn] (maíz).

panocha; panoja *f* ear (de maíz).

panoli; panolis *adj* FAM stupid, foolish.
◆ *m/f* fool.

panoplia *f* panoply (armadura) || arms *o* weapon collection.

panorama *m* panorama || FIG panorama; *el panorama de la situación económica* the panorama of the economic situation | scene, view (vista) || FIG *cambio de panorama* change of scenery.

panorámico, ca *adj* panoramic || *pantalla panorámica* panoramic screen.
◆ *f* panorama, view (en un cine).

panqué; panqueque *m* AMER pancake (hojuela).

pantagruélico, ca *adj* Pantagruelian.

pantagruelismo *m* Pantagruelism.

pantaleta *f*; **pantaletas** *f pl* AMER knickers *pl*, panties *pl*.

pantalón *m*; **pantalones** *m pl* trousers *pl* (de hombre) || panties *pl*, knickers *pl* (interiores de mujer) || trousers *pl*, slacks *pl* (de mujer) || — FAM *bajarse los pantalones* to give in to, to crawl to || *falda pantalón* culotte-skirt || FIG & FAM *llevar* or *ponerse los pantalones* to wear the trousers (mandar la mujer) || *pantalón bombacho* knickerbockers *pl* (de hombre), knickers *pl* (de niño), plus fours *pl* (de jugador de golf, etc.), baggy trousers *pl* (de zuavo, etc.) || *pantalón corto* shorts *pl* (de deporte), short trousers *pl* (de niño) || *pantalón tubo* slacks *pl* || *pantalón vaquero* jeans *pl*.

pantalonero, ra *m/f* trouser maker.

pantalla *f* shade, lampshade (de lámpara) || screen (cine); *en la pantalla* on the screen || fireguard (de chimenea) || TECN screen; *pantalla de radar* radar screen | screen, shield, guard (para proteger) || FIG front, cover, blind; *servir de pantalla* to serve as *o* to be a front (una persona) || AMER fan (abanico) || — *hacer pantalla con la mano* to shade one's eyes with one's hand || *la pequeña pantalla* the small screen, the television (la televisión) || *llevar a la pantalla* to screen, to film || INFORM *mostrar en pantalla* to display || *pantalla acústica* baffle || INFORM *pantalla de cristales líquidos* LCD, Liquid Crystal Display || *pantalla de radar* radar screen || INFORM *pantalla de visualización* visual display unit, display screen | *pantalla táctil* touch screen.

pantanal *m* marsh, bog, marshland.

pantano *m* marsh, bog (natural) || reservoir, dam (embalse).

pantanoso, sa *adj* marshy, boggy || FIG difficult, thorny (negocio).

panteísmo *m* pantheism.

panteísta *adj* pantheistic.
◆ *m/f* pantheist.

panteístico, ca *adj* pantheistic.

panteón *m* pantheon || mausoleum (sepultura) || *panteón de familia* family vault.

pantera *f* ZOOL panther || *pantera negra* black panther.

pantimedias *f pl* AMER tights, panty hose (panty, leotardo).

pantógrafo *m* pantograph.

pantomima *f* pantomime.

pantomimo *m* mime.

pantoque *m* MAR bilge.

pantorrilla *f* calf [of the leg].

pantorrillera *f* padded stocking.

pantufla *f*; **pantuflo** *m* slipper.

panza *f* FAM belly (barriga) || rumen (de rumiante) || belly (de vasija) || FAM *aterrizar sobre la panza* to make a belly landing.

panzada *f* blow in the belly (golpe) || FAM bellyful (hartazgo) || — FAM *darse una panzada* to eat *o* to have one's fill (saciarse), to be fed up (*de* with), to have had a bellyful (*de* of) (estar harto), to do a bellyflop (al tirarse al agua) | *darse una panzada de reír* to collapse laughing *o* with laughter | *una panzada de* a lot of.

panzazo *m* FAM *darse un panzazo* to do a bellyflop, to bellyflop (en el agua).

panzón, ona; panzudo, da *adj* paunchy, potbellied, big-bellied, fat (hombre), round (cosa).

pañal *m* nappy [*US* diaper] (de recién nacido) || shirttail (de camisa).
◆ *pl* nappies [*US* diapers]; *niño en pañales* baby in nappies || — FIG *criarse en buenos pañales* to be born with a silver spoon in one's mouth, to have a good start in life | *dejar en pañales a uno* to leave s.o. standing || *estar en pañales* to be in nappies (niño), to be wet behind the ears, to be green (ser novato), to be still in one's infancy; *la aviación estaba entonces en pañales* aviation was still in its infancy; *una industria en pañales* an industry which is still in its infancy.

pañería *f* draper's shop [*US* dry-goods store] (tienda) || drapery [*US* dry goods *pl*] (paños).

pañero, ra *adj* textile, cloth; *industria pañera* textile industry.
◆ *m/f* draper [*US* dry-goods dealer].

pañito *m* → **paño.**

paño *m* wool, woollen cloth [*US* woolen cloth] (tela de lana) || cloth, material (tela) || dishcloth (trapo de cocina) || duster (trapo para quitar el polvo) || cloth (para limpiar) || width (ancho de una tela) || drapery, hanging (colgadura) || MED towel; *paño higiénico* sanitary towel || dullness (falta de brillo) || mist, cloud (en un cristal) || flaw (de un diamante) || pebble dash (enlucido) || wall, panel (pared) || MAR sails *pl* (velas) || — *al paño* aside || FIG *conocer el paño* to know one's stuff | *el buen paño en el arca se vende* good merchandise needs no publicity || *paño de altar* altar cloth || *paño de billar* billiard cloth || *paño de manos* hand towel (toalla) || *paño fúnebre* or *mortuorio* or *de tumba* pall || FIG & FAM *ser del mismo paño* to be tarred with the same brush, to be two of a kind | *ser el paño de lágrimas de alguien* to give s.o. a shoulder to cry on, to be s.o.'s consoler || *traje de paño negro* black woollen suit.
◆ *pl* hangings || ARTES drapery *sing* || — FIG *estar en paños menores* to be in one's undies *o* underclothes | *jugar a dos paños* to play a double game, to run with the hare and hunt with the hounds | *no andarse con paños calientes* not to use half measures || *paños calientes* packing (remedio), half measures (paliativo) || *paños menores* underwear *sing*, underclothes, undies.

pañol *m* MAR storeroom, store || *pañol de municiones* ammunition room.

pañoleta *f* fichu (para los hombros) || necktie, tie (del torero).

pañolón *m* shawl || large handkerchief (pañuelo).

pañosa *m* TAUR «muleta» [cloth cape].

pañuelo *m* handkerchief (para las narices) || scarf (en la cabeza), fichu (en los hombros) || — *pañuelo de bolsillo* pocket handkerchief || *pañuelo de papel* paper handkerchief, paper tissue || FIG *ser grande como un pañuelo* to be as small as can be, to be tiny *o* minute.

papa *m* pope (sumo pontífice).

papa *f* potato (patata) || FAM hoax (noticia falsa) || — FIG *no saber ni papa de* not to have a clue about, to know nothing whatsoever about; *de esto no sé ni papa* I haven't a clue about this || AMER *papa del aire* yam | *papa dulce* sweet potato (batata).

papá *m* FAM daddy, papa, dad (padre) || AMER *papá grande* grandfather (abuelo) || *Papá Noel* Father Christmas.

papable *adj* papable (un cardenal).

papachador, ra *adj* AMER comforting (reconfortante).

papachar *vt* AMER to cuddle (mimar).

papada *f* double chin (de una persona) || dewlap (del buey).

papado *m* papacy.

papafigo *m* figpecker (ave) || golden oriole (oropéndola).

papagayo *m* parrot (ave) || AMER kite (cometa) || FIG & FAM parrot, magpie, chatterbox (parlanchín) || FIG & FAM *repetir como un papagayo* to repeat parrot-fashion, to parrot.

papahígo *m* figpecker (ave).

papaína *f* QUÍM papain.

papaíto *m* FAM daddy, dad.

papal *adj* papal; *decretos papales* papal decrees.
◆ *m* AMER potato field.

papalina *f* cap which covers the ears (gorra) || bonnet (cofia) || FAM *coger una papalina* to get sozzled *o* canned (emborracharse).

papalote *m* AMER kite (cometa).

papamoscas *m inv* flycatcher (ave) || FIG simpleton, fool (tonto).

papamóvil *m* popemobile.

papanatas *m inv* FAM simpleton, fool (tonto) | gaper (mirón).

papanatería *f*; **papanatismo** *m* FAM simplicity, silliness (idiotez) | gaping (mirada).

papar *vt* to swallow (tragar) || FIG & FAM *papar moscas* to catch flies, to gape, to daydream.

paparrucha; paparruchada *f* FAM hoax (mentira) | worthless thing (cosa inútil) | piece of nonsense, silly thing (tontería).

papaveráceas *f pl* BOT papaveraceae.

papaverina *f* QUÍM papaverine.

papaya *f* papaya fruit (fruto).

papayo *m* papaya tree (árbol).

papel *m* paper; *papel corriente* ordinary paper || paper (escrito) || piece of paper, sheet of paper (hoja) || piece of paper (pedazo); *dame un papel para apuntar esto* give me a piece of paper to write this down || TEATR role, part; *primer papel* first role, leading part; *segundo papel* second role, minor part || FIG role; *tu papel es obedecer* your role is to obey || COM paper money, banknotes *pl* || — FIG *blanco como el papel* as white as a sheet || *desempeñar* or *representar el papel* to play a role *o* a part || FIG *emborronar papel* to scribble | *encajar muy bien en un papel* to fit the part || *fábrica de papel* paper mill || FIG *hacer buen, mal papel* to do well, badly; to cut a good figure, a bad figure || *hacer el papel de* to play, to play the part of || FIG *hacer papel de* to act as (servir de) || *hacer un pobre papel* to give a poor show || *papel atrapamoscas* flypaper || *papel autográfico* autographic paper || *papel biblia* bible paper, India paper || *papel carbón* carbon paper || *papel cebolla* pelure paper || *papel cuadriculado* squared paper, graph paper || *papel cuché* coated paper || *papel de barba* untrimmed paper || *papel de calcar* tracing paper || *papel de cartas* writing paper, notepaper || *papel de dibujo* drawing paper || *papel de embalar* or *de envolver* wrapping paper || *papel de empapelar* wallpaper || *papel de escribir* notepaper, writing papper || *papel de estaño* or *de aluminio* tinfoil , aluminium foil || *papel de estraza* or *de añafea* wrapping *o* brown paper || *papel de filtro* filter paper || *papel de fumar* cigarette paper || *papel del Estado* government bonds || *papel de lija* or *de vidrio* sandpaper || *papel de marca* foolscap paper || *papel de música* or *pautado* music paper || *papel de pagos* stamp, stamped paper || *papel de pegar* sticky *o* gummed paper || *papel de periódico* newsprint (papel de baja calidad), newspaper; *envuelto en papel de periódico* wrapped in newspaper || *papel de plata* silver paper || *papel de pruebas* paper used for proofs || *papel de seda* or *de culebrilla* tissue paper || *papel de tornasol* litmus paper || *papel en blanco* clean *o* fresh sheet of paper || *papel engomado* sticky *o* gummed paper || *papel esmerilado* emery paper || FIG *papel estelar* leading role || *papel glaseado* or *de brillo* glossy paper || *papel higiénico* or *sánico* toilet paper || *papel kraft* kraft || AMER *papel madera* brown paper (papel de estraza) || FIG *papel mojado* worthless piece of paper (documento) || *papel moneda* paper money, banknotes *pl* || *papel pintado* wallpaper || *papel secante* blotting paper || *papel sellado* stamp, stamped paper || *papel sin sellar* unstamped paper || *papel tela* cloth finish writing paper (para carta) || *papel timbrado* stamped paper || *papel vegetal* grease-proof paper || *papel vergé* or *verjurado* laid paper || *papel vitela* vellum paper || *papel volante* leaflet || FIG *se cambiaron los papeles* the roles have been reversed | *ser papel mojado* to be worthless | *sobre el papel* on paper.
◆ *pl* papers (documentación) || newspapers, papers (periódicos) || — *papeles de a bordo* ship's papers || *venir a uno con papeles* to tease *o* to torment s.o.

papelear *vi* to rummage through papers || FIG & FAM to show off (querer aparentar).

papeleo *m* rummaging through papers || *el papeleo administrativo* red tape, paper work.

papelera *f* wastepaper basket (cesto) || paper mill (fábrica) || writing desk (mueble).

papelería *f* stationer's (tienda) || pile *o* mess of papers (papeles en desorden).

papelero, ra *adj* paper || FIG pretentious, showy (ostentoso).
◆ *m/f* stationer, paper manufacturer *o* seller || FIG show-off (ostentoso).
◆ *m* AMER newspaper seller.

papeleta *f* ticket; *papeleta de rifa* draw ticket || file card (ficha) || ballot paper, voting paper; *papeleta en blanco* blank ballot paper || pawn ticket (de monte de piedad) || question paper (papel que lleva una pregunta en un examen) || question (pregunta) || report (calificación de un examen) || FIG problem, poser (problema) | tough *o* unpleasant job (incordio) | drag (pesadez); *¡menuda papeleta!* what a drag! || — FIG *le ha tocado una mala papeleta* yours is a tough job | *plantear una papeleta difícil* to pose a problem.

papelillo; papelito *m* sachet (de medicina) || confetti || cigarette (cigarro) || piece of paper (trozo de papel).

papelón, ona *adj* FAM pretentious, showy (presumido).
◆ *m/f* FAM show-off, pretentious *o* showy person.
◆ *m* scrap of paper (papelucho) || bristol board (cartulina) || cornet (cucurucho) || AMER brown sugar | ridiculous role | blunder (plancha).

papelote; papelucho *m* FAM scrap of paper.

papera *f* MED goitre [*US* goiter] (bocio).
◆ *pl* mumps *sing* (enfermedad).

papero, ra *adj* AMER potato.

papi *m* FAM daddy, dad (papá).

papiamento *m* dialect spoken en Curaçao.

papila *f* ANAT papilla.

papilar *adj* ANAT papillary.

papilionáceo, a *adj* papilionaceous.
◆ *f pl* papilonaceae.

papiloma *m* MED papilloma.

papilla *f* pap (para niños) || — FIG & FAM *echar la primera papilla* to be as sick as a dog, to be violently sick | *hacer papilla a uno* to make mince-meat of s.o. | *hecho papilla* fagged out, shattered (muy cansado), a mess, a write-off (destrozado).

papillote *m* curl paper (para el pelo).

Papiniano *npr m* Papinian.

papiro *m* papyrus.

pápiro *m* FAM banknote.

papirología *f* study of papyri.

papirólogo, ga *m/f* person who studies papyri.

papirotada; papirotazo *m* fillip (golpe) || AMER stupid thing (sandez).

papirote *m* fillip (golpe).

papirusa *f* AMER FAM good looker [*US* doll] (muchacha).

papisa *f* *la papisa Juana* Pope Joan.

papismo *m* papistry, popery.

papista *adj* papist, popish || FIG *ser más papista que el papa* to out-Herod Herod.
◆ *m/f* papist.

papo *m* dewlap (de los animales) || double chin, jowl (sotabarba) || craw, maw (buche de las aves) || MED goitre [*US* goiter] (bocio).

paprika *f* paprika.

papú; papúa *adj/s* Papuan.

Papúa Nueva Guinea *npr f* GEOGR Papua New Guinea.

Papuasia *npr f* GEOGR Papua.

paquear *vi* to snipe (un soldado aislado).
◆ *vt* to snipe at.

paquebote *m* MAR packet boat, packet.

paquete *m* packet (caja); *un paquete de cigarrillos* a packet of cigarettes || package (lío), parcel (de mayor bulto) || packet boat (buque) || passenger in a sidecar (moto) || FAM dandy | joke, trick (embuste); *dar un paquete* to play a trick || POP task, job (cosa pesada); *¡vaya un paquete!* what a job! || — MIL & FAM *meter un paquete* to bawl out || *paquete bomba* parcel bomb, mail bomb || INFORM *paquete de programas* software package || *paquete postal* parcel.

paquete, ta *adj* AMER elegant, spruce, smart.

paquetería *f* small business || AMER affectation.

paquidermo *adj m* ZOOL pachydermatous.
◆ *m* ZOOL pachyderm.

Paquistán *npr m* GEOGR Pakistan.

paquistaní *adj/s* Pakistani.

par *adj* even; *número par* even number || equal, like (semejante).
◆ *m* pair (dos unidades); *un par de zapatos* a pair pf shoes || peer (dignidad) || pair, couple; *un par de huevos* a couple of eggs || couple; *por un par de pesetas* for a couple of pesetas || equal (igual) || ARQ rafter || MAT even number || FÍS couple (electricidad) || TECN couple (de fuerzas).
◆ *f* COM par.
◆ *f pl* MED placenta *sing* || — *abierto de par en par* wide open || *abrir de par en par* to open wide || *a la par, al par* at par (monedas); *cambio a la par* exchange at par || *a la par* together (conjuntamente), at the same time (igualmente); *es alto y gordo a la par* he is tall and at the same time fat || *a la par que* at the same time as, as, while; *cantaba a la par que bailaba* he sang as he danced; and, cum; *es sabio a la par que artista* he is a wise man and an artist *o* a wise man cum artist; both, at the same time; *éste es un vestido moderno a la par que elegante* this dress is both modern and elegant || *al par de* on an equal footing with || *a pares* in pairs, in twos, two by two || *ir a la par de* to go with, to match || *jugar a pares y nones* to play odds and evens || FAM *le dio un par de bofetadas* she slapped his face || *no tener par* to have no parallel, to be unique || *sin par* without equal *o* par, matchless, peerless || *voy a decirte un par de palabras* I am going to tell him a thing or two.

para *prep*

> **1.** DESTINO **2.** SITIO, DIRECCIÓN **3.** TIEMPO **4.** RELACIÓN, COMPARACIÓN **5.** LOCUCIONES

1. DESTINO For: *este libro es para ti* this book is for you; *es importante para la salud* it is important for the health; *ha sido muy desagradable para nosotros* it was very unpleasant for us; *bueno para la garganta* good for the throat || to, in order to: *para cantar bien* in order to sing well || to: *nombrar para un cargo* to appoint to a post; *no tengo tiempo para comer* I have no time to eat; *no tengo permiso para salir* I am not allowed to go out; *eso no tiene utilidad para mí* that is of no use to me; *es primordial para la industria* it is vital to industry || as: *le han con-*

tratado para secretario they have engaged him as secretary.
2. SITIO, DIRECCIÓN Towards (hacia): *caminó para el árbol, para el coche* he walked towards the tree, towards the car || to: *voy para el pueblo* I am going to the village.
3. TIEMPO For: *tiene pan para dos días* he has enough bread for two days; *me voy para una semana* I am going away for a week || by, at: *volverá para Navidad* he will come back by Christmas || — *faltaban diez días para Navidad* there were ten days till Christmas || *para Navidades hará dos años* it will be two years ago this Christmas || *va para dos años que* it is nearly two years since.
4. RELACIÓN, COMPARACIÓN As for, as regards, in regard to (por lo que toca) || for (comparación): *hace buen tiempo para la estación* the weather is good for the season; *para un hombre normalmente tan antipático se ha portado muy amablemente* for a man who is normally so unpleasant he has been very nice || compared with to: *eso es mucho para lo que él suele dar* that is a lot compared with what he usually gives.
5. LOCUCIONES *Dar para* to give enough money for: *dar para pan* to give enough money for bread; *dar para vestirse* to give enough money to dress o.s.; to be enough for (ser bastante para) || *decir para sí* to say to o.s. || *este hombre es para matarle* this man ought to be put away || *haber nacido para pintar* to have been born to paint || *haber nacido para ser pintor* to be a born painter || *ir para los cuarenta años* to be about forty [age] || *ir para casa* to go home || *ir para la taberna* to go to *o* towards the tavern || *ir para viejo* to grow old || *lo leyó para él* he read it to himself || *no es para tanto* there is no need to make such a fuss || *para abajo* downward, downwards, down || *para arriba* upward, upwards, up || *para atrás* behind (detrás), backwards (hacia atrás) || *para con* to, towards: *ingrato para con sus padres* ungrateful to one's parents || *para concluir* in conclusion, to conclude || *para eso* for that || *para mí* in my opinion, as far as I am concerned (a mi parecer) || *para que* so that, in order that: *para que venga* so that he should come || *¿para qué?* why?: *¿para qué vienes?* why are you coming?; what... for?: *¿para qué sirve esto?* what is this for?; what for? (¿y de qué me serviría?) || *¿para qué te voy a contar?* there is no need to tell you || *para siempre* for ever || *ser para nada* to be good for nothing, to be useless || *ser para todo* to be good for everything || *ser para volverse loco* to be enough to drive one mad || *tener para sí que* to think that, to believe that.

parabellum *m* automatic pistol (pistola).

parabién *m* congratulations *pl* || greeting || *dar el parabién* to congratulate.

parábola *f* parable (de Cristo) || MAT parabola.

parabólico, ca *adj* parabolic.

parabolizar *vt* to parabolize.

parabrisas *m inv* windscreen [US windshield].

paraca *f* AMER wind [blowing from the Pacific].

paracaídas *m inv* parachute || — *lanzamiento en paracaídas* parachuting || *lanzar en paracaídas* to parachute || *tirarse* or *lanzarse en paracaídas* to parachute.

paracaidismo *m* parachuting, parachute jumping; *practicar el paracaidismo* to go in for parachuting.

paracaidista *adj* *tropas paracaidistas* paratroopers.
◆ *m/f* parachutist || MIL paratrooper.

parachispas *m inv* spark arrester.

parachoques *m inv* bumper [US fender] (de coche) || buffer (de vagón).

parada *f* stop (sitio); *parada discrecional* request stop; *parada del autobús* bus stop || stopping (acción) || stop, halt (en el camino); *una parada de cinco minutos* a five-minute stop || rank, stand (de taxis) || pause, break (detención) || pen (para rebaños) || stud farm (acaballadero) || relay, relay post (para caballos de reemplazo) || relay (caballos de reemplazo) || parade (espectáculo) || stake (en el juego) || parry (esgrima) || MIL parade || MÚS pause || dam (presa de un río) || DEP save, stop (en fútbol) || AMER boasting || — *hacer parada* to stop || *parada en firme* dead stop *o* halt (equitación) || *parada en seco* dead stop *o* halt || *parada y fonda* stop-restaurant facilities (en una estación).

paradera *f* sluice gate (de molino) || seine net (red).

paradero *m* whereabouts *pl* (sitio) || destination (destino) || home, residence (morada) || FIG end (término); *tendrá mal paradero* she'll come to a bad end || AMER station (apeadero) || — *averiguar el paradero de* to ascertain the whereabouts of, to locate || *no conozco su paradero* I do not know where he is *o* where he lives.

paradigma *m* GRAM paradigm (modelo).

paradigmático, ca *adj* GRAM paradigmatic.

paradisiaco, ca; paradisíaco, ca *adj* paradisiac, paradisiacal, heavenly; *un sitio paradisiaco* a heavenly place.

parado, da *adj* stationary; *estaba parado en medio de la calle* he was stopped in the middle of the road || still, motionless (quieto) || idle, at rest (cosa, máquina) || unemployed, out of work (sin trabajo) || closed, at a standstill (una fábrica) || FIG slow, indolent (poco activo) | idle, unoccupied (desocupado) | lazy (perezoso) || AMER standing (de pie) || — FIG *dejar algo, a alguien mal parado* to leave sth., s.o. in a sorry state; *la enfermedad le ha dejado mal parado* his ilness has left him in a sorry state; *Francisco dejó mal parado a Juan* Frank left, John in a sorry state | *quedarse parado* to be dumbfounded *o* struck dumb | *salir bien, mal parado* to manage *o* to come off well, badly (una persona), to turn out well, badly (un asunto).
◆ *m* unemployed person || *el número de parados ha incrementado mucho* the number of unemployed has greatly increased.

paradoja *f* paradox.

paradójico, ca *adj* paradoxical.

parador, ra *adj* stopping || heavy-betting (en los juegos).
◆ *m/f* heavy better *o* bettor (en los juegos).
◆ *m* inn (mesón) || «parador» [State hotel].

paraestatal *adj* which cooperates with the State, semi-official.

parafernal *adj* JUR paraphernal || *bienes parafernales* paraphernalia, wife's personal property as distinct from her dowry.

parafernalia *f* paraphernalia.

parafina *f* paraffin || *aceite de parafina* mineral oil.

parafinado *m* paraffining, oiling with paraffin.

parafinar *vt* to paraffin.

parafraseador, ra *m/f* paraphraser.

parafrasear *vt* to paraphrase.

paráfrasis *f inv* paraphrase.

parafrástico, ca *adj* paraphrastic.

paragoge *f* GRAM paragoge.

paragógico, ca *adj* paragogic.

paragolpes *m inv* AMER bumper [US fender] (parachoques).

parágrafo *m* (p us) paragraph (párrafo).

paragranizo *adj m* antihail (cañón).

paraguas *m inv* umbrella.

Paraguay *npr m* GEOGR Paraguay (país y río).

paraguaya *f* kind of peach.

paraguayo, ya *adj/s* Paraguayan.

paraguazo *m* blow from *o* with an umbrella.

paragüería *f* umbrella shop.

paragüero, ra *m/f* umbrella dealer (vendedor).
◆ *m* umbrella stand (para poner paraguas).
◆ *f* AMER umbrella stand.

parahúso *m* drill.

paraíso *m* paradise || FIG paradise, heaven || TEATR gods, gallery [US peanut gallery] || — *ave del paraíso* bird of paradise || ECON *paraíso fiscal* tax haven || *paraíso terrenal* earthly paradise.

paraje *m* place, spot; *paraje desconocido* unknown place *o* spot || area, region; *paraje salvaje* wild area *o* region || state (estado).
◆ *pl* MAR waters || *¿qué haces por estos parajes?* what are you doing in these parts?

paralaje *f* ASTR parallax.

paralelamente *adv* parallel, in a parallel direction.

paralela *f* parallel (línea) || trench, parallel (foso).
◆ *pl* parallel bars (gimnasia).

paralelepípedo *m* MAT parallelepiped.

paralelismo *m* parallelism.

paralelo, la *adj* parallel; *paralelo a* or *con* parallel to; *correr paralelo a* to run parallel to || — DEP *barras paralelas* parallel bars (en gimnasia) || *las «Vidas paralelas» de Plutarco* Plutarch's «Parallel Lives».
◆ *m* parallel; *el paralelo treinta y tres* the thirty-third parallel || *establecer un paralelo entre* to compare, to parallel, to draw a parallel between.

paralelogramo *m* MAT parallelogram.

parálisis *f* MED paralysis, palsy; *parálisis infantil, parcial* infantile, partial paralysis; *parálisis progresiva* creeping paralysis; *parálisis cerebral* cerebral palsy || FIG paralysis.

paralítico, ca *adj/s* paralytic.

paralización *f* MED paralysis || FIG paralysis.

paralizador, ra; paralizante *adj* paralysing.
◆ *m/f* paralyser.

paralizar *vt* to paralyse, to paralyze; *paralizado de una pierna, de terror* paralysed in one leg, with fright.
◆ *vpr* to become paralysed || FIG to be paralysed, to come to a standstill.

paralogismo *m* paralogism, fallacy.

paramagnético, ca *adj* ELECTR paramagnetic.

paramagnetismo *m* ELECTR paramagnetism.

paramento *m* adorning, decoration (acción) || adornment, ornamental covering || facing (de una pared) || caparison (de caballo).
◆ *pl* paraments, vestments (del altar).

paramera *f* barren region.

paramétrico, ca *adj* parametric.

parámetro *m* MAT parameter.

paramilitar *adj* paramilitary, semi-military.

paramnesia *f* paramnesia.

páramo *m* wide barren plain.

parangón *m* pattern, model (dechado) || comparison || *sin parangón* incomparable, matchless.

parangonable *adj* comparable (*con* to).

parangonar *m* to compare (*con* to) (comparar) ‖ IMPR to justify.

paranéfrico, ca *adj* MED paranephric.

paraninfo *m* auditorium, assembly hall (en una universidad) ‖ best man (en una boda).

paranoia *f* MED paranoia.

paranoico, ca *adj/s* paranoiac.

paranomasia *f* paranomasia.

paranormal *adj* paranormal.

parapente *m* DEP paragliding.

parapetarse *vt* to take shelter, to take cover ‖ FIG to barricade o.s.; *se ha parapetado en su habitación* he has barricaded himself in his room | to take refuge; *parapetarse tras el silencio* to take refuge in silence.

parapeto *m* parapet, railing, railings *pl* (de un puente) ‖ MIL breastwork, parapet ‖ FIG wall, barricade.

paraplejía *f* MED paraplegia.

parapléjico, ca *adj/s* paraplegic.

parapsicología *f* parapsychology.

parar *vi* to stop; *ha parado la lluvia, ha parado de llover* the rain has stopped, it has stopped raining ‖ to stop, to halt; *pararon en medio de la calle* they stopped in the middle of the street ‖ to end, to lead; *este camino va a parar al bosque* this road ends at *o* leads to the wood ‖ to end up (llegar a) ‖ to get; *parar en las manos de* to get into the hands of ‖ to give up (abandonar); *no pararé hasta lograrlo* I won't give up until I succeed ‖ to stay; *pararé en casa de mi tío* I shall stay at my uncle's ‖ to stay, to stop, to put up; *actualmente paro en el hotel X* at the moment I am staying at the X hotel ‖ FIG to decide; *pararon en que se marcharían al día siguiente* they decided to leave the next day ‖ to point (el perro) ‖ — *¿adónde vamos a parar?* where are we going? ‖ FIG *ir a parar* to get at; *¿dónde quiere usted ir a parar?* what are you getting at?; to get to, to be; *¿dónde ha ido a parar este libro?* where is that book?, where has that book got to?; to end up, to land up; *el hombre fue a parar a la cárcel* the man ended up in jail ‖ *mis esfuerzos pararon en nada* my efforts came to nothing ‖ *no paró hasta que obtuvo lo que quería* he did not stop until he had got what he wanted ‖ *parar en seco* to stop dead *o* suddenly ‖ *sin parar* without stopping, nonstop, continuously ‖ *trabajaba, hablaba sin parar* he never stopped working, talking ‖ *trabajamos sin parar* we worked nonstop ‖ *venir a parar* to come to, to end (up); *sus ilusiones han venido a parar esto* his illusions have come to that; to result in, to lead to (dar lugar a), to reach, to arrive at, to come to; *venir a parar a la misma conclusión* to reach the same conclusion; to end (up), to stop; *la pelota vino a parar a mis pies* the ball ended up at my feet ‖ *y pare usted de contar* and that is as far as it goes.

◆ *vt* to stop; *pare el coche aquí* stop the car here ‖ to point (perro de caza) ‖ to parry, to ward off [a blow, a thrust] (boxeo, esgrima) ‖ to stop (un balón) ‖ to fix (la atención) ‖ — FIG *parar los pies* or *el carro a uno* to put s.o. in his place | *parar mientes en* to think of, to consider; *sin parar mientes en las consecuencias* without thinking of *o* considering the consequences.

◆ *vpr* to stop; *aquí no nos podemos parar* we cannot stop here ‖ AMER to stand up (ponerse de pie) | to get up (de la cama) ‖ — *no pararse en barras* to stop at nothing ‖ *pararse a pensar* to stop to think ‖ *pararse en algo* to pay attention to something ‖ *pararse en seco* to stop dead *o* in one's tracks ‖ *pararse en tonterías* to mess about ‖ *sin pararse en detalles* without going into details.

pararrayo *m*; **pararrayos** *m inv* lightning conductor [US lightning rod] (en edificios) ‖ lightning arrester (en aparatos eléctricos).

paraselene *f* ASTR paraselene.

parasicología *f* parapsychology.

parasimpático, ca *adj* parasympathetic.

◆ *m* parasympathetic nervous system.

parasitario, ria *adj* parasitic, parasitical.

parasiticida *adj/sm* parasiticide.

parasítico, ca *adj* parasitic, parasitical.

parasitismo *m* parasitism.

parásito, ta *adj* parasitic, parasitical (*de* on).

◆ *m* parasite ‖ FIG parasite.

◆ *pl* interference *sing*, atmospherics, static *sing* (en la radio).

parasol *m* parasol, sunshade (quitasol) ‖ FOT sunshade.

paratífico, ca *adj* MED paratyphoid.

paratifoidea *adj f/s/f* paratyphoid.

paratiroides *adj* parathyroid.

◆ *f pl* parathyroids.

paratopes *m inv* AMER buffer (de tren).

paratuberculosis *f* MED paratuberculosis.

paratuberculoso, sa *adj* MED paratuberculous.

Parcas *npr fpl* MIT Fates, Parcae.

parcela *f* plot, piece of ground, parcel (de tierra) ‖ particle (átomo) ‖ *división en parcelas* division into plots, parcelling out.

parcelable *adj* divisible into plots.

parcelación *f* division into plots, parcelling out (de un terreno).

parcelar *vt* to divide into plots, to parcel out; *parcelar un bosque* to parcel out a forest.

parcelario, ria *adj* divided into plots *o* parcels (parcelado) ‖ *concentración parcelaria* land consolidation [regrouping of lands].

parcial *adj* partial (incompleto); *vista parcial* partial view ‖ partial (injusto); *juicio parcial* partial judgment.

◆ *adj/s* partisan.

parcialidad *f* partiality, prejudice, bias (prejuicio) ‖ clique, faction, party (grupo).

parcialmente *adv* partially, partly, part (en parte) ‖ partially (injustamente).

parcimonia *f* parsimony (parsimonia).

parco, ca *adj* sparing; *parco en el hablar* or *en palabras* sparing in words ‖ mean (mezquino) ‖ moderate, scanty; *parco en el comer* a moderate *o* a scanty eater ‖ frugal, scanty (comida, etc.) ‖ — *parco en cumplidos* sparing in compliments ‖ *parco en gastar* economical (que gasta poco), mean, tightfisted (fam) (avaro).

parcómetro *m* parking meter.

parche *m* patch (en un neumático) ‖ plaster (emplasto) ‖ patch (para remendar) ‖ patch (colorete) ‖ botch, daub (pintura) ‖ FIG person *o* thing which is out of place ‖ TAUR cockade, knot of ribbons stuck onto the bull's forehead ‖ drumhead (de un tambor) ‖ FIG drum (tambor) ‖ MED specially coated plaster used to detect tuberculosis, skin test ‖ — *bolsillo de parche* patch pocket ‖ FIG & FAM *¡oído al parche!* be careful!, look out!, watch your step! | *pegar un parche a uno* to put one over on s.o. (engañar).

parchís; parchesi *m* parcheesi.

pardear *vi* to be *o* to stand out *o* to look brown.

¡pardiez! *interj* FAM goodness me!, good Lord!

pardillo, lla *adj/s* peasant, yokel (palurdo).

◆ *m* linnet (pájaro).

pardo, da *adj* brown; *oso pardo* brown bear ‖ dark, grey (tiempo, cielo, etc.) ‖ flat, dull (voz) ‖ AMER mulatto ‖ FIG *tener gramática parda* to have plenty of gumption.

pardusco, ca *adj* brownish, greyish.

pareado, da *adj* matching (emparejado) ‖ *versos pareados* rhyming couplets.

◆ *m pl* rhyming couplets.

parear *vt* to match, to pair, to put together (formar pares) ‖ to mate, to pair (animales) ‖ TAUR to place *o* to stick the banderillas in [a bull].

parecer *m* opinion, view; *a mi parecer* in my opinion *o* view; *tomar parecer de uno* to ask for s.o.'s opinion *o* view ‖ appearance, looks *pl* (aspecto); *buen parecer* pleasant appearance ‖ JUR expert opinion *o* advice (dictamen) ‖ — *al parecer* to all appearances, apparently ‖ *arrimarse al parecer de uno* to adopt s.o.'s opinion ‖ *de buen parecer* good-looking, nice-looking ‖ *de mal parecer* ugly, plain ‖ *mudar de parecer* to change one's mind ‖ *parecer de peritos* expert opinion ‖ *por el buen parecer* to keep up appearances, for form's sake ‖ *según el parecer de* according to ‖ *ser del parecer que...* to be of the opinion that...

parecer* *vi/v impers* to seem, to look, to appear; *parece cansado* he seems *o* he looks tired; *parece que va a llover* it seems that *o* it looks as if it is going to rain ‖ to seem; *parece imposible a su edad* it seems impossible at his age ‖ to be like, to look like, to seem like; *parece seda* it is like silk ‖ to appear (aparecer) ‖ to think (juzgar); *¿qué te parece?* what do you think? ‖ to be all right with (consentir); *iremos ahora si te parece* we shall go now if it is all right with you ‖ to be convenient (ser conveniente); *podemos trabajar en mi casa si te parece* we can work in my house if it is convenient for you ‖ to like (querer); *si te parece te lo llevo a tu casa* if you like I shall take it home for you ‖ — *a lo que parece* to all appearances, apparently ‖ *así parece* so it seems ‖ *aunque no lo parezca* incredible as it may seem ‖ *como le parezca* as you like ‖ *me ha parecido verle* I thought I saw him ‖ *me parece que* I think (that), it seems to me that ‖ *me parece que sí, que no* I think so, I don't think so ‖ *no parece tener la edad que tiene* he doesn't look his age ‖ *parece como si desease* it looks as if he wanted to ‖ *parece mentira que...* it hardly seems possible that..., who would have thought that...? ‖ *parece ser que...* it seems that... ‖ *según lo que parece* to all appearances ‖ *si le parece bien* if it is all right with you, if you like ‖ *si le parece mal* if you disagree, if you don't like the idea.

◆ *vpr* to look like, to resemble; *se parece mucho a su padre* he looks a lot like his father, he resembles his father a great deal ‖ to be alike, to look like *o* to resemble each other (aspecto); *los dos hermanos no se parecen nada* the two brothers are not at all alike, the two brothers do not look at all like each other ‖ to be alike, to resemble each other; *se parecen en el carácter, en las facciones* they are alike in character, in their features ‖ *ni nada que se le parezca* nor anything of the sort, far from it.

parecido, da *adj* alike; *los dos hermanos son muy parecidos* the two brothers are very alike ‖ like; *es muy parecido a su hermano* he is a lot like his brother ‖ of the kind, one like it; *éste o uno parecido* this one or one of the kind *o* or one like it ‖ similar (semejante) ‖ lifelike; *un retrato muy parecido* a very lifelike portrait ‖ — *algo parecido* sth. of the kind *o* of the sort, sth. like that ‖ FAM *bien parecido* good-looking, nice-looking, not bad (una persona) ‖ *ser parecido a* to be like.

◆ *m* resemblance, likeness; *parecido de familia* family likeness *o* resemblance ‖ similarity (semejanza) || *tener parecido con uno* to bear a resemblance to s.o.

pared *f* wall (de casa, etc.); *pared de ladrillos* brick wall || ANAT wall || — FIG *blanco como la pared* white as a sheet *o* as a ghost || FIG & FAM *como si hablara a una pared* like talking to a (brick) wall | *darse contra las paredes* to tear one's hair out || *dejar pegado a la pared* to nonplus (dejar confuso), to ruin (arruinar) || *entre cuatro paredes* between four walls || FIG *estar entre la espada y la pared* to go between the devil and the deep blue sea || FIG & FAM *está que se sube por las paredes* he is hopping mad | *estar pegado a la pared* to be flat broke (sin un cuarto) || FIG *las paredes oyen* walls have ears || *lienzo de pared* stretch of wall || *pared divisoria* or *intermedia* internal *o* dividing wall || *pared maestra* main *o* supporting wall || *pared medianera* party wall || FIG & FAM *subirse por las paredes* to go up the wall, to hit the roof (enfadarse), to be hopping mad (estar furioso) || *vivir pared por medio* to live in adjoining rooms *o* houses.

paredón *m* thick wall || piece of wall (en ruinas) || place of execution || — *¡al paredón!* to the firing squad! || *llevar al paredón* to send before the firing squad!

pareja *f* pair (par) || couple (hombre y mujer); *ser una buena pareja* to make a good couple || pair, couple; *una pareja de amigos* a pair *o* a couple of friends; *una pareja de palomas* a pair *o* a couple of pigeons || boy and girl (hijo e hija) || pair of Civil Guards (guardias) || partner (de baile y juego) || brace (caza) || pair (de naipes) || — *doble pareja* two pairs (póker) || FIG *hacer pareja con* to be two of a kind; *hace pareja con su amiga* she and her friend are two of a kind.
◆ *pl* two pairs, doublet *sing* (dados) || *por parejas* two by two, in pairs.

parejo *adv* AMER at the same time, together.

parejo, ja *adj* similar, the same, alike || even, smooth, flush (regular) || — *correr parejo con* to be on an equal footing with, to be on a par with, to be paralleled by || *ir parejos* to be equal || DEP *van parejos* they are neck and neck.

parénquima *m* ANAT & BOT parenchyma.

parentela *f* relations *pl*, relatives *pl* (conjunto de parientes).

parentesco *m* relationship, kinship || — FIG *parentesco espiritual* spiritual bond || *parentesco político* relationship by marriage.

paréntesis *m inv* parenthesis (frase) || brackets *pl* (signo) || FIG interruption, break || — *abrir, cerrar el paréntesis* to open, to close brackets || *entre paréntesis* in parentheses, in brackets || *sea dicho entre paréntesis* incidentally, be it said parenthetically.

pareo *m* pairing off, matching (unión) || loincloth (taparrabos) || mating (de las aves).

paresa *f* peeress.

pargo *m* porgy (pez).

parhelia *f*; **parhelio** *m* ASTR parhelion, mock sun.

parhilera *f* ARQ ridgepole.

paria *m* pariah || FIG outcast, pariah.

parida *adj f* who, which has given birth || *recién parida* woman who has just given birth.
◆ *f* FAM crap.

paridad *f* equality, parity (igualdad) || parity (de las monedas) || comparison (comparación).

paridígito *adj* whose toes form pairs (animal).

pariente, ta *m/f* relative, relation (miembro de la familia); *pariente cercano* close relative || — *medio pariente* distant cousin || *pariente político* in-law, relative by marriage.
◆ *m* FAM old man (esposo).
◆ *f* FAM missus (esposa).
— OBSERV *Parents* (mother and father) is translated in Spanish by *padres*.

parietal *adj* parietal.
◆ *m* parietal bone.

parietaria *f* BOT pellitory.

parihuelas *f pl* stretcher *sing*.

paripé *m* FAM *dar el paripé* to trick, to fool (engañar) | *hacer el paripé* to put on airs (presumir), to put on an act; *se detestan, pero en público hacen el paripé* they detest each other, but in public they put on an act; to pretend; *no entiende ni palabra de inglés, pero hace el paripé* he doesn't understand a word of English, but he pretends to.

parir *vi* to give birth (mujer y animales) || to calve (la vaca) || to foal (los solípedos) || FIG & FAM *por si fuéramos pocos parió la abuela* that's all we needed, that's the last straw.
◆ *vt* to bear (mujer), to give brith to (mujer y animales) || FIG & FAM to produce, to cause || FAM *poner a parir* to bitch about s.o., to slag off s.o. *o* sth.

Paris *npr m* MIT Paris.

París *n pr* GEOGR Paris.

parisién; parisino, na parisiense *adj/s* Parisian.

parisilábico, ca; parisílabo, ba *adj* parisyllabic.

paritario, ria *adj* joint; *comisión paritaria* joint committee.

parkerización *f* TECN parkerization.

parking *m* car park [*US* parking lot].

parlamentar *vi* to parley, to hold a parley (dos enemigos) || FAM to chatter, to gossip (conversar).

parlamentario, ria *adj* parliamentary; *sistema parlamentario* parliamentary system.
◆ *m* member of parliament [*US* congressman] (miembro) || parliamentarian || negotiator (que parlamenta).

parlamentarismo *m* parliamentarianism (doctrina) || parliamentary government (gobierno parlamentario).

parlamento *m* parliament (asamblea) || parley, negotiation (negociación) || speech (discurso) || TEATR tirade || FAM chatter (charla).

parlanchín, ina *adj* chatty, talkative.
◆ *m/f* chatterbox.

parlante *adj* HERÁLD canting, allusive; *armas parlantes* canting *o* allusive arms || talking (sonoro).

parlar *vi* to chat, to gossip (charlar) || to talk, to speak (hablar).

parlotear *vi* FAM to chatter, to prattle.

parloteo *m* FAM gossip, small talk, chatter, prattle.

parmesano, na *adj/s* Parmesan || *queso parmesano* Parmesan cheese.

parnasianismo *m* Parnassian School (literatura).

parnasiano, na *adj/s* Parnassian.

Parnaso *npr m* Parnassus (montaña).

parné; parnés *m* POP cash, loot, dough (dinero).

paro *m* tit (ave) || stoppage, standstill (suspensión en el trabajo) || unemployment (desempleo); *paro estacional* seasonal unemployment; *paro cíclico* cyclical unemployment || — *estar en paro forzoso* to be unemployed || ZOOL *paro carbonero* coal tit, coletit || *paro encubierto* underemployment || *paro forzoso* unemployment || *paro técnico* technological unemployment.

parodia *f* parody.

parodiar *vt* to parody.

paródico, ca *adj* parodic, parodical.

parodista *m* parodist.

parón *m* EQUIT refusal || sudden *o* dead stop (parada en seco).

paronimia *f* paronymy.

paronímico, ca *adj* paronymous.

parónimo, ma *adj* paronymous.
◆ *m* paronym (vocablo).

paronomasia *f* paronomasia (en retórica).

parótida *f* ANAT parotid.

parotiditis *m* MED parotitis.

paroxismo *m* paroxysm || FIG paroxysm, climax.

paroxítono, na *adj/sm* GRAM paroxytone.

parpadear *vi* to blink, to wink (los ojos) || to flicker, to blink (la luz) || to twinkle (las estrellas).

parpadeo *m* blinking, winking, blink, wink (ojos) || flickering, blinking, flicker (luz) || twinkling, twinkle (estrellas).

párpado *m* ANAT eyelid.

parque *m* park, gardens *pl* || garden; *parque zoológico* zoological garden || playground (de niños) || — *parque automóvil* or *móvil* number of cars on the road (en un país) || *parque de artillería* artillery park || *parque de atracciones* fairground, fun fair || *parque de bomberos* fire station || *parque de coches* or *de estacionamiento* car park [*US* parking lot] || *parque nacional* national park || *parque tecnológico* industrial park.

parqué *m* parquet.

parqueadero *m* AMER car park [*US* parking lot].

parquear *vt* AMER to park (aparcar).

parquedad *f* parsimony, frugality (sobriedad) || moderation, temperance (templanza) || scantiness, paucity; *la parquedad de las raciones* the scantiness of the rations.

parqueo *m* AMER parking (acción) || car park [*US* parking lot] (para estacionar).

parquet *m* parquet.

parquímetro *m* parking meter.

parra *f* grapevine (vid) || — *hoja de parra* fig leaf (en esculturas, etc.) || *parra virgen* Virginia creeper || FIG & FAM *subirse a la parra* to blow one's top, to hit the roof (enfadarse).

parrafada *f*; **parrafeo** *m* FAM chat (charla) | speech (perorata) || FAM *echar una parrafada* to have a chat.

parrafear *vi* to chat, to have a chat.

párrafo *m* paragraph || — FAM *echar un párrafo* to have a chat || *hacer párrafo aparte* to start a new paragraph (escribiendo) || *párrafo aparte* new paragraph (punto y aparte), to change the subject (cambio de conversación).

parral *m* gravepine (vid) || vine arbour [*US* vine arbor] (parra en una armazón).

parrampán *m* AMER FAM poseur (cursi).

parranda *f* FAM party, spree (juerga) || band of musicians *o* singers (cuadrilla) || — FAM *andar* or *estar de parranda* to be out of a binge *o* for a good time | *irse de parranda* to go out on a binge *o* for a good time.

parrandear *vi* FAM to go out on a binge *o* for a good time (irse de parranda).

parrandeo *m* FAM fling, party, binge (juerga).

parrandista *m* FAM reveller (juerguista).

parricida *m/f* parricide, patricide (criminal).
◆ *adj* parricidal, patricidal.

parricidio *m* parricide, patricide (crimen).

parrilla *f* grill, gridiron ‖ grate, grating (de locomotora, de horno) ‖ grillroom (en un restaurante) ‖ earthenware jug (recipiente) ‖ AMER roof rack, luggage rack (baca) ‖ — *bistec a la parrilla* grilled steak ‖ *carne asada en la parrilla* grilled meat ‖ DEP *parrilla de salida* starting grid ‖ *parrilla eléctrica* electric grill.

parrillada *f* barbecue ‖ CULIN grilled seafood dish.

párroco *m* parish priest ‖ *cura párroco* parish priest.

parroquia *f* REL parish church (iglesia) | parish, parishioners *pl* (gente) | parish (territorio) ‖ customers *pl*, clients *pl*, clientele (de comerciante) ‖ supporters *pl* (de equipo deportivo).

parroquial *adj* parish, parochial; *iglesia parroquial* parish church.

parroquiano, na *m/f* (regular) customer, client (de un comerciante) ‖ regular (customer) (de un bar) ‖ REL parishioner.

parsec *m* ASTR parsec.

parsimonia *f* parsimony (parquedad) ‖ moderation, temperance (templanza) ‖ calmness (calma) ‖ *con parsimonia* calmly, unhurriedly.

parsimonioso, sa *adj* parsimonious ‖ calm, unhurried (tranquilo).

parte *f* part; *como parte del pago* in part payment; *parte de la oración* part of speech; *parte del ejército quedó allí* part of the army remained there ‖ section (sección) ‖ share, part, portion (de un reparto) ‖ share, interest (comercio) ‖ MAT part (véase OBSERV) ‖ spot, point; *parte sensible* sensitive spot ‖ side (lado) ‖ place, spot (lugar); *en aquella parte* in that place ‖ way (camino); *echar por otra parte* to go a different way ‖ faction, party (parcialidad, bando) ‖ side (rama de parentesco); *primos de* or *por parte de mi madre* cousins on my mother's side ‖ TEATR part, role (papel); *hacer su parte* to play one's part | actor, actress (actor) ‖ side (en una contienda); *¿por qué parte estás?* which side are you on? ‖ JUR party, part (contratante, litigante) | portion (de herencia) ‖ MÚS part ‖ — *a* or *en otra parte* somewhere else, elsewhere ‖ *a una y otra parte* on both sides ‖ *constituirse parte en contra de alguien* to bring a civil action against s.o. ‖ *cuarta parte* quarter, fourth part ‖ *dar parte en* to give a share in ‖ *de algún, poco, mucho tiempo a esta parte no le hemos visto* we haven't seen him for some, a short, a long time ‖ *de mi parte* on my behalf, for me (en nombre mío) ‖ *de parte a parte* back and forth, from one side to the other (de un lado a otro), from top to bottom, completely (sin omitir nada), right through (atravesar) ‖ *de parte de* from, on behalf of (en nombre de), on the side of (a favor de) ‖ *¿de parte de quién?* who is calling? (teléfono), your name, please? (hablando) ‖ *de una parte a otra* back and forth, to and fro ‖ *de una y otra parte* from both sides (movimiento), on both sides (en, de los dos lados), on *o* from all sides (por todas partes) ‖ *echar algo a buena parte, a mala parte* to take sth. the right way, the wrong way ‖ *en alguna* or *en cierta parte de España* somewhere in Spain ‖ *en cualquier otra parte* anywhere else ‖ *en cualquier parte donde* anywhere ‖ *en esta parte* here, around here, hereabouts ‖ *en gran parte* to a large extent, in large measure ‖ *en ninguna parte* nowhere ‖ *en otra parte* somewhere else ‖ *en parte* partly, in part ‖ *¿en qué parte de?* in which part of?, where in? ‖ FAM *en salva sea la parte* where it hurts most, you know where (las posaderas) ‖ *entrar a formar parte de* to be a part of, to form a part of ‖ *entrar* or *ir a la parte en* to take a share in, to go shares in ‖ *ir a otra parte* to go somewhere else ‖ *la mayor parte* the majority, most (con el verbo en plural) ‖ *la mayor parte de* most, the majority of (cuando hay varios); *la mayor parte de los españoles* most Spaniards, the majority of Spaniards; most of, the greater part of (de un entero); *la mayor parte de España* most of Spain ‖ FIG *la parte del león* the lion's share | *la parte en la que la espalda pierde su casto nombre* the you know what ‖ *llevar la mejor parte* to have the advantage ‖ *llevarse la mejor parte* to come off best, to get the best of it, to get the best of the bargain ‖ *mirar a otra parte* to look the other way *o* in another direction ‖ FIG *no ir a ninguna parte* to have no importance, to be nothing (no tener importancia) ‖ *no llevar a ninguna parte* not to get one anywhere, to get one nowhere ‖ *no ser* or *no tener parte en* to have nothing to do with ‖ *parte alícuota* aliquot part ‖ JUR *parte civil* plaintiff claiming damages [in a criminal case] ‖ *parte contraria* opposing party (en pleito), opposing team (equipo) ‖ *parte del mundo* continent ‖ *parte por parte* piece by piece, step by step, systematically ‖ *poner* or *hacer de su parte* to do one's bit ‖ *ponerse de parte de* to side with ‖ *por cualquier parte que lo vea* from whichever side he looks at it ‖ *por mi parte* for my part, as for me, as far as I am concerned (en cuanto a mí), on my side (por mi lado) ‖ *por otra parte* (and) on the other hand, moreover (además) ‖ *por parte de* on the part of ‖ *por una parte y por otra* on the one hand and on the other ‖ *saber de buena parte* to have heard from a reliable source ‖ *ser juez y parte* to be judge in one's own case ‖ *ser parte en* to take part in (participar), to be a party to (en un juicio) ‖ *tener a uno de su parte* to have s.o. on one's side ‖ *tener* or *tomar parte en* to take part in, to participate in, to have a part in (colaborar), to receive a share of (compartir) ‖ *tercera parte* third; *disminuir algo en una tercera parte* to reduce sth. by a third ‖ *tomar en mala parte* to take in a bad part *o* badly.

◆ *pl* private parts, privates (órganos genitales) ‖ *a partes iguales* into equal parts *o* shares ‖ *en dos partes iguales* in half, into two equal parts ‖ *en todas las partes del mundo* in the four corners of the earth ‖ *en todas partes* everywhere, all over the place (fam) ‖ FIG & FAM *en todas partes cuecen habas* it's the same the whole world over ‖ *partes pudendas* or *vergonzosas* private parts, privates ‖ *por ambas partes* on both sides ‖ *por partes* bit by bit, stage by stage ‖ *por todas partes* everywhere, from all sides ‖ FIG *por todas partes se va a Roma* all roads lead to Rome ‖ *¡vayamos por partes!* first things first.

◆ *m* report (informe); *parte facultativo, meteorológico* progress, weather report ‖ despatch (telegrama oficial) ‖ communiqué (comunicado) ‖ news report (diario hablado) ‖ — *dar parte* to give notice ‖ *dar parte de algo* to announce sth., to let know of sth., to inform of sth. ‖ *dar parte de uno* to report s.o. ‖ MIL *ir al parte* to be reported ‖ *parte de boda* wedding card ‖ *parte médico* medical report.

— OBSERV *Parte* is also used to express fractions: *las dos terceras partes de nueve son seis* six is two thirds of nine; *la tercera parte de nueve* a third of nine.

parteluz *m* mullion (de ventana).

partenogénesis *f inv* parthenogenesis.

Partenón *npr m* Parthenon.

partenueces *m inv* nutcracker.

partera *f* midwife.

partero *m* male midwife, obstetrician.

parterre *m* flower bed (de jardín) ‖ stalls *pl*, orchestra stalls *pl* [US orchestra] (de cine, teatro).

partición *f* sharing out, division, distribution (reparto) ‖ partition, division (de un territorio) ‖ partition (de una herencia) ‖ MAT division (división) ‖ HERÁLD quarter, partition.

participación *f* participation (parte); *participación en un crimen* participation in a crime ‖ contribution (contribución); *su participación en los sucesos* his contribution to the events ‖ COM interest; *su participación en la empresa* his interest in the firm | share (acción) | investment (inversión) ‖ notice (aviso); *dar participación de sus propósitos* to give notice of one's intentions ‖ part of a lottery ticket (en la lotería) ‖ DEP entry (en un torneo) ‖ — *participación de boda* wedding card ‖ *participación en los beneficios* profit sharing.

participante *adj* participating, participant (que toma parte).

◆ *m/f* informant, informer, notifier (que comunica) ‖ participant, participator (que toma parte) ‖ competitor, participant (en un concurso).

participar *vt* to announce (una noticia); *participar la buena noticia* to announce the good news ‖ to inform of (con sustantivo); *nos participó los sucesos de aquel día* he informed us of the events of that day ‖ to inform, to notify (con locución verbal); *nos participa nuestro corresponsal que se ha casado X* our correspondent informs us that X has married.

◆ *vi* to participate, to take part; *participar en el trabajo* to take part in the work ‖ to enter, to go in (un concurso); *participar en un concurso* to enter (for) *o* to go in for a competition ‖ to partake; *el mulo participa del burro y del caballo* the mule partakes of the ass and the horse ‖ to have a share; *participar en los beneficios* to have a share in *o* of the profits ‖ to invest (invertir) ‖ to share (compartir); *participar de la misma opinión* to share the same opinion; *participar en una herencia* to share in an inheritance.

partícipe *adj* participating, participant (que colabora) ‖ interested (que tiene interés).

◆ *m/f* participant (que colabora) ‖ interested party (que tiene interés) ‖ beneficiary (beneficiario) ‖ — *hacer partícipe a uno de una cosa* to give s.o. a share in sth. (compartir), to inform s.o. of sth. (informar), to make s.o. a party to sth. (implicar) ‖ *ser partícipe en* to take part in ‖ *ser partícipes en* to be partners in (un negocio, un crimen).

participio *f* GRAM participle ‖ — *participio activo* or *de presente* present participle ‖ *participio pasivo* or *de pretérito* past participle.

partícula *f* particle.

particular *adj* particular; *en ciertos casos particulares* in some particular cases ‖ peculiar (propio); *particular a* or *de un país* peculiar to a country ‖ peculiar (raro); *un sabor particular* a peculiar taste ‖ individual; *el interés particular debe ser sacrificado en aras del interés colectivo* individual interest must be sacrificed to the common interest ‖ personal, private; *asuntos particulares* personal *o* private affairs; *correspondencia particular* personal *o* private correspondence ‖ — *alojarse en una casa particular* to live with a family ‖ *casa particular* private house *o* home ‖ *clase particular* private lesson ‖ *en particular* in particular ‖ *nada de particular* nothing special ‖ *no venga a mi despacho sino a mi casa particular* do not come to my office but to my home *o* to my house.

◆ *m* matter, subject, point (asunto); *no sé nada de este particular* I know nothing about this matter ‖ member of the public (persona cualquiera) ‖ private individual, individual (individuo) ‖ civilian; *vestido de particular* dressed as a civilian, in civilian dress.

particularidad *f* peculiarity, particularity.

particularismo *m* particularism.

particularización *f* particularization.

particularizar *vt* to specify, to particularize (especificar) ‖ to prefer, to favour [US to favor]

(preferir) || to distinguish (diferenciar) || to give details about (detallar).
◆ *vpr* to stand out, to be distinguishable (destacar); *se particulariza por su color* it stands out because of *o* it is distinguishable by its colour || to distinguish o.s.; *se particularizó en la batalla de* he distinguished himself in the battle of.

particularmente *adv* particularly, in particular.

partida *f* departure (salida) || band, gang (cuadrilla); *partida de ladrones* band of thieves || certificate (de nacimiento, de matrimonio, de defunción) || COM entry, item (asiento en una cuenta) | item, heading, entry (en un presupuesto); *partida arancelaria* tariff item; *el comercio de exportación tiene como principales partidas* the principal items under exports are || consignment, batch (remesa); *una partida de muebles* a consignment of furniture || party; *partida de caza* hunting party || MIL party; *partida de reconocimiento* reconnaissance party || game, hand (juego); *echar una partida de naipes* to have a game of cards || hand (manos de juego) || — *contabilidad por partida doble* double-entry bookkeeping || *dar la partida por ganada* to think it is all over || *jugar una mala partida* to have a bad game (jugar mal), to play a dirty trick on (hacer una mala jugada) || *las Siete Partidas* laws compiled by Alfonso X the Wise [13th century] || *partida de campo* picnic || *partida de gente* a crowd of people || COM *partida doble* double entry || FAM *partida serrana* dirty trick || COM *partida simple* single entry.

partidario, ria *adj* partisan || partisan, guerrilla.
◆ *m/f* follower, supporter, partisan (seguidor) || advocate (defensor) || guerrilla, partisan (en la guerra) || AMER sharecropper (aparcero).

partidismo *m* favouritism [*US* favoritism] (por uno) || party spirit (en opiniones).

partidista *adj* partisan.

partido, da *adj* divided, split || HERÁLD party.
◆ *m* party (político); *régimen de partido único* single-party system || side (lado) || camp (posición ideológica); *abandonar el partido de la oposición* to leave the opposition camp || backing, support (apoyo) || support, supporters *pl*, followers *pl* (partidarios) || advantage, profit, benefit (ventaja) || course [of action] (proceder) || measure, step (medida) || team (equipo); *el partido contrario* the opposing team || game; *partido amistoso* friendly game; *partido de pelota* game of pelota || match (encuentro organizado); *partido de desempate* deciding match; *partido de vuelta* return match || district (distrito) || match (de matrimonio); *un buen partido* a good match || AMER small farm (finca) | parting [*US* part] (crencha) || — *darse a partido* to give in || *partido judicial* judicial district || *sacar partido de* to benefit by, to profit from, to take advantage of || FIG *ser un partido* to be eligible (un soltero) || *tener partido* to have supporters (partidarios), to be successful (tener éxito) || *tomar el partido de* to decide on (una cosa), to decide to (con verbo) || *tomar partido por* to side with || *venirse a partido* to give in.

partidor *m* distributor (repartidor).

partir *vt* to divide, to split (dividir); *partir algo en dos* to divide sth. in two || to share (compartir); *partir entre cuatro* to share between four; *partir como hermanos* to share like brothers || to distribute (distribuir) || to crack; *partir nueces* to crack nuts || to cut, to chop; *partir leña* to cut wood || to cut (con un cuchillo); *partir una manzana por la mitad* to cut an apple in two || to break (con las manos); *partir el pan* to break the bread || FIG to break (el corazón) || MAT to divide || to cut (cortar las cartas) || — FIG *estar a partir un piñón* to be hand in glove | *partir a uno por el eje* or *por en medio* or *por la mitad* to mess things up for s.o. (fastidiar) | FAM *partir la cara a uno* to break s.o.'s neck, to smash s.o.'s face in || *partir la diferencia* to split the difference (dividir), to compromise (transigir) || FIG *¡que le parta un rayo!* to hell with him!
◆ *vi* to set off *o* out, to leave (marcharse); *partir para Laponia* to set off for Lapland; *partir con rumbo a* to set out in the direction of || FIG to begin, to start; *partir de un supuesto falso* to begin with a false supposition || — *a partir de* starting from || *a partir de hoy* as of today, from today on, starting today || *es el quinto a partir de la derecha* he is the fifth one from the right || *partiendo de la base de que...* assuming that... || FIG *quien parte y reparte se lleva la mejor parte* he who cuts the cake takes the biggest slice.
◆ *vpr* to set off *o* out, to leave (irse) || to break (romperse) || to split (dividirse) || — FIG *partirse de risa* to split one's sides laughing, to die laughing | *partirse el pecho* to break one's back, to slave away | *partirse el pecho por uno* to go out of one's way for s.o., to do one's utmost for s.o.

partitivo, va *adj/sm* GRAM partitive.

partitura *f* MÚS score.

parto *m* delivery, childbirth (de una mujer); *parto sin dolor* painless delivery; *parto prematuro* premature delivery || parturition (de un animal) || FIG giving birth (producción) | brainchild, creation (obra de ingenio, resultado) || — *asistir en un parto* to deliver a baby || *estar de parto* to be in labour (una mujer), to be parturient (animales) || *mal parto* miscarriage || *morir de parto, quedarse en el parto* to die in childbirth (la madre), to be stillborn (el niño) || *parto de la oveja* lambing || *parto de la yegua* foaling || FIG *ser el parto de los montes* to be an anticlimax.

parto, ta *adj/s* Parthian; *la flecha del parto* the Parthian shaft.

parturienta *adj f/s/f* parturient.

parva *f* AGR unthreshed corn.

parvedad *f* smallness, minuteness, tiny size (pequeñez) || *hacer algo con la parvedad de medios* to barely have the means to do sth. (una acción), to barely have the means to make sth. (fabricar algo).

parvo, va *adj* small, little.

parvulario *m* infant school.

párvulo, la *adj* small, little (pequeño) || simple, naïve, innocent (ingenuo).
◆ *m/f* child, infant (niño) || *escuela* or *colegio de párvulos* infant school.

pasa *f* raisin (uva seca) || MAR channel, pass (canal estrecho) || pass (en los juegos) || — FIG & FAM *estar hecho una pasa* to be completely wizened || *pasas de Corinto* currants.

pasable *adj* passable.

pasabocas *m* AMER savoury tidbits, appetizers (tapas).

pasacalle *m* MÚS passacaglia.

pasacintas *m inv* bodkin.

pasada *f* passage, passing (acción de pasar) || flight (de aves) || TECN operation (de máquina herramienta) || row [of stitches] (línea de puntos) || tacking stitch (hilvanado) || EQUIT passade || — *a la primera pasada no lo vi* the first time I went past I did not see it || *dar una pasada con la plancha a un pantalón* to run *o* to pass the iron over a pair of trousers || *de pasada* in passing; *dicho sea de pasada* let it be said in passing || FAM *hacer una mala pasada a* to play a nasty *o* dirty trick on.

pasadero, ra *adj* passable (mediano) || bearable (aguantable) || fair (salud) || passable (transitable).
◆ *m/f* stepping stone.

pasadizo *m* corridor, passage (pasillo) || alley (en las calles, etc.).

pasado, da *adj* past; *tiempos pasados* past times || last; *el viernes pasado* last Friday || old-fashioned, outmoded (anticuado) || faded (descolorido) || worn (usado) || rotten, overripe, bad (fruta) || off, bad (carne) || overdone (comida guisada) || stale (una noticia, etc.) || GRAM past || — *el pasado día 3* the third of last month (hablando), the 3rd ult (en cartas comerciales) || *en los años pasados* in years gone by, in years past || *huevo pasado por agua* boiled egg || *pasadas las 12* after twelve || *pasado de moda* old-fashioned, out of date || *pasado mañana* the day after tomorrow.
◆ *m* past; *olvidar el pasado* or *lo pasado* to forget the past || GRAM past (tiempo) || — *lo pasado, pasado está* let bygones be bygones (hay que olvidarlo), what is done is done (no hay que lamentarse).

pasador, ra *m/f* smuggler (contrabandista).
◆ *m* colander (colador para alimentos grandes), strainer (para té, café, etc.) || filter (filtro) || espagnolette (de ventana) || bolt (pestillo) || bodkin (pasacintas) || slide (para el pelo) || tie clip, tie pin (de corbata) || brochette (para condecoraciones) || clasp (broche) || stud (para el cuello de la camisa) || TECN pin || MAR marlinspike, marlinespike (especie de punzón) || *pasador de seguridad* safety lock.
◆ *pl* cuff links (gemelos).

pasadores *mpl* AMER shoe laces (cordones).

pasaje *m* passage (paso) || passage (de un libro) || passage (derecho) || fare, passage (precio del viaje) || ticket, passage (billete de avión o barco) || passengers *pl* (pasajeros) || MAR voyage, crossing, passage (viaje) || alleyway, passageway (calle) || MAR channel, strait, pass (estrecho) || MÚS change of key.

pasajero, ra *adj* passing, fleeting, transient, temporary (que dura poco) || busy (sitio frecuentado).
◆ *adj/s* passenger (viajero) || — *ave pasajera* migratory bird, bird of passage (sentido propio), rolling stone, bird of passage (sentido figurado) || *capricho pasajero* passing fancy.

pasamanería *f* passementerie || passementerie factory (fábrica) || passementerie shop (tienda).

pasamanero, ra *m/f* passementerie maker (fabricante) || passementerie seller (vendedor).

pasamano *m*; **pasamanos** *m inv* handrail, rail (de una escalera exterior, etc.) || banister, banisters *pl* (de la escalera de una casa) || strap (para agarrarse) || MAR gangway.

pasamontañas *m inv* balaclava.

pasante *adj* passing || HERÁLD passant.
◆ *m* assistant (de abogado, de médico, etc.) || clerk (de notario); *primer pasante* head clerk.

pasantía *f* assistantship (función de pasante) || probationary period (tiempo que dura).

pasapalos *m* AMER savoury tidbits, appetizers (tapas).

pasapasa *m* sleight of hand (prestidigitación).

pasaportar *vt* FAM to deal with, to dispatch, to account for (matar) | to rush off (despachar); *pasaportar un trabajo* to rush off a job | to pack off (mandar); *pasaportó a su hijo a Francia* he packed his son off to France.

pasaporte *m* passport; *expedir un pasaporte* to issue a passport || MIL travel documents *pl* || FIG free hand, carte blanche; *dar pasaporte para* to give s.o. a free hand to | passport; *pasaporte a la fama* passport to fame || FIG *dar pasaporte a uno* to give s.o. his marching orders (despedir).

pasapurés *m inv* potato masher.

pasar *vt* to pass (en sentido general) ‖ to move (trasladar) ‖ to take (llevar) ‖ to give, to hand, to pass (dar); *pásame el azúcar* pass me the sugar ‖ to pass on, to give (un mensaje) ‖ to hand over; *pasar los poderes a* to hand over one's powers to ‖ to send (una cuenta) ‖ to take, to lead (llevar a una persona) ‖ to give; *le he pasado mi constipado* I have given him my cold ‖ to get over (curarse de una enfermedad) ‖ to run; *pasar la mano por el pelo* to run one's fingers through one's hair ‖ to sit, to take, to pass (un examen) ‖ to cross, to pass, to go over (un río, una calle) ‖ to pass through (atravesar) ‖ to go over, to cross (la sierra) ‖ to strain, to pass through (colar) ‖ to slip, to pass; *pasar un papel por debajo de la puerta* to slip a piece of paper under the door ‖ to put (poner); *pasar el brazo por la ventana* to put one's arm out of the window ‖ to smuggle, to pass (de contrabando) ‖ to pass off (falsa moneda) ‖ to go through (traspasar) ‖ to swallow (tragar) ‖ to overtake, to pass (un coche) ‖ FIG to go beyond, to overstep (los límites) | to outdo, to be better than (superar) | to last (durar) | to suffer, to go through, to endure (desgracias, dolor físico); *¡lo que he pasado!* the things I have been through! | to bear (tolerar, soportar) | to be (seguido de un adjetivo); *pasar mucho frío* to be very cold | to suffer from, to know; *pasar hambre* to suffer from hunger | to put up with; *no hay que pasarle todas sus tonterías* we must not put up with all his nonsense | to overlook, to let go *o* pass (una falta) ‖ to spend, to pass (el tiempo); *pasar la noche fuera* to spend the night outside; *pasa el tiempo divirtiéndose* he spends his time enjoying himself ‖ to leave out, to pass over, to bypass (omitir) ‖ to turn over; *pasar la página* to turn over the page ‖ COM to charge (en cuenta) ‖ — *¿cómo lo pasas?* how are you getting on? ‖ *pasar a alguien a cuchillo* to put s.o. to the sword ‖ *pasar algo en limpio* to make a fair copy of sth. ‖ *pasar al toro con la muleta* to make a pass with the muleta ‖ *pasar el balón a* to pass the ball to, to pass to ‖ *pasar el rato* to while away the time, to kill time ‖ *pasar en blanco* to leave out, to miss out (omitir) ‖ *pasar en silencio* to make no mention of, to keep quiet about ‖ *pasar la noche en blanco* to have a sleepless night ‖ FAM *pasarlas canutas* or *negras* or *moradas, pasar las de Caín* or *las negras* to go through hell *o* murder, to have a rough time ‖ *pasar las cuentas del rosario* to tell one's beads ‖ *pasar lista* to call the roll ‖ *pasar lista a los alumnos* to take *o* to call the register ‖ *pasarlo bien* to have a good time ‖ FAM *pasarlo bomba* to have a great time *o* a ball *o* a whale of a time ‖ *pasarlo mal* not to enjoy o.s. (aburrirse), to have a hard time *o* a bad time (tener dificultades) ‖ FIG *pasar por alto* to leave out, to skip, to miss out, to omit (omitir), to miss out, to forget about (olvidar) ‖ *pasar por encima* to look *o* to glance through (un escrito), to overlook, to turn a blind eye to (hacer la vista gorda) ‖ FIG *pasar por la piedra a uno* to leave s.o. standing (vencer) ‖ *pasar por las armas a* to shoot, to execute ‖ *pasar revista a* to inspect (en el cuartel), to review (en un desfile), to review (problemas, etc.) ‖ *pasar un mal rato* to have a bad time of it ‖ *¡que lo pase bien!* have a good time! ‖ *¿qué tal lo pasó en la fiesta?* how did you enjoy the party? ‖ *ya te he pasado muchas* I have already put up with enough from you.

◆ *vi* to pass (en sentido general) ‖ to go, to pass, to move; *pasar de un sitio a otro* to go from one place to another ‖ to pass, to get through *o* past *o* by; *déjame pasar* let me pass, let me get past ‖ to pass; *los enemigos no pasarán* the enemy shall not pass ‖ to call *o* to drop in, to come round; *pasaré por tu casa* I shall call in at your house, I shall come round to your house ‖ to go through; *pasar con el disco cerrado* to go through a red light ‖ to go, to pass; *este tren pasa por Londres* this train goes through London ‖ to pass, to go past; *el tren pasó muy rápidamente* the train went pass at a great speed; *el autobús pasa por tu casa* the but goes past your house ‖ to come in, to go in; *¡pase!* come in!; *dígale que pase* tell him to come in ‖ to go; *ha pasado de empleado a director* he has gone from employee to director ‖ to be legal tender, to pass (moneda) ‖ to go (off) (transcurrir); *¿cómo pasó la sesión?* how did the session go? ‖ to happen (ocurrir); *y el accidente ¿cómo pasó?* how did the accident happen?; *¿qué pasa?* what's happening? ‖ to be the matter; *¿qué te pasa?* what's the matter with you? ‖ to go by, to pass; *a medida que pasan los años* as the years go by; *¡cómo pasa el tiempo!* how time passes! ‖ to come to an end, to be over (acabarse); *ya pasarán los malos momentos* the bad times will soon come to an end ‖ to go *o* to be out (of fashion) (no estar de moda) ‖ to wash, to do; *esta excusa no pasa* this excuse will not wash ‖ to pass (ser aprobado) ‖ to be passed *o* carried (una moción) ‖ to be accepted (una propuesta) ‖ to pass (cartas, juegos) ‖ — *aquí no pasó nada* it is nothing to worry about, it is alright ‖ *de ahí no pasa* that's all (esto es todo), that's as far as he can go (es lo más que puede hacer) ‖ *de ésta no pasa* this is the very last time ‖ *de hoy no pasa que lo haga* I'll do it this very day ‖ *hacerse pasar por* to pass o.s. off as ‖ *ir pasando* to get by, to make out, to manage ‖ *lo mismo pasa con él* it's the same with him ‖ *lo que pasa es que...* the thing is that... ‖ *pasar a* to proceed; *pasemos al punto 3 del orden del día* let us proceed to item 3 on the agenda; to come to; *paso ahora a su pregunta* I now come to your question; to start to (con infinitivo), to start (con gerundio); *pasó a recitar otra poesía* he started reciting another poem ‖ *pasar a decir algo* to go on to say sth. ‖ *pasar adelante* to go on, to proceed ‖ *pasar a mejor vida* to pass away, to pass on to better things ‖ *pasar a ser* to become, to come to be ‖ *pasar con* to make do with, to get by with, to manage with (arreglarse), to be under instruction with (abogado, médico) ‖ *pasar con poco* to get along with very little, to manage on very little, to make do with very little ‖ *pasar de* to be more than, to be over (cierto número); *pasan de los veinte* there are more than twenty; *no pasa de los cuarenta años* he is not more than *o* no more than forty; *pasa de los cuarenta años* he is over forty years old ‖ FIG *pasar de castaño oscuro* to be going too far, to be a bit much | *pasar de la raya* or *de los límites* to go too far ‖ *pasar de largo* to go straight past, to pass by (sin pararse), to pass over (un detalle) ‖ *pasar (de las palabras) a las manos* to come to blows ‖ *pasar de moda* to be out of fashion; *ha pasado, pasará de moda* it is, it will be out of fashion; to go out of fashion; *el sombrero pasa de moda cada tres años* hats go out of fashion every three years ‖ *pasar de vida a muerte* to pass away, to give up the ghost ‖ *pasar por* to be considered; *pasa por el científico más importante* he is considered the most important scientist; to be taken for, to pass for; *pasó por invitado* he passed for a guest ‖ *pasar por casa de uno* to call in at *o* to drop in at *o* to come round to s.o.'s house ‖ *pasar por ello* to know what it is like (saber lo duro que es), to put up with it (aguantarlo), to go through with it (hacerlo) ‖ *pasar por la imaginación* or *por la cabeza* to occur to one, to cross one's mind; *ni siquiera me pasó por la cabeza* it did not even occur to me *o* cross my mind ‖ *pasar por todo con tal que...* to put up with anything as long as... ‖ *pasar por un puente* to go over *o* to cross a bridge ‖ *pasar sin* to do *o* to go without (prescindir) ‖ *pase lo que pase* whatever happens, happen what may, come what may ‖ *pase (por una vez)* just don't let it happen again ‖ *paso* I pass (naipes) ‖ *y que pase lo que pase* and we shall see what happens (ya veremos).

◆ *v impers* to happen (ocurrir).

◆ *vpr* to pass, to pass off (en general) ‖ to be over; *se ha pasado la primavera* Spring is over ‖ to miss; *se me pasó el turno* I missed my turn ‖ to go over; *pasarse al enemigo, al otro cuarto* to go over to the enemy, to the other room ‖ to go too far (excederse) ‖ to get over; *ya se me pasará* I'll get over it ‖ to forget; *se me ha pasado lo que me dijiste* I have forgotten what you said ‖ to do *o* to go without (prescindir) ‖ to fade, to wither (flores) ‖ to fade (la belleza) ‖ to wear out (tela) ‖ to go bad *o* off (frutas, legumbres, etc.) ‖ to be overdone (guisado) ‖ to leak (recipiente) ‖ to be porous (ser poroso) ‖ to spend, to pass (tiempo); *se pasó seis meses allí* he spent six months there ‖ to be loose (tener juego, estar holgado) ‖ — *pasarse de* to be too; *pasarse de bueno* to be too good ‖ FIG *pasarse de la raya* or *de los límites* to go too far | *pasarse de listo* or *de vivo* to be too clever by half | *pasarse de rosca* to go too far (pasarse de los límites), to lose its thread (un tornillo) ‖ *pasarse el peine* to run a comb through one's hair ‖ *pasarse el tiempo cantando* to be always singing ‖ *pasárselo en grande* to have a whale of a time, to have a fabulous time ‖ *pasarse por* to call in at, to pass by; *pasarse por la oficina* to call in at the office.

pasarela *f* footbridge (puentecillo) ‖ MAR gangway, gangplank (de embarcación) ‖ catwalk (en los teatros).

pasatiempo *m* pastime, hobby, amusement.

pascal *m* pascal (unidad de presión).

pascua *f* passover (fiesta judía) ‖ Christmas (Navidad); *¡felices Pascuas y próspero Año Nuevo!* merry Christmas and a happy New Year! ‖ Easter (pascua de Resurrección) ‖ Epiphany (los Reyes) ‖ Pentecost (Pentecostés) ‖ — FIG & FAM *cara de pascua* cheerful *o* smiling face ‖ *comulgar por Pascua florida* to do one's Easter duty, to take the Sacrament at Easter ‖ *dar las pascuas* to wish s.o. a merry Christmas ‖ FIG *estar como unas pascuas* to be as happy as a lark, to be as pleased as Punch ‖ FAM *hacer la pascua a alguien* to mess things up for s.o. (fastidiar) ‖ FIG *ocurrir de Pascuas a Ramos* to happen once in a blue moon ‖ *pasar las Pascuas en familia* to spend Christmas with one's family *o* at home ‖ *Pascua del Espíritu Santo* Whitsunday, Pentecost ‖ *Pascua de Navidad* Christmas ‖ *Pascua de Resurrección* Easter ‖ *Pascua florida* Easter ‖ FAM *y santas pascuas* and that's all there is to it, and that's that.

Pascua (isla de) *npr f* GEOGR Easter Island.

pascual *adj* paschal.

pase *m* pass (autorización) ‖ permission (permiso) ‖ invitation ‖ showing (de una película) ‖ DEP & TAUR pass ‖ feint (en esgrima) ‖ COM permit ‖ pass (de prestidigitador, etc.) ‖ AMER passport (pasaporte) ‖ — DEP *pase adelantado* or *adelante* forward pass ‖ *pase de favor* safe-conduct (salvoconducto) ‖ DEP *pase hacia atrás* backward pass, back pass.

paseante *adj* passing, going past (transeúnte).

◆ *m/f* passer-by, walker, stroller (transeúnte) ‖ FIG *paseante en corte* loafer.

◆ *pl* people out for a walk, strollers.

— OBSERV El plural de *passer-by* es *passers-by*.

pasear *vt* to take for a walk (dar un paseo) ‖ FIG to parade, to show off (exhibir, fanfarronear).

◆ *vi/vpr* to go for a walk; *pasearse por el campo* to go for a walk in the country ‖ to take a walk (dar un paseo) ‖ to go for a ride (en bicicleta, en coche, a caballo) ‖ to go for a trip (en barco) || to run; *las chinches se paseaban por todas partes* bugs were running all over the place || FIG to idle, to loaf about (holgazanear).

paseíllo *m* opening parade (de toreros).

paseo *m* walk (a pie), drive, ride (en coche), ride (en bicicleta, a caballo), trip, row, sail (en barco); *dar un paseo* to go for a walk, for a ride, etc. || excursion || walking (acción) || promenade, walk, public walk, avenue (avenida) || parade (de toreros) || — FIG *dar el paseo* to take s.o. out to be shot (fusilar) | *mandar* or *enviar a uno a paseo* to send s.o. away, to send s.o. packing, to tell s.o. to go to blazes | *mandarlo todo a paseo* to chuck it all in, to give up | *¡váyase a paseo!* go to blazes! go to hell!

pasicorto, ta *adj* who *o* which takes short steps.

pasiego, ga *adj/s* [of *o* from the] Pas Valley [in the Spanish province of Santander]
◆ *f* FAM nurse (ama de cría).

pasiflora *f* BOT passionflower.

pasillo *m* corridor, passage (corredor) || TEATR promenade (en la sala) | short play, sketch (obra corta) || FIG lobby || AMER mat (estera) || — *pasillo aéreo* air corridor || *pasillo rodante* public walkway [US moving sidewalk].

pasión *f* passion; *dejarse llevar por la pasión* to give way to passion, to let passion take over; *tener pasión por la música* to have a passion for music || REL Passion; *la Pasión según San Mateo* the Passion according to St. Matthew || *tener pasión por alguien* to be passionately fond of s.o., to have a passion for s.o.

pasional *adj* passional || *crimen pasional* crime of passion, crime passionel.

pasionaria *f* BOT passionflower.

pasito *adv* gently, softly.

pasitrote *m* short trot.

pasividad *f* passivity, passiveness.

pasivo, va *adj* passive || — *clases pasivas* pensioners || *pensión pasiva* State pension, pension || GRAM *voz pasiva* passive voice, passive.
◆ *m* COM liabilities *pl* || *en el pasivo* on the debit side.

pasma *f* POP fuzz, cops.

pasmado, da *adj* flabbergasted, astounded, amazed, completely astonished (de asombro) || frozen stiff, perished (de frío) || stupefied, openmouthed (atontado) || frozen (plantas) || — *mirar con cara de pasmado* to look in astonishment at, to look flabbergasted at || *pasmado de admiración* overwhelmed with wonder, flabbergasted, astounded, amazed.

pasmar *vt* to leave flabbergasted, to flabbergast, to astound, to amaze, to astonish (asombrar); *su respuesta me ha pasmado* his answer left me flabbergasted || to freeze to death (enfriar mucho a uno) || to freeze, to blight (helar las plantas) || to make (s.o.) faint (causar desmayo).
◆ *vpr* to be flabbergasted *o* astounded *o* amazed *o* astonished (quedarse asombrado) || to be frozen stiff, to be perished (estar helado) || to be frozen (las plantas) || to faint (desmayarse) || MED to get lockjaw || to tarnish, to fade (colores, barniz).

pasmarota *f* FAM fuss.

pasmarote *m* FAM dape, dunce (necio).

pasmo *m* chill (enfriamiento) || MED lockjaw || amazement, astonishment, shock (asombro) | marvel, wonder (lo que produce asombro).

pasmoso, sa *adj* amazing, astounding, astonishing.

paso *m* step, pace; *dar tres pasos* to take three steps || walk, gait (modo de andar) || gait (del caballo) || pace (ritmo); *aminorar el paso* to slow down one's pace || step, pace (distancia); *a tres pasos* three steps away || passing, passage (acción); *al paso del tren* on the train's passing; *el paso del tiempo* the passage of time || crossing, passage (cruce); *el paso del mar Rojo por los judíos* the crossing of the Red Sea by the Jews || path, way, way through, passage; *el paso está libre* the path is clear || passage (derecho) || clearing, surmounting (de un obstáculo) || step, stair (de escalera) || footprint, track (huella) || footstep (ruido del paso) || track, trail (rastro de la caza) || pass (naipes) || step (de baile) || deed (aventura) || FIG advance, advances *pl*, progress; *la industria aeronáutica ha dado un gran paso últimamente* the aircraft industry has made great progress *o* great advances lately | transition (transición) | step, move (trámite); *dar pasos para* to take steps *o* to make moves towards || passage, migration (de las aves) || stitch (en costura) || GEOGR pass (entre montañas) | strait, straits *pl* (estrecho); *Paso de Calais* Straits of Dover || «Paso», stage [each important stage in the Passion of Christ, and the platforms bearing sculptured scenes from the Passion, carried through the streets in Holy Week] || TEATR sketch, short play || pitch (de hélice, de tornillo) || — *abrir paso a* to make way for || *abrirse* or *hacerse paso entre* to force *o* to fight one's way through (en una muchedumbre, etc.), to break through (las tropas) || *abrirse paso a codazos, a tiros* to elbow, to shoot one's way through || *abrirse paso en la vida* to make one's way in life (triunfar) || *a buen paso* at a good pace, smartly, quickly || FIG *a cada paso* at every step *o* turn || *adelantar cuatro pasos* to take four steps forward, to go forward *o* to advance four steps || FIG *a dos pasos* a few steps away, a short way away || FIG *a ese paso* at this *o* that rate || FIG *a grandes pasos* by leaps and bounds (avanzar) || *alargar el paso* to lengthen one's stride, to step out || *al paso* in passing, on the way, when one passes by (al pasar), at a walking pace; *ir al paso* to go at a walking pace; slowly (lentamente) || *al paso que* at the same time as, while (al mismo tiempo), as (como) || *al paso que va* at this rate || *a mi paso* as I went by *o* passed, in passing || *a mi paso por Londres* when I pass through London || *andar al mismo paso que* to keep pace with || FIG *andar a paso de buey* or *de carreta* to go at a snail's pace || *andar a paso largo* to stride || FIG *andar con pasos contados* to tread warily, to watch one's step | *andar en malos pasos* to go astray, to get into bad ways || MIL *a paso de ataque* or *de carga* or *gimnástico* or *ligero* at the double | *a paso de maniobra* at ease || FIG *a paso de tortuga* at a snail's pace || *a paso lento* at a slow pace || *a pasos agigantados* with giant strides (con paso largo), by leaps and bounds (muy rápidamente) || *a pocos pasos* a few steps away || *apretar* or *acelerar* or *aligerar el paso* to quicken one's pace || *ave de paso* migratory bird, bird of passage (sentido propio), rolling stone, bird of passage (sentido figurado) || *ceda el paso* give way (señal de tráfico) || *ceder el paso a* to make way for, to let (s.o.) pass (dejar pasar), to give way to, to give place to (dar lugar a) || *cerrar el paso* to block the way (interceptar el camino), to put a stop to (impedir) || *coger algo al paso* to collect sth. on one's way *o* in passing || *coger el paso* to get *o* to fall into step (sentido propio), to get into the swing of things, to get the hang of it (adaptarse) || *coger un peón al paso* to take a pawn in passing (ajedrez) || *con paso alegre* gaily, happily || *cortar el paso a uno* to block s.o.'s path, to cut s.o. off, to intercept s.o., to bar s.o.'s way || *dar (el) paso a uno* to let s.o. pass || FIG *dar los primeros pasos* to take the first steps, to make the first moves | *dar* or *dejar paso a* to open the way to | *dar un buen paso* to take a great step | *dar un mal paso* to make a wrong move, to take a false step || *dar un paso adelante* to step forward, to take a step forward (al andar), to make progress, to gain ground; *ha dado un paso adelante en su vida* he has made progress in life; *las negociaciones han dado un paso adelante* progress has been made in the negociations || *dar un paso atrás* to step back, to take a step backwards (al andar), to lose ground (retroceder) || *dar un paso en falso* to stumble, to trip (andando), to make a wrong move, to take a false step (obrar desacertadamente) || *dejar (el) paso libre* to get out of the way of; *dejar el paso libre a los bomberos* to get out of the way of the firemen; to let pass; *los aduaneros dejaron paso libre al automovilista* the customs officers let the motorist pass; to keep the way clear (no obstruir el paso) || *de paso* in passing, on the way; *de paso iré a ver a mi tía* on the way I shall call in and see my aunt; passing through, stopping off; *estaba de paso en Madrid* I was just passing through Madrid *o* stopping off in Madrid; in passing; *de paso habló del Cid* in passing he talked about El Cid || *dicho sea de paso* incidentally, by the way || *enderezar sus pasos a* to direct one's steps towards, to make one's way towards || *entrar de paso* to drop in, to call in || FIG *estar a dos pasos de la muerte* to be at death's door || MIL *ir al paso* to keep *o* to march in step || *lo difícil es el primer paso* the first step is the most difficult || FIG *ir por sus pasos contados* to go one's own sweet way, to jog along at one's own pace | *llevar a buen paso* to speed along || MIL *llevar el paso* or *ir con paso acompasado* to keep *o* to march in step || *mal paso* fix, tight spot; *sacarle a uno de un mal paso* to get s.o. out of a fix || MIL *marcar el paso* to mark time || *medir a pasos* to pace (a room), to pace, to pace off, to pace out (a distance) || FIG *medir sus pasos* to watch one's step | *no podemos dar un paso sin...* we cannot do anything *o* we cannot make a move without... || *¡paso!, ¡paso libre!* gangway!, make way! || FIG *paso adelante* breakthrough, step forward, step in the right direction; *este descubrimiento ha sido un gran paso adelante* this discovery was a great breakthrough || *paso a nivel* level crossing [US railroad *o* grade crossing] || *paso a paso* step by step || *paso atrás* step backwards (andando), backward step (retroceso) || EQUIT *paso de ambladura* or *de andadura* amble || AUT *paso de cebra* zebra crossing || EQUIT *paso de costado* passage || *paso de cuatro* pas de quatre (danza) || MIL *paso de la oca* goose step || *paso del ecuador* crossing the line (línea ecuatorial), half-way point [in a course of study] (mitad de la carrera) || *paso de peatones* pedestrian crossing [US crosswalk] || MAR *paso de popa a proa* fore-and-aft gangway || MÚS *paso doble* paso doble || *paso elevado* flyover || *paso firme* sure step || *paso franco* or *libre* free passage *o* access || *paso protegido* right-of-way (señal de tráfico) || *paso subterráneo* subway (para peatones), underpass (para coches) || *primeros pasos* first steps (de un niño, de una ciencia), début; *dar sus primeros pasos en la diplomacia* to make one's début as a diplomat || *prohibido el paso* no entry, no trespassing (para personas), no entry, no throughfare (para los automóviles) || *quitar algo del paso* to move sth. out of the way || *romper el paso* to break step || FIG *salir al paso de* to forestall; *salir al paso de las críticas* to forestall one's critics; to waylay; *hoy Pablo me salió al paso* Paul waylayed me today; to go to meet (salir al encuentro de) | *salir del paso* to get out of trouble *o* out of the fix || *seguir los pasos a uno* to watch s.o.'s every move (observar) || *seguir los pasos de uno* to follow *o* to trail s.o. (seguir), to follow in s.o.'s footsteps (imitar) || JUR *servidumbre de paso* right-of-way || MIL *¡un paso al frente, ar!* one step forward, march! || *volver sobre sus pasos* to retrace one's steps, to go back (desandar lo andado), to re-

tract *o* to withdraw *o* to take back a statement (desdecirse).
◆ *adv* gently, softly; *hable paso* speak softly.

paso, sa *adj* dried (fruta) ‖ — *ciruela pasa* prune ‖ *uvas pasas* raisins.

pasodoble *m* paso doble.

pasoso, sa *adj* AMER porous.

pasota *m/f* waster, non-conformist.

pasquín *m* (ant) pasquinade, lampoon (epigrama) ‖ poster (cartel) ‖ tract (octavilla).

passing-shot *m* passing shot (tenis).

pasta *f* CULIN paste, dough (masa sin cocer) | pastry (masa cocida); *pasta de hojaldre* puff pastry ‖ paste; *pasta de gambas* shrimp paste ‖ full binding (de un libro) ‖ ARTES impasto (empaste) ‖ FIG makings *pl* (madera); *tiene pasta de torero* he has the makings of a bullfighter ‖ FAM dough, cash, loot (dinero) ‖ — *libro en pasta* bound book ‖ *media pasta, pasta holandesa* quarter binding ‖ *pasta de dientes* or *dentífrica* toothpaste ‖ *pasta de hígado* pâté de foie, liver paste ‖ *pasta de madera* wood pulp ‖ *pasta de papel* paper pulp ‖ FIG & FAM *ser de buena pasta* to be a good soul, to be good-natured | *tiene muy buena pasta* he's got what it takes, there is good stuff in him.
◆ *pl* pasta *sing* (tallarines, etc.) ‖ petits fours, small cakes [*US* cookies] (pastelillos).

pastaca *f* AMER pork stew (guiso).

pastaflora *f* sponge cake ‖ FIG & FAM *ser de pastaflora* to be a good soul.

pastaje; pastal *m* AMER pasture.

pastar *vt/vi* to pasture, to graze.

pasteca *f* MAR snatch block.

pastel *m* cake; *pastel de crema, de almendras* cream, almond cake ‖ pie; *pastel de carne* meat pie; *pastel de frutas* fruit pie ‖ pastel (color, dibujo, lápiz) ‖ FIG & FAM crooked *o* sharp dealing (trampa) | mess (lío) ‖ IMPR pie (letras confundidas) ‖ — *azul pastel* pastel blue ‖ FIG & FAM *descubrir el pastel* to get wise, to cotton on (adivinar), to spill the beans, to squeal (chivarse) ‖ *dibujo al pastel* pastel, pastel drawing ‖ *hierba pastel* woad (planta) ‖ *pintar* or *dibujar al pastel* to do pastel drawings, to draw in pastels ‖ FIG *repartirse el pastel* to share out the profits, benefits, winnings.
◆ *pl* pastry *sing.*

pastelear *vi* FIG & FAM to play for time, to stall (temporizar) | to be a bootlicker (adular).

pasteleo *m* FIG & FAM stalling, playing for time (temporización) | licking, bootlicking (adulación).

pastelería *f* cakes *pl*, pastries *pl* (pasteles) ‖ confectionery (dulces) ‖ confectioner's, cake shop (tienda).

pastelero, ra *m/f* pastrycook (repostero) ‖ person who sells cakes (vendedor) ‖ FIG & FAM staller (que temporiza) | bootlicker, licker (adulador).

pastelista *m/f* pastellist (pintor).

pastense *adj* [of *o* from] Pasto.
◆ *m/f* inhabitant *o* native of Pasto (ciudad de Colombia).

pasterización; pasteurización *f* pasteurization.

pasterizado, da; pasteurizado, da *adj* pasteurized.

pasterizar; pasteurizar *vt* to pasteurize (esterilizar por pasterización).

pastiche *m* pastiche, imitation (de una obra).

pastilla *f* bar, cake, tablet (de jabón) ‖ piece, square (de chocolate) ‖ pastille, lozenge (de menta, etc.) ‖ MED tablet (tableta) ‖ — FIG & FAM *a toda pastilla* like a bat out of hell, at full tilt ‖ *pastilla de café con leche* toffee ‖ INFORM *pastilla de silicio* silicon chip | *pastilla electrónica* electronic chip ‖ *pastilla para la tos, para la garganta* cough drop, throat lozenge.

pastinaca *f* whip-tailed sting ray (pez) ‖ BOT parsnip.

pastizal *m* pasture *o* grazing land, pasture.

pasto *m* pasture, pasture *o* grazing land, pasturage (sitio) ‖ grazing (acción) ‖ pasture, pasturage (hierba) ‖ food, fodder, feed (pienso para el ganado) ‖ FIG food, nourishment (alimento) ‖ AMER grass, lawn (césped) ‖ — FIG & FAM *a pasto* in plenty | *a todo pasto* without limit, freely, in great quantity | *dar algo de pasto a los cerdos* to feed sth. to the pigs ‖ FIG *dar pasto a* to give cause for (causar) ‖ *de pasto* table (vino) ‖ *derecho de pasto* grazing rights ‖ FIG *el incidente sirvió de pasto a los periódicos* the newspapers thrived on the incident | *las novelas son su pasto* he thrives on novels ‖ *pasto comunal* common pasturage, common pasture ‖ FIG *pasto espiritual* spiritual food *o* sustenance *o* nourishment ‖ *pasto seco* fodder ‖ FIG *ser pasto de la actualidad* to be a headline story | *ser pasto del fuego* or *de las llamas* or *del incendio* to be fuel for the flames, to be consumed by the fire *o* the flames | *su nombre sirve de pasto al chismorreo* his name is food for gossip.

pastón *m* FAM a lot of dough (mucho dinero).

pastor, ra *m/f* shepherd (hombre), shepherdess (mujer), (que cuida el ganado).
◆ *m* protestant minister, clergyman, pastor (sacerdote) ‖ — *el Buen Pastor* the Good Shepherd ‖ *perro pastor* sheepdog.

pastoral *adj* pastoral ‖ *anillo pastoral* pastoral ring.
◆ *f* pastoral (poema, del obispo) ‖ MÚS pastorale.

pastorear *vt* to graze, to pasture, to put out to pasture (apacentar) ‖ FIG to lead, to guide (el sacerdote).
◆ *vi* to graze, to pasture.

pastorela *f* pastourelle.

pastoreo *m* shepherding.

pastoril *adj* pastoral.

pastosidad *f* pastiness ‖ furring, furriness (de la lengua) ‖ pastosity, thickness (de pintura).

pastoso, sa *adj* pasty, doughy (blando, suave) ‖ pastose, thick, impasto (pintura) ‖ — *boca, lengua pastosa* coated *o* furry mouth, tongue ‖ *voz pastosa* rich *o* mellow voice.

pasturaje *m* pasture, pasture *o* grazing land ‖ grazing rights *pl* (derecho).

pata *f* leg (pierna de animal) ‖ foot (pie de animales bípedos) ‖ paw (pie de animales cuadrúpedos con garras) ‖ hoof (pie de caballo, vaca, cerdo, oveja, etc.); *pata hendida* cloven hoof ‖ FAM leg (pierna del hombre) ‖ leg (de mueble); *una mesa de cuatro patas* a table with four legs ‖ tab, strap (de vestidos) ‖ duck (hembra del pato) ‖ AMER leg, lap (etapa) ‖ — FAM *¡abajo las patas!* hands off! (hablando a una persona), down!, get down! (a un animal) | *a cuatro patas* on all fours (a gatas) ‖ FIG *a la pata coja* blindfold (muy fácilmente) ‖ FIG *a la pata la llana* simply, without ceremony *o* formalities ‖ *andar a la pata coja* to hop (along) ‖ FAM *a pata* on foot (a pie) ‖ *de pata hendida* cloven-hoofed ‖ FIG & FAM *echar las patas por alto* to blow one's top, to go mad (con enfado) | *¡en cada pata!* and the rest! [said of a person who claims to be younger than he or she is] | *enseñar la pata* to show the cloven hoof, to reveal one's true self | *estirar la pata* to kick the bucket (morir) | *mala pata* tough *o* bad luck | *metedura de pata* bloomer, blunder | *meter la pata* to put one's foot in it | *pata de banco* clanger; *salir con una pata de banco* to drop a clanger ‖ *pata de cabra* heel-glazing iron (herramienta de zapatero) ‖ *pata de gallina* starshake (enfermedad de los árboles) ‖ *pata de gallo* goose foot (planta), broken check material (tela), clanger (fam) (despropósito) ‖ MAR *pata de ganso* crowfoot ‖ *pata de mosca* scrawl (garabatos) ‖ *pata de palo* wooden leg, peg leg ‖ CULIN *pata negra* cured Spanish ham ‖ FAM *patas arriba* flat on one's back (caer), upside down, topsy turvy (desordenado) ‖ *patas de gallo* crow's feet (arrugas) ‖ FIG & FAM *poner a uno de patas en la calle* to kick s.o. out, to throw s.o. out on his ear (echar) | *tener mala pata* to be unlucky ‖ AMER *tener patas* to have a nerve, to have a lot of brass neck (caradura).

pataca *f* BOT Jerusalem artichoke.

patada *f* kick (puntapié) ‖ stamp (en el suelo) ‖ — FIG & FAM *a patadas* loads of, thousands of; *hay pasteles a patadas* there are loads of cakes | *dar la patada a alguien* to give s.o. the boot | *darle cien patadas a uno* to get on one's nerves (molestar) ‖ *dar patadas en el suelo* to stamp one's feet ‖ FIG & FAM *darse (de) patadas* to clash; *el verde se da de patadas con el azul* green clashes with blue ‖ *dar una patada a* to kick ‖ FIG & FAM *echar a alguien a patadas* to kick s.o. out | *hacer algo a patadas* to make a botch of sth., to botch sth. | *hacer algo en dos patadas* to do sth. in two ticks *o* in two shakes | *largar una patada en el trasero* to kick s.o. in the pants *o* up the behind *o* up the backside | *le costará muchas patadas lograrlo* you will have to push for it | *sentar algo como una patada en el estómago* to take sth. really badly | *tratar a patadas* to kick *o* to push around.

patagón, ona *adj/s* Patagonian.

Patagonia *npr f* GEOGR Patagonia.

patagónico, ca *adj* Patagonian.

patalear *vi* to hop about with rage, to stamp one's feet with rage (de rabia) ‖ to kick (el niño en la cuna).

pataleo *m* stamping (en el suelo) ‖ kicking (en el aire) ‖ FIG & FAM *el derecho de* or *al pataleo* the right to kick *o* to protest.

pataleta *f* tantrum, fit; *a Pedro le dio una pataleta* Peter went into *o* threw a tantrum, Peter had a fit.

patán *m* FAM country bumpkin, yokel (rústico) | duffer, lout, boor (tonto).

patanería *f* FAM churlishness, boorishness.

¡pataplún! *interj* crash!, bang!

patarráez *m* MAR preventer shroud.

Patas *npr m* FAM Old Nick (el demonio).

patata *f* potato; *patata temprana* early *o* new potato; *puré de patatas* mashed potatoes ‖ potato (batata); *patatas dulces* sweet potatoes ‖ — *patata de caña* Jerusalem artichoke (pataca) ‖ *patatas al vapor* boiled potatoes ‖ *patatas fritas* chips [*US* French fries] ‖ *patatas fritas a la inglesa* crisps [*US* potato chips] ‖ *patatas paja* potato straws.

patatal; patatar *m* potato field.

patatero, ra *adj* potato, of the potato ‖ FAM risen from the ranks (oficial del ejército).
◆ *m/f* potato grower (cultivador), potato seller (vendedor).

patatín patatán (que) FAM and so on and so forth.

patatús *m inv* FAM faint, fainting fit (desmayo) ‖ FAM *le dio un patatús* he went out like a light.

pateador, ra *adj* AMER which kicks, vicious (animal) ‖ *ser pateador* to kick, to be a kicker.

patear *vt* FAM to kick (dar patadas a), to stamp on (pisar) ‖ FIG to tread on, to trample

on (pisotear) | to boo, to jeer, to give the bird (una obra de teatro).
◆ *vi* FAM to stamp one's feet (en el suelo) | to bustle about, to chase about all over the place (para conseguir algo) || DEP to kick, to punt (en rugby) || to kick (animal) || to kick (arma).

paté *m* CULIN pâté.

patena *f* REL paten || FIG *limpio como una patena* as clean as a whistle *o* as a new pin.

patentado, da *adj* patent, patented.
◆ *m/f* patentee.

patentar *vt* to patent (invento) || to register, to patent; *marca patentada* registered trade mark.

patente *adj* patent, obvious (evidente) || *letras patentes* letters patent.
◆ *f* licence [*US* license] (autorización) || patent (de invención) || MAR sea letter || *AMER* licence plate (de automóvil) || — *hacer patente* to show clearly, to make evident || MAR *patente de corso* letter *o* letters of marque | *patente de navegación* ship's certificate of registration | *patente de sanidad* bill of health | *patente limpia, sucia* clean, foul bill of health.

patentemente *adv* patently, obviously.

patentizar *vt* to make evident *o* obvious, to show.

pateo *m* FAM stamping (de impaciencia, rabia) || trampling (pisoteo) || jeers *pl* (en el teatro).

paterfamilias *m inv* paterfamilias.

paternal *adj* paternal; *autoridad paternal* paternal authority || fatherly; *amor paternal* fatherly love.

paternalismo *m* paternalism.

paternalista *adj* paternalistic.

paternidad *f* paternity, fatherhood; *la paternidad acarrea muchas responsabilidades* paternity entails many responsibilities || FIG paternity (de una idea) || — *atribuir la paternidad de un libro a* to father a book on || *investigación de paternidad* affiliation suit.

paterno, na *adj* paternal (autoridad) || fatherly (cariño) || paternal, on one's father's side; *mi abuelo paterno* my paternal grandfather, my grandfather on my father's side.

paternóster *m* Lord's Prayer, Paternoster (oración).

patético, ca *adj* pathetic, moving, touching, poignant (conmovedor).

patetismo *m* pathos.

patiabierto, ta *adj* FAM bandy, bowlegged.

patibulario, ria *adj* sinister, harrowing; *rostro patibulario* sinister expression.

patíbulo *m* scaffold, gallows *pl* (cadalso) || FIG *carne de patíbulo* gallows bird.

paticojo, ja *adj* FAM gammy-legged, lame.
◆ *m/f* FAM cripple, lame person.

paticorto, ta *adj* short-legged.

patidifuso, sa *adj* FAM flabbergasted, dumbfounded, nonplussed; *quedarse patidifuso* to be flabbergasted.

patilargo, ga *adj* long-legged.

patilla *f* scar (de un arma de fuego) || arm, side (de gafas) || MÚS position of the left hand on guitar-like instruments.
◆ *pl* sideburns, sideboards, sidewhiskers (pelo en las sienes) || kiss curls (peinado femenino).

Patillas *n pr* FAM Old Nick (el demonio).

patilludo, da *adj* with long thick sideburns.

patín *m* skate (para patinar); *patín de hielo* or *de cuchilla* ice skate; *patín de ruedas* roller skate || shoe (calzado de niños pequeños) || scooter (patineta) || paddle boat (hidropedal) || runner (de un trineo) || AVIAC skid (de aterrizaje); *patín de cola* tail skid || TECN shoe, block (del freno).

pátina *f* patina || — *dar pátina a* to patinate, to coat with a patina || *la pátina del tiempo* weathering.

patinador, ra *m/f* skater.

patinaje *m* skating; *patinaje sobre ruedas* roller skating; *patinaje artístico* figure skating; *patinaje sobre hielo* ice skating || skidding (de un coche).

patinar *vi* to skate (un patinador) || to skid (un vehículo) || to slide (resbalar voluntariamente) || to slip, to slide (resbalar sin querer) || FIG to slip up, to make a blunder *o* a slip (meter la pata).
◆ *vt* to patinate, to coat with a patina, to give a patina to (dar pátina).

patinazo *m* skid (de un vehículo) || FIG & FAM slip, boob, blunder (planchazo) || *dar* or *pegar un patinazo* to skid, to go into a skid (resbalar), to make a slip *o* a boob *o* a blunder, to slip up (meter la pata).

patineta *f*; **patinete** *m* scooter.

patinillo *m* small yard (de una casa).

patio *m* yard (de una casa) || patio (en una casa española) || — TEATR *butaca de patio* seat in the stalls [*US* seat in the orchestra] || FAM *¡cómo está el patio!* what a carry-on! || TEATR *patio de butacas* stalls [*US* orchestra] || *patio de escuela* or *de recreo* schoolyard, playground || *patio de Monipodio* den of thieves.

patiquebrar *vt* to break the leg of [an animal].

patita *f* FIG & FAM *poner a uno de patitas en la calle* to kick s.o. out, to throw s.o. out on his ear (echar).

patitieso, sa *adj* stiff-legged (con las piernas paralizadas) || FIG & FAM paralysed [with cold, fear, etc.] | stiff, starchy, stuck-up (estirado) || — FIG & FAM *dejar patitieso* to dumbfound, to astound, to astonish (asombrar) | *quedarse patitieso* to be bowled over *o* astounded *o* astonished *o* flabbergasted (asombrarse).

patituerto, ta *adj* crooked-legged || FIG & FAM crooked, lopsided, misshapen (torcido).

patizambo, ba *adj* knock-kneed || cowhocked (caballo).

pato *m* duck; *pato salvaje* or *silvestre* wild duck || drake (pato macho) || FAM drip, bore, dull person (persona sosa y tonta) || — FIG & FAM *la edad del pato* an awkward age | *pagar el pato* to carry the can, to foot the bill || *pato de flojel* eider (ave).

patochada *f* blunder, bloomer (disparate) || — *decir patochadas* to talk nonsense || *hacer patochadas* to play the fool.

patogenia; patogenesia *f* MED pathogenesis.

patogénico, ca *adj* MED pathogenetic, pathogenic.

patógeno, na *adj* MED pathogenic.

patología *f* MED pathology.

patológico, ca *adj* MED pathologic, pathological.

patólogo, ga *m/f* pathologist.

patoso, sa *adj* FAM clumsy, awkard (torpe) || tiresome, wearisome (cargante).
◆ *m/f* bore.

patraña *f* FAM hoax, fabrication (mentira).

patria *f* mother country, homeland, fatherland, native land; *volver a la patria* to return to one's mother country || — *la madre patria* mother country, motherland || *la patria chica* home, one's home town *o* area || *merecer bien de la patria* to have served one's country well || *patria adoptiva* country of adoption || *patria celestial* heaven, paradise.

patriarca *m* patriarch.

patriarcado *m* patriarchate || patriarchate, patriarchy (régimen).

patriarcal *adj* patriarchal.
◆ *f* patriarchal church || patriarchate (territorio).

patriciado *m* patriciate.

Patricio *npr m* Patrick.

patricio, cia *adj* patrician || aristocratic, noble.
◆ *m/f* patrician || aristocrat, noble.

patrimonial *adj* patrimonial, hereditary.

patrimonio *m* patrimony, heritage || — *patrimonio del Estado* national heritage || *patrimonio forestal del Estado* crown forests (en inglaterra), State forests (en otros países) || *patrimonio nacional* national heritage || *patrimonio real* crown land.

patrio, tria *adj* native, home; *suelo patrio* native soil || paternal (del padre); *patria potestad* paternal authority || *AMER* army, belonging to the army (caballo).

patriota *adj* patriotic.
◆ *m/f* patriot.

patriotería *f* chauvinism, jingoism.

patriotero, ra *adj* chauvinistic, jingoistic.
◆ *m/f* chauvinist, jingoist.

patriótico, ca *adj* patriotic.

patriotismo *m* patriotism.

patrístico, ca *adj* patristic.
◆ *f* patristics.

patrocinador, ra *adj* sponsoring.
◆ *m/f* sponsor, patron (hombre), patroness (mujer).

patrocinar *vt* to sponsor, to patronize; *campaña patrocinada por* campaign sponsored by.

patrocinio *m* patronage, sponsorship (amparo).

patrón *m* patron || captain, skipper, master (de un barco) || landlord (de pensión) || master (de esclavos) || pattern (en costura) || standard (modelo); *patrón oro* gold standard || REL patron || FIG master, boss (jefe) || — FIG *cortado por el mismo patrón* cast in the same mould, tarred with the same brush | *donde hay patrón no manda marinero* the boss is the boss || BOT *patrón de injerto* stock || REL *santo patrón* patron saint.

patrona *f* patroness (protectora) || landlady (de casa de huéspedes) || employer (jefe) || owner (dueña) || REL patron saint, patroness.

patronal *adj* employers', of employers; *sindicato patronal* employers' association *o* union || REL patronal || *cierre patronal* lockout.

patronato *m* patronage, sponsorship (protección); *bajo el patronato de* under the patronage of || board of trustees (de una obra benéfica) || board, organization (organización); *patronato de turismo* tourist board || employers *pl* (patronos) || trust, foundation (fundación) || centre (centro) || society; *patronato de los Amigos de...* society of the Friends of... || — *patronato de apuestas mutuas* pari-mutuel || *patronato real* royal patronage.

patronazgo *m* patronage; *bajo el patronazgo de* under the patronage of || *a Santa Bárbara corresponde el patronazgo de la artillería* Saint Barbara is the patron saint *o* the patroness of artillerymen.

patronímico, ca *adj/sm* patronymic.

patrono, na *m/f* boss (jefe) || patron saint, patron (santo), patron saint, patroness (santa) | patron (hombre), patroness (mujer), (de una obra benéfica) || owner, employer (empresario).

patrulla *f* patrol; *estar de patrulla* to be on patrol || FIG band, group (cuadrilla) || — *coche patrulla* patrol car || *estar de patrulla en* or *por* to patrol; *unos soldados están de patrulla en la frontera* soldiers patrol the border || *jefe de patrulla* patrol leader.

patrullar *vi* to patrol, to go on patrol.

patrullero, ra *adj* patrol (avión, buque).
◆ *m* patrol boat (barco) || patrol car (coche) || patrol plane (avión).

patulea *f* FAM bunch of kids (chiquillos) | disorderly soldiers *pl* (soldadesca) | mob (muchedumbre).

Paúl *adj/s* REL Vincentian (de San Vicente de Paúl).

paular *vi* FAM to chat, to talk (hablar) || — FAM *ni paula ni maula* he doesn't even open his mouth | *sin paular ni maular* without saying a word.

paulatinamente *adj* slowly, little by little, gradually.

paulatino, na *adj* slow, gradual || *de un modo paulatino* gradually.

paulina *f* decree of excommunication || FIG & FAM scolding, reprimand (reprensión).

paulista *adj* [of *o* from] São Paulo [Brazil].
◆ *m/f* native *o* inhabitant of São Paulo.
◆ *m* Paulinist (miembro de una congregación).

Paulo *npr m* Paul.

pauperismo *m* pauperism.

pauperización *f* pauperization.

paupérrimo, ma *adj* very poor, poverty-stricken.

pausa *f* pause, break (interrupción) || slowness (lentitud) || MÚS rest || — *a pausas* at intervals || *con pausa* calmly, unhurriedly.

pausado, da *adj* slow, calm || *pausado en el hablar* deliberate in one's speech.
◆ *adv* slowly, calmly, unhurriedly.

pauta *f* rule, guide (regla) || line, lines *pl* (rayas) || FIG model, example (dechado); *servir de pauta a* to act as a model for || MÚS staff (del papel) || AMER writing guide (falsilla) || FIG *dar* or *marcar la pauta* to set the example, to lay down the norm *o* the guideline.

pautar *vt* to rule || FIG to regulate; *vida pautada* regulated life || MÚS to rule (pentagrama) || *papel pautado* ruled paper (para escribir), music paper.

pava *f* turkey-hen (ave) || FIG bore, dull woman (mujer sosa) || furnace bellows *pl* (fuelle) || FAM butt (colilla) || AMER kettle (para el mate) || — *pava real* peahen || FIG & FAM *pelar la pava* to court, to woo.

pavada *f* flock of turkeys || FIG & FAM silliness, foolishness, stupidity (tontería).

pavana *f* pavan (danza).

pavés *m* large shield (escudo grande).

pavesa *f* spark, ember (chispa) || cinder (ceniza) || — FIG & FAM *estar hecho una pavesa* to be a shadow of one's former self | *pavesa humana* human torch.

pavía *f* clingstone peach (fruto).

Pavía *n pr* GEOGR Pavia.

pávido, da *adj* terrified.

pavimentación *f* paving [of a street, of a road] (revestimiento) || tiling, flooring (con losas, losetas).

pavimentar *vt* to pave (con adoquines, asfalto, etc.) || to tile, to floor (con losas, losetas).

pavimento *m* paving, pavement (de adoquines, asfalto, etc.) || tiling, flooring (de losas o losetas).

pavipollo *m* young turkey || FAM dunce, fool (bobo).

pavisoso, sa; pavitonto, ta *adj* silly, stupid, foolish (mentecato).
◆ *m/f* ninny, nincompoop, fool; *este chico es un pavitonto* this boy is a fool.

pavo *m* turkey (ave) || FIG & FAM ninny, drip (necio) | five pesetas (un duro) || AMER stowaway (polizón) || — FIG & FAM *comer pavo* to be a wallflower (en un baile) | *edad del pavo* awkward age | *encendido como un pavo* as red as a beetroot | *hincharse como un pavo real, ser más orgulloso que un pavo* to be as proud as a peacock | *no es moco de pavo* it's no trifle; *este trabajo no es moco de pavo* this job is no trifle || *pavo real* peacock || FIG & FAM *subírsele a uno el pavo* to blush, to go as red as a beetroot | *tener pavo* to be shy *o* timid.

pavón *m* peacock (pavo real) || peacock butterfly (mariposa) || TECN bluing, bronzing (del acero).

pavonado, da *adj* dark blue || blued, bronzed (acero).
◆ *m* bluing, bronzing (del acero).

pavonar *vt* to blue, to bronze (acero).

pavonear *vt* to deceive, to delude (engañar).
◆ *vi/vpr* to strut, to peacock, to show off (presumir).

pavoneo *m* strutting, showing off.

pavor *m* fear, terror, panic, dread.

pavorosamente *adj* fearfully, frightfully (de una manera espantosa) || trembling with fear (con pavor).

pavoroso, sa *adj* fearful, frightful, dreadful, terrifying (espantoso).

paya *f* AMER improvised song of a travelling minstrel.

payada *f* AMER improvised song of a travelling minstrel (canción) | party at which travelling minstrels perform and compete with each other (fiesta).

payador; pallador *m* AMER travelling minstrel.

— OBSERV The word *payador* was used in the 19th century, notably in the countries of the River Plate, to designate the travelling minstrels who improvised songs to the accompaniment of their guitars. Santos Vega is the outstanding example of the Argentinan *payador*.

payadura *f* AMER improvised song.

payar *vi* to improvise songs accompanying o.s. on the guitar.

payasada *f* clownery, buffoonery, clowning || *hacer payasadas* to clown about, to act the clown.

payasear *vi* to clown, to clown about.

payaso *m* clown (del circo) || FIG clown, boffoon, joker (persona poco seria) || *hacer el payaso* to act the clown.

payés, esa *m/f* peasant [in Catalonia and the Balearic Islands] || *payeses de remensa* serfs bound to the soil (en la Cataluña medieval).

payo, ya *adj* peasant, rustic || who is not a Gypsy (en el lenguaje de los gitanos).
◆ *m/f* peasant (campesino) || FAM fool, dunce (mentecato) || AMER albino.

paz *f* peace; *pedir la paz* to sue for peace; *mantener la paz* to keep the peace || peacefulness, tranquillity, peace and quiet (tranquilidad) || REL pax (imagen que besaban los fieles) || — *¡a la paz de Dios!* God be with you! || *dejar en paz* to leave alone, to leave be; *déjame en paz* leave me alone; *deja en paz esa silla, a tu hermano* leave that chair, your brother alone || *descansar en paz* to rest in peace || *estar en paz* to be at peace (no estar en guerra), to be even, to be quits (no deberse nada) || *firmar la paz* to sign a peace treaty (estados) || *hacer las paces* to make (it) up, to make peace || *mantenimiento de la paz* peace-keeping || *no dar paz a la lengua* not to stop talking, not to shut up (fam) || *no dejar en paz a uno* to give s.o. no peace, to plague s.o. || *¡paz a sus cenizas!* peace to his ashes! || *paz octaviana* Octavian peace || *pipa de la paz* pipe of peace, peace pipe || *poner paz* to make peace, to reconcile; *poner paz entre varias personas* to make peace between *o* to reconcile several people || *quedar en paz* to make peace (no estar más en guerra), to get even (saldar la deuda) || *que en paz descanse* may he rest in peace; *mi marido, que en paz descanse, era militar* my husband, may he rest in peace, was a serviceman || *tener la conciencia en paz* to have a clear conscience || *¡vaya en paz!* go in peace! || *¡y aquí paz y después gloria!, ¡y en paz!* it's as simple as that!, that's all there is to it!, and that's final!
◆ *pl* peace *sing*; *firmar las paces* to make peace (individuos).

pazguatería *f* silliness, simplicity, doltishness (simpleza) || prudishness (mojigatería).

pazguato, ta *adj* silly, simple, doltish (simple) || old-maidish, prudish (mojigato).
◆ *m/f* simpleton, dolt (tonto) || prude (gazmoño).

pazo *m* country manor (en Galicia).

PCC *abrev de Partido Comunista Cubano* Cuban Communist Party.

PCE *abrev de Partido Comunista Español* Spanish Communist Party.

¡pche!; ¡pchs! *interj* pshaw!, bah!

pe *f* p [name of the letter «p»[|| *de pe a pa* from beginning to end, from A to Z.

pea *f* POP drunkeness (borrachera) || — POP *agarrar una pea* to get blink drunk, to get pissed | *tener una pea encima* to be blind drunk *o* pissed.

peaje *m* toll (derecho de paso).

peal *m* AMER lasso *m* (lazo).

pealar *vt* AMER to lasso (el caballo).

peana *f* stand, pedestal (zócalo) || platform (del altar) || window sill (de una ventana) || FIG *adorar el santo por la peana* to court the mother in order to marry the daughter.

peatón *m* pedestrian (transeúnte); *paso de peatones* pedestrian crossing [*US* crosswalk].

pebe *m* AMER kid, youngster (niño).

pebeta *f* AMER young girl.

pebete *m* joss stick (sustancia aromática) || FIG & FAM stink (mal olor) || fuse, touch paper (de cohete) || AMER kid, youngster (niño).

pebetero *m* incense burner.

peca *f* freckle (en la piel).

pecadillo *m* peccadillo.

pecado *m* sin; *pecado mortal, venial, original* mortal *o* deadly, venial, original sin || defect (defecto en una cosa) || FIG & FAM shame, crying shame (lástima); *¡qué pecado!* what a shame!, it's a crying shame! || — FIG & FAM *de mis pecados* of mine; *esta niña de mis pecados* this child of mine || FIG *en el pecado va la penitencia* every sin carries its own punishment || *estar en pecado* to be in sin || *los siete pecados capitales* the seven deadly sins || FIG & FAM *más feo que un pecado* as ugly as sin || *morir en pecado* to die unrepentant || *no hay pecado sin remisión* there is no sin without remission || *pecado confesado es medio perdonado* a fault confessed is half redressed || *pecado nefando* sodomy || *por mis pecados* for my sins || *todo pecado merece perdón* there is forgiveness for every sin.

pecador, ra *adj* sinful, sinning.
◆ *m/f* sinner, transgressor || *pecador de mí* sinner that I am.

pecaminoso, sa *adj* sinful.

pecar *vi* to sin || FIG to be at fault (razonamiento) | to do *o* to be wrong (una persona)

|| — *no pecar de generoso* not to be guilty of generosity, not to be exactly overgenerous || *pecar con la intención* or *de intención* to have sinful *o* evil thoughts || *pecar de palabra, de obra* to sin by word, by deed || *pecar de severo, de confiado* to be too *o* overly severe, confident || *pecar por defecto* to fall short of the mark || *pecar por exceso* to overdo it, to go too far || *pecar por omisión* to sin by omission.

pecarí; pécari *m* peccary (mamífero).

pecblenda *f* MIN pitchblende.

peccata minuta *loc lat* FAM peccadillo.

pecera *f* fishbowl (redonda), aquarium (acuario).

pecio *m* flotsam, wreckage (de un naufragio).

pecíolo; peciolo *m* BOT petiole.

pécora *f* head of sheep (res lanar) || FIG *mala pécora* wicked woman (mujer mala), tramp (prostituta).

pecoso, sa *adj* freckled, freckly; *cara pecosa* freckled face || *niña pecosa* freckle-faced girl.
◆ *m/f* freckle-faced person.

pectíneo, a *adj* ANAT pectineal (músculo).

pectoral *adj* pectoral; *músculos pectorales* pectoral muscles || cough; *pastillas pectorales* cough drops.
◆ *m* pectoral cross (de obispo) || pectoral, cough medicine || breastplate (de sacerdote judío) || pectoral (adorno).

pecuario, ria *adj* (of) livestock.

peculado *m* JUR peculation, embezzlement.

peculiar *adj* peculiar, particular, characteristic; *traje peculiar de una región* costume peculiar to *o* characteristic of a region.

peculiaridad *f* peculiarity.

peculio *m* peculium || FIG own *o* private *o* personal money; *lo tuve que pagar de mi peculio* I had to pay in out of my own money.

pecuniariamente *adv* pecuniarily, financially (económicamente) || cash (en metálico).

pecuniario, ria *adj* pecuniary || *pena pecuniaria* fine.

pechada *f* AMER push [with the chest] (empujón) | touch for a loan (sablazo) || FAM *darse una pechada de trabajar* to work a lot.

pechar *vt* to pay as a tax (pagar) || AMER FAM to push [with the chest] (empujar) | to sponge off (s.o.), to touch (s.o.) for a loan (pedir dinero).
◆ *vi* FAM *pechar con* to shoulder, to take on, to bear; *pechar con el trabajo más difícil* to shoulder the most difficult job || FAM *siempre tengo que pechar con la más gorda* I always get stuck with the fattest girl.

pechblenda *f* MIN ⟶ **Pecblenda.**

pechera *f* shirtfront (de camisa de hombre) || front (de otras prendas de vestir) || jabot (chorrera) || breast collar (arnés del caballo) || FAM breast, bosom (de la mujer) || AMER apron (mandil) || *pechera postiza* dicky.

pechero, ra *adj* taxable || plebeian (plebeyo).
◆ *m* bib (babero) || plebeian, commoner (plebeyo) || taxpayer (que paga tributo).

pechina *f* shell (venera) || ARQ pendentive (de bóveda).

pecho *m* ANAT chest; *en el pecho* on the chest | breast, bosom, bust (de la mujer) || breast (de un animal) || slope, gradient (repecho) || tax, tribute (tributo) || FIG heart (ánimo) | courage, spirit (valor, esfuerzo) | voice (calidad de la voz) || — FIG *abrir su pecho a alguien* to unbosom o.s. *o* to open one's heart to s.o. | *a lo hecho, pecho* it is no use crying over spilt milk || MED *angina de pecho* angina pectoris || FIG *a pecho descubierto* unprotected, defenceless (sin protección), with an open heart (con franqueza) || *apretar contra su pecho* to hug to one's breast || FIG *criar a sus pechos* to take s.o. under one's wing || *dar el pecho* to breast-feed, to nurse, to suckle (a un niño), to face (up to), to confront (a un peligro) || FIG *descubrir el pecho* to open one's heart || FIG & FAM *echarse entre pecho y espalda* to put *o* to tuck away || *enfermo del pecho* consumptive || FIG *no caberle a alguien la alegría, el orgullo en el pecho* to be bursting with happiness, pride | *partirse el pecho* to break one's back, to slave away | *partirse el pecho por uno* to go out of one's way for s.o., to do one's utmost for s.o. || *sacar el pecho* to stick out one's chest || *tomar el pecho* to nurse, to suck (un niño) || *tomar* or *tomarse una cosa a pecho* to take sth. to heart.

pechuga *f* breast [of fowl] (pecho de ave); *una pechuga de pollo* a breast of chicken || FIG & FAM slope, gradient (cuesta) | bosom (de mujer) || AMER sangfroid, nerve.

pechugona *adj* FAM big-breasted, big-bosomed, buxom.
◆ *f* FAM big-breasted girl *o* woman, buxom lass.

pedagogía *f* pedagogy.

pedagógico, ca *adj* pedagogic, pedagogical, teaching.

pedagogo *m* pedagogue [US pedagog] || teacher, educator (educador) || tutor (ayo) || schoolmaster (maestro de escuela) || FAM pedant.

pedal *m* pedal; *los pedales de una bicicleta* the pedals of a bicycle; *pedal de embrague, de freno* clutch, brake pedal || MÚS pedal (de piano, órgano); *pedal fuerte* loud pedal || *dar a los pedales* to pedal.

pedalear *vi* to pedal.

pedaleo *m* pedalling.

pedáneo *adj m* JUR *juez pedáneo* justice of the peace.

pedanía *f* AMER district.

pedante *adj* pedantic.
◆ *m/f* pedant.

pedantear *vi* to be pedantic.

pedantería *f* pedantry.

pedazo *m* piece; *un pedazo de pan* a piece of bread || — *a pedazos* in pieces, in bits || *caerse a pedazos* to fall to pieces *o* to bits || FIG *caerse uno a pedazos, estar hecho pedazos* to be worn out, to be all in, to be dead beat | *ganarse un pedazo de pan* to earn one's living || *hacer pedazos* to break *o* to smash to pieces (romper), to tear to pieces (desgarrar), to tear to pieces (a una persona) || *hacerse pedazos* to fall to pieces || FIG & FAM *morirse* or *estar (muerto) por los pedazos de alguien* to be madly in love with s.o. | *pedazo de alcornoque, de animal, de bruto* you dope, you beast, you brute | *pedazo del alma* or *del corazón* apple of one's eye || *romperse en mil pedazos* to smash to pieces || *saltar algo en pedazos* to blow to pieces || FIG *ser un pedazo de pan* to be kindness itself | *tener el corazón hecho pedazos* to be heartbroken.

pederasta *m* paederast [US pederast].

pederastia *f* paederasty [US pederasty].

pedernal *m* silex || flint (piedra de chispa) || FIG *duro como el* or *como un pedernal* as hard as a rock.

pederse *vpr* POP to fart.

pedestal *m* pedestal (de estatua); *pedestales de mármol* marble pedestals || stand, pedestal (peana) || FIG stepping-stone (apoyo) || *a su madre la tiene (puesta) en un pedestal* he has placed his mother on a pedestal.

pedestre *adj* pedestrian || FIG pedestrian, commonplace | vulgar || *carrera pedestre* footrace.

pedestrismo *m* DEP footrace.

pedíatra; pediatra *m* MED paediatrician, paediatrist [US pediatrician, pediatrist].

pediatría *f* MED paediatrics [US pediatrics].

pedicular *adj* pedicular.

pedículo *m* BOT peduncle (pedúnculo).

pedicuro, ra *m/f* chiropodist (callista).
◆ *f* chiropody (cuidado de los pies).

pedido *m* COM order; *entregar, hacer un pedido* to fill, to make an order; *los pedidos pendientes* (the) pending orders || request (petición); *hacer, atender un pedido* to make, to grant a request || — *a pedido de* at the request of || *hoja de pedido* order form.

pedidor, ra *adj* demanding (exigente) || who is always asking for sth.
◆ *m/f* petitioner || client, customer (cliente).

pedigree; pedigrí *m* pedigree.

pedigüeño, ña *adj* FAM persistent.
◆ *m/f* FAM pest, nuisance.

pedimento *m* petition, request || JUR suit, petition | claim of ownership (en derecho inmobiliario) || JUR *pedimento del fiscal* indictment of the public prosecutor.

pedir* *vt* to ask for, to request (*seguido de sustantivo*); *pedir dinero, un libro* to ask for money, for a book || to ask (*seguido de un verbo*); *me pidió que le pagase la deuda* he asked me to pay off the debt || to ask for, to order (encargar); *pedir un café* to order a cup of coffee || to beg (pedir limosna) || COM to order (hacer un pedido) || to require, to demand (requerir); *tal oficio pide paciencia* such a job requires patience || to ask (poner precio); *pide demasiado por el piso* he is asking too much for the flat || to ask for s.o.'s hand in marriage (a una mujer) || — FIG *a pedir de boca* to one's heart's content, for the asking || *no hay más que pedir* what more do you want? || *no se puede pedir más* one couldn't ask for more || *pedir disculpas* to apologize || JUR *pedir en justicia* to sue || *pedir la Luna* to ask the earth, to ask for the moon || *pedir la paz* to sue for peace || *pedir limosna* to ask for alms, to beg || FIG *pedir peras al olmo* to ask for the impossible || *pedir prestado* to borrow; *tuve que pedir prestado diez libras* I had to borrow ten pounds; to ask (s.o.) to lend, to ask for a loan of, to ask to borrow; *me pidió prestado el coche* he asked me to lend him my car, he asked to borrow my car || *pedir socorro* or *auxilio* to ask for help.

pedo *m* POP fart (ventosidad) | drunkenness (borrachera) || — POP *estar pedo* to be canned, to be pissed (estar borracho) || *pedo de lobo* puffball (hongo) || POP *pegarse* or *tirarse un pedo* to fart, to break wind.

pedología *f* pedology.

pedorrera *f* POP string of farts.

pedrada *f* blow with *o* from a stone (golpe) || — *a pedradas* by stoning || *matar a pedradas* to stone to death || *pegar una pedrada a uno* to throw a stone at s.o. || FIG & FAM *venir* or *caer como pedrada en ojo de boticario* to come in the nick of time, to come just right.

pedrea *f* stoning (con piedras) || fight with stones, stone-throwing fight (combate) || hail (granizo) || FIG & FAM small prizes *pl* (en la lotería).

pedregal *m* stony *o* rocky ground.

pedregoso, sa *adj* stony, rocky.

pedrería *f* precious stones *pl*, jewels *pl*.

pedrisca *f* hail (granizo) || hailstorm (granizada).

pedriscal *m* stony *o* rocky ground.

pedrisco *m* hail (granizo) || hailstorm (granizada) || stony ground (pedregal).

Pedro *npr m* Peter || FIG *como Pedro por su casa* as if he owned the place.

pedrusco *m* rough stone.

pedunculado, da *adj* BOT pedunculate, pedunculated.

peduncular *adj* BOT peduncular.

pedúnculo *m* BOT & ANAT peduncle.

peerse *vpr* POP to fart, to break wind.

pega *f* ZOOL magpie (urraca) | remora (pez) || sticking (acción de pegar con cola) || pitch, coating (baño de pez) || FAM hoax, trick (chasco) | difficulty; *aclarar una pega a un alumno* to clear up a difficulty for a student | but, snag; *hay una pega* there is a but (hay un pero) | snag (engorro); *asunto lleno de pegas* job full of snags | difficulty, problem; *hoy no hay ninguna pega para conseguir un pasaporte* today there is no problem in getting a passport | inconvenience (inconveniente) | beating, thrashing (zurra) || MIN firing of a blast (de barreno) || — FAM *de pega* sham, fake | *ésa es la pega* that's the catch *o* snag | *poner pegas a* to find fault with (criticar), to put up obstacles to, to raise objections to (poner dificultades).

pegada *f* DEP stroke, hit (en pelota, en tenis, etc.) | punch, blow (en boxeo).

pegadizo, za *adj* sticky (pegajoso) || FIG sponging (gorrón) | contagious, catching; *tener una risa pegadiza* to have a contagious laugh | catchy (música, etc.) | false, imitation (falso).

pegado, da *adj* stuck (con cola) || burnt; *la leche está pegada* the milk is burnt || FAM bad, hopeless, useless; *estar pegado en matemáticas* to be hopeless at mathematics || *oler a pegado* to smell of burning.
◆ *m* patch, sticking plaster.

pegador *m* MIN blaster || puncher (boxeador).

pegadura *f* sticking, gluing, glueing (acción de pegar) || joint (unión).

pegajoso, sa *adj* sticky (que se pega) || viscous, sticky (viscoso) || contagious, catching (contagioso) || FIG & FAM mellow (meloso) | tiresome, boring (cargante).

pegamento *m* glue (para pegar) || rubber solution (para los parches).

pegar *vt* to stick (*término más general*); *pegar un sello en un sobre* to stick a stamp on an envelope || to glue, to paste (con cola) || to put up, to post (carteles) || to sew on (coser); *pegar un botón* to sew on a button || to fire; *pegar un tiro* to fire a shot || to put flush against *o* right up against; *pegar el piano a la pared* to put the piano flush against the wall || to give, to strike (golpes); *pegar un palo* to strike a blow with a stick || to hit, to strike; *pegar a un niño* to hit a child || to let out; *pegar un grito* to let out a yell || to hit (al balón) || to give; *le he pegado mi enfermedad* I have given him my illness || — MIL *codos pegados al cuerpo* elbows in || *goma de pegar* glue || *iban pegados uno a otro* they walked along side by side *o* arm in arm || *no pegar ojo* not to sleep a wink || *papel de pegar* sticking paper || FAM *pegarle cuatro gritos a alguien* to give s.o. a piece of one's mind, to haul s.o. over the coals || *pegar fuego a algo* to set fire to sth. || *pegar saltos de alegría* to jump for joy || *pegar un salto* to jump || *pegar un susto a uno* to give s.o. a fright, to frighten s.o. || *pelo pegado* plastered-down hair || *sin pegar un tiro* without firing a shot.
◆ *vi* to stick (adherir) || to go, to match (sentar bien o mal); *dos colores que no pegan uno con otro* two colours which don't go together || to fit, to go (well), to look right; *este cuadro no pega aquí* this picture doesn't go here *o* doesn't look right here || to touch, to adjoin (estar contiguo) || to hit (dar un golpe) || to beat (dar una paliza) || to strike, to hit (dar en un punto, en el blanco, etc.) || to trip, to stumble (tropezar) || to beat down, to be hot (el sol) || — *no me pega que haya sido él* I don't think *o* believe that it was he || *no pega* it's not right (no conviene), it won't hold, it won't wash (no venga con cuentos) || *pegar duro* or *fuerte* to hit hard || *quien pega primero pega dos veces* the first blow is half the battle.
◆ *vpr* to stick (fijarse, adherir en general) || to get close to, to press o.s. against; *pegarse a la pared* to get close to the wall || to burn, to stick to the pan (un guiso); *el arroz se ha pegado* the rice has burnt || to lie down on; *pegarse al suelo* to lie down on the ground || to hit each other *o* one another, to fight (pelearse varias personas) || FIG to hang around s.o., to stick to s.o. (estar siempre con una persona) | to be catching *o* catchy; *el acento del Sur se pega fácilmente* the Southern accent is very catching | to be contagious, to be catching (una enfermedad) | to pass on (una costumbre) || FAM to lead (llevar); *¡hay que ver la vida que se pega!* you should see the life he leads! | to get through (una comilona, un trabajo) | to go on (hacer un viaje, dar un paseo) | to have (tener, pasar) | to become fond of, to take a liking to (aficionarse) || — FIG *coche que se pega muy bien a la carretera* car which holds the road well || *el coche se pegó a la acera* the car pulled over to the curb || FIG *¡es para pegarse un tiro!* it's enough to make you scream! | *esta canción se me ha pegado al oído* I can't get this song out of my mind || FIG & FAM *pegarse como una lapa* to stick like glue *o* like a leech | *pegársela a uno* to take s.o. in, to put one over on s.o. (engañar); *se la pegó a su socio* he took his partner in; to deceive; *se la pegaba a su marido* she was deceiving her husband; to fool, to trick, to catch (hacer picar con una broma o un engaño) | *pegársele a uno las sábanas* to oversleep; *ha llegado tarde esta mañana porque se le pegaron las sábanas* he arrived late this morning because he overslept || *pegarse un tiro* to shoot o.s.

pegaso *m* pegasus (pez).

Pegaso *npr m* MIT Pegasus.

pegatina *f* sticker.

pego *m* FAM *dar el pego* to fool, to take in (engañar).

pegote *m* plaster, sticking plaster (emplasto) || FIG & FAM sticky mess, stodgy mess (guiso apelmazado) | compact mass (cosa espesa) | sponger (gorrón) | patch, botch (parche) | tasteless addition (en una obra de arte) || FAM *¡qué pegote!* what a pest *o* a nuisance! (persona), what a sight! (cosa).

pegual *m* AMER cinch, girth (sobrecincha).

peinado, da *adj* combed.
◆ *m* hairstyle (del pelo); *peinado afro* Afro hairstyle || combing, carding (de textiles).

peinador, ra *m/f* hairdresser (el que peina).
◆ *m* peignoir, bathrobe (bata) || AMER dressing table (tocador).
◆ *f* wool-combing machine.

peinadura *f* combing [the hair] (acción).
◆ *pl* combings.

peinar *vt* to comb s.o.'s hair; *peinar a un niño* to comb a child's hair || to comb; *peino mi peluca a diario* I comb my wig daily || to do s.o.'s hair; *¿quién peina a la reina?* who does the queen's hair? || to comb out (desenredar) || to brush, to touch (rozar ligeramente) || to comb, to card (la lana) || — FIG & FAM *peinar canas* to be getting old, to be going grey | *peinar los naipes* to stack the cards.
◆ *vpr* to comb one's hair || to have one's hair done (hacerse peinar).

peinazo *m* lintel (de puerta o de ventana).

peine *m* comb (para el pelo) || comb, card (para la lana) || reed (de telar) || FIG & FAM sly fellow (hombre astuto), sly minx (mujer astuta) || TEATR gridiron (telar) || — *pasarse el peine* to comb one's hair || *peine de balas* cartridge clip || *peine espeso* toothcomb [US fine-tooth comb] || FAM *¡te vas a enterar de lo que vale un peine!* that'll teach you a thing or two!

peineta *f* back comb [large ornamental comb] || AMER toothcomb [US fine-tooth comb] (lendrera) || FIG & FAM *¡mira qué peineta!* you must be joking!
— OBSERV The *peineta* is a large curved comb usually made of shell. It is worn in the chignon and serves to hold the mantilla in place.

peje *m* fish (pez) || FIG & FAM crafty devil (astuto) || — *peje araña* stingfish (pez) || *peje diablo* scorpion fish (pez).

pejepalo *m* stockfish, dried cod.

pejesapo *m* toadfish, angler.

pejiguera *f* FAM nuisance, bind, drag (fastidio).

Pekín *n pr* GEOGR Peking.

pekinés, esa *adj/s* Pekingese *inv*, Pekinese *inv*.
◆ *m* Pekingese, pekinese (perro).

pela *f* peeling (de frutas o de legumbres) || FAM peseta; *dame cinco pelas* give me five pesetas.

pelada *f* AMER haircut (corte de pelo) | bald head (calva) | blunder (tontería) || AMER FAM *la pelada* death (muerte).

peladar *m* AMER bare land (páramo).

peladera *f* MED alopecia, baldness || AMER gossip (crítica).

peladilla *f* sugared almond (almendra confitada) || FIG pebble (guijarro) || FAM bullet (proyectil).

pelado, da *adj* bald, hairless (cabeza) || peeled (la piel) || bare, barren (terreno) || peeled, pared (mondado) || fleshless, clean (hueso) || plain (estilo) || round (número); *un número pelado* a round number || FIG bare; *nos pagaron el sueldo pelado* they paid us the bare salary || smooth (guijarro) || AMER insolent (insolente) | coarse (grosero) || — FAM *dejar a uno pelado, estar pelado* to leave s.o. broke, to be broke | *tengo cien pesetas peladas* I've only got a hundred pesetas.
◆ *m* bare patch (terreno) || haircut (corte de pelo) || FAM pauper, poor man (pobre) | poor devil (pobre diablo) || AMER fellow, guy (individuo) | child (niño).

pelador *m* barker (que descorteza).

peladura *f* barking (de árboles) || peeling (de frutas) || peelings *pl* (mondaduras).

pelafustán *m* FAM idler, ne'er-do-well (perezoso) | poor devil (pobre hombre).

pelagatos *m inv* FAM poor devil, ragamuffin (pobre hombre) || FAM *había cuatro pelagatos* there was hardly anybody.

pelagianismo *m* Pelagianism (herejía).

pelagiano, na *adj/s* Pelagian.

pelágico, ca *adj* pelagic (de alta mar); *fauna pelágica* pelagic fauna.

Pelagio *npr m* Pelagius (hereje).

pelagra *f* MED pellagra.

pelaje *m* coat, fur (de un animal) || FIG & FAM appearance, looks *pl* (apariencia) || FAM *y otros del mismo pelaje* and others like him.

pelambre *m* hair, fur, coat (pelo del animal) || lime pit (baño de cal) || MED alopecia, baldness (caída del pelo).
◆ *f* FAM mop (cabellera), long hair (pelo largo), thick hair (pelo espeso).
— OBSERV This word is often used in the feminine.

pelambrera *f* mob (cabellera), long hair (pelo largo), thick hair (pelo espeso) ‖ baldness (calvicie).

pelamen *m* FAM hair (pelambre).

pelana *m*; **pelanas** *m inv* FAM poor devil, ragamuffin (pelagatos).

pelandusca *f* FAM prostitute, whore (ramera).

pelapatatas *m inv* potato peeler.

pelar *vt* to cut (el pelo) ‖ to peel; *pelar patatas, un melocotón* to peel potatoes, a peach ‖ to shell (mariscos, guisantes, habas) ‖ to pluck (ave) ‖ to strip (un árbol, un hueso, etc.) ‖ FIG & FAM to clean out, to fleece (ganar a otro todo el dinero) | to strip, to despoil (despojar) | to pull to pieces, to slate (criticar) ‖ *AMER* to beat ‖ — FIG & FAM *duro de pelar* a hard nut | *hace un frío que pela* it is freezing cold, it is icy ‖ FIG *pelar la pava* to court, to woo ‖ *AMER pelar los ojos* to open one's eyes wide, to goggle, to stare wide-eyed.
➡ *vpr* FAM to get one's hair cut ‖ to peel (la piel) ‖ *AMER* to become confused (confundirse) ‖ — FAM *correr que se las pela* to run like mad ‖ FAM *pelárselas* to do sth. speedily | *pelárselas por una cosa* to be dying for sth (desear), to do one's utmost to get sth (hacer todo lo posible).

pelásgico, ca *adj* pelasgic, pelasgian.

pelasgo, ga *adj/s* pelasgian.

peldaño *m* step (de escalera) ‖ rung (de escalera de mano).

pelea *f* battle, fight, combat, scuffle (*fam*), battle, fight, combat, scuffle (contienda) ‖ fight (de animales, en deportes) ‖ quarrel, row, fight (riña) ‖ FIG struggle (por conseguir una cosa) ‖ — FAM *buscar pelea* to be looking for a fight ‖ *gallo de pelea* gamecock, fighting cock ‖ *pelea de gallos* cockfight.

peleado, da *adj* *estar peleado con alguien* to have fallen out with s.o., not to be on speaking terms with s.o.

peleador, ra *adj* quarrelsome, pugnacious (aficionado a pelear) ‖ *gallo peleador* gamecock, fighting cock.
➡ *m* fighter.

pelear *vi* to fight (luchar) ‖ to battle (batallar) ‖ to quarrel (con palabras) ‖ to war, to battle, to fight; *el Cid peleó contra los moros* the Cid warred against the Moors ‖ FIG to war (elementos, cosas) | to struggle; *peleaba por vencer su pasión* he struggled to control his passion ‖ FIG *pelear por* to struggle for (afanarse por algo).
➡ *vpr* to fight; *pelearse a puñetazos* to fight with one's fists ‖ FAM to quarrel, to fall out (*con* with), to quarrel, to fall out (enemistarse).

pelechar *vi* to moult (mudar el pelo o la pluma) ‖ to grow hair (echar pelos), to grow feathers (echar plumas) ‖ FIG & FAM to begin to prosper (prosperar) | to take a turn for the better (salud).

pelele *m* rag doll, puppet (muñeco) ‖ rompers *pl* (de un niño) ‖ FIG & FAM puppet, tool; *era un pelele en sus manos* he was a puppet in his hands.

pelendengue *m* ⟶ **perendengue.**

peleón, ona *adj* quarrelsome, pugnacious ‖ *vino peleón* cheap wine, plonk (pirriaque).
➡ *m/f* troublemaker.

pelerina *f* pelerine (capa femenina).

peletería *f* furriery (oficio y comercio) ‖ furrier's shop, fur shop (tienda) ‖ furs *pl*, peltry (pieles).

peletero, ra *adj* fur; *la industria peletera* the fur industry.
➡ *m* furrier (vendedor de pieles).

peliagudo, da *adj* FIG & FAM arduous; *un trabajo peliagudo* an arduous task | thorny, tricky, ticklish; *un asunto peliagudo* a thorny affair.

pelícano; pelicano *m* pelican (ave) ‖ forceps (de dentista).

pelicorto, ta *adj* short-haired.

película *f* pellicle (piel) ‖ TECN film (de fotos) | pellicle (hoja de gelatina sensible) ‖ CINEM film, picture [*US* movie, motion picture] (cine); *película muda, de miedo* silent, horror film ‖ — FAM *de película* extraordinary, sensational ‖ *echar* or *poner una película* to show a film ‖ *película de dibujos animados* cartoon film, animated cartoon ‖ *película del Oeste* western ‖ *película en colores* colour film (para sacar fotos), film in colour (en el cine) ‖ *película de vídeo* video film ‖ *película en jornadas* or *de episodios* serial.

peliculado *m* FOT stripping.

pelicular *adj* pellicular.

peliculero, ra *adj* FAM film (de cine) | keen on films, keen on the cinema (aficionado) ‖ FIG & FAM dreamy and highly imaginative (fantasioso).
➡ *m/f* FAM film fan, film enthusiast (aficionado) | film maker (director), film actor (actor) ‖ FIG & FAM dreamer, dreamy and highly imaginative person.
➡ *m pl* film people (gente de cine).

peligrar *vi* to be in danger; *usted peligra en una región tan apartada* you are in danger in such an isolated region ‖ to be in danger, to be threatened; *actualmente peligran gravemente los valores eternos de la persona humana* at present the eternal values of the human being are gravely threatened *o* are in grave danger ‖ *hacer peligrar* to menace, to threaten; *las tensiones internas hacen peligrar el equilibrio del país* (the) internal tensions menace the stability of the country.

peligro *m* danger, peril; *huir del peligro* to flee from danger; *arrostrar el peligro* to face the peril ‖ risk, danger (riesgo) ‖ — *con peligro de su vida* at the risk of one's life ‖ *corramos el peligro* let's risk it ‖ *correr (el) peligro de* to run the risk of; *corremos (el) peligro de perder el tren* we run the risk of missing the train ‖ *correr peligro, estar en peligro* to be in danger ‖ *correr un peligro* to run *o* to take a risk ‖ *en peligro* in danger ‖ MAR *en peligro de naufragio* in distress, in danger of shipwreck ‖ *estar enfermo de peligro* to be critically ill ‖ *fuera de peligro* out of danger ‖ *peligro de muerte* deadly danger ‖ *poner en peligro* to endanger ‖ FIG *quien busca el peligro, en él perece* if you play with fire you will be burnt ‖ *vivir entre peligros* to live dangerously.

peligrosidad *f* dangerousness, danger.

peligroso, sa *adj* dangerous; *peligroso de manejar* dangerous to handle; *es peligroso jugar con armas* it is dangerous to play with weapons ‖ dangerous, risky, hazardous, perilous; *empresa peligrosa* perilous enterprise ‖ *es peligroso asomarse al exterior* do not lean out of the window (letrero).

pelilargo, ga *adj* long-haired.

pelillo *m* short hair (pelo corto) ‖ down (vello) ‖ FIG & FAM trifle, a mere nothing (nadería) ‖ — FIG & FAM *echar pelillos a la mar* to let bygones be bygones, to say no more about it, to bury the hatchet | *no reparar en pelillos* not to bother with details (no reparar en detalles), to stop at nothing (no tener escrúpulos) | *no tener pelillos en la lengua* not to mince one's words, to be outspoken | *pararse en pelillos* to be easily offended (enfadarse), to worry about trifles (pararse en pequeñeces).

pelirrojo, ja *adj* ginger, red-haired, redheaded.
➡ *m/f* redhead.

pelirrubio, bia *adj* blond, fair-haired.
➡ *m* blond, fair-haired man *o* boy.
➡ *f* blonde, fair-haired girl *o* woman.

pelitre *m* BOT pyrethrum.

pelma; pelmazo *adj* FIG & FAM boring.
➡ *m/f* FIG & FAM bore (persona pesada); *¡no seas pelma!* don't be such a bore!
➡ *m* stodgy mass.

pelo *m* hair (de hombre o de animal) ‖ hair (un cabello) ‖ hair (cabellos); *cortarle el pelo a uno* to cut s.o.'s hair ‖ whisker (del bigote o de la barba) ‖ fur, hair, coat (pelos o color de un animal) ‖ down (de ave) ‖ hair, down, bristle (de planta) ‖ bristle (del cepillo) ‖ strand, thread (hebra de una tela) ‖ pile, nap (de un tejido) ‖ flaw, defect (en un diamante) ‖ raw silk (seda cruda) ‖ TECN flaw (defecto) | fretsaw (sierra fina) ‖ DEP kiss (en el billar) ‖ — *a contra pelo* the wrong way, against the nap ‖ FIG *agarrarse* or *asirse de un pelo* to clutch at a straw *o* at straws ‖ *al pelo* to a tee, perfectly (perfectamente), with the nap, the right way (en las telas), just at the right moment (en el momento oportuno) ‖ FIG *a pelo* bareheaded, hatless (sin sombrero), bareback (equitación) | *buscar pelos en la sopa* to find fault with everything | *coger la ocasión por los pelos* to seize the opportunity by the scruff of the neck | *con pelos y señales* in the minutest detail ‖ *cortarse el pelo* to have one's hair cut (por otro), to cut one's hair (uno mismo) ‖ FIG *cortar un pelo en el aire* to be as sharp as a razor (cuchillo, persona perspicaz) ‖ FIG & FAM *cuando las ranas crien pelos* when pigs fly *o* have wings ‖ FIG *dar para el pelo a uno* to leave s.o. in a sorry state (pegar) | *estuvieron a un pelo de ganarnos el partido, faltó un pelo para que nos ganasen el partido* they came within an inch *o* within a hairbreadth of beating us | *estar hasta la punta del pelo de, estar hasta los pelos de* to be fed up with, to be sick and tired of | *faltó un pelo para que se cayese* he very nearly fell | *hombre de pelo en pecho* real man | *lucirle a uno el pelo* to be as fit as a fiddle (bien de salud) ‖ *montar a pelo* to ride bareback (a caballo) ‖ FIG *no tener pelo de tonto* to be no fool | *no tener pelos en la lengua* not to mince one's words, to be outspoken | *no verle el pelo a uno* not to see hide nor hair of s.o. ‖ *pelo de camello* camel hair (tela) ‖ FIG & FAM *pelo de la dehesa* uncouth ways, rusticity | *por el pelo de una hormiga* by a hairbreadth | *por los pelos* by the skin of one's teeth | *por un pelo* by a whisker; *se libró por los pelos* he escaped by the skin of his teeth | *quitar el pelo de la dehesa a alguien* to rub the corners off s.o. | *relucirle a uno el pelo* to be glowing with health | *se le pusieron los pelos de punta* his hair stood on end ‖ *sin pelos en la barba* beardless, smooth-faced | *soltarse el pelo* to take one's hair down (despeinarse), to let one's hair down (hacer su santa voluntad) | *tirarse de los pelos* to tear one's hair (de desesperación), to tear each other's hair out (pelearse) | *tomarle el pelo a uno* to pull s.o.'s leg (burlarse) | *traído por los pelos* farfetched | *venir al pelo* to come in very handy (ser muy útil), to suit (s.o.) to a tee, to suit (s.o.) down to the ground (convenirle), to come just at the right moment (ser oportuno).

pelón, ona *adj* with a crew cut *o* a brush cut (con el pelo al rape); *un chico pelón* a boy with a crew cut ‖ hairless (sin pelo o con poco pelo) ‖ bald (calvo) ‖ FIG & FAM empty-headed, stupid (de escaso entendimiento) | broke, skint (sin dinero).
➡ *m* FAM poor devil (desgraciado) ‖ *AMER* child (niño).
➡ *f* MED alopecia (alopecia) ‖ FAM *la pelona* death (la muerte).

peloponense *adj/s* Peloponnesian.

Peloponeso *npr m* GEOGR Peloponnese.

pelota *f* ball; *jugar a la pelota* to play ball ‖ ball (de manteca, etc.) ‖ pelota (juego vasco) ‖ FIG & FAM bonce, nut (cabeza) ‖ *AMER* cowhide raft ‖ — FIG & FAM *dejar a uno en pelota* to clean s.o. out (quitar todo el dinero), to leave s.o. stark naked (dejar desnudo) | *en pelota* starkers | *estar en pelota* to be in one's birthday suit ‖ FIG & FAM *jugar a la pelota con uno* to play around with s.o., to use s.o. | *la pelota está aún en el tejado* it is still in the air ‖ *pelota base* baseball ‖ *pelota bombeada* lob (fútbol) ‖ *pelota corta* short ball (tenis) ‖ *pelota rasante* drive (tenis) ‖ FIG & FAM *rechazar* or *devolver la pelota a alguien* to give s.o. a taste of his own medicine, to give s.o. tit for tat.
◆ *pl* POP balls (testículos) ‖ POP *estar hasta las pelotas de* to be sick to death of.
◆ *m* FAM creeper, toady (adulador).

pelotari *m/f* pelota player.

pelotazo *m* blow with a ball ‖ *le dio un pelotazo en la cara* the ball hit him in the face.

pelotear *vt* to audit, to check (una cuenta).
◆ *vi* to knock up (tenis) ‖ to kick a ball around (en fútbol, etc.) ‖ to throw *o* to toss about (lanzar) ‖ FIG to argue, to quarrel (reñir) ‖ *AMER* to cross (a river) in a cowhide raft.

peloteo *m* knock-up (tenis) ‖ warm-up (en fútbol, etc.) ‖ crawling, sucking up (adulación) ‖ FIG exchange; *peloteo de notas diplomáticas* exchange of diplomatic notes.

pelotera *f* FAM quarrel, squabble, row (pelea) ‖ FAM *armar una pelotera* to kick up a rumpus | *armar una pelotera a uno* to have a go at s.o.

pelotilla *f* pellet (pelota pequeña) ‖ FIG & FAM soft soap (adulación) ‖ FIG & FAM *hacerle a alguien la pelotilla* to soft-soap s.o., to butter s.o. up (adular).

pelotilleo *m* FAM soft soap.

pelotillero, ra *m/f* FAM creeper, toady, fawner (adulador).
◆ *adj* FAM fawning.

pelotón *m* big ball ‖ bundle (de pelos o de hilos) ‖ MIL squad; *pelotón de ejecución* firing squad | picket (de guardia) ‖ crowd (muchedumbre).

pelotudo, da *adj* *AMER* bloody stupid, idiot.

peluca *f* wig (cabellera postiza); *llevar (una) peluca* to wear a wig ‖ FIG & FAM scolding, dressing down (reprensión).

pelucón, ona *m/f* conservative (en Chile).

pelucona *f* FAM doubloon (moneda).

peluche *f* plush.
— OBSERV This word is a Gallicism for *felpa*.

peludo, da *adj* hairy (de mucho pelo) ‖ long-haired (de pelo largo).

peluquería *f* hairdresser's shop (para señoras), barber's shop (para caballeros); *comprar una peluquería* to buy a hairdresser's shop ‖ hairdresser's (para señoras), barber's (para caballeros); *ir a la peluquería* to go to the hairdresser's.

peluquero, ra *m/f* hairdresser (para señoras), barber (para caballeros).

peluquín *m* toupee (peluca pequeña) ‖ — FIG & FAM *ni hablar del peluquín* out of the question | *tomarle el peluquín a uno* to pull s.o.'s leg.

pelusa *f* down (de planta) ‖ choke (de alcachofa) ‖ fluff (de telas) ‖ fluff, dust (suciedad) ‖ FAM jealousy (entre niños) ‖ — *soltar pelusa* to shed fluff (una tela) ‖ FAM *tener pelusa* to be jealous.

pelusilla *f* mouse-ear (planta) ‖ FAM jealousy (envidia).

pelviano, na; pélvico, ca *adj* ANAT pelvic.

pelvis *f* ANAT pelvis.

pella *f* round mass (masa redonda) ‖ lump, trowelful (de yeso, etc.) ‖ blob (de merengue) ‖ block; *pella de mantequilla* block of butter ‖ raw lard (manteca de cerdo) ‖ head (de coliflor) ‖ — FIG & FAM *hacer pella* to play truant [US to play hooky] (no asistir a clase) | *tener una pella de dinero* to have a pile of money.

pelleja *f* skin (pellejo) ‖ FAM bag of bones (persona flaca) | whore (ramera) ‖ — FIG & FAM *jugarse la pelleja* to risk one's neck | *salvar la pelleja* to save one's skin.

pellejería *f* tannery (curtiduría) ‖ skins *pl* (pieles).
◆ *pl* *AMER* trouble *sing* (dificultad).

pellejo *m* skin (piel) ‖ skin, hide (de animal) ‖ skin, peel (de fruta) ‖ wineskin (odre) ‖ FIG & FAM drunkard, boozer (borracho) ‖ — FIG & FAM *dar* or *dejar* or *perder el pellejo* to give *o* to lose one's life | *defender el pellejo* to defend one's life | *jugarse el pellejo, arriesgar el pellejo* to risk one's neck | *no caber en el pellejo* to be good and fat (estar muy gordo) | *no caber en el pellejo de gozo, de orgullo* to be overflowing with joy, to be bursting with pride | *ni quisiera estar* or *hallarme en su pellejo* I wouldn't want to be in his shoes | *no tener más que el pellejo* to be all skin and bones | *quitar a uno el pellejo* to bump s.o. off (matar), to gossip about s.o. (murmurar), to fleece s.o., to clean s.o. out (dejar sin dinero) | *salvar el pellejo* to save one's skin.

pellejudo, da *adj* loose-skinned, flabby-skinned.

pelliza *f* pelisse (de pieles) ‖ MIL dolman.

pellizcar *vt* to pinch; *pellizcarle a uno en la mejilla* to pinch s.o. on the cheek, to pinch s.o.'s cheek ‖ to take a pinch of (tomar un poco de) ‖ to nibble (at) (comer sin apetito).

pellizco *m* pinch (acción de pellizcar) ‖ bruise (hematoma) ‖ pinch, bit (pequeña porción) ‖ FIG sharp pain; *pellizco en el corazón* sharp pain in the heart ‖ — *dar* or *tirar un pellizco a uno* to give s.o. a pinch ‖ *darse* or *cogerse un pellizco* to get pinched ‖ *pellizco de monja* hard twisting pinch (con las uñas), macaroon (dulce).

pena *f* sorrow, grief (pesadumbre); *la muerte de su amigo le causó mucha pena* the death of his friend caused him great sorrow ‖ difficulty; *lo he hecho con mucha pena* I did it with great difficulty ‖ penalty, pain, punishment (castigo); *pena de muerte* death penalty ‖ FAM pain (dolor físico) ‖ penna (pluma de ave) ‖ MAR peak ‖ (ant) necklace, ribbon (cinta) ‖ *AMER* uneasiness, discomfort (malestar) ‖ — *ahorrarse la pena de* to save o.s. the trouble *o* the bother of ‖ *alma en pena* soul in torment ‖ *bajo* or *so pena de* under penalty of, under pain of ‖ *da pena que* it's a shame *o* a pity that ‖ *estar que da pena* to be in a sorry state *o* in a pitiful state ‖ *estos pobrecitos huérfanos me dan tanta pena* I feel so sorry for these poor little orphans ‖ *¡es una pena!, ¡qué pena!* it's a shame!, it's a pity!, what a shame!, what a pity!; *¡qué pena que no hayas venido antes!* what a shame you didn't arrive sooner; *es una pena que esté tan enferma* it's a pity that she is so ill ‖ *me da pena que no pueda venir a cenar con nosotros* I'm sorry that you can't come to dinner with us ‖ *me da pena verte tan triste* I'm sorry to see you so sad, it grieves me to see you so sad ‖ *merecer* or *valer la pena* to be worthwhile, to be worth it; *merece la pena* it is worth it; to be worth, to be worth the trouble; *merece la pena visitar la catedral* the cathedral is worth visiting *o* worth a visit, it is worth the trouble to pay a visit to the cathedral ‖ *morir de pena* to die of a brokenheart ‖ *no merece la pena molestarse* it's not worth bothering, it's not worth it ‖ FAM *pasar la pena negra* to go through hell ‖ *pena capital* capital punishment ‖ *pena infamante* penalty involving loss of civil rights ‖ *se lo di porque me dio pena* I gave it to him because I felt sorry for him ‖ *ser de pena* to be lamentable *o* pitiful ‖ *sería una pena dejarlo* it seems a shame to leave it ‖ *vale la pena verlo* it is worth seeing ‖ *vivir sin pena ni gloria* to live an uneventful life.
◆ *pl* hardships, toils (dificultades) ‖ torments (del infierno) ‖ — *a duras penas* with great difficulty ‖ *¡allá penas!* that's not my worry! ‖ *a penas* hardly, barely, scarcely.

penacho *m* tuft, crest (de aves) ‖ plume (de un morrión) ‖ FIG trail, plume (de humo) | arrogance, haughtiness (soberbia) ‖ MIL *penacho de plumas* plume.

penado, da *m/f* convict (delincuente).
◆ *adj* grieved, sad, sorrowful (triste) ‖ difficult (difícil).

penal *adj* penal; *código penal* penal code.
◆ *m* penitentiary, prison (penitenciaría).

penalidad *f* suffering, hardship (trabajos); *pasar muchas penalidades* to go through much hardship ‖ DEP penalty ‖ JUR penalty, punishment.

penalista *m/f* criminal lawyer (abogado) ‖ expert in criminal law (especialista en derecho penal).

penalización *f* sanction (castigo) ‖ penalty (deporte).

penalizar *vt* to penalize.

penalti *m* DEP penalty | penalty kick (rugby) ‖ *punto de penalti* penalty spot ‖ *casarse de penalti* to have a shotgun wedding.

penar *vt* to punish, to chastise.
◆ *vi* to suffer, to toil (padecer) ‖ — FIG *penar de amores* to be unhappy in love | *penar por una cosa* to long *o* to pine *o* to yearn for sth.

penates *m pl* penates (dioses) ‖ FAM *volver a los penates* to return home.

penca *f* BOT fleshy leaf | joint (hoja del nopal) ‖ whip (azote) ‖ *AMER* prickly pear (chumbera) | agave (pita).

penco *m* FAM hack, nag (jamelgo) ‖ agave (pita) ‖ FAM dope, ass (tonto).

pencón, ona *adj/s* [of *o* from] Concepción (Chile).
◆ *m/f* native *o* inhabitant of Concepción.

pendejada *f* FAM *AMER* foolishness, stupidity (tontería) ‖ cowardliness (cobardía).

pendejear *vi* to act the fool, to fool around.

pendejo *m* pubic hair ‖ *AMER* FIG & FAM coward (cobarde) | idiot, fool (imbécil).

pendencia *f* fight, quarrel, trouble (contienda); *armar una pendencia* to start a fight, to stir up trouble ‖ *se armó una pendencia* a fight broke out.

pendenciero, ra *adj* quarrelsome, pugnacious.
◆ *m/f* troublemaker.

pender *vi* to hang; *los frutos penden de las ramas* the fruit hangs from the branches ‖ to depend; *esto pende de su decisión* this depends on *o* upon his decision ‖ FIG to be pending (pleito, negocio) ‖ FIG *pender de un hilo* or *de un pelo* to be hanging by a thread.

pendiente *adj* hanging; *pendiente de una rama* hanging from a branch ‖ FIG pending; *problemas pendientes* pending problems; *pedidos pendientes* pending orders ‖ outstanding; *asuntos pendientes* outstanding business; *deudas pendientes* outstanding debts; *asignaturas pendientes* outstanding subjects ‖ sloping (inclinado) ‖ — FIG *dejar pendiente a uno* to fail s.o. (en un examen) | *estar pendiente* to be pending (no estar resuelto) | *estar pendiente de* to depend on (depender), to be waiting for; *estoy pendiente de su decisión* I am waiting for your decision; to be always glued to; *estar pendiente*

de la televisión to be always glued to the television; to be on the watch for; *estar pendiente de los errores de uno* to be on the watch for s.o.'s mistakes | *estar pendiente de los labios de alguien* to hang on s.o.'s every word | *estar pendiente de un cabello* to be hanging by a thread.
◆ *f* slope, gradient (cuesta); *pendiente suave, pronunciada* or *empinada* gentle *o* slight, steep slope || slope (de un monte) || pitch (de un tejado) || — *en pendiente* sloping || FIG *estar en la pendiente del vicio* to be sinking into vice || FIG & FAM *remontar la pendiente* to get back on one's feet.
◆ *m* earring (joya para las orejas) || pendant (colgante) || MIN top.

péndola *f* pendulum (péndulo) || pendulum clock (reloj) || ARQ queen post (de un tejado) | suspension cable (de un puente colgante) || quill, pen (pluma).

pendolón *m* ARQ king post.

pendón *m* banner, standard (insignia militar o de cofradía) || pennon (insignia feudal) || tiller, shoot (de un árbol) || FIG & FAM whore, tart (mujer de mala vida) | lanky woman (mujer desgarbada) | rat, rotter (sinvergüenza).

pendona *f* FIG & FAM whore, tart.

pendonear *vi* FAM to gallivant, to gad about.

pendular *adj* pendular.

péndulo, la *adj* hanging (colgante).
◆ *m* pendulum (cuerpo oscilante, de reloj).

pene *m* ANAT penis.

penene *m/f* school or university teacher working without tenure.

peneque *adj* FAM drunk (borracho).

penetrabilidad *f* penetrability.

penetrable *adj* penetrable || FIG understandable (fácil de entender).

penetración *f* penetration || MIL breakthrough || FIG insight (sagacidad).

penetrante *adj* penetrating || deep (herida) || FIG piercing, shrill (voz) | sharp, keen, acute (inteligencia) | biting, piercing (frío) | searching, penetrating (mirada) | sharp (arma).

penetrar *vt* to penetrate, to pierce || FIG to pierce; *la respuesta penetró en su corazón* the answer pierced him to the heart | to find out, to penetrate; *penetrar un secreto* to find out a secret | to fathom, to penetrate (un misterio) || FIG *estar penetrado de las ideas de* to be imbued with the ideas of.
◆ *vi* to penetrate, to go into; *penetrar en la selva* to penetrate into the forest || to enter, to go in; *penetrar en un cuarto* to enter a room || FIG *el frío penetra en los huesos* the cold gets right into one's bones.
◆ *vpr* to become aware; *penetrarse de la realidad de un hecho* to become aware of the reality of a fact || to steep o.s. (*de* in) (un tema) || to imbibe (de unas ideas).

penicilina *f* MED penicillin.

penicillium *m* penicillium (moho).

penillanura *f* GEOGR peneplain, peneplane.

Peninos *npr mpl* GEOGR Pennines || *montes Peninos* Pennine Chain, Pennines.

península *f* GEOGR peninsula; *la península Ibérica* the Iberian Peninsula || isthmus (istmo).

peninsular *adj/s* peninsular.

penique *m* penny (moneda inglesa, que desde 1971 representa la centésima parte de la libra esterlina en vez de la doscientas cuarentava parte anteriormente).
— OBSERV *Penny* hace en plural *pence* cuando se trata del valor de la moneda y *pennies* si se refiere a la misma moneda. Dos peniques se traduce por *two pennies, twopence* o *tuppence* según el caso: tres peniques por *three pennies, threepence* o *thruppence*; medio penique se dice *half penny* o *ha'penny* y medios peniques *half-pennies, ha'pennies, halfpence* o *ha'pence*. Por otra parte, la palabra *pence* va siempre unida con las cifras de la decena: *fivepence, ninepence*, etc. Ejemplo: *there are four pennies on the table* (cuatro monedas de un penique), *there is fourpence on the table* (monedas por un valor de cuatro peniques).

penitencia *f* penitence (sentimiento) || penance (castigo) || *como penitencia* as penance || *cumplir la penitencia* to do penance || *en penitencia* as a penance || *hacer penitencia* to do penance (un pecador), to share a modest meal; *venga a casa a hacer penitencia* come over to my place to share a modest meal || *imponer una penitencia a uno* to give s.o. a penance.

penitenciado, da *adj* condemned by the Inquisition || AMER imprisoned (encarcelado).

penitencial *adj* penitential.

penitenciar *vt* to impose penance on.

penitenciaría *f* penitentiary (tribunal eclesiástico en Roma, cárcel) || office of penitentiary (cargo de penitenciario).

penitenciario, ria *adj* penitentiary; *régimen penitenciario* penitentiary system.
◆ *m* REL penitentiary, confessor.

penitente *adj/s* penitent.

Penjab *npr m* Punjab.

penol *m* MAR yardarm (de verga) | peak (de antena).

penoso, sa *adj* laborious, toilsome, arduous, hard; *un trabajo penoso* a laborious job || distressing, sorry, lamentable (lamentable) || burdensome (pesado) || grieved, distressed (afligido).

penquisto, ta *adj* [of *o* from] Concepción [Chile].
◆ *m/f* native *o* inhabitant of Concepción.

pensado, da *adj* thought || thought-out (reflexionado) || — *bien pensado* well-intentioned (persona), considered, well thought-out (cosa) || *bien pensado, no vale la pena* after thinking it over, *o* all things considered, it's not worth it || *de pensado* on purpose (de intento) || *el día menos pensado* when least expected, any day || *en el momento menos pensado* when least expected || *¡no seas mal pensado!* don't be so evil-minded || *tener pensado algo* to have sth. in mind, to be planning sth., to be thinking of sth || *una solución mal pensada* a poorly thought-out solution, an unthinking solution.

pensador, ra *adj* thinking.
◆ *m/f* thinker || *libre pensador* freethinker.

pensamiento *m* thought (facultad) || thought (ideas); *el pensamiento de Platón* Plato's thought || mind (mente) || maxim, saying (sentencia) || FIG suspicion (sospecha) || BOT pansy (flor) || — *adivinar los pensamientos de uno* to read s.o.'s thoughts || FIG *como el pensamiento* in a flash || *con el pensamiento puesto en* with the idea of || *libertad de pensamiento* freedom of thought || *libre pensamiento* free thought || *ni por pensamiento* I wouldn't think of it || *no pasarle a uno por el pensamiento* not to cross one's mind, not to occur to one || *venirle a uno al pensamiento* to come to mind.

pensante *adj* thinking.

pensar* *vt/vi* to think; *¿pensarán los animales?* are animals able to think?; *pensar mucho* to think hard; *pensar en todo* to think of everything || to think (over), to think (about); *piensa bien este problema* think this problem over well, think carefully about this problem; *piénsalo* think it over, think about it || to think (about); *¿en qué piensas?* what are you thinking about? || to intend, to think (tener intención); *pienso salir mañana* I intend to go out *o* I am thinking of going out tomorrow || to devise, to design, to plan (concebir); *pensado para durar mucho* planned to last a long time || — *dar (a uno) que pensar* to make one think || *llegó cuando menos se pensaba* he arrived when least expected || *¡ni lo piense!* forget it, don't dream of it || *¡ni pensarlo!* not by any means!, not a bit of it! || *pensándolo mejor* or *bien* on second thoughts, on reflection || *pensar bien, mal de* to think well, badly of || FIG & FAM *pensar con los pies* to talk through one's hat || *pensar en lo peor* to think the worst || *pensarlo mucho* to think it over || *pensar que* to think that || *piense lo que piense* whatever you think || *pienso, luego existo* I think, therefore I am || *sin pensar, sin pensarlo* without thinking, without stopping to think || *sólo con pensarlo* just thinking about it || *tendría que pensarlo dos veces antes de hacerlo* you should think twice before doing that.

pensativo, va *adj* pensive, thoughtful.

Pensilvania *npr f* GEOGR Pennsylvania.

pensilvano, na *adj/s* Pennsylvanian.

pensión *f* pension; *pensión de retiro* retirement pension || board and lodging (en un hotel), charge for board and lodging (precio) || boardinghouse (casa de huéspedes) || boarding school (colegio) || FIG & FAM burden (gravamen) || — *cobrar la pensión* to draw one's pension (persona jubilada) || *media pensión* partial board || *pensión alimenticia* alimony, allowance for necessities || *pensión completa* full board || *pensión de viudedad* widow's pension || *pensión pasiva* State pension, pension || *pensión vitalicia* life annuity.

pensionado, da *adj* pensioned.
◆ *m/f* pensioner.
◆ *m* boarding school (colegio).

pensionar *vt* to pension, to give a pension.

pensionista *m/f* boarder (de colegio) || pensioner (del Estado) || *medio pensionista* day pupil, day student, student who has lunch at school.

pentaedro *m* pentahedron.

pentagonal *adj* pentagonal.

pentágono, na *adj* MAT pentagonal.
◆ *m* pentagon.

pentagrama; pentágrama *m* MÚS stave, staff.

pentarquía *f* pentarchy.

pentasílabo, ba *adj* pentasyllabic.
◆ *m* pentasyllable.

Pentateuco *m* Pentateuch (libro sagrado).

pentatlón *m* DEP pentathlon.

Pentecostés *m* Whitsun, Whitsuntide; *en* or *por Pentecostés* at Whitsun || Pentecost (fiesta hebraica) || *Domingo de Pentecostés* Whitsunday, Pentecost.

pentedecágono *m* MAT pentadecagon.

pentodo *m* FÍS pentode.

pentotal *m* MED Pentothal.

penúltimo, ma *adj/s* penultimate, last but one, next to last.

penumbra *f* ASTR penumbra || semi-obscurity, shadow, semi-darkness, half light.

penuria *f* penury, shortage, scarcity (escasez) || poverty, need (miseria).

peña *f* rock (roca) || circle, group (de amigos) || FIG *ser una peña* to have a heart of stone.

peñaranda (en) *loc* FAM in pawn [*US* in hock] (empeñado).

peñascal *m* rocky ground.

peñasco *m* large rock, crag (roca) || ANAT petrosal bone (del oído) || ZOOL murex (molusco).

peñascoso, sa *adj* rocky, craggy.

péñola *f* quill, pen.

peñón *m* rock; *el peñón de Gibraltar* the Rock of Gibraltar.

peo *m* POP fart (pedo).

peón *m* unskilled labourer [*US* unskilled laborer] (obrero no especializado) || farm labourer, farmhand (en una granja o en una hacienda) || pawn (ajedrez) || piece, man (damas) || TECN spindle (árbol) || MIL foot soldier (infante) || TAUR assistant || (p us) pedestrian (peatón) || — *peón caminero* navvy, roadman || *peón de albañil* hod carrier, hodman, building labourer.

peonada *f* day's work [of a labourer] (trabajo) || *AMER* gang of workers *o* labourers (obreros).

peonaje *m* MIL fot soldiers *pl* || gang of workers (obreros).

peonar *vi* *AMER* to be a labourer.

peonería *f* day's ploughing (tierra labrada).

peonía *f* peony (planta).

peonza *f* top (trompo) || — FIG & FAM *bailar como una peonza* to spin like a top | *ser una peonza* to be always on the move, to be fidgety, not to be able to keep still.

peor *adj* worse (comparativo); *tu ejercicio es peor que el suyo* your exercise is worse than his || worst (superlativo); *llevarse la peor parte* to get the worst part.
◆ *adv* worse; *peor que nunca* worse than ever || — *cada vez peor* worse and worse, from bad to worse || *en el peor de los casos, poniéndose en el peor de los casos* at worst, if the worst comes to the worst || *lo peor* the worst thing || *peor para ti, para él* that's too bad; that's your, his lookout || *peor que peor* worse still, so much the worse, worse and worse || *tanto peor* too bad, so much the worse || *y lo que es peor* and what is more *o* worse.

Pepa *npr f* (diminutivo de *Josefa* Josephine) Josie || *¡viva la Pepa!* hurrah! (expresa alegría), I'll be damned! (expresa desaprobación).

Pepe *npr m* (diminutivo de *José* Joseph) Joe.

pepinar *m* cucumber patch.

pepinazo *m* FIG & FAM explosion, blast (explosión) | shell (obús) | cannonball shot (en fútbol).

pepinillo *m* gherkin (planta y fruto).

pepino *m* BOT cucumber || FAM shell (obús) || — FIG & FAM *no importar un pepino* not to matter | *(no) me importa un pepino* or *tres pepinos* I couldn't care less, I don't give a hang | *no valer un pepino* not to be worth a brass farthing *o* a damn || BOT *pepino del diablo* squirting cucumber.

pepita *f* seed, pip (de fruto) || nugget (de oro) || pip (enfermedad de las gallinas) || *AMER* seed (de cacao).

Pepita *npr f* (diminutivo de *«Pepa»*) Josie.

pepito *m* small meat sandwich (bocadillo).

Pepito *npr m* (diminutivo de *«Pepe»*) Joey.

pepitoria *f* fricassee [prepared with egg yolk]; *pollo en pepitoria* chicken fricassee || FIG jumble (desorden).

pepla *f* FAM nuisance; *¡qué pepla tener que salir ahora!* what a nuisance having to go out now!

peplo *m* peplum (túnica antigua).

pepona *f* large paper doll (muñeca) || FIG *se pinta como una pepona* she paints herself like a doll.

pepsina *f* QUÍM pepsin.

peque *m/f* FAM child.

pequeñajo, ja *adj* FAM small.
◆ *m/f* small person; *es una pequeñaja* she's a small girl || child (niño).

pequeñez *f* smallness, littleness, small size (tamaño) || infancy (infancia) || tender age (corta edad) || FIG meanness (mezquindad) | slightest thing (cosa insignificante); *una pequeñez le asusta* the slightest thing frightens him | trifle; *no pararse* or *no reparar en pequeñeces* not to stop at trifles || *pequeñez de miras* narrow-mindedness.

pequeñín, ina; pequeñuelo, la *adj* very small, very little, tiny.
◆ *m/f* child, tot.

pequeño, ña *adj* small, little (persona, cosa) || young (de poca edad) || short (bajo, corto).
◆ *m/f* child (niño) || youngest; *en casa soy el pequeño* in my family I am the youngest || small person (persona pequeña) || — *de pequeño* as a child, when one was small || FIG *dejar pequeño* to put in the shade || *el hijo más pequeño* the youngest son || *los infinitamente pequeños* the infinitely small || *pequeño burgués* petit bourgeois, lower middle-class || *reproducción en pequeño* scale model.
— OBSERV *Pequeño* generally follows the noun: *un libro pequeño* a small book.

pequeñuelo, la *adj/s* → **pequeñín.**

Pequín *n pr* GEOGR Peking.

pequinés, esa *adj/s* Pekinese, Pekingese.

per *prep* *per cápita* per capita.

pera *f* pear (fruto); *pera de agua* juicy pear || goatee (barba) || pear-shaped switch (interruptor eléctrico) || FIG sinecure, cushy job (empleo) || — FIG & FAM *estar como pera* or *como perita en dulce* to be pampered like a baby | *no partir peras con nadie* not to become overfriendly with anybody | *partir peras con uno* to be very friendly with s.o. | *pedir peras al olmo* to ask for the impossible | *ponerle a uno las peras al cuarto* to clamp down on s.o.
◆ *adj* smartly dressed (elegante).

peral *m* pear tree (árbol).

peraleda *f* pear orchard.

peraltar *vt* ARQ to stilt (un arco) || TECN to bank (carreteras); *curva peraltada* banked curve.

peralte *m* ARQ superelevation || superelevation, banking (en las carreteras).

perborato *m* QUÍM perborate.

perca *f* ZOOL perch (pez).

percal *m* percale, calico (tejido) || FIG *conocer bien el percal* to know one's stuff.

percalina *f* percaline (tela).

percance *m* mishap, setback, misfortune (contratiempo) || perquisite, profit (provecho) || *los percances del oficio* the drawbacks of the job.

percatarse *vpr* to notice, to perceive; *me he percatado del peligro* I have noticed the danger || to realize (comprender); *se percató de la importancia del asunto* he realized the importance of the matter.

percebe *m* goose barnacle (molusco) || FIG & FAM fool, dope (necio).

percepción *f* perception (sensación), idea, notion (idea) || collection (de dinero).

percepcionismo *m* perceptionism.

perceptibilidad *f* perceptibility (sensación).

perceptible *adj* perceptible, perceivable, noticeable (que se siente o que es visible) || payable, receivable, collectable (que se cobra).

perceptivo, va *adj* perceptive; *facultades perceptivas* perceptive faculties.

percibible *adj* payable, collectable (cobrable).

percibir *vt* to perceive, to notice, to sense (sentir); *percibió un ruido leve* he perceived a faint sound || to collect, to receive (cobrar dinero).

perclorato *m* QUÍM perchlorate.

percloruro *m* QUÍM perchloride.

percolador *m* percolator.

percusión *f* percussion; *instrumentos de percusión* percussion instruments; *arma de percusión* percussion gun || MED percussion.

percusor; percutor *m* hammer, firing pin (de un arma) || MED plexor || striker, hammer (en general).

percutir *vt* to strike, to hit || MED to percuss.

percutor *m* → **percusor.**

percha *f* hanger, clothes hanger, coat hanger (para colgar ropa, etc.) || clothes rack (colgador fijo en la pared) || perch (de las aves) || rack (para utensilios) || perch (perca, pez) || FIG & FAM *tener buena percha* to have a good physique, to be well-built.

perchero *m* clothes rack (percha).

percherón, ona *adj/s* Percheron (caballo de tiro).

perdedor, ra *adj* losing.
◆ *m/f* loser; *buen, mal perdedor* good, bad loser.

perder* *vt* to lose (un libro, una fortuna, la vida, un combate, etc.); *perdió mucho dinero en el juego* he lost a lot of money gambling; *perder a su padre* to lose one's father; *he perdido mi monedero* I have lost my purse || to waste (malgastar, desperdiciar, no aprovechar); *perder el tiempo en detalles* to waste time on details; *sin perder un momento* without wasting a moment; *no pierdas energía con esto* don't waste your energy on that || to miss (el tren, el avión, etc.); *si no nos damos prisa perderemos el barco* if we do not hurry we shall miss the boat || to miss, to waste (una oportunidad); *perdí la ocasión* I missed my chance; *no debes perder una oportunidad tan buena* you mustn't waste such a good opportunity || to lose (el respeto) || to forget (la cortesía) || to get out of, to get rid of, to shake, to break (una costumbre) || to damage, to harm (dañar) || to spoil (estropear) || to ruin (arruinar) || — FIG & FAM *andar* or *estar perdido por uno* to be crazy about s.o., to be head over heels in love with s.o. || *dar algo por perdido* to give sth. up as lost || *el que todo lo quiere, todo lo pierde* the more you want, the less you get || *hasta perder la respiración* until one is out of breath; *corrió hasta perder la respiración* he ran until he was out of breath || *no hay tiempo que perder* there is *o* we have no time to lose || *no perder de vista a alguien* not to lose sight of s.o., not to let s.o. out of one's sight, not to take one's eyes off s.o. || *no tener nada que perder* to have nothing to lose || FIG *perder el color* to turn pale, to grow pale (una persona) | *perder el juicio* or *la razón* to take leave of one's senses, to go out of one's mind, to lose one's mind || *perder la esperanza* to lose hope || FIG *perder la cabeza* to lose one's head | *perder los estribos* or *el dominio de sí mismo* to lose one's temper, to fly off the handle (perder el control), to lose one's head (perder la serenidad) || *perder pie* to lose one's footing, to slip (caerse), to go out of one's depth (en el agua), to lose one's way (confundirse) || *perder terreno* to lose ground || *perder unos kilos* to lose a little weight (una persona) || JUR *perder un pleito* to lose a case.
◆ *vi* to lose (no ganar); *perdimos* we lost || to leak (un recipiente) || to depreciate, to lose its value (el dinero) || *salir perdiendo* to lose, to lose out, to be the loser, to come off worst.
◆ *vpr* to get lost, to lose one's way (una persona) || to be lost (una cosa) || to lose, to mislay; *se le pierde todo* he loses everything || to be lost (no oírse, no verse) || to disappear, to die out (desaparecer) || to be wasted, to go

to waste (desperdiciarse) || to get lost *o* confused (enmarañarse) || to be ruined *o* spoiled (estropearse) || to go to the bad (corromperse una persona) || — *el barco se alejó hasta perderse de vista* the boat (moved off and) disappeared into the distance || *es capaz de perderse por el dinero* there is nothing he wouldn't do for money || *los tulipanes se extendían hasta perderse de vista* tulips stretched as far as the eye could see || *¡no te lo pierdas!* don't miss it! || FIG *perderse por alguien* to be crazy about s.o. | *¡tú te lo pierdes!* that's your lookout, that's your hard luck.

perdición *f* loss || FIG ruin, undoing; *ir uno a su perdición* to go to one's ruin | ruin, undoing, ruination; *será tu perdición* it will be the ruin of you, it will be your undoing *o* your ruination | dissipation (disipación) || REL perdition, damnation.

pérdida *f* loss; *la pérdida del paraguas* the loss of the umbrella; *sentir la pérdida de alguien* to regret the loss of s.o. || waste (de tiempo, de esfuerzos) || leak, leakage (de un líquido, del aire) || ruin, destruction (ruina) || damage, harm (daño) || — *no tiene pérdida* you can't miss it (al indicar una dirección) || *pérdida del sentido* or *del conocimiento* loss of consciousness | *vender con pérdida* to sell at a loss.
◆ *pl* MIL losses, casualties (bajas) || COM *pérdidas y ganancias* profit and loss.

perdidamente *adv* madly, desperately, hopelessly (con exceso); *perdidamente enamorado (de)* madly in love (with) || uselessly (inútilmente).

perdido, da *adj* lost || stray (una bala) || idle, spare, odd (momentos, ratos) || isolated (lugar) || wasted (esfuerzo, tiempo) || lost, ruined (cosecha) || loose (mujer) || wrapped up, lost, absorbed (en los pensamientos) || hopelessly ill (enfermo) || FAM filthy (muy sucio) || covered; *estar perdido de barro* to be covered with mud || confirmed, inveterate, incorrigible; *un borracho perdido* a confirmed drunkard || — *a fondo perdido* at one's own expense, with no hope of retrieving it || *a ratos perdidos* in one's spare moments || *depósito* or *oficina de objetos perdidos* lost property office [US lost and found office] || FIG *estar perdido por* to be crazy about || FIG & FAM *estar más perdido que Carracuca* to have no way out, to be doomed, to be hopelessly lost || *loco perdido* raving mad || *trabajo perdido* wasted effort *o* work.
◆ *m* FAM scamp, rake (golfo) || IMPR overplus printing || *hacerse el perdido* to hide.

perdigón *m* young partridge (pollo de perdiz) || decoy (perdiz que sirve de reclamo) || small shot (munición) || FAM spendthrift, wastrel, waster (derrochador) | loser (en juegos) | saliva (saliva) | bit of snot (moco) | failure, failed student (suspendido) || FAM *echar perdigones* to splutter, to spray saliva.

perdigonada *f* discharge of small shot, shot (tiro de perdigones) || shot wound (herida).

perdigonera *f* ammunition *o* shot pouch.

perdiguero, ra *adj* partridge-hunting || *perro perdiguero* setter.
◆ *m* game dealer (el que vende caza).

perdis *m* FAM rake (calavera).

perdiz *f* partridge || — *perdiz blanca* rock ptarmigan || FIG *y vivieron felices, comieron perdices y a mí no me dieron* and they lived happily ever after (al final de un cuento).

perdón *m* pardon, forgiveness; *pedir perdón de* to beg pardon for || REL pardon || — *con perdón, con perdón de los presentes* by your leave, if you don't mind || *con perdón sea dicho* no offense meant, if you will pardon my saying so || *pedir perdón a uno* to apologize to s.o. || *¡perdón!* sorry!, I beg your pardon!

perdonable *adj* pardonable, forgivable.

perdonar *vt/vi* to excuse, to pardon, to forgive (dispensar, disculpar); *perdone la molestia* excuse me for bothering you; *perdone, pero creo que no es así* excuse me but I think you are mistaken || to miss (perder, dejar); *no perdonar un baile, una ocasión* not to miss a dance, a chance || to overlook (omitir); *no perdonar un detalle* not to overlook a detail || to spare (un esfuerzo) || to shirk from, to let go by (no aprovechar); *no perdonar medio de enriquecerse* not to shirk from any means of getting rich || to forgo, to renounce (renunciar) || to exempt, to excuse (exceptuar) || — *perdonarle la vida a uno* to spare s.o.'s life || *¡perdone usted!* pardon me!, I beg your pardon!, sorry! || *que Dios lo haya perdonado* may God have mercy on him.

perdonavidas *m inv* FIG & FAM bully, braggart (valentón).

perdulario, ria *adj* careless, negligent (descuidado) || forgetful (olvidadizo) || vicious (vicioso).
◆ *m/f* sloven (descuidado) || rogue (pillo) || rake (disoluto).

perdurabilidad *f* eternal nature, unending nature, everlasting nature (de lo eterno) || perdurability, durability (de lo duradero).

perdurable *adj* eternal, everlasting, unending, imperishable (eterno) || lasting, perdurable (duradero) || incessant, endless (incesante).

perdurablemente *adj* eternally.

perdurar *vi* to last a long time, to last (durar) || to subsist (subsistir).

perecedero, ra *adj* perishable; *bienes perecederos* perishable goods || mortal (mortal) || temporal, transient, transitory (que ha de acabarse).

perecer* *vi* to perish || to die (morir).
◆ *vpr perecerse por* to be dying to (seguido de infinitivo), to be dying for (seguido de sustantivo).

perecimiento *m* disappearance (desaparición) || death (muerte) || end (fin).

perecuación *f* proportional distribution (de las cargas).

peregrinación *f* pilgrimage (viaje) || pilgrimage (a un santuario); *ir en peregrinación a Santiago de Compostela* to go on a pilgrimage to Santiago de Compostela.

peregrinaje *m* (p us) pilgrimage.

peregrinamente *adv* peculiarly, strangely (de un modo raro).

peregrinante *adj* travelling [US traveling].
◆ *m* pilgrim (peregrino).

peregrinar *vi* to go on a pilgrimage || to travel, to journey, to peregrinate (por tierras extrañas) || FIG to go to and fro.

peregrino, na *adj* travelling [US traveling] (que viaja) || migrating (aves) || exotic, strange (exótico) || FIG peculiar, singular, odd, strange (extraño); *una idea peregrina* a peculiar idea.
◆ *m/f* pilgrim (que va a un santuario).

perejil *m* BOT parsley.

perendengue; pelendengue *m* cheap ornament, trinket (adorno) || earring (arete).

Perengano, na *m/f* so-and-so || *Mengano y Perengano* so-and-so and what's-his-name.
— OBSERV The word *Perengano* is only used after the nouns *Fulano* and *Mengano* to indicate a name which one has forgotten.

perenne *adj* BOT perennial (planta) | evergreen (hojas) || perennial (manantial) || FIG perennial, everlasting; *belleza perenne* perennial beauty.

perennemente *adv* perennially, perpetually || forever, for ever (siempre, constantemente).

perennidad *f* perenniality, perpetuity.

perentoriamente *adv* peremptorily (terminantemente) || urgently, pressingly (urgentemente).

perentoriedad *f* peremptoriness || urgency.

perentorio, ria *adj* peremptory (terminante); *con tono perentorio* in a peremptory tone || peremptory, pressing, urgent (apremiante) || — JUR *excepción perentoria* peremptory plea, demurrer || *plazo perentorio* strict time limit.

pereza *f* laziness, sloth, indolence, idleness (holgazanería) || ZOOL sloth (perezoso) || — *me da pereza ir a* I can't be bothered *o* it's too much trouble going to || *pereza mental* mental laziness, sluggishness of mind || *sacudir la pereza* to shake off one's laziness || *tener pereza* to feel *o* to be lazy.

perezosamente *adv* lazily || sluggishly, slowly, without hurrying, unhurriedly (lentamente).

perezoso, sa *adj* lazy, slothful, indolent, idle (holgazán) || FIG sluggish, slow-moving, slow (lento); *arroyo perezoso* sluggish stream.
◆ *m/f* lazybones, loafer, idler, sluggard, lazy person (holgazán).
◆ *m* ZOOL sloth (desdentado) || FIG *ni corto ni perezoso* without thinking twice.

perfección *f* perfection; *canta a la perfección* she sings to perfection || *a la perfección* to perfection, perfectly.

perfeccionador, ra *adj* perfectioning || improving (que mejora).

perfeccionamiento *m* perfection, perfecting || improvement, betterment (mejora) || further training (estudios).

perfeccionar *vt* to perfect, to bring to perfection (hacer perfecto) || to improve, to (make) better (mejorar) || to brush up (sus conocimientos) || to finish off (acabar).

perfeccionismo *m* perfectionism.

perfeccionista *m/f* perfectionist.

perfectamente *adv* perfectly.
◆ *interj* right!, quite!, agreed!, of course!

perfecto, ta *adj* perfect (excelente) || FIG perfect (absoluto); *un perfecto imbécil* a perfect idiot || — GRAM *futuro perfecto* future perfect | *pretérito perfecto* perfect, present perfect.

perfidia *f* perfidy, treachery.

pérfido, da *adj* perfidious, treacherous.

perfil *m* profile (parte lateral); *perfil izquierdo* left profile; *ver a uno de perfil* to see s.o. in profile || profile, contour, outline, silhouette (contorno); *el perfil de un caballo* the outline of a horse || upstroke, thin stroke (de las letras) || FIG profile, portrait (retrato moral) || section, cross section (de un plano) || profile, vertical section (geología) || TECN profile || — *de perfil* in profile, from the side || *perfil del puesto* job description || *retrato de medio perfil* three-quarter-face *o* semi-profile portrait || *vista de perfil* side view, profile.
◆ *pl* FIG attentions, courtesies (miramientos) | refinement *sing* (delicadeza) | finishing touches (retoques) | features, characteristics (aspectos) || *tomar perfiles* to trace.

perfilado, da *adj* in profile (de perfil) || outlined (dibujado) || long and thin (rostro) || perfect, well-shaped, regular (boca, nariz, etc.) || TECN streamlined (coche, etc.).
◆ *m* profile (perfil) || TECN streamlining.

perfilar *vt* to profile, to draw in profile || to outline (contorno) || FIG to shape (dar forma) | to polish, to apply the finishing touches to (rematar) || TECN to streamline (coche, avión, etc.).
◆ *vpr* to present one's profile, to turn sideways || FIG to take shape *o* definite form; *los proyectos se perfilan* the plans are taking shape | to be outlined, to stand out; *el campanario se*

perfilaba en el cielo the belfry was outlined *o* stood out against the sky | to titivate o.s. (aderezarse) || TAUR to prepare for the kill.

perfoliado, da *adj* BOT perfoliate.

perforación *f* perforation, piercing || TECN punch hole, perforation (taladro en tarjetas, etc.) | boring, drilling (de barrenos, pozos de petróleo, etc.) || MED perforation.

perforado *m* perforation || TECN punching, perforating (de tarjetas) | boring, drilling (minería).

perforador, ra *adj* perforating || TECN punching, perforating (de tarjetas) | boring, drilling (minería).
◆ *m/f* perforator || TECN puncher (de tarjetas) | borer, driller (minería).
◆ *f* borer, drill, drilling machine (minería) || punch, punching machine (de tarjetas, etc.).

perforante *adj* perforating.

perforar *vt* to perforate, to pierce || to go *o* to pass *o* to run through, to pierce; *un túnel que perfora una montaña* a tunnel which runs through a mountain || TECN to punch, to perforate (tarjetas, etc.) | to bore, to drill; *perforar un agujero en la pared, un túnel en el monte* to bore a hole in the wall, a tunnel through the mountain || MED *úlcera perforada* perforating ulcer.

performance *f* performance (resultado notable).

perfumadero *m* perfume pan, cassolette (pebetero).

perfumador *m* perfume pan (pebetero) || perfume atomizer (pulverizador).

perfumar *vt* to perfume, to scent.
◆ *vi* to be fragrant, to perfume.
◆ *vpr* to perfume o.s., to scent o.s. || *se perfuma demasiado* she uses too much perfume.

perfume *m* perfume, scent (de tocador) || perfume, fragance, aroma, scent (aroma).

perfumería *f* perfumery (fabricación, tienda) || perfumery, perfume (productos).

perfumero, ra; perfumista *m/f* perfumer.

perfusión *f* MED perfusion.

pergamino *m* parchment.
◆ *pl* FIG & FAM titles of nobility, title deeds (títulos de nobleza) | diploma *sing* [US sheepskin *sing*] (diploma).

pergeñar *vt* to rough out, to sketch out (diseñar) || to prepare (un texto) || to arrange (arreglar).

pergeño *m* look, appearance (apariencia).

pérgola *f* pergola (emparrado) || rooftop garden (sobre la techumbre).

periantio *m* BOT perianth.

pericardio *m* ANAT pericardium.

pericarpio *m* BOT pericarp.

pericia *f* expertness, expertise (saber) || skill, expertise, dexterity (práctica).

pericial *adj* expert, expert's, experts'; *dictamen, tasación pericial* expert's advice, appraisal; *informe pericial* expert report.

periclitar *vi* to be in danger *o* in jeopardy (peligrar) || to decline (decaer).

perico *m* parakeet, parrakeet (ave) || toupee (peluca) || chamberport, jerry (*fam*), chamberport, jerry (orinal) || MAR mizzen topgallant mast (palo) *o* sail (vela).

Perico *npr m* (diminutivo de «*Pedro*») FAM Pete || — FIG & FAM *más duro que la pata de Perico* as hard as iron (en general), as tough as leather (carne) || FAM *Perico el de los palotes* John Smith [US Joe Doe], any Tom, Dick or Harry || *Perico entre ellas* lady's man, ladies' man.

pericón *m* popular Argentinian dance (baile).

pericráneo *m* ANAT pericranium.

peridoto *m* MIN peridot.

periferia *f* MAT periphery | periphery, outskirts *pl* (de una población).

periférico, ca *adj* peripheric, peripheral || outlying (barrio).
◆ *m* INFORM peripheral.

perifollo *m* BOT chervil.
◆ *pl* FIG & FAM frills, trimmings, frippery *sing* (adorno).

perifrasear *vi* to periphrase.

perífrasis *f inv* periphrasis (circunloquio).

perifrástico, ca *adj* periphrastic.

perigeo *m* ASTR perigee.

perilla *f* goatee [beard] (barbilla) || (pear-shaped) switch (interruptor eléctrico) || pear-shaped ornament (adorno) || lobe (de oreja) || pommel (de silla de montar) || — FIG & FAM *¡de perilla!, ¡de perillas!* great!, splendid! | *venirle a uno de perilla* or *de perillas* to come in very handy (ser muy útil), to suit s.o. to a tee, to suit s.o. down to the ground (convenirle), to come just at the right moment for s.o. (en el momento oportuno).

perillán *m* FAM rascal, little monkey, rogue.

perimétrico, ca *adj* perimetric.

perímetro *m* MAT perimeter || *perímetro de caderas* hip measurement.

perinatal *adj* perinatal.

perinatología *f* MED perinatology.

perineo *m* ANAT perineum.

perinola *f* teetotum (juguete).

periodicidad *f* periodicity.

periódico, ca *adj* periodic, periodical; *el movimiento periódico de los planetas* the periodic motion of the planets || recurrent (fiebre) || periodical (publicación) || MAT *fracción periódica* recurring decimal.
◆ *m* newspaper (diario); *puesto de periódicos* newspaper stand; *periódico de la tarde* evening newspaper || periodical (revista, etc.).

periodicucho *m* FAM rag (periódico malo).

periodismo *m* journalism.

periodista *m/f* journalist, newspaperman (hombre), journalist, newspaperwoman (mujer), reporter, pressman (hombre), reporter, presswoman (mujer).

periodístico, ca *adj* journalistic (estilo, etc.) || *artículo periodístico* newspaper article.

período; periodo *m* period, time; *el período de (las) vacaciones* the holiday period || period, era, age (época) || ASTR period; *período lunar* lunar period || GEOL period, cycle || MED period (menstruación, fase de una enfermedad) || MAT period || MÚS & GRAM period || FÍS period || — *período de arrendamiento* duration *o* term of a lease || ECON *período de carencia* qualifying period || *período de prácticas* probationary period, period of instruction, training || *período de sesiones* session, sitting (de una asamblea).

periostio *m* ANAT periosteum.

peripatético, ca *adj* FIL peripatetic || FIG & FAM ridiculous [in one's opinions or assertions].
◆ *m/f* FIL peripatetic.
◆ *f* FAM streetwalker (ramera).

peripatetismo *m* peripateticism.

peripecia *f* peripeteia, peripetia, vicissitude (cambio de fortuna) || incident (incidente) || adventure (aventura) || drama.

periplo *m* periplus (p us), tour.

peripuesto, ta *adj* FAM spruced up, dressed up, dolled up (ataviado) || FIG *estar muy peripuesto* to be dressed up to the nines, to be all dolled up.

periquete *m* FAM *en un periquete* in a tick, in a jiffy, in no time.

periquito *m* parakeet, parrakeet (ave).

periscópico, ca *adj* periscopic.

periscopio *m* periscope.

perisístole *f* MED perisystole.

perista *m/f* receiver [of stolen goods].

peristáltico, ca *adj* ANAT peristaltic.

peristilo *m* ARQ peristyle.

peritación *f*; **peritaje** *m* expert *o* expert's opinion *o* report *o* work (informe) || expert's fee (honorarios) || engineering studies *pl* [aeronautical, industrial, etc.] (carrera).

peritar *vt* to give an expert appraisal of sth. (hacer un peritaje).

perito, ta *adj* expert (especialista) || expert, skilled, skilful (hábil) || experienced (experimentado) || qualified, proficient (calificado) || *ser perito en la materia* to be an expert on the subject.
◆ *m* expert || — *a juicio de peritos* according to expert opinion || *perito aeronáutico, agrónomo* aeronautical, agricultural engineer [qualified from an «escuela de peritos», school of aeronautics, agricultural college] || *perito electricista* qualified electrician || *perito en contabilidad, perito mercantil* chartered *o* qualified accountant [US certified civil accountant] || *perito tasador* expert appraiser.

peritoneo *m* ANAT peritoneum.

peritonitis *f* MED peritonitis.

perjudicado, da *adj* damaged || injured, harmed (persona, fama, etc.) || wronged (moralmente).

perjudicar *vt* to damage (causar daño material) || to harm, to injure, to cause detriment to (la salud, la fama, etc.) || to wrong (en lo moral) || to detract from the looks of, to spoil the appearance of, not to suit (desfavorecer) || *perjudicar los intereses de uno* to prejudice *o* to be prejudicial to s.o.'s interests.

perjudicial *adj* prejudicial, harmful, injurious, detrimental.

perjuicio *m* damage (daño) || harm, injury, detriment (en la salud) || wrong, moral injury, prejudice (daño moral); *reparar el perjuicio que se ha hecho* to redress the wrong one has done || (financial) loss (económico) || — *causar perjuicio a* to damage, to cause damage to (causar daño material), to harm, to injure, to cause detriment to (la salud, la fama, etc.), to wrong, to do (s.o.) wrong (en lo moral) || *con* or *en perjuicio de* to the prejudice of, to the detriment of || *en perjuicio suyo* to his detriment || *sin perjuicio de* or *de que* or *que* even though, without dismissing the possibility that || *sin perjuicio de sus derechos* without prejudice to *o* without detriment to *o* without prejudicing his rights.

perjurar *vi* to perjure o.s., to forswear o.s., to commit perjury (jurar con falsedad) || to swear, to curse (jurar mucho).
◆ *vpr* to perjure o.s.

perjurio *m* perjury (juramento en falso).

perjuro, ra *adj* perjured, forsworn.
◆ *m/f* perjurer.

perla *f* pearl; *perla cultivada* cultured pearl; *perla fina* real pearl || IMPR pearl, four-point type (carácter) || HERÁLD pall (palio) || FIG pearl, gem, jewel, treasure (persona o cosa excelente) || — FIG & FAM *baila, canta de perlas* she dances, she sings a treat *o* like a dream | *de perlas* perfectly (*adverbio*), excellent, marvellous (*adjetivo*) | *hablar de perlas* to speak words of gold | *me parece de perlas* it seems fine to me || *pesca de perlas* pearl fishing || *pescador de perlas* pearl diver *o* fisher || FIG *venirle a uno de perlas* to come in very handy (ser muy útil),

to suit s.o. to a tee, to suit s.o. down to the ground (convenirle), to come just at the right moment (ser oportuno).
◆ *adj inv* pearl; *gris perla* pearl grey.

perlado, da *adj* pearl-shaped, pearly (en forma de perla) ‖ pearly, pearl-coloured (de color de perla) ‖ *cebada perlada* pearl barley.

perlé *adj m* *algodón perlé* crochet *o* corded cotton.

perlería *f* pearls *pl*, collection of pearls.

perlero, ra *adj* pearl; *industria perlera* pearl industry.

perlesía *f* MED paralysis, palsy | muscular atony [especially in the aged].

perlífero, ra *adj* pearl-producing ‖ *ostra perlífera* pearl oyster.

permanecer* *vi* to remain; *permanecer inmóvil* to remain motionless; *la situación permanece grave* the situation remains serious ‖ to stay (residir); *Juan permaneció dos años en Londres* John stayed two years in London.

permanencia *f* permanence (duración constante); *la permanencia de las leyes* the permenance of laws ‖ stay (estancia); *durante mi permanencia en el extranjero* during my stay abroad; *los cosmonautas han batido el récord de permanencia en el espacio* the cosmonauts have broken the record for the longest stay in space ‖ constancy, perseverance (perseverancia).

permanente *adj* permanent, lasting ‖ standing (ejército, comisión, etc.) ‖ *servicio permanente* all-day service.
◆ *f* permanent wave, perm (*fam*) (de los cabellos) ‖ *hacerse la permanente* to have one's hair permed.

permanentemente *adv* permanently.

permanganato *m* QUÍM permanganate.

permeabilidad *f* permeability, perviousness; *permeabilidad del terreno* permeability of the land.

permeable *adj* permeable, pervious ‖ FIG pervious (influenciable).

permi *m* FAM leave (permiso militar); *tener un permi de quince días* to have fifteen day's leave.

pérmico, ca; permiano, na *adj/sm* GEOL Permian.

permisible *adj* permissible.

permisión *f* ⟶ **permiso.**

permisivo, va *adj* permissive.

permiso *m* permission (autorización); *pedir, dar, tener permiso* to ask, to give, to have permission ‖ permit, licence [*US* license] (documento); *permiso para* or *de caza, de construir* hunting licence, building permit ‖ leave, furlough (del soldado); *estar de* or *con permiso* to be on leave ‖ tolerance [in coinage] (moneda) ‖ — *con permiso, con su permiso, con permiso de usted* if I may, with your permission, if you don't mind, by *o* with your leave ‖ MIL *licencia con permiso ilimitado* long leave ‖ *permiso al país de origen* home leave (diplomático) ‖ *permiso de conducir* or *de conducción* driving licence [*US* driver's license] ‖ *permiso de residencia* residence permit ‖ *permiso de trabajo* work permit.

permitido, da *adj* permitted, allowed.

permitir *vt* to permit, to allow (dejar); *permitir que desembarque un pasajero* to permit a passenger to disembark ‖ to permit, to put up with, to tolerate (tolerar) ‖ to permit, to enable, to allow (hacer posible); *su fortuna le permite viajar mucho* his wealth permits him to do a lot of travelling ‖ — *mis recursos no me lo permiten* I can't afford it ‖ *¡permítame!* excuse me (perdone), allow me! (para ayudar a uno) ‖ *permítame que le diga* allow me to tell you *o* to say ‖ *si el tiempo lo permite* weather permitting ‖ *¿usted permite?* may I?
◆ *vpr* to be permitted *o* allowed (estar permitido); *no se permite fumar aquí* smoking is not allowed in here ‖ to permit o.s., to allow o.s.; *permitirse el lujo de* to permit o.s. the luxury of ‖ to take the liberty of *o* to (tomarse la libertad de); *me permito escribirle* I am taking the liberty of writing to you ‖ — *me permito recordarle que...* allow me to remind you that... ‖ *me permito rogarle que* may I make so bold as to ask you to ‖ *si se me permite la expresión* if you will forgive the expression.

permuta *f* exchange ‖ MAT permutation.

permutabilidad *f* exchangeability ‖ MAT permutability.

permutable *adj* exchangeable ‖ MAT permutable.

permutación *f* exchange ‖ MAT permutation.

permutador *m* changeover switch (conmutador).

permutar *vt* to exchange, to barter, to swap (cambiar) ‖ to exchange, to switch (empleos) ‖ MAT to permute.

pernada *f* kick (golpe) ‖ kicking *o* thrashing about [with one's legs] (movimiento violento) ‖ — *dar pernadas* to kick, to thrash about [with one's legs] ‖ JUR *derecho de pernada* droit du seigneur, jus primae noctis.

pernear *vi* to kick, to kick one's legs, to thrash about [with one's legs].

pernera *f* trouser leg (pernil).

perniabierto, ta *adj* open-legged (con las piernas abiertas) ‖ bandy-legged (defecto físico).

pernicioso, sa *adj* pernicious.

pernil *m* ham, haunch and thigh (de un animal) ‖ ham (de cerdo) ‖ leg (de pantalón) ‖ haunch (de caza mayor).

pernio *m* strap hinge (de gozne).

perniquebrar* *vt* to break (s.o.'s) leg *o* legs.
◆ *vpr* to break a *o* one's leg.

pernituerto, ta *adj* crooked-legged.

perno *m* bolt (tornillo).

pernoctar *vi* to sleep out, to stay out all night (pasar la noche fuera de su propio domicilio) ‖ to spend *o* to stay the night; *pernoctaremos en Burgos* we shall stay the night in Burgos.

pero *m* apple tree [producing elongated fruit] (árbol) ‖ (elongated variety of) apple (fruto) ‖ AMER pear tree (peral).

pero *conj* but; *pero no quiero ir* but I don't want to go; *es bonito pero caro* it is nice, but expensive; *¿pero no ibas a ver a tu abuelo?* but weren't you going to see your grandfather? ‖ but, yet (sin embargo); *la casa era pequeña pero cómoda* the house was small yet comfortable ‖ then, now (objeción, desaprobación); *¿pero qué hace usted aquí?* what are you doing here, then?, now what are you doing here? ‖ — *¡pero bueno!* why!, now look! ‖ *pero dígame* come on, tell me ‖ *¡pero qué chica más simpática!* why, what a friendly girl!, isn't she a friendly girl! ‖ *¡pero qué muy bien hecho!* very well done indeed! ‖ *¿pero quieres dejarme en paz?* leave me alone, will you! ‖ *¡pero si está más guapa que nunca!* why *o* well, if she isn't prettier than ever! ‖ *¿pero te vas a callar?* are you going to be quiet or aren't you? ‖ *pero vamos a ver* let's see now.
◆ *m* FAM fault (defecto); *poner* or *encontrar peros a* to find fault with | snag (dificultad); *tener muchos peros* to have a lot of snags | objection (reparo); *poner peros a* to raise objections to ‖ — *no hay pero que valga* no buts, there are no buts about it ‖ *sin un pero* faultless.

perogrullada *f* FAM platitude, truism.

Perogrullo *npr m* *verdad de Perogrullo* platitude, truism.

perol *m* pot (vasija de metal) ‖ saucepan (cacerola).

peroné *m* ANAT fibula (hueso).

peroneo, a *adj* ANAT peroneal, fibular.

peroración *f* peroration, speech.

perorador, ra *m/f* perorator.

perorar *vi* to perorate, to make *o* to deliver a speech.

perorata *f* long-winded speech, tiresome speech ‖ *echar una perorata* to hold forth, to spout.

peróxido *m* QUÍM peroxide.

perpendicular *adj* perpendicular, at right angles (*a* to).
◆ *f* perpendicular.

perpendicularidad *f* perpendicularity.

perpetración *f* perpetration.

perpetrador, ra *adj* perpetrating.
◆ *m/f* perpetrator.

perpetrar *vt* to perpetrate (un delito).

perpetua *f* BOT everlasting, everlasting flower.

perpetuación *f* perpetuation.

perpetuar *vt* to perpetuate; *las pirámides perpetúan el recuerdo de los faraones* the pyramides perpetuate the memory of the pharaohs.
◆ *vpr* to be perpetuated.

perpetuidad *f* perpetuity; *a perpetuidad* in perpetuity ‖ *trabajos forzados a perpetuidad* penal servitude for life.

perpetuo, tua *adj* perpetual, everlasting ‖ life, for life (que dura toda la vida); *exilio perpetuo* exile for life; *cadena perpetua* life imprisonment ‖ *nieves perpetuas* perpetual snow.

perpiaño *adj m* ARQ *arco perpiaño* ribbed arch.
◆ *m* ARQ bondstone, parpen [*US* perpend] (piedra).

perplejidad *f* perplexity (confusión), hesitancy (indecisión).

perplejo, ja *adj* perplexed, puzzled (confuso), hesitant (vacilante) ‖ *dejar perplejo* to perplex.

perquirir* *vt* to investigate, to inquire into.

perquisición *f* inquiry, investigation (pesquisa).

perquisidor, ra *adj* inquiring, investigating.
◆ *m* investigator.

perra *f* bitch (animal) ‖ FAM penny [*US* cent, dime] (dinero); *no tengo ni una perra, estoy sin una perra* I haven't a penny to my name | tantrum (rabieta); *coger una perra* to go into a tantrum | pigheadedness (obstinación) ‖ — FAM *ha cogido* or *esta con* or *tiene la perra de un coche deportivo* he's got this thing *o* an obsession about a sports car ‖ *perra chica* (copper) five-cent piece ‖ *perra gorda* (copper) ten-cent coin.
◆ *pl* FAM cash *sing*, lolly *sing* (dinero); *tiene muchas perras* he's got lots of cash.

perrada *f* pack of dogs (jauría) ‖ FIG & FAM dirty trick (mala jugada).

perramente *adv* FIG & FAM very badly.

perrera *f* kennel, doghouse (casita del perro) ‖ pound, kennels *pl* (de perros sin dueño) ‖ dogcatcher's wagon (camión) ‖ dog box [on a train] (de tren) ‖ FAM grind, fag, drag (trabajo) | bad payer (mal pagador) | tantrum (rabieta).

perrería *f* pack of dogs (jauría) || gang [of thieves, villains, etc.] || FIG & FAM dirty trick (mala acción); *hacerle una perrería a uno* to play a dirty trick on s.o. || FAM *decir perrerías a uno* to talk dirt about s.o., to say nasty things about s.o.

perrero *m* dogcatcher (que recoge perros vagabundos) || houndman, keeper of hounds (que cuida los perros de caza) || dog lover (a quien le gustan los perros).

perrilla *f* FAM penny, farthing, copper [*US* cent, dime] || *AMER* sty, stye (orzuelo) || FAM *no tener una perrilla* not to have a penny to one's name [*US* not to have a cent], to be stony-broke, to be flat broke.

perrillo *m* little dog, pup, puppy (perro).

***perro** *m* dog (animal) || FAM penny, copper, farthing [*US* cent, dime] (moneda) | dog, cur (hombre despreciable) || — FIG *allí no atan los perros con longanizas* money does not grow on trees there || FIG & FAM *andar* or *llevarse como el perro y el gato* or *como perros y gatos* to fight like cat and dog || FIG *¡a otro perro con ese hueso!* pull the other one!, don't give me that!, tell it to the Marines! (no me lo creo), no chance, you'll be lucky!, come off it! (para rechazar una proposición desagradable) | *a perro flaco todo son pulgas* misfortunes rain upon the wretched || *cuidado con el perro* beware of the dog | *como un perro apaleado* beaten up || FIG & FAM *dar perro a uno* to keep s.o. waiting (dar un plantón) | *darse a perros* to get mad, to go up the wall, to blow one's top (irritarse) | *de perros* lousy, filthy; *tiempo de perros* filthy weather; *estar de un humor de perros* to be in a filthy mood; lousy, hell of a; *hemos tenido un día de perros* we've had a hell of a day | *echar a perros* to waste, to idle away [time] | *el perro del hortelano (que ni come ni deja comer)* the dog in the manger | *estar como los perros* to be very salty [food] | *estar más malo que los perros* to be as sick as a dog | *llevar una vida de perros* to lead a dog's life | *morir como un perro* to die without receiving extreme unction (sin los auxilios de la religión), to die a lonely *o* a forgotten man (solo o abandonado) | *muerto el perro se acabó la rabia* dead dogs don't bite || *perro alano* mastiff || *perro caliente* hot dog || *perro callejero* stray dog || *perro cobrador* retriever || *perro corredor* hound || *perro danés* Great Dane || *perro de aguas* or *de lanas* water spaniel || *perro de casta* pedigree dog || *perro de muestra* pointer || *perro de presa, perro dogo* bulldog || *perro de Terranova* Newfoundland dog || *perro faldero* lapdog || *perro galgo* or *lebrel* greyhound || *perro ganadero* sheepdog || FIG *perro ladrador poco mordedor* his bark is worse than his bite || *perro lobo* Alsatian || *perro marino* dogfish (cazón) || *perro mastín* mastiff || *perro pachón, perro tranvía* (*fam*) basset hound, basset || *perro pastor* sheepdog || *perro pekinés* Pekinese, Pekingese || *perro perdiguero* setter || *perro podenco* spaniel || *perro policía* police dog || *perro raposero* foxhound || *perro rastrero* tracker || FIG *perro sarnoso* mangy cur || *perro sin dueño* stray *o* ownerless dog || *perro sabueso* bloodhound | FIG *perro viejo* old hand, sly old fox, wily bird (hombre astuto) | *por dinero baila el perro* there is nothing money cannot buy (con dinero se consigue todo), you never get sth. for nothing | *tratar a alguien como a un perro* to treat s.o. like dirt *o* like a dog.

perro, rra *adj* FAM hell of a, rotten, lousy; *pasé una noche perra* I had a hell of a night || — FAM *esta vida perra* this wretched life | *¡qué suerte más perra!* what rotten luck!

perroquete *m* MAR topgallant mast (juanete).

perruno, na *adj* dog, dog's canine.
◆ *f* dog biscuit (pan).

persa *adj/s* Persian (de la Persia antigua y moderna).

persecución *f* persecution (tormento) || pursuit (acoso, seguimiento); *ir en persecución de uno* to set off in pursuit of s.o. || *carrera de persecución* pursuit (en ciclismo).

persecutorio, ria *adj* pursuing (que acosa o que sigue) || persecutory, persecuting (que atormenta) || *manía persecutoria* persecution mania, persecution complex.

perseguidor, ra *adj* pursuing (que acosa o que sigue) || persecuting (que atormenta) || JUR prosecuting.
◆ *m* pursuer (que acosa o que sigue) || persecutor (que atormenta) || JUR prosecutor, plaintiff || pursuit rider (en ciclismo).

perseguimiento *m* persecution (tormento) || pursuit (acoso, seguimiento).

perseguir* *vt* to pursue, to chase, to be *o* to go *o* to run after (seguir) || to persecute; *Diocleciano persiguió a los cristianos* Diocletian persecuted the Christians || JUR to prosecute || FIG to pursue, to hound (acosar); *perseguir a sus deudores* to pursue one's debtors | to pursue, to aim at, to go after, to strive after (intentar conseguir); *perseguir el bienestar del pueblo, un puesto en el ministerio* to pursue the well-being of the people, a post in the ministry | to pester, to harass (importunar); *perseguir con sus demandas* to pester with one's demands | to persecute, to torment (los remordimientos, etc.) || *me persigue la mala suerte* I am dogged by ill luck.

perseverancia *f* perseverance; *perseverancia en el trabajo, en estudiar* perseverance in one's work, in studying.

perseverante *adj* persevering.

perseverar *vi* to persevere; *perseverar en una empresa* to persevere in an enterprise || to persist (*en* in), to continue (*en* to), to continue (con infinitivo); *persevera en callarse* he persists in saying nothing.

Persia *npr f* GEOGR Iran, Persia (hoy), Persia (en la Antigüedad).

persiana *f* persienne, slatted shutter (postigo) || blind (enrollable); *persiana veneciana* Venetian blind || persienne (tela).

pérsico *m* peach (tree) (árbol) || peach (fruto).

Pérsico *adj* GEOGR *golfo Pérsico* Persian gulf.

persignar *vt* to cross, to make the sign of the cross over.
◆ *vpr* to cross o.s.

persistencia *f* persistence; *persistencia en el error, en rehusar* persistence in error, in refusing.

persistente *adj* persistent.

persistir *vi* to persist; *persistir en creer* to persist in believing.

persona *f* person (hombre o mujer) || personage, personality, figure (hombre importante) || character, personage (en una obra literaria) || GRAM person; *la tercera persona del singular* the third person singular || person (en teología) || — *dárselas de persona importante* to act important, to put on airs || *de persona a persona* man to man (de hombre a hombre), between ourselves (entre nosotros) || *enciclopedia en persona* walking encyclopaedia || *en la persona de* in the person of || *en persona* in person; *es el diablo en persona* he is the devil in person || JUR *persona física* natural person | *persona jurídica* or *social* or *civil* artificial person, body corporate, legal entity || *persona mayor* adult, grown-up || JUR *persona natural* natural person || *por persona* each, per person, per head || *ser muy buena persona* to be very nice *o* kind || JUR *tercera persona* third person, third party.

◆ *pl* people; *convidar a ocho personas* to invite eight people; *varias personas* several people || *sin acepción de personas* without respect of persons.

personaje *m* personage, person of mark, important person (persona importante) || character, personage (en una obra literaria).

personal *adj* personal; *un asunto personal* a personal affair || private, personal; *habitación, entrevista personal* private room, interview || GRAM personal (pronombre) || *los intereses general y personal* public and private interests.
◆ *m* personnel, staff, employees *pl* (empleados) || FAM bods *pl*, people (gente) || ancient tax (tributo) || — *el personal dirigente* the managerial staff || *el personal docente* the teaching staff || *personal de tierra* ground crew *o* staff.

personalidad *f* personality; *culto a la personalidad* personality cult; *desdoblamiento de la personalidad* split personality || — JUR *personalidad jurídica* legal status || *tener personalidad* to have personality *o* character.

personalismo *m* personalism || personal remark (observación) || preference, partiality (parcialidad).

personalista *adj* personalist, personalistic.
◆ *m/f* personalist.

personalización *f* personalization.

personalizar *vt* to personalize || to personify, to embody (personificar) || GRAM to make personal (un verbo).
◆ *vi* to make a personal reference *o* remark.

personarse *vpr* to come *o* to appear in person (presentarse); *se personó en mi casa* he came in person to my house, he appeared in person at my house || to go to *o* to visit (the scene of the occurrence); *la policía se personó rápidamente en el lugar del crimen* the police quickly went to the scene of the crime || to meet (reunirse) || JUR to appear.

personero *m* procurator.

personificación *f* personification.

personificar *vt* to personify; *Nerón personificaba la crueldad* Nero personified cruelty; *personificar los animales* to personify animals || *es la avaricia personificada* he is avarice personified.

perspectiva *f* perspective; *perspectiva aérea, lineal* aerial, linear perspective || perspective, scene, view (vista) || FIG perspective, prospect, outlook; *buenas perspectivas económicas* good economic perspectives | perspective (distancia); *no tenemos suficiente perspectiva para juzgar estos acontecimientos* we do not have sufficient perspective to judge these events, we cannot yet judge these events in the proper perspective || *en perspectiva* in perspective (dibujo), in perspective, in prospect, in view (proyecto).

perspectivo, va *adj* perspective.

perspicacia; perspicacidad *f* keen eyesight, keenness of sight (agudeza de vista) || FIG perspicacity, perspicaciousness, insight (penetración).

perspicaz *adj* keen, sharp (vista) || FIG perspicacious, sharp, shrewd (sagaz).

perspicuo, cua *adj* clear, transparent || FIG perspicuous (estilo, orador).

persuadir *vt* to persuade; *le persuadí de mi sinceridad, de que no mentía* I persuaded him of my sincerity, that I was not lying || — *dejarse persuadir* to allow o.s. to be persuaded *o* prevailed upon || *persuadido que* convinced that.
◆ *vpr* to persuade o.s., to become persuaded *o* convinced.

persuasión *f* persuasion || firm belief (convicción).

persuasiva *f* persuasive power, persuasiveness.

persuasivo, va *adj* persuasive, convincing.
◆ *m/f* persuasive person.

persulfato *m* QUÍM persulphate [*US* persulfate].

pertenecer* *vi* to belong, to be; *estas casas pertenecen a mi padre* these houses belong to my father *o* are my father's ‖ to belong; *el pino pertenece a la familia de las coníferas* the pine belongs to the family of conifers ‖ — *a mí no me pertenece decidir* it is not for me *o* it is not up to me to decide ‖ *eso pertenece al pasado* that is a thing of the past.

perteneciente *adj* belonging, which belongs; *una finca perteneciente al Estado* a property belonging to the State ‖ JUR belonging.

pertenencia *f* possession, ownership, property (propiedad); *reivindicar la pertenencia de algo* to lay claim to the possession of sth. ‖ possession (territorio) ‖ outbuilding, annex (de una finca, de un palacio, etc.) ‖ membership (*a* of), membership (a un partido, etc.) ‖ MIN claim [of one square acre].

pértiga *f* pole (vara) ‖ DEP *salto de pértiga* pole vault.

pértigo *m* shaft (de carro).

pertiguero *m* verger (de iglesia).

pertinacia *f* pertinacity, obstinacy (terquedad) ‖ FIG persistence (larga duración).

pertinaz *f* pertinacious, obstinate (obstinado) ‖ FIG persistent.

pertinazmente *adv* pertinaciously, obstinately ‖ FIG persistently.

pertinencia *f* pertinence, relevance ‖ opportuneness (oportunidad).

pertinente *adj* pertinent, relevant (que viene al caso) ‖ opportune, apt, appropriate (oportuno).

pertinentemente *adv* pertinently, relevantly ‖ opportunely (oportunamente).

pertrechar *vt* MIL to supply with stores and ammunition, to equip, to munition ‖ FIG to prepare, to arrange (disponer) | to supply (proveer).
◆ *vpr* to equip *o* to provide o.s. (*de*, *con* with).

pertrechos *m pl* MIL stores and ammunition, munitions ‖ equipment *sing*, implements; *pertrechos de labranza* farming equipment, farm implements ‖ *pertrechos de pesca* fishing tackle *sing*.

perturbación *f* perturbation, disturbance (disturbio); *perturbaciones sociales* social perturbations ‖ disorder, unsettlement (desorden) ‖ perturbation (de la mente) ‖ perturbation (de un astro, de una aguja magnética) ‖ MED upset, disorder, disturbance ‖ *perturbación del orden público* disturbance *o* breach of the peace.

perturbado, da *m/f* mentally unbalanced person.

perturbador, ra *adj* disturbing (alborotador) ‖ perturbing (que desasosiega).
◆ *m/f* disturber.

perturbar *vt* to disturb (trastornar); *perturbar el orden público* to disturb the peace ‖ to perturb (desasosegar a uno) ‖ to unsettle, to upset (el tiempo) ‖ to upset (un proyecto) ‖ MED to upset, to unsettle, to disturb (el organismo) | to disturb (la mente).

Perú *npr m* GEOGR Peru ‖ — FIG *valer un Perú* to be worth a fortune (cosa), to be a treasure, to be worth one's weight in gold (persona).

peruanismo *m* peruvianism, Peruvian word (vocablo) *o* expression (giro).

peruano, na *adj/s* Peruvian.

perulero, ra *adj/s* (p us) Peruvian (peruano).
◆ *m/f* emigrant returned from Peru with a fortune.
◆ *m* earthenware jar (vasija).

perversidad *f* perversity.

perversión *f* perversion, corruption, depravation.

perverso, sa *adj* perverse, depraved ‖ evil (malo).
◆ *m/f* pervert ‖ evil doer (persona mala).

pervertido, da *adj* perverted.
◆ *m/f* pervert.

pervertidor, ra *adj* perversive, perverting.
◆ *m/f* perverter.

pervertimiento *m* perversion, perverting.

pervertir* *vt* to pervert, to deprave, to corrupt (corromper) ‖ to distort (un texto) ‖ to corrupt (el gusto).
◆ *vpr* to be *o* to become perverted.

pervinca *f* periwinkle.

pervivencia *f* survival (supervivencia).

pervivir *vi* to survive (supervivir).

pesa *f* weight; *una balanza y sus pesas* a balance and its weights ‖ weight (de un reloj) ‖ handset (microteléfono).
◆ *pl* weights, dumbbells (gimnasia) ‖ — DEP *levantamiento de pesas* weight-lifting ‖ *pesas y medidas* weights and measures.

pesabebés *m inv* baby-weighing scales *pl*.

pesacartas *m inv* letter-weighing scales *pl*.

pesada *f* weighing.

pesadamente *adv* heavily ‖ slowly (lentamente) ‖ FIG tiresomely, annoyingly.

pesadez *f* heaviness, weight (peso); *la pesadez de un bulto* the heaviness of a bundle ‖ FIG heaviness (del estómago, de la cabeza, etc.) | sluggishness, slowness (lentitud); *la pesadez de sus movimientos* the sluggishness of his movements | pigheadedness (terquedad) | bind, bore (persona molesta); *¡qué pesadez!* what a bore! | nuisance, bore, bind, drag (fastidio); *es una pesadez tener que ir a ese sitio ahora* it is a drag having to go there now ‖ (p us) FÍS gravity (gravedad) ‖ — FIG & FAM *este hombre ¡qué pesadez!* what a bore that man is! ‖ *sentir pesadez de cabeza, de estómago* to feel heavy-headed, to have a heavy feeling in one's stomach.

pesadilla *f* nightmare ‖ FIG nightmare, bugbear, pet aversion; *es mi pesadilla* it is my bugbear ‖ *de pesadilla* nightmarish.

pesado, da *adj* heavy, weighty; *una maleta pesada* a heavy suitcase ‖ heavy; *metal pesado* heavy metal ‖ FIG sluggish, slow (movimiento) | heavy (paso) | heavy, ungainly (torpe) | heavy, deep (sueño) | heavy (cabeza, ojos, etc.) | sultry, heavy (tiempo) | heavy (terreno, comida) | tough, hard (trabajo) | heavy, wearisome (penoso) | boring, tedious, tiresome, dull (molesto) | in bad taste (broma) ‖ stiff (mecanismo) ‖ QUÍM heavy (aceite, hidrógeno) ‖ MIL heavy (artillería) ‖ — *agua pesada* heavy water ‖ FIG & FAM *más pesado que un saco de plomo* deadly boring, as dull as ditchwater.
◆ *m/f* FIG & FAM bore, drag, bind, pest; *ser un pesado* to be a bore.

pesador, ra *adj* (used for) weighing.
◆ *m/f* weigher, weighman (hombre), weighwoman (mujer).

pesadumbre *f* heaviness (pesadez) ‖ FIG bind, bother (molestia) | sorrow, grief (sentimiento); *tener mucha pesadumbre* to be in great sorrow, to be filled with grief | disagreement, upset (riña).

pesaje *m* DEP weighing-in; *el pesaje de los dos boxeadores* the weighing-in of the two boxers.
— OBSERV This is a Gallicism for *peso*.

pesaleche *m* milk hydrometer.

pesalicores *m inv* FÍS alcoholometer (alcohómetro) | aerometer (aerómetro).

pésame *m* condolences *pl*, sympathy; *dar el pésame* to express one's condolences, to send one's sympathy ‖ *mi más sentido pésame* my deepest sympathy.

pesante *adj* weighty (que pesa) ‖ sad (triste).

pesantez *f* gravity (gravedad).

pesar *m* sorrow, grief (pena) ‖ regret (remordimiento) ‖ — *a pesar de* in spite of, despite; *a pesar de sus padres* in spite of one's parents ‖ *a pesar de los pesares* in spite of everything ‖ *a pesar de que* in spite of *o* despite (the fact that), although; *a pesar de estar malo* or *de que estaba malo* despite being ill, despite the fact that he was ill, although he was ill ‖ *a pesar de todo* in spite of *o* despite everything, for all that (a pesar de los pesares), all the same; *me lo han prohibido, pero lo haré a pesar de todo* they have forbidden me to do it, but I shall all the same ‖ *a pesar de todos* in spite of everyone ‖ *a pesar mío, suyo* against my will, against his will; despite me, despite him ‖ *con gran pesar mío* much to my sorrow ‖ *sentir* or *tener pesar por haber...* to regret having..., to feel *o* to be sorry for having.

pesar *vt* to weigh ‖ to weigh in (a jockeys, a boxeadores) ‖ to weigh down; *me pesan los zapatos* my shoes weigh me down ‖ FIG to weigh (examinar); *pesar el pro y el contra* to weigh the pros and the cons ‖ FIG *pesar sus palabras* to weigh one's words.
◆ *vi* to weigh; *un paquete que pesa tres kilos* a parcel weighing three kilos ‖ to be heavy *o* weighty, to weigh a lot (tener mucho peso) ‖ FIG to weigh heavily (*a* on, upon), to be a burden (*a* on, upon), to be a burden (ser una carga) | to fall (recaer); *muchas obligaciones pesan sobre él* many obligations fall upon him | to be sorry, to regret (sentir); *me pesa que no haya venido* I regret *o* I am sorry that he has not come | to grieve (entristecer) | to carry a lot of weight, to play an important part, to count for a lot (influir); *mis argumentos pesaron mucho en su decisión* my arguments played an important part in his decision ‖ — FIG *mal que te pese* whether you like it or not ‖ *pesar corrido* to give good measure ‖ FIG *pesarle a uno en el alma* to weigh on *o* upon s.o.'s mind | *pesarle a uno los años* to be weighed down by the years ‖ *pesar menos que* to be lighter than ‖ *pesar poco* to be light ‖ *pese a* despite, in spite of; *pese a sus muchas tareas vino* he came in spite of his many duties ‖ *pese a que* in spite of, despite (a pesar de que) ‖ *pese a quien pese* come what may ‖ *¡ya te pesará!* you'll be sorry!, you'll regret it!

pesario *m* MED pessary.

pesaroso, sa *adj* sorry, regretful (que se arrepiente) ‖ sorrowful, sad (triste, afligido).

pesca *f* fishing, angling; *ir, estar de pesca* to go, to be fishing; *la pesca del salmón* salmon fishing ‖ fish *pl* (peces); *aquí hay mucha pesca* there are a lot of fish in these parts ‖ catch (lo pescado); *buena pesca* a good catch ‖ — FIG *andar a la pesca de cumplidos* to fish for compliments ‖ *pesca con caña, con red* angling, netting ‖ *pesca de bajura* or *de litoral, de altura* coastal *o* inshore fishing, deep-sea fishing ‖ *pesca de la ballena* whaling ‖ *pesca de perlas* pearl diving *o* fishing ‖ *pesca submarina* underwater fishing ‖ FIG & FAM *y toda la pesca* and Uncle Tom Cobley and all, and all the rest of the crew (personas), and what not, and what have you (y todo lo demás).

pescada *f* hake (pez, manjar).

pescadería *f* fish shop, fishmonger's.

pescadero, ra *m/f* fishmonger.

pescadilla *f* whiting (pez) ‖ FIG *es la pescadilla mordiéndose la cola* I am (you are, he is, etc.), right back where I (you, he, etc.), started.

pescado *m* fish ‖ *día de pescado* day of abstinence, fish day ‖ CULIN *pescado a la plancha* grilled fish ‖ *pescado azul* bluefish ‖ *pescado blanco* whitefish.

— OBSERV *Pescado* is a fish that has been caught, considered as food; *pez* is a live fish still in water.

pescador, ra *adj* fishing.
◆ *m/f* fisher, fisherman (hombre), fisherwoman (mujer) ‖ — *pescador de caña* angler ‖ *pescador de perlas* pearl diver *o* fisher.
◆ *m* ZOOL angler.
◆ *f* sailor blouse (camisa).

pescante *m* coachman's seat, driver's seat (en los carruajes) ‖ shelf, support (tabla), hanger (palo, barra), hanger (en la pared) ‖ TEATR hoist [for apparitions] (tramoya) ‖ MAR davit ‖ jib, boom (construcción).

pescar *vt* to fish, to fish for (tratar de coger) ‖ to catch (coger) ‖ FIG & FAM to land, to get (lograr); *pescar un buen puesto, un marido* to land a good job, a husband | to pick up, to get, to get hold of (encontrar); *¿dónde has pescado esta noticia?* where did you pick up this piece of news? | to grasp, to get (comprender) | to catch, to get (coger); *pescar un resfriado* to catch a cold | to catch, to nab, to cop (a un desprevenido) | to catch out; *estudiante difícil de pescar en historia* student hard to catch out in history | to fish for, to tout for (clientes).
◆ *vi* to fish ‖ — *ir a pescar* to go fishing ‖ FIG *pescar a* or *en río revuelto* to fish in troubled waters ‖ *pescar con caña* to angle.

pescozón *m* cuff round the scruff of the neck.

pescuezo *m* neck (de un animal) ‖ FAM scruff of the neck (de las personas) ‖ FIG pride, haughtiness (soberbia) ‖ — FIG & FAM *apretar* or *estirar* or *torcer* or *retorcer a uno el pescuezo* to wring s.o.'s neck | *ser más malo que la carne de pescuezo* to be a load of rubbish, to be worse than bad (en general), not to be fit for the pigs (comida), to be as rotten as they come (persona), to be a horrid little beast (niño) | *torcer el pescuezo* to break one's neck (morir).

pesebre *m* rack, manger, crib (de una cuadra).

pesebrera *f* row of racks *o* mangers.

pesero *m* AMER fixed-fare taxi.

peseta *f* peseta (moneda española) ‖ AMER twenty-five centavos [in Mexico] ‖ FIG & FAM *cambiar la peseta* to throw up, to be sick (vomitar).

pesetero, ra *adj* FAM peseta, one peseta (que cuesta una peseta) | penny-pinching, stingy (avaro).
◆ *m/f* skinflint (avaro).

pesimismo *m* pessimism.

pesimista *adj* pessimistic.
◆ *m/f* pessimist.

pésimo, ma *adj* very bad, abominable, terrible.

peso *m* weight (fuerza de gravitación y su medida); *el peso del aire* the weight of air; *un peso de diez kilos* a weight of ten kilos ‖ FÍS weight; *peso atómico* atomic weight ‖ weight (cosa pesada, de una balanza) ‖ weight (carga); *el suelo no puede resistir el peso de tantos muebles* the floor cannot bear the weight of so much furniture ‖ balance, scales *pl* (balanza) ‖ weighing (acción de pesar) ‖ weighing-in (de los jockeys, de los boxeadores) ‖ peso (moneda) ‖ DEP shot, weight; *lanzamiento del peso* shot put; *lanzar el peso* to put the shot ‖ FIG weight (importancia o influencia); *argumentos de peso* arguments that carry weight | weight, burden (carga); *el peso de los años, de la responsabilidad* the weight of years, of responsibility ‖ — *al peso* by the weight ‖ FIG *a peso de oro* for its weight in gold, at a ransom price (a precio muy subido); *vender algo a peso de oro* to sell sth. for its weight in gold | *caerse de* or *por su peso* to go without saying, to be self-evident, to stand to reason ‖ *coger* or *tomar una cosa en peso* to feel the weight of sth., to try sth. for weight (sopesar) ‖ *dar buen peso* to give good weight ‖ FIG *de peso* influential; *gente, persona de peso* influential people, person | *de poco peso* lightweight ‖ *hacer peso* to give *o* to add weight, to make heavy ‖ DEP *levantamiento de pesos* weight-lifting ‖ *levantar en peso* to lift bodily ‖ *lleva la dirección de la empresa en peso* he runs the firm entirely on his own, the running of the firm rests entirely upon his shoulders ‖ FIG *no tener mucho peso, ser cosa de poco peso* to carry little weight ‖ *peso atómico, molecular* atomic, molecular weight ‖ *peso bruto* gross weight ‖ *peso de baño* bathroom scales *pl* ‖ *peso en vivo* live weight (carnicería) ‖ *peso específico* specific weight ‖ *peso mosca, gallo, pluma, ligero, mediano ligero, medio, semipesado, pesado* flyweight, bantamweight, featherweight, lightweight, welterweight, middleweight, light heavyweight *o* cruiser, heavyweight (boxeo) ‖ *peso muerto* deadweight ‖ *peso neto* net weight ‖ FIG *quitarle a uno un peso de encima* to take a load off s.o.'s mind | *valer su peso en oro* to be worth its *o* one's weight in gold ‖ *vender al peso* to sell by weight.

pespuntar *vt* backstitch.

pespunte *m* backstitch ‖ *medio pespunte* running stitch.

pespuntear *vt* to backstitch.

pesquera *f* fishery, fishing ground.

pesquería *f* fishing, fishery (actividad) ‖ fishery, fishing ground (sitio).

pesquero, ra *adj* fishing; *buque, puerto pesquero* fishing boat, port.
◆ *m* fishing boat.

pesquis *m* FIG & FAM insight (perspicacia) | sense, gumption (inteligencia).

pesquisa *f* inquiry; *hacer una pesquisa judicial sobre* to conduct a judicial inquiry into ‖ (house) search (en casa de uno).
◆ *m* AMER detective.

pesquisar *vt* to inquire into, to investigate ‖ to search (en casa de uno).

pesquisidor, ra *adj* inquiring, investigating ‖ searching.
◆ *m/f* inquirer, investigator ‖ searcher ‖ examining magistrate (juez).

pestaña *f* eyelash, lash (del ojo) ‖ fringe, edging (adorno de una tela) ‖ hem (en una costura) ‖ rim, edge (borde saliente) ‖ TECN flange (de rueda, etc.), rim (de llanta) ‖ tongue (de una lata de sardinas) ‖ joint (ceja de un libro) ‖ — FIG *no mover pestaña* not to bat an eyelid | *no pegar pestaña* not to sleep a wink, not to get a wink of sleep.
◆ *pl* BOT cilia ‖ FIG *quemarse las pestañas* to swot hard (estudiar mucho), to burn the midnight oil (por la noche).

pestañear *vi* to blink, to wink ‖ FIG *sin pestañear* without batting an eyelid, without turning a hair.

pestañeo *m* blinking, winking.

pestazo *m* FAM stink, stench (hedor).

peste *f* plague; *peste bubónica* bubonic plague ‖ FIG & FAM stink, stench (mal olor) | pestilence, evil (cosa mala) | corruption, rottenness (depravación) | poison (persona malvada); *esta mujer es una peste* this woman is poison | plague, pest (niño); *¡estos niños son la peste!* what a plague *o* what pests these children are! | plague (plaga, exceso); *una peste de ratas* a plague of rats ‖ — FIG & FAM *huir de uno como de la peste* to avoid *o* to shun s.o. like the plague | *¡mala peste se lo lleve!* a plague of him! ‖ *peste aviar* fowl pest ‖ *peste negra* Black Death.
◆ *pl* curses, words of execration ‖ — FIG & FAM *decir* or *echar pestes de uno* to drag s.o. through the mud, to heap abuse upon s.o., to run s.o. down.

pesticida *m* pesticide.

pestífero, ra *adj* pestiferous ‖ foul, fetid, stinking, foul-smelling (que tiene mal olor) ‖ plague-stricken (enfermo de la peste).
◆ *m/f* plague victim (enfermo).

pestilencia *f* pestilence (epidemia) ‖ stink, fetid smell, stench (hedor).

pestilencial *f* pestilential, pestilent ‖ fetid, stinking, foul-smelling (que tiene mal olor).

pestilente *adj* pestilent, pestilential (pestífero) ‖ fetid, stinking, foul-smelling (que huele mal).

pestillo *m* bolt (cerrojo) ‖ bolt (de la cerradura); *pestillo de golpe* spring bolt.

pestiño *m* honey-coated pancake.

pestorejo *m* nape of the neck.

pestoso, sa *adj* foul-smelling, stinking, foul.

pesuña *f* hoof.

petaca *f* tobacco pouch (de cuero), tobacco tin (de metal) (para el tabaco) ‖ cigar case (para cigarros puros) ‖ cigarette case (para cigarrillos) ‖ leather covered chest (baúl) ‖ AMER suitcase (maleta).
◆ *m/f* AMER lazy person.
◆ *adj inv* AMER idle, lazy (perezoso).

pétalo *m* BOT petal.

petanca *f* French bowls *pl* (juego).

petardear *vt* MIL to blow down (a door) with a petard *o* with petards (derribar con petardos) | to hurl a petard *o* petards at (disparar petardos).
◆ *vi* to backfire (un automóvil).

petardista *m/f* FAM sponger, cadger (sablista) | swindler (estafador).

petardo *m* cracker, firecracker; *tirar petardos* to fire crackers ‖ MIL petard (explosivo) ‖ FIG & FAM swindle (estafa) | horror, crow, ugly old bag (mujer fea); *¡qué petardo!* what a horror! ‖ FIG & FAM *pegarle a uno un petardo* to touch s.o. for a loan, to cadge a loan off s.o.

petate *m* palm matting (estera) ‖ bed roll (de ropa de la cama) ‖ FAM luggage (de pasajero) | crook, swindler (embustero) | runt, squirt (hombre insignificante) ‖ AMER sleeping mat ‖ FIG & FAM *liar el petate* to pack up (and go) (marcharse), to kick the bucket (morir).

petatearse *vpr* AMER FAM to peg out (morir).

petatería *f* AMER mat making (fábrica), mat shop (tienda).

petenera *f* Andalusian popular song ‖ FIG *salirse* or *salir por peteneras* to go off at a tangent, to say sth. completely irrelevant.

petición *f* request, demand (acción de pedir); *hacer una petición* to make a request ‖ petition (a una autoridad); *elevar una petición al Gobierno* to get up a petition to the Government ‖ JUR petition, claim (pedimento) ‖ petition (oración) ‖ — *a petición* by request ‖ *a petición de* at the request of ‖ *consulta previa petición de hora* consultation by appointment ‖ *petición de divorcio* petition for divorce ‖ *petición de indulto* appeal for a reprieve ‖ *petición de mano* proposal ‖ *petición de más* plus petitio, demand for more than is due ‖ *petición de principio* petitio principii, begging the question.

peticionar *vt* AMER to petition.

peticionario, ria *adj* AMER petitioning (solicitante).
◆ *m/f* petitioner.
petifoque *m* MAR flying jib.
petigrís *m* squirrel (fur).
petimetre *m* dandy, fop, dude.
petirrojo *m* redbreast, robin (pájaro).
petiso, sa; petizo, za *adj* AMER short, squat.
◆ *m* AMER small horse (caballo).
petisú *m* cream puff (pastelillo).
petitoria *f* request, petition.
petitorio, ria *adj* petitionary.
◆ *m* FAM insistent and tiresome demand *o* request ‖ medicine catalogue (en una farmacia) ‖ *medicamento incluido en el petitorio del Seguro* medicine paid for by the health service.
petizo, za *adj/sm* AMER → **petiso.**
peto *m* breastplate, plastron (de armadura) ‖ plastron, ornamental front (of bodice) (de vestido) ‖ bib (babero, de un delantal) ‖ TAUR (horse's) protective padding (de caballo de los picadores) ‖ plastron (de tortuga) ‖ *peto de trabajo* work apron.
petral *m* breastplate (correa).
Petrarca *npr m* Petrarch.
petrarquismo *m* Petrarchism.
petrarquista *adj* Petrarchan.
◆ *m/f* Petrarchist.
petrel *m* petrel (ave).
pétreo, a *adj* stone, of stone (de piedra) ‖ stony (pedregoso) ‖ rocky, stone-like, petrous (p us); *dureza pétrea* rocky hardness | *Arabia Pétrea* Arabia Petraea.
petrificación *f* petrification, petrifaction.
petrificante *adj* petrifying.
petrificar *vt* to petrify, to turn into stone ‖ FIG to petrify, to root to the spot.
◆ *vpr* to petrify, to be petrified.
petrífico, ca *adj* petrifying.
petrografía *f* petrography.
petroleado *m* AUT spraying (of underchassis) with oil.
petrolear *vt* AUT to spray with oil.
petróleo *m* petroleum, oil, mineral oil; *petróleo crudo* or *en bruto* crude *o* base oil ‖ — *petróleo lampante* paraffin, paraffin oil, kerosene ‖ *pozo de petróleo* oil well.
petrolero, ra *adj* oil, petroleum, mineral-oil; *la industria petrolera* the oil industry ‖ AMER petroliferous, oil-bearing.
◆ *m* oil tanker (buque).
◆ *m/f* incendiary ‖ petroleum retailer (vendedor).
petrolífero, ra *adj* oil-bearing, petroliferous, petroleum-bearing, petroleum-producing.
petrología *f* petrology.
petroquímica *f* petrochemistry.
petroquímico, ca *adj* petrochemical ‖ *producto petroqu'imico* petrochemical.
petulancia *f* arrogance (presunción).
— OBSERV *Petulance* en inglés significa *mal humor, irritabilidad.*
petulante *adj* arrogant (presumido).
— OBSERV *Petulant* en inglés significa *malhumorado, irritable.*
petunia *f* petunia (flor).
peyorativo, va *adj* pejorative, deprecatory.
peyote *m* peyote, peyotl (cacto).
pez *m* fish; *pez de agua dulce* freshwater fish; *pez marino* salt-water fish ‖ — FIG *buen pez* wily bird, foxy person ‖ FIG & FAM *el pez grande se come al chico* the big fish swallow up the little ones | *estar como pez en el agua* to be in one's element, to feel completely at home | *estar pez* to be a dunce (*en* at, in), not to have a clue (*en* about), not to have a clue (ignorar todo) ‖ *peces de colores* goldfish ‖ FIG & FAM *pez de cuidado* nasty customer ‖ *pez de san Pedro* John dory ‖ *pez espada* swordfish ‖ FIG & FAM *pez gordo* big shot, bigwig (persona importante) ‖ *pez luna* moonfish, sunfish ‖ *pez martillo* hammerhead ‖ *pez mujer* manatee, sea cow (manatí) ‖ *pez piloto* pilot fish ‖ *pez sierra* sawfish ‖ *pez volador* or *volante* flying fish ‖ FIG & FAM *por la boca muere el pez* the least said the better, silence is golden, least said is soonest mended.
— OBSERV *Pez* is a live fish; *pescado* is a fish that has been caught, considered as food.
pez *f* pitch, tar (para pegar) ‖ MED meconium ‖ *pez griega* colophony, rosin (colofonia).
pezón *m* BOT stalk, stem (de flores, de frutos), stem (de hojas) ‖ nipple (de la teta) ‖ knob (protuberancia) ‖ TECN tip (de ejes).
pezonera *f* linchpin (de eje) ‖ nipple shield (de rueda).
pezpita *f*; **pezpítalo** *m* wagtail (aguzanieves).
pezuña *f* hoof.
— OBSERV *Pezuña* is a cloven hoof (cows, sheep, etc.). *Casco* is the hoof of a horse.
phi *f* phi (letra griega).
Phnom Penh *n pr* GEOGR Phnom Penh.
pi *f* pi (letra griega) ‖ MAT pi (número).
piache (tarde) *loc* FAM too late (for the fair).
piada *f* cheep, chirp (de pájaro) ‖ FIG & FAM expression, saying (borrowed from someone else).
piador, ra *adj* cheeping, chirping.
piadosamente *adv* compassionately (con lástima) ‖ piously (con devoción).
piadoso, sa *adj* compassionate, pitiful (que compadece) ‖ pious, devout (devoto); *alma piadosa* pious soul ‖ *mentira piadosa* white lie.
piafador, ra *adj* pawing, stamping (caballo).
◆ *m* pawer, stamper.
piafar *vi* to paw the ground (rascar el suelo), to stamp (dar patadas).
pialar *vt* AMER to lasso (an animal) by its feet.
piamadre; piamáter *f* ANAT pia mater.
Piamonte *npr m* GEOGR Piedmont.
piamontés, esa *adj/s* Piedmontese.
pian, pian; pian, piano *loc adv* FAM ever so slowly, little by little, nice and easy.
pianillo *m* barrel organ (organillo).
pianísimo *adv* MÚS pianissimo.
pianista *m/f* pianist (músico) ‖ piano maker, piano manufacturer (fabricante), piano dealer (vendedor).
pianístico, ca *adj* pianistic.
piano *m* MÚS piano; *tocar el piano* to play the piano ‖ — *afinador de pianos* piano tuner ‖ *piano de cola* grand piano ‖ *piano de manubrio* street piano, hurdy gurdy ‖ *piano de media cola* baby grand piano ‖ *piano recto* or *vertical* upright piano ‖ *taburete de piano* piano stool.
◆ *adv* MÚS piano.
pianoforte *m* pianoforte.
pianola *f* pianola.
piante *m/f* FAM grouser.
piar *m* cheeping, chirping, peeping (de las aves).
piar *vi* to cheep, to chirp, to peep (las aves) ‖ FIG & FAM to grouse (protestar) ‖ FAM *piar por* to cry for.
piara *f* herd (de cerdos, ovejas, caballos).
piastra *f* piastre, piaster (moneda).
PIB *abrev de Producto Interior Bruto* GDP, gross domestic product.
pibe, ba *m/f* AMER FAM kid.
piberío *m* AMER kids *pl*, bunch of kids (chiquillos).
pica *f* pike (arma) ‖ pick (herramienta) ‖ pikeman (soldado) ‖ TAUR goad, picador's lance *o* pike ‖ MED pica ‖ ZOOL magpie (urraca) ‖ stonemason's hammer (escoda) ‖ AMER tapping (de hevea) | pique, resentment (pique) | narrow path (sendero) ‖ FIG & FAM *poner una pica en Flandes* to pull off sth. very difficult.
picacera *f* AMER pique, resentment.
picacho *m* peak (de una montaña).
picada *f* → **picadura.**
picadero *m* riding school, manège (para aprender a montar) ‖ ring [for training wild horses] (para caballos salvajes) ‖ MAR stock, block (madero) ‖ FAM bachelor pad (cuarto) ‖ AMER slaughterhouse (matadero).
picadillo *m* minced meat, mince (de carne) ‖ chopped onion (de cebolla) ‖ sort of hash (guiso) ‖ FIG *hacer picadillo* to cut to pieces, to make mincemeat of (a un ejército, a una persona), to smash to pieces (algo).
picado *m* mincing (de la carne) ‖ pricking-out (de una cartulina de encaje) ‖ diving (acción), dive (resultado), dive (de un avión, de un pájaro) ‖ knocking, pinking [*US* pinging] (de un motor) ‖ punching, clipping (de un billete) ‖ cutting (de las piedras) ‖ MÚS staccato ‖ mince (picadillo).
picado, da *adj* sour (bebida) ‖ bad, off (fruta, alimento) ‖ high (carne mala) ‖ bitten (por araña, pulga, serpiente) ‖ stung (por una avispa) ‖ CULIN minced (carne) | chopped (cebolla) ‖ cut (tabaco) ‖ choppy (mar) ‖ FIG piqued, nettled, narked (*fam*), (ofendido) ‖ AMER FAM picked, sozzled (achispado) ‖ — *diente picado* decayed *o* bad tooth ‖ MÚS *nota picada* staccato note ‖ *picado de viruelas* pockmarked.
picador *m* TAUR «picador» ‖ horsebreaker (de caballos) ‖ miner (minero) ‖ CULIN chopping board.
picadora *f* mincer, mincing machine (para picar).
picadura; picada; picotada; picotazo *m* bite (de araña, pulga, serpiente) ‖ sting (de avispa) ‖ peck (de pájaro) ‖ spot (en las frutas) ‖ cut tobacco, loose tobacco (tabaco) ‖ pockmark (de viruela) ‖ moth hole (de polilla) ‖ decay, caries (en las muelas) ‖ *tener una picadura en un diente* to have a bad tooth *o* a decayed tooth.
picafigo *m* figpecker (ave).
picaflor *m* hummingbird (ave) ‖ AMER FIG Romeo, flirt (mariposón).
picajón, ona; picajoso, sa *adj* FAM touchy, peevish.
picamaderos *m inv* woodpecker (ave).
picana *f* AMER goad (del boyero).
picanear *vt* AMER to goad.
picante *adj* hot, piquant, pungent; *salsa picante* piquant sauce ‖ spicy, highly seasoned (comida) ‖ sour, tart (vino) ‖ FIG spicy, racy, risqué; *chiste picante* spicy joke | pungent, pointed, biting, cutting, stinging; *palabras picantes* pungent words | sharp, biting (contestación).
◆ *m* piquancy (de la pimienta, de una salsa, etc.), spiciness (de un manjar) ‖ FIG pungency, pointedness (mordacidad) | spice, zest (de un relato, de un chiste) ‖ pepper (pimienta) ‖ AMER piquancy, highly-seasoned dish.
picantería *f* AMER cheap restaurant (restaurante modesto).
picapedrero *m* stonecutter.

picapica *f* AMER plant with itch-producing leaves or stalk || *polvillos de picapica* itching powder.

picapleitos *m inv* FAM litigitious fellow (pleitista) | caseless *o* briefless lawyer (abogado sin pleitos).

picaporte *m* doorhandle (tirador de la puerta) || latch (barrita) || latchkey (llave) || doorknocker (aldaba).

picar *vt* to prick, to pierce (con instrumento punzante) || to peck, to peck at (morder o comer las aves) || to bite (araña, pulga, serpiente) || to sting (avispa) || to eat into (los gusanos) || to prickle (barba, espinas) || TAUR to prick, to goad [the bull] || to bite (el pez); *picar el anzuelo* to bite the hook || to burn, to sting, to be hot on (ser picante); *la pimienta pica la lengua* pepper burns the tongue, pepper is hot on the tongue || to pick at, to nibble at (comer poco) || to mince, to chop up, to hash (hacer picadillo con la carne) || to chop up (la cebolla) || to cut up (el tabaco) || to spur on (espolear un caballo), to break (in) (adiestrar) || to punch, to clip (los billetes) || to perforate (perforar) || to cut (piedras) || to roughen (una pared, una piedra de molino) || to crush, to pound (hacer pedazos) || FIG to pique, to nettle, to nark (*fam*), to pique, to nettle, to nark (enojar) | to wound (el amor propio) | to pique, to arouse (la curiosidad) | to prick; *le pica la conciencia* his conscience pricks him | to spur on, to goad on (estimular) || to spin (una bola de billar, un balón) || MIL to harass (acosar) || MAR to cut; *picar un cable* to cut a cable | to speed up (the rowing) (remar más deprisa) || MÚS to strike (a note) briefly and sharply || to add the finishing touches to, to touch off [a painting] (pintura) || to pink (perforar para adorno), to prick out (el dibujo de un encaje) || — FIG & FAM *a quien le pique que se rasque* if the cap fits, wear it || *me pica la espalda, la herida* my arm, the wound itches (escuece) || *me pica mucho la boca* my mouth is on fire || *me pican los ojos con el humo* the smoke is making my eyes smart *o* sting || FIG & FAM *¿qué mosca le ha picado?* what's eating him?, what's biting him?

◆ *vi* to prick (agujerear) || to peck (morder las aves) || to bite (araña, pulga, serpiente) || to sting (la avispa) || to prickle (la barba, espinas) || to bite (un pez) || to bite (el frío) || to bite, to cut (el viento) || to nibble, to have a nibble (comer muy poco) || to burn, to be hot [on the tongue o palate] (ajo, pimienta, etc.) || to be sharp *o* tart (el vino) || to itch, to sting (la piel) || to smart, to sting (una herida) || to dive, to nosedive (un avión) || to blaze down, to scorch (el sol) || to pick (con un pico) || to knock, to rap (at the door) (llamar a la puerta) || to pick a page at random (abrir un libro al azar) || to knock, to pink [US to ping] (un motor) || to cut (cortar piedra) || FIG to swallow it (dejarse atraer o engañar) | to slip up, to let the cat out of the bag (dejar escapar un secreto) | to bite, to nibble (dejarse atraer los compradores, etc.) || — FIG *picar en* to dabble in (aprender nociones superficiales), to be something of a; *picar en poeta* to be something of a poet; to border on; *picar en insolencia* to border on insolence; to be quite; *picar en gracioso* to be quite witty; to swallow, to fall for, to be taken in by (creerse una cosa) || FIG & FAM *picar (muy) alto* to aim (very) high.

◆ *vpr* to become moth-eaten (por la polilla) || to get worm-eaten (la madera por la carcoma) || to spot, to mildew (la ropa por la humedad) || to rust (un metal) || to spot, to go rotten (una fruta) || to turn sour (el vino, la leche) || to go bad, to decay (dientes) || to get choppy (el mar) || to be in rut (los animales machos) || FIG to get piqued *o* nettled *o* narked (*fam*) (ofenderse) | to get cross (enfadarse) || AMER FAM to get pickled *o* sozzled || — FIG & FAM *el que se pica* or *quien se pica ajos come* if the cap fits, wear it || FIG *picarse con* to be piqued by, to be set on one's mettle by (sentirse estimulado), to be dead set on sth. (desear) | *picarse de* to think o.s., to think one is; *se pica de gracioso* he thinks himself funny; *se pica de poeta* he thinks he is a poet | *picarse en el juego* to get the gambling itch.

pícaramente *adv* slyly, wilily (con astucia) || mischievously (de manera traviesa) || despicably (con vileza) || *mirar pícaramente a uno* to give s.o. a mischievous *o* a coy look.

picaraza *f* ZOOL magpie (urraca).

picarazado, da *adj* AMER pockmarked (picado de viruela).

picardear *vt* to corrupt, to teach bad ways.

◆ *vi* to be a rogue || to play up, to get up to mischief (niño) || to say rude things (decir).

◆ *vpr* to go to the bad, to become corrupted.

picardía *f* despicable action, dirty trick, vile deed (acción baja) || crookedness, roguishness (bribonería) || craftiness, slyness (astucia) || naughty *o* mischievous trick, prank, mischief (travesura) || rude thing, naughty thing (palabra o acción licenciosa) || gang of rogues (grupo) || FIG *tener mucha picardía* to be a real scamp, to be full of mischief (niño), to have many a trick up one's sleeve (hombre).

◆ *pl* (p us) insults (insultos).

picaresca *f* gang of rogues (pandilla) || roguery, roguish life (vida) || picaresque novel; *la picaresca es una creación literaria española* the picaresque novel is a Spanish literary creation.

picaresco, ca *adj* picaresque; *novela picaresca* picaresque novel || roguish, arch, mischievous; *una mirada picaresca* an arch look || picaresque (literatura).

pícaro, ra *adj* despicable, base (vil) || rascally, roguish, crooked (bribón) || crafty, sly, wily (astuto) || evil-minded (malicioso) || naughty, mischievous (niño) || FIG scampish, rascally, saucy (calificativo cariñoso) || *este pícaro mundo* this damned world.

◆ *m/f* rascal, crook, rogue (bribón) || crafty *o* sly person (astuto) || villain (malicioso) || FIG scamp, rascal (pillo, sinvergüenza).

◆ *m* «pícaro», rogue (tipo de la literatura española) || — *a pícaro, pícaro y medio* diamond cut diamond || *pícaro de cocina* kitchen boy, scullion (ant) (pinche).

picarón, ona *adj* FAM roguish, rascally, mischievous.

◆ *m/f* rogue, rascal.

picatoste *m* round of fried bread (pan frito) || round of toast (pan tostado).

picaza *f* magpie (urraca).

picazón *f* tingling, itch, itching (leve), stinging, sting, smarting (escozor fuerte) || FIG & FAM annoyance, pique (enfado) | anxiety, uneasy feeling (desazón moral).

picea *f* spruce (abeto).

Picio *npr m* FAM *más feo que Picio* as ugly as sin.

picnic *m* picnic (comida campestre).

pícnico, ca *adj* pyknic.

picnómetro *m* pycnometer, pyknometer.

pico *m* beak, bill (de ave) || beak (de insecto) || beak, sharp point (parte saliente) || corner (de un mueble); *golpearse contra el pico de la mesa* to bump into the corner of the table || corner (de sombrero, pañuelo, cuello) || pick, pickaxe (herramienta) || lip (de cazuela), spout, beak (de tetera, etc.) || peak (cima, montaña) || piece (of a skirt hem) that dips (de una falda) || nappy (de niño) || FIG crust (extremo del pan) | bread stick (panecillo de forma alargada) | odd money (suma) || FIG & FAM gift of the gab (habladuría) | mouth, lips *pl*, trap (boca) || socket (de candil) || MAR gaff || AMER acorn barnacle (bálano) | kiss (beso) || — FIG & FAM *callar* or *cerrar el pico* to shut one's trap, to belt up (callarse), to shut (s.o.) up (hacer callar) | *costar un pico* to cost a pretty penny, to cost quite a bit | *darse el pico* to kiss (besarse), to get on very well (llevarse muy bien) | *hincar el pico* to peg out, to kick the bucket (morirse), to throw in the sponge, to give in (darse por vencido) | *irse del pico* to shoot one's mouth off, to talk too much | *perderse por el pico* to talk too much, to talk o.s. into trouble || *pico carpintero* woodpecker || *pico de cigüeña* geranium || TECN *pico de colada* nose (of Bessemer converter) | *pico de cuervo* bird's beak (instrumento) || AMER *pico de frasco* or *de canoa* toucan (tucán) || *pico verde* green woodpecker (ave) || FIG & FAM *ser* or *tener un pico de oro* to have the gift of the gab | *trabajar de pico y pala* to work like a slave, to work with pick and shovel || *y pico* -odd; *cien pesetas y pico* a hundred-odd pesetas; just after, a little after; *son las tres y pico* it is just after three.

◆ *pl* spades (en los naipes) || — FIG & FAM *andar* or *irse de picos pardos* to go on a binge [US to go have a blast] (irse de juerga), to gad about, to lead a gay life (ser amigo de juergas) || *sombrero de dos picos* two cornered hat, cocked hat || *sombrero de tres picos* three cornered hat, tricorn.

picón, ona *adj* with protruding upper teeth (animal) || FAM touchy, peevish (susceptible).

◆ *m* small coal (carbón) || stickleback (pez).

piconero *m* coalman, small-coal merchant.

picor *m* itch, itching, prickling (escozor), smarting, stinging (en los ojos) || *dar picor* to itch, to smart.

picoso, sa *adj* AMER spicy, hot (picante).

picota *f* pillory (suplicio) || spire (de torre) || peak (de montaña) || boy's game (juego) || MAR support rod (de guimbalete) || bigarreau cherry (cereza) || FIG *poner a uno en la picota* to hold s.o. up to obloquy, to pillory s.o.

picotada *f*; **picotazo** *m* ⟶ **picadura.**

picoteado, da *adj* pecked.

picotear *vt* to peck, to peck at (morder o comer las aves) || FIG to pick at, to nibble at (comer un poco).

◆ *vi* to toss its head (el caballo) || FIG to pick at one's food (comer poco) || FIG & FAM to patter, to prattle (hablar).

◆ *vpr* FIG to squabble, to bicker (reñir).

picoteo *m* pecking (de pájaros) || FIG nibble, nibbling (acción de comer).

picotón *m* AMER ⟶ **picadura.**

pícrico *adj m* QUÍM picric (ácido).

picto, ta *adj* Pictish, Pict.

◆ *m/f* Pict (de Escocia).

◆ *m* Pictish (lengua).

pictografía *f* pictography, picture writing (escritura) || pictograph (imagen aislada).

pictográfico, ca *adj* pictographic.

pictórico, ca *adj* pictorial; *interés, motivo pictórico* pictorial interest, motif || painting (para pintar).

picudilla *f* rail (ave).

picudo, da *adj* pointed, with a point (puntiagudo) || lipped; *cazuela picuda* lipped pan || spouted, beaked (tetera, etc.) || long-beaked, long-billed (ave) || long-snouted, long-nosed (hocicudo) || peaked (montaña).

picha *f* POP cock, prick.

pichichi *m* DEP top-goal scorer.

pichilingo *m* AMER kid.

pichincha *f* AMER bargain, good deal (ganga).

pichón *m* young pigeon (pollo de paloma) ‖ pigeon; *tiro de pichón* pigeon shooting ‖ FIG & FAM dove, pet (término cariñoso); *ven acá pichón* come here, my dove ‖ AMER novice (novicio).

pichona *f* hen pigeon (ave) ‖ FAM dove, pet (término cariñoso).

pichonear *vt* AMER to swindle (estafar).

pichula *f* AMER prick (picha).

pídola *f* leapfrog (juego) ‖ *saltar a pídola* to leapfrog.

pidón, ona *adj* FAM always asking for things.
◆ *m/f* FAM *es un pidón* he's always asking for things.

pie *m* foot (de hombre, de animal) ‖ foot (de mueble, escalera, montaña); *al pie de la colina* at the foot of the hill ‖ foot (de las medias) ‖ stand (de una máquina de fotografiar, de un telescopio, etc.) ‖ base, foot (de una columna) ‖ stem (de una copa) ‖ BOT stalk, stem (tallo) | plant (planta entera); *mil pies de lechugas* a thousand lettuce plants | stock (de viña) ‖ sediment (poso) ‖ foot (de un escrito); *al pie de la página* at the foot of the page ‖ legend, caption (de foto o de dibujo) ‖ ending (de un documento) ‖ name of signatory (firma) ‖ foot (medida); *de dos pies de altura* two feet high, two foot high ‖ foot (de verso) ‖ FIG foundation, basis (fundamento) ‖ MAT foot, base (de una recta) ‖ residue of pressed grapes (de uvas) ‖ — *a cuatro pies* on all fours (a gatas) ‖ FIG *a los pies de alguien* at s.o.'s service (al servicio de), at s.o.'s beck and call (bajo el dominio de) ‖ *a los pies de la cama* at the foot of the bed ‖ *al pie de* at the foot of; *al pie de un árbol* at the foot of a tree; next to (junto), almost (casi) ‖ *al pie de fábrica* at factory price (precio) ‖ *al pie de la escalera* at the foot of the stairs ‖ *al pie de la letra* to the letter; *cumplió mis instrucciones al pie de la letra* he carried out my instructions to the letter; literally; *tomó al pie de la letra lo que dije y se enfadó* he took what I said literally and got angry; word for word; *copió el artículo al pie de la letra* he copied the article word for word ‖ *al pie de la obra* delivered on site ‖ *a pie* on foot (andando) ‖ *a pie enjuto* dryshod, without getting one's feet wet ‖ *a pie firme* steadfastly ‖ *a pie juntillas* or *juntillo, con los pies juntos* with one's feet together; *saltar a pie juntillas* to jump with one's feet together; firmly; *cree a pie juntillas todo lo que le dicen* he firmly believes everything they tell him ‖ FIG *atado de pies y manos* bound hand and foot | FIG *besar los pies* (*véase* OBSERV) | *buscar cinco* or *tres pies al gato* to split hairs (hilar muy fino), to make life more difficult than it is, to complicate matters (complicarse la vida) | *caer de pie como los gatos* to fall *o* to land on one's feet | *cojear del mismo pie* to have the same faults | *con el pie en el estribo* about to *o* ready to leave | *con pies de plomo* carefully, warily ‖ *dar con el pie* to tap one's foot [on the ground] (en el suelo), to kick (tropezar, dar una patada) ‖ FIG *dar pie a* to give cause for ‖ *de pie* standing; *estar de pie* to be standing; full-length (retrato, foto) ‖ *de pies a cabeza* from head to foot (enteramente), to the hilt (armado) ‖ *echar pie a tierra* to dismount (caballería), to get out, to alight (coche) ‖ *en pie* standing; *estaba en pie* he was standing; up and about, on one's feet (curado), standing (las cosechas), on the hoof (ganado) ‖ *en pie de guerra* on a war footing ‖ FIG *entrar con el pie derecho* or *con buen pie* to start off on the right foot *o* footing, to make a good start | *en un pie de igualdad* on an equal footing | *esperar a pie firme* to wait resolutely | *esta frase no tiene ni pies ni cabeza* I can't make head or tail of this sentence (no la entiendo) | *estar con un pie en el aire* to be a rolling stone | *estar en pie* to be still there (problema) | *fallarle a uno los pies* to lose one's balance, to overbalance ‖ *gente de a pie* foot soldiers *pl*, infantry (soldados) ‖ *golpear el suelo con el pie* to stamp *o* to tap one's foot on the ground ‖ *hacer pie* to be in one's depth (en el agua) ‖ FIG *hacerle un pie agua a uno* to mess things up for s.o. ‖ FIG *hacer una cosa con los pies* to botch *o* to bungle sth., to do sth. in a slapdash way (hacerla muy mal) ‖ *ir a pie* to walk, to go on foot ‖ FIG *írsele los pies a uno* to slip; *se le fueron los pies* he slipped | *levantarse con el pie izquierdo* to get up on the wrong side of the bed ‖ *ligero de pies* light-footed ‖ FIG *meter un pie en algún sitio* to get a foothold somewhere | *morir al pie del cañón* to die with one's boots on, to die in harness | *nacer de pie* to be born under a lucky star | *no da pie con bola* he can't do a thing right | *no levanta dos pies del suelo* he is tiny | *no poner los pies más en un sitio* not to set foot in a place again | *no tener ni pies ni cabeza* to be ridiculous *o* absurd, to be nonsense ‖ *no tenerse de pie* not to be able to stand up; *desde su enfermedad no se tiene de pie* since his illness he cannot stand up; not to hold water; *la historia no se tiene de pie* your story does not hold water ‖ FIG *pararle a uno los pies* to put s.o. in his *o* her place (poner a alguien en su sitio) | *pensar con los pies* to talk through one's hat ‖ *perder pie* to lose one's footing, to slip (caerse), to go out of one's depth (en el agua), to lose one's way (confundirse) ‖ *pie a pie* little by little ‖ MIL *pie a tierra* dismount (orden) ‖ *pie de altar* surplice fees (emolumentos) ‖ *pie de amigo* support, prop (estaca) ‖ MED *pie de atleta* athlete's foot (dolencia) ‖ FIG & FAM *pie de banco* stupid thing (necedad) ‖ BOT *pie de becerro* cuckoo pint (aro) ‖ *pie de burro* acorn barnacle ‖ *pie de cabra* crowbar (palanca), goose barnacle (crustáceo) ‖ *pie de imprenta* publisher's imprint, imprint ‖ *pie de liebre* kind of clover (trébol) ‖ ARQ *pie derecho* upright ‖ *pie de rey* slide calliper ‖ POÉT *pie forzado* forced rhyme ‖ *pie plano* flatfoot; *tener los pies planos* to have flatfeet ‖ *pie prensatelas* foot (costura) ‖ POÉT *pie quebrado* a line of four or five syllables [alternating with other longer lines] ‖ *pie zambo* clubfoot ‖ *pies contra cabeza* head to tail ‖ CULIN *pies de cerdo* pigs' trotters ‖ *poner el pie en tierra firme* to set foot on dry land ‖ FIG *poner en pie* to set up, to establish ‖ *poner los pies en* to set foot in ‖ *poner pie en* to set foot on (desembarcar) ‖ FIG *poner pies en polvorosa* to take to one's heels [US to take a powder] ‖ *ponerse en* or *de pie* to stand up, to rise to one's feet ‖ FIG *quedar en pie* to be still there, to remain (una dificultad), to remain standing, to be left standing (un edificio) | *saber de qué pie cojea uno* to know s.o.'s weak spots | *sacar los pies del plato* to overstep the mark (ir demasiado lejos), to come out of one's shell (dejar de ser tímido) | *ser más viejo que el andar a pie* to be as old as the hills | *ser pies y mano de uno* to be s.o.'s right hand | *soldado de a pie* foot soldier | *tener buenos* or *muchos pies* to be a good walker | *tener el estómago en los pies* to be faint with hunger, to be starving ‖ *tener los pies hacia fuera* to have splay feet ‖ FIG *tener* or *estar con un pie en el sepulcro* or *en la sepultura* or *en el hoyo* to have one foot in the grave | *trabajar con los pies* to be all thumbs, to work clumsily | *tratar a alguien con la pluma del pie* to kick s.o. around ‖ *volver pie atrás* to turn back, to go back (desandar lo andado), to go back on *o* to take back what one has said (desdecirse), to back down (ceder).
— OBSERV The Spanish expression *besar los pies*, like *besar las manos*, is a formal expression of respect used in letters, and may be translated by *Yours respectfully*.
— OBSERV El plural de la palabra inglesa *foot* es *feet*.

piececito *m* little foot, tootsie (*fam*).

piedad *f* pity, compassion (compasión); *mover a uno a piedad* to move s.o. to pity; *hombre sin piedad* man without pity ‖ piety, piousness (religiosa) ‖ respect (filial) ‖ ARTES Pietà (la Virgen) ‖ — *con piedad* with pity, pityingly (sentimiento); *mirar a alguien con piedad* to look at s.o. with pity ‖ *dar piedad* to be pitiful ‖ *me dan piedad* I feel sorry for them ‖ *por piedad* out of pity ‖ *¡por piedad!* for pity's sake! ‖ *tener piedad de* to take pity on ‖ *¡tenga un poco de piedad!* show some sympathy!

piedra *f* stone ‖ hailstone (granizo) ‖ MED stone (en el riñón) ‖ flint (de encendedor) ‖ millstone (de molino) ‖ place where foundlings were left (de inclusa) ‖ FIG stone; *corazón de piedra* heart of stone ‖ — FIG *ablandar las piedras* to melt a heart of stone | *a tiro de piedra* a stone's throw away | *cerrar a piedra y lodo* to shut tight | *es un día señalado con piedra blanca* it is a red-letter day | *hasta las piedras lo saben* the whole world knows it | *menos da una piedra* it is better than nothing | *no dejar piedra por mover* to leave no stone unturned | *no dejar piedra sobre piedra* to raze to the ground, not to leave a stone standing | *pasar a uno por la piedra* to leave s.o. standing (vencer) ‖ *piedra amoladera* or *de amolar* grindstone ‖ *piedra angular* or *fundamental* cornerstone ‖ *piedra arenisca* sandstone ‖ *piedra berroqueña* granite ‖ *piedra de afilar* hone, whetstone ‖ *piedra de cal* or *caliza* limestone ‖ *piedra de construcción* stone (used in building) ‖ *piedra de chispa* flint (pedernal) ‖ *piedra de encendedor* or *de mechero* flint ‖ FIG *piedra de* or *del escándalo* cause *o* source of scandal ‖ *piedra del altar* altar stone ‖ *piedra de molino* millstone ‖ *piedra de sillería* or *sillar* ashlar ‖ *piedra de toque* touchstone ‖ *piedra filosofal* philosopher's stone ‖ *piedra fina* semi-precious stone ‖ *piedra imán* lodestone ‖ *piedra infernal* lunar caustic ‖ *piedra meteórica* meteoric stone ‖ *piedra molar* millstone grit ‖ FIG *piedra movediza, nunca moho la cobija* a rolling stone gathers no moss ‖ *piedra pómez* pumice stone ‖ *piedra preciosa* precious stone ‖ *poner la primera piedra* to lay the cornerstone, to lay the foundation stone ‖ FIG *quedarse de piedra* to be thunderstruck | *tirar la piedra y esconder la mano* to hit and run | *tirar la primera piedra* to cast the first stone | *tirar piedras al tejado ajeno* to blame s.o. else ‖ *tirar piedras contra uno* to throw stones at s.o., to stone s.o. (apedrear), to criticize s.o. (censurar).

piedrecita *f* pebble.

piel *f* skin (del cuerpo) ‖ leather, skin (cuero); *piel de Rusia* Russian leather ‖ fur, skin, pelt (de animal con pelo largo) ‖ fur (para prenda de vestir) ‖ skin, peel (de las frutas) ‖ — *artículos de piel* leather goods ‖ FIG & FAM *dar la piel para obtener algo* to give one's right arm for sth. ‖ *piel de gallina* goose pimples *pl*, gooseflesh ‖ *piel de zapa* shagreen ‖ FIG & FAM *ser de la piel del diablo* to be a little devil (niño) ‖ FIG *un piel roja* a redskin | *vender la piel del oso antes de haberlo matado* to count one's chickens before they are hatched.
◆ *pl* fur *sing*; *un abrigo de pieles* a fur coat ‖ *suavizar las pieles* to stake skins.

piélago *m* POÉT sea, ocean ‖ high sea (alta mar) ‖ FIG sea (abundancia).

pielitis *f* MED pyelitis.

pienso *m* fodder, feed; *piensos compuestos* mixed feed ‖ FIG & FAM *¡ni por pienso!* I wouldn't dream of it!

pierna *f* leg; *pierna de madera* wooden leg ‖ leg, drumstick (de ave) ‖ leg (de compás) ‖ downstroke (de letra) ‖ lobe (de nuez) ‖ — FIG & FAM *cortarle a uno las piernas* to stop s.o. in his tracks ‖ FIG *dormir a pierna suelta* or *tendida* to sleep like a log, to sleep soundly ‖

FIG & FAM *estirar las piernas* to stretch one's legs.

pierrot *m* pierrot (payaso).

pietismo *m* REL pietism (doctrina).

pieza *f* part, piece; *las piezas de un motor* the parts of a motor ‖ play (de teatro) ‖ piece (de música) ‖ patch (remiendo) ‖ roll, piece (de tejido) ‖ piece, head (de caza) ‖ piece, coin (moneda) ‖ man, piece (ajedrez) ‖ room (habitación) ‖ piece (de vajilla) ‖ unit of pressure (unidad de presión) ‖ ordinary heraldic bearing (heráldica) ‖ FIG specimen (ejemplar); *ha cazado una buena pieza* he has bagged a fine specimen ‖ — FIG & FAM *dejar de una pieza* to leave speechless; *esta noticia me dejó de una pieza* this news left me speechless ‖ *de una pieza* in one piece (cosa), upright (persona) ‖ FIG *¡es una buena* or *linda pieza!* a fine one he is!, he is a right one! | *me he quedado de una pieza* I was speechless *o* flabbergasted ‖ *pieza corta* sketch (de teatro) ‖ *pieza de artillería* piece of artillery ‖ *pieza de autos* file on a case ‖ *pieza de convicción* vital evidence ‖ *pieza de museo* museum exhibit, show piece, museum piece ‖ *pieza de recambio* or *de repuesto* spare part ‖ *pieza oratoria* speech ‖ *poner una pieza* to patch (remendar) ‖ *por piezas* in pieces, piece by piece ‖ *un dos piezas* a suit (traje de mujer), a bikini (bikini).

piezoelectricidad *f* FÍS piezoelectricity.

piezoeléctrico, ca *adj* FÍS piezoelectric.

piezometría *f* piezometry.

piezómetro *m* FÍS piezometer.

pífano *m* MÚS fife.

pifia *f* miscue (en el billar) ‖ FIG & FAM blunder, bloomer (descuido); *cometer una pifia* to make a bloomer ‖ AMER mockery, joke (burla).

pifiar *vi* to miscue (en el billar) ‖ FIG & FAM to blunder, to make a bloomer (meter la pata) ‖ AMER to mock (burlarse).

pigargo *m* osprey, fish hawk (ave).

Pigmalión *npr m* Pygmalion.

pigmentación *f* pigmentation.

pigmentar *vt* to pigment.

pigmentario, ria *adj* pigmentary.

pigmento *m* pigment.

pigmeo, a *m/f* pygmy.
◆ *adj* pygmean, pygmy.

pignoración *f* pledge (en el monte de piedad).

pignorar *vt* to pawn, to pledge.

pignoraticio, cia *adj* JUR pignoratious, of *o* pertaining to a pledge.

pigricia *f* laziness (pereza) ‖ AMER trifle (trivialidad).

pija *f* POP prick (miembro viril).

pijada *f* FAM knick-knack, trinket (objeto) | silly thing (cosa estúpida) | trifle (menudencia) ‖ FAM *no me vengas con pijadas* don't bother me.

pijama *m* pyjamas *pl* [*US* pajamas *pl*] ‖ CULIN FAM kind of knickerbocker glory.

pije *adj* AMER FAM ridiculous ‖ pretentious, haughty (cursi).

pijo, ja *adj* FAM daft (tonto).
◆ *m/f* FAM fool (tonto).
◆ *m* POP prick.

pijota *f* codling (pescadilla) ‖ *hacer pijotas* to play ducks and drakes, to skim stones across the water.

pijotada *f* → **pijotería.**

pijotería *f* FAM bother, nuisance (molestia) | silly thing (cosa estúpida) | trifle (menudencia) ‖ AMER meanness (tacañería).

pijotero, ra *adj* FAM bothersome, tiresome (pesado) | damned, damn; *este pijotero niño* this damned child ‖ AMER FAM mean, stingy (tacaño).
◆ *m/f* FAM bore, pest, nuisance, drag (pesado) ‖ AMER FAM skinflint, miser (tacaño).

pila *f* heap (rimero), pile (montón); *una pila de leña* a pile of wood ‖ FIG loads *pl* (serie); *tiene una pila de niños* he has loads of children | loads *pl*, heaps *pl*, stacks *pl*, piles *pl* (gran cantidad) ‖ basin (de fuente) ‖ sink (de cocina) ‖ stoup (de agua bendita) ‖ font (para bautizar) ‖ trough (bebedero) ‖ ARQ pier (machón de un puente) ‖ FÍS battery, cell; *pila seca* dry battery ‖ AMER fountain (fuente) ‖ — *nombre de pila* Christian name, first name ‖ *pila atómica* atomic pile ‖ *sacar de pila* to be a godparent.

pilar *m* ARQ pillar (columna) | pier (de un puente) ‖ milestone (mojón) ‖ basin, bowl (de fuente) ‖ FIG pillar, prop (apoyo) ‖ prop (forward) (rugby).

pilar *vt* to pound [grain].

pilastra *f* ARQ pilaster.

Pilato (Poncio) *npr m* Pontius Pilate.

pilcha *f* AMER FAM (peasant's) clothes *pl*.

píldora *f* pill ‖ FIG & FAM bad news ‖ — FIG & FAM *dorar la píldora* to gild the pill | *se tragó la píldora* he swallowed it, he fell for it (se lo creyó), he swallowed the bitter pill (tuvo que aguantarlo).

pileta *f* small stoup (de agua bendita) ‖ small basin (fuente) ‖ sink (de cocina) ‖ AMER swimming pool (piscina).

pilífero, ra *adj* piliferous.

piliforme *adj* piliform.

pilón *m* basin (de fuente) ‖ trough (bebedero) ‖ mortar (mortero) ‖ sugarloaf (azúcar) ‖ ARQ pylon (puerta monumental) | pillar, post (columna) ‖ *martillo pilón* drop hammer.

pilongo, ga *adj* thin (flaco) ‖ *castaña pilonga* dried chestnut.

pilórico, ca *adj* pyloric.

píloro *m* ANAT pylorus.

pilorriza *f* BOT calyptra.

pilosidad *f* pilosity.

piloso, sa *adj* pilose; *sistema piloso* pilose system.

pilotaje *m* MAR & AVIAC pilotage, piloting ‖ ARQ piles *pl* (conjunto de pilotes) ‖ *pilotaje sin visibilidad* blind flying.

pilotar; pilotear *vt* MAR to pilot, to steer, to navigate ‖ AVIAC to pilot, to fly ‖ to drive (un coche) ‖ FIG to guide, to lead, to show the way to (guiar).

pilote *m* pile, stake (estaca).
◆ *pl* piles; *construido sobre pilotes* built on piles.

pilotear *vt* → **pilotar.**

piloto *m* MAR pilot; *piloto práctico* coastal *o* harbour pilot | pilot, mate, second in command (de un buque) ‖ pilot (de un avión) ‖ driver (conductor de un coche) ‖ AUT rear light (luz posterior), sidelight, parking light (luz de posición) ‖ pilot lamp (para indicar el funcionamiento de un aparato) ‖ pilot light (en los aparatos de gas) ‖ FIG guide (guía) ‖ — *avión sin piloto* pilotless plane ‖ *piloto automático* automatic pilot ‖ *piloto de altura* high-sea pilot ‖ *piloto de línea* or *civil* airline pilot ‖ *piloto de pruebas* test pilot.
◆ *adj* pilot (que sirve de modelo); *fábrica piloto* pilot plant.

piltra *f* FAM bed, pit, sack (cama).

piltrafa *f* FAM gristly meat (carne mala) ‖ FAM wretch, poor specimen (persona) ‖ AMER bargain (ganga).
◆ *pl* scraps (residuos) ‖ FIG & FAM *hacer piltrafas* to make mincemeat of (destrozar).

pillaje *m* plunder, pillage (saqueo).

pillapilla *m* *jugar al pillapilla* to play tag, to play tick, to play it.

pillar *vt* to pillage, to plunder, to loot (saquear) ‖ FAM to catch; *pillar a un ladrón* to catch a thief; *pillar el tren* to catch the train; *pillar un resfriado* to catch a cold | to run over; *cuidado que no te pille un coche* be careful that a car does not run you over | to get (obtener) ‖ — FAM *me pilla bastante lejos* it's quite a way | *me pilla de camino* it's on my way | *me pilló un dedo la puerta del coche* I caught my finger *o* I got my finger caught in the car door | *no me pilla de camino* it's out of my way.

pillastre; pillastrón *m* FAM scoundrel, rogue, rascal (bribón) | rascal (niño).

pillear *vi* FAM to lead the life of a scoundrel, to get up to roguery | to play tricks, to be mischievous (los niños).

pillería *f* FAM gang of scoundrels | trick (engaño) | rascality, knavery (carácter de pillo).

pillete; pillín *m* FAM little rascal, little scamp (pilluelo).

pillo, lla *m/f* FAM rogue, scoundrel (persona mayor) | rascal, scamp (niño) ‖ — FIG *a pillo, pillo y medio* set a thief to catch a thief ‖ *dárselas de pillo* to try to be smart *o* big, to think o.s. big.
◆ *adj* naughty (malo).

pilluelo, la *m/f* FAM scallywag, little rascal, urchin, little scamp (chico malo).

¡pim! *interj* bang!, boom! ‖ *pim, pam, pum* Aunt Sally (pimpampún).

pimental *m* pepper patch.

pimentar *vt* FIG to season (sazonar).

pimentero *m* pepper plant (arbusto).

pimentón *m* CULIN paprika (polvo).

pimienta *f* pepper; *pimienta blanca, negra* white, black pepper ‖ FIG & FAM spice ‖ — *echar pimienta* to pepper ‖ FIG & FAM *sal y pimienta* charm.

pimiento *m* pimiento (planta) ‖ pimiento, pepper (fruto) ‖ paprika (pimentón) ‖ pepper plant ‖ — FIG & FAM *me importa un pimiento* I couldn't care less, I don't give a hoot ‖ *pimiento chile* chilli ‖ *pimiento morrón* sweet pepper.

pimpampúm *m* Aunt Sally (en las ferias).

pimpante *adj* smart, trim, spruce (peripuesto) ‖ self-assured, pleased with o.s. (seguro de sí mismo).

pimpi *m* FAM fool, idiot (bobo) | bighead, snob (presumido).

pimpinela *f* BOT burnet (rosácea), pimpernel (umbelífera), pimpernel (planta).

pimplar *vt* FAM to down (beber).
◆ *vi* FAM to booze, to tipple.
◆ *vpr* FAM to down.

pimpollo *m* shoot (vástago) ‖ young tree (árbol nuevo) ‖ rosebud (capullo) ‖ FIG & FAM angel, cherub (niño) | handsome boy (joven), good-looker, pretty girl (chica).

pinabete *m* fir (tree) (abeto).

pinacoteca *f* art *o* picture gallery, pinacotheca.

pináculo *m* pinnacle ‖ FIG pinnacle, acme, peak; *estar en el pináculo de la gloria* to be at the peak of one's glory ‖ FIG *poner a alguien en el pináculo* to extol s.o., to praise s.o. to the skies.

pinado, da *adj* pinnate, pinnated (hoja).

pinar *m* pine grove, pinewood.

pinaza *f* pinnace (embarcación).

pincel *m* paintbrush, brush ‖ FIG style [of painting] (modo de pintar) | painter, artist (pintor) | work, painting (obra).

pincelada *f* stroke of a brush, brushstroke || MED painting (en la garganta) || FIG touch (rasgo); *pincelada fuerte* firm touch || FIG *dar la última pincelada* to put the finishing *o* final touch.

pinciano, na *adj* [of *o* from] Valladolid.
◆ *m/f* native *o* inhabitant of Valladolid.

pinchadiscos *m inv* disc jockey.

pinchadura *f* prick (con una espina, etc.).

pinchar *vt* to prick; *las espinas pinchan* thorns prick || to punture (neumático) || FIG to tease, to goad, to annoy (irritar) | to goad, to push, to prod (incitar) | to wound (mortificar) | to stir up (provocar) | to annoy, to rile (enojar) || MED to inject.
◆ *vi* to get punctured, to puncture (neumático) || FIG & FAM *ni pincha ni corta* he cuts no ice.
◆ *vpr* to prick o.s. (con un alfiler) || to get punctured, to puncture (neumático) || FIG & FAM to tease *o* to taunt one another (meterse uno con otro).

pinchaúvas *m inv* FAM good-for-nothing.

pinchazo *m* prick || puncture, blowout (de neumático) || FIG scathing remark (dicho malicioso).

pinche *m* kitchen boy, scullion (de cocina) || FIG & FAM *haber sido pinche antes de cocinero* to be nobody's fool, to know all the tricks.
◆ *adj* AMER bloody, damned (maldito, miserable).

pinchito *m* CULIN small skewer, brochette (para asar) | skewer (de carne) || *pinchitos morunos* shish kebab.

pincho *m* point || prickle, thorn (de planta) || spine (de animal) || CULIN skewer (asador) || AMER hatpin || *pincho moruno* shish kebab.

Píndaro *npr m* Pindar.

pindonga *f* FAM gadabout (mujer).

pindonguear *vi* FAM to gallivant, to gad [about].

pindongueo *m* FAM gallivanting, gadding (about).

pineal *adj* ANAT pineal; *cuerpo pineal* pineal body.

pineda *f* pine grove, pinewood (pinar).

pínfano *m* MÚS dulcimer.

pingajo *m* FAM rag, tatter.

pinganilla *f* AMER dandy (currutaco) || AMER *en pinganillas* crouching (en cuclillas), on tiptoe (de puntillas), on tenterhooks (en situación incierta).

pingo *m* FAM rag, tatter (pingajo) | gadabout (mujer) || AMER horse (caballo) | devil (diablo).
◆ *pl* FAM togs, gear *sing* [clothes] (trapos viejos).

pingonear *vi* FAM to gallivant, to gad (about).

ping-pong *m* table tennis, ping-pong.

pingüe *adj* fatty (graso) || FIG fat, big, large; *obtener pingües beneficios* to make fat profits | profitable, fat (negocio) | abundant, plentiful (abundante).

pingüino *m* ZOOL penguin.

pinitos *m pl* FAM first steps [of a convalescent, a child, etc.]; *hacer pinitos* to take one's first steps.

pinnado, da *adj* BOT pinnate.

pinnípedo, da *adj/s* ZOOL pinniped.

pino, na *adj* steep (pendiente).
◆ *m* BOT pine (árbol) || FIG & POÉT bark, vessel, craft, boat (nave) || first step; *hacer pinos* to take one's first steps || — FIG & FAM *en el quinto pino* at the back of beyond, in the middle of nowhere (muy lejos) || *hacer el pino* to stand on one's head || *pino albar* or *rayo* or *silvestre* Scotch pine || *pino alerce* larch || *pino carrasco* Aleppo pine || *pino piñonero* or *real* stone pine, umbrella pine || *pino rodeno* or *marítimo* pinaster, cluster pine.

pinol; pinole; pínole *m* AMER roasted maize flour, pinole.

pinolero, ra *m/f* AMER FAM Nicaraguan.

pinreles *m pl* POP hooves [US dogs] (pies).

pinsapar *m* grove of Spanish firs.

pinsapo *m* Spanish fir [tree] (árbol).

pinta *f* stain, mark, spot (mancha) || spot (lunar) || drop (gota) || mark [on playing cards] || pint (medida) || trump (triunfo en cartas) || FIG appearance, aspect, look (aspecto) || AMER colour [of an animal] (color) | race, pedigree, stock (casta) || — FIG *con esa pinta no le recibirán en ningún sitio* the way he looks they will not accept him anywhere | *tener buena pinta* to look good | *tener mala pinta* to look bad (la situación), to look off-colour, to look under the weather (parecer enfermo) | *tener pinta de* to look like; *tener pinta de pícaro* to look like a rogue.
◆ *m* scoundrel, rogue (golfo)
◆ *f pl* typhoid *sing* (tabardillo).

pintada *f* guinea fowl (ave) || graffito.

pintado, da *adj* painted; *pintado de azul* painted blue || painted, made-up [face] (rostro) || speckled (la piel de los animales) || — FIG & FAM *eso le puede pasar al más pintado* that could happen to the best of us | *es su padre pintado* he's the spitting image of his father | *ir* or *sentar que ni pintado* to suit to a tee | *no puedo verle ni pintado* I can't bear *o* stand *o* stick him, I can't bear the sight of him, I hate the very sight of him || *papel pintado* wallpaper || FIG & FAM *venir como pintado* or *que ni pintado* to suit to a tee, to suit down to the ground.
◆ *m* painting (acción de pintar).

pintalabios *m inv* lipstick.

pintamonas *m inv* FAM dauber (mal pintor).

pintar *vt* to paint (con pintura); *pintar un retrato* to paint a portrait; *pintar de rojo una habitación* to paint a room red || to draw, to sketch (dibujar); *píntame un caballo* draw me a horse || FIG to describe, to depict, to paint (describir) || — FIG *no pintar nada* not to fit in, to be out of place (estar fuera de su ámbito), not to have a say, to cut no ice (no tener influencia) || *pintar al fresco, al óleo* to paint in fresco, in oils || *pintar al temple* to paint in tempera || *pintar con pistola* to spray || FIG & FAM *pintarla* to put it on, to put on airs and graces.
◆ *vi* to paint || to ripen (las frutas) || FIG to come out, to show (mostrarse).
◆ *vpr* to put one's makeup on, to make up (el rostro) || to put one's lipstick on (los labios) || to make one's eyes up (los ojos) || FIG to appear, to show (o.s.); *la felicidad se pintaba en su rostro* his happiness showed in his face || — FIG & FAM *para esto me las pinto solo* this is right up my street | *se las pinta solo* there's no one like him.

pintarrajar; pintarrajear *vt* FAM to daub, to bedaub.
◆ *vpr* FAM to put on layers of makeup.

pintarroja *f* ZOOL dogfish (lija).

pintiparado, da *adj* exactly the same, identical (semejante) || just right, just at the right time; *llegar pintiparado* to arrive just at the right time || perfectly (well); *esta corbata viene pintiparada con este traje* this tie goes perfectly with this suit || — *es pintiparado a su hermano* he is the spitting image of his brother || *venir pintiparado* to come just right (ser oportuno), to suit (s.o.) to a tee (convenirle a uno).

pintiparar *vt* FAM to compare (comparar) | to make alike (asemejar).

Pinto *n pr* FAM *estar entre Pinto y Valdemoro* to be tipsy (medio borracho), to be undecided, to sit on the fence (estar indeciso).

pinto, ta *adj* *caballo pinto* pinto || *judía pinta* pinto bean.

pintor, ra *m/f* painter || AMER haughty *o* conceited *o* boastful person (fachendoso) || — *pintor de brocha gorda* (house) painter (de puertas, de ventanas, etc.), dauber, bad painter (mal pintor) || *pintor de cuadros* painter, artist || *pintor decorador* decorator || TEATR *pintor escenógrafo* painter of scenery, scenery painter.

pintoresco, ca *adj* picturesque || colourful [US colorful] (estilo).

pintoresquismo *m* picturesqueness || colour [US color] (del estilo).

pintorrear *vt* FAM to daub; *pintorrear de azul y rojo* to daub in blue and red.

pintura *f* paint (color); *cuidado con la pintura* wet paint (letrero) || painting; *pintura rupestre* cave painting; *la pintura de la casa* the painting of the house || picture, painting (cuadro) || FIG description, picture, portrayal (descripción) || — FIG & FAM *no poder ver a uno ni en pintura* not to be able to stand *o* to bear *o* to stick s.o., not to be able to bear the sight of s.o. || *pintura a la acuarela* watercolour || *pintura a la aguada* gouache || *pintura al fresco* fresco || *pintura al temple* tempera painting || *pintura con pistola* spray painting.

pinturero, ra *adj* FAM dressy, showy | haughty, conceited (presumido).
◆ *m* dandy (elegante) | haughty man (presumido).
◆ *f* showy woman | haughty woman.

pinza *f* pincer, nipper, claw (de cangrejo, etc.) || dart (costura) || TECN pincers *pl* || peg, pin (para colgar la ropa lavada) || *pinza sujetapapeles* paper clip.
◆ *pl* tweezers; *pinzas para* or *de depilar* eyebrow tweezers || — *pinzas de dentista* forceps || *pinzas para el azúcar* sugar tongs (tenacillas) || FIG & FAM *sacársele a uno con pinzas* to drag it out of s.o.

pinzón *m* chaffinch (ave) || *pinzón real* bullfinch.

piña *f* (pine) cone (del pino) || fruit, cone (de otros árboles) || pineapple (ananás) || FAM blow (puñetazo) || FIG clan, clique (grupo cerrado) | cluster, group (de personas) | cluster, bunch (de cosas).

piñata *f* *domingo de piñata* the first Sunday of Lent.

— OBSERV The *piñata* is a pot full of sweets which is broken with sticks during a masked ball on the first Sunday of Lent.

piñón *m* pine seed *o* nut (simiente del pino) || pinion (rueda); *piñón de cambio* bevel pinion || ass at the rear of the herd (burro) || rear sprocket wheel (de bicicleta) || — FIG & FAM *estar a partir un piñón con uno* to be hand in glove with s.o. || TECN *piñón fijo* fixed wheel | *piñón libre* freewheel | *piñón mayor* sprocket wheel (de bicicleta) | *piñón planetario* planet gear.

piñonata *f*; **piñonate** *m* candied pine nut.

piñonero *adj m* *pino piñonero* stone pine, umbrella pine (árbol).
◆ *m* ZOOL bullfinch (pinzón real).

pío *m* chirping, cheeping (de las aves) || clucking (del pollo) || FAM desire, yearning (deseo) || FIG & FAM *no decir ni pío* not to say a word.

Pío *npr m* Pius; *Pío nono* (IX), Pius IX [the ninth].

pío, a *adj* pious (devoto) || charitable (compasivo) || piebald (caballo) || *obra pía* religious foundation (fundación religiosa), charity, charitable institution (institución de beneficiencia).

piocha *f* pickaxe [US pickax] (zapapico).

pioftalmia *f* MED pyophthalmia.

piogenia *f* MED pyogenesis.

piojo *m* louse || — *piojo de mar* whale louse (crustáceo) || FIG & FAM *piojo resucitado* upstart.

piojoso, sa *adj* lousy (lleno de piojos) || FIG stingy, mean (mezquino) | dirty (sucio).

piola *f* MAR houseline || leapfrog (juego); *jugar a la piola* to play leapfrog || AMER string (bramante).

piolar *vi* to cheep, to chirp (pájaro).

piolet *m* ice axe, piolet (alpinismo).

piolín *m* AMER string (bramante).

pión, ona *adj* cheeping, chirping || FIG peevish, crabbed (protestón).

pionero *m* pioneer (precursor, adelantado).

piorrea *f* MED pyorrhoea [US pyorrhea].

pipa *f* pipe; *fumar en pipa* to smoke a pipe || barrel, cask (tonel) || pipe (medida) || pip (pepita) || seed (de girasol, de melón, etc.) || MÚS pipe (flauta) | reed (lengüeta) || — FIG & FAM *eso es el cuento de la buena pipa* it goes on and on || *pipa de la paz* pipe of peace, peace pipe || TECN *pipa del distribuidor* distributor arm (automóvil).

piperáceas *f pl* BOT piperaceae.

pipería *f* barrels *pl.*

pipermín *m* peppermint.

pipeta *f* pipette.

pipi *m* POP ass, clot (tonto) | squaddy, soldier (soldado).

pipí *m* FAM wee-wee || *hacer pipí* to wee-wee, to wee.

pipiar *vi* to cheep, to chirp (piar).

pípila *f* AMER turkey.

pipiolo *m* FAM novice, newcomer [US greenhorn] (inexperto), new boy (de una escuela) | little boy (niño) | youngster (joven).

pipirigallo *m* BOT sainfoin.

pipiritaña *f* flute, pipe (caramillo).

pipirrana *f* cucumber and tomato salad (en Andalucía).

pipistrelo *m* pipistrelle, small bat (murciélago).

pipón, ona *m/f* AMER FAM nipper, kiddie (chiquillo).

pipote *m* AMER rubbish bin [US trash can].

pipudo, da *adj* FAM fantastic, terrific, wonderful, great (espléndido).

pique *m* pique, resentment (resentimiento) || self-esteem (amor propio) || MAR crotch || AMER chigoe (nigua) | pepper (ají) | path (senda) || — *a pique* sheer [cliff] (a plomo) || *a pique de* on the point of (a punto de) || *echar a pique* to sink (un barco, un negocio), to ruin (los proyectos, una empresa) || *estar a pique de hacer algo* to almost do sth., to be about to do sth.; *he estado a pique de caerme* I almost fell || *irse a pique* to sink (un barco), to fail (fracasar), to be ruined (arruinarse, frustrarse) || *tener un pique con alguien* to have a grudge against s.o.

piqué *m* piqué (tela).

piquera *f* entrance hole [in beehive] (de colmenas) || bunghole (de tonel) || TECN taphole (altos hornos) | barrel (de lámpara) || AMER dive (taberna barata).

piquero *m* pikeman (soldier) || miner (minero).

piqueta *f* pickaxe [US pickax] || ice axe, piolet (de montañero) || AMER weak wine (aguapié).

piquete *m* picket; *piquete de huelga* strike picket || squad; *piquete de ejecución* firing squad || sting (pinchazo) || small hole (agujero) || stake, post (jalón) || AMER yard (corral).

pira *f* pyre (hoguera) || FIG & FAM *irse de pira* to play truant [US to play hooky] (no ir a clase).

piragua *f* pirogue (embarcación) || canoe (de madera) || kayak (de tela).

piragüismo *m* canoeing.

piragüista *m/f* canoeist.

piramidal *adj* pyramidal.

pirámide *f* pyramid; *pirámide truncada* truncated pyramid || — *pirámide de las edades* pyramid-shaped graph showing the age of the population || *tronco de pirámide* trunk of a pyramid.

piramidión *m* ARQ pyramidion.

piraña *f* AMER piranha (pez).

pirarse *vpr* FAM to buzz off, to hop it, to clear off (marcharse); *estoy deseando pirarme* I'd like to buzz off.

pirata *m* pirate || FIG hard-hearted man, brute (hombre despiadado) || *pirata aéreo* or *del aire* hijacker.

◆ *adj* FIG pirate (clandestino); *edición, emisión pirata* pirate edition, broadcast.

piratear *vi* to pirate, to practise piracy || FIG to pirate (copiar) | to steal (robar).

piratería *f* piracy || *piratería aérea* high-jacking.

piraya *f* AMER piranha (pez).

pirca *f* AMER dry-stone wall.

pirenaico, ca *adj/s* Pyrenean.

Pireo (El) *npr m* GEOGR Piraeus.

pirético, ca *adj* pyretic.

pírex *m* Pyrex (vidrio).

pirexia *f* MED pyrexia.

piri *m* POP *darse el piri* to buzz off, to hop it.

pirindola *f* (spinning) top (perinola).

pirindolo *m* FAM thing, thingummyjig.

Pirineos *npr mpl* GEOGR Pyrenees.

piripi *adj* FAM merry, tipsy (un poco ebrio).

pirita *f* MIN pyrites | pyrite, iron pyrites (de hierro).

piro *m* FAM *darse el piro* to buzz off, to hop it (marcharse).

pirofosfato *m* QUÍM pyrophosphate.

pirofosfórico *adj m* QUÍM pyrophosphoric; *ácido pirofosfórico* pyrophosphoric acid.

pirógeno *adj* pyrogenic, pyrogenous.

pirograbado *m* pyrogravure, pyrography.

pirolisis *f* pyrolisis.

piromancia *f* pyromancy.

piromanía *f* pyromania.

pirómano, na *adj* pyromaniacal.

◆ *m/f* pyromaniac.

pirometría *f* pyrometry.

pirómetro *m* pyrometer (termómetro).

piropear *vt* FAM to compliment, to pay flirtatious compliments to.

piropo *m* FAM compliment, amorous compliment, flirtatious remark [especially in the street] || FAM *decir* or *echar piropos a* to compliment, to pay flirtatious compliments to.

piróscafo *m* steamship (barco de vapor).

pirosfera *f* pyrosphere.

pirosis *f* MED pyrosis.

pirotecnia *f* pyrotechnics.

pirotécnico, ca *adj* pyrotechnical, pyrotechnic, firework.

◆ *m* pyrotechnist (obrero).

piroxeno *m* MIN pyroxene.

pirrarse *vpr* FAM *pirrarse por* to rave about, to be crazy about (estar loco por).

pirriaque *m* POP plonk (vino).

pírrico, ca *adj/s* Pyrrhic (danza) || *victoria pírrica* Pyrrhic victory.

pirriquio *m* POÉT pyrrhic.

Pirro *npr m* Pyrrhus.

pirueta *f* pirouette || *con una hábil pirueta evitó la pregunta* he neatly sidestepped the question, he cleverly dodged the question.

pirulí *m* lollipop (caramelo).

pirulo *m* earthenware pitcher (botijo) || AMER slim child.

pis *m* FAM wee-wee (orina) || FAM *hacer pis* to wee.

pisa *f* fulling (del paño) || pressing, treading (aceituna o uva) || mating (de los animales) || FAM hiding (zurra).

pisada *f* track, trace, footprint, trail [of steps] (huella) || step, footstep; *se oían sus pisadas* his steps were heard || pressing, treading (de la fruta) || trampling (aplastamiento) || fulling (de paños) || *seguir las pisadas de uno* to follow s.o.'s tracks *o* trail, to trail s.o. (seguir el rastro), to follow in s.o.'s footsteps (hacer igual que otro).

pisapapeles *m inv* paperweight.

pisar *vt* to stand on, to tread on; *pisarle el pie a uno* to stand on s.o.'s foot || to step on (poner el pie casualmente) || to full; *pisar paños* to full cloth || to tread, to press; *pisar uvas* to press grapes || to tread down (tierra) || MÚS to pluck (las cuerdas) | to strike [the keys] (las teclas) || to cover (el macho) || FIG to trample on, to abuse, to humiliate (pisotear) | to take away (quitar); *pisarle el puesto a uno* to take away s.o.'s job, to take s.o.'s job away from him | to pinch, to steal (robar) || — FIG *ir* or *andar pisando huevos* to walk carefully | *no se deja pisar por nadie* he does not let anyone tread on him || *no vuelvo a pisar más esa casa* I shall not set foot in that house again || *pisar el acelerador* to put one's foot on *o* to step on *o* to press the accelerator, to put one's foot down || *pisar el escenario* or *las tablas* to be on the stage, to tread the boards; *es la primera vez que este actor pisa el escenario* it is the first time that this actor has been on the stage || FIG *pisar fuerte* to know where one is at, to make a strong start || *pisar las huellas de alguien* to follow s.o.'s track *o* trail || FIG *pisarle a uno el terreno* to beat s.o. to it || *prohibido pisar el césped* keep off the grass.

◆ *vi* to tread, to step || to be one above the other [storeys of a building].

pisaúvas *m inv* grape treader.

pisaverde *m* FAM dandy (joven presumido).

piscícola *adj* piscicultural.

piscicultor *m* piscicultivator.

piscicultura *f* pisciculture.

piscifactoría *f* fish hatchery.

pisciforme *adj* pisciform.

piscina *f* swimming pool (para bañarse) || fishpond (estanque) || piscina (de iglesia).

Piscis *npr m* ASTR Pisces.

piscívoro, ra *adj* piscivorous.

◆ *m/f* piscivorous animal.

pisco *m* AMER pisco brandy (aguardiente) | earthenware picher (botijo).

piscolabis *m inv* FAM snack; *tomar un piscolabis* to have a snack.

pisiforme *adj* ANAT pisiform (hueso).

piso *m* floor, storey (de una casa); *casa de seis pisos* six-floor building || floor; *vive en el sexto piso* he lives on the sixth floor || flat [US apartment] (vivienda); *piso de tres habitaciones* three-roomed flat || deck (de un autobús) || stage (de un cohete) || tread (de un neumático) || sole (suela de un zapato) || layer (capa) || ground (suelo) || floor (de madera) || surface (de la calle) ‖ seam, layer (capa geológica) ‖ MIN level ‖ — *autobús de dos pisos* double-decker bus ‖ *casa de pisos* block of flats [US apartment building] ‖ *piso bajo* ground floor [US first floor] ‖ *piso franco* hideout ‖ *piso principal* main floor, first floor [US second floor] (de una casa), dress circle (de teatro).

pisón *m* beetle (de cantero).

pisotear *vt* to trample on, to trample underfoot (aplastar) ‖ to stamp on (dar pisotones a) ‖ FIG to trample on (desconsiderar).

pisotón *m* FAM stamp on the foot ‖ *darle a uno un pisotón* to tread *o* to stamp on s.o.'s foot.

pispar *vt* POP to pinch, to nick [US to hook] (robar) ‖ AMER to watch (acechar).

pisqueño, ña *adj* [of *o* from] Pisco (Perú).
◆ *m/f* native *o* inhabitant of Pisco.

pista *f* trail, track (huella) ‖ track (de carreras) ‖ runway (de aviones) ‖ court (de tenis) ‖ run, slope (de esquí) ‖ rink (de hielo, de patinaje) ‖ ring (de circo) ‖ trail; *pista falsa* false trail ‖ — *corredor en pista* cyclist who races only on indoor tracks ‖ *estar sobre la pista* to be on the scent, to be on the track ‖ *pista de aterrizaje* runway, landing strip ‖ *pista de baile* dance floor ‖ *pista de ceniza* dirt track ‖ *pista para ciclistas* cycle path ‖ *seguir la pista* to follow the trail *o* track, to be on the trail *o* track, to trail, to track.

pistachero *m* pistachio (alfóncigo).

pistacho *m* pistachio [nut] (fruto).

pistilo *m* BOT pistil.

pisto *m* dish of fried vegetables (fritada) ‖ FIG & FAM *darse pisto* to put on airs.

pistola *f* pistol (arma); *tiro de pistola* pistol shot ‖ spray gun, sprayer (para pintar) ‖ *pistola ametralladora* submachine gun ‖ *pistola de agua* water pistol.

pistolera *f* hoslter.

pistolero *m* gangster, gunman (bandolero) ‖ hired killer (asesino pagado).

pistoletazo *m* pistol shot.

pistón *m* piston (émbolo); *el recorrido del pistón* the stroke of the piston ‖ percussion cap, cartridge cap (de arma de fuego) ‖ MÚS piston [valve] (de instrumento) | cornet (corneta de llaves).

pistonudo, da *adj* POP great, fantastic, terrific.

pita *f* BOT agave (planta) ‖ pita [thread] (hilo) ‖ whistling, hissing (en el teatro) ‖ (glass) marble (canica) ‖ *recibir una pita* to be hissed.

pitada *f* whistle ‖ whistling, hissing (en el teatro) ‖ AMER puff (de cigarro) ‖ FIG & FAM *dar una pitada* to hiss, to boo (en el teatro).

Pitágoras *npr m* Pythagoras; *tabla de Pitágoras* Pythagorean table.

pitagórico, ca *adj/s* Pythagorean.

pitanza *f* (daily) ration, dole (ración de comida) ‖ FAM daily bread (alimento cotidiano).

pitar *vi* to whistle, to blow a whistle ‖ FIG & FAM to work, to go well (marchar) ‖ to hoot (un coche) ‖ AMER to smoke ‖ FAM *salir pitando* or *de estampía* to go *o* to be off like a shot *o* like a rocket.
◆ *vt* to whistle at, to hiss, to boo; *pitar una obra de teatro* to whistle at a play ‖ to whistle; *el árbitro pitó al jugador* the referee whistled the player ‖ (p us) to pay (pagar) ‖ AMER to smoke (fumar).

pitarra *f* sleep, rheum (p us) (legaña).

pitarroso, sa *adj* with sleep *o* rheum in one's eyes.

pitecántropo *m* ZOOL pithecanthropus.

pitejo *m* FAM undertaker.

pitia *f* pythoness (de Delfos).

Pitias *npr m* Pythias.

pítico, ca *adj* Pythian (de Delfos); *juegos píticos* Pythian games.

pitido; pitío *m* whistling (ruido producido por el aire, etc.) ‖ whistle (con el pito); *le llamó con un pitido* he called him with a whistle ‖ hooting (del klaxon).

pitillera *f* cigarette case (petaca).

pitillo *m* FAM cigarette; *liar, echar un pitillo* to roll, to smoke a cigarette ‖ AMER straw (para tomar bebidas).

pítima *f* MED poultice ‖ FAM drunkenness (borrachera) ‖ FAM *coger una pítima* to get plastered *o* sozzled.

pitiminí *m* fairy rose bush (rosal) ‖ *rosa de pitiminí* fairy rose.

pitio, tia *adj* Pythian.

pitío *m* ⟶ **pitido.**

pito *m* whistle (instrumento) ‖ hooter (de un automóvil) ‖ whistle (del tren) ‖ spout (de vasija) ‖ FAM fag, ciggy (cigarrillo) ‖ jack, jackstone (taba) ‖ ZOOL tick (insecto) | woodpecker (pájaro) ‖ POP prick (miembro viril) ‖ AMER pipe ‖ — FAM *cuando pitos, flautas, cuando flautas, pitos* if it's not one thing it's another | *entre pitos y flautas hemos perdido la mañana* what with one thing and another we have wasted the morning | *me oyes como quien oye el pito del sereno* it's like talking to a brick wall | *no me importa un pito, no se me da un pito* I couldn't care less, I don't give a damn *o* a hang | *no valer un pito* or *tres pitos* not to be worth a tinker's cuss | *pitos flautos* foolery, fooling | *por pitos o flautas* for some reason (or another) | *ser el pito del sereno* to be a nobody.

pitoche *m* FAM whistle (pito).

pitón *m* python (serpiente) ‖ horn (de toros, etc.) ‖ spout (de botijos) ‖ shoot (de árbol) ‖ AMER hose pipe (de riego) ‖ *pitón de escalada* piton, peg (alpinismo).

pitonazo *m* butt (golpe) ‖ gore (herida).

pitonisa *f* pythoness.

pitorrearse *vpr* FAM to make fun of, to scoff at.

pitorreo *m* FAM joke (broma) | farce (farsa) | fuss, to-do (alboroto) ‖ — FAM *tomarlo todo a pitorreo* to take everything as a big joke | *traerse un pitorreo con* to make fun of.

pitorro *m* spout (de vasija).

pitpit *m* pipit (ave).

pituita *f* ANAT pituita.

pituitario, ria *adj* ANAT pituitary; *membrana pituitaria* pituitary membrane.

pituso, sa *adj* FAM sweet, cute, lovely (niños).
◆ *m/f* FAM kid, child.

pivotante *adj* BOT tap-rooted (raíz).

pivote *m* TECN pivot (gorrón) ‖ pivot (baloncesto).

píxide *f* pyx (copón).

piyama *m* pyjamas *pl* [US pajamas *pl*].

pizarra *f* slate (piedra y tablilla para escribir) ‖ blackboard (encerado); *salir a la pizarra* to go up *o* out to the blackboard.

pizarral *m* slate quarry.

pizarrería *f* slate quarry.

pizarrero *m* slater.

pizarrín *m* slate pencil.

pizarrón *m* AMER blackboard (encerado) scoreboard (marcador en deportes).

pizarroso, sa *adj* slated, slaty, slatey.

pizca *f* FAM tiny piece (trozo pequeño); *yo sólo como una pizca de pan* I eat only a tiny piece of bread | pinch (de sal, etc.) | drop (cosa líquida) | just a little bit; *con una pizca de suerte hubiera ganado yo* with just a little bit of luck I should have won; *se parece una pizca a su padre* he looks just a little bit like his father ‖ AMER harvest (cosecha) ‖ — FAM *ni pizca* not at all, not in the least, not a bit; *eso no me gusta ni pizca* I don't like that at all; *no tiene ni pizca de autoridad* he has no authority at all | *no hay pizca de vino* there is no wine at all.

pizpireta *adj f* FAM bright, lively, cheerful (alegre).

pizpita; pizpitilla *f* ZOOL wagtail.

pizza *f* CULIN pizza.

pizzería *f* pizzeria, pizza parlour.

pizzicato *m* MÚS pizzicato.

placa *f* plate; *placa de matrícula* number plate [US license plate] ‖ badge [of an order] (insignia) ‖ plaque (medalla conmemorativa) | sign (para señalar) ‖ FOT plate ‖ plate (rótulo) ‖ record (de gramófono) ‖ *placa giratoria* turntable (de ferrocarriles) ‖ INFORM *placa madre* motherboard ‖ *placa solar* solar panel.

placaje *m* tackle (rugby) ‖ *hacer un placaje* to tackle, to bring down (rugby).

placear *vt* to market (vender).

pláceme *m* congratulations *pl* ‖ *dar el pláceme a uno* to congratulate s.o.

placenta *f* ANAT & BOT placenta.

placentario, ria *adj* placental.

placentero, ra *adj* charming, pleasant (agradable); *es un jardín placentero* it is a charming garden ‖ amusing (entretenido).

placer* *m* pleasure (diversión, gusto); *los placeres de la vida* the pleasures of life; *tengo el placer de anunciar* I have pleasure in announcing; *será un placer para mí* it will be a pleasure for me ‖ will (voluntad); *tal es mi placer* such is my will ‖ amusement, enjoyment (entretenimiento) ‖ delight; *placeres de la carne* carnal delights ‖ MAR sandbank (arena) ‖ MIN placer ‖ AMER pearl fishing ground ‖ — *a placer* as much as one wants (en la cantidad que uno quiere), at one's leisure (lentamente) ‖ *mentir a placer* to lie for the sake of lying ‖ *un viaje a placer* a holiday trip.

placer *vi* to like; *me place estudiar* I like studying ‖ *si me place* if I like, if I want to.
— OBSERV The Spanish verb *placer* is little used and usually appears in an impersonal form.

plácet *m* placet (diplomático).

placidez *f* placidity.

plácido, da *adj* calm, still, peaceful (quieto) ‖ placid, tranquil (tranquilo) ‖ pleasant (grato).

plácito *m* opinion (parecer).

plafón *m* ARQ soffit (sofito).

plaga *f* scourge (de un pueblo) ‖ plague, calamity, catastrophe (infortunio) ‖ disaster, catastrophe (daño) ‖ BOT pest, blight ‖ plague (de langostas) ‖ plague, epidemic (abundancia de cosas malas) ‖ glut, surfeit (de cosas buenas); *hay plaga de frutas* there is a surfeit of fruit ‖ *las diez plagas de Egipto* the ten plagues of Egypt.

plagal *adj* MÚS plagal.

plagar *vt* to cover (cubrir); *plagar de heridas* to cover with wounds ‖ to fill; *carta plagada de faltas* letter full of mistakes ‖ — *estar plagado de* to be overburdened *o* plagued with; *plagado de hijos* overburdened with children; *plagado de deudas* plagued with debts ‖ *plagado de ratas* rat-infested.
◆ *vpr* to become covered in.

plagiar *vt* to plagiarize (copiar).

plagiario, ria *adj* plagiaristic.
◆ *m/f* plagiarist ‖ AMER kidnapper (raptor).

plagio *m* plagiarism ‖ pastiche (imitación) ‖ AMER kidnapping (rapto).

plagióstomos *m pl* ZOOL plagiostomi.

plan *m* plan, project (proyecto); *hacer planes* to make plans ‖ scheme, skeleton, framework, plan (esquema); *el plan de un libro* the plan of a book ‖ plan; *plan quinquenal* five-year plan; *plan de construcción* building plan ‖ idea, intention (propósito) ‖ programme (programa) ‖ date (cita) ‖ way (modo) ‖ attitude (actitud) ‖ level (nivel) ‖ height (altura) ‖ FIG & FAM boyfriend (novio), girlfriend (novia) ‖ MAR bilge ‖ MED diet; *estar a plan para adelgazar* to be on a slimming diet | course of treatment; *seguir un plan para engordar* to be on a course of treatment to put on weight ‖ MIN floor (piso) ‖ AMER plain (planicie) ‖ — *a todo plan* on a grand scale ‖ *en plan de* as; *en plan de vencedor* as the winner ‖ *en plan de broma* as a joke, for a laugh *o* a joke; *meterse con alguien en plan de broma* to tease s.o. for a laugh ‖ *en plan grande* on a grand scale ‖ *en plan político* from the political point of view ‖ *en un plan de intimidad* on an intimate footing ‖ *plan de ataque* plan of attack ‖ *plan de estudios* course of study, curriculum, syllabus ‖ *plan de paz* peace plan ‖ ECON *plan de pensiones* pension scheme ‖ *¿tienes plan para mañana?* are you booked for tomorrow?, are you doing anything tomorrow?

plana *f* page (página) ‖ side, page of paper (en la escuela) ‖ plain (llanura) ‖ TECN drawknife (de carpintero) | trowel (llana) ‖ — *a plana y renglón* line for line the same (imprenta), perfectly, exactly (perfectamente) ‖ *a toda plana* full spread (titular), full page (página entera) ‖ FIG *corregir* or *enmendar la plana* to criticize (criticar), to surpass, to outdo (superar) ‖ *en primera plana* on the front page (en los periódicos) ‖ *estar en la primera plana de la actualidad* to be in the headlines *o* in the news ‖ MIL *plana mayor* staff.

planador *m* TECN planisher.

planton *m* plankton.

plancha *f* plate (de metal) ‖ iron (utensilio); *plancha eléctrica* electric iron ‖ ironing (ropa planchada, acción de planchar) ‖ IMPR plate ‖ FIG & FAM boob, bloomer, blunder (error) ‖ dangerous play (fútbol) ‖ MAR gangplank (pasarela) ‖ — *hacer la plancha* to float (on one's back) ‖ *plancha de blindaje* armour plate ‖ FIG & FAM *tirarse una plancha* to boob, to put one's foot in it.

planchada *f* MAR gangplank (puentecillo) ‖ AMER FAM boob, bloomer, blunder.

planchado *m* ironing, pressing ‖ *camisa que no necesita planchado* non-iron *o* drip-dry shirt.

planchado, da *adj* ironed ‖ FAM broke (sin dinero) ‖ AMER FAM very smart.

planchador, ra *m/f* ironer ‖ *máquina planchadora* ironing machine.

planchar *vt* to iron, to press ‖ AMER to flatter (adular) ‖ *mesa de planchar* ironing board.
◆ *vi* to iron, to do the ironing.

planchazo *m* FAM boob, bloomer, blunder (metedura de pata) ‖ dangerous play (en fútbol) ‖ FAM *tirarse un planchazo* to boob, to put one's foot in it.

planchón *m* large plate ‖ FAM boob, bloomer, blunder (planchazo).

planeador *m* glider (avión).

planeadora *f* leveller (máquina de nivelar).

planear *vt* to plan; *planear un viaje* to plan a journey; *planear una reforma* to plan a reform ‖ to draw up a plan of (hacer un plano de).
◆ *vi* to glide (avión) ‖ *vuelo planeado* gliding.

planeo *m* gliding (aviación).

planeta *m* ASTR planet.

planetario, ria *adj* planetary ‖ TECN *piñón planetario* planet gear.
◆ *m* planetarium ‖ TECN planet gear.

planetarium *m* planetarium.

planetoide *m* planetoid.

planicie *f* plain (llanura) ‖ plateau (meseta).

planificación *f* planning; *planificación económica* economic planning; *planificación familiar* family planning.

planificador, ra *adj* planning.
◆ *m/f* planner.

planificar *vt* to plan.

planilla *f* AMER list (lista) | table (cuadro) | ticket (billete) | form, application form, blank (formulario) | ballot paper (papeleta de voto).

planimetría *f* planimetry, surveying.

planímetro *m* planimeter.

planisferio *m* planisphere.

planning *m* planning.

plano, na *adj* flat, level, even, smooth; *terreno plano* flat land; *superficie plana* flat surface ‖ flat; *zapatos planos* flat shoes ‖ MAT plane (geometría) | straight; *ángulo plano* straight angle.
◆ *m* map, plan (mapa); *he comprado un plano de la ciudad* I have bought a map of the city ‖ ARQ plan, draught [US draft] (de construcción) ‖ MAT plane ‖ shot (cine, foto) ‖ plane (de avión) ‖ flat (de la espada) ‖ — *caer de plano* to fall flat (on one's face), to fall full length ‖ *dar de plano* to strike with the flat of a sword (con el sable), to shine straight; *el sol daba de plano en la habitación* the sun was shining straight into the room ‖ *de plano* straightforwardly, directly ‖ *de primer plano* of the first rank, of the utmost importance ‖ *en el primer, en el segundo, en el último plano* in the foreground, in the middle distance, in the background; *en el primer plano del cuadro* in the foreground of the picture ‖ FIG *estar en primer plano* to be in the limelight ‖ *hacer* or *alzar* or *levantar un plano* to make a survey (topografía) ‖ *plano acotado* contour map ‖ *plano americano* three-quarter view *o* shot, view *o* shot from the knees up (cine) ‖ *plano de cola* tailplane (de avión) ‖ *plano de fondo* background (en pintura) ‖ *plano de incidencia* plane of incidence ‖ *plano de tiro* line *o* plane of sight *o* fire ‖ *plano general* or *largo* or *de conjunto* overall plan *o* survey ‖ *plano inclinado* chute ‖ FIG *poner en primer plano* to bring to the fore | *ponerse en primer plano* to come to the fore ‖ CINEM *primer plano* close-up, close shot ‖ *segundo plano* middle distance.

planocóncavo, va *adj* plano-concave.

planoconvexo, xa *adj* plano-convex.

planta *f* plant (vegetal); *planta de adorno, forrajera, carnosa, trepadora* decorative, forage, fleshy, climbing plant ‖ ground plan (plano); *planta de la casa* ground plan of the house ‖ floor, storey; *vivo en la primera planta* I live on the first floor ‖ sole (del pie) ‖ factory, plant (fábrica); *planta siderúrgica* iron and steel plant ‖ plant; *planta eléctrica* electricity plant ‖ field (plantío) ‖ MAT foot (de una perpendicular) ‖ FIG plan (plan) ‖ stance, position of the feet (danza, esgrima) ‖ — FIG & FAM *buena planta* good appearance ‖ *construir una casa de nueva planta* to build a new building ‖ *planta baja* ground floor [US first floor] ‖ FIG *ser una planta de estufa* to be a hothouse person | *tener buena planta* to look good, to be good-looking (ser apuesto).

plantación *f* plantation; *plantación de plátanos* banana plantation ‖ planting (acción).

plantado, da *adj* planted ‖ — FIG & FAM *bien plantado* good-looking, well turned out | *dejar a uno plantado* to stand s.o. up, not to turn up (no acudir a una cita), to leave s.o. standing there (dejar solo), to walk out on s.o. (abandonar), to finish with s.o. (entre novios), to let s.o. down (no prestar ayuda) | *dejarlo todo plantado* to drop everything, to leave everything where it is | *quedarse plantado* to stand (permanecer), to be left standing there (quedarse solo).

plantador, ra *adj* who plants, planting.
◆ *m* planter (el que planta) ‖ dibble, dibber (instrumento agrícola).
◆ *f* AGR planter (máquina).

plantaina *f* BOT plantain (llantén).

plantar *adj* ANAT plantar.

plantar *vt* AGR to plant (plantas, un terreno) ‖ FIG to found, to set up, to establish (establecer) ‖ to set, to put, to place (poner) ‖ to put in (un poste, una estaca) ‖ FIG & FAM to land, to plant (un golpe), to give, to land (una bofetada) | to throw; *plantar en la calle* to throw out; *plantar en la cárcel* to throw into prison | to give up, to finish with, to chuck (abandonar) | to shut up (dejar callado).
◆ *vpr* FIG & FAM to stand o.s.; *se plantó ante la puerta, en la calle* he stood himself in the doorway, in the street | to stand firm (aguantarse) | to get, to be; *en dos horas me plantaré en su casa* I'll get to *o* I'll be at your house in two hours | to stop (pararse) | to settle, to install o.s.; *plantarse en Cádiz* to settle in Cádiz | AMER to dress up (ataviarse) ‖ *me planto* I stick (cartas).

plante *m* strike, stoppage (huelga) ‖ mutiny (motín) ‖ *dar un plante a alguien* to put s.o. in his place.

planteamiento *m* exposition (exposición) ‖ raising (de un problema) ‖ institution, introduction (de sistemas, de reformas, etc.) ‖ MAT laying out, layout, setting out (enfoque de un problema), phrasing (formulación de un problema).

plantear *vt* to expound, to set forth, to state (exponer) ‖ to create, to raise (causar); *la reforma planteó muchas dificultades* the reform created many difficulties ‖ to raise, to bring up, to introduce (introducir un tema, un pleito, etc.) ‖ to plan, to plan out, to think out (planear) ‖ to institute, to introduce (sistemas, reformas, instituciones) ‖ to start (empezar) ‖ MAT to lay out, to set out (enfocar un problema), to phrase (formular un problema) ‖ *plantear la cuestión de confianza* to ask for a vote of confidence.
◆ *vpr* to arise; *se nos plantea el problema de la devaluación* there arises the question of devaluation, the question of devaluation arises.

plantel *m* nursery, seedbed (de plantas) ‖ FIG nursery, training establishment (institución).

planteo *m* MAT laying out, setting out, layout (de un problema).

plantificación *f* institution, introduction, establishment (de instituciones, sistemas, reformas).

plantificar *vt* to institute, to introduce, to establish (establecer) ‖ FIG & FAM to put, to stick (plantar algo o a uno en cierto sitio) | to land, to plant (un golpe).
◆ *vpr* FAM to install o.s., to plant o.s.; *se plantificó en la casa sin avisarnos* he installed himself in the house without warning us | to get; *con el coche nos plantificamos allí en dos minutos* in the car we got there in no time.

plantígrado, da *adj/s* ZOOL plantigrade.

plantilla *f* insole (suela interior) ‖ sole (de calcetín) ‖ payroll, staff, personnel, employees *pl* (empleados); *estar en plantilla en una empresa* to be on the payroll of a firm ‖ payroll, list of staff *o* personnel *o* employees (lista del personal) ‖ model, pattern (modelo) ‖ plan, design (plano) ‖ French curve (de los dibujantes) ‖ — *empleado de plantilla* member of the permanent staff ‖ *plantilla de estarcir* stencil.

plantío, a *adj* cultivable (labrantío) || cultivated, planted (labrado).
◆ *m* field (campo); *plantío de patatas* field of potatoes || patch (labrantío pequeño); *plantío de lechugas* lettuce patch || planting (acción).

plantón *m* seedling (planta joven para trasplantar) || — FIG & FAM *dar (un) plantón a uno* to stand s.o. up (si se trata de la novia), not to turn up (no acudir), to keep s.o. waiting (tardar mucho) || *estar de plantón* to be on extra guard duty (centinela), to cool one's heels, to stand waiting (estar esperando).

plañidero, ra *adj* plaintive, mournful; *voz plañidera* plaintive voice.
◆ *f* hired mourner.

plañido; plañimiento *m* moan, lamentation.

plañir* *vi* (p us) to wail, to moan, to lament.

plaqué *m* gold *o* silver plate.

plaqueta *f* plaquette (placa pequeña) || BIOL blood platelet (de sangre).

plasma *m* BIOL plasma.

plasmar *vt* to shape, to mould [US to mold] || FIG to capture; *el artista plasmó su pena* the artist captured her grief.
◆ *vpr* FIG to materialize; *el descontento popular se plasmó en una huelga general* popular discontent materialized into a general strike.

plasta *f* thick paste || FAM botch (cosa mal hecha) || — *al llegar al suelo se hizo una plasta* when it hit the ground it was completely flattened || FIG & FAM *el arroz está hecho una plasta* the rice has gone all sticky *o* gooey.
◆ *m/f* FAM drag, bore.
◆ *adj* FAM boring.

plasticidad *f* plasticity.

plástico, ca *adj* plastic; *materias plásticas* plastic materials.
◆ *m* plastic; *plásticos industriales* industrial plastics || plastic explosive (explosivo) || — *bomba de plástico* plastic bomb || *voladura con plástico* demolition with plastic explosives.
◆ *f* plastic art.

plastificación *f* plasticization.

plastificado, da *adj* plasticized.
◆ *m* plasticization.

plastificar *vt* to plasticize, to plastify.

plastrón *m* breastplate (pechera) || plastron (en esgrima) || dicky, shirtfront (de camisa) || wide tie, kipper (corbata) || plastron (de quelonios).

plata *f* silver (metal); *estatua de plata* silver statue || silver, silverware (vajilla u objetos de plata); *limpiar la plata* to clean the silver || FIG money (dinero); *tener mucha plata* to have a lot of money || — FIG *hablar en plata* to put it plainly | *hacer plata* to make a mint *o* a fortune | *la Tacita de Plata* Cádiz || *limpio como la plata* shining bright, as clean as a whistle *o* as a new pin || *plata alemana* German *o* nickel silver || *plata sobredorada* silver gilt || AMER *sin plata* broke (sin dinero) || FIG *tender* or *hacer un puente de plata a uno* to present s.o. with a golden opportunity.

platabanda *f* BOT flower bed || ARQ flat moulding.

platada *f* AMER dish, plateful.

plataforma *f* platform || open goods wagon, flatcar (vagón de mercancías) || FIG stepping-stone; *le va a servir de plataforma para la fama* it will serve him as a stepping-stone to fame || — *plataforma continental* continental shelf || *plataforma de lanzamiento* launching pad || *plataforma de perforación* drilling rig || *plataforma de salida* starting block (natación) || *plataforma giratoria* turntable (ferrocarril) || *plataforma móvil* moving pavement *o* carpet [US moving sidewalk] (pasillo rodante) || *plataforma rodante* dolly (cine).

platal *m* AMER FAM fortune (dineral).

platanal; platanar *m* banana plantation.

platanazo *m* AMER FAM fall (caída) | downfall, collapse, fall (caída de un gobierno).

platanera *f* banana plantation (plantación) || banana seller (vendedora).

platanero *m* banana tree (plátano) || banana seller (vendedor).

plátano *m* banana tree (árbol frutal) || banana (fruta) || plane tree (árbol).

platea *f* TEATR stalls *pl* [US orchestra] (patio) | parterre box (palco de platea).

plateado, da *adj* silvered, silver-plated (cubierto de plata) || silver, silvery (de color de plata) || AMER wealthy (adinerado).
◆ *m* silver plate, silver plating (baño de plata).

platear *vt* to silver, to silver-plate.

plateau *m* CINEM set, film set (plató).

platelmintos *m pl* ZOOL platyhelminthes.

platense *adj* of the Plate River (río), [of *o* from] La Plata [town in Argentina].
◆ *m/f* native *o* inhabitant of La Plata *o* of the Plate River.

plateresco, ca *adj* ARQ plateresque (estilo).

platería *f* silversmithing (oficio de platero) || silversmith's workshop (taller) || silversmith's, jeweller's (tienda) || *artículos de platería* silverware *sing*.

platero *m* silversmith (artista) || jeweller (joyero).

plática *f* talk, chat (charla) || sermon (religioso) || — *estar de plática* to be chatting || MAR *libre plática* pratique || *se pasaron la tarde de plática* they spent the afternoon chatting.

platicar *vi* to talk, to chat, to converse (conversar) || AMER to talk, to speak (hablar) | to say, to tell (decir).

platija *f* flounder, plaice (pez).

platillo *m* saucer (de una taza) || small plate (plato) || disc (pieza) || pan, tray, scale (de balanza) || plate (de mendigos) || MÚS cymbal (instrumento) || AMER course, dish (plato) || — *pasar el platillo* to pass round the hat, to take a collection || *platillo volante* flying saucer.

platina *f* TECN stage, slide (de microscopio) | worktable (de máquina herramienta) || IMPR platen (de la máquina de imprimir).

platinado *m* TECN platinizing.

platinar *vt* to platinize.

platinífero, ra *adj* platiniferous.

platino *m* platinum (metal); *esponja de platino* platinum sponge || — *rubia platino* platinum blonde || *teñir de rubio platino* to dye platinum blond.
◆ *pl* AUT points, contact points (motor).

platirrino *m* ZOOL platyrrhine (mono).

plato *m* plate (plato llano) || dish (plato hondo); *plato sopero* soup dish; *plato frutero* fruit dish || dish (guiso); *plato exquisito* exquisite dish; *plato del día* dish of the day || course (parte de una comida); *comida de tres platos* three course meal || plateful, plate, dish (contenido de un plato) || pan, scale, tray (de balanza) || plate (del embrague) || FIG butt (objeto de críticas) | talking point, subject for gossip (tema de habillas) || ARQ metope (metopa) || DEP clay pigeon (tiro) || — FIG *comer en el mismo plato* to be very close friends | *¿desde cuándo hemos comido en el mismo plato?, ¿en qué plato hemos comido juntos?* please remember whom you are talking to [reproof of familiarity] || *huevos al plato* fried eggs || *lavar* or *fregar los platos* to wash the dishes, to wash up || FIG *pagar los platos rotos* to carry the can, to pay the consequences | *parece que no ha roto un plato en su vida* butter wouldn't melt in his mouth || *plato combinado* one-course meal || *plato de segunda mesa* warmed-up leftovers *pl* (restos de comida), second best, stand-in (persona designada para sustituir a otra), old hat (lo ya conocido), second hand (ya usado) || *plato fuerte* or *de resistencia* main course || *plato giratorio* turntable (de tocadiscos) || *plato montado* tiered cake || *plato preparado* ready-cooked meal, convenience food || *primer plato* first course || *ser plato del gusto de uno* to be the spice of life for s.o. || *tiro al plato* trapshooting || FIG *vender por un plato de lentejas* to sell for a mess of pottage.

plató *m* CINEM set, film set.

Platón *npr m* Plato.

platónico, ca *adj* Platonic.
◆ *m/f* Platonist.

platonismo *m* Platonism.

platudo, da *adj* AMER FAM rich, wealthy (rico).

plausibilidad *f* plausibility || praiseworthiness.

plausible *adj* plausible, acceptable (admisible) || praiseworthy, commendable (laudable).

playa *f* beach; *en la playa* on the beach || seaside resort (estación balnearia) || AMER *playa de estacionamiento* car park (aparcamiento).

play back *m* CINEM playback.

playboy *m* playboy.

playera *f* t-shirt (camisa) || popular Andalusian song (canto).
◆ *pl* plimsolls [US sneakers] (zapatos de lona).

playero, ra *adj* beach (de playa).

plaza *f* square; *plaza mayor* main square || parvis, square (de una iglesia) || market, market place (mercado); *ir a la plaza* to go to (the) market || COM place, town, market || town (población) || place, seat (asiento); *reservar una plaza* to reserve a seat || place, space; *estacionamiento de quinientas plazas* car park with five hundred places || post, position, job (empleo); *cubrir una plaza* to fill a post || MIL fortified town, stronghold, fortress (ciudad fortificada) || bullring (de toros) || TECN hearth (de un horno) || — *hacer plaza* to make room || *¡plaza!* make way! || *plaza de abastos* market || *plaza de armas* parade ground (campo de instrucción) || *plaza de toros* bullring || *plaza fuerte* fortified town, stronghold, fortress || *plaza vacante* situation vacant, vacancy || FIG *sacar a la plaza* to tell the world about, to shout from the rooftops || MIL *sentar plaza* to enlist, to join up || FIG *sentar plaza de* to confirm o.s. to be.

plazo *m* period (período); *tenemos un plazo de tres meses para pagar la cuenta* we have a period of three months to pay the bill || date (fecha); *letra pagadera a plazo fijo* bill payable at a fixed date || time (tiempo) || instalment [US installment] (parte de un pago); *lo pagamos en doce plazos* we payed for it in twelve instalments || term (de una letra) || time limit (límite de tiempo) || — *a corto plazo* forthwith, within a short time, as soon as possible (pronto), short-dated (efectos comerciales), short-term; *un préstamo a corto plazo, una inversión a corto plazo* a short-term loan, a short-term investment; *esta medicina hace efecto a corto plazo* this medicine has a short-term effect || *a largo plazo* long-dated (efectos comerciales), long-term (préstamo, inversión, etc.), in the long run (más tarde) || *antes del vencimiento del plazo* before maturity, prior maturity || *a plazo vencido* on maturity, on the expiry date || *comprar, vender a plazos* to buy, to sell on hire-purchase *o* on credit [US on the installment plan] || *dar* *a uno un mes de plazo para pagar* to give s.o. a month to pay || *el plazo vence mañana* the payment is due tomorrow || *en breve plazo* within a short time, at short notice (dentro de muy poco) || *en el plazo de un año* within a year || *en un plazo de quince días* at a fortnight's notice || *fuera de plazo* beyond closing date, beyond payment date || *operación a plazo* credit transaction, transaction for the account (en la Bolsa) || *plazo de despedida* notice || COM *plazo de entrega* delivery period, lead time || *plazo de respiro* grace, respite || *plazo suplementario* extension || *vencimiento del plazo* maturity date.

plazoleta; plazuela *f* small square.

pleamar *f* MAR high tide, high water.

plebe *f* common people *pl*, masses *pl*, plebeians *pl* || FAM plebs *pl* (despectivo).

plebeyez *f* plebeianism, plebianism || FIG plebianism, vulgarity, commonness.

plebeyo, ya *adj/s* plebeian, plebian.

plebiscitar *vt* to submit to a plebiscite (someter a plebiscito) || to approve by plebiscite (aprobar).

plebiscitario, ria *adj* plebiscitary.

plebiscito *m* plebiscite.

plectognatos *m pl* ZOOL plectognaths.

plectro *m* plectrum, pick (púa).

plegable *adj* pliable (flexible) || folding, collapsible; *silla plegable* folding chair.

plegadera *f* paper knife (para cortar) || folder, bone blade (para plegar).

plegado *m*; **plegadura** *f* folding (acción de plegar) || pleating (tableado de una tela) || pleats *pl*, folds *pl* (conjunto de pliegues) || bending (encorvamiento).

plegador, ra *adj* folding.
◆ *m* bone blade (para plegar papel).
◆ *f* IMPR folding machine.

plegadura *f* ⟶ **plegado.**

plegamiento *m* GEOL folding.

plegar* *vt* to fold (hacer un doblez) || to bend (doblar) || to pleat (tablear una tela) || GEOL to fold.
◆ *vpr* to bend (doblarse) || FIG to bow, to give way, to submit (someterse).

plegaria *f* prayer.

pleistoceno, na *adj/sm* GEOL Pleistocene.

pleita *f* plaited strand of esparto grass.

pleiteador, ra; pleiteante *adj* pleading || *las partes pleiteantes* the litigants.
◆ *m/f* litigant.

pleitear *vi* to litigate, to plead || FIG to argue (discutir).

pleitesía *f* hommage, tribute (homenaje); *rendir pleitesía a* to pay hommage to, to pay a tribute to.

pleitista *adj* litigious (litigioso) || pettifogging (aficionado a pleitos) || quarrelsome (pendón).
◆ *m/f* litigious person || pettifogger.

pleito *m* JUR lawsuit, case; *ganar un pleito* to win a lawsuit || case (caso); *el pleito de X contra Y* the case of X against Y || feud, dispute (disputa) || — JUR *armar pleito* to go to law | *entablar pleito* to bring an action, to bring suit | *poner pleito a uno* to bring an action against s.o., to sue s.o. | *tener un pleito con alguien* to be at law with s.o.
◆ *pl* FAM pettifogging *sing*; *ser aficionado a pleitos* to be fond of pettifogging.

plenamar *f* high tide, high water (pleamar).

plenario, ria *adj* plenary; *indulgencia, sesión plenaria* plenary indulgence, session.

plenilunio *m* full moon (luna llena).

plenipotencia *f* full *o* unlimited powers *pl*.

plenipotenciario, ria *adj/s* plenipotentiary.

plenitud *f* plenitude, fullness; *en la plenitud de* in the fullness of || FIG prime (de una persona); *alcanzar la plenitud* to reach one's prime.

pleno, na *adj* full; *en plena actividad* in full activity; *en plena posesión de sus facultades* in full possession of his faculties || — *a plena vista* in full view || *a pleno sol* in the sunshine, under the sun || *en plena calle* in the middle of the street || *en plena cámara de los lores* in the House of Lords itself || *en plena cara* straight in the face, right in the face || *en plena rebeldía* in open revolt || *en pleno día* in broad daylight || *en pleno invierno, plena selva* in the heart of (the) winter, of the jungle || *hacer algo con pleno derecho* to have every right to do sth. || *la asamblea en pleno* the entire assembly || *pleno empleo* full employment || *plenos poderes* full powers.
◆ *m* plenary meeting, plenum (reunión).
— OBSERV The adjective *pleno* is used mainly in the abstract.

pleonasmo *m* GRAM pleonasm (repetición).

pleonástico, ca *adj* pleonastic.

plepa *f* FAM nuisance.

plesiosauro *m* plesiosaur (fósil).

pletina *f* iron plate (metalurgia).

plétora *f* plethora, abundance.

pletórico, ca *adj* plethoric, abundant || *pletórico de* full of.

pleura *f* ANAT pleura.

pleural *adj* ANAT pleural.

pleuresía *f* MED pleuresy.

pleurítico, ca *adj/s* MED pleuritic.
◆ *adj* pleural; *derrame pleurítico* pleural effusion.

pleuritis *f inv* MED pleuritis.

plexiglás *m* perspex, plexiglass, plexiglas.

plexo *m* ANAT plexus; *plexo solar* solar plexus.

pléyade *f* Pléiade (poetas franceses) || pleiad, group, number (conjunto).
◆ *pl* ASTR & MIT Pleiades.

plica *f* sealed envelope (sobre cerrado) || escrow (documento legal).

pliego *m* sheet *o* piece *o* leaf of paper (hoja de papel) || sealed letter (documento cerrado) || sealed orders *pl* (documento militar) || IMPR signature, gathering || — *pliego de cargos* list of charges || *pliego de condiciones* specifications *pl* || *pliego de descargos* statement in defence.

pliegue *m* fold (doblez) || pleat (tabla); *los pliegues de una falda* the pleats of a skirt || GEOL fold (ondulación del terreno).

Plinio *npr m* Pliny; *Plinio el Viejo, el Joven* Pliny the Elder, the Younger.

plinto *m* ARQ plinth (de columna) || horse (en gimnasia).

plioceno *m* GEOL Pliocene.

plisado *m* pleating (acción y efecto de plisar) || pleats *pl*, pleating (tablas, tableado).

plisar *vt* to pleat; *plisar una falda* to pleat a skirt.

plomada *f* plumb line (de albañil) || sinker (de red) || MAR sounding line (sonda) || lead pencil (lápiz).

plomar *vt* to seal with lead.

plomazo *m* lead shot wound.

plombagina *f* MAR plumbago, graphite.

plombaginácea *f* BOT ⟶ **plumbaginácea.**

plomear *vi* to score a bull's-eye *o* a hit.

plomería *f* plumbing (oficio de plomero) || lead roofing (de tejado).

plomero *m* plumber.

plomífero, ra *adj* MIN plumbiferous || FIG & FAM boring, dull (pesado).

plomizo, za *adj* leaden.

plomo *m* lead (metal) || lead weight (peso) || plumb line (plomada) || slug, lead shot (de fusil) || sinker (de red) || fuse (electricidad) || FAM super (gasolina) | drag, bore, pest (pesado) || — FIG *andar con pies de plomo* to tread warily || *a plomo* straight down, vertically, plumb (verticalmente) || FIG & FAM *caer a plomo* to fall flat (una persona) || *caer como un plomo* to fall *o* to drop like a stone || ELECTR *se fundieron los plomos* the fuses have gone, the fuses have blown || FIG & FAM *ser un plomo* to be a bore *o* a drag || *soldadito de plomo* tin soldier || FIG *tener un sueño de plomo* to be dog-tired.

plomo, ma *adj* leaden, lead-coloured.

plotter *m* INFORM plotter (trazador de gráficos).

pluma *f* feather, plume (p us); *pluma de ganso* goose feather; *colchón de plumas* feather bed || plume, feather (de adorno) || MAR & TECN derrick || pen (para escribir, de metal) || quill (para escribir, de ave) || FIG writer (escritor) | pen, style (estilo) | pen; *el periodista vive de su pluma* a journalist lives by his pen || AMER tap (grifo) || — *escribir al correr de la pluma* or *a vuela pluma* to let one's pen run on || *peso pluma* featherweight (boxeador) || *pluma estilográfica* fountain pen || *tomar la pluma* to put pen to paper.
◆ *pl* flight *sing* (de una flecha) || FIG & FAM *vestirse* or *engalanarse con plumas ajenas* to strut in borrowed plumes *o* feathers.

plumada *f* stroke of a pen, flourish.

plumafuente *f* AMER fountain pen (estilográfica).

plumaje *m* plumage, feathers *pl* (de aves) || plume, crest (de casco).

plumajería *f* plumage.

plumajero, ra *m/f* plumassier.

plumaria *adj f* *arte plumaria* art of decorating with ornamental plumes.

plumazo *m* stroke of one's pen; *lo tachó de un plumazo* he crossed it out with a stroke of his pen.

plumazón *f* plumage (plumaje).

plumbagina *f* MIN plumbago, graphite.

plumbaginácea; plombaginácea *f* BOT plumbago.
◆ *pl* BOT plumbaginaceae.

plúmbeo, a *adj* leaden, heavy as lead || FIG deep (sueño) | boring, dull (aburrido).

plumeado *m* hatching (en pintura).

plumear *vt* to hatch, to hatch in (en pintura) || AMER to write (escribir).

plumería *f*; **plumerío** *m* bunch *o* pile of feathers.

plumero *m* feather duster (para quitar el polvo) || pencil box *o* case (estuche) || MIL plume (penacho) || AMER penholder (portaplumas) || FIG & FAM *vérsele a uno el plumero* to see through s.o., to be able to see through s.o.

plumetís *m* plumetis (tela).

plumier *m* pencil box *o* case.
— OBSERV This word is a Gallicism for *plumero*.

plumífero, ra *adj* plumed, feathered.
◆ *m* FAM pen-pusher (chupatintas).

plumilla *f*; **plumín** *m* small feather || nib (de estilográfica) || BOT plumule.

plumista *m* clerk (empleado).

plumón *m* down (de las aves) || eiderdown (edredón).

plumoso, sa *adj* feathery.
plúmula *f* BOT plumule.
plural *adj/sm* plural; *poner una palabra en plural* to put a word into the plural.
pluralidad *f* plurality ‖ — *a pluralidad de votos* by a majority of votes ‖ *una pluralidad de personas* a great number of people.
pluralismo *m* pluralism.
pluralista *m* pluralist.
pluralizar *vt* GRAM to pluralize, to put into the plural ‖ FIG to use the plural, to generalize.
pluricelular *adj* pluricellular.
pluridisciplinar *adj* pluridisciplinary, multidisciplinary.
pluriempleo *m* moonlighting.
plurilingüe *adj/s* polyglot.
◆ *adj* multilingual.
pluripartidismo *m* multi-partyism.
pluripartidista *adj* multi-party.
plurivalencia *f* QUÍM polyvalence ‖ versatility.
plurivalente *adj/sm* QUÍM polyvalent ‖ versatile.
plus *m* bonus (gratificación) ‖ — *plus de carestía de vida* cost-of-living bonus ‖ *plus de peligrosidad* danger-money ‖ *plus petición* plus petitio.
pluscafé *m* AMER liqueur [taken after coffee].
pluscuamperfecto *m* GRAM pluperfect.
plusmarca *f* record; *batir la plusmarca* to break the record.
plusmarquista *m/f* record holder.
plusvalía *f* appreciation, increased value, gain in value.
plúteo *m* shelf (anaquel).
Plutarco *npr m* Plutarch.
plutocracia *f* plutocracy.
plutócrata *m/f* plutocrat.
Plutón *npr m* ASTR Pluto.
plutonio *m* MIN plutonium (metal).
pluvial *adj* pluvial, rain; *erosión pluvial* pluvial erosion ‖ REL *capa pluvial* pluvial, cope.
pluviógrafo *m* pluviograph.
pluviometría *f* pluviometry.
pluviómetro *m* pluviometer, rain gauge.
pluviosidad *f* pluviosity.
pluvioso, sa *adj* pluvious, rainy (lluvioso).
p. m. *abrev de post-meridiem a las tres p. m.* at three p. m.
PNB *abrev de Producto Nacional Bruto* GNP, gross national product.
pneumococo *m* MED pneumococcus.
PNV *abrev de Partido Nacionalista Vasco* Basque nationalist political party.
Po *n pr* GEOGR the Po.
poa *f* poa (hierba) ‖ MAR bridle.
población *f* population (acción de poblar, habitantes); *población activa* working population ‖ town, city (ciudad) ‖ village (pueblo) ‖ centre of population (núcleo urbano) ‖ built-up area (en el código de la circulación) ‖ BIOL population.
poblacho; pueblacho *m* FAM hole, dump (pueblo).
poblada *f* AMER rebellion, revolt, riot, uprising (sedición) | crowd (gentío).
poblado, da *adj* populated, inhabited (con gente o conanimales) ‖ wooded (con árboles); *paisaje poblado* wooded countryside ‖ thick (la barba) ‖ bushy (cejas) ‖ FIG full of; *composición poblada de faltas* composition full of mistakes ‖ *poblado de* peopled with, populated with.
◆ *m* built-up area (lugar); *atravesar un poblado* to go through a built-up area ‖ town, city (ciudad) ‖ centre of population (núcleo urbano).
poblador, ra *adj* resident, inhabitant (que reside).
◆ *m/f* settler, inhabitant (habitante) ‖ colonist, settler, founder (fundador de una colonia).
poblano, na *m/f* villager (aldeano).
◆ *adj* [of *o* from] Puebla [town in Mexico].
◆ *m/f* inhabitant, native of Puebla.
poblar* *vt* to populate, to people (con gente) ‖ to populate (con animales) ‖ to plant (con plantas) ‖ to stock; *poblar un río de peces* to stock a river with fish ‖ to inhabit (habitar) ‖ to colonize, to found, to settle (fundar) ‖ FIG to people, to stock, to fill.
◆ *vpr* to become peopled ‖ to become crowded, to fill (*de* with), to become crowded, to fill (llenarse) ‖ to bud, to leaf (plantas).
pobre *adj* poor; *una familia pobre* a poor family; *pobre en minerales* poor in minerals ‖ FIG poor; *el pobre de tu padre* your poor father ‖ little, no; *pobre consuelo* little consolation ‖ — FIG *hacer un pobre papel* to give a poor perfomance | *¡pobre de él!* poor fellow!, the poor thing! | *¡pobre de mí!* poor old me!, poor me! | *¡pobre desgraciado!* poor devil!, poor thing! | *¡pobre de ti!* you poor thing! | *¡pobre de ti si...!* you'll be sorry if...! | *ser más pobre que Carracuca* or *que una rata* or *que las ratas* to be as poor as a church mouse.
◆ *m/f* poor person *o* man *o* woman; *un pobre* a poor man.
◆ *pl* poor people, poor; *hay demasiados pobres en el mundo* there are too many poor people in the world; *los pobres* the poor ‖ JUR *abogacía de pobres* legal aid.
pobrecito, ta *m/f* poor little thing.
◆ *adj* poor little.
pobrete, ta *m/f* poor devil, poor thing.
pobretear *vi* to play the poor man, to put on the agony.
pobretón, ona *adj* wretched, very poor.
◆ *m/f* poor wretch, poor thing.
pobreza *f* poverty, indigence, need (falta de dinero) ‖ penury (penuria) ‖ poorness; *pobreza de espíritu* poorness of spirit ‖ scarcity (escasez); *pobreza de metales* scarcity of metals ‖ lack (falta); *pobreza de recursos* lack of resources ‖ barrenness, sterility (de la tierra) ‖ FIG meanness (falta de magnanimidad) ‖ — JUR *beneficio de pobreza* legal aid ‖ FIG *pobreza no es vileza* poverty is no crime, it is no crime to be poor.
pocero *m* well digger (el que hace pozos) ‖ sewerman (alcantarillero).
pocilga *f* pigsty, piggery (de cerdos) ‖ FIG & FAM pigsty.
pocillo *m* sump (para recoger líquidos) ‖ cup (jícara).
pócima; poción *f* potion ‖ FIG concoction, brew.
poción *f* potion ‖ FIG concoction, brew.
poco, ca *adj sing* not much, little (no mucho) (véase OBSERV); *tiene poco dinero* he has not much money; *queda poca leche* there is not much milk left; *con poco respeto* with little respect ‖ little, small; *de poco interés* of small interest.
◆ *adj pl* not many, few; *pocos árboles* not many trees; *aquí son pocas las casas antiguas* there are not many old houses here ‖ — *hay pocos que* there are not many who ‖ *lo poco* how little; *y ya sabes lo poco que me gusta leer* and you know how little I like reading ‖ *muchos pocos hacen un mucho* every little (bit) helps, many a little makes a mickle ‖ *poca cosa* nothing much; *¿qué hicisteis? —poca cosa* what did you do? —nothing much ‖ *pocas palabras pero buenas* let us be brief but to the point ‖ *pocas veces* not very often ‖ *poco tiempo* just a short time, just a little while; *salió hace poco tiempo* he went out *o* he left just a short time ago ‖ *tiene poca inteligencia* he is not very intelligent ‖ *tiene poca memoria* he has not a very good memory ‖ *unos pocos* a few, some; *unas pocas casas* a few houses; *unos pocos de los que quedan* a few of those which remain.
◆ *adv* not very much, little; *bebo poco* I do not drink very much, I drink little ‖ not very (con adjetivo); *es poco inteligente* he is not very intelligent ‖ not long (poco tiempo); *se quedó poco allí* he did not stay there long ‖ — *a poco de* shortly after, a short time after; *a poco de llegar aquí murió* shortly after he arrived here he died ‖ *a poco que* if... at all (por poco que) ‖ *dentro de poco* shortly, soon ‖ FAM *de poco más o menos* of little *o* no account ‖ *equivocarse por muy poco* not to be far out *o* wrong; *me equivoqué por muy poco* I was not far out ‖ *es poco* it's not much ‖ *estar en poco* to almost do sth., to very nearly do sth.; *estuvo en poco que le pegase* he very nearly hit him ‖ *hace poco* a short time ago, not long ago ‖ *muy poco* very little (no bastante) ‖ *no es poco* that's not bad ‖ *no poco* a lot (con verbo), a lot of (con sustantivo), very (con adjetivo) ‖ *o poco menos* or something like that ‖ *poco antes, después* shortly before, after ‖ *poco a poco* little by little, gradually ‖ *¡poco a poco!* easy does it!, gently now! ‖ *poco falta para* it is not long before (indica tiempo), a little more and (indica cantidad); *poco falta para llenarlo* a little more and it will be full ‖ *poco ha faltado* or *poco faltó para que perdiese el tren* he nearly missed *o* he almost missed the train ‖ *poco más, poco menos* not much more, not much less; *tiene poco más de treinta años* he is not much more than thirty years old; *poco más viejo que yo* not much older than I ‖ *poco más o menos* more or less ‖ *poco o nada* little or nothing ‖ *por poco* nearly, almost; *por poco me caigo* I nearly fell over ‖ *por poco que* if... at all; *por poco que te muevas romperás la silla* if you move at all you will break the chair; *por poco inteligente que sea lo entenderá* if he is at all intelligent he will understand ‖ *por poco que sea* little as it is, little as it might seem ‖ *tener en poco* to think little of, not to think much of ‖ *un poco más* a little more, not much more; *un poco más caro que el tuyo* not much more expensive than yours ‖ *un poco más joven que yo* a little younger *o* not much younger than I ‖ *un poco menos* a little less ‖ *vivir con muy poco* to live on very little ‖ *y por si fuera poco* and to top it all.
◆ *m* *un poco* a little ‖ *un poco de* a little; *un poco de pan* a little bread; *un poco más de vino* a little more wine.

— OBSERV Cuando el adjetivo *poco* acompaña un sustantivo abstracto el inglés suele sustituir *not much* (seguido del sustantivo) por *not very* (seguido del adjetivo correspondiente): *tiene poca importancia* it is not very important.

pochismo *m* AMER way of speaking of Mexicans in the southeast of the United States.
pocho, cha *adj* faded, discoloured (flores, colores) ‖ pale, off-colour (personas) ‖ overripe, soft (fruta).
pochocho, cha *adj* AMER chubby, plump (gordo).
pochola *f* FAM nice girl.
poda *f* AGR pruning (acción) ‖ pruning season (temporada).
podadera *f* AGR pruning shears *pl* (tijeras), pruning knife (cuchillo).
podador *m* pruner.
podagra *f* MED podagra, gout.

podar *vt* to prune, to trim (árboles) ‖ FIG to prune, to trim (quitar lo inútil).

podenco, ca *adj/sm* spaniel (perro).

poder *m* power (dominio, autoridad) ‖ possession (posesión); *pasar a poder de* to pass into the possession of ‖ capacity (capacidad); *tiene un gran poder de trabajo* he has a great capacity for work ‖ strength (fuerza física) ‖ power, ability (facultad) ‖ JUR power ‖ TECN power ‖ — *bajo el poder de* under the power of, in the hands of (caer, estar, etc.) ‖ *dar a uno poder para* to authorize *o* to allow s.o. to, to give s.o. the power to ‖ *de poder a poder* man to man (discutir, hablar, etc.) ‖ *estar en el poder* to be in power (un gobierno) ‖ *estar en poder de alguien* to be in the power *o* in the hands of s.o. (una persona), to be in s.o.'s hands *o* possession (una cosa) ‖ FIG *hacer un poder* to make an effort (un esfuerzo) ‖ *llegar a poder de uno* to reach s.o. ‖ *obrar en poder de uno* to be in s.o.'s hands *o* possession ‖ *ocupar el poder* to be in power ‖ *poder absoluto, ejecutivo, judicial, legislativo* absolute, executive, judicial, legislative power ‖ *poder adquisitivo* purchasing power ‖ *poder de convocatoria* crowd-pulling capacity ‖ MIL *poder disuasivo* deterrent ‖ *tener en su poder* to have, to have in one's possession (una cosa), to have it in one's power to (tener la posibilidad de).
◆ *pl* powers, power *sing*; *con plenos poderes* with full powers ‖ *casarse por poderes* to marry by proxy ‖ *dar poderes* to give proxy ‖ *división* or *separación de poderes* separation of powers ‖ *entrega* or *transmisión de poderes* handing over of power ‖ *entregar los poderes* to hand over power ‖ *obrar por poderes* to act by proxy ‖ *plenos poderes* full powers, full power ‖ *por poderes* by proxy.

poder* *vt* to be able to, can (presente), could (pretérito), could (capacidad física) (véase OBSERV); *este animal no puede nadar* this animal cannot *o* can't swim; *le dolía tanto que no podía andar* it hurt him so much that he could not *o* couldn't walk *o* that he was unable to walk; *hubiéramos podido ir si* we could have gone if, we should have been able to go if ‖ may, might (pidiendo o dando permiso); *¿puedo salir esta noche?* may I go out tonight?; *su padre dijo que podía ir al baile* her father said that she might go to the dance (véase OBSERV) ‖ to be allowed to (permiso ya dado); *no puede salir después de las diez* she is not allowed to go out after ten o'clock; *no pudo ir* he was not allowed to go (no le dejaron ir) ‖ may, might (posibilidad); *ha podido pasar sin ser visto* he may have passed without being seen; *puede venir en cualquier momento* he may come at any moment ‖ might (sugerencia); *por lo menos podría saludarnos* he might at least say hello (to us) ‖ — *a más no poder* as much (fast, hard, etc.) as possible *o* as can be *o* as one can; *están trabajando a más no poder* they are working as hard as can be; *correr a más no poder* to run as fast as possible; *es tonto a más no poder* he is as silly as can be; *comimos a más no poder* we ate as much as we could ‖ *a poder ser* if possible ‖ *aquellos que pueden* those who can, those who are able ‖ *el que puede lo más puede lo menos* once difficult things are mastered easy things are all the easier ‖ *hasta más no poder, hasta no poder más* as much (hard, long, etc.) as possible *o* as can be *o* as one can; *están trabajando a más no poder* they are working as hard as can be; *comimos a más no poder* we ate as much as we could; *corrimos hasta más no poder* we ran as fast *o* as far as we could ‖ *no poder con* not to be able to do anything with, not to be able to cope with (no poder dominar); *no puedo con este niño* I cannot do anything with this child; not to be able to stand (no aguantar); *no puedo con la hipocresía* I cannot stand hypocrisy ‖ *no poder más* to be exhausted, to be all in (agotado), not to be able to stand any more; *¡no puedo más!* I cannot stand any more! ‖ *no poder más que* can only; *no puedo más que decírselo a mis superiores* I can only tell my superiors ‖ *no poder menos que* or *de, no poder sino* not to be able to help; *no pude menos que invitarle a cenar* I could not help asking him to dinner ‖ *no puede ser* it *o* that is impossible ‖ *por lo que pudiera ocurrir* because of what might happen ‖ *puede ser* maybe, perhaps ‖ *puede ser que* it may be that, it is possible that, perhaps, maybe ‖ *¿se puede?* may I (we)?

— OBSERV El verbo *can* no tiene infinitivo ni participios ni tiempo futuro. Para expresar estas ideas hay que emplear el verbo *to be able: no podremos ir* we shall not be able to go; *no pudiendo correr* being unable to run, not being able to run. El pasado del verbo *may* es *might*. No obstante *might* es de por sí un verbo auxiliar que se emplea para pedir permiso y también para expresar una posibilidad. Aunque el único sentido normal de *can* sea el de tener la capacidad física de hacer algo, se emplea cada día más este verbo para todos los significados de *poder*.

poderdante *m/f* principal.

poderhabiente *m/f* manager, managing director, signing clerk (que firma) ‖ agent (que representa) ‖ proxy (que tiene el poder de otro).

poderío *m* power.

poderosamente *adv* powerfully.

poderoso, sa *adj* powerful ‖ good, effective (remedio) ‖ strong, powerful (motivo, razón) ‖ rich, wealthly (rico).

podio *m* podium.

podología *f* MED podology.

podómetro *m* pedometer.

podre *f* pus (humor).

podredumbre *f* putrefaction, rottenness ‖ pus (humor) ‖ FIG corruption, rot, rottenness | uneasiness (desasosiego).

podridero *m* compost heap.

podrido, da *adj* rotten ‖ — *oler a podrido* to smell rotten ‖ FIG & FAM *estar podrido de dinero* to be filthy rich *o* stinking rich.

podrir* *vt* ⟶ **pudrir.**

podzol *m* podzol.

poema *m* poem ‖ MÚS poem; *poema sinfónico* symphonic poem ‖ — FIG *es un poema* it is quite something ‖ *poema en prosa* prose poem.

poemario *m* book of poems *o* of verse.

poemático, ca *adj* poematic, poetic.
◆ *f* theme.

poesía *f* poetry (género literario) ‖ poem (poema).

poeta *m* poet.

poetastro *m* FAM poetaster, would-be poet.

poético, ca *adj* poetic, poetical.
◆ *f* poetics (arte).

poetisa *f* poetess.

poetizar *vt* to poetize, to poeticize.

pogrom; pogromo *m* pogrom.

poise *m* poise (unidad de viscosidad).

póker; póquer *m* poker (juego) ‖ poker (dados); *póker de ases* poker of aces ‖ four of a kind (naipes); *tengo un póker* I have four of a kind ‖ *póker de ases* four aces (naipes).

polaco, ca *adj* Polish.
◆ *m/f* Pole (habitante).
◆ *m* Polish (lengua).

polaina *f* gaiter (en las pantorrillas).

polar *adj* polar; *círculo polar* polar, circle ‖ — *casquete polar* polar cap ‖ *clima polar* polar climate ‖ *estrella polar* polestar ‖ *oso polar* polar bear.

polaridad *f* polarity.

polarímetro *m* FÍS polarimeter.

polariscopio *m* FÍS polariscope.

polarización *f* polarization.

polarizador, ra *adj* polarizing.
◆ *m* polarizer.

polarizar *vt* FÍS to polarize ‖ FIG to concentrate on (concentrar).
◆ *vpr* to polarize.

polaroid *m* Polaroid.

polca *f* polka (música y baile).

pólder *m* polder.

polea *f* pulley.

poleadas *f pl* porridge *sing* (gachas).

polémico, ca *adj* polemic, polemical.
◆ *f* polemic, controversy (controversia) ‖ polemics (arte de la discusión).

polemista *m/f* polemist, polemicist.

polemizar *vi* to indulge in a polemic, to argue.

polen *m* BOT pollen.

polenta *f* CULIN polenta.

poli *m* FAM cop (policía).
◆ *f* FAM police, cops *pl* (cuerpo de policía).

poliandra *adj* polyandrous.

poliandria *f* polyandry.

policéfalo, la *adj* polycephalous.

policía *f* police, police force; *policía antidisturbios, militar, secreta, urbana* riot, military, secret, urban police ‖ courtesy (cortesía) ‖ — *policía judicial* Criminal Investigation Department ‖ MIL *revista de policía* kit check *o* inspection ‖ *viene la policía* the police are coming.
◆ *m* policeman (agente).

policiaco, ca; policíaco, ca; policial *adj* police ‖ detective; *película, novela policiaca* detective film, story.

policlínica *f* MED polyclinic.

policroísmo *m* FÍS polychroism.

policromado, da *adj* polychrome.

policromía *f* polychromy.

policromo, ma; polícromo, ma *adj* polychromatic.

policultivo *m* mixed farming.

Polichinela *npr m* Punchinello, Punch.

polidactilo, la *adj/s* polydactyl.

poliédrico, ca *adj* polyhedral, polyhedric, polyhedrical.

poliedro *adj m* MAT polyhedral.
◆ *m* MAT polyhedron.

poliéster *m* QUÍM polyester.

poliestireno *m* QUÍM polystyrene.

polietileno *m* QUÍM polyethylene, polythene.

polifacético, ca *adj* many-sided, versatile.

polifásico, ca *adj* FÍS polyphase.

polifonía *f* MÚS polyphony.

polifónico, ca *adj* polyphonic.

poligalia *f* MED polygalactia.

poligamia *f* polygamy.

polígamo, ma *adj* polygamous.
◆ *m* polygamist.

poliginia *f* polygyny.

poliglotía *f* polyglotism.

polígloto, ta; poligloto, ta *adj/s* polyglot.

poligonáceo, a *adj* BOT polygonaceous.
◆ *f pl* BOT polygonaceae.

poligonal *adj* MAT polygonal.

polígono *m* MAT polygon ‖ MIL rifle range ‖ — *polígono de desarrollo* development area ‖ *polígono industrial* industrial estate.

poligrafía *f* polygraphy.

polígrafo *m* polygraph.

polilla *f* moth (insecto).

polimería *f* QUÍM polymerism.

polimérico, ca *adj* polymeric.

polimerización *f* polymerization.

polimerizar *vt* QUÍM to polymerize.

polímero, ra *adj* QUÍM polymeric.
◆ *m* QUÍM polymer.

polimórfico, ca *adj* polymorphic.

polimorfismo *m* polymorphism.

polimorfo, fa *adj* polymorphic, polymorphous.

Polinesia *npr f* GEOGR Polynesia.

polinesio, sia *adj/s* Polynesian.

polinífero, ra *adj* polliniferous.

polinización *f* BOT pollination.

polinizar *vt* to pollinate.

polinómico, ca *adj* MAT polynomial.

polinomio *m* MAT polynomial.

polio *f* MED polio.

poliomielitis *f* MED poliomyelitis.

poliomielítico, ca *adj* poliomyelitic.
◆ *m/f* person affected with poliomyelitis.

polipasto *m* (hoisting) tackle, rigging (poleas).

polipéptido *m* QUÍM polypeptide.

polípero *m* ZOOL polypary.

polipétalo, la *adj* polypetalous.

pólipo *m* ZOOL polyp ‖ MED polypus, polyp.

polisacárido *m* QUÍM polysaccharide.

polisílabo, ba; polisilábico, ca *adj* GRAM polysyllabic, polysyllabical.
◆ *m* polysyllable.

polisón *m* crinoline (de faldas).

polispasto *m* (hoisting) tackle, rigging (poleas).

politburó *m* politburo.

politécnico, ca *adj* polytechnic, polytechnical ‖ *escuela politécnica* polytechnic [school].
◆ *m* polytechnician.

politeísmo *m* polytheism.

politeísta *adj* polytheistic.
◆ *m/f* polytheist.

política *f* politics (arte de gobernar); *dedicarse a la política* to devote o.s. to politics; *la política partidista* party politics; *meterse en política* to get mixed up in politics ‖ policy (manera de obrar); *política exterior, agraria* foreign, agricultural policy; *política hábil* skilful policy; *política de buena vecindad* good neighbour policy ‖ — *política de no intervención* policy of non-intervention ‖ *política económica* economic policy ‖ *política monetaria* monetary policy ‖ *política restrictiva* restraint policy.

politicastro, tra *m/f* petty politician, politicaster.

político, ca *adj* political; *partido político* political party ‖ courteous, polite (cortés) ‖ politic, tactful, wary (prudente) ‖ -in-law (pariente); *padre político* father-in-law; *hermana política* sister-in-law; *hija política* daughter-in-law ‖ by marriage (para tíos, primos y sobrinos); *es pariente político suyo* he is a relative of his by marriage ‖ — *economía política* economics ‖ *por parte política* by marriage.
◆ *m* politician, statesman.

politicón, ona *adj* keenly interested in politics ‖ ceremonious, obsequious (ceremonioso).
◆ *m/f* person who is keenly interested in politics ‖ ceremonious person.

politiquear *vi* FAM to play at politics, to dabble in politics (interesarse superficialmente) | to job (con fines deshonestos).

politiqueo *m*; **politiquería** *f* FAM dabbling in politics (interés superficial) | political jobbery (corrupción).

politización *f* politization.

politizar *vt* to politicize.

polivalencia *f* QUÍM polyvalence ‖ FIG versatility.

polivalente *adj* QUÍM polyvalent, multivalent ‖ FIG multivalent, versatile.

polivinilo *m* polyvinyl.

póliza *f* policy (de seguros); *suscribir, rescindir una póliza* to take out, to cancel a policy ‖ contract (contrato) ‖ stamp (sello de impuesto) ‖ papers *pl* (de mercancías) ‖ *póliza adicional* additional clause (seguro).

polizón *m* stowaway (en un buque).

polizonte *m* FAM cop, bobby (policía).

poljé *m* GEOL polje (depresión).

polo *m* pole; *polo Norte, Sur* North, South Pole ‖ ELECTR pole; *polo negativo, positivo* negative, positive pole ‖ popular Andalusian tune (canto) ‖ iced lolly [US eskimo pie] (helado) ‖ sportshirt (camisa) ‖ polo (juego) ‖ FIG pole (término opuesto) | pole, focus (centro) | zone, area; *polo de desarrollo* development area ‖ — *polo acuático* water polo ‖ FIG *polo de atracción* centre of attention ‖ FIG *ser el polo opuesto de* to be the complete opposite of | *ser polos opuestos* to be poles apart.

polola *f* AMER FAM flirt (muchacha coqueta).

pololear *vt* AMER to annoy (molestar) | to court (requebrar).
◆ *vi* to flirt.

pololos *m pl* bloomers.

polonés, esa *adj* (p us) Polish.
◆ *m/f* (p us) Pole.
◆ *f* MÚS polonaise.

Polonia *npr f* GEOGR Poland.

polonio *m* QUÍM polonium.

poltrón, ona *adj* lazy, idle.
◆ *f* easy chair (silla poltrona).

poltronear *vi* FAM to slack, to idle.

poltronería *f* laziness, idleness.

polución *f* pollution.

poluto, ta *adj* stained, soiled (manchado).

Pólux *npr m* MIT Pollux.

polvareda *f* dust cloud, cloud of dust; *levantar una polvareda* to raise a dust cloud ‖ FIG storm, to-do (escándalo).

polvera *f* (powder) compact, powder box.

polvero *m* AMER dust cloud, cloud of dust (polvareda) | handkerchief (pañuelo).

polvo *m* dust (de la tierra) ‖ dust (suciedad); *hacer* or *levantar polvo* to raise dust ‖ powder (medicina, química, cocina) ‖ pinch (porción pequeña) ‖ FIG remains *pl* (cenizas de los muertos) ‖ POP screw ‖ — *café en polvo* instant coffee ‖ *convertirse en polvo* to turn to dust ‖ *en polvo* powdered; *chocolate en polvo* powdered chocolate; *leche en polvo* powdered milk ‖ FIG & FAM *estar hecho polvo* to be worn out, to be exhausted (cansado), to be depressed (deprimido) | *hacer polvo* to annihilate (vencer), to pulverize, to beat to a pulp (pegar), to smash to smithereens (hacer añicos), to reduce to dust (destruir), to wear out, to exhaust (dejar sin fuerzas), to depress (deprimir), to ruin; *tu decisión ha hecho polvo todos mis proyectos* your decision has ruined all my plans | *hacerse polvo* to be ruined (estropearse), to smash to smithereens (hacerse añicos) | *hacerse polvo la vista* to ruin one's sight; *con tanto trabajo la vista se le ha hecho polvo* so much work has ruined his sight | *limpio de polvo y paja* clear, net (precio y sueldo) ‖ *nieve en polvo* powdery snow ‖ *oro en polvo* gold dust ‖ FIG *morder el polvo* to bite the dust ‖ *polvo cósmico* cosmic dust ‖ *polvo de carbón* coal dust ‖ *quitar el polvo* to dust ‖ FIG *reducir a polvo* to reduce to dust ‖ *sacudir el polvo* to shake off the dust, to dust (traje), to dust (muebles) ‖ *sacudir el polvo a uno* to tan s.o.'s hide, to give s.o. a beating (dar una paliza) ‖ *tabaco en polvo* snuff.
◆ *pl* powder *sing* (cosmético); *polvos de talco* talcum powder; *polvos de arroz* rice *o* face powder ‖ FIG & FAM *polvos de la madre Celestina* magical cure-all ‖ *ponerse polvos* to powder one's face.

pólvora *f* gunpowder, powder (explosivo) ‖ fire-works *pl* (pirotecnia) ‖ FIG bad temper (mal genio) | vivacity, liveliness (vivacidad) ‖ — *algodón pólvora* guncotton ‖ *correr la pólvora* to perform a fantasia ‖ *fábrica de pólvora y explosivos* gunpowder factory ‖ FIG & FAM *gastar la pólvora en salvas* to waste one's efforts *o* one's ammunition | *has descubierto la pólvora* and Queen Ann's dead | *no ha inventado la pólvora* he didn't invent gunpowder, he's as thick as two short planks [US he doesn't know enough to come in out of the rain] | *propagarse como un reguero de pólvora* to spread like wildfire.

polvoriento, ta *adj* dusty; *cuarto polvoriento* dusty room; *carretera polvorienta* dusty road.

polvorilla *m/f* FAM *ser un* or *una polvorilla* to be touchy *o* quick-tempered.

polvorín *m* very fine gunpowder (explosivo) ‖ powder flask (frasco) ‖ powder magazine, gunpowder arsenal (almacén de pólvora) ‖ FIG spitfire (persona de genio vivo) | powder keg; *este país es un polvorín* this country is like a powder keg ‖ AMER tic (garrapata).

polvorista *m* firework maker (de fuegos artificiales) ‖ gunpowder maker (de explosivos).

polvorón *m* very dry Spanish sweet of a floury consistency (pastelillo).

polvoso, sa *adj* AMER dusty.

polla *f* pullet, young hen (gallina joven) ‖ stake (juegos) ‖ bet (en las carreras) ‖ FIG & FAM girl, lass (muchacha) ‖ POP prick (miembro viril) ‖ AMER horse race (carrera de caballos) ‖ — ZOOL *polla cebada* fattened chicken | *polla de agua* marsh hen, water hen, moorhen.

pollada *f* brood (de una gallina).

pollastre *m* chick, chicken (pollo) ‖ FIG & FAM kid, youngster (joven).

pollastro, tra *m/f* young cock (macho), young hen (hembra) ‖ FIG & FAM kid, youngster (joven).
◆ *m* FIG & FAM sly old fox (persona astuta).

pollear *vi* FAM to become *o* to get interested in girls *o* in the opposite sex; *mi hijo empieza ya a pollear* my son is already beginning to get interested in girls | to act like a youngster (una persona mayor).

pollera *f* baby walker (para niños) ‖ hen-house (gallinero) ‖ chicken coop (caja de pollos) ‖ petticoat (falda interior) ‖ AMER skirt (falda).

pollería *f* poultry shop, poulterer's (tienda).

pollero, ra *m/f* poulterer, poultry seller.

pollerón *m* AMER riding skirt.

pollino, na *m/f* young ass, young donkey.

pollito, ta *m/f* FIG & FAM kid, youngster ‖ chick (pollo), young pullet (polla).

pollo *m* chick (cría de la gallina al nacer) ‖ chicken (ya más crecido); *pollo asado* roast chicken ‖ young (de las aves) ‖ POP spit (gargajo) | frog [in the throat] ‖ FIG & FAM boy, kid, youngster (hasta los 15 años), boy, young

man (después) | chap, fellow (individuo) || — FAM *pollo pera* dandy, spiv [US dude] (lechuguino) || AMER *pollo rostizado* roast chicken || *pollo tomatero* tender young fryer.
◆ *pl* FIG & FAM young men.

polluelo *m* chicken, chick.

pomáceo, a *adj* BOT pomaceous.

pomada *f* ointment (medicina) || pomade (cosmético).

pomar *m* orchard (de árboles frutales) || apple orchard (manzanar).

pomelo *m* BOT grapefruit (fruta) | grapefruit tree (árbol).

pómez *adj f* *piedra pómez* pumice stone.

pomo *m* pommel (de espada, de bastón) || knob (de puerta) || flagon (licores) || bottle of perfume, scent bottle (frasco).

pompa *f* pomp (esplendor); *con gran pompa* with great pomp || display (ostentación) || bubble; *pompa de jabón* soap bubble || billow, puff (en la ropa) || spread of a peacock's tail (del pavo real) || MAR pump (bomba) || — FIG *hacer pompa de* to make a show of (ostentar).
◆ *pl* FIG pomps (vanidades) || *pompas fúnebres* funeral (ceremonia), undertaker's, funeral director's (funeraria).

Pompeya *n pr* GEOGR Pompeii.

pompeyano, na *adj/s* Pompeian.

Pompeyo *npr m* Pompey (el Magno) || Pompeius (Sexto).

pompi *m* FAM bottom, backside.

pomposamente *adv* pompously (con arrogancia) || with great pomp, splendidly.

pomposidad *f* pomp, display, splendour || pomposity (de una persona).

pomposo, sa *adj* pompous (persona) || splendid, magnificent, sumptuous.

pómulo *m* ANAT cheekbone (hueso) | cheek (mejilla).

poncha *f* AMER blanket (manta).

ponchada *f* AMER pile, great quantity, lot.

ponche *m* punch [drink].

ponchera *f* punch bowl.

poncho *m* AMER poncho (prenda de vestir) || AMER FAM *estar a poncho* to be in the dark (estar pez).

ponderable *adj* praiseworthy (elogiable) || ponderable (que se puede pesar).

ponderación *f* weighing, pondering, deliberation (consideración) || deliberation, calm; *habla con ponderación* he speaks with deliberation || exagerated *o* excessive praise, eulogy (encarecimiento) || balance (equilibrio) || weighing (acción de pesar) || *estar por encima de toda ponderación* to be above praise, to be inestimable, to be too good for words.

ponderado, da *adj* measured (cosa) || prudent, tactful (persona) || calm, steady, well-balanced (mentalidad).

ponderar *vt* to weigh up, to ponder over, to deliberate on, to consider (examinar) || to balance (equilibrar) || to speak highly of, to praise highly (elogiar); *ponderar un libro* to speak highly of a book || to weigh (sopesar).

ponderativo, va *adj* excessive (que encarece) || thoughtful, meditative (reflexivo) || deliberative || eulogistic, highly favourable (elogioso).

ponedero *m* nest box.

ponedora *adj f* egg-laying, laying (gallina).

ponencia *f* position of reporter *o* of rapporteur (cargo) || report (informe) || rapporteur (ponente) || JUR reporter.

ponente *adj* reporting.
◆ *m* JUR reporter || rapporteur (en una conferencia).

poner* *vt* to put; *pon este libro en la mesa* put this book on the table; *estaría mejor poner este cuadro aquí* it would be better to put this painting here || to place (colocar) || to set; *pon derecha la lámpara* set the lamp straight || to put in, to drive in (un clavo) || to set, to lay (disponer); *poner la mesa* to set the table || to put on (ropa); *poner un abrigo a un niño* to put a coat on a child, to put a child's coat on || to put; *poner dinero en la caja de ahorros* to put money in the savings bank || to put, to invest (invertir dinero) || to contribute, to give, to put (dar dinero) || to stake, to bet, to put (en el juego) || to bet (apostar); *pongo diez pesetas a que lo hago* I bet ten pesetas that I do it || MAT to put down (una cifra) || to put (inscribir); *poner un nombre en una lista* to put a name on a list || to translate, to put (escribir); *puse la frase en francés* I translated the sentence into French || to send (enviar); *le puse un telegrama, una carta* I sent him a telegram, a letter || to send, to put; *poner a un niño interno* to send a child to a boarding school, to put a child in a boarding school || to make (con adjetivos); *poner triste, rojo* to make sad, red || to state (enunciar); *poner sus condiciones* to state one's conditions || to raise (objeciones) || to cause, to provoke (causar, provocar) || to put, to place, to leave, to get; *eso me puso en un apuro* it put me in a difficult situation, it got me into a fix || to impose (un impuesto) || to give (una multa) || to give, to assign (señalar un trabajo) || to pose, to raise, to set (un problema) || to suppose, to say (suponer); *pongamos que no dije nada* let us suppose that I said nothing || to take (tardar); *puso dos horas en venir* he took two hours coming, it took him two hours to come || to take, to exercise; *poner gran cuidado en* to take great care to || to appoint, to make (nombrar para un puesto); *a Juan lo han puesto de secretario* they have appointed John secretary || to give, to call (un nombre, un mote) || to call (calificar); *poner a alguien de embustero* to call s.o. a liar || to put, to expose; *poner en peligro* to put in danger, to expose to danger || to get, to take (llevar); *el avión te pone en Madrid en una hora* the plane will get you to Madrid in an hour || to fit up, to equip (amueblar una casa) || to open, to set up, to equip (amueblar una casa) || to open, to set up (abrir una tienda, etc.) || to install; *poner el gas* to install gas || to switch on, to turn on, to put on (la radio, la televisión) || to show, to put on (una película); *ponen esta película en el cine Médicis* they are showing this film in the Médicis cinema || to put on (en el teatro) || to connect, to put through (*con*, to), to connect, to put through (poner al habla por teléfono) || to set, to adjust (un reloj en hora) || to lay (las gallinas) || — *ir muy bien puesto* to be very well dressed || *llevar puesto* to wear || *¿me puede usted poner con X?* may I speak to X, please?, can you put me through to X, please? || *poner a asar la carne* to put the meat on to roast || *poner a buen recaudo* to put in safekeeping (a salvo) || *poner a fuego y a sangre* to put to fire and sword || *poner al día* to bring up to date || *poner a mal tiempo buena cara* to keep a stiff upper lip, to keep one's chin up || *poner* or *someter a prueba* to put to the test, to test, to try out (la amistad, un empleado, un avión, etc.) || *poner a punto* to tune up (un motor, una máquina, etc.), to finish off, to round off, to put the finishing touch to (dar el último toque) || *poner a* or *de un lado* to put on one side || *poner a secar la ropa* to put the washing out to dry || *poner a uno a contribución* to make s.o. contribute || FIG *poner a uno como un trapo* to haul s.o. over the coals, to give s.o. a dressing down (reprender), to call s.o. all the names under the sun (insultar) | *poner a uno de vuelta y media* to call s.o. all the names under the sun || *poner a votación* to put to the *o* a vote || *poner bien a uno* to praise s.o. || FIG *poner buena cara a algo* to take sth. well | *poner buena cara a alguien* to be nice to s.o. || *poner cara de* to look like (con sustantivo), to look as if (con verbo) || *poner casa* to move (into a house) (para uno mismo), to give a house to (para otra persona) || *poner ceño* to frown || *poner colorado a uno* to make s.o. blush || FIG & FAM *poner como nuevo* to make as good as new || *poner cuidado en* to be careful *o* to take care in || *poner de comer* to feed || *poner de mal humor* to put in a bad mood || *poner de nombre* to name, to call; *mis padres me pusieron de nombre Miguel* my parents named me Michael || *poner de su bolsillo* to put in [money] out of one's own pocket || *poner de su lado a uno* to put s.o. on one's side, to win s.o. over || *poner de su parte* or *de su lado* to do one's bit || *poner en claro* to clarify, to make clear; *poner en claro un asunto* to clarify a matter || *poner en condiciones de* to put in a position to, to enable to || *poner en duda* to doubt, to question (dudar), to put in doubt (poner en tela de juicio) || *poner en ejecución* or *en práctica* to put into practice || *poner en guardia a uno* to put s.o. on his guard || *poner en la calle* to throw out || *poner en limpio* to make a fair copy of (un escrito), to clarify, to clear up (un asunto) || *poner en pie* to set up || *poner en tela de juicio* to put in doubt, to put in question || *poner entre la espada y la pared* to put between the devil and the deep blue sea (lío) || *poner en venta* to put up for sale || *poner los ojos en* to set eyes on || *poner los pelos de punta* to make s.o.'s hair stand on end || *poner mal a uno* to illtreat s.o. (maltratar), to speak ill of s.o. (hablar mal) || *poner mala cara* to be sulky (*a uno*, with s. o), to sulk (*a una cosa*, about sth.) || *poner malo a uno* to make s.o. ill || *poner manos a la obra* to set to work, to start work || *poner música a* to set to music; *poner música a versos* to set verse to music || FIG *poner por las nubes* to praise to the skies || *poner por testigo a* to call to witness, to take to witness || *poner término a* to put an end to || *poner tierra por medio* to make o.s. scarce || *poniendo que* supposing that || *¿qué ponen en el cine hoy?* wath's on at the pictures today.
◆ *vpr* to place o.s., to put o.s. (colocarse) || to become, to get (volverse); *ponerse furioso* to become furious || to turn (colores); *ponerse colorado* to turn red || to dress, to wear (vestirse); *ponerse de azul* to dress in blue, to wear blue || to put on (para abrigarse); *¡ponte un abrigo!* put on a coat! || to put on (cosméticos) || to set (lo astros) || to get down to; *no es que sea un trabajo difícil, pero hay que ponerse* it is not that it is difficult work, it is just a case of getting down to it || to bet (apostar); *me pongo contigo a que termino este trabajo* I bet you I finish this work || to be, to arrive (llegar); *en media hora nos ponemos en tu casa* we shall be at your house in half an hour || to take a job; *ponerse de chófer* to take a job as a chauffeur || to point (un perro) || to land (avión), to light, to alight (aves) || — *¡no se ponga así!* don't be like that! || *ponerse a* to start; *se puso a llorar* he started to cry || *ponerse a bien con alguien* to get on good terms with s.o. || *ponerse a cubierto* to get under cover || *ponerse a dieta* to put s.o. on a diet || *ponerse al corriente* to find out (enterarse), to keep up to date (mantenerse al día) || *ponerse al teléfono* to answer the telephone (al descolgar el aparato), to come to the phone (después de descolgarlo) || *ponerse a régimen* to put o.s. on a diet || *ponerse a servir* to get a job as a servant, to go into service || *ponerse bueno* to recover || *ponerse cómodo* or *a sus anchas* to make o.s. at home *o* comfortable || FAM *ponerse como el Quico* to stuff o.s. (hincharse de comer) || *ponerse de acuerdo* to come to an agreement, to agree || *ponerse de grasa, de lodo hasta los pelos* to get grease, mud all over o.s. || *ponerse delante* to get in the way (estorbar) ||

ponerse or *vestirse de largo* to wear a long dress (para salir de noche), to come out, to make one's début in society AMER (sentido figurado) || *ponerse de luto* to go into mourning || *ponerse de mal en peor* to go from bad to worse || *ponerse de pie* to stand (up) || FAM *ponerse de tiros largos* to put on one's Sunday best, to dress up || *ponerse en camino* to set out, to start out || *ponerse en contacto* or *en relación con* to get in touch with, to contact || *ponerse en contra de* to oppose || *ponerse en el lugar de uno* to put o.s. in s.o.'s place || *ponerse enfermo* to fall ill || *ponerse en filas* to line up to form ranks (alinearse) || *ponerse guapo* to smarten o.s. up || AMER FAM *ponérsela* to get stoned *o* sloshed (emborracharse) || *ponerse malo* to fall ill, to be ill || *ponerse trágico* to get melodramatic (una persona), to become a tragedy (una cosa).

poney *m* pony (caballo).

poniente *m* west (oeste) || west wind (viento).

pontaje; pontazgo *m* bridge toll.

pontear *vt* to make a bridge over.

pontificado *m* pontificate.

pontifical *adj* pontifical.
◆ *m* pontifical (libro) || pontificals *pl* (ornamentos) || FIG *de pontifical* in pontifical dress (con ornamentos litúrgicos de obispo), in one's Sunday best (bien vestido).

pontificar *vi* to pontificate.

pontífice *m* REL pontiff || HIST Pontifex (en Roma) || *El Sumo Pontífice* the Sovereign Pontiff.

pontificio, cia *adj* pontifical.

pontón *m* MAR lighter, pontoon (buque) | pontoon (puente) || float (de un avión).

pontonero *m* MIL pontoneer, pontonier.

ponzoña *f* venom, poison (de los animales) || poison (de los vegetales o de los minerales) || FIG poison; *la ponzoña de una doctrina mala* the poison of an evil doctrine | venom (malevolencia).

ponzoñoso, sa *adj* poisonous.

pool *m* COM pool.

pop *adj/sm* MÚS pop || *pop art* pop art.

popa *f* MAR stern || — *a popa* astern, abaft || FIG *de popa a proa* from top to bottom, through and through | *todo va viento en popa* everything is going smoothly, everything is going well | *vamos viento en popa* we are in luck, it is all systems go, the wind is with us.

popayaneso, sa; popayanense *adj* [of *o* from] Popayán (Colombia).
◆ *m/f* native o inhabitant of Popayán.

pope *m* pope (sacerdote ruso).

popelín *m*; **popelina** *f* poplin (tela).

popí *m* AMER manioc (mandioca).

poplíteo, a *adj* ANAT popliteal.

popote *m* AMER straw (paja) || FIG *estar hecho un popote* to be as thin as a rake.

populachería *f* cheap popularity.

populachero, ra *adj* cheap (barato) || vulgar, common (vulgar) || popular; *drama populachero* popular drama.

populacho *m* populace, masses *pl*, plebs *pl*.

popular *adj* popular; *un artista popular* a popular artist || of the people; *la educación popular* the education of the people || folk, popular (música, etc.) || colloquial (lenguaje) || *República Popular* People's Republic.

popularidad *f* popularity.

popularización *f* popularization.

popularizar *vi* to popularize.
◆ *vpr* to become popular.

populismo *m* populism.

populista *m/f* populist.

populoso, sa *adj* populous.

popurrí *m* MÚS potpourri.

póquer *m* —→ **póker.**

poquitín *m* FAM a tiny little bit.

poquito, ta *adj* a little bit of.
◆ *pl* a few.
◆ *adv* a little, a bit.
◆ *m* a little bit || — *a poquito(s)* little by little, bit by bit || *poquito a poco* little by little.

por *prep*

> 1. CAUSA, MEDIO, AGENTE 2. DESTINO, DESIGNIO 3. SITIO 4. TIEMPO 5. CON UN INFINITIVO 6. MODO 7. DISTRIBUTIVA 8. SENTIDOS DIVERSOS 9. LOCUCIONES

1. CAUSA, MEDIO, AGENTE By (agente); *la carta fue escrita por él* the letter was written by him || because of (motivo); *por su mucha edad no trabaja* he does not work because of his old age || from, out of, because of; *por necesidad* out of necessity || for; *por miedo a* for fear of || for, because of; *lo han despedido por perezoso* he was dismissed for laziness *o* because of his laziness || about; *inquieto por* worried about || because (seguido de un participio pasado); *cayó por herido* he fell because he was wounded || — *por causa tuya* because of you, thanks to you || *por tu culpa he perdido el tren* I missed the train because of you *o* thanks to you, you made me miss the train.

2. DESTINO, DESIGNIO For; *lo hice por ti* I did it for you; *iré por ti* I'll go for you || to; *lo hice por ayudarte* I did it to help you || for, as; *tomar por jefe, por esposa* to take for one's chief, for one's wife || in; *interesarse por alguien* to be interested in s.o. || *lo digo por ti* I'm telling you for your own sake, I'm only thinking of you.

3. SITIO Via, by; *ir a Madrid por Burgos* to go to Madrid via Burgos || through; *al pasar por Madrid* passing through Madrid; *pasamos por el túnel* we went through the tunnel || on, along; *por el lado derecho* on the right side || at; *atravesó la frontera por Irún* he crossed the frontier at Irún || towards, around (cerca de); *eso está por Pamplona* that is towards Pamplona || throughout; *por toda la ciudad* throughout the whole town || in, along, through; *pasearse por la calle* to walk in the street || in; *por mi barrio* in my district.

4. TIEMPO About, towards (fecha aproximada); *vendré por el 5 de marzo* I shall come about the 5th of March || at (fecha); *llegó por Navidad* he arrived at Christmas || on; *llegó por San Juan* he arrived on St John's Day || in, during; *por el verano, por la mañana* in *o* during the summer, the morning || for (plazo); *vendré por tres días* I shall come for three days || — *por ahora* for the time being, for the moment || *por la noche* in *o* during the night, at night.

5. CON UN INFINITIVO In order to, so as to (con vistas a); *por no equivocarse* in order not to make a mistake || for, because (a causa de); *le han castigado por haber mentido* they punished him for having lied *o* for lying *o* because he had lied || because, as, since; *no vine por tener mucho trabajo* I did not come because I had a lot of work; *por no saber qué hacer, me fui* as I did not know what to do, I went away || in; *por hacer una fortuna, perdió su dignidad* in making a fortune he lost his dignity || to be [with past participle] (sin); *todo está aún por hacer* everything is still to be done.

6. MODO By; *por señas* by signs; *viajar por tren* to travel by train || by, because of; *la conocí por el sombrero* I recognized her by her hat || by, according to (conforme); *juzgar por* to judge by || by; *amable por naturaleza* kind by nature || in; *por escrito* in writing; *por orden alfabético* in alphabetical order; *cortado por la mitad* cut in half.

7. DISTRIBUTIVA Per, for each; *a diez pesetas por persona* ten pesetas per person || by the; *comprar por metros, por docenas, por cientos* to buy by the metre, by the dozen, by the hundred || a, per; *una libra por hora* a pound an hour; *cien kilómetros por hora* a hundred kilometres per hour *o* an hour.

8. SENTIDOS DIVERSOS For, in exchange for; *trocar una cosa por otra* to swap one thing for another || for, instead of (en vez de); *pagar por otro* to pay for s.o. else || on behalf of (en nombre de) || for; *tener un tugurio por casa* to have a slum for a house || out of, through, for (a favor de) || for (precio); *por cien pesetas* for a hundred pesetas || for (con ir, con mandar, etc.); *vino por fósforos* he came for matches; *lo mandé por vino* I sent him for wine || as for, for (en cuanto a); *por lo que dijiste ya veremos* as for what you said, we shall see about that later || as for, for, as far as; *por mí* as for me, for my part, as far as I am concerned || times (multiplicación); *tres por cuatro, doce* three times four, twelve || by (superficie); *dos metros por cuatro* two metres by four || for; *diez ciudadanos por cada labrador* ten city dwellers for each agricultural worker.

9. LOCUCIONES *Agradecer por* to thank for || *empezar por* to start by (*con verbo*); *empezó por reírse* he started by laughing; to start with (persona); *empezaron por su padre* they started with his father || *ir por* to go and fetch, to go for || *juzgar a uno por las apariencias* to judge s.o. by appearances | *por allá* over there, that way || *por ciento* percent; *un interés del tres por ciento* three percent interest || *por cierto* of course, indeed, certainly || *por cierto...* by the way...; *por cierto ayer fui al cine y no te encontré* by the way I went to see you yesterday and you weren't in || *por cuanto* since, in as much as || *¡por Dios!* for goodness' sake!, for God's sake! || *por donde* by where, wherever; *por donde voy los encuentro* wherever I go I meet them; from which (de lo cual) || *por ejemplo* for instance, for example (verbigracia), as an example; *tomar a uno por ejemplo* to take s.o. as an example || *por el honor* on one's honour || *por el mundo* all over the world || *por entre* through, between || *por eso, por eso mismo* that is why, for that reason; *por eso lo hago, lo hago por eso* that is why I do it, I do it for that reason; exactly; *pero él no viene* =m *¡por eso!* but he is not coming =m exactly! || *por eso es por lo que* that is why || *por esta vez* this time || *por favor* please || *por fuera* outside (exteriormente), on the outside (en apariencia) || *por lo cual* (and) so, (and) that is why, (and) that is the reason || *por lo largo y por lo ancho* to and fro || *por lo menos* at least || *por lo... que* so (con adjetivo); *no pude moverlo por lo pesado que era* he was so heavy that I could not move him || *por mandato de* on the orders of || *por más, por mucho, por muy que* however much, no matter how much véase OBSERV || *por medio de* through (the middle of); *el río pasa por medio del pueblo* the river passes through the middle of the town; by means of, with the help of (mediante), through (por el intermedio de) || *por menos que* however little || *por... que* however; *por buena que sea* however good she is *o* she may be; *por mucha prisa que tenga* however much of a hurry he is in *o* he may be in; *por poco que sea* however little it is *o* it may be || *por que* because («que» in this sense, has no written accent) || *por qué* why; *no sé por qué viene tan a menudo* I don't know why he comes so often || *por si acaso* just in case, in case; *por si acaso vienes* just in case you come || *por sí mismo* by himself || *por sí solo* all by himself, all on his own || *por tanto* (and) so || *por uno que calla, diez gritan* for every one who keeps quiet there are ten who shout || *por un sí o por un no* for nothing, over nothing

|| *preguntar por* to ask about *o* after, to ask for news of; *preguntar por alguien* to ask after s.o.; to ask for (querer ver o hablar).

— OBSERV Hay que distinguir tres casos en la traducción de *por más, por mucho, por muy que:*
a) Con un adjetivo: *por más* or *por muy guapa que es* or *sea* however pretty *o* no matter how pretty she is.
b) Con un verbo: *por más* or *por mucho que trabaje* however much *o* no matter how much he works.
c) Con un sustantivo: *por más libros que tenga, no sabe nada* however many *o* no matter how many books he has, he knows nothing; *por mucho dinero que tenga* however much *o* no matter how much money he has.

porcachón, ona; porcallón, ona *adj* FAM filthy, dirty.
◆ *m/f* FAM pig.

porcelana *f* porcelain, china || chinaware, china (vajilla).

porcentaje *m* percentage; *le dan cierto porcentaje sobre las ventas* he is given a certain percentage of what he sells || rate (índice); *porcentaje de modulación* modulation rate || ratio (proporción, relación).

porcentual *adj* porcentage.

porcino, na *adj* porcine, pig, of *o* relating to pigs || *pan porcino* sowbread (planta).
◆ *m* small pig (cochinillo).
◆ *pl* swine, pigs (ganado porcino).

porción *f* share, part, portion; *la porción de cada uno* each person's share || part, portion; *le dio una porción de lo que tenía* he gave him part of what he had || piece, portion; *dame una porción de este pastel* give me a piece of this cake | portion (en una comunidad) || sum (de dinero) || FIG quantity; *una porción reducida de frutas* a small quantity of fruit | lot, crowd, number; *llegó una porción de gente* a crowd of people arrived.

porcuno, na *adj* porcine, pig.
◆ *m pl* pigs.

porche *m* arcade (soportal) || porch (de una casa) || porch (atrio).

pordiosero, ra *adj* begging.
◆ *m/f* beggar.

porfía *f* persistence (persistencia) || obstinacy, stubbornness (obstinación) || dispute, struggle (lucha) || *a porfía* emulously, in competition.

porfiado, da; porfiador, ra *adj* persistent (persistente) || obstinate, stubborn (obstinado); *un representante porfiado* a stubborn salesman || keen; *una discusión porfiada* a keen argument || fierce, bitter (enemigo).
◆ *m/f* obstinate person.

porfiar *vi* to persist (continuar); *porfiar en negar* to persist in denying || to persist in trying (intentar porfiadamente) || to argue stubbornly (discutir obstinadamente) || to wrangle (disputarse) || to vie (rivalizar) || — *porfiar en que* to insist on (querer), to insist that (afirmar) || *porfiar sobre* or *acerca de* to wrangle over.

pórfido *m* MIN porphyry.

porfírico, ca; porfídico, ca *adj* MIN porphyritic.

pórfiro *m* MIN porphyry.

pormenor *m* detail (not to be confused with *«por menor»* in detail); *los pormenores de un asunto* the details of a subject.

pormenorizar *vt* to give a detailed account of, to detail, to go into the details of.
◆ *vi* to go into detail.

pornografía *f* pornography.

pornográfico, ca *adj* pornographic.

pornógrafo *m* pornographer.

poro *m* pore (en la piel) || AMER maté gourd.

porongo *m* AMER gourd (calabaza).

pororó *m* AMER popcorn (roseta de maíz).

porosidad *f* porosity, porousness.

poroso, sa *adj* porous.

porotada *f* AMER CULIN dish of beans.

porotal *m* AMER beanfield (plantación) || AMER FIG *un porotal de* a lot of.

poroto *m* AMER bean (judía, frijol) | food (comida).

porque *conj* because (motivo); *no vino porque no quiso* he did not come because he did not want to || so that (para que); *porque viniese* so that he came || *porque no, porque sí* just because (para negar o afirmar tajantemente).

porqué *m* reason, the whys and the wherefores *pl* (motivo); *saber el porqué de cada cosa* to know the whys and the wherefores of *o* the reason for everything.

porquería *f* FAM filth (suciedad) | rubbish (basura, cosa de poco valor); *quítame esta porquería* take this rubbish away; *este reloj es una porquería* this watch is rubbish | dirty story *o* joke; *siempre cuenta porquerías* he's always telling dirty stories | nastiness (indecencia) | dirty trick (jugarreta) | nasty *o* awful food (comida mala) | trifle, worthless thing (cosa de poco valor) || — *esta calle es una porquería* this street is foul *o* filthy (muy sucia) || *tu cuarto está hecho una porquería* your room is like a pigsty.

porqueriza *f* pigsty (pocilga).

porquerizo, za; porquero, ra *m/f* swineherd.

porra *f* club, cudgel, bludgeon (arma) || baton (de guardia de circulación) || truncheon (arma de caucho) || TECN sledgehammer (de fragua) || bank (en los juegos de naipes) || last player (en los juegos de muchachos) || TEATR claque || fritter (churro de Madrid) || FIG & FAM bore, pest (persona pesada) | vanity (presunción) || — FAM *guardia de la porra* traffic cop || FIG & FAM *irse a la porra* to fall flat (un proyecto), to be ruined (estropearse) | *mandar a la porra* to send packing | *¡qué porra!* what a drag *o* a bore! | *¡vete a la porra!* go to the devil!, go to blazes!, go to hell!
◆ *interj* FAM damn!

porrada *f* blow (golpe) || blow with a club (con la porra) || FIG & FAM nonsense, twaddle (necedad) | pile, heap, loads *pl*; *una porrada de cosas* a pile of *o* loads of things || FAM *una porrada de dinero* lots *o* loads of money.

porrazo *m* blow || bump (golpe, choque) || AMER pile, heap, loads, *pl* (montón) || — *de golpe y porrazo* suddenly (de repente), very hurriedly (precipitadamente) || *obligar a uno a porrazos a hacer algo* to bludgeon s.o. into doing sth. || *pegarse un porrazo contra* to bump into, to bang into, to crash into; *se pegó un porrazo contra un árbol* he bumped into a tree.

porreta *m/f* FAM head (fumador de hachís) || FAM *en porreta* starkers.

porrillo *m* mason's hammer (maza de cantero) || FAM *a porrillo* by the ton, galore.

porrita *f* bank (en los juegos de naipes).

porro, rra *adj* FAM dull, stupid thick (torpe) || FAM *m* idiot, dope, fool | joint (marihuana).

porrón, ona *adj* dull, stupid (torpe) || FAM *a porrones* by the ton, galore, in abundance.
◆ *m* wineskin with a long spout || earthenware jug (botijo) || garlic sauce (salsa).

porrudo, da *adj* FAM dull, stupid.

porta *m* MAR port, porthole || TAUR *a porta gayola* pass made when the bull enters the ring.
◆ *adj f* ANAT portal; *vena porta* portal vein.

portaagujas *m inv* needle holder.

portaaviones *m inv* aircraft carrier.

portabandera *f* flag holder (cosa) || standard bearer, banner bearer, colour bearer (persona).

portabilidad *f* INFORM portability.

portabombas *m inv* bomb carrier.

portabotellas *m inv* bottle rack.

portabustos *m pl* AMER bra (sostén).

portacartas *m inv* briefcase (cartera).

portacruz *m* cross bearer.

portachuelo *m* gorge (entre montañas).

portada *f* façade, front (de casa, de iglesia) || porch (puerta) || IMPR title page (de un libro) | cover (de una revista) || FIG façade (fachada).

portadilla *f* IMPR half *o* bastard title (anteportada).

portadocumentos *m inv* briefcase (cartera).

portador, ra *adj* carrying, bearing.
◆ *m/f* carrier; *portador de gérmenes* germ carrier.
◆ *m* COM bearer; *pagar al portador* to pay the bearer; *el portador de la carta* the bearer of the letter.

portaequipajes *m inv* boot [*US* trunk] (en un coche) || carrier (de bicicleta) || luggage rack (de tren).

portaestandarte *m* standard bearer (oficial).

portafirmas *m inv* folder containing documents to be signed.

portafolio *m* portfolio.

portafusil *m* sling (for a rifle).

portaguión *m* MIL standard bearer.

portahelicópteros *m inv* helicopter carrier.

portaherramientas *m inv* TECN toolholder.

portaje *m* toll (portazgo).

portal *m* entrance hall (zaguán) || porch (de edificio) || arcade (soportal) || creche, crib (de navidad).

portalámparas *m inv* socket [for a bulb].

portalápiz *m* pencil holder.

portalibros *m inv* book straps *pl*.

portaligas *m inv* suspender belt.

portalón *m* monumental gate *o* door (puerta) || MAR gangway.

portamaletas *m inv* boot [*US* trunk] (de un coche).

portamantas *m inv* straps *pl* for carrying travelling rugs.

portaminas *m inv* propelling pencil.

portamonedas *m inv* purse.

portante *m* amble (del caballo) || FIG & FAM *tomar el portante* to go, to leave, to make o.s. scarce.

portanuevas *m/f inv* bearer of news.

portañica; portañuela *f* fly (de los pantalones).

portañola *f* MAR porthole (portal).

portaobjetos *m inv* slide (de microscopio).

portaplumas *m inv* penholder.

portar *vi* MAR to stand up to bad weather.
◆ *vt* to carry, to bear (llevar).
◆ *vpr* to behave; *portarse bien* to behave well, to behave o.s.

portarretrato *m* photograph frame.

portatacos *m inv* cue rack (en el billar).

portátil *adj* portable || INFORM transportable (transportable), portable (que se lleva a mano).

portaviandas *m inv* food can [*US* dinner pail, dinner bucket] (fiambrera).

portaviones *m inv* aircraft carrier.

portavoz *m* megaphone (bocina) || spokesman (persona autorizada).

portazgo *m* toll (impuesto).

portazguero *m* tollkeeper.

portazo *m* bang, slam of a door || — FIG *dar a uno un portazo* to slam the door in s.o.'s face || *dar un portazo* to slam the door || *oír un portazo* to hear a door slam.

porte *m* transport, carriage (transporte) || carriage transport charges *pl* (precio) || conduct, behaviour [*US* behavior] (comportamiento) || bearing (compostura) || air, appearance (aspecto) || — *franco de porte* carriage paid (transporte), post-free, postpaid (correos) || *porte debido* carriage forward || *porte pagado* carriage paid (en comercio), postage paid (en correos).

porteador, ra *adj/s* carrier.

portear *vt* to carry (llevar) || to slam (la puerta).
◆ *vi* to slam (una puerta) || *AMER* to go away (marcharse).

portento *m* marvel, wonder || *es un portento de inteligencia* he is exceptionally intelligent.

portentoso, sa *adj* prodigious, marvellous.

porteño, ña *adj* [of *o* from] Puerto de Santa María [Spain] *o* Buenos Aires [Argentina] *o* Puerto Cortés [Honduras] *o* Valparaíso [Chile] *o* Puerto Barrios [Guatemala].
◆ *m/f* native *o* inhabitant of Puerto de Santa María [Spain], of Buenos Aires [Argentina], of Puerto Cortés [Honduras], of Valparaíso [Chile], of Puerto Barrios [Guatemala].

porteo *m* transport, carriage.

portería *f* caretaker's lodge, doorman's lodge (habitación) || caretaker's job, doorman's job (empleo) || REL gate house (conventos) || goal (line) (fútbol).

portero, ra *m/f* caretaker, janitor (de casa de vivienda) || doorman, doorkeeper (que vigila) || concierge (en Francia, España).
◆ *m* DEP goalkeeper (guardameta) || — *portero de estrados* court usher (de tribunal) || *portero eléctrico* interphone, intercom.
◆ *adj* REL *hermano portero* monk who acts as doorkeeper.

portezuela *f* small door || door (de coche).

pórtico *m* portico; *un pórtico griego* a Greek portico || porch; *el pórtico de la Gloria en Santiago de Compostela* the porch of the Gloria in Santiago de Compostela || portal; *los pórticos de la catedral de Chartres* the portals of Chartres cathedral || arcade (soportales) || FIG gateway.

portilla *f* MAR porthole || gate [in a field].

portillo *m* opening, gap (de muro) || chip (de plato) || small door (puerta pequeña) || gate (en una muralla) || wicket (postigo) || pass (entre montañas) || FIG weak spot (punto vulnerable) | opening (posibilidad).

portland *m* Portland cement (cemento).

Port-Louis *n pr* GEOGR Port-Louis.

portón *m* large door || hall door (del vestíbulo).

portorriqueño, ña *adj/s* Puerto Rican.

portuario, ria *adj* harbour, port, of *o* pertaining to a port || *trabajador portuario* docker.

portuense *adj* [of *o* from] Puerto de Santa María [Spain] || [of *o* from] Ostia [Italy].
◆ *m/f* native *o* inhabitant of Puerto de Santa María [Spain], native o inhabitant of Ostia [Italy].

Portugal *npr m* GEOGR Portugal.

portugués, esa *adj/s* Portuguese.
◆ *m* Portuguese (lengua).

portulano *m* MAR portolano, portulan (mapa).

porvenir *m* future; *un joven con porvenir* a young man with a future; *un porvenir espléndido* a fine future || — *en el* or *en lo porvenir* in future (de hoy en adelante), in the future (en el futuro) || *sin porvenir* with no future, with no prospects.

pos (en) *adj* *en pos de* behind, after (detrás) || *ir en pos de* to be looking for, to pursue.

posada *f* inn (mesón) || guest house, boarding house (casa de huéspedes) || home, dwelling (morada) || hospitality, shelter; *dar posada* to offer hospitality, to give shelter.

posadeño, ña *adj* [of *o* from] Posadas [Argentina].
◆ *m/f* native o inhabitant of Posadas.

posaderas *f pl* FAM backside *sing*, behind *sing*, buttocks (trasero).

posadero, ra *m/f* landlord, landlady (de casa de huéspedes) || innkeeper (de mesón).

posar *vi* to alight, to settle (un pájaro) || to pose, to sit (para foto o para pintura) || to put on airs (darse importancia) || to lodge (alojarse).
◆ *vt* to put, to lay; *posó su mano sobre mi cabeza* he put his hand on my head || to put down (dejar en el suelo, etc.).
◆ *vpr* to settle (depositarse) || to alight, to settle (un pájaro) || to land (un avión).
— OBSERV *Posar* is a Gallicism in the sense of *servir de* or *como modelo a un pintor* and of *darse importancia.*

posavasos *m inv* drinks mat.

poscomunión *f* REL post-communion.

posdata *f* postscript.

pose *f* FOT exposure (exposición) || airs *pl*, pose, affectation (afectación) || pose (de un modelo).
— OBSERV *pose* is a Gallicism.

poseedor, ra; posesor, ra *adj* who possesses.
◆ *m/f* owner, possessor; *ella es la poseedora* she is the possessor || holder; *el poseedor de un récord* the holder of a record.

poseer *vt* to possess, to have, to own || to have, to enjoy (disfrutar) || to hold (un récord) || to master, to know perfectly (un idioma, un tema) || to possess (una mujer) || to haunt (obsesionar).
◆ *vpr* to keep o.s. under control, to control o.s.

poseído, da *adj* possessed || possessed, overcome (por un afecto, etc.) || full of o.s. (engreído) || *está muy poseída de sus conocimientos* she is very conscious of her knowledge.
◆ *m/f* possessed person (por el demonio) || *gritaba como un poseído* he was screaming like one possessed.

Poseidón *npr m* MIT Poseidon.

posesión *f* possession, property, ownership (propiedad) || possession (colonia de un Estado) || possession (del demonio) || *AMER* property, estate (finca rústica) || — *dar posesión de un cargo a uno* to hand over a post to s.o. || *estar en posesión de* to hold; *está en posesión del récord de los 110 metros vallas* he holds the record for the 110 metres hurdles || *toma de posesión* taking over (en un cargo), investiture (investidura) || *tomar posesión de* to take over, to take possession of (una casa), to take up (un cargo).
◆ *pl* property *sing*, estate *sing*.

posesionar *vt* to hand over, to give possession of.
◆ *vpr* to take possession, to take over || to seize (apoderarse).

posesivo, va *adj/sm* possessive.

poseso, sa *adj* possessed; *poseso del demonio* possessed by the devil.
◆ *m/f* possessed person (poseído).

posesor, ra *adj/s* ⟶ **poseedor.**

posesorio, ria *adj* JUR possessory.

posfecha *f* postdate.

posfechar *vt* to postdate.

posfranquismo *m* post-Franco period.

posfranquista *adj* post-Franco.

posguerra *f* postwar years *pl*, postwar period.

posibilidad *f* possibility || opportunity, chance, possibility (oportunidad) || *quizás no tenga la posibilidad de verle* it may not be possible for me to see him, I may not be able to see him, I may not get a chance to see him.
◆ *pl* chances, possibilities; *calcular las posibilidades de éxito* to calculate the chances of success.

posibilitar *vt* to make possible, to facilitate (hacer posible) || to allow, to permit (permitir).

posible *adj* possible; *es posible que venga* it's possible that he will come; *hacer posible* to make possible || — *de ser posible* if possible || *en* or *dentro de lo posible* as far as possible, as much as possible || *en la medida de lo posible* as far as possible, insofar as it is possible || *hacer todo lo posible para* to do everything within one's power *o* everything possible to, to do one's best *o* one's utmost to || *¡no es posible!* really! (exclamación de disgusto), well I never! (de incredulidad) || *¿será posible que no te lo haya dicho?* is it possible that he didn't tell you? || *si es posible* if possible, if it is possible || *si me es posible* if I possibly can || *tan pronto como sea posible* as soon as possible.
◆ *m pl* FAM means, resources (fortuna).

posiblemente *adv* possibly || probably (probablemente).

posición *f* position, place (sitio) || position, attitude, posture (postura) || position, standing, status; *posición social* social position || position; *ocupar una posición honorable* to occupy an honourable position || MIL position || — *entrar en posición* to position, to line up (cañón) || FIG *hallarse en una mala posición* to be in a bad way || INFORM *posición de memoria* storage location.

positivado *m* FOT printing.

positivismo *m* FIL positivism || realism (realismo).

positivista *adj* FIL positivist || realistic (realista).
◆ *m/f* FIL positivist || realist.

positivo, va *adj/sm* positive.
◆ *f* FOT positive, (positive) print.

pósito *m* communal granary (granero) || cooperative.

positón; positrón *m* positron (electrón positivo).

posma *adj* FAM dull, sluggish (lento) | bothersome, tiresome (latoso) | nonchalant (sin entusiasmo).
◆ *m/f* FAM dullard, dull person | nonchalant person | pest, nuisance, bore (persona latosa).
◆ *f* FAM dullness (lentitud) | nuisance (lata).

poso *m* sediment, lees *pl*, dregs *pl* (de vino o de otro líquido) || grounds *pl* (de café) || FIG vestige, trace (huella) || *formar poso* to settle (líquido).

posología *f* dosage (dosis) || posology (en terapéutica).

posponer* *vt* to put in second place, to put behind *o* below, to value less (estimar menos) || to postpone, to put off (diferir) || GRAM to postpone, to place after || *posponer el interés personal al general* to put the public interest before one's personal interest.

posposición *f* subordination, putting after ‖ postponement ‖ GRAM postposition.

posta *f* relay of post horses (de caballos) ‖ piece (pedazo) ‖ pellet of buckshot (perdigón) ‖ stake (envite) ‖ ARQ volute ‖ — *a posta* on purpose, intentionally (adrede) ‖ *caballo de posta* relay horse, post horse ‖ *silla de posta* post chaise.
◆ *pl* ARQ scroll *sing* (adorno).

postal *adj* postal ‖ — *giro postal* money order, postal order ‖ *paquete postal* parcel (sent by post) ‖ *tarjeta postal* postcard.
◆ *f* postcard (tarjeta).

postbalance *m* *venta postbalance* stocktaking sale [*US* post-inventory sale].

postcombustión *f* TECN reheating, afterburning.

postdata *f* postscript.

postdiluviano, na *adj* postdiluvian.

poste *m* pole; *poste telegráfico* telegraph pole ‖ pillar (columna) ‖ post (estaca) ‖ picket (para caballos) ‖ TECN pylon ‖ DEP post (de una portería) ‖ — FAM *más tieso que un poste* as stiff as a board ‖ *poste indicador* signpost ‖ FAM *quedarse parado como un poste* to stand dead still.

postema *f* MED abscess (absceso).

poste restante *f* *AMER* poste restante [*US* general delivery] (lista de correos).

postergación *f* postponement, delay (retraso) ‖ adjournment (aplazamiento oficial) ‖ passing over (relegación) ‖ omission (olvido).

postergar *vt* to postpone, to put off (aplazar) ‖ to adjourn (caso oficial) ‖ to pass over (a un empleado) ‖ to leave on one side (dejar de lado).

posteridad *f* posterity (descendencia).

posterior *adj* posterior, rear, back (trasero) ‖ subsequent (ulterior) ‖ later; *su cumpleaños fue posterior al mío* his birthday was later than mine.

posteriori (a) *loc* a posteriori.

posterioridad *f* posteriority ‖ *con posterioridad* later, subsequently.

posteriormente *adv* subsequently, later (on).

postescolar *adj* after school (después de la escuela), postgraduate (después de la universidad).

postfijo *m* suffix, postfix (sufijo).

postglacial *adj* postglacial.

postguerra *f* postwar years *pl*, postwar period.

postigo *m* shutter (de ventana) ‖ secret *o* hidden door (puerta falsa) ‖ door (puerta) ‖ wicket (puerta abierta en otra mayor) ‖ gate (de ciudad).

postilla *f* MED scab (en la piel) ‖ annotation, note (aclaración).

postillón *m* postilion, postillion (conductor).

postilloso, sa *adj* MED scabby.

postimpresionismo *m* postimpressionism.

postimpresionista *adj/s* postimpressionist.

postín *m* FAM airs *pl* (presunción) | elegance ‖ — FAM *darse postín* to put on airs, to show off, to swank | *un traje de mucho postín* a very chic *o* elegant dress.

postinear *vi* FAM *darse postín* to put on airs, to show off, to swank.

postinero, ra *adj* FAM snooty, swanky (presumido) | chic, elegant, posh (elegante).

postizo, za *adj* false; *cabellos postizos* false hair; *diente postizo* false tooth ‖ artificial; *pierna postiza* artificial leg ‖ detachable (cuello) ‖ assumed (nombre).
◆ *m* hairpiece, switch (de pelo).

postmeridiano, na *adj* postmeridian, afternoon.

postnatal *adj* postnatal.

postoperatorio, ria *adj* postoperative.

postor *m* bidder (en una subasta) ‖ *al mayor* or *mejor postor* to the highest bidder.

postpalatal *adj* postpalatal.

postración *f* prostration.

postrado, da *adj* prostrate.

postrar *vt* to prostrate, to overcome; *postrado por la calentura* prostrated by fever; *postrado por la desgracia* overcome by unhappiness ‖ to prostrate, to humiliate (humillar).
◆ *vpr* to prostrate o.s., to kneel down (arrodillarse) ‖ to weaken (debilitarse) ‖ to be overcome (por las desgracias).

postre *adj* last (postrero).
◆ *m* dessert, sweet; *tomar de postre fruta* to have fruit for dessert ‖ *a los postres* at the dessert.
◆ *f* *a la postre* in the end, at last, finally.

postremo, ma *adj* last, ultimate.

postrer *adj m* last (postrero); *el postrer suspiro* the last sigh.

— OBSERV This word is the apocopated form of *postrero* and is used before masculine singular nouns.

postrero, ra *adj* last; *el día postrero* the last day.

postrimer *adj* last (apocopated form of «*postrimero*»).

postrimería *f* end (of life, etc.) ‖ REL death ‖ *en las postrimerías del siglo* towards *o* at the end of the century.

— OBSERV This word is mainly used in the plural form.

postrimero, ra *adj* last.

post scriptum *m inv* postscript (posdata).

postsincronización *f* CINEM postsynchronization.

postsincronizar *vt* CINEM to postsynchronize.

postulación *f* collection [in the streets, for a charity] (colecta) ‖ REL postulation.

postulado *m* postulate.

postulador *m* REL postulator.

postulante, ta *m/f* postulant, applicant (candidato) ‖ collector [for a charity] (el que hace una colecta).

postular *vt* to postulate ‖ to request, to ask for, to demand; *postular medidas* to ask for measures ‖ to apply for (un cargo) ‖ to be a candidate for (ser candidato).
◆ *vi* to collect [for charity] (hacer una colecta).

póstumo, ma *adj* posthumous.

postura *f* position, posture, attitude (situación); *una postura incómoda* an uncomfortable position ‖ FIG attitude, position; *no saber qué postura tomar* not to know what attitude to take | position, stand; *su postura no es muy clara* his position is not very clear ‖ laying (de los huevos) ‖ egg (huevo) ‖ sapling (arbolillo) ‖ price fixed by the authorities (de mercancías) ‖ bid (en una almoneda) ‖ pact, agreement (convenio) ‖ bet, wager (apuesta) ‖ stake (en los juegos).

postventa; posventa *adj* after-sale; *servicio postventa* after-sale service.

potable *adj* drinkable, potable ‖ FAM palatable, decent, acceptable (aceptable) ‖ *agua potable* drinking water.

potaje *m* dish of dried vegetables ‖ FIG jumble, muddle (mezcla confusa).

potasa *f* QUÍM potash.

potásico, ca *adj* QUÍM potassic.

potasio *m* potassium (metal).

pote *m* pot (tarro) ‖ pan, pot (para cocer) ‖ jar (de farmacia) ‖ stew (cocido en Galicia) ‖ FIG & FAM pout (gesto) ‖ *AMER* tin, can (lata) | flowerpot (maceta) ‖ — FIG & FAM *a pote* in abundance (mucho) | *darse pote* to put on airs, to swank.

potencia *f* FÍS & MAT power; *la potencia de un motor* the power of an engine ‖ power (nación); *las grandes potencias* the great powers ‖ potency, virility (de un hombre) ‖ — MAT *elevar un número a la cuarta potencia* to raise a number to the fourth power ‖ *en potencia* potential, in the making, potentially ‖ *potencia al freno* brake horsepower ‖ INFORM *potencia de cálculo* computing power ‖ *potencia nuclear* nuclear power ‖ MAT *tres elevado a la segunda potencia, a la tercera potencia, a la cuarta potencia* three squared, cubed, to the power of four.
◆ *pl* faculties [of memory, understanding and will] (del alma).

potenciación *f* MAT involution.

potencial *adj* potential ‖ — GRAM *modo potencial* conditional [tense] | *potencial simple* present conditional [tense].
◆ *m* potentiality, potential ‖ *potencial humano* manpower.

potencialidad *f* potentiality, potential.

potenciar *vt* to give power to ‖ to increase the power of ‖ to make possible, to allow (facultar) ‖ to increase the possibilities of.

potenciómetro *m* FÍS potentiometer.

potentado *m* potentate.

potente *adj* powerful; *una máquina potente* a powerful machine ‖ virile (capaz de engendrar) ‖ powerful, strong, mighty (persona, voluntad) ‖ leading (empresa).

potenza *f* HERÁLD potent cross.

potenzado, da *adj* *cruz potenzada* potent cross.

poterna *f* postern (en las fortificaciones).

potestad *f* power (poder) ‖ podesta (gobernador en Italia) ‖ JUR *patria potestad, potestad paternal* paternal authority, patria potestas.
◆ *pl* REL powers, sixth order *sing* of angels.

potestativo, va *adj* JUR facultative ‖ optional.

potingue *m* FAM concoction.

Potosí *m* FIG *no vale un Potosí* it (he, she, etc.) is not worth a thing | *ser un Potosí, valer un Potosí* to be worth one's weight in gold *o* its weight in gold.

— OBSERV From the town of Potosí, in Bolivia, which is famous for its silver mines.

potosino, na *adj* [of *o* from] Potosí [in Bolivia].
◆ *m/f* native *o* inhabitant of Potosí.

potra *f* filly (caballo) ‖ FAM hernia (hernia) ‖ FIG & FAM luck (suerte) ‖ FIG & FAM *tener potra* to be lucky.

potrada *f* herd of colts.

potranca *f* young filly.

potranco *m* colt (potro).

potrero *m* *AMER* field (campo).

potrillo *m* young colt ‖ *AMER* tumbler (vaso grande).

potro *m* colt (caballo) ‖ rack, instrument of torture (de tormento) ‖ stanchion [for branding] (para veterinarios o herradores) ‖ (vaulting) horse (gimnasia) ‖ *potro con arzón* pommelled horse, side horse.

potroso, sa *adj* MED ruptured ‖ FAM lucky (afortunado).
◆ *m/f* MED person suffering from a hernia ‖ FAM lucky person.

poyete *m* small stone bench ‖ FIG & FAM *quedarse en el poyete* to be left on the shelf, to be an old maid (solterona), to be a wallflower (en el baile).

poyo *m* stone bench (banco).

poza *f* large puddle (charca).

pozal *m* bucket, pail (cubo) || rim of a well (brocal) || jar (tinaja).

pozo *m* well (de agua, de petróleo) || shaft (de mina) || hole, deep part (en un río) || pit (hoyo seco) || bank (en los naipes) || MAR hold (bodega) | bilge (sentina) | fish tank [on a boat] (de peces) || FIG well, fountain (fuente) || *AMER* spring (manantial) | large puddle (charca) || — FAM *mi gozo en un pozo* that's just my luck || *pozo artesiano* artesian well || FIG *pozo de ciencia* well *o* fountain of knowledge || *pozo negro* cesspool.

PPA *abrev de Partido Peronista Auténtico* Argentinian political party.

pracrito; prácrito *m* prakrit (idioma de la India).

práctica *f* practice; *aprender con la práctica* to learn by practice || experience, knowledge || method || — *es práctica establecida* it is the custom, it is standard practice || *poner en práctica* to put into practice.

◆ *pl* practical studies (clases) || training *sing* (preparación) || devotions (devociones) || *período de prácticas* practical training period.

practicabilidad *f* practicability.

practicable *adj* practicable || passable [road, etc.] (transitable).

◆ *m* practicable (en el teatro).

practicaje *m* pilotage [in a port].

practicante *adj* practising (en religión).

◆ *m/f* nurse (auxiliar de medicina) || assistant chemist (de botica) || practitioner, person who practises his *o* her religion (en religión).

practicar *vt* to practise [*US* to practice]; *practicar un idioma* to practise a language || to practise, to make a practice of; *practicar la virtud* to practise virtue || to go in for; *practicar los deportes* to go in for sport || to play; *practicar el fútbol* to play football || to make (un agujero) || to perform, to do (hacer) || *practicar la esgrima* to fence.

◆ *vi* REL to practise, to be practising.

práctico, ca *adj* practical (cómodo) || handy (cosa) || useful, convenient (medida, medio) || expert, experienced (ejercitado) || *clases prácticas* practical lessons, practicals.

◆ *m* coastal pilot || *barco del práctico* pilot boat.

pradera *f* meadow (pequeña) || prairie (grande, especialmente en Estados Unidos).

prado *m* meadow || promenade (paseo).

Praga *n pr* GEOGR Prague.

pragmático, ca *adj* pragmatic.

◆ *m/f* pragmatist.

pragmatismo *m* pragmatism.

pragmatista *adj* pragmatic.

◆ *m/f* pragmatist.

praseodimio *m* praseodymium (metal).

preacuerdo *m* agreement in principle.

preamplificador *m* RAD preamplifier.

prebenda *f* prebend (de canónigo) || FIG & FAM sinecure (oficio lucrativo).

prebendado *m* prebend, prebendary.

prebendar *vt* to bestow a prebend on.

◆ *vi* to obtain a prebend.

prebostazgo *m* (ant) provostship.

preboste *m* provost.

precalentador *m* TECN preheater.

precalentamiento *m* TECN preheating.

precalentar *vt* to preheat.

precambriano, na; precámbrico, ca *adj* GEOL Precambrian.

◆ *m* Precambrian era.

precampaña *f* run-up [to the electoral campaign].

precandidato, ta *m/f* possible candidate.

precariedad *f* precariousness.

precario, ria *adj* precarious.

precaución *f* precaution (medida) || precaution, foresight, caution (prudencia) || — *con precaución* cautiously, carefully, warily || *por precaución* as a precaution, as a safety measure.

precaucionarse *vpr* to take precautions.

precaver *vt* to guard against, to take precautions against (tomar precauciones) || to prevent (impedir).

◆ *vpr* to be on one's guard, to take precautions; *precaverse de un peligro* to be on one's guard against danger | to forestall; *precaverse contra la miseria* to forestall poverty.

precavidamente *adv* cautiously, warily.

precavido, da *adj* cautious, prudent, wary, careful (prudente) || provident (previsor) || cunning (astuto).

precedencia *f* precedence, priority (de fecha, de importancia).

precedente *adj* preceding; *los años precedentes a éste* the preceding years, the years preceding this one || previous (previo) || earlier (anterior).

◆ *m* precedent (antecedente); *sentar un precedente* to establish *o* to set a precedent || *sin precedentes* unprecedented.

preceder *vt/vi* to precede, to go before.

preceptista *adj* preceptive.

◆ *m/f* preceptist, theorist.

preceptivo, va *adj* mandatory.

◆ *f* precepts *pl*, rules *pl* (literaria).

precepto *m* precept (de un arte, etc.) || order, rule (orden) || — *cumplir con el precepto* to fulfill one's obligations || *fiestas de precepto* days of obligation.

preceptor, ra *m* (private) tutor.

◆ *f* governess.

preceptorado *m* tutorship, post of tutor || post of governess.

preces *f pl* prayers.

precesión *f* ASTR precession; *precesión de los equinoccios* precession of the equinoxes || reticence.

preciado, da *adj* valuable, precious (de valor) || esteemed, appreciated (estimado); *una obra muy preciada* a highly esteemed work.

preciar *vt* to appreciate, to esteem (apreciar) || to value, to appraise (tasar).

◆ *vpr* to be conceited, to be vain (estar engreído) || to boast (jactarse) || to think o.s.; *se precia de inteligente* he thinks himself clever || — *como cualquier español que se precie* like any self-respecting Spaniard || *preciarse de orador* to boast of being an orator, to consider o.s. a great orator.

precinta *f* official seal (en las aduanas).

precintado, da *adj* sealed.

◆ *m* sealing (de un paquete).

precintar *vt* to seal, to place a seal on (un paquete) || JUR to seal, to seal off.

precinto *m* placing of seals || lead seal (marchamo) || JUR official seal || seal (de una botella) || — JUR *colocación de precinto* sealing off | *violación* or *quebrantamiento de precinto* breaking of seals.

precio *m* price; *precio ofrecido, al contado, de coste, de lista, neto* asking, cash, cost, list, net price || fare (de un viaje) || rate, charge (de un hotel) || value, worth (valor) || — *a cualquier precio* whatever the price *o* the cost (cualquiera que sea el precio), at any cost (cualesquiera que sean las circunstancias) || FIG *al precio de* at the cost of || *control de precios* price control || *de gran* or *de mucho precio* expensive, dear, costly (cosa), valuable (persona) || *fijación de precio* or *de precios* price fixing || *fuera de precio* priceless, beyond price || *lista de precios* price list || *lo compraría a precio de oro* I would pay a fortune for it || *mantenimiento de los precios* price support || *no tener precio* to be priceless || *poner a precio la cabeza de uno* to put a price on s.o.'s head || *poner precio a* to put a price on || *precio alambicado* or *estudiado* rock-bottom price, cheapest possible price || *precio al por mayor* wholesale price || *precio al por menor* retail price || *precio barato* or *bajo* low price || *precio corriente* or *de mercado* market price || *precio de compra* purchase price || *precio de fábrica* factory price, ex-works price || *precio de lanzamiento* special launch price, introductory offer price || *precio de oferta* offering price, put price || *precio de tasa* fixed price || *precio de venta* sale price || *precio fijo* fixed price || *precio fuerte* full price || *precio por unidad* unit price || *precio tope* top price, ceiling price || *subida de precio* price rise || *subida de precios* rise in price, rising prices || *tener en gran precio* to esteem highly.

preciosidad *f* great value (valor) || charm, beauty (encanto); *la preciosidad de esta joya* the charm of this jewel || beauty, marvel (cosa preciosa); *esta pulsera es una preciosidad* this bracelet is a beauty || jewel, beauty, darling (mujer, niño) || preciosity (culteranismo) || *¡qué preciosidad de niña!* what a delightful *o* a darling *o* a lovely *o* a gorgeous child!

preciosismo *m* preciosity (afectación).

preciosista *adj* precious, affected (afectado) || precious, of *o* pertaining to the «précieux».

◆ *m* «précieux», precious writer.

◆ *f* «précieuse» (literata).

precioso, sa *adj* precious, valuable (de gran precio) || FIG delightful, beautiful, lovely, wonderful (hermoso); *una mujer preciosa* a beautiful woman | wonderful, beautiful; *un coche precioso* a wonderful car | witty (chistoso, festivo) || *piedra preciosa* precious stone.

preciosura *f* *AMER* → **preciosidad.**

precipicio *m* precipice (corte) || abyss; *caer al precipicio* to fall into the abyss || FIG ruin, downfall (ruina).

precipitación *f* precipitation, rainfall (lluvia) || haste, precipitation (prisa) || QUÍM precipitation || *con precipitación* hastily, hurriedly, precipitately.

precipitadamente *adv* hastily, hurriedly (muy rápidamente) || precipitately (con demasiada prisa).

precipitadero *m* precipice (corte) || abyss (abismo).

precipitado, da *adj* hasty, hurried, rapid (rápido) || rash, reckless, precipitate (imprudente) || headlong (huida).

◆ *m* QUÍM precipitate, deposit (sedimento).

precipitar *vt* to hurl down, to throw, to cast down (algo, alguien) || to push headlong, to hurl *o* to throw headlong (a una persona empujándola) || to hasten, to rush, to hurry on, to speed along, to accelerate (apresurar) || QUÍM to precipitate.

◆ *vpr* to throw *o* to hurl s.o.; *precipitarse contra el enemigo* to hurl o.s. against the enemy || to pounce (*sobre*, on) (sobre una presa) || to rush [headlong]; *precipitarse hacia la salida* to rush towards the exit || to hurry, to hasten (darse prisa) || FIG to gather momentum (acontecimientos, etc.) | to be hasty (actuar apresuradamente) || QUÍM to precipitate || *no precipitarse* to take one's time, not to hurry.

precisamente *adv* precisely, exactly, just (justamente); *por esto precisamente* precisely because of that || really (realmente) || specially; *vino precisamente para verte* he came specially to see you || *¡precisamente!* exactly!, precisely!

precisar *vt* to specify, to state exactly (indicar) || to define exactly (definir) || to state clearly; *precisa tu idea* state your idea clearly || to need (necesitar); *preciso datos* I need information || to force (forzar) || — *se precisa un contable* accountant needed *o* required || *verse precisado a* to be forced to, to be obliged to.
◆ *v impers* to be necessary (ser necesario).

precisión *f* precision; *instrumento de precisión* precision instrument || accuracy, exactness (exactitud) || need (necesidad); *tengo precisión de tu ayuda* I have need of your help || *tirar con precisión* to hit the *o* one's target (dar en el blanco), to aim accurately *o* well (apuntar bien).
◆ *pl* details, particulars.

preciso, sa *adj* precise, clear, concise (claro) || necessary, essential (necesario); *las cualidades precisas* the essential qualities; *es preciso tener coche* it is essential to have a car || precise, very, exact; *el día preciso de nuestra marcha* the precise day of our departure || accurate, exact (exacto) || — *cuando sea preciso* when necessary || *ser preciso* to be necessary, must; *es preciso que vengas* it is necessary for you to come, you must come || *tener tiempo preciso para ir* to have just enough time to go.

precitado, da *adj* aforementioned, abovementioned, aforesaid.

preclaro, ra *adj* outstanding, illustrious.

precocidad *f* precocity, precociousness || earliness (de una planta).

precocinado, da *adj* ready-cooked.

precognición *f* precognition, foreknowledge.

precolombino, na *adj* pre-Columbian, before Columbus (anterior a Colón).

precombustión *f* precombustion (de motor diesel).

precompresión *f* precompression.

preconcebir* *vt* to preconceive.

preconización *f* recommendation (recomendación) || suggestion, proposal (sugerencia) || advice (consejo) || praising (alabanza) || REL preconization (de un prelato).

preconizador, ra *adj* advising, advisory.
◆ *m/f* adviser (consejero) || advocate, partisan (partidario) || praiser (que alaba).

preconizar *vt* to praise (alabar) || to recommend, to advise (recomendar) || to advise (aconsejar) || to suggest, to propose (proponer) || to advocate (ser partidario de) || REL to preconize.

precoz *adj* precocious (persona) || early (fruta).

precursor, ra *adj* precursory, premonitory || *los signos precursores de la desgracia* the forerunners of misfortune.
◆ *m* precursor, forerunner.

predecesor, ra *m/f* predecessor.

predecir* *vt* to predict, to forecast, to foretell.

predestinación *f* predestination.

predestinado, da *adj* predestined.
◆ *m/f* predestinate.

predestinar *vt* to predestine, to predestinate.

predeterminación *f* predetermination.

predeterminante *adj* predetermining.

predeterminar *vt* to predetermine.

predial *adj* predial, praedial.

prédica *f* sermon (sermón protestante).
◆ *pl* FIG preaching *sing.*

predicable *adj* which can be preached, predicable.
◆ *m* GRAM predicable.

predicación *f* preaching || sermon.

predicaderas *f pl* FAM eloquence *sing.*

predicado *m* GRAM predicate.

predicador, ra *m/f* preacher.
◆ *m* ZOOL praying mantis (insecto).

predicamento *m* FIL predicament || FIG influence, weight (influencia) | prestige (prestigio).

predicante *m* predicant.

predicar *vt/vi* to preach; *el cura predicaba la virtud* the vicar preached virtue || FIG to sermonize, to preach to, to lecture (amonestar o reprender) || — *predicar con el ejemplo* to set an example || *predicar en el desierto* to preach in the wilderness || *una cosa es predicar y otra es dar trigo* it is easy to talk, actions speak louder than words.

predicativo, va *adj* GRAM predicative.

predicción *f* prediction, forecast || forecast (del tiempo).

predicho, cha *adj* aforesaid, aforementioned.

predigerido, da *adj* predigested.

predigestión *f* predigestion.

predilección *f* predilection.

predilecto, ta *adj* favourite; *mi hijo predilecto* my favourite son || favourite, preferred; *ciudad predilecta de los pintores* favourite town of painters, town preferred by painters.

predio *m* estate, property (heredad) || — *predio rústico* country estate *o* property || *predio urbano* town property.

predisponer* *vt* to predispose || *predisponer contra* to prejudice against.

predisposición *f* predisposition || *predisposición contra* prejudice against.

predispuesto, ta *adj* predisposed || *predispuesto contra* prejudiced against.

predominación; predominancia *f* predominance, predominancy, predomination.

predominante *adj* predominant, predominating, prevailing.

predominar *vt* to predominate over || FIG to overlook (una casa, etc.).
◆ *vi* to predominate, to prevail.

predominio *m* predominance, predominancy, prevalence.

preelectoral *adj* pre-election; *campaña preelectoral* pre-election campaign.

preelegir* *vt* to choose *o* to select beforehand *o* in advance, to preselect (escoger) || to elect beforehand (por elección) || *preelegido* preselected, previously chosen *o* selected; previously elected.

preeminencia *f* preeminence.

preeminente *adj* preeminent.

preempción *f* preemption.

preescolar *adj* preschool.

preestablecer *vt* to preestablish.

preestablecido, da *adj* preestablished.

preexcelencia *f* preeminence.

preexistencia *f* preexistence.

preexistente *adj* preexistent, preexisting.

preexistir *vi* to preexist.

prefabricación *f* prefabrication.

prefabricar *vt* to prefabricate.

prefacio *m* preface, foreword || *hacer un prefacio a un libro* to preface a book.

prefecto *m* prefect.

prefectura *f* prefecture.

preferencia *f* preference || predilection || terraces *pl* in front of the stands (localidad en un campo de fútbol) || — *con preferencia a* with preference to || *de preferencia* preferably || *preferencia de paso* right of way, priority (en una carretera).

preferente *adj* prefering (que prefiere) || preferential; *trato preferente* preferential treatment || preference, preferential (acción de una sociedad) || preferable (que se prefiere) || excellent; *ocupar un lugar preferente* to occupy an excellent place || superior, better (superior).

preferible *adj* preferable.

preferiblemente *adv* preferably.

preferido, da *adj* preferred, favourite.
◆ *m/f* favourite.

preferir* *vt* to prefer; *prefiero con mucho* or *mucho más* I much prefer || to like; *el que menos prefiero* the one I like the least || *prefiere quedarse dos días* he prefers to stay two days, he would rather stay two days.

prefiguración *f* prefiguration.

prefigurar *vt* to prefigure, to foreshadow.

prefijar *vt* GRAM to prefix || to arrange before-hand, to prearrange, to fix in advance (fijar de antemano).

prefijo, ja *adj* prefixed.
◆ *m* GRAM prefix || area code (teléfonos).

prefloración *f* BOT vernation, aestivation [US estivation].

preformación *f* preformation.

preformar *vt* to preform.

preglaciar *adj* GEOL preglacial.

pregón *m* public announcement (noticia) || street vendor's cry *o* shout *o* call (de vendedor) || bann (para un matrimonio).

pregonar *vt* to proclaim, to shout *o* to cry out (publicar en voz alta) || to hawk [one's wares] (un vendedor) || FIG to reveal, to tell, to make public (revelar); *pregonar una noticia* to reveal a piece of news | to praise (alabar) || (p us) to proscribe, to outlaw (proscribir) || FIG *pregonar a bombo y platillos* or *a voz en grito* to shout from the rooftops.

pregonero, ra *adj* proclaiming, divulging.
◆ *m/f* proclaimer (que proclama) || divulger (que revela) || street vendor (que vende).
◆ *m* town crier (empleado municipal).

preguerra *f* prewar period.

pregunta *f* question (interrogación); *pregunta indiscreta, capciosa* indiscreet, catch question; *hacer preguntas* to ask questions; *no contestó a mi pregunta* he didn't answer my question || — *a pregunta necia, oídos sordos* or *oídos de mercader* ask a silly question, (and you will) get a silly answer || FIG & FAM *estar* or *andar a la cuarta pregunta* to be flat broke | *estrechar a preguntas* to ply with questions || *hacer una pregunta a alguien* to ask s.o. a question, to put a question to s.o. || FIG & FAM *quedarse a la cuarta pregunta* to be cleaned out, to be left penniless.

preguntador, ra *adj* inquisitive.
◆ *m/f* questioner (el que hace una pregunta) || inquisitive person (curioso).

preguntar *vt* to ask; *pregúntaselo a él* ask him || to question; *preguntar a un candidato* to question a candidate || *preguntar por* to ask about *o* after, to ask for news of; *preguntar por alguien* to ask after s.o.; to ask for (querer ver o hablar); *preguntan por usted en el teléfono* s.o. is asking for you on the telephone.
◆ *vpr* to wonder; *me pregunto qué hora es* I wonder what time it is || to ask o.s.

— OBSERV Do not confuse *preguntar* with *pedir,* which means *to ask for* in the sense of *to request.*

preguntón, ona *adj* FAM inquisitive, nosey; *un niño preguntón* an inquisitive child.
◆ *m/f* FAM nosey parker, inquisitive person.

prehistoria *f* prehistory.

prehistoriador, ra *m/f* prehistorian.

prehistórico, ca *adj* prehistoric.

preincaico, ca *adj* HIST pre-Incan.

prejudicial *adj* JUR interlocutory (cuestión, etc.) || pre-judicial (acción).

prejuicio *m* prejudice; *prejuicio racial* racial prejudice || bias (falta de objetividad) || prejudgment (acción de prejuzgar) || — *crearle a uno un prejuicio* to prejudice s.o. || *tener prejuicios* to be prejudiced; *tiene prejuicios raciales* he is racially prejudiced; to be biassed; *no lo encuentras inteligente porque tienes prejuicios* you do not think he is intelligent because your are biassed.

prejuzgar *vt* to prejudge.

prelacía *f* prelature, prelacy.

prelación *f* preference, priority, precedence; *orden de prelación* order of preference || *tener prelación sobre* to take preference over, to come before; *haría falta que la generosidad tuviese prelación sobre el egoísmo* generosity should come before egoism.

prelado *m* prelate.

prelatura *f* prelature, prelacy.

preliminar *adj/sm* preliminary.

preludiar *vi/tr* MÚS to prelude || FIG to prelude, to lead up to.

preludio *m* prelude.

premarital *adj* premarital.

prematuramente *adv* prematurely.

prematuro, ra *adj* premature.
◆ *m/f* premature baby.

premeditación *f* premeditation || JUR *con premeditación* with malice aforethought, with premeditation.

premeditadamente *adv* with premeditation, deliberately.

premeditado, da *adj* premeditated, deliberate.

premeditar *vt* to premeditate.

premiado, da *adj* winning, prize-winning; *número premiado* winning number || rewarded; *premiado por su heroísmo* rewarded for his heroism || prize; *novela premiada* prize novel.
◆ *m/f* winner, prizewinner.

premiar *vt* to reward; *premiar a uno por su heroísmo* to reward s.o. for his heroism || to give *o* to award a prize to (en un certamen) || *salir premiado* to win a prize.

premilitar *adj* premilitary.

premio *m* reward, recompense (recompensa) || prize, award; *llevarse el premio* to win the prize; *premio de consolación* consolation prize || COM premium || — *como premio a* as a reward for || *premio en metálico* cash prize, prize money || *premio gordo* first prize, grand prize || *reparto* or *distribución de premios* prizegiving.

premiosidad *f* tightness (estrechez) || awkwardness (molestia, dificultad) || awkwardness, clumsiness (torpeza).

premioso, sa *adj* tight (ajustado) || urgent (urgente) || heavy; *una carga premiosa* a heavy burden || awkward (movimientos, habla, etc.) || strict (estricto) || awkward, clumsy (estilo, lenguaje, etc.).

premisa *f* premise (en lógica).

premolar *m* premolar (diente).

premonición *f* premonition.

premonitorio, ria *adj* MED premonitory || indicative, warning.

premura *f* urgency (urgencia) || haste (prisa) || lack [of time, of space] (falta de tiempo, espacio).

prenatal *adj* prenatal, antenatal.

prenda *f* pledge, security, guarantee (garantía) || token pledge (prueba de amistad) || deposit (señal) || article of clothing, garment (ropa) || linen (de mesa y de cama) || darling (apelativo cariñoso) || COM security || — *dar* or *dejar en prenda* to pledge || *en prenda de* as a token of, as a pledge of || FIG & FAM *no soltar prenda* not to commit o.s., to be noncommittal || *prenda interior* undergarment || FIG & FAM *soltar prenda* to commit o.s.
◆ *pl* forfeits (juego) || qualities, gifts, talents (buenas cualidades) || *no dolerle prendas a uno* not to mind admitting one's faults (admitir sus errores), to spare no expense *o* effort (no escatimar gastos o esfuerzos).

prendarse *vpr* to fall in love (*de* with), to fall in love (una persona) || to take a fancy (*de* to) (un objeto) || to be captivated (*de* by), to be enchanted (*de* with) (estar cautivado por).

prendedor *m* pin, clasp, brooch (broche) || clip (de una estilográfica).

prender *vt* to seize, to grasp (asir) || to arrest, to apprehend (detener a uno) || to put in prison, to imprison (encarcelar) || to catch, to capture, to take prisoner (capturar) || to fasten (sujetar algo) || to set (fuego); *han prendido fuego a la casa* they have set fire to the house || AMER to light (encender) | to switch on (la luz) || *prender con alfileres* to pin.
◆ *vi* to take root (arraigar) || to take (un injerto, una vacuna) || to take, to catch (fuego); *el fuego no prende* the fire is not taking *o* will not take || FIG to catch.
◆ *vpr* to dress up (engalanarse una mujer) || to catch fire (encenderse) || to mate (los animales) || AMER to get drunk (embriagarse).
— OBSERV The verb *prender* has two past participles: *prendido* and *preso*. *Prendido* usually means *fastened*, and *preso* means *arrested, imprisoned*.

prendería *f* secondhand shop.

prendero, ra *m/f* secondhand dealer (comerciante).
◆ *m* skirt hanger (percha).

prendido, da *adj* enchanted, captivated (encantado).

prendimiento *m* capture, arrest, seizure.

prenombrado, da *adj* AMER aforementioned, aforesaid.

prenombre *m* Christian name, first name.
— OBSERV *Christian name* is usually translated by *nombre* or *nombre de pila*.

prensa *f* press, printing press (máquina para imprimir) || TECN press; *prensa hidráulica* hydraulic press || press (publicaciones, periódicos); *libertad de prensa* freedom of the press || — *dar a la prensa* to publish, to print || *entrar en prensa* to go to press || *prensa amarilla* tabloids || *prensa del corazón* romance magazines || FIG *tener buena, mala prensa* to have a good, a bad press.

prensado *m* calendering, lustre (de los tejidos) || pressing (acción de prensar).

prensador, ra *adj* pressing.
◆ *m/f* press operator, presser.

prensaestopas *m inv* TECN stuffing box.

prensar *vt* to press.

prensatelas *adj inv* *pie prensatelas* foot.

prensil *adj* prehensile; *cola prensil* prehensile tail.

prensilla *f* presser foot (de máquina de coser).

prensor *adj m* ZOOL zygodactyl (aves).

prenupcial *adj* antenuptial, prenuptial.

preñado, da *adj* pregnant || bulging, sagging (pared) || full, charged (lleno); *palabras preñadas de amenazas* words full of *o* charged with menace.

preñar *vt* to get pregnant (mujer) || to impregnate (animal).

preñez *f* pregnancy.

preocupación *f* preoccupation, worry, care, concern || *tiene la preocupación de que le va a pasar algo* he is worried that sth. is going to happen to him.

preocupado, da *adj* worried, concerned, preoccupied.

preocupar *vt* to worry, to preoccupy (inquietar) || to bother (molestar) || to bias, to prejudice (predisponer) || to previously occupy (ocupar antes) || *es lo que menos me preocupa* that is the least of my worries.
◆ *vpr* to worry, to get worried; *preocuparse por su salud* to worry about one's health || to be worried *o* concerned (estar preocupado) || — *no se preocupa por nada* he doesn't worry about anything, nothing worries him || *¡no se preocupe!* don't worry! || *se preocupó de que todo estuviera acabado a tiempo* he saw to it that everything was finished in time.

preolímpico, ca *adj* DEP pre-Olympic.

prepalatal *adj* prepalatal (en fonética).

preparación *f* preparation || training (entrenamiento) || preparation (en farmacia) || cooking, preparation (en cocina) || MED *preparación anatómica* anatomic specimen.

preparado, da *adj* prepared, ready || CULIN ready cooked.
◆ *m* preparation (en farmacia).

preparamiento *m* preparation || training (entrenamiento).

preparar *vt* to prepare; *está bien preparado para la vida* he is well prepared for life; *le estamos preparando una sorpresa* we are preparing a surprise for him || to prepare, to get ready; *estoy preparando la cena* I am getting dinner ready || to prepare for; *preparar un examen* to prepare for an examination || DEP to train, to coach.
◆ *vpr* to get ready, to prepare (o.s.); *nos estamos preparando para las vacaciones* we are getting ready for the holidays, we are preparing (ourselves) for the holidays.

preparativo, va *adj* preparatory, preliminary.
◆ *m* preparation (preparación).

preparatorio, ria *adj* preparatory, preliminary.
◆ *m* preparatory studies *pl*.

preponderancia *f* preponderance.

preponderante *adj* preponderant || *voto preponderante* casting vote.

preponderar *vi* to preponderate, to predominate || to prevail (una opinión).

preponer* *vt* to put before (anteponer).

preposición *f* GRAM preposition || *preposición inseparable* prefix.

prepositivo, va *adj* GRAM prepositive.

prepotencia *f* prepotency.

prepotente *adj* prepotent, very powerful.

prepucio *m* ANAT prepuce, foreskin.

prerrafaelismo *m* pre-Raphaelitism.

prerrafaelista; prerrafaelita *adj/s* pre-Raphaelite.

prerrogativa *f* prerogative (privilegio).

prerromanticismo *m* preromanticism.

presa *f* capture, seizure (acción de prender) || catch, prize (cosa apresada); *una buena presa* a good catch || quarry (animal o persona que se caza) || prey, catch (animal cazado); *el zorro*

se llevó su presa the fox carried off its prey || FIG victim (víctima); *presa de los calumniadores* victim of slanderers || prey; *ser presa de pesadillas* to be a prey to nightmares || hold, grip (lucha, alpinismo) || dam (embalse) || millrace [US flume] (de molino) || MAR prize (barco capturado) || AMER slice (tajada), piece (pedazo) || — *ave de presa* bird of prey || *hacer presa en una cosa* to seize sth. || *presa de contención* reservoir.
◆ *pl* fangs (colmillos) || talons, claws (de ave de rapiña).

presagiar *vt* to presage, to portend, to forebode, to betoken.

presagio *m* omen, portent (señal de suerte o de desgracia); *buen, mal presagio* good, bad omen || premonition, foreboding (premonición).

presagioso, sa *adj* foreboding.

presbicia *f* MED longsightedness, farsightedness, presbyopia.

présbita; présbite *adj* longsighted, farsighted, presbyopic.

presbiterado; presbiterato *m* priesthood.

presbiteral *adj* presbyteral, presbyterial, priestly.

presbiterianismo *m* presbyterianism.

presbiteriano, na *adj/s* presbyterian.

presbiterio *m* presbytery.

presbítero *m* presbyter, priest (clérigo).

presciencia *f* prescience, foreknowledge.

presciente *adj* prescient.

prescindible *adj* dispensable.

prescindir *vi* to ignore, to disregard (hacer caso omiso) || to do without; *ya no puedo prescindir de su ayuda* I can no longer do without his help || to omit, to leave out (omitir) || to forget (olvidar) || to get rid (*de* of), to get rid (desembarazarse) || to manage *o* to do without (arreglárselas sin algo).

prescribir *vt* to prescribe, to lay down (ordenar) || MED to prescribe (recetar) || JUR to prescribe.
◆ *vi* JUR to prescribe || FIG to expire, to lapse.

prescripción *f* prescription || MED *prescripción facultativa* medical prescription.

prescriptible *adj* prescriptible.

prescripto, ta; prescrito, ta *adj* prescribed (señalado) || JUR annulled, null and void (juicio).

preselección *f* RAD preselection || DEP seeding.

preseleccionar *vt* DEP to seed.

preselector *m* RAD preselector.

presencia *f* presence || bearing, presence (porte); *mujer de buena presencia* woman of good bearing || — *en presencia del rey* in the presence of the king, in the king's presence || *hacer acto de presencia* to be present, to put in an appearance || *presencia de ánimo* presence of mind.

presencial *adj* *testigo presencial* eyewitness.

presenciar *vt* to witness, to see, to watch; *presenciar un accidente* to witness an accident || to attend, to be present at; *el presidente presenció una corrida* the president attended a bullfight.

presentable *adj* presentable.

presentación *f* presentation || appearance (aspecto); *su presentación es siempre impecable* his appearance is always impeccable || presentation, appearance (aspecto de una mercancía) || display (exposición) || parade, show (de moda) || introduction (de dos personas por una tercera); *carta de presentación* letter of introduction || — INFORM *presentación en pantalla* (on-screen) display || *presentación en sociedad* coming out || *todavía no ha hecho las presentaciones* you still have not introduced us.

presentador, ra *m/f* compère [US master of ceremonies] (en el teatro, en la televisión, etc.).

presentante *adj* presenting.

presentar *vt* to present || to present, to give, to offer (ofrecer) || to put forward, to submit (un proyecto, una propuesta, etc.) || to present (un informe) || to file (una queja, una denuncia) || to introduce (una persona a otra) || to propose, to nominate, to present; *presentar a uno para un puesto* to propose s.o. for a post || to have (tener) || to show, to display (mostrar) || to tender; *presentar la dimisión* to tender one's resignation || to put on (una obra de teatro) || to show (una película) || JUR to produce (testigos) | to submit (pruebas) || — *le presento a mi madre* may I introduce you to my mother, I would like you to meet my mother || *le presento el testimonio de mi consideración* I remain yours faithfully (al final de una carta) || *presentar armas* to present arms || *presentar la cuestión de confianza* to ask for a vote of confidence || *presentar los respetos* to pay one's respects || JUR *presentar una demanda contra uno* to bring an action against s.o., to sue s.o. || *ser presentado en sociedad* to come out.
◆ *vpr* to present o.s. || to arise, to come up (una dificultad, una cuestión) || to turn up, to come up, to arise (una oportunidad) || to report (ante una autoridad, para empezar a trabajar); *tengo que presentarme ante el jefe a las tres* I have to report to the boss at three o'clock || to appear, to look (un negocio) || to go (ir) || to come (venir) || to appear, to turn up (aparecer); *se presentó en mi casa a las doce de la noche* he appeared at my house at midnight || to turn up (acudir a una cita) || to introduce o.s. (darse a conocer); *permita que me presente* allow me to introduce myself || to stand, to run (como candidato); *presentarse a presidente* to stand for president || to sit, to take (a un examen) || to apply (*a* for), to apply (para conseguir un empleo) || *presentarse en sociedad* to come out.

presente *adj* present || — *estar presente en* to be present at || *hacer presente* to notify, to inform, to tell, to let know (avisar), to impart, to disclose, to announce (dar a conocer), to state (declarar) || *las personas presentes* those present || *tener presente* to bear in mind, to remember, not to forget; *hay que tener presente esta posibilidad* we must bear this possibility in mind.
◆ *m* present (regalo) || GRAM present || — *en el presente* at present, at the present time || *hasta el presente* up to the present || *la presente (carta)* this letter || *lo presente* the present || *los presentes* those present || *mejorando lo presente* present company excepted || GRAM *participio de presente* present participle.

presentimiento *m* presentiment, foreboding, premonition.

presentir* *vt* to have a presentiment of, to have a foreboding of.

preservación *f* preservation || protection.

preservador, ra *adj* preservative, preserving || protective.

preservar *vt* to preserve (*contra* from) || to protect (proteger).

preservativo, va *adj* preservative.
◆ *m* contraceptive sheath, condom.

presidario *m* convict (presidiario).

presidencia *f* presidency (de una nación) || chairmanship (de una reunión) || — *asumir la presidencia* to take over as president || *ocupar la presidencia* to take *o* to occupy the chair (en una reunión).

presidencial *adj* presidential.

presidenta *f* president || chairwoman (de una asamblea) || president's wife (esposa del presidente).

presidente *m* president (de la nación) || chairman, president (de una asamblea) || Speaker (del Parlamento) || premier (del Consejo de Ministros) || JUR presiding magistrate (de un tribunal) || *presidente de la mesa electoral* polling station principal clerk.

presidiario *m* convict (prisionero).

presidio *m* prison (prisión) || convicts *pl* (prisioneros) || hard labour; *diez años de presidio* ten years' hard labour || fortress, stronghold (fortaleza) || garrison (guarnición) || praesidium (en la U. R. S. S.).

presidir *vt* to preside over *o* at || to chair, to be chairman of (debate, reunión) || FIG to reign over; *la tristeza presidió la reunión* sadness reigned over the party | to dominate, to prevail in (dominar) || *presidir el duelo* to be chief mourner.
◆ *vi* to preside || to take *o* to occupy the chair (en una reunión).

presidium *m* praesidium, presidium (presidencia del Consejo Supremo de los Soviets).

presilla *f* loop (en el borde de una prenda) || fastener (para cerrar) || loop (vuelta hecha en una cuerda, un hilo o un alambre) || loop (del cinturón) || buttonhole stitch (punto de ojal).

presión *f* pressure; *ejercer presión* to exert pressure || — *a presión* under pressure || *ejercer* or *hacer presión* to press || *grupo de presión* pressure group || *olla de presión* pressure cooker || MED *presión arterial* or *sanguínea* blood pressure || *presión atmosférica* atmospheric pressure || *presión fiscal* tax burden.

presionar *vt* to press, to push (apretar) || FIG to put pressure on, to press.
◆ *vi* to press.

preso, sa *adj* imprisoned, under arrest (detenido) || stricken (bajo los efectos de) || *preso de pánico* panic-stricken.
◆ *m/f* prisoner.

prestación *f* contribution (aportación) || help (ayuda) || services *pl* (servicios) || benefit; *prestación por maternidad* maternity benefit; *prestaciones sociales* social benefits || JUR prestation || — JUR *prestación de juramento* swearing in || *prestación personal* compulsory communal work.

prestado, da *adj* lent (a alguien) || borrowed (de alguien); *una chaqueta prestada* a borrowed jacket || lent, loaned (dinero) || — *dar prestado* to lend, to loan || *el único ejemplar que tenemos está prestado* the only copy we have is on loan || *pedir* or *tomar prestado* to borrow || *vivir de prestado* to live on what one can borrow.

prestador, ra *adj* lending.
◆ *m/f* lender.

prestamente *adv* quickly, rapidly.

prestamista *m/f* moneylender.

préstamo *m* lending (acción de prestar) || borrowing (acción de pedir prestado) || loan (cantidad o cosa que se presta) || — COM *ley de préstamo y arriendo* lend-lease act || *pedirle a uno un préstamo* to ask s.o. for a loan, to borrow sth. from s.o. || JUR & MAR *préstamo a la gruesa* bottomry loan.

prestancia *f* excellence || distinction, elegance.

prestar *vt* to lend; *prestar dinero* to lend money || to lend, to give (ayuda, etc.) || to do, to render (un favor) || to pay, to lend; *prestar atención* to pay attention, to lend one's attention || — *prestar auxilio* or *socorro* or *ayuda* to give help *o* aid *o* assistance || *prestar juramento* to take the oath || *prestar oídos* to lend one's ear || *prestar servicio* to be of service *o* assistance ||

prestar testimonio to bear witness || *prestar una declaración jurada* to make a statement *o* a declaration under oath || *tomar prestado* to borrow.
◆ *vi* to lend; *prestar con interés* to lend at interest || to stretch (estirarse) || to serve (servir).
◆ *vpr* to consent (consentir) || to lend o.s. (persona), to lend itself (cosa) || to be suitable *o* favourable (*a* for) (ser adecuado para) || *prestarse a discusión* to be debatable.

preste *m* (ant) priest || *Preste Juan* Prester John (personaje fabuloso de la Edad Media).

presteza *f* promptness || *con presteza* promptly, quickly.

prestidigitación *f* conjuring, prestidigitation, sleight of hand, magic.

prestidigitador *m* conjurer, conjuror, prestidigitator, magician.

prestigiado, da *adj* prestigious, famous.

prestigiar *vt* to give prestige to (dar prestigio a).

prestigio *m* prestige || sleight of hand (magia) || trick (engaño).

prestigioso, sa *adj* prestigious, famous.

presto, ta *adj* prompt, quick (pronto); *presto en las respuestas* prompt to answer || ready, prepared (dispuesto) || MÚS presto.
◆ *adv* promptly, quickly || MÚS presto.

presumible *adj* presumable, probable, likely || *era presumible* it was to be presumed.

presumido, da *adj* presumptuous || pretentious, conceited.

presumir *vt* to presume, to assume, to suppose (conjeturar) || AMER to court (cortejar).
◆ *vi* to be vain *o* conceited (ser vanidoso) || to swank, to show off (jactarse) || to be presumptuous (ser presumido) || to think o.s., to think one is (creerse); *presume de poeta* he thinks he is a poet; *presume de listo, de valiente* he thinks himself clever, brave || — *es de presumir que* it is to be supposed that, presumably, supposedly || *presumir demasiado de su fuerza* to overestimate one's strength || *según cabe presumir* presumably, as may be presumed.

presunción *f* conceit, vanity, presumptuousness (vanidad) || presumption, supposition (suposición) || JUR presumption; *presunción legal* legal presumption.

presuntamente *adv* presumably, supposedly, presumedly.

presunto, ta *adj* presumed, supposed; *es el presunto autor del crimen* he is the presumed author of the crime || presumptive; *heredero presunto* presumptive heir || would-be, so-called, supposed; *el presunto poeta* the would-be poet.

presuntuosidad *f* vanity, presumptuousness, conceit.

presuntuoso, sa *adj* presumptuous, conceited, vain.

presuponer* *vt* to presuppose || —> **presupuestar.**

presuposición *f* presupposition.

presupuestar; presuponer* *vt* to work out (calcular) || to work out the cost of, to cost (calcular el precio de) || to draw up the budget for, to budget (elaborar el presupuesto de).

presupuestario, ria *adj* budgetary, budget.

presupuestívoro, ra *m/f* FAM person living off the State.

presupuesto, ta *adj* presupposed || estimated (calculado) || *presupuesto que* assuming *o* supposing that.
◆ *m* budget (de ingresos y gastos); *equilibrar el presupuesto* to balance the budget || estimate (estimación); *hacer un presupuesto* to make an estimate || motive, reason (motivo) || assumption, supposition.

presurización *f* pressurization.

presurizar *vt* to pressurize.

presuroso, sa *adj* in a hurry, anxious (que tiene prisa); *presuroso de marcharse* in a hurry to leave || prompt, speedy (rápido) || quick, light (pasos).

pretal *m* breast strap (de caballo).

pretencioso, sa; pretensioso, sa *adj* pretentious, presumptuous, conceited (persona) || pretentious (estilo, cosas).

pretender *vt* to seek, to try for, to be after (intentar conseguir) || to apply for (solicitar) || to aspire to (honores) || to want (querer); *pretende llegar a la cima* he wants to reach the top || to intend to (tener la intención de) || to try to, to seek to (intentar) || to aim at (una meta, un objetivo) || to claim (afirmar); *pretender poder hacer algo* to claim to be able to do sth.; *pretende haber conocido al presidente* he claims to have known the president || to claim, to pretend to (el trono) || to court (cortejar) || to pretend (fingir) || *¿qué pretende decir con eso?* what does he mean by that?

pretendido, da *adj* so-called (llamado) || would-be, so-called, supposed (presunto) || pretended, supposed (simulado); *pretendida amabilidad* pretended kindness.

pretendiente *adj* pretending, aspiring.
◆ *m* pretender (al trono) || suitor (a una mujer) || applicant, candidate (*a* for), applicant, candidate (un puesto) || claimant (de una herencia).

pretensado, da *adj* prestressed.

pretensar *vt* TECN to prestress.

pretensión *f* pretension, claim (reivindicación); *tener pretensiones de* to lay claim to || aim, object (finalidad, propósito) || aspiration || pretentiousness (vanidad) || pretence (para engañar) || — *sin pretensiones* unpretentious || *tiene la pretensión de casarse conmigo* he expects *o* he thinks he is going to marry me.

pretensioso, sa *adj* —> **pretencioso.**

preterición *f* preterition, omission || JUR preterition.

preterir* *vt* to leave out, to miss out, to pass over || JUR not to mention, to pretermit [an heir in a will].

pretérito, ta *adj* past || FIG past, former.
◆ *m* past || GRAM past || — GRAM *pretérito anterior* past anterior | *pretérito imperfecto* imperfect || *pretérito indefinido* past historic, preterite, preterit | *pretérito perfecto* perfect, present perfect || *pretérito pluscuamperfecto* pluperfect.
— OBSERV The Spanish *pretérito* is not to be confused with the English *preterite,* which is translated by *pretérito indefinido.*

pretexta *f* praetexta, pretexta (toga).

pretextar *vt* to pretext, to allege, to put forward as a pretext, to plead, to claim.

pretexto *m* pretext || — *con el* or *so pretexto de* under the pretext of || *con el pretexto de que* under the pretext that, with the excuse that, pretending that, on the pretence that.

pretil *m* parapet (de puente, de balcón).

pretina *f* belt, waistband (correa).

pretor *m* praetor, pretor (magistrado romano).

pretoría *f* praetorship.

pretorial *adj* praetorial, pretorial.

pretorianismo *m* praetorianism.

pretoriano, na *adj/s* praetorian.

pretorio, ria *adj* praetorian.
◆ *m* praetorium.

pretura *f* praetorship.

preu *m* FAM —> **preuniversitario.**

preuniversitario *m* formerly an advanced level course of study lasting one year, and the ensuing examination. Those who pass the examination may go on to study at university.

prevalecer* *vi* to prevail (*sobre* against, over) (dominar, sobresalir) || to take root (arraigar plantas) || FIG to thrive (prosperar).
◆ *vpr* to take advantage of, to use (aprovechar).

prevaleciente *adj* prevailing, prevalent.

prevaler* *vi* to prevail.
◆ *vpr* to take advantage (*de* of), to use (aprovecharse de).

prevaricación *f* abuse of trust, breach of trust, prevarication.

prevaricador, ra *adj* dishonest.
◆ *m/f* prevaricator.

prevaricar *vi* to betray one's trust.

prevención *f* prevention (para impedir); *prevención del crimen* crime prevention || precaution (precaución) || preparation, provision (preparativo); *las prevenciones para el viaje* preparations for the journey || warning (aviso) || prejudice (prejuicio) || police station (de policía); *llevar a alguien a la prevención* to take s.o. to the police station || MIL guard (soldado) | guardhouse (cuerpo de guardia) || JUR preventive detention (detención preventiva) || *tener prevención contra uno* to be prejudiced against s.o.

prevenido, da *adj* prepared, ready (dispuesto) || precautious, cautious, prudent (precavido) || warned, forewarned (advertido) || *hombre prevenido vale por dos* forewarned is forearmed.

prevenir* *vt* to prepare, to make ready (preparar) || to prevent, to forestall (impedir) || to foresee, to anticipate, to provide for (prever) || to avoid (evitar) || to warn, to forewarn (avisar, advertir) || to prejudice, to bias, to predispose (predisponer) || *más vale prevenir que curar* prevention is better than cure.
◆ *vpr* to make ready, to get ready, to prepare o.s. (prepararse) || to take precautions (against sth.) (tomar precauciones) || to provide for; *prevenirse contra toda eventualidad* to provide for every eventuality.

preventivo, va *adj* preventive; *medicina preventiva* preventive medicine || JUR *detención preventiva* protective custody, remand in custody.

preventorio *m* MED preventorium (sanatorio).

prever* *vt* to foresee, to forecast || to anticipate, to provide for (prevenirse) || to expect (esperar).

previamente *adv* previously, beforehand.

previo, a *adj* previous; *cuestión previa* previous question || preliminary (preparatorio) || — *previa consulta a los interesados* the interested parties having been consulted || *previa enmienda al texto* an amendment having been made to the text, the text having been amended || *previo acuerdo de los demás* subject to the agreement of the others || *previo aviso* notice, prior notice; *previo aviso de un mes* a month's notice || *previo pago* after payment.

previsible *adj* foreseeable, predictable.

previsión *f* forecast (lo que se prevé) || estimate (evaluación) || foresight (clarividencia) || prudence, precaution (prudencia) || — *caja de previsión* social security || *en previsión de* as a precaution against || *previsión del tiempo* weather forecast || *previsión social* social security.

previsivo, va *adj* farsighted, thoughtful, provident.

previsor, ra *adj* provident, thoughtful, farsighted ‖ *poco previsor* improvident, imprudent.

previsto, ta *adj* foreseen, predicted; *tenía previsto su fracaso* I had foreseen his failure ‖ provided; *previsto por los estatutos* provided by the statutes ‖ — *como previsto* as anticipated *o* planned ‖ *estaba previsto su fracaso* his failure was predictable *o* foreseeable, it was evident that he would fail ‖ *no es un caso previsto por la ley* there is no provision in the law for a case such as this.

prez *m* honour [US honor], glory.

PRI *abrev de Partido Revolucionario Institucional* Mexican political party.

prieto, ta *adj* firm (carne) ‖ tight (apretado) ‖ very dark, black (color) ‖ stingy (tacaño).

prima *f* prime (hora canónica) ‖ MÚS first string (cuerda) ‖ cousin; *prima carnal* first cousin ‖ COM premium; *prima de seguro* insurance premium | bonus, bounty (gratificación); *prima de rendimiento* output bonus | subsidy (subvención) ‖ MIL first quarter of the night ‖ MAR *prima de flete* primage.

primacía *f* primacy (superioridad, dignidad de primado).

primada *f* FAM *es una primada pagar tanto* it is stupid to pay so much.

primado *m* REL primate.

primar *vi* to have *o* to take priority.

primario, ria *adj* primary; *escuela, enseñanza primaria* primary school, education; *instintos primarios* primary instincts ‖ — POÉT *acento primario* primary accent ‖ GEOL *era primaria* primary era.

◆ *m* ELECTR primary.

◆ *f* primary school.

primate *m* ZOOL primate ‖ FIG important figure *o* person (prócer).

primavera *f* spring (estación) ‖ spring, springtime (época) ‖ BOT primrose ‖ silk cloth printed with a flower pattern (tela) ‖ FIG prime, springtime; *en la primavera de su vida* in the prime of (his) life.

◆ *m/f* FIG & FAM drip (despistado).

primaveral *adj* spring; *un vestido primaveral* a spring dress ‖ springlike.

primazgo *m* cousinhood, cousinship (parentesco) ‖ primacy (primacía).

primer *adj* first; *primer piso* first floor ‖ *primer ministro* Prime Minister, Premier.

— OBSERV *Primer* is the apocopation of *primero* used before a masculine singular noun.

primera *f* AUT first, first gear, low gear (velocidad) ‖ first class; *viajar en primera* to travel first class ‖ — *a la primera* first time; *conseguirlo a la primera* to succeed first time ‖ FIG *a las primeras de cambio* at the first opportunity | *de primera* first-class, first-rate (muy bueno), first-rate (muy bien), really well (muy bien hecho) | *venirle a uno de primera* to come in very handy (ser muy útil), to suit s.o. to a tee, to suit s.o. down to the ground (convenir), to come just at the right moment (ser oportuno).

primerizo, za *adj* novice (principiante) ‖ MED primiparous.

◆ *m/f* novice, beginner (novicio).

◆ *f* primipara.

primero, ra *adj* first; *el primer hombre* the first man; *la primera empleada* the first employee ‖ front, first (página) ‖ primary; *primera enseñanza* primary education ‖ former (anterior) ‖ best (mejor) ‖ leading, principal (más importante) ‖ — *artículos de primera necesidad* basic necessities ‖ *página primera* page one ‖ *primera actriz* leading lady, star ‖ *primera línea* front line ‖ *primeras materias* raw materials ‖ *vino por la mañana a primera hora* he came early in the *o* first thing in the morning.

◆ *m/f* first; *es la primera de su clase* she is first in her class ‖ number one (el número uno) ‖ best (mejor) ‖ — *a primeros de mes* at the beginning of the month ‖ *lo primero es lo primero* first things first ‖ *primero de año* New Year's day ‖ *primero de cordada* leader, first on the rope (alpinismo) ‖ *primero entre sus pares* the best man in his field ‖ *ser el primero en* to be the first to (con verbo).

◆ *f* → **primera.**

◆ *adv* first; *haz esto primero* do this first ‖ firstly (en una enumeración) ‖ before; *llegaré primero que tú* I shall arrive before you ‖ better, sooner (mejor); *primero morir que vivir en la esclavitud* it is better to die than to live in slavery, I would sooner die than live in slavery.

primicias *f pl* first fruits; *las primicias del campo* the first fruits of the countryside ‖ FIG first fruits ‖ *tener las primicias de una noticia* to be the first to hear a piece of news.

primigenio, nia *adj* primitive, original.

primípara *adj f* MED primiparous.

◆ *f* primipara.

primitivismo *m* primitivism.

primitivo, va *adj* primitive ‖ original; *a su estado primitivo* to its original state.

◆ *m* primitive.

primo, ma *adj* MAT prime; *número primo* prime number ‖ *materia prima* raw material.

◆ *m/f* cousin; *primo hermano* or *carnal* first cousin; *primo segundo* second cousin ‖ FIG & FAM drip, dunce, dope; *este pobre chico es un primo* this poor lad is a drip ‖ — FIG & FAM *hacer el primo* to be taken for a ride (dejarse engañar) | *tiene cara de primo* he looks a right drip.

primogénito, ta *adj* first-born, eldest.

◆ *m/f* first-born.

primogenitura *f* primogeniture, birthright ‖ *vender su primogenitura por un plato de lentejas* to sell one's birthright *o* heritage for a mess of pottage.

primor *m* delicacy (finura) ‖ fine thing, lovely thing (cosa bonita) ‖ skill (destreza) ‖ — *esta chica, este bordado es un primor* this girl, this embroidery is exquisite *o* beautiful ‖ *hacer con primor* to do most skilfully ‖ *que es un primor* marvellously, wonderfully; *canta que es un primor* she sings wonderfully.

primordial *adj* fundamental, essential, basic, primordial (fundamental) ‖ prime, primary (interés, importancia); *es de importancia primordial* it is of prime importance.

primoroso, sa *adj* exquisite, beautiful, fine (hermoso) ‖ skilful [US skillful] (diestro).

prímula *f* BOT primula.

primuláceas *f pl* BOT primulaceae.

princeps *adj* first, original; *edición princeps* first edition.

princesa *f* princess.

principado *m* principality, princedom (territorio y título) ‖ primacy (primacía).

◆ *pl* principalities (séptimo coro de los ángeles).

principal *adj* principal, main (más importante) ‖ illustrious (noble) ‖ very important; *un asunto principal* a very important matter ‖ — *carretera principal* main road ‖ GRAM *oración principal* main clause ‖ *piso principal* main floor, first floor [US second floor] (de una casa), dress circle (de teatro) ‖ *puerta principal* front *o* main door.

◆ *m* principal (capital) ‖ chief, head boss (jefe de una fábrica, etc.) ‖ main floor, first floor [US second floor] (de una casa) ‖ dress circle (de teatro, de cine) ‖ COM & JUR principal ‖ *lo principal* the main thing *o* point.

príncipe *adj* first, original; *edición príncipe* first edition.

◆ *m* prince; *príncipe consorte* prince consort; *príncipe heredero* crown prince; *príncipe real* prince royal ‖ — *el príncipe azul* prince charming ‖ *Príncipe de Asturias* crown prince of Spain ‖ *vivir como un príncipe* to live like a king, to live it up.

principesco, ca *adj* princely.

principianta *f* beginner, novice, learner.

principiante *adj* novice ‖ who is beginning.

◆ *m/f* beginner, novice, learner.

principiar *vt/vi* to start, to begin.

principio *m* start, beginning; *el principio de las negociaciones* the start of (the) negotiations ‖ origin, source (origen) ‖ principle, idea (idea) ‖ principle (teorema); *el principio de Arquímedes* Archimedes' principle ‖ principle (moral); *mis principios no me permiten hacerlo* my principles will not allow me to do it ‖ entrée (comidas) ‖ principle, rudiment, first notion; *principios de metafísica* principles of metaphysics ‖ — *al principio* at first; *al principio no sabía qué decir* at first he did not know what to say; *al principio no sabía nada, pero ahora trabaja bien* at first he knew nothing, but now he works well; at the start, at the beginning; *al principio de la obra* at the start of the play ‖ *a principios de* or *del mes* at the beginning of the month ‖ *dar principio a* to start off ‖ *del principio al fin, desde el principio hasta el fin* from beginning to end, from start to finish ‖ *desde el principio* from the first, from the outset ‖ *el principio de conservación* the instinct of self-preservation ‖ *en principio* in *o* on principle ‖ *en un principio* at first, to start with ‖ *es el principio del fin* it is the beginning of the end ‖ *por principio, por principios* on principle ‖ *principio quieren las cosas* it is a start ‖ *sin principios* unprincipled ‖ *tener por principio* to make a point of ‖ *tener principio* to start, to begin.

pringada *f* bread dipped in gravy *o* dripping.

pringar *vt* to get grease on, to stain with fat (ensuciar) ‖ to dip in the dripping (pan) ‖ FAM to wound (herir) | to drag, to involve; *pringarle a uno en un asunto* to drag s.o. into an affair | to slander, to run down (deshonrar) ‖ FIG & FAM *¡ya la has pringado!* now you've done it!, that's torn it!

◆ *vi* FAM to work, to get stuck in (trabajar) | to make a packet (sacar tajada) | to get mixed up (mezclarse) ‖ AMER to drizzle (lloviznar).

◆ *vpr* to get grease on, to stain with fat (mancharse) ‖ FIG to get mixed up (en un asunto feo).

pringoso, sa *adj* greasy.

pringue *m/f* dripping (que suelta el tocino al freírlo) ‖ grease stain (mancha).

prior, ra *m/f* REL prior (hombre), prioress (mujer).

priorato *m* priory (comunidad) ‖ priorate (cargo).

priori (a) *loc lat* a priori.

prioridad *f* priority.

prioritario, ria *adj* priority, having priority ‖ *ser prioritario* to take *o* to have priority.

prisa *f* haste, hurry (apresuramiento) ‖ urgency (urgencia) ‖ speed (velocidad) ‖ rush (afluencia de gente o de trabajo) ‖ — *a prisa* or *de prisa* quickly, swiftly, fast (rápidamente), hastily, hurriedly, in a hurry (apresuradamente) ‖ *a toda prisa* as quickly as possible, posthaste ‖ *correr prisa* to be urgent ‖ *darse prisa* to hurry, to hurry up ‖ *¡date prisa!* hurry up! ‖ *¡de prisa!* hurry up! ‖ *de prisa y corriendo* in a hurry, with utmost speed, at full speed ‖ *estar* or *andar con prisas* to be in a hurry, to be pressed for time ‖ *hay prisas* we are in a hurry, we are pressed for time, it is urgent || *meter* or *dar prisa a uno* to hurry s.o., to rush s.o. || *¿por qué tantas prisas?* why all the hurry?, what's the big hurry *o* rush? || *tener prisa* to be in a hurry || *tener prisa por* or *en* to be in a hurry to.

prisión *f* prison (cárcel) || imprisonment (encarcelamiento) || capture, arrest, seizure (acción de prender) || bond (atadura moral) || — JUR *prisión por deudas* imprisonment for debts | *prisión preventiva* remand in custody | *reducir a uno a prisión* to imprison s.o., to put s.o. in prison.
◆ *pl* irons, shackles, chains (grilletes).

prisionero, ra *m/f* prisoner; *hacer prisionero a uno* to take s.o. prisoner; *prisionero de guerra* prisoner of war.

prisma *m* MAT prism.

prismático, ca *adj* MAT prismatic.
◆ *m pl* binoculars.

prístino, na *adj* pristine, original.

privación *f* deprivation, deprival (acción) || loss (pérdida) || privation (falta) || *pasar privaciones* to suffer privation.

privadamente *adv* privately, in private; *discutir privadamente de algo* to discuss sth. in private.

privado, da *adj* private; *clase privada* private lesson || personal || confidential || — *privado de* bereft of, without || *vida privada* privacy; *no tener vida privada* to have no privacy; private life; *no tiene por qué meterse en mi vida privada* my private life is no concern of his.
◆ *m* favourite [US favorite] (del rey) || private; *en público y en privado* in public and in private.

privanza *f* favour [US favor].

privar *vt* to deprive; *privar a uno de algo* to deprive s.o. of sth. || to forbid (prohibir) || to prevent; *esto me privó de verte* this prevented me from seeing you || *el médico le privó de tabaco* the doctor told him to stop smoking.
◆ *vi* to be in favour [US favor] (tener privanza); *privar con uno* to be in s.o.'s favour || to be popular, to be in fashion (tener aceptación) || to be present, to prevail (prevalecer).
◆ *vpr* to deprive o.s., to go without; *privarse de tabaco* to deprive o.s. of cigarettes, to go without cigarettes || to abstain from (abstenerse) || *no privarse de nada* to lack nothing.

privativo, va *adj* GRAM privative || particular (propio) || *ser privativo de* to be exclusive to.

privilegiado, da *adj* privileged || — *memoria privilegiada* exceptionally good memory || *unos pocos privilegiados* a privileged few.
◆ *m/f* privileged person.

privilegiar *vt* to grant a privilege to, to privilege, to favour [US to favor].

privilegio *m* privilege.

pro *m* profit, advantage, benefit (ventaja) || — *en pro de* for, on behalf of, for the benefit of; *campaña en pro de los subnormales* campaign for the mentally handicapped || *hombre de pro* upright *o* honest man || *los pros y los contras* the pros and cons || *no estar ni en pro ni en contra* to be neither for nor against.
◆ *prep* in favour of [US in favor of], on behalf of, for.

proa *f* MAR prow, bows *pl*, bow || — *mascarón de proa* figurehead || FIG *poner la proa a algo* to aim at sth., to set one's sights on sth. | *poner la proa a alguien* to turn against s.o. || MAR *poner proa a* to set sail for, to make for, to head for.

probabilidad *f* probability, likelihood; *según toda probabilidad* in all probability || chance, hope, prospect; *tener poca probabilidad de ganar* to have little chance of winning || *probabilidades de vida* life expectancy *sing.*

probabilismo *m* probabilism.

probabilista *adj/s* probabilist.

probable *adj* probable, likely (casi cierto); *apenas probable* hardly likely; *es poco probable que venga* he is not likely to come || *provable* (demostrable).

probablemente *adv* probably, in all likelihood.

probación *f* proof (prueba) || probation (noviciado).

probado, da *adj* proven, proved (demostrado) || proven (acreditado); *es remedio probado* it is a proven remedy.

probador, ra *adj* testing, test || proving.
◆ *m* fitting room (en una tienda).

probar* *vt* to test, to put to the test (poner a prueba); *probar su fuerza* to test one's strength || to try (experimentar) || to prove (demostrar) || to try on; *probar un vestido* to try on a dress || to taste, to try; *probar el vino* to taste the wine || to try, to attempt (intentar); *probó levantarse* he tried to get up || — *no probar ni bocado* not to eat a bite || *probar de todo* to try a little of everything || *probar ventura* to try one's luck.
◆ *vi* to try (intentar) || to suit (sentar) || — *probar a* to try to, to attempt to || *probar bien* to suit; *vivir en el campo me prueba bien* living in the country suits me || *probar no cuesta nada* there is no harm in trying.
◆ *vpr* to try on; *me probé un abrigo* I tried on a coat; *ya me lo probé* I have already tried it on.

probatorio, ria *adj* probative, probatory.

probeta *f* QUÍM graduated test tube *o* flask, graduate || MIL eprouvette (para la pólvora).

probidad *f* probity, integrity (honradez).

problema *m* problem; *resolver* or *solucionar un problema* to solve a problem.

problemático, ca *adj* problematic, problematical.
◆ *f* problems *pl.*

probo, ba *adj* honest, upright.

probóscide *f* ANAT proboscis.

proboscidios *m pl* ZOOL proboscideans, proboscidians.

procacidad *f* insolence, impudence (insolencia) || indecency (indecencia).

procaína *f* QUÍM procaine.

procaz *adj* insolent, impudent (insolente) || shameless (sinvergüenza) || indecent (indecente).

procedencia *f* origin, source || port of origin (de un barco) || JUR merits *pl* (de una petición, de una demanda, etc.) || cogency (de una idea).

procedente *adj* reasonable, sensible (sensato) || fitting, proper (adecuado) || JUR admissible || — *el tren procedente de Madrid* the train from Madrid || *palabras procedentes del latín* words which come from Latin, words derived from Latin || *procedente de* coming from, proceeding from.

proceder *m* conduct, behaviour [US behavior].

proceder *vi* to come, to proceed; *esta palabra procede del latín* this word comes from Latin || to behave, to act (portarse) || to proceed, to go ahead, to get on (*a* with), to proceed, to go ahead, to get on (pasar a); *proceder a la elección* to proceed with the election || to be advisable (ser conveniente); *procede hacerlo con método* it is advisable to do it methodically || to be fitting, to be right (ser apto o justo) || to be sensible (ser sensato) || JUR to be admissible *o* relevant *o* pertinent || — JUR *proceder contra uno* to institute *o* to take proceedings against s.o. || *proceder de consuno* to work in concert || JUR *según proceda* as befitting.

procedimiento *m* method, procedure, process (método) || procedure (en asambleas) || JUR procedure (serie de trámites), proceedings *pl* (acción judicial).

proceloso, sa *adj* tempestuous, stormy.

prócer *adj* eminent, noble, illustrious || FIG majestic, noble, lofty (árboles, etc.).
◆ *m* member of the Upper Chamber (en el Parlamento) || eminent person (persona importante).

procesado, da *adj* JUR procedural, of the proceedings (del proceso) | accused (acusado).
◆ *m/f* accused, defendant.

procesador *m* INFORM processor; *procesador de red* network processor; *procesador de textos* word processor; *procesador vectorial* array processor.

procesal *adj* JUR procedural, of the proceedings || — *costas procesales* legal costs || *derecho procesal* procedural law.

procesamiento *m* JUR prosecution || INFORM processing || — *auto de procesamiento* indictment || INFORM *procesamiento de datos* data processing | *procesamiento de textos* word processing | *procesamiento por lotes* batch processing | *procesamiento secuencial* serial *o* sequential processing.

procesar *vt* JUR to prosecute (*por* for).

procesión *f* procession || — FIG *la procesión va por dentro* still waters run deep | *no se puede repicar y andar en la procesión* one cannot do two things at once.

procesional *adj* processional.

procesionaria *adj f* processionary.

procesionario *m* processional (libro).

proceso *m* process (método); *proceso químico, industrial* chemical, industrial process || JUR trial, lawsuit, action (pleito) | procedure (serie de trámites) || process; *proceso mental* thought *o* mental process || course (transcurso); *en el proceso de una vida* in the course of a lifetime || MED course, progress (de una enfermedad) || ANAT process || INFORM *proceso de datos* data processing | *proceso de textos* word processing | *proceso de textos* word processing.

proclama *f* proclamation.
◆ *pl* banns (amonestaciones); *correr las proclamas* to publish the banns.

proclamación *f* proclamation (notificación pública) || acclamation (alabanza pública).

proclamar *vt* to proclaim (anunciar) || to acclaim (aclamar).
◆ *vpr* to proclaim o.s.

proclítico, ca *adj/sm* GRAM proclitic.

proclive *adj* inclined, disposed (inclinado).

proclividad *f* proclivity (propensión).

procomún; procomunal *m* public service *o* utility.

procónsul *m* proconsul.

proconsulado *m* proconsulate (cargo) || proconsulship (tiempo).

proconsular *adj* proconsular.

procreación *f* procreation.

procreador, ra *adj* procreant, procreative.
◆ *m/f* procreator, begetter.

procrear *vt* to procreate.

proctológico, ca *adj* MED proctological, proctologic.

proctólogo, ga *m/f* MED proctologist.

proctoscopia *f* MED proctoscopy.

proctoscopio *m* MED proctoscope.

procumbente *adj* BOT procumbent.

procura *f* power of attorney, proxy, procuration (poder dado) || AMER search (busca) | obtaining (obtención).

procuración *f* power of attorney, proxy || office of a lawyer *o* procurator (oficio) || *por procuración* by procuration, by proxy.

procurador, ra *m/f* procurator, lawyer (abogado) || REL procurator (hombre), procuratrix (mujer) || procurator (magistrado romano) || — *procurador a* or *de* or *en Cortes* member of Parliament || FIG & FAM *procurador de pobres* busybody.

procuraduría *f* procurator's *o* lawyer's office.

procurar *vt* to try (intentar); *procura venir temprano* try to arrive early || to get (obtener) || to procure, to manage to get; *le procuré un piso* I procured a flat for him || to give, to bring; *este niño sólo me procura satisfacciones* this child gives me nothing but satisfaction || *procurar que* to make sure that.
◆ *vpr* to procure o.s.

prodigalidad *f* prodigality.

prodigar *vt* to lavish (dar mucho) || to squander (malgastar) || FIG to lavish; *prodigar cuidados* to lavish care || *no prodigar* to be mean with.
◆ *vpr* to do one's best to please *o* to help (intentar agradar) || to be generous (*en* with), to be generous (ser generoso) || to make an exhibition of o.s., to show off (presumir).

prodigio *m* prodigy || prodigy, miracle, wonder; *hacer prodigios* to work wonders || *niño prodigio* child prodigy.

prodigiosidad *f* prodigiousness.

prodigioso, sa *adj* prodigious, wonderful (maravilloso) || FAM fabulous, enormous.

pródigo, ga *adj* prodigal, wasteful (despilfarrador) || generous, lavish; *pródigo de* or *en alabanzas* generous with praise; *pródigo con todos* generous to *o* with everyone || *el hijo pródigo* the prodigal son.

pródromo *m* prodrome (síntoma).

producción *f* production; *producción en serie* mass production || ECON *producción limitada* limited output.

producir* *vt* to produce || to produce, to bear (frutos) || COM to produce | to bear, to yield (interés) || *producir beneficios* to yield profits, to be profitable.
◆ *vpr* to appear (aparecer); *producirse en público* to appear in public || to come out, to take place, to happen, to occur (un suceso).

productibilidad *f* productibility.

productividad *f* productivity.

productivo, va *adj* productive || lucrative, profitable (negocio).

producto, ta *adj* (p us) produced.
◆ *m* product; *productos manufacturados* manufactured products || AGR produce; *productos agrícolas* farm produce (véase OBSERV) || proceeds *pl*; *el producto de una venta* the proceeds of a sale || COM yield, profit | product; *producto nacional bruto* gross national product || MAT product || — *producto derivado* by-product || *productos alimenticios* foodstuffs || *productos de belleza* cosmetics || *productos de consumo* consumer goods || *productos químicos* chemicals.

— OBSERV La palabra inglesa *produce* se refiere a los productos agrícolas y hortícolas en general (*los productos agrícolas de Irlanda* Ireland's farm produce). Cuando se trata de un solo producto se emplea *product* (*un producto hortícola* a horticultural product).

productor, ra *adj* producing.
◆ *m/f* producer || worker (trabajador).
◆ *m* CINEM producer.

proemio *m* preface, introduction, proem.

proeza *f* exploit, heroic deed, feat (hazaña).

profanación *f* profanation, desecration.

profanador, ra *adj* profanatory || irreverent.
◆ *m/f* profaner || irreverent person.

profanar *vt* to profane, to desecrate (un lugar sagrado) || to show insufficient respect for (tener poco respeto) || to violate (una tumba) || to defile, to pollute (la inocencia) || to blacken (el recuerdo de alguien).

profano, na *adj* profane, wordly (no sagrado) || profane, irreverent (que no respeta lo sagrado) || uninitiated, lay, ignorant (ignorante) || (p us) irreverent || indecent (indecente).
◆ *m/f* uninitiated *o* ignorant person, layman || (p us) irreverent person || *los profanos* the profane, the uninitiated.

profase *f* BIOL prophase.

profecía *f* prophecy.

proferir* *vt* to utter, to speak (palabras) || to hurl (insultos).

profesar *vt* to profess (una doctrina, una religión) || to teach (enseñar); *profesar la medicina* to teach medicine || to profess, to practise (ejercer una profesión) || to profess, to declare, to put forth (una opinión) || to have, to profess, to feel; *profesar un amor profundo* to have a deep love for.
◆ *vi* to profess [vows] (religión) || to profess, to teach (enseñar).

profesión *f* profession || REL taking of vows (de votos) | profession, declaration (de fe) || — *de profesión escritor* a writer by profession || — *hacer profesión de* to profess, to make a profession of.

profesional *adj/s* professional || *un profesional del crimen* a professional criminal.

profesionalismo *m* professionalism.

profesionalizar *vt* to professionalize.

profesionista *m/f* AMER professional.

profeso, sa *adj* professed.
◆ *m* professed monk.
◆ *f* professed nun.

profesor, ra *m/f* teacher (en la escuela) || lecturer (en la universidad) || — *profesor asociado* associate professor || *profesor auxiliar* assistant (teacher) || *profesor de canto, de esgrima* singing, fencing teacher *o* master || *profesor de gimnasia* gym instructor *o* teacher || *professor titular* titular *o* full professor.

profesorado *m* teaching profession (profesión) || (teaching) staff, teachers *pl* (escuela), staff, lecturers *pl* (universidad), staff, lecturers *pl* (cuerpo docente) || post of teacher (escuela), post of lecturer (universidad) (cargo).

profesoral *adj* teaching (escuela), lecturing (universidad); *trabajos profesionales* teaching work.

profeta *m* prophet || *nadie es profeta en su tierra* a prophet is without honour in his own country.

profético, ca *adj* prophetic.

profetisa *f* prophetess.

profetizador, ra *adj* prophesying.
◆ *m/f* prophesier.

profetizar *vt/vi* to prophesy.

profiláctico, ca *adj* MED prophylactic.
◆ *f* MED prophylaxis.

profilaxis; profilaxia *f* MED prophylaxis.

prófugo, ga *adj/s* fugitive (fugitivo).
◆ *m* deserter (del servicio militar) || JUR refractory person.

profundamente *adv* deeply || FIG profoundly, deeply | soundly (dormir).

profundidad *f* depth; *trescientos pies de profundidad* three hundred feet in depth || FIG profundity (del pensamiento) | soundness (del sueño) | profoundness, deepness (de un misterio) | profundity, depth, extent (del saber) || — *poca profundidad* shallowness || FOT *profundidad de campo* depth of field.

profundizar *vt* to deepen, to make deeper || to study in depth, to go *o* to delve deeply into, to examine thoroughly || *profundizar las cosas* to get to the bottom of things.
◆ *vi* to deepen || FIG to deepen (volverse más profundo) | to go deeply into a subject, to study a subject in depth | *tenemos que profundizar más* we must go into it more deeply.

profundo, da *adj* deep; *un pozo profundo* a deep well || FIG profound; *pensamientos profundos* profound thoughts; *miseria profunda* profound poverty | utter (ignorancia) | deep, heartfelt (respeto) | deep, sound (sueño) | pitch, inky, thick (oscuridad) || — *en la desesperación más profunda* in the depths of despair || *en lo más profundo de mi ser* in the bottom of my heart, in my heart of hearts.

profusión *f* profusion || *con profusión* profusely.

profuso, sa *adj* profuse.

progenie *f* line, lineage, family (generación) || progeniture, progeny, offspring (descendientes).

progenitor *m* progenitor.
◆ *pl* ancestors (antepasados) || parents (padres).

progenitura *f* progeniture, offspring (progenie).

progesterona *f* progesterone.

progestina *f* progestin.

prognatismo *m* prognathism.

prognato, ta *adj* prognathous, prognathic.
◆ *m/f* prognathous person.

programa *f* programme [*US* program] (de espectáculos, en la televisión, etc.) || schedule, programme (de actividades) || INFORM program, software || programme, platform (de un partido político) || curriculum, programme (de estudios) || — INFORM *programa aplicativo* applications program || *programa de intercambio* exchange programme || INFORM *programa de juegos* game-playing program | *programa del sistema* systems program | *programa de utilidad* utility program || *programa de vuelo* flight programme || INFORM *programa didáctico* courseware || *programa espacial* space programme || INFORM *programa fuente* source program | *programa gráfico* graphics software | *programa integrado* integrated program.

programación *f* programming.

programador, ra *adj* programming.
◆ *m/f* programmer || INFORM programmer.
◆ *m* programmer (electrónica).

programar *vt* to programme [*US* to program] || to programme, to plan; *programar una reforma* to programme a reform.

progre *adj* FAM trendy liberal.

progresar *vi* to progress, to make progress.

progresión *f* progression (adelanto) || MÚS progression || MAT *progresión aritmética, geométrica* arithmetic, geometric progression.

progresismo *m* progressivism (doctrina política) || progressionism (creencia en el progreso).

progresista *adj/s* progressive; *periódico progresista* progressive newspaper.

progresividad *f* progressiveness.

progresivo, va *adj* progressive.

progreso *m* progress *inv* || *hacer progresos* to make progress, to progress.

prohibición *f* prohibition || prohibition (de bebidas alcohólicas en los Estados Unidos) || *levantar la prohibición de* to lift the ban on.

prohibicionismo *m* prohibitionism.

prohibicionista *adj/s* prohibitionist.

prohibido, da *adj* forbidden, prohibited; *terminantemente prohibido* strictly forbidden || — *dirección prohibida* no entry (calle) || *prohibido aparcar* no parking || *prohibido el paso* no entry, no trespassing (para personas), no entry, no thoroughfare (para los automóviles) || *prohibido fijar carteles* stick no bills || *prohibido fumar* no smoking, smoking prohibited.

prohibir *vt* to forbid, to prohibit (vedar); *te prohibo que salgas* I forbid you to go out; *prohibir a uno que haga algo* to prohibit s.o. from doing sth. || — *se prohibe fumar* no smoking || *se prohibe la entrada* no entry.

prohibitivo, va *adj* prohibitive; *ley prohibitiva* prohibitive law; *precio prohibitivo* prohibitive price.

prohibitorio, ria *adj* prohibitory.

prohijamiento *m* adoption.

prohijar *vt* to adopt (a un niño, opiniones).

prohombre *m* great figure *o* man, outstanding man (persona notable) || leader (dirigente).

proindivisión *f* JUR joint possession.

pro indiviso *loc lat* JUR pro indiviso.

proís; proíz *m* MAR mooring post (noray).

prójima *f* FAM woman (mujer) | tart (mujer libertina) | better half (esposa).

prójimo *m* one's fellow man, neighbour [US neighbor] || FAM bloke (sujeto) || — *amar al prójimo como a sí mismo* to love one's neighbour as o.s. || *ser bueno con su prójimo* to be good to others *o* to one's fellow man.

prolapso *m* MED prolapse, prolapsus.

prole *f* offspring, progeny.

prolegómenos *m pl* prolegomena (introducción).

prolepsis *f* prolepsis (anticipación).

proletariado *m* proletariat.

proletario, ria *adj/s* proletarian.

proletarización *f* proletarianization.

proletarizar *vt* to proletarianize.

proliferación *f* proliferation.

proliferar *vi* to proliferate.

prolífero, ra *adj* proliferous.

prolífico, ca *adj* prolific.

prolijidad *f* prolixity, tediousness, verbosity, long-windedness (pesadez) || meticulousness, thoroughness (meticulosidad) || extensiveness.

prolijo, ja *adj* prolix, long-winded, tedious, verbose; *estilo prolijo* prolix style || exhaustive, thorough (exhaustivo) || meticulous (meticuloso).

prologar *vt* to prologue, to preface, to write a preface *o* prologue to.

prólogo *m* prologue, preface, introduction, foreword || FIG prelude.

prologuista *m* writer *o* author of a prologue *o* preface.

prolonga *f* MIL prolonge.

prolongación *f* prolongation || extension (de una ciudad, de una calle).

prolongado, da *adj* prolonged || oblong, long (apaisado) || lengthy (de mucho tiempo).

prolongamiento *m* prolongation.

prolongar *vt* to prolong, to extend.
◆ *vpr* to be prolonged || to extend (extenderse) || to last longer; *la sesión se prolongó más de lo previsto* the meeting lasted longer than expected || *la reunión se ha prolongado* the meeting ended late *o* went on late *o* lasted longer than expected.

promediar *vt* to divide in two || to average out (sacar el promedio).
◆ *vi* to mediate || *al promediar el mes de junio* in the middle of June.

promedio *m* middle (punto de división en dos) || average; *el promedio es de mil toneladas* the average is one thousand tons || — *calcular el promedio de las exportaciones* to calculate average exports || *el promedio de las exportaciones fue de X libras* exports averaged X pounds || *el promedio de sus ingresos es de* their average income is || *en* or *como promedio* on average || *ganan un promedio de cien libras* they earn one hundred pounds on average.

promesa *f* promise; *cumplir su* or *con su promesa* to keep one's promise; *faltar a una promesa* to break a promise || vow (religioso) || FIG hope; *este joven bailarín es la promesa de la compañía* this young dancer is the hope of the company.

prometedor, ra *adj* promising, full of promise.
◆ *m/f* promiser.

prometeo *m* QUÍM promethium.

Prometeo *npr m* MIT Prometheus.

prometer *vt* to promise; *prometer hacer algo* to promise to do sth. || FIG *prometer el oro y el moro* to promise the earth, to promise the moon and stars.
◆ *vi* to promise || — *este niño promete* this child shows promise *o* promises much || *es un tenista que promete* he is a promising tennis player.
◆ *vpr* to promise o.s. || to expect (esperarse) || to get engaged (*con* to), to get engaged (desposarse) || FAM *prometérselas felices* to have high hopes.

prometido, da *adj* promised (futuro) || engaged (novios); *prometido con* engaged to || — *cumplir con lo prometido* to keep one's promise || *lo prometido es deuda* a promise is a promise.
◆ *m* fiancé (novio).
◆ *f* fiancée (novia).

prominencia *f* protuberance, projection, bulge || rise (del terreno) || FIG prominence, prominency.

prominente *adj* prominent, projecting, protruding (saliente) || FIG prominent.

promiscuidad *f* promiscuity, promiscuousness.

promiscuo, cua *adj* promiscuous.

promisión *f* promise || *Tierra de Promisión* Promised Land.

promisorio, ria *adj* JUR promissory; *juramento promisorio* promissory oath || promising (alentador).

promoción *f* promotion || — *partido de promoción* promotion match (deportes) || *promoción de ventas* sales promotion || *ser de la misma promoción universitaria* to graduate in the same year, to be in the same year.

promocionar *vt* COM to promote.

promontorio *m* promontory, headland (punta) || small hill (colina) || ANAT promontory.

promotor, ra; promovedor, ra *adj* promotive.
◆ *m/f* promoter, originator, cause (origen) || COM promoter || instigator (instigador) || *promotor inmobiliario* real estate developer.

promover* *vt* to promote (elevar); *promover a uno a capitán* to promote s.o. to captain || to promote (promocionar) || to foster, to favour (fomentar) || to provoke, to cause (provocar) || to start (empezar) || to instigate, to stir up (sublevaciones, etc.) || to cause, to give rise to (dar lugar a).

promovido, da *adj* promoted.

promulgación *f* promulgation, enactment || FIG announcement.

promulgador, ra *adj* promulgating.
◆ *m/f* promulgator.

promulgar *vt* to promulgate to enact (una ley, etc.) || FIG to promulgate, to proclaim, to make public (divulgar una cosa).

pronación *f* ANAT pronation.

pronador, ra *adj* ANAT pronating.
◆ *m* ANAT pronator.

pronaos *m* pronaos (de templo griego).

prono, na *adj* prone (to) || prone (echado sobre el vientre) || *decúbito prono* prone decubitus.

pronombre *m* GRAM pronoun; *pronombre personal* personal pronoun.

pronominado, da; pronominal *adj* GRAM pronominal.

pronosticación *f* prognostication, forecasting.

pronosticador, ra *m/f* prognosticator, forecaster.

pronosticar *vt* to forecast, to foretell, to predict, to prognosticate || MED to give the prognosis of.

pronóstico *m* prognostication, prediction, forecast (predicción) || forecast (del tiempo) || MED prognosis || — MED *de pronóstico leve* not serious | *pronóstico reservado* prognosis that has not yet been disclosed.

prontamente *adv* quickly.

prontitud *f* speed, promptness, quickness (rapidez) || quickness, sharpness (de la inteligencia).

pronto, ta *adj* quick, fast, rapid (rápido); *pronto a enfadarse* quick to anger || ready (dispuesto); *pronto para salir* ready to go out || — *ser pronto de genio* to be quick-tempered || *una pronta curación* a speedy recovery.
◆ *m* sudden movement, start; *le dio un pronto* he gave a start, he made a sudden movement || sudden impulse, urge (arrebato repentino) || sudden feeling (sentimiento inesperado).
◆ *adv* fast, quickly (de prisa) || early (temprano); *llegó muy pronto* he arrived very early || AMER suddenly (de pronto) || — *al pronto* at first || *cuanto más pronto mejor* the sooner the better || *de pronto* suddenly, all at once (de repente), hastily, hurriedly, quickly (apresuradamente) || *¡hasta pronto!* see you soon! || *lo más pronto (posible)* as soon as possible, as fast as possible || *por de* or *por lo pronto* for the moment, for the time being (por ahora), at least, anyway (al menos), meanwhile (mientras tanto) || *tan pronto... como* as soon as (en cuanto), no sooner... than; *tan pronto ríe como llora* he no sooner laughs than he cries.

prontuario *m* summary || handbook (compendio) || notebook (libro de apuntes).

pronunciable *adj* pronounceable.

pronunciación *f* pronounciation || JUR passing (de una sentencia) || *pronunciación figurada* phonetic transcription.

pronunciado, da *adj* pronounced || FIG pronounced (marcado) | sharp (curva) | marked, noticeable (acentuado).

pronunciamiento *m* rising, insurrection (alzamiento) || JUR pronouncement, pronouncing (of sentence).

pronunciar *vt* to pronounce; *pronunciar bien una palabra* to pronounce a word well || to pronounce, to speak; *pronunció dos palabras* he pronounced two words || to deliver; *pronun-*

ciar un discurso to deliver a speech || JUR to pronounce, to pass; *pronunciar un fallo* to pronounce sentence.
◆ *vpr* to be pronounced || to rise up (sublevarse) || to pronounce o.s., to declare o.s. (declararse).
— OBSERV *Pronunciarse* is a Gallicism when used as a synonym of *declararse, manifestarse.*

propagación *f* propagation, spreading.

propagador, ra *adj* propagating, propagative.
◆ *m/f* propagator, spreader; *propagador de noticias falsas* propagator of false rumours.

propaganda *f* propaganda (a favor de una idea, de una opinión, etc.) || advertising, publicity (comercial) || COM *hacer propaganda* to advertise.

propagandista *adj/s* propagandist.

propagandístico, ca *adj* [of o pertaining to] propaganda || COM advertising, publicity.

propagar *vt* to propagate || FIG to spread, to propagate; *propagar una noticia* to spread a piece of news | to divulge (algo secreto) || FÍS to propagate, to convey (la luz, el sonido).
◆ *vpr* to propagate, to spread (noticias) || FÍS to be conveyed (la luz, el sonido) || to spread (una epidemia).

propagativo, va *adj* propagative.

propalación *f* spreading, propagation.

propalador, ra *adj* propagating, propagative.
◆ *m/f* propagator, spreader || divulger (divulgador).

propalar *vt* to spread, to propagate; *propalar una noticia* to spread a piece of news || to divulge (divulgar).

propano *m* QUÍM propane (gas).

proparoxítono, na *adj* proparoxytone.

propasar *vt* to go beyond, to overstep.
◆ *vpr* to go too far, to overstep the limits (excederse).

propender *vi* to tend, to be inclined (inclinarse); *propende a la tristeza* he tends towards sadness, he is inclined to sadness || to have a leaning towards (estar aficionado).
— OBSERV The regular past participle of this verb is *propendido.* The irregular past participle *propenso* is used only as an adjective.

propensión *f* propensity (*a* for), tendency (*a* to, towards), inclination (*a* to) || MED predisposition, susceptibility.

propenso, sa *adj* inclined, prone; *ser propenso a la ira* to be inclined to anger.

propergol *m* propellant.

propi *f* FAM tip (propina).

propiamente *adv* exactly, really || — *el centro propiamente dicho* the centre proper, the centre itself || *no es un oficial propiamente dicho* strictly speaking he is not an officer, he is not really an officer, he is not an officer in the true sense of the word.

propiciación *f* propitiation.

propiciador, ra *adj* propitious.
◆ *m/f* propitiator.

propiciar *vt* to placate, to appease; *propiciar la ira divina* to placate the anger of the gods || to propitiate (hacer propicio) || AMER to patronize, to favour [US to favor] (auspiciar).

propiciatorio, ria *adj* propitiatory.

propicio, cia *adj* propitious, favourable; *ocasión propicia* propitious moment || suitable; *es la persona más propicia para este trabajo* he is the most suitable person for this job || *ser propicio a* to be inclined *o* prone to.

propiedad *f* property (lo que posee uno) || property, estate (terreno, casa) || ownership, proprietorship (hecho de poseer) || property, quality (característica) || perfect likeness (semejanza) || FÍS & QUÍM property || — *de la propiedad de* belonging to || *emplear una palabra con propiedad* to use a word correctly || JUR *nuda propiedad* bare ownership, ownership without usufruct || *pertenecer en propiedad* to rightfully belong || *propiedad horizontal* or *de casa por pisos* joint-ownership of a block of flats || *propiedad industrial* patent rights *pl* || *propiedad inmobiliaria* real estate || *propiedad intelectual* copyright || *propiedad literaria* copyright || *propiedad privada* private property.

propietario, ria *adj* proprietary.
◆ *m* owner (de cualquier cosa) || proprietor, owner (de casa, de fábrica, etc.) || AGR landowner, landlord, property owner (de tierras) || — JUR *nudo propietario* bare owner, owner without usufruct | *propietario de bienes inmuebles* property owner || *ser propietario de* to own.
◆ *f* owner, proprietress, landlady.

propileo *m* ARQ propylaeum.

propina *f* tip, gratuity (gratificación) || — *dar una propina a un camarero* to tip a waiter || *dejar una propina* to leave a tip || FAM *de propina* as a tip (como propina), in addition, extra (por añadidura).

propinar *vt* to give (dar); *propinar una paliza* to give a hiding.

propincuidad *f* proximity, propinquity.

propincuo, cua *adj* near.

propio, pia *adj* own (que pertenece); *su propio hijo* his own son || own (característico); *su carácter propio* his own character; *en su propio interés* in your own interest || particular, peculiar (particular) || natural; *propio de su edad* natural for his age || GRAM proper; *nombre propio* proper noun | proper, strict, real; *sentido propio* strict meaning || suitable, correct (conveniente) || own, real; *su pelo propio* his own hair || himself, herself, etc.; *el propio interesado debe firmar* the interested party himself must sign || same; *hacer lo propio* to do the same || — AMER *al propio* on purpose (expresamente) || *al propio tiempo* at the same time || *de propio* on purpose || *en propias manos* personally, in person || FAM *es muy propio de él* it's very typical of him, it's just like him || *lo propio* the same (thing) (lo mismo); *haré lo propio que tú* I shall do the same as you || *lo propio sucede con* it is the same with, the same thing happens with || *ser propio de* to be characteristic of *o* peculiar to; *la irreflexión es propia de los niños* thoughtlessness is characteristic of children; *la llovizna es propia de esta región* drizzle is characteristic of this region.
◆ *m* messenger (mensajero); *despachar un propio* to send a messenger || REL proper.
◆ *pl* communal *o* public property *sing.*

propóleos *m* propolis (sustancia cérea).

proponente *adj* proposing.
◆ *m/f* proposer.

proponer* *vt* to propose, to put forward, to suggest; *proponer un parecer* to propose an idea || to propound (una teoría) || to move, to propose (en una reunión); *propongo que se levante la sesión* I move that the meeting be adjourned.
◆ *vpr* to propose; *se propone salir mañana para Madrid* he proposes to leave for Madrid tomorrow || to mean, to intend, to propose (tener intención de) || *tú te has propuesto que lleguemos tarde* you are determined to make us arrive late.

proporción *f* proportion; *guardar las proporciones* to keep a sense of proportion; *en proporción con* in proportion to; *las proporciones del cuerpo humano* the proportions of the human body; *guardar proporción con* to be in proportion with; *fuera de proporción* out of proportion || chance, opportunity (oportunidad) || opportunity (coyuntura); *esperar una buena proporción* to wait for the right opportunity || MAT proportion, ratio (razón) || — *a proporción de* according to (según) || *no hay ninguna proporción* there is no comparison || *no sabemos en qué proporción intervino él* we do not know to what extent he was involved || MAT *proporción aritmética, geométrica* arithmetic, geometric proportion.
◆ *pl* size *sing* (tamaño) || extent *sing* (extensión) || *en grandes proporciones* greatly, to a great extent, on a large scale.

proporcionable *adj* proportionable.

proporcionado, da *adj* proportionate, in proportion || suitable (adecuado) || *bien proporcionado* well proportioned.

proporcional *adj* proportional.

proporcionalidad *f* proportionality || proportion.

proporcionar *vt* to proportion; *proporcionar sus gastos a sus recursos* to proportion one's expenditure to one's means || to furnish, to provide (facilitar); *proporcionar trabajo a alguien* to provide s.o. with work || to give (dar) || to lend (prestar) || to procure, to bring (procurar); *proporcionar provecho* to procure a benefit || to adapt; *proporcionar los medios al objeto* to adapt the means to the end.
◆ *vpr* to procure, to obtain, to get; *proporcionarse dinero* to procure money.

proposición *f* proposition, proposal (sugerencia) || proposal, offer (oferta) || MAT proposition || GRAM clause (oración).

propósito *m* intention (intención); *buenos propósitos* good intentions || purpose, aim, object (objetivo) || subject [matter] (tema) || — *a propósito* by the way (por cierto), opportunely, at the right time (oportunamente), useful, handy (útil); *el dinero que me enviaste me vino muy a propósito* the money that you sent me came in very handy; on purpose, intentionally (a posta); *perdona, no lo hice a propósito* excuse me, I didn't do it on purpose; suitable, fitting, appropriate (adecuado); *ese vestido no es a propósito para ir de excursión* that dress is not very suitable for an excursion || *a propósito de* with regard to, on the subject of, speaking of; *a propósito de dinero ¿cuándo me vas a pagar?* speaking of money, when are you going to pay me?; because of (con motivo de) || *con el propósito de* in order to || *con este propósito* to this end || *de propósito* on purpose, intentionally, deliberately (a posta) || *fuera de propósito* irrelevant, beside the point || *poco a propósito* rather unsuitable, rather inadequate || *tener el propósito de aprender* to intend to *o* to propose to *o* to mean to learn.

propretor *m* propraetor, propretor.

propretura *f* propraetorship, propretorship.

propuesta *f* proposal, proposition, suggestion; *a propuesta de* at the proposal of || offer, proposal (oferta) || tender (de obras públicas).

propugnación *f* defence [US defense], advocacy.

propugnar *vt* to defend, to advocate.

propulsar *vt* to propel, to drive (impeler) || to reject, to refuse (rechazar) || FIG to foster, to promote (fomentar).

propulsión *f* propulsion; *propulsión a chorro* or *por reacción* jet propulsion || *con propulsión a chorro* jet-propelled.

propulsivo, va *adj* propulsive.

propulsor, ra *adj* propulsive || *cohete propulsor* rocket propulsor.
◆ *m* propulsor.

prorrata *f* quota, share [US prorate] || *a prorrata* pro rata, proportionally.

prorratear *vt* to apportion [*US* to prorate], to share out *o* to divide proportionally.

prorrateo *m* apportionment [*US* proration], sharing || *a prorrateo* pro rata, proportionally.

prórroga *f* prorogation, prolongation, extension || COM extension || MIL deferment || DEP extra time [*US* overtime] (de un partido) || *prórroga tácita* tacit extension (de un acuerdo, etc.).

prorrogable *adj* that can be prolonged *o* extended.

prorrogación *f* prorogation, extension.

prorrogar *vt* to prorogue, to prolong || to extend (ampliar) || MIL to defer.

prorrumpir *vi* to shoot forth, to spring up (brotar) || FIG to burst out, to burst; *prorrumpir en llanto, en sollozos, en carcajadas* to burst out crying, sobbing, laughing, to burst into tears, sobs, laughter || to break out; *prorrumpían las críticas por todos los lados* criticism broke out on all sides || — *los espectadores prorrumpieron en aplausos* the spectators burst into applause || *prorrumpir en gritos de alegría, de dolor* to shout for *o* with joy, to scream *o* to yell with pain || *prorrumpir en insultos* to unleash a shower of insults, to hurl abuse || *prorrumpir en lágrimas* to burst into tears.

prosa *f* prose || FIG prosaicness, prosaic nature, prose (aspecto vulgar de las cosas) | hot air (palabrería) || FIG & FAM *gastar mucha prosa* to talk and talk, to go on and on.

prosador, ra *m/f* prosaist, prose writer || FIG & FAM chatterbox, talker, windbag (hablador).

prosaico, ca *adj* prosaic.

prosaísmo *m* prosaism || FIG prosaicness, prosaic nature; *el prosaísmo de las tareas cotidianas* the prosaicness of everyday tasks.

prosapia *f* ancestry, lineage (alcurnia).

proscenio *m* TEATR proscenium || *palco de proscenio* proscenium box, stage box.

proscribir *vt* to proscribe, to banish (echar) || FIG to proscribe, to prohibit (prohibir) || to outlaw (a un criminal).

proscripción *f* proscription, banishment (destierro) || FIG proscription, prohibition (prohibición) || outlawing (de criminales).

proscriptor, ra *adj* proscriptive.
◆ *m* proscriber.

proscrito, ta *adj* proscribed, banished || outlawed (criminal).
◆ *m/f* exile || outlaw (criminal).

prosecución *f*; **proseguimiento** *m* pursuit, pursuance; *la prosecución de un negocio, de un ideal* the pursuit of a business deal, of an ideal || continuation (continuación).

proseguimiento *m* → **prosecución.**

proseguir* *vt* to pursue; *proseguir sus estudios* to pursue one's studies || to proceed, to carry on with, to continue with; *proseguiremos el trabajo mañana* we shall carry on with the work tomorrow || to continue, to go on, to carry on; *prosiguió hablando* he went on talking || *proseguir su camino* to continue on one's way.
◆ *vi* to continue, to go on, to proceed (seguir); *proseguir con* or *en su tarea* to go on with one's task || to continue, to persist (el mal tiempo).
— OBSERV One should not confuse *proseguir* with *perseguir*.

proselitismo *m* proselytism.

proselitista *adj* proselytizing.

prosélito *m* proselyte, convert.

prosénquima *m* BOT prosenchyma.

prosificar *vt* to put into prose.

prosimios *m pl* ZOOL prosimii.

prosista *m* prosist, prose writer.

prosístico, ca *adj* prosaic, of *o* pertaining to prose.

prosodia *f* GRAM prosody.

prosódico, ca *adj* GRAM prosodic.

prosopopeya *f* prosopopeia || FIG pomposity.

prospección *f* prospecting, prospection (del subsuelo) || canvassing, survey, prospection (del mercado).

prospectar *vt* to prospect.

prospectivo, va *adj* prospective.

prospecto *m* prospectus.

prospector *m* prospector.

prosperar *vt* to prosper, to make prosperous.
◆ *vi* to prosper, to thrive, to flourish; *los negocios prosperan* business is prospering || to thrive (un país) || to prosper, to be successful (una persona).

prosperidad *f* prosperity || success (éxito).

próspero, ra *adj* prosperous, thriving, flourishing; *comercio próspero* prosperous business || prosperous, wealthy, well-to-do, well-off (persona) || *feliz y próspero Año Nuevo* happy and prosperous New Year.

próstata *f* ANAT prostate (gland).

prostático, ca *adj* MED prostate, prostatic.
◆ *m* prostate sufferer.

prostatitis *f* MED prostatitis.

prosternación *f* prostration.

prosternarse *vpr* to prostrate o.s.

próstesis *f* GRAM prosthesis.

prostíbulo *m* brothel (lupanar).

próstilo *m* ARQ prostyle.

prostitución *f* prostitution.

prostituir* *vt* to prostitute || FIG to prostitute; *prostituir su talento* to prostitute one's talent.
◆ *vpr* to prostitute o.s.

prostituta *f* prostitute.

protactinio *m* QUÍM protactinium.

protagonista *m/f* protagonist, main character, hero (hombre), heroine (mujer), heroine (de novela, drama, película, etc.) || TEATR & CINEM *ser el protagonista* to play the lead, to star (un actor).

protagonizar *vt* to play the lead in, to star in; *¿quién protagoniza la película?* who plays the lead in the film?, who stars in the film?

protargol *m* QUÍM protargol.

protección *f* protection || INFORM *protección de datos* data protection || *sistema de protección* protective *o* safety system.

proteccionismo *m* protectionism.

proteccionista *adj/s* protectionist.

protector, ra; protectriz *adj* protective, protecting || FIG patronizing (actitud) || *sociedad protectora de animales* Society for the Prevention of Cruelty to Animals.
◆ *m* protector, defender (defensor) || patron (de las artes, etc.) || mouthpiece (boxeo) || stocking protector (de las medias) || HIST protector (de Inglaterra) || *protector labial* lipsalve.
◆ *f* protectress || patroness.

protectorado *m* protectorate.

proteger *vt* to protect; *¡que Dios le proteja!* may God protect you!

protegido, da *adj* protected, favoured || TECN guarded.
◆ *m/f* protégé (hombre), protégée (mujer) || *paso protegido* right-of-way.

proteico, ca *adj* protean (cambiante) || QUÍM proteinic, proteic, proteinaceous.

proteido *m* QUÍM proteid.

proteína *f* QUÍM protein.

proteínico, ca *adj* QUÍM proteinic.

proteles *m* ZOOL proteles.

Proteo *npr m* MIT Proteus.

protervidad *f* perversity, wickedness.

protervo, va *adj* perverse, wicked.
◆ *m/f* pervert.

protésico, ca *adj* MED prosthetic.

prótesis *f* GRAM prosthesis, prothesis || MED prosthesis; *prótesis dental* dental prosthesis || REL prothesis.

protesta *f* protest; *hacer una protesta* to raise a protest || protestation (de inocencia) || COM protest (de letras) || JUR *bajo protesta* under protest.

protestación *f* protestation.

protestador, ra *adj* protestating, protestant.
◆ *m/f* protester.

protestante *adj* protesting, protestant (que protesta) || REL protestant.
◆ *m/f* Protester || REL Protestant.

protestantismo *m* protestantism.

protestar *vi* to protest (reclamar) || FAM to grumble (refunfuñar); *siempre está protestando* he is always grumbling || *protestar de su inocencia* to protest one's innocence.
◆ *vt* COM to protest, to give notice of a protest (una letra).

protesto *m* protestation (protesta) || COM protest.

protestón, ona *m/f* FAM moaner, grumbler.

prótidos *m pl* QUÍM protides.

protocolar *vt* to protocol, to protocolize.

protocolar; protocolario, ria *adj* established by protocol || FIG formal; *invitación protocolaria* formal invitation.

protocolización *f* JUR probate (de un testamento).

protocolizar *vt* to protocol, to protocolize || JUR to probate.

protocolo *m* protocol || medical record || FIG etiquette, formalities *pl* || *jefe de protocolo* chief of protocol || INFORM *protocolo de comunicación* link *o* communications protocol.

protohistoria *f* protohistory.

protohistórico, ca *adj* protohistoric.

protomártir *m* protomartyr.

protón *m* FÍS proton.

protónico, ca *adj* FÍS protonic.

protonotario *m* REL protonotary, prothonotary || *protonotario apostólico* protonotary apostolic.

protoplasma *m* BIOL protoplasm.

protoplasmático, ca; protoplásmico, ca *adj* BIOL protoplasmic.

protoplasto *m* BIOL protoplast.

protórax *m* ZOOL prothorax.

prototipo *m* prototype.

protóxido *m* QUÍM protoxide.

protozoario; protozoo *m* ZOOL protozoon.
— OBSERV El plural inglés de esta palabra es *protozoa*.

protráctil *adj* protractile; *lengua protráctil* protractile tongue.

protractor, ra *adj* ANAT *músculo protractor* protractor.

protrombina *f* QUÍM prothrombin.

protuberancia *f* protuberance.

protuberante *adj* protuberant.

protutor, ra *m/f* JUR protutor.

provecto, ta *adj* old (antiguo) || advanced; *edad provecta* advanced age.

provecho *m* profit, benefit; *sin provecho alguno* without any profit || progress (adelanto) || advantage (ventaja) || — FAM *¡buen provecho!* enjoy your meal! || *de provecho* useful (útil), profitable (provechoso) || *en provecho de* in favour of, to the advantage of, to the profit of || *no le será de ningún provecho* it will be of no use to him || *para su provecho* for one's own good, to one's own advantage || *sacar provecho de* to benefit from, to profit by (beneficiarse de), to take advantage of (aprovecharse de), to make the most of (aprovecharse al máximo).

provechoso, sa *adj* beneficial, good; *provechoso a* or *para la salud* beneficial to *o* good for one's health || profitable; *venta, experiencia provechosa* profitable sale, experience || useful (útil) || advantageous (ventajoso).

proveedor, ra *adj* purveying, supplying.
◆ *m/f* supplier, purveyor (abastecedor) || *proveedor de fondos* financial backer.

proveer *vt* to supply, to provide, to furnish; *proveer a uno de ropa, de alimentos* to provide s.o. with clothes, with food || to attend; *ella proveía a sus necesidades* she attended to his needs || to decide, to resolve (disponer) || to fill (una vacante).
◆ *vi* JUR to make a ruling, to rule (decidir) || JUR *para mejor proveer* until further enquiries have been made.
◆ *vpr* to provision o.s. (aprovisionarse) || to provide o.s. (*de* with), to provide o.s. (proporcionarse).

proveniente *adj* arising, originating, resulting (procedente).

provenir* *vi* to come from, to arise from, to issue from, to originate in (proceder).

Provenza *npr f* GEOGR Provence (Francia).

provenzal *adj/s* Provençal.

proverbial *adj* proverbial.

proverbio *m* proverb (refrán) || saying (dicho).
◆ *pl* Proverbs (libro de la Biblia).

providencia *f* providence; *la Divina Providencia* Divine Providence || measure, step (disposición); *tomar las providencias necesarias para* to take the necessary measures in order to || FIG providence || JUR ruling, judgment (resolución) || *tomar una providencia* to make a decision.

providencial *adj* providential.

providencialismo *m* providential philosophy.

providencialista *m/f* providential philosopher.

providenciar *vt* to take (steps) || JUR to decide on, to rule on.

providente *adj* provident (próvido) || prudent (previsor).

próvido, da *adj* provident (prevenido) || propitious, favourable (propicio).

provincia *f* province || — *capital de provincia* county town [*US* county seat] || *vivir en la provincia* to live in the provinces.

provincial *adj* provincial || *diputación provincial* county council.
◆ *m* REL provincial.

provinciala *f* REL provincial.

provincialato *m* REL provincialate.

provincialismo; provincianismo *m* provincialism.

provinciano, na *adj/s* provincial.

provisión *f* provision (acción) || provision, supply; *hacer provisión de azúcar* to get in a supply of sugar || measure (medida) || cover, deposit, funds *pl* (en banco) || — *provisión de fondos* reserve funds *pl*, financial cover.
◆ *pl* provisions, food *sing* (comida) || *provisiones de boca* provisions, victuals, food *sing*.

provisional *adj* provisional || *gerente provisional* acting manager.

provisionalidad *f* provisional state.

provisor *m/f* purveyor, supplier, caterer (proveedor) || REL vicar-general.

provisora *f* cellaress [of a convent].

provisorio, ria *adj* AMER provisional, provisory.

provisto, ta *adj* supplied, provided; *provisto de* provided with.

provocación *f* provocation, incitement, instigation.

provocador, ra *adj* provocative, provoking || *una mirada provocadora* a provocative glance.
◆ *m/f* provoker.

provocar *vt* to provoke; *provocar a uno* to provoke s.o. || to rouse (despertar) || to cause; *provocar la risa* or *a risa* to cause laughter || to cause, to start; *una chispa provocó el incendio* a spark started the fire; *el incidente que provocó la guerra* the incident which started the war || to cause, to bring about (ocasionar) || to make one feel sick (dar ganas de vomitar) || AMER to feel like (apetecer); *no me provoca ir hoy* I don't feel like going today.

provocativo, va *adj* provocative.

proxeneta *m* procurer, pimp, pander.
◆ *f* procuress.

proxenetismo *m* procuring, pandering.

próximamente *adv* soon, shortly, before long (dentro de poco) || approximately, more or less (aproximadamente).

proximidad *f* nearness, closeness, proximity (cercanía) || *en las proximidades de* close to, near, in the vicinity of.

próximo, ma *adj* near, close (cerca); *próximos unos a otros* near (to) *o* close to one another || nearby, neighbouring [*US* neighboring] (vecino) || next; *el año próximo* next year; *el mes próximo* next month; *la próxima vez* the next time; *el próximo 31 de agosto* on the 31th August next || — *en fecha próxima* shortly, at an early date || *estar próximo a* to be near, to be close to (al lado de), to be about to, to be on the point of (a punto de) || *més próximo pasado* last month.

proyección *f* projection || showing (de una película) || projection (de diapositivas) || FIG diffusion; *la proyección de la cultura* the diffusion of culture || *proyección cónica* conic projection.

proyectar *vt* to project || to plan, to be thinking of; *proyecto salir para los Estados Unidos* I plan to leave *o* I am thinking of leaving for the United States || to project, to hurl, to throw (lanzar) || to cast, to shed, to project (una luz) || to project, to cast (una sombra) || to emit, to pour, to gush (un líquido) || to show, to project (una película) || to project (fotos) || MAT & FÍS to project || ARQ to plan || TECN to design.

proyectil *m* projectile, missile || missile; *proyectil teledirigido* or *teleguiado* guided missile; *proyectil balístico* ballistic missile.

proyectista *m/f* planner, schemer (planificador) || designer, planner (diseñador).

proyecto *m* project, plan, scheme; *no es más que un proyecto* it is just a project; *proyectos ambiciosos* ambitious plans || TECN plan, design || draft; *proyecto de acuerdo* draft agreement; *proyecto de resolución* draft resolution || — *estar en proyecto* to be in the planning stage || *proyecto de ley* bill; *presentar un proyecto de ley* to introduce a bill || *tener en proyecto* to be planning || *tener proyectos* to have plans || *tengo un viaje en proyecto* I am planning a trip.

proyector, ra *adj* projecting.
◆ *m* projector (para proyectar imágenes) || condenser (óptico) || searchlight (reflector) || spotlight (en teatro, en cine).

prudencia *f* prudence, caution (cuidado) || moderation (templanza) || wisdom (sagacidad) || discretion (cordura) || *con prudencia* cautiously, prudently.

prudencial *adj* prudential || FAM moderate; *una cantidad prudencial* a moderate amount | approximate, rough (cálculo).

prudenciarse *vpr* AMER to control o.s.

prudente *adj* prudent, wise; *un consejero prudente* a wise adviser || cautious, wary, prudent (circunspecto) || reasonable; *acostarse a una hora prudente* to go to bed at a reasonable hour || careful (conductor, etc.) || *lo más prudente sería* it would be advisable to, it would be wisest *o* best to.

prudentemente *adv* prudently, wisely || carefully (cuidadosamente).

prueba *f* proof; *dar una prueba de lo que se afirma* to give proof of what one says; *salvo prueba en contrario* or *en contra* if there is no proof to the contrary; *con las pruebas en la mano* with the proof in hand || proof, sign, token (señal); *dar pruebas de devoción* to give a proof of one's devotion || test, examination (parte de un examen); *mañana tenemos la prueba de inglés* tomorrow we have the English test || event (en deportes) || tasting (de bebidas) || fitting (de prenda de vestir); *sala de pruebas* fitting room || TECN test, trial | test (ensayo); *pruebas nucleares* nuclear tests; *piloto de prueba* test pilot || MAT proof || QUÍM experiment, test || JUR evidence, proof || IMPR proof || FOT proof, print || FIG trial, hardship, ordeal; *ha tenido que pasar duras pruebas en su vida* he has lived through a lot of hardship *o* trials || — *a guisa de prueba* by way of proof || *a prueba* on trial; *llevarse una radio a prueba* to take a radio home on trial || *a prueba de* proof against || *a prueba de agua, de bomba, de bala, de choques, etc.* waterproof, bombproof, bulletproof, shockproof, etc. || *a toda prueba* unyielding, unwearying || *dar prueba de* to give *o* to produce proof of || *en prueba de* in proof of, to prove || MAT *hacer prueba de* to prove the accuracy of (un cálculo) || *hacer la prueba del nueve* to cast out the nines || CINEM *hacer una prueba* to screen-test (a una persona), to shoot a trial take (hacer un ensayo) || *poner* or *someter a prueba* to put to the test, to test, to try out (la amistad, un empleado, un avión, etc.) || *prueba absoluta* proof positive || *prueba de acceso* entrance exam || *prueba de ello es que* the proof of it is that || *prueba de inteligencia* intelligence test || *prueba mixta* mixed trials *pl* (esquí) || FOT *prueba negativa* negative proof | *prueba positiva* positive, print || *someter a uno a una prueba de aptitud* to give s.o. an aptitude test || *tomar a prueba* to take on trial.
◆ *pl* acrobatics (ejercicios acrobáticos) || *banco de pruebas* testing bench || IMPR *corregir pruebas* to proofread || *dar pruebas de inteligencia* to show intelligence || *dar pruebas de su aptitud* to prove one's ability || *los empleados están dando pruebas de descontento* the employees are showing signs of discontent || FAM *pruebas al canto* with evidence to prove it.

prurigo *m* MED prurigo.

prurito *m* MED pruritus, itch (comezón) || FIG itch, eagerness, urge (deseo excesivo).

Prusia *npr f* GEOGR Prussia.

prusiano, na *adj/s* Prussian || *azul de Prusia* Prussian blue.

prusiato *m* QUÍM prussiate.

prúsico, ca *adj* QUÍM *ácido prúsico* prussic acid.

PSC *abrev de Partit dels Socialistes de Catalunya* Catalan socialist party («los socialistas catalanes»).

psi *f* psi (letra griega).

psicastenia *f* MED psychasthenia.

psicasténico, ca *adj* MED psychasthenic.

psicoanálisis *m inv* psychoanalysis.

psicoanalista *m/f* psychoanalyst.

psicoanalítico, ca *adj* psychoanalytic, psychoanalytical.

psicoanalizar *vt* to psychoanalyse, to psychoanalyze.

psicodélico, ca *adj* psychedelic.

psicodrama *m* psychodrama.

psicofármaco *m* psychoactive drug.

psicogeriatría *f* MED psychogeriatrics.

psicología *f* psychology.

psicológico, ca *adj* psychological; *momento psicológico* psychological moment || *guerra psicológica* psychological warfare.

psicologismo *m* psychologism.

psicólogo, ga *adj* psychological.
◆ *m/f* psychologist.

psicometría *f* psychometry.

psicomotor, ra *adj* psychomotor.

psiconeurosis *f inv* MED psychoneurosis.

psicópata *m/f* MED psychopath.

psicopatía *f* MED psychopathy.

psicopático, ca *adj* MED psychopathic.

psicopatología *f* MED psychopathology.

psicosis *f inv* MED psychosis || FIG psychosis; *psicosis de guerra* war psychosis.

psicosomático, ca *adj* psychosomatic.

psicotecnia *f* psychotechnology.

psicotécnico, ca *adj* psychotechnological.

psicoterapia *f* MED psychotherapy.

psicótropo, pa *adj* psychotropic.
◆ *m* psychotropic drug (medicamento).

Psique; Psiquis *f* psyche.

Psique; Psiquis *npr f* MIT Psyche.

psiquiatra *m/f* MED psychiatrist.

psiquiatría *f* MED psychiatry.

psiquiátrico, ca *adj* MED psychiatric.

psíquico, ca *adj* psychic, psychical.

psiquismo *m* psychism.

psitacosis *f inv* MED psittacosis.

psoas *m inv* psoas (músculo).

PSOE *abrev de Partido Socialista Obrero Español* Spanish Socialist Party.

psoriasis *f inv* MED psoriasis.

PSUC *abrev de Partit Socialista Unificat de Catalunya* Catalan socialist party («los comunistas catalanes»).

Ptas *abrev de pesetas* Ptas, pesetas.

pteridofita *f* BOT pteridophyte.

pterodáctilo *m* ZOOL pterodactyl.

pterópodo *m* ZOOL pteropod.

pterosaurio *m* ZOOL pterosaur.

ptialina *f* ptyalin.

ptialismo *m* ptyalism.

ptolemaico, ca *adj* Ptolemaic.

Ptolomeo *npr m* Ptolemy.

ptomaína *f* BOT ptomaine.

ptosis *f inv* MED ptosis.

púa *f* sharp point (punta aguda) || quill (de erizo o de puerco espín) || tooth (de peine) || prong, tine (del tenedor) || barb (de alambrada) || thorn (de rosa, etc.) || AGR graft, scion (de injerto) || MÚS plectrum (plectro) || needle (de gramófono) || *AMER* spur (espolón de ave).

púber, ra *adj* pubescent, adolescent, who has reached puberty.
◆ *m/f* pubescent youth, adolescent.

pubertad *f* puberty.

pubescencia *f* pubescence.

pubescente *adj* pubescent.

pubiano, na; púbico, ca *adj* ANAT pubic.

pubis *m* ANAT pubes (parte inferior del vientre) || ANAT *hueso pubis* pubis.

publicable *adj* publishable.

publicación *f* publication (obra publicada, acción de publicar) || *se ruega la publicación* for the favour of publication in your columns.

publicador, ra *adj* publishing.
◆ *m/f* publisher.

publicano *m* HIST publican.

publicar *vt* to publish; *publicar un libro* to publish a book | to announce, to proclaim (proclamar) || to publicize, to make public, to divulge (hacer público) || to publish (los bandos) || MED to issue (un parte facultativo).
◆ *vpr* to be published (libro); *acaba de publicarse* it has just been published.

publicidad *f* publicity (en general) || COM advertising; *agencia de publicidad* advertising agency || CINEM & RAD advertisement, advert (anuncio publicitario) || — *dar publicidad a* to give publicity to || *hacer publicidad por* to advertise || FAM *publicidad a bombo y platillos* noisy *o* loud publicity.

publicista *m/f* publicist || *AMER* COM publicity agent.

publicitario, ria *adj* advertising, publicity; *empresa publicitaria* advertising firm.

público, ca *adj* public; *opinión pública* public opinion || — *deuda pública* national debt, public debt || *es público que* it is common knowledge that, it is well known that, everybody knows that || *hacer pública una cosa* to publicize *o* to make public *o* to publish sth. || *ser público y notorio* to be common knowledge.
◆ *m* public; *aviso al público* notice to the public; *se ruega al público* the public are requested; *hablar en público* to speak in public || FIG people *pl*; *la sala estaba llena de público* the room was full of people || audience (en un espectáculo, en una sala) || spectators *pl* (en deportes) || viewers *pl* (de la televisión) || readers, followers *pl*; *cada escritor tiene su público* every writer has his followers || — FIG *dar al público* to publish (una novela, etc.), to present (obra de teatro) || *público en general* or *gran público* general public || *sacar al público* to publicize, to make public, to publish.

publirreportaje *m* promotional film (en televisión, cine) || special advertising section (en una publicación).

pucallpeño, ña *adj* [from] Pucallpa (Perú).
◆ *m/f* native *o* inhabitant of Pucallpa.

pucará *m* *AMER* small fort (fortaleza incaica) | archaeological site.

pucha *interj* *AMER* good heavens! (¡caramba!).

pucherazo *m* blow with a pot || FIG & FAM *dar pucherazos* to rig the elections, to count votes that were not cast.

puchero *m* pot, cooking pot (vasija) || stew (guisado) || FIG & FAM daily bread (alimento diario) || — FIG & FAM *calentar* or *hacer cocer el puchero* to keep the pot boiling | *ganarse el puchero* to earn one's daily bread, to earn a living | *hacer pucheros* to pout (un niño).

puches *mpl/fpl* gruel *sing*, porridge *sing* (gachas).

puchito, ta *m/f* *AMER* child.

pucho *m* cigar *o* cigarette butt (colilla) || *AMER* leftover (resto de algo) | baby, youngest (hijo más joven).

pudding *m* pudding.

pudelado *m* puddling.

pudelar *vt* TECN to puddle.

pudendo, da *adj* shameful (vergonzoso) || *partes pudendas* pudenda, private parts.

pudibundez *f* affected modesty, prudishness, prudery.

pudibundo, da *adj* bashful, modest (pudoroso) || prudish (mojigato).

pudicicia *f* pudicity, modesty, chastity.

púdico, ca *adj* chaste, modest.

pudiente *adj* rich, wealthy, well-to-do (rico).
◆ *m/f* wealthy person || *los pudientes* the wealthy.

pudín *m* pudding.

pudor *m* modesty || shame (vergüenza) || decency (decencia) || chastity (castidad) || — *atentado contra el pudor* indecent assault || *sin pudor* shameless || *ultraje contra el pudor* indecent exposure.

pudoroso, sa *adj* bashful, modest || prudish (mojigato) || chaste, virtuous (casto).

pudrición *f* putrefaction, rotting.

pudridero *m* rubbish dump (vertedero) || temporary vault (para cadáveres).

pudrimiento *m* rotting, putrefaction (acción) || rottenness, rot (efecto).

pudrir* *vt* to rot, to putrefy, to decay.
◆ *vpr* to rot, to putrefy || FIG to be spoilt || — FIG & FAM *¡ahí te pudras!* to hell with you! | *pudrirse de aburrimiento* to be bored stiff | *pudrírsele la sangre a uno* to get worked up | *un por ahí te pudras* a dicky [US a rumble seat] (de coche).

puebla *f* town (población).

pueblacho *m* FAM ⟶ **poblacho.**

pueblada *f* *AMER* uprising, riot (motín).

pueblerino, na *adj* village || FIG rustic; *gustos pueblerinos* rustic tastes.
◆ *m/f* villager.

pueblo *m* town (población) || village (población pequeña) || people (nación); *todos los pueblos de Europa* all the peoples of Europe; *el pueblo español* the Spanish people || people *pl*, common people *pl*, masses *pl* (el vulgo); *hacer un llamamiento al pueblo* to call on the people || — *de pueblos* from the country || *hombre del pueblo* man of the people || *pueblo bajo* lower class people || FAM *pueblo de mala muerte* dump, hole [US hick town].

puente *m* bridge (sobre un río) || FIG long weekend (entre dos fiestas); *hacer puente* to take *o* to have a long weekend | gap (espacio de tiempo) || ELECTR bridge; *puente de Wheatstone* Wheatstone bridge || MÚS bridge (de violín) || MAR bridge (plataforma sobre la cubierta) | deck (cubierta) || MED bridge (en las muelas) || — *cabeza de puente* bridgehead || FIG *hacer* or *tender un puente de plata a uno* to present s.o. with a golden opportunity || *puente aéreo* airlift (para abastecimiento), air shuttle (para viajeros) || *puente basculante* bascule bridge || *puente colgante* suspension bridge || *puente de aterrizaje* or *de despegue* flight deck (en los portaaviones) || *puente de barcas* or *de pontones* pontoon bridge || FIG *puente de los asnos* pons asinorum || MAR *puente de mando* bridge || *puente en esviaje* skew bridge || *puente ferroviario* railway bridge || *puente giratorio* swing bridge || *puente grúa* bridge crane || *puente levadizo* drawbridge || *puente para peatones* footbridge || *puente transbordador* transporter bridge || AUT *puente trasero* rear axle || *tender un puente sobre* to throw a bridge over.

puerco, ca *adj* dirty, filthy (sucio) || FIG nasty, disgusting (asqueroso) | smutty, bawdy (obsceno).
◆ *m* pig, swine (cerdo).
◆ *f* sow (cerda).
◆ *m/f* FIG & FAM pig, sloven (persona sucia) | swine, rogue (sinvergüenza) || — FIG & FAM *a cada puerco le llega su San Martín* every dog has his day | *echar margaritas a los puercos* to cast pearls before swine || *puerco espín* porcupine.

puericia *f* childhood.

puericultor, ra *m/f* specialist in puericulture.

puericultura *f* puericulture.

pueril *adj* puerile, childish.

puerilidad *f* puerility, childishness.

puerilismo *m* puerilism, childishness.

puerperal *adj* MED puerperal.

puerperio *m* puerperium (sobreparto).

puerro *m* leek (planta).

puerta *f* door; *abrir una puerta* to open a door; *escuchar detrás de las puertas* to listen behind doors || door (de coche, vagón, mueble, etc.) || gate (de una ciudad) || gate (del infierno) || FIG gateway, doorway (medio de acceso); *la puerta de la fama* the gateway to fame || DEP goal (en fútbol, en hockey, etc.) || — FIG *abrir la puerta a* to open the door to | *a las puertas de* on the verge of; *estar a las puertas de un conflicto* to be on the verge of a conflict | *a las puertas de la muerte* at death's door || *a puerta cerrada* in camera (jurisprudencia), behind closed doors || FIG *cerrar la puerta a* to close the door on || *coche de dos puertas* 2-door car || FIG *coger* or *tomar la puerta* to leave, to go | *cuando una puerta se cierra, cien se abren* when one door closes another always opens | *dar a uno con* or *cerrar la puerta en las narices* to slam *o* to shut the door in s.o.'s face | *dejar* or *reservarse una puerta abierta* to leave a door open || *de puerta en puerta* from door to door || *de puertas adentro* at home || *echar la puerta abajo* to break the door down || FIG *encontrar todas las puertas cerradas* to find all doors closed | *en puertas* just around the corner | *llamar a la puerta de alguien* to call on s.o. for help (pedir ayuda) | *poner a uno en la puerta de la calle* to throw *o* to turn s.o. out (expulsar), to sack s.o., to fire s.o., to turn s.o. out (a un empleado) | *poner puertas al campo* to try to stem the tide || *puerta accesoria* side door || *puerta a puerta* door-to-door transport (transporte), house-to-house canvassing (venta, reparto) || *puerta automática* automatic door (en el metro) || *puerta blindada* reinforced door || *puerta cochera* carriage *o* car entrance || *puerta de corredera* sliding door || *puerta de entrada* front door || *puerta de servicio* tradesmen's entrance || *puerta excusada* or *falsa* concealed door || *puerta giratoria* revolving door || *puerta principal* main entrance || *puerta secreta* secret door || *puerta trasera* back door || *puerta vidriera* glass door (puerta), French window (que da al balcón) || FIG *tener puerta abierta* to have an open door.

puertaventana *f* french window.

puerto *m* port, harbour [*US* harbor] (abrigo para la navegación) || port; *puerto pesquero* fishing port || seaport (marítimo); *Cádiz es un puerto* Cádiz is a seaport || mountain pass, col (paso entre montañas) || INFORM port || FIG haven, refuge, shelter (amparo) || — *llegar a buen puerto* to reach port, to get safely into port || *puerto aéreo* airport || MAR *puerto comercial* commercial *o* trading port | *puerto de amarre* or *de matrícula* port of registry || FIG & FAM *puerto de arrebatacapas* den of thieves || *puerto de arribada* or *de escala* port of call || *puerto de carga* commercial port || *puerto deportivo* pleasure harbour || *puerto de salvación* haven of refuge || *puerto franco* or *libre* free port || INFORM *puerto paralelo* parallel port | *puerto serial* serial port || *tomar puerto* to reach *o* to make port.

Puerto España *n pr* GEOGR Port of Spain.

Puerto Príncipe *n pr* GEOGR Port-au-Prince (Haití).

Puerto Rico *npr m* GEOGR Puerto Rico.

puertorriqueño, ña *adj/s* Puerto Rican.

pues *adv/conj* since, as (ya que); *póntelo tú, pues lo compraste* since you bought it, you wear it || because; *no pude salir, pues vino mi abuela* I couldn't go out because my grandmother came || so (así) || then (entonces) || well (consecuencia); *pues te arrepentirás* well you'll regret it || yes (afirmación) || well, of course (interjección familiar) || hum! (duda) || what? (interrogación) || — *así pues* therefore, so therefore || *pues bien* thus (por lo tanto), good, OK, right then (bueno) || *¡pues claro!* of course! || *pues que* being that, since (puesto que) || *¿pues qué?* so what? || *¿y pues?* so?, so what?
— OBSERV This particle used at the beginning of a sentence reinforces the idea which one wishes to express (*¡pues no faltaba más!* now that's all we needed!). It may also have various meanings depending on the intonation: *pues peor* even worse; *pues mejor* so much the better; *¡pues no!* certainly not!

puesta *f* setting (de un astro) || bet (cantidad que se apuesta) || laying (de huevos) || putting; *puesta en cultivo, en órbita, en servicio* putting into cultivation, into orbit, into service || — *puesta al día* bringing up to date || *puesta a punto* tuning (de un motor), adjusting (arreglo) || *puesta de espaldas* fall, pinfall (en una lucha) || *puesta de largo* début, coming out || *puesta de Sol, puesta del Sol* sunset || *puesta en escena* staging || *puesta en marcha* starting (de una máquina), beginning (de un proyecto).

puestear *vi* to set up a stall.

puestero *m* AMER salesman, stallholder, vendor (el que tiene o atiende un puesto) || ranch hand, herdsman (en las estancias).

puesto, ta *adj* placed, set put (colocado) || worn (la ropa) || dressed (persona); *bien, mal puesto* well, badly dressed || laid (la mesa) || *tener puesto* to have on, to be wearing; *tenía puesta una chaqueta nueva* he had a new jacket on, he was wearing a new jacket; *tenía el sombrero puesto* he had his hat on, he was wearing his hat.
◆ *m* small shop (tiendecita); *puesto de flores* small flower shop || stall (en el mercado) || stand (en una exposición) || post, job, position (empleo); *tener un buen puesto* to have a good job || seat (sitio); *el puesto del piloto* the pilot's seat || place (lugar); *déjame tu puesto* let me have your place || place, position (de un alumno) || hide [*US* blind] (en la caza) || MIL post; *puesto avanzado* advanced post; *puesto de mando* command post || — MIL *¡a sus puestos!* action stations! || *copar los dos primeros puestos* to win the first two places (en deportes) || FIG *escalar puestos* to move up || *incorporarse a su puesto de trabajo* to take up one's duties || *puesto de abastecimiento* supply station || *puesto de periódicos* newsstand, newspaper stand || *puesto de socorro* first-aid station *o* post.
◆ *conj* *puesto que* since, as (ya que).

puf *m* pouf (taburete bajo).
— OBSERV This word is a Gallicism.

pufo *m* FAM trick (engaño) || debt (deuda); *dejar de pufo mil pesetas* to leave a debt of a thousand pesetas || FAM *dar el pufo* to trick.

púgil; pugilista *m* pugilist (gladiador que combatía a puñetazos) || boxer, pugilist, fighter (boxeador).

pugilato *m* pugilism, boxing (boxeo) || brawl (pelea) || dispute (discusión).

pugilismo *m* pugilism.

pugilístico, ca *adj* pugilistic.

pugna *f* fight, battle, struggle (lucha) || *entrar, estar en pugna con* to clash with.

pugnacidad *f* pugnacity, aggressiveness (belicosidad).

pugnar *vi* to fight, to struggle (luchar) || FIG to insist || *pugnar por entrar* to struggle to get in.

pugnaz *adj* pugnacious, aggressive.

puja *f* bid (en una subasta) || struggle, fight (lucha) || — *hacer una puja* to make a bid (en una subasta), to make an effort (esforzarse) || *se hicieron pujas fuertes* the bidding was high.

pujador, ra *m/f* bidder.

pujamen *m* MAR foot of a sail.

pujante *adj* strong, vigorous (vigoroso) || powerful (poderoso).

pujanza *f* strength (fuerza), vigour [*US* vigor] (robustez), power (poder).

pujar *vt* to bid up, to raise.
◆ *vi* to bid higher (en una subasta) || to bid (en las cartas) || to struggle (luchar) || FIG & FAM to pout (hacer pucheros) || to grope for words (expresarse con dificultad) | to hesitate (vacilar) || FAM to strain (al hacer de vientre).

pujavante *m* butteris (de herrador).

pujido *m* scream (lamento).

pujo *m* MED tenesmus || FIG longing, yearning (ansia) | irresistible urge (gana incontenible) | aspiration; *tenía pujos de ser pintor* he had aspirations to be a painter | attempt, try (intento).

pulcritud *f* neatness, tidiness, cleanliness (esmero) || care (cuidado) || *vestir con pulcritud* to dress neatly.

pulcro, cra *adj* neat, tidy, clean || exquisite (estilo).

pulga *f* ZOOL flea (insecto) || tiddlywink (peón para jugar) || — FIG & FAM *a perro flaco todo son pulgas* misfortunes rain upon the wretched | *buscarle a uno las pulgas* to taunt s.o., to pick a fight with s.o. || FIG *estar con* or *tener la mosca* or *la pulga detrás de la oreja* to be suspicious *o* uneasy || FIG & FAM *hacer de una pulga un elefante* to make a mountain out of a molehill | *no aguantar pulgas* to stand for no nonsense | *sacudirse uno las pulgas* to stand for no nonsense | *tener malas pulgas* to be touchy *o* bad-tempered.

pulgada *f* inch (medida).

pulgar *m* thumb (dedo) || shoot (viña) || *dedo pulgar* thumb.

pulgarada *f* fillip, flick (papirote) || pinch (pizca); *una pulgarada de tabaco* a pinch of tobacco || inch (pulgada).

Pulgarcito *npr m* Tom Thumb.

pulgón *m* ZOOL plant louse.

pulguillas *m/f inv* FAM touchy person.

pulidez *f* refinement, polish, elegance (refinamiento) || neatness (pulcritud) || shine, polish (brillo).

pulido, da *adj* polished; *metal pulido* polished metal || smooth (liso) || refined, polished, elegant (refinado) || neat, smart, trim (pulcro).
◆ *m* polishing (pulimento) || shine, polish (brillo).

pulidor, ra *adj* polishing.
◆ *m* polisher (instrumento) || TECN polishing machine (máquina).

pulimentar *vt* to polish (pulir).

pulimento *m* polishing (acción) || polish, shine (brillo).

pulir *vt* to polish; *pulir el mármol, el vidrio, un metal* to polish marble, glass, metal ‖ to smooth (alisar) ‖ to put the final touch to, to finish off (perfeccionar una cosa) ‖ FIG to polish, to refine; *pulir el estilo* to polish one's style | to refine, to give polish to, to civilize; *pulir a un lugareño* to refine a peasant ‖ FAM to sell off (vender) | to steal, to pinch (hurtar) ‖ to adorn, to embellish (adornar).
◆ *vpr* to become polished ‖ FIG to acquire polish (una persona).

pulmón *m* lung; *gritar con todas las fuerzas de los pulmones* to scream at the top of one's lungs; *pulmón artificial* artificial lung; *pulmón de acero* iron lung.

pulmonado, da *adj/sm* ZOOL pulmonate.

pulmonar *adj* pulmonary, lung.

pulmonía *f* MED pneumonia.

pulóver *m* jumper, pullover (jersey).

pulpa *f* pulp (tejidos animales o vegetales); *pulpa dental* or *dentaria* dental pulp; *pulpa de un fruto* pulp of a fruit ‖ *pulpa de madera* wood pulp.

pulpejo *m* soft flesh ‖ soft part of the hoof (del caballo).

pulpería *f* AMER grocer's shop [US grocery store] (tienda) | tavern (taberna).

pulpero *m* AMER grocer, owner of a «pulpería» (de una tienda) | tavern keeper (de una taberna).

pulpitis *f* MED pulpitis.

púlpito *m* pulpit (de un predicador).

pulpo *m* octopus (cefalópodo) ‖ octopus luggage elastic (para fijar paquetes).

pulposo, sa *adj* pulpy, fleshy.

pulque *m* AMER «pulque» [Mexican drink].

pulquería *f* AMER pulque bar, «pulquería».

pulquero, ra *m/f* AMER keeper of a «pulquería».

pulquérrimo, ma *adj* immaculate, impeccable.

pulsación *f* pulsation (acción) ‖ beat, throb (del corazón) ‖ stroke, tap, touch (mecanografía).
— OBSERV In Spanish the expression *pulsaciones por minuto* is used to determine the efficiency rate of a typist. In English the equivalent would be *words per minute*.

pulsador, ra *adj* pulsating.
◆ *m* button (de timbre eléctrico); *pulsador del timbre* bell button.

pulsar *vt* to play (tocar); *pulsar un instrumento músico* to play a musical instrument ‖ to press, to push; *pulsar un botón* to press a button ‖ to take *o* to feel the pulse of (tomar el pulso) ‖ FIG to sound out (tantear un asunto); *pulsar la opinión pública* to sound out public opinion.
◆ *vi* to beat, to throb (latir el pulso).

pulsátil *adj* pulsating, beating, pulsatile.

pulsativo, va *adj* pulsatory.

pulsear *vi* to Indian-wrestle.

pulsera *f* bracelet (joya) ‖ watch strap (de reloj) ‖ — *pulsera de pedida* engagement bracelet (véase OBSERV) ‖ *reloj de pulsera* wristwatch.
— OBSERV In Spanish-speaking countries the equivalent to the *engagement ring* is the *pulsera de pedida*.
— OBSERV En los países de habla inglesa se suele ofrecer una *sortija de pedida* (engagement ring).

pulsímetro *m* pulsimeter.

pulso *m* ANAT pulse | wrist (muñeca) ‖ strength in one's wrist (fuerza) ‖ steady hand (para hacer trabajos delicados) ‖ FIG prudence, care, caution; *obrar con pulso* to proceed with caution ‖ AMER bracelet (pulsera) ‖ — *a pulso* with one's own bare hands, all alone ‖ *dibujo a pulso* freehand drawing ‖ *echar un pulso* to Indian-wrestle ‖ *ganarse, conseguir algo a pulso* to earn sth. (haciendo esfuerzos) ‖ *pulso arrítmico* or *irregular* irregular pulse ‖ *pulso sentado* or *normal* regular pulse ‖ *tomar el pulso a la opinión* to sound out opinion ‖ *tomarle el pulso a alguien* to take *o* to feel s.o.'s pulse.

pulsómetro *m* TECN pulsometer.

pulsorreactor *m* AVIAC pulse-jet engine.

pululación *f* pullulation.

pulular *vi* to pullulate, to swarm, to teem.

pulverizable *adj* pulverizable.

pulverización *f* pulverization (de sólidos) ‖ atomization (de líquidos).

pulverizador *m* pulverizer ‖ jet (del carburador) ‖ spray gun (para pintar) ‖ atomizer, spray (de perfume).

pulverizar *vt* to pulverize ‖ to atomize, to spray (un líquido) ‖ FIG to shatter, to smash; *pulverizar un vaso* to shatter a glass | to pulverize, to smash; *pulverizar al enemigo, un récord* to smash the enemy, a record | to tear to pieces; *pulverizar una teoría* to tear a theory to pieces | to dissipate, to waste; *pulverizó su fortuna* he dissipated his fortune.
◆ *vpr* to pulverize.

pulverulencia *f* pulverulence.

pulverulento, ta *adj* pulverulent.

pulla *f* taunt, gibe (expresión aguda y picante) ‖ dig, cutting remark (observación mordaz) ‖ obscenity, obscene word (palabra grosera) ‖ FAM insinuation; *tirar pullas a uno* to make insinuations about s.o. ‖ AMER machete.

pullman *m* pullman.

pull-over *m* pullover.

¡pum! *interj* boom!, bang!

puma *m* ZOOL puma.

puna *f* AMER «puna» (páramo) | «puna», mountain sickness (soroche).

punción *f* MED puncture; *punción lumbar* lumbar puncture ‖ sharp pain (punzada).

puncionar *vt* to puncture.

punching ball *m* punchball [US punching bag].

pundonor *m* honour, dignity.

pundonoroso, sa *adj* honourable, honest (honrado) ‖ conscientious (concienzudo).

puneño, ña *adj* [of *o* from] Puno (Perú).
◆ *m/f* native *o* inhabitant of Puno.

pungente *adj* sharp, stabbing (dolor).

pungimiento *m* prick (punzada).

pungir *vt* to prick, to punch (punzar).

punible *adj* punishable (castigable).

punición *f* punishment.

púnico, ca *adj* Punic (cartaginés); *las Guerras Púnicas* the Punic wars ‖ FIG *fe púnica* bad faith.

punir *vt* (p us) to punish.

punitivo, va *adj* punitive.

punitorio, ria *adj* AMER punitive.

Punjab *npr m* GEOGR Punjab.

punk *adj* punk.

punki *m/f* punk.

punta *f* point (extremo agudo) ‖ tip (extremo); *punta del pie* tip of the toe ‖ head, point (de una flecha) ‖ end (final) ‖ horn (asta del toro) ‖ point (lengua de tierra) ‖ sourness (sabor agrio del vino) ‖ pointing, point (del perro de caza) ‖ butt (colilla) ‖ nib (de una herramienta) ‖ nail (clavo) ‖ FIG bit, streak; *tener una punta de loco* to have a streak of madness, to be a bit crazy ‖ MIL point ‖ small bunch (de ganado) ‖ AMER group (de personas) | bunch (de cosas) | source (cabecera de río) ‖ — AMER *a punta de* by means of ‖ FAM *a punta de pala* or *a punta pala* in large quantity, a lot ‖ *con el escote en punta* V-neck ‖ *de punta* on end ‖ *de punta a cabo, de punta a punta* from one end to the other, from A to Z ‖ *de punta en blanco* dressed up to the nines (muy bien vestido), in full armour (con la armadura completa) ‖ FIG *estar de punta con* to be at odds with (enfadados) | *estar hasta la punta de los pelos de* to be fed up with ‖ *horas punta* rush hours, peak hours ‖ FIG *poner los nervios de punta* to set one's nerves on edge, to get on one's nerves | *poner los pelos de punta a uno* to make one's hair stand on end | *ponerse de punta* to stand on end (el pelo) | *ponerse de punta con uno* to get angry with s.o. ‖ *sacar punta a* to sharpen (afilar), to find fault with (interpretar maliciosamente); *sacan punta a todo lo que digo* they find fault with everything I say ‖ FIG *tener algo en la punta de la lengua* to have sth. on the tip of one's tongue | *tener los nervios de punta* to be (all) on edge ‖ FIG *tratar a alguien con la punta del pie* to kick s.o. around ‖ *velocidad punta* top speed.
◆ *pl* point lace *sing*, needlepoint *sing* (encaje) ‖ *bailar de puntas* to dance on tiptoe.

puntada *f* stitch; *coser a puntadas largas* to sew with long stitches ‖ FIG note (apunte) | sharp pain (punzada) | insinuation (indirecta) ‖ FIG & FAM *no dar puntada* not to do a thing.

puntal *m* prop, shore, strut (madero) ‖ FIG support (sostén) | foundation, base (elemento principal) | pillar; *este chico es el puntal del equipo* this boy is the pillar of the team ‖ MAR depth (altura del barco) | stanchion.

puntano, na *adj* [of *o* from] San Luis [Argentina].
◆ *m/f* native *o* inhabitant of San Luis.

puntapié *m* kick ‖ *echar a puntapiés* to kick out.

puntarenense *adj* [of *o* from] Punta Arenas [Chile], [of *o* from] Puntarenas [Costa Rica].
◆ *m/f* native *o* inhabitant of Punta Arenas [Chile] *o* Puntarenas [Costa Rica].

puntazo *m* sligh gore (cornada).

punteado *m* MÚS plucking (de guitarra) ‖ dotted line (serie de puntos) ‖ dotting, stippling (acción).

puntear *vt* MÚS to pluck (las cuerdas) | to dot (una nota) ‖ to check (en una lista) ‖ to dot, to mark with dots (trazar puntos) ‖ to check (una cuenta) ‖ to dot (hacer puntos) ‖ AMER to lead, to walk at the front of.

puntel *m* punty (en fábricas de vidrio).

punteo *m* plucking (de guitarra) ‖ COM checking (de una cuenta).

puntera *f* toe (de media) ‖ toecap (de calzado) ‖ cap, top (para lápices) ‖ FAM kick (puntapié) ‖ *de puntera* with the tip of the toe (fútbol).

puntería *f* aiming, aim (de un arma) ‖ aim; *enmendar la puntería* to change one's aim ‖ FIG marksmanship (destreza) ‖ — *dirigir la puntería* to aim (*hacia* at), to aim (sin disparar), to shoot at (disparando) ‖ *tener buena, mala puntería* to be a good, bad shot, to be a good, bad marksman.

puntero, ra *adj* outstanding; *un médico, un equipo puntero* an outstanding physician, team.
◆ *m* pointer (para señalar) ‖ TECN puncheon (de herrero) | chisel (de cantero) ‖ INFORM pointer.

punterola *f* MIN small pick.

puntiagudo, da *adj* pointed, sharp.

puntilla *f* fine lace, picot (encaje) ‖ nib (de una pluma) ‖ tack (tachuela) ‖ TAUR «puntilla», dagger [for finishing off the bull] ‖ FIG the final blow, the last straw (remate) ‖ TECN tracing point || AMER penknife (cortaplumas) || — *andar de puntillas* to walk on tiptoe, to tiptoe || *dar la puntilla a* to kill, to finish off (un toro), to finish (una persona) || *de puntillas* on tiptoe.

puntillazo *m* kick (puntapié) || coup de grâce (al toro).

puntillero *m* TAUR bullfighter who deals the coup de grâce.

puntillismo *m* pointillism (pintura).

puntillista *adj/s* pointillist (pintor).

puntillo *m* punctilio, unimportant point (nimiedad) || MÚS dot || honour (pundonor).

puntilloso, sa *adj* ticklish, punctilious (quisquilloso) || finical, punctilious (detallista y exigente).

punto *m* dot, point (señal) || sight (del fusil) || place, spot, point (lugar) || stitch (costura); *punto por encima, de cadeneta, de cruz, de dobladillo* overcast, chain, cross, hem stitch; *escapársele a uno un punto* to drop a stitch || mark (de las notas escolares) || taxi rank *o* stand || point (que se gana en toda clase de juegos) || point (de una pluma) || point (en una discusión); *en ese punto no estamos de acuerdo* we differ on that point || subject, matter (asunto) || item (del orden del día) || honour, dignity (pundonor) || punter (que juega contra la banca en los juegos de azar) || moment (momento) || hole (agujero) || dot (de la *i* y la *j*) || full stop [*US* period] (al final de la frase) || MED stitch (en cirugía) || IMPR point (medida tipográfica) || FÍS point; *punto de fusión, de congelación* melting, freezing point || FIG & FAM rascal, rogue (sinvergüenza) || MAR reckoning, position; *echar* or *señalar* or *hacer el punto* to plot the reckoning || GEOGR point; *puntos cardinales* cardinal points || MÚS dot, point (señal) | pitch (tono) || — *al llegar a este punto* at this point, having come thus far || *al punto* at once, immediately || *al punto que* at the very moment that || *a punto* ready (preparado), on time (a la hora); *llegar a punto* to arrive on time; just right, just at the right time, just in time (en el momento oportuno) || FIG *a* or *en punto de caramelo* at a perfect moment, just at the right time || *a punto fijo* exactly, for sure, precisely || ARQ *arco de medio punto* semicircular arch || *bajar de punto* to decline, to decrease || *coger los puntos* to mend, to pick up the stitches || FIG *con puntos y comas* in detail, in minute detail, in every detail | *conocer los puntos que calza uno* to know what s.o. is capable of, to know where one stands with s.o. | *dar el punto a algo* to do sth. to a turn, to do sth. just right | FIG *dar en el punto* to hit the nail on the head || *dar veinte puntos de ventaja* to give a twenty point advantage || *de punto* knitted || *de todo punto* absolutely; *es de todo punto imposible* it's absolutely impossible || *dos puntos* colon || *en punto* sharp, on the dot; *son las dos en punto* it's two on the dot; *ven a las dos en punto* come at 2 sharp || *en su punto* done to a turn, just right, perfect, ready; *el arroz está en su punto ahora* the rice is done to a turn || *estar a punto de* to be about to, to be on the point of; *estoy a punto de salir* I am about to go out; to be on the verge of; *estar a punto de caerse* to be on the verge of falling || *hacer punto* to knit || *hasta cierto punto* up to a point, to a certain extent || *hasta el punto de* to the point of, to the extent of || *hasta tal punto* to such a point *o* an extent || *labores de punto* knitting || *línea de puntos* dotted line, stippled line || FIG *no perder punto* not to miss a thing || *poner a punto* to tune up (un motor, una máquina, etc.), to finish off, to round off, to put the finishing touch to (dar el último toque) || FIG *poner en su punto* to get into shape | *poner los puntos a alguien* or *algo* to have got one's eye on s.o. *o* sth. | *poner los puntos sobre las íes* to dot the i's and cross the t's | *poner punto en boca* to shut up || *poner punto final a* to put a stop to (suprimir), to finish (acabar) || *por puntos* on points; *victoria por puntos* a win on points (en boxeo) || AMER *punto acápite* full stop, new paragraph [*US* period, new paragraph] || *punto crítico* critical point || *punto culminante* climax, high point (culminación), highest peak *o* mountain (de un país) || *punto de apoyo* fulcrum (física), base; *establecer un punto de apoyo para una red comercial* to set up a base for a commercial network || *punto de arranque* starting point || FIG *punto débil* weak spot *o* point || MED *punto débil* weak spot *o* point || MED *punto de costado* stitch (dolor) || *punto de ebullición* boiling point || *punto de honor* point of honour || *punto de interrogación, de admiración* question, exclamation mark || *punto de mira* front sight (de arma), target (objetivo) || *punto de partida* starting point || *punto de penalty* penalty spot (en fútbol) || *punto de referencia* point of reference || *punto de venta* sales outlet || *punto de vista* point of view, viewpoint; *desde este punto de vista* from this point of view || FIG *¡punto en boca!* mum's the word!, don't say a word! || FAM *es un punto filipino* he is a scoundrel *o* a rogue || *punto final* full stop || *punto flaco* weak spot *o* point || *punto menos que* a shade less than, not quite || *punto muerto* neutral (automóvil), dead centre (en mecánica), deadlock, stalemate, impasse; *las negociaciones han llegado a un punto muerto* the negociations have reached a deadlock || *punto por punto* point by point || *puntos de sutura* stitches || *puntos suspensivos* suspension marks *o* points || *punto y aparte* full stop, new paragraph [*US* period, new paragraph] (escritura), another story; *eso ya es punto y aparte* that's another story || *punto y coma* semicolon.

puntuable *adj* counting.

puntuación *f* punctuation (escribiendo) || scoring (acción de marcar puntos) || score, number of points (en deportes, recuentos, etc.) || mark [*US* grade] (calificación) || *signos de puntuación* punctuation marks.

puntual *adj* punctual; *es muy puntual* he is very punctual || precise, accurate, reliable, punctual; *un puntual relato* an accurate account || exact.
◆ *adv* on time, punctually; *llegó puntual a la cita* he arrived on time for the appointment.

puntualidad *f* punctuality || exactness, preciseness, accuracy (precisión).

puntualizar *vt* to arrange, to fix (concretar); *puntualicemos el lugar de la cita* let us arrange a meeting place || to fix in mind (grabar en la memoria) || to settle, to determine (determinar) || to describe in detail, to give a detailed account of (referir detalladamente) || to perfect, to put the finishing touches to (perfeccionar).

puntualmente *adv* punctually (con puntualidad) || on time, punctually; *llegó puntualmente* he arrived on time || in detail (punto por punto); *me contó puntualmente lo sucedido* he told me what happened in detail.

puntuar *vt* to punctuate (al escribir) || to mark [*US* to grade] (poner notas).
◆ *vi* to score (points) (en deportes).

punzada *f* prick (herida) || FIG sharp pain (dolor agudo) | pang (de conciencia) || — *me da punzadas el pie* I have sharp pains in my foot || *punzada en el costado* stitch, sharp pain in the side.

punzador, ra *adj* pricking.

punzante *adj* prickly, pricking (que pincha) || sharp, shooting (dolor físico) || sharp (agudo, en punta) || FIG cutting, biting (mordaz) | caustic, biting (mortificante).

punzar *vt* to prick || TECN to punch || FIG to give shooting pains (un dolor) | to prick (la conciencia) | to torment (atormentar).

punzó *adj* flame-red, ponceau (rojo muy vivo).

punzón *m* TECN needle (de válvula de aguja) | burin (buril) | punch (para marcar monedas) | pricker (dibujo).

punzonar *vt* TECN to punch.

puñada *f* punch (puñetazo) || *dar de puñadas* to punch.

puñado *m* handful (porción); *un puñado de arena* a handful of sand || FIG handful; *un puñado de gente* a handful of people || FIG *a puñados* by the handful, lots of; *gasta dinero a puñados* he spends lots of money, he spends money by the handful.

puñal *m* dagger || FIG *poner el puñal en el pecho* to hold a knife at s.o.'s throat.

puñalada *f* stab [of a dagger] || FIG blow, shock; *la pérdida de su hijo fue para ella una puñalada* the loss of her son was a blow to her | sudden stab of pain (dolor) || — FIG & FAM *coser a puñaladas a uno* to cut s.o. to pieces | *dar una puñalada trapera* to stab (s.o.) in the back || *murió de una puñalada* he was stabbed to death, he died of a stab wound || FIG & FAM *¡no es puñalada de pícaro!* there is no great rush.

puñeta *f* POP *hacer la puñeta* to get on (s.o.'s) nerves, to pester, to annoy (molestar), to mess things up (for s.o.) (estropearlo todo) || AMER POP to masturbate || POP *¡qué puñeta!* hell! | *ser la puñeta* to be a drag *o* a bind *o* a bore | *¡vete a hacer puñetas!* get lost!, go to hell!

puñetazo *m* punch || — *a puñetazos* with one's fist *o* fists || *dar a uno de puñetazos* to punch s.o. || *dar puñetazos en* to hammer on, to pound on (la mesa, etc.).

puñetero, ra *adj* POP rotten, lousy, stinking; *un trabajo puñetero* a rotten job | bloody; *no cuenta más que el puñetero dinero* money is the only bloody thing that counts || POP *vida puñetera* dog's life.

puño *m* fist (mano cerrada) || handful (puñado) || cuff (de una camisa) || handle (mango) || handlebar (de bicicleta) || MAR tack (de una vela); *puño de la amura* tack of a sail || hilt (de una espada) || — *amenazar a alguien con el puño* to threaten s.o. with one's fist, to shake one's fist at s.o. || FIG *apretar los puños* to try one's best || *a puño cerrado* with one's fists || FIG & FAM *caber en un puño* to fit in the palm of one's hand | *comerse los puños* to be starving, to be famished | *como puños* great big, whopping great (enorme) | *como un puño* as big as your fist; *un huevo como un puño* an egg as big as your fist; tiny, very small; *una habitación como un puño* a very small room || *de su puño y letra* by (his, her, etc.) own hand || FIG & FAM *es una verdad como un puño* it's as plain as a pikestaff | *hombre de puños* strong man | *meter a uno en un puño* to get s.o. in the palm of one's hand | *morderse los puños* to kick o.s. | *por puños* on one's own | *tener a alguien en un puño* to have s.o. under one's thumb, to have s.o. eating out of one's hand.

pupa *f* pustule, pimple || cold sore (en los labios) || scab (postilla) || hurt, sore (en lenguaje infantil) || FIG & FAM *hacer pupa a uno* to hurt s.o.

pupila *f* pupil (del ojo) || prostitute (de una casa de trato) || ward, pupil, orphan (huérfano) || boarder (huésped) || FIG ward (protegido) || FAM *tener pupila* to be sharp.

pupilaje *m* JUR pupilage, pupillage (condición de pupilo) || tutelage, guardianship (tutela) || boarding-house (casa de huéspedes) || fee, board (precio).

pupilar *adj* pupillar.

pupilo, la *m/f* ward, pupil, orphan (huérfano) || boarder (huésped) || FIG ward (protegido) || *casa de pupilos* boardinghouse (casa de huéspedes).

pupitre *m* desk (mueble de madera) || INFORM console.

pupo *m* AMER navel (ombligo).

puquial; puquio *m* AMER spring, source.

puramente *adv* purely, simply (simplemente).

puré *m* purée; *puré de tomates* tomato purée || — FIG & FAM *estar hecho puré* to be shattered (hecho añicos, muy cansado, muy abatido) || FIG *puré de guisantes* pea-souper [*US* pea soup], thick fog (niebla) || *puré de patatas* mashed potatoes.

pureza *f* purity, pureness (calidad de puro) || virginity (doncellez) || FIG innocence.

purga *f* purgative, purge (medicina) || FIG purge (eliminación) || TECN residue (restos).

purgación *f* MED purgation (acción de purgarse) || period (menstruación) || REL purgation.
◆ *pl* MED FAM gonorrhoea *sing*, the clap *sing (fam)*.

purgador, ra *adj* TECN purging.
◆ *m* TECN purge cock.

purgamiento *m* purgation, purging.

purgante *adj* purgative || *iglesia purgante* church suffering.
◆ *m* purgative, purge.

purgar *vt* to purge (a un enfermo) || to cleanse, to clean (limpiar) || FIG to purify (purificar) | to purge, to liquidate (eliminar) | to expiate, to purge, to atone for; *purgar una culpa* to expiate an error || TECN to drain, to vent || *purgar los caracoles* to clean snails.
◆ *vpr* to take a purgative.

purgativo, va *adj* purgative (que purga).

purgatorio *m* purgatory; *ánima* or *alma del purgatorio* soul in purgatory || FIG purgatory.

puridad *f* purity (pureza).

purificación *f* purification || *la fiesta de la Purificación* the Purification.

purificador, ra *adj* purifying, cleansing.
◆ *m/f* purifier (persona que purifica).
◆ *m* REL purificator (para el cáliz y para los dedos).

purificar *vt* to purify || to cleanse (limpiar).
◆ *vpr* to become purified, to purify.

purificatorio, ria *adj* purificatory.

Purísima *npr f* REL the Immaculate Conception.

purismo *m* purism.

purista *adj* puristical, puristic.
◆ *m/f* purist.

puritanismo *m* puritanism.

puritano, na *adj* puritan, puritanical.
◆ *m/f* puritan.

puro, ra *adj* pure (sin mezcla); *oro puro, ciencias puras* pure gold, pure sciences || sheer; *la vi por pura casualidad* I saw her by sheer chance; *por puro aburrimiento* out of sheer boredom || simple, plain; *la pura verdad* the plain truth || pure; *puro castellano* pure Castilian || chaste, pure (casto) || neat, straight (bebida alcohólica) || clear (el cielo) || AMER only, just (solamente) || — *a puro* by means of, by dint of || *de puro cansado se desmayó* he collapsed from sheer tiredness, he was so tired that he just collapsed || *de puro gordo no cabe por la puerta* he is so fat that he can't get through the door || *un pura sangre* a thoroughbred (caballo).

puro *m* cigar (cigarro puro).

púrpura *f* purple (molusco) || purple (colorante, tela) || purple (color) || POÉT blood (sangre) || FIG purple (dignidad) || MED purpura || HERÁLD purpure.

purpurado *m* cardinal (prelado).

purpurar *vt* to dye purple (teñir de púrpura) || to dress in purple.

purpurear *vi* to have a purple hue.

purpúreo, a *adj* purple.

purpurina *f* purpurin (sustancia colorante roja) || metallic paint (pintura).

purpurino, na *adj* purple (purpúreo).

purulencia *f* MED purulence.

purulento, ta *adj* purulent.

purria *f* FAM riff-raff.

pus *m* MED pus, matter.

pusilánime *adj* pusillanimous, fainthearted (tímido).

pusilanimidad *f* pusillanimity, faintheartedness, cowardliness (cobardía).

pústula *f* MED pustule, pimple.

pustuloso, sa *adj* MED pustular; *erupción pustulosa* pustular eruption || pustulous, pustulate, pimply; *cara pustulosa* pimply face.

puta *f* POP whore.

putada *f* POP dirty trick (faena).

putativo, va *adj* putative, supposed.

putear *vt* POP to piss s.o. about, to mess s.o. about.
◆ *vi* POP to go whoring (andar de putas) | to solicit (una prostituta).

puto *m* POP bugger (cabrón).

putrefacción *f* putrefaction, rotting, decay.

putrefacto, ta *adj* putrefied, rotten.

putrescente *adj* putrescent, rotting.

putridez *f* putrefaction, rotting.

pútrido, da *adj* putrid, putrified, rotten.

putsch *m* putsch (alzamiento).

puya *f* TAUR steel point, goad [of the lance] | jab *o* blow with the lance || FIG dig, gibe, cutting remark (pulla).

puyazo *m* blow *o* jab with the lance || FIG dig, gibe, cutting remark.

puzle *m* jigsaw, jigsaw puzzle.

puzolana *f* pozzolana (roca volcánica).

PVP *abrev de Precio de Venta al Público* published price.

Pza *abrev de plaza* sq, square.

Q

q *f* q.

— OBSERV This letter in Spanish is always followed by a silent *u* and has the sound of the *c* in the English word *cave.*

quantum *m* FÍS quantum || *teoría de los quanta* quantum theory.

— OBSERV pl *quanta.*

Qatar *n pr* GEOGR Katar, Qatar.

que *pron rel* who, that (sujeto para personas); *el hombre que vive aquí* the man who lives here || whom, who, that (complemento para personas); *el hombre que vi* the man (whom) I saw véase OBSERV || that, which (sujeto y complemento para cosas); *el libro que está sobre la mesa* the book that is on the table; *el libro que estoy leyendo* the book (that) I am reading || which (se puede omitir cambiando el orden de la frase); *el cuchillo con (el) que corto el pan* the knife with which I cut the bread, the knife I cut the bread with; *la silla en (la) que estoy sentado* the chair in which I am sitting, the chair I am sitting in || what; *es lo que pensaba* that is what I was thinking of || — *al que, a la que* to (whom); *la mujer a la que me dirigí* the woman to whom I spoke, the woman I spoke to; to (which); *el libro al que me refiero* the book to which I am referring, the book I am referring to || *dar que pensar* to make one think || *de que, del que, de la que, de los que, de las que* of whom; *el hombre del que hablo* the man of whom I am speaking; of which (para cosas); *estas revistas, de las que varias son nuestras* these magazines, several of which are ours || *de que se trata* in question; *el asunto de que se trata* the matter in question || *el día que llegaste* the day you arrived *o* of your arrival || *en el momento en que* the moment (that) (en cuanto); *en el momento en que llegue* the moment he arrives; just as (justo cuando) || *es por lo que* that is why || *es su padre el que manda* it is his father who commands || *lo que es peor* what is more *o* worse || FAM *¡lo que faltaba!* that's all we needed! || *lo que quieras* anything you like || *yo que tú* if I were you.

◆ *conj* (no se traduce); *quiero que vengas* I want you to come; *te dije que volvieras más tarde* I told you to come back later; *le ruego que venga* I beg you to come || that (se omite con frecuencia); *me temo que lo haya echado todo a perder* I'm afraid (that) he may have ruined everything; *¿sabes que me caso mañana?* do you know (that) I'm getting married tomorrow? || because (se omite con frecuencia); *hable más fuerte, que oigo mal* speak louder (because) I can't hear you; *no podemos, que no tenemos dinero* we can't, we have no money || or; *queramos que no* whether we like it or not; *dámelo que te pego* give it to me or I'll hit you || if; *que viene, bien, que no viene, nos arreglamos sin él* if he comes, fine, if he doesn't, we'll manage without him || — *antes que* before; *no iré antes que todo esté listo* I'll not leave before everything is ready; *antes que yo* before me || *a que* I bet that; *¡a que llego primero! ¡a que no!* I bet (that) I get there first I bet you don't! || *¡claro que no!* of course not! || *¡claro que sí!* of course! || *corre que te corre* in a hurry, fast || *cualquier otro que no fuese él* anyone but him || *decir que no, que sí* to say no, yes || *el que* the fact that, that; *me extraña el que no me hayan dicho nada* I am surprised (that) they haven't said anything, the fact that they haven't said anything surprises me || *está que parece otro* he seems another person || *más, menos que* more, less than || *no hay más que apretar el botón* you only have to press the button || *no hay más que hablar* there's nothing more to be said || *que da asco* disgusting (adj), disgustingly (adv) || *que da gloria* or *gusto* marvellously, beautifully (adv), lovely, wonderful (adj) || *que da* or *que mete miedo* fearsome, frightful (adj), frighteningly, fearsomely, frightfully, dreadfully (adv); *de un feo que mete miedo* dreadfully ugly || *¡que lo echen!* throw him out! || *¡que me dejen en paz* or *tranquilo!* leave me alone!, stop pestering me! (vds), tell them to leave me alone (ellos) || *que no no; dijo que no* he said no; of course not (claro que no), no, no (enérgicamente), not; *era su tía que no su madre* it was his aunt not his mother; without; *no hay día que no me acuerde de ella* not a day goes by without my thinking of her || *¡que se divierta!* enjoy yourself!, have fun! | *que sí* yes (sí), of course (claro que sí) || *¡que si era él!* yes it was him || *que tengan ustedes mucha suerte* I wish you (good) luck || *tan... que* so... that || *tanto más cuanto que* all the more so since || *ya que* since.

— OBSERV En inglés, el pronombre relativo con función de complemento se omite muy frecuentemente: *el libro que estoy leyendo* the book I am reading; *el chico que vi* the boy I saw.

— OBSERV Cuando *que* se refiere a personas y tiene función de complemento directo, la forma *who* sustituye con frecuencia *whom*, en la lengua hablada, aunque sea incorrecto desde un punto de vista puramente gramatical.

qué *adj interr y exclamat* what (con sustantivo); *¿qué hora es?* what time is it?; *¡qué suerte!* what luck!; *¡qué chico más simpático!* what a nice boy!; *¡qué idea tan rara!* what a strange idea! || which (entre varios); *¿qué color prefieres?* which colour do you prefer? || how (con adj. o adv); *¡qué despacio va este tren!* how slow this train is going!; *¿qué edad tienes?* how old are you?; *¡qué calor hace!* how hot it is!; *¡qué guapa estás!* how pretty you look! || — *¿de qué tamaño?* what size?, how big? || *¡qué bien!* how marvellous! || *¡qué de!* what a lot of; *¡qué de gente!* what a lot of people! || *¡qué divertido!* what fun! || *¡qué miedo!* what a fright! (¡qué susto!), how scary!, how frightening! (¡qué espantoso!).

◆ *pron interr* what; *¿qué pasa?* what's happening?; *¿qué dijiste?* what did you say?; *¿qué es esto?* what is this?; *¿en qué piensa usted?* what are you thinking about?; *¿para qué sirve esto?* what is this for? || — *¿de qué le sirve tener un coche si no sabe conducir?* what good is a car to you if you don't know how to drive? || *¿de qué se trata?* what's it all about? || *el qué dirán* what people say || *¿qué dice?* what did you say? || *¿qué es de Pedro?* how is Peter? || *¿qué es de su vida?* how are you? || *¿qué es lo que ocurre?* what is the matter? || *¿qué hay?* how are you?, what's new? (¿qué tal?), what's up?, what's the matter? (¿qué pasa?) || *¿qué le parece?* what do you think of it? || *¿qué más da?* what difference does it make? || *¿qué sé yo?* how should I know? || *¿qué tal?* how?; *¿qué tal le pareció la película?* how did you like the film?; *¿qué tal el viaje?* how was the trip? || FAM *¿qué tal?* how are you? | *¡qué va!* come off it!, nonsense!, rubbish! || *un no sé qué* a certain something || *¿y a mí qué?* what about me? (¿y para mí?), what's that got to do with me? (¿qué tiene que ver conmigo?) || *¿y qué?* so what?

Québec *n pr* *m* GEOGR Quebec.

quebracho *m* quebracho (árbol) || breakaxe [*US* breakax] (madera).

quebrada *f* narrow pass (paso entre montañas) || ravine, gorge (hondonada) || *AMER* stream.

quebradero *m* FIG & FAM *quebradero de cabeza* headache; *ya tengo suficientes quebraderos de cabeza* I've got enough headaches already.

quebradizo, za *adj* fragile, brittle; *el cristal es quebradizo* crystal is fragile || FIG fragile, frail, delicate; *salud quebradiza* fragile health | feeble, weak (voz).

quebrado, da *adj* broken (roto) || broken, rough, uneven (terreno) || MED herniary || FIG dull, dim (color) | hoarse, faltering; *voz quebrada por la emoción* voice hoarse with emotion || COM bankrupt || — *línea quebrada* broken line || *número quebrado* fraction.

◆ *m* MAT fraction; *quebrado decimal* decimal fraction || MED hernia || COM bankrupt.

quebradura *f* fracture, break (fractura) || crack, fissure, split (grieta) || MED hernia, rupture.

quebrantador, ra *adj* contravening (de la ley) || crushing (que machaca).

◆ *m/f* offender, violator, transgressor (de la ley).

quebrantahuesos *m inv* ZOOL lammergeyer [*US* lammergeier] (ave que vive en regiones montañosas) | osprey, fish hawk (pigargo) || FIG & FAM bore (pesado).

quebrantamiento *m* breaking, breaking up || FIG violation, contravention, infringement; *quebrantamiento de la ley* violation of the law | breaking, breach (de un compromiso, del ayuno) | weakening, deterioration (de la salud) | broken health (salud quebrantada) | exhaustion (agotamiento) || — *quebrantamiento de destierro* violation of exile || JUR *quebrantamiento de forma* faulty drafting | *quebrantamiento de sellos* breaking of seals.

quebrantaolas *m inv* MAR breakwater.

quebrantar *vt* to break; *quebrantar un vaso* to break a glass || to crush (machacar); *quebrantar aceitunas* to crush olives || to split (hender) || to crack (resquebrajar) || FIG to break, to violate, to transgress; *quebrantar la ley* to break the law | to break (promesa, sello, ayuno) | to lower, to break; *quebrantar el ánimo, la moral (a uno)* to lower (s.o.'s) spirits, morale | to weaken (debilitar) | to shake; *quebrantar*

una convicción to shake s.o.'s conviction | to harm, to injure (salud) | to warm (templar un líquido) | to tone down, to soften (color) | to force open (abrir forzando) | to break into (entrar sin derecho) || *quebrantar el destierro* to violate one's exile.
◆ *vpr* to break, to crack, to split (romperse) || FIG to crack up (una persona).

quebranto *m* weakening, deterioration (deterioro) || exhaustion (agotamiento) || broken health (salud quebrantada) || discouragement (del ánimo) || loss (pérdida) || damage, harm (daño) || affliction, distress (dolor profundo) || *quebranto de fortuna* severe financial setback.

quebrar* *vt* to break; *quebrar un vaso* to break a glass || to bend, to twist (doblar, torcer); *quebrar el cuerpo* to bend one's body || FIG to put an end to (acabar con) | to tone down, to soften (templar un color).
◆ *vi* to break (romperse) || COM to go bankrupt.
◆ *vpr* to break, to be broken (romperse) || MED to rupture o.s. (herniarse) || FIG to break, to become hoarse; *se le quebró la voz con la emoción* her voice became hoarse with emotion || — FAM *no quebrarse* not to overdo it | *quebrarse la cabeza* to rack one's brains.

queche *m* MAR ketch.

quechemarín *m* AMER coasting lugger (lugre).

quechua *adj* Quechuan.
◆ *m/f* Quechua.

quechuismo; quichuismo *m* Quechuan word *o* expression.

queda *f* curfew; *tocar a queda* to sound the curfew || *toque de queda* curfew [bell].

quedar *vi* to remain, to stay (permanecer); *la chica quedó en casa* the girl stayed at home || to remain; *al final quedaron muy amigos* in the end they remained good friends || to arrange to meet; *quedé con ellos a las ocho* I arranged to meet them at eight o'clock || to be; *queda lejos* it is a long way away; *la junta quedó constituida tras la segunda votación* the board was constituted after the second vote; *su segunda novela queda muy por debajo de la primera* his second novel is quite inferior to his first; *quedé extrañadísimo* I was astonished; *quedar fuera de peligro* to be out of danger || to stand; *así queda la cosa* that's how it stands || to end, to stop, to leave off; *ahí quedó la conversación* the conversation ended there || to be left; *quedan cinco minutos* there are five minutes left || — *¿dónde habíamos quedado?* where were we? (¿qué decíamos?) || *¿en qué quedamos?* what is it to be?, what shall we do? (¿qué hacemos?), so; *¿en qué quedamos?, ¿vienes o no vienes?* so, are you coming or not? || *eso queda a mi cuidado* I'll take care of that || *he quedado con ella a las ocho* I have a date with her at eight || *la carta quedó sin contestar* the letter remained unanswered *o* was left unanswered || *la chaqueta queda corta* the jacket is too short for him || *me quedan sólo cinco pesetas* I've only got five pesetas left || *por mí que no quede* do as you please, don't let me stop you || *queda de usted atentamente* I remain, yours faithfully, Yours faithfully (en una carta) || *queda de usted su affmo, y s. s.* Yours faithfully (en una carta) || *quedan cinco días para los exámenes* there are five days to go before the exams || *¿queda pan?* is there any bread left? || *queda por saber si* it remains to || *algo que ni pintado* to fit like a glove; *el traje le queda que ni pintado* the suits fits him like a glove; to be *o* to look perfect; *este cuadro queda aquí que ni pintado* this painting looks perfect here || *quedar bien* to look good; *el cuarto queda muy bien con su nuevo empapelado* the room looks very good with the new wallpaper; to go well; *quedan bien tus nuevos zapatos con tu traje gris* your new shoes go well with your grey suit; to go down well, to perform well; *el cantante ha quedado bien* the singer performed well; to make a good impression; *regalando flores siempre quedas bien* you always make a good impression with flowers || *quedar ciego* to go blind (por viejo, etc.), to be blinded (por un accidente) || *quedar cojo* to be lamed *o* crippled || *quedar con vida* to survive || *quedar de acuerdo* to agree, to reach an agreement || *quedar en* to agree to, to decide to; *quedamos en salir mañana* we have agreed to go out tomorrow; *quedaron en ir todos de negro* they all agreed to go dressed in black; to agree, to say (that); *quedó en venir a las siete* he agreed to come at seven, he said he was coming at seven || *quedar mal* to come out badly, to look bad; *la foto quedó muy mal* the photo came out very badly; to perform badly; *el cantante quedó tan mal que le pitaron* the singer performed so badly that he was booed; to make a bad impression; *he quedado muy mal con sus padres* I made a very bad impression on her parents || *quedar para* to arrange to meet; *hemos quedado para mañana* we have arranged to meet tomorrow || *quedar por* to remain to be, to have still to be; *queda mucho por hacer* much remains to be done; *queda por pagar el teléfono* the telephone bill has still to be paid || *quedar todo en casa* to remain in the family; *metiendo al niño en el negocio, todo quedará en casa* if we put our son in the business it will remain in the family || FAM *ya le queda poco* he doesn't have much longer, he doesn't have much time left.
◆ *vpr* to stay, to remain; *se quedó un año en Lima* he stayed a year in Lima; *quedarse en la cama, en casa* to stay in bed, at home; *quedarse silencioso* to remain silent || to stay (en un hotel, etc.) || to go, to become; *quedarse cojo, ciego, sordo* to go lame, blind, deaf || to remain, to stay; *quedarse soltero* to stay single || to be left; *quedarse huérfano* to be left an orphan || — FAM *me quedé de una pieza* I was speechless *o* flabbergasted || *no saber con qué quedarse* not to know what to choose || FIG *quedarse ahí* to die (morir) || *quedarse anticuado* to go out of fashion *o* style || FIG *quedarse a oscuras* or *in albis* to remain *o* to be left in the dark || *quedarse atrás* to stay behind (queriendo), to be left behind (sin querer) || *quedarse boquiabierto* or *con la boca abierta* to stand agape, gaping, openmouthed; *me quedé boquiabierto cuando la vi* I stood agape *o* gaping when I saw her || FIG & FAM *quedarse como quien ve visiones* to look as if one has seen a ghost || *quedarse (con)* to keep; *se quedó con mi libro* he kept my book; *si te gusta tanto quédatelo* if you like it so much, keep it; to take (tomar); *me quedo con éste* I'll take this one; to have left; *después de haber comprado este vestido me quedé con cien pesetas* after buying this dress I had a hundred pesetas left; to be left with (cargar con) || FIG *quedarse con un palmo* or *dos palmos de narices* to be out of luck || *quedarse con hambre* to still be hungry || FIG *quedarse con las ganas* to have to do without, to have to go without, to have to forget the idea, not to get what one wanted | *quedarse con uno* to fool s.o. (engañar) | *quedarse cortado* not to know what to say || *quedarse corto* to fall short (un tiro), to be *o* to go short (dinero), to underestimate, to miscalculate (calcular mal), not to say all one could, to be unable to say enough (en un relato) || *quedarse de piedra* to be thunderstruck || *quedarse encima* to have the last word || *quedarse en el poyete* or *poyetón* to be a wallflower (en un baile), to be left on the shelf (quedar solterona) || FIG & FAM *quedarse en la calle* to be homeless, to be in the street (sin casa), to be left jobless (sin empleo) || FIG *quedarse helado* to be dumb-founded *o* flabbergasted (sorpresa), to be scared stiff (miedo) || *quedarse limpio* to be cleaned out || *quedarse pálido* to turn pale || FIG *quedarse para vestir santos* to be left on the shelf || FIG & FAM *quedarse plantado* to stand (permanecer), to be left standing there (quedarse solo) || *quédate quieto* keep quiet (cállate), keep still (no te muevas) || *quedarse sin* to run out of (acabársele a uno); *me he quedado sin tinta* I have run out of ink; to be left (without); *quedarse sin habla* to be left speechless; *quedarse sin esperanzas* to be left in despair *o* without hope; *quedarse sin trabajo* to be left jobless *o* without work; *quedarse sin una gorda* to be left penniless *o* without a penny; not to, to go without (con verbo); *quedarse sin comer* not to eat || *se me quedó mirando* he just stared at me.

quedo, da *adj* calm, tranquil, still || quiet (silencioso); *el niño está muy quedo* the child is very quiet || low, soft (voz); *en voz queda* in a low voice || soft, gentle (ruido).
◆ *adv* softly, quietly; *hablar muy quedo* to speak very quietly.

quehacer *m* duty, task; *nuestro quehacer cotidiano* our daily duty.
◆ *pl* tasks, chores, duties; *los quehaceres domésticos* the household chores || business *sing*; *ir a sus quehaceres* to go about one's business.

queja *f* moan, groan (de dolor); *las quejas de un enfermo* the moans of a sick person || complaint; *las quejas de los vecinos* the complaints of the neighbours; *las quejas de un acreedor* the complaints of a creditor || JUR complaint; *presentar una queja* to lodge a complaint || — *dar motivo de queja* to give reason for complaint || *dar quejas* or *queja de uno, de algo* to complain about s.o., about sth. || *tener queja de* to have a complaint about.

quejarse *vpr* to moan, to groan (gemir); *quejarse lastimosamente* to moan pitifully || to complain; *quejarse de uno* to complain about s.o. || — *no me puedo quejar* I can't complain || *quejarse de algo a uno* to complain to s.o. about sth. || *quejarse de hambre* to complain that one is hungry || *quejarse de vicio* to complain for the sake of it.

quejica; quejicoso, sa; quejón, ona *adj* grumpy, querulous, hard to please || *no seas tan quejica* stop moaning, don't be such a grouse.
◆ *m/f* grouse, moaner.

quejido *m* moan, groan; *los quejidos de un herido* the moans of a wounded person || *dar* or *lanzar quejidos* to moan, to groan.

quejigal *m* gall oak grove.

quejigo *m* BOT gall oak (roble).

quejón, ona *adj/s* ⟶ **quejica.**

quejoso, sa *adj* displeased, angry, annoyed (enfadado); *estoy quejoso de tu comportamiento* I am annoyed at your behaviour.

quejumbre *f* moaning, groaning (gemidos) || grumbling, complaining, moaning (de descontento).

quejumbrón, ona *adj* whining, plaintive.
◆ *m/f* moaner.

quejumbroso, sa *adj* whining, plaintive, complaining.
◆ *m/f* moaner.

quelonios *m pl* ZOOL chelonians.

quema *f* burning (acción de quemar); *la quema de los herejes, de los conventos* the burning of heretics, of the convents || death by fire, the stake; *condenado a la quema* condemned to death by fire || COM clearance sale (liquidación de géneros) || AMER burning of fields || FIG *huir de la quema* to flee from danger.

quemadero *m* stake (para los sentenciados) || incinerator (para basuras).

quemado, da *adj* burnt [US burned] || FIG burnt-out [US burned-out]; *un futbolista, un equipo quemado* a burnt-out footballer, team | embittered, resentful (amargado, resentido).

◆ *m* burning; *huele a quemado* I can smell burning || patch of burnt land (chamicera).

quemador, ra *adj* burning.
◆ *m* burner; *quemador de gas* gas burner.

quemadura *f* burn (herida); *quemadura de tercer grado* third-degree burn || scald (causado por un líquido caliente) || AGR smut (tizón) | cold blight (de las plantas heladas) || *quemadura de sol* sunburn.

quemar *vt* to burn; *quemar papeles* to burn papers || to burn down *o* out (destruir con fuego) || to set fire to (prender fuego a) || FAM to burn; *el sol nos quemó* the sun burnt us | to burn (el dinero) || to sell at a reduction, to sell cheap (malbaratar) || AGR to nip, to blight (desecar las plantas heladas) || FIG to overtrain; *un entrenador que quema a sus jugadores* a trainer who overtrains his players | to wear out; *un exceso de actuaciones quema a los actores* too many performances wear out the actors || — *a quema ropa* at point-blank rage, point-blank || FIG *para mí es un político quemado* as far as I am concerned he is a has-been | *quemar cartuchos* to fire shots | *quemar etapas* to get on in leaps and bounds | *quemar la sangre* to make one's blood boil; *su cachaza me quema la sangre* his calmness makes my blood boil | *quemar las naves* to burn one's boats [*US* to burn one's bridges] || *quemar una colección de fuegos artificiales* to let off fireworks.
◆ *vi* to burn || to be burning hot *o* boiling hot (estar muy caliente).
◆ *vpr* to burn o.s.; *quemarse con una cerilla* to burn o.s. with a match || to burn (up) (papeles, etc.) || to burn (down), to be burnt down (una casa, etc.) || to burn (un asado) || — FIG *quemarse la sangre* to fret (preocuparse mucho) | *quemarse las cejas* or *las pestañas (estudiando)* to burn the midnight oil | *¡que te quemas!* you're boiling (en juegos).

quemarropa (a) *loc adv* point-blank, at point-blank range (disparo y contestación).

quemazón *f* burning (acción de quemar) || burn (quemadura) || intense heat (calor excesivo) | FIG sore, sting (dolor) | itch (comezón) || FIG *sentía una gran quemazón por haber sido tan mal tratado* I felt annoyed *o* resentful at having been treated so badly.

quena *f* AMER quena, Indian flute.
— OBSERV The *quena* is a reed flute generally with five finger holes. It is used mainly by the Indians of Peru and Bolivia.

quenopodiáceas *f pl* BOT chenopodiaceae.

quepis *m* kepi (gorro).

queque *m* AMER cake.

queratina *m* BIOL keratin.

querella *f* (ant) moan, groan (queja) || JUR complaint || quarrel, dispute (riña).

querellante *adj* complaining.
◆ *m/f* JUR complainant, plaintiff.

querellarse *vpr* JUR to lodge a complaint (against).

querelloso, sa *adj* querulous (quejica).

querencia *f* homing instinct (instinto de los animales) || favourite place (sitio preferido) || FAM home (hogar) || (p us) affection, attachment (cariño) || TAUR tendency of the bull to go towards a certain part of the ring.

querencioso, sa *adj* homing, which tends to return to the same spot.

querer* *vt* to want (desear); *quiero un helado* I want an ice cream; *¿cuánto quiere por el cuadro?* how much does he want for the picture?; *se lo ofrecí pero no lo quiso* I offered it to him, but he didn't want it; *le dije que viniese, pero no quiso* I told him to come but he didn't want to; *quiero ir al cine* I want to go to the pictures; *quiero que lo hagas tú* I want you to do it; *quería que lo hicieses tú* I wanted you to do it || to want, to like; *¿quiere un cigarrillo?* would you like a cigarette?, do you want a cigarette? || to wish, to like, to want; *haga lo que quiera* do as you wish, do what you like; *si usted quiere* if you like *o* wish *o* want || to love (con amor); *me quiere, no me quiere* she loves me, she loves me not; *te quiero con todo mi corazón* I love you with all my heart; *quiere mucho a sus hijos* she loves her children dearly || to be fond of (tener cariño a) || to like (encontrar simpático) || to hope (esperar); *quisiera que no lloviese mañana* I hope it doesn't rain tomorrow || to wish, to like; *quisiera que estuviera aquí* I wish he were here, I would like him to be here || to try (intentar); *me quiso matar* he tried to kill me || to be about to (estar a punto de); *quería amanecer* dawn was about to break || to need (necesitar); *esta planta quiere agua* this plant needs water || to require, to demand (requerir); *la urbanidad quiere que se ceda el asiento a las señoras* politeness requires that one should give up one's seat to a lady || to be looking for *o* asking for (buscar); *se le ve que quiere pelea* he is obviously looking for trouble || to claim (pretender); *su teoría quiere que* his theory claims that || — *como quien no quiere la cosa* quite nonchalantly *o* offhandedly, just like that || *como quiera* as you like || *como quiera que* since, inasmuch as (dado que) || *cuando quiera* whenever you like, any time || *cuando quiera que* whenever || *donde quiera* anywhere (en cualquier parte), everywhere (en todas partes); *dondequiera que* wherever, anywhere || FAM *gente de quiero y no puedo* people who live above their means || *¡no lo quiera Dios!* Heaven forbid!, God forbid! || *no quiero sus excusas* I don't want your excuses || *¡por lo que más quieras!* for Heaven's sake! || *¿qué más quieres?* what more do you want? || FAM *¡qué más quisieras tú!* you'd like that, wouldn't you? || *que quiera que no quiera, quiera o no quiera* (whether you) like it or not || *¿qué quiere decir con eso?* what do you mean by that? || *¿qué quiere decir esto?* what does this mean?, what is the meaning of this? || *¿qué quieres?* what do you want? || *¿qué quieres que yo le haga?* what do you want me to do (about it)? || *que si quieres (arroz, Catalina)* it is *o* was useless || *querer bien a uno* to like s.o., to be fond of s.o. (tenerle afecto) || *querer decir* to mean || *querer es poder* where there's a will there's a way || *querer mal a uno* not to like s.o., to have it in for s.o. (fam) || *querer más* to prefer || *quería saber si* I wanted to know if || *queriendo* on purpose, deliberately, intentionally || *quien bien te quiere te hará llorar* you have to be cruel to be kind, spare the rod and spoil the child || *quiérase o no* like it or not || *quieras que no* like it or not (a la fuerza) || *¿quiere darme las tijeras, por favor?* would you give me the scissors, please? || *quiere llover* it's trying to rain, it looks like rain || *quisiera ir contigo* I'd like to go with you || *sin querer* unintentionally, without meaning to; *lo hice sin querer* I did it unintentionally, I didn't mean to do it || *sí quiero* I will (en la boda).
◆ *vpr* to love each other || FAM *quererse como tórtolos* to be like turtledoves.

querer *m* affection, love, fondness.

queretano, na *adj* [of *o* from] Querétaro [Mexico].
◆ *m/f* native *o* inhabitant of Querétaro.

querido, da *adj* loved; *querido por sus hijos* loved by his children || dear; *querido tío* dear uncle; *mi querida prima* my dear cousin || darling, dear; *sí, querida* yes, darling || — *fórmula tan querida por* favourite formula of, formula so much liked by || *mi querido amigo* my dear *o* beloved friend.
◆ *m* lover (amante).
◆ *f* lover, mistress; *echarse una querida* to take a mistress.

querindongo, ga *m/f* FAM lover.

quermes *m* kermes (insecto).

quermese *f* kermis.

queroseno; kerosén *m* kerosene.

querubín *m* cherubim.

quesadilla *f* AMER cheesecake (pastel).

quesera *f* cheese factory (fábrica) || cheese dish (plato) || cheese mould [*US* cheese mold].

quesería *f* cheese shop (tienda).

quesero, ra *adj* cheese; *industria quesera* cheese industry.
◆ *m/f* cheese maker *o* seller || lover of cheese (aficionado).

queso *m* cheese || — FIG & FAM *dársela con queso a uno* to take s.o. in, to put one over on s.o. (engañar) || *queso de bola* Edam cheese || *queso de cabra* goat cheese || *queso de cerdo* or *de cabeza* headcheese || *queso de Chester* Cheshire cheese || *queso manchego* Manchego cheese [cheese from La Mancha].

quetzal *m* quetzal (ave) || quetzal (moneda).

quevedos *m pl* pince-nez *sing.*

¡quiá! *interj* FAM come off it!, nonsense!, rubbish!, never!

quiasma *m* ANAT chiasma (cruce).

quicial *m* TECN hinging post (de puerta o de ventana).

quicio *m* TECN pivot hole (gozne) | frame (marco de puerta o de ventana) || — FIG *fuera de quicio* beside o.s. (persona), out of order (cosa) | *sacar de quicio a uno* to make s.o. wild, to infuriate s.o. (enfurecer) | *sacar de quicio una cosa* to carry sth. to extremes | *salir de quicio* to fly off the handle.

Quico *m* FAM *ponerse como el Quico* to stuff o.s. (hincharse de comer).

quiché *adj/s* Quiche [Indian of Guatemala].

quichua *adj* Quechuan.
◆ *m* Quechua, Quechuan.

quichuismo *m* ⟶ **quechuismo.**

quid *m* gist, crux, main point; *¡ahí está el quid!* there is the gist || — *dar en el quid* to hit the nail on the head || *quid pro quo* misunderstanding (malentendido), mistake (error).

quídam *m* FAM somebody or other (fulano) | nobody (don nadie).

quiebra *f* break (rotura) || crack, fissure (grieta) || COM bankruptcy (bancarrota) | crash (crac) || FIG collapse; *la quiebra de los valores humanos* the collapse of human values || — COM *declararse en quiebra* to declare bankruptcy | *estar en quiebra* to be bankrupt.

quiebro *m* dodge (ademán) || dribbling (fútbol) || MÚS grace notes *pl* || TAUR dodge || *dar un quiebro* to dribble (fútbol), to dodge (el torero).

quien *pron rel (sujeto)* who; *fue su padre quien lo dijo* it was his father who said it; *su madre, quien estaba escuchando, dijo* his mother, who was listening, said || anyone who, whoever; *quien no sabe eso es tonto* anyone who doesn't know that is stupid; *quien acabe el último paga* whoever finishes last pays || someone (who); *ya encontraré quien me haga este trabajo* I shall find s.o. who will do this job *o* s.o. to do this job for me || — *a quien* whom, that (complemento directo); *la persona a quien quiero* the person whom I love véase OBSERV to whom (complemento indirecto); *las personas a quienes* or *a quien hablo* the people to whom I am speaking || *a quien se tiene que dirigir usted es a ese señor* that is the man you must speak to || *como quien* like he who (she who, etc.), like the one who; *se porta como quienes le han educado* he acts like those who raised him; as if; *hace como quien no oye* he acts as if he doesn't hear || *como quien dice* as it were, so to speak || *como quien no quiere la cosa* quite nonchalantly *o* offhandedly, just like that || *de quien* of anyone who, of whoever, of he who (she who, etc.); *el alma de quien muere sin bautismo va al limbo* the soul of he who dies unbaptized goes to limbo; whose (cuyo); *en casa de quien* in whose house || *es... quien* it is... who; *es su madre quien manda* it is his mother who rules || *habrá quien lo sepa* there will surely be s.o. who knows || *hay quien dice* there are people who say, there are those who say, some say || *la gente con quien vive* the people he lives with || *no es quien para hacer esto* he is not one to do this, it is not his place to do this || *no hay quien se ocupe de él* there is no one to take care of him || *quien más quien menos* everybody.

— OBSERV En el lenguaje hablado *whom* se suprime a menudo: *the person I love; the people I am speaking to.*

quién *pron interr o exclam* who (sujeto); *¿quién es?* who is it?; *¿quiénes son estos dos chicos?* who are these two boys?; *dime quién es* tell me who it is || whom, who (con preposición); *¿para quién trabajas?* for whom do you work?, who do you work for?; *¿con quién ibas ayer?* who were you with *o* with whom were you yesterday (véase OBSERV) || — *¿de quién?* whose?; *¿de quién es este abrigo?* whose is this coat?, whose coat is this?; *no sé de quién es* I don't know whose it is || *dime con quién andas y te diré quién eres* a man is known by the company he keeps || *¡quién pudiera!* if only I could! || *quién... quién* some... some || *¿quién sabe?* who knows? || *¿quién vive?* who goes there?.

— OBSERV En la lengua hablada *who* sustituye con frecuencia a *whom* cuando va acompañado por una preposición o cuando es complemento directo del verbo, aunque, desde un punto de vista puramente gramatical, *whom* sea la única forma correcta.

quienquiera *pron indef* whoever, anyone, anybody; *quienquiera que lo vea* whoever sees him, anyone *o* anybody who sees him || *quienquiera que sea* whoever it may be, whoever it is.

— OBSERV The plural *quienesquiera* is rare.

quietismo *m* FIL quietism (doctrina) || FIG immobilism.

quietista *adj/s* quietist.

quieto, ta *adj* still (sin ruido) || motionless, still (inmóvil) || calm, quiet (persona, vida, mar, etc.); *por el momento todo está quieto* everything is quiet at the moment || — *¡déjame quieto!* leave me alone! || *¡estate quieto!* keep still! || *no sabe estarse quieto* he can't keep still || *¡quieto!* don't move, keep still! (no te muevas), down, boy! (a un perro), whoa, boy! (a un caballo) || *¡todo el mundo quieto!* nobody move! (en un asalto, etc.).

quietud *f* stillness, calm, quietude.

quijada *f* ANAT jawbone.

quijera *f* cheek strap (de los arriendos).

quijotada *f* quixotic deed, quixotism.

quijote *m* cuisse (de la armadura) || rump, croup (del caballo) || FIG & FAM *un quijote* a quixote.

Quijote (Don) *npr m* Don Quixote || *el Quijote* Don Quixote (obra de Cervantes).

quijotería *f* Quixotism.

quijotesco, ca *adj* Quixotic.

quijotismo *m* Quixotism.

quilatador *m* assayer (de oro).

quilate *m* carat [US carat, karat]; *oro de 18 quilates* 18 carat gold || ancient coin || — FIG & FAM *de muchos quilates* of great value | *no tiene dos quilates de juicio* he's got no sense at all, he hasn't got an ounce of sense.

quilo *m* BIOL chyle || FIG & FAM *sudar el quilo* to sweat blood.

quilo *m* kilogram, kilogramme, kilo.

quilombo *m* AMER brothel (lupanar) | hut (choza).

quilla *f* MAR keel; *quilla de balance* bilge keel || breastbone, keel (de las aves) || *dar de quilla a un barco* to keel a boat, to keel a boat over.

quillay *m* AMER quillaja (palo de jabón).

quillotra *f* FAM concubine (manceba).

quillotrar *vt* (p us) FAM to stir up, to rouse, to excite, to stimulate (excitar) | to woo, to court (galantear) | to mediate, to ponder (meditar) | to adorn, to embellish (engalanar).
◆ *vpr* to grumble (quejarse).

quillotro *m* (p us) FAM stimulus (estímulo) | sign (señal) | love affair (amorío) | headache, worry (quebradero de cabeza) | wooing, courting (requiebro) | adornment (gala) | friend (amigo).

quimera *f* MIT chimera || FIG quarrel, argument (contienda); *buscar quimera* to be looking for a quarrel || daydream, pipe dream (sueño); *vivir de quimeras* to live on daydreams || chimera, wild idea (idea absurda).

quimérico, ca *adj* chimerical, unrealistic.

quimerista *adj* dreaming || quarrelsome.
◆ *m/f* dreamer (soñador) || troublemaker (pendenciero).

química *f* chemistry; *química general, mineral* or *inorgánica, orgánica* general, inorganic, organic chemistry.

químico, ca *adj* chemical; *productos químicos* chemical products.
◆ *m/f* chemist.

quimioterapia *f* MED chemotherapy.

quimista *m* alchemist (alquimista).

quimo *m* BIOL chyme.

quimono *m* kimono.

quina *f* cinchona bark (corteza) || MED quinine || galbanum (gálbano) || — FIG & FAM *más malo que la quina* revolting, disgusting (una cosa), horrible, nasty (una persona) | *tragar quina* to put up with murder (aguantarse).

quinario, ria *adj* quinary, consisting of five elements.
◆ *m* five-day devotion (cultos durante cinco días).

quincalla *f* hardware, ironmongery (objetos).

quincallería *f* hardware shop, ironmongery.

quincallero, ra *m/f* hardware dealer, ironmonger.

quince *adj num* fifteen; *quince chicos* fifteen boys || — *quince días* a fortnight; *hace quince días* a fortnight ago || *unos quince libros* about fifteen books.
◆ *adj ord* *Luis XV (quince)* Louis XV [the fifteenth]; *el día quince* the fifteenth; *el siglo XV (quince)* the 15th [fifteenth] century.
◆ *m* fifteen (número) || fifteen, team [in rugby union] (equipo de rugby) || — FIG & FAM *dar quince y raya a* to run rings round s.o., to knock spots off s.o. || *el quince no sale nunca* (number) fifteen never comes up.

quincena *f* fortnight || MÚS fifteenth || *recibir su quincena* to receive one's fortnightly pay.

quincenal *adj* fortnightly, twice monthly (que se hace cada quincena) || fortnight-long (que dura una quincena).

quincenalmente *adv* every fortnight, fortnightly.

quinceno, na *adj* fifteenth.
◆ *m/f* fifteen-month-old mule.

quincuagenario, ria *adj* made up of fifty units *o* parts || fifty-year-old, quinquagenarian, in one's fifties (cincuentón).
◆ *m/f* fifty-year-old (person), quinquagenarian, man (*o* woman) in his (*o* her) fifties (cincuentón).

quincuagésimo, ma *adj/sm* fiftieth.
◆ *f* REL quincuagesima.

quincha *f* AMER reed binding (para techos, para muros).

quinchar *vt* AMER to build (mud or cane walls, etc.) using reeds to strengthen them.

quingentésimo, ma *adj/s* five hundredth.

quinielas *f pl* football pools (fútbol).

quinielista *m/f* person who does the pools (fútbol).

quinientos, tas *adj* five hundred; *quinientos hombres* five hundred men; *quinientos veinte* five hundred and twenty; *el año quinientos* the year five hundred || *mil quinientos* one thousand five hundred, fifteen hundred (número), fifteen hundred (año).

quinina *f* quinine.

quino *m* BOT cinchona (árbol).

quinoa *f* BOT quinoa (planta).

quínola *f* card game in which the best hand is a four-card flush (juego de naipes).

quinona *f* QUÍM quinone.

quinqué *m* oil lamp (lámpara) || FAM *tener mucho quinqué* to be very sharp *o* bright.

quinquefolio *m* BOT & ARQ cinquefoil.

quinquenal *adj* quinquennial, five-year || *plan quinquenal* five-year plan.

quinquenio *m* quinquennium, five-year period.

quinqui *m* FAM hardware dealer, ironmonger (vendedor de quincalla) || FAM villain, rogue.

quinquina *f* cinchona (quina).

quinta *f* villa, country house, manor (casa) || MIL call-up, conscription (reclutamiento) | contingent of troops called up in one year (reemplazo) || quinte (esgrima) || MÚS fifth || — MIL *entrar en quintas* to reach call-up age | *es de la misma quinta que yo* we were called up in the same year | *librarse de quintas* to be exempted from military service.

quintaesencia *f* quintessence.

quintaesenciar *vt* to quintessence, to quintessentialize.

quintal *m* quintal (peso) || *quintal métrico* a hundred kilogrammes, quintal (peso de cien kilos).

— OBSERV The former Spanish *quintal* weighed one hundred pounds.

quintana *f* villa, country house.

quintar *vt* to take one in five (uno de cada cinco) || MIL to call up, to conscript, to draft || AGR to plough for the fifth time.
◆ *vi* to reach its fifth day [the moon] (la luna) || to bid a fifth higher, to raise the bid by a fifth.

quinteo *m* drawing of lots (*de* for).

quintería *f* farm, property (finca).

quintero *m* farmer (arrendatario) || farm labourer, farmhand (mozo de labranza).

quinteto *m* MÚS quintet, quintette.

quintilla *f* five-line stanza (estrofa de cinco versos).

quintillizos, zas *mpl/fpl* quintuplets, quins (*fam*).

quintillón *m* quintillion.

Quintín *npr m* Quentin || → **San Quintín.**

quinto, ta *adj* fifth || — *en quinto lugar* fifthly, in fifth place || *la quinta columna* the fifth column || *la quinta parte* a fifth || *quinto* fifthly (en una enumeración).
◆ *m* fifth || MIL conscript, recruit.

quintuplicación *f* quintupling.

quintuplicar *vt* to quintuple.
◆ *vpr* to quintuple.

quíntuplo, pla *adj/sm* quintuple.

quinua *f* BOT quinoa (planta).

quinzavo, va *adj/sm* fifteenth.

quiñón *m* piece *o* plot of land.

quiosco *m* kiosk (en general) ‖ summerhouse (en el jardín) ‖ — *quiosco de música* bandstand ‖ *quiosco de periódicos* newspaper stand *o* stall, newsstand.

quipos; quipus *m pl* quipus.
— OBSERV The *quipus* are knotted threads used by the Incas for recording information. The meaning was interpreted according to the colour of the threads, the number of knots, etc.

quiquiriquí *m* cock-a-doodle-doo (canto del gallo).

quirófano *m* operating theatre [US operating room].

quiromancia *f* chiromancy, palmistry.

quiromántico, ca *adj* chiromantic, palmist.
◆ *m/f* chiromancer, palmist.

quiromasaje *m* chiropractic.

quiromasajista *m/f* chiropractor.

quiropodia *f* chiropody.

quiropráctica *f* MED chiropractic.

quiropráctico *m* MED chiropractor.

quiróptero, ra *adj/sm* ZOOL chiropteran.

quirquincho *m* (kind of) armadillo (armadillo).

quirúrgico, ca *adj* surgical.

quiscal *m* grackle (ave).

quisicosa *f* FAM puzzle, riddle.

quisque *pron* FAM *cada* or *todo quisque* everyone, absolutely everybody *o* everyone.

quisquilla *f* trifle, triviality (pequeñez) ‖ shrimp (camarón).
◆ *adj/s* ⟶ **quisquilloso** ‖ *color quisquilla* light pink.

quisquilloso, sa *adj* finical [US finicky] fastidious, punctilious, fussy; *jefe quisquilloso* fastidious boss ‖ touchy, sensitive (susceptible).
◆ *m/f* fastidious person ‖ touchy person.

quiste *m* MED cyst.

quisto, ta *adj* ⟶ **bienquisto, malquisto.**

quistoso, sa *adj* cystic.

quita *f* release from a debt (de una deuda) ‖ *de quita y pon* detachable, removeable.

quitación *f* income, salary, wage.

quitaesmalte *m* nail varnish *o* nail polish remover.

quitaipón *m* ⟶ **quitapón.**

quitamanchas *adj inv* stain removing.
◆ *m inv* stain remover.

quitanieves *m inv* snowplough [US snowplow].

quitapesares *m inv* FAM consolation (consuelo) | distraction (que distrae).

quitapiedras *m inv* cowcatcher (de locomotora).

quitapón; quitaipón *m* headstall ornament for mules (adorno) ‖ *de quitapón* detachable, removeable.

quitar *vt* to take off, to remove; *quitar el abrigo a alguien* to take s.o.'s coat off; *quitar la tapa, la piel* to remove *o* to take off the lid, the peel ‖ to take, to take away; *quítale ese cuchillo al niño* take that knife (away) from the baby; *le quitaron el pasaporte* they took his passport away (from him) ‖ to take; *quitar la vida a alguien* to take s.o.'s life ‖ MAT to take (away), to substract (restar); *quitar a uno de tres* to take one from three ‖ to free, to relieve; *quitar a uno la preocupación* to free s.o. of a worry ‖ to relieve, to stop, to take away (un dolor) ‖ to get rid of, to remove (una mancha) ‖ to extract, to remove, to separate; *quitar las impurezas a un mineral* to extract the impurities from a mineral ‖ to remove, to take off (una pieza) ‖ to snatch (con violencia); *le quitó el bolso de las manos* he snatched the bag from her hands ‖ to take, to steal (robar); *me han quitado el bolso* s.o. has taken my bag ‖ to stop, to prevent (impedir); *eso no quita que sea un holgazán* that does not stop his being lazy ‖ FIG to detract; *su fracaso no le quita nada de sus cualidades* his failure does not detract from his qualities ‖ to reduce, to detract from; *quitarle valor a una cosa* to reduce the value of sth. ‖ — *de quita y pon* detachable, removeable; *impermeable con capucha de quita y pon* raincoat with a detachable hood ‖ FIG *en un quítame allá esas pajas* in the wink of an eye, in a jiffy | *me has quitado las palabras de la boca* you took the words right out of my mouth ‖ FIG & FAM *no quito ni pongo rey* it's none of my business, it's nothing to do with me | *por un quítame allá esas pajas* for no reason at all | *¡que me quiten lo bailado!* nothing can take away the good times I've had | *¡quita!* get off!, get away! | *¡quita, hombre!* come, now!, come off it! ‖ *quitando el primero me gustan todos* apart from *o* except for the first one I like them all ‖ *quitar de encima* or *de en medio* to get rid of, to get out of the way; *me lo han quitado de en medio* they have got rid of it *o* him for me ‖ FIG & FAM *quitar el hipo* to take one's breath away ‖ *quitar la idea de* to dissuade, to persuade not to; *le he quitado la idea de irse* I have dissuaded him from going, I have persuaded him not to go ‖ *quitar la mesa* to clear the table ‖ FIG & FAM *quitar la vida* to be the death of; *este niño me quita la vida* this child will be the death of me ‖ *quitarle el sueño a uno* to prevent *o* to stop one's sleeping ‖ *quitarle la razón a alguien* to show that s.o. is wrong (culpar a uno de error), to drive s.o. mad (volverle a uno loco) ‖ *quitarle mucho tiempo a uno* to take up a lot of one's time ‖ FIG *no quitar ojo a* or *no quitar los ojos de encima* not to take one's eyes off, to keep watching (no dejar de mirar), not to let out of one's sight, to keep on *o* one's eye on (vigilar) | *quitar un peso de encima* to take a load off one's mind.
◆ *vpr* to be removed; *el molde se quita a los dos días* the mould is removed after two days ‖ to come out *o* off (una mancha); *esa mancha no se quita con agua* that stain won't come out with water ‖ to take off, to remove; *quitarse la boina* to take off one's beret; *quitarse los zapatos* to take off one's shoes ‖ to get rid of (deshacerse de) ‖ — *consiguió quitarse de la bebida* he managed to give up drinking ‖ *eso quíteselo usted de la cabeza* you can get that idea out of your head ‖ *quitarse años* to lie about one's age ‖ FAM *quitarse de encima* to clear o.s. of (deudas), to get out of (un problema, dificultades), to get rid of (una cosa), to get rid of, to shake off (una persona); *creía que no podría nunca quitármelo de encima* I thought I would never be able to get rid of him ‖ *quitarse de en medio* to get out of the way (cambiar de sitio); *¡quítate de en medio!* get out of the way!; to disappear, to make o.s. scarse (irse) ‖ *quitarse el sombrero ante* to take one's hat off to (de admiración) | *¡quítate de bobadas!* stop messing about!, enough of this nonsense! | *¡quítate de en medio!* get out of the way! | *¡quítate de mi vista!* get out of my sight! | *¡quítese de ahí!* get away with you!

quitasol *m* parasol, sunshade.

quitasueño *m* FAM nightmare, worry.

quite *m* removal (acción de quitar) ‖ parry (esgrima) ‖ dodge (movimiento evasivo) ‖ TAUR «quite», movement to attract the bull's attention away from a man in danger ‖ — TAUR *dar el quite* to draw the bull away ‖ *estar al quite* to be ready to draw the bull away (tauromaquia), to be ready to come to s.o.'s aid (en defensa de uno).

quiteño, ña *adj* [of *o* from] Quito [Ecuador].
◆ *m/f* native *o* inhabitant of Quito.

quitina *f* QUÍM chitin.

quitinoso, sa *adj* chitinous.

Quito *n pr* GEOGR Quito.

quitrín *m* AMER two-wheeled open carriage.

quizá; quizás *adv* perhaps, maybe; *quizá venga* perhaps he will come.

quórum *m* quorum (de una asamblea).

R

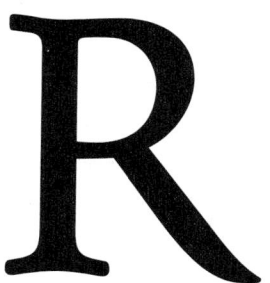

r *f* r.
— OBSERV The Spanish *r* must be rolled. Initial *r*, *r* after the letters *l*, *n*, *s*, and the double *r* (*rr*) are the strongest and several trills must be produced in pronouncing them. In writing, the double *r* must not be split at the end of a line.

ra *m inv* roll, drum roll (redoble del tambor).

Ra *n pr* Ra (dios egipcio).

rabadilla *f* FAM rump, parson's nose (de pollo) | back (de conejo, de liebre) || ANAT coccyx.

rabanal *m* radish bed, radish patch.

rabanera *f* radish seller (vendedora) || FIG & FAM coarse woman, fishwife (mujer grosera).

rabanero, ra *adj* FIG & FAM short (vestidos) | coarse (grosero, descarado).

rabanillo *m* wild radish (planta crucífera) || small radish.

rabanito *m* radish.

rabaniza *f* radish seed (simiente) || wall rocket (planta).

rábano *m* radish (planta) || — FAM *me importa un rábano* I couldn't care less || *rábano blanco* horseradish || *rábano silvestre* wild horseradish || FAM *tomar el rábano por las hojas* to get hold of the wrong end of the stick.

Rabat *n pr* GEOGR Rabat.

rabear *vi* to wag its tail (un perro) || MAR to swing her stern (un barco).

rabel *m* rebec (instrumento de música).

rabí *m* rabbi (título) || rabbi, rabbin (rabino).

rabia *f* MED rabies (enfermedad) || FIG rage, fury, anger || — FIG *dar rabia* to make furious, to infuriate, to make one's blood boil; *me da rabia leer tales mentiras* it makes me furious to read such lies | *muerto el perro se acabó la rabia* dead dogs don't bite | *que da rabia* maddening, infuriating (adjetivo), maddeningly, infuriatingly (adverbio) | *rabia, rabieta; rabia, rabiña* yah!, yah! | *reventar de rabia* to foam at the mouth | *tener rabia a uno* to have it in for s.o., not to be able to stand (the sight of) s.o. | *tomarle rabia a uno* to take a dislike to s.o.

rabiar *vi* MED to have rabies (padecer rabia) || FIG to be furious, to rage, to rave || — FIG *a rabiar* rabid; *republicano a rabiar* rabid republican; wildly, without restraint (sin parar); *aplaudir a rabiar* to applaud wildly | *está que rabia* he is furious, he is seething, he is hopping mad | *estar a rabiar con uno* to be at daggers drawn with s.o. | *hacer rabiar a uno* to make s.o. see red, to make s.o. furious, to make s.o.'s blood boil | *me gusta a rabiar* I am mad about it, I adore it | *pica que rabia* it is as hot as the devil | *rabiar de dolor* to writhe in agony *o* in pain | *rabiar de hambre, de sed* to be dying of hunger, of thirst | *rabiar por* to long to, to be dying to; *está rabiando por irse* he is dying to go | *rabiar por algo* to long for sth., to be dying for sth. | *soy más alto que tú, ¡rabia!* I am taller than you, so there!

rabiatar *vt* to tie by the tail.

rábico, ca *adj* MED rabid.

rabicorto, ta *adj* with a short tail, short-tailed || FIG & FAM wearing a short skirt *o* a miniskirt, in a short skirt *o* a miniskirt; *una chiquilla rabicorta* a girl in a short skirt.

rabieta *f* FAM tantrum, paddy (de un niño) || FAM *coger una rabieta* to fly into a tantrum.

rabietas *m/f inv* FAM little terror.

rabihorcado *m* frigate bird (ave).

rabilargo, ga *adj* with a long tail, long-tailed.
◆ *m* kind of magpie (ave).

rabillo *m* small tail (cola corta) || stalk, stem (de una hoja o de un fruto) || tab, strap (de pantalón o de chaleco) || BOT darnel (cizaña) || mildew spot [on cereals] (mancha en los cereales) || corner (del ojo) || FAM *mirar con el rabillo del ojo* to look out of the corner of one's eye (at).

rabinismo *m* rabbinism (doctrina de los rabinos).

rabino *m* rabbi, rabbin || *gran rabino* chief rabbi.

rabión *m* rapids *pl*.

rabioso, sa *adj* rabid; *perro rabioso* rabid dog || FIG furious (enojado); *estar rabioso con alguien* to be furious with s.o. | rabid (fanático) | gaudy, shocking, loud (color) | very strong *o* hot (sabor) || — *dolor rabioso* agony, torment || *rabioso de ira* furious, livid, foaming at the mouth, seething.

rabiza *f* tip (de la caña de pescar) || MAR short lashing rope (de cordaje).

rabo *m* tail; *el rabo del perro* the dog's tail || stalk, stem (de una hoja o de un fruto) || corner (del ojo) || tail (de una letra) || FIG tail, train (cosa que cuelga) || — *rabo de buey* oxtail || FIG & FAM *aún está el rabo por desollar* the worst is yet to come | *irse, volver con el rabo entre las piernas* to go away, to come back with one's tail between one's legs.

rabón, ona *adj* bobtail, tailless.
◆ *f* AMER camp follower || FAM *hacer rabona* to play truant, to skive [*US* to play hooky or *hookey*].

racamenta *f*; **racamento** *m* MAR parrel.

racanear *vi* FAM to slack (no trabajar) | to be stingy (ser tacaño).

rácano, na *adj* FAM idle (holgazán) | stingy (tacaño).

racial *adj* racial; *problemas raciales* racial problems || race, racial; *odio racial* race hatred.

racimo *m* BOT raceme || bunch, cluster; *racimo de uvas* bunch of grapes || FIG bunch, cluster (conjunto).

raciocinar *vi* to ratiocinate, to reason.

raciocinio *m* reason (razón); *carecer de raciocinio* to lack reason || reasoning (razonamiento).

ración *f* ration, share (parte) || helping, portion (en una fonda, en un bar); *una ración de gambas* a helping of shrimps || MIL ration || REL prebend (prebenda) || — FIG *a ración* meanly, stingily | *poner a media ración* to put on short rations | *tener su ración de* to get one's share *o* one's fill of.

racionabilidad *f* judgment, reason.

racional *adj* rational; *método racional* rational method; *un ser racional* a rational being.
◆ *m* rational being.

racionalidad *f* rationality.

racionalismo *m* rationalism.

racionalista *adj* rationalist, rationalistic.
◆ *m/f* rationalist.

racionalización *f* rationalization.

racionalizar *vt* to rationalize.

racionamiento *m* rationing || MIL rationing out || *cartilla de racionamiento* ration card, ration book.

racionar *vt* to ration; *racionar el pan* to ration bread || MIL to ration out.

racionista *m/f* person who lives on an allowance || person who is rationed (racionado) || TEATR bit-part actor (actor).

racismo *m* racialism.

racista *adj* racialistic, racialist.
◆ *m/f* racialist.

racor *m* connecter, adapter || AUT hose.

racha *f* gust of wind (ráfaga de viento) || spell; *una racha de frío* a cold spell || FIG series, run, wave; *una racha de triunfos* a series of successes || — FIG *a rachas* by fits and starts || FIG & FAM *estar de racha, tener una buena racha* to have a run of good luck | *tener una mala racha* to be out of luck, to have a run of bad luck.

rada *f* MAR roadstead, bay.

radar *m* radar || *pantalla de radar* radar screen.

radiación *f* FÍS radiation || broadcasting (en la radio).

radiactividad *f* radioactivity.

radiactivo, va *adj* radioactive.

radiado, da *adj* BOT & ZOOL radiate || RAD broadcast, transmitted || *un programa radiado* a radio programme.
◆ *m* BOT radiate plant || ZOOL radiate animal.

radiador *m* radiator; *radiador de gas* gas radiator.

radial *adj* radial; *neumáticos radiales* radial tyres; *carretera radial* radial road || AMER radio (de la radio).

radián *m* MAT radian (unidad angular).

radiante *adj* FÍS radiant; *calor radiante* radiant heat || FIG radiant, shining, bright; *rostro radiante* radiant face || — FIG *radiante de alegría* radiant with joy || *superficie radiante* radiating surface, surface of radiation.

radiar *vi* to radiate.
◆ *vt* to irradiate, to radiate || RAD to broadcast, to transmit || MED to treat with X rays.

radicación *f* MAT evolution [extraction of roots from an expression] || FIG establishment, taking root, setting in [of a custom, of a vice, etc.].

radical *adj/s* radical; *medios radicales* radical measures.
◆ *m* GRAM & MAT radical, root ‖ CHEM radical, radicle.

radicalismo *m* radicalism (política radical).

radicalización *f* radicalization.

radicalizar *vt* to radicalize.

radicalsocialismo *m* radical socialism.

radicalsocialista *adj/s* radical socialist.

radicante *adj* rooted, taking root ‖ FIG emanating, issuing.

radicar *vi* to reside, to live; *radicado en Madrid* residing in Madrid ‖ to be, to be situated; *una finca que radica en la provincia de Guadalajara* a farm which is situated in the province of Guadalajara ‖ BOT to take root ‖ FIG *radicar en* to lie in, to stem from.
◆ *vpr* to settle (down) (domiciliarse) ‖ to take root (arraigarse).

radícula *f* BOT radicle.

radiestesia *f* water divining.

radiestesista *m/f* water diviner.

radio *m* radius; *radio de curvatura* radius of curvature ‖ spoke (de una rueda) ‖ RAD wireless *o* radio operator ‖ FIG radius; *en un radio de cien kilómetros* within a radius of a hundred kilometres ‖ MIL range (alcance); *de largo radio de acción* long-range ‖ ANAT radius (hueso) ‖ QUÍM radium (metal) ‖ AMER radio (la radio) ‖ — *radio de acción* jurisdiction, sphere, field (sector) ‖ *radio de giro* turning circle (de un vehículo) ‖ BOT *radio medular* medullary ray.
◆ *f* radio, wireless ‖ radio (set), wireless (set) (aparato) ‖ — *dirección por radio* radio control ‖ *por radio* by radio, on *o* over the radio ‖ *radio galena* crystal detector set.

radioactividad *f* radioactivity.

radioactivo, va *adj* radioactive.

radioaficionado, da *m/f* radio ham, radio amateur.

radioaltímetro *m* radio altimeter.

radioastronomía *f* radio astronomy.

radiobiología *f* radiobiology.

radiocasete *m* radio cassette player.

radiocobalto *m* radiocobalt.

radiocompás *m* radio compass.

radiocomunicación *f* radio communication.

radioconductor *m* radioconductor.

radiocontrol *m* radiocontrol.

radiodespertador *m* radio alarm clock.

radiodiagnosis *f*; **radiodiagnóstico** *m* X-ray diagnosis.

radiodifundir *vt* to broadcast.

radiodifusión *f* broadcasting ‖ *estación de radiodifusión* radio station, transmitter.

radiodifusor, ra *adj* broadcasting ‖ *estación radiodifusora* radio station, transmitter.

radioelectricidad *f* radioelectricity.

radioelemento *m* radioelement.

radioemisora *f* radio station, transmitter.

radioescucha *m/f* listener [*US* auditor].

radiofaro *m* radio beacon.

radiofonía *f* radiotelephony, radio.

radiofónico, ca *adj* radio, wireless.

radiófono *m* radiophone.

radiofotografía *f* radiophotograph, radiophoto.

radiofrecuencia *f* radio frequency.

radiogoniometría *f* radiogoniometry.

radiogoniómetro *m* radiogoniometer, direction finder.

radiografía *f* radiography (técnica) ‖ radiograph, X-ray [photograph] (imagen) ‖ *hacerse una radiografía* to have an X-ray, to be X-rayed.

radiografiar *vt* to X-ray, to radiograph (con rayos X).

radiográfico, ca *adj* radiographic, X-ray.

radiógrafo *m* radiographer.

radiograma *m* radiogram.

radioisótopo *m* FÍS radioisotope.

radiolarios *m pl* ZOOL radiolaria.

radiolocalización *f* radiolocation.

radiología *f* radiology.

radiólogo *m* radiologist.

radiometría *f* radiometry.

radiométrico, ca *adj* radiometric.

radiómetro *m* ASTR & FÍS radiometer.

radiomicrómetro *m* radiomicrometer.

radionavegación *f* radio navigation.

radionavegante *m* radio officer.

radionovela *f* serial [broadcast on the radio].

radioquímica *f* radiochemistry.

radiorreceptor *m* radio receiver, wireless (set), radio (set).

radiorreloj *m* clock radio.

radioscopia *f* radioscopy.

radioscópico, ca *adj* radioscopic.

radiosensibilidad *f* radiosensitivity.

radiosonda *f* radiosonde.

radiotaxi *m* radiocab, radiotaxi.

radiotécnica *f* radiotechnology.

radiotécnico, ca *adj* radiotechnological.
◆ *m* radio engineer.

radiotelefonía *f* radiotelephony.

radiotelefonista *m/f* radio operator.

radioteléfono *m* radiotelephone.

radiotelegrafía *f* radiotelegraphy.

radiotelegrafiar *vt* to radiotelegraph.

radiotelegráfico, ca *adj* radiotelegraphic ‖ *despacho radiotelegráfico* radiotelegram.

radiotelegrafista *m/f* radio *o* wireless operator.

radiotelegrama *m* radiotelegram.

radiotelescopio *m* radio telescope.

radiotelevisión *f* radio and television.

radioterapia *f* radiotherapy.

radiotorio *m* radiothorium.

radiotransmisión *f* radiotransmission, broadcasting.

radiotransmisor *m* radio transmitter.

radiotransmitir *vt* to broadcast [by radio].

radioyente *m/f* listener.

radiumterapia *f* radiotherapy.

radón *m* QUÍM radon (gas).

RAE *abrev de Real Academia Española* Spanish Royal Academy.

raedera *f* scraper ‖ trowel (llana) ‖ shovel (azada).

raedor, ra *adj* scraping.
◆ *m/f* scraper.
◆ *m* strickle, leveller (rasero).

raedura *f* scraping (acción de raer) ‖ scrapings *pl* (parte raída) ‖ worn part *o* patch (de un traje).

raer* *vt* to scrape (raspar) ‖ to scrape off (quitar raspando) ‖ FAM to wear out (traje) ‖ to level (nivelar) ‖ to extirpate, to eradicate (extirpar).

Rafael *npr m* Raphael.

rafaelesco, ca *adj* Raphaelesque.

ráfaga *f* gust (de viento) ‖ flash (de luz) ‖ burst [of machine-gun fire] (de ametralladora).

rafia *f* BOT raffia.

raglán *adj/sm* raglan; *mangas raglán* raglan sleeves.

ragú *m* CULIN ragout.

raid *m* raid (incursión) ‖ AVIAC long-distance flight.

raído, da *adj* worn, threadbare, trayed; *traje raído* threadbare suit ‖ shameless (desvergonzado).

raigambre *f* roots *pl* (de una planta) ‖ FIG deep-rootedness | tradition; *familia de raigambre republicana* family of republican tradition ‖ FIG *costumbre de honda raigambre en Castilla* deep-rooted Castilian custom.

raigón *m* thick root (tocón) ‖ root (de un diente) ‖ FAM stump (de un diente cariado).

raíl; rail *m* rail ‖ *rail guía* runner, curtain rail.

raimiento *m* scraping (acción) ‖ scraping, scrapings *pl* (resultado).

Raimundo *npr m* Raymond.

raíz *f* BOT root ‖ ANAT root (de un diente) ‖ GRAM root ‖ MAT root; *raíz cuadrada, cúbica* square, cube root ‖ origin, source (origen) ‖ — FIG *a raíz de* straight after, immediately after, as a result of ‖ *arrancar* or *cortar de raíz* to uproot (árbol), to wipe out, to eradicate, to uproot (suprimir completamente), to nip in the bud (hacer abortar) ‖ *echar raíces* to take root (una planta, una costumbre, etc.), to settle (down) (instalarse) ‖ BOT *raíz adventicia, pivotante* or *columnar* or *napiforme* adventitious, napiform root ‖ *sacar de raíz* to pull up by the roots (plantas), to wipe out, to eradicate, to uproot (acabar con) ‖ FIG *tener raíces* to be deep-rooted; *la virtud tiene raíces profundas en su corazón* virtue is deep-rooted in his heart.

raja *f* slice (de melón, de sandía, etc.); *hacer rajas* to cut slices ‖ cut (cortadura) ‖ crack, split (hendidura) ‖ slit (en costura) ‖ vent (de chaqueta) ‖ crack (en un plato).

rajá *m* rajah (soberano de la India).

rajado, da *adj* split, cracked (hendido) ‖ FIG & FAM yellow.
◆ *m/f* FIG & FAM chicken, funk, coward, person who backs out ‖ FAM *te lo mereciste por rajado* it's your own fault for backing out.

rajadura *f* split, crack (hendidura).

rajamiento *m* FAM backing out.

rajar *vt* to slice, to cut into slices; *rajar un melón* to cut a melon into slices ‖ to split, to crack (hender) ‖ to slit (hacer una raja en) ‖ to chop, to split (leña).
◆ *vi* FAM to boast, to brag (jactarse) | to chatter (parlotear) | to moan, to grumble (refunfuñar).
◆ *vpr* to crack, to split ‖ FAM to back out, to quit, to chicken out (desistir).

rajatabla (a) *adv* vigorously, strictly ‖ *cumplir una orden a rajatabla* to carry out an order to the letter.

rajeta *f* coarse coloured cloth (tela).
◆ *m/f* FAM chicken (miedoso).

rajón *m* rip, tear (rasguño) ‖ chicken (cobarde) ‖ braggart (jactancioso).

ralea *f* type, sort (raza) ‖ prey (de las aves de cetrería) ‖ — *es un hombre de baja ralea* he is a low sort ‖ *gente de la misma ralea* birds of a feather.

ralentí *m* CINEM slow motion (cámara lenta); *escena al ralentí* slow motion sequence, sequence in slow motion ‖ *funcionar al ralentí* to tick over (motor).

ralo, la *adj* sparse, thin (pelo, árboles) ‖ with gaps between them (dientes) ‖ thin, fine (tela fina) || threadbare (tela desgastada) || loosely woven (de tejido muy separado) || scattered (diseminado) || rare (aire).

rallado, da *adj* grated; *queso rallado* grated cheese.

◆ *m* grating.

rallador *m* grater (utensilio de cocina).

ralladura *f* gratings *pl* || *ralladuras de queso* grated cheese.

rallar *vt* to grate; *rallar zanahorias* to grate carrots || FIG & FAM to grate on (molestar).

rallo *m* grater (rallador) || earthenware jug (vasija).

rallye *m* AUT rally.

rama *f* branch, bough (de árbol) || FIG branch; *las diferentes ramas del saber* the different branches of knowledge | branch (de una familia) || IMPR chase || — FIG & FAM *andarse por las ramas* to beat about the bush || *en rama* raw; *algodón en rama* raw cotton || FIG & FAM *no andarse por las ramas* not to beat about the bush, to get *o* to go straight to the point.

ramada *f* branches *pl* (ramaje) || AMER shelter, shed (cobertizo).

ramadán *m* ramadan (noveno mes musulmán).

ramaje *m* branches *pl* (ramas) || floral pattern *o* design (de una tela).

ramal *m* branch (parte secundaria) || branch line, branch (de ferrocarril) || foothill (de una cordillera) || branch (tramo) || flight (de escalera) || strand (de una cuerda) || halter (ronzal) || secondary gallery (de mina) || RAD wire || — *de la carretera principal arranca un ramal hacia Burgos* a branch of the main road goes off to Burgos || MIL *ramal de trinchera* secondary trench, side trench.

ramalazo *m* lash (golpe) || FIG weal, mark (señal dejada) | sharp pain (dolor) | fit (de locura, de depresión) | gust (de viento) | lash (de lluvia) || FIG *tener un ramalazo de loco* to be a little mad, to have a streak of madness in one.

rambla *f* gully (cauce) || torrent (torrente) || avenue, boulevard (paseo) || TECN tenter (para los paños) || AMER dock (muelle).

rameado, da *adj* flowery, with a floral pattern *o* design (tejido).

ramera *f* prostitute, whore.

rami *m* rummy (juego de naipes).

ramificación *f* ramification || FIG consequence, repercussion (consecuencia) | branch, subdivision (rama).

ramificarse *vpr* to ramify, to branch || FIG to branch out *o* off, to ramify.

ramilla *f* twig.

ramillete *m* bunch (ramo de flores), bouquet (artísticamente hecho), posy (más pequeño) || FIG collection; *ramillete de máximas* collection of maxims | bunch, group; *ramillete de muchachas* bunch of girls.

ramilletero, ra *m/f* florist.

◆ *m* vase.

ramiza *f* branches *pl.*

ramnáceas *f* BOT rhamnaceae.

ramo *m* (small) branch (rama pequeña) || bouquet, posy, bunch (ramillete); *ramo de flores* bouquet of flowers || COM branch, department, line (sección) || field (sector) || sheaf (manojo de hierbas) || FIG branch (subdivisión) || — *Domingo de Ramos* Palm Sunday || FIG *tener un ramo de locura* to be a little mad, to have a streak of madness in one.

ramojo *m* loose branches *pl.*

ramón *m* twigs *pl* cut for use as fodder.

Ramón *npr m* Raymond.

ramonear *vt* to prune (los árboles) || to browse on (los animales).

ramoneo *m* pruning (poda) || pruning season (época).

ramoso, sa *adj* ramose, with many branches.

rampa *f* MED cramp (calambre) || ramp (plano inclinado) || *rampa de lanzamiento* launching pad.

rampante *adj* HERÁLD rampant.

rampla *f* AMER tow, trailer (remolque).

ramplón, ona *adj* common, vulgar; *artículo ramplón* vulgar article; *tío ramplón* common type | dull, heavy; *versos ramplones* dull poetry.

◆ *m* calk (de herradura).

ramplonería *f* vulgarity (vulgaridad) || poor taste (falta de gusto).

rampojo *m* grape stem (escobajo).

rampollo *m* cutting [of a tree].

rana *f* frog; *ancas de rana* frogs' legs || game resembling Aunt Sally [consisting of throwing coins into the mouth of a model frog] (juego) || — FIG & FAM *cuando las ranas críen* or *tengan pelos* when pigs fly *o* have wings | *no ser rana* to be no fool || *rana de zarzal* tree frog || *rana marina* or *pescadora* anglet (pejesapo) || *rana mugidora* bullfrog || FIG & FAM *salir rana* to fall through, to fail, to misfire, to go wrong *o* amiss; *mi proyecto ha salido rana* my plan has fallen through; to be a disappointment (un hijo, etc.), to let (s.o.) down (una persona a otra).

rancajo *m* splinter (espina, astilla).

ranciar *vt* to make rancid.

◆ *vpr* to become rancid *o* stale.

ranciedad *f* rancidity, rancidness, rankness, staleness.

rancio, cia *adj* rancid, stale (la comida, etc.) || rancio (licor) || FIG old-fashioned, antiquated; *una solterona un poco rancia* an old-fashioned spinster | ancient; *de rancio abolengo* from an ancient family.

◆ *m* rancidity, rancidness, rankness || grease (del paño) || rancio wine (vino) || *oler a rancio* to smell rancid.

rancheadero *m* settlement.

ranchear *vi/vpr* to form a settlement, to make a camp, to camp.

◆ *vt* AMER to pillage, to loot.

rancheo *m* AMER pillage, pillaging, sacking.

ranchera *f* AMER popular song.

ranchería *f* settlement, camp (conjunto de ranchos).

ranchero *m* cook, camp cook (el que guisa el rancho) || leader of a settlement (de un campamento) || AMER farmer, rancher (dueño de un rancho).

rancho *m* mess, communal meal (comida) || FAM bad food, swill (comida mala) || farm (finca) || ranch (finca en Norteamérica) || camp, settlement (campamento); *rancho de gitanos* Gipsy camp || AMER hut (choza) || MAR crew's quarters *pl* (alojamiento) || FIG *hacer rancho aparte* to keep to o.s., to go one's own way.

randa *f* lace, lace trimming.

◆ *m* FAM pickpocket.

randera *f* lacemaker.

rangífero *m* reindeer (reno).

rango *m* rank (categoría) || AMER luxury (lujo) | pomp (pompa) | generosity (generosidad) | nag (rocín) || — *conservar* or *mantener su rango* to maintain one's standing || *de alto* or *de mucho rango* high-ranking || *tener rango de* to have the position of.

Rangún *n pr* GEOGR Rangoon.

ránidos *m pl* ZOOL ranidae.

ranilla *f* frog (del caballo).

ranking *m* ranking (clasificación, lista).

ranunculáceas *f pl* BOT ranunculaceae.

ranúnculo *m* BOT ranunculus, buttercup.

ranura *f* groove || slot (de un teléfono público, de una máquina tragaperras) || — *hacer una ranura en* to make a groove in, to groove || TECN *ranura de engrase* lubrication groove.

rapabarbas *m inv* FAM barber (barbero).

rapacejo *m* band of a fringe (alma de fleco) || fringe (fleco) || lad, youngster (muchacho).

rapacería *f* rapacity || childish prank (muchachada).

rapacidad *f* rapacity.

rapador *m* FAM barber (barbero).

rapadura *f*; **rapamiento** *m* shave, shaving (de la barba) || crop, cropping (del pelo) || AMER brown sugar.

rapapiés *m inv* jumping jack (petardo).

rapapolvo *m* FAM dressing down, telling off; *echar un rapapolvo a alguien* to give s.o. a dressing down.

rapar *vt* to shave (afeitar) || to crop, to give a close haircut (cortar el pelo al rape) || FIG & FAM to pinch, to lift, to nick (hurtar).

◆ *vpr* to shave, to have a shave (afeitarse) || to have a close haircut (cortarse el pelo).

rapaz *adj* rapacious || ZOOL predatory || *ave rapaz* bird of prey.

◆ *m/f* rapacious person.

◆ *m pl* ZOOL predators | birds of prey (aves).

rapaz; rapazuelo *m* lad, boy, youngster.

rapaza; rapazuela *f* lass, girl, youngster.

rape *m* ZOOL angler (pez) || quick shave (afeitado) || — *al rape* close; *pelo cortado al rape* close-cropped hair || FIG & FAM *dar un rape* to give a dressing down *o* a telling off (reprender).

rapé *m* snuff, rappee (tabaco en polvo).

rapidez *f* rapidity, speed.

rápido, da *adj* rapid, fast, swift, quick, speedy || express, fast (tren).

◆ *m* express (tren).

◆ *pl* rapids (río).

◆ *adv* quickly || FAM *¡venga, rápido!* make it snappy!, hurry up!, look lively!

rapiña *f* robbery, stealing, theft (hurto) || *ave de rapiña* bird of prey.

rapiñador, ra *m/f* sneak thief, robber.

rapiñar *vt/vi* FAM to pinch, to steal, to thieve.

rapónchigo *m* rampion (planta).

raposa *f* fox (zorro) || vixen, female fox, she-fox (zorra) || FIG & FAM sly fox.

raposear *vi* to be sly *o* cunning.

raposeo *m* cunning, artfulness, guile.

raposera *f* foxhole.

raposería; raposía *f* (sly) trick (ardid) || cunning, artfulness, guile (astucia).

raposo *m* fox (zorro) || FIG fox (astuto).

rapsoda *m* rhapsodist.

rapsodia *f* rhapsody.

rapsódico, ca *adj* rhapsodic, rhapsodical.

raptar *vt* to abduct, to kidnap (una persona).

rapto *m* abduction, kidnapping (de personas) || ecstasy, rapture (éxtasis) || impulse (impulso) || burst, fit, upsurge [of anger, etc.] (de cólera) || MED swoon, faint || *el rapto de las Sabinas* the rape of the Sabine women.

raptor, ra *m/f* abductor, kidnapper.

raque *m* beachcombing.

raquear *vi* to beachcomb.

Raquel *npr f* Rachel.

raquero, ra *adj/s* pirate (pirata).
◆ *m* beachcomber ‖ thief [who operates in ports] (ratero).

raqueta *f* racket (de tenis, etc.) ‖ (croupier's) rake (de croupier) ‖ snowshoe (para andar por la nieve) ‖ hedge mustard (jaramago).

raquialgia *f* MED rachialgia.

raquídeo, a *adj* rachidian; *bulbo raquídeo* rachidian bulb.

raquis *m* ANAT & BOT rachis.

raquítico, ca *adj* MED rachitic, rickety (persona) ‖ stunted (plantas) ‖ weak (débil) ‖ FIG rickety (destartalado).
◆ *m/f* rachitic person.

raquitismo *m* MED rachitis, rickets.

raramente *adv* rarely, seldom (rara vez) ‖ strangely, oddly (extrañamente).

rareza *f* rarity, scarcity (poca frecuencia) ‖ FIG oddity (peculiaridad) ‖ FIG *tener sus rarezas* he is a bit odd.

rarificar *vt* to rarefy.

rarificativo, va; rarificante *adj* rarefactive.

raro, ra *adj* rare (poco frecuente) ‖ rare, scarce (escaso) ‖ FIG strange, odd, bizarre, weird (extraño); *una manera muy rara de expresarse* a very strange way of expressing o.s.; *¡qué raro!* how odd! ‖ QUÍM rare, rarefied (gas) ‖ — FIG *me miró como a un bicho raro* he looked at me as if I came from outer space | *¡qué cosa más rara!* how very strange! ‖ *rara vez* rarely, seldom ‖ FIG *sentirse raro* to feel out of sorts, to feel a bit odd ‖ *son raros los estudiantes que terminan la carrera* very few students finish their course.

ras *m* *a ras de* (on a) level with ‖ *a ras de tierra* on ground level ‖ *lleno* or *llena al ras* full to the brim (recipiente), level (cucharada) ‖ *ras con ras* level ‖ *volar a ras de tierra* to skim the ground, to fly low, to hedgehop.

rasa *f* threadbare *o* thin patch (en una tela).

rasadura *f* levelling.

rasamente *adv* clearly, openly.

rasante *adj* grazing, close; *tiro rasante* grazing shot ‖ low, skimming (vuelo).
◆ *f* slope (de un camino) ‖ *cambio de rasante* brow of a hill.

rasar *vt* to graze, to skim; *rasar el vuelo* to graze the ground ‖ to level (pasar el rasero) ‖ to raze, to rase (arrasar) ‖ AVIAC *rasando el suelo* flying low, skimming the ground, hedgehopping.

rasca *f* AMER drunkenness (borrachera).

rascacielos *m inv* skyscraper (edificio).

rascacio *m* scorpion fish (pez).

rascada *f* AMER scraping, scratching.

rascadera *f* scraper ‖ FAM currycomb (almohaza).

rascado, da *adj* scraped, scratched (rajado) ‖ irascible, irritable ‖ FAM drunk (borracho).

rascador *m* scraper (raedera) ‖ ornamental hair slide (en el pelo) ‖ strip on a matchbox for striking matches, striking surface (para los fósforos) ‖ sheller, husker (para desgranar) ‖ MIL sheller (de una granada) ‖ AUT *rascador de aceite* scraper ring.

rascadura *f* scratch (en la piel) ‖ scratching (acción) ‖ scraping, scrubbing (para quitar algo).

rascamiento *m* scratching (en la piel) ‖ scraping, scrubbing (para quitar algo).

rascar *vt* to scratch (con la uña) ‖ to scrape (raspar) ‖ FAM to scratch away at (la guitarra) ‖ — FIG *el comer y el rascar, todo es empezar* the first step is the hardest ‖ FIG & FAM *vámonos, que aquí no hay nada que rascar* let's go, there's nothing doing around here.
◆ *vpr* to scratch (o.s.) ‖ AMER to get drunk (emborracharse) ‖ FIG *a quien le pique que se rasque* if the cap fits, wear it.

rascatripas *m inv* FAM third-rate fiddle player (violinista malo).

rascón, ona *adj* sour, sharp, rough, tart (vino).
◆ *m* water rail (polla de agua).

rasera *f* spatula, fish slice.

rasero *m* leveller ‖ strickle (para el grano) ‖ FIG *medir por el mismo rasero* to treat impartially, to give the same treatment.

rasete *m* satinet, satinette (tela).

rasgado, da *adj* torn ‖ FIG wide (boca) | almond (ojos).
◆ *m* tear, rip, rent (rasgadura).

rasgadura *f* tear, rip, rent.

rasgar *vt* to tear, to rip, to rent (romper).
◆ *vpr* AMER to die.

rasgo *m* characteristic, feature, trait ‖ stroke (pintando) ‖ feat, act (de heroísmo, etc.) ‖ *rasgo de ingenio* stroke of genius, flash of wit.
◆ *pl* features [of the face] ‖ characteristics (de la escritura) ‖ *explicar a grandes rasgos* to outline, to explain briefly.

rasgón *m* tear, rip, rent.

rasgueado *m* strumming.

rasguear *vt* to strum ‖ FIG to write (escribir).
◆ *vi* to make flourishes [with a pen].

rasgueo *m* strumming (de la guitarra).

rasguñar *vt* to scratch (arañar) ‖ to sketch (un boceto).

rasguño *m* scratch (arañazo) ‖ sketch (boceto).

rasilla *f* kind of serge (tela) ‖ tile (ladrillo).

raso, sa *adj* smooth (liso) ‖ flat, level (llano) ‖ level; *una cucharada rasa* a level spoonful ‖ clear, cloudless; *cielo raso* clear sky ‖ backless (sin respaldo) ‖ low (pelota, vuelo) ‖ — *al raso* in the open air (al aire libre), cropped (muy corto) ‖ *cielo raso* ceiling (techo) ‖ *en campo raso* in the open country ‖ FIG & FAM *hacer tabla rasa de* to make a clean sweep of ‖ MIL *soldado raso* private.
◆ *m* satin (tela).

raspa *f* backbone, bone (de un pescado) ‖ BOT beard (eje) | stalk (de un racimo de uvas).

raspado *m* MED scrape, scraping ‖ scraping (raedura) ‖ scratching out (para borrar).

raspador *m* erasing knife, scraper (para raspar lo escrito) ‖ TECN scraper, scraping knife.

raspadura *f*; **raspamiento** *m* scratching ‖ scraping (raspado) ‖ grating (rallado) ‖ scratching out (para borrar) ‖ scrapings *pl* (residuo del raspado) ‖ scratch (huella) ‖ AMER brown sugar.

raspamiento *m* ⟶ **raspadura.**

raspante *adj* scraping, which scrapes ‖ sharp, rough, tart (vino).

raspar *vt* to scrape ‖ to scratch (arañar) ‖ to graze (la piel) ‖ to scrape off (pintura) ‖ to be sharp *o* rough on; *vino que raspa la boca* wine which is sharp on the palate ‖ to steal (hurtar) ‖ to scratch out (algo escrito) ‖ TECN to scrape ‖ to graze, to skim (rasar) ‖ AMER to tell off (reprender) ‖ FIG *raspando* just, by the skin of one's teeth; *aprobar raspando* to pass by the skin of one's teeth.
◆ *vi* to be rough (la piel) ‖ to be sharp *o* rough (vino).

raspear *vi* to scratch (la pluma).

raspetón (de) *loc* AMER sideways (de lado) | askance (mirar) | in passing (de pasada).

raspilla *f* BOT forget-me-not.

raspón *m* AMER telling off, scolding, dressing down (reconvención) | graze, scratch (desolladura).

rasposo, sa *adj* rough, sharp (áspero).

rasqueta *f* MAR scraper ‖ AMER currycomb (almohaza).

rasquetear *vt* AMER to currycomb, to brush down (almohazar).

rastacuero *m* upstart, parvenu (advenedizo).

rastra *f* trail, track (huella) ‖ cart (carro) ‖ harrow (grada) ‖ string [of onions, of garlic, etc.] (ristra) ‖ trawl (net) (para pescar) ‖ AMER decorative buckle of a gaucho's belt ‖ — *a la rastra* or *a rastras* dragging, trailing (arrastrando), grudgingly, unwillingly (de mal grado) ‖ FAM *andar a rastras* to have a hard time of it | *ir a rastras de uno* to depend on s.o. | *llevar a rastras* to drag (along); *llevar a alguien a rastras al médico* to drag s.o. along to the doctor's; to have still to do; *llevo dos asignaturas a rastras* I still have two subjects to do.

rastreador, ra *adj* tracker, tracking ‖ — MAR *barco rastreador* trawler ‖ *rastreador de minas* minesweeper.

rastrear *vt* to track, to trail, to trace (seguir las huellas) ‖ to trawl (en la pesca) ‖ to sweep (minas) ‖ to drag (un río para buscar algo) ‖ to sell (meat) in the market.
◆ *vi* to fly low, to skim the ground (un avión) ‖ AGR to rake ‖ to trawl (pescar) ‖ FIG to make inquiries.

rastreo *m* dragging ‖ tracking (seguimiento) ‖ AGR raking (con el rastrillo) | harrowing (con la grada) ‖ trawling (en la pesca) ‖ sweeping (minas).

rastrera *f* MAR lower studding sail.

rastreramente *adv* basely.

rastrero, ra *adj* creeping, crawling; *animal rastrero* creeping animal ‖ BOT creeping (tallo) ‖ low (vuelo) ‖ trailing (vestido, etc.) ‖ FIG cringing (persona) | creeping (conducta) | base, vile; *ambiciones rastreras* base ambitions ‖ *perro rastrero* tracker.

rastrillada *f* rake (con el rastrillo) ‖ AMER track, trail (pista).
◆ *pl* rakings.

rastrillado *m* raking ‖ combing, dressing, hackling (de textiles).

rastrillador, ra *m/f* raker ‖ comber (de textiles).
◆ *f* AGR harrow.

rastrillaje *m* AGR raking.

rastrillar *vt* to rake; *rastrillar las avenidas de un jardín* to rake the paths of a garden ‖ AGR to harrow (con la grada) ‖ TECN to hackle, to dress, to comb (cáñamo, lino) ‖ AMER to fire (disparar) | to strike (un fósforo).

rastrillo *m* AGR rake (rastro) ‖ hackle, comb (para el cáñamo, el lino) ‖ MIL portcullis (de fortificación) ‖ small flea market (mercado) ‖ TEATR light batten ‖ TECN ward (de cerradura).

rastro *m* AGR rake (para recoger hierba, paja, etc.) | harrow (grada) | layer (mugrón) ‖ abattoir, slaughterhouse (matadero) ‖ FIG trace, sign; *ni rastro de* no trace of; *no encontrar rastro de* to find no trace of | trail, tracks *pl*, track; *seguir el rastro* to follow the trail | scent (olor) | path (de una tormenta) ‖ — *el Rastro* the flea market in Madrid ‖ *perder el rastro de alguien* to lose track of s.o., to lose s.o.'s scent.

rastrojar *vt* AGR to clear of stubble, to glean.

rastrojera *f* stubble field (tierras) ‖ season during which cattle graze on stubble (temporada).

rastrojo *m* stubble (paja) ‖ stubble field (campo segado) ‖ AMER waste, remains *pl*.

rasurador *m* electric razor.

rasurar *vt* (p us) to shave (afeitar).
◆ *vpr* to shave (afeitarse).

rata *f* rat (mamífero roedor); *rata de alcantarilla* brown rat ‖ — FIG & FAM *más pobre que las ratas* or *que una rata* as poor as a church mouse | *no había ni una rata* there was not a living soul | *no mataría ni a una rata* he wouldn't hurt a fly | *no se salvó ni una rata* no one escaped, the same happened to everyone ‖ *rata blanca* white mouse ‖ *rata de agua* water rat ‖ FIG & FAM *rata de hotel* hotel thief | *rata de sacristía* bigoted churchwoman.
◆ *m* FAM thief (ratero).

ratafía *f* ratafia (licor).

ratania *f* rhatany (planta).

rata parte *loc lat* pro rata (prorrata).

rataplán *m* rub-a-dub, ra-ta-ta (del tambor).

rata por cantidad *loc adv* pro rata.

rateado, da *adj* pro rata.

ratear *vi* to crawl, to creep (arrastrarse).
◆ *vt* to steal (robar) ‖ to give out pro rata, to share out proportionally (repartir).

rateo *m* pro rata distribution.

ratería *f* petty theft, pilfering.

raterismo *m* petty thieving, petty thefts *pl*.

ratero, ra *adj* creeping (rastrero) ‖ FIG cringing, creeping (despreciable) ‖ thieving (ladrón) ‖ — *perro ratero* tracker ‖ *un tío ratero* a thief.
◆ *m/f* thief, petty thief (ladrón) ‖ pickpocket (carterista) ‖ *ratero de hotel* hotel thief.

raticida *m* raticide, rat poison.

ratificación *f* ratification.

ratificar *vt* to ratify.
◆ *vpr* to be ratified.

ratificatorio, ria *adj* ratifying, confirmatory.

ratina *f* ratteen (tela).

rato *adj m* *matrimonio rato* unconsummated marriage.

rato *m* while, time, moment; *salió hace un rato* he went out a while ago ‖ — *a cada rato* all the time, every couple of minutes ‖ *al poco rato* a short time after, shortly after ‖ *a ratos* from time to time, at times ‖ *a ratos perdidos, en los ratos perdidos* in odd moments ‖ *a ratos... y a ratos* one moment... the next; *a ratos está sonriente y a ratos serio* one moment he is smiling, the next he is serious ‖ *de rato en rato* from time to time ‖ *hace mucho rato que* it is a long time since ‖ *hacerle pasar un mal rato a alguien* to give s.o. a rough time ‖ AMER *¡hasta cada rato!* see you soon!, see you later! [US so long!] (hasta luego) ‖ FAM *¡hasta otro rato!* cheerio!, I'll be seeing you! [US so long!] (hasta la vista) | *hay para rato* it'll take quite a while ‖ *llevarse un mal rato* to have a bad time ‖ *para pasar el rato* to pass the time, to kill time, to while away the time ‖ *pasar un buen rato* to have a good time ‖ *pasar un mal rato* to have a rough *o* a bad time of it ‖ *ratos libres* or *de ocio* free *o* spare time ‖ FAM *saber un rato de* to know quite a bit *o* a lot about | *tener ratos* to have one's moments (persona) ‖ *un buen rato* a good time (momento agradable), a good while, some time, quite a while (mucho tiempo) ‖ FIG & FAM *un rato* really (muy); *esta película es un rato buena* this film is really good; loads, heaps, piles (gran cantidad).

ratón *m* mouse (animal) ‖ INFORM mouse ‖ — *el ratón Mickey* Mickey Mouse ‖ FAM *es un ratón de biblioteca* he is a bookworm ‖ *más vale ser cabeza de ratón que cola de león* it is better to reign in hell than to serve in heaven ‖ *ratón almizclero* muskrat ‖ *ratón campesino* field mouse.
— OBSERV El plural de *mouse* es *mice*.

ratoncito *m* AMER blind-man's buff (juego) ‖ FAM *el ratoncito Pérez* the good fairy (personaje infantil).

ratonera *f* mousetrap (trampa para ratones) ‖ mousehole (madriguera del ratón) ‖ AMER hovel (casucha) ‖ FIG & FAM *caer en la ratonera* to fall into the trap.

ratonero, ra; ratonesco, ca; ratonil *adj* mousy ‖ — *la raza ratonil* the mouse tribe ‖ *música ratonera* caterwauling.

rauco, ca *adj* POÉT raucous, harsh.

raudal *m* torrent (corriente de agua) ‖ FIG floods *pl*; *un raudal de lágrimas* floods of tears; *raudales de luz* floods of light ‖ — *a raudales* in torrents ‖ *entrar a raudales* to stream in, to flood in.

raudo, da *adj* rapid, swift (veloz).

ravioles; raviolis *m pl* ravioli.

raya *f* line (línea) ‖ parting [US part] (del peinado) ‖ stripe (lista) ‖ crease (del pantalón) ‖ rifling (de un arma de fuego) ‖ dash (en un escrito, en el alfabeto morse) ‖ limit (límite) ‖ line (de la mano) ‖ scratch (trozo raspado) ‖ ZOOL ray (pez) ‖ line (drogas) ‖ AMER wages *pl*, pay (sueldo) | pitching pennies (juego) ‖ — *camisa a rayas* striped shirt ‖ FIG & FAM *cruz y raya* that's the end of that, that's that | *dar ciento y raya* or *quince y raya a* to run rings round s.o., to knock spots off s.o. ‖ *hacerse la raya* to part one's hair ‖ FIG & FAM *mantener a raya a un inferior* to keep an inferior in his place ‖ *pasar la raya* to go over the line (atletismo) ‖ FIG *pasarse de la raya* to go too far, to overstep the mark ‖ *raya de puntos* dotted line ‖ *tener a raya* to keep at bay *o* in check.

rayadillo *m* striped cotton (tela).

rayado, da *adj* striped; *tela rayada* striped cloth ‖ ruled, lined; *papel rayado* ruled paper ‖ rifled; *cañón rayado* rifled barrel.
◆ *m* stripes *pl*, stripe (rayadura) ‖ lines *pl*, ruled lines *pl* (pauta) ‖ rifling (de un cañón).

rayano, na *adj* bordering, adjacent ‖ on the border (frontera) ‖ *rayano en* bordering on.

rayar *vt* to rule, to line, to draw lines on (el papel) ‖ to stripe (la tela) ‖ to cross *o* to strike out (borrar) ‖ to rifle (un arma de fuego) ‖ to underline (subrayar) ‖ to scratch, to score (una superficie dura).
◆ *vi* to border on; *su jardín raya con el mío* his garden borders on mine ‖ FIG to border on, to verge on; *este acto raya en la locura* this action borders on madness | to be nearly, to be going on for, to be pushing (*fam*); *rayar en los cuarenta* to be nearly forty ‖ to dawn (el día, el alba) ‖ FIG *rayar a gran altura* to shine, to distinguish o.s., to excel.

rayero *m* AMER judge [at a horse-race meeting].

rayo *m* ray; *los rayos del Sol* the sun's rays ‖ ray, beam; *un rayo de luz* a ray of light ‖ lightning (en una tormenta); *ser alcanzado por un rayo* to be struck by lightning ‖ spoke (de una rueda) ‖ FÍS ray; *rayos catódicos* cathode rays ‖ thunderbolt; *los rayos de Júpiter* Jupiter's thunderbolts ‖ FIG live wire; *esta niña es un rayo* this child is a live wire ‖ — FIG *caer como un rayo* to be a bombshell (noticias) ‖ *caer fulminado por un rayo* to be struck by lightning ‖ FIG *con la velocidad del rayo* as quick as a flash, in a flash, like lightning | *echaba rayos por los ojos* his eyes flashed with rage | *echar rayos y centellas* to be furious | *mal rayo me parta si* may I be struck down if | *más vivo que un rayo* as quick as lightning | *¡que le parta un rayo!* to hell with him!, damn him! ‖ *rayo de luna* moonbeam ‖ *rayo de sol* sunbeam ‖ *rayos cósmicos* cosmic rays ‖ *rayos gamma* gamma rays ‖ *rayos infrarrojos* infrared rays ‖ *rayos ultravioleta* ultraviolet rays ‖ FAM *rayos uva* U V A ‖ *rayo verde* green flash, green ray ‖ *rayos X* X rays ‖ FIG *salir como un rayo* to fly out, to shoot out | *temer a uno como al rayo* to fear s.o. like the devil | *¡y a mí que me parta un rayo!* and what about me?

rayón *m* rayon (tejido).

rayuela *f* pitch and toss (juego) ‖ AMER hopscotch (tejo).

raza *f* race; *raza negra* Negro race; *raza humana* human race ‖ breed, strain (de animales) ‖ FAM tribe; *la raza ratonil* the mouse tribe ‖ ray, beam (de luz) ‖ VET sand crack ‖ AMER FAM cheek, nerve (descaro) ‖ *de raza* thoroughbred (caballo), pedigree (perro).

razón *f* reason ‖ reason, cause (motivo); *tener razón para* to have cause to ‖ message (recado); *llevar una razón* to take a message ‖ MAT ratio (proporción) ‖ — *a razón de* at the rate of ‖ *asistirle a uno la razón* to have right on one's side, to be in the right ‖ *atenerse* or *avenirse a razones* to give way *o* to listen *o* to bow to reason ‖ *cerrado por vacaciones —Razón: café la Perla* closed for holidays —Inquiries to La Perla ‖ *con mayor razón* with all the more reason ‖ *con razón* quite rightly, with good reason; *se ha quejado con razón* he quite rightly complained ‖ *con razón o sin ella* rightly or wrongly ‖ *con razón que le sobra, con toda la razón, con mucha razón* quite *o* very rightly ‖ *dar la razón a uno* to say that s.o. is right, to agree with s.o. ‖ *dar razón de* to inform about, to give information about, to tell about ‖ *dar razón de sí* to show signs of life ‖ *en razón a* or *de* because of ‖ *entrar en razón* to listen to reason, to see sense ‖ *¡eso es ponerse en razón!* now you're being reasonable! ‖ *estar cargado de razón* to be completely right (persona, argumento) ‖ *lo hizo con mucha razón* he was very right to do it ‖ *meter* or *poner* or *hacer entrar en razón* to make listen to reason, to make see sense ‖ *no hay razón que valga* there is no excuse *o* no valid reason ‖ *no tener razón* to be wrong, not to be right ‖ *obras son amores, que no buenas razones* actions speak louder than words ‖ *perder la razón* to take leave of one's senses, to go out of one's mind ‖ *ponerse en razón* to be reasonable, to listen to reason ‖ *por una razón o por otra* for some reason, for some reason or another ‖ *quitar la razón a alguien* to say that s.o. is wrong, to disagree with s.o. (no estar de acuerdo), to prove s.o. wrong (demostrar que se equivoca) ‖ *razón de estado* reason of state ‖ *razón de más para* all the more reason for [doing sth.], another reason for, one more reason for ‖ FAM *razón de pie de banco* preposterous talk ‖ *razón de ser* raison d'être ‖ MAT *razón directa, inversa* direct, inverse ratio ‖ *razón social* trade name ‖ *reducirse a la razón* to listen to reason ‖ *sin razón* wrongly ‖ *tener razón* to be right; *usted tiene toda la razón* you are quite *o* so right ‖ *tener razón en hacer algo* to be right to do sth. ‖ *uso de razón* power of reasoning.

razonable *adj* reasonable; *pretensión razonable* reasonable claim; *precio razonable* reasonable price.

razonadamente *adv* reasonably, rationally.

razonado, da *adj* reasoned, well-reasoned, considered.

razonador, ra *adj* reasoning.
◆ *m/f* reasoner, person who reasons.

razonamiento *m* reasoning.

razonar *vi* to reason; *razonar bien* to reason well ‖ to talk (hablar).
◆ *vt* to reason out (problema).

razzia *f* razzia, foray, raid.

re *m* MÚS re, ray.

Rea *npr f* MIT Rhea.

reabastecer *vt* to revictual.

reabsorbente *adj* reabsorbent.

reabsorber *vt* to reabsorb.

reabsorpción *f* reabsorption.

reacción *f* reaction; *reacción en cadena* chain reaction || — *avión de reacción* jet (plane), jet-propelled aeroplane || *propulsión por reacción* jet propulsion.

reaccionar *vi* to react || QUÍM to react.

reaccionario, ria *adj/s* reactionary.

reacio, cia *adj* stubborn (obstinado) || reticent; *se mostró reacio a mi propuesta* he was reticent about my proposal || *estar reacio a hacer algo* to be reluctant to do sth.

reacondicionar *vt* to recondition.

reactancia *f* ELECTR reactance.

reactivación *f* reactivation (de un suero) || recrudescence, reactivation (recrudescencia) || recovery (de la Bolsa, de la economía).

reactivar *vt* to reactivate (la economía, etc.).

reactivo, va *adj* reactive.
◆ *m* QUÍM reagent.

reactor *m* FÍS reactor; *reactor nuclear* nuclear reactor || jet, jet plane, jet-propelled aircraft (avión).

reactorista *m* AVIAC jet pilot.

reacuñación *f* recoinage, remintage.

readaptación *f* readaptation || retraining; *readaptación profesional* industrial retraining || rehabilitation (de un enfermo).

readaptar *vt* to readapt || to retrain (trabajadores) || to rehabilitate (a un enfermo).

readmisión *f* readmission.

readmitir *vt* to readmit || to reemploy (a un empleado).

reafirmar *vt* to reaffirm, to reassert.

reagravarse *vpr* to get worse again.

reagrupación *f*; **reagrupamiento** *m* regrouping.

reagrupar *vt* to regroup.
◆ *vpr* to regroup.

reajustar *vt* to readjust.
◆ *vpr* to readjust.

reajuste *m* readjustment; *reajuste de los salarios* readjustment of salaries || change, reshuffle; *reajuste de un gobierno* government reshuffle.

real *adj* real (efectivo); *necesidades reales* real necessities || royal (del rey); *palacio real* royal palace; *estandartes reales* royal standards || royal; *águila real* royal eagle || FIG splendid, fine (regio) | handsome, fine (hermoso); *un real mozo* a handsome boy || — *camino real* main road (carretera), the shortest way (lo más corto) || FAM *no me da la real gana* I don't feel like it, I don't want to || *una real moza* a lovely girl.
◆ *m* one quarter of a peseta (moneda de 25 céntimos); *diez reales* two and a half pesetas || fairground (ferial) || MIL camp; *alzar* or *levantar el real* or *los reales* to break camp || — *lo real* reality || FAM *no tener un real* not to have a penny to one's name | *no vale un real* it is not worth a red cent | *sentar sus reales* to settle down, to establish o.s.

realce *m* relief; *bordar a realce* to embroider in relief || FIG sparkle (touch of), splendour (esplendor); *dar realce a una fiesta* to give a sparkle *o* a touch of splendour to an occasion | importance || — FIG *dar realce a su estilo* to enhance one's style | *poner de realce* to bring out, to highlight.

realejo *m* MÚS small organ (órgano).

realengo, ga *adj* royal, regal || *bienes de realengo* possessions of the crown (real), possessions of the State (del Estado).

realeza *f* royalty.

realidad *f* reality || truth (verdad) || — *en realidad* in fact, actually || *la realidad es que* the fact of the matter is that || *tenemos que atenernos a la realidad* we must face the facts.

realismo *m* realism (doctrina filosófica y artística) || royalism (fidelidad a la monarquía) || — POÉT *realismo mágico* magic realism || *realismo socialista* socialist realism.

realista *adj* realistic (en arte, en filosofía) || royalist (partidario de la monarquía).
◆ *m/f* realist (en arte, en filosofía) || royalist (partidario de la monarquía).

realizable *adj* attainable (meta) || feasible, practical (factible) || COM saleable, realizable (activo).

realización *f* realization || fulfilment, execution, carrying out (ejecución) || fulfilment (de las esperanzas) || COM selling, sale (venta) | realization (del activo) || production (cine, televisión) || broadcast (radio).

realizar *vt* to carry out, to accomplish, to effect; *realizar un proyecto* to carry out a plan || to accomplish, to attain, to achieve (la meta) || to fulfil; *realizar sus esperanzas* to fulfil one's hopes || to make; *realizar un viaje* to make a journey || COM to realize, to sell; *realizar sus bienes* to sell one's belongings | to make, to realize (beneficio, contrato) || *realizar gestiones* to negotiate.
◆ *vpr* to be fulfilled; *sus esperanzas se realizaron* his hopes were fulfilled || to come true (los sueños, los deseos) || to be carried out, to be accomplished (un plan) || to take place (tener lugar).

realmente *adv* really, truly (de verdad) || really, actually, in fact (en realidad).

realquilado, da *adj* sublet (subarrendado) || relet (alquilado de nuevo).

realquilar *vt* to sublet (subarrendar) || to relet (alquilar de nuevo).

realzado, da *adj* raised.

realzar *vt* to raise, to lift (levantar) || to highlight (en pintura) || FIG to give sparkle *o* colour to (una fiesta) | to enhance, to heighten, to bring out (belleza).

reanimación *f* revival.

reanimar *vt* to revive || to relight (la llama olímpica) || FIG to revive (vigorizar) || *reanimar la conversación* to bring back a bit of life into the conversation, to liven up the conversation.
◆ *vpr* to revive (personas) || to liven up again (fiesta, conversación, etc.).

reanudación *f*; **reanudamiento** *m* renewal, resumption, reestablishment; *reanudación de las relaciones diplomáticas* reestablishment of diplomatic relations || resumption (de conversaciones) || renewal (de una amistad) || reopening (del Parlamento) || return; *reanudación de las clases* return to school.

reanudar *vt* to renew; *reanudar una amistad* to renew a friendship || to resume; *reanudar conversaciones* to resume talks; *reanudar un debate* to resume a debate; *reanudar un servicio de autobuses* to resume a bus service || — *reanudar el paso* or *la marcha* to set off again || *reanudar las clases* to go back to school (los alumnos).
◆ *vpr* to start again, to resume; *se reanudaron las conversaciones* the talks started again.

reaparecer* *vi* to reappear (volver a aparecer) || to make a comeback (un artista, un político) || to recur (un fenómeno).

reaparición *f* reappearance || comeback (de actor, político) || recurrence (de un fenómeno).

reapertura *f* reopening.

rearmar *vt* to rearm.
◆ *vpr* to rearm.

rearme *m* rearmament.

reasegurar *vt* to reinsure.

reaseguro *m* reinsurance.

reasentamiento *m* move, transfer (de colonos, de refugiados).

reasumir *vt* to reassume, to resume.

reasunción *f* reassumption, resumption.

reata *f* rope *o* strap used to keep animals in single file (correa) || packtrain (de caballos, de mulas, etc.) || lead mule (que va en cabeza) || — *de reata* in single file || *enganche de reata* tying (of mules) in single file.

reatar *vt* to reattach, to retie (volver a atar) || to tie tightly (atar firmemente) || to tie in single file [horses or mules].

reavivar *vt* to revive (reanimar) || to rekindle, to revive (sentimientos, etc.).

rebaba *f* rough edge || burr (de un metal fundido).

rebaja *f* discount, reduction (descuento) || lowering (del nivel) || — *grandes rebajas* big reductions (saldos) || *vender con rebaja* to sell at a discount.

rebajado, da *adj* lowered || reduced (precios) || FIG humiliated || ARQ depressed (arco en general) | basket-handle (arco apainelado) || softened, toned down (color).
◆ *m* person exempted from military service.

rebajador *m* FOT reducer.

rebajamiento *m* lowering || FIG humiliation || ARQ depressing || softening, toning down (de los colores) || FOT reduction.

rebajar *vt* to lower (bajar) || to deduct, to make a reduction of; *rebajar mil pesetas* to make a reduction of one thousand pesetas || to cut, to reduce (precios) || to reduce (mercancías, etc.) || to reduce, to diminish, to cut; *rebajarle a uno el sueldo* to reduce s.o.'s wages || to diminish (intensidad) || FIG to humiliate, to deflate || ARQ to depress || to tone down, to soften (colores) || FOT to reduce || *estar rebajado de gimnasia* to be excused *o* let off gym.
◆ *vpr* to be lowered || to go off sick (un empleado) || MIL to be let off; *Pérez se rebajó de la faena de cocina* Perez was let off mess duty || FIG *rebajarse a* to stoop to, to descend to.

rebaje *m* MIL exemption.

rebajo *m* TECN groove, rabbet || ARQ batter (derrame del basamento).

rebalsa *f* pool, pond, puddle || MED engorgement.

rebalsar *vt* to dam, to dam up.
◆ *vpr* to become dammed, to collect in a pool.

rebalse *m* dam (presa) || pool of stagnant water (agua estancada).

rebanada *f* slice; *rebanada de pan* slice of bread.

rebanar; rebanear *vt* to slice, to cut into slices (cortar en rebanadas) || to slice off, to cut off (cortar).

rebañadera *f* grapnel.

rebañadura *f* remains *pl*, leftovers *pl* [of food in a saucepan, etc.].

rebañar *vt* to finish off (comida) || FIG to clean out || to glean (el trigo) || *rebañar el plato con pan* to wipe one's plate clean with bread.

rebaño *m* flock (de ovejas) || herd (de otros animales) || FIG flock (congregación de fieles).

rebasadero *m* MAR safe place [for passing].

rebasar *vt* to exceed, to pass; *rebasar una cantidad* to exceed an amount || to go beyond (una marca) || to surpass; *el éxito rebasó nuestros pronósticos* the success surpassed our forecasts || MAR to pass (un cabo) || to overtake (adelan-

tar) || *rebasar los límites* to overstep the mark, to go too far (exagerar).
◆ *vi* to overflow (un líquido).

rebatimiento *m* refutation.

rebatiña *f* fight, scramble (pelea).

rebatir *vt* to refute (un argumento, etc.); *rebatir una teoría* to refute a theory || to reject, to rebuff (rechazar propuestas, etc.) | to repel, to ward off, to drive back (un ataque) || to stop (un golpe) || to parry (en esgrima) || to resist (una tentación) || to reduce, to lower (rebajar) || to deduct (descontar).

rebato *m* alarm; *tocar a rebato* to sound the alarm || MIL surprise attack (ataque repentino).

rebautizar *vt* to rebaptize, to rechristen.

rebeca *f* cardigan (jersey).

Rebeca *npr f* Rebecca.

rebeco *m* chamois (gamuza).

rebelarse *vpr* to rebel, to revolt; *rebelarse contra el gobierno* to rebel against the government.

rebelde *adj* rebellious || JUR defaulting || rebellious, unruly, unmanageable (indócil) || *ser rebelde a* to be in revolt against (rebelarse contra), to resist.
◆ *m/f* rebel || JUR defaulter.

rebeldía *f* rebelliousness || JUR default || — JUR *condenado en rebeldía* judged by default || *declararse en rebeldía* to rebel, to revolt (sublevarse), to default (en un juicio) || *estar en rebeldía* to be in revolt || *sentencia en rebeldía* judgment by default *o* in contumacy.

rebelión *f* rebellion, revolt || *la rebelión de las masas* The Revolt of the Masses (obra de Ortega y Gasset).

rebencazo *m*; **rebenqueada** *m* lash [of a whip] (golpe) || crack [of a whip] (chasquido).

rebenque *m* whip (látigo) || MAR lashing || MAR *sujetar con rebenques* to lash.

rebenqueada *f* ⟶ **rebencazo.**

rebenquear *vt* AMER to whip.

rebién *adv* very well indeed.

rebina *f* AGR third dressing [of land].

rebinar *vt* AGR to give the third dressing.

rebisabuelo, la *m/f* great-great-grandfather (hombre), great-great-grandmother (mujer).

rebisnieto, ta *m/f* great-great-grandson (chico), great-great-granddaughter (chica).

reblandecer* *vt* to soften (ablandar).
◆ *vpr* to soften, to become soft.

reblandecimiento *m* softening || MED softening; *reblandecimiento cerebral* softening of the brain.

rebobinado *m* rewinding.

rebobinar *vt* to rewind.

rebonito, ta *adj* FAM lovely, gorgeous.

reborde *m* edge, flange; *en el reborde* on the edge.

rebordeador *m* TECN flanger.

rebordear *vt* to flange.

rebosadero *m* overflow || spillway (de embalse).

rebosadura *f*; **rebosamiento** *m* overflowing, overflow (de un líquido).

rebosante *adj* brimming, overflowing, bursting; *estar rebosante de vitalidad* to be overflowing with vitality.

rebosar *vi* to overflow, to brim over (un recipiente) || FIG to be overflowing *o* brimming *o* bursting; *rebosar de entusiasmo* to be overflowing with enthusiasm | to abound (ser abundante) || — FIG *rebosar de riquezas* to be rolling in money | *rebosar de salud, de alegría* to be brimming *o* glowing with health, with joy.

rebotadura *f* bounce (rebote) || napping (de las telas).

rebotar *vi* to bounce, to rebound; *la pelota rebotó en el suelo* the ball bounced on the ground || to ricochet (bala) || *hacer rebotar una pelota contra la pared* to bounce a ball against the wall.
◆ *vt* to clinch (un clavo) || to nap (los paños) || to drive *o* to push back, to repel (rechazar) || FAM to annoy, to get on s.o.'s nerves.
◆ *vpr* to worry, to get upset (turbarse) || to get angry (irritarse).

rebote *m* bounce, rebound (de la pelota) || ricochet (balas o piedras) || *de rebote* on the rebound.

rebotica *f* back room of a chemist's shop.

rebozar *vt* to muffle with *o* to wrap in a cloak || CULIN to cover with batter *o* breadcrumbs, to fry in batter *o* breadcrumbs (pescado, frituras).
◆ *vpr* to muffle o.s. with one's cloak.

rebozo; arrebozo *m* wrap, shawl, cloak (prenda de vestir) || mantilla (mantilla) || FIG dissimulation || — *de rebozo* secretly, in secret || *sin rebozo* openly, frankly.

rebrotar *vi* to shoot, to sprout (retoñar).

rebrote *m* shoot || FIG renewal.

rebueno, na *adj* FAM very good, marvellous.

rebufar *vi* to snort loudly (un animal).

rebujar *vt* ⟶ **arrebujar.**

rebujina; rebujiña *f* FAM bustle (alboroto) | crowd (muchedumbre).

rebullicio *m* bustle (movimiento) || hubbub, commotion, stir (ruido y movimiento).

rebullir* *vi* to stir, to come to life.
◆ *vpr* to stir.

rebusca *f* search (búsqueda) || gleaning (de uvas, de cereales) || gleanings *pl* (espigueo) || FIG leavings *pl*, leftovers *pl* (desecho).

rebuscado, da *adj* recherché, pedantic, affected, elaborate (estilo, palabra, etc.).

rebuscador, ra *adj* searching || gleaning (de uvas, de cereales).
◆ *m/f* searcher || gleaner (de uvas, de cereales, etc.).

rebuscamiento *m* affectation (afectación).

rebuscar *vt* to search thoroughly (un sitio) || to search for (una cosa) || AGR to glean (uvas, cereales).

rebusco *m* search (rebusca).

rebuznador, ra *adj* braying.

rebuznar *vi* to bray.

rebuzno *m* braying, bray.

recabar *vt* to obtain [by entreaty]; *recabar fondos para* to obtain funds for || to ask for (solicitar) || to claim (reclamar) || *recabar toda la atención* to require all one's attention.

recadero, ra *m/f* messenger.
◆ *m* errand boy (niño que lleva los recados) || delivery man (hombre que lleva los pedidos).

recado *m* errand; *le haré el recado* I shall run the errand for him; *le mandé a un recado* I sent him on an errand || message (mensaje); *¿quiere dejarle un recado?* would you like to leave him a message? || materials *pl*, gear, tackle; *recado de escribir* writing materials || AMER saddle and trappings *pl*.
◆ *pl* shopping *sing*, errands (compras); *voy a hacer los recados* I'm going to do the shopping.

recaer* *vi* to fall again, to fall back (caer de nuevo) || to backslide, to relapse (en vicios, en errores, etc.) || to have a relapse, to relapse (un enfermo) || FIG to fall; *la culpa recae sobre él* the blame falls on him; *el premio recayó en el más digno* the prize fell to the worthiest | to hit (afectar) | to come back *o* round; *la conversación recae siempre sobre el mismo tema* the conversation always comes back to the same topic.

recaída *f* backsliding, relapse (en vicios, en errores, etc.) || relapse (de un enfermo).

recalada *f* MAR landfall, sighting of land.

recalar *vt* to soak, to saturate.
◆ *vi* to swim underwater (bucear) || MAR to sight land || AMER to end up, to arrive (llegar).

recalcadura *f* pressing, squeezing, packing || FIG repetition.

recalcar *vt* to press, to squeeze (apretar) || to pack, to cram (rellenar) || FIG to stress, to underline, to emphasize; *recalcar la importancia* to stress the importance | to stress, to accent, to emphasize; *recalcar una frase, una sílaba* to accent a sentence, a syllable | to agree; *siempre he pensado lo mismo, recalcó su primo* that is what I have always thought, agreed his cousin | to insist on (insistir) || *siempre está recalcando lo mismo* he is always coming out with the same thing, he is always saying the same thing.
◆ *vi* MAR to list, to heel.
◆ *vpr* to sit back (arrellanarse).

recalcificación *f* recalcification.

recalcitrante *adj* recalcitrant.

recalcitrar *vi* to back away *o* up, to step back (retroceder) || FIG to be recalcitrant, to resist.

recalentador *m* boiler (calentador de agua) || TECN superheater.

recalentamiento *m* superheating || overheating (calentamiento excesivo) || reheating (recocido).

recalentar* *vt* to superheat || to reheat, to warm up (comida) || to overheat (calentar demasiado) || FIG to excite (excitar).
◆ *vpr* to be superheated || to overheat (calentarse demasiado) || to be on heat (estar en celo) || to spoil (ciertas sustancias) || to rot (maderas) || FIG to get excited (excitarse).

recalmón *m* MAR lull.

recalzar *vt* AGR to ridge, to bank up earth around [*US* to hill] (plantas) || ARQ to underpin, to reinforce.

recalzo *m* extra felloe (de la llanta) || ARQ reinforcement, underpinning || AGR ridging, banking up of earth around plants [*US* hilling].

recamado *m* (relief) embroidery.

recamador, ra *m/f* embroiderer.

recamar *vt* to embroider in relief (bordar).

recámara *f* dressing room (vestuario) || chamber (de arma de fuego) || blast hole (de mina) || reserve (timidez) || AMER bedroom (alcoba) || FIG *Antonio tiene mucha recámara* Anthony is very reserved.

recamarera *f* AMER maid (criada).

recambiable *adj* refillable, able to be refilled.

recambiar *vt* to change again (cambiar de nuevo) || to change, to change over (una pieza) || COM to draw [a redraft].

recambio *m* change (acción de cambiar) || refill (de estilográfica) || spare, spare part (pieza) || *de recambio* spare; *rueda de recambio* spare wheel.

recancamusa *f* FAM ruse, trick.

recancanilla *f* kind of hopping game (juego de niños) || FIG & FAM emphasis, stress || *hablar con recancanilla* to emphasize one's words, to speak emphatically.

recapacitar *vt/vi* to think over, to consider; *recapacitar sobre una cosa* to think sth. over, to consider sth.
◆ *vi* to think things over, to reflect (reflexionar).

recapitulación *f* recapitulation, summing up, summary.

recapitulador, ra *m/f* recapitulator.

recapitular *vt* to recapitulate, to sum up.

recapitulativo, va *adj* recapitulative, recapitulating.

recarga *f* refill.

recargable *adj* refillable, able to be refilled.

recargar *vt* to reload (cargar de nuevo) ‖ to overload (sobrecargar) ‖ to increase, to raise; *recargar los impuestos* to increase taxes; *recargar del diez por ciento* to increase by ten percent ‖ to put a strain on; *esto recarga mi presupuesto* that is putting a strain on my budget ‖ to recharge (una batería) ‖ to lengthen [a sentence] (una condena) ‖ FIG to overburden, to load down; *recargar de obligaciones* to load down with duties ‖ — *estilo recargado* overelaborate style ‖ *recargado de adornos* overornate, overadorned ‖ FIG *recargar el cuadro* or *las tintas* to exaggerate, to overdo it.

recargo *m* new load *o* burden, additional load *o* burden (nuevo cargo) ‖ increase (de impuestos, de precios) ‖ refill (recarga) ‖ additional payment, surcharge (sobretasa); *un recargo del diez por ciento* a ten percent surcharge, an additional payment of ten percent ‖ JUR increase, lengthening (de pena) ‖ MED temperature rise ‖ MIL extra period [of service] (tiempo suplementario).

recatadamente *adv* prudently, cautiously (con prudencia) ‖ becomingly, modestly, fittingly (decentemente) ‖ humbly (humildemente).

recatado, da *adj* prudent, cautious (prudente) ‖ reserved (reservado) ‖ modest, demure, decent (mujer).

recatar *vt* to hide, to cover up (encubrir).
◆ *vpr* to take care, to be careful (andar con cuidado) ‖ to act discreetly (actuar sin ostentación) ‖ to hesitate (vacilar) ‖ — *recatarse de la gente* to hide o.s. away ‖ *sin recatarse* openly.

recato *m* prudence, caution (prudencia) ‖ modesty (pudor) ‖ reserve.

recauchutado *m* retreading (de un neumático).

recauchutar *vt* to retread (un neumático).

recaudación *f* takings *pl*, take (cobro); *la recaudación ascendió a 2.000 pesetas* the takings amounted to 2,000 pesetas; *hacer una buena recaudación* to have good takings ‖ collection, collecting (acción de recaudar) ‖ receipts *pl*, returns *pl* (contribuciones, tasas, impuestos) ‖ tax collector's office (sitio).

recaudador *m* tax collector; *oficina del recaudador* tax collector's office ‖ *recaudador de contribuciones* tax collector.

recaudar *vt* to take, to collect (recibir) ‖ to collect (contribuciones) ‖ to put in a safe place (asegurar) ‖ to recover (una deuda).

recaudo *m* precaution (precaución) ‖ collection (recaudación) ‖ care (cuidado) ‖ JUR deposit (fianza) ‖ *estar a buen recaudo* to be in safekeeping *o* in a safe place.

recazo *m* guard (de espada) ‖ back (del cuchillo).

recelar *vt/vi* to suspect (barruntar); *recelo que va a venir hoy* I suspect he is going to come today ‖ to fear, to be afraid (temer); *recelo que me suceda alguna desgracia* I fear that some misfortune may befall me ‖ to be suspicious (desconfiar); *recelar de todo* to be suspicious of everything ‖ to excite (a una yegua).

recelo *m* distrust, mistrust (desconfianza); *acoger con cierto recelo* to greet with a certain amount of distrust ‖ suspicion (suspicacia) ‖ fear (temor) ‖ — *mirar con recelo* to look suspiciously at ‖ *tener recelo de* to distrust.

receloso, sa *adj* distrustful, suspicious; *receloso con sus amigos* suspicious of his friends ‖ fearful, apprehensive (temeroso).

recensión *f* review, write-up (*fam*) (reseña de una obra) ‖ recension (obra revisada), .

recental *adj* sucking, unweaned; *ternero recental* sucking calf.
◆ *m* suckling.

recentar* *vt* to leaven.
◆ *vpr* to be renewed (renovarse).

recepción *f* receipt (de un paquete, etc.) ‖ reception, reception desk (en un hotel) ‖ reception (fiesta) ‖ admission ‖ JUR examination [of witnesses].

recepcionista *m/f* receptionist.

receptáculo *m* receptacle.

receptividad *f* receptivity, receptiveness.

receptivo, va *adj* receptive.

receptor, ra *adj* receiving ‖ *aparato receptor* receiver, receiving set.
◆ *m* receiver, recipient (persona) ‖ receiver, receiving set (radio, televisión) ‖ ANAT & BIOL receptor ‖ — *receptor de control* monitor ‖ *receptor de televisión* television set *o* receiver ‖ *receptor universal* universal recipient.
◆ *f* receiver (máquina).

receptoría *f* tax collector's office.

recesión *f* recession (en economía).

recésit *m* holiday (recle).

recesivo, va *adj* recessive (en biología).

receso *m* (p us) recession ‖ AMER recess (vacaciones) ‖ AMER *entrar en receso* to recess (una asamblea).

receta *f* CULIN recipe ‖ MED prescription, recipe (p us) ‖ FIG recipe (fórmula); *tener una receta para hacer fortuna* to have a recipe for making a fortune ‖ FIG & FAM *receta de vieja* old wive's tale.

recetar *vt* MED to prescribe.

recetario *m* prescription (del médico) ‖ prescription book *o* record (en un hospital) ‖ pharmacopoeia (farmacopea).

recibí *m* *poner el recibí a* or *en una factura* to sign a receipt.

recibidor, ra *adj* receiving.
◆ *m* receiver, recipient (persona) ‖ entrance hall (entrada) ‖ antechamber (antesala).

recibimiento *m* reception ‖ welcome, reception (acogida); *tuvo muy mal recibimiento* he got a very bad welcome ‖ reception (fiesta) ‖ entrance hall (vestíbulo) ‖ antechamber (antesala).

recibir *vt/vi* to receive, to entertain; *siendo mujer de ministro tiene que recibir a menudo* being a minister's wife she often has to entertain ‖ to receive, to welcome; *el ministro fue recibido con gran pompa* the minister was received with great pomp ‖ to receive; *el Presidente no pudo recibirme* the President couldn't receive me ‖ to receive, to welcome, to take; *no recibieron muy bien su propuesta* his proposal was not very well received ‖ to accept; *reciba mi sincera enhorabuena* accept my sincere congratulations ‖ TAUR (*véase* OBSERV) ‖ — *reciba un atento saludo de* Yours sincerely ‖ COM *recibí* or *recibimos* received with thanks ‖ *recibir con los brazos abiertos* to welcome with open arms ‖ *recibir una negativa* to be refused, to meet with a refusal ‖ *ser recibido como los perros en misa* to be as welcome as a bull in a china shop.
◆ *vpr* to graduate ‖ *recibirse de doctor* to receive one's doctor's degree, to qualify as a doctor.

— OBSERV In bullfighting terminology this verb is used mainly in the expression *matar recibiendo*; this entails the bullfighter thrusting as the bull charges. The alternative is *matar a volapié*, the bullfighter moving towards the stationary bull to kill it.

recibo *m* receipt (documento) ‖ reception, receiving (recibimiento) ‖ small living room (sala) ‖ antechamber (antesala) ‖ — *acusar recibo* to acknowledge receipt ‖ *estar de recibo* to be acceptable (un traje, etc.), to be decent *o* presentable (una persona).

reciclado *m* retraining.

reciclar *vt* to retrain.

recidiva *f* MED relapse.

reciedumbre *f* strength.

recién *adv* recently, newly; *casa recién construida* recently built house; *una flor recién abierta* a newly opened flower ‖ — *estar recién* to have just; *estar recién llegado* to have just arrived; *está recién hecho* it has just been done; *estaba recién comido* he had just eaten ‖ *los recién casados* the newlyweds ‖ *los recién llegados* the newcomers ‖ *los turistas recién llegados* the tourists who have just arrived ‖ *recién salido del colegio* just out of school, fresh from school ‖ *un niño recién nacido* a newborn baby.

— OBSERV In Spain, *recién* which is the apocopation of *recientemente*, is used only before past participles. In Latin America it is very common with the active mood of the verb, in the sense of *not long ago* (*recién hemos llegado* we have just arrived; *recién en 1886* as early as 1886).

reciente *adj* recent; *una noticia reciente* recent news ‖ fresh; *queso reciente* fresh cheese ‖ *construida en fecha reciente* newly *o* recently built.

recientemente *adv* recently, of late, lately.

recinto *m* enclosure ‖ precinct, precincts *pl*, grounds *pl* (zona delimitada); *el recinto de la escuela* the school precinct ‖ area (área).

recio, cia *adj* strong, vigorous, robust (vigoroso) ‖ sturdy, strong (grueso) ‖ loud (voz) ‖ rigorous, harsh, severe (frío, temperatura) ‖ heavy (lluvia) ‖ wild, violent (tempestad, corriente de agua, etc.) ‖ *en lo más recio del combate, del invierno, del verano* in the thick of the battle, in the dead of (the) winter, at the height of (the) summer.
◆ *adv* loudly, loud; *hablar recio* to speak loudly ‖ heavily, hard; *llover recio* to rain hard ‖ *de recio* strongly, vigorously, violently.

récipe *m* FAM prescription (receta) ‖ scolding, telling off (reprimenda).

recipiendario *m* newly elected member.

recipiente *adj* receiving, recipient.
◆ *m* recipient (persona) ‖ vessel, receptacle, container (vasija, etc.) ‖ TECN bell glass ‖ QUÍM receiver.

reciprocación *f* GRAM reciprocity ‖ reciprocation.

reciprocarse *vpr* to reciprocate.

reciprocidad *f* reciprocity.

recíproco, ca *adj/sf* reciprocal ‖ *a la recíproca* vice versa.

recitación *f* recitation, recital.

recitado *m* MÚS recitative ‖ recitation (recitación).

recitador, ra *adj* reciting.
◆ *m/f* reciter.

recital *adj* recital; *músico que ha dado recitales por todo el mundo* musician who has given recitals throughout the world ‖ reading (de poesías).

recitar *vt* to recite.

recitativo *m* MÚS recitative.

reclamación *f* claim, demand (petición) || protest, complaint (queja); *hacer una reclamación* to lodge *o* to make a complaint.

reclamador, ra *m/f* JUR claimant.

reclamar *vt* to claim, to demand (pedir); *reclamar lo que se le debe a uno* to claim what is due to one || to require, to demand, to need (exigir) || to call (las aves) || *la multitud reclamaba que saliese el presidente al balcón* the crowd clamoured for the president (to appear).
◆ *vi* JUR to appeal (protestar); *reclamar contra un fallo* to appeal against a sentence || to protest, to complain; *reclamar contra una decisión* to protest against a decision || — MAR *izar a reclamar* to hoist home || JUR *reclamar en juicio* to appeal.

reclamo *m* decoy bird (ave amaestrada) || birdcall (pito) || call (llamada) || COM advertisement (anuncio) | advertising slogan (frase publicitaria) || JUR claim || IMPR catchword || FIG inducement || *acudir al reclamo* to answer the call.

recle *m* holiday (en los conventos).

reclinación *f* leaning.

reclinar *vt* to lean.
◆ *vpr* to lean; *reclinarse en* or *sobre* to lean on.

reclinatorio *m* prie-dieu (para arrodillarse).

recluido, da *adj* shut *o* locked in (encerrado).

recluir* *vt* to imprison (encarcelar) || to confine (en un manicomio) || to shut *o* to lock in (encerrar) || to shut away (apartar).
◆ *vpr* to shut o.s. off *o* away.

reclusión *f* seclusion || prison, imprisonment, confinement (prisión) || retreat (lugar de retiro) || — JUR *reclusión mayor* maximum-term rigorous imprisonment | *reclusión menor* long-term rigorous imprisonment | *reclusión perpetua* ordinary imprisonment for life.

recluso, sa *adj* imprisoned || *población reclusa* prison population.
◆ *m/f* prisoner (en una prisión).

recluta *m* MIL recruit | conscript (quinto).
◆ *f* conscription, recruitment (reclutamiento) (*véase* OBSERV en RECLUTAR).

reclutador *m* MIL recruiting officer (*véase* OBSERV en RECLUTAR).

reclutamiento *m* recruitment, conscription | recruits *pl*, conscripts *pl* (conjunto de reclutas) (*véase* OBSERV en RECLUTAR).

reclutar *vt* MIL to recruit, to conscript || to recruit (trabajadores) || *AMER* to round up (reunir el ganado).

— OBSERV Las palabras inglesas *recruit* y *conscript* no son sinónimas. *To recruit* es alistar reclutas voluntarios, *to conscript* es obligarlos a alistarse.

recobrar *vt* to recover; *recobrar la salud, el buen humor, la confianza* to recover one's health, one's good humour, one's confidence || to recapture (una ciudad) || to make up (for) (tiempo perdido) || to get back; *recobrar aliento, sus derechos* to get one's breath back, one's rights back || to regain; *recobrar la esperanza, las fuerzas* to regain hope, strength || — *recobrar el espíritu* or *el sentido* to come round, to regain consciousness, to come to || *recobrar su dinero* to find one's money (encontrar), to get one's money back (cubrir gastos).
◆ *vpr* to get one's money back (desquitarse) || to come round *o* to (volver en sí) || to recover, to recuperate, to get better (recuperarse).

recobro *m* recovery || convalescence.

recocer* *vt* to recook, to warm up (volver a cocer) || to cook for a long time (cocer mucho tiempo) || to overcook (cocer demasiado) || TECN to anneal (el acero, el vidrio).
◆ *vpr* to cook for a long time (cocer mucho) || FIG to be consumed (*de* with).

recocido, da *adj* recooked (vuelto a cocer) || overcooked, overdone (demasiado cocido) || cooked for a long time (muy cocido).
◆ *m* annealing (vidrio, acero).

recocina *f* scullery.

recochinearse *vpr* FAM to make fun of, to mock (burlarse) | to ogle (viendo un espectáculo licencioso) | to have fun *o* a good time (divertirse).

recochineo *m* FAM mocking, mockery (burla) | fun, lark; *¡qué recochineo!* what a lark!, what fun! || FAM *y encima con recochineo* and not only that, he laughed about it.

recodadero *m* elbow rest.

recodar *vi* to wind, to twist, to turn (un río).
◆ *vi/vpr* to lean (one's elbows) (*en* on).

recodo *m* twist, turn (de río) || bend (de carretera) || angle (ángulo) || nook, recess; *casa con muchos recodos* house with many nooks.

recogedero *m* place where things are collected (sitio) || dustpan (pala para la basura).

recogedor, ra *adj* collecting.
◆ *m/f* collector || AGR harvester (de la cosecha) | picker (de frutas, de patatas, etc.).
◆ *m* dustpan (para la basura) || AGR kind of rake (instrumento).

recogemigas *m inv* crumb scoop [for sweeping up crumbs].

recogepelotas *m inv* ball boy.

recoger *vt* to take again, to take back (coger de nuevo) || to collect, to gather; *recoger datos, leña* to collect information, wood || to save, to collect; *recoger sellos de correo* to save postage stamps || to collect (dinero) || to gather (el polvo) || to wipe up (agua, etc., en el suelo) || to pick up; *recoge el libro que se ha caído* pick up the book which has fallen; *recoger dos entradas de teatro* to pick up two theatre tickets || to gather, to stop (la pelota) || to pick up, to fetch, to go for (a uno); *le recogeré a las ocho* I shall pick you up at eight o'clock || AGR to gather in, to bring in (poner al abrigo); *recoger las mieses* to gather in the harvest | to harvest (cosechar) || to pick (fruta, flores) || to put away (poner en su sitio) || to take in, to shelter, to welcome (dar asilo) || to seize (retirar de la circulación); *recoger un periódico* to seize a newspaper || to lift *o* to pick up (la falda) || to roll up (las mangas) || to take in, to shorten (en costura) || MAR to take in (las velas) || FIG to reap; *recoger el fruto de su trabajo* to reap the fruit of one's work | to get (obtener) || — *quien siembra vientos recoge tempestades* he who sows the wind shall reap the whirlwind || *recoger el caballo* to draw up one's horse || FIG *recoger el guante* to take up the gauntlet *o* the challenge | *recoger laureles* to reap *o* to win laurels || *recoger los platos de la mesa* to clear the table, to clear the dishes away.
◆ *vpr* to withdraw within o.s. (ensimismarse) || REL to recollect o.s. || to go home (retirarse a su casa); *se recoge temprano* he goes home early || to go to bed (irse a la cama) || to gather together (los animales) || to pick *o* to lift up (la falda) || — *recogerse el pelo* to put one's hair up || *recogerse en sí mismo* to withdraw within o.s.

recogida *f* collection (del correo, de la basura, etc.) || AGR harvest, harvesting (cosecha) || seizure (de un periódico) || (ant) withdrawal (retirada) || *recogida de firmas* petition, gathering of signatures.

recogidamente *adv* retiringly (apartado) || solitarily, alone (en soledad) || quietly (tranquilamente) || devoutly (con devoción).

recogido, da *adj* short (animal) || small (pequeño) || withdrawn (apartado del mundo) || secluded; *vida recogida* secluded life || quiet (tranquilo) || pinned *o* tied back (pelo).

recogimiento *m* withdrawal (del espíritu) || AGR roundup (del ganado) || REL recollection || *vivir con gran recogimiento* to lead a very withdrawn *o* secluded life.

recolar* *vt* to refilter, to filter *o* to strain again.

recolección *f* AGR harvest, harvesting, picking (acción) | harvest time (temporada) || collection, gathering; *recolección de informaciones estadísticas* collection of statistical information || REL retreat (retiro) | strict observance (de la regla en los conventos).

recolectar *vt* to harvest, to gather in (cosechar) || to collect (colectar).

recolector *m* collector.

recoleto, ta *adj* quiet, peaceful (calle, plaza) || withdrawn, retiring (una persona).
◆ *m/f* recollet (religioso).

recomendable *adj* recommendable || commendable (laudable) || *no ser recomendable* to be unwise, to be inadvisable.

recomendación *f* recommendation (consejo, etc.) || references *pl*, testimonial (referencias) || — *carta de recomendación* recommendation, letter of introduction || *recomendación del alma* prayers for the dying || *valerse de la recomendación de alguien* to give s.o. as a reference.

recomendado, da *adj* recommended.
◆ *m/f* protégé, protégée.

recomendador, ra *adj* recommendatory.

recomendante *m* person who recommends, recommender.

recomendar* *vt* to recommend, to advise (aconsejar) || to commend (alabar) || to confide (confiar) || *te lo recomiendo* I recommend it to you.

recomendatorio, ria *adj* recommendatory.

recomenzar *vt* to recommence, to begin *o* to start again.

recomerse; reconcomerse *vpr* FIG to be consumed (*de* with, by).

recompensa *f* recompense, reward || *en recompensa de* in return for, as a reward for.

recompensable *adj* rewardable, recompensable.

recompensar *vt* to recompense, to reward; *recompensar por un trabajo* to recompense for a job || to compensate (compensar).

recomponer* *vt* to recompose | to repair (arreglar) || to dress up, to doll up (*fam*), (acicalar).
◆ *vpr* to dress up, to doll o.s. up (*fam*), (acicalarse).

recomposición *f* recomposition.

recompuesto, ta *adj* recomposed || repaired (arreglado) || dressed up, dolled up (acicalado).

reconcentración *f*; **reconcentramiento** *m* concentration.

reconcentrar *vt* to concentrate || to conceal (el odio, etc.) || to bring together (reunir).
◆ *vpr* to concentrate (abstraerse) || to withdraw into o.s. (ensimismarse) || to build up (el odio, etc.).

reconciliación *f* reconciliation.

reconciliador, ra *adj* reconciling, reconciliatory.
◆ *m/f* reconciler.

reconciliar *vt* to reconcile.
◆ *vpr* to be reconciled.

reconcomerse *vpr* FIG → **recomerse.**

reconcomio *m* FIG longing, urge, itch (deseo) | grudge (rencor) | remorse (remordimiento) | doubt, suspicion, misgiving (sospecha).

recondenado, da *adj* FAM damn, damned; *¡recondenada vida!* this damn life!

reconditez *f* heart of hearts ‖ bottom; *la reconditez del alma* the bottom of the soul.

recóndito, ta *adj* secret, hidden ‖ — *en lo más recóndito de* in the depths of ‖ *en lo más recóndito del alma* deep inside ‖ *lo más recóndito del asunto* the heart of the matter ‖ *lo más recóndito del corazón* one's heart of hearts, the bottom of one's heart.

reconducción *f* JUR renewal, extension (prórroga).

reconducir* *vt* JUR to renew, to extend (prorrogar).

reconfirmar *vt* to reconfirm.

reconfortación *f* comfort.

reconfortante *adj* comforting.
◆ *m* MED tonic.

reconfortar *vt* to comfort (confortar) ‖ to cheer up (animar) ‖ MED to strengthen, to fortify.

reconocer* *vt* to recognize; *no te reconocí a primera vista* I didn't recognize you at first sight ‖ to distinguish, to identify (distinguir) ‖ to admit, to acknowledge; *reconocer sus faltas* to admit one's mistakes; *lo reconozco* I admit it ‖ to recognize (un gobierno) ‖ to recognize; *reconocer por hijo* to recognize as one's son ‖ to face; *reconozcamos los hechos* let's face the facts ‖ to survey (el terreno) ‖ MED to examine ‖ MIL to reconnoitre [*US* to reconnoiter], to make a reconnaissance ‖ to check, to go through (registrar) ‖ to be grateful for (mostrarse agradecido) ‖ — FIG *reconocer el terreno* to see how the land lies ‖ *reconocer la evidencia* to bow to the evidence.
◆ *vpr* to be recognized *o* known ‖ to admit; *reconocerse culpable* to admit one's guilt.

reconocible *adj* recognizable.

reconocidamente *adv* gratefully, with gratitude (con gratitud) ‖ obviously, clearly (evidentemente) ‖ avowedly (por confesión propia).

reconocido, da *adj* grateful (agradecido) ‖ recognized ‖ confessed, acknowledged (confesado).

reconocimiento *m* recognition; *el reconocimiento de un error, de un amigo* the recognition of a mistake, of a friend; *el reconocimiento de un niño* the recognition of a child ‖ recognition (de un gobierno) ‖ confession, acknowledgement, admission (confesión) ‖ check, inspection (registro) ‖ gratitude (gratitud) ‖ MIL reconnaissance; *avión de reconocimiento* reconnaissance plane ‖ — *en reconocimiento a los servicios prestados* in appreciation of services rendered, for services rendered ‖ *reconocimiento de deuda* acknowledgement of debt ‖ INFORM *reconocimiento de formas* pattern recognition | *reconocimiento de la voz* voice *o* speech recognition ‖ MED *reconocimiento médico* medical examination, checkup ‖ INFORM *reconocimiento óptico de caracteres* optical character recognition.

reconquista *f* reconquest.
— OBSERV The name *Reconquista* applies especially to the period from 718 (battle of Covadonga) to 1492 (the taking of Granada by Ferdinand and Isabel), during which the Spanish people fought the Moslem invaders who had occupied a large part of the peninsula.

reconquistar *vt* to reconquer (un país) ‖ to reconquer, to recapture (una ciudad) ‖ FIG to recover, to win back.

reconsiderar *vt* to reconsider.

reconstitución *f* reconstitution ‖ JUR reconstruction.

reconstituir* *vt* to reconstitute ‖ JUR to reconstruct (un crimen).

reconstituyente *adj/sm* reconstituent.

reconstrucción *f* reconstruction, rebuilding.

reconstructivo, va *adj* reconstructive.

reconstruir* *vt* to reconstruct, to rebuild.

recontar* *vt* to recount, to count again (una cuenta) ‖ to retell, to tell again (una historia).

¡recontra! *interj* damn!, blast!

reconvención *f* reproach, reprimand (censura) ‖ JUR counterclaim, cross action.

reconvenir* *vt* to reproach, to reprimand, to rebuke; *reconvenir a uno por alguna cosa* to reproach s.o. with sth. ‖ JUR to counterclaim.

reconversión *f* reconversion ‖ retraining (nueva formación).

reconvertir* *vt* to reconvert ‖ to retrain (dar nueva formación).
◆ *vpr* to be reconverted *o* retrained.

recopilación *f* summary, résumé, compendium (compendio) ‖ compilation; *recopilación de poemas* compilation of poems ‖ code; *recopilación de leyes* code of laws.
— OBSERV The name *Recopilación* is given to the official code of Spanish laws which was established in 1567. The *Nueva Recopilación* and the *Novísima Recopilación* are two more modern versions, which were compiled in 1775 and 1805 respectively.

recopilador *m* compiler.

recopilar *vt* to compile (reunir) ‖ to summarize (resumir) ‖ to codify, to compile (leyes).

récord *m* record (marca); *batir, tener, establecer un récord* to break *o* to beat, to hold, to set up a record; *el poseedor del récord* the record holder.
◆ *adj* record; *en un tiempo récord* in record time.

recordable *adj* memorable.

recordación *f* memory (recuerdo) ‖ remembering (acción de recordar) ‖ *un presidente de feliz recordación* a president who left a happy memory.

recordar* *vt* to remind of; *recordar un hecho a uno* to remind s.o. of a fact; *esta muchacha me recuerda a su madre* this girl reminds me of her mother ‖ to remember, to recall (acordarse de); *recuerdo tu visita* I remember your visit; *recuerdo que llegó muy tarde* I remember that he arrived very late ‖ to recall, to bring to mind, to be reminiscent of (hacer pensar en); *este paisaje recuerda un cuadro de Turner* this scenery is reminiscent of a painting by Turner ‖ to commemorate; *hacer algo para recordar un acontecimiento* to do sth. to commemorate an event ‖ (ant) AMER to wake up (despertar) ‖ *para recordar* in memory *o* remembrance of (una persona), to commemorate (un acontecimiento).
◆ *vi* to wake up (despertarse) ‖ to reminisce (pensar en o hablar de los viejos tiempos) ‖ to remember (acordarse) ‖ — *que yo recuerde* as far as I can recall *o* remember ‖ *si mal no recuerdo* if my memory serves me well, if I remember rightly, as far as I can remember.
◆ *vpr* to wake up (despertarse).

recordativo, va *adj* reminiscent.

recordatorio *m* notice of death (estampa en recuerdo de los difuntos) ‖ reminder (medio para hacer recordar) ‖ reminder (advertencia) ‖ lesson; *para que te sirva de recordatorio* as a lesson to you.

recordman; recordwoman *m/f* record holder.
— OBSERV Although these words are often used, there does exist the Spanish equivalent *plusmarquista*.

recorrer *vt* to go *o* to travel through *o* over, to cross; *recorrer una ciudad* to go through a city ‖ to tour, to travel round *o* through (un país) ‖ to cover, to scour (buscando algo) ‖ to cover, to go, to come, to travel (una distancia); *llegaron aquí después de haber recorrido miles de kilómetros* they arrived here having covered *o* travelled thousands of kilometres; *hemos recorrido una gran distancia* we have come *o* covered a great distance ‖ to look over, to run through (un escrito) ‖ to inspect, to examine, to check, to go through (registrar) ‖ IMPR to overrun ‖ *recorrer mundo* to see the world.

recorrida *f* AMER → **recorrido.**

recorrido *m* journey; *es un recorrido precioso* it is a beautiful journey; *un recorrido por España* a journey through Spain ‖ journey, run; *es un recorrido muy largo* it is a long journey ‖ distance covered (distancia recorrida) ‖ route (trayecto); *el recorrido del autobús, de una procesión* the bus route, the route of a procession ‖ path, flight path (trayectoria de proyectil) ‖ round; *el recorrido del cartero* the postman's round ‖ DEP run (en esquí) | round (en golf, en equitación, etc.); *un recorrido sin faltas* a clear round ‖ IMPR overrun ‖ TECN stroke (del émbolo) | overhaul (repaso, arreglo general) ‖ FAM good talking-to (reprensión larga); *darle un recorrido a alguien* to give s.o. a good talking-to.

recortable *adj* cutout.

recortado, da *adj* cut out ‖ jagged (un borde) ‖ uneven, irregular (una superficie).

recortadura *f* cutting.
◆ *pl* cuttings.

recortar *vt* to cut (imágenes, etc.) ‖ to recut, to cut again (volver a cortar) ‖ to trim, to cut *o* to even off (el borde de una pieza) ‖ to outline (pintura) ‖ to trim (el pelo).
◆ *vpr* to stand out, to be outlined; *la torre se recortaba en el cielo* the tower stood out against the sky.

recorte *m* cutting (out) (acción) ‖ trim (de pelo) ‖ cutting (fragmento cortado); *recorte de prensa* press cutting ‖ cutout (para los niños) ‖ piece [that has been cut] (metales, telas) ‖ TAUR dodge (del torero) ‖ ECON *recorte de presupuesto* budget cutback.
◆ *pl* cuttings (de metal, cuero, papel) ‖ FIG *estar hecho de recortes* to be a scissors-and-paste job.

recoser *vt* to resew, to sew again (volver a coser) ‖ to darn, to mend (zurcir).

recosido *m* darning, mending (acción de recoser) ‖ mend, darn (zurcido).

recostado, da *adj* recumbent, reclining (en un sofá, etc.) ‖ leaning (en la mesa, etc.).

recostar* *vt* to lean (apoyar) ‖ to lean, to bend (inclinar).
◆ *vpr* to lean; *recostarse en* or *sobre* to lean on ‖ to lean back, to recline (hacia atrás) ‖ to lie down (tumbarse).

recova *f* poultry business (comercio) ‖ poultry market (mercado) ‖ pack [of dogs] (jauría) ‖ AMER market.

recovar *vi* to trade in poultry and eggs.

recoveco *m* bend, turn, twist (vuelta) ‖ nook, odd corner (en casas) ‖ FIG cunning (artificio) | recess; *los recovecos del alma, del corazón* the recesses of the mind, of the heart ‖ — *sin recovecos* frank (franco), frankly (sinceramente) || *un asunto con muchos recovecos* a complicated business.

recovero, ra *m/f* poultry merchant.

recre *m* holiday (recle).

recreable *adj* recreational.

recreación *f* recreation.

recrear *vt* to amuse, to entertain (divertir) || to recreate (crear de nuevo) || *recrear la vista* to be a joy to behold.

◆ *vpr* to amuse o.s., to enjoy o.s. (entretenerse) || to relax (solazarse); *recrearse en leer* to relax with a book *o* by reading || FAM to enjoy, to delight, to take pleasure; *recrearse con un hermoso espectáculo* to enjoy a magnificent show; *recrearse con el mal ajeno* to delight in *o* to take pleasure in the misfortune of others.

recreativo, va *adj* recreational; *velada recreativa* recreational evening || entertaining (que distrae).

recrecer* *vi* to rise (el río) || to increase (aumentar).

◆ *vpr* to recover one's spirits, to cheer up (reanimarse).

recrecimiento *m* increase (aumento) || rise (de un río) || FIG new zeal.

recremento *m* recrement.

recreo *m* break, playtime [*US* recess] (en el colegio) || recreation, amusement (entretenimiento) || — *casa de recreo* country house || *de recreo* pleasure; *barco de recreo* pleasure boat; *viaje de recreo* pleasure trip || *ser un recreo para la vista* to be a joy to behold || *tren de recreo* miniature railway (en parques, en zoos, etc.).

recría *f* breeding.

recriador *m* breeder.

recriar *vt* to breed (animales).

recriminación *f* recrimination, reproach.

recriminador, ra *adj* recriminative.

recriminar *vt* to recriminate, to make a recrimination against; *recriminar a uno* to make a recrimination against s.o. || to reproach; *recriminar a uno su conducta* to reproach s.o. with his conduct.

◆ *vpr* to recriminate each other *o* one another.

recriminatorio, ria *adj* recriminatory.

recrudecer* *vi* to be rising *o* increasing again, to be on the rise *o* increase again; *recrudece la criminalidad* the crime rate is on the rise again || to worsen, to deteriorate (empeorar) || *el frío recrudece* it is getting colder again.

◆ *vt* to cause to break out again || to worsen (empeorar).

◆ *vpr* to break out again, to recrudesce.

recrudecimiento *m*; **recrudescencia** *f* worsening; *recrudecimiento del frío* worsening of the cold || rise; *recrudecimiento de la criminalidad* rise of the crime rate || recrudescence, new outbreak; *recrudecimiento de una enfermedad* recrudescence of an illness.

recrudescente *adj* worsening, deteriorating (tiempo) || rising (criminalidad) || recrudescent, worsening (enfermedad).

recta *f* ⟶ **recto**.

rectal *adj* ANAT rectal.

rectamente *adv* in a straight line || FIG rightly, justly (con justicia) | wisely (con juicio) | correctly, rightly (con exactitud).

rectangular *adj* MAT rectangular.

rectángulo *adj* MAT rectangular || MAT *triángulo rectángulo* right-angled *o* rectangular triangle.

◆ *m* rectangle.

rectificable *adj* rectifiable.

rectificación *f* rectification || correction.

rectificado *m* TECN rebore.

rectificador, ra *adj* rectifying.

◆ *m* ELECTR rectifier (de corriente) || QUÍM rectifier.

◆ *f* grinder (máquina).

rectificar *vt* to rectify, to right (un error, un mal) || to change (su voto) || to correct (corregir) || ELECTR to rectify || TECN to rebore (un cilindro).

◆ *vi* to correct o.s.

rectificativo, va *adj* rectifying.

◆ *m* rectifying document.

rectilíneo, a *adj* rectilinear.

rectitis *f* MED proctitis.

rectitud *f* straightness || FIG rectitude, uprightness (justicia).

recto, ta *adj* straight; *línea recta* straight line || FIG just, fair; *juez recto* just judge | sound (juicio) | upright, honest, honourable (honrado); *hombre recto* upright man | lawful, proper (intención) || true, proper, literal (sentido) || *ángulo recto* right angle.

◆ *adv* straight on; *siga recto* go straight on.

◆ *m* ANAT rectum (del intestino) | rectus (músculo); *recto del abdomen* rectus abdominis || recto (de una página).

◆ *f* MAT straight line (línea) || straight stretch, straight (de una carretera, etc.) || DEP straight.

rector, ra *adj* principal, main; *idea rectora* principal idea || guiding (principio, etc.) || driving, leading; *fuerza rectora* driving force || leading (persona) || *país rector del mundo occidental* leading Western country.

◆ *m* rector (de universidad, de colegios religiosos) || FIG leader, head, chief (dirigente) | line; *rector del pensamiento* line of thought.

— OBSERV In Spain the rector of a University receives the title of *Magnífico* (Rector Magnífico de la Universidad de Salamanca).

rectorado *m* rectorate, rectorship (cargo).

rectoral *adj* rectorial.

◆ *f* REL rectory.

rectoría *f* rectorate, rectorship (cargo) || REL rectory (casa del rector).

rectoscopia *f* MED proctoscopy.

rectoscopio *m* MED proctoscope.

recua *f* drove (de caballos o de mulas) || FIG & FAM gang, band.

recuadrar *vt* to frame (enmarcar) || to grid, to divide into squares (cuadricular).

recuadro *m* frame (marco) || box (en un periódico) || square (cuadro).

recubrir *vt* to cover || to coat (con pintura).

recuelo *m* strong bleach (lejía) || FAM *café de recuelo* weak coffee.

recuento *m* recount || count (enumeración) || — *hacer el recuento de los libros* to count (up) the books || *hacer el recuento de votos* to recount the votes.

recuerdo *m* memory, recollection; *un recuerdo confuso* a vague recollection; *un recuerdo desagradable* an unpleasant memory || memory, remembrance; *en recuerdo de* in memory of || booster (vacuna) || souvenir; *tienda de recuerdos* souvenir shop || keepsake (objeto para recordar algo o a alguien); *guarda esto como recuerdo* take this as a keepsake || — *dele recuerdos a* remember me to, give my regards *o* best wishes to || MED *dosis de recuerdo* booster injection || *guardar un feliz recuerdo de* to have happy memories of || *muchos recuerdos* kindest regards.

reculada *f* backing, reversing (de un vehículo) || backward movement (retroceso) || recoil, recoiling (de un arma) || FIG backdown.

recular *vi* to back, to reverse (un vehículo) || to go back, to back (un animal) || to move back (moverse hacia atrás) || to retreat (un ejército) || to recoil (un arma) || FIG to back down (rajarse).

reculones (a) *loc* FAM backwards.

recuperable *adj* recuperable, recoverable, retrievable.

recuperación *f* recuperation, recovery || making up (de un retraso) || recovery, picking up (de un astronauta) || recovery (de un país); *recuperación económica* economic recovery.

recuperador, ra *adj* recuperative.

◆ *m* recuperator.

recuperar *vt* to recuperate, to retrieve, to recover (un objeto) || to recuperate, to recover (la salud) || to recover (la vista, etc.) || to get back (un puesto) || to regain; *recuperar el conocimiento* to regain consciousness || to win back, to get back; *recuperar la confianza, el cariño de uno* to win back s.o.'s confidence, s.o.'s affection || to make up for (compensar); *recuperar el tiempo perdido* to make up for lost time || to make up (ganar); *recuperar una hora de trabajo* to make up an hour's work || TECN to reclaim (los subproductos) | to salvage (metales) || — *hallarse totalmente recuperado* to have made a complete recovery, to be completely well again || *recuperar el sentido* to come round, to regain consciousness.

◆ *vpr* to recuperate, to recover; *recuperarse de una enfermedad* to recuperate from an illness || to feel better; *después de haber dormido tanto me he recuperado* I feel better after such a long sleep || to get over (de una emoción); *recuperarse de su tristeza* to get over one's sadness || to recover, to pick up (los negocios) || *recuperarse de una pérdida* to recoup a loss.

recurrencia *f* MED recurrence.

recurrente *adj* recurrent.

◆ *adj/s* JUR appellant.

recurrir *vi* to turn, to appeal; *recurrir a alguien* to turn to s.o. || to have recourse, to resort; *recurrir a la astucia* to resort to cunning || to appeal; *recurro a su generosidad* I appeal to your generosity || JUR to appeal.

recurso *m* recourse, resort (acción de recurrir) || recourse (medio) || resource; *recursos económicos, naturales* economic, natural resources || JUR appeal || — *carecer de recursos económicos* to lack funds, to be short of funds || *como* or *en último recurso* as a last resort || *haber agotado todos los recursos* to be at the end of one's resources || *hombre de recursos* resourceful man || *no hay otro recurso* it is the only way, there is no alternative || JUR *recurso de casación* high-court appeal.

recusable *adj* objectionable.

recusación *f* rejection || JUR recusation, challenge.

recusante *adj/s* recusant.

recusar *vt* to reject, to refuse || JUR to recuse, to challenge.

rechazable *adj* refusable.

rechazamiento *m* refusal, repulse; *rechazamiento de una oferta* refusal of an offer || rejection; *rechazamiento de una petición* rejection of a petition || repelling, beating off (del enemigo) || denial (negación).

rechazar *vt* to refuse, to reject, to turn down; *rechazar una oferta* to refuse an offer || to repulse, to repel, to drive back; *rechazar un ataque, al enemigo* to repel an attack, the enemy || to push back, to push away (empujar hacia atrás) || to reject; *rechazar una petición, un pretendiente* to reject a petition, a suitor || to refute (refutar) || to deny (negar) || to refuse (rehusar); *rechazar un regalo* to refuse a present || to resist (una tentación) || to reflect (la luz).

rechazo *m* rebound (rebote) || recoil (de un arma) || FIG refusal, rejection (de una oferta) |

denial (negación) || MED rejection (de un trasplante) || *de rechazo* indirectly, consequently (como consecuencia), as it richocheted (una bala), on the rebound (una pelota).

rechifla *f* long whistle (sonido) || FIG derision, mockery (burla) | booing, jeering (abucheo) || FIG *se retiró en medio de una rechifla* he withdrew amidst booing and jeering.

rechiflar *vt* to whistle hard (silbar) || to hiss, to boo (abuchear).
◆ *vi* to whistle, to hiss.
◆ *vpr* to make fun, to mock (burlarse).

rechinador, ra; rechinante *adj* squeaky (rueda de carro, etc.) || creaky (puerta, de escalera, etc.) || clanking, grinding, grating (máquina) || grating, grinding, gnashing (dientes).

rechinamiento *m* squeaking (de una rueda, etc.) || creak, creaking (de puerta, escalera, etc.) || clanking, grinding (de máquina) || grating, grinding, gnashing (de dientes).

rechinante *adj* ⟶ **rechinador.**

rechinar *vi* to squeak (chirriar) || to creak (una puerta, etc.) || to clank, to grate, to grind (máquinas) || to grind, to grate, to gnash (los dientes) || FIG to do *o* to accept sth. reluctantly.

rechistar *vi* to whisper (chistar) || *sin rechistar* without replying, without saying a word (sin contestar), without a murmur, without saying a word (sin protestar).

rechoncho, cha *adj* FAM tubby, chubby, plump.

rechupete (de) *loc* FAM delicious, scrumptious (comida) | marvellous, fabulous (muy bueno).
◆ *adv le salió de rechupete* he got on just fine, everything went really well for him || *pasarlo de rechupete* to have a whale of a time.

red *f* net (para pescar, cazar) || net; *red de tenis* tennis net || network (ferroviaria, de carreteras, de radio, de teléfono, de distribución) || ELECTR mains *pl* [*US* house current] || network, netting, mesh (de hilos entrelazados) || hairnet (redecilla) || rack (de tren) || chain (de almacenes) || graph; *red de estadísticas* graph of statistics || FIG trap (trampa); *caer en la red* to fall into the trap; *caer en las propias redes* to be caught in one's own trap; *tender una red a uno* to set a trap for s.o. | ring, network; *red de espionaje* spy ring || INFORM network; *red local* local area network || — *echar* or *tender las redes* to cast one's net || *red barredera* trawl || *red de alambre* wire mesh *o* netting || *red de carreteras* or *viaria* road network *o* system || *red de emisoras* broadcasting network || COM *red de ventas* sales network || ANAT *red vascular* vascular system.

redacción *f* writing (acción de escribir) || wording (palabras empleadas) || editing, redaction (preparación para publicar) || drafting, drawing up (de un tratado, etc.) || editorial staff (conjunto de redactores) || editorial office (oficina) || essay, composition (ejercicio).

redactar *vt* to write (escribir) || to word (formular); *un texto mal redactado* a badly-worded text || to edit, to redact (preparar para publicar) || to draft, to draw up (un tratado, etc.) || to write, to compose (un ejercicio).

redactor, ra *m/f* writer (escritor) || editor (que prepara algo para publicación) || subeditor (de periódico) || *redactor jefe* editor in chief (de cualquier publicación), editor (de periódico).

redada *f* MAR casting (of nets) | catch, haul (pescado) || FIG raid, roundup (de la policía) | gang, band (de ladrones) || FIG *hacer una redada en un sitio* to raid a place.

redaño *m* ANAT mesentery.
◆ *pl* FAM guts (valor).

redecilla *f* net, mesh, netting (tejido) || hairnet (para el pelo) || string bag (para la compra) || luggage rack (para el equipaje) || ZOOL reticulum (de rumiantes).

rededor *m* surroundings *pl* (contorno) || ⟶ **alrededor.**

redención *f* redemption.

redentor, ra *adj* redeeming.
◆ *m/f* redeemer || — *el Redentor* the Redeemer || FIG *meterse a redentor* to intervene (entrometerse).

redentorista *m* redemptorist.

redescuento *m* COM rediscount.

redhibición *f* JUR redhibition.

redhibir *vt* to cancel the sale of [merchandise].

redhibitorio, ria *adj* JUR redhibitory.

redicho, cha *adj* repeated || hackneyed (trillado) || FAM affected, pretentious, stilted (pedante).

rediente *m* redan (en fortificaciones).

¡rediez! *interj* good heavens!, good God!

redil *m* fold, sheepfold || FIG fold; *hacer volver al redil a una oveja descarriada* to bring a lost sheep back to the fold.

redilear *vt* to round up (el ganado).

redimible *adj* redeemable.

redimidor, ra *m/f* redeemer.

redimir *vt* to redeem; *redimir cautivos* to redeem captives || FIG & JUR to redeem.
◆ *vpr* to buy one's liberty || FIG to redeem o.s.

redingote *m* redingote.

rédito *m* interest, yield || *prestar dinero a rédito* to lend money at interest.

redituable *adj* interest yielding, which yields interest.

redituar *vt* to yield, to produce (una renta).

redivivo, va *adj* resuscitated, revived.

redoblado, da *adj* intensified, redoubled || TECN reinforced || MIL *paso redoblado* double-quick march.

redobladura *f*; **redoblamiento** *m* intensification, redoubling || TECN reinforcing | clinching (de un clavo).

redoblante *m* side drum (tambor).

redoblar *vt* to intensify, to redouble (reiterar); *redoblar sus esfuerzos* to redouble one's efforts || to clinch (un clavo) || to bend back, to fold (doblar) || to double; *redoblar una consonante* to double a consonant || to redouble (bridge) || *redoblar sus gritos* to scream even louder.
◆ *vi* to roll, to beat (los tambores) || to play a roll on the drum (persona).

redoble *m* intensification, redoubling (redoblamiento) || roll (del tambor) || redouble (bridge) || *hacer redoble* to redouble (bridge).

redoblón *m* rivet.

redoma *f* flask (de química).

redomado, da *adj* sly, artful (astuto) || utter, out-and-out, proper; *pícaro redomado* utter scoundrel.

redomón, ona *adj* AMER half broken-in, half-tamed.
◆ *m* AMER horse which is half broken-in *o* half-tamed.

redonda *f* (p us) region (comarca) || pasture (dehesa) || round hand (letra manuscrita) || Roman type (letra de imprenta) || MAR square sail (vela) || MÚS semibreve || — *a la redonda* around; *diez leguas a la redonda* ten leagues around || FIG *se oía a un kilómetro a la redonda* you could hear it a mile off.

redondamente *adv* in a circle || FIG categorically, flatly (rotundamente).

redondear *vt* to round (off), to make round || FIG to round off, to make up to a round number; *redondear una cantidad* to make a sum up to a round number || *redondear los bajos* to level off the hem (de un traje).
◆ *vpr* to be *o* to become round (ser redondo) || FIG to start living comfortably (enriquecerse).

redondel *m* circle (círculo) || short cape (capa) || arena, ring (en la plaza de toros).

redondez *f* roundness || *en toda la redondez de la Tierra* on the face of the Earth, in the whole wide world.

redondilla *f* quatrain (poesía) || round hand (letra).

— OBSERV The *redondilla* is made up of four octosyllabics, rhyming in the pattern a b b a.

redondo, da *adj* round; *una mesa redonda* a round table; *letra redonda* round letter || FIG whose four grandparents are of noble families | clear, straightforward (sin rodeos) | flat (negativa) | complete, all-round; *triunfo redondo* complete success || — FIG & FAM *caerse redondo* or *en redondo* to collapse, to fall in a heap (caerse de repente), to drop dead (morir) || *cuenta redonda* round sum || *dar una vuelta en redondo* to turn right round || *en redondo* around (a la redonda) || *negarse en redondo* to refuse point-blank, to flatly refuse || *negocio redondo* excellent deal *o* piece of business || *número redondo* round number *o* figure || *tener cinco metros en redondo* to be five metres round || FIG *virar en redondo* to turn round (volverse), to change completely *o* radically (cambiar completamente) || MAR *virar en redondo* to veer.
◆ *m* circle.

redopelo *m* brushing against the nap || *a* or *al redopelo* against the nap.

redorar *vt* to gild again, to regild.

reducción *f* reduction (aminoración) || MED setting (de un hueso) || AMER village of Indians converted to Christianity.

— OBSERV The *reducciones* were Indian villages created by the Spanish missionaries during the colonization. The most famous were those of the *Misiones jesuíticas del Paraguay*.

reducibilidad *f* reducibility.

reducible *adj* reducible.

reducido, da *adj* reduced || limited (limitado) || small (pequeño) || limited, small, poor; *un rendimiento muy reducido* a very poor yield || confined (espacio) || low (precio) || narrow (estrecho) || MIL *quinta de efectivos reducidos* year in which there are few conscripts.

reducimiento *m* reduction.

reducir* *vt* to reduce; *reducir en una cuarta parte* to reduce by a quarter; *reducir a polvo* to reduce to dust; *reducir al silencio* to reduce to silence || to reduce, to cut down (cantidad, duración, etc.) || to abridge (un texto) || to reduce, to bring down; *la tasa ha sido reducida del 10 al 5 por ciento* the rate has been reduced from 10 to 5 percent || to subdue (al enemigo, etc.) || QUÍM & MAT to reduce || to convert (convertir) || MED to set || — *reducir a la razón* to make see reason || *reducir a prisión* to send to prison || *reducir a su más mínima expresión* to reduce to its lowest terms *o* simplest expression (matemáticas), to reduce to almost nothing.
◆ *vpr* to be reduced; *reducirse a lo más preciso* to be reduced to the bare essentials || to come (down) to, to boil down to, to amount to; *todo esto se reduce a nada* all this comes down to nothing || FIG to limit *o* to confine o.s.; *tú te reduces a cumplir tu obligación* you limit yourself to carrying out your duty || FIG *esto se re-*

duce a decir that is like saying, that boils down to saying.

reductibilidad *f* reductibility.

reducible *adj* reducible.

reducto *m* redoubt.

reductor, ra *adj* TECN & QUÍM reducing.
◆ *m* QUÍM reducer, reducing agent || reducer (de velocidad).

redundancia *f* redundancy.

redundante *adj* redundant.

redundar *vi* (p us) to overflow (rebosar) || to abound; *redundar en citas* to abound with quotations || — *esto redundará en perjuicio de usted* that will turn against you || *esto redundará en provecho de usted* that will be *o* redound to your advantage || *redundar en* to redound to.

reduplicación *f* intensification, redoubling (acción de reduplicar) || BOT & GRAM reduplication.

reduplicado, da *adj* reduplicated || BOT & GRAM reduplicate.

reduplicar *vt* to intensify, to redouble (redoblar) || to reduplicate.

reduplicativo, va *adj* reduplicative.

reedición *f* reissue.

reedificación *f* reconstruction, rebuilding.

reedificador, ra *adj* reconstructing, rebuilding.

reedificar *vt* to reconstruct, to rebuild.

reeditar *vt* to reprint, to reissue.

reeducación *f* reeducation.

reeducar *vt* to reeducate.

reelección *f* reelection.

reelecto, ta *adj* reelected.
◆ *m/f* reelected person.

reelegible *adj* reeligible.

reelegido, da *adj* reelected.
◆ *m/f* reelected person.

reelegir* *vt* to reelect.

reembarcar *vt* to reembark.
◆ *vpr* to reembark.

reembarco *m* reembarkation (de personas).

reembargar *vt* JUR to seize again.

reembarque *m* reshipment (de cosas).

reembolsable *adj* reimbursable, repayable || returnable (depósito).

reembolsar; rembolsar *vt* to reimburse, to repay (a una persona) || to repay (dinero) || to refund, to return (depósito).
◆ *vpr* to recover (recuperar).

reembolso; rembolso *m* repayment, reimbursement || refund (de un depósito) || *enviar algo contra reembolso* to send sth. cash on delivery *o* C. O. D.

reemplazable *adj* replaceable.

reemplazante *m/f* replacement, substitute.

reemplazar; remplazar *vt* to replace, to substitute.

reemplazo; remplazo *m* replacement || annual draft of recruits (quinta) || replacement (en la milicia) || MIL *de reemplazo* reserve, from the reserve.

reemprender *vt* to start again.

reencarnación *f* reincarnation.

reencarnarse *vpr* to be reincarnated.

reencuadernación *f* rebinding.

reencuadernar *vt* to rebind (un libro).

reencuentro *m* collision (de cosas) || MIL clash, skirmish.

reenganchado *m* MIL reenlisted soldier.

reenganchar *vt* MIL to reenlist.
◆ *vpr* MIL to reenlist.

reenganche *m* MIL reenlistment | reenlistment bonus (gratificación).

reengendrar *vt* to regenerate.

reensayar *vt* to test again, to retest, to try out again || TEATR to re-rehearse, to rehearse again.

reensayo *m* retesting (de máquina) || TEATR rehearsal, second rehearsal.

reenviar *vt* to send back, to return (al sitio de procedencia) || to forward (reexpedir).

reenvidar *vt* to raise (the bid) (juegos).

reenvío *m* forwarding (reexpedición) || return (al sitio de procedencia).

reenvite *m* raised bid.

reestrenar *vt* to revive, to put on again (teatro, cine).

reestreno *m* revival (teatro, cine).

reestructuración *f* reorganization.

reestructurar *vt* to reorganize.

reexaminación *f* reexamination.

reexaminar *vt* to reexamine.

reexpedición *f* forwarding || *se ruega la reexpedición* please forward.

reexpedir* *vt* to forward, to send on || *se ruega reexpedir al destinatario* please forward.

reexportación *f* reexport.

reexportar *vt* to reexport.

refacción *f* refection, snack (comida ligera) || repair, repairs *pl* (reparación) || extra, bonus (gratificación) || COM allowance.

refaccionaria *f* AMER garage, repair workshop (taller de reparaciones).

refacciones *fpl* AMER spare parts (piezas de repuesto).

refajo *m* petticoat, underskirt, slip (enagua) || skirt (falda).

refección *f* refection (comida ligera) || repair, repairs *pl* (reparación).

refectorio *m* refectory, dining hall.

referencia *f* reference || account, report (de un suceso) || — *con referencia a* with reference to, concerning || *hacer referencia a* to refer to, to make a reference to.
◆ *pl* references (informes) || *por referencias* by hearsay.

referendario *m* countersigner.

referéndum *m* referendum.

referente *adj* *referente a* concerning, regarding.

referible *adj* referable.

referir* *vt* to recount, to tell of; *referir hechos interesantes* to tell of interesting facts || to refer (remitir) || to refer, to relate (relacionar) || to place, to refer; *refiere el suceso al primer mes de la guerra* he places the event in the first month of the war.
◆ *vpr* to refer (remitirse); *esto se refiere a lo que te dije ayer* this refers to what I told you yesterday || to refer, to mean, to be speaking about (aludir); *no me refiero a usted* I am not referring to you || GRAM to agree || *por lo que se refiere a eso* as for that, as regards that.

refilado *m* IMPR trimming (con la guillotina).

refilar *vt* IMPR to trim.

refilón (de) *loc* briefly (de pasada); *ver algo de refilón* to see sth. briefly || obliquely, sideways (de soslayo) || — *chocar de refilón contra un coche* to graze a car || *mirar de refilón* to look at out of the corner of one's eye, to look askance at.

refinación *f* refining (refinado).

refinadera *f* stone roller for refining chocolate.

refinado, da *adj* refined; *azúcar refinado* refined sugar || FIG refined (distinguido).
◆ *m* TECN refining; *el refinado del petróleo* oil refining.

refinador, ra *adj* refining.
◆ *m/f* refiner.

refinadura *f* refining.

refinamiento *m* refinement (esmero).

refinar *vt* TECN to refine (metal, azúcar, etc.) || FIG to refine, to polish (el estilo).
◆ *vpr* to become refined || TECN to be refined.

refinería *f* refinery; *refinería petrolífera* oil refinery.

refino, na *adj* very fine, extra fine (muy fino).
◆ *m* refining (refinado) || grocer's (tienda de comestibles).

reflectancia *f* FÍS reflectance.

reflectante *adj* reflecting; *superficie reflectante* reflecting surface.

reflectar *vt* FÍS to reflect (reflejar).

reflector, ra *adj* FÍS reflecting, reflective.
◆ *m* reflector || projector (proyector) || ELECTR spotlight || MIL & AVIAT searchlight.

reflectorizado, da *adj* reflecting, reflective (placa).

reflejado, da *adj* reflected; *rayo reflejado* reflected ray.

reflejante *adj* reflecting, reflective; *superficie reflejante* reflecting surface.

reflejar *vt* to reflect; *el espejo refleja la luz* the mirror reflects light || FIG to reflect, to reveal; *nuestros ojos reflejan nuestros sentimientos* our eyes reflect our feelings | to show, to reveal; *una cara que refleja bondad* a face which shows goodness.
◆ *vpr* to be reflected || FIG to be reflected; *la felicidad se reflejaba en su rostro* his happiness was reflected in his face; *el precio de la materia prima se refleja en el del producto acabado* the price of the raw material is reflected in that of the finished product.

reflejo, ja *adj* reflected; *rayo reflejo* reflected ray || reflexivo (verbo) || reflex (movimiento).
◆ *m* reflection; *reflejos en el agua* reflections in the water || reflex; *reflejo condicionado* conditioned reflex || FIG reflection (imagen) || gleam, glint (brillo) || rinse; *darse un reflejo rojizo* to give one's hair a red rinse || streak (efecto del sol en el pelo).

reflexibilidad *f* reflexibility.

reflexible *adj* reflexible.

reflexión *f* FÍS reflection || FIG reflection (acción de reflexionar) || — *con reflexión* on reflection || *sin reflexión* without thinking, unthinkingly.

reflexionar *vi* to reflect, to think; *reflexionar sobre un asunto* to reflect on *o* to think about a matter; *reflexionar antes de actuar* to think before acting.

reflexivamente *adv* GRAM in the reflexive form, reflexively || reflectively, thoughtfully (reflexionando).

reflexivo, va *adj* reflective, reflecting (que refleja) || reflective, thoughtful; *un niño reflexivo* a reflective child || considered (acción) || GRAM reflexive.

reflorecer* *vi* to flower *o* to blossom *o* to bloom again || FIG to flourish again, to reflourish.

reflorecimiento *m* second flowering *o* blossoming *o* blooming || FIG renaissance.

refluir* *vi* to flow back (un líquido) || to redund (*en* in), to lead (*en* to), (dar lugar a).

reflujo *m* ebb (marea).

refocilación *f*; **refocilo** *m* enjoyment, delight.

refocilar *vt* to amuse, to delight.
◆ *vpr* to enjoy o.s., to delight (alegrarse) ‖ *refocilarse con* to enjoy, to delight in.

refocilo *m* ⟶ **refocilación.**

reforma *f* reform; *reforma agraria* land reform ‖ REL reformation ‖ ARQ modification, change, alteration (modificación) ‖ *cerrado por reformas* closed for repairs *o* improvements.

reformable *adj* reformable.

reformación *f* reform, reformation.

reformado, da *adj* reformed ‖ modified, altered (cambiado) ‖ improved (mejorado).

reformador, ra *adj* reforming.
◆ *m/f* reformer.

reformar *vt* to reform ‖ to improve, to carry out improvements in, to renovate; *reformar una cocina* to improve a kitchen ‖ to modify, to alter, to change (modificar) ‖ to reorganize (una empresa, etc.) ‖ to modify (un texto) ‖ to alter (en costura).
◆ *vpr* to reform, to mend one's ways.

reformatorio, ria *adj/sm* reformatory ‖ *reformatorio de menores* remand home.

reformismo *m* reformism.

reformista *adj/s* reformist.

reforzado, da *adj* reinforced, strengthened.
◆ *m* tape, binding, ribbon.

reforzador, ra *adj* reinforcing, strengthening.
◆ *m* FOT intensifier, intensifying agent ‖ ELECTR booster.

reforzar* *vt* to reinforce, to strengthen; *reforzar un tubo, una pared* to reinforce a tube, a wall ‖ FOT to intensify ‖ MIL to reinforce ‖ ELECTR to boost ‖ *reforzar el ánimo a* to comfort, to encourage.
◆ *vpr* to be reinforced, to be strengthened.

refracción *f* FÍS refraction; *ángulo de refracción* angle of refraction ‖ *índice de refracción* refractive index.

refractar *vt* FÍS to refract.

refractario, ria *adj* refractory, heat-resistant (mal conductor del calor) ‖ fireproof (resistente al fuego) ‖ FIG refractory ‖ — *ser refractario a los cambios* to be opposed *o* unamenable to change, to resist change ‖ *ser refractario a los idiomas* to be a hopeless case where languages are concerned.

refractivo, va *adj* refractive.

refractómetro *m* refractometer.

refractor *m* refractor.

refrán *m* saying, proverb ‖ — FIG *según reza el refrán* as the saying goes, as the proverb says | *tener refranes para todo* to have an answer for everything.

refranero *m* collection of sayings *o* proverbs.

refranesco, ca *adj* proverbial.

refrangibilidad *f* refrangibility.

refrangible *adj* refrangible.

refranista *m/f* person who is fond of quoting proverbs.

refregadura *f*; **refregamiento** *m* ⟶ **refregón.**

refregar*; **refrotar** *vt* to rub (frotar) ‖ FIG & FAM to throw back at (un reproche) ‖ FIG *refregar algo a alguien* to go on at s.o. about sth., to rub sth. in.

refregón *m*; **refregadura** *f*; **refregamiento** *m* FAM rubbing, rub | mark (señal).

refreír* *vt* to refry, to fry again (freír de nuevo) ‖ to overfry (patatas, etc.), to overcook (carne).

refrenable *adj* suppressible, controllable.

refrenado, da *adj* in check, restrained (un caballo, las pasiones).

refrenamiento *m* suppression, restraint, repression.

refrenar *vt* to rein (in), to check (a un caballo) ‖ FIG to restrain, to keep in check, to curb, to suppress, to repress (las pasiones).
◆ *vpr* to restrain o.s.

refrendación *f* visa (de un pasaporte) ‖ countersigning (acción) ‖ countersignature (firma).

refrendador, ra *adj* countersigning.

refrendar *vt* to visa, to stamp (un pasaporte) ‖ to countersign, to endorse (legalizar) ‖ to approve (una ley).

refrendario *m* countersigner.

refrendata *f* countersignature.

refrendo *m* visa (de un pasaporte) ‖ countersigning (acción de firmar) ‖ countersignature (firma) ‖ approval; *ley sometida al refrendo popular* law submitted to popular approval.

refrescante *adj* refreshing.

refrescar *vt* to refresh, to cool (líquidos, etc.) ‖ FIG to revive (recuerdos) | to brush up; *refrescar el inglés* to brush up one's English ‖ FIG *refrescar la memoria* to refresh one's memory.
◆ *vi* to turn fresh; *el tiempo refresca* the weather is turning fresh ‖ to freshen (el viento) ‖ to be refreshing (un líquido) ‖ *esta tarde ha refrescado un poco* the afternoon has turned a bit fresh.
◆ *vpr* to take some refreshment, to refresh o.s., to take a refreshing drink (beber algo fresco) ‖ to get some fresh air, to take the air (tomar el fresco).

refresco *m* soft drink, cool drink (bebida) ‖ refreshment, snack (refrigerio) ‖ — FIG *de refresco* fresh ‖ *refresco de limón* lemonade.
◆ *pl* refreshments.

refresquería *f* AMER refreshment room (bar).

refriega *f* clash, skirmish, fray (combate) ‖ scuffle (riña).

refrigeración *f* refrigeration ‖ air conditioning (aire acondicionado) ‖ snack (comida) ‖ cooling (de un motor) ‖ chilling (de la carne) ‖ *refrigeración por aire* air-cooling.

refrigerador, ra *adj* refrigerating.
◆ *m* refrigerator.

refrigerante *m* QUÍM refrigerant (sustancia) | cooler (recipiente) | condenser (condensador).
◆ *adj* refreshing (refrescante) ‖ refrigerating, cooling (que enfría).

refrigerar *vt* to cool, to refrigerate (enfriar) ‖ to refresh (refrescar) ‖ to chill; *carne refrigerada* chilled meat ‖ to air-condition (habitación, casa, etc.) ‖ TECN to cool (motor) | to refrigerate.
◆ *vi/vpr* to refresh o.s. (una persona).

refrigerio *m* refreshing drink (bebida) ‖ snack, refreshment (comida) ‖ FIG rest; *lugar de refrigerio* place of rest | rest, peace; *refrigerio eterno* eternal peace | relief (alivio) ‖ *se servirá un refrigerio durante el descanso* refreshments will be served in the interval.

refringencia *f* FÍS refringence.

refringir *vt* FÍS to refract.

refrito, ta *adj* refried (frito de nuevo) ‖ overfried (demasiado frito).
◆ *m* FIG & FAM rehash; *esta obra de teatro es un refrito* this play is a rehash.

refrotar *vt* ⟶ **refregar.**

refucilo; refusilo *m* AMER lightning (relámpago).

refuerzo *m* reinforcement, strengthening ‖ welt (en costura) ‖ FOT intensifying (proceso) | intensification (resultado) ‖ TECN brace, support ‖ MIL reinforcement; *enviar refuerzos* to send reinforcements.

refugiado, da *adj/s* refugee.

refugiar *vt* to give refuge to.
◆ *vpr* to take refuge (de una tormenta, de un peligro) ‖ to take shelter (a causa de la lluvia).

refugio *m* refuge, shelter ‖ refuge (de montaña) ‖ traffic island (en la calle) ‖ FIG refuge ‖ — *refugio antiaéreo* air-raid shelter ‖ *refugio atómico* fallout shelter ‖ MIL *refugio de invierno* winter quarters *pl* | *refugio subterráneo* underground shelter, dugout.

refulgencia *f* refulgence, brightness, brilliance.

refulgente *adj* refulgent, shining, bright, brilliant.

refulgir *vi* to shine, to glitter.

refundición *f* recasting ‖ FIG adaptation.

refundidor, ra *m/f* adaptor, revisor (de libro, de ley).

refundir *vt* to recast; *refundir un cañón* to recast a cannon ‖ FIG to adapt, to rewrite; *refundir una obra* to adapt a work.

refunfuñador, ra *adj* grumbling, grumpy, moaning.
◆ *m/f* grumbler, moaner.

refunfuñadura *f* grumbling, moaning.

refunfuñar *vi* FIG & FAM to grumble, to moan.

refunfuño *m* grumble, moan.
◆ *pl* grumbling *sing*, moaning *sing* ‖ *déjate de refunfuños* stop moaning, stop your moaning.

refunfuñón, ona *adj* FAM grumbling, grumpy, moaning.
◆ *m/f* FAM grumbler, moaner, grouch.

refusilo *m* AMER ⟶ **refucilo.**

refutable *adj* refutable.

refutación *f* refutation.

refutar *vt* to refute; *refutar un argumento* to refute an argument.

regadera *f* watering can; *alcachofa de regadera* rose of a watering can ‖ irrigation ditch (reguera) ‖ AMER shower (ducha) ‖ FAM *está como una regadera* he's as mad as a hatter.

regadero *m* irrigation ditch.

regadío, a *adj* irrigable; *tierras regadías* irrigable lands.
◆ *m* irrigated camp (campo) ‖ irrigation (de un terreno) ‖ — *cultivo de regadío* irrigation farming ‖ *de regadío* irrigable, irrigated.

regador, ra *m/f* waterer.

regadura *f* watering, sprinkling.

regala *f* MAR gunwale.

regaladamente *adv* comfortably; *estar regaladamente instalado en un sillón* to be sitting comfortably in an armchair ‖ extremely well (muy bien); *comer regaladamente* to eat extremely well ‖ in luxury (vivir).

regalado, da *adj* given as a present ‖ soft, delicate, dainty (suave) ‖ comfortable (con comodidades) ‖ FIG & FAM delicious, delightful (delicioso) | dirt cheap (barato); *estos zapatos están regalados* these shoes are dirt cheap ‖ — FIG *no la quieren ni regalada* they don't want it at any price, they don't want to know | *no lo quiero ni regalado* I wouldn't want it even as a gift | *tener* or *llevar vida regalada* to lead a pleasant life (agradable), to live a life of luxury (lujosa).

regalar *vt* to give; *¿qué le podemos regalar para su cumpleaños?* what can we give him for his birthday?; *me regaló su reloj* he gave me his

watch ‖ to give away; *ya que no lo quería lo regalé* I gave it away since I didn't want it any more ‖ to present, to present with; *le regalaron un cuadro al rey* they presented the king with a painting, they presented a painting to the king ‖ to give, to give away; *con cada paquete regalan un vaso* with each packet they are giving a free glass *o* they are giving away a glass ‖ to flatter (halagar) ‖ to treat royally (tratar muy bien) ‖ — *¿qué te regalaron para tu cumpleaños?* what did you get *o* what presents did you get for your birthday? ‖ *regalar a alguien con atenciones* to lavish attentions on s.o. ‖ *regalar a alguien con un banquete* to entertain s.o. with *o* to treat s.o. to a banquet ‖ *regalar el oído* to flatter; *cumplidos que regalan el oído* flattering compliments; to be a pleasure to hear, to be a joy to the ear (música, etc.) ‖ *regalar la vista* to be a pleasure to see, to be a joy to behold.
◆ *vpr* to regale o.s., to feast on; *regalarse con pasteles* to regale o.s. with cakes, to feast on cakes ‖ to regale o.s., to indulge o.s., to look after o.s. (cuidarse bien) ‖ *regálate la vista con eso* feast your eyes on that.

regalía *f* royal prerogative (prerrogativa real) ‖ FIG privilege, prerogative ‖ bonus (sueldo) ‖ *AMER* present, gift (regalo).

regalismo *m* regalism.

regalista *m* regalist.

regaliz *m*; **regaliza** *f* liquorice, licorice; *barra de regaliz* licorice stick.

regalo *m* present, gift (obsequio); *dar de regalo* to give as a present ‖ pleasure, joy (placer); *esta música es un regalo para el oído* this music is a joy to the ear ‖ feast (festín) ‖ treat (alimento exquisito) ‖ comfort, ease (comodidad) ‖ *vivir con gran regalo* to live a life of ease *o* of luxury.

regalonear *vt* *AMER* FAM to spoil, to pamper (mimar).

regalón, ona *adj* FAM comfort-loving (cómodo) | delicate (delicado) ‖ spoilt, pampered (mimado) ‖ *vida regalona* easy life, life of ease *o* of luxury.

regante *m* farmer who has the right to irrigate his fields from a certain ditch (dueño) ‖ labourer who waters the fields, waterer (empleado).

regañadientes (a) *loc* reluctantly, grudgingly, against one's will; *obedecer a regañadientes* to obey reluctantly.

regañar *vi* to argue, to quarrel (enfadarse) ‖ to finish (entre novios); *he regañado con mi novio* I have finished with my boyfriend ‖ to fall out (entre amigos) ‖ to moan, to complain, to grumble (quejarse) ‖ to split (open) (frutas) ‖ *estar regañados* to have fallen out (dos personas).
◆ *vt* to tell off, to scold (reprender); *regañar a un niño* to tell a child off ‖ to nag, to go on at (insistentemente).

regañina *f* scolding, telling off.

regaño *m* scolding, telling off.

regañón, ona *adj* FAM grumpy, grouchy (que se queja) | nagging (criticón) | touchy, irritable (enfadadizo).
◆ *m/f* FAM moaner, grouch, grumbler.

regañuza *f* scolding, telling off (represión) ‖ quarrel (pelea).

regar* *vt* to water (las plantas); *regar las flores* to water the flowers ‖ to water, to irrigate (un campo) ‖ to water (un río) ‖ to wash (bañar la costa) ‖ to hose down, to wash down, to water (la calle, etc., para limpiar) ‖ to bathe; *regar una herida* to bathe a wound; *regar con lágrimas* to bathe with tears ‖ FIG to pour (desparramar) | to sprinkle (rociar).

regata *f* MAR & DEP regatta, boat race | sailing; *aficionado a la regata* fond of sailing ‖ irrigation ditch (reguera).

regate *m* dodge, duck (del cuerpo) ‖ DEP dribbling (con el balón), dodging (del cuerpo) ‖ FIG & FAM dodge.

regateador, ra *adj* haggling.
◆ *m/f* haggler.

regatear *vt* to haggle over (el precio) ‖ to be mean *o* sparing with (dar con parsimonia); *regatear el vino* to be sparing with the wine ‖ FIG to deny; *no le regateo inteligencia* I don't deny he is intelligent ‖ — *no les regatea ningún disgusto* he gives them no end of trouble ‖ *no regatear esfuerzos* to spare no effort.
◆ *vi* to be awkward (poner dificultades) ‖ to haggle (*sobre* over), (el precio) ‖ DEP to dribble (con el balón), to dodge, to duck (con el cuerpo) ‖ MAR to race.

regateo *m* haggling, bargaining (entre comprador y vendedor) ‖ DEP dribbling (balón), dodging (del cuerpo) ‖ FIG & FAM awkwardness (dificultad) | dodge (escapatoria).

regato *m* pool (charco) ‖ stream (arroyo).

regatón *m* tip (contera) ‖ ferrule (de un bastón, de un tubo).

regazo *m* lap; *el regazo materno* the mother's lap ‖ FIG lap (refugio).

regencia *f* regency.
◆ *adj inv* regency; *estilo Regencia* Regency style.

regeneración *f* regeneration (transformación) ‖ TECN regeneration (del caucho) | reclaiming, processing for re-use (de desechos).

regenerador, ra *adj* regenerative.
◆ *m/f* regenerator.

regenerar *vt* to regenerate (transformar) ‖ TECN to regenerate (caucho) | to reclaim, to process for re-use (desechos).

regenta *f* manager's wife ‖ regent's wife ‖ judge's wife ‖ teacher (profesora).

regentar *vt* to manage (dirigir) ‖ to hold (cátedra) ‖ to hold temporarily (un cargo) ‖ FIG to guide, to preside over (destino) ‖ FAM to boss.

regente *adj* ruling, governing ‖ — *Príncipe regente* Prince Regent ‖ *reina regente* regent.
◆ *m/f* regent (de un estado).
◆ *m* manager (director) ‖ IMPR foreman ‖ magistrate (magistrado).

regentear *vt* to rule (con autoridad).

regiamente *adv* regally, royally.

regicida *f* regicidal.
◆ *m/f* regicide (asesino).

regicidio *m* regicide (crimen).

regidor, ra *adj* governing, ruling (gobernante) ‖ managing (dirigente).
◆ *m* manager (director) ‖ town councillor (concejal) ‖ stage manager (teatro) ‖ assistant director (en cine).
◆ *f* manageress ‖ town councillor's wife (concejala).

regidoría; regiduría *f* town councillorship ‖ CINEM assistant directorship.

régimen *m* rules *pl*, regulations *pl* (reglas) ‖ system (sistema) ‖ MED diet, regimen (p us); *ponerse a régimen* to go on a diet ‖ régime, regime, system; *régimen político* political régime ‖ rule (gobierno) ‖ GEOGR régime ‖ GRAM government ‖ TECN speed (velocidad); *régimen máximo* top *o* full speed | normal running rate (marcha normal) ‖ — MED *poner a alguien a régimen* to put s.o. on a diet ‖ TECN *régimen de crucero* optimum running speed (de máquina), cruising speed (de vehículo) ‖ *régimen de vida* way of life.
— OBSERV The plural of the word *régimen* is *regímenes*.

regimentar* *vt* to regiment.

regimiento *m* MIL regiment ‖ town council (concejo) ‖ town councillorship (oficio) ‖ management (dirección) ‖ government (gobierno).

regio, gia *adj* royal, regal ‖ FIG royal, splendid.

región *f* GEOGR region ‖ district, area, zone (zona) ‖ ANAT region.

regional *adj* regional.

regionalismo *m* regionalism.

regionalista *adj* regionalistic, regionalist.
◆ *m/f* regionalist.

regionalización *f* regionalization.

regionalizar *vt* to regionalize.

regir* *vt* to govern, to rule (una nación) ‖ to direct, to manage, to control (una empresa) ‖ to run, to be in charge of (un colegio) ‖ to govern; *la ley de la oferta y la demanda rige el mercado* the law of supply and demand governs the market ‖ JUR to govern ‖ GRAM to govern ‖ *este verbo rige el acusativo* this verb takes the accusative.
◆ *vi* to be in force, to apply; *aún rige este decreto* this decree is still in force ‖ MAR to steer ‖ TECN to work (funcionar) ‖ — *el mes que rige* the present month ‖ FIG & FAM *no regir* to be crackers, not to be right in the head (estar loco); *este tipo no rige* this bloke is crackers *o* is not right in the head; not to work (no funcionar); *mi reloj no rige* my watch doesn't work ‖ *que rigen* prevailing (condiciones, precios, etc.).
◆ *vpr* to navigate, to be guided; *regirse por las estrellas* to navigate by the stars ‖ FIG to follow, to be guided; *se rige por su buen sentido* he follows his common sense, he is guided by common sense.

registrado, da *adj* registered; *marca registrada* registered trade mark.

registrador, ra *adj* registering ‖ inspecting, examining, checking (que inspecciona) ‖ *caja registradora* cash register.
◆ *m/f* inspector, checker (que inspecciona).
◆ *m* TECN recorder ‖ registrar (fielato) ‖ *registrador de la propiedad* person in charge of the registration of land.

registrar *vt* to search; *registrar a un ladrón* to search a thief; *me registraron todo el equipaje* they searched all my luggage ‖ to search, to go through (cajón, bolsillos) ‖ to inspect, to examine, to check (inspeccionar) ‖ to register, to enter, to record (anotar en un registro) ‖ to enter, to note, to write down (inscribir) ‖ to register (matricular) ‖ to record (grabar) ‖ FIG to note, to notice; *hemos registrado un aumento de la criminalidad* we have noted a rise in the crime rate ‖ *la policía registró el barrio a fondo* the police carried out a complete search of the area.
◆ *vi* to search; *registró en el armario* he searched in the wardrobe.
◆ *vpr* to search, to go through; *registrarse los bolsillos* to go through one's pockets ‖ to be reported; *se han registrado disturbios* disturbances have been reported ‖ to happen (ocurrir) ‖ to enrol (matricularse) ‖ to register (hacerse anotar).

registro *m* registration, registry, recording (transcripción) ‖ entry (en un libro) ‖ register (libro); *registro de hotel* hotel register ‖ roll, list (lista) ‖ record office (oficina) ‖ inspection, examination, checking (inspección) ‖ search, searching (en la aduana, de un lugar) ‖ bookmark (para señalar las páginas) ‖ MÚS register (extensión de la voz o de un instrumento) | stop (de órgano), pedal (de piano) ‖ TECN inspection *o* observation hole (trampilla) | manhole (abertura en el suelo) | regulator (de reloj) ‖ INFORM register (de datos) ‖ — *registro central* main register ‖ *registro central de penados y re-*

beldes (police) records (servicio) || *registro civil* births, marriages and deaths register (libro), registry office, registry [US register office] (oficina) || *registro de antecedentes penales* police record (boletín) || *registro de erratas* list of errata || *registro de la propiedad* land register *o* records (libro) || *registro de la propiedad industrial* industrial property register || *registro del sonido* sound recording || *registro de patentes y marcas* patents office || *registro electoral* voting register || *registro genealógico* pedigree (animales) || *registro mercantil* business register || *registro parroquial* parish record *o* register || MÚS *registros de lengüeta* reed stops || FIG *tocar todos los registros* to pull out all the stops, to try everything *o* every possibility (intentarlo todo).

regla *f* ruler, rule (utensilio) || rule, regulation (reglamento, norma) || MAT rule; *regla de tres* rule of three || (set) pattern, rule (modelo); *responder a una regla* to follow a (set) pattern || REL rule, order || instruction; *reglas para utilizar una máquina de escribir* instructions for using a typewriter || MED period (menstruación) || (p us) moderation (moderación) || — *con todas las reglas del arte* according to the book || *en regla* according to the book; *batalla en regla* battle fought according to the book; in order; *tener sus papeles en regla* to have one's papers in order; *todo está en regla* everything is in order || *estar en regla con las autoridades* to be on the right side of the law *o* the authorities || *hacerse una regla de ser puntual* to make a point of being punctual || *la excepción confirma la regla* the exception proves the rule || *obrar según las reglas* to play by the rules || *por regla general* generally, usually, as a rule || *regla de aligación* alligation (rule) || *regla de cálculo* slide rule || *reglas de la circulación* traffic regulations || *reglas del juego* rules of the game, laws of the game || FIG *salir de regla* to go too far, to go beyond the limits || *trazar una línea con la regla* to rule a line || *una excepción a la regla* an exception to the rule.

reglado, da *adj* temperate, moderate || *papel reglado* ruled *o* lined paper.

reglaje *m* TECN checking (comprobación) | overhaul (revisión) | adjustment, adjusting (ajuste) || MIL correction (de la puntería).

reglamentación *f* regulation || regulations *pl*, rules *pl* (reglas).

reglamentar *vt* to regulate.

reglamentario, ria *adj* required, prescribed, regulation || obligatory, compulsory (obligatorio).

reglamento *m* rules *pl*, regulations *pl* (en general) || standing orders *pl* (de comisión, etc.) || bylaw (estatuto).

reglar *adj* regular (religioso).

reglar *vt* to rule (lines) (pautar) || to rule, to rule lines on (papel) || to regulate (someter a reglas) || TECN to adjust, to regulate (ajustar) | to overhaul (revisar) | to check (comprobar) || MIL to correct (puntería).
◆ *vpr* to be guided (*por* by), to follow (dejarse guiar por) || to conform (*a* to), (acomodarse).

regleta *f* IMPR lead || (small) ruler (regla).

regletear *vt* IMPR to lead.

reglón *m* mason's rule (de albañil).

regocijado, da *adj* joyful, delighted, merry, happy.

regocijar *vt* to delight, to gladden, to cheer (dar alegría) || to amuse (divertir).
◆ *vpr* to be happy *o* delighted, to rejoice (ante una noticia, etc.) || to laugh (reír) || to make merry, to enjoy o.s. (divertirse) || to delight, to take pleasure (*de* in) (de las desgracias ajenas).

regocijo *m* happiness, joy, delight (felicidad) || merriment, rejoicing (alegría general) || *con gran regocijo mío* much to my delight.
◆ *pl* festivities, celebrations.

regodearse *vpr* FAM to get immense enjoyment *o* pleasure (*con* out of), to delight (*con* in); *regodearse con la lectura* to get immense enjoyment out of reading || to ogle (at) (con un espectáculo licencioso) || FIG to delight, to get great satisfaction; *regodearse en* or *con la desgracia ajena* to delight in other people's misfortunes, to get great satisfaction out of other people's misfortunes.

regodeo *m* FAM delight, pleasure, joy; *comerse una perdiz con regodeo* to eat a partridge with great delight || FIG cruel delight (satisfacción maligna).

regoldar *vi* FAM to belch, to burp.

regoldo *m* wild chestnut.

regordete, ta *adj* FAM tubby, plump.

regresar *vi* to return, to come *o* to go back.
◆ *vt* AMER to return, to give back (devolver).
◆ *vpr* AMER to return, to come *o* to go back.

regresión *f* regression, decline; *epidemia en regresión* epidemic on the decline *o* in regression || drop (disminución); *regresión de las exportaciones* drop in exports || return; *regresión a procedimientos antiguos* return to former ways || BIOL & GEOL regression.

regresivo, va *adj* regressive (propenso a la regresión) || backward (que hace retroceder).

regreso *m* return journey (viaje de vuelta); *un regreso fácil* an easy return journey || return (vuelta) || *estar de regreso* to be back, to be home, to have come home (*de* from).

regüeldo *m* FAM belch, burp.

reguera *f* irrigation ditch || MAR cable, mooring rope.

reguero *m* trail, trickle (señal); *un reguero de sangre* a trail of blood || irrigation ditch (reguera) || *la noticia se propagó como un reguero de pólvora* the news spread like wildfire.

regulación *f* regulation || adjustment || control; *regulación de los precios, de los nacimientos* price, birth control; *regulación del volumen, del tráfico* volume, traffic control || *regulación de un curso de agua* regulation of a water course.

regulado, da *adj* arranged, orderly, in order (ordenado) || regular (regular) || regulated, adjusted (un aparato) || controlled (precios, etc.).

regulador, ra *adj* regulating.
◆ *m* regulator || TECN regulator, governor | throttle (de locomotora) | control, control knob (de una radio o de una televisión); *regulador de volumen* volume control.

regular *adj* regular; *movimiento, ritmo regular* regular movement, rhythm; *clero regular* regular clergy || FAM not bad, reasonable, average (no tan malo); *es una película regular* it is not a bad film; *¿qué tal está? —regular* what's it like? not bad | in between (entre los dos); *¿te gusta el chocolate espeso o líquido? regular* do you like your chocolate thick *o* runny? in between | not too; *el agua estaba regular de fría* the water was not too cold | average, run-of-the-mill; *un alumno regular* an average student || — FAM *estar regular* to be so-so (ni bien ni mal) || *por lo regular* as a rule, generally || FAM *¿y ella, qué tal es? regular* and what is she like? so-so *o* nothing special.

regular *vt* TECN to regulate, to adjust (un mecanismo) || to regulate (caudal, flujo) || to regulate (reglamentar) || to control (precios, el mercado) || to regulate, to control (cambios, etc.) || *regular la circulación* to control *o* to direct traffic.

regularidad *f* regularity || *con regularidad* regularly.

regularización *f* regularization.

regularizar *vt* to regularize.

regularmente *adv* regularly || not too badly (medianamente) || usually, generally, as a rule; *regularmente voy al cine dos veces por semana* I usually go to the cinema twice a week.

regulativo, va *adj* regulative.

régulo *m* regulus, kinglet, petty king (reyezuelo) || basilisk (basilisco) || QUÍM regulus.

regurgitación *f* regurgitation.

regurgitar *vi* to regurgitate.

regusto *m* aftertaste.

rehabilitable *adj* deserving of rehabilitation (que lo merece), capable of being rehabilitated (a quien se puede rehabilitar).

rehabilitación *f* rehabilitation || reinstatement (en un puesto).

rehabilitador, ra *adj* rehabilitative.

rehabilitar *vt* to rehabilitate || to reinstate (en un puesto).

rehacer* *vt* to redo, to do again, to do over (volver a hacer) || to repeat (repetir) || to remake, to rebuild (reconstruir) || to repair, to mend (reparar) || to renew, to do up (renovar).
◆ *vpr* MED to recover || MIL to rally.

rehacimiento *m* remaking, rebuilding (reconstrucción) || repairing, mending (reparación) || recovery.

rehala *f* herd *o* flock belonging to various owners.

rehecho, cha *adj* thickset (persona) || FIG rested (descansado) | recovered (de una enfermedad o de una desgracia).

rehén *m* hostage; *lo tienen como rehén* they are holding him hostage.

rehilandera *f* whirligig [US pinwheel] (juguete).

rehilar *vi* to shake, to quiver (temblar) || to whizz, to whiz (flecha).
◆ *vt* to twist (retorcer).

rehilete *m* dart (flechilla) || shuttlecock (juguete y juego) || banderilla (banderilla) || FIG gibe, dig (dicho malicioso).

rehiletero *m* TAUR banderillero.

rehogar *vt* CULIN to brown (dorar).

rehuir* *vt* to avoid, to shun, to shy away from, to shrink from (evitar, esquivar).
— OBSERV When the *u* in *rehuir* is stressed it has a written accent: *rehúyo, rehúyes, rehúye, rehúyen.*

rehumedecer* *vt* to soak.

rehusable *adj* refusable.

rehusar *vt* to decline, to refuse, to turn down (no aceptar) || to refuse (negarse); *rehusar trabajar* to refuse to work || to deny (negar).
◆ *vi* to refuse.

Reikiavik *n pr* GEOGR Reykjavik.

reimportación *f* reimportation.

reimportar *vt* to reimport.

reimposición *f* COM reimposition (de impuestos).

reimpresión *f* reprinting (operación) || reprint (resultado).

reimpreso, sa *adj* reprinted.

reimprimir *vt* to reprint.

reina *f* queen; *reina madre* queen mother; *reina viuda* dowager queen || queen (bee) (abeja reina) || queen (dama en el ajedrez) || — *reina claudia* greengage (ciruela) || *reina de belleza* beauty queen || *reina de los prados* meadowsweet (flor).

reinado *m* reign; *bajo el reinado de Enrique VIII* in the reign of Henry VIII ‖ FIG reign.

reinante *adj* reigning, ruling ‖ FIG prevailing, reigning.

reinar *vi* to reign, to rule; *reinar en* or *sobre España* to reign over Spain ‖ FIG to reign, to prevail ‖ — *dividir para reinar* to divide to rule ‖ *el rey reina pero no gobierna* the king reigns, but does not rule ‖ *reinaba un desorden total* complete confusion reigned, the place was in utter chaos.

reincidencia *f* relapse.

reincidente *adj/s* recidivist.

reincidir *vi* to relapse, to fall back (*en* into).

reincorporación *f* reincorporation.

reincorporar *vt* to reincorporate.
◆ *vpr reincorporarse a* to rejoin.

reineta *f* pippin (manzana).

reingresar *vi* to return, to reenter.

reingreso *m* return, reentry.

reino *m* kingdom (de un rey) ‖ kingdom; *el reino de los animales* the animal kingdom ‖ — *el reino de los cielos* the kingdom of heaven ‖ GEOGR *Reino Unido* United Kingdom.

reinserción *f* reintegration ‖ *reinserción social* social rehabilitation.

reinstalación *f* reinstatement (en un puesto) ‖ reinstallation (en un lugar).

reinstalar *vt* to reinstate (en un puesto) ‖ to reinstall.

reintegrable *adj* able to be reintegrated ‖ COM refundable, reimbursable, repayable.

reintegración *f* reintegration ‖ reimbursement, refund, repayment (de dinero, etc.).

reintegrar *vt* to reintegrate ‖ to reimburse, to refund, to pay back (dinero que se ha gastado); *reintegrar una suma a uno* to reimburse s.o. with a sum of money, to refund *o* to pay back a sum of money to s.o. ‖ to reinstate, to reincorporate (reincorporar).
◆ *vpr* to rejoin (volver a formar parte de) ‖ to return; *reintegrarse a su trabajo, a la patria* to return to one's job, to one's native country ‖ to be paid back, to recover; *te reintegrarás de lo que me adelantaste* you will be paid back what you lent me.

reintegro *m* reintegration ‖ refund, repayment, reimbursement (de dinero) ‖ official stamps *pl* (pólizas) ‖ return of one's stake (lotería) ‖ *cobrar el reintegro* to have the price of one's lottery ticket refunded.

reír* *vi* to laugh; *echarse a reír* to start laughing, to burst out laughing ‖ FIG to laugh, to sparkle (los ojos) ‖ — *al freír será el reír, quien ríe el último, ríe mejor* he who laughs last laughs longest ‖ *dar que reír* to be laughable *o* ridiculous ‖ *reír a carcajadas* or *como un descosido* to split one's sides laughing ‖ FAM *reír a mandíbula batiente* to laugh till one's sides ache, to laugh one's head off, to laugh until one's jaws ache ‖ *reír con ganas* to laugh heartily ‖ *reír con risa de conejo, reír de dientes afuera* to force a laugh *o* a smile ‖ *reír para su capote* or *para su sayo* or *para su coleto* or *para sus adentros* or *a solas* to laugh *o* to chuckle to o.s., to laugh *o* to chuckle up one's sleeve.
◆ *vt* to laugh at; *reírle a uno las gracias* to laugh at s.o.'s jokes.
◆ *vpr* to laugh; *no hay de que reírse* there is nothing to laugh about ‖ to have a good laugh; *anoche me reí mucho con él* I had a good laugh with him last night ‖ to laugh, to make fun of s.o. ‖ FIG to split (abrirse) ‖ — *¡déjeme que me ría!* that's a good one! ‖ FIG *me río yo de los peces de colores* I'm alright, I'm laughing, I don't give a damn ‖ *reírse de uno en su cara* or *en sus barbas* to laugh in s.o.'s face.

reiteración *f* reiteration.

reiteradamente *adv* repeatedly.

reiterar *vt* to reiterate, to repeat ‖ *reiteradas veces* repeatedly.

reiterativo, va *adj* reiterative ‖ repetitive, repetitious ‖ GRAM frequentative.

reivindicación *f* claim (reclamación) ‖ vindication.

reivindicar *vt* to claim (reclamar) ‖ to vindicate (vindicar) ‖ to restore (restablecer) ‖ to recover (recuperar).

reivindicatorio, ria; reivindicativo, va *adj* vindicative.

reja *f* grating (alambrera) ‖ grill, grille (de ventana) ‖ AGR ploughshare [US plowshare] (del arado) ‖ — AGR *dar una reja* to plough [US to plow] ‖ FAM *entre rejas* behind bars (en la cárcel).

rejalgar *m* MIN realgar.

rejego, ga *adj* AMER wild (rebelde, terco).

rejilla *f* latticework (de ventana) ‖ screen (contra los insectos, etc.) ‖ grating (de una abertura, de la chimenea) ‖ grill, gridiron (de un horno) ‖ wickerwork (de una silla) ‖ brazier (para calentarse) ‖ grill (del ventilador) ‖ grid (de radio) ‖ luggage rack (para equipaje) ‖ — *de rejilla* wickerwork; *una silla de rejilla* a wickerwork chair ‖ *rejilla del radiador* radiator grille (de un coche).

rejón *m* TAUR lance ‖ goad (garrocha).

rejonazo *m* thrust *o* jab of a lance.

rejoncillo *m* lance (rejón).

rejoneador *m* bullfighter on horseback.

rejonear *vt* to fight on horseback (torear a caballo) ‖ to wound with the lance (clavar el rejón al toro).
◆ *vi* to fight (the bull) on horseback.

rejoneo *m* bullfight on horseback (corrida).

rejuvenecedor, ra *adj* rejuvenating.

rejuvenecer* *vt/vi* to rejuvenate.
◆ *vpr* to be rejuvenated, to rejuvenate.

rejuvenecimiento *m* rejuvenation.

relación *f* relation, relationship, connection (conexión); *guardar relación con* to bear relation to ‖ relation; *mantener relaciones amistosas* to maintain friendly relations; *romper las relaciones diplomáticas* to break off diplomatic relations ‖ list (lista) ‖ record (oficial) ‖ account, statement, report, relation (narración, relato) ‖ tale (de dificultades); *les hizo una relación de sus desgracias* he told them his tale of woe ‖ report (ponencia) ‖ JUR summing-up, summary (de un juez) ‖ MAT ratio (razón), proportion (proporción) ‖ FIG relationship; *la relación entre la causa y el efecto* the relationship between cause and effect ‖ GRAM relation ‖ — *con relación a* in *o* with regard *o* relation to (por lo que se refiere a), in relation to (en comparación con) ‖ *estar en relación con* to be in contact with, to have dealings with (tener tratos con) ‖ *hacer relación a algo* to refer to *o* to make reference to sth. ‖ *no guardar relación alguna con* to be out of all proportion to ‖ *ponerse en relación* to get in touch (entrar en contacto) ‖ TECN *relación de compresión* pressure ratio ‖ *sacar a relación* to make reference to.
◆ *pl* acquaintances (personas conocidas) ‖ connections, contacts, powerful friends (personas influyentes) ‖ — *estar en buenas relaciones con* to be on good terms with ‖ *ponerse en relaciones* to start courting (los novios); *se pusieron en relaciones hace un año* they started courting a year ago; *se puso en relaciones con ella* he started courting her ‖ *relaciones comerciales* trade relationship ‖ *relaciones de parentesco* relationship, kinship, blood relationship ‖ *relaciones públicas* public relations ‖ *tener buenas relaciones* to be well connected, to have powerful friends ‖ *tener relaciones con* to be in contact with, to have dealings with ‖ *tener relaciones (con)* to be courting, to be going out (with) (ser novio de, ser novios).

relacionable *adj* relatable.

relacionado, da *adj* concerning, regarding (que se refiere) ‖ related (*con* to), connected (*con* with), (que está ligado) ‖ — *estar bien relacionado* to have good connections, to be well connected ‖ *todo lo relacionado a* everything concerning *o* which concerns.

relacionar *vt* to relate, to connect; *relacionar un hecho con otro* to relate one fact to another, to connect one fact with another ‖ to put in touch; *relacionar a uno con otro* to put s.o. in touch with s.o. else ‖ to relate, to give an account of, to report (hacer relación de un hecho).
◆ *vpr* to be related *o* connected (tener conexión) ‖ to refer (referirse) ‖ to get in touch (ponerse en contacto) ‖ *en lo que se relaciona con* with regard to.

relajación *f*; **relajamiento** *m* FIG laxity, looseness, slackness (efecto de relajar costumbres, disciplina, moral, etc.) ‖ relaxation (diversión) ‖ slackening, loosening (aflojamiento) ‖ MED relaxing (de músculo) ‖ hernia (hernia) ‖ easing, relaxation; *relajación de la tensión internacional* easing of international tension ‖ *relajación de la autoridad* slackening of authority.

relajado, da *adj* loose.

relajador, ra *adj* relaxing ‖ MED laxative.

relajamiento *m* → **relajación.**

relajante *adj* relaxing ‖ MED laxative.
◆ *m* MED laxative.

relajar *vt* to relax, to loosen; *relajar los músculos* to relax one's muscles ‖ to slacken (una cuerda) ‖ FIG to relax, to slacken (autoridad, disciplina) ‖ to weaken (moralidad) ‖ to ease, to relieve (la tensión) ‖ to be relaxing; *esta música relaja* this music is relaxing.
◆ *vpr* to become lax, to weaken, to wane (la moralidad, disciplina, etc.) ‖ to let o.s. go (viciarse) ‖ to relax (descansar) ‖ to slacken, to loosen (aflojarse) ‖ MED to sprain; *relajarse un tobillo* to sprain one's ankle.

relajo *m* AMER depravity, debauchery (depravación).

relamer *vt* to lick.
◆ *vpr* to lick one's lips (una persona) ‖ to lick its chops (un animal) ‖ FIG to put on one's warpaint, to paint one's face (pintarse las mujeres) ‖ to smack one's lips (de júbilo) ‖ to gloat, to brag (jactarse).

relamido, da *adj* prim and proper, affected (persona) ‖ affected (manera, estilo, etc.) ‖ finical, finicky (cuadro).

relámpago *m* lightning (fenómeno) ‖ flash of lightning (relámpago aislado) ‖ eclair (pastel) ‖ VET leucoma (en el ojo) ‖ — FIG *como un relámpago* as quick as a flash, like greased lightning ‖ FOT *luz relámpago* flash ‖ FIG *pasar como un relámpago por* to flash through, to shoot through.
◆ *adj* lightning; *visita relámpago* lightning visit ‖ *guerra relámpago* blitzkrieg.

relampagueante *adj* sparkling, flashing, gleaming.

relampaguear *vi* FIG to sparkle, to flash, to gleam (brillar).
◆ *v impers* to thunder ‖ *cuando relampaguea* when there is lightning *o* a thunderstorm.
— OBSERV Para traducir el verbo *relampaguear*, que no existe en inglés, se suelen emplear locuciones con los sustantivos *lightning* (relámpago) y *thunderstorm* (tormenta).

relampagueo *m* lightning (relámpagos) ‖ flash, glint, spark (centelleo).

relance *m* accident, coincidence (suceso casual) || second round *o* hand (en los juegos de envite) || *de relance* by chance.

relapso, sa *adj* who relapses [into crime, etc.] || REL relapsed.
◆ *m/f* backslider || REL relapsed heretic.

relatador, ra *m/f* narrator, teller.

relatar *vt* to report, to relate, to recount (un suceso) || to tell, to narrate, to recount (un cuento).

relatividad *f* relativity; *teoría de la relatividad* theory of relativity.

relativismo *m* FIL relativism.

relativo, va *adj* relative || — *en lo relativo a* in *o* with regard to, as regards, as for, with relation to || *relativo a* relative to.
◆ *m* GRAM relative.

relato *m* story, tale (cuento) || report, account (informe) || narration, relating (acción de narrar).

relator *m/f* narrator, teller (de un cuento).
◆ *m* rapporteur (ponente) || reporter (en los tribunales).

relatoría *f* reportership (cargo de relator) || reporter's office (oficina).

relé *m* ELECTR & RAD relay.

relectura *f* second reading, rereading.

releer *vt* to reread, to read again.

relegación *f* relegation.

relegar *vt* to relegate || *relegar al olvido una cosa* to consign sth. to oblivion, to banish sth. from one's mind, to forget all about sth.

relente *m* evening dew (humedad) || chill of the night air (frescura).

relevación *f* JUR exoneration, exemption (de una obligación) | release (de un contrato) || MIL relief.

relevador *m* ELECTR relay.

relevante *adj* outstanding.

relevar *vt* to paint in relief (pintar) || to carve in relief, to emboss (tallar) || to substitute for, to take the place of, to replace (sustituir a uno) || to relieve, to take over from (tomar el relevo de) || to exempt, to exonerate; *relevar a uno de una obligación* to exonerate s.o. from an obligation || MIL to relieve (un centinela) || *ser relevado de su mando* to be relieved of one's command.
◆ *vpr* to take turns (turnarse).

relevo *m* MIL relief, change || relay (deportes); *carrera de relevos* relay race || — *caballos de relevo* relay horses || *100 metros relevos* 100 metres relay || *relevo estilos* medley relay (natación) || *tomar el relevo de* to relieve, to take over from.

relicario *m* reliquary, shrine (caja con reliquias) || locket (medallón).

relieve *m* relief || embossing (estampado) || FIG prominence (importancia) | social standing (categoría social) || — *alto relieve* high relief || *bajo relieve* low relief, bas-relief || FIG *de relieve* prominent, important || *en relieve* in relief || *formar relieve* to stand out || *mapa en relieve* relief map, map in relief || *medio relieve* half relief, mezzo-rilievo || *película en relieve* three-dimensional film || *poner en relieve* to emphasize, to underline.
◆ *pl* leavings, leftovers, scraps (de comida).

religión *f* religion || religiousness, piety (cualidad de religioso) || FIG religion, cult || *entrar en religión* to take vows.

religiosamente *adv* religiously || FIG religiously, scrupulously.

religiosidad *f* religiousness, religiosity, piety || FIG religiousness, thoroughness, punctiliousness.

religioso, sa *adj* religious || religious, pious (piadoso); *hombre religioso* religious man || FIG conscientious, scrupulous, punctilious, religious (concienzudo, escrupuloso) || — *cumplir con sus deberes religiosos* to fulfil one's religious duties || *hacerse religioso, religiosa* to become a monk, a nun, to take vows.
◆ *m* monk, religious (monje).
◆ *f* nun, religious (monja).

relimpio, pia *adj* spick-and-span, as clean as a new pin.

relinchar *vi* to neigh, to whinny.

relincho *m* neigh, whinny || FIG & FAM whoop (of joy) (grito de alegría) || *dar relinchos* to neigh, to whinny (el caballo).

relinga *f* MAR boltrope (de las velas) | balk, baulk, headline (de una red de pescar).

relingar *vt* MAR to rope (una vela).
◆ *vi* MAR to flap (las velas).

reliquia *f* relic || MED aftereffect, result (de una enfermedad) || *reliquia de familia* family heirloom.
◆ *pl* FIG remains, relics (restos, vestigios).

reloj *m* clock; *el reloj de la estación* the station clock; *el reloj de la torre* the clock on the tower; *dar cuerda a un reloj* to wind up a clock || watch (reloj de pulsera) || INFORM clock || — DEP *carrera contra reloj* race against the clock || FIG *marchar como un reloj* to run *o* to work like clockwork (una cosa) || *poner en hora un reloj* to put a clock right || *reloj automático* timer || *reloj de agua* water clock || *reloj de arena* sandglass, hourglass || *reloj de bolsillo* pocket watch || *reloj de caja* grandfather clock || *reloj de campana* chiming clock || *reloj de cuarzo* quartz watch, quartz clock || *reloj de cuco* cuckoo clock || *reloj de péndulo* pendulum clock || *reloj de pulsera* wristwatch, watch || *reloj de sol* or *solar* sundial || *reloj despertador* alarm clock || *reloj digital* digital watch, digital clock || *reloj parlante* talking clock || *reloj registrador* time clock.

relojería *f* watchmaking, clockmaking (arte) || watchmaker's, clockmaker's, jeweller's (tienda) || — *bomba con mecanismo de relojería* time bomb || *mecanismo de relojería* clockwork.

relojero, ra *m/f* watchmaker, clockmaker.

reluciente *adj* shining, glittering, sparkling, gleaming (brillante) || bonny, healthy-looking (sano).

relucir* *vi* to shine; *el sol reluce* the sun is shining || to glitter, to gleam, to sparkle; *el agua reluce bajo el sol* the water glitters in the sunlight || FIG to shine (destacarse) || — *no es oro todo lo que reluce* all that glitters is not gold || *sacar a relucir* to bring out (poner en relieve), to bring up (mencionar); *siempre saca a relucir todos los favores que me ha hecho* he always brings up all the favours he has done me || *salir a relucir* to come to light.

reluctancia *f* ELECTR reluctance.

reluctante *adj* reluctant, unwilling (reacio).

relumbrante *adj* dazzling, resplendent, brilliant.

relumbrar *vi* to shine, to sparkle, to gleam, to glitter || to shine (el sol) || to dazzle (deslumbrar).

relumbrón *m* flash, glare (golpe de luz) || FIG flashiness, ostentation || — FIG *de relumbrón* flashy || *vestirse de relumbrón* to wear flashy clothes, to dress flashily.

rellanar *vt* to level again.
◆ *vpr* to sit back (en un sillón).

rellano *m* landing (de escalera) || shelf (en una vertiente).

rellenar *vt* to fill in *o* out; *rellenar un formulario* to fill in a form || to fill (un pastel) || to stuff; *rellenar un pollo* to stuff a chicken; *rellenar un sillón* to stuff an armchair || to pack, to stuff, to cram (un armario, una maleta, etc.) || to pad (en costura) || to fill in (un hueco) || to fill up (llenar completamente) || to refill, to replenish (llenar de nuevo) || to top up (algo parcialmente vacío) || AVIAC to refuel || FAM to feed (s.o.) up (hartar de comida) | to pad out (un discurso, un escrito, etc.); *¿por qué no cuentas unos chistes para rellenar?* why don't you tell some jokes to pad it out?
◆ *vpr* to be filled in *o* up || FAM to stuff o.s.

relleno, na *adj* packed, stuffed, crammed, full up (completamente lleno) || full; *cara rellena* full face || CULIN stuffed; *aceitunas rellenas* stuffed olives || soft-centered (caramelos) || cream (pasteles).
◆ *m* stuffing, filling (cocina) || filling (acción de llenar) || padding, stuffing, wadding (de un asiento) || padding, wadding (en costura) || filling-in (de un hueco) || filler (material para rellenar) || ullage (de los toneles) || FIG padding (parte superflua) || *material de relleno* filler.

remachado *m* riveting (acción).

remachador *m* riveter.

remachadora *f* riveting machine *o* hammer, riveter.

remachar *vt* to rivet (un metal) || to clinch (un clavo) || FIG to stress, to drive home; *remachar sus palabras* to stress one's words | to crown; *remachar su victoria* to crown one's victory.

remache *m* riveting (del metal) || clinching (de un clavo) || rivet (roblón).

remallar *vt* to mend.

remanencia *f* FÍS remanence.

remanente *adj* FÍS residual, remanent (corriente, etc.) || leftover, remaining, residual (que queda) || COM surplus.
◆ *m* remainder, remnants *pl*, remains *pl*, rest || balance (saldo) || surplus (de la producción).

remangar *vt* to turn *o* to roll up (el pantalón o las mangas) || to pull *o* to tuck up, to bunch (las faldas, etc.) || *con la camisa remangada* with one's shirt sleeves rolled up, in one's shirt sleeves.
◆ *vpr* to roll up one's sleeves (las mangas) || to tuck up; *se remangó las faldas* she tucked up her skirt.

remansarse *vpr* to slow right down, to flow very slowly (río).

remanso *m* pool of still water (charca) || backwater (agua estancada) || FIG sluggishness (lentitud) || FIG *un remanso de paz* a haven of peace.

remar *vi* to row; *remar contra la corriente* to row against the current || FIG *remar en la misma galera* to be in the same boat.

remarcable *adj* remarkable.
— OBSERV This word is a Gallicism for *muy notable.*

remarcar *vt* to mark again (marcar otra vez).
— OBSERV En inglés *to remark* significa sobre todo *observar.*

rematadamente *adv* absolutely, utterly; *rematadamente malo* absolutely awful.

rematado, da *adj* out-and-out, absolute, utter; *un pillo rematado* an out-and-out rascal || JUR convicted || *loco rematado* as mad as March hare *o* as a hatter, as mad as they come.

rematador *m* goal scorer (en fútbol).

rematamiento *m* ⟶ **remate.**

rematante *m* highest bidder.

rematar *vt* to put out of its misery (para que no sufra más); *rematar un caballo herido* to put a wounded horse out of its misery || to kill

(matar) || to use up (agotar) || to finish off (en costura) || COM to knock down (subasta) | to sell off cheap (venta) || FIG to add the finishing touches to (perfeccionar); *rematar una labor* to add the finishing touches to a piece of work | to finish off (terminar); *remató su discurso con una anécdota* he finished off his speech with an anecdote || to crown; *el éxito remató sus esfuerzos* his efforts were crowned by success | to finish off (a alguien) || AMER to pull up sharply (el caballo) || ARQ to be at the top of, to top, to crown.
◆ *vi* to end up; *el campanario remataba en punta* the bell tower ended up in a point || DEP to shoot (at goal), to take *o* to have a shot (at goal) (en fútbol) || DEP *rematar de cabeza* to head a goal || FIG *rematar en* to end in.

remate; rematamiento *m* end (término) || finishing touch (toque final) || ARQ finial, top || DEP shot (fútbol) || last stitch (en costura) || FIG crowning; *el remate de su carrera política* the crowning of his political career || JUR highest bid (puja) || AMER auction (subasta) || — *como remate* to top it all; *y como remate perdí mis papeles* and to top it all I lost my papers || *como remate de* to round off; *como remate de su actuación* to round off his act || FIG *dar remate a* to round off; *dio remate a su viaje con la visita al centro de investigaciones nucleares* he rounded off his journey with a visit to the nuclear research centre || *de remate* utterly (completamente), utter (completo) || *loco de remate* as mad as March hare *o* as a hatter, as mad as they come || *para remate* to top it all || *por remate* finally.

rematista *m* AMER auctioneer.

rembolsar *vt* ⟶ **reembolsar.**

rembolso *m* ⟶ **reembolso.**

remecer *vt* AMER to shake (sacudir).

remedable *adj* imitable, mimicable.

remedador, ra *adj* imitating, mimicking.
◆ *m/f* imitator, mimic.

remedar *vt* to imitate, to copy (imitar); *remedar la voz de uno* to imitate s.o.'s voice || to mimic, to ape (para burlarse).

remediable *adj* remediable || *fácilmente remediable* easily remedied.

remediador, ra *adj* remedial.

remediar *vt* to remedy, to put right, to repair (daño, perjuicio) || FIG to solve (resolver); *gritando no remedias nada* you will not solve anything by shouting; *tu venida no remediará nada* your coming will not solve anything | to put a stop to, to do sth. about (evitar que continúe); *el gobierno debe remediar este estado de anarquía* the government must put a stop to this state of anarchy | to help (ayudar); *siento no poder remediarte* I am sorry I cannot help you || *no poder remediar* not to be able to help; *no pude remediar el echarme a reír* I could not help laughing out loud; *no lo puedo remediar* I can't help it.

remedio *m* remedy, cure (contra la enfermedad); *remedio casero* household remedy || FIG remedy, solution | help, consolation, relief (ayuda, consuelo) || JUR recourse, remedy (recurso) || — *a grandes males, grandes remedios* desperate ills call for desperate measures || *como último remedio* as a last resort || *el remedio es peor que la enfermedad* the remedy is worse than the disease || *ella no tiene remedio* she's a hopeless case || FIG *ni para un remedio* none at all; *no se encontraba una habitación ni para un remedio* no rooms were to be found at all || *no hay más remedio que* all we (you, etc.) can do is, there is nothing left to do but || *no hay remedio* there is nothing we (you, etc.) can do about it || *no hay más remedio* to have no alternative *o* choice || *no tiene remedio* it's unavoidable (es inevitable), there's nothing we (you, etc.) can do about it (no tiene solución) || *poner remedio a* to put a stop to, to do sth. about || *¿qué remedio me queda?* what else can I do? || FIG *remedio heroico* drastic measure || *sin remedio* without fail (sin falta).

remedo *m* imitation (acción) || imitation, copy || travesty, parody (plagio).

remembranza *f* memory, remembrance.

rememoración *f* recollection, remembrance.

rememorar *vt* to recall, to remember.

rememorativo, va *adj* commemorative.

remendado, da *adj* patched; *pantalones remendados* patched trousers || patchy (animales).

remendar* *vt* to mend, to repair (arreglar) || to patch (echando remiendos) || to mend (zurcir) || to darn (calcetines) || to mend (una red) || FIG to correct.

remendón, ona *adj* mending || *zapatero remendón* cobbler, shoemender.
◆ *m/f* mender || cobbler, shoemender (zapatero).

remensa *f* ⟶ **payés.**

remera *f* remex, quill feather || AMER T-shirt (camiseta).
— OBSERV El plural de *remex* es *remiges*.

remero, ra *m/f* rower.

remesa *f* COM shipment, consignment (de mercancías) || remittance (de dinero).

remesar *vt* COM to ship, to send, to consign (mercancías) | to remit (dinero) || (p us) to tear out, to pull out (la barba, el pelo).

remeter *vt* to put back (volver a meter) || to tuck in; *remeter las sábanas, la camisa* to tuck in the sheets, one's shirt.

remezón *m* AMER shake, jolt (sacudón).

remiendo *m* mending, repairing (acción de remendar) || mend (parte remendada) || patching (con un pedazo nuevo) || patch; *echar un remiendo a un pantalón* to put a patch on a pair of trousers || IMPR job, piece of work || FIG improvement (mejora) || — *a remiendos* piecemeal || FAM *echar un remiendo a una cosa* to patch sth. up || *no hay mejor remiendo que el del mismo paño* if you want a thing done well do it yourself.

remige *f* remex (pluma).
— OBSERV El plural es *remiges* en ambos idiomas.

remigio *m* crapette (juego de naipes).

remilgado, da *adj* fussy, finicky (con la comida) || fastidious (exigente) || affected (en el hablar, el vestir) || prudish (moralmente) || *hacer el remilgado* to make a great fuss.

remilgarse *vpr* to be fussy *o* affected *o* prudish *o* fastidious (ser remilgado) || to put on an act (hacer gestos afectados).

remilgo *m* fastidiousness (exigencia) || affectation || *andar con* or *hacer remilgos* to make a fuss, to be fussy (ser melindroso), to be fastidious (ser exigente).

remilgoso, sa *adj* AMER ⟶ **remilgado.**

remilitarización *f* remilitarization.

remilitarizar *vt* to remilitarize.

reminiscencia *f* reminiscence.

remirado, da *adj* cautious, careful (prudente) || prudish (moralmente) || affected (afectado) || fussy (con la comida).

remirar *vt* to look over, to look at again, to have another look at (mirar de nuevo) || to look again and again at (mirar repetidas veces) || to take a close look at, to examine (mirar detenidamente).
◆ *vpr* to take great pains (*en* over).

remisamente *adv* remissly, carelessly (negligentemente) || begrudgingly (con poca voluntad).

remisibilidad *f* remissibility.

remisión *f* sending (envío) || delivery (entrega); *la remisión de un paquete* the delivery of a parcel || REL remission, forgiveness; *la remisión de los pecados* the remission of sins || MED remission (de una enfermedad) || JUR remission (de una pena) || reference; *texto lleno de remisiones* text full of references || postponement (diferimiento) || — *no hay pecado sin remisión* there is no sin without remission || FIG *sin remisión* without fail (sin remedio).

remisivo, va *adj* reference; *nota remisiva* reference mark || remissive (que perdona).

remiso, sa *adj* remiss, slack (negligente) || reluctant, unenthusiastic (reacio); *muchedumbre remisa a la hora de aplaudir* a reluctant crowd when it comes to applauding || *no ser remiso en* to be ready and willing to.

remisor, ra *m/f* AMER sender.

remisorias *f pl* JUR transfer of a case to another court.

remisorio, ria *adj* remissive.

remite *m* sender's name and address.

remitencia *f* MED remission.

remitente *adj* who sends || MED remittent.
◆ *m/f* sender; *devuélvase al remitente* return to sender.

remitido *m* advertisement, announcement (en el periódico).

remitir *vt* to send, to ship, to consign (enviar mercancías) || to remit (dinero) || to deliver (entregar) || to postpone (aplazar) || to remit, to forgive; *remitir los pecados* to remit sins || to refer; *el autor nos remite a la primera parte* the author refers us to the first part || JUR to transfer (un caso) | to remit (una pena).
◆ *vi* to subside; *ha remitido el temporal* the storm has subsided || to remit, to subside (fiebre) || to refer; *remitir a la página diez* to refer to page ten.
◆ *vpr* to abandon o.s.; *remitirse a la Providencia* to abandon o.s. to Providence || to leave it; *remitirse a la decisión de otro* to leave it to s.o. else's decision || to refer; *me remito a las pruebas existentes* I refer to the existing evidence; *remítanse a la primera página* refer to the first page.

remo *m* oar (grande) || paddle (pequeño) || rowing (deporte) || (ant) galley || — *barca de remo* rowing boat [US rowboat] || *ir a remo* to row.
◆ *pl* FIG limbs (del hombre) | legs (de los cuadrúpedos) | wings (de aves) | hardships (dificultades).

Remo *npr m* Remus.

remoción *f* removal || shake-up, reshuffle (cambio de personal) || AMER dismissal (cese, destitución) || *remoción de tierras* earthworks.

remojar *vt* to soak, to steep; *remojar garbanzos en agua* to soak chickpeas in water || to soak (la colada, el cáñamo) || to dip, to dunk; *remojar una galleta en el té* to dip a biscuit in one's tea || to soak again (volver a mojar) || to soak, to drench (involuntariamente) || FIG & FAM to celebrate, to drink to; *remojar un éxito* to celebrate a success || AMER to tip (dar una propina) || FIG & FAM *esto hay que remojarlo* this calls for a celebration *o* for a drink.
◆ *vpr* to soak; *garbanzos que se remojan en el agua* chickpeas soaking in water || FIG to get soaked *o* drenched.

remojo *m* soaking || FIG & FAM dip (baño); *darse un remojo* to take a dip || AMER tip (propina) || *echar* or *dejar* or *poner a* or *en remojo* to soak, to leave to soak (garbanzos, ropa, etc.), to let ride (un asunto).

remojón *m* FAM soaking (acción de mojar mucho) | cloudburst (lluvia); *¡qué remojón!* what a cloudburst! || CULIN sop, piece of bread [soaked in milk, gravy, etc.].

remolacha *f* beet; *remolacha azucarera* sugar beet || beetroot [*US* beet] (encarnada y comestible) || *remolacha forrajera* mangel-wurzel.

remolachero, ra *adj* beet; *la industria remolachera* the beet industry.
◆ *m/f* beet grower (cultivador) || worker in a beet factory (obrero).

remolcador *m* MAR tug, tugboat || AUT breakdown lorry.

remolcar *vt* to tow, to take in tow || FIG to rope in; *remolcar a uno* to rope s.o. in || MAR *remolcar abarloado* to tow alongside.

remoler* *vt* to grind up.

remolinar; remolinear *vi/vpr* to swirl, to eddy (agua) || to whirl, to spin (en el aire) || to mill around (la gente) || to crowd together, to throng (amontonarse).

remolino *m* swirl, eddy, whirlpool (del agua) || whirl, whirlwind (del aire) || whirl, cloud (de polvo, etc.) || cowlick (de pelo) || throng (masa de gente) || milling (movimiento de la muchedumbre).

remolón, ona *adj* lazy, slack.
◆ *m* upper tusk (del jabalí).
◆ *m/f* shirker, idler, slacker || *hacerse el remolón* to shirk, to slack (eludir el trabajo), to refuse to budge (no moverse).

remolonear *vi* to shirk, to slack.

remoloneo *m* shirking, slacking.

remolque *m* towing (acción de remolcar) || towline, towrope (cabo) || trailer (detrás de un coche) || caravan [*US* trailer] (de turismo) || — *a remolque* on tow || *dar remolque a* to tow || *grúa remolque* breakdown truck || *ir a remolque de* to be towed by (ser remolcado por), to be roped in by (ir forzado) || *llevar a uno a remolque* to take s.o. in tow (sentido propio), to rope s.o. in (obligar a seguir).

remonta *f* repair (reparación) || leather patch (del pantalón de montar) || MIL remount.

remontar *vt* to mend, to repair (remendar) || to overcome, to beat, to master (un obstáculo) || to beat up (la caza) || MIL to remount (proveer de caballos) || *remontar el vuelo* to soar.
◆ *vpr* to go back; *remontarse hasta la época prehistórica* to go back to prehistoric times || to soar (pájaro) || HIST to take to the hills (esclavos) || FIG to soar (espíritu) || COM to amount to (cantidad) || *el castillo se remonta al siglo XIV* the castle dates back to *o* dates from the 14th century.

remontista *m* MIL remount serviceman.

remoquete *m* FIG nickname (apodo) | cutting remark, dig (dicho punzante) || punch (puñetazo).

rémora *f* ZOOL remora (pez) || FIG hindrance; *las viejas estructuras constituyen una rémora para el progreso* old structures are a hindrance to progress.

remorder* *vt* to gnaw (morder insistentemente) || FIG to trouble, to worry, to give cause for remorse || *el recuerdo de su crimen le remuerde la conciencia* his crime preys on his mind, he has a guilty conscience *o* he is full of remorse when he remembers the crime he committed.
◆ *vpr* to suffer remorse (sentir remordimiento) || to fret (preocuparse).

remordimiento *m* remorse; *estar torturado por el remordimiento* to be tortured by remorse || *tener remordimientos* to feel remorse.

remosquearse *vpr* FAM to be wary (escamarse) || IMPR to mackle.

remotamente *adv* remotely, vaguely; *lo recuerdo remotamente* I can remotely remember it.

remoto, ta *adj* remote; *países remotos* remote lands; *peligro remoto* remote danger || vague (vago) || — *la remota antigüedad* the far-distant past || *ni la más remota posibilidad* not the remotest chance.

remover* *vt* to move (mover) || to remove (quitar) || to stir (el café, etc.) || to shake up (agitar) || to turn over, to dig up (la tierra) || FIG to revive, to rake up; *remover recuerdos* to revive memories | to remove (a uno de su empleo) | to stir up (un asunto).

remozamiento *m* rejuvenation || FIG brightening up (de un vestido, etc.) | bringing up to date, modernization (de las instituciones).

remozar *vt* to rejuvenate || FIG to brighten up (una fachada, un vestido, etc.) | to bring up to date, to modernize (actualizar).
◆ *vpr* to be rejuvenated || to look much younger (parecer más joven) || FIG to be brightened up; *se ha remozado toda la ciudad para las fiestas* the whole town has been brightened up for the celebrations.

remplazable *adj* replaceable.

remplazante *m/f* substitute.

remplazar *vt* → **reemplazar.**

remplazo *m* → **reemplazo.**

rempujar *vt* FAM to shove, to push.

rempujón *m* FAM shove, push.

remunerable *adj* remunerable.

remuneración *f* remuneration.

remunerador, ra *adj* remunerating (que remunera) || remunerative (rentable) || rewarding (que da satisfacción).
◆ *m/f* remunerator.

remunerar *vt* to remunerate, to pay (pagar).
◆ *vi* to be remunerative (ser rentable) || to be rewarding (ser satisfactorio).

remunerativo, va *adj* remunerative.

remuneratorio, ria *adj* remuneratory.

renacentista *adj inv* Renaissance; *estilo renacentista* Renaissance style.

renacer* *vi* to be reborn (nacer de nuevo) || BOT to grow again (las plantas) | to bloom again (flores) || FIG to revive (recobrar fuerzas) | to reappear (reaparecer) || FIG *el día renace* a new day is dawning.

renaciente *adj* renascent; *paganismo renaciente* renascent paganism || *el día renaciente* the dawn of a new day.

renacimiento *m* HIST Renaissance || rebirth, revival (acción de renacer) || FIG recovery, rebirth (recuperación); *el renacimiento de una nación* the recovery of a nation | revival (reaparición).
◆ *adj inv* Renaissance (estilo).

renacuajo *m* ZOOL tadpole || FIG & FAM shrimp (persona pequeña).

renal *adj* renal, kidney.

Renania *npr f* GEOGR Rhineland.

renano, na *adj* Rhenish, [of *o* from the] Rhineland, [of *o* from] the Rhine.
◆ *m/f* Rhinelander.

rencilla *f* quarrel (riña).
◆ *pl* arguing *sing*, bickering *sing*, arguments (discusiones).

rencilloso, sa *adj* quarrelsome, peevish || resentful (rencoroso).

renco, ca *adj* lame (cojo).

rencor *m* rancour [*US* rancor] || resentment (resentimiento) || *guardar rencor a uno por algo* to hold a grudge against s.o. *o* to bear s.o. malice because of sth.

rencoroso, sa *adj* rancourous [*US* rancorous] (propenso a sentir rencor) || resentful (dominado por el rencor).

rendajo *m* ZOOL jay (arrendajo).

rendibú *m* *hacer el rendibú a uno* to flatter s.o. (lisonjear), to treat s.o. well (obsequiar).

rendición *f* surrender; *la rendición de Breda* the surrender of Breda || yield (rendimiento).

rendido, da *adj* surrendered (ciudad, pueblo, etc.) || submissive (que se somete voluntariamente) || obsequious, humble, submissive (obsequioso) || worn-out, exhausted (muy cansado) || — *admirador rendido* devoted admirer || *rendido de amor por* madly in love with.

rendija *f* crack; *mirar por la rendija de la puerta* to look through the crack in the door.

rendimiento *m* yield; *este terreno tiene un rendimiento bajo* this land has a low yield || COM yield, return || output (lo que produce una máquina, un obrero, una fábrica) || TECN efficiency | performance (de un motor) || FIG obsequiousness (obsequiosidad) | submission, submissiveness (sumisión) | fatigue, exhaustion (gran cansancio).

rendir* *vt* to defeat, to subdue, to conquer (derrotar) || to take (una fortaleza) || to surrender (entregar); *rendir la ciudad* to surrender the town || to dip (la bandera) || to produce, to yield (producir) || to yield (ganancia) || to yield, to bear (interest) || to bear (fruto) || to give, to render (las gracias) || to pay, to do (homenaje) || to give (una cuenta) || to hand over (la guardia) || to wear out, to exhaust (agotar); *este paseo me ha rendido* this walk has worn me out || to dominate (dominar) || to overcome (superar) || to vomit, to throw up (*fam*) || — FIG *rendir cuentas* to account for one's actions || *rendir culto a* to worship (un santo, una persona), to pay homage *o* tribute to; *rendir culto a la valentía de una persona* to pay homage to a person's courage || *rendir el alma* to give up the ghost || *rendir pleitesía a* to pay tribute *o* hommage to.
◆ *vi* to pay; *este trabajo no rinde* this work does not pay || to produce; *el negocio rinde para mantener una familia* the business produces enough to support a family.
◆ *vpr* to surrender, to submit, to give in; *rendirse al enemigo* to surrender to the enemy || to give in, to submit (darse por vencido) || to wear o.s. out (cansarse) || MAR to snap, to break (la verga) || — *rendirse a la evidencia* to bow to the evidence || *rendirse a la razón* to listen to reason.

renegado, da *adj* renegade || FAM gruff, bad-tempered (de mal carácter).
◆ *m/f* renegade || FAM nasty piece of work (de mal carácter).

renegador, ra *adj* blasphemous, profane.
◆ *m/f* blasphemer.

renegar* *vi* to renounce, to deny, to abjure; *renegar de su fe* to renounce one's faith || to disown; *renegar de su familia* to disown one's family; *todos tus amigos renegarían de ti* all your friends would disown you || to blaspheme (blasfemar) || FAM to swear (decir groserías) | to grumble (refunfuñar) | to complain (quejarse).
◆ *vt* to deny strongly.

renegón, ona *adj* FAM grumpy, grumbling (refunfuñón).
◆ *m/f* FAM moaner.

renegrido, da *adj* black (negro) || blackened (ennegrecido).

RENFE *abrev de Red Nacional de los Ferrocarriles Españoles* Spanish national railway company.

rengífero *m* ZOOL reindeer (reno).

renglón *m* line (escrito) || item, heading (de una cuenta) || — FIG *a renglón seguido* straight away, immediately afterwards | *leer entre renglones* to read between the lines || *poner unos renglones a alguien* to drop s.o. a line.

renglonadura *f* ruled lines *pl*, ruling.

rengo, ga *adj* lame (cojo).
◆ *m/f* cripple.

renguear *vi* AMER to limp (renquear).

renguera *f* AMER limp (cojeo) | lameness (cojera).

reniego *m* curse, oath (dicho injurioso) || moaning *inv* (protestas).

renio *m* rhenium (metal).

reno *m* ZOOL reindeer.

renombrado, da *adj* renowned, famous (famoso).

renombre *m* renown, fame (fama) || nickname (sobrenombre) || *de renombre* of renown, renowned, famous.

renovable *adj* renewable.

renovación *f* renewal (de un pasaporte, un contrato, un arriendo, votos, etc.) || renovation (de una cosa en mal estado) || decorating, redecoration (de una habitación) || reorganization, shake-up (de personal).

renovar* *vt* to renew; *renovar un pasaporte, votos, un contrato* to renew a passport, vows, a contract || to renew, to replace (el personal de una casa, el mobiliario, etc.) || to renovate (una cosa en mal estado) || to redecorate (volver a decorar); *renovar una habitación* to redecorate a room || to reorganize (una organización, etc.) || FIG *renovar la herida* to open up an old wound.
◆ *vpr* to be renewed.

renquear *vi* to limp, to hobble || FIG & FAM to dither (vacilar).

renqueo *m* limp.

renta *f* income; *impuesto sobre la renta* income tax; *renta per cápita* per capita income || rent; *la renta del piso* the rent for the flat; *renta de bienes raíces* or *de la tierra* or *del suelo* ground rent || national debt (deuda pública) || interest, return (beneficio) || — *a renta* on lease || *distribución de la renta* distribution of wealth || *renta bruta* gross income || *renta de una finca urbana* rental value || *renta nacional* national income || *renta pagada por el Estado* interest on Government bonds || *renta pública* national revenue || *renta vitalicia* life annuity || *vivir de sus rentas* to live on one's private income.

rentabilidad *f* profitability.

rentabilizar *vt* to make profitable.

rentable *adj* profitable; *un negocio rentable* a profitable business || *ya no es rentable* it is no longer economic.

rentado, da *adj* of independent means.

rentar *vt* to yield, to produce (rendir) || AMER to let (alquilar).

rentero, ra *m/f* tenant farmer (colono).

rentista *m/f* bondholder, holder of Government bonds (accionista) || person of independent means (que vive de sus rentas).

rentístico, ca *adj* financial; *reforma rentística* financial reform.

renuente *adj* reluctant (reacio a).

renuevo *m* BOT shoot, sprout || renewal (renovación) || BOT *echar renuevos* to sprout.

renuncia *f* renunciation (*a* of) || JUR waiver, renunciation (a un derecho, a una queja, etc.) || resignation (a un puesto) || *hacer renuncia de* to renounce.

renunciable *adj* renounceable.

renunciación *f*; **renunciamiento** *m* renunciation.

renunciante *adj* renunciant, renunciative.
◆ *m/f* renunciant.

renunciar *vi* to give up, to abandon; *renunciar a un proyecto* to give up a project; *renunciar a la lucha* to give up the struggle || JUR to renounce (a una herencia, a la corona, etc.) | to waive, to drop (una demanda) || to resign; *renunciar a su puesto* to resign one's post || to renounce, not to follow suit (en los naipes) || to withdraw (*a* from), (en una competición).
◆ *vt* to relinquish, to give up; *renunciar sus derechos en otro* to give up one's rights in favour of s.o. else.
◆ *vpr* to deny o.s.

renuncio *m* renounce, failure to follow suit (naipes) || — FIG & FAM *coger en renuncio* to catch out || *hacer renuncio* to renounce, not to follow suit (naipes).

renvalsar *vt* TECN to rabbet.

renvalso *m* TECN rabbet (en carpintería).

reñidamente *adv* bitterly (luchar).

reñidero *m* cockpit, cockfighting pit, pit.

reñido, da *adj* on bad terms, at odds; *estar reñido con un amigo* to be on bad terms with a friend || bitter, hard-fought (lucha, batalla) || tough, hard-fought; *un partido muy reñido* a very tough match || incompatible; *lo útil no está reñido con lo bello* usefulness and beauty are not incompatible || *en lo más reñido de la lucha* in the thick of the struggle.

reñidura *f* FAM scolding, telling off, dressing down.

reñir* *vi* to quarrel, to argue (disputar) || to fight (pelearse) || to fall out (enemistarse); *he reñido con mi novio, con mi familia* I have fallen out with my boyfriend, with my family || *reñir por* to fight for *o* over.
◆ *vt* to tell off, to scold (reprender); *reñir a un niño* to tell a child off || to fight, to wage (una batalla).

reo *m/f* JUR defendant, accused (acusado); *absolver a un reo* to acquit a defendant | culprit (persona culpable) | criminal || *reo de Estado* person accused of treason.
◆ *m* sea trout (pez).
— OBSERV Note that the feminine form is *la reo* and not *la rea*.

reoca; repanocha *f* FAM *es la reoca* that's the limit *o* the last straw (es el colmo), that's priceless (es muy gracioso).

reóforo *m* FÍS rheophore.

reojo (mirar de) *loc* to look (at s.o. or at sth.) out of the corner of one's eye || FIG to look askance at (con enfado).

reómetro *m* rheometer.

reordenar *vt* to rearrange.

reorganización *f* reorganization || *reorganización ministerial* cabinet reshuffle.

reorganizador, ra *adj* reorganizing.
◆ *m/f* reorganizer.

reorganizar *vt* to reorganize || to reshuffle (el gobierno).

reostático, ca *adj* FÍS rheostatic.

reóstato; reostato *m* FÍS rheostat.

repanchingarse; repantigarse *vpr* to loll, to sprawl out; *repantigarse en un sillón* to loll in an armchair.

repanocha *f* FAM → **reoca.**

reparable *adj* repairable; *daño reparable* repairable damage || noteworthy (digno de atención).

reparación *f* repair; *taller de reparaciones* repair shop || repairing, mending (acción) || FIG reparation (compensación, satisfacción) || — *en reparación* being repaired, undergoing repair || *hacer una reparación a* to repair, to do a repair job on.

reparador, ra *adj* FIG reparative (de una ofensa) | refreshing; *sueño reparador* refreshing sleep | fortifying (alimento, medicina) | faultfinding (criticón).
◆ *m* repairman.
◆ *m/f* FIG faultfinder.

reparar *vt* to repair, to mend, to fix (arreglar); *reparar un reloj* to repair a clock || FIG to make amends for (una ofensa) | to make up for (remediar una falta) | to correct (corregir una falta) | to renew, to restore (las fuerzas) || to notice (notar); *reparar un error* to notice a mistake || to parry (un golpe).
◆ *vi* to notice (ver); *no reparé en su presencia* I did not notice his presence || to pay attention (*en* to), to take notice (*en* of) (hacer caso); *nadie reparó en lo que decía* nobody took any notice of what he was saying || to think (reflexionar) || to realize (darse cuenta) || — *no repara en nada* he stops at nothing || *no reparar en gastos* to spare no expense || *reparar en detalles* to pay attention to details || *reparar en pelillos* or *en pormenores* to be a stickler for details.

reparativo, va *adj* reparative.

reparo *m* repair || fault (falta); *Noel está siempre poniendo reparos a la cocina de Jill* Noel is always finding fault with Jill's cooking || objection (objeción) || parry (en esgrima) || reservation, reserve; *aprobar una decisión con cierto reparo* to approve a decision with some reservation || MED remedy || — *no andes con reparos* no buts (no vaciles) || *no tener reparo en* not to be afraid to, not to hesitate to; *no tenga nunca reparo en decir lo que usted piensa* never be afraid to say what you think; *no tiene reparo en hacer cualquier cosa* he is not afraid to do anything || *poner reparos a todo* to raise objections to everything, to find fault with everything || *sin reparo* without consideration.

repartición *f* sharing out (reparto) || division || parcelling out (de un terreno) || distribution.

repartidor, ra *m/f* distributor (el que reparte).
◆ *m* delivery man *o* boy (de compras) || — *repartidor de leche* milkman || *repartidor de periódicos* paperboy.

repartimiento *m* sharing out (reparto) || distribution (distribución) || JUR assessment (del impuesto).

repartir *vt* to share out, to apportion; *repartir una suma entre tres hombres* to share out a sum of money between three men || to partition (un país) || to give out, to hand out, to distribute; *repartir los premios* to give out the prizes || to deliver; *el cartero reparte el correo* the postman delivers the mail; *repartir la leche* to deliver the milk || to serve out (comida) || to hand out, to deal out; *repartir golpes* to hand out blows || to deal (naipes) || to space out, to spread out (colocar en varios sitios) || to parcel out (un terreno) || TEATR to cast || FIG & FAM *repartir leña* to play rough (deportes), to lash out (pegar).

reparto *m* sharing out; *el reparto del dinero* the sharing out of the money || division || parcelling out (de terrenos) || distribution (distribución) || partition, partitioning; *el reparto de Polonia* the partition of Poland || delivery; *reparto del correo, de la leche* delivery of the mail, milk delivery || TEATR & CINEM cast (actores) | casting (distribución de papeles) || deal (naipes) || — *coche de reparto* delivery van || *hacer el reparto del dinero* to share out the money || *le tocó poco en el reparto* he did not get a very big share || *reparto de premios* prize-giving.

repasador *m* AMER tea towel (paño de cocina).

repasar *vt* to go over (again), to reexamine (examinar de nuevo) || to revise, to go over (lección) || to go *o* to look over; *el actor repasó su papel* the actor went over his part || to

check, to look over (para corregir) || to polish up (dar los últimos toques) || to glance over *o* through (leer superficialmente) || to mend (la ropa) || to check, to overhaul (una máquina) || to go over (pasar de nuevo); *repasar el cepillo por la madera* to go over the wood with the plane.
◆ *vi* to go back; *repasar por una calle* to go back through a street.

repasata *f* FAM scolding, telling off (reprimenda); *dar una repasata a uno* to give s.o. a scolding.

repaso *m* revision (de una lección) || check (de un aparato) || mending (de la ropa) || FAM scolding, telling off (repasata) || — *curso de repaso* refresher course || *dar un repaso a* to look over *o* through; *el actor dio un repaso a su papel* the actor looked over his part; to mend (la ropa), to glance over *o* through (leer superficialmente), to add the finishing touches to (dar la última mano), to check, to overhaul (una máquina).

repatriación *f* repatriation.

repatriar *vt* to repatriate.
◆ *vpr* to be repatriated || to return to one's country (volver a su patria).

repechar *vi* to go uphill.

repecho *m* steep slope (cuesta) || *a repecho* uphill.

repelente *adj* repulsive, repellent, disgusting || *niño repelente* little know-all.

repeler *vt* to repulse, to repel (rechazar) || to reject (un argumento) || to repel (un ataque) || to throw out; *repeler a intrusos de su domicilio* to throw intruders out of one's home || to reflect; *el color blanco repele el calor* white reflects heat || to repel; *esta pintura repele el agua* this paint repels water || FIG to repel (disgustar) | to disgust, to repel (asquear); *las arañas me repelen* spiders disgust me.
◆ *vpr* to be incompatible.

repelo *m* the wrong way [opposite direction to the nap] (de una tela) || fibre [*US* fiber] (de la madera) || ANAT hangnail || FIG repugnance, disgust (repugnancia) || *darle repelo a uno* to make one sick.

repeluco; repelús; repeluzno *m* shiver || *darle a uno repeluzno* to give s.o. the shivers.

repellado *m* plastering-up.

repellar *vt* to plaster up.

repensar *vt* to reconsider, to think over.

repente *m* FAM start (movimiento) | fit; *un repente de ira* a fit of rage *o* temper | sudden feeling; *me dio el repente que iba a suicidarse* I had the sudden feeling that he was going to commit suicide || *de repente* suddenly.

repentinamente *adv* suddenly.

repentino, na *adj* sudden; *muerte repentina* sudden death.

repentizar *vi* MÚS to sight-read, to play at sight || to ad-lib, to improvise, to extemporize (improvisar).

repercusión *f* repercussion || — *de amplia repercusión* far-reaching || *un discurso que ha tenido mucha repercusión en el país* a speech which had great repercussions in the country (consecuencias), a speech which caused a great stir in the country (reacciones).

repercutida *f* → **repercusión.**

repercutir *vi* to resound, to re-echo, to reverberate (el sonido) || to rebound (rebotar) || *repercutir en* to have repercussions on, to affect (tener repercusiones).
◆ *vt* to reflect.
◆ *vpr* to reverberate (el sonido).

repertorio *m* index, repertory (list) || TEATR repertoire, repertory; *poner en el repertorio* to include in the repertoire.

repesar *vt* to reweigh.

repesca *f* second chance to qualify [given to those eliminated in a competition].

repescar *vt* to give a second chance to qualify.

repetición *f* repetition || MÚS repeat || — *fusil de repetición* repeater, repeating rifle || *reloj de repetición* repeater, repeating watch.

repetido, da *adj* repeated; *repetidas ausencias* repeated absences *o* absence || — *en repetidas ocasiones* on many occasions, many times || *repetidas veces* many times, repeatedly, again and again.

repetidor, ra *adj* repeating || *alumno repetidor* student who is repeating a year.
◆ *m/f* lecturer (en la universidad) || private tutor, coach (en privado) || TECN relay, booster station; *repetidor de televisión* television relay | repeater (de teléfono).

repetir* *vt* to repeat; *repetir una frase* to repeat a sentence; *repetir un curso* to repeat a year || to recite; *repetir la lección* to recite the lesson || to do again (hacer de nuevo) || to start again (comenzar de nuevo) || to have a second helping of (un plato) || TEATR to revive (reestrenar) || to re-echo (las palabras de otro).
◆ *vi* to take a second helping (de un plato) || to repeat (on one;) *la sardina repite* sardines repeat [on one] || *estar repetido* to be duplicated (estar hecho dos veces), to be a double; *este sello está repetido* this stamp is a double.
◆ *vpr* to repeat o.s. || to recur; *la epidemia se ha repetido tres veces este año* the epidemic has recurred three times this year || to come, to fall; *fiesta que se repite siempre en la misma fecha* celebration which always comes on the same date || to repeat (on one) (un sabor) || — *no ha habido que repetírselo dos veces* he did not need to be told twice || *¡que no se repita!* don't let it happen again! || *¡que se repita!* encore!, more!

repicar *vt* to ring, to peal, to sound (las campanas) || to prick *o* to sting again (picar de nuevo) || to repique (en los naipes) || to mince finely (cortar).
◆ *vi* to peal, to ring out, to chime (las campanas) || to beat (el tambor).

repintar *vt* to repaint.
◆ *vpr* to make up, to lay on the makeup (maquillarse excesivamente) || IMPR to mackle.

repipi *adj* FAM la-di-dah || *niño repipi* precocious little horror.

repique *m* peal, ringing, chiming (de las campanas) || repique (en los naipes).

repiquete *m* lively peal (de campanas).

repiquetear *vi* to peal out (campanas) || to beat (tambor) || FIG to pitter-patter; *la lluvia repiqueteaba en el tejado* the rain pitter-pattered on the roof | to drum (con los dedos en la mesa).

repiqueteo *m* lively peal (de campanas) || beating (de tambor) || FIG pitter-patter (de la lluvia) | rattle, clatter (de ametralladora, etc.).

repisa *f* ARQ corbel || shelf (estante) || *repisa de chimenea* mantelpiece.

replantación *f* replanting.

replantar *vt* AGR to replant | to transplant (trasplantar).

replantear *vt* to lay out a ground plan of (un edificio) || to restate (un problema).

repleción *f* repletion.

replegable *adj* folding || AVIAC retractable (tren de aterrizaje).

replegado, da *adj* replicate (doblado).

replegar* *vt* to fold up (doblar) || AVIAC to retract (el tren de aterrizaje).
◆ *vpr* MIL to fall back.

repleto, ta *adj* crammed full, packed; *calle repleta de gente* street crammed full of *o* packed with people || plump, chubby (rechoncho) || full, full up, replete (ahíto) || *bolsa repleta* well-lined purse.

réplica *f* retort, rejoinder (contestación) || replica (copia) || JUR replication || *sin réplica* unquestionably (indiscutiblemente), speechless (cortado); *se quedó sin réplica* he was left speechless.

replicar *vt* to answer (contestar).
◆ *vi* to retort, to answer, to rejoin (p us) || to argue, to answer back; *los niños deben obedecer sin replicar* children should do as they are told without answering back.

replicón, ona *adj* argumentative (respondón).

repliegue *m* fold, crease || MIL withdrawal || FIG recess; *los repliegues del alma humana* the recesses of the human mind.

repoblación *f* repopulation (de un país) || restocking (de un río, de un estanque) || *repoblación forestal* reafforestation [*US* reforestation].

repoblar* *vt* to repopulate (un país) || to restock (un río, un estanque) || to reafforest [*US* to reforest] (con árboles).

repollo *m* cabbage (col) || head (de lechuga).

repolludo, da *adj* round-headed (plantas) || FIG tubby (rechoncho).

reponer* *vt* to put back, to replace (poner de nuevo) || to replace (sustituir) || to revive, to bring back, to put on again (obra de teatro) || to restore (salud) || to reply, to retort (replicar) || to replenish; *reponer las existencias* to replenish one's stocks || to restore (en un cargo).
◆ *vpr* to recover (salud) || *reponerse de* to recover from, to get over.

reportaje *m* report, article (en el periódico); *reportaje gráfico* illustrated report || RAD report, item.

reportamiento *m* restraint, control.

reportar *vt* to transfer (en litografía) || to bring (proporcionar); *su participación sólo le ha reportado desgracias* his taking part has only brought him misfortune || *AMER* to report (informar) || *reportarle beneficio a uno* to benefit s.o.
◆ *vpr* to calm down (serenarse) || to restrain *o* to control o.s. (moderarse).

reporte *m* news report *o* item || (piece of) gossip (chisme) || transfer (litografía).

reporterismo *m* reporting, journalism, news reporting.

reportero, ra *m/f* reporter, news reporter.

reportista *m* IMPR lithographer.

reposadamente *adj* calmly.

reposadero *m* ladle (en los hornos).

reposado, da *adj* rested, relaxed (descansado) || calm (el mar) || calm, peaceful (tranquilo) || unhurried, steady (pausado).

reposapiés *m inv* footrest (de moto, etc.).

reposar *vi* to lie, to rest, to be buried (yacer) || to rest, to take a rest, to repose (p us); *después de comer suele reposar un rato* after lunch he usually rests a while *o* he usually takes a little rest || to relax (solazándose).
◆ *vi/vpr* to settle (un líquido).

reposera *f* *AMER* deck chair (tumbona).

reposición *f* replacement || revival (teatro, cine) || replenishment; *reposición de existencias* replenishment of stocks || MED recovery.

reposo *m* rest; *gozar de un bien merecido reposo* to enjoy a well-earned rest; *un mes de reposo absoluto* a month's complete rest || — *cuerpo en reposo* body at rest || *tierra en reposo* fallow land.

repostar *vi/vpr* to stock up (reponer provisiones) || to refuel (buque, avión, etc.) || to fill up (coche).

repostería *f* confectioner's, cake shop (tienda) || pantry (despensa) || pastrymaking (arte u oficio).

repostero *m* pastrycook (pastelero) || butler to the king (cargo palaciego) || cloth ornamented with a coat of arms (paño) || AMER larder, pantry (despensa).

repotente *adj* FAM *me da la repotente gana de salir* I really feel like going out | *no me da la repotente gana* I just don't feel like it.

reprender *vt* to reprehend, to reprimand; *le reprendió su mala conducta* he reprehended him for his bad behaviour.

reprensible *adj* reprehensible.

reprensión *f* reprimand, reprehension.

reprensivo, va; reprensor, ra *adj* reproachful, reprehensive.

represa *f* dam (en un río) || millpond (para un molino).

represalia *f* reprisal, retaliation || *tomar* or *ejercer represalias contra* to take reprisals *o* to retaliate against.

represar *vt* to dam (un río) || to hold back (las aguas) || FIG to contain, to repress (reprimir).

representable *adj* representable || performable (obra de teatro).

representación *f* representation || JUR representation || TEATR performance || — *en representación de* as a representative of, representing || JUR *heredero por representación* representative heir || *hombre de representación* man of some importance *o* some standing.

representante *adj/s* representative; *representante comercial, diplomático* commercial, diplomatic representative.
◆ *m/f* actor, actress (comediante).

representar *vt* to present again (volver a presentar) || to represent; *este dibujo representa una casa* this drawing represents a house; *representar un país* to represent a country || to stand for, to represent; *este símbolo representa el infinito* this symbol stands for infinity || TEATR to play, to act (un papel); *representó muy bien su papel* he played his part very well | to perform, to play (una obra de teatro) || to look (aparentar); *no representa la edad que tiene* he does not look his age; *representa unos cuarenta años* he looks about forty (years old) || to represent (equivaler); *libro que representa diez años de trabajo* book which represents ten years' work || to look worth; *este mueble no representa lo que te ha costado* this piece of furniture does not look worth what you paid for it.
◆ *vpr* to imagine, to picture (imaginarse).

representativo, va *adj* representative.

represión *f* suppression || repression (psicológica).

represivo, va *adj* repressive.

reprimenda *f* reprimand, reprehension.

reprimible *adj* repressible, suppressible.

reprimir *vt* to repress, to suppress || to suppress, to quell (un levantamiento) || to hold back, to repress, to suppress (risa, llanto, etc.) || to repress (en psicología).
◆ *vpr reprimirse de hacer algo* to stop o.s. *o* to refrain from doing sth.

reprise *f* AUT acceleration (poder de aceleración).

reprobable *adj* reproachable, reprehensible, reprovable.

reprobación *f* reprobation, reproof, reproval.

reprobado, da *adj* reprobate, damned (réprobo).

reprobador, ra *adj* reproachful, reproving, reprehensive.

reprobar* *vt* to condemn, to reprobate (una acción); *repruebo toda clase de violencia* I condemn violence of any kind || to reproach, to reprove, to rebuke (a una persona); *reprobar a uno su comportamiento* to reproach s.o. with his behaviour || to disapprove (of) (desaprobar) || REL to damn, to reprobate.

reprobatorio, ria *adj* reprobative, reprobatory.

réprobo, ba *adj/s* reprobate, damned.

reprochable *adj* reproachable.

reprochador, ra *m/f* reproachful person.

reprochar *vt* to reproach; *reprochar algo a alguien* to reproach s.o. for *o* with sth.
◆ *vpr* to reproach o.s.

reproche *m* reproach, reproof; *aguantar reproches injustos* to suffer unjust reproach.
— OBSERV *Reproach* y *reproof* suelen emplearse en singular.

reproducción *f* reproduction || MED recurrence (de una enfermedad) || *derechos de reproducción* copyright.

reproducible *adj* reproducible.

reproducir* *vt* to reproduce; *reproducir un cuadro* to reproduce a painting || to reproduce, to breed (criar animales).
◆ *vpr* to reproduce || MED to recur (una enfermedad) || to reoccur, to happen again (ocurrir de nuevo).

reproductividad *f* reproductivity.

reproductor, ra *adj* ANAT reproductive || breeding (animal) || reproducing; *máquina reproductora* reproducing machine.
◆ *m/f* breeder (animal).

reprografía *f* reproduction (de documentos, etc.).

repropio, pia *adj* balky, stubborn, restive (caballo).

reps *m* rep, repp (tela).

reptación *f* slither, crawl.

reptante *adj* slithering, crawling || BOT creeping.

reptar *vi* to slither, to snake, to crawl.

reptil *adj* reptilian, reptile.
◆ *m* reptile.

república *adj* republic || — *la República Argentina* the Argentine Republic || *la República Dominicana* the Dominican Republic || *república bananera* banana republic || *república de las letras* republic of letters.

República Centroafricana *npr f* GEOGR Central African Republic.

republicanismo *m* republicanism.

republicanizar *vt* to republicanize.
◆ *vpr* to be republicanized.

republicano, na *adj/s* republican.

repudiable *f* repudiable.

repudiación *f* repudiation || JUR *repudiación de la herencia* renunciation *o* relinquishment of one's inheritance.

repudiar *vt* to repudiate (a una mujer, una doctrina, etc.) || JUR to renounce, to relinquish.

repudio *m* repudiation.

repudrir *vt* to rot completely.
◆ *vpr* to rot away || FIG & FAM to eat one's heart out, to pine away.

repuesto, ta *adj* replaced, put back (puesto de nuevo) || restored (en un cargo) || recovered (de salud).
◆ *m* provisions *pl*, food supplies *pl* (comestibles) || supply; *tenemos buen repuesto de gasolina* we have a good supply of petrol || spare part, spare (pieza) || sideboard (mueble) || *de repuesto* in reserve (en reserva), spare (de recambio); *rueda de respuesto* spare wheel.

repugnancia *f* repugnance, aversion, disgust; *sentir repugnancia a* or *hacia* to feel repugnance towards; *sentir repugnancia por* to feel repugnance at || contradiction, opposition, incompatibility; *repugnancia entre dos teorías* contradiction between two theories || reluctance (desgana) || *las arañas me dan repugnancia* I loathe *o* detest spiders.

repugnante *adj* disgusting, repugnant, repulsive, revolting.

repugnar *vi* not to be able to stand, to loathe, to detest; *los sapos me repugnan* I cannot stand *o* I loathe toads || to disgust; *me repugnó su comportamiento* his behaviour disgusted me || to hate; *me repugna tener que hacerlo* I hate having to do it.
◆ *vt* to hate (tener aversión).
◆ *vpr* to contradict each other.
— OBSERV Nótese que para traducir el verbo intransitivo hace falta invertir la construcción en inglés.

repujado, da *adj* TECN repoussé, embossed.
◆ *m* TECN repoussé [work], embossing.

repujar *vt* TECN to emboss.

repulir *vt* to repolish, to polish up (pulir de nuevo) || FIG to spruce up, to dress up to the nines (acicalar).
◆ *vpr* FIG to dress up to the nines, to spruce o.s. up.

repulsa *f* refusal, rejection (negativa) || rebuff (a una persona).

repulsar *vt* to reject (una pretensión) || to rebuff (a una persona).

repulsión *f* repulsion, repugnance (aversión) || rejection (repulsa).

repulsivo, va *adj* repulsive (repelente).

repullo *m* jump, start (sobresalto) || *dar un repullo* to jump, to start.

repunta *f* headland, cape, point (cabo) || FIG slight sign, inkling (indicio).

repuntar *vi* to turn (la marea).
◆ *vt* AMER to round up (el ganado).
◆ *vpr* to turn sour (el vino) || FIG & FAM to fall out (enfadarse).

repunte *m* turn (de la marea) || AMER roundup, rounding up (del ganado).

reputación *f* reputation.

reputado, da *adj* reputed; *bien reputado* highly reputed || *mal reputado* of ill repute.

reputar *vt* to deem, to consider, to repute, to think (considerar); *le reputan de experto* he is considered *o* deemed an expert, he is reputed *o* thought to be an expert.

requebrar* *vt* to court (cortejar) || to flatter (lisonjear) || to break in tiny pieces (quebrar mucho).

requemado, da *adj* scorched, burnt, charred (quemado) || tanned, brown, bronzed (la tez).

requemar *vt* to scorch, to burn, to char (quemar) || to scorch, to parch (las plantas) || to burn (la lengua, el paladar) || MED to inflame || to tan, to bronze (la tez).
◆ *vpr* to scorch || to scorch, to parch (las plantas) || FIG to harbour resentment (reconcomerse).

requerible *adj* requisite.

requerido, da *adj* required, requisite || JUR summoned, summonsed.

requeridor, ra; requeriente *adj* requiring.
◆ *m/f* requirer || JUR summoner.

requerimiento *m* JUR injuction, summons (intimación) | request (demanda).

requerir* *vt* to urge, to beg, to call on, to ask, to request; *requerir a alguien para que haga algo* to ask s.o. to do sth. ‖ to need, to require, to call for (necesitar); *esto requiere mucha atención* this needs a lot of attention ‖ to require, to call for; *las circunstancias lo requieren* the circumstances require it; *esta conducta requiere castigo* this behaviour calls for punishment ‖ to order (ordenar) ‖ JUR to summon (intimar) | to notify (avisar) ‖ *requerir de amores* to court, to woo.

requesón *m* cottage cheese (queso) ‖ curd (cuajada).

requete *pref* FAM this prefix is often added to an adjective in Spanish to intensify it; *requetebueno* really good; *es un requetetonto* he is a complete fool; *requetelleno* brimful, full to the top.

requeté *m* «requeté», Carlist volunteer ‖ Carlist forces *pl* (organización militar carlista).

requetebién *adv* marvellously, wonderfully.

requiebro *m* flattering *o* flirtatious remark, compliment (a mujeres) ‖ MIN stamped *o* crushed ore ‖ *decir requiebros a* to flatter (lisonjear), to court (cortejar).

réquiem *m* requiem.

requirente *adj* requiring.
◆ *m/f* requirer ‖ JUR summoner.

requisa *f* requisition (requisición) ‖ inspection.

requisar *vt* to requisition.

requisición *f* requisition.

requisito, ta *adj* required, requisite ‖ JUR summoned.
◆ *m* requirement, requisite; *este documento satisface todos los requisitos* this document fulfils all the requirements ‖ — *requisito previo* prerequisite ‖ *ser requisito indispensable* to be absolutely essential.

requisitoria *f* JUR requisition, demand.

res *f* beast, animal; *reses de matadero* animals for slaughter ‖ head *inv*; *rebaño de veinte reses* flock of twenty head ‖ — AMER *carne de res* beef ‖ *res vacuna* head of cattle.
— OBSERV *Res* is applied only to large animals.

resabiado, da *adj* vicious (animales) ‖ TAUR experienced (por haber sido toreado).

resabiarse *vpr* to become vicious (animales) ‖ to fall into bad habits (personas).

resabido, da *adj* well-known (perfectamente sabido) ‖ pedantic (que se precia de sabio) ‖ *es sabido y resabido que...* it is a perfectly well-known fact that...

resabio *m* bad habit (vicio) ‖ unpleasant aftertaste (sabor desagradable).

resaca *f* MAR undertow, undercurrent ‖ COM redraft ‖ FAM hangover; *tener resaca* to have a hangover.

resalado, da *adj* FIG & FAM witty, charming.

resalir* *vi* to protrude, to jut out.

resaltar *vi* to stand out (destacarse); *las flores rojas resaltaban sobre el césped* the red flowers stood out against the lawn ‖ to jut out (un balcón) ‖ to rebound, to bounce (rebotar) ‖ *hacer resaltar* to emphasize, to stress (subrayar hablando), to bring out, to set off; *el marco hacía resaltar la belleza del cuadro* the frame set off the beauty of the picture.

resalte *m* ledge, projection (en la pared).

resalto *m* bounce, rebound (rebote) ‖ projection, protrusion (parte que sobresale).

resalvo *m* BOT sapling.

resarcible *adj* indemnifiable ‖ repayable (reembolsable).

resarcimiento *m* indemnification, compensation ‖ repayment (reembolso).

resarcir *vt* to indemnify, to compensate (indemnizar); *resarcir a alguien de una pérdida* to indemnify s.o. for a loss ‖ to repay (reembolsar); *resarcir a uno de sus gastos* to repay s.o.'s expenses.
◆ *vpr* to make up for; *resarcirse de una pérdida* to make up for a loss.

resbalada *f* AMER slide (resbalón).

resbaladero, ra *adj* slippery (resbaladizo).
◆ *m* skating rink, slippery spot (sitio resbaladizo) ‖ chute, slide (para la madera).

resbaladizo, za *adj* slippery ‖ FIG ticklish, delicate (delicado).

resbaladura *f* skid *o* slide mark.

resbalamiento *m* ⟶ **resbalón.**

resbalar *vi/vpr* to slide (deslizarse); *resbalar en el hielo* to slide on the ice ‖ to slip (over) (involuntariamente); *resbaló y se cayó* he slipped and fell ‖ AUT to skid (un coche) | to slip (el embrague) ‖ to trickle (caer lentamente un líquido); *las gotas de lluvia resbalaban por los cristales* the raindrops trickled down the windows ‖ FIG to slip up (incurrir en un desliz).

resbalón; resbalamiento *m* slide (voluntario) ‖ slip, slide (involuntario) ‖ skid (de un coche) ‖ FIG slip, slipup (desliz) ‖ *dar un resbalón* to slide, to slip.

rescaldar *vt* to scald.

rescatable *adj* redeemable.

rescatador, ra *m/f* redeemer ‖ rescuer.

rescatar *vt* to recapture, to recover; *rescatar una ciudad* to recapture a town ‖ to recover, to rescue (a prisioneros) ‖ to ransom (pagar por la libertad) ‖ to save, to rescue (algo o alguien que está en peligro) ‖ to pick up (astronautas) ‖ to recover (recuperar) ‖ to make up (for) (el tiempo perdido) ‖ FIG to rescue; *rescatar del olvido* to rescue from oblivion.

rescate *m* recapture, recovery (de una ciudad) ‖ recovery, rescue (de prisioneros) ‖ ransom (dinero) ‖ picking up (de los astronautas) ‖ rescue (de gente en peligro) ‖ recovery (recuperación) ‖ COM redemption ‖ *exigir* or *imponer rescate por alguien* to hold s.o. to ransom [US to hold s.o. in ransom], to ransom s.o.

rescaza *f* ZOOL scorpion fish, hogfish (pez).

rescindible *adj* rescindable, rescissible.

rescindir *vt* to cancel, to rescind, to annul (un contrato).

rescisión *f* rescission, cancellation.

rescisorio, ria *adj* rescissory (que rescinde).

rescoldo *m* embers *pl* ‖ FIG misgiving, lingering doubt (recelo).

rescripto; rescrito *m* rescript.

resecación *f* thorough drying, drying up, drying out.

resecar *vt* MED to resect (un órgano) ‖ to dry up *o* out (secar mucho) ‖ to parch, to scorch (las plantas).
◆ *vpr* to dry up, to parch ‖ *se me reseca la boca* my mouth is dry *o* parched.

resección *f* MED resection.

reseco, ca *adj* very dry, parched ‖ FIG skinny (flaco).

reseda *f* BOT reseda, mignonette (planta).

resedáceas *f pl* BOT resedaceae.

resentido, da *adj* resentful ‖ — *estar resentido contra uno* to bear resentment towards s.o., to be annoyed with s.o. ‖ *estar resentido por* to resent, to be resentful of.
◆ *m/f* resentful person.

resentimiento *m* resentment.

resentirse* *vpr* to feel the effects; *resentirse de una antigua herida* to feel the effects of an old wound ‖ to be weakened (debilitarse); *la casa se resintió con la explosión* the building was weakened by the explosion ‖ — *resentirse con* or *contra uno* to bear s.o. resentment, to be annoyed with s.o. ‖ *resentirse de* or *por algo* to take offence at sth., to resent sth. ‖ *resentirse de la pierna* to still have a bad leg, to still have trouble with one's leg.

reseña *f* description (descripción) ‖ account (relación); *reseña histórica* historical account ‖ review, report, account (de periódico); *reseña de los libros recientemente publicados* review of recently published books.

reseñar *vt* to give a description of, to describe (describir) ‖ to give an account of, to report on (dar informaciones sobre) ‖ to review (una obra).

reserva *f* reservation, booking (en un hotel, tren, etc.); *reserva de habitaciones* room reservation, reservation of rooms ‖ reserve, stock (cosa reservada); *reservas de comida* food reserves, stock of food ‖ COM reserves *pl*; *reserva de divisas* foreign currency reserves ‖ reservation; *reserva de indios* Indian reservation ‖ reserve (de animales) ‖ REL reservation ‖ MIL reserve, reserves *pl* ‖ reservedness, reserve (de carácter); *nos acogió con su reserva habitual* he received us with his usual reserve ‖ reservation (salvedad); *acepto con ciertas reservas* I accept, but with certain reservations ‖ — *a reserva de* except for ‖ *a reserva de que* unless | *con la mayor reserva* in the strictest confidence (confidencialmente) ‖ *con reserva* reservedly ‖ *de* or *en reserva* reserve, in reserve; *tropas de reserva* reserve troops, troops in reserve; reserve; *provisiones de reserva* reserve food supply ‖ *guardar* or *tener en reserva* to keep in reserve ‖ *guardar reserva* not to commit o.s. ‖ *reserva mental* mental reservation ‖ *reserva natural* nature reserve ‖ *sin reserva* unreservedly, without reservation.
◆ *pl* reserves.
◆ *m/f* DEP reserve.

reservable *adj* reservable.

reservación *f* reservation.

reservadamente *adv* confidentially, in confidence.

reservado, da *adj* reserved; *tener plazas reservadas* to have reserved seats ‖ confidential (asunto) ‖ reserved (carácter).
◆ *m* reserved *o* private room (en un restaurante, etc.) ‖ reserved compartment (en un tren) ‖ REL host kept in the ciborium.

reservar *vt* to reserve; *reservar una parte de los beneficios para obras pías* to reserve part of the profits for charity ‖ to reserve, to save, to keep; *reservó la mejor noticia para el final* he saved the best news until last; *reserva tus consejos para ti* keep your advice to yourself ‖ to reserve, to book (una habitación, un asiento en un tren, en el teatro, etc.) ‖ to withhold, to reserve; *reservar su opinión* to withhold one's opinion ‖ REL to reserve.
◆ *vpr* to save o.s.; *me reservo para mañana* I am saving myself for tomorrow ‖ to take it easy (cuidarse) ‖ to reserve, to withhold; *reservarse el juicio acerca de algo* to reserve one's judgment on sth.

reservativo, va *adj* reserve.

reservista *m* MIL reserve, reservist.

reservón, ona *adj* FAM very quiet *o* reserved ‖ TAUR hesitant, reluctant (el toro).

resfriado, da *adj* cooled, cold ‖ *estar resfriado* to have a cold (estar constipado).

◆ *m* cold (catarro); *coger un resfriado* to catch a cold | chill (enfriamiento).

resfriadura *f* VET cold.

resfriamiento *m* cooling (acción de enfriar) || MED chill (enfriamiento).

resfriar *vt* to cool (enfriar) || FIG to cool (moderar) || MED to give (s.o.) a cold.
◆ *vi* to cool (down).
◆ *vpr* MED to catch *o* to get a cold (acatarrarse) | to catch *o* to get a chill (enfriarse) || FIG to cool off (la amistad, las relaciones, etc.).

resfrío *m* → **resfriado.**

resguardar *vt* to protect, to shelter; *esta mampara nos resguarda del viento* this screen shelters us from the wind || to protect (amparar) || to safeguard (salvaguardar).
◆ *vpr* to protect o.s. || FIG to be careful, to be wary, to take precautions (obrar con cautela).

resguardo *m* protection || safeguard, guarantee; *este documento le servirá de resguardo* this document will be your safeguard || guarantee (bancario) || counterfoil [*US* stub] (de un talonario) || receipt (recibo) || voucher (vale) || frontier guard (aduana) || MAR sea room.

residencia *f* residence; *residencia veraniega* summer residence || hall of residence [*US* dormitory]; *residencia de estudiantes* students' hall of residence || residential hotel (hotel) || home (asilo); *residencia de ancianos* old people's home || headquarters *pl* (de una organización) || head office (de una compañía) || JUR impeachment (de un funcionario) || — *interdicción de residencia* prohibition from entering an area || *permiso de residencia* residence permit || *tener su residencia* to reside.

residencial *adj* residential.

residenciar *vt* to impeach, to hold an enquiry into (s.o.'s) conduct (a un funcionario) || to call to account (a un particular).

residente *adj* resident, residing; *residente en París* residing in Paris || resident; *médico residente* resident doctor || — *ministro residente* minister resident || *no residente* non-resident.
◆ *m/f* resident.

residir *vi* to reside, to live; *residir en Londres, en el campo* to reside in London, in the country || FIG to lie, to reside; *ahí es donde reside la dificultad* that is where the difficulty lies || FIG *residir en* to reside in, to rest with, to be vested in; *el poder legislativo reside en el Parlamento* legislative power resides in Parliament.

residual *adj* residual, residuary || — *aguas residuales* sewage || *aire residual* residual air.

residuo *m* residue (desecho, sobra) || QUÍM residuum || MAT remainder.
◆ *pl* waste *sing*, refuse *sing* (materiales inservibles) || remains (restos).

resiembra *f* replanting, resowing.

resignación *f* resignation.

resignado, da *adj* resigned.

resignar *vt* to resign (un cargo) || to hand over (el mando).
◆ *vpr* to resign o.s.; *resignarse a vivir modestamente* to resign o.s. to a modest life.

resignatario *m* resignee.

resiliencia *f* FÍS resilience, resiliency.

resina *f* resin.

resinar *vt* to tap (a tree) for resin (un árbol).

resinero, ra *adj* resin.
◆ *m* resiner (obrero).

resinoso, sa *adj* resinous.

resistencia *f* resistance; *resistencia pasiva* passive resistance; *resistencia a la infección* resistance to infection || ELECTR resistance || endurance, stamina (aguante) || strength (de los materiales) || resistance, opposition (hostilidad); *el proyecto encontró mucha resistencia* the plan met with a lot of resistance || — *la Resistencia* the Resistance (política) || *oponer resistencia* to offer resistance, to resist.

resistente *adj* resistant, resistent (que resiste) || strong (material) || hard-wearing (tela, superficie, etc.) || BOT hardy || indefatigable (incansable) || *resistente a la presión* resistant to pressure, pressure-resistant.
◆ *m* Resistance fighter, member of the Resistance.

resistir *vi* to resist; *resistir al ataque* to resist the attack || to have endurance *o* stamina; *¿ya estás cansado? tú no resistes nada* tired already? you have no stamina || to last, to wear well (durar) || *el secador resiste todavía* the hairdryer is still working.
◆ *vt* to resist; *resistir la tentación* to resist temptation || to resist; *este producto no resiste el calor* this product does not resist heat || to bear, to endure, to stand (soportar); *no resisto el calor* I cannot bear the heat || to stand up to; *este libro no resistirá la crítica* this book will not stand up to the critics || to withstand (peso, presión, etc.) || to defy; *precio que resiste toda competencia* price which defies all competition.
◆ *vpr* to struggle, to resist, to offer resistance (forcejear) || to refuse (negarse); *me resisto a hacer una cosa tan desagradable* I refuse to do such an unpleasant thing || — *me resisto a creerlo* I find it hard to believe || *se le resiste el inglés* English gives him trouble.

resistividad *f* ELECTR resistivity.

resma *f* ream (de papel).

resmilla *f* one fifth of a ream, four quires (de papel).

resobado, da *adj* hackneyed, trite (trillado).

resol *m* glare *o* reflection of the sun.

resoluble *adj* soluble, solvable.

resolución *f* solution (de un problema) || resolution (en una asamblea); *adoptar una resolución* to adopt a resolution; *un proyecto de resolución* a draft resolution || resolution, resolve, determination (determinación) || decision || — *en resolución* in short, in summary, to sum up || *hombre de resolución* man of decision.

resolutivo, va *adj/sm* resolvent || *parte resolutiva* operative part (de una resolución, de una ley).

resoluto, ta *adj* resolute (determinado).

resolutorio, ria *adj* JUR resolutive, resolutory.

resolvente *adj/sm* resolvent.

resolver* *vt/vi* to solve, to resolve; *resolver un problema* to solve a problem || to resolve, to settle (conflicto) || to overcome (dificultad) || to resolve, to decide; *resolvió marcharse* he resolved to leave || to resolve (descomponer) || MED to resolve || QUÍM to dissolve || JUR to decide; *resolver a favor de uno* to decide in s.o.'s favour || *resolver por unanimidad* to resolve unanimously.
◆ *vpr* to be solved; *el problema se resolvió sin mucha dificultad* the problem was solved without much difficulty || to work out; *todo se resolverá con el tiempo* everything will work out in time || to end up; *las negociaciones se resolvieron en un compromiso* the talks ended up in a compromise || to resolve, to make up one's mind, to decide; *resolverse a salir* to resolve to go out || MED to resolve.

resollar* *vi* to breathe heavily, to breathe noisily (respirar con ruido) || to puff and blow (jadear) || FIG & FAM to show signs of life; *hace mucho tiempo que no resuella* it's a long time since he showed any signs of life || FIG & FAM *sin resollar* without a word (sin hablar).

resonador, ra *adj* resounding, resonant.
◆ *m* resonator.

resonancia *f* resonance || echo (eco) || MÚS harmony || FIG importance | renown (fama) | repercussions *pl* (consecuencias) || FIG *tener resonancia* to cause a stir (un suceso).

resonante *adj* resounding, resonant (sonoro) || FIG resounding; *una victoria resonante* a resounding victory.

resonar *vi* to resound, to re-echo, to ring || to resound (un cuarto vacío).

resoplar *vi* to puff and blow, to breathe heavily (respirar con ruido) || to pant (por cansancio) || to snort, to puff and blow (por enfado).

resoplido; resoplo *m* heavy breathing (respiración fuerte) || panting (jadeo) || snort (de un caballo) || snort (de enfado) || FIG sharp retort (contestación brusca) || — *el coche iba dando resoplidos* the car chugged along || *llegamos a la cima dando resoplidos* we arrived panting at the top.

resorber *vt* to reabsorb.
◆ *vpr* to be reabsorbed.

resorción *f* reabsorption, resorption.

resorte *m* spring (muelle); *resorte espiral* coil spring || springiness, elasticity (elasticidad).
◆ *pl* FIG strings; *tocar todos los resortes* to pull all the strings one can || FIG *conocer todos los resortes de algo* to know all the ins and outs of sth.

respaldar *m* back (respaldo).

respaldar *vt* to endorse, to indorse (escribir en el respaldo de) || FIG to support, to back (up) (apoyar) | to back, to cover; *depósitos respaldados por el oro* deposits backed by gold.
◆ *vpr* to lean (back); *respaldarse contra un árbol* to lean against a tree || FIG *respaldarse en* to base o.s. on.

respaldo *m* back (de silla) || back, reverse side, verso (de un papel) || endorsement, indorsement (lo escrito en el dorso) || FIG backing, endorsement, support (apoyo) | backing (financiero).

respectar *vi* to concern, to regard; *por lo que respecta a tu hermano, nos arreglaremos* we shall sort sth. out as regards your brother *o* as far as your brother is concerned.
— OBSERV Not to be confused with *respetar* (to respect).

respectivamente; respective *adv* respectively.

respectivo, va *adj* respective || *en lo respectivo a* as regards, with regard to.

respecto *m* respect || — *al respecto, a este respecto* about *o* on the matter, in this respect; *me pidieron aclaraciones al respecto* they asked me to shed some light on the matter || *con respecto a, respecto a, respecto de* with regard to, as regards (en cuanto a), in relation to (con relación a) || *respecto a mí* as for me, as far as I am concerned.

résped *m* (forked) tongue (de las serpientes) || sting (de la abeja).

respetabilidad *f* respectability.

respetable *adj* respectable || *a respetable distancia* from *o* at a respectable distance.
◆ *m* FAM audience (público).

respetar *vt* to respect; *respetar a los superiores, la ley* to respect one's superiors, the law || to spare (conservar) || — *hacerse respetar* to command respect || AUT *respetar la prioridad* to give way.
◆ *vpr* to respect o.s., to have self-respect || to be respected (la ley, etc.).

respeto *m* respect (*a* for); *infundir respeto* to inspire respect; *respeto a la ley* respect for the law || consideration || — *de respeto* respectable

(respetable), spare (reservado) || *faltar al respeto a uno* to lack respect for s.o., to be disrespectful towards s.o. || *por respeto a* out of consideration for || *respeto a sí mismo* self-respect.
◆ *pl* respects; *presentar sus respetos a uno* to pay one's respects to s.o. || *campar por sus respetos* to do as one pleases.

respetuosidad *f* respect, respectfulness.

respetuoso, sa *adj* respectful || *dirigir sus saludos respetuosos a* to pay one's respects to.

respingado, da *adj* turned-up; *nariz respingada* turned-up nose.

respingar *vi* to shy, to start (un animal) || to kick (persona) || to be higher on one side, to be lopside (la falda, el abrigo).

respingo *m* start, jump; *pegar* or *dar un respingo* to give a start.

respingón, ona *adj* FAM *nariz respingona* turned-up nose.

respirable *adj* breathable, respirable.

respiración *f* breathing, respiration; *respiración ruidosa* noisy *o* loud breathing || breath (aliento); *perder la respiración* to lose one's breath || ventilation (ventilación) || — *cortarle a uno la respiración* to take s.o.'s breath away, to leave s.o. breathless (un susto, una noticia, etc.), to wind s.o., to knock the breath out of s.o. (un golpe) || *faltarle a uno la respiración* to be breathless *o* out of breath; *al llegar al séptimo piso me faltaba la respiración* when I got to the seventh floor I was out of breath || *respiración artificial* artificial respiration || *respiración boca a boca* mouth-to-mouth respiration, kiss of life || *sin respiración* breathless.

respiradero *m* ventilator || air vent *o* valve (orificio de aeración) || snorkel (para pesca submarina) || ventilation shaft (en una mina) || FIG breather, respite, rest (descanso).

respirador, ra *adj* breathing || respiratory; *músculos respiradores* respiratory muscles.
◆ *m* respiratory muscle.

respirar *vi* to breathe, to respire (p us); *todavía respira* he is still breathing || to breathe a sigh of relief, to breathe again (con alivio) || to get one's breath back; *dejar respirar a los caballos* to let the horses get their breath back || — FIG *no dejar respirar a alguien* not to give s.o. a moment's peace | *no poder respirar* to be up to one's neck (de trabajo) | *no respirar* not to breathe a word | *sin respirar* without stopping for breath, non-stop (sin descansar), without a word (sin hablar).
◆ *vt* to breathe (in), to respire (p us) || to inhale || FIG to exude (olor) || FIG *respirar felicidad* to ooze happiness.

respiratorio, ria *adj* respiratory || *aparato respiratorio* respiratory system.

respiro *m* breathing (respiración) || FIG rest, breather, break (descanso); *tomarse un respiro* to take a breather | break (tregua) | peace, respite; *no dar respiro* to give no peace || — *plazo de respiro de tres días* three days' grace || *respiro de alivio* sigh of relief.

resplandecer* *vi* to shine; *el sol resplandece* the sun shines || to blaze, to glow (un fuego) || to glitter, to gleam (plata, etc.) || FIG to shine, to glow; *su rostro resplandecía de felicidad* her face shone with joy | to shine, to stand out (sobresalir).

resplandeciente *adj* shining, resplendent || FIG outstanding (sobresaliente) | glowing, radiant, shining; *resplandeciente de salud* glowing with health.

resplandecimiento *m* brilliance, brightness, resplendence.

resplandor *m* brightness, brilliance, resplendence; *el resplandor del sol* the brightness of the sun || flash (momentáneo) || blaze, glow (de llamas) || glitter, gleam (de vidrieras, etc.) || FIG splendour.

responder *vt* to answer.
◆ *vi* to reply, to answer; *responder a una carta, una pregunta* to reply to *o* to answer a letter, a question || to answer, to respond to (a un llamamiento) || to answer; *responder a la amistad con grosería* to answer friendliness with rudeness || to answer back (replicar) || to answer (el eco) || to respond; *responder a un tratamiento* to respond to a treatment; *no responde a mis súplicas* he does not respond to my pleas || to answer; *esta medida responde a una necesidad* this measure answers a need || to correspond (*a* with) (corresponder) || to be responsible (ser responsable); *son los padres los que deben responder de la conducta de sus hijos* the parents are responsible for their children's behaviour || to take the responsibility (aceptar la responsabilidad) || to vouch (apoyar, confirmar); *yo puedo responder de lo que dice* I can vouch for what he says || — *los mandos no responden* the controls don't respond || *responder a las especificaciones, las necesidades* to meet the specifications, the needs || *responder al nombre de* to go by the name of, to be called || *responder a una descripción* to fit a description || *responder a una obligación* to honour an obligation || *responder por* to vouch for, to guarantee (garantizar).

respondón, ona *adj* argumentative, cheeky, saucy.

responsabilidad *f* responsibility || — *cargar a uno con la responsabilidad de* to make s.o. responsible for || *cargar con la responsabilidad de* to take the responsibility for, to answer for || *responsabilidad civil* civil liability || *responsabilidad limitada* limited liability || *sociedad de responsabilidad limitada* private company.

responsabilizarse *vpr* to take the responsibility.

responsable *adj* responsible (*de* for) || JUR liable (*de* for) | responsible (de su conducta) || — *hacerse responsable de algo* to assume responsibility for sth. || *la persona responsable* the person in charge (el encargado).

responso *m* REL prayer for the dead.

responsorio *m* REL responsory, response.

respuesta *f* answer, reply (contestación) || response (reacción) || — *dar la callada por respuesta* no to deign to answer, to say nothing in reply | *tener siempre respuesta* to have an answer for everything.

resquebradura *f* crack (grieta).

resquebrajadizo, za *adj* easily cracked, fragile, brittle.

resquebrajadura *f*; **resquebrajamiento** *m* crack (grieta).

resquebrajar *vt* to crack (barro, loza, etc.).
◆ *vpr* to crack.

resquebrar *vt* to crack (resquebrajar).

resquemor *m* sting (en la boca) || FIG inner torment, uneasiness (desasosiego) | remorse (remordimiento) | resentment (resentimiento).

resquicio *m* chink, crack (abertura) || FIG opening, chance (ocasión) | slight chance (posibilidad pequeña) || FIG *un resquicio de esperanza* a glimmer of hope.

resta *f* MAT subtraction (operación aritmética) | remainder (resto).

restablecer* *vt* to reestablish || to restore (orden, monarquía).
◆ *vpr* to recover (de una enfermedad) || to be reestablished (una institución) || to be restored (orden, monarquía).

restablecimiento *m* reestablishment || restoration (del orden, de la monarquía) || recovery (de salud).

restallar *vi* to crack (el látigo) || to crack (crujir) || to crackle (el fuego) || to click (la lengua).

restallido *m* crack (de látigo) || crackle (del fuego) || click (de la lengua).

restante *adj* remaining || *lo restante* the remainder, the rest.

restañadero *m* estuary (estuario).

restañadura *f*; **restañamiento** *m* retinning (con estaño) || stanching (de la sangre).

restañar *vt* to retin (volver a estañar) || to resilver (espejo) || to stanch (sangre, herida).
◆ *vi* to crack (restallar).
◆ *vi/vpr* to stop bleeding (una herida).

restaño *m* stanching (de herida).

restar *vt* MAT to subtract, to take (away); *restar dos de cinco* to take two (away) from five, to subtract two from five || to deduct, to take away (deducir) || FIG to reduce, to lessen (autoridad, importancia, etc.) || to return (la pelota en el tenis).
◆ *vi* to subtract, to do subtraction || to remain, to be left; *es todo lo que resta de su capital* it is all that is left of his capital; *no nos resta más que marcharnos* it only remains for us to leave.

restauración *f* restoration.

restaurador, ra *adj* restorative, restoring.
◆ *m/f* restorer.

restaurante *m* restaurant || *coche restaurante* restaurant car (de tren).

restaurar *vt* to restore.

restinga *f* MAR bank, shoal.

restingar *m* MAR shoals *pl.*

restitución *f* restitution, return.

restituible *adj* restorable, returnable.

restituidor, ra *adj* restoring.
◆ *m/f* restorer.

restituir* *vt* to restitute || to return, to restore, to give back (devolver) || to restore (restaurar).

restitutorio, ria *adj* restitutory.

resto *m* rest, remainder; *el resto de su fortuna* the rest of his fortune || remainder, balance (saldo de una cuenta) || stake (cantidad que se juega) || all one has (todo lo que se tiene); *apostar el resto* to bet all one has || DEP return (devolución) | receiver (jugador) || MAT remainder || FIG *echar el resto* to put all one has into it, to give it all one has got (trabajar mucho), to stake everything one has got, to put one's shirt on it (naipes).
◆ *pl* ruins (de un monumento) || remains; *restos mortales* mortal remains || leftovers (de comida).

restón *m* DEP receiver (tenis).

restorán *m* restaurant.

restregadura *f*; **restregamiento** *m* rubbing (refregamiento) || rub mark (señal).

restregar* *vt* to rub hard (frotar) || to scrub (el suelo).

restregón *m* rub (acción de frotar) || scrub (del suelo) || rub mark (señal).

restricción *f* restriction; *restricciones a las importaciones* import restrictions.

restrictivo, va *adj* restrictive.

restricto, ta *adj* restricted (limitado).

restringente *adj* restrictive.

restringible *adj* restrainable.

restringir *vt* to restrict, to limit || MED to contract.
◆ *vpr* to reduce, to cut down on; *restringirse en los gastos* to reduce (one's) spending.

restriñidor, ra *m* MED astringent.

restriñimiento *m* MED astringency.

restriñir* *vt* to astringe, to constrict (astringir) || to constipate (estreñir).

resucitación *f* MED resuscitation.

resucitado, da *adj* resuscitated.
◆ *m/f* resuscitated person || FIG person who suddenly appears after a long absence.

resucitar *vi* MED to resuscitate || REL to rise from the dead.
◆ *vt* MED to resuscitate, to bring back to life || to raise (a los muertos) || to revive; *el vino me resucitó* the wine revived me || to revive, to bring back; *resucitar un recuerdo* to bring back a memory.

resudar *vi* to perspire *o* to sweat slightly || to exude (los árboles).

resuelto, ta *adj* resolute, determined || firm; *tono resuelto* firm tone.

resuello *m* breathing (acción de resollar) || — *perder el resuello, quedarse sin resuello* to get out of breath, to be out of breath || FIG *quitarle a uno el resuello* to take one's breath away.

resulta *f* result, effect, consequence (efecto) || decision, outcome (de una deliberación) || *de resultas* as a result; *se quedó ciego de resultas de una enfermedad* he went blind as a result of an illness.

resultado *m* result; *se colocarán los resultados en el tablón de anuncios* the results will be posted on the notice board || result, outcome; *el resultado del pleito* the result of a lawsuit; *la operación tuvo resultado satisfactorio* the operation had a satisfactory outcome || answer; *el resultado de una multiplicación* the answer to a multiplication || — *dar buen resultado* to work (una maniobra) || *tener por resultado* to have the effect of, to lead to.

resultando *m* JUR *los resultandos* the whereases.

resultante *adj/s f* resultant.

resultar *vi* to result; *de tantas medidas discriminatorias resultó un descontento general* general discontent resulted from so many discriminatory measures || to turn out, to come out, to work out; *el experimento no ha resultado como esperábamos* the experiment didn't turn out as we expected || to be; *aquí la vida resulta muy barata* the cost of living here is very low, living here is very cheap; *resultó herido en el accidente* he was injured in the accident; *resulta difícil comprenderlo* it is difficult to understand; *sus esfuerzos resultaron vanos* his efforts were in vain || to happen, to occur; *resulta que no tenemos dinero* it so happens that we don't have any money || to turn out to be (ser finalmente); *las negociaciones resultaron un fracaso* the negociations turned out to be a failure || to seem; *ella me resulta muy simpática* she seems very nice to me || to go; *este collar resulta muy bien con este vestido* this necklace goes very well with this dress || to be worth (ser conveniente); *no resulta comer a la carta* it is not worth eating à la carte || to come to (costar); *el traje completo resulta por unas tres mil pesetas* the complete suit comes to about three thousand pesetas || — *de esto resulta que...* from this we can deduce *o* infer that..., it follows from this that... || *esta broma me está resultando ya un poco pesada* this joke is beginning to annoy me || *la habitación nos resulta pequeña* we find the room small || *no resultó* it didn't work || *parecía que iba a quedarse soltera pero resulta que al final se casó* it looked like she was going to remain single, but in fact she finally got married || *resulta que cuando llegamos a la estación el tren había salido* it turned out that when we arrived at the station the train had already left || *resulta que no tengo dinero* the thing *o* the fact is that I haven't got any money || *resultar en* to result in || *resultar ser* to happen to be, to turn out to be; *resultó ser el hijo de un amigo mío* he turned out to be the son of a friend of mine || *si resulta ser verdadero* if it proves to be true || *viene a resultar lo mismo* it amounts to the same thing.

resumen *m* summary, résumé || abstract (sumario) || — *en resumen* in short || *hacer un resumen de* to make a summary of, to summarize.

resumidamente *adv* in summary form (de manera resumida) || briefly (en pocas palabras).

resumidero *m* AMER drain, sewer (alcantarilla).

resumido, da *adj* summarized || *en resumidas cuentas* in short, in a word.

resumir *vt* to summarize; *resumir un libro* to summarize a book || to sum up (recapitular) || to abbreviate (abreviar) || to abridge, to shorten (cortar).
◆ *vpr* to be summarized, to be summed up; *esto se puede resumir en cuatro palabras* this can be summed up in four words || to amount to, to boil down to (venir a ser).

resurgimiento *m* reappearance (de un curso de agua) || FIG resurgence, revival (reaparición) | recovery; *el resurgimiento de la economía nacional* the recovery of the national economy || *el resurgimiento de Italia* the Risorgimento of Italy.

resurgir *vi* to reappear (un río, etc.) || FIG to rise up again, to reappear (aparecer de nuevo).

resurrección *f* resurrection || — *Domingo de Resurrección* Easter Sunday || *Pascua de Resurrección* Easter.

retablo *m* retable, altarpiece.

retacar *vt* to hit (the ball) twice (en billar).

retacería *f* remmants *pl* (de tejidos).

retaco *m* short shotgun (arma) || FIG & FAM shorty (persona) || short cue (en billar).

retador, ra *adj* challenging.
◆ *m/f* challenger.

retaguardia *f* rearguard || *quedarse a retaguardia* to bring up the rear.

retahíla *f* string; *una retahíla de niños* a string of children; *una retahíla de triunfos, de desgracias* a string of victories, of misfortunes || stream, string (de insultos).

retal *m* remnant, left-over piece, scrap.

retama *f* BOT broom.

retamal; retamar *m* BOT broom field.

retar *vt* to challenge || to accuse (acusar) || FIG to reproach | to scold (reprender) || *retar en duelo* to challenge to a duel.

retardación *f* delay, retardation.

retardado, da *adj* retarded, delayed (retrasado) || *bomba de efecto retardado* delayed-action bomb, time bomb.

retardar *vt* to slow down; *retardar el avance de una enfermedad* to slow down the advance of a disease || to delay, to hold up (retrasar).

retardatriz *adj f* *fuerza retardatriz* retardative force.

retardo *m* delay || *bomba de retardo* delayed-action bomb, time bomb.

retasa; retasación *f* reappraisal.

retasar *vt* to reappraise.

retazo *m* remnant, piece, scrap (tela) || FIG fragment, portion, piece.

rete *adv* AMER FAM very (muy).

retejar *vt* to retile, to repair the tiling of.

retejer *vt* to weave closely.

retemblar* *vi* to shake, to tremble; *el piso retembló* the flat shook.

retemplar *vt* AMER to enliven (dar vigor).

retén *m* reserves *pl*, reserve corps (de bomberos, de soldados en el cuartel) || reinforcements *pl* (refuerzo) || TECN stop || *de retén* in reserve.

retención *f*; **retenimiento** *m* retention (acción de retener) || stoppage, deduction (parte deducida) || MED retention; *retención de orina* urine retention || *capacidad de retención* power of retention (memoria).

retenedor *adj* retaining.
◆ *m* *retenedor de puerta* safety chain (para que no se abra enteramente), door catch (para mantenerla abierta).

retener* *vt* to hold (impedir que se vaya); *retén este caballo para que no se escape* hold this horse so that he doesn't escape || to keep (guardar); *siempre retiene los libros prestados más de lo debido* he always keeps books he has borrowed longer than he should || to hold back, to keep back; *quería emigrar pero su familia le retuvo* he wanted to emigrate but his family kept him back || to hold; *la esponja retiene el agua* sponge holds water || to retain, to remember (en la memoria) || COM to deduct, to withhold; *retienen veinte dólares semanales de mi sueldo* they deduct twenty dollars a week from my salary || — *retener el aliento* to hold one's breath || *retener la atención de alguien* to hold s.o.'s attention || *retener la lengua* to hold one's tongue.
◆ *vpr* to hold o.s. back, to restrain o.s.

retenida *f* MAR guy (cable).

retenimiento *m* → **retención.**

retentiva *f* memory (memoria).

retentivo, va *adj* retentive.

reticencia *f* insinuation, innuendo; *un discurso lleno de reticencias* a speech full of insinuation *o* of innuendos.

reticente *adj* insinuating.

rético, ca *adj/s* Rhaetian.
◆ *m* Rhaeto-Romanic (lengua).

reticulado, da *adj* reticulated.

retícula *f* reticle (óptica) || ARTES tint.

reticular *adj* reticular.

retículo *m* reticle (óptica) || ZOOL reticulum || net, network (tejido en forma de red).

retina *f* ANAT retina.

retinal; retiniano, na *adj* ANAT retinal.

retinitis *f* MED retinitis (enfermedad).

retintín *m* ringing (en los oídos) || FIG & FAM sarcastic tone; *preguntar algo con retintín* to ask sth. in a sarcastic tone.

retiración *f* IMPR form for backing.

retirada *f* MIL withdrawal; *la retirada de las tropas de un país* the withdrawal of troops from a country | retreat; *tocar retirada* to sound the retreat; *batir en retirada* to beat a retreat || withdrawal; *retirada del carnet de conducir* withdrawal of one's driving licence || ebbing; *la retirada de las aguas* the ebbing of the tide || retirement; *la retirada de un actor* an actor's retirement || removal, clearing (away); *retirada de la nieve* snow clearing || recall (de un embajador) || retreat, refuge (lugar seguro) || — *cubrir la retirada* to cover the retreat (tropas) || MIL *emprender la retirada* to retreat.

retiradamente *adv* in seclusion; *vivir retiradamente* to live in seclusion || FIG secretly, in secret.

retirado, da *adj* remote (lejano); *barrio retirado* remote neighbourhood || secluded; *vida retirada* secluded life || retired (jubilado).
◆ *m* retired person.

retirar *vt* to remove; *retirar los platos de la mesa* to remove the plates from the table ‖ to move away (un mueble) ‖ to draw back (la mano, las sábanas, etc.) ‖ to withdraw; *retirar dinero del banco* to withdraw money from the bank; *retirar un proyecto de ley* to withdraw a bill from Parliament ‖ to take away; *retirar el carnet de conducir a alguien* to take away s.o.'s driving licence ‖ to take back, to retract; *retirar su palabra* to take back one's promise; *retirar lo dicho* to retract what one has said ‖ IMPR to print the back of a sheet ‖ to recall, to withdraw; *retirar a un embajador* to recall an ambassador ‖ to withdraw (una moneda) ‖ to pension off, to retire (a un empleado) ‖ DEP to withdraw.
◆ *vpr* to draw back, to move back, to withdraw; *retirarse de la ventana* to draw back from the window ‖ to retire, to go into retirement (jubilarse) ‖ MIL to withdraw, to retreat (tropas) ‖ DEP to withdraw, to retire ‖ to retire; *retirarse a su cuarto* to retire to one's room ‖ to ebb (la marea) ‖ to go into seclusion (apartarse del mundo) ‖ — *no se retire* hold on [*US* don't hang up] (al teléfono) ‖ *puede usted retirarse* you may leave ‖ *retirarse a dormir* to go to bed, to retire to one's bedroom.

retiro *m* retirement; *llegar a la edad del retiro* to reach retirement age ‖ (retirement) pension (pensión); *cobrar el retiro* to receive one's pension ‖ retreat (lugar tranquilo); *un retiro campestre* a country retreat ‖ withdrawal (retirada) ‖ REL retreat.

reto *m* challenge (desafío); *aceptar el reto* to accept the challenge ‖ threat (amenaza); *echar retos* to make threats ‖ *lanzar un reto* to challenge, to throw a challenge.

retobado, da *adj* AMER saucy, impudent (respondón) | stubborn, obstinate (obstinado) | sly, crafty (astuto).

retobar *vt* AMER to cover with leather (forrar con cuero) | to cover with sackcloth (con arpillera).

retobo *m* AMER refuse, junk (deshecho) | sackcloth (arpillera).

retocador, ra *m/f* FOT retoucher.

retocar *vt* to touch up, to retouch; *retocar una fotografía* to retouch a photograph ‖ to alter (la ropa).

retoñar; retoñecer* *vi* BOT to shoot, to sprout (una planta) ‖ FIG to reappear.

retoño *m* BOT sprout, shoot (de planta) ‖ FAM kid (niño).

retoque *m* retouching, touching up (de fotografía, maquillaje, etc.) ‖ alteration (de la ropa).

retor *m* twisted cotton fabric (tela).

retorcedor *m* twister.

retorcedura *f* ⟶ **retorcimiento.**

retorcer* *vt* to twist; *retorcer un alambre* to twist a wire ‖ to twine (cabos) ‖ to wring; *retorcer la ropa* to wring the clothes; *retorcer el pescuezo a uno* to wring s.o.'s neck ‖ to twirl (el bigote) ‖ FIG to twist; *retorcer un argumento* to twist an argument | to alter, to twist, to distort (un sentido).
◆ *vpr* to writhe; *retorcerse de dolor* to writhe in pain ‖ to double up; *retorcerse de risa* to double up with laughter.

retorcido, da *adj* twisted ‖ FIG twisted; *tenía la mente retorcida* he had a twisted mind | involved; *lenguaje retorcido* involved style | devious (taimado).
◆ *m* twisting.

retorcimiento *m*; **retorcedura** *f*; **retorsión** *f* twisting (del hilo) ‖ twining (de cabos) ‖ wringing (de la colada) ‖ FIG involved nature (del estilo) | twistedness (de la mente) | deviousness (de una persona).

retórica *f* rhetoric.
◆ *pl* FAM talk *sing*, verbiage *sing* (palabrería) ‖ FAM *no me vengas con retóricas* do me a favour (déjame tranquilo).

retórico, ca *adj* rhetorical.
◆ *m* rhetorician (especialista en retórica).

retornar *vt* to return, to give back (devolver).
◆ *vi/vpr* to return, to go back; *retornaron a su patria* they returned to their country ‖ *retornar en sí* to regain consciousness.

retornelo *m* MÚS ritornello.

retorno *m* return; *retorno al campo* return to the country ‖ exchange (cambio) ‖ INFORM *retorno de carro* carriage return ‖ *retorno de llama* backfire.

retorromano, na *adj/s* Rhaetian (rético).
◆ *m* Rhaeto-Romanic (lengua).

retorsión *f* ⟶ **retorcimiento.**

retorta *f* retort.

retortero *m* turn (vuelta) ‖ — FAM *andar al retortero* to be extremely busy, to have a million things to do | *traer a uno al retortero* to keep s.o. busy *o* on the move *o* on the go (baquetear), to be on one's mind (preocupar).

retortijón *m* twist ‖ stomach cramp (de tripas).

retostar* *vt* to toast again (volver a tostar) ‖ to toast too much ‖ to tan (broncear).

retozador, ra *adj* frolicsome, playful (juguetón).

retozar *vi* to frolic, to romp (juguetear).

retozo *m* frolic, romp (jugueteo) ‖ playfulness.
◆ *pl* frolicking *sing*.

retozón, ona *adj* frolicsome, playful.

retracción *f* retraction.

retractable *adj* retractable.

retractación *f* retraction, recantation, retractation ‖ withdrawal (en la Bolsa) ‖ *retractación pública* public retraction.

retractar *vt* to recant, to retract, to withdraw; *retractar una opinión* to recant an opinion.
◆ *vpr* to retract, to recant; *retractarse de una declaración* to retract a statement ‖ *me retracto* I take that back.

retráctil *adj* retractile ‖ retractable (tren de aterrizaje).

retractilidad *f* retractility.

retractivo, va *adj* retractive.

retracto *m* retraction, withdrawal; *retracto de autorización* withdrawal of authorization ‖ JUR *derecho de retracto* right of repurchase.

retractor *adj* retractive.
◆ *m* retractor.

retraer* *vt* to bring back, to bring again (volver a traer) ‖ to dissuade (disuadir) ‖ JUR to repurchase.
◆ *vpr* to withdraw (retirarse) ‖ to take refuge (*a* in), (refugiarse).

retraído, da *adj* solitary ‖ FIG reserved, shy (tímido) | unsociable (insociable).

restraimiento *m* retirement, withdrawal (acción) ‖ seclusion (vida aislada) ‖ FIG reserve, shyness (timidez).

retranca *f* breeching (del arnés) ‖ AMER brake (de coche) ‖ — *correa de retranca* breeching strap ‖ FIG *tener mucha retranca* to have a lot of experience.

retranquear *vt* to sight [with one eye].

retransmisión *f* passing on (de un mensaje) ‖ RAD (live) broadcast | repeat (segunda difusión).

retransmisor *m* TECN transmitter.

retransmitir *vt* to pass on (un mensaje) ‖ RAD to broadcast (live) | to repeat (dar una emisión por segunda vez) | to relay (servir de repetidor).

retrasado, da *adj* late; *un tren retrasado* a late train ‖ slow; *reloj retrasado* slow clock ‖ backward, underdeveloped; *países retrasados* backward countries ‖ late, behind; *estoy retrasado en el pago del alquiler* I'm behind with the rent ‖ retarded, backward; *un niño retrasado* a retarded child ‖ behind; *estar retrasado en gramática* to be behind in grammar; *tener trabajo retrasado* to be behind in one's work ‖ *voy cinco minutos retrasado* my watch is five minutes slow.
◆ *m/f* mentally retarded person.

retrasar *vt* to delay; *la lluvia nos ha retrasado* the rain has delayed us; *he retrasado mi viaje* I have delayed my trip ‖ to postpone, to put off (aplazar) ‖ to put back (un reloj) ‖ to retard, to slow down (progreso) ‖ to hold up; *la producción fue retrasada por la huelga* production was held up by the strike.
◆ *vi* to be slow; *mi reloj retrasa* my clock is slow ‖ to fall behind (en el trabajo, etc.).
◆ *vpr* to be late, to arrive late, to be delayed; *perdón por haberme retrasado* excuse me for being late; *el avión se retrasó* the aeroplane was late ‖ to fall behind (en el trabajo, los estudios, el pago) ‖ to lose (un reloj) ‖ to be put off (ser aplazado).

retraso *m* delay; *el retraso del tren* the delay of the train ‖ underdevelopment, backwardness (poco desarrollo) ‖ slowness (de un reloj) ‖ deficiency, retardation; *retraso mental* mental retardation ‖ — *el tren llegó con retraso* the train arrived late ‖ *llegué con diez minutos de retraso* I arrived ten minutes late ‖ *llevamos un retraso de un mes en el trabajo* we are a month behind in our work.

retratador, ra *m/f* portrait painter.

retratar *vt* to paint a portrait of, to portray (un pintor) ‖ to photograph, to take a photograph of (fotografiar) ‖ FIG to portray, to depict; *un escritor que retrata fielmente las costumbres de la época* a writer who faithfully portrays the customs of the era ‖ *hacerse retratar* to have one's portrait painted.
◆ *vpr* to have one's photograph taken (fotografiarse) ‖ to have one's picture painted (por un pintor) ‖ to be reflected; *la imagen de Narciso se retrataba en el agua* the image of Narcissus was reflected in the water ‖ FAM to cough up (pagar).

retratista *m/f* portrait painter (pintor) ‖ FOT photographer.

retrato *m* portrait; *hacer un retrato de cuerpo entero* to do a full-length portrait; *retrato de tamaño natural* life-size portrait | photograph | FIG portrayal, portrait, description (descripción) ‖ FIG *es el vivo retrato de su padre* he is the living image of his father.

retrechar *vi* to back (el caballo).

retrechería *f* FAM attractiveness, charm (encanto) | slyness, cunning (astucia) | crafty trick (subterfugio).

retrechero, ra *adj* FAM attractive, charming; *cara retrechera* attractive face | crafty, artful (astuto) | slippery (hábil para escurrir el bulto).

retrepado, da *adj* lounging; *cómodamente retrepado en su mecedora* comfortably lounging in his rocking chair.

retreparse *vpr* to lean back; *retreparse en una silla* to lean back in a chair | to lounge back (ponerse cómodo).

retreta *f* MIL retreat; *tocar retreta* to sound the retreat ‖ AMER open-air band concert | series (retahíla).

retrete *m* lavatory, toilet.

retribución *f* retribution, payment (remuneración) || fee (de un artista) || reward (recompensa).

retribuir* *vt* to pay (pagar); *un empleo bien retribuido* a well-paid job || to recompense, to reward (recompensar) || AMER to return, to repay (corresponder a un favor).

retributivo, va; retribuyente *adj* repaying, rewarding.

retro JUR *venta con pacto de retro* sale subject to right of vendor to repurchase.

retroacción *f* retroaction || retrocession (retroceso).

retroactividad *f* retroactivity.

retroactivo, va *adj* retroactive; *una ley con efecto retroactivo* a retroactive law.

retrocarga (de) *adv* breech-loading (arma).

retroceder *vi* to go back; *retroceder un paso* to go back a step || to go back, to move back, to turn back; *como la calle estaba cortada tuvimos que retroceder* as the street was blocked we had to go back || to go down, to drop (el nivel de agua) || FIG to go back, to look back; *para comprender los acontecimientos de hoy, hay que retroceder al siglo pasado* in order to understand the events of today, one must look back to last century | to back down (echarse atrás) || MIL to give ground, to fall back, to retreat || to recoil (arma de fuego) || AUT to change down [US to gear down] (velocidades) || — *hacer retroceder* to force back || FIG *no retroceder* to stand firm.

retrocesión *f* JUR retrocession || *hacer retrocesión de* to retrocede.

retroceso *m* retrocession, backward movement || recoil; *el retroceso de un arma de fuego* the recoil of a firearm || FIG recession; *un retroceso en la economía* a recession in the economy || MED aggravation (de una enfermedad) || TECN back stroke (de pistón) || screwback (en el billar) || MIL withdrawal, retreat || return (de una máquina de escribir).

retrocohete *m* retrorocket.

retroflexión *f* MED retroflexion.

retrogradación *f* ASTR retrogradation, regression (de un planeta).

retrogradar *vi* to retrograde.

retrógrado, da *adj* retrograde; *movimiento retrógrado* retrograde movement || FIG reactionary.

◆ *m/f* reactionary (reaccionario).

retrogresión *f* retrogression.

retropropulsión *f* AVIAC jet propulsion.

retroproyector *m* overhead projector.

retropulsión *f* MED retropulsion.

retrospección *f* retrospection.

retrospectivo, va *adj* retrospective; *una exposición retrospectiva* a retrospective exhibition || *mirada retrospectiva* look back.

retrotraer* *vt* to antedate, to predate || to take *o* to carry back; *recuerdo que nos retrotrae a nuestra infancia* memory that takes us back to our childhood.

retrovender *vt* to sell back [to the original vendor].

retrovendición; retroventa *f* JUR selling back to the vendor.

retroversión *f* MED retroversion.

retrovisor *m* AUT rearview mirror, driving mirror (interior) | wing mirror, rearview mirror (exterior).

retrucar *vi* to kiss (bolas de billar).

◆ *vt* to throw back at s.o. (un argumento).

retruco *m* kiss (en el billar).

retruécano *m* pun, play on words.

retruque *m* kiss (billar).

retumbante *adj* resonant, resounding || bombastic, pompous (estilo).

retumbar *vi* to resound, to echo; *la sala retumbaba con los aplausos* the hall resounded with applause || to thunder, to boom (el cañón, el trueno).

retumbo *m* resounding, echoing (acción) || echo (sonido) || thunder, boom (cañón, trueno).

reúma; reuma *m* MED rheumatism.

reumático, ca *adj/s* rheumatic; *anciano reumático* rheumatic old man; *dolor reumático* rheumatic pain.

reumatismo *m* MED rheumatism.

reumatoideo, a *adj* MED rheumatoid.

reunificación *f* reunification.

reunificar *vt* to reunify.

reunión *f* reunion (de gente que se había separado) || gathering; *reunión social* social gathering || assembly, gathering, crowd (de mucha gente) || meeting (conversación); *el director tuvo una reunión con sus empleados* the director had a meeting with his employees; *celebrar una reunión* to hold a meeting || meeting; *punto de reunión* meeting place || session [US meeting] (período de sesiones).

reunir *vt* to assemble; *reunir las tropas* to assemble the troops || to join together; *reunir dos pisos* to join two flats together || to put together; *podríamos reunir nuestros ahorros* we could put our savings together || to fulfil; *los que reúnen estos requisitos pueden venir* those who fulfil these requirements may come || to assemble, to collect, to gather (datos) || to make (una colección) || to collect (fondos) || to assemble, to get together; *reunir unos amigos* to assemble some friends || *reunir sus fuerzas* to summon one's strength (una persona), to join forces (dos personas, dos países, etc.).

◆ *vpr* to join together || to meet; *me reuniré con vosotros a las ocho* I'll meet you at 8 || to meet (una asamblea).

reumatalgia *f* MED rheumatalgia.

revacunación *f* MED revaccination.

revacunar *vt* to revaccinate.

reválida *f* final examination (examen de fin de estudios) || revalidation (revalidación).

revalidación *f* JUR revalidation.

revalidar *vt* JUR to revalidate || to take a final examination in (unos estudios).

revalorar *vt* to revalue.

revalorización *f* revaluation || revaluation, revalorization (de una moneda).

revalorizar *vt* to revalue || to revalue, to revalorize (una moneda).

revaluación *f* revaluation, revalorization.

revancha *f* revenge || *tomar* or *tomarse la revancha* to take revenge, to get one's own back.

— OBSERV *Revancha* is a Gallicism often used instead of *desquite*.

revanchismo *m* revanchism.

revanchista *adj* revengeful.

◆ *m/f* revenger, avenger.

revelación *f* revelation || FIG revelation, surprise (equipo, deportista, cantante, etc.) || *esa noticia fue una revelación para todos nosotros* that news was an eye-opener for *o* a revelation to all of us.

revelado *m* FOT developing.

revelador, ra *adj* revealing.

◆ *m/f* revealer.

◆ *m* FOT developer.

revelar *vt* to reveal, to disclose (secreto) || to reveal; *Dios reveló su deseo a los israelitas* God revealed His will to the Israelites || to show (enseñar) || FOT to develop.

◆ *vpr* to reveal o.s.

revellín *m* ravelin (fortificación) || mantelpiece (de chimenea).

revendedor, ra *adj* reselling.

◆ *m/f* reseller (persona que revende) || retailer (detallista) || *revendedor de entradas* ticket tout.

revender *vt* to resell || to retail (el detallista) || to tout (billetes).

revenimiento *m* cave-in (de una mina) || shrinkage (encogimiento).

reventa *f* resale || retail (venta al por menor) || *comprar una entrada en la reventa* to buy a ticket off a tout.

reventadero *m* rugged *o* rough ground || FIG & FAM grind (trabajo penoso).

reventador *m* TEATR catcaller.

reventar* *vi* to burst; *las burbujas reventaban en la superficie del agua* the bubbles burst on the surface of the water; *el neumático reventó* the tyre burst || to give way, to burst; *la presa ha reventado* the dam has given way || to break (romperse) || FIG & FAM to be dying to; *está que revienta por ir al cine* he's dying to go to the cinema | to burst; *reventar de orgullo* to be bursting with pride | to hate; *me revienta tener que pedirle perdón* I hate having to ask his pardon | to disgust, to make sick; *ese tío me revienta* that fellow disgusts me *o* makes me sick | to kick the bucket, to peg out (morirse) || — FIG & FAM *comer hasta reventar* to eat until one bursts | *reventar de cansancio* to be dead tired | *reventar de gordo* to be as fat as a pig | *reventar de rabia* to hit the roof (saltar), to be fighting mad (estar furioso) | *reventar de risa* to split one's sides laughing, to die laughing.

◆ *vt* to burst (un globo, un neumático, etc.) || to crush, to smash (aplastar) || to break (romper) || FIG & FAM to tire (s.o.) out, to kill (s.o.) (fatigar) | to ride hard (un caballo).

◆ *vpr* to burst || to burst, to burst open (absceso) || to crush (aplastarse), to burst, to blow (neumático) || FIG to tire o.s. out, to kill o.s. (de cansancio).

reventón *adj m* *clavel reventón* large carnation.

◆ *m* burst || blowout, flat tyre (de un neumático) || FIG & FAM jam, difficulty (apuro, dificultad) || AMER outcrop (de mineral) || — *darse un reventón de trabajar* to kill o.s. working || *darse* or *pegarse un reventón para hacer algo* to make an all-out effort to get sth. done.

reverberación *f* reflection, reverberation.

reverberante *adj* reflecting, reverberating.

reverberar *vi* to be reflected, to reverberate (reflejarse) || to glint (destellar).

reverbero *m* reflection, reverberation (reverberación) || reflector || reflecting lamp (farol) || AMER cooking stove || *horno de reverbero* reverberatory furnace.

reverdecer* *vi* to grow green again || FIG to revive, to acquire new vigour (remozarse).

reverdecimiento *m* growing green again, turning green again.

reverencia *f* reverence || bow (de hombre), curtsy (de mujer) || — *hacer una reverencia* to bow (hombre), to curtsy (mujer) || *Su Reverencia* Your Reverence.

reverenciable *adj* venerable.

reverencial *adj* reverential.

reverenciar *vt* to revere, to venerate.

reverendísimo, ma *adj* REL Most Reverend.

reverendo, da *adj/s* REL Reverend.

◆ *adj* FAM huge, enormous; *una reverenda tontería* an enormous blunder.

reverente *adj* reverent, respectful.

reversibilidad *f* reversibility.

reversible *adj* reversible.

reversión *f* reversion.

reversivo, va *adj* reversive.

reverso *m* reverse || FIG *el reverso de la medalla* the other side of the coin (el aspecto opuesto), the complete opposite (la antítesis).

revertir* *vi* to revert, to return (volver) || JUR to revert || to result, to turn out (resolverse en) || — *poner una conferencia a cobro revertido* to make a reverse-charge call || *revertir en beneficio de* to be to the advantage of || *revertir en perjuicio de* to be to the detriment of.

revés *m* wrong side; *el revés de un tejido* the wrong side of a cloth || back; *el revés de la mano* the back of the hand || backhander, blow with the back of the hand (golpe) || slap (bofetada) || backhand [stroke] (en tenis) || FIG misfortune; *los reveses de la vida* the misfortunes of life | setback, reverse (fracaso) || — *al revés* inside out (con lo de dentro fuera), back to front (con lo de delante atrás); *ponerse el jersey al revés* to put one's pullover on inside out *o* back to front; backwards (invertido el orden), the other way round (en sentido inverso), the wrong way (mal); *comprender, ir al revés* to understand, to go the wrong way; vice versa || *al revés de* contrary to; *al revés de lo que se dice* contrary to what is said || *del revés* upside down (con lo de arriba abajo), inside out (con lo de dentro fuera), back to front (con lo de delante detrás) || *es el mundo al revés* it's a topsy-turvy world || *reveses de fortuna* setbacks, reverses of fortune || *todo le sale al revés* everything he does turns out wrong || *volver algo del revés* to turn sth. round (cambiar de posición), to turn sth. inside out (sacar lo de dentro fuera).

revesado, da *adj* complex, intricate, complicated (un asunto) || unruly, mischievous (niños).

revestido; revestimiento *m* covering (del suelo, etc.) || TECN coating (con un metal) | lining (de un tubo) | sheathing (de un cable).

revestir* *vt* to cover, to surface; *revestir el suelo con linóleo* to cover the floor with lino || TECN to line (una tubería) | to sheathe (un cable) | to coat (con metal) || to put on (poner un vestido) || to wear (llevar un vestido) || FIG to take on, to acquire; *revestir nuevas dimensiones* to take on new dimensions || — FIG *el acto revistió gran solemnidad* it was a solemn occasion | *la ceremonia revistió gran brillantez* the ceremony went off splendidly, it was a splendid ceremony.
◆ *vpr* to put on (la ropa) || to put on one's vestments (el sacerdote) || — FIG *revestirse de energía* to summon up one's energy | *revestirse de paciencia* to be patient.

revigorizar *vt* to revigorate, to reinvigorate.

revirada *f* MAR tacking.

revisación; revisada *f* AMER ⟶ **revisión.**

revisar *vt* to revise, to go through; *revisar un texto* to revise a text || to check, to revise; *revisar una traducción* to check a translation || to overhaul [US to check]; *hacer revisar el coche* to have the car overhauled || to review (volver a ver) || to inspect (billetes) || to check, to audit (cuentas).

revisión *f* revision, review || checking, revision (de una traducción, etc.) || inspection (de billetes) || TECN overhaul, check || *revisión de cuentas* audit, auditing.

revisionismo *m* revisionism.

revisionista *adj/s* revisionist.

revisor, ra *adj* revisory.
◆ *m* reviser, revisor || inspector || ticket inspector, inspector [US conductor] (de billetes) || *revisor de cuentas* auditor.

revisoría *f* post of inspector || post of auditor (de cuentas).

revista *f* magazine, review, journal; *revista científica* scientific magazine || inspection || MIL review || revue (espectáculo) || review (artículo); *revista teatral* stage review || — *pasar revista a* to inspect (en el cuartel), to review (en un desfile), to review (problemas, etc.) || *revista comercial* trade paper || *revista del corazón* romance magazine || *revista de modas* fashion magazine.

revistar *vt* to review.

revistero *m* reviewer, critic (de un periódico) || magazine rack (para colocar revistas).

revivificación *f* revivification.

revivificar *vt* to revivify.

revivir *vi* to revive || to be renewed, to break out again; *revivió la discordia* discord broke out again || *hacer revivir* to bring back to life.
◆ *vt* to bring back to life (evocar).

revocabilidad *f* revocability.

revocable *adj* revocable.

revocación *f* revocation || recall (de un embajador).

revocador *m* plasterer (albañil).

revocadura *f* ARQ ⟶ **revoque.**

revocar *vt* to revoke; *revocar una orden, una ley, un decreto* to revoke an order, a law, a decree || to cancel (anular) || to dismiss, to remove from office (destituir a un funcionario) || to dissuade (disuadir) || ARQ to resurface (poner nueva fachada) | to plaster, to stucco (enlucir) | to whitewash (encalar) || to blow back; *el viento revoca el humo* the wind blows the smoke back.

revocatorio, ria *adj* revocatory.

revoco *m* ARQ ⟶ **revoque.**

revolcadero *m* wallow (de animales).

revolcar* *vt* to knock down, to knock over (tirar al suelo) || FIG to defeat, to floor (derrotar) || FAM to fail (en un examen).
◆ *vpr* to roll; *revolcarse en el suelo* to roll on the ground || to wallow (animales); *revolcarse en el fango* to wallow in the mud || FAM *revolcarse de dolor, de risa* to double up with pain, with laughter.

revolcón *m* fall; *sufrir un revolcón sin consecuencias* to have a minor fall || TAUR tumble || FIG & FAM *dar un revolcón a uno* to wipe the floor with s.o. (en una discusión).

revolotear *vi* to fly about, to flutter about.

revoloteo *m* fluttering (de pájaros) || FIG stir, commotion (revuelo).

revoltijo; revoltillo *m* mess, jumble, clutter; *un revoltijo de papeles* a jumble of papers || heap, pile (montón) || *revoltillo de huevos* scrambled eggs.

revoltoso, sa *adj* mischievous (travieso); *niño revoltoso* mischievous child || unruly (difícil de gobernar) || restless (turbulento) || seditious, rebelious (sedicioso).
◆ *m/f* mischievous child, scamp || rebel (rebelde) || troublemaker (alborotador).

revolución *f* revolution; *la revolución industrial* the Industrial Revolution; *la revolución francesa* the French Revolution || ASTR & TECN revolution; *40 revoluciones por minuto* 40 revolutions per minute.

revolucionar *vt* to revolutionize.

revolucionario, ria *adj/s* revolutionary.

revolver* *vt* to mix (mezclar) || to toss; *revolver la ensalada* to toss the salad || to stir (un líquido) || to rummage through; *revolver sus papeles* to rummage through one's papers || to rummage in (un cajón, etc.) || to turn upside down, to disarrange; *revolver la casa* to turn the house upside down || to entangle, to confuse (confundir, mezclar) || to stir up; *revolver los ánimos* to stir up the people || to irritate, to annoy (irritar) || to upset, to turn; *esto me revuelve el estómago* this upsets my stomach || to roll (los ojos) || to turn (la cabeza) || — *revolver algo en la cabeza* to turn sth. over in one's mind || *revolver la sangre* to make one's blood boil.
◆ *vpr* to toss and turn; *revolverse en la cama* to toss and turn in bed || to turn round (dar la vuelta) || to turn; *el toro se revolvió contra el torero* the bull turned on the bullfighter || to roll; *revolverse en la hierba* to roll in the grass || to turn stormy (el tiempo) || to get rough (el mar) || to turn cloudy (un líquido) || *revolverse contra alguien* to turn against s.o.

revólver *m* revolver.

revoque *m*; **revocadura** *f*; **revoco** *m* ARQ resurfacing (limpieza, reparación, etc.) | plastering (enlucido) | whitewashing (encalado) | plaster, stucco (material).

revuelco *m* fall (caída) || TAUR tumble || roll (en la hierba) || wallow (en el fango).

revuelo *m* second flight || fluttering (revoloteo) || FIG stir, commotion; *la noticia produjo gran revuelo en los medios taurinos* the news caused a great stir in bullfighting circles || AMER blow that a fighting cock gives with its spur || FIG *de revuelo* in passing.

revuelta *f* revolt, rebellion (motín) || disturbance (alteración del orden) || quarrel (riña) || turn, bend (vuelta) || corner (esquina) || *dar vueltas y revueltas* to go round and round.

revueltamente *adv* in a disorderly way, higgledy-piggledy, pell-mell.

revuelto, ta *adj* jumbled, in a mess, in disorder, in disarray (papeles, etc.) || tangled (enredado) || cloudy (líquidos) || rough, stormy (mar) || variable, unsettled, changeable (tiempo) || excited, agitated, worked up (*fam*), annoyed; *la gente está revuelta a causa de la subida de precios* people are annoyed at the rise in prices || turbulent, stormy; *vivimos en tiempos revueltos* we are living in turbulent times || mischievous (travieso) || restless (turbulento) || docile, easy to handle (caballo) || — *huevos revueltos* scrambled eggs || *pelo revuelto* dishevelled hair.

revulsión *f* MED revulsion.

revulsivo, va *adj/sm* MED revulsive.

rey *m* king (monarca) || king (en juegos) || FIG king; *el león es el rey de la selva* the lion is the king of the jungle || — FIG *a cuerpo de rey* like a king; *tratar a uno a cuerpo de rey* to treat s.o. like a king; *vivir a cuerpo de rey* to live like a king | *a rey muerto, rey puesto* off with the old, on with the new | *cada uno es rey en su casa* a man's home is his castle | *del tiempo del rey que rabió* as old as the hills || *hablando del rey de Roma, por la puerta asoma* talk of the devil (and he will appear) || FIG *ni quito ni pongo rey* it's none of my business, it's nothing to do with me | *no temer ni rey ni roque* to fear nothing and nobody || *rey de armas* king of arms || *rey de codornices* corncrake (ave) || *rey de gallos* mock king in a carnival || *Rey de reyes* King of Kings || *Rey Sol* Sun King.
◆ *pl* king and queen (rey y reina) || — *día de Reyes* Epiphany, Twelfth-Day || *libro de los Reyes* Book of Kings || *los Reyes Católicos* the Catholic Monarchs [Ferdinand and Isabella] || *los Reyes Magos* the three Magi, the three Wise Men of the East, the three Kings.

reyerta *f* quarrel, wrangle (disputa).

reyezuelo *m* kinglet (rey, ave).

rezado, da *adj* said, spoken ‖ *misa rezada* low Mass.

rezagado, da *m/f* MIL straggler ‖ latecomer (que llega tarde) ‖ — *ir rezagado* to lag behind ‖ *quedar rezagado* to be left behind.

rezagar *vt* to leave behind (dejar atrás) ‖ to delay, to postpone, to put off (retrasar).
◆ *vpr* to fall behind (retrasarse) ‖ to lag behind (quedarse atrás).

rezar *vi* to pray; *rezar a Dios* to pray to God ‖ to say, to go; *según reza el refrán* as the saying goes ‖ to say (un escrito) ‖ to apply; *esta ley no reza para los ex combatientes* this law does not apply to ex-servicemen ‖ *esto no reza conmigo* that does not concern me.
◆ *vt* to say; *rezar una oración* to say a prayer ‖ to say (misa, el rosario) ‖ to say, to read; *el escrito reza lo siguiente* the document says the following *o* reads as follows ‖ FIG & FAM *ser más fácil que rezar un credo* to be as easy as pie.

rezno *m* bot, bott (larva) ‖ BOT castor-oil plant.

rezo *m* praying (acción de rezar) ‖ prayer (oración) ‖ office (oficio litúrgico).

rezón *m* MAR grapnel, grappling iron.

rezongador, ra; rezongón, ona; rezonguero, ra; rezonglón, ona *adj* FAM grumbling, grouchy, grumpy.
◆ *m/f* grumbler, moaner, grouch.

rezongar *vi* FIG & FAM to grumble, to moan, to complain.

rezongo; rezongueo *m* grumbling, moaning.

rezongón, ona; rezonguero, ra; rezonglón, ona *adj/s* —→ **rezongador.**

rezumar *vt* to ooze, to exude; *la pared rezuma humedad* the wall oozes moisture ‖ FIG to ooze; *canción que rezuma tristeza* song which oozes sadness.
◆ *vi* to seep, to ooze (el contenido); *el aceite rezuma a través de la loza* the oil seeps through the pot ‖ to leak (una vasija) ‖ to bead; *el sudor le rezumaba por la frente* the seat beaded on his forehead ‖ *le rezuma el orgullo* he oozes pride.
◆ *vpr* to leak; *el botijo se rezuma* the pitcher leaks ‖ to ooze, to seep (el contenido).

rezumo *m* sweating.

Rhodesia; Rodesia *npr f* GEOGR Rhodesia.

ría *f* estuary, river mouth (desembocadura) ‖ GEOGR ria (valle invadido por el mar).

riachuelo; riacho *m* brook, stream.

Riad *n pr* GEOGR Riyadh.

riada *f* flood (crecida) ‖ flood, inundation (inundación) ‖ FIG flood; *riada de visitantes* flood of visitors.

ribazo *m* embankment, slope.

ribera *f* bank (de un río) ‖ shore, seashore (del mar).

riberano, na *adj/s* AMER —→ **ribereño.**

ribereño, ña *adj* riparian (p us), on the bank, along the bank (en general) ‖ riverside (al lado de un río) ‖ waterfront (que da al mar) ‖ *los países ribereños del Danubio* the countries which lie along the Danube.
◆ *m/f* Riverside dweller (al lado de un río) ‖ waterfront dweller (junto al mar).

ribete *m* border, edging, trimming (orla) ‖ — FIG *tener ribetes cómicos* to have a comical side | *tener ribetes de poeta* to be sth. of a poet.

ribeteado, da *adj* bordered, edged ‖ *tener los ojos ribeteados de rojo* to have red-ringed eyes.

ribetear *vt* to border, to edge, to trim (una tela) ‖ FIG to border.

ribonucleico, ca *adj* ribonucleic (ácido).

ricacho, cha; ricachón, ona *m/f* FAM money-bags.

ricadueña; ricahembra *f* wife or daughter of a nobleman, noblewoman.

ricamente *adv* richly (con opulencia) ‖ marvellously, wonderfully (muy bien).

Ricardo *npr m* Richard.

ricino *m* BOT castor-oil plant ‖ *aceite de ricino* castor oil.

rico, ca *adj* rich, wealthy; *un rico propietario* a rich property owner ‖ rich; *persona rica de virtudes* person rich in virtues ‖ fertile, rich; *tierra rica* fertile land ‖ full; *viaje rico en aventuras* a trip full of adventures ‖ rich, magnificent; *adornado con ricos bordados* adorned with rich embroidery ‖ delicious; *pastel muy rico* delicious cake ‖ adorable, lovely; *¡qué niño más rico!* what an adorable child! ‖ — FAM *estar muy rica* to be a nice bit of stuff, to be a gorgeous piece (una chica) ‖ *hacerse rico* to get rich ‖ FAM *oye rico, ¿qué te has creído?* hey!, what's the big idea? ‖ *¡rico!* love, dear | *¡un momento, rico!* just a minute, mate!
◆ *m/f* rich person ‖ *nuevo rico* nouveau riche.
◆ *pl* the rich.

rictus *m* grin ‖ *rictus de dolor* wince (of pain).

ricura *f* deliciousness ‖ *¡qué ricura de niño!* what a darling child!, what an adorable child!

ridiculez *f* ridiculousness, absurdity (cualidad de absurdo) ‖ ridiculous thing (cosa ridícula o insignificante) ‖ nothing, triviality; *se han peleado por una ridiculez* they fought over nothing ‖ *es una ridiculez hacer eso* it's ridiculous to do that.

ridiculizar *vt* to ridicule, to deride (burlarse) ‖ to make a fool of, to ridicule (dejar en ridículo).

ridículo *m* reticule (bolso de señora).

ridículo, la *adj* ridiculous, ludicrous, absurd; *decir cosas ridículas* to say ridiculous things ‖ ridiculously small, minute; *una ganancia ridícula* a ridiculously small profit.
◆ *m* ridiculous ‖ — *caer en el ridículo* to become ridiculous ‖ *hacer el ridículo, quedar en ridículo* to make a fool of o.s. ‖ *poner en ridículo* to make a fool of, to ridicule.

riego *m* irrigation (irrigación) ‖ watering (en el jardín) ‖ — *boca de riego* hydrant | *canal de riego* irrigation canal ‖ *riego asfáltico* cutback ‖ *riego por aspersión* sprinkling ‖ ANAT *riego sanguíneo* circulation of the blood.

riel *m* rail, track; *los rieles del tranvía* the tram rails; *riel de cortina* curtain rail ‖ ingot, bar (de metal).

rielar *vi* POÉT to glitter; *la Luna en el mar riela* the moon glitters on the sea ‖ to twinkle (las estrellas).

rielera *f* ingot mould [US ingot mold].

rienda *f* rein (correa) ‖ — *a rienda suelta* with a free rein (sin freno), at full speed (muy rápidamente) ‖ *dar rienda suelta a* to give free rein to ‖ *tirar de la rienda a* to tighten the reins on.
◆ *pl* FIG reins, control *sing*; *las riendas del gobierno* the reins of government ‖ — FIG *aflojar las riendas* to slacken the rein, to ease up | *coger* or *tomar las riendas de* to take in hand | *empuñar las riendas* to take the reins, to take control | *llevar las riendas* to hold the reins, to be in control.

riente *adj* laughing ‖ FIG bright, cheerful; *riente jardín* cheerful garden.

riesgo *m* risk, danger; *correr un riesgo* to run a risk ‖ — *a* or *con riesgo de* at the risk of ‖ *correr (el) riesgo de* to run the risk of ‖ *por su cuenta y riesgo* at one's own risk ‖ *seguro a todo riesgo* fully comprehensive insurance.

riesgoso, sa *adj* AMER risky, dangerous.

Rif *npr m* GEOGR Rif.

rifa *f* raffle (tómbola) ‖ quarrel (riña).

rifado, da *adj* raffled ‖ FIG *este chico está rifado* this young man is highly sought-after.

rifar *vt* to raffle, to raffle off ‖ to draw lots for (echar a suertes).
◆ *vpr* MAR to split (una vela) ‖ FIG & FAM *todo el mundo se rifa su compañía* everyone vies for her company.

rifirrafe *m* FAM row, scuffle (riña).

rifle *m* rifle (arma).

riflero *m* AMER rifleman.

Riga *n pr* GEOGR Riga.

rigidez *f* rigidity, stiffness ‖ FIG strictness (severidad) | inflexibility ‖ *rigidez cadavérica* rigor mortis.

rígido, da *adj* rigid, stiff; *una barra de acero rígida* a rigid steel bar ‖ stiff; *pierna rígida* stiff leg ‖ FIG strict, rigorous; *disciplina rígida* strict discipline; *moral rígida* strict morals | inflexible | expressionless (inexpresivo) ‖ *quedarse rígido* to get stiff (de frío), to go rigid (un cadáver).

rigodón *m* rigadoon.

rigor *m* severity, strictness, rigour [US rigor] (severidad); *el rigor de un juez* the severity of a judge ‖ exactness, precision, rigorousness (exactitud) ‖ rigour, severity, harshness; *el rigor del clima polar* the harshness of the polar climate ‖ — *de rigor* de rigueur ‖ *después del discurso de rigor* after the inevitable speech ‖ *en el rigor del verano* in the height of (the) summer ‖ *en rigor* strictly speaking ‖ FIG *ser el rigor de las desdichas* to be born under an unlucky star.

rigorismo *m* rigorism, strictness ‖ austerity; *el rigorismo de los puritanos* the austerity of the Puritans.

rigurosamente *adv* severely (con severidad) ‖ rigorously, accurately (con exactitud) ‖ meticulously (minuciosamente) ‖ strictly, absolutely; *rigurosamente exacto* absolutely exact.

riguroso, sa *adj* rigorous, accurate, exact (exacto) ‖ harsh (actitud) ‖ severe, tough (severo) ‖ strict (estricto) ‖ harsh, severe (tiempo) ‖ meticulous (minucioso).

rijoso, sa *adj* quarrelsome (camorrista) ‖ sensitive, touchy (susceptible) ‖ sensual, lustful (sensual) ‖ in rut; *caballo rijoso* horse in rut.

rilar *vi* to tremble, to shake, to shudder (de miedo) ‖ to shiver, to shudder (de frío).

rima *f* rhyme.
◆ *pl* poems, poetry *sing*.

rimador, ra *adj* rhyming.
◆ *m/f* rhymer, rhymester.

rimar *vi/tr* to rhyme.

rimbombancia *f* grandiloquence, pomposity, bombast (del estilo).

rimbombante *adj* resounding, ringing ‖ grandiloquent, pompous, bombastic, highflown; *estilo rimbombante* grandiloquent style ‖ showy, ostentatious; *vestido rimbombante* showy dress.

rímel *m* mascara (para los ojos).

rimero *m* heap, pile (montón).

Rimini *n pr* GEOGR Rimini.

rin *m* AMER telephone token (ficha telefónica) | wheel rim (llanta).

Rin *npr m* Rhine; *valle del Rin* Rhine valley.

rincón *m* corner; *en un rincón de la habitación* in a corner of the room ‖ FIG corner, nook, remote place (lugar apartado) ‖ *poner* or *castigar en el rincón* to put in the corner (a un niño castigado).
— OBSERV *Rincón* applies exclusively to reentrant angles, as opposed to *esquina* which indicates a salient angle.

rinconada *f* corner.

rinconera *f* corner table (mueble) ‖ ARQ wall between a corner and the nearest recess.

ring *m* DEP ring (de boxeo y lucha).

ringlera *f* row, line.

ringorrango *m* curlicue, flourish (en la escritura) || frill, adornment (adorno).

rinitis *f* MED rhinitis.

rinoceronte *m* ZOOL rhinoceros.

rinofaringe *f* ANAT rhinopharynx.

rinofaringitis *f* MED rhinopharyngitis.

rinología *f* MED rhinology.

rinólogo *m* MED rhinologist.

rinoplastia *f* MED rhinoplasty.

riña *f* brawl, fight (pelea); *una riña sangrienta* a bloody brawl || quarrel, argument (discusión); *riña de niños* childish quarrel || *riña de gallos* cockfight.

riñón *m* ANAT kidney || CULIN kidney; *riñones al jerez* kidney in sherry sauce || FIG heart, centre; *vivo en el mismo riñón de Madrid* I live right in the heart of Madrid; *el riñón del asunto* the heart of the matter || MIN nodule, kidney ore || ARQ spandrel || — FIG *costar un riñón* to cost a fortune *o* a mint | *cubrirse el riñón* to feather one's nest | *pegarse al riñón* to be very nutritious (un alimento) | *tener el riñón bien cubierto* to be well off *o* well heeled.
◆ *pl* loins (lomos) || FIG *tener riñones* to have guts, to have nerve.

riñonada *f* ANAT cortical tissue of the kidney (tejido) || loin (de res); *chuleta de riñonada* loin chop || CULIN kidney stew (guiso) || FIG & FAM *costar una riñonada* to cost the earth.

río *m* river; *el río Misisipí* the River Mississippi, the Mississippi river || FIG river, stream (de lágrimas, sangre) || — FIG *a río revuelto ganancia de pescadores* it's an ill wind that blows nobody good | *cuando el río suena agua lleva* there's no smoke without fire | *pescar en* or *a río revuelto* to fish in troubled waters || *río abajo* downstream || *río arriba* upstream || *río de lava* stream of lava || FIG *todavía ha de correr mucha agua por el río* a lot of water has still to flow under the bridge.

riobambeño, ña *adj* [of *o* from] Riobamba (Ecuador).
◆ *m/f* native *o* inhabitant of Riobamba.

Río de Janeiro *n pr* GEOGR Rio de Janeiro.

Río de la Plata *npr m* GEOGR River Plate.

riojano, na *adj* [of *o* from] La Rioja (argentina y españa).
◆ *m/f* native *o* inhabitant of La Rioja.

rioplatense *adj* of *o* from the River Plate region.
◆ *m/f* native *o* inhabitant of the River Plate region.

riostra *f* ARQ brace, strut.

ripia *f* lath, batten (tabla delgada) || rough surface (de un madero aserrado).

ripio *m* rubble filling, broken stone (relleno de albañilería) || residue (residuo) || refuse (escombros) || FIG padding (palabrería inútil); *meter ripio* to do a lot of padding | word used to fill in a verse (palabra superflua) || FIG *no perder ripio* not to miss a trick.

ripioso, sa *adj* filled with unnecessary words (versos).

riqueza *f* riches *pl*, wealth.
◆ *pl* riches; *amontonar riquezas* to pile up riches.

riquísimo, ma *adj* extremely rich || FIG absolutely delicious (comida).

risa *f* laugh || laughter; *la risa del público* the laughter of the audience || laughingstock (hazmerreír); *ser la risa de todo el mundo* to be the laughingstock of everyone || — *caerse* or *desternillarse* or *mondarse* or *morirse* or *reventar* or *troncharse de risa* to split one's sides laughing, to die laughing || *contener la risa* to keep a straight face || *dar risa* to make one laugh || *es (cosa) de risa* it's laughable, it's enough to make one laugh || *llorar de risa* to cry laughing || *me entró* or *me dio la risa* I began to laugh, I couldn't help laughing || *¡qué risa!* how very funny!, what a laugh! (*fam*) || *risa burlona* or *socarrona* mocking laugh, horselaugh || *risa de conejo* forced laugh *o* smile || *risa nerviosa* or *loca* hysterical laughter || *ser motivo de risa* to be sth. to laugh about || *soltar la risa* to burst out laughing || *tener un ataque de risa* to have a fit of laughter || *tomar una cosa a risa* to take sth. as a joke, to laugh sth. off.

risco *m* crag, cliff.

risible *adj* laughable.

risilla; risita *f* giggle, titter || false laugh (risa falsa).

risión *f* derision, mockery (mofa) || laughingstock (hazmerreír) || *objeto de risión* laughingstock.

risorio *m* ANAT risorius (músculo).

risotada *f* guffaw, boisterous laugh || — *dar risotadas* to guffaw || *soltar una risotada* to burst out laughing.

rispidez *f* harshness.

ristra *f* string; *una ristra de ajos, de cebollas* a string of garlic, of onions || FIG & FAM string, pack; *una ristra de mentiras* a string of lies || *en ristra* in single file.

ristre *m* *en ristre* at the ready (lanza).

ristrel *m* wooden moulding.

risueño, ña *adj* smiling; *cara risueña* smiling face || FIG happy, gay (contento) | pleasant, cheerful; *pradera risueña* pleasant meadow | bright (prometedor); *un porvenir risueño* a bright future.

Rita *npr f* Rita || — FIG & FAM *¡cuéntaselo a Rita!* tell it to the marines! | *¡que lo haga Rita!* I'm not going to do it, let s.o. else do it!

ritmar *vt* to put rhythm into (dar ritmo).

rítmico, ca *adj* rhythmic, rhythmical.

ritmo *m* rhythm || FIG pace, rate; *el ritmo de trabajo* the rate of work || *dar ritmo* to put rhythm (*a* into).

rito *m* rite || FIG ritual (costumbre); *los ritos de la vida familiar* the rituals of family life.

ritornelo *m* MÚS ritornello.

ritual *adj* ritual || *libro ritual* ritual.
◆ *m* ritual || FIG *ser de ritual* to be a ritual *o* a custom, to be customary.

ritualidad *f* ritualism, rituality.

ritualista *adj* ritualistic.
◆ *m/f* ritualist.

rival *adj/s* rival.

rivalidad *f* rivalry.

rivalizar *vi* to rival; *rivalizar en simpatía, en belleza* to rival in kindness, in beauty.

rivera *f* brook (arroyo).

rizado, da *adj* curly; *tener el pelo rizado* to have curly hair || curled (artificialmente) || ripply (la superficie del agua) || choppy, wavy; *mar rizada* choppy sea.
◆ *m* curling (acción).

rizador *m* curling iron.

rizar *vt* to curl (el pelo) || to ripple (la superficie del agua) || to make choppy (el mar) || to crease, to crumple (tela, papel).
◆ *vpr* to curl || to go curly, to curl; *se me rizó el pelo con la lluvia* my hair has gone curly with the rain || to ripple (la superficie del agua) || to become *o* to get choppy (el mar).

rizo, za *adj* curly; *pelo rizo* curly hair.
◆ *m* curl, lock (de cabellos) || ripple (del agua) || terry velvet (terciopelo) || AVIAC loop; *rizar el rizo* to loop the loop || MAR reef point || — *nudo de rizo* reef knot || MAR *tomar rizos* to take in sail, to reef.

rizófago, ga *adj* rhizophagous (animal).

rizoma *m* BOT rhizome.

rizópodo *m* ZOOL rhizopod.
◆ *pl* rhizopoda.
◆ *adj* rhizopodous.

rizoso, sa *adj* (naturally) curly (el pelo).

RNE *abrev de Radio Nacional de España* Spanish broadcasting company.

ro *interj* rock-a-by, hushaby.

roa *f* MAR stem.

roano, na *adj/sm* roan.

robador, ra *adj* robbing, thieving.
◆ *m/f* robber, thief.

róbalo; robalo *m* ZOOL bass (pez).

robar *vt* to steal, to rob (algo); *robar mil pesetas* to steal a thousand pesetas; *le han robado el reloj* s.o. robbed him of his watch, s.o. stole his watch from him || to rob (a una persona); *me han robado* I've been robbed || to break into, to burgle (una casa) || to kidnap, to abduct (raptar) || to eat away (el mar) || to carry away (los ríos) || to draw (juego de cartas) || FIG to rob; *en esta tienda te roban* in this shop they rob you | to steal, to capture (la atención) | to steal (away); *robar el corazón* to steal one's heart (away) | to take (la vida) || *robar con fractura* or *efracción* to burgle, to commit burglary.

robín *m* rust (orín).

robinia *f* BOT robinia, acacia.

robladura *f* clinching (de un clavo).

roblar *vt* to clinch (un clavo).

roble *n* oak, oak tree (árbol) || FIG & FAM robust *o* strong person (persona) || — *de roble* oak || FIG *más fuerte que un roble* as strong as an ox (fuerte), as solid as a rock (resistente).

robledal *m*; **robleda** *f*; **robledo** *m* oak grove.

roblón *m* rivet; *roblón de cabeza plana, fresada, redonda* flathead, countersunk, buttonhead rivet.

roblonar *vt* to rivet.

robo *m* robbery, theft; *cometer un robo* to commit a robbery; *robo a mano armada* armed robbery || stolen article (cosa robada) || draw (en los juegos de cartas) || FIG robbery (estafa) || — *robo con agravante* aggravated theft || *robo con fractura* or *efracción* burglary.

roborar *vt* to fortify, to strengthen (reforzar) || FIG to corroborate (corroborar).

robot *m* robot || FIG puppet (pelele) || *robot de cocina* food processor.
— OBSERV The plural of *robot* in Spanish is *robots*, as in English.

robótica *f* robotics.

robustecer* *vt* to strengthen, to make strong *o* robust.
◆ *vpr* to become strong, to gain strength.

robustecimiento *m* strenghtening, fortifying.

robustez *f* robustness, strength (de personas) || strength; *la robustez de un puente* the strength of a bridge || sturdiness, solidness; *la robustez de un coche* the sturdiness of a car.

robusto, ta *adj* robust, strong (persona) || strong, sturdy, solid (una construcción, etc.).

roca *f* rock; *roca sedimentaria* sedimentary rock; *escalar una roca* to climb a rock || FIG stone; *corazón de roca* heart of stone || — *cristal de roca* rock crystal || FIG *firme como una roca* as solid as a rock || *roca viva* bare rock.

rocadero *m* distaff head (de la rueca).

rocalla *f* stone chippings *pl* (al tallar la piedra) || rubble (desprendida de la roca) || large glass bead (abalorio grueso).

rocalloso, sa; rocoso, sa *adj* rocky, rubbly (lleno de trozos de roca) || stony (lleno de piedras).

roce *m* rubbing, chafing; *roce de los zapatos, del cuello* rubbing of one's shoes, of one's collar || touch (ligero); *el roce de su mano le dio escalofríos* the touch of her hand made him shiver || rub, mark, scuff (en la pared, un mueble, etc.) || chafe mark (en la piel) || FIG contact (trato entre personas) | friction; *roces entre dos naciones vecinas* friction between two neighbouring countries || TECN friction.

rociada *f* sprinkling, spraying (acción y efecto de rociar) || dew (rocío) || FIG shower, hail; *una rociada de golpes, de insultos* a shower of blows, of insults.

rociadera *f* watering can (regadera).

rociador *m* sprayer, clothes sprinkler.

rociadura *f* sprinkling, spraying.

rociar *vt* to sprinkle, to spray; *rociar con agua* to sprinkle with water || to water, to sprinkle; *rociar las flores* to water the flowers || FIG to wash down; *una comida rociada con una botella de clarete* a meal washed down with a bottle of claret | to scatter, to strew (arrojar cosas dispersas) || to moisten (humedecer).

◆ *vi* *ha rociado durante la noche* dew has formed *o* has fallen during the night.

rocín *m* hack, nag (caballo) || FIG stupid fellow, clodhopper.

rocinante *m* worn-out nag.

rocino *m* hack, nag (caballo).

rocío *m* dew || drizzle (llovizna).

rococó *m* rococo (estilo).

Rocosas (Montañas) *npr fpl* GEOGR Rocky Mountains.

rocoso, sa *adj* ⟶ **rocalloso.**

roda *f* MAR stem.

rodaballo *m* ZOOL turbot (pez) || FIG & FAM sly dog, crafty devil (hombre taimado).

rodado, da *adj* dappled (caballo) || smooth (piedra) || FIG experienced (experimentado) || run-in (automóvil) || — *canto rodado* boulder (grande), pebble (pequeño) || *tránsito rodado, circulación rodada* vehicular *o* road traffic || FIG & FAM *venir rodado* to come *o* to arrive just at the right time *o* moment.

◆ *m* AMER vehicle.

◆ *f* imprint, tyre mark.

rodadura *f* rolling.

rodaja *f* disc (de metal u otra materia) || slice (de limón, salchichón) || rowel (estrellita de la espuela) || small wheel (ruedecilla) || roll, fold (de grasa) || TECN cutting *o* perforating wheel || *en rodajas* sliced, in slices.

rodaje *m* wheels *pl* (conjunto de ruedas) || filming, shooting (de una película) || running in (de un motor, de un coche) || — *en rodaje* running in (coche) || *secretaria de rodaje* continuity girl, script girl (cine).

rodamiento *m* bearing; *rodamiento de bolas, de rodillos* ball, roller bearing.

Ródano *npr m* GEOGR Rhone.

rodante *adj* rolling.

rodapelo *m* brushing against the nap.

rodapié *m* skirting board [US baseboard] (zócalo de una pared) || dust ruffle (de cama, de mesa).

rodaplancha *f* ward (de la llave).

rodar* *vi* to roll; *la pelota rueda* the ball rolls || to turn (una rueda) || to run; *coche que rueda bien* car that runs well || to travel, to go; *rodar a cien kilómetros por hora* to go at a hundred kilometres per hour || to roll (accidentalmente); *el coche rodó cuesta abajo* the car rolled downhill || to fall; *rodar escaleras abajo* to fall down the stairs || CINEM to shoot, to film || FIG to roam; *rodar por las calles, por el mundo* to roam the streets, the world | to move about (ir de acá para allá) | to go around; *mil proyectos rodaban en su cabeza* a thousand ideas were going around in his head || AMER to stumble, to fall (un caballo) || — FIG & FAM *andar rodando* to be scattered around; *no quiero que mis libros anden rodando por la casa* I don't want my books to be scattered around the house | *echarlo todo a rodar* to ruin everything (estropear), to give up (abandonar) || *rodar por el mundo* to roam the world over (viajar), to exist (existir).

◆ *vt* to film, to shoot; *rodar una película* to film a picture || to run in (un motor, un coche) || to roll (un objeto redondo) || to travel; *haber rodado todo el mundo* to have travelled all over the world.

Rodas *n pr* GEOGR Rhodes.

rodear *vt* to enclose, to inclose; *rodear un huerto con una cerca* to enclose a garden with a fence || to wrap; *rodear la cabeza con una venda* to wrap one's head in a bandage || to surround; *la policía rodeó la casa* the police surrounded the house || to go around; *el camino rodea la montaña* the road goes around the mountain || AMER to round up (el ganado) || *le rodeé el cuello con mis brazos* I threw my arms round his neck.

◆ *vpr* to surround o.s.; *rodearse de los mejores consejeros* to surround o.s. with the best advisors || *rodearse de lujo* to lavish luxury on o.s.

rodela *f* buckler, round shield || AMER pad (rodete).

rodeno, na *adj* red, reddish (rojo, rojizo) || BOT *pino rodeno* cluster, pinaster.

rodeo *m* detour, roundabout way; *dar un rodeo* to make a detour, to go by a roundabout way || roundup (del ganado) || rodeo (fiesta de rancheros) || corral (lugar donde se celebra) || AMER Mexican bullfight.

◆ *pl* FIG evasiveness *sing* (al hablar) || — FIG *andar* or *andarse con rodeos* to beat about the bush | *dejémonos de rodeos* let's get to the point | *no andarse con rodeos* to get straight to the point, not to beat about the bush.

rodera *f* rut, track (carril).

Rodesia *npr f* GEOGR ⟶ **Rhodesia .**

rodesiano, na *adj/s* Rhodesian.

rodete *m* bun, chignon (de pelo) || pad, cushion, padded ring (para cargar algo sobre la cabeza) || ward (de cerradura) || roll [of fat] (de grasa en una persona) || fifth wheel (de carruaje).

rodilla *f* ANAT knee || pad (para llevar algo sobre la cabeza) || floorcloth, cloth (para fregar suelos) || — *caer de rodillas* to fall on one's knees || *de rodillas* keeling (de hinojos), on bended knees (humildemente); *pedir algo de rodillas* to ask for sth. on bended knees || *doblar la rodilla* to go down on one knee (arrodillarse), to humble o.s. (humillarse) || *estar de rodillas* to be keeling, to kneel || *hincar la rodilla* to go down on one knee, to kneel || *hincarse de rodillas* to go down on one's knees, to kneel (down).

rodillazo *m* blow given with the knee || blow on the knee || *dar un rodillazo a alguien* to knee s.o.

rodillazo *m* TAUR kneeling pass.

rodillera *f* knee guard (protección) || knee patch (refuerzo en los pantalones) || pad (para llevar pesos sobre la cabeza) || *hacer rodilleras* to go baggy *o* to bag at the knees (un pantalón).

rodillo *m* roller || platen, roller (de la máquina de escribir) || rolling pin (de cocina) || mangle (de lavadora) || IMPR *rodillo entintado* inking roller.

rodio *m* QUÍM rhodium.

rododendro *m* BOT rhododendron.

rodomiel *m* rose honey.

rodrigar *vt* to prop up, to stake (una planta).

rodrigazón *f* season when plants are propped up.

rodríguez *m* FIG & FAM grass widower.

rodrigón *m* prop, stake (para las plantas) || FIG & FAM chaperon.

roedor, ra *adj* rodent, gnawing.

◆ *m* rodent.

roedura *f* gnawing (acción) || gnaw mark (marca dejada al roer) || gnawed part (porción roída).

roel *m* HERÁLD roundel.

roela *f* blank, planchet (en numismática).

roentgen *m* FÍS roentgen, röntgen.

roentgenoterapia *f* MED roentgenotherapy.

roer* *vt* to nibble (at); *roer una galleta* to nibble (at) a biscuit || to gnaw; *el perro está royendo un hueso* the dog is gnawing a bone || FIG to gnaw, to nag (atormentar); *su conciencia le roe* he is gnawed by pangs of conscience, his conscience nags him | to nibble away at, to eat away (quitar poco a poco) || — FIG & FAM *dar que roer a uno* to give s.o. a tough time | *un problema duro de roer* a hard problem to solve, a hard nut to crack.

◆ *vpr* to bite; *roerse las uñas* to bite one's fingernails.

rogación *f* request (petición).

◆ *pl* REL rogations (letanías).

rogador, ra; rogante *adj* supplicatory.

rogar* *vt/vi* to request, to ask (pedir); *le rogué que viniera en seguida* I requested him to come at once || to beg, to plead (con humildad); *le ruego un poco de compasión* I beg you *o* I beg of you *o* I plead with you to take pity on me || to implore (implorar) || to pray; *rogar a Dios* to pray to God || — *hacerse de rogar* to take a lot of asking, to play hard to get, to have to be coaxed || *no se hace de rogar* he doesn't have to be asked twice || *ruega por nos* pray for us || *se ruega no fumar* no smoking please, you are requested to refrain from smoking || *se ruega la publicación* for the favour of publication in your columns.

rogativa *f* rogation || *hacer rogativas para que llueva* to pray for rain.

rogativo, va *adj* supplicatory.

rogatorio, ria *adj* JUR rogatory; *comisión rogatoria* rogatory commission.

roído, da *adj* gnawed, eaten (carcomido) || miserable.

rojete *m* rouge (colorete).

rojez *f* redness.

rojizo, za *adj* reddish.

rojo, ja *adj* red; *pelo rojo* red hair || ruddy (las mejillas) || — FAM *estar más rojo que un cangrejo* to be as red as a beetroot || VET *mal rojo* swine fever || *ponerse rojo* to blush, to go red (ruborizarse), to turn red (cualquier cosa) || *ponerse rojo de ira* to get fighting mad.

◆ *adj/sm* FAM red, communist (comunista) | republican.

◆ *m* red || — *el disco está en rojo* the lights are red, the traffic light is on red || FIG *la discusión se puso al rojo vivo* the discussion became heated | *la situación está al rojo vivo* the situation is electric *o* is very tense || *poner al rojo* to heat until red hot, to make red hot || *rojo blanco* white hot || *rojo cereza* cherry red || *rojo de labios* lipstick.

Rojo (mar) *npr m* GEOGR Red Sea.

rol *m* roll (lista) || MAR muster roll.

roldana *f* pulley wheel.

rollizo, za *adj* round (cilíndrico) || chubby, plump; *niño rollizo* chubby child.
◆ *m* round log (madero).

rollo *m* roll; *rollo de papel* roll of paper || rolling pin (de pastelero) || coil (de cuerda) || roll (carrete de película) || round log (de madera) || scroll (de pergamino) || FAM roll, layer (carne) | bore, drag; *ese tío, la conferencia es un rollo* that fellow, the lecture is a bore || (ant) stone pillar || — FAM *¡largue el rollo!* speech! | *perdón por todo este rollo* forgive me for boring you to death | *¡qué mal rollo!* what a drag! | *soltó su rollo clásico* he came out with his usual boring tale, he said what he always says | *¡vaya rollo!* what a bore!

Roma *n pr* GEOGR Rome || — FIG & FAM *cuando a Roma fueres, haz lo que vieres* when in Rome do as the Romans do | *por todas partes se va a Roma, todos los caminos van a Roma* all roads lead to Rome | *revolver Roma con Santiago* to leave no stone unturned, to move heaven and earth.

romadizo *m* MED head cold.

romana *f* steelyard (balanza).

romance *adj* romance; *las lenguas romances* Romance languages.
◆ *m* Romance (lengua) || Spanish, Castilian (castellano) || romance (composición poética con versos octosílabos) || — FIG *en buen romance* clearly, plainly || *romance de ciego* ballad sung on the street by a blind man.

romancero, ra *m/f* author or singer of Spanish romances.
◆ *m* collection of Spanish romances.

romanear *vt* to weigh on a steelyard.

romanesco, ca *adj* Roman (de los romanos) || novelesque.

románico, ca *adj/sm* ARQ & ARTES Romanesque || *lenguas románicas* Romance languages.

romanilla *adj* round.
◆ *f* round hand (letra).

romanismo *m* Romanism.

romanista *m/f* Romanist.

romanizar *vt* to Romanize.

romano, na *adj/s* Roman || — *el Imperio Romano* the Roman Empire || *lechuga romana* cos lettuce [US romaine lettuce] || *números romanos* Roman numerals || FIG *obra de romanos* Herculean task.

romanticismo *m* romanticism.

romántico, ca *adj/s* romantic.

romanticón, ona *adj* romantic; *espíritu romanticón* romantic spirit.

romanza *f* MÚS romance.

rombal *adj* rhombic.

rómbico, ca *adj* rhombic.

rombo *m* MAT rhombus || turbot (rodaballo).

romboédrico, ca *adj* rhombohedral.

romboedro *m* rhombohedron.

romboidal *adj* rhomboidal.

romboide *m* MAT rhomboid.

romboideo, a *adj* rhomboid.

Romeo *npr m* Romeo.

romería *f* pilgrimage (peregrinación); *ir de romería* to go on a pilgrimage || festival at a local shrine (fiesta popular).

romero, ra *adj* who goes on a pilgrimage, pilgrim.
◆ *m/f* pilgrim (peregrino).
◆ *m* rosemary (arbusto) || pilot fish (pez).

romo, ma *adj* blunt, dull; *punta roma* blunt point || snub (nariz) || snub-nosed (persona) || FIG dull (torpe).

rompecabezas *m inv* puzzle (juego) || jigsaw (puzzle) (de tacos de madera) || FIG puzzle, riddle (problema complicado).

rompedera *f* TECN punch.

rompedor, ra *adj* destructive || hard on one's clothes.
◆ *m/f* destructive person, breaker.

rompehielos *m inv* icebreaker (barco).

rompehuelgas *m inv* FAM strikebreaker, blackleg, scab (esquirol).

rompelotodo *m inv* destructive person.

rompenueces *m inv* nutcracker (cascanueces).

rompeolas *m inv* breakwater, jetty.

romper *vt* to break; *romper una silla* to break a chair | to smash, to shatter, to break; *romper la vajilla* to smash the dishes || to break down (una valla) || to snap, to break (una cuerda) || to tear (papel, tela) || to wear out; *romper el calzado* to wear out one's shoes || FIG to interrupt, to break; *romper la monotonía* to break the monotony | to break off (las relaciones, la amistad) | to initiate, to begin (empezar); *romper las hostilidades* to initiate hostilities | to cut through, to cleave; *el barco rompe las aguas* the boat cuts through the water | to violate, to break (una ley) || — MIL to open; *romper el fuego* to open fire | to break through (el frente enemigo) || DEP to break [service] (tenis) || FIG & FAM to smash in; *romperle la cara* or *las narices a uno* to smash s.o.'s face in || — MIL *¡rompan filas!* fall out!, dismiss! || *romper el ayuno* to break one's fast || FIG *romper el hielo* to break the ice || MIL *romper filas* to break ranks, to fall out || *romper la marcha* to lead the way || FIG & FAM *romper una lanza por* to fight for, to defend.
◆ *vi* to break (las olas) || FIG to break off relations, to break off, to break up; *ha roto con su novia* he has broken up with his girlfriend | to break; *romper con el pasado* to break with the past | to burst out, to burst into; *rompió a hablar* he burst out talking; *romper en llanto* to burst out crying, to burst into tears || to bloom, to blossom (las flores) || — *al romper el alba* or *el día* at dawn, at daybreak || FIG *de rompe y rasga* determined, resolute | *quien rompe paga* one must pay the consequences (of one's actions).
◆ *vpr* to break; *se rompió la silla* the chair broke || to break, to smash (una vasija) || to snap (una cuerda) || to tear (un papel, una tela) || to break, to fracture; *romperse una pierna* to break one's leg || to break down; *se me rompió el coche* my car broke down || to wear out (zapatos) || — FIG & FAM *romperse las narices* to fall flat on one's face | *romperse los cascos* or *la cabeza* to rack one's brains.

rompible *adj* breakable, fragile.

rompiente *m* reef, shoal (escollo).

rompimiento *m* ⟶ **ruptura.**

Rómulo *npr m* Romulus.

ron *m* rum.

ronca *f* bellow [of a buck deer in rut] (bramido) || rutting season (época) || halberd (arma).

roncador, ra *adj* snoring (que ronca).
◆ *m/f* snorer.

roncamente *adv* hoarsely || coarsely, roughly (toscamente).

roncar *vi* to snore (durmiendo) || to bellow [a buck deer in the rutting season] || FIG to roar (el mar) | to roar, to howl (el viento).

roncear *vi* to dawdle (remolonear) || FAM to flatter, to soft-soap (halagar).

roncería *f* dawdling, slowness (lentitud) || FAM flattery, soft soap (halago).

roncero, ra *adj* dawdling (remolón) || grouchy (regañón) || flattering, soft-soaping (halagador) || MAR slow (embarcación).

ronco, ca *adj* hoarse, raucous (áspero); *voz ronca* hoarse voice || hoarse (que tiene ronquera); *estar ronco* to be hoarse || raucous, harsh (sonido).

roncha *f* swelling, lump, bump (en la piel) || slice (rodaja).

ronda *f* round (vuelta dada para vigilar) || watch (vigilancia) || patrol (patrulla) || round (del cartero) || beat (de la policía) || group of young minstrels (conjunto musical) || hand (en juegos de cartas) || ring road (camino de circunvalación) || FAM round (convidada); *pagar una ronda* to stand a round || FIG round (de negociaciones) || AMER circle (corro) || *camino de ronda* parapet walk, rampart walk || *ronda de reconocimiento* reconnaissance mission.

rondador, ra *adj* making rounds || serenading.
◆ *m/f* patrolman, night watchman (vigilante) || serenader || AMER Ecuadorian panpipe (flauta).

rondalla *f* group of serenaders *o* minstrels || tale, story (patraña).

rondar *vi* to patrol, to go the rounds (para vigilar) || to prowl (merodear).
◆ *vt* to go around (dar vueltas) || FIG to threaten; *la gripe le está rondando* the flu is threatening him | to be about; *rondar la cincuentena* to be about fifty | to pursue (andar en pos de) | to court (a una mujer) | to walk up and down; *rondar la calle* to walk up and down the street | to serenade || FIG *me está rondando el sueño* I am feeling very sleepy.

rondel *m* rondel (poema).

rondeño, ña *adj* [of *o* from] Ronda [town in Spain].
◆ *m/f* native *o* inhabitant of Ronda.
◆ *f* fandango of Ronda.

rondín *m* AMER watchman (vigilante) | harmonica (armónica).

rondó *m* MÚS rondo.

rondón (de) *loc* unannounced, without warning (sin avisar); *entrar de rondón* to enter without warning || unexpectedly (inesperadamente).

ronquear *vi* to be hoarse.

ronquedad *f* hoarseness (de la voz) || raucousness (de un ruido).

ronquera *f* hoarseness || *tener* or *padecer ronquera* to be hoarse.

ronquido *m* snore || snoring || FIG howling; *el ronquido del viento* the howling of the wind.

ronronear *vi* to purr (un gato).

ronroneo *m* purring (del gato).

ronzal *m* halter.

ronzar *vt* to crunch (al comer) || MAR to lever.

roña *f* VET mange (del ganado) || dirt, filth (mugre) || rust (orín) || FAM stinginess (tacañería).
◆ *adj* FAM stingy, tight (roñoso).
◆ *m/f* FAM skinflint, scrooge.

roñería *f* FAM ⟶ **roñosería.**

roñica *adj* FAM stingy, tight.
◆ *m/f* FAM skinflint, scrooge.

roñosería; roñería *f* FAM stinginess.

roñoso, sa *adj* VET mangy; *carnero roñoso* mangy sheep || dirty, filthy (mugriento) || rusty (oxidado) || FAM stingy, tight (avaro) || AMER rancorous (rencoroso).

ropa *f* clothes *pl*, clothing, dress, garments *pl* || — *a quema ropa* at point-blank range, point-blank || *con la ropa hecha jirones* in tatters, with one's clothes in tatters || FIG *hay ropa tendida* be careful what you say | *la ropa sucia se* *lava en casa* one should not wash one's dirty linen in public | *nadar y guardar la ropa* to have the best of both worlds || *ropa blanca* linen, drapery (sábanas, etc.), lingerie (de mujer), underwear (de hombre) || *ropa de cama* bed linen || *ropa hecha* ready-made *o* ready-to-wear clothes || *ropa interior* underclothes, underwear || *ropa lavada* or *por lavar* washing || *ropa planchada* ironing || CULIN *ropa vieja* meat stew (guiso) || FIG *tentarse la ropa* to think about it, to hesitate.

ropaje *m* robes *pl*, vestments *pl* (ropa suntuosa) || heavy clothes *pl* (ropa excesiva) || ARTES drapery || FIG *traicionar a uno bajo el ropaje de la amistad* to betray s.o. under the banner of friendship.

ropavejería *f* old-clothes shop.

ropavejero, ra *m/f* second-hand dealer (de baratijas) || old-clothesman (de ropa vieja).

ropería *f* clothes shop, clothing store (tienda) || clothier's trade (industria) || old-clothes shop (ropavejería) || linen room (en comunidades).

ropero *m* wardrobe [*US* clothes closet] (para guardar la ropa) || charitable organization that distributes clothes to the poor (institución de caridad).

ropero, ra *m/f* clothier.

roque *m* rook (ajedrez) || FIG & FAM *estar, quedarse roque* to be, to fall asleep.

roqueda *f*; **roquedal** *m* rocky place.

roquedo *m* crag, rock (peñasco).

roquefort *m* roquefort (queso).

roqueño, ña *adj* rocky || hard as a rock (duro).

roqueta *f* turret (fortificación).

roquete *m* rochet (vestidura eclesiástica).

rorcual *m* ZOOL rorqual, finback (ballena).

rorro *m* baby (niño pequeñito) || AMER doll (muñeca).

ros *m* MIL cap.

rosa *f* rose; *ramo de rosas* bouquet of roses || red spot [on the body] (mancha) || rosette (hecha con cintas de colores) || ARQ rose window (rosetón) || pink, rose (color); *un rosa claro* a pale pink || — *agua de rosas* rose water || FIG *color de rosa* pink, rose, rose-coloured || FIG & FAM *estar como las propias rosas* to feel as fit as a fiddle || FIG *la vida no es un lecho de rosas* life is not a bed of roses | *no hay rosa sin espinas* every rose has its thorn | *novela rosa* novelette, romantic novel | *pintar las cosas de color de rosa* to paint everything in the garden rosy || *rosa de Jericó* rose of Jericho || *rosa de los vientos* or *náutica* compass card || *rosa de pitiminí* fairy rose || *rosa de té* tea rose || *rosa silvestre* dog rose || FIG *verlo todo de color de rosa* to see everything through rose-coloured glasses.
◆ *adj inv* pink; *un traje rosa* a pink dress.

rosáceo, a *adj* rosy || MED *acné rosácea* acne rosacea.

rosado, da *adj* pink, rosy, rose-coloured (color de rosa) || rose-flavoured; *miel rosada* rose-flavoured honey || AMER red-roan (caballo) || *color rosado* pink.
◆ *adj/sm* rosé (vino).

rosal *m* rosebush || — *rosal silvestre* dog rose || *rosal trepador* rambling rose.

rosaleda; rosalera *f* rose garden.

rosarino, na *adj* [of *o* from] Rosario (Argentina).
◆ *m/f* native *o* inhabitant of Rosario.

rosario *m* rosary, beads *pl*; *rezar el rosario* to tell one's beads, to say the rosary || FIG series, string; *un rosario de imprecaciones, de desdichas* a series of imprecations, of misfortunes || FIG & FAM backbone (columna vertebral) || TECN chain [of buckets] || — FIG *acabar como el rosario de la aurora* to end abruptly (una reunión) || TECN *rosario hidráulico* chain pump.

rosbif *m* roast beef.

rosca *f* thread (de un tornillo) || roll (pan) || doughnut (bollo) || roll of fat (de gordura) || ring (de humo) || AMER pad, round pad (rodete para llevar pesos en la cabeza) || — FIG & FAM *hacer la rosca a uno* to suck up to s.o. || *hacerse una rosca* to curl up [in a ball] || *pasarse de rosca* to go too far (pasarse de los límites), to lose its thread (un tornillo) || *paso de rosca* pitch || *rosca de Arquímedes* Archimedes' screw || *tapón de rosca* screw-on cap.

roscado, da *adj* spiral-shaped || threaded (tornillo).
◆ *m* TECN threading.

roscar *vt* to thread.

rosco *m* ring-shaped cake (roscón) || doughnut (bollo) || roll (pan) || ring (flotador) || FIG & FAM zero; *me han puesto un rosco en física* I got zero in physics.

roscón *m* ring-shaped cake || *roscón de Reyes* twelfth-cake, twelfth-night cake.

Rosellón *npr m* GEOGR Roussillon.

roséola *f* MED roseola.

roseta *f* small rose (rosa pequeña) || flush (en las mejillas) || rosette (de cintas de colores) || AMER rowel (de espuela).
◆ *pl* popcorn *sing* (maíz).

rosetón *m* ARQ rose window | rosette (adorno).

rosicler *m* rosy hue of dawn.

rosillo, lla *adj* pink, rosy (rosado) || reddish (rojizo) || roan (caballo).

rosquete *m* AMER FAM queer (marica).

rosquilla *f* doughnut || grub, caterpillar (larva) || FIG & FAM *venderse como rosquillas* to sell like hot cakes (fácilmente).

rosquillero, ra *m/f* doughnut maker (fabricante) || doughnut seller (vendedor).

rostrado, da; rostral *adj* rostral; *columna, corona rostral* rostral column, crown.

rostro *m* face, countenance; *un rostro alegre, sonriente* a happy, smiling face || beak (pico del ave) || MAR rostrum, beak || — FIG *hacer rostro a* to face || FIG & FAM *tener mucho rostro* to have a lot of cheek *o* nerve | *torcer el rostro* to pull a face, to grimace || *volver el rostro* to turn one's head aside.

rota *f* rout, defeat (derrota) || BOT rattan || REL rota (tribunal).

rotáceo, a *adj* BOT rotate.

rotación *f* rotacion || — COM *fondo de rotación* revolving fund || AGR *por rotación* in rotation | *rotation de cultivos* crop rotation.

rotacismo *m* rhotacism (fonética).

rotatorio, ria *adj* rotatory.

rotativo, va *adj* rotary, revolving (giratorio).
◆ *f* IMPR rotary press.
◆ *m* newspaper (periódico); *rotativo matutino* morning newspaper.

roten *m* rattan, ratan (planta) || rattan cane (bastón).

rotería *f* AMER poor *pl*, rabble (pobres).

rotífero *m* ZOOL rotifer.

roto, ta *adj* broken; *juguete roto* broken toy; *cuerda rota* broken string || shattered, broken; *cristal roto* broken glass || torn (tela, papel) || FIG broken (hombre) | shattered, ruined; *una vida rota por los desengaños* a life shattered by bitter experiences.
◆ *m* hole (en tela) || AMER common man, poor man | FAM Chilean (chileno) || FIG *nunca falta un roto para un descosido* birds of a feather flock together.

rotograbado *m* IMPR rotogravure.

rotonda *f* ARQ rotunda.

rotor *m* AVIAC & TECN rotor.

rotoso, sa *adj* AMER tattared, ragged (roto, harapiento).

Rotterdam *n pr* GEOGR Rotterdam.

rótula *f* ANAT kneecap, patella, rotula || TECN ball-and-socket joint.

rotulación *f* lettering.

rotulador *m* felt-tipped pen (lápiz) || letterer (pintor).

rotular *vt* to letter || to mark in the names on, to label, to letter; *rotular un plano* to mark in the names on a map.

rotular; rotuliano, na *adj* ANAT rotulian.

rótulo *m* sign; *rótulo luminoso* electric sign || poster, sign, notice (letrero) || label (etiqueta) || title (título) || lettering (de un mapa).
◆ *pl* CINEM subtitles.

rotundamente *adv* flatly, categorically; *se negó rotundamente* he flatly refused || emphatically; *dijo rotundamente que sí* he emphatically agreed.

rotundidad *f* firmness; *la rotundidad de su negativa me descorazonó* the firmness of his refusal disheartened me || rotundity (redondez) || polish (del lenguaje).

rotundo, da *adj* flat, categorical, resounding, firm (negativa); *un no rotundo* a resounding no || emphatic, categorical (afirmación) || round (redondo) || well-rounded (frase) || resounding (éxito).

rotura *f* breaking, breakage (acción de romper) || break (parte quebrada) || fracture, break (de un hueso) || tear, rip, rent (de un tejido).

roturación *f* AGR ploughing [*US* plowing], breaking up [of untilled ground].

roturador, ra *adj* ploughing [*US* plowing].
◆ *f* AGR plough [*US* plow].

roturar *vt* AGR to plough [*US* to plow], to break up.

round *m* DEP round (asalto de boxeo).

roya *f* BOT mildew, rust, blight.

royalty *f* royalty.

roza *f* groove, hollow (en la pared) || cleared ground (tierra rozada).

rozadora *f* MIN coal-cutting machine (máquina).

rozadura *f* scratch; *la bala le hizo una rozadura en el casco* the bullet made a scratch on his helmet || abrasion, sore (desolladura) || chafe (caballos).

rozagante *adj* showy (persona, vestido) || spirited, lively (caballo) || splendid, magnificent.

rozamiento *m* rubbing (roce) || TECN friction || AGR clearing [of the ground] (desbroce) || FIG friction.

rozar *vt* to graze; *la rueda rozó el bordillo de la acera* the wheel grazed the curb || to rub against; *la silla roza la pared* the chair rubs against the wall || to touch, to brush against; *mi mano le rozó la cara* my hand touched her face || to skim (una superficie) || to scratch (causando un arañazo) || to dirty (ensuciar) || AGR to clear (un terreno) | to graze (el ganado); *rozar la hierba* to graze the grass || FIG to be bordering on; *rozar la cuarentena* to be bordering on forty; *su actitud roza el descaro* his attitude borders on impudence | to touch on; *es un asunto que roza la religión* it's a subject which touches on religion || FIG *rozamos el accidente* we nearly had an accident.

◆ *vi* to rub || *rozar con* to border on, to touch on.
◆ *vpr* to rub, to brush; *se rozó con el alambre* he rubbed against the wire || FIG to rub shoulders; *rozarse con artistas* to rub shoulders with artists || MAR to chafe (desgastarse).

RTVE *abrev de Radiotelevisión Española* Spanish broadcasting company.

rúa *f* street (calle).

ruano, na *adj* roan (caballo).
◆ *f* AMER poncho.

rubefacción *f* MED rubefaction.

rubefaciente *adj/sm* MED rubefacient.

rúbeo, a *adj* reddish.

rubéola *f* MED German measles, rubella.

rubescente *adj* rubescent.

rubeta *f* tree frog (rana de zarzal).

rubí *m* ruby || jewel (de un reloj) || — *rubí balaje* balas ruby || *rubí de Bohemia* rose quartz.
— OBSERV pl *rubíes*.

rubia *f* BOT madder (granza) || estate car, shooting brake [US station wagon] (coche) || blonde (mujer de pelo rubio) || FAM peseta (moneda) || FAM *rubia de frasco* peroxide blonde.

rubiáceas *f pl* BOT rubiaceae.

rubial *m* madder field (campo de granzas).

rubiales *m/f inv* FAM blond (hombre rubio) | blonde (mujer rubia).

rubicán *adj* roan.

rubicela *f* MIN rubicelle.

Rubicón *npr m* GEOGR Rubicon || *atravesar* or *pasar el Rubicón* to cross the Rubicon.

rubicundez *f* rubicundity || reddishness (del pelo) || MED rubefaction.

rubicundo, da *adj* rubicund || reddish (pelo) || ruddy (rebosante de salud).

rubidio *m* rubidium (metal).

rubificar *vt* to redden || MED to rubefy.

rubio, bia *adj* blond, blonde, fair; *tiene el pelo rubio* she has blond hair || *tabaco rubio* Virginia tobacco.
◆ *m* blond, blonde (color); *rubio ceniza* ash blond || blond (hombre con pelo rubio) || ZOOL red gurnard (pez).
◆ *f* ⟶ **rubia.**

rublo *m* rouble (moneda rusa).

rubor *m* bright red (color) || blush, flush (en las mejillas) || FIG shame (vergüenza) | abashment, bashfulness (pudor) || — FIG *causar* or *producir rubor* to make blush | *sentir rubor* to be ashamed (avergonzarse).

ruborizado, da *adj* blushing; *cara ruborizada* blushing face || FIG ashamed (avergonzado) | abashed (por el pudor).

ruborizar *vt* to make blush.
◆ *vpr* to blush, to turn red || FIG to feel ashamed *o* bashful *o* abashed (avergonzarse).

ruboroso, sa *adj* blushing, bashful.

rúbrica *f* rubric, section (sección de periódico) || heading, title (título) || flourish, paraph (trazo añadido a la firma) || initials *pl* (del nombre) || red mark (señal roja) || *ser de rúbrica* to be customary.

rubricante *adj* signatory, who signs.

rubricar *vt* to initial (un documento, etc.) || FIG to round off; *el torero rubricó su faena con una gran estocada* the bullfighter rounded off his display with an impressive sword thrust || *firmado y rubricado* signed and sealed.

rubro, bra *adj* red (encarnado).
◆ *m* AMER heading, title (rúbrica) | item, entry (en contabilidad).

rucio, cia *adj* grey (animal) || grey-haired (persona) || AMER blond (rubio).
◆ *m* donkey (asno).

ruco, ca *adj* AMER worn-out.

ruche (estar) *loc* FAM to be flat broke *o* stony broke.

rucho *m* donkey, jackass (borrico).

ruda *f* BOT rue (planta) || FIG & FAM *es más conocido que la ruda* everybody knows him.

rudeza *f* roughness, coarseness, rudeness.

rudimentario, ria *adj* rudimentary.

rudimento *m* rudiment.

rudo, da *adj* coarse, rough, unpolished (tosco) || hard, difficult (difícil); *trabajo duro* hard job || rude, crude; *franqueza ruda* rude frankness.

rueca *f* distaff (para hilar).

rueda *f* wheel || castor (de un mueble) || circle, ring (de personas) || spread (de un pavo) || slice; *rueda de merluza* slice of hake || rack (suplicio) || — *barco de ruedas* paddle steamer || FIG & FAM *comulgar con ruedas de molino* to swallow *o* to believe anything, to be very gullible || *de* or *con dos ruedas* two-wheeled || FIG & FAM *hacer comulgar con ruedas de molino* to pull the wool over s.o.'s eyes, to take s.o. in || *hacer la rueda* to spread its tail (pavo), to court (cortejar), to cajole (lisonjear) || FIG *ir sobre ruedas* to go *o* to run smoothly || *la rueda de la fortuna* the wheel of fortune || *patinaje sobre ruedas* roller-skating || *patines de ruedas* roller skates || *rueda catalina* Catherine wheel (relojería) || *rueda delantera, trasera* front, rear wheel || *rueda de molino* millstone || *rueda dentada* cog, cogwheel || *rueda de paletas* or *álabes* paddle wheel || *rueda de prensa* press conference || *rueda de recambio* or *de repuesto* spare wheel || *rueda de trinquete* ratchet wheel || *rueda hidráulica* waterwheel; mill wheel (de molino) || *rueda libre* freewheel || *ruedas gemelas* dual wheels.

ruedo *m* round mat (esterilla) || edge, border (borde) || hem (de la falda) || TAUR bullring (redondel) || — *dar la vuelta al ruedo* to go round the ring receiving applause [the matador] || FIG *echarse al ruedo* to enter the fray.

ruego *m* request (petición); *a ruego mío* at my request || entreaty, plea (súplica) || *le envío estos datos con el ruego de que los publique* I am sending you this information in the hope that you will publish it.

rufián *m* pimp (chulo) || villain, rogue (granuja).

rufianear *vi* to pander.

rufianesco, ca *adj* villainous.
◆ *f* underworld (hampa).

rufo, fa *adj* blond (rubio) || red-haired (pelirrojo) || curly (rizado) || self-satisfied, smug (ufano).

rugby *m* DEP rugby || *rugby a trece* rugby league.

rugido *m* roar || FIG shout, bellow (grito) | howl, howling (de dolor, del viento).

rugidor, ra; rugiente *adj* roaring, bellowing.

ruginoso, sa *adj* rusty (mohoso).

rugir *vi* to roar, to bellow || FIG to shout, to bellow (dar gritos) | to howl (el viento).

rugosidad *f* rugosity.

rugoso, sa *adj* wrinkled, rugose || rough (áspero).

Ruhr *npr m* GEOGR River Ruhr.

ruibarbo *m* BOT rhubarb.

ruido *m* noise; *los ruidos de la calle* the noises of the street || sound (sonido) || din, row (alboroto); *hacer* or *meter ruido* to make a din || FIG stir; *esta noticia va a hacer mucho ruido* this news is going to cause a big stir | row, rumpus (escándalo) || — *mucho ruido y pocas nueces, mucho ruido por nada* much ado about nothing || *ruido ambiental* noise || *ruido de fondo* background noise || *sin ruido* without making a noise, noiselessly, silently.

ruidosamente *adv* noisily || loudly; *aplaudir ruidosamente* to applaud loudly.

ruidoso, sa *adj* noisy, loud || FIG sensational; *noticia ruidosa* sensational piece of news.

ruin *adj* vile, base, foul, despicable; *gente, acción ruin* base people, deed || mean, stingy (avaro) || miserable; *persona de ruin aspecto* miserable-looking person || puny (raquítico) || vicious, mean (caballo) || *en nombrando al ruin de Roma, asoma* talk of the devil.

ruina *f* ruin, collapse (acción de hundirse) || FIG wrack and ruin; *vamos a la ruina* we are going to wrack and ruin | ruin, downfall; *va a ser su ruina* it will be the ruin of him *o* his downfall | fall; *la ruina del Imperio Romano* the fall of the Roman Empire | destruction (de las ilusiones) || — *el negocio le llevó a la ruina* the business ruined him || *lo encontré hecho una ruina* I found him a shadow of his former self *o* a wreck || *un edificio que amenaza ruina* a building on the verge of collapse.
◆ *pl* ruins; *una casa en ruinas* a house in ruins; *las ruinas de una ciudad* the ruins of a city.

ruindad *f* vileness, meanness (vileza) || mean act, piece of villainy (acción ruin) || meanness, stinginess (tacañería).

ruinoso, sa *adj* ruinous; *un negocio ruinoso* a ruinous business || tumbledown, in ruins; *castillo ruinoso* castle in ruins || dilapidated; *casas ruinosas* dilapidated houses || *en estado ruinoso* ramshackle, run-down, dilapidated.

ruiponce *m* BOT rampion.

ruiseñor *m* nightingale (pájaro).

ruleta *f* roulette (juego de azar) || *ruleta rusa* Russian roulette.

ruletear *vi* AMER to drive a taxi (conducir un taxi).

ruletero *m* AMER taxi driver (taxista).

rulo *m* roller, land leveller || roller (para el pelo) || rolling pin (para la cocina).

Rumania *npr f* GEOGR Rumania, Roumania, Romania.

rumano, na *adj/s* Rumanian, Roumanian.

rumazón *f* MAR overcast horizon.

rumba *f* rumba (baile).

rumbeador; rumbero *m* AMER pathfinder, guide.

rumbear *vi* AMER to head (*hacia* for) | to get one's bearings (orientarse).

rumbo *m* direction (dirección) || AVIAC & MAR course; *corregir el rumbo* to correct the course || FIG course; *tomar otro rumbo* to take another course; *marcar el rumbo* to set the course | lavishness (generosidad) | pomp || — MAR *abatir el rumbo* to fall to leeward | *cambiar de rumbo* to change course || FIG *celebrar una boda con mucho rumbo* to have a very lavish wedding || *hacer rumbo a un sitio* to head for a place || MAR *navegar rumbo a* to be bound for, to be on course for || FIG *perder el rumbo* to lose one's bearings || *poner rumbo a* to head for || *rumbo a* heading for, bound for || FIG *tomar buen rumbo* to take a turn for the better (un asunto).

rumboso, sa *adj* generous, lavish (generoso) || lavish, splendid (magnífico); *una fiesta rumbosa* a lavish party.

rumí *m* Roumi, Christian.
— OBSERV Term used by Moslems to refer to Christians.

rumia *f* rumination.

rumiante *adj/sm* ruminant.

rumiar *vt* to ruminate, to chew (masticar) || FIG to ruminate, to think over; *rumiar un proyecto* to think a plan over | to grumble, to growl (refunfuñar), .
◆ *vi* to rumiate, to chew the cud (un animal).

rumor *m* rumour [US rumor] || murmur; *se oía un rumor de voces* a murmur of conversation could be heard; *el rumor de las aguas* the murmur of the water || rustle, whisper (de los árboles) || — *el rumor general* popular rumour || *según los rumores* rumour has it that.

rumorear *vt/vi* to rumour [US to rumor].
◆ *vpr* to be rumoured; *se rumorea que...* it is rumoured that...

rumoroso, sa *adj* murmuring, babling; *arroyo rumoroso* murmuring stream, babbling brook.

runrún *m* rumour [US rumor] (hablilla); *corre el runrún* the rumour is going around || murmur, buzz (de voces).

runrunearse *vpr* to be rumoured [US to be rumored], to be said; *se runrunea que van a subir los precios* it is said that prices are going to rise.

rupestre *adj* rupestrian, rupestral || rock; *planta rupestre* rock plant || *pintura rupestre* cave *o* rupestrian painting.

rupia *f* rupee (moneda).

rupicabra; rupicapra *f* chamois (gamuza).

ruptor *m* ELECTR contact breaker.

ruptura *f*; **rompimiento** *m* breaking (acción de romper) || break (parte rota) || fracture (fractura) || breaking-off (de relaciones) || breakup (de dos personas) || breaking (de un contrato) || MIL breakthrough || ELECTR *corriente de ruptura* breaking current.

rural *adj* rural; *los problemas rurales* rural problems || country, rural; *cura, médico rural* country priest, doctor || — *éxodo rural* depopulation of rural areas || *finca rural* country estate.

Rusia *npr f* GEOGR Russia.

rusificación *f* Russianization, Russification.

rusificar *vt* to Russianize, to Russify.

ruso, sa *adj/s* Russian.
◆ *m* Russian (idioma).

rusófilo, la *adj/s* Russophile.

rusticidad *f* rusticity || uncouthness (patanería).

rústico, ca *adj* rustic, rural, country || uncouth (tosco).
◆ *f en rústica* paperback, paperbound; *edición en rústica* paperbound edition.
◆ *m* countryman, peasant (campesino) || rustic, yokel (palurdo).

rustiquez *f* rusticity.

Rut *npr f* Ruth.

ruta *f* route, itinerary (itinerario); *la ruta de Don Quijote* the route of Don Quixote || road, way (camino); *señalar la ruta de la victoria* to point out the road to victory || MAR course || — *hoja de ruta* waybill || *ruta aérea* air lane.

rutáceas *f pl* BOT rutaceae.

rutenio *m* QUÍM ruthenium.

rutilante *adj* shining, brilliant, rutilant.

rutilar *vi* to shine.

rutilo *m* MIN rutile.

rutina *f* routine; *apartarse de la rutina diaria* to get away from the daily routine; *por mera rutina* as a matter of mere routine.

rutinario, ria *adj* routine; *procedimiento rutinario* routine procedure || unimaginative (persona).

ruzafa *f* garden (jardín de recreo).

S

s *f* s (letra); *una s mayúscula, minúscula* a capital, a small s.

S.A. *abrev de Sociedad Anónima* PLC, plc, Public Limited Company.

Saba *n pr* GEOGR Sheba; *la reina de Saba* the Queen of Sheba.

sábado *m* Saturday; *vendré el sábado* I shall come on Saturday; *el sábado pasado* last Saturday; *el sábado que viene* next Saturday || REL Sabbath (de los judíos) || — FIG *hacer sábado* to do the weekly cleaning || *Sábado de Gloria* or *Santo* Easter Saturday || *tener sábado inglés* to work only half a day on Saturday.

sabalera *f* fire grate (de un horno) || shad net (red).

sábalo *m* shad (pez).

sabana *f* savannah, savanna (llanura).

sábana *f* sheet (de cama); *sábana bajera, encimera* bottom, top sheet || altar cloth (del altar) || FIG sheet (de nieve, etc.) || FIG & FAM thousand-peseta note || FIG & FAM *pegársele a uno las sábanas* to oversleep; *ha llegado tarde esta mañana porque se le pegaron las sábanas* he arrived late his morning because he overslept.

sabandija *f* bug (bicho) || FIG louse, slob (persona despreciable).

sabanear *vi* AMER to round up *o* to herd cattle [on the savannah].

sabanilla *f* altar cloth (del altar).

sabañón *m* chilblain || FIG & FAM *comer como un sabañón* to eat like a horse.

sabático, ca *adj* sabbatical.

sabatino, na *adj* Saturday || REL sabbatine; *bula sabatina* sabbatine bull.

◆ *f* REL Saturday religious service || Saturday lesson (lección).

sabedor, ra *adj* informed, aware || *ser sabedor de algo* to be aware of sth., to know sth.

sabelotodo *m/f inv* FAM know-all [*US* know-it-all].

sabeo, a *adj/s* Sabaean, Sabean.

saber *m* knowledge, learning; *persona de gran saber* person of great learning || — *el saber no ocupa lugar* one never knows too much || *según mi leal saber y entender* to the best of my knowledge.

saber* *vt* to know; *saber griego, la lección* to know Greek, the lesson; *no querer saber nada* not to want to know || to know how to, to be able to; *saber leer y escribir* to know how to read and write; *no sabe nadar* he cannot swim || to be good at; *sabe muchas matemáticas* he is very good at mathematics || to learn, to find out (enterarse); *supe que habías venido* I found out that you had come || to know (conocer); *yo sé muy bien la historia de Francia* I know French history very well || — *a saber si lo que dice es verdad* I wonder if what he says is true || *cada uno sabe dónde le aprieta el zapato* everyone knows his own weaknesses, everyone knows where the shoe pinches || *¡conque ya lo sabes!* so now you know! || *¡cualquiera sabe!* it's anybody's guess || *¡de haberlo sabido antes!* if only I'd known! || *dejar a alguien sin saber qué decir* to leave s.o. speechless || *hacer saber* to inform, to let know || *¡lo sabré yo!* I ought to know!, I know better than anyone! || *lo sé* I know || *me dio no sé qué pastel* he gave me some cake or other || *no saber alguien lo que se pesca* or *dónde se mete* not to know what one is letting o.s. in for || *no saber a qué atenerse* not to know what to think *o* to believe, not to know where *o* how one stands || *no saber a qué carta quedarse* to be all at sea, to be in a dilemma || FAM *no saber a qué santo encomendarse* to be at one's wit's end, not to know where to turn || *no saber dónde meterse* not to know what to do with o.s., to wish o.s. a hundred miles away || *no saber nada de nada* not to know anything about anything || FAM *no saber ni jota* or *ni papa* or *ni pío de algo* not to know the first thing about sth., not to have a clue about sth. | *no saber por dónde se anda* not to know what one is doing | *no saber uno dónde tiene las narices* not to know left from right | *no sé cuántos* sth. or other || *para que lo sepas* let me tell you, for your information || *¿qué sé yo?* how do I know?, how should I know? || *que yo sepa* as far as I know, to my knowledge || *sabe Dios* God only knows || *sabe Dios si* God knows if || FAM *sabe más que Lepe* he's got no flies on him, he's nobody's fool || FIG *saber al dedillo* or *de corrido* or *de carrerilla* to have at one's fingertips, to know by heart, to know backwards | *saber algo como el Padre Nuestro* to know sth. backwards *o* by heart *o* backwards and forwards | *saber algo de buena tinta* to have sth. on good authority, to get sth. straight from the horse's mouth || FAM *saber arreglárselas* to be able to look after o.s., to know what one is doing | *saber cuántas son cinco* to know what's what || *saber de fijo* or *a punto fijo* to know for sure *o* for certain || *saber de memoria* to know by heart || *saber de sobra que...* to know only too well that... || *saber ir a un sitio* to know the way to a place, to know how to get to a place || *saber lo que se quiere* to know one's own mind || FAM *saber más de la cuenta* to know too much || *saber mucho* or *un rato de* to know a lot aboutFAM *se las sabe todas* he is nobody's fool, he knows all the tricks || *¡si lo sabré!* I should know!, I ought to know! || *sin saberlo yo (tú, etc.)* without my (your, etc.) knowledge, without my (your, etc.) knowing it || *te lo haré saber cuanto antes* I'll let you know as soon as possible || *¿tú qué sabes?* what do you know? || *un no sé qué* a certain sth. || FAM *van a saber quién soy yo* they're going to hear from me | *¡vete a saber!* who knows!, your guess is as good as mine || *¡vete a saber lo que ha hecho!* goodness knows what he has done! || *¡ya lo sabía yo!* that's what I thought!, I thought as much! || *¿yo qué sé?* how am I supposed to know?, how should I know? || *¡y qué sé yo!* and how should I know!

◆ *vi* to know || to taste (tener sabor) || — *a saber* namely, that is, that is to say || *queda por saber* it remains to be seen; *queda por saber si vendrá o no* it remains to be seen whether he will come or not || *¿quién sabe?* who knows?, who can tell? || FAM *¿sabe?* you know? || *saber a* to taste of *o* like; *esto sabe a miel* this tastes of honey; to smack of, to be like; *los consuelos le saben a injurias* consolation is like an insult to him || *saber a gloria* to taste divine, to be delicious || *saber de* to hear from, to have news from; *hace un mes que no sé de mis padres* I haven't heard from my parents in a month; to know (of); *sé de sitios que son muy tranquilos* I know of some very quiet places || *saber mal* to taste bad; *esta sopa sabe mal* this soup tastes bad; to be embarrassing; *me sabe muy mal ir a verle después de lo que ha pasado* it is very embarrassing to go and see him after what happened; not to appreciate; *lo que has hecho me sabe muy mal* I don't appreciate what you did at all; to upset, to annoy (molestar).

◆ *vpr* to be discovered (ser descubierto) || to know (por haber estudiado), to have learned (por experiencia); *yo me sé la lección* I know the lesson, I have learnt my lesson || — *no se sabe* nobody knows || *se lo sabe todo* he knows everything || *¡sépase cuántas veces fui!* I went goodness knows how many times || *sépase que...* let it be known that... || *se puede saber si...* can you tell me if... *o* whether... || *se sabe que...* it is known that..., it is a known fact that... || *todo llega a saberse* everything comes to light in the end || *¿y se puede saber por qué?* might one ask why?

sabiamente *adv* expertly (con ciencia) || wisely, sensibly, sagely (sensatamente).

sabido, da *adj* known; *sabido es que...* it is known that... || learned, knowledgeable (que sabe mucho) || — *como es sabido* as is well known, as everyone knows (como todos lo saben), that goes without saying (no hace falta decirlo) || *de sabido* of course (por supuesto) || *es cosa sabida que...* it is well known that... || *tener sabido que...* to know (that)...

sabiduría *f* wisdom (prudencia) || knowledge, wisdom, learning (instrucción) || REL wisdom || — *la sabiduría eterna* or *increada* eternal wisdom || *Libro de la Sabiduría* Book of Wisdom.

sabiendas (a) *loc adv* knowingly, on purpose (a propósito) || knowingly, consciously (con conocimiento de causa) || *a sabiendas de que...* knowing full well that..., fully aware that...

sabihondez *f* FAM pedantry, pedantism.

sabihondo, da *adj* pedantic, know-all [*US* know-it-all].

◆ *m/f* know-all [*US* know-it-all], pedant.

sabino, na *adj/s* HIST Sabine || *el rapto de las sabinas* the rape of the Sabine women.

sabio, bia *adj* learned (que posee sabiduría) || wise, sensible (prudente) || trained (animal); *perro sabio* trained dog || FIG & FAM know-all [*US* know-it-all] (pedante).

◆ *m/f* learned man, learned woman, learned person (que posee sabiduría) || scholar (que tiene conocimientos profundos de una disciplina) || sage (prudente) || FIG & FAM know-all [*US* know-it-all] || — *de sabios es mudar de opinión* only fools never change their minds ||

los Siete Sabios de Grecia the Seven Sages *o* Wise Men of Greece.

sabiondo, da *adj* ⟶ **sabihondo.**

sablazo *m* blow with a sabre (golpe) ‖ sabre wound (herida) ‖ FIG & FAM sponging, cadging, scrounging ‖ FIG & FAM *dar un sablazo a uno* to cadge *o* to scrounge money off s.o., to tap s.o. (pedir dinero).

sable *m* sabre [US saber] (arma); *desenvainar el sable* to draw *o* to unsheathe one's sabre ‖ HERÁLD sable (negro) ‖ FIG sponging, cadging, scrounging (arte de sacar dinero) ‖ *tirar el sable* to fence (esgrima).

sableador, ra *m/f* FAM sponger, cadger, scrounger.

sablear *vi* FAM to sponge, to cadge, to scrounge (pedir dinero prestado).

sablista *adj* FAM sponging, cadging, scrounging.
◆ *m/f* FAM sponger, cadger, scrounger.

saboneta *f* hunter [watch].

sabor *m* taste, flavour [US flavor], savour [US savor] (p us); *un sabor a naranja* an orange flavour ‖ FIG flavour; *un poema de sabor clásico* a poem with a classical flavour ‖ — *con sabor a naranja* orange-flavoured ‖ *mal sabor de boca* bad taste in one's mouth (alimento, mala impresión) ‖ FIG *sabor local* local colour | *sin sabor* flat, dull, insipid, tasteless.
◆ *pl* beads (del bocado del caballo).

saborcillo *m* slight taste.

saborear *vt* to taste (percibir el sabor) ‖ to flavour (dar sabor) ‖ FIG to savour, to relish (apreciar).
◆ *vpr* to relish, to savour (deleitarse) ‖ FIG to relish, to savour.

saboreo *m* savouring [US savoring].

sabotaje *m* sabotage.

saboteador, ra *m/f* saboteur.

sabotear *vt* to sabotage.

Saboya *npr f* GEOGR Savoy.

saboyano, na *adj/s* Savoyard.

sabroso, sa *adj* delicious, tasty, savoury ‖ FIG pleasant, delightful | meaty (libro) | racy; *una broma sabrosa* a racy joke.

sabuco *m* BOT elder (saúco).

sabueso, sa *adj/s* *perro sabueso* bloodhound.
◆ *m* FIG detective, sleuth (investigador).

saburra *f* fur (en la lengua).

saburral; saburroso, sa *adj* MED coated, furry (lengua).

saca *f* taking out, withdrawal, removal (efecto de sacar) ‖ big sack (costal) ‖ mailbag (del correo) ‖ COM export | supply, stock (de efectos estancados) ‖ authorized copy *o* duplicate (de un documento) ‖ group of prisoners executed in reprisal.

sacabala *f* bullet-extracting forceps.

sacabalas *m inv* worm (para armas de fuego).

sacabocados *m inv* punch.

sacabotas *m inv* bootjack.

sacabrocas *m inv* nail puller, pincers *pl* (de zapatero).

sacabuche *m* MÚS sackbut.

sacaclavos *m inv* nail puller, pincers *pl.*

sacacorchos *m inv* corkscrew.

sacacuartos *m inv* ⟶ **sacadinero.**

sacadinero *m*; **sacadineros** *m inv*; **sacacuartos** *m inv*; **sacaperras** *m inv* bauble (bisutería) ‖ swindle, fiddle (espectáculo sin valor).
◆ *m/f* sponger, cadger, scrounger (sablista) | swindler (estafador).

sacador, ra *adj* pulling, extracting (que saca).
◆ *m/f* person who pulls *o* extracts, remover (que saca) ‖ server (tenis).

sacaliña *f* pointed stick, goad (garrocha) ‖ FIG cunning (socaliña).

sacamanchas *m inv* stain remover, spot remover (quitamanchas).

sacamantecas *m inv* FAM ripper, criminal who cuts open his victims.

sacamuelas *m/f inv* FAM dentist (dentista).
◆ *m inv* charlatan (vendedor) ‖ chatterbox (hablador) ‖ *mentir más que un sacamuelas* to lie through one's teeth.

sacaperras *m inv* ⟶ **sacadinero.**

sacapuntas *m inv* pencil sharpener.

sacar *vt/vi* to stick out (la lengua, el pecho, etc.), to get out, to take out; *sacar un pañuelo del bolsillo* to take a handkerchief out of one's pocket ‖ to pull out, to extract, to take out; *sacar un diente* to pull a tooth out ‖ to draw; *sacó la pistola* he drew his gun; *sacar la espada* to draw one's sword; *sacar agua* to draw water ‖ to draw (out); *sacar una papeleta* to draw (out) a slip of paper ‖ to remove, to take out; *sacar un armario de un cuarto* to remove a wardrobe from a room ‖ to remove, to get out *o* off; *sacar una mancha* to remove a stain ‖ to put out (un ojo) ‖ to remove, to take off (suprimir); *saqué dos nombres de la lista* I took two names off the list ‖ to get, to obtain; *ha sacado mucho dinero de sus cuadros* he has got a lot of money from his paintings; *ha sacado el pasaporte en Madrid* he got his passport in Madrid; *sacar un buen número en la lotería* to get a winning number in the lottery ‖ to get, to win (un premio) ‖ to get (una entrada, un billete) ‖ to take out; *le han sacado del colegio para las vacaciones* they have taken him out of school for the holidays ‖ to bring out (nuevo modelo) ‖ to take (muestras) ‖ to make (hacer); *sacar fichas* to make file cards ‖ to set, to start (una moda) ‖ to win, to obtain, to get; *sacar la mayoría en las elecciones* to win a majority in the elections ‖ to take; *una película sacada de una novela* a film taken from a novel ‖ to deduce, to conclude (deducir) ‖ to extract (extraer); *el azúcar se saca de la remolacha* sugar is extracted from sugar beet ‖ to show (enseñar); *sacar los dientes* to show one's teeth; *¿me puede sacar ese abrigo negro?* would you show me that black coat? ‖ to give (un apodo) ‖ to find (encontrar); *el profesor sacó tres faltas en el dictado* the teacher found three mistakes in the dictation ‖ to reach, to find, to get (respuesta, solución) ‖ to solve (un problema) ‖ to take out, to withdraw, to draw; *sacar dinero del banco* to withdraw money from the bank ‖ to get out; *sacar de prisión* to get out of prison ‖ FOT to take; *me sacó una foto* he took a photograph of me; *sacar fotografías* to take photographs | to have made, to make (una copia) ‖ MAT to extract, to find (una raíz cuadrada) ‖ to take out; *tienes que sacar a tu hermana más, la pobrecita se aburre* you should take your sister out more, the poor girl gets bored ‖ COM to produce, to turn out (producir) ‖ FIG to get out; *no se le puede sacar una palabra* you can't get a word out of him | to come out with; *siempre nos saca la historia de su vida* he always comes out with the story of his life | to mention, to bring up (mencionar) | to draw; *saqué fuerzas de flaqueza* I drew strenght from nowhere | to let out (en costura) | to make, to form; *del grupo de chicos sacaron dos equipos* they formed two teams from the group of boys ‖ MIN & QUÍM to extract (extraer) ‖ DEP to serve (tenis) | to throw in [to play] (desde la banda), to kick off (desde el centro), to take a goal kick (de la puerta), to clear (despejar), to take (un córner) (fútbol) ‖ — FAM *a mí me saca medio metro* he's half a metre taller than me ‖ *sacar a bailar* to ask to dance ‖ *sacar a colación* to bring up, to mention ‖ *sacar adelante* to give a good education to, to bring up well; *el padre sacó adelante a sus diez hijos* the father gave a good education to his ten children; to make prosper (un negocio) ‖ *sacar a flote* to refloat, to set afloat (un barco), to put on its feet (un negocio) ‖ *sacar a la venta* to put on sale *o* up for sale ‖ *sacar a la vergüenza pública* to put to public shame ‖ *sacar algo a* or *por suerte* to draw (lots) for sth. ‖ *sacar a luz* to publish (publicar), to bring to light (descubrir), to throw light on (dar aclaraciones sobre) ‖ *sacar a pasear a uno* to take s.o. for a walk ‖ *sacar apuntes* or *datos* to take notes ‖ *sacar a relucir* to bring out (poner en relieve), to bring up (mencionar); *siempre saca a relucir todos los favores que me ha hecho* he always brings up all the favours he has done me ‖ *sacar a subasta* to put up for auction ‖ *sacar a uno de sus costumbres* to make s.o. change his ways, to change s.o.'s ways ‖ *sacar brillo a los zapatos* to polish *o* to shine one's shoes ‖ *sacar cuartos* to make money; *sólo le interesa sacar cuartos* he is only interested in making money; to get money (*a* out of) (obtener dinero) ‖ *sacar de banda* to throw in, to take a throw-in (fútbol) ‖ *sacar defectos a todos* to find fault with *o* faults in everyone ‖ FIG *sacar del arroyo a uno* to drag s.o. from the gutter ‖ *sacar del olvido* to rescue from oblivion ‖ *sacar de mentira verdad* to lie in order to get at the truth ‖ *sacar de pila a uno* to be s.o.'s godparent ‖ *sacar de pobre* to save from poverty ‖ *sacar de puerta* to take a goal kick (fútbol) ‖ FIG *sacar de raíz* to pull up by the roots (plantas), to wipe out, to eradicate, to uproot (acabar con) | *sacar de sí a uno* to infuriate s.o., to make s.o. mad *o* furious | *sacar de un mal paso a uno* to get s.o. out of a fix, to help s.o. out ‖ *sacar el cuello* to stretch one's neck ‖ *sacar el dobladillo* to let the hem down *o* out ‖ FIG *sacar el jugo a uno* to bleed s.o. dry *o* white ‖ *sacar en claro* or *en limpio de* to get out of, to solve; *hablé con él pero no saqué nada en claro* I talked with him but got nothing out of him *o* but solved nothing; to clear up (aclarar) ‖ *sacar en* or *a hombros a uno* to carry s.o. shoulder-high *o* on one's shoulders ‖ *sacar la conclusión de que...* to come to the conclusion that... (llegar a la conclusión), to draw the conclusion that... (inferir) ‖ *sacar la mano* to put one's hand out ‖ *sacar la verdad a uno* to get the truth from *o* out ot s.o. ‖ *sacarle a uno una idea de la cabeza* or *del magín* to get an idea out of s.o.'s head ‖ FIG *sacar los colores a la cara de alguien* to make s.o. blush | *sacar los pies del plato* to overstep the mark (ir demasiado lejos), to come out of one's shell (dejar de ser tímido) ‖ *sacar pajas* to draw straws ‖ FIG *sacar punta a* to find fault with (criticar) ‖ *sacar punta a un lápiz* to sharpen a pencil ‖ MED *sacar sangre* to take *o* to draw blood ‖ *sacar una buena media* to have a good average; *sacar una buena, mala nota* to get a good, bad mark ‖ *sacar una conclusión* to draw a conclusion ‖ *sacar un beneficio de* to profit by ‖ *sacar veinte metros de ventaja* to be twenty metres ahead (un corredor).
◆ *vpr* to take off; *sácate los zapatos* take off your shoes ‖ to have taken; *me he sacado una foto en casa del fotógrafo* I had a photograph of myself taken at the photographer's.

sacarífero, ra *adj* sacchariferous.

sacarificación *f* QUÍM saccharification.

sacarificar *vt* QUÍM to saccharify.

sacarímetro *m* QUÍM saccharimeter, saccharometer.

sacarino, na *adj* saccharine.
◆ *f* QUÍM saccharin.

sacaroideo, a *adj* saccharoid.

sacaromicetos *m pl* saccharomyces.

sacarosa *f* QUÍM saccharose, sucrose.

sacatacos *m inv* worm (de una escopeta).

sacatrapos *m inv* MIL worm.

sacerdocio *m* priesthood.

sacerdotal *adj* sacerdotal, priestly.

sacerdote *m* priest; *sumo sacerdote* high priest.

sacerdotisa *f* priestess.

saciar *vt* to satiate, to sate, to satisfy (hartar) || FIG to satiate, to satisfy one's desire for; *saciar su venganza* to satisfy one's desire for vengeance || *saciar la sed* to quench *o* to slake one's thirst.
◆ *vpr* to satiate o.s. (hartarse) || FIG to be satisfied; *saciarse con poco* to be satisfied with little || *saciarse de sangre* to slake one's thirst for blood.

saciedad *f* satiety, satiation || — *comer, beber hasta la saciedad* to eat, to drink one's fill || *repetir algo hasta la saciedad* to say sth. over and over again.

saco *m* sack, bag (costal) || sack, bag, sackful, bagful (contenido) || smock, coarse dress (vestidura) || sack, plunder, pillage (saqueo) || ANAT sac || MAR bight (ensenada) || AMER jacket (chaqueta) | handbag, bag [US pocketbook] (bolso) || — FIG *caer en saco roto* to go in one ear and out the other, to fall upon deaf ears || *carrera de sacos* sack race || *entrar a saco* to pillage, to plunder, to sack || *la avaricia rompe el saco* a rich man and his money are soon parted || FIG *no echar una cosa en saco roto* to take good note of sth. || *saco de dormir* sleeping bag || FIG *saco de huesos* bag of bones | *saco de malicias* or *de prestidigitador* bag of tricks | *saco de mentiras* pack of lies || *saco de noche* or *de viaje* overnight bag || FIG *saco roto* spendthrift (manirroto) || MIL *saco terrero* or *de arena* sandbag || FIG *tenía dinero a sacos* he had bags of money *o* stacks of money | *vaciaron el saco* they got it out of their system.

sacramentado, da *adj* having received the Extreme Unction *o* the last sacraments (con el viático) || consecrated (la hostia) || — *Jesús sacramentado* the Host || *ser sacramentado* to receive the Extreme Unction *o* the last sacraments.

sacramental *adj* sacramental || — *auto sacramental* «auto sacramental», mystery play || *especies sacramentales* Eucharistic species || *palabras sacramentales* ritual words.
◆ *m* sacramental.
◆ *f* brotherhood devoted to the worship of the sacrament || *la Sacramental de San Isidro* the Cementery of the Brotherhood of Saint Isidorus [in Madrid].

sacramentar *vt* to administer the last sacraments *o* the Extreme Unction to || to consecrate (la hostia).

sacramentario *m* REL sacramentarian.

sacramento *m* REL sacrament; *administrar los últimos sacramentos* to administer the last sacraments || — *el sacramento del altar* the Eucharist || *El Santísimo Sacramento* the Blessed Sacrament || *recibir los sacramentos* to receive the last sacraments.

sacrificable *adj* sacrificeable.

sacrificadero *m* sacrificial altar.

sacrificado, da *adj* sacrificed || self-sacrificing; *es una persona muy sacrificada* he is a very self-sacrificing person || COM *vender a un precio sacrificado* to sacrifice, to sell at a sacrificial price.

sacrificador, ra *m/f* sacrificer.

sacrificar *vt* to sacrifice || to slaughter (una res para el consumo).
◆ *vpr* to sacrifice o.s.; *sacrificarse por uno* to sacrifice o.s. for s.o.

sacrificatorio, ria *adj* sacrificial.

sacrificio *m* sacrifice || slaughter (de una res) || *ofrecer un sacrificio* to offer *o* to make a sacrifice, to sacrifice; *ofrecer un sacrificio a los dioses* to make a sacrifice to the gods.

sacrilegio *m* sacrilege.

sacrílego, ga *adj* sacrilegious.
◆ *m/f* sacrilegious person, sacrilegist (ant).

sacrismoche; sacrismocho *m* FAM poor man dressed in black (hombre vestido de negro).

sacristán *m* sacristan, verger, sexton.

sacristana *f* sacristan's *o* verger's *o* sexton's wife (mujer del sacristán) || vestry nun (religiosa).

sacristanía *f* office of sexton *o* verger *o* sacristan.

sacristía *f* sacristy, vestry (en las iglesias) || office of sacristan *o* verger *o* sexton (sacristanía).

sacro, cra *adj* sacred; *la vía sacra* to Sacred Way || holy; *Sacra Familia* Holy Family || ANAT sacral (del sacro) || — REL *el Sacro Colegio* the Sacred College, the College of Cardinals || *el Sacro Imperio Romano* the Holy Roman Empire || *fuego sacro* sacred fire || *historia sacra* sacred history, Bible history || ANAT *hueso sacro* sacrum || *música sacra* sacred music.
◆ *m* ANAT sacrum.

sacroilíaco, ca *adj* ANAT sacroiliac.

sacrosanto, ta *adj* sacrosanct.

sacudida *f* shake, shaking (agitación) || shake, jolt, jerk (movimiento brusco) || jolt, jerk (de un vehículo) || shock, tremor (de un terremoto) || jerk, toss (de la cabeza) || FIG shock (emoción fuerte) | upheaval (en la política) || FIG & FAM good hiding, beating (paliza); *darle una sacudida a su hijo* to give one's son a good hiding || — *avanzar dando sacudidas* to jolt *o* to bump *o* to jerk along || *dar una sacudida a una alfombra* to beat a carpet || *sacudida eléctrica* electric shock.

sacudido, da *adj* shaken (movido) || FIG surly, ill-disposed; *un muchacho sacudido* a surly boy | self-assured (desenvuelto) || FIG *está más sacudido que una estera* he is completely shameless.

sacudidor, ra *adj* shaking, beating.
◆ *m* whisk, beater (instrumento para sacudir las alfombras, etc.).

sacudimiento *m* shaking, shake, jolt (sacudida) || MED succussion.

sacudir *vt* to shake (agitando) || to beat (dando golpes); *sacudir una alfombra* to beat a carpet || to jerk, to tug (una cuerda) || to toss, to shake (la cabeza) || to wag (la cola) || to jolt (coche, tren) || to chase away (ahuyentar) || FIG to give; *sacudir una bofetada, una paliza* to give a slap in the face, a beating | to beat, to spank (a un niño) | to beat up (dar una paliza) | to scold (reñir) | to shake (conmocionar) || — *sacudir el polvo* to shake off the dust, to dust (traje), to dust (muebles), to tan s.o.'s hide, to give s.o. a beating (dar una paliza) || FIG *sacudir el yugo* to throw off the yoke || FAM *sacudir la mosca* to fork out, to cough up, to pay up (pagar) || FIG *sacudir los nervios* to shatter s.o.'s nerves.
◆ *vpr* to shake, to shake o.s. || FIG to shake off, to get rid of; *se sacudió de su amigo fácilmente* he shook off his friend easily || FAM to fork out, to cough up, to pay up (dinero); *¡sacúdase!* cough up!

sachar *vt* to weed.

sádico, ca *adj* sadistic.
◆ *m/f* sadist.

sadismo *m* sadism.

saduceo, a *adj* Sadducean.
◆ *m/f* Sadducee.

saeta *f* arrow (grande), dart (pequeña) (arma) || hand [of a watch] (manecilla) || magnetic needle (brújula) || religious song, «saeta» (copla).
— OBSERV The *saeta* is a short and fervent prayer of popular origin that is sung at the passing of a procession, especially in Andalusia, during Holy Week.

saetada *f*; **saetazo** *m* shot from a bow, arrow shot (disparo) || arrow wound (herida).

saetear *vt* to shoot an arrow at (asaetear).

saetera *f* loophole (aspillera) || FIG narrow window (ventanilla).

saetero *m* archer, bowman (soldado).

saetilla *f* dart, small arrow (saeta pequeña) || hand [of a watch] (manecilla) || BOT sagittaria, arrowhead.

saetín *m* millcourse, millrace (de molino) || brad, tack (clavito).

safari *m* safari (cacería); *está de safari* he is on safari.

safena *adj f* ANAT saphenous; *vena safena* saphenous vein.
◆ *f* ANAT saphena.

sáfico, ca *adj/sm* sapphic; *verso sáfico* sapphic verse || *poesía sáfica* sapphics, sapphic verse.

Safo *npr f* Sappho.

saga *f* sorceress, witch (bruja) || saga (leyenda escandinava).

sagacidad *f* sagacity (perspicacia) || astuteness, shrewdness (astucia).

sagaz *adj* sagacious (perspicaz) || astute, shrewd (astuto).

sagitario *m* archer, bowman (saetero) || ASTR Sagittarius (constelación y signo del zodiaco).

sagrado, da *adj* sacred, holy, consecrated (dedicado a Dios) || holy; *Sagrada Familia* Holy Family; *Sagrada Comunión* Holy Communion || — *fuego sagrado* sacred fire || *historia sagrada* sacred history, Bible history || *Sagrada Escritura* Holy Scripture || *Sagrado Corazón* Sacred Heart.
◆ *m* asylum, sanctuary, place of refuge (asilo) || — *acogerse a sagrado* to take holy sanctuary || *estar acogido a sagrado* to be given sanctuary *o* asylum.

sagrario *m* shrine, sanctuary (parte del templo) || tabernacle (para el santísimo) || chapel that serves as a parish church in some cathedrals.

saguntino, na *adj/s* Saguntine.

Sagunto *n pr* GEOGR Sagunto.

Sáhara; Sahara *npr m* GEOGR Sahara.

saharaui *adj/n* Saharan.

sahariana *f* bush shirt *o* jacket.

sahariano, na *adj/s* Saharan, Saharian.

sahino *m* ZOOL peccary, Mexican hog.

sahornarse *vpr* to get chafed *o* sore.

sahumadura *f*; **sahumerio** *m* perfuming with incense || aromatic smoke (humo) || aromatic substance (sustancia aromática).

sahumar *vt* to perfume with incense.

sahumerio *m* —› **sahumadura.**

saimirí *m* ZOOL squirrel monkey (mono).

saín *m* animal fat, fat (grasa).

sainete *m* TEATR short comedy, one-act farce (pieza jocosa y corta) | curtain raiser (que se representa al principio de las funciones teatrales) || titbit, choice morsel (bocadillo sabroso).

sainetear *vi* to act in farces.

sainetero; sainetista *m* writer of farces.

sainetesco, ca *adj* farcical, burlesque.

saíno *m* ZOOL peccary, Mexican hog.

sajadura *f* MED incision.

sajar *vt* MED to lance (un absceso, etc.) | to make an incision in, to cut open (abrir).

sajón, ona *adj/s* Saxon.

Sajonia *npr f* GEOGR Saxony || *Baja Sajonia* Lower Saxony.

sajú *m* ZOOL sapajou (mono).

sajuriana *f* AMER traditional Peruvian dance.

sakí *m* ZOOL saki (mono) || sake, saki (bebida).

sal *f* salt; *una pizca de sal* a pinch of salt; *sal marina* sea salt; *sal gema* or *pedrés* rock salt || FIG wit, spice (gracia) | charm, liveliness (encanto) || — FIG *con su sal y pimienta* with a lot of wit || FIG & FAM *echar en sal una cosa* to put sth. on ice | *echarle sal en la mollera a uno* to quieten s.o. down || *echar sal a* to salt || FIG *la sal de la tierra* the salt of the earth | *la sal de la vida* the spice of life || QUÍM *sal amoniaco* or *amoniaca* salammoniac || *sal común* common salt || *sal de frutas* fruit salts || *sal de la Higuera* Epsom salts, liver salts || *sal de mesa* table salt || *sal de plomo* or *de Saturno* lead acetate || *sal morena* or *de cocina* kitchen salt, cooking salt || FIG *tener mucha sal* to be great fun (persona), to be very funny (chiste).
◆ *pl* smelling salts (para reanimar) || salts; *sales de baño* bath salts.

sala *f* room (cuarto); *sala de comisiones* committee room || large room (cuarto grande) || living room, sitting room, lounge (sala de estar) || house (de un teatro) || ward (en un hospital) || JUR court (tribunal); *sala de lo criminal* criminal court || — *deporte en sala* indoor sport || *sala capitular* chapter house || JUR *sala de apelación, de justicia* court of appeal, of justice || *sala de batalla* sorting room (en correos) || *sala de clase* classroom || *sala de conferencias* lecture theatre *o* room, lecture hall (en una universidad), conference room, conference hall (para reuniones) || *sala de espectáculos* theatre [U. S., theater]; cinema || *sala de espera* waiting room || *sala de estar* living room, sitting room, lounge || *sala de estreno* first-run cinema [US first-run picture theater] (cine) || *sala de exposición* showroom || *sala de fiestas* ballroom, dance hall (de baile), reception hall (en un ayuntamiento), nightclub, cabaret (con espectáculo) || *sala del consejo* or *de la junta* boardroom || *sala de lectura* reading room || *sala del trono* throne room || *sala de máquinas* engine room || *sala de prevención* guardroom || *sala de recibir* drawing room || *sala de subastas* auction room.

salacidad *f* salaciousness, prurience.

salacot *m* topee, topi (casco).

saladar *m* salt marsh (marismas) || salt meadow (terreno).

saladería *f* meat-salting industry.

saladero *m* salting tub (lugar para salar) || salting factory (casa para salar) || «salting tub», former prison in Madrid (cárcel) || AMER slaughterhouse that salts its meat.

saladillo *adj m* *tocino saladillo* half-salted bacon.

salado, da *adj* CULIN salt, salted, salty (carne, etc.) | salty; *demasiado salado* too salty || salt (agua) || FIG witty, funny (gracioso) | spirited, sharp (ingenioso) | darling, cute, lovely; *tiene dos niños muy salados* she has two lovely children | winsome, attractive, charming (atractivo) || AMER unfortunate (desgraciado).

salador, ra *m/f* salter.
◆ *m* salting tub (sitio).

saladura *f* salting.

salamanca *f* ZOOL salamander (salamandra) | small lizard (lagartija).

Salamanca *n pr* GEOGR Salamanca.

salamandra *f* ZOOL salamander || salamander stove (calorífero) || *salamandra acuática* newt, triton.

salamanqués, esa *adj* [of *o* from] Salamanca.
◆ *m/f* native *o* inhabitant of Salamanca.

salamanquesa *f* gecko (lagarto).

salamanquino, na *adj* [of *o* from] Salamanca.
◆ *m/f* native *o* inhabitant of Salamanca.
◆ *f* AMER lizard (lagartija).

salame *m* AMER salami (salchichón).

salar *m* AMER salt marsh.

salar *vt* CULIN to salt (para sazonar o conservar) || AMER to dishonour (deshonrar) | to spoil (echar a perder) | to bring bad luck to (causar mala suerte a).

salarial *adj* wage, salary; *incremento salarial* wage increase.

salariar *vt* to pay a wage *o* a salary to (asalariar).

salario *m* wages *pl*, wage, pay, salary; *deducir del salario* to deduct from one's wages || — *fijación de salarios máximos* fixing of maximum wage || *salario a destajo* piece rate || *salario base* or *básico* basic wage || *salario colectivo* collective wage || *salario de convenio colectivo* conventional wage || *salario de hambre* starvation wages || *salario mínimo* minimum wage || *salario por hora* hourly rate || *salario por unidad de tiempo* wage *o* rate per unit of time || *salario tope* or *máximo* top *o* maximum wage.

salaz *adj* salacious, prurient.

salazón *f* salting (acción) || salting industry (industria).
◆ *pl* salted meat *sing* (carne salada) || salted fish *sing* (pescado salado).

salceda *f*; **salcedo** *m* willow grove.

salcochar *vt* to boil in salt water.

salchicha *f* pork sausage.

salchichero, ra *m/f* pork butcher.

salchichón *m* highly-seasoned sausage (embutido).

saldar *vt* to liquidate, to pay, to settle (una cuenta) || to sell off (vender a bajo precio) || FIG to settle (divergencias) || *el accidente se saldó con 10 muertos* the death toll of the accident rose to 10 || FIG *saldar una cuenta* to pay s.o. back, to get even with s.o.

saldista *m* dealer in clearance lines.

saldo *m* COM balance; *saldo acreedor, deudor* credit, debit balance; *saldo a favor* or *positivo* favourable balance; *saldo en contra* or *negativo* adverse balance, overdraft || (bargain) sale (liquidación de mercancías) || liquidation, settlement, payment (pago); *saldo de una cuenta* settlement of an account || FIG remnant, leftover (cosa de poco valor).

saledizo, za *adj* projecting.
◆ *m* ARQ projection (parte que sobresale) | ledge (en un muro) | corbelling, overhang (balcón, etc.) || *en saledizo* projecting.

salero *m* saltcellar (para echar sal) || salt warehouse (almacén) || TECN salt mine || FIG & FAM charm, allure (en una mujer); *esa chica tiene mucho salero* that girl has a lot of charm | elegance (elegancia) | wit (ingenio) || *un actor con mucho salero* a very funny *o* witty actor.

saleroso, sa *adj* FIG & FAM charming, winsome; *chica salerosa* charming girl | funny, amusing, witty (divertido).

salesa *f* nun of the Order of the Visitation || *las Salesas* the Law Courts [in Madrid].

salesiano, na *adj/s* REL Salesian.

saleta *f* court of appeal (sala de apelación) || royal antechamber (antecámara).

salicilato *m* QUÍM salicylate.

salicílico, ca *adj* QUÍM salicylic.

sálico, ca *adj* Salic; *ley sálica* Salic law.

salicor *m* BOT saltwort.

salida *f* departure, leaving (partida); *a su salida de Madrid* on his leaving Madrid, on his departure from Madrid || departure; *la salida del tren* the departure of the train, the train's departure || exit, way out (puerta) || leak (de gas, de líquido) || projection (parte saliente) || rising (de un astro) || publication (de un libro, una revista) || appearance (de un periódico) || lead (en juegos de cartas) || FIG way out (medio) | excuse (pretexto) | loophole (escapatoria) | opening; *los licenciados en ciencias tienen muchas salidas* there are many openings for science graduates | way out, solution (solución); *no veo salida a este problema* I can't see any way out of *o* any solution to this problem | outcome, result (resultado) || FAM witticism, witty remark (ocurrencia) | comeback, repartee (réplica) || AVIAC recovery (después de un picado) || COM production, output (producción) | sale (venta) | outlet, market (posibilidad de venta); *encontrar salida para un producto* to find an outlet *o* a market for a product | shipment (transporte de mercancías) | debit (de una cuenta) | outlay (dinero gastado) || DEP start; *salida lanzada, parada* flying, standing start || TECN outlet, vent (orificio de salida) || MIL sortie, sally || TEATR entrance [of an actor]; *salida a escena* entrance on stage || INFORM output (de datos) || — *a la salida del cine* coming out of the cinema || *calle sin salida* cul-de-sac, dead-end street || *dar la salida* to give the starting signal || COM *dar salida a* to sell, to find an outlet *o* a market for; *hemos dado salida a todas nuestras existencias* we have sold all our stocks || *de salida* from the start, to begin with || *dio salida a su cólera* he gave vent to his anger || DEP *línea de salida* starting line || FIG *no tengo otra salida que aceptar su propuesta* I have no option but to accept his proposal | *prepararse una salida* to arrange a way out for o.s. || *salida de artistas* stage door || *salida de baño* bathrobe (para casa), beach robe (para la playa) || *salida de caja* debit || *salida de divisas* outflow of currency || *salida de emergencia* or *de incendio* emergency *o* fire exit || *salida del cascarón* or *del huevo* hatching || *salida del Sol* sunrise || FAM *salida de pata de banco* clanger || *salida de tono* improper remark (observación inoportuna), silly remark (tontería) || DEP *salida nula* false start || *tener salida* to come out (acabar); *una calle que tiene salida a* a street that comes out on to; to open; *la casa tiene salida al bulevar* the house opens on to the boulevard; to have an outlet; *un país que no tiene salida al mar* a country which has no outlet to the sea; to sell well (mercancías) || FIG *tener salida para todo* to have an answer to everything.

salidizo *m* ARQ ⟶ **saledizo.**

salido, da *adj* bulging (ojos) || prominent (frente, mentón, etc.) || projecting (que sobresale) || on heat (animales).

saliente *adj* ARQ projecting, overhanging || rising (Sol) || retiring, outgoing (que abandona sus funciones) || FIG salient (importante) | outstanding (persona) || — *ángulo saliente* salient angle || MIL *guardia saliente* retiring *o* outgoing guard.
◆ *m* (p us) east (oriente) || projection, overhang, ledge (parte que sobresale) || peak (pico) || MIL salient.

salífero, ra *adj* GEOL saliferous.

salificación *f* QUÍM salification.

salificar *vt* QUÍM to salify.
◆ *vpr* QUÍM to salify.

salina *f* salt mine.
◆ *pl* saltworks, saltern *sing*.

salinero *m* salter, salt merchant.

salinero, ra *adj* salt; *industria salinera* salt industry || with red and white spots (un toro).

salinidad *f* salinity.

salino, na *adj* saline.

salio, lia *adj/s* HIST Salian.

salir* *vi* to leave; *para llegar a tiempo tendremos que salir a las cinco* to get there on time we will have to leave at five o'clock; *el tren salió de la estación* the train left the station; *el rápido sale a las dos* the express leaves at two || to depart, to leave; *el tren para París sale de la estación de Chamartín* the Paris train departs from Chamartin station *o* leaves from Chamartin station || to go out; *salir de casa* to go out of the house; *salir a la calle* to go out into the street; *salir con amigos* to go out with friends || to come out; *si no sales en seguida entro yo* if you don't come out at once I'm coming in || to be out (no estar); *la señora ha salido* madam is out || to go; *salir de viaje* to go on a trip || to get out; *el pájaro no puede salir de su jaula* the bird can't get out of its cage || to appear; *le gusta mucho salir en los periódicos, en la televisión* he likes to appear in the newspapers, on television || to rise, to come up *o* out (un astro) || to come up (vegetales) || to come out (flores) || to grow (crecer el pelo) || to stick out, to project, to jut out (relieve) || to come out, to be published (publicarse); *¿cuándo salió su última novela?* when did his last novel come out? || to come in; *acaba de salir una nueva moda* a new fashion has just come in || to be raised, to speak *o* to come out; *una voz salió en su defensa* a voice spoke out in his defence || to spring (aparecer inesperadamente); *¿de dónde sales?* where have you sprung from? || to start, to make the first move (juegos) || to open (al principio de un juego de cartas), to lead (después de una baza) || to come up, to be drawn (en la lotería) || to be elected (ser elegido) || to come out *o* off (una mancha) || DEP to start (corredores) || TEATR to enter, to come on (un actor) || MAR to sail || FIG to get over, to get out of; *por fin hemos salido de ésta* we have finally got out of that | to turn out (to be); *salió muy inteligente* he turned out (to be) very intelligent; *el melón salió muy sabroso* the melon turned out very tasty | to go, to turn out; *¿cómo le salió el examen?* how did his exam go? | to spring to mind (ocurrírsele a uno de repente) | to be able to think of; *no me sale su apellido* I can't think of his surname | to come to light, to come out (descubrirse) | to turn up, to come up (una oportunidad); *me ha salido una colocación muy buena* a very good job has turned up for me || — *al niño le salió un diente* the baby cut a tooth || FIG *a lo que salga, a lo que saliere* trusting to luck (al buen tuntún) || *ha salido cara, cruz* it's heads, tails (echando suertes) || *me ha salido una cana* I have got a grey hair || *no conseguiré nunca salir de pobre* I'll always be poor || *no me sale este problema* I can't work this problem out || *Pedro salió airoso de la prueba* Peter passed the test with flying colours || *recién salido de la universidad* just out of university, fresh from university || *salga lo que saliere, salga lo que salga* come what may || *salir a* to take after; *el niño ha salido a su madre* the boy takes after his mother; to come to, to cost; *la comida me salió a cuarenta pesetas* the meal came to forty pesetas, the meal cost me forty pesetas; to come out into, to lead to; *la calle sale a la plaza* the street comes out into the square || FIG *salir adelante* to get on *o* by, to make out || *salir a flote* to get back on one's feet, to get out of difficulty (después de un apuro), to become solvent again, to get out of the red (*fam*) (después de una crisis financiera) || FIG *salir a la calle* to come out (publicarse) || *salir a la pizarra* to go to the blackboard || *salir a la superficie* to come *o* to float to the surface (objeto), to surface (submarino) || *salir al encuentro de* to go to meet (ir a buscar), to contradict (contradecir), to oppose, to make a stand against (oponer), to anticipate (anticiparse), to face (afrontar una dificultad) || *salir al escenario* or *a escena* to come on stage, to enter || FIG *salir al paso de* to forestall; *salir al paso de las críticas* to forestall one's critics; to waylay; *hoy Pablo me salió al paso* Paul waylayed me today; to go to meet (salir al encuentro de) || *salir a pasear* or *de paseo* to go (out) for a walk || *salir barato, caro* to be *o* to work out cheap, expensive || *salir bien* to work, to turn out well; *la estratagema le salió bien* his stratagem worked *o* turned out well; to turn out *o* to come out well; *este dibujo me ha salido bien* this picture I drew come out well; to come out well (en una foto, retrato, etc.), to come *o* to pull through well; *la operación era grave, pero el enfermo ha salido bien* the operation was serious but the patient has come through well; to come out all right (de un mal paso), to pass (de un examen), to go off well (fiesta, reunión, etc.); *la primera representación salió muy bien* the first performance went off very well || *salir bien librado* to come out unscathed to get off lightly || *salir con* to come out with (decir); *ahora sales tú con eso* and now you come out with this; to get (obtener); *ha salido con lo que quería* he has got what he wanted; to go out with [*US* to date] (los novios), to lead, to play (en juegos de cartas); *salir con el rey de espadas* to lead the king of spades; to get done (hacer); *es capaz de salir con todo el trabajo* he will probably get all the work done || FIG & FAM *salir con las orejas gachas* to come out with one's tail between one's legs || *salir de* to leave (un sitio); *al salir del trabajo lo haré* I'll do it when I leave work; to cease to be (dejar de ser); *ha salido de ministro* he has ceased to be minister; to come out as; *sale de teniente* he comes out as a lieutenant; to dispose of, to sell (vender), to come from; *el azúcar sale de la remolacha* sugar comes from sugar beet || *salir de apuros* to get out of trouble *o* out of a tight spot *o* out of a difficult situation || *salir de dudas* to shed one's doubts || *salir de la habitación* to be up and about (un enfermo) || *salir del cascarón* or *del huevo* to hatch || *salir del coma* to come out of *o* to emerge from a coma || FIG *salir del paso* to get out of trouble *o* out of the fix || *salir de madre* to overflow (un río) || FIG *salir de Málaga para entrar en Malagón* to jump out of the frying pan into the fire || FIG *salir de sus casillas* to come out of one's shell (cambiar de costumbres), to lose one's temper, to fly off the handle (enfurecerse) || *salir de una enfermedad* to get over *o* to pull through an illness || *salir de un compromiso* to break an engagement || *salir empatados* to tie, to draw || *salir en defensa de alguien, algo* to come out in defence of s.o., sth. || *salir mal* not to do very well, to do badly, to come unstuck (una persona); *me salió mal el examen* I did badly in the exam; not to work, to go wrong, to misfire; *la estratagema le salió mal* his stratagem did not work; not to be very good, not to come out very well (fotografía, dibujo, retrato, etc.), to come out badly (de un mal paso), to be a failure (ser un fracaso) || *salir mal parado* to come out the worse for wear || *salir perdiendo* to lose out, to come off worst || FAM *salir pitando* or *de estampía* to go *o* to be off like a shot *o* like a rocket || *salir para* to leave for (dirigirse a) || FIG *salir con alguien* to come to s.o.'s defence (en una contienda), to vouch for s.o. (salir fiador de) || FIG & FAM *salir por peteneras* to go off at a tangent, to say sth. completely irrelevant | *salir que ni pintado* to come out beautifully || *¡tiene a quien salir!* like father, like son! || *todavía no le ha salido novio* she still hasn't got a boyfriend.
◆ *vpr* to leak (out) (líquido); *el agua se sale por el agujero* the water is leaking out of the hole || to leak (un recipiente) || to leak, to escape; *el gas se sale* the gas is leaking | to overflow; *río que se ha salido de su cauce* river that has overflowed its banks || to leave; *salirse de un club* to leave a club || to get out; *el pájaro se salió de la jaula* the bird got out of the cage || to escape (evadirse) || to go off; *salirse de la carretera* to go off the road (un coche) || to boil over, to spill over, to overflow (rebosar); *la leche se ha salido* the milk has boiled over || to come off, to become disconnected (desconectarse) || — *no salirse de la legalidad* to keep within the law || *no se saldrá de pobre* he will always be poor || FIG *salirse con la suya* to get *o* to have one's own way; *Tomás siempre se sale con la suya* Thomas always gets his own way || *salirse de las reglas* to break the rules || *salirse de la vía* to go off *o* to leave the rails || *salirse de lo corriente* to be out of the ordinary || *salirse de los límites* to go beyond the limits || *salirse del tema* to get off the subject, to digress || *salirse de madre* to overflow (río), to lose one's self-control (enfadarse) || *salirse de tono* to make an improper remark || FIG & FAM *salirse por la tangente* to fly off *o* to go off at a tangent (hacer una digresión), to evade the issue, to dodge the question (esquivar una pregunta) || *se le salieron los colores a la cara* his face turned red, he blushed.

salitrado, da *adj* saltpetrous.

salitral *adj* saltpetrous.
◆ *m* salpetre works *pl*, nitre works *pl* (explotación) || salpetre deposit *o* bed (yacimiento).

salitre *m* saltpetre [*US* salpeter], nitre [*US* niter].

salitrería *f* saltpetre works *pl*, nitre works *pl*.

salitrero, ra *adj* saltpetrous.
◆ *m* saltpetre worker.
◆ *f* saltpetre deposit *o* bed (yacimiento).

salitroso, sa *adj* saltpetrous.

saliva *f* saliva || — FIG *estoy gastando saliva en balde* I'm wasting my breath | *tragar saliva* to swallow one's feelings, to hold one's peace.

salivación *f* salivation.

salivadera *f* AMER spittoon.

salivajo *m* spit, spittle.

salival; salivar *adj* salivary; *glándulas salivales* salivary glands.

salivar *vi* to salivate || AMER to spit (escupir).

salivazo *m* spit || *echar un salivazo* to spit.

salivoso, sa *adj* salivous.

salmanticense; salmantino, na *adj* [of *o* from] Salamanca.
◆ *m/f* native *o* inhabitant of Salamanca.

salmer *m* ARQ skewback.

salmista *m* psalmist (autor de salmos).

salmo *m* psalm; *el Libro de los Salmos* the Book of Psalms.

salmodia *f* psalmody || FAM drone (ruido monótono).

salmodiar *vi* to sing psalms || FAM to drone.

salmón *m* salmon (pez) || *cría de salmones* salmon breeding.

salmonado, da *adj* salmon-like || *trucha, trucha salmonada* salmon trout.

salmoncillo *m* samlet (pez).

salmonero, ra *adj* salmon; *escala salmonera* salmon ladder.

salmonete *m* red mullet, surmullet (pez).

salmónidos *m pl* ZOOL salmonidae.

salmuera *f* brine ‖ *salazón en salmuera* brining.

salobral *adj* saline (terreno).

salobre *adj* brackish (ligeramente salado) ‖ briny (muy salado) ‖ salty (salado).

salobreño, ña *adj* saline (tierra).

salobridad *f* saltiness, brackishness.

Salomón *npr m* Solomon.

salomónico, ca *adj* Solomonic ‖ ARQ *columna salomónica* wreathed column.

salón *m* lounge, sitting room ‖ drawing room (para recibir visitas) ‖ hall; *salón de actos* or *de reuniones* assembly hall ‖ show, exhibition (exposición); *salón del automóvil* Motor Show ‖ salon, coterie (literario, etc.) ‖ common room (de colegio, etc.) ‖ — *salón de baile* ballroom, dance hall ‖ *salón de belleza* beauty parlour ‖ *salón de conferencias* lecture room ‖ *salón de demostraciones* show-room ‖ *salón de fiestas* dance hall ‖ *salón de peluquería* hairdressing salon ‖ *salón de pintura* art gallery ‖ *salón de té* tearoom, teashop.

salpicaderas *f pl* AMER mudguard (guardabarros).

salpicadero *m* dashboard, fascia, facia (de un coche).

salpicadura *f* splashing spattering (acción) ‖ splash (de algo líquido); *salpicaduras de pintura* splashes of paint ‖ spatter (de barro).

salpicar *vt* to splash (con un líquido) ‖ to spatter (con barro) ‖ to sprinkle (rociar) ‖ to dot (con puntos) ‖ to scatter; *mesa salpicada de flores* table scattered with flowers ‖ FIG to sprinkle, to intersperse; *una conversación salpicada de chistes* a conversation sprinkled with jokes; *texto salpicado de citas* text sprinkled with quotations ‖ — *salpicado de estrellas* star-spangled ‖ *traje salpicado de motas* spotted dress.

salpicón *m* CULIN salmagundi ‖ (ant) leftover beef with onion sauce ‖ splash, spatter (salpicadura) ‖ AMER fruit juice (bebida) ‖ *salpicón de mariscos* seafood cocktail.

salpimentar* *vt* to season (sazonar) ‖ FIG to spice, to season (amenizar).

salpresar *vt* to salt down.

salpullido *m* rash (erupción) ‖ fleabite (de la pulga).

salsa *f* sauce; *salsa blanca* white sauce; *salsa tártara* tartare sauce, tartar sauce ‖ gravy (de la carne) ‖ dressing (para la lechuga) ‖ FIG sauce, appetizer; *no hay mejor salsa que el apetito* hunger is the best sauce ‖ FAM sauce, zest (salero) ‖ — FIG *cocerse en su propia salsa* to stew in one's own juice | *en su (propia) salsa* in one's element | *la salsa de la vida* the spice of life ‖ *media salsa* court bouillon ‖ *salsa bechamel* or *besamel* béchamel *o* white sauce ‖ *salsa de tomate* tomato sauce ‖ *salsa mahonesa* or *mayonesa* mayonnaise ‖ *trabar una salsa* to thicken a sauce.

salsera *f* sauceboat, gravy boat (para salsa) ‖ small saucer (salserilla).

salsereta; salserilla *f* small saucer (de pintor).

salsifí *m* BOT salsify.

salsoláceas *f pl* BOT salsolaceae.

saltabanco *m/f*; **saltabancos** *m/f inv* FIG & FAM mountebank, charlatan (que vende medicinas) ‖ tumbler, acrobat (saltimbanqui) ‖ Punch and Judy showman (titiritero).

saltabardales; saltabarrancos *m/f inv* FIG & FAM harum-scarum, scatterbrain, happy-go-lucky.

saltadero *m* jumping place ‖ jet of water (surtidor).

saltadizo, za *adj* fragile, brittle (quebradizo).

saltador, ra *adj* jumping.
◆ *m/f* jumper ‖ *saltador de pértiga* pole vaulter.
◆ *m* skipping rope (comba).

saltadura *f* chip.

saltamontes *m inv* ZOOL grasshopper.

saltaojos *m inv* BOT peony.

saltar *vi* to jump, to leap; *saltó desde la azotea* he jumped from the terrace; *saltó en el caballo* he leapt on to the horse; *saltó en la silla* he jumped up on (to) the chair ‖ to jump (en paracaídas) ‖ to fidget (brincar); *saltaba de impaciencia* he fidgeted impatiently ‖ to hop, to skip (dar saltitos) ‖ to bounce (pelota) ‖ to break (romperse) ‖ to burst (estallar) ‖ to burst, to explode (explotar) ‖ to come off, to come loose, to come out (desprenderse) ‖ to come off (un botón) ‖ to spring *o* to dash *o* to bound *o* to leap forward (salir con ímpetu) ‖ to spring, to spurt, to gush (brotar) ‖ to pop out *o* off; *el tapón ha saltado* the cork has popped out ‖ to break off, to come off (deshacerse una pieza) ‖ to fly (off) (virutas, trozos de madera) ‖ FIG to jump, to skip; *saltar de un tema a otro* to jump from one subject to another; *alumno que ha saltado de una clase a otra* pupil who jumped from one year to another | to blow up (enfadarse); *saltó al oír tales insultos* he blew up on hearing such insults ‖ — FIG *cuando* or *donde menos se piensa salta la liebre* things always happen when you least expect them to | *estar a la que salta* to be ready for the first thing that pops up ‖ *hacer saltar* to blow up (destruir), to jump (un caballo) ‖ *hacer saltar la banca* to break the bank ‖ *hacer saltar las lágrimas a uno* to bring tears to s.o.'s eyes, to make one cry ‖ *saltar a la comba* to skip ‖ FIG *saltar a la palestra* to enter the fray *o* the arena | *saltar a la vista* or *a los ojos* to be obvious, to be as plain as a pikestaff ‖ *saltar al agua* to jump into the water ‖ *saltar a tierra* to leap ashore (de un barco) ‖ *saltar con pértiga* to pole-vault ‖ FIG *saltar con una impertinencia* to come out with an impertinent remark | *saltar de alegría* to jump for *o* with joy ‖ *saltar de la cama* to leap out of bed ‖ FIG & FAM *saltar la tapa de los sesos a alguien* to blow s.o.'s brains out ‖ *saltar sobre* to pounce on ‖ *saltó y dijo* he suddenly said, he upped and said ‖ FIG & FAM *y ahora saltas tú con eso* and now you come out with that.
◆ *vt* to jump (over), to leap (over); *saltar un arroyo* to jump over a brook ‖ to jump (over), to leap (over), to vault (over); *saltar una tapia* to jump over a wall ‖ to blow up (con un explosivo) ‖ to put out (un ojo) ‖ to knock out (dientes, etc.) ‖ to pull off (arrancar) ‖ to break (romper) ‖ to jump (en el juego de damas) ‖ to cover (el macho a la hembra) ‖ FIG to jump, to skip (omitir) ‖ — FIG & FAM *saltar la tapia* to go over the wall | *saltarle la tapa de los sesos a uno* to blow s.o.'s brains out.
◆ *vpr* to skip, to jump (en un escrito, un escalafón); *me he saltado una página* I have skipped a page ‖ to miss, to skip (una comida) ‖ — FIG & FAM *saltarse algo a la torera* to completely ignore sth. | *saltarse la tapa de los sesos* to blow one's brains out (suicidarse) | *saltarse un semáforo* to jump the lights ‖ *se le saltaron las lágrimas* tears welled up in his eyes, tears came to his eyes.

saltarín, ina *adj* jumping, skipping (que salta) ‖ dancing (que baila) ‖ restless (agitado) ‖ FIG scatterbrained, harum-scarum (atolondrado).
◆ *m/f* dancer.

salteado *m* CULIN sauté.

salteador *m* highwayman, holdup man.

salteamiento *m* holdup, highway robbery (robo) ‖ assault, surprise attack (asalto).

saltear *vt* to holp up, to rob, to waylay (robar) ‖ to pounce on (atacar por sorpresa) ‖ to make less frequent, to space out (espaciar); *saltear las visitas* to make one's visits less frequent ‖ to do (sth.) in fits and starts, to skip through *o* over (sth.) (hacer algo saltándose partes) ‖ CULIN to sauté ‖ FIG to take by surprise ‖ *hilera de chopos y sauces salteados* row of alternating black poplars and willows.

salteño, ña *adj* [of *o* from] Salto (Uruguay) ‖ [of *o* from] Salta (Argentina).
◆ *m/f* native *o* inhabitant of Salto (Uruguay) ‖ native *o* inhabitant of Salta (Argentina).

salterio *m* REL psalter, psalmbook (libro) ‖ MÚS psaltery (instrumento).

saltimbanqui *m* member of a travelling circus ‖ acrobat, tumbler (acróbata).

salto *m* jump, leap, bound; *de un salto* in a bound ‖ falls *pl*, waterfall, cascade (de agua) ‖ precipice (despeñadero) ‖ unevenness (desnivel) ‖ omission (omisión) ‖ DEP jump; *salto de altura, de longitud* high, long jump | vault; *salto de* or *con pértiga,* AMER *garrocha* pole vault | dive; *salto del ángel* swan dive ‖ FIG springboard; *la televisión ha sido para él un salto a la fama* television has been his springboard to fame ‖ TECN chute ‖ — *a salto de mata* from hand to mouth, from one day to the next (vivir al día), like a shot (con mucha velocidad), as it bolts from cover (liebre), haphazardly (de cualquier manera) ‖ *a saltos* by leaps and bounds, in leaps and bounds ‖ *bajar de un salto* to jump down ‖ *cruzar de un salto* to leap over, to jump over ‖ *dar saltos de alegría* to jump for *o* with joy ‖ *dar* or *pegar un salto* to jump, to leap, to bound ‖ FAM *dar* or *pegar un salto por casa de alguien* to drop by s.o.'s house, to pop over to s.o.'s house ‖ *dar un salto atrás* to jump back *o* backwards ‖ FIG *dar un salto en el vacío* to take a shot in the dark, to do sth. blindly ‖ *de un salto* with one bound, with one jump ‖ FIG *el corazón me dio un salto* my heart skipped a beat | *en un salto* in a jiffy, in a flash (rápidamente) ‖ *ir* or *avanzar a saltos* to jump along ‖ FIG *ir en un salto a, plantarse en un salto en* to pop *o* to nip over to ‖ *salto de cama* négligé [US negligee] ‖ FIG *salto de carnero* buck (de un caballo) ‖ DEP *salto de la carpa* jackknife ‖ *salto de lobo* sunk fence ‖ DEP *salto de trampolín* springboard dive ‖ MAR *salto de viento* shift *o* change of wind ‖ DEP *salto mortal* somersault ‖ *subir de un salto* to jump up ‖ DEP *triple salto* hop, step and jump.

saltón, ona *adj* jumping, hopping (que anda a saltos) ‖ bulging (ojos).
◆ *m* ZOOL grasshopper (saltamontes).

salubre *adj* salubrious, healthy.

salubridad *f* salubrity, healthiness.

salud *f* health (del cuerpo); *salud delicada* delicate health ‖ REL salvation; *la salud eterna* eternal salvation ‖ welfare (bienestar) ‖ — *beber a la salud de uno* to drink to s.o.'s health ‖ *Comité de Salud Pública* Public Safety Committee ‖ FIG *curarse en salud* to take precautions (precaverse) ‖ *estar bien, mal de salud* to be in good, in bad health ‖ *estar rebosante de salud, vender salud* to be brimming *o* glowing with health ‖ *gastar salud* to be in *o* to enjoy good health, to be healthy ‖ *gozar de buena salud* to be in *o* to enjoy good health ‖ *jurar por la salud de uno* to swear on one's mother's grave ‖ *mirar por su salud* to look after *o* to take care of one's health ‖ *recobrar la salud* to recover one's health ‖ *salud de hierro* iron constitution ‖ *tener poca salud* not to be very healthy.
◆ *interj* FAM greetings! ‖ *¡a su salud!, ¡salud y pesetas!, ¡salud!* cheers!, good health!

saludable *adj* healthy (sano) || good, healthy (provechoso, benéfico) || salutary, wholesome; *un castigo saludable* a salutary punishment.

saludar *vt* to greet (muestra de cortesía) || to acknowledge, to say hello to; *no me saluda nunca por la calle* he never acknowledges me in the street || MIL to salute || FIG to salute, to hail; *saludar el advenimiento de la libertad* to hail the arrival of freedom || FAM to look at; *este alumno no ha saludado siquiera la lección* this pupil hasn't even looked at the lesson || FIG to cure by magic (curar por ensalmo) || — *ir a saludar a alguien* to call in and see s.o., to go and say hello to s.o. || *le saluda atentamente (su seguro servidor)* Yours faithfully, Yours truly (cartas) || *salude de mi parte a* give my regards to *o* my best to.
◆ *vi* MIL to salute.

saludo *m* MIL salute || bow (inclinación) || greeting, salutation || — *reciba un atento saludo de* Yours sincerely || *¡un saludo a María!* give my regards *o* my best to Mary!, say hello to Mary for me!
◆ *pl* regards, best wishes || — *atentos saludos* or *saludos cordiales de* best wishes (from) || *saludos respetuosos* respectfully yours, Yours faithfully.

Salustio *n pr* Sallust.

salustista *m/f* salvationist, member of the Salvation Army (miembro del Ejército de Salvación).

salutación *f* salutation, greeting || REL *la Salutación angélica* the Hail Mary.

salutífero, ra *adj* salutary, wholesome.

salva *f* MIL salvo, volley; *tirar una salva* to fire a volley | salute (en honor de alguien) || thunder, storm; *salva de aplausos* thunder of applause || tasting (prueba de la comida) || ordeal (de un acusado) || tray, salver (bandeja) || oath, vow, solemn promise (juramento) || — *cartucho para salvas* blank cartridge || FIG *gastar la pólvora en salvas* to waste one's efforts *o* one's ammunition.

salvación *f* rescue, delivery, salvation || REL salvation; *la salvación eterna* eternal salvation || — *Ejército de Salvación* Salvation Army || *este enfermo no tiene salvación* there is no hope for this patient || FIG *tabla de salvación* last hope (último recurso), salvation (salvación).

salvadera *f* sandbox (para secar la tinta).

salvado *m* bran (afrecho).

Salvador (El) *npr m* GEOGR El Salvador.

salvador, ra *adj* saving.
◆ *m/f* saviour [*US* savior], rescuer || MAR salvager, salvor || *El Salvador* the Saviour [*US* the Savior], Jesus Christ.

salvadoreño, ña *adj/s* Salvadoran.

salvaguarda *f* INFORM saving, backup || → **salvaguardia.**

salvaguardar *vt* to safeguard.

salvaguardia; salvaguarda *f* safeguard || FIG guardian; *la ONU es la salvaguardia de la paz* the UN is the guardian of peace.

salvajada; salvajería *f* savage *o* brutal act *o* deed, savagery (acto) || horror, atrocity; *las salvajadas de la guerra* the horrors of war.

salvaje *adj* savage (feroz) || wild (no domesticado); *animal salvaje* wild animal || wild (plantas, paisaje) || savage (sin cultura) || uncivilized, primitive (primitivo).
◆ *m/f* savage (persona en estado primitivo) || FIG savage, boor (bruto).

salvajería *f* → **salvajada.**

salvajino, na *adj* wild, savage || *carne salvajina* game, meat from wild animals.
◆ *m/f* savage.
◆ *f* furs *pl*, skins *pl*, pelts *pl* (pieles) || wild animals *pl* (fieras montesas) || game (carne).

salvajismo *m* savagery.

salvamanteles *m inv* tablemat.

salvamento *m* rescue, saving (acción de salvar) || REL salvation (salvación) || salvage (de naufragios) || FIG refuge (refugio) || — *bote de salvamento* lifeboat || *equipo de salvamento* rescue party || *operaciones de salvamento* rescue operations || *Sociedad de salvamento de náufragos* Lifeboat Association.

salvar *vt* to save, to rescue (de un peligro); *salvar a un náufrago* to save a shipwrecked person || to salvage (un barco) || to save; *salvar su honor* to save one's honour; *salvó a su hijo de la ruina* he saved his son from ruin || to jump over; *salvar un arroyo* to jump over a stream || to clear (un obstáculo) || to negotiate; *los montañeros salvaron la cadena de montañas en dos días* the mountaineers negotiated the mountain range in two days || to cover (una distancia) || to span, to cross; *el puente salva el río* the bridge spans the river || to get round (evitar); *salvar una dificultad* to get round a difficulty || to overcome (resolver) || to exclude, to except (excluir); *salvando la posibilidad de* excepting the possibility of || to notarize (autorizar un documento) || FIG to make up for, to compensate for; *su simpatía lo salva todo* her kindness makes up for everything || *el honor está salvado* honour is saved.
◆ *vpr* REL to save one's soul, to be saved || to survive, to escape; *salvarse de un accidente terrible* to survive a nasty accident || to recover (un enfermo) || — FAM *salvarse por los pelos* to escape by the skin of one's teeth || *¡sálvese quien pueda!* every man for himself!

salvavidas *m inv* life preserver (cualquier dispositivo) || life buoy (boya) || life belt (cinturón) || lifeboat (bote, lancha) || fender, guard (en tranvías).
◆ *adj* life-saving || — *bote salvavidas* lifeboat || *chaleco salvavidas* life jacket.

salvedad *f* condition, proviso (condición) || exception (excepción) || reservation, qualification (reserva) || distintion (distinción).

salvia *f* BOT salvia, sage.

salvilla *f* salver, tray (bandeja).

salvo, va *adj* safe || FAM *le dio en salva sea la parte* it hit him you know where *o* in the you-know-what, it hit him where it hurts most.
◆ *adv/prep* except (for), save; *todos vinieron salvo él* everyone came except for him || — *a salvo* safe and sound (ileso), safe, out of danger (fuera de peligro); *a salvo de* safe from; safe; *su reputación está a salvo* her reputation is safe || *dejar a salvo* to safeguard (salvaguardar), to spare; *la revolución no dejó a salvo ningún convento* the revolution didn't spare a single convent || *poner a salvo* to put in a safe place || *ponerse a salvo* to reach safety || *salvo casos en que...* except for cases where... *o* in which... || *salvo el parecer de usted* unless I hear to the contrary, unless otherwise notified || *salvo que* unless (a no ser que).

salvoconducto *m* safe-conduct.

Salzburgo *n pr* GEOGR Salzburg.

samario *m* samarium (metal).

samario, ria *adj* [of *o* from] Santa Marta [Colombia].
◆ *m/f* native *o* inhabitant of Santa Marta.

samaritano, na *adj/s* Samaritan.

samba *f* samba (baile).

sambenito *m* sanbenito [cloak worn by those condemned by the Inquisition] (capotillo) || FIG disgrace, dishonour (mala fama) | taboo (tabú) || — FIG *a mí me han colgado ese sambenito* they have given me a bad name | *le han colgado el sambenito de embustero* they have branded him a liar.

samnita *adj/s* HIST Samnite.

Samotracia *n pr* GEOGR Samothrace.

samovar *m* samovar (tetera rusa).

sampaguita *f* kind of jasmine.

sampán *m* MAR sampan (embarcación china).

samurai *m* samurai (guerrero japonés).

samuro *m* AMER turkey buzzard (ave).

san *adj* apocopated form of («santo») Saint, St; *San Pedro* Saint Peter || *¿a qué hora dicen la misa en San Pedro?* at what time is mass at St Peter's.
— OBSERV *San* is used before all masculine names of saints except Tomás, Tomé, Toribio and Domingo.

sanable *adj* curable.

sanador, ra *adj* healing, curing.
◆ *m/f* healer, person who cures.

sanalotodo *m* cure-all (emplasto) || FIG panacea (remedio útil para todo).

sanar *vt* to heal, to cure.
◆ *vi* to recover (un enfermo) || to heal (una herida).

sanatorio *m* sanatorium, sanitarium (para tuberculosis) || clinic, nursing home; *mi mujer ha dado a luz en el sanatorio* my wife has just given birth in the clinic || hospital (hospital) || *sanatorio psiquiátrico* psychiatric clinic.

San Bernardo (perro de) *m* Saint-Bernard.

sanción *f* sanction.

sancionador, ra *adj* sanctioning.
◆ *m/f* sanctioner.

sancionar *vt* to sanction; *sancionar una ley* to sanction a law || to sanction, to penalize; *este comerciante ha sido sancionado por venta ilícita de mercancías* this merchant has been penalized for the illegal sale of merchandise.

sanco *m* AMER gruel (gachas) | thick mud (barro).

sancochar *vt* CULIN to parboil.

sancocho *m* AMER stew made with meat, yucca and bananas.

sancta *m* REL forepart of the tabernacle.

sanctasanctórum *m* sanctum sanctorum, holy of holies || FIG sanctum, sanctum sanctorum.

sancho *m* AMER ram (carnero) | domestic animal.

Sancho *npr m* Sancho || FIG *al buen callar llaman Sancho* discretion is the better part of valour.

sanchopancesco, ca *adj* like Sancho Panza, down-to-earth.

sandalia *f* sandal.

sándalo *m* BOT sandal, sandalwood (árbol y madera).

sandáraca *f* sandarac (resina, mineral).

sandez *f* nonsense (palabra) || silly thing (acto) || silliness (cualidad) || — *decir sandeces* to talk nonsense || *es una sandez* it's silly.

sandía *f* BOT watermelon.

sandio, dia *adj* silly, nonsensical.
◆ *m/f* fool, dolt.

sanducero, ra *adj* [of *o* from] Paysandú [Uruguay].
◆ *m/f* native *o* inhabitant of Paysandú.

sandunga *f* FAM charm (encanto) | wit (gracia) || AMER party (parranda) | typical Mexican dance.

sandunguero, ra *adj* FAM charming (encantador) | witty (gracioso).

sandwich *m* sandwich (emparedado).
— OBSERV In Spanish the plural is *sandwiches* or *sandwichs*.

saneado, da *adj* drained (el terreno) ‖ stabilized (la moneda) ‖ reorganized (las finanzas) ‖ sound; *tiene una posición muy saneada* he has a very sound position.

saneamiento *m* drainage (desecación de un terreno) ‖ stabilization (de la moneda) ‖ reorganization (de las finanzas) ‖ JUR guarantee | indemnification ‖ *artículos de saneamiento* sanitary ware, bathroom goods *o* fixtures.

sanear *vt* to drain, to dry out (el terreno) ‖ to rid of damp (una casa) ‖ to put right, to mend (reparar) ‖ to stabilize (la moneda) ‖ to reorganize (las finanzas) ‖ JUR to guarantee (garantizar) | to indemnify (indemnizar).

sanedrín *m* HIST Sanhedrin, Sanhedrim.

sanfasón *m* AMER cheek (*fam*), nerve (*fam*), insolence (desfachatez) ‖ AMER *a la sanfasón* nonchalantly (despreocupadamente), carelessly (descuidadamente).

sanforizado, da *adj* sanforized (textiles).

sangradera *f* MED lancet (lanceta) | basin for blood (vasija para la sangre) ‖ sluice, sluiceway, irrigation ditch (caz) ‖ sluice, sluice gate, floodgate (compuerta).

sangrador *m* bloodletter (el que sangra) ‖ sluice gate, outlet (compuerta).

sangradura *f* ANAT inner part of the elbow (sangría) ‖ MED incision into a vein (corte) ‖ FIG drain, outlet (en un canal).

sangrante *adj* bleeding (herida) ‖ FIG flagrant (injusticia, etc.).

sangrar *vt* to bleed; *sangrar a un enfermo* to bleed a sick person ‖ to drain (un terreno) ‖ to tap, to draw resin from (un pino) ‖ IMPR to indent ‖ FIG & FAM to bleed dry *o* white (sacar todo el dinero) | to filch (robar) ‖ TECN to tap (una tubería).
◆ *vi* to bleed ‖ — FIG *estar sangrando* to be still fresh (ser reciente) ‖ *estás sangrando por la nariz* your nose is bleeding ‖ FAM *sangrar como un cochino* or *un toro* to bleed profusely, to gush blood, to bleed like a pig.
◆ *vpr* MED to have o.s. bled.

sangraza *f* contamined blood.

sangre *f* blood ‖ FIG blood; *tener sangre de reyes* to have royal blood (linaje, parentesco); *sangre azul* blue blood ‖ — *a sangre fría* in cold blood ‖ *a sangre y fuego* mercilessly ‖ *azotar a alguien hasta hacerle sangre* to beat s.o. black and blue ‖ FIG & FAM *calentarle la sangre a alguien* to rub s.o. up the wrong way, to irritate s.o. ‖ FIG *chorrear sangre* to cry out to heaven (una acción monstruosa) | *chupar la sangre a uno* to bleed s.o. white *o* dry | *dar la sangre* or *la sangre de las venas por algo* or *alguien* to give one's right arm for sth. *o* s.o. ‖ MED *dar sangre* to give blood ‖ *derramar sangre* to shed blood ‖ ZOOL *de sangre caliente, fría* warm-blooded, cold-blooded ‖ *donante de sangre* blood donor ‖ *echar sangre* to bleed ‖ FAM *echar sangre como un cochino* or *un toro* to bleed like a pig *o* profusely ‖ *echar sangre por las narices* to have a nosebleed, to bleed from the nose ‖ FIG *estar bañado en sangre* to be bathed in blood ‖ *estar chorreando sangre* to be gushing blood ‖ *hacer sangre* to draw blood ‖ FIG *helarle la sangre a uno* to make s.o.'s blood run cold | FIG & FAM *la letra con sangre entra* spare the rod and spoil the child | FIG *lavar con sangre* to avenge with blood (un agravio, una afrenta) | *la voz de la sangre* the call of blood | *le bulle* or *hierve la sangre* he is hot-blooded | *lo lleva en la sangre* it is *o* it runs in his blood | *llevar* or *tener en la sangre, llevar en la masa de la sangre* to have in one's blood (algo), to have got in one's blood (alguien) ‖ *naranja de sangre* blood orange ‖ FIG *no llegó la sangre al río* it wasn't too serious | *no quedar sangre en el cuerpo* or *en las venas* to be scared stiff ‖ *pura sangre* thoroughbred (caballo) ‖ FIG *quemarle* or *freírle a uno la sangre* to make s.o.'s blood boil | *sangre fría* coolness, sangfroid | *se le quemó la sangre* his blood boiled, it made his blood boil | *subírsele a uno la sangre a la cabeza* to see red | *sudar sangre* to sweat blood | *tener la sangre gorda* to be sluggish | *tener las manos manchadas de sangre* to have blood on one's hands | *tener mala sangre* to be evil-minded | *tener sangre de artistas* to come from a line of artists | *tener sangre de horchata, no tener sangre en las venas* to have water in one's veins, to have no blood in one's veins ‖ *tracción de* or *a sangre* animal traction.

sangregorda *m/f* FAM sluggard, oaf.

sangría *f* ANAT inner part of the elbow ‖ MED bleeding, bloodletting ‖ draining outlet (en un canal) ‖ tap (en un árbol) ‖ «sangría», sangaree (p us) [refreshing sweet drink made from red wine, oranges and lemons] ‖ FIG drain, outflow; *una sangría en el capital* a drain on capital, an outflow of capital ‖ IMPR indentation ‖ TECN tapping [of molten metal] (en los altos hornos) ‖ FIG *sangría monetaria* monetary drain.

sangriento, ta *adj* bloody, bloodstained, covered with blood; *manos sangrientas* bloody hands ‖ bleeding (herida) ‖ FIG bloody; *batalla sangrienta* bloody battle | cruel; *una broma sangrienta* a cruel joke ‖ crying, outrageous (injusticia) ‖ cruel, cutting, deadly (injuria).

sanguaraña *f* popular Peruvian dance (baile).

sanguijuela *f* ZOOL leech, bloodsucker ‖ FIG leech, sponger, bloodsucker.

sanguina *f* sanguine (lápiz y dibujo) ‖ blood orange, sanguine orange (naranja).

sanguinario, ria *adj* bloodthirsty.
◆ *f* bloodstone (piedra preciosa) ‖ BOT bloodroot.

sanguíneo, a *adj* sanguineous ‖ blood; *grupo sanguíneo* blood group; *vasos sanguíneos* blood vessels.

sanguino, na *adj* sanguineous ‖ bloodthirsty (sanguinario) ‖ *naranja sanguina* blood orange, sanguine orange.
◆ *m* BOT red dogwood (cornejo).
◆ *f* blood orange, sanguine orange (naranja).

sanguinolencia *f* bloodiness, sanguinolence (p us).

sanguinolento, ta *adj* bloody, bleeding (que echa sangre) ‖ bloodstained, sanguinolent (p us) (manchado de sangre) ‖ FIG bloodred (color) ‖ *ojos sanguinolentos* bloodshot eyes.

sánico *adj m* *papel sánico* toilet paper.

sanidad *f* health (salud); *sanidad pública* public health ‖ sanitation; *problemas de sanidad* sanitation problems ‖ — *certificado* or *patente de sanidad* health certificate ‖ MIL *cuerpo de Sanidad Militar* medical corps ‖ *Dirección General de Sanidad* Ministry of Health ‖ *inspector de Sanidad* sanitary inspector ‖ *medidas de sanidad* sanitary measures.

sanie; sanies *f* MED sanies.

sanitario, ria *adj* sanitary; *cordón sanitario* sanitary cordon; *medidas sanitarias* sanitary measures.
◆ *m* MIL military health officer.

San José *n pr* GEOGR San José.

sanjuanada *f* festival of Saint John's Day.

sanjuanero, ra *adj* ripe by Saint John's Day (frutas) ‖ (of) Saint John's Day ‖ [of *o* from] San Juan (Cuba).
◆ *m/f* native *o* inhabitant of San Juan.

sanjuanista *adj* of the Order of Saint John of Jerusalem.
◆ *m* knight of the Order of Saint John of Jerusalem.

sanluisero, ra *adj* [of *o* from] San Luis.
◆ *m/f* native *o* inhabitant of an Luis [Argentina].

San Marino *n pr* GEOGR San Marino.

sanmartiniano, na *adj* of *o* like San Martín [Argentine general].

sano, na *adj* healthy; *persona sana* healthy person; *clima sano* healthy climate ‖ healthy, wholesome; *un alimento sano* a wholesome food ‖ FIG sound; *una filosofía sana* a sound philosophy ‖ good; *no queda un plato sano en toda la casa* there is not one good plate left in the entire house ‖ good, sound; *una manzana sana* a good apple ‖ sound (saneado); *un negocio sano* a sound business ‖ FIG healthy, wholesome (sin vicios); *tiene ideas muy sanas* he has very healthy ideas ‖ — FIG *cortar por lo sano* to take drastic action, to settle things once and for all ‖ *estar en su sano juicio* to be in one's right mind ‖ *estar más sano que una manzana* or *una pera* to be as fit as a fiddle ‖ *sano de cuerpo y alma* sound in mind and body ‖ *sano y salvo* safe and sound.

San Quintín *n pr* GEOGR Saint Quentin ‖ — FIG & FAM *se armó la de San Quintín* all hell broke loose | *se va a armar la de San Quintín* there's going to be a real trouble *o* a hell of a row.

sánscrito, ta *adj/sm* Sanskrit.

sanseacabó *loc* FAM *y sanseacabó* and that's the end of it, and that's all there is to it.

sansimoniano, na *adj* FIL Saint-Simonian.
◆ *m/f* Saint-Simonian, Saint-Simonist.

sansimonismo *m* FIL Saint-Simonism.

sansirolé *m* FAM nincompoop, simpleton (bobo).

Sansón *npr m* Samson ‖ FIG *ser un Sansón* to be as strong as an ox.

santabárbara *f* MAR magazine.

santacruceño, ña *adj* [of *o* from] Santa Cruz [Argentina].
◆ *m/f* native *o* inhabitant of Santa Cruz.

santafecino, na *adj* [of *o* from] Santa Fe [Argentina].
◆ *m/f* native *o* inhabitant of Santa Fe.

santafereño, ña *adj* [of *o* from] Santa Fe [Colombia].
◆ *m/f* native *o* inhabitant of Santa Fe.

santamente *adv* *vivir santamente* to live like a saint, to live a saintly life.

santandereano, na *adj* [of *o* from] Santander [Colombia].
◆ *m/f* native *o* inhabitant of Santander.

santanderino, na; santanderiense *adj* [of *o* from] Santander [Spain].
◆ *m/f* native *o* inhabitant of Santander.

santateresa *f* ZOOL praying mantis.

santero, ra *adj* sanctimonious (beato).
◆ *m/f* caretaker of a sanctuary (que cuida un santuario) ‖ alms collector [who carries the image of a saint] (que pide limosna).

Santiago *n pr* Santiago [city in Chile, Cuba, etc.].

Santiago *npr m* James (persona) ‖ Saint James (orden) ‖ — *Camino de Santiago* Milky Way (Vía Láctea), the road to Santiago de Compostela (peregrinación) ‖ *¡Santiago!, ¡Santiago y cierra España!, ¡Santiago y a ellos!* ancient Spanish war cry ‖ *Santiago de Compostela* Santiago de Compostela (ciudad), St. James the Greater (apóstol).

santiagueño, ña *adj* ripe by Saint James' Day (frutas) || [of *o* from] Santiago del Estero [Argentina].
◆ *m/f* native *o* inhabitant of Santiago del Estero.

santiaguero, ra *adj* [of *o* from] Santiago de Cuba.
◆ *m/f* native *o* inhabitant of Santiago de Cuba.

santiagués, esa *adj* [of *o* from] Santiago de Compostela [Spain].
◆ *m/f* native *o* inhabitant of Santiago de Compostela.

santiaguino, na *adj* [of *o* from] Santiago de Chile.
◆ *m/f* native *o* inhabitant of Santiago de Chile.

santiaguista *adj* of the order of Saint James.
◆ *m/f* knight of the order of Saint James.

santiamén *m* instant || FAM *en un santiamén* in a jiffy, in an instant, in no time at all; *hizo su trabajo en un santiamén* he did his work in a jiffy; *llegué a Madrid en un santiamén* I arrived in Madrid in no time at all.

santidad *f* saintliness, holiness || — *olor de santidad* odour of sanctity || *Su Santidad* His Holiness.

santificación *f* sanctification.

santificar *vt* to sanctify || to consecrate (un lugar) || to keep, to observe (los domingos y fiestas) || FIG to excuse, to forgive (disculpar) || REL *santificado sea Tu Nombre* hallowed be Thy Name.

santiguada *f* sign of the cross.

santiguamiento *m* making the sign of the cross (acción de santiguar) || crossing o.s., making the sign of the cross (acción de santiguarse).

santiguar *vt* to bless, to make the sign of the cross over (bendecir) || to make the sign of the cross over (los curanderos) || FIG to slap (abofetear).
◆ *vpr* to cross o.s., to make the sign of the cross (persignarse).

santísimo, ma *adj* very *o* most holy || — FAM *hacerle a uno la santísima pascua* to mess things up for s.o. (fastidiar), to play a dirty trick on s.o. (hacer una mala jugada) || *la Virgen Santísima* the Holy Virgin || *Santísimo Sacramento* Holy Sacrament || FAM *todo el santísimo día* all the livelong day, all day long.
◆ *m* the Holy Sacrament.

santo, ta *adj* holy; *Semana Santa* Holy Week; *la santa Iglesia católica* the holy Catholic Church || saintly, holy; *una persona santa* a saintly person || holy; *la Tierra Santa* the Holy Land | consecrated, holy (consagrado); *tierra santa* holy ground || FAM blessed; *me tuvo esperando toda la santa tarde* he kept me waiting all the blessed afternoon; *tuve que dormir en el santo suelo* I had to sleep on the blessed floor || saint; *Santo Tomás* Saint Thomas; *Santa Ana* Saint Ann || — *Ciudad Santa* Holy City || *Espíritu Santo* Holy Spirit *o* Ghost || *guerra santa* holy war || FAM *hacer su santa voluntad* or *su santo gusto* to do as one jolly well *o* damn well pleases || *Jueves Santo* Holy Thursday, Maundy Thursday || *la Santa Sede* the Holy See || *Padre Santo, Santo Padre* Holy Father || *Sábado Santo* Holy Saturday || HIST *Santa Alianza* Holy Alliance || *Santa Biblia* Holy Bible || *Santa Faz* Holy Face || *Santo Grial* Holy Grail || *Santo Oficio* Holy Office, Inquisition || *santo óleo* holy oil || FIG *santo y bueno* all well and good || FAM *todo el santo día* all the livelong day, all day long || *un santo varón* a saint || *Viernes Santo* Good Friday || FIG *¡y santas Pascuas!* and that's that!, and that's all there is to it!
◆ *m/f* saint (véase OBSERV) || FAM image of a saint (grabado) || FIG saint (persona muy buena).
◆ *m* name day; *hoy es mi santo* today is my name day; *felicitar a uno (por) su santo* to congratulate s.o. on his name day || — FIG & FAM *adorar el santo por la peana* to court the mother in order to marry the daughter || FAM *alabar a su santo* to look after one's own interests | *alzarse* or *cargar con el santo y la limosna* to clear off with everything | *aquello fue llegar y besar el santo* it was as easy as pie, it was a piece of cake, it was like taking candy from a baby | *¿a santo de qué...?* why on earth...?, why the devil...? || FIG *comerse los santos* to be sanctimonious || FAM *desnudar a un santo para vestir a otro* to rob Peter to pay Paul || *el día* or *la fiesta de Todos los Santos* All Saints' Day || FAM *hacerse el santo* to play the little saint | *írsele a uno el santo al cielo* to lose one's train of thought (en una conversación), to clear forget, to completely forget; *ayer fue tu cumpleaños y se me fue el santo al cielo* yesterday was your birthday and I completely forgot | *no es santo de mi devoción* I'm not exactly fond of him | *no saber a qué santo encomendarse* to be at one's wits' end, not to know where to turn || *por todos los santos (del cielo)* by the gods (juramento), for goodness sake (exclamación) || FAM *quedarse para vestir santos* to be left on the shelf, to remain an old maid || *santo patrón* or *titular* patron saint || *santo y seña* password || FAM *ser bueno como un santo* to be as good as gold | *tener el santo de espaldas* to have hard luck, to be unlucky | *todos los santos tienen novena* my (your, our, etc.) time will come.
— OBSERV *Saint* se suele abreviar en *St* delante de un nombre propio: *Santo Tomás* St Thomas.

Santo Domingo *n pr* GEOGR Santo Domingo || REL Saint Dominic.

santón *m* Mohammedan monk (mahometano) || FIG & FAM sanctimonious hypocrite, bigot (hipócrita) | big shot, big wheel (persona influyente).

santoral *m* book of life stories of the saints (vidas de santos) || sanctorale (libro de coro) || sanctoral calendar (lista) || *santoral del día* saint of the day.

Santo Tomé y Príncipe *n pr* GEOGR São Tomé and Principé.

santuario *m* sanctuary, shrine || AMER buried treasure (tesoro).

santurrón, ona *adj* sanctimonious (beato) || hypocritical (hipócrita).
◆ *m/f* sanctimonious person (beato) || hypocrite.

santurronería *f* sanctimoniousness || hypocrisy.

saña *f* rage, fury (furor) || cruelty (porfía) || *con saña* cruelly, viciously.

sañoso, sa; sañudo, da *adj* furious, enraged (enfurecido) || cruel, vicious (encarnizado).

São Paulo *n pr* GEOGR São Paulo.

sapajú *m* ZOOL sapajou (mono).

sapan *m* BOT sapanwood.

sapidez *f* sapidity, taste, savouriness [*US* savoriness].

sápido, da *adj* sapid, savoury.

sapiencia *f* wisdom, sapience (sabiduría) || book of Wisdom [in the Apocrypha] (de la Biblia) || knowledge (conocimientos); *la sapiencia de este chico me admira* this boy's knowledge amazes me.

sapiencial *adj* sapiential || *libros sapienciales* sapiential books.

sapiente *adj* wise, sapient (sabio).

sapo *m* ZOOL toad (batracio) || FIG beast, animal (animalito) || AMER game resembling Aunt Sally [consisting in throwing coins into the mouth of a model frog] (juego) || FIG & FAM *echar sapos y culebras* or *gusarapos* to rant and rave.

saponáceo, a *adj* saponaceous.

saponaria *f* BOT soapwort.

saponificación *f* QUÍM to saponify.
◆ *vpr* to saponify.

saponita *f* MIN saponite.

sapote *m* BOT sapodilla (zapote).

saprófito, ta *adj* BOT saprophytic.
◆ *m* saprophyte.

saque *m* serve, service (tenis) || kickoff (fútbol) || server (jugador) || AMER distillery (de aguardiente) || — *hacer* or *tener el saque* to kick off (fútbol), to serve (tenis) || *hacer el saque de puerta* to take a goal kick (fútbol) || *línea de saque* service line (tenis) || *romper el saque* to break (the) serve *o* service (tenis) || *saque de banda* throw-in (fútbol), line-out (rugby) || *saque de castigo* free kick || *saque de centro* kickoff || *saque de esquina* corner kick, corner || *saque de puerta* goal kick || FIG & FAM *tener un buen saque* to be a big eater (comer mucho).

saqueador, ra *adj* plundering, pillaging, looting, sacking.
◆ *m/f* plunderer, pillager, looter, sacker.

saqueamiento *m* plunder, looting, pillage, sacking.

saquear *vt* to plunder, to loot, to pillage, to sack || FIG to loot, to plunder.

saqueo *m* plunder, looting, pillage, sacking; *el saqueo de Roma* the sacking of Rome.

saquería *f* manufacture of sacks (fabricación) || sacks *pl* (sacos).

saquero, ra *m/f* person who makes or sells sacks.

saquete *m* small bag *o* sack || cartridge bag (del cañón).

Sara *npr f* Sarah.

saraguate; saraguato *m* AMER species of ape.

sarampión *m* MED measles || FIG cancer, malady; *el amor es el sarampión de todas las edades* love is a cancer of all ages.

sarandí *m* AMER BOT waterside bush of the family euphorbiaceae.

sarao *m* soirée (reunión).

sarape *m* AMER serape, sarape (capote de monte).

sarapico *m* ZOOL curlew (zarapico).

sarasa *m* FAM queer, fairy (marica).

sarazo *adj m* AMER ripening, half-ripe (maíz) | tipsy (achispado) | rancid (agua de coco, coco).

sarcasmo *m* sarcasm.

sarcásticamente *adv* sarcastically.

sarcástico, ca *adj* sarcastic.

sarcocele *m* MED sarcocele.

sarcófago *m* sarcophagus.

sarcoma *m* MED sarcoma (tumor).

sarcomatosis *f* MED sarcomatosis.

sarcomatoso, sa *adj* MED sarcomatous.

sardana *f* sardana (danza catalana).

sardanapalesco, ca *adj* Sardapanalian || FIG *llevar una vida sardanapalesca* to live it up.

Sardanápalo *npr m* Sardanapalus.

sardanés, esa *adj* [of *o* from the] Cerdagne Valley (Cataluña).
◆ *m/f* native *o* inhabitant of the Cerdagne Valley.

sardina *f* ZOOL sardine; *sardinas en espetones* sardines on a spit *o* skewer || FIG *estar como sardinas en banasta* or *en lata* to be (packed) like sardines.

sardinal *m* sardine net (red).

sardinel *m* ARQ rowlock (obra de ladrillos).

sardinero, ra *adj* sardine; *barco sardinero* sardine boat.
◆ *m/f* sardine seller.

sardineta *f* small sardine || MIL pointed chevron (galón).

sardo, da *adj* spotted (el ganado).
◆ *adj/s* Sardinian (de Cerdeña).
◆ *m* Sardinian (lengua).

sardónico, ca *adj* sardonic; *risa sardónica* sardonic laugh.

sarga *f* serge, twill (tela).

sargazo *m* BOT sargasso, gulfweed || GEOGR *mar de los Sargazos* Sargasso Sea.

sargenta *f* halberd, halbert (alabarda) || sergeant's wife (mujer) || FIG & FAM tyrant, dragon, grouch; *su mujer es una sargenta* his wife is a tyrant.

sargentear *vt* FIG & FAM to boss about.
◆ *vi* FIG & FAM to be bossy.

sargentería *f* sergeantship.

sargentía *f* sergeancy, sergeantship, rank of sergeant.

sargento *m* MIL sergeant || FIG & FAM tyrant, grouch; *su director es un sargento* his director is a tyrant || *sargento mayor* quartermaster-sergeant, sergeant major.

sargentona *f* FAM tyrant, dragon.

sargo *m* sargo (pez).

sari *m* sari (traje femenino en la India).

sariga *f* AMER opossum (zarigüeya).

sarmentoso, sa *adj* sarmentose (relativo o parecido a un sarmiento) || climbing, twining (árbol, planta) || FIG bony, scrawny (miembros).

sarmiento *m* vine shoot || FIG *el pobre está ya hecho un sarmiento* the poor man is already a bag of bones.

sarna *f* MED itch, scabies || VET mange || FIG & FAM *más viejo que la sarna* as old as the hills.

sarniento, ta *adj* AMER ⟶ **sarnoso.**

sarnoso, sa *adj* itchy, scabby || VET mangy.
◆ *m/f* person suffering from the itch *o* scabies.

sarpullido *m* rash.

sarraceno, na *adj/s* HIST Saracen || *trigo sarraceno* buckwheat, Saracen corn.

Sarre *npr m* GEOGR Saar (región industrial) | Saarland (territorio).
— OBSERV The words *Sarre* in Spanish and *Saar* in English take the definite article.

sarrillo *m* death rattle (estertor) || tartar (sarro) || BOT arum (aro).

sarro *m* deposit, incrustation, crust (en una vasija) || scale, fur (de una caldera) || tartar (de los dientes) || BOT rust, mildew, blight (roya) || MED fur, coating (de la lengua).

sarroso, sa *adj* incrusted (vasija) || scaly, furry (caldera) || covered with tartar, tartarous (dientes) || coated, furry, saburral (lengua) || BOT rusted, mildewed, blighted (planta).

sarta *f* string; *sarta de cebollas* string of onions || FIG string, line (de personas) | string; *en medio de su discurso soltó toda una sarta de citas* in the middle of his speech he came out with a whole string of quotations; *soltó una sarta de mentiras* he came out with a string of lies || FIG *esta carta es una sarta de embustes* this letter is a tissue *o* a web of lies.

sartén *m* frying plan || FIG oven, furnace; *este cuarto es una sartén* it is like an oven in here || FIG & FAM *tener la sartén por el mango* to have the whip hand, to run the show.

sartenada *f* panful, pan.

sartenazo *m* blow with a frying pan || FIG & FAM belting, beating (paliza).

sarteneja *f* small frying pan || AMER dried-out hollow (depresión) | crack (grieta).

sartenejal *m* AMER dry cracked land.

sartorio *adj m* ANAT sartorial (músculo).
◆ *m* ANAT sartorius.

sasafrás *m* BOT sassafras.

sasánida *adj/s* HIST Sassanian.

sastra *f* woman tailor, tailoress (que hace trajes de hombre) || mender (que arregla los trajes) || seamstress (costurera) || tailor's wife (mujer del sastre).

sastre *m* tailor || costumier (de teatro) || — FIG & FAM *cajón de sastre* muddle, jumble, mess (objetos en desorden) || FAM *entre sastres no se pagan hechuras* what's a favour between friends? || *sastre, traje sastre* tailored suit (de mujer) || *sastre de señoras* dressmaker || *sastre de viejo* mending tailor || FIG & FAM *ver algo desde el tendido de los sastres* to have a full view *o* a bird's eye view of sth.

sastrería *f* tailoring (oficio) || tailor's [shop] (tienda); *ir a la sastrería* to go to the tailor's.

Satán; Satanás *npr m* Satan.

satánico, ca *adj* satanic, diabolical.

satanismo *m* Satanism.

satélite *adj* satellite; *país satélite* satellite country; *ciudad satélite* satellite town.
◆ *m* ASTR satellite; *satélite artificial* artificial satellite || TECN planet wheel, loose pinion (piñón) || FIG satellite (persona) | satellite (país, ciudad) || *satélite de comunicaciones* communications satellite || *satélite de Satán* fiend.

satelización *f* putting into orbit.

satelizar *vt* to put into orbit.

satén *m* sateen (raso).

satín *m* satinwood.

satinado, da *adj* satiny, satin-like, shiny || *papel satinado* glossy paper.
◆ *m* gloss, shine.

satinar *vt* to satin, to satinize || to gloss (el papel).

sátira *f* satire.

satírico, ca *adj* satirical, satiric (de la sátira) || satyrical, satyric (del sátiro).
◆ *m* satirist.

satirizar *vt/vi* to satirize.

sátiro *m* MIT satyr || ZOOL satyr butterfly || FIG satyr, lecher (hombre lascivo).

satisdación *f* JUR bail (fianza).

satisfacción *f* satisfaction; *dar entera satisfacción* to give complete satisfaction || satisfying, sating (del apetito) || satisfaction, fulfilment (de un deseo) || — *a satisfacción de* to the satisfaction of || *pedir satisfacción de una ofensa* to demand satisfaction for an offence || *satisfacción de sí mismo* self-satisfaction || *tener mucha satisfacción de sí mismo* to be very self-satisfied.

satisfacer* *vt* to satisfy || to pay (pagar); *satisfacer una deuda* to pay a debt || to give satisfaction, to make amends; *satisfacer de* or *por una ofensa* to give satisfaction for an offence || to compensate (compensar) || to meet, to satisfy; *satisfacer (a) la demanda* to meet the demand; *satisfacer todos los requisitos* to meet all the requirements || to meet (gastos) || MAT to satisfy || COM to honour (letra de cambio) || to expiate (expiar) || JUR *satisfacer una demanda* to accede to a request.
◆ *vpr* to be satisfied, to satisfy o.s. (contentarse) || to avenge o.s., to take vengeance (vengarse) || to obtain satisfaction (considerarse desagraviado).

satisfactoriamente *adv* satisfactorily.

satisfactorio, ria *adj* satisfactory; *contestación satisfactoria* satisfactory answer || REL satisfactory.

satisfecho, cha *adj* satisfied, content || smug, self-satisfied || — *darse por satisfecho con* to be satisfied with || *dejar satisfecho a* to satisfy || FAM *me he quedado satisfecho* I'm full, I've had enough (comida).

sátrapa *m* HIST satrap.

satrapía *f* HIST satrapy.

saturabilidad *f* QUÍM saturability.

saturable *adj* saturable.

saturación *f* saturation.

saturado, da *adj* satured || FIG tired, sick, saturated (harto); *estoy saturado de derecho civil* I'm sick *o* tired of civil law, I'm saturated with civil law.

saturador *m* saturator, saturater.

saturar *vt* to saturate.

saturnal *adj* Saturnian.

saturnales *f pl* HIST Saturnalia.

saturnino, na *adj* saturnine (triste) || saturnine (del plomo) || *cólico saturnino* lead *o* painter's colic.

saturnio, nia *adj* Saturnian.

saturnismo *m* MED lead poisoning, saturnism.

Saturno *npr m* ASTR & MIT Saturn.

sauce *m* BOT willow (árbol) || — BOT *sauce cabruno* goat willow | *sauce llorón* weeping willow.

sauceda *f*; **saucedal** *m*; **saucera** *f* BOT willow grove.

saúco *m* BOT elder (arbusto).

saudade *f* nostalgia (añoranza).

saudí; saudita *adj f* Saudi; *Arabia Saudita* Saudi Arabia.

saudoso, sa *adj* nostalgic.

sauna *f* sauna.

saurio, ria *adj/sm* ZOOL saurian.
◆ *pl* sauria.

savia *f* BOT sap || FIG sap, vitality || FIG *infundir nueva savia en una empresa* to infuse new blood in an undertaking.

saxífraga *f* BOT saxifrage.

saxofón; saxófono *m* MÚS saxophone, sax (*fam*).

saya *f* skirt (falda) || petticoat (enaguas).

sayal *m* sackcloth (tela).

sayo *m* cassock, cloak (casaca) || smock, loose garment (vestido amplio) || tunic (abrigo de los soldados romanos) || — FIG & FAM *cortarle a uno un sayo* to run s.o. down (criticar) | *decir para su sayo* to say to o.s. || FIG *hacer de su capa un sayo* to do as one pleases | *hasta el cuarenta de mayo no te quites el sayo* ne'er cast a clout till May is out.

sazón *f* ripeness, maturity (madurez) || flavour [US flavor] (sabor) || seasoning (aderezo) || FIG time (momento) || — *a la sazón* at that time, then || *en sazón* in season, ripe (fruta), at the right moment, opportunely (oportunamente) || *fuera de sazón* inopportunely (inoportunamente), out of season (fruta).
◆ *adj* AMER ripe, mature; *plátano sazón* ripe banana.

sazonado, da *adj* ripe (maduro) || seasoned (aderezado) || tasty (sabroso) || FIG witty (gracioso).

sazonar *vt* to season, to flavour (manjares) || to ripen, to mature (madurar) || FIG to add spice *o* relish to (amenizar); *sazonar un relato*

con salidas ingeniosas to add spice to a tale with witty remarks.
◆ *vpr* to ripen, to mature (madurar).

scooter *m* scooter (motocicleta).

scout *m* scout (explorador).

script girl *f* CINEM continuity girl, script girl (secretaria de rodaje).

scherzo *m* MÚS scherzo.

schnorchel *m* MAR snorkel.

se *pron pers*
1. oneself, himself, herself, itself, yourself, yourselves, themselves (acción reflexiva); *vengarse* to avenge oneself; *se cuidan bien* they take good care of themselves; *ella se alaba* she flatters herself ‖ each other, one another (el uno al otro); *ellos se odian* they hate one another; *se están hablando* they are talking to each other ‖ muchos verbos pierden su forma reflexiva en inglés; *sentarse* to sit down; *acostarse* to go to bed; *levantarse* to rise, to get up; *quejarse* to complain; *casarse* to get married; *pasearse* to take a walk, etc. ‖ algunos verbos pueden tomar la forma reflexiva en inglés o no tomarla; *lavarse* to wash, to wash oneself; *se compró un perro* he bought himself a dog, he bought a dog.
2. subject + to be + past participle (voz pasiva); *se siega el trigo en agosto* the wheat is cut in August; *se me entregaron dos cartas* two letters were given to me; *se piden voluntarios* volunteers are called for (in this case, the construction in Spanish is reflexive although its meaning is not).
3. it + to be + past participle (uso impersonal); *se sabe que...* it is know that...; *se dice que...* it is said that...
4. one, s.o., you, people, we, they (indefinido); *nunca se sabe* one never knows; *el domingo no se trabaja* we do not work on Sunday; *se dice que...* people say that...; *Señor, se le llama* Sir, s.o. is calling you ‖ — *aquí se habla demasiado* there is too much talking here ‖ *se bailaba y se cantaba* there was dancing and singing, people danced and sang.
5. to him, to her, to it, to you, to them (dativo) (dirigiéndose a); *se lo diré (a él)* I will tell him; *se lo diremos (a usted* or *a ustedes)* we will tell you (in Spanish the indirect object precedes the direct object) ‖ for him, for her, for it, for you, for them (para él, etc.); *se lo compraré (a ella)* I'll buy it for her ‖ from him, from her, from it, from you, from them (de él, etc.); *se lo arrancó bruscamente* he tore it from him ‖ *se ha roto una muela* he broke his tooth.
— OBSERV The pronoun *se* is enclitic when it is the object of an infinitive (callarse), of a gerund (quejándose), or of an imperative (siéntese).
— OBSERV One should note that in Spanish the reflexive frequently replaces the passive voice: *se resolvió el problema* the problem was solved; *se felicitó a los vencedores* the winners were congratulated.
— OBSERV La forma reflexiva de cada uno de los verbos se ha tratado por separado en el artículo del verbo correspondiente (véase PASEARSE en pasear).

sebáceo, a *adj* sebaceous; *glándulas sebáceas* sebaceous glands.

sebo *m* tallow (para velas, jabón) ‖ suet (para guisar) ‖ grease, fat (grasa) ‖ fat (gordura) ‖ grease, grime, filth (suciedad grasienta) ‖ ANAT sebum ‖ FAM drunkenness (borrachera) ‖ — *AMER* FAM *hacer sebo* to idle, to loaf (holgazanear) ‖ FAM *¡vaya sebo que cogió anoche!* the state he was in last night! (¡qué borrachera!).

seborrea *f* MED seborrhea.

seboso, sa *adj* tallowy (untado de sebo) ‖ suety (guiso) ‖ greasy, fatty (grasiento) ‖ greasy, grimy, filthy (sucio).

seca *f* drought (sequía) ‖ dry season (época) ‖ sandbank, sandbar (secano) ‖ MED swollen gland (hinchazón de las glándulas).

secadal *m* dry land (tierra seca) ‖ non-irrigable land (no irrigable).

secadero, ra *adj* that can be dried (frutas).
◆ *m* drying room *o* place (lugar).

secado *m* drying ‖ seasoning (de maderas).

secador *m* dryer, drier ‖ hair dryer (de pelo) ‖ AMER towel (toalla) ‖ *secador centrífugo* spin dryer (centrifugadora).

secadora *f* clothes dryer, dryer, drier (máquina para secar la ropa).

secamente *adv* dryly, drily.

secano *m* unirrigated land (no regado) ‖ dry land, dry region (por escasez de lluvia) ‖ sandbank, sandbar (banco de arena) ‖ — *campo de secano* land used for dry farming ‖ *cultivo de secano* dry farming.

secante *adj* drying (que seca) ‖ blotting (para tinta) ‖ siccative, quick-drying; *pintura secante* quick-drying paint ‖ MAT secant.
◆ *m* blotting paper, blotter (papel) ‖ siccative (sustancia) ‖ DEP marker, player who marks an opponent (jugador).
◆ *f* MAT secant.

secar *vt* to dry (la ropa, etc.) ‖ to dry, to wipe (enjugar); *secar los platos* to dry the dishes ‖ to blot (con papel secante) ‖ to mop, to wipe dry (el suelo) ‖ to wipe (la mesa, etc.) ‖ to wipe up, to mop up (un líquido derramado) ‖ to dry up (la tierra, las frutas, una úlcera, una fuente, un pozo) ‖ to dry up, to wither (las plantas) ‖ to season (la madera) ‖ FIG to wipe away, to dry (las lágrimas) ‖ to harden [one's heart] (el alma) ‖ to annoy, to bore (aburrir) ‖ DEP to mark.
◆ *vpr* to dry; *espera que se seque* wait until it dries ‖ to dry o.s.; *secarse al sol después de un baño* to dry o.s. in the sun after a swim ‖ to dry up (suelo, líquido, úlcera) ‖ to run dry, to dry up (río, fuente, pozo) ‖ to dry up, to wither, to wilt (planta) ‖ FIG to waste away (persona o animal) ‖ to become hardhearted (el alma) ‖ to dry, to wipe away; *sécate las lágrimas* dry your tears ‖ *secarse el sudor de la frente* to mop one's brow.

sección *f* section, cutting (cortadura); *la sección de un hueso* the cutting of a bone ‖ section (parte o grupo) ‖ section (dibujo) ‖ department (de un almacén); *sección de caballeros* men's department ‖ MAT & MIL section ‖ IMPR page, section (en un periódico); *la sección deportiva* the sports page ‖ — *sección de anuncios* or *de publicidad* advertising section ‖ *sección de trabajo* labour department ‖ *sección transversal* cross section.

seccionador *m* ELECTR (disconnecting) switch.

seccionamiento *m* sectioning.

seccionar *vt* to divide into sections, to section.

secesión *f* secession (de un Estado).

secesionista *adj/s* secessionist.

seco, ca *adj* dry (sin humedad); *la ropa está seca* the clothes are dry; *terreno, tiempo seco* dry land, weather ‖ dry (sin agua); *río seco* dry river ‖ dried up, withered (flores ajadas) ‖ dried (flores de herbario, frutas) ‖ dry (pan, leña) ‖ FIG skinny (flaco) ‖ dry (no dulce); *champaña seca* dry champagne ‖ pure (puro) ‖ sharp (ruido, golpe); *un ruido seco* a sharp sound ‖ dry, hacking (tos) ‖ curt, sharp, dry (contestación) ‖ dry (genio, estilo, etc.) ‖ hard (corazón) ‖ plain (explicación) ‖ dead (árbol) ‖ — *ama seca* dry nurse ‖ *a palo seco* under bare poles (barco), simply, on its own, just, nothing else (sin acompañamiento); *comimos pan a palo seco* we ate bread on its own, we just ate bread ‖ *a secas* simply, just; *se llama Pedro a secas* he is just called Peter; by itself, on its own; *emplear una palabra a secas* to use a word by itself ‖ FIG & FAM *dejar seco* to bump off (matar), to leave speechless (sin saber qué decir) ‖ *en seco* dry; *limpieza en seco* dry cleaning; dead, suddenly; *parar en seco* to stop dead; sharply; *frenar en seco* to pull up sharply; high and dry (fuera del agua) ‖ FIG *estar seco* to be parched *o* thirsty (tener sed) ‖ *hojas secas* dead leaves ‖ FIG *más seco que una pasa* or *un higo* or *un ripio* as thin as a rake, completely wizened ‖ *parar a uno en seco* to cut s.o. short.

secoya *f* BOT sequoia (árbol).

secreción *f* secretion.

secreta *f* JUR secret investigation ‖ REL secret (oración) ‖ water closet (excusado) ‖ FAM secret police.

secretar *vt* to secrete.

secretaría *f* secretaryship (cargo de un secretario) ‖ secretary's office (oficina de un secretario) ‖ secretariat, secretariate (oficina administrativa) ‖ Government department (del gobierno) ‖ *Secretaría de Estado* State Department (en el Vaticano y en los Estados Unidos).

secretariado *m* secretariat, secretariate (oficina) ‖ secretaryship (cargo).

secretario, ria *adj* (ant) entrusted with secrets, confidential (persona).
◆ *m/f* secretary; *secretaria particular* private secretary; *secretario general* secretary general ‖ — *secretaria de rodaje* continuity girl, script girl ‖ *Secretario de Estado* Secretary of State ‖ *secretario municipal* town clerk.
◆ *m* secretary bird (ave).

secretear *vi* FAM to talk confidentially, to whisper.

secreteo *m* FAM whispering ‖ *andar con secreteos* to whisper to each other.

secreter *m* secretaire, writing desk, escritoire (mueble).

secretina *f* secretin (hormona).

secreto, ta *adj* secret, hidden (oculto) ‖ secret (información, agente, sociedad) ‖ secret, confidential (confidencial) ‖ secretive (persona) ‖ *votación secreta* secret ballot.
◆ *m* secret; *revelar un secreto* to reveal *o* to tell a secret ‖ secrecy (condición); *hecho en secreto* done in secrecy ‖ MÚS soundboard ‖ combination (de una cerradura) ‖ — *bajo secreto de confesión* under the seal of confession *o* of the confessional ‖ *de* or *en secreto* in secret, in secrecy, secretly ‖ *estar en el secreto* to be in on the secret ‖ *guardar un secreto* to keep a secret ‖ FAM *secreto a voces* open secret ‖ *secreto de Estado* state secret ‖ *secreto de fabricación* trade secret ‖ *secreto profesional* professional secrecy.

secretor, ra; secretorio, ria *adj* ANAT secretory.

secta *f* sect.

sectario, ria *adj/s* sectarian.

sectarismo *m* sectarianism.

sector *m* MAT & ECON sector; *sector esférico* spherical sector; *sector económico* economic sector; *sector público, privado* public, private sector ‖ MIL sector ‖ INFORM sector (de disco) ‖ FIG area (zona) ‖ section (parte) ‖ — ECON *sector empresarial* business sector ‖ *sector primario* primary industry ‖ *sector secundario* secondary industry ‖ *sector terciario* tertiary industry.

sectorial *adj* MAT & COM sectorial.

secuaz *m* underling, henchman; *Al Capone y sus secuaces* Al Capone and his henchmen ‖ follower, partisan (partidario).
— OBSERV This word usually has a pejorative meaning.

secuela *f* consequence, sequel, result (consecuencia) ‖ MED sequela.

secuencia *f* sequence (en la misa) ‖ CINEM sequence.

secuencial *adj* INFORM sequential, serial.

secuestrador, ra *adj* JUR sequestrating ‖ kidnapping ‖ hijacking, high-jacking.
◆ *m/f* JUR sequestrator ‖ kidnapper (de una persona) ‖ hijacker, high-jacker (de aviones).

secuestrar *vt* JUR to confiscate, to seize, to sequester (embargar bienes, retirar un periódico, etc.) ‖ to kidnap, to abduct (una persona) ‖ to high-jack, to hijack (un avión) ‖ FIG to sequester, to sequestrate (aislar a alguien).

secuestro *m* confiscation, seizure, sequestration (de bienes, periódicos, etc.) ‖ kidnapping, abduction; *el secuestro de una persona* the kidnapping of a person ‖ high-jacking, hijacking (de un avión) ‖ MED sequestrum.

secular *adj* secular (seglar); *clero secular* secular clergy; *brazo secular* secular arm ‖ century-old (de cien años o más); *árbol secular* century-old tree ‖ secular (que se repite cada siglo o que dura un siglo) ‖ FIG age-old, century-old; *un prejuicio secular* an age-old prejudice.
◆ *m* REL secular.

secularización *f* secularization.

secularizar *vt* to secularize.

secundar *vt* to second, to support (apoyar) ‖ to assist (ayudar).

secundario, ria *adj* secondary.
◆ *m* secondary.

secundinas *f pl* MED afterbirth *sing.*

sed *f* thirst; *sed insaciable* unquenchable thirst ‖ FIG thirst, hunger; *la sed del oro* the thirst for gold ‖ AGR drought (de las tierras) ‖ — *apagar* or *quitar la sed* to quench one's thirst; *una bebida que quita la sed* a drink that quenches one's thirst ‖ *dar sed* to make thirsty ‖ *rabiar de sed* to be dying of thirst ‖ *tener sed* to be thirsty ‖ FIG *tener sed de* to be thirsty for, to thirst for, to long for.

seda *f* silk (textil); *seda cruda, floja* raw, floss silk ‖ bristle (cerda de puerco o jabalí) ‖ — FIG *aunque la mona se vista de seda, mona se queda* you can't make a silk purse out of a sow's ear ‖ *de seda* silk; *un traje de seda* a silk dress; silken, silky (como la seda) ‖ FIG *entrar como una seda* to enter *o* to go in quite easily ‖ *gusano de seda* silkworm ‖ FIG *hecho una seda* like a lamb, as meek as a lamb (persona) | *ir* or *marchar como una seda* to go *o* to run like clockwork, to go smoothly, to go like a charm ‖ *seda artificial* artificial silk ‖ *ser como una seda* to be as meek as a lamb (dócil), to be as smooth as silk (suave).

sedación *f* MED sedation ‖ soothing, calming (mitigación).

sedal *m* fishing line (para la pesca) ‖ MED seton.

sedán *m* sedan (automóvil de carrocería cerrada).

sedante *adj* MED sedative ‖ FIG soothing.
◆ *m* MED sedative.

sedar *vt* (p us) to sedate, to quiet, to soothe.

sedativo, va *adj/sm* MED sedative.

sede *f* see (episcopal) ‖ seat (de un gobierno) ‖ headquarters *pl* (de una organización); *la sede de la ONU* the headquarters of the UN ‖ — *Santa Sede* Holy See ‖ *sede social* head office (sociedad).

sedear *vt* to brush (joyas).

sedentario, ria *adj* sedentary.

sedentarismo *m* sedentariness.

sedente *adj* (p us) seated, sitting, sedentary (estatua).

sedeño, ña *adj* silken, silky (sedoso) ‖ bristly (animal).

sedera *f* bristle brush (del joyero).

sedería *f* silk trade (cría, elaboración y comercio) ‖ silk shop (tienda donde se vende seda) ‖ drapery, draper's (tienda de tejidos).

sedero, ra *adj* silk; *industria sedera* silk industry.
◆ *m* silk dealer (negociante en seda) ‖ draper (negociante en tejidos).

sedicente; sediciente *adj* so-called, would-be.

— OBSERV Este adjetivo es un barbarismo en español empleado en lugar de su equivalente *supuesto*.

sedición *f* sedition (rebelión).

sedicioso, sa *adj* seditious.
◆ *m/f* rebel (rebelde) ‖ mutineer (amotinado) ‖ troublemaker (que provoca disturbios).

sediente *adj* JUR *bienes sedientes* real estate.

sediento, ta *adj* thirsty ‖ FIG dry, parched (campos) | thirsty, hungry; *sediento de poder* power hungry, power thirsty.

sedimentación *f* sedimentation.

sedimentar *vt* to deposit, to settle (un sedimento) ‖ FIG to settle (calmar).
◆ *vpr* to settle (depositarse) ‖ FIG to settle down, to calm down (sosegarse).

sedimentario, ria *adj* sedimentary.

sedimento *m* sediment, deposit.

sedoso, sa *adj* silky, silken.

seducción *f* seduction ‖ seductiveness, charm, fascination, allure (atractivo).

seducir* *vt* to seduce, to tempt; *seducir con hermosas promesas* to seduce with attractive promises ‖ to seduce (a una mujer) ‖ to captivate, to fascinate ‖ to attract, to seduce; *esta idea me seduce* this idea attracts me.

seductor, ra *adj* seductive (que seduce) ‖ seductive, tempting (cosa) ‖ captivating, fascinating (fascinante).
◆ *m/f* seducer (que seduce) ‖ charmer (que encanta).

sefardí; sefardita *adj* Sephardic.
◆ *m/f* Sephardi.

— OBSERV El plural de la palabra inglesa es Sephardim.

— OBSERV *Sefardí* is the name given to the Spanish and Portuguese Jews in the Balkans and North Africa who have conserved their manner of speech from the XVth century when they were expelled from the Peninsula.

segadera *f* sickle (hoz) ‖ scythe (guadaña).

segador *m* harvester, reaper (trabajador) ‖ ZOOL harvestman.

segadora *adj f* mowing, reaping (máquina).
◆ *f* mower, reaper, mowing machine, reaping machine (máquina) ‖ lawnmower (para el césped) ‖ harvester, reaper (mujer) ‖ — *segadora atadora* binder ‖ *segadora trilladora* combine harvester.

segar* *vt* to reap, to cut (la mies) ‖ to mow, to cut (la hierba) ‖ FIG to cut off (cortar) | to cut down, to mow down; *segados en plena juventud* cut down in their prime | to ruin (frustrar).

seglar *adj* secular, lay (laico); *el apostolado seglar* the secular apostolate.
◆ *m/f* layman (hombre), laywoman (mujer).

segmentación *f* segmentation.

segmentar *vt* to segment.
◆ *vpr* to segment.

segmentario, ria *adj* segmentary, segmental.

segmento *m* MAT segment ‖ TECN ring; *segmento del émbolo* piston ring ‖ ZOOL segment.

segoviano, na; segoviense *adj/s* Segovian.

segregación *f* segregation; *segregación racial* racial segregation ‖ BIOL secretion.

segregacionismo *m* segregationism.

segregacionista *adj/s* segregationist.

segregar *vt* to segregate (apartar) ‖ BIOL to secrete (secretar).

segregativo, va *adj* segregative.

segueta *f* fretsaw.

seguida *f* rhythm ‖ (p us) continuation ‖ — *coger la seguida* to get into the swing of things ‖ *de seguida* without a break, continuously (seguidamente), at once, right away (inmediatamente) ‖ *en seguida* at once, straight away, immediately, right away (sin esperar); *lo llamé y vino en seguida* I called him and he came right away; *lo haré en seguida* I'll do it at once ‖ *en seguida termino* I'm nearly finished *o* through ‖ *voy en seguida* I'm just coming, I'll be right there.

seguidamente *adv* continuously, without a break (sin interrupción) ‖ straight away, straight afterwards, next (inmediatamente después).

seguidilla *f* MÚS «seguidilla».

seguido, da *adj* continuous ‖ successive, consecutive; *nuestro equipo ha ganado seis partidos seguidos* our team has won six successive games ‖ in succession, in a row, running; *seis días seguidos* six days in a row, six days running ‖ in a row; *ha tenido dos niños seguidos* she has had two boys in a row ‖ one straight after the order; *ha tenido tres niños muy seguidos* she has had three children one straight after the other ‖ straight, direct (camino, carretera) ‖ *acto seguido* immediately, immediately afterwards, straight away, at once.
◆ *adv* straight on *o* ahead; *vaya seguido* go straight on ‖ behind, after (detrás) ‖ AMER often (a menudo) ‖ *todo seguido* straight ahead; *siga usted, es todo seguido* keep on going, it is straight ahead.

seguidor, ra *adj* following (que sigue).
◆ *m/f* follower.
◆ *m* DEP supporter, fan, follower (aficionado) | follower (en ciclismo) ‖ guide lines *pl* [for writing] (pauta) ‖ suitor (pretendiente).

seguimiento *m* continuation (continuación) ‖ pursuit (perseguimiento) ‖ TECN tracking (de un satélite); *estación de seguimiento* tracking station ‖ FIG follow-up ‖ *ir en seguimiento de* to go in pursuit of.

seguir* *vt* to follow (ir detrás o después) ‖ to chase, to pursue (perseguir) ‖ to continue, to pursue, to carry on; *sigamos nuestras investigaciones* let's continue our investigations ‖ to follow (un consejo, una doctrina) ‖ to do, to take; *estuve siguiendo un cursillo de tres semanas* I did a three-week training course ‖ to follow; *es difícil seguir sus explicaciones* it is difficult to follow his explanations ‖ to take (marcha, curso, etc.); *la enfermedad sigue su curso* the illness is taking its course ‖ to hound (acosar) ‖ to follow (la pista) ‖ to follow up (un indicio) ‖ to court (cortejar) ‖ to track (un satélite) ‖ — FIG *el que la sigue la mata* perseverances gives results ‖ *seguir con los ojos a uno* to follow s.o. with one's eyes ‖ *seguir de cerca a uno* to follow s.o. closely ‖ *seguir la carrera de* to study; *seguir la carrera de médico* to study medicine ‖ FIG *seguir la corriente* to swim with the stream, to follow the tide *o* the crowd (ser conformista) ‖ *seguir las huellas* or *las pisadas de alguien* to follow s.o.'s tracks *o* trail, to trail s.o. (seguir el rastro), to follow in s.o.'s footsteps (hacer igual que otro) ‖ *seguir su camino*

to continue on one's way (continuar adelante), to carry on, to get on with it (continuar con lo que se está haciendo); *tú sigue tu camino y no te preocupes de lo que dicen* you carry on and don't worry about what they say.
◆ *vi* to follow, to come after, to come next (venir después) ‖ to follow on, to continue; *este artículo sigue en la página 7* this article follows on on page 7 ‖ to carry on, to go on, to continue; *¡sigue!* carry on!, go on!; *¡sigamos!* let's continue! ‖ to go on (con una idea) ‖ to remain (permanecer); *siguió de pie* he remained standing ‖ to be still (estar todavía); *sigue en París* he is still in Paris; *mi tío sigue enfermo* my uncle is still sick; *sigue trabajando* he is still working ‖ (to still) + verb; *sigo sin comprender* I still don't understand; *sigo sin recibir noticias* I still haven't received any news ‖ — *como sigue* as follows ‖ *¿cómo sigue?* how is he?, how is he doing?, how is he getting on? (¿qué tal está?), what comes next?, how does it go on? (intentando recordar algo) ‖ *¡que siga bien!* keep well ‖ *seguir* (con verbo en gerundio), to keep on (gerundio), to go on (gerundio), to continue (gerundio); *seguir leyendo* to keep on reading ‖ *seguir adelante* to go on, to carry on (en un trabajo), to go straight on (en un camino) ‖ *seguir con su trabajo* to carry on working, to carry on with one's work ‖ *seguir en su error* to persist *o* to continue in one's error ‖ FIG & FAM *seguir en sus trece* to stick to one's guns ‖ *seguir en su trabajo* to be still in the same job ‖ *seguir por una carretera* to go along a road ‖ *seguir siendo* to be still, to continue to be; *a pesar de su edad sigue siendo guapa* in spite of her age she is still good-looking ‖ *¡sigamos!* on with the show! (en el teatro) ‖ *sigue* continued (folletín), PTO, please turn over (carta, documento).
◆ *vpr* to follow (ir a continuación) ‖ to ensue, to follow (ocurrir como consecuencia) ‖ to deduce, to infer (inferirse) ‖ to spring, to issue, to be derived (derivarse) ‖ *de esto se sigue que...* it follows that...

seguiriya *f* MÚS «seguidilla» (seguidilla flamenca).

según *prep* according to, depending on; *según la edad que tienes* according to how old you are, according to your age; *según las circunstancias* depending on the circumstances ‖ in accordance with, according to (de conformidad con); *te pagaré según tu trabajo* I will pay you in accordance with your work; *según el Tratado de Roma* according to the Treaty of Rome ‖ depending on; *según te encuentres mañana* depending on how you feel tomorrow; *según el tiempo* depending on the weather ‖ according to; *según lo que me dijo* according to what he told me; *según ellos* according to them; *evangelio según San Lucas* Gospel according to Saint Luke; *según las últimas noticias* according to the latests news.
◆ *adv* so; *no podía moverse, según estaba de cansado* he couldn't move he was so tired ‖ it all depends, it depends; *vendrá o no, según* he may or may not come, it depends ‖ depending on; *según me diga que sí o que no* depending on whether he says yes or no ‖ according to; *según me dijo* according to what he told me ‖ just as (igual que); *sigue todo según estaba* everything is just as it was ‖ as (a medida que); *según nos acercábamos el ruido aumentaba* as we approached the noise grew louder ‖ — *es según* it all depends, it depends ‖ *según cómo vayamos* depending on how we go ‖ *según están las cosas* the way things are at present ‖ *según estén las cosas* depending on *o* according to how things stand ‖ *según que haga frío o calor* depending on whether is hot or cold ‖ *según se frotaba las manos debía de estar contento* he must have been pleased judging by the way be rubbed his hands together ‖ *según y como, según y conforme* just as, exactly as (igual que); *te lo diré según y como me lo dijeron* I will tell you it just as it was told to me; depending on how; *vendré según y cómo me encuentre* I'll come depending on how I feel; it all depends, it depends (depende).

segunda *f* double turn of a lock (cerradura) ‖ second class; *viajar en segunda* to travel in second class ‖ second (velocidad) ‖ seconde (de esgrima) ‖ FIG double *o* veiled *o* hidden meaning; *hablar con segundas* to talk with double meanings ‖ MÚS second.

segundar *vt* to repeat (repetir) ‖ to help, to second (ayudar).
◆ *vi* to come second, to be second.

segundario, ria *adj* secondary.

segundero, ra *adj* of the second crop of the year (fruto).
◆ *m* second hand (en un reloj).

segundo, da *adj* second ‖ — FIG *de segunda mano* secondhand (ventas), at second hand (informaciones) ‖ *en segundo lugar* secondly (en conversación), in second place (en una competición) ‖ *segunda enseñanza* secondary education ‖ *segunda intención* double meaning; *hablar con segundas intenciones* to talk with double meanings ‖ *segundas nupcias* second marriage ‖ *segundo jefe* assistant chief ‖ *segundo piso* second floor [US third floor] ‖ *sobrino segundo* first cousin once removed.
◆ *adv* second (en segundo lugar).
◆ *m/f* second [one] (segunda persona).
◆ *m* second (del reloj) ‖ second in command *o* in authority (en una jerarquía) ‖ second floor [US third floor] (piso) ‖ MAT second ‖ DEP second (en boxeo) ‖ — MAR *el segundo de a bordo* the first mate ‖ FIG *sin segundo* peerless, unrivalled.

segundogénito, ta *adj/s* second-born.

segundón *m* second son (segundo hijo) ‖ younger son (hijo que no es el primogénito).

segur *f* axe (hacha) ‖ sickle (hoz).

seguramente *adv* for sure, for certain (con certidumbre) ‖ probably (probablemente) ‖ surely (muy probablemente) ‖ securely, safely (sujetar, etc.).

seguridad *f* security, safety; *la seguridad del país está en peligro* the security of the country is in danger ‖ security; *las mujeres buscan seguridad* women long for security; *las pensiones dan la seguridad para la vejez* pensions give security in old age; *medidas de seguridad para proteger un arma secreta* security measures to protect a secret weapon ‖ safety; *la seguridad en carretera depende del estado de la calzada* road safety depends upon the state of the road surface ‖ reliability; *la seguridad del frenado* the reliability of the brakes ‖ safety, safeness; *la seguridad de un puente* the safety of a bridge ‖ surety, certainty (certidumbre) ‖ conviction; *hablar con seguridad* to speak with conviction ‖ sureness (destreza, firmeza) ‖ — *con seguridad* securely (con fijeza), for sure, for certain (seguramente) ‖ *consejo de Seguridad* Security Council (de la ONU) ‖ *con toda seguridad* with complete *o* absolute certainty (sin riesgo), for sure, for certain (seguramente) ‖ *de seguridad* safety; *cerradura de seguridad* safety lock; *cinturón de seguridad* safety belt ‖ *Dirección General de Seguridad* police headquarters ‖ *en la seguridad de que...* knowing that..., with the surety that... ‖ *en seguridad* in safety ‖ *para mayor seguridad* for safety's sake, to be on the safe side ‖ *seguridad en sí mismo* self-confidence ‖ *Seguridad Social* Social Security ‖ AUT *seguridad vial* road safety ‖ *tener la seguridad de que...* to be sure *o* certain that... ‖ *tengan la seguridad de que...* rest assured that...

seguro, ra *adj* sure, certain (cierto); *estoy seguro de que ha venido* I am sure that he has come ‖ secure; *nuestra victoria es segura* our victory is secure ‖ safe; *un sitio seguro* a safe place; *inversión segura* safe investment ‖ solid, firm, secure (firme) ‖ secure, steady, stable (estable) ‖ firm, definite (fecha) ‖ reliable, dependable, trustworthy (de fiar) ‖ reliable; *fuentes seguras* reliable sources ‖ reliable, trustworthy; *informaciones seguras* reliable information ‖ — *dar por seguro* to take for granted ‖ *lo más seguro es irse* the safest thing *o* the best thing is to go.
◆ *adv* for sure, for certain.
◆ *m* insurance; *seguro a todo riesgo* fully comprehensive insurance; *seguro contra accidentes* accident insurance; *seguro contra robo* insurance against theft, theft insurance; *seguro contra terceros* third-party insurance; *seguro contra incendios* fire insurance; *seguro sobre la vida, seguro de vida* life insurance; *compañía de seguros* insurance company; *prima de seguro* insurance premium ‖ safety device (dispositivo de seguridad) ‖ safety catch (de armas) ‖ AMER safety pin (imperdible) ‖ — *a buen seguro* surely, without a doubt *o* any doubt ‖ *de seguro* surely, without a doubt *o* any doubt ‖ *en seguro* in safekeeping, in a safe place (a salvo) ‖ *ir sobre seguro* to be on safe ground ‖ *póliza de seguro* insurance policy ‖ *saber a buen seguro* to know for certain ‖ *seguros sociales* social *o* national insurance, social security ‖ *sobre seguro* without any risk, safely.

seibo *m* AMER BOT ceibo.

seis *adj/s* six; *el seis de corazones* the six of hearts ‖ — *el reloj dio las seis* the clock struck six ‖ *son las seis* it is six o'clock.
◆ *m* sixth (fecha); *el seis de enero* the 6th [sixth] of January, January 6th [the sixth].

seisavo, va *adj/s* sixth.
◆ *m* hexagon.

seiscientos, tas *adj/s* six hundred; *dos mil seiscientos* two thousand six hundred; *el año seiscientos* the year six hundred ‖ *seiscientos veinte* six hundred and twenty.

seise *m* one of six choir boys who sing and dance in the cathedral of Seville during certain festivals.

seisillo *m* MÚS sextuplet.

seísmo *m* earthquake, seism (p us) (terremoto).

selacio *m* ZOOL selachian.

selección *f* selection; *selección natural* natural selection ‖ selection (conjunto de cosas seleccionadas); *una selección de libros* a selection of books.

seleccionado, da *adj* DEP selected.
◆ *m/f* player selected for a team.

seleccionador, ra *m/f* DEP selector.

seleccionar *vt* to select, to choose, to pick (out) (elegir) ‖ DEP to select.

selectividad *f* RAD selectivity.

selectivo, va *adj* selective ‖ *(curso) selectivo* selective course taken before one begins technical studies at university.

selecto, ta *adj* selected; *poesías selectas* selected poems ‖ FIG choice, select (superior); *vinos selectos* select wines | select; *sociedad selecta* select society ‖ *ser de lo más selecto* to be of the very best.

selector *m* selector.

selenio *m* QUÍM selenium.

selenita *f* selenite.
◆ *m/f* moon dweller.

selenografía *f* ASTR selenography.

selenógrafo *m* ASTR selenographer.

seleúcidas *npr mpl/fpl* HIST Seleucids.

self *f* ELECTR self-induction coil.

selfinducción *f* self-induction.

selfservice *m* self-service.

Seltz *n pr* *agua de Seltz* seltzer (water).

selva *f* forest; *selva virgen* virgin forest ‖ jungle (jungla) ‖ — *la ley de la selva* the law of the jungle ‖ GEOGR *Selva Negra* Black Forest | *selva tropical* tropical forest.

selvático, ca; silvático, ca *adj* forest, woodland (de las selvas); *árboles selváticos* woodland trees ‖ FIG crude, incouth (inculto).

selvoso, sa *adj* forest, forested, wooded ‖ jungle (con jungla).

sellado, da *adj* sealed ‖ stamped; *carta, papel sellado* stamped letter, paper ‖ AUT *circuito sellado* sealed circuit.
◆ *m* sealing, affixing of seals ‖ stamping (de una carta).

sellador, ra *adj* stamping (que franquea) ‖ sealing.
◆ *m/f* stamper (franqueador) ‖ sealer (de documentos oficiales, etc.).

selladura *f* sealing (de un documento oficial) ‖ stamping (de una carta) ‖ sealing (lacrado).

sellar *vt* to seal (un documento oficial) ‖ to stamp (estampar el sello); *me sellaron este papel en el consulado* they stamped this paper for me in the consulate ‖ to seal (cerrar); *sellar con lacre* to seal with wax ‖ to stamp (timbrar) ‖ to hallmark, to stamp (joyas, monedas) ‖ FIG to brand, to stamp (marcar) | to seal (la amistad) | to seal (cerrar); *sellar los labios* to seal one's lips | to close, to end (concluir).

sello *m* stamp (viñeta de papel); *sello fiscal* revenue stamp; *poner un sello en un sobre* to put a stamp on an envelope ‖ seal (de documento oficial) ‖ seal (de metal) ‖ stamp, seal (señal impresa) ‖ rubber stamp, rubber seal (de caucho) ‖ signet ring (sortija) ‖ stamp office (oficina) ‖ MED capsule ‖ hallmark, stamp (de joyas y monedas) ‖ FIG mark; *sus obras llevan su sello* his works carry his mark | stamp, mark; *el sello del genio* the mark of genius | hallmark, seal; *sello de distinción* hallmark of distinction ‖ — FIG *echar el sello a una cosa* to put the finishing touches to sth., to finish sth. off ‖ *estampar* or *poner el sello* to stamp, to seal ‖ FIG *marcar a alguien con el sello de* to brand s.o.; *le han marcado con el sello de mentiroso* they have branded him a liar ‖ *sello de correo* postage stamp ‖ *sello de Salomón* Solomon's seal ‖ *sello discográfico* record label.
◆ *pl* seals; *quebrantamiento* or *violación de sellos* breaking of seals.

semáforo *m* semaphore (martítimo) ‖ traffic lights *pl* (de tráfico urbano) ‖ signal (de ferrocarril).

semana *f* week; *Semana grande* or *mayor* or *Santa* Holy Week; *dos veces a la semana* twice a week ‖ week's wages *pl* (salario semanal) ‖ game similar to hopscotch (juego) ‖ — *días entre semana* week-days ‖ *entre semana* during the week ‖ *fin de semana* weekend (sábado y domingo), weekend case (maletín) ‖ *la semana pasada, que viene* last, next week ‖ FAM *la semana que no tenga viernes* never in a month of Sundays, when pigs have wings *o* begin to fly ‖ *semana inglesa* five and a half day week ‖ *semana laboral* working week.

semanal *adj* weekly; *salario semanal* weekly wage ‖ *descanso semanal* weekly closing day (de una tienda).

semanalmente *adv* weekly.

semanario, ria *adj* weekly.
◆ *m* weekly (periódico) ‖ set of seven razors (navajas de afeitar) ‖ set of seven bracelets (pulseras).

semántico, ca *adj* semantic.
◆ *f* semantics.

semasiología *f* semantics, semasiology.

semblante *m* countenance, visage, face; *semblante risueño* smiling face ‖ FIG look (aspecto) ‖ — *componer el semblante* to regain one's composure ‖ *en su semblante* in one's face ‖ *mudar de semblante* to change colour (personas), to take on a different aspect (cosas) ‖ *tener buen, mal semblante* to look well, bad (salud), to be in a good, a bad mood; to be in good, bad humour (humor).

semblanza *f* portrait, biographical sketch.

sembradera *f* drill, seed drill (máquina).

sembradío, a *adj* cultivable, cultivatable.

sembrado *m* sown field *o* land.

sembrador, ra *adj* sowing, seeding.
◆ *m/f* sower.
◆ *f* drill, seed drill (sembradera).

sembradura *f* sowing, seeding ‖ sown land (sembrado).

sembrar* *vt* AGR to sow, to seed (un campo); *un terreno sembrado de patatas* a piece of land sown with potatoes | to sow (las semillas) ‖ FIG to sow, to spread; *sembrar el pánico* to sow panic | to spread, to diffuse (una doctrina) | to scatter, to strew (un camino con flores, palmas) ‖ — FIG *quien siembra recoge* one reaps what one has sown | *quien siembra vientos recoge tempestades* he who sows the wind shall reap the whirlwind | *sembrar la discordia* to sow discord.

sembrío *m* AMER sown land.

semejante *adj* similar, alike; *dos objetos semejantes* two similar objects ‖ similar, such; *en semejante caso* in a similar case, in such a case ‖ such, like that; *nunca he visto a semejante tonto* I have never seen such a fool; *cuando oigo cosas semejantes* when I hear things like that ‖ MAT similar ‖ — *es muy semejante a ti* he is quite like you ‖ *son muy semejantes* they are very much alike *o* very similar ‖ *una cosa semejante* sth. of the sort, sth. like that.
◆ *m* fellow man (prójimo) ‖ *no tiene semejante* it has no equal.

semejanza *f* resemblance, likeness (parecido) ‖ similarity; *la semejanza de los métodos* the similarity of methods ‖ simile (símil) ‖ MAT similarity ‖ — *a semejanza de* after, in the manner of, like ‖ *tener semejanza con* to bear a resemblance to, to resemble.

semejar *vi* to seem to be, to seem (parecer) ‖ to look like (parecerse a).
◆ *vpr* to resemble each other, to be similar, to be *o* to look alike ‖ *semejarse a* to be like, to resemble.

semen *m* BIOL semen, sperm ‖ BOT seed (semilla).

semental *adj m* breeding, stud (animal macho) ‖ seed (de la semilla) ‖ sowing (de la siembra).
◆ *m* sire, stud animal (caballo).

sementera *f* sowing, seeding (acción) ‖ sowing time, seedtime (temporada) ‖ sown land (tierra) ‖ FIG hotbed (*de* of), breeding ground (*de* for).

sementero *m* seedbag (saco) ‖ seeding, sowing (sementera).

semestral *adj* half-yearly, biannual.

semestre *m* period of six months ‖ semester (en una universidad americana) ‖ COM half-yearly payment (pago).

semianual *adj* semiannual.

semiárido, da *adj* semiarid.

semiautomático, ca *adj* semiautomatic.

semibreve *f* MÚS semibreve [US whole note].

semicilíndrico, ca *adj* semicylindrical.

semicilindro *m* semicylinder.

semicircular *adj* semicircular.

semicírculo *m* MAT semicircle.

semicircunferencia *f* MAT semicircumference.

semiconductor *m* ELECTR semiconductor.

semiconsciente *adj* semiconscious, half-conscious.

semiconsonante *adj* GRAM semiconsonantal.
◆ *f* GRAM semiconsonant.

semicorchea *f* MÚS semiquaver [US sixteenth note].

semicromático, ca *adj* MÚS semichromatic.

semicualificado, da *adj* semiskilled.

semiculto, ta *adj* half-learned (palabra)

semidesierto, ta *adj* half-deserted.

semidesnudo, da *adj* half-naked.

semidiámetro *m* MAT semidiameter.

semidifunto *adj* half-dead.

semidiós *m* demigod.

semidirecto, ta *adj* semidirect.

semidoble *adj* BOT & REL semi-double.

semidormido, da *adj* half-asleep.

semieje *m* semiaxis.

semiesfera *f* hemisphere.

semiesférico, ca *adj* hemispherical.

semifallo *m* singleton (bridge).

semifinal *f* semifinal.

semifinalista *adj* semifinal.
◆ *m/f* semifinalist.

semifino, na *adj* semifine.

semifusa *f* MÚS hemidemisemiquaver [US sixty-fourth note].

semilunar *adj* semilunar.

semilla *f* BOT seed ‖ FIG source, cause, seed, seeds *pl* (origen) ‖ FIG *echar la semilla de la discordia* to sow the seeds of discord.

semillero *m* nursery, seedbed ‖ FIG seedbed (cantera); *esta universidad es un semillero de estadistas* this university is a seedbed of statesmen | hotbed, breeding ground (de criminales, etc.) | source; *esto ha sido un semillero de disturbios* this has been a source of disturbances.

semimanufacturado, da *adj* semi-manufactured.

semimedio *m* DEP welterweight (en boxeo).

seminal *adj* BIOL seminal; *líquido seminal* seminal fluid.

seminario *m* seminary (colegio eclesiástico) ‖ nursery, seedbed (semillero) ‖ seminar (de investigaciones) ‖ — *seminario de teología* theological seminary *o* college ‖ *seminario mayor* Roman Catholic seminary, training college [for priesthood] ‖ *seminario menor* secondary school [staffed by priests].

seminarista *m* seminarist.

seminífero, ra *adj* ANAT & BOT seminiferous.

seminómada *adj* seminomadic.
◆ *m/f* seminomad.

seminuevo, va *adj* almost new.

semioculto, ta *adj* half-hidden.

semioficial *adj* semiofficial.

semiología *f* MED semeiology, semiology.

semiológico, ca *adj* MED semeiologic, semiologic.

semiólogo *m* MED semeiologist, semiologist.

semiótico, ca *adj* semeiotic, semiotic.
◆ *f* semeiotics, semiotics.

semipesado *adj m/sm* light heavyweight (boxeo).

semipleno, na *adj* JUR incomplete, imperfect.

semiprecioso, sa *adj* semiprecious.

semiproducto *m* by-product.

semirrecto *adj m* forty-five degree (ángulo).

semirrefinado, da *adj* semi-refined.

semirremolque *m* semitrailer.

semirrígido, da *adj* semirigid.

semisalvaje *adj* half-savage.

semisólido, da *adj/sm* semisolid.

semita *adj* Semitic.
◆ *m/f* Semite.

semítico, ca *adj* Semitic.

semitismo *m* Semitism.

semitista *m/f* Semitist.

semitono *m* MÚS semitone, halftone.

semitransparente *adj* semitransparent.

semivivo, va *adj* half-alive.

semivocal *adj* GRAM semivocalic.
◆ *f* GRAM semivowel.

sémola *f* semolina.

semoviente *adj* *bienes semovientes* livestock.

sempiterno, na *adj* sempiternal, everlasting, eternal (eterno) ‖ FIG everlasting, unending (fastidioso).
◆ *f* BOT everlasting flower, immortelle.

Sena *npr m* GEOGR Seine.

senado *m* senate ‖ FIG assembly.

senador *m* senator.

senaduría *f* senatorship.

senatorio, ria; senatorial *adj* senatorial.

sencillamente *adv* simply.

sencillez *f* simplicity; *hablar con mucha sencillez* to speak with great simplicity ‖ unaffectedness, simplicity, naturalness (falta de afectación) ‖ — *con sencillez* simply ‖ *un mecanismo de una gran sencillez* a very simple mechanism.

sencillo, lla *adj* simple, easy (fácil); *no hay cosa sencilla en este mundo* nothing is easy in this world ‖ single; *una escopeta de un cañón sencillo* a single barrel shotgun; *billete sencillo* single ticket ‖ BOT single ‖ plain (sin adorno); *una fachada sencilla* a plain façade ‖ simple, unpretentious; *una comida sencilla* a simple meal ‖ plain, simple; *un vestido sencillo* a plain dress ‖ simple, harmless, guileless (sin malicia) ‖ natural, unaffected, unsophisticated (natural) ‖ gullible, naïve (ingenuo) ‖ — *no hay cosa más sencilla* there is nothing simpler ‖ *sencillo a la par que elegante* simple but elegant.
◆ *m* AMER small change (suelto).

sencillote, ta *adj* FAM simple.

senda *f* path, track, footpath ‖ FIG road, way, path; *tomar la mala senda* to take the wrong road, to go the wrong way.

sendero *m* path, track, footpath (senda).

sendos, das *adj pl* each; *los niños recibieron sendos regalos* the children each received a present; *los tres hombres llevaban sendos sombreros* the three men were each wearing a hat.

Séneca *npr m* Seneca ‖ FIG man of wisdom.

senectud *f* old age.

Senegal *npr m* GEOGR Senegal.

senegalés, esa *adj/s* Senegalese.

senescal *m* seneschal.

senescencia *f* aging, ageing, senescence.

senestrado, da *adj* HERÁLD sinister.

senil *adj* senile (de la vejez).

senilidad *f* senility.

senior *m* senior.

seno *m* ANAT breast (pecho) | womb (matriz) | sinus (de un hueso); *seno frontal* frontal sinus ‖ bosom; *guardó la carta en el seno* she put the letter in her bosom ‖ FIG bosom; *en el seno del mar* in the bosom of the sea; *el seno de la iglesia* the bosom of the church ‖ MAR bay, gulf (bahía pequeña) | belly (de una vela) | trough (entre las olas) ‖ MAT sine ‖ ARQ spandrel ‖ cavity, recess (cavidad) ‖ *el seno de Abrahán* the bosom of Abraham.

sensación *f* sensation; *causar sensación* to cause a sensation; *este número ha sido la sensación de la noche* this act was the sensation of the evening ‖ feeling, sensation; *sensación de calor* feeling of warmth.

sensacional *adj* sensational.

sensacionalismo *m* sensationalism.

sensacionalista *adj* sensationalistic, sensational.
◆ *m/f* sensationalist.

sensatez *f* good sense, sensibleness (buen sentido) ‖ sensibleness, wisdom; *la sensatez de una respuesta* the sensibleness of an answer.

sensato, ta *adj* sensible.

sensibilidad *f* sensibility ‖ sensitivity, feeling (perceptibilidad de sensaciones); *tiene muy poca sensibilidad en el brazo* he has very little feeling in his arm; *pinta con sensibilidad* he paints with feeling ‖ sensitivity (de aparatos, etc.) ‖ *tiene mucha sensibilidad* he is very sensitive (impresionable), he is very softhearted *o* compassionate (compasivo).

sensibilización *f* FOT & MED sensitization.

sensibilizar *vt* FOT & MED to sensitize.

sensible *adj* sentient, feeling (capaz de tener sensaciones); *un ser sensible* a sentient being ‖ sensitive (impresionable); *una mujer sensible* a sensitive woman ‖ tenderhearted (compasivo) ‖ sensible, perceptible (perceptible) ‖ tangible; *el mundo sensible* the tangible world ‖ noticeable, appreciable; *sensibles adelantos* noticeable advances ‖ sensitive; *un aparato sensible* a sensitive device; *sensible a la luz* sensitive to light ‖ FOT sensitive ‖ lamentable, deplorable (lamentable) ‖ — FIG *corazón sensible* tender heart ‖ *sensible al tacto* tender, sensitive to the touch (que duele todavía), which can be felt, perceptible to the touch, tangible (que se nota tocando) ‖ *sitio sensible* tender *o* sore spot ‖ *un oído sensible* a sensitive ear.

sensiblemente *adv* appreciably, noticeably.

sensiblería *f* sentimentality, sentimentalism ‖ schmaltz (*fam*), sloppiness (*fam*) (peyorativo).

sensiblero, ra *adj* schmaltzy (*fam*), oversentimental, sloppy (*fam*).

sensitiva *f* BOT sensitive plant, mimosa.

sensitivo, va *adj* sensitive, susceptible (sensible) ‖ sense; *órgano sensitivo* sense organ ‖ sentient (que tiene facultades sensoriales).

sensorial; sensorio, ria *adj* sensorial, sensory.

sensual *adj* sensual; sensuous.

sensualidad *f* sensuality.

sensualismo *m* sensualism.

sensualista *adj* sensualistic.
◆ *m/f* sensualist.

sentada *f* sitting (asentada) ‖ sit-in (huelga de estudiantes) ‖ sit-down strike (huelga de empleados) ‖ AMER reining in [of a horse in full gallop] ‖ *de una sentada* in one sitting.

sentado, da *adj* seated, sitting (down); *estar sentado* to be seated *o* sitting (down) ‖ established, settled (asentado) ‖ stable (estable) ‖ FIG sensible, steady (sesudo, reflexivo) | sedate (sosegado) ‖ BOT sessile ‖ — FIG *dar algo por sentado* to take sth. for granted, to assume sth. | *haber sentado la cabeza* to have settled down ‖ *pan sentado* stale bread ‖ *quiero dejar sentado que...* I want to make it clear that... ‖ *sentado esto* having established this.

sentadura *f* sore (en la piel).

sentamiento *m* ARQ settling.

sentar* *vt* to seat, to sit (a alguien) ‖ to set (poner firme) ‖ to press (una costura) ‖ to establish, to set up, to lay (down) (establecer algo) ‖ to state, to affirm (una conclusión) ‖ to pitch (una tienda) ‖ AMER to rein in sharply (un caballo) ‖ — FIG *sentar cabeza* to settle down, to calm down (volverse razonable) | *sentar las bases de* to lay the foundations of ‖ *sentar plaza* to enlist, to join up (un soldado) ‖ *sentar por escrito* to put (down) in writing ‖ FIG & FAM *sentar sus reales* to settle down, to establish o.s. ‖ *sentar un precedente* to establish *o* to set a precedent.
◆ *vi* to suit, to become (favorecer); *no te sienta nada bien el amarillo* yellow doesn't suit you at all; *te sienta muy bien este peinado* this hairstyle really suits you; *esa actitud no te sienta nada bien* that attitude doesn't become you at all ‖ to fit (las medidas de la ropa, etc.); *me sienta bastante bien la chaqueta, pero el pantalón me está pequeño* the jacket fits me quite well, but the trousers are too small ‖ to agree with (digerirse bien o mal); *los caracoles me sientan fatal* snails don't agree with me at all ‖ to suit (convenir) ‖ — *sentar bien* to do good, to be good for (hacer buen efecto); *bébete este té, que te sentará bien para el dolor de vientre* drink this tea, it will be good for your tummy ache *o* it will do your tummy good; to like, to appreciate (gustar a uno); *los cumplidos siempre sientan bien* people always like to be flattered; to take well (tomar bien); *le sentó bien lo que le dije* he took what I said well ‖ *sentar como anillo al dedo* to fit like a glove (estar bien ajustado), to suit down to the ground (convenir o favorecer mucho) ‖ FIG & FAM *sentar como un tiro* to come as a blow *la noticia le sentó como un tiro* the news came as a blow to him, he took the news very badly ‖ *sentar mal* not to appreciate; *la broma le sentó muy mal* he didn't appreciate the joke; to take badly (tomar a mal) ‖ *te habrá sentado mal algo que comiste* sth. you ate must have disagreed with you.
◆ *vpr* to sit (down); *se sentó en una silla* he sat down in a chair; *siempre me siento aquí* I always sit here ‖ to settle; *el poso del café se ha sentado en el fondo de la taza* the coffee dregs have settled in the bottom of the cup ‖ to settle down, to clear up (el tiempo, etc.) ‖ ARQ to settle ‖ to rub (los zapatos) ‖ FIG *sentársele a uno el juicio* to come to one's senses.

sentencia *f* maxim (máxima) ‖ FIG ruling, decision (decisión) ‖ JUR sentence; *pronunciar la sentencia* to pronounce *o* to pass sentence; *cumplir la sentencia* to serve one's sentence ‖ — JUR *sentencia en rebeldía* judgment by default *o* in contumacy | *sentencia firme* final judgment | *visto para sentencia* ready for judgment.

sentenciar *vt* to judge (juzgar) ‖ to sentence (condenar); *sentenciar al exilio* to sentence to exile.

sentencioso, sa *adj* sententious.

sentido *m* meaning, sense (significado); *esta frase tiene varios sentidos* this sentence has various meanings ‖ sense; *sentido común* common sense; *buen sentido* good sense; *el sentido de la vista, del olfato* the sense of sight, of smell ‖ consciousness (conocimiento) ‖ direction; *en sentido contrario* in the opposite direction ‖ sense; *los negros tienen un buen sentido del ritmo* Negroes have a good sense of rhythm; *sentido del humor* sense of humour ‖ feeling (sentimiento); *lo leyó con mucho sentido* he read it with a lot of feeling ‖ — *aguzar el sentido* to prick up one's ears, to listen attentively ‖ *calle* *de sentido único* one-way street || *con los cinco sentidos* for all one is worth; *escuché con los cinco sentidos* I listened for all I was worth || FAM *costar un sentido* to cost the earth *o* a fortune || *dar mal sentido a algo* to take sth. the wrong way || *dar sentido torcido a* to twist the meaning of || *de doble sentido* with double meaning || FIG *dejar sin sentido* to stun || *embargar los sentidos* to take one's breath away (de admiración) || *en cierto sentido* in a sense || *en contra del sentido común* against common sense, in defiance of common sense || *en el buen sentido de la palabra* in the best sense of the word || *en el sentido amplio de la palabra* in the broad sense of the word || *en tal sentido* to this effect || *en todos los sentidos* in every sense (una palabra), in all directions (en todas direcciones), in every way (en todos los aspectos) || *esto no tiene sentido* this doesn't make sense || FIG *hacerle perder el sentido a uno* to drive s.o. insane || FAM *llevar* or *pedir un sentido* to ask the earth || *no le encuentro sentido alguno* I can't make any sense (out) of it || *perder el sentido* to faint, to lose consciousness (desmayarse), to go out of one's mind, to lose one's senses (volverse loco) || FAM *poner sus cinco sentidos en una cosa* to give one's undivided attention to sth., to put everything one has into sth. || FAM *quitar el sentido* to take one's breath away, to knock s.o. out; *esta mujer me quita el sentido* this woman knocks me out || *recobrar el sentido* to come round, to regain consciousness, to come to || *sentido de la orientación* sense of direction || *sentido figurado* figurative sense || *sin sentido* meaningless (palabra, etc.), senseless, unconscious (inconsciente) || *tener sentido* to make sense || *tomar una cosa en buen, en mal sentido* to take sth. the right, the wrong way.

sentido, da *adj* deeply felt, deepest, heartfelt, sincere; *sentido pésame* sincere condolences, deepest sympathy || deeply felt; *una muerte muy sentida* a very deeply felt death || moving, touching (conmovedor) || tender; *un sentido recuerdo* a tender memory || FIG sensitive, touchy (sensible).

sentimental *adj* sentimental || — *aventura sentimental* love affair || *vida sentimental* love life.

◆ *m/f* sentimentalist.

sentimentalismo *m* sentimentalism, sentimentality.

sentimentaloide *adj* FAM schmaltzy, oversentimental.

sentimiento *m* feeling; *tener sentimentos cariñosos* to have affectionate feelings; *un sentimiento de alegría* a feeling of joy || sentiment; *sentimientos nobles, liberales* noble, liberal sentiments || regret, sorrow (pesar) || grief, sorrow (aflicción) || sense (sentido); *sentimiento del deber* sense of duty || — *con mi mayor sentimiento* with my deepest regret || *herir los sentimientos de alguien* to hurt s.o.'s feelings || *le acompaño en el sentimiento* my deepest sympathy, I sympathize with you.

sentina *f* MAR bilge || FIG sewer, cesspool (albañal) | den of iniquity (donde hay vicio).

sentir *m* sentiment, feeling; *el sentir de la nación* national sentiment || judgment, opinion, view (parecer) || *en mi sentir* in my opinion.

sentir* *vt/vi* to feel; *¿no sientes frío, hambre?* don't you feel cold, hungry?; *yo nunca siento el frío* I never feel the cold || to hear (oír); *sentimos una fuerte explosión* we heard a loud explosion || to sense, to feel, to have the feeling that (barruntar); *sentí que alguien me seguía* I sensed s.o. was following me || to have a feeling for; *sentir la poesía* to have a feeling for poetry || to feel (en lo moral); *sintió mucha pena* he felt a great deal of sorrow || to regret, to feel *o* to be sorry (afligirse); *siento que se vaya* I am sorry that you're going; *siento no haberle visto* I regret not having seen him, I'm sorry I didn't see him || to feel (opinar) || to feel the effect of (una enfermedad, etc.) || to be affected by, to feel the effect of; *muchas flores sienten la falta de lluvia* many flowers are affected by the lack of rain || — *dar que sentir* to give cause for regret || *dejarse sentir* to begin to make itself felt || *dejarse sentir el calor, el frío* to begin to get hot, cold (el tiempo) || *lo siento* I'm sorry || *lo siento mucho* I'm very sorry, I'm so sorry || *marcharse sin sentir* to leave unnoticed, to slip out || *sentir en el alma* to be deeply sorry, to regret deeply || *sin sentir* just like that, without noticing; *se nos pasó la mañana sin sentir* the morning went by just like that *o* without our noticing it; just like that; *se tragó la pastilla sin sentir* he swallowed the pill just like that.

◆ *vpr* to feel; *sentirse enfermo, obligado a* to feel ill, obliged to || to suffer (*de* from), to suffer (de una enfermedad) || — *comienza a sentirse el frío en noviembre* it starts to get cold in November || *me siento mal* I feel ill *o* sick || FIG *no se siente una mosca* it is dead silent, you could hear a pin drop || *sentirse como en su casa* to feel at home || FIG *sentirse como un pez en el agua* to be in one's element, to feel completely at home || *sentirse con ánimos para hacer algo* to feel like doing sth., to feel up to doing sth.

sentón *m* AMER reining in || *dar un sentón* to rein in sharply.

seña *f* sign, signal; *hacer señas* to make signs || mark (marca) || MIL password *santo y seña* password.

◆ *pl* address *sing*; *le di mis señas* I gave him my address || description *sing* (filiación) || — *dar señas de satisfacción* to show signs of satisfaction || *hablar por señas* to talk in sign language || *las señas son mortales* it's perfectly clear || *me hizo señas para que empezara* he signalled to me to start || *por más señas* more specifically || || *señas personales* description.

señal *f* mark (marca) || signal; *al ver su señal nos paramos* when we saw his signal, we stopped; *señal de alarma* alarm signal; *dar la señal* to give the signal || sign, indication (signo, indicio); *buena, mala señal* good, bad sign || sign (letrero) || mark, scar (cicatriz) || proof, sign (prueba) || bookmark (en un libro) || landmark (mojón) || COM deposit, token payment (dinero); *dejar una señal* to leave a deposit || dialling tone (teléfono) || token, indication; *dar una señal de su talento* to give an indication of one's talent || trace, track (rastro) || reminder (recordatorio) || mark of distinction (de distinción) || — *código de señales* signal code || *¿da la señal de llamada?* is it ringing? (el teléfono) || *en señal de* as a token of (como muestra de), as proof of (como prueba de) || *explicar algo con pelos y señales* to explain sth. in the minutest detail || *me hacía señales* he was signalling to me || *ni señal* not a trace || *no dar señales de vida* not to show any signs of life || *señal de ataque* signal to attack || REL *señal de la Cruz* sign of the Cross || *señal del casco* bottle receipt (de las botellas) || *señal de ocupado* engaged tone [US busy signal] || *señal de peligro* danger signal || *señal de prohibición de estacionamiento* no parking sign || *señal de tráfico* traffic *o* road sign (placa) || *señales de socorro* distress signals || *señales urbanas* urban traffic signs *o* signals || *señal para marcar* dialling tone [US dial tone] || *sin dejar señal* without a trace, without leaving a trace || AUT *utilizar las señales acústicas* to sound one's horn.

señaladamente *adv* expressly, especially, specifically (especialmente) || distinctly (claramente).

señalado, da *adj* outstanding, distinguished (insigne) || exceptional; *un señalado favor* an exceptional favour || appointed, set, fixed, arranged; *en el día señalado* on the appointed day || noticeable, marked; *una ausencia señalada* a noticeable absence || confirmed; *un señalado anarquista* a confirmed anarchist || marked, scarred; *el accidente le ha dejado señalado para toda la vida* the accident left him marked for life || FIG *un día señalado* a special day, a red-letter day.

señalamiento *m* signalling (acción de señalar) || JUR designation.

señalar *vt* to mark (poner una señal); *señalar las faltas con lápiz* to mark the mistakes with a pencil || to point to; *las manecillas del reloj señalan las tres y media* the hands of the clock are pointing to half past three || to point out, to call *o* to draw s.o.'s attention to (hacer observar); *me señaló un error* he pointed out a mistake to me, he drew my attention to a mistake || to point out; *señalar algo a la atención del público* to point sth. out to the public || to arrange, to make (una cita) || to set, to fix (una fecha, un precio) || to set (un trabajo) || to give, to show; *el reloj señala la hora* the clock gives the time || to mark; *eso señaló el fin del imperio romano* this marked the end of the Roman Empire || to indicate (indicar) || to scar, to mark (dejar cicatriz) || to announce (anunciar) || to signpost (carretera, trayecto) || to mark down (puntos en el juego de naipes) || to mark (baraja) || to sign and seal (rubricar) || to appoint, to designate; *señalar a alguien para hacer algo* to appoint s.o. to do sth. || *señalar algo con el dedo* to point at *o* to sth.

◆ *vpr* FIG to stand out (perfilarse) | to stand out; *señalarse por su elegancia* to stand out by one's elegance | to distinguish o.s. (distinguirse).

señalización *f* signposting (colocación de señales) || road signs *pl* (señales de tráfico) || railway signals *pl* (de ferrocarriles).

señalizar *vt* to signpost.

señero, ra *adj* alone, solitary (solo) || unique, unequalled, unrivalled (sin par) || FIG *figura señera* outstanding figure.

señor, ra *adj* distinguished, noble (distinguido) || FIG some, fine; *una señora herida* a fine wound, some wound; *¡es una señora calabaza!* that's some pumpkin!

◆ *m* man, gentleman; *un señor mayor* an elderly gentleman || Mister, Mr; *el señor Pérez* Mr. Pérez; *Señor Presidente* Mr. Chairman, Mr. President (en una asamblea) || Sir; *buenos días, señor* good morning, Sir || lord; *señor feudal* feudal lord || master (amo); *el siervo mató a su señor* the serf killed his master || owner (propietario) || Sir (título real) || my Lord (dirigiéndose a lores, jueces, etc.) || — *a lo gran señor* in grand style || *a tal señor, tal honor* honour to whom honour is due *darle a uno una paliza de padre y muy señor mío* to give s.o. a hell of a beating (pegarle fuerte) || *dárselas* or *echárselas de señor* to put on airs, to give o.s. airs || || *el Señor, Nuestro Señor* The Lord, Our Lord || *el señor conde, marqués* my lord, your lordship (dirigiéndose a la persona), my lord, his lordship (hablando a un tercero) || *el señor de la casa* the master of the household || *el señor no está* the master is not in || *el señor obispo* my Lord Bishop || *es mi dueño y señor* he is my lord and master || *estimado señor* Dear Sir || *los señores de Tarazona* Mr. and Mrs. Tarazona, the Tarazonas || *muy señores nuestros* gentlemen || *muy señor mío* Dear Sir || FIG *¡no señor!* definitely not! || *pues sí señor* yes indeed || *¡señor!* good Lord! || *señor de horca y cuchillo* feudal lord invested with civil and criminal jurisdiction (sentido propio), Grand Pajandrum (sentido irónico) (déspota) || REL *Señor de los Ejércitos* Lord of Hosts || *señor don Miguel de Unamuno* Mr. M. de Unamuno, M. de Unamuno, Esq (en un sobre) || *¡señores!* gentlemen! || *ser siempre señor de sus actos* to be master of one's ac-

tions ‖ *ser todo un señor* to be a real *o* a perfect gentleman ‖ *¡sí señor!* yes, Sir! (es así), bravo! (en el cante flamenco) ‖ *su señor padre* your (dear) father.
◆ *f* lady, woman; *una señora mayor* an elderly lady ‖ Mrs; *la señora de Pérez* Mrs. Pérez; *Señora Doña Isabel Martín de Ibarra* Mrs. Isabel Martin Ibarra ‖ Madam (tratamiento de cortesía); *buenos días, señora* good morning, Madam ‖ FAM wife (esposa); *recuerdos a su señora* my regards to your wife ‖ — *la señora condesa, marquesa* my *o* your ladyship ‖ *la señora de Tal* Mrs. So-and-So ‖ *la señora no está* Madam is out ‖ *muy señora mía* Dear Madam ‖ *Nuestra Señora* Our Lady ‖ *peluquería de señoras* ladies' hairdresser ‖ *señora de compañía* lady's companion ‖ *señoras y señores* ladies and gentlemen ‖ *ser toda una señora* to be a real *o* a perfect lady ‖ *sí señora* yes, Madam ‖ *su señora madre* your (dear) mother.
— OBSERV Obsérvese que cuando la palabra *señor* antecede un título profesional no suele traducirse en inglés en la mayoría de los casos: *el señor alcalde* the mayor; *el señor cura* the priest.

señorear *vt/vi* to dominate, to control, to rule (mandar) ‖ FIG to tower over, to dominate (desde lo alto) | to master, to control (las pasiones) ‖ FAM to lord it (dárselas de señorito) | to keep calling (s.o.) Sir, to sir.
◆ *vpr* to seize, to seize control of, to take over (apoderarse de).

señoría *f* lordship (hombre), ladyship (mujer) (título) ‖ lordship (terreno) ‖ rule, sway, dominion (gobierno) ‖ seigniory, seignory (en Italia) ‖ *su Señoría* your *o* his lordship, my lord (a un señor), your *o* her ladyship, my lady (a una señora).

señorial; señoril *adj* lordly (relativo a un señorío) ‖ FIG stately (imponente); *una casa señorial* a stately home | aristocratic (aristocrático) | elegant; *un barrio señorial* an elegant district ‖ gentlemanly (comportamiento).

señorilmente *adv* in a lordly *o* gentlemanly fashion.

señorío *m* dominion, rule, sway (mando) ‖ seigniory (derecho y territorio del señor) ‖ manor, estate (propiedad) ‖ nobility, lordliness (calidad de señor) ‖ FIG dignity (dignidad) | distinction (distinción) | stateliness (majestuosidad) | mastery, control (de las pasiones) | distinguished people *pl* (gente distinguida) ‖ *señorío feudal* suzerainty, lordship.

señorita *f* young lady ‖ miss (tratamiento de cortesía); *señorita Pelayo* Miss Pelayo ‖ FAM Miss (nombre que dan los criados a sus amas); *señorita, le llaman* Miss, you're wanted ‖ *la señorita Isabel me lo dio* Miss Isabel gave it to me.
— OBSERV Spanish servants frequently call their mistress *señorita* even if she is married.
— OBSERV En inglés la palabra *Miss* va seguida del apellido de la persona a quien uno se refiere: *¿está la señorita en casa?* is Miss Jones at home?

señoritingo, ga *m/f* FAM rich little daddy's boy, rich little daddy's girl.

señoritismo *m* privileges *pl* of the rich.

señorito *m* young gentleman ‖ FAM master [of the house] (nombre que dan los criados a sus amos); *el señorito ha salido* the master has gone out ‖ rich little daddy's boy (hijo de un padre influyente y rico).

señorón, ona *adj* distinguished, lordly (muy señor) ‖ FAM *no seas tan señorón* don't be so lordly *o* so high and mighty.
◆ *m/f* FAM big shot.

señuelo *m* lure (para halcones) ‖ decoy (reclamo) ‖ lark mirror (para alondras) ‖ FIG bait (espejuelo) | trap (trampa); *caer en el señuelo* to fall into the trap ‖ AMER lead steer (buey guía) | group of tame young bulls that lead wild cattle (mansos) | lead mare (madrina de la tropilla) ‖ FIG *la juventud se marcha a otros países tras el señuelo de los salarios altos* young people are lured abroad by the prospect of high wages.

seo *f* cathedral (en Aragón).

sépalo *m* BOT sepal.

separación *f* separation (acción, duración, etc.) ‖ space, gap (distancia) ‖ TECN removal (de una pieza) ‖ JUR *separación matrimonial* legal separation.

separadamente *adv* separately.

separado, da *adj* separated, separate ‖ separated; *está separada de su marido* she is separated from her husband ‖ — *por separado* separately; under separate cover (correos) ‖ *tiene los dientes separados* he has gaps between his teeth, he has gappy teeth.

separador, ra *adj* separative.
◆ *m* separator.

separar *vt* to separate (una cosa o una persona de otra) ‖ to move away (apartar); *separa la silla del radiador* move the chair away from the radiator ‖ to keep away; *su trabajo le separa de la familia* his work keeps him away from his family ‖ FIG to put *o* to set aside, to keep (guardar); *separa una tajada de sandía para mí* put a slice of watermelon aside for me ‖ to divide, to break up, to split (palabras, sílabas) ‖ to separate, to sort (out); *separar los cuchillos de los tenedores* to separate the knives from the forks ‖ to dismiss, to remove; *separar a un funcionario de su puesto* to dismiss a civil servant from his job ‖ TECN to detach ‖ — *bajo las piernas separadas de Gulliver pasó todo el pueblo* the whole town passed between Gulliver's open legs ‖ *no se le puede separar de sus libros* he and his books are inseparable, nothing will drag him away from his books.
◆ *vpr* to separate (un matrimonio) ‖ to part company, to separate (dos o más personas) ‖ to part with; *nunca me separaré de esta joya* I'll never part with this jewel ‖ to move away from; *el barco se iba separando cada vez más de la costa* the ship moved farther and farther away from the coast ‖ to cut o.s. off (romper las relaciones); *se ha separado de toda la familia* he has cut himself off from all his family ‖ to retire; *se ha separado de su negocio* he has retired from his business ‖ to leave; *Pedro se ha separado de la pandilla* Peter has left the gang ‖ JUR to waive [a right] ‖ TECN to come off *o* away ‖ *se ha separado de su mujer* he and his wife have separated.

separata *f* IMPR offprint, separate.

separatismo *m* separatism.

separatista *adj/s* separatist.

separativo, va *adj* separative.

separo *m* AMER cell (celda).

sepedón *m* ZOOL seps (lagarto).

sepelio *m* interment, burial.

sepia *f* ARTES sepia (tinta) ‖ ZOOL cuttlefish.

seps *m* ZOOL seps (lagarto).

septembrino, na *adj* September, of September.

septenado; septenato *m* septennate.

septenal *adj* septennial.

septenario, ria *adj/sm* septenary.

septenio *m* septennium, septennate.

septentrión *m* north (norte) ‖ ASTR Great Bear (Osa Mayor).

septentrional *adj* northern, north.

septenviro *m* septemvir.

septeto *m* MÚS septet, septette.

septicemia *f* MED septicaemia.

septicémico, ca *adj* MED septicaemic.

septicidad *f* septicity.

séptico, ca *adj* septic.

septiembre *m* September; *nació el 4 de septiembre* he was born on the 4th of September.
— OBSERV The dictionary of the Spanish Academy of the language admits the spelling *setiembre*, which is used by the majority of South American authors, and even by certain Spanish authors (Unamuno, Cela) who alternate between the two spellings. One should note that in the pronunciation the *p* is scarcely sounded.

septillo *m* MÚS septimole.

séptima *f* MÚS seventh; *séptima menor, aumentada* minor, augmented seventh ‖ septime (esgrima) ‖ MÚS *séptima de dominante* dominant seventh.

séptimo, ma *adj/s* seventh; *el séptimo cielo* the seventh heaven ‖ the Seventh; *Carlos VII (séptimo)* Charles VII [the Seventh] ‖ — *en séptimo lugar* in seventh place, seventh ‖ *la séptima parte* one seventh, a seventh.

septingentésimo, ma *adj/s* seven hundredth.

septotomía *f* MED septotomy.

septuagenario, ria *adj* septuagenarian, seventy-year-old.
◆ *m/f* septuagenarian, man (*o* woman) in his (*o* her) seventies, seventy-year-old.

septuagésima *f* REL Septuagesima (fiesta).

septuagésimo, ma *adj/s* seventieth.

septuplicar *vt* to septuple.

séptuplo, pla *adj* septuple, sevenfold.
◆ *m* septuple.

sepulcral *adj* sepulchral ‖ — *lápida sepulcral* gravestone, tombstone ‖ FIG *silencio sepulcral* deathly silence ‖ *voz sepulcral* sepulchral voice.

sepulcro *m* sepulchre [US sepulcher], grave, tomb ‖ — *el Santo Sepulcro* the Holy Sepulchre ‖ *sepulcro blanqueado* whited sepulchre ‖ FIG *ser un sepulcro* to be as silent as the grave | *tener un pie en el sepulcro* to have one foot in the grave.

sepultamiento *m* burial, entombment.

sepultar *vt* to bury, to entomb (enterrar) ‖ to trap; *mineros sepultados* trapped miners ‖ FIG to bury (olvidar); *recuerdos sepultados* buried memories | to conceal, to bury (ocultar); *una caja sepultada bajo varios objetos* a box concealed under several objects | to bury; *sepultado en sus pensamientos* buried in thought; *pueblo sepultado bajo las rocas* town buried under the rocks.

sepulto, ta *adj* buried.

sepultura *f* burial, sepulture (acto) ‖ grave, tomb, sepulchre [US sepulcher] (tumba) ‖ — *dar sepultura* to bury ‖ *dar sepultura cristiana* to give a Christian burial ‖ FAM *estar con un pie aquí y otro en la sepultura* to have one foot in the grave | *genio y figura hasta la sepultura* the leopard cannot change his spots.

sepulturero *m* gravedigger.

sequedad *f* dryness (cualidad de seco) ‖ FIG curtness, abruptness (en el trato) | dryness (del estilo).

sequedal; sequeral *m* dry land.

sequía *f* drought.

séquito *m* entourage, retinue (de personas) ‖ FIG aftermath, train (consecuencias); *la guerra y su séquito de horrores* war and its aftermath of horror.

ser *m* being; *los seres humanos* human beings ‖ existence, life (vida) ‖ essence, substance (esencia) ‖ — *dar el ser* to give life, to bring into the world ‖ *en lo más íntimo de su ser* deep down, deep inside himself, in his heart of hearts ‖ *Ser Supremo* Supreme Being.

ser* *vi*

1. SENTIDOS GENERALES 2. SER DE 3. SER PARA 4. USOS DIVERSOS

1. SENTIDOS GENERALES to be; *ser o no ser* to be or not to be; *soy español* I am Spanish; *somos dos* there are two of us; *son las ocho* it is eight o'clock; *serán las diez* it will be about ten o'clock; *serían las diez cuando nos fuimos* it would be ten o'clock when we left; *es fácil* it is easy; *soy yo* it's me, it is I || to be, to happen (suceder); *¿qué ha sido?* what was it?; *¿cómo fue eso?* how did that happen?, how was that? || to be, to take place; *la toma de Granada fue en 1492* the conquest of Granada was in 1492 || to be (costar); *¿cuánto es la carne?* how much is the meat? || to be, to belong to (pertenecer); *este libro es mío* this book is mine, this book belongs to me || to be, to make; *dos y dos son cuatro* two and two is four || to be; *soy yo el que lo hice* or *quien lo hizo* I am the one who did it, it was I who did it.
2. SER DE to be made of, to be of (materia); *la mesa es de madera* the table is made of wood || to be from, to come from; *¿de dónde eres?* where are you from?, where do you come from? || to be, to belong to (pertenecer); *es de Juan* it is John's, it belongs to John; *¿de quién es?* whose is it?, who does it belong to? || to be by, to be written by (un autor) || to be like (ser característico); *es muy de él* that is just like him || to be with *o* for, to be on s.o.'s side (ser partidario); *soy de Juan* I am with John *o* on John's side || to be; *¡hay que ver cómo es de goloso!* what a glutton he is!, how greedy he is! || to be, to be worth (deber); *es de ver* it should be seen, it is worth seeing || to become of, to happen to; *¿qué habría sido de mí?* what would have become of me?; *¿qué ha sido de tu novia?* what has happened to your girlfriend? || *es de creer, esperar que...* it is to be believed, hoped that... || *este comportamiento no es de un caballero* that is not a gentlemanly way to behave, such behaviour does not become a gentleman.
3. SER PARA to be for; *esta carta es para ti* this letter is for you || to be fitting for, to suit (apto para) || — *es para morirse de risa* it is hilarious, it is enough to make you die laughing || *esta clase de vida no es para mí* this kind of life isn't for me || *ser para poco* to be of next to no use, to be of little account.
4. USOS DIVERSOS *ahora soy todo suyo* right, I'm all yours || *a no ser por* had it not been for, if it were not for, but for || *a no ser que* unless; *a no ser que él llegue antes* unless he arrives *o* should arrive first || *¡así sea!* so be it! || *aun cuando fuera* even if one *o* it were || *aunque fuese* even if one *o* it were; *aunque fuese verdad* even if it were true || *¿cómo es eso?* how's that? || *¿cómo es que...?* how is it that...?, how come...?; *¿cómo es que no me lo has dicho antes?* how come you didn't tell me sooner? || *¡cómo ha de ser!* what can you expect? || *¿cómo puede ser?* how come? || *como sea* any way at all, one way or another (de cualquier manera), anyway (de todas maneras) || *con ser* in spite of being (a pesar de ser) || *de no ser así* if not, otherwise || *de no ser por* had it not been for, but for, if it were not for || *érase que se era, érase una vez* once upon a time (there was) (en cuentos) || *es decir* that is to say, in other words || *es más* what is more || *eso es* that's it, that's right || *esto es* that is to say (es decir) || *lo que sea* anything, anything at all || FAM *¡no es para menos!* and rightly so!, I should think so, too! || *no puede ser* that can't be, that's impossible || *no sea que, no vaya a ser que* unless (a menos que), in case, lest (ant) (por si acaso) || *no somos nada* or *nadie* it just goes to show how insignificant we are || *o sea, en otros términos* in other words, that is to say, that is || *o sea que* in other words, so, that is to say (en conclusión) || *o somos o no somos* let's get on with it, what are you waiting for? || *por si fuera poco* and on top of that, and to top it all (para colmo) || *que no sea* except, but (salvo); *cualquiera que no sea Juan* anyone but John || *¿quién es?* who is it?; who is speaking? (en el teléfono) || *sea* right, agreed (de acuerdo) || *sea como sea* one way or another (de todas maneras) || *sea lo que Dios quiera* God's will be done || *sea lo que fuere* or *lo que sea* be that as it may || *sea o no sea* anyway || *sea... sea* either... or || *ser de lo que no hay* to be unique || *ser el no va más* to be the last word || *ser muy suyo* to keep very much to o.s., to be very independent (ser independiente), to be very selfish (ser muy egoísta), to be different (ser especial) || *siendo así que* since || *si no es por* if it were not for, if it hadn't been for, but for; *si no es por mí se mata* if it were not for me he would have killed himself || *si no es que* unless || *si yo fuera usted* if I were you || FAM *un si es no es* a bit, somewhat || *ya sea... ya sea* either... or || *yo soy la madre* I'll be mother (en juegos de niños).

— OBSERV *Ser*, in contrast to *estar*, indicates an essential or permanent quality of the subject: *es una mujer* she is a woman; *es joven, española, simpática, secretaria* she is young, Spanish, nice, a secretary. *Ser* is also used as an auxiliary verb in the passive voice: *el carbón es extraído por los mineros* the coal is extracted by the miners; *fue asesinado* he was murdered.

sera *f* pannier, basket, frail (espuerta).

sérac *m* GEOL serac (en un glaciar).

seráfico, ca *adj* seraphic, angelic || Franciscan (orden) || — *Doctor Seráfico* Seraphic Doctor [St. Bonaventura] || *sueño seráfico* peaceful sleep *o* slumber.

serafín *m* REL seraph || FAM angel (ángel) || FIG angel, beauty (persona hermosa).
◆ *pl* REL seraphim.

serbal *m* service tree (árbol).

Serbia *npr f* GEOGR Serbia.

serbio, bia *adj/s* Serb, Serbian.

serbocroata *adj/s* Serbo-Croatian.

serena *f* serenade.

serenar *vt* to calm (el mar, etc.) || FIG to calm down, to pacify (a uno) || to settle, to clear (un líquido).
◆ *vpr* to calm o.s., to calm down (persona) || to grow calm (el mar) || to settle, to clear (un líquido).

serenata *f* MÚS serenade || FIG & FAM *dar la serenata* to pester (molestar).

serenero *m* AMER headscarf (pañuelo).

serenidad *f* serenity (sosiego) || calm, calmness, tranquillity (tranquilidad) || peacefulness (quietud) || clearness (del cielo) || serenity (título) || *conservó la serenidad* he remained calm *o* unruffled.

serenísimo, ma *adj* *Su Alteza Serenísima* His Serene Highness.

sereno, na *adj* cloudless, clear (cielo) || fine; *tiempo sereno* fine weather || FIG calm, serene, tranquil (apacible); *no sé cómo puede permanecer tan sereno* I don't know how you can stay so calm | serene (sosegado) | calm, peaceful, quiet; *el ambiente en la oficina está muy sereno ahora* the atmosphere in the office is very peaceful now | sober (no borracho) || — FIG *ponerse sereno* to sober up || *se mantuvo sereno* he remained calm.
◆ *m* night watchman (vigilante) || cool night air (humedad nocturna) || *al sereno* in the open air, out in the open.

— OBSERV The *sereno* was a man who kept watch during the night after the street doors of the blocks of flats had been locked. He had the keys to these doors and opened them to people who returned home late.

sereta *f*; **serete** *m* small basket *o* frail.

sergas *f pl* deeds, exploits (hazañas); *Las sergas de Esplandián* The Exploits of Esplandian.

serial *m* serial (en radio o televisión).

seriamente *adv* seriously.

seriar *vt* to arrange in series, to seriate.

sericícola *adj* sericultural.

sericicultor; sericultor *m* sericulturist.

sericicultura; sericultura *f* sericulture.

serie *f* series || instalment (de un empréstito) || break (en el billar) || MAT series || FIG series, string; *toda una serie de acontecimientos* a whole series of events | succession || — *artículo fuera de serie* oddment || *coches fabricados en serie* mass-produced cars || ELECTR *en serie* in series || FIG *fuera de serie* out of the ordinary, unusual || *novela por serie* novel in serial form || *producción en serie* mass production || FIG *se ha publicado una serie de artículos sobre este tema* a series of articles has been published on this subject.

seriedad *f* seriousness; *me lo dijo con toda seriedad* he told me in all seriousness || gravity (gravedad) || staidness (gravedad excesiva) || reliability, trustworthiness, dependability (comportamiento digno de confianza) || honesty, uprightness (honradez) || sense of propriety (decencia) || sense of responsibility (formalidad) || seriousness, gravity; *la seriedad de una enfermedad* the seriousness of an illness || — *falta de seriedad* lack of seriousness, irresponsibility, levity || *¡qué poca seriedad tienes!* how frivolous you are! || *un hombre de gran seriedad* a very serious man || *¡un poco de seriedad!* let's be serious now!

serigrafía *f* serigraphy, silk-screen process.

serijo; serillo *m* small basket *o* frail.

seringa *f* AMER BOT seringa.

serio, ria *adj* serious; *lo dijo en tono serio* he said it in a serious voice || grave (grave) || staid (excesivamente grave) || reliable, trustworthy, dependable (confiable) || honest, upright (honrado) || proper (decente) || responsible (formal) || sober (sobrio); *color serio* sober colour || formal; *traje serio* formal suit || grave, serious (enfermedad, etc.) || — *mantenerse serio* to stay serious, to keep a straight face || *ponerse serio* to become serious, to look serious.
◆ *adv* *en serio* seriously || *¿en serio?* seriously?, really? || *hablar en serio* to be serious, to speak seriously; *¿hablas en serio?* are you serious? || *no hablar en serio* not to be serious, to be joking, not to mean it || *tomar en serio* to take seriously || *va en serio* it's looking *o* becoming *o* getting serious (es grave), it's true, seriously (es verdad).

sermón *m* REL sermon; *Sermón de la Montaña* Sermon of the Mount || FIG & FAM sermon, lecture (reprimenda); *echarle un sermón a uno* to give s.o. a lecture.

sermoneador, ra *adj* fault-finding.
◆ *m/f* fault-finder (criticón) || sermonizer (que reprende).

sermonear *vt* FAM to lecture, to sermonize (reprender insistentemente) || to sermonize, to preach (predicar).
◆ *vi* to sermonize.

sermoneo *m* FAM sermon, lecture.

serología *f* serology.

serón *m* large basket *o* frail || FAM *es más basto que un serón* he's as crude as they come.

serosidad *f* serosity.

seroso, sa *adj* serous.

seroterapia *f* MED serotherapy.

serpa *f* AGR sterile shoot (de la vid).

serpentaria *f* BOT green dragon.

serpentario *m* ZOOL serpent eater, secretary bird.

Serpentario *npr m* ASTR Serpens.

serpenteante *adj* winding, twisting (camino) || meandering, winding (río).

serpentear *vi* to slither, to crawl, to wriggle (culebrear) || to wind, to twist and turn (un camino) || to wind, to meander (un río).

serpenteo *m* slithering, crawling, wriggling (culebreo) || winding, twisting (de un camino) || winding, meandering (de un río).

serpentín *m* worm (de alambique) || coil (espiral) || MIL serpentine (parte del arcabuz, pieza de artillería) | cock [of gun].

serpentina *f* (paper) streamer (de papel) || MIN serpentine || MIL serpentine (parte del arcabuz, pieza de artillería) | cock [of gun].

serpentino, na *adj* serpentine, snaky (relativo a las serpientes) || winding, serpentine (camino, río).

serpiente *f* ZOOL snake, serpent || FIG & FAM snake, snake in the grass (persona pérfida) || — *serpiente de anteojo* cobra || *serpiente de cascabel* rattlesnake || FIG *serpiente de verano* make-believe news [used to fill newspapers in the summer].

serpol *m* BOT wild thyme, mother of thyme (tomillo).

serpollar *vi* to shoot, to sprout (un árbol).

serpollo *m* BOT shoot, sprout.

serrado, da *adj* sawed || serrate, serrated, toothed (dentado).

serrador, ra *adj* sawing.
◆ *m* sawyer.

serraduras *f pl* sawdust *sing* (serrín).

serrallo *m* seraglio (harén) || FIG brothel.

serranía *f* mountain range, mountains *pl*.

serraniego, ga *adj* mountain, highland.

serranil *m* knife.

serranilla *f* lyric composition generally on a romantic theme.

serrano, na *adj* mountain, highland || — *jamón serrano* cured ham || FAM *mi cuerpo serrano* yours truly, myself | *partida serrana* rotten *o* dirty trick (mala jugada).
◆ *m/f* highlander.
◆ *f* lyric composition generally on a romantic theme (serranilla).

serrar* *vt* to saw (aserrar) || to saw off (quitar con la sierra) || to saw up (en pedazos).

serrátil *adj* ANAT irregular (pulso) || *juntura serrátil* serrated suture.

serrato *adj* serrated (serrado).
◆ *m* serratus (músculo).

serrería *f* sawmill.

serreta *f* small saw (sierra pequeña).

serrijón *m* secondary chain (de montañas).

serrín *m* sawdust (partículas de madera).

serrucho *m* handsaw, saw.

Servia *npr f* GEOGR Serbia.

servible *adj* serviceable, usable.

servicial *adj* obliging, accommodating, helpful.
◆ *m* AMER servant (criado).

servicio *m* service; *estar al servicio de uno* to be in the service of s.o. || servants *pl*; *es cada día más difícil encontrar servicio* it gets harder every day to find servants || domestic help (asistenta) || favour [US favor], service (favor) || service; *servicio de reparaciones* repair service || service, set (juego); *servicio de té* tea service || servicio; *servicio de mesa* dinner service || service (en los restaurantes, hoteles) || service charge; *servicio incluido* service charge included || maid's room, servant's quarters; *un piso de cuatro habitaciones y servicio* a four-roomed flat with servant's quarters || serve, service (en el tenis) || REL service || chamber pot (orinal) || enema (lavativa) || — MAR *barco de servicio* harbour craft, tender || *el lunes será puesto en servicio* or *entrará en servicio el nuevo teleférico* the new cable car will be put into operation on Monday *o* will go into operation on Monday || *en acto de servicio* in the service of one's country, in action (morir) || *en condiciones de servicio* operational || *estar al servicio del gobierno* to be on government service || *estar de* or *en servicio* to be on duty || *galería de servicio* underground gallery *o* works (obras públicas) || MIL *galón de servicio* service stripe || *hacer un flaco servicio* to be of little use (ser de poco uso), to play a dirty trick on (hacer una mala jugada) || *prestar servicio* to serve (criado, funcionario) || *prestar un servicio* to do a favour, to do a service (persona), to do a service (cosa) || MIL *servicio activo* active service || *servicio a domicilio* home delivery service || *servicio de café* coffee set || *servicio de comunicaciones* communications service || *servicio de paquetería* parcel service || *servicio de urgencias* emergency service || *servicio militar* military service || *servicio permanente* 24-hour service || *servicio postventa* after-sales service || *servicio público* public service (autobuses, etc.), civil service (funcionarios) || *servicio secreto* secret service || *servicio social* social service (véase OBSERV).
◆ *pl* services || toilet *sing*, lavatory *sing* [US rest room *sing*] || *hoja de servicios* service record (de los militares), record (de los deportistas).

— OBSERV The *servicio social* was a Spanish institution, similar to militar service for men, which was required of unmarried Spanish women under Franco's dictatorship. During three months of full-time duty or six months of part-time duty they took courses in politics, religion, sociology, art, etc.

servidor, ra *m/f* servant.
◆ *m* MIL gunner || INFORM server || — *servidor de usted* at your service, your servant || *su seguro servidor* Yours faithfully *o* truly (en una carta), your humble servant || FAM *un servidor* yours truly (yo) || *¡un servidor!* your servant, Sir!
◆ *interj* present! (cuando se pasa lista).

servidumbre *f* servitude || staff of servants, servants *pl* (conjunto de criados); *tomar una nueva servidumbre* to take on a new staff of servants || obligation (obligación) || — *servidumbre de paso* right-of-way || *servidumbre de vistas* right to open windows overlooking another person's property.

servil *adj* servile || FIG subservient | grovelling, abject, base (rastrero) || menial (oficio) || slavish (imitación).
◆ *adj m/sm* HIST absolutist [name given by the Liberals to the Conservatives in Spain at the beginning of the 19th century].

servilismo *m* servility || FIG subservience || HIST absolutism.

servilón, ona *adj m/sm* HIST absolutist.

servilleta *f* table napkin, serviette (de mesa) || FAM *doblar la servilleta* to kick the bucket (morir).

servilletero *m* napkin ring.

servio, via *adj/s* Serbian, Serb.

serviola *f* MAR cathead.

servir* *vt* to serve, to wait on; *servir a su amo* to serve one's master || to serve (with); *servir vino a alguien* to serve s.o. (with) wine || to serve; *servir a la patria* to serve one's country || MIL to man (artillería) || to tend, to mind (una máquina) || DEP & COM to serve || REL to serve || to follow suit (naipes) || to help, to assist, to be of service (ayudar) || — *¿en qué puedo servirle?* what can I do for you?, may *o* can I help you? || *me sirven, gracias* I am being served, thank you || *no se puede servir a Dios y al diablo* you can't serve God and the devil at the same time || *para servirle* at your service || FAM *¡pues sí que le sirve de mucho!* that will do him a lot of good! || *servir en la mesa* to serve *o* to wait at table || *servir una causa* to serve a cause || *un whisky bien servido* a well-poured whisky.
◆ *vi* to be a servant, to be in service (criado) || to serve, to wait (camarero) || to be of use, to be useful (ser útil) || MIL to do one's military service (hacer el servicio militar) | to serve (en el ejército) || DEP to serve || to work (funcionar) || to follow suit (naipes) || — *eso no sirve* that's no good || *no servir para nada* to be of no use at all, to be no good at all, to be useless; *esto no me sirve para nada* this is of no use at all to me; to be no use; *llorar no sirve para nada* it is no use crying || *¿para qué sirve llorar, ganar tanto dinero?* what is the use *o* the good of crying, of earning so much money? || *servir de* to serve as || *servir de estorbo* to get in the way; *este piano sólo sirve de estorbo* this piano just gets in the way; to be too much trouble; *si no le sirve de estorbo* if it is not too much trouble || *servir de intérprete* to act as interpreter || *servir para* to be used for; *un bolígrafo sirve para escribir* a Biro is used for writing; to be for; *¿para qué podría servir esto?* what could this be for? || *yo no sirvo para esta clase de cosas* I am no good at this sort of thing.
◆ *vpr* to serve *o* to help o.s.; *sírvase usted mismo* help yourself || to help o.s.; *sírvete queso* help yourself to cheese || to use; *servirse de un diccionario* to use a dictionary || to be kind enough to; *sírvase usted decirme su nombre* would you be kind enough to tell me your name? || *sírvase sentarse* do take a seat, do sit down, please take a seat, would you like to take a seat?

servita *m* REL servite.

servoasistido, da *adj* power-assisted.

servocroata *adj/s* Serbo-Croatian.

servodirección *f* MECÁN power steering.

servofreno *m* servo brake.

servomando *m* TECN servo control.

servomecanismo *m* TECN servomechanism.

servomotor *m* TECN servomotor.

sesada *f* brains *pl* (de animal) || CULIN fried brains.

sésamo *m* BOT sesame (alegría) || *¡Sésamo ábrete!* open sesame!

sesamoideo, a *adj* ANAT sesamoid (hueso).

sesear *vi* to pronounce the Spanish *c* [before *e* or *i* and *z* as an *s*] (véase SESEO).

sesenta *adj/sm inv* sixty || sixtieth (sexagésimo) || — *sesenta y uno, y dos, etc.* sixty-one, sixty-two, etc. || *tiene unos sesenta años* he is about sixty years old || *unos sesenta* about sixty.

sesentavo, va *adj/s* sixtieth.

sesentón, ona *adj* sixty-year-old, in one's sixties.
◆ *m/f* sixty-year-old, person in his (*o* her) sixties.

seseo *m* pronunciation of the Spanish *c* [before *e* or *i* and *z* as *s*].

— OBSERV The *seseo* is common in Andalusia, the Canary Islands and in the Spanish-speaking countries of Latin America.

sesera *f* brainpan (de animal) || FAM grey matter, brains *pl* (inteligencia); *este chico no tiene mucha sesera* that boy hasn't got much grey matter.

sesgado, da *adj* slanting, slanted (inclinado) || cut on the bias, cut on the skew (cortado).

sesgadura *f* cutting on the bias *o* on the skew (acción) || cut on the bias *o* on the skew (corte al sesgo).

sesgar *vt* to cut on the bias *o* on the skew (cortar) || to slant, to skew, to put askew (colocar).

sesgo, ga *adj* slanting, slanted (inclinado).
◆ *m* slant (inclinación) || bias (en costura) || FIG subterfuge (quiebro) | turn (rumbo); *tomar un mal sesgo* to take a turn for the worse || *al sesgo* on the bias (cortar), askew, awry, slanting (no en la posición debida).

sesión *f* session, sitting (de un tribunal, etc.) || meeting, session (reunión); *sesión a puerta cerrada* closed session; *sesión de apertura, plenaria* opening, plenary session; *en sesión pública* in public meeting; *reanudar la sesión* to resume the meeting || session (de concilio) || show, performance (de teatro) || showing, session (de cine) || sitting (pintor o escultor) || — *abrir, levantar la sesión* to open, to adjourn the meeting (una asamblea) || *celebrar una sesión* to hold a meeting || *período de sesiones* session (de una asamblea) || *se abre la sesión* the meeting is open, the meeting is declared open || CINEM *sesión continua* continuous showing || ECON *sesión de bolsa* Stock Exchange session || *sesión de clausura* closing *o* final meeting, closing *o* final session || *sesión de espiritismo* séance.

seso *m* ANAT brain || FIG brains *pl*, grey matter, sense (juicio); *tienes muy poco seso* you have very little sense || — FIG & FAM *perder el seso* to lose one's head, to go out of one's mind | *Tomás le sorbe el seso a María* Mary is head over heels in love with Thomas, Mary is mad about Thomas.
◆ *pl* CULIN brains; *sesos de carnero* lamb brains || — FIG & FAM *beberle los sesos a uno* to have s.o. bewitched *o* under one's spell | *calentarse* or *devanarse* or *estrujarse los sesos* to rack one's brains.

sesquicentenario, ria *adj/sm* sesquicentennial.

sesquióxido *m* QUÍM sexquioxide.

sesteadero *m* shady resting place for cattle.

sestear *vi* to have a nap, to take a siesta (descansar) || to rest in the shade (el ganado).

sesteo *m* AMER nap, siesta | shady resting place for cattle.

sestercio *m* sesterce (moneda romana).

sesudamente *adv* wisely, sensibly (sensatamente) || intelligently, cleverly (inteligentemente).

sesudo, da *adj* brainy (inteligente) || wise, sensible (sensato).

set *m* set (en tenis, cine).

seta *f* BOT mushroom (hongo).

setal *m* mushroom patch.

setecientos, tas *adj/sm* seven hundred; *dos mil setecientos veinte* two thousand seven hundred and twenty; *el año setecientos* the year seven hundred || *mil setecientos* one thousand seven hundred, seventeen hundred.

setenta *adj/sm* seventy || seventieth (septuagésimo) || *setenta y uno, setenta y dos* seventy-one, seventy-two.

setentavo, va *adj/s* seventieth.

setentón, ona *adj* seventy-year-old, in one's seventies.
◆ *m/f* seventy-year-old, person in his (*o* her) seventies.

setiembre *m* september (*véase* OBSERV en SEPTIEMBRE).

seto *m* fence (cercado) || hedge (seto vivo) || *seto vivo* hedge, quickset hedge.

setter *m* setter (perro).

seudo *adj inv/pref* pseudo.

seudónimo, ma *adj* pseudonymous.
◆ *m/f* pseudonym, pen name; *escribir con un seudónimo* to write under a pen name.

seudópodo *m* ZOOL pseudopod, pseudopodium.

severidad *f* severity, strictness (en el trato) || sternness (de aspecto) || severity (de un estilo, etc.) || — *castigar con severidad* to punish severily || *obrar con severidad* to be severe *o* strict.

severo, ra *adj* strict; *una disciplina severa* strict discipline; *un profesor muy severo* a very strict teacher || harsh, severe; *un castigo severo* a harsh punishment || severe, harsh (críticas) || FIG harsh, bleak, severe (invierno) | harsh, stern (cara) | stark, severe, harsh (estilo, traje); *la severa fachada del monasterio* the stark façade of the monastery.

sevicia *f* cruelty, brutality.

Sevilla *n pr* GEOGR Seville || *quien fue a Sevilla perdió* or *quien va a Sevilla pierde su silla* he who goes to the fair loses his chair.

sevillano, na *adj/s* Sevillian.
◆ *f pl* Sevillian music and dance.

sexagenario, ria *adj* sexagenarian.

Sexagésima *f* REL Sexagesima.

sexagesimal *adj* sexagesimal.

sexagésimo, ma *adj/s* sixtieth || *sexagésimo primero, segundo* sixty-first, sixty-second.

sex appeal *m* sex appeal.

sexcentésimo, ma *adj/s* six hundredth.

sexenio *m* (period of) six years.

sexo *m* sex || — *bello sexo* fair sex || *sexo débil, fuerte* gentle *o* weaker, stronger sex || *sin sexo* sexless.

sexología *f* sexology.

sexólogo *m* sexologist.

sexta *f* REL sext (hora) || MÚS sixth.

sextante *m* MAR sextant || sextans (moneda romana).

sexteto *m* MÚS sextet, sextette.

sextillo *m* MÚS sextuplet (seisillo).

sextina *f* sestina (en poesía).

sexto, ta *adj* sixth || the Sixth; *Alfonso VI* (sexto) Alphonse VI [the Sixth] || — *en sexto lugar* in sixth place, sixth || *la sexta parte* one sixth, a sixth.
◆ *m* sixth || FAM the sixth commandment (del decálogo).

sextuplicar *vt* to sextuple, to increase sixfold, to multiply by six.
◆ *vpr* to sextuple, to increase sixfold.

séxtuplo, pla *adj* sextuple, sixfold.
◆ *m* sextuple.

sexuado, da *adj* sexed.

sexual *adj* sexual (relaciones) || sex; *vida sexual* sex life; *órganos sexuales* sex organs.

sexualidad *f* sexuality.

sexualmente *adv* sexually.

sexy *adj* sexy.

Seychelles *npr f* GEOGR the Seychelles.

shah *m* shah (soberano persa).

shakespeariano, na *adj* Shakespearian, Shakespearean.

Shanghai *n pr* GEOGR Shanghai.

shantung *m* shantung (tela).

sheriff *m* sheriff.

sherry *m* sherry (vino de Jerez).

shimmy *m* shimmy (danza) || AUT shimmy.

shock *m* MED shock.

shorts *m pl* shorts (pantalón corto).

shrapnel *m* MIL shrapnel (granada).

shunt *m* ELECTR shunt (derivación).

si *m* MÚS ti, si, B.

si *conj* if; *si viene mañana, avísame* if he comes tomorrow, let me know; *si no lloviera saldríamos a pasear* if it weren't raining we would go for a walk || whether, if; *dime si vendrás mañana* tell me whether you are coming tomorrow; *no sé si iré o no* I don't know whether I'll go or not || when, if; *¿por qué lo aceptas ahora si ayer lo rechazaste?* why do you accept now when yesterday you refused || what if, supposing, suppose, I wonder if (con duda); *¿si me habrá mentido?* what if he lied to me?, supposing he lied to me? || but; *¡si en esta habitación no hay nadie!* but there's no one in this room!; *¡si te digo que no lo quiero!* but I tell you I don't want it! || how much (cuánto); *¡sabes si lo estimo!* you know how much I think of him! || — *como si* as if; *quiero a este niño como si fuera mi hijo* I love this boy as if he were my own son || *como si nada* as if it were nothing at all || *incluso si* even if; *incluso si me amenazaran, no lo haría* even if they threatened me I wouldn't do it || *por si, por si acaso* just in case, in case || FAM *que si esto que si lo otro* this that and the other || *si acaso* if (by chance *o* by any chance) || *si bien* even though; *si bien no sabía nada* even though he didn't know anything || *¡si fuera verdad!* if only it were true || *si no* if not, otherwise || *¡si será posible!* it's not possible! || *¿si será verdad?* what if it's true? || *si... si* whether... or; *no supo decir si ocurrió de noche si de día* he couldn't say whether it happened at night or during the day || *si supieran* if (only) they knew.

sí *pron pers refl 3ª persona* himself, herself, itself *sólo piensa en sí* he only thinks of himself (él), she only thinks of herself (ella); *la luz se apagó por sí misma* the light went out by itself || yourself (refiriéndose a usted); *Ud. sólo piensa en sí mismo* you only think of yourself || oneself (impersonal); *hay cosas que uno tiene que hacer por sí mismo* there are certain things one has to do by oneself; *hablar de sí* to talk of *o* about oneself || each other (el uno con el otro); *hablaban entre sí* they were talking to each other || *themselves* (cuando hay más de dos personas); *hablaban entre sí* they were talking among themselves || — *decir para sí* to say to o.s. || *de por sí, en sí* in itself, per se; *un libro bueno de por sí* a good book in itself || *entre sí* to himself, to herself, to o.s., etc. (para sí); *dijo entre sí* he said to himself || *estar en sí* to be in one's right mind, to be quite rational || *estar fuera de sí* to be beside o.s. (de furia o de alegría) || *estar sobre sí* to be on one's guard, to keep one's wits about one (estar alerta), to control o.s. (dominarse) || *mirar para sí mismo* to look after o.s. || *poner a uno fuera de sí* to make s.o. mad *o* wild (de furia), to make s.o. jump for joy (de alegría) || *por sí y ante sí* oneself, of one's own accord || *sí misma* herself; itself; yourself || *sí mismo* himself; itself; yourself || *volver en sí* to come to, to come round, to regain consciousness.

— OBSERV La forma plural de *himself, herself* y *itself* es *themselves.* La forma plural de *yourself* (refiriéndose a usted) es yourselves.

sí *adv* yes; *¿vienes conmigo? —sí* are you coming with me? —yes || — *claro que sí, sí por cierto* of course; yes, of course; certainly || *contestar sí o no* to answer yes or no || *creo que sí* I think so || *decir que sí* to say yes; *no decir ni que sí ni que no* to say neither yes nor no || *ella no irá pero yo sí* she won't go but I shall || *ella no lee pero yo sí* she doesn't read but I do || FAM *¡eso sí que no!* certainly not! || *hablar porque sí* to talk for the sake of it || *pero sí* but (después de una frase negativa); *no tiene hermanos pero sí cuatro hermanas* he has no brothers, but he has four sisters || *porque sí* because, because I (he, she) feel *o* felt like it (porque

me da or *me dio la gana), because that's the way it is (porque es así)* || *por sí o por no* just in case || *¡pues sí!* well, yes!, of course!, by all means! || *¡que sí, hombre!* yes, I tell you!, I tell you it is! || *sí que* really, certainly (for emphasis); *ahora sí que nos vamos a reír* we are really going to laugh now; *ése sí que sabe lo que quiere* that fellow certainly knows what he wants || *¡sí lo es!* it certainly is!, I'll say it is! || *un día sí y otro no* every other day, on alternate days || *yo sí vendré* I'll certainly come.
◆ *m* yes; *un sí categórico* a definite yes || consent, approval, agreement (consentimiento) || — *dar el sí* to say yes, to accept (para casarse), to agree, to give one's consent *o* approval, to say yes (asentir) || *los síes y los noes* the ayes and the nays; *contar los síes y los noes* to count the ayes and the nays || *sin que falte ni un sí ni un no* in minute detail.

sial *m* GEOL sial.

sialagogo, ga *adj* MED sialogogue, sialagogue.

sialoadenitis *f* MED sialadenitis, sialodenitis.

sialografía *f* MED sialography.

Siam *npr m* GEOGR Siam.

siamés, esa *adj/s* Siamese || *hermanos siameses* Siamese twins.

sibarita *adj* Sybaritic.
◆ *m/f* Sybarite.

sibaritismo *m* sybaritism.

Siberia *npr f* GEOGR Siberia.

siberiano, na *adj/s* Siberian.

sibila *f* sibyl.

sibilante *adj/s f* sibilant.

sibilino, na *adj* sibylline.

sic *adv* sic.

sicalíptico, ca *adj* suggestive, erotic (escabroso).

sicamor *m* Judas tree (ciclamor).

sicario *m* hired assassin.

sicastenia *f* psychasthenia.

sicasténico, ca *adj* psychasthenic.

sicigia *f* ASTR syzygy.

Sicilia *npr f* GEOGR Sicily.

siciliano, na *adj/s* Sicilian.

siclo *m* shekel.

sicoanálisis *m* psychoanalysis.

sicoanalista *m/f* psychoanalyst.

sicoanalítico, ca *adj* psychoanalytic, psychoanalytical.

sicoanalizar *vt* to psychoanalyze, to psychoanalyse.

sicodélico, ca *adj* psychedelic.

sicodrama *m* psychodrama.

sicofanta; sicofante *m* (ant) sycophant.

sicología *f* psychology.

sicológico, ca *adj m* psychological.

sicólogo, ga *m/f* psychologist.

sicometría *f* psychometric.

sicómoro; sicomoro *m* BOT Egyptian sycamore (árbol exótico) | sycamore, maple (plátano falso).

siconeurosis *f* MED psychoneurosis.

sicópata *m/f* MED psychopath.

sicopatía *f* MED psychopathy.

sicopático, ca *adj* MED psychopathic.

sicopatología *f* MED psychopathology.

sicosis *f* psychosis.

sicoterapia *f* MED psychotherapy.

sidecar *m* sidecar.
— OBSERV In Spanish the plural of *sidecar* is *sidecares.*

sideral; sidéreo, a *adj* ASTR sidereal, astral.

siderita *f* MIN siderite.

siderosa *f* MIN siderite.

siderosis *f* MED siderosis.

siderurgia *f* iron and steel industry, siderurgy.

siderúrgico, ca *adj* iron and steel; *industria siderúrgica* iron and steel industry; *fábrica siderúrgica* iron and steel works.

sidra *f* cider (bebida).

siega *f* reaping (acción de segar) || harvesting (acción de segar y recoger) || harvest (temporada) || harvest (mies segada).

siembra *f* sowing (acción de sembrar) || sowing time (temporada) || sowed *o* sown field (sembrado).

siempre *adv* always; *siempre tendrá dinero* he will always have money || all the time, always, forever (sin descanso); *siempre habla* he talks all the time, he is always talking || certainly (seguramente) || — *como siempre* as usual, as always || *de siempre* same old, usual; *es el cuento de siempre* it is the same old story; usual; *a la hora de siempre* at the usual time; old; *un amigo de siempre* an old friend || *eso se viene haciendo desde siempre* this has always been done || *estar siempre con* to be always with (ir con) || FAM *está siempre con la misma monserga* he's always singing the same tune || *lo de siempre* the same old thing, the same old story || *para* or *por siempre* for ever [*US* forever] || *para* or *por siempre jamás* for ever and ever [*US* forever and ever] || *siempre pasa lo mismo* it's always the same || *siempre que, siempre y cuando* provided that, as long as (con que), every time that, whenever (cada vez que).

siempretieso *m* tumbler, roly-poly (juguete).

siempreviva *f* BOT everlasting flower, immortelle.

sien *f* temple; *con las sienes entrecanas* with greying temples.

sierpe *f* serpent (serpiente).

sierra *f* TECN saw; *sierra abrazadera, de arco, de cinta, de contornar, eléctrica* rip pit saw, bow saw, band *o* belt *o* ribbon saw, compass *o* scroll saw, electric saw || sierra, mountain range (cordillera) || mountains *pl*, sierra; *pasar las vacaciones en la sierra* to spend one's holidays in the mountains || ZOOL sawfish (pez) || — *en forma de sierra* sawlike, saw-shaped || TECN *sierra para metales* hacksaw.

Sierra Leona *n pr* GEOGR Sierra Leone.

siervo, va *m/f* slave (esclavo) || serf (en la Edad Media) || servant; *siervo de Dios* servant of God.

síes *m pl* ayes, yeas; *contar los síes y los noes* to count the ayes and the nays.

sieso *m* ANAT rectum.

siesta *f* siesta (afternoon), nap; *dormir* or *echar una siesta* to have a siesta, to have one's afternoon nap || hottest part of the day (calor del mediodía) || *siesta del carnero* or *del fraile* nap before lunch.

siete *adj* seven.
◆ *m* seven; *el siete de corazones* the seven of hearts || seventh; *el siete de abril* the seventh of April || FAM L-shaped tear (rasgón) || TECN dog (de un banco de carpintero) || *AMER* anus (ano) || — *AMER* FAM *de la gran siete* fantastic (de aúpa) || FIG & FAM *hablar más que siete* to talk nineteen to the dozen, to be a real chatterbox, to talk the hind leg off a donkey || *AMER* FAM *hijo de la gran siete* bastard (hijo de puta) | *¡la gran siete!* good lord! || FIG & FAM *saber más que siete* to know a lot | *ser más embustero que siete* to be a big liar || *son las siete* it is seven o'clock.

sietemesino, na *adj* seven-month.
◆ *m* seven-month baby || FIG & FAM little squirt.

sieteñal *adj* seven-year-old.

sífilis *f* MED syphilis.

sifilítico, ca *adj/s* syphilitic.

sifón *m* siphon (para trasvasar líquidos) || U-bend, trap (tubería) || siphon (de agua gaseosa) || FAM soda water, soda; *échame un poco de sifón en el vaso* pour a little soda water in my glass.

sigilar *vt* to seal, to stamp (sellar) || to conceal (ocultar).

sigilo *m* seal, stamp (sello) || FIG secret (secreto) | discretion (discreción) || stealthiness (cautela) || — *con gran sigilo* with *o* in great secrecy || *sigilo sacramental* secrecy of the confessional.

sigilografía *f* sigillography.

sigiloso, sa *adj* secret (secreto) || discreet (discreto) || stealthy (cauteloso).

sigla *f* abbreviation, initials *pl* (inicial); *ONU es la sigla de la Organización de las Naciones Unidas* UNO is the abbreviation of the United Nations Organization.

siglo *m* century; *ser del siglo X* (diez) to date from *o* to be from *o* to belong to the 10th [tenth] century || FIG world; *fuera del siglo* apart from the world; *retirarse del siglo* to withdraw from the world | ages *pl*; *hace un siglo que no le he visto* I haven't seen him for ages | time, century; *al correr de los siglos* with the passing of time *o* of the centuries || — *dentro de un siglo* in a hundred years' time, in a century || REL *en el siglo* in the world; *Santa Teresa de Jesús, en el siglo Teresa de Cepeda y Ahumada* Saint Theresa of Ávila, in the world Theresa de Cepeda y Ahumada || *por los siglos de los siglos* for ever and ever [*US* forever and ever] (para siempre), world without end (en oraciones) || *siglo de las luces* Age of Enlightenment || *Siglo de Oro* Golden Age.

sigma *f* sigma (letra griega).

sigmoideo, a *adj* sigmoid.

signar *vt* to sign (firmar) || to mark, to put a seal on (sellar) || to make the sign of the Cross over, to sign (persignar).
◆ *vpr* to cross o.s. (persignarse).
— OBSERV In Spanish the usual word for *to sign* [a letter, etc.] is *firmar.*

signatario, ria *adj/s* signatory (firmante).

signatura *f* stamp, mark, sign (señal) || signature (firma) || IMPR & MÚS signature || catalogue number (para clasificar un libro).

significación *f* meaning (significado) || FIG significance (importancia); *un hecho de gran significación* a fact of great significance.

significado, da *adj* signified, indicated (señalado) || FIG well-known (conocido).
◆ *m* meaning (sentido); *no conozco el significado de esta palabra* I don't know the meaning of this word || significance (de un acontecimiento).

significante *adj* significant.

significar *vt* to mean, to signify; *en latín «magister» significa maestro* in Latin «magister» means teacher || to indicate, to make known; *significar a uno sus intenciones* to make one's intentions known to s.o. || to express, to make known (hacer presente) || FIG to mean; *esto significa mucho para mí* this means a lot to me | to be important; *él significa mucho en el ayuntamiento* he is very important at the town hall.
◆ *vpr* to stand out (destacar) || to distinguish o.s. (distinguirse) || to declare o.s., to come out as (declararse); *se significó como monárquico* he declared himself a monarchist.

significativo, va *adj* significative (*de* of) (indicativo) || FIG significant (importante); *es significativo que...* it is significant that... | meaningful, meaning (mirada, etc.).

signo *m* sign; *las golondrinas son el signo de la llegada de la primavera* swallows are the sign of the arrival of spring || IMPR & MÚS sign || mark; *signo de puntuación, de admiración, de interrogación* punctuation, exclamation, question mark || symbol; *signo fonético* phonetic symbol || ASTR sign (del zodíaco) || MAT sign; *signo igual, más, menos* equals, plus, minus sign | tendency (tendencia); *signo político* political tendency || flourish, mark (de los notarios) || fate, destiny (destino) || — *bajo el signo de* under the sign of || *signo de la Cruz* sign of the Cross || *signos monetarios* monetary units || *signos Morse* Morse code.

siguemepollo *m* ribbon [on a dress] (en el vestido) || choker, neckband (collar).

siguiente *adj* following, after, next; *el año siguiente* the following year, the year after || following; *nos ayudaron las personas siguientes* the following people helped us || — *anunció lo siguiente* he announced the following || *¡que pase el siguiente!* next please!

sij *adj* Sikh.
— OBSERV pl *sijs* Sikh.

sil *m* yellow ochre (ocre).

sílaba *f* syllable; *sílaba abierta, aguda* or *tónica, cerrada* or *trabada* open, accentuated *o* stressed *o* accented, closed syllable.

silabar *vi* to syllable.

silabario *m* spelling book, syllabary.

silabear *vt/vi* to syllable, to pronounce syllable by syllable (pronunciar) || to syllabicate, to divide into syllables.

silabeo *m* syllabication, division into syllables.

silábico, ca *adj* syllabic.

silba *f* hissing, catcalls *pl* (rechifla) || *dar una silba* to hiss, to whistle.

silbante *adj* whistling (que silba) || sibilant (sibilante) || MED sibilant, wheezing || FIG catcalling, jeering, hissing (que desaprueba).

silbar *vt* to whistle (una melodía) || to whistle to; *silbar al perro* to whistle to the dog || to blow (un pito) || FIG to hiss, to boo (en el teatro, etc.).
◆ *vi* to whistle || to whistle (el viento) || to whine, to whistle, to whizz (una bala) || to whizz (una flecha) || MED to wheeze || FIG to hiss, to catcall, to boo (en el teatro, etc.) | to ring, to buzz (los oídos).

silbatina *f* AMER catcalls *pl*, hissing (silba).

silbato *m* whistle (pito).

silbido *m* whistle, whistling || hissing, catcalls *pl* (abucheo) || whistle (del viento) || whizz (de bala, de flecha) || MED wheeze || *dar un silbido* to whistle.

silbo *m* whistle, whistling || FIG & FAM *estar más flaco que un silbo* to be as skinny as a rake.

silbón *m* ZOOL widgeon (ave).

silenciador *m* TECN silencer (de arma) || AUT silencer, muffler.

silenciar *vt* to muffle, to silence (ahogar un ruido) || to hush up (ocultar un acontecimiento) || to keep quiet about, to make no mention of (no hablar de un acontecimiento) || to silence (callar).

silencio *m* silence; *silencio sepulcral* deathly silence; *sufrir en silencio* to suffer in silence || MÚS rest (pausa) || — *en silencio* in silence || FIG *entregar al silencio* to cast into oblivion || *guardar silencio* to keep silent *o* quiet || *imponer silencio a uno* to keep s.o. quiet, to order s.o. to be silent, to call for silence || *pasar algo en silencio* to keep quiet about sth., to make no mention of sth. || *reducir al silencio* to silence || *romper el silencio* to break the silence || MÚS *silencio de corchea* quaver rest.

silencioso, sa *adj* quiet; *persona, casa silenciosa* quiet person, house || silent, quiet, noiseless (máquina).
◆ *m* silencer, muffler (en un automóvil).

silepsis *f* GRAM syllepsis.

sílex *m* silex, flint (pedernal).

sílfide *f* sylph.

silfo *m* MIT sylph.

silicato *m* QUÍM silicate.

sílice *f* QUÍM silica (roca).

silíceo, a *adj* siliceous.

silícico, ca *adj* QUÍM silicic.

silicio *m* QUÍM silicon.

silicona *f* QUÍM silicone.

silicosis *f* MED silicosis.

silo *m* silo (almacén de grano).

silogismo *m* syllogism.

silogístico, ca *adj* syllogistic, syllogistical.

silogizar *vi* to syllogize.

silueta *f* silhouette || figure (figura) || outline (contorno) || ARTES outline sketch, silhouette.

siluetear *vt* to silhouette.

siluriano, na; silúrico, ca *adj/sm* GEOL Silurian.

siluro *m* catfish (pez) || MAR self-propelling torpedo.

silva *f* miscellany (colección).

silvanita *f* MIN sylvanite.

silvano *m* sylvan, silvan (divinidad de la selva).

silvático, ca *adj* → **selvático.**

silvestre *adj* wild; *plantas silvestres* wild plants; *fruta silvestre* wild fruit || FIG rustic (rústico).

silvicultor *m* forestry expert, silviculturist.

silvicultura *f* sylviculture, silviculture, forestry.

silvoso, sa *adj* forested, wooded.

silla *f* chair; *sentarse en una silla* to sit down in a chair || saddle (de jinete) || REL see (sede) || FIG dignity (dignidad) || — *caballo de silla* saddle horse || *juez de silla* umpire (tenis) || FIG & FAM *pegársele a uno la silla* to overstay one's welcome || *silla arzobispal* archbishopric, archdiocese, archsee || *silla curul* curule || *silla de coro* choir stall || *silla de la reina* chair (entre niños) || *silla de manos* sedan chair || *silla de montar* riding saddle || *silla de posta* post chaise || *silla de rejilla* cane chair || *silla de ring* ringside seat || *silla de ruedas* wheelchair || *silla de tijera* or *plegable* folding chair || *silla eléctrica* electric chair || REL *silla episcopal* or *obispal* see || *silla gestatoria* gestatorial chair (del papa) || *silla giratoria* swivel chair || *silla inglesa* English saddle, hunting saddle || *silla poltrona* easy chair.

sillar *m* ashlar (piedra) || horse's back (lomo).

sillería *f* chairs *pl*, set of chairs (asientos) || seating, seats *pl* (en los auditorios, etc.) || choir stalls *pl* (del coro) || chairmaker's workshop, chair factory (taller) || ARQ ashlar.

sillero, ra *m/f* chairmaker (fabricante de sillas) || chair seller (vendedor) || chair mender (reparador) || saddler (que hace sillas de montar).

silleta *f* small chair (silla).

sillín *m* saddle, seat (de bicicleta o motocicleta) || light riding saddle (silla de montar).

sillón *m* armchair (butaca) || sidesaddle (de montar) || — *sillón de orejas* wing chair || *sillón de ring* ringside seat || *sillón de ruedas* wheelchair (para un inválido) || *sillón giratorio* swivel chair.

sima *f* chasm, abyss || FIG depths *pl* (abismo).
— OBSERV Do not confuse *sima* chasm, with *cima* top.

simbiosis *f* BIOL symbiosis.

simbiótico, ca *adj* BIOL symbiotic.

simbólico, ca *adj* symbolic, symbolical.

simbolismo *m* symbolism.

simbolización *f* symbolization.

simbolizar *vt* to symbolize.

símbolo *m* symbol; *el símbolo del hierro es Fe* Fe is the symbol of iron || *el símbolo de los apóstoles* or *de la Fe* the Apostles' Creed, the Creed.

simetría *f* symmetry.

simétrico, ca *adj* symmetrical, symmetric.

símico, ca *adj* ZOOL simian, apish, apelike.

simiente *f* AGR seed (semilla).

simiesco, ca *adj* simian, apish, apelike.

símil *adj* similar, alike.
◆ *m* similarity, resemblance (semejanza) || comparison; *hacer un símil entre dos países* to make a comparison between two countries || simile (figura retórica).

similar *adj* similar.

similicuero *m* imitation leather.

similigrabado *m* process-engraving, halftone engraving.

similitud *f* similitude, similarity.

simio *m* ZOOL simian (mono).

simón *m* horse-drawn *o* hackney carriage.

simonía *f* simony.

simoniático, ca *adj* simoniac.
◆ *m/f* simoniac, simonist.

simpa *f* AMER plait (trenza de pelo).

simpatía *f* liking; *le tengo mucha simpatía* I have a great liking for him; *le he cogido simpatía* I have taken a liking to him || affection, fondness (cariño) || friendship (amistad) || friendliness, congeniality (amabilidad) || charm (encanto) || friend (amigo); *no tiene simpatías en la oficina* he has no friends in the office || sympathy, solidarity (solidaridad) || MED sympathy || — *dolores de simpatía* sympathy pains || *no me tiene simpatía* he doesn't like me || *simpatías y antipatías* likes and dislikes || *una persona que tiene mucha simpatía* a very likeable *o* pleasant *o* nice person.
— OBSERV One should not confuse *simpatía* with *sympathy* (compasión).

simpático, ca *adj* nice, likeable (amable); *es muy simpático* he is very nice || pleasant (agradable) || kind, nice, friendly; *fue muy simpático conmigo* he was very kind to me || charming (encantador) || — *él no me ha caído simpático* I didn't take to him, I didn't like him much || *intentar hacerse simpático* to try to ingratiate o.s. || *me es simpática esta chica* I like that girl || *tinta simpática* invisible ink, sympathetic ink.
◆ *m* ANAT *gran simpático* sympathetic nervous system.

simpatizante *adj* sympathizing.
◆ *m/f* sympathizer.

simpatizar *vi* to get on; *no sé si van a simpatizar* I don't know if they are going to get on || to hit it off; *simpatizaron en seguida* they hit it off at once || to take to, to hit it off; *simpaticé con ella en seguida* I took to her at once, we hit it off at once || to sympathize (*con algo* with sth.).

simple *adj* simple (no compuesto, sin adorno) || single (sencillo, único); *una simple capa de pintura* a single coat of paint || simple, easy (fácil) || just one, one single (que basta por sí solo); *con una simple palabra* with just one

word ‖ GRAM simple; *tiempo simple* simple tense ‖ simple, plain, unpretentious (no afectado) ‖ simple, guileless (incauto) ‖ simple, half-witted (tonto) ‖ mere (mero); *esto es un simple trámite* this is a mere formality ‖ BOT single ‖ — QUÍM *cuerpo simple* simple body ‖ *es un simple carpintero* he is just a carpenter *o* a simple carpenter ‖ *por simple descuido* out of sheer *o* through sheer carelessness, through pure carelessness.
◆ *m* simpleton, half-wit (bobo) ‖ singles *inv* (en tenis); *un simple caballeros* a men's singles ‖ MED simple (planta medicinal).

simplemente *adv* simply ‖ *pura y simplemente* purely and simply.

simpleza *f* simpleness, simplicity (cualidad de simple) ‖ naïvety (ingenuidad) ‖ stupid thing (tontería) ‖ trifle (cosa de poco valor).
◆ *pl* nonsense *sing* (tonterías).

simplicidad *f* simplicity, simpleness (de una cosa) ‖ naïvety (candor).

simplificable *adj* simplifiable.

simplificación *f* simplification.

simplificador, ra *adj* simplifying.
◆ *m/f* simplifier.

simplificar *vt* to simplify.

simplismo *m* oversimplification, simplism.

simplista *adj* simplistic, over-simple.

simplón, ona *adj* gullible, simple, naïve.
◆ *m/f* simpleton, half-wit.

simposio; simpósium *m* symposium.

simulación *f* simulation ‖ sham (fingimiento) ‖ malingering (fingiendo enfermedad).

simulacro *m* simulacrum (representación) ‖ mockery (farsa); *el pleito no fue más que un simulacro* the trial was no more than a mockery ‖ idol, image (imagen) ‖ show, sham, pretence [US pretense] (fingimiento) ‖ semblance (apariencia) ‖ — *hacer el simulacro de* to pretend to ‖ *un simulacro de ataque* a simulated *o* sham attack.

simulado, da *adj* feigned; *tristeza simulada* feigned sorrow ‖ simulated; *miedo simulado* simulated fear; *vuelo simulado* simulated flight; *fue un accidente simulado* it was a simulated accident.

simulador, ra *adj* simulative.
◆ *m/f* shammer, pretender ‖ malingerer (que finge estar enfermo) ‖ *es un hábil simulador* he is a good shammer *o* pretender.

simular *vt* to feign; *simula sentimientos que no tiene* he feigns feelings he doesn't have ‖ to simulate, to feign, to pretend; *simula que tiene miedo* he simulates *o* feigns fear, he pretends to be afraid ‖ to pretend; *simula que trabaja* he pretends that he is working ‖ to sham, to rig; *simularon el accidente* they rigged the accident ‖ *pasarse la vida simulando* to spend one's life pretending *o* in pretence, to live a life of pretence.
◆ *vi* to malinger, to feign illness.

simultáneamente *adv* simultaneously.

simultanear *vt* to do simultaneously *o* at the same time (dos cosas) ‖ to combine; *simultanea el trabajo con la diversión* he combines work and pleasure ‖ — *simultanea la carrera de derecho y la de ciencias* he is studying law and science at the same time ‖ *simultanear la risa con las lágrimas* to smile through one's tears.

simultaneidad *f* simultaneity.

simultáneo, a *adj* simultaneous.

simún *m* simoon, simoon (viento).

sin *prep* without; *sin él no podría hacer nada* without him I couldn't do anything; *sin hacerlo tú* without your doing it ‖ without, with no; *me quedé sin carbón* I was left with no coal ‖ not counting (sin contar) ‖ — *dejar algo sin terminar* to leave sth. unfinished ‖ *estar sin* (con un infinitivo) not to have been; *el cuarto está sin hacer* the room has not been made ‖ *estoy sin desayunar* I haven't had any breakfast ‖ *hijas sin casar* unmarried daughters ‖ *quedarse sin cenar* to go without dinner ‖ *quedarse sin provisiones* to run out of provisions ‖ FIG *sigue sin levantar cabeza* he hasn't got his head above water yet ‖ *sin ambages ni rodeos* without any beating about the bush ‖ FAM *sin blanca* or *cinco* or *gorda* or *linda* or *un céntimo* or *un cuarto* or *una perra* stony *o* flat broke ‖ *sin cesar* unceasingly, ceaselessly, nonstop ‖ *sin compromiso* without obligation (sin obligación), unattached (sin obligaciones matrimoniales) ‖ FAM *sin decir esta boca es mía* or *ni pío* without saying a word, without opening one's mouth | *sin decir oxte ni moxte* without a word, without warning ‖ *sin demora* or *dilación* without delay ‖ *sin Dios* godless ‖ *sin embargo* nevertheless, however ‖ *sin entrada* no down payment ‖ *sin escala* non-stop; *vuelo sin escala* nons-top flight ‖ *sin eso, sin lo cual* otherwise ‖ *sin falta* without fail ‖ *sin hogar* homeless ‖ *sin inconvenientes* without inconvenience ‖ FIG *sin levantar cabeza* without looking up *o* stopping (sin dejar de trabajar) ‖ *sin más ni más* without more ado, without further ado ‖ *sin pies ni cabeza* ridiculous, absurd, nonsensical, without rhyme or reason ‖ *sin que* without; *los niños se comieron el pastel sin que los viera* the children ate the cake without my seeing them ‖ JUR *sin recurso* unappealable ‖ *sin sellar* unsealed.
— OBSERV En muchos casos la preposición *sin* seguida por un sustantivo se puede traducir al inglés sea mediante el sufijo *-less*, cuando se trata de una locución adjetival: *sin piedad* merciless; *sin casa* homeless; *sin vergüenza* shameless, sea con el sufijo *-lessly*, en los casos en que corresponde a una locución adverbial: *castigar sin compasión* to punish mercilessly.
— OBSERV Cuando *sin* va seguido por un infinitivo se puede traducir al inglés con el prefijo *un-* colocado delante del participio pasivo del verbo: *trabajo sin acabar* unfinished work.

sinagoga *f* synagogue.

Sinaí *npr m* GEOGR Sinai.

sinalagmático, ca *adj* JUR synallagmatic.

sinalefa *f* GRAM synaloepha [US synalepha].

sinalgia *f* MED synalgia.

sinántropo *m* sinanthropus, Peking man.

sinapismo *m* MED mustard plaster ‖ FIG & FAM bore, drag, nuisance (persona o cosa pesada).

sinartrosis *f* ANAT synarthrosis.

sincerar *vt* to exonerate.
◆ *vpr* to exonerate o.s., to vindicate o.s. (justificarse) ‖ to open one's heart; *sincerarse con sus amigos* to open one's heart to one's friends ‖ to tell the truth, to come out into the open (decir la verdad).

sinceridad *f* sincerity; *decir algo con toda sinceridad* to say sth. in all sincerity.

sincero, ra *adj* sincere.

sinclinal *adj* GEOL synclinal.
◆ *m* GEOL syncline.

síncopa *f* MÚS syncopation, syncope ‖ GRAM syncope.

sincopar *vt* GRAM & MÚS to syncopate ‖ FIG to abridge (abreviar).

síncope *m* MED & GRAM syncope.

sincrético *adj* syncretic.

sincretismo *m* syncretism.

sincretista *m/f* syncretist.

sincrociclotrón *m* FÍS synchrocyclotron.

sincronía *f* synchrony.

sincrónico, ca *adj* synchronous, synchronic, synchronistic ‖ simultaneous; *dos hechos sincrónicos* two simultaneous events ‖ synchronic (lingüística).

sincronismo *m* synchronism ‖ simultaneity.

sincronización *f* synchronization.

sincronizado, da *adj* synchronized ‖ AUT syncromesh.

sincronizador *m* CINEM synchronizer ‖ AUT synchromesh.

sincronizar *vt* to synchronize.
◆ *vi* RAD to tune in (*con* to).

síncrono, na *adj* synchronous.

sincrotrón *m* FÍS synchrotron.

sindáctilo, la *adj/sm* ZOOL syndactyl, syndactyle.

sindéresis *f* good judgment.

sindesmofito *m* MED syndesmophyte.

sindesmografía *f* MED syndesmography.

sindesmopexia *f* MED syndesmopexy.

sindesmotomía *f* MED syndesmotomy.

sindicado, da *adj* who belongs to a trade union.
◆ *m* syndicate, body of trustees (junta de síndicos).

sindical *adj* union, trade-union [US labor union]; *problemas sindicales* trade-union problems ‖ syndical.

sindicalismo *m* trade unionism, unionism (sistema) ‖ syndicalism (teoría política).

sindicalista *adj* union, trade-union [US labor union] ‖ syndicalist (partidario del sindicalismo).
◆ *m/f* trade unionist, unionist ‖ syndicalist.

sindicar *vt* to unionize.
◆ *vpr* to join a union (afiliarse a un sindicato) ‖ to form a trade union [US a labor union] (formar un sindicato).

sindicato *m* trade union [US labor union] (de trabajadores) ‖ syndicate (grupo).

síndico *m* syndic, trustee.

sindineritis *f* FAM *tener sindineritis* to be broke.

síndrome *m* MED syndrome ‖ — *síndrome de abstinencia* withdrawal symptoms ‖ *síndrome de Estocolmo* Stockholm syndrome ‖ *síndrome tóxico* toxic syndrome.

sinécdoque *f* synecdoche.

sinecura *f* sinecure.

sine die *loc adv* sine die (sin fijar fecha ni día).

sine qua non *loc adv* *condición sine qua non* prerequisite, essential condition.

sinéresis *f* GRAM synaeresis, syneresis.

sinergia *f* synergy.

sinérgico, ca *adj* synergic.

sinestesia *f* synaesthesia [US synesthesia].

sinfín *m* no end, an endless number ‖ *citó un sinfín de nombres* he quoted countless names *o* an endless number of names *o* no end of names.

sinfinidad *f* FAM multitude, endless number ‖ *una sinfinidad de* countless, no end of.

sínfisis *f* ANAT symphysis.

sinfonía *f* symphony; *sinfonía incompleta* unfinished symphony.

sinfónico, ca *adj* symphonic.
◆ *f* symphony orchestra.

sinfonista *m* symphonist.

singladura *f* MAR day's run (recorrido) | day (día).

singlar *vi* MAR to steer, to navigate.

single *m* singles *inv* (tenis) || single (coche cama).

singleton *m* singleton (semifallo en el bridge).

singracia *adj* dull, insipid (soso).
◆ *f* dullness.

singular *adj* singular, unique (único) || outstanding (excepcional) || FIG odd, peculiar, singular; *una persona singular* a peculiar person || *combate singular* single combat.
◆ *m* GRAM singular; *en singular* in the singular || FIG *en singular* in particular.

singularidad *f* singularity.

singularizar *vt* to single out, to distinguish, to singularize (distinguir) || GRAM to use in the singular.
◆ *vi* to speak in the singular.
◆ *vpr* to stand out, to distinguish o.s. (distinguirse).

sinhueso *f* FAM tongue (lengua) || FAM *darle a la sinhueso* to chin-wag.

siniestra *f* left hand (mano izquierda).

siniestrado, da *adj* damaged || HERÁLD sinister.
◆ *m/f* victim [of an accident, etc.].

siniestro, tra *adj* left; *mano siniestra* left hand || left, left-hand; *lado siniestro* left-hand side || FIG sinister, ominous; *mirada siniestra* sinister look | fateful, disastrous (funesto) | evil (malo) || *a diestro y siniestro* right and left (por todas partes), at random (sin método).
◆ *m* catastrophe, disaster (catástrofe) || accident (accidente) || fire (incendio).

sinnúmero *m* endless number, no end || *hubo un sinnúmero de víctimas* there were countless victims *o* no end of victims.

sino *m* fate, destiny (hado, destino).

sino *conj* but (para contraponer un concepto afirmativo a uno negativo); *no era él sino su hermano* it wasn't him but his brother || but, except; *nadie ha venido sino su hermano* no one has come but your brother || — *no parece sino que es idiota* he looks a complete idiot || *no... sino* not... but; *no es militar sino abogado* he is not a soldier but a lawyer; nothing but; *no hace sino criticar* he does nothing but criticize; just, only (sólo) || *no sólo... sino* not only... but || *no sólo... sino que* or *sino que también* not only... but (also); *no sólo pide, sino que exige* he not only asks but demands || *sino que* but (pero); *no lo leí sino que lo hojeé* I didn't read it but flicked through it; except that, but (salvo); *fue todo muy bien sino que llovió un poco* everything went well except that it rained a little.
— OBSERV A veces la expresión *sino que* no se traduce al inglés: *no basta que usted lo diga, sino que quiero verlo* it isn't enough that you say so, I want to see it.

sinodal *adj* synodal.

sinódico, ca *adj* synodical, synodal || ASTR synodic, synodical.

sínodo *m* synod (junta) || *el Santo Sínodo* the Holy Synod (en Rusia).

sinojaponés, esa *adj* Sino-Japanese.

sinología *f* sinology.

sinólogo, ga *m/f* Sinologist, Sinologue.

sinonimia *f* synonymity, synonymy.

sinonímico, ca *adj* synonymic.

sinónimo, ma *adj* synonymous.
◆ *m* synonym.

sinopsis *f inv* synopsis.
◆ *pl* synopses.

sinóptico, ca *adj* synoptic, synoptical || *cuadro sinóptico* chart, diagram.

sinovia *f* ANAT synovia.

sinovial *adj* ANAT synovial || *cápsula sinovial* synovial capsule.

sinovitis *f* MED synovitis.

sinrazón *f* wrong, injustice; *las sinrazones de la política* the injustices of politics || absurdity, foolish thing, nonsense (disparate).

sinsabor *m* displeasure, unpleasantness (disgusto) || FIG trouble, worry; *este trabajo me ha causado muchos sinsabores* this job has brought me a lot of troubles | sorrow (pena).

sinsonte *m* mockingbird.

sinsustancia *m/f* FAM nonentity.

sintáctico, ca *adj* GRAM syntactic, syntactical.

sintaxis *f* GRAM syntax.

sinterización *f* TECN sintering.

sinterizar *vt* TECN to sinter.

síntesis *f* synthesis.

sintético, ca *adj* synthetic; *caucho sintético* synthetic rubber.

sintetizar *vt* to synthesize, to synthetize.

sintoísmo *m* Shintoism, Shinto (religión).

sintoísta *m/f* Shintoist.

síntoma *m* symptom.

sintomático, ca *adj* symptomatic || FIG significant (que revela algo).

sintomatología *f* MED symptomatology.

sintonía *f* ELECTR syntony || RAD signature tune (de una emisión) || FIG harmony || RAD *bobina de sintonía* tuning coil.

sintónico, ca *adj* syntonic.

sintonismo *m* syntony.

sintonización *f* syntonization, tuning || *mando de sintonización* tuner, tuning knob.

sintonizador *m* RAD tuner, tuning knob.

sintonizar *vt* to syntonize, to tune || RAD to tune in || *sintonizan ustedes con Radio San Sebastián* you are tuned to *o* tuned in to Radio San Sebastián.

sinuosidad *f* sinuosity || bend, curve (curva) || FIG tortuosity (rodeo); *las sinuosidades de la diplomacia* the tortuosities of diplomacy.

sinuoso, sa *adj* sinuous, winding; *una carretera sinuosa* a winding road || wavy; *línea sinuosa* wavy line || FIG devious (retorcido).

sinusitis *f* MED sinusitis.

sinusoidal *adj* MAT sinusoidal.

sinvergonzón, ona *adj/s* ⟶ **sinvergüenza.**

sinvergüencería *f* shamelessness (desvergüenza) || dirty trick (*fam*), rotten thing to do (*fam*) (acto).

sinvergüenza; sinvergonzón, ona *adj* brazen, shameless (granuja) || cheeky (descarado).
◆ *m/f* scoundrel (granuja) || rotter (canalla) || brat (gamberro) || cheeky devil (descarado) || — *¡qué sinvergüenza eres!* you've got a nerve! || FAM *un tío sinvergüenza* a real rotter.

sinvergüenzada *f* AMER dirty trick, rotten thing to do.

sinvivir *m* unbearable situation.

Sión *n pr* Zion.

sionismo *m* Zionism.

sionista *adj/s* Zionist.

siquíatra; siquiatra *m* MED psychiatrist.

siquiatría *f* MED psychiatry.

síquico, ca *adj* psychic.

siquiera *conj* even if *o* though (aunque); *préstame el coche, siquiera sea por unos días* lend me the car, even if only for a few days || *siquiera... siquiera* whether... or whether; *siquiera venga, siquiera no venga* whether he comes or whether he doesn't.
◆ *adv* at least (por lo menos); *dame siquiera las gracias* you might at least thank me; *déjame siquiera acabar* at least let me finish || just; *¡si ganáramos siquiera para comer!* if we just earned enough to eat! || even, just; *si pudiera irme siquiera una semana* if I could just go for a week, if I could go even for a week || even; *sin enterarse siquiera de lo que pasaba* without even realizing what was happening || — *ni siquiera* or *no... siquiera* not even; *no tiene siquiera zapatos* he hasn't even got any shoes; *ni siquiera me lo dijo* he didn't even tell me || *¿y te ayudó? ni siquiera* and did he help you? not at all, by no means.

siquismo *m* psychism.

Siracusa *n pr* GEOGR Syracuse.

siracusano, na *adj/s* Syracusan.

sirena *f* MIT siren (ninfa) || mermaid (de los cuentos de hadas) || siren (señal acústica).

sirénido; sirenio *m* ZOOL sirenian.
◆ *pl* sirenia.

sirga *f* MAR towrope || *camino de sirga* towpath.

sirgar *vt* MAR to tow.

Siria *npr f* GEOGR Syria.

siriaco, ca *adj* Syrian.
◆ *m* Syriac (idioma antiguo).

sirimbo, ba *adj* AMER stupid, silly.
◆ *f* AMER fainting fit.

sirimiri *m* drizzle (llovizna).

siringa *f* AMER rubber tree || MÚS syrinx, flute.

siringe *m* syrinx (de las aves).

sirio, ria *adj/s* Syrian.

siroco *m* sirocco (viento).

sirope *m* AMER syrup (jarabe).

sirvienta *f* maid, servant (criada).

sirviente *adj* serving.
◆ *m* servant (criado) || waiter (camarero) || MIL gunner (de artillería).

sisa *f* FAM pilfering, petty theft (hurto) || dart (en un vestido) || armhole (de la manga).

sisador, ra *adj* pilfering.
◆ *m/f* pilferer, petty thief.

sisal *m* BOT sisal (pita).

sisar *vt* to pilfer, to filch (en las compras) || to take in, to dart (un vestido).
◆ *vi* to pilfer.

sisear *vt/vi* to hiss.

siseo *m* hiss, hissing.

sísmico, ca *adj* seismic.

sismo *m* earthquake, seism (seísmo).

sismógrafo *m* seismograph.

sismograma *m* seismogram.

sismología *f* seismology.

sismológico, ca *adj* seismologic, seismological.

sismómetro *m* seismometer.

sisón *m* ZOOL little bustard.

sisón, ona *adj* FAM pilfering, filching.
◆ *m/f* FAM pilferer, petty thief.

sistema *m* system; *sistema político* political system || method (método) || — *por sistema* as a rule || *proceder con sistema* to proceed systematically || *sistema cegesimal* centimetre-gram-second system || *sistema cristalino* or *cristalográfico* crystalline system || *sistema de altavoces* public address system || INFORM *sistema de entrada salida* input/output system | *sistema de gestión de base de datos* data base management system || *sistema de numeración* number system || *sistema decimal* decimal system || MAT *sistema de ecuaciones* simultaneous equations || INFORM *sistema de proceso de datos* data processing system | *sistema experto* expert system || *sistema métrico* metric system || *sistema montañoso* mountain chain || *sistema nervioso* nervous system || INFORM *sistema operativo* operating system || *sistema planetario* planetary system || *sistema solar* solar system || *sistema tributario* tax system.

sistemar *vt* AMER to systematize.

sistemáticamente *adv* systematically.

sistemático, ca *adj* systematic.
◆ *f* systematics.

sistematización *f* systematization.

sistematizar *vt* to systematize, to systemize.

sístole *f* ANAT systole.

sitiado, da *adj* besieged.
◆ *m/f* besieged.

sitiador, ra *adj* besieging.
◆ *m/f* besieger.

sitial *m* seat of honour || seat (asiento).

sitiar *vt* MIL to besiege, to lay siege to; *sitiar una ciudad* to lay siege to a town, to besiege a town || FIG to surround, to hem in; *sitiaron al ladrón* they surrounded the thief.

sitio *m* place; *vete a tu sitio* go to your place || spot, place; *es un sitio precioso* it's a lovely spot || space, room (espacio); *ocupar mucho sitio* to take up *o* to occupy a lot of space; *hay sitio de sobra* there's plenty of room || MIL siege (cerco) || location, site (para un edificio) || AMER lot, building site (solar para edificar) | small farm (granja pequeña) || — FIG & FAM *cada cosa en su sitio y un sitio para cada cosa* there is a time and a place for everything || *cambiar de sitio* to move || *cambiar de sitio con* to change places with || *cualquier sitio* anywhere || FIG & FAM *dejar a alguien en el sitio* to kill s.o. on the spot || *dejar* or *ceder el sitio* to give up one's place || *en cualquier sitio* anywhere || MIL *en estado de sitio* in a state of siege || *en todos los sitios* everywhere || *hacer sitio* to make room || MIL *levantar el sitio* to raise the siege || FIG & FAM *ponerle a alguien en su sitio* to put s.o. in his place || MIL *poner sitio a* to lay siege to, to besiege || FIG *quedarse en el sitio* to die (on the spot) || *real sitio* royal residence.

sitios *adj pl* JUR *bienes sitios* real estate.

sito, ta *adj* located (colocado) || situated; *una casa sita en Madrid* a house situated in Madrid || JUR *bienes sitos* real estate *sing.*

situación *f* situation; *una situación peligrosa* a dangerous situation || location, site (sitio); *la situación de una casa* the location of a house || condition, state; *no está en situación de hacer un viaje* he is in no condition to travel || position, standing (posición social) || — *estar en situación de* to be in a position to; *está en situación de conseguir un puesto en el ministerio* he is in a position to get a job in the ministry || AMER *precios de situación* reduced prices || *ser dueño de la situación* to be in control of the situation, to have the situation under control || *situación acomodada* sound financial position || *situación activa* active service || *situación social* social position.

situado, da *adj* situated || FIG *estar bien situado* to be in a comfortable position, to be comfortably off.

situar *vt* to place, to put (poner) || to situate, to site, to locate; *una ciudad situada a orillas del mar* a town located on the coast || COM to place, to invest (invertir) | to earmark (asignar fondos).
◆ *vpr* to be successful, to do well for o.s., to make o.s. a good position (alcanzar una buena posición) || to be situated (estar) || to take (a stand), to adopt (a position) (adoptar una posición).

siútico, ca *adj* AMER FAM terribly posh, affected (cursi).

siux *adj/s* Sioux (indio norteamericano).

sixtino, na *adj* sistine || *la Capilla Sixtina* the Sistine Chapel.

Sixto *npr m* Sixtus.

sketch *m* sketch (en cine y teatro).

S.L. *abrev de Sociedad Limitada* Ltd co, Limited Company.

slalom *m* DEP slalom (prueba de habilidad).

slam *m* slam (en bridge).

slip *m* pants *pl*, underpants *pl*, briefs *pl*.

slogan *m* slogan (lema publicitario).

sloop *m* MAR sloop (balandro).

smash *m* DEP smash (mate en tenis).

SME *abrev de Sistema Monetario Europeo* EMS, European Monetary System.

smoking *m* dinner jacket [*US* tuxedo].

snack-bar *m* snack bar (cafetería).

snipe *m* MAR snipe (barco).

snob *adj* snobbish.
◆ *m/f* snob.

snobismo *m* snobbery, snobbishness.

so *m* FAM you; *¡so tonto!* you idiot!

so *prep* under; *so pena de* under penalty of.

¡so! *interj* whoa! [to stop a horse].

soasar *vt* to roast lightly.

soba *f* kneading (del pan) || FAM thrashing, hiding (paliza); *le dieron una soba* they gave him a thrashing || FIG fulling (pieles) || POP fondling, pawing (manoseo).

sobaco *m* ANAT armpit.

sobadero *m* fulling mill (de pieles).

sobado, da *adj* kneaded (pan) || FIG worn, shabby; *el cuello de la camisa está muy sobado* the collar of the shirt is very worn | shabby, dog-eared; *un libro muy sobado* a very shabby book || FIG & FAM well-worn, hackneyed (tema, asunto) || CULIN short (torta).

sobadura *f* kneading (pan) || fulling (de las pieles) || POP fondling, pawing (manoseo).

sobaquera *f* armhole (del vestido) || dress shield (para no manchar el vestido de sudor) || underarm *o* body odour (olor).

sobaquillo (de) *adv* TAUR on the side.

sobaquina *f* body *o* underarm odour.

sobar *vt* to knead (pan) || to full (pieles) || FIG to thrash, to give a hiding, to wallop (zurrar) | to handle, to finger (manosear) | to pester (molestar) || POP to caress, to fondle (acariciar) | to paw (acariciar pesadamente).
◆ *vpr* POP to pet, to cuddle (acariciarse).

sobarda *f* noseband (de la brida) || double chin (papada).

sobeo *m* strap used to attach the yoke to the pole of the cart (de un carro) || POP fondling, pawing.

soberanamente *adv* extremely, supremely (muy).

soberanía *f* sovereignty || *plaza de soberanía* territory under the sovereignty of another country (Ceuta, Melilla).

soberano, na *adj* sovereign; *poder, estado soberano* sovereign power, state || FIG sovereign, supreme; *la belleza soberana* the supreme beauty; *soberano desprecio* sovereign contempt | excellent || FIG & FAM *dar una soberana paliza* to give a real good hiding.
◆ *m/f* sovereign || *los soberanos* the King and Queen.

soberbia *f* pride (orgullo, pecado capital) || arrogance, haughtiness, excessive pride (altivez) || FIG anger (ira).

soberbiamente *adv* arrogantly || FIG superbly, magnificently.

soberbio, bia *adj* proud (orgulloso) || arrogant, haughty (altivo) || FIG magnificent, superb, splendid (magnífico) | spirited (caballo) | angry, furious (colérico) || FIG & FAM *le dieron una soberbia paliza* they gave him a real good hiding.

sobón, ona *adj* POP randy, fresh (chico) | randy, fruity (chica) || FIG skiving, idle (remolón) || POP *es muy sobón* he's all hands, he's ever so randy.
◆ *m* POP randy bloke | skiver, slacker (remolón).
◆ *f* POP randy girl | skiver, slacker (remolona).

sobordo *m* MAR inspection (de la carga) | manifest (relación de cargamento).

sobornable *adj* bribable, venal.

sobornal *m* overload.

sobornar *vt* to bribe.

soborno *m* bribery, bribing (acción) || bribe (dinero dado) || AMER overload (sobrecarga) || AMER *de soborno* in addition, additional.

sobra *f* surplus, excess || — *de sobra* more than enough, to spare, plenty of (mucho); *tengo dinero de sobra* I have more than enough money; spare, extra; *¿tienes algún lápiz de sobra?* have you got a spare pencil? || FIG *estás de sobra* you are not wanted, you are in the way || *saber de sobra* to know only too well.
◆ *pl* leftovers (de comida) || trash *sing* (desperdicios).

sobradamente *adv* extremely (muy) || *estar sobradamente satisfecho* to be more than happy.

sobradero *m* overflow pipe (desagüe).

sobradillo *m* penthouse (sobre ventana o puerta).

sobrado, da *adj* more than enough, plenty of; *tiene sobrados motivos de queja* he has more than enough reason to complain || plenty of; *estoy sobrado de amistades* I have plenty of friends || — *tener sobrada razón* to be quite right || *y con sobrada razón* and quite rightly so.
◆ *adv* too (demasiado).
◆ *m* ARQ attic, garret (desván) || AMER kitchen shelf (vasar).
◆ *pl* AMER leftovers (sobras).

sobrante *adj* remaining (que queda) || leftover, spare (que sobra) || surplus (excedente).
◆ *m* surplus.

sobrar *vi* to have left over, to be left over; *me sobran cien pesetas* I have one hundred pesetas left over; *sobra vino* there is some wine left over || to have more than enough, to be more than enough; *me sobra dinero* I have more than enough money; *aquí sobra pan* there is more than enough bread here || to have plenty of; *te sobra tiempo* you have plenty of time || to be one (two, three, etc.) too many; *sobran cuatro libros* there are four books too many || to be too much (haber demasiado) || to be in the way (estorbar); *tú sobras* you are in the way || not to be necessary, to be unnecessary (ser inútil); *sobran los detalles* the details are not necessary || — *basta y sobra* that's more than enough || *no estar sobrado de* to be a little short of || *sobrarle a uno la gracia* to be ever so funny.

sobrasada; sobreasada *f* Majorcan sausage (embutido).

sobre *m* envelope (de carta); *poner en un sobre* to put in an envelope || packet; *sobre de sopa* packet of soup || — *bajo sobre* under cover || *por sobre separado* under separate cover.

sobre *prep* on, upon (véase OBSERV); *sobre la mesa* on the table || on top of (encima de); *poner un libro sobre otro* to put one book on top of another || on; *imponer un gravamen sobre* to levy a tax on || on, about; *hablar sobre un tema* to talk about a subject; *un libro sobre el arte* a book on art || around, round about, about; *ten-*

go sobre mil pesetas I have around 1000 pesetas; *vendré sobre las ocho* I will come about eight o'clock || upon; *dice insulto sobre insulto* he says insult upon insult || above (por encima de); *sobre nosotros veíamos un cielo tempestuoso* above us we saw a stormy sky || over; *el avión pasó sobre nosotros* the plane passed over our heads || onto; *las ventanas dan sobre la plaza* the windows look onto the square || down on *o* upon; *el ejército vino sobre los campesinos* the army came down upon the farmers || in addition to, on top of (además de); *le dio tres mil pesetas sobre lo estipulado* he gave him three thousand pesetas in addition to the agreed sum; *sobre los problemas que ya tenía, ahora tiene otros* he has got other problems now in addition to the ones he already had || over, above (en una jerarquía); *sobre él sólo tiene un jefe* he has only got one boss over him || above; *tres grados sobre cero* three degrees above zero || near (cerca de); *está sobre la calle de Goya* it is near Goya Street || — FIG & FAM *sobre ascuas* on tenterhooks || *sobre aviso* on one's guard, forewarned || *sobre gustos no hay nada escrito* everyone to his own taste, there's no accounting for tastes || *sobre manera* or *modo* exceedingly || *sobre poco más o menos* more or less, just about || *sobre ser rica es hermosa* not only is she rich, but she is also beautiful; she is beautiful as well as rich || *sobre todo* especially, above all; *me gusta España, sobre todo Andalucía* I like Spain, especially Andalusia; chiefly (principalmente).

— OBSERV Aunque *upon* tiene el mismo sentido que *on* su uso es menos frecuente.

sobreabundancia *f* superabundance, overabundance.

sobreabundante *adj* superabundant, overabundant.

sobreabundar *vi* to superabound (*en* with).

sobreagudo, da *adj* MÚS high-pitched.

sobrealimentación *f* overfeeding.

sobrealimentar *vt* to overfeed || TECN to supercharge.

sobrealzar *vt* to raise up.

sobreañadir *vt* to superadd, to add on.

sobreasada *f* ⟶ **sobrasada.**

sobrebota *f* AMER legging.

sobrecalentar *vt* to overheat.

sobrecama *f* bedspread.

sobrecaña *f* VET splint.

sobrecarga *f* overload (exceso de carga) || packing strap (cuerda o soga) || COM surcharge (en un sello) || FIG additional burden.

sobrecargar *vt* to overload || to weigh down, to overburden (una persona) || to fell (una costura) || to surcharge (un sello).

sobrecargom *m* MAR supercargo.

sobreceja *f* brow.

sobrecejo; sobreceño *m* frown.

sobrecincha *f* surcingle, girth (del caballo).

sobrecogedor, ra *adj* frightening (que asusta) || overwhelming (que conmueve).

sobrecoger *vt* to startle (miedo) || to take by surprise (frío) || to frighten (asustar).
◆ *vpr* to startle, to give a start (asustarse) || to give a start (de horror) || *sobrecogerse de miedo* to be seized with fear.

sobrecomprimir *vt* AVIAC to pressurize.

sobrecubierta *f* dust cover, jacket (de libro) || extra cover.

sobredicho, cha *adj* aforesaid, aforementioned, above-mentioned.

sobredorar *vt* to gild (los metales) || FIG to gloss over (disimular).

sobredosis *f* overdose.

sobreedificar *vt* to build over *o* on.

sobreentender*; sobrentender* *vt* to understand (comprender) || to guess, to deduce (deducir).
◆ *vpr* to be understood, to be implied.

sobreentendido, da *adj* implied, implicit.

sobreentrenamiento *m* DEP overtraining.

sobreentrenar *vt* DEP to overtrain.

sobreesdrújulo, la *adj* ⟶ **sobresdrújulo.**

sobreestadía *f* ⟶ **sobrestadía.**

sobreexceder *vt* to exceed.

sobreexcitación *f* overexcitement.

sobreexcitar *vt* to overexcite.
◆ *vpr* to get overexcited.

sobreexponer *vt* to overexpose.

sobreexposición *f* overexposure.

sobrefalda *f* overskirt.

sobrefaz *f* surface.

sobrefusión *f* QUÍM supercooling.

sobrehaz *f* surface.

sobrehilado *m* whipstitching.

sobrehilar *vt* to whipstitch.

sobrehílo *m* whipstitch.

sobrehumano, na *adj* superhuman.

sobreimpresión *f* FOT & CINEM superimposition.

sobrejuanete *m* MAR royal mast.

sobrelecho *m* ARQ underside of a stone.

sobrellenar *vt* to overfill.

sobrellevar *vt* FIG to bear, to endure (aguantar) | to help to bear, to share (ayudar a otro).

sobremanera *f* exceedingly, excessively.

sobremesa *f* table cover, table covering (tapete) || dessert (postre) || chat *o* conversation after dinner; *tuvimos una agradable sobremesa ayer* we had a nice chat after dinner yesterday || — *de sobremesa* after-dinner; *charla de sobremesa* after-dinner chat || *estar de sobremesa* to be sitting round the table after dinner.

sobremesana *f* MAR mizzen topsail.

sobrenatural *adj* supernatural || REL *vida sobrenatural* life after death.

sobrenaturalismo *m* supernaturalism.

sobrenombre *m* nickname || *dar a uno el sobrenombre de* to nickname s.o.

sobrentender* *vt* ⟶ **sobreentender.**

sobrepaga *f* bonus.

sobreparto *m* postnatal confinement || — *dolores de sobreparto* afterpains || *morir de sobreparto* to die in childbirth.

sobrepasar *vt* to surpass, to exceed || to exceed (unos límites) || AVIAC to overshoot [the runway] (la pista) || DEP to beat (vencer).
◆ *vpr* *sobrepasarse a sí mismo* to surpass o.s.

sobrepelo *m* AMER saddlecloth.

sobrepelliz *f* REL surplice.

sobrepeso *m* overload (exceso de carga) || *sobrepeso de equipaje* excess baggage.

sobreponer* *vt* to superimpose (*en* on), to put on top (*en* of) || to put before (anteponer).
◆ *vpr* to overcome; *sobreponerse a su dolor* to overcome one's pain || to pull o.s. together; *te tienes que sobreponer* you must pull yourself together || to triumph (*a* over) (vencer).

sobreporte *m* extra postage.

sobreprecio *m* surcharge.

sobreprima *f* extra premium (seguros).

sobreproducción *f* overproduction, excess production.

sobrepuerta *f* pelmet [over a door].

sobrepuesto, ta *adj* superimposed.
◆ *m* appliqué work (ornamentación) || basket *o* clay covering for a beehive.

sobrepuja *f* overbid, overbidding (en las subastas).

sobrepujar *vt* to surpass; *ella sobrepuja a todas sus hermanas en belleza* she surpasses all her sisters in beauty || to overbid, to outbid (subasta).

sobrequilla *f* MAR keelson.

sobrero *adj* extra, spare (sobrante) || TAUR spare [bull] (toro).
◆ *m* TAUR spare bull (toro).

sobresalienta *f* TEATR understudy.

sobresaliente *adj* projecting, overhanging || outstanding; *una de las personas más sobresalientes de su época* one of the most outstanding figures of his time.
◆ *m* high mark, excellent mark (nota superior) || first class honours *pl* (en un examen de licenciatura) || TAUR substitute bullfighter || understudy (actor que reemplaza a otro).

sobresalir* *vi* to project, to jut out, to stick out (resaltar) || to stick out, to jut out; *hay un adoquín que sobresale de la acera* there is a paving stone sticking out of the pavement || FIG to excel, to stand out; *él sobresale entre todos sus amigos* he stands out from all his friends | to stand out, to be conspicuous (diferenciarse).

sobresaltar *vt* to startle, to give a fright, to make (s.o.) jump.
◆ *vpr* to be startled (*con, por* by), to start (*con, por* at).

sobresalto *m* start (movimiento) || fright, scare (susto); *me dio un sobresalto* he gave me a fright.

sobresaturación *f* supersaturation.

sobresaturar *vt* to supersaturate.

sobresdrújulo, la; sobreesdrújulo, la *adj* GRAM accented on the syllable preceding the antepenultimate one [as in *devuélvemelo* give it back to me].

sobreseer *vt* JUR to stay; *sobreseer la causa* to stay proceedings.

sobreseimiento *m* JUR stay (provisional); *el sobreseimiento de una causa* the stay of proceedings || JUR *sobreseimiento libre* nonsuit.

sobresello *m* second seal, double seal.

sobrestadía; sobreestadía *f* MAR demurrage (días de prórroga e indemnización).

sobrestante *m* foreman (capataz).

sobrestimación *f* overestimate.

sobrestimar *vt* to overestimate.

sobresueldo *m* bonus.

sobretasa *f* surcharge.

sobretensión *f* ELECTR surge.

sobretodo *m* overcoat (abrigo) || overall (para proteger un traje).

sobrevenir* *vi* to happen, to occur, to take place (ocurrir) || *les sobrevino una catástrofe* disaster befell them, disaster struck (them).

sobrevidriera *f* screen (tela metálica) || second window (segunda vidriera).

sobreviviente *adj* surviving.
◆ *m/f* survivor.

sobrevivir *vi* to survive || *sobrevivir a* to outlive, to survive (una persona), to survive (una epidemia).

sobrevolar* *vt* AVIAC to fly over, to overfly.

sobrexcedente *adj* excess.

sobrexceder *vt* to exceed.

sobrexcitación *f* overexcitement.

sobrexcitar *vt* to overexcite.
◆ *vpr* to overexcite o.s., to become *o* to get overexcited.

sobriedad *f* soberness, restraint, sobriety.

sobrino, na *m/f* nephew (hombre), niece (mujer) ‖ — *sobrino carnal* nephew ‖ *sobrino político* nephew by marriage ‖ *sobrino segundo* first cousin once removed.

sobrio, bria *adj* sober; *es muy sobrio en sus costumbres* he has very sober habits; *color, estilo, discurso sobrio* sober colour, style, speech ‖ light (comida) ‖ — *ser sobrio de palabras* to speak with restraint ‖ *sobrio en la bebida* temperate in one's drinking habits.

socaire *m* MAR lee ‖ — MAR *al socaire* leeward ‖ FIG *al socaire de* protected by.

socaliña *f* cunning (ardid).

socaliñar *vt* to get (sth.) through cunning (conseguir con maña).

socaliñero, ra *adj* cunning, crafty.
◆ *m/f* cunning *o* crafty person, sly dog.

socapa *f* pretext, pretence [*US* pretense] ‖ *a socapa* surreptitiously.

socarrar *vt* to scorch, to singe (chamuscar).

socarrón, ona *adj* sarcastic, ironical ‖ sly (taimado) ‖ *una sonrisa socarrona* a sly smile.

socarronería *f* sarcasm, irony ‖ slyness (carácter taimado).

socavar *vt* to undermine, to dig under ‖ FIG to undermine.

socavón *m* excavation ‖ gallery (galería) ‖ subsidence (hundimiento) ‖ hollow (hueco).

sociabilidad *f* sociability.

sociable *adj* sociable.

social *adj* social ‖ COM *razón social* trade name.

socialdemócrata *adj* social-democratic.
◆ *m/f* social democrat.

socialdemocracia *f* social democracy.

socialismo *m* socialism.

socialista *adj/s* socialist.

socialización *f* nationalization ‖ socialization.

socializar *vt* to nationalize ‖ to socialize.

socialmente *adv* socially.

sociedad *f* society; *la sociedad en que vivimos* the society in which we live; *sociedad protectora de animales* society for the prevention of cruelty to animals ‖ company, society (comercial) ‖ — *alta* or *buena sociedad* high society ‖ *ecos de sociedad* society news, society column ‖ *entrar* or *presentarse en la sociedad* to make one's début, to come out ‖ *sociedad anónima* public limited company [*US* corporation] ‖ *sociedad civil* general partnership ‖ *sociedad comanditaria* or *en comandita* limited partnership ‖ *sociedad cooperativa* cooperative, cooperative society ‖ *sociedad conyugal* marriage partnership ‖ *Sociedad de Naciones* League of Nations ‖ *sociedad industrial* industrial society ‖ *sociedad (de responsabilidad) limitada* limited liability company ‖ *sociedad mercantil* trading company ‖ *sociedad secreta* secret society.

socio, cia *m/f* member (de una asociación); *socio de un club* member of a club ‖ partner, associate (de una sociedad comercial); *¿cuántos socios hay en el negocio?* how many partners are there in the business? ‖ FAM chap, fellow, guy ‖ — *hacerse socio* to become a member ‖ *socio capitalista* capitalist partner ‖ *socio comanditario* sleeping partner [*US* silent partner] ‖ *socio de número* full member ‖ *socio fundador* founding partner.

socioeconómico, ca *adj* socioeconomic.

sociología *f* sociology.

sociológico, ca *adj* sociological.

sociólogo, ga *m/f* sociologist.

socolor *m* pretext, pretence [*US* pretense] ‖ *socolor de* under the pretext of.

socorrer *vt* to help, to assist, to relieve; *socorrer a los pobres* to help the poor ‖ to relieve (una ciudad).

socorrido, da *adj* helpful (dispuesto a socorrer) ‖ well stocked (abastecido) ‖ FAM handy, useful; *es un traje muy socorrido* it is a very handy dress.

socorrismo *m* first aid ‖ life saving (en una piscina, una playa).

socorrista *m/f* person trained in first aid ‖ life-saver (en piscina, playa).

socorro *m* help, aid, assistance; *prestar socorro* to give aid ‖ MIL relief (soldados) ‖ supplies *pl*, provisions *pl* (provisiones) ‖ — *agua de socorro* emergency baptism (bautismo) ‖ *casa de socorro* emergency *o* casualty hospital, first-aid post ‖ *fuerzas de socorro* reinforcements ‖ *ir en socorro de alguien* to go to s.o.'s aid ‖ *puesto de socorro* first-aid post ‖ *señal de socorro* distress signal.
◆ *interj* help!

Sócrates *npr m* Socrates.

socrático, ca *adj* Socratic.

sochantre *m* REL succentor.

soda *f* QUÍM soda (sosa) ‖ soda water (bebida).

sódico, ca *adj* QUÍM (of) sodium; *carbonato, bicarbonato sódico* sodium carbonate, bicarbonate.

sodio *m* QUÍM sodium; *cloruro de sodio* sodium chloride.

Sodoma *n pr* HIST Sodom.

sodomía *f* sodomy.

sodomita *adj/s* sodomite.

sodomítico, ca *adj* sodomite.

soez *adj* rude, vulgar, dirty.

sofá *adj* sofa ‖ *sofá cama* studio couch.

Sofía *npr f* Sophia (nombre de pila) ‖ GEOGR Sofia.

sofión *m* snort, bellow (bufido) ‖ rebuff (negación) ‖ scolding (reprensión) ‖ blunderbuss (trabuco).

sofisma *m* sophism.

sofista *adj* sophistic.
◆ *m/f* sophist.

sofistería *f* sophistry.

sofisticación *f* use of sophistry (de un razonamiento) ‖ sophistication (afectación) ‖ adulteration.

sofisticado, da *adj* sophisticated (afectado) ‖ adulterated (falsificado).

sofisticar *vt* to adulterate (falsificar) ‖ to sophisticate (quitar naturalidad).

sofístico, ca *adj* sophistical, sophistic.

sofito *m* ARQ soffit.

soflama *f* flicker (del fuego) ‖ FIG blush (en el rostro) | harangue (discurso ardoroso) | deceit (engaño) | cajolery (zalamería).

soflamar *vt* to scorch, to singe (quemar ligeramente) ‖ FIG to make blush (abochornar) | to deceive (engañar) | to cajole (zalamear).
◆ *vpr* to burn (quemarse).

sofocación *f* suffocation (pérdida del aliento) ‖ choking sensation (ahogo) ‖ FIG suppression (de una revolución) | hushing up (de un escándalo) | blushing (rubor) | embarrassing situation (situación molesta).

sofocador, ra; sofocante *adj* suffocating (humo, gas) ‖ stifling, suffocating (calor, clima) ‖ stuffy (atmósfera).

sofocar *vt* to suffocate, to stifle (hacer perder la respiración) ‖ to put out, to smother (un incendio) ‖ FIG to suppress, to put down, to stifle (una revolución) | to stop (una epidemia) | to make (s.o.) blush (avergonzar) | to anger, to upset (irritar).
◆ *vpr* to suffocate, to stifle (de calor) ‖ to get out of breath (al hacer un esfuerzo) ‖ to choke (atragantarse) ‖ FIG to blush (ruborizarse) | to get angry, to get upset (irritarse).

Sófocles *npr m* Sophocles.

sofoco *m* suffocation ‖ choking sensation (ahogo) ‖ FIG shame (vergüenza) | embarrassing situation (vergüenza) ‖ FIG & FAM *le dio un sofoco* it gave him quite a turn.

sofocón *m* FAM shock (gran disgusto) ‖ FAM *me llevé un gran sofocón* I was beside myself.

sofoquina *f* FAM shock (sofocón) | suffocating heat (calor sofocante) ‖ FAM *¡vaya sofoquina que hace aquí!* it's stifling here!

sofreír* *vt* to fry lightly.

sofrenada *f* sharp jerk on the reins (caballo) ‖ FIG talking-to, dressing down (reprimenda).

sofrenar *vt* to rein in sharply (al caballo) ‖ FIG to give a good talking-to *o* a good dressing down (reprender) | to restrain (las pasiones).

software *m* INFORM software ‖ — *software de aplicación* application software ‖ *software de juegos* games software ‖ *software didáctico* courseware ‖ *software integrado* integrated software ‖ *software gráfico* graphics software ‖ *software operativo* operating software.

soga *f* rope, cord (cuerda) ‖ AMER leather strap (tira de cuero) ‖ — FIG *dar soga a uno* to get s.o. to speak (darle cuerda), to make fun of s.o. (burlarse) | *echar la soga tras el caldero* to throw helve after hatchet | *estar con la soga al cuello* to have one's neck in a noose, to have a knife at one's throat | *siempre se quiebra la soga por lo más delgado* the weakest goes to the wall.

soja *f* BOT soya bean, soja bean [*US* soybean].

sojuzgador, ra *adj* subjugating, subduing.
◆ *m/f* subjugator, subduer.

sojuzgar *vt* to subjugate, to subdue (someter) ‖ to rule tyrannically (tratar tiránicamente).

sol *m* sun; *sol poniente, naciente, de medianoche* setting, rising, midnight sun ‖ sun, sunlight, sunshine (luz solar); *el sol descolora la pintura* the sunlight takes the colour out of the paintwork ‖ sol (unidad monetaria del Perú) ‖ FIG darling; *¡qué sol de niño!* what a darling child! ‖ TAUR seats *pl* in the sun (en la plaza de toros) ‖ QUÍM sol (coloide) ‖ MÚS sol (nota) ‖ — *al ponerse el sol* at sunset ‖ *al salir el sol* at sunrise ‖ *al sol* in the sun ‖ FIG & FAM *arrimarse al sol que más calienta* to get on the winning side ‖ *bajo el sol* in the sun; *estoy a gusto bajo el sol* I like being in the sun; under the sun; *no hay nada nuevo bajo el sol* there is nothing new under the sun ‖ FIG & FAM *como el sol que nos alumbra* as clear as the light of day ‖ *da el sol de pleno* the sun beats down directly ‖ *de sol* sunny; *una tarde de sol* a sunny afternoon ‖ *de sol a sol* from sunrise to sunset ‖ *el Rey Sol* the Sun King ‖ *el sol aprieta* the sun is hot *o* strong ‖ *hace sol* it is sunny, the sun is shining ‖ FIG & FAM *más hermoso que un sol* as pretty as a picture, divine (chica, niño), fine-looking, handsome (adolescente) | *no dejar a uno ni a sol ni a sombra* not to leave s.o. alone *o* in peace, to pester *o* to hound s.o. ‖ FIG *pegársele el sol a alguien* to get suntanned ‖ *quemadura de sol* sunburn ‖ *rayo de sol* sunbeam ‖ *reloj de sol* sundial ‖ FIG & FAM *¡salga el sol por Antequera!* come what may! ‖ BOT *sol de las Indias* sunflower ‖ *sol y sombra* stands in the bullring which are first in the sun and then in the shade (plaza de toros), drink of brandy and anisette (bebida) ‖ *tendido de sol* stands in the sun (plaza de toros) || *tomar el sol* to sunbathe, to bask in the sun (tumbado), to take the sun (paseándose, etc.).

solado *m* flooring.

solador *m* floorer.

soladura *f* flooring.

solamente *adv* only; *no solamente* not only || — *con solamente que* or *solamente con que no me moleste* provided (that) he does not bother me, as long as he does not bother me || *estoy muy agradecido, solamente que no sé expresarlo* I am very grateful, but I do not know how to show it || *solamente que fuese un poco menos caro, lo compraría* if only it were a little cheaper I would buy it.

solana *f* sunny place *o* spot || sunshine; *ahora hay mucha solana* there is a lot of sunshine now || veranda (de una casa).

solanácea *f* BOT solanum.
◆ *pl* solanaceae.

solanera *f* sunstroke, sunburn (insolación) || scorching sun (sol fuerte).

solano *m* east wind (viento) || BOT nightshade.

solapa *f* lapel (de una chaqueta) || flap (de bolsillo, de libro, de sobre) || FIG pretext.

solapadamente *adv* slyly, in an underhand way.

solapado, da *adj* sly, underhand.

solapar *vt* to overlap (cubrir parcialmente) || to put lapels on (una chaqueta) || FIG to hide, to cover up (ocultar).

solar *adj* solar, of the sun || — *año solar* solar year || ANAT *plexo solar* solar plexus || *rayos solares* sun's rays, rays of sunlight || *sistema solar* solar system.
◆ *m* lot, plot (terreno); *acaban de comprar un solar para hacerse una casa* they have just bought a lot to build a house on || building site (terreno donde se está construyendo) || family, lineage, line (linaje) || family seat, country seat, ancestral home (casa solariega).

solar* *vt* to resole (calzado) || to floor (suelo).

solariego, ga *adj* family (del patrimonio) || noble || *casa solariega* ancestral home, family seat, country seat.

solario *m* solarium.

solaz *m* recreation, entertainment (diversión) || solace, consolation, relief (alivio) || relaxation (descanso) || *a solaz* with pleasure.

solazar *vt* to divert, to amuse, to entertain (divertir) || to solace, to console (aliviar).
◆ *vpr* to amuse o.s., to enjoy o.s.

solazo *m* FAM scorching sun.

soldada *f* salary (sueldo) || pay (de soldado, de marinero).

soldadesca *f* military profession, soldiering || soldiery (grupo de soldados) || undisciplined troops *pl* (soldados indisciplinados).

soldadesco, ca *adj* soldier-like, soldierly || barrack-room (lenguaje, etc.).

soldadito *m* soldier; *soldadito de plomo* tin *o* toy soldier.

soldado *m* soldier || — *soldado bisoño* raw recruit || *soldado cumplido* discharged soldier || *soldado de artillería* artilleryman || *soldado de caballería* trooper, cavalryman || *soldado de infantería* infantryman || *soldado de infantería de marina* marine || *soldado de primera, de segunda clase* private first class, private || *soldado desconocido* unknown warrior *o* soldier || *soldado montado* cavalryman || *soldado raso* private, private soldier || *soldado romano* Róman soldier [in the Holy Week processions] || *soldado voluntario* volunteer.

soldador *m* welder (obrero) || soldering iron (instrumento).

soldadora *f* welder, welding machine.

soldadura *f* welding, soldering (acción) || soldered joint, weld || — *soldadura a tope* butt welding || *soldadura autógena* (oxyacetylene) welding || *soldadura blanda* soft soldering || *soldadura fuerte* hard soldering || *soldadura oxiacetilénica* oxyacetylene welding || *soldadura por puntos* spot welding.

soldar* *vt* to weld, to solder || FIG to mend (una falta) || *soldar por puntos* to spot-weld.
◆ *vpr* FIG to join together (unirse) | to knit (huesos).

soleá *f* melancholy Andalusian song and dance.
— OBSERV pl *soleares*.

soleado, da *adj* sunny.

soleamiento *m* exposure to the sun.

solear *vt* to expose to the sun, to put in the sun.

soleares *f pl* → **soleá.**

solecismo *m* GRAM solecism.

soledad *f* solitude (estar solo) || loneliness (sentirse solo) || grieving (nostalgia) || lonely place (sitio) || melancholy Andalusian song and dance (soleá).

solemne *adj* solemn || FIG downright; *es una solemne tontería* it is downright madness | terrible; *un solemne error* a terrible mistake.

solemnidad *f* solemnity (seriedad) || ceremony (acto) || formality (trámite) || FAM *pobre de solemnidad* penniless.

solemnizar *vt* to solemnize, to celebrate (celebrar) || to commemorate (conmemorar).

solenoide *m* FÍS solenoid.

sóleo *m* ANAT soleus (músculo).

soler* *vi* to usually (do, etc.), to be in the habit of (acostumbrar); *suele venir el lunes* he usually comes on Mondays, he is in the habit of coming on Mondays || to (be, do, etc.) usually *o* frequently *o* often *o* generally (ser frecuente); *los españoles suelen ser morenos* the Spanish are usually dark; *suele equivocarse* he is frequently mistaken; *aquí suele hacer mucho frío* it is generally very cold here || to use to (sólo empleado en pasado); *solía leer por la tarde* he used to read in the afternoon || *suele llover mucho aquí* it usually *o* frequently *o* often *o* generally rains a lot here, it tends to rain a lot here.

solera *f* prop (soporte) || lower millstone (de molino) || bottom (de un canal) || TECN floor (de horno) | stone pavement (de un puente o alcantarilla) || lees *pl* (heces del vino) || reserve (reserva de vino) || flat stone base (para postes, etc.) || FIG tradition (tradición) | lineage (linaje) || — *familia de mucha solera* old-established family || *marca de solera* old-established brand, prestige brand || *vino de solera* vintage wine.

solería *f* leather for soles || flooring (suelo).

soleta *f* patch (remiendo) || FIG & FAM *picar* or *tomar soleta* to beat it (irse).

solevantar *vt* to lift || FIG to stir up.

solfa *f* MÚS solfeggio, sol-fa (solfeo) || FIG & FAM thrashing (paliza) || — FIG & FAM *echar una solfa a uno* to give s.o. a good talking-to | *poner en solfa* to ridicule | *tomar a solfa* not to take seriously.

solfatara *f* GEOL solfatara.

solfear *vt* to sol-fa || FIG & FAM to give a good thrashing (zurrar) | to give a good talking-to (reprender).

solfeo *m* MÚS solfeggio (arte) || FIG & FAM thrashing (paliza) | talking-to (acción de reprender).

solicitación *f* requesting (acción de pedir) || request (petición) || invitation (para salir) || canvassing (de votos) || temptation (tentación) || *solicitación de fondos* call for funds.

solicitador, ra; solicitante *m/f* petitioner (el que pide) || applicant (el que hace una solicitud).

solicitar *vt* to request; *solicitar una entrevista* to request an interview || to ask for, to seek (un permiso) || to apply for; *solicitar un empleo* to apply for a job || to attract (llamar la atención) || to pursue, to chase after (*fam*) (a una persona) || to court (a una mujer) || to canvass for (votos) || FÍS to attract || *es una chica muy solicitada* she is very much in demand, she is a very popular girl.

solícito, ta *adj* solicitous, obliging (amable); *es muy solícito conmigo* he is very solicitous with me || — *el camarero se acercó solícito* the waiter came over attentively || *mostrarse solícito con* to be obliging with || *un hijo solícito* an affectionate son.

solicitud *f* solicitude, care (cuidado) || application (para un puesto) || request (petición); *dirigir una solicitud* to make a request || petition (instancia) || *a solicitud* on request.

solidar *vt* to consolidate, to strengthen, to reinforce (reforzar) || to prove (demostrar).

solidaridad *f* solidarity || *por solidaridad con* out of solidarity with, in simpathy with.

solidario, ria *adj* solidary || JUR jointly responsible *o* liable (persona) | mutually binding (obligación) | common (responsabilidad) || TECN integral (pieza).

solidarizar *vt* JUR to render jointly liable *o* responsible.
◆ *vpr* to make common cause, to line up; *solidarizarse con los huelguistas* to make common cause with the strikers || to support (apoyar).

solideo *m* skullcap (de eclesiástico).

solidez *f* strength, firmness, solidity (resistencia) || solidity (naturaleza sólida) || FIG soundness (de un argumento) || fastness (de un color).

solidificación *f* solidification.

solidificar, solidificarse *vpr/vt* to solidify.

sólido, da *adj* solid; *cuerpo, alimento sólido* solid body, food || strong (resistente) || firm (firme) || solid, secure (seguro, estable) || FIG sound (argumento, principio, base) || fast (color).
◆ *m* MAT & FÍS solid || solidus (moneda romana).

soliloquiar *vi* to soliloquize, to talk to o.s.

soliloquio *m* soliloquy, monologue.

solio *m* (canopied) throne (trono).

solípedo, da *adj/sm* ZOOL soliped.

solista *m/f* MÚS soloist.

solitaria *f* tapeworm; *tener la solitaria* to have a tapeworm || post chaise (carruaje).

solitario, ria *adj* solitary (persona) || solitary, lonely, deserted, secluded (lugar).
◆ *m/f* hermit, recluse (ermitaño) || solitary person (persona que busca la soledad).
◆ *m* solitaire (juego de naipes) || solitaire (diamante).

sólito, ta *adj* usual, customary.

soliviantar *vt* to rouse, to stir up (excitar a una actitud rebelde) || to irritate (irritar) || to worry (preocupar) || *soliviantado por los celos* eaten up *o* consumed with envy.

solo, la *adj* alone, by o.s.; *hacer algo solo* to do sth. by o.s.; *vivir solo* to live alone || lonely; *sentirse solo* to feel lonely || only, sole (único); *su sola preocupación* his only worry || single; *ni una sola crítica* not a single criticism || unique (sin par) || MÚS solo; *violín solo* solo violin || — *a solas* alone, by o.s.; *él come a solas* he eats

alone || *café solo* black coffee || *como él solo* as only he can || FIG *de solo a solo* alone || *eso marcha solo* that's no trouble at all || *quedarse solo* to have no equal (no tener rival), to be left alone in the world (quedarse huérfano, viudo, etc.) || *se presenta una sola dificultad* there is just one *o* only one difficulty.
◆ *m* solitaire, solo (naipes) || solo; *un solo de tambor* a drum solo; *un solo para soprano* a soprano solo.

sólo *adv* only, solely, merely, just; *sólo quiero que vengas* I only want you to come || — *aunque sólo sea por un día* even if it is only for one day || *con sólo, sólo con* (con infinitivo) just by (con gerundio); *con sólo decir esta palabra* just by saying this word || *con sólo que..., sólo con que...* provided that..., as long as... (con tal que) || *con sólo que, sólo con que falte una persona, no podemos hacer nada* it just needs one person to be missing and we cannot do anything; if just one person is missing, we cannot do anything || *no sólo... sino* not only... but; *no sólo en este pueblo sino en toda la provincia* not only in this village, but in all the province; *no sólo canta sino que también baila* she not only sings, but she also dances || *sólo que* only, but; *me gustó la blusa, sólo que era demasiado pequeña* I liked the blouse, only it was too small; *yo iré, sólo que no me divierte nada* I'll go, but I won't enjoy it at all || *sólo un momento* just a minute, just a moment || *tan sólo* only, merely, just; *tan sólo quiero que me dejen en paz* I only want them to leave me alone || *tan sólo con* (con infinitivo), just by (con gerundio); *tan sólo con decirme la verdad* just by telling me the truth || *tan sólo con que* (con subjuntivo), if only; *tan sólo con que vayas a verle* if only you go to see him || *tan sólo te pido que me dejes tranquilo* all I want is to be left alone, the only thing I ask of you is that you leave me alone.

solomillo *m* sirloin.

solomo *m* sirloin (solomillo) || loin of pork (de cerdo).

solsticio *m* ASTR solstice; *solsticio de invierno, de verano* winter, summer solstice.

soltar* *vt* to release || to let go of, to drop; *soltó un plato* he dropped a plate || to free, to set free, to release (un preso) || to let loose (los animales) || to unleash (un perro) || to untie, to undo; *soltar un nudo* to untie a knot || to loosen, to slacken, to ease (aflojar) || to pay out; *soltar un poco de cuerda* to pay out a little rope || to drop (puntos) || to give off (desprender); *esto suelta mucho humo* this gives off a lot of smoke || to loosen (el vientre) || FIG to resolve; *soltar una dificultad* to resolve a difficulty | to give up (ceder, abandonar) || MAR to cast off; *suelta las amarras* cast off the ropes || AUT to release (el freno) || AVIAC to release, to drop; *soltar una bomba* to release a bomb || FAM to tell, to come out with (contar) | to say, to come out with, to hurl; *me soltó una grosería* he hurled a nasty remark at me | to give; *nos soltó un discurso pesadísimo* he gave us a very boring speech | to blurt out, to let out (un secreto) | to break; *soltar la noticia* to break the news | to heave (un suspiro) | to utter, to let out (un grito) | to give, to land, to deal; *soltar un puñetazo* to land a punch | to cough up; *soltar diez dólares* to cough up ten dollars || to shed; *la culebra suelta la piel* the snake sheds its skin || — FAM *no soltar prenda* not to commit o.s., to be noncommital | *sin soltar un cuarto* without spending a penny || FIG & FAM *soltar coces* to lash out || *soltar la lengua* to loosen s.o.'s tongue || FAM *soltar la pasta* to fork up, to cough up || *soltar la risa* to burst out laughing || *soltar una andanada* to fire a broadside (marítimo), to lash out (injurias) || *soltar una carcajada* or *una risotada* to burst out laughing || FAM *¡suelta!* out with it! (dilo) || *¡suéltame!* let me go!
◆ *vpr* to come unfastened, to come untied (desanudarse) || to get loose, to break loose; *el perro se soltó de la correa* the dog got loose from the leash || to break, to come undone (puntos) || to come off (desprenderse) || to come out, to come unscrewed (tornillo) || to loosen (vientre) || FIG to get the knack; *soltarse en el trabajo* to get the knack of the job | to lose one's shyness, to become more self-confident (desenvolverse una persona); *ya era hora de que se soltara este chico* it is about time this boy lost his shyness | to start (un niño); *hasta hace unos días no andaba, acaba de soltarse ahora* a few days ago he could not walk, he has just started now | to become *o* to get fluent *o* proficient; *ya empiezo a soltarme en francés* I am just beginning to get fluent in French || — FAM *soltarse a su gusto* to let off steam || MAR *soltarse de las amarras* to cast off || *soltarse de manos* to take one's hands off the handlebars (de un manillar de bicicleta) || *soltarse el pelo* to take one's hair down (despeinarse), to let one's hair down (hacer su santa voluntad) || *soltársele a uno la lengua* to become very talkative.
— OBSERV The past participle of *soltar* is irregular: *suelto, suelta*.

soltería *f* celibacy.

soltero, ra *adj* unmarried, single; *él está soltero* he is unmarried; *quedarse soltero* to stay single.
◆ *m* bachelor, unmarried man || *despedida de soltero* stag party.
◆ *f* single woman, spinster || — *apellido de soltera* maiden name || *despedida de soltera* hen party || *la Sra. López, de soltera Gómez* Mrs. López, née *o* nee Gómez.

solterón *m* old bachelor.

solterona *f* spinster, old maid.

soltura *f* looseness, slackness || agility (agilidad) || FIG ease, fluency (al hablar); *hablar con mucha soltura* to speak with great ease || confidence, assurance (seguridad) || JUR release (de un preso) || shamelessness (descaro) || — FIG *con soltura* fluently, with ease; *hablar un idioma con soltura* to speak a language fluently; with ease, gracefully (moverse) | *soltura de palabras* fluency | *soltura de vientre* looseness of the bowels.

solubilidad *f* solubility.

soluble *adj* soluble (que se disuelve) || solvable, soluble (que se resuelve).

solución *f* solution; *la solución de un problema* the solution to a problem || QUÍM solution || ending, dénouement; *la solución del drama* the dénouement of the drama || *solución de continuidad* interruption, solution of continuity.

solucionar *vt* to solve, to resolve; *solucionar un problema* to solve a problem || *solucionar una huelga* to settle a strike.

solvencia *f* solvency (capacidad para pagar deudas) || settlement (pago).

solventar *vt* to settle (una deuda) || to solve, to resolve (una dificultad) || to settle (un asunto).

solvente *adj* solvent.
◆ *m* QUÍM solvent.

solla *f* plaice (pez).

sollado *m* MAR orlop.

sollamar *vt* to scorch, to singe.

sollastre *m* scullion, kitchen boy (pinche) || FIG rascal, rogue.

sollo *m* ZOOL sturgeon (pez) || FIG & FAM *estar gordo como un sollo* to be as fat as a pig.

sollozar *vi* to sob.

sollozo *m* sob; *estallar* or *prorrumpir en sollozos* to burst into sobs || *decir algo entre sollozos* to say sth. sobbing, to sob sth.

soma *m* soma.

somalí *adj/s* Somali.

Somalia *npr f* GEOGR Somalia.

somanta *f* FAM beating, licking (tunda) | spanking (a los niños) || FAM *le dio una somanta de palos* he gave him a real thrashing.

somatén *m* militia [in Catalonia] (milicia) || tocsin, alarm (rebato); *tocar a somatén* to sound the alarm || FIG & FAM disorder, uproar (alboroto).
◆ *interj* Catalan war cry.

somático, ca *adj* MED somatic.

somatología *f* MED somatology.

sombra *f* shade; *está sentado en la sombra del árbol* he is sitting in the shade of the tree; *luz y sombra* light and shade || shadow; *la sombra del árbol se proyecta en la pared* the shadow of the tree is cast on the wall || FIG ghost, shade (fantasma); *las sombras de los muertos* the ghosts of the dead | wit (agudeza) | luck (suerte) || shadow (en televisión) || TAUR shady section of the bullring || ASTR umbra || FIG darkness; *bruscamente las sombras de la noche cayeron sobre el castillo* suddenly the darkness of night fell upon the castle; *no veo nada más que sombras a mi alrededor* all I see is darkness around me | shadow (acompañante) | spot, stain (mancha) | bit, trace, shade (un poco) || AMER sunshade (quitasol) | awning (toldo) | underlines *pl* (falsilla) || — *a la sombra* in the shade; *los viejos se sentaron a la sombra* the old men sat in the shade; in jail (en chirona), undercover, secretly; *los contrabandistas trabajan a la sombra* smugglers work undercover || FIG *burlarse* or *reírse de su sombra* to laugh at everything || *dar sombra* to give shade (un árbol) || *dar sombra a* to shade || FIG *desconfía hasta de su sombra, no se fía ni de su sombra* he does not even trust his own shadow || *hacer sombra* to cast a shadow (dar sombra), to put in the shade (exceder en calidad) || FIG *mala sombra* bad luck | *ni por sombra* in the least (lo más mínimo); *no sospecharon de él ni por sombra* they didn't suspect him in the least; by no means (de ninguna manera) | *no dejar a uno ni a sol ni a sombra* not to leave s.o. alone *o* in peace, to pester *o* to hound s.o. | *no ser más que la sombra* or *ni sombra de lo que era* to be a mere shadow of one's former self | *no tiene ni sombra de gracia* that's not the slightest bit funny | *sombra de duda* shadow of a doubt || MAT *sombra proyectada* cast shadow || *sombras chinescas* shadow theatre || FIG & FAM *tener buena sombra* to be witty (ser ocurrente), to be lucky (tener suerte) | *tener mala sombra* to be unpleasant (ser antipático), to be unlucky (no tener suerte), to bring bad luck, to be a jinx (traer mala suerte) | *tener miedo hasta de su sombra* to be afraid of one's own shadow | *tener una sombra de parecido con* to bear a faint resemblance to.

sombraje; sombrajo *m* shelter from the sun, sunshade || FIG *se le cayeron los palos del sombrajo* he was discouraged.

sombrar *vt* to shade.

sombreado *m* shading (gradación del color).

sombreador *m* eyeshadow.

sombrear *vt* to cast a shadow upon (dar sombra) || to shade (árboles) || to strengthen (un color) || to shade (un dibujo).

sombrerera *f* milliner, hatter || hatbox (caja para sombreros).

sombrerería *f* hatter's (tienda para caballeros) || milliner's (tienda para señoras) || hat factory (fábrica).

sombrerero *m* hatter (de sombreros para caballeros) || milliner (de sombreros para señoras).

sombrerete *m* small hat || BOT pileus, cap (de los hongos) || cowl (de chimenea) || TECN cap (de carburador, etc.) | bonnet (de válvula).

sombrerillo *m* BOT pileus, cap (de los hongos) | Venus's-navelwort (ombligo de Venus).

sombrero *m* hat; *ponerse el sombrero* to put on one's hat || sounding board (del púlpito) || (ant) Spanish grandee's privilege [of keeping his hat on in the presence of the king] || cowl, hood (de chimenea) || BOT pileus, cap (de los hongos) || MAR head (del cabrestante) || TECN cap || — *calarse el sombrero* to jam *o* to put one's hat firmly on one's head || *con el sombrero puesto* or *en la cabeza* with one's hat on || *quitarse el sombrero ante* to take one's hat off to (para saludar o admirar) || *sin sombrero* hatless, bareheaded || *sombrero calañés* Andalusian hat with an upturned brim || *sombrero canotier* straw hat, boater || *sombrero cordobés* or *de ala ancha* wide-brimmed Andalusian hat || *sombrero chambergo* soft hat with a wide brim upturned on one side || *sombrero de campana* cloche hat || *sombrero de canal* or *de canoa* or *de teja* priest's hat || *sombrero de copa* top hat || *sombrero de jipijapa* Panama hat || *sombrero de muelles* opera hat, crush hat || *sombrero de paja* straw hat || *sombrero de tres picos, sombrero de candil, sombrero de tres candiles* three-cornered hat, cocked hat || *sombrero flexible* soft felt hat, trilby || *sombrero hongo* bowler hat (bombín) || *sombrero jíbaro* peasant hat.

sombrilla *f* sunshade, parasol (quitasol).

sombrío, a *adj* sombre [US somber], gloomy (lóbrego) || dark (oscuro) || shaded (sombreado) || FIG sullen, gloomy (melancólico).

someramente *adv* briefly, superficially.

somero, ra *adj* shallow (de poca profundidad) || FIG brief (corto) | shallow, superficial; *un estudio somero* a shallow study.

someter *vt* to subdue, to put down; *someter a los rebeldes* to subdue the rebels || to subject; *someter a los rebeldes a cinco años de cárcel* to subject the rebels to five years in prison; *someter el producto a análisis* to subject the product to analysis || to master, to overcome, to subdue (las pasiones) || to subordinate (subordinar) || to submit, to present (entregar) || — *someter algo a la aprobación de alguien* to submit sth. for s.o.'s approval || *someter a prueba* to test, to put to the test || *someter a tratamiento* to put under treatment (a un enfermo) || *someter a una autoridad* to refer to an authority for a decision || *someter a votación* to put to the vote.
◆ *vpr* to surrender, to yield (en una lucha) || to undergo; *someterse a una operación* to undergo an operation || *someterse a la opinión de la mayoría* to bow to the opinion of the majority.

sometimiento *m* submission, submissiveness, subjection (de una persona) || submission, presentation (de una propuesta, etc.).

somier *m* spring mattress (de cama).

somnambulismo *m* somnambulism, sleepwalking.

somnámbulo, la *adj* somnambulistic, somnambulant.
◆ *m/f* somnambulist, sleepwalker.

somnífero, ra *adj* somniferous, soporific, sleep-inducing.
◆ *m* sleeping pill.

somnolencia *f* somnolence, sleepiness, drowsiness.

somnolento, ta; somnoliento, ta *adj* somnolent, sleepy, drowsy (soñoliento).

somorgujar; somormujar *vt* to plunge, to submerge, to duck.
◆ *vi/vpr* to dive, to plunge (bucear).

somorgujo *m* loon, diver, grebe (ave).

somormujar *vt* ⟶ **somorgujar.**

son *m* sound (sonido); *al son del acordeón* to the sound of the accordion || FIG news, word, rumour [US rumor] (noticia); *corre el son de que le han matado* the news is going around that they have killed him | manner, mode, way (modo); *en este son* in this manner || MÚS name of an Afro-Antillean dance || — FIG *¿a qué son?, ¿a son de qué?* why?, for what reason?, for what motive? | *¿a qué son viene esa pregunta?* what is the reason for that question? || FIG *bailar al son que tocan* to toe the line, to run with the pack | *en son de* in a... tone *o* way *o* manner *o* mood; *en son de burla* in a humourous tone | *en son de broma* jokingly | *no saber a qué son bailar* not to know what road to take, to be in a quandary | *sin ton ni son* without rhyme or reason | *venir en son de paz* to come in peace, to come in the spirit of peace.

sonadero *m* handkerchief (pañuelo).

sonado, da *adj* famous (famoso) || talked-about; *un escándalo muy sonado* a much talked-about scandal || — FAM *hacer una que sea sonada* to cause a scandal *o* a sensation *o* a great stir || *los días sonados* holidays.

sonaja *f* rattle (de niño).
◆ *pl* jingling metal disks || (type of) tambourine *sing* (pandereta).

sonajero *m* rattle.

sonambulismo *m* somnambulism, sleepwalking.

sonámbulo, la *adj* somnambulistic, somnambulant.
◆ *m/f* somnambulist, sleepwalker.

sonante *adj* sonant (que suena) || resounding (que resuena) || sonorous (sonoro).

sonar *m* MAR sonar (aparato de detección por el sonido).

sonar* *vi* to sound; *sonar a hueco* to sound hollow; *esta trompeta suena raro* this trumpet sounds funny || to ring; *la campana suena* the bell rings || to strike (reloj); *acaban de sonar las dos* it has just struck two || to ring (teléfono) || to be pronounced, to be sounded (una letra); *en la palabra «que» la «u» no suena* in the word «que» the «u» is not pronounced || FIG & FAM to sound familiar, to ring a bell; *no me suena ese nombre* that name does not sound familiar (to me) to look familiar, to ring a bell; *me suena su cara* his face rings a bell || to be mentioned (mencionarse); *su nombre suena entre los de los posibles ministros* his name is mentioned among those of the possible ministers || — *como suena* as it is pronounced (como se pronuncia), just as I am telling you (literalmente) || FIG *cuando el río suena agua lleva* there's no smoke without fire | *sonar a* to sound like; *eso me suena a burla* that sounds like a joke to me | *sonar bien, mal* to sound right, wrong (parecer correcto, incorrecto).
◆ *vt* to blow (las narices); *no me deja que le suene las narices* he won't let me blow his nose || to sound (el claxon, etc.) || to ring (el timbre, una campana) || to sound, to tap, to bang; *sonó la moneda en el mostrador* he sounded the coin on the counter || MÚS to sound, to play (un instrumento).
◆ *vpr* to blow one's nose (las narices) || *sonarse las narices* to blow one's nose.

sonata *f* MÚS sonata.

sonatina *f* MÚS sonatina.

sonda *f* MAR sounding (acción) | sounding line *o* lead || MED sound, probe || MIN drill, bore || TECN sounding balloon (en meteorología) | probe (en aeronáutica); *sonda espacial* space probe || MAR *sonda acústica* sonic depth finder, echo sounder.

Sonda (islas de la) *f* GEOGR Sunda Islands.

sondador *m* MAR sonic depth finder, echo sounder.

sondaje *m* ⟶ **sondeo.**

sondaleza *f* MAR sounding line *o* lead.

sondar *vt* ⟶ **sondear.**

sondear; sondar *vt* MAR to sound, to take soundings in || MED to probe, to sound || MIN to drill, to bore || FIG to investigate, to explore (el terreno) | to probe, to sound; *sondear la opinión pública* to probe public opinion | to sound out (a una persona).

sondeo; sondaje *m* MAR sounding || MED probing, sounding || MIN boring, drilling || TECN wind observation (meteorología) || FIG poll, inquiry || — TECN *muestra de sondeo* drilling sample | *sondeo de la opinión pública* public opinion poll, Gallup poll || MIN *sondeo del petróleo* drilling for oil.

sonetista *m* sonneteer.

soneto *m* sonnet.

songa *f* AMER sarcasm, irony || *a la songa* slyly.

sónico, ca *adj* sonic, sound.

sonido *m* sound; *sonido estereofónico* stereophonic sound; *el sonido de un disparo* the sound of a shot || MED murmur || sound (fonético) || — *luz y sonido* son et lumière || *velocidad del sonido* speed of sound.

soniquete *m* ⟶ **sonsonete.**

sonómetro *m* sonometer.

sonoridad *f* sonority, sonorousness.

sonorización *f* recording the sound track of a film || voicing (en fonética) || installation of amplifying equipment.

sonorizar *vt* to record the sound track of [a film] || to voice (en fonética) || to install amplifying equipment in.

sonoro, ra *adj* sonorous || sonorous, loud, resounding; *una voz sonora* a resounding voice || sonant, voiced (en fonética) || — *banda sonora* sound track || *efectos sonoros* sound effects || *onda sonora* sound wave || *película sonora* talking picture, talkie (*fam*).

sonreír *vi* to smile; *ella sonríe siempre* she is always smiling; *me sonrió* she smiled at me || FIG to smile on; *la vida le sonríe* life smiles on him.
◆ *vpr* to smile.

sonriente *adj* smiling.

sonrisa *f* smile; *tiene una sonrisa bonita* she has a pretty smile || — *no perder la sonrisa* to keep smiling || *sonrisa abierta* broad smile.

sonrojar *vt* to make blush (avergonzar).
◆ *vpr* to blush (avergonzarse).

sonrojo *m* blush, blushing (rubor) || shame (vergüenza).

sonrosado, da *adj* rosy, pink.

sonrosar; sonrosear *vt* to colour *o* to turn pink.
◆ *vpr* to blush, to turn pink.

sonsacamiento *m* wheedling, coaxing, cajoling.

sonsacar *vt* to wheedle, to coax, to cajole (sacar algo con palabras amables); *sonsacarle algo a alguien* to wheedle sth. out of s.o. || to worm out (un secreto) || to entice away (atraer engatusando).

sonsear *vi* AMER to behave stupidly, to act the fool.

sonsera; sonsería *f* AMER silliness (estupidez) | mere trifle (nadería).

sonso, sa *adj* AMER silly, stupid, inane.
◆ *m/f* AMER silly person, fool, bore.

sonsonete; soniquete *m* rhythmic tapping (golpecitos) || FIG song, tune (cantinela) | monotonous tone, singsong (voz monótona) | mocking tone (tono de burla).

soñación *f* FAM *¡ni por soñación!* not on your life!, not likely!

soñado, da *adj* dream, of one's dreams; *su casa soñada* the house of her dreams, her dream house || *que ni soñado* marvellous, wonderful; *fue un espectáculo que ni soñado* it was a marvellous show.

soñador, ra *adj* dreamy, given to dreaming.
◆ *m/f* dreamer.

soñar* *vt/vi* to dream; *soñó que era rico* he dreamed he was rich || to daydream, to dream (despierto); *ella siempre está soñando* she is always daydreaming; *¿en qué estás soñando?* what are you dreaming about? || — *¡ni lo sueñes!, ¡ni soñarlo!* not on your life!, not likely! || *soñar con* to dream of *o* about; *sueño con ir a Grecia* I dream of going to Greece || FAM *soñar con los angelitos* to have sweet dreams || *soñar con quimeras* to build castles in the air || *soñar despierto* to daydream, to dream || *soñar en un mundo mejor* to dream of a better world || *soñar en voz alta* to talk in one's sleep.

soñarrera; soñera *f* deep sleep (sueño profundo) || sleepiness, drowsiness (ganas de dormir).

soñolencia *f* somnolence, sleepiness, drowsiness.

soñolientamente *adv* sleepily, drowsily.

soñoliento, ta *adj* somnolent, sleepy, drowsy.

sopa *f* soup (plato); *sopa de fideos, de cebolla* noodle, onion soup || food served to the poor (comida repartida entre los pobres) || sop (trozo de pan mojado) || — FIG *de la mano a la boca se pierde la sopa* there is many a slip 'twixt the cup and the lip | *estar hecho una sopa* to be soaked through, to be sopping wet | *está hasta en la sopa* there's no getting away from him (al estar harto de alguien), I am tired of hearing about him (harto de oír hablar de alguien) || *sopa de ajo* garlic soup || *sopa de cangrejos* crab bisque || *sopa de sobre* packet soup || *sopa de tomate* tomato soup || *sopa de verduras* vegetable soup || *sopa juliana* julienne soup || FIG *tenerle a uno hasta en la sopa* to be fed up with s.o. (estar harto de uno), to be tired of hearing about s.o. (harto de oír hablar de uno) || FIG *vivir* or *comer de la sopa boba* to live off others, to be a parasite.
◆ *pl* dish consisting of pieces of bread soaked in a liquid (pan mojado en líquido) || FIG *dar sopas con honda a alguien* to leave s.o. standing, to outshine s.o.

sopapear *vt* FAM to slap (dar una bofetada).

sopapo *m* slap (bofetada) || chuck under the chin.

sopar; sopear *vt* to dip, to sop, to dunk (el pan).

sopero, ra *adj* soup; *plato sopero* soup dish; *cuchara sopera* soup spoon.
◆ *m* soup dish (plato).
◆ *f* soup tureen (fuente).

sopesar *vt* to try the weight of (pesar) || FIG to weigh up (examinar); *sopesar las posibles dificultades* to weigh up the possible difficulties.

sopetón *m* toast soaked in oil (pan tostado) || FAM slap (golpe) || *de sopetón* unexpectedly, suddenly.

sopicaldo *m* thin soup.

sopita *f* light soup (sopa ligera) || finger, sop (trozo de pan).

sopitipando *m* FAM fainting spell (desmayo) || *le dio un sopitipando* he fainted.

¡sopla! *interj* good gracious!, good heavens!

sopladero *m* vent.

soplado, da *adj* FIG & FAM drunk, tight (borracho) | overdressed (acicalado) | conceited (vanidoso).
◆ *m* glassblowing (del vidrio) || MIN deep fissure.

soplador, ra *m/f* blower || troublemaker (incitador).
◆ *m* glassblower (de vidrio) || fan (aventador) || AMER prompter (teatro).

sopladura *f* blowing (acción) || glassblowing (del vidrio) || air hole *o* bubble (defecto).

soplagaitas *m/f inv* FAM blockhead.

soplamocos *m inv* FAM slap, punch.

soplapollas *adj inv* POP ⟶ **jilipolla.**

soplar *vi* to blow; *soplar con la boca* to blow with the mouth; *el viento sopla* the wind blows || FAM to squeal (denunciar) | to whisper the answer (apuntar) | to booze (beber).
◆ *vt* to blow out (apagar); *soplar una vela* to blow out a candle || to blow off; *soplar los polvos de encima del libro* to blow the dust off the book || to blow up; *soplar un globo* to blow up a balloon || to blow on; *soplar la sopa para que se enfríe* to blow on the soup to cool it || to fan (el fuego) || FIG to inspire (la musa) | to whisper; *soplar la respuesta a uno* to whisper the answer to s.o. || TECN to blow (vidrio) || FIG to huff (juego de damas) || FIG & FAM to split on, to squeal on (delatar) | to tell on, to tell tales on, to tattle on (entre niños) | to deal, to fetch (golpes) | to steal, to snitch, to pinch (birlar) | to rush (cobrar); *¿cuánto te soplaron por eso?* what did they rush you for that? || — FIG & FAM *el negocio ya no sopla como antes* business is not as good as it used to be | *saber de qué lado sopla el viento* to know which way the wind blows | *soplar una torta a alguien* to slap s.o.
◆ *vpr* to blow on; *soplarse los dedos para calentárselos* to blow on one's fingers to warm them || FAM to down (comida); *soplarse una botella de vino* to down a bottle of wine | to spend (tiempo).

soplete *m* blowlamp [*US* blowtorch] (de soldador) || blowtube (de vidrieros).

soplido *m* blow, puff || blast (muy fuerte).

soplillo *m* fan (aventador).

soplo *m* blow, puff (con la boca) || gust (de viento) || FIG second, minute, moment; *llego en un soplo* I'll be with you in a moment || FIG & FAM sneak, telltale (niño soplón) | informer (de la policía) | tip-off (delación) || — FIG & FAM *dar el soplo* to squeal, to split (denunciar), to inform (informar) || FIG *la vida es un soplo* life is short || MED *soplo cardíaco* heart murmur.

soplón, ona *adj* FAM tattletale, telltale, sneaky (entre niños).
◆ *m/f* FAM tattletale, telltale, sneak (entre niños) | informer, squealer (de la policía) || AMER prompter (apuntador) | policeman (policía).

soplonear *vi* FAM to squeal, to split.

soplonería *f* FAM taletelling, sneaking.

soponcio *m* FAM faint, swoon || FAM *me dio un soponcio* I fainted.

sopor *m* sleepiness, drowsiness.

soporífero, ra; soporífico, ca *adj* soporiferous, soporific, sleep-inducing.
◆ *m/f* soporific, sleeping pill.

soportable *adj* bearable.

soportal *m* portico, porch (de una casa).
◆ *pl* arcade, colonnade (de una calle).

soportar *vt* to support, to bear, to carry, to hold up; *las columnas soportan el arco* the columns support the arch || FIG to bear, to endure, to stand; *no puedo soportar a mi primo* I can't stand my cousin; *soportó bien la operación* he bore the operation well | to weather (una tormenta, un huracán).

soporte *m* support || HERÁLD supporter (de blasón) || base, stand (de una figura) || holder (de maceta, de lápiz, etc.) || stand (atril de libro, partituras musicales) || hanger, bracket (de repisa) || prop (para muros) || rest (para herramientas, escopetas, tacos de billar) || FIG support, pillar (apoyo) || — INFORM *soporte de datos* data medium, data carrier || *soporte publicitario* advertising medium.

soprano *m/f* MÚS soprano.

sor *m* sister (religiosa); *Sor María* Sister Mary.

sorber *vt* to suck (un huevo, la sangre, etc.) || to sip (un líquido) || FIG to soak up, to absorb (absorber) | to swallow up (el mar) | to breath in, to inhale (por la nariz) || — FIG & FAM *sorber el seso a uno* to be head over heels in love with s.o., to be mad about s.o.; *Tomás le sorbe el seso a María* Mary is head over heels in love with Thomas *o* Mary is mad about Thomas | *sorberse los vientos por alguien* to be crazy about s.o.
◆ *vpr* to soak up, to absorb.

sorbete *m* sherbet, water ice; *sorbete de limón* lemon sherbet || AMER top hat (chistera).

sorbetera *f* freezer (heladora).

sorbetón *m* gulp (de líquido).

sorbito *m* little sip.

sorbo *m* sip; *sólo tomé un sorbo de leche* I only took a sip of milk || gulp (trago) || — *beber a sorbos* to drink in small sips, to sip one's drink || *de un sorbo* in one swallow.

sorche; sorchi *m* FAM soldier (soldado), recruit (recluta).

sordamente *adv* silently || secretly.

sordera *f* deafness.

sordidez *f* squalor (suciedad) || meanness (avaricia).

sórdido, da *adj* sordid, squalid (sucio) || mean, miserable (avaro).

sordina *f* MÚS damper (piano) | mute (instrumentos de viento) || *en sordina* muted (música), secretly, on the quiet (en secreto).

sordino *m* MÚS fiddle.

sordo, da *adj* deaf; *sordo de nacimiento* deaf from birth; *quedarse sordo* to go deaf || voiceless, unvoiced (en fonética) || FIG dull (dolor) | muffled, dull (voz, ruido) | pent-up, held back; *una cólera sorda* pent-up anger | deaf, indifferent, unmoved; *permaneció sordo a mis ruegos* he remained unmoved by *o* deaf to my pleas | secret, undeclared (guerra) | dim, dull (linterna) || — FIG & FAM *a la sorda, a lo sordo, a sordas* silently, on the quiet || *a palabras necias, oídos sordos* I'll treat that remark with the contempt it deserves.
◆ *m/f* deaf person || — *hacerse el sordo* to turn a deaf ear, to pretend not to hear || *los sordos* deaf people, the deaf.

sordomudez *f* deaf-muteness.

sordomudo, da *adj* deaf-and-dumb, deaf-mute.
◆ *m/f* deaf-mute.

sorgo *m* BOT sorghum.

sorianense *adj* [of *o* from] Soriano (Uruguay).
◆ *m/f* native *o* inhabitant of Soriano (Uruguay).

soriano, na *adj* [of *o* from] Soria [Old Castile].
◆ *m/f* native *o* inhabitant of Soria.

soriasis *f* MED psoriasis.

sorites *m* sorites (raciocinio).

sorna *f* sarcasm (mofa) || calmness, coolness, deliberation (calma) || — *hablar con sorna* to talk sarcastically || *mirar con sorna* to look mockingly *o* slyly at.

sorocharse *vpr* AMER to get mountain sickness | to blush (avergonzarse).

soroche *m* AMER mountain sickness | blush (rubor) | galena (piedra).

sorocho, cha AMER unripe (fruta).

sorprendente *adj* surprising, amazing, astonishing.

sorprender *vt* to surprise, to amaze, to astonish (causar sorpresa); *¿le sorprende la noticia?* does the news surprise you? || to catch unawares, to surprise, to take by surprise (coger desprevenido); *sorprendió al ladrón* he caught the thief unawares || to discover (descubrir); *sorprendimos su secreto* we discovered his secret || to abuse, to deceive (engañar); *sorprender su buena fe* to abuse one's good faith || to overhear (una conversación).
◆ *vpr* to be surprised, to be amazed; *se sorprendió al verme* he was surprised to see me.

sorprendido, da *adj* surprised, amazed, astonished; *quedarse sorprendido ante* to be surprised at *o* by || caught (cogido) || discovered (descubierto) || abused (engañado).

sorpresa *f* surprise; *¡vaya sorpresa!* what a surprise! || surprise (del roscón de reyes) || surprise (regalo inesperado) || astonishment, surprise, amazement; *se le notó la sorpresa en la cara* you could see the astonishment in his face || — *ataque por sorpresa* surprise attack || *coger de sorpresa* to catch unawares, to take by surprise || *con gran sorpresa suya* much to his surprise, to his great surprise || *dar* or *causar* or *producir una sorpresa a alguien* to surprise s.o., to give s.o. a surprise.

sorpresivo, va *adj* AMER unexpected (inesperado) | surprising (que sorprende).

sorrostrada *f* insolence.

sorteamiento *f* raffle, casting *o* drawing of lots.

sortear *vt* to draw *o* to cast lots for (echar a suertes); *no sabían a quién darlo, y lo sortearon* they did not know who to give it to, so they drew lots for it || to allot (asignar o repartir puestos, trabajos, etc.) || to decide by lot (decidir) || to choose by lot (escoger) || to draft (los quintos) || to toss up for (echar a cara o cruz) || to raffle (rifar) || FIG to avoid (evitar) | to overcome, to get round (un obstáculo, una dificultad) | to elude (eludir) | to dodge (esquivar) | to evade, to get round (las preguntas) || DEP to dribble (driblar) | to dodge (esquivar) || *hoy sortean los premios de la lotería* they are drawing the winning numbers in the lottery today.
◆ *vi* to draw lots (echar a suertes) || to toss up (echar a cara o cruz).

sorteo *m* draw; *el ganador del sorteo* the winner of the draw || allotment (de puestos) || toss (a cara o cruz) || draw (en la lotería); *sorteo extraordinario de Navidad* special Christmas draw || raffle (rifa) || FIG dodging, evading (acción de evitar o esquivar) || *por sorteo* by lot; *elegido por sorteo* chosen by lot.

sortija *f* ring (anillo) || curl, ringlet (de pelo) || hunt the thimble (juego) || *sortija de sello* signet ring.

sortilegio *m* sorcery, witchcraft, witchery (hechicería) || spell; *echar un sortilegio a* to cast a spell on || charm (encanto).

sortílego, ga *m/f* sorcerer, wizard (hechicero) || soothsayer (adivino).

SOS. *m* SOS (señal de socorro); *lanzar un SOS* to send out an SOS.

sosa *f* BOT saltwort || QUÍM soda; *sosa cáustica* caustic soda.

sosaina *m/f* dull person, bore.

sosamente *adv* in a dull *o* uninteresting way, boringly.

sosegadamente *adv* calmly, quietly.

sosegado, da *adj* calm, quiet.

sosegar* *vt* to calm, to quieten, to tranquilize (calmar) || to reassure; *la noticia me ha sosegado* the news has reassured me.
◆ *vi* to rest (descansar).
◆ *vpr* to calm down (tranquilizarse).

sosera *f* boring thing (cosa sosa).

sosería *f* insipidity, insipidness || FIG insipidity, insipidness, dullness || *ser una sosería* to be dull *o* boring.

sosia *m* double.

sosiego *m* tranquility, calmness, quietness || *con sosiego* calmly.

soslayar *vt* to put sideways, to tip on its side, to put on a slant (inclinar) || FIG to avoid, to dodge, to evade (eludir) | to get round (una dificultad, un obstáculo).

soslayo (al); soslayo (de) *loc* sideways, aslant, on a slant || FIG *mirar de soslayo* to look sideways (at), to look out of the corner of one's eye (at) (mirar de lado), to look askance (at) (con desaprobación).

soso, sa *adj* tasteless, insipid (de poco sabor) || saltless, unsalted (sin sal) || FIG dull, boring, uninteresting (sin gracia) | silly (tonto) | dull, flat; *chiste soso* dull joke; *estilo soso* flat style.

sospecha *f* suspicion; *despertar las sospechas* to arouse suspicion; *la policía tiene sospechas de él* the police have suspicions about him || — *fuera* or *por encima de toda sospecha* above suspicion || JUR *tener en sospecha* to hold under suspicion || *tener la sospecha de que...* to have a suspicion that... || *tener sospechas de que...* to have one's suspicions that..., to suspect that... || *vehementes* or *vivas sospechas* a strong suspicion.

sospechar *vt/vi* to suspect; *sospecho que Pedro miente* I suspect that Pedro is lying || to think, to imagine, to suppose; *lo sospechaba* I imagined as much || *sospechar de* to suspect, to be suspicious of.

sospechosamente *adv* suspiciously.

sospechoso, sa *adj* suspicious; *un tipo sospechoso* a suspicious character || suspect (dudoso).
◆ *m/f* suspicious person, suspect; *han detenido a varios sospechosos* several suspects have been detained.

sostén *m* support (soporte) || ARQ support, prop || MAR steadiness (de un barco) || bra, brassière (prenda de mujer) || FIG support, pillar (apoyo) | sustenance (sustento) || — *sostén de* or *con cuerpo, sostén largo* long-line brassière || FIG *sostén de familia* breadwinner.

sostenedor, ra *adj* supporting, sustaining.
◆ *m/f* supporter, upholder (defensor).

sostener* *vt* to support, to hold up; *sostener con una viga* to support with a beam; *columnas que sostienen una bóveda* columns that support a vault || to hold (sujetar) || to hold up; *el agua de mar nos sostiene más que el agua dulce* salt water holds us up more than fresh water; *estabas tan borracho que te tuvimos que sostener* you were so drunk that we had to hold you up || to bear (ataque, peso) || to carry, to bear (carga) || to keep up, to maintain (la velocidad, la categoría, los precios) || FIG to defend, to uphold (defender); *sostener la causa* to defend the cause | to endure, to tolerate, to stand, to bear; *sostener una situación muy desagradable* to tolerate a very disagreeable situation | to carry on, to hold, to keep up (conversación) | to support, to keep, to maintain, to provide for (una familia) | to maintain, to carry on, to keep up; *sostener una correspondencia con alguien* to maintain correspondence with s.o.; *sostener buenas relaciones* to maintain good relations | to hold (entrevista) | to maintain, to affirm; *él sostiene que el gobierno va a caer* he maintains that the government is going to fall | to support, to back (apoyar) | to keep going (dar fuerza); *al final lo único que le sostenía era el deseo de vivir* in the end it was just his will to live which kept him going || *sostener la mirada de alguien* to stare s.o. out, to look s.o. unflinchingly in the eye.
◆ *vpr* to hold o.s. up, to support o.s. (agarrándose a algo) || to stand up (mantenerse de pie); *no podía sostenerme de cansado que estaba* I was so tired I could not stand up || FIG to remain (continuar) | to stay, to remain; *sostenerse en el poder* to stay in power | to support o.s., to earn a living; *me sostengo dando clases* I earn a living giving lessons | to keep going, to live; *se sostiene a base de inyecciones* he lives on injections || — FIG *sostenerse en* to stand firm in; *se sostiene en su actitud liberal* he stands firm in his liberal attitude | *sostenerse mutuamente* to support one another *o* each other.

sostenidamente *adv* steadily.

sostenido, da *adj* MÚS sharp; *fa sostenido* F sharp || sustained; *esfuerzo sostenido* sustained effort || continuous || steady (en la Bolsa).
◆ *m* MÚS sharp; *doble sostenido* double sharp.

sostenimiento *m* support (apoyo) || maintenance (mantenimiento) || sustenance; *el padre se encarga del sostenimiento de la familia* the father is responsible for the sustenance of the family || keeping, maintaining (de relaciones) || defence (de una tesis).

sota *f* jack, knave (naipe).

sotabanco *m* attic, garret (buhardilla) || ARQ springer (de arco).

sotabarba *f* newgate frill (barba) || double chin (papada).

sotana *f* soutane, cassock.

sótano *m* basement || cellar (bodega).

sotavento *m* MAR leeward.

sotechado *m* shed.

soterrado, da *adj* buried, underground (enterrado) || FIG hidden, concealed (oculto).

soterramiento *m* burying.

soterraño, ña *adj* subterranean, underground.

soterrar* *vt* to bury.

sotileza *f* (ant) subtlety (sutileza).

soto *m* grove (arboleda) || thicket (matorral).

soufflé *m* CULIN soufflé.

soul *m* MÚS soul, soul music.

soviet *m* soviet.

soviético, ca *adj* Soviet.
◆ *m/f* Soviet.

sovietización *f* sovietization.

sovietizar *vt* to sovietize.

sovjoz *m* state farm in the USSR.

spaghettis *m pl* spaghetti, *sing.*

sparring *m* DEP sparring partner.

spleen *m* spleen.

sport *m* sports; *chaqueta de sport* sports jacket; *coche de sport* sports car || *ir vestido de sport* to be dressed casually.

— OBSERV In Spanish, *sport* is used only to qualify certain cars or pieces of clothing. *Sport* (football, etc.) is translated by *deporte: I like sport,* me gusta el deporte.

sprint *m* DEP sprint.

sprintar *vi* DEP to sprint.

sprinter *m* DEP sprinter (velocista).

sputnik *m* sputnik (satélite artificial).

squash *m* DEP squash.
Sr. *abrev de Señor* Mr, Mister.
Sra. *abrev de Señora* Mrs, Mistress.
Sres. *abrev de Señores* Messrs, Messieurs.
Srta. *abrev de Señorita* Miss.
Sta. *abrev de Santa* St, Saint.
staccato *adj/sm* MÚS staccato.
stajanovismo *m* Stakhanovism.
stajanovista *m/f* Stakhanovite.
staliniano, na *adj/s* Stalinist.
stalinismo *m* Stalinism.
stalinista *adj/s* Stalinist.
stand *m* stand (caseta).
standard *adj* standard; *modelo standard* standard model.
standardización *f* standardization.
standardizar *vt* to standardize.
standing *m* standing (posición social) ‖ DEP balancing [on a stationary bicycle].
starter *m* AUT choke ‖ DEP starter (juez de salida).
statu quo *m* status quo.
steeplechase *m* steeplechase (carrera de obstáculos).
esténcil *m* stencil (cliché de multicopista).
steward *m* steward (auxiliar de vuelo).
stick *m* DEP stick (hockey).
Sto. *abrev de Santo* St, Saint.
stock *m* stock (existencias).
stock-car *m* stock car (para competiciones).
stop *m* stop sign (señal de tráfico) ‖ stop (en un telegrama).
strip-tease *m* striptease.
su *adj pos de la 3ª persona* his (de él); *su padre* his father ‖ her (de ella); *su padre* her father ‖ its (neutro); *su color* its colour (del cuadro) ‖ one's (de uno) ‖ your (de usted, de ustedes); *su hermano* your brother ‖ their (de ellas, de ellos, neutro); *su padre* their father; *sus ejércitos* their armies.
— OBSERV El plural de *su* es *sus*.
suabo, ba *adj/s* swabian.
suasorio, ria *adj* persuasive.
suave *adj* soft, smooth; *cutis suave* soft skin ‖ smooth, even; *carretera suave* smooth road ‖ FIG mild, clement (el tiempo) | gentle, soft (el viento) | mild, lenient (castigo, regla, ley) | mild, smooth (sabor, tabaco) | gentle, mild, sweet (de carácter) | soft, gentle, subdued (luz, color) | gentle, soft, smooth (voz, música, sonido, movimiento) | easy, smooth; *paso suave* easy pace | gentle (pendiente, curva) ‖ — FIG *más suave que un guante* as meek as a lamb | *suave como el terciopelo* or *la piel de un niño* or *la piel de una manzana* (as) smooth as silk *o* as a baby's skin.
suavidad *f* smoothness, softness, suavity (p us); *la suavidad de su cutis* the softness of her skin ‖ smoothness, evenness; *la suavidad de la carretera* the smoothness of the road ‖ FIG mildness (del tiempo) | leniency (de castigo, regla, ley) | mildness, smoothness (de sabor) | gentleness, mildness, sweetness (del carácter) | softness (de color, luz) | gentleness, softness, smoothness (de voz, música, sonido, movimiento) | ease, smoothness; *la suavidad de su paso* the smoothness of his gait | gentleness (de pendiente, curva).
suavizador, ra *adj* smoothing, softening.
◆ *m* razor strop.
suavizante *adj* softener (para la ropa) ‖ conditioner (para el pelo)
suavizar *vt* to soften; *suaviza la piel* it softens the skin ‖ to make smoother (una pasta) ‖ to smooth (out); *suavizar la superficie* to smooth the surface | to strop (navaja de afeitar) ‖ FIG to soften, to temper, to sweeten (carácter) | to temper, to ease (castigo, regla, ley) | to temper (caballo) | to soften, to tone down, to subdue (luz, color) | to soften (sonido, voz) | to ease; *suavizar el paso* to ease the pace | to make more gentle (curva, pendiente) ‖ FIG *suavizar asperezas* to smooth things over.
subacuático, ca *adj* subaqueous, underwater.
subafluente *m* tributary.
subalimentado, da *adj* undernourished, underfed.
subalimentar *vt* to undernourish, to underfeed.
subalterno, na *adj* subordinate, subaltern ‖ auxiliary (personal) ‖ secondary (secundario).
◆ *m* subordinate, subaltern.
subarrendador, ra *m/f* subtenant (subarrendatario) ‖ subletter (que da en arrendamiento).
subarrendamiento *m* sublease.
subarrendar* *vt* to sublet, to sublease.
subarrendatario, ria *m/f* subtenant.
subarriendo *m* sublease.
subártico, ca *adj* subartic.
subasta *f* JUR auction (venta) | tender (para la ejecución de una obra) ‖ — *sacar a subasta* to auction ‖ *salir a subasta* to be on auction ‖ *vender en pública subasta* to put up for auction, to sell at auction, to auction, to auction off.
subastador, ra *m/f* auctioneer.
subastar *vt* to auction (off), to sell at auction.
subcampeón *m* runner-up.
subcarpeta *f* folder (para documentos).
subclase *f* BOT & ZOOL subclass.
subclavio, via *adj* ANAT suclavian.
subcomisión *f*; **subcomité** *m* subcommittee.
subconjunto *m* MAT subset.
subconsciencia *f* subconscious.
subconsciente *adj/sm* subconscious.
subcontinente *m* subcontinent.
subcontratación *f* subcontracting.
subcontratista *m* subcontractor.
subcontrato *m* subcontract ‖ *ceder, tomar en subcontrato* to subcontract.
subcutáneo, a *adj* subcutaneous; *inyección subcutánea* subcutaneous injection.
subdelegación *f* subdelegation.
subdelegado, da *adj/s* subdelegate.
subdelegar *vt* to subdelegate.
subdesarrollado, da *adj* underdeveloped.
subdesarrollo *m* underdevelopment.
subdiaconado; subdiaconato *m* REL subdiaconate.
subdiácono *m* REL subdeacon.
subdirección *f* assistant *o* deputy managership (cargo) ‖ assistant *o* deputy manager's office (oficina).
subdirector *m* assitant manager, deputy manager.
súbdito, ta *adj* subject (de un monarca).
◆ *m/f* citizen (de un país) ‖ subject (de un monarca).
subdividir, subdividirse *vt/vpr* to subdivide.
subdivisión *f* subdivision.
subdominante *f* MÚS subdominant.
subempleo *m* underemployment.
suberoso, sa *adj* suberous, suberose.
subespecie *f* BOT & ZOOL subspecies.
subestación *f* ELECTR substation.
subestimación *f* underestimation.
subestimar *vt* to underestimate.
subexponer *vt* FOT to underexpose.
subexposición *f* FOT underexposure.
subexpuesto, ta *adj* FOT underexposed.
subfamilia *f* BOT & ZOOL subfamily.
subfluvial *adj* subfluvial.
subgénero *m* BOT & ZOOL subgenus.
subgobernador *m* lieutenant *o* deputy governor.
subibaja *m* seesaw (columpio).
subida *f* ascent; *la subida de la montaña* the ascent of the mountain ‖ climb; *una subida peligrosa* a dangerous climb ‖ slope, hill (pendiente) ‖ FIG rise, increase (precios) | rise (temperatura) | increase (aumento) ‖ *luchar contra la subida de precios* to combat rising prices.
subido, da *adj* FIG high; *precios subidos* high prices | intense, bright, strong (color) | strong (olor) ‖ — FIG *subido de color, de color subido* strong in colour (un cuadro), off-colour, strong (chiste, etc.) | *subido de precio* high-priced, expensive | *subido de tono* daring, risqué.
subíndice *m* MAT subindex.
subinquilino, na *m/f* subtenant.
subir *vt* to go up, to climb (una calle, una cuesta) ‖ to go up, to climb, to climb up, to ascend (escalera) ‖ to put (poner); *subir el equipaje al tren* to put the luggage on the train ‖ to carry up, to bring up, to take up; *sube la maleta al piso* carry the suitcase up to the apartment ‖ to raise (una pared) ‖ to lift, to raise (cabeza) ‖ FIG to turn up (radio, televisión) | to increase (sonido) | to strengthen, to tone up (color) | to increase, to put up, to raise (sueldo, precio) | to increase *o* to put up *o* to raise the price of (una mercancía) | to promote (promocionar) ‖ MÚS to raise (tono).
◆ *vi* to go up, to come up; *subir al quinto piso* to go up to the fifth floor; *subir en ascensor* to go up in a lift ‖ to get into; *subir a un coche* to get into a car ‖ to get in; *¡anda, sube!* come on!, get in! ‖ to get on, to board (barco, tren, avión); *subir al avión* to get on the plane ‖ to mount, to get on (animales, bicicleta); *subir a caballo* to mount one's horse ‖ to rise, to climb, to go up; *el avión sube* the plane climbs ‖ to rise (río, marea, sol) ‖ to slope up (terreno) ‖ FIG to increase; *la curiosidad de todo el mundo sube* everyone's curiosity is increasing | to rise, to go up; *suben los precios* prices are rising; *sube la temperatura* the temperature rises | to get worse (la fiebre) | to get on, to get ahead, to advance; *ha subido mucho en su profesión* he has got on well in his profession ‖ to rise, to grow (higher) (una pared al construirse) ‖ to climb (trepar); *subir a un árbol* to climb up a tree ‖ COM to total, to come to, to amount to; *la cuenta sube a 1000 pesetas* the bill comes to 1000 pesetas ‖ MÚS to go up, to rise (tono) ‖ — *es más fácil bajar que subir* it's easier coming down than going up ‖ *subir a bordo* to go *o* to come aboard, to board ‖ FIG *subir a las tablas* to go on the stage | *subir al trono* to come to *o* to ascend (to) the throne | *subir de categoría* to better one's position (una persona), to become more select (un barrio, etc.) | *subir* or *de tono* to warm up (una conversación), to become louder (la voz, etc.), to become arrogant *o* haughty (adoptar un aire arrogante).
◆ *vpr* to climb up (implica dificultad o esfuerzo); *subirse a un árbol* to climb up a tree; *subirse al muro, al tejado* to climb up on the wall, up on the roof ‖ to go up (por una es-

calera, etc.); *subirse a su cuarto* to go up to one's room ‖ to rise (los precios) ‖ to get into (a un coche) ‖ to get on, to board (barco, avión) ‖ to mount, to get on (a caballo) ‖ to pull up; *súbete los calcetines* pull your socks up ‖ — FIG & FAM *subirse a la parra* to blow one's top, to hit the roof (enfadarse) | *subirse a las barbas de* to treat disrespectfully | *subirse a* or *por las paredes* to go up the wall, to hit the roof (enfadarse), to be hopping mad (estar furioso) ‖ FIG *subírsele a la cabeza a uno* to go to one's head (vino honores, cargos); *el vino se le subió a la cabeza* the wine went to his head | *subírsele el pavo a uno, subírsele los colores a la cara a uno* to blush, to go as red as a beetroot | *subírsele la sangre a la cabeza a uno* to see red | *subírsele los humos a la cabeza a alguien* to get s.o. on one's high horse, to become conceited; *se le subieron los humos a la cabeza* he got on his high horse, he became conceited.

súbitamente *adv* suddenly, all of a sudden, unexpectedly.

súbito, ta *adj* sudden, unexpected; *cambio súbito de temperatura* sudden change in temperature; *una súbita llamada* an unexpected call ‖ *de súbito* suddenly, unexpectedly, all of a sudden.
◆ *adv* suddenly.

subjefe *m* assistant chief.

subjetividad *f* subjectivity.

subjetivismo *m* FIL subjectivism.

subjetivo, va *adj* subjective.

subjuntivo, va *adj/sm* GRAM subjunctive.

sublevación *f* revolt, rebellion, rising.

sublevar *vt* to incite *o* to rouse to rebellion (excitar) ‖ FIG to infuriate, to upset; *tanta injusticia me subleva* all this injustice infuriates me.
◆ *vpr* to revolt, to rebel, to rise (up) (rebelarse).

sublimación *f* sublimation.

sublimado *m* QUÍM sublimate.

sublimar *vt* to sublimate, to sublime ‖ to sublime, to praise, to exalt (ensalzar a alguien).
◆ *vpr* to sublime.

sublime *adj* sublime ‖ noble, lofty (noble, elevado) ‖ *lo sublime* the sublime.

sublimidad *f* sublimity.

subliminal *adj* subliminal.

sublunar *adj* sublunary, sublunar, earthly.

submarinismo *m* scuba diving.

submarinista *m* submarine crew member.

submarino *adj* submarine, underwater.
◆ *m* submarine (buque).

submaxilar *adj* ANAT submaxillary; *glándula submaxilar* submaxillary gland.

submúltiplo, pla *adj/sm* MAT submultiple.

subnormal *adj* MED subnormal (anormal); *niños subnormales* subnormal children.
◆ *m* MAT subnormal (de una curva).

suboficial *m* MIL non-commissioned officer, warrant officer ‖ MAR petty officer.

suborbitario, ria *adj* ANAT suborbital.

suborden *m* BOT & ZOOL suborder.

subordinación *f* subordination.

subordinado, da *adj* subordinate ‖ GRAM *oración subordinada* subordinate clause.
◆ *m/f* subordinate.

subordinante *adj* GRAM subordinating.

subordinar *vt* to subordinate; *subordinar la razón a la fe* to subordinate reason to faith.
◆ *vpr* to subordinate o.s.

subproducción *f* underproduction.

subproducto *m* by-product.

subprograma *m* INFORM subprogram.

subrayable *adj* noteworthy, worth emphasizing.

subrayado, da *adj* underlined ‖ in italics (en bastardilla).
◆ *m* underlining (con una línea) ‖ italics *pl.*

subrayar *vt* to underline, to underscore ‖ FIG to emphasize, to underline (poner énfasis); *subrayar cada palabra con un ademán* to emphasize each word with a gesture.

subreino *m* ZOOL subkingdom.

subrepción *f* subreption.

subrepticio, cia *adj* surreptitious.

subrigadier *m* MIL lance corporal.

subrogación *f* JUR subrogation.

subrogar *vt* JUR to subrogate, to substitute.
◆ *vpr* to be subrogated *o* substituted.

subrutina *f* INFORM subroutine.

subsanable *adj* excusable (disculpable) ‖ reparable, repairable, mendable (reparable).

subsanar *vt* to excuse, to overlook (disculpar) ‖ to repair, to mend (reparar) ‖ FIG to rectify, to put right, to remedy, to correct, to mend (remediar); *subsanar un error* to correct an error | to get round, to overcome (una dificultad, un obstáculo) | to make up for (compensar).

subscribir *vt* ⟶ **suscribir.**

subscripción *f* ⟶ **suscripción.**

subscripto, ta *adj* ⟶ **suscrito.**

subscriptor, ra *m/f* ⟶ **suscriptor.**

subsecretaría *f* undersecretaryship (cargo) ‖ undersecretary's office (oficina).

subsecretario, ria *m/f* undersecretary ‖ *subsecretario de Estado* undersecretary of State.

subsecuente *adj* subsequent.

subseguir*, subseguirse *vi/vpr* to follow.

subsidiar *vt* to subsidize.

subsidiario, ria *adj* subsidiary ‖ JUR ancillary.

subsidio *m* subsidy, grant, aid ‖ — *subsidio de enfermedad* sick pay *o* benefit ‖ *subsidio de paro* unemployment benefit ‖ *subsidio de vejez* old age pension ‖ *subsidio de vivienda* housing allowance ‖ *subsidios familiares* family allowance.

subsiguiente *adj* subsequent.

subsistencia *f* subsistence (vida) ‖ sustenance (lo necesario para vivir).

subsistente *adj* surviving, lasting, subsisting (still), existing.

subsistir *vi* to subsist, to survive, to last, to remain, to still exist (perdurar); *subsiste la costumbre* the custom survives ‖ to subsist, to live (vivir).

subsónico, ca *adj* subsonic.

substancia *f* ⟶ **sustancia.**
— OBSERV The spelling *sustancia* (without *b*) is at present the more common. This applies to all Spanish words beginning with *subst*, except *substrato.*

substanciación *f* JUR ⟶ **sustanciación.**

substancial *adj* ⟶ **sustancial.**

substancialismo *m* FIL ⟶ **sustancialismo.**

substanciar *vt* ⟶ **sustanciar.**

substancioso, sa *adj* ⟶ **sustancioso.**

substantivar *vt* GRAM ⟶ **sustantivar.**

substantividad *f* GRAM ⟶ **sustantividad.**

substantivo, va *adj/sm* ⟶ **sustantivo.**

substitución *f* ⟶ **sustitución.**

substituible *adj* ⟶ **sustituible.**

substituidor, ra *adj/s* ⟶ **sustituidor.**

substituir* *vt* ⟶ **sustituir.**

substitutivo, va *adj/sm* ⟶ **sustitutivo.**

substituto, ta *m/f* ⟶ **sustituto.**

substracción *f* ⟶ **sustracción.**

substraendo *m* MAT ⟶ **sustraendo.**

substraer* *vt* ⟶ **sustraer.**

substrato *m* GEOL & FIL substratum ‖ FIG substratum.

subsuelo *m* subsoil.

subtangente *f* MAT subtangent.

subte *m* AMER underground, tube [US subway] (metro).

subtender *vt* MAT to subtend.

subteniente *m* MIL second lieutenant.

subterfugio *m* subterfuge.

subterráneo, a *adj* subterranean, underground.
◆ *m* cellar (bodega) ‖ underground passage *o* tunnel (conducto) ‖ AMER underground [US subway] (metro).

subtipo *m* subtype.

subtitular *vt* to subtitle.

subtítulo *m* subtitle.

subtotal *m* COM subtotal.

subtropical *adj* subtropical.

suburbano, na *adj* suburban.
◆ *m/f* suburbanite.
◆ *m* suburban train.

suburbio *m* suburb (arrabal) ‖ slums *pl* (barrio pobre).

subvalorar *vt* to underrate, to underestimate.

subvención *f* subsidy, subvention, grant.

subvencionar *vt* to subsidize.

subvenir* *vt* to help, to assist (*a* with, in) (ayudar) ‖ to meet, to defray (los gastos) ‖ to pay for, to defray the cost of (proveer).

subversión *f* subversion ‖ revolution (revolución).

subversivo, va *adj* subversive; *literatura subversiva* subversive literature.

subvertir* *vt* to subvert ‖ to disturb (el orden).

subyacente *adj* subjacent, underlying.

subyacer *vi* to underlie.

subyugación *f* subjugation.

subyugador, ra *adj* FIG captivating (cautivador).

subyugar *vt* to subjugate ‖ FIG to master, to subdue (sus pasiones) | to captivate, to charm (encantar).

succínico, ca *adj* succinic (ácido).

succión *f* suction.

succionar *vt* to suck, to suck in.

sucedáneo, a *adj* substitute, succedaneous.
◆ *m* substitute, succedaneum.

suceder *vi* to succeed, to follow; *Juan sucede a Carlos en el puesto* John succeeds Charles in the job; *la noche sucede al día* night follows day ‖ to suceed (a un rey) ‖ to be the heir of (ser el heredero de); *los hijos suceden a sus padres* the sons are the heirs of their fathers ‖ to happen, to occur (ocurrir); *sucedió que...* it happened that...; *eso sucede a menudo* that often happens ‖ — *lo más que puede suceder* the worst that can happen ‖ *lo que sucede es que...* the fact is that... ‖ *por lo que pueda suceder* just in case ‖ *¿qué sucede?* what is the matter?, what is going on? ‖ *suceda lo que suceda* come what may, whatever happens ‖ *sucede con el fútbol lo mismo que con el baloncesto* it is the same with football as it is with basketball.
◆ *vpr* to follow each other *o* one another.

sucedido *m* FAM happening, event (suceso) || *lo sucedido* what happened; what has happened; what had happened.

sucesión *f* succession, series (serie); *una sucesión de desgracias* a succession of misfortunes || JUR issue, heirs *pl*; *se murió sin sucesión* he died without issue | inheritance (herencia); *sucesión intestada, testada* intestate, testate inheritance | succession; *en la línea de sucesión al trono* in the line of succession to the throne || — JUR *derecho de sucesión* inheritance rights | *derechos de sucesión* probate duties (al legalizar un testamento), death duty, death tax (al heredar) | *sucesión forzosa* forced inheritance, inheritance-at-law | *sucesión universal* universal succession (la del heredero universal).

sucesivamente *adv* successively || *y así sucesivamente* and so forth, and so on.

sucesivo, va *adj* successive, following || consecutive; *ha tenido tres operaciones sucesivas* he had three consecutive operations || running; *cinco días sucesivos* five days running || — *en días sucesivos* in days to come || *en lo sucesivo* henceforth (de ahora en adelante), thenceforth (a partir de entonces).

suceso *m* event, happening, occurrence (acontecimiento) || incident (incidente) || outcome, issue (resultado) || *el lugar del suceso* the scene of the accident (accidente), the scene of the crime (crimen), the site of the disaster (siniestro) || *sección de sucesos* accident and crime reports (en los periódicos).

sucesor, ra *adj* succeeding.
◆ *m/f* successor (el que viene después) || heir (heredero).

sucesorio, ria *adj* JUR successory || *comunidad sucesoria* community of heirs.

suciedad *f* dirt, filth (cosa que ensucia) || dirtiness, filthiness; *la suciedad de un cuarto* the dirtiness of a room || FIG obscenity | foul deed (acción innoble) | vileness (ruindad) || DEP unfairness.

sucintamente *adv* briefly, succintly, concisely.

sucinto, ta *adj* brief, concise, succint || FIG brief (muy corto).

sucio, cia *adj* dirty; *trapo sucio* dirty rag || filthy (muy sucio) || DEP dirty, foul, unfair; *juego sucio* foul play || unfair (poco honrado) || FIG dirty, filthy, nasty; *siempre me dan el trabajo sucio* they always give me the dirty work | dirty, shady (negocio) | dirty, filthy; *lenguaje sucio* dirty language | despicable, vile (ruin) || which dirties easily; *el blanco es un color sucio* white is a colour which dirties easily || FIG off, dirty; *un rojo sucio* an off red | smudged; *un dibujo sucio* a smudged drawing || — FIG *conciencia sucia* guilty conscience | *en sucio* in rough, in rough draft || FIG & FAM *estar más sucio que el palo de un gallinero* to be filthy dirty || FIG *jugar sucio* to play dirty *o* foul || FIG & FAM *lengua sucia* coated *o* furred tongue (de indigestión) | *tener una lengua sucia* to be foulmouthed.

sucre *m* sucre (unidad monetaria del Ecuador).

sucrense *adj* [of *o* from] Sucre (Venezuela, Bolivia).
◆ *m/f* native o inhabitant of Sucre (Venezuela, Bolivia).

sucreño, ña *adj* [of *o* from] Sucre (Bolivia).
◆ *m/f* native *o* inhabitant of Sucre.

sucrosa *f* QUÍM sucrose.

suculencia *f* succulence.

suculento, ta *adj* succulent.

sucumbir *vi* to succumb, to yield; *el castillo sucumbió a los ataques* the castle succumbed to the attacks || to succumb, to die (morir) || FIG to succumb, to yield; *sucumbir a la tentación* to yield to temptation | to be defeated; *sucumbió en las elecciones* he was defeated in the elections | to fall (imperio, país) || JUR to lose a suit.

sucursal *adj* branch.
◆ *f* branch office, branch; *la sucursal de un banco* the branch of a bank || subsidiary; *la sucursal de una empresa* the subsidiary of a company.

sud *m* AMER south.

sudaca *m/f* FAM South American.

sudación *f* sweating.

sudadera *f* sweat || —→ **sudadero** || FAM *pegarse una sudadera* to sweat buckets, to get covered with sweat.

sudadero *m* handkerchief, sweating cloth (paño) || saddlecloth (debajo de la silla de montar) || sweating room (sitio para baños de sudor) || damp patch (sitio húmedo).

sudado *m* AMER stew (cocido).

Sudáfrica *npr f* GEOGR South Africa.

sudafricano, na *adj/s* South African.

Sudamérica *npr f* GEOGR South America.

sudamericano, na *adj/s* South American.

Sudán *npr m* GEOGR Sudan.

sudanés, esa *adj/s* Sudanese (del Sudán) || *los sudaneses* the Sudanese.

sudar *vi* to perspire, to sweat; *sudo mucho* I perspire a lot || to sweat; *las paredes sudan* the walls sweat || FIG to work hard (trabajar mucho) || FIG & FAM *sudar a chorros* or *a mares* to drip with sweat.
◆ *vt* to make sweaty (mojar); *sudó la ropa de la cama* he made the bed linens sweaty || FIG & FAM to make a great effort for, to work hard for; *he sudado el premio* I worked hard for the prize | to make a great effort to, to work hard to; *sudó el aprobado del examen* he worked hard to pass the exam || FIG to exude, to ooze, to give off; *los pinos sudan resina* pine trees exude sap || — FIG & FAM *sudar la gota gorda* or *el quilo* or *tinta* to be dripping with sweat (transpirar mucho), to sweat blood (para hacer un trabajo) | *sudar sangre* to sweat blood.

sudario *m* shroud (para cadáveres) || REL *el Santo Sudario* the Holy Shroud.

sudestada *f* southeaterly wind.

sudeste; sureste *adj* southeast, southeastern (parte) || southeasterly (dirección) || southeast (viento).
◆ *m* southeast || southeast wind (viento).

Sudetes *npr mpl* Sudeten Mountains.

sudista *adj* HIST Southern.
◆ *m/f* HIST Southerner.

sudoeste; suroeste *adj* southwest, southwestern (parte) || southwesterly (dirección) || southwest (viento).
◆ *m* southwest || southwest wind (viento).

sudor *m* sweat, perspiration || FIG moisture, sweat (en una pared, etc.) || — FIG *con el sudor de su frente* by the sweat of one's brow || — FIG & FAM *chorrear de sudor, estar bañado en* or *empapado en sudor* to be dripping with sweat *o* bathed in sweat, to be in a sweat || *tener la frente cubierta* or *perlada de sudor* to have perspiration on one's brow.
◆ *pl* hard work *sing*, sweat *sing* (trabajo) || — FIG & FAM *costarle a uno muchos sudores* to cause s.o. a lot of sweat || FIG *tener sudores fríos* to be in a cold sweat.

sudorífero, ra *adj* sudoriferous.

sudorífico, ca *adj/sm* sudorific.

sudoríparo, ra *adj* ANAT sudoriferous, sudoriparous || *glándula sudorípara* sweat gland.

sudoroso, sa *adj* sweaty, sweating.

sudsudeste *m* south-southeast, south-southeast wind (viento).

sudsudoeste *m* south-southwest || south-southwest wind (viento).

Suecia *npr f* GEOGR Sweden.

sueco, ca *adj* Swedish.
◆ *m* Swedish (idioma).
◆ *m/f* Swede || FIG & FAM *hacerse el sueco* to pretend not to understand, to play dumb, to turn a deaf ear.

suegra *f* mother-in-law.

suegro *m* father-in-law || *los suegros* one's parents-in-law, one's in-laws.

suela *f* sole || strong leather (cuero) || leather tip (del taco de billar) || washer (del grifo) || ZOOL sole (lenguado) || ARQ socle (zócalo de un muro) | skirting board (madero en la parte inferior de la pared) || — FIG & FAM *duro como la suela de un zapato* tough as leather || FIG & FAM *no llegarle a uno a la suela del zapato* not to hold a candle to s.o.
◆ *pl* sandals (sandalias) || *medias suelas* half soles || FIG & FAM *un pícaro de siete suelas* an out-and-out villain.

sueldo *m* salary, pay (retribución); *sueldo mensual* monthly salary || — *a sueldo* paid; *un espía a sueldo* a paid spy; hired; *asesino a sueldo* hired assassin || *estar a sueldo* to be on a salary || *estar a sueldo (de)* to be employed (by) (un empleado), to be in the pay (of) (espías, asesinos, etc.) || *sueldo atrasado* back pay || *sueldo base* basic pay || *sueldo de hambre* starvation pay.

suelo *f* ground; *los niños estaban jugando en el suelo* the children were playing on the ground; *se cayó al suelo* he fell to the ground || soil, land; *suelo fértil* fertile soil; *en suelo extranjero* on foreign soil || floor, flooring (interior); *el suelo de esta habitación* the floor of this room || FIG bottom (de un recipiente) || surface; *el suelo de la carretera está resbaladizo* the road surface is slippery || — FIG *arrastrar a uno por el suelo* or *por los suelos* to drag s.o. though the mud, to run s.o. down | *arrastrarse* or *echarse por los suelos* to grovel, to humble o.s., to crawl | *besar el suelo* to fall flat on one's face | *dar consigo* or *con los huesos en el suelo* to fall, to come a cropper || FIG *¡del suelo no pasa!* it won't hurt (cuando se cae algo) | *echar al suelo* to demolish | *echar por los suelos* to ruin (hacer fracasar un plan, etc.) | *en el santo suelo* on the (blessed) floor *o* ground | *estar por los suelos* to be held in low esteem (cosas, personas), to be rock-bottom (precios), to be very low (moral) | *irse al suelo* to fall through; *todas mis esperanzas se han ido al suelo* all my hopes have fallen through | *medir el suelo* to fall full-length | *poner por los suelos* to run down || *suelo patrio* or *natal* native land, homeland || *venirse al suelo* to fall down (derrumbarse), to fail (fracasar).

suelta *f* release (de palomas, de presos) || fetter (de los animales) || reserve team of oxen (bueyes) || place where oxen are released to graze || *dar suelta* to give time off (dar tiempo libre).

suelto, ta *adj* loose; *los caballos están sueltos en el prado* the horses are loose in the meadow; *el tornillo está suelto* the screw is loose; *venden el arroz suelto* they sell rice loose || loose, down (pelo); *ella lleva el pelo suelto* she wears her hair down || undone (cordones) || untied (sin atar) || odd; *tengo dos tomos sueltos de la enciclopedia* I have two odd volumes of the encyclopedia; *un zapato suelto* an odd shoe || free, released, out; *ha estado en la cárcel, pero ya está suelto* he was in jail, but he has been released *o* he is out now || loose, at large; *el asesino anda suelto todavía* the killer is still at large || loose (el vientre) || fluid, thin (líquido) || loose, loose-fitting (prendas de vestir) || FIG isolated; *esos son hechos sueltos* those are isolated facts | fluent, easy-flowing (conversación, estilo) | free; *movimientos sueltos* free movements | agile, nimble (ágil) | daring (atrevido) | free and easy (desembarazado); *una mujer suelta* a free and easy woman | blank (verso) || — FIG *cabo suelto* loose end; *no dejes ningún cabo suelto en este asunto* don't leave any loose ends in this affair | *dar rienda suelta (a)* to give free rein (to) || *dinero suelto* loose change || FIG *estar muy suelto en* to be good *o* quite fluent in; *ya está muy suelto en inglés* he is good at English now || *estos artículos no se venden sueltos* these articles are not sold separately *o* singly *o* loose || *hojas sueltas* loose sheets [of paper] (de papel) || *piezas sueltas* parts || FIG *ser suelto de manos* to be free with one's hands.

◆ *m* change, small *o* loose change; *no tengo suelto* I haven't any small change || item (de periódico).

sueño *m* sleep; *sueño pesado* heavy sleep || drowsiness, sleepiness (cansancio, ganas de dormir) || dream; *anoche tuve un sueño horrible* last night I had a horrible dream || FIG dream, illusion (ilusión); *esos son sueños de juventud* those are the dreams of youth | dream (encanto); *es un sueño* he's a dream; *he visto un niño que es un sueño* I saw a dream of a baby || — FIG *caerse de sueño* to be falling asleep on one's feet || *coger* or *conciliar el sueño* to get to sleep || *dar sueño* to make sleepy; *este discurso me da sueño* this speech is making me sleepy || FIG & FAM *descabezar un sueño* to take forty winks, to have a nap || FIG *dormir el sueño de los justos* to sleep the sleep of the just | *dulce sueño* beloved (amado) || *echar un sueño* to take a nap || MED *enfermedad del sueño* sleeping sickness || FIG *en sueños* in one's dreams || *entregarse al sueño* to abandon o.s. to sleep, to sink into sleep || *entre sueños* half asleep || FIG *eso lo has visto en sueños* you must have been dreaming | *espantar el sueño* to ward off sleep || *la clave de los sueños* the key to dream interpretation || FIG *la vida es sueño* life is a dream | *mundo de sueños* dream world | *¡ni en* or *por sueños!* not on your life! || *perder el sueño por algo* to lose sleep over sth. || *quitar el sueño* to keep awake; *el café te quitará el sueño* the coffee will keep you awake; *los problemas de la oficina me quitan el sueño* office problems keep me awake || FIG *sueño de una noche de verano* midsummer night's dream | *sueño dorado* life's dream, greatest dream; *mi sueño dorado es vivir en el campo* my greatest dream *o* my life's dream is to live in the country | *sueño eterno* eternal rest *o* sleep | *sueño hecho realidad* dream come true || *sueño hipnótico* hypnotic sleep || *tener el sueño ligero* to be a light sleeper || *tener sueño* to be *o* to feel tired *o* sleepy || *tengo un sueño que no veo* I am falling asleep on my feet.

suero *m* whey (de la leche) || serum (de la sangre) || MED *suero fisiológico* physiological salt solution, physiological saline solution.

sueroterapia *f* MED serotherapy, serum therapy.

suerte *f* fate, destiny; *así lo quiso la suerte* fate willed it so || luck, fortune (buena o mala fortuna); *tener mala suerte* to have bad luck || destiny, fate, lot (porvenir); *tu suerte está decidida* your destiny is decided || lot, situation, conditions *pl* (condiciones); *mejorar la suerte de los campesinos* to improve the lot of the rural population || lot (elección); *elegir por* or *a suerte* to decide by lot || kind, sort; *conoce a toda suerte de personas* he knows all kinds of people || quality, class (calidad); *primera suerte* first class || manner, way (manera) || trick (de prestidigitador) || lot (parcela) || TAUR stage, «suerte» [one of the divisions of the bullfight] || AMER lottery ticket (billete de lotería) || — *¡buena suerte!*, *¡suerte!* good luck! || *caerle* or *tocarle a uno en suerte* to fall to s.o.'s lot; *me ha caído en suerte nacer rico* it fell to my lot to be born rich || *confiar en la suerte* to trust to luck || *con un poco de suerte ganaremos* with a bit of luck we'll win || *dar* or *traer buena, mala suerte* to bring good, bad luck; to be lucky, unlucky || *de otra suerte* otherwise || *de suerte que* so (that); *te hemos tratado muy bien de suerte que no tienes por qué quejarte* we have treated you very well, so you have no reason to complain || *de tal suerte que...* in such a way that... || *echar suertes, echar a suertes* to draw lots; *echar algo a suertes* to draw lots for sth.; to toss (for sth.) (a cara o cruz) || *estar de mala suerte* to be out of luck || *estar de suerte* to be in luck || *golpe de suerte* stroke of luck || *hombre de suerte* lucky man || FIG *la suerte es ciega* luck is blind || *la suerte está echada* the die is cast || *leerle la suerte a uno* to tell s.o.'s fortune || *¡mala suerte!* hard luck!, bad luck! || TAUR *poner en suerte (el toro)* to place [the bull] || *por suerte* luckily, fortunately; *por suerte vino* fortunately he came || *probar (la) suerte* to try one's luck || *¡qué suerte más negra* or *más perra!* what rotten luck! || *¡que tengas (mucha) suerte!* good luck!, the best of luck! || *quiso la suerte que...* as fate would have it..., as luck would have it... || *salir a suerte* to be drawn || *tener buena, mala suerte* to be lucky, unlucky; to have good, bad luck || *tener la suerte de* to be lucky enough to || *tener suerte* to be lucky || *tener una suerte loca* or *de mil demonios* to have the luck of the devil || *tentar la suerte* to push one's luck, to tempt fate || *traer buena, mala suerte* to be lucky, unlucky, to bring good luck, bad luck; *el número que me trae buena suerte* my lucky number.

suertero, ra *adj* AMER lucky.

◆ *m* AMER seller of lottery tickets.

suertudo, da *adj* lucky, jammy (*fam*).

sueste *m* southeast || MAR sou'wester, southwester (sombrero).

suéter *m* sweater.

Suez *m pr* GEOGR Suez; *canal de Suez* Suez canal.

suficiencia *f* sufficiency (capacidad) || adequancy (conveniencia) || FIG competence, capability | self-importance, smugness, complacency (presunción) || FIG *tener aire de suficiencia* to look smug, to look cocksure.

suficiente *adj* sufficient, enough (bastante) || suitable (apto) || FIG self-important, cocksure, self-satisfied, smug, complacent (engreído) || — *lo suficiente* sufficient, enough; *tengo lo suficiente para vivir* I have enough to live on || *no tiene suficiente anchura* it is not wide enough.

suficientemente *adv* sufficiently, enough; *suficientemente grande* sufficiently big, big enough.

sufijo, ja *adj* GRAM suffixal.

◆ *m* GRAM suffix.

sufra *f* backband (del harnés).

sufragáneo, a *adj/sm* suffragan.

sufragar *vt* to help, to support (ayudar) || to pay, to defray, to cover; *sufragar los gastos de un pleito* to pay the cost of a suit || to finance, to pay for; *sufragar un proyecto* to finance a project.

◆ *vi* *sufragar por* to vote for.

sufragio *m* suffrage; *sufragio universal* universal suffrage || vote (voto); *recuento de sufragios* counting of the votes || help, aid (ayuda) || REL service for the redemption of souls from purgatory.

sufragismo *m* suffragettism.

sufragista *m* suffragist (adicto al sufragismo).

◆ *f* suffragette.

sufrido, da *adj* long-suffering, patient (paciente) || FIG & FAM complaisant (marido) || FIG serviceable, hard-wearing (tela) || FIG *un color poco sufrido* an easily soiled colour.

◆ *m* complaisant husband.

sufridor, ra *adj* suffering.

sufrimiento *m* suffering (dolor) || misery (miseria) || FIG tolerance (tolerancia) | patience (paciencia) | sufferance (capacidad para sufrir).

sufrir *vt* to suffer; *sufrir persecuciones* to suffer persecutions || to have, to suffer (experimentar); *ha sufrido un grave accidente* he has had a bad accident; *sufrir un ataque de corazón* to have a heart attack || to undergo; *sufrir una operación, un cambio* to undergo an operation, a change || to do, to sit, to take (un examen) || to suffer; *sufrir una derrota, las consecuencias* to suffer defeat, the consequences; *sufrir reveses de fortuna, un fracaso* to suffer setbacks, a failure || to tolerate; *no sufriré tus insultos* I will not tolerate your insults || FAM to bear, to stand, to put up with (tolerar a una persona); *no puedo sufrir a Juan* I can't stand John || FIG *sufrir su* or *un calvario* to carry one's cross.

◆ *vi* to suffer; *durante su vida sufrió mucho* during his life he suffered a lot || — FIG *sufrir como un condenado* to go through hell || *sufrir de* to suffer from *o* with; *sufro de dolores de cabeza* I suffer from headaches; *sufrir del corazón* to suffer with one's heart, to suffer from heart trouble.

sugerencia *f* suggestion.

sugerente; sugeridor, ra *adj* suggestive.

sugerir* *vt* to suggest.

sugestión *f* suggestion (sugerencia) || autosuggestion || hypnotic power (poder hipnótico).

sugestionable *adj* suggestible, impressionable, easily influenced.

sugestionar *vt* to influence || to have a hypnotic power over (dominar, fascinar).

sugestivo, va *adj* suggestive, stimulating || attractive.

suicida *adj* suicidal.

◆ *m/f* suicide (persona) || FIG daredevil, madcap (intrépido).

suicidarse *vpr* to commit suicide, to take one's life.

suicidio *m* suicide; *intento de suicidio* attempted suicide.

sui géneris *adj* sui generis.

suite *f* suite (en un hotel) || MÚS suite.

Suiza *npr f* GEOGR Switzerland.

suizo, za *adj/s* Swiss; *suizo alemán* Swiss German.

◆ *m* (ant) foot soldier || bun (bollo).

— OBSERV El plural de *Swiss* es *Swiss*.

sujeción *f* subjection (acción de sujetar) || subjection, subordination; *sujeción a las leyes* subordination to the law || fastening (ligadura) || obligation; *no me gustan las sujeciones* I don't like obligations.

sujetador, ra *adj* fastening, binding.

◆ *m* brassière, bra (prenda femenina) || fastener (objeto para sujetar) || clip (para el pelo, papeles).

sujetalibros *m inv* bookend.

sujetapapeles *m inv* paper clip.

sujetar *vt* to secure, to fasten, to hold, to fix, to attach (fijar); *este cuadro está sujetado* or *sujeto por un clavo* this picture is held by a nail to hold (sostener); *sujeta el libro un momento* hold the book a moment || to keep hold of, to hold down (a la fuerza); *los guardias lo sujetaban para que no se escapase* the guards held him down so that he wouldn't escape || to seize (agarrar) || to hold up; *unos tirantes le sujetan el delantal* straps hold up her apron || to tie tightly (atar); *sujeta bien el nudo* tie the knot tightly || to hold in place, to keep in place (el

pelo) || to fasten together (papeles) || to subdue (someter) || to subordinate (subordinar) || FIG to restrain, to control, to keep in check, to hold down *o* back; *este chico necesita a alguien que le sujete* this boy needs s.o. to restrain him; *hay que sujetar al pueblo para evitar la revolución* the people must be held down *o* kept in check to avoid revolution | to tie down; *los quehaceres de la casa la sujetan mucho* the housework ties her down a lot || DEP to tackle (rugby) || *sujetar con grapas, con clavos* to staple, to nail.
◆ *vpr* to hold on, to hang on; *para no caer me sujeté a las ramas* so as not to fall I hung on to the branches; *¡sujétate bien!* hold on tight! || to stay up; *sin tirantes este pantalón no se sujeta* without braces these trousers won't stay up || to subject o.s. (*a* to) (someterse) || FIG to abide by, to respect, to stick to; *hay que sujetarse a la constitución* one must abide by the constitution | to act in accordance with (ajustarse a).

sujeto, ta *adj* subject, liable (susceptible); *este proyecto está sujeto a cambios* this plan is subject to changes || fastened, secure; *la cuerda está bien sujeta* the rope is securely fastened *o* quite secure || attached, fixed; *¿está el cuadro bien sujeto?* is the painting firmly fixed? || FIG subject (sometido); *sujeto a derechos arancelarios* subject to customs duties | tied down (ocupado); *está muy sujeto al trabajo de la oficina* he is very tied down by office work || — *sujeto a la aprobación de* subject to the approval of || FIG *tener a alguien muy sujeto* to keep s.o. well in check, to keep s.o. under close control.
◆ *m* fellow, individual (persona); *la policía detuvo a un sujeto sospechoso* the police detained a suspicious fellow || GRAM & FIL subject.

sulfamida *f* MED sulphonamide [*US* sulfonamide].

sulfatación *f* QUÍM sulphating [*US* sulfating].

sulfatado *m* QUÍM sulphating [*US* sulfating].

sulfatador, ra *adj* which sulphates, sulphating [*US* sulfating].
◆ *f* sulphating machine [*US* sulfating machine].

sulfatar *vt* QUÍM to sulphate [*US* to sulfate].

sulfato *m* QUÍM sulphate [*US* sulfate]; *sulfato de hierro* iron sulphate.

sulfhídrico, ca *adj* QUÍM sulphuretted [*US* sulfuretted] || *ácido sulfhídrico* hydrosulphuric acid, hydrogen sulphide.

sulfito *m* QUÍM sulphite [*US* sulfite].

sulfurado, da *adj* QUÍM sulphuretted [*US* sulfuretted] || FIG infuriated.
◆ *m* AGR sulphuration, sulphurization [*US* sulfuration, sulfurization].

sulfurar *vt* QUÍM to sulphurate, to sulphurize [*US* to sulfurate, to sulfurize] || FIG to infuriate (irritar).
◆ *vpr* FIG to lose one's temper; *¡no te sulfures!* don't lose your temper!

sulfúrico, ca *adj* QUÍM sulphuric [*US* sulfuric]; *ácido sulfúrico* sulphuric acid.

sulfuro *m* QUÍM sulphide [*US* sulfide].

sulfuroso, sa *adj* QUÍM sulphurous, sulphureous [*US* sulfurous, sulfureous] || *agua sulfurosa* sulphur water [*US* sulfur water].

sultán *m* sultan.

sultana *f* sultana.

sultanato *m*; **sultanía** *f* sultanate.

suma *f* sum; *la suma de tres y cuatro es siete* the sum of three and four is seven || sum, total; *la factura llegó a la suma de cinco mil pesetas* the bill came to a sum *o* a total of five thousand pesetas || sum, amount (de dinero) || MAT addition; *hacer una suma* to do *o* to make an addition || FIG summary (recopilación) | substance, essence (lo más sustancial de una cosa) || — *en suma* in short || MAT *hacer sumas* to do sums, to add up.

sumador *m* INFORM adder.

sumamente *adv* extremely, highly.

sumando *m* MAT addend.

sumar *vt* to add, to add up; *sumar dos números* to add two numbers || to amount to, to total; *sus ingresos suman diez mil pesetas* his income amounts to ten thousand pesetas || to total; *tres países que suman cien millones de habitantes* three countries which total one hundred million inhabitants || FIG to gather (recopilar) | to summarize, to sum up (compendiar) || *máquina de sumar* adding machine.
◆ *vi* MAT to add up || *suma y sigue* carried forward (en contabilidad), and that's not all (y hay más).
◆ *vpr* to join (in); *me sumé a la conversación* I joined in the conversation; *sumarse a un partido* to join a party || *otras ventajas que se suman a la rapidez son...* advantages other than speed which come into play *o* which must be taken into account are...

sumaria *f* JUR indictment.

sumarial *adj* JUR pertaining to an indictment.

sumariamente *adv* JUR summarily.

sumariar *vt* JUR to indict.

sumario, ria *adj* summary, brief (breve) || JUR summary; *proceso sumario* summary proceedings.
◆ *m* summary (resumen) || JUR indictment || FIG *pertenece al secreto de sumario* it should be kept secret.

sumarísimo, ma *adj* JUR swift, expeditious.

Sumatra *npr f* GEOGR Sumatra.

sumergible *adj* submersible.
◆ *m* submarine (embarcación).

sumergimiento *m* submersion, submergence.

sumergir *vt* to submerge || FIG to overwhelm (*en* with) (agobiar) | to plunge (hundir).
◆ *vpr* to sink, to submerge || FIG *sumergirse en* to become immersed in.

sumerio, ria *adj/s* Sumerian.

sumersión *f* submersion, submergence.

sumidero *m* drain, sewer (alcantarilla) || cesspool (pozo negro).

sumiller *m* (ant) chamberlain.

suministrador, ra *adj* which supplies, supplying.
◆ *m/f* supplier (proveedor).

suministrar *vt* to supply, to provide, to furnish (proveer); *suministrar algo a alguien* to supply s.o. with sth., to supply sth. to s.o.

suministro *m* supply || supply, supplying, provision (acción de suministrar) || *suministro a domicilio* home delivery.
◆ *pl* supplies (víveres) || supply *sing*; *nuestros suministros de municiones* our ammunition supply.

sumir *vt* to sink, to submerge (hundir) || REL to receive (consumir) || FIG to plunge; *sumir a alguien en la duda* to plunge s.o. into doubt; *sumir a alguien en la miseria* to plunge s.o. into misery.
◆ *vpr* to sink (hundirse) || to run away (las aguas residuales, etc.) || FIG to immerse o.s., to become immersed; *se sumió en los estudios* he immersed himself in his studies || to be sunken (las mejillas, el pecho) || FIG *sumirse en el sueño* to sink into a deep sleep.

sumisión *f* submission || submissiveness (carácter sumiso).

sumiso, sa *adj* submissive.

súmmum *m* summit; *el súmmum de la sabiduría* the summit of knowledge || height; *el súmmum de la desvergüenza* the height of shamelessness || *ser el súmmum* to be the limit (ser el colmo).

sumo, ma *adj* greatest, highest; *la suma felicidad* the greatest happiness || supreme, highest; *suma autoridad* supreme authority || extreme; *con sumo cuidado* with extreme care || — *a lo sumo* at (the) most || *de sumo* completely || *El Sumo Sacerdote* the High Priest || *en sumo grado* in the extreme, extremely || *Sumo Pontífice* Sovereign Pontiff.

suní *adj* Sunni [orthodox Muslim].
— OBSERV pl *suníes* Sunni.

sunlight *m* CINEM sunlight.

sunna *f* Sunna, Sunnah (ortodoxia musulmana).

sunnita *m* Sunnite (musulmán ortodoxo).

suntuario, ria *adj* sumptuary.

suntuosidad *f* sumptuousity (lujo) || sumptuousness (magnificencia).

suntuoso, sa *adj* sumptuous; *una casa suntuosa* a sumptuous house.

supeditación *f* subjection, subordination.

supeditar *vt* to subdue (avasallar) || to subordinate (subordinar) || FIG to subject; *supedito mi viaje a la decisión de mis padres* I subject my trip to my parents' decision || *estar supeditado a* to be subject to, to depend on; *todo está supeditado a la venta de la casa* everything is subject to the sale of the house.
◆ *vpr* to subject o.s. to, to bow to; *no estoy dispuesta a supeditarme a sus caprichos* I will not subject myself to his whims.

súper *adj* FAM super.
◆ *f* super (gasolina).

superable *adj* superable, surmountable.

superabundancia *f* superabundance.

superabundante *adj* superabundant.

superabundar *vi* to superabound.

superación *f* overcoming; *la superación de dificultades* the overcoming of difficulties, overcoming difficulties || excelling (de uno mismo) || *afán de superación* urge to improve o.s. *o* to better o.s.

superactividad *f* superactivity.

superalimentación *f* overfeeding.

superalimentar *vt* to overfeed.

superar *vt* to surpass (ser superior); *este producto supera a todos* this product surpasses all others || to outshine, to beat, to outdo (a una persona) || to overcome (al adversario) || to overcome; *he superado todas las dificultades* I have overcome all the difficulties || to break, to beat (una plusmarca) || — *estar superado* to be over; *la época del colonialismo está superada* the age of colonialism is over || *hemos superado lo más difícil* we are over the most difficult part, the worst is behind us now.
◆ *vpr* to surpass o.s., to excel o.s.; *se ha superado en el examen* he excelled himself in the exam || to better o.s., to do better; *en la vida hay que intentar superarse* one must always try to better o.s.

superávit *m* COM surplus, superavit.
— OBSERV According to the Spanish Academy the word *superávit* is invariable. In practice, however, the plural forms *superávit* and *superávits* are both used.

supercapitalización *f* overcapitalization.

supercapitalizar *vt* COM to overcapitalize.

supercarburante *m* high-octane fuel.

superciliar *adj* ANAT superciliary; *arco superciliar* superciliary arch *o* ridge.

supercompresión *f* TECN supercharging.

supercomprimir *vt* TECN supercharge.

superchería *f* fraud, trick.

superdesarrollado, da *adj* overdeveloped.

superdesarrollo *m* overdevelopment.

superdirecta *f* AUT overdrive.

superdominante *f* MÚS superdominant.

supereminencia *f* supereminence.

supereminente *adj* supereminent.

superempleo *m* overemployment.

supererogación *f* supererogation.

superestructura *f* superstructure.

superfetación *f* superfetation, superfoetation.

superficial *adj* superficial || — *aguas superficiales* surface waters || *herida superficial* flesh wound, superficial injury.

superficialidad *f* superficiality.

superficialmente *adv* superficially.

superficie *f* surface; *la superficie del agua* the surface of the water || area (extensión); *la superficie de una ciudad* the area of a city || MAT area (área) || — *de superficie* surface; *transporte de superficie* surface transport || MAR *salir a la superficie* to surface (un submarino, buceador), to come *o* to float to the surface (un objeto) || AGR *superficie aprovechable* cultivable land || AUT *superficie de rodadura* tread (del neumático) || *superficie de rozamiento* friction surface || AVIAC *superficie sustentadora* lifting surface || *superficie terrestre* land surface.

superfino, na *adj* superfine.

superfluidad *f* superfluity, superflousness.

superfluo, a *adj* superfluous.

superfortaleza *f* AVIAC superfortress (avión).

superfosfato *m* QUÍM superphosphate.

superheterodino *m* superheterodyne (radio).

superhombre *m* superman.

superhumeral *m* REL superhumeral.

superintendencia *f* superintendence.

superintendente *m* superintendent.

superior *adj* superior, high; *de calidad superior* high quality || upper; *mandíbula superior* upper jaw; *los pisos superiores* the upper floors || upper, top: *la parte superior de la biblioteca* the upper part of the bookcase || higher, above; *todos los números superiores a diez* all numbers above ten *o* higher than ten || superior; *es superior a todos* he is superior to everybody || better (mejor) || *enseñanza superior* higher education.

superior *m* superior; *tienes que obedecer a tu superior* you must obey your superior || REL superior (de convento o monasterio).

superiora *f* REL mother superior.

superioridad *f* superiority || advantage; *el púgil tuvo una clara superioridad sobre su adversario* the boxer had a clear advantage over his opponent || *la superioridad* a higher authority.

superlativo, va *adj* superlative (excelente) || GRAM superlative.
◆ *m* GRAM superlative.

superligero, ra *adj* DEP light weight.
◆ *m* DEP light-welter weight.

supermercado *m* supermarket.

supernumerario, ria *adj* supernumerary || MIL on leave without pay.
◆ *m/f* supernumerary.

superorden *m* ZOOL superorder.

superpoblación *f* overpopulation (del mundo, de un país) || overcrowding, overpopulation (de las ciudades).

superpoblado, da *adj* overpopulated (mundo, país) || overcrowded, overpopulated (ciudad).

superponer* *vt* to superpose, to superimpose || FIG to put before; *él superpone la ambición a la tranquilidad* he puts ambition before tranquility.
◆ *vpr* FIG to come before (anteponerse); *al miedo se superpone el sentido del deber* the sense of duty comes before fear.

superposición *f* superposition.

superpotencia *f* superpower, great power.

superpresión *f* TECN overpressure.

superproducción *f* overproduction || CINEM mammoth production (película).

superpuesto, ta *adj* superimposed, superposed.

superrealismo *m* surrealism.

supersaturación *f* QUÍM supersaturation.

supersaturar *vt* to supersaturate.

supersecreto, ta *adj* top secret.

supersónico, ca *adj* AVIAC supersonic; *avión supersónico* supersonic aircraft.

superstición *f* superstition.

supersticioso, sa *adj* superstitious.

supérstite *adj* JUR surviving.
◆ *m/f* JUR survivor.

supervaloración *f* overvaluing, overrating.

supervalorar *vt* to overvalue, to overrate.

supervisar *vt* to supervise.

supervisión *f* supervision.

supervisor, ra *m/f* supervisor.

supervivencia *f* survival || JUR survivorship.

superviviente *adj* surviving.
◆ *m/f* survivor.

supervivir *vi* to survive.

supervoltaje *m* ELECTR boosting (de la corriente) | overruning (de una lámpara).

supinación *f* supination.

supinador *adj* ANAT supinating.
◆ *m* ANAT supinator.

supino, na *adj* supine, face up (boca arriba) || — *en posición supina* in a supine position, face up, on one's back || *ignorancia supina* supine *o* crass ignorance.
◆ *m* GRAM supine.

súpito, ta *adj* AMER flabbergasted, dumbfounded (perplejo).

suplantación *f* supplantation, supplanting (reemplazo) || supposition, forgery (falsificación).

suplantar *vt* to supplant, to take the place of (reemplazar) || to forge, to falsify (falsificar).

suplementario, ria *adj* supplementary, additional || supplementary (ángulos) || relief, extra (tren) || — *crédito suplementario* extension of credit || *empleo suplementario* sideline.

suplemento *m* supplement, additional supply; *necesitamos un suplemento de papel* we need an additional supply of paper || supplement (a una revista, libro, periódico); *suplemento dominical* Sunday colour suplement || extra charge (cantidad de dinero); *sin suplemento* without extra charge || supplement, excess fare (de un billete de ferrocarril) || MAT supplement.

suplencia *f* substitution, replacement.

suplente *adj* substitute, deputy || DEP reserve (jugador).
◆ *m/f* substitute || DEP reserve || TEATR understudy.

supletorio, ria *adj* additional, supplementary, extra.

súplica *f* supplication, entreaty (ruego) || request (petición) || JUR petition || *a súplica de* at the request of, by request of.

suplicación *f* supplication || rolled wafer (barquillo) || JUR appeal.

suplicante *adj* beseeching, supplicating, imploring, entreating.
◆ *m/f* supplicant.

suplicar *vt* to supplicate, to implore, to beseech, to beg (rogar); *le suplico que venga* I beg you to come || JUR to appeal to || *carta suplicada (a)* to be forwarded (to) || *se suplica no hacer ruido* please be quiet.

suplicatoria *f* JUR letters *pl* rogatory.

suplicio *m* torture (tortura) || FIG torment, torture; *llevar zapatos estrechos es un suplicio* tight shoes are a torment *o* are torture | anguish (padecimiento moral) || — *el suplicio eterno* eternal torment || *suplicio de Tántalo* torment of Tantalus || *último suplicio* death penalty (pena de muerte), death; *someter a alguien al último suplicio* to put s.o. to death.

suplir *vt* to replace, to substitute (reemplazar); *suplir a un profesor* to replace a teacher || to make up for (compensar); *tenemos que suplir la falta de este jugador* we have to make up for the absence of this player || to cover up (for) (ocultar); *supliremos su error* we will cover up for his error || to make up (poner); *yo supliré lo demás* I'll make up the rest || to add (añadir) || to remedy (remediar) || to fill in; *súplanse los espacios en blanco con las respuestas* fill in the blank spaces with the answers.

suponer *m* FAM supposition.

suponer* *vt* to suppose, to assume; *supongamos que lo dice que es mentira* let's suppose that what he says is false || to believe (creer); *puedes suponer lo que quieras* you can believe what you want || to imagine (imaginar) || to guess (adivinar) || to mean, to involve, to entail; *este proyecto supone grandes gastos* this plan means *o* entails a considerable outlay || to mean (significar); *su negativa no supone nada* his refusal does not mean anything || — *como es de suponer* as is to be expected || *le supongo cincuenta años* I suppose *o* I would say he must be about fifty years old || *ser de suponer* to be possible *o* likely || *supongo que sí* I suppose so || *suponiendo que...* assuming *o* supposing that... || *valor se le supone* he is supposed to be brave, he is credited with courage.
◆ *vi* to count for; *su padre supone mucho en la familia* his father counts for a great deal in the family.

suposición *f* supposition, assumption || slander (calumnia) || JUR *suposición de parto, de infante* setting up a child [to displace the real heir].

supositorio *m* suppository.

supranacional *adj* supranational.

suprarrealismo *m* surrealism.

suprarrenal *adj* suprarenal; *glándula suprarrenal* suprarenal gland.

suprasensible *adj* supersensible, supersensory, supersensitive.

supremacía *f* supremacy.

supremo, ma *adj* supreme; *la autoridad suprema* the supreme authority || decisive; *tu hora suprema ha llegado* the decisive moment has come for you || — *Ser Supremo* Supreme Being || *hora suprema, momento supremo* dying moments || *sacrificio supremo* supreme sacrifice || *tribunal supremo* supreme court.

supresión *f* suppression, elimination; *la supresión de un artículo* the suppression of an article || deletion (de una palabra) || lifting (de una restricción).

suprimir *vt* to suppress; *suprimir la libertad de expresión* to suppress freedom of speech ‖ to abolish, to suppress (abolir) ‖ to omit, to leave out, to skip (*fam*) (omitir); *suprima los detalles* skip the details ‖ to eliminate, to remove (eliminar) ‖ to delete (una palabra) ‖ to lift (una restricción) ‖ INFORM to delete.

supuesto, ta *adj* so-called, self-styled, would-be; *un supuesto pintor* a so-called painter ‖ supposed (que se supone); *su supuesto suicidio* his supposed suicide ‖ imaginary; *una supuesta enfermedad* an imaginary illness ‖ hypothetical (hipotético) ‖ — *dar por supuesta una cosa* to take sth. for granted ‖ *¡por supuesto!* of course!, naturally! ‖ *por supuesto que* of course ‖ *supuesto que* since (ya que), if (si) ‖ *un nombre supuesto* an assumed name.
◆ *m* hypothesis, supposition, assumption (hipótesis) ‖ — *en el supuesto de que...* supposing that... ‖ MIL *supuesto táctico* military manoeuvre.
◆ *pl* data; *carecemos de los supuestos más elementales* we are lacking the most elementary data.

supuración *f* MED suppuration.

supurante *adj* MED suppurating.

supurar *vi* MED to suppurate.

supurativo, va *adj* suppurative.

sur *m* south; *más al sur* further south ‖ south wind (viento).
◆ *adj* south, southern (parte) ‖ south, southerly (viento) ‖ southerly (dirección).

sura *f* sura (del Corán).

surá *m* surah (tela).

surafricano, na *adj/s* South African.

suramericano, na *adj/s* South American.

surata *f* sura (del Corán).

surcar *vt* AGR to plough, to furrow (con el arado) ‖ FIG to plough, to cleave (el agua) | to fly through (el aire) ‖ — FIG *frente surcada de arrugas* furrowed brow | *surcar los mares* to ply the seas.

surco *m* AGR furrow ‖ FIG wrinkle; *una frente llena de surcos* a forehead full of wrinkles | rut; *las ruedas del carro dejan surcos en la tierra* the wheels of the cart leave ruts in the ground | groove (de disco) | wake (estela del barco).

surcoreano, na *adj/s* South Korean.

sureño, ña; surero, ra *adj* AMER Southern.
◆ *m/f* AMER Southerner.

surero *m* AMER cold south wind.

surestada *f* AMER southeasterly wind.

sureste *adj/sm* → **sudeste.**

surgir *vi* to spurt up, to spout up, to come out, to spring up (agua) ‖ MAR to anchor (fondear) ‖ to appear, to tower, to loom up, to rise; *la torre de la catedral surge entre las casas* the cathedral tower looms up above the houses ‖ to appear unexpectedly (aparecer de repente) ‖ to emerge (de la sombra) ‖ FIG to appear, to emerge, to appear on the scene; *ha surgido una nueva actriz* a new actress has appeared on the scene | to arise, to crop up, to come up; *han surgido muchas dificultades* many difficulties have arisen.

Surinam *n pr* GEOGR Surinam.

suripanta *f* FAM chorus girl ‖ POP slut (mujer de mal vivir).

surmenaje *m* overwork (físico) ‖ mental strain *o* fatigue (mental).

suroeste *adj/sm* → **sudoeste.**

surrealismo *m* surrealism.

surrealista *adj* surrealist, surrealistic.
◆ *m/f* surrealist.

sursudoeste *m* south-southwest ‖ south-southwest wind (viento).

sursuncorda *m* FAM The Pope, the king (imaginary authority) ‖ FAM *no lo hago aunque me lo mande el sursuncorda* I wouldn't do it for all the tea in China.

surtidero *m* outlet (de un estanque) ‖ jet (chorro de agua).

surtido, da *adj* assorted; *caramelos surtidos* assorted sweets ‖ well stocked; *estamos surtidos en géneros para esta temporada* we are well stocked with goods for this season.
◆ *m* assortment; *un surtido de galletas* an assortment of biscuits ‖ selection; *tener un gran surtido de corbatas* to have a large selection of ties ‖ stock, supply (provisión).

surtidor, ra *adj* supplying, providing.
◆ *m* jet, spout (chorro de agua) ‖ fountain (fuente) ‖ petrol pump [*US* gas pump], petrol station [*US* gas station] (de gasolina) ‖ carburettor jet (del carburador).

surtir *vt* to supply, to provide, to stock (proveer); *surtir de carbón* to supply with coal ‖ — *surtir efecto* to have an effect (medicina), to work, to have the desired effect (una estratagema), to come into force, to take effect (ley) ‖ *surtir el mercado* to supply the market ‖ *surtir un pedido* to fill an order.
◆ *vi* to spout, to spurt, to gush (brotar).
◆ *vpr* to provide *o* to supply o.s. (*de* with), to get in; *surtirse de carbón* to get some coal in ‖ to be supplied by, to get one's supplies from (en cierto sitio).

surto, ta *adj* MAR anchored.

survietnamita *adj/s* South Vietnamese.

surumpe; surupí *m* AMER inflammation of the eyes [caused by the reflection of the sun on the snow].

¡sus! *interj* cheer up! (para animar) ‖ shoo!, go away! (para ahuyentar) ‖ come on!, go on! (para excitar).

susceptibilidad *f* susceptibility ‖ sensitivity (sensibilidad) ‖ touchiness (propensión a ofenderse).

susceptible *adj* susceptible ‖ sensitive (sensible) ‖ touchy (propenso a sentirse ofendido) ‖ — *susceptible de educación* educable, capable of being educated ‖ *susceptible de fluctuaciones* liable to fluctuate, subject *o* liable to fluctuation ‖ *susceptible de mejora* improvable.

suscitar *vt* to provoke, to cause; *su discurso suscitó una rebelión* his speech caused a revolt ‖ to stir up; *hizo todo lo posible para suscitar una rebelión* he did his utmost to stir up a rebellion ‖ to raise, to cause; *esta medida puede suscitar muchos problemas* this measure is liable to raise a lot of problems ‖ to arouse (interés) ‖ to provoke, to cause, to start (una discusión).

suscribir; subscribir *vt* to sign (firmar); *suscribir la petición* to sign the petition ‖ to take out an option on (acciones y valores de Bolsa) ‖ to take out a subscription for; *suscribir a alguien a una revista* to take out a subscription to a magazine for s.o. ‖ FIG to endorse, to subscribe to; *no suscribo su conducta* I don't endorse his conduct ‖ *el que suscribe* the undersigned.
◆ *vpr* to subscribe; *suscribirse a una revista* to subscribe to a magazine.

suscripción; subscripción *f* subscription; *abrir una suscripción* to take out a subscription.

suscriptor, ra; subscriptor, ra *m/f* subscriber.

suscrito, ta; subscripto, ta *adj* subscribed ‖ undersigned (infrascrito).
◆ *m/f* undersigned.

susodicho, cha *adj* above-mentioned, afore-said.

suspender *vt* to suspend, to hang; *suspender del techo* to hang from the ceiling ‖ FIG to adjourn; *suspender la sesión* to adjourn the meeting | to delay, to postpone (aplazar); *han suspendido el trabajo hasta nueva orden* they have delayed work until new orders | to discontinue, to suspend; *el servicio de trenes ha sido suspendido* the train service has been discontinued | to interrupt (interrumpir) | to fail; *le han suspedido en tres asignaturas* they have failed him in three subjects | to astonish, to astound, to amaze (admirar) ‖ *suspender a uno de empleo y sueldo* to suspend s.o. without pay.
◆ *vpr* FIG to stop (parar) ‖ to rear (un caballo).

suspense *m* CINEM suspense.

suspensión *f* suspension, hanging ‖ suspension; *la suspensión de las pruebas nucleares* suspension of nuclear tests ‖ AUT & MÚS & QUÍM suspension ‖ interruption (interrupción) ‖ adjournment (de una reunión) ‖ postponement (aplazamiento) ‖ amazement, astonishment (asombro) ‖ JUR stay ‖ — *suspensión de garantías constitucionales* suspension of constitutional rights ‖ *suspensión de hostilidades* cease-fire ‖ *suspensión de pagos* suspension of payments.

suspensivo, va *adj* suspensive ‖ *puntos suspensivos* suspension points *o* marks.

suspenso, sa *adj* hanging, suspended; *suspenso en el aire* hanging in the air ‖ FIG baffled, bewildered (confuso) | amazed, astonished (pasmado) ‖ failed (alumno).
◆ *m* fail, failure (en un examen) ‖ — *dar un suspenso a alguien* to fail s.o. (en un examen) ‖ *en suspenso* pending, outstanding (cuestiones), outstanding (trabajo), in abeyance (pleito) ‖ *tener el corazón en suspenso* to be in suspense ‖ *tener un suspenso* to fail, to be failed.

suspensores *m pl* AMER braces [*US* suspenders] (tirantes).

suspensorio, ria *adj* suspensory.
◆ *m* suspensory bandage (vendaje) ‖ jockstrap (para deportistas).

suspicacia *f* distrust, mistrust, suspicion.

suspicaz *adj* suspicious, distrustful, untrusting.

suspirado, da *adj* FIG longed-for.

suspirar *vi* to sigh ‖ FIG *suspirar por* to long for, to sigh for; *suspira por un abrigo de visón* she longs for a mink coat.

suspiro *m* sigh; *dar un suspiro* to heave *o* to give a sigh ‖ breath (respiro) ‖ MÚS crotchet rest [*US* quarter rest] ‖ BOT pansy ‖ FIG sigh (del viento) ‖ glass whistle (pito) ‖ — FIG *deshacerse en suspiros* to heave deep sighs | *exhalar* or *dar el último suspiro* to breathe one's last | *lo que no va en lágrimas va en suspiros* she does nothing but weep and sigh.

sustancia; substancia *f* substance (materia); *¿de qué sustancia están hechos?* what substance are they made of ‖ extract; *sustancia de carne* meat extract ‖ FIL substance ‖ FIG substance, value; *sus argumentos tienen poca sustancia* his arguments have little value | substance, essence (lo esencial) ‖ importance (importancia) ‖ — FIG *en sustancia* in substance | *persona sin sustancia* or *de poca sustancia* uninteresting *o* dull person | *sin sustancia* lacking in substance ‖ ANAT *sustancia blanca* white matter | *sustancia gris* grey matter.

sustanciación; substanciación *f* JUR substantation.

sustancial; substancial *adj* substantial (grande, nutritivo, etc.) ‖ substantial, important; *no dijo nada sustancial* he didn't say anything important ‖ fundamental, essential, vital; *es el punto sustancial del discurso* it is the fundamental point of the speech.

sustancialismo; substancialismo *m* FIL substantialism.

sustanciar; substanciar *vt* to abridge, to condense (compendiar) || JUR to substantiate.

sustancioso, sa; substancioso, sa *adj* substantial, wholesome (comida, etc.) || FIG meaty (de mucha enjundia).

sustantivar; substantivar *vt* GRAM to use as a noun, to substantivate, to substantivize.

sustantividad; substantividad *f* GRAM substantiveness.

sustantivo, va; substantivo, va *adj* substantive || GRAM substantive, substantial, noun.

◆ *m* GRAM noun, substantive.

sustentación *f*; **sustentamiento** *m* sustenance || support (base) || suspension (retórica) || AVIAC lift.

sustentador, ra *adj* sustaining || AVIAC *superficie sustentadora* lifting surface.

sustentamiento *m* ⟶ **sustentación.**

sustentante *adj* sustaining || supporting (que apoya).

◆ *m* defender (de una tesis) || support (apoyo) || ARQ support, prop.

sustentar *vt* to support, to hold up (sostener) || to sustain, to nourish (alimentar) || to sustain, to support, to maintain, to feed (mantener); *sustentar una familia* to maintain a family || to maintain (afirmar) || to defend (teoría) || to feed, to foster (esperanzas).

◆ *vpr* to sustain o.s., to nourish o.s. (alimentarse) || to feed (*con* on), to live (*con* on), to live (comer) || to subsist (subsistir) || to be held up, to be supported (*con* by),(apoyarse en) || *sustentarse del aire* to live on air.

sustento *m* sustenance, food (alimento) || support (apoyo) || FIG livelihood, living (medios de subsistencia) || — *ganarse el sustento* to earn one's living || FIG *sustento principal* mainstay.

sustitución; substitución *f* substitution.

sustituible; substituible *adj* replaceable.

sustituidor, ra; substituidor, ra *adj/s* substitute.

sustituir*; substituir* *vt/vi* to substitute, to replace; *sustituyeron la bicicleta por la moto* they substituted the motorcycle for the bicycle, they replaced the bicycle with *o* by the motorcycle || to replace; *la República sustituyó a la Monarquía* the Republic replaced the Monarchy || to change, to replace (cambiar) || to stand in for, to take over from, to replace; *el vicepresidente sustituye al presidente cuando éste está de viaje* the vicepresident stands in for the president in his absence.

sustitutivo, va; substitutivo, va *adj* substitutive, substitute.

◆ *m* substitute (*de* for).

sustituto, ta; substituto, ta *m/f* substitute || TEATR understudy.

susto *m* fright, scare, shock; *me dio un susto horrible* it (*he, etc.*), gave me such a fright, I got such a fright || — FIG *caerse del susto* to be frightened to death, to get the fright of one's life || FIG & FAM *darle un susto al miedo* to be as ugly as sin, to be frightfully ugly, to be hideous || *dar un susto a alguien* to give s.o. a fright, to frighten *o* to scare s.o. || *darse* or *llevarse* or *pegarse un susto* to get a fright || FAM *llevarse un susto padre* to get the fright of one's life || FIG *no pasó del susto* I was more frightened than hurt || *¡qué susto me has dado!* you frightened the life out of me!

sustracción; substracción *f* theft (robo) || removal (extracción) || deduction || MAT subtraction (resta).

sustraendo; substraendo *m* MAT subtrahend (en una sustracción).

sustraer*; substraer* *vt* to steal (robar) || to remove (quitar) || to remove, to extract (extraer) || MAT to subtract || to deduct (deducir).

◆ *vpr* to elude, to evade; *se sustrajo a las preguntas indiscretas* he evaded the indiscreet questions || to resist; *sustraerse a la tentación* to resist temptation || to get out of *o* away from (compromisos, etc.).

susurrar *vi* to whisper, to murmur (hablar bajo); *susurrar al oído* to whisper in s.o.'s ear || FIG to murmur (el agua) | to rustle (hojas).

◆ *vpr* to be rumoured [*US* to be rumored], to be whispered; *se susurra que está casado* it is rumoured that he is married.

susurro *m* whisper, murmur || FIG murmur (del agua) | rustle (de las hojas).

susurrón, ona *adj* whispering, murmuring.

◆ *m/f* whisperer.

sutil *adj* thin, fine, light; *una sutil gasa* a thin gauze || gentle (viento) || FIG subtle; *una diferencia sutil* a subtle difference | keen, sharp (ingenioso).

sutileza; sutilidad *f* fineness, thinness (finura) || FIG subtlety (penetración) | sharpness, keenness (ingenio) | subtlety (dicho penetrante) | instinct (de los animales) || *sutileza de manos* dexterity (agilidad), light-fingeredness, deftness (del carterista).

sutilizar *vt* to make fine, to thin down (adelgazar) || FIG to polish, to refine (pulir) | to subtilize (hacer distinciones sutiles) | to quibble about (discutir) | to sharpen (agudizar).

◆ *vi* FIG to subtilize (actuar con sutileza) | to quibble, to split hairs (hilar fino).

sutra *m* sutra.

sutura *f* seam (unión) || MED suture || MED *punto de sutura* stitch.

suturar *vt* MED to suture, to stitch up.

suyo, ya *adj/pron pos* his (de él), hers (de ella), its (de cosas, animales, etc.), yours (de usted, de ustedes), theirs (de ellos, de ellas) (cuando va acompañado por el artículo o el verbo «ser»); *suyo no puede ser* it can't be his (hers, etc.); *él tiene el suyo en la mano* he's got his in his hand; *éste es el suyo* this is yours; *no encontraba los suyos* she couldn't find hers || his, of his (de él), her, of hers (de ella), its (de cosas, animales, etc.), your, of yours (de usted, de ustedes), their, of theirs (de ellos, de ellas) (con un sustantivo); *varios amigos suyos* several friends of theirs, several of their friends; *no vino ningún amigo suyo* none of his friends came, no friends of his came; *no es culpa suya* it is not your fault, it is no fault of yours || of his, of hers, of yours, of theirs (con un adjetivo demostrativo); *aquella idea suya* that idea of his; *ese amigo suyo* that friend of yours || one's own (de uno mismo) || — *aguantar lo suyo* to put up with a lot || *cada cual* or *cada uno a lo suyo* it is best to mind one's own business || *de suyo* in itself, by its very nature, intrinsically; *el asunto es de suyo complicado* the affair is complicated in itself || *AMER eso cae de suyo* that goes without saying || FIG *estar haciendo de las suyas* to be up to one's tricks | *hacer suyo* to echo (una opinión, etc.) | *ir a lo suyo* to go one's own way (ser independiente), to take care of one's own way (ser independiente), to take care of one's own interests, to look after number one (preocuparse por uno mismo) || *la culpa es suya* it's his (your, etc.) fault || *los suyos* his (her, etc.) family *o* friends *o* people *o* men *o* supporters *o* side; *los suyos vienen a pasar el fin de semana* his people are coming over for the weekend || *lo suyo* one's share (su parte), what one deserves; *recibirá lo suyo* he will get what he deserves || *muy suyo* typical of one; *una broma muy suya* a typical joke of his; very much his (hers, etc.) very like him (her, etc.); *el estilo es muy suyo* the style is very much his; aloof, reserved (reservado); *es muy suyo* he is very aloof || FIG & FAM *salirse con la suya* to get *o* to have one's own way; *Tomás siempre se sale con' la suya* Thomas always gets his own way || *suyo afectísimo* Yours faithfully *o* sincerely || FIG & FAM *una de las suyas* one of his (her, etc.) tricks | *ver la suya* to get one's chance.

svástica; swástica *f* swastika.

swing *m* swing (boxeo y jazz).

T

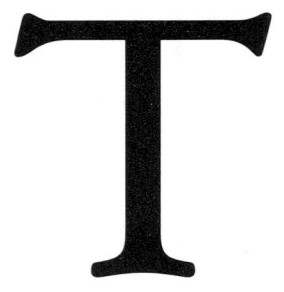

t *f* t (letra); *una t minúscula* a small t.

taba *f* ANAT astragalus, anklebone.
◆ *pl* knucklebones (juego).

tabacal *m* tobacco plantation.

tabacalero, ra *adj* tobacco; *la industria tabacalera* the tobacco industry.
◆ *m/f* tobacco grower (plantador) ‖ tobacconist (vendedor de tabaco).
◆ *f* Spanish state tobacco monopoly.

tabaco *m* tobacco ‖ BOT tobacco plant ‖ cigar (puro) ‖ cigarettes *pl* (cigarrillos); *¿tienes tabaco?* have you any cigarettes? ‖ snuff (rapé); *tomar tabaco* to take snuff ‖ tobacco (color) ‖ black rot (enfermedad de algunos árboles) ‖ — AMER FIG & FAM *acabársele el tabaco a uno* to run out of money ‖ *tabaco de hebra* long-cut tobacco ‖ *tabaco de hoja* leaf tobacco ‖ *tabaco de mascar* chewing tobacco ‖ *tabaco de pipa* pipe tobacco ‖ *tabaco en polvo* or *rapé* snuff ‖ *tabaco habano* Havana tobacco ‖ *tabaco negro* black *o* dark tobacco ‖ *tabaco picado* cut tobacco ‖ *tabaco rubio* Virginia tobacco.

tabalear *vt* to swing (balancear) ‖ to rock (mecer).
◆ *vi* to drum (con los dedos).

tabanco *m* stand, stall, booth (puesto de venta) ‖ AMER loft, attic (desván).

tábano *m* horsefly, gadfly (insecto).

tabaqueada *f* AMER fight, brawl (riña).

tabaquera *f* snuffbox (caja para rapé) ‖ tobacco box, tobacco jar (caja para tabaco) ‖ pipe bowl (de la pipa) ‖ AMER tobacco pouch (bolsa para tabaco).

tabaquería *f* tobacconist's, tobacco shop (tienda).

tabaquero, ra *adj* tobacco.
◆ *m/f* cigar maker (fabricante) ‖ tobacconist (vendedor).

tabaquismo *m* nicotinism.

tabardillo *m* typhoid fever (enfermedad) ‖ sunstroke (insolación) ‖ FIG & FAM pain in the neck (persona pesada).

tabardo *m* tabard.

tabarra *f* FAM pain in the neck ‖ *dar la tabarra* to be a pain in the neck.

tabarro *m* wasp (avispa) ‖ horsefly, gadfly (tábano).

tabasco *m* tabasco [sauce].

tabasqueño, ña *adj* [of *o* from] Tabasco (México).
◆ *m/f* native *o* inhabitant of Tabasco.

taberna *f* tavern (antiguamente), pub, bar (hoy).

tabernáculo *m* tabernacle.

tabernario, ria *adj* tavern ‖ FIG *lenguaje tabernario* taproom language.

tabernera *f* tavernkeeper (antiguamente) ‖ barmaid (camarera) ‖ landlady, publican (la que lleva la taberna).

tabernero *m* tavernkeeper (antiguamente) ‖ bartender, barman (barman) ‖ landlord, publican (el que lleva la taberna).

tabernucho *m*; **tabernucha** *f* FAM dive.

tabes *f* MED consumption, tabes.

tabica *f* rise, riser (de escalera).

tabicar *vt* to partition off (cerrar con tabique) ‖ to wall up, to brick up (una puerta, ventana).
◆ *vpr* to get stopped up, to get bunged up (las narices).

tabique *m* partition, (thin) wall ‖ *tabique nasal* nasal bone.

tabla *f* plank, board (de madera) ‖ slab (de piedra, de mármol) ‖ sheet (de metal) ‖ shelf (anaquel) ‖ ARTES panel ‖ pleat, box pleat (de un vestido) ‖ notice board [US bulletin board] (para anuncios) ‖ drawing board (de dibujante) ‖ index (de un libro) ‖ MAT table; *tabla de logaritmos* logarithm table; *tabla de multiplicar* multiplication table ‖ flat (de una parte del cuerpo) ‖ calm part [of a river] ‖ table, list (lista, catálogo) ‖ scale (de salarios) ‖ meat counter (mostrador de carnicero) ‖ AGR strip of land, plot, bed ‖ (ant) geographical map (mapa) | customs house ‖ — FIG & FAM *a raja tabla* vigorously, strictly; *cumplir una orden a raja tabla* to carry out an order to the letter ‖ *Caballeros de la Tabla Redonda* Knights of the Round Table ‖ FIG & FAM *hacer tabla rasa de* to make a clean sweep of ‖ FIG *salvarse en una tabla* to have a narrow escape, to escape by a hairsbreadth *o* by the skin of one's teeth ‖ DEP *tabla a vela* or *de windsurf* windsurfing board, sailboard ‖ *tabla de cocina* chopping board ‖ *tabla de dibujo* drawing board ‖ *tabla de juego* gambling den (casa de juego) ‖ *tabla de lavar* washboard ‖ *tabla de planchar* ironing board ‖ FIG *tabla de salvación* last hope (último recurso), salvation (salvación) ‖ DEP *tabla deslizadora* or *de surf* surfboard.
◆ *pl* TEATR stage *sing*, boards; *pisar las tablas* to go on the stage ‖ TAUR barrier *sing* (barrera) | part *sing* of the bullring closest to the barrier FIG & FAM *escaparse por tablas* to have a narrow escape *o* a close shave, to escape by the skin of one's teeth ‖ TEATR *pisar bien las tablas* to act well ‖ *quedar en tablas, hacer tablas* to draw (en ajedrez), to tie (empatar) ‖ *tablas alfonsinas* astronomical tables prepared by order of Alfonso X of Castile ‖ REL *Tablas de la Ley* Tables of the Law ‖ *tablas reales* backgammon (juego) ‖ FIG *tener muchas tablas* to have a lot of presence (actor), to be an old hand (sabérselas todas).

tablada *f* AMER AGR stockyard.

tablado *m* platform (suelo de tablas) ‖ stage (para representaciones teatrales) ‖ flooring (suelo de carro) ‖ scaffold (cadalso) ‖ bed frame (de cama) ‖ flamenco show ‖ — *sacar al tablado* to bring out (actor) ‖ *salir* or *subir al tablado* to go on the stage.

tablaje *m* planks *pl*, boards *pl* (conjunto de tablas) ‖ gambling den (garito).

tablajería *f* butcher's (carnicería) ‖ gambling (vicio de jugar).

tablajero *m* butcher (carnicero).

tablao *m* flamenco show.
— OBSERV *Tablao* is an Andalusian deformation of *tablado*.

tablazón *m* planking ‖ MAR decking (de la cubierta) | planking (del casco).

tableado, da *adj* pleated (falda, etc.).
◆ *m* pleats *pl* ‖ sawing into planks (de un madero) ‖ division into plots (de un huerto) ‖ levelling (del suelo) ‖ lamination, rolling (del hierro).

tablear *vt* to saw into planks (un madero) ‖ to divide into plots (un huerto) ‖ to level (el suelo) ‖ to pleat (la ropa) ‖ to laminate, to roll (hierro).

tableo *m* sawing into planks (de un madero) ‖ division into plots (de un huerto) ‖ levelling (del suelo) ‖ lamination, rolling (del hierro).

tablero, ra *adj* suitable for cutting into planks ‖ *madero tablero* timber.
◆ *m* panel, board ‖ blackboard (encerado) ‖ notice board [US bulletin board] (para anuncios) ‖ dashboard (de coche) ‖ instrument panel (de avión) ‖ chessboard (para jugar al ajedrez) ‖ draughtboard [US checkerboard] (para las damas) ‖ backgammon board (de tablas reales) ‖ floor, road (de puente) ‖ table top (de una mesa) ‖ gambling den (garito) ‖ beds *pl*, plots *pl* (de huerto) ‖ panel (de puerta) ‖ cutting table (del sastre) ‖ MAR partition, bulkhead (mamparo) ‖ ARQ panel ‖ ELECTR switchboard ‖ INFORM display board ‖ — *tablero de dibujo* drawing board ‖ FIG *tablero político* political scene.

tableta *f* block (de madera) ‖ tablet (pastilla); *una tableta para dolor de cabeza* a headache tablet ‖ — *tableta de chocolate* bar *o* tablet *o* slab of chocolate ‖ *tabletas de San Lázaro* rattle [used by lepers].

tableteado *m* rattling, rattle (sonido).

tabletear *vi* to rattle (con tablillas) ‖ FIG to rattle; *las ametralladoras tabletearon* the machine guns rattled.

tableteo *m* rattling, rattle.

tablilla *f* small board (tabla pequeña) ‖ small notice board [US bulletin board] ‖ cushion between pockets (billar) ‖ MED splint ‖ HIST tablet ‖ *tablillas de San Lázaro* rattle [used by lepers].

tablón *m* plank ‖ notice board [US bulletin board] ‖ springboard (trampolín) ‖ — FAM *agarrar* or *coger un tablón* to get drunk (emborracharse) ‖ *tablón de anuncios* notice board [US bulletin board].

tabor *m* MIL Spanish army unit of regular Moroccan troops.

tabú *m* taboo.

tabuco *m* hovel (tugurio).

tábula rasa *f* FIL tabula rasa.

tabulador *m* tabulator (de máquina de escribir).

tabuladora *f* tabulator, tabulating machine.

tabular *adj* tabular.

tabular *vt* to tabulate.

taburete *m* stool.

tac *m* tick (onomatopeya).

tacada *f* stroke (billar) ‖ break (carambolas en el billar) ‖ MAR wedges *pl.*

tacañear *vi* FAM to be stingy *o* mean *o* miserly (obrar con avaricia).

tacañería *f* stinginess, miserliness, meanness (avaricia) ‖ cunning (astucia).

tacaño, ña *adj* mean, stingy, miserly (avaro) ‖ cunning, sly, crafty (engañoso).
◆ *m/f* miser, skinflint (*fam*) (avaro) ‖ sly fox, crafty devil (engañoso).

tacatá; tacataca *m* baby walker.

tacita *f* small cup ‖ — FAM *la tacita de plata* the city of Cádiz ‖ FIG *ser una tacita de plata* to be as bright as a new pin.

tácito, ta *adj* tacit.

Tácito *npr m* Tacitus.

taciturno, na *adj* taciturn, silent (callado) ‖ melancholy, sullen (triste).

taco *m* plug, stopper (tarugo) ‖ wedge (cuña) ‖ plug (para sujetar algo en la pared) ‖ cue (de billar) ‖ ramrod (baqueta) ‖ plug, wad (cartucho, mina) ‖ writing pad (para escribir) ‖ book [of tickets]; *taco de billetes de metro* book of underground tickets ‖ wad [of notes]; *un taco de billetes de cinco libras* a wad of five-pound notes ‖ stub (parte que queda de un billete, etc.) ‖ snack, bite to eat (refrigerio) ‖ piece, cube (trocito); *un taco de jamón* a piece of ham ‖ drink of wine (de vino) ‖ peashooter (juguete de niños) ‖ stud (de la bota de fútbol) ‖ FIG & FAM swearword (palabrota) | mess, mix-up (lío) ‖ fritter (churro) ‖ AMER heel (del zapato) | «taco», rolled-up tortilla with filling ‖ — *calendario de taco* tear-off calendar ‖ FIG & FAM *estar hecho un taco* to be all mixed up | *hacerse* or *armarse un taco* to get all mixed up | *soltar tacos* to curse, to swear.

tacómetro *m* tachometer.

tacón *m* heel; *tacones altos* high heels; *tacón aguja* stiletto heel ‖ *de tacón alto* high-heeled (zapato).

taconazo *m* kick with the heel ‖ *dar un taconazo* to click one's heels.

taconear *vi* to tap one's heels.

taconeo *m* heel tapping.

táctico, ca *adj* tactical; *el uso táctico de los aviones* the tactical use of aircraft.
◆ *m* tactician.
◆ *f* MIL tactics (arte) | tactic (maniobra) ‖ FIG tactic.

táctil *adj* tactile.

tactismo *m* taxis (tropismo).

tacto *m* touch (sentido) ‖ touching, touch (acción de tocar) ‖ FIG tact (delicadeza); *falta de tacto* lack of tact ‖ — *al tacto* to the touch ‖ *mecanografía al tacto* touch-typing ‖ FIG *no tener tacto* to be tactless ‖ MIL *tacto de codos* elbows touching ‖ FIG *tener tacto* to be tactful.

tacuara *f* AMER bamboo.

tacurú *m* AMER small ant (hormiga) | anthill (hormiguero).

tacha *f* flaw, blemish, fault (defecto) ‖ blemish (descrédito) ‖ — *poner tachas a* to find fault with ‖ *sin tacha* flawless (cosa), unblemished (persona).

tachadura *f* erasure, crossing out (acción) ‖ crossing out; *esta página está llena de tachaduras* this page is full of crossings out.

tachar *vt* to erase (borrar); *tacha esta palabra* erase this word ‖ to cross out (con una raya) ‖ JUR to challenge ‖ to censure, to find fault with (censurar) ‖ FIG *tachar de* to accuse of; *le tachan de cobardía* they accuse him of cowardliness; to accuse of being; *le tachan de cobarde* they accuse him of being a coward.

tachero *m* AMER sugar factory worker (en una fábrica de azúcar) | tinsmith (hojalatero).

tacho *m* AMER boiler (caldero) | pan (paila) | bucket (cubo) ‖ AMER *irse al tacho* to fail (fracasar).

tachón *m* crossing out, erasure (tachadura) ‖ large stud (clavo).

tachonar *vt* to stud, to decorate with studs (adornar con clavos) ‖ to trim (con cintas) ‖ FIG to dot, to stud; *el cielo estaba tachonado de estrellas* the sky was dotted with stars.

tachuela *f* tack, stud (clavo) ‖ AMER metal pan (cacerola).

tafetán *m* taffeta (tela) ‖ sticking plaster (para heridas) ‖ *tafetán inglés* sticking plaster.
◆ *pl* FIG colours, flags, standards (bandera) | finery *sing*, frills (galas de mujer).

tafia *f* tafia, rum (aguardiente).

tafilete *m* Morocco leather (cuero).

tafiletear *vt* to cover *o* to decorate with Morocco leather.

tafiletería *f* Morocco leatherwork (arte de curtir) ‖ Morocco leather tannery (taller) ‖ Morocco leather shop (tienda).

tafiletero, ra *m/f* Morocco leather seller.

tagalo, la *adj/s* Tagalog (indígena de las Filipinas).
◆ *m* Tagalog (lengua de los tagalos).

tagarnina *f* BOT golden thistle ‖ FIG poor quality cigar ‖ FIG & FAM AMER drunkenness (borrachera).

tagarote *m* sparrow hawk (halcón) ‖ FIG & FAM longlegs (hombre alto) | scribe, clerk, pen-pusher (escribiente) | gentleman sponger (hidalgo que vive a expensas de los demás).

tagua *f* AMER coot (ave) | ivory palm, corozo palm (palmera) | corozo nut semilla.

tahalí *m* baldric.

Tahití *n pr* GEOGR Tahiti.

tahitiano, na *adj/s* Tahitian.
◆ *m* Tahitian (idioma).

tahona *f* bakery (panadería) ‖ flour mill (molino).

tahonero, ra *m/f* baker.

tahúlla *f* land measurement in southeast Spain of 11. 18 ares [= 0. 28 acres].

tahúr *m* cardsharper (fullero).

taicún *m* shogun, tycoon (título japonés).

taifa *f* faction, party (facción) ‖ FIG & FAM gang of ruffians (gente despreciable) ‖ *reyes de taifa* Moorish kings who ruled Spain after the breaking up of the caliphate of Cordova in 1031.

taiga *f* taiga (selva).

tailandés, esa *adj/s* Thai.

Tailandia *npr f* GEOGR Thailand.

taimado, da *adj* sly, shrewd, astute (disimulado) ‖ sullen, bad-humoured (malhumorado) ‖ AMER lazy (perezoso).

taimería *f* slyness, cunning, shrewdness, astuteness.

taino, na *adj/s* Taino (indio).
◆ *m* Taino (idioma).

Taipei *n pr* GEOGR Taipei.

taita *m* daddy (en lenguaje infantil).
— OBSERV In Argentina and Chile *taita* is used to address not only one's father but also other people worthy of respect; in the Caribbean it is used to address elderly Negro men, whilst among the gauchos of Argentina it means *matón* (bully).

Taiwan *npr f* GEOGR Taiwan.

tajada *f* cut, slice (porción); *tajada de melón* slice of melon ‖ — FIG & FAM *agarrar* or *coger una tajada* to get plastered (borracho) | *hacer tajadas* to cut to pieces | *llevarse la tajada del león, llevarse la mejor tajada* to take the lion's share *o* the largest part | *sacar tajada* to get one's share (sacar provecho) | *sacar tajada de todas partes* to do o.s. proud, to look after number one (aprovecharse de todo).

tajadera *f* chopper (cuchillo) ‖ cold chisel (cortafrío).

tajadero *m* chopping block (de carnicero).

tajado, da *adj* FIG & FAM canned, stewed, plastered (borracho).

tajamar *m* cutwater (de puente, barco) ‖ AMER dike, seawall (malecón) | dam (presa).

tajante *adj* cutting (que corta) ‖ FIG sharp, emphatic, categorical; *me dio un «no» tajante* he gave me a categorical «no».
◆ *m* butcher.

tajaplumas *m inv* penknife (cortaplumas).

tajar *vt* to cut, to chop, to slice (cortar) ‖ to trim, to sharpen (pluma de ave).

tajo *m* cut, incision (corte) ‖ slash (con espada, con cuchillo) ‖ cutting edge (filo) ‖ chopping block (para picar la carne) ‖ job, work (tarea y sitio de la tarea); *vamos al tajo* let's get on with the job ‖ steep cliff (escarpa alta) ‖ gorge (valle profundo); *el tajo de Ronda* the gorge of Ronda ‖ three-legged stool (taburete) ‖ executioner's block (del verdugo) ‖ AMER small path (caminito) ‖ — *mina a tajo abierto* opencast mine [US opencut mine] ‖ *tirar tajos y estocadas* to cut and thrust.

Tajo *npr m* GEOGR Tagus (río).

tal *adj* such; *tal es mi punto de vista* such is my point of view ‖ such, so great, so large (tan grande); *tal es su poder que todo el mundo le obedece* so great is his power that everyone obeys him ‖ such a, this, that; *no conozco a tal hombre* I don't know such a man ‖ a similar, such a (semejante); *en mi vida he visto tal espectáculo* I have never in my life seen such a thing ‖ such and such; *la calle tal* such and such a street ‖ — *como si tal cosa* just like that ‖ *de tal manera que* in such a way that, so that ‖ *el tal* that, that fellow; *el tal Juan* that fellow John ‖ *nunca te dije tal cosa* I never said any such thing, I said no such thing ‖ *tal como* such as (como por ejemplo) ‖ *tal cual* an occasional, one or two, a few; *la policía paró tal cual coche* the police stopped an occasional car; fair, so-so; *he comprado una tela tal cual* I have bought some fair material ‖ *tal vez* perhaps ‖ *tal y tal* one or two, a few (alguno que otro) ‖ *un tal* a certain, a man called; *un tal Rodríguez* a certain Rodríguez.
◆ *pron* such a thing (cosa); *no haré tal* I will do no such thing ‖ someone, someone or other (persona); *tal habrá que ya lo sepa* someone is bound to know ‖ — *como tal* as such ‖ *con tal que, con tal de que* provided that, as long as; *con tal de que vengas, todo irá bien* provided that you come all will go well ‖ *el tal* that one, that fellow, he; *el tal es muy astuto* that fellow is very cunning ‖ *fulano de tal* John Smith, Mr. So-and-So, Mr. what's his name ‖ *¡no hay tal!* no such thing! (es falso) ‖ *no hay tal como* there is nothing like; *no hay tal como pasar el día en el campo* there is nothing like spending a day in the country ‖ *otro que tal* another one ‖ *si tal hubiera* if that were true (si fuera verdad) ‖ *tal hay que* some people; *tal hay que opina igual* some people hold the same opinion ‖ *tal o cual* someone or other (personas indeterminadas) ‖ *tal para cual* two of a kind, birds of a feather ‖ FAM *una tal* a prostitute, a whore | *¡voto a tal!* damn it!, confound it! ‖ *y tal y cual* and so on and so forth, and so on (etcétera).
◆ *adv* so; *tal estaba de emocionado que no me vio* he was so excited that he didn't see me ‖ in such a way, as though; *tal hablaba que parecía que lo había visto* he talked in such a way that it seemed he had seen it, he talked as though he had seen it ‖ — *¿qué tal?* how; *¿qué tal le pareció la película?* how did you like the

film?; *¿qué tal el viaje?* how was the trip? ‖ FAM *¿qué tal?* how are you? ‖ *tal como, tal cual* the way; *tal como me lo dijo me pareció un insulto* the way he said it I took it as an insult; just as; *lo encontré tal como lo había dejado* I found it just as I had left it ‖ *tal cual* just as it is *o* as it was; *lo dejé todo tal cual* I left everything just as it was ‖ *tal... cual* like... like ‖ *tal y como están las cosas* the way things are at present.

tala *f* felling (de árboles) ‖ pruning (poda) ‖ destruction, desolation, ruin (destrucción) ‖ MIL abatis, defence made with tree trunks (defensa).

talabarte *m* sword belt (cinturón).

talabartería *f* saddlery (taller, tienda).

talabartero *m* saddler.

talache; talacho *m* AMER hoe (azada).

talador, ra *adj* cutting, felling (que tala) ‖ pruning (que poda).
◆ *m/f* cutter, feller (que tala) ‖ pruner (que poda).

taladrador, ra *adj* drilling, boring ‖ piercing.
◆ *m/f* driller, borer.
◆ *f* drill (máquina).

taladrar *vt* to bore, to drill (horadar) ‖ to pierce (perforar) ‖ to punch (billete) ‖ FIG to pierce (herir los oídos).

taladro *m* drill (taladradora) ‖ drill, bit (punta) ‖ gimlet (barrena) ‖ drill hole (agujero).

talamete *m* MAR foredeck.

tálamo *m* nuptial bed (lecho conyugal) ‖ nuptial chamber (alcoba conyugal) ‖ BOT thalamus (receptáculo de una flor) ‖ ANAT thalamus; *tálamos ópticos* optic thalami.

talán *m* clang, dingdong (de campana).

talanquera *f* fence (valla) ‖ barrier, barricade (de defensa) ‖ FIG refuge, shelter (refugio).

talante *m* humour, mood, disposition, temper (humor); *estar de buen, de mal talante* to be in good, in a bad mood ‖ will (voluntad) ‖ — *hacer algo de buen talante* to do sth. willingly, to do sth. with good grace ‖ *hacer algo de mal talante* to do sth. unwillingly, to do sth. reluctantly, to do sth. with ill grace.

talar *adj* full-length, long (largo).
◆ *m pl* MIT talaria (alas de Mercurio).

talar *vt* to fell, to cut (cortar) ‖ to prune (podar) ‖ FIG to destroy, to ruin, to lay waste (destruir).

talareño, ña *adj* [of *o* from] Talara (Perú).
◆ *m/f* native *o* inhabitant of Talara (Perú).

talasocracia *f* thalassocracy.

talasoterapia *f* MED thalassotherapy, salt water *o* sea air cure.

talavera *m* Talavera pottery (cerámica).

talayote *m* talayot, prehistoric stone tower [in the Balearics].

talco *m* talc (mineral) ‖ tinsel (lámina metálica) ‖ *polvos de talco* talcum powder.

talcualillo *adj* FAM fair, so-so (regular) | so-so, no so bad (de salud).

taled *m* tallith (velo judío).

talega *f* bag, sack; *talega de ropa sucia* laundry bag ‖ bagful, sackful, bag, sack (contenido); *una talega de arroz* a bagful of rice ‖ nappy [*US* diaper] (pañal) ‖ hairnet (para proteger el peinado) ‖ FIG & FAM wealth, money (dinero) | sins *pl* (pecados).

talegada *f* bagful, suckful (contenido).

talegazo *m* fall (caída) ‖ blow (golpe).

talego *m* bag, sack (saco).

taleguilla *f* small sack *o* bag (talega pequeña) ‖ TAUR bullfighter's breeches *pl* (calzón).

talento *m* talent; *un hombre de mucho talento* a man of great talent ‖ talent, gift; *tiene talento para pintar* he has a gift for painting ‖ aptitude (capacidad) ‖ intelligence, cleverness (inteligencia) ‖ talent (moneda, peso).

talentoso, sa; talentudo, da *adj* talented, gifted.

talero *m* AMER short whip.

Tales *npr m* Thales.

Talgo *abrev de Tren Articulado Ligero Goicoechea-Oriol* Talgo [articulated train of Spanish invention].

Talía *npr f* MIT Thalia.

talio *m* thallium (metal).

talión *m* talion, retaliation.

talismán *m* talisman, amulet, (lucky) charm.

talmente *adv* FAM exactly like (exactamente como) | so (tan).

Talmud *npr m* Talmud.

talmúdico, ca *adj* Talmudic, Talmudical.

talo *m* BOT thallus.

talófitas *f pl* BOT thallophytes.

talón *m* heel (de pie, calzado, media) ‖ MÚS heel (del arco del violín) ‖ heel (de las caballerías) ‖ MAR heel (de la quilla) ‖ flange (del neumático) ‖ ARQ talon, ogee moulding (moldura) ‖ voucher, receipt, coupon (bono, recibo, etc.) ‖ cheque [*US* check] (cheque) ‖ monetary standard (patrón monetario) ‖ — FIG & FAM *apretar los talones* to take to one's heels, to show a clean pair of heels | *ir pegado a* or *pisarle a uno los talones* to be on s.o.'s heels, to follow close on s.o.'s heels, to tread on s.o.'s heels (seguir, competir) ‖ ECON *talón bancario* counter cheque | *talón confirmado* certified cheque ‖ *talón de Aquiles* Achilles' heel ‖ ECON *talón devuelto* bounce cheque | *talón en blanco* blank cheque | *talón sin fondos* dud *o* bad cheque [*US* rubber cheque].

talonada *f* kick with the heel [to spur one's horse].

talonador *m* DEP hooker (rugby).

talonaje *m* DEP heeling, heeling out (rugby).

talonar *vt* DEP to heel out (rubgy).

talonario, ria *adj* with stubs ‖ *libro talonario* stub book.
◆ *m* book of vouchers, book of coupons, book of receipts, stub book (de vales, de recibos) ‖ chequebook [*US* checkbook] (de cheques).

talonazo *m* kick with the heel.

talonera *f* heel piece (de medias, de calcetines) ‖ binding (de pantalones).

talquera *f* powder box (para polvos de talco).

talud *m* talus, slope.

talla *f* carving (en madera) ‖ engraving (del metal) ‖ cutting (de piedras preciosas) ‖ height, stature (estatura); *hombre de poca talla* man of small stature ‖ size (de ropa) ‖ tally, measuring stick (palo para medir) ‖ hand (juego de baraja) ‖ tallage (tributo antiguo) ‖ MED lithotomy, removal of gallstones (operación de vejiga) ‖ reward (premio) ‖ MAR purchase block ‖ AMER chat (charla) ‖ — FIG *dar la talla* to be up to scratch | *de talla* prominent, outstanding | *ser de talla para, tener talla para* to be cut out for (ser capaz de).

tallado, da *adj* carved (madera) ‖ cut (piedra) ‖ engraved (metal) ‖ shaped, formed.
◆ *m* carving (en madera) ‖ engraving (en metal) ‖ cutting (de piedras preciosas).

tallador *m* engraver (grabador) ‖ MIL man who measures recruits.

tallar *adj* ready for cutting; *leña tallar* wood ready for cutting.
◆ *m* forest ready for cutting (bosque).

tallar *vt* to carve (madera) ‖ to engrave (metal) ‖ to cut (piedras preciosas) ‖ to measure the height of (medir) ‖ to deal (en los juegos de azar) ‖ to tax (imponer tributos) ‖ to appraise (tasar).
◆ *vi* AMER to chat (charlar) | to court (cortejar).

tallarín *m* noodle.

talle *m* waist (cintura); *talle de avispa* wasp waist ‖ figure, shape (de mujer); *talle esbelto* svelte figure ‖ physique, build (de hombre) ‖ measurement from shoulder to waist (en costura).

tallecer* *vi* BOT to sprout, to shoot (entallecer).

taller *m* workshop, shop; *taller de cerámica, de montaje* ceramic, assembly workshop ‖ studio, atelier (de pintor, escultor) ‖ garage, repair shop (de reparaciones de coche) ‖ factory, plant (fábrica).

tallo *m* BOT stem, stalk (de la planta) | sprout, shoot (renuevo) ‖ AMER BOT cabbage (col).

tamal *m* AMER tamale, minced meat and red peppers wrapped in corn husk or banana leaves | package (bulto) ‖ AMER FAM intrigue (intriga).

tamalería *f* AMER tamale shop.

tamalero, ra *m/f* AMER tamale maker (que hace tamales) | tamale seller (vendedor).

tamandúa *m* tamandua, tree-dwelling anteater.

tamango *m* AMER (gaucho's) boot (calzado).

tamañito, ta *adj* FIG & FAM confused (confundido) ‖ *dejarle a uno tamañito* to make s.o. feel small.

tamaño, ña *adj* such a big, so big a (tan grande); *no se puede superar tamaña dificultad* we cannot overcome so big an obstacle ‖ such a small, so small a (tan pequeño) ‖ — FAM *abrir tamaños ojos* to open one's eyes wide ‖ *tamaño como* as large as (tan grande como), as small as (tan pequeño como).
◆ *m* size; *¿de qué tamaño son los zapatos?* what size are the shoes? ‖ dimensions *pl* (dimensión) ‖ volume, capacity (volumen) ‖ FIG importance (importancia) ‖ — *del tamaño de* as large as ‖ INFORM *tamaño de la memoria* memory size ‖ *tamaño natural* life size.

támara *f* date palm (palmera) ‖ date palm grove (terreno poblado de palmeras).
◆ *pl* cluster *sing* of dates.

tamarao *m* tamarau, Philippine buffalo.

tamarindo *m* BOT tamarind (árbol, fruta).

tamarisco; tamariz *m* BOT tamarisk (taray).

tamarugal *m* AMER grove of carob trees.

tamarugo *m* AMER carob tree.

tamba *f* AMER Indian wrap-around skirt.

tambaleante *adj* staggering, tottering, reeling ‖ wobbly (mueble) ‖ FIG unstable, shaky; *instituciones tambaleantes* shaky institutions.

tambalear *vpr* to stagger, to totter, to reel ‖ to wobble (mueble) ‖ FIG to be unstable *o* shaky; *las estructuras de esta organización se tambalean* the foundations of this organization are shaky.

tambaleo *m* staggering, tottering, unsteadiness, reeling (de persona) ‖ wobbliness (de mueble).

tambarria *f* AMER rave, good time [*US* blast, ball] (jolgorio).

tambero, ra *adj* AMER tame (manso) | dairy (ganado).
◆ *m/f* AMER innkeeper (ventero) | dairy farmer (granjero).

también *adv* also, too, as well, likewise (igualmente) ‖ — *¿también?* that as well? ‖ *yo* *también* me too, so am I (so do I, so was I, etc.).

tambo *m* AMER inn (parador) | dairy farm (vaquería).

tambor *m* drum (instrumento) || drummer (persona) || ANAT eardrum (tímpano del oído) || sieve, sifter (para el azúcar) || revolving drum (de rifa o lotería) || tambour, embroidery frame (para bordar) || roaster (para tostar café) || ARQ drum, tambour (de cúpula o columna) | small room, cubicle (aposento) || cylinder (de revólver) || TECN cylinder, barrel (cilindro) | drum (de lavadora) | brake drum (del freno) || MAR paddle box (en los vapores) | capstan (para enrollar un cable) || FIG *a tambor batiente* in triumph, triumphantly (triunfalmente) || INFORM *tambor magnético* magnetic drum.

tamborear *vi* ⟶ **tamborilear.**

tamboril *m* MÚS small drum, tabor.

tamborilear; tamborear *vi* to drum (con los dedos) || to beat (el tamboril) || FIG to patter, to pitter-patter (la lluvia).

◆ *vt* to praise, to extol (alabar) || IMPR to plane (down).

tamborileo *m* drumming, beating.

tamborilero *m* drummer.

tamborilete *m* IMPR planer || MÚS small drum.

tamborín; tamborino *m* MUS tabor.

Támesis *npr m* GEOGR Thames.

tamil *adj* Tamil.

tamiz *m* sieve, sifter || — FIG *pasar por el tamiz* to screen, to sift || *tamiz vibratorio* vibrating screen.

tamizar *vt* to sieve, to sift, to pass through a sieve; *tamizar harina* to sift flour || to filter (luz) || FIG to screen (seleccionar).

tampoco *adv* not either, nor, neither; *tampoco va Juan* John is not going either, nor is John going, neither is John going; *mi madre no contestó y yo tampoco* my mother didn't answer and I didn't either *o* neither did I.

tampón *m* ink pad (para entintar).

tam tam *m* MÚS tom-tom.

tamujal *m* buckthorn patch.

tamujo *m* BOT buckthorn.

tamul *adj/s* Tamil.

◆ *m* Tamil (idioma).

tan *m* rat-a-tat-tat, rub-a-dub (del tambor) || clang, dong (de la campana).

tan *adv* (apócope de tanto) so; *no seas tan necio* don't be so stupid || such, so; *no necesito un piso tan grande* I do not need such a large flat, I do not need so large a flat || — *cuan... tan* as... as; *cuan bueno el padre, tan malo el hijo* the father is as good as the son is bad || *de tan bueno, acaba por parecer tonto* he is so good-natured that he appears stupid || *de tan... como* because... so, so... that; *no podía dormir de tan preocupado como estaba* I was so worried that I could not sleep, I could not sleep because I was so worried || *ni tan siquiera* even || *¡qué... tan!* what a...; *¡qué chica tan guapa!* what a pretty girl! || *tan... como* as... as; *tan malo como su hermano* as bad as his brother; *tan fácilmente como usted dice* as easily as you say || *tan es así que...* so much so that... || *tan pronto como* as soon as || *tan... que* so (that); *el viento es tan fuerte que rompe las ramas* the wind is so trong (that) it breaks the branches || *tan siquiera* just, only; *si tuviera tan siquiera mil pesetas* if I had just *o* if only I had a thousand pesetas || *tan sólo* only, merely, just; *tan sólo quiero que me dejen en paz* I only want them to leave me alone || *tan sólo con* (con infinitivo) just by (con gerundio); *tan solo con decirme la verdad* just by telling me the truth || *tan sólo con que* (con subjuntivo) if only; *tan sólo con que vayas a verla* if only you go to see him || *tan sólo te pido que me dejes tranquilo* all I want is to be left alone, the only thing I ask of you is that you leave me alone.

— OBSERV The from *tan* can only precede adjectives, adverbs and nouns used as adjectives: *me encuentro tan a gusto aquí* I feel so comfortable here; *soy tan poeta como tú* I am just as much a poet as you. When *tan* and an adjective precede a noun, the indefinite article is not used in Spanish: *tan importante negocio* such an important business.

tanagra *f* tanagra (estatuita) || ZOOL tanager, tanagra (ave).

Tananarivo *n pr* GEOGR Antananarivo.

tanate *m* AMER leather bag (zurrón de cuero) || FIG & FAM AMER *cargar con los tanates* to pack one's bags.

tanda *f* group (grupo) || layer (capa); *una tanda de ladrillos* a layer of bricks || series *inv* (serie) || shower (de golpes) || batch (cantidad); *¿cuándo sale la próxima tanda de pan?* when will the next batch of bread be ready? || job (tarea) || shift (grupo de obreros, período de trabajo); *tiene la tanda de diez a seis* he is on the ten till six shift || turn (turno) || AGR turn to use the water (disfrute del agua) || game (partida); *una tanda de billar* a game of billiards || AMER performance (representación) | bad habit (resabio).

tándem *m* tandem.

tandeo *m* distribution of irrigation water by turns.

Tanganica *npr m* GEOGR Lake Tanganyica.

tanganillas (en) *adj* shaky, insecure, unsteady, unsafe.

tanganillo *m* support, prop.

tángano, na *adj* AMER short, squat (bajito).

tangará *m* ZOOL tanager, tanagra (ave).

tangencia *f* tangency.

tangencial *adj* tangential.

tangente *adj/sf* tangent || FIG & FAM *salirse por la tangente* to fly off *o* to go off at a tangent (hacer una digresión), to evade the issue, to dodge the question (esquivar una pregunta).

Tánger *n pr* GEOGR Tangier.

tangerino, na *adj* [of *o* from] Tangier, Tangerine.

◆ *m/f* native *o* inhabitant of Tangier, Tangerine.

tangible *adj* tangible, palpable.

tango *m* MÚS tango.

tangón *m* MAR boom (botalón).

tanguear *vi* to tango.

tanguista *f* cabaret girl [US taxi girl].

tánico, ca *adj* QUÍM tannic.

tanino *m* QUÍM tannin.

tanque *m* tank, resevoir (depósito) || MIL tank (carro de combate) || tanker (barco cisterna) || road tanker (camión cisterna).

tanquista *m* MIL tanker.

tanrec *m* ZOOL tenrec, tanrec.

tanta *f* AMER cornbread.

tantalio *m* QUÍM tantalum.

tántalo *m* QUÍM tantalum || ZOOL wood stork.

Tántalo *npr m* MIT Tantalus.

tantán tom-tom (tambor) || gong (batintín).

tantarán; tantarantán *m* rat-a-tat-tat, rub-a-dub (sonido del tambor) || FIG & FAM bang (golpe).

tanteador *m* scorekeeper, scorer (persona) || scoreboard (marcador) || scorer (goleador).

tantear *vt* to work out roughly, to estimate, to guess (calcular aproximadamente) || to size up, to gauge (medir); *estoy tanteando la tela a ver si hay bastante para una blusa* I am sizing up the material to see if there is enough for a blouse || FIG to try out, to test (ensayar, probar) | to sound out (la actitud de una persona) | to examine, to study (un proyecto) || to keep the score of (el juego) || to sketch, to outline (un dibujo) || FIG *tantear el terreno* to see how the land lies.

◆ *vi* to grope, to feel one's way (titubear) || DEP to keep score, to score.

tanteo *m* rough estimate, approximate calculation (cálculo aproximado) || sizing up (medida) || test (prueba) || study, examination (examen) || sounding (sondeo) || groping, feeling one's way (titubeo) || DEP score || ARTES outline, sketch.

1. ADJETIVO **2.** ADVERBIO **3.** SUSTANTIVO **4.** PRONOMBRE.

1. ADJETIVO so much (singular), so many (plural); *no bebas tanto vino* don't drink so much wine; *¡tengo tantos amigos!* I have so many friends! || as much (singular), as many (plural) (comparación): *tengo tanto dinero como él* I have as much money as he; *tengo tantos amigos como ella* I have as many friends as she || — *de* or *con tanto* through so much, with so much, because of so much: *me he vuelto ronco de tanto hablar* I have become hoarse with talking so much || *no ser como para* to be not enough *o* not as many to: *la diferencia no fue tanta como para hacer variar el resultado* the difference was not enough to alter the result || *otros tantos, otras tantas* so many more, as many more: *las estrellas son otros tantos soles* the stars are so many more suns || *tanto tiempo* such a long time, so long || *y tantos, y tantas* just over, odd: *mil pesetas y tantas* just over a thousand pesetas; something: *el año mil novecientos setenta y tantos* the year nineteen seventy something.

2. ADVERBIO so much:*no hables tanto* don't talk so much; *trabaja tanto que nunca tiene tiempo para descansar* he works so much that he never has time to rest || such a long time, so long: *para venir aquí no tardará tanto* he won't take such a long time to get here; *hace tanto que no lo veo* it has been so long since I last saw him || so often: *tanto me has dicho su nombre que ya me acuerdo* you have told me his name so often that it has stuck || — *a tanto* to such an extent, to such a degree: *a tanto había llegado la decadencia* things had deteriorated to such a degree || *cuanto más... tanto más* the more... the more: *cuanto más sufro tanto más me hacen sufrir* the more I suffer, the more they make me suffer || *en tanto, entre tanto, mientras tanto* in the meantime, meanwhile || *en tanto que* as long as, while, whilst (mientras que), until (hasta que) | *eso es tanto como* that is like, that is as good as: *eso es tanto como decir que es estúpido* that is like saying he's stupid || *hasta tanto que* as long as || *ni tanto así* not even this much || *ni tanto ni tan calvo, ni tanto ni tan poco* neither one extreme nor the other || *no es tanto como para* it is nothing to *o* not enough to, it is not worth: *no es tanto como para enfadarte* it is nothing to get angry about, it is not worth losing your temper over || *no tanto... como* not so much... as: *su fracaso no se debe tanto a su ignorancia como a su pereza* his failure is due not so much to his ignorance as to his lazyness || *no... tanto como para* not... enough to: *no ha bebido tanto como para ponerse enfermo* he didn't drink enough to make him ill || *por lo tanto, por tanto* so, therefore || *tanto así* just like that || *tanto bueno, tanto bueno por aquí* so good to see you || *tanto... como* both, as well as: *tanto aquí como allí* here as well as there, both here

and there; as much... as: *de eso sé tanto como él* I know as much about this as he || *¡tanto como eso!* as much as that! || *tanto como una belleza no es, pero mona sí* I wouldn¡t go so far as to say she's beautiful, but she's certainly pretty || *tanto cuanto* as much as: *tiene tanto cuanto dinero necesita* he has as much money as he needs || *tanto más* the more, all the more || *tanto más... cuanto más* the more... the more || *tanto más... cuanto que* all the more... since *o* because || *tanto mejor* all the better, so much the better || *tanto menos* all the less || *tanto peor* so much the worse, too bad || *tanto si... como si* whether... or: *tanto si como como si no come, se va a morir* he will die whether he eats or not || FIG & FAM *tanto vales cuanto tienes* a man is worth as much as he owns || *tanto y más* as much and more || *¡y tanto!* and how!, you can say that again!
2. SUSTANTIVO point (en un juego) || DEP goal (en el fútbol): *marcar un tanto* to score a goal || counter (ficha) || chip (en el póker) || certain sum *o* amount (suma): *se paga un tanto al contado y el resto a plazos* a certain amount is paid in cash and the rest in instalments || percentage, part: *me darás un tanto de la ganancia* you will give me a percentage of the profit || — *algún tanto* somewhat, a bit: *el calor ha cedido algún tanto* the heat has let up somewhat || *apuntar* or *señalar los tantos* to keep score || *apuntarse un tanto* to score a point || COM *a tanto alzado* on a lump sum basis || *estar al tanto* to be up to date (estar al día): *estoy al tanto de las noticias* I am up to date on the news; tobe on the alert (estar a la expectativa) || *¿estás al tanto? do you know anything about it?, do you know the latest?, have you heard?* || *las tantas* late: *son las tantas* it is late; *vino a las tantas de la noche* he came late at night || *poner al tanto* to bring up to date (poner al corriente), to let know, to inform: *le pondré al tanto de lo que hayamos decidido* I'll let you know what we decide || COM *tanto alzado* overall price, lump sum || *tanto por ciento* percentaje || *tener al tanto* to keep up to date || FIG *un tanto* somewhat, a little, rather: *es un tanto perezoso* he is somewhat lazy | *un tanto a favor de alguien* a point in s.o.'s favour | *un tanto en contra de alguien* a point against s.o., a black mark.
4. PRONOMBRE so much (singular), so many (plural): *cada uno tiene que pagar tanto* each has to pay so much; *vinieron tantos que no sabíamos cómo alojarlos* so many people came that we did not know where to put them all || this, that: *a tanto conduce el vicio* that is where vice gets you || — *a tantos de* one day iň, sometime in: *llegaron a tantos de agosto* they arrived sometime in August || *no es para tanto* there is no need to make such a fuss || *otros tantos* just as many, as many more; *se marcharon veinte y otros tantos llegaron* twenty left and just as many arrived || *otro tanto* the same (lo mismo), as much again (el doble) || *uno de tantos* nothing special, one of many: *él es uno de tantos* he is nothing special.

tanto, ta copie ci-jointe.

tanza *f* line (pesca).

Tanzania *n pr* GEOGR Tanzania.

tañer* *vt* to play; *tañer un instrumento* to play an instrument.
◆ *vi* to toll (las campanas) || to drum (tabalear).

tañido *m* sound (de un instrumento) || tolling (de las campanas).

tao *m* tau [badge of the orders of St Anthony and St John].

taoísmo *m* Taoism.

taoísta *adj/s* Taoist.

tapa *f* lid; *la tapa de un baúl* the lid of a trunk; *la tapa de un pupitre* the lid of a desk || top; *la tapa de una botella* a bottle top || cover (de libro) || AUT head (de cilindro) || lift (capa del tacón) || savoury tidbit, appetizer (para tomar con bebidas) || gate (compuerta de canal) || horny part (casco del caballo) || round [of beef] (de las reses) || — FIG & FAM *levantar* or *saltar la tapa de los sesos a alguien* to blow s.o.'s brains out | *levantarse* or *saltarse la tapa de los sesos* to blow one's brains out (suicidarse) || *tapa blanda* flexible paper binding.
— OBSERV *Tapas* are savoury tidbits (olives, salted nuts, pieces of cheese or sausage, etc.) served in Spanish bars to accompany a drink.

tapabarro *m* AMER mudguard (guardabarros).

tapaboca *f* scarf, muffler (bufanda).

tapabocas *m inv* scarf, muffler (bufanda) || MIL tampion (del cañón).

tapacubos *m inv* AUT hubcap.

tapaculo *m* ZOOL fish resembling sole (pez) || BOT hip (escaramujo).

tapada *f* veiled woman || AMER denial (mentís).

tapadera *f* cover, lid, top; *la tapadera de un cazo* the lid of a pot || plug, stopper (para un agujero) || FIG cover, front (encubridor).

tapadillo *m* covering one's face with a veil *o* scarf || MÚS flute stop (del órgano) || FAM *de tapadillo* secretly.

tapado, da *adj* covered (cubierto) || wrapped (envuelto) || AMER all the same colour (caballo, yegua).
◆ *m* AMER coat (abrigo) | buried treasure (tesoro enterrado).

tapador, ra *adj* covering.
◆ *m* cover, lid, top (tapa) || plug, stopper (para agujeros) || FIG cover.

tapadura *f* covering (cobertura) || plugging, stopping up (de un agujero).

tapafunda *f* flap (de pistolera).

tapagujeros *m inv* FIG & FAM botcher, bad brick-layer *o* mason | stand-in (sustituto).

tapajuntas *m inv* ARQ fillet [sealing door or window joints].

tápalo *m* AMER shawl, cloak (chal o mantón).

tapanco *m* AMER loft (desván) | bamboo awning (toldo).

tapar *vt* to cover; *la colcha tapa las mantas* the bedspread covers the blankets || to wrap up (con ropa) || to cover (en la cama) || to hide, to cover (up); *las nubes tapaban el sol* clouds hid the sun || to plug, to stop, to stop up (un agujero) || to put the top on (una botella) || to put the lid on (una lata, cacerola, etc.) || FIG to conceal, to hide (un criminal) | to cover up (una falta) | to obstruct, to block (la vista) || AMER to fill (empastar) || MIL to stop up (una brecha) || *tener la nariz tapada* to have a blocked-up nose.
◆ *vpr* to cover up, to wrap up (abrigarse) || to cover (up); *taparse los oídos* to cover (up) one's ears.

tapara *f* AMER gourd.

taparo *m* AMER gourd tree.

taparrabo *m* loincloth (de salvaje) || bathing trunks *pl* (bañador).

tape *m* AMER Guarani Indian.

tapera *f* AMER ruined village (pueblo) | hovel, shack (vivienda).

tapete *m* runner (de mesa) || rug (alfombra) || — FIG *estar sobre el tapete* to be under consideration, to be on the carpet | *poner sobre el tapete* to put on the carpet, to bring up || *tapete verde* gambling table.

tapia *f* adobe *o* mud wall (de adobe) || wall (muro de cerca) || — FIG & FAM *mas sordo que una tapia* as deaf as a post | *saltar la tapia* to go over the wall.

tapiar *vt* to wall in, to enclose (cerrar con tapias) || FIG to brick up, to wall up, to close up; *tapiar una ventana* to wall up a window.

tapicería *f* tapestry making (arte o industria de hacer tapices) || tapestries *pl* (tapices) || upholstery material (tela para tapizar) || upholsterer's (tienda de tela para muebles) || draper's (tienda de cortinajes) || upholstery (de coche, de muebles).

tapicero, ra *m/f* tapestry maker (que hace tapices) || upholsterer (que tapiza muebles, etc.).

tapioca *f* tapioca.

tapir *m* ZOOL tapir.

tapisca *f* AMER corn harvest.

tapiscar *vt* AMER to harvest [corn].

tapiz *m* tapestry.

tapizar *vt* to tapestry, to hang with tapestries (una pared) || to upholster (muebles, un coche) || to carpet (el suelo).

tapón *m* stopper, cork (de las botellas) || bung (de tonel) || top (tapa) || MED tampon || FIG & FAM shorty, shorthouse (persona) || FIG obstruction (obstrucción) || — FIG & FAM *al primer tapón, zurrapa* unlucky from the beginning || FIG *estado tapón* buffer state || *tapón corona* cap, top || FIG & FAM *tapón de alberca* or *de cuba* shorty, shorthouse (persona) || *tapón de cerumen* wax in the ear || *tapón de desagüe* drain plug || *tapón de espita* spigot || *tapón de rosca* or *de tuerca* screw-on cap.

taponamiento *m* MED tamponage, tamponade || traffic jam (de coches) || closing (de una brecha) || plugging, stopping up (de un agujero).

taponar *vt* to plug, to stop up (un orificio) || to close up; *taponar la brecha* to close up the gap || to cork, to stopper (una botella) || MED to tampon.

taponazo *m* pop (ruido) || FAM shot (fútbol) || *recibir un taponazo en el ojo* to be hit in the eye by a flying cork.

taponería *f* corks *pl*, stoppers *pl* (tapones) || cork *o* stopper factory (fábrica) || cork *o* stopper store (tienda) || cork *o* stopper industry (industria).

taponero, ra *adj* cork, stopper; *industria taponera* stopper industry.
◆ *m/f* cork *o* stopper maker, cork *o* stopper seller.

tapujo *m* muffler (para la cara) || FIG deceit (engaño) | secrecy (secreto).

taqué *m* TECN stopper, stop.

taquear *vt* AMER to ram (un arma) | to fill (llenar).
◆ *vi* AMER to tap one's heels (taconear).

taquera *f* rack for billiard cues.

taquería *f* AMER «taco» shop.

taquero, ra *m/f* AMER «taco» seller.

taquicardia *f* MED tachycardia.

taquigrafía *f* shorthand, stenography.

taquigrafiar *vt* to write in shorthand, to stenograph.

taquigráficamente *adv* in shorthand.

taquigráfico, ca *adj* shorthand || *actas taquigráficas* verbatim record (de una reunión).

taquígrafo, fa *m/f* stenographer, shorthand writer || verbatim reporter (de una conferencia).

taquilla *f* filing cabinet (archivador) || set of pigeon-holes (mueble de casillas) || booking office, ticket office (en las estaciones, etc.) || TEATR box office || locker (armario) || FIG takings *pl*, returns *pl* box office (dinero cobrado)

|| FIG *hacer taquilla, tener buena taquilla, ser un éxito de taquilla* to be good box office (una película, un artista, etc.).

taquillero, ra *adj* good box office (película, actor) || *éxito taquillero* box-office success.
◆ *m/f* ticket clerk, booking clerk.

taquimeca *f* FAM shorthand typist.

taquimecanógrafa *f* shorthand typist.

taquimetría *f* tachymetry.

taquímetro *m* tachymeter.

tara *f* tare (peso) || defect (defecto) || tally, tally stick (tarja).

tarabilla *f* millclapper (de molino) || catch, latch (de ventana, de puerta) || wooden peg [used to tighten the cord of a frame saw] (de sierra) || FIG & FAM chatterbox (persona) | jabber, chatter (retahíla de palabras desordenadas) || AMER bull roarer (juguete).

tarabita *f* tongue (de la cincha) || AMER rope [of a cableway].

taracea *f* marquetry, intarsia.

taracear *vt* to inlay; *taraceado con marfil* inlaid with ivory.

tarado, da *adj* defective, damaged (mercancía) || handicapped (persona).

tarambana *adj* mad, wild (alocado).
◆ *m/f* crackpot, madcap.

taranta *f* type of flamenco song (canto) || AMER fit (locura pasajera) | whim (idea pasajera) | fainting spell (desmayo) | drunkenness (borrachera).

tarantela *f* tarantella (baile y música).

tarántula *f* tarantula (araña) || FIG *picado de la tarántula* nervous, jumpy.

tarar *vt* to tare.

tarará *f* tantara, tantarara [trumpet blast].

tararear *vt* to hum.

tarareo *m* humming.

tarasca *f* monster (monstruo) || FIG & FAM hag, battle-axe (mujer de carácter violento) || AMER big mouth.

tarascada *f* bite (mordedura) || scratch (arañazo) || FIG & FAM sharp retort (contestación).

tarascar *vt* to bite.

tarascón *m*; **tarascona** *f* monster (monstruo) || AMER bite (mordedura).

taray *m* BOT salt cedar, tamarisk.

tarazana *f*; **tarazanal** *m* dockyard (atarazana).

tardanza *f* delay (retraso) || slowness (lentitud).

tardar *vi* to take; *este trabajo tardará una hora* this work will take an hour; *¿cuánto tarda el tren de París a Madrid?* how long does the train from Paris to Madrid take? || to take *o* to be a long time; *el tren tarda en llegar* the train is taking a long time to arrive; *¡cuánto tardas en vestirte!* what a long time you take to get dressed! || to delay, to linger; *no tardo ni un minuto* I won't delay a minute || — *a más tardar* at the latest || *no tardaré mucho* I won't be long, I won't take long, it won't take me long || *no tardé nada en terminarlo* I finished it in no time || *no tardes en decírmelo* tell me at once.

tarde *f* afternoon (desde mediodía hasta las cinco o las seis) || evening (después) || — *a la caída de la tarde* at dusk, at nightfall || *a las cuatro de la tarde* at four o'clock in the afternoon, at four p.m. || *buenas tardes* good afternoon (hasta las seis), good evening (después de las seis) || *dar las buenas tardes* to say good afternoon *o* good evening || *de tarde en tarde* now and then, from time to time || *función de la tarde* matinée || *por la tarde* in the afternoon, in the evening || *tarde de toros* bullfight; *hoy es tarde de toros* today there is a bullfight.
◆ *adv* late; *levantarse tarde* to get up late; *llegó tarde a la oficina* he arrived late at the office || too late (demasiado tarde); *ya es tarde para marcharse* it is too late now to leave || — *hacerse tarde, hacérsele tarde a uno* to grow *o* to get late; *se me hizo tarde y no pude ir al teatro* it grew late and I couldn't go to the theatre || *lo más tarde* at the latest || *luego es tarde* later on is too late || *más tarde o más temprano* sooner or later || *más vale tarde que nunca, nunca es tarde si la dicha es buena* better late than never || *tarde o temprano* sooner or later || FAM *tarde piache* too late [for the fair].

tardecer* *vi* to get *o* to grow dark.

tardíamente *adv* too late, tardily, belatedly.

tardígrado, da *adj/sm* ZOOL tardigrade.
◆ *m pl* tardigrada.

tardío, a *adj* late, overdue, belated, tardy; *llegada tardía* belated arrival || slow; *tardío en decidirse* slow to decide || *fruto tardío* late fruit.

tardísimo *adv* very late.

tardo, da *adj* slow (lento) || late (retrasado) || slow; *tardo en comprender* slow to understand || slow, dull, dense (torpe).

tardón, ona *adj* FAM very slow (que tarda mucho) | slow, dull (torpe).
◆ *m/f* FAM slowcoach.

tarea *f* task, job, piece of work; *dar una tarea a alguien* to assign s.o. a piece of work, to give s.o. a job to do || work; *agobiado de tarea* overburdened with work || — *eso no es tarea de unos días* it's no small job || *tareas escolares* schoolwork, homework || FIG *tarea le mando* you'll have your work cut out there.

tarifa *f* tariff, rate; *tarifa reducida* reduced rate; *tarifa completa* full tariff; *tarifa de fuera de temporada* off-season tariff || fare (transportes) || price list (tabla de precios).

tarifar *vt* to tariff, to fix a tariff for.
◆ *vi* FIG to quarrel (enfadarse).

tarima *f* platform, stand (tablado) || stool, footstool (para los pies) || bench (banquillo).

tarja *f* shield, buckler (escudo) || tally, tally stick (palo) || FAM belt, blow (golpe) || AMER (visiting) card [US calling card].

tarjar *vt* to tally || AMER to cross out (tachar).

tarjeta *f* card; *el abogado me dio su tarjeta* the lawyer gave me his card || ARQ cartouche, tablet with inscription || title and imprint (mapas) || — DEP *tarjeta amarilla, roja* yellow, red card || INFORM *tarjeta con chip, tarjeta chip* chip card || *tarjeta de crédito* credit card || *tarjeta de embarque* boarding pass *o* card || *tarjeta de identidad* identity card || INFORM *tarjeta de memoria* chip card || *tarjeta de Navidad* Christmas card || *tarjeta de visita* visiting card [US calling card] || INFORM *tarjeta inteligente* smart card [chip card] | *tarjeta madre* motherboard | *tarjeta magnética* magnetic card || *tarjeta multiviaje* travel card [for use on public transport] || *tarjeta perforada* punch card || *tarjeta postal* postcard.

tarjetera *f* AMER ⟶ **tarjetero.**

tarjetero *m* card case, small wallet for carrying cards.

tarlatana *f* tarlatan (tela).

Tarpeya *npr m* Tarpeia || *Roca Tarpeya* Tarpeian Rock.

tarquín *m* slime, ooze (cieno).

Tarquino *npr m* HIST Tarquin.

tarquino, na *adj* AMER thoroughbred (animal vacuno).
◆ *m/f* thoroughbred animal.

tarraconense *adj* [of *o* from] Tarragona.
◆ *m/f* native *o* inhabitant of Tarragona.

Tarraconense *n pr* HIST Tarraconensis [province of Roman-occupied Spain].

tárraga *f* 17th century Spanish dance.

tarraja *f* diestock (para tornillos) || modelling board [US modeling board] (para yeso) || AMER leather tally.

tarreña *f* clay castanet (castañuela).

tarro *m* jar; *un tarro de mermelada* a jam jar || AMER horn (cuerno) | top hat (sombrero de copa).

tarsiano, na *adj* ANAT tarsal.

tarso *m* ANAT tarsus.

tarta *f* cake, tart (pastel) || baking pan (tartera) || *tarta de boda* wedding cake || *tarta de cumpleaños* birthday cake.

tártago *m* BOT spurge.

tartajear *vi* to stutter, to stammer.

tartajeo *m* stuttering, stammering (acción) || stutter, stammer (defecto).

tartajoso, sa *adj* stuttering, stammering.
◆ *m/f* stutterer, stammerer.

tartamudear *vi* to stutter, to stammer.

tartamudeo *m* stuttering, stammering.

tartamudo, da *adj* stuttering, stammering || *es tartamudo* he stutters.
◆ *m/f* stutterer, stammerer.

tartán *m* tartan, Scotch plaid (tela).

tartana *f* MAR tartan (barco) || trap, light carriage (carro).

tartáreo, a *adj* POÉT Tartarean.

Tartaria *npr f* GEOGR Tartary.

tartárico, ca *adj* QUÍM tartaric.

tártaro, ra *adj* Tartar (de Tartaria).
◆ *m* QUÍM tartar || tartar (sarro) || POÉT Tartarus, hell.

tartera *f* baking pan (para hacer tartas) || lunch box [US dinner pail *o* bucket] (fiambrera).

tartesio, sia *adj/s* HIST Tartessian.

tartrato *m* QUÍM tartrate.

tártrico, ca *adj* QUÍM tartaric.

tartufería *f* hypocrisy.

tartufo *m* hypocrite (mojigato).

tarugo *m* chunk, piece (de madera, etc.) || piece of stale bread (pan duro) || wooden peg *o* plug (clavija) || wooden paving block (para pavimentar calles) || FIG & FAM blockhead, dolt (zoquete).

tarumba *adj* FAM confused (confuso) || — FAM *volver tarumba* to drive mad (volver loco), to confuse, to rattle (aturdir) | *volverse tarumba* to go mad (volverse loco), to get confused (confundirse).

tas *m* anvil (yunque pequeño).

tasa *f* appraisal, valuation (valoración) || tax (impuesto); *tasa de importación* import tax || limit (límite); *poner una tasa a los gastos mensuales* to put a limit on one's monthly outlay || measure, standard (medida, regla) || rate (tipo, índice); *tasa de crecimiento* growth rate; *tasa de desempleo* or *de paro* unemployment rate; *tasa de mortalidad* mortality rate; *tasa de natalidad* birth rate | *sin tasa, sin tasa ni medida* without limit, limitless (sin límites), without any moderation (sin moderación).

tasación *f* appraisal, valuation (valoración) || calculation (cálculo).

tasador, ra *adj* appraising.
◆ *m/f* valuator, valuer [US appraiser].

tasajear *vt* AMER to jerk (la carne).

tasajo *m* jerked meat (carne seca y salada) || piece of meat (trozo de carne).

tasajudo, da *adj* AMER tall and thin.

tasar *vt* to appraise, to value (valorar); *tasar un cuadro* to appraise a painting || to fix *o* to set the price of (fijar el precio de) || to regulate (los precios) || to tax (gravar) || FIG to limit, to ration; *tasar la comida a un enfermo* to limit a patient's food; *en la pensión tasan hasta el agua* in the boardinghouse they even ration the water.

tasca *f* bar, pub (taberna) ‖ gambling den (timba) ‖ AMER MAR crosscurrent ‖ FAM *ir de tascas* to go on a pub crawl [US to go barhopping].

tascar *vt* to scutch, to swingle (cáñamo) ‖ FIG to munch, to champ (la hierba) ‖ FIG & FAM *tascar el freno* to champ at the bit.

Tasmania *npr f* GEOGR Tasmania.

tasugo *m* ZOOL badger.

tata *m* FAM AMER daddy (papá).
◆ *f* nurse, nanny (niñera) ‖ FAM maid (criada).

tataibá *m* AMER mulberry.

tatarabuela *f* great-great-grandmother.

tatarabuelo *m* great-great-grandfather.
◆ *pl* great-great-grandparents.

tataranieta *f* great-great-granddaughter.

tataranieto *m* great-great-grandson.
◆ *pl* great-great-grandchildren.

tátaro, ra *adj/s* Tatar.

tatas *f pl* *andar a tatas* to begin to walk, to take one's first steps (empezar a andar), to crawl [on all fours] (andar a gatas).

¡tate! *interj* be careful!, take care!, look out! (cuidado) ‖ slowly!, steady! (para detener) ‖ I see!, so that's it! (ya comprendo).

tatetí *m* AMER naughts-and-crosses [US ticktacktoe].

tatito *m* FAM AMER daddy, papa (papá).

tato, ta *adj* lisping [who pronounces *c* and *s* like *t*].
◆ *m* FAM little brother, kid brother (hermano pequeño).

tatú *m* ZOOL tatouay, giant armadillo.

tatuaje *m* tattooing (acción) ‖ tattoo (dibujo).

tatuar *vt* to tattoo.

tatusa *f* AMER little woman (mujercilla).

tau *m* tau cross, tau (cruz).
◆ *f* tau, nineteenth letter in the Greek alphabet.

taumaturgia *f* thaumaturgy.

taumaturgo *m* thaumaturge.

Taúride *n pr* GEOGR Tauris.

taurino, na *adj* taurine (del toro) ‖ bullfighting (de la corrida).
◆ *f* QUÍM taurine, taurin.

Tauro *npr m* GEOGR Taurus ‖ ASTR Taurus.

taurófilo, la *adj* fond of bullfighting.
◆ *m/f* bullfighting fan.

taurómaco, ca *adj* bullfighting, tauromachian ‖ knowledgeable about bullfighting.
◆ *m/f* bullfighting connoisseur *o* expert.

tauromaquia *f* bullfighting, tauromachy.

tauromáquico, ca *adj* bullfighting, tauromachian; *término tauromáquico* bullfighting term.

tautología *f* GRAM tautology (pleonasmo).

tautológico, ca *adj* GRAM tautological.

taxativamente *adv* limitatively ‖ precisely.

taxativo, va *adj* limitative, restrictive ‖ precise.

taxi *m* taxi, taxicab, cab.

taxia *f* BIOL taxis.

taxidermia *f* taxidermy.

taxidermista *m/f* taxidermist.

taxímetro *m* taximeter (contador) ‖ taxi, taxicab (coche).

taxis *f* BIOL & MED taxis.

taxista *m/f* taxi driver, cab driver, cabby.

taxonomía *f* taxonomy.

taxonómico, ca *adj* taxonomic, taxonomical.

taylorismo *m* taylorism, scientific management.

taylorización *f* introduction of scientific management techniques.

tayuyá *f* AMER BOT type of watermelon.

taza *f* cup; *una taza de porcelana* a porcelain cup ‖ bowl (de retrete) ‖ cup, cupful; *ha tomado tres tazas de café* he has had three cups of coffee ‖ basin (de una fuente) ‖ basket hilt (de la espada) ‖ AMER basin ‖ *taza de té* cup of tea (llena de té), teacup (que sirve para el té).

tazón *m* bowl, large cup (taza grande).

te *pron pers* you, to you; *te veo* I can see you; *te hablo* I speak to you; *te lo di* I gave it to you ‖ you, for you; *te he traído unas flores* I have brought you some flowers, I have brought some flowers for you ‖ REL Thee, to Thee.
◆ *pron refl* yourself; *lávate* wash yourself ‖ REL Thyself ‖ *te lo puedes quedar* you can keep it (for yourself).

te *f* t (letra t) ‖ T square (escuadra).

té *m* tea (planta, bebida); *té con limón* lemon tea ‖ tea (reunión); *convidar a alguien para el té* to invite s.o. to tea; *té baile* tea dance ‖ — FAM *dar el té* to bore, to bother ‖ *salón de té* tearoom ‖ *té de Méjico* Mexican tea ‖ *té de los jesuitas* or *del Paraguay* maté, Paraguay tea.

tea *f* torch (antorcha) ‖ FIG & FAM *coger una tea* to get plastered (emborracharse).

teatino, na *m/f* REL theatine.

teatral *adj* theatre, drama; *grupo teatral* drama group ‖ theatrical, melodramatic (exagerado); *en tono teatral* in a theatrical tone ‖ *obra teatral* play, dramatic work.

teatralidad *f* theatricality.

teatro *m* theatre [US theater] (sitio); *vamos al teatro esta noche* we're going to the theatre tonight ‖ theatre, drama, dramatic works *pl* (literatura dramática); *el teatro de Lope de Vega* the theatre of Lope de Vega ‖ theatre, acting, theatrical profession (profesión); *dedicarse al teatro* to go into the theatre ‖ stage; *dejar el teatro* to give up the stage; *escribe para el teatro* he writes for the stage ‖ FIG theatre; *el teatro de la batalla* the theatre of the battle | scene (lugar de un acontecimiento) ‖ FIG *echarle teatro* to playact, to exaggerate | *hacer teatro* to playact, to be dramatic ‖ *obra de teatro* play, theatrical work ‖ *teatro de la ópera* opera house ‖ MIL *teatro de operaciones* battlefield ‖ *teatro de variedades* variety theatre ‖ *teatro experimental* experimental theatre ‖ FIG *tener mucho teatro* to be theatrical *o* melodramatic.

tebaico, ca *adj* Theban (de Tebas).

Tebaida *npr f* Thebaid.

tebano, na *adj/s* Theban (de Tebas).

Tebas *n pr* GEOGR Thebes.

tebeo *m* comic [US comic book].

teca *m* teak (árbol) ‖ ANAT & BOT theca ‖ relicary (relicario).

tecali *m* Mexican alabaster, tecali.

tecla *f* key (de instrumento de música, de máquina de escribir) ‖ — FIG & FAM *dar en la tecla* to strike the right note (acertar) ‖ INFORM *tecla de anclaje* or *de bloqueo* caps lock | *tecla de anulación* cancel key | *tecla de borrado* delete key | *tecla de control* control key | *tecla de función* function key | *tecla de retorno* return key ‖ *tecla de retroceso* back spacer, back space key ‖ FIG *tocar la tecla sensible* to find s.o.'s soft *o* weak spot | *tocar una tecla* or *teclas* to pull strings.

teclado *m* keyboard ‖ INFORM *teclado alfanumérico* alphanumeric keyboard | *teclado expandido* expanded keyboard | *teclado numérico* numeric *o* digital keyboard.

tecleado *m* fingering.

teclear *vi* to finger the keyboard ‖ to type (escribir a máquina) ‖ to play the piano (tocar el piano) ‖ FIG & FAM to drum [one's fingers].
◆ *vt* FIG to sound out, to feel out.

tecleo *m* fingering (de instrumento) ‖ drumming (con los dedos) ‖ *se oía el tecleo de las máquinas de escribir* you could hear the clatter of the typewriters.

tecnecio *m* QUÍM technetium.

técnica *f* technique (método); *técnica de fabricación* manufacturing technique ‖ technique (habilidad) ‖ technology (tecnología) ‖ engineering; *técnica hidráulica* hydraulic engineering ‖ *los progresos de la técnica* the technological advances.

técnicamente *adv* technically.

tecnicidad *f* technicality.

tecnicismo *m* technicality (carácter técnico) ‖ technical word *o* term (palabra).

técnico, ca *adj* technical; *diccionario técnico* technical dictionary; *terminología técnica* technical terms ‖ technological (tecnológico).
◆ *m/f* technician.

tecnicolor *m* technicolor; *en tecnicolor* in technicolor.

tecnocracia *f* technocracy.

tecnócrata *m/f* technocrat.
◆ *adj* technocratic.

tecnología *f* technology ‖ *tecnología punta* hich technology [high tech].

tecnológico, ca *adj* technological.

tecnólogo, ga *m/f* technologist.

tecol *m* AMER maguey worm.

tecolines *m pl* FAM AMER dough *sing*, money *sing*.

tecolote *m* AMER owl.

tecomate *m* AMER gourd (calabaza) | earthenware cup (vasija de barro).

tectónico, ca *adj* tectonic.
◆ *f* tectonics.

tectrices *f pl* ZOOL tectrices.

techado *m* roof, roofing (techo) ‖ shed (cobertizo) ‖ *bajo techado* under cover, indoors.

techador *m* roofer.

techar *vt* to roof.

techo *m* ceiling (parte interior) ‖ roof (tejado); *techo de paja* straw *o* thatched roof ‖ AUT roof ‖ AVIAC ceiling ‖ FIG roof, house; *acoger a uno bajo su techo* to take s.o. under one's roof, to take s.o. into one's house ‖ — *techo corredizo* sliding *o* sun roof ‖ *vivir bajo el mismo techo* to live under the same roof.

techumbre *m* roof, roofing (cubierta).

tedéum; Te Deum *m* REL Te Deum.

tediar *vt* to loathe (odiar).

tedio *m* boredom, tedium (aburrimiento) ‖ annoyance (fastidio) ‖ loathing (repugnancia).

tedioso, sa *adj* tedious, boring (fastidioso) ‖ bothersome, annoying (molesto).

tegmen *m* BOT tegmen.

Tegucigalpa *n pr* GEOGR Tegucigalpa.

tegucigalpense *adj* [of *o* from] Tegucigalpa (Honduras).
◆ *m/f* native o inhabitant of Tegucigalpa.

tegumentario, ria *adj* tegumentary.

tegumento *m* tegument.

Teherán *m pr* GEOGR Teheran, Tehran.

teína *f* QUÍM theine.

teísmo *m* theism.

teísta *adj* theistic.
◆ *m/f* theist.

teja *f* tile; *teja plana* plain *o* flat tile; *teja de cumbrera* ridge tile ‖ FAM priest's shovel hat (sombrero de cura) ‖ steel facing (de la espada) ‖ MAR notch (muesca) ‖ — FIG & FAM *a toca teja* cash | *de tejas abajo* in this world (en la tierra) | *de tejas arriba* in heaven (en el cielo) ‖ *teja flamenca* pantile.

tejadillo *m* small roof (tejado) ‖ top, roof, cover (de un carruaje).

tejado *m* roof, tile roof ‖ — FIG *hasta el tejado* full, packed | *la pelota está aún en el tejado* it is still in the air | *tiene el tejado de vidrio* he is no one to talk, people who live in glass houses shouldn't throw stones.

tejamaní; tejamanil *m* AMER shingle.

tejano, na *adj/s* Texan.

tejar *m* tile works.

tejar *vt* to tile.

Tejas *npr m* GEOGR Texas.

tejavana *f* shed (cobertizo) ‖ building with a plain tile roof.

tejedera *f* weaver (tejedora) ‖ water strider (araña).

tejedor, ra *adj* weaving (que teje) ‖ AMER FIG & FAM intriguing, sheming (intrigante).
◆ *m/f* weaver (que teje).
◆ *m* water strider (araña) ‖ weaverbird (ave).

tejedura *m* weaving (acción de tejer) ‖ texture (textura).

tejeduría *f* art of weaving, weaving (arte de tejer) ‖ weaving mill (taller).

tejemaneje *m* FAM to-do, fuss (actividad) | trickery, scheming, goings-on *pl* (intriga) ‖ FAM *¿qué tejemaneje te traes?* what are you up to?, what are you cooking up?

tejer *vt* to weave (entrelazar) ‖ to spin; *la araña teje su tela* the spider spins its web ‖ to knit (hacer punto) ‖ FIG to weave, to prepare; *está tejiendo su futuro* he is preparing his future | to plot, to weave, to concoct; *le están tejiendo una trampa* they are concocting a trap for him ‖ AMER to scheme (intrigar) ‖ FIG *tejer y destejer* to chop and change.

tejería *f* tile works (tejar).

tejeringo *m* fritter (churro).

tejero *m* tile maker.

tejido *m* weave; *un tejido muy apretado* a very tight weave ‖ weaving (acción) ‖ material, fabric (tela) ‖ textile ‖ ANAT tissue; *tejido muscular* muscle tissue ‖ FIG tissue, web; *un tejido de embustes* a tissue of lies ‖ — *fábrica de tejidos* textile factory ‖ *tejido de punto* jersey.

tejo *m* disk, quoit (plancha metálica circular) ‖ quoits *pl* (juego) ‖ TECN step bearing (tejuelo) ‖ gold ingot (lingote de oro) ‖ blank (para hacer una moneda) ‖ hopscotch (juego de niñas) ‖ yew (árbol).

tejocote *m* AMER hawthorn (planta).

tejoleta *f* piece of tile (pedazo de teja) ‖ clay castanet (tarreña).

tejón *m* ZOOL badger.

tejonera *f* badger burrow.

tejuelo *m* small disk *o* quoit (plancha circular metálica) ‖ TECN step bearing ‖ label (en el lomo de un libro).

tela *f* material, cloth, fabric; *he comprado la tela para el vestido* I have bought the material for the dress ‖ web, cobweb (de araña) ‖ film, skin (de nata) ‖ skin, membrane (de las frutas) ‖ ANAT membrane | film (en el ojo) ‖ ARTES canvas (lienzo) | painting (cuadro) ‖ FIG & FAM dough (dinero) ‖ FIG conversation material, sth. to talk about; *tienen tela para rato* they have plenty to talk about ‖ — *encuadernación en tela* cloth binding ‖ FIG *estar en tela de juicio* to be in doubt ‖ FAM *¡esto es tela marinera!* it's a tall order!, we'll have our work cut out with this! ‖ FIG *hay tela de que cortar* there is an awful lot to be done | *poner en tela de juicio* to question, to put in doubt ‖ *tela de araña* spider's web, cobweb ‖ *tela de cebolla* onion skin ‖ *tela de saco* burlap ‖ *tela metálica* wire netting.

telamón *m* ARQ telamon.

telar *m* loom (máquina) ‖ sewing press (de los encuadernadores) ‖ ARQ frame (de puerta o ventana) ‖ FIG *tener algo en el telar* to have sth. in the making.
◆ *pl* textile mill *sing* (fábrica) ‖ TEATR flies.

telaraña *f* web, spider's web, cobweb ‖ FIG trifle, bagatelle, nothing (cosa de poca importancia) ‖ — FIG *mirar las telarañas* to stargaze | *tener telarañas en los ojos* to be blind.

tele *f* FAM telly, TV (televisión).

teleadicto, ta *adj* addicted to television.
◆ *m/f* telly addict.

telecabina *f* cable car.

telecarga *m* INFORM downloading, uploading.

telecine; telecinematógrafo *m* telecine.

teleclub *m* television club.

telecomunicación *f* telecommunication.

telecontrol *m* remote control, telecontrol.

telecopia *f* INFORM facsimile transmission, fax.

teledebate *m* televised debate.

telediario *m* television news bulletin, news; *el telediario de las nueve* the nine o'clock news.

teledifusión *f* telecast, television broadcast.

teledinámico, ca *adj* telodynamic.

teledirección *f* remote control.

teledirigido, da *adj* remote-controlled ‖ *proyectil teledirigido* guided missile.

teledirigir *vt* to operate *o* to guide by remote control.

telefax *m inv* telefax, fax.

teleferaje *m* telpherage.

teleférico *m* cable car *o* railway.

telefilm *m* telefilm.

telefonazo *m* FAM ring, telephone call ‖ *dar un telefonazo a alguien* to ring s.o. up, to give s.o. a ring, to call s.o.

telefonear *vt/vi* to telephone, to phone.

telefonema *m* telephoned telegram.

telefonía *f* telephony; *telefonía sin hilos* wireless telephony.

telefónicamente *adv* by telephone.

telefónico, ca *adj* telephone, phone, telephonic ‖ — *cabina telefónica* telephone box *o* booth ‖ *central telefónica* telephone exchange ‖ *compañía telefónica* telephone company ‖ *llamada telefónica* telephone call, phone call.

telefonista *m/f* telephone operator.

teléfono *m* telephone, phone ‖ — *guía de teléfonos* telephone directory *o* book ‖ *le llaman por teléfono* you're wanted on the telephone ‖ *llamar a alguien por teléfono* to telephone s.o., to phone s.o., to ring s.o. up, to call s.o. ‖ FIG *teléfono rojo* hot line.

telefoto *m* phototelegraph, telephotograph, telephoto.

telefotografía *f* telephotography.

telefotográfico, ca *adj* telephoto, telephotographic.

telegrafía *f* telegraphy; *telegrafía sin hilos* wireless telegraphy.

telegrafiar *vt/vi* to telegraph, to wire.

telegráficamente *adv* by telegraph, by telegram, telegraphically.

telegráfico, ca *adj* telegraphic ‖ *giro telegráfico* money order.

telegrafista *m/f* telegrapher, telegraph operator, telegraphist.

telégrafo *m* telegraph; *telégrafo sin hilos* wireless telegraph.

telegrama *m* telegram, wire (*fam*).

teleguiar *vt* to operate *o* to guide by remote control.

teleimpresor *m* teleprinter, teletype, teletypewriter.

telejuego *m* video game.

telele *m* fainting spell (desmayo).

Telémaco *npr m* Telemachus.

telemando *m* remote control.

telemantenimiento *m* INFORM remote maintenance.

telemática *f* INFORM telematics, data communications.

telemecánico, ca *adj* telemechanic.
◆ *f* telemechanics.

telemetría *f* telemetry.

telemétrico, ca *adj* telemetric.

telémetro *m* range finder, telemeter.

telencéfalo *m* ANAT telencephalon.

telenovela *f* soap opera.

telenque *adj* AMER silly, foolish (bobo).

teleobjetivo *m* FOT telephoto lens, telelens.

teleología *f* teleology.

teleológico, ca *adj* teleological, teleologic.

teleósteo *adj* ZOOL teleostean, teleost.
◆ *m* teleost.

telépata *m/f* telepathist.

telepatía *f* telepathy.

telepático, ca *adj* telepathic.

teleprocesamiento; teleproceso *m* INFORM teleprocessing.

teleprocesar *vt* to teleprocess.

teleproceso *m* INFORM → **teleprocesamiento.**

telequinesia *f* telekinesis.

telera *f* plough pin (del arado) ‖ transom, crosspiece (del carro) ‖ MIL transom (de cureña) ‖ jaw (de prensa) ‖ MAR rack block ‖ sheep pen (redil) ‖ AMER rectangular biscuit | oval loaf of bread.

telerón *m* transom.

telescópico, ca *adj* telescopic.

telescopio *m* telescope.

telesilla *f* chair lift.

telespectador, ra *m/f* televiewer, viewer.

telesquí *m* ski lift.

telestesia *f* telesthesia.

teletexto *m* Teletext.

teletipo *m* teletype, teleprinter, teletypewriter.

teletonta *f* FAM goggle-box.

teletratamiento *m* INFORM teleprocessing.

televidente *m/f* viewer, televiewer.

televisar *vt* to televise.

televisión *f* television; *ver la televisión* to watch television ‖ FAM television set (televisor) ‖ — *televisión en blanco y negro* black and white television ‖ *televisión en colores* colour television ‖ *televisión por cable* cable television ‖ *televisión vía satélite* satellite television ‖ *transmitir por televisión* to televise.

televisivo, va *adj* telegenic (apto para ser televisado) ‖ television (de televisión).

televisor *m* television, television set.

télex *m* telex.

telilla *f* light camlet (tela) ‖ film, skin (en líquidos).

telón *m* curtain, drop curtain ‖ — FIG *telón de acero* iron curtain ‖ TEATR *telón de boca* house *o* drop curtain | *telón de fondo* or *de foro* backdrop, backcloth | *telón metálico* safety curtain.

telonero, ra *adj* first on (artista) ‖ *combate telonero* preliminary bout (boxeo).
◆ *m/f* first act (en los espectáculos).

telúrico, ca *adj* telluric.

telurio *m* QUÍM tellurium (metal).

telurismo *m* influence of the Earth [on the inhabitants of a region].

tema *m* topic, subject, theme (asunto); *el tema de la conversación* the subject of the conversation ‖ theme, subject (de un libro, de un discurso) ‖ GRAM stem ‖ MÚS theme ‖ translation into a foreign language (traducción inversa) ‖ obsession, mania (manía) ‖ grudge, ill will (antipatía) ‖ question (en un examen) ‖ subject (en oposiciones) ‖ — *atenerse al tema* to keep to the point ‖ FAM *cada loco con su tema* everyone has his hobbyhorse ‖ *salirse del tema* to get off the subject, to digress ‖ *tema de actualidad* topical subject, current talking point ‖ *tener tema para un rato* to have plenty to talk about.

temario *m* programme [*US* program] (lista de temas) ‖ agenda (de una conferencia).

temático, ca *adj* thematic ‖ GRAM stem.
◆ *f* theme, subject (conjunto de temas) ‖ doctrine (doctrina) ‖ ideology (ideología) ‖ philosophy (filosofía).

tembetá *m* AMER stick worn by some Indians in the lower lip.

tembladal *m* quaking bog, quagmire (tremedal).

tembladera *f* shaking fit (temblor) ‖ thin two-handled bowl (vasija) ‖ jewel mounted on a spiral (joya) ‖ AMER quaking bog, quagmire (tremedal) ‖ ZOOL torpedo, electric ray (pez) ‖ BOT quaking grass.

tembladeral *m* AMER quaking bog, quagmire.

tembladero, ra *adj* trembling, shaking.
◆ *m* quaking bog, quagmire.

temblar* *vi* to shake, to tremble, to shudder, to quiver; *el miedo le hizo temblar* he trembled with fear; *durante el terremoto todas las casas temblaban* during the earthquake all the houses were shaking ‖ to shiver (de frío) ‖ to tremble (la voz) ‖ FIG to tremble *o* to shake with fear (tener miedo) ‖ FIG & FAM *dejó temblando la botella* he nearly finished off the whole bottle.

tembleque *m* shaking fit (temblor intenso); *le dio un tembleque* he had a shaking fit ‖ trembler (persona) ‖ jewel mounted on a spiral (joya).

temblequear *vi* to shake, to tremble, to quiver (temblar) ‖ FIG & FAM to pretend to tremble.

temblequeo *m* FAM shivers *pl*, shakes *pl*.

tembletear *vi* to shake, to tremble, to quiver.

temblón, ona *adj* shaking, trembling, quivering, tremulous (que tiembla).

temblor *m* tremor, shudder ‖ shivering, shivers *pl* (de frío) ‖ trembling (de la voz) ‖ FIG shiver; *me da temblores pensar en lo que va a pasar* it gives me the shivers to think what is going to happen ‖ AMER earthquake ‖ *temblor de tierra* earthquake, earth tremor.

tembloroso, sa *adj* shaking, trembling, quivering, tremulous (que tiembla) ‖ trembling, tremulous (voz).

temer *vt* to be afraid of, to fear; *teme a su padre* he is afraid of his father ‖ to be afraid, to fear (sospechar con inquietud); *temo que no me lo devuelva* I am afraid he won't give it back to me ‖ REL to fear; *temer a Dios* to fear God ‖ *no temer ni a Dios ni al diablo* to fear neither man nor beast.
◆ *vi* to be afraid ‖ — *ser de temer* to be dangerous ‖ *temer por* to fear for, to be afraid for; *temo por su vida* I fear for his life.
◆ *vpr* to be afraid; *me temo que no venga* I am afraid he won't come; *me lo temo* I am afraid so.

temerario, ria *adj* rash, reckless, bold, foolhardy, temerarious; *un joven temerario* a reckless youth; *un acto temerario* a rash act ‖ *un juicio temerario* a rash judgment.

temeridad *f* temerity, recklessness.

temerosamente *adv* fearfully.

temeroso, sa *adj* frightful, fearful (que causa terror) ‖ fearful, timorous, timid (medroso) ‖ — *temeroso de* afraid of; *temeroso de sus superiores* afraid of his superiors ‖ *temeroso de Dios* God-fearing.

temible *adj* fearsome, fearful, dreadful, frightful; *un arma temible* a fearful weapon.

Temis *npr f* MIT Themis.

Temístocles *npr m* Themistocles.

temor *m* fear; *el temor al castigo* fear of punishment ‖ dread, apprehension (recelo) ‖ — *por temor a* or *de* for fear of; *por temor de herirle, no le dije la verdad* I didn't tell him the truth for fear of hurting him ‖ *temor de Dios* fear of God ‖ *tener mucho temor a* to be terrified of.

témpano *m* floe (de hielo) ‖ FIG *ser un témpano* to be as cold as ice *o* as an iceberg.

temperamental *adj* temperamental.

temperamento *m* temperament, disposition, nature (manera de ser); *tiene un temperamento tranquilo* he has a quiet temperament ‖ weather (temperie) ‖ MÚS temperament ‖ *tener temperamento* to be temperamental, to have a temperament.

temperancia *f* temperance, moderation.

temperante *adj* calming (que tempera) ‖ MED sedative ‖ AMER teetotal.
◆ *m/f* teetotaller [*US* teetotaler].

temperar *vt* to temper, to moderate (moderar) ‖ to mitigate ‖ MED to calm (calmar) ‖ MÚS to temper.
◆ *vi* AMER to have a change of air.
◆ *vpr* to warm up (el tiempo).

temperatura *f* temperature; *temperatura máxima* maximum temperature ‖ MED temperature, fever (fiebre, calentura); *tener temperatura* to have a temperature ‖ *temperatura absoluta, crítica* absolute, critical temperature.

temperie *f* weather [conditions].

tempero *m* favourable condition of the land [for sowing].

tempestad *f* storm, tempest (tormenta) ‖ FIG storm; *una tempestad de aplausos, de insultos* a storm of applause, of insults; *levantó una tempestad de protestas* it raised a storm of protest ‖ — FIG *levantar tempestades* to produce turmoil ‖ *tempestad de arena, de nieve* sandstorm, snowstorm ‖ FIG *una tempestad en un vaso de agua* a storm in a teacup.

tempestear *vi* to storm ‖ FIG & FAM to rant and rave (estar furioso).

tempestuoso, sa *adj* turbulent, stormy, tempestuous; *tiempo tempestuoso* stormy weather ‖ FIG stormy; *el ambiente tempestuoso de la asamblea* the stormy atmosphere at the assembly.

tempisque *m* AMER BOT ironwood.

templa *f* distemper (pintura).

templado, da *adj* temperate, moderate (sobrio) ‖ lukewarm, warm (tibio); *agua templada* lukewarm water ‖ temperate, mild (clima, tiempo) ‖ temperate (región) ‖ MÚS tuned, in tune ‖ FIG restrained (estilo) | moderate (moderado) ‖ brave, courageous (valiente) | bright (listo) ‖ TECN tempered (cristal, metal) ‖ AMER drunk (borracho) | tipsy (achispado) ‖ — FIG & FAM *estar bien, mal templado* to be in a good, in a bad mood | *nervios bien templados* nerves of steel, steady nerves.

templador, ra *adj* tempering ‖ MÚS tuning.
◆ *m* MÚS tuning fork (diapasón) | tuner (el que templa) ‖ TECN temperer (obrero) | turnbuckle (tensor).

templadura *f* tempering (metal) ‖ MÚS tuning.

templanza *f* temperance (virtud) ‖ moderation ‖ mildness, temperateness (del clima) ‖ harmony [of colours] (en pintura).

templar *vt* to temper, to moderate (moderar) ‖ to make temperate (volver templado) ‖ to warm up (agua fría) ‖ to cool down (agua caliente) ‖ to restrain, to control (reprimir) ‖ to calm down (apaciguar) ‖ to appease (la cólera) ‖ MÚS to tune, to temper ‖ TECN to temper (acero, vidrio) ‖ to blend (armonizar los colores) ‖ to soften (color, luz) ‖ to tighten (atirantar, apretar).
◆ *vi* to warm up (el tiempo).
◆ *vpr* to be moderate, to control o.s. (moderarse) ‖ to warm up (ponerse templado) ‖ AMER to fall in love (enamorarse) | to get tipsy (bebiendo).

templario *m* knight Templar, Templar.

temple *m* temper (metal, vidrio) ‖ atmospheric conditions *pl*, weather (tiempo) ‖ temperature (temperatura) ‖ FIG temper, humour, mood; *estar de buen, de mal temple* to be in a good, in a bad mood | spirit, energy (energía) | resoluteness (entereza) ‖ ARTES tempera, tempera paint (pintura) ‖ MÚS tuning, tempering ‖ FIG average, mean ‖ — *dar temple* to temper ‖ ARTES *pintar al temple* to paint in tempera.

Temple *m* REL order of the knights Templar.

templete *m* small temple (templo pequeño) ‖ niche (para imágenes) ‖ kiosk (pabellón).

templo *m* temple ‖ church (iglesia) ‖ FIG temple (de sabiduría, justicia, etc.) ‖ — FIG & FAM *como un templo* huge, enormous; *una mentira como un templo* a huge lie; real; *una mujer como un templo* a real woman | *es una verdad como un templo* it is the patent truth.

tempo *m* MÚS tempo (movimiento).

temporada *f* season; *temporada de verano* summer season; *temporada teatral* theatre season; *temporada de toros* bullfighting season ‖ period of time, spell; *pasamos una temporada en Málaga* we spent a period of time in Malaga ‖ period, time; *la mejor temporada de mi vida* the best time of my life ‖ — *de fuera de temporada* off-season; *tarifas de fuera de temporada* off-season rates ‖ *en plena temporada* at the height of the season ‖ *estar de temporada* to be on holiday ‖ *hace una temporada que no trabaja* he has been out of work for a while ‖ *por temporadas* on and off ‖ *temporada baja* off season ‖ *temporada de calma* or *de poca venta* or *de venta reducida* slack season.

temporal *adj* temporal (contrapuesto a espiritual o eterno); *el poder temporal de los papas* the temporal power of the Popes ‖ temporary, provisional (de poca duración); *un empleo temporal* a temporary job ‖ worldly (material); *los bienes temporales* worldly goods ‖ ANAT temporal (de la sien) ‖ GRAM temporal.
◆ *m* storm, tempest (tempestad) ‖ rainy spell (lluvia) ‖ seasonal worker (obrero) ‖ ANAT temporal bone ‖ — *capear el temporal* to

weather the storm || *correr un temporal* to go through a storm (en el mar).

temporalidad *f* temporality.
◆ *pl* temporalities (beneficios eclesiásticos).

temporalizar *vt* to make temporal.

temporáneo, a; temporario, ria *adj* temporary, provisional.

Témporas *f pl* REL Ember days.

temporero, ra *adj* seasonal, temporary.
◆ *m* seasonal *o* temporary worker (obrero).

temporizar *vi* to temporize (contemporizar) || to pass the time, to kill time (matar el tiempo).

tempranal *adj* early-yielding (tierra, plantío).

tempranamente *adv* early (temprano) || too early (prematuramente).

tempranero, ra *adj* early-rising (persona) || AGR early || *ser tempranero* to be an early riser (persona).

temprano, na *adj* early (plantas).
◆ *m* early crop; *recoger los tempranos* to gather in the early crops.
◆ *adv* early; *levantarse temprano* to get up early || *más temprano* earlier.

ten *m* FAM *tener mucho ten con ten* to be very careful.

tenacidad *f* tenacity || perseverance || TECN tensile strength.

tenacillas *f pl* small pliers *o* tongs (tenazas pequeñas) || sugar tongs (para el azúcar) || curling iron *sing* (para rizar el pelo) || tweezers (de depilar) || cigarette holder *sing* (para tener cogido el cigarrillo) || snuffers (despabiladeras).

tenallón *m* MIL tenail, tenaille (fortificación).

tenante *m* supporter (de un escudo).

tenar *adj/sm* ANAT thenar.

tenaz *adj* tenacious (persona) || persistent (dolor) || hard to remove (mancha) || adhesive, sticky (pegajoso); *la pez es muy tenaz* pitch is very sticky || stubborn (resistencia).

tenaza *f*; **tenazas** *f pl* pliers, pincers (herramienta) || tongs (para el fuego) || claws, pincers (de crustáceos) || tenail, tenaille (fortificación) || tongs (para hielo, pasteles) || MED forceps || TECN jaws (del torno) || tenace (juego de baraja) || — FIG & FAM *eso no se puede coger ni con tenazas* I wouldn't touch it with a barge pole || DEP *hacer tenaza* to get *o* to put a scissors hold on (lucha libre) || FIG & FAM *no hay manera de* or *no se puede sacárselo ni con tenazas* wild horses couldn't drag it out for him.

tenazón (a); tenazón, (de) *loc adv* without taking aim, blindly.

tenca *f* ZOOL tench (pez).

tendal *m* awning (toldo) || canvas used to catch olives (para recoger aceitunas) || drying place (tendedero) || AMER shearing shed (para esquilar los animales) | drying floor (para secar café, cacao) | lot, heap (gran cantidad).

tendedero *m* drying place (sitio para tender ropa).

tendejón *m* little shop.

tendel *m* levelling line (cuerda) || layer of mortar (capa de mortero).

tendencia *f* tendency, trend; *la tendencia al aumento de precios* the tendency for prices to rise, the trend towards rising prices || — ECON *tendencia del mercado* market trend || *tendencia política* political tendency || *tener tendencia a hacer algo* to tend to do sth., to have a tendency to do sth.

tendencioso, sa *adj* tendentious [*US* tendencious].

tendente *adj* directed, aimed; *medidas tendentes a una mejora económica* measures directed towards economic improvement.

ténder *m* tender (de la locomotora).

tender* *vt* to spread, to spread out, to lay out; *tender el mantel sobre la mesa* to spread the tablecloth over the table; *tender la ropa en el suelo para que se seque* to spread clothes on the ground to dry || to lay (poner en posición horizontal) || to put out, to stretch out (la mano) || to hang out (ropa en una cuerda) || to stretch (cuerda) || to lay (vía, cable) || to cast (redes) || to build, to throw (puente) || to set, to lay (emboscada) || to draw (un arco) || to plaster (revestir las paredes con una capa de cal) || MAR to spread (velas).
◆ *vi* to tend, to have a tendency; *tiende a ser perezoso* he tends towards laziness, he tends to be lazy, he has a tendency to be lazy.
◆ *vpr* to stretch out, to lie down; *tenderse en* or *por el suelo* to stretch out on the floor || to lay down, to throw one's cards on the table (naipes) || to run at full gallop (caballo) || to droop (las mieses).

tenderete *m* stall, stand (puesto de venta) || display (exposición de mercancías) || pile, heap (montón desordenado).

tendero, ra *m/f* shopkeeper.
◆ *m* tent maker (que fabrica tiendas de campaña).

tendido, da *adj* spread out, laid out (extendido) || hung out (ropa) || lying down (persona) || — *a galope tendido* at full gallop (un caballo), at full speed, with utmost haste (muy rápidamente) || FIG & FAM *dejar tendido a uno* to floor s.o. | *dormir a pierna tendida* to sleep soundly, to sleep like a log | *hablar largo y tendido de algo* to talk sth. over | *llorar a moco tendido* to cry bitterly, to cry one's eyes out, to sob one's heart out, to weep buckets.
◆ *m* construction, building (de un puente) || laying (de un cable) || wash, washing (ropa puesta a secarse) || batch of bread (tanda de pan) || coat of plaster (capa de yeso) || TAUR lower tiers *pl* of seats excluding the first row || slope [of a roof from ridge to eaves] (del tejado) || run (de encaje) || AMER bed linen || FIG *para el tendido* for the masses.

tendiente *adj* tending (*a* to).

tendón *m* tendon || *tendón de Aquiles* Achilles' tendon.

tenducha *f*; **tenducho** *m* FAM small rundown shop.

tenebrosidad *f* darkness, gloom || FIG shadiness.

tenebroso, sa *adj* dark, gloomy, tenebrous (oscuro) || FIG dark, gloomy; *un porvenir muy tenebroso* a very dark future | shady, sinister; *maquinaciones tenebrosas* shady dealings.

tenedor *m* fork (utensilio de mesa); *un tenedor de plata* a silver fork || COM bearer, holder || owner (el que posee) || — *tenedor de acciones* stockholder || *tenedor de libros* bookkeeper.

teneduría *f* bookkeeping || *teneduría de libros* bookkeeping.

tenencia *f* possession; *tenencia ilícita de armas* illicit possession of arms || MIL lieutenancy (cargo de teniente) || *tenencia de alcaldía* position of deputy mayor.

tener* *vt* to have, to have got; *tener dinero* to have money; *tener buenas cualidades* to have good qualities; *el ministro tiene una entrevista esta tarde* the minister has an interview this afternoon || to have, to have got, to own, to possess (ser propietario de); *tiene dos casas en Madrid* he owns two houses in Madrid || to hold, to have; *tenía el sombrero en la mano* he was holding his hat in his hand || to hold, to contain (contener) || to weigh (pesar) || to be, to measure (medir); *la habitación tiene seis metros por diez* the room is six metres by ten || to keep (mantener); *el ruido me ha tenido despierto toda la noche* the noise kept me awake all night || to hold (celebrar); *tener una asamblea* to hold an assembly || to take (coger); *ten tu billete* take your ticket; *tenga Vd. la vuelta* take the change || to keep, to be in charge of (ocuparse de); *tener los libros* to keep the books || to have, to spend (pasar); *hemos tenido un día muy bueno* we have had a very good day || to have, to receive (recibir) || to keep, to maintain (conservar); *tener en buen estado* to keep in good shape || to have (dar a luz); *acaba de tener un niño* she has just had a baby || — *¡ahí lo tienes!* you see!, so there you are! (ya ves), there it is (allí está) || *allí tiene...* there is..., there are... || *aquí tiene...* here is... || *¿conque ésas tenemos?* is that so?, so that's the way it is || *¿cuántos años tienes?* how old are you? || *¡él tenía que ser!* it would be him!, it had to be him! || *eso no tiene nada que ver* that has nothing to do with it, that is irrelevant || FIG *no sabe lo que tiene* he doesn't realize how lucky he is || *no tendremos ni para empezar con esto* we won't go far with this || FAM *no tenerlas todas consigo* not to rate one's chances, to have one's doubts (no estar muy seguro de algo), to have the wind up (tener miedo) || *no tener más que* to have only to; *no tienes más que llamar para que vaya enseguida* you have only to call and I shall be there at once || FIG *no tener más que lo puesto* to have only the shirt on one's back || *no tener nada de particular* to be nothing extraordinary *o* unusual || *no tener nada que ver con* to have nothing to do with; *yo no tengo nada que ver con eso* I have nothing to do with that || *no tener razón* to be wrong || *¿qué tiene de particular?* what is so unusual about that? || *¿qué tienes?* what's the matter (with you)?, what's wrong (with you)? || *quien más tiene más quiere* the more one has the more one wants || *quien tuvo retuvo* one always retains something of one's past glory *o* splendour *o* fortune || *tener a bien* to see fit, to think it better; *tuve a bien quedarme más tiempo* I saw fit to stay longer; to be so good *o* so kind as to (tener la amabilidad de) || *tener a la vista* or *ante los ojos* to have before one's eyes || *tener al corriente* to keep informed || *tener al día* to keep up to date || *tener algo de beber, de comer* to have (got) sth. to drink, to eat || *tener a mano* to have at *o* to hand, to have handy || *tener a menos* to consider it beneath o.s.; *tiene a menos trabajar* he considers it beneath himself to work || *tener ante sí* to have before one; *el comité tiene ante sí un informe* the committee has before it a report || *tener... años* to be... (years old); *tiene cuarenta años* he is fourty (years old) || FIG & FAM *tener a alguien atravesado* not to be able to stand *o* to bear *o* to abide s.o.; *le tengo atravesado* I can't stand him || *tener calor* to be hot || *tener cinco pies de alto y tres de ancho* to be five feet high and three feet wide || *tener con que* or *para vivir* to have enough to live on || *tener... de retraso* to be... late; *tenemos una hora de retraso* we are an hour late || *tener el genio atravesado* to be bad-humoured *o* bad-tempered || FIG *tener encima* to be loaded down with, to have on; *tengo una cantidad enorme de trabajo encima* I have an enormous amount of work on || *tener envidia* to be envious || *tener fama* to be famous, to be well known || *tener frío* to be cold || *tener hambre* to be hungry || *tener la cara atravesada* to be grim-faced *o* glum-faced *o* surly || *tenerla tomada con uno* to have it in for s.o. || *tener paciencia* to be patient || *tener para sí* to think, to believe; *tengo para mí que ya ha llegado* I think he has arrived || *tener por* to consider, to regard as (considerar); *le tengo por inteligente* I consider him intelligent || *tener por seguro* to rest assured; *ten por seguro que te llamará* rest assured he will call you || *tener puesto*

to wear, to have on || *tener que* to have to, must; *tengo que irme* I have to go, I must go || *tener razón* to be right || *tener sed* to be thirsty || *tener sobre sí* to be in charge of || FIG & FAM *tener una encima* to be drunk *o* canned *o* plastered || *tiene mucho de su padre* he takes after his father || *tienen el jardín hecho un barrizal* their garden is like a swamp || *ya tiene años, ya tiene sus añitos* he's no spring chicken.
◆ *vi* to have money (tener dinero) || *yo no tengo* I haven't got any.
◆ *vpr* to stop, to halt (detenerse); *¡tente!* stop! || to catch o.s. (al caerse) || to stay, to keep (mantenerse); *tente quieto* keep still || to stand up; *el niño se tiene solo* the child stands up alone || — FIG & FAM *estar uno que no se tiene* to be so tired that one cannot stand up (de cansado), to be so drunk that one cannot walk straight (de borracho) || *tenerse de* or *en pie* to stand up || *tenerse en mucho* to think highly of o.s. || *tenerse en poco* to underrate o.s., to underestimate o.s. || FIG *tenerse firme* to stand firm, to stand one's ground || *tenerse por* to consider o.s.

— OBSERV Como existen muchas expresiones con el verbo *tener* se han tratado generalmente en el artículo correspondiente al sustantivo de la frase considerada.

— OBSERV The auxiliary verb *to have* is usually translated by *haber*. If, however, one wishes to stress the result obtained, the verb *tener* may replace *haber* as the auxiliary. In this case the past participle agrees in number and gender with the object of the verb: *tengo ahorradas unas veinte mil pesetas* I have (got) some twenty thousand pesetas saved up (*he ahorrado veinte mil pesetas* I have saved twenty thousand pesetas). This usage of *tener* as an auxiliary verb does not necessarily affect the English translation: *no tengo acabado el trabajo* I haven't finished the work.

— OBSERV Cuando el verbo *to have* significa *to possess* va seguido muy frecuentemente en el habla corriente por el participio pasivo *got* sin que sea modificado el sentido: *tengo una casa* I have got a house.

— OBSERV El pretérito y el participio pasivo de este verbo son irregulares: *had*, así como la tercera persona del singular del presente de indicativo: *has*.

tenería *f* tannery (curtiduría).

tenguerengue (en) *loc adv* unstable; *estar en tenguerengue* to be unstable.

tenia *f* tapeworm, taenia (gusano) || ARQ taenia (moldura).

tenida *f* meeting (reunión) || *AMER* clothes (ropa), suit (traje), uniform (uniforme).

tenienta *f* lieutenant's wife (mujer del teniente).

teniente *adj* holding, owning, possessing, having (que tiene) || unripe (fruta) || FIG & FAM hard of hearing | stingy, tightfisted, tight (tacaño).
◆ *m* lieutenant || — *segundo teniente* second lieutenant || *teniente coronel* lieutenant colonel || *teniente de alcalde* deputy mayor || *teniente general* lieutenant general.

tenífugo, ga *adj/sm* taeniafuge, teniafuge.

tenis *m* tennis (juego) || tennis court (campo de tenis) || *tenis de mesa* ping-pong, table tennis.

tenista *m/f* tennis player.

Tenochtitlán *n pr* GEOGR Tenochtitlan.

tenor *m* tenor; *a juzgar por el tenor de su discurso* judging by the tenor of his speech || MÚS tenor || — FIG *a este tenor* at this rate, if this continues || *a tenor* likewise, in the same fashion; *comimos mucho y bebimos a tenor* we ate a lot and drank likewise || *a tenor de* in accordance with.

tenorio *m* Don Juan, lady-killer.

tenrec *m* ZOOL tenrec, tanrec.

tensar *vt* to tauten (un cable) || to draw (un arco) || *tensado* taut, tense, tautened (cable), drawn (arco).

tensión *f* tension || tautness, tightness (de una cuerda) || TECN stress || ELECTR tension, voltage; *alta tensión* high tension *o* voltage || FIG tension, strained relations *pl*; *tensión entre dos países* strained relations between two countries | tenseness (de la situación) | tension, stress, strain; *mi madre está bajo una tensión enorme* my mother is under enormous strain || — *cable de alta tensión* high-tension cable || *tener la tensión alta* to suffer from high blood pressure || *tensión arterial* blood pressure || *tensión nerviosa* nervous tension *o* stress || *tensión superficial* surface tension.

tenso, sa *adj* tense, tight, taut (tirante) || FIG tense, strained; *relaciones tensas entre las dos familias* tense relations between the two families.

tensor, ra *adj* tightening, tensile (que tensa).
◆ *m* ANAT tensor || tightener (dispositivo que sirve para tensar) || TECN turnbuckle (aparato) | tension (de máquina de coser) | stiffener (de camisa) || MAT tensor.

tentación *f* temptation; *ceder a la tentación* to yield to temptation; *no nos dejes caer en la tentación* lead us not into temptation.

tentaculado, da *adj* tentacled.

tentacular *adj* tentacular.

tentáculo *m* ZOOL tentacle.

tentadero *m* pen where the bravery of young bulls is tested.

tentador, ra *adj* tempting, enticing; *proposición tentadora* tempting proposal.
◆ *m* tempter || *el Tentador* the Devil.
◆ *f* temptress.

tentadura *f* mercury test of silver ore.

tentalear *vt* to feel.

tentar* *vt* to touch, to feel (examinar por medio del tacto) || to tempt, to entice; *la serpiente tentó a Eva* the serpent tempted Eve || to tempt, to attract (atraer) || to attempt, to try (intentar) || to try, to test (someter a prueba) || MED to probe || — FIG *tentar a Dios* to tempt Providence (intentar algo muy peligroso) | *tentar al diablo* to tempt the devil, to look for trouble.
◆ *vpr* to feel o.s. || FIG *tentarse la ropa* to think about it, to hesitate.

tentativa *f* attempt, try; *tentativa infructuosa* unsuccessful attempt || (ant) entrance examination (en la universidad) || JUR *tentativa de asesinato* attempted murder.

tentemozo *m* prop (puntal) || pole prop (del carro) || tumbler, roly-poly (juguete) || cheek strap (quijera del caballo).

tentempié *m* bite to eat, snack (refrigerio) || tumbler, roly-poly (dominguillo).

tentenelaire *m/f* child of a quadroon and a mulatto.
◆ *m* *AMER* hummingbird (colibrí).

tentetieso *m* tumbler, roly-poly (juguete).

tenue *adj* thin, tenuous, delicate; *los hilos tenues del gusano de seda* the tenuous threads of the silkworm || thin, light (niebla) || weak, subdued, faint (voz, luz) || flimsy (tela) || simple, natural (estilo) || insignificant (de poca importancia).

tenuidad *f* tenuity, delicacy, thinness (poco grosor) || thinness (de la niebla) || weakness, faintness (de luz, de voz) || flimsiness (de la tela) || simplicity (estilo) || trifle (cosa de poca entidad).

tenuirrostro *m* ZOOL tenuiroster.
◆ *pl* ZOOL tenuirostres.

teñido, da *adj* dyed; *un abrigo teñido de azul* a coat dyed blue || tinted, dyed (pelo) || FIG tinged.
◆ *m* dyeing (acción) || dye (color).

teñir* *vt* to dye; *teñir un abrigo de verde* to dye a coat green || to stain (manchar) || to tone down (un color) || FIG to tinge.
◆ *vpr* to dye one's hair; *se ha teñido de rubio* she has dyed her hair blond.

teocali *m* teocalli (templo mejicano).

teocracia *f* theocracy.

teocrático, ca *adj* theocratic.

Teócrito *npr m* Theocritus.

teodicea *f* theodicy.

teodolito *m* theodolite.

Teodorico *npr m* Theodoric.

teodosiano, na *adj* Theodosian; *el código teodosiano* the Theodosian Code.

Teodosio *npr m* Theodosius.

teogonía *f* theogony.

teologal *adj* theological, theologic || *virtudes teologales* theological virtues.

teología *f* theology; *la teología católica* Catholic theology || IG *teología de la liberación* liberation theology || FIG & FAM *no meterse en teologías* not to get into deep water.

teológico, ca *adj* theological, theologic.

teologizar *vi* to theologize.

teólogo, ga *adj* theological (teologal).
◆ *m/f* theologian.

teorema *m* theorem; *teorema de Pitágoras* Pythagoras theorem.

teoría *f* theory || — *en teoría* theoretically, in theory || *teoría del conocimiento* theory of knowledge || *teoría de los quanta* quantum theory.

teóricamente *adv* theoretically.

teórico, ca *adj* theoretical.
◆ *m/f* theoretician.
◆ *f* theoretics, theory.

teorizar *vi* to theorize.
◆ *vt* to theorize on.

teosofía *f* theosophy.

teosófico, ca *adj* theosophical, theosophic.

teósofo *m* theosophist.

tepache *m* *AMER* Mexican drink made from pulque, water, pineapple and cloves.

tepe *m* sod.

tepeizcuinte *m* *AMER* ZOOL spotted cavy, paca (roedor).

tepetate *m* *AMER* rock used in construction.

teponascle *m* *AMER* teponaxtle, Mexican slit-drum.

tequila *f* tequila (bebida).

tequio *m* *AMER* nuisance.

terapeuta *m/f* MED therapist.

terapéutica *f* therapeutics, therapy; *terapéutica ocupacional* occupational therapy.

terapéutico, ca *adj* therapeutic, therapeutical.

terapia *f* MED therapy; *terapia de grupo* group therapy.

teratología *f* teratology.

terbio *m* QUÍM terbium (metal).

tercamente *adv* obstinately, stubbornly.

tercelete *adj* ARQ *arco tercelete* tierceron.

tercena *f* government tobacco warehouse || *AMER* butcher's shop (carnicería).

tercer *adj* (apócope de tercero), third; *vivo en el tercer piso* I live on the third floor || *Tercer Mundo* Third World.

— OBSERV *Tercero* is always apocopated before a masculine singular noun even if another adjective comes between it and the noun. It is occasionally apocopated before a feminine noun: *la tercer noche.*

tercera *f* tierce, sequence of three cards (juegos de naipes) || procuress (alcahueta) || MÚS third || AUT third (velocidad) || third class (en el tren) || tierce (en esgrima).

terceramente *adv* thirdly, in the third place.

tercería *f* mediation, arbitration (de un tercero) || procuring (de los alcahuetes) || JUR right of third party.

tercerilla *f* triplet (poesía).

tercero, ra *adj* third; *la tercera calle a la derecha* the third street on the right || — *Carlos III* (tercero) Charles III [the third] || REL *orden tercera* third order || *por tercera persona* by a third party || *seguro contra tercera persona* third party insurance || *ser tercero* to be the odd man out (en una reunión) || *tercera parte* third (división); *cinco es la tercera parte de quince* five is the third of fifteen.
◆ *m/f* third, third one.
◆ *m* third party, third person; *causar daño a un tercero* to harm a third party || REL tertiary || third floor; *vivo en el tercero* I live on the third floor || third year (tercer curso) || pimp, procurer (alcahuete) || go-between (intermediario) || mediator, arbitrator (que zanja una cuestión) || *ser el tercero en discordia* to be the arbitrator *o* the mediator.
— OBSERV Véase OBSERV en TERCER.

tercerol *m* MAR third [any object situated in third position].

tercerola *f* musketoon (arma) || small flute (flauta) || medium-sized barrel (barril) || FAM third class (en los trenes).

terceto *m* tercet (estrofa) || MÚS trio.

tercia *f* third (tercio) || third of a «vara» (medida) || REL tierce || tierce (en los juegos de naipes) || AGR third digging.

terciado, da *adj* crosswise (atravesado) || medium-sized (toro) || *azúcar terciado* brown sugar.
◆ *m* broadsword (espada) || wide ribbon (cinta).

terciador, ra *adj* mediating, arbitrating.
◆ *m/f* mediator, arbitrator.

terciana *f*; **tercianas** *f pl* MED tertian fever, tertian.

terciar *vt* to divide into three parts (dividir) || to place diagonally *o* crosswise (poner en diagonal) || to wear across one's chest (una prenda de ropa) || AGR to plough for the third time | to cut (a plant) near the roots || to balance [the weight] (sobre la acémila) || AMER to water down (aguar).
◆ *vi* to arbitrate, to mediate (mediar) || to make up the number (completar el número) || to participate, to take part (participar) || to reach the third day (la luna).
◆ *vpr* to occur, to arise, to present itself (una posibilidad) || *si se tercia* should the occasion arise.

terciario, ria *adj* third (tercero en orden).
◆ *adj/sm* GEOL Tertiary.
◆ *m/f* REL tertiary.

tercio, cia *adj* third (tercero).
◆ *m* third (tercera parte) || each of the three parts of a rosary || MIL infantry regiment [in the 16th and 17th centuries] | legion; *tercio extranjero* foreign legion || division (de la guardia civil) || TAUR stage, phase, part [of the bullfight]; *tercio de varas* opening stage, picador stage; *tercio de banderillas* banderilla stage | each of the three concentric zones of the bullring || each of the three stages of the horse race (en equitación) || pack (de una acémila) || MAR harbour guild || — TAUR *el tercio de muerte* the kill || JUR *tercio de libre disposición* disposable portion [of estate].

terciopelado, da *adj* velvety.

terciopelo *m* velvet; *cortinas de terciopelo* velvet curtains.

terco, ca *adj* stubborn, obstinate (obstinado).

terebenteno *m* QUÍM terebenthene.

terebintáceas *f pl* BOT terebinthaceae.

terebinto *m* BOT terebinth, turpentine tree.

Terencio *npr m* Terence.

Teresa *npr f* Theresa.

teresiano, na *adj* of Saint Theresa of Avila.
◆ *f* MIL cap || REL Teresian.

tergal *m* (*nombre registrado*) French polyester fabric (tejido).

tergiversable *adj* which can be misrepresented *o* twisted *o* distorted.

tergiversación *f* distortion, twisting, misrepresentation.

tergiversador, ra *adj* distorting.
◆ *m/f* person who distorts *o* misrepresents the facts.

tergiversar *vt* to distort, to twist, to misrepresent (palabras, sentido).

terliz *m* ticking (tela).

termal *adj* thermal

termas *f pl* thermae, hot baths, hot springs.

termes *m* ZOOL termite.

termia *f* FÍS therm.

térmico, ca *adj* thermal, thermic, heat; *energía térmica* thermal power.

terminación *f* termination, ending (acción de acabarse) || completion; *la terminación de la obra duró dos meses* the completion of the work took two months || finish (acabado) || end, final part (parte final) || GRAM ending.

terminacho *m* FAM vulgar expression, rude word (palabra indecente o poco culta) | barbarism (término bárbaro).

terminal *adj* terminal, final, ultimate || BOT terminal || *estación terminal* terminus (de transportes).
◆ *m* ELECTR terminal || INFORM terminal; *terminal conversacional* conversational *o* interactive terminal; *terminal gráfico* graphic terminal; *terminal vídeo* video terminal; *terminal videotex* videotex terminal.
◆ *f* *terminal, terminal aérea* air terminal.

terminante *adj* categorical; *una negativa terminante* a categorical refusal || peremptory; *una orden terminante* a peremptory command || conclusive, definite; *resultados terminantes* conclusive results || strict (prohibición).

terminantemente *adv* categorically || peremptorily || conclusively, definitely || strictly; *queda terminantemente prohibido* it is strictly forbidden.

terminar *vt* to finish, to complete; *terminar la carrera* to finish one's studies || to end (poner fin a) || to conclude (concluir) || *dar algo por terminado* to finish sth. (acabar), to consider sth. finished (considerar acabado).
◆ *vi* to finish, to end; *el espectáculo termina a las once* the show finishes at eleven || to end, to finish, to close; *la reunión terminó a medianoche* the meeting ended at midnight || to draw to a close, to end, to finish (llegar a su fin); *la conferencia se está terminando* the conference is drawing to a close || to conclude (concluir) || to finish; *no he terminado de comer* I haven't finished eating || to have just (acabar de); *termino de llegar* I have just arrived || to end up; *terminó yéndose a América, terminó por irse a América* he ended up going to America; *terminé rendido* I ended up exhausted || FIG to break up (reñir); *mi hermana y su novio han terminado* my sister and her boyfriend have broken up || MED to come to the final stage (una enfermedad) || — *éramos muy amigos pero terminamos mal* we were good friends but we ended up on bad terms || *este chico terminará mal* this boy will come to a sticky end *o* will come to no good || *no termino de comprender* I still cannot understand || *terminar loco* to go mad || *¡termina ya!* get it finished.
◆ *vpr* to end (llegar a su fin) || to run out (agotarse); *se ha terminado el vino* the wine has run out || *se terminó la reunión* the meeting is over.

término *m* end, finish, conclusion; *llegamos al término del viaje* we reached the end of the trip; *poner término a* to put an end to || term, word (palabra); *término técnico* technical term || GRAM & MAT & FIL term || terminus (de una línea de transporte) || boundary (frontera) || boundary marker (mojón) || period, term (plazo); *dentro de un término de ocho días* within a period of eight days || district, area; *término municipal* municipal district || place (lugar señalado) || object, aim goal (objetivo) || condition, state (estado de una persona o de una cosa) || place (en una enumeración); *en primer término* in the first place || ARQ term || — *dar término a* to finish off || *en último término* as a last resort || *llevar a buen término* to see through *o* to carry out successfully || *llevar a término* to see [sth.] through, to carry out || *mantenerse en el término medio* to be moderate || ARTES *primer término* foreground | *segundo término* middle distance || *término medio* average; *por término medio* on the average; in-between; *no hay término medio* there is no in-between; compromise (compromiso).
◆ *pl* conditions, terms; *los términos del tratado* the terms of the treaty || terms (relaciones); *está en malos términos con sus padres* he is on bad terms with his parents || — *en términos de* in terms of || *en términos generales* in general, generally speaking || *en términos propios* clearly || FIG *invertir los términos* to get it the wrong way round || *medios términos* evasions || *términos del intercambio* terms of trade, terms of exchange.

terminología *f* terminology.

terminológico, ca *adj* terminological.

términus *m* terminus (estación terminal).

termita; termite *m* ZOOL termite (comején).

termitero *m* termite nest.

termo; termos *m* Thermos flask *o* bottle, Thermos || boiler, water heater (termosifón).

termoaislante *adj* insulating.

termocauterio *m* MED thermocautery.

termodinámico, ca *adj* thermodynamic.
◆ *f* thermodynamics.

termoelectricidad *f* thermoelectricity.

termoeléctrico, ca *adj* thermoelectric || *par termoeléctrico* thermocouple, thermoelectric couple.

termoelemento *m* thermoelement.

termoendurecible; termoestable *adj* thermosetting.

termógeno, na *adj* thermogenous, thermogenic.

termógrafo *m* thermograph.

termoiónico, ca *adj* thermionic.

termología *f* thermology.

termometría *f* thermometry.

termométrico, ca *adj* thermometric, thermometrical.

termómetro *m* thermometer; *termómetro clínico* clinical thermometer; *termómetro de máxima y mínima* maximum and minimum thermometer.

termonuclear *adj* thermonuclear.

termopar *m* FÍS thermocouple.

termopila *f* ELECTR thermopile.

Termópilas *npr fpl* Thermopylae.

termoplástico, ca *adj* thermoplastic.

termoquímica *f* thermochemistry.

termoquímico, ca *adj* thermochemical.

termorregulación *f* thermoregulation.

termorregulador *m* thermoregulador, thermostat.

termos *m* ⟶ **termo.**

termosifón *m* boiler, water heater (calentador de agua) || FÍS thermosiphon.

termostato *m* thermostat.

termoterapia *f* MED thermotherapy.

terna *f* list of three candidates for a post || pair of threes (en los dados) || set of dice (juego de dados).

ternario, ria *adj* ternary || MÚS *compás ternario* ternary form.
◆ *m* three days' devotion.

terne *adj m* FAM bullying.

ternera *f* calf (animal) || veal (carne); *chuleta de ternera* veal chop.

ternero *m* calf; *ternero recental* sucking calf.

terneza *f* tenderness.
◆ *pl* FAM sweet nothings.

ternilla *f* gristle, cartilage.

ternilloso, sa *adj* gristly, cartilaginous.

ternísimo, ma *adj* very tender.

terno *m* set of three (tres cosas) || three-piece suit (traje) || FAM curse, swearword (voto) || IMPR three sheets folded together || tern (en la lotería) || AMER set of jewellery [consisting of earrings, necklace and brooch] (joyas) || *echar ternos* to curse, to swear.

ternura *f* tenderness || sweet nothing (palabra cariñosa).

tero *m* AMER ZOOL South American lapwing.

terpeno *m* QUÍM terpene.

Terpsícore *npr f* MIT Terpsichore.

terquedad *f* stubbornness, obstinacy.

terracota *f* terra-cotta.

terrado *m* flat roof, roof terrace (azotea).

terraja *f* diestock (para tornillos) || modelling board (para molduras).

terraje *m* rent [paid on arable land].

terrajero *m* tenant farmer.

terral *adj m* land; *viento terral* land wind.
◆ *m* land wind.

terramicina *f* MED terramycin.

terranova *m* Newfoundland dog (perro).

Terranova *n pr* GEOGR Newfoundland.

terraplén *m* embankment (de la carretera y de la vía de ferrocarril) || MIL terreplein, earthwork, embankment || slope (pendiente).

terraplenar *vt* to level off (nivelar) || to embank, to bank up (hacer terraplén).

terráqueo, a *adj* terraqueous || *globo terráqueo* globe, earth.

terrateniente *m/f* landowner, landholder.

terraza *f* terrace, roof terrace (azotea) || terrace, balcony (balcón) || terrace; *sentarse en la terraza de un café* to sit down on a café terrace || AGR terrace (bancal) || AGR *cultivo en terrazas* terracing.

terrazgo *m* arable land, field (tierra) || land rent (arrendamiento).

terrazo *m* ground (en pintura) || terrazzo (revestimiento para el suelo).

terremoto *m* earthquake.

terrenal *adj* worldly; *bienes terrenales* worldly goods || *paraíso terrenal* earthly paradise.

terreno, na *adj* earthly, worldly; *vida terrena* earthly life.
◆ *m* ground, land, terrain; *terreno desigual* rough land || piece of land; *comprar un terreno en el campo* to buy a piece of land in the country || plot, site (solar); *se venden terrenos para la construcción* building plots for sale || FIG field, sphere (esfera); *en el terreno de la medicina* in the field of medicine || GEOL terrain, terrane || soil, ground, earth (suelo); *terreno pedregoso* stony ground || DEP field, ground; *terreno de fútbol* football ground || — FIG *ceder terreno* to give way || *coche todo terreno* jeep || FIG *el país es terreno abonado para tal ideología* the country is ready for such an ideology | *ganar, perder terreno* to gain, to lose ground | *meterse en el terreno de otro* to interfere | *minarle a uno el terreno* to cut the ground from under s.o.'s feet | *preparar el terreno* to pave the way || MIL *reconocer el terreno* to reconnoitre || FIG *saber alguien el terreno que pisa* to know what's what | *sobre el terreno* on the spot | *tantear el terreno* to see how the land lies | *terreno abonado* breeding ground, hotbed | *terreno conocido* familiar ground (tema) || *terreno de camping* camping site, camping ground || *terreno de honor* duelling ground || FIG *terreno vedado* taboo || *terreno urbanizable* property development site, building site.

terrero, ra *adj* earth (de tierra) || low, skimming (vuelo de algunas aves) || FIG humble (humilde) || AMER one-storey (casa).
◆ *m* pile of earth, mound (montón de tierra) || terrace (terraza) || public square (plaza pública) || target, mark (blanco de tiro) || alluvium (tierra de aluvión) || MIN spoil heap.

terrestre *adj* terrestrial, earthly.

terrible *adj* terrible, awful, dreadful (atroz) || *hace un calor terrible* it's terribly hot.

terrícola *m/f* Earth dweller (habitante de la tierra) || earthling (en ciencia ficción).
◆ *adj* terricolous.

terrier *m* terrier (perro).

terrígeno, na *adj* terrigenous.

territorial *adj* territorial; *límites territoriales* territorial limits; *aguas territoriales* territorial waters || — *código territorial* area code, code number (teléfonos) || *impuesto territorial* land tax.

territorialidad *f* territoriality.

territorio *m* territory || AMER region, district.

terrizo, za *adj* earthenware (hecho de tierra).
◆ *m/f* bowl (barreño).

terrón *m* clod (de tierra) || lump (de sal, azúcar, harina) || marc (residuo de aceitunas).
◆ *pl* farmland *sing.*

terror *m* terror || HIST terror.

terrorífico, ca *adj* terrifying, dreadful, awful, frightful.

terrorismo *m* terrorism.

terrorista *m/f* terrorist.

terrosidad *f* earthiness.

terroso, sa *adj* earthy || brown, earth-coloured.

terruño *m* country, native land, native soil (país, patria) || clod (terrón) || piece of land (parcela de tierra) || land (tierra que se trabaja).

terso, sa *adj* clear, clean (claro) || smooth (liso); *piel tersa* smooth skin || polished, glossy, shiny (brillante) || FIG smooth, flowing, easy (estilo).

tersura; tersidad *f* smoothness; *la tersura de la piel* the smoothness of one's skin || skininess, glossiness (brillo) || FIG smoothness, easiness, polish (del estilo).

tertulia *f* gathering of friends, get-together (reunión) || circle, group (peña) || back room (de un café) || upper gallery (del antiguo teatro) || — *tener tertulia* to have a get-together, to meet || *tertulia literaria* literary circle, coterie (grupo), literary gathering (reunión).

Tertuliano *npr m* Tertullian.

tertuliano, na; tertuliante; tertulio, lia *m/f* participant in a social or literary gathering || *uno de los tertulianos* one of the people present.

tertuliar *vi* AMER to have a get-together, to meet.

tertulio, lia *m/f* ⟶ **tertuliano.**

terutero; teruteru *m* AMER ZOOL South American lapwing.

terylene *m* Terylene.

Tesalia *npr f* GEOGR Thessaly.

tesaliense; tesalio, lia *adj/s* Thessalian.

Tesalónica *npr f* GEOGR Thessalonica.

tesar *vt* MAR to tauten, to tighten.
◆ *vi* to back, to back up, to pull back (bueyes).

tesina *f* project.

tesis *f* thesis (de universidad) || theory, idea (opinión); *él y yo sostenemos la misma tesis* he and I hold the same theory || theory (opinión) || FIL thesis || — *novela de tesis* novel with a message || *tesis doctoral* doctoral thesis.

tesitura *f* MÚS tessitura || frame of mind, mood (estado de ánimo) || situation, circumstances *pl* (circunstancia); *en esta tesitura* in this situation.

tesón *m* firmness, inflexibility (firmeza) || tenacity, perseverance (perseverancia) || *sostener con tesón una opinión* to firmly maintain an opinion.

tesonero, ra *adj* persevering, tenacious (perseverante).

tesorería *f* treasury, treasurer's office (oficina) || treasurership (cargo).

tesorero, ra *m/f* treasurer || REL custodian [of a church's valuables].

tesoro *m* treasure; *tesoro escondido* buried treasure || treasury, exchequer (del Estado) || REL valuables *pl*, collection of relics and ornaments (de una iglesia) || thesaurus (libro) || FIG treasure, gem, jewel; *la muchacha es un verdadero tesoro* the maid is really a treasure || FIG & FAM dear, treasure, precious; *mi tesoro* my treasure || — *bono del Tesoro* Treasury bond || *Tesoro público* Treasury.

Tespis *npr m* Thespis.

test *m* test.

testa *f* front (frente) || head (cabeza) || BOT testa || *testa coronada* crowned head.

testáceo, a *adj* ZOOL testacean, testaceous.

testado, da *adj* testate.

testador *m* testator, testate.

testadora *f* testatrix, testate.

testaferro *m* front man, man of straw.

testamentaría *f* testamentary execution (gestiones) || estate, inheritance (herencia) || meeting of executors (junta).

testamentario, ria *adj* testamentary.
◆ *m* executor.
◆ *f* executrix.

testamento *m* will, testament; *hacer* or *otorgar testamento* to make one's will || — REL *Antiguo* or *Viejo Testamento* Old Testament | *Arca del Testamento* Ark of the Covenant | *Nuevo Testamento* New Testament || JUR *testamento abierto* nuncupative will | *testamento auténtico* legal will | *testamento cerrado* sealed will | *testamento ológrafo* holograph will | *testamento público* public will.

testar *vi* to make one's will *o* one's testament.
◆ *vt* to erase (tachar).

testarada *f* knock on the head ‖ FAM obstinacy, stubbornness (terquedad).

testarazo *m* knock on the head (golpe en la cabeza) ‖ butt (golpe dado con la cabeza) ‖ header, head (en fútbol).

testarudez *f* obstinacy, stubbornness.

testarudo, da *adj* stubborn, obstinate.
◆ *m/f* stubborn *o* obstinate person.

teste *m* ANAT testis.

testera *f* front, front part (parte delantera) ‖ forehead (de un animal) ‖ frontstall (de la armadura de un caballo) ‖ forward-facing seat (en un carruaje) ‖ wall (de horno de fundición).

testero *m* front, front part (testera) ‖ wall (pared) ‖ MIN stope.

testicular *adj* ANAT testicular.

testículo *m* ANAT testicle.

testificación *f* testification ‖ testimony (testimonio).

testifical *adj* JUR witness.

testificante *adj* testifying.

testificar *vt/vi* to testify.

testigo *m/f* JUR witness; *esta mujer es la primera testigo* this woman is the first witness.
◆ *m* evidence, witness, proof (prueba); *las catedrales antiguas son testigos de la fe de nuestros antepasados* our old cathedrals are evidence of *o* bear witness to the faith of our ancestors ‖ DEP stick, baton (en carrera de relevos) ‖ TECN core (de sondeo) ‖ — *lámpara testigo* pilot light, warning light ‖ *poner* or *tomar por testigo a uno* to call *o* to take s.o. to witness ‖ *pongo por testigo al cielo* I swear to God, as God is my witness ‖ JUR *testigo de cargo* witness for the prosecution | *testigo de descargo* witness for the defence | *testigo de vista, testigo ocular* eyewitness ‖ REL *testigos de Jehová* Jehovah's Witnesses.

testimonial *adj* JUR testimonial.
◆ *f pl* JUR documentary evidence *sing* ‖ REL testimonial *sing*.

testimoniar *vt* to be evidence *o* proof of, to testify to, to bear witness to; *estas ruinas testimonian la existencia de una civilización* these ruins testify to the existence of a civilization.

testimonio *m* JUR testimony, evidence | attestation, affidavit (hecho por escribano) ‖ mark, token; *testimonio de amistad* token of friendship ‖ — *falso testimonio* perjury, false evidence ‖ *levantar falsos testimonios* to bear false witness, to commit perjury; to slander (calumniar) ‖ FIG *según el testimonio de* according to ‖ *testimonio de pésame* condolences.

testosterona *f* BIOL testosterone.

testuz *m* forehead (frente) ‖ nape (nuca del toro, de la vaca).

tesura *f* rigidity, stiffness (rigidez).

teta *f* teat, nipple (pezón) ‖ breast, tit (*fam*), boob (*fam*), (pecho) ‖ udder, teat (de animales) ‖ FIG hillock, knoll (montículo) ‖ — *dar la teta a* to suckle, to breast-feed, to nurse ‖ *niño de teta* babe-in-arms ‖ *quitar la teta a* to wean ‖ FIG *teta de vaca* meringue (merengue), viper's grass (escorzonera).

tetania *f* MED tetany.

tetánico, ca *adj* MED tetanic.

tetanizar *vt* to tetanize.

tétano; tétanos *m* MED tetanus.

tetera *f* teapot ‖ AMER nipple (del biberón).

tetero *m* AMER baby's bottle, feeding bottle (biberón).

tetilla *f* nipple (de los mamíferos machos) ‖ nipple (del biberón).

Tetis *npr f* MIT Thetis.

tetón *m* stub (de una rama).

tetona *adj* FAM busty, buxom, large-breasted.
◆ *f* POP busty *o* buxom wench.

tetraédrico, ca *adj* MAT tetrahedral.

tetraedro *m* MAT tetrahedron.

tetragonal *adj* MAT tetragonal.

tetralogía *f* tetralogy.

tetrámero, ra *adj* tetrameral, tetramerous.

tetramotor *adj* four-engined.
◆ *m* four-engined aircraft.

tetraplejía *f* MED tetraplegia.

tetrápodo, da *adj/sm* ZOOL tetrapod.

tetrarca *m* tetrarch.

tetrarquía *f* tetrarchy, tetrarchate.

tetrasílabo, ba *adj* tetrasyllabic.
◆ *m* tetrasyllable.

tetrástrofo *adj* having four lines, four-line.
◆ *m* quatrain.

tetravalente *adj* tetravalent.

tétrico, ca *adj* gloomy, sullen (sombrío).

tetrodo *m* ELECTR tetrode.

Tetuán *n pr* GEOGR Tetuan.

tetuda *adj/s* FAM → **tetona.**

teucali *m* teocalli (templo mexicano).

teúrgia *f* theurgy.

teúrgico, ca *adj* theurgic, theurgical.

teutón, ona *adj* Teutonic.
◆ *m/f* Teuton.

teutónico, ca *adj* Teutonic.
◆ *m* Teutonic (idioma).

textil *adj/sm* textile; *industria textil* textile industry.

texto *m* text ‖ *libro de texto* textbook.

textual *adj* textual.

textualmente *adv* textually ‖ *lo que dijo textualmente fue lo siguiente* his exact words were, this is exactly what he said.

textura *f* texture (trama de un tejido) ‖ weaving (acción de tejer) ‖ structure (de un mineral).

teyú *m* AMER ZOOL iguana.

tez *f* complexion (cutis).

tezontle *m* AMER volcanic rock [used for building].

thai *adj/s* Thai, Tai.

theta *f* theta (letra griega).

ti *pron pers* you; *a ti* to you; *para* or *por ti* for you ‖ yourself; *¿lo has hecho para ti?* did you make it for yourself? ‖ REL Thee, Thyself (dirigiéndose a Dios) ‖ — FAM *de ti para mí* between you and me | *hoy por ti, mañana por mí* you can do the same for me sometime ‖ *para ti mismo* for youself.

tía *f* aunt ‖ FAM old; *la tía María* old Mary | bird [US gal, dame] (mujer cualquiera) | tart, whore (prostituta) ‖ — FAM *a tu tía, cuéntaselo a tu tía* tell it to the marines | *no hay tu tía* there's nothing doing ‖ *tía abuela* great-aunt, grandaunt ‖ *tía carnal* aunt ‖ *tía segunda* first cousin once removed.

tialina *f* BIOL ptyalin.

tiamina *f* thiamine, thiamin.

tiangue; tiánguez; tianguis *m* AMER market.

tiara *f* tiara.

Tíber *npr m* GEOGR Tiber.

Tiberíades *n pr* GEOGR Tiberias.

tiberio *m* FAM row, uproar, shindy; *armar un tiberio* to kick up a shindy *o* a row, to make an uproar.

Tiberio *npr m* Tiberius.

Tibet (El) *npr m* GEOGR Tibet.

tibetano, na *adj/s* Tibetan.

tibia *f* ANAT tibia, shinbone.

tibial *adj* tibial (de la tibia).

tibiamente *adv* FIG unenthusiastically, tepidly.

tibieza *f* lukewarmness, tepidity ‖ FIG lack of enthusiasm, coolness, tepidity.

tibio, bia *adj* lukewarm, tepid; *agua tibia* lukewarm water ‖ FIG lukewarm, unenthusiastic, cool, tepid (poco fervoroso); *recibimiento tibio* lukewarm reception ‖ FIG & FAM *ponerle tibio a alguien* to call s.o. all the names under the sun.

Tibulo *npr m* Tibullus.

tiburón *m* ZOOL shark ‖ FIG shark ‖ AMER egotist, self-seeker (egoísta).

tic *m* tic, twitch; *tiene un tic nervioso* he has a nervous tic ‖ FIG habit, mannerism (manía).

Ticiano *npr m* Titian.

ticket *m* ticket.

tico, ca *adj/s* AMER Costa Rican (costarriqueño).

tictac *m* ticktock, tick, ticking (de reloj) ‖ tapping (de máquina de escribir).

tiemblo *m* BOT aspen (álamo temblón).

tiempo *m* time; *no tengo tiempo para hacerlo* I have no time to do it; *tardó mucho tiempo en hacerlo* it took him a long time to do it ‖ time, times *pl*, age, epoch, days *pl*, era; *en tiempo de César* in the time of Caesar ‖ season, time (estación); *no es tiempo de naranjas* it is no the orange season ‖ weather; *hace buen tiempo* the weather is fine; *¿qué tiempo hace?* what's the weather like?; *tiempo cargado* overcast weather ‖ FAM age (edad); *tu hijo y el mío son del mismo tiempo* your son and mine are of the same age ‖ moment, time (momento); *no era tiempo de llorar* it was no time for crying; *se acerca el tiempo* the moment is drawing near; *cuando sea tiempo* when the time is right ‖ MAR stormy weather ‖ GRAM tense; *tiempo simple, compuesto* simple, compound tense ‖ MÚS movement (parte) | time (compás) ‖ DEP half (período); *primer, segundo tiempo* first, second half ‖ stage (fase) ‖ TECN stroke; *motor de cuatro tiempos* four-stroke engine ‖ — *aclararse* or *alzarse el tiempo* to clear; *cuando se alza el tiempo* when the weather clears ‖ FIG *acomodarse* or *adaptarse al tiempo* to adapt o.s. to the circumstances ‖ *ahora no es tiempo* it's too late ‖ *algún tiempo atrás* some time ago ‖ *al mismo tiempo* at the same time ‖ *al poco tiempo* a short time after, soon after ‖ *¡al tiempo!, y, si no, al tiempo* time will tell! ‖ *andando el tiempo* in the course of time, as time goes by *o* passes ‖ *andar con el tiempo* to keep up with the times ‖ *antes de tiempo* early, before time (con anticipación), at the wrong time *o* moment (inoportunamente), prematurely (parto) ‖ *a su debido tiempo* in due course, in due time ‖ *a su tiempo* at the right moment; *hazlo a su tiempo* do it at the right moment; in due time, in due course; *todo vendrá a su tiempo* everything will come in due time ‖ *a tiempo* in time, just in time (en el momento oportuno); *has llegado a tiempo* you have arrived just in time; on time; *nunca llega a su casa a tiempo* he never gets home on time ‖ *a través de los tiempos* through the ages ‖ *a un tiempo* at the same time ‖ *breve* or *corto tiempo* short while ‖ *cierto tiempo* a while, a certain time ‖ *¡cómo pasa* or *vuela el tiempo!* how time flies! ‖ *con el tiempo* in the course of time, in time, with time; *con el tiempo lo conseguiremos* we shall succeed in time ‖ *confiar* or *dejar* *algo al tiempo* to let things take their course || *con tiempo* in advance (por adelantado); *hay que sacar las entradas con tiempo* you have to get the tickets in advance; unhurriedly (sin prisa), in plenty of time (con tiempo de sobra), in time (en el momento oportuno) || *¿cuánto tiempo?* how long? || *darle a uno tiempo de* or *para* to have enough time to; *no me da tiempo de ir allí* I don't have enough time to go there; to give s.o. time to; *nunca me das tiempo para hacer las cosas como es debido* you never give me time to do things properly || *dar tiempo al tiempo* to give it time || *de algún tiempo a esta parte, de un tiempo a esta parte* for some time now || FIG *del tiempo de Maricastaña* or *del rey que rabió* as old as the hills || *demasiado tiempo* too long || *desde hace (mucho) tiempo* for a long time; *no le he visto desde hace tiempo* I haven't seen him for a long time || *de tiempo en tiempo* from time to time || *de tiempo inmemorial* from time immemorial || *el tiempo corre* time flies, time passes quickly || *el tiempo dirá* time will tell || FIG *el tiempo es oro* time is money || *el tiempo se me hace largo* time seems to drag by *o* to pass very slowly || *en el tiempo en que* when, in the days when || FIG *engañar el tiempo* to kill time || *en la noche de los tiempos* in the mists of time || *en los buenos tiempos* in the good old days || *en los tiempos que corren, en estos tiempos* nowadays || *en mis tiempos* in my time, in my day || *en otros tiempos, en un tiempo* in the past, in former times || *en tiempos de* at the time of, in the days of || FIG *en tiempos del rey que rabió, en tiempos de Maricastaña* in the days of good Queen Bess, in days of yore || *en tiempos remotos* in the distant past || *estar a tiempo de* to still have time to || *fuera de tiempo* out of season (fuera de su estación), untimely, inopportune, at the wrong moment (inoportuno) || *ganar tiempo* to save time (para adelantar), to gain time; *introducir toda clase de dificultades para ganar tiempo* to create all sorts of difficulties so as to gain time || *gastar el tiempo* to waste time || *hace bastante tiempo que nos conocemos* we have known each other for quite a while || *hace (mucho) tiempo* a long time ago; *me lo pediste hace tiempo* you asked me for it a long time ago || *hace (mucho) tiempo que no pasas por aquí* you haven't been round for a long time, it has been a long time since you last came round || *hacer tiempo* to kill time || *haga buen o mal tiempo* come rain or shine || FIG *le faltó tiempo para decirlo* it didn't take him long to say it || *malgastar el tiempo* to waste (one's) time || *más tiempo* longer (frase afirmativa), any longer (frase negativa o interrogativa) || FAM *más vale llegar a tiempo que rondar un año* it's best to be in the right place at the right time || *matar el tiempo* to kill time || *no hay tiempo que perder* there is no time to lose || *pasar el tiempo* to pass the time || *pasarse el tiempo leyendo* to spend one's time reading || *perder el tiempo* to waste time || FIG *poner a mal tiempo buena cara* to keep a stiff upper lip, to keep one's chin up, to look on the bright side || *por aquel tiempo* at that time || *¡qué tiempos los actuales!* what times we live in! || *¿qué tiempo tiene este niño?* how old is this boy? || *requerir* or *tomar tiempo* to take time || *ser de su tiempo* to be in step with the times; to be one's age; *Juan era de mi tiempo* John was my age || *sin perder tiempo* at once || *tener tiempo para todo* to find time for everything || *tiempo atrás* some time ago; *tiempo atrás solíamos ir allí* we used to go there some time ago || INFORM *tiempo compartido* time-sharing | *tiempo de acceso* access time || FOT *tiempo de exposición* exposure, exposure time || *Tiempo de Pasión* Passion Week || FAM *tiempo de perros* lousy *o* filthy weather || INFORM *tiempo de respuesta* response time || *tiempo ha* a long time ago || *tiempo libre* spare *o* free time || *tiempo límite de aceptación* closing date (concurso), deadline (trabajo) || ASTR *tiempo medio* mean time || INFORM *tiempo real* real-time|| *tiempos actuales* or *modernos* modern times || ASTR *tiempo verdadero* true time || *todo el tiempo* all the time, always (siempre), all the time; *todo el tiempo que estuvimos allí* all the time we were there || *tomarse tiempo, tomarlo con tiempo* to take one's time || *ya es tiempo de* or *para* it is time to.

tienda *f* shop [US store]; *tienda de antigüedades* antique shop; *abrir tienda* to set up shop, to open a shop || grocer's [US grocery store] (de comestibles) || tent (de campaña); *dormir en la tienda* to sleep in the tent || awning, canvas cover (de un barco) || cover (de carro) || AMER draper's (de telas) || — MIL *batir tiendas* to strike camp || *ir de tiendas* to go shopping, to go round the shops || *tienda de comestibles* grocer's [US grocery store] || *tienda de campaña* tent; *armar una tienda de campaña* to pitch a tent || *tienda de modas* boutique || MED *tienda de oxígeno* oxygen tent || *tienda de ultramarinos* grocer's, grocer's shop, grocery [US grocery store] || *tienda libre de impuestos* duty-free shop.

tienta *m* MED probe || TAUR test of bravery of young bulls || FIG artfulness, sagacity, cleverness || — *andar a tientas* to grope along || *a tientas* feeling one's way, gropingly.

tientaguja *f* sounding rod.

tiento *m* touch (sentido del tacto) || blind man's cane *o* stick (de los ciegos) || ropewalker's pole (contrapeso) || FIG tact, prudence (miramiento) | caution, care (prudencia) || ARTES maulstick || steady hand, sureness of hand (pulso) || FIG & FAM blow, punch (golpe) | swig (trago) | bite (bocado) || MÚS preliminary notes *pl* [before playing] || ZOOL tentacle, feeler || AMER strip of leather (tira de cuero) || — FIG *andar con tiento* to tread carefully, to watch one's step || *a tiento* gropingly, feeling one's way || FAM *coger el tiento* to get the knack | *dar un tiento a* to test, to try (intentar), to take a swig from; *dar un tiento a la botella* to take a swig from the bottle.

tientos *m pl* flamenco dance and song.

tiernamente *adv* tenderly.

tierno, na *adj* tender; *carne tierna* tender meat || soft (blando) || FIG young; *un tierno niño* a young child || tender, affectionate, loving; *corazón tierno* tender heart; *esposa tierna* affectionate wife || FIG sensitive, tender (sensible) | soft, delicate; *un color tierno* a soft colour || AMER green, unripe (frutos) || — FIG *edad tierna* tender age || *pan tierno* fresh bread.

tierra *f* Earth (planeta) || land (superficie no cubierta por el mar); *ver tierra* to see land || earth, soil; *un saco de tierra* a bagful of soil || ground (suelo); *durmió en la tierra* he slept on the ground || AGR land; *cultivar la tierra* to cultivate the land || native country (país), native region (región); *mi tierra* my native country; *nunca salió de su tierra* he never left his native region || soil (comarca); *tierra española* Spanish soil || ELECTR earth [US ground] || — FIG & FAM *besar la tierra* to fall flat on one's face || FIG *besar uno la tierra que otro pisa* to worship the ground s.o. walks on | *caer por tierra* to crumble (las ilusiones, etc.) || *dar en tierra, dar consigo en tierra* to fall [down] || *dar en tierra con* to drop *o* to throw on the ground || *echar a tierra* to knock down, to demolish (un edificio) || FIG *echar por tierra* to wreck, to dash to the ground, to crush, to destroy; *una objeción que echa por tierra un razonamiento* an objection which destroys an argument || FIG *echarse por tierra* to humiliate o.s. | *echar tierra a* to hush up (ocultar) | *en tierra de ciegos el tuerto es rey* in the land of the blind the one-eyed man is king | *en toda tierra de garbanzos* everywhere, all over the world | *estar comiendo* or *mascando tierra* to be pushing up daisies || FAM *la tierra de María Santísima* Andalusia || *poner pie en tierra* to dismount (de caballo), to get out *o* off, to disembark (de un vehículo) || FIG & FAM *poner tierra por medio* to make o.s. scarce || *por tierra* overland, by land || *tierra adentro* inland || *tierra de batán* fuller's earth || *tierra de cultivo* or *de labor* or *de labranza* farmland, arable land, agricultural land || *tierra de Jauja* land of milk and honey, land of plenty, Never-Never land || *tierra de nadie* no man's land || *tierra de pan llevar* or *paniega* wheatland || *Tierra de Promisión* or *Prometida* Promised Land || *tierra firme* terra firma || *tierra rara* rare earth || *Tierra Santa* Holy Land || *tierra vegetal* humus, mold, topsoil || AVIAC *tocar tierra* to touch down || *tomar tierra* to land (avión, barco, pasajeros) || FIG *tragársele a uno la tierra* to disappear into nowhere; *a Juan se le ha tragado la tierra* John has disappeared into nowhere || *venirse a tierra* to collapse (hundirse), to collapse, to crumble (ilusiones), to fall through (planes) || *ver tierras* to travel, to see the world (viajar mucho).
◆ *pl* land *sing*; *tiene tierras en el norte* he has land in the north || *por estas tierras* in these parts.

Tierra del Fuego *n pr* GEOGR Tierra del Fuego.

tierruca *f* country, native land (terruño) || FAM *la Tierruca* the province of Santander.

tieso, sa *adj* stiff, rigid (rígido); *pierna tiesa* stiff leg || erect, straight, upright (erguido) || firm (firme) || taut, tight (tenso) || FIG proud, arrogant, stuck-up (engreído) | stiff, starchy (envarado) | brave, courageous (valiente) | stubborn, unbending (terco) | well, in good shape; *está muy tieso a pesar de sus años* he is in good shape in spite of his years || FIG & FAM dead, stiff (muerto) || — FIG & FAM *dejar tieso* to leave penniless (sin dinero) | *estar tieso* to be stony-broke [US to be stone-broke] | *estar* or *ser más tieso que un ajo* or *que un huso* or *que el palo de la escoba* to be as stiff as a board *o* as a poker || *poner las orejas tiesas* to prick up its ears (perro) || *tener las orejas tiesas* to be prick-eared (perro) || FIG & FAM *tenérselas tiesas a* or *con alguien* to stand up to s.o., not to budge, to hold firm.
◆ *adv* hard, strongly.

tiesto *m* flowerpot (maceta) || potsherd, broken piece of earthenware (pedazo de vasija) || AMER pot, bowl (vasija).

tiesura *f* rigidity, stiffness (rigidez) || FIG stiffness, starchiness (gravedad exagerada).

tífico, ca *adj* MED typhous.
◆ *m/f* person suffering from typhus.

tiflitis *f* MED typhlitis.

tifo *m* ⟶ **tifus.**

tifogénico, ca *adj* MED typhogenic.

tifoideo, a *adj* typhoid; *fiebre tifoidea* typhoid fever.

tifón *m* typhoon.

tifus; tifo *m* MED typhus; *tifus icteroides* icteric typhus || FIG & FAM claque, people *pl* with free seats || — MED *tifus asiático* cholera, Asiatic cholera | *tifus de América* yellow fever || *tifus de Oriente* bubonic plague.

tigra *f* tigress (tigre hembra) || AMER female jaguar (jaguar hembra).

tigre *m* tiger || AMER jaguar || FIG tiger, bloodthirsty person (persona cruel) || *tigre hembra* tigress || FIG & FAM *oler a tigre* to stink of sweat.

tigrero, ra *adj* AMER brave.
◆ *m* AMER jaguar hunter.

tigresa *f* tigress.
— OBSERV *Tigresa* is a Gallicism for *tigra*.

tigrillo *m* AMER ocelot.

Tigris *npr m* GEOGR the (River) Tigris.

TIJ *abrev de Tribunal Internacional de Justicia* ICJ, International Court of Justice.

tija *f* stem (de la llave).

tijera *f* scissors *pl* (para cortar) ‖ sawbuck, sawhorse (para aserrar madera) ‖ first feather of a hawk's wing (pluma) ‖ DEP scissors, scissors hold (en la lucha libre) | scissors (salto) ‖ drainage ditch (para desagüe) ‖ sheepshearer (esquilador) ‖ brace (de carro) ‖ — *asiento* or *silla de tijera* folding chair ‖ *cama de tijera* folding bed ‖ FIG *cortado con la misma tijera* tarred with the same brush, cast in the same mould ‖ *echar* or *meter la tijera en* to start cutting (cortar) ‖ *escalera de tijera* stepladder ‖ DEP *salto de tijera* scissors.
◆ *pl* scissors; *tijeras para las uñas* nail scissors ‖ shears (de jardín, etc.) ‖ FIG & FAM backbiter *sing*, gossip *sing* (murmurador).

tijereta *f* small scissors *pl*, pair of small scissors ‖ BOT tendril (de la viña) ‖ ZOOL earwig (insecto) ‖ DEP *salto de tijereta* scissors.

tijeretada *f*; **tijeretazo** *m* snip.

tijeretear *vt* to cut, to snip (dar tijeretazos) ‖ FIG & FAM to meddle in.

tijereteo *m* cutting, snipping (acción de tijeretear) ‖ click, snip, snip-snipping (ruido).

tijerilla; tijeruela *f* BOT tendril (de la viña).

tila *f* lime, linden (árbol) ‖ linden blossom, lime blossom (flor) ‖ linden-blossom tea, lime-blossom tea (infusión).

tílburi *m* tilbury.

tildado, da *adj* with an accent (con acento) ‖ with a tilde (ñ).

tildar *vt* to put an accent on (poner acento) ‖ to put a tilde on (la n) ‖ to cross out (tachar) ‖ FIG to call, to brand, to label; *le tildan de avaro* they call him a miser.

tilde *m* tilde (sobre la n) ‖ accent (acento) ‖ fault, flaw, blemish (tacha) ‖ iota, dot, tittle (cosa insignificante) ‖ FIG *poner tilde a* to criticize.

tiliáceas *f pl* BOT tiliaceae.

tiliche *m* AMER trinket.

tilichero *m* AMER pedlar [US peddler].

tilín *m* ting-a-ling (de la campanilla) ‖ — AMER FIG & FAM *en un tilín* in a flash ‖ FAM *hacer tilín* to appeal | *le hizo tilín* he liked it (*o* her, etc.).

tilingo, ga *adj* AMER silly (tonto).

tilma *f* AMER blanket, poncho.

tilo *m* BOT lime, linden (árbol).

tilla *f* MAR deck.

tillado *m* MAR planking, boarding.

timador, ra *m/f* FAM swindler, cheat.

tímalo *m* grayling (pez).

timar *vt* FAM to swindle, to cheat (estafar); *le timaron mil pesetas* they swindled him out of a thousand pesetas | to cheat, to trick (engañar); *en esa tienda me timaron* they cheated me in that shop.
◆ *vpr* FAM to make eyes at each other ‖ FAM *timarse con* to make eyes at.

timba *f* FAM hand [of cards] (partida de juego) | gambling den (garito).

timbal *m* MÚS kettledrum, timbal | small drum (pequeño) ‖ meat pie, timbale (empanada).
◆ *pl* MÚS timpani.

timbalero *m* kettledrummer.

timbiriche *m* AMER alcoholic drink (bebida) | small shop (tiendecilla).

timbrado, da *adj* stamped ‖ *papel timbrado* stamped paper (sellado), letterhead stationery (con membrete).

timbrar *vt* to stamp (poner un sello) ‖ to seal (sellar) ‖ HERÁLD to crest (un escudo de armas) ‖ *máquina de timbrar* stamper, stamping machine.

timbrazo *m* loud *o* long ring (ruido) ‖ *dar un timbrazo* to ring the bell.

timbre *m* stamp, seal (sello) ‖ COM fiscal *o* revenue stamp (fiscal) ‖ bell, electric bell (de la puerta); *tocar el timbre* to ring the bell ‖ timbre, ring (sonido característico); *timbre metálico* metallic ring ‖ MÚS timbre ‖ HERÁLD crest, timbre; *timbre de nobleza* crest of nobility ‖ — *timbre de alarma* alarm bell ‖ FIG *timbre de gloria* title *o* claim to fame ‖ *timbre móvil* fiscal *o* revenue stamp.

timeleáceo, a *adj* thymelaeaceous.

timidez *f* shyness, timidity, bashfulness.

tímido, da *adj* timid, shy, bashful ‖ *venga, no seas tan tímido* come on, don't be shy.

timo *m* grayling (pez) ‖ FAM swindle, confidence trick (estafa); *un timo de mil pesetas* a one thousand peseta swindle | trick (engaño) | ANAT thymus ‖ — FIG & FAM *dar un timo a* to swindle | *esta película es un timo* this film is a swindle *o* a waste of money | *timo del sobre* envelope trick.

timón *m* MAR & AVIAC rudder ‖ beam (del arado) ‖ pole (de carro) ‖ FIG helm; *manejar el timón* to be at the helm ‖ AMER AUT steering wheel (volante) ‖ — AVIAC *timón de dirección* rudder | *timón de profundidad* elevator.

timonear *vi* to steer, to be at the helm.

timonel *m* MAR steersman, helmsman.

timonera *f* ZOOL rectrix, tail feather ‖ MAR wheelhouse.

timonero *adj* beam; *arado timonero* beam plough.
◆ *m* MAR steersman, helmsman.

timorato, ta *adj* timid, shy (tímido) ‖ God-fearing (que teme a Dios) ‖ prudish, priggish (mojigato).

timpánico, ca *adj* tympanic.

timpanismo *m*; **timpanitis** *f*; **timpanización** *f* MED tympanites.

timpanizarse *vpr* MED to become distended with gases.

tímpano *m* MÚS kettledrum (timbal) | type of dulcimer ‖ ANAT tympanum, eardrum ‖ ARQ tympanum ‖ IMPR tympan ‖ top, bottom (tapa de tonel).
◆ *pl* MÚS tympani.

tina *f* large earthen vat (tinaja) ‖ vat, tub, tank, copper (recipiente); *tina de tintorero* cleaner's vat ‖ bathtub (para bañarse).

tinaja *f* large earthen vat (recipiente) ‖ vat (cantidad).

tinajero *m* potter [who makes and sells large earthen vats] (fabricante o vendedor) ‖ stand for large earthen jars (donde se colocan).

tinamú *m* ZOOL tinamou (ave).

tindalización *f* FÍS Tyndall effect.

Tíndaro *npr m* MIT Tyndareus.

tinerfeño, ña *adj* [of *o* from] Tenerife.
◆ *m/f* native *o* inhabitant of Tenerife.

tingitano, na *adj* [of *o* from] Tangier, Tangerine.
◆ *m/f* native *o* inhabitant of Tangier, Tangerine.

tinglado *m* shed (cobertizo) ‖ platform, raised floor (tablado) ‖ FIG intrigue, plot, mystery (intriga) | mix-up, muddle (embrollo) ‖ AMER sea turtle ‖ — FIG & FAM *conocer el tinglado* to see through it, to know exactly what is going on | *manejar el tinglado* to pull the strings | *¡menudo tinglado se ha formado!* what a fuss!, what a to-do!

tinieblas *f pl* darkness *sing*, obscurity *sing*; *las tinieblas de la noche* the darkness of night ‖ REL tenebrae ‖ FIG confusion, darkness, ignorance ‖ — FIG *ángel de tinieblas* prince of darkness | *estoy en tinieblas sobre sus verdaderas intenciones* I am in the dark about his true intentions, I am ignorant of his true intentions.

tino *m* FIG skill, dexterity (habilidad) | good judgment (juicio) | common sense, sense (buen sentido) | moderation (moderación) ‖ good aim (puntería con un arma) ‖ metal *o* stone vat (tina) ‖ wine *o* olive press (lagar) ‖ — *a tino* gropingly, feeling one's way ‖ FIG *obrar con tino* to act wisely | *perder el tino* to take leave of one's senses | *sacar de tino a uno* to make s.o. lose his temper, to infuriate s.o., to make s.o. mad | *sin tino* stupidly (insensatamente), immoderately (sin moderación), madly, headlong, recklessly (correr, etc.).

tinta *f* ink (de la pluma); *escribir con tinta* to write in ink ‖ tint, hue (color) ‖ ink (de los calamares, etc.) ‖ — FIG *de buena tinta* on good authority, from a reliable source, straight from the horse's mouth ‖ *media tinta* half tone, half tint (que une los claros con los oscuros), first coat of a fresco painting (de fresco) ‖ *saber de buena tinta* to have it on good authority *o* from a reliable source, to get it straight from the horse's mouth ‖ FIG & FAM *sudar tinta* to sweat blood ‖ *tinta china* Indian ink [US India ink] ‖ *tinta de imprenta* printer's ink ‖ *tinta simpática* invisible *o* sympathetic ink.
◆ *pl* colours, hues; *pintar con tintas azules* to paint with blue hues ‖ FIG shades; *pintar el futuro con tintas negras* to paint the future in shades of black ‖ — FIG & FAM *medias tintas* vague words, generalities (soluciones o respuestas indeterminadas), half measures (medidas inadecuadas) | *recargar las tintas* to exaggerate, to lay it on, to overdo it.

tintar *vt* to tint, to dye (teñir).

tinte *m* dye (colorante) ‖ dyeing, dyeing process (operación de teñir) ‖ dyer's [shop] (tienda donde se tiñe) ‖ dry cleaner's (tienda donde se limpia en seco) ‖ stain (para la madera) ‖ FIG shade, colouring, overtones *pl*; *tener un tinte político* to have political overtones | veneer, gloss (barniz).

tinterillo *m* FIG & FAM pen-pusher (chupatintas) ‖ AMER pettifogger.

tintero *m* inkwell, inkstand (recipiente) ‖ age mark in horse's tooth (del caballo) ‖ IMPR ink fountain ‖ FIG & FAM *se le dejó en el tintero, se le quedó en el tintero* it completely slipped his mind, he clean forgot about it.

tintillo *adj* light red (vino).
◆ *m* light red wine.

tintín *m* clink, clinking, chink (vasos) ‖ jingle, jingling, tinkle, tinkling, ting-a-ling (campanilla).

tintinar; tintinear *vi* to clink (vasos) ‖ to jingle, to tinkle, to ting-a-ling (campanilla).

tintineo *m* clink, clinking (vasos) ‖ jingle, jingling, tinkle, tinkling, ting-a-ling (campanilla).

tinto, ta *adj* dyed, stained (teñido) ‖ red; *vino tinto* red wine ‖ AMER dark red | black (café) ‖ FIG tinged.
◆ *m* red wine; *una botella de tinto* a bottle of red wine ‖ AMER black coffee.

tintóreo, a *adj* tinctorial.

tintorería *f* dyeing (acción de teñir) ‖ dry cleaning (limpieza en seco) ‖ dyer's [shop] (taller donde se tiñe) ‖ dry cleaner's (taller donde se limpia en seco).

tintorero, ra *m/f* dyer (que tiñe) ‖ dry cleaner (que limpia en seco).
◆ *f* AMER female shark.

Tintoreto *npr m* Tintoretto.

tintorro *m* FAM plonk, rough red wine.

tintura *f* dye, tint ‖ FIG notion, slight knowledge, smattering; *tengo una tintura de historia literaria* I have a smattering *o* some notion of literature ‖ MED tincture; *tintura de yodo* tincture of iodine.

tiña *f* ZOOL honeycomb moth ‖ MED tinea, ring-worm ‖ FIG & FAM misery, poverty (pobreza) | meanness, stinginess (tacañería).

tiñoso, sa *adj* scabby ‖ FAM mean, stingy (tacaño).

tío *m* uncle ‖ FAM old, uncle; *el tío Juan* old John | fellow, bloke, chap, guy; *un tío estupendo* a fantastic fellow | so-and-so (peyorativo); *¡qué tío más idiota!* the silly so-and-so! ‖ *AMER* uncle, old [before the name of an elderly Negro] (negro viejo) ‖ — FIG & FAM *el tío del saco* the bogyman | *el Tío Sam* Uncle Sam | *tener un tío en las Indias* to have a rich uncle ‖ *tío abuelo* great uncle ‖ *tío segundo* first cousin once removed.
◆ *pl* uncle and aunt.

tiovivo *m* roundabout, merry-go-round [*US* merry-go-round, carousel, carrousel].

tipa *f* *AMER* wicker basket (cesta) | trollop (mujer despreciable).

tiparraco, ca; tipejo, ja *m/f* FAM wretch, twerp, blighter, heel (persona despreciable).

típico, ca *adj* typical ‖ characteristic ‖ traditional ‖ picturesque (pintoresco).

tipificación *f* classification (clasificación) ‖ standardization (uniformización).

tipificar *vt* to standardize (uniformizar) ‖ to typify (caracterizar).

tipismo *m* local colour; *lleno de tipismo* full of local colour ‖ traditional *o* characteristic nature (carácter típico) ‖ *el tipismo andaluz* all the things characteristic of Andalusia, everything one associates with Andalusia.

tiple *m* MÚS soprano [voice] (voz) | treble guitar (guitarrita).
◆ *m/f* MÚS soprano, soprano singer.

tipo *m* type (modelo) ‖ type, kind, class (clase); *¿qué tipo de coche tiene?* what kind of car does he have? ‖ rate; *tipo de cambio, de interés* rate of exchange, of interest; *tipo de interés fijo* fixed interest rate; *tipo de interés preferencial* prime rate; *tipo impositivo* tax rate ‖ percentage (descuento) ‖ type, type of person; *es un tipo deportivo* he is the sporting type ‖ figure, shape (de mujer), physique, build (de hombre); *esta chica tiene un tipo bonito* that girl has a pretty figure ‖ appearance (facha) ‖ FAM fellow, chap, character; *¡qué tipo más extraordinario!* what an extraordinary fellow!; *es un tipo malo* he is a nasty character ‖ IMPR type ‖ type; *tipo ario* Aryan type ‖ — FIG & FAM *aguantar el tipo* to bear up | *jugarse el tipo* to risk one's neck | *me juego el tipo a que* I bet anything you like that.

tipografía *f* typography, printing (arte) ‖ printing works *o* press (lugar).

tipográfico, ca *adj* typographical, typographic, printing.

tipógrafo, fa *m/f* typographer.

tipología *f* typology.

tipómetro *m* type gauge.

tipoy *m* tunic [worn by South American Indians].

típula *f* crane fly, daddy longlegs.

tíquet; tiquete *m* ticket.

tiquismiquis *m pl* FAM silly scruples (reparos nimios) | bowing and scraping, affected manners (cortesías afectadas) | bickering, silly little fights, quarrelling (peleas) ‖ FAM *andarse con tiquismiquis* to be fussy.

tira *f* strip (de tela, papel, etc.) ‖ strap; *las tiras de los zapatos* the straps of the shoes ‖ comic strip, strip cartoon (del periódico) ‖ MAR fall ‖ — FIG & FAM *esperé la tira para coger el autobús* I waited ages *o* an eternity for the bus | *quitar la piel a tiras, sacar las tiras del pellejo* to tear (s.o.) to pieces (criticar).

tirabala *m* blowpipe, peashooter.

tirabeque *m* tender pea (guisante mollar) ‖ catapult [*US* slingshot] (tiragomas).

tirabotas *m inv* boot hook.

tirabuzón *m* corkscrew (sacacorchos) ‖ FIG ringlet, curl (rizo de cabello) ‖ AVIAC spin ‖ DEP twist (del trampolín) ‖ FIG & FAM *sacarle a uno las palabras con tirabuzón* to drag *o* to twist the words out of s.o.

tirada *f* long distance, stretch (distancia) ‖ series; *nos leyó una tirada de versos* he read us a series of verses ‖ IMPR printing (acción) | edition; *segunda tirada* second edition; *una tirada de veinte mil ejemplares* a twenty thousand copy edition ‖ FAM tart (fulana) ‖ — *de* or *en una tirada* in one go ‖ IMPR *tirada aparte* offprint.

tiradero *m* *AMER* rubbish dump (vertedero).

tirado, da *adj* FAM dead easy, as easy as pie; *este trabajo está tirado* this work is dead easy | dirt cheap (barato); *este reloj está tirado* this watch is dirt cheap ‖ streamlined (embarcación) ‖ TECN drawn.
◆ *m* TECN wiredrawing (de los metales) ‖ printing.

tirador, ra *m/f* shooter, marksman (hombre), markswoman (mujer) ‖ drawer (de metales) ‖ — *es buen tirador* he is a good shot *o* a good marksman ‖ *tirador de arco* archer, bowman ‖ *tirador de fusil* rifleman.
◆ *m* handle, knob (de puerta, de cajón) ‖ bellpull, rope (de campanilla) ‖ catapult [*US* slingshot] (tiragomas) ‖ IMPR pressman ‖ TECN drawplate (para los metales) ‖ *AMER* gaucho's belt [frequently decorated with silver coins] ‖ *tirador de oro* gold wiredrawer.
◆ *pl* braces (tirantes).

tirafondo *m* MED forceps, surgical pincers *pl* ‖ screw (tornillo).

tiragomas *m inv* catapult [*US* slingshot].

tiralevitas *m inv* FAM bootlicker, crawler.

tiralíneas *m inv* drawing pen, ruling pen ‖ FIG *con tiralíneas* with great precision.

tiramollar *vt* MAR to slacken.

Tirana *n pr* GEOGR Tirana.

tiranía *f* tyranny.

tiranicida *m/f* tyrannicide (asesino).

tiranicidio *m* tyrannicide (crimen).

tiránico, ca *adj* tyrannic, tyrannical.

tiranización *f* tyrannizing.

tiranizar *vt* to tyrannize.

tirano, na *adj* tyrannic, tyrannical.
◆ *m/f* tyrant.

tirante *adj* tight, taut, tense (tenso) ‖ FIG tense, strained; *relaciones tirantes* strained relations ‖ FIG *estar tirante* to be on bad terms, to be at odds; *estamos tirantes* we are on bad terms; *Juan está tirante con su hermano* John is at odds with *o* on bad terms with his brother.
◆ *m* trace, harness trace (de caballería) ‖ strap (de falda, delantal, ropa interior) ‖ ARQ tie, tie beam ‖ TECN brace, stay, strut.
◆ *pl* braces [*US* suspenders] (del pantalón).

tirantez *f* tenseness, tautness, tightness ‖ FIG tension, strained relations *pl*, tenseness, strain; *tirantez entre el presidente y sus ministros* tension between the president and his ministers ‖ FIG *tirantez de las relaciones* strained relations.

tirapié *m* stirrup (del zapatero).

tirar *vt* to throw, to toss, to sling (*fam*); *tirar un libro al suelo* to throw a book to the ground; *tirar piedras a uno* to throw stones at s.o. ‖ to drop (dejar caer) ‖ to spill (un líquido); *tirar el agua en la mesa* to spill the water on *o* over the table ‖ to knock over (volcar); *tirar un vaso de vino* to knock over a glass of wine ‖ to pull down, to knock down (derribar); *tirar un árbol* to pull down a tree; *tirar una casa* to pull a house down ‖ to pull (traer hacia sí); *tirar la puerta* to pull the door ‖ to stretch, to draw, to pull (estirar) ‖ to throw away *o* out, to discard (desechar); *este abrigo está ya para tirarlo* this coat is ready to be thrown away ‖ to waste, to throw away, to squander (disipar); *tirar dinero* to squander money ‖ IMPR to print, to run off (imprimir) ‖ FOT to print | to take (tomar); *tira una foto del niño* take a photo of the child | to make (fotocopia) ‖ to reproduce ‖ TECN to draw, to draw out (estirar un metal) ‖ to fire (un cañonazo, un cohete) ‖ AVIAC to drop (paracaidista, bomba) ‖ FAM to run down (criticar); *me está siempre tirando* he is always running me down | to sell for a giveaway price, to give away (vender barato) ‖ DEP to take; *tirar un saque de esquina* to take a corner ‖ MAT to draw (línea, curva) | to drop (perpendicular) ‖ to give; *le tiró un pellizco* he gave him a pinch ‖ *AMER* to carry, to transport (transportar) ‖ — FIG & FAM *lanzaron* or *tiraron indirectas sobre la infidelidad de su esposa* they alluded to *o* insinuated *o* hinted at his wife's infidelity | *tirar abajo* to pull down, to knock down, to demolish (un edificio), to break down (una puerta) *tirar coces* to kick, to lash out | *tirar la casa por la ventana* to spare no expense, to go overboard, to lash out (*fam*) | *tirar la piedra y esconder la mano* to hit and run | *tirar la primera piedra* to cast the first stone ‖ *tirar piedras al tejado ajeno* to blame s.o. else ‖ *tirar piedras contra uno* to throw stones at s.o., to stone s.o. (apedrear), to criticize s.o. (censurar) ‖ *tirar un beso a alguien* to blow s.o. a kiss ‖ *tirar un mordisco a alguien* to bite s.o., to give s.o. a bite.
◆ *vi* to pull, to draw (una chimenea); *esta chimenea tira bien* this chimney draws well ‖ to fire, to shoot; *tirar con rifle* to fire a rifle; *tirar al aire* to fire *o* to shoot into the air; *¡no tire!* don't shoot! ‖ to pull, to tug; *tirar de una cuerda* to pull (on) a rope; *tirar a alguien de la manga* to tug at s.o.'s sleeve ‖ to draw, to attract; *el imán tira del hierro* the magnet attracts iron ‖ to pull, to draw; *el caballo tira del carro* the horse draws the cart ‖ FAM to work, to run, to pull (funcionar); *este motor tira bien* this motor works well ‖ FIG to attract, to appeal to (atraer); *no le tira la pintura* painting does not attract him | to turn (torcer); *tira a la derecha* turn right | to go; *tira adelante* go straight on | to take, to go (*por* by), (coger); *si tirásemos por este camino llegaríamos antes* if we took this road we would arrive sooner | to last (durar); *esta falda tirará todo el invierno* this skirt will last all winter | to make do (with), to get by *o* along (on) (mantenerse); *él tira con diez mil pesetas al mes* he makes do with ten thousand pesetas a month | to tend towards; *este color tira a rojo* this colour tends towards red | to be rather; *él tira a tacaño* he is rather miserly | to be attracted to *o* inclined towards; *tira para cura* he is attracted to the priesthood | to take after, to look like (parecerse a); *ella tira más bien a su padre* she takes more after her father ‖ to draw, to pull out (sacar un arma); *tiraron de las espadas* they pulled out their swords ‖ to pull out, to take out (sacar cualquier cosa) ‖ DEP to shoot (chutar) ‖ — FIG *a más tirar, a todo tirar, tirando por alto* at the most, at the outside | *dejar tirado a uno* to abandon s.o. (abandonar), to leave s.o. behind, to surpass s.o. (superar), to astonish s.o. (dejar asombrado) ‖ FIG & FAM *ir tirando* to get along, to get by, to cope, to manage; *vamos tirando* we are managing ‖ FIG *la cabra siempre tira al monte* what's bred in the bone will come out in the flesh |

la patria siempre tira one always feels drawn by one's homeland || *naranja que tira a rojo* reddish orange || FAM *tirando* so-so || FIG *tirando por bajo* at least || *tirar al blanco* to shoot at a target | *tirar a matar, tirar con bala* to shoot to kill (con un arma de fuego), to pull (s.o.) to pieces (criticar mucho) || FIG *tirar de la lengua* to draw s.o. out || FIG & FAM *tirar de la levita* to butter up, to flatter (adular) || FIG *tirar largo* or *de largo* or *por largo* to spend lavishly (dinero), to use (etc.) freely; *si tiras de largo la pintura* if you put the paint on freely; to estimate high (calcular) | *tirar por lo alto* to have high ambitions, to aim high (ser ambicioso), to do things in style *o* in a big way (no escatimar los gastos) || *tira tú ahora* it's your turn *o* go now || FIG & FAM *tira y afloja* give and take (toma y daca), tact, diplomacy (tacto).
◆ *vpr* to jump, to throw *o* to hurl o.s. (arrojarse); *se tiró al agua* he jumped into the water || to spring, to jump, to rush (abalanzarse); *el perro se tiró sobre él* or *al niño* the dog jumped on *o* rushed at the child || to lie down (tumbarse); *se tiró en la cama* he lay down on the bed || FIG to spend; *se tiró un día entero pescando* he spent a whole day fishing | to have to put up with (tener que aguantar); *se tiró un viaje muy largo* he had to put up with a very long trip || DEP to dive (a la pelota) || POP to lay, to have (a una chica) || — FIG & FAM *tirarse al suelo de risa* to roll about laughing | *tirarse a matar* to pull each other to pieces || *tirarse de cabeza a la piscina* to dive into the swimming pool || FIG & FAM *tirarse del moño* to tear each other's hair out | *tirarse los trastos a la cabeza* to have a flaming row, to throw pots and pans at one another (reñir) | *tirarse un planchazo* or *una plancha* to boob, to put one's foot in it.

tiricia *f* FAM jaundice (ictericia).

tirilla *f* strip, band (tira pequeña) || neckband (de camisa).

tirio, ria *adj/s* Tyrian || FIG *tirios y troyanos* opposing parties.

tirita *f* MED plaster.

tiritar *vt* to shiver, to shake, to tremble (*de* with) || FIG & FAM *dejar un plato tiritando* to almost completely polish off a dish.

tiritera *f* shivers *pl*, shivering, shaking, trembling || *le dio la tiritera* he started shivering.

tiritón *m* shiver || *dar tiritones* to make one shiver; *de pensarlo me dan tiritones* it makes me shiver to think about it.

tiritona *f* FAM shivers *pl*, shivering, shaking, trembling || — FAM *dar una tiritona* to make shiver | *tener una tiritona* to have the shivers, to shiver.

tiro *m* throw (lanzamiento) || shot, discharge (disparo, ruido); *tiro de pistola* pistol shot; *se oyen tiros* shots are heard || shooting (acción o arte); *tiro al blanco* target shooting || shot (herida, huella) || shot, bullet (bala) || load, charge (carga) || range (sitio); *tiro al blanco* target *o* rifle range || MIL gun (pieza de artillería) | firing, fire (manera de disparar); *tiro directo* direct firing; *tiro oblicuo* oblique fire || range (alcance); *a tiro de escopeta* within rifle range || throw (distancia); *a tiro de piedra* within a stone's throw; *un tiro de 55 metros* a 55-metre throw || length (de un tejido) || distance between crotch and waist of trousers (de pantalón) || shoulder width (de vestido) || flight (de escalera) || draught [US draft] (de chimenea) || team (de animales); *tiro de caballos* team of horses || FIG blow (golpe duro) | petty theft (robo) | joke, prank, trick (chasco) || pulley *o* hoisting rope, pull chain *o* rope (cuerda de garrucha) || harness trace (tirante) || DEP shot (fútbol, etc.); *tiro a gol* shot at goal || MIN shaft (pozo) | depth (profundidad) || VET stable vice (de los caballos) || AMER edition (tirada) || — *a tiro* within range (de arma), within reach (asequible); *se me puso a tiro* he came within my reach || FIG *a tiro de ballesta* at a glance || *a tiro hecho* with precision (apuntando bien), deliberately, purposely, intentionally (adrede) || *a tiro limpio* firing, guns blazing | *animal de tiro* draught animal || *campo de tiro* shooting range || *dar* or *pegar un tiro* to fire a shot, to shoot || FAM *darse* or *pegarse un tiro* to shoot o.s., to commit suicide || FIG *errar el tiro* to miss the mark, to fail || FIG & FAM *la noticia le sentó como un tiro* the news came as a blow to him, he took the news very badly | *le salió el tiro por la culata* it backfired on him || FIG & FAM *matar dos pájaros de un tiro* to kill two birds with one stone | *poner el tiro muy alto* to aim high || *sin pegar un tiro* without firing a shot || DEP *tiro al plato* trapshooting || *tiro de* or *con arco* archery || *tiro de gracia* coup de grâce, death blow || DEP *tiro de pichón* pigeon shooting.
◆ *pl* belt *sing* (para la espada) || AMER braces [US suspenders] (tirantes) || FAM *de tiros largos* all dressed up, dressed to kill || FAM *liarse a tiros* to start shooting, to have a shoot-out || *matar a alguien a tiros* to shoot s.o. dead || FIG & FAM *ni a tiros* not for love nor money || FIG *pegar cuatro tiros* to shoot.

Tiro *npr m* Tyre.

tiroideo, a *adj* ANAT thyroid.

tiroides *m* ANAT thyroid, thyroid gland.
◆ *adj* ANAT thyroid.

tiroidina *f* MED thyroid extract.

tiroiditis *f* MED thyroiditis.

Tirol *npr m* GEOGR Tyrol.

tirolés, esa *adj/s* Tyrolese, Tyrolean.

tirón *m* tug, pull, jerk (en una cuerda, etc.) || jerk, jolt (sacudida) || cramp (de estómago, de músculo) || tyro, novice (aprendiz) || FAM good distance, long stretch *o* way (distancia); *hay un tirón de aquí a tu casa* there's a good distance between your house and here || FIG pull (atracción) || — *a tirones* jerkily (avanzar, etc.) || *dar un tirón a* to tug *o* to pull at, to give a tug || *dar un tirón de orejas* to pull *o* to tweak s.o.'s ear || *de un tirón* straight off (al primer intento), all at once, in one go (de una sola vez); *leer una novela de un tirón* to read a novel in one go; at a stretch, at one stretch, in one go; *hacer cincuenta kilómetros de un tirón* to do fifty kilometres at a stretch || *me lo arrancó de un tirón* he pulled *o* yanked it away from me || *ni a dos tirones* never in a million years.

tirotear *vt* to snipe at, to fire at, to take shots at, to shoot at; *le tirotearon desde el tejado* they shot at him from the roof.
◆ *vpr* to exchange shots *o* fire, to shoot at each other, to fire at each other.

tiroteo *m* firing, shooting (acción de tirotear) || shooting, firing, shots *pl* (ruido); *se oía un tiroteo a lo lejos* shooting was heard in the distance || skirmish (escaramuza).

tirotricina *f* QUÍM tyrothricin.

Tirreno (mar) *npr m* Tyrrhenian Sea.

tirria *f* FAM dislike || — FAM *tener tirria a* to have a grudge against, to have it in for, to dislike | *tomar tirria a uno* to take a dislike to s.o.

tisana *f* infusion, ptisan, tisane.

tisanuro *adj/sm* ZOOL thysanuran.
◆ *pl* ZOOL thysanura.

tísico, ca *adj* phthisical, tubercular, consumptive.
◆ *m/f* consumptive.

tisiología *f* MED phthisiology.

tisiólogo *m* MED phthisiologist.

tisis *f* MED phthisis, tuberculosis, consumption.

tisú *m* lamé (tela).
— OBSERV pl *tisúes* o *tisús*.

tita *f* FAM auntie, aunty.

titán *m* titan.

titánico, ca *adj* titanic || QUÍM titanic || FIG *un trabajo titánico* a titanic *o* gigantic task *o* job.

titanio *m* titanium (metal).

títere *m* puppet, marionette || FIG weakling, puppet (persona que se deja dominar) || — FIG *no dejar títere con cabeza* to turn everything upside down, to break everything in sight | *no queda títere con cabeza* there's not a plate in the house left unbroken.
◆ *pl* puppet show *sing* || *teatro de títeres* puppet show.

tití *m* ZOOL titi (mono).

titilador, ra; titilante *adj* quivering || twinkling (estrella) || flickering (fuego).

titilar; titilear *vi* to quiver (temblar) || to twinkle (estrella) || to flicker, to twinkle (luz).

titileo *m* twinkling (de una estrella).

titirimundi *m* cosmorama.

titiritaina *f* FAM row, din, racket (bulla).

titiritar *vi* to tremble, to shiver, to shake.

titiritero, ra *m/f* puppeteer (que maneja los títeres) || tightrope walker (volatinero) || acrobat, juggler, mountebank (saltimbanqui).

tito *m* FAM uncle (tío).

Tito *npr m* Titus.

Tito Livio *npr m* Livy.

titubeante *adj* shaky, staggering, unsteady, tottering; *un andar titubeante* a shaky walk || stammering (que farfulla) || FIG hesitant (que duda).

titubear *vi* to stagger, to totter (oscilar) || FIG to hesitate, to waver; *titubea en venir* he hesitates to come; *titubeaba si lo haría* he hesitated about doing it || to falter, to stammer (farfullar).

titubeo *m* staggering, tottering, stagger, unsteadiness (al andar) || hesitation, hesitancy, wavering (vacilación) || stammering (acción de farfullar).

titulación *f* QUÍM titration.

titulado, da *adj* entitled (un libro, etc.) || qualified; *enfermera titulada* qualified nurse || FIG so-called; *un titulado pintor* a so-called painter || *ser titulado en medicina* to have a degree in medicine.

titular *adj* titular; *profesor, obispo titular* titular professor, bishop || DEP regular; *jugador titular* regular player || *juez titular* regular judge.
◆ *m/f* holder (de pasaporte, etc.) || *hacer titular* to confirm (s.o.) in his post.
◆ *m pl* headlines (de periódico).

titular *vt* to title, to entitle, to call (poner un título) || QUÍM to titrate.
◆ *vi* to receive a title of nobility.
◆ *vpr* to be titled, to be called (un libro, etc.) || to call o.s.

titularizar *vt* to confirm (s.o.) in his post.

titulillo *m* IMPR running head, running title.

título *m* title (de una obra) || title (dignidad); *título de nobleza* title of nobility || titled person (dignatario) || degree; *título de licenciado* bachelor's degree || diploma (diploma) || qualification; *tener los títulos necesarios* to have the necessary qualifications || COM security, bond (valor); *título al portador* bearer bond || FIG quality (calidad) | right (derecho) || JUR title; *título de propiedad* title deed | heading (de un texto legal) | item (de un presupuesto) || IMPR title (de libro, etc.) | headline (en periódicos) | QUÍM titre [US titer] || — *a título de* in the capacity of, as (en calidad de), by way of (en concepto de) || *conceder un título* to give *o* to grant a title || *con el mismo título* with the same title (igual), with the same motive (por el mismo motivo) || *¿con qué título?* by what right? || *títulos cotizables* listed shares || *título de pago* title of payment || *título de renta* government bond || *título de piloto* pilot's certificate.

tiza *f* chalk; *escribir con tiza* to write with chalk || chalk (de billar) || *una tiza* a piece of chalk.

Tiziano *npr m* Titian.

tizna *f* grime, dirt.

tiznado, da *adj* dirty, blackened, sooty (manchado) || *AMER* drunk (ebrio).

tiznadura *f* blackening, smudging (acción) || smudge, smut (tiznón).

tiznajo *m* smudge.

tiznar *vt* to blacken, to smudge with black, to soil with soot (manchar de negro) || to soil, to dirty (manchar, ensuciar) || to blacken [with soot]; *tiznar una pared* to blacken a wall [with soot] || FIG to blacken, to soil, to stain; *tiznar la reputación de alguien* to blacken s.o.'s reputation.
◆ *vpr* to get dirty (mancharse) || to blacken; *se tiznaron la cara* they blackened their faces || *AMER* to get drunk (emborracharse).

tizne *m/f* soot (hollín) || grime, soot, black, dirt (suciedad) || FIG stain.

tiznón *m* smudge, smut.

tizón *m* half-burnt stick, smouldering brand (palo a medio quemar) || half-burnt log (leño a medio quemar) || FIG stain (mancha en la fama) || BOT smut (parásito) || ARQ header (del sillar) || FAM *negro como un tizón* as black as soot *o* as coal.

tizona *f* FAM sword.
— OBSERV *Tizona* was the name of the Cid's sword.

tizonadas *f pl*; **tizonazos** *m pl* FIG & FAM hellfire *sing* (infierno).

tizoncillo *m* smut (enfermedad de los vegetales).

tizonear *vi* to poke, to stir up (el fuego).

tlacoyo *m* *AMER* omelet made with kidney beans.

tlacuache *m* *AMER* opossum (zarigüeya).

tlapalería *f* *AMER* hardware shop.

tlaspi *m* candytuft (planta).

tlazol *m* *AMER* tops of sugar cane or corn used as fodder.

toa *f* *AMER* towrope, rope (maroma).

toalla *f* towel; *toalla de baño* bath towel; *toalla de manos* hand towel || *toalla de felpa* Turkish towel.

toallero *m* towel rail, towel rack.

toar *vt* MAR to tow (remolcar).

toba *f* tufa (piedra) || tartar (sarro) || BOT cotton thistle (cardo borriquero).

tobáceo, a *adj* tufaceous, tuffaceous.

tobar *m* tufa quarry.

tobera *f* nozzle.

tobillera *adj f* FAM *niña tobillera* teenager [*US* bobby-soxer].
◆ *f* ankle support.

tobillo *m* ANAT ankle || FIG *no le llega ni al tobillo* he is no match for him, he can't hold a candle to him.

tobogán *m* slide, chute (para niños, mercancías) || toboggan (para deslizarse por la nieve).

toca *f* headdress || wimple, cornet (de religiosa) || hat (sombrero).

tocadiscos *m inv* record player, gramophone.

tocado *adj* wearing [on one's head]; *tocado con un sombrero negro* wearing a black hat || FIG & FAM touched, crazy (loco) || FAM *tocado en la cabeza* touched in the head, not all there.
◆ *m* hat, headdress (sombrero) || coiffure, hairdo (peinado) || touch (esgrima).

tocador, ra *m/f* MÚS player || — *tocador de arpa* harpist, harp player || *tocador de guitarra* guitarist, guitar player.
◆ *m* dressing table (mueble para mujer) || boudoir, dressing room (cuarto) || vanity case (neceser) || FAM powder room, ladies' room (servicios) || *artículos de tocador* cosmetics.

tocamiento *m* touching.

tocante *adj* touching || — *dijo unas palabras tocantes a la economía* he touched on the economy, he briefly mentioned the economy, he said a few words about the economy || *en lo tocante a* with reference to || *tocante a* about, concerning, with reference to; *no diré nada tocante a la economía* I won't say anything about the economy.

tocar *vt* to touch; *tocar algo con el dedo* to touch sth. with one's finger; *le tocó el hombro* he touched him on the shoulder; *las montañas parecían tocar las nubes* the mountains seemed to touch the clouds || MÚS to play; *tocar la guitarra, el piano, los discos* to play the guitar, the piano, the records | to play, to beat (el tambor) | to play, to blow (la trompeta) || to touch, to feel, to handle; *se ruega no tocar la mercancía* please do not handle the goods; *tócalo a ver cómo te parece* feel it and see what you think || to chime, to strike (dar la hora el reloj) || to ring; *tocar la campana* to ring the bell || MIL to sound; *tocar diana, la retirada* to sound reveille, the retreat || to touch, to hit (esgrima) || to hit (un blanco, etc., con un tiro) || to essay, to test with a touchstone, to touch (metal precioso) || to stop at, to put in at, to call at; *el barco tocará los siguientes puertos* the boat will stop at the following ports || to touch up (una pintura) || FIG to touch on, to mention briefly (mencionar); *tocar un tema* to touch on a subject | to touch, to reach (impresionar); *me has tocado el corazón* you've touched my heart || — *a toca teja* cash, cash down (pagar) || FIG *toca madera* touch wood || *tocar el timbre* to ring the bell || FIG *tocar en lo vivo* to cut to the quick || *tocar la bocina* or *el claxon* to sound *o* to blow the horn || FIG *tocar por encima* to briefly touch on (un asunto) | *tocar todos los registros* to pull out all the stops, to try everything *o* every possibility (intentarlo todo).
◆ *vi* to knock; *tocar a la puerta* to knock on the door || to ring (una campana) || to be up to; *me toca decirlo* it is up to me to say it; *no le toca a usted hacer este trabajo* it is not up to you to do this job || to win (en suerte); *le tocó el gordo* he won first prize || to fall; *tocar a uno en un reparto* to fall to one, to fall to one's lot *o* share; *le tocó a él ir a buscarlo* it fell to him to go and fetch it || to be one's turn; *a usted le toca tomar la palabra* it is your turn to speak; *a ti te toca jugar* it is your turn to play; *¿a quién le toca ahora?* whose turn is it now? || to be related to, to be a relation of (ser pariente); *Antonio no me toca nada* Anthony is not related to me at all; *¿qué te toca Clemente?* how is Clement related to you?, what relation of yours is Clement? || to have to, to be time to; *ahora toca pagar* now we have to pay, now it is time to pay || to stop, to put in, to call (barco, avión); *el avión tocará en Palma* the plane will stop at Palma || FIG to touch, to reach; *le tocó Dios en el corazón* God reached his heart | to concern; *este asunto me toca de cerca* this matter concerns me deeply || — *no es a ti a quien le toca aguantar a los niños* you're not the one who has to put up with the children || *por lo que a mí me toca* as far as I am concerned || *tocar a misa* to ring the bell for mass || *tocar a muerto* to toll (the knell) || *tocar a rebato* to sound the alarm || *tocar a su fin* to be coming to an end (estar a punto de acabar), to be on the point of death (estar a punto de morir) || *tocar con* to be next to; *mi casa toca con la suya* my house is next to yours || FIG *tocar en* to verge on (rayar en).
◆ *vpr* to touch o.s. || to touch (each other) (dos cosas o personas) || to cover one's head (cubrirse la cabeza) || to put on *o* on one's head; *tocarse con un sombrero* to put a hat on || to do one's hair (peinarse).

tocata *f* MÚS toccata || FAM thrashing, spanking (paliza).

tocateja (a) *adv* cash, cash down; *pagar a tocateja* to pay cash down.

tocay *m* tokay (vino).

tocayo, ya *m/f* namesake.

tocinería *f* pork butcher's.

tocinero, ra *m/f* pork butcher.

tocineta *f* *AMER* bacon (tocino).

tocino *m* bacon || fat, lard || — *tocino del cielo* sweet made of eggs and syrup || *tocino entreverado* (streaky) bacon || *tocino gordo* fat bacon.
◆ *interj* pepper! (en el juego de la comba).

toco *m* *AMER* niche (hornacina).

tocología *f* tocology, obstetrics.

tocólogo *m* tocologist, obstetrician.

tocomate *m* *AMER* pumpkin (calabaza).

tocón *m* stump (de un árbol o miembro).

toconal *m* land covered with tree stumps || olive grove (olivar).

tocuyo *m* *AMER* coarse cotton cloth.

tocho *m* iron ingot.

todavía *adv* still; *duerme todavía, todavía duerme* he is still sleeping; *¿trabajas todavía en la misma oficina?* do you still work in the same office? || still, yet; *no ha venido todavía* he still hasn't come, he hasn't come yet || — *todavía más* even more (con adjetivo), even (con adjetivo comparativo); *el rico quiere enriquecerse todavía más* the rich man wants to become even richer; still more, even more; *éste cuesta todavía más* this one costs even more || *todavía no* not yet.

todito, ta *adj* FAM all; *ha llorado todita la noche* he cried all night (long); *se ha comido toditos los pasteles* he has eaten all the cakes || — *se lo ha bebido todito todo* he has drunk every single drop of it || *se lo ha comido todito todo* he has eaten it all up, he has eaten every single bit of it.

todo, da *adj/pron indef* all; *lo saben todos los hombres* all men know it; *han venido todos* they have all come || every (cada); *todo buen cristiano* every good Christian; *todos los días, los meses* every day, month || everything; *todo está preparado* everything is ready; *me gusta todo* I like everything || all; *mi falda está toda manchada* my shirt is all dirty; *este pescado es todo espinas* this fish is all bones || full of (lleno de); *la calle era toda baches* the street was full of holes || all of, all, the whole of; *España toda aprueba la decisión* all Spain *o* all of Spain *o* the whole of Spain approves the decision || every inch, every bit, a real (un verdadero); *es todo un hombre* he's a real man, he's every inch *o* every bit a man || exactly like, the image of (igual que); *eres todo tu padre* you are exactly like your father, you are the image of your father || — *ante todo* above all, first and foremost, first of all || *a pesar de todo* in spite of *o* despite everything, for all that (a pesar de los pesares), all the same; *me lo han prohibido, pero lo haré a pesar de todo* they have forbidden me to do it, but I shall all the same || *así y todo* even so, in spite of everything, just the same || *a toda velocidad* or *marcha* or *mecha, a todo correr* (at) full speed, (at) top speed || *a todo esto* in the meantime (mientras tanto), by the way, speaking of that (hablando de esto) || *a todo riesgo* fully comprehensive (seguro) || *a todo vapor* at full steam (barco), at great speed || *considerándolo todo* all things considered || *con toda mi alma, de todo corazón* with all my heart || *con todas sus fuerzas* with all his might *o* strength || *con todo, con todo y con eso* in spite of everything, nevertheless, even so || *después de todo* after all || *de todas formas, en todo caso* anyway || *de todo hay en la viña del Señor* it takes all sorts *o* all kinds to make a world || *en todo el día no lo he visto* I haven't seen him all day || *en todo el mundo no hay uno parecido* there is not another one like it anywhere in the world || *eso es todo* that's all || *es todo uno* it's all the same || *fue todo uno* it all happened at once || *hacer todo lo posible* to do everything within one's power *o* everything possible to, to do one's best *o* one's utmost to || *ha viajado por toda España* he has travelled all over Spain || *hay de todo* there are all sorts of things (toda clase de cosas), there are all sorts (varios tipos de la misma cosa) || *lo... todo* it all, everything; *lo sabe todo* he knows it all; *lo he dicho todo* I have said everything; *lo estás estropeando todo* you are ruining everything || *lo he buscado en* or *por toda la casa* I have searched for it all over the house || *o todo o nada* (it is) all or nothing || *ser toda sonrisa* to be all smiles || *ser todo ojos, todo oídos* to be all eyes, all ears || *sobre todo* above all, especially || *todo aquel que* anyone who, whoever || FAM *todo Cristo, todo Dios* absolutely everybody || *todo cuanto* everything (cosas); *te dará todo cuanto quieras* he will give you everything you want || *todo el mundo* everybody, everyone; *lo sabe todo el mundo* everybody knows that || *todo el que* anyone who, whoever; *todo el que quiera venir que me siga* anyone who wants to come *o* whoever wants to come, follow me || *todo eran quejas* it was all complaints, there were nothing but complaints || *todo incluido* everything included, all in || *todo lo contrario* quite the contrary *o* the opposite || *todo lo demás* everything else, all the rest || *todo lo más* at the most (como mucho), at the latest (como muy tarde) || *todo lo que* anything *o* everything (which), whatever; *todo lo que te parezca útil* anything (which) you think might be useful || *todo lo... que, todo cuanto* as... as; *no estuvo todo lo simpático que yo esperaba* he wasn't as nice as I hoped || *todo o nada* (it is) all or nothing || *todo quisque* (absolutely) everybody || *todos* everybody, everyone (todo el mundo), all; *somos todos hermanos* we are all brothers; all of; *todos nosotros* all of us || *todos cuantos* everybody, everyone, all (personas), all (cosas); *el cuadro les gusta a todos cuantos lo ven* everybody who sees the painting likes it || *todos los días* every day || *todos los que puedan* all those who can || *todos ustedes* all of you || *todos y cada uno* all and sundry, each and every one || *y todo* and all, and everything; *perdió su perro y todo* he lost his dog and all; although; *cansado y todo siguió trabajando* although he was tired he carried on working.

todo *m* whole; *una parte del todo* a part of whole; *considerado como un todo* taken as a whole || all, everything (cada cosa) || — *del todo* entirely, wholly, all; *no es del todo antipático* he's not entirely unpleasant; quite, absolutely; *estamos decididos del todo* we are absolutely determined; quite, really, very (muy); *está triste del todo* he is very sad; right; *arriba del todo, abajo del todo* right at the top, right at the bottom || *el todo* my all, my whole (en las charadas) || *jugarse el todo por el todo* to stake everything one has (apostar), to go the whole hog, to take the plunge (tomar una acción drástica) || *quien todo lo quiere todo lo pierde* the more you want the less you get || *ser el todo* to be the most important thing (cosa), to be the mastermind, to run the show (persona).

◆ *adv* completely, entirely, all, totally.

todopoderoso, sa *adj/s* all-powerful, omnipotent, almighty || *el Todopoderoso* the Almighty (Dios).

toffee *m* toffee (pastilla de café con leche).

tofo *m* MED tophus (nodo).

toga *f* toga (de los romanos) || gown, robe (de magistrado).

togado, da *adj* togaed, togated (romanos) || robed (magistrados).

◆ *m* gentleman of the robe, lawyer.

◆ *pl* *los togados* the gentlemen of the robe, the legal profession, the lawyers.

Togo *npr m* GEOGR Togo.

toisón *m* fleece || *Orden del Toisón de Oro* Order of the Golden Fleece.

— OBSERV The Golden Fleece that was captured by Jason and the Argonauts is called *vellocino de oro*.

tojal *m* furze-covered place.

tojo *m* BOT furze.

tokai *m* tokay (vino).

Tokio *n pr* GEOGR Tokyo.

tolanos *m pl* short hairs on the nape of the neck.

toldería *f* AMER Indian camp, Indian village.

toldero *m* salt retailer.

toldilla *f* MAR poop deck.

toldo *m* awning (en un patio, una tienda, una calle, etc.) || tilt, awning, canvas cover (en un carro o un camión) || sunshade (en la playa) || AMER tent, tepee (de los indios).

tole *m* FIG hubbub, uproar, clamour [US clamor] || — FAM *armar un tole* to cause uproar, to cause a commotion (causar protestas), to kick up a fuss *o* a stink (protestar) | *tomar el tole* to beat it (irse).

toledano, na *adj/s* Toledan || FIG *pasar una noche toledana* to have *o* to spend a sleepless night.

Toledo *n pr* GEOGR Toledo.

tolemaico, ca *adj* Ptolemaic.

tolerable *adj* tolerable.

tolerancia *f* tolerance || tolerance, toleration; *tolerancia religiosa* religious tolerance || TECN tolerance.

tolerante *adj* tolerant.

tolerantismo *m* toleration, religious tolerance.

tolerar *vt* to tolerate (permitir) || — *¿cree que tolerará el peso?* do you think it will take *o* stand *o* bear the weight? || *mi hígado no tolera este tipo de comida* my liver cannot take this kind of food || *película tolerada por la censura* film approved by the censor || *tolerada para menores* suitable for children, U-certificate (película cinematográfica) || *tolerar demasiado a alguien* to be too tolerant *o* lenient with s.o.

tolete *m* MAR thole, tholepin || AMER (short) club *o* stick, cudgel (garrote).

toletole *m* FAM hubbub, uproar, commotion (jaleo).

tolita *f* tolite (explosivo).

Tolomeo *npr m* Ptolemy.

tolondro, dra *adj* scatterbrained.

◆ *m/f* scatterbrain.

◆ *m* bump, lump, swelling (chichón).

tolondrón *m* bump, lump, swelling (chichón) || FIG *a tolondrones* by fits and starts.

Tolosa *n pr* GEOGR Tolosa [Spain] | Toulouse [France].

tolteca *adj/s* Toltec.

tolueno *m* QUÍM toluene.

tolva *f* hopper, chute.

tolvanera *f* dust storm.

tollina *f* FAM hiding, thrashing, beating.

toma *f* taking (over), assumption; *toma de control* assumption of control || taking, capture, seizure (conquista); *la toma de Granada* the capture of Granada || dose (medicamentos); *una toma de quinina* a dose of quinine || tap, outlet (de agua) || inlet, intake (de aire) || socket, plug, terminal (enchufe) || lead, wire [US cord] (cable) || CINEM take, shot || AMER irrigation ditch, channel (acequia) || — *toma de conciencia* awareness || *toma de corriente* power point, A. C. outlet, plug || *toma de decisiones* decision making || *toma de hábito* take of vows || *toma de mando* taking (over) *o* assumption of command || *toma de muestras* sampling || *toma de posesión* taking over (en un cargo), investiture (investidura) || *toma de rapé* pinch of snuff || *toma de sangre* blood sample || *toma de sonido* sound recording || *toma de tierra* earth [US ground] (de una antena), landing, touchdown (de un avión), landing (de un paracaidista) || CINEM *toma de vistas* shooting, filming.

tomadero *m* handle (agarradero) || outlet, tap (de agua).

tomado, da *adj* AMER drunk || *voz tomada* hoarse voice.

tomador, ra *adj* taking (que toma) || stealing, thieving (que roba) || AMER drunken (que bebe) || *perro tomador* retriever.

◆ *m/f* taker (que toma) || thief (ladrón) || AMER drinker, drunkard (bebedor).

◆ *m* COM drawee (de una letra de cambio) || MAR gasket.

tomadura *f* taking (toma) || dose (de una medicina) || MIL taking, capture (de una ciudad) || FAM *tomadura de pelo* joke, big hoax *o* joke (burla); *fue todo una tomadura de pelo* it was all a big hoax; daylight robbery, rip-off (precio abusivo).

tomahawk *m* tomahawk (hacha de guerra).

tomaína *f* QUÍM ptomaine.

tomar *vt* to take (coger con la mano) || to take (un taxi, apuntes, una curva, etc.); *tomar una foto, un baño, un pedido* to take a photo, a bath, an order || to catch (el autobús, etc.); *no pude tomar el tren porque llegué tarde* I couldn't catch the train because I arrived too late || to go by (ir en) || to take, to go by; *tomamos el camino más corto* we took the shortest road || to take, to accept (un regalo, etc.) || to have, to eat; *tomar el desayuno* to have breakfast || to have, to drink (beber); *¿qué quieres tomar?* what would you like to drink? || MIL to take, to capture (conquistar) || MED to take (el pulso, la temperatura, una medicina) || to get into, to acquire; *tomar malas costumbres* to acquire bad habits || to take, to adopt, to make (adoptar); *tomar decisiones* to make decisions || to take (empezar a tener); *tomar forma* to take shape || to take on, to adopt (un aspecto) || to take on, to hire (contratar); *tomar un criado* to take on a servant || to rent, to take (alquilar); *han tomado una casa en la playa* they have taken a house by the beach || to take over (un negocio) || to buy, to get (comprar); *tomar las entradas* to get the tickets || to take; *tomar una cita de un autor* to take a quotation from an author || to take, to steal (robar) || to get back (recobrar) || to cover (el macho a la hembra) || — *a toma y daca* on a give and take basis || FAM *haberla tomado con alguien* to have it in for s.o. || *lo toma o lo deja* take it or leave it || FIG *más vale un toma que dos te daré* a bird in the hand is worth two in the bush || *¡toma!* here!, here you are!; *toma, aquí tienes el lápiz* here, here's the pencil; fancy that! (asombro o sorpresa), no!, really? (incredulidad), take that! (tómate ésa), huh!, poo! (¡eso no es nada!), well!, so!, aha! (exclamación de entendimiento); *¡toma! ¡aho-*

ra lo comprendo! well! now I understand!, you see! I told you so! (¡ya ves!), it serves you right (tienes tu merecido), here! (para llamar a un perro) ‖ *tomar a broma* to make fun of, to deride (ridiculizar), to take as a joke (tomar a guasa) ‖ *tomar afecto a alguien* to become attached to *o* fond of s.o. ‖ *tomar algo a bien, a mal* to take sth. well, badly ‖ *tomar algo sobre sí* to take sth. upon o.s. ‖ *tomar aliento* to catch one's breath, to get one's breath back ‖ *tomar a medias* to split, to share ‖ *tomar a pecho* to take to heart ‖ *tomar asiento* to take a seat, to sit down ‖ *tomar a una persona por otra* to take s.o. for s.o. else; *te tomé por tu hermano* I took you for your brother ‖ *tomar como ejemplo* to take as an example ‖ *tomar de la mano* to take by the hand ‖ *tomar el fresco* to get some fresh air ‖ *tomar el pecho* to nurse, to suck ‖ FIG *tomar el pelo a uno* to pull s.o.'s leg ‖ FAM *tomar el portante* to go, to leave, to make o.s. scarce ‖ *tomar en cuenta* to take into account, to bear in mind (tomar en consideración), to mind; *no tomes en cuenta que no venga a visitarte* don't mind if I don't come and visit you ‖ *tomar en serio* to take seriously ‖ *tomar estado* to marry (casarse), to take holy orders (profesar) ‖ *tomar frío* to catch a cold ‖ *tomar fuerzas* to get back *o* to recover one's strength ‖ *tomar a uno la delantera* to take the lead over s.o., to get ahead of s.o. (en una carrera), to get there before s.o., to beat s.o. to it (anticiparse); *fui a solicitar un trabajo pero me cogieron la delantera* I went for a job but s.o. beat me to it ‖ *tomar la palabra* to speak, to take the floor (hablar), to take (s.o.) at his word (creer) ‖ *tomar las aguas* to take the waters ‖ *tomar armas* to take up arms (armarse), to present arms (hacer los honores militares) ‖ FIG & FAM *tomarlas* or *tomarla con uno* to pick on s.o., to have a go at s.o. (tomar tirria, criticar) | *tomar las de Villadiego* to beat it, to take to one's heels ‖ *tomar las lecciones* to make (s.o.) recite his lessons ‖ *tomar medidas* to take measures *o* steps ‖ *tomar nota* to take note ‖ *tomar odio a* to get to hate ‖ *tomar partido por* to side with, to take sides with ‖ *tomar por* to take for; *¿por quién me tomas?* who do you take me for? ‖ *tomar por escrito* to take down, to write down ‖ *tomar prestado* to borrow ‖ *tomar sangre* to take blood ‖ *tomar tiempo* to take time (requerir tiempo) ‖ AVIAC *tomar tierra* to land ‖ FAM *¡tómate ésa!* take that!

◆ *vi* to turn, to go; *tome a la derecha* turn right ‖ to take (una planta, un injerto, etc.) ‖ AMER to drink (beber) ‖ FAM *tomar y...* to go and..., to up and...; *tomó y se fue* he upped and left, he went and left.

◆ *vpr* to take; *tomarse unas vacaciones* to take a holiday; *tomarse la libertad de* to take the liberty to (con infinitivo) *o* of (con gerundio) ‖ to eat (comer) ‖ to drink (beber) ‖ to take (medicina) ‖ to get rusty (cubrirse de moho) ‖ to go bad (vino) ‖ — *tomarse el trabajo* or *la molestia de* to take the trouble to ‖ *tomárselo con calma* to take it easy ‖ *tomarse por alguien* to think one is somebody.

Tomás *npr m* Thomas ‖ — *Santo Tomás de Aquino* Saint Thomas Aquinas ‖ *Tomás Moro* Thomas More.

tomatada *f* fried tomatoes *pl*.

tomatal *m* tomato patch *o* bed *o* field.

tomatazo *m* blow with a tomato ‖ *le recibieron a tomatazos* the people threw rotten tomatoes at him.

tomate *m* tomato (fruto y planta) ‖ FAM hole, spud (en las medias, etc.) ‖ — FIG *colorado como un tomate* as red as beetroot ‖ *salsa de tomate* tomato sauce (casera), ketchup, catsup (embotellada) ‖ FAM *tener tomate* to be difficult *o* awkward *o* bothersome; *este trabajo tiene mucho tomate* this job is really difficult.

tomatera *f* tomato (planta) ‖ FAM *tener tomatera* to put on airs.

tomatero, ra *m/f* tomato seller (vendedor), *o* tomato grower (cultivador) ‖ *pollo tomatero* tender young fryer.

tomavistas *m inv* cinecamera [*US* movie camera] ‖ television camera.

tómbola *f* tombola.

tomillar *m* field of thyme.

tomillo *m* thyme (planta).

tomineja *f*; **tominejo** *m* hummingbird.

tomismo *m* REL & FIL Thomism.

tomista *adj* REL & FIL Thomistic, Thomist.
◆ *m/f* REL & FIL Thomist.

tomiza *f* esparto rope.

tomo *m* volume (de un libro) ‖ FIG size (tamaño) | importance (importancia) ‖ FIG *de tomo y lomo* out-and-out, utter, first rate; *es un sinvergüenza de tomo y lomo* he's an out-and-out cad.

tomógrafo *m* MED scanner.

ton *m* *sin ton ni son* without rhyme or reason.

tonada *f* song, tune (canción) ‖ tune (música) ‖ AMER accent (dejo).

tonadilla *f* ditty (canción) ‖ «tonadilla» [short musical piece popular in the 18th century].

tonadillero, ra *m/f* writer of popular songs.
◆ *f* songstress, singer [of «tonadillas»].

tonal *adj* MÚS tonal.

tonalidad *f* tonality ‖ RAD *control de tonalidad* tone control.

tonante *adj* thundering.

tonar *vi* to thunder.

tonca *adj f* BOT *haba tonca* tonka bean.

tondino *m* ARQ astragal.

tondo *m* ARQ round moulding (mediacaña).

tonel *m* barrel, cask, keg (cuba y contenido) ‖ AVIAC barrel roll (acrobacia) ‖ FIG *Juan está como un tonel* John is ever so fat.

tonelada *f* ton (peso) ‖ MAR ton (medida); *tonelada de arqueo* register ton ‖ barrels *pl*, casks *pl* (toneles) ‖ *tonelada larga, métrica, corta* long, metric, short ton.

tonelaje *m* tonnage (de un navío); *tonelaje bruto* gross tonnage.

tonelería *f* barrelmaking, cooperage (fabricación) ‖ barrel shop, cooperage, coopery (taller) ‖ barrels *pl*, casks *pl* (toneles).

tonelero, ra *adj* barrel, cask.
◆ *m* cooper, barrelmaker.

tonelete *m* small barrel, keg, cask (tonel) ‖ child's short skirt (traje de niño) ‖ piece of armour protecting the body between the waist and the knees (armadura) ‖ short silk skirt [worn by men] (vestidura antigua) ‖ ballet skirt, tutu (faldilla de bailarina).

tonga *f* layer (capa) ‖ AMER pile, heap | task, job, work (tarea).

tongada *f* layer (capa).

tongo *m* DEP bribery [in sports] ‖ AMER FAM bowler hat (bombín, sombrero hongo) ‖ — DEP *aquí hay tongo* it's been fixed *o* rigged, it's a fix | *hubo tongo en el combate* the fight was fixed *o* rigged.

tongonearse *vpr* AMER ⟶ **contonearse.**

tongoneo *m* AMER ⟶ **contoneo.**

tonicidad *f* tonicity.

tónico, ca *adj* tonic, accented, stressed; *sílaba tónica* accented syllable ‖ MED & MÚS tonic.
◆ *m* tonic; *la quina es un tónico* quinine is a tonic ‖ *tónico cardíaco* cardiotonic.
◆ *f* MÚS tonic ‖ FIG tendency, trend; *la tónica general* the general tendency; *la tónica de la Bolsa* the trend of the Stock Market ‖ FIG *marcar la tónica* to set the pace *o* the trend.

tonificación *f* toning up, invigoration.

tonificante *adj* invigorating, tonic.

tonificar *vt* MED to tone up, to invigorate.

tonillo *m* singsong, monotone (tono monótono) ‖ accent (dejo) ‖ sarcastic tone (retintín).

tonina *f* tunny, tuna (atún) ‖ dolphin (delfín).

Tonkín *npr m* GEOGR Tonkin.

tono *m* tone (de voz, color, etc.); *su tono de voz* his tone of voice; *el tono de una carta* the tone of a letter ‖ MÚS tone (de un sonido) | key; *tono mayor, menor* major, minor key | pitch (altura) | key (tecla) | slide (vara) ‖ ANAT & MED tone (de un músculo) ‖ FIG class, social standing (de una familia, etc.) | conceit (presunción) | tone (carácter) ‖ FAM energy (energía) ‖ — *a este tono* like this, this way ‖ *a tono con* in tune *o* harmony with ‖ FIG *bajar el tono* to lower one's voice, to tone down | *bajarle el tono a uno* to take s.o. down a peg | *cambiar de tono* to change one's tune *o* one's tone | *dar buen tono* to give tone *o* class *o* prestige (dar prestigio) | *dar el tono* to set the tone *o* standard | *darse tono* to put on airs | *de buen tono* elegant, fashionable, stylish | *de mal tono* common, vulgar | *decir en todos los tonos* to tell (sth. to s.o.) time and again ‖ *en tono airado* in an angry tone [of voice] ‖ FIG *estar a tono con* to be in proportion with; *paga un alquiler que no está a tono con sus ingresos* the rent he pays is out of proportion with his income; to be on a level with (estar al mismo nivel), to be on the same wavelength as (entenderse muy bien con otra persona) | *fuera de tono* inappropriate, out of place | *mudar de tono* to change one's tune *o* one's tone | *ponerse a tono con alguien* to adapt o.s. to s.o. | *salida de tono* improper remark (observación inoportuna), silly remark (tontería) ‖ *subir* or *subirse de tono* to warm up (una conversación), to become louder (la voz, etc.), to become arrogant *o* haughty (adoptar un aire arrogante).

Tonquín *npr m* GEOGR Tonkin.

tonquinés, esa *adj/s* Tonkinese.

tonsila *f* ANAT tonsil (amígdala).

tonsilar *adj* ANAT tonsillar.

tonsilectomía *f* MED tonsillectomy.

tonsilitis *f* MED tonsillitis.

tonsura *f* tonsure ‖ *prima tonsura* tonsure (ceremonia).

tonsurado *adj m* tonsured (clérigo).
◆ *m* cleric, priest.

tonsurar *vt* to tonsure (un clérigo) ‖ to cut (el pelo) ‖ to shear (la lana).

tontada *f* ⟶ **tontería.**

tontaina; tontainas *adj* FAM foolish, silly.
◆ *m/f* FAM fool, idiot.

tontamente *adv* foolishly, stupidly.

tontarrón, ona *adj* FAM idiotic, stupid.
◆ *m/f* FAM blockhead, numbskull, fool.

tontear *vi* to act the fool, to fool about (hacer tonterías) ‖ to talk nonsense (decir tonterías) ‖ to flirt (flirtear).

tontedad; tontera *f* foolishness, silliness.

tontería; tontada *f* foolishness, stupidity, idiocy (cualidad) ‖ silly thing (acción, dicho) ‖ stupid remark (dicho) ‖ FIG trifle, foolish thing (nadería); *gastarse el dinero en tonterías* to spend one's money on trifles ‖ — *decir tonterías* to talk nonsense ‖ *¡déjate de tonterías!* don't be stupid! (al hablar), stop messing *o* fooling about! (al actuar) ‖ *dejémonos de tonterías* let's be serious

|| *hacer tonterías* to mess about, to fool about || *he hecho una tontería* I've done a stupid thing || *lo compré por una tontería* I got it for next to nothing || *no es ninguna tontería* it's serious (va en serio), it's no bad at all (no está nada mal).

tontillo *m* farthingale (de una falda).

tontina *f* tontine (asociación) || FAM fool || FAM *no seas tontina* don't be silly.

tontito *m* maternity dress (prenda de maternidad) || smock (bata corta).

tontivano, na *adj* pretentious, conceited, foppish.
◆ *m/f* fop.

tonto, ta *adj* foolish, stupid, silly, dumb, idiotic; *una idea tonta* a foolish idea || *es lo bastante tonto para creerlo* he's fool enough to believe it.
◆ *m/f* fool, dolt, idiot; *¡qué tonto!* what a fool!; *¡tonto tú!* you're the fool || — *a tontas y a locas* haphazardly, any old how || *hablar a tontas y a locas* to talk without rhyme or reason, to talk foolishly || *hacer el tonto* to act the fool (hacer el idiota), to flirt (tontear) || *hacerse el tonto* to play *o* to act dumb | *hasta los tontos lo saben* any fool knows that || *¡no tan tonto!* he's not as stupid as you think *o* as he looks || *ponerse tonto* to do (sth.) too much (exagerar), to flirt (tontear), to put on airs (presumir) || *¡qué tonto es!* what a fool he is! || *ser tonto de capirote* or *de remate, ser más tonto que Abundio* or *una mata de habas* to be a prize idiot, to be as mad as a hatter *o* as daft as a brush || FAM *tonto del bote* the biggest twit of all.
◆ *m* clown (payaso).

tontuelo, la *adj* FAM naïve, silly.
◆ *m/f* FAM little fool, silly thing (persona).

tontuna; tontura *f* foolishness, silliness (tontería).

toña *f* tipcat (juego) || tipcat, cat, catty (palo) || FAM blow (golpe) || FAM *coger una toña* to get drunk *o* plastered *o* canned.

¡top! *interj* stop!, whoa!

topacio *m* topaz.

topada *f* butt (topetada).

topadora *f* AMER bulldozer (buldózer).

topar *vt* to butt (los carneros) || to bump against (tropezar) || to run into, to bump into (encontrar a alguien) || to come across, to find (encontrar algo) || to run into, to bump into (chocar) || FIG to run into, to encounter (dificultades) || MAR to butt (dos maderos) || AMER to try out (dos gallos).
◆ *vi* to butt (los carneros) || to take a bet (en el juego) || FIG to work (salir bien); *lo dije a ver si topaba* I said it to see if it would work || FIG *la dificultad topa en esto* this is the difficulty *o* the trouble *o* the problem.
◆ *vpr* to meet (encontrarse) || to butt [each other] (los carneros) || *toparse con* to encounter, to run into, to bump into.

tope *m* butt, end (extremo) || bump, knock, bang (golpe) || butt (con la cabeza) || stop, check, catch (mecanismo) || buffer (de locomotora) || buffer stop [US bumping post] (de línea férrea) || bumper (de tranvía) || bumper guard, overrider (de coche) || FIG difficulty, snag, rub (obstáculo); *ahí está el tope* there's the rub | limit; *poner tope a sus ambiciones* to put a limit to one's ambitions | quarrel (riña) | scuffle (reyerta) || MAR masthead (del mastelero) | butt-end of a plank (extremo de un tablón) | topman (marinero de vigía) || AMER simulated cock fight (pelea de gallos) || — *a* or *al tope* end to end || *de tope a tope* from end to end || FIG *estar hasta los topes* to be loaded to the gunwales (un barco), to be crammed full (estar muy lleno), to be fed up *o* browned off (estar harto) || *hasta el tope* to the brim || FIG *llegar al tope* to reach one's limit | *rebasar el tope* to go too far *o* beyond the limits || *repostar a tope* to fill up, to fill to the brim (gasolina) || *tope de puerta* doorstop || *tope de retención* stop.
◆ *adj* top, maximum; *precio tope* top price || *fecha tope* deadline, closing date.

topear *vt* AMER to unhorse.

topetada *f* butt (de un carnero) || butt, bump (con la cabeza).

topetar *vt/vi* to butt || FIG to bump into.

topetazo; topetón *m* butt (de los carneros) || butt, bump (con la cabeza) || crash, bump, bang, collision (de dos cosas) || *darse un topetazo* to bump *o* to bang *o* to crash into each other (dos cosas).

tópico, ca *adj* MED topical, local || commonplace, trite.
◆ *m* MED external local application || cliché, commonplace, trite saying (lugar común) || AMER topic, subject (tema de conversación).

topinambur *m* BOT Jerusalem artichoke.

topless *m* topless fashion || *en topless* topless.

topo *m* ZOOL mole (mamífero) || FIG & FAM awkward person, blunderer (torpe) || AMER league and a half (medida) | large pin (alfiler) || FIG & FAM *ver menos que un topo* to be as blind as a bat.

topocho, cha *adj* FAM AMER chubby (rechoncho).

topografía *f* topography (configuración) || surveying, topography (levantamiento de planos).

topográfico, ca *adj* topographic, topographical.

topógrafo *m* topographer || surveyor (agrimensor).

topolino *m/f* teenager, youngster (joven).
◆ *m* wedge-heeled shoe (zapato).

topología *f* topology.

toponimia *f* toponymy, study of place-names (ciencia) || place-names *pl* (nombres).

toponímico, ca *adj* toponymic, toponymical.

topónimo *m* toponym, place-name.

toque *m* touch; *toque de varita mágica* touch of the magic wand; *dale un toque* give him a touch || peal, pealing, ringing (de campanas) || blare, blaring, sound, sounding (de trompetas, etc.) || hoot, blast (de sirena, claxon) || beat, beating (de tambores) || ARTES touch (pincelada ligera) || test (ensayo de metales preciosos) || FIG warning (advertencia) | blow (golpe), tap (golpecito) || DEP touch (en esgrima) || MIL bugle call || AMER turn (turno) || — FIG *dar el toque de alarma* to sound the alarm | *dar el último toque a* to put the finishing touch to | *dar otro toque a un cliente* to have another attempt at convincing a client | *darse un toque* to see to one's makeup | *dar un toque a uno* to put s.o. to the test (probar), to take s.o. to task (llamar al orden), to sound s.o. out (sondear) || MED *dar unos toques en la garganta* to paint one's throat || *piedra de toque* touchstone || *toque de alarma* alarm signal (rebato), warning (aviso) || FIG *toque de atención* warning, warning note || DEP *toque de balón* ball control || *toque de diana* reveille || *toque de difuntos* knell, passing bell (de campanas), last post (de trompeta) || *toque del alba* Angelus bell || ARTES *toque de luz* highlight || *toque de oración* Angelus bell, call to prayer || *toque de queda* curfew [bell] || *toque de timbre* ring of a bell || *último toque* final *o* finishing touch.

toquetear *vt* FAM to fiddle with, to finger, to play about with || MÚS FAM to mess about on (un instrumento) || FAM to pet, to caress, to fondle (a una persona).
◆ *vi* FAM to rummage.

toqueteo *m* FAM handling, fiddling, touching (de una cosa) | petting, fondling (de una persona).

toqui *m* AMER Araucan Indian chief.

toquilla *f* knitted shawl (prenda de punto) || kerchief, headscarf (pañuelo) || gauze *o* ribbon adornment for a man's hat (adorno antiguo) || AMER straw hat (sombrero de paja) | low palm tree (palmera).

tora *f* Torah (de los israelitas) || ancient tax (tributo) || BOT nutgall (agalla).

torácico, ca *adj* ANAT thoracic || *caja* or *cavidad torácica* thoracic *o* chest cavity.

torada *f* drove *o* herd of bulls.

toral *adj* main, principal; *arco toral* main arch.
◆ *m* TECN mould [US mold] (molde) | copper bar (barra de cobre).

tórax *m* ANAT thorax.

torbellino *m* whirlwind (viento) || dust cloud (de polvo) || FIG whirl, turmoil, swirl (de cosas) | whirlwind (persona) || FIG *irrumpir como un torbellino* to burst in like a whirlwind.

torcaz; torcazo, za *adj/sf* *paloma torcaz* ringdove, wood pigeon.

torcecuello *m* wryneck (ave).

torcedor, ra *adj* twisting.
◆ *m/f* twister (que tuerce lana, seda, etc.).
◆ *m* spindle (huso) || FIG torment, torture (tormento) || AMER tobacco twister.

torcedura *f* twist, twisting || MED sprain, twist, strain || bad wine (vino malo).

torcer* *vt* to twist; *torcer una cuerda, el brazo de uno* to twist a rope, s.o.'s arm || to change (desviar); *torcer el rumbo* to change course; *torcer el curso de un razonamiento* to change one's line of reasoning || to turn, to round (dar la vuelta); *le vi al torcer la esquina* I saw him as I turned the corner || to bend (doblar) || to warp (alabear) || to move (round), to move slightly (desplazar ligeramente) || to slant (un cuadro) || FIG to twist, to distort; *torcer el sentido de una frase* to distort the meaning of a sentence | to bend (la justicia, la verdad) | to pervert (pervertir) | to corrupt (corromper) | to screw up, to contort (la cara) || MED to twist, to sprain (un miembro) | to strain, to pull (un músculo) || DEP to spin (una pelota) || — FIG & FAM *dar su brazo a torcer* to give in || *torcer el gesto* or *el semblante* to grimace, to pull a face || *torcer los ojos* to squint (bizquear).
◆ *vi* to turn; *el camino, el coche tuerce a la derecha* the road, the car turns (to the) right || to swerve (desviarse bruscamente).
◆ *vpr* to twist (una cuerda, etc.) || to bend (doblarse) || to become slanted (ladearse) || to warp (alabearse la madera) || to buckle, to bend (el metal) || to screw up, to contort (la cara) || FIG to go sour (el vino) | to curdle (la leche) | to take a turn for the worse (la salud) | to go astray, to turn bad; *este muchacho se ha torcido* this boy has gone astray | to go awry, to go wrong (frustrarse) | to take a sudden turn (los acontecimientos, la historia) | to be corrupted, to go crooked (un juez) || — FIG *se me ha torcido la suerte* my luck has gone bad, my luck has turned (for the worse) || *se me torció el tobillo* I sprained *o* I twisted my ankle || *torcerse un músculo* to pull a muscle.

torcida *f* wick (mecha) || fans *pl* (partidarios).

torcido, da *adj* twisted || twisting, winding (camino) || twisted, sprained, strained (un miembro) || crooked, slanted (oblicuo) || buckled, bent (metal, rueda) || warped (madera) || crossed (ojos) || FIG twisted (mente) | devious, crooked (tramposo) | hypocritical || *llevas la corbata torcida* your tie is crooked.

◆ *m* roll of candied fruits (frutas en dulce) || bad wine (vino malo) || strong silk thread (hebra de seda).

torcijón *m* twisting (retorcimiento) || MED stomach cramp (retortijón) || VET gripes *pl.*

torcionario *m* torturer.

tórculo *m* screw press.

tordillo, lla *adj* dapple-grey (caballo).
◆ *m/f* dapple-grey horse.

tordo, da *adj* grey, gray (gris) || dapple-grey (caballo).
◆ *m/f* dapple-grey horse (caballo) || thrush (ave).
◆ *m* AMER starling (estornino).

toreador, ra *m* (p us) toreador, bullfighter.
— OBSERV The usual term in Spanish is *torero.*

torear *vt* TAUR to fight (lidiar un toro) || FIG to avoid, to dodge, to sidestep (evitar algo o a alguien) | to handle well (manejar bien) | to put (s.o.) off, to keep (s.o.) at bay (entretener) | to confuse [with contradictions] | to banter, to mock, to tease (burlarse) || AMER to goad (azuzar) || — *llevar el toro toreado* to have complete control of the bull || FIG & FAM *no se deja torear por nadie* he doesn't let anyone mess him about || *toro toreado* vicious bull.
◆ *vi* TAUR to fight bulls (lidiar toros) || to fight; *¡qué bien ha toreado hoy!* he really fought well today || AMER to bark (ladrar) || *Romero toreaba mejor que nadie* Romero was the best bullfighter of them all.

toreo *m* TAUR bullfighting (arte y acción) || FIG & FAM banter (burla) || FIG & FAM *¡se acabó el toreo!* that's enough!, no more fooling around! (se acabó la burla).

torera *f* bolero (chaquetilla) || FIG & FAM *saltarse algo a la torera* to completely ignore sth.

torero, ra *adj* TAUR bullfighting.
◆ *m* TAUR bullfighter.

torete *m* young bull (toro joven).

toribio *m* FAM Simple Simon, simpleton (tonto).
◆ *pl* reformatory *sing* (para niños indisciplinados).

tórico, ca *adj* toric.

toril *m* TAUR bullpen [where bulls are kept before a bullfight].

torillo *m* dowel (espiga) || ARQ torus (moldura) || blenny (pez).

torio *m* QUÍM thorium.

torito *m* small bull.

tormenta *f* storm || FIG storm (riña, discusión, etc.); *la tormenta ha pasado ya* the storm is over now | misfortune (adversidad, desgracia) || — *hacer frente a la tormenta* to brave the storm || FIG *una tormenta en un vaso de agua* a storm in a teacup.

tormento *m* torture, torment (dolor) || torture (del reo) || FIG torment, anguish (angustia) || — *dar tormento* to torture, to put to torture (a un reo), to torment (molestar) || *estas botas son un tormento* these boots are agony.

tormentoso, sa *adj* stormy.

torna *f* return (vuelta) || weir (presa) || — *cuando se vuelvan las tornas* when the tables turn, when our luck changes || *volverle a uno las tornas* to give s.o. tit for tat (corresponder uno al proceder de otro), to turn the tables on s.o. (hacer sufrir a otro lo que uno ha sufrido).

tornaboda *f* day after the wedding.

tornadizo, za *adj* changeable, fickle (cambiadizo) || renegade (renegado).
◆ *m/f* turncoat.

tornado *m* tornado (huracán).

tornaguía *f* receipt.

tornapunta *f* prop, stay (puntal).

tornar *vt* to return, to give back (devolver) || to turn, to make (volver); *la tinta tornó el agua negra* the ink made the water black || to turn, to change, to transform (convertir); *tornar una cosa en otra* to turn one thing into another.
◆ *vi* to return, to go back (regresar) || to begin again; *tornó a hablar* he began to talk again || *tornar en sí* to come to, to regain consciousness (volver en sí).
◆ *vpr* to turn, to become (ponerse); *el cielo se tornó azul* the sky became blue || to return (regresar) || *tornarse en* to turn into *o* to, to become.

tornasol *m* BOT sunflower || litmus (materia colorante); *papel de tornasol* litmus paper || iridescence (viso).

tornasolado, da *adj* iridescent (color) || shot (tejido); *seda tornasolada* shot silk.

tornasolar *vt* to make iridescent.
◆ *vi* to become iridescent, to look iridescent.

tornatrás *m/f* throwback.

tornavía *f* turntable.

tornavoz *m* sounding board.

torneado, da *adj* turned (hecho a torno) || FIG shapely, nicely rounded (cuerpo).
◆ *m* TECN turning [on the lathe].

torneador, ra *m* turner, lathe operator (tornero) || jouster (en un torneo).

torneadura *f* shaving (viruta) || TECN turning [on the lathe].

tornear *vt* to turn [on the lathe]; *tornear una pata de mesa* to turn a table leg.
◆ *vi* to revolve, to spin, to go round (dar vueltas) || to tourney, to joust (en un torneo).

torneo *m* HIST tourney, joust, tournament || tournament, competition (competición).

tornera *f* nun in attendance at the revolving window of a convent.

tornería *f* turnery (arte y taller).

tornero *m* turner, lathe operator (que hace obras en el torno) || errand boy, messenger (recadero de monjas).

tornillo *m* screw (rosca) || small lathe (torno pequeño) || — FIG & FAM *apretarle a uno los tornillos* to put the screws *o* the pressure on s.o. || MIL *hacer tornillo* to desert || FIG & FAM *le falta un tornillo, tiene flojos los tornillos* he has a screw loose || *tornillo de banco* vice [US vise], clamp || *tornillo de mordazas* jaw vice || *tornillo de orejas* thumbscrew || *tornillo micrométrico* micrometer screw || *tornillo sin fin* worm gear, endless screw.

torniquete *m* turnstile (barra giratoria) || MED tourniquet.

torniscón *m* FAM slap (golpe dado en la cara) | pinch (pellizco).

torno *m* lathe (máquina herramienta); *labrar a torno* to turn on the lathe || winch, windlass, winding drum (para levantar pesos) || revolving window (en los conventos) || revolving food stand (de comedor) || bend, turn (recodo) || turn, revolution (movimiento circular) || — *en torno a* around, round, about (alrededor), with regard to, as far as (sth.) is concerned, about (en cuanto a) || *torno de alfarero* potter's wheel || *torno de banco* vice [US vise], clamp || *torno de hilar* spinning wheel || *torno elevador* winch.

toro *m* ZOOL bull; *toro bravo* or *de lidia* fighting bull || ARQ torus (moldura) || ASTR Taurus (Tauro) || MAT tore, torus || — FIG *coger al toro por los cuernos* to take the bull by the horns | *echarle* or *soltarle a uno el toro* to give s.o. a piece of one's mind (decir las cuatro verdades) | *estar hecho un toro* to be a strong *o* a strapping lad | *ir al toro* to get to the point | *¡otro toro!* let's change the subject | *ser fuerte como un toro* to be as strong as an ox | *ser un toro corrido* to be nobody's fool, to be an old hand, to be no easy mark || *toro de fuego* fireworks on a bull-shaped frame.
◆ *pl* bullfights, bullfighting *sing*; *¿le gustan los toros?* do you like bullfights? || bullfight *sing* (corrida); *ir a los toros* to go to a *o* to the bullfight || bullfighting *sing* (arte, negocio, etc.) || FIG *ver los toros desde la barrera* to sit on the fence, to be an onlooker.

toronja *f* Seville orange, bitter orange (naranja) || grapefruit (pomelo).

toronjil *m*; **toronjina** *f* lemon balm.

toronjo *m* Seville orange tree, bitter orange tree || grapefruit tree.

torozón *m* VET gripes *pl.*

torpe *adj* awkward, clumsy (falto de habilidad) || ungainly (desgarbado) || stupid, dim (necio) || slow, heavy, sluggish, torpid (movimientos) || slow (en comprender) || lewd, indecent; *torpes instintos* lewd instincts || crude, obscene (conducta) || — FIG & FAM *más torpe que un arado* as thick as two short planks || *torpe de oídos* hard of hearing.

torpedear *vt* to torpedo.

torpedeo *m* torpedoing.

torpedero *m* torpedo boat (barco).

torpedista *m* torpedoist, torpedoman.

torpedo *m* MIL torpedo || ZOOL electric ray, torpedo (raya).

torpemente *adv* clumsily, awkwardly (sin destreza) || heavily, sluggishly (pesadamente) || slowly (lentamente).

torpeza *f* clumsiness, awkwardness (falta de destreza) || ungainliness (desgarbo) || slowness, stupidity, dimness (necedad) || heaviness, torpidity (pesadez) || crudeness, obscenity (obscenidad) || *cometer una torpeza* to make a blunder.

torpón, ona *adj* very clumsy *o* stupid.

torques *f* torque (collar antiguo).

torrado *m* toasted chick-pea.

torrar *vt* to toast (tostar).

torre *f* tower; *la torre Eiffel* the Eiffel tower; *la Torre de Londres* the Tower of London || castle, rook (ajedrez) || bell tower (campanario) || turret (de buque de guerra) || villa, country house (quinta) || ELECTR pylon (poste) || — *torre albarrana* or *flanqueante* turret || *Torre de Babel* Tower of Babel || *torre de control* or *de mando* control tower (aeropuerto), conning tower (portaviones) | *torre de extracción* derrick, oil derrick (de petróleo), headgear (de una mina) || *torre del homenaje* donjon, keep || FIG *torre de marfil* ivory tower (aislamiento) || *torre de perforación* derrick || MAR *torre de vigía* crow's nest.

torrefacción *f* torrefaction, roasting.

torrefactar *vt* to torrefy, to torrify (en general) || to roast (el café).

torrefacto, ta *adj* torrefied, roasted.

torrefactor *m* roaster.

torrencial *adj* torrential; *lluvia torrencial* torrential rain.

torrente *m* torrent (curso de agua) || ANAT bloodstream (la sangre) || FIG flood, torrent (abundancia); *un torrente de injurias* a flood of insults || — *a torrentes* in torrents || *llover a torrentes* to rain torrents, to rain cats and dogs.

torrentera *f* course of a torrent (cauce).

torrentoso, sa *adj* torrential.

torreón *m* large fortified tower.

torrero *m* lighthouse keeper (de faro) || keeper of a villa (de una casa).

torreta *f* ARQ turret || conning tower (en los submarinos) || AVIAT & MAR & MIL turret (de un tanque, etc.).

torreznada *f* dish of fried bacon.

torreznero, ra *adj* idle, loafing (holgazán).
◆ *m/f* loafer, idler (holgazán).

torrezno *m* fried bacon.

tórrido, da *adj* torrid.

torrija *f* bread soaked in milk and egg and fried [US French toast].

torsión *f* torsion ‖ TECN torsion; *barra de torsión* torsion bar ‖ — FÍS *balanza de torsión* torsion balance | *momento de torsión* torque.

torso *m* ANAT torso ‖ ARTES bust.

torta *f* CULIN cake, tart ‖ FIG cake (masa aplastada) ‖ FAM slap, wallop (bofetada) | drunkenness (borrachera) ‖ IMPR fount, font (paquete de caracteres) | form kept for distribution ‖ AGR oil cake (tortada) ‖ AMER sandwich ‖ — FIG *la torta costó un pan* it was more trouble than it was worth | *ni torta* not a thing; *no ve ni torta* he can't see a thing | *pegarse una torta* to come a cropper (caerse, chocar) | *son tortas y pan pintado* that's child's play (no es difícil), that's nothing (no es nada) ‖ FAM *tener una torta* to be drunk *o* sozzled *o* sloshed.

tortada *f* meat *o* chicken pie (pastel) ‖ AGR oil cake.

tortazo *m* FAM hard slap, wallop (bofetada) ‖ — FIG & FAM *pegarse un tortazo* to come a cropper (caerse), to have a crash (en coche) | *pegarse un tortazo contra un árbol* to bash *o* to crash into a tree.

tortedad *f* blindness in one eye.

tortícolis; torticolis *m* o *f* stiff neck [US wryneck], crick in one's neck, torticollis; *tener tortícolis* to have a stiff neck.
— OBSERV This word is generally used in the feminine.

tortilla *f* omelet, omelette; *tortilla de jamón, de patatas* ham, potato omelet; *tortilla a la francesa* French omelet ‖ AMER tortilla, corn cake ‖ — FIG *hacerse una tortilla* to be flattened *o* squashed flat | *hacer tortilla a* to flatten | *se ha vuelto la tortilla* the tables have turned, the boot is on the other foot (la situación ha cambiado).

tortillero, ra *m/f* tortilla maker, tortilla seller.
◆ *f* POP lesbian.

tortita *f* pancake.

tórtola *f* turtledove (pájaro).

tortolito, ta *adj* inexperienced.

tórtolo *m* male turtledove.
◆ *pl* FIG lovebirds (pareja enamorada).

tortuga *f* tortoise (de tierra) ‖ turtle (de mar) ‖ MIL testudo ‖ FIG *andar a paso de tortuga* to walk at a snail's pace.

tortuosidad *f* tortuosity.

tortuoso, sa *adj* tortuous, winding; *una carretera tortuosa* a tortuous road ‖ FIG devious, tortuous; *métodos tortuosos* tortuous means.

tortura *f* torture (tormento) ‖ FIG torment, torture, anguish (angustia).

torturar *vt* to torture.
◆ *vpr* to torture o.s. (atormentarse).

torus *m* ANAT torus.

torva *f* snow storm (nieve) ‖ rain storm *o* squall (lluvia).

torviscal *m* field of spurge flax.

torvisco *m* BOT spurge flax.

torvo, va *adj* grim, fierce; *mirada torva* grim look.

tory *adj/sm* tory (conservador).

torzadillo *m* fine silk twist.

torzal *m* silk twist (hilo de seda) ‖ twine, twist (de cualquier tipo de hebras) ‖ AMER leather lasso.

torzón *m* VET gripes *pl*.

tos *f* cough; *tener tos* to have a cough ‖ coughing; *su tos no me dejó dormir* his coughing prevented me from sleeping ‖ — *acceso de tos* coughing fit *o* spell *o* bout ‖ MED *tos ferina* whooping cough, hooping cough.

tosca *f* tufa, tuff (piedra).

Toscana *npr f* GEOGR Tuscany.

toscano, na *adj/s* Tuscan.
◆ *m* Tuscan (dialecto).

tosco, ca *adj* rustic, crude; *una silla tosca* a rustic chair ‖ rough, coarse; *tela tosca* coarse cloth ‖ FIG uncouth, crude (persona).

toser *vi* to cough ‖ — FIG & FAM *a mí nadie me tose* no one pushes me around, no one tells me what to do | *no hay quien le tosa* nobody can compete with him.

tósigo *m* poison ‖ FIG grief, sorrow (pena).

tosquedad *f* coarseness, crudeness, roughness.

tostada *f* piece *o* slice of toast ‖ AMER nuisance, bore (lata) ‖ — FIG & FAM *dar* or *pegar la tostada a uno* to trick *o* to cheat s.o., to put one over on s.o. | *olerse la tostada* to smell a rat.
◆ *pl* toast; *¿cuántas tostadas quieres?* how much toast do you want?

tostadero *m* *tostadero de café* coffee roaster.

tostado, da *adj* roasted (el café) ‖ toasted (el pan) ‖ FIG tanned, brown (la tez) | brown (color).
◆ *m* roasting (del café) ‖ toasting (del pan) ‖ FIG tan (de la piel) ‖ AMER toasted maize (maíz).

tostador, ra *adj* roasting (el café, etc.) ‖ toasting (el pan).
◆ *m/f* roaster ‖ toaster.
◆ *m* roaster (de café) ‖ toaster (de pan).

tostar* *vt* to roast (el café, etc.) ‖ to toast (el pan) ‖ CULIN to brown ‖ FIG to roast, to burn (calentar demasiado) | to tan, to brown (la piel) | to beat, to tan, to give a beating *o* a hiding (dar una paliza).
◆ *vpr* FIG to tan, to turn brown (ponerse moreno) ‖ to roast (el café, etc.) ‖ to toast (el pan).

tostón *m* toasted chick-pea (torrado) ‖ crouton (pan frito) ‖ toast soaked in oil (pan empapado en aceite) ‖ roast sucking pig (cochinillo) ‖ FAM bore, drag, bind (persona o cosa pesada) | silver coin (moneda) ‖ — FIG & FAM *dar el tostón a uno* to get on s.o.'s nerves | *¡qué tostón!* what a bore!

total *adj* total, complete; *fue un triunfo total* it was a total triumph.
◆ *adv* so; *total, que me marché* so I left ‖ after all (al fin y al cabo).
◆ *m* total, sum (suma) ‖ whole (totalidad) ‖ — *en total* in a word (en una palabra), as a whole (en conjunto).

totalidad *f* totality, whole ‖ — *en su totalidad* as a whole ‖ *la totalidad de la obra* the whole of the work ‖ *la totalidad de las familias* all the families.

totalitario, ria *adj* totalitarian.

totalitarismo *m* totalitarianism.

totalización *f* totalization.

totalizador, ra *adj* totalizing.
◆ *m* totalizer, totalizator (máquina de sumar).

totalizar *vt* to totalize, to total, to add up (sumar) ‖ to add up to, to total (ascender a).

totalmente *adv* totally, wholly, completely.

totay *m* AMER palm tree.

tótem *m* totem.
— OBSERV pl *tótemes* o *tótems*.

totémico, ca *adj* totemic, totemistic.

totemismo *m* totemism.

totilimundi *m* cosmorama ‖ FAM everybody.

totoneca; totonaca *adj* Totonac.
◆ *m/f* Totonac, Totonaco, Totonaca (pueblo indio).
◆ *m* Totonacan (idioma).

totora *f* AMER cattail (planta) ‖ boat made of cattail (en el lago Titicaca).

totoral *m* place overgrown with cattails.

totuma *f*; **totumo** *m* AMER calabash (fruto y vasija).

toxicidad *f* toxicity.

tóxico, ca *adj* toxic, toxicant, poisonous.
◆ *m* toxicant, poison.

toxicología *f* toxicology.

toxicológico, ca *adj* toxicological.

toxicólogo *m* toxicologist.

toxicomanía *f* drug addiction, toxicomania.

toxicómano, na *adj* addicted to drugs.
◆ *m/f* drug addict.

toxicosis *f* MED toxicosis.

toxina *f* toxin.

tozudez *f* stubbornness, obstinacy.

tozudo, da *adj* stubborn, obstinate.
◆ *m/f* stubborn *o* obstinate person.

tozuelo *m* (back of the) neck (cerviz).

traba *f* tie, bond (unión) ‖ hobble, trammel (para caballos) ‖ FIG obstacle, hindrance (estorbo) ‖ JUR seizure (embargo) ‖ TECN lock.
◆ *pl* fetters (de un preso) ‖ FIG *poner trabas a* to hinder, to put obstacles in the way of.

trabacuenta *f* mistake (error) ‖ FIG dispute.

trabadero *m* pastern (de caballos).

trabado, da *adj* hobbled (animales) ‖ fettered (un preso) ‖ with two white stockings (caballo) ‖ robust (robusto) ‖ wiry, sinewy (nervudo) ‖ sound, coherent (discurso).

trabajado, da *adj* worked ‖ FIG worn-out (cansado) | elaborate (estilo).

trabajador, ra *adj* working (que trabaja) ‖ hard-working, industrious (que trabaja mucho).
◆ *m/f* worker, labourer ‖ *trabajador estacional* seasonal worker ‖ *trabajador eventual* casual worker.
◆ *m* workman, workingman.
◆ *f* workwoman, workingwoman.

trabajar *vi* to work; *trabajar en una obra* to work on a construction site; *trabajar mucho* to work hard ‖ to act (un actor) ‖ to be under stress, to be stressed (una viga) ‖ to warp (la madera) ‖ FIG to work (obrar) | to work at, to strive to (esforzarse por); *trabajar en imitar a su maestro* to strive to imitate one's master ‖ MAR to work ‖ — FIG *hacer trabajar* to make work (el dinero) ‖ FIG & FAM *matarse trabajando* to work o.s. to death ‖ *poner a trabajar* to put to work ‖ *trabajar a destajo* to be on piecework ‖ FIG *trabajar como un condenado* or *una bestia* or *un negro* or *un mulo* to work like a slave *o* a Black *o* a horse *o* a dog ‖ *trabajar de* to be, to work as (oficio); *trabajar de sastre* to be a tailor; to play the role of, to play (actor); *trabaja de Don Juan* he plays the role of Don Juan ‖ *trabajar de balde* to work for nothing ‖ *trabajar en balde* to work in vain ‖ *trabajar en el teatro* to work in the theatre ‖ FIG & FAM *trabajar para el obispo* to work for nothing ‖ *trabajar por horas* to be paid by the hour.
◆ *vt* to work; *trabajar la madera* to work wood ‖ CULIN to knead (la masa) ‖ FIG to bother, to disturb (molestar) ‖ AGR to till, to work (la tierra) ‖ to work in, to be in (tener como oficio) ‖ to train, to work out (un caballo) ‖ FIG to work on, to persuade (intentar convencer

a uno) | to work on *o* at (sus lecciones, una novela, una idea, etc.) | to bring out, to play up (acentuar); *necesitamos trabajar más el lado melodramático* we must play up the melodramatic side.

◆ *vpr* to work on, to study; *me estoy trabajando el asunto* I'm working on the matter || FIG to work on, to persuade (a una persona).

trabajo *m* work, labour [US labor]; *trabajo manual* manual labour || work (obra) || effort, labour [US labor] (esfuerzo); *es trabajo perdido* it's a waste of effort, it's wasted effort || job, task (tarea) || work, job, employment; *trabajo de jornada entera, de media jornada* full-time, part-time employment || job, position, post (puesto) || labour [US labor], workers *pl* (los obreros) || work, study (estudio) || work, acting (de un actor) || FÍS work || — *accidente de* or *del trabajo* industrial accident || *ahorrarse el trabajo de* to spare o.s. the trouble *o* the bother of || *con mucho* or *con gran trabajo* with great difficulty || *costar trabajo* to take a lot, to be difficult, to find it difficult; *me ha costado trabajo rehusar* it took a lot to refuse it, it was difficult for me to refuse; *me cuesta trabajo creerlo* it takes a lot of believing, I find it difficult to believe || *darle duro al trabajo* to work hard at it, to put one's nose to the grindstone || *darse el trabajo de* to take the trouble to || *dar trabajo* to make work, to give work (proporcionar una ocupación), to give trouble (ser difícil) || *día de trabajo* workday, working day || *estar sin trabajo* to be out of work *o* unemployed || *ir al trabajo* to go to work || *lengua de trabajo* working language || *programa de trabajo* work schedule || *puesto de trabajo* job || *ropa de trabajo* working clothes || *sin trabajo* easily (sin dificultad), unemployed, out of work (obrero) || *tomarse el trabajo de* to take the trouble to || *trabajo a destajo* piecework || *trabajo a jornal* work paid by the day || *trabajo clandestino* illegal work || *trabajo de encargo* work done to order || FIG *trabajo de chinos* very delicate and tedious work || *trabajo de equipo* teamwork || *trabajo en el terreno* fieldwork || *trabajo estacional* seasonal work || *trabajo intelectual* brainwork || *trabajo por horas* work paid by the hour, timework || *trabajo por turno* shift work || FIG *trabajo te* or *le mando* it will take some doing, you will have your work cut out.

◆ *pl* hardships (penas) || — *Trabajos de Hércules* Labours of Hercules || *trabajos forzados* or *forzosos* hard labour [US hard labor] || *trabajos manuales* manual work (en general), handicraft (en la escuela).

trabajosamente *adv* laboriously.

trabajoso, sa *adj* hard, laborious (que cuesta trabajo) || hard, difficult (difícil); *trabajoso de hacer* hard to do || laboured [US labored] (falto de espontaneidad) || AMER demanding (exigente) | bothersome (molesto).

trabalenguas *m inv* tongue twister.

trabamiento *m* joining, uniting.

trabanco *m* yoke (trangallo).

trabar *vt* to lock, to fasten (sujetar) || to join, to link, to unite (juntar) || to jam (inmovilizar) || to hobble (un animal) || to shackle, to fetter (a una persona) || to thicken (espesar una salsa, un líquido) || FIG to start (empezar) | to strike up (conversación) | to hinder, to impede, to obstruct (obstaculizar) || to grasp, to seize (asir) || — FIG *trabar amistad* to strike up a friendship, to become friends || *trabar batalla* to join battle, to do battle.

◆ *vpr* to become entangled, to get tangled (enmarañarse) || to thicken (una salsa, etc.) || to lock, to jam (un mecanismo) || *se le trabó la lengua* he got tongue-tied.

trabazón *f* joining, joints *pl* (ensambladura) || FIG link, bond, connection (enlace entre cosas) | consistency, coherence (coherencia) || CULIN thickness, consistency (de una salsa, etc.).

trabe *f* beam.

trabilla *f* foot strap (del pie de un pantalón) || half belt (de chaqueta, etc.) || dropped stitch (punto que queda suelto).

trabucación *f* upset || FIG confusion, jumble, mix-up (confusión) | mistake (error).

trabucaire *adj m* FAM bold, blustering.

◆ *m* HIST Catalonian rebel.

trabucar *vt* to disarrange, to jumble, to mess up, to upset (desordenar) || FIG to mix up, to confuse (confundir) | to mix up (mezclar).

◆ *vpr* FIG to get all mixed up (al hablar o al escribir) || *se me trabucó la lengua* I got tongue-tied.

trabucazo *m* shot from a blunderbuss (de trabuco) || FIG shock.

trabuco *m* catapult (catapulta) || blunderbuss (arma de fuego) || peashooter (juguete) || *trabuco naranjero* blunderbuss.

traca *f* jumping jack, string *o* fireworks || MAR strake.

trácala *f* AMER trick (trampa).

tracalada *f* AMER crowd, mob (muchedumbre) | string (sarta).

tracalero, ra *adj* AMER tricky.

◆ *m/f* AMER trickster.

tracción *f* traction || pulling (de un cable) || *tracción delantera* front-wheel drive (de un coche).

Tracia *npr f* GEOGR Thrace.

tracio, cia *adj/s* Thracian.

tracoma *m* MED trachoma.

tractivo, va *adj* tractive.

tracto *m* lapse of time, interval || REL tract (en la misa) || ANAT tract; *tracto intestinal* intestinal tract.

tractor, ra *adj/sm* tractor; *hélice tractora* tractor propeller; *tractor oruga* caterpillar tractor.

tractorista *m/f* AGR tractor driver.

tradición *f* tradition || JUR delivery (entrega).

tradicional *adj* traditional.

tradicionalismo *m* traditionalism.

tradicionalista *adj* traditionalistic.

◆ *m/f* traditionalist.

tradicionalmente *adv* traditionally.

tradicionista *m/f* writer *o* collector of stories relating local traditions.

traducción *f* translation || — INFORM *traducción asistida por ordenador* or *automática* machine translation || *traducción directa* translation out of the foreign language || *traducción inversa* translation into the foreign language.

traducible *adj* translatable.

traducir* *vt* to translate; *traducir del español al inglés* to translate from Spanish into English || to interpret (interpretar) || to express (expresar) || — *traducir directamente* or *de corrido* to translate at sight || *traducir literalmente* to translate literally.

◆ *vpr* to translate; *esta expresión se traduce fácilmente* this phrase translates easily || to result in, to bring about (ocasionar) || to mean in practice (significar).

traductor, ra *adj* translating.

◆ *m/f* translator; *traductor jurado* sworn translator.

traer* *vt* to bring; *traer una carta, noticias* to bring a letter, news; *trajeron a un prisionero* they brought a prisoner; *¿qué le trae por aquí?* what brings you here? || to wear (la ropa); *hoy trae un traje nuevo* today is wearing a new suit || to carry about (llevar encima) || to attract, to draw, to pull (atraer) || to bring, to cause (acarrear); *eso le trajo muchos disgustos* that caused him a lot of misfortune || to have; *su retraso nos traía muy preocupados* their delay had us very worried || to put forward, to adduce (argumento, testimonio) || to have; *el mes de abril trae treinta días* the month of April has thirty days || to contain, to carry, to print; *el periódico traía un artículo sobre las elecciones* the paper carried an article about the elections || — FAM *me trae sin cuidado* I don't care, I don't give me a damn, I couldn't care less || *¡trae!, ¡traiga!* here!, give it here!, give it to me!, give me it! || *traer aguas* to supply with water || *traer a las mientes* to recall, to bring to mind || *traer a mal traer* to treat badly, to maltreat (maltratar), to keep s.o. busy *o* on the go *o* on the move *o* on his toes (dar trabajo), to get (s.o.) down, to pester (molestar) || *traer a uno al retortero* to keep s.o. busy *o* on the move *o* on the go (baquetear), to be on one's mind (preocupar) || *traer de aquí para allá* to order s.o. about (baquetear), to keep s.o. busy *o* on the go *o* on the move (mantener ocupado) || *traer a uno de cabeza* to worry s.o. (preocupar), to get on s.o.'s nerves (molestar), to be on s.o.'s mind (ocupar los pensamientos), to drive s.o. mad (volver loco) || *traer buena, mala suerte* to bring good, bad luck || FAM *traer cola* to have serious consequences, to bring trouble || FIG & FAM *traer frito a uno* to get on s.o.'s nerves || *traer loco a uno* to drive one mad || FIG *traer por la calle de la amargura* to give a hard time || *traer puesto* to be wearing; *trae puesta su chaqueta nueva* he is wearing his new jacket || FIG *traer y llevar a uno* to gossip about s.o.

◆ *vpr* to bring; *tráete el libro que te pedí* bring the book I asked you for || to be up to, to be planning (estar tramando) || — *traerse entre manos* to plan (planear), to plot, to scheme (tramar), to have in hand *o* on one's hands, to be engaged in (estar ocupándose en), to be up to; *¿qué te traes entre manos?* what are you up to? || FAM *traérselas* to be terrible *o* shocking (persona, cosa), to be really difficult (ser difícil).

tráfago *m* traffic, trade (tráfico) || hustle and bustle, comings and goings *pl* (trajín).

traficante *adj* dealing, trading.

◆ *m/f* dealer, trader (negociante) || trafficker (en productos ilegales).

traficar *vi* to deal, to trade (*con* with; *en* in) || to traffic; *traficar en drogas* to traffic in drugs || FIG to deal illegally in, to make money illegally from | to keep on the move, to travel a lot (viajar).

tráfico *m* traffic, trade; *tráfico de divisas* traffic of foreign currency || traffic (tránsito); *calle de mucho tráfico* street with a lot of traffic || slave trade (de esclavos); *tráfico de negros* black slave trade || — *accidente de tráfico* road accident || *guardia de tráfico* traffic policeman || *policía de tráfico* traffic police || *tráfico de influencias* corrupt practice (política), insider dealing *o* trading (Bolsa) || *tráfico rodado* vehicular *o* road traffic.

tragabolas *m inv* Aunt Sally (juego).

tragacanto *m* BOT tragacanth.

tragaderas *f pl* FAM throat *sing*, gullet *sing* (esófago) || FIG *tener buenas tragaderas* to swallow *o* to believe anything (ser crédulo); *tiene buenas tragaderas* he will believe anything; to be very easygoing *o* excessively tolerant (ser muy tolerante), to really put it away (beber o comer mucho).

tragadero *m* FAM throat, gullet (garganta) | hole, drain (agujero).

tragahombres *m inv* FAM bully.

trágala *m* song sung by Liberal opponents of the Spanish absolutists in 1820 || FAM *cantar a uno el trágala* to laugh in s.o.'s face.

tragaldabas *m/f inv* FAM glutton, pig.

tragaleguas *m/f inv* FAM keen walker, good walker.

tragaluz *m* skylight (en el tejado) || transom (de puerta o ventana).

tragamillas *m/f inv* FAM keen walker, good walker.

tragante *adj* swallowing.
◆ *m* TECN mouth, throat (de un alto horno) | flue (de un horno de reverbero).

tragantón, ona *adj* gluttonous.
◆ *f* FAM tuck-in, feast, spread (comilona) || gulp (trago) || FAM *darse una tragantona* to have a feast, to tuck in (comiendo).

tragaperras *adj* *máquina tragaperras* slot machine, fruit machine, one-armed bandit (de juego), slot machine, vending machine (expendedora automática).

tragar *vi* to swallow; *tragar con dificultad* to swallow with difficulty.
◆ *vt/vpr* to swallow (comer o beber) || FIG to put away, to devour, to down (comer vorazmente) | to swallow up (hacer desaparecer); *tragado por el mar* swallowed up by the sea | to swallow (creer); *se traga cuanto le dicen* he swallows everything they tell him | to swallow, to take (soportar); *tragarse un insulto* to swallow *o* to take an insult | to soak up (absorber) | to swallow up, to eat up (consumir) || — FIG & FAM *duro de tragar* hard to swallow (difícil de creer), hard to take *o* to swallow (difícil de aceptar) | *no hay quien se lo trague* no one will swallow that | *no poder tragar a uno* not to able to stand *o* to stomach s.o.; *no le puedo tragar* I can't stand him | *tenerse tragado algo* to see it coming | *tragar la píldora, tragársela* to swallow it (creérselo), to swallow the bitter pill (aguantar) | *tragar quina* to put up with murder (aguantarse) | *tragar saliva* to swallow one's feelings, to hold one's peace.

tragasables *m inv* swordswallower.

tragasantos *m inv* FAM overpious person.

tragedia *f* tragedy || *parar* or *terminar en tragedia* to have a tragic *o* a sad ending.

trágicamente *adv* tragically || *tomar algo trágicamente* to make a tragedy out of sth.

trágico, ca *adj* tragic, tragical (funesto) || — *actor trágico* tragedian || *actriz trágica* tragedienne || *lo trágico es que...* the tragedy of it is that..., the tragic part is that... || *ponerse trágico* to become *o* to get tragic *o* serious (situación), to become all serious, to put on the agony (persona) || *tomar algo por lo trágico* to make a tragedy *o* a big thing (out) of sth.
◆ *m* tragedian (autor).

tragicomedia *f* tragicomedy.

tragicómico, ca *adj* tragicomic.

trago *m* drop, swig (porción de líquido); *echar un trago de vino* to take a swig of wine || gulp, swallow; *beber de un trago* to drink in one gulp || ANAT tragus (de la oreja) || FAM bottle, drink (bebida); *ser aficionado al trago* to be given to drink, to be fond of the bottle | drink, drop; *echemos un trago* let's have a drink || FIG & FAM hard blow (adversidad), bad time (mal momento) || — FIG *a tragos* little by little || *beber a tragos* to sip, to nurse (*fam*) || FIG *de un trago* in one go || FAM *echarse un trago al coleto* to take a swig || FIG & FAM *fue un mal trago* it was a hard blow, it was hard to take | *pasar un trago amargo* to have a rough *o* a bad time of it, to go through a rough patch.

tragón, ona *adj* FAM gluttonous, greedy.
◆ *m/f* FAM glutton, big eater.

tragonería *f* FAM gluttony.

traición *f* treason (delito); *alta traición* high treason || treachery (perfidia) || — *a traición* treacherously || *hacer traición a su patria* to betray one's country || *una traición* a betrayal, an act of treachery.

traicionar *vt* to betray; *traicionar a su país* to betray one's country || FIG to betray; *su rostro traicionó sus intenciones* his face betrayed his intentions; *le traicionó su corazón* his heart betrayed him.

traicionero, ra *adj* treacherous, traitorous, treasonous || FIG treacherous.
◆ *m/f* traitor.

traída *f* bringing (acción de traer) || — *canal de traída* headrace || *traída de aguas* water supply.

traído, da *adj* brought (véase traer) || FIG threadbare, worn-out (vestidos) | hackneyed, trite (repetido) || — FAM *bien traído* clever, witty (chiste) | *traído por los pelos* farfetched | *traído y llevado* hackneyed, well-worn.

traidor, ra *adj* treasonous, traitorous (delictuoso) || treacherous (pérfido) || restive, tricky, bad-tempered (caballo).
◆ *m* traitor || FIG betrayer | restive *o* tricky *o* bad-tempered horse.
◆ *f* traitress || FIG betrayer.

traidoramente *adv* treacherously, traitorously.

trailer *m* CINEM trailer [*US* preview, prevue] (avance).

traílla *f* leash, lead (para atar los perros) || team *o* pack of dogs (conjunto de perros trabados) || lash (del látigo) || TECN leveller (para igualar terrenos) | scraper (de tractor).

traillar *vt* to level (land).

traína *f* dragnet (red).

trainera *f* trawler (barco).

traiña *f* sardine net (red).

Trajano *npr m* Trajan.

trajano, na *adj* Trajan || *Columna Trajana* Trajan's Column.

traje *m* suit; *traje de hombre* man's suit; *traje a la medida* made-to-measure suit, tailor-made suit; *traje de confección* ready-made *o* ready-to-wear suit, off-the-peg suit || dress (vestido de mujer); *traje de seda* silk dress || costume, dress; *traje regional* regional dress || — FIG & FAM *cortar trajes* to gossip, to criticize people, to backbite | *cortar un traje a uno* to slate s.o., to pull s.o. to pieces, to run s.o. down || *traje camisero* shirtwaist dress || *traje cruzado* double-breasted suit || *traje de baño* bathing suit *o* costume, swimsuit || *traje de calle* town clothes; plain clothes (de un policía) || *traje de campaña* battledress || *traje de casa* casual clothes || *traje de ceremonia* full dress (de un militar), formal dress || *traje de cuartel* undress || *traje de chaqueta* (woman's) tailored suit || *traje de diario* everyday clothes || *traje de domingo* Sunday clothes *o* dress, Sunday best (*fam*) || MIL *traje de faena* fatigue clothes || *traje de luces* bullfighter's costume (de un torero) || *traje de malla* tights || *traje de montar* riding habit || *traje de noche* evening dress *o* gown || *traje de novia* wedding dress, bridal gown || *traje de paisano* civilian clothes || *traje de primera comunión* first communion dress *o* suit || *traje de vuelo* or *espacial* spacesuit || *traje largo* evening gown || *traje sastre* (woman's) tailored suit.

trajear *vt* to dress, to clothe.

trajín *m* transport, haulage, carriage (transporte) || work, chores *pl*; *el trajín de la casa* household chores || FAM comings and goings *pl*, hustle and bustle (ajetreo) | work (trabajo) | lover (amiguita) || *el trajín cotidiano* the daily round.

trajinante *adj* transporting.
◆ *m* carrier, haulage contractor.

trajinar *vt* to transport, to carry || AMER to search (registrar).
◆ *vi* to come and go, to bustle about (ajetrearse) || FAM to slave away, to toil away (trabajar) || FIG & FAM *¿qué está usted trajinando por ahí?* what are you cooking up over there?

trajinería *f* transport, carriage, haulage.

trajinero *m* carrier.

tralla *f* rope, cord (cuerda) || whiplash, lash (del látigo).

trallazo *m* lash [of a whip] (golpe) || crack (restallido) || FIG tongue-lashing, telling off (reprensión).

trama *f* weft, woof (de un tejido) || tram (hilo de seda) || screen (en fotograbado) || blossoming (florecimiento del olivo) || FIG plot (argumento) | plot, scheme (enredo, intriga).

tramador, ra *m/f* weaver.

tramar *vt* to weave (tejer) || FIG & FAM to scheme, to plot, to cook up (maquinar) | to hatch, to weave (un complot) || FIG & FAM *¿qué estás tramando?* what are you up to?, what are you cooking up?
◆ *vi* to blossom (olivos).
◆ *vpr* to be afoot, to be going on.

tramitación *f* transaction (de un asunto) || procedure, steps *pl* (trámites) || negotiation.

tramitar *vt* to take the necessary steps to obtain, to attend to; *tramitar su pasaporte* to take the necessary steps to obtain one's passport || to negotiate, to transact (un negocio, un asunto) || to convey, to transmit (facilitar); *respuesta tramitada a través del embajador* response transmitted through the ambassador || to make a study of, to study (un expediente).

trámite *m* step (diligencia); *hay que hacer muchos trámites para conseguir el permiso* many steps must be taken to obtain the licence || formality, requirement (requisito); *cumplir con los trámites necesarios* to go through the necessary formalities || passage, transit (paso).
◆ *pl* procedure *sing*; *los trámites para la obtención del permiso* the procedure for obtaining the licence || JUR proceedings.

tramo *m* lot, tract, stretch, plot (de terreno) || flight (de escalera) || ARQ span || section, stretch (de carretera, ferrocarril, canal).

tramojo *m* stalk used to tie a sheaf || AMER yoke (trangallo).

tramontana *f* tramontane, north wind (viento del norte) || north (norte) || haughtiness, conceit, pride (soberbia).

tramontano, na *adj* tramontane.

tramontar *vi* to go over the mountains || to sink behind the mountains (el sol).
◆ *vt* to help escape (ayudar a escapar).

tramoya *f* TEATR piece of stage machinery (máquina) | stage machinery (conjunto de máquinas) || FIG & FAM scheme, plot (enredo) || FIG & FAM *una fiesta con mucha tramoya* a very showy party.

tramoyista *m* TEATR stagehand, sceneshifter || FIG & FAM schemer, trickster, swindler (que usa engaños).

trampa *f* trap, snare (caza); *poner una trampa* to set *o* to lay a trap || trapdoor, hatch (abertura en el suelo) || hatch (de mostrador) || fly (de pantalón) || cheating (en el juego) || ambush (celada) || debt (deuda) || trick (de prestidigitación) || MAR & CULIN hatch || FIG trap, snare, pitfall | trick, fiddle, hoax (engaño) | trick (estratagema); *era una trampa para ver si me diría la verdad* it was a trick to get him to tell me the truth || — FIG *caer en la trampa* to fall *o* to walk into the trap | *coger en la trampa* to catch red-handed || *ganar con trampas* to win by cheating || *hacer trampas* to cheat; *hacer trampas en el juego* to cheat at cards; to be on the fiddle (cometer fraude) || *hecha la ley hecha la trampa* laws are made to be broken || *no hay trampa ni cartón, sin trampa ni cartón* there is nothing up my sleeve || FIG *tiene trampa* there's a catch (hay un truco o una pega) ‖ *trampa adelante* out of one debt and into another, constantly in debt ‖ MIL *trampa explosiva* booby trap.

trampear *vi* to cheat (en el juego) ‖ to live by one's wits (vivir de su ingenio) ‖ FIG to get by, to make out, to manage; *va trampeando* he gets by.
◆ *vt* to swindle, to cheat (estafar).

trampero, ra *adj* AMER cheating.
◆ *m* trapper (cazador).

trampilla *f* trapdoor, hatch (puerta al nivel del suelo) ‖ oven door *o* window (de un horno) ‖ fly (del pantalón).
◆ *pl* TEATR cuts and slots.

trampista *adj/s* → **tramposo.**

trampolín *m* springboard, diving board (en la piscina) ‖ ski jump (en la pista de nieve) ‖ FIG springboard (base para obtener algo) ‖ *salto de trampolín* dive.

tramposo, sa; trampista *adj* cheating (en el juego) ‖ lying (embustero) ‖ swindling, crooked (petardista).
◆ *m/f* cheat, cardsharper (en el juego) ‖ liar (embustero) ‖ swindler, crook, trickster (petardista).

tranca *f* cudgel (garrote) ‖ bar (de puerta) ‖ binge, drunken spree (borrachera) ‖ — *a trancas y barrancas* in spite of all the obstacles ‖ FAM *coger una tranca* to get drunk.

trancada *f* stride (tranco); *en dos trancadas* in two strides.

trancanil *m* MAR waterway.

trancazo *m* blow with a cudgel (golpe dado con la tranca) ‖ FIG & FAM flu (gripe).

trance *m* moment, juncture; *un trance desagradable* a disagreeable moment ‖ critical moment (dificultad) ‖ tight corner *o* spot, fix, awkard situation (mal paso); *sacar a uno de un trance* to get s.o. out of a fix ‖ trance (del medium) ‖ JUR distraint, seizure ‖ — *a todo trance* at all costs, at any cost ‖ *el último* or *postrer trance* or *trance mortal* one's last moments (de la vida) ‖ *en trance de desarrollo* developing ‖ *en trance de muerte* on the point of death ‖ *estar en trance de* to be on the point of *o* in the process of ‖ *salió del trance* he pulled through ‖ *trance de armas* feat of arms.

tranco *m* stride (paso largo) ‖ leap, jump (salto) ‖ threshold (umbral) ‖ — *andar a trancos* to take big steps, to stride along ‖ AMER *a tranco* at a gallop (un caballo) ‖ FIG *a trancos* in a slapdash way ‖ *en dos trancos* in a jiffy, in the wink of an eye.

trangallo *m* yoke.

tranquera *f* palisade (estacada).

tranquero *m* ARQ lintel (piedra).

tranquil *m* ARQ plumb line ‖ ARQ *arco por tranquil* flying arch.

tranquilidad *f* tranquillity, calmness (quietud, sosiego) ‖ respite, peace and quiet *o* tranquillity (descanso); *un momento de tranquilidad* a moment's peace and quiet ‖ — *con toda tranquilidad* with one's mind at ease (sin preocupaciones); *descansar con toda tranquilidad* to rest with one's mind at ease; at one's leisure; *estudiar algo con toda tranquilidad* to study sth. at one's leisure; calmly; *contestó con toda tranquilidad* he answered calmly ‖ *dormir con toda tranquilidad* to sleep peacefully *o* soundly ‖ *para mayor tranquilidad* to put one's mind at ease, to be sure *o* safe; *para mayor tranquilidad llamaremos a un médico* to put your mind at ease we shall call a doctor ‖ *perder la tranquilidad* to become anxious *o* uneasy *o* restless.

tranquilizador, ra *adj* tranquillizing [US tranquilizing], reassuring ‖ soothing (música, etc.).

tranquilizante *adj* MED tranquillizing [US tranquilizing].
◆ *m* MED tranquillizer [US tranquilizer].

tranquilizar *vt* to tranquillize [US to tranquilize], to calm (down) (sosegar) ‖ to reassure, to put one's mind at ease; *la noticia me ha tranquilizado* the news has reassured me.
◆ *vpr* to calm down, to calm o.s. ‖ to be reassured (*con* by) ‖ to calm down (tormenta, mar, etc.) ‖ *¡tranquilízate!* don't worry!, calm down!, calm yourself!

tranquilo, la *adj* tranquil, calm, peaceful ‖ reassured (libre de preocupación) ‖ calm, still, quiet; *mar tranquilo* calm sea ‖ quiet; *tono tranquilo* quiet tone ‖ clear (conciencia) ‖ — *¡déjame tranquilo!* leave me alone! ‖ *estate tranquilo hasta que vuelva* stay put *o* stay right there until I get back ‖ *se quedó tan tranquilo* he didn't bat an eyelid ‖ *tú, tranquilo* don't (you) worry, calm down, take it easy; *tú, tranquilo, que todo saldrá bien* don't you worry, everything will be all right; don't worry; *tú, tranquilo, yo me ocuparé de esto* don't worry, I'll see to it.

tranquilla *f* small peg, pin (pasador) ‖ FAM trap, catch, stratagem.

tranquillo *m* FAM knack; *coger* or *dar con el tranquillo* to get the knack.

trans *pref* trans.
— OBSERV *Trans* often changes to *tras* in Spanish: *transcendental* or *trascendental.*

transacción *f* COM transaction (acción y efecto) | transaction deal (negocio) ‖ settlement, compromise (acuerdo).

transaccional *adj* INFORM transactional.

transalpino, na *adj* transalpine.

transandino, na; trasandino, na *adj* of *o* from *o* on the other side of the Andes, trans-Andean.
◆ *m* train that goes from Chile to Argentina, trans-Andean train (tren).

transar *vi* AMER → **transigir.**

transatlántico, ca *adj* transatlantic.
◆ *m* MAR (Atlantic) liner, ocean liner.

transbordador *m* ferry ‖ — *puente transbordador* transporter bridge ‖ *transbordador aéreo* telpher [US telfer] ‖ *transbordador de ferrocarril* train ferry ‖ *transbordador espacial* space shuttle ‖ *transbordador funicular* cable railway, funicular railway.

transbordar; trasbordar *vt* to transfer ‖ MAR to transship ‖ to ferry across (en un río).
◆ *vi* to change [US to transfer].

transbordo; trasbordo *m* ferrying ‖ change, transfer (de un tren a otro) ‖ transshipment (de un tren o barco a otro) ‖ *hacer transbordo* to change [US to transfer] (de tren, de barco, etc.).

transcaspiano, na *adj* transcaspian.

Transcaucasia *npr f* GEOGR Transcaucasia.

transcaucásico, ca *adj/sm* Transcaucasian.

transcendencia *f* → **trascendencia.**

transcendental *adj* → **trascendental.**

transcendentalismo; trascendentalismo *m* FIL transcendentalism.

transcendente *adj* → **trascendente.**

transcender *vt/vi* → **trascender.**

transcodificación *f* INFORM transcoding.

transcontinental *adj* transcontinental.

transcribir; trascribir *vt* to transcribe.

transcripción; trascripción *f* transcription, transcribing (acción) ‖ MÚS transcription (acción y resultado) ‖ transcription, transcript (cosa escrita).

transcripto, ta *adj* transcribed.

transcriptor *m* transcriber (aparato).

transcrito, ta *adj* 'transcribed.

transcurrir; trascurrir *vi* to pass, to elapse (el tiempo); *transcurrieron diez años* ten years passed ‖ to be, to pass; *el día transcurrió tranquilo* the day passed peacefully, the day was peaceful ‖ to take place, to go off; *la ceremonia transcurrió sin incidente* the ceremony went off without incident.

transcurso *m* course (del tiempo); *en el transcurso de los años* in the course of the years ‖ period, space; *pinté este cuadro en el transcurso de dos meses* I painted this picture in *o* over a period *o* the space of two months ‖ *en el transcurso de un mes* in the space *o* the course of a month.

transeúnte *m/f* passer-by (en una calle) ‖ temporary resident, transient (que reside transitoriamente).

transexual *adj* transsexual, transexual.

transferencia; trasferencia *f* transfer, transference (de una propiedad) ‖ transfer (de fondos); *transferencia de crédito* credit transfer ‖ DEP transfer ‖ transference (en psicología).

transferidor, ra; trasferidor, ra *adj* transferential.
◆ *m/f* transferrer.

transferir*; trasferir *vt* to transfer ‖ to postpone (aplazar).

transfiguración *f* transfiguration.

transfigurar *vt* to transfigure.
◆ *vpr* to become transfigured.

transfijo, ja *adj* transfixed.

transfixión *f* transfixion.

transformación *f* transformation ‖ DEP *transformación de ensayo* conversion of a try (rugby).

transformador, ra *adj* transforming.
◆ *m/f* transformer.
◆ *m* ELECTR transformer.

transformar; trasformar *vt* to transform, to change ‖ DEP *transformar un ensayo* to convert a try.
◆ *vpr* to become transformed, to change.

transformismo *m* transformism, evolution.

transformista *adj* transformist.
◆ *m/f* transformism ‖ TEATR quick-change artist.

tránsfuga; trásfuga *m/f* deserter (desertor) ‖ turncoat (en política).

transfundir; trasfundir *vt* to transfuse (líquidos) ‖ to spread (noticias).
◆ *vpr* to spread (propagarse).

transfusión *f* transfusion; *hacerle a uno una transfusión de sangre* to give s.o. a blood transfusion.

transfusor, ra; trasfusor, ra *adj* transfusing.
◆ *m* transfuser.

transgredir* *vt* to transgress; *transgredir la ley* to transgress the law.

transgresión *f* transgression (infracción).

transgresor, ra; trasgresor, ra *adj* transgressing.
◆ *m/f* transgressor (de una ley, etc.).

transiberiano, na *adj* Trans-Siberian.
◆ *m* Trans-Siberian railway.

transición *f* transition ‖ *gobierno de transición* transitional government.

transido, da *adj* overcome (*de* with) (de angustia, pena, etc.) ‖ — *transido de dolor* racked with pain ‖ *transido de frío* freezing cold, chilled to the marrow ‖ *transido de hambre* starving, weak with hunger ‖ *transido de miedo* terrified, seized with fear, panic-stricken.

transigencia *f* compromise (acuerdo) ‖ spirit of compromise (actitud) ‖ tolerance.

transigente *adj* accomodating, compromising (acomodaticio) || tolerant.

transigible *adj* acceptable.

transigir *vi* to compromise || to give in (ceder) || — *transigir con* to agree to (aceptar), to tolerate || *yo no transijo con nadie* I refuse to accept a compromise.

Transilvania *npr f* GEOGR Transylvania.

transilvano, na *adj/s* Transylvanian.

transistor *m* ELECTR & RAD transistor; *radio de transistores* transistor radio || FAM transistor (aparato de radio) || INFORM *transistor discreto* discrete transistor.

transistorizado, da *adj* transistorized.

transitable *adj* passable; *camino transitable* passable road.

transitar *vi* to travel || to pass || — *calle transitada* busy street || *transitar por las calles* to go along *o* through the streets.

transitivo, va *adj/sm* GRAM transitive.

tránsito *m* transit, movement, traffic (paso); *el tránsito de peatones* pedestrian transit || transit (de mercancías, de viajeros) || stopping place (sitio) || traffic (tráfico) || passageway (camino) || passing (muerte); *tránsito de la Virgen* passing of the Virgin || Assumption (Asunción) || — COM *agente de tránsito* transit agent, forwarding agent || *cerrado al tránsito* road closed (por obras, etc.), no thoroughfare (reservado a los peatones) || *de mucho tránsito* busy (calle) || *de tránsito* passing through; *estar de tránsito en una ciudad* to be passing through a city; in transit (viajeros, mercancías) || *hacer* or *llevar en tránsito* to convey (goods) in transit || *país de tránsito* country of transit || *tránsito rodado* vehicular *o* road traffic.

transitoriedad *f* transience, transitoriness.

transitorio, ria *adj* transitory || provisional (provisional) || transitional (período).

Transjordania *npr f* GEOGR Transjordania.

translación *f* ⟶ **traslación.**

translaticio, cia *adj* figurative.

translativo, va *adj* ⟶ **traslativo.**

translimitación *f* overstepping, going too far.

translimitar *vt* to overstep (derechos) || to cross (over) (fronteras).

translucidez *f* translucence.

translúcido, da; transluciente *adj* translucent.

translucir *vt/vpr* ⟶ **traslucir.**

transmediterráneo, a *adj* transmediterranean.

transmigración *f* transmigration.

transmigrar *vi* to transmigrate.

transmigratorio, ria *adj* transmigratory.

transmisibilidad *f* transmissibility.

transmisible *adj* transmissible.

transmisión; trasmisión *f* transmission || JUR transfer, transference (de bienes) || TECN transmission || — *correa de transmisión* driving belt || JUR *derechos de transmisión de herencia* succession duty || *transmisión delantera, trasera* front-wheel, rearwheel drive || *transmisión del pensamiento* telepathy, thought transmission || *transmisión del poder* transfer of power || RAD *transmisión en directo* live broadcast || *transmisión por cadena, por fricción* chain, friction drive || INFORM *transmisión remota de datos* remote data transmission.
◆ *pl* MIL signals || MIL *cuerpo de transmisiones* signal corps.

transmisor, ra *adj* transmitting (que transmite).
◆ *m* transmitter (telegráfico o telefónico).

transmitir; trasmitir *vt* RAD to transmit, to broadcast || to transmit (por morse, etc.) || to hand down (bienes) || JUR to transfer || MED to transmit (una enfermedad).

transmudar; trasmudar *vt* to move, to transfer (trasladar) || to change, to transform (transformar) || to transmute (transmutar).

transmutabilidad *f* transmutability.

transmutable *adj* transmutable.

transmutación *f* transmutation.

transmutar *vt* to transmute.

transoceánico, ca *adj* transoceanic.

transónico, ca *adj* transsonic, transonic.

transpacífico, ca *adj* transpacific.

transparencia; trasparencia *f* transparency, transparence || FOT slide, transparency || ECON *transparencia fiscal* flow-through taxation.

transparentar *vt* to reveal (dejar ver); *su cara transparentaba su alegría* her face revealed her happiness.
◆ *vpr* to be transparent, to show through (ser transparente); *este vestido se transparenta* this dress is transparent || FIG to show through, to be *o* to become clear (dejarse ver o adivinar); *sus intenciones se transparentan* his intentions show through | to be worn thin, to be threadbare (un vestido viejo) | to be as thin as a rake (ser flaco).

transparente; trasparente *adj* transparent || clear, transparent (agua, etc.) || see-through, transparent (vestido, etc.) || FIG transparent, clear, plain (evidente).
◆ *m* transparency (colocado ante una luz) || curtain (cortina) || shade, blind (pantalla) || stained-glass window (vidriera) || «Transparency» [sculpture by Narciso Tomé in Toledo cathedral].

transpiración; traspiración *f* transpiration || perspiration (sudor).

transpirar; traspirar *vi* BOT to transpire || to perspire (sudar).

transpirenaico, ca; traspirenaico, ca *adj* Trans-Pyrenean, of *o* from *o* on the other side of the Pyrenees || Trans-Pyrenean, crossing the Pyrenees.

transplantar *vt* ⟶ **trasplantar.**

transponer* *vt* to move (mudar de sitio) || to cross over (atravesar) || to disappear behind; *el sol transpuso la montaña* the sun disappeared behind the mountain || to disappear round (una esquina) || to transplant (trasplantar).
◆ *vpr* to disappear (desaparecer) || to set, to go down (el sol) || *quedarse transpuesto* to doze *o* to nod off (dormitar).

transportable *adj* INFORM transportable (ordenador).

transportador, ra *adj* transporting || MÚS transposing || *cinta transportadora* conveyor belt.
◆ *m* transporter, conveyor || MAT protractor (instrumento) || — *transportador aéreo* cableway || *transportador mecánico* or *de cinta* conveyor belt, belt conveyor.

transportar *vt* to transport, to carry (llevar); *transportar a lomo* to carry on one's back || MAR to ship (mercancías) | to transport, to carry (pasajeros) || MÚS to transpose || MAT to transfer, to lay off (un ángulo) || ELECTR to carry, to transmit (corriente).
◆ *vpr* to be carried away || *transportarse de alegría* to be carried away with joy, to go into transports.

transporte *m* transport || COM transport, freight, freightage || MÚS transposition || FIG transport (éxtasis) || — *buque de transporte* transport ship || *transporte a flote* floating (de la madera) || *transportes colectivos* or *públicos* public transport.

transportista *m* transporter, carrier.

transposición; trasposición *f* transposition || setting (del sol) || disappearance (ocultación).

transubstanciación *f* REL transubstantiation.

transuránico, ca *adj* QUÍM transuranic.

transvasar *vt* ⟶ **trasvasar.**

transvase *m* decanting.

transverberación *f* ⟶ **trasverberación.**

transversal; trasversal *adj* transversal, transverse || collateral (pariente) || side; *camino transversal* side road || *una calle transversal de la Gran Vía* a street which crosses the Gran Vía.
◆ *f* MAT transversal || side road (calle).

transverso, sa; trasverso, sa *adj* transverse; *músculo transverso* transverse muscle.

tranvía *f* tramcar, tram [*US* streetcar] || tramway, tram (sistema) || (stopping) train (tren).

tranviario, ria; tranviero, ra *adj* tramway, tram; *red tranviaria* tramway system.
◆ *m* tramway employee (empleado) || tram driver (conductor).

tranzadera *f* braid.

trapa *f* MAR spilling line (cabo) || REL *la Trapa* the Trappist order.
◆ *pl* MAR tackle used to fasten lifeboats on ships.

trapacear *vi* to swindle (en ventas) || to deceive, to cheat (engañar) || to play tricks.

trapacería *f* swindle, con, fiddle (en ventas, etc.) || trick, ruse (pillería) || hoax, trick, fraud (engaño).

trapacero, ra; trapacista *adj* swindling, fiddling (en ventas) || wily, tricky (pillo) || deceitful (engañoso).
◆ *m/f* swindler, fiddler (petardista) || trickster, rogue (pillo) || deceiver, liar, cheat (que engaña).

trapajo *m* rag, tatter.

trapajoso, sa *adj* ragged, shabby, tattered (andrajoso).

trápala *f* FAM racket, uproar, din, hullabaloo (jaleo) | lie, fib (embuste) | trick (engaño) || hoofbeat, clatter of hooves, clip-clop (de caballo).
◆ *m* FAM chatterbox (hablador) | swindler, trickster, cheat (embustero) | liar (mentiroso).

trapalear *vi* FAM to chatter, to jabber (parlotear) | to fib, to lie (mentir) || to clatter, to clip-clop (un caballo) || to clatter along, to walk *o* to run noisily (una persona).

trapalón, ona *adj* FAM talkative, garrulous (hablador) | dishonest, cheating, swindling (embustero) | lying (mentiroso).
◆ *m/f* FAM trickster, cheat (embustero) || liar (mentiroso).

trapatiesta *f* FAM racket, hullaballo, din, uproar (jaleo) | row, fight, rumpus, brawl (pelea) | mess (desorden) || FAM *armar una trapatiesta* to kick up a rumpus.

trapeador *m* AMER floor mop.

trapear *vt* AMER to mop (el suelo).

trapecio *adj* trapezius; *músculo trapecio* trapezius muscle || *vestido trapecio* A-line dress.
◆ *m* MAT trapezium [*US* trapezoid] || MED trapezium (hueso) | trapezius (músculo) || trapeze (gimnasia).

trapecista *m/f* trapeze artist.

trapense *adj/s* Trappist (religioso).

trapería *f* rags *pl* (trapos) || old-clothes shop (tienda).

trapero, ra *adj* FAM *puñalada trapera* stab in the back.

◆ *m/f* ragman, ragpicker.

trapezoedro *m* trapezohedron.

trapezoidal *adj* MAT trapezoidal, trapezoid.

trapezoide *m* MAT trapezoid [*US* trapezium].

trapiche *m* sugar mill (de azúcar) ‖ press (para aceitunas) ‖ *AMER* crusher (molino para pulverizar minerales).

trapichear *vi* FAM to scheme, to plot (ingeniarse) | to buy and sell on a small scale (comerciar) | to be mixed up in shady dealings, to be on the fiddle (tener actividades poco claras).

trapicheo *m* FAM jiggery-pokery *inv*, shady dealing, trickery; *trapicheos electorales* electoral jiggery-pokery ‖ *andar con trapicheos* to scheme, to be mixed up in shady dealings, to be on the fiddle (tener actividades poco claras).

trapichero *m* sugar mill worker.

trapillo *m* small rag (trapo) ‖ FIG nest egg, savings *pl* (ahorrillos) ‖ *de trapillo* casually dressed (en traje de casa), shabbily dressed (mal vestido).

trapío *m* FIG & FAM charm, elegance (garbo) ‖ TAUR fighting spirit (gallardía del toro) | good stance, surefootedness (buena planta del toro) ‖ *tener buen trapío* to carry o.s. well, to move elegantly.

trapisonda *f* FIG & FAM to-do, commotion, uproar, fuss (jaleo); *armar trapisondas* to cause a to-do | swindle, fiddle (estafa) | scheme, plot, trick (enredo) ‖ choppy sea (agitación del mar).

trapisondear *vi* FAM to cause a to-do, to kick up a fuss (armar jaleo) | to scheme, to plot (enredar).

trapisondista *m/f* FAM troublemaker, rowdy person (alborotador) | trickster (tramposo) | schemer, plotter (enredador).

trapito *m* small rag.
◆ *pl* FAM clothes (ropa) ‖ — FAM *es elegante con cuatro trapitos* she looks good whatever she wears | *los trapitos de cristianar* one's Sunday best.

trapo *m* rag (pedazo de tela) ‖ dishcloth (de cocina); *secar los platos con un trapo* to dry the dishes with a dishcloth ‖ duster (del polvo) ‖ MAR canvas (velamen) ‖ FAM red cape (del torero) | curtain (del teatro) ‖ — *a todo trapo* (under) full sail (a toda vela) ‖ FIG *poner a uno como un trapo* to haul s.o. over the coals, to give s.o. a dressing down (reprender), to call s.o. all the names under the sun (insultar) | *soltar el trapo* to burst out crying, to burst into tears (echarse a llorar), to burst out laughing (echarse a reír) | *tener manos de trapo* to be a butterfingers.
◆ *pl* FAM clothes (ropa) | rags, tatters (ropa vieja) ‖ — FIG *hablar de trapos* to talk about clothes | *los trapos sucios se lavan en casa* one should not wash one's dirty linen in public ‖ *sacar los trapos sucios a relucir* to rake up the past, to throw the past in s.o.'s face.

traque *m* bang, crack (estallido) ‖ fuse (guía de pólvora).

tráquea *f* trachea, windpipe.

traqueal *adj* tracheal.

traquearteria *f* ANAT trachea, windpipe.

traqueítis *f* MED tracheitis.

traqueo *m* ⟶ **traqueteo.**

traqueotomía *f* MED tracheotomy.

traquetear *vi* to explode, to go bang, to go off (la traca) ‖ to rattle, to clatter (hacer ruido); *coche que traquetea* car that rattles ‖ to bump *o* to jerk *o* to jolt along, to shake (moverse con sacudidas).
◆ *vt* to shake (agitar); *traquetear una botella* to shake a bottle ‖ to handle, to finger (manosear).

traqueteo; traqueo *m* bang, crack (ruido de la traca) ‖ jolting, bumping (movimiento) ‖ clatter, rattle, banging (ruido).

traquido *m* crack, bang (ruido).

traquita *f* trachyte.

tras *pref* trans (*véase* OBSERV en TRANS).

tras *prep* behind (detrás); *tras la puerta* behind the door; *caminaban uno tras otro* they were walking one behind the other ‖ after, in pursuit of (en pos de); *corrieron tras el ladrón* they ran after the thief ‖ after; *una desgracia tras otra* one misfortune after another; *tras dos meses de ausencia* after two months of absence ‖ on the other side of, beyond (más allá); *tras los Pirineos* beyond the Pyrenees ‖ behind, on the other side of; *el sol descendió tras la montaña* the sun sank behind the mountain ‖ behind; *dejó un buen recuerdo tras él* he left a good memory behind him ‖ besides, as well as, in addition to (además); *tras ser inteligente, es guapo* besides being intelligent, he's good looking ‖ *día tras día* day after day, day in day out.
◆ *m* FAM backside (trasero).

trasalcoba *f* dressing room.

trasalpino, na *adj* transalpine.

trasandino, na *adj/m* ⟶ **transandino.**

trasanteanoche *adv* three nights ago.

trasanteayer; trasantier *adv* three days ago.

trasañejo, ja *adj* over three years old (vino).

trasatlántico, ca *adj* transatlantic.
◆ *m* (Atlantic) liner, ocean liner.

trasbordar *vt* ⟶ **transbordar.**

trasbordo *m* ⟶ **transbordo.**

trasbotica *f* back shop, back room.

trascendencia; transcendencia *f* transcendence, transcendency ‖ FIG importance, significance, consequence; *un asunto de gran trascendencia* a matter of great importance ‖ *sin trascendencia* unimportant, insignificant.

trascendental; transcendental *adj* FIL transcendental ‖ far-reaching (de gran alcance) ‖ transcendent (superior) ‖ FIG extremely important *o* significant (sumamente importante).

trascendentalismo *m* FIL ⟶ **transcendentalismo.**

trascendente; transcendente *adj* FIL transcendent ‖ transcendent (superior) ‖ FIG extremely important *o* significant (sumamente importante) ‖ MAT *número trascendente* transcendental number.

trascender*; transcender *vi* to smell (*a* of), (oler); *el jardín trasciende a jazmín* the garden smells of jasmine ‖ to float across, to reach; *el olor trascendía hasta nosotros* the smell floated across to us ‖ to become known, to come *o* to leak out, to transpire (divulgarse); *ha trascendido la noticia, su secreto* the news, his secret has leaked out ‖ to extend, to spread (extenderse); *la huelga ha trascendido a todas las ramas de la industria* the strike has spread to all branches of the industry ‖ FIL to be transcendent ‖ — *ha trascendido que...* we have heard *o* learned that..., it has transpired that... ‖ *según ha trascendido* according to what we have heard.
◆ *vt* FIL to transcend.

trascocina *f* scullery, back kitchen.

trascolar* *vpr* to strain, to filter.

trasconejarse *vpr* to squat (la caza) ‖ to get lost *o* mislaid *o* misplaced (perderse) ‖ *se me ha trasconejado tu carta* I have mislaid your letter.

trascordarse* *vpr* to forget (olvidar).

trascoro *m* retrochoir (espacio detrás del coro) ‖ back of the choir (parte posterior del coro).

trascribir *vt* ⟶ **transcribir.**

trascripción *f* ⟶ **transcripción.**

trascurrir *vi* ⟶ **transcurrir.**

trasdós *m* ARQ extrados (bóveda) | pilaster (pilastra).

trasegador *m* person who decants wine.

trasegar* *vt* to upset, to mix up (trastornar) ‖ to move (cambiar de sitio) ‖ to decant (cambiar de recipiente) ‖ to draw off, to rack (para eliminar las heces).
◆ *vi* FAM to drink, to booze (beber).

trasero, ra *adj* back, rear ‖ — *parte trasera* back, rear; *en la parte trasera* on the back ‖ *puente trasero* rear axle (de coche) ‖ *rueda trasera* rear wheel.
◆ *m* ANAT bottom, buttocks *pl* (de persona) ‖ hindquarters *pl*, rump (de animal).
◆ *pl* FAM ancestors (antepasados).

trasferencia *f* ⟶ **transferencia.**

trasferidor, ra *adj/s* ⟶ **transferidor.**

trasferir *vt* ⟶ **transferir.**

trasfiguración *f* transfiguration.

trasfigurar *vt* to transfigure.

trasfixión *f* transfixion.

trasfondo *m* background (fondo) ‖ FIG undertone (en las intenciones, etc.).

trasformar *vt/vpr* ⟶ **transformar.**

trásfuga *m/f* ⟶ **tránsfuga.**

trasfundir *vt/vpr* ⟶ **transfundir.**

trasfusor, ra *adj/sm* ⟶ **transfusor.**

trasgo *m* goblin, imp (duende) ‖ FIG imp (niño).

trasgredir* *vt* to transgress.

trasgresión *f* transgression.

trasgresor, ra *adj/s* ⟶ **transgresor.**

trasguear *vi* to get up to mischief, to play impish tricks.

trasguero, ra *m/f* mischievous imp, practical joker (persona).

trashoguero, ra *adj* lazy, stay-at-home.
◆ *m/f* stay-at-home.
◆ *m* fireback (de chimenea) ‖ large log (leña).

trashojar *vt* to leaf through (hojear).

trashumación; trashumancia *f* transhumance, seasonal migration.

trashumante *adj* transhumant.

trashumar *vi* to move to new pastures.

trasiego *m* decanting (de líquidos) ‖ drawing off, racking (para eliminar las heces) ‖ moving (cambio de sitio).

traslación; translación *f* transfer; *traslación de un preso* transfer of a prisoner ‖ moving (desplazamiento) ‖ translation (traducción) ‖ metaphor (metáfora) ‖ ASTR passage, movement (de un astro) ‖ MAT & TECN translation.

trasladador, ra *adj* moving, carrying.
◆ *m/f* carrier, mover.

trasladar *vt* to move (mudar de sitio) ‖ to carry, to take, to transport (llevar) ‖ to transfer (a un empleado, etc.); *trasladar a un preso* to transfer a prisoner; *le trasladaron a Barcelona* they transferred him to Barcelona ‖ to postpone (aplazar) ‖ to translate (traducir) ‖ to copy, to transcribe (copiar).
◆ *vpr* to go; *el ministro se trasladó a Madrid* the minister went to Madrid ‖ to move (cam-

biar de residencia); *la organización va a trasladarse a otro país* the organization is going to move to another country.

traslado *m* copy, transcript (copia) || transfer, transferring (de un funcionario) || moving; *el traslado de un enfermo al hospital* the moving of a patient to the hospital || removal (cambio de residencia) || transfer, transferring (de restos mortales) || JUR communication, notification || *dar traslado* to send a copy.

traslapar *vt* to overlap (cubrir).

traslapo *m* overlap, overlapping.

traslativo, va; translativo, va *adj* translative.

traslúcido, da; trasluciente *adj* translucent.

traslucir*; translucir *vt* to show, to betray, to reveal (revelar) || *dejar traslucir* to insinuate, to suggest, to hint.
◆ *vpr* to be translucent *o* transparent; *la porcelana se trasluce* porcelain is translucent || to show through (dejarse ver) || FIG to show through, to be plain, to be revealed (inferirse); *se trasluce la verdad en sus palabras* the truth shows through his words | to be written (en el rostro) | to leak out, to come to light (algo secreto).

traslumbramiento *m* dazzling (acción) || dazzlement (efecto).

traslumbrar *vt* to dazzle (deslumbrar).

trasluz *m* diffused light (luz que pasa a través de un cuerpo traslúcido) || reflected light (luz reflejada) || — *al trasluz* against the light || *mirar una diapositiva al trasluz* to hold a slide up to the light.

trasmallo *m* trammel net (red).

trasmano *m* second hand (en ciertos juegos) || *a trasmano* out of reach (fuera de alcance), out of the way (apartado).

trasmigración *f* transmigration.

trasmigrar *vi* to transmigrate.

trasminar *vt* to make a tunnel in (una galería) || to penetrate, to seep through (pasar a través).

trasmisible *adj* transmissible.

trasmisión *f* ⟶ **transmisión.**

trasmitir *vt* ⟶ **transmitir.**

trasmudar *vt* ⟶ **transmudar.**

trasmutable *adj* transmutable.

trasmutación *f* transmutation.

trasmutar *vt* to transmute.

trasnochado, da *adj* stale, old (comida) || FIG haggard, run-down, pale (macilento) | stale, hackneyed (antiguo); *chiste trasnochado* stale joke.

trasnochador, ra *adj* who stays up late, who keeps late hours (que se acuesta tarde) || who stays up all night (que no se acuesta).
◆ *m/f* night bird, night owl (persona).

trasnochar *vi* to stay up all night (no acostarse) || to spend a sleepless night (pasar la noche sin dormir) || to spend the night (pernoctar) || to stay up late, to keep late hours; *le gusta trasnochar* he likes to keep late hours.

trasoñar* *vt* to dream, to imagine.

trasovado, da *adj* BOT *hoja trasovada* obovate leaf.

traspapelado, da *adj* mislaid, misplaced.

traspapelar *vt* to mislay, to misplace [a piece of paper].
◆ *vpr* to get mislaid *o* misplaced *o* lost.

trasparencia *f* ⟶ **transparencia.**

trasparentarse *vpr* ⟶ **transparentar.**

trasparente *adj/m* ⟶ **transparente.**

traspasable *adj* portable, transportable (que se puede llevar) || crossable, passable (que se puede atravesar) || transferable (negocio).

traspasación *f* transfer, transference.

traspasador, ra *adj* transgressing.
◆ *m/f* transgressor.

traspasar *vt* to transfix, to run through; *le traspasó con la espada* he transfixed him *o* he ran him through with his sword || to pierce, to go through; *la bala le traspasó el brazo* the bullet went through his arm || to transfer, to make over (un derecho, un comercio); *traspasar su negocio* to transfer one's business || to sell (vender) || to transgress, to break, to violate (una ley, un reglamento) || DEP to transfer (un jugador profesional a otro equipo) || to go beyond (ciertos límites) || FIG to transfix (de dolor físico) | to soak through, to go *o* to come through; *la lluvia traspasa su abrigo* the rain soaks through his coat || to cross (over); *traspasar el arroyo* to cross the stream || — *se traspasa tienda* shop for sale || FIG *traspasar el corazón* to pierce one's heart | *traspasar el oído* to pierce one's ears.

traspaso *m* transfer, sale (de un local comercial) || take-over fee (precio de la cesión) || property transferred (local traspasado) || DEP transfer (de un jugador) || JUR conveyance (de una propiedad) | transfer (de un derecho) | transgression, infringement (de la ley) || FIG grief (pena).

traspatio *m* AMER backyard.

traspié *m* trip, stumble, slip (tropezón) || trip (zancadilla) || FIG faux pas, blunder (equivocación, indiscreción) || *dar un traspié* to trip, to stumble, to slip (al andar), to slip up, to make a blunder (cometer un error).

traspiración *f* ⟶ **transpiración.**

traspirar *vi* ⟶ **transpirar.**

traspirenaico, ca *adj* ⟶ **transpirenaico, ca.**

trasplantable *adj* transplantable.

trasplantación *f* transplantation.

trasplantar *vt* to transplant || MED to transplant.
◆ *vpr* FIG to uproot o.s., to move (cambiar de residencia).

trasplante *m* transplanting || MED transplant, transplantation; *trasplante de corazón, de córnea* heart, corneal transplant.

trasponer *vt* ⟶ **transponer.**

traspontín *m* folding seat [in a taxi, etc.] || FAM backside (trasero).

trasportín *m* folding seat [in a taxi, etc.].

trasposición *f* ⟶ **transposición.**

traspuesta *f* transposition || rise (del terreno) || flight (huida) || outbuildings *pl* (de una casa).

traspunte *m* TEATR callboy (que llama a los actores) | prompter (apuntador).

traspuntín *m* folding seat (asiento).

trasquila *f* ⟶ **trasquiladura.**

trasquilado, da *adj* sheared (ovejas) || cropped (el pelo) || FIG & FAM cut down, curtailed (mermado) || — FIG *ir por lana y volver trasquilado* to go for wool and come home shorn || FIG & FAM *salir trasquilado* to come out a loser.
◆ *m* FAM priest (tonsurado).

trasquilador *m* shearer.

trasquiladura; trasquila *f* shearing (de ovejas) || cropping (del pelo) || FIG & FAM cutting down, curtailment (merma).

trasquilar *vt* to shear (esquilar) || to crop (el pelo) || FIG & FAM to cut down, to curtail (mermar).

trasquilón *m* FAM slash, hole (desigualdad en el corte de pelo) || FIG & FAM big hole *o* dent; *dar un trasquilón a su fortuna* to make a big hole in one's fortune || — *a trasquilones* unevenly (el pelo), haphazardly (sin orden ni concierto) || *hacer trasquilones en el pelo* to hack one's hair, to cut one's hair very badly.

trastabillar *vi* ⟶ **titubear.**

trastada *f* FAM dirty trick (jugarreta); *hacerle una trastada a uno* to play a dirty trick on s.o. | prank (travesura) | practical joke (broma pesada).

trastajo *m* FAM piece of junk.

trastazo *m* FAM whack, thump, bang (porrazo) || — FAM *darse* or *pegarse un trastazo* to come a cropper | *darse un trastazo contra algo* to bash *o* to crash *o* to bump into sth.

traste *m* fret (de guitarra, etc.) || wine taster (vaso) || AMER FAM bottom, backside (trasero) || — FAM *dar al traste con* to mess up, to spoil (proyectos), to squander (dinero), to put an end to (paciencia, esperanzas) | *ir al traste* to fall through, to be ruined, to be messed up.

trastear *vt* to rummage in, to turn upside down (revolver) || MÚS to play (un instrumento) || TAUR to work *o* to play (the bull) with the muleta || FIG & FAM to twist (s.o.) round one's little finger, to manœuvre (a uno).
◆ *vi* to rummage around (hurgar).

trastejar *vt* to re-tile (retejar).

trasteo *m* TAUR working *o* playing (the bull) with the muleta || FIG & FAM manœuvring.

trastería *f* junk (trastos).

trastero, ra *adj* junk (cuarto).
◆ *m/f* junk room.

trastienda *f* back room (de una tienda) || FIG & FAM canniness, cunning (astucia) | reserve (reserva) || FIG & FAM *tiene mucha trastienda* he's very canny (astuto), he's a dark horse (reservado).

trasto *m* piece of furniture (mueble) || utensil || FAM piece of junk (cosa inútil) | good-for-nothing, dead loss (persona inútil) | thingumajig, thing (chisme) || TEATR flat, wing (bastidor) || FIG & FAM *quita ese trasto de en medio* get that thing out of the way.
◆ *pl* junk (cosas inútiles) || weapons (armas) || tackle *sing*, gear *sing*; *los trastos de pescar* fishing tackle || bullfighter's equipment *sing* (de torear) || — FIG & FAM *con todos sus trastos* with the whole caboodle [US with kit and caboodle] || *llevarse los trastos* to pack up and leave || FIG & FAM *tirarse los trastos a la cabeza* to have a flaming row, to throw pots and pans at one another (reñir) | *trastos viejos* junk, old lumber *sing*.

trastocar* *vt* to disarrange, to upset (trastornar) || to change around completely (cambiar completamente).
◆ *vpr* to go mad (trastornarse).

trastornado, da *adj* unbalanced (persona, mente).

trastornador, ra *adj* upsetting.
◆ *m/f* troublemaker.

trastornamiento *m* ⟶ **trastorno.**

trastornar *vt* to upset, to disrupt, to ruin (proyecto, etc.) || to drive mad, to unhinge (volver loco) || to upset, to trouble (inquietar) || to make dizzy (dar mareo) || to drive crazy; *una mujer que trastorna a los hombres* a woman who drives men crazy || to turn upside down (desordenar); *Pedro lo ha trastornado todo aquí* Peter has turned everything upside down here || to disturb (el orden, la paz) || to disrupt (alterar) || to change completely (cambiar) || — *trastornarle la mente a alguien* to drive s.o. mad, to unhinge s.o. || *trastornarle la salud a alguien* to be bad for one, to be injurious to one's health.

◆ *vpr* to get *o* to become upset, to upset o.s. (estar conmovido) ‖ FIG to go mad, to go out of one's mind (turbarse).

trastorno; trastornamiento *m* inconvenience (inconveniente) ‖ trouble (molestia) ‖ upheaval; *la crisis económica causó un trastorno en el país* the economic crisis cause an upheaval in the country ‖ disorder, disturbance (mental, político) ‖ trouble, disorder, upset; *padecer trastornos estomacales* to have stomach troubles ‖ upset; *la instalación de la nueva máquina supondrá un gran trastorno en la fábrica* the installation of the new machine will mean a major upset in the factory ‖ — *causar profundos trastornos en la economía* to severely disrupt the economy ‖ *si no le sirve de trastorno* if it is not too much trouble.

trastrabillar *vi* AMER to stagger, to totter.

trastrocamiento *m* switch, reversal, change.

trastrocar* *vt* to change, to transform (transformar) ‖ to switch *o* to change round (cosas) ‖ to reverse, to invert (el orden) ‖ to change (el significado).

trastrueco; trastrueque *m* switch, reversal, change.

trasudación *f* transudation ‖ perspiration.

trasudar *vt/vi* to transude ‖ to perspire *o* to sweat slightly (sudar) ‖ *tiene la camisa trasudada* his shirt is soaked through with sweat.

trasudor *m* perspiration.

trasuntar *vt* to copy, to transcribe (copiar) ‖ to summarize (compendiar) ‖ FIG to exude; *su rostro trasuntaba serenidad* his face exuded serenity.

trasunto *m* copy ‖ FIG carbon copy, replica (cosa idéntica) | representation.

trasvasar; transvasar *vt* to decant, to transvase (vino) ‖ to transfer (agua de un río a otro, etc.).

trasvase *m* decanting (de vino, etc.) ‖ transfer (de grandes cantidades de agua, etc.).

trasvenarse *vpr* to extravasate ‖ FIG to spill (derramarse).

trasver* *vt* to distinguish, to perceive, to make out (distinguir) ‖ to see through (ver a través) ‖ not to see properly (ver mal).

trasverberación; transverberación *f* transverberation, transfixion.

trasversal *adj/f* → **transversal.**

trasverso, sa *adj* → **transverso.**

trasverter* *vi* to run over, to overflow.

trasvolar* *vt* to fly over.

trata *f* slave trade *o* traffic, slavery; *trata de blancas* white slave trade, white slavery.

tratable *adj* easy to get along with, amiable, sociable, friendly.

tratadista *m* writer (of treatises).

tratado *m* treatise; *tratado de matemáticas* treatise on mathematics ‖ treaty (convenio); *tratado de paz, de alianza* peace, alliance treaty.

tratamiento *m* treatment; *malos tratamientos* bad treatment ‖ title; *tratamiento de señoría* title of nobility ‖ MED treatment ‖ TECN processing, treatment; *el tratamiento de materias primas* the processing of raw materials | treatment; *tratamiento magnético* magnetic treatment ‖ — FIG *apear el tratamiento a uno* to drop s.o.'s formal title, to address s.o. informally ‖ *dar tratamiento a uno* to address s.o. by his title ‖ *dar tratamiento de tú, de usted* to address s.o. as «tú», as «usted» ‖ INFORM *tratamiento automático del lenguaje* automatic language processing | *tratamiento de datos* data processing ‖ *tratamiento de la información* data processing ‖ INFORM *tratamiento de textos* word processing | *tratamiento por lotes* batch processing | *tratamiento secuencial* sequential *o* serial processing.

tratante *adj* dealer; *tratante en automóviles* car dealer.

tratar *vt* to deal with, to discuss (un tema) ‖ to handle, to deal with (ocuparse de) ‖ to treat, to handle, to deal with; *tratar un asunto, un problema con delicadeza* to treat a matter, a problem with delicacy ‖ to treat, to handle (manejar); *hay que tratar las cosas con más cuidado* you should handle things more carefully ‖ MED to treat ‖ TECN to treat, to process (metal, madera, etc.) ‖ to entertain; *nos trató opíparamente* he entertained us lavishly ‖ to treat (a una persona); *tratar a los vencidos con clemencia* to treat the vanquished mercifully ‖ to address as, to give the title of (dar cierto tratamiento a uno) ‖ — *tratar a alguien* to know s.o., to associate with s.o., to have dealings with s.o. (tener trato con, conocer) ‖ FIG & FAM *tratar a alguien a puntapiés* or *con la punta del pie* to kick s.o. around ‖ FAM *tratar a alguien como a un perro* to treat s.o. like dirt *o* like a dog ‖ *tratar a alguien con guante blanco* to handle s.o. with kid gloves ‖ *tratar a alguien de ladrón* to call s.o. a thief ‖ *tratar a alguien de tú, de usted* to address s.o. as «tú», as «usted» ‖ FIG & FAM *tratar a alguien de tú a tú* to be very informal with s.o. (tratar con naturalidad), to prove to be s.o.'s equal (valer tanto como otro) ‖ FIG & FAM *tratar a alguien por encima del hombro* to look down on s.o. ‖ *tratar a alguien sin contemplaciones* to be very abrupt with s.o. ‖ *tratar a alguien sin miramientos* to be impolite to *o* inconsiderate towards s.o. ‖ *tratar algo por separado* to deal with sth. separately, to treat sth. apart.

◆ *vi* *tratar con* to associate with, to have dealings with, to know (tener trato con personas), to treat with, to negotiate with (negociar con), to deal with (hablar con), to deal with, to work with, to handle (en el trabajo); *el taxidermista trata con animales muertos* the taxidermist deals with dead animals ‖ *tratar de* to try to, to attempt to (intentar); *tratar de salir de un apuro* to try to get out of a jam ‖ *tratar de* or *sobre* to be about, to deal with, to talk about; *¿de qué (tema) trata el libro?* what is the book about?, what subjects does the book deal with?; to talk about, to discuss, to deal with (discutir, hablar de) ‖ *tratar en* to deal in (en comercio).

◆ *vpr* to take care of o.s., to look after o.s. (cuidarse); *se trata muy bien* he takes good care of himself ‖ to treat each other (dos personas) ‖ to call each other, to address each other; *se tratan de tú* they address each other as «tú» ‖ to be about; *¿de qué se trata?* what is it (all) about? ‖ to talk to each other; *a pesar de la riña que tuvieron, todavía se tratan* in spite of the quarrel they had they still talk to each other ‖ — *el asunto de que se trata* the matter in question ‖ *luego se trata sencillamente de encenderlo* then it's just a question of switching it on ‖ *si no se trata más que de eso* if that's all it is ‖ *tratarse con alguien* to have dealings with s.o., to associate with s.o. ‖ *ya no se tratan* they don't have anything to do with each other any more.

tratativas *fpl* AMER negotiations.

trato *m* treatment; *trato inhumano* inhuman treatment ‖ manners *pl*, behaviour (modales) ‖ agreement, bargain, deal (en negocios); *cerrar un trato* to strike a bargain, to make an agreement, to make *o* to close a deal ‖ title (título) ‖ — *casa de trato* brothel ‖ *deshacer el trato* to break an agreement ‖ *no tener trato con alguien* not to have anything to do with s.o. ‖ *romper el trato con alguien* to break off relations with s.o. ‖ *tener trato agradable* to have a pleasant personality, to be easy to get on with ‖ *tener trato con* to associate with, to know, to be friendly with ‖ *tener trato de gentes* to have a way with people ‖ *tengo un trato superficial con Pedro* Peter is a casual acquaintance of mine ‖ *trato carnal* sexual intercourse ‖ *¡trato hecho!* it's a deal! ‖ *trato preferente* preferential treatment.

◆ *pl* dealings ‖ — *estar en tratos con* to be negotiating with ‖ *malos tratos* ill treatment; cruelty; *acusó a su marido de malos tratos* she accused her husband of cruelty.

trauma *m* MED trauma.

traumático, ca *adj* MED traumatic.

traumatismo *m* MED traumatism.

traumatología *f* MED traumatology.

travelín; travelling *m* CINEM travelling [*US* traveling], dollying (procedimiento) | dolly (plataforma).

través *m* inclination, slant (de un cuadro, etc.) ‖ bias; *la tela está cortada a través* the material is cut on the bias ‖ setback, reverse, upset (contratiempo, revés) ‖ ARQ crossbeam (viga) ‖ MAR beam ‖ traverse (en fortificaciones) ‖ — *al través* crossways ‖ *a través de, al través de* across, over; *había un árbol colocado a través de la carretera* there was a tree lying across the road; through; *la monja miró a través de la celosía* the nun looked through the lattice; through, from; *lo sé a través de mi hermano* I heard about it through my brother ‖ MAR *dar al través* to hit broadside on ‖ *de través* crossways, crosswise (al través), sideways (de lado), askew, crooked (mal colocado) ‖ MAR *ir de través* to drift off course ‖ *mirar de través* to squint (defecto físico), to look askance *o* out of the corner of one's eyes at (mirar de reojo).

travesaño *m* crosspiece ‖ crosspiece, crossbeam, strut (de un tejado) ‖ bolster (almohada) ‖ DEP crossbar (en fútbol) ‖ AMER sleeper [*US* crosstie] (de ferrocarril).

travesear *vi* to get up to mischief, to be naughty (los niños) ‖ to lead a dissolute life.

travesero, ra *adj* cross.

◆ *m* bolster (almohada).

travesía *f* crossing; *la travesía del Pacífico* the crossing of the Pacific ‖ voyage, crossing (viaje marítimo) ‖ distance (distancia) ‖ passage (que comunica dos calles) ‖ crossroad, cross street (entre dos carreteras) ‖ urban section of a road, section of a road which crosses a town ‖ MIL traverse wind, crosswind ‖ AMER broad arid plain [between two mountain ranges] (páramo).

travesío, a *adj* traverse (viento).

travestido *m* transvestite.

travestir* *vt* to dress as a member of the opposite sex.

◆ *vpr* to be a transvestite.

travestismo *m* transvestism.

travesura *f* mischief (diablura); *el niño ha estado haciendo travesuras todo el día* the child has been (getting) up to mischief all day long ‖ prank (picardía); *fue una travesura de niño* it was a childish prank ‖ *hacer travesuras* to get up to mischief, to be up to mischief.

traviesa *f* sleeper [*US* crosstie] (de ferrocarril) ‖ ARQ crossbeam (del tejado) | wall (muro) ‖ MIN transverse gallery ‖ bet (apuesta) ‖ raise on a bet (algo añadido a la puesta).

travieso, sa *adj* mischievous (que hace diabluras) ‖ naughty (malo) ‖ sly, cunning, crafty (astuto) ‖ sharp, witty (ingenioso) ‖ — *a campo traviesa* across country ‖ DEP *carrera a campo traviesa* cross-country race.

trayecto *m* distance (distancia) ‖ stretch (tramo de carretera) ‖ way; *nos paramos en el trayecto* we stopped on the way ‖ itinerary, route (recorrido); *el trayecto de la procesión* the procession route ‖ trip, journey (viaje); *tene-*

mos un trayecto de cinco horas it is a five-hour journey || walk (camino hecho a pie) || hike (en el campo a pie) || route, run (de un autobús, etc.).

trayectoria *f* trajectory, path || FIG course, line, path, direction, tendency (orientación).

traza *f* plan, design (de una obra) || looks *pl*, appearance (aspecto); *me gusta su traza* I like his looks; *no me gusta la traza que tiene* I don't like the looks of him (una persona) *o* of it (una cosa) || trace, sign (señal) || MAT trace (en geometría) || — FIG *darse trazas para* to manage to, to contrive to; *se dio trazas para llegar a tiempo a la estación* he managed to arrive at the station on time || FIG & FAM *este trabajo tiene trazas de no acabar nunca* this work looks as if *o* as though it will never end | *la chica tiene trazas de no querer estudiar* the girl doesn't seem to want to study || *tener buena traza* to be good-looking (una persona), to look promising *o* good (un asunto, un proyecto, etc.) || *tener buena, mala, poca, mucha traza para algo* to be good, no good, not very good, very good at sth.

trazado *adj* laid out, made, designed; *el camino está mal trazado* the road is badly laid out || — *bien trazado* good-looking, nice-looking (de buen ver) || *mal trazado* unattractive, ungainly.
◆ *m* layout (disposición) || plan, design (proyecto de edificio, puente, etc.) || drawing, sketch (dibujo) || outline (contorno) || course (de una carretera).

trazador, ra *adj* tracer, tracing || planning, designing || *bala trazadora* tracer (bullet).
◆ *m/f* planner, designer.
◆ *m* INFORM plotter; *trazador de gráficos* graph plotter.

trazar *vt* to draw (up) (un plano, dibujo, etc.) || to sketch, to outline (bosquejar) || to plot, to lay out (un jardín, un parque, etc.) || to draw, to trace (una línea) || to trace, to plot (el itinerario) || ARQ to design (puentes, edificios, etc.) || — FIG *trazar las líneas generales de un proyecto* to draw up the broad outlines of a project | *trazar una semblanza de alguien* to draw a picture of s.o., to depict s.o., to describe s.o. (con palabras).

trazo *m* line; *trazo rectilíneo* straight line || stroke, line (de lápiz, pincel) || stroke (de una letra) || sketch, outline (bosquejo) || FIG feature, line (de la cara); *el capitán tiene trazos enérgicos* the captain has energetic features || fold (del ropaje) || *dibujar al trazo* to draw in outline.

trazumarse *vpr* to ooze, to seep, to exude.

trébede *f*; **trébedes** *f pl* trivet *sing* (utensilio) || raised part of a room under which straw is burnt to provide heat (habitación).

trebejo *m* utensil; *los trebejos de la cocina* (the) kitchen utensils || chessman, chess piece (ajedrez).
◆ *pl* equipment *sing*, gear *sing*; *los trebejos de matar* the matador's equipment.

trébol *m* BOT clover, trefoil || club (naipe) || ARQ trefoil (adorno) || cloverleaf junction (en carreteras).
◆ *pl* clubs (palo de la baraja).

trebolado, da *adj* trefoil.

trebolar *AMER* clover field.

trece *adj* thirteen; *trece libros* thirteen books || thirteenth; *León XIII (trece)* Leo XIII [the thirteenth]; *el día 13 (trece) de febrero* the 13th [thirteenth] of Frebruary.
◆ *m* thirteenth; *el 13 (trece) de septiembre* the 13th [thirteenth] of September || thirteen, number thirteen; *ganó el trece* thirteen won; *vivo en el trece* I live at number thirteen || — FIG *mantenerse en sus trece* to stick to one's guns | *martes y trece* unlucky day (corresponde a «Friday the thirteenth» en inglés).

treceno, na *adj* thirteenth.

trecentista *adj* [of *o* in the] fourteenth century.

trecésimo, ma *adj* thirtieth.

trecha *f* sommersault (voltereta) || trick (ardid).

trecho *m* distance, way; *hay un gran trecho entre las dos ciudades* there is a great distance between the two cities, the two cities are a long way apart; *anduvimos un buen trecho* we walked a good *o* a long way || stretch; *un trecho muy malo en el camino* a very rough stretch in the road || spell, while, time (espacio de tiempo); *esperé largo trecho* I waited quite a spell || AGR plot, patch || FAM bit, piece (pedazo) || — *a trechos* in places, in parts, at times (en ciertas partes), now and again (con discontinuidad en el tiempo) || *de trecho a trecho, de trecho en trecho* at intervals, every so often; *árboles plantados de trecho en trecho* trees planted at intervals.

tredécimo, ma *adj* thirteenth || *una tredécima parte* a thirteenth.

trefilado *m* TECN wiredrawing.

trefilador *m* TECN wiredrawer.

trefiladora *f* TECN wiredrawing machine.

trefilar *vt* to draw (wire).

trefilería *m* wireworks, wiredrawing factory.

tregua *f* MIL truce; *acordar una tregua* to declare a truce || FIG rest, respite (descanso); *sus acreedores no le dan tregua* his creditors give him no respite | lull, letup (período de actividad menos intensa) || HIST *tregua de Dios* truce of God.

treinta *adj* thirty; *treinta hombres* thirty men || *vino el día treinta de mayo* he came on the thirtieth of May.
◆ *m* thirty, number thirty; *juego siempre al treinta* I always bet on the thirty || thirtieth; *el treinta de mayo* the 30th [thirtieth] of May || — *los años treinta* the thirties || *treinta y uno* thirty-one (número), thirty-first (fecha) || *unos treinta* about thirty.

treintadosavo, va *adj* thirty-second || IMPR *en treintadosavo* in 32mo, in thirty-twomo.

treintañal *adj* thirty-year-old.

treintavo, va *adj/s* thirtieth.

treintena *f* thirty (treinta unidades); *envíeme una treintena* send me thirty (of them) || thirtieth (treintava parte).

treinteno, na *adj* thirtieth (trigésimo).

tremadal *m* ⟶ **tremedal.**

trematodo *m* ZOOL trematode, fluke.

tremebundo, da *adj* terrible, dreadful, frightful.

tremedal; tremadal *m* quaking bog, quagmire.

tremendo, da *adj* terrible, frightful, dreadful; *un espectáculo, un crimen tremendo* a terrible sight *o* spectacle, crime; *un porrazo tremendo* a terrible bang || tremendous, terrific (grandísimo, fortísimo, etc.); *una paliza, un golpe, un disparo tremendo* a tremendous hiding, blow, shot || terrific, terrible (muy grande); *un calor tremendo* terrible heat; *un disparate tremendo* a terrible blunder || FAM marvellous, fantastic (persona) || FAM *tomarlo por la tremenda* to take it hard.

trementina *f* turpentine; *esencia de trementina* oil of turpentine.

tremés; tremesino, na *adj* three-month-old || *trigo tremés* or *tremesino* summer wheat.

tremielga *f* crampfish, torpedo fish (pez).

tremolar *vi* to flutter, to wave.
◆ *vt* to wave (banderas) || FIG to flaunt (ostentar).

tremolina *f* gusty wind (viento) || FIG & FAM uproar, rumpus, fuss; *armar la tremolina* to kick up a rumpus *o* a fuss, to create uproar.

trémolo *m* MÚS tremolo.

tremor *m* tremor (temblor).

tremulante; trémulo, la *adj* trembling, tremulous || flickering (luz).

tren *m* train; *tren expreso, ómnibus, rápido, correo* express, stopping *o* slow, fast, mail train; *tren mixto* passenger and goods train || luggage, equipment, gear (bagaje) || FIG pace, speed; *ir a buen tren* to go at a good pace *o* speed || convoy, line (convoy); *un tren de camiones* a convoy of lorries || MIL convoy || — *cambiar de tren* to change (trains) || FIG & FAM *estar como un tren* to be a bit of allright || FIG *ir a un tren endiablado* to go at breakneck speed || *ir en tren* to go by train || FIG *perder el tren* to miss the boat (perder la ocasión) || *poner un tren suplementario* to put on an extra *o* a relief train || *por tren* by train || *tomar el tren* to catch a train || *tren ascendente, descendente* up train, down train || FAM *tren botijo* or *de recreo* excursion train || *tren de alta velocidad* high-speed train || *tren de aterrizaje* undercarriage, landing gear || *tren de cercanías* commuter *o* suburban train || *tren de circunvalación* peripheral train || *tren de engranajes* gear train || MIL *tren de equipajes* supply train || TECN *tren de laminación* or *laminador* rolling mill || AUT *tren delantero, trasero* front wheel, rear wheel assembly || *tren de mercancías* goods *o* freight train || TECN *tren desbastador* roughing mill || FIG *tren de vida* way of life || *tren directo* through train || *tren nocturno* night train || FIG *vivir a todo tren, llevar un gran tren de vida* to live in style *o* on a grand scale.

trena *f* FAM clink (cárcel) || MIL sash.

trenca *f* crosspiece [in a beehive] (de colmena) || main root (de una cepa) || duffle coat (abrigo).

trencilla *f* braided *o* plaited ribbon, braid.

trencillar *vt* to braid.

treno *m* threnody || lamentation; *los trenos de Jeremías* the lamentations of Jeremiah.

Trento *n pr* GEOGR Trent, Trento.

trenza *f* braid (en costura) || plait (de cabello) || *trenza postiza* switch.

trenzado, da *adj* braided (en costura) || plaited (cabello) || intertwined (entrelazado).
◆ *m* braid (trenza, en costura) || plait (trenza de pelo) || braiding, plaiting (trenzas, acción de trenzar) || entrechat (en la danza) || crossover step (de caballo).

trenzador, ra *m/f* braider, plaiter.
◆ *f* TECN braiding machine.

trenzar *vt* to braid, to plait || to plait (el cabello).
◆ *vi* to perform entrechats (los bailarines) || to walk with crossover steps (el caballo).
◆ *vpr AMER* to wrestle (luchar) | to begin to quarrel (reñir).

trepa *f* climb, climbing (subida) || drilling, boring (acción de taladrar) || trimming, edging (guarnición) || grain (de la madera) || forward roll, somersault (voltereta) || FIG trick, ruse (ardid).

trepado, da *adj* leaning back, reclined (retrepado) || strong (animales).
◆ *m* perforation (línea de puntos taladrados) || trimming, edging (adorno) || drilling, boring (acción de taladrar).

trepador, ra *adj* climbing, rambling; *planta trepadora* climbing plant || ZOOL *ave trepadora* creeper.

◆ *f pl* BOT climbers, ramblers ‖ ZOOL creepers ‖ climbing irons (garfios para trepar).

trepanación *f* MED trepanation.

trepanar *vt* MED to trephine, to trepan.

trépano *m* MED trephine (instrumento) ‖ TECN trepan, boring bit (perforadora).

trepar *vt/vi* to climb; *trepar a un árbol* to climb (up) a tree ‖ to scale; *trepar por una roca* to scale a rock ‖ to climb, to creep; *la hiedra trepa por las paredes* ivy creeps up walls ‖ to drill, to bore (taladrar) ‖ to trim, to edge (adornar).

trepatroncos *m inv* blue titmouse (pájaro).

trepidación *f* vibration.

trepidante *adj* vibrating, shaking.

trepidar *vi* to vibrate, to shake (temblar).

treponema *m* ZOOL treponema.

tres *adj* three; *tiene tres hermanos* he has three brothers ‖ third; *el día tres de junio* the third of June.

◆ *m* third; *el tres de junio* the third of June ‖ three, number three (número) ‖ — *como tres y dos son cinco* as sure as eggs are eggs (segurísimo), perfectly clear (evidente) ‖ MÚS *compás de tres por dos, tres por ocho, tres por cuatro* three-two, three-eight, three-four time ‖ FIG & FAM *de tres al cuarto* cheap, of little value; *un vestido de tres al cuarto* a cheap dress; third-rate; *un político de tres al cuarto* a third-rate politician ‖ MIL *en formación de a tres* three abreast ‖ *las tres de la mañana* or *de la madrugada, de la tarde* three o'clock in the morning, in the afternoon ‖ FIG *ni a la de tres* not for the life of me (of him, etc.); *no consigo que lo haga ni a la de tres* I cannot get him to do it for the life of me | *no ver tres en un burro* to be as blind as a bat ‖ MAT *regla de tres* rule of three ‖ *son las tres y media* it is half past three ‖ *tres en raya* noughts-and-crosses [*US* ticktacktoe].

tresañal; tresañejo, ja *adj* three-year-old.

tresbolillo (al) *adv* in quincunxes; *plantación al tresbolillo* plantation in quincunxes.

trescientos, tas *adj/sm* three hundred; *trescientos veinte* three hundred and twenty; *en el año trescientos* in the year three hundred ‖ *mil trescientos* thirteen hundred, one thousand three hundred.

tresdoblar *vt* to treble, to triple.

tresillo *m* ombre (juego de naipes) ‖ MÚS triplet ‖ three-piece suite (muebles) ‖ ring with three stones (sortija).

treta *f* trick (ardid); *valerse de una treta* to use a trick ‖ feint (en esgrima).

Tréveris *n pr* GEOGR Trier.

trezavo, va *adj/sm* thirteenth.

tría *f* sorting.

triaca *f* MED theriaca, antidote ‖ cure, remedy (cura).

triácido, da *adj/sm* triacid.

tríada *f* triad.

trial *m* DEP trial.

triangulación *f* triangulation.

triangulado, da *adj* triangulated (dividido en triángulos) ‖ triangular (en forma de triángulo).

triangular *adj* triangular; *pirámide, músculo triangular* triangular pyramid, muscle.

triangular *vt* to triangulate.

triángulo *m* triangle; *triángulo equilátero, isósceles, escaleno* equilateral, isosceles, scalene triangle ‖ MÚS triangle.

trías *m* GEOL trias.

triásico, ca *adj* GEOL Triassic.

◆ *m* GEOL Trias, Triassic.

triates *mpl* AMER triplets (trillizos).

triatómico, ca *adj* triatomic.

tribal *adj* tribal.

tribásico, ca *adj* QUÍM tribasic.

tribu *f* tribe.

tribulación *f* tribulation.

tribuna *f* rostrum, platform (de un orador); *subir a la tribuna* to go up to the rostrum ‖ tribune (para un espectáculo) ‖ DEP grandstand ‖ gallery (en una iglesia) ‖ — JUR *tribuna del acusado* dock ‖ *tribuna de la prensa* press box ‖ JUR *tribuna del jurado* jury box.

tribunado *m* tribunate, tribuneship.

tribunal *m* JUR court; *tribunal de apelación, supremo, tutelar de menores* court of appeal, High Court [*US* Supreme Court], juvenile court ‖ tribunal; *tribunal de Dios* tribunal of God; *tribunal militar* military tribunal ‖ board; *tribunal de examen* board of examiners; *tribunal de conciliación laboral* conciliation board in industrial disputes ‖ — *Tribunal de Cuentas* National Audit Office [*US* Committee on Public Accounts] ‖ *Tribunal de Justicia Internacional* International Court of Justice.

tribuno *m* tribune.

tributable *adj* tributary (sujeto a tributo).

tributación *f* tax, tribute (tributo) ‖ payment of taxes (pago) ‖ tax system (régimen tributario).

tributante *adj* taxpaying.

◆ *m/f* taxpayer.

tributar *vt* to pay (pagar) ‖ FIG to pay; *tributar respeto, homenaje* to pay respect, tribute | to show; *tributar cariño* to show affection.

tributario, ria *adj* tax, taxation; *sistema* or *régimen tributario* tax system ‖ tributary (que paga tributo) ‖ tributary (corriente de agua).

tributo *m* tribute ‖ tax (impuesto) ‖ FIG price; *el tributo de la gloria* the price of fame | tribute; *el respeto es el tributo debido a la virtud* respect is the tribute one pays to virtue.

tricéfalo, la *adj* tricephalous.

tricenal *adj* thirty-year.

tricentenario *m* tercentenary, tricentennial.

tricentésimo, ma *adj/s* three hundredth.

tríceps *m* ANAT triceps.

triciclo *m* tricycle.

tricípite *adj* tricephalous.

triclínico, ca *adj* MIN triclinic (cristal).

triclinio *m* triclinium.

tricología *f* MED trichology.

tricólogo, ga *m/f* MED trichologist.

tricolor *adj* tricolour [*US* tricolor], three-coloured [*US* three-colored] ‖ *bandera tricolor* tricolour [*US* tricolor].

tricorne *adj* POÉT three-cornered.

tricornio *adj m* three-cornered.

◆ *m* tricorn, three-cornered hat.

tricotar *vt* to knit ‖ *máquina de tricotar* knitting machine.

tricotomía *f* trichotomy.

tricotosa *f* knitting machine.

tricromía *f* three-colour process, trichromatism.

tricromo, ma *adj* three-colour, three-coloured [*US* three-color, three-colored].

tricúspide *adj* ANAT tricuspid; *válvula tricúspide* tricuspid valve.

◆ *m* ANAT tricuspid.

tridáctilo, la *adj* tridactyl.

tridente *m* trident.

tridentino, na *adj* of Trent, Tridentine; *el Concilio tridentino* the Council of Trent.

tridimensional *adj* three-dimensional, tridimensional.

triduo *m* REL triduo, triduum.

triedro, dra *adj* MAT trihedral.

◆ *m* MAT trihedron.

trienial *adj* triennial.

trienio *m* triennium.

trifásico, ca *adj* three-phase, triphase (corriente).

trifenilmetano *m* QUÍM triphenylmethane.

trifoliado, da *adj* BOT trifoliate, trifoliated.

triforio *m* ARQ triforium.

trifulca *f* system of three levers [for working the bellows] ‖ FIG & FAM squabble, rumpus, row; *armar una trifulca* to kick up a rumpus.

trifurcarse *vpr* to divide into three.

trigal *m* wheat field.

trigémino, na *adj m/sm* ANAT trigeminal.

trigésimo, ma *adj/s* thirtieth ‖ *trigésimo primero, segundo, etc.* thirty-first, thirty-second, etc.

triglifo *m* ARQ triglyph.

trigo *m* BOT wheat ‖ — FIG & FAM *meterse en trigo ajeno* to meddle in s.o. else's affairs | *no es trigo limpio* he's a shady character (persona), it's a fishy business (asunto) | *nunca es mal año por mucho trigo* you can't have too much of a good thing ‖ *trigo atizonado* or *con tizón* blighted wheat ‖ *trigo candeal* white wheat ‖ *trigo chamorro* or *mocho* summer *o* beardless wheat ‖ *trigo duro* or *fanfarrón* hard wheat ‖ *trigo en cierne* wheat in the blade ‖ *trigo marzal* spring wheat ‖ *trigo sarraceno* buckwheat.

◆ *pl* BOT wheat *sing*.

trígono, na *adj* MAT trigonal.

trigonometría *f* trigonometry.

trigonométrico, ca *adj* trigonometric, trigonometrical.

trigueño, ña *adj* olive-skinned (persona, rostro) ‖ golden, dark blond (pelo).

triguero, ra *adj* wheat; *campos trigueros* wheat fields.

◆ *m* wheat merchant ‖ wheat sieve (criba).

trilateral; trilátero, ra *adj* trilateral, three-sided.

trilingüe *adj* trilingual.

trilita *f* tolite (explosivo).

trilito *m* trilithon, dolmen.

trilobites *m pl* trilobites.

trilobulado, da *adj* trilobate ‖ trefoil (arco).

trilogía *f* trilogy.

trilógico, ca *adj* of *o* pertaining to a trilogy.

trilla *f* threshing (acción) ‖ threshing time *o* season (temporada) ‖ thresher (trillo) ‖ ZOOL gurnard (pez) ‖ FAM thrashing (tunda).

trillado *adj* AGR threshed ‖ FIG worn-out, hackneyed, played out; *un tema trillado* a worn-out subject | beaten; *camino trillado* beaten path.

trillador, ra *adj* threshing.

◆ *f* threshing machine (máquina) ‖ *trilladora segadora* combine harvester.

trilladura *f* AGR threshing.

trillar *vt* AGR to thresh ‖ FIG to wear out, to play out (emplear mucho) | to beat (maltratar).

trillizos, zas *m/f pl* triplets.

trillo *m* thresher [drawn by a horse, mule, etc.] ‖ AMER path, lane.

trillón *m* trillion [*US* quintillion].

trimestral *adj* quarterly, three-monthly ‖ *exámenes trimestrales* end-of-term exams.

trimestralmente *adv* quarterly, every three months.

trimestre *m* quarter, trimester || term (en la universidad) || quarterly payment (pago).

trimielga *f* torpedo fish (pez).

trimorfismo *m* trimorphism.

trimorfo, fa *adj* trimorphic, trimorphous.

trimotor *adj m* three-engined.
◆ *m* three-engined aircraft.

trinado *m* warble (de un pájaro) || trill (de un cantante).

trinar *vi* to warble (un pájaro) || MÚS to trill || FIG & FAM *está Juan que trina* John is fuming *o* furious.

trinca *f* trio, group of three, threesome (reunión de tres personas o cosas) || MAR lashing.

trincar *vt* to tie securely, to bind (atar) || MAR to lash || to break up, to smash (romper) || FAM to catch (apresar) | to hold down (inmovilizar) | to steal (robar) | to drink, to put away, to down (beber) || FAM *trincar una trompa* to get plastered *o* tight.

trincha *f* strap.

trinchado *m* carving (de la carne).

trinchador, ra *adj* carving (de carne).
◆ *m/f* carver (de carne).
◆ *m* carving knife (cuchillo).

trinchante *adj* carving.
◆ *m* servant [who carved meat in olden times] || carving knife (cuchillo) || meat fork (tenedor) || stonecutter's hammer (escoda) || serving table, side table, sideboard (mueble).

trinchar *vt* to carve, to cut (la carne).

trinchera *f* trench (para defenderse) || cutting (de ferrocarril) || ditch (para cables, tuberías, etc.) || trench coat (abrigo impermeable) || *guerra de trincheras* trench warfare.

trinchero *m* carving (plato).
◆ *m* serving table, side table, sideboard (mueble) || carving dish (plato).

trinchete *m* shoemaker's knife || *AMER* (table) knife.

trineo *m* sledge [*US* sled] (pequeño) || sleigh (grande).

trinidad *f* trinity.

Trinidad y Tobago *n pr* GEOGR Trinidad and Tobago.

trinitaria *f* BOT heartsease, wild pansy.

trinitario, ria *adj/s* Trinitarian.

trinitrotolueno, na *m* QUÍM trinitrotoluene.

trino, na *adj* REL triune, three in one || trine (triple) || ASTR trine.

trino *m* MÚS trill || warble, trill (del pájaro).

trinomio *m* trinomial.

trinquetada *f* MAR sailing under foresail.

trinquete *m* MAR foremast (palo) | foresail (vela) || DEP pelota court (frontón) || TECN pawl, ratchet (de rueda dentada).

trinquetilla *f* MAR fore-topmast staysail | small jib.

trinquis *m* FAM swig, drink (trago) | bottle; *le gusta mucho el trinquis* he is fond of the bottle | drink; *echar un trinquis* to have a drink.

trío *m* trio.

tríodo *m* FÍS triode.

trióxido *m* QUÍM trioxide.

tripa *f* gut, intestine (intestino) || FAM stomach, tummy, belly (vientre); *dolor de tripa* stomachache | paunt, gut; *echar tripa* to put on a paunch; *tener tripa* to have a paunch | belly (panza de una vasija) || filling (de un cigarro puro) || catgut; *cuerda de tripa* catgut string || FIG & FAM *llenar* or *llenarse la tripa* to eat one's fill.
◆ *pl* FAM innards, works (de una máquina) | inside *sing*, core *sing* (de una fruta, etc.) || — FIG & FAM *echar las tripas* to throw up (vomitar) | *hacer de tripas corazón* to keep a stiff upper lip, to pluck up courage | *quitar las tripas a un animal* to gut an animal || *revolver las tripas* to turn one's stomach | *tener malas tripas* to be cruel o ruthless.

tripada *f* FAM *darse una tripada* to have one's fill (saciarse), to have had a bellyful (*de* of) (estar harto).

tripanosoma *f* MED trypanosome.

tripanosomiasis *f* MED trypanosomiasis.

tripartición *f* tripartition.

tripartir *vt* to divide into three.

tripartito, ta *adj* tripartite; *acuerdo tripartito* tripartite agreement.

tripería *f* tripe shop, butcher's shop where offal is sold.

tripero, ra *m/f* tripe *o* offal butcher.
◆ *m* flannel waistband.

tripétalo, la *adj* BOT tripetalous.

tripicallero, ra *m/f* tripe seller.

tripicallos *m pl* CULIN tripe *sing*.

triplano *m* triplane (avión).

triplaza *adj* three-seater.

triple *adj* triple || triple, three times || triple thickness (de tres espesuras).
◆ *m* triple || — *ahora cuesta el triple de lo que costaba* it costs three times as much as it used to || *ser el triple de grande que...* to be three times as big as...

triplicación *f* triplication.

triplicado *adj* triplicate.
◆ *m* triplicate; *por triplicado* in triplicate.

triplicar *vt* to triplicate (producir tres copias idénticas) || to triple, to treble.
◆ *vpr* to triple, to treble; *la población de Los Angeles se ha triplicado* the population of Los Angeles has tripled.

tríplice *adj* triple.

triplicidad *f* triplicity.

triplo, pla *adj* triple.

trípode *m* tripod.

tripón, ona *adj* FAM potbellied.

tríptico *m* triptych.

triptongo *m* GRAM triphthong.

tripudo, da *adj* FAM potbellied.

tripulación *f* crew (de un barco, avión).

tripulante *m* crew member.
◆ *pl* crew *sing*.

tripular *vt* to man; *satélite tripulado* manned satellite; *vuelo tripulado* manned flight.

triquina *f* trichina.

triquinosis *f* MED trichinosis.

triquinoso, sa *adj* trichinous.

triquiñuela *f* FAM trick, dodge; *las triquiñuelas del oficio* the tricks of the trade || *andar con triquiñuelas* to be a trickster.

triquitraque *m* clatter, clackety-clack (de un tren) || bang, crash (ruido fuerte) || firework similar to a jumping jack (en pirotecnia).

trirrectángulo, la *adj* MAT trirectangular.

trirreme *m* trireme.

tris *m* crack (estallido) || rip (de algo al rasgarse) || — FIG & FAM *en un tris* in a jiffy | *estuvo en un tris que le pillara el coche* he was very nearly run over by the car | *he estado en un tris de llamar a la policía* I was on the point of calling *o* I very nearly called the police | *no lo alcanzó por un tris* it missed him by a hairsbreadth, it very nearly hit him.

trisagio *m* REL trisagion.

trisca *f* crunch (crujido) || FIG uproar, rumpus, racket (bulla, jaleo).

triscador, ra *adj* rowdy, uproarious.
◆ *m* saw set (sierra).

triscar *vt* to mingle, to mix (enredar) || to set (una sierra).
◆ *vi* to stamp (patear) || to gambol, to frisk (retozar, un animal) || FIG to romp, to frollick (persona).

trisecar *vt* MAT to trisect.

trisección *f* MAT trisection.

trisemanal *adj* triweekly.

trisemanalmente *adv* thrice weekly, three times a week (tres veces por semana) || every three weeks (cada tres semanas).

trisílabo, ba *adj* trisyllabic.
◆ *m* trisyllable.

triste *adj* sad, unhappy, sorrowful; *triste por la muerte de su padre* sad because of the death of his father || sad, melancholy, gloomy; *tiene un carácter triste* he has a gloomy character || dismal, dreary, gloomy; *un día triste* a gloomy day; *una calle triste* a dismal street || sad, unfortunate, sorry (situación) || sad (noticia, canción, etc.) || FIG sorry, measly, paltry, miserable; *un triste sueldo* a sorry salary; *sólo me queda un triste cigarrillo* I've only got one measly cigarette left || — FIG *es la triste verdad* it's the sad truth *o* the sorry truth || *es triste que no haya ganado* it's a shame *o* a pity he didn't win.
◆ *m* AMER sad popular song.

tristeza *f* sadness, sorrow (de una persona) || sadness, desolation, gloominess, dreariness (de un sitio) || *siempre me viene a contar sus tristezas* she always comes to me with her problems.

tristón, ona *adj* melancholy, somewhat sad, gloomy.

trisulfuro *m* QUÍM trisulphide [*US* trisulfide].

tritio *m* QUÍM tritium.

tritón *m* ZOOL newt.

Tritón *m* MIT Triton.

trituración *f* trituration, grinding, crushing.

triturador, ra *adj* triturating, crushing, grinding.
◆ *f* crusher, triturator (máquina).
◆ *m* garbage disposal (unit) (de basura).

triturar *vt* to grind, to triturate, to crush (moler) || to chew (mascar) || FIG to make suffer (hacer sufrir) | to tear to pieces (criticar severamente) || FIG & FAM *triturar a palos* to beat (s.o.) up.

triunfador, ra *adj* triumphant, victorious.
◆ *m/f* winner, victor, triumpher.

triunfal *adj* triumphal (arco, etc.) || triumphant.

triunfalmente *adv* triumphantly.

triunfante *adj* triumphant || *salir triunfante* to emerge victorious.

triunfar *vi* to triumph (*sobre, de* over) || FIG to win, to triumph; *triunfar en un certamen* to win a contest, to triumph in a contest | to succeed; *triunfar en la vida* to succeed in life || DEP to win || to play a trump, to trump (en los juegos de cartas).

triunfo *m* triumph, victory (victoria) || triumph (en la Roma antigua) || FIG success; *triunfo teatral* theatrical success; *triunfo en la vida* success in life || trump (naipes) || DEP win, victory || *AMER* popular dance || — *en triunfo* in triumph || FIG *tener todos los triunfos en la mano* to hold all the trumps.

triunviral *adj* triumviral.

triunvirato *m* triumvirate.

triunviro *m* triumvir.

trivalencia *f* trivalence, trivalency.

trivalente *adj* QUÍM trivalent.

trivial *adj* trivial, trite (insustancial); *conversación trivial* trivial conversation ‖ commonplace, trite (corriente).

trivialidad *f* triviality (cosa trivial) ‖ triteness, triviality (cualidad).
◆ *pl* trivia, trivialities ‖ *decir trivialidades* to talk trivially.

trivio; trivium *m* trivium (estudios) ‖ junction (of three roads).

triza *f* bit, piece (pedazo pequeño); *hacer trizas* to smash to pieces ‖ shred (jirón); *hacer trizas* to tear to shreads ‖ MAR halyard ‖ FIG *hacer trizas a uno* to pull s.o. to pieces, to tear s.o. to shreds (criticar severamente).

trocánter *m* ANAT trochanter.

trocar *m* MED trocar.

trocar* *vt* to exchange, to barter; *trocar un caballo por una mula* to exchange a horse for a mule ‖ to change, to convert; *trocar el amor en odio* to convert love into hate ‖ FIG to confuse, to mix up (confundir, mezclar) ‖ to vomit.
◆ *vpr* to change (*en* into).

trocear *vt* to cut up.

troceo *m* cutting up.

trocla *f* pulley (polea).

tróclea *f* ANAT trochlea.

trocoide *adj/s f* trochoid.

trócola *f* pulley.

trocha *f* narrow path, trail (sendero) ‖ shortcut (atajo) ‖ *AMER* gauge, gage (del ferrocarril).

trochemoche (a); troche y moche (a) *adv* helter-skelter, pellmell (rápida y confusamente), haphazardly (al azar).

trochuela *f* narrow path.

trofeo *m* trophy ‖ victory, triumph (triunfo).

troglodita *adj* troglodytical, troglodytic, cave-dwelling ‖ FIG coarse, brutish (bárbaro) | gluttonous (comilón).
◆ *m/f* troglodyte, caveman, cave dweller ‖ FIG brute (bruto) | glutton (comilón).
◆ *m* ZOOL troglodyte (pájaro).

troglodítico *adj* troglodytic, troglodytical.

troica *f* troika.

troj; troje *f* granary, barn (granero).

trola *f* FAM lie, fib (mentira).

trole *m* trolley, trolly, trolley pole.

trolebús *m* trolleybus.

trolero, ra *adj* FAM lying (mentiroso).
◆ *m/f* FAM liar, fibber.

tromba *f* waterspout ‖ — FIG *en tromba* like a whirlwind | *una tromba de agua* a heavy downpour (aguacero).

trombina *f* thrombin.

trombo *m* MED thrombus.

trombocito *m* thrombocyte.

trombón *m* MÚS trombone (instrumento) | trombonist (músico) ‖ — *trombón de pistones* or *de llaves* valve trombone ‖ *trombón de varas* slide trombone.

trombosis *f* MED thrombosis.

trompa *f* horn; *trompa de caza* hunting horn ‖ trunk (del elefante) ‖ snout (hocico) ‖ proboscis (de insecto) ‖ top, spinning top (trompo) ‖ humming top (trompo que zumba) ‖ ARQ squinch, pendentive ‖ trompe (de forja) ‖ scape (de la cebolla) ‖ FAM hooter, snout, conk (nariz) | thump, bash, bang (puñetazo) ‖ — FAM *coger una trompa* to get tight *o* plastered | *estar trompa* to be tight *o* sozzled *o* plastered ‖ ANAT *trompa de Eustaquio* Eustachian tube | *trompa de Falopio* Fallopian tube.
◆ *m* horn player.

trompada *f*; **trompazo** *m* FAM bump, bang, bash (choque) | thump, bash, punch (puñetazo) ‖ — FAM *andar a trompazo limpio, darse de trompazos* to be fighting | *darse un trompazo con una puerta* to bash *o* to bump into a door | *darse un trompazo con un coche contra* to crash into.

trompear *vi* to spin a top.
◆ *vt* *AMER* to punch, to thump.

trompeta *f* MÚS trumpet | bugle (clarín) ‖ *tocar la trompeta* to play the trumpet.
◆ *m* MÚS trumpet player, trumpeter | bugler (del clarín).

trompetada *f* FAM blunder (necedad).

trompetazo *m* trumpet blast (sonido) ‖ blow with a trumpet (golpe) ‖ FIG & FAM blunder (trompetada).

trompetear *vi* FAM to play the trumpet.

trompeteo *m* trumpet playing.

trompetería *f* trumpets *pl*, trumpet section (de una orquesta) ‖ trumpets *pl* (de un órgano).

trompetero *m* trumpet player, trumpeter (el que toca la trompeta) ‖ trumpet maker (el que hace trompetas) ‖ MIL bugler, trumpeter ‖ boarfish (pez).

trompetilla *f* ear trumpet (para oír mejor).

trompetista *m/f* trumpet player, trumpeter.

trompicar *vt* to trip, to trip up, to make stumble (hacer tropezar).
◆ *vi* to trip, to trip up, to stumble; *trompicó al subir la escalera* he tripped on the stairs.

trompicón *m* stumble, trip ‖ FIG & FAM punch (golpe) ‖ FIG *a trompicones* by fits and starts.

trompillar *vt/vi* to trip, to trip up (trompicar).

trompillón *m* ARQ keystone of a squinch *o* circular vault.

trompito *m* FAM chick-pea (garbanzo).

trompo *m* top, spinning top (juguete) ‖ FIG dolt, oaf (persona torpe) ‖ FIG & FAM *ponerse como un trompo* to stuff o.s. silly (de comer), to drink like a fish (de beber).

tronada *f* storm.

tronado, da *adj* FAM broken-down, old, worn-out (viejo) | broke, flat broke (sin dinero).

tronador, ra *adj* thundering (que truena) ‖ detonating.

tronar* *v impers* to thunder; *tronó toda la noche* it thundered all night.
◆ *vi* to thunder; *el cañón truena* the cannon thunders ‖ FIG to thunder, to boom; *tronó la voz del capitán* the captain's voice thundered | to thunder, to fulminate; *tronar contra el vicio* to thunder against vice ‖ — FIG & FAM *¡está que truena!* he is hopping mad *o* fuming | *por lo que pueda tronar* just in case.
◆ *vt* *AMER* to shoot (fusilar).

tronazón *f* *AMER* thunderstorm.

troncal *adj* trunk.

troncar *vt* to truncate.

tronco *m* trunk (de árbol, persona, animal) ‖ ARQ trunk, drum (de columna) ‖ team (dos caballerías) ‖ MAT frustum (de cono, pirámide, prisma) ‖ FIG stock, lineage (de una familia) | blockhead (zoquete) ‖ — FIG & FAM *dormir como un tronco* to sleep like a log ‖ MAT *tronco de cono* truncated cone.

troncocónico, ca *adj* shaped like a truncated cone.

troncha *f* *AMER* slice | cushy job (trabajo bien remunerado).

tronchar *vt* to bring down, to fell (árboles); *el viento ha tronchado varios árboles* the wind has brought down several trees ‖ FIG to wear out (rendir de cansancio) | to break (up) (romper) | to break off (quitar, arrancar) | to destroy (las esperanzas) | to cut short (la vida).
◆ *vpr* FIG & FAM *troncharse de risa* to split one's sides laughing.

troncho *m* stem, stalk.

tronera *f* loophole (de fortificación) ‖ porthole (de barco) ‖ small window (ventanilla) ‖ pocket (billar).
◆ *m/f* FIG & FAM harum-scarum (persona de poco juicio).

tronido *m* thunderclap ‖ FIG boom, roar (de cañón, etc.).
◆ *pl* thunder *sing*.

trono *m* throne; *el trono real* the royal throne ‖ crown; *heredar el trono* to inherit the crown; *lealtad al trono* loyalty to the crown ‖ REL tabernacle (del Santo Sacramento) | shrine (para un santo).
◆ *pl* REL thrones.

tronzador *m* two-handed saw (sierra).

tronzar *vt* to cut up (cortar) ‖ to smash, to shatter (quebrar) ‖ to pleat, to put small pleats in (poner pliegues) ‖ FIG to wear out, to exhaust (cansar).

tropa *f* troop, flock, crowd (reunión de gente) ‖ MIL troops *pl*; *la tropa necesita nuevos uniformes* the troops need new uniforms | rank and file, ranks *pl* (no oficiales) | assembly (toque) ‖ *AMER* herd, drove (de animales) ‖ — MIL *procede de la clase de tropa* he came up from the ranks ‖ FAM *ser de tropa* to be in the army.
◆ *pl* troops ‖ — MIL *tropas aerotransportadas* airborne troops | *tropas de asalto* storm troops | *tropas de línea* line troops.

tropear *vi* *AMER* to divide into herds (el ganado).

tropel *m* throng, mob, rush, crush (muchedumbre) ‖ hurry, rush (prisa) ‖ jumble, heap, hodgepodge (montón) ‖ *en tropel* in a mad rush.

tropelía *f* (p us) mad rush (prisa confusa) ‖ outrage (ultraje) ‖ *actos de tropelía* acts of violence.

tropero *m* *AMER* cowboy, cattle driver.

tropezadura *f* stumble.

tropezar* *vi* to stumble, to trip; *tropecé al entrar en el cuarto* I tripped coming into the room ‖ FIG to slip up, to go wrong (cometer un error) ‖ — *tropezar con* or *en* to stumble on, to trip over (una piedra, etc.) ‖ FIG *tropezar con* to run into, to bump into (chocar), to run into, to bump into, to come across (encontrar a una persona), to run into, to come up against (dificultad), to fall out with, to quarrel with (reñir) ‖ FIG & FAM *tropezar con un hueso* to hit a snag.
◆ *vpr* to run *o* to bump into one another (encontrarse).

tropezón *m* stumble, trip (traspiés) ‖ FIG slipup, slip (desacierto) ‖ *dar un tropezón* to stumble, to trip (al andar), to slip up, to go wrong (equivocarse).
◆ *pl* small pieces of food ‖ FIG *a tropezones* by fits and starts.

tropical *adj* tropical.

trópico, ca *adj* tropic, tropical ‖ FIG tropical (de tropo).
◆ *m* tropic ‖ — *Trópico de Cáncer* Tropic of Cancer ‖ *Trópico de Capricornio* Tropic of Capricorn.

tropiezo *m* stumble, trip ‖ FIG slip, slipup (desliz) | setback, mishap (revés) | obstacle, snag, stumbling block, hitch (impedimento) | argument, quarrel (discusión) ‖ *dar un tropiezo* to stumble, to trip.

tropismo *m* tropism.

tropo *m* trope, figure of speech.

tropología *f* tropology.

troposfera *f* troposphere.

troquel *m* TECN die || FIG *formados en el mismo troquel* cast in the same mould.

troqueladora *f* TECN stamping press.

troquelar *vt* to stamp out || to coin, to mint (acuñar moneda).

troquilo *m* trochilus.

trotacalles *m/f inv* FAM gadabout, saunterer (persona callejera).

trotaconventos *f inv* FAM procuress, go-between (alcahueta).

trotada *f* distance, way, walk (trayecto) || *dar una trotada* to walk a good distance.

trotamundos *m/f inv* globetrotter.

trotar *vi* to trot || FIG & FAM to run *o* to chase about, to be on the go || — *empezar a trotar* to break into a trot || *hacer trotar un caballo* to trot a horse.

trote *m* trot (paso); *a trote corto* at an easy *o* slow trot || FIG & FAM chasing about, running backwards and forwards (actividad) || — *al trote* trotting, at a trot (trotando), in a rush, quickly (de prisa) || FIG *de* or *para todo trote* for everyday wear *o* use (vestido).
◆ *pl* FIG & FAM affairs, business *sing* (enredo); *no te debes meter en esos trotes* you shouldn't get mixed up in such affairs || FIG & FAM *ya no estoy yo para estos trotes* I can't dash about like that any more, I can't keep up the pace any more.

trotón, ona *adj* trotting (caballo) || FIG everyday (de uso diario).
◆ *m* trotter (caballo).

trotskista *adj/s* Trotskyist, Trotskyite.

trova *f* verse (verso) || poem.

trovador, ra *adj* versifying.
◆ *m* poet || troubadour, minstrel (en la Edad Media).
◆ *f* poetess.

trovadoresco, ca *adj* troubadour; *una canción trovadoresca* a troubadour song.

trovar *vi* to write verse.

trovero *m* trouvère.

Troya *n pr* Troy || — FIG & FAM *allí* or *aquí fue Troya* then the trouble began, that was when it started (se armó un escándalo) | *arda Troya* come what may, whatever the consequences || *caballo de Troya* Trojan horse.

troyano, na *adj/s* Trojan.

trozo *m* piece; *un trozo de papel, de madera* a piece of paper, of wood || part (parte) || passage (obra literaria o musical) || MAR detail || — MIL *trozo de retaguardia* rear guard (de un ejército) | *trozo de vanguardia* or *de San Felipe* advance guard (de un ejército) || *trozos escogidos* selected passages, selections (de un escritor).

trucaje *m* CINEM trick photography.

trucar *vi* to make the first bet (hacer el primer envite) || to pocket the opponent's ball (en el billar).

trucidar *vt* to kill [cruelly] (matar).

truco *m* knack (habilidad, tranquillo) || trick (engaño); *truco de naipes* card trick || CINEM trick shot || pocketing of the opponent's ball (en billar) || card game (juego de naipes) || FAM *cogerle el truco a algo* to get the hang of sth., to get the knack | *cogerle el truco a alguien* to twig s.o., to cotton on to s.o. | *tener mucho truco* to be tricky.
◆ *pl* billiards *sing*, pool *sing* (billar) || FAM *andarse con trucos* to resort to trickery.

truculencia *f* horror, cruelty || FIG & FAM *déjate de truculencias* stop dramatizing.

truculento, ta *adj* horrifying, terrifying, ghastly.

trucha *f* trout (pez) || — FIG & FAM *no se cogen* or *pescan truchas a bragas enjutas* nothing ventured nothing gained || *trucha arco iris* rainbow trout || *trucha asalmonada* salmon trout || *trucha de mar* scorpion fish.

truchero, ra *adj* trout; *río truchero* trout river.
◆ *m* trout fisherman (pescador) || trout seller (vendedor).

truchimán, ana *m/f* dragoman, interpreter (trujamán) || FIG & FAM rascal, scoundrel.

truchuela *f* small trout (trucha pequeña) || smoked codfish (bacalao curado).

trudgeon *m* DEP trudgeon (natación).

trueno *m* thunder || thunderclap, clap of thunder (estampido) || boom, bang, report (de arma o cohete) || FAM young tearaway *o* madcap, reckless young fellow (atolondrado) || — *trueno gordo* finale (juegos artificiales) || *voz de trueno* booming *o* thundering voice.

trueque *m* barter, exchange || AMER change || — *a trueque de* in exchange for || *aun a trueque de perder la fama* even if it costs me my reputation.

trufa *f* truffle (hongo) || FIG lie, fib (mentira).

trufar *vt* CULIN to stuff with truffles.
◆ *vi* FIG to fib, to lie (decir mentiras).

truhán, ana *adj* roguish, crooked (desvergonzado) || FAM clownish, buffoonish (gracioso).
◆ *m* rogue, crook (granuja) || FAM buffoon, clown (gracioso).

truhanear *vi* to cheat, to swindle (engañar) || FAM to play the buffoon, to jest, to clown.

truhanería *f* roguery, crookedness || FAM buffoonery, clowning.

truhanesco, ca *adj* roguish, crooked (desvergonzado) || FAM clownish, buffoonish (gracioso).

truismo *m* truism.

trujamán, ana *m/f* dragoman, interpreter.
◆ *m* expert adviser.

trujamanear *vi* to interpret, to be an interpreter, to work as an interpreter.

trulla *f* racket, uproar, noise.

trullo *m* POP clink, slammer.

truncado, da *adj* MAT truncated; *cono truncado* truncated cone.

truncar *vt* to truncate || to mutilate (estatua) || to cut short, to cut down (un libro) || FIG to cut short (interrumpir); *carrera truncada por la muerte* career cut short by death.

truquillo *m* FAM knack.

trusa *f* AMER bathing trunks *pl.*

trust *m* COM trust.

tsé-tsé *f* tsetse [fly] (mosca del sueño).

tu, tus *adj pos* your; *tu sombrero* your hat; *tus zapatos* your shoes || REL Thy, Thine.

tú *pron pers* you (*sujeto*); *tú vas* you go || REL Thou || — *a tú por tú* disrespectfully || *hablar* or *llamar* or *tratar de tú* to address as «tú», to address familiarly; to be on friendly terms with (ser amigos) || FIG *llamar a Dios de tú* to be disrespectful || FAM *más eres tú* who are you to talk!, look who's talking! || *¡tú!* hey you!, hey! || *tú y yo* tea set for two (servicio de té), place mat for two (mantel).

tuareg *m* Tuareg.

tuba *f* tuba, Philippine liquor (licor) || MÚS tuba (instrumento).

tuberculina *f* MED tuberculin.

tubérculo *m* BOT tuber, tubercle || MED & ANAT tubercle.

tuberculosis *f* MED tuberculosis.

tuberculoso, sa *adj* tuberous (tuberoso) || MED tuberculous, tubercular.
◆ *m/f* MED person who suffers from tuberculosis, tubercular.

tubería *f* piping, pipes *pl*, tubing (conjunto de tubos) || plumbing (instalación) || pipe, tube (conducto) || pipe factory *o* store (fábrica, comercio de tubos).

tuberosa *f* BOT tuberose.

tuberosidad *f* tuberosity, swelling.

tuberoso, sa *adj* tuberous, tuberose; *raíz tuberosa* tuberous root.

tubo *m* pipe; *el tubo del agua* the water pipe || ANAT tube; *tubo capilar* capillary tube || tube (recipiente alargado); *tubo de pasta dentífrica* tooth-paste tube || chimney (de lámpara) || MÚS pipe (de órgano) || FÍS tube; *tubo de rayos catódicos* cathode-ray tube || — *falda tubo* tight skirt || *tubo acústico* speaking tube || *tubo de desagüe* drainpipe (para lluvia), wastepipe (del lavabo) || *tubo de drenaje* drainage tube || *tubo de ensayo* test tube || *tubo de escape* exhaust pipe || *tubo de órgano* organ pipe || *tubo de vacío* vacuum tube || ANAT *tubo digestivo* alimentary canal | *tubo intestinal* intestinal tract || *tubo lanzallamas* flamethrower || *tubo lanzacohetes* rocket launcher || *tubo lanzatorpedos* torpedo tube.

tubulado, da *adj* tubulate.

tubular *adj* tubular || *caldera tubular* fire-tube boiler.
◆ *m* bicycle tyre [*US* bicycle tire].

tucán *m* ZOOL toucan (ave).

tuco, ca *adj* AMER one-armed, one-handed (manco de brazo, de mano).
◆ *m* AMER firefly (insecto) | stump (muñón).

tucumano, na *adj* [of *o* from] Tucumán.
◆ *m/f* native *o* inhabitant of Tucumán (Argentina).

tucutucu *m* AMER tuco-tuco (topo).

tucuyo *m* AMER coarse cotton cloth.

tudesco, ca *adj/s* German || — FIG & FAM *beber como un tudesco* to drink like a fish | *comer como un tudesco* to eat like a horse.
◆ *m* German cloak (capote).

Tudor *n pr* Tudor.

tuera *f* BOT colocynth, bitter apple || FIG *más amargo que la tuera* as bitter as gall.

tuerca *f* nut || *tuerca de aletas* or *de orejas* or *de mariposa* wing nut.

tuerto, ta *adj* one-eyed, blind in one eye; *quedarse tuerto* to become blind in one eye || twisted, bent (torcido) || *a tuertas o a derechas* rightly or wrongly (con razón o sin ella), by hook or by crook (por las buenas o por las malas).
◆ *m/f* one-eyed person.
◆ *m* injustice, wrong (ofensa).
◆ *m pl* MED afterpains (entuertos).

tueste *m* toasting (tostadura).

tuétano *m* ANAT marrow (médula) || FIG essence, heart, core, substance (sustancia) || — FIG & FAM *calado hasta los tuétanos* drenched to the bone | *enamorado hasta los tuétanos* head over heels in love | *hasta los tuétanos* through and through | *sacar los tuétanos a uno* to wring s.o.'s neck.

tufarada *f* strong smell (olor) || waft (racha de olor) || gust (racha de aire).

tufo *m* fume (emanación) || foul odour *o* smell, stink; *tufo de una alcantarilla* foul odour of a sewer || fug (en un cuarto lleno de gente) || curl (mechón de pelo) || tufa (toba).
◆ *pl* FIG airs; *tener tufos* to put on airs.

tugurio *m* hovel, slum, shack (casucha); *vivir en un tugurio* to live in a shack || small room (habitación pequeña) || shepherd's hut (choza).

tuición *f* JUR custody, protection.

tuitivo, va *adj* JUR protective, defensive.

tul *m* tulle (tela).

tulio *m* QUÍM thulium.

tulipa *f* (tulip-shaped) lampshade.

tulipán *m* BOT tulip.

tulipanero; tulipero *m* tulip tree.

tullecer *vt* to cripple, to maim (incapacitar) || to paralyse (paralizar).
◆ *vi* to be crippled *o* maimed *o* paralysed (lisiarse).

tullidez *f* paralysis || disability, disablement.

tullido, da *adj* crippled, disabled, maimed || paralysed || FIG exhausted, worn-out (cansado).
◆ *m/f* cripple, disabled person.

tullimiento *m* paralysis || disability, disablement.

tullir* *vt* to cripple, to maim (incapacitar) || to paralyse (paralizar) || FIG to exhaust, to wear out (cansar mucho).
◆ *vpr* to be crippled *o* paralysed.

tumba *f* tomb, grave (sepultura) || jolt, lurch (sacudida) || somersault (voltereta) || arched top (cubierta arqueada) || AMER tree clearing || — FIG *abrir su tumba* to dig one's own grave | *ser como una tumba* to be as silent as the grave.

tumbaga *f* tombac, tomback (aleación) || tombac ring (sortija de tumbaga) || ring (sortija).

tumbal *adj* tomb || *piedra tombal* tombstone.

tumbar *vt* to knock down *o* over (derribar); *lo tumbó de un golpe* he knocked him down with one blow || to knock *o* to bend over (inclinar mucho); *el viento ha tumbado el poste* the wind has knocked the post over || FIG & FAM to fail; *me tumbaron en latín* they failed me in Latin | to knock out (un olor fuerte, etc.) | to overwhelm, to stun; *la visión lo dejó tumbado* the sight overwhelmed him || MAR to keel || AMER to fell, to clear (los árboles) || POP to lay (a una mujer) || — *estar tumbado* to lie, to be lying down || FIG & FAM *tumbar de espaldas* to bowl over; *la noticia me tumbó de espaldas* the news bowled me over.
◆ *vi* to tumble, to fall over (desplomarse) || MAR to keel || FIG & FAM *que tumba* overwhelming; *hay un olor a gasolina que tumba* there is a overwhelming smell of petrol.
◆ *vpr* to lie down; *tumbarse en la cama* to lie down on the bed || to sprawl, to lounge (repantigarse); *tumbarse en una butaca* to lounge in an armchair || FIG & FAM to let up, to take it easy (dejar de hacer esfuerzos).

tumbo *m* jolt, bump, jerk (sacudida) || FIG difficulty || *dar tumbos* to bump, to lurch, to jerk, to jolt; *el coche daba tumbos por el camino* the car bumped along the road.

tumbón, ona *adj* lazy, idle (perezoso) || sly (socarrón).

tumbona *f* sofa, lounge (diván) || deckchair (silla de lona).

tumefacción *f* MED tumefaction, swelling.

tumefacer* *vt* MED to tumefy, to cause to swell.

tumefacto, ta *adj* MED swollen.

tumescencia *f* MED tumescence, swelling.

tumescente *adj* MED tumescent.

túmido, da *adj* tumid || ARQ swollen.

tumor *m* tumour [US tumor]; *tumores malignos* malignant tumours.

tumulario, ria *adj* tumular, sepulchral; *inscripción tumularia* sepulchral inscription.

túmulo *m* tumulus, barrow, burial mound (montecillo artificial) || catafalque (catafalco) || tomb (sepultura).

tumulto *m* tumult, turmoil, commotion || FIG uproar.

tumultuoso, sa *adj* tumultuous.

tuna *f* BOT tuna, prickly pear (fruta y árbol) || group of student minstrels (estudiantina) || student minstrel (estudiante) || *correr la tuna* to lead an idle and vagrant life.

tunal *m* tuna, prickly pear (nopal) || tuna grove (sitio).

tunante *adj* crooked, roguish, rascally (granuja).
◆ *m/f* rogue, crook, rascal.

tunantear *vi* to be crooked *o* roguish.

tunantería *f* crookedness, roguishness (cualidad) || mean trick (acción).

tunantuelo, la *m/f* little rascal.

tunda *f* shearing || FAM beating, licking, thrashing; *dar una tunda a uno* to give s.o. a thrashing.

tundición; tundido *m* cloth shearing.

tundidor, ra *adj* cloth shearing.
◆ *m/f* cloth shearer.
◆ *f* cloth shearing machine.

tundidura *f* cloth shearing.

tundir *vt* to shear (cortar) || FAM to give a licking *o* a beating *o* a thrashing.

tundra *f* tundra.

tunear *vi* to lead a vagrant life.

tunecí; tunecino, na *adj/s* Tunisian.

túnel *m* tunnel || *túnel aerodinámico* wind tunnel || AUT *túnel de lavado* car wash.

tunería *f* roguishness, rascality.

Túnez *n pr* GEOGR Tunis (ciudad) | Tunisia (país).

tungstato *m* QUÍM tungstate.

tungsteno *m* QUÍM tungsten, wolfram.

túnica *f* tunic || ANAT tunic, tunica.

tunicado, da *adj/sm* tunicate.

tunicela *f* REL tunicle.

tuno, na *adj* roguish, wicked.
◆ *m/f* rogue, villain, rascal.
◆ *m* student minstrel (de la tuna).

tuntún (al); tuntún (al buen) *adv* FAM haphazardly, any old how.

tupaya *f* ZOOL tupaia.

tupé *m* toupee || FIG & FAM cheek, nerve (descaro).

tupí *adj* Tupian.
◆ *m/f* Tupi.
◆ *m* Tupi (idioma).

tupido, da *adj* thick; *un paño tupido* a thick cloth || dense, thick; *niebla tupida* dense fog || FIG dense, dim, stupid (torpe).

tupinambo *m* BOT Jerusalem artichoke.

tupir *vt* to pack tightly (apretar).
◆ *vi* to thicken (hierba).
◆ *vpr* FIG & FAM to stuff o.s. (comer mucho).

turba *f* peat, turf (combustible) || mob, crowd (muchedumbre).

turbación *f* confusion || disorder (desorden) || upset, disturbance (trastorno).

turbado, da *adj* upset, disturbed (preocupado, etc.) || confused (confuso).

turbador, ra *adj* disturbing, upsetting || confusing.
◆ *m/f* disturber.

turbamulta *f* FAM mob.

turbante *m* turban.

turbar *vt* to stir up (enturbiar) || FIG to disturb; *turbar la paz* to disturb the peace | to upset, to disturb, to worry; *la noticia le turbó visiblemente* the news visibly upset him | to confuse (confundir) | to embarrass (dejar perplejo).
◆ *vpr* to be stirred up *o* disturbed (enturbiarse) || FIG to be upset *o* worried *o* disturbed; *al oír la pregunta se turbó visiblemente* he was visibly upset by the question | to get confused *o* embarrassed.

turbelarios *m pl* ZOOL turbellaria.

turbera *f* peat bog.

túrbido, da *adj* turbid, cloudy (falto de transparencia) || turbid, muddy (sucio).

turbiedad *f* cloudiness, turbidity, turbidness (de líquidos) || opacity (opacidad) || FIG confusion.

turbina *f* turbine; *turbina hidráulica* hydraulic *o* water turbine || *turbina de vapor* steam turbine.

turbinto *m* pepper shrub.

turbio, bia *adj* turbid, cloudy, muddy; *líquido turbio* cloudy liquid || FIG shady, suspicious, suspect, fishy; *un negocio turbio* a shady business | troubled, turbulent (agitado); *período turbio* troubled period | blurred, dim, cloudy, unclear; *vista turbia* blurred vision *o* view | confused (confuso) | obscure, unclear (manera de hablar).
◆ *m pl* dregs, sediment *sing* (sedimentos).

turbión *f* squall, heavy shower || FIG shower, avalanche, torrent (gran cantidad).

turboalternador *m* ELECTR turboalternator.

turbobomba *m* TECN turbopump.

turbocompresor *m* TECN turbocompressor.

turbodinamo *m* ELECTR turbodynamo.

turbogenerador *m* ELECTR turbogenerator.

turbohélice *m* TECN turboprop.

turbomotor *m* TECN turbomotor.

turbonada *f* squall, downpour (aguacero) || AMER strong wind (vendaval).

turbopropulsor *m* TECN turboprop.

turborreactor *m* TECN turbojet.

turbosoplante *f* TECN turboblower.

turboventilador *m* TECN turboventilator.

turbulencia *f* turbulence; *la turbulencia del agua* the turbulence of the water || FIG turbulence, disorder, disturbance, commotion (disturbio) | unruliness (rebeldía) || turbulence (atmosférica).

turbulento, ta *adj* turbulent, troubled (agitado); *aguas turbulentas* turbulent waters || FIG boisterous, unruly, disorderly (bullicioso); *alumnos turbulentos* boisterous pupils | troubled, turbulent; *en esta época turbulenta* in these troubled times.

turco, ca *adj* Turkish || — *baño turco* Turkish bath || *cama turca* divan.
◆ *m/f* Turk.
◆ *m* Turkish (idioma) || — *cabeza de turco* scapegoat || *el Gran turco* the Grand Turk || FIG & FAM *más celoso que un turco* consumed with jealousy.
◆ *f* FIG & FAM booze-up [US drunk] || FIG & FAM *coger una turca* to get canned *o* plastered.

turcomano, na *adj/s* Turcoman, Turkoman (gente o idioma).

turf *f* DEP racecourse (pista) | horse racing, turf (deporte).

turfista *m* turfman.

turgencia *f* turgidity, turgescence.

turgente *adj* turgid.

túrgido, da *adj* turgid.

turibulario *m* thurifer.

turiferario *m* thurifer.

turificar *vt* to incense, to cense.

turismo *m* tourism; *el turismo todavía no ha afectado la isla* the tourism has not yet affected the island || tourism, the tourist trade *o* industry; *el turismo es la primera industria* tourism is the major industry; *desarrollar el turismo en un país* to develop a country's tourist industry || private car (coche) || — *el turismo ha estropeado la costa* the tourist invasion has ruined the coast || *hacer turismo* to go touring (en un país), to go sightseeing (en una ciudad) || *turismo de masas* mass tourism.

turista *m/f* tourist.

turístico, ca *adj* tourist; *una atracción turística* a tourist attraction.

Turkmenistán *npr m* GEOGR Turkmenistan, Turkomen.

turma *f* truffle (hongo) || ANAT testicle (testículo).

turmalina *f* MIN tourmaline.

túrmix *f* mixer.

turnar, turnarse *vi/vpr* to take turns; *turnarse para hacer algo* to take turns to do sth.

turno *m* shift; *turno de día* day shift || shift (cuadrilla) || turn, go; *es tu turno* it is your turn || — *¿a quién le toca el turno?* whose turn *o* whose go is it?, who is next? || *estar de turno* to be on duty || *lavamos los platos por turno* we take turns *o* we take it in turn to do the washing up || *trabajar por turnos* to work in shifts, to work shifts || *turno de noche* night shift.

turolense *adj* [of *o* from] Teruel.
◆ *m/f* native *o* inhabitant of Teruel.

turón *m* polecat (animal).

turquesa *f* turquoise (piedra preciosa) || mould [*US* mold] (molde) || *azul turquesa* turquoise blue, turquoise.

turquesco, ca *adj* Turkish.

Turquestán *npr m* GEOGR Turkestan.

turquí; turquino *adj m* *azul turquí* indigo.

Turquía *npr f* GEOGR Turkey.

turrar *vt* to toast, to roast (tostar).

turrón *m* nougat (dulce) || FIG & FAM cushy number (cargo).
— OBSERV The *turrón* is eaten especially at Christmas.

turronería *f* nougat shop, confectioner's.

turronero, ra *m/f* nougat maker *o* seller, confectioner.

turulato, ta *adj* FAM flabbergasted, dumbfounded (pasmado) | dazed (aturdido).

turumba *f* AMER calabash, gourd (vasija).

tururú *m* three of a kind, brelan (en las cartas) || — FAM *está tururú* he is touched in the head | *¡tururú!* that's what you think!

tus *m* *sin decir tus ni mus* without a word.
◆ *interj* here, boy! (a un perro).

tusa *f* AMER corncob, cob of maize (carozo) | husk of maize [*US* corn husk] | cigar rolled in a corn husk (cigarro) | mane (del caballo) | pockmark (hoyo de viruela) | streetwalker, tart (prostituta).

tusar *vt* AMER to shear.

tusilago *f* BOT coltsfoot.

tuso, sa *adj* AMER bobtail, tailless, docked (rabón) | pockmarked (por la viruela).
◆ *interj* FAM here, boy! (para llamar al perro).

tusona *f* FAM tart.

tusor *m* tussore [*US* tussah] (tela).

tute *m* card game || FAM beating, licking (paliza) || FIG & FAM *darse un tute* to work o.s. into the ground (trabajando), to walk *o* to run o.s. into the ground (andando, corriendo), to stuff o.s. (comiendo).

tuteamiento *m* use of the familiar «tú» form of address.

tutear *vt* to address as «tú».
◆ *vpr* to address one another using the familiar «tú» form.

tutela *f* JUR guardianship (de personas) | trusteeship (de territorios) || FIG protection (protección) | guidance (dirección) || — *bajo tutela* in ward (persona) || *territorio bajo tutela* territory in trusteeship, trust territory.

tutelar *adj* tutelary; *acción tutelar* tutelary action || protecting; *divinidad tutelar* protecting divinity || *ángel tutelar* guardian angel.

tuteo *m* use of the familiar «tú» form of address.

tutilimundi *m* cosmorama.

tutiplén (a) *adv* FAM galore; *repartían caramelos a tutiplén* they were giving out sweets galore | a lot (mucho) || — FAM *comer a tutiplén* to stuff o.s. | *llovía a tutiplén* it was raining buckets.

tutor, ra *m/f* JUR guardian || guardian, protector (protector).
◆ *m* AGR stake, prop (rodrigón).

tutoría *f* guardianship.

tutorial *m* INFORM tutorial.

tutú *m* South American bird of prey || tutu (de bailarina).

tutuma *f* AMER FAM block (cabeza).

tuyo, ya *adj pos* of yours, one of your; *un hermano tuyo* a brother of yours, one of your brothers || — *lo tuyo* what is yours, what belongs to you (lo que te pertenece), your business (lo que te concierne) || *siempre tuyo* Yours truly (en una carta).
◆ *pron pos* yours, your own; *tú tienes el tuyo en la mano* you have yours *o* your own in your hand || REL Thine || — FIG & FAM *hiciste de las tuyas* you got up to your old tricks || *los tuyos* your family *o* friends *o* people *o* men *o* supporters *o* side; *los tuyos están aquí* your family is here.
— OBSERV The familiar forms *tuyo, tuya* are generally used to address family members or friends.

tuyu *m* AMER nandu, rhea (ñandú).

tuyuyú *m* AMER type of stork (ave).

TVE *abrev de Televisión Española* Spanish broadcasting company.

tweed *m* tweed (tejido).

tyndalización *f* Tyndall effect.

U

u *f* u; *una u mayúscula* a capital u || *la U consonante* the V.

— OBSERV The Spanish *u* is a vowel or semiconsonant and is pronounced rather like the English *oo*. In the groups *gue, gui* and *que, qui* the *u* is silent; but when it bears a diaeresis, or occurs in the group *gua, guo,* it is pronounced like the English *oo*: *vergüenza, guasa, antiguo.*

u *conj* or.

— OBSERV U is used instead of *o* before words beginning with *o* or *ho*: *diez u once* ten or eleven; *belga u holandés* Belgian or Dutch.

Úbeda *n pr* GEOGR Úbeda [Andalusia] || FIG & FAM *irse por los cerros de Úbeda* to wander from the subject, to go off at a tangent (salirse del tema).

ubérrimo, ma *adj* very fertile; *tierra ubérrima* very fertile land || abundant, luxuriant; *vegetación ubérrima* luxuriant vegetation.

ubicación *f* position, situation, location.

ubicar *vi* to be, to be situated *o* located *o* placed.

◆ *vt* AMER to put, to place | to nominate (a un candidato) | to park (un coche).

◆ *vpr* to be, to be situated *o* located *o* placed || to place o.s.

ubicuidad *f* ubiquity || *no tengo el don de la ubicuidad* I can't be everywhere at once.

ubicuo, cua *adj* ubiquitous.

ubre *f* udder.

ucase; ukase *m* ukase (edicto del zar) || FIG dictation (decisión autoritaria).

UCD *abrev de Unión de Centro Democrático* Spanish political party of the centre.

Ucrania *npr f* GEOGR Ukraine; *Kiev es la capital de Ucrania* Kiev is the capital of the Ukraine.

ucraniano, na *adj/s* Ukrainian.

ucranio, nia *adj/s* Ukrainian.

Ud. *pron pers (abreviatura de «usted»),* ⟶ **usted.**

Uds. *pron pers (abreviatura de «ustedes»),* ⟶ **usted.**

ued *m* wadi.

UEFA *abrev de Unión de Asociaciones Europeas de Fútbol* UEFA, Union of European Football Associations.

¡uf! *interj* phew! (alivio, cansancio) || ugh! (repugnancia).

ufanarse *vpr* to be proud; *ufanarse con* or *de sus riquezas* to be proud of one's riches || to boast (*de* of), to pride o.s. (*de* on) (jactarse).

ufano, na *adj* proud.

Uganda *n pr* GEOGR Uganda.

UGT *abrev de Unión General de los Trabajadores* Spanish trade union [with Socialist affiliations].

ujier *m* usher.

UIT *abrev de Unión Internacional de Telecomunicaciones* ITU, International Telecommunication Union.

ukase *m* ⟶ **ucase.**

ukelele; ukulele *m* MÚS ukelele, ukulele.

Ulan-Bator *n pr* GEOGR Ulan Bator.

ulano *m* MIL uhlan.

úlcera *f* MED ulcer.

ulceración *f* ulceration.

ulcerado, da *adj* ulcerated.

ulcerar, ulcerarse *vt/vpr* to ulcerate.

ulema *m* ulema, ulama (sabio musulmán).

Ulises *npr m* MIT Ulysses.

ulmáceas *f pl* BOT ulmaceae.

ulterior *adj* ulterior, farther, further (más allá) || subsequent, later (que ocurre después) || following (siguiente).

ulteriormente *adv* subsequently, later, later on.

ultimación *f* conclusion, completion.

ultimador, ra *m/f* AMER killer (asesino).

últimamente *adv* ultimately, finally (por último) || lately (recientemente).

ultimar *vt* to conclude, to complete, to finalize, to finish, to end; *ultimar un trato* to conclude a deal || to finalize; *ultimar los detalles* to finalize the details || AMER to kill (matar).

ultimátum *m* ultimatum; *dirigir un ultimátum* to give an ultimatum.

último, ma *adj* last, final; *diciembre es el último mes del año* December is the last month of the year; *la última palabra* the last word || latter (de dos) || latest (más reciente); *última moda* latest fashion || furthest, farthest, utmost (más lejano) || back, last (de atrás) || top, last (de arriba); *en el último piso* on the top floor || bottom, last (de abajo) || final (definitivo); *su última decisión* his final decision || lowest (precio).

◆ *m/f* last one, last || latter (de dos) || — *a la última* up to date || *a últimos de mes* at *o* towards the end of the month || *como* or *en último recurso* or *en última instancia* as a last resort || *dar el último toque* or *la última mano* to put the finishing touches to, to finish off || FIG *el último grito, la última palabra* the latest thing *o* craze || *en último lugar* as a last resort (si no hay otro remedio), finally (para concluir) || FIG *¡es lo último!* that's the best yet!, that really is the limit! | *¡es lo último que me faltaba por oír!* now I've heard everything!, that's the best yet! || FAM *estar en las últimas* to be at death's door, to be on the deathbed (moribundo), to be down to one's last penny (sin dinero) || *estos últimos meses* these *o* the last few months || FAM *¡has hecho las diez de últimas!* you've had it! || *llegar el último* to arrive last || *por último* finally || *quedarse con la última palabra* to have the last word || *ser el último en llegar* to be the last one *o* to be the last *o* to be last to arrive.

ultra *adj/s* ultra (extremista).

ultracentrifugadora *f* ultracentrifuge.

ultraconservador, ra *adj* ultraconservative (en política).

ultracorto, ta *adj* ultrashort.

ultraísmo *m* «ultraism».

— OBSERV *Ultraísmo* (1919-1923) was a literary movement created by Spanish and Spanish-American poets in search of pure poetry. Its principal representatives were Guillermo de Torre, Jorge Luis Borges, Eugenio Montes and Gerardo Diego.

ultrajador, ra *adj* outrageous || insulting (insultante) || offensive (ofensivo).

ultrajante *adj* outrageous || offensive.

ultrajar *vt* to outrage, to do outrage; *ultrajarle a alguien* to outrage s.o., to do s.o. an outrage || to insult (insultar) || to offend (ofender).

ultraje *m* outrage || outrage, insult (insulto) || offence (delito) || *ultraje a las buenas costumbres* indecent behaviour, moral offence.

ultramar *m* overseas countries *pl* || — *azul de ultramar* ultramarine || *ir a ultramar* to go abroad *o* overseas || *provincias de ultramar* overseas provinces.

ultramarino, na *adj* overseas || *azul ultramarino* ultramarine.

◆ *m pl* foreign products *o* foodstuffs (géneros de ultramar) || groceries, foodstuffs (comestibles) || *ultramarinos, tienda de ultramarinos* grocer's, grocer's shop, grocery [US grocery store].

ultramicroscopio *m* ultramicroscope.

ultramoderno, na *adj* ultramodern.

ultramontanismo *m* ultramontanism.

ultramontano, na *adj/s* ultramontane.

ultramundano, na *adj* ultramundane.

ultranza (a) *loc* to the death (a muerte) || decisively (con decisión) || extreme, out-and-out, uncompromising; *un pacifista a ultranza* an extreme pacifist || at any price, whatever the cost (cueste lo que cueste).

ultrapasar *vt* to go beyond, to surpass.

ultrarrápido, da *adj* extra-fast.

ultrarrojo, ja *adj/sm* FÍS ultrared, infrared.

ultrasensible *adj* hypersensitive.

ultrasónico, ca *adj* ultrasonic.

ultrasonido *m* FÍS ultrasound, supersound.

ultrasonoterapia *f* MED ultrasound therapy.

ultratumba *f* beyond the grave; *una voz de ultratumba* a voice from beyond the grave.

ultraviolado, da; ultravioleta *adj/sm* ultraviolet.

ultravirus *m inv* BIOL ultravirus.

úlula *f* tawny owl (ave).

ululación *f* howl, howling (del viento, de un animal) || hoot, hooting (del búho) || ululation (p us).

ulular *vi* to howl (viento, animal) || to hoot (búho).

ululato *m* howl, howling (del viento, de un animal) || hoot, hooting (del búho).

ulva *f* BOT ulva (alga).

ulluco *m* AMER ullucu, ulluco (planta).

umbelífero, ra *adj* BOT umbelliferous.

◆ *f* BOT umbellifer.

◆ *pl* BOT umbelliferae.

umbeliforme *adj* BOT umbelliform.

umbilical *adj* ANAT umbilical; *cordón umbilical* umbilical cord.

umbral *m* threshold; *en el umbral* on the threshold || FIG threshold; *el umbral de la vida* the threshold of life; *umbral de audibilidad* just within hearing || — FIG *en los umbrales de la muerte* at death's door | *estar en los umbrales de una nueva era* to be on the threshold of a new era || *pisar los umbrales* to cross the threshold.

umbrela *f* ZOOL umbrella (de medusa).

Umbría *npr f* GEOGR Umbria.

umbrío, a *adj* shady (umbroso).

umbroso, sa *adj* shady.

un *art indef* a; *un hombre* a man || a, one; *un amigo mío* one of my friends, a friend of mine.
◆ *adj num* one; *un águila* one eagle.
— OBSERV La *a* inglesa se transforma en *an* delante de una vocal *(an egg)*, y de una *h* no aspirada *(an hour)*.
— OBSERV *Un* is the apocopated form of *uno* used before a masculine noun, and of *una* before a feminine noun beginning with an accented *a* or *ha* (véase uno).

una *art indef/adj num* ⟶ **uno.**

unánime *adj* unanimous.

unanimidad *f* unanimity || *aprobar por unanimidad* to approve unanimously.

unción *f* unction.

uncir *vt* to yoke; *uncir los bueyes a un carro* to yoke the oxen to a cart.

undecágono *m* MAT undecagon.

undécimo, ma *adj/s* eleventh || *en undécimo lugar* eleventhly, in eleventh place.

undulación *f* undulation || wave (onda).

undulante *adj* undulant, undulating.

undular *vi* to undulate.

undulatorio, ria *adj* undulatory.

Unesco *abrev de Organización de las Naciones Unidas para la Educación, la Ciencia y la Cultura* UNESCO, United Nations Educational, Scientific and Cultural Organization.

ungido *adj m* anointed (sacerdote, etc.).

ungimiento *m* unction.

ungir *vt* to anoint.

ungüento *m* ointment, unguent.

unguiculado, da *adj/sm* ZOOL unguiculate.

unguis *m* unguis (hueso de la órbita).

ungulado, da *adj/sm* ZOOL ungulate.

ungular *adj* ungular, nail, of the nail (de la uña).

únicamente *adv* only, solely.

unicameral *adj* unicameral.

Unicef *abrev de Fondo Internacional de las Naciones Unidas para la Infancia* UNICEF, United Nations International Children's Emergency Fund.

unicelular *adj* unicellular, single-cell.

unicidad *f* unicity, uniqueness.

único, ca *adj* only, sole; *el único culpable* the only guilty person; *la única persona que ha sido simpática conmigo* the only person who was nice to me || FIG unique; *un acontecimiento único en la historia* an event unique in history; *único en su género* unique in *o* of its kind || — *hijo único* only child || *sistema de partido único* one party *o* single-party system.
◆ *m/f* only one; *es el único que me queda* it is the only one I have left || — *lo único* the only thing; *lo único que puedo hacer* the only thing I can do || *¡lo único que faltaba!* that's all I (he, she, etc.) needed!

unicolor *adj* of one colour, all one colour.

unicornio *m* unicorn (animal fabuloso) || *unicornio marino* narwhal, narwal.

unidad *f* unit; *unidad métrica, monetaria* metric, monetary unit || unity (literaria); *unidad de acción, de lugar, de tiempo* unity of action, of place, of time || harmony (armonía) || branch (de tren, de metro) || unity; *la unidad política* political unity || MAT & MIL unit; *columna de unidades* units column; *unidad de combate* combat unit || COM *coste por unidad* unit cost || INFORM *unidad de control* control unit | *unidad de disco* disk unit | *unidad de salida* output unit *o* device || *unidad de vigilancia intensive* intensive care unit (en el hospital) || RAD *unidad móvil* outside broadcast unit.

unidireccional *adj* RAD unidirectional.

unido, da *adj* united; *familia muy unida* very united family || *unidos venceremos* united we stand.

unifamiliar *adj* semi-detached (vivienda).

unificación *f* unification.

unificador, ra *adj* unifying.
◆ *m/f* unifier.

unificar *vt* to unify.

uniformación *f* uniformizing || standardization.

uniformar *vt* to make wear a uniform, to give a uniform to; *uniformar a los empleados de la casa* to make the employees of the firm wear a uniform || to uniformize, to make uniform (uniformizar) || to standardize (normalizar).
◆ *vpr* to become uniform.

uniforme *adj* uniform || plain; *color uniforme* plain colour || even, level (superficie) || steady, uniform (velocidad) || *hacer uniforme* to uniformize, to make uniform.

uniforme *m* uniform; *el uso del uniforme* the wearing of the uniform || *uniforme de gala* full-dress uniform, dress uniform, ceremonial dress, full regimentals.

uniformidad *f* uniformity || smoothness, evenness (de una superficie).

uniformizar *vt* to uniformize, to make uniform || to standardize (normalizar).

unigénito, ta *adj* only; *hijo unigénito* only child || REL only begotten.
◆ *m* the Son of God (Hijo de Dios).

unilateral *adj* unilateral; *contratos unilaterales* unilateral contracts || BOT unilateral.

unilateralmente *adv* unilaterally.

unilocular *adj* BOT unilocular.

uninominal *adj* uninominal.

unión *f* union; *la unión del alma y del cuerpo* the union of body and soul; *la unión de Castilla y León* the union of Castile and León || union; *unión de cooperativas* cooperative union; *unión aduanera* customs union || meeting (up), joining; *la unión de dos ejércitos* the meeting up of two armies || union, wedding (casamiento) || union, harmony (armonía) || MED closing; *la unión de los labios de una herida* the closing of the lips of a wound || TECN coupling, joining (acción) | coupler (manguito) | coupler (electricidad) | joint (junta) || — *en unión de* in the company of (en compañía de), together with (con la participación de) || *la unión hace la fuerza* united we stand || *la Unión Soviética* the Soviet Union || *manguito de unión* coupler.

unionismo *m* unionism.
— OBSERV *Trade unionism* is translated by *sindicalismo.*

unionista *adj/s* unionist.

uníparo, ra *adj* uniparous.

unipersonal *adj* GRAM unipersonal || individual, for one, single.

unipolar *adj* unipolar.

unir *vt* to unite, to join (together); *unir dos familias por un matrimonio* to unite two families by a marriage; *unir un país con otro* to join one country with another || to join (together), to combine; *unir dos campos para hacer uno solo* to join together two fields to make one || to link (up); *una carretera que une Madrid con Alcalá* a road which links Madrid with Alcalá || FIG to combine; *unir la bondad con la firmeza* to combine goodness with firmness | to attach; *estamos muy unidos uno con otro* we are very attached to one another | to bind; *estar unidos por el mismo interés* to be bound by the same interest | to unite; *la desdicha une a los que sufren* unhappiness unites those who suffer || COM to merge (compañías) | to pool (los recursos) || MED to close (los labios de una herida) || TECN to join, to attach (juntar) || to mix (mezclar líquidos, etc.).
◆ *vpr* to unite, to join together (reunirse) || to join, to meet (encontrarse) || to marry (casarse) || FIG to be combined, to combine (aliarse) | to unite, to be united | to be attached (afecto) | to associate o.s. with, to second; *me uno a las palabras anteriormente pronunciadas* I second what has already been said || COM to merge, to amalgamate, to combine (compañías).

unisex *adj* unisex.

unisexo *adj inv* unisex.

unisexual *adj* unisexual.

unisón *m* MÚS unison.

unisonancia *f* unison.

unísono, na *adj* unisonous, in harmony.
◆ *m* unison || FIG unison, harmony; *al unísono* in unison.

unitario, ria *adj* unitary || unit; *precio unitario* unit price || REL Unitarian.
◆ *m/f* REL Unitarian.

unitarismo *m* REL Unitarianism.

universal *adj* universal || FIG world, of the world; *historia universal* world history | worldwide (en todo el mundo) || *de fama universal* world-famous.
◆ *m* FIL *los universales* the universals.

universalidad *f* universality.

universalización *f* universalization.

universalizar *vt* to universalize.

universalmente *adv* universally || all over the world (en el mundo entero).

universidad *f* university; *la Universidad de Madrid* the University of Madrid || universality (universalidad) || *universidad a distancia* university course by correspondence [Open University] || *Universidad laboral* college of advanced technology.

universitario, ria *adj* university, of *o* pertaining to a university; *reforma universitaria* university reform.
◆ *m/f* (university) lecturer (profesor) || (university) student (estudiante).

universo *m* universe.

unívoco, ca *adj* FIL univocal.

uno, na *art indef* a, an⟶ (*véase* OBSERV en UN).
◆ *adj* one || — *a un tiempo* at the same time || *de una vez* in one go || *el día uno de mayo* the first of May || *el tomo uno* volume one, the first volume || *es todo uno, todo es uno* it is one and the same, it is all the same || *no ser más que uno* to be the same thing, to be one and the same, to be all the same || *uno que otro* the occasional, the odd, a few; *se veía uno que otro árbol* the occasional *o* the odd tree *o* a few trees could be seen.
◆ *pl* some; *unos libros* some books; *unos años después* some years later; *unas tijeras*

some scissors || about, some (aproximadamente); *unos cien kilómetros* some hundred kilometres.
◆ *pron* one; *él tiene dos hermanos y yo uno* he has two brothers and I have one; *una de mis hermanas* one of my sisters || one, you; *uno tiene sus costumbres* one has one's habits; *aquí uno no tiene derecho a protestar* here you have no right to protest; *el ruido acaba por aturdirle a uno* in the end the noise stuns one || someone, somebody (alguien); *preguntar a uno* to ask someone; *vi a uno que se te parecía mucho* I saw someone who looked just like you || — *cada uno a lo suyo* it is best to mind one's own business || *cada uno, cada una* each one, every one || MIL *de uno en fondo* in single *o* Indian file || *de uno en uno* one by one || *los unos... los otros* some... the others || *ni uno ni otro* neither (one), neither the one nor the other, neither of them || *no me gusta ni uno ni otro* I don't like either of them || *¿quiere dos? —no, quiero uno solo* do you want two? —no, I just want *o* I only want one || *una de dos* one of the two || *una y no más* once is enough || *uno a otro, unos a otros* (to, at, etc.) each other, one another (reciprocidad); *mirarse uno a otro* to look one at one another || *uno a uno, uno por uno* one by one || *uno con otro* taking one thing with another, all things considered, all in all || *uno... el otro* one... the other || *uno más, uno de tantos* just another face in the crowd, one of many || *uno mismo* oneself, yourself; *esto puede hacerlo uno mismo* one can do this oneself, you can do this yourself || *uno por uno* one by one || *unos cuantos* a few, some || *unos u otros* somebody; *tienen que quedarse unos u otros* somebody has to stay || *unos y otros* all; *empezaron a hablar unos y otros* they all started to speak || *uno tras otro* one after *o* behind the other (en fila), one after the other (todos) || *uno u otro* one or the other, either || *uno y otro* both; *uno y otro son muy simpáticos* they are both very nice.
◆ *m* one; *uno y uno son dos* one and one is two || first; *el uno de abril* the 1st [first] of April || number one, one; *apostar al uno* to bet on number one || — *lo uno... lo otro* on the one hand... on the other hand || *ni lo uno ni lo otro* neither one thing nor the other.
◆ *f* *es la una* it is one o'clock || *quedarse más solo que la una* to be completely alone.
◆ *m/f* FAM some fellow, some woman; *ahora Lola sale con uno* Lola is going out with some fellow now.
— OBSERV Véase OBSERV en UN.

untador, ra *adj* greasing, oiling.
◆ *m/f* greaser, oiler.

untadura *f* greasing, oiler (con aceite) || smearing, rubbing (con ungüento) || TECN grease, oil (aceite) || MED ointment (ungüento).

untar *vt* to grease, to oil (con aceite) || MED to smear, to rub, to anoint (con ungüento); *untar con bálsamo* to anoint with balm || to smear, to stain (manchar) || to spread; *untar el pan con mantequilla* to spread butter on one's bread || FIG & FAM *untar la mano a alguien* to grease s.o.'s palm (sobornar).
◆ *vpr* to smear o.s., to smudge o.s. (*con* with) (mancharse) || FIG & FAM to line one's pockets, to feather one's nest (sacar provecho).

unto *m* grease (grasa) || ointment (ungüento) || AMER polish (betún) || FIG & FAM *unto de México* lolly, cash (dinero).

untuosidad *f* greasiness, oiliness.

untuoso, sa *adj* greasy, oily.

untura *f* greasing || anointing (a un enfermo) || ointment (unto).

uña *f* nail (*palabra general*), fingernail (de la mano), toenail (del pie); *morderse las uñas* to bite one's nails *o* fingernails; *uña encarnada* ingrowing nail *o* toenail || claw (garra de los animales) || hoof (casco) || sting (de alacrán) || MED pterygium (del ojo) || TECN notch, nick (muesca) | claw (arrancaclavos) | clutch, grab (en mecánica) || MAR fluke (del ancla) || pointed hook (saliente) || — *arreglarse las uñas* to manicure one's nails (hacerse la manicura) || FIG *enseñar* or *mostrar las uñas* to show one's claws, to bare one's teeth | *esconder las uñas* to hide one's feelings | *estar de uñas* to be at daggers drawn | *hacer una cosa a uña de caballo* to do sth. at full speed (muy rápidamente) | *ser uña y carne* to be inseparable, to be hand in glove | *tener las uñas largas* or *afiladas* to be light-fingered || *uña de vaca* cow's trotter (carnicería).

uñero *m* MED felon, whitlow (panadizo) | ingrowing nail (uña encarnada).
◆ *pl* thumb index *sing* (de un libro) || *con uñeros* thumb-indexed (libro).

uñeta *f* small nail (uña pequeña) || TECN chisel.

¡upa! *interj* up!, up you go!

upar *vt* to lift (up) (aupar).

Ural *npr m* GEOGR Ural (río) || *los Montes Urales, los Urales* the Ural Mountains, the Urals.

uraloaltaico, ca *adj* Ural-Altaic.

uranato *m* QUÍM uranate.

uránico, ca *adj* uranic.

uranífero, ra *adj* uraniferous.

uranio *m* uranium (metal).

uranio, nia *adj* uranic (del cielo).

uranita *f* uranite.

urano *m* uranium oxide (óxido de uranio).

Urano *n pr* MIT & ASTR Uranus.

uranografía *f* uranography (cosmografía).

urbanidad *f* politeness, courtesy, urbanity (cortesía).

urbanismo *m* town planning [*US* city planning], urbanism.

urbanista *adj* urbanistic.
◆ *m/f* town planner [*US* city planner], urbanist.

urbanístico, ca *adj* urban, city, town (de la ciudad) || town-planning [*US* city planning] (del urbanismo) || *conjunto urbanístico* development; housing estate.

urbanización *f* town planning [*US* city planning] (urbanismo) || development; *obras de urbanización de una ciudad* development works in a city || new town (pueblo nuevo) || urbanization (fenómeno demográfico) || upbringing (educación).

urbanizar *vt* to urbanize (dar carácter urbano) || to develop (los terrenos); *urbanizar una ciudad* to develop a city || to civilize, to educate; *urbanizar a un paleto* to civilize a peasant || — *zona sin urbanizar* undeveloped *o* underdeveloped area || *zona urbanizada* built-up area.

urbano, na *adj* urban, city, town; *población urbana* urban population || FIG polite, courteous, urbane (cortés) || *guardia urbano* policeman.

urbe *f* large city.

urca *f* MAR hooker (embarcación) || ZOOL orc (cetáceo).

urchilla *f* BOT archil.

urdidor, ra *adj* warping.
◆ *m/f* warper.
◆ *m* warping machine, warper.

urdidura *f* warping || FIG plotting, scheming.

urdimbre; urdiembre *f* warp (de un tejido) || warping (urdidura) || FIG intrigue, scheme.

urdir *vt* to warp || FIG to plot, to scheme || FIG *urdir una conspiración* to intrigue, to plot, to scheme.

urea *f* urea.

uremia *f* MED uraemia, uremia.

urémico, ca *adj* uraemic, uremic.

uréter *m* ANAT ureter.

ureteral *adj* ANAT ureteral.

urétera *f* ANAT → **uretra.**

uretra; urétera *f* ANAT urethra.

uretral *adj* ANAT urethral.

urgencia *f* urgency; *con toda urgencia* with the utmost urgency || urgent need (necesidad) || — *con urgencia* urgently || *cura de urgencia* first aid || *curar de urgencia* to give first aid to || JUR *recurso de urgencia* summary procedure.

urgente *adj* urgent; *necesidad urgente* urgent need || express [*US* special delivery]; *correo urgente* express mail || — *poner una carta urgente* to send a letter express || *recibir una carta urgente* to receive an express letter [*US* to receive a special delivery].

urgentemente *adv* urgently.

urgir *vi* to be urgent, to be pressing; *el asunto urge* the matter is urgent || — *me urge tenerlo* I need it urgently, it is urgent that I have it as soon as possible || *nos urge el tiempo* we are pressed for time, time is short.
◆ *v impers* to be urgent, to require immediate attention || *urge terminar con el chabolismo* the slum problem *o* slum clearance requires immediate attention.
◆ *vt* to urge; *los delegados urgieron al congreso para que tomara esta medida* the delegates urged the congress to take this measure.

úrico, ca *adj* uric; *ácido úrico* uric acid.

urinario, ria *adj* urinary; *vías urinarias* urinary tract.
◆ *m* urinal.

urinífero, ra *adj* ANAT uriniferous.

urna *f* urn (vasija) || ballot box (electoral) || glass case (caja de cristal) || *ir a las urnas* to go to the polls.

uro *m* ZOOL urus, aurochs.

urodelos *m pl* ZOOL urodela.

urogallo *m* capercaillie.

urogenital *adj* urogenital.

urografía *f* urography.

urología *f* MED urology.

urólogo, ga *m/f* urologist.

uroscopia *f* MED uroscopy.

urraca *f* magpie (ave) || FIG chatterbox, magpie (hablador).

URSS *abrev de Unión de Repúblicas Socialistas Soviéticas* USSR, Union of Soviet Socialist Republics.

ursulina *f* Ursuline (monja).

urticáceas *f pl* BOT urticaceae.

urticante *adj* urticant.

urticaria *f* urticaria, hives.

urubú *m* black vulture, urubu.

Uruguay *npr m* GEOGR Uruguay.

uruguayo, ya *adj/s* Uruguayan.

urunday; urundey *m* urunday (árbol).

usado, da *adj* worn-out, worn (deteriorado) || used (que ha servido ya) || worn (ropa) || secondhand (de segunda mano) || used; *palabra poco usada* rarely used word || used (utilizado) || (p us); *usado a hacer algo* used to doing sth. (ejercitado).

usagre *m* MED infantile impetigo.

usanza *f* usage (uso) || style, fashion; *a la antigua usanza* in the old style || *a la usanza de la Corte* according to Court custom, in the fashion of the Court.

usar *vt* to use; *uso tinta negra* I use black ink; *billete que no se puede usar* ticket that cannot

be used || to wear; *usa camisas de seda* he wears silk shirts; *usar gafas* to wear glasses || *estar sin usar* to be unused.
◆ *vi* to use, to make use (hacer uso de) || to exercise; *usar de su derecho* to exercise one's right || — *usa dormir después del almuerzo* he usually sleeps after lunch, he is in the habit of sleeping after lunch || *usar mal de* to misuse.
◆ *vpr* to be used; *esta palabra ya no se usa* this word is no longer used || to be worn, to be in fashion; *ya no se usan miriñaques* crinolines are no longer worn || *esas cosas ya no se usan* that sort of thing is not done any more.

Usatges *npr mpl* List of Laws and customs made in Catalonia in the 11th century by Ramón Berenguer.

usía *pron pers* your lordship.

usina *f* factory.
— OBSERV *Usina* is a Gallicism frequently used in Uruguay.

uso *m* use (empleo); *el uso de la violencia* the use of violence || use; *perdió el uso de una pierna* he lost the use of one leg || custom, usage (costumbre); *es el uso del país* it is the custom of the country || use; *instrucciones para su uso* instructions for use || exercise; *el uso de la autoridad, de un privilegio* the exercise of authority, of a privilege || wearing (de ropa, etc.); *uso indebido de condecoraciones* illegal wearing of decorations || — *al uso* in fashion, in style (que se estila), in the style *o* fashion *o* way of; *al uso aragonés* in the Aragonese way || *con el uso* with wear; *los zapatos dan de sí con el uso* shoes stretch with wear || *de mucho uso* hard-wearing || *deteriorado por el uso* worn || *deterioro por el uso* wear and tear || *de uso* in use || *de uso corriente* in common use, in everyday use || *el uso hace al maestro* practice makes perfect || *en buen uso* in good condition || *en uso* in use; *palabra en uso* word in use || *en uso de* making use of, using; *en uso de sus prerrogativas* making use of his prerogatives; by virtue of; *en uso de las facultades que me han sido conferidas* by virtue of the powers vested in me || *hacer buen uso de* to make good use of, to put to good use, to use well || *hacer mal uso de* to misuse, to use badly || *hacer uso de* to make use of (utilizar), to exercise (autoridad, etc.) || *hacer uso de la palabra* to take the floor, to speak, to address the meeting || *para uso de* to be used by || MED *para uso externo* for external use || *según la moda al uso* as is customary || *ser de uso* to be used (emplearse), to be worn (llevarse) || *usos y costumbres de un país* ways and customs of a country.

usted *pron pers* you; *usted y sus hermanos* you and your brothers || — *¡a usted!* thank you! (devolviendo las gracias) || *¿es de usted este sombrero?* is this hat yours? || *hablar* or *tratar de usted* to address as «usted», to use the polite form of address with || *la casa de usted* your house || *la de usted ¿dónde está?* where is yours?
◆ *pl* you; *ustedes y su hija* you and your daughter.
— OBSERV The personal pronoun *usted* is the polite form of address used with strangers and with people who deserve one's respect.
Usted is a contraction of *Vuestra merced* (your honour) and all verbs, pronouns or possessive adjectives qualified by it are construed in the third person (*usted es alto, señor doctor, pero su hijo lo es aún más*, you are tall, doctor, but your son is even taller).
Usted can be written in the abbreviated forms *Ud.* or *Vd.*, and *ustedes Uds.* or *Vds.*

ustorio *adj m* *espejo ustorio* burning glass.

usual *adj* usual, common; *términos usuales* usual terms || habitual, usual, customary (habitual).

usualmente *adv* usually.

usuario, ria *m/f* user; *los usuarios de la carretera* road users || JUR usufructuary.

usucapión *f* JUR usucapion, usucaption.

usucapir *vt* JUR to usucapt.

usufructo *m* JUR usufruct, use.

usufructuar *vt* to have the usufruct of, to usufruct.

usufructuario, ria *adj/s* usufructuary.

usura *f* interest, usury (ant) (interés) || usury, profiteering || FIG *pagar con usura* to repay a thousandfold.

usurario, ria *adj* usurious; *beneficio usurario* usurious profit.

usurero, ra *adj* usurious.
◆ *m/f* usurer || FIG profiteer.

usurpación *f* usurpation; *usurpación de estado civil* usurpation of civil status || encroachment, usurpation (intrusión).

usurpador, ra *adj* usurping.
◆ *m/f* usurper.

usurpar *vt* to usurp; *usurpar un título* to usurp a title || FIG to usurp on *o* upon, to encroach upon; *usurpar derechos ajenos* to usurp on the rights of others.

usurpatorio, ria *adj* usurpatory, usurpative.

usuta *f* AMER sandal (ojota).

ut *m inv* MÚS do, doh (do).

utensilio *m* utensil; *utensilios de cocina* kitchen utensils || tool (herramienta) || device, implement (aparato).

uterino, na *adj* uterine; *hermano uterino* uterine brother || *furor uterino* nymphomania.

útero *m* ANAT uterus, womb.

útil *adj* useful (*para* to) || fit (apto) || working (día) || — *¿en qué puedo serle útil?* can I help you? || *es muy útil saberlo* it is a useful thing to know.
◆ *m* tool (herramienta) || utensil || — *unir lo útil con lo agradable* to combine *o* to mix business with pleasure || *útiles de escritorio, de pintor* writing, painter's materials || *útiles de labranza* agricultural implements || *útiles de matar* matador's equipment || *útiles de pesca* fishing tackle.

utilidad *f* usefulness, utility || COM profit (beneficio) || *impuesto de utilidades* income tax.

utilitario, ria *adj* utilitarian || utility (coche, etc.).
◆ *m* utility car.

utilitarismo *m* utilitarianism.

utilitarista *adj/s* utilitarian.

utilizable *adj* utilizable, useable, usable || fit for use (que puede servir) || ready for use (en condiciones de ser utilizado).

utilización *f* use, utilization, using.

utilizar *vt* to use, to make use of, to utilize (emplear) || TECN to harness (la energía, etc.).

útilmente *adv* usefully || profitably (con provecho).

utillaje *m* tools *pl*, equipment.

utopía *f* Utopia.

utópico, ca *adj/s* Utopian.

utopista *adj/s* Utopian.

utrero, ra *m/f* young bull, young heifer.

uva *f* grape; *racimo de uvas* bunch of grapes || — FIG & FAM *entrar por uvas* to take the risk (arriesgarse) | *estar de mala uva* to be in a bad mood || *tomar las uvas* or *las uvas de la suerte* New Year's Eve custom of eating twelve grapes at midnight which is supposed to bring happiness in the new year || *uva albilla* white grape || *uva de mesa* (table) grape || *uva moscatel* muscatel, muscat || *uvas pasas* raisins.

uve *f* V [name of the letter V] || *en forma de uve* V-shaped || *uve doble* W [name of the letter W].

uvero, ra *m/f* grape seller.
◆ *m* sea grape (árbol de América).
◆ *adj* grape, of *o* pertaining to grapes; *exportación uvera* grape exportation.

úvula *f* ANAT uvula (campanilla).

uvular *adj* uvular.

¡uy! *interj* ouch! (dolor), ugh! (repugnancia), oh! (sorpresa).

V

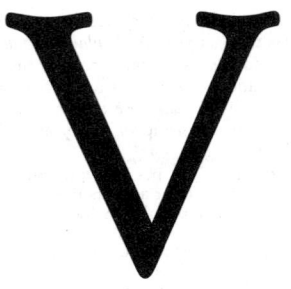

v *f* v (uve); *una v mayúscula* a capital v || *v doble* w.
— OBSERV The *v* is pronounced like the Spanish *b*.

vaca *f* cow; *vaca lechera* milk cow, milch cow || beef (carne); *estofado de vaca* beef stew || cowhide (cuero) || stake (dinero jugado a las cartas) || — *carne de vaca* beef || FIG & FAM *parece una vaca* she's like an elephant || *vaca de San Antón* ladybird [US ladybug] || *vaca marina* sea cow (manatí) || FIG *vaca sagrada* sacred cow | *vacas flacas* lean years | *vacas gordas* years of plenty | *ya vendrán las vacas gordas* my (our, etc.) ship will come in.

vacaciones *f pl* holidays, holiday *sing*, vacation *sing*; *vacaciones de verano* summer holidays; *vacaciones escolares* school holidays; *vacaciones retribuidas* or *pagadas* paid holidays || vacation *sing*, recess *sing* (de un tribunal) || — *estar de vacaciones* to be on holiday || *irse de vacaciones* to go on holiday || *pasamos las vacaciones en Ibiza* we went to Ibiza for our holidays, we spent our holidays *o* we holidayed in Ibiza.

vacada *f* herd of cows.

vacante *adj* vacant; *puesto vacante* vacant post.
◆ *f* vacancy, vacant post; *en caso de producirse una vacante* should there be a vacancy; *cubrir las vacantes en una empresa* to fill the vacancies in a firm.

vacar *vi* to fall vacant (quedarse vacante un puesto) || to be vacant (estar vacante) || not to work (no trabajar) || to stop working (dejar de trabajar) || to devote o.s. (*a, en* to) (dedicarse a) || to be without (carecer de).

vacarí *adj* leather.

vaccíneo, a *adj* MED vaccinal.

vaccinostilo *m* MED vaccinator (lanceta).

vaccinoterapia *f* MED vaccine therapy.

vaciadero *m* dumping ground, rubbish tip (lugar) || sewer (conducto).

vaciado *m* casting, moulding [US molding] (acción y resultado); *vaciado de yeso* plaster casting; *vaciado en molde* casting in a mould || hollowing out (formación de un hueco) || emptying (de un depósito) || sharpening (de un cuchillo) || INFORM dumping (de memoria) || *orificio de vaciado* tapping hole.

vaciador *m* TECN caster, moulder [US molder] (de figuras en molde) || foundry worker (obrero fundidor) || emptier (instrumento para vaciar).

vaciante *f* ebb tide (menguante).

vaciar *vt* to empty (out) (un líquido, un recipiente); *vaciar un tonel* to empty a barrel || to cast, to mould [US to mold]; *vaciar una estatua en bronce* to cast a statue in bronze || to drain (un líquido) || to clean; *vaciar un pollo* to clean a chicken || to hollow out (ahuecar) || to sharpen (un cuchillo) || to expound at length (una teoría) || to copy out (un texto).
◆ *vi* to flow; *río que vacía en el mar* river which flows into the sea.
◆ *vpr* to empty || FIG to unburden o.s.

vaciedad *f* emptiness (estado de vacío) || FIG emptiness (de la conversación, etc.) || *decir vaciedades* to talk nonsense.

vacilación *f* hesitation, hesitancy, vacillation (duda) || irresolution (falta de determinación) || vacillation, swaying (balanceo) || *sin vacilaciones* without hesitation, unhesitatingly.

vacilante *adj* unsteady, shaky (paso, mano, etc.) || faltering, halting; *voz vacilante* faltering voice || flickering; *luz vacilante* flickering light || hesitant (que tarda en decidirse) || irresolute (falto de determinación).

vacilar *vi* to vacillate, to rock, to sway, to wobble (moverse por falta de estabilidad) || to flicker (la luz) || to falter (al hablar) || to fail (la memoria) || to totter, to stumble (al andar) || FIG to hesitate; *vacilar en su resolución* to hesitate over one's decision; *vacilar en la elección* to hesitate about one's choice; *no vaciló en contestar* he did not hesitate to answer || *AMER* to go on a spree || — FIG *hacer vacilar* to shake; *hacer vacilar las convicciones de uno* to shake one's convictions | *memoria que vacila* shaky memory | *sin vacilar* without hesitation, unhesitatingly | *una persona que vacila mucho* an indecisive *o* irresolute person, a very hesitant person.

vacilón, ona *m/f* FAM joker, teaser.
◆ *m* *AMER* FAM wild party (juerga).

vacío, a *adj* empty; *cajón vacío* empty drawer; *sala vacía* empty room || vacant, unoccupied, empty; *vivienda vacía* vacant house || unfurnished (sin amueblar) || vacant, unoccupied (puesto de trabajo) || FIG empty; *una conversación vacía* an empty conversation || barren (hembra) || — FIG *tener el estómago vacío* to feel hungry | *tener la cabeza vacía* to be empty-headed | *volver con las manos vacías* to come back empty-handed.
◆ *m* emptiness, void; *su grito resonó en el vacío* his cry resounded in the void || hole, gap (cavidad) || space, empty space (espacio) || blank space (espacio en blanco) || FÍS vacuum; *hacer el vacío* to create a vacuum; *en vacío* in a vacuum || ANAT flank (ijada) || FIG emptiness, void (sentimiento); *sintió un vacío en el corazón* he felt an emptiness in his heart | gap (hueco) | vacancy (vacante) || — FIG *caer en el vacío* to fall on deaf ears (no ser escuchado) || *envasar al vacío* to vacuum pack || *estar suspendido en el vacío* to be suspended *o* hanging in mid air || FIG *hacer el vacío a uno* to send s.o. to Coventry, to cold-shoulder s.o. | *ha quedado un vacío en el despacho desde que se fue* the office seems empty since he left, the office has not been the same since he left | *tener un vacío en el estómago* to feel hungry || *volver de vacío* to come back empty (un vehículo), to come back empty-handed (una persona).

vacuidad *f* vacuity.

vacuna *f* MED vaccine || VET cowpox, vaccinia (de la vaca).

vacunación *f* MED vaccination.

vacunar *vt* MED to vaccinate || FIG to inure.
◆ *vpr* to be vaccinated.

vacuno, na *adj* bovine || *el ganado vacuno* cattle.

vacuo, cua *adj* empty (vacío) || vacant (vacante) || vacuous, empty (frívolo, insubstancial).
◆ *m* void.

vacuola *f* vacuole.

vacuolar *adj* vacuolar.

vade *m* folder (para guardar papeles) || (school) satchel (cartera).

vadear *vt* to ford || FIG to overcome, to surmount (una dificultad) | to sound out (el ánimo de uno).

vademécum *m inv* vademecum (libro) || (school) satchel (de colegial).

vado *m* ford (de un río) || FIG way out, solution (salida, solución).

vagabundear; vagamundear *vi* to wander, to roam, to lead a vagrant life.

vagabundeo *m* vagabondage.

vagabundo, da *adj* vagrant; *vida vagabunda* vagrant life.
◆ *m/f* rover, wanderer (trotamundos) || vagabond, vagrant (más despectivo) || tramp (muy despectivo) || JUR vagrant.

vagamundear *vi* ⟶ **vagabundear.**

vagamundo, da *adj/s* FAM ⟶ **vagabundo.**

vagancia *f* vagrancy (delito) || laziness, idleness (ociosidad).

vagar; vaguear *vi* to wander (about), to roam (about); *vagar por el pueblo* to wander through the village; *se pasó todo el día vagando* he spent all day just wandering about || to loaf about, to idle (andar ocioso).

vagido *m* cry, wail [of a newborn baby] || *dar vagidos* to cry.

vagina *f* ANAT vagina.

vaginal *adj* ANAT vaginal.

vaginitis *f inv* MED vaginitis.

vago, ga *adj* vague; *promesas vagas* vague promises; *perfil vago* vague outline || FOT & ARTES blurred, indistinct || lazy, idle (perezoso) || FIG vague; *idea vaga* vague idea || ANAT *nervio vago* vagus nerve, vagus.
◆ *m/f* loafer, idler, slacker (perezoso) || tramp (vagabundo) || JUR vagrant || — *hacer el vago* to laze about || *ley de vagos y maleantes* vagrancy act.

vagón *m* carriage, coach, car (para viajeros); *vagón de primera, de segunda* first-class, second-class carriage || truck, wagon; *vagón para ganado* cattle truck, cattle wagon || wagonload (contenido de un vagón) || — *vagón cerrado* van, closed *o* covered wagon || *vagón cisterna* tank wagon, tanker || *vagón cuba* tank wagon, tanker || *vagón de mercancías* goods van *o* wagon [US freight car] || *vagón restaurante* dining car || *vagón tolva* hopper wagon.

vagoneta *f* small wagon.

vagotomía *f* MED vagotomy.

vagotonía *f* MED vagotonia, vagotony.

vaguada *f* lowest part of a valley.

vagueación *f* wandering.

vaguear *vi* ⟶ **vagar.**

vaguedad *f* vagueness; *la vaguedad de sus palabras* the vagueness of his words || indistinctness (de una imagen).
◆ *pl* vague remarks; *no ha dicho nada preciso sino sólo vaguedades* he said nothing definite, he only made vague remarks || — *andarse con vaguedades* to be vague, to speak vaguely || *decir vaguedades* to make vague remarks, to be vague || *hablar sin vaguedades* not to beat about the bush, to get straight to the point.

vaguemaestre *m* MIL baggage master.

vaharada *f* puff, breath.

vahído *m* dizzy *o* giddy spell (mareo) || *le dio un vahído* he felt dizzy *o* giddy.

vaho *m* breath || steam, vapour (vapor) || *hay vaho en los cristales* the windows are steamed up.
◆ *pl* MED inhalation *sing* || fumes (emanaciones).

vaída *adj f* *bóveda vaída* truncated dome.

vaina *f* sheath, scabbard (de espada) || sheath, case (de navaja) || BOT pod; *vaina de guisantes* pod of peas | sheath (del tallo) || ANAT sheath || MAR tabling (de vela) || case (de cartucho) || *AMER* FAM thing (cosa) | nuisance, bother, bore (molestia) | luck (suerte).
◆ *m* good-for-nothing, oaf.

vainazas *m inv* FAM slob, lout.

vainica *f* hemstitch.

vainilla *f* vanilla; *helado de vainilla* vanilla ice cream || vanilla (planta).

vaivén *m* swinging, swaying (balanceo) || rocking (de un tren, una mecedora, etc.) || coming and going, bustle (de la gente, de los coches, etc.) || FIG exchange; *un vaivén de ideas nuevas* an exchange of new ideas | fluctuation, change; *los vaivenes de la vida política* the fluctuations of political life | change of fortune (cambio de fortuna) || back and forth movement; *el vaivén de la lanzadera* the back and forth movement of the shuttle || up and down movement (movimiento vertical).
◆ *pl* FIG ups and downs (altibajos).

vajilla *f* dishes *pl*, crockery || — *lavar la vajilla* to wash up || *regalar una vajilla* to give a set of dishes *o* a dinner service || *vajilla de plata* silverware || *vajilla de porcelana* chinaware.

val *m* (p us) valley (valle).

valaco, ca *adj/s* Walachian.

Valaquia *npr f* GEOGR Walachia.

Valdemoro *n pr* FAM *estar entre Pinto y Valdemoro* to be tipsy (medio borracho), to be undecided, to sit on the fence (estar indeciso).

valdepeñas *m* Valdepeñas wine.

vale *m* voucher; *vale por diez pesetas* voucher for ten pesetas || receipt (recibo) || promissory note, IOU (pagaré) || star (en el colegio) || *AMER* FAM mate [*US* buddy] (compañero).

valedero, ra *adj* valid.

valedor, ra *m/f* protector (protector) || *AMER* mate [*US* buddy] (compañero).

valemadrista *adj* *AMER* FAM cynical (apático, cínico).

valencia *f* QUÍM valency, valence.

Valencia *n pr* GEOGR Valencia.

valenciano, na *adj* [of *o* from] Valencia, Valencian.
◆ *f* *AMER* turn-up (vuelta de pantalón).
◆ *m/f* inhabitant *o* native of Valencia, Valencian.

valentía *f* courage, valour [*US* valor], bravery (valor); *la valentía de un general* the valour of a general || bragging, boasting (ostentación de valor) || boldness, dash; *pintor que maneja el pincel con gran valentía* artist who paints with great dash || brave deed, act of bravery (acción valerosa).

valentón, ona *adj* bragging, boastful.
◆ *m/f* braggart.

valentona; valentonada *f* bragging, boasting, brag, boast.

valer *m* value, worth, merit.

valer* *vt* to be worth (tener un valor de); *la casa vale más de lo que pagaste* the house is worth more than you paid for it || to cost, to be (costar); *valen seis pesetas el kilo* they cost *o* they are six pesetas a kilo; *¿cuánto vale?* how much is it?, how much does it cost? || to mean, to be worth; *este recuerdo vale mucho para mí* this memory means a lot to me || to win, to gain, to earn (ganar); *la gloria que le han valido sus hazañas* the glory which his exploits won (for) him || to cause (causar); *me ha valido muchos disgustos* it caused me a lot of trouble || to cost, to result in; *esa táctica les valió la derrota* that move cost them defeat, that move resulted in their defeat; *su pereza le valió un suspenso en el examen* his laziness cost him (failure in) the exam, his laziness resulted in his failing the exam || to get, to earn; *su comportamiento le valió una paliza* his behaviour earned him a beating || MAT to equal || to protect, to help, to defend (proteger) || — FAM *no valer nada* not to be worth a thing, to be worthless (no tener valor), to be useless (ser muy malo) || *valer la pena* to be worth it, to be worth the trouble; *no vale la pena hacerlo* it is not worth doing, it is not worth it, it is not worth the trouble || *valer lo que cuesta* to be worth the money, to be worth it || FIG *valer lo que pesa en oro* or *tanto oro como pesa* or *un Perú* or *un Potosí* to be worth one's *o* its weight in gold, to be worth a fortune || *¡válgame Dios!* by Jove!, bless my soul! (sorpresa), Lord, give me strength!
◆ *vi/v impers* to be worth; *cada ficha vale por una comida* each disc is worth a meal || to cost, to be (costar); *valen a seis pesetas el kilo* they cost six pesetas a kilo || to be valuable (tener valor) || to be valid; *el billete me vale aún* my ticket is still valid; *sus argumentos no valen* his arguments are not valid || to count (contar); *este partido no vale* this match does not count || to be of use, to help; *no le valió esa astucia* that trick was of no use to him *o* did not help him || to do (bastar); *este mismo papel me vale* this paper will do (me) || to be suitable, to be right (ser conveniente); *este chico no vale para el cargo* this boy is not suitable for the job || to serve (servir); *todavía me valen estos zapatos* these shoes still serve me || to be of use, to be useful (ser útil) || to be good; *yo no valgo para esta clase de trabajo* I am no good at this sort of work; *este año no hay ningún alumno que valga* not one of the students is any good this year; *¿este martillo te vale?* is this hammer any good to you? || to be legal tender (monedas) || — *hacerse valer* to assert o.s. || *hacer valer sus derechos* to exercise one's rights (emplearlos), to assert one's rights (hacerlos prevalecer) || *hacer valer sus razones* to assert one's opinions || *la primera impresión es la que vale* the first impression is the one that counts || *lo que mucho vale, mucho cuesta* you have to pay for quality || *más vale* it is better (es preferible); *más vale hacerlo ahora* it is better to do it now; *más vale así* it is better like that || *más vale no hacerlo* it's better not do it, I (we, etc.) had better not do it || *más vale que lo hagas* you had better do it || *más vale tarde que nunca* better late than never || *más vale un toma que dos te daré* a bird in the hand is worth two in the bush || *no hay excusa que valga* no excuses || *no hay pero que valga* no buts || *no vale* it does not count (no cuenta), you cannot do that (no hay derecho), that is not right, I do not agree (no estoy conforme) || *no vale para nada* it (he, she) is useless || *sin que valgan excepciones* without exception || *su hermana no vale gran cosa* his sister is not up to much || *tanto vale el uno como el otro* the one is as good as the other, they are as good as each other || *tanto vale hacerlo ahora mismo* I (you, she, etc.) had better *o* best do it right now || *tanto vales cuanto tienes* a man is worth as much as he owns || *un médico que vale (mucho)* a (very) good doctor || FAM *¡vale!* O. K., all right (está bien), that's enough (basta) | *¿vale?* is that all right?, will that do?, O. K.? || *vale mucho tener una buena recomendación* it is very useful to have good references || *valer por* to be worth; *vale por dos kilos de patatas* it is worth two kilos of potatoes; to be as good as, to equal; *ese gesto vale por un discurso* that gesture is as good as a speech || *valer tanto como* to be as good as; *Juan vale tanto como su hermano* John is as good as his brother || *válgame la frase* if I may say so, if you will pardon *o* excuse the expression.
◆ *vpr* to be as good as one another || to use; *valerse de un bastón para andar* to use a stick for walking; *valerse de un diccionario* to use a dictionary || to exercise; *valerse de sus derechos* to exercise one's rights || to make use of, to use; *valerse de sus relaciones* to make use of one's connections || — *no poder valerse* to be unable to manage on one's own || *valerse de todos los medios* to try everything || *valerse por sí mismo* to manage by o.s.

valeriana *f* BOT valerian (planta).

valeroso, sa *adj* valiant, courageous, brave; *un soldado valeroso* a valiant soldier || valuable, precious (de mucho precio).

valet *m* jack (sota o jota en la baraja francesa).

valetudinario, ria *adj/s* valetudinarian.

valía *f* value, worth; *joya de mucha valía* jewel of great value || merit, worth (de personas) || favour [*US* favor] (confianza).

validación *f* validation.

validar *vt* to validate.

validez *f* validity || *dar validez a* to validate.

valido, da *adj/sm* favourite [*US* favorite].

válido, da *adj* robust, strong; *un hombre válido* a robust man || FIG valid (que satisface los requisitos); *elección válida* valid election; *recibo válido* valid receipt.

valiente *adj* valiant, courageous, brave; *un soldado valiente se expone en los combates* a brave soldier takes risks in battle || boastful, bragging (valentón) || FIG & FAM a fine, some; *¡valiente amigo eres!* a fine friend *o* some friend you are! || — *¡valiente amigo tienes!* you've a fine friend there! || *¡valiente frío!* it's freezing! || *¡valiente tonto!* what a fool!, what an idiot!
◆ *m/f* brave man (valeroso) || braggart (bravucón).

valija *f* suitcase, case (maleta) || mailbag (del cartero) || *valija diplomática* diplomatic bag *o* pouch.

valimiento *m* favour [*US* favor], good graces *pl*; *hombre que tiene valimiento con el rey* man who is in favour with the king *o* in the good graces of the king || worth, value, merit (mérito).

valioso, sa *adj* precious, valuable; *una joya valiosa* a precious jewel; *tesoro valioso* valuable treasure || highly esteemed (estimado) || useful (útil) || rich, wealthy (rico) || FIG valuable; *un asesoramiento valioso* a valuable piece of advice | excellent; *¡valiosa idea!* excellent idea.

valisoletano, na *adj/s* ⟶ **vallisoletano.**

Valkiria *f* MIT Valkyrie.

valón, ona *adj/s* Walloon.

valona *f* vandyke [collar] || AMER cropped mane (de los caballos).

valor *m* value, worth, merit; *artista de gran valor* artist of great merit || courage, bravery, valiance, valour [US valor]; *el valor de un soldado* the courage of a soldier || value, denomination (de monedas, sellos, etc.) || courage, heart; *no tengo valor para ir a verle* I have not got the courage to go and see him || importance (importancia) || efficacy (eficacia) || FIG credit; *no doy valor a sus palabras* I do not give credit to his words || FAM nerve, cheek (cara); *tuvo valor para pedir que le pagaran* he had the nerve to ask them to pay him || COM value; *valor comercial* or *de mercado* market *o* commercial value; *valor en oro* value in gold; *por el valor de* to the value of || MAT value; *valor absoluto, relativo* absolute, relative value || — FAM *¿cómo va ese valor?* how are things? || *dar* or *conceder valor a* to attach importance to, to take notice of || *de valor* valuable; *objeto de valor* valuable object || *objetos de valor* valuables || FAM *¡qué valor!* what a nerve!, of all the cheek! (qué caradura) || *quitar valor a algo* to reduce the value of sth. (reducir el valor), to minimize the importance of, to play down (quitar importancia) || *sin valor* worthless || FIG *tener más valor que un torero* not to be afraid of anything || *valor adquisitivo* purchasing power || *valor alimenticio* food value || ECON *valor añadido* value added || COM *valor contable* book value || *valor recibido* value received.
◆ *pl* COM securities || values (principios) || — *depósito de valores* stock deposit || COM *valores en cartera* or *habidos* share portfolio | *valores inmuebles* real estate.

valoración *f* valuation, appraisal (estimación) || appreciation (aumento de valor).

valorar *vt* to value; *valorar una cosa en alto precio* to value sth. at a high price || to appreciate, to raise the value of (aumentar el valor) || *valorar a alguien en mucho* to value s.o. highly, to hold s.o. in high esteem.

valorización *f* valuation, valuing (valoración) || appreciation (revalorización).

valorizar *vt* to value | to raise the value of (aumentar el valor).

vals *m* waltz || — *bailar el vals* to waltz || *bailar un vals* to dance a waltz.

valsar *vi* to waltz.

valuación *f* valuation, appraisal.

valuar *vt* to value.

valva *f* BOT & ZOOL valve.

valvolina *f* jelly-like grease.

válvula *f* ANAT valve (de las venas) || RAD valve [US tube]; *válvula rectificadora* rectifying valve || TECN valve; *válvula de admisión* inlet valve; *válvula de seguridad* safety valve; *esmerilado de válvulas* grinding of valves || *válvula de mariposa* butterfly valve.

valvular *adj* valvular.

valla *f* fence (cerca) || MIL barricade, stockade (fortificación) || FIG obstacle, hindrance, barrier (obstáculo) || DEP hurdle; *100 metros vallas* 100 metres hurdles || AMER cockpit [for cockfights] || *valla publicitaria* hoarding.

valladar *m* fence (cerca) || FIG obstacle, barrier, hindrance.

vallado *m* fence (cerca) || defensive wall.

Valladolid *n pr* GEOGR Valladolid.

vallar *vt* to fence, to put a fence round.

valle *m* valley || FIG *valle de lágrimas* vale *o* valley of tears.

vallejo *m* glen.

vallico *m* BOT ryegrass.

vallisoletano, na; valisoletano, na *adj* [of *o* from] Valladolid.
◆ *m/f* native *o* inhabitant of Valladolid.

vampiresa *f* CINEM vamp (mujer fatal).

vampirismo *m* vampirism.

vampiro *m* vampire (murciélago y espectro) || FIG vampire.

vanadato *m* QUÍM vanadate.

vanadio *m* vanadium (metal).

vanagloria *f* vainglory.

vanagloriarse *vpr* to boast; *vanagloriarse de sus conocimientos* to boast of one's knowledge.

vanaglorioso, sa *adj* vainglorious.

vanamente *adj* vainly, in vain, uselessly (en vano) || without reason (sin razón) || vainly (con presunción).

vandálico, ca *adj* vandal, vandalic.

vandalismo *m* vandalism.

vándalo *adj/s* Vandal.

vanguardia *f* vanguard || — *de vanguardia* of the vanguard (soldados), avant-garde (en arte, música, etc.) || FIG *ir a la vanguardia del progreso* to be in the van of *o* at the forefront of progress.

vanguardismo *m* avant-garde movement.

vanguardista *adj* avant-garde; *una película vanguardista* an avant-garde film.

vanidad *f* vanity; *hacer algo por pura vanidad* to do sth. out of sheer vanity || *vanidad de vanidades y todo es vanidad* vanity of vanities, all is vanity.

vanidoso, sa *adj* vain, conceited.
◆ *m/f* vain person.

vanilocuencia *f* verbosity.

vanílocuo, cua *adj* verbose.
◆ *m/f* prattler.

vaniloquio *m* verbosity.

vano, na *adj* vain; *excusas vanas* vain excuses; *vanas esperanzas* vain hopes || vain, useless (inútil); *esfuerzos vanos* useless efforts || groundless, unfounded, idle (infundado) || empty, hollow (vacío) || vain, conceited (vanidoso) || frivolous (frívolo) || — *en vano* in vain, vainly || *promesas vanas* empty promises.
◆ *m* ARQ opening, bay (hueco) | span (distancia).

vapor *m* vapour [US vapor]; *vapor de agua* water vapour || steam (vaho) || MAR steamer, steamship (barco) || — FIG *a todo vapor* at full steam (barco), at great speed || *caldera de vapor* steam boiler || *máquina de vapor* steam engine || *patatas al vapor* steamed potatoes || *vapor de ruedas* paddle steamer.
◆ *pl* MED vapours, hysteria *sing*, hysterics || *los vapores del vino* vapour *o* fumes given off by wine.

vaporización *f* vaporization || decating, decatizing (de tejidos).

vaporizador *m* vaporizer, atomizer, spray.

vaporizar, vaporizarse *vt/vpr* to vaporize.

vaporoso, sa *adj* vaporous || sheer, diaphanous (tejido).

vapulear *vt* to give a hiding *o* a thrashing; *vapulear a un niño* to give a child a hiding || to beat (una alfombra) || FIG to slate (criticar).

vapuleo *m* hiding, thrashing || beating (de una alfombra) || FIG slating (crítica).

vaqueiro *m* cowherd.

vaquería *f* cowshed (sitio) || dairy (lechería) || herd of cows (vacada).

vaquerizo, za *adj* cattle, cow; *corral vaquerizo* cattle enclosure.
◆ *m/f* cowherd.
◆ *f* cowshed.

vaquero, ra *adj* cattle, cow || of *o* pertaining to cowherds or cowboys || *pantalón vaquero* jeans, pair of jeans.
◆ *m/f* cowherd (pastor) || cowboy (en Estados Unidos); *película de vaqueros* cowboy film.
◆ *m* AMER whip (látigo).
◆ *m pl* jeans (pantalones).

vaqueta *f* cowhide (cuero).

vaquetón, ona *adj* AMER daring.

vaquillona *f* AMER heifer.

vaquita *f* small cow || stake (apuesta) || *vaquita de San Antón* ladybird [US ladybug].

var *m* ELECTR var.

vara *f* staff, pole (palo largo) || pole; *derribar nueces con una vara* to knock nuts down with a pole || staff, wand (insignia de autoridad) || stick (palo) || switch (para azotar) || shaft (varal de un coche) || yard [approximately] (medida de longitud) || TAUR picador's lance (pica) | thrust, lunge (garrochazo) || MÚS slide (de trombón) || — TAUR *poner una vara* to thrust at [the bull] || FIG *temer como una vara verde* to be scared stiff of | *tener mucha vara alta* to be very influential | *tener vara alta en un negocio* to have the upper hand in an affair.

varada *f* MAR running aground | beaching (sacando el barco a la playa) || gang of farm labourers || MIN three months' work (trabajo) | three months' wages (pago).

varadera *f* MAR skid.

varadero *m* MAR dry dock.

varado, da *adj* MAR beached (en la playa) | aground, stranded (encallado) | at anchor (anclado).

varadura *f* running aground (encallamiento) | beaching.

varal *m* staff, pole (vara) || shaft (de un carruaje) || TEATR batten || FIG & FAM beanpole (persona muy alta) || AMER wooden structure upon which meat is dried.

varano *m* ZOOL monitor (lagarto).

varapalo *m* long staff *o* pole (palo) || blow with a stick (golpe) || FIG & FAM setback, blow (contratiempo).

varar *vt* MAR to launch (botar) | to beach (poner en seco) | to run aground (encallar).
◆ *vi* MAR to run aground (encallar) | to drop anchor (anclar) || FIG to come to a standstill (un asunto).

varazo *m* blow with a stick *o* pole || TAUR thrust.

vareado *m* knocking down [of fruit, etc.].

vareador *m* beater (de árboles).

varear *vt* to knock down, to beat down; *varear nueces* to knock nuts down [from the trees] || to measure in «varas» (medir por varas) || to beat (lana, alfombras, etc.) || COM to sell by the yard (vender) || TAUR to jab with the lance (al toro).

varec *m* BOT kelp, varec (alga).

varenga *f* MAR floor timber.

vareo *m* knocking down (de nueces) || measuring in «varas» (medición por varas).

vareta *f* small pole *o* staff (vara pequeña) || limetwig (para cazar pájaros) || taunt, gibe (insinuación molesta) || stripe (lista de color) || FIG & FAM *irse de vareta* to have diarrhoea.

varetazo *m* TAUR sideways butt (paletazo).

Vargas *n pr* *averígüelo Vargas* goodness knows.

variabilidad *f* variability.

variable *adj* variable, changeable; *tiempo variable* changeable weather || MAT variable.
◆ *f* MAT variable.

variación *f* variation ‖ *variación magnética* magnetic declination.

variante *f* version, variant; *una variante de esa canción* one version of this song ‖ difference.

◆ *adj* variable, changeable; *tiempo variable* changeable weather ‖ MAT variable.

variar *vt* to vary; *variar el menú* to vary the menu ‖ to switch about, to change round (de posición) ‖ *galletas variadas* assorted biscuits.

◆ *vi* to vary; *sus respuestas varían* his answers vary ‖ to change; *variar de opinión* to change one's mind *o* opinion; *el viento ha variado* the wind has changed ‖ to differ, to be different (ser diferente); *su versión varía de la del vecino* his version differs from *o* is different from his neighbour's ‖ MAT to vary ‖ *por no variar* as usual.

— OBSERV The *i* in variar bears a written accent in the first, second and third person singular and in the third person plural of the present indicative and subjunctive, and also in the second person singular of the imperative.

varice *f* MED varicose vein, varix.

varicela *f* MED chicken pox, varicella.

varicocele *m* MED varicocele.

varicoso, sa *adj* varicose.

◆ *m/f* person suffering from varicose veins.

variedad *f* variety, diversity ‖ BOT & ZOOL variety ‖ FIG *en la variedad está el gusto* variety is the spice of life.

◆ *pl* (variety) show *sing* (espectáculo).

varilarguero *m* TAUR picador.

varilla *f* small stick, rod (vara pequeña) ‖ rail (de cortinas) ‖ rib (de abanico, paraguas) ‖ perch (en una jaula) ‖ stay (de corsé) ‖ ANAT jawbone ‖ TECN rod ‖ — *varilla de la virtud* or *de las virtudes* or *encantada* or *mágica* magic wand ‖ *varilla de zahorí* divining rod ‖ *varilla indicadora* or *graduada* gauge.

varillaje *m* ribs *pl*, ribbing (de abanico, de paraguas).

vario, ria *adj* different, diverse (distinto); *tela de varios colores* material of different colours ‖ various, several; *tratar de varios asuntos* to discuss various subjects ‖ variable, changeable (cambiadizo) ‖ varying, varied (que varía) ‖ several (unos cuantos); *tiene varios amigos* he has several friends ‖ *asuntos varios* or *cuestiones varias* (any) other business (en el orden del día).

◆ *pron indef pl* several, some (people); *varios piensan que* some (people) think that.

variólico, ca *adj* variolous.

varita *f* wand; *varita de la virtud* or *de las virtudes* or *mágica* or *encantada* magic wand ‖ small stick, rod (pequeña vara).

varón *m* man; *esclarecidos varones* great men ‖ boy; *familia compuesta de una hija y tres varones* family of one girl and three boys ‖ — *hijo varón* male child, son, boy ‖ *santo varón* saint ‖ *sexo: varón* sex: male (en un pasaporte) ‖ *varón de Dios* saint.

varonía *f* male issue, male descent.

varonil *adj* virile, manly; *carácter varonil* virile character ‖ mannish; *una mujer varonil* a mannish woman.

varraco *m* boar (verraco).

Varsovia *n pr* GEOGR Warsaw.

varsoviano, na *adj* [of *o* from] Warsaw.

◆ *m/f* native *o* inhabitant of Warsaw.

vasallaje *m* vassalage ‖ subjection, servitude ‖ *rendir vasallaje* to pay homage.

vasallo, lla *adj/s* vassal ‖ subject (súbdito).

vasar *m* kitchen shelf.

vasco, ca *adj/s* Basque ‖ *País vasco* Basque Country (francés y español).

◆ *m* Basque (lengua).

vascófilo *m* bascologist.

vascón *adj m*; **vascónico, ca** *adj* of *o* pertaining to the Vascons (pueblo antiguo).

vascongado, da *adj/s* Basque ‖ *las provincias vascongadas* the (Spanish) Basque Country, the Basque Provinces.

— OBSERV The *provincias vascongadas* are: *Álava, Guipúzcoa* and *Vizcaya*; their capitals are *Vitoria, San Sebastián* and *Bilbao*.

Vasconia *npr f* GEOGR the Basque Country.

vascónico, ca *adj* → **vascón.**

vascuence *adj/sm* Basque (lengua).

vascular *adj* vascular; *tejido vascular* vascular tissue.

vascularidad *f* vascularity.

vascularización *f* vascularization.

vasectomía *f* MED vasectomy.

vaselina *f* MED vaseline ‖ FIG & FAM *dar mucha vaselina a alguien* to soft-soap s.o.

vasera *f* large tray for glasses (bandeja para vasos) ‖ kitchen shelf (vasar).

vasija *f* pot; *vasija de barro* earthenware pot ‖ vase; *una vasija precolombina* a pre-Columbian vase ‖ vessel, recipient, container (recipiente).

vaso *m* glass; *vaso de cristal* crystal glass; *beberse un vaso de agua* to drink a glass of water ‖ glass, glassful (cantidad) ‖ vase (florero); *vaso de porcelana* porcelain vase ‖ ANAT vessel; *vaso capilar* capillary vessel; *vasos sanguíneos* blood vessels ‖ BOT vessel ‖ — FIG *ahogarse en un vaso de agua* to make a mountain out of a molehill ‖ FÍS *vasos comunicantes* communicating vessels ‖ REL *vasos sagrados* sacred vessels.

vasoconstricción *f* vasoconstriction.

vasoconstrictor *adj* vasoconstrictive.

◆ *m* vasoconstrictor.

vasodilatación *f* vasodilatation.

vasodilatador *adj/sm* vasodilator.

vasomotor, ra *adj* vasomotor (nervios).

vástago *m* shoot (de planta, árbol) ‖ TECN rod (del émbolo) ‖ descendent, scion, offspring; *el último vástago de una ilustre familia* the last descendent of an illustrious family ‖ *vástago de perforación* drill stem.

vastedad *f* vastness.

vasto, ta *adj* vast, huge.

vate *m* poet (poeta) ‖ prophet (adivino).

vaticanista *adj* Vatican, of the Vatican.

Vaticano *npr m* GEOGR Vatican.

vaticano, na *adj* Vatican, of the Vatican.

vaticinar *vt/vi* to prophesy, to foretell.

vaticinio *m* prophecy, prediction.

vatímetro *m* ELECTR wattmeter.

vatio *m* ELECTR watt (unidad) ‖ *potencia en vatios* wattage.

vatio-hora *n* ELECTR watt-hour.

vaudeville *m* comedy, vaudeville (comedia ligera).

— OBSERV En inglés la palabra *vaudeville* se aplica más particularmente a un espectáculo de variedades.

vaudevillesco, ca *adj* comedy, vaudeville.

vaudevillista *m* comedy writer, vaudevillist.

vaya *f* FAM mockery (burla) ‖ *dar vaya a* to make fun of, to mock.

Vº Bº *abrev de Visto Bueno* O. K.

Vd. *abrev de usted* → **usted.**

ve *f* v (nombre de la letra *v*).

vecero, ra *adj* alternating ‖ biennial (planta).

vecinaje *m* neighbourhood [US neighborhood].

vecinal *adj* local, vicinal; *camino vecinal* local road.

vecindad *f* neighbourhood [US neighborhood], vicinity; *vive en la vecindad* he lives in the neighbourhood ‖ population (de una ciudad) ‖ neighbourhood, inhabitants *pl* (de un barrio) ‖ neighbours *pl* (los vecinos) ‖ residents *pl* ‖ nearness, proximity (proximidad) ‖ similarity (semejanza) ‖ — *casa de vecindad* block of flats [US apartment building] ‖ *política de buena vecindad* good neighbour policy.

vecindario *m* population, inhabitants *pl*; *el vecindario de una ciudad* the population of a city ‖ neighbourhood, neighbours *pl* [US neighborhood, neighbors] (los vecinos); *acudió todo el vecindario* the whole neighbourhood came ‖ residents *pl*.

vecino, na *adj* neighbouring [US neighboring]; *país vecino* neighbouring country ‖ nearby (cerca) ‖ next door, next; *vive en la casa vecina de la mía* he lives in the house next door to *o* next to mine ‖ FIG similar (semejante) ‖ *nuestras casas son vecinas* our houses are next (door) to each other, we live next (door) to each other.

◆ *m/f* neighbour [US neighbor]; *nuestros vecinos son muy ruidosos* our neighbours are very noisy ‖ resident (residente) ‖ inhabitant; *los vecinos de Madrid* the inhabitants of Madrid ‖ — *cada* or *cualquier hijo de vecino* everyone, anyone, every mother's son ‖ *los vecinos de esta calle* the residents in *o* the people who live in this street ‖ *ser vecino de Soria* to live in Soria ‖ *son vecinos del mismo piso* or *de la misma planta* they live on the same floor.

vector *adj/sm* vector; *radio vector* radius vector.

vectorial *adj* vectorial.

veda *f* close season [US closed season] (pesca, caza) ‖ prohibition (prohibición) ‖ *levantamiento de la veda* opening of the season.

Veda *m* Veda (libro sagrado de la India).

vedado *m* private preserve ‖ — *cazar en vedado* to poach, to hunt on a private preserve ‖ *vedado de caza* (game) preserve.

vedar *vt* to prohibit, to forbid, to ban; *vedar la entrada en un sitio* to prohibit people from entering a place, to ban people from entering a place, to forbid people to enter a place ‖ to prevent (impedir) ‖ *coto vedado* (game) preserve.

vedegambre *m* white hellebore (planta).

vedeja *f* long hair.

védico, ca *adj* REL Vedic.

vedija *f* tuft of wool (de lana) ‖ matted lock [of hair] (de pelo).

vedijoso, sa *adj* having matted wool.

veedor *m* (ant) supervisor, inspector; *veedor de caminos* road inspector ‖ (ant) *veedor de vianda* royal caterer.

veeduría *f* supervisorship, inspectorship (cargo) ‖ inspector's *o* supervisor's office (oficina).

vega *f* fertile plain, fertile valley ‖ AMER tobacco plantation [in Cuba].

vegetación *f* vegetation.

vegetal *adj* vegetal; *medicamentos vegetales* vegetal medicines ‖ plant, vegetable; *el reino vegetal* the vegetable kingdom.

◆ *m* vegetable.

vegetalina *f* vegetable butter.

vegetar *vi* to grow, to vegetate (plantas) ‖ FIG to vegetate (las personas).

vegetarianismo *m* vegetarianism.

vegetariano, na *adj/s* vegetarian.

vegetativo, va *adj* vegetative.

veguer *m* magistrate [in Aragon, Catalonia and Majorca] (magistrado).

veguería *f*; **veguerío** *m* jurisdiction of a «veguer».

veguero, ra *adj* lowland, of the plains.
◆ *m* farmer (labrador) ‖ FAM cigar (puro).

vehemencia *f* vehemence, passion ‖ impetuosity (irreflexión).

vehemente *adj* vehement, passionate (apasionado) ‖ impetuous (irreflexivo).

vehículo *m* vehicle ‖ FIG vehicle (modo de transmisión) ‖ transmitter, carrier (de microbios); *las monedas son vehículo de microbios* coins are transmitters of germs ‖ *vehículo espacial* spacecraft.

veintavo, va *adj/sm* twentieth (vigésimo).

veinte *adj num* twenty; *veinte personas* twenty people; *página veinte* page 20 [twenty] ‖ twentieth; *en el siglo veinte* in the 20th [twentieth] century; *el día veinte* (on) the 20th [twentieth] ‖ — *los años veinte* the twenties ‖ FIG *son las menos veinte, son las y veinte* silence reigns (silencio en una conversación) ‖ *unos veinte* about twenty.
◆ *m* twenty (número) ‖ twentieth; *el veinte de mayo* the twentieth of May ‖ twenty, number twenty; *apostar en el veinte* to bet on number twenty.

veintena *f* about twenty, score; *una veintena de personas* about twenty people, a score of people.

veinteno, na *adj/sm* twentieth.

veinteñal *adj* twenty-year, of twenty years.

veintésimo, ma *adj/sm* twentieth.

veinticinco, ca *adj num/sm* twenty-five (cardinal) ‖ twenty-fifth (ordinal); *el veinticinco de mayo* the twenty-fifth of May.

veinticuatro *adj num/sm* twenty-four (cardinal) ‖ twenty-fourth (ordinal); *el veinticuatro de junio* the twenty-four of June.
◆ *m* (ant) town councillor [in Andalusia].

veintidós *adj num/sm* twenty-two (cardinal) ‖ twenty-second (ordinal); *el veintidós de enero* the twenty-second of January.

veintinueve *adj num/sm* twenty-nine (cardinal) ‖ twenty-ninth (ordinal); *el veintinueve de julio* the twenty-ninth of July.

veintiocho *adj num/sm* twenty-eight (cardinal) ‖ twenty-eighth (ordinal); *el veintiocho de abril* the twenty-eighth of April.

ventiséis *adj num/sm* twenty-six (cardinal) ‖ twenty-sixth (ordinal); *el veintiséis de marzo* the twenty-sixth of March.

veintisiete *adj num/sm* twenty-seven (cardinal) ‖ twenty-seventh (ordinal); *el veintisiete de diciembre* the twenty-seventh of December.

veintitantos, tas *adj* about twenty, twenty-odd; *veintitantas personas* about twenty *o* twenty-odd people ‖ about the twentieth; *sucedió hacia el veintitantos de abril* it happened about the twentieth of April.

veintitrés *adj num/sm* twenty-three (cardinal) ‖ twenty-third (ordinal); *el veintitrés de noviembre es mi cumpleaños* my birthday is on the twenty-third of November.

veintiún *adj num* twenty-one; *tener veintiún libros* to have twenty-one books.
— OBSERV This adjective is the apocopated form of *veintiuno* before masculine nouns.

veintiuno, na *adj num/sm* twenty-one (cardinal) ‖ twenty-first (ordinal); *el veintiuno de octubre* the twenty-first of October.
◆ *f* twenty-one, blackjack, vingt-et-un (juego de azar).

vejación *f*; **vejamen** *m* vexation (maltratamiento) ‖ humiliation (humillación).

vejancón, ona *adj* very old, doddery (*fam*).
◆ *m* old man.
◆ *f* old woman.

vejar *vt* to vex, to annoy, to hurt (ofender).

vejatorio, ria *adj* humiliating; *condiciones vejatorias* humiliating conditions ‖ hurtful, vexatious, offensive; *palabras vejatorias* hurtful words.

vejestorio *m* FAM old crock.

vejete *adj m* old.
◆ *m* old man, old boy.

vejez *f* old age.

vejiga *f* ANAT bladder ‖ blister (en la piel) ‖ — *vejiga de la bilis* gall bladder ‖ *vejiga natatoria* air *o* swimming bladder (de los peces).

vejigazo *m* blow with an air-filled bladder ‖ FAM *darse un vejigazo* to fall flat on one's face.

vejiguilla *f* blister (en la piel).

vela *f* MAR sail; *vela latina* lateen sail ‖ candle; *vela de estearina* tallow candle ‖ wakefulness (desvelo) ‖ vigil, watch (de un muerto) ‖ vigil, watching over (de un enfermo) ‖ FIG horn (del toro) ‖ — MAR *hacerse a la vela* to set sail | *a toda vela* under full sail | *barco de vela* sailing ship | *cambiar la vela* to shift sail | *dar la vela* to set sail ‖ FIG & FAM *encender* or *poner una vela a Dios y otra al diablo* to run with the hare and hunt with the hounds ‖ FIG *no tener vela en un entierro* to have no say in the matter ‖ *pasar la noche en vela* to have a sleepless night, not to get a wink of sleep all night ‖ FIG *¿quién te dio vela en este entierro?* who asked you to poke your nose in? | *ser más derecho que una vela* to be as straight as a die ‖ MAR *vela al tercio* lugsail | *vela de abanico* or *tarquina* spritsail | *vela de estay* staysail | *vela mayor* mainsail.
◆ *pl* FAM snot *sing* (mocos) ‖ — MAR *alzar velas* to set sail | *a velas desplegadas* or *tendidas* under full sail ‖ FIG & FAM *estar a dos velas* to be broke ‖ MAR *largar las velas* to set sail ‖ FIG *recoger velas* to back down.

velación *f* vigil, watching over (de un enfermo) ‖ vigil, wake (de un muerto).
◆ *pl* ceremony *sing* of the veil [with which the bride and groom are covered during the wedding].

velacho *m* MAR fore-topsail (vela).

velada *f* evening; *quedarse de velada con unos amigos* to spend the evening with a few friends; *velada literaria* literary evening ‖ party [held at night] (reunión de personas).

velado, da *adj* veiled (cubierto con un velo) ‖ FIG veiled; *alusión velada* veiled reference; *ojos velados por lágrimas* eyes veiled in *o* by tears ‖ BOT blurred ‖ *voz velada* muffled voice.

velador, ra *adj* who watches, watching.
◆ *m* vigil-keeper (que vela) ‖ watchman (que hace guardia) ‖ pedestal table (mesita) ‖ candlestick (candelero) ‖ AMER bedside table (mesita de noche).

veladura *f* glaze (en pintura) ‖ FOT fog.

velamen *m* MAR canvas, sails *pl* ‖ ANAT velamen.

velar *vi* to stay awake, not to sleep (no dormir) ‖ to stay up (no acostarse) ‖ to keep watch (hacer guardia) ‖ REL to keep vigil ‖ to work late (trabajar tarde) ‖ FIG to watch over, to look after; *velar por la salud de un enfermo* to watch over a sick person ‖ *velar por la observancia de las leyes* to make sure *o* to ensure that the laws are observed.
◆ *vt* to watch over, to sit up with; *velar a un enfermo* to watch over a sick person ‖ to stand vigil over (a un muerto) ‖ to veil (cubrir con un velo) ‖ FIG to veil, to hide (disimular) ‖ FOT to fog, to blur ‖ to glaze (en pintura) ‖ *velar las armas* to carry out the vigil of arms.
◆ *vpr* FOT to be fogged *o* blurred.

velar *adj/sf* ANAT & GRAM velar.

velatorio *m* vigil, wake.

velazqueño, ña *adj* of Velazquez, typical of Velazquez.

veleidad *f* caprice, whim (deseo vano) ‖ fickleness, inconstancy (versatilidad).

veleidoso, sa *adj* inconstant, fickle.

velero, ra *adj* sailing; *barco velero* sailing ship *o* boat.
◆ *m* MAR sailing ship (barco grande) | sailing boat (pequeño) | sailmaker (que hace velas para barcos) ‖ chandler (de velas de cera).

veleta *f* weather vane, weathercock (para el viento) ‖ float (de caña de pescar).
◆ *m/f* FIG weathercock, inconstant person (persona).

velilla *f* match (cerilla).

velo *m* veil; *velo de novia* bride's veil ‖ FIG veil, shroud ‖ confusion (confusión) ‖ ANAT velum, veil ‖ — FIG *correr* or *echar un velo* or *un tupido velo sobre algo* to hush sth. up, to draw a veil over sth., to keep sth. quiet | *descorrer el velo* to draw back the veil ‖ REL *tomar el velo* to take the veil ‖ ANAT *velo del paladar* velum, soft palate ‖ REL *velo humeral* humeral veil.

velocidad *f* speed, velocity; *la velocidad de la luz* the speed of light ‖ TECN & AUT gear; *tiene cuatro velocidades* it has four gears; *cambiar de velocidad* to change gear ‖ MÚS speed (rapidez de ejecución) ‖ INFORM speed ‖ — *a gran velocidad* at a high speed ‖ *a toda velocidad* (at) full speed ‖ AUT *caja de velocidades* gearbox ‖ FIG *confundir el tocino con la velocidad* not to know one's left hand from one's right ‖ *con gran velocidad* very fast, with great speed ‖ FIG *con la velocidad del rayo* like lightning, as quick as a flash ‖ TECN *de alta velocidad* high-speed ‖ *disminuir la velocidad* to reduce speed, to slow down ‖ *en gran velocidad* by express (ferrocarril) ‖ *en pequeña velocidad* by goods train [US by freight] (ferrocarril) ‖ *Europa de dos velocidades* two-speed Europe ‖ *ganar velocidad* to pick up speed, to gather speed ‖ *meter la segunda velocidad* to change into second gear (automóvil) ‖ *multado por exceso de velocidad* fined for speeding *o* for exceeding the speed limit ‖ *perder velocidad* to lose speed (un avión, un vehículo), to lose its hold (una moda) ‖ *primera velocidad* first *o* bottom *o* low gear ‖ *velocidad de crucero* cruising speed ‖ *velocidad de liberación* escape velocity (de un vehículo espacial) ‖ *velocidad límite* speed limit ‖ *velocidad máxima* or *tope* or *punta* top speed.

velocímetro *m* speedometer.

velocípedo *m* velocipede.

velocista *m* DEP sprinter.

velódromo *m* cycle track [US velodrome].

velomotor *m* moped, small motorcycle.

velón *m* oil lamp (lámpara de aceite) ‖ AMER thick candle (vela grande).

velonero *m* lamp maker.

velorio *m* wake, vigil (velatorio) ‖ party, celebration (fiesta) ‖ REL taking of the veil (de una monja).

veloz *adj* quick, fast, rapid, swift; *veloz como un rayo* as quick as lightning *o* as a flash.
◆ *adv* fast, quickly, rapidly, swiftly; *corre muy veloz* he runs very fast.

velozmente *adv* fast, quickly, rapidly, swiftly.

veludillo *m* velveteen (tela).

vello *m* down.

vellocino *m* fleece ‖ MIT *Vellocino de oro* Golden Fleece.

vellón *m* fleece (de carnero u oveja) ‖ tuft of wool (vedija) ‖ copper coin (monedas).

vellosidad *f* downiness, fluffiness || down (vello).

velloso, sa *adj* downy, hairy, fluffy.

velludillo *m* velveteen (tela).

velludo, da *adj* hairy, shaggy.
◆ *m* plush (felpa).

vena *f* ANAT vein || vein, streak (de piedras, maderas) || BOT vein, rib || GEOL & MIN vein, seam || — FIG & FAM *coger a alguien en vena* to catch s.o. in the right mood | *estar en vena para* to be in the mood for | *estar en vena* to be on form | *le ha dado la vena de ir al Polo* he has taken *o* got it into his head to go to the Pole | *tener una vena de loco* to have a streak *o* a vein of madness | *tener vena de pintor* to have a gift for painting || FIG & FAM *trabajar por venas* to work in fits and starts || ANAT *vena cava* vena cava | *vena porta* portal vein.

venablo *m* javelin, dart (arma) || FIG *echar venablos* to roar with anger.

venadero *m* place frequented by deer (del ciervo).

venado *m* deer, stag (ciervo) || CULIN venison.

venal *adj* venal; *funcionario venal* venal official || ANAT venous (venoso) || venal, purchasable (que se puede comprar).

venalidad *f* venality.

venático, ca *adj* fickle, inconstant.

venatorio, ria *adj* hunting.

vencedero, ra *adj* COM falling due (pago).

vencedor, ra *adj* conquering, victorious; *el ejército vencedor* the conquering army || winning, victorious (equipo, jugador).
◆ *m/f* conqueror, victor || winner, victor (ganador).

vencejo *m* bond (atadura) || ZOOL swift (pájaro).

vencer *vt* to conquer, to vanquish, to defeat, to beat; *vencer a los enemigos* to defeat the enemy || DEP to beat || FIG to overcome, to surmount; *vencer un obstáculo* to surmount an obstacle | to master (pasiones) | to overcome (tentación, sueño) | to outdo, to surpass, to beat; *vencer a uno en generosidad* to outdo s.o. in generosity | to cover (recorrer); *vencer una distancia* to cover a distance | to conquer; *el Aconcagua fue vencido en 1897* the Aconcagua was conquered in 1897 | to break (romper); *el peso de los libros ha vencido la mesa* the books were so heavy that they broke the table || *dejarse vencer* to give up the fight, to give in.
◆ *vi* to win, to triumph (ganar, triunfar) || to fall due, to be payable; *la cuenta vence mañana* the bills falls due tomorrow || to expire (plazo) || to fall due, to mature (deuda).
◆ *vpr* FIG to control o.s. (controlarse) | to bend, to sag (doblarse) | to break, to collapse (romperse).

vencetósigo *m* BOT white swallowwort.

vencible *adj* conquerable, vanquishable (país, enemigo) || beatable (adversario) || FIG surmountable, which can be overcome (superable).

vencida *f* *a la tercera va la vencida* third time lucky (para animar), let that be the last time.

vencido, da *adj* defeated, beaten || losing (que pierde) || due, payable (un pagaré, etc.) || mature, falling due (deuda) || expired (plazo).
◆ *m/f* conquered *o* vanquished person || DEP loser || — *¡ay* or *guay de los vencidos!* woe betide the conquered! || *darse por vencido* to give up, to admit defeat || *la tormenta va de vencida* the worst of the storm is over || *los vencidos* the conquered, the vanquished (en una guerra), the losers (en deportes, etc.).

vencimiento *m* falling due (de un pagaré, etc.) || maturity (de una deuda) || expiration, expiry (de un plazo) || FIG overcoming, surmounting (de un obstáculo) || victory (victoria) || defeat (derrota) || FIG bending (torsión) | collapse (al romperse).

venda *f* bandage; *venda de gasa* gauze bandage || dressing (vendaje) || band, fillet (de cabeza) || — FIG *quitar a uno la venda de los ojos* to open s.o.'s eyes | *se le cayó la venda de los ojos* his eyes were opened | *tener una venda en los ojos* to go around blindfolded *o* with one's eyes closed, to be blind.

vendaje *m* MED dressing || *vendaje enyesado* plaster cast (para un miembro roto).

vendar *vt* to bandage (una herida) || — FIG *la pasión le venda los ojos* he is blinded by passion || *vendar los ojos a alguien* to blindfold s.o.
◆ *vpr* to bandage; *vendarse el brazo* to bandage one's arm.

vendaval *m* gale, strong wind || FIG storm.

vendedor, ra *adj* selling.
◆ *m* salesman (en una tienda de muebles, coches, etc.) || seller; *vendedor de periódicos* newspaper seller || shop assistant (dependiente) || — *vendedor ambulante* pedlar [US peddler], hawker || *vendedor ambulante de periódicos* newsboy || *vendedor callejero* street hawker.
◆ *f* salesgirl, saleswoman, shop assistant.

vendehúmos *m/f inv* FAM braggart, show-off.

vendeja *f* public sale (feria).

vender *vt* to sell; *vender naranjas* to sell oranges; *vender un cuadro en* or *por diez mil pesetas* to sell a painting for ten thousand pesetas || FIG to sell; *vender su alma* to sell one's soul | to sell (out), to betray (traicionar); *vender a un amigo* to sell a friend || — *artículo sin vender* unsold article || FIG *el enemigo ha vendido cara su derrota* the enemy put up a good fight || *vender al contado* to sell for cash || *vender al descubierto* to sell short (en la Bolsa) || *vender al por mayor* to wholesale, to sell wholesale || *vender al por menor* to retail || *vender a plazos* or *a cuota (amer)* to sell on credit || *vender cara su vida* to sell one's life dearly, to put up a good fight || *vender caro* to sell at a high price, to be expensive (un comerciante) || *vender con pérdida* to sell at a loss || *vender de contrabando* to sell illegally || *vender en pública subasta* to auction || FIG *vender la piel del oso antes de haberlo matado* to count one's chickens before they are hatched || *vender por las casas* to sell from door to door || *vender salud* to be glowing *o* brimming with health.
◆ *vpr* to cost; *actualmente el terreno se vende caro* land costs a lot these days || FIG to sell o.s. (dejarse sobornar) | to give o.s. away (traicionarse) || — *«se vende»* «for sale» || *se vende en las principales librerías* it is on sale in the main bookshops || *se vende un coche deportivo* sports car for sale || *venderse a* or *por* to sell for *o* at, to cost, to fetch; *los huevos se venden a veinte pesetas la docena* eggs are selling at twenty pesetas a dozen || FIG *venderse caro* to play hard to get | *venderse como rosquillas* or *como pan caliente* to sell like hot cakes.

vendí *m* certificate of sale.

vendido, da *adj* sold || FIG lost.

vendimia *f* grape harvest, vintage (recolección) || vintage; *la vendimia de 1944* the 1944 vintage.

vendimiador, ra *m/f* vintager, grape harvester.

vendimiar *vt* to harvest, to gather (las uvas).

vendo *m* selvedge (de la tela).

venduta *f* AMER auction (subasta).

Venecia *n pr* GEOGR Venice (ciudad) | Venetia (región).

veneciano, na *adj/s* Venetian (de Venecia).

venencia *f* tube [for sampling sherry].

veneno *m* poison (químico o vegetal); *la estricnina es un veneno violento* strychnine is a powerful poison || venom, poison (de los animales) || FIG poison (que causa daño moral) | venom, spite (malevolencia) || FIG *sus palabras destilan veneno* his words are venomous *o* full of venom.

venenoso, sa *adj* poisonous, poison; *seta venenosa* poisonous mushroom || venomous, poison, poisonous; *serpiente venenosa* venomous snake || FIG poisonous (que causa daño moral) | venomous (malevolente).

venera *f* scallop (concha) || spring (manantial).

venerabilísimo, ma *adj* very *o* most venerable.

venerable *adj/s* venerable.

veneración *f* veneration || worship (adoración).

venerar *vt* to venerate, to revere; *venerar a uno por santo* to venerate s.o. as a saint || to worship (adorar).

venéreo, a *adj* MED venereal.
◆ *m* MED venereal disease.

venero *m* spring (manantial) || MIN seam, vein (yacimiento) || FIG source (origen) | mine; *venero de informaciones* mine of information.

véneto, ta *adj/s* Venetian.

venezolanismo *m* Venezuelan expression (giro) *o* word (voz).

venezolano, na *adj/s* Venezuelan.

Venezuela *npr m* GEOGR Venezuela.

vengador, ra *adj* avenging.
◆ *m/f* avenger.

venganza *f* vengeance, revenge; *clamar venganza* to demand vengeance; *tomar venganza de alguien* to take revenge on s.o.

vengar *vt* to avenge.
◆ *vpr* to avenge o.s., to take revenge; *vengarse de una afrenta en uno* to avenge o.s. *o* to take revenge on s.o. for an insult.

vengativo, va *adj* vindictive, vengeful.

venia *f* forgiveness, pardon (perdón) || permission, leave, consent; *con la venia del profesor* with the teacher's permission || greeting (saludo).

venial *adj* venial; *pecado venial* venial sin.

venialidad *f* veniality.

venida *f* coming (acción de venir); *idas y venidas* comings and goings || arrival, coming (llegada); *la venida de la primavera* the arrival of spring || flooding (de un río) || attack (esgrima) || *me alegro de tu venida* I am delighted (that) you have come.

venidero, ra *adj* future, coming; *los años venideros* future years || *en lo venidero* in the future.
◆ *m pl* future generations, descendants.

venilla *f* ANAT small vein.

venir* *vi* to come; *él va a venir* he is going to come; *¡ven aquí!* come here; *dile que venga* tell him to come || to arrive (llegar); *vino muy cansado* he arrived very tired || to come (proceder); *este té viene de Ceilán* this tea comes from Ceylon; *su mala conducta viene de su educación* his ill conduct comes from his upbringing || to come (suceder); *la primavera viene después del invierno* spring comes after winter || to have been; *lo vengo diciendo desde hace diez años* I have been saying it for the last ten years || to happen (ocurrir) || to be, to come; *su foto viene en la primera página* his photograph is on the first page || to be, to be written; *el texto viene en inglés* the text is written in English || to be; *este piso nos viene ancho* this flat is too big for us; *me viene un poco estrecho* it is rather tight

for me || to be; *vengo triste* I am sad || — *¿a dónde quieres venir a parar?* what are you getting at?, what do you mean by that? || *a mal venir* at the worst || *¿a qué viene esto?* what is that doing here? (un objeto), what is the point of that? (una acción) || *¿a qué viene llorar?* what is the good *o* the point of crying? || *¿a qué vienes?* what are you doing here?, what do you want here? || *como le venga en gana* as you like, as it suits you, just as you wish || *de ahí viene que...* so it is that..., thus it is that... || *depende de cómo venga la cosa* that will depend on the circumstances || *el año que viene* next year, the coming year || *en el periódico de hoy viene un reportaje muy interesante* in today's paper there is a very interesting report || *en lo por venir* in future (de aquí en adelante), in the future (en lo futuro) || *eso no viene a cuento* that has nothing to do with it, that is irrelevant (no tiene nada que ver), there is no sense in it (no es oportuno) || *eso vengo diciendo desde hace tiempo* that's what I've been saying all along || *hacer venir a uno* to summon s.o., to bring s.o., to send for s.o. || *le vino en gana marcharse al extranjero* he took it into his head *o* he got the urge to go abroad || FIG *lo veía venir* I could see it coming, I was expecting it || *me vinieron ganas de reír* I felt like laughing, I could have laughed || *me vino un dolor de muelas terrible* I got terrible toothache || FAM *no le va ni le viene* it has nothing to do with him, it is none of his business (no le importa), he doesn't care one way or the other, he couldn't care less (le da igual) || *no me viene su nombre a la memoria* I cannot remember his name, his name escapes me || *se le vino* or *le vino a la boca un disparate* he put his foot in it || *si a mano viene* should the occasion arise || *vendrá a tener cincuenta años* he must be about fifty || *¡venga!* come on!; *¡venga!, que vamos a llegar tarde* come on, we shall be late; go on! (anda), give it to me!, give it here! (dámelo) || *venga como venga la cosa* come what may, whatever happens, whatever may happen || *venga lo que venga* come what may || *venga o no venga a cuento* without rhyme or reason (a tontas y a locas), rightly or wrongly (con razón o sin ella) || *venir a* to reach, to arrive at (alcanzar); *vinieron a un acuerdo* they reached an agreement; to end up (by) (acabar por); *vinieron a firmar las paces* they ended up signing the treaty || *venir a cuento* to be opportune (ser oportuno), to be relevant (ser pertinente) || *venir a la cabeza* to come to mind || *venirle a la memoria a uno* to remember, to occur to; *me vino a la memoria que...* I remembered that..., it occurred to me that... || *venir a la mente* to cross one's mind; *la sospecha no me vino a la mente* the suspicion did not cross my mind; to come to mind; *me vienen a la mente tristes pensamientos* sad thoughts come to my mind || *venir a las manos* to arrive, to reach; *tu carta llegó a mis manos ayer* your letter reached me yesterday *o* arrived yesterday; to come to blows (pegarse) || *venir al mundo* to come into the world || FAM *venir a punto* to come in handy, to come at a good moment, to come just right || *venir a menos* to go downhill (una empresa), to lose status, to come down in the world (personas) || *venir a parar* to come to, to end (up) *sus ilusiones han venido a parar en eso* his illusions have come to that; to result in, to lead to (dar lugar a), to reach, to arrive at, to come to; *venir a parar a la misma conclusión* to reach the same conclusion; to end (up), to stop; *la pelota vino a parar a mis pies* the ball ended up at my feet || *venir a ser* to boil down to, to amount to; *venir a ser lo mismo* to boil down to the same thing; to turn out (resultar); *viene a ser más molesto de lo que pensábamos* it is turning out to be more bothersome than we expected; to be, to amount to; *esto viene a ser una mera estafa* this is a downright swindle || *venir con cuentos* to tell stories || *venir en decretar, en nombrar* to decree, to appoint || FAM *venirle al pelo a uno* to suit s.o. down to the ground || *venirle bien a uno* to suit s.o.; *el verde te viene bien* green suits you; to fit; *¿te viene bien el abrigo? no, es un poco largo* does the coat fit you? no, it is a little long; to come in handy (ser útil); *esas diez mil pesetas me vendrían muy bien* those ten thousand pesetas would come in very handy for me; to suit (convenir); *me vendría muy bien ir a las siete* it would suit me to go at seven || *venirle mal a uno* not to suit s.o., not to fit s.o. (traje), to be inconvenient for s.o., to be a nuisance for s.o. (no convenir); *me viene mal ir esta tarde* it is inconvenient for me to go this afternoon || *venir mejor* to suit *o* to fit better (convenir o ir mejor), to be better (ser mejor) || FAM *venir que ni pintado* to suit down to the ground, to suit to a tee | *venir rodado* to come *o* to arrive just at the right time *o* moment || FIG *verle venir a uno* to see s.o. coming || *vino una inundación a estropear la cosecha* a flood destroyed *o* came and destroyed the crop || *voy y vengo* I'll be right back.
◆ *vpr* to come back, to go back (volver) || to ferment (el vino) || — *la sala se venía abajo con los aplausos* the applause shook the hall || *todo se nos vino encima a la vez* everything came upon us at once, everything went wrong at once || *venirse abajo* to fall down, to collapse (un edificio), to fall through, to collapse (un proyecto) || *venirse al suelo* or *a tierra* to fall down (derrumbarse), to fail (fracasar), to collapse (hundirse), to collapse, to crumble (ilusiones), to fall through (planes).

venosidad *f* ANAT venosity.

venoso, sa *adj* venous; *sangre venosa* venous blood || veinly, veined; *manos venosas* veined hands || veined, ribbed; *hoja venosa* veined leaf.

venta *f* sale, selling; *la venta de la leche* the sale of milk; *la compra y la venta de muebles* the buying and selling of furniture, the purchase and sale of furniture || sales *pl*; *servicio de venta* sales department || — *contrato de venta* bill of sale || *de venta en todas las librerías* on sale in all bookshops || *estar a la venta* or *en venta* to be on sale || *poner en venta* to put on sale (un producto), to put up for sale; *no tiene más remedio que poner su casa en venta* he has no choice but to put his house up for sale || *precio de venta* selling price || *precio de venta al público* retail price || *ser un artículo de fácil venta* to sell || *venta a crédito* sale on credit || *venta a domicilio* or *a puerta fría* door-to-door selling || *venta al contado* cash sale || *venta al por menor* retail || *venta a plazos*, AMER *por cuotas* hire purchase [US sale on the installment plan] || *venta callejera* street-selling, peddling || *venta CF (coste y flete)* cost and freight sale || *venta de localidades de 7 a 9* the ticket office *o* the booking office is open from 7 to 9 || *venta en firme* firm sale || *venta por catálogo* catalogue sale | *venta por correo* or *por correspondencia* mail-order selling || *venta postbalance* stocktaking sale [US post-inventory sale] || *venta pública* public sale.

ventaja *f* advantage; *tiene la ventaja de ser fuerte* he has the advantage of being strong || benefit; *ventajas sociales* social benefits || profit (provecho) || advantage (en deportes) || headstart, start (en una carrera) || — *dar dos metros de ventaja a uno* to give s.o. a two-metre start || *llevar ventaja a* to have the advantage over *o* the edge on (s.o.) || *sacar ventaja a* to be ahead of; *sacó ventaja de 20 metros or de 20 segundos a su competidor* he was 20 metres *o* 20 seconds ahead of his opponent; *sacar gran* or *mucha ventaja* to be well ahead; to leave behind (ser superior) || *sacar ventaja de* to profit *o* to benefit from.

ventajero, ra; ventajista *m/f* AMER advantage-taker, opportunist.
◆ *adj* opportunist.

ventajoso, sa *adj* advantageous; *me ofrecieron condiciones muy ventajosas* they offered me very advantageous conditions || profitable (rentable); *fue un negocio muy ventajoso* it was a very profitable deal.

ventalla *f* valve [of a legume].

ventana *f* window || nostril (de la nariz) || INFORM window || — FIG *tirar algo por la ventana* to waste sth., to throw sth. away | *tirar la casa por la ventana* to spare no expense, to go overboard, to lash out (*fam*) || *ventana de guillotina* sash window || *ventana vidriera* picture window.

ventanal *m* large window.

ventanilla *f* window (en los trenes, coches, aviones) || porthole (en los barcos) || window (taquilla) || ANAT nostril (de la nariz).

ventanillo *m* wicket, small window (postigo pequeño) || peephole (mirilla) || ventilator (de un sótano) || window (de un avión).

venteado, da *adj* windy.

ventarrón *m* gale, strong wind (viento fuerte).

ventear *v impers* to be windy.
◆ *vt/vi* to air, to air out (una habitación, un vestido, etc.) || to sniff (olfatear) || FIG to snoop (investigar) | to smell (sospechar).
◆ *vpr* to split (agrietarse) || to blister (los ladrillos al cocerse) || to spoil (estropearse) || FAM to break wind (ventosear).

ventero, ra *m/f* innkeeper.
◆ *adj* *perro ventero* pointer.

ventilación *f* ventilation; *la ventilación de un túnel* the ventilation of a tunnel || — *conducto de ventilación* air duct, ventilation shaft || MAR *manguera de ventilación* windsail (de lona), air intake (de metal) || *sin ventilación* unventilated || *ventilación pulmonar* pulmonary ventilation.

ventilador *m* ventilator (para ventilar) || fan (para refrescar o mover el aire) || window fan (en una ventana).

ventilar *vt* to ventilate; *ventilar un túnel* to ventilate a tunnel || to air, to ventilate, to air out; *ventilar la habitación abriendo la ventana* to air the room by opening the window || FIG to air (hacer público) | to clear up [US to take care of] (discutir y resolver).
◆ *vpr* to be aired, to be aired out (un cuarto, etc.) || to be ventilated (túnel, etc.) || FIG to be cleared up, to be discussed (resolverse) | to be at stake (estar en juego); *se ventila su porvenir* his future is at stake || FIG & FAM to knock off, to polish off; *este trabajo me lo ventilo en una hora* I'll knock off this job in an hour || to get some fresh air (tomar el aire) || — *el resultado del partido se ventiló en los últimos cinco minutos* the outcome of the match was decided in the last five minutes || FAM *ventilárselas* to take care of o.s. (arreglárselas).

ventisca *f* blizzard, snowstorm.

ventiscar *v impers* to blow a blizzard; *está ventiscando* it is blowing a blizzard.
◆ *vi* to swirl (la nieve).

ventisco *m* blizzard, snowstorm.

ventisquear *vi* → **ventiscar.**

ventisquero *m* glacier (helero) || snowdrift (nieve acumulada) || slope *o* part of a mountain most exposed to snowstorms || blizzard, snowstorm (ventisca).

ventolera *f* gust of wind, blast (ráfaga) || whirligig [US pinwheel] (molinillo de juguete) || — FIG & FAM *darle a uno la ventolera de hacer algo* to take it into one's head to do sth. | *darle a uno la ventolera por alguien* to take a fancy to s.o. | *tener mucha ventolera* to be bigheaded, to have a big head (ser muy vanidoso).

ventolina *f* light and variable wind.

ventor, ra *adj* tracking.
◆ *m* pointer (perro).

ventorrillo *m* roadhouse (merendero).

ventorro *m* small inn (venta pequeña).

ventosa *f* MED cupping glass || suction cup (objeto que se adhiere) || sucker (de los animales) || vent, air hole (abertura).

ventosear *vi* to break wind.

ventosidad *f* wind, flatulence.

ventoso, sa *adj* windy; *día ventoso* windy day.

ventral *adj* ventral.

ventregada *f* litter (camada).

ventrera *f* cinch (cincha) || abdominal support (faja) || (skirt of) tasses (de la armadura).

ventricular *adj* ventricular.

ventrículo *m* ANAT ventricle.

ventrílocuo, cua *adj* ventriloquistic.
◆ *m/f* ventriloquist.

ventroloquia *f* ventriloquy, ventriloquism.

ventrudo, da *adj* FAM potbellied.

ventura *f* happiness (felicidad) || good fortune; *tienes la ventura de tener a tus hijos contigo* you have the good fortune of having your children with you || (good) luck; *le deseo mucha ventura en su nuevo trabajo* I wish you lots of (good) luck in your new job || fate, fortune (casualidad); *la ventura quiso que me encontrara con ella* fate led me to meet her || hazard (riesgo) || — *a la ventura, a la buena ventura* at random (al azar), without a fixed plan (sin nada previsto) || *echar la buena ventura a alguien* to tell s.o.'s fortune || *mala ventura* bad *o* ill luck || *por ventura* by chance (por casualidad), luckily, fortunately (afortunadamente) || *probar ventura* to try one's luck.

venturina *f* aventurine (piedra).

venturo, ra *adj* future.

venturosamente *adv* fortunately.

venturoso, sa *adj* happy (feliz) || fortunate, lucky (afortunado) || successful (que tiene éxito).

venus *f* ZOOL venus (género de moluscos) || FIG venus (mujer muy bella).

Venus *npr f* MIT Venus (diosa) || *monte de Venus* mount of Venus.

Venus *npr m* ASTR Venus.

ver *m* sight, vision (sentido de la vista) || looks *pl*, appearance (de una persona) || appearance (de una cosa) || opinion; *a mi ver* in my opinion || *un hombre de buen ver* a good-looking man.

ver* *vt/vi* to see; *lo he visto con mis propios ojos* I saw it with my own eyes; *no le vi marcharse* I didn't see him leave; *no le veo* I can't see him; *no veo muy bien por qué lo hiciste* I can't really see why you did it; *vea Vd. si le va este traje* see if this suit fits you; *ir a ver a un amigo* to go to see a friend; *voy a ver si puedo* I'm going to see if I can || to know (saber); *no veo la decisión que he de tomar* I don't know what decision to make || to look at (mirar); *está viendo un documento muy importante* he's looking at a very important document || to watch (la televisión) || to find; *te veo cansado* I find you tired || JUR to hear, to try (una causa) || — *¡a más ver!, ¡hasta más ver!* I'll be seeing you!, so long! || *a mi modo de ver* in my opinion, to my way of thinking, the way I see it || *aquí donde me ve usted* as sure as I am standing here now, surprising though it may seem || *a ver* let's see, let's have a look (con curiosidad); *a ver qué película echan* let's see what film they're showing; all right, now then (con tono imperioso); *¡a ver! ¿qué pasa aquí?* all right, what's going on here? || *¡a ver qué pasa!* so what! (desafío) || *a ver si* how about; *a ver si estudias un poco más* how about studying a little more; I hope (that); *a ver si puedo acabar este trabajo hoy* I hope I can finish this job today; what if, supposing; *a ver si es que se ha perdido* what if he got lost? || *como si lo viera* as if I were seeing it with my own eyes || *darse a ver* to show o.s. || *dejarse ver* to show up, to show one's face (una persona), to show (manifestarse) || *dejar ver* to make it clear *o* understood || *deje que vea* let me see || *dígame a ver* tell me || *echar de ver* to realize, to see (darse cuenta) || *echa un poco de sal a la sopa a ver qué pasa* put a little salt in the soup to see what happens || *estar viendo* to be beginning to think (sospechar), to see (imaginarse); *te estoy viendo hacer el equipaje* I can just see you packing your bags || *esto está por ver, esto habrá que verlo* that remains to be seen || *¡habría que ver que lo hicieses!* you wouldn't dare (do it), I'd like to see you (do it) || *hacer ver algo a alguien* to point sth. out to s.o., to make s.o. see sth. || *hay que ver* you should see, it's amazing; *hay que ver lo que ha crecido* you should see how much he's grown, it's amazing how much he's grown || *¡hay que ver!* it just goes to show! || *hay que verlo* it's worth seeing || *hay que verlo para creerlo* it has to be seen to be believed || *le haré ver quien soy yo* I'll show him || *lo estaba viendo* I could see it coming || *¿lo ves?* see!, you see! || *manera de ver las cosas* way of looking at things || *mire a ver* have a look || *mire a ver si puede hacerlo* see if you can do it || *no dejarse ver* to keep out of sight (esconderse), to make o.s. scarce (desaparecer) || *no hay quien te vea* you've been making yourself scarce || *no le veo la gracia* I don't think that's funny || *no puedo verle, no puedo verle ni pintado* I can't bear *o* stand *o* stick him, I can't bear the sight of him, I hate the very sight of him || *no tener nada que ver con* to have nothing to do with || *no ver más allá de sus narices* not to be able to see further than the end of one's nose || *no ver ni jota, no ver tres en un burro* to be as blind as a bat (ser miope), not to be able to see a thing (en un sitio oscuro) || *nunca he visto cosa igual* I've never seen anything like it, I've never seen such a thing || *¡para que veas!* so there!, you see! || *por lo que veo, por lo que se ve, por lo visto* apparently, it seems that || FIG & FAM *que no veo* ever so, terribly; *tengo un hambre que no veo* I'm ever so hungry; rotten; *tengo un constipado que no veo* I've got a rotten cold || *ser de ver* to be worth seeing || *si no lo veo no lo creo* I would never have believed it || FIG *si te he visto no me acuerdo* you (he, etc.) just don't want to know | *te lo veo en la cara* I can see it in your eyes | *tener que ver con* to have to do with, to concern | *tener que ver en* to have a hand in | *te veo venir* I see you coming, I know what you're after || *vamos a ver* let's see || *verás* you'll see || *ver de* to try to (*con infinitivo*), to see about (*con gerundio*) || *veremos* we'll see || *ver es creer* seeing is believing || FIG *ver las estrellas* to see stars | *verlas venir* to catch on quickly || *ya lo veo, ya se ve* that's obvious, that's easy to see || *ya veremos* we'll see || *ya ves* you see.
◆ *vpr* to be seen (ser visto) || to be, to find o.s. (estar); *me veo en un apuro* I am in a jam || to see each other (visitarse) || to meet (encontrarse); *¿dónde nos vamos a ver?* where shall we meet? || to imagine o.s.; *esta chica ya se ve estrella de cine* this girl already imagines herself a film star || to remember (recordar); *me veo en mi juventud* I remember when I was young || to see o.s. (imaginar algo futuro); *ya me veo en la playa* I can already see myself on the beach || to look (parecer) || — *con tantas torres ya no se ve el cielo* with so many tower blocks you can't even see the sky || *¿cuándo se vio cosa igual?* did you ever see such a thing? || *es digno de verse, merece verse* it's worth seeing || *¡habrase visto!* did you ever! || FIG *se ve a la legua* or *de lejos* you can see it a mile away || *se ve que...* it is obvious that... || *véase el capítulo siguiente* see the following chapter || *verse con alguien* to see s.o. || FIG *vérselas con uno* to deal with s.o.

vera *f* edge, side || — *a la vera de* beside, next to || *a mi vera* beside me, at *o* by my side.

veracidad *f* truthfulness, veracity.

veranada *f* AGR summer season.

veranadero *m* summer pasture.

veranda *f* veranda.

veraneante *m/f* holidaymaker [*US* summer vacationist].

veranear *vi* to spend one's summer holidays [*US* to spend one's summer vacation]; *voy a veranear a Miami* I'm going to spend my summer holidays in Miami || *¿dónde veraneas este año?* where are you holidaying *o* where are you going for your holidays this summer?, where are you spending your summer holidays this year?

veraneo *m* summer holidays *pl* [*US* summer vacation]; *organizar el veraneo* to make all the arrangements for one's summer holidays || — *ir de veraneo* to go on holiday [*US* to take one's vacation] || *lugar de veraneo* summer resort.

veranero *m* summer pasture.

veraniego, ga *adj* summer; *temporada veraniega* summer season; *vestido veraniego* summer dress || *vas muy veraniego hoy* you look very summery today.

veranillo *m* *veranillo de San Juan* warm spell in June || *veranillo de San Martín* or *de San Miguel* or *del membrillo* Indian summer.

verano *m* summer; *vacaciones de verano* summer holidays || *vestirse de verano* to put on one's summer clothes.

veras *f pl* *ahora va de veras que me marcho* now I am really going || *de veras* really (realmente), seriously (seriamente) || *esto va de veras* this is serious, this is no joke || *lo siento de veras* I am truly sorry || *¿me lo dices de veras?* do you really mean that?

veraz *adj* truthful, veracious; *relato veraz* truthful account || reliable; *historiador veraz* reliable historian.

verbal *adj* verbal; *acuerdo verbal* verbal agreement; *sustantivo verbal* verbal noun.

verbalismo *m* verbalism.

verbalista *adj* verbalistic.
◆ *m/f* verbalist.

verbasco *m* BOT mullein.

verbena *f* BOT verbena, vervain || fair (fiesta popular) || dance [held on the eve of a saint's day] (baile).

verbenáceas *f pl* BOT verbenaceae.

verbenero, ra *adj* of the fair.

verbigracia; verbi gratia *loc* for example, for instance, e. g.

verbo *m* GRAM verb; *verbo auxiliar* auxiliary verb; *verbo transitivo* transitive verb || language, style (lenguaje, estilo) || — GRAM *verbo activo* active verb | *verbo impersonal* impersonal verb | *verbo intransitivo* intransitive verb | *verbo neutro* neutral verb | *verbo pasivo* passive verb | *verbo recíproco* reciprocal verb.

Verbo *npr m* REL Word.

verborrea *f* verbosity (verbosidad) || verbiage, wordiness (palabrería) || *tener mucha verborrea* to be verbose.

verbosidad *f* verbosity, wordiness.

verboso, sa *adj* verbose, wordy.

verdad *f* truth; *juró que diría toda la verdad* he swore that he would tell the whole truth; *acento de verdad* ring of truth; *verdad matemática* mathematical truth || *— a decir verdad, la verdad sea dicha* to tell the truth, actually || *bien es verdad que...* it is of course true that... || *cantarle* or *decirle a uno cuatro verdades* or *las verdades del barquero* to give s.o. a piece of one's mind, to tell s.o. a few home truths || *decir la verdad* to tell the truth || *de verdad* really (*adverbio*); *entonces me enfadé de verdad* then I really got angry; real (*adjetivo*); *un torero de verdad* a real bullfighter || *¿de verdad?* really? || FAM *de verdad de la buena* honest to God, honest to goodness || *de verdad que sí, que no* honestly, really || *en honor a la verdad* for truth's sake || *en verdad* verily (en la Biblia); *en verdad os digo* verily I say unto you || *es la pura verdad* it's the gospel truth || *eso es una verdad como un puño* or *como un templo* it's the patent truth || *es verdad* it is true || *faltar a la verdad* to lie || *hora de la verdad* momento of truth || *jurar decir la verdad, sólo la verdad y nada más que la verdad* to swear to tell the truth, the whole truth, and nothing but the truth || *la pura verdad* the plain truth || *las verdades amargan* the truth hurts || *la verdad* to tell the truth, actually; *la verdad no lo sé* actually I don't know || *la verdad escueta* or *al desnudo* the naked truth || *la verdad es que...* the truth is..., actually... || *no es verdad* it is not true || *¿no es verdad?* isn't that so? || *no hay más que los niños y los locos que dicen las verdades* out of the mouths of babes and fools || *no todas las verdades son para dichas* it is sometimes better not to tell the truth || *se lo digo de verdad* I really mean it || *si bien es verdad que* although (aunque) || *sólo la verdad ofende* nothing hurts like the truth || *tan de verdad* or *tan verdad como que Dios existe* it's the gospel truth || *uno de verdad* a real one || *¿verdad?* véase OBSERV || *verdad a medias* half-truth || *verdad de Perogrullo* truism, platitude || *verdad es que...* it is true that...

— OBSERV *Verdad* is also used as an invariable adjective to mean *real, true*: *los aristócratas verdad* the real aristocrats.

— OBSERV La expresión *¿verdad?* no tiene una traducción única sino que varía según la forma y la naturaleza del verbo. En cuanto a la forma, si el verbo se encuentra en una frase afirmativa, la expresión equivalente a *¿verdad?* tiene que ponerse en forma negativa (*estás contento, ¿verdad?* you are happy, aren't you?) y viceversa (*no estás contento, ¿verdad?* you are not happy, are you?). Por lo que se refiere a la naturaleza, cuando el verbo es un auxiliar, *¿verdad?* se traduce empleando el mismo auxiliar (*sabes nadar, ¿verdad?* you can swim, can't you?), pero en el caso en que se trate de un verbo transitivo, intransitivo, pronominal o defectivo hay que utilizar el auxiliar *do* (*trabaja muy bien, ¿verdad?* he works very well, doesn't he?). Hay que señalar además que el verbo, cualquiera que sea, tiene que ir en el tiempo y persona correspondientes a los del verbo de la frase inicial (*trabajaba muy bien, ¿verdad?* he worked very well, didn't he?).

verdaderamente *adv* truly, really.

verdadero, ra *adj* true, real; *historia verdadera* true story || real, genuine; *un diamante verdadero* a real diamond || truthful, veracious (veraz) || real, true; *un verdadero amigo* a real friend || ASTR true; *mediodía, norte verdadero* true noon, north || *— es el verdadero retrato de su padre* he is the spit and image *o* spitting image of his father || *lo verdadero* the true, what is true; *distinguir lo verdadero de lo falso* to distinguish the true from the false.

verdal *adj* green [even when ripe].

verdasca *f* switch, green stick (vara).

verde *adj* green; *un sombrero verde* a green hat || green, unripe (fruta) || green, unseasoned (leña) || FIG dirty, blue (licencioso); *contar chistes verdes* to tell dirty jokes | young, in the early stages; *el negocio está aún verde* the deal is still in the early stages || *— cuero en verde* green hide || FIG *estar verde de envidia* to be green with envy || *forraje verde* green fodder || *los Verdes* the Greens (militantes ecologistas) || FIG & FAM *pasar las verdes y las maduras* to have a really rough time || FAM *poner verde a uno* to call s.o. all the names under the sun || *tapete verde* gaming table || FAM *un viejo verde* a dirty old man.

◆ *m* green (color); *me gusta el verde* I like green || foliage (de las plantas) || grass (hierba) || FIG impropriety; *lo verde de sus palabras* the impropriety of his remarks || AMER maté, Paraguay tea || *verde esmeralda* emerald green.

verdear *vi* to look green (tirar a verde) || to grow *o* to turn green; *el campo empieza a verdear* the countryside is beginning to grow green.

verdeceledón *m* celadon (color).

verdecer *vi* to grow *o* to turn green.

verdecillo *m* greenfich (pájaro).

verdegal *m* green patch (en un campo) || green field (campo verde).

verdemar *adj* sea-green.

◆ *m* sea green.

verdeo *m* olive harvest.

verdeoscuro, ra *adj* dark green.

verderón *m* greenfinch (pájaro) || cockle (molusco).

verdete *m* verdigris.

verdezuelo *m* greenfinch (pájaro).

verdín *m* verdure, fresh green (de las plantas) || mildew, mould (moho) || verdigris (verdete, cardenillo) || moss (musgo) || green stain, grass stain (mancha en la ropa).

verdinegro, gra *adj* dark green.

verdolaga *f* purslane (planta).

verdor *m* verdure, greenness, verdancy (color) || FIG youth (juventud) | vigour, strength (vigor).

verdoso, sa *adj* greenish.

verdugado *m* hoopskirt, crinoline.

verdugal *m* hill covered with young plants.

verdugazo *m* lash [with a whip].

verdugo *m* executioner, hangman (ejecutor de la justicia) || BOT twig, shoot (vástago) || whip (látigo) || weal (verdugón) || bruise (cardenal) || FIG tyrant (tirano) | scourge (tormento); *ser un verdugo para sus alumnos* to be the scourge of one's pupils || ARQ horizontal layer of bricks || TAUR sword for accomplishing the «descabello».

verdugón *m* weal (hecho por un látigo) || bruise (cardenal) || twig, shoot (renuevo).

verduguillo *m* weal-like swelling [on leaves] (en las hojas) || small razor (navaja de afeitar) || TAUR sword for accomplishing the «descabello».

verdulería *f* greengrocer's (tienda); *ir a la verdulería* to go to the greengrocer's || FIG coarse word *o* expression (dicho grosero) | coarseness (grosería).

verdulero, ra *m/f* greengrocer.

◆ *f* FIG & FAM fishwife (mujer desvergonzada) || FAM *hablar como una verdulera* to speak like a fishwife.

verdura *f* verdure, greenery, greenness; *la verdura de los prados* the verdure of the meadows || greenness (color verde).

◆ *pl* vegetables, greens (hortalizas); *comer verduras* to eat greens || *verduras tempranas* early vegetables *o* greens.

verdusco, ca *adj* dirty green, greenish.

verecundia *f* bashfulness, timidity, shyness (vergüenza).

verecundo, da *adj* bashful, timid, shy (vergonzoso).

vereda *f* path, lane (senda) || AMER pavement [US sidewalk] (acera) || FIG & FAM *meter en vereda a uno* to bring s.o. into line.

veredicto *m* JUR verdict; *veredicto de inculpabilidad* verdict of not guilty.

verga *f* ANAT penis || MAR yard.

vergajo *m* pizzle whip, pizzle.

vergé *adj* *papel vergé* laid paper.

vergel *m* orchard (huerto).

vergeteado, da *adj* HERÁLD paly.

vergonzante *adj* shameful || *pobre vergonzante* poor but too proud to beg.

vergonzoso, sa *adj* shameful, disgraceful; *huida vergonzosa* shameful flight || shy, timid, bashful (tímido) || ANAT *partes vergonzosas* private parts, privates.

◆ *m/f* shy *o* timid *o* bashful person || *El vergonzoso en palacio* The Timid Youth at Court (de Tirso de Molina).

◆ *m* ZOOL variety of armadillo.

verguear *vt* to beat (varear).

vergüenza *f* shame (humillación, arrepentimiento); *por vergüenza no quiso confesar que estaba embarazada* shame prevented her from admitting that she was pregnant || embarrassment (confusión, bochorno) || bashfulness, shyness, timidity (timidez) || FIG disgrace, shame (oprobio); *eres la vergüenza de tu familia* you are a disgrace to your family || modesty (pudor) || honour [US honor], dignity (pundonor); *un hombre con vergüenza* a man of honour || *— con* or *para gran vergüenza suya* much to his shame (humillación), much to his embarrassment (confusión) || *¡es una vergüenza!* it is disgraceful *o* shameful!, it is a disgrace! || *me da vergüenza hablar en público* I don't like speaking *o* I'm shy about speaking in public, it embarrasses me to speak in public || *me da vergüenza su conducta* your behaviour shames me *o* makes me ashamed || *me da vergüenza tener que pedírselo* I am ashamed to have to ask you for it || *¿no le da a usted vergüenza?* aren't you ashamed?, have you no shame? || *pasé mucha vergüenza* I was so ashamed (humillación), I was so embarrassed (confusión) || *perder la vergüenza* to lose all sense of shame || *¡qué poca vergüenza tiene!* the man has no shame!, he is quite shameless! || *sacar a alguien a la vergüenza pública* to put s.o. to public shame || *se le cayó la cara de vergüenza* he blushed with shame *o* died of shame || *sin vergüenza* shameless (desvergonzado), shamelessly (de manera desvergonzada) || *tener vergüenza* to be ashamed (*de* to, of), to be shy; *no tengas vergüenza, cántame algo* don't be shy, sing me a song || *vergüenza para quien piense mal* honni soit qui mal y pense || *vergüenza torera* dignity (dignidad).

◆ *pl* ANAT private parts, privates (partes pudendas).

vergueta *f* twig, small switch.

vericueto *m* rough *o* rugged path.

verídico, ca *adj* truthful; *hombre verídico* truthful man || true (verdadero); *lo que digo es verídico* what I am saying is true; *relato verídico* true story.

verificación *f* checking, inspection, testing (de una máquina, etc.) || verification, checking (de un resultado) || carrying out, fulfilment (ejecución).

verificador, ra *adj* checking, inspecting, testing (de una máquina) || verifying, checking (de un resultado).

◆ *m/f* tester, inspector.

verificar *vt* to check, to inspect, to test (máquinas, etc.) || to check, to verify (un resultado) || to carry out, to perform, to effect; *la aviación verificó un bombardeo* the air force carried out a bombing raid.
◆ *vpr* to take place, to be held (tener lugar); *la boda se verificará mañana* the wedding will take place tomorrow || to come true (una predicción).

verisímil *adj* probable, likely.

verisimilitud *f* → **verosimilitud.**

verismo *m* verism.

verja *f* grating, grille (de puerta, de ventana) || railings *pl* (cerca).

verjurado, da *adj* laid; *papel verjurado* laid paper.

verme *m* MED intestinal worm.

vermicida *adj* vermicidal.
◆ *m* vermicide.

vermiculado, da *adj* ARQ vermiculate.

vermicular *adj* vermicular.

vermiforme *adj* vermiform.

vermífugo, ga *adj/sm* vermifuge, anthelmintic.

verminoso, sa *adj* MED accompanied by intestinal worms.

vermívoro, ra *adj* ZOOL vermivorous.

vermut; vermú *m* vermouth; *vermut con ginebra* gin and vermouth || AMER matinée (de teatro o cine).
— OBSERV pl *vermús.*

vernáculo, la *adj* vernacular || *lengua vernácula* vernacular.

vernier *m* TECN vernier (nonio).

vero *m* (p us) vair (animal) || HERÁLD vair (blasón).

verónica *f* veronica, speedwell (planta) || TAUR veronica [pass with the cape].

verosímil *adj* probable, likely || credible (relato).

verosimilitud; verisimilitud *f* probability, likelihood || credibility (de un relato).

verosímilmente *adv* probably.

verraco *m* boar, hog (cerdo) || FAM *gritar como un verraco* to squeal like a pig.

verraquear *vi* FAM to grumble, to growl, to moan (gruñir) | to wail, to scream, to howl (berrear).

verraquera *f* FAM tantrum (rabieta); *agarrar una verraquera* to throw a tantrum.

verriondo, da *adj* on heat (los cerdos, etc.).

verrón *m* boar, hog (cerdo).

verruga *f* MED & BOT wart || FIG & FAM pain in the neck (pesadez).

verrugosidad *f* wart-like swelling.

verrugoso, sa *adj* warty.

versado, da *adj* versed; *versado en lenguas* versed in languages.

versal *adj/s/f* IMPR capital (letra).

versalilla; versalita *adj/s/f* IMPR small capital (letra).

Versalles *n pr* Versailles.

versallés; versallesco, ca *adj* in the style of Versailles || FIG & FAM old-world; *modos muy versallescos* very old-world manners | princely (principesco).
◆ *m/f* native *o* inhabitant of Versailles.

versar *vi* to go *o* to turn round (girar) || FIG *versar sobre* to deal with, to be about (tratar de).

versátil *adj* BOT & ZOOL versatile || FIG fickle, inconstant, changeable (inconstante).

versatilidad *f* BOT & ZOOL versatility || FIG fickleness, inconstancy, changeableness.

versícula *f* place where hymnbooks are kept.

versiculario *m* person who sings versicles || keeper of hymnbooks.

versículo *m* versicle.

versificación *f* versification.

versificar *vi* to versify, to write verse.
◆ *vt* to versify, to put into verse.

versión *f* version; *dos versiones de un suceso* two versions of an event || translation, version (traducción) || INFORM version.

verso *m* verse; *verso blanco* or *suelto* blank verse || line; *un poema de veinte versos* a poem with twenty lines || versicle (versículo) || — *comedia en verso* comedy in verse (form) || *hacer versos* to write poetry || *poner en verso* to put into verse || *verso libre* free verse.

verso *m* verso (reverso de una hoja) || MIL small culverin (pieza de artillería).

vértebra *f* ANAT vertebra.

vertebrado, da *adj/sm* ZOOL vertebrate.

vertebral *adj* vertebral; *discos vertebrales* vertebral discs || ANAT *columna vertebral* vertebral *o* spinal column, spine, backbone (espinazo).

vertedera *f* mouldboard [*US* moldboard] (de un arado).

vertedero *m* drain (desaguadero) || spillway, overflow (para que no rebose) || rubbish dump, rubbish tip (de basuras) || FAM pigsty (estercolero) || *vertedero de basuras* rubbish chute [*US* garbage disposal].

vertedor, ra *adj* pouring.
◆ *m/f* pourer.
◆ *m* spillway, overflow (desagüe) || drain (para aguas residuales) || MAR bailer, bale, bail (achicador) || scoop (en una tienda).

verter* *vt* to pour (out); *verter el trigo en el depósito* to pour the wheat into the container || to spill (derramar); *verter vino en el mantel* to spill wine on the tablecloth || to empty (out) (vaciar) || to upset (volcar) || to shed; *verter lágrimas* to shed tears || to tip, to dump (basuras) || to translate, to put into (traducir); *verter al francés* to put *o* to translate into French || FIG to pronounce (decir) || FAM *verter aguas menores* to relieve o.s.
◆ *vi/vpr* to flow (*a* into) (un líquido) || to slope, to fall (una vertiente).

vertical *adj* vertical; *líneas verticales* vertical lines || vertical, upright (posición) || *formato vertical* lengthwise format (ilustración).
◆ *f* MAT vertical (línea).
◆ *m* ASTR vertical *o* azimuth circle.

verticalidad *f* verticality.

verticalmente *adv* vertically.

vértice *m* MAT vertex (de un ángulo) | apex (de un cono) || ANAT vertex.

verticilo *m* BOT verticil.

vertido *m* discharge, dumping; *vertido de substancias tóxicas* dumping of toxic waste.

vertiente *adj* pouring, which pours || *aguas vertientes* rainwater flowing off a roof (del tejado).
◆ *f* slope; *en la vertiente sur de la montaña* on the south slope of the mountain || versant (término geográfico) || slope (de un tejado) || FIG aspect || AMER spring (manantial).

vertiginosamente *adv* vertiginously, giddily, dizzily || *subir vertiginosamente* to spiral upwards, to soar (precios).

vertiginosidad *f* vertiginousness.

vertiginoso, sa *adj* vertiginous || FIG giddy, vertiginous (velocidad).

vértigo *m* MED vertigo, giddiness, dizziness || giddiness, dizziness (mareo) || FIG frenzy (arrebato); *le dio un vértigo* he went into a frenzy; *una actividad de vértigo* a frenzy of activity | whirl; *dejarse envolver en el vértigo de las fiestas* to get caught up in the whirl of parties || — *de vértigo* frenzied (actividad, etc.), stunning (belleza, etc.) || *la altura me da vértigo* heights make me giddy *o* dizzy || *tener vértigo* to feel dizzy *o* giddy.

vesanía *f* MED insanity (locura) || rage, fury (cólera).

vesánico, ca *adj* MED insane, demented || furious.
◆ *m/f* madman, madwoman, insane *o* demented person.

vesical *adj* MED vesical.

vesicante *adj/sm* MED vesicant.

vesicatorio, ria *adj/sm* MED vesicatory.

vesícula *f* vesicle || *vesícula biliar* gall bladder.

vesicular *adj* vesicular.

vesperal *m* vesperal (libro).

vespertino, na *adj* vespertine, evening || *estrella vespertina, lucero vespertino* evening star.

Vespucio *npr m* Vespucci.

vestal *f* vestal [virgin] (sacerdotisa de Vesta).
◆ *adj* vestal.

vestibular *adj* ANAT vestibular.

vestíbulo *m* ARQ hall (de una casa particular) | vestibule, foyer (de un edificio público) || ANAT vestibule.

vestido, da *adj* dressed; *estar bien vestido* to be well dressed || dressed, wearing; *vestido de negro* dressed in *o* wearing black; *vestido con una chaqueta roja* dressed in *o* wearing a red jacket.
◆ *m* clothes *pl*, garments *pl* (ropa); *los primitivos utilizaban la piel de los animales para su vestido* primitive man used animal skins as clothes || costume; *historia del vestido* history of costume || dress (de mujer); *un vestido de seda* a silk dress || — FIG & FAM *cortarle a uno un vestido* to slate s.o., to pull s.o. to pieces, to criticize s.o. | *cortar vestidos* to gossip, to criticize people, to backbite, to tittle-tattle || *vestido cruzado* high-necked dress || *vestido de noche* evening dress *o* gown || *vestido tubo* or *tubular* sheath dress.

vestidor *m* dressing room.

vestidura *f* piece of clothing, garment (prenda de vestir) || clothing, clothes *pl* (ropa).
◆ *pl* REL vestments || FIG *rasgarse las vestiduras* to make a great to-do.

vestigio *m* vestige (resto) || FIG trace (huella).
◆ *pl* vestiges, remains (restos); *los vestigios de una civilización* the vestiges of a civilization.

vestimenta *f* clothes *pl*, garments *pl*; *llevaba una vestimenta extraña* he was wearing strange clothes || *vestimenta ridícula* ridiculous garb.
◆ *pl* REL vestments.

vestir* *vt* to dress, to clothe; *vestir a un niño* to dress a child || to dress; *este sastre viste a todos mis hermanos* this tailor dresses all my brothers || to buy (s.o.'s) clothes, to clothe; *sus padres le visten todavía* his parents still buy his clothes, his parents still clothe him || to wear; *la novia vestía un traje blanco* the bride was wearing a white dress || to cover; *vestir de cuero un sillón* to cover a chair with leather || to hang; *vestir las paredes con tapices* to hang the walls with tapestries || FIG to embellish (un discurso) | to hide, to cover (la realidad) || — FIG *vestir al desnudo* to help the destitute *o* the poor | *vísteme despacio que tengo prisa* more haste less speed | *vistió un rostro de severidad* he took on *o* he adopted a serious air || *yo fui vestido de torero* I went dressed as a bullfighter.
◆ *vi* to dress; *viste bien* he dresses well || to wear, to dress in (llevar); *vestir de negro, de uniforme* to dress in *o* to wear black, uniform || FIG to be dressy; *la seda viste mucho* silk is very

dressy || FIG & FAM to be classy *o* smart; *tener un coche deportivo viste mucho* it is very classy to have a sports car || — FIG *el mismo que viste y calza* the very same, none other || *un traje de vestir* a formal suit *o* dress.
◆ *vpr* to get dressed, to dress; *está tardando mucho en vestirse* she's taking a long time to get dressed || to wear, to dress; *vestirse de negro* to wear black, to dress in black || to buy one's clothes; *se viste en las mejores tiendas* she buys her clothes in the best shops || FIG to turn; *los campos se visten de verde* the fields are turning green || — FIG *vestirse con plumas ajenas* to strut in borrowed feathers *o* in borrowed plumes || *vestirse de* to dress up as (disfrazarse de) || *vestirse de largo* to wear a long dress (para salir de noche), to come out, to make one's début in society (sentido figurado) || *vestirse de máscara* to disguise o.s., to dress up || FAM *vestirse de tiros largos* to put on one's Sunday best, to dress up || *vestirse de verano* to put on one's summer clothes.

vestuario *m* wardrobe, clothes *pl* (conjunto de trajes); *tengo que renovar mi vestuario* I must renew my wardrobe || dressing room (donde se visten los actores, etc.) || costumes *pl* (trajes de teatro, de cine) || MIL uniform || DEP changing room || cloakroom (en un teatro, cine, club, etc.) || *encargado* or *encargada del vestuario* dresser (de un actor de teatro), cloakroom attendant (para los abrigos del público).

Vesubio *npr m* GEOGR Vesuvius.

veta *f* vein, streak (de piedra, de madera) || streak, stripe (raya) || MIN vein (de oro, etc.) | seam (de carbón).

vetar *vt* to veto, to put a veto on.

vetear *vt* to grain, to streak (madera, piedra) || to streak (con rayas).

veteranía *f* long experience || seniority (antigüedad).

veterano, na *adj* veteran; *un periodista, un soldado veterano* a veteran reporter, soldier.
◆ *m* veteran || FIG old hand.

veterinaria *f* veterinary medicine *o* science.

veterinario, ria *adj* veterinary; *medicina veterinaria* veterinary medicine.
◆ *m* veterinary surgeon, vet, veterinary [*US* veterinarian].

veto *m* veto; *derecho de veto* power *o* right of veto || — *poner el veto a* to veto, to put a veto on || *veto absoluto, suspensivo* absolute, suspensory veto.

vetusto, ta *adj* ancient, very old.

vez *f* time; *tres veces al mes* three times a month; *cuatro veces seguidas* four times in a row || turn (turno); *hablar a su vez* to speak in one's turn; *perder la vez* to lose one's turn; *tengo la vez* it is my turn || — *a la vez* at the same time, at once (al mismo tiempo), together (juntos) || *a la vez que...* at the same time as... || *algunas veces, a veces* at times, sometimes, occasionally || *alguna vez* sometimes (en alguna ocasión), ever (en preguntas); *¿has estado alguna vez en Roma?* have you ever been to Rome? || *a veces... y otras veces* sometimes... sometimes; *a veces está sonriente y otras veces serio* he is sometimes smiling and sometimes serious || *cada vez* every time, each time || *cada vez más* more and more (véase OBSERV) || *cada vez menos* (*seguido de un adjetivo o de un sustantivo en singular*), less and less; *es cada vez menos difícil* it gets less and less difficult (*seguido de un sustantivo en plural*), less and less, fewer and fewer; *hay cada vez menos oportunidades* there are fewer and fewer opportunities || *cada vez mejor, peor* better and better, worse and worse || *cada vez que...* whenever, every *o* each time (that)... || *contadas veces* seldom, rarely || *demasiadas veces* too often || *de una (sola) vez* in one go || *de una vez, de una vez para siempre* once and for all || *de vez en cuando* from time to time, occasionally || *dos veces* twice || *dos veces más rico* twice as rich || *en vez de* instead of || *érase una vez* once upon a time (there was) || *estar cada vez peor* to get worse and worse, to go from bad to worse || *hacer las veces de* to act as, to serve as || *hacer otra vez algo* to do sth. again || *infinitas veces* an infinite number of times || *las más de las veces, la mayoría de las veces* usually, most times, more often than not || *más de una vez* more than once || *miles de veces* thousands of times, over and over again || *muchas veces* often, many times || *otra vez* once more (una vez más), again (de nuevo), more, encore (espectáculo); *¡otra vez!* encore! || *otras veces* other times || *pase por una vez* it is all right this once *o* this time || *pocas* or *raras veces* seldom, rarely || *por enésima vez* for the umpteenth time || *por última vez* for the last time || *rara vez* seldom || *repetidas veces* repeatedly, again and again, many times || *tal cual vez* rarely, on rare occasions || *tal vez* perhaps, maybe || *toda vez que...* since..., seeing that... (ya que, dado que) || *una vez* once || *una vez al año no hace daño* once in a while never hurt anyone || *una vez dice que sí y otra que no* first he says yes and then he says no || *una vez más* once more, again, once again || *una vez que lo hubo hecho* once he had done it || *una vez que otra, una que otra vez* from time to time, occasionally, now and then || *una vez tras otra* over and over again (sin parar) || *una (vez) y otra vez, una vez y cien veces* time and time again || *varias veces* several times.

— OBSERV Nótese que la forma *more and more* se sustituye por el comparativo en *-er* cuando el adjetivo que sigue la expresión *cada vez más* se traduce al inglés por una palabra corta: *es cada vez más mona* she gest prettier and prettier.

vía *f* road, way; *vía romana* Roman road || railway line, line, rail, track (ferrocarril) || route; *vía marítima* sea route || lane (de autopista) || ANAT track, passage; *vías urinarias* urinary tract || QUÍM way, process; *vía húmeda, seca* wet, dry process || TECN track (automóvil) || FIG way, means | channel; *vía ordinaria* usual channel || JUR procedure || INFORM channel || — *cuaderna vía* verse form with four alexandrines (del mester de clerecía) || *de vía estrecha* narrow-gauge || *el tren está en la vía primera* the train is at platform one || *estar en vías de* to be in the process of || *países en vías de desarrollo* developing countries || *por vía aérea* by air (personas, cargamento, etc.), (by) airmail (correo) || *vía de acceso* slip road || *por vía oral* orally || FIG *por vía de* by means of; *por vía de sufragios* by means of votes; by way of, as; *por vía de ensayo* as an experiment || *por vía de buen gobierno* as a cautionary measure || *por vía interna* internally || *por vía marítima* by sea || *por vía oficial* through official channels || *recurrir a la vía judicial* to go to law || *vía aérea* by airmail (correo) || *vía de acceso* slip road || MAR *vía de agua* leak; *abrirse una vía de agua* to spring a leak || *vía de circunvalación* ring road || *vía de comunicación* communication channel, means of communication || *vía de maniobra* (railway) siding || *vía férrea* railway [*US* railroad] || *vía fluvial* waterway || ASTR *Vía Láctea* Milky Way || *vía muerta* siding (ferrocarril) || *vía pública* public thoroughfare, public way || JUR *vías de hecho* acts of violence, assault and battery.

vía *prep* via; *Madrid-Londres vía París* Madrid-London via Paris.

viabilidad *f* viability || feasibility, practicableness (posibilidad de realizarse).

viable *adj* viable || feasible, practicable (posible).

viacrucis; vía crucis *m* way of the Cross, Stations *pl* of the Cross || FIG calvary (tormento).

viaducto *m* viaduct.

viajante *adj* travelling [*US* traveling].
◆ *m/f* traveller [*US* traveler] || *viajante (de comercio)* commercial traveller [*US* traveling salesman].

viajar *vi* to travel; *viajar por España* to travel through Spain.

viaje *m* journey, trip; *¿habéis tenido buen viaje?* did you have a nice journey?; *hacer un viaje a Inglaterra* to go on a trip to England; *los peregrinos hicieron un viaje muy largo* the pilgrims went on a long journey || travel; *durante sus viajes se encontró con su profesor* on his travels he met his teacher || drive, journey (en coche); *el viaje por la autopista fue algo aburrido* the drive along the motorway was rather boring || load (carga); *echar un viaje de leña* to go for a load of wood || FAM jab, slash (con una navaja, etc.) | punch (puñetazo) || TAUR butt || FAM trip (con drogas) || — *agencia de viajes* travel agency, travel agent's || *¡buen viaje!* bon voyage!, have a good journey! || *estar de viaje* to be away, to be away on a journey, to be travelling || *hacer un viaje por toda Escocia* to tour Scotland, to travel all round Scotland || *ir* or *irse de viaje* to go away, to go on a journey *o* trip || *no me gustan los viajes* I don't like travelling || FIG & FAM *¡para este viaje no se necesitan alforjas!* a fat lot of good that is! || *se ha ido de viaje* he is away on a journey, he has gone away || *viaje de buena voluntad* goodwill visit || *viaje de ida* outward journey || *viaje de ida y vuelta* return journey *o* trip, round trip || *viaje de novios* honeymoon; *fueron en viaje de novios a* they went on their honeymoon to, they spent their honeymoon in, they honeymooned in || *viaje de prueba* trial *o* test run || *viaje de recreo* pleasure trip || MAR *viaje en barco* boat trip (corto), voyage (largo) || *viaje todo comprendido* all-in trip, inclusive *o* package tour.

viajero, ra *adj* travelling [*US* traveling] (pasajero).
◆ *m/f* traveller [*US* traveler] || passenger || *¡viajeros al tren!* all aboard!

vial *adj* road (de la carretera) || traffic (de la circulación).
◆ *m* (p us) avenue.

vianda *f* food (alimento).
◆ *pl* food *sing.*

viandante *m/f* traveller [*US* traveler] (viajero) || passerby (transeúnte) || vagabond (vagabundo).

viaraza *f* AMER fit of anger, fit of temper.

viaticar *vt* to administer the viaticum to.

viático *m* HIST viaticum || REL viaticum, Eucharist || per diem, daily expense allowance (dietas).

víbora *f* viper (reptil) || FAM snake (persona maldiciente).

viborezno *m* young viper (víbora pequeña).

vibración *f* vibration || TECN vibration (del cemento).

vibrado *m* vibration (del cemento).

vibrador, ra *adj* vibrant, vibrating.
◆ *m* vibrator.

vibráfono *m* MÚS vibraphone.

vibrante *adj* vibrant, vibrating || GRAM vibrant (sonido).
◆ *f* GRAM vibrant.

vibrar *vt/vi* to vibrate.

vibrátil *adj* vibratile.

vibrato *m* MÚS vibrato.

vibratorio, ria *adj* vibratory.

vibrión *m* vibrio (bacteria).

vibromasaje *m* MED vibromassage.

vicaria *f* deputy of the Mother Superior.

vicaría *f* vicariate || vicarage (residencia) || FAM *pasar por la vicaría* to get married [in church].

vicarial *adj* vicarial.

vicariato *m* vicariate.

vicario *m* vicar; *el Papa es el vicario de Jesucristo* the Pope is the Vicar of Christ || *vicario general* vicar-general.

vicealmirantazgo *m* vice-admiralty.

vicealmirante *m* vice-admiral.

vicecanciller *m* vice-chancellor.

vicecancillería *f* vice-chancellorship (cargo) || vice-chancellor's office (oficina).

vicecónsul *m* vice-consul.

viceconsulado *m* vice-consulate.

vicegobernador *m* vice-governor.

Vicente *npr m* Vincent || *¿dónde va Vicente?, donde va la gente* he (she, etc.) just follows the crowd.

vicepresidencia *f* vice-presidency (en un país) || vice-chairmanship (en comité, reunión, compañía).

vicepresidente, ta *m/f* vice-president (de un país) || vice-chairman (de comité, reunión, compañía).

vicerector *m* vice-rector (de Universidad).

vicesecretaría *f* assistant secretaryship.

vicesecretario, ria *m/f* assistant secretary.

vicetiple *f* chorus girl.

viceversa *adv* vice versa.

vicia *f* BOT vetch (arveja).

viciado, da *adj* corrupt (corrompido) || contaminated, polluted, vitiated, foul (aire) || stuffy (atmósfera).

viciar *vt* to vitiate, to corrupt (corromper) || to adulterate (adulterar) || to falsify (falsificar) || JUR to vitiate, to nullify; *error que vicia un contrato* mistake which nullifies a contract || to contaminate, to pollute, to vitiate (el aire) || to spoil (estropear) || to distort, to twist (el sentido de algo).
◆ *vpr* to spoil, to become spoiled (estropearse) || to warp (madera) || to become twisted, to go out of shape (cualquier objeto) || to become contaminated *o* polluted *o* vitiated (el aire) || to be corrupted, to take to vice (enviciarse).

vicio *m* vice; *antro de vicio* den of vice || bad habit (mala costumbre) || JUR fault; *vicios ocultos* hidden faults || spoiling (mimo) || warp, buckle (alabeo) || defect (defecto) || incorrect usage (en el lenguaje) || — *contra el vicio de pedir hay la virtud de no dar* it is sometimes better to say no [to a person who asks too much] || *de vicio* for no reason at all, without reason; *llorar de vicio* to cry for no reason at all || *vicio de forma* faulty drafting.

viciosamente *adv* badly, wrongly, incorrectly || viciously.

vicioso, sa *adj* vicious (persona, animal) || faulty, defective (cosa) || vicious, incorrect; *una locución viciosa* a vicious expression || FAM spoiled (mimado) || *círculo vicioso* vicious circle.
◆ *m/f* vicious person || addict.

vicisitud *f* vicissitude.

víctima *f* victim; *ser la víctima de* to be the victim of || — *hubo cuatro víctimas en el accidente* there were four casualties in the accident || FIG *víctima propiciatoria* scapegoat.

victimar *vt* AMER to kill (matar).

victimario *m* person who bound and held the victim during the sacrifice || AMER murderer, killer (asesino).

victorear *vt* to acclaim, to cheer, to applaud.

victoria *f* victoria (coche).

victoria *f* victory || win, victory, triumph (en un deporte, concurso) || — *cantar victoria* to proclaim a victory || *victoria aplastante* or *rotunda* resounding *o* overwhelming victory || *victoria moral* moral victory || *victoria pírrica* Pyrrhic victory || BOT *victoria regia* victoria regia, victoria.

Victoria *npr m* GEOGR Lake Victoria.

victoriano, na *adj/s* Victorian.

victorioso, sa *adj* victorious.
◆ *m/f* victor, winner (triunfador).

vicuña *f* vicuna, vicugna, vicuña (mamífero).

vichar *vt* AMER to spy on (espiar) | FIG to devour with one's eyes.

vichy *m* kind of gingham (tela).

vid *f* vine, grapevine (planta).

vida *f* life; *vida y muerte* life and death || life, life-time (duración) || living; *nivel de vida* standard of living || trump (triunfo en los naipes) || — *cambiar de vida* to turn over a new leaf, to change one's way of live || *costarle la vida a uno* to cost s.o. his life || *cuéntenos su vida y milagros* tell us all about yourself, tell us your life history || *dar la vida* to give one's life || *dar mala vida a uno* to make s.o.'s life a misery, to give s.o. a bad time || *darse buena vida* to have a good life, to live well *o* comfortably || *dar vida a* to give birth to (un hijo), to bring to life (un retrato, etc.) || *de mala vida, de vida airada* loose-living || *de por vida* for life, for ever || *de toda la vida* lifelong; *un amigo de toda la vida* a lifelong friend || *durante toda la vida* one's whole life long *o* through || FIG & FAM *echarse a la vida* to go on the game (una mujer) || *en esto le va la vida* his life depends on it, his life is at stake || FIG *¡en la vida!* never!, never in a million years! || *en mi vida* never in my life || *enterrarse en vida en un pueblucho* to bury o.s. in a tiny village || *en vida* alive, living; *estar en vida* to be alive || *en vida de* during the life *o* lifetime of || *en vida de mi padre* during the lifetime of my father, when my father was alive || *escapar con vida de un accidente* to come out of an accident alive *o* safe and sound *o* with one's life || *¡esto es vida!* this is living! || *ganarse la vida* to earn one's living || *hacerle a uno la vida imposible* to make life impossible for s.o. || FIG & FAM *hacer por la vida* to eat || *hacer vida ascética* to lead an ascetic life || *hacer vida con uno* to live with s.o. || *hacer vida nueva* to turn over a new leaf, to change one's way of life || *hija de mi vida* my darling daughter || *jugarse la vida* to risk one's life, to take one's life in one's hand || *la otra vida* the next life, the life to come || *¡la vida!* that's life || *la vida es así* that's life || *la vida es sueño* life is a dream || *lleno de vida* lively, full of life || *llevar una vida alegre* to lead *o* to live *o* to have a happy life || *mala vida* loose life || FIG *media vida* right arm, eyeteeth; *daría media vida por* I should give my right arm for || *meterse en vidas ajenas* to interfere *o* to meddle [in other people's affairs] || *¡mi vida!, ¡vida mía!* or *¡vida!* my love!, darling! || *mientras dura, vida y dulzura* enjoy life while you can, make the most of it while it lasts || *mientras hay vida hay esperanza* while there's life there's hope || FIG & FAM *mujer de la vida* or *de mala vida* or *de vida alegre* prostitute, whore || *no hubo pérdidas de vida* no lives were lost, there was no loss of life || *pagar con su vida* to pay with one's life || *para toda la vida* for life, for the whole of one's life || *pasar a mejor vida* to pass away || *pasar de vida a muerte* to pass away || FAM *pegarse la vida padre* or *una buena vida* or *la gran vida* to live it up, to live like a king || *perder la vida* to lose one's life || *¡por mi vida!* upon my soul! || *¿qué es de tu vida?* how are things?, how are you going on?, how is life? || *¡qué vida ésta!* what a life! || *quitarse la vida* to take one's own life || *seguro de vida* life insurance || FIG & FAM *ser de la vida* to be on the game (mujer) || *si Dios nos da vida* if God is willing || *sin vida* lifeless || *su vida está pendiente de un hilo* his life is hanging by a thread || FIG & FAM *tener siete vidas como los gatos* to have nine lives || *vender cara su vida* to sell one's life dearly, to put up a good fight || FIG *vida de perros* dog's life || *vida de soltero* bachelor's life || *vida familiar* family life || *vida y milagros* life story *o* history.

vidalita *f* AMER melancholic folk song.

videncia *f* clear-sightedness.

vidente *m/f* seer (que adivina el porvenir).

vídeo *m* RAD video || *vídeo comunitario* shown without copyright permission.

videocámara *f* video camera.

videocasete *f* videocassette.

videocinta *f* videotape.

videoclub *m* video club.

videodisco *m* videodisc [*US* videodisk].

videojuego *m* video game.

videoteca *f* video library.

videotexto *m* INFORM videotex.

vidorra *f* FAM cushy life.

vidriado, da *adj* glazed (cerámica).
◆ *m* glazing, glaze (barniz para cerámica) || glazed earthenware (cerámica).

vidriar *vt* TECN to glaze (la cerámica).
◆ *vpr* to be glazed || to become glassy, to become glazed, to glaze over (los ojos).

vidriera *f* glass window (ventana) || glass door (puerta) || stained-glass window (vitral) || AMER shopwindow [*US* show window] (escaparate) || *puerta vidriera* glass door (puerta), French window (que da al balcón).

vidriería *f* glassworks (taller) || glass shop (tienda) || *vidriería de color* stained-glass making.

vidriero *m* glassworker (obrero) || glassmaker (fabricante) || glazier (que fabrica o coloca cristales).

vidrio *m* glass; *vidrio de ventanas* glass for windows; *vidrio de color* stained glass || — *fibra de vidrio* glass fibre || *lana de vidrio* glass wool || FIG & FAM *pagar los vidrios rotos* to carry the can || *vidrio cilindrado* plate glass || *vidrio deslustrado* or *esmerilado* ground glass, frosted glass.

vidrioso, sa *adj* glazed, glassy; *ojos vidriosos* glazed eyes || brittle (frágil) || slippery (suelo) || FIG delicate, tricky (difícil de tratar); *tema vidrioso* delicate subject.

vieira *f* scallop (molusco, concha).

vieja *adj/s/f* ⟶ **viejo.**

viejales *m inv* FAM old boy.

viejito, ta *m/f* little old man, little old woman (viejo) || AMER FAM mate (amigo).

viejo, ja *adj* old; *soy más viejo que tú* I am older than you; *un hombre viejo* an old man; *una vieja gabardina* an old gabardine || — *hacerse viejo* to grow old, to get old || FIG & FAM *más viejo que andar a gatas* or *a pie* as old as the hills | *más viejo que Matusalén* as old as Methuselah || *morir de viejo* to die of old age || FAM *no llegará a viejo, no hará huesos viejos* he will not make old bones || *Plinio el Viejo* Pliny the Elder.
◆ *m/f* old man (hombre), old lady, old woman (mujer); *una vieja muy arrugada* a very wrinkled old woman || FAM old man (padre, marido) | old lady *o* woman (madre, esposa) || — FIG *hacer la cuenta de la vieja* to count on one's fingers | *poquito a poco* or *poco a poco hila la vieja el copo* every little bit helps || FAM *una viejita* a little old lady | *un viejo coquetón* or *verde* a dirty old man || *vamos a tirar todo lo viejo* we are going to throw out all the old things.

◆ *pl* old people, old folks || FIG & FAM old folks (padres) || *cuento de viejas* old-wive's tale.

viella *f* MÚS hurdy-gurdy.

Viena *n pr* GEOGR Vienna (Austria).

vienés, esa *adj/s* Viennese.

viento *m* wind; *viento del oeste* west wind; *vientos alisios* trade winds; *viento en popa* stern wind; *corre bastante viento* there is quite a wind; *ráfaga de viento* gust of wind || scent (olfato) || guy (tirante de cuerda) || MÚS wind; *instrumentos de viento* wind instruments || FAM wind (ventosidad) || — MAR *a favor del viento* before the wind || *al capricho del viento* at the mercy of the wind || *azotado por los vientos* windswept || FIG & FAM *beber los vientos por* to be dying to (*con verbo*), to be dying for (*con sustantivo*), to be head over heels in love with (una mujer) || MAR *contra el viento* against the wind, in the teeth of the wind, in the wind's eye || FIG *contra viento y marea* through *o* come hell and high water, against all odds | *corren malos vientos* the time is not right || *corre* or *hace viento* it is windy || FIG *darle a uno el viento de una cosa* to get wind of sth. (barruntar) | *despedir* or *echar con viento fresco* to send packing, to throw out (echar) || *el viento ha cambiado* the wind has turned *o* changed || MAR *ganar el viento* to sail with the wind || FAM *gritar a los cuatro vientos* to shout from the rooftops | *hace un viento de mil demonios* it's blowing a gale || MAR *hurtar el viento* to sail against the wind || FIG *ir al amparo del viento, irse con el viento que corre* to follow the tide | *ir más rápido que el viento* to go like the wind || MAR *ir viento en popa* to sail before the wind | *lo que el viento se llevó* gone with the wind | *lleno de viento* empty (vacío), conceited (vanidoso) | *mandar a uno con viento fresco* to send s.o. packing || *molino de viento* windmill || FIG *moverse a todos los vientos* to change with the wind, to be as fickle as the wind || FAM *¿qué viento te trae?* what brings you here? || FIG *quien siembra vientos recoge tempestades* he who sows the wind shall reap the whirlwind | *tener viento en contra* to be sailing against the wind | *tener viento favorable* to have the wind behind one | *todo va viento en popa* everything is going smoothly, everything is going well || *tomar el viento* to take the scent (caza) || *viento de cola* tail wind || FIG *vamos viento en popa* we are in luck, it is all systems go, the wind is with us || *viento de costado* crosswind || *viento en contra* or *contrario* or *en proa* headwind, foul wind.

vientre *m* ANAT belly, abdomen | womb; *llevar un niño en el vientre* to carry a child in one's womb || belly (de vasija, barco) || FIG bowels *pl* || FÍS antinode, loop || — *bajo vientre* lower abdomen || FAM *echar vientre* to put on weight, to get a pot-belly || REL *el fruto de tu vientre* the fruit of thy womb || *evacuar* or *exonerar el vientre, hacer de vientre* to have a bowel movement.

viernes *m* Friday; *el viernes pasado, que viene* last, next Friday; *Viernes Santo* Good Friday || — *cara de viernes* gloomy *o* dismal face || *comer de viernes* to fast, to abstain from eating meat || FAM *¿te lo has aprendido en viernes?* change the record!, you're always on about the same thing!, give it a rest!

Vietnam *npr m* GEOGR Vietnam || *Vietnam del Norte, del Sur* North, South Vietnam.

vietnamita *adj/s* Vietnamese.

viga *f* beam, rafter; *viga principal* main beam || girder (metálica) || — *viga de apuntalamiento* needle || *viga maestra* main beam || *viga transversal* crossbeam.

vigencia *f* validity (cualidad de vigente) || — *entrar en vigencia* to come into force || *estar en vigencia* to be in force || *tener vigencia* to be valid.

vigente *adj* in force; *la ley vigente* the law in force; *estar vigente* to be in force || prevailing (existente).

vigesimal *adj* vigesimal.

vigésimo, ma *adj/sm* twentieth || *vigésimo primero, segundo* twenty-first, twenty-second.

vigía *m* lookout, watchman || MAR watch.
◆ *f* watchtower, lookout post (atalaya) || watch, lookout (acción de vigilar) || MAR reef.

vigilancia *f* surveillance (acción de vigilar); *sometido a vigilancia* under surveillance || vigilance, watchfulness (cuidado en el vigilar) || vigilance committee (servicio).

vigilante *adj* vigilant, watchful (que vigila) || alert (alerta) || wakeful (que no duerme).
◆ *m* watchman (en un edificio) || guard (de documentos secretos, etc.) || AMER policeman || superviser (en el colegio, trabajo, etc.) || *vigilante de noche* or *nocturno* night watchman.

vigilar *vt* to watch (over), to look after (cuidar de) || to supervise; *vigilar un trabajo* to supervise a job || to keep an eye on; *vigilar la comida para que no se queme* to keep an eye on the dinner so that it doesn't burn || to guard (presos, frontera).
◆ *vi* to keep watch (el vigía) || to be vigilant, to be watchful (ser vigilante) || *vigilar por* or *sobre* to watch over, to look after.

vigilia *f* vigil (de quien no duerme) || eve (víspera) || mass for the dead (de difuntos) || meatless meal (comida) || REL vigil || — *día de vigilia* day of abstinence || *hacer* or *comer de vigilia* to abstain from meat || *pasar la noche de vigilia* to stay awake all night.

vigor *m* force, effect; *entrar en vigor* to come into force, to take effect; *estar en vigor* to be in force; *poner en vigor* to put into effect || vigour [US vigor], strength, force (fortaleza) || *estilo lleno de vigor* vigorous *o* forceful style.

vigorar *vt* to invigorate, to fortify (vigorizar).

vigorizador, ra *adj* invigorating, fortifying.

vigorizar *vt* to invigorate, to fortify.
◆ *vpr* to be invigorated, to be fortified.

vigorosidad *f* vigour [US vigor], strength.

vigoroso, sa *adj* vigorous, strong.

vigota *f* MAR deadeye (polea).

viguería *f* framework, beams *pl.*

vigueta *f* small beam (viga pequeña de madera) || small girder (metálica) || joist (cabio).

vihuela *f* MÚS kind of guitar.
— OBSERV The *vihuela* is a small guitar which was very fashionable in the 16th century before it was superseded by the guitar.

vihuelista *m/f* «vihuela» player.

vikingo *m* viking.

vil *adj* vile, base, despicable.

vilayato *m* vilayet (división territorial en Turquía).

vileza *f* vileness, baseness || despicable act, vile deed (acción vil) || *pobreza no es vileza* it is no crime to be poor, poverty is no crime.

vilipendiador, ra *adj* vilifying, abusive, comptemptuous, vilipending (p us).
◆ *m/f* vilifier, vilipender.

vilipendiar *vt* to vilify, to vilipend (p us) || to despise, to scorn (despreciar).

vilipendio *m* scorn, contempt (desprecio) || vilification (acción) || humiliation (humillación).

vilipendioso, sa *adj* vilifying, abusive, contemptuous.

Vilna *n pr* GEOGR Vilnius.

vilo (en) *loc adv* in the air (suspendido) || FIG on tenterhooks (intranquilo, impaciente) | in suspense; *esta novela nos tiene en vilo* this novel keeps us in suspense.

vilordo, da *adj* lazy, idle.

vilorta *f*; **vilorto** *m* wooden ring (aro) || washer (arandela) || kind of lacrosse (juego) || BOT clematis.

vilote, ta *m/f* AMER coward.
◆ *adj* AMER cowardly.

villa *f* town (ciudad) || villa (casa) || small town (pueblo) || *la Villa del Oso y el Madroño, la Villa y Corte* Madrid.

Villadiego *n pr* FIG & FAM *tomar las de Villadiego* to beat it, to take to one's heels.

villanada *f* villainy, villainous *o* despicable act.

villancejo; villancete; villancico *m* (Christmas) carol (canción de Navidad).

villanería *f* villainy, villainous *o* despicable act (villanía) || villeinage (villanaje).

villanesca *f* country dance accompanied by singing.

villanesco, ca *adj* of the common folk, country.

villanía *f* villainy, villainous *o* despicable act (acción ruin) || coarse remark *o* expression (dicho) || HIST villeinage (estado).

villano, na *adj* lowly, common, peasant, of *o* pertaining to a villein (que no es noble) || FIG rustic (rústico) | coarse (grosero).
◆ *m/f* HIST villein (que no es noble) || FIG villain (persona vil).
◆ *m* country dance.

villar *m* village (pueblo).

villorrio *m* dump, hole (poblacho).

vinagrada *f* drink of vinegar, water and sugar.

vinagre *m* vinegar || FIG & FAM sour puss (persona malhumorada) || *cara de vinagre* sour expression.

vinagrera *f* vinegar bottle (vasija) || vinegar seller (vendedora) || sorrel (acedera) || AMER heartburn, acidity (acedía).
◆ *pl* cruet *sing* (angarillas).

vinagrero, ra *adj* vinegar, of *o* pertaining to vinegar.
◆ *m* vinegar maker, vinegar seller.

vinagreta *f* vinaigrette [sauce] (salsa).

vinagroso, sa *adj* vinegary || FIG & FAM sour, grouchy.

vinajera *f* REL altar cruet.

vinario, ria *adj* wine, of *o* pertaining to wine.

vinate *m* FAM wine.

vinatera *f* MAR rope joining two cables *o* spars.

vinatería *f* wine shop (tienda) || wine trade (comercio).

vinatero, ra *adj* wine, of *o* pertaining to wine; *industria vinatera* wine industry.
◆ *m* wine merchant, vintner (comerciante).

vinaza *f* poor wine [drawn from the dregs].

vinazo *m* FAM rough wine.

vincapervinca *f* BOT large periwinkle.

vinculación *f* linking (acción) || bond, link (lo que vincula) || JUR entailment.

vincular *vt* to link, to bind, to tie; *dos familias vinculadas entre sí* two families which are linked together || to bind; *vinculado por el reconocimiento* bound by gratitude || to relate, to connect (relacionar) || to tie, to attach; *los campesinos están vinculados a la tierra* peasants are attached to the land || JUR to entail (los bienes) || FIG to base; *vincular sus esperanzas en* to base one's hopes on || *estar vinculado con* to be related *o* connected with.

◆ *vpr* to be bound, to be tied.

vínculo *m* tie, link, bond; *vínculos matrimoniales* matrimonial ties ‖ JUR entail (propiedad) | entailment (acción de vincular) ‖ FIG link; *España sirve de vínculo entre Europa y África* Spain serves as a link between Europe and Africa.

vincha *f* AMER band [for the hair].

vindicación *f* vengeance, revenge (venganza) ‖ vindication (defensa).

vindicador, ra *adj* avenging, revenging (que venga) ‖ vindicatory (que defiende).
◆ *m/f* avenger.

vindicar *vt* to avenge, to revenge (vengar) ‖ to vindicate (defender) ‖ JUR to claim, to vindicate (reivindicar).

vindicativo, va *adj* vindictive ‖ vindicatory.

vindicatorio, ria *adj* vindicatory.

vindicta *f* vengeance, revenge (venganza).

vinería *f* AMER wineshop.

vínico, ca *adj* wine, of *o* pertaining to wine, vinic.

vinícola *adj* wine-producing, wine, winegrowing.

vinicultor, ra *m/f* wine producer, winegrower.

vinicultura *f* wine growing, wine production, viniculture.

vinificación *f* vinification, fermentation.

vinílico, ca *adj* vinyl, of *o* pertaining to vinyl.

vinilo *m* QUÍM vinyl.

vinillo *m* FAM thin wine (demasiado flojo) | light wine (ligero).

vino *m* wine; *echar vino* to pour out wine; *vino de la tierra* rough wine ‖ — FAM *ahogar las penas en vino* to drown one's sorrows | *bautizar el vino* to water down wine | *dormir el vino* to sleep it off | *tiene el vino alegre* he is happy when he is drunk | *tiene el vino triste* he is sad when he is drunk ‖ *vino a granel* wine from the barrel ‖ *vino aguado* watered down wine ‖ *vino aloque* rosé wine ‖ *vino añejo* vintage wine ‖ *vino blanco* white wine ‖ *vino de aguja* rough wine ‖ *vino de cava* Catalan wine similar to champagne ‖ *vino de coco* spirit made from fermented coconut milk ‖ *vino de consagrar* communion *o* altar wine ‖ *vino de dos orejas* good wine ‖ *vino de garrote* wine which needs much pressing ‖ *vino de honor* special wine ‖ *vino de Jerez* sherry ‖ *vino de lágrima* juice which comes from the grapes before they are pressed ‖ *vino de mesa* table wine ‖ *vino de Oporto* port (wine) ‖ *vino de pasto* ordinary wine ‖ *vino de quina* wine laced with cinchona ‖ *vino dulce* sweet wine ‖ *vino espumoso* sparkling wine ‖ *vino generoso* full-bodied *o* generous *o* fortified wine ‖ FAM *vino peleón* cheap wine, plonk ‖ *vino seco* dry wine ‖ *vino tinto* red wine.

vinoso, sa *adj* wine, of *o* pertaining to wine, vinous (p us) ‖ *de color vinoso* wine-coloured, vinaceous.

viña *f* vineyard ‖ — AGR *arropar las viñas* to bank up the earth around the vines ‖ FIG *de todo hay en la viña del Señor* it takes all sorts *o* all kinds to make a world ‖ *viña loca* or *virgen* Virginia creeper.

viñador *m* viticulturist, vine grower (cultivador).

viñal *m* AMER vineyard (viñedo).

viñatero *m* viticulturist, vine grower (viñador).

viñedo *m* vineyard.

viñero *m* viticulturist, owner of a vineyard (propietario).

viñeta *f* IMPR vignette.

viñetero *m* IMPR cupboard in which vignette moulds are kept.

viola *f* MÚS viola ‖ *viola de gamba* viola da gamba.
◆ *m/f* viola player.

violáceo, a *adj* violaceous, violet.
◆ *f pl* BOT violaceae.

violación *f* violation, infringement (de las leyes) ‖ rape, violation (p us) (de una mujer) ‖ violation (de un territorio, etc.) ‖ JUR *violación de sellos* or *de precinto* breaking of seals.

violador, ra *m/f* violator (de las leyes).
◆ *m* rapist (de una mujer).

violar *vt* to violate, to infringe (las leyes) ‖ to rape, to ravish, to violate (p us) (a una mujer) ‖ to violate (un territorio).

violencia *f* violence ‖ rape (violación) ‖ embarrassment (embarazo) ‖ JUR violence ‖ force (fuerza) ‖ *no violencia* nonviolence.

violentar *vt* to force (forzar) ‖ to break into (el domicilio) ‖ to use force on (obligar por la fuerza) ‖ to distort, to twist (el sentido de un texto).
◆ *vpr* to force o.s.

violentismo *m* AMER uproar (agitación).

violentista *adj* AMER subversive (agitador).

violento, ta *adj* violent; *tempestad violenta* violent storm; *muerte violenta* violent death; *persona violenta* violent person ‖ DEP rough ‖ embarrassed, awkward, ill at ease (molesto); *me sentía muy violento en su presencia* I felt very awkward in his presence ‖ embarrassing, awkward, difficult; *me es violento decírselo* it is embarrassing for me to tell you this.

violeta *f* violet (flor).
◆ *m* violet (color).
◆ *adj inv* violet; *un vestido violeta* a violet dress; *luces violeta* violet lights.

violetera *f* violet seller.

violetero *m* vase for violets.

violín *m* MÚS violin (instrumento); *tocar el violín* to play the violin | violin (violinista de una orquesta); *primer violín* first violin | violinist, violin player (violinista) ‖ — AMER FIG & FAM *embolsar el violín* to come back with one's tail between one's legs ‖ FIG *violín de Ingres* hobby, favourite passtime.

violinista *m/f* violinist, violin player.

violón *m* MÚS double bass (instrumento) | double bass player (músico) ‖ FIG & FAM *tocar el violón* to talk through one's hat (hablar), to do silly things (obrar), to make a fool of o.s. (hacer el ridículo).

violonchelista; violoncelista *m/f* MÚS cellist, violoncellist.

violonchelo; violoncelo *m* MÚS cello, violoncello.

vipéreo, a *adj* viperous.

viperino, na *adj* viperine ‖ FIG viperish ‖ *lengua viperina* poisonous tongue.

vira *f* dart (saeta) ‖ welt [of a shoe] (zapatería).

virada *f* MAR putting about, tack.

virador *m* FOT toning liquid ‖ MAR toprope | messenger [of capstan] (del cabrestante) ‖ FOT *baño virador* toning bath.

virago *f* mannish woman, virago.

viraje *m* turn, bend (curva) ‖ FOT & FÍS toning ‖ MAR putting about, tack ‖ turn (en coche, etc.) ‖ turning point; *la Revolución Francesa marca un viraje decisivo en la historia* the French Revolution marks a decisive turning point in history.

virar *vt/vi* MAR to put about, to tack ‖ FOT & MED & QUÍM to tone ‖ to turn (round) (coche) ‖ — MAR *virar a babor* to turn to port | *virar de bordo* to put about, to tack ‖ FIG *virar en redondo* to turn round (volverse), to change completely *o* radically (cambiar completamente) ‖ MAR *virar en redondo* or *con viento en popa* to veer.

virgen *adj* virgin ‖ FIG virgin; *selva, cera virgen* virgin forest, wax.
◆ *f* virgin ‖ guide (en lagares) ‖ — *islas Vírgenes* Virgin Isles ‖ *la Virgen Santísima* the Blessed Virgin Mary ‖ FAM *un viva la Virgen* a happy-go-lucky *o* devil-may-care type.

Virgilio *npr m* Virgil, Vergil.

virginal *adj* virginal ‖ REL of the Virgin.

virgíneo, a *adj* virginal.

Virginia *npr f* GEOGR Virginia.

virginiano, na *adj/s* Virginian.

virginidad *f* virginity.

virgo *m* virginity ‖ ANAT hymen ‖ ASTR Virgo (zodíaco).

virguería *f* FAM marvel; *hacer virguerías* to perform marvels (with), to work wonders.

vírgula *f* small rod (pequeña vara) ‖ virgule (rayita) ‖ MED cholera *o* comma bacillus.

virgulilla *f* small punctuation mark.

viril *adj* virile ‖ *miembro viril* male member, penis.
◆ *m* small monstrance within a large one (custodia) ‖ glass (vidrio).

virilidad *f* virility.

virilizar *vt* to virilize.

virola *f* ferrule.

virolento, ta *adj* suffering from smallpox ‖ pockmarked (picado de viruela).
◆ *m/f* person suffering from smallpox.

virote *m* arrow, dart (arma) ‖ iron rod [attached to a slave] ‖ stuffed shirt (*fam*) (persona seria).

virotillo *m* ARQ short upright brace, strut.

virreina *f* viceroy's wife, vicereine (mujer del virrey) ‖ vicereine (que gobierna).

virreinato *m* viceroyalty.

virrey *m* viceroy.

virtual *adj* virtual ‖ potential ‖ FÍS *imagen virtual* virtual image.

virtualidad *f* potentiality, possibility ‖ virtuality.

virtualmente *adv* virtually.

virtud *f* virtue (cualidad de una persona) ‖ ability (capacidad) ‖ — *en virtud de* by virtue of ‖ *tener la virtud de* to have the virtue of (*con gerundio*), to have the power to (*con infinitivo*).

virtuosidad *f*; **virtuosismo** *m* virtuosity.

virtuoso, sa *adj* virtuous; *una conducta virtuosa* virtuous conduct ‖ skilled (artista).
◆ *m/f* virtuous person ‖ virtuoso (artista).

viruela *f* smallpox (enfermedad) ‖ pockmark (cicatriz) ‖ *viruela del ganado vacuno* cowpox.
◆ *pl* smallpox *sing* ‖ — *¡a la vejez viruelas!* there's no fool like an old fool ‖ *picado de viruelas* pockmarked (cara) ‖ MED *viruelas locas* chicken pox.

— OBSERV In Spanish the plural form is the more frequently used.

virulé (a la) *loc adv* FAM *a la virulé* crooked, twisted (torcido) | *ojo a la virulé* black eye.

virulencia *f* virulence.

virulento, ta *adj* virulent.

virus *m inv* virus; *virus filtrable* filterable virus ‖ FIG poison, venom ‖ INFORM virus.

viruta *f* shaving (de madera, metales).

vis *f vis cómica* comic sense, comicality, humour.

visa *f* AMER visa.

visado, da *adj* endorsed with a visa.
◆ *m* visa (de un pasaporte).

visaje *m* grimace (mueca) || *hacer visajes* to pull *o* to make faces, to grimace.

visar *vt* to endorse (un documento) || to visa, to endorse with a visa (un pasaporte).

vísceras *f pl* ANAT viscera.

visceral *adj* visceral.

visco *m* birdlime (liga).

viscosa *f* QUÍM viscose.

viscosidad *f* viscosity.

viscoso, sa *adj* viscous.

visera *f* visor || peak (de gorra) || eyeshade (de jokey) || ARQ gutter overhang (goterón) || *calar* or *calarse la visera* to lower one's visor.

visibilidad *f* visibility; *hay una visibilidad de tres metros* visibility is down to three metres || — *una curva con poca visibilidad* a blind bend || *visibilidad cero* zero visibility || *vuelo sin visibilidad* blind flying.

visible *adj* visible || FIG decent (presentable); *¿puedo entrar?, ¿estás visible?* can I come in?, are you decent?

visiblemente *adv* visibly, perceptibly || *engorda visiblemente* yo can see him getting fatter.

visigodo, da *adj* Visigothic.
◆ *m/f* Visigoth.

visigótico, ca *adj* Visigothic.

visillo *m* curtain (cortinilla).

visión *f* vision || sight; *perdió la visión de un ojo* he lost his sight in one eye || view; *visión de conjunto* overall view || REL vision || FIG & FAM sight, fright (persona fea) || — FIG & FAM *quedarse como quien ve visiones* to look as if one has seen a ghost | *ver visiones* to see things, to be deluded.

visionadora *f* FOT viewer.

visionario, ria *adj* visionary || FIG deluded, subject to hallucinations.
◆ *m/f* visionary || FIG person who imagines things.

visir *m* vizier, vizir; *gran visir* grand vizier.

visirato *m* vizierate.

visita *f* visit; *visita de pésame* visit of condolence || visitors *pl* (invitados); *mañana tenemos visita* we are having visitors tomorrow || inspection || — *devolver a alguien una visita* to return a visit *o* a call || *estar de visita en casa de una tía* to be visiting one's aunt *o* paying a visit to one's aunt || *ir de visita a casa de uno* to pay s.o. a call *o* a visit || FAM *no me hagas la visita* don't stand on ceremony || *tarjeta de visita* visiting card || *visita de cumplido* or *de cortesía* courtesy visit *o* call || FAM *visita de médico, visita relámpago* short *o* hurried visit *o* call, flying visit.

visitación *f* REL visitation.

visitador, ra *adj* fond of visiting.
◆ *m/f* person fond of visiting || visitor (visitante).
◆ *m* inspector.

Visitandina *f* REL Visitandine (nun).

visitante *adj* visiting.
◆ *m/f* visitor.

visitar *vt* to visit; *visitar un monumento* to visit a monument || to visit, to call on, to go and see; *visitar a un amigo* to visit a friend || to visit, to inspect (inspeccionar).

visiteo *m* visiting, visits *pl*; *le gusta mucho el visiteo* he enjoys visiting.

vislumbrar *m* to glimpse, to catch a glimpse of || FIG to begin to see (una solución).

vislumbre *f* glimmer (claridad tenue) || glimpse, brief view (vista momentánea) || FIG glimmer; *una vislumbre de esperanza* a glimmer of hope || *tener vislumbres de* to have an inkling *o* a suspicion of.

viso *m* shimmer, sheen; *tela de seda azul con visos morados* blue silk with a violet shimmer || slip, underslip [of a transparent dress or skirt] (forro suelto) || FIG appearance, aspect (aspecto) | glimmer; *bajo unos visos de verdad* beneath a glimmer of truth || eminence (eminencia) || — *dar visos a una tela* to put a sheen on a material || *de viso* important, prominent; *persona de viso* prominent person || *hacer visos* to shimmer || *tener visos de* to seem, to appear (parecer) || *viso cambiante* shimmer.

visón *m* ZOOL mink.

visor *m* sight || FOT viewfinder.

visorio, ria *adj* visual.
◆ *m* expert examination *o* inspection (examen pericial).

víspera *f* day before; *el jueves es la víspera del viernes* Thursday is the day before Friday || eve, day before (de una fiesta).
◆ *pl* vespers (oficio religioso) || — *día de mucho víspera de nada* no two days are alike || *en vísperas de* on the eve of || HIST *vísperas sicilianas* Sicilian Vespers.

vista *f* sight, eyes *pl*, vision; *vista aguda* or *penetrante* sharp sight; *tener buena vista* to have good sight || view; *esta habitación tiene una vista espléndida* this room has a wonderful view; *vista panorámica* panoramic view || glance, look (vistazo) || view (cuadro, foto) || appearance, aspect (apariencia) || JUR trial, hearing || — *agradable a la vista* pleasing to the eye || *a la vista* visible (visible), at *o* on sight; *pagadero a la vista* payable at sight; on show, on display; *poner a la vista* to put on show; in sight; *un barco a la vista* a boat in sight; in view (previsto) || *a la vista de* at the sight of (al ver), within view of, within sight of; *estábamos a la vista del puerto* we were within view of the port; in view of, because of; *a la vista de las dificultades* in view of the difficulties; in the light of (a la luz de), in the presence of; *a la vista de mucha gente* in the presence of many people || *a la vista de todos* openly, publicly || *a la vista, no son ricos* you wouldn't think they were rich to look at them || *alzar la vista* to look up, to raise one's eyes || *apartar la vista de* to look away from || *a primera vista* at first sight || *a simple vista* at first sight, at first (primeramente), at a glance, with the naked eye (fácilmente) || COM *a tantos días vista* so many days after sight || *a vista de ojos* visibly || *bajar la vista* to look down || *clavar* or *fijar la vista en* to gaze *o* to stare at || FIG *comerse con la vista* to devour with one's eyes || *conocer de vista* to know by sight || *dar una vista a* to have a look at, to glance at || *desde el punto de vista de* from the point of view of || *desde mi punto de vista* from my point of view || *dirigir la vista a* to turn towards, to look towards || *echar la vista a una cosa* to have one's eye on; *ha echado la vista a ese abrigo* he has his eye on that coat || *el barco se alejó hasta perderse de vista* the boat disappeared into the distance || *en vista de* in view of, considering; *en vista de las circunstancias* in view of the circumstances || *en vista de que...* in view of the fact that..., since... || *estar a la vista* to be obvious *o* evident *o* clear (evidente); *los resultados están a la vista* the results are obvious; to be in the public eye (una personalidad), to keep an eye on things (vigilar) || *fijar la vista en* to stare at || FIG *hacer la vista gorda* to turn a blind eye, to close one's eyes || *hasta donde alcanza la vista* as far as the eye can see || *¡hasta la vista!* good-bye!, see you! || *írsele a uno la vista tras algo* to be dying for sth. (desear) || *la vista engaña* one should not trust appearances, appearances are deceptive || *leer con la vista* to read silently *o* to o.s. || *medir a uno con la vista* to look s.o. up and down, to size s.o. up || *no perder de vista* not to lose sight of, not to let out of one's sight || *no quitar la vista de encima* not to take one's eyes off || *no ser agradable a la vista* not to be a pretty sight || *observar la ciudad a vista de pájaro* to get a bird's-eye view of the town || *perder de vista* to lose sight of || *perderse de vista* to go out of sight || *se le nubló la vista* his eyes became glazed, his eyes glazed over || FIG *saltar a la vista* to be obvious, to be as plain as a pikestaff || *ser corto de vista* to be shortsighted || FIG *ser largo de vista* to be farseeing || FIG *tener a la vista* to have in mind, to plan (un proyecto), to have one's eye on (vigilar), to have within sight (ver) || *tener mucha vista* to be farsighted (una persona), to look very nice, to be very pretty *o* attractive (una cosa) || *tener poca vista* to be shortsighted, to have bad sight *o* eyes (ver poco), to be shortsighted (no ser perspicaz) || *tener una vista de lince* or *de águila* to have eyes like a hawk || *torcer la vista* to squint || *traducción a la vista* unseen *o* sight translation || *una foto de la ciudad a vista de pájaro* a bird's-eye view of the town || FAM *uno de la vista baja* a pig (cerdo) || MIL *¡vista al frente!* eyes front! || *vista cansada* failing eyesight || FIG *vista de conjunto* overall view || *vista general* panorama, panoramic view || *volver la vista atrás* to look back || *ya se ha perdido de vista ése que dices* the one you are talking about has completely disappeared.
◆ *pl* ARQ windows and doors (en los edificios) | view *sing*; *casa con vistas al mar* house with a sea view *o* a view onto the sea || meeting *sing* (reunión) || — *a ojos vistas* visibily || *con vistas a* in anticipation of, as a provision for; *con vistas al frío compré una tonelada de carbón* as a provision for the cold weather I bought a ton of coal; with a view to; *negociaciones con vistas a una alianza* negotiations with a view to an alliance || *servidumbre de vistas* right to open windows over-looking another person's property.

vista *m* customs man, customs officer, customs official (aduanero).

vistavisión *f* wide screen (cine).

vistazo *m* glance || — *dar* or *echar un vistazo* to have a (quick) look || *dar* or *echar un vistazo a* to glance at, to take a glance at, to have a (quick) look at.

vistesantos *f inv* old maid (solterona).

vistillas *f pl* viewpoint *sing*.

visto, ta *pp* → **ver.**
◆ *adj* in view of, considering (en vista de) || — *cosa nunca vista* sth. quite unheard-of || *estaba visto* it was to be expected, what can you expect? || *está muy visto* it is very common (muy corriente), that is old hat (nada original) || *estar bien visto* to be well looked on || *estar mal visto* to be frowned on || FAM *estar más visto que el tebeo* to be all over the place, to be old hat || *está visto que...* it is obvious *o* evident *o* clear that... || *este espectáculo es algo nunca visto* this show is unique || *ladrillo visto* uncovered brickwork || *¡lo nunca visto!* you've never seen anything like it! || *no visto ni oído* in a flash || *por lo visto* obviously (por lo que se ve), apparently (según parece) || *visto bueno, visto y conforme* seen and approved *o* passed || *visto que...* in view of the fact that..., seeing that..., being that...
◆ *m* *visto bueno* approval, O. K. || *dar el visto bueno a* to give one's approval to, to approve, to okay.

vistosamente *adv* colourfully, brightly; *sala vistosamente engalanada* colourfully decorated room || flashily, showily (de modo llamativo).

vistosidad *f* colourfulness [US colorfulness], brightness || showiness, flashiness (aspecto llamativo).

vistoso, sa *adj* colourful [US colorful], bright; *llevar un vestido muy vistoso* to wear a very colourful dress || showy, flashy (llamativo).

Vístula *npr m* GEOGR the Vistula.

visual *adj* visual || *campo visual* visual field, field of vision.
◆ *f* line of sight || *tirar visuales* to take measurements *o* readings, to survey (topografía).
◆ *m* INFORM visual display unit.

visualización *f* visualization || INFORM display.

visualizar *vt* to visualize || INFORM to display.

vital *adj* vital; *órganos vitales* vital organs || FIG vital (fundamental); *de importancia vital* of vital importance || — *espacio vital* living space || FIL *impulso* or *elan vital* vital force, élan vital.

vitalicio, cia *adj* life; *pensión vitalicia* life annuity; *miembro vitalicio* life member || — *cargo vitalicio* post held for life || *renta vitalicia* life annuity.
◆ *m* life annuity.

vitalidad *f* vitality.

vitalismo *m* vitalism (doctrina biológica).

vitalista *adj* vitalistic.
◆ *m/f* vitalist.

vitalización *f* vitalization.

vitalizar *vt* to vitalize.

vitamina *f* vitamin.

vitaminado, da *adj* vitaminized, enriched with vitamins, vitamin-enriched.

vitamínico, ca *adj* vitaminic || vitamin; *contenido vitamínico* vitamin content.

vitando, da *adj* to be avoided || FIG odious, hateful.

vitela *f* vellum.

vitelino, na *adj* BIOL vitelline.

vitelo *m* vitellus, yolk (del huevo).

vitícola *adj* viticultural, vine, vine growing.
◆ *m* viticulturist, vinegrower.

viticultor *m* viticulturist, vinegrower.

viticultura *f* viticulture, vine growing.

vitíligo *m* MED vitiligo (despigmentación de la piel).

vitivinícola *adj* viticultural [associated with vine growing and the production of wine].

vitivinicultor *m* winegrower, viticulturist.

vitivinicultura *f* wine growing.

vito *m* Andalusian dance and song.

Vito *npr m* MED *baile de San Vito* St. Vitus' dance.

vitola *f* band, cigar band (de puros) || calibrator (para calibrar) || FIG appearance (aspecto) || MAR scantling, model.

vítor *m* cheer || — *dar vítores al presidente* to cheer *o* to acclaim the president || *¡vítor!* bravo!, hurrah!

vitorear *vt* to acclaim, to cheer, to applaud.

Vitoria *n pr* GEOGR Vitoria.

vitral *m* stained-glass window (de iglesia).

vítreo, a *adj* vitreous; *electricidad vítrea* vitreous electricity; *humor vítreo* vitreous humour || vitreous (de vidrio).

vitrificación *f*; **vitrificado** *m* vitrification.

vitrificador, ra *adj* vitrifying.

vitrificar, vitrificarse *vt/vpr* to vitrify.

vitrina *f* showcase, glass case (en tiendas) || display cabinet (en una casa) || AMER shopwindow [US show window] (escaparate).

vitriolar *vt* to vitriol.

vitriólico, ca *adj* vitriolic.

vitriolo *m* vitriol; *aceite de vitriolo* oil of vitriol.

vituallar *vt* to provision, to victual (p us).

vituallas *f pl* provisions, victuals.

vituperación *f* vituperation, reprehension, censure.

vituperador, ra *adj* vituperative, reproachful.

vituperar *vt* to vituperate, to reprehend, to censure.

vituperio *m* vituperation, reprehension, censure (vituperación) || shame, disgrace (vergüenza).
◆ *pl* insults, abuse *sing*.

viudedad *f* widowerhood (estado de viudo) || widowhood (de viuda) || widow's pension (pensión).

viudez *f* widowerhood (estado de viudo) || widowhood (estado de viuda).

viudita *f* young widow (mujer) || AMER widow monkey (mono) | kind of parrot (loro).

viudo, da *adj* widowed.
◆ *m* widower.
◆ *f* widow; *viuda alegre* merry widow || widow bird (ave).

viva *m* cheer || — *dar vivas* to cheer || *¡viva!* hurrah! || *¡viva el rey!* long live the king!, hurrah for the king!

vivac *m* bivouac.

vivacidad *f* vivacity, liveliness, vivaciousness || sharpness (inteligencia).

vivales *m/f inv* FAM crafty devil, sly one.

vivamente *adv* vividly (brillar o destacarse) || quickly (rápidamente) || smartly, briskly (moverse) || sincerely (sinceramente) || deeply; *lo siento vivamente* I am deeply sorry || vividly (narrar, recordar) || sharply (protestar).

vivaque *m* bivouac.

vivaquear *vi* to bivouac.

vivar *m* warren (de conejos) || fishpond (estanque para los peces) || fish hatchery (donde se crían peces).

vivaracho, cha *adj* lively, sprightly, vivacious, bouncy.

vivaz *adj* long-lived (que dura) || quick-witted, sharp (agudo) || vigorous (vigoroso) || lively, vivacious (lleno de vida) || BOT perennial.

vivencia *f* (personal) experience.

víveres *m pl* supplies, provisions; *cortarle los víveres a alguien* to cut off s.o.'s supplies.

vivero *m* nursery (para plantas) || fishpond (estanque para peces) || fish hatchery (donde se crían) || farm; *vivero de ostras* oyster farm || cloth made in Vivero (Galicia) || FIG nursery, breeding ground; *esta ciudad es un vivero de atletas* this town is a nursery for athletes.

viveza *f* vividness (de colores, narraciones) || sharpness (de espíritu) || keenness, acuteness (de un sentimiento) || sincerity (sinceridad) || vivacity, liveliness (de una persona) || quickness (de movimiento) || sparkle (de ojos) || passion, feeling (pasión).

vivido, da *adj* true, true life, which actually happened [to one].

vívido, da *adj* vivid.

vividor, ra *adj* living, live, alive (que vive) || shrewd, adept, capable (que sabe manejarse).
◆ *m/f* person who makes the most of life || opportunist (oportunista).

vivienda *f* housing; *escasez de vivienda* housing shortage; *problema de la vivienda* housing problem || dwelling (morada) || habitant (de animales) || house (casa) || flat (piso) || *vivienda de protección oficial* government subsidized housing [council housing] || *vivienda plurifamiliar* block of flats [US apartment block] || *viviendas de renta limitada* or *protegidas* council houses *o* flats [US low cost housing].

viviente *adj* living; *seres vivientes* living beings || — *cuadro viviente* tableau vivant || *los vivientes* the living.

vivificante *adj* vivifying, life-giving || comforting.

vivificar *vt* to vivify, to give life to || to comfort.

viviparidad *f* ZOOL & BOT viviparity.

vivíparo, ra *adj* ZOOL & BOT viviparous.

vivir *m* life (vida) || living (sustento) || way of life (modo de vivir) || — *gente de mal vivir* bad people, shady characters *pl* || *tener un vivir decente* to live reasonably well.

vivir *vi* to live; *los loros viven mucho tiempo* parrots live a long time; *vivir en el campo* to live in the country; *vive en Madrid desde hace tres años* he has been living in Madrid for three years || to be alive (estar vivo) || FIG & FAM to last (durar) || — *alegría de vivir* joy of living, joie de vivre || *como se vive se muere* as we live so shall we die || *ir viviendo* to get by, to get along || *mientras yo viva* as long as I live; *mientras yo viva no te faltará nada* as long as I live you will want for nothing; over my dead body; *mientras yo viva no lo harás* you'll do it over my dead body || *no dejar vivir a uno* not to give s.o. any peace, not to leave s.o. alone (una persona), to be a constant torment to s.o. (problemas, etc.) || *no vive del miedo que tiene* he is scared to death, he is tormented *o* plagued by fear || *¿quién vive?* who goes there? (centinela) || *saber vivir* to enjoy life to the full || *se vive bien en este país* it's a good life *o* life is good in this country || *tener con que vivir* to have enough to live on || *¡viva!* hurrah!, hurray! || *¡viva España!* long live Spain! || *¡vivan los novios!* hurray for *o* three cheers for the bride and groom! || *¡vive Dios!* good God!, good heavens! (sorpresa) || FIG & FAM *vivir a cuerpo de rey* to live like a king || *vivir al día* to live from hand to mouth *o* from one day to the next || *vivir bien* to live well (teniendo bastante dinero), to lead an honest life (vivir honestamente), to get along well together (vivir en armonía varias personas) || *vivir con poco* to live on very little || *vivir del aire* to live on next to nothing || *vivir de ilusiones* or *de quimeras* to live in a dream world || *vivir de sus ahorros* to live off one's savings || *vivir de sus rentas* to live on one's private income || *vivir muy justo* to scrape a bare living || *vivir para ver* to live and learn || *vivir por encima de sus posibilidades* to live beyond one's means || *vivir sin pena ni gloria* to lead an uneventful life || *y vivieron felices, comieron perdices, y a mí no me dieron* and they all lived happily ever after (final de los cuentos).
◆ *vt* to go *o* to live through; *vivir momentos difíciles* to go through difficult times.

vivisección *f* vivisection.

vivisector, ra *m/f* vivisector.

vivismo *m* doctrine of Luis Vives [16th century Spanish philosopher].

vivista *m* follower of Luis Vives.

vivito, ta *adj* FAM *vivito y coleando* alive and kicking, going strong (una persona), not over yet; *el asunto queda vivito y coleando* the matter is not over yet.

vivo, va *adj* living; *seres vivos* living beings || alive; *está todavía vivo* he is still alive || living (lengua) || vivid (descripción, color, recuerdo, imaginación, etc.) || sharp, quick (inteligencia) || sharp, intense (dolor) || deep, keen, intense (emociones) || quick (movimiento) || strong (protesta) || lively, vivacious (lleno de vida) || bright, quick-witted (listo) || alert (perspicaz) || quick-tempered (que se enfada fácilmente) || FIG cunning, sly, shrewd (astuto) | unscrupulous (aprovechón) || sharp (arista, ángulo) || — *agua viva* springwater || *al* or *a lo vivo* vividly || *a viva fuerza* by main force || *de viva actualidad*

much talked about, much discussed || *de viva voz* personally, in person (personalmente); *decir algo a alguien de viva voz* to tell s.o. sth. personally; viva voce, orally, by word of mouth || *Dios vivo* the living God || *en carnes vivas, en cueros vivos* (stark) naked (desnudo) || *en carne viva* raw, red raw (la espalda, la piel, etc.), like an unhealed wound; *un recuerdo que está en carne viva* a memory which is like an unhealed wound || *en roca viva* in *o* out of *o* from living *o* solid rock (tallar, etc.) || *en vivo* on the hoof (ganadería), with live animals; *experimentar en vivo* to experiment with live animals || *fuerzas vivas* life *o* driving force [of a town's or nation's economy] || FIG *hay una diferencia como de lo vivo a lo pintado* there is no comparison | *herir en carne viva* to cut *o* to touch to the quick (ofender), to rub salt in a wound (volver a herir) | *herir* or *tocar en lo vivo* to cut *o* to touch to the quick | *llegar a lo vivo* to cut to the quick (a una persona), to reach the quick *o* the heart (de un asunto) | *llorar a lágrima viva* to cry bitterly, to cry one's eyes out, to sob one's heart out, to weep buckets || MAR *obra viva* quickwork || FIG *pasarse de vivo* to try to be too clever | *ser el vivo retrato de alguien* to be the spitting image *o* the living image of s.o. | *ser más vivo que un rayo* to be as quick as lightning | *ser vivo de genio* to be quick-witted | *ser vivo de imaginación* to have a vivid imagination || *seto vivo* quickset hedge || FIG *tener el genio vivo* to be quick-tempered *o* easily excitable.
◆ *m* living person || FIG & FAM crafty devil (astuto) || trimming (en costura) || — JUR *donación entre vivos* gift inter vivos || *los vivos y los muertos* the quick *o* the living and the dead.

vizcacha *f* viscacha (roedor).

vizcachera *f* viscacha's warren.

vizcaínada *f* typically Basque expression || typically Basque action.

vizcaíno, na *adj/s* Biscayan (de la provincia de Vizcaya) || Basque (del País Vasco).

vizcaitarra *adj/s* Basque nationalist.

Vizcaya *npr f* GEOGR Biscay; *la bahía de Vizcaya* the Bay of Biscay.

vizcondado *m* viscountcy, viscounty (dignidad) || viscounty (jurisdicción).

vizcondal *adj* of *o* pertaining to a viscount.

vizconde *m* viscount.

vizcondesa *f* viscountess.

vocablo *m* word, vocable (p us) || FIG *jugar del vocablo* to make a play on words *o* a pun.

vocabulario *m* vocabulary.

vocación *f* vocation, calling; *errar la vocación* to miss one's vocation.

vocal *adj* vocal; *cuerdas vocales* vocal chords; *órganos vocales* vocal organs.
◆ *f* GRAM vowel.
◆ *m/f* member; *vocal de una comisión* committee member.

vocálico, ca *adj* vocalic, vowel.

vocalismo *m* vocalism.

vocalista *m/f* vocalist (en una orquesta).

vocalización *f* vocalization.

vocalizar *vi/vt* to vocalize.

vocativo *m* vocative.

voceador, ra *adj* vociferous, loud-mouthed.
◆ *m/f* shouter (que grita).
◆ *m* town crier (pregonero).

vocear *vi* to shout *o* to cry *o* to yell (out).
◆ *vt* to cry *o* to shout (out) (un vendedor) || to shout from the rooftops, to proclaim (publicar) || to shout to, to hail (llamar) || to acclaim, to hail (aclamar).

vocería *f*; **vocerío** *m* shouting, yelling (gritería) || uproar, clamour [US clamor] (clamor).

vocero *m* spokesman (portavoz).

vociferador, ra *adj* vociferous, vociferant.

vociferante *adj* vociferant, vociferous.

vociferar *vi/vt* to vociferate, to scream, to shout.

vocinglería *f* shouting (gritería) || hubbub, uproar, clamour [US clamor] (clamor).

vocinglero, ra *adj* loud-mouthed (que habla mucho y en voz alta).

vodevil *m* vaudeville, music hall.

vodka *m* o *f* vodka.

vodú *m* voodoo.

volada *f* flight, short flight || AMER ⟶ **bolada.**

voladera *f* paddle, blade (paleta).

voladero, ra *adj* flying || able to fly.

voladizo, za *adj* ARQ projecting, jutting out; *cornisa voladiza* projecting cornice.
◆ *m* projection || *en voladizo* projecting.

volado, da *adj* IMPR superior || projecting (voladizo) || — FIG & FAM *estar volado* to be uneasy (inquieto), not to know where to put o.s. (de vergüenza), to be pressed for time (tener prisa) || FIG *hacer algo volado* to do sth. in a hurry.

volador, ra *adj* flying (que vuela); *pez volador* flying fish; *aparato volador* flying machine.
◆ *m* rocket (cohete) || flying fish (pez) || AMER symbolic Mexican game in which men swing on ropes round the top of a very high pole.

voladura *f* blowing-up; *la voladura de un puente* the blowing-up of a bridge || blasting (en una cantera, de una mina).

volandas (en); volandillas (en) *loc* off the ground, in the air || FIG & FAM *llevar a uno en volandas al hospital* to rush s.o. off to hospital.

volandera *f* grindstone, millstone (de molino) || washer (arandela) || FIG & FAM lie, fib (mentira).

volandero, ra *adj* newly fledged, ready to fly (volantón) || FIG unexpected (imprevisto) | restless, wandering (que no se queda en un lugar) | loose (que no está sujeto) | hanging (suspendido).

volandillas (en) *loc* ⟶ **volandas (en).**

volante *adj* flying; *escuadrón, pez, platillo volante* flying squad, fish, saucer || FIG mobile, itinerant (que va de un sitio a otro); *equipo volante* mobile team *o* crew | temporary (temporal); *campamento volante* temporary camp || DEP *medio volante* wing half, half back.
◆ *m* shuttlecock (rehilete) || badminton (juego) || flounce (en vestidos) || frill (adorno) || note (comunicación no oficial) || leaflet (hoja suelta) || AUT (steering) wheel || MED card || TECN flywheel (para regularizar el movimiento) | balance wheel (de reloj) | coin press (para acuñar moneda) || AMER volante, two-wheeled carriage (vehículo).

volantín *m* AMER kite.

volapié *m* TAUR «volapié» [method of killing a bull in which the matador runs at the stationary animal and drives the blade between the shoulders].

volapuk *m* Volapük (lengua).

volar* *vi* to fly (aves, aviones); *este avión vuela a diez mil metros* this aeroplane flies at an altitude of ten thousand metres || to be blown away (con el viento); *los papeles volaron* the papers were blown away || FIG to fly (correr); *volar en auxilio de uno* to fly to s.o.'s aid; *¡cómo vuela el tiempo!* how time flies! || FAM to disappear (desaparecer) || ARQ to project, to jut out (balcón) || — *echarse a volar* to fly away *o* off, to take wing (los pájaros), to leave home (dejar el hogar) || FIG *el pájaro ha volado* or *voló* the bird has flown | *hacer algo volando* to do sth. as quick as a flash | *ir volando* to fly along, to hurble along, to speed along (coche, etc.), to go at once, to fly (ir en seguida) | *ir volando a hacer algo* to run and do sth. | *las noticias vuelan* news spreads fast | *pasar, salir volando* to fly past, out | *¡volando!* jump to it!, on the double!, make it snappy! | *volar con sus propias alas* to stand on one's own two feet || *volar por encima* or *sobre* to fly over.
◆ *vpr* to blow up, to demolish (edificios, etc.) || to blast (en una cantera, una mina) || to flush (las aves en la caza) || to fly (el halcón).
◆ *vpr* to be blown away, to fly away (con el viento); *los papeles se volaron* the papers were blown away || AMER to lose one's temper, to blow up (encolerizarse).

volatería *f* falconry (caza) || birds *pl*, fowl *pl* (aves de corral).

volátil *adj* volatile || FIG fickle, changeable, inconstant.

volatilidad *f* volatility || FIG inconstancy, fickleness, changeableness.

volatilización *f* volatilization.

volatilizar *vt* to volatize || FIG to spirit away (hacer desaparecer).
◆ *vpr* to volatilize || FIG to vanish into thin air (desaparecer).

volatín *m*; **volatinero, ra** *m/f* flier [US aerialist].

volcán *m* volcano.

volcanada *f* AMER FAM puff (bocanada).

volcanicidad *f* volcanicity || volcanism (volcanismo).

volcánico, ca *adj* volcanic.

volcanismo *m* volcanism.

volcanista *m* volcanist, vulcanist.

volcanizar *vt* to volcanize.

volcar* *vt* to tip over, to knock over, to upset; *volcar un vaso* to knock a glass over || to knock down (un adversario) || to empty out, to pour out (vaciar) || FIG to make (s.o.) dizzy (turbarle la cabeza a uno) | to make (s.o.) change his mind (hacer que uno cambie de opinión) | to upset, to get on (s.o.'s) nerves (irritar).
◆ *vi* to turn over, to overturn (vehículo) || to capsize (barco) || *volqué con el coche* I turned the car over.
◆ *vpr* to fall over (vaso, etc.) || to turn over, to overturn (vehículo) || to capsize (barco) || FIG to do one's utmost, to bend over backwards; *volcarse para conseguir fondos* to do one's utmost to raise funds.

volea *f* swingletree, whippletree (carruajes) || DEP volley (en el juego de pelota) | lob (en el tenis y el fútbol).

volear *vt* to volley (pelota) || AGR to broadcast, to scatter (semillas).
◆ *vi* DEP to volley.

voleibol *m* AMER DEP volleyball (balonvolea).

voleo *m* volley (en el juego de pelota) || hard slap (bofetón) || high kick (en la danza) || — *a* or *al voleo* at random, randomly, haphazardly (arbitrariamente) || *del primer* or *de un voleo* first go, first time || *sembrar a* or *al voleo* to broadcast seed, to scatter seed.

volframina *f* QUÍM wolframine.

volframio *m* QUÍM wolfram (tungsteno).

volframita *f* QUÍM wolframite.

Volga *npr m* GEOGR the Volga.

volición *v* volition.

volitivo, va *adj* volitive.

volován *m* vol-au-vent.

volquete *m* tipcart (carro) || tip-up lorry [*US* dump truck] (camión).

volquetero *m* lorry driver [*US* truck driver].

volscos *m pl* Volsci.

Volta *npr m* GEOGR the Volta.

voltaico, ca *adj* ELECTR voltaic.

voltaje *m* ELECTR voltage.

voltámetro *m* ELECTR voltameter.

voltamperímetro *m* ELECTR voltammeter.

voltamperio *m* ELECTR volt-ampere.

voltariedad *f* inconstancy, fickleness, changeableness.

voltario, ria *adj* inconstant, fickle, changeable.

volteada *f AMER* method of isolating chosen animals from a herd by galloping a horse through the herd.

voltear *vt* to swing; *voltear una honda* to swing a sling || to turn, to turn over, to toss (la tierra, el heno, una tortilla, etc.) || to turn round (dar una vuelta) || to overturn (volcar) || to ring out loud, to peal out (las campanas) || to toss *o* to throw up in the air; *el toro volteó al torero* the bull tossed the bullfighter up in the air || FIG & FAM to fail (en un examen) | to topple (un gobierno).

◆ *vi* to roll over (caerse redondo) || to do *o* to turn a somersault [o a cartwheel, etc.], to somersault (un volteador) || to peal out, to be at full peal (las campanas).

◆ *vpr AMER* to turn one's coat, to desert one's party (cambiar de chaqueta) | to turn round (dar la vuelta).

volteo *m* trick riding (equitación) || peal (de las campanas).

voltereta *f* somersault || handspring (poniendo las manos en el suelo) || *dar volteretas* to do somersaults, to turn somersaults, to somersault.

volterianismo *m* Voltairianism.

volteriano, na *adj/s* Voltairean, Voltairian.

voltímetro *m* voltmeter.

voltio *m* ELECTR volt.

volubilidad *f* inconstancy, fickleness, changeableness, volubility (p us) || BOT volubility.

volúbilis *m* BOT convolvulus.

voluble *adj* inconstant, changeable, fickle, voluble (p us) || BOT voluble, twining.

volumen *m* volume (de recipiente, cantidad, sonido) || size (tamaño) || bulk, bulkiness (gran tamaño) || volume, tome (libro) || — *de mucho volumen* important, sizeable (importante) || *poner la radio a todo volumen* to turn the radio up full || ECON *volumen de contratación* trading volume | *volumen de negocios* turnover.

volumetría *f* volumetry.

volumétrico, ca *adj* volumetric, volumetrical.

volúmetro *m* volumeter.

voluminoso, sa *adj* voluminous || bulky, cumbersome (que ocupa mucho sitio); *paquete voluminoso* bulky parcel.

voluntad *f* will; *los reflejos no dependen de la voluntad* one's reflexes are independent of one's will; *lo hago contra mi voluntad* I am doing it against my will; *tiene mucha voluntad* he has a strong will || wishes *pl* (deseos); *hacer algo contra la voluntad de otro* to do sth. against s.o. else's wishes || wish (deseo); *su voluntad es meterse a cura* his wish is to become a priest || willpower (fuerza de voluntad); *es muy listo pero le falta voluntad* he is very clever, but he lacks willpower || affection, liking (cariño) || — *a voluntad* at will, as one wishes || *buena voluntad* goodwill; *visita de buena voluntad* goodwill visit; good intentions (buenas intenciones); *tiene buena voluntad* his intentions are good || *con poca voluntad* reluctantly || *fuerza de voluntad* willpower || *ganar la voluntad de uno* to win s.o. over || FAM *hacer su santa voluntad* to do exactly as one pleases *o* likes || *hágase tu voluntad* Thy will be done (oración) || *mala voluntad* ill will, malice || *me atengo a su voluntad* I leave it to your discretion || *no tener voluntad propia* to have no will of one's own || *por causas ajenas a nuestra voluntad* for reasons beyond our control || *por su propia voluntad* of one's own free will || *tenerle buena, mala voluntad a uno* to like, not to like s.o. || JUR *última voluntad* last wish (de un condenado a muerte), last will and testament, will (de un moribundo) || *voluntad divina* Divine will || *voluntad férrea* or *de hierro* will of iron || *zurcir voluntades* to pander.

voluntariado *m* MIL voluntary enlistment.

voluntariedad *f* voluntariness || wilfulness [*US* willfulness] (de una persona obstinada).

voluntario, ria *adj* voluntary || wilful [*US* willful] (obstinado).

◆ *m/f* volunteer.

voluntarioso, sa *adj* willing (deseoso de hacer las cosas bien) || wilful [*US* willful] (testarudo).

voluptuosidad *f* voluptuousness.

voluptuoso, sa *adj* voluptuous; *vida voluptuosa* voluptuous life.

◆ *m/f* voluptuary.

voluta *f* ARQ volute, spiral, scroll || spiral, column (de humo) || ZOOL volute.

volver* *vt* to turn; *volver la cabeza* to turn one's head; *volver la esquina* to turn the corner || to turn, to turn over (poniendo lo de arriba abajo); *volver una tortilla, la tierra* to turn an omelette, the earth; *volver la página* to turn (over) the page || to turn (*a* on) (un arma de fuego) || to turn inside out (poniendo lo de dentro afuera); *volver un calcetín* to turn a sock inside out || to make; *el éxito le ha vuelto presumido* success has made him arrogant || to turn (convertir); *volver el agua en vino* to turn water into wine; *el tinte lo volvió verde* the dye turned it green || to turn back, to return, to restore; *producto que vuelve el pelo a su color natural* product which turns hair back to its natural colour || FIG to turn; *han vuelto contra él sus propios argumentos* they turned his own arguments against him || to put; *volver una frase en la forma pasiva* to put a sentence into the passive || to turn (en costura) || — *volver a la vida a uno* to bring s.o. back to life, to revive s.o. || *volver algo a su sitio* to put sth. back || *volver boca abajo* to turn upside down (una cosa), to turn over (a una persona) || *volver del revés* to turn (sth.) inside-out || FIG *volver casaca* or *la casaca* to turn one's coat, to change sides || *volver la espalda* to turn round (volverse) || *volver la espalda a uno* to turn one's back on s.o. (*sentido propio*), to give s.o. (*sentido figurado*) || FIG *volver la hoja* to change the subject (cambiar de conversación), to turn over a new leaf (cambiar de vida) || *volver la mirada* or *los ojos a* to look round at, to turn one's eyes towards || *volver la vista atrás* to look back || *volver loco a uno* to drive s.o. mad.

◆ *vi* to go back, to return (estando lejos del sitio de que se habla); *volver a su patria* to go back to one's homeland || to come back, to return (estando en el sitio de que se habla); *no vuelvas muy tarde* don't come back too late || to go back, to go again, to return (ir de nuevo); *este verano volveremos a París* this summer we shall go back to Paris *o* we shall go to Paris again || FIG to return; *la juventud no vuelve nunca* one's youth never returns | to return, to revert; *volvamos a nuestro tema* let us return to the subject in hand | to revert; *la tribu ha vuelto al paganismo* the tribe has reverted to paganism || — *hacer volver al buen camino* to put back on the right road || *no lo vuelva a hacer* don't do it again || *volver a* to start to... again; *volvió a llover* it started to rain again (*véase* OBSERV) || *volver a la carga* or *al ataque* to renew the attack *o* the assault, to charge again (las tropas), to keep at it (insistir) || *volver a la infancia* to be in one's second childhood || *volver a las andadas* to fall back into *o* to revert to one's old habits *o* ways || *volver al orden* or *a la normalidad* to return to normal || *volver a lo de siempre* to get back to the same old thing || *volver al redil* to return to the fold || *volver a llevar* to take back || *volver a meter* to put back || *volver a ponerse* to put back on || *volver atrás* to go back, to turn back || *volver con las manos vacías* to come *o* to go back *o* to return empty-handed || *volver en sí* to come to, to come round, to regain consciousness || *volver sobre sus pasos* to retrace one's steps, to go back (desandar lo andado), to retract *o* to withdraw *o* to take back a statement (desdecirse) || *vuelva a llenar* the same again (al convidar a otra copa).

◆ *vpr* to turn round (dar la vuelta) || to turn; *se volvió hacia mí* he turned to me || to go back, to come back, to return (regresar) || to turn over; *se ha vuelto la página* the page has turned over || to turn inside out (ponerse al revés) || to become, to turn; *el tiempo se vuelve bueno* the weather is turning fine; *volverse triste* to become sad || to turn (sour) (agriarse) || *volverse contra alguien* or *en contra de alguien* to turn against s.o. || *volverse loco* to go mad.

— OBSERV La mayoría de las veces la expresión española *volver a* seguida de un infinitivo se traduce al inglés por el verbo acompañado del adverbio *again* cuando se trata de la repetición de una acción (*volver a cantar* to sing again) y del adverbio *back* si implica la vuelta al objeto mencionado al sitio donde estaba (*volver a poner un libro en la biblioteca* to put a book back in the bookcase).

vólvulo *m* MED volvulus.

vómer *m* ANAT vomer.

vómica *f* MED vomica.

vómico, ca *adj* vomitive, emetic || *nuéz vómica* nux vomica.

vomitar *vi* to be sick, to vomit || *dar a uno ganas de vomitar* to make one feel sick.

◆ *vt* to vomit, to bring up || FIG to belch, to spew out, to spit; *los cañones vomitaban fuego* the cannons belched fire | to hurl; *vomitar injurias* to hurl abuse || FIG & FAM to spit out, to cough up (revelar) || *vomitar sangre* to spit blood.

vomitera *f* sickness || *le ha dado la vomitera* she feel sick.

vomitivo, va *adj/sm* MED emetic.

vómito *m* vomiting, vomit (acción) || vomit (resultado) || — *vómito de sangre* hemoptysis || *vómito negro* black vomit, yellow fever.

vomitón, ona *adj* FAM who often vomits [suckling child].

◆ *f* FAM *echar una vomitona* to be violently sick, to throw up.

vomitorio *adj/sm* emetic (vomitivo).

◆ *m* vomitory (de los circos romanos).

vorace *adj* POÉT voracious (voraz).

voracidad *f* voracity, voraciousness.

vorágine *f* vortex, maelstrom, whirlpool.

voraz *adj* voracious || FIG raging (llamas, etc.).

vórtice *m* vortex, whirlpool || centre of a cyclone (centro de un ciclón) || hurricane (huracán).

vorticela *f* ZOOL vorticella.

vortiginoso, sa *adj* vortical, swirling.

vos *pron pers de la 2.ª pers del sing y del pl* You || Thou (dirigiéndose a Dios).

— OBSERV *Vos* is used instead of *usted* in poetic and oratorical style to address God or an eminent person: *Señor, Vos sois nuestra Providencia* Lord, Thou art our Providence. In the seventeenth century *vos* was an intermediate form of address between *tú* and *Vuestra Merced*. In many parts of Latin America *vos* has replaced *tú* as the formula for addressing one's equals or inferiors. The accusative form *te* has however survived, and is often used with *vos*: *a vos te parece bien* that seems all right to you; *vos te comeréis* or *te comerás este pastel* you will eat this cake.

vosear *vt* to address as «vos» (*véase* OBSERV) en VOS.

voseo *m* use of «vos» to address s.o. (*véase* OBSERV) en VOS.

vosotros, tras *pron pers de la 2.ª pers del plural* you; *¿cuándo venís vosotros?* when are you coming?; *lo hice por vosotros* I did it for you || yourselves; *¿lo habéis discutido entre vosotros?* have you discussed it amongst yourselves? || — *el coche de vosotros* your car || *el de vosotros* yours.

— OBSERV This pronoun is the plural form of the familiar *tú* form of address: *a vosotros, hijos míos, os diré lo mismo* I shall say the same thing to you, my sons.

— OBSERV This second person plural may also be used by a speaker to address his audience, by an author to address his readers, etc.

votación *f* voting (acción de votar); *modo de votación* method of voting; *votación a mano alzada* voting by a show of hands || vote; *la votación tuvo lugar ayer* the vote was taken yesterday; *poner* or *someter a votación* to put to the vote; *votación unánime* unanimous vote; *votación nula* unconclusive vote || ballot; *votación adicional* or *de desempate* second ballot || — *por votación popular* by popular vote || *proponer la votación por separado* to move that a separate vote be taken || *votación masiva* heavy voting || *votación nominal* vote *o* voting by roll call || *votación por levantados y sentados* vote by sitting and standing [US rising vote] || *votación secreta* secret ballot *o* vote.

votante *adj* voting.
◆ *m/f* voter.

votar *vt/vi* to vote; *votar a mano alzada* to vote by a show of hands; *votar por uno* to vote for s.o.; *votar la candidatura de* to vote for || to pass (aprobar); *una moción votada por unanimidad* a motion passed unanimously || to vote; *votar diez mil libras para la investigación* to vote ten thousand pounds for research || to vote on (someter a votación) || to curse, to swear (blasfemar) || REL to vow || — *proceder a votar* to proceed to a vote || *votar puestos en pie* or *por levantados y sentados* to vote by sitting and standing || *¡voto a tal!* damn it!, confound it!

votivo, va *adj* votive; *misa votiva* votive Mass.

voto *m* vote; *explicar el voto* to account for *o* to explain one's vote; *moción aprobada por doce votos a favor y nueve en contra* motion passed by twelve votes to nine; *dar su voto a* to give one's vote to || vow; *voto de castidad* vow of chastity; *pronunciar sus votos* to take vows || wish (deseo); *formular votos por el éxito de algo* to express one's sincere wishes for the success of sth. || curse (reniego) || — *acciones de voto plural* shares with plural voting rights || *depositar un voto* to cast a vote || *derecho al voto* the right to vote, suffrage, franchise || FAM *no tener ni voz ni voto* to have no say in the matter || *tener voto* to have the right to vote || *tener voz y voto* to be a voting member (en una asamblea) || *voto de calidad* casting vote || *voto de castigo* vote-splitting || *voto de censura* vote of censure || *voto de confianza* vote of confidence || *voto de gracias* vote of thanks || *voto de obediencia* vow of obedience || *voto de pobreza* vow of poverty || *voto de silencio* vow of silence || *voto por correspondencia* or *por correo* postal vote *o* ballot || *voto por poderes* vote by proxy || *voto secreto* vote *o* ballot || *voto solemne* solemn vow.
◆ *pl* vote *sing*, votes (conjunto de los votos) || — *echar votos* to curse, to swear (blasfemar) || *hacer votos por* or *por que* to earnestly hope for *o* that || *por una mayoría de votos* by a majority vote || *votos de felicidad* best wishes || *votos emitidos* votes cast || *votos indecisos* floating votes.

vox *f* *ser vox pópuli* to be common knowledge || *vox pópuli* rumour.

¡vóytelas! *interj* AMER good heavens! (¡caramba!).

voz *f* voice; *voz cavernosa* hollow voice; *tener buena voz* to have a good voice || shout, cry (grito) || GRAM voice; *voz pasiva, activa* passive, active voice | word (vocablo); *voz culta* learned word || rumour (rumor) || vote, support (voto) || MÚS tone (de un instrumento) | voice (en un fuga) | voice (cada cantante) | part, voice; *una canción para dos voces* a two-part song || FIG voice; *la voz de la conciencia* the voice of one's conscience | sound (sonido) | noise (ruido) || — *aclararse la voz* to clear one's throat || *alzar* or *levantar la voz* to raise one's voice || *a media voz* in a low voice, softly (en voz baja), under one's breath (con insinuación) || MÚS *apagar la voz* to dampen [the sound] (de un instrumento) || *a una voz* with one voice, unanimously || *a voz en cuello* or *en grito* at the top of one's voice || *con voz pero sin voto* without a right to vote, non-voting || *con voz y voto* with a right to vote, voting || *corre la voz que...* rumour has it that..., it is rumoured that... || *dar la voz de alarma* to raise the alarm || *dar una voz a uno* to give s.o. a shout *o* a call || *decir algo en voz alta* to say sth. aloud *o* out loud || *de viva voz* personally, in person (personalmente); *decir algo a alguien de viva voz* to tell s.o. sth. personally; viva voce, orally, by word of mouth || FIG & FAM *donde Cristo dio las tres voces* miles from anywhere, at the back of beyond || MÚS *educar la voz* to train one's voice || *en voz alta* aloud, in a loud voice, out loud || *en voz baja* in a low voice, softly, quietly || *en voz queda* in a soft voice, softly || *estar en voz* to be in good voice || *forzar la voz* to strain one's voice || *hablar en voz baja, en voz alta* to speak softly, loudly || *hacer correr la voz* to spread the rumour || FIG *llevar la voz cantante* to rule the roost | *no tener voz ni voto* to have no say in the matter || *perder la voz* to lose one's voice || *se le está mudando la voz* his voice is breaking || *ser voz pública* to be common knowledge || *tener la voz tomada* to be hoarse || *tener voz consultiva* to have a voice but no vote || *tener voz y voto* to be a voting member (en una asamblea) || *voz aguda* high *o* high-piched voice (de una persona), word with the stress on the last syllable (palabra) || *voz apagada* weak voice || MÚS *voz cantante* principal *o* main voice || *voz de alarma* alarm, alarm call || *voz del cielo* voice from the sky || *voz del pueblo* voice of the people || MIL *voz de mando* order, command || *voz de trueno* thunderous *o* thundering voice || *voz en off* voice-over || *voz estentórea* stentorian voice || *voz pública* public opinion.
◆ *pl* voices || shouting *sing* (gritos) || — *a voces* shouting || *cantar a dos voces* to sing a duet || *dar voces* to shout || FIG *dar voces al viento* to be wasting one's breath || *decir algo a voces* to shout sth. out loud || *estar pidiendo a voces* to be crying out for || *secreto a voces* open secret.

vozarrón *m*; **vozarrona** *f* powerful *o* booming voice.

vuecelencia; vuecencia *pron pers* Your Excellency [term used, especially in former times, to address a superior].

vuelco *m* upset || FIG change, shake-up (cambio) || capsizing (de una embarcación) || — *dar un vuelco* to overturn (coche), to capsize (barco), to change (cambiar), to go to ruin (ir a la ruina) || *dar un vuelco a una cosa* to knock sth. over || FIG *le dio un vuelco el corazón* his heart skipped a beat.

vuelo *m* flying (acción de volar); *vuelo a ciegas* or *ciego* or *sin visibilidad* blind flying || flight (acto de volar una vez, distancia volada, modo de volar); *ha sido un vuelo excelente* it has been an excellent flight; *vuelo sin escala* nonstop flight || fullness, flare (de un vestido) || wing (ala) || flight feathers *pl*, flights *pl* (plumas) || wingspan, wingspread (envergadura) || lace ruffle (volante) || ARQ projection || — *al vuelo* in flight (aves, moscas, etc.); *coger moscas al vuelo* to catch flies in flight; on the wing (aves), very quickly (rápidamente) || *alzar* or *emprender* or *levantar* or *tomar el vuelo* to take flight, to take off (aves), to clear off (marcharse) || *a vuelo de pájaro* as the crow flies (distancia) || FIG & FAM *cogerlas* or *cazarlas al vuelo* to catch on quickly, to be quick on the uptake | *coger* or *cazar una cosa al vuelo* to catch on to sth. quickly | *cortar los vuelos a uno* to clip s.o.'s wings || *de mucho vuelo* ambitious, far-reaching (persona, proyecto, etc.), full (vestido) || FIG *de* or *en un vuelo* quickly, in a trice, in a jiffy || *echar las campanas a vuelo* to set all the bells ringing, to ring all the bells full peal (*sentido propio*), to shout from the rooftops (cacarear), to be overcome with joy, to rejoice (alegrarse) || FIG *¡no tantos vuelos!* don't be so ambitious! || *personal de vuelo* flight staff || *remontar el vuelo* to soar (up) || FIG *se hubiera podido oír el vuelo de una mosca* one could have heard a pin drop | *tomar vuelo* to grow (crecer) || *vuelo a ras de tierra* or *rasante* hedgehopping, low flying || *vuelo a vela* or *sin motor* gliding || *vuelo de prueba* test flight || *vuelo en picado* dive || *vuelo espacial* space flight || *vuelo nocturno* night flight || *vuelo planeado* gliding.

vuelta *f* walk, stroll (paseo); *dar una vuelta por la ciudad* to go for a walk round the town; *dar una vuelta por la tarde* to go for an afternoon walk || return (regreso); *celebrar la vuelta de alguien* to celebrate s.o.'s return || return, return journey, journey back (viaje de regreso) || return (retorno); *la vuelta de la primavera* the return of spring || return (devolución) || round (turno en un concurso, un torneo, etc.); *elegido a la primera vuelta* elected in the first round || bend, curve, turn (recodo) || turn-up (de un pantalón) || ruffle (adorno en el puño, etc.) || row (de un collar, haciendo punto) || loop, coil (de una cuerda, un cabo, etc.) || back (de una tela, de una hoja de papel) || change (dinero); *dar la vuelta al comprador* to give the customer his change; *se quedó con la vuelta* he kept the change || revolution, turn (revolución) || rotation, turn (rotación) || DEP lap (en una carrera); *sólo quedan cuatro vueltas* there are only four laps to go || ARQ vault (bóveda) | curve (del intradós) || EQUIT volte, volt (del caballo) || revolution (unidad de ángulo) || hiding (paliza, tunda); *le dio una vuelta* he gave him a hiding || FIG & FAM round (ronda de bebidas) || — *a la vuelta de* once back from; *a la vuelta de España* once back from Spain || FIG *a la vuelta de diez años* after *o* at the end of ten years || *a la vuelta de la esquina* just round the corner || *a la vuelta de las vacaciones* after the holidays || FIG *andar a vueltas con un problema* to try to come to terms with a problem || *a vuelta de correo* by return of post || FIG & FAM *buscarle a uno las vueltas* to look for faults in everything s.o. does, to find fault with s.o. || *cerrar con dos vueltas* to double-lock || FIG *coger las vueltas* to get the hang *o* the knack of it (el tranquillo) | *cogerle las vueltas a uno* to know how to handle s.o. || FAM *¡con vuelta!* I want it back! (cosa prestada) || FIG *dar la vuelta* to change radically (cambiar) || *dar la vuelta a* to go round (alrededor); *dar la vuelta al mundo* to go round the world; to turn; *dar la vuelta a la llave* to turn the key; to turn round (girar), to turn upside down (poniendo lo de arriba abajo), to turn inside out (poniendo fuera lo de dentro), to turn over (cambiándolo de lado) || *dar la* or *una vuelta de campana* to overturn, to turn over (un coche) || FIG *darle cien vueltas a uno* to knock spots off s.o., to run rings round s.o. || *dar media vuelta* to walk out (irse), to about turn [*US* to about-face] (soldado), to turn round (para volverse atrás), to do a U-turn (coche, etc.) || *dar* or *darse un vuelta* to go for a walk *o* a stroll (andando), to go for a ride *o* for a drive *o* for a run (en coche), to make a short trip (hacer un viaje corto) || *dar vueltas* to turn round, to go round and round, to spin, to rotate (alrededor de un eje), to twist and turn (un camino), to revolve; *la Tierra da vueltas alrededor del Sol* the Earth revolves around the Sun; to go round in circles (no llegar a ninguna parte) || *dar vueltas a* to turn (llave, etc.), to spin (hacer girar), to turn over; *dar vueltas a una idea en la cabeza* to turn an idea over in one's mind; to thoroughly examine (examinar), to go round; *dimos dos vueltas a la manzana* we went twice round the block || FIG *el mundo da muchas vueltas* anything might happen || *estar de vuelta (de)* to be back (from) || FAM *estar de vuelta de todo* to be blasé || *¡hasta la vuelta!* see you when you came back! || FIG *las vueltas de la vida* the ups and downs of life | *le estás dando demasiadas vueltas* you are worrying too much about it || *me da vueltas la cabeza* my head is swimming, I feel dizzy || *media vuelta* about turn [*US* about-face] (los soldados), short walk (paseo corto) || FIG & FAM *no andar con vueltas* not to beat about the bush | *no hay que darle vueltas* that's all there is to it, there's nothing more to be said about it | *no le des más vueltas a este asunto* let the matter lie, don't think about it any more | *no tiene vuelta de hoja* there's no doubt about it (está claro), there is no alternative (no hay otra solución) || *partido de vuelta* return match (deportes) || FIG & FAM *poner a uno de vuelta y media* to call s.o. all the names under the sun | *tener muchas vueltas* to be very tricky *o* complicated || *tener vuelta* to be reversible (la ropa) || *véase a la vuelta* please turn over, P. T. O. (continúa al dorso), overleaf (vea en la página siguiente) || *vuelta a escena* comeback (de un artista) || TAUR *vuelta al ruedo* lap of honour || *vuelta atrás* backward step || *vuelta ciclista* long-distance cycle race || *vuelta ciclista a Francia* Tour de France || *vuelta de campana* somersault (voltereta con el cuerpo) || *vuelta sobre el ala* roll (de un avión) || FAM *¡y vuelta!* not again!

vuelto, ta *pp de volver* || — *cuello vuelto* roll neck, polo neck [*US* turtleneck] || *sombrero con las alas vueltas* hat with the brim turned up *o* with a turned-up brim.
◆ *m* AMER change (vuelta de dinero).

vuesamerced *pron pers* You (vuestra merced).

vuestro, tra *adj pos de la 2.ª pers del pl* your; *vuestro hijo y vuestras hijas* your son and (your) daughters || of yours, your; *uno de vuestros amigos* a friend of yours, one of your friends.
◆ *pron pos* yours; *mis amigos y los vuestros* my friends and yours || — *los vuestros* yours, your people (vuestra familia) || *lo vuestro* what is yours, what belongs to you.

vulcanismo *m* GEOL volcanism, vulcanism.

vulcanita *f* vulcanite.

vulcanización *f* TECN vulcanization.

vulcanizado, da *adj* TECN vulcanized; *caucho vulcanizado* vulcanized rubber.

vulcanizador *m* TECN vulcanizer.

vulcanizar *vt* TECN to vulcanize.

Vulcano *npr m* MIT Vulcan.

vulcanología *f* volcanology, vulcanology.

vulcanologista; vulcanólogo *m* volcanologist, volcanist, vulcanologist, vulcanist.

vulgar *adj* common, general; *opinión vulgar* common opinion || ordinary, common; *el hombre vulgar* the common man || commonplace, trite, banal; *idea vulgar* commonplace idea || ordinary, humdrum (vida) || vulgar, common (poco refinado); *gustos vulgares* vulgar tastes || lay, layman's (no técnico); *término vulgar* lay term || vulgar (no sabio); *latín vulgar* vulgar Latin.

vulgaridad *f* triviality, banality (cosa sabida) || vulgarity (grosería) || *decir vulgaridades* to talk small talk (cosas sabidas), to use bad language, to be rude (groserías).

vulgarismo *m* vulgarism (expresión popular).

vulgarización *f* popularization, vulgarization, extension; *la vulgarización de una ciencia* the vulgarization of a science.

vulgarizar *vt* to vulgarize (hacer vulgar) || to popularize, to vulgarize (exponer algo en forma asequible al vulgo) || to extend (difundir).
◆ *vpr* to be vulgarized *o* popularized || to become common *o* ordinary || to become vulgar *o* common (grosero).

Vulgata *npr f* Vulgate (Biblia).

vulgo *m* common people *pl*, masses *pl*, vulgus (p us) (pueblo) || laymen *pl* (profanos).

vulnerabilidad *f* vulnerability.

vulnerable *adj* vulnerable.

vulneración *f* violation; *vulneración de un tratado* violation of a treaty || wounding, injuring (herida).

vulnerar *vt* to injure, to wound (herir) || to harm, to injure (perjudicar) || to violate (tratado, ley, contrato).

vulnerario, ria *adj/sm* MED vulnerary.
◆ *f* BOT lady's finger (planta).

vulpeja *f* vixen, she-fox (zorra).

vulpino, na *adj* vulpine.
◆ *m* foxtail (planta).

vulva *f* ANAT vulva.

vulvar *adj* vulvar, vulval.

vulvitis *f inv* MED vulvitis.

W

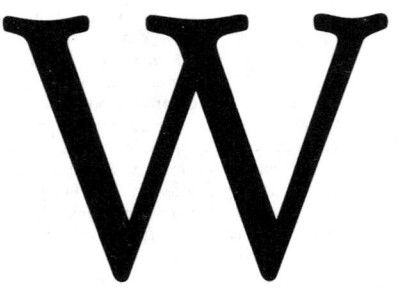

w *f* w (uve doble).
— OBSERV The letter *w* is not proper to the Spanish language and it is used only in words of foreing origin.

wagneriano, na *adj/s* Wagnerian.

wahabita *adj/s* Wahhabi, Wahabi.

walhalla *m* Walhalla.

walkiria *f* Walkyrie (divinidad escandinava).

walk-over *m* walkover (abandono).

wapití *m* ZOOL wapiti (ciervo).

warrant *m* COM warrant (recibo de depósito).

Washington *n pr* GEOGR Washington DC (capital).

water *m* FAM toilet, lavatory (retrete).

waterballast *m* water ballast (tanque de agua).

watercloset *m* water closet (retrete).

watergang *m* water gang (canal en Holanda).

water-polo *m* water polo (polo acuático).

watt *m* ELECTR watt (vatio).

weber; weberio *m* ELECTR weber (unidad).

welter *m* welterweight (peso semimedio en boxeo).

western *m* western (película del Oeste).

Westfalia *npr f* GEOGR Westphalia.

whisky *m* whisky (bebida).

wigwam *m* wigwam (choza de indios).

winchester *m* winchester (fusil de repetición).

wintergreen *m* BOT wintergreen.

wolframio *m* wolfram (metal).

X

x *f* x (equis) ‖ MAT x ‖ — *el señor X* Mr. X ‖ *rayos X* X rays.

xantato *m* QUÍM xanthate.

xanteno *m* QUÍM xanthene.

xantina *f* QUÍM xanthin, xanthine.

xantofila *f* xanthophyll.

xantoma *m* MED xanthoma.

xenofilia *f* xenophilia.

xenófilo, la *adj* xenophilous.
◆ *m/f* xenophile.

xenofobia *f* xenophobia.

xenófobo, ba *adj* xenophobic.
◆ *m/f* xenophobe.

xenogénesis *f* xenogenesis.

xenón *m* QUÍM xenon (gas).

xerocopia *f* Xerox copy.

xerófilo, la *adj* BOT xerophilous.

xerografía *f* xerography.

xerosis *f inv* MED xerosis.

xi *f* xi (letra griega).

xifoideo, a *adj* ANAT xiphoid, xiphoidal.

xifoides *adj* ANAT xiphoid, xiphoidal.
◆ *m* xiphoid.

xifosuro *adj/sm* ZOOL xiphosuran.
◆ *pl* xiphosura.

xileno *m* QUÍM xylene (hidrocarburo).

xilófago, ga *adj* ZOOL xylophagous.
◆ *m pl* xylophaga.

xilofonista *m/f* MÚS xylophonist.

xilófono *m* MÚS xylophone (instrumento).

xilografía *f* xylography, wood engraving (arte) ‖ xylograph (impresión).

xilográfico, ca *adj* xylographic, xylographical.

xilógrafo, fa *m/f* xylographer.

Y

y *f* y (i griega).

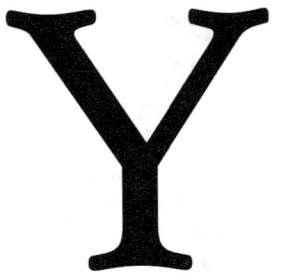

— OBSERV *Y* is a semiconsonant. When it stands on its own, i.e. when it is a conjunction, it is pronounced as a Spanish *i*. At the end of a syllable it diphtongizes the preceding vowel: *rey* [rɛj]. Between two vowels it has the same sound as the English *y*: *raya* [raja]. Moreover, in certain regions of Spain and several Latin American countries, particularly Argentina, it resembles more a weak English *j* as in beige [beiʒ].

y *conj* and; *padre y madre* father and mother ‖ after (repetición); *cartas y cartas* letter after letter ‖ and; *¡y no me lo habías dicho!* and you didn't even tell me! ‖ — *y eso que* although; *no está cansado, y eso que ha trabajado mucho* he's not tired although he has worked a lot ‖ *¿y qué?* so what?

ya *adv*

> **1.** TIEMPO **2.** AFIRMACIÓN **3.** LOCUCIONES Y EMPLEOS DIVERSOS

1. TIEMPO already (*con una acción en el pasado*); *llegó ya* he has already arrived; *ya he acabado* I've already finished; *ya lo sabía* I already knew ‖ already, ever (antes); *¿ya has estado en Francia?* have you already been to France? ‖ now (ahora); *ya es rico* he is rich now; *ya los días van siendo más largos* the days are getting longer now ‖ now, nowadays (actualmente, hoy en día) ‖ later (más adelante); *ya hablaremos de eso* we'll speak about that later ‖ right away, immediately (en seguida) ‖ soon (pronto); *ya lo encontrarás, no te preocupes* you'll soon find it, don't worry ‖ any more (*negativo*); *ya no me gustan esas cosas* I don't like that sort of thing any more.

2. AFIRMACIÓN well (insistencia); *ya lo creo* I well believe it ‖ now (por fin); *ya me acuerdo* now I remember ‖ right, all right (bien, de acuerdo); *¿mañana vendrás a mi casa? —ya* come over to my house tomorrow. —all right.

3. LOCUCIONES Y EMPLEOS DIVERSOS *ahora ya no hace nada* now he doesn't do anything ‖ *eso ya no se hace* that is not done any more ‖ *no ya* not only ‖ *pues ya* of course, naturally ‖ *si ya* if ‖ *¡ya!* at last! (por fin), that's it (eso es), quite, of course, yes (sí), right! (entendido) ‖ *¡ya caigo!* now I remember! (ya recuerdo), now I see (ya comprendo) ‖ *¡ya está!* that's it! ‖ *ya es hora* it is (high) time ‖ *ya mismo* right away ‖ *ya no me queda más que una libra* (now) I only have one pound left ‖ *ya que* since, as (puesto que), now that (ahora que) ‖ *ya se ve* that's obvious, that's easy to see ‖ *ya verás, ya* you just wait and see ‖ *ya veremos* we shall see, we shall see about it ‖ *ya ves* you see, you know ‖ *¡ya, ya!* yes, yes! ‖ *ya... ya* sometimes... sometimes (a veces) ‖ *ya... ya, ya sea... ya sea* whether... or; *ya en el campo, ya en casa* whether in the country or at home.

— OBSERV Very often *ya* serves only to emphasize the action expressed in the verb and is not translated in English: *ya voy* I'm coming.

yaacabó *m* insectivorous bird (ave).

yaba *f* AMER cabbage tree (árbol).

yac *m* ZOOL yak (búfalo).

yacamar *m* AMER jacamar.

yacaré *m* AMER alligator, caiman, cayman.

yacente *adj* lying ‖ — *estatua yacente* recumbent statue ‖ *herencia yacente* unclaimed estate, estate in abeyance.
◆ *m* MIN floor of a vein (cara inferior de un criadero).

yacer* *vi* to be lying, to be lying down (estar tendido) ‖ to lie (los muertos) ‖ to be located, to be (estar en algún lugar) ‖ to graze at night (los caballos) ‖ — *aquí yace* here lies (un muerto) ‖ *yacer con* to lie with.

yaciente *adj* lying.

yacija *f* bed, couch (lecho) ‖ sepulchre, tomb, grave (sepultura) ‖ *ser de mala yacija* to be a poor sleeper.

yacimiento *m* GEOL bed, deposit ‖ *yacimiento petrolífero* oil field.

yaco *m* AMER variety of otter (nutria).

yactura *f* damage, loss.

yacht *m* yacht (yate).

yachting *m* yachting (navegación a vela).

yagual *m* AMER head pad (rodete).

yaguar *m* AMER jaguar (animal).

yaguareté *m* AMER jaguar (jaguar).

yaguarú *m* AMER otter (nutria).

yaguarundi *m* AMER eyra.

yaguasa *f* AMER yaguaza, tree duck.

yaguré *m* AMER skunk (mamífero).

yak *m* yak (búfalo).

Yakarta *n pr* GEOGR Djakarta, Jakarta.

yámbico, ca *adj* iambic; *verso yámbico* iambic verse.

yambo *m* iamb (poesía) ‖ jambo (árbol).

yanacón; yanacona *m* AMER Indian tenant farmer (colono) | Indian servant (criado indio).

yanqui *adj/s* FAM Yankee, Yank.

yantar *m* (ant) food.

yantar *vt* (ant) to eat.

Yaoundé *n pr* GEOGR Youndé.

yapa *f* AMER little extra, bonus (adehala) | mercury [added to silver ore to facilitate extraction] (azogue) | tip (propina) | thick end (del lazo).

yapú *m* AMER ZOOL variety of thrush (tordo).

yarará *f* AMER viper (víbora).

yaraví *m* melancholic Indian song.

yarda *f* yard (medida).

yare *m* poisonous juice extracted from yucca.

yaro *m* arum (planta).

yatagán *m* yataghan (sable).

yatay *m* AMER palm.

yate *m* yacht.

yaya *f* AMER lancewood (planta) ‖ AMER *dar yaya* to beat, to thrash (apalear).

yaz *m* jazz.

ye *f* (p us) name of the letter y.

yedra *f* ivy (planta).

yegua *f* mare ‖ AMER cigar butt (colilla del puro).

yeguada *f* herd of horses ‖ AMER foolish act *o* remark (disparate).

yeguar *adj* (of) mares.
◆ *m* herd of mares.

yegüería *f* herd of horses.

yegüero *m* keeper of a herd of mares.

yeísmo *m* phenomenon which consists in pronouncing the Spanish letter *ll* like the Spanish *y*.

— OBSERV This phenomenon is widespread in Spain (Madrid an other towns, Andalusia, the Balearic and Canary Islands) and in much of Latin America. Though increasingly common, this pronunciation is considered colloquial.

yelmo *m* helmet ‖ *el yelmo de Mambrino* Mambrino's helmet (en El Quijote).

yema *f* BOT & ZOOL bud (renuevo) ‖ yolk (del huevo) ‖ tip (del dedo) ‖ sweet made of sugar and egg yolk ‖ FIG the cream, the best (lo mejor) | middle (medio) ‖ — *vinagre de yema* vinegar made with the wine taken from the centre of the barrel ‖ *yema del dedo* fingertip ‖ *yema mejida* eggnog.

Yemen *npr m* GEOGR Yemen.

yemení; yemenita *adj/s* Yemenite.

yen *m* yen (unidad monetaria del Japón).

yente *m* *los yentes y vinientes* people coming and going; passersby (en la calle).

yerba *f* grass (hierba) ‖ herb (medicinal, etc.) ‖ AMER maté (yerba mate).

yerbajo *m* weed.

yerbal *m* AMER maté field ‖ pasture (herbazal).

yerbatero, ra *adj* AMER (of) maté; *industria yerbatera* maté industry.
◆ *m/f* AMER maté plantation worker *o* owner.
◆ *m* AMER quack doctor (curandero).

yerbear *vi* AMER to drink maté.

yermo, ma *adj* uninhabited (despoblado) ‖ uncultivated (sin cultivar) ‖ barren (sin vegetación).
◆ *m* wilderness, desert (sitio deshabitado) ‖ barren land, waste land (sitio inculto).

yerno *m* son-in-law (hijo político).

yero *m* lentil vetch (planta).

yerra *f* AMER branding.

yerro *m* error, mistake; *enmendar* or *deshacer un yerro* to correct an error.
◆ *pl* errors (extravíos).

yerto, ta *adj* rigid (tieso) ‖ stiff (un cadáver) ‖ — FIG *quedarse yerto* to be petrified ‖ *yerto de frío* frozen stiff.

yervo *m* lentil vetch (yero).

yesal; yesar *m* gypsum pit (cantera).

yesca *f* tinder [US amadou, punk] ‖ FIG stimulus, fuel (de pasión o afecto) | dynamite (situación explosiva) ‖ — FIG & FAM *arrimar yesca* to give a hiding *o* a licking ‖ *echar una yesca* to strike a light.
◆ *pl* tinderbox *sing*, tinder *sing*.

yesera *f* gypsum pit (yesal).

yesería *f* gypsum kiln (fábrica de yeso).

yesero, ra *adj* plaster; *industria yesera* plaster industry.
◆ *m* plasterer.

yeso *m* GEOL gypsum ‖ chalk (polvo) ‖ plaster (empleado en construcción y arte) ‖ plaster cast (escultura) ‖ — *dar de yeso* to plaster (una pared) ‖ *yeso blanco* superfine white plaster ‖ *yeso mate* or *de París* plaster of Paris ‖ *yeso negro* rough plaster.

yesón *m* chunk of plaster.

yesoso, sa *adj* gypseous ‖ chalky; *terreno yesoso* chalky soil ‖ *alabastro yesoso* translucent gypsum.

yesquero *adj* *hongo yesquero* tinder fungus.
◆ *m* tinder vendor *o* maker ‖ pouch (bolsa).

yeti *m* yeti.

ye-yé *adj* POP [fashion and music of the sixties].

yeyuno *m* ANAT jejunum.

yezgo *m* danewort, dwarf elder (planta).

ylang-ylang *m* ylang-ylang (planta).

yo *pron pers de la 1.ª pers del sing* I; *yo soy* I am ‖ — *soy yo* it is I, it's me (*fam*) ‖ *soy yo el que habla* I am the one who is speaking ‖ *yo mismo* I myself ‖ *yo que usted, yo en su lugar, si yo fuera usted* if I were you, if I were in your place.
◆ *m* FIL *el yo* the I, the ego.

yod *f* yod (i griega).

yodado, da *adj* iodized.

yodar *vt* to iodize.

yodato *m* QUÍM iodate.

yodhídrico *adj m* QUÍM hydriodic (ácido).

yódico, ca *adj* QUÍM iodic.

yodismo *m* MED iodism (intoxicación por el yodo).

yodo *m* QUÍM iodine; *tintura de yodo* tincture of iodine.

yodoformo *m* MED iodoform.

yoduración *f* QUÍM iodization.

yodurado, da *adj* QUÍM iodized.

yoduro *m* QUÍM iodide.

yoga *m* yoga.

yogui; yogi; yoghi *m* yogi.

yogur *m* yogurt, yoghurt, yoghourt.

yohimbina *f* QUÍM yohimbine.

yola *f* MAR yawl.

yonqui *m/f* FAM junkie, junky.

yoquey *m* DEP jockey.

yoyo *m* yo-yo (juguete).

yperita *f* yperite (gas).

ypsilón *f* upsilon (letra griega).

yterbio *m* ytterbium (metal).

yuambú *m* AMER tinamou.

yubarta *f* finback (cetáceo).

yuca *f* BOT yucca (planta liliácea) ‖ cassava, manioc (mandioca).

yucal *m* yucca grove *o* plantation ‖ cassava *o* manioc field.

Yucatán *npr m* GEOGR Yucatán.

yucateco, ca *adj* Yucatecan.
◆ *m/f* Yucatec.
◆ *m* Yucatec (lengua).

yugada *f* yoke of land (espacio de tierra labrada en un día) ‖ land measurement of about 32 hectares ‖ yoke of oxen (yunta de bueyes).

yugo *m* yoke (de bueyes, de campana) ‖ FIG yoke; *sacudir el yugo* to throw off the yoke ‖ MAR transom ‖ FIG *yugo de matrimonio* marriage bond, yoke of marriage.

Yugoslavia *npr f* GEOGR Yugoslavia.

yugoslavo, va *adj/s* Yugoslavian, Yugoslav.

yuguero *m* ploughman [US plowman].

yugular *adj/sf* ANAT jugular; *vena yugular* jugular vein.

yugular *vt* FIG to nip in the bud.

yumbo, ba *m/f* Indian of Ecuador.

yungas *f pl* AMER name given to the warm valleys of Peru, Bolivia and Ecuador.

yungla *f* jungle.

yunque *m* anvil ‖ FIG stoic, long-suffering person (en las adversidades) | tireless worker, plodder (en el trabajo) ‖ ANAT incus, anvil (del oído).

yunta *f* yoke, team [of oxen] ‖ yoke of land (tierra labrada).

yuntería *f* beasts *pl* of burden ‖ stable (establo).

yuntero *m* ploughman [US plowman].

yunto, ta *adj* close (junto).

¡yupi! *interj* FAM yippee!

yuppie *m/f* yuppie.

yurta *f* tent (choza).

yuruma *f* AMER heart of a palm.

yurumí *m* AMER anteater (oso hormiguero).

yusera *f* nether millstone.

yusión *f* JUR jussive, order.

yuso *adv* (ant) below (abajo).

yuta *f* AMER slug (babosa) ‖ AMER FAM *hacer la yuta* to play truant [US to play hooky].

yute *m* jute (material textil).

yuxtalineal *adj* juxtalinear.

yuxtaponer* *vt* to juxtapose.

yuxtaposición *f* juxtaposition.

yuxtapuesto, ta *adj* juxtaposed.

yuyal *m* AMER weed-covered ground.

yuyo *m* AMER weed (yerbajo).

yuyú *m* MAR dinghy (chinchorro).

yuyuba *f* BOT jujube (azufaifa).

Z

z *f* z (zeda, zeta); *una z mayúscula* a capital z.
— OBSERV The *z* is an interdental fricative which is pronounced like the English *th* (as in *thank*) by placing the tip of the tongue between the teeth.

¡za! *interj* shoo! (a un perro).

zabarcera *f* greengrocer, woman who sells fruit and other food.

zaborda *f*; **zabordamiento** *m* MAR running aground.

zabordar *vi* MAR to run aground.

zabordo *m* MAR running aground (zaborda).

zabro *m* zabrus, caraboid beetle (insecto).

zabullir *vt* ⟶ **zambullir.**

zaca *f* leather bucket for bailing (en minas).

zacatal *m* AMER pasture.

zacate *m* AMER fodder, hay.

zacatón *m* AMER tall pasture grass.

zadorija *f* BOT scarlet pimpernel.

zafacón *m* AMER dustbin [*US* trashcan] (cubo de basura).

zafada *f* MAR unbending.

zafado, da *adj* AMER cheeky, brazen (descarado) | sharp, alert (vivo) | dislocated (huesos).

zafadura *f* AMER dislocation (de un hueso).

zafaduría *f* AMER cheek (descaro).

zafar *vt* to undo, to untie, to unfasten (soltar); *zafar un nudo* to undo a knot || MAR to unbend (cabos, velas, etc.) || (p us) to adorn (adornar).
◆ *vi* AMER to leave, to go away.
◆ *vpr* to escape, to get away (escaparse) || FIG to get out, to evade; *zafarse de un compromiso* to get out of a commitment, to evade a commitment | to get away, to shake off; *zafarse de una persona* to get away from s.o. | to get out; *zafarse de una situación delicada* to get out of a delicate situation || to come off (una correa) || AMER to be dislocated (un hueso) || FAM *zafarse con* to run off with.

zafarrancho *m* MAR clearing for action || FIG & FAM mess (estropicio) | row, rumpus (riña) || — FIG & FAM *armar un zafarrancho* to kick up a rumpus, to cause uproar || *zafarrancho de combate* call to action stations.

zafiedad *f* coarseness, uncouthness.

zafio, fia *adj* coarse, uncouth.

zafirino, na *adj* sapphirine.

zafiro *m* sapphire.

zafo, fa *adj* MAR free, clear | unscathed, unharmed, safe and sound (ileso).

zafra *f* sugar cane harvest (cosecha de caña) || sugar cane crop (cantidad cosechada) || sugar making (fabricación) || sugar cane harvest season (temporada) || harvest (cosecha, recolección) || oil jar, oil can (recipiente) || MIN rubbish (escombros).

zafre *m* MIN zaffer, zaffre (óxido de cobalto).

zafrero *m* rubbish carrier (en las minas).

zaga *f* rear (parte posterior) || load carried in the rear of a vehicle (carga) || DEP defence [*US* backline] (fútbol) || — *a la zaga, en zaga* behind, in *o* at the rear || FIG *no irle a la zaga a nadie* to be second to none | *no irle a uno a la zaga* or *en zaga* to be every bit as good as s.o. | *no quedarse* or *no ir a la zaga* not to be left behind, not to be outdone.
◆ *m* last player (en el juego).

zagal *m* boy, youth, young man (adolescente) || shepherd boy (pastor mozo).

zagala *f* girl, lass || shepherdess (pastora).

zagalejo *m* petticoat (refajo) || shepherd boy (pastor).

zagalón *m* big boy, strapping lad.

zagalona *f* big girl.

zagual *m* paddle (remo pequeño).

zaguán *m* hall.

zaguanete *m* hall (zaguán) || room for the royal guard (aposento de la guardia) || royal guard (guardia).

zaguero, ra *adj* rear, back (trasero) || bottom (último) || lagging behind (que está atrasado) || overloaded in the rear (cargado en la parte trasera).
◆ *m* back (en deportes).

zagüí *m* AMER squirrel monkey (mono).

zahareño, ña *adj* unsociable (arisco) || wild (intratable) || haggard (ave de rapiña).

zahén *adj* of fine gold (moneda).

zahena *f* doubloon (moneda).

zaherimiento *m* upbraiding, reprimand (reprimenda) || reproach (censura) || mockery (mofa) || mortification (mortificación) || sarcastic criticism (crítica).

zaherir* *vt* to upbraid, to reprimand (reprender) || to reproach (censurar) || to mock (escarnecer) || to mortify, to hurt one's feelings (mortificar) || to criticize sarcastically.

zahína *f* sorghum (planta).

zahinar *m* sorghum field.

zahonado, da *adj* whose front legs differ in colour from the rest of the body (animal).

zahondar *vt* to deepen (ahondar).
◆ *vi* to sink (hundirse).

zahones *m pl* chaps.

zahorí *m* seer, clairvoyant (adivino) || water diviner (de manantiales) || FIG mind reader (que sabe adivinar los pensamientos) | very perceptive person (persona perspicaz).

zahorra MAR ballast (lastre).

zahúrda *f* pigsty [*US* pigpen] (pocilga) || FIG hovel (tugurio) | pigsty (casa sucia).

zaida *f* ZOOL demoiselle (ave).

zaino, na *adj* treacherous, false, deceitful (persona) || vicious (animal) || pure black (negro); *toro zaino* pure black bull || chestnut (caballo) || *mirar a lo zaino* to look sideways.

Zaire *npr m* GEOGR Zaire.

zairense *adj/s* Zairian.

zalagarda *f* ambush, ambuscade (emboscada) || skirmish (escaramuza) || trap, snare (trampa) || FIG & FAM rumpus, to-do (alboroto).

zalama *f*; **zalamelé** *m*; **zalamería** *f* cajolery, coaxing by flattery (engatusamiento) || flattery, adulation (adulación).

zalamero, ra *adj* flattering, fawning (adulador) || cajoling (engatusador).
◆ *m/f* flatterer (adulador) || cajoler (engatusador).

zalea *f* sheepskin.

zalear *vt* to shake (sacudir).

zalema *f* FAM salaam (saludo oriental) | cajolery, coaxing by flattery (engatusamiento) | flattery (adulación).
◆ *pl* bowing and scraping (coba).

zaleo *m* sheepskin (piel) || shaking (acción de zalear).

zalmedina *m* ancient magistrate of Aragon.

zamacuco *m* FAM dolt (tonto) | sly one (hombre solapado) || FIG & FAM drunkenness [*US* drunk] (borrachera).

zamacueca *f* popular Chilian and Peruvian dance.

zamarra *f* sheepskin jacket (vestidura hecha de piel) || sheepskin (piel de carnero).

zamarrear *vt* to shake (sacudir) || FIG & FAM to push (s.o.) about, to knock (s.o.) about (zarandear) | to corner (en una discusión).

zamarreo *m* shaking, shake (sacudimiento) || FIG & FAM rough treatment (trato malo).

zamarreón *m* FAM shaking, shake.

zamarrico *m* sheepskin bag.

zamarrilla *f* BOT mountain germander.

zamarro *m* sheepskin jacket (zamarra) || sheepskin (piel de carnero) || FIG & FAM peasant [*US* hick] (hombre tosco) | bore (hombre pesado) | cunning fellow (hombre astuto).
◆ *pl* AMER leather chaps.

zamarrón *m* thick sheepskin jacket (zamarra) || leather apron (mandil).

zamba *f* popular South American dance || samba (samba).

zambaigo, ga *adj/s* AMER descendant of a Chinese and an Indian | Zambo (descendiente de negro e india o viceversa).

zambarco *m* broad breast strap (parte de los arreos) || strap with a buckle (cincha con hebilla).

zambardo *m* AMER chance (casualidad).

Zambeze *npr m* GEOGR Zambezi.

Zambia *npr f* GEOGR Zambia.

zambo, ba *adj* knock-kneed (de piernas torcidas).
◆ *m/f* AMER zambo (hijo de negro e india o viceversa).
◆ *m* ZOOL spider monkey (mono).

zambomba *f* kind of drum.
◆ *interj* Gosh!
— OBSERV The *zambomba* is a cylinder covered at one end by a tightly stretched skin with a stick fastened to the centre. A deep

and monotonous sound is produced by moving the stick up and down. This instrument is used generally during the Christmas season.

zambombazo *m* FAM punch, thump, hard blow (golpe) | boom, bang (ruido) | explosion (explosión).

zambombo *m* FAM boor, brute.

zamborondón, ona; zamborrotudo, da *adj* FAM clumsy (tosco) | slapdash (chapucero).
◆ *m/f* boorish and clumsy person || bungler (chapucero).

zambra *f* Moorish festival (fiesta) || FAM uproar, rumpus (jaleo) || *zambra gitana* Andalusian gipsy dance.

zambullida *f* dive, plunge || lunge (treta de la esgrima) || — *darle a uno una zambullida* to give s.o. a ducking || *darse una zambullida* to dive into the water (tirarse al agua), to go for a swim, to take a dip (bañarse).

zambullir*; zabullir *vt* to plunge, to dip (un objeto) || to duck (persona).
◆ *vpr* to go for a swim, to go for a dip (bañarse) || to dive, to plunge, to take a dive *o* a plunge (tirarse al agua de cabeza) || FIG to plunge; *zambullirse en el trabajo* to plunge into one's work | to hide (esconderse).

zambullo *m* AMER big dustbin [*US* garbage can].

zambumbia *f* AMER kind of drum.

Zamora *n pr* GEOGR Zamora || FIG *no se ganó Zamora en una hora* Rome wasn't built in a day.

zamorano, na *adj* [of *o* from] Zamora.
◆ *m/f* native *o* inhabitant of Zamora.

zampa *f* ARQ pile.

zampabodigos; zampabollos *m/f inv* FAM glutton, greedy pig.

zampalimosnas *m/f inv* FIG & FAM beggar.

zampar *vt* to hide (esconder) || to gobble down, to wolf down (la comida) || to hurl, to throw, to dash (arrojar); *zampó la jarra de vino en el suelo* he threw the wine pitcher to the floor || to dip; *zampó el bizcocho en el café* he dipped the cake into the coffee || to deal, to give (una bofetada).
◆ *vpr* to gobble, to wolf; *se zamparon el almuerzo en un santiamén* they gobbled down their lunch in a trice || to dash, to dart (*en* into) (entrar rápidamente) || to fall (dejarse caer).

zampatortas *m/f inv* FAM glutton, greedy pig (persona glotona) || FIG & FAM thickhead (torpe).

zampeado *m* piling, piles *pl*.

zampear *vt* to drive piles into (un terreno).

zampón, ona *adj* greedy (glotón).
◆ *m/f* glutton, greedy pig (*fam*).

zampoña *f* panpipe (caramillo) || FIG & FAM nonsense (necedad).

zanahoria *f* carrot (planta).

zanca *f* leg (pierna de las aves) || FIG & FAM shank, leg (pierna) || ARQ stringpiece of a staircase (de una escalera) | leg of a scaffold (de un andamio) || large pin (alfiler).

zancada *f* stride (paso largo); *dar grandes zancadas* to take long strides || — FIG & FAM *en dos zancadas* in a jiffy || *irse a zancadas* to stride off, to go off with long strides || FIG *seguir las zancadas de* to follow in the footsteps of.

zancadilla *f* trip || FIG trap, trick (trampa) || *echar la zancadilla* or *poner la zancadilla a uno* to trip s.o. up, to make s.o. trip (hacerle caer), to put the skids under s.o., to trip s.o. up.

zancadillear *vt* to trip up, to make trip || FIG to set a trap for (armar una trampa), to put the skids under (s.o.), to trip (s.o.) up (perjudicar).

zancado *adj* which has spawned (salmón).

zancajear *vi* to rush about.

zancajera *f* coach step (del estribo del coche).

zancajo *m* heel bone (hueso) || heel (del pie, del zapato) || FAM lean bone (zancarrón) | runt (persona fea).

zancajoso, sa *adj* bowlegged.

zancarrón *m* FAM lean bone (hueso) || FIG & FAM skinny old man, old bag of bones (hombre viejo y flaco) | bad teacher (mal profesor).

zanco *m* stilt (para andar).

zancón, ona *adj* FAM lanky, long-legged || AMER too short (vestido).

zancudo, da *adj* long-legged, lanky || ZOOL wading || *aves zancudas* waders.
◆ *m* AMER mosquito (mosquito).
◆ *f pl* ZOOL waders.

zanfonía *f* hurdy-gurdy (instrumento).

zángara *f* FAM lazy woman, lazybones (holgazana).

zanganada *f* FAM stupid remark (majadería).

zangandongo, ga; zangandullo, lla; zangandungo, ga *m/f* FAM lazybones, idler, loafer.

zanganear *vi* FAM to idle, to loaf *o* to laze around (holgazanear) || | to make stupid remarks (decir majaderías).

zanganería *f* FAM idleness, laziness.

zángano *m* drone (insecto) || FIG & FAM lazybones, idler, loafer (holgazán) | fool (tonto).

zangarilleja *f* FAM sloven, slut.

zangarrear *vi* FAM to strum a guitar.

zangarriana *f* VET staggers *pl* (modorra) || FAM slight recurrent ailment (achaque) || FIG & FAM blues *pl*, sadness (tristeza).

zangarullón *m* FAM big lazybones, lanky loafer.

zangolotear *vt* to jiggle, to fiddle with, to shake.
◆ *vi* FAM to fidget (una persona).
◆ *vpr* FAM to rattle (una puerta, etc.).

zangoloteo *m* jiggling, shaking || FIG & FAM fidgeting, stirring (de una persona) | rattling, rattle (de una puerta, etc.).

zangolotino, na *adj* FAM who does not act his age, childish || *niño zangolotino, niña zangolotina* big baby.

zangón *m* FAM lanky lazybones, lanky loafer.

zangotear *vi* to fidget.

zanguanga *f* FAM malingering, feigning illness || FAM *hacer la zanguanga* to feign illness, to malinger.

zanguango, ga *adj* FAM idle, slack (gandul).
◆ *m/f* FAM shirker, loafer, slacker.

zanja *f* ditch, channel, trench; *zanja de desagüe* drainage channel || trench (para los cimientos) || AMER ravine, gully (arroyada) || *abrir las zanjas* to lay the foundations.

zanjar *vt* to dig a ditch *o* a trench in (abrir una zanja) || FIG to settle, to clear up; *zanjó el asunto* he settled the matter || to surmount, to overcome, to obviate (obstáculos); *zanjar una dificultad* to obviate a difficulty.

zanjear *vt* AMER to dig a ditch in.

zanjón *m* large ditch *o* trench.

zanquear *vi* to waddle (andar torciendo las piernas) || to stride along (dar zancadas) || to rush about (de un lado para otro).

zanquilargo, ga *adj* FAM long-legged, lanky.
◆ *m/f* FAM lanky person, long-legged person, spindleshanks.

zanquituerto, ta *adj* FAM knock-kneed.

zanquivano, na *adj* FAM spindle-legged, spindle-shanked.

Zanzíbar *npr m* GEOGR Zanzibar.

zapa *f* spade (pala de zapador) || sapping, trenching, digging (acción de zapar) || shagreen, sharkskin (lija) || *piel de zapa* shagreen, sharkskin.

zapador *m* MIL sapper.

zapallo *m* AMER calabash.

zapapico *m* mattock, pickaxe.

zapar *vt* MIL to sap.

zaparrastrar *vi* FAM to let one's gown trail behind.

zaparrastroso, sa *adj/s* FAM ⟶ **zarrapastrón.**

zapata *f* TECN track, shoe (de oruga) | washer (arandela) || ARQ lintel || MAR false keel (falsa quilla) | shoe (del ancla) || AMER socle (zócalo) || *zapata de freno* brake shoe, brake lining.

zapatazo *m* blow [with a shoe] (golpe) || MAR flapping (de una vela).
◆ *pl* stamping *sing o* pounding *sing* of feet (ruido) || — *dar zapatazos* to stamp one's feet || FIG *mandar a zapatazos* to rule with an iron hand | *tratar a zapatazos* to kick around, to treat like a dog.

zapateado *m* «zapateado» [Spanish heel-tapping dance].

zapatear *vt* to tap with one's feet || FIG to tread on (pisotear) || to touch with the button of the foil (en esgrima).
◆ *vi* to paw the ground (el caballo) || to thump (el conejo) || to flap (las velas) || to stamp *o* to tap one's feet (en el baile) || to dance the «zapateado».
◆ *vpr* FIG & FAM to get rid of (s.o.) (quitarse de encima) | to polish off (liquidar rápidamente) || FAM *saber zapateárselas* to know how to look after o.s., to be able to take care of o.s.

zapateo *m* «zapateo», stamping *o* tapping with the feet (en el baile) || tap dance (con música de jazz) || pawing (del caballo).

zapatera *f* shoemaker || shoemaker's *o* cobbler's wife (mujer del zapatero).

zapatería *f* shoe shop (taller) || shoe shop [*US* shoe store] (tienda) || shoemaking (oficio) || *zapatería de viejo* cobbler's, shoe shop, shoe repair shop, shoemender's.

zapatero, ra *adj* tough; *bistec zapatero* tough steak || hard, underdone; *patatas zapateras* hard potatoes.
◆ *m/f* shoe seller *o* dealer (vendedor).
◆ *m* shoemaker (el que hace zapatos) || shoemender, cobbler (el que los remienda) || — *dejar zapatero* to leave s.o. with no tricks (naipes) || *quedarse zapatero* to lose all the tricks (naipes) || *zapatero a la medida* bootmaker, shoemaker || FIG *¡zapatero a tus zapatos!* mind your own business!, the cobbler should stick at his last || *zapatero de viejo* or *remendón* cobbler, shoemender.

zapateta *f* jump accompanied by a slap on the shoe.

zapatiesta *f* FAM rumpus; *armar una zapatiesta* to kick up a rumpus.

zapatilla *f* slipper (para estar en casa) || shoe; *zapatilla de baile* dancing shoe || slipper (de torero) || tip (billar) || button (del florete) || hoof (pezuña) || TECN washer (arandela).

zapatillero, ra *m/f* slipper dealer (vendedor) || slipper manufacturer (fabricante).

zapato *m* shoe; *un par de zapatos* a pair of shoes; *zapatos de tacón* high-heeled shoes; *za-*

patos de color brown shoes || — FIG *encontrar la horma de su zapato* to find just what the doctor ordered (lo deseado), to find Mr *o* Miss Right, to meet one's perfect match (a un novio o una novia conveniente), to meet one's match (a alguien con quien medirse) | *saber dónde le aprieta el zapato* to know where the shoe pinches, to know one's own weaknesses.

zapatón *m* FAM heavy shoe, clodhopper (zapato grande).

zape *m* FAM gay, queer (afeminado).
◆ *interj* shoo!, scat! (para ahuyentar a los gatos) || *¡zape de aquí!* get out of here!

zapear *vt* to shoo away (gatos) || to scare off *o* away (personas).

zapotal *m* grove of sapodilla trees.

zapote *m* sapodilla (árbol) || sapodilla plum (fruto).

zapoteco, ca *adj* Zapotecan.
◆ *m/f* Zapotec.

zapotillo *m* BOT sapodilla.

zaque *m* small wineskin *o* goatskin || FIG & FAM old soak, drunk (borracho).

zaquizamí *m* attic, garret (desván) || poky hole, cubbyhole (cuchitril).
— OBSERV pl *zaquizamíes*.

zar *m* czar, tzar, tsar.

zarabanda *f* MÚS saraband, sarabande || FAM whirl, turmoil, confused rush (jaleo).

zarabandista *m/f* person who dances, plays or composes sarabands.

zaragata *f* FAM rumpus, row, squabble (riña) | hubbub (confusión, jaleo, ruido).

zaragate *m* AMER rogue.

zaragatero, ra *adj* quarrelsome, rowdy, troublemaking.
◆ *m/f* troublemaker, rowdy person (pendenciero).

zaragatona *f* BOT ribgrass, fleawort.

zaragocí *m* variety of yellow plum.

Zaragoza *n pr* GEOGR Saragossa [Spain].

zaragozano, na *adj/s* Saragossan.
◆ *m* calendar which gives meteorological forecasts.

zaragüelles *m* wide-legged overalls (calzones) || wide-legged breeches (pantalones).

zarambeque *m* Negro dance.

zaranda *f* sieve, screen (criba) || small sieve, strainer (colador) || AMER spinning top (trompo).

zarandajas *f pl* FAM trivialities, trifles.

zarandear *vt* to sieve, to sift (cribar); *zarandear el trigo* to sieve the wheat || to strain (colar) || to shake (sacudir) || to knock about, to jostle; *ser zarandeado por la multitud* to be knocked about by the crowd || to keep on the go (mandar de un sitio para otro).
◆ *vpr* to sway the hips (contonearse).

zarandeo *m* sifting, sieving (con la criba) || straining (con el colador) || shaking (meneo) || AMER swaying of the hips.

zarandillo *m* small sieve *o* screen (zaranda) || FIG & FAM fidget || FIG & FAM *llevar a uno como un zarandillo* to keep s.o. on the go.

zarape *m* sarape, serape (sarape) || FAM gay, queer (afeminado).

zarapito *m* curlew (ave).

zaraza *f* chintz (tela de algodón).

zarazo, za *adj* AMER half-ripe (fruto).

zarcear *vt* to clean out (las cañerías).
◆ *vi* to flush out game from the undergrowth (el perro) || FIG to rush about (ajetrearse).

zarceño, ña *adj* brambly.

zarcero *adj* *perro zarcero* terrier.
◆ *m* terrier (perro).

zarceta *f* garganey (ave).

zarcillo *m* earring (pendiente) || BOT tendril || hoe (escardillo).

zarco, ca *adj* light blue; *ojos zarcos* light blue eyes.

zarevitz *m* czarevitch, tsarevitch.

zariano, na *adj* czaristic, tsaristic.

zarigüeya *f* ZOOL opossum.

zarina *f* czarina, tsarina.

zarismo *m* czarism, tsarism.

zarista *adj* czaristic, tsaristic.
◆ *m/f* czarist, tsarist.

zarpa *f* claw, paw (de un animal) || MAR weighing anchor || FIG *echar la zarpa a algo* to claw at sth. (un animal), to grab sth. (una persona), to get hold of sth. (apoderarse).

zarpanel *adj* ARQ *arco zarpanel* basket-handle arch.

zarpar *vi* MAR to weigh anchor || *zarpar del puerto* to sail out of port.

zarpazo *m* lash of a claw *o* paw || *dar un zarpazo* to lash out with the claws, to claw.

zarpear *vt* AMER to bespatter, to dirty [with mud].

zarposo, sa *adj* bespattered.

zarracatería *f* FAM insincere flattery.

zarracatín *m* FAM bargainer, haggler.

zarraspastrón, ona; zarrapastroso, sa; zaparrastroso, sa *adj* FAM slovenly, shabby, untidy.
◆ *m/f* FAM sloven, ragamuffin, tramp.

zarria *f* leather thong *o* strap (tira de cuero).

zarza *f* BOT blackberry bush, bramble || *zarza ardiente* burning bush (en la Biblia).

zarzagán *m* cold wind (cierzo).

zarzal *m* blackberry *o* bramble patch, clump of brambles || bush, thicket (matorral).

zarzaleño, ña *adj* [of *o* from the] bramble.

zarzamora *f* blackberry (fruto) || blackberry bush (zarza).

zarzaparrilla *f* BOT sarsaparilla.

zarzaparrillar *m* sarsaparilla field.

zarzaperruna *f* BOT dog rose (escaramujo).

zarzarrosa *f* BOT dog rose.

zarzo *m* wattle.

zarzoso, sa *adj* brambly, covered with blackberry *o* bramble bushes.

zarzuela *f* «zarzuela» (*véase* OBSERV) || CULIN fish dish prepared with spicy sauce.
— OBSERV The *zarzuela* is a Spanish operetta having a spoken dialogue and usually a comic theme.

zarzuelero, ra *adj* of *o* from the «zarzuela».
◆ *m* author of «zarzuelas».

zarzuelista *m* author *o* composer of «zarzuelas».

¡zas! *interj* bang!, whack!, crash!

zascandil *m* FAM scatterbrain (tarambana) | busybody, meddler (entrometido).

zascandilear *vi* FAM to snoop, to pry, to meddle (curiosear); *andar zascandileando* to be snooping around | to idle, to waste time (vagar).

zeda *f* zed [US zee] (letra).

zedilla *f* cedilla (letra antigua) || cedilla (signo ortográfico).

zéjel *m* «zejel» [a medieval Spanish poetic composition of Mozarabic origin].

Zelanda; Zelandia *npr f* GEOGR Zeeland || *Nueva Zelanda* New Zealand.

zelandés, esa *adj* Zeeland.
◆ *m/f* Zeelander.

zendo, da *adj* Zend, Zendic.
◆ *m* Zend (lengua).

zenit *m* zenith (cenit).

Zenón *npr m* Zeno.

zeolita *f* MIN zeolite.

zepelín *m* zeppelin (dirigible).

zeta *f* zed [US zee] (letra) || zeta (letra griega).

zeugma; zeuma *f* GRAM zeugma.

zigoma *m* ANAT zygoma (hueso).

zigomático, ca *adj* ANAT zygomatic.

zigoto *m* BIOL zygote.

zigzag *m* zigzag.
— OBSERV The plural of the Spanish word *zigzag* is *zigzags* or *zigzagues*.

zigzaguear *vi* to zigzag.

zigzagueo *m* zigzagging.

zimasa *f* QUÍM zymase.

Zimbabue *n pr* GEOGR Zimbabwe.

zinc *m* zinc (cinc).

zíngaro, ra *adj/s* gypsy, tzigane.

zíper *m* AMER zip (cremallera).

zipizape *m* FAM row, scuffle, rumpus, set-to.

zircón *m* zircon.

¡zis zas! *interj* biff! baff!

ziszás *m* zigzag.

zloty *m* zloty (moneda polaca).

zoantarios *m pl* ZOOL zoantharia.

zoantropía *f* MED zoanthropy.

zócalo *m* ARQ socle (de un edificio) || plinth, socle (pedestal) || skirting board (en la parte inferior de una pared) || GEOL insular shelf || AMER square (plaza).
— OBSERV In certain towns and cities of Mexico the name *zócalo* denotes the centre of the (plaza) or public square, and by extension the entire square.

zocato, ta *adj* left-handed (zurdo) || rubbery (frutas, verduras).
◆ *m/f* left-handed person.

zoclo *m* clog, wooden shoe (zueco) || overshoe (chanclo).

zoco, ca *adj* left-handed (zurdo).
◆ *m/f* left-handed person (zurdo).
◆ *m* Moroccan market place (mercado marroquí).

zodiacal *adj* ASTR zodiacal.

zodiaco *m* ASTR zodiac; *los signos del zodiaco* the signs of the zodiac.

zolocho, cha *adj* FAM simple, dozy.
◆ *m/f* FAM simpleton, dope.

zollipar *vi* FAM to sob.

zollipo *m* FAM sob.

zombi; zombie *m/f* zombi, zombie.

zona *f* zone; *zona glacial, templada, tórrida* glacial, temperate, torrid zone || region, area; *zona vinícola* wine-growing region || MED shingles || FIG area, zone; *zona de influencia* area of influence || — *zona azul* restricted parking zone || *zona catastrófica* disaster area || *zona de ensanche* development area || *zona del dólar, del franco, de la libra esterlina* dollar, franc, sterling area || *zona de libre cambio* or *de libre comercio* free trade area || *zona edificada* built-up area || *zona franca* free zone || *zona fronteriza* frontier *o* border zone || *zona urbana* urban area || *zonas verdes* recreational areas, park and garden areas (en una ciudad), greenbelt (alrededor de una ciudad).

zonal *adj* zonal.

zoncear *vi* AMER to play the fool, to behave stupidly.

zoncera; zoncería *f* AMER silliness (idiotez).

zonda *f* AMER zonda.
— OBSERV The *zonda* is a hot enervating north wind which sweeps down from the Andes over the Argentine pampas.

zonzo, za *adj* AMER stupid, silly, inane (tonto) || insipid (soso).
◆ *m/f* AMER silly person, fool, bore.

zoo *m* zoo (parque zoológico).

zoófago, ga *adj* zoophagous.
◆ *m/f* zoophagan.
◆ *m pl* zoophaga.

zoófito *m* zoophyte.
◆ *pl* zoophyta.

zoofobia *f* zoophobia.

zoóforo *m* ARQ zoophorus.

zoogeografía *f* zoogeography.

zooide *adj* zooidal.
◆ *m* zooid.

zoólatra *adj* zoolatrous.
◆ *m/f* zoolater.

zoolatría *f* zoolatry.

zoolito *m* petrified animal, animal fossil.

zoología *f* zoology.

zoológico, ca *adj* zoological || *parque zoológico* zoological garden, zoological gardens *pl*, zoo.
◆ *m* zoo.

zoólogo *m* zoologist.

zoom *m* CINEM zoom || FOT zoom, zoom lens.

zoomorfismo *m* zoomorphism.

zoopsia *f* MED hallucination in which one sees animals.

zoospora *f* BOT zoospore.

zoosporangio *m* BOT zoosporangium.

zootecnia *f* zootechny.

zootécnico, ca *adj* zootechnic, zootechnical.
◆ *m/f* zootechnician.

zooterapia *f* zootherapy.

zoótropo *m* zootrope.

zopas *m/f inv* FAM lisper.

zope *m* ZOOL buzzard (zopilote).

zopenco, ca *adj* FAM daft, dopey.
◆ *m/f* FAM dope, idiot, fool.

zopilote *m* ZOOL buzzard (ave de rapiña).

zopo, pa *adj* crippled, maimed (persona) || crooked (mano, pie) || clumsy (torpe).

zoquete *m* block *o* chunk of wood (de madera) || piece of stale bread (de pan) || FIG & FAM dope, blockhead (persona estúpida).
◆ *m pl* AMER ankle socks (calcetines).

zorcico *m* basque song and dance.

zorito, ta *adj* wild || *paloma zorita* rock pigeon, rock dove (de color apizarrado), wood pigeon, ringdove (torcaz).

zoroástrico, ca *adj/s* Zoroastrian.

zoroastrismo *m* Zoroastrianism.

Zoroastro *npr m* Zoroaster.

zorollo *adj m* *trigo zorollo* wheat reaped while unripe.

zorongo *m* kerchief [worn on the head] || bun (moño) || «zorongo» [popular Andalusian dance].

zorra *f* ZOOL vixen, she-fox (hembra) | fox (macho) || dray, truck (carro) || FIG & FAM whore (prostituta) || FIG & FAM *coger una zorra* to get drunk *o* canned.

zorrastrón, ona *adj* sly, foxy, cunning (astuto).
◆ *m* sly fox, sly old fox (hombre).
◆ *f* sly *o* crafty woman (mujer).

zorrear *vi* FAM to use guile, to resort to trickery (ser astuto) | to lead a life of debauchery (llevar una vida disoluta).

zorrera *f* fox hole, earth (madriguera) || FIG smoke-filled room | drowsiness, heaviness (amodorramiento).

zorrería *f* FAM foxiness, slyness, cunning (astucia) | dirty trick, sly trick (cochinada).

zorrero, ra *adj* slow-sailing (barco) || last (que va el último) || FIG foxy, sly, cunning (astuto) || *perro zorrero* fox terrier.

zorrilla *f* rail inspection car.

zorrillo *m* fox cub.

zorrillo; zorrino *m* AMER ZOOL skunk.

zorro *m* fox, he-fox (raposo) || fox (fur), foxskin (piel) || FIG & FAM old fox, cunning fellow (hombre astuto) | idler, lazybones (perezoso) || AMER ZOOL skunk (mofeta) || FIG & FAM *hacerse el zorro* to play dumb.
◆ *pl* duster *sing* [made of strips of cloth or leather] (sacudidor).

zorrón *m* FAM old fox, cunning fellow (hombre astuto) | drunkenness [US drunk] (borrachera).

zorrona *f* FAM whore (prostituta).

zorronglón, ona *adj* FAM grumbling, complaining, grumpy.
◆ *m/f* FAM grumbler, complainer (refunfuñador).

zorruno, na *adj* fox-like, foxy, vulpine || FIG & FAM *oler a zorruno* to smell of old socks *o* of sweaty feet.

zorullo *m* FAM turd.

zorzal *m* ZOOL thrush (ave) || FIG old fox (hombre astuto) || *zorzal marino* black wrasse (pez).

zote *adj* doltish, dull, dopey (*fam*).
◆ *m/f* dolt, dullard, dope (*fam*).

zozobra *f* shipwreck, capsizing (naufragio) || sinking (hundimiento) || very bad weather (mal tiempo) || FIG anxiety, anguish; *vivir en una perpetua zozobra* to live in constant anxiety.

zozobrar *vi* MAR to be shipwrecked, to capsize (naufragar) | to be in danger (estar en peligro) | to sink, to go down (irse a pique) || FIG to be ruined (unos planes) | to collapse, to be ruined (negocio) | to be worried *o* anxious, to worry (estar intranquilo).

zuavo *m* zouave.

zueco *m* clog, sabot, wooden shoe (de madera) || galosh (de cuero con suela de madera).

Zuinglio *n pr* Zwingli (Zwinglio).

zulacar *vt* TECN to cover with lute.

zulaque *m* TECN lute (betún).

zulo *m* hideout.

zulú *adj/s* Zulu.

Zululandia *npr f* GEOGR Zululand.

zulla *f* sulla, French honeysuckle || excrement.

zullarse *vpr* FAM to dirty o.s.

zumacal *m* sumach field.

zumaque *m* BOT sumach, sumac.

zumaya *f* ZOOL night heron (ave zancuda) | tawny owl (autillo) | nightjar (chotacabras).

zumba *f* bell [worn by the lead mule or ox] (cencerro grande) || FIG teasing, joking (broma) || AMER beating, thrashing (tunda).

zumbador, ra *adj* buzzing, humming.
◆ *m* buzzer (aparato).

zumbar *vi* to buzz, to hum, to ring; *me zumban los oídos* my ears are buzzing || to buzz, to hum (los insectos) || to purr (un motor) || — FIG & FAM *ir zumbando* to be streaking *o* whizzing *o* zooming along (un coche, etc.) | *salir zumbando* to shoot off, to zoom off | *¡zumbando!* make it snappy! | *zumbarle a uno* to give s.o. a beating *o* a thrashing.
◆ *vt* FAM to land, to fetch, to give; *zumbarle a uno una bofetada* to land s.o. a slap *o* a smack | to rag, to tease (tomar el pelo) | to make fun of (burlarse de) || AMER to throw, to fling (arrojar).
◆ *vpr* FAM to hit one another, to lash out, to let fly (pegarse) | to laugh at, to make fun of (burlarse).

zumbido; zumbo *m* buzzing, humming, ringing; *zumbido de oídos* buzzing of the ears, ringing in the ears || buzz, buzzing, hum, humming (insectos) || purr, purring (motor) || hum, humming, whir, whirring (peonza).

zumbón, ona *adj* FAM joking, teasing (burlón) | funny (divertido).
◆ *m/f* FAM clown, joker, tease.

zumo *m* juice; *zumo de tomate* tomato juice || juice, squash; *zumo de naranja, de limón* orange, lemon squash || FIG profit (provecho) || — FIG *sacarle el zumo a uno* to bleed s.o. dry || *zumo de cepas* or *de parras* wine.

zunchar *vt* to fasten with a metal hoop *o* band.

zuncho *m* metal hoop *o* band (anillo de metal).

zupia *f* dregs *pl*, lees *pl*, sediment of wine (poso) || muddy *o* cloudy wine (vino turbio).

zurcido *m* darning, mending (acción de zurcir) || mend, darn; *un zurcido en la chaqueta* a mend in the jacket || FIG *un zurcido de mentiras* a tissue of lies.

zurcidor, ra *m/f* darner, mender || fine-drawer (de zurcido invisible) || — FIG *zurcidora de voluntades* bawd, procuress, go-between | *zurcidor de voluntades* pimp, procurer, go-between.

zurcir *vt* to darn, to mend; *zurcir calcetines* to darn socks || to fine-draw (de modo invisible) || to sew up (lo muy roto) || FIG to join *o* to put together (unir) | to concoct, to spin (mentiras) || — FIG & FAM *¡anda y que te zurzan!* go jump in the lake!, go to hell! | FIG *zurcir voluntades* to pander.

zurdo, da *adj* left; *mano zurda* left hand || left-handed (persona) || FIG & FAM *no ser zurdo* to have one's head screwed on, to be no fool.
◆ *m/f* left-handed person, left-hander, southpaw (*fam*).
◆ *f* left hand (mano).

zurear *vi* to coo, to bill and coo (paloma).

zureo *m* cooing, billing and cooing (arrullo).

Zurich *n pr* GEOGR Zurich.

zurito, ta *adj* wild || *paloma zurita* rock pigeon, rock dove (de color apizarrado), wood pigeon, ringdove (torcaz).

zuro, ra *adj* wild (paloma).
◆ *m* cob (del maíz).

zurra *f* TECN currying, dressing, tanning (del cuero) | curriery (arte del zurrador) || FIG & FAM beating, thrashing (paliza) | brawl, scuffle (contienda).

zurrador, ra *m* currier, tanner, dresser.

zurrapa *f* lees *pl*, dregs *pl*, sediment (poso) || grounds *pl* (del café) || FIG & FAM trash, rubbish (cosa despreciable).
— OBSERV This word is frequently used in the plural.

zurrapelo *m* FAM dressing down; *dar un zurrapelo a uno* to give s.o. a dressing down.

zurrapiento, ta; zurraposo, sa *adj* full of dregs, muddy (que tiene posos) || turbid (turbio).

zurrar *vt* to curry, to dress, to tan (el cuero) || FIG & FAM to beat up, to give a thrashing *o* a beating, to lay into (dar una paliza) | to whip, to flagellate (con azotes) | to give (s.o.) a tongue-lashing (reprender) || FIG & FAM *zurrarle a uno la badana* to tan s.o.'s hide (pegar), to give s.o. a dressing down (con palabras).
◆ *vpr* FAM to wet o.s. (irse del vientre o tener temor) || FAM *zurrarse la badana* to thump each other, to lay into each other.

zurriaga *f* whip (látigo).

zurriagar *vt* to whip, to flog, to lash, to flagellate.

zurriagazo *m* lash [of a whip] || FIG stroke of bad luck, blow, mishap (desgracia).

zurriago *m* whip || *zurriago oculto* or *escondido* hunt the thimble (juego).

zurribanda *f* FAM beating, thrashing (zurra) | scuffle, brawl, rumpus (pendencia).

zurriburri *m* FAM despicable type, scum (sujeto vil) | shady bunch (grupo) | uproar, turmoil, confusion (jaleo).

zurrido *m* whack [with a stick] (golpe) || grating noise (sonido).

zurrón *m* shepherd's pouch *o* bag (bolsa de pastor) || leather bag (bolsa de cuero) || husk [of certain fruits] (cáscara).

zurullo *m* lump (grumo) || FAM turd (excremento).

zurupeto *m* FAM unregistered broker (corredor de bolsa) || unauthorized notary (notario intruso).

zutano, na *m/f* FAM what's-his-name || *Fulano, Mengano y Zutano* Tom, Dick and Harry.
— OBSERV The noun *zutano* is only used after the words *fulano* and *mengano* to designate a third person whose name is unknown.

¡zuzo! *interj* shoo!, scat! (para espantar al perro).

zuzón *m* groundsel.

zwinglianismo *m* REL Zwinglianism.

zwingliano, na *adj/s* Zwinglian.

Zwinglio *npr m* Zwingli.

ENGLISH - SPANISH
INGLÉS - ESPAÑOL

ABBREVIATIONS

abbrev	abbreviation	abreviatura
adj	adjective	adjetivo
adv	adverb	adverbio
adv phr	adverbial phrase	locución adverbial
AGR	agriculture, rural economy	agricultura, economía rural
AMER	americanism	americanismo
ANAT	anatomy	anatomía
ant	antiquated, obsolete	anticuado
ARCH	architecture, building	arquitectura, construcción
art	article	artículo
ARTS	arts	artes
ASTR	astronomy	astronomía
AUT	automobile	automóvil
aux	auxiliary	auxiliar
AVIAT	aviation	aviación
BIOL	biology	biología
BOT	botany	botánica
CHEM	chemistry	química
CINEM	cinematography	cinematografía
COMM	commerce, finance	comercio, finanzas
comp	comparative	comparativo
compl	complement	complemento
conj	conjunction	conjunción
CULIN	culinary, cooking	culinario, cocina
def	definite	definido
dem	demonstrative	demostrativo
dim	diminutive	diminutivo
ECON	economics	economía
ELECTR	electricity	electricidad
exclamat	exclamatory	exclamativo
f	feminine	femenino
FAM	familiar, colloquial	familiar
FIG	figurative	figurado
GEOGR	geography	geografía
GEOL	geology	geología
GRAMM	grammar	gramática
HERALD	heraldry	heráldica
HIST	history	historia
impers	impersonal	impersonal
indef	indefinite	indefinido
INFORM	computing	informática
infr	infrequent	poco usado
inter	interjection	interjección
interr	interrogative	interrogativo
inv	invariable	invariable
JUR	jurisprudence	jurisprudencia
lat phr	latin phrase	locución latina
m	masculine	masculino
MAR	maritime	marítimo
MATH	mathematics	matemáticas
MED	medicine	medicina
MIL	military	militar
MIN	mining, mineralogy	minería, mineralogía
MUS	music	música
MYTH	mythology	mitología
n	noun	nombre
NUCL	nuclear	nuclear
num	numeral	numeral
o.s.	oneself	se
pers	personal	personal
PHIL	philosophy	filosofía
PHOT	photography	fotografía
PHYS	physics	física
pl	plural	plural
POET	poetry	poético
POP	popular	popular
poss	possessive	posesivo
pp	past participle	participio pasivo
pref	prefix	prefijo
prep	preposition	preposición
pret	preterite	pretérito
PRINT	printing	imprenta
pron	pronoun	pronombre
pr n	proper noun	nombre propio
RAD	radio, television	radio, televisión
rel	relative	relativo
REL	religion	religión
s	substantive	sustantivo
s.o.	someone	alguien, uno
SP	sports	deportes
sth.	something	algo
superl	superlative	superlativo
TAUR	tauromachy	tauromaquia
TECH	technology, mechanical engineering, industry	tecnología, mecánica, industria
THEATR	theatre	teatro
US	United States	Estados Unidos
v	verb	verbo
vi	intransitive verb	verbo intransitivo
vpr	pronominal verb	verbo pronominal
vt	transitive verb	verbo transitivo
VET	veterinary science	veterinaria
ZOOL	zoology	zoología

ALFABETO FONÉTICO INTERNACIONAL

Sonidos ingleses

Consonantes

Símbolos	*Ejemplos*
[b]	bat [bæt]
[d]	dot [dɔt], begged [begd]
[dʒ]	jam [dʒæm], edge [edʒ]
[f]	fat [fæt], phrase [freiz], laugh [lɑ:f]
[g]	goat [gout], ghastly ['gɑ:stli], guard [gɑ:d]
[gw]	language ['læŋgwidʒ]
[gz]	exact [ig'zækt]
[ʒ]	measure ['meʒə*], azure ['eiʒə*], garage ['gærɑ:ʒ]
[h]	hat [hæt]
[k]	cat [kæt], keen [ki:n], Christmas ['krisməs], antique [æn'ti:k]
[ks]	taxi ['tæksi], access ['ækses], eczema ['eksimə]
[kw]	quack [kwæk]
[l]	lap [læp]
[m]	mat [mæt]
[n]	natter ['nætə*]
[ŋ]	blank [blæŋk]
[t]	tatter ['tætə*], fixed [fikst], thyme [taim]
[tʃ]	chat [tʃæt], match [mætʃ], nature ['neitʃə*]
[θ]	thatch [θætʃ]
[ð]	that [ðæt], father ['fɑ:ðə*]
[v]	vat [væt], Stephen ['sti:vn]
[z]	haze [heiz], disease [di'zi:z], scissors ['sizəz], xebec ['zi:bek]

Semivocales

Símbolos	*Ejemplos*
[j]	yet [jet], onion ['ɔnjən], extraneous [eks'treinjəs]
[w]	war [wɔ:*], quite [kwait]; (cf. [kw], [gw])

Semivocales y vocales

Símbolos	*Ejemplos*
[ju:]	unit ['ju:nit], new [nju:], suit [sju:t], adieu [ə'dju:], beauty ['bju:ti], yule [ju:l], yew, you [ju:], deuce [dju:s]
[juə]	fewer ['fjuə*], pure ['pjuə*]
[wʌ]	one, won [wʌn]; (cf. [w], [kw], [gw])

Vocales

Símbolos	*Ejemplos*
[æ]	cat [kæt], plait [plæt]
[e]	hen [hen], head [hed], any [eni], bury ['beri], leisure ['leʒə*], said [sed], leopard ['lepəd], friend [frend]
[i]	pig [pig], English ['iŋgliʃ], women ['wimin], palace ['pælis], business ['bizinis], pyx [piks], barley ['bɑ:li], sieve [siv], build [bild], carriage ['kæridʒ], Greenwich ['grinidʒ], captain ['kæptin], Sunday ['sʌndi], foreign ['fɔrin], forehead ['fɔrid]
[ɔ]	cock [kɔk], wash [wɔʃ], because [bi'kɔz], Gloucester ['glɔstə*], knowledge ['nɔlidʒ]
[u]	bull [bul], book [buk], wolf [wulf], could [kud], worsted ['wustid]
[ʌ]	duck [dʌk], come [kʌm], courage ['kʌridʒ], blood [blʌd]
[ə]	again [ə'gein], verandah [və'rændə], bacon ['beikən], tortoise ['tɔ:təs], famous ['feiməs], suggest [sə'dʒest], collar ['kɔlə*], cover ['kʌvə*], tapir ['teipə*], motor ['moutə*], cupboard ['kʌbəd], vigour ['vigə*], chauffeur ['tʃɔ:fə*], figure ['figə*], litre ['litə*]
[ə:]	bird [bə:d], hermit ['hə:mit], earn [ə:n], amateur ['æmətə:*], word [wə:d], courteous ['kə:tiəs], nurse [nə:s], myrtle ['mə:tl], colonel ['kə:nl]
[ɑ:]	calf [kɑ:f], far [fɑ:*], farm [fɑ:m], aunt [ɑ:nt], clerk [klɑ:k], heart [hɑ:t]
[i:]	sheep [ʃi:p], tea [ti:], scene [si:n], seize [si:z], litre [li:tr], fiend [fi:nd], Caesar ['si:zə*], quay [ki:], people ['pi:pl]
[ɔ:]	off [ɔ:f], lawn [lɔ:n], caught [kɔ:t], war [wɔ:*], broad [brɔ:d], born [bɔ:n], thought [θɔ:t], source [sɔ:s], all [ɔ:l], more [mɔ:*], floor [flɔ:*], boar [bɔ:*], your [jɔ:*]
[u:]	goose [gu:s], rule [ru:l], who [hu:], wound [wu:nd], blue [blu:], juice [dʒu:s], screw [skru:], shoe [ʃu:], manœuvre [mə'nu:və*]

Diptongos

Símbolos	*Ejemplos*
[ai]	ice [ais], fly [flai], aye, eye [ai], height [hait], pie [pai, rye [rai, buy [bai], island ['ailənd], light [lait]
[ei]	snake [sneik], maid [meid], play [plei], veil [veil], great [greit], phaeton ['feitn], gauge [geidʒ], gaol [dʒeil], grey [grei], weigh [wei]
[ɔi]	coin [kɔin], joy [dʒɔi], buoy [bɔi]
[au]	mouse [maus], cow [kau], plough [plau]
[ou]	go [gou], goat [gout], doe [dou], soul [soul], blow [blou], brooch [broutʃ], mauve [mouv], bureau [bjuə'rou], yeoman ['joumən], sew [sou], dough [dou], owe [ou]
[ɛə]	bear [bɛə*], care [kɛə*], pair [pɛə*], there [ðɛə*], prayer ['prɛə*], mayor [mɛə*], aerial ['ɛəriəl], heir [hɛə*], vary ['vɛəri]
[iə]	deer [diə*], here [hiə*], tier [tiə*], beard [biəd], weird [wiəd], theory ['θiəri], idea ['aidiə]
[uə]	poor [puə*], sure [suə*], tour [tuə*], pleurisy ['pluərisi], cruel [kruəl], Boer [buə*]

Triptongos

Símbolos	*Ejemplos*
[aiə]	science ['saiəns], via ['vaiə], liar ['laiə*], lion ['laiən], pious ['paiəs], higher ['haiə*], fire ['faiə*], choir ['kwaiə*], buyer ['baiə*], dryer ['draiə*], pyre ['paiə*]
[auə]	flower [flauə*], vowel ['vauəl], hour [auə*], coward ['kauəd]

— Observ. El signo (:) colocado después de una vocal indica que ésta es larga. El asterisco (*) señala que la *r* escrita en posición final no se pronuncia en Gran Bretaña, excepto cuando la palabra siguiente empieza por vocal. En los Estados Unidos esta *r* se pronuncia siempre.

Además de los símbolos incluidos en el cuadro se han utilizado otros tres para representar sonidos nasales existentes en palabras tomadas del francés que son ɑ (vol-au-vent ['vɔləu'vɑŋ]), ɛ (lingerie ['lɛʒəri]) y ɔ (wagon-lit ['vægɔn'li:]).

Para conocer la relación entre los sonidos ingleses y los castellanos es preciso consultar el apartado del «Resumen de gramática inglesa» dedicado a la pronunciación.

A

a [ei] *n* a *f* (letter); *a small a* una a minúscula || MUS la *m*; *A minor* la menor; *A major* la mayor; *A flat* la bemol; *A sharp* la sostenido || — FAM *from A to Z* de cabo a rabo || *number 20 A, Villiers Street* calle Villiers número 20 duplicado.
◆ *indef art* un, una; *a man* un hombre; *a woman* una mujer || un tal, una tal; un cierto, una cierta; *a Mr Jones* un tal Sr Jones || el mismo, la misma; *to be of a size* tener el mismo tamaño || (not translated in Spanish); *to make a noise* hacer ruido; *as a taxpayer* como contribuyente; *my father is a doctor* mi padre es médico; *my friend, a teacher of languages* mi amigo, profesor de idiomas; *what a surprise!* ¡qué sorpresa!; *a fine answer!* ¡menuda contestación!; *have you got a flat?* ¿tienes piso?; *you haven't got a flat* no tienes piso || (distributive use); *two shillings a head* dos chelines por persona; *pears at three shillings a pound* peras a tres chelines por libra || (expressing time); *twice a day* dos veces al día *or* por día; *one hundred miles an hour* cien millas por hora || — *a few* unos pocos, unas pocas; unos, unas; *in a few minutes* dentro de unos minutos || *a great many* muchísimos, muchísimas || *half an hour* media hora || *so great a man* un hombre tan grande || *such a* tal; *I don't like such a book* no me gusta tal libro || *too cautious a man* un hombre demasiado prudente || *to set an example* dar ejemplo, dar el ejemplo.
— OBSERV Se emplea el artículo *a* cuando antecede una palabra que empieza por una consonante (*a boat* un barco), una «h» aspirada (*a house* una casa) o una «u» con el sonido [ju] (*a use* un empleo). Se sustituye por *an* delante de vocal (*an eye* un ojo) o «h» muda (*an hour* una hora).

AA *abbr of* *Automobile Association* automóvil club británico.

A-1 [ei-wʌn] *adj* FAM de primera categoría | en plena forma (in good health).

Aachen ['ɑːkən] *pr n* GEOGR Aquisgrán.

aardvark ['ɑːdvɑːk] *n* cerdo *m* hormiguero.

aback [ə'bæk] *adv* MAR en facha || FIG *to be taken aback* quedar sorprendido *or* estupefacto.

abacus ['æbəkəs] *n* ARCH & MATH ábaco *m*.
— OBSERV El plural de *abacus* es *abaci* o *abacuses*.

abaft [ə'bɑːft] *adv* MAR a popa (towards stern) | en popa (in stern).
◆ *prep* detrás de.

abalone [æbə'ləuni] *n* ZOOL oreja *f* de mar.

abandon [ə'bændən] *n* abandono *m* || desenfado *m* (ease).

abandon [ə'bændən] *vt* abandonar (to leave) || renunciar a (to give up) || *to abandon o.s. to* abandonarse a, entregarse a.

abandoned [-d] *adj* abandonado, da || perdido, da (immoral).

abandoning [-iŋ]; **abandonment** [-mənt] *n* abandono *m*.

abase [ə'beis] *vt* rebajar, degradar.

abasement [-mənt] *n* degradación *f*, rebajamiento *m*.

abash [ə'bæʃ] *vt* avergonzar (to make ashamed) || desconcertar (to disconcert).

abashment [-mənt] *n* vergüenza *f*.

abate [ə'beit] *vt* JUR abolir || disminuir, reducir (to reduce) || debilitar (to weaken) || rebajar, descontar (to deduct).
◆ *vi* reducirse, disminuir || calmarse (storm, pain) || amainar (wind) || bajar (flood) || moderarse (violence).

abatement [ə'beitmənt] *n* JUR abolición *f*, supresión *f* || disminución *f* || alivio *m* (of a pain) || rebaja *f*, descuento *m* (deduction).

abattoir ['æbətwɑː*] *n* matadero *m*.

abbacy ['æbəsi] *n* REL abadía *f*.

Abbasids ['æbəsidz] *pl prn* HIST Abasidas *m*.

abbatial [æ'beiʃəl] *adj* abacial || *abbatial lands* tierras abadengas.

abbé ['æbei] *n* REL abate *m*.

abbess ['æbis] *n* REL abadesa *f*.

abbey ['æbi] *n* REL abadía *f*.

abbot ['æbət] *n* REL abad *m*.

abbreviate [ə'briːvieit] *vt* abreviar || MATH simplificar.

abbreviation [əˌbriːvi'eiʃən] *n* abreviación *f* (action of abbreviating) || abreviatura *f* (shortened form); *table of abbreviations* cuadro de abreviaturas.

A B C ['eibiː'siː] *n* abecé *m*, alfabeto *m*, abecedario *m* (alphabet).

ABC *abbr of* *American Broadcasting Company* cadena de radiotelevisión norteamericana.

abdicate ['æbdikeit] *vt* abdicar (the throne) || dimitir de (a function) || renunciar a (one's rights).
◆ *vi* abdicar; *to abdicate from the throne* abdicar el trono.

abdication [æbdi'keiʃən] *n* abdicación *f* || renuncia *f* (of rights) || dimisión *f* (of a function).

abdomen ['æbdəmən] *n* ANAT abdomen *m*.

abdominal [æb'dəminl] *adj* ANAT abdominal; *abdominal muscles* músculos abdominales.

abducent [æb'djuːsnt] *adj* ANAT abductor.

abduct [æb'dʌkt] *vt* secuestrar (to kidnap).

abduction [æb'dʌkʃən] *n* rapto *m*, secuestro *m* || ANAT abducción *f*.

abductor [æb'dʌktə*] *n* raptor, ra; secuestrador, ra (kidnapper) || ANAT abductor *m*.

abeam [ə'biːm] *adv* MAR de través.

abed [ə'bed] *adv* en cama.

Abel ['eibəl] *pr n* Abel *m*.

abelmosk [-məusk] *n* BOT algalia *f*.

aberrant [æ'berənt] *adj* aberrante || ANAT anormal, anómalo, la.

aberration [æbə'reiʃən] *n* aberración *f*.

abet [ə'bet] *vt* incitar || JUR *to aid and abet* ser cómplice de.

abetment [-mənt] *n* incitación *f* || JUR complicidad *f*.

abettor [-ə*] *n* JUR cómplice *m* & *f* || instigador, ra.

abeyance [ə'beiəns] *n* suspensión *f* || — *in abeyance* en suspenso || *inheritance in abeyance* herencia *f* yacente || *into abeyance* en desuso.

abhor [əb'hɔː*] *vt* aborrecer, odiar, abominar.

abhorrence [əb'hɔrəns] *n* aborrecimiento *m*, odio *m* || *to hold in abhorrence* odiar, aborrecer.

abhorrent [əb'hɔrənt] *adj* aborrecible, detestable, abominable.

abidance [ə'baidəns] *n* acatamiento *m*, respeto *m* (*by* de) (the law, etc.).

abide* [ə'baid] *vt* tolerar, soportar, aguantar; *I can't abide him* no le aguanto || esperar (to await).
◆ *vi* permanecer (to stay) || acatar, someterse a, atenerse a; *to abide by the rules* acatar las reglas || cumplir; *to abide by a promise* cumplir una promesa || morar (to dwell).
— OBSERV Pret y pp *abode, abided*.

Abidjan [æbiː'dʒɑːn] *pr n* GEOGR Abiyán.

abiding [-iŋ] *adj* duradero, ra || *law abiding* respetuoso de las leyes.

ability [ə'biliti] *n* habilidad *f* (skill) || capacidad *f* || aptitud *f*.
◆ *pl* talento *m sing* || inteligencia *f sing*.

abject ['æbdʒekt] *adj* abyecto, ta; vil, despreciable (despicable) || miserable (wretched).

abjection [æb'dʒekʃən] *n* bajeza *f*, abyección *f*.

abjuration [æbdʒuə'reiʃən] *n* abjuración *f*.

abjure [əb'dʒuə*] *vt* abjurar (de) (one's faith) || retractarse de (one's opinion).

ablation [æb'leiʃən] *n* ablación *f*.

ablative ['æblətiv] *n* GRAMM ablativo *m*; *ablative absolute* ablativo absoluto.
◆ *adj* en ablativo | ablativo (case).

ablaut ['æblaut] *n* GRAMM apofonía *f*.

ablaze [ə'bleiz] *adj/adv* en llamas, ardiendo (on fire) || encendido, da (lit up) || FIG inflamado, da | brillante || *ablaze with anger* furibundo, da.

able ['eibl] *adj* listo, ta; inteligente (clever) || capaz (capable) || bien hecho (work) || *to be able to* poder.

able-bodied [-'bɔdid] *adj* sano, na; fuerte.

able-bodied seaman [-bɔdidsiːmən] *n* MAR marinero *m* de primera.

abloom [ə'bluːm] *adj/adv* en flor.

ablution [ə'bluːʃən] *n* ablución *f*.

ably ['eibli] *adv* hábilmente.

abnegate ['æbnigeit] *vt* renunciar a (rights, etc.) || REL abjurar.

abnegation [æbni'geiʃən] *n* renuncia *f* (of rights) || abnegación *f* (self-denial) || REL abjuración *f*.

abnormal [æb'nɔːməl] *adj* anormal.

abnormality [æbnɔː'mæliti] *n* anormalidad *f*.

aboard [ə'bɔːd] *adv* a bordo || — *all aboard!* ¡viajeros al tren! (on a train), ¡pasajeros a bordo! (on a boat) || *to go aboard* ir a bordo,

embarcarse || *to take aboard* llevar a bordo, embarcar.
◆ *prep* a bordo de.

abode [ə'bəud] *n* residencia *f*, domicilio *m*; *of no fixed abode* sin domicilio fijo || *to take up one's abode* domiciliarse, fijar domicilio.

abode [ə'bəud] *pret/pp* ⟶ **abide.**

abolish [ə'bɔliʃ] *vt* abolir.

abolishment [-mənt]; **abolition** [ˌæbə'liʃən] *n* abolición *f*.

abolitionism [æbəliʃənizəm] *n* abolicionismo *m*.

abolitionist [ˌæbə'liʃənist] *n* abolicionista *m* & *f*.

abomasum [ˌæbəu'meisəm] *n* ANAT abomaso *m*, cuajar *m*.
— OBSERV El plural de *abomasum* es *abomasa*.

A-bomb ['eibɔm] *n* PHYS bomba *f* A.

abominable [ə'bɔminəbl] *adj* abominable, detestable || *the abominable snowman* el abominable hombre de las nieves.

abominate [ə'bɔmineit] *vt* abominar, aborrecer, detestar.

abomination [əˌbɔmi'neiʃən] *n* aborrecimiento *m*, abominación *f* (loathing) || FIG *this wine is an abomination* este vino es horrible.

aboriginal [ˌæbə'ridʒənl] *adj/n* aborigen, indígena.

Aborigine [ˌæbə'ridʒini] *n* aborigen *m* & *f* de Australia.

aborigines [ˌæbə'ridʒini:z] *pl n* aborígenes *m* & *f*.

abort [ə'bɔ:t] *vi* MED abortar || FAM fracasar (to fail).
◆ *vt* abortar, hacer abortar.

abortion [ə'bɔ:ʃən] *n* aborto *m* provocado || FIG engendro *m*, aborto *m* (sth. badly developed) | fracaso *m* (failure) || *to have an abortion* abortar.

abortive [ə'bɔ:tiv] *adj* abortivo, va || FIG fracasado, da; frustrado, da || *abortive medicine* abortivo *m*.

abound [ə'baund] *vi* abundar (*in, with* en).

about [ə'baut] *adv* por aquí y por allá; *he was walking about* andaba por aquí y por allá || por aquí; *there is a lot of flu about* hay mucha gripe por aquí || MIL media vuelta; *about turn!*, US *about face!* ¡media vuelta! || a punto de; *I am about to do it* estoy a punto de hacerlo || más o menos; *that's about right* eso es más o menos exacto || casi, unos, alrededor de; *about three thousand men* alrededor de tres mil hombres; *about two years ago* hace unos dos años || casi, más o menos; *it's just about finished* está casi acabado || — *all about* por todas partes, en todos lados || *I'm happy to see you up and about* me alegro de verte de nuevo en pie || *to be about* estar a mano.
◆ *prep* sobre; *a book about aeroplanes* un libro sobre aviones || acerca de, con respecto a, sobre; *he told me all about him* me dijo todo acerca de él || por; *he worries about his health* se preocupa por su salud || en; *he only thinks about him* piensa sólo en él || alrededor de, cerca de (around); *somewhere about Pamplona* alrededor de Pamplona || a eso de, hacia; *at about 4 o'clock* a eso de las cuatro || por; *his toys were spread about the garden* sus juguetes estaban esparcidos por el jardín || junto a; *about the fire* junto al fuego || — *he has no money about him* no lleva dinero encima *or* consigo || *how about me?* ¿y yo? || *how about that?* ¿qué te parece? || *what are you about?* ¿qué hace? || *there is sth. strange about that girl* esta chica tiene algo (de) extraño || *what is it about?* ¿de qué se trata? || *what's that book about?* ¿de qué trata ese libro?

about-face [-feis] *n* US MIL media vuelta *f* || FIG cambio *m* rotundo.

about-face [-feis] *vi* US MIL dar media vuelta.

about-ship [-ʃip] *vi* MAR virar.

about turn [-tə:n] *n* MIL media vuelta *f*.

about turn [-tə:n] *vi* MIL dar media vuelta.

above [ə'bʌv] *adv* arriba (higher); *it is above* está arriba || anteriormente (before in a printed passage) || de arriba; *the flat above* el piso de arriba || más arriba, más allá (further) || *see above* véase más arriba.
◆ *prep* encima de (higher than); *above your house* encima de su casa || más allá de (beyond); *the road above the village* la carretera más allá del pueblo || más de (more than); *we cannot admit above 25 people* no se admiten más de 25 personas || más arriba de (river) || sobre; *above sea level* sobre el nivel del mar; *fifteen degrees above zero* quince grados sobre cero || superior a; *any number above 100* cualquier número superior a 100 || — *above all* sobre todo || *above and beyond* mucho más allá de, por encima de || *over and above* además de || *people above 18 years of age* mayores de 18 años || *to be above all suspicion* estar por encima de toda sospecha || *to be above deception* ser incapaz de engañar.
◆ *adj* susodicho, cha; citado anteriormente.

aboveboard [ə'bʌv'bɔ:d] *adj* honrado, da (honest) || franco, ca; sincero, ra || leal.
◆ *adv* abiertamente.

above-mentioned [ə'bʌv'menʃənd] *adj* anteriormente citado, anteriormente mencionado.

abracadabra [ˌæbrəkə'dæbrə] *n* abracadabra *m*.

abrade [ə'breid] *vt* raer, desgastar.

Abraham ['eibrəhæm] *pr n* Abrahán *m*.

abrasion [ə'breiʒən] *n* GEOL erosión *f* || MED & TECN abrasión *f*.

abrasive [ə'breisiv] *adj* abrasivo, va.
◆ *n* abrasivo *m*.

abreast [ə'brest] *adv* uno al lado del otro || MIL de frente (to march) || — *four abreast* en fila de a cuatro || *to be abreast of the times* andar con el tiempo || *to keep abreast of* mantenerse informado de, estar al tanto *or* al corriente de (news, etc.), estar al día con (all one's work), seguir [el ritmo de] (to keep up with), correr parejo con (in a race).

abridge [ə'bridʒ] *vt* condensar, abreviar (a book) || limitar, reducir (rights) || privar (to deprive) || acortar (to shorten).

abridgement; abridgment [-mənt] *n* compendio *m*, resumen *m* || limitación *f*, reducción *f* || JUR privación *f* (of rights).

abroad [ə'brɔ:d] *adv* en el extranjero (in a foreign place) || al extranjero (to a foreign place) || fuera, fuera de casa (outside) || *how did the news get abroad?* ¿cómo se divulgó la noticia? || FIG *the rumour is abroad that...* corre el rumor de que...

abrogate ['æbrəugeit] *vt* abrogar.

abrogation [ˌæbrəu'geiʃən] *n* abrogación *f*.

abrupt [ə'brʌpt] *adj* abrupto, ta; escarpado, da (steep) || brusco, ca (people) || brusco, ca (sudden); *an abrupt halt* una parada brusca || entrecortado, da (jerky).

Abruzzi [ə'brutsi:] *pl prn* GEOGR Abruzos *m*.

abscess ['æbsis] *n* MED absceso *m*.

abscissa [æb'sisə] *n* MATH abscisa *f*.
— OBSERV El plural es *abscissae* o *abscissas*.

abscission [æb'siʒən] *n* MED abscisión *f*.

abscond [əb'skɔnd] *vi* fugarse, huir.

abseil ['æbseil] *vt* hacer rappel.

absence ['æbsəns] *n* ausencia *f* (of a person) || falta *f* (lack) || JUR incomparecencia *f* || — *absence of mind* distracción *f* || *in the absence of* en ausencia de, a falta de.

absent ['æbsənt] *adj* ausente || distraído, da (not attentive) || MIL *to declare s.o. absent without leave* declararle a uno ausente sin permiso.

absent [æb'sent] *vt* *to absent o.s.* ausentarse.

absentee [ˌæbsən'ti:] *n* ausente *m* & *f* || absentista *m* & *f* (landlord, worker).

absenteeism [-izəm] *n* absentismo *m*.

absentee landlord [-'lændlɔ:d] *n* absentista *m*.

absentminded ['æbsənt'maindid] *adj* distraído, da.

absentmindedness [-nis] *n* distracción *f*.

absinth; absinthe ['æbsinθ] *n* ajenjo *m*.

absolute ['æbsəlu:t] *adj* absoluto, ta || rotundo, da (denial) || JUR irrevocable || FAM completo, ta | perfecto, ta (liar, idiot, etc.) || *to obtain an absolute majority* obtener la mayoría absoluta.
◆ *n* lo absoluto.

absolute scale [-skeil] *n* PHYS escala *f* de Kelvin.

absolution [ˌæbsə'lu:ʃən] *n* absolución *f*; *to grant absolution* dar la absolución.

absolutism [ˌæbsəlu:tizəm] *n* absolutismo *m*.

absolutist ['æbsəlu:tist] *adj/n* absolutista.

absolve [əb'zɔlv] *vt* absolver || liberar (from a promise).

absorb [əb'zɔ:b] *vt* absorber || amortiguar (a shock) || FIG absorber || *to be absorbed in* estar absorto en.

absorbency [əb'zɔ:bənsi] *n* absorbencia *f*.

absorbent [əb'zɔ:bənt] *adj* absorbente.
◆ *n* absorbente *m*.

absorbent cotton [-'kɔtn] *n* US algodón *m* hidrófilo.

absorbing [əb'zɔ:biŋ] *adj* absorbente (work, etc.).

absorption [əb'zɔ:pʃən] *n* absorción *f* || FIG ensimismamiento *m* || AUT amortiguamiento *m*.

absorptive [əb'zɔ:ptiv] *adj* absorbente.

absorptivity [əb'zɔ:p'tiviti] *n* PHYS absorción *f*.

abstain [əbstein] *vi* abstenerse; *to abstain from comment* abstenerse de comentarios.

abstemious [æb'sti:mjəs] *adj* abstemio, mia.

abstention [æb'stenʃən] *n* abstención *f* (from voting) || abstinencia *f*.

abstentionism [-izəm] *n* abstencionismo *m*.

abstentionist [-ist] *n* abstencionista *m* & *f*.

abstinence ['æbstinəns] *n* abstinencia *f*.

abstinent ['æbstinənt] *adj* abstinente.

abstract ['æbstrækt] *adj* abstracto, ta.
◆ *n* resumen *m* (summary) || extracto *m* (extract) || abstracción *f* || *in the abstract* en abstracto.

abstract [æb'strækt] *vt* extraer (to extract) || resumir (to summarize) || hacer caso omiso de (an idea) || sustraer (to steal) || *to abstract o.s.* abstraerse, ensimismarse.

abstracted [æb'stræktid] *adj* abstraído, da; ensimismado, da.

abstraction [æb'strækʃən] *n* abstracción *f* (generalization) || extracción *f* (extraction) || distracción *f* (of mind) || sustracción *f* (of papers, etc.) || malversación *f* (of funds).

abstruse [æb'stru:s] *adj* abstruso, sa.

abstruseness [-nis] *n* carácter *m* abstruso.

absurd [əb'zə:d] *adj* absurdo, da || ridículo, la.

absurdity [-iti] *n* absurdo *m*.

Abu Dhabi [,æbu'dɑ:bi] *pr n* GEOGR Abu Dhabi.

abulia [ə'bu:liə] *n* abulia *f.*

abulic [ə'bu:lik] *adj* abúlico, ca.

abundance [ə'bʌndəns] *n* abundancia *f* ‖ *in abundance* en abundancia.

abundant [ə'bʌndənt] *adj* abundante.

abundantly [ə'bʌndəntli] *adv* abundantemente.

abuse [ə'bju:s] *n* abuso *m* (misuse); *abuse of confidence* abuso de confianza ‖ insultos *m pl* (insults).

abuse [ə'bju:z] *vt* abusar de (to mistreat, to misuse) ‖ insultar (to insult) ‖ denigrar (to disparage) ‖ *he has been abused* le han engañado.

Abu Simbel [,æbu'simbl] *pr n* GEOGR Abu Simbel.

abusive [ə'bju:siv] *adj* abusivo, va (misusing) ‖ injurioso, sa (insulting).

abut [ə'bʌt] *vi* lindar (*on* con) (to border) ‖ apoyarse (*on against* en) (to lean against).

abutment [-mənt] *n* límite *m* (limit) ‖ ARCH contrafuerte *m* ‖ empalme *m* (in carpentry).

abutting [-iŋ] *adj* lindante con.

abysm [ə'bizəm] *n* abismo *m.*

abysmal [ə'bizməl] *adj* abismal, abismático, ca ‖ FIG profundo, da | pésimo, ma (very bad).

abyss [ə'bis] *n* abismo *m*, sima *f.*

abyssal [-əl] *adj* abisal.

Abyssinia [,æbi'siniə] *pr n* GEOGR Abisinia *f.*

Abyssinian [-n] *adj n* abisinio, nia.

acacia [ə'keiʃə] *n* BOT acacia *f.*

academic [,ækədemik] *adj* académico, ca (scholarly) ‖ bizantino, na (too speculative) ‖ universitario, ria; escolar; *academic year* curso escolar.
◆ *n* universitario *m.*

academical [-əl] *adj* académico, ca (scholarly).
◆ *pl n* vestidura *f sing* académica.

academic freedom [-'fri:dəm] *n* libertad *f* de cátedra *or* de enseñanza.

academician [ə,kædə'miʃən] *n* académico, ca.

academicism [,ækə'demisizəm] *m* academicismo *m.*

academy [ə'kædəmi] *n* academia *f* (a specialized institute); *military, naval academy* academia militar, naval ‖ instituto *m* de enseñanza media (in Scotland) ‖ US internado *m* ‖ conservatorio *m* (of music).

acaleph [,ækə'li:f] *n* ZOOL acalefo *m.*
— OBSERV El plural de *acaleph* es *acalepha.*

acanthopterygii [,ækænθɔptə'ridʒi] *pl n* ZOOL acantopterigios *m.*

acanthus [ə'kænθəs] *n* ARCH & BOT acanto *m.*
— OBSERV El plural de la palabra inglesa *acanthus* es *acanthuses* o *acanthi.*

acaridae [ə'kæridi:] *pl n* ZOOL acáridos *m.*

acarus ['ækərəs] *n* ZOOL ácaro.
— OBSERV El plural de *acarus* es *acari.*

acaulescent ['ækɔ:'lesənt]; **acauline** ['ækɔ:lain] *adj* BOT acaule.

accede [æk'si:d] *vi* acceder a (to agree) ‖ subir a (to the throne) ‖ tomar posesión de (to a post) ‖ afiliarse a (to affiliate) ‖ adherirse a (to a treaty).

accelerant [æk'selərənt] *n* CHEM acelerador *m*, acelerante *m.*

accelerate [æk'seləreit] *vt/vi* acelerar.

accelerating [-iŋ] *adj* acelerador, ra ‖ *accelerating force* fuerza aceleratriz.

acceleration [æk,selə'reiʃən] *n* aceleración *f* ‖ *acceleration of* o *due to gravity* aceleración terrestre.

accelerative [æk'selərətiv] *adj* acelerador, ra.

accelerator [ək'seləreitə*] *n* acelerador *m.*

accent ['æksent] *n* acento *m*; *written accent* acento gráfico ‖ — *in broken accents* con voz entrecortada ‖ *to put the accent on* acentuar, subrayar, hacer hincapié en, recalcar.

accent [æk'sent] *vt* acentuar.

accentuate [æk'sentjueit] *vt* acentuar.

accentuation [æk,sentju'eiʃən] *n* acentuación *f* (stress).

accept [ək'sept] *vt* aceptar; *to accept an invitation, a bill of exchange* aceptar una invitación, una letra de cambio ‖ admitir (to admit).

acceptability [ək,septə'biliti] *n* aceptabilidad *f.*

acceptable [ək'septəbl] *adj* aceptable ‖ adecuado, da; oportuno, na (appropriate) ‖ admisible.

acceptance [ək'septəns] *n* aceptación *f* ‖ aprobación *f* (approval).

acceptation [,æksep'teiʃən] *n* acepción *f* (of a word) ‖ aceptación *f* (of an invitation, a bill, etc.).

accepted [ək'septid] *adj* aceptado, da ‖ corriente, normal (widely used) ‖ reconocido, da (s.o. with a quality).

acceptor [ək'septə*] *n* aceptador, ra; aceptante *m* & *f*

access ['ækses] *n* acceso *m* ‖ MED ataque *m*, acceso *m* ‖ — INFORM *access time* tiempo *m* de acceso ‖ *easy of access* de fácil acceso (place), muy abordable (person) ‖ *to give access to* dar entrada a.

accessibility [æk,sesi'biliti] *n* accesibilidad *f.*

accessible [æk'sesəbl] *adj* accesible, asequible (place) ‖ abordable (person) ‖ comprensible (understandable) ‖ *accessible to pity* capaz de compasión.

accession [æk'seʃən] *n* acceso *m*, entrada *f* ‖ aumento *m* (increase) ‖ accesión *f* (to power) ‖ subida *f*, accesión *f* (of a king) ‖ entrada *f* en posesión (to a post) ‖ adhesión *f* (to a party, a treaty) ‖ asentimiento *m*, accesión *f* (assent).

accessit [æk'sesit] *n* accésit *m.*

accessory [æk'sesəri] *adj* accesorio, ria.
◆ *n* accesorio *m* (sth. additional, equipment) ‖ JUR cómplice *m* & *f* (accomplice) ‖ *toilet accesories* artículos *m pl* de tocador.

accessory after the fact [-ɑ:ftə*-ðə-fækt] *n* JUR encubridor, ra; cómplice *m* & *f.*

accessory before the fact [-bi'fɔ:*-ðə-fækt] *n* JUR cómplice *m* & *f* [por instigación], instigador, ra.

accidence ['æksidəns] *n* GRAMM accidente *m.*

accident ['æksidənt] *n* accidente *m* (mishap, catastrophe); *accident insurance* seguro contra accidentes; *accident to a third party* accidente contra terceros; *motoring, traffic, road accident* accidente de coche, de circulación, de carretera; *aircraft accident* accidente de aviación; *to meet with an accident* sufrir un accidente ‖ casualidad *f*; *we met by accident* nos encontramos por casualidad ‖ GEOL, PHIL & REL accidente *m* ‖ *industrial accident* accidente de trabajo.

accidental [,æksi'dentl] *adj* accidental, fortuito, ta ‖ accidental (not essential).
◆ *n* MUS accidente *m*, accidental *m.*

acclaim [ə'kleim] *n* aclamación *f* (enthusiastic praise) ‖ ovación *f* (loud applause).

acclaim [ə'kleim] *vt* aclamar; *to acclaim a minister* aclamar a un ministro; *they acclaimed him leader* le aclamaron jefe ‖ ovacionar (to applaud).

acclamation [,æklə'meiʃən] *n* aclamación *f.*

acclimate [ə'klaimət] *vt* US aclimatar.

acclimation [,æklai'meiʃən] *n* US aclimatación *f.*

acclimatization [ə,klaimətai'zeiʃən] *n* aclimatación *f.*

acclimatize [ə'klaimətaiz] *vt* aclimatar.
◆ *vi* aclimatarse.

acclivity [ə'kliviti] *n* cuesta *f*, subida *f*, pendiente *f.*

accolade ['ækəleid] *n* acolada *f*, espaldarazo *m* (investment of knighthood) ‖ panegírico *m* (recognition of merit) ‖ MUS corchete *m.*

accommodate [ə'kɔmədeit] *vt* acomodar, adaptar (to adjust to circumstances) ‖ alojar, hospedar (to lodge) ‖ resolver (a dispute) ‖ reconciliar (to reconcile) ‖ caber, haber sitio para; *the car accommodates three people* en el coche caben tres personas ‖ proveer, suministrar (to supply) ‖ complacer (to do a favour) ‖ ANAT & PHYS acomodar.
◆ *vi* acomodarse.

accommodating [-iŋ] *adj* acomodadizo, za ‖ servicial (obliging) ‖ complaciente (husband).

accommodation [ə,kɔmə'deiʃən] *n* alojamiento *m* (lodging) ‖ habitación *f* (room) ‖ cabida *f*, capacidad *f* (capacity) ‖ sitio *m*, espacio *m* (space) ‖ préstamo *m* (loan of money) ‖ reconciliación *f* (reconciliation) ‖ adaptación *f* ‖ acuerdo *m*, convenio *m*, arreglo *m* (agreement) ‖ ANAT & PHYS acomodación *f* ‖ comodidad *f* (commodity) ‖ favor *m* (favour) ‖ ayuda *f* (help) ‖ *to book accommodation at the hotel* reservar habitación en el hotel.

accommodation ladder [-'lædə*] *n* MAR escala *f* real.

accompaniment [ə'kʌpənimənt] *n* acompañamiento *m.*

accompanist [ə'kʌmpənist] *n* MUS acompañante *m* & *f.*

accompany [ə'kʌmpəni] *vt* acompañar (*with, by* de).
◆ *vi* MUS acompañar (*on* con).

accomplice [ə'kɔmplis] *n* cómplice *m* & *f.*

accomplish [ə'kɔmpliʃ] *vt* realizar, ejecutar, llevar a cabo (to carry out) ‖ alcanzar, llegar a, lograr (an end) ‖ terminar, acabar (to complete) ‖ recorrer (a distance) ‖ cumplir (a forecast).

accomplished [-t] *adj* realizado, da; ejecutado, da ‖ consumado, da (fact, dancer, etc.) ‖ competente, experto, ta (skilled).

accomplishment [-mənt] *n* talento *m* (talent) ‖ realización *f*, ejecución *f* ‖ logro *m* (achievement) ‖ cumplimiento *m* (completion).

accord [ə'kɔ:d] *n* acuerdo *m* (agreement); *in accord with* de acuerdo con ‖ armonía *f* (harmony) ‖ — *of one's own accord* de motu propio, espontáneamente ‖ *out of accord with* en desacuerdo con ‖ *with one accord* de común acuerdo.

accord [ə'kɔ:d] *vt* conceder, otorgar.
◆ *vi* concordar.

accordance [-əns] *n* conformidad *f* ‖ *in accordance with* de acuerdo con, según, conforme a, con arreglo a, de conformidad con.

accordant [-ənt] *adj* conforme.

according [-iŋ] *adv* *according as* según, a medida que ‖ *according to* según.

accordingly [-iŋli] *adv* por consiguiente (therefore) ‖ en consecuencia, como corresponde (correspondingly).

accordion [ə'kɔ:djən] *n* MUS acordeón *m* ‖ *accordion pleating* plisado *m* de acordeón.

accordionist [-ist] *n* MUS acordeonista *m* & *f.*

accost [ə'kɔst] *vt* abordar, dirigirse a ‖ abordar (prostitute).

account [ə'kaunt] *n* cuenta *f*; *bank account* cuenta en el banco ‖ cuenta *f* (bill) ‖ estado *m* de cuenta (statement) ‖ informe *m*, relación *f* (report) ‖ importancia *f* (importance) ‖ — *by all accounts* al decir de todos ‖ *current account* cuenta corriente ‖ *deposit account* cuenta a plazo fijo ‖ *joint account* cuenta indistinta ‖ *of no account* de ninguna manera, bajo ningún concepto (not at all), de poca importancia ‖ *on account* a cuenta ‖ *on account of* a causa de, por motivo de ‖ *on account of s.o.* por alguien ‖ *on every account* en todos los aspectos ‖ *on his own account* por su cuenta ‖ *on many accounts* por muchos motivos ‖ *on no account* bajo ningún concepto ‖ *on one's own account* por su propia cuenta ‖ *to bring to account* pedir cuentas a ‖ *to buy on account* comprar a plazos *or* a crédito ‖ *to call to account* pedir cuentas a ‖ *to give a good account of o.s.* causar buena impresión ‖ *to keep the accounts* llevar las cuentas ‖ *to leave out of account* no tener en cuenta ‖ *to make little account of* hacer caso omiso de, tener poco en cuenta ‖ *to pay into the account of* abonar en cuenta de ‖ FIG *to settle accounts with s.o.* ajustar las cuentas a uno ‖ *to settle an account* liquidar una cuenta ‖ *to square accounts* ajustar cuentas ‖ *to take into account, to take account of* tener en cuenta ‖ *to turn to account* sacar provecho de.

account [ə'kaunt] *vt* considerar; *I account him handsome* lo considero guapo ‖ *to account for* dar cuenta de, justificar (to justify), explicar (to explain), responder de (to answer for), acabar con, liquidar (to kill).

accountability [əkauntə'biliti] *n* responsabilidad *f.*

accountable [ə'kauntəbl] *adj* responsable (*for* de; *to* ante) ‖ explicable.

accountancy [ə'kauntənsi] *n* contabilidad *f.*

accountant [ə'kauntənt] *n* contable *m* & *f* ‖ *accountant's office* contaduría *f.*

accounting [ə'kauntiŋ] *n* contabilidad *f.*

accoutre; US accouter [ə'ku:tə*] *vt* equipar.

accoutrement; US accouterment [ə'ku:təmənt] *n* equipo *m.*

accredit [ə'kredit] *vt* acreditar (diplomatically) ‖ reconocer (to recognize) ‖ atribuir (to attribute).

accretion [æ'kri:ʃən] *n* unión *f* (joining together) ‖ crecimiento *m* (organic growth) ‖ GEOL acreción *f* ‖ JUR acrecencia *f*, acrecimiento *m.*

accrue [ə'kru:] *vi* derivarse, proceder (to derive) ‖ acumularse (to accumulate) ‖ *to accrue to* corresponder a.

accrued interest [-'intrist] *n* interés *m* acumulado *or* devengado.

accumulate [ə'kju:mjuleit] *vt* acumular; *to accumulate riches* acumular riquezas; *to accumulate interest on the capital* acumular intereses al capital.

◆ *vi* acumularse.

accumulation [əˌkju:mju'leiʃən] *n* acumulación *f.*

accumulative [ə'kju:mjulətiv] *adj* acumulativo, va.

accumulator [ə'kju:mjuleitə*] *n* acumulador, ra ‖ ELECTR & INFORM acumulador *m.*

accuracy ['ækjurəsi] *n* precisión *f*, exactitud *f.*

accurate ['ækjurit] *adj* preciso, sa; exacto, ta ‖ fiel (memory, translation) ‖ certero, ra (shot) ‖ exacto, ta (answer) ‖ de precisión (instrument).

accursed [ə'kə:sid]; **accurst** [ə'kə:st] *adj* condenado, da; maldito, ta ‖ odioso, sa (odious).

accusal [ə'kju:zəl] *n* acusación *f.*

accusation [ækju'zeiʃən] *n* acusación *f* ‖ *to bring an accusation against* formular una acusación contra.

accusative [ə'kju:zətiv] *adj* GRAMM acusativo, va.

◆ *n* GRAMM acusativo *m.*

accusatorial [əˌkju:zə'tɔriəl]; **accusatory** [ə'kju:zətəri] *adj* acusatorio, ria.

accuse [ə'kju:z] *vt* acusar; *to accuse of robbery* acusar de robo; *to accuse s.o. of doing sth.* acusar a alguien de hacer algo.

accused [-d] *adj/n* acusado, da.

accuser [-ə*] *n* acusador, ra.

accustom [ə'kʌstəm] *vt* acostumbrar ‖ *to accustom o.s. to, to become accustomed to* acostumbrarse a.

accustomed [-d] *adj* acostumbrado, da.

ace [eis] *n* as *m* (in dice, cards, etc.) ‖ un poco *m*; *an ace lower* un poco más bajo ‖ «ace» *m* (golf, tennis) ‖ — FIG *as black as the ace of spades* negro como el carbón | *he is an ace* es un as | *to have an ace up one's sleeve* tener un triunfo en la mano | *within an ace of* a dos dedos de.

acephalous [ə'sefələs] *adj* acéfalo, la.

acerb [ə'sə:b] *adj* acerbo, ba.

acerbic [ə'sə:bik] *adj* acerbo, ba.

acerbity [ə'sə:biti] *n* acerbidad *f*, acritud *f.*

acetate ['æsitit] *adj* CHEM acetato *m.*

acetic [ə'si:tik] *adj* CHEM acético, ca.

acetify [ə'setifai] *vt* acetificar.

acetone ['æsitəun] *n* CHEM acetona *f.*

acetyl ['æsitil] *n* CHEM acetilo *m.*

acetylene [ə'setili:n] *n* CHEM acetileno *m* ‖ *acetylene torch* soplete oxiacetilénico.

Achaean [ə'kiən] *adj/n* aqueo, a.

ache [eik] *n* dolor *m* ‖ *aches and pains* achaques *m.*

ache [eik] *vi* doler (to hurt); *my head aches* me duele la cabeza ‖ *to ache for, to be aching to* anhelar, ansiar.

achene [ə'ki:n] *n* BOT aquenio *m.*

achievable [ə'tʃi:vəbl] *adj* realizable, factible, hacedero, ra.

achieve [ə'tʃi:v] *vt* llevar a cabo, ejecutar, realizar (to carry out) ‖ conseguir, lograr (to manage to get) ‖ alcanzar (an aim, a level).

◆ *vi* US alcanzar su objetivo.

achievement [-mənt] *n* realización *f*, ejecución *f* (carrying out) ‖ consecución *f* (of an aim) ‖ éxito *m*, logro *m* (thing achieved) ‖ hazaña *f* (feat) ‖ HERALD escudo *m.*

Achilles [ə'kili:z] *pr n* Aquiles ‖ — *Achilles heel* talón *m* de Aquiles ‖ *Achilles tendon* tendón *m* de Aquiles.

aching ['eikiŋ] *adj* dolorido, da ‖ FIG compungido, da (heart) ‖ FAM *aching all over* molido.

◆ *n* dolor *m.*

achromatic [ækrəu'mætik] *adj* acromático, ca.

acid ['æsid] *adj* ácido, da (taste, smell, etc.) ‖ FIG mordaz, agrio, gria; áspero, ra; *an acid remark* una observación áspera.

◆ *n* CHEM ácido *m* ‖ FAM LSD *m*, alucinógeno *m.*

acidic [ə'sidik] *adj* CHEM ácido, da ‖ FIG ácido, da; agrio, gria (taste, etc.).

acidification [əˌsidifi'keiʃən] *n* acidificación *f.*

acidify [ə'sidifai] *vt* acidificar.

◆ *vi* acidificarse.

acidity [ə'siditi] *n* acidez *f.*

acidosis [æsi'dəusis] *n* MED acidosis *f.*

acid-proof ['æsid-pru:f]; **acid-resisting** ['æsid-ri'zistiŋ] *adj* a prueba de ácidos.

acid rain ['æsid rein] *n* lluvia *f* ácida.

acid test ['æsid-test] *n* CHEM prueba *f* del ácido ‖ FIG prueba *f* decisiva.

acidulate [ə'sidjuleit] *vt* acidular.

acidulous [ə'sidjuləs] *adj* acídulo, la; acidulado, da.

acinus ['æsinəs] *n* BOT & ANAT ácino *m.*
— OBSERV El plural de *acinus* es *acini.*

ack-ack ['æk'æk] *n* defensa *f* antiaérea *or* contra aviones.

acknowledge [ək'nɔlidʒ] *vt* admitir, reconocer (to admit sth. as true) ‖ reconocer (to recognize officially) ‖ acusar recibo de (a letter) ‖ saludar (to greet) ‖ confesar (to avow) ‖ agradecer, estar agradecido por (a favour) ‖ *to acknowledge o.s. beaten* darse por vencido.

acknowledgement; acknowledgment [-mənt] *n* admisión *f* (admission) ‖ reconocimiento *m* (recognition) ‖ acuse *m* de recibo (of receipt) ‖ agradecimiento *m*, reconocimiento *m* (gratefulness) ‖ confesión *f* (of a misdeed) ‖ contestación *f* (of a greeting) ‖ recompensa *f* (reward) ‖ *in acknowledgement of* en reconocimiento de.

acme ['ækmi] *n* cumbre *f*, cima *f*, apogeo *m*; *the acme of glory* el apogeo de la gloria.

acne ['ækni] *n* MED acné *m.*

acolyte ['ækəulait] *n* REL acólito *m.*

aconite ['ækənait] *n* BOT acónito *m.*

aconitine [ə'kɔniti:n] *n* CHEM aconitina *f.*

acorn ['eikɔ:n] *n* BOT bellota *f.*

acotyledon [æˌkɔti'li:dən] *n* acotiledónea *f* (plant without cotyledons).

acoustic [ə'ku:stik] *adj* acústico, ca.

acoustics [-s] *pl n* acústica *f sing.*

acquaint [ə'kweint] *vt* informar, poner al corriente (*with* de) ‖ — *to acquaint o.s. with* informarse sobre (to get information), familiarizarse con (to familiarize o.s.) ‖ *to be acquainted with* conocer (s.o.), estar al corriente *or* al tanto de, conocer (sth.) ‖ *to be acquainted with the fact that...* saber que... ‖ *to become acquainted with* conocer a (s.o.), ponerse al corriente de (a fact), aprender (to learn) ‖ *they have long been acquainted* se conocen desde hace mucho tiempo.

acquaintance [-əns] *n* conocido, da (person) ‖ conocimiento *m* (knowledge); *further acquaintance* mayor conocimiento ‖ relaciones *f pl*, amistades *f pl*; *a wide acquaintance* muchas relaciones ‖ — *to improve upon acquaintance* ganar con el trato ‖ *to make acquaintance with* conocer a ‖ *to make s.o.'s acquaintance* conocer a uno.

acquaintanceship [ə'kweintənsʃip] *n* conocimiento *m* ‖ relaciones *f pl.*

acquiesce [ækwi'es] *vi* consentir (*in* en), asentir (*in* a) (to assent) ‖ conformarse (*in* con), aceptar (to conform to).

aquiescence [-ns] *n* aquiescencia *f*, asentimiento *m*, conformidad *f* (agreement) ‖ consentimiento *m* (consent).

aquiescent [-nt] *adj* condescendiente, conforme.

acquire [ə'kwaiə*] *vt* conseguir (to manage to get) ‖ adquirir (to get) ‖ contraer, tomar (a habit) ‖ aprender (a language) ‖ — *to acquire a taste for* tomar gusto a ‖ *to be an acquired taste* ser un gusto *or* una afición que se adquiere con el tiempo.

acquirement [-mənt] *n* adquisición *f.*

◆ *pl* conocimientos *m* (knowledge).

acquiring [-riŋ] *adj* adquisidor, ra; adquiridor, ra.

acquisition [ˌækwi'ziʃən] *n* adquisición *f*.

acquisitive [ə'kwizitiv] *adj* codicioso, sa.

acquit [ə'kwit] *vt* JUR absolver (an accused) || liquidar, pagar, satisfacer (a debt) || cumplir (a promise) || liberar (of an obligation) || *to acquit o.s.* defenderse; *he acquitted himself well in the exam* se defendió bien en el examen.

acquittal [-əl] *n* JUR absolución *f* || cumplimiento *m* (of a duty) || pago *m*, satisfacción *f* (of a debt).

acquittance [-əns] *n* liquidación *f*, pago *m* (of a debt) || comprobante *m*, recibo *m* (receipt).

acre ['eikə*] *n* acre *m* [medida de aproximadamente 4 000 metros cuadrados].

acreage ['eikəridʒ] *n* superficie *f* en acres.

acrid ['ækrid] *adj* acre (smell, taste) || FIG cáustico, ca.

acridity [æ'kriditi] *n* acritud *f* || FIG causticidad *f*.

acrimonious [ˌækri'məunjəs] *adj* cáustico, ca; mordaz.

acrimony ['ækriməni] *n* acrimonia *f*, acritud *f*.

acrobat ['ækrəbæt] *n* acróbata *m* & *f*.

acrobatic [ˌækrə'bætik] *adj* acrobático, ca.

acrobatics [-s] *n* acrobacia *f*.

acrocephalic [ˌækrəse'fælik]; **acrocephalous** [ˌækrə'sefələs] *adj* acrocéfalo, la.

acromegalia [ˌækrəmə'geiljə]; **acromegaly** [ˌækrə'megəli] *n* MED acromegalia *f*.

acronym ['ækrənim] *n* siglas *f pl*.

Acropolis [ə'krɔpəlis] *n* Acrópolis *f inv*.

across [ə'krɔs] *adv* a través || — *to be two feet across* tener dos pies de ancho || *to go across* atravesar, cruzar || *to swim across* cruzar a nado.
◆ *prep* del otro lado de (on the other side); *the house across the road* la casa del otro lado de la calle || a través de (from one side to the other); *across the fields* a través de los campos.
— OBSERV El adverbio *across* no se suele traducir literalmente en español; en efecto la mayoría de las veces se expresa por un verbo que contiene la idea implicada por el adverbio.
— OBSERV Hay casos en los cuales *across*, preposición, no se traduce literalmente, incluyéndose en el verbo: *to walk across the street* cruzar la calle.

across-the-board [-ðəbɔːd] *adj* ECON general, lineal, por categorías; *an across-the-board reduction* una reducción general; *an across-the-board pay rise* un aumento lineal de salarios.

acrostic [ə'krɔstik] *adj* POET acróstico, ca.
◆ *n* acróstico *m*.

acroter ['ækrətə*] *n* ARCH acrotera *f*, acrótera *f*.

acrylic [ə'krilik] *adj* acrílico, ca.

act [ækt] *n* acto *m* (deed, part of a play, etc.) || acción *f*; *act of justice, of war* acción de justicia, de guerra || número *m* (artist's routine) || JUR acta *f* || ley *f*, decreto *m* (of Parliament) || acto *m* (of faith) || — *act of bankruptcy* declaración *f* de quiebra || *act of God* caso *m* de fuerza mayor || JUR *act on petition* recurso *m* de urgencia || *caught in the act* cogido in fraganti *or* con las manos en la masa *or* en el acto || *in the act of* en el momento de || *they were in the act of stealing* estaban robando || FIG *to get in on the act* sacar tajada, subirse al carro || *to get one's act together* organizarse || *to put on an act* simular.
◆ *pl* hechos *m* (of the Apostles).

act [ækt] *vt* desempeñar el papel de (to play the part of) || desempeñar (a part) || representar (a play) || hacer (to act like); *don't act the fool* no hagas el tonto.
◆ *vi* actuar, obrar (to do a thing) || comportarse, actuar (to behave) || obrar, tomar medidas (to take steps) || actuar (to fulfil a function); *to act as referee* actuar de árbitro || actuar (to intervene, to have an effect); *the police acted quickly* la policía actuó pronto; *acid acts on metal* el ácido actúa sobre el metal || actuar (to perform) || fingirse (to pretend); *to act dead* fingirse muerto || TECH funcionar || — *to act as* hacer de, actuar de || *to act for* obrar en representación de || *to act on* guiarse por || *to act on* o *upon* actuar sobre.
◆ *phr v* ***to act out*** exteriorizar (feelings), representar (an event) || FAM ***to act up*** fallar (machine).

acting [-iŋ] *adj* interino, na (provisional) || en funciones, en ejercicio (in office).
◆ *n* interpretación *f*, actuación *f* (performance) || profesión *f* de actor || acción *f* (act).

actinia [æk'tiniə] *n* ZOOL actinia *f* (sea anemone).
— OBSERV El plural de la palabra inglesa es *actinias* o *actiniae*.

actinium [æk'tiniəm] *n* CHEM actinio *m*.

action ['ækʃən] *n* acción *f* (deed, act) || movimiento *m* (movement); *to put in action* poner en movimiento || argumento *m*, acción *f*, intriga *f* (plot of a story or play) || MIL acción *f* (combat) || acto *m* de servicio; *he died in action* murió en acto de servicio || medida *f*; *disciplinary action* medida de disciplina || TECH mecanismo *m* || funcionamiento *m* || JUR acción *f*, demanda *f*; *to bring an action* presentar una demanda || proceso *m* || — *action!* ¡acción! (cinematography) || *actions speak louder than words* obras son amores, que no buenas razones || *a man of action* un hombre de acción || *field of action* esfera *f* de acción || *reflex action* acto reflejo || *to be out of action* estar estropeado *or* averiado (sth.), estar imposibilitado (s.o.) || *to put into action* poner en práctica (a plan) || *to put out of action* estropear, volver inutilizable (sth.) || *to suit the action to the word* unir la acción a la palabra || *to take action* tomar medidas (to intervene), intentar una acción judicial (in justice).

actionable ['ækʃnəbl] *adj* procesable.

action replay [ˌækʃən'riːplei] *n* repetición *f* de la jugada, replay *m*.

activate ['æktiveit] *vt* activar || INFORM activar || *activated carbon, sludge* carbón, lodo activado.

activation [ˌækti'veiʃən] *n* activación *f*.

activator ['æktiveitə*] *n* CHEM activador *m*.

active ['æktiv] *adj* activo, va || vigente (a law) || vivo, va (interest) || — *active volcano* volcán en actividad || *on active service* en servicio activo.

active list [-list] *n* MIL escala *f* activa.

activism ['æktivizəm] *n* activismo *m*.

activist ['æktivist] *adj/n* activista *m* & *f*.

activity [æk'tiviti] *n* actividad *f*; *field of activity* esfera de actividad; *activity of a volcano, of an acid* actividad de un volcán, de un ácido.

actor ['æktə*] *n* actor *m* || JUR demandante *m* & *f* || *leading actor* primer actor.

actress ['æktris] *n* actriz *f* || *leading actress* primera actriz.

actual ['æktjuəl] *adj* verdadero, ra; real (true) || concreto, ta (case) || mismo, ma; *I'd like to have the actual figures* me gustaría tener las cifras mismas || actual (present) || *in actual fact* en realidad.

actuality [ˌæktju'æliti] *n* realidad *f*.
— OBSERV *Actuality* no significa nunca *actualidad*.

actualization [ˌæktjuəlai'zeiʃən] *n* realización *f* || PHIL actualización *f*.

actualize ['æktjuəlaiz] *vt* realizar || actualizar, describir con realismo || PHIL actualizar.

actually ['æktjuəli] *adv* en realidad, realmente, verdaderamente (really) || en realidad (as a matter of fact) || incluso (even) || actualmente (at present).
— OBSERV *Actually* no se emplea mucho con el sentido de *actualmente*.

actuarial [ˌæktju'ɛərjəl]; **actuarian** [ˌæktju'ɛərjən] *adj* actuarial.

actuary ['æktjuəri] *n* actuario *m*.

actuate ['æktjueit] *vt* accionar, hacer funcionar, poner en movimiento (an engine) || mover, impulsar (to motivate); *actuated by anger, he killed his friend* movido por la rabia, mató a su amigo.

acuity [ə'kjuːiti] *n* agudeza *f*, acuidad *f*.

acumen [a'kjuːmen] *n* perspicacia *f*.

acupuncture ['ækjuˌpʌŋktʃə*] *n* acupuntura *f*.

acute [ə'kjuːt] *adj* agudo, da (sharp) || MATH, MED & GRAMM agudo, da || FIG agudo, da; perspicaz (shrewd) || grave (crucial, critical).

acute-angled [-'æŋgld] *adj* acutángulo, la.

acutely [ə'kjuːtli] *adv* extremadamente (extremely) || con perspicacia (shrewdly).

acuteness [ə'kjuːtnis] *n* agudeza *f*, perspicacia *f* || MED carácter *m* agudo || agudeza *f* (of ear).

acyclic [ə'saiklik] *adj* acíclico, ca.

ad [æd] *n* US FAM anuncio *m*.

adage ['ædidʒ] *n* adagio *m*, refrán *m*.

adagio [ə'dɑːdʒiəu] *adj/adv* MUS adagio.
◆ *n* adagio *m*.

Adam ['ædəm] *pr n* Adán *m*; *Adam and Eve* Adán y Eva || — *I do not know him from Adam* no le conozco ni por asomo || FAM *Adam's ale* agua *f* || *Adam's apple* nuez *f*.

adamant ['ædəmənt] *n* diamante *m* (diamond).
◆ *adj* inexorable, inflexible (unyielding).

adamantine [ˌædə'mæntain] *adj* adamantino, na.

adapt [ə'dæpt] *vt* adaptar; *to adapt a novel for the theatre* adaptar una novela al teatro || *to adapt o.s. to sth.* adaptarse a algo.

adaptability [əˌdæptə'biliti] *n* adaptabilidad *f*, facultad *f* de adaptación.

adaptable [ə'dæptəbl] *adj* adaptable.

adaptation [ˌædæp'teiʃən] *n* adaptación *f*; *the adaptation of a novel for the theatre* la adaptación de una novela al teatro.

adapter; adaptor [ə'dæptə*] *n* ELECTR enchufe *m* múltiple (plug) || adaptador *m* (for connecting) || adaptador, ra (person).

add [æd] *vt* añadir || — *to add in* incluir || *to add insult to injury* empeorar las cosas || *to add on* añadir || *to add together* sumar || *to add up* sumar.
◆ *vi* sumar || — *to add to* aumentar || *to add up* sumar (to do addition), tener sentido; *his explanation does not add up* su explicación no tiene sentido || *to add up to* alcanzar (to reach), significar (to mean).

addend ['ædend] *n* MATH sumando *m*.

addendum [ə'dendəm] *n* apéndice *m*, addenda *m*.
— OBSERV El plural de *addendum* es *addenda*.

adder ['ædə*] *n* ZOOL víbora *f* (viper) || INFORM sumador *m* || US culebra *f* (non-poisonous snake).

addict ['ædikt] *n* adicto, ta (s.o. addicted to sth. harmful) || entusiasta, fanático, ca (fanatic) || *drug addict* toxicómano, na; drogadicto, ta.

addicted [ə'diktid] *adj* adicto, ta (*to* a) (drugs, drink, etc.) || fanático, ca (fanatic).

addiction [ə'dikʃən] *n* vicio *m* (habitual inclination) || afición *f* (liking).

addictive [ə'diktiv] *adj* adictivo, va.

adding machine ['ædiŋməʃi:n] *n* máquina *f* calculadora.

Addis Ababa [,ædis 'æbəbə] *pr n* GEOGR Addis Abeba.

addition [ə'diʃən] *n* adición *f* (action) || añadido *m*, adición *f*, añadidura *f* (sth. added) || MATH suma *f* || *in addition to* además de.

additional [-l] *adj* adicional || suplementario, ria.

additionally [ə'diʃnəli] *adv* además (furthermore) || más aún (still more).

additives ['æditivz] *pl n* aditivos *m*.

addle ['ædl] *adj* podrido, da (rotten) || huero, ra (sterile).

addle ['ædl] *vt* pudrir.
◆ *vi* pudrirse.

addled [-d] *adj* podrido (egg).

address [ə'dres] *n* dirección *f*, señas *f pl* (place of abode); *home adress* dirección privada || súplica *f*, petición *f* (request) || habilidad *f*, destreza *f* (skill) || discurso *m*, alocución *f* (speech) || tratamiento *m*, título *m* (title) || INFORM dirección *f*; *address space* espacio de dirección || (ant) modales *m pl* (manners) || *to pay one's adresses to* cortejar.

address [ə'dres] *vt* hablar a (to speak to) || dirigirse a; *to address the king* dirigirse al rey || dirigir (letter, remarks) || poner la dirección en (on a letter, parcel, etc.) || tomar la palabra; *to address the House* tomar la palabra en el Parlamento || INFORM direccionar || — *to address o.s. to a job* ponerse a trabajar || *to adress s.o. as* dar a uno el tratamiento de || *to be adressed to* estar dirigido a.

addressee [ædre'si:] *n* destinatario, ria.

addressing [iŋ] *n* INFORM direccionamiento *m*.

adduce [ə'dju:s] *vt* citar (to quote) || aducir, alegar (to evoke) || dar (a proof).

adducent [-nt] *adj* ANAT aductor.

adduct [ə'dʌkt] *vt* MED efectuar la aducción.

adduction [ə'dʌkʃən] *n* MED aducción *f* || JUR alegato *m*.

adductor [ə'dʌktə*] *n* ANAT aductor *m*.

adenoid ['ædinɔid] *adj* adenoideo, a.

adenoids ['ædinɔidz] *pl n* adenoides *m*.

adept ['ædept] *adj/n* experto, ta (*at* en) || adepto, ta (of a sect).

adequacy ['ædikwəsi] *n* adecuación *f* (suitability) || suficiencia *f* || exactitud *f* (of an idea).

adequate ['ædikwit] *adj* adecuado, da; suficiente.

adhere [əd'hiə*] *vi* adherirse (*to* a).

adherence [əd'hiərəns] *n* adherencia *f* || adhesión *f* (to a cause, party).

adherent [əd'hiərənt] *adj* adhesivo, va (sticky).
◆ *n* adepto, ta; adherente *m* & *f*, partidario, ria.

adhesion [əd'hi:ʒən] *n* adhesión *f*.

adhesive [əd'hi:siv] *adj* adhesivo, va.
◆ *n* adhesivo *m*.

adhesive tape [-teip] *n* MED esparadrapo *m* cinta *f* adhesiva.

ad hoc [,æd'hɔk] *adj/adv* *ad hoc* a propósito.

adiabatic [,ædiə'bætik] *adj* PHYS adiabático, ca.

adieu [ə'dju:] *interj* ¡adiós!
◆ *n* despedida *f*, adiós *m* || — *to bid adieu* decir adiós *to take adieu* despedirse.
— OBSERV El plural de *adieu* es *adieus* o *adieux*.

Adige ['ɑ:didʒe] *pr n* GEOGR Adigio *m*.

ad infinitum ['ædinfi'naitəm] *adv* sin fin (without end) || indefinidamente (indefinitely).

adipose ['ædipəus] *adj* adiposo, sa.

adiposity [,ædi'pɔsiti] *n* adiposidad *f*.

adjacency [ə'dʒeisənsi] *n* proximidad *f*.

adjacent [ə'dʒeisənt] *adj* adyacente.

adjectival [,ædʒek'taivəl] *adj* adjetival, adjetivo, va.

adjective ['ædʒiktiv] *n* GRAMM adjetivo *m*.

adjoin [ə'dʒɔin] *vt* estar contiguo a, lindar con (to be next to) || unir (to join) || añadir (to add).
◆ *vi* estar contiguo.

adjoining [-iŋ] *adj* contiguo, gua; limítrofe.

adjourn [ə'dʒə:n] *vt* suspender (to suspend) || aplazar (to postpone) || suspender, levantar (a meeting).
◆ *vi* suspenderse (a meeting) || suspender la sesión (the delegates) || *to adjourn to* pasar a.

adjournment [-mənt] *n* suspensión *f* (of a meeting) || aplazamiento *m* (postponement).

adjudge [ə'dʒʌdʒ] *vt* JUR juzgar, decidir (to decide) | declarar (to find) | adjudicar (to award) || otorgar, atribuir, conceder (a prize).

adjudicate [ə'dʒu:dikeit] *vt* juzgar (to judge); *to adjudicate on sth.* juzgar algo || declarar (to declare).
◆ *vi* actuar como juez || sentenciar (to sentence).

adjudication [ə,dʒu:di'keiʃən] *n* JUR sentencia *f*, fallo *m* (judge's decision).

adjunct ['ædʒʌŋkt] *adj* adjunto, ta.
◆ *n* adjunto *m*.

adjunction [æ'dʒʌŋkʃən] *n* adición *f*, añadidura *f*.

adjuration [,ædʒuə'reiʃən] *n* (ant) adjuración *f*.

adjure [ə'dʒuə*] *vt* (ant) adjurar.

adjust [ə'dʒʌst] *vt* ajustar (a mechanism, etc.) || adaptar (to adapt) || arreglar (to arrange) || resolver (a difference).

adjustable [-əbl] *adj* ajustable.

adjusted [-id] *adj* equilibrado, da; *to be well, badly adjusted* ser equilibrado, poco equilibrado (mentally, emotionally).

adjuster; *US* **adjustor** [-ə*] *n* ajustador *m*.

adjustment [-mənt] *n* ajuste *m* (action or means of adjusting) || adaptación *f* || arreglo *m*, solución *f*, liquidación *f* (settlement) || modificación *f*, cambio *m* (change) || arreglo *m* (arrangement) || MIL regulación *f* (of fire).

adjutancy ['ædʒutənsi] *n* MIL ayudantía *f*.

adjutant ['ædʒutənt] *n* MIL ayudante *m* || ZOOL marabú *m* || ayudante *m* (a helper).

adjuvant ['ædʒuvənt] *n* auxiliar *m* & *f*.

ad lib ['æd'lib] *n* improvisación *f*, morcilla *f* (fam).

ad-lib ['æd'lib] *vt/vi* improvisar.

ad-lib ['æd'lib] *adv* a discreción, a voluntad.

admin ['ædmin] *n* FAM administración *f*.

administer [əd'ministə*]; *US* **administrate** *vt* administrar; *to administer justice* administrar justicia; *to administer medical aid* administrar ayuda médica || aplicar; *to administer a punishment* aplicar un castigo || formular, hacer (questions, etc.) || *to administer an oath to* tomar juramento a.
◆ *vi* administrar || *to administer to* prestar ayuda a (to a person), atender a (to satisfy).

administration [əd,minis'treiʃən] *n* administración *f*; *public administration* administración pública || *US* gobierno *m*; *the wartime Administration* el gobierno de la época de la guerra || toma *f* (of an oath).

administrative [əd'ministrətiv] *adj* administrativo, va.

administrator [əd'ministreitə*] *n* administrador, ra.

admirable ['ædmərəbl] *adj* admirable.

admiral ['ædmərəl] *n* MIL almirante *m*.

admiral of the fleet [-əv-ðə-fli:t] *n* MIL capitán *m* de la Armada.

admiralty ['ædmərəlti] *n* MIL almirantazgo *m* (the office of admiral) || Ministerio *m* de Marina.

admiration [,ædmə'reiʃən] *n* admiración *f*.

admire [əd'maiə*] *vt* admirar.

admirer [-rə*] *n* admirador, ra || enamorado, da (suitor).

admiring [-riŋ] *adj* admirativo, va.

admissibility [əd,misə'biliti] *n* admisibilidad *f*.

admissible [əd'misəbl] *adj* admisible, aceptable.

admission [əd'miʃən] *n* admisión *f* (the action of admitting) || entrada *f*; *admission five francs* entrada cinco francos; *free admission* entrada gratuita || confesión *f*; *by his own admission* por confesión suya || reconocimiento *m* (acknowledgment) || *the management reserves the right to refuse admission* reservado el derecho de admisión.

admit [əd'mit] *vt* admitir; *to admit s.o. in a society* admitir a alguien en una sociedad; *this place admits five hundred people* este local admite quinientas personas || dejar entrar (to allow to enter) || aceptar, admitir (to accept) || reconocer, admitir (to recognize); *he admits (to) stealing the car* reconoce haber robado el coche || confesar (to confess) || — *ticket which admits two* entrada *f* para dos personas || *to be admitted to* ingresar en (an academy).
◆ *vi* *to admit of* admitir, dar lugar, permitir; *his actions admit of no other interpretation* sus actos no admiten otra interpretación.

admittance [-əns] *n* entrada *f* || ELECTR admitancia *f* || *no admittance* prohibida la entrada, se prohibe la entrada.

admittedly [-idli] *adv* cierto es que.

admix [əd'miks] *vt* mezclar.

admixture [-tʃə*] *n* ingrediente *m* (ingredient) || mezcla *f* (mixture) || dosis *f* (dose).

admonish [əd'mɔniʃ] *vt* amonestar, reprender (to reprove) || advertir (to warn) || exhortar (to exhort) || aconsejar (to advise).

admonishment [-mənt]; **admonition** [,ædməu'niʃən] *n* amonestación *f*, reprensión *f* (reproof) || advertencia *f*, consejo *m* (advice).

admonitory [əd'mɔnitəri] *adj* admonitorio, ria.

ad nauseam [æd 'nɔ:ziəm] *adv* interminablemente, hasta el hastío.

ado [ə'du:] *n* *much ado about nothing* mucho ruido y pocas nueces || *with much ado* con gran dificultad || *without further* o *more ado* sin más ni más.

adobe [ə'dəubi] *n* adobe *m* (a sun-dried brick) || casa *f* de adobe (building).

adolescence [,ædə'lesns] *n* adolescencia *f*.

adolescent [,ædə'lesnt] *adj/n* adolescente.

Adolph ['ædɔlf] *pr n* Adolfo *m*.

Adonis [ə'dəunis] *pr n* Adonis *m*.

adopt [ə'dɔpt] *vt* adoptar; *to adopt Western dress* adoptar la vestimenta occidental; *to adopt a child* adoptar a un niño || aceptar (to accept) || aprobar (the agenda, etc.) || *adopted child* hijo adoptivo.

adoption [ə'dɔpʃən] *n* adopción *f* (of a child, custom) || aprobación *f* (approval) || *country of adoption* patria adoptiva.

adoptive [ə'dɔptiv] *adj* adoptivo, va.

adorable [ə'dɔ:rəbl] *adj* adorable.

adoration [,ædɔ:'reiʃən] *n* adoración *f*.

adore [ə'dɔ:*] *vt* adorar (to worship).

adoring [-riŋ] *adj* lleno, na de adoración (look) || cariñoso, sa; que adora (person).

adorn [ə'dɔ:n] *vt* adornar.

adornment [-mənt] *n* adorno *m*.

adrenal [ə'dri:nl] *adj* suprarrenal.
◆ *m* glándula *f* suprarrenal.

adrenalin [ə'drenəlin] *n* adrenalina *f*.

Adrian ['eidriən] *pr n* Adrián *m*.

Adriatic Sea [,eidri'ætik'si:] *pr n* mar *m* Adriático.

adrift [ə'drift] *adj/adv* a la deriva || — FIG *to be all adrift* ir a la deriva, no saber por dónde se anda || *to break adrift* romper las amarras || FIG *to come adrift* desprenderse | *to turn s.o. adrift* abandonar a uno a su suerte.

adroit [ə'drɔit] *adj* diestro, tra; hábil.

adroitness [-nis] *n* destreza *f*, habilidad *f*, maña *f*.

adsorb [æd'zɔ:b] *vt* adsorber.

adsorbent [-ənt] *adj* adsorbente.
◆ *n* adsorbente *m*.

adsorption [-ʃən] *n* adsorción *f*.

adulate ['ædjuleit] *vt* adular.

adulation [,ædju'leiʃən] *n* adulación *f*.

adulatory ['ædjuleitəri] *adj* adulador, ra.

adult ['ædʌlt] *adj/n* adulto, ta (mature) || JUR mayor de edad.

adulterate [ə'dʌltərit] *adj* adulterado, da (adulterated) || adulterino, na (adulterine).

adulterate [ə'dʌltəreit] *vt* adulterar.

adulteration [ə,dʌltə'reiʃən] *n* adulteración *f*.

adulterer [ə'dʌltərə*] *n* adúltero *m*.

adulteress [ə'dʌltəris] *n* adúltera *f*.

adulterine [ə'dʌltərain] *adj* adulterino, na; espurio, ria.

adulterous [ə'dʌltərəs] *adj* adúltero, ra.

adultery [ə'dʌltəri] *n* adulterio *m*.

adumbrate ['ædʌmbreit] *vt* bosquejar (to give a shadowy account of) || presagiar (to foreshadow).

advance [əd'vɑ:ns] *n* adelanto *m*, progreso *m*; *the advance of civilization* el progreso de la civilización; *a technical advance* un adelanto técnico || anticipo *m*, adelanto *m* (payment before it is due) || subida *f*, aumento *m* (rise in price or value) || TECH avance *m* (car); *advance of the ignition, spark advance* avance al encendido || FIG paso; *to make the first advances to* dar los primeros pasos hacia || MIL avance *m* || — *advance booking office* despacho *m* de venta por adelantado || *in advance* con anticipación, con antelación; adelantado, da; por anticipado, de antemano || *the advance guard* la vanguardia || *to arrive in advance of* llegar antes que || *to be in advance of* adelantarse a || *to let s.o. know two days in advance* avisar a uno con dos días de anticipación || *to pay in advance* pagar por adelantado *or* con anticipación || *thanks in advance* gracias anticipadas.
◆ *pl* insinuaciones *f* [amorosas].

advance [əd'vɑ:ns] *vt* avanzar, adelantar (to move forward) || adelantar (watch, hour, date); *they advanced the wedding date* adelantaron la fecha de la boda || proponer; *to advance a theory* proponer una teoría || exponer, emitir (an opinion) || presentar, formular (a claim) || aumentar; *he advanced his price by fifty per cent* aumentó el precio en un cincuenta por ciento || adelantar, anticipar; *his employer advanced him a month's salary* el empresario le adelantó el salario de un mes || hacer progresar (sciences, etc.) || ayudar; *his election will advance our cause* su elección ayudará a nuestra causa || MIL ascender; *they advanced him to general* le ascendieron a general.
◆ *vi* avanzar, adelantarse (to go forward) || progresar (to progress) || avanzar (troops) || ascender (to go up in rank, status) || subir, aumentar (prices) || *to advance on* acercarse a *or* hacia.

advanced [-t] *adj* avanzado, da; *advanced ideas* ideas avanzadas; *advanced stage of pregnancy* estado avanzado de gestación || adelantado, da; anticipado, da (money) || adelantado, da; *he is very advanced for his age* está muy adelantado para su edad || adelantado, da (country) || superior (studies) || *advanced in years* entrado en años, de edad avanzada.

advancement [-mənt] *n* adelanto *m*, progreso *m*; *the advancement of science* el avance de la ciencia || ascenso *m* (promotion).

advantage [əd'vɑ:ntidʒ] *n* ventaja *f*; *he has the advantage of me* me saca ventaja || provecho *m*, beneficio *m*; *for whose advantage?* ¿en provecho de quién? || ventaja *f* (in tennis) || — *to be in s.o.'s advantage* ser ventajoso para uno || *to have the advantage* jugar con ventaja || *to have the advantage of numbers* aventajar en número || *to take advantage of s.o., of sth.* aprovecharse *or* sacar partido de alguien, de algo || *to turn sth. to advantage* sacar provecho de algo.

advantage [əd'vɑ:ntidʒ] *vt* ser ventajoso para, favorecer.

advantageous [,ædvən'teidʒəs] *adj* ventajoso, sa.

advent ['ædvənt] *n* advenimiento *m*, venida *f*.

Advent ['ædvənt] *n* REL Adviento *m*.

Adventist ['ædvəntist] *n* REL adventista *m*.

adventitious [,ædven'tiʃəs] *adj* adventicio, cia.

adventure [əd'ventʃə*] *n* aventura *f*.

adventure [əd'ventʃə*] *vt* aventurar.
◆ *vi* aventurarse.

adventure playground [-'pleigraund] *n* parque *m* infantil.

adventurer [-rə*] *n* aventurero *m*.

adventuresome [-səm] *adj* ⟶ **adventurous.**

adventuress [-ris] *n* aventurera *f*.

adventurous [-rəs]; **adventuresome** [-səm] *adj* aventurero, ra (people) || aventurado, da; arriesgado, da (thing).

adverb ['ædvə:b] *n* GRAMM adverbio *m*.

adverbial [əd'və:bjəl] *adj* GRAMM adverbial; *adverbial phrase* locución adverbial.

adversary ['ædvəsəri] *n* adversario, ria.

adversative [əd'və:sətiv] *adj* GRAMM adversativo, va.

adverse ['ædvə:s] *adj* adverso, sa; opuesto, ta (opposing) || contrario, ria (wind) || desfavorable, adverso, sa (unfavourable) || negativo, va (balance).

adversity [əd'və:siti] *n* adversidad *f*, infortunio *m*.

advert ['ædvə:t] *n* FAM anuncio *m*.

advert [æd'və:t] *vi* referirse, hacer alusión (*to* a).

advertise; *US* **advertize** ['ædvətaiz] *vt* anunciar.
◆ *vi* hacer publicidad *or* propaganda || poner un anuncio || *to advertise for* buscar por medio de anuncios.

advertisement [əd'və:tismənt]; *US* **advertizement** [,ædvə'taizmənt] *n* anuncio *m* || *classified advertisements* anuncios *m* por palabras.

advertiser; *US* **advertizer** ['ædvətaizə*] *n* anunciante *m* & *f*.

advertising; *US* **advertizing** ['ædvətaiziŋ] *n* publicidad *f*, propaganda *f*; *television advertising* la publicidad en televisión || *advertising campaing* campaña publicitaria || *advertising company* empresa de publicidad *or* anunciadora.

advice [əd'vais] *n* consejo *m*; *to seek advice* pedir consejo || asesoramiento *m*; *with the technical advice of* con el asesoramiento técnico de || COMM informe *m* (report) || — *a piece of advice* un consejo || *as per advice from* siguiendo el consejo de || *to take advice* consultar; *to take medical advice* consultar al médico; seguir un consejo; *I took his advice* seguí su consejo || *to take legal advice* consultar a un abogado.
◆ *pl* noticias *f*.

advice note [-nəut] *n* notificación *f*.

advisability [əd,vaizə'biliti] *n* conveniencia *f*, oportunidad *f*.

advisable [əd'vaizəbl] *adj* conveniente, aconsejable || juicioso, sa; prudente || — *if we think it advisable* si nos parece bien || *it would be advisable to say so* sería aconsejable *or* mejor decirlo.

advise [əd'vaiz] *vt* aconsejar (to give advice); *I advise you to travel* le aconsejo viajar *or* que viaje || asesorar (as paid adviser) || informar (to inform) || COMM notificar (to notify).
◆ *vi* aconsejar || — *to advise on* ser asesor en || *to advise with* consultar.

advised [-d] *adj* aconsejado, da || reflexionado, da; pensado, da (considered) || *to keep advised* tener al tanto *or* al corriente.

advisedly [-idli] *adv* deliberadamente (deliberately) || con conocimiento de causa (with due consideration).

adviser; *US* **advisor** [əd'vaizə*] *n* consejero, ra; asesor, ra (someone who advises) || *US* tutor *m* || — *adviser's office* asesoría *f* || *legal adviser* asesor jurídico.

advisory [əd'vaizəri] *adj* consultivo, va; asesor, ra; *advisory committee* comisión consultiva || *in an advisory capacity* como asesor.

advocacy ['ædvəkəsi] *n* JUR defensa *f* | abogacía *f* (the work of advocates) || recomendación *f* (recommendation of a line of action) || apoyo *m* (support).

advocate ['ædvəkit] *n* JUR abogado *m* || defensor, ra; abogado, da (of a cause) || *the devil's advocate* el abogado del diablo.

advocate ['ædvəkeit] *vt* defender, abogar por || recomendar, preconizar.

advowson [əd'vauzən] *n* JUR derecho *m* de patronato || REL colación *f* de un beneficio.

adze; **adz** [ædz] *n* azuela *f*.

AEA *abbr of Atomic Energy Authority* comisariado británico para la energía nuclear.

aedile ['i:dail] *n* edil *m*.

Aegean [i:'dʒi:ən] *adj* Egeo, a; *Aegean Sea* mar Egeo.

aegis; **egis** ['i:dʒis] *n* égida *f* || patrocinio *m*, tutela *f* (sponsorship) || *under the aegis of* bajo los auspicios de.

Aegisthus ['i:dʒisθəs] *pr n* MYTH Egisto *m*.

Aeneas [i:'ni:æs] *pr n* MYTH Eneas *m*.

Aeneid ['i:niid] *pr n* MYTH Eneida *f*.

aeolian [i:'əuliən] *adj* eolio, lia || eólico, ca (wind).

aeolotropic ['i:ɔlətrɔpik] *adj* CHEM alotrópico, ca.

Aeolus ['i:əuləs] *pr n* MYTH Eolo *m*.

aeon; eon [ˈiːən] *n* eón *m*.

aerate [ˈeiəreit] *vt* airear, ventilar (to ventilate) || gasificar (to charge a liquid with gas) || MED oxigenar || *aerated water* agua gaseosa.

aeration [ˌeiəˈreiʃən] *n* aeración *f*, ventilación *f* || gasificación (with gas) || MED oxigenación *f*.

aerial [ˈɛəriəl] *adj* aéreo, a (of or in the air); *aerial photography* fotografía aérea || etéreo, a (ethereal) || *aerial beacon* aerofaro *m*.
◆ *n* antena *f* (radio, TV); *indoor aerial* antena interior; *transmitting aerial* antena transmisora.

aerialist [-ist] *n* US equilibrista *m* & *f*, volatinero, ra.

aerie [ˈɛəri] *n* aguilera *f* (nest of bird of prey).

aeriform [-fɔːm] *adj* gaseoso, sa; aeriforme (gaseous) || inmaterial (unsubstantial).

aerify [-fai] *vt* airear (to aerate) || CHEM aerificar.

aerobatics [ˌɛərəˈbætiks] *n* acrobacia *f* aérea.

aerobe [ˈɛərəub] *n* BIOL aerobio *m*.

aerobic [ɛəˈrəubik] *adj* BIOL aerobio, bia.

aerobics [-s] *n* aerobic *m*.

aerodrome [ˈɛrədrəum] *n* AVIAT aeródromo *m*.

aerodynamic [ˈɛərəudaiˈnæmik] *adj* aerodinámico, ca.

aerodynamics [-s] *n* aerodinámica *f*.

aerodyne [ˈɛərəudain] *n* AVIAT aerodino *m*.

aerofoil [ˈɛərəufɔil] *n* AVIAT superficie *f* sustentadora.

aerogram [ˈɛərəugræm] *n* aerograma *m*, radiograma *m*.

aerograph [ˈɛərəugrɑːf] *n* aerógrafo *m*.

aerolite [ˈɛərəlait] *n* aerolito *m*.

aeromarine [ˈɛərəmæˈriːn] *adj* aeromarítimo, ma.

aeromechanic [ˈɛərəməˈkænik] *n* AVIAT mecánico *m* de aviación.

aerometer [ɛəˈrɔmitə*] *n* aerómetro *m*.

aeromodelling [ˈɛərəˈmɔdliŋ] *n* aeromodelismo *m*.

aeromotor [ˈɛərəuməutə*] *n* aeromotor *m*.

aeronaut [ˈɛərənɔːt] *n* aeronauta *m* & *f*.

aeronautic [ˌɛərəˈnɔːtik]; **aeronautical** [-əl] *adj* aeronáutico, ca.

aeronautics [ˌɛərəˈnɔːtiks] *n* aeronáutica *f*.

aeronaval [ˌɛərəˈneivəl] *adj* aeronaval.

aerophagia [ˌɛərəˈfeidʒiə] *n* aerofagia *f*.

aeroplane [ˈɛərəplein] *n* AVIAT avión *m* || — *aeroplane modeller* aeromodelista *m* & *f* || *aeroplane modelling* aeromodelismo *m* || *model aeroplane* aeromodelo *m*.

aerosol [ˈɛərəsɔl] *n* CHEM aerosol *m* || pulverizador *m* (spray).

aerospace [ˈɛərəuspeis] *n* espacio *m* extraterrestre.
◆ *adj* aeroespacial; *the aerospace industry* la industria aeroespacial.

aerostat [ˈɛərəstæt] *n* aeróstato *m*.

aerostatic [ˌɛərəˈstætik] *adj* aerostático, ca.

aerostatics [-s] *n* PHYS aerostática *f*.

aerostation [ˌɛərəˈsteiʃən] *n* aerostación *f*.

aerotechnical [ɛərəˈteknikəl] *adj* aerotécnico, ca.

aerotherapeutics [ˌɛərəuˌθerəˈpjuːtiks] *n* aeroterapia *f*.

aerotherapy [ˌɛərəuˈθerəpi] *n* aeroterapia *f*.

aerothermodynamics [ˈɛərəuˈθəːməudaiˈnæmiks] *n* aerotermodinámica *f*.

aery [ˈɛəri] *n* aguilera *f*.

Aeschines [ˈiːskiniːz] *pr n* Esquines *m*.

Aeschylus [ˈiːskiləs] *pr n* Esquilo *m*.

Aesculapius [ˌiːskjuˈleipjəs] *pr n* Esculapio *m*.

Aesop [ˈiːsɔp] *pr n* Esopo *m*.

aesthete [ˈiːsθiːt] *n* esteta *m* & *f*.

aesthetic [iːsˈθetik] *adj* estético, a.

aesthetician [iːsθəˈtiʃən] *n* estético *m*.

aestheticism [iːsˈθetisizəm] *n* esteticismo *m*.

aesthetics [iːsˈθetiks] *n* estética *f*.

aestival [iːsˈtaivəl] *adj* estival.

aestivate [ˈiːstiveit] *vi* ZOOL pasar el verano en estado de letargo.

aetiology [ˌiːtiˈɔlədʒi] *n* etiología *f*.

Aetna [ˈetnə] *pr n* Etna *m*.

afar [əˈfɑː*] *adv* lejos || *from afar* desde lejos.

affability [ˌæfəˈbiliti] *n* afabilidad *f*.

affable [ˈæfəbl] *adj* afable.

affair [əˈfɛə*] *n* asunto *m*; *this is no affair of yours* esto no es (un) asunto tuyo; *affair of state* asunto de estado || asunto *m*, cuestión *f* (matter); *family affairs* cuestiones familiares || acontecimiento *m*; *social affair* acontecimiento social || asunto *m*, incidente *m* (an incident) || duelo *m* (duel) || caso *m* (case) || lance *m*; *affair of honour* lance de honor || aventura *f* (love); *she had an affair with her boss* tuvo una aventura con su jefe.
◆ *pl* negocios *m* (business) || — *current affairs* actualidad *f sing* || *Foreign Affairs* Asuntos Exteriores (in Spain), Relaciones Exteriores (in Latin America).

affect [əˈfekt] *n* sentimiento *m*.

affect [əˈfekt] *vt* afectar; *to affect great elegance* afectar suma elegancia; *this law affects all citizens* esta ley afecta a todos los ciudadanos; *his mother's death affected him deeply* la muerte de su madre le afectó profundamente; *the injury affected the whole leg* la herida afectó a toda la pierna || lucir; *to affect a dress* lucir un traje || dárselas de, echárselas de (to pretend to be) || fingir (to feign).

affectation [ˌæfekˈteiʃən] *n* simulación *f* (a pretence) || afectación *f*, amaneramiento *m* (artificiality).

affected [əˈfektid] *adj* afectado, da; amanerado, da.

affecting [əˈfektiŋ] *adj* conmovedor, ra (moving).

affection [əˈfekʃən] *n* afecto *m*, cariño *m* (*for, towards* por, hacia) (fondness) || MED afección *f*.

affectionate [-it] *adj* afectuoso, sa; cariñoso, sa.

affective [əˈfektiv] *adj* afectivo, va.

affectivity [ˌæfekˈtiviti] *n* afectividad *f*.

afferent [ˈæfərənt] *adj* ANAT aferente.

affiance [əˈfaiəns] *vt* dar palabra de casamiento.

affidavit [ˌæfiˈdeivit] *n* JUR declaración *f* jurada || *affidavit by process server* atestiguación *f* forense.

affiliate [əˈfilieit] *n* asociado, da (an associate) || US filial *f* (a subsidiary organization).

affiliate [əˈfilieit] *vi* afiliarse (*to, with* a) || asociarse (*to, with* con).
◆ *vt* afiliar || asociar (to add as an associate) || legitimar (a child) || atribuir (a piece of work).

affiliation [əˌfiliˈeiʃən] *n* afiliación *f* || asociación *f* || JUR legitimación *f* (of a child) || *action for affiliation* investigación *f* de la paternidad.

affinity [əˈfiniti] *n* afinidad *f*.

affirm [əˈfəːm] *vt* afirmar.

affirmation [ˌæfəːˈmeiʃən] *n* afirmación *f*.

affirmative [əˈfəːmətiv] *adj* afirmativo, va.
◆ *n an answer in the affirmative* una respuesta afirmativa.

affirmatory [əˈfəːmətəri] *adj* afirmativo, va.

affix [ˈæfiks] *n* GRAMM afijo *m* || añadido *m*.

affix [əˈfiks] *vt* sujetar; *he affixed his tie with a pin* se sujetó la corbata con un alfiler || pegar; *to affix an advert to the wall* pegar un anuncio en la pared || poner; *to affix a seal to a document* poner un sello a un documento; *to affix one's signature to a document* poner la firma a un documento || añadir, agregar (to add) || echar, atribuir (a blame).

affixed [əˈfikst] *adj* GRAMM afijo, ja.

afflict [əˈflikt] *vt* afligir; *his death afflicted me* su muerte me afligió || *to be afflicted with* estar aquejado de, sufrir de.

affliction [əˈflikʃən] *n* pesar *m*, aflicción *f* (grief) || sufrimiento *m* (suffering) || achaque *m* (of old age) || MED enfermedad *f*, aflicción *f*.

afflictive [əˈfliktiv] *adj* doloroso, sa.

affluence [ˈæfluəns] *n* opulencia *f* || abundancia *f*.

affluent [ˈæfluənt] *adj* opulento, ta; acaudalado, da (wealthy); *affluent society* sociedad opulenta || abundante.
◆ *n* afluente *m* (a tributary stream).

afflux [ˈæflʌks] *n* afluencia *f* || MED aflujo *m*.

afford [əˈfɔːd] *vt* permitirse; *can we afford to speak out?* ¿podemos permitirnos el hablar libremente? || costearse; *can we afford a new car?* ¿podemos costearnos un coche nuevo? || permitirse el lujo; *I can't afford to relax* no me puedo permitir el lujo de descansar || dar, proporcionar; *these trees afford little shelter* estos árboles dan poca protección || *the tower affords a nice view* desde la torre hay una buena vista.
— OBSERV Excepto cuando significa *dar*, el verbo *afford* se emplea precedido de *can* o de *be able*.

affordable [-əbəl] *adj* asequible (price).

afforest [æˈfɔrist] *vt* repoblar con árboles.

afforestation [æˌfɔrisˈteiʃən] *n* repoblación *f* forestal.

affranchise [əˈfræntʃaiz] *vt* manumitir.

affranchisement [əˈfræntʃizmənt] *n* manumisión *f*.

affray [əˈfrei] *n* JUR reyerta *f*, refriega *f*.

affricate [ˈæfrikit] *n* africada *f* (consonant).

affricative [æˈfrikətiv] *adj* GRAMM africado, da.

affront [əˈfrʌnt] *n* afrenta *f* || insulto *m* (verbal).

affront [əˈfrʌnt] *vt* afrentar || insultar (verbally).

affusion [əˈfjuːʒən] *n* afusión *f*.

afghan [ˈæfgæn] *n* US colcha *f* de punto.

Afghan [ˈæfgæn] *adj/n* afgano, na.

Afghanistan [æfˈgænistæn] *pr n* Afganistán *m*.

afield [əˈfiːld] *adv* al campo || *far afield* muy lejos.

afire [əˈfaiə*] *adj/adv* ardiendo, en llamas.

aflame [əˈfleim] *adj/adv* en llamas.
◆ *adj* FIG inflamado, da.

afloat [əˈfləut] *adj/adv* MAR flotando; *the ship was afloat* el barco estaba flotando | a flote; *the ship managed to keep afloat after the collision* el barco consiguió mantenerse a flote tras el choque | a bordo (on board ship) || inundado, da (flooded) || FIG solvente (free of debt) || *rumours were afloat that he would resign* circulaban rumores de que iba a dimitir.

afoot [əˈfut] *adj/adv* a pie (walking) || en marcha (beginning to make progress) || FIG *there is sth. afoot* se está tramando algo.

afore [əˈfɔː*] *adv/prep* MAR a proa.

aforementioned [-menʃənd]; **aforesaid** [-sed] *adj* susodicho, cha; antedicho, cha; anteriormente mencionado.

aforethought [-θɔːt] *n* premeditación *f*.
◆ *adj* premeditado, da ‖ *with malice aforethought* con premeditación.

afraid [əˈfreid] *adj* asustado, da; *go with her because she is afraid* vete con ella porque está asustada ‖ — *I am afraid she is out* lo siento pero ha salido ‖ *I am afraid I can't come* me temo que no pueda ir ‖ *to be afraid for* temer por ‖ *to be afraid of* tener miedo a *or* de (see OBSERV under FEAR *vt*) ‖ *to feel afraid to speak* no atreverse a hablar.
— OBSERV See OBSERV under FEAR *vt*.

afresh [əˈfreʃ] *adv* de nuevo, otra vez.

Africa [ˈæfrikə] *pr n* África *f* ‖ *South Africa* África del Sur.

African [ˈæfrikən] *adj/n* africano, na.

Africanist [-ist] *n* africanista.

Africanize [ˈæfrikənaiz] *vt* africanizar.

Afrikaans [ˌæfriˈkɑːns] *n* afrikaans *m* & *f*.

Afrikaner [ˌæfriˈkɑːnə*] *n* afrikánder *m* & *f*.

Afro-American [ˌæfrəuəˈmerikən] *adj/n* afroamericano, na.

Afro-Asian [ˈæfrəuˈeiʃən] *adj/n* afroasiático, ca.

Afro-Cuban [-ˈkjubən] *adj/n* afrocubano, na.

aft [ɑːft] *adv* MAR a popa; en popa ‖ *fore and aft* de proa a popa.

after [ˈɑːftə*] *adj* posterior; *in the after years* en los años posteriores ‖ siguiente (next) ‖ trasero, ra; *the after parts of a bull* los cuartos traseros de un toro ‖ MAR de popa.
◆ *prep* tras (in pursuit of); *she ran after the postman* corrió tras el cartero; *one after the other* uno tras otro ‖ detrás de (behind); *the police are after her* la policía está detrás de ella ‖ después de; *after a week we went home* después de una semana nos fuimos a casa ‖ en busca de (in search of); *she is after a husband* va en busca de marido ‖ a la manera de; *paintings after the Dutch masters* pinturas a la manera de los maestros holandeses ‖ a imitación de, según el estilo de; *engraving after Poussin* grabado hecho a imitación de Poussin ‖ por, acerca de; *to ask after s.o.* preguntar por alguien ‖ — *after all is said and done* al fin y al cabo ‖ *after hours* fuera de horas ‖ *after you!* ¡usted primero! ‖ *day after day* día tras día ‖ *he read page after page* leyó página tras página ‖ *I am after a red dress* estoy buscando un traje rojo ‖ *I have been after that for years* estoy buscando eso desde hace años ‖ *it's after five o'clock* son las cinco pasadas ‖ US *it's half after four* son las cuatro y media ‖ *named after* llamado como; llamado en honor a ‖ *the day after the battle* el día siguiente de la batalla ‖ *the day after tomorrow* pasado mañana ‖ *they called me John after my father* me pusieron Juan por mi padre ‖ FIG *to be after s.o.'s blood* querer matar a alguien ‖ *to look after* (see LOOK) ‖ *what's he after?* ¿qué es lo que busca?
◆ *adv* después; *before and after* antes y después; *long after* mucho tiempo después ‖ detrás (behind).
◆ *conj* una vez que, después de que; *after he left the room, we started talking* una vez que salió de la habitación, nos pusimos a hablar.

afterbirth [-bəːθ] *n* ANAT placenta *f* ‖ JUR nacimiento *m* póstumo.

aftercare [-kɛə*] *n* MED vigilancia *f* postoperatoria.

afterdamp [-dæmp] *n* MIN mofeta *f*.

afterdeck [-dek] *n* MAR cubierta *f* de popa.

after-dinner [-ˈdinə*] *adj* de sobremesa.

aftereffect [-iˈfekt] *n* consecuencia *f*, efecto *m* secundario.

afterglow [-gləu] *n* resplandor *m* crepuscular (of sky).

afterlife [-laif] *n* vida *f* futura ‖ resto *m* de la vida.

aftermath [-mæθ] *n* repercusiones *f pl*, secuelas *f pl* (consequences) ‖ AGR renadío *m*, segundo corte *m*.

aftermost [-məust] *adj* MAR de popa.

afternoon [-ˈnuːn] *n* tarde *f* (part of the day) ‖ FIG atardecer *m*; *he is in the afternoon of life* está en el atardecer de la vida ‖ *good afternoon* buenas tardes.
◆ *adj* de la tarde.

afterpains [-peinz] *pl n* dolores *m* después del parto, entuertos *m* (pain following childbirth).

aftertaste [-teist] *n* regusto *m*, mal sabor *m* de boca, resabio *m*, gustillo *m*.

afters [-z] *n* FAM postre *m*.

aftershave [-ʃeiv] *n* loción *f* para después del afeitado.

afterthought [-θɔːt] *n* ocurrencia *f* tardía, idea *f* tardía.

afterward [-wəd]; **afterwards** [-wədz] *adv* después, más tarde (at a later time) ‖ *long afterward* mucho después.

afterworld [-wəːld] *n* el más allá, el otro mundo.

again [əˈgen] *adv* otra vez, nuevamente, de nuevo (once more) ‖ además (in addition) ‖ por otra parte (on the other hand) ‖ — *again and again, time and again* una y otra vez ‖ *as much again* otro tanto más ‖ *never again* nunca más ‖ *now and again* de vez en cuando ‖ *once again* otra vez ‖ *to say again and again* decir una y otra vez ‖ *what's his name again?* ¿cómo ha dicho que se llama? ‖ *would you do it again?* ¿lo volverías a hacer?

against [əˈgenst] *prep* contra; *to fight against the enemy* luchar contra el enemigo; *precautions against cold* precauciones contra el frío; *hailstones against the window* granizos contra la ventana; *they were warned against the danger* se les puso en guardia contra el peligro ‖ en contra de, contra; *I was against him* estaba en contra de él ‖ a cambio de; *he gave me his football against my bicycle* me dio la pelota de fútbol a cambio de la bicicleta ‖ para (for) ‖ al lado de, cerca de (near) ‖ — FIG *against all odds* o *all the odds* contra viento y marea ‖ *as against this* frente a eso ‖ *to put it against expenses* ponerlo en la nota de gastos ‖ *to run up against* tropezar con.

agami [əˈgæmi] *n* ZOOL agamí *m*.

agamic [eiˈgæmik]; **agamous** [ˈægəməs] *adj* BIOL asexuado, da; asexual ‖ BOT ágamo, ma.

agape [ˈægəpi] *n* ágape *m* (christian banquet) ‖ amor *m* espiritual.

agape [əˈgeip] *adj/adv* boquiabierto, ta.

agar-agar [ˈeigɑːeigɑː] *n* agar agar *m*.

agaric [ˈægərik] *n* BOT agárico *m*.

agate [ˈægət] *n* ágata *f* (stone) ‖ bruñidor *m* (bookbinder's tool) ‖ US tipo *m* de 5,5 puntos (in printing) ‖ canica *f* (marble).

Agatha [ˈægəθə] *pr n* Águeda *f*.

agave [əˈgeivi] *n* BOT agave *f*, pita *f*.

age [eidʒ] *n* edad *f*; *ten years of age* diez años de edad; *of school age* en edad escolar; *at the age of ten* a la edad de diez años; *Middle Ages* Edad Media; *the Stone Age* la Edad de Piedra ‖ era *f*; *the motor car age* la era del automóvil ‖ época *f*; *the age of the impressionists* la época de los impresionistas; *the age I live in* la época en que vivo ‖ FIG siglo *m*, eternidad *f*, mucho tiempo *m* (long time) ‖ — *be o act your age* no seas niño ‖ *Golden Age* Siglo de Oro (in Spain) ‖ *it's an age since we last met* hace un siglo que no nos vemos ‖ *middle age* mediana edad ‖ *old age* vejez *f* ‖ *the age of consent* la edad núbil ‖ *the age of discretion* la edad del juicio, el uso de razón ‖ *the age of reason* la edad de la razón *or* del juicio ‖ *the awkward age* la edad del pavo [AMER la edad del chivateo] ‖ *to be of age* ser mayor de edad ‖ *to be over age* ser demasiado viejo ‖ *to be under age* ser menor de edad (minor), ser demasiado joven (too young) ‖ *to come of age* alcanzar la mayoría de edad ‖ *to look one's age* representar la edad que se tiene ‖ *what age are you?* ¿qué edad tiene?
◆ *pl n* FIG siglos *m* (a long time); *I haven't seen him for ages* hace siglos que no lo veo.

age [eidʒ] *vt/vi* envejecer; *she hasn't aged a bit* no ha envejecido nada.

aged [-id] *adj* anciano, na; viejo, ja; de edad avanzada; *a very aged man* un hombre muy anciano ‖ *a boy aged ten* un niño de diez años de edad.

age group [ˈeidʒgruːp] *n* grupo *m* de personas de la misma edad ‖ *to be of different age groups* no tener la misma edad.

ageing [ˈeidʒiŋ] *adj* → **aging**.

ageing [ˈeidʒiŋ] *n* envejecimiento *m*.

ageless [ˈeidʒlis] *adj* eterno, na ‖ siempre joven.

agelong [ˈeidʒlɔŋ] *adj* secular.

agency [ˈeidʒənsi] *n* agencia *f*; *travel agency* agencia de viajes; *advertising agency* agencia de publicidad ‖ mediación *f*; *through his doctor's agency he received compensation* por mediación del médico recibió una indemnización ‖ acción *f* ‖ agente *m*; *natural agency* agente natural ‖ — *free agency* libre albedrío *m* ‖ *real estate agency* agencia inmobiliaria ‖ *specialized agencies* organismos especializados (of UN).

agenda [əˈdʒendə] *n* orden *m* del día (of a meeting) ‖ *what's on the agenda?* ¿qué tenemos previsto?

agent [ˈeidʒənt] *n* agente *m* (a representative); *insurance agent* agente de seguros ‖ COMM agente *m*, representante *m* ‖ apoderado *m* (law) ‖ instrumento *m* (instrument) ‖ agente *m* (cause) ‖ CHEM agente *m*; *cooling agent* agente refrigerante ‖ GRAMM agente *m* ‖ — *business agent* agente de negocios ‖ *estate agent* agente inmobiliario.

agent provocateur [ˈæʒɑ̃ːprəvɔkəˈtəː*] *n* agente *m* provocador.

age-old [ˈeidʒəuld] *adj* secular (centuries old) ‖ antiguo, gua (ancient).

agglomerate [əˈglɔmərit] *n* aglomeración *f* (a mass or collection) ‖ GEOL aglomerado *m*.
◆ *adj* aglomerado, da.

agglomerate [əˈglɔməreit] *vt* aglomerar.
◆ *vi* aglomerarse.

agglomeration [əglɔməˈreiʃən] *n* aglomeración *f*.

agglutinate [əˈgluːtinit] *adj* aglutinado, da.

agglutinate [əˈgluːtineit] *vt* aglutinar.
◆ *vi* aglutinarse.

agglutination [əgluːtiˈneiʃən] *n* aglutinación *f*.

agglutinative [əˈgluːtinətiv] *adj* aglutinante (language) ‖ MED aglutinativo, va.

aggrandize [əˈgrændaiz] *vt* ampliar, agrandar (to make greater in power, rank) ‖ FIG exagerar (to exaggerate) ‖ engrandecer (to magnify).

aggrandizement [əˈgrændizmənt] *n* ampliación *f*, agrandamiento *m* ‖ FIG engrandecimiento *m*.

aggravate [ˈægrəveit] *vt* agravar (to make worse) ‖ FAM exasperar, irritar (to exasperate) ‖ JUR *aggravated theft* robo *m* con agravante.

aggravating [-iŋ] *adj* irritante, molesto, ta ‖ JUR agravante.

aggravation [ægrə'veiʃən] *n* agravación *f* (a making worse) ‖ FAM exasperación *f*, irritación *f* ‖ JUR circunstancia *f* agravante.

aggregate ['ægrigit] *n* agregado *m* (mass of different things) ‖ conjunto *m* (whole) ‖ *in the aggregate* en conjunto, en total, globalmente.
◆ *adj* global, colectivo, va; total ‖ acumulado, da (amassed) ‖ BOT & GEOL agregado, da.

aggregate ['ægrigeit] *vt* agregar, reunir, unir.
◆ *vi* ascender a, totalizar, sumar.

aggregation [ægri'geiʃən] *n* agregación *f* ‖ reunión *f* ‖ agregado *m* (aggregate).

aggression [ə'greʃən] *n* agresión *f*.

aggressive [ə'gresiv] *adj* agresivo, va; *an aggressive person* una persona agresiva ‖ MIL de ataque, ofensivo, va; *an aggressive move* un movimiento de ataque ‖ llamativo, va; *an aggressive advertisement* un anuncio llamativo ‖ US emprendedor, ra | dinámico, ca; enérgico, ca.
◆ *n* ofensiva *f*.

aggressiveness [-nis] *n* agresividad *f*, acometividad *f*.

aggressor [ə'gresə*] *n* agresor, ra.

aggrieved [ə'gri:vd] *adj* agraviado, da.

aggro ['ægrəu] *n* POP agresividad *f*.

aghast [ə'gɑ:st] *adj* espantado, da; horrorizado, da (*at* de) (horrified) ‖ pasmado, da (amazed).

agile ['ædʒail] *adj* ágil.

agility [ə'dʒiliti] *n* agilidad *f*.

aging; ageing ['eidʒiŋ] *adj* que envejece.

agio ['ædʒiəu] *n* agio *m*.

agiotate ['ædʒətidʒ] *n* agiotaje *m*.

agitate ['ædʒiteit] *vt* agitar (to shake up, to move) ‖ discutir, debatir (a question).
◆ *vi* *to agitate for* hacer una campaña en favor de.

agitation [ædʒi'teiʃən] *n* agitación *f* ‖ excitación *f*, nerviosismo *m* (excitement) ‖ discusión *f*, debate *m* ‖ campaña *f* (of an agitator).

agitator ['ædʒiteitə*] *n* agitador, ra ‖ agitador *m* (apparatus).

aglet ['æglit] *n* herrete *m* (of a lace) ‖ MIL cordón *m* ‖ BOT candelilla *f*, amento *m* (of birch, hazel).

aglow [ə'gləu] *adv/adj* radiante (*with* de).

agnail ['ægneil] *n* padrastro *m*.

agnate ['ægneit] *n* agnado *m*, consanguíneo *m*.

Agnes ['ægnis] *pr n* Inés *f*.

agnostic [æg'nɔstik] *adj/n* agnóstico, ca.

agnosticism [æg'nɔstisizəm] *n* agnosticismo *m*.

ago [ə'gəu] *adj* hace; *a year ago* hace un año.
◆ *adv* *as long ago as 1920* ya en 1920 ‖ *long ago* hace mucho tiempo ‖ *not long ago* hace poco tiempo.

agog [ə'gɔg] *adj* ansioso, sa (eager) ‖ *to set s.o. agog* infundir curiosidad a uno, intrigar a uno.

agonize ['ægənaiz] *vt* atormentar.
◆ *vi* luchar, hacer esfuerzos desesperados (*after* por) (to struggle) ‖ sufrir horriblemente ‖ preocuparse mucho (*over, about* por).

agony ['ægəni] *n* dolor *m* (physical pain) ‖ angustia *f*, congoja *f* (mental suffering) ‖ — *the Agony* la Agonía de Cristo ‖ *the last agony* la agonía ‖ *to go through agonies* pasarlas moradas ‖ *to suffer* o *to be in agonies* sufrir atrozmente.

agony aunt [-a:nt] *n* consejero, ra sentimental [en la prensa].

agony column [-'kɔləm] *n* FAM anuncios *m pl* personales [relativos a personas u objetos perdidos].

agora ['ægərə] *n* ágora *f*.
— OBSERV El plural de la palabra inglesa es *agorae*.

agoraphobia [ægərə'fəubjə] *n* agorafobia *f*.

agouti; agouty [ə'gu:ti] *n* ZOOL agutí *m*.

agraffe [ə'græf] *n* grapa *f*.

agrarian [ə'grɛəriən] *adj* agrario, ria.

agrarianism [-izəm] *n* agrarismo *m*.

agree [ə'gri:] *vi* consentir; *she will never agree to it* nunca lo consentirá ‖ acceder a, aceptar; *to agree to a proposal* aceptar una propuesta ‖ aprobar (to approve) ‖ ponerse de acuerdo (to come to an agreement) ‖ estar de acuerdo; *we don't agree about the dog* no estamos de acuerdo respecto al perro ‖ estar de acuerdo, reconocer; *he agreed that it was stupid* reconoció que aquello era estúpido ‖ sentar bien; *this climate agrees with me* este clima me sienta bien ‖ coincidir, concordar; *these two figures don't agree* estas dos figuras no coinciden ‖ GRAMM concordar ‖ — *don't you agree?* ¿no le parece? ‖ *it is agreed* de acuerdo ‖ *to agree on* convenir en ‖ *it was agreed that...* se resolvió que..., se acordó que... ‖ *to agree upon* o *on* acordar; *to agree upon a price* acordar un precio ‖ *to agree with* estar de acuerdo con.
◆ *vt* acordar; *both statesmen have agreed to increase cooperation* ambos estadistas han acordado estrechar la cooperación ‖ quedar en; *he agreed to come* quedó en venir ‖ estar de acuerdo con; *do you agree the bill?* ¿está de acuerdo con la cuenta?

agreeable [ə'griəbl] *adj* agradable, placentero, ra (pleasant) ‖ conforme; *to be agreeable to a plan* estar conforme con un plan ‖ conforme, dispuesto; *to be agreeable to doing sth.* estar conforme en *or* dispuesto a hacer algo ‖ *its that agreeable to you?* ¿está de acuerdo?

agreed! [ə'gri:d] *interj* ¡de acuerdo!, ¡conforme!

agreement [ə'gri:mənt] *n* acuerdo *m*; *to come to* o *to reach (an) agreement* llegar a un acuerdo ‖ acuerdo *m*; *general agreement on tariffs and trade* acuerdo general sobre tarifas arancelarias y comercio ‖ JUR contrato *m* (contract) | convenio *m*; *collective agreements* convenios colectivos ‖ concordancia *f*, coincidencia *f* (of figures) ‖ GRAMM concordancia *f* ‖ — *a poor agreement is better than a good court case* más vale mala avenencia que buena sentencia ‖ *as per agreement* según lo convenido ‖ *by mutual agreement* de común acuerdo ‖ *in agreement* de acuerdo, acorde ‖ *to conclude an agreement* concertar un acuerdo.

agricultural [ægri'kʌltʃərəl] *adj* agrícola; *agricultural product, equipment, community* producto, maquinaria, comunidad agrícola ‖ — *agricultural college* escuela *f* de peritos agrícolas ‖ *agricultural engineer* perito agrícola *or* agrónomo ‖ *agricultural expert* ingeniero agrónomo.

agriculturalist [ægri'kʌltʃərəlist]; **agriculturist** [ægri'kʌltʃərist] *n* agricultor, ra (farmer) ‖ agrónomo *m*, ingeniero *m* agrónomo (expert).

agriculture ['ægrikʌltʃə*] *n* agricultura *f*.

agriculturist [ægri'kʌltʃərist] *n* → **agriculturalist.**

Agrigento [ɑ:grid'ʒentəu] *pr n* GEOGR Agrigento.

agrimony [ægriməni] *n* BOT agrimonia *f*, agrimoña *f*.

Agrippina [ægri'pi:nə] *pr n* Agripina *f*.

agronomist [ə'grɔnəmist] *n* agrónomo *m*.

agronomy [ə'grɔnəmi] *n* agronomía *f*.

aground [ə'graund] *adj* MAR encallado, da (on rock) | varado, da (in mud, sand).
◆ *adv* MAR *to run aground* encallar, varar.

ague ['eigju:] *n* MED fiebre *f* intermitente (of malaria) | escalofrío *m* (chill, shivering).

ahead [ə'hed] *adv* delante (*of* de) (in front) ‖ MAR avante (direction); *full steam ahead!* ¡avante a toda máquina! ‖ antes de; *ahead of schedule* antes de lo previsto ‖ antes que; *to arrive ahead of s.o.* llegar antes que alguien ‖ — *go ahead!* ¡adelante! ‖ *straight ahead* todo seguido, todo derecho ‖ *to be ahead* ir ganando, llevar ventaja (in sports) ‖ *to be ahead of* llevar ventaja a ‖ *to be ahead of one's time* anticiparse a su época ‖ *to get ahead* adelantar, progresar; *one must work hard to get ahead* para adelantar uno debe trabajar mucho ‖ *to get* o *to go ahead of s.o.* adelantarse a alguien ‖ *to go on ahead* adelantarse ‖ *to go ahead with* llevar adelante ‖ *to look ahead* mirar el futuro ‖ *to send on ahead* mandar por delante.

ahem! [h'mm] *interj* ¡ejem!

ahoy! [ə'hɔi] *interj* MAR ¡ah!; *ahoy there!* ¡ah del barco! ‖ MAR *ship ahoy!* ¡barco a la vista!

ai [ai] *n* ZOOL ai *m* (sloth).

aid [eid] *n* ayuda *f*; *he was a great aid to me* fue una gran ayuda para mí; *to give aid* prestar ayuda ‖ auxilio *m*, socorro *m*, ayuda *f*; *to go to the aid of a drowning person* ir en auxilio de una persona que se ahoga ‖ ayudante *m* & *f* (helper) ‖ — *by* o *with the aid of* con la ayuda de ‖ *first aid* primeros auxilios ‖ *hearing aid* aparato *m* para sordos ‖ *in aid of* en pro de, a beneficio de ‖ *medical aid* asistencia médica ‖ *state aid* ayuda estatal ‖ *that will be of aid to you* eso será de utilidad para ti, eso te será útil ‖ *to come to the aid of* acudir en ayuda de ‖ *what's all this in aid of?* ¿a qué viene todo eso?

aid [eid] *vt/vi* ayudar, auxiliar.

AID *abbr of Agency for International Development* ODI, Organismo para el Desarrollo Internacional.

aide [eid] *n* asistente, ta; ayudante *m* & *f* (in government or the armed forces).

aide-de-camp ['eiddə'kɑ:] *n* MIL ayudante *m* de campo, edecán *m*.
— OBSERV El plural es *aides-de-camp*.

aide-mémoire ['eidmeim,wɑ:] *n* memorándum *m*.
— OBSERV El plural de *aide-mémoire* es *aides-mémoire*.

aidman ['eidmən] *n* US enfermero *m* militar.

Aids [eɪdz] *n* sida *m*.

AIDS [eɪdz] *abbr of acquired immune deficiency syndrome* SIDA, síndrome de inmunodeficiencia adquirida.

aid station ['eid,steiʃən] *n* US MIL puesto *m* de socorro.

aigrette ['eigret] *n* ZOOL garceta *f* ‖ penacho *m* (of feathers) ‖ diadema *f* (of gems).

aiguille ['eigwi:l] *n* picacho *m* (of rock) ‖ barrena *f* (drill).

aiguillette [eigwi'let] *n* MIL cordón *m*.

ail [eil] *vt* afligir, doler, hacer sufrir.
◆ *vi* estar enfermo, sufrir.

ailanthus [ei'lænθəs] *n* BOT ailanto *m* (tree).

aileron ['eilərɔn] *n* alerón *m* (of aeroplane).

ailing ['eiliŋ] *adj* enfermo, ma.

ailment ['eilmənt] *n* indisposición *f*, malestar *m*.

aim [eim] *n* puntería *f* (when firing a gun); *to take accurate aim* afinar la puntería; *to have a good aim* tener buena puntería ‖ blanco *m*, objetivo *m* (target) ‖ intención *f*, propósito *m*, objetivo *m*, meta *f*, fin *m* (intention); *what is the aim of these questions?* ¿cuál es la intención de estas preguntas? ‖ meta *f* (goal); *his aim was to* *be a doctor* su meta era ser médico || — *missiles which fall short of their aim* proyectiles que no alcanzan su objetivo || FIG *to fall short of one's aim* no conseguir su propósito || *to miss one's aim* errar el tiro || *to spoil one's aim* estropearle a uno el tiro || *to take aim (at s.o.)* apuntar (a alguien) || *with the aim of* con la intención de, con el propósito de, con el objetivo de.

aim [eim] *vt* asestar, lanzar (a blow); *he aimed a punch at him* le asestó un puñetazo || apuntar con; *to aim one's gun at s.o.* apuntar a alguien con la pistola || FIG dirigir (a question, a statement, measures) || *that shot was aimed at you* ese tiro iba dirigido a ti.
◆ *vi* apuntar; *to aim at s.o.* apuntar a alguien || aspirar, tener el propósito de, pretender; *I aim to become a doctor* aspiro a ser médico || *to aim high* picar muy alto, aspirar a mucho.

aimless [-lis] *adj* sin objeto, sin propósito fijo.

ain't [eint] FAM (contraction of «is not», «are not», «am not», «has not», «have not»).

air [εə*] *n* aire *m* (atmosphere, breeze, the space above us); *to throw a ball up into the air* echar una pelota al aire; *compressed, liquid air* aire comprimido, líquido || aire *m*; *he wore an air of sadness* tenía un aire de tristeza || cara *f*, semblante *m* (face) || MUS aire *m*, canción *f* (tune); *he sang a merry air* entonó un aire alegre || — *by air* en avión (to travel), por avión (to send) || FIG *conceited air* aire de suficiencia || *foul air* aire viciado || *fresh air* aire fresco || FIG *in the air* en el aire; *our plans are in the air* nuestros planes están en el aire; *rumours are in the air that...* hay rumores en el aire de que... || *in the open air* al aire libre || *into the air* al aire || *to be on the air* hablar por la radio || *to be put on the air* radiarse || *to build castles in the air* levantar castillos en el aire || *to get fresh air* tomar el fresco || *to have a change of air* cambiar *or* mudar de aires || *to have the air of a gentleman* tener aires de gran señor || *to leave pending in the air* dejar en el aire || FIG *to live on air* vivir del aire | *to rend the air* herir el aire || FIG *to vanish into thin air* evaporarse | *to walk on air* no caber en sí de gozo || *up in the air* en el aire.
◆ *pl* aires *m*; *to put on airs, to put on airs and graces* darse aires.
◆ *adj* aéreo, a || atmosférico, ca (flow, pressure).

air [εə*] *vt* airear, ventilar (to expose to the air) || orear (to hang out to dry) || FIG publicar, hacer público (to make known) | lucir, hacer gala *or* alarde de (one's knowledge) || *to air one's views, one's grievances* exponer sus opiniones, sus quejas.

air attaché [-ə'tæʃei] *n* agregado *m* aéreo.

air base [-beis] *n* base *f* aérea.

air bladder [-ˌblædə*] *n* ZOOL vejiga *f* natatoria || BOT vesícula *f*.

airborne [-bɔːn] *adj* aerotransportado, da (troops) || transportado *or* llevado por el aire (bacteria, etc.) || en el aire, volando.

air brake [-breik] *n* freno *m* de aire comprimido || AVIAT freno *m* aerodinámico.

airbrick [-brik] *n* ladrillo *m* hueco.

airbrush [-brʌʃ] *n* aerógrafo *m*.

airburst [-bəːst] *n* explosión *f* en el aire.

airbus [-bʌs] *n* aerobús *m*.

air chamber [-ˌtʃeimbə*] *n* cámara *f* de aire.

air-condition [-kənˌdiʃən] *vt* climatizar, instalar aire acondicionado en.

air-conditioned [-kən'diʃənd] *adj* con aire acondicionado.

air conditioner [-kən'diʃənə*] *n* acondicionador *m* de aire.

air conditioning [-kən'diʃəniŋ] *n* aire *m* acondicionado || climatización *f*, acondicionamiento *m* del aire.

air-cool [-kuːl] *vt* refrigerar por aire.

air corridor [-ˌkɔridɔː*] *n* pasillo *m* áereo.

aircraft [-krɑːft] *n* aeronave *f* (any flying machine) || avión *m* (aeroplane); *long-range aircraft* avión de larga distancia *or* transcontinental; *medium-haul aircraft* avión de distancias medias *or* continental.
— OBSERV El plural de *aircraft* es *aircraft*.

aircraft carrier [-krɑːft'kæriə*] *n* portaaviones *m inv*, portaviones *m inv*.

aircraftman [-krɑːftmən]; **aircraftsman** [-krɑːftsmən] *n* MIL cabo *m* segundo.

aircrew [-kruː] *n* tripulación *f* [de un avión].

air cushion [-kuʃən] *n* colchón *m* de aire.

airdrome [-drəum] *n* AVIAT aeródromo *m*.

air duct [-dʌkt] *n* tubo *m* de ventilación.

airfield [-fiːld] *n* AVIAT aeródromo *m*, campo *m* de aviación.

airfoil [-fɔil] *n* AVIAT superficie *f* sustentadora.

air force [-fɔːs] *n* MIL fuerzas *f pl* aéreas, aviación *f*.

airframe [-freim] *n* estructura *f* de avión.

airfreight [-freit] *n* flete *m* por avión.

air gap [-gæp] *n* ELECTR entrehierro *m*.

air gun [-gʌn] *n* pistola *f* de aire comprimido.

air hammer [-'hæmə*] *n* martillo *m* neumático.

air hole [-həul] *n* respiradero *m* || US bache *m*.

air hostess [-ˌhəustis] *n* azafata *f*.

airily [-fili] *adv* alegremente, a la ligera.

airiness [-rinis] *n* ligereza *f*.

airing [-riŋ] *n* ventilación *f* || oreo *m* (for drying) || paseo *m* para tomar el aire || FIG publicación *f* (of views, opinions).

airing cupboard [-'kʌbəd] *n* armario *m* para secar la ropa.

air intake [-inteik] *n* toma *f* de aire.

air lane [-lein] *n* ruta *f* aérea.

airless [-lis] *adj* cargado, da; mal ventilado, da (room) || sin aire *or* viento.

air letter [-ˌletə*] *n* carta *f* aérea.

airlift [-lift] *n* puente *m* aéreo.

airlift [-lift] *vt* transportar por un puente aéreo, aerotransportar.

airline [-lain] *n* línea *f* aérea || compañía *f* aérea.

airliner [-lainə*] *n* avión *m* de línea.

airlock [-lɔk] *n* burbuja *f* de aire (in a pipe, etc.) || compartimiento *m* estanco, esclusa *f* de aire (sealed chamber).

airmail [-meil] *n* correo *m* aéreo || *by airmail* por avión, por correo aéreo.

airman [-mən] *n* aviador *m*.
— OBSERV El plural es *airmen*.

air marshal [-ˌmɑːʃəl] *n* MIL teniente *m* general.

air mattress [-ˌmætris] *n* colchón *m* neumático.

airplane [-plein] *n* US AVIAT avión *m* || US *airplane modelling* aeromodelismo *m*.

airplay [-plei] *n* RAD salida *f* en antena.

air pocket [-ˌpɔkit] *n* bache *m*.

airport [-pɔːt] *n* aeropuerto *m*.

air pressure [-ˌpreʃə*] *n* presión *f* atmosférica.

airproof [-pruːf] *adj* hermético, ca.

air pump [-pʌmp] *n* bomba *f* de aire.

air raid [-reid] *n* MIL ataque *m* aéreo || *air raid shelter* refugio antiaéreo.

air route [-ruːt] *n* aerovía *f*, ruta *f* aérea.

airscrew [-skruː] *n* AVIAT hélice *f*.

air-sea base [-'siːbeis] *n* base *f* aeronaval.

air shaft [-ʃɑːft] *n* MIN pozo *m* de ventilación.

airship [-ʃip] *n* AVIAT dirigible *m*, aeronave *f*.

air shuttle [-ʃʌtl] *n* puente *m* aéreo.

airsick [-sik] *adj* mareado, da [en avión].

airsickness [-nis] *n* mareo *m*.

airspace [-speis] *n* espacio *m* aéreo.

airspeed [-spiːd] *n* AVIAT velocidad *f* aerodinámica.

airspraying [-spreiiŋ] *n* fumigación *f* aérea.

air stewart [-stjuəd] *n* auxiliar *m* de vuelo.

airstream [-striːm] *n* corriente *f* de aire.

airstrip [-strip] *n* AVIAT pista *f* de aterrizaje.

airtight [-tait] *adj* hermético, ca || US FIG irrecusable, seguro, ra; *an airtight alibi* una coartada irrecusable.

airtime [-taim] *n* RAD tiempo *m* en antena.

air-to-air [-tə–] *adj* MIL aire-aire, de avión a avión.

air traffic control [-'træfik kən'trəul] *n* control *m* de tráfico aéreo.

air valve [-vælv]; **air vent** [-vent] *n* respiradero *m* [orificio de aeración].

airwaves [-weivz] *pl n* RAD ondas *f*.

airway [-wei] *n* aerovía *f*, ruta *f* aérea (route) || línea *f* aérea (airline) || conducto *m* de ventilación (in mine).

airwoman [-ˌwumən] *n* aviadora *f*.
— OBSERV El plural es *airwomen*.

airworthiness [-ˌwəːðinis] *n* AVIAT navegabilidad *f*.

airworthy [-ˌwəːði] *adj* AVIAT en condiciones de vuelo.

airy ['εəri] *adj* aireado, da; ventilado, da (open to the air) || espacioso, sa (large) || ligero, ra (step) || alegre (cheerful) || ligero, ra; frívolo, la (lacking proper seriousness) || vanidoso, sa (self-complacent) || airoso, sa (graceful, delicate) || etéreo, a (immaterial).

aisle [ail] *n* ARCH nave *f* lateral (of a church) | pasillo *m* (between rows of seats) || *to lead* o *take s.o. up the aisle* llevar a alguien al altar.

aitch [eitʃ] *n* hache *f* (letter).

aitchbone ['eitʃbəun] *n* cadera *f* (of animals) || cadera *f* (cut of beef).

Aix-la-Chapelle ['eikslɑːʃæ'pel] *pr n* GEOGR Aquisgrán.

ajar [ə'dʒɑː*] *adj/adv* entreabierto, ta; entornado, da.

akimbo [ə'kimbəu] *adv* en jarras, en jarra.

akin [ə'kin] *adj* consanguíneo, a (related by blood) || semejante (*to* a) (similar).

Alabama [ˌælə'bæmə] *pr n* GEOGR Alabama *m*.

alabaster ['æləbɑːstə*] *n* alabastro *m*.
◆ *adj* alabastrino, na.

alabastrine [ˌælə'bɑːstrin] *adj* alabastrino, na.

alack [ə'læk] *interj* ¡ay de mí!, ¡ay!

alacrity [ə'lækriti] *n* diligencia *f*, prontitud *f*, alacridad *f* (infr).

Aladdin [ə'lædin] *pr n* Aladino *m*.

Alan ['ælən] *pr n* Alano *m*.

Alans ['eilənz]; **Alani** ['eiləni] *pl prn* alanos *m*.

alar ['eilə*] *adj* del ala || MED axilar.

Alaric ['ælərik] *pr n* Alarico *m*.

alarm [ə'lɑːm] *n* alarma *f* (signal, warning, call to arms); *alarm signal* señal de alarma | susto *m*, alarma *f* (fear) || timbre *m* del despertador (in the alarm clock) || — *alarm call* voz *f* de alarma || *burglar alarm* dispositivo antirrobo || *false alarm* falsa alarma || *to cry out in alarm* dar un toque de alarma || *to raise o to give the alarm* dar la alarma.

alarm [ə'lɑːm] *vt* asustar, alarmar (to frighten) | dar la alarma, alertar (to warn).

alarm bell [-bel] *n* timbre *m* de alarma.

alarm clock [-klɔk] *n* reloj *m* despertador, despertador *m*.

alarming [ə'lɑːmiŋ] *adj* alarmante.

alarmist [ə'lɑːmist] *n* alarmista *m* & *f*.

alary [eiləri] *adj* del ala.

alas [ə'læs] *interj* ¡ay de mí!, ¡ay!

Alaska [ə'læskə] *pr n* GEOGR Alaska *m*.

alated ['eileitid] *adj* alado, da; con alas.

alb [ælb] *n* REL alba *f*.

albacore ['ælbəkɔː*] *n* ZOOL albacora *f*.

Albania [æl'beinjə] *n* GEOGR Albania *f*.

Albanian [-n] *adj* albanés, esa.
◆ *n* albanés, esa (people) || albanés *m* (language).

albata [æl'beitə] *n* metal *m* blanco, alpaca *f*, plata *f* alemana.

albatross ['ælbətrɔs] *n* ZOOL albatros *m*.

albeit [ɔːl'biːit] *conj* bien que, aunque (although); *an intelligent, albeit quiet child* un niño inteligente, bien que callado.

Albert ['ælbət] *pr n* Alberto *m*.

Albigenses [ælbi'gensiːz] *pr pr n* Albigenses *m*.

Albigensian [ælbi'gensjən] *adj* albigense | *Albigensian Crusade* cruzada de los albigenses.

albinism ['ælbinizəm] *n* albinismo *m*.

albino [æl'biːnəu] *adj/n* albino, na.

Albion ['ælbjən] *pr n* Albión *f*.

albite ['ælbait] *n* MIN albita *f*.

album ['ælbəm] *n* álbum *m*.

albumen ['ælbjumin] *n* albúmina *f* (white of an egg) | BOT albumen | BIOL albúmina *f*.

albumin ['ælbjumin] *n* BIOL albúmina *f*.

albuminoid [æl'bjuːminɔid] *n* CHEM albuminoide *m*.
◆ *adj* albuminoideo, a.

albuminose [æl'bjuːminəus]; **albuminous** [æl'bjuːminəs] *adj* albuminoso, sa.

albuminuria [æl'bjuːmiː'njuəriə] *n* MED albuminuria *f*.

alburnum [æl'bəːnəm] *n* alburno *m*, alborno *m*, albura *f* (sapwood).

alcaic [æl'keiik] *adj* alcaico, ca.
◆ *n* alcaico *m*.

alcazar [ælkə'zɑː] *n* alcázar *m*.

alchemist ['ælkimist] *n* alquimista *m*.

alchemy ['ælkimi] *n* alquimia *f*.

alcohol ['ælkəhɔl] *n* alcohol *m*.

alcoholate [-eit] *n* alcoholato *m*.

alcoholic [ælkə'hɔlik] *adj/n* alcohólico, ca.

alcoholism ['ælkəhɔlizəm] *n* alcoholismo *m*.

alcoholize ['ælkəhɔlaiz] *vt* alcoholizar.

alcoholometer [ælkəhɔ'lɔmitə*] *n* alcoholímetro *m*.

alcove ['ælkəuv] *n* nicho *m*, hueco *m*.

Alcyone [æl'saiəni] *pr n* Alción *f*.

aldehyde ['ældihaid] *n* aldehído *m*.

alder ['ɔːldə*] *n* BOT aliso *m* || *alder grove* alisar *m*, aliseda *f*.

alderman ['ɔːldəmən] *n* concejal *m*.

ale [eil] *n* ale *m*, cerveza *f* inglesa; *light o pale ale* cerveza inglesa ligera.

aleatory ['æliətəri] *adj* aleatorio, ria.

alembic [ə'lembik] *n* alambique *m*.

alert [ə'ləːt] *adj* alerta, vigilante (vigilant) || despierto, ta; despabilado, da (awake) || activo, va || *alert to* atento, a.
◆ *n* alerta *f*, alarma *f*; *to give the alert* dar la alerta || — *on the alert* alerta || *red alert* alerta roja || *to be on the alert* estar alerta, estar ojo alerta.

alert [ə'ləːt] *vt* alertar || *to alert s.o. to sth.* alertar *or* avisar a alguien de algo.

aleurone [ə'ljuərən] *n* BOT aleurona *f*.

A-level ['eilevl] *abbr of* *Advanced level* crédito *m* de enseñanza secundaria en Gran Bretaña.

Alexander [ælig'zɑːndə*] *pr n* Alejandro *m*; *Alexander the Great* Alejandro Magno.

Alexandria [ælig'zɑːndriə] *pr n* GEOGR Alejandría.

alexandrine [ælig'zændrain] *n* alejandrino *m*.
◆ *adj* alejandrino, na.
— OBSERV See ALEJANDRINO.

alexia [æ'leksiə] *n* MED alexia *f*.

alexipharmic [æ,leksi'fɑːmik] *n* alexifármaco *m*.

alfa ['ælfə] *n* esparto *m*.

alfalfa [æl'fælfə] *n* BOT alfalfa *f*.

Alfred ['ælfrid] *pr n* Alfredo *m*.

alfresco [æl'freskəu] *adj/adv* al aire libre.

alga ['ælgə] *n* BOT alga *f*.
— OBSERV El plural de la palabra inglesa es *algae* o *algas*.

algebra ['ældʒibrə] *n* álgebra *f*.

algebraic [ældʒi'breiik]; **algebraical** [-əl] *adj* algebraico, ca; algébrico, ca.

Algeria [æl'dʒiəriə] *pr n* GEOGR Argelia *f*.

Algerian [-n] *adj/n* argelino, na.

algid ['ældʒid] *adj* álgido, da; *algid fever* fiebre álgida.

algidity [æl'dʒiditi] *n* algidez *f*, frialdad *f*.

Algiers [æl'dʒiəz] *pr n* GEOGR Argel.

algorithm ['ælgəriðəm] *n* INFORM algoritmo *m*.

alguazil [ælgwə'sil] *n* alguacil *m*.

alias ['eiliæs] *adv* alias.
◆ *n* alias *m inv*.
— OBSERV El plural de la palabra inglesa es *aliases*.

alibi ['ælibai] *n* JUR coartada *f*; *to provide an alibi* presentar una coartada | FAM excusa *f*, pretexto *m*.

Alice ['ælis] *pr n* Alicia *f*; *Alice in Wonderland* Alicia en el país de las maravillas.

alidad ['ælidæd]; **alidade** ['ælideid] *n* alidada *f*.

alien ['eiljən] *adj* extranjero, ra || — *alien from* distinto de (differing in character) || *alien to* ajeno a (opposed in nature).
◆ *n* extranjero, ra (foreigner) || extraño, ña (outsider).
— OBSERV *Alien* se aplica sobre todo a los súbditos de otro país que el de uno mismo. *Foreigner* se dice del extranjero por su lengua y su cultura. *Stranger* forastero o desconocido, se dice del que viene de otro sitio o de la persona a quien no se conocía antes.

alienable ['eiljənəbl] *adj* enajenable, alienable.

alienate ['eiljəneit] *vt* enajenar, alienar (property) || apartar (from one's friends).

alienation [eiljə'neiʃən] *n* alienación *f*, enajenación *f* (transfer, insanity) || apartamiento *m* (from one's friends).

alienist ['eiljənist] *n* MED alienista *m* & *f*.

aliform ['eilifɔːm] *adj* aliforme.

alight [ə'lait] *vi* apearse, bajar (*from* de) (to get down) || posarse (birds) || aterrizar, posarse (aircraft).

alight [ə'lait] *adj/adv* ardiendo, da (on fire) || encendido, da (lit up) || FIG encendido, da; *a face alight with happiness* una cara encendida de alegría | encandilado, da; *eyes alight with love* ojos encandilados de amor || *to set alight* incendiar, pegar fuego a.

align; aline [ə'lain] *vt* alinear (to line up, to bring into line) || *to align o.s. with* ponerse al lado de.
◆ *vi* alinearse.

alignment; alinement [-mənt] *n* alineación *f*, alineamiento *m* || — *in alignment* alineados | US AUT *wheel alignment* convergencia *f* de las ruedas delanteras.

alike [ə'laik] *adv* de la misma forma *or* manera *or* modo; *we think alike* pensamos del mismo modo || *winter and summer alike* en invierno como en verano, lo mismo en invierno que en verano.
◆ *adj* semejante, parecido, da; *they are all alike* todos son parecidos || — *it's all alike to me* todo me da igual || *to look alike* parecerse.

aliment ['ælimənt] *n* alimento *m*.

aliment ['ælimənt] *vt* alimentar.

alimentary [æli'mentəri] *adj* alimenticio, cia || *alimentary canal* tubo digestivo.

alimentation [ælimen'teiʃən] *n* alimentación *f*.

alimony ['æliməni] *n* pensión *f* alimenticia.

aline [ə'lain] *vt/vi* ⟶ **align.**

alinement [ə'lainmənt] *n* ⟶ **alignment.**

aliped ['æliped] *adj* quiróptero, ra.
◆ *n* quiróptero *m*.

aliquant ['ælikwənt] *adj* alicuanta.

aliquot ['ælikwɔt] *adj* alícuota.
◆ *n* parte *f* alícuota.

alive [ə'laiv] *adj* vivo, va (living, lively, in existence) || lleno de, rebosante de (swarming) || sensible (to an impression) || atento, ta (to one's interests) || consciente (conscious) || FIG activo, va; enérgico, ca | ardiendo (fire) || del mundo; *the fastest man alive* el hombre más rápido del mundo || — *alive and kicking* vivito y coleando || *any man alive* cualquier hombre (existente) || *dead or alive* vivo o muerto || *it's good to be alive!* ¡qué bueno es vivir! || *look alive!* ¡muévete!, ¡menéate! || FAM *man alive!* ¡hombre!, ¡por Dios! | *to be alive to* darse cuenta de, ser consciente de (to be conscious of) || *to come alive* cobrar vida | *to come alive again* revivir | *to keep alive* hacer perdurar (memory), sobrevivir (s.o.).

alkalescence [ælkə'lesns] *n* CHEM alcalescencia *f*.

alkalescent [ælkə'lesnt] *adj* alcalescente.

alkali ['ælkəlai] *n* CHEM álcali *m* || *alkali metals* metales alcalinos.
— OBSERV El plural de *alkali* es *alkalis* o *alkalies*.

alkalify ['ælkælifai] *vt* CHEM alcalinizar.

alkaline ['ælkəlain] *adj* CHEM alcalino, na.

alkaline earth [-əːθ] *n* CHEM alcalinotérreo *m*.

alkalinity [ælkə'liniti] *n* CHEM alcalinidad, *f*.

alkalinization [ælkalini'zeiʃn] *n* CHEM alcalización *f*, alcalinización *f*.

alkalinize ['ælkəlinaiz]; **alkalize** ['ælkəlaiz] *vt* alcalizar, alcalinizar.

alkaloid ['ælkəlɔid] *n* CHEM alcaloide *m*.
◆ *adj* alcaloideo, a; alcaloide.

alkalosis [ælkə'ləusis] *n* MED alcalosis *f*.

all [ɔ:l] *adj* todo, da; *all the harvest* toda la cosecha; *all our friends* todos nuestros amigos; *all the others* todos los demás; *beyond all doubt* fuera de toda duda ‖ cualquiera (any whatever); *at all hours* a cualquier hora ‖ — *all day* todo el día ‖ *all men* todos los hombres ‖ *all people* todos ‖ FIG *all this and heaven too* el oro y el moro ‖ *all told* todo incluido ‖ *and all that* y todo lo demás ‖ *for all* con todo, da; *for all his wealth, he was not happy* con toda su riqueza no era feliz ‖ *in all sincerity* con toda sinceridad ‖ *of all people* precisamente; *you, of all people!* ¡tú precisamente!
◆ *adv* completamente, todo, da; *he was all alone* estaba completamente solo; *she was all covered in mud* estaba toda cubierta de barro ‖ — *all along* constantemente, siempre (all the time), desde el principio (from the beginning) ‖ *all along the line* en toda la línea ‖ *all at once* de repente ‖ *all but* casi; *he was all but dead* estaba casi muerto ‖ *all in* exhausto, ta; rendido, da ‖ *all of* nada menos que; *to cost all of 1,000 pesetas* costar nada menos que 1 000 pesetas ‖ *all out* a toda velocidad (full speed), a fondo, completamente, con todas sus fuerzas; *to go all out* entregarse a fondo ‖ *all over* por todas partes (everywhere), por todo; *all over the house* por toda la casa; completamente (completely), terminado, da; acabado, da (finished), muy; *that is you all over* eso es muy tuyo; cien por cien; *he is his father all over* es su padre cien por cien ‖ *all set* listo, ta; dispuesto, ta ‖ *all the* mucho; *you'll be all the better for a night's sleep* estarás mucho mejor después de haber dormido ‖ *all the more* más aún ‖ *all the same* a pesar de todo ‖ *all the worse* tanto peor ‖ *at all* algo; *did you know him at all?* ¿le conocías algo? ‖ SP *five all* cinco a cinco, empatado a 5 ‖ *for good and all* para siempre, de una vez ‖ *if he comes at all* si es que viene ‖ *it's all but impossible* es punto menos que imposible ‖ *not at all* nada en absoluto; *did you like it? not at all* ¿te gustó? nada en absoluto; no hay de qué; *thank you not at all* gracias no hay de qué; nada; *it's not at all easy* no es nada fácil; de ninguna manera, en absoluto (certainly not) ‖ SP *score of 15 all* un tanteo de 15 iguales ‖ *that's all very well but...* me parece muy bien pero... ‖ *to be all for* estar a favor de, parecerle a uno muy bien que... ‖ *to be all the same* ser igual, dar lo mismo.
◆ *pron* todo, da; *when all had been sold* una vez que se vendió todo; *all decided to go* todos decidieron ir ‖ lo único; *that's all I could do to help him* es lo único que pude hacer para ayudarle ‖ — *above all* sobre todo ‖ *after all* después de todo ‖ *all because of you* todo por tu culpa ‖ *all but three of them came along* vinieron todos excepto tres ‖ *all for one, one for all* uno para todos y todos para uno ‖ *all in all* considerándolo todo ‖ *all manner of...* todo tipo de... ‖ *all of* todo, da; *all of the books* todos los libros ‖ *all of us* todos nosotros ‖ *all one* todo uno ‖ *all's well that ends well* bien está lo que bien acaba ‖ *all that* todo lo que; *all that I have* todo lo que tengo ‖ *all who* todos aquellos que ‖ *and all* y todo; *there he was hat and all* allí estaba con sombrero y todo ‖ *first of all* ante todo, primero ‖ *for all* a pesar de; *for all he may say, I don't believe him* a pesar de lo que diga no lo creo; en lo que; *for all I care* en lo que a mí concierne ‖ *for all I know* que yo sepa ‖ *in all* en total ‖ *is that all?* ¿nada más? ‖ *it's all one* es igual ‖ *it was all I could do not to laugh* faltó poco para que me echase a reír ‖ *most of all* sobre todo, más que nada ‖ *one and all* todos y cada uno ‖ *that's all* eso es todo ‖ *when all is said and done* a fin de cuentas.
◆ *n* todo *m*, todos *m pl*, todas *f pl*; *to stake one's all* jugárselo todo.

Allah ['ælə] *pr n* REL Alá *m*.

all-American ['ɔ:lə'merikən] *adj* típicamente americano, na ‖ *the all-American team* el mejor equipo americano.

Allan ['ælən] *pr n* Alano *m*.

allantois [ə'læntəuis] *n* ANAT alantoides *f*.
— OBSERV El plural de *allantois* es *allantoides*.

all-around ['ɔ:lə'raund] *adj* US completo, ta.

allay [ə'lei] *vt* aliviar (pain) ‖ calmar (fear, suspicion).

all-clear ['ɔ:l'kliə*] *n* final *m* de la alarma.

allegation [,æle'geiʃən] *n* JUR alegato *m*, alegación *f*.

allege [ə'ledʒ] *vt* JUR alegar ‖ pretender.

alleged [-d] *adj* pretendido, da; supuesto, ta.

allegiance [ə'li:dʒəns] *n* lealtad *f*, devoción *f* ‖ vasallaje *m*.

allegoric [,æle'gɔrik] *adj* alegórico, ca.

allegorical [-əl] *adj* alegórico, ca.

allegorize ['æligəraiz] *vt* alegorizar.

allegory ['æligəri] *n* alegoría *f*.

allegretto [æli'gretəu] *adv* MUS allegretto, alegreto.
◆ *n* allegretto *m*, alegreto *m*.

allegro [ə'leigrəu] *adv* MUS allegro, alegro.
◆ *n* allegro *m*, alegro *m*.

alleluia [,æli'lu:jə] *n* REL aleluya *f*.

all-embracing [ɔ:lim'breisiŋ] *adj* global, que lo abarca todo.

Allen ['ælin] *pr n* Alano *m*.

allergic [ə'lə:dʒik] *adj* MED alérgico, ca; *allergic to cats* alérgico a los gatos.

allergist ['ælədʒist] *n* médico *m* especialista en alergias.

allergy ['ælədʒi] *n* MED alergia *f*.

alleviate [ə'li:vieit] *vt* aliviar, mitigar.

alleviation [ə,li:vi'eiʃən] *n* alivio *m*.

alleviative [ə'li:viətiv] *adj* aliviador, ra.
◆ *n* paliativo *m*.

alley ['æli] *n* callejón *m* (narrow lane) ‖ paseo *m* (in a park) ‖ SP bolera *f* (for bowling) ‖ canica *f* de alabastro (marble) ‖ — *blind alley* callejón *m* sin salida ‖ FIG *that is right up* o *down my alley* eso es lo mío.

alley cat [-kæt] *n* US gato *m* callejero.

alleyway [-wei] *n* callejón *m*.

All Fools' Day [ɔ:lfu:lzdei] *n* día *m* de los Inocentes.
— OBSERV En Inglaterra este día es el uno de abril y no el veintiocho de diciembre como en España.

Allhallows ['ɔ:l'hæləuz] *n* día *m* de Todos los Santos.

alliance [ə'laiəns] *n* alianza *f*; *alliance treaty* pacto de alianza ‖ *the Holy Alliance* la Santa Alianza.

allied [ə'laid] *adj* aliado, da (joined in alliance) ‖ conexo, xa; relacionado, da (related).

Allies (the) ['ælaiz] *pl n* los aliados *m*.

alligation [æli'geiʃən] *n* aligación *f*, regla *f* de aligación.

alligator ['æligeitə*] *n* ZOOL caimán *m*.

alligator pear [-pɛə*] *n* BOT aguacate *m*.

all-in ['ɔ:l-in] *adj* global ‖ — *all-in charge* precio *m* todo incluido ‖ SP *all-in wrestling* lucha *f* libre.

alliterate [ə'litəreit] *vi* escribir o hablar usando aliteraciones.

alliteration [ə,litə'reiʃən] *n* aliteración *f*.

alliterative [ə'litərətiv] *adj* aliterado, da.

all-knowing ['ɔ:l'nəuiŋ] *adj* omnisciente.

all-night ['ɔ:l'nait] *adj* abierto toda la noche (bar) ‖ que dura toda la noche (meeting, etc.).

allocate ['æləkeit] *vt* asignar ‖ repartir (to distribute).

allocation [,ælə'keiʃən] *n* asignación *f* ‖ reparto *m* (distribution) ‖ lo asignado (thing allocated).

allocution [,æləu'kju:ʃən] *n* alocución *f*.

allodium [ə'ləudjəm] *n* JUR alodio *m*.

allopathic [,æləu'pæθik] *adj* MED alopático, ca.

allopathist [ə'lɔpəθist] *n* MED alópata *m* & *f*.

allopathy [ə'lɔpəθi] *n* MED alopatía *f*.

allot [ə'lɔt] *vt* asignar.

allotment [-mənt] *n* asignación *f* (allocation) ‖ parcela *f* (ground) ‖ reparto *m* ‖ parte *f* (share) ‖ US parte *f* del sueldo de un miembro de las fuerzas armadas que se envía a una persona designada por él.

allotropic [,ælə'trɔpik] *adj* alotrópico, ca.

allotropy [ə'lɔtrəpi] *n* CHEM alotropía *f*.

all-out ['ɔ:l'aut] *adj* acérrimo, ma; incondicional (unreserved) ‖ máximo, ma; supremo, ma (effort).

allover [ɔ:l'əuvə*] *adj* repetido por toda la tela [dibujo].

allow [ə'lau] *vt* permitir, dejar (to permit); *to allow s.o. to do sth.* permitir que alguien haga algo ‖ autorizar, permitir; *smoking is allowed* se permite fumar ‖ conceder, dar (to grant as a concession, to permit to have) ‖ dar (time) ‖ admitir, conceder (to admit) ‖ admitir, reconocer; *to allow sth. to be true* reconocer que algo es verdad ‖ asignar (to pay regularly) ‖ dejar; *allow one inch for the margin* deja una pulgada para el margen ‖ — *allow me* permítame ‖ *to allow o.s.* permitirse.
◆ *vi* *to allow for* tener en cuenta; *allowing for his stupidity* teniendo en cuenta su estupidez; dejar un margen para (to leave a margin for); *to allow for unexpected expenses* dejar un margen para gastos imprevistos ‖ *to allow of* admitir.

allowable [ə'lauəbl] *adj* admisible.

allowance [ə'lauəns] *n* pensión *f*, renta *f* (sum of money paid to a dependant) ‖ COMM rebaja *f*, descuento *m* ‖ ayuda *f*, subsidio *m*; *family allowance* subsidios familiares ‖ subvención *f* (subsidy) ‖ concesión *f* ‖ dinero *m* de bolsillo ‖ permiso *m*, autorización *f* ‖ TECH tolerancia *f* ‖ — *subsistence allowance* dietas *f pl* ‖ *to make allowances for* tener en cuenta (to take into consideration), ser indulgente con (person).

alloy ['ælɔi] *n* CHEM aleación *f* ‖ FIG mezcla *f*.

alloy [ə'lɔi] *vt* CHEM alear ‖ FIG alterar.

all-powerful ['ɔ:l'pauəful] *adj* omnipotente.

all-purpose ['ɔ:l'pə:pəs] *adj* para todo uso, universal.

all right ['ɔ:l'rait] *adj* ⟶ **right.**

all-round ['ɔ:l'raund] *adj* completo, ta.

all-rounder ['ɔ:l'raundə*] *n* SP jugador, ra versátil *or* polifacético, ca.

All Saints' Day ['ɔ:l'seintsdei] *n* día *m* de Todos los Santos.

All Souls' Day ['ɔ:l'səulzdei] *n* día *m* de los Difuntos.

allspice ['ɔ:lspais] *n* pimienta *f* de Jamaica.

all-star ['ɔ:lsta:*] *adj* de primeras figuras.

all-time ['ɔ:ltaim] *adj* nunca visto, ta; *an all-time success* un éxito nunca visto ‖ nunca alcanzado, da; *an all-time record* un récord nunca alcanzado.

allude [ə'lu:d] *vi* aludir.

allure [ə'ljuə*] *n* atractivo *m*.

allure [ə'ljuə*] *vt* atraer ‖ seducir (to seduce) ‖ apartar (from one's duty).

allurement [-mənt] *n* atractivo *m*.

alluring [-iŋ] *adj* atractivo, va; seductor, ra.

allusion [ə'lu:ʒən] *n* alusión *f*; *she said in allusion to* dijo haciendo alusión a.

allusive [ə'lu:siv] *adj* alusivo, va.

alluvial [ə'lu:vjəl] *adj* GEOL aluvial, de aluvión.

alluvion [ə'lu:vjən] *n* GEOL aluvión *m*.

alluvium [ə'lu:vjəm] *n* GEOL aluvión *m*.
— OBSERV El plural de *alluvium* es *alluviums* o *alluvia*.

all-weather ['ɔ:l'weðə*] *adj* para todo tiempo.

ally ['æli] *n* canica *f* de alabastro (marble).

ally ['ælai] *n* aliado, da.

ally [ə'lai] *vi* aliarse.
◆ *vt* emparentar con ‖ hacer alianza con.

almagest ['ælmədʒest] *n* almagesto *m*.

alma mater ['ælmə'meitə*] *n* alma máter *f*.

almanac ['ɔ:lmənæk] *n* almanaque *m*.

almandine ['ælməndi:n] *n* MIN almandina *f*.

almemar [æl'mi:mɑ:*] *n* REL almimbar *m*.

almemor [æl'mi:mɔ:*] *n* REL almimbar *m*.

almightiness [ɔl'maitinəs] *n* omnipotencia *f*.

almighty [ɔ:l'maiti] *adj* todopoderoso, sa; omnipotente ‖ FAM imponente, enorme ‖ REL *the Almighty* el Todopoderoso, el Altísimo.

almond ['ɑ:mənd] *n* BOT almendro *m* (tree) | almendra *f* (nut) ‖ — *burnt almonds* almendras tostadas ‖ *sugar* o *sugared almond* peladilla *f*.

almond-eyed [-aid] *adj* de ojos rasgados.

almond tree [-tri:] *n* almendro *m*.

almoner ['ɑ:mənə*] *n* asistenta *f* social ‖ limosnero *m* (of church).

Almoravid; Almoravide [ˌælmə'rævid] *adj/n* almorávide.

almost ['ɔ:lməust] *adv* casi.

alms [ɑ:mz] *pl n* limosna *f sing*.

alms box [-bɔks] *n* cepillo *m* para los pobres.

almshouse [-haus] *n* asilo *m* de ancianos.

alodium [ə'ləudjəm] *n* JUR alodio *m*.

aloe ['æləu] *n* BOT áloe *m* ‖ *aloe juice* acíbar *m*.
◆ *pl* MED áloe *m sing*.

aloft [ə'lɔft] *adj/adv* arriba (up) ‖ en el aire, en alto (up in the air) ‖ MAR en la arboladura ‖ en vuelo (plane).

alone [ə'ləun] *adj* solo, la; *I was alone* estaba solo; *all alone* completamente solo ‖ único, ca; *is he alone in speaking so?* ¿es el único en hablar así? ‖ — *let alone* y mucho menos; *I have not twopence, let alone two pounds* no tengo dos peniques y mucho menos dos libras; sin hablar de ‖ *to leave* o *to let alone* dejar en paz (to leave in peace), dejar solo (to leave unaccompanied) ‖ *to stand alone* ser único (to be unique).
◆ *adv* sólo, solamente (exclusively); *that alone can help us* sólo eso nos puede ayudar.

along [ə'lɔŋ] *prep* por; *I was walking along the street* iba por la calle ‖ a lo largo de; *a hedge grows along the path* hay un seto a lo largo del sendero ‖ según (according to).
◆ *adv all along* constantemente, siempre (all the time), desde el principio (from the beginning) ‖ *along with* junto con ‖ *bring your guitar along* tráete la guitarra ‖ *come along with me* venga conmigo ‖ *move along, please!* ¡circulen, por favor! ‖ *to carry along* llevar consigo ‖ *to get along* poder arreglárselas ‖ *to get along (well) with s.o.* llevarse bien con alguien ‖ US *to get along with sth.* seguir, continuar; *get along with your work!* ¡sigue trabajando! | *to go along with* estar de acuerdo con (to agree), acompañar.

alongshore [-ʃɔ:*] *adv* a lo largo de la costa.

alongside [-'said] *prep* junto a, al lado de.
◆ *adv* al lado ‖ MAR de costado ‖ *to come alongside* atracar.

aloof [ə'lu:f] *adv* lejos (apart) ‖ a distancia (at a distance) ‖ *to keep aloof* mantenerse apartado (*from* de).
◆ *adj* reservado, da.

aloofness [-nis] *n* reserva *f*.

alopecia [ælə'pi:ʃiə] *n* MED alopecia *f*.

aloud [ə'laud] *adv* alto, en voz alta ‖ *to cry aloud for* pedir a gritos; *this situation is crying aloud for a solution* esta situación está pidiendo a gritos una solución.

alow [ə'ləu] *adv* MAR abajo.

alp [ælp] *n* montaña *f* (mountain).

alpaca [æl'pækə] *n* alpaca *f*.

alpenstock ['ælpinstɔk] *n* alpenstock *m*, bastón *m* de montañero.

alpha ['ælfə] *n* alfa *f*; *alpha rays* rayos alfa.

alphabet ['ælfəbit] *n* alfabeto *m*.

alphabetic [ˌælfə'betik]; **alphabetical** [-əl] *adj* alfabético, ca; *in alphabetical order* por orden alfabético.

alphanumeric [ˌælfənju'merik] *adj* alfanumérico, ca ‖ INFORM alfanumérico, ca; *alphanumeric keyboard* teclado alfanumérico.

Alphonsine [æl'fɔnsi:n] *adj* *Alphonsine tables* tablas alfonsinas.

alpine ['ælpain] *adj* alpino, na; alpestre.

alpinism ['ælpinizəm] *n* alpinismo *m*.

alpinist ['ælpinist] *n* alpinista *m* & *f*.

alpist ['ælpist] *n* BOT alpiste *m* (canary grass).

Alps [ælps] *pl prn* GEOGR Alpes *m*.

already [ɔ:l'redi] *adv* ya.

alright ['ɔ:l'rait] *adv* → **right (all).**

Alsace ['ælsæs] *pr n* GEOGR Alsacia *f*.

Alsatian [æl'seiʃjən] *adj* alsaciano, na.
◆ *n* alsaciano, na (inhabitant of Alsace) ‖ pastor *m* alemán (dog).

also ['ɔ:lsəu] *adv* también (too, as well) ‖ además (moreover).

also-ran [-ræn] *n* caballo *m* que no se coloca en una carrera (horse racing) ‖ candidato *m* vencido en una elección (in an election) ‖ FAM nulidad *f* (nonentity).

Altaic [æl'teiik] *adj* altaico, ca.

altar ['ɔ:ltə*] *n* REL altar *m* ‖ — *altar boy* monaguillo *m* ‖ *altar cloth* sabanilla *f*, mantel *m* ‖ *high altar* altar mayor ‖ FIG *on the altars of* en aras de.

altarpiece ['ɔ:ltəpi:s] *n* retablo *m*.

altar stone ['ɔ:ltəstəun] *n* ara *f*.

alter ['ɔ:ltə*] *vt* cambiar, modificar, alterar ‖ retocar (a garment) ‖ ARCH reformar ‖ MAR *to alter course* cambiar de rumbo.
◆ *vi* cambiar (to change) ‖ *to alter for the worse* ir cada vez peor, empeorar.

alterability [ˌɔ:ltərə'biliti] *n* alterabilidad *f*.

alteration [ˌɔ:ltə'reiʃən] *n* cambio *m*, modificación *f*, transformación *f* ‖ ARCH reforma *f* ‖ retoque *m* (of a garment).

altercate ['ɔ:ltə:keit] *vi* altercar.

altercation [ˌɔ:ltə:'keiʃən] *n* altercado *m*.

alter ego [æltər'i:gəu] *n* álter ego *m*.

alternant [ɔ:l'tə:nənt] *adj* alternante.

alternate [ɔ:l'tə:nit] *adj* alterno, na; *alternate leaves* hojas alternas; *alternate angles* ángulos alternos ‖ *on alternate days* en días alternos, cada dos días.
◆ *n* sustituto *m*, suplente *m* (substitute).

alternate ['ɔ:ltə:neit] *vt/vi* alternar.

alternately [ɔ:l'tə:nitli] *adv* alternativamente.

alternating ['ɔ:ltə:neitiŋ] *adj* alternativo, va; *the alternating swing of the pendulum* el movimiento alternativo del péndulo ‖ alterno, na (current).

alternation [ˌɔ:ltə:'neiʃən] *n* alternancia *f*, alternación *f* ‖ *in alternation* alternativamente.

alternative [ɔ:l'tə:nətiv] *adj* alternativo, va ‖ — GRAMM *alternative conjunction* conjunción disyuntiva ‖ *alternative energy* energía alternativa ‖ *alternative theatre* teatro alternativo.
◆ *n* alternativa *f* (choice between two things) ‖ *we have no alternative* no tenemos más remedio.

alternator ['ɔ:ltə:ˌneitə*] *n* ELECTR alternador *m*.

although [ɔ:l'ðəu] *conj* aunque, a pesar de que; *although very old, he is still very active* aunque muy viejo aún es muy activo; *I'll do it although it cost me my life* lo haré aunque me cueste la vida; *although it was raining I went out* salí aunque estaba lloviendo.
— OBSERV See THOUGH.

altimeter ['æltimi:tə*] *n* altímetro *m*.

altitude ['æltitju:d] *n* altitud *f* (height above sea level) ‖ MATH & ASTR altura *f*.
◆ *pl* alturas *f*.

alto ['æltəu] *n* MUS contralto *m*.

altogether [ˌɔ:ltə'geðə*] *adv* completamente, del todo (completely); *altogether different* completamente distinto ‖ en total, en conjunto (on the whole) ‖ FAM *in the altogether* en cueros vivos.

altruism ['æltruizəm] *n* altruismo *m*.

altruist ['æltruist] *adj/n* altruista.

altruistic [ˌæltru'istik] *adj* altruista.

alum ['æləm] *n* CHEM alumbre *m*.

alumina [ə'lju:minə] *n* CHEM alúmina *f*.

aluminate [ə'lju:mineit] *vt* TECH aluminar.

aluminium [ˌælju'minjəm] *n* aluminio *m*.

aluminothermy [ə'lju:minəˌθə:mi] *n* CHEM aluminotermia *f*.

aluminous [ə'lju:minəs] *adj* CHEM aluminoso, sa.

aluminum [ə'lu:minəm] *n* US aluminio *m*.

alumna [ə'lʌmnə] *n* US antigua alumna *f*.
— OBSERV El plural de la palabra inglesa es *alumnae*.

alumnus [ə'lʌmnəs] *n* US antiguo alumno *m*.
— OBSERV El plural de la palabra inglesa es *alumni*.

alunite ['æljunait] *n* MIN alunita *f*.

alveolar [æl'viələ*] *adj* alveolar.

alveolate [æl'viəlit] *adj* alveolado, da.

alveolus [æl'viələs] *n* alveolo *m*, alvéolo *m*.
— OBSERV El plural de *alveolus* es *alveoli*.

always ['ɔ:lweiz] *adv* siempre.

am [æm] *pres* → **be.**

a. m. ['ei'em] *adv* de la mañana.

AM *abbr of amplitude modulation* AM, modulación de amplitud.

Amadeus [æmə'di:əs] *pr n* Amadeo *m*.

amadou ['æmədu:] *n* yesca *f*.

amalgam [ə'mælgəm] *n* amalgama *f*.

amalgamate [ə'mælgəmeit] *vt* amalgamar.
◆ *vi* amalgamarse.

amalgamation [əˌmælgə'meiʃən] *n* amalgamación *f*.

amanita [æmə'naitə] *n* amanita *f* (fungus).

amanuensis [əˌmænju'ensis] *n* amanuense *m*.
— OBSERV El plural de *amanuensis* es *amanuenses*.

amaranth ['æmərænθ] *n* BOT amaranto *m*.

amaryllis [æmə'rilis] *n* BOT amarilis *f*.

amass [ə'mæs] *vt* amontonar, acumular.

amateur ['æmətə*] *adj/n* aficionado, da; amateur.

amateurish ['æmə'tə:riʃ] *adj* aficionado, da; amateur ‖ de aficionado.

amateurism [æmə'tə:rizəm] *n* calidad *f* de aficionado *or* de no profesional.

amative ['æmətiv] *adj* apasionado, da; amatorio, ria.

amatory ['æmətəri] *adj* amoroso, sa (feelings) ‖ amatorio, ria (letter) ‖ erótico, ca (poem).

amaurosis [,æmɔ:'rəusis] *n* MED amaurosis *f*.

amaze [ə'meiz] *vt* asombrar.

amazed [-d] *adj* asombrado, da ‖ *to be amazed at* estar *or* quedarse asombrado de.

amazement [-mənt] *n* asombro *m*.

amazing [-iŋ] *adj* asombroso, sa.

amazon ['æməzən] *n* amazona *f* ‖ FIG marimacho *m* (virago).

Amazon ['æməzən] *pr n* GEOGR Amazonas *m*.

Amazonian ['æmə'zəunjən] *adj* amazónico, ca.

ambages ['æmbidʒi:z] *pl n* ambages *m* (circumlocution).

ambassador [æm'bæsədə*] *n* embajador *m*; *ambassador extraordinary, plenipotentiary* embajador extraordinario, plenipotenciario.

ambassadorship [æm'bæsədəʃip] *n* embajada *f*.

ambassadress [æm'bæsədris] *n* embajadora *f*.

amber ['æmbə*] *n* BOT ámbar *m* ‖ ámbar *m* (colour of traffic light).
◆ *adj* ambarino, na.

ambergris ['æmbəgris] *n* ámbar *m* gris.

ambidexter [,æmbi'dekstə*] *adj/n* ambidextro, tra ‖ FIG falso, sa; hipócrita.

ambidextrous [,æmbi'dekstrəs] *adj* ambidextro, tra ‖ FIG doble, falso, sa (two-faced).

ambience ['æmbjəns] *n* ambiente *m*.

ambient ['æmbjənt] *adj* ambiente.

ambiguity ['æmbi'gju:iti] *n* ambigüedad *f*.

ambiguous [æm'bigjuəs] *adj* ambiguo, gua.

ambit ['æmbit] *n* ámbito *m* ‖ límites *m pl* (of a land) ‖ casco *m* (of a town).

ambition [æm'biʃən] *n* ambición *f*; *to have ambition* tener ambición.

ambitious [æm'biʃəs] *adj* ambicioso, sa ‖ *to be ambitious of* ambicionar.

ambivalence [æm'bivələns] *n* ambivalencia *f*.

ambivalent [æm'bivələnt] *adj* ambivalente.

amble ['æmbl] *n* ambladura *f* (of a horse).

amble ['æmbl] *vi* amblar (a horse) ‖ andar sin prisa, deambular (a person).

amblyopia [,æmbli'əupjə] *n* MED ambliopía *f*.

ambo ['æmbəu] *n* ARCH ambón *m* (pulpit).

ambrosia [æm'brəuzjə] *n* ambrosía *f*.

ambrosial [-l] *adj* ambrosíaco, ca.

Ambrosian [-n] *adj* REL ambrosiano, na.

ambry ['æmbri] *n* armario *m* (cupboard).

ambulance ['æmbjuləns] *n* ambulancia *f* ‖ *ambulance man* ambulanciero *m*.

ambulatory ['æmbjulətəri] *adj* ambulatorio, ria ‖ US MED no encamado, da.
◆ *n* ARCH deambulatorio *m*.

ambuscade [,æmbəs'keid] *n* MIL emboscada *f*.

ambush ['æmbuʃ] *n* MIL emboscada *f*; *to lay an ambush* tender una emboscada ‖ FIG asechanza *f*, emboscada *f* ‖ *to lie in ambush* estar emboscado.

ambush ['æmbuʃ] *vt* tender una emboscada ‖ *to be ambushed* caer en una emboscada.
◆ *vi* emboscarse.

ameba [ə'mi:bə] *n* ZOOL ameba *f*, amiba *f*.

ameer [e'miə] *n* emir *m*.

ameliorate [ə'mi:ljəreit] *vt/vi* mejorar (to improve).

amelioration [ə,mi:ljə'reiʃən] *n* mejora *f*, mejoría *f*, mejoramiento *m*.

amen ['ɑ:'men] *interj* amén.

amenability [ə,mi:nə'biliti] *n* sensibilidad *f* (responsiveness) ‖ responsabilidad *f* (responsibility) ‖ docilidad *f* (docility).

amenable [ə'mi:nəbl] *adj* sensible (responsive); *amenable to advice* o *to suggestions* sensible a los consejos *or* a las sugerencias ‖ que se puede someter; *amenable to high temperatures* que se puede someter a temperaturas elevadas ‖ responsable (answerable); *amenable to the law* responsable ante la ley ‖ sujeto, ta; *amenable to a fine* sujeto a multa ‖ dócil, sumiso, sa (obedient) ‖ — *amenable to argument* que se deja convencer ‖ *amenable to reason* capaz de avenirse a razones.

amend [ə'mend] *vt* enmendar; *to amend the constitution, a law, a text* enmendar la constitución, una ley, un texto ‖ rectificar, corregir (to rectify) ‖ mejorar (to improve).
◆ *vi* enmendarse (to improve).

amendable [-əbl] *adj* enmendable.

amendment [-mənt] *n* enmienda *f*; *to propose an amendment* proponer una enmienda; *the amendment of a text, a law* la enmienda de un texto, una ley ‖ rectificación *f*, corrección *f*.

amends [-z] *pl n* reparación *f sing*, compensación *f sing* ‖ — *to make amends for sth.* compensar algo (to compensate for), reparar (to put right); *to make amends for an offence* reparar una ofensa ‖ *to make amends to s.o. for sth.* compensar a alguien de algo (to compensate), indemnizar a alguien por algo (to indemnify).

amenity [ə'mi:niti] *n* amenidad *f* (pleasantness) ‖ amabilidad *f* (of a person) ‖ comodidad *f*; *shower, telephone and other amenities* ducha, teléfono y otras comodidades.
◆ *pl* etiqueta *f sing* (etiquette) ‖ formalidades *f* (formalities) ‖ normas *f* (rules of conduct) ‖ entretenimientos *m* (entertainments) ‖ *the amenities of life* las cosas agradables de la vida.

amenorrhoea [æ'menə'ri:ə] *n* MED amenorrea *f*.

ament [ə'ment] *n* BOT amento *m* ‖ MED débil mental *m* & *f*, subnormal *m* & *f*.

amentaceous [,æmən'teiʃəs] *adj* BOT amentáceo, a.

amentia [ei'menʃjə] *n* MED debilidad *f* mental.

amentiferous [,æmən'tifərəs] *adj* BOT amentífero, ra.

amerce [ə'mə:s] *vt* multar (to fine).

America [ə'merikə] *pr n* GEOGR América *f*; *North America* América del Norte; *South America* América del Sur; *Central America* América Central ‖ (los) Estados *m pl* Unidos (the United States).

American [-n] *adj/n* americano, na (in general) ‖ americano, na; estadounidense, norteamericano, na (of the United States).
◆ *n* americano *m* (language).

Americanism [ə'merikənizəm] *n* americanismo *m*.

Americanist [ə'merikənist] *n* americanista *m* & *f*.

Americanize [ə'merikənaiz] *vt* americanizar.
◆ *vi* americanizarse.

americium [,æmə'risiəm] *n* americio *m*.

Amerind ['æmərind] *n* amerindio, dia.

Amerindian [,æmər'indjən] *adj* amerindio, dia.

amethyst ['æmiθist] *n* amatista *f*.
◆ *adj* amatista.

ametropia ['æme'trəupiə] *n* MED ametropía *f*.

Amex ['æmeks] *abbr of American Stock Exchange* segunda plaza bursátil norteamericana.

amiability [,eimjə'biliti] *n* amabilidad *f*, afabilidad *f*.

amiable ['eimjəbl] *adj* amable, afable.

amianthus [æmi'ænθəs] *n* amianto *m*.

amicability [,æmikə'biliti] *n* amabilidad *f* ‖ amistad *f* (friendship).

amicable ['æmikəbl] *adj* amistoso, sa; amigable.

amice ['æmis] *n* REL amito *m*.

amid [ə'mid] *prep* entre.

amide ['æmaid] *n* CHEM amida *f*.

amidol ['æmidɔl] *n* CHEM amidol *m*.

amidships [ə'midʃips] ; US **amidship** [ə'midʃip] *adv* MAR en medio del barco.

amidst [ə'midst] *prep* entre.

amine [ə'mi:n] *n* CHEM amina *f*.

amino [ə'mi:nəu] *adj* aminado, da.

amino acid [-'æsid] *n* CHEM aminoácido *m*.

amir [ə'miə] *n* emir *m*.

amiss [ə'mis] *adj* inoportuno, na (inopportune) ‖ malo, la (bad) ‖ — *it would not be amiss for him* no le vendría mal ‖ *there is nothing amiss* no pasa nada ‖ *there is sth. amiss* hay algo que no va (bien) ‖ *what is amiss (with him)?* ¿qué (le) pasa?, ¿qué hay?
◆ *adv* mal (badly, wrongly); *to judge, to play amiss* juzgar, jugar mal ‖ inoportunamente; *to speak amiss* hablar inoportunamente ‖ — *to come amiss* venir mal ‖ *to go amiss* salir mal ‖ *to take amiss* tomar a mal.

amity ['æmiti] *n* amistad *f*.

ammeter ['æmitə*] *n* amperímetro *m*.

ammo ['æməu] *n* FAM munición *f*.

ammonia [ə'məunjə] *n* CHEM amoniaco *m*, amoníaco *m*.

ammoniac [a'məunjæk] *adj* CHEM amoniaco, ca; amoníaco, ca; *sal ammoniac* sal amoniaca.

ammoniated [ə'məunieitid] *adj* amoniacado, da.

ammonite ['æmənait] *n* ZOOL amonita *f* (fossil).

ammonium [ə'meunjəm] *n* CHEM amonio *m*.

ammunition [,æmju'niʃən] *n* munición *f*, municiones *f pl* ‖ FIG argumento *m*, argumentos *m pl*.

amnesia [æm'ni:zjə] *n* MED amnesia *f*.

amnesic [æm'ni:zik] *adj/n* MED amnésico, ca.

amnesty ['æmnesti] *n* amnistía *f*.

amnion ['æmniɔn] *n* ANAT amnios *m*.
— OBSERV El plural de *amnion* es *amnions* o *amnia*.

amniotic [æmni'ɔtik] *adj* ANAT amniótico, ca.

amoeba [ə'mi:bə] *n* ZOOL ameba *f*, amiba *f*.
— OBSERV El plural de *amoeba* es *amoebas* o *amoebae*.

amok [ə'mɔk] ; **amuck** [ə'mʌk] *adv* FIG *they ran amok through the town* atravesaron la ciudad destruyéndolo todo | *to run amok* volverse loco (to go mad).

among [ə'mʌŋ]; **amongst** [-st] *prep* entre; *a house among the trees* una casa entre los árboles; *a king among kings* un rey entre reyes; *they argued among themselves* discutían entre ellos ‖ — *from among* de entre ‖ *to be among those who* ser de los que.

amontillado [əˌmɔntiˈlɑːdəu] *n* amontillado *m* (sherry).

amoral [ˌeiˈmɔrəl] *adj* amoral.

amoralism [-izəm] *n* amoralismo *m*.

amorality [ˌeiməˈræliti] *n* amoralidad *f*.

amorist [ˈæmərist] *n* tenorio *m*.

amorous [ˈæmərəs] *adj* amoroso, sa; *amorous looks* miradas amorosas || enamorado, da (in love) || enamoradizo, za (who falls in love easily) || cariñoso, sa (affectionate).

amorphism [əˈmɔːfizəm] *n* amorfismo *m*.

amorphous [əˈmɔːfəs] *adj* amorfo, fa.

amortization [əˌmɔːtiˈzeiʃən] *n* amortización *f*.

amortize [əˈmɔːtaiz] *vt* amortizar.

amount [əˈmaunt] *n* cantidad *f* (quantity); *a large amount of books* una gran cantidad de libros; *to pay a great amount* pagar una gran cantidad || COMM importe *m* [AMER monto *m*] || *to the amount of* por valor de, hasta un total de.

amount [əˈmaunt] *vi* alcanzar, ascender a, llegar a (to reach); *production amounted to three hundred tons* la producción ascendió a *or* alcanzó trescientas toneladas || sumar, hacer (to add up to); *that amounts to fifteen shillings* eso suma quince chelines || valer; *his argument does not amount to much* su argumento no vale mucho || equivaler a, venir a ser, significar; *his action amounts to treason* su acción equivale a *or* viene a ser una traición.

amour [əˈmuə*] *n* aventura *f* amorosa, amorío *m*.

amp [æmp] *n* ELECTR amperio *m*.

amperage [ˈæmpəridʒ] *n* ELECTR amperaje *m*.

ampere [ˈæmpɛə] *n* ELECTR amperio *m*.

amperemeter [-ˌmiːtə*] *n* amperímetro *m*.

ampere-turn [-təːn] *n* ELECTR amperio vuelta *m*.

ampersand [-sænd] *n* nombre que se da al signo &.

amphetamine [æmˈfetəmin] *n* anfetamina *f*.

amphibian [æmˈfibiən] *n* anfibio *m*.
◆ *adj* anfibio, bia.

amphibious [æmˈfibiəs] *adj* anfibio, bia.

amphibole [ˈæmfibəul] *n* MIN anfíbol *m*.

amphibological [ˌæmfibəˈlɔdʒikəl] *adj* anfibológico, ca.

amphibology [ˌæmfiˈbɔlədʒi] *n* anfibología *f*.

amphictyon [æmˈfiktiən] *n* anfictión *m*.

anphioxus [ˈæmfiɔksəs] *n* ZOOL anfioxo *m*.

amphisbaena [æmfisˈbiːnə] *n* ZOOL anfisbena *f*.

amphiscians [æmˈfiʃiənz] *pl n* anfiscios *m*.

amphitheatre; *US* **amphitheater** [ˈæmfiˌθiətə*] *n* anfiteatro *m* (in hospital, university, theatre, roman games) || GEOL circo *m*.

Amphitrite [ˈæmfitraiti] *pr n* Anfitrita *f*.

Amphitryon [æmˈfitriən] *pr n* Anfitrión *m*.

amphora [ˈæmfərə] *n* ánfora *f*.
— OBSERV El plural es *amphoras* o *amphorae*.

ample [ˈæpl] *adj* amplio, plia; *an ample garden* un jardín amplio; *an ample biography* una biografía amplia || grande; *an ample helping* una porción grande || suficiente, bastante (enough); *it will fit, there's ample room* cabrá, hay bastante sitio || abundante; *an ample meal* una comida abundante || de sobra (more than enough); *to have ample time* tener tiempo de sobra.

ampleness [-nis] *n* amplitud *f* || abundancia *f*.

amplification [ˌæmplifikeiʃən] *n* amplificación *f* (of sound) || aclaración *f*, explicación *f* (explanation).

amplifier [ˈæmplifaiə*] *n* amplificador *m*.

amplify [ˈæmplifai] *vt* amplificar (a sound) || desarrollar (una idea) || aumentar (one's authority).

amplitude [ˈæmplitjuːd] *n* amplitud *f*.

amply [ˈæmpli] *adv* bien; *amply rewarded* bien recompensado || ampliamente || abundantemente.

ampoule [ˈæmpuːl]; **ampule** [ˈæmpjuːl] *n* ampolla *f*.

amputate [ˈæmpjuteit] *vt* amputar.

amputation [ˈæmpjuˈteiʃən] *n* amputación *f*.

Amsterdam [ˈæmstəˈdæm] *pr n* GEOGR Amsterdam.

amuck [əˈmʌk] *adv* ⟶ **amok.**

amulet [ˈæmjulit] *n* amuleto *m*.

amuse [əˈmjuːz] *vt* entretener; *to amuse one's guests* entretener a sus invitados || divertir; *the joke amused everyone* el chiste divirtió a todo el mundo || distraer, entretener (to occupy the attention of) || — *I am not amused* no le veo la gracia || *to amuse o.s.* distraerse, divertirse || *to be amused at* o *by* divertirse con, entretenerse con || *to keep s.o. amused* entretener *or* distraer a uno.

amusement [-mənt] *n* distracción *f*, diversión *f*, entretenimiento *m*; *my favorite amusements* mis distracciones preferidas || pasatiempo *m* (pastime) || regocijo *m* (laughter); *much to my amusement* con gran regocijo mío || — *amusement arcade* sala *f* de juegos recreativos || *amusement park* parque *m* de atracciones || *look of amusement* mirada divertida || *place of amusement* lugar *m* de recreo || *to do sth. for one's amusement* hacer algo para entretenerse || *to try to hide one's amusement* aguantar la risa.
◆ *pl* atracciones *f* (at the fair).

amusing [-iŋ] *adj* divertido, da; gracioso, sa (funny) || entretenido, da (entertaining) || *to be amusing* tener gracia, ser divertido.

amygdala [əˈmigdələ] *n* ANAT amígdala *f*.
— OBSERV El plural de *amygdala* es *amygdalae*.

amygdalaceous [əˌmigdəˈleiʃəs] *adj* amigdaláceo, a.

amygdalin [æˈmigdəlin] *n* amigdalina *f*.

amyl [ˈæmil] *n* CHEM amilo *m*; *amyl acetate* acetato de amilo || *amyl alcohol* alcohol amílico.

amylaceous [ˌæmiˈleiʃəs] *adj* amiláceo, a.

amylase [ˈæmileis] *n* amilasa *f*.

amylene [ˈæmiliːn] *n* CHEM amileno *m*.

amylic [əˈmilik] *adj* amílico, ca.

amyloid [ˈæmilɔid] *adj* amiloide.

amyloidosis [ˈæmilɔiˈdəusis] *n* MED amilosis *f*.

an [æn] *indef art* un, una.
— OBSERV See A, indefinite article.

Anabaptism [ˌænəˈbæptizəm] *n* anabaptismo *m*.

Anabaptist [ˌænəˈbæptist] *adj/n* anabaptista.

anabasis [əˈnæbəsis] *n* anábasis *f*.

anabolic steroid [ænəˈbɔlik ˈsterɔid] *n* MED esteroide anabolizante *m*.

anabolism [əˈnæbəlizəm] *n* anabolismo *m*.

anachronism [əˈnækrənizəm] *n* anacronismo *m*.

anachronistic [əˌnækrəˈnistik] *adj* anacrónico, ca.

anacoluthon [ˌænəkəˈluːθɔn] *n* GRAMM anacoluto *m*.
— OBSERV El plural es *anacolutha* o *anacoluthons*.

anaconda [ˌænəˈkɔndə] *n* ZOOL anaconda *f*.

Anacreon [əˈnækriən] *pr n* Anacreonte *m*.

Anacreontic [əˌnækriˈɔntik] *adj* anacreóntico, ca.

anacrusis [ˌænəˈkruːsis] *n* anacrusis *f*.

anaemia [əˈniːmjə] *n* MED anemia *f*.

anaemic [əˌniːmik] *adj* anémico, ca.

anaerobe [ˈænərəub] *n* anaerobio *m*.

anaerobic [ˈænəˈrəubik] *adj* anaerobio, bia.

anaesthesia [ˌænisˈθiːzjə] *n* anestesia *f*.

anaesthetic [ˌænisˈθetik] *adj* anestésico, ca.
◆ *n* anestésico *m*; *to be under the effect of an anaesthetic* estar bajo los efectos de un anestésico.

anaesthetist [æˈniːsθitist] *n* anestesista *m* & *f*.

anaesthetization [æˌniːsθitiˈzeiʃən] *n* anestesia *f*.

anaesthetize [æˈniːsθitaiz] *vt* anestesiar.

anaglyph [ˈænəglif] *n* anáglifo *m*.

anagoge; anagogy [ˈænəgɔdʒi] *n* anagoge *m*, anagogía *f*.

anagram [ˈænəgræm] *n* anagrama *m*.

anagrammatic [ænəgrəˈmætik]; **anagrammatical** [-al] *adj* anagramático, ca.

anal [ˈeinəl] *adj* ANAT anal.

analecta [ˈænəlektə]; **analects** [ˈænəlekts] *pl n* analectas *f*.

analeptic [ˌænəˈleptik] *adj* analéptico, ca.
◆ *n* analéptico *m*.

analgesia [ˌænælˈdʒiːzjə] *n* MED analgesia *f*.

analgesic [ˈænælˈdʒiːzik] *adj* analgésico, ca.
◆ *n* analgésico *m*.

analog [ˈænəlɔg] *n* ⟶ **analogue.**

analog computer [-kamˈpjuːtə*] *n* INFORM ordenador *m* analógico.

analogic [ænəˈlɔdʒik]; **analogical** [-əl] *adj* analógico, ca || INFORM analógico, ca.

analogism [əˈnælədʒizəm] *n* analogismo *m*.

analogize [əˈnælədʒaiz] *vi* raciocinar basándose en analogías (to use analogy) || *to analogize with* presentar analogías con.
◆ *vt* comparar (to compare).

analogous [əˈnæləgəs] *adj* análogo, ga.

analogue; analog [ˈænəlɔg] *n* cosa *f* análoga (thing) || término *m* análogo (word) || BIOL órgano *m* análogo.

analogy [əˈnælədʒi] *n* analogía *f* || — *on the analogy of* por analogía con || *to make* o *draw an analogy between* trazar una anlogía entre.

analysable; analyzable [ˈænəlaizəbl] *adj* analizable.

analysand [əˈnæləˌsænd] *n* persona *f* que sigue un tratamiento de psicoanálisis.

analyse [ˈænəlaiz] *vt* analizar || psicoanalizar.

analyser [-ə*] *n* analizador *m* || INFORM analizador *m*.

analysis [əˈnæləsis] *n* análisis *m* || psicoanálisis *m* || *in the final* o *last analysis* después de considerar todos los aspectos.
— OBSERV El plural de *analysis* es *analyses*.

analyst [ˈænəlist] *n* analista *m* & *f* || psicoanalista *m* & *f*.

analytic [ˌænəˈlitik]; **analytical** [-əl] *adj* analítico, ca; *analytic language* lengua analítica; *analytical geometry* geometría analítica.

analytics [-s] *n* analítica *f*.

analyzable [ˈænəlaizəbl] *adj* analizable.

analyze [ˈænəlaiz] *vt* analizar || psicoanalizar.

analyzer [-ə*] *n* analizador *m*.

anapaest; *US* **anapest** [ˈænəpiːst] *n* anapesto *m* (metrical foot).

anapaestic; *US* **anapestic** [ænəˈpiːstik] *adj* anapéstico, ca.

anaphase [ˈænəfeiz] *n* anafase *f*.

anaphora [ə'næfərə] *n* anáfora *f.*

anaphrodisia [ˌænæfrə'diziə] *n* anafrodisia *f.*

anaphrodisiac ['ænæfrə'diziæk] *n* anafrodisíaco *m.*
◆ *adj* anafrodisíaco, ca.

anaphylactic [ˌænəfi'læktik] *adj* anafiláctico, ca.

anaphylaxis [ˌænəfi'læksis] *n* MED anafilaxia *f*, anafilaxis *f.*

anarchic [æ'nɑːkik]; **anarchical** [-əl] *adj* anárquico, ca.

anarchism ['ænəkizəm] *n* anarquismo *m.*

anarchist ['ænəkist] *adj/n* anarquista.

anarchy ['ænəki] *n* anarquía *f.*

anastigmatic [ˌænəstig'mætik] *adj* anastigmático, ca.

anastomose [ə'næstəməuz] *vi* BIOL anastomosarse.

anastomosis [ˌænəstə'məusis] *n* BIOL anastomosis *f.*
— OBSERV El plural de la palabra inglesa es *anastomoses.*

anathema [ə'næθimə] *n* REL anatema *m* || FIG *it is anathema to him* le es odioso.

anathematize [ə'næθimətaiz] *vt* anatematizar.

Anatolia [ˌænə'təuljə] *pr n* GEOGR Anatolia *f.*

anatomic [ˌænə'tɔmik]; **anatomical** [-əl] *adj* anatómico, ca.

anatomist [ə'nætəmist] *n* anatomista *m* & *f.*

anatomize [ə'nætəmaiz] *vt* anatomizar || FIG analizar.

anatomy [ə'nætəmi] *n* anatomía *f.*

anatoxin [ˌænə'tɔksin] *n* MED anatoxina *f.*

anatropal [ə'nætrəpəl]; **anatropous** [ə'nætrəpəs] *adj* BOT anátropo, pa.

Anaxagoras [ˌænæk'sægəræs] *pr n* Anaxágoras *m.*

ANC *abbr of African National Congress* CNA, Congreso Nacional Africano.

ancestor ['ænsistə*] *n* antepasado *m*, ascendiente *m* || *ancestor worship* el culto de los antepasados.

ancestral [æn'sestrəl] *adj* ancestral || *ancestral home* casa solariega.

ancestry ['ænsistri] *n* ascendencia *f*, linaje *m.*

anchor ['æŋkə*] *n* MAR ancla *f* || TECH áncora *f* (of watch, walls) || FIG pilar *m* (reliable person) || — MAR *at anchor* al ancla, anclado || FIG *he had been the anchor of all my hopes* había puesto todas mis esperanzas en él | *sheet anchor* ancla de salvación || MAR *to cast* o *to drop anchor* echar el ancla, anclar | *to weigh anchor* levar anclas, zarpar.

anchor ['æŋkə*] *vt* MAR anclar || FIG sujetar, afianzar (to secure).
◆ *vi* MAR echar el ancla, fondear, anclar.

anchorage [-ridʒ] *n* MAR ancladero *m*, fondeadero *m*, anclaje *m* (place) | derechos *m pl* de anclaje (fee) | anclaje *m* (action).

anchoress [-ris] *n* anacoreta *f.*

anchoret [-ret]; **anchorite** [-rait] *n* anacoreta *m.*

anchorman [-mæn] *n* RAD comunicador *m* coordenador [de un programa en multiplex].

anchovy ['æntʃəvi] *n* boquerón *m* (fresh or live) || anchoa *f* (salted, in tins).

anchylose ['æŋkiləus] *vt* anquilosar.
◆ *vi* anquilosarse.

anchylosis ['æŋki'ləusis] *n* MED anquilosis *f.*

ancient ['einʃənt] *adj* antiguo, gua; *ancient Greece* Grecia antigua; *ancient customs* costumbres antiguas; *an ancient copy of a newspaper* un número antiguo de un periódico || anticuado, da (old-fashioned).
◆ *n* antiguo *m*; *the ancients* los antiguos || anciano, na (old person).

ancillary [æn'siləri] *adj* auxiliar; *surgery and ancillary services* cirugía y servicios auxiliares || subordinado, da || anexo, xa; *ancillary plants* fábricas anexas || secundario, ria || afín (related).

ancon ['æŋkɔn] *n* ancón *m.*

ancylostomiasis [ˌæŋkiləustəu'maiəsis] *n* MED anquilostomiasis *f.*

and [ænd] *conj* y, e (see OBSERV); *men and women* hombres y mujeres; *thousands and thousands* miles y miles || a; *go and look for him* vete a buscarle || (omitted in Spanish); *two hundred and thirty* doscientos treinta; *try and come* intente venir || — *and so* y entonces || *and so on, and so forth* etcétera || *and so on, and so forth* etcétera, etcétera || *colder and colder* cada vez más frío || *more and more* cada vez más || *now and then* de vez en cuando || *to try and do sth.* tratar de *or* intentar hacer algo || *you can't come and go without showing the pass* no puede entrar ni salir sin enseñar el permiso.
— OBSERV The conjunction *e* replaces *y* before words beginning with *i* or *hi* (vocalic i): *Federico e Isabel* Frederick and Isabella; *madre e hija* mother and daughter. However, at the beginning of an interrogative or exclamatory sentence, or before a word beginning with *y* or *hi* followed by a vowel (consonantal i), the *y* is retained: *¿y Ignacio?* and Ignatius?; *vid y hiedra* vine an ivy; *tú y yo* you and I.

Andalusia [ˌændə'luːzjə] *pr n* GEOGR Andalucía *f.*

Andalusian [-n] *adj/n* andaluz, za.

andante [æn'dænti] *adv* MUS andante.
◆ *n* MUS andante *m.*

andantino [ændæn'tiːnəu] *adv* MUS andantino.
◆ *n* MUS andantino *m.*

Andean [æn'diːən] *adj* andino, na.

Andes ['ændiːz] *pl prn* GEOGR Andes *m* || GEOGR *the Andes Mountain Ranges* la cordillera de los Andes.

andesite ['ændəzait] *n* andesita *f.*

andiron ['ændaiən] *n* morillo *m.*

Andorra [æn'dɔrə] *pr n* GEOGR Andorra *f.*

Andorran [-n] *adj/n* andorrano, na.

Andrew ['ændruː] *pr n* Andrés *m* || *St Andrew's cross* cruz *f* de San Andrés, aspa *f.*

androecium [æn'driːsjəm] *n* BOT androceo *m.*
— OBSERV El plural de *androecium* es *androecia.*

androgen ['ændrəudʒən] *n* BOT andrógeno *m.*

androgynous [æn'drɔdʒinəs] *adj* andrógino, na.

android ['ændrɔid] *n* androide *m.*

Andromache [æn'drɔməki] *pr n* Andrómaca *f.*

Andromeda [æn'drɔmidə] *pr n* ASTR Andrómeda *f.*

anecdotal [ˌænek'dəutl] *adj* anecdótico, ca.

anecdote ['ænikdəut] *n* anécdota *f.*

anecdotical ['ænək'dɔtikl] *adj* anecdótico, ca.

anecdotist ['ænikˌdəutist] *n* anecdotista *m* & *f.*

anemia [ə'niːmjə] *n* US MED anemia *f.*

anemic [ə'niːmik] *adj* US MED anémico, ca.

anemograph [ə'neməugrɑːf] *n* PHYS anemógrafo *m.*

anemometer [ˌæni'mɔmitə'] *n* PHYS anemómetro *m.*

anemometry [ˌæni'mɔmitri] *n* PHYS anemometría *f.*

anemone [ə'neməni] *n* BOT anémona *f*, anémone *f* (plant) || *sea anemone* anémona de mar.

anemophilous [ˌænə'mɔfələs] *adj* BOT anemófilo, la.

aneroid ['ænərɔid] *adj* PHYS aneroide; *aneroid barometer* barómetro aneroide.

anesthesia [ˌænis'θiːzjə] *n* US MED anestesia *f.*

anesthetic [ˌænis'θetik] *adj* US anestésico, ca.
◆ *n* anestésico *m.*

anesthetist [æ'niːsθitist] *n* US anestesista *m* & *f.*

anesthetize [æ'niːsθitaiz] *vt* US MED anestesiar.

aneurysm; aneurism ['ænjuərizəm] *n* MED aneurisma *m.*

anew [ə'njuː] *adv* otra vez, de nuevo (again) || de nuevo (afresh).

anfractuosity [ˌænfræktju'ɔsiti] *n* anfractuosidad *f.*

angaria [æn'gæriə] *n* angaria *f.*

angel ['eindʒəl] *n* ángel *m*; *guardian angel* ángel custodio, ángel de la guarda; *fallen angel* ángel caído || FIG cielo *m*; *what an angel you are!* ¡qué cielo eres! || THEATR & FAM productor *m* de una obra || HIST moneda *f* de oro || *to sing like an angel* cantar como los ángeles.

angelfish [-fiʃ] *n* ZOOL angelote *m.*

angelic [æn'dʒelik] *adj* angelical; angélico, ca.

angelica [æn'dzelikə] *n* BOT angélica *f.*

angelical [-l] *adj* angelical; angélico, ca.

Angelus ['ændʒələs] *n* ángelus *m* (prayer, bell).

anger ['æŋgə*] *n* ira *f*, cólera *f*, enojo *m*; *to vent one's anger on s.o.* desahogar su ira en alguien; *to act in anger* dejarse llevar por la cólera || *to speak in anger* hablar furioso.

anger ['æŋgə*] *vt* enojar, enfadar, encolerizar, airar.
◆ *vi* encolerizarse, enfadarse, enojarse.

Angevin; Angevine ['ændʒivin] *adj/n* angevino, na; de Anjou.

angina [æn'dʒainə] *n* MED angina *f*; *angina pectoris* angina de pecho.

angiography [ændʒi'ɔgrəfi] *n* angiografía *f.*

angiology [ændʒi'ɔlədʒi] *n* angiología *f.*

angioma [ændʒi'əumə] *n* MED angioma *m.*
— OBSERV El plural de la palabra inglesa es *angiomata* o *angiomas.*

angiosperm ['ændʒjəuˌspəːm] *n* BOT angiosperma *f.*

angle ['æŋgl] *n* ángulo *m*; *alternate angles* ángulos alternos; *at right angles* en ángulo recto || ángulo *m* (of solid) || punto *m* de vista, aspecto *m* (point of view); *that is another angle to the problem* ése es otro aspecto del problema || — *at an angle* al bies (crooked) || *to be at an angle to* formar ángulo con || FIG *to try to look at a problem from another angle* intentar enfocar el problema de otra manera *or* desde otro punto de vista.

angle ['æŋgl] *vi* pescar con caña (to fish) || FIG & FAM *to angle for* ir a la caza de.
◆ *vt* US formar ángulo con | FAM presentar bajo cierto punto de vista, enfocar (a report).

angled [-d] *adj* angular, angulado, da || al bies.

angle iron [-ˌaiən] *n* angular *m*, ángulo *m.*

angler [-ə*] *n* pescador *m* de caña || pejesapo *m*, rape *m* (fish).

Angles [-z] *pl prn* anglos *m.*

anglesite [-sait] *n* MIN anglesita *f.*

Anglian ['æŋgliən] *adj/n* anglo, gla.

Anglican ['æŋglikən] *adj/n* REL anglicano, na.

Anglicanism [-izəm] *n* REL anglicanismo *m*.

Anglicism ['æŋglisizəm] *n* anglicismo *m*.

Anglicist ['æŋglisist] *n* anglicista *m* & *f*.

anglicize ['æŋglisaiz] *vt* anglicanizar, hacer inglés.

angling ['æŋgliŋ] *n* pesca *f* con caña.

Anglo-American ['æŋgləuə'merikən] *adj/n* angloamericano, na.

Anglo-Arab ['æŋgləu'ærəb] *n* angloárabe *m* & *f*.

Anglo-Arabian ['æŋgləuə'reibjən] *adj* angloárabe.

Anglomania ['æŋgləu'meinjə] *n* anglomanía *f*.

Anglomaniac ['æŋgləu'meiniæk] *n* anglómano, na.

Anglo-Norman ['æŋgləu'nɔːmən] *adj/n* anglonormando, da.

Anglophil; Anglophile ['æŋgləufail] *adj/n* anglófilo, la.

Anglophilia [æŋgləu'filiə] *n* anglofilia *f*.

Anglophobe ['æŋgləufəub] *adj/n* anglófobo, ba.

Anglophobia [æŋgləu'fəubjə] *n* anglofobia *f*.

Anglo-Saxon ['æŋgləu'sæksən] *adj/n* anglosajón, ona.

Angola [æŋ'gaulə] *pr n* GEOGR Angola *f*.

Angolese [æŋgəu'liːz] *adj/n* angolés, esa.

angora [æŋ'gɔːrə] *n* lana *f* de angora.

Angora [æŋ'gɔːrə] *pr n* HIST Angora ‖ *Angora cat, goat, rabbit* gato, cabra, conejo de Angora.

angostura [æŋgɔs'tjuərə] *n* BOT angostura *f*.

angrily ['æŋgrili] *adv* con enojo, airadamente.

angry ['æŋgri] *adj* enfadado, da; enojado, da; airado, da; *to be angry at* o *with s.o.* estar enfadado con alguien; *to be angry at sth.* estar enfadado por algo ‖ FIG amenazador, ra (menacing) | tormentoso, sa; borrascoso, sa (sky) | enfurecido, da; embravecido, da; desencadenado, da (sea) ‖ MED inflamado, da (sore) ‖ — *I will be angry* me enfadaré ‖ *to get angry* enfadarse, enojarse, enfurecerse ‖ *to make angry* enfadar, enojar, enfurecer, airar.

angst [æŋst] *n* angustia *f*, ansiedad *f*.

angstrom ['æŋstrəm] *n* PHYS angström *m*.

anguillule [æŋ'gwlijul] *n* ZOOL anguílula *f*.

anguish ['æŋgwiʃ] *n* angustia *f*, congoja *f* ‖ dolor *m* (pain) ‖ MED angustia *f* ‖ *to be in anguish* estar angustiado.

angular ['æŋgjulə*] *adj* angular (shape, distance, etc.) ‖ anguloso, sa (features).

angularity ['æŋgju'læriti] *n* forma *f* angular, angularidad *f*.

angulate ['æŋgjuleit] *adj* angulado, da; anguloso, sa.

anhydride [æn'haidraid] *n* CHEM anhídrido *m*.

anhydrite [æn'haidrait] *n* MIN anhidrita *f*.

anhydrous [æn'haidrəs] *adj* CHEM anhidro, dra.

anil ['ænil] *n* añil *m*, índigo *m*.

anile ['einail] *adj* senil ‖ FAM imbécil.

anilin ['ænilin]; **aniline** ['æniliːn] *n* CHEM anilina *f*.

animadversion [ænimæd'vəʃən] *n* animadversión *f* (ill will) ‖ censura *f*, reprobación *f* (blame).

animadvert [ænimæd'vəːt] *vi* *to animadvert on s.o.'s action* censurar *or* reprobar la acción de alguien.

animal ['æniməl] *adj* animal; *the animal kingdom* el reino animal ‖ *animal charcoal* carbón *m* animal.

◆ *n* animal *m*; *domestic animal* animal doméstico; *wild animal* animal salvaje ‖ FIG animal *m* (brute).

animalcule ['æni'mælkjuːl] *n* ZOOL animálculo *m*.

animal husbandry ['ænimәl'hʌzbəndri] *n* ganadería *f*, cría *f* de animales.

animalism ['ænimәlizəm] *n* animalismo *m*.

animality [æni'mæliti] *n* animalidad *f* ‖ reino animal (animal kingdom).

animalize ['ænimәlaiz] *vt* animalizar.

animal power ['ænimәl,pauə*] *n* fuerza *f* de tracción animal.

animal spirits ['ænimәl'spirits] *pl n* vitalidad *f sing*, animación *f sing*, vigor *m sing*.

animate ['ænimit] *adj* animado, da; vivo, va; *animate beings* seres animados.

animate ['ænimeit] *vt* animar (to give life to); *the soul animates the body* el alma anima el cuerpo ‖ alentar, animar (to motivate) ‖ animar (to liven up); *to animate the conversation* animar la conversación.

animated [-id] *adj* animado, da; *an animated street, person, discussion* una calle, una persona, una discusión animada ‖ vivo, va (lively) ‖ que tiene vida (painting, sculpture) ‖ *animated cartoons* dibujos animados.

animation [æni'meiʃən] *n* animación *f*.

animator ['ænimeitə*] *n* animador, ra.

animism ['ænimizəm] *n* animismo *m*.

animist ['ænimist] *n* animista *m* & *f*.

animistic ['æni'mistik] *adj* animista.

animosity [æni'mɔsiti] *n* animosidad *f*.

animus ['æniməs] *n* animosidad *f* ‖ ánimo *m*, intención *f* (will).

anion ['ænaiən] *n* PHYS anión *m*.

anise ['ænis] *n* BOT anís *m* ‖ *star anise* anís estrellado.

aniseed ['ænisiːd] *n* BOT anís *m*.

anisette [æni'zet] *n* anisete *m*, licor *m* de anís.

anisopetalous [ə,naisə'pətələs] *adj* BOT anisopétalo, la.

anisophyllous [ə,naisə'filəs] *adj* BOT anisófilo, la.

anisotropic [ə,naisə'trɔpik] *adj* anisótropo, pa.

Ankara ['æŋkərə] *pr m* GEOGR Ankara.

ankle ['æŋkl] *n* ANAT tobillo *m* ‖ — *ankle socks* calcetines *m* ‖ *ankle support* tobillera *f*.

anklebone [-bəun] *n* hueso *m* del tobillo.

anklet ['æŋklit] *n* ajorca *f* para el tobillo ‖ US calcetín *m* (sock).

ankylose ['æŋkiləuz] *vt* anquilosar.

◆ *vi* anquilosarse.

ankylosis [æŋki'ləusis] *n* MED anquilosis *f*.

ankylostomiasis ['æŋkiləstə'maiəsis] *n* MED anquilostomiasis *f*.

Ann [æn] *pr n* Ana *f*.

annalist ['ænəlist] *n* analista *m* & *f*.

annals ['ænlz] *pl n* anales *m*.

Annam ['ænæm] *pr n* GEOGR Anam *m*.

Annamite ['ænəmait] *adj/n* anamita.

Anne [æn] *pr n* Ana *f*.

anneal [ə'niːl] *vt* TECH recocer ‖ FIG endurecer.

annealing [-iŋ] *n* TECH recocido *m*.

annelid ['ænəlid] *n* ZOOL anélido *m*.

annex [ə'neks] *vt* anexionar, anexar (territory) ‖ añadir, adjuntar (to add) ‖ adjuntar (to a document).

annex; annexe ['æneks] *n* anexo *m*, dependencia *f* (of a building) ‖ anexo *m*, apéndice *m* (of a document).

◆ *pl* JUR anexidades *f*.

annexation [ænek'seiʃən] *n* anexión *f*.

annexationism [ænek'seiʃənizəm] *n* anexionismo *m*.

annexationist [ænek'seiʃənist] *adj/n* anexionista.

annexed [ə'nekst] *adj* anexo, xa; anejo, ja.

annihilate [ə'naiəleit] *vt* aniquilar.

annihilation [ənaiə'leiʃən] *n* aniquilación *f*, aniquilamiento *m*.

anniversary ['æni'vəːsəri] *n* aniversario *m*; *wedding anniversary* aniversario de boda; *the anniversary of an event* el aniversario de un suceso ‖ *gold, silver anniversary* bodas *f pl* de oro, de plata.

annona [ə'nəunə] *n* BOT anona *f* (soursop).

annotate ['ænəuteit] *vt* anotar (to write explanatory notes in) ‖ comentar (to comment on).

◆ *vi* poner notas, hacer anotaciones.

annotation ['ænəu'teiʃən] *n* anotación *f*, nota *f* ‖ comentario *m*.

annotator ['ænəuteitə*] *n* anotador, ra.

announce [ə'nauns] *vt* anunciar; *to announce a piece of news* anunciar una noticia; *to announce a guest* anunciar a un invitado; *he suddenly announced that he was leaving* de repente anunció que se iba a marchar ‖ comunicar, hacer saber (to inform).

◆ *vi* ser locutor (on the radio, television).

announcement [-mənt] *n* anuncio *m* ‖ declaración *f* ‖ aviso *m*; *to make an announcement to the public* dar un aviso al público.

announcer [-ə*] *n* locutor, ra (on the radio, television) ‖ anunciador, ra.

annoy [ə'nɔi] *vt* molestar, fastidiar (to bother) ‖ enfadar, enojar (to anger) ‖ MIL acosar (the enemy) ‖ *to be annoyed about, at* estar enfadado por, con.

annoyance [ə'nɔiəns] *n* enfado *m*, enojo *m* (anger) ‖ molestia *f*, fastidio *m* (annoying thing) ‖ *what an annoyance!* ¡qué molesto!, ¡qué fastidio!

annoying [ə'nɔiiŋ] *adj* molesto, ta; fastidioso, sa; *how annoying you are!* ¡qué molesto eres!; *annoying requirements* requisitos molestos.

annual ['ænjuəl] *adj* anual; *annual income* renta anual; *annual ceremony* ceremonia anual; *annual plant* planta anual ‖ BOT *annual ring* capa *f* cortical (of a tree).

◆ *n* anuario *m* (publication) ‖ BOT planta *f* anual.

annuitant [ə'njuitənt] *n* rentista *m* & *f*, censualista *m* & *f*.

annuity [ə'njuiti] *n* anualidad *f* ‖ renta *f* vitalicia (life annuity).

annul [ə'nʌl] *vt* anular (marriages, wills, contracts, etc.) ‖ cancelar, abrogar (laws) ‖ denunciar (a treaty).

annular ['ænjulə*] *adj* anular.

annulate ['ænjuleit] *adj* anillado, da.

annulet ['ænjulet] *n* anillito *m* (small ring) ‖ ARCH collarino *m*.

annulment [ə'nʌlmənt] *n* anulación *f* (of marriages, wills, contracts, etc.) ‖ cancelación *f*, abrogación *f* (of laws) ‖ denuncia *f* (of a treaty).

annum ['ænəm] *n* año *m* (year) ‖ *per annum* por año, al año, anualmente.

annunciate [əˌnʌnʃieit] *vt* anunciar.

Annunciation [əˌnʌnsiˈeiʃən] *n* REL Anunciación *f.*

annunciator [əˈnʌnʃieitə*] *n* anunciador, ra (person) || cuadro *m* indicador (electric indicator).

anode [ˈænəud] *n* ELECTR ánodo *m.*

anodic [əˈnɔdik] *adj* PHYS anódico, ca.

anodon [ˈænədɔn]; **anodont** [ˈænədɔnt] *n* ZOOL anodonte *m.*

anodontia [ænəˈdɔnʃə] *n* anodontia *f.*

anodyne [ˈænəudain] *adj* MED anodino, na || FIG anodino, na.
◆ *n* MED anodino *m*, calmante *m.*

anodynia [ænəˈdiniə] *n* MED anodinia *f.*

anoint [əˈnɔint] *vt* untar, ungir || REL ungir || FAM *to anoint the palm* untar la mano (to bribe).

anointment [-mənt] *n* ungimiento *m.*

anomalous [əˈnɔmələs] *adj* anómalo, la.

anomaly [əˈnɔməli] *n* anomalía *f.*

anon [əˈnɔn] *adv* POET luego, dentro de poco tiempo || *ever and anon* de vez en cuando.

anona [əˈnəunə] *n* BOT anona *f* (soursop).

anonym [ˈænənim] *n* anónimo *m* (person) || seudónimo *m* (pseudonym).

anonymity [ˌænəˈnimiti] *n* anónimo *m*, anonimato *m.*

anonymous [əˈnɔniməs] *adj* anónimo, ma || *to remain anonymous* conservar el anónimo.

anopheles [əˈnɔfiliːz] *n* anofeles *m.*

anorak [ˈænəræk] *n* anorak *m.*

anorexia [ænəˈreksiə]; **anorexy** [ˈænəreksi] *n* MED anorexia *f.*

anorexic [ˌænəˈreksik] *adj* MED anoréxico, ca.

anosmia [əˈnɔzmjə] *n* MED anosmia *f.*

another [əˈnʌðə*] *adj* otro, tra; *another cup of coffee* otra taza de café || más (more); *it will take another three years* tardará tres años más; *another ten pounds* diez libras más || — *another one* otro, otra || *another time* otro día (some other day), otra vez (again) || *in another way* de otra manera || *many another* otros muchos || *one another* unos y otros || *such another* otro igual || *that is another matter* eso es otra cosa || *to feel another person* sentirse distinto, no ser el mismo || *to help one another* ayudarse unos a otros || *without another word* sin más palabras, sin decir nada más.
◆ *pron* otro, tra; *may I have another?* ¿puedo tomar otro? || *another would have done it in a different way* cualquier otro lo hubiese hecho de manera diferente.

anouran [əˈnurən] *adj/n* ⟶ **anuran.**

anoxemia [ˌænɔkˈsiːmiə] *n* MED anoxemia *f.*

anserine [ˈænsərain] *adj* ansarino, na || FIG estúpido, da.

answer [ˈɑːnsə*] *n* contestación *f*, respuesta *f*; *a negative answer* una contestación negativa || réplica *f* (to an insult) || solución *f*; *the answer is to study harder* la solución es estudiar más || JUR réplica *f* || MATH solución *f* (of a problem); *what do you make the answer?* ¿qué solución tiene? | resultado *m* (of a sum) || razón *f*, explicación *f* (reason) || — *in answer to* en respuesta a, contestando a || *the answer to one's dreams* la realización de sus sueños || *to have an answer for everything* tener una respuesta para todo, tener siempre respuesta || *to make no answer* no contestar || *to write s.o. an answer* contestar a uno por escrito.

answer [ˈɑːnsə*] *vt* contestar a, responder a (door, etc.) || contestar (a), responder a (a letter) || contestar (to one's name) || contestar a, atender a, responder a (the telephone) || satisfacer, responder a (one's needs) || servir para, convenir para (a purpose) || corresponder a, responder a, cuadrar con; *to answer the description* corresponder a la descripción || escuchar, oír (the prayers) || — JUR *to answer a charge* defenderse contra una acusación || *to answer one's dreams* realizar los sueños de uno || *to answer one's expectations* colmar las esperanzas de uno || *to answer s.o. back* replicarle a uno || MAR *to answer the helm* obedecer al timón || *to answer the requirements* cumplir *or* satisfacer los requisitos.
◆ *vi* contestar, responder; *to answer correctly* contestar bien; *to answer to one's name* contestar al ser llamado; *to answer with a counterattack* contestar con un contraataque || replicar (to retort) || obedecer; *the car would not answer to the wheel* el coche no obedecía al volante || corresponder; *to answer to a description* corresponder a una descripción || satisfacer; *to answer to one's requirements* satisfacer los requisitos de uno || — *don't answer back!* ¡no replique!, ¡no sea respondón! || *to answer for* responder de (sth.), responder por, salir fiador de (s.o.) || *to answer to the name of* responder al nombre de, tener por nombre.

answerable [ˈɑːnsərəbl] *adj* responsable (*for* de) (responsible) || refutable (objection) || que admite una respuesta (question) || MATH solucionable.

answerer [ˈɑːnsərə*] *n* JUR fiador *m*, garante *m.*

answering machine [ˈɑːnseriŋməˈʃiːn]; **answer phone** [ˈɑːnserfəun] *n* contestador *m* automático.

ant [ænt] *n* ZOOL hormiga *f.*

anta [ˈæntə] *n* ARCH anta *f* || ZOOL tapir *m* [AMER anta *f*].
— OBSERV El plural de *anta* en inglés es *antae.*

antagonism [ænˈtægənizəm] *n* antagonismo *m.*

antagonist [ænˈtaegənist] *adj/n* antagonista.

antagonistic [ænˌtægəˈnistik] *adj* antagónico, ca || ANAT antagonista.

antagonize [ænˈtægənaiz] *vt* contrariar (to counteract, to annoy) || suscitar el antagonismo de (to provoke hostility) || enemistarse con (to become an enemy).

Antananarivo [ˈæntaˌnænəˈriːvəu] *pr n* GEOGR Tananarivo.

Antarctic [ænˈtɑːktik] *adj* antártico, ca.
◆ *pr m* GEOGR Antártico *m.*

Antarctica [ænˈtɑːktikə] *pr n* GEOGR Antártida *f.*

ant bear [ˈæntˌbɛə*] *n* ZOOL oso *m* hormiguero.

ante [ˈænti] *n* apuesta *f* inicial (poker) || FAM cuota *f* (the share one pays).

ante [ˈænti] *vi* apostar || *to ante up* contribuir.

anteater [ˈæntˌiːtə*] *n* ZOOL oso *m* hormiguero.

antecedence [ˌæntiˈsiːdəns] *n* precedencia *f*, anterioridad *f* || ASTR antecedencia *f.*

antecedent [ˌæntiˈsiːdənt] *adj* precedente, anterior, antecedente || GRAMM antecedente.
◆ *n* antecedente *m*; *the antecedents and consequences of the war* los antecedentes y las consecuencias de la guerra || GRAMM & MATH & MUS antecedente *m.*
◆ *pl* antepasados *m*, antecesores *m* (ancestors).

antechamber [ˈæntiˌtʃeimbə*] *n* antecámara *f.*

antechapel [ˈæntiˌtʃæpəl] *n* antecapilla *f.*

antechoir [ˈæntiˌkwaiə*] *n* antecoro *m.*

antedate [ˈæntiˌdeit] *n* antedate *f.*

antedate [ˈæntiˈdeit] *vt* antedatar (to backdate) || preceder, ser anterior a.

antediluvian [ˈæntidiˈluːvjən] *adj* antediluviano, na || FIG antediluviano, na; anticuado, da.
◆ *n* FIG cavernícola *m* (person) | antigualla *f* (thing).

antefix [ˈætifiks] *n* ARCH antefijo *m.*

antelope [ˈæntiləup] *n* ZOOL antílope *m.*

antemeridian [ˈæntiməˈridiən] *adj* antemeridiano, na.

ante meridiem [ˈæntiməˈridiəm] *adj* de la mañana, ante meridiem.
— OBSERV La expresión *ante meridiem* se usa normalmente en la forma abreviada *a.m.*: *seven a.m.* las siete de la mañana.

antenatal [ˈæntiˈneitl] *adj* antenatal, prenatal.

antenna [ænˈtenə] *n* antena *f.*
— OBSERV El plural de *antenna* es *antennae* o *antennas* cuando tiene un sentido zoológico y *antennas* en los demás casos.

antenuptial [ˈæntiˈnqipʃəl] *adj* prenupcial.

antepenult [ˈæntipiˈnʌlt] *n* antepenúltima *f* (antepenultimate syllable).

antepenultimate [ˈæntipiˈnʌltimit] *adj* antepenúltimo, ma.
◆ *n* antepenúltimo, ma || antepenúltima *f* (syllable).

anterior [ænˈtiəriə*] *adj* anterior (*to* a).

anteriority [æntiəriˈɔriti] *n* anterioridad *f.*

anteroom [ˈæntirum] *n* antecámara *f*, antesala *f* (antechamber) || sala *f* de espera (waiting room).

anthelmintic [ænθelˈmintik] *adj* vermífugo, ga; antihelmíntico, ca.
◆ *n* vermífugo *m*, antihelmíntico *m.*

anthem [ˈænθəm] *n* himno *m*; *national anthem* himno nacional || REL antífona *f.*

anther [ˈænθə*] *n* BOT antera *f.*

antheridium [ˌænθəˈridjəm] *n* BOT anteridia *f.*
— OBSERV El plural de *antheridium* es *antheridia.*

anthill [ˈænthil] *n* hormiguero *m.*

anthological [ˌænθəˈlɔdʒikəl] *adj* antológico, ca.

anthology [ænˈθɔlədʒi] *n* antología *f.*

Anthony [ˈæntəni] *pr n* Antonio *m.*

anthozoa [ˈænθəuˈzəuə] *pl n* ZOOL antozoarios *m.*

anthracene [ˈænθrəsiːn] *n* antraceno *m.*

anthracite [ˈænθrəsait] *n* antracita *f.*

anthrax [ˈænθræks] *n* MED ántrax *m.*
— OBSERV El plural de *anthrax* es *anthraces.*

anthrenus [ænˈθriːnəs] *n* ZOOL antreno *m* (insect).

anthropocentric [ˌænθrəpəuˈsentrik] *adj* antropocéntrico, ca.

anthropoid [ˈænθrəpɔid] *adj* antropoide, antropoideo, a (manlike in appearance).
◆ *n* antropoide *m.*

anthropologic [ˌænθrəpəˈlɔdʒik]; **anthropological** [ˌænθrəpəˈlɔdʒikəl] *adj* antropológico, ca.

anthropologist [ˌænθrəˈpɔlədʒist] *n* antropólogo, ga.

anthropology [ˌænθrəˈpɔlədʒi] *n* antropología *f.*

anthropometric [ˌænθrəpəuˈmetrik]; **anthropometrical** [-əl] *adj* antropométrico, ca.

anthropomorphic [ˌænθrəpəuˈmɔːfik] *adj* antropomórfico, ca.

anthropomorphism [ˌænθrəpəuˈmɔːfizəm] *n* antropomorfismo *m.*

anthropomorphist [ˌænθrəpəu'mɔːfist] *n* antropomorfita *m* & *f*.

anthropomorphous [ˌænθrəpəu'mɔːfəs] *adj* antropomorfo, fa.

anthroponymy [ˌænθrə'pɔnimi] *n* antroponimia *f*.

anthropophagite [ˌænθrə'pɔfədʒait] *n* antropófago, ga.

anthropophagy [ˌænθrə'pɔfədʒi] *n* antropofagia *f*.

anthropopithecus [ˌænθrəpəupi'θiːkəs] *n* antropopiteco *m*.

anti ['ænti] *pref* anti [con el sentido de «contra», «contrario a» u «opuesto a»].
— OBSERV La lista de palabras construidas con este prefijo que damos a continuación no pretende ser exhaustiva. Existen en efecto otras muchas palabras de esta índole tanto en español como en inglés.

antiaircraft ['ænti'ɛkrɑːft] *adj* antiaéreo, a; *antiaircraft gun* cañón antiaéreo.

antialcoholism ['ænti'ælkəhɔlizəm] *n* antialcoholismo *m*.

anti-American ['æntiə'merikən] *adj* antiamericano, na.

antiballistic missile ['æntibə'listik ˌmisɑil] *n* MIL misil *m* antibalístico.

antibiotic ['æntibai'ɔtik] *adj* MED antibiótico, ca.
◆ *n* antibiótico *m*; *to be on antibiotics* tomar antibióticos.

antibody ['æntiˌbɔdi] *n* BIOL anticuerpo *m*.

anticancerous ['ænti'kænsərəs] *adj* anticanceroso, sa.

anticathode ['ænti'kæθəud] *n* PHYS anticátodo *m*.

antichresis [ˌænti'kriːsis] *n* JUR anticresis *f*.
— OBSERV El plural de *antichresis* es *antichreses*.

Antichrist ['æntikraist] *n* antecristo *m*, anticristo *m*.

antichristian ['ænti'kristjən] *adj* anticristiano, na.

anticipate [æn'tisipeit] *vt* esperar, contar con, prever (to foresee, to expect) || prometerse (to look forward to) || anticiparse a, adelantarse a (to forestall); *to anticipate s.o.* anticiparse a alguien || anticiparse a; *he anticipated my wish* se anticipó a mi deseo || salir al paso de; *to anticipate criticism* salir al paso de las críticas || anticipar, adelantar (payment) || gastar de antemano (to use or spend in advance).

anticipation [ænˌtisi'peiʃən] *n* previsión *f* (forecast) || esperanza *f* (hope) || anticipación *f* (of wishes, reactions, etc.) || gasto *m* anticipado (spending in advance) || expectación *f* || MUS anticipación *f* || — *in anticipation* de antemano || *in anticipation of the future* pensando en el futuro || *to thank s.o. in anticipation* agradecerle a alguien por anticipado *or* por adelantado.

anticipatory [æn'tisipeitəri] *adj* previsor, ra.

anticlerical ['ænti'klerikl] *adj/n* anticlerical.

anticlericalism [-izəm] *n* anticlericalismo *m*.

anticlimax ['ænti'klaimæks] *n* decepción *f* (disappointment).

anticlinal ['ænti'klainəl] *adj* anticlinal.

anticline ['æntiklain] *n* GEOL anticlinal *m*.

anticlockwise [ˌænti'klɔkwaiz] *adj/adv* en sentido contrario a las agujas del reloj.

anticoagulant ['æntikəu'ægjulənt] *adj* anticoagulante.
◆ *n* anticoagulante *m*.

anticolonialism ['æntikə'ləunjəlizəm] *n* anticolonialismo *m*.

anticolonialist ['æntikə'ləunjəlist] *adj/n* anticolonialista.

anticommunist ['ænti'kɔmjunist] *adj/n* anticomunista.

antics ['æntiks] *pl n* payasadas *f*, bufonadas *f* (clowning) || travesuras *f* (tricks) || cabriolas *f* (capers) || *to be up to one's antics* estar haciendo de las suyas.

anticyclone ['ænti'saikləun] *n* anticiclón *m*.

anticyclonic ['æntisai'klɔnik] *adj* anticiclonal.

antidazzle ['ænti'dæzl] *adj* antideslumbrante.

antidemocrat ['ænti'deməkræt] *n* antidemócrata *m* & *f*.

antidemocratic ['æntiˌdemə'krætik] *adj* antidemocrático, ca.

antidotal ['æntidəutl] *adj* alexifármaco, ca.

antidote ['æntidəut] *n* antídoto *m* (*to, for, against* contra).

antiemetic ['æntii'metik] *adj* MED antiemético, ca.
◆ *n* MED antiemético *m*.

antifascism ['ænti'fæʃizəm] *n* antifascismo *m*.

antifascist ['ænti'fæʃist] *adj/n* antifascista.

antifebrile ['ænti'fiːbrail] *adj* MED antifebrífugo, ga; antifebril.

antifederalist ['ænti'fedərəlist] *n* antifederalista *m* & *f*.

antifeminism ['ænti'feminizəm] *n* antifeminismo *m*.

antifeminist ['ænti'feminist] *adj/n* antifeminista.

antiferment ['ænti'fəːmənt] *n* antifermento *m*.

antifreeze ['æntifriːz] *n* anticongelante *m*.

antifriction ['ænti'frikʃən] *n* antifricción *f*.

antigen ['æntidʒən] *n* MED antígeno *m*.

antiglare ['æntiglɛə*] *adj* antideslumbrante.

Antigone [æn'tigəni] *pr n* Antígona *f*.

anti-government ['ænti'gʌvmənt] *adj* antigubernamental.

Antigua and Barbuda [æn'tiːgə and bɑː'buːdə] *pr n* GEOGR Antigua y Barbuda.

anti-hero ['ænti'hiərəu] *n* antihéroe *m*.

antihistamine ['ænti'histəmiːn] *adj* antihistamínico, ca.
◆ *n* antihistamínico *m*.

antihysteric ['æntihis'terik] *adj* antihistérico, ca.

antiinflationary ['æntiin'fleiʃnəri] *adj* antiinflacionista.

antiknock ['æntinɔk] *adj* antidetonante.
◆ *m* antidetonante *m*.

Antillean [æn'tiliən] *adj/n* antillano, na.

Antilles [æn'tiliːz] *pl prn* GEOGR Antillas *f*.

antilogarithm ['ænti'lɔgəriθəm] *n* MATH antilogaritmo *m*.

antilogy [æn'tilədʒi] *n* antilogía *f*.

antimacassar ['æntimə'kæsə*] *n* antimacasar *m*, macasar *m*.

antimagnetic ['æntimæg'netik] *adj* antimagnético, ca.

antimalarial ['æntimə'lɛəriəl] *adj* antipalúdico, ca.

anti-masonic ['æntimə'sɔnik] *adj* antimasónico, ca.

antimatter ['æntiˌmætə*] *n* antimateria *f*.

antimilitarism ['ænti'militərizəm] *n* antimilitarismo *m*.

antimilitarist ['ænti'militərist] *adj/n* antimilitarista.

antimonarchical ['æntimɔ'nɑːkikəl] *adj* antimonárquico, ca.

antimonial [ˌænti'məunjəl] *adj* CHEM antimonial.

antimoniate [ænti'məunieit] *n* CHEM antimoniato *m*.

antimony ['æntiməni] *n* CHEM antimonio *m*.

antinational ['ænti'næʃənl] *adj* antinacional.

antineuralgic ['æntinjuə'rældʒik] *adj* MED antineurálgico, ca.

antinode ['æntinəud] *n* antinodo *m* (in acoustics).

antinomic [ˌænti'nɔmik]; **antinomical** [-əl] *adj* antinómico, ca.

antinomy [æn'tinəmi] *n* antinomia *f*.

Antioch ['æntiɔk] *pr n* Antioquía.

Antiochus [æn'taiəkəs] *pr n* Antíoco *m*.

antiparliamentarianism ['æntiˌpɑːləmen'tɛəriənizem] *n* antiparlamentarismo *m*.

antiparticle ['ænti'pɑːtikl] *n* PHYS antipartícula *f*.

antipathetic ['æntipə'θetik]; **antipathetical** [-əl] *adj* antipático, ca (causing antipathy) || contrario, ria; opuesto, ta (against).

antipathy [æn'tipəθi] *n* antipatía *f*, hostilidad *f* || repugnancia *f* (*to* hacia) (repugnance).

antipatriotism ['ænti'pætriətizəm] *n* antipatriotismo *m*.

antiperistaltic ['æntiˌperi'stæltik] *adj* antiperistáltico, ca.

antipersonnel ['æntipəːsə'nel] *adj* MIL antipersonal.

antiperspirant ['æntipəs'pairənt] *n* antitranspirante *m*.

antiphilosophic ['æntiˌfilə'sɔfik]; **antiphilosophical** [-əl] *adj* antifilosófico, ca.

antiphlogistic ['æntifləu'dʒistik] *adj* MED antiflogístico, ca.
◆ *n* antiflogístico *m*.

antiphon ['æntifən] *n* REL antífona *f*.

antiphonal [æn'tifənl] *n* antifonario *m*.

antiphonary [æn'tifənəri] *n* antifonario *m*.

antiphrasis [æn'tifrəsis] *n* antífrasis *f*.

antipodal [æn'tipədl] *adj* antípoda.

antipodes [æn'tipədiːz] *pl n* GEOGR antípodas *f*.

antipope ['æntipəup] *n* antipapa *m*.

antiprogressive ['æntiprə'gresiv] *adj/n* antiprogresista.

antiprohibitionist ['æntiˌprəui'biʃənist] *adj/n* antiprohibicionista.

antiprotectionist ['æntiprə'tekʃənist] *adj/n* antiproteccionista.

antiproton ['ænti'prəutɔn] *n* PHYS antiprotón *m*.

antiputrefactive ['æntiˌpjuːtri'fæktiv] *adj* BIOL antipútrido, da.
◆ *n* antipútrido *m*.

antipyretic ['æntipai'retik] *adj* MED antipirético, ca.
◆ *n* antipirético *m*.

antipyrine [ænti'pairiːn] *n* MED antipirina *f*.

antiquarian [ˌænti'kwɛəriən] *n* anticuario *m*.

antiquary ['ætikwəri] *n* anticuario *m*.

antiquated ['æntikweitid] *adj* anticuado, da.

antique [æn'tiːk] *adj* antiguo, gua; viejo, ja (old) || anticuado, da (antiquated).
◆ *n* antigüedad *f* || FIG antigualla *f* (pejorative) || — *antique dealer* anticuario *m* || *antiques* antigüedades || *antique shop* anticuario *m*, tienda *f* de antigüedades.

antiquity [æn'tikwiti] *n* antigüedad *f*.
◆ *pl* antigüedades *f*.

antirabic [ænti'ræbik] *adj* antirrábico, ca.

antirachitic ['æntiræ'kitik] *adj* MED antirraquítico, ca.

antiradar ['ænti'reidɑː*] *adj* antirradar.

antireligious ['æntiri'lidʒəs] *adj* antirreligioso, sa.

antirepublican ['æntiri'pʌblikən] *adj/n* antirrepublicano, na.

antirevolutionary ['ænti,revə'luːʃnəri] *adj/n* antirrevolucionario, ria.

antirust ['ænti'rʌst] *adj* antioxidante.

antiscians [æn'tiʃənz] *pl n* antiscios *m.*

antiscorbutic ['æntiskɔː'bjuːtik] *adj* MED antiescorbútico, ca.
◆ *n* antiescorbútico *m.*

anti-Semite ['ænti'siːmait] *n* antisemita *m & f.*

anti-Semitic ['æntisi'mitik] *adj* antisemítico, ca.

anti-Semitism ['ænti'semitizəm] *n* antisemitismo *m.*

antisepsis [,ænti'sepsis] *n* MED antisepsia *f.*

antiseptia [,ænti'septik] *adj* MED antiséptico, ca.
◆ *n* antiséptico *m.*

antiskid ['æntiskid] *adj* antideslizante.

antislavery ['ænti'sleivəri] *adj* antiesclavista.

antisocial ['ænti'səuʃəl] *adj* antisocial.

antispasmodic ['æntispæz'mɔdik] *adj* MED antiespasmódico, ca.
◆ *n* MED antiespasmódico *m.*

antistrophe [æn'tistrəfi] *n* antistrofa *f.*

antisubmarine ['ænti,sʌbmə'riːn] *adj* antisubmarino, na.

antitank ['ænti'tæŋk] *adj* MIL antitanque, contra carros de combate.

antitetanic ['æntite'tænik] *adj* MED antitetánico, ca.

anti-theft device ['ænti'θeftdi,vais] *n* antirrobo *m.*

antithesis [æn'tiθisis] *n* antítesis *f.*
— OBSERV El plural de *antithesis* es *antitheses.*

antithetic [,ænti'θetik]; **antithetical** [-əl] *adj* antitético, ca.

antitoxic [,ænti'tɔksik] *adj* antitóxico, ca.

antitoxin [,ænti'tɔksin] *n* MED antitoxina *f.*

antitrades ['ænti'treidz] *pl n* contraalisios *m* (winds).

antitrust ['ænti'trʌst] *adj* antimonopolista.

antitubercular ['æntitju'bəːkjulə*] *adj* MED antituberculoso, sa.

antitype ['æntitaip] *m* antitipo *m,* prototipo *m.*

antivenin ['ænti'venin] *n* US antitoxina *f.*

antivenereal [æntivi'niəriəl] *adj* antivenéreo, a.

antler ['æntlə*] *n* mogote *m,* cornamenta *f.*

antlered [-d] *adj* astado, da.

ant lion ['ænt,laiən] *n* hormiga *f* león (insect).

Antoinette [,æntuɑ'net] *pr n* Antonia *f.*

Antoninus [,æntəu'nainəs] *pr n* Antonino *m.*

antonomasia [,æntɔnə'meiziə] *n* antonomasia *f.*

Antony ['æntəni] *pr n* Antonio *m.*

antonym ['æntənim] *n* antónimo *m.*

antrum ['æntrəm] *n* ANAT cavidad *f.*
— OBSERV El plural de *antrum* es *antra.*

Antwerp ['æntwəːp] *pr n* GEOGR Amberes.

anuran [ə'jurən]; **anouran** [ə'nurən] *n* ZOOL anuro *m.*
◆ *adj* anuro, ra.

anury [ə'njuːri] *n* MED anuria *f.*

anus ['einəs] *n* ANAT ano *m.*

anvil ['ænvil] *n* yunke *m* || ANAT yunque *m* || FIG *on the anvil* sobre el tapete (under discussion), en el telar (in preparation).

anxiety [æŋ'zaiəti] *n* inquietud *f,* ansiedad *f,* preocupación *f* (worry); *anxiety about one's health* inquietud por su salud; *anxiety for s.o.'s safety* inquietud por la seguridad de alguien || anhelo *m,* ansia *f* (yearning); *his anxiety to make a good impression* su ansia de dar una buena impresión || ansia *f* (intense dread) || MED ansiedad *f.*

anxious ['æŋkʃəs] *adj* inquieto, ta; preocupado, da (worried); *an anxious glance* una mirada inquieta; *anxious about the future* preocupado por el futuro || de inquietud; *I spent two very anxious hours* pasé dos horas de mucha inquietud || lleno de preocupaciones; *an anxious job* un trabajo lleno de preocupaciones || deseoso, sa (desirous); *he is anxious to see you* está deseoso de verte || ansioso, sa (yearning); *anxious for riches* ansioso de riqueza.

anxiously [-li] *adv* con inquietud (worriedly) || con ansia, ansiosamente; *waiting anxiously for the results* esperando con ansia los resultados.

anxiousness [-nis] *n* inquietud *f,* preocupación *f.*

any ['eni] *adj* alguno, na; *is there any reason?* ¿hay alguna razón?; *is there any Englishman here?* ¿hay algún inglés aquí? || ninguno, na; alguno, na; *there isn't any problem* no hay ningún problema, no hay problema alguno || cualquiera (whatever, whichever); *any book will do* cualquier libro vale; *any woman will tell you that* cualquier mujer te lo dirá || todo, da; cualquiera (all); *any lack of discipline will be punished* toda indisciplina será castigada; *to avoid any contact with* evitar todo contacto con || (not translated); *have you got any cigarettes?* ¿tienes cigarrillos?; *is there any bread?* ¿hay pan?; *don't bring any friends* no traigas a amigos (see OBSERV) || — *any amount of* una gran cantidad de || *any and every* todos, todas || *any... at all* algo de; *is there any bread at all?* ¿hay algo de pan?; cualquiera (no matter which); *any day at all* un día cualquiera, cualquier día || *any day now* cualquier día de éstos || *any minute, any moment, any time now* de un momento a otro || *any old thing* cualquier cosa || *at any cost* a toda costa || *at any rate* de todas formas || *at any time* en cualquier momento || *in any case* en todo caso || *not any... at all* ninguno, na; alguno, na; *I couldn't find any paper at all* no podía encontrar papel alguno *or* ningún papel.
◆ *adv* algo; *are you any better?* ¿estás algo mejor?; *did it hurt you any?* ¿te ha dolido algo? || nada (in negative constructions); *he isn't any better* no está nada mejor; *it didn't hurt me any* no me ha dolido nada || (not translated); *I can't go any further* no puedo ir más lejos; *don't do it any more* no lo hagas más (see OBSERV) || — *any longer* más tiempo || *any the* algo; *is he any the happier?* ¿está algo más contento? || *not any the* nada; *not any the worse* nada peor.
◆ *pron* alguno, na; *can you see any?* ¿ves alguno?; *if any of you should arrive late* si alguno de vosotros llega tarde || ninguno, na (in negative sentences); *I don't know any of them* no conozco a ninguno de ellos || cualquiera; *any of them would do it for you* cualquiera de ellos lo haría por ti || (not translated); *I can't offer you any wine, there isn't any* no te puedo ofrecer vino, no hay || — FAM *any more for any more?* ¿alguien quiere algo más? || *if any, I would have chosen the big one* de haber cogido uno hubiera escogido el grande || *there are few men, if any, who would be brave enough* pocos hombres, si los hay, tendrían bastante valor.
— OBSERV Since *any* is a normal feature of negative and interrogative constructions in English, it is often not translated into Spanish.
— OBSERV The adverb *any,* when followed by a comparative, is often translated into Spanish by a simple comparative.
— OBSERV *Alguno,* and *ninguno* are apocopated to *algún* and *ningún* in Spanish when they precede a masculine singular noun. Similarly *cualquiera* becomes *cualquier* before a singular masculine or feminine noun.

anybody [-,bɔdi] *pron* cualquiera, cualquier persona; *anybody could do it* lo podría hacer cualquiera, lo podría hacer cualquier persona || alguien; *did you see anybody?* ¿viste a alguien?; *if anybody calls* si alguien llama || nadie (nobody); *I don't know anybody here* no conozco a nadie aquí || *better, worse than anybody* mejor, peor que nadie.

anyhow [-hau] *adv* de cualquier manera, de cualquier modo (carelessly, in any manner) || de todos modos, de todas maneras (in any case).

anymore [-'mɔː*] *adv* nunca más, ya.

anyone [-wʌn] *pron* → **anybody.**

anything [-θiŋ] *pron* algo; *did you say anything?* ¿has dicho algo? || nada; *I didn't say anything* no dije nada; *without saying anything* sin decir nada || cualquier cosa; *he eats anything* come cualquier cosa; *anything will do* cualquier cosa valdrá || todo; *anything is possible* todo es posible; *she likes anything classical* le gusta todo lo clásico || — *anything else?* ¿algo más? || *have you seen anything of David lately?* ¿has visto a David últimamente? || *if anything* de (+ infin +) algo; *what would you do? if anything I'd take a holiday* ¿qué harías? de hacer algo me iría de vacaciones || *if he were anything of a gentleman* si fuera realmente un caballero || *is there anything I can do for you?* ¿en qué puedo servirle? (in a shop), ¿puedo hacer algo por ti? || *I would give anything for* daría cualquier cosa por || *like anything* como nadie; *to work like anything* trabajar como nadie; como nunca; *it is raining like anything* llueve como nunca || *to be anything but stupid* no ser nada tonto || *to be as easy as anything* ser coser y cantar, estar tirado (fam).
◆ *adv* algo; *is he anything like his brother?* ¿se parece algo a su hermano? || ni mucho menos, muy lejos de; *it isn't anything like as easy as I thought* no es, ni mucho menos, tan fácil como pensaba; está muy lejos de ser tan fácil como pensaba || *anything but* todo menos; *he is anything but clever* es todo menos inteligente.

anyway [-wei] *adv* → **anyhow.**

anywhere [-wɛə*] *adv* en cualquier sitio, en cualquier parte, donde sea, dondequiera; *put in down anywhere* ponlo en cualquier sitio || en algún sitio, en alguna parte; *can you see it anywhere?* ¿lo ves en algún sitio? || a cualquier sitio, dondequiera, a donde sea (with a verb of motion); *take me anywhere* llévame a cualquier sitio || en todas partes (everywhere); *anywhere in the world* en todas partes del mundo || — *anywhere from five to ten pounds* entre cinco y diez libras || *anywhere else* en cualquier otro sitio || *are you anywhere near finished?* ¿os falta mucho para acabar? || *miles from anywhere* muy lejos, en el quinto pino || *not anywhere* en ningún sitio, en ninguna parte; a ninguna parte (motion).

anywise [-waiz] *adv* de cualquier manera, de cualquier modo, de cualquier forma (anyhow) || en cierta manera, en cierto modo (in any way) || *not anywise* de ninguna manera, de ningún modo (in no way).

Anzac ['ænzæk] *n* soldado *m* australiano o neocelandés.

Anzac ['ænzæk] *abbr of Australia-New Zealand Army Corps* Fuerzas Armadas de Australia y Nueva Zelanda.

AOB; a.o.b. *abbr of any other business* cualquier otro negocio.

aorist ['ɛərist] *n* GRAMM aoristo *m.*

aorta [ei'ɔːtə] *n* ANAT aorta *f.*

aortic [ei'ɔːtik] *adj* aórtico, ca.

aortitis [eiɔː'taitis] *n* MED aortitis *f.*

apace [ə'peis] *adv* aprisa, rápidamente.

Apache [ə'pætʃi] *n* apache *m.*

apanage; appanage ['æpənidʒ] *n* HIST infantado *m* || herencia *f* (inheritance) || dependencia *f* (territory) || *to be the apanage of* ser privativo de, ser el patrimonio de.

apart [ə'pɑːt] *adj* aparte; *he is a man apart* es un hombre aparte.
◆ *adv* aparte; *he stood apart* se mantuvo aparte; *to put sth. apart* poner algo aparte; *to treat a matter apart* tratar un asunto aparte || separado por; *ten centimetres apart* separados por diez centímetros || separadamente, por separado; *to consider each topic apart* examinar cada tema separadamente || — *apart from* aparte de, aparte (except for); *apart from the style I quite like it* aparte del estilo *or* el estilo aparte, me gusta bastante; aparte de, además de (as well as) || *joking apart* bromas aparte || FIG *to be miles apart* estar a kilómetros de distancia || *to come apart* desprenderse (to come off), ser desmontable (able to be dismantled), estropearse; *this chair is coming apart* esta silla se está estropeando || *to get o to pull two things apart* separar dos cosas || *to keep apart* apartar (to isolate), apartarse (to isolate o.s.), separar (to separate); *to keep the boys apart from the girls* separar a los chicos de las chicas || *to live apart* vivir apartado || *to move apart to let s.o. pass* apartarse para dejar pasar a alguien || *to set apart* apartar, reservar || *to stand apart* mantenerse apartado || *to stand with one's legs apart* estar con las piernas separadas || *to take apart* desmontar (to dismantle), ser desmontable (able to be dismantled), tomar aparte (a person) || *to tear apart* destrozar (sth.), hacer trizas (s.o.) || *to tell two things apart* distinguir dos cosas una de otra.

apartheid [ə'pɑːtheit] *n* «apartheid» *m*, segregación *f* racial.

apartment [ə'pɑːtmənt] *n* piso *m*, apartamento *m* (flat) || cuarto *m*, habitación *f* (room) || *apartment house* casa *f* de pisos.
◆ *pl* piso *m sing*, apartamento *m sing.*

apathetic [ˌæpə'θetik] *adj* apático, ca.

apathy ['æpəθi] *n* apatía *f* || indiferencia *f*, falta *f* de interés (indifference).

apatite ['æpətait] *n* MIN apatito *m.*

APB *abbr of all points bulletin* orden de busca y captura (United States).

ape [eip] *n* ZOOL mono *m* || FIG imitamonos *m* & *f inv* || FIG *to play the ape* dárselas de gracioso.

ape [eip] *vt* imitar, remedar.

apeak [ə'piːk] *adj/adv* MAR a pique.

apelike ['eiplaik] *adj* simiesco, ca.

Apennines ['æpinainz] *pl pr m* GEOGR Apeninos *m.*

apepsy [ə'pepsi] *n* MED apepsia *f.*

aperient [ə'piəriənt] *adj* MED laxante.
◆ *n* laxante *m.*

aperiodic ['eipiəri'ɔdik] *adj* aperiódico, ca.

apéritif [əˌperitiːf] *n* aperitivo *m* (drink).

aperitive [ə'peritiv] *adj* MED laxante.
◆ *n* laxante *m.*

aperture ['æpətjuə*] *n* abertura *f* || rendija *f*, resquicio *m* (crack).

apery ['eipəri] *n* mímica *f* (mimicking).

apetalous [ei'petələs] *adj* BOT apétalo, la; sin pétalos.

apex ['eipeks] *n* ápice *m*, cima *f* (highest point) || FIG cumbre *f*, cúspide *f* (height) || ASTR ápex *m* || vértice *m* (of a triangle).
— OBSERV La palabra inglesa *apex* tiene dos plurales: *apices* y *apexes.*

aphaeresis [æ'fiərisis] *n* GRAMM aféresis *f.*

aphasia [æ'feizjə] *n* afasia *f.*

aphasiac [ə'feisiək]; **aphasic** [ə'feizik] *adj/n* MED afásico, ca.

aphelion [æ'fiːljən] *n* ASTR afelio *m.*

aphesis ['æfisis] *n* GRAMM aféresis *f.*

aphid ['eifid] *n* áfido *m* (inseet).

aphis ['eifis] *n* áfido *m* (insect).
— OBSERV El plural de *aphis* es *aphides.*

aphonia [æ'fəunjə] *n* MED afonía *f.*

aphonic [æ'fɔnik] *adj* afónico, ca; áfono, na.

aphony ['æfəni] *n* MED afonía *f.*

aphorism ['æfərizəm] *n* aforismo *m.*

aphorismic [ˌæfə'rizmik]; **aphoristic** [ˌæfə'ristik] *adj* aforístico, ca.

aphrodisiac [ˌæfrəu'diziæk] *adj* afrodisiaco, ca.
◆ *n* afrodisiaco *m.*

Aphrodite [ˌæfrə'daiti] *pr n* Afrodita *f.*

aphtha ['æfθə] *n* MED afta *f.*

aphthous ['æfθəs] *adj* MED aftoso, sa; *aphthous fever* fiebre aftosa.

apiarian [ˌeipi'ɛəriən] *adj* apícola.

apiarist ['eipjərist] *n* apicultor, ra.

apiary ['eipjəri] *n* colmenar *m*, abejera *f.*

apical ['æpikəl] *adj* apical || que está en la cumbre.

apices ['eipisiːz] *pl n* ⟶ **apex.**

apiculture ['eipikʌltʃə*] *n* apicultura *f.*

apiece [ə'piːs] *adv* cada uno; *we had two blankets apiece* teníamos dos mantas cada uno; *they cost a pound apiece* cuestan una libra cada uno; *he gave them one apiece* les dio uno a cada uno || por persona, por cabeza (per person).

apish ['eipiʃ] *adv* simiesco, ca (apelike) || FIG necio, cia; tonto, ta (stupid) | imitador, ra; remedador, ra (imitative).

aplanatic [ˌæplə'nætik] *adj* PHYS aplanético, ca.

aplenty [ə'plenti] *adv* en abundancia.

aplomb [ə'plɔm] *n* aplomo *m*, sangre *f* fría.

apnoea; apnea ['æpniə] *n* MED apnea *f.*

Apocalypse [ə'pɔkəlips] *n* Apocalipsis *m.*

apocalyptic[əˌpɔkə'liptik]; **apocalyptical** [-əl] *adj* apocalíptico, ca.

apocopate [ə'pɔkəpeit] *vt* GRAMM apocopar.

apocopation [ə'pɔkə'peiʃən] *n* GRAMM apócope *m.*

apocope [ə'pɔkəpi] *n* GRAMM apócope *f.*

Apocrypha [ə'pɔkrifə] *pl n* Libros *m* apócrifos.

apocryphal [-l] *adj* apócrifo, fa.

apod ['æpɔd] *n* ZOOL ápodo *m.*

apodal ['æpədəl] *adj* ZOOL ápodo, da.

apodictic [ˌæpəu'diktik] *adj* apodíctico, ca (incontestable).

apodosis [ə'pɔdəusis] *n* apódosis *f.*
— OBSERV El plural de *apodosis* es *apodoses.*

apogee ['æpəudʒiː] *n* ASTR & FIG apogeo *m.*

apolitical [æpɔ'litikəl] *adj* apolítico, ca.

Apollo [ə'pɔləu] *pr n* MYTH Apolo *m.*

Apollonian [ˌæpə'ləunjən] *adj* apolíneo, a.

apologetic [əˌpɔlə'dʒetik] *adj* apologético, ca; *an apologetic treatise* un tratado apologético || *he was very apologetic about the incident* me ofreció toda clase de disculpas por el incidente.

apologetically [-əli] *adv* excusándose, disculpándose.

apologetics [-s] *n* apologética *f.*

apologia [ˌæpə'ləudʒiə] *n* apología *f.*

apologist [ə'pɔlədʒist] *n* apologista *m* & *f.*

apologize [ə'pɔlədʒaiz] *vi* disculparse (*for* de, por; *to* con), pedir perdón (*for* por; *to* a).

apologue ['æpəlɔg] *n* apólogo *m.*

apology [ə'pɔlədʒi] *n* disculpa *f*, excusa *f*; *my apologies* mis disculpas || apología *f*, defensa *f* (defence) || FAM birria *f*; *what an apology for a house!* ¡vaya birria de casa! || *to make an apology, to offer one's apologies* disculparse, presentar sus excusas.

aponeurosis [ˌæpənju'rəusis] *n* aponeurosis *f.*

apophthegm ['æpəuθem] *n* apotegma *m.*

apophysis [ə'pɔfisis] *n* ANAT apófisis *f.*
— OBSERV El plural de la palabra inglesa *apophysis* es *apophyses.*

apoplectic [ˌæpəu'plektik] *adj/n* apoplético, ca || FIG *to get apoplectic* ponerse furioso.

apoplexy ['æpəpleksi] *n* MED apoplejía *f.*

aporia [ə'pɔːriə] *n* PHIL aporía *f.*

apostasy [ə'pɔstəsi] *n* apostasía *f.*

apostate [ə'pɔstit] *adj/n* apóstata.

apostatize [ə'pɔstətaiz] *vi* apostatar.

apostemate [ə'pɔstəmeit] *vt* MED apostemar.

aposteme [ə'pɔstiːm] *n* MED apostema *f.*

a posteriori ['eipɔsˌteri'ɔːrai] *adj/adv* a posteriori.

apostil [ə'pɔstil] *n* apostilla *f*, nota *f* marginal.

apostle [ə'pɔsl] *n* apóstol *m*; *the Acts of the Apostles* los Hechos de los Apóstoles || FIG apóstol *m.*

apostleship [-ʃip]; **apostolate** [ə'pɔstəlit] *n* apostolado *m.*

apostolic [ˌæpəs'tɔlik]; **apostolical** [-əl] *adj* apostólico, ca || *apostolic see* sede apostólica.

apostrophe [ə'pɔstrəfi] *n* apóstrofo *m* (punctuation mark) || apóstrofe *m* (in rhetoric).

apostrophize [ə'pɔstrəfaiz] *vt* apostrofar.

apothecary [ə'pɔθikəri] *n* boticario *m.*

apothegm ['æpəθem] *n* apotegma *m.*

apothem ['æpəθem] *n* MATH apotema *f.*

apotheosis [əˌpɔθi'əusis] *n* apoteosis *f.*

apotheosize [ə'pɔθiəusaiz] *vt* deificar (to deify) || glorificar (to glorify) || idealizar (to idealize).

appal; appall [ə'pɔːl] *vt* horrorizar, espantar (to frighten) || horrorizar, repugnar (to repulse) || asombrar (to amaze).

Appalachians [ˌæpə'leitʃjənz] *pr n* Apalaches *m pl* (mountains).

appalling [ə'pɔːliŋ] *adj* espantoso, sa; horrible, horroroso, sa (frightening) || pésimo, ma (very bad) || asombroso, sa (amazing).

appanage ['æpənidʒ] *n* ⟶ **apanage.**

apparatus [ˌæpə'reitəs] *n* aparato *m* (system); *digestive apparatus* aparato digestivo || equipo *m*; *climbing apparatus* equipo de montañismo; *breathing apparatus* equipo de respiración || aparatos *m pl* (in gymnastics) || FIG *the apparatus of government* el aparato del gobierno.
— OBSERV El plural de apparatus es *apparatuses* o *apparatus.*

apparel [ə'pærəl] *n* POET atavío *m*, indumentaria *f* (attire) || ropa *f* (clothes) || MAR aparejo *m.*

apparel [ə'pærəl] *vt* POET ataviar, vestir || MAR aparejar.

apparent [ə'pærənt] *adj* aparente; *his apparent coldness is only shyness* su aparente frialdad es sólo timidez || evidente, claro, ra; manifiesto, ta (obvious); *his sadness was very ap-*

parent su tristeza era muy evidente || — *for no apparent reason* sin motivo aparente || JUR *heir apparent* presunto heredero || *it is apparent that...* es obvio que..., es evidente que...

apparently [-li] *adv* por lo visto, aparentemente, al parecer (seemingly) || evidentemente, claramente (obviously).

apparition [,æpə'riʃən] *n* aparición *f.*

apparitor [ə'pæritɔː*] *n* JUR ordenanza *m.*

appeal [ə'piːl] *n* JUR apelación *f*; *to make an appeal* presentar *or* interponer una apelación; *without appeal* sin apelación || llamamiento *m* (to the masses); *an appeal for rebellion* un llamamiento a la sublevación; *an appeal on behalf of the blind* un llamamiento en favor de los ciegos || llamada *f*; *an appeal for help* una llamada de socorro || súplica *f*, ruego *m*, petición *f* (petition) || atractivo *m*, interés *m*; *this has no appeal for the younger generation* esto no tiene atractivo para los jóvenes || solicitación *f*; *appeal for funds* solicitación de fondos || cuestación *f* (of charity) || — JUR *appeal for annulment* recurso *m* de nulidad | *court of appeal* tribunal *m* de apelación | *right of appeal* derecho *m* de apelación.

appeal [ə'piːl] *vt* US JUR apelar de || US JUR *to appeal a case* interponer apelación, presentar apelación.
◆ *vi* JUR apelar (*to* a; *against* contra, de); *to appeal against a decision* apelar de una decisión || suplicar, rogar (to beg); *he appealed to the crowd to calm down* suplicó a la multitud que se calmase || recurrir, apelar; *to appeal to s.o.'s kindness* apelar a la bondad de uno; *to appeal to arms* recurrir a las armas || hacer un llamamiento; *to appeal on behalf of the blind* hacer un llamamiento en favor de los ciegos || gustar (to please); *the idea doesn't appeal to me* la idea no me gusta || interesar, atraer (to interest); *this will appeal to all the readers* esto interesará a todos los lectores.

appealable [ə'piːləbl] *adj* JUR apelable.

appealing [ə'piːliŋ] *adj* suplicante (beseeching) || atrayente, atractivo, va (pleasing) || conmovedor, ra (touching).

appear [ə'piə*] *vi* aparecer (to come into sight); *the town appeared on the horizon* la ciudad apareció en el horizonte; *he was the last to appear* fue el último en aparecer; *this custom appears in the tenth century* esta costumbre aparece en el siglo diez || aparecer, publicarse (a book) || parecer (to seem); *he appears to be very nice* parece ser muy simpático; *so it appears* según parece || THEATR actuar (to act) || — JUR *to appear in court* comparecer ante un tribunal || *to appear on the stage* aparecer en escena.

appearance [-rəns] *n* aparición *f* (act of appearing); *the appearance of smoke on the horizon raised the sailors' hopes* la aparición de humo en el horizonte dio esperanza a los marineros; *his sudden appearance startled me* su aparición súbita me sobresaltó || aspecto *m*, apariencia *f* (looks); *his dishevelled appearance* su aspecto desaliñado || aparición *f*, publicación *f* (of a book) || COMM presentación *f* || JUR comparecencia *f* || — *at first appearance* a primera vista || THEATR *first appearance* primera presentación, début *m* || *to make an appearance* aparecer, dejarse ver (at a meeting, party, etc.), tener una actuación, salir (in theatre) || *to put in an appearance* aparecer, dejarse ver, hacer acto de presencia || *to put on an appearance of surprise* simular *or* fingir la sorpresa.
◆ *pl* apariencias *f*; *one should not judge by appearances* no se debe juzgar por las apariencias || — *appearances are deceptive* las apariencias engañan || *to all appearances* según parece, al parecer, por lo visto, aparentemente || *to keep up appearances* guardar *or* salvar las apariencias.

appease [ə'piːz] *vt* apaciguar (to pacify, to calm down) || aplacar (anger) || aplacar, mitigar (thirst, hunger).

appeasement [-mənt] *n* apaciguamiento *m.*

appellant [ə'pelənt] *adj/n* JUR apelante.

appellate [ə'pelit] *adj* JUR de apelación (court).

appellation [,æpə'leiʃən] *n* título *m*, denominación *f*, nombre *m* (name) || apodo *m* (nickname).

appellative [ə'pelətiv] *adj* GRAMM apelativo, va.
◆ *n* apelativo *m.*

append [ə'pend] *vt* añadir, adjuntar (to add, to join) || adjuntar (sth. to a document) || poner (one's signature).

appendage [-idʒ] *n* ANAT apéndice *m* || accesorio *m* (accessory, accompaniment) || añadidura *f* (sth. added) || anexo *m* (of building).

appendant [-ənt] *adj* anexo, xa (annexed) || adjunto, ta (accompanying) || JUR accesorio, ria.
◆ *n* dependencia *f* || ANAT anexo *m* || JUR derecho *m* accesorio.

appendectomy [,æpin'dektəmi]; **appendicectomy** [ə,pendi'sektəmi] *n* MED apendectomía *f.*

appendicitis [ə,pendi'saitis] *n* MED apendicitis *f.*

appendicular [,æpen'dikjulə*] *adj* apendicular.

appendix [ə'pendiks] *n* ANAT apéndice *m* || apéndice *m* (of book).
— OBSERV El plural de *appendix* es *appendices* o *appendixes.*

apperceive [,æpə'siːv] *vt* percibir, apercibir.

appertain [,æpə'tein] *vi* pertenecer (to belong) || relacionarse (*to* con) (to be related to) || atañer, incumbir (to be incumbent) || corresponder (to correspond).

appetence ['æpitəns]; **appetency** [-i] *n* apetencia *f* || afinidad *f* (between things).

appetent ['æpitənt] *adj* ávido, da; codicioso, sa.

appetite ['æpitait] *n* apetito *m*; *to whet one's appetite* abrir *or* dar *or* despertar el apetito; *to have a good appetite* tener mucho apetito || FIG apetito *m*, apetencia *f* (desire, longing); *appetite for power* apetito de poder || — *sexual appetite* apetito carnal || *to eat with an appetite* comer con mucho apetito.

appetitive [æ'petitiv] *adj* apetitivo, va.

appetizer ['æpitaizə*] *n* aperitivo *m* (drink) || tapa *f* (food).

appetizing ['æpitaiziŋ] *adj* apetitoso, sa; apetecedor, ra.

Appian Way ['æpiən'wei] *pr n* Vía *f* Apia.

applaud [ə'plɔːd] *vi* aplaudir.
◆ *vt* aplaudir || FIG alabar, celebrar, aplaudir (to praise).

applause [ə'plɔːz] *n* aplauso *m*; *to the applause of* con el aplauso de || aplausos *m pl*; *a thunder of applause* una salva de aplausos || FIG alabanza *f* (praise) | aprobación *f* (approval) || *a round of applause* una salva de aplausos.

apple ['æpl] *n* BOT manzano *m* (tree) | manzana *f* (fruit); *apple pie* pastel *or* tarta de manzana; *stewed apples* compota de manzanas || — *apple brandy* aguardiente *m* de manzana || *apple green* verde manzana || FIG *the apple of discord* la manzana de la discordia | *to be the apple of one's eye* ser la niña de los ojos de uno.

applecart [-kɑːt] *n* FIG *to upset s.o.'s applecart* desbaratar los planes de uno.

applejack [-dʒæk] *n* US aguardiente *m* de manzana.

apple-pie bed [-pai'bed] *n* *to make s.o. an apple-pie bed* hacer la petaca a uno.

apple-pie order [-pai'ɔːdə*] *n* *in apple-pie order* en perfecto orden.

appliance [ə'plaiəns] *n* aparato *m*, dispositivo *m*, artefacto *m* (apparatus) || aplicación *f* (action) || MIL artefacto *m* || *electrical appliance, home appliance* electrodoméstico *m*, aparato electrodoméstico.
◆ *pl* accesorios *m.*

applicability [,æplikə'biliti] *n* aplicabilidad *f* || pertinencia *f* (relevance).

applicable ['æplikəbl] *adj* aplicable || pertinente (relevant).

applicant ['æplikənt] *n* aspirante *m* & *f*, pretendiente *m*; *applicant for a job* aspirante *or* pretendiente a un puesto || candidato, ta (candidate) || JUR demandante *m* & *f.*

application [,æpli'keiʃən] *n* aplicación *f*; *the application of a theory* la aplicación de una teoría; *the application of an ointment* la aplicación de una pomada; *to show application in one's studies* mostrar aplicación en los estudios || aplicación *f* (putting into practice) || solicitud *f* (for a job, etc.); *the closing date for application* la fecha tope para las solicitudes || petición *f*, solicitud *f* (request, petition) || INFORM aplicación *f* || — *application form* formulario *m* || INFORM *application program* aplicativo *m*, programa *m* de aplicación || MED *for external application only* para uso externo || *to make an application for* solicitar || *to make an application to* dirigirse a || *to submit an application for membership of an organization* pedir su ingreso en una organización.

applied [ə'plaid] *adj* aplicado, da || *applied for* solicitado, da.

appliqué [æ'pliːkei] *n* aplicación *f* (fabric decoration).

apply [ə'plai] *vt* aplicar; *to apply a coat of paint, a theory, a bandage* aplicar una capa de pintura, una teoría, una venda || destinar, afectar, asignar (funds) || JUR aplicar (law, rule) || TECH accionar || *to apply o.s. to one's job* aplicarse en su trabajo.
◆ *vi* aplicarse; *this rule applies to everyone* esta regla se aplica a todos || solicitar; *to apply for a job* solicitar un trabajo || — *apply within* razón aquí || *to apply to* referirse a, ser relativo a (to refer to), dirigirse a, acudir a (to/go).

appogiattura [ə,pɔdʒə'tuərə] *n* MUS apoyatura *f.*

appoint [ə'pɔint] *vt* señalar, fijar, designar (a time, date, etc.); *at the appointed time* a la hora fijada || nombrar, designar; *to appoint s.o. as mayor* nombrar a uno alcalde; *to appoint s.o. to a post* nombrar a uno para un puesto || designar (one's heirs) || aparejar (to fit out) || amueblar (to furnish).

appointee [əpɔin'tiː] *n* persona *f* designada *or* nombrada.

appointment [ə'pɔintmənt] *n* cita *f* (date); *he broke the appointment* faltó a la cita || nombramiento *m*, designación *f*; *the appointment of a secretary* el nombramiento de un secretario || cargo *m*, empleo *m* (post) || — *appointment book* agenda *f* de entrevistas || *by appointment to* proveedores de || *to keep an appointment* acudir a una cita || *to make an appointment* pedir hora (at the doctor's, hairdresser's, etc.), quedar, citarse (*with* con) (a friend).
◆ *pl* equipo *m sing* (equipment) || mobiliario *m sing* (furniture).

apportion [ə'pɔːʃən] *vt* prorratear (a sum) || asignar, conceder (to assign) || desglosar (expenses) || repartir (to share).

apportionment [-mənt] *n* prorrateo *m* (of a sum) || desglose *m* (of expenses) || reparto *m* (sharing).

appose [æ'pəuz] *vt* añadir.

apposite ['æpəzit] *ajd* apropiado, da; conveniente.

apposition [æpə'ziʃən] *n* yuxtaposición *f* ‖ añadidura *f*, añadido *m* (addition) ‖ GRAMM aposición *f*; *in apposition* en aposición.

appositional [æpə'ziʃənl]; **appositive** [æ'pɔzitiv] *adj* apositivo, va; en aposición.

appraisal [ə'preizəl] *n* evalución *f*, estimación *f*, valoración *f*, tasación *f*.

appraise [ə'preiz] *vt* valorar, evaluar, estimar, tasar.

appraiser [-ə*] *n* US tasador *m* ‖ *official appraiser* perito *m* tasador.

appreciable [ə'pri:ʃəbl] *adj* apreciable, estimable; *an appreciable difference* una diferencia apreciable ‖ considerable, grande (considerable).

appreciate [ə'pri:ʃieit] *vt* comprender (to understand); *I appreciate your point of view* comprendo su punto de vista ‖ apreciar, estimar; *to appreciate a good film* apreciar una buena película; *one cannot fully appreciate wealth without having known poverty* uno no puede apreciar la riqueza sin haber conocido la pobreza ‖ agradecer (to be grateful for); *I really appreciate your help* le agradezco mucho su ayuda ‖ apreciar, estimar, tasar, valorar, evaluar (to evaluate) ‖ aumentar el valor de (to raise the value of) ‖ — *I fully appreciate that...* me doy perfectamente cuenta de que... ‖ *to appreciate sth. for its true value* apreciar algo en su justo valor.
◆ *vi* valorizarse, subir.

appreciation [ə'pri:ʃi'eiʃən] *n* aprecio *m*, apreciación *f* (understanding, enjoyment) ‖ agradecimiento *m*, reconocimiento *m*, gratitud *f* (gratitude) ‖ apreciación *f*, valoración *f* (appraisal) ‖ plusvalía *f*, subida *f*, aumento *m* de valor (rise in value) ‖ crítica *f* (literary).

appreciative [ə'pri:ʃjətiv]; **appreciatory** [ə'pri:ʃjətəri] *adj* apreciativo, va ‖ agradecido, da (grateful) ‖ sensible (sensitive) ‖ elogioso, sa (flattering) ‖ atento, ta (audience).

apprehend [æpri'hend] *vt* prender, detener, aprehender (to arrest) ‖ percibir, comprender (to perceive, to understand) ‖ temer (to fear).
◆ *vi* comprender.

apprehensible [æpri'hensəbl] *adj* comprensible ‖ perceptible.

apprehension [æpri'henʃən] *n* aprensión *f*, temor *m*, recelo *m* (fear); *although he is healthy he has the apprehension that he is going to die* aunque está sano tiene la aprensión de que se va a morir ‖ detención *f*, prendimiento *m*, arresto *m* (arrest) ‖ perception *f* (perception) ‖ comprensión *f* (understanding).

apprehensive [æpri'hensiv] *adj* aprensivo, va (fearful) ‖ inquieto, ta (worried); *apprehensive for s.o.'s safety* inquieto por la seguridad de alguien ‖ de comprensión; *apprehensive capacity* capacidad de comprensión ‖ inteligente (intelligent) ‖ *to be apprehensive for, that...* temer por, que...

apprehensiveness [-nis] *n* temor *m*, recelo *m*, aprensión *f* (fear) ‖ comprensión *f*.

apprentice [ə'prentis] *n* aprendiz, za; *shoemaker's apprentice* aprendiz de zapatero ‖ principiante, novicio, cia (beginner).

apprentice [ə'prentis] *vt* colocar de aprendiz ‖ *to be apprenticed to* estar de aprendiz con.

apprenticeship [-ʃip] *n* aprendizaje *m*; *to serve one's apprenticeship with* hacer el aprendizaje con.

apprise; apprize [ə'praiz] *vt* informar, avisar.

approach [ə'prəutʃ] *n* acercamiento *m*; *the approach of the troops* el acercamiento de las tropas ‖ acceso *m*, vía *f* or camino *m* de acceso; *the approach to the plateau was perilous* el camino de acceso a la meseta era peligroso ‖ acceso *m*; *difficult of approach* de difícil acceso ‖ FIG manera de abordar *or* de empezar (way of beginning) | aproximación *f* | planteamiento *m*, enfoque *m* (way of looking at a problem) | propuesta *f*, proposición *f*; *we have made several approaches but he will not sell the picture* le hemos hecho varias proposiciones pero no quiere vender el cuadro | oferta *f* (offer).
◆ *pl* MIL aproches *m* ‖ *to make approaches to a country* intentar entrar en contacto con un país.

approach [ə'prəutʃ] *vi* acercarse, aproximarse; *the appointed hour was approaching* se acercaba la hora señalada.
◆ *vt* acercarse a, aproximarse a; *the train was fast approaching the town* el tren se iba acercando rápidamente a la ciudad ‖ FIG enfocar (to look at); *to approach a problem* enfocar un problema | considerar (to consider) | parecerse a, ser semejante a (to look like) | acercarse a, rayar en (to border on); *a passion which approaches madness* una pasión que se acerca a la locura *or* que raya en locura | abordar (to accost a person, to tackle a problem) | dirigirse a; *to approach s.o. for a loan* dirigirse a uno para pedirle un préstamo | entrar en contacto; *to approach a foreign power in view of a trade agreement* entrar en contacto con una potencia extranjera con vistas a un acuerdo comercial ‖ *a man who is easy to approach* un hombre de fácil acceso *or* abordable.

approachability [əprəutʃə'biliti] *n* accesibilidad *f*.

approachable [ə'prəutʃəbl] *adj* accesible (place) ‖ abordable, accesible (person).

approaching [ə'prəutʃiŋ] *adj* próximo, ma ‖ semejante, parecido, da (similar) ‖ que se acerca.

approachless [ə'prəutʃlis] *adj* inaccesible, inabordable.

approbate ['æprəubeit] *vt* US aprobar.

approbation [æprəu'beiʃən] *n* aprobación *f*.

approbative ['æprəubeitiv] *adj* aprobativo, va.

approbatory ['æprəubeitəri] *adj* aprobatorio, ria.

appropriate [ə'prəupriit] *adj* apropiado, da; conveniente.

appropriate [ə'prəuprieit] *vt* apropiarse de (to take for o.s.) ‖ asignar, destinar (to set aside); *to appropriate funds* asignar fondos.

appropriateness [ə'prəupriitnis] *n* conveniencia *f*.

appropriation [ə'prəupri'eiʃən] *n* apropiación *f* ‖ asignación *f* (of a sum of money).

appropriator [ə'prəuprieitə*] *n* apropiador, ra ‖ usurpador, ra.

approvable [ə'pru:vəbl] *adj* digno de aprobación.

approval [ə'pru:vəl] *n* aprobación *f*; *to give one's approval* dar su aprobación ‖ *on approval* a prueba (on trial), previa aceptación (previous acceptance).

approve [ə'pru:v] *vt* aprobar; *to approve a plan unanimously* aprobar un proyecto por unanimidad ‖ probar, demostrar (one's quality) ‖ *to be approved by* tener la aprobación de, ser aprobado por.
◆ *vi* aprobar, dar su aprobación ‖ *to approve of* aprobar.

approved school [ə'pru:vd,sku:l] *n* reformatorio *m*, correccional *m*.

approving [ə'pru:viŋ] *adj* aprobatorio, ria; de aprobación.

approximate [ə'prɔksimit] *adj* aproximado, da.

approximate [ə'prɔksimeit] *vt* aproximarse a, acercarse a; *the result approximates the forecast* el resultado se aproxima al pronóstico.
◆ *vi* aproximarse, acercarse.

approximately [ə'prɔksimitli] *adv* aproximadamente.

approximation [əprɔksi'meiʃən] *n* aproximación *f*.

appurtenance [ə'pə:tinəns] *n* accesorio *m* (accessory) ‖ ARCH dependencia *f*.
◆ *pl* JUR anexidades *f*.

appurtenant [ə'pə:tinənt] *adj* accesorio, ria ‖ JUR anexo, xa.

après-ski ['æpreiski:] *n* vida *f* nocturna en una estación de esquí.

apricot ['eiprikət] *n* BOT albaricoquero *m* (tree) | albaricoque *m* (fruit) ‖ color *m* albaricoque.

April ['eiprəl] *n* abril ‖ — *April fool* inocente *m* & *f* (victim of a joke) ‖ *April Fool's Day* día *m* de los Inocentes ‖ *April showers bring May flowers* en abril, aguas mil ‖ *to make an April fool of* dar una inocentada a.
— OBSERV En Inglaterra el **día de los Inocentes** es el 1 de abril y no el 28 de **diciembre** como en España.

a priori ['eiprai'ɔ:rai] *adj/adv* a priori.

apriority [eiprai'ɔriti] *n* apriorismo *m*.

apron ['eiprən] *n* delantal *m*, mandil *m* (garment) ‖ salpicadero *m* (of a car) ‖ TECH placa *f* de distribución ‖ THEATR proscenio *m* ‖ AVIAT pista *f* delante de los hangares ‖ FIG *tied to his mother's apron strings* agarrado a las faldas de su madre.

apropos ['æprəpəu] *adj* oportuno, na.
◆ *adv* a propósito, oportunamente ‖ *apropos of* respecto a.

apse [æps] *n* ARCH ábside *m* ‖ ASTR ápside *m* ‖ *apse aisle* deambulatorio *m*.

apsidal ['æpsidl] *adj* absidal.

apsidiole [æp'sidiəul] *n* ARCH absidiolo *m*.

apsis ['æpsis] *n* ápside *m* (in astronomy).
— OBSERV El plural de *apsis* es *apsides*.

apt [æpt] *adj* apropiado, da; conveniente (appropriate) ‖ apto, ta (fitted) ‖ listo, ta; dotado, da (gifted) ‖ acertado, da; oportuno, na (remark) ‖ exacto, ta; atinado, da (description) ‖ dispuesto, ta (ready) ‖ susceptible (liable) ‖ propenso, sa (inclined).

apterous ['æptərəs] *adj* ZOOL áptero, ra.
◆ *n* ZOOL áptero *m*.

apteryx ['æptəriks] *n* ZOOL ápterix *m*.

aptitude ['æptitju:d] *n* aptitud *f*; *aptitude test* prueba de aptitud ‖ capacidad *f* ‖ inclinación *f*, propensión *f* (natural tendency) ‖ *to have an aptitude for* tener aptitudes para.

aptness ['æptnis] *n* lo apropiado ‖ → **aptitude.**

Apuleius [æpju'li:jəs] *pr m* Apuleyo *m*.

apyretic [æpai'retik] *adj* MED apirético, ca.

apyrexy [æ'paireksi] *n* MED apirexia *f*.

aquafortis ['ækwə'fɔ:tis] *n* CHEM agua *f* fuerte.

aqualung ['ækwəlʌŋ] *n* escafandra *f* autónoma.

aquamarine [ækwəmə'ri:n] *n* aguamarina *f* (stone) ‖ color *m* de aguamarina.
◆ *adj* de color de aguamarina, de color verde mar.

aquaplane ['ækwəplein] *n* acuaplano *m*, hidropatín *m*.

aqua regia ['ækwə'ri:dʒjə] *n* CHEM agua *f* regia.

aquarelle [ækwə'rel] *n* ARTS acuarela *f*.

aquarium [ə'kwɛəriəm] *n* acuario *m*.
— OBSERV El plural es *aquaria* o *aquariums*.

Aquarius [ə'kwɛəriəs] *pr n* Acuario *m*.

aquatic [ə'kwætik] *adj* acuático, ca.
◆ *n* BOT planta *f* acuática || ZOOL animal *m* acuático.
◆ *pl* deportes *m* acuáticos.

aquatint ['ækwətint] *n* ARTS acuatinta *f*.

aqua vitae ['ækwə'vaiti:] *n* aguardiente *m*.

aqueduct ['ækwidʌkt] *n* acueducto *m*.

aqueous ['eikwiəs] *adj* acuoso, sa; ácueo, a || GEOL sedimentario, ria (rock) || ANAT *aqueous humour* humor acuoso.

aquiferous [ə'kwifərəs] *adj* acuífero, ra.

Aquila ['ækwilə] *pr n* ASTR Águila *f* (constellation).

aquiline ['ækwilain] *adj* aquilino, na || aguileño, ña; aquilino, na (nose) || de águila.

Aquitaine [,ækwi'tein] *pr n* GEOGR Aquitania *f*.

Aquitania [,ækwi'teinja] *pr m* HIST Aquitania *f*.

ara ['ærə] *n* ZOOL guacamayo *m*.

Ara ['ærə] *n* ASTR Ara *m* (constellation).

Arab ['æreb] *adj* árabe.
◆ *n* árabe *m* & *f* (inhabitant of Arab country) || árabe *m* (language) || FAM *street Arab* golfillo *m*, pilluelo *m*.

arabesque [,ærə'besk] *adj* arabesco, ca.
◆ *n* arabesco *m*.

Arabia [ə'reibjə] *pr n* GEOGR Arabia *f*.

Arabian [-n] *adj* árabe, arábigo, ga || de Arabia (desert) || — GEOGR *Arabian Gulf* golfo Arábico || *Arabian Nights* Las mil y una noches || *Arabian Sea* mar *m* de Omán.
◆ *n* árabe *m* & *f*.

Arabic ['ærəbik] *adj* árabe, arábigo, ga || *Arabic numerals* numeración arábiga.
◆ *n* árabe *m*.

Arabicism [æ'ræbisizəm] *n* arabismo *m*.

Arabist ['ærəbist] *n* arabista *m* & *f*.

arabize ['ærəbaiz] *vt* arabizar.

arable ['ærəbl] *adj* arable, cultivable.
◆ *n* tierra *f* cultivable *or* de cultivo.

arachnid [ə'ræknid]; **arachnidan** [-ən] *adj* ZOOL arácnido, da.
◆ *n* ZOOL arácnido *m*.

arachnoid [ə'ræknɔid] *adj* ANAT aracnoideo, a.
◆ *n* ANAT aracnoides *f inv* || ZOOL arácnido *m*.

Aragon ['ærəgən] *pr n* GEOGR Aragón *m*.

Aragonese [ærəgə'ni:z] *adj/n* aragonés, esa.

aragonite [ə'rægənait] *n* MIN aragonito *m*.

Aral Sea ['a:rəl] *pr n* GEOGR mar *m* de Aral.

Aramaean; Aramean [,ærə'mi:ən] *adj/n* arameo, a.

Aramaic [,ærə'meiik] *n* arameo *m* (language).

arapaima [,ærə'paimə] *n* ZOOL arapaima *m*.

Araucan [ə'rɔ:kən]; **Araucanian** [,ærɔ:'keinjən] *adj* araucano, na.
◆ *n* araucano, na (person) || araucano *m* (language).

araucaria [,ærɔ:'kɛəriə] *n* BOT araucaria *f*.

arbalest ['a:bəlest]; **arbalist** ['a:bəlist] *n* ballesta *f* (crossbow).

arbiter ['a:bitə*] *n* árbitro *m*; *Petronius, arbiter of elegance* Petronio, árbitro de la elegancia.

arbitral ['a:bitrəl] *adj* arbitral.

arbitrarily ['a:bitrərili] *adv* arbitrariamente.

arbitrariness ['a:bitrərinis] *n* arbitrariedad *f*.

arbitrary ['a:bitrəri] *adj* arbitrario, ria.

arbitrate ['a:bitreit] *vt/vi* arbitrar.

arbitration [,a:bi'treiʃən] *n* arbitraje *m*; *to go to arbitration* recurrir al arbitraje || *judgment by arbitration* sentencia *f* arbitral.

arbitrator ['a:bitreitə*] *n* árbitro *m*.

arbor ['a:bə*] *n* TECH árbol *m* || US TECH mandril *m* || US emparrado *m*, cenador *m* || US *Arbor Day* día *m* del árbol.

arboreal [a:'bɔ:riəl] *adj* arbóreo, a.

arborescence [,a:bə'resns] *n* arborescencia *f*.

arboriculture ['a:bərikʌltʃə*] *n* arboricultura *f*.

arborization [,a:bəri'zeiʃən] *n* arborización *f*.

arborvitae ['a:bə'vaiti] *n* BOT árbol *m* de la vida, tuya *f* || ANAT árbol *m* de la vida.

arbour ['a:bə*] *n* emparrado *m*, cenador *m*.

arbutus [a:'bju:təs] *n* BOT madroño *m*.

arc [a:k] *n* arco *m*; *arc of a circle* arco de círculo || ELECTR *electric arc* arco voltaico.

arcade [a:'keid] *n* arcada *f* || soportales *m pl* (in a square) || *shopping arcade* galería *f* comercial.

Arcadia [a:'keidjə] *pr n* Arcadia *f*.

Arcadian [a:'keidjən] *adj/n* árcade.

arcana [a:'keinə] *pl n* arcanos *m*.

arcane [a:'kein] *adj* arcano, na; secreto, ta.

arch [a:tʃ] *adj* grande; *his arch rival* su gran rival || malicioso, sa; *an arch look* una mirada maliciosa.
◆ *n* arco *m* || — ARCH *arch behind a lintel* arco capialzado || *arch of heaven* bóveda *f* celeste || ARCH *basket-handle arch* arco carpanel *or* apainelado *or* rebajado || ANAT *dental arch* arco alveolar || ARCH *flat arch* arco adintelado *or* a nivel | *flying arch* arco por tranquil | *gothic arch* arco de todo punto *or* ojival | *horseshoe* o *Moorish arch* arco de herradura *or* morisco *or* arábigo | *inflected arch* arco de cortina | *lancet arch* arco apuntado *or* lanceolado | *ogee arch* arco conopial | *segmental arch* arco escarzano | *semicircular arch* arco de medio punto | *splayed arch* arco abocinado | *stilted arch* arco peraltado | *trefoil arch* arco trebolado *or* trilobulado || *triumphal arch* arco de triunfo *or* triunfal.

arch [a:tʃ] *vt* arquear || *to arch one's eyebrows* arquear *or* enarcar las cejas.
◆ *vi* arquearse.

archaeological [,a:kiə'lɔdʒikəl] *adj* arqueológico, ca.

archaeologist [,a:ki'ɔlədʒist] *n* arqueólogo, ga.

archaeology [,a:ki'ɔlədʒi] *n* arqueología *f*.

archaeopteryx [,a:ki'ɔptəriks] *n* ZOOL arqueoptérix *m*.

archaic [a:'keiik] *adj* arcaico, ca.

archaism ['a:keiizəm] *n* arcaísmo *m*.

archaist [a:keiist] *n* arcaísta *m* & *f*.

archaistic [a:kei'istik] *adj* arcaizante.

archaize ['a:keiaiz] *vt/vi* arcaizar.

archangel ['a:k,eindʒəl] *n* arcángel *m*.

archangelic ['a:kein'dʒelik] *adj* arcangélico, ca.

archbishop ['a:tʃ'biʃəp] *n* REL arzobispo *m*.

archbishopric [a:tʃ'biʃəprik] *n* REL arzobispado *m*, archidiócesis *f*.

archconfraternity ['a:tʃ,kɔnfrə'tə:niti] *n* archicofradía *f*.

archdeacon ['a:tʃ'di:kən] *n* REL arcediano *m*, archidiácono *m*.

archedeaconate ['a:tʃ'di:kənit] *n* REL arcedianato *m*.

archdeaconry ['a:tʃ'di:kənri]; **archdeaconship** ['a:tʃ'di:kənʃip] *n* REL arcedianato *m*.

archdiocesan ['a:tʃdai'ɔsisən] *adj* REL archidiocesano, na.

archdiocese ['a:tʃdaiəsis] *n* archidiócesis *f*.

archducal ['a:tʃ'dju:kəl] *adj* archiducal.

archduchess ['a:tʃ'dʌtʃis] *n* archiduquesa *f*.

archduchy ['a:tʃ'dʌtʃi] *n* archiducado *m*.

archduke ['a:tʃ'dju:k] *n* archiduque *m*.

archegonium [,a:ki'gəunjəm] *n* BOT arquegonio *m*.
— OBSERV El plural de *archegonium* es *archegonia*.

archenemy ['a:tʃ'enimi] *n* enemigo *m* jurado (the direst enemy) || el diablo *m*, Satanás *m* (Satan).

archer ['a:tʃə*] *n* arquero *m* || ASTR *the Archer* el Sagitario.

archery ['a:tʃəri] *n* tiro *m* al arco (sport) || equipo *m* para tiro al arco (equipment).

archetypal [,a:ki'taipl] *adj* arquetípico, ca.

archetype ['a:kitaip] *n* arquetipo *m*.

archfiend ['a:tʃ'fi:nd] *n* → **archenemy.**

archidiaconal [,a:kidai'ækənl] *adj* del arcediano.

archiepiscopal [,a:kii'piskəpəl] *adj* arzobispal.

archiepiscopate [,a:kii'piskəpit] *n* REL arzobispado *m* (archbishopric).

archil ['a:tʃil] *n* BOT urchilla *f*.

archimandrite [,a:ki'mændrait] *n* REL archimandrita *m*.

Archimedes [,a:ki'mi:di:z] *pr n* Arquímedes || *Archimedes' screw* tornillo *m* de Arquímedes.

arching ['a:tʃiŋ] *n* arqueo *m* (of the body).

archipelago [,a:ki'peligəu] *n* archipiélago *m*.

archips ['a:kips] *pl n* ZOOL arquípteros *m*.

architect ['a:kitekt] *n* arquitecto *m*; *landscape architect* arquitecto paisajista || FIG artífice *m*, autor *m*.

architectonic ['a:kitek'tɔnik] *adj* ARCH arquitectónico, ca.
◆ *n* arquitectura *f*, arquitectónica *f*.

architectural [,a:ki'tektʃərəl] *adj* ARCH arquitectónico, ca.

architecture ['a:kitektʃə*] *n* ARCH arquitectura *f*.

architrave [a:kitreiv] *n* ARCH arquitrabe *m*.

archives [a:kaivz] *pl n* archivo *m sing*; *National Archives* Archivo Nacional.

archivist [a:kivist] *n* archivero, ra; archivista *m* & *f*.

archivolt ['a:kivəult] *n* ARCH archivolta *f*, arquivolta *f*.

archlute [a:tʃlu:t] *n* MUS archilaúd *m*.

archly ['atʃli] *adv* maliciosamente.

archness ['a:tʃnis] *n* malicia *f* || socarronería *f*.

archon ['a:kən] *n* HIST arconte *m*.

archonship [-ʃip]; **archontate** [-teit] *n* arcontado *m*.

archpriest ['a:tʃpri:st] *n* REL arcipreste *m*.

archpriesthood [-hud]; **archpriestship** [-ʃip] *n* arciprestazgo *m*.

archway ['a:tʃwei] *n* arco *m*, arcada *f*.

arc lamp ['a:k-læmp] *n* ELECTR lámpara *f* de arco.

Arctic ['a:ktik] *adj* GEOGR ártico, ca || FAM helado, da; glacial.
◆ *n* ártico *m* || FAM el Polo *m*; *it's like the Arctic here* aquí se está como en el Polo || — *Arctic Circle* Círculo Polar Ártico || *Arctic Ocean* Océano Ártico.

arctics [-s] *pl n* US botas *f* impermeables.

arcuate ['a:kjuit] *adj* arqueado, da.

arc welding ['a:k'weldiŋ] *n* soldadura *f* por arco.

ardency [ˈɑːdənsi] *n* ardor *m*.

ardent [ˈɑːdənt] *adj* ardiente.

ardour; US **ardor** [ˈɑːdə*] *n* ardor *m*.

arduous [ˈɑːdjuəs] *adj* escarpado, da (slope) || arduo, dua (strenous).

arduousness [-nis] *n* dificultad *f*.

are [ɑː*] *pres indic* → **be.**

are [ɑː*] *n* área *f* (100 square metres).

area [ˈɛəriə] *n* área *f*, superficie *f* (exact measure) || superficie *f*, extensión *f* || región *f* (region) || zona *f* (zone) || distrito *m* postal (mail) || campo *m*, terreno *m*, esfera *f* (academic field) || patio *m* (yard) || — SP *goal area* área de gol || *metropolitan area* área metropolitana *or* urbana || SP *penalty area* área de castigo || *sterling area* zona de la libra esterlina.

area code [-kəud] *n* prefijo *m* (telephone).

areaway [ˈɛəriəwei] *n* US patio *m*.

areca [ˈærikə] *n* BOT areca *f*.

arena [əˈriːnə] *n* arena *f* || ruedo *m*, redondel *m* (of a bullring) || pista *f* (circus) || FIG campo *m*, esfera *f* (field).

arenaceous [ˌæriˈneiʃəs] *adj* arenoso, sa; arenáceo, a.

arenicolous [ˌæriˈnikələs] *adj* ZOOL arenícola.

aren't [ɑːnt] (contraction of «are not»).

areola [æˈriələ] *n* areola *f*, aréola *f*.
— OBSERV El plural en inglés es *areolae* o *areolas*.

areole [ˈæriəul] *n* areola *f*, aréola *f*.

areometer [æriˈɔmitə*] *n* areómetro *m*.

areometry [æriˈɔmitri] *n* areometria *f*.

areopagite [ˌæriˈɔpəgait] *n* areopagita *m*.

Areopagus [ˌæriˈɔpəgəs] *pr n* Areópago *m*.

arête [æˈreit] *n* arista *f*.

argent [ˈɑːdʒənt] *adj* HERALD argénteo, a.
◆ *n* argén *m* (silver).

argentiferous [ˌɑːdʒənˈtifərəs] *adj* argentífero, ra.

Argentina [ˌɑːdʒənˈtiːnə] *pr n* GEOGR Argentina *f*.

argentine [ˈɑːdʒəntain] *adj* argentino, na.
◆ *n* metal *m* plateado (metal).

Argentine [ˈɑːdʒəntain] *adj/n* argentino, na || *the Argentine* Argentina *f*.

Argentinean [ˌɑːdʒənˈtinjən] *adj/n* argentino, na.

argillaceous [ˌɑːdʒiˈleiʃəs] *adj* arcilloso, sa.

Argive [ˈɑːgaiv] *adj/n* HIST argivo, va.

argon [ˈɑːgɔn] *n* CHEM argón *m*.

argonaut [ˈɑːgənɔːt] *n* ZOOL argonauta *m*.

Argonaut [ˈɑːgənɔːt] *n* MYTH Argonauta *m*.

argosy [ˈɑːgəsi] *n* MAR carraca *f*.

argot [ˈɑːgəu] *n* argot *m*.

arguable [ˈɑːgjuːəbl] *adj* defendible (that can be supported) || discutible (open to doubt).

argue [ˈɑːgjuː] *vt* razonar (to apply reason to) || discutir (to discuss); *to argue with s.o. about sth.* discutir con alguien, discutir con alguien sobre algo || sostener, mantener, argüir (to maintain) || persuadir (to persuade) || demostrar (to indicate).
◆ *vi* discutir (to wrangle); *don't argue!* ¡no discutas! || abogar (*for* por) (to plead) || argüir, argumentar (to adduce) || razonar.

argument [ˈɑːgjumənt] *n* razón *f* (reason) || discusión *f*, debate *m* (discussion) || discusión *f*, disputa *f* (quarrel) || razonamiento *m* (reasoning) || sumario *m* (summary) || JUR alegato *m* || — *for the sake of argument* como hipótesis || *it is beyond argument* es indiscutible || *let's not have any argument* no discutamos.

argumentation [ˌɑːgjumenˈteiʃən] *n* argumentación *f*, razonamiento *m* (reasoning) || discusión *f*, debate *m* (discussion).

argumentative [ˌɑːgjuˈmentətiv] *adj* sujeto a controversia *or* a discusión (matter) || discutidor, ra; argumentador, ra (person).

argus [ˈɑːgəs] *n* ZOOL & FIG argos *m*.

Argus [ˈɑːgəs] *pr n* Argos *m*.

aria [ˈɑːriə] *n* MUS aria *f*.

Ariadne [ˌæriˈædni] *pr n* MYTH Ariana *f*.

Arian [ˈɛəriən] *adj/n* REL arriano, na.

Arianism [-izəm] *n* REL arrianismo *m*.

arid [ˈærid] *adj* árido, da.

aridity [æˈriditi] *n* aridez *f*.

Aries [ˈɛəriːz] *n* ASTR Aries *m* (ram).

aright [əˈrait] *adv* (ant) correctamente.

aril [ˈæril] *n* BOT arilo *m*.

arise* [əˈraiz] *vi* originarse (*from* en), resultar (*from* de) (to result) || surgir, presentarse, aparecer (to come up) || plantearse (a problem) || levantarse (person, sun, storm, building) || elevarse (cry) || resucitar (from the dead).
— OBSERV Pret ***arose***; pp ***arisen***.

arisen [əˈrizən] *pp* → **arise.**

arista [əˈristə] *n* BOT arista.
— OBSERV El plural de la palabra inglesa es *aristae*.

aristarch [ˈæristɑːk] *n* aristarco *m*.

Aristides [ˌærisˈtaidiːz] *pr n* Arístides *m*.

aristocracy [ˌærisˈtɔkrəsi] *n* aristocracia *f*.

aristocrat [ˈæristəkræt] *n* aristócrata *m* & *f*.

aristocratic [ˌæristəˈkrætik] *adj* aristocrático, ca.

aristolochia [ˌæristəˈləukjə] *n* BOT aristoloquia *f*.

Aristophanes [ˌærisˈtɔfəniːz] *pr n* Aristófanes *m*.

Aristotelian [ˌæristɔˈtiːljən] *adj/n* aristotélico, ca.

Aristotle [ˈæristɔtl] *pr n* Aristóteles *m*.

arithmetic [əˈriθmətik] *n* MATH aritmética *f* || *mental arithmetic* cálculo *m* mental.

arithmetic [ˌæriθˈmetik] *adj* aritmético, ca || — MATH *arithmetic mean* media aritmética || MATH *arithmetic progression* progresión aritmética || INFORM *arithmetic operator* operador *m* aritmético.

arithmetical [ˌæriθˈmetikəl] *adj* aritmético, ca.

arithmetician [əˌriθməˈtiʃən] *n* aritmético, ca.

Arizona [ˌæriˈzaunə] *pr n* GEOGR Arizona *m*.

ark [ɑːk] *n* REL arca *f* || — REL *Ark of the Covenant* Arca de la Alianza || *Noah's Ark* arca de Noé.

Arkansas [ˈɑːkənsɔː] *pr n* GEOGR Arkansas *m*.

arm [ɑːm] *n* ANAT brazo *m*; *to give s.o. one's arm* dar el brazo a uno || FIG brazo *m* (of sea, of chair, etc.) || pata *f* delantera, brazo *m* (of animals) || tentáculo *m* (of octopus) || manga *f* (sleeve) || astil *m*, brazo *m* (beam of a balance) || aguilón *m*, brazo *m* (of a crane) || radio *m* (of a wheel) || uña *f* (of a anchor) || brazo *m* (of record player) || arma *f* (weapon) || MIL arma *f*; *the infantry arm* el arma de infantería || — *right arm* brazo derecho || *the long arm of the law* el brazo de la justicia || FIG *to keep s.o. at arm's length* mantener a uno a distancia | *to let one's arm be twisted* dar su brazo a torcer || *to walk arm in arm* ir del brazo *or* cogidos del brazo.
◆ *pl* HERALD escudo *m sing*, armas *f* || — *arms race* carrera *f* de armamentos || *coat of arms* escudo *m* de armas || *feat of arms* hecho *m* de armas || *in arms* en armas || *infant in arms* niño *m* de pecho || *in one's arms* en brazos || *order arms!* ¡descansen armas! || *present arms!* ¡presenten armas! || *to arms!* ¡a las armas!, ¡a formar con armas! || *to bear arms* servir [como soldado] || *to be up in arms* haberse levantado en armas (to fight), poner el grito en el cielo, sublevarse (against an abuse) || *to carry arms* ir armado || *to carry out the vigil of arms* velar las armas || *to order arms* descansar las armas || *to present arms* presentar armas || *to rise up in arms* alzarse *or* levantarse en armas || *to surrender one's arms, to lay down one's arms* rendir las armas || *to take up arms* tomar las armas || *to throw one's arms around s.o.'s neck* echar los brazos al cuello a alguien || FIG *to throw one's arms in the air* levantar los brazos al cielo || *under arms* sobre las armas || *with one's arms folded* con los brazos cruzados || *with open arms* con los brazos abiertos.

arm [ɑːm] *vt* armar (to provide with arms); *armed forces* fuerzas armadas || proteger (to protect); *armed against the cold* protegido contra el frío || armar (to provide with); *armed with a hammer* armado de un martillo || equipar (to fit with some device) || — *armed robbery* robo *m* a mano armada || *armed to the teeth* armado hasta los dientes || *to arm o.s.* armarse.
◆ *vi* armarse.

armada [ɑːˈmɑːdə] *n* MAR armada *f* || HIST *the Spanish Armada* la Armada Invencible.

armadillo [ˌɑːməˈdiləu] *n* ZOOL armadillo *m*.

Armageddon [ˌɑːməˈgedn] *pr n* Armagedón *m*.

armament [ˈɑːməmənt] *n* MIL armamento *m*.
◆ *pl* MIL armas *f*, armamento *m sing* (military equipment) | fuerzas *f* (military forces).

armature [ˈɑːmətjuə*] *n* TECH armadura *f* || armazón *f* (metal supporting structure) || ELECTR inducido *m*.

armband [ˈɑːmˈbænd] *n* brazalete *m*.

armchair [ˈɑːmˈtʃɛə*] *adj* de sillón || FIG *armchair strategist* estratega *m* de café.
◆ *n* sillón *m*, butaca *f*.

Armenia [ɑːˈmiːnjə] *pr n* Armenia *f*.

Armenian [-n] *adj/n* armenio, nia || *Armenian bole* bol arménico.

armful [ˈɑːmful] *n* brazada *f*.

armhole [ˈɑːmhəul] *n* sisa *f* (in sewing).

armillary [ˈɑːmiləri] *adj* armilar; *armillary sphere* esfera armilar.

Arminian [ɑːˈminiən] *adj/n* arminiano, na.

armistice [ˈɑːmistis] *n* armisticio *m*.

armlet [ˈɑːmlit] *n* brazalete *m* || brazo *m* (of sea, etc.).

armor [ˈɑːmə*] *n/vt* US → **armour.**

armorial [ɑːˈmɔːriəl] *adj* HERALD nobiliario, ria; heráldico, ca || *armorial bearings* blasón *m*, escudo *m* de armas.
◆ *n* HERALD armorial *m*.

armorist [ˈɑːmərist] *n* HERALD heraldista *m* & *f*.

armory [ˈɑːməri] *n* HERALD blasón *m*, heráldica *f* (study) | armorial *m* (book).

armour; US **armor** [ˈɑːmə*] *n* armadura *f* (suit of mail, leather, etc.) || blindaje *m* (on tanks, ships, etc.) || fuerzas *f pl* blindadas (armed vehicles) || ZOOL armadura *f* || HERALD blasón *m* escudo *m* de armas.

armour; US **armor** [ˈɑːmə*] *vt* blindar, acorazar || *armoured car* vehículo blindado.

armour-clad; US **armor-clad** [ˈɑːmə*klæd] *adj* acorazado, da; blindado, da.

armourer; US **armorer** [ˈɑːmərə*] *n* armero *m*.

armour-plate; US **armor-plate** [ˈɑːmə*pleit] *n* blindaje *m*.

armour-plate; US **armor-plate** ['ɑːmə*pleit] *vt* blindar, acorazar.

armour-plating; armor-plating [-iŋ] *n* blindaje *m*, acorazamiento *m*.

armoury; US **armory** ['ɑːməri] *n* arsenal *m* (arms store, factory) || US FAM armas *f pl* de fuego (guns).

armpit ['ɑːmpit] *n* ANAT axila *f*, sobaco *m*.

armrest ['ɑːmrest] *n* brazo *m* (of an armchair).

army ['ɑːmi] *n* MIL ejército *m* || FIG multitud *f* (crowd) || — MIL *army chaplain* capellán *m* castrense | *army corps* cuerpo *m* de ejército | *army of occupation* ejército de ocupación | *army register* escalafón *m*.

arnica ['ɑːnikə] *n* BOT árnica *f* || MED tintura *f* de árnica.

aroma [ə'rəumə] *n* aroma *m*.

aromatic [ˌærəu'mætik] *adj* aromático, ca.
◆ *n* planta *f* aromática.

aromatize [ə'rəumətaiz] *vt* aromatizar.

arose [ə'rəuz] *pret* → **arise.**

around [ə'raund] *adv* por aquí (round here) || por allá (round there) || alrededor (in the vicinity) || por todos lados (on all sides) || cerca, aproximadament (near) || — *I don't get around much these days* no salgo mucho actualmente || *the other way around* al revés || *the word is going around that...* corre el rumor de que... || *the year around* durante todo el año || *to come around* venir; *he came around to see us* vino a vernos; volver en sí; *he came around one hour after the accident* volvió en sí una hora después del accidente; restablecerse (from an illness); cambiar de dirección; MAR virar (a ship); ceder (to yield); hacer una visita (to visit) || *to come around to one's point of view* darle la razón a uno, dejarse convencer, aceptar el punto de vista de alguien || *to get around* viajar (to travel), salir (to go out), divulgarse, propalarse (a rumour, news) || *to have been around* haber viajado mucho (to have done much travelling), tener mucha experiencia, haber corrido mundo (to have much experience).
◆ *prep* alrededor de (encircling) || a eso de; *around five o'clock* a eso de las cinco || por; *to go around town* ir por la ciudad || cerca de (near).

arousal [ə'rauzəl] *n* despertar *m*.

arouse [ə'rauz] *vt* despertar.
◆ *vi* despertarse.

arpeggio [ɑː'pedʒiəu] *n* MUS arpegio *m*.

arpeggio [ɑː'pedʒiəu] *vi* MUS arpegiar.

arquebus ['ɑːkwibəs] *n* arcabuz *m*.

arraign [ə'rein] *vt* acusar (accuse) || atacar, criticar (an opinion, s.o.) || JUR hacer comparecer.

arraignment [-mənt] *n* acusación *f* (accusation).

arrange [ə'reindʒ] *vt* arreglar, poner en orden (to put in order), || arreglar (one's hair) || arreglar (to fix up) || disponer (to dispose) || fijar, señalar (to fix upon) || decidir (to decide) || planear (to plan) || MUS arreglar, adaptar.
◆ *vi* ponerse de acuerdo, acordar (to agree) || tomar medidas (to see to the details of) || *to arrange to meet s.o.* quedar *or* citarse con alguien.

arranged marriage [-d'mæridʒ] *n* matrimonio *m* concertado.

arrangement [-mənt] *n* arreglo *m* (act of arranging or putting in order) || orden *m* (way in which things are arranged) || arreglo *m* (of a dispute) || convenio *m*, arreglo *m*, acuerdo *m* (agreement); *to make an arrangement* llegar a un acuerdo || plan *m* (plan) || FAM combinación *f* (combination) || MUS arreglo *m*, adaptación *f*.
◆ *pl* planes *m* || disposiciones *f*, medidas *f* (measures).

arrant ['ærənt] *adj* redomado, da; de marca mayor.

arras ['ærəs] *n* tapiz *m*.

array [ə'rei] *n* MIL formación *f*, orden *m*; *in battle array* en orden de batalla || FIG colección *f*, serie *f* (collection) || gala *f*, atavío *m* (ceremonial dress) || pompa *f* (pomp).

array [ə'rei] *vt* MIL formar; *to array the troops* formar las tropas || ataviar (to dress magnificently) || JUR formar; *to array the jury* formar el jurado.

array processor [ə'reiprəusesə*] *n* INFORM procesador *m* vectorial.

arrears [ə'riəz] *pl n* atrasos *m* || *to be in arrears* estar atrasado.

arrest [ə'rest] *n* arresto *m*, detención *f* (seizure by police) || paro *m* (checking of forward movement) || — *close arrest* arresto mayor || *to be under arrest* estar detenido, estar bajo arresto || *under house arrest* bajo arresto domiciliario || MIL *under open arrest* bajo arresto simple *or* menor.

arrest [ə'rest] *vt* detener, arrestar (to seize legally) || detener, parar (to check) || atraer, llamar; *her beauty arrested the attention of all present* su belleza atrajo la atención de todos los presentes.

arresting [ə'restiŋ] *adj* que llama la atención, llamativo, va.

arrhythmia [ə'riðmiə] *n* arritmia *f*.

arris ['æris] *n* ARCH arista *f* (of a beam) | lima *f* tesa (of a roof).

arrival [ə'raivəl] *n* llegada *f* (act of arriving) || — *new arrival* recién llegado || *the first arrivals* los primeros en llegar *or* llegados.

arrive [ə'raiv] *vi* llegar (to reach a destination) || aparecer (to appear) || lograr *or* alcanzar éxito, triunfar (to succeed) || *to arrive at* llegar a (a destination, a conclusion), alcanzar (an objective).

arrivism ['ærivizəm] *n* arribismo *m* (unscrupulous ambition).

arriviste; arrivist [ˌæri'viːst] *n* arribista *m* & *f*.

arrogance ['ærəgəns]; **arrogancy** [-i] *n* arrogancia *f*.

arrogant ['ærəgənt] *adj* arrogante.

arrogate ['ærəugeit] *vt* *to arrogate to o.s.* arrogarse, atribuirse.

arrogation [ˌærəu'geiʃən] *n* arrogación *f*.

arrow [ˌærəu] *n* flecha *f*.

arrowhead [-hed] *n* punta *f* de flecha || BOT saetilla *f*.

arrowroot [-ruːt] *n* arrurruz *m*.

arroyo [ə'rɔiə] *n* US cauce *m* seco de un río.

arse [ɑːs] *n* POP culo *m*, trasero *m*.

arsehole ['ɑːshəul] *n* POP gilipollas *m* & *f inv*.

arsenal ['ɑːsinəl] *n* arsenal *m*.

arsenate ['ɑːsinit]; **arseniate** ['ɑːsinieit] *n* arseniato *m*.

arsenic ['ɑːsnik] *n* CHEM arsénico *m*.
◆ *adj* CHEM arsénico, ca.

arsenide ['ɑːsinaid] *n* arseniuro *m*.

arsenious [ɑː'siːnjəs]; **arsenous** ['ɑːsənəs] *adj* CHEM arsenioso, sa.

arsine ['ɑːsiːn] *n* arsina *f*.

arsis ['ɑːsis] *n* POET sílaba *f* acentuada, arsis *f*.
— OBSERV El plural de la palabra inglesa es *arses*.

arson ['ɑːsn] *n* JUR incendio *m* premeditado.

arsonist [-ist] *n* incendiario, ria.

art [ɑːt] → **BE.**
— OBSERV *Art* es la forma antigua de la segunda persona del singular del verbo *to be* (*are*).

art [ɑːt] *n* arte *m* & *f*; *a work of art* una obra de arte; *the art of cooking* el arte culinario || *art for art's sake* el arte por el arte.
◆ *pl* letras *f*; *bachelor of Arts* licenciado en letras || — *arts and crafts* artes y oficios || *fine arts* Bellas Artes.
— OBSERV In Spanish *arte* is usually feminine in the plural and masculine in the singular, but with certain adjectives it remains feminine: *arte poética, arte cisoria*, etc.

Artaxerxes [ˌɑːtəg'zəːksiːz] *pr n* Artajerjes *m*.

artefact ['ɑːtifækt] *n* artefacto *m*.

arterial [ɑː'tiəriəl] *adj* arterial || nacional (road).

arteriole [ɑː'teriəul] *n* arteriola *f*.

arteriosclerosis [ɑː'tiəriəuskliə'rəusis] *n* MED arteriosclerosis *f*.

arteritis [ˌɑːtə'raitis] *n* MED arteritis *f*.

artery ['ɑːtəri] *n* ANAT arteria *f* || arteria *f* (road, street).

artesian [ɑː'tiːzjən] *adj* artesiano, na; *artesian well* pozo artesiano.

artful ['ɑːtful] *adj* ingenioso, sa.

artfulness [-nis] *n* ingenio *m*.

art gallery ['ɑːtˌgæləri] *n* galería *f* de arte.

arthralgia [ɑː'θrældʒiə] *n* MED artralgia *f*.

arthritic [ɑː'θritik] *adj/n* MED artrítico, ca.

arthritis [ɑː'θraitis] *n* MED artritis *f* || *rheumatoid arthritis* reúma *m* articular.

arthritism ['ɑːθritizəm] *n* MED artritismo *m*.

arthropod ['ɑːθrəpɔd] *n* ZOOL artrópodo *m*.
— OBSERV El plural es *arthropoda* o *arthropods*.

Arthur ['ɑːθə*] *pr n* Arturo *m* || Artús *m*, Arturo *m* (king).

artichoke ['ɑːtitʃəuk] *n* BOT alcachofa *f* || *Jerusalem artichoke* topinambur *m*, aguaturma *f*, pataca *f*.

article ['ɑːtikl] *n* artículo *m* (item) || artículo *m* (of newspaper) || cláusula *f* (clause) || REL artículo *m*; *articles of faith* artículos de fe || GRAMM artículo *m* || ZOOL artejo *m* || — *article of clothing* prenda *f* de vestir || *leading article* artículo de fondo, editorial *m*.
◆ *pl* articulado *m sing*, artículos *m* (of a law) || — *articles and conditions* pliego *m sing* de condiciones || *articles of apprenticeship* contrato *m sing* de aprendizaje || *articles of incorporation* estatutos *m* de una sociedad comercial || *articles of war* código *m sing* de justicia militar || MAR *ship's articles* rol *m sing* || *toilet articles* artículos de tocador, objetos *m* de tocador.

article ['ɑːtikl] *vt* formular || colocar de aprendiz || US JUR acusar.

articled clerk [-d klaːk] *n* pasante *m* [en prácticas].

articular [ɑː'tikjulə*] *adj* ANAT articular.

articulate [ɑː'tikjulit] *adj* articulado, da.

articulate [ɑː'tikjuleit] *vt/vi* articular.

articulation [ɑːˌtikju'leiʃən] *n* articulación *f*.

artifact ['ɑːtifækt] *n* artefacto *m*.

artifice ['ɑːtifis] *n* artificio *m* (trickery) || arte *m*, ingeniosidad *f*, habilidad *f* (skill).

artificial [ˌɑːti'fiʃəl] *adj* artificial; *an artificial lake* un lago artificial || sintético, ca; artificial (synthetic) || químico, ca (manure) || artificial, afectado, da (affected) || postizo, za (teeth) || — *artificial insemination* inseminación *f* artificial || INFORM *artificial intelligence* inteligencia *f* artificial || *artificial leg* pierna *f* artificial || MED *artificial respiration* respiración *f* artificial.

artificiality [ˌɑːtifiʃiˈæliti] *n* lo artificial, carácter *m* artificial || afectación *f*.

artificier [ɑːˈtifisə*] *n* artífice *m*.

artillery [ɑːˈtiləri] *n* MIL artillería *f*; *heavy artillery* artillería pesada.

artilleryman [-mən] *n* MIL artillero *m*.

artisan [ˌɑːtizæn] *n* artesano, na.

artist [ˈɑːtist] *n* artista *m* & *f*.

artiste [ɑːˈtiːst] *n* artista *m* & *f*.

artistic [ɑːˈtistik] *adj* artístico, ca.

artistry [ˈɑːtistri] *n* arte *m* & *f*.

artless [ˈɑːtlis] *adj* simple, natural (simple) || cándido, da (guileless) || torpe, poco habilidoso (unskilful) || inculto, ta (ignorant).

artlessness [-nis] *n* naturalidad *f* || candidez *f*.

Art Nouveau [ɑː nuːˈvəu] *n* ARTS Art Nouveau *m*.

artsy-craftsy [ˈɑːtsiˈkræftsi] *adj* US que se las da de artista.

arty [ˈɑːti]; **arty-crafty** [ˈɑːtiˈkrɑːfti] *adj* que se las da de artista.

arum [ˈɛərəm] *n* BOT aro *m*.

Aryan [ˈɛəriən] *adj/n* ario, ria.

as [æz] *conj/adv* como (like); *do as you like* haga como guste; *heavy as stone* pesado como una piedra || mientras, cuando (while); *he arrived as you were leaving* llegó cuando se estaba marchando || como, lo que; *do as I tell you* haz lo que te digo || como, lo mismo que; *as you and I* como tú y yo || ya que, puesto que (because); *as he objects, I won't read* no leeré puesto que él se opone || como; *as I said yesterday, it is very easy* como le dije ayer, es muy fácil || aunque; *sick as he was, he came to work* aunque estaba enfermo, vino a trabajar || — *as... as* tan... como; *as tall as a mountain* tan alto como una montaña || *as far as I am concerned* en lo que a mí se refiere || *as far as I know* que yo sepa || *as for* en cuanto a, en *or* por lo que se refiere a || *as from* a partir de || *as if* como si || *as if to* como para || *as it is* tal (y) como están las cosas || *as it seems* según parece || *as it were* por decirlo así || *as long as* mientras || *as much as, as many as* tanto... como, tantos... como; *I have as much money as you* tengo tanto dinero como tú || *as many as* cuantos; *to as many as are present I would say...* a cuantos están presentes afirmo que... || US *as of* a partir de || *as regards* con respecto a || *as... so* como... también *or* lo mismo || *as soon as* tan pronto como || *as the case may be* según sea el caso || *as though* como si || *as to* en cuanto a, en *or* por lo que se refiere a || *as well* también || *as well as* así como || *as yet* hasta ahora || *so as to* para; *I did it so as to give him an idea of how hard it is* lo hice para darle una idea de lo difícil que es || *such as* tal como.

◆ *prep* en calidad de, como (in the capacity of); *he came as an observer* vino en calidad de observador || como (like) || por; *as a rule* por regla general.

ASA *abbr of American Standards Association* asociación norteamericana de normalización.

asafoetida; asafetida [æsəˈfetidə] *n* asa *f* fétida.

asbestos [æzˈbestəs] *n* amianto *m*, asbesto *m*.

◆ *adj* de amianto || — *asbestos cement* fibrocemento *m* || *asbestos fiber* fibra de amianto.

ascend [əˈsend] *vt* ascender (a), subir (to climb) || subir a; *to ascend the throne* subir al trono || subir, remontar (towards the source of a river, etc.).

◆ *vi* subir, ascender || elevarse (smoke, balloon).

ascendancy; ascendency [-i] *n* ascendiente *m*, ascendencia *f*.

ascendant; ascendent [əˈsendənt] *adj* ascendente, ascendiente || *in the ascendant* en auge.

◆ *pl n* ascendientes *m*, antepasados *m*.

ascension [əˈsenʃən] *n* ascensión *f* || REL *the Ascension* la Ascensión.

ascent [əˈsent] *n* subida *f*, ascensión *f*, ascenso *m* (act of ascending) || ascenso *m* (promotion) || cuesta *f* (slope) || subida *f* (way up) || *line of ascent* ascendencia *f*.

ascertain [ˌæsəˈtein] *vt* comprobar (to verify) || averiguar (to find out); *I am going to ascertain what happened* voy a averiguar lo que ha sucedido.

ascertainable [-əbl] *adj* comprobable || averiguable.

ascertainment [-mənt] *n* comprobación *f* (verification) || averiguación *f*.

ascesis [əˈsisəs] *n* ascesis *f*.

ascetic [əˈsetik] *adj* ascético, ca.

◆ *n* asceta *m* & *f*.

asceticism [əˈsetisizəm] *n* ascetismo *m*, ascética *f*.

ASCII [ˈæski] *abbr of American Standard Code for Information Interchange* ASCII, código estándar norteamericano para el intercambio de información [entre sistemas de proceso de datos] || *ASCII code* código *m* ASCII.

ascomycete [æskəuˈmaisiːt] *n* BOT ascomiceto *m*.

ascot [ˈæskət] *n* US fular *m*, pañuelo *m*.

ascribable [əsˈkraibəbl] *adj* atribuible, imputable.

ascribe [əsˈkraib] *vt* atribuir, imputar.

ascription [əsˈkripʃən] *n* atribución *f*, imputación *f*.

ascus [ˈæskəs] *n* BOT asca *f*.

— OBSERV El plural de *ascus* es *asci*.

ASE *abbr of American Stock Exchange* plaza bursátil norteamericana.

asepsis [æˈsepsis] *n* MED asepsia *f*.

aseptic [æˈseptik] *adj* MED aséptico, ca.

asepticize [æˈseptisaiz] *vt* esterilizar, volver aséptico, aseptizar.

asexual [æˈseksjuəl] *adj* asexual, asexuado, da.

ash [æʃ] *n* ceniza *f*; *to burn to ashes* reducir a cenizas || BOT fresno *m* (tree) || *Ash Wednesday* Miércoles *m* de Ceniza.

ASH [æʃ] *abbr of Action on Smoking and Health* asociación británica contra el tabaco.

ashamed [əˈʃeimd] *adj* avergonzado, da || — *to be ashamed of* avergonzarse de, estar avergonzado por || *to be ashamed to do sth.* avergonzarse de hacer algo.

ash bin [ˈæʃbin] *n* cubo *m* de la basura.

ash can [ˈæʃkæn] *n* US cubo *m* de la basura.

ashen [ˈæʃn] *adj* BOT de fresno (of ash tree) || pálido, da; ceniciento, ta (palid).

ashlar; US **ashler** [ˈæʃlə*] *n* sillar *m* (building stone) || sillería *f* (stonework).

ashore [əˈʃɔː*] *adv* MAR a tierra (towards land) || en tierra (on land) || — *to go ashore* desembarcar || *to run ashore* encallar, varar.

ashtray [ˈæʃtrei] *n* cenicero *m*.

ashy [ˈæʃi] *adj* ceniciento, ta.

Asia [ˈeiʒə] *pr n* Asia *f*; *Asia Minor* Asia Menor.

Asian [ˈeiʃən] *adj/n* asiático, ca.

Asiatic [ˌeiʒiˈætik] *adj/n* asiático, ca.

aside [əˈsaid] *adv* al lado (to one side) || aparte; *joking aside* bromas aparte || — *aside from* además de (as well as), aparte de (apart from) || *to lay aside* dejar a un lado (sth. that is unwanted); guardar (to save); dejar de lado (scruples, prejudices) || *to set aside* anular || *to step aside* hacerse a un lado || *to take aside* llevar aparte || *to throw o to cast aside* echar a un lado, desechar.

◆ *n* THEATR aparte *m* || digresión *f*.

asinine [ˈæsinain] *adj* asnal || FAM estúpido, da.

ask [ɑːsk] *vt* preguntar; *ask the way home* pregunta el camino de casa; *ask him about mealtimes* pregúntale las horas de las comidas || hacer (a question) || pedir; *may I ask a favour of you?* ¿te puedo pedir un favor?; *to ask to be allowed to speak* pedir la palabra; *he asked me to come* me pidió que viniese || invitar (to invite); *I asked them round to dinner* les invité a cenar || JUR publicar (the banns) || — *don't ask me!* ¿yo qué sé? || *asking price* precio *m* inicial || *if you ask me* en mi opinión || *to ask s.o. in* decir a alguien que entre.

◆ *vi* preguntar || — *for the asking* a pedir de boca || *this asks for great prudence* esto requiere mucha prudencia || *to ask after* o *about* o *for* preguntar por || *to ask for it* buscársela || *to ask for sth. back* pedir que se devuelva algo || FIG *to ask for the moon* pedir la luna || *to ask for trouble* buscarse problemas.

askance [əsˈkæns] *adj* oblicuamente || de reojo, de soslayo || *to look askance at* mirar con desconfianza *or* recelo *or* con mala cara.

askew [əsˈkjuː] *adv* de reojo, de soslayo (to look).

◆ *adj* torcido, da; ladeado, da.

aslant [əˈslɑːnt] *adv* oblicuamente.

◆ *prep* a través de.

asleep [əˈsliːp] *adj* dormido, da (sleeping); *he was fast asleep* estaba profundamente dormido || adormecido, da (numb) || *to fall asleep* quedarse dormido, dormirse; *he was so tired that he fell asleep* estaba tan cansado que se quedó dormido.

aslope [əsˈləup] *adv/adj* en pendiente.

asp [æsp] *n* ZOOL áspid *m*, áspide *m*.

asparagus [əsˈpærəgəs] *n* BOT espárrago *m* (vegetable) || asparagus *m* (fern).

ASPCA *abbr of American Society for the Prevention of Cruelty to Animals* sociedad norteamericana para la prevención de la crueldad con los animales.

aspect [ˈæspekt] *n* aspecto *m* (outward appearance) || punto *m* de vista; *from a personal aspect* desde un punto de vista personal || aspecto *m*; *this problem has various aspects* este problema tiene varios aspectos || exposición *f*, orientación *f* (of a house) || ASTR aspecto *m* || *flat with a westerly aspect* piso orientado al oeste.

aspen [ˈæspən] *n* BOT álamo *m* temblón.

asperges [əsˈpəːdʒiːz] *n* REL asperges *m*.

aspergillum [ˌæspəˈdʒiləm] *n* REL hisopo *m*, aspersorio *m*.

— OBSERV El plural de *aspergillum* es *aspergilla*.

aspergillus [ˌæspəˈdʒiləs] *n* BOT aspergilo *m*.

— OBSERV El plural de *aspergillus* es *aspergilli*.

asperity [æsˈperiti] *n* aspereza *f*.

asperous [ˈæspərəs] *adj* áspero, ra (rough).

asperse [əsˈpəːs] *vt* difamar, calumniar (to malign) || hisopear, asperjar (to sprinkle).

aspersion [əsˈpəːʃən] *n* difamación *f*, calumnia *f* (defamation) || aspersión *f* (sprinkling) || *to cast aspersions on s.o.* difamar *or* calumniar a alguien.

aspersorium [ˌæspəˈsɔːrjəm] *n* REL hisopo *m*.

— OBSERV El plural es *aspersoria* o *aspersoriums*.

asphalt [ˈæsfælt] *n* asfalto *m*.

asphalt [ˈæsfælt] *vt* asfaltar.

asphalting [-iŋ] *n* asfaltado *m*.

asphodel ['æsfədel] *n* BOT asfódelo *m*, gamón *m*.

asphyxia [æs'fiksiə] *n* asfixia *f*.

asphyxiate [æs'fiksieit] *vt* asfixiar.
◆ *vi* asfixiarse.

asphyxiation [æs,fiksi'eiʃən] *n* asfixia *f*.

aspic ['æspik] *n* gelatina *f* de carne *or* de tomate ‖ ZOOL áspid *m* ‖ BOT espliego *m*.

aspidistra [,æspi'distrə] *n* BOT aspidistra *f*.

aspirant [əs'paiərənt] *n* aspirante *m* & *f*, candidato, ta.

aspirate ['æspərit] *n* GRAMM aspiración *f* (sound made by the letter «h») ‖ aspirada *f* (a consonant).
◆ *adj* GRAMM aspirado, da.

aspirate ['æspəreit] *vt* GRAMM & MED aspirar.

aspiration [,æspə'reiʃən] *n* aspiración *f*, ambición *f* ‖ MED & GRAMM aspiración *f*.

aspirator ['æspəreitə*] *n* MED aspirador *m*.

aspiratory [-ri] *adj* aspiratorio, ria.

aspire [əs'paiə*] *vi* aspirar, ambicionar; *to aspire to high positions* aspirar a *or* ambicionar altos cargos.

aspirin ['æspərin] *n* MED aspirina *f*.

aspiring [əs'pairiŋ] *adj* ambicioso, sa; en potencia.

asquint [ə'skwint] *adv/adj* de soslayo, de reojo.

ass [æs] *n* ZOOL asno *m*, burro *m* ‖ FAM burro *m* (a stupid person) ‖ US POP culo *m* ‖ — FAM *to be like Buridan's ass* parecerse al asno de Buridán ‖ *to make an ass of o.s.* ponerse en ridículo.

assagai ['æsəgai] *n* azagaya *f*.

assail [ə'seil] *vt* asaltar; *the beggars assailed him* los mendigos le asaltaron ‖ atacar, acometer (to attack) ‖ abrumar (with questions).

assailant [-ənt] *n* agresor, ra; asaltante *m* & *f*.

assassin [ə'sæsin] *n* asesino, na; *hired assassin* asesino pagado.

assassinate [ə'sæsineit] *vt* asesinar.

assassination [ə,sæsi'neiʃən] *n* asesinato *m* (murder).

assault [ə'sɔ:lt] *n* ataque *m* (vigorous attack); *bayonet assault* ataque a la bayoneta ‖ ultraje *m* (violent criticism) ‖ MIL & SP asalto *m* ‖ JUR amenaza *f* ‖ — JUR *assault and battery* lesiones *f pl*, vías *f pl* de hecho ‖ *criminal assault* intento *m* de violación ‖ *indecent assault* atentado *m* contra el pudor ‖ *to make an assault on* asaltar a, dar el asalto a.

assault [ə'sɔ:lt] *vt* asaltar, atacar; *the thief assaulted him* el ladrón le asaltó ‖ JUR agredir ‖ violar (to rape).

assault course [-kɔ:s] *n* MIL pista *f* de entrenamiento.

assay [ə'sei] *n* TECH aquilatamiento *m* (of gold), ensaye *m* (of a metal) ‖ muestra *f* de ensaye (sample of metal).

assay [ə'sei] *vt* TECH ensayar (metals) ‖ aquilatar (gold) ‖ FIG probar, intentar.

assegai ['æsigai] azagaya *f*.

assemblage [ə'semblidʒ] *n* colección *f* (of things) ‖ reunión *f* (of persons) ‖ TECH montaje *m*, ensambladura *f*.

assemble [ə'sembl] *vt* reunir (to bring together) ‖ armar, montar, ensamblar (to fit together) ‖ JUR convocar ‖ INFORM ensamblar.
◆ *vi* reunirse, juntarse.

assembler [-ə*] *n* montador *m* ‖ INFORM ensamblador *m*.

assembly [ə'sembli] *n* asamblea *f* (parliament) ‖ reunión *f*, asamblea *f* (a gathering of people) ‖ TECH montaje *m* ‖ MIL formación *f* ‖ — *assembly hall* salón *m* de actos ‖ *assembly line* cadena *f or* línea *f* de montaje ‖ *assembly line production* producción *f* en cadena ‖ *assembly shop* taller *m* de montaje.

assemblyman [-mən] *n* asembleista *m* ‖ US miembro *m* de la cámara baja de un Estado.

assent [ə'sent] *n* asentimiento *m*, consentimiento *m* ‖ sanción *f* (of a law).

assent [ə'sent] *vi* asentir, consentir.

assert [ə'sə:t] *vt* afirmar (to state as true) ‖ mantener, sostener (to maintain) ‖ hacer valer (rights, claims) ‖ *to assert o.s.* imponerse.

assertion [ə'sə:ʃən] *n* afirmación *f*, aserción *f*, reivindicación *f* (of a right).

assertive [ə'sə:tiv] *adj* perentorio, ria ‖ positivo, va (positive) ‖ afirmativo, va; asertivo, va (affirmative).

assertor [ə'sə:tə*] *n* asertor, ra ‖ FIG defensor *m*, campeón *m* (of a cause).

assertory [-ri] *adj* asertorio, ria.

assess [ə'ses] *vt* evaluar, valorar (*at* en) (to set an estimated value on) ‖ gravar (to impose a tax) ‖ repartir (expenses) ‖ juzgar (to consider).

assessment [-mənt] *n* valoración *f*, evaluación *f*, tasación *f*; *the assessment came to twenty pounds* la valoración fue de veinte libras ‖ gravamen *m* (tax) ‖ juicio *m* (judgment).

assessor [-ə*] *n* tasador, ra (who estimates values for insurance, taxation, etc.) ‖ asesor *m* (adviser).

asset ['æset] *n* ventaja *f* (advantage); *having a car is an asset in my profession* tener coche es una ventaja en mi profesión ‖ baza *f* (trump).
◆ *pl* bienes *m*; *personal assets* bienes muebles; *real assets* bienes raíces ‖ COMM haber *m sing*, activo *m sing* (positive items on a balance sheet) ‖ activo *m sing* (total property); *assets in hand* activo disponible.

asseverate [ə'sevəreit] *vt* aseverar, asegurar, afirmar.

asseveration [ə,sevə'reiʃən] *n* aseveración *f*, afirmación *f*.

asshole ['æshaul] *n* US POP gilipollas *m* & *f inv*.

assiduity [,æsi'dju:iti] *n* asiduidad *f*.

assiduous [ə'sidjuəs] *adj* asiduo, dua.

assign [ə'sain] *n* JUR cesionario, ria.

assign [ə'sain] *vt* asignar (to allot) ‖ designar, nombrar (to nominate) ‖ ceder (property, right) ‖ atribuir (to attribute) ‖ fijar (a date) ‖ señalar, indicar (a reason).

assignation [,æsig'neiʃən] *n* asignación *f* (the act of assigning) ‖ atribución *f* ‖ designación *f*, nombramiento *m* ‖ cita *f* (meeting) ‖ JUR cesión *f*.

assignee [,æsi'ni:] *n* JUR cesionario, ria (beneficiary) ‖ apoderado, da (proxy).

assignment [ə'sainmənt] *n* asignación *f* ‖ JUR cesión *f* (transference of property or rights) ‖ escritura *f* de cesión (document) ‖ misión *f* (mission) ‖ tarea *f*, trabajo *m* (task).

assimilable [ə'similəbl] *adj* asimilable.

assimilate [ə'simileit] *vt* asimilar; *to assimilate food* asimilar la comida; *to assimilate knowledge* asimilar conocimientos.
◆ *vi* asimilarse.

assimilation [ə,simi'leiʃən] *n* asimilación *f*.

assimilatory [ə'similətəri] *adj* asimilativo, va.

assist [ə'sist] *vt/vi* asistir, ayudar (to help); *he assists him in his work* le asiste en su trabajo ‖ asistir, presenciar (to be present) ‖ *to assist in* tomar parte en.

assist [ə'sist] *n* asistencia *f*, ayuda *f*.

assistance [ə'sistəns] *n* ayuda *f*, asistencia *f* ‖ *to be of assistance to* ayudar a.

assistant [ə'sistənt] *n* ayudante *m* & *f*, auxiliar *m* & *f*.
◆ *adj* ayudante ‖ — *assistant cameraman* ayudante de operador ‖ *assistant director* regidor *m* de escena ‖ *assistant manager* subdirector *m* ‖ *assistant teacher* profesor *m* auxiliar *or* adjunto ‖ *assistant secretary* subsecretario *m*, secretario adjunto.

assistantship [-ʃip] *n* ayudantía *f*.

assize [ə'saiz] *n* JUR jurado *m* (in Scotland) ‖ *Assize Court* Audiencia *f* de lo criminal.
◆ *pl* sesión *f sing* judicial.

associable [ə'səuʃjəbl] *adj* asociable.

associate [ə'səuʃiit] *adj* asociado, da; *associate publishers* editores asociados; *associate member* miembro asociado ‖ adjunto, ta (professor) ‖ *war and its associate horrors* la guerra y los horrores que la acompañan.
◆ *n* socio *m* (partner) ‖ compañero, ra (friend) ‖ cómplice *m* (in crime).

associate [ə'səuʃieit] *vt* asociar ‖ *to associate o.s. with an idea* adherir a una opinión.
◆ *vi* unirse, asociarse (to join together) ‖ tratarse, tratar; *I refuse to associate with them* me niego a tratar con ellos.

association [ə,səusi'eiʃən] *n* asociación *f*; *religious association* asociación religiosa; *European Free Trade Association* Asociación Europea de Libre Cambio ‖ COMM sociedad *f* ‖ recuerdo *m*; *Paris has happy associations for her* París tiene recuerdos felices para ella ‖ relación *f* (relationship) ‖ — *association of ideas* asociación de ideas ‖ — *in association with* en colaboración con.

association football [-'futbɔ:l] *n* SP fútbol *m*.

associative [ə'səuʃjətiv] *adj* de asociación.

assonance ['æsənəns] *n* asonancia *f*.

assonant ['æsənənt] *adj/n* asonante.

assonate ['æsəuneit] *vi* asonantar, asonar.

assort [ə'sɔ:t] *vt* clasificar, ordenar (to classify).
◆ *vi* cuadrar (to fit) ‖ corresponder, concordar (to agree).

assorted [-id] *adj* clasificado, da (classified) ‖ variado, da; surtido, da (miscellaneous) ‖ — *ill-assorted couple* matrimonio mal avenido ‖ *well-assorted couple* matrimonio bien avenido.

assortment [ə'sɔ:tmənt] *n* surtido *m*, variedad *f* ‖ clasificación *f*.

assuage [ə'sweidʒ] *vt* aliviar, mitigar (pain) ‖ saciar (hunger, thirst) ‖ satisfacer (desire) ‖ calmar (anger).

Assouan [æs'wa:n] *pr n* GEOGR → **Aswan.**

assume [ə'sju:m] *vt* asumir; *we assume his guilt* asumimos su culpabilidad; *he assumed the responsibility* asumió la responsabilidad ‖ tomar, asumir (power) ‖ tomar, usurpar (to usurp) ‖ arrogarse (right) ‖ tomar (an appearance) ‖ dar por; *we assume him dead* le damos por muerto ‖ adoptar, tomar; *he assumed a foreign accent* adoptó un acento extranjero; *he assumed a posture of arrogance* adoptó una postura arrogante ‖ manifestarse; *the disease assumes many forms* la enfermedad se manifiesta de muchas maneras ‖ suponer; *I assume you will be there* supongo que estarás allí ‖ tomar, servirse de, utilizar (a name) ‖ afectar, fingir (a virtue) ‖ darse (air).

assumed [-d] *adj* supuesto, ta (taken for granted) ‖ fingido, da; simulado, da (pretended) ‖ ficticio, cia (fictitious).

assuming [-iŋ] *adj* arrogante, presumido, da ‖ *assuming that...* suponiendo que..., en el supuesto de que...

assumption [ə'sʌmpʃən] *n* suposición *f*, supuesto *m* (supposition) ‖ toma *f* (of power) ‖ apropiación *f*, usurpación *f* ‖ pretensión *f*, presunción *f* (vanity) || — *on the assumption that...* suponiendo que... || REL *the Assumption* la Asunción.

assurance [əˈʃuərəns] *n* seguridad *f* (certainty, self-confidence) || COMM seguro *m* (insurance) || garantía *f* (guarantee) || FIG descaro *m*, desfachatez *f* (impudence) || — *I gave my assurance that I would go* le di palabra de que iría, le prometí que iría || *to make assurance doubly sure* para mayor seguridad.

assure [əˈʃuə*] *vt* asegurar (to insure) || garantizar, asegurar (to make certain) || asegurar (to promise).

assured [-d] *adj* asegurado, da (certain, safe) || seguro, ra (self-confident) || *rest assured that...* tenga la seguridad de que...

assuredly [-ridli] *adv* ciertamente, seguramente.

assuredness [-ridnis] *n* certeza *f* (certainty) || seguridad *f* (self-confidence).

assurer [-ə*] *n* asegurador, ra.

Assyria [əˈsiriə] *pr n* GEOGR Asiria *f*.

Assyrian [-n] *adj/n* asirio, ria.

astatic [eiˈstætik] *adj* PHYS astático, ca.

aster [ˈæstə*] *n* BOT aster *m*.

asterisk [ˈæstərisk] *n* asterisco *m*.

asterisk [ˈæstərisk] *vt* poner un asterisco a.

asterism [ˈæstərizəm] *n* ASTR & MIN asterismo *m*.

astern [əsˈtəːn] *adv* MAR a popa, de popa, por popa || hacia atrás (backwards) || *astern of* detrás de.

asteroid [ˈæstərɔid] *n* ASTR asteroide *m*.
◆ *adj* asteroide.

asthenia [æsˈθiːnjə] *n* MED astenia *f*.

asthenic [æsˈθenik] *adj/n* asténico, ca.

asthma [ˈæsmə] *n* MED asma *f*.

asthmatic [æsˈmætik] *adj/n* asmático, ca.

astigmat [ˈæstigmæt] *n* astigmático, ca.

astigmatic [ˌæstigˈmætik] *adj* astigmático, ca.

astigmatism [æsˈtigmətizəm] *n* astigmatismo *m*.

astir [əˈstəː*] *adj* levantado, da (out of bed) || en movimiento (in motion) || en efervescencia (in excitement).

astonish [əsˈtɔniʃ] *vt* asombrar || *to be astonished at* o *by* quedarse asombrado *or* asombrarse de *or* por.

astonishing [-iŋ] *adj* asombroso, sa.

astonishment [-mənt] *n* asombro *m*.

astound [əsˈtaund] *vt* aterrar (with fear) || asombrar, pasmar (with wonder, amazement).

astounding [-iŋ] *adj* asombroso, sa; pasmoso, sa.

astraddle [əˈstrædl] *adv/adj* a horcajadas.

astragal [ˈæstrəgəl] *n* ANAT & ARCH astrágalo *m*.

astragalus [əsˈtrægələs] *n* ANAT & BOT astrágalo *m*.
— OBSERV El plural de *astragalus* es *astragali*.

astrakhan [ˌæstrɔˈkæn] *n* astracán *m*.

astral [ˈæstrəl] *adj* astral; *astral bodies* cuerpos astrales.

astray [əsˈtrei] *adv* por mal camino || — *to go astray* extraviarse (to get lost), errar el blanco (bullets, etc.) || *to lead astray* despistar (to mislead), descarriar, llevar por mal camino.

astrict [əˈstrikt] *vt* constreñir.

astricted [əˈstriktid] *adj* astricto, ta.

astriction [əˈstrikʃən] *n* astricción *f*.

astride [əsˈtraid] *adv/adj* a horcajadas.
◆ *prep* a horcajadas sobre.

astringe [əsˈtrindʒ] *vt* astreñir.

astringency [əsˈtrindʒənsi] *n* astringencia *f* || FIG austeridad *f*.

astringent [əsˈtrindʒənt] *adj* astringente || FIG austero, ra (style) | severo, ra (criticism).
◆ *n* astringente *m*.

astrobiology [ˈæstrəuˌbaiˈɔlɔdʒi] *n* astrobiología *f*.

astrolabe [ˈæstrəuleib] *n* ASTR astrolabio *m*.

astrologer [əsˈtrɔlədʒə*] *n* astrólogo, ga.

astrologic [ˌæstrəˈlɔdʒik]; **astrological** [-əl] *adj* astrológico, ca.

astrology [əsˈtrɔlədʒi] *n* astrología *f*.

astronaut [ˈæstrənɔːt] *n* astronauta *m* & *f*.

astronautics [ˌæstrəˈnɔːtiks] *n* astronáutica *f*.

astronavigation [ˈæstrəuˌnæviˈgeiʃən] *n* navegación *f* interplanetaria *or* espacial.

astronomer [əsˈtrɔnəmə*] *n* astrónomo *m* || *Astronomer Royal* director *m* del observatorio astronómico de Greenwich.

astronomic [ˌæstrəˈnɔmik] *adj* astronómico, ca; *astronomic unit* unidad astronómica || FIG astronómico, ca.

astronomical [-əl] *adj* astronómico, ca; *astronomical clock, telescope* reloj, telescopio astronómico || FIG astronómico, ca.

astronomy [əsˈtrɔnəmi] *n* astronomía *f*.

astrophysicist [ˈæstrəuˈfizisist] *n* astrofísico, ca.

astrophysics [ˈæstrəuˈfiziks] *n* astrofísica *f*.

Asturian [æsˈtjuəriən] *adj/n* asturiano, na.

Asturianism [æsˈtjuəriænizəm] *n* asturianismo *m*.

Asturias [æsˈtjuəriæs] *pl n* GEOGR Asturias *f*.

astute [əsˈtjuːt] *adj* astuto, ta.

astuteness [-nis] *n* astucia *f*.

asunder [əˈsʌndə*] *adv* en pedazos || — *to come asunder* separarse || *to tear asunder* hacer pedazos.

Aswan; Assouan [æsˈwɑːn] *pr n* GEOGR Asuán.

asylum [əˈsailəm] *n* refugio *m*, asilo *m* (place of refuge) || asilo *m*; *to seek political asylum* pedir asilo político; *to afford asylum to* dar asilo a || asilo *m*, hospicio *m* (for aged people, etc.) || manicomio *m* (mental house).

asymmetric [ˌæsiˈmetrik]; **asymmetrical** [-əl] *adj* asimétrico, ca.

asymmetry [æˈsimitri] *n* asimetría *f*.

asymptote [ˈæsimptəut] *n* MATH asíntota *f*.

asymptotic [ˌæsimpˈtɔtik]; **asymptotical** [-əl] *adj* asintótico, ca.

asynchronous [əˈsinkrənəs] *adj* asincrónico, ca.

asyndetic [ˌæsinˈdetik] *adj* asindético, ca.

asyndeton [æˈsinditən] *n* GRAMM asíndeton *m*.
— OBSERV El plural de *asyndeton* es *asyndetons* o *asyndeta*.

at [æt] *prep* en (expressing position, time, manner and condition); *at home* en casa; *at Peter's* en casa de Pedro; *at Easter* en Semana Santa; *good at arithmetic* bueno en aritmética; *at work* en el trabajo; *at war* en guerra || a (expressing time, position, direction, state and price); *at six o'clock* a las seis; *at the table* a la mesa; *at them!* ¡a ellos!; *sad at leaving* triste al partir; *at five pesetas a kilogramme* a cinco pesetas el kilo || de; *what is he laughing at?* ¿de qué se ríe?; *attempt at escape* tentativa de evasión || por (through); *to go in at one door and come out at the other* entrar por una puerta y salir por la otra; *at Christmas* por Navidades || — *angry at* enfadado con || *at best* en el mejor de los casos || *at first* al principio || *at his cries we rushed* acudimos al oír sus gritos || *at last* por fin || *at least* al menos, por lo menos || *at most* a lo más, a lo sumo, como mucho || *at once* en seguida || *at night* de noche, por la noche || *at play* jugando || *at present* actualmente || *at random* al azar || *at sea* en el mar || *at that* además; *he is a footballer and a good one at that* es futbolista y muy bueno además; sin más; *we have left it at that* lo hemos dejado sin más; en ese, en esa; *at that moment* en ese momento; ante eso (because of that); *he laughed and at that they all left* se rió y ante eso se marcharon todos || *at your request* a petición suya || *to be at* estar haciendo; *what are you at?* ¿qué estás haciendo?; *they have been at it a long time* ya llevan mucho tiempo con ello; *while we are at it* de paso, ya que estamos || *to look at o.s. in the mirror* mirarse en el espejo || *two at a time* de dos en dos.

ataraxia [ætəˈræksiə]; **ataraxy** [ˈætəˌræksi] *n* ataraxia *f*.

atavism [ˈætəvizəm] *n* atavismo *m*.

atavistic [ˌætəˈvistik] *adj* atávico, ca.

ataxia [əˈtæksiə]; **ataxy** [əˈtæksi] *n* MED ataxia *f*.

ate [eit] *pret* ⟶ **eat**.

ateles [ˈætəliːz] *n* ZOOL ateles *m* (monkey).

atellans [əˈtelənz] *pl n* atelanas *f* (Latin comedy).

atelier [ˈætəljei] *n* estudio *m* (artist's studio) || taller *m* (workroom).

atheism [ˈeiθiizəm] *n* ateísmo *m*.

atheist [ˈeiθiist] *n* ateo, a.

atheistic [ˌeiθiˈistik]; **atheistical** [-əl] *adj* ateo, a.

athenaeum [ˌæθiˈniːəm] *n* ateneo *m*.

Athenian [əˈθiːnjən] *adj/n* ateniense.

Athens [ˈæθinz] *pr n* GEOGR Atenas.

athermanous [æˈθəːmənəs] *adj* PHYS atérmano, na.

athirst [əˈθəːst] *adj* sediento, ta || FIG ávido, da.

athlete [ˈæθliːt] *n* atleta *m*.

athlete's foot [-s fut] *n* MED pie *m* de atleta.

athletic [æθˈletik] *adj* atlético, ca.

athletics [-s] *n* atletismo *m*.

at home [ətˈhəum] *n* recepción *f*.

athwart [əˈθwɔːt] *prep* a través de (across) || contra (against).
◆ *adv* de través, transversalmente.

athwartships [-ʃips] *adv* MAR de babor a estribor.

atlantes [ətˈlæntiːz] *pl n* ARCH atlantes *m*.

Atlantic [ətˈlæntik] *pr n* GEOGR Atlántico *m*.
◆ *adj* Atlántico, ca; *Atlantic Ocean* Océano Atlántico.

Atlantis [ətˈlæntis] *pr n* Atlántida *f*.

atlas [ˈætləs] *n* ANAT atlas *m* || atlas *m* (of maps) || atlante *m* (pillar).
— OBSERV El plural de *atlas*, cuando significa *atlante* es *atlantes*.

atmosphere [ˈætməsfiə*] *n* atmósfera *f* || FIG ambiente *m*; *an intellectual atmosphere* un ambiente intelectual.

atmospheric [ˌætməsˈferik] *adj* atmosférico, ca.

atmospherics [-s] *pl n* RAD perturbaciones *f* atmosféricas, parásitos *m*, interferencias *f*.

atoll [ˈætɔl] *n* atolón *m*.

atom [ˈætəm] *n* átomo *m* || FIG átomo *m* || — *atom bomb* bomba atómica || *atom smasher* acelerador *m* de partículas atómicas.

atomic [əˈtɔmik] *adj* atómico, ca; *atomic age* era atómica || — *atomic bomb* bomba atómica || *atomic dust* polvo radiactivo || *atomic energy* energía atómica || *atomic mass* masa atómica

|| *atomic number* número atómico || *atomic pile* pila atómica || *atomic warhead* cabeza atómica || *atomic weight* peso atómico.

atomicity [ˌætəˈmisiti] *n* CHEM atomicidad *f*.

atomics [əˈtɔmiks] *n* atomística *m*.

atomism [ˈætəmizəm] *n* atomismo *m*.

atomist [ˈætəmist] *n* atomista *m* & *f*.

atomistic [ˌætəˈmistik] *adj* atomístico, ca.

atomization [ˌætəmaiˈzeiʃən] *n* atomización *f*, pulverización *f*.

atomize [ˈætəmaiz] *vt* atomizar, pulverizar.

atomizer [-ə*] *n* atomizador *m*, pulverizador *m*, vaporizador *m*.

atonal [eiˈtəunl] *adj* MUS atonal (toneless).

atonality [ˈeitəuˈnæliti] *n* MUS atonalidad *f*.

atone [əˈtəun] *vt/vi* expiar, reparar; *to atone for sth.* expiar algo || *to atone with* reconciliarse con.

atonement [-mənt] *n* expiación *f*, reparación *f* || REL *Day of Atonement* día *m* de la Expiación.

atonic [æˈtɔnik] *adj* átono, na; atónico, ca (phonetics) || MUS atonal || MED atónico, ca (weak).

atony [ˈætəni] *n* MED atonía *f*.

atop [əˈtɔp] *adv* encima.
◆ *prep* encima de.

atrabilious [ˌætrəˈbiljəs] *adj* atrabiliario, ria.

atrip [əˈtrip] *adj* MAR *with anchor atrip* con el ancla levada.

atrium [ˈɑːtriəm] *n* ARCH atrio *m* || MED aurícula *f* (of the heart).
— OBSERV El plural de *atrium* es *atria*.

atrocious [əˈtrəuʃəs] *adj* atroz.

atrociousness [-nis] *n* atrocidad *f*.

atrocity [əˈtrɔsiti] *n* atrocidad *f*.

atrophy [ˈætrəfi] *n* MED atrofia *f*.

atrophy [ˈætrəfi] *vt* atrofiar.
◆ *vi* atrofiarse.

atropine [ˈætrəpin] *n* CHEM atropina *f*.

attach [əˈtætʃ] *vt* atar, ligar (to bind, to connect to) || sujetar (to fasten) || pegar (to stick) || FIG unir, ligar, vincular (to connect) || unir (to bind by love); *we are very attached to one another* estamos muy unidos el uno al otro || adjuntar (in a letter) || agregar (to work with); *an expert attached to a delegation* un experto agregado a una delegación || MIL destinar (to appoint to); *attached to a regiment as a special instructor* destinado a un regimiento como instructor especial || JUR embargar, incautar || imputar (to attribute); *to attach blame* imputar la responsabilidad || dar, atribuir, conceder (to give value to); *to attach importance to* dar importancia a || aplicar, dar (an epithet) || poner (a seal) || enganchar (to hook) || — *to be attached to* corresponder a (to accompany), tener cariño a (to love), estar apegado a, tener apego a; *to be attached to customs* estar apegado a las costumbres || *to attach o.s. to* entrar a formar parte de (to join), coger cariño a (to become fond of).
◆ *vi* colocarse (to be fastened) || incumbir; *no blame attaches to him* no le incumbe ninguna responsabilidad || corresponder a, pertenecer a (to belong).

attaché [əˈtæʃei] *n* agregado *m*.

attaché case [əˈtæʃikeis] *n* maletín *m*.

attachment [əˈtætʃmənt] *n* colocación *f*, fijación *f* (act of attaching); *the attachment of the door to its frame was not easy* la colocación de la puerta en el marco no fue fácil || sistema *m* de unión (device or method for attaching) || TECH acoplamiento *m* || accesorio *m* (attached object) || cariño *m*, apego *m*, afecto *m* (affection); *there is a strong attachment between them* se tienen mucho apego || adhesión *f* || lazo *m*, vínculo *m* (bond) || JUR incautación *f*, embargo *m* (*on* de).

attack [əˈtæk] *n* ataque *m* (*on* a, contra); *to launch an attack* iniciar un ataque; *surprise attack* ataque por sorpresa || agresión *f*, ataque *m* (on a person) || MED ataque *m*.

attack [əˈtæk] *vt/vi* atacar || luchar contra, combatir (to fight) || FIG asaltar; *attached by doubts* asaltado por las dudas || acometer, atacar (to undertake) || MED aquejar.

attacker [-ə*] *n* atacador, ra.

attacking [-iŋ] *adj* agresor, ra; *attacking army* ejército agresor.

attain [əˈtein] *vt* alcanzar, conseguir || alcanzar, llegar a (an age, happiness, knowledge, a rank).
◆ *vi* *to attain to* alcanzar, conseguir; *to attain to perfection* alcanzar la perfección.

attainability [əˌteinəˈbiliti] *n* accesibilidad *f*.

attainable [əˈteinəbl] *adj* accesible (*by* a, para), alcanzable (*by* por).

attainder [əˈteində*] *n* JUR muerte *f* civil.

attainment [əˈteinmənt] *n* logro *m*, obtención *f*, consecución *f*, realización *f*.
◆ *pl* conocimientos *m* (acquired skill).

attaint [əˈteint] *vt* condenar a muerte civil || MED aquejar, afectar.

attar of roses [ˈætə*əvˈrəuziz] *n* esencia *f* de rosas.

attempt [əˈtempt] *n* intento *m*, tentativa *f* (endeavour, try) || atentado *m* (attack); *attempt upon the security of the State* atentado contra la seguridad del Estado || *to make an attempt on s.o.'s life* atentar contra la vida de *or* a la vida de alguien, cometer un atentado contra alguien.

attempt [əˈtempt] *vt* intentar, tratar de (to try to); *he attempted to jump the wall* intentó saltar el muro || intentar, tratar de [hacer] (to try sth.); *he attempted a smile* intentó sonreír; *they attempted the fortress* intentaron asaltar la fortaleza; *they attempted a rescue* intentaron rescatarle || — *attempted murder* tentativa *f* de asesinato || *to attempt the life of* atentar contra la vida de *or* a la vida de.

attend [əˈtend] *vt* asistir a (to be present at) || ir a, asistir a (to go regularly to); *he attends evening classes* asiste a clases nocturnas || acompañar (to accompany); *she attended the princess during her tour of the country* acompañó a la princesa durante su viaje por el país || acompañar (to accompany as a result); *success attended his every effort* el éxito acompañaba todos sus esfuerzos || atender (to see to the needs of customers) || tratar, asistir, atender (to visit and treat); *Mr. X is being attended by his personal physician* al Sr. X le está tratando su médico particular || servir (a maid) || *well-attended conference* conferencia muy concurrida.
◆ *vi* atender || — *to attend at* asistir a || *to attend to* cumplir (one's duties), prestar atención a (to pay attention to), ocuparse de (to apply o.s. to); *I must attend to my work now* tengo que ocuparme de mi trabajo ahora; atender; *are you being attended to, Sir?* ¿le atienden, señor?; tener en cuenta (to bear in mind), ejecutar (an order) || *to attend upon* acompañar.

attendance [-əns] *n* asistencia *f*; *attendance is compulsory* la asistencia es obligatoria || compañía *f* (company) || MED asistencia *f*, cuidados *m pl* || — *cabs in attendance* taxis *m* en la parada || *to be in attendance* estar de servicio || *to dance attendance on* desvivirse por alguien.

attendant [-ənt] *adj* concomitante (circumstances, etc.) || asistente, presente (present) || — *attendant on s.o.* que sirve *or* acompaña a uno || *war and its attendant horrors* la guerra y su secuela de horrores.
◆ *n* encargado, da (employee in charge) || acompañante *m* & *f* (companion) || asistente *m* & *f* (person present) || acomodador, ra (in cinema, theatre) || sirviente, ta (servant) || secuela *f*; *ignorance and its attendants, fear and prejudice* la ignorancia y sus secuelas, el miedo y los prejuicios.

attention [əˈtenʃən] *n* atención *f*; *to pay attention to* prestar atención a || atención *f*; *to attract* o *to draw* o *to call s.o.'s attention* llamar la atención de uno || cuidado *m*; *he received medical attention* recibió cuidados médicos; *attention!* ¡cuidado! || servicio *m* (service in a shop, restaurant) || — MIL *attention!* ¡firmes! || *for the attention of* a la atención de || *it has come to my attention that...* me he enterado de que... || *to be all attention* estar muy atento || MIL *to bring to attention* dar la orden de cuadrarse || *to call s.o.'s attention to* llamar la atención de alguien sobre || MIL *to come to attention* ponerse firme, cuadrarse || *to shower attention on s.o.* tener mil atenciones con uno || MIL *to stand at attention* estar en posición de firme | *to stand to attention* cuadrarse || *you must pay attention to my advice* tienes que hacer caso de mi consejo || *your attention, please!* ¡atención!
◆ *pl* atenciones *f*; *his constant attentions annoy me* sus constantes atenciones me molestan.

attentive [əˈtentiv] *adj* atento, ta; *attentive to the slightest sound* atento al menor ruido || aplicado, da; atento, ta (industrious); *an attentive pupil* un alumno aplicado || atento, ta (considerate, thoughtful).

attentiveness [-nis] *n* atención *f*.

attenuate [əˈtenjueit] *vt* atenuar.
◆ *vi* atenuarse.

attenuation [əˌtenjuˈeiʃən] *n* atenuación *f*.

attest [əˈtest] *vt* atestiguar (to affirm, to bear witness to) || dar fe (to confirm as authentic) || legalizar (document or signature) || juramentar (to place on oath).
◆ *vi* dar testimonio (*to* de).

attestant [əˈtestənt] *n* testigo *m* & *f*.

attestation [ˌætesˈteiʃən] *n* atestación *f*, testimonio *m* (act of bearing witness) || testimonio *m* (testimony) || atestación *f*, atestado *m* (document) || garantía *f*; *that signature is sufficient attestation for us* esa firma es garantía suficiente para nosotros || prestación *f* de juramento (oath).

attic [ˈætik] *n* ático *m* (top floor) || desván *m* (loft).

Attic [ˈætik] *adj/n* ático, ca.

Attica [ˈætikə] *pr n* GEOGR Ática *f*.

Attila [ˈætilə] *pr n* Atila *m*.

attire [əˈtaiə*] *n* traje *m*, atavío *m* || HERALD astas *f pl* de ciervo.

attire [əˈtaiə*] *vt* vestir, ataviar.

attitude [ˈætitjuːd] *n* postura *f* (position) || actitud *f* (mental state); *attitude of mind* actitud mental || AVIAT posición *f* || *to strike an attitude* adoptar una postura teatral, tener una actitud estudiada.

attitudinize [ˈætiˈtjuːdinaiz] *vi* adoptar una postura teatral, tener una actitud estudiada.

attorney [əˈtəːni] *n* JUR procurador *m* || apoderado *m* (proxy) || US JUR abogado *m* || — *attorney general* fiscal *m* del Tribunal Supremo (in Great Britain), Ministro *m* de Justicia (in United States) || *district attorney* fiscal *m*.
— OBSERV El *attorney* es un asesor de derecho consuetudinario y el *attorney general* miembro del Parlamento, es también presidente del Colegio de Abogados en Inglaterra. Sus funciones son parecidas a las que tiene el fiscal del Tribunal Supremo. En los

Estados Unidos el cargo de *attorney general* equivale al de ministro de Justicia.

attract [ə'trækt] *vt* atraer || — *to attract s.o.'s attention* llamar la atención de alguien || *to be attracted to* sentirse atraído por.

attraction [ə'trækʃən] *n* atracción *f*; *molecular attraction* atracción molecular; *the main attraction of the fair* la atracción principal de la feria || atractivo *m* (of a person).

attractive [ə'træktiv] *adj* atractivo, va; *attractive offer* oferta atractiva || atrayente (interesting) || atractivo, va (person) || halagüeño, ña (prospect).

attractiveness [-nis] *n* atracción *f*, atractivo *m*.

attributable [ə'tribjutəbl] *adj* atribuible.

attribute ['ætribju:t] *n* atributo *m*; *reason is the attribute of man* la razón es el atributo del hombre || GRAMM atributo *m*.

attribute [ə'triju:t] *vt* atribuir.

attribution [,ætri'bju:ʃən] *n* atribución *f*.

attributive [ə'tribjutiv] *adj* atributivo, va.

attrite [ə'trait] *adj* REL atrito, ta || TECH desgastado por el roce.

attrition [ə'triʃən] *n* roce *m* (rubbing) || desgaste *m* (wearing away, exhausting) || REL atrición *f*.

attune [ə'tju:n] *vt* MUS afinar || FIG adaptar (to adapt) | armonizar (to bring into harmony).

ATV *abbr of Associated Television* canal de televisión británico.

atypical [,ei'tipikəl] *adj* anormal.

aubade [əu'bɑ:d] *n* MUS & POET alborada *f*.

aubergine ['əubəʒi:n] *n* BOT berenjena *f*.

auburn ['ɔ:bən] *adj* castaño, ña.
◆ *n* color *m* castaño.

auction ['ɔ:kʃən] *n* subasta *f* || — *to be on auction* salir a subasta || *to put up for auction, to sell at auction* subastar, poner *or* vender en pública subasta.

auction ['ɔ:kʃən]; **auction off** [[-ɔf] *vt* subastar.

auctioneer [,ɔ:kʃə'niə*] *n* subastador *m*.

auction room ['ɔ:kʃənrum] *n* sala *f* de subastas.

audacious [ɔ:'deiʃəs] *adj* audaz (daring) || atrevido, da (too daring).

audaciousness [-nis]; **audacity** [ɔ:'dæsiti] *n* audacia *f* (boldness); *to show* o *to display audacity* demostrar audacia || atrevimiento *m* (impudence).

audibility [,ɔ:di'biliti] *n* audibilidad *f*.

audible ['ɔ:dəbl] *adj* audible.

audience ['ɔ:djəns] *n* público *m*, auditorio *m* (at show, etc.) || radioyentes *m pl* (of radio) || telespectadores *m pl* (of television) || lectores *m pl* (of writer) || audiencia *f* (official reception).

audio ['ɔ:diəu] *adj* audio.

audio frequency ['ɔ:diəu'fri:kwənsi] *n* PHYS audiofrecuencia *f*.

audiogram ['ɔ:diəgræm] *n* audiograma *m*.

audiometer [,ɔ:di'ɔmitə*] *n* audiómetro *m*.

audio-visual ['ɔ:diəu'vizjuəl] *adj* audiovisual || *audio-visual aids* medios *m pl* audiovisuales.

audit ['ɔ:dit] *n* revisión *f or* intervención *f* de cuentas || *Audit Office* Tribunal *m* de Cuentas.

audit ['ɔ:dit] *vt/vi* verificar *or* revisar la contabilidad || US ser oyente (to a class).

auditing [-iŋ] *n* intervención *f or* revisión *f* de cuentas.

audition [ɔ:'diʃən] *n* audición *f*.

audition [ɔ:'diʃən] *vt/vi* dar una audición.

auditive ['ɔ:ditiv] *adj* auditivo, va.

auditor ['ɔ:ditə*] *n* interventor *m* de cuentas (accounts) || US radioyente *m* & *f* | estudiante *m* & *f* libre, oyente *m* & *f*.

auditorium [,ɔ:di'tɔ:riəm] *n* sala *f* (theatre) || paraninfo *m* (lecture hall, assembly hall) || nave *f* (of church) || locutorio *m*, sala *f* de visitas (of a convent).

auditory ['ɔ:ditəri] *adj* auditivo, va.

au fait [,əu 'fei] *adj* familiarizado, da.

Augean [ɔ:'dʒiən] *adj* de Augias || FIG asqueroso, sa; inmundo, da.

auger ['ɔ:gə*] *n* TECH barrena *f*, taladro *m*.

aught [ɔ:t] *n* algo (in affirmative sentences) || nada (in negations) || — *for aught I care* por mí || *for aught I know* que yo sepa.

augite ['ɔ:dʒait] *n* MIN augita *f*.

augment [ɔ:g'mənt] *vt/vi* aumentar.

augmentation [,ɔ:gmen'teiʃən] *n* aumento *m*.

augmentative [ɔ:g'mentətiv] *adj* aumentativo, va.
◆ *n* GRAMM aumentativo *m*.

augur ['ɔ:gə*] *n* augur *m*.

augur ['ɔ:gə*] *vt/vi* augurar, pronosticar || *to augur ill, well* ser de mal, de buen agüero.

augural ['ɔ:gjurəl] *adj* augural.

augury ['ɔ:gjuri] *n* augurio *m*, presagio *m*.

August ['ɔ:gəst] *pr n* agosto *m*; *on the 15th of August* el 15 de agosto.

august [ɔ:'gʌst] *adj* augusto, ta.

auguste ['ɔ:gəst] *n* augusto *m* (clown).

Augustine [ɔ:'gʌstin] *pr n* Agustín *m*.

Augustinian [,ɔ:gəs'tiniən] *adj* REL agustino, na (religious order) || agustiniano, na (doctrine).
◆ *n* REL agustino, na.

Augustinism [ɔ:'gʌstinizəm] *n* REL agustinianismo *m*.

Augustus [ɔ:'gʌstəs] *pr n* Augusto *m*.

auk [ɔ:k] *n* ZOOL alca *f*.

auld lang syne ['əuld læŋ zɑin] *n* canción *f* escocesa tradicional de despedida.

aulic ['ɔ:lik] *adj* áulico, ca.

aunt [ɑ:nt] *n* tía *f* | *aunt-in-law* tía política.

aunty; auntie ['ɑ:nti] *n* tía *f*.

au pair ['ə'pɛə*] *adj/adv* «au pair».
◆ *n* chica *f* «au pair», ayuda *f* familiar.

aura ['ɔ:rə] *n* REL aureola *f* || aura *f*, ambiente *m* (atmosphere) || MED aura *f* || emanación *f* (of flowers, etc.).

aural ['ɔ:rəl] *adj* auricular.

aureate ['ɔ:riit] *adj* dorado, da.

aureola [ɔ:'riələ]; **aureole** ['ɔ:riəul] *n* aureola *f*.

aureomycin ['ɔ:riəu'maisin] *n* MED aureomicina *f*.

auric ['ɔ:rik] *adj* áurico, ca.

auricle ['ɔ:rikl] *n* aurícula *f*.

auricula [ə'rikjulə] *n* aurícula *f*.
— OBSERV El plural de la palabra inglesa es *auriculas* o *auriculae*.

auricular [ɔ:'rikjulə*] *adj* auricular.

auriculate [ɔ:'rikjulit] *adj* auriculado, da.

auriferous [ɔ:'rifərəs] *adj* aurífero, ra.

Auriga [ɔ:'raigə] *n* ASTR Auriga *m* (Waggoner).

aurochs ['ɔ:rɔks] *n* ZOOL uro *m*, auroch *m*.

aurora [ɔ:'rɔ:rə] *n* aurora *f* || — *aurora australis* aurora austral || *aurora borealis* aurora boreal.

aurous ['ɔ:rəs] *adj* áurico, ca.

auscultate ['ɔ:skəlteit] *vt/vi* MED auscultar.

auspice ['ɔ:spis] *n* auspicio *m*; *under the auspices of* bajo los auspicios de.

auspicious [ɔ:s'piʃəs] *adj* propicio, cia; favorable.

auspiciously [-li] *adv* favorablemente, con buenos auspicios.

auspiciousness [-nis] *n* buenos *m pl* auspicios, carácter *m* propicio.

Aussie ['ɔzi] *adj/n* FAM australiano, na.

austere [ɔs'tiə*] *adj* austero, ra.

austerity [ɔs'teriti] *n* austeridad *f*.

Austin Friar ['ɔstin'fraiə*] *n* REL fraile *m* agustino.

austral ['ɔ:strəl] *adj* austral.

Australasia [ɔstrə'leiʒjə] *pr n* GEOGR Australasia *f*.

Australia [ɔs'treiljə] *pr n* GEOGR Australia *f*.

Australian [-n] *adj/n* australiano, na.

Austrasia [ɔs'treiʒjə] *pr n* GEOGR Austrasia *f*.

Austria ['ɔstriə] *pr n* GEOGR Austria *f*.

Austrian [-n] *adj/n* austríaco, ca.

autarchic [ɔ:'tɑ:kik]; **autarchical** [-əl] *adj* autárquico, ca.

autarchy ['ɔ:tɑ:ki] *n* autarquía *f*, autarcía *f*.

authentic [ɔ:'θentik] *adj* auténtico, ca.

authenticate [-eit] *vt* autenticar, autentificar.

authentication [ɔ:,θenti'keiʃən] *n* autenticación *f*, autentificación *f*.

authenticity [,ɔ:θen'tisiti] *n* autenticidad *f*.

author ['ɔ:θə*] *n* autor, ra || *author's royalties* derechos *m* de autor.

authoress [-ris] *n* autora *f*.

authoritarian [ə'θɔri'tɛərjən] *adj/n* autoritario, ria.

authoritarianism [ə'θɔri'tɛərjənizəm] *n* autoritarismo *m*.

authoritative [ɔ:'θɔritətiv] *adj* autoritario, ria (with an air of command) || que es una autoridad (book, document) || autorizado, da (source).

authority [ɔ:'θɔriti] *n* autoridad *f*; *to have authority over one's employees* tener autoridad sobre sus empleados || — *authority of father* patria potestad || *he has no authority to act* no está autorizado para obrar || *I have it on good authority* lo sé de fuente fidedigna || *in authority* al mando || *on his own authority* por su propia autoridad || *on the authority of Cervantes* con la autoridad de Cervantes || *to act on the authority of* obrar por poder de || *to apply to the proper authority* dirigirse a la autoridad competente | *to be an authority* ser una autoridad || *to give s.o. authority to* autorizar a uno para que || *to have the authority to* tener autoridad para || *with complete authority* con plena autoridad || *without authority* sin autorización.

authorization [,ɔ:θərai'zeiʃən] *n* autorización *f*.

authorize ['ɔ:θəraiz] *vt* autorizar.

authorized [-d] *adj* autorizado, da || REL *the Authorized Version* la versión *f* autorizada (of the Bible).

authorless ['ɔ:θəlis] *adj* anónimo, ma.

authorship ['ɔ:θəʃip] *n* profesión *f* de escritor || paternidad *f* literaria || — *I claim authorship of this book* sostengo que soy el autor de este libro || *of unknown authorship* de autor desconocido.

autistic [ɔ:'tistik] *adj* autístico, ca.
◆ *n* autista.

auto ['ɔ:təu] *n* US FAM coche *m*, auto *m* [AMER carro *m*].

autobiographer [,ɔ:təubai'ɔgrəfə*] *n* autobiógrafo *m*.

autobiographic ['ɔ:təu,baiəu'græfik]; **autobiographical** [-əl] *adj* autobiográfico, ca.

autobiography [ˌɔːtəubaiˈɔgrəfi] *n* autobiografía *f*.

autochthon [ɔːtɔkθən] *n* autóctono, na.
— OBSERV El plural es *autochthons* o *autochthones*.

autochthonous [ɔːˈtɔkθənəs] *adj* autóctono, na.

autoclave [ˈɔːtəkleiv] *n* autoclave *f*.

autocracy [ɔːˈtɔkrəsi] *n* autocracia *f*.

autocrat [ˈɔːtəkræt] *n* autócrata *m* & *f*.

autocratic [ˈɔːtəˈkrætik]; **autocratical** [-əl] *adj* autocrático, ca.

autocue [ˈɔːtəukjuː] *n* RAD apuntador *m*.

auto-da-fé; auto de fé [ˈɔːtəudɑːˈfei] *n* REL auto de fe *m*.

autodidact [ˈɔːtədidækt] *n* autodidacto, ta.
— OBSERV See OBSERV at SELF-TAUGHT.

autodidactic [ˌɔːtədiˈdæktik] *adj* autodidáctico, ca; autodidacto, ta.
— OBSERV See OBSERV at SELF-TAUGHT.

autogamy [ɔːˈtɔgəmi] *n* BOT autogamia *f*.

autogenous [ɔːˈtɔdʒənəs] *adj* autógeno, na || *autogenous vaccine* autovacuna *f*.

autogiro [ˈɔːtəuˈdʒaiərəu] *n* AVIAT autogiro *m*.

autograph [ˈɔːtəgrɑːf] *n* autógrafo *f* (signature).

autograph [ˈɔːtəgrɑːf] *vt* poner un autógrafo a || firmar (to sign).

autographic [ˌɔːtəˈgræfik]; **autographical** [-əl] *adj* autográfico, ca || autógrafo, fa (letter, etc.).

autography [ɔːˈtɔgrəfi] *n* autografía *f*.

autogyro [ˈɔːtəuˈdʒaiərəu] *n* AVIAT autogiro *m*.

autoinduction [ˈɔːtəuinˈdʌkʃən] *n* autoinducción *f*.

autoinfection [ˈɔːtəuinˈfekʃən] *n* autoinfección *f*.

autointoxication [ˈɔːtəuinˌtɔksiˈkeiʃən] *n* autointoxicación *f*.

autolysis [ɔːˈtɔlisis] autólisis *f*.

automat [ˈɔːtəmæt] *n* US restaurante *m* en que la comida es distribuida por máquinas automáticas (restaurant) || aparato *m* mecánico (machine).

automate [ˈɔːtəmeit] *vt* automatizar.

automatic [ˌɔːtəˈmætik] *adj* automático, ca || — INFORM *automatic justification* justificación *f* automática | *automatic language processing* tratamiento *m* automático del lenguaje.
◆ *n* arma *f* automática.

automaticity [ˌɔːtəməˈtisiti] *n* automaticidad *f*.

automatic pilot [ˌɔːtəˈmætik ˈpailət] *n* AVIAT piloto *m* automático || FIG *on automatic pilot* por rutina, como un robot.

automation [ˌɔːtəˈmeiʃən] *n* automatización *f*.

automatism [ɔːˈtɔmətizəm] *n* automatismo *m*.

automaton [ɔːˈtɔmətən] *n* autómata *m*.
— OBSERV El plural es *automatons* o *automata*.

automobile [ˈɔːtəməubiːl] *n* automóvil *m*.

automotive [ˌɔːtəˈməutiv] *adj* US automotor, ra.

autonomist [ɔːˈtɔnəmist] *n* autonomista *m* & *f*.

autonomous [ɔːˈtɔnəməs] *adj* autónomo, ma.

autonomy [ɔːˈtɔnəmi] *n* autonomía *f*.

autoplasty [ˈɔːtəˈplæsti] *n* autoplastia *f*.

autopsy [ˈɔːtɔpsi] *n* autopsia *f*.

autopsy [ˈɔːtɔpsi] *vt* MED autopsiar.

autosuggestion [ˈɔːtəusəˈdʒestʃən] *n* autosugestión *f*.

autotomy [ɔːˈtɔtəmi] *n* autotomía *f*.

autovaccine [ˈɔːtəuˈvæksiːn] *n* autovacuna *f*.

autumn [ˈɔːtəm] *n* otoño *m*.

autumnal [ɔːˈtʌmnəl] *adj* otoñal, de otoño.

autumn crocus [ˈɔːtəmˈkrəukəs] *n* BOT cólquico *m*.

auxiliary [ɔːgˈziljəri] *adj* auxiliar || — INFORM *auxiliary store* memoria *f* auxiliar || *auxiliary verb* verbo *m* auxiliar.
◆ *n* verbo *m* auxiliar.
◆ *pl* MIL tropas *f* auxiliares.

avail [əˈveil] *n* ventaja *f*, utilidad *f* || — *of no avail* sin efecto, inútil || *of what avail is it?* ¿de qué sirve? || *to be of little avail* no servir para mucho || *to no avail, without avail* en vano.

avail [əˈveil] *vt/vi* valer, servir || — *it avails nothing to* de nada sirve || *to avail o.s. of* aprovecharse de, sacar partido de (an opportunity), valerse de (a right, a weapon), utilizar (a service).

availability [əˌveiləˈbiliti] *n* disponibilidad *f*.

available [əˈveiləbl] *adj* disponible, que sirve (ready for use) || que se puede conseguir, obtenible (obtainable) || válido, da (ticket) || realizable (assets) || asequible || — *by all available means* por todos los medios posibles || *to make available to* poner a la disposición de || *when will he be available?* ¿cuándo estará libre?

avalanche [ˈævəlɑːnʃ] *n* avalancha *f*, alud *m*.

avant-garde [ˈævɑːŋgɑːd] *n* vanguardia *f*.

avarice [ˈævəris] *n* avaricia *f*.

avaricious [ˌævəˈriʃəs] *adj* avaro, ra; avaricioso, sa; avariento, ta.

avatar [ˌævəˈtɑː*] *n* avatar *m* (in Hindu religion) || FAM manifestación *f*, materialización *f*.

ave [ˈɑːvi] *n* avemaría *f*.

Ave *abbr of avenue* AV, Avda., avenida.

Ave Maria [ˈɑːvimәˈriә] *n* Avemaría *f*.

avenge [əˈvendʒ] *vt* vengar || *to avenge o.s.* vengarse.
◆ *vi* vengarse.

avenger [-ə*] *n* vengador *m*.

aventurine [əˈventjuriːn] *n* MIN venturina *f*.

avenue [ˈævinjuː] *n* avenida *f* || FIG vía *f*, senda *f*, camino *m*.

aver [əˈvəː*] *vt* afirmar, declarar || JUR establecer la prueba de.

average [ˈævəridz] *n* media *f*, promedio *m* || MAR avería *f* || *on average* por término medio, como promedio, como media.
◆ *adj* medio, dia (in statistics); *the average price* el precio medio || regular (so-so) || mediano, na (middling); *a man of average build* un hombre de estatura mediana || *the average age of the pupils* el promedio de edad *or* la edad media de los alumnos.

average [ˈævəridʒ] *vt* calcular *or* sacar la media de, calcular el promedio de (to work out the average) || US repartir proporcionalmente, prorratear || — *he averaged 50 kilometres per hour* hizo una media de cincuenta kilómetros por hora || *he averages ten hours of work a day* trabaja una media de diez horas diarias || *the age of the class averages 15* la edad media de la clase es quince años || *sales average 1,000 copies a week* las ventas arrojan un promedio de 1 000 ejemplares por semana.
◆ *vi to average out at, to average up to* ser por término medio, alcanzar un promedio de.

averment [əˈvəːmənt] *n* afirmación *f*.

Averrhoes; Averroes [əˈverəuiːz] *pr n* Averroes.

averse [əˈvəːs] *adj* contrario, ria (*to* a); enemigo, ga (*to* de); *I am averse to drinking* soy enemigo de la bebida.

aversión [əˈvəːʃən] *n* aversión *f*, repugnancia *f*; *aversion for work* aversión al trabajo || — *pet aversion* pesadilla *f* || *to take an aversion to s.o.* tomar antipatía a alguien.

avert [əˈvəːt] *vt* apartar, alejar.

avian [ˈeivjən] *adj* aviar.

aviary [ˈeivjəri] *n* pajarera *f*.

aviation [ˌeiviˈeiʃən] *n* aviación *f*.

aviator [ˈeivieitə*] *n* aviador, ra.

aviculture [ˈeivikʌltʃə*] *n* avicultura *f*.

avid [ˈævid] *adj* ávido, da.

avidity [əˈviditi] *n* avidez *f*.

Avignon [ˈævinjɔn] *pr n* GEOGR Aviñón.

aviso [əˈvaizəu] *n* MAR aviso *m* (boat).

avitaminosis [ˈeivitəmiˈnəusis] *n* avitaminosis *f*.
— OBSERV El plural de la palabra inglesa es *avitaminoses*.

avocado [ˌævəˈkɑːdəu] *n* BOT aguacate *m* [AMER palta *f*] || — *avocado pear* aguacate *m* || *avocado plantation* aguacatal *m*.

avocation [ˌævəˈkeiʃən] *n* distracción *f*, ocupación *f*, pasatiempo *m*.

avocet [ˈævəuset] *n* ZOOL avoceta *f*.

avoid [əˈvɔid] *vt* evitar; *I can't very well avoid asking him to stay to dinner* no puedo evitar pedirle que se quede a cenar || eludir (a duty) || huir (to shun) || JUR anular.

avoidable [-əbl] *adj* evitable || JUR anulable.

avoidance [-əns] *n* el evitar *m* || JUR anulación *f*.

avoirdupois [ˌævədəˈpɔiz] *n* sistema *f* de pesas en países de habla inglesa.

avoset [ˈævɔuset] *n* ZOOL avoceta *f*.

avouch [əˈvautʃ] *vt* afirmar, sostener (to state) || garantizar (to guarantee) || reconocer, confesar (to avow).

avow [əˈvau] *vt* reconocer, admitir, confesar.

avowal [-əl] *n* confesión *f*.

avowed [-d] *adj* declarado, da; reconocido, da.

avulsion [əˈvʌlʃən] *n* avulsión *f*.

avuncular [əˈvʌŋkjulə*] *adj* de tío.

await [əˈweit] *vt* esperar.

awake [əˈweik] *adj* despierto, ta (not asleep) || alerta (alert) || — *to be awake to* ser consciente de || *to keep s.o. awake* impedir dormir a uno, desvelar a uno.

awake* [əˈweik] *vi* despertarse (to stop sleeping) || darse cuenta (*to* de) (to realize).
◆ *vt* despertar.
— OBSERV Pret ***awoke***; pp ***awoken, awaked, awoke***.

awaken [əˈweikən] *vt* despertar.
◆ *vi* despertarse.

awakening [-iŋ] *n* despertar *m* || FIG *a rude awakening* un brusco despertar.

award [əˈwɔːd] *n* JUR concesión *f*, adjudicación *f* | sentencia *f*, fallo *m* (judgment) || premio *m*, recompensa *f* (prize) || MIL condecoración *f*.

award [əˈwɔːd] *vt* conceder, otorgar || JUR adjudicar.

awardee [əˈwɔːˈdiː] *n* adjudicatario, ria.

awarder [əˈwɔːdə*] *n* adjudicador, ra.

awarding [-iŋ] *n* atribución *f*, concesión *f*, otorgamiento *m*.

aware; ware [əˈwɛə*] *adj* consciente (conscious) || al corriente (up to date) || — *are you aware of the risk involved?* ¿se da cuenta del riesgo que corre? || *are you aware of the time?* ¿sabe Vd. la hora que es? || *as far as I am aware* que yo sepa || *I am aware of that* lo sé, me doy cuenta de ello || *not that I am aware of* no que yo sepa || *to become aware of* enterarse de (to find out), darse cuenta de, llegar a tener conciencia de (to realize).

awareness [-nis] *n* conciencia *f*, conocimiento *m*.

awash [ə'wɔʃ] *adj/adv* inundado, da (flooded) || a flor de agua || flotando (floating).

away [ə'wei] *adv* fuera (in a different place); *I am sorry, my father is away* lo siento, mi padre está fuera || a; *we are five miles away from the station* estamos a cinco millas de la estación; *the house is ten miles away* la casa está a diez millas || lejos; *away from the din* lejos del bullicio; *from away* desde lejos || incesantemente, sin parar (continuously); *he worked away for two days* trabajó sin parar durante dos días; *they fired away till they ran out of ammunition* dispararon incesantemente hasta que se les acabaron las municiones || en sentido opuesto (in the opposite direction); *the arrow pointed away from the door* la flecha apuntaba en sentido opuesto a la puerta || — *away with you!* ¡fuera de aquí! || *far and away* sin la menor duda, sin ninguna duda || *far away* lejos; *the house is not far away* la casa no está lejos || *I must go away* tengo que irme *or* marcharme || *right away* inmediatamente, en seguida; *I will do it right away* lo haré inmediatamente || *sing, dance, talk away!* ¡sigan cantando, bailando, hablando! || SP *to play away* jugar fuera, jugar en campo contrario.

◆ *adj* SP *away ground* campo *m* contrario | *away match* partido *m* de ida | *away team* equipo *m* de fuera.

◆ *n* SP partido *m* jugado fuera.

— OBSERV Hay muchos casos en los cuales el adverbio *away* no se traduce literalmente, sino que se incluye en el verbo español: *to go away* irse; *to throw away* tirar; *to take away* quitar. Por lo tanto hay que consultar los verbos correspondientes.

awe [ɔ:] *n* temor *m* (fear and respect); *awe of God* temor de Dios || asombro *m*, admiración *f* (wonder); *he looked in awe at the mountain* contempló la montaña con admiración; *to fill with awe* llenar de admiración || — *to go* o *to stand in awe of* temer pavorosamente a, tener un miedo pavoroso a; *he stands in awe of his father* tiene un miedo pavoroso a su padre || *to hold* o *to keep in awe* tener sometido por el temor.

awe [ɔ:] *vt* atemorizar; *he was awed by his solemn words* sus solemnes palabras le atemorizaron.

awe-inspiring [-in,spaiəriŋ] *adj* impresionante.

awesome [-səm] *adj* impresionante.

awestruck [-strʌk] *adj* atemorizado, da.

awful ['ɔ:ful] *adj* horrible, espantoso, sa; terrible (appalling) || atroz, horrible (ugly) || FAM enorme, tremendo, da (tremendous) || — *an awful lot* un montón, muchísimo, ma || *how awful!* ¡qué horror!

awfully ['ɔ:fuli] *adv* terriblemente, atrozmente; *he is awfully stupid* es terriblemente estúpido || muchísimo; *I am awfully sorry* lo siento muchísimo; *it has been awfully hot today* ha hecho muchísimo calor hoy || muy; *awfully good* muy bueno; *that's awfully good of you* es usted muy amable.

— OBSERV En muchos casos el adverbio *awfully* se traduce en español por un adjetivo en grado superlativo: *she is awfully nice* es simpatiquísima; *it is awfully easy* es facilísimo.

awfulness ['ɔ:fulnis] *n* horror *m*, atrocidad *f*.

awhile [ə'wail] *adv* durante un rato, un rato || *not yet awhile* no tan pronto.

awkward ['ɔ:kwəd] *adj* difícil (difficult); *an awkward problem* un problema difícil || torpe, torpón, ona (clumsy); *she is very awkward on her feet* es muy torpe andando || desgarbado, da (graceless) || inoportuno, na; inadecuado, da (inconvenient); *an awkward time to meet* una hora inadecuada para encontrarse || embarazoso, sa; molesto, ta (embarrassing); *an awkward situation* una situación embarazosa || incómodo, da; violento, ta (ill at ease) || poco manejable (tool) || pesado, da (style) || FAM *the awkward age* la edad del pavo [*AMER* la edad del chivateo].

awkwardness [-nis] *n* dificultad *f* || molestia *f*, carácter *m* molesto, incomodidad *f* (of a situation) || torpeza *f* (clumsiness).

awl [ɔ:l] *n* lezna *f*.

awn [ɔ:n] *n* BOT arista *f*.

awning ['ɔ:niŋ] *n* toldo *m* || marquesina *f* (at hotel door) || MAR toldilla *f*.

awoke [ə'wəuk] *pret/pp* → **awake.**

awoken [ə'wəuken] *pp* → **awake.**

AWOL ['eiwol] *adv/adj* ausente sin permiso.

awry [ə'rai] *adj/adv* torcido, da || — *to go awry* salir mal || *to look awry* mirar de soslayo.

ax; axe [æks] *n* hacha *f* (tool) || FIG reducción *f* (of prices) || — FAM *to get the ax* ser despedido | *to have an axe to grind* tener intereses personales.

ax; axe [æks] *vt* cortar (to cut) || FIG reducir (to reduce) | suprimir (to do away with) | despedir (personnel).

axial ['æksiəl] *adj* axial, del eje.

axil ['æksil] *n* BOT axila *f*.

axilla [æk'silə] *n* ANAT axila *f* (armpit).

— OBSERV El plural de *axilla* es *axillae* o *axillas*.

axillary [-ri] *adj* axilar.

axiology [,æksi'ɔlədʒi] *n* axiología *f*.

axiom ['æksiəm] *n* axioma *m*.

axiomatic [,æksiə'mætik] *adj* axiomático, ca || FAM evidente, patente.

axis ['æksis] *n* eje *m* || BOT eje *m* || ANAT axis *m*.

— OBSERV El plural de la palabra inglesa es *axes*.

axle ['æksl] *n* eje *m*; *rear axle* eje trasero.

axle box [-bɔks] *n* TECH caja *f* del eje.

axletree [-tri:] *n* eje *m*.

axolotl [,æksə'lɔtl] *n* ZOOL ajolote *m*.

ayatollah [,ɑiə'tɔlə] *n* ayatollah *m*.

aye [ei] *adv* (ant) siempre || *for aye* para siempre.

aye; ay [ai] *adv* sí.

◆ *n* *ayes and noes* votos *m* a favor y en contra || *the ayes have it* hay una mayoría de votos a favor.

Aymara [aimə'rɑ:] *n* aimara *m* & *f*, aimará *m* & *f* (people) || aimara *m*, aimará *m* (language).

Aymaran [-n] *adj* aimara, aimará.

◆ *n* aimara *m*, aimará *m* (language).

A-Z (guide) [,ɑy tə 'zed (gɑid)] *n* guía *f* callejera alfabética (guide), callejero *m* (street plan).

azalea [ə'zeiljə] *n* BOT azalea *f*.

azimuth ['æziməθ] *n* acimut *m*.

azoic [ə'zəuik] *adj* azoico, ca.

Azores [ə'zɔ:z] *pl prn* GEOGR Azores *f*.

azote [ə'zəut] *n* CHEM ázoe *m*, nitrógeno *m*.

Aztec ['æztek] *adj/n* azteca.

azure ['æʒə*] *adj* azul *m* celeste || HERALD azur.

◆ *n* azul *m* celeste || HERALD azur *m*.

azygous ['æzigəs] *adj* ANAT ácigos.

azygous ['æzigəs] *adj* BIOL ácigos.

◆ *n* ácigos *f*.

azyme ['æzaim] *n* pan *m* ázimo.

B

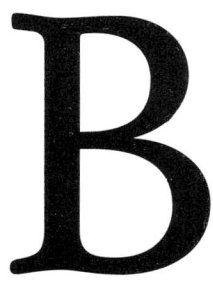

b [biː] *n* b *f* (letter) ‖ segundo, da (in a series) ‖ MUS si *m*.

BA *abbr of Bachelor of Arts* licenciado, da en Letras.

baa [bɑː] *n* balido *m*.

baa [bɑː] *vi* balar, dar balidos.

babbitt [ˈbæbit] *vt* TECH revestir de metal antifricción.

Babbitt [ˈbæbit] *n* burgués *m*, tradicionalista.

babbitt metal [-metl] *n* metal *m* antifricción.

babble [ˈbæbl]**; babbling** [-iŋ] *n* balbuceo *m* (of a baby) ‖ murmullo (of a brook) ‖ charloteo *m*, parloteo *m* (of people) ‖ farfulla *f* (confused speech) ‖ cháchara *f* (idle talk).

babble [ˈbæbl] *vi* murmurar (brook) ‖ charlotear, parlotear (people) ‖ cotillear (to gossip) ‖ balbucear (baby) ‖ ladrar fuera de la pista (hound).
◆ *vt* farfullar (to utter incoherently) ‖ soltar; *to babble nonsense* soltar necedades ‖ revelar (a secret).

babbler [ə*] *n* charlatán, ana; parlanchín, ina (chatterer) ‖ cotilla *m* & *f* (gossiper).

babe [beib] *n* nene *m*, nena *f*, bebé *m* (baby) ‖ niño *m*, niña *f* (naïve person) ‖ US POP monada *f* (attractive girl) ‖ *babe in arms* niño *f* de pecho.

babel [ˈbeibəl] *n* jaleo *m* (confused noise) ‖ *tower of Babel* torre *f* de Babel.

babirusa; babiroussa [ˌbæbiˈruːsə] *n* ZOOL babirusa *f*.

Babism [ˈbɑːbizm] *n* babismo *m* (Persian religion).

baboon [bəˈbuːn] *n* ZOOL zambo *m*, babuino *m* (monkey).

babouche [bəˈbuːʃ] *n* babucha *f* (slipper).

baby [ˈbeibi] *n* nene *m*, nena *f*, bebé *m* (infant) ‖ niño *m*, niña *f* (young child) ‖ cría *f* (of an animal) ‖ benjamín *m* (youngest member of a family) ‖ niño *m*, niña *f* (childish person) ‖ FAM hijo *m* (product) ‖ US POP monada *f* (attractive girl) ‖ FAM *to be left holding the baby* cargar con el muerto *or* con el mochuelo.
◆ *adj* de niño (of a baby) ‖ infantil (like a baby); *baby face* cara infantil ‖ pequeño, ña (small); *a baby car* un coche pequeño.

baby carriage [-ˌkæridʒ] *n* US coche *m* de niño.

baby farm [-fɑːm] *n* US guardería *f* infantil.

baby grand [-grænd] *n* MUS piano *m* de media cola.

babyhood [-hud] *n* infancia *f*, niñez *f*.

babyish [-iʃ] *adj* de niño, infantil (infantile) ‖ pueril (childish).

Babylon [ˈbæbilən] *pr n* Babilonia *f* (town).

Babylonia [ˌbæbiˈləunjə] *pr n* Babilonia *f* (kingdom).

Babylonian [-n] *adj* babilónico, ca; babilonio, nia.
◆ *n* babilonio, nia.

baby-sit [ˈbeibiˌsit] *vi* cuidar a los niños.

baby-sitter [-ə*] *n* persona *f* que cuida a los niños.

baby sitting [-iŋ] *n* vigilancia *f* de los niños.

baby tooth [ˈbeibiˌtuːθ] *n* diente *m* de leche.

baby walker [ˈbeibiˌwɔːkə*] *n* tacataca *m*, tacatá *m*, pollera *f*.

baby-weighing scales [ˈbeibiˌweiiŋˌskeilz] *n* pesabebés *m inv*.

bacca [ˈbækə] *n* baya *f*.
— OBSERV El plural de *bacca* es *baccae*.

baccalaureate [ˌbækəˈlɔːriit] *n* bachillerato *m*.

baccarat [ˈbækərɑː] *n* cristal *m* de Baccarat.

baccarat; baccarra [ˈbækərɑː] *n* bacarrá *m*, bacará *m* (gambling game).

baccate [ˈbækeit] *adj* abayado, da (berry-shaped).

bacchanal [ˈbækənəl] *n* bacante *f* (follower of Bacchus) ‖ bacanal *f* (orgy) ‖ juerguista *m* & *f* (carouser).
◆ *adj* báquico, ca.

Bacchanalia [ˌbækəˈneiljə] *pl n* bacanales *f*.

bacchanalian [-n] *adj* báquico, ca.

bacchante [bəˈkæntiː] *n* bacante *f*, ménade *f*.

Bacchus [ˈbækəs] *pr n* Baco *m*.

bach [bætʃ] *vi* US FAM llevar una vida de soltero.

bachelor [ˈbætʃələ*] *n* soltero *m* (unmarried man); *bachelor flat* piso de soltero ‖ bachiller, ra (student) ‖ — *bachelor of Arts* licenciado *m* en letras ‖ *bachelor of Laws* licenciado *m* en derecho ‖ *bachelor of Science* licenciado *m* en ciencias ‖ BOT *bachelor's button* botón *m* de oro, ranúnculo *m* (yellow flower), aciano *m* (blue flower in USA) ‖ *in my bachelor days* en mi época de soltero ‖ *old bachelor* solterón *m*.
— OBSERV No hay equivalencia exacta entre los títulos otorgados por las universidades de lengua española y los de Gran Bretaña y Estados Unidos.

bachelor girl [-gəːl] *n* soltera *f*.

bachelorhood [-hud] *n* soltería *f*, celibato *m*.

bacillar [bəˈsilə*]**; bacillary** [bəˈsiləri] *adj* MED bacilar.

bacilliform [bəˈsilifɔːrn] *adj* MED baciliforme.

bacillus [bəˈsiləs] *n* MED bacilo *m*.

back [bæk] *n* espalda *f*, espaldas *f pl* (of person) ‖ lomo *m* (of animal, book, sword) ‖ canto *m* (of knife) ‖ respaldo *m*, espaldar *m*, respaldar *m* (of chair) ‖ dorso *m*, revés *m*, envés *m* (of hand) ‖ dorso *m*, reverso *m*, respaldo *m* (of sheet of paper) ‖ revés *m* (of fabric) ‖ reverso *m* (of medal) ‖ forzal *m*, canto *m* (of comb) ‖ parte *f* posterior *or* de atrás (of head, house, car, mountain) ‖ fondo *m* (of room) ‖ SP defensa *f*, zaga *f* (defensive position) ‖ defensa *m*, zaguero *m* (player) ‖ dorso *m*, respaldo *m* (of cheque) ‖ foro *m* (of stage) ‖ ARCH extradós *m* (of vault) ‖ — *at one's back* detrás de uno ‖ *at the back of* en la parte de atrás de ‖ FAM *at the back of beyond* en el quinto pino ‖ *back to back* de espaldas ‖ *behind one's back* por detrás de uno, a espaldas de uno ‖ *excuse my back* perdone que le vuelva las espaldas ‖ US *in back of* detrás de ‖ *in the back of one's mind* en lo más recóndito del pensamiento ‖ *to be on one's back* estar acostado boca arriba (to be lying), estar encamado (to be ill) ‖ *to break one's back* deslomarse (to fall down, to overwork) ‖ FIG *to break the back of a task* hacer la parte más difícil de un trabajo ‖ *to carry on one's back* llevar a cuestas ‖ *to carry sth. across one's back* llevar algo terciado ‖ *to fall (flat) on one's back* caerse de espaldas ‖ FIG *to get one's back up* picarse (to become annoyed) ‖ *to have a broad back* tener anchas las espaldas ‖ FIG *to have one's back to the wall* estar entre la espada y la pared ‖ *to have s.o. at one's back* estar respaldado por alguien ‖ *to have s.o. on one's back* tener a uno encima, tener que cargar con uno ‖ *to know like the back of one's hand* conocer como la palma de la mano ‖ *to lend a back to* aupar ‖ FIG *to put one's back into it* echar el resto ‖ *to put s.o.'s back up* picar a uno (to annoy) ‖ *to see the back of* librarse de, deshacerse de ‖ *to stand with one's back to* dar la espalda a ‖ FIG *to turn one's back on* o *to* volver la espalda a.
◆ *adj* trasero, ra; posterior; *the back seat of a car* el asiento trasero de un coche ‖ de vuelta (on returning) ‖ atrasado, da (in arrears); *back rent* alquiler atrasado ‖ TECH de retroceso ‖ GRAMM velar (vowel) ‖ US del interior (remote) ‖ *back pay* o *wages* atrasos *m pl*.
◆ *adv* detrás, atrás (to the rear) ‖ atrás; *to step back a pace* dar un paso atrás ‖ de vuelta; *he is back* está de vuelta; *journey back* viaje de vuelta ‖ de nuevo, otra vez (again) ‖ — *back from* de vuelta *or* de regreso de (on returning), no alineado con (house) ‖ *back in* allá por; *back in the forties* allá por los años cuarenta ‖ US *back of* detrás de ‖ *to answer s.o. back* replicar a uno ‖ *to bow back to* devolver el saludo a ‖ *to get back* volver (to return), recobrar (to recover) ‖ *to give back* devolver ‖ *to hold back* retener ‖ *to make one's way back* volver ‖ *to pay back* devolver, reembolsar ‖ *to pay s.o. back* devolverle el dinero a uno (to return money), pagarle a uno con la misma moneda (to avenge o.s.) ‖ *to put back* poner en su sitio ‖ *to walk back* volver andando ‖ *two years back* hace dos años ‖ *years back* años atrás.
— OBSERV Además de todos los sentidos que indicamos en el artículo, tenemos que señalar que el adverbio *back* puede dar al verbo que acompaña una idea de devolución (*to send back a letter* devolver una carta) o de repetición (*to fall back into the water* volver a caer al agua).

back [bæk] *vt* apoyar, respaldar (to support); *to back a colleague* apoyar a un colega; *to back a venture* respaldar una empresa ‖ reforzar (to line, to strengthen) ‖ hacer retroceder, dar marcha atrás a (to cause to move backwards) ‖ dominar (to lie at the back of); *the hills that back the town* las colinas que dominan la ciudad ‖ dar (*onto* a); *the church backs onto the Field* la iglesia da al campo ‖ apostar por (to bet on) ‖ montar (to mount a horse) ‖ enlomar (a book) ‖ endosar (a cheque) ‖ avalar (a bill) ‖ hacer marcha atrás con (a car) ‖ — *foam-backed raincoat* impermeable con un forro de

espuma || *leather-backed chair* silla con un respaldo de cuero || *to back up* apoyar || MAR *to back water* ciar.
◆ *vi* retroceder (to move backwards) || dar marcha atrás (a car) || — *to back down* echarse atrás, volverse atrás || *to back out* salir dando marcha atrás (in a car), retractarse, volverse atrás (of a commitment) || *to back up* retroceder.

backache [-eik] *n* dolor *m* de espalda.

back and forth [-ənd'fɔːθ] *adv phr* de acá para allá (to walk) || para adelante y para atrás (to sway) || — *back and forth motion* movimiento de vaivén || *to go back and forth* ir y venir, ir de un sitio para otro.

backband [-bænd] *n* sufra *f* (of harness) || lomera *f* (of book).

back bench [-'bentʃ] *n* una de las filas traseras de los escaños en el Parlamento donde se sientan los diputados que no pertenecen ni al gabinete en el poder ni al de la oposición.

backbencher [-'benʃə*] *n* miembro *m* del Parlamento que ocupa un escaño en una de las filas traseras.

backbite [-bait] *vt* maldecir de, hablar mal de.
◆ *vi* murmurar.

backbiting [-baitiŋ] *n* maledicencia *f*, murmuración *f*.

backboard [-bɔːd] *n* respaldo *m*, espaldar *m* (of bench) || tabla *f* trasera (of bookshelves, etc.).

backbone [-bəun] *n* ANAT columna *f* vertebral, espina *f* dorsal, espinazo *m* || FIG carácter *m* (strength of character) | elemento *m* principal, pilar *m* (mainstay); *farmers are the backbone of the nation* los campesinos son el elemento principal de la nación || lomo *m* (of book) || FIG *English to the backbone* inglés hasta la médula *or* los tuétanos.

backbreaking [-ˌbreikiŋ] *adj* FAM matador, ra; deslomador, ra; *backbreaking task* trabajo matador.

backchat [-tʃæt]; *US* **back talk** [-tɔːk] *n* impertinencia *f* || *I want none of your backchat!* ¡déjate de impertinencias!, ¡no seas tan respondón!

back-cloth [-klɔθ] *n* telón *m* de foro.

back comb [-kəum] *n* peineta *f*.

back copy [-'kɔpi] *n* número *m* atrasado (of publication).

back current [-ˌkʌrent] *n* ELECTR contracorriente *f*.

backdate [-'deit] *vt* antedatar (a document) || dar efecto retroactivo a (to make retroactive).

back door [-'dɔː*] *n* puerta *f* trasera || puerta *f* falsa *or* trasera.

back door [-'dɔː*] *adj* de la puerta trasera || FIG clandestino, na; secreto, ta (surreptitious).

backdown [-daun] *n* FAM retractación *f*.

backdrop [-drɔp] *n* telón *m* de foro (of theatre) || FIG fondo *m* (background).

backer ['bækə*] *n* comanditario, ria (financial supporter) || fiador, ra (guarantor) || apostante *m* & *f* (who bets) || partidario, ria (supporter).

backfire [-faiə*] *n* AUT petardeo *m*, explosión *f* || encendido *m* prematuro (of engine) || retorno *m* de llama (of Bunsen burner) || contrafuego *m* (to stop a fire).

backfire [-'faiə*] *vi* AUT petardear || encenderse prematuramente (engine) || dar retorno de llama (burner) || FIG fallar, salir rana (to fail) || FIG *the scheme backfired on us* nos salió el tiro por la culata.

back-formation [-fɔː'meiʃən] *n* derivación *f* regresiva.

backgammon [-'gæmən] *n* chaquete *m*, tablas *f pl* reales.

background [-graund] *n* fondo *m*; *red triangles on a green background* triángulos rojos en un fondo verde || último plano *m* (of picture, photograph) || FIG segundo plano *m*, segundo término *m* (less prominent position) | antecedentes *m pl* (events leading up to); *the background to the revolution* los antecedentes de la revolución | ambiente *m*, medio *m* (atmosphere) | bases *f pl* (basic knowledge) | origen *m* (origin); *he has an English background* es de origen inglés | conocimientos *m pl*, experiencia *f* (experience) | educación *f* | pasado *m* (past life) || *background music, noise* música, ruido de fondo.

backhand [hænd] *adj* dado con el dorso de la mano || *backhand stroke* revés (in tennis, etc.).
◆ *n* revés *m* (blow, stroke) || letra *f* inclinada hacia la izquierda (handwriting).

backhanded ['hændid] *adj* dado con el revés de la mano (blow) || inclinado hacia la izquierda (handwriting) || FIG ambiguo, gua; equívoco, ca (compliment) | que vacila (hesitant); *he is not backhanded in asking for more* no vacila en pedir más.

backhander [-'hændə*] *n* FIG & FAM soborno *m*.

backing [-iŋ] *n* apoyo *m* (support) || refuerzo *m*; *a cloth belt with a leather backing* un cinturón de tela con un refuerzo de cuero || entretela *f* (in sewing) || soporte *m* (of picture) || *financial backing* respaldo financiero.

back issue [-'iʃuː] *n* número *m* atrasado (of publication).

backlash [læʃ] *n* TECH retroceso *m* (backward movement) | holgura *f*, juego *m* (looseness) | sacudida *f* (jarring reaction) || FIG reacción *f* (antagonistic reaction).

backless ['bækləs] *adj* escotado por detrás (dress).

backlighting [-laitiŋ] *n* contraluz *m*.

backlog [lɔg] *n* leño *m* en el fondo del hogar (of a fire) || reserva *f* (reserve); *this backlog of orders assures the continued growth of the company* esta reserva de pedidos garantiza el constante desarrollo de la compañía || atrasos *m pl* (outstanding work) | acumulación *f* (accumulation).

back number [-'nʌmbə*] *n* número *m* atrasado (of a publication) || FIG cosa *f* or persona *f* anticuada (old-fashioned) | vieja gloria *f* (has-been).

back of beyond [-əvbi'jɔnd] *n* FAM quinto pino *m* (remote place); *he lives in the back of beyond* vive en el quinto pino.

backpack ['bækˌpæk] *n* *US* mochila *f*.

backpacker ['bækˌpækə*] *n* *US* mochilero, ra.

back pay ['bæk pei] *n* atrasos *m pl* en la paga.

backpedal [-'pedl] *vi* pedalear hacia atrás || FIG volverse atrás (to back down).

backplate [-pleit] *n* espaldar *m*.

backrest [-rest] *n* respaldo *m* (of chair).

back room [-ruːm] *n* cuarto *m* trasero || FIG *decisions taken in the back room* decisiones tomadas entre bastidores.

back scratcher [-ˌskrætʃə*] *n* rascador *m*.

back seat [-'siːt] *n* asiento *m* trasero || — *back-seat driver* persona *f* que abruma de consejos al conductor (in a car), persona entrometida (meddler) || FIG *to take a back seat* pasar al segundo plano; estar en el segundo plano.

backset [-set] *n* revés (setback) || contracorriente *f* (of water).

back shop [-'ʃɔp] *n* trastienda *f*.

backside [-said] *n* FAM trasero *m*.

backslapper [-ˌslæpə*] *n* persona *f* campechana.

backslapping [-ˌslæpiŋ] *n* FIG felicitaciones *f pl*.

backslide [-'slaid] *vi* desviarse, salir del buen camino (to become corrupted) || reincidir, volver a caer (to relapse).

backslider [-'slaidə*] *n* reincidente *m* & *f* || REL apóstata *m* & *f*.

backsliding [-'slaidiŋ] *n* reincidencia *f* || REL apostasía *f*.

backspacer [-ˌspeisə*] *n* tecla *f* de retroceso (of typewriter).

backspin [-spin] *n* efecto *m*; *to put a backspin on a ball* dar efecto a una pelota.

backstage [-steidʒ] *n* bastidores *m pl*.
◆ *adj* de bastidores || FIG de la vida privada (of theatre people) | oculto, ta; secreto, ta; *backstage deals* acuerdos ocultos || — *backstage noises* ruidos *m* que vienen de los bastidores || *backstage workers* hombres *m* que trabajan entre bastidores.
◆ *adv* entre bastidores || a *or* en los camerinos (to or in the dressing rooms).
— OBSERV *Entre bastidores* may not be used with a verb of motion (*they went backstage* se fueron a los camerinos: but *it happened backstage* ocurrió entre bastidores).

back stairs [-'stɛəz] *pl n* escalera *f sing* de servicio.

backstairs [-'stɛəz] *adj* FIG secreto, ta (secret) | barato, ta; *backstairs novels* novelas baratas | sórdido, da (sordid) || FIG *to get a job through backstairs influence* conseguir un puesto por enchufe.

backstay [-stei] *n* MAR estay *m*, brandal *m* || soporte *m* (support) || contrafuerte *m* (of shoe).

backstitch [-stitʃ] *n* pespunte *m* (in sewing).

back street [-striːt] *n* calle *f* pequeña, callejuela *f*.

backstreet abortion [-ə'bæːʃən] *n* aborto *m* ilegal.

backstroke [-strəuk] *n* braza *f* de espalda (in swimming) || revés *m* (in tennis).

backsword [-sɔːd] *n* sable *m* (sword) || bastón *m* (singlestick).

back talk [-tɔːk] *n* *US* ⟶ **backchat.**

backtrack [-træk] *vi* volver hacia atrás || FIG volverse atrás.

backward [-wəd] *adj* hacia atrás; *a backward glance* una mirada hacia atrás || atrasado, da; *a backward country, child* un país, un niño atrasado || tardío, a (fruit) || — *backward in* tímido para (shy), remiso en (reluctant), tardo en (slow) || *backward motion* retroceso *m*.
◆ *adv* ⟶ **backwards.**

backwardness [-wədnis] *n* atraso *m*, retraso *m* (mental, economic) || timidez *f* (shyness) || falta *f* de entusiasmo (reluctance) || tardanza *f* (slowness).

backwards [-wədz] *adv* hacia atrás; *to lean backwards* inclinarse hacia atrás || de espaldas; *to fall backwards* caerse de espaldas || al revés; *to do things backwards* hacer las cosas al revés || — *backwards and forwards* de acá para allá || *to know sth. backwards* o *backwards and forwards* saber algo al dedillo *or* como el padre nuestro || FIG *to look backwards in time* mirar hacia atrás || *to move backwards* retroceder || *to read backwards* leer al revés || *to stroke the cat backwards* acariciar el gato a contrapelo.

backwash [-wɔʃ] *n* remolinos *m pl* de agua ‖ resaca *f* (of waves) ‖ FIG repercusión *f*.

backwater [-ˌwɔːtə*] *n* agua *f* estancada (behind an obstruction) ‖ remanso *m* (still water) | brazo *m* de mar (of sea) ‖ FIG lugar *m* apartado (remote place) | lugar *m* atrasado (backward place).

backwoods [-wudz] *pl n* selvas *f* del interior (de América del Norte) ‖ FIG región *f sing* apartada (remote area) | lugar *m* apartado *or* perdido (remote place).
◆ *adj* tosco, ca; rústico, ca.

backwoodsman [-wudzmən] *n* persona *f* que vive en un lugar perdido ‖ patán *m* (peasant) ‖ lord *m* que no presencia casi nunca las sesiones del Parlamento.
— OBSERV El plural es *backwoodsmen*.

backyard [-ˈjɑːd] *n* traspatio *m*, patio *m* interior.

bacon [ˈbeikən] *n* tocino *m* entreverado, «bacon» *m* ‖ — FAM *to bring home the bacon* ganarse el cocido *or* el pan (to earn a living), llevarse la palma (to succeed) | *to save one's bacon* salvar el pellejo.

Baconian [beiˈkəunjən] *adj/n* baconiano, na.

bacterial [bækˈtiəriəl] *adj* bacteriano, na.

bactericide [bækˈtiərisaid] *n* bactericida *m*.

bacteriological [bækˌtiəriːəˈlɔdʒikəl] [bækˌtiəriəˈlɔdʒikəl] *adj* bacteriológico, ca; *bacteriological warfare* guerra bacteriológica.

bacteriologist [bækˌtiəriːˈɔlədʒist] *n* bacteriólogo, ga.

bacteriology [bækˌtiːəriˈɔlədʒi] *n* bacteriología *f*.

bacterium [bækˈtiəriəm] *n* bacteria *f*.
— OBSERV El plural de *bacterium* es *bacteria*.

bad [bæd] *adj* malo, la; *bad habits* malas costumbres; *bad blood* mala sangre; *to keep bad company* tener malas compañías; *a bad light for reading* una luz mala para leer; *these apples are bad* estas manzanas están malas; *bad news* malas noticias; *I have got a bad taste in my mouth* tengo mal sabor de boca; *smoking is bad for the health* el fumar es malo para la salud; *to be bad at arithmetic* ser malo en aritmética; *a bad boy* un niño malo ‖ fuerte (headache) ‖ severo, ra; intenso, sa (cold) ‖ grave (mistake, accident, disease) ‖ falso, sa (coin) ‖ incobrable (debt) ‖ viciado, da (blood) ‖ cruel (defeat) ‖ — *a bad type* un mal tipo ‖ FAM *bad egg, bad lot* mala persona ‖ *bad form* mala educación ‖ *bad language* palabrotas *f pl* ‖ *from bad to worse* de mal en peor ‖ FAM *he is a bad one* es un tipo de cuidado, es un mal sujeto ‖ US *I am in bad with my friend* mi amigo está enfadado conmigo ‖ *in a bad sense* en mal sentido ‖ *in a bad way* en mal estado (in a bad state), en un mal paso (in a tight spot) ‖ *it's not bad* no está mal ‖ *to be bad* estar malo (to be ill) ‖ *to be bad for* ser malo para ‖ *to feel bad* encontrarse mal ‖ FIG *to feel bad abouth sth. one has done* sentir haber hecho algo ‖ *to go bad* echarse a perder, estropearse ‖ *to have a bad leg* dolerle a uno la pierna ‖ *to look bad* tener mala cara ‖ FAM *too bad!* ¡qué pena! (what a shame!), ¿qué le vamos a hacer? (never mind) ‖ *to use bad language* ser mal hablado.
◆ *n* lo malo ‖ gente *f* mala (bad people) ‖ — *I am ten pounds to the bad* tengo un déficit de diez libras ‖ *to go to the bad* echarse a perder.

bad debt [-ˈdet] *n* ECON deuda *f* incobrable.

bade [beid] *pret* → **bid**.

badge [bædʒ] *n* insignia *f* (of office) ‖ distintivo *m* (distinctive device) ‖ medalla *f* (award) ‖ FIG símbolo *m* ‖ *Red Cross badge* brazalete *m* de la Cruz Roja.

badger [-ə*] *n* ZOOL tejón *m*.

badger [-ə*] *vt* importunar, acosar [con preguntas].

badinage [ˈbædinɑːʒ] *n* discreteo *m* (playful teasing) ‖ broma *f* (joking).

badlands [ˈbædˌlændz] *pl n* páramos *m*, tierras *f* yermas.

bad-looking [ˈbædˈlukiŋ] *adj* feo, a.

badly [ˈbædli] *adv* mal; *to behave badly* portarse mal ‖ gravemente; *badly hurt* gravemente herido ‖ mucho; *to miss s.o. badly* echar mucho de menos a alguien ‖ — *he needs money badly* tiene mucha necesidad de dinero ‖ *to be badly off* andar mal de dinero (hard up) ‖ *to be badly off for* andar mal de.

badminton [ˈbædmintən] *n* bádminton *m*, juego *m* del volante.

badness [ˈbædnis] *n* maldad *f* (of a person) ‖ rigor *m* (of climate, of weather) ‖ mal estado *m* (of a road) ‖ COMM mala calidad *f*.

bad-tempered [ˈbædˈtempəd] *adj* de mal genio (permanently) ‖ de mal humor, malhumorado, da (occasionally).

baffle [ˈbæfl] *n* deflector *m* ‖ «baffle» *m*, pantalla *f* acústica (of loudspeaker) ‖ *baffle plate* deflector *m*.

baffle [ˈbæfl] *vt* desconcertar (to puzzle) ‖ frustrar (to frustrate) ‖ impedir (to hamper) ‖ TECH desviar (to deflect) | detener (to stop) ‖ *to baffle all description* escapar a cualquier descripción.

baffling [-iŋ] *adj* desconcertante.

bag [bæg] *n* bolsa *f*; *shopping bag* bolsa para la compra; *paper bag* bolsa de papel ‖ saco *m* (sack) ‖ bolso *m* (handbag) ‖ cartera *f* (satchel) ‖ chistera *f* (for carrying fish) ‖ morral *m* (for carrying game) ‖ caza *f* (animals taken in a hunt) ‖ pesca *f* (fish caught) ‖ bolsa *f* (of animals); *poison, ink bag* bolsa de veneno, de tinta ‖ bolsa *f* (under the eye) ‖ bolsa *f*, rodillera *f* (in trousers) ‖ ANAT bolsa *f* ‖ — FIG & FAM *bag of bones* costal *m* de huesos ‖ *diplomatic bag* valija diplomática ‖ FAM *it's in the bag* está en el bote ‖ *laundry bag* bolsa para la ropa sucia ‖ FIG *the whole bag of tricks* todo ‖ FAM *to be a bag of bones* estar en los huesos ‖ US FAM *to be left holding the bag* cargar con el muerto ‖ FAM *to pack up bag and baggage* liar el petate ‖ *travelling bag* bolsa de viaje.
◆ *pl* pantalón *m sing*, pantalones *m* ‖ FIG & FAM *bags of* montones de; *bags of money* montones de dinero; mucho, mucha; *there's bags of room* hay mucho sitio.

bag [bæg] *vt* empaquetar, ensacar (to put in bags) ‖ cazar (animals) ‖ pescar (fish) ‖ FIG pescar, coger; *the police bagged the whole gang* la policía pescó toda la banda | coger; *he bagged the best seat* cogió el mejor sitio; *who has bagged my matches?* ¿quién ha cogido mis fósforos?
◆ *vi* hacer bolsas (clothing) ‖ hincharse (to swell).

bagasse [bæˈgæs] *n* bagazo *m* (of grapes).

bagatelle [bægəˈtel] *n* bagatela *f*, fruslería *f* (triple) ‖ billar *m* inglés (game).

bagful [ˈbægful] *n* bolsa *f*, saco *m*; *they picked three bagfuls of apples* recogieron tres sacos de manzanas ‖ montón *m*; *bagfuls of money* montones de dinero.
— OBSERV El plural es *bagfuls* o *bagsful*.

baggage [ˈbægidʒ] *n* equipaje *m* (luggage) ‖ MIL bagaje *m* ‖ (ant) picaruela *f* (saucy girl) | ramera *f* (prostitute) ‖ — US *baggage car* furgón *m* de equipajes | *baggage check* talón *m* de equipajes | *baggage rack* redecilla *f* ‖ *baggage room* consigna *f* de equipajes.

baggy [ˈbægi] *adj* que hace bolsas; *a baggy suit* un traje que hace bolsas ‖ holgado, da (loose) ‖ *trousers baggy at the knees* pantalón con rodilleras.

Baghdad [bægˈdæd] *pr n* GEOGR Bagdad.

bagpiper [ˈbægpaipə*] *n* gaitero, ra.

bagpipes [ˈbægpaips] *pl n* gaita *f sing*, cornamusa *f sing*.

baguette [bæˈget] *n* ARCH junquillo *m*.

bah! [bɑː] *interj* ¡bah!

Bahamas [bəˈhɑːməz] *pl n* GEOGR Bahamas *f*.

Baikal Lake [baiˈkæl] *pr n* GEOGR lago *m* Baikal.

bail [beil] *n* JUR fianza *f*; *a bail of two hundred dollars* una fianza de doscientos dólares; *on bail* bajo fianza; *to admit to bail* libertar bajo fianza ‖ asa *f* (of pail, kettle) ‖ arco *m* [que sostiene un toldo] ‖ achicador *m* (for scooping water) ‖ barra *f* que separa los compartimientos de un establo ‖ muro *m* exterior (of castle) ‖ — *to be on bail* estar en libertad bajo fianza ‖ *to forfeit bail* perder la fianza ‖ *to go bail* o *to put up bail* o *to stand bail for s.o.* salir fiador por uno, dar fianza por uno ‖ *to jump bail* huir estando bajo fianza.

bail [beil] *vt* JUR poner en libertad bajo fianza (to free) | dar fianza por, salir fiador por (to put up bail for) ‖ achicar (water out of a boat) ‖ FIG *to bail out* sacar de apuro.
◆ *vi* achicar (in a boat) ‖ *to bail out (of an aeroplane)* saltar en paracaídas de un avión.

bailee [beiˈliː] *n* JUR depositario *m*.

bailer [ˈbeilə*] *n* MAR achicador *m* ‖ JUR fiador, ra.

bailey [ˈbeili] *n* muralla *f* exterior.

bailie [ˈbeili] *n* magistrado *m* municipal escocés.

bailiff [ˈbeilif] *n* administrador *m*, mayordomo *m* (of estate) ‖ alguacil *m* (debt collector) ‖ (ant) baile *m* (magistrate).

bailiwick [ˈbeiliwik] *n* (ant) bailía *f*.

bailment [ˈbeilmənt] *n* JUR puesta *f* en libertad bajo fianza | entrega *f* de bienes al depositario.

bailor [ˈbeilə*]; **bailsman** [ˈbeilzmən] *n* JUR fiador *m*.

bain-marie [ˌbɛ̃mæˈri] *n* baño *m* maría, baño *m* de maría.

bairn [bɛən] *n* niño, ña.

bait [beit] *n* cebo *m*, carnada *f* (in fishing and hunting) ‖ FIG cebo *m*, señuelo *m* (enticement) ‖ — *to lay the bait* poner el cebo ‖ *to take the bait* picar, tragar el anzuelo.

bait [beit] *vt* poner el cebo en, cebar; *to bait the hook* poner el cebo en el anzuelo ‖ (ant) azuzar (bears, etc.) ‖ FIG hostigar (to torment).

baize [beiz] *n* bayeta *f* ‖ *green baize* tapete *m* verde (in games).

bake [beik] *n* cocción *f* (baking).

bake [beik] *vt* cocer en el horno (in an oven); *to bake a cake* cocer un pastel en el horno ‖ secar (to dry) ‖ endurecer (to harden) ‖ — *baked bricks* ladrillos cocidos ‖ *baked potato* patata *f* al horno.
◆ *vi* cocer, cocerse ‖ FIG & FAM *it's baking hot* hace un calor achicharrante.

baked beans [-tˈbiːnz] *pl n* alubias *f* guisadas con tomate.

Bakelite [-əlait] *n* baquelita *f*.

baker [-ə*] *n* panadero, ra (who makes and sells bread) ‖ pastelero, ra (who makes and sells cakes) ‖ — *baker's* panadería *f* ‖ FIG *baker's dozen* docena *f* del fraile.

bakery [-əri] *n* panadería *f*.

baking [-iŋ] *n* cocción *f* ‖ hornada *f* (batch) ‖ TECH cochura *f* (of bricks) ‖ — *baking powder* levadura *f* en polvo ‖ *baking soda* bicarbonato *m* de sosa ‖ *baking tin* molde *m* para el horno.

baksheesh [ˈbækʃiːʃ] *n* gratificación *f*, guante *m* (tip).

balaclava [ˌbæləˈklɑːvə] *n* *balaclava helmet* pasamontañas *m inv.*

balalaika [ˌbæləˈlaikə] *n* MUS balalaica *f.*

balance [ˈbæləns] *n* balanza *f* (scales) ‖ equilibrio *m* (physical, mental, artistic); *to lose one's balance* perder el equilibrio ‖ volante *m* (of clock) ‖ COMM saldo *m* (difference between the debit and credit sides); *credit balance* saldo positivo | balance *m* (financial statement) | balanza *f*; *balance of payments, of trade* balanza de pagos, comercial ‖ resto *m* (remainder) ‖ — COMM *balance due* saldo deudor ‖ *balance in hand* saldo disponible ‖ *balance of power* equilibrio de fuerzas ‖ *balance pole* balancín *m* (of acrobat) ‖ MAR *balance reef* faja *f* de rizos ‖ *balance sheet* balance *m*, estado *m* de cuentas ‖ *balance spring* espiral *f* del volante (of clock) ‖ *balance wheel* volante *m* (of clock) ‖ *off one's balance* desequilibrado, da ‖ *on balance* mirándoio bien ‖ FIG *to be* o *to hang in the balance* estar en juego; *his reputation is in the balance* su reputación está en juego; estar en la balanza; *love and duty were in the balance* el amor y el deber estaban en la balanza; estar pendiente de un hilo (in a critical position) ‖ *to hold one's balance* mantener *or* guardar el equilibrio ‖ FIG *to hold the balance* llevar la voz cantante ‖ *to throw s.o. off his balance* hacerle a uno perder el equilibrio (to topple), desconcertar a uno (to bewilder).

balance [ˈbæləns] *vt* pesar (to weigh) ‖ comparar; *to balance the advantages against the disadvantages* comparar las ventajas con los inconvenientes ‖ poner en equilibrio; *to balance a plate on the end of a stick* poner un plato en equilibrio en la punta de un palo ‖ equilibrar (to equilibrate) ‖ compensar (to compensate) ‖ contrarrestar (s.o.'s power) ‖ sopesar (to ponder) ‖ COMM equilibrar; *to balance the budget* equilibrar el presupuesto | saldar (to settle) ‖ igualar (an equation) ‖ COMM *to balance the books* hacer el balance.
◆ *vi* hacer equilibrios (an acrobat); *to balance on a tightrope* hacer equilibrios en la cuerda floja ‖ guardar el equilibrio, quedarse en equilibrio (to remain in equilibrium) ‖ equilibrarse (to weigh the same) ‖ COMM cuadrar; *the accounts do not balance* las cuentas no cuadran ‖ FIG compensarse (to compensate each other) ‖ balancearse (to swing) ‖ vacilar, dudar (to hesitate).

balanced [-t] *adj* equilibrado, da; *a balanced mind* una mente equilibrada; *a balanced diet* una alimentación equilibrada.

balancer [-ə*] *n* equilibrista *m* & *f* (acrobat) ‖ TECH balancín *m* | fiel *m* de la balanza (of scales).

balancing act [-iŋ ækt] *n* FIG malabarismos *m pl.*

balas [ˈbæləs] *n* balaje *m* (ruby).

balboa [bælˈbəuə] *n* balboa *m* (Panamanian currency).

balcony [ˈbælkəni] *n* balcón *m* (of house) ‖ anfiteatro *m* (of theatre) ‖ entresuelo *m* (of cinema).

bald [bɔːld] *adj* calvo, va (people); *I am going bald* me estoy quedando calvo ‖ pelado, da (countryside, landscape) ‖ FIG franco, ca; *bald statement* declaración franca | desnudo, da; escueto, ta (style) | sencillo, lla; simple, sin adornos (straightforward) ‖ — *bald patch* calva *f* ‖ *bald tyre* neumático desgastado ‖ FAM *to be as bald as a coot* estar calvo como una bola de billar.

baldachin; baldaquin [-əkin] *n* baldaquín *m*, baldaquino *m.*

balderdash [-ədæʃ] *n* tonterías *f pl*, disparates *m pl.*

bald-headed [-ˈhedid] *adj* calvo, va ‖ FIG *to go at it bald-headed* lanzarse ciegamente a ello.

balding [-iŋ] *adj* que se está quedando calvo, va.

baldness [-nis] *n* calvicie *f* ‖ FIG lo pelado (of countryside, landscape) | lo escueto (of style).

bald-pated [-ˌpeitid] *adj* calvo, va.

baldric [-rik] *n* tahalí *m.*

bale [beil] *n* bala *f*, fardo *m* (of goods) ‖ bala *f*, paca *f* (of cotton) ‖ MAR achicador *m* (bail) ‖ dolor *m*, pena *f* (suffering) ‖ desgracia *f* (misfortune).

bale [beil] *vt* embalar (to pack) ‖ empacar, embalar (cotton) ‖ MAR achicar (water).

Bâle [bɑːl] *pr n* GEOGR Basilea.

Balearic [ˌbæliˈærik] *adj* balear, baleárico, ca ‖ *the Balearic Islands* las islas Baleares, las Baleares.

baleen [bəˈliːn] *n* ballena *f* (whalebone).

baleful [ˈbeilful] *adj* funesto, ta; pernicioso, sa; siniestro, tra; *baleful influence* influencia funesta ‖ tétrico, ca (sight).

baler [ˈbeilə*] *n* achicador *m* (for scooping water) ‖ embaladora *f* (for packing).

balk [bɔːk] *n* AGR caballón *m* ‖ viga *f* (beam) ‖ relinga *f or* cuerda *f* superior (of fishing net) ‖ cabaña *f* (billiards) ‖ FIG obstáculo *m.*

balk [bɔːk] *vt* frustrar (to frustrate) ‖ obstaculizar, poner obstáculos a (to hinder) ‖ evitar, esquivar (to evade) ‖ perder (to miss).
◆ *vi* plantarse, repropiarse (a horse) ‖ negarse (to refuse); *to balk at doing sth.* negarse a hacer algo ‖ — *to balk at a difficulty* echarse atrás ante una dificultad ‖ *to balk at the work* resistirse *or* negarse a hacer el trabajo.

Balkan [ˈbɔːlkən] *adj* balcánico, ca ‖ *the Balkan Mountains* los Balcanes.

Balkans [-z] *pl prn* GEOGR Balcanes *m.*

balkline [ˈbɔːklain] *n* línea *f* que separa la cabaña del resto de la mesa (billiards).

balky [ˈbɔːki] *adj* repropio, pia (a horse) ‖ reacio, cia; recalcitrante (people).

ball [bɔːl] *n* bola *f* (spherical object) ‖ pelota *f* (used in games); *to play ball* jugar a la pelota ‖ SP balón *m* (football, etc.) | pelota *f* (tennis, baseball) | bola *f* (billiards, golf, hockey) ‖ bola *f* (of snow) ‖ borla *f* (of a fringe) ‖ esfera *f*, globo *m* (planetary body) ‖ bola *f* (used in voting) ‖ ovillo *m* (wool, string) ‖ MIL bala *f* (of cannon, rifle) ‖ MED globo *m* ocular (of the eye) ‖ CULIN albóndiga *f* (of meat) ‖ ANAT eminencia *f* tenar (of thumb) | eminencia *f* metatarsiana (of foot) ‖ baile *m* (dance); *dress ball* baile de etiqueta; *fancy dress ball* baile de disfraces ‖ FIG responsabilidad *f* ‖ POP huevo *m* (testicle) ‖ — FIG *to be on the ball* estar atento, estar ojo avizor (to be alert), ser espabilado *or* despierto (to be lively) | *to catch the ball on the bounce* coger la ocasión al vuelo ‖ FAM *to have a ball* pasarlo en grande ‖ FIG *to have the ball at one's feet* tenerlo todo resuelto | *to keep the ball rolling, to keep the ball up* mantener [conversación, etc.] | *to play ball* cooperar | *to start* o *to get* o *to set the ball rolling* empezar [conversación, etc.].

ball [bɔːl] *vt* hacer una bola de (to make into a ball) ‖ hacer un ovillo con *or* de (wool, string) ‖ apelotonarse alrededor de (bees) ‖ FAM *to ball up* hacer un lío, embrollar.
◆ *vi* hacerse una bola ‖ hacer bolitas (wool).

ballad [ˈbæləd] *n* POET balada *f*, romance *m* ‖ MUS balada *f*, copla *f.*

ballade [bæˈlɑːd] *n* POET balada *f.*

ball-and-socket joint [ˈbɔːlændˈsɔkitˌdʒɔint] *n* TECH articulación *f* de rótula.

ballast [ˈbæləst] *n* lastre *m* (in boats and balloons) ‖ balasto *m* (on roads, for railway lines) ‖ — *ballast bed* firme *m* (roads) ‖ MAR *to be in ballast* ir en lastre.

ballast [ˈbæləst] *vt* lastrar (boats, balloons) ‖ balastar (roads, railway lines) ‖ FIG estabilizar.

ball bearing [ˈbɔːlˈbɛəriŋ] *n* TECH cojinete *m* de bolas, rodamiento *m* de bolas | bola *f* (steel ball).

ball boy [ˈbɔːlbɔi] *n* recogepelotas *m inv.*

ball cock [ˈbɔːlkɔk] *n* TECH llave *f* de bola, grifo *m* de flotador.

ballerina [ˌbæləˈriːnə] *n* bailarina *f.*

ballet [ˈbælei] *n* ballet *m*, baile *m* clásico ‖ *ballet skirt* tutú *m.*

ballet dancer [-ˌdɑːnsə*] *n* bailarín, ina.

balletomane [ˈbælitəumein] *n* aficionado *m* al ballet, aficionada *f* al ballet.

ball game [ˈbɔːl geim] *n* US partido *m* de béisbol. ‖ FIG & FAM *it's a whole new ball game* es otra historia.

ballista [bæˈlistə] *n* balista *f* (weapon).
— OBSERV El plural de *ballista* es *ballistae.*

ballistic [bəˈlistik] *adj* balístico, ca; *ballistic missiles* proyectiles balísticos.

ballistics [-s] *n* balística *f.*

ballocks [ˈbɔləks] *pl n* POP cojones *m*, huevos *m.*

balloon [bəˈluːn] *n* AVIAT globo *m*; *to go up in a balloon* montar en globo ‖ globo *m* (toy) ‖ CHEM matraz *m*, balón *m* ‖ ARCH bola *f* ‖ copa *f* (drinking glass) ‖ balón *m*, bocadillo *m* (in cartoons) ‖ — *balloon barrage* barrera *f* de globos ‖ *balloon sleeves* mangas *f pl* de jamón ‖ *barrage balloon* globo de barrera ‖ *captive balloon* globo cautivo ‖ *sounding balloon* globo sonda.

balloon [bəˈluːn] *vi* ir *or* montar en globo (to fly) ‖ hincharse (to swell out) ‖ subir rápidamente (to increase).

balloonist [-ist] *n* aeronauta *m* & *f.*

balloon tyre; US **balloon tire** [bəˈluːnˌtaiə*] *n* neumático *m* balón *or* de baja presión.

ballot [ˈbælət] *n* papeleta *f* (voting paper) | balota *f* (voting ball) ‖ votación *f* (vote); *secret ballot* votación secreta ‖ lista *f* de candidatos ‖ sorteo *m* (drawing of lots) ‖ — *ballot box* urna *f* ‖ *to take a ballot on* someter *or* poner a votación.

ballot [ˈbælət] *vi* votar (to vote); *to ballot for s.o.* votar por alguien ‖ sortear (to draw lots); *to ballot for a place* sortear un puesto.
◆ *vt* invitar a votar.

ballotade [ˌbæləˈteid] *n* balotada *f* (of a horse).

ballot paper [ˈbælətˌpeipə*] *n* papeleta *f.*

ball-point [ˈbɔːlpɔint]; **ball-point pen** [-ˈpen] *n* bolígrafo *m.*

ballroom [ˈbɔːlrum] *n* sala *f or* salón *m* de baile ‖ *ballroom dancing* baile *m* de salón.

balls up [ˈbɔːlz ʌp] *n* FIG & POP cagada *f.*

ball valve [ˈbɔːlvælv] *n* válvula *f* de bola.

ballyhoo [ˌbæliˈhuː] *n* propaganda *f or* publicidad *f* exagerada *or* sensacionalista, bombo *m* publicitario (blatant publicity) ‖ tontería *f* (nonsense) ‖ jaleo *m* (fuss).

balm [bɑːm] *n* bálsamo *m* (resin, ointment) ‖ BOT melisa *f*, citronela *f*, toronjil *m* ‖ FIG bálsamo *m* (soothing influence).

balmy [-i] *adj* balsámico, ca (of or like balm) ‖ FIG balsámico, ca (soothing) | fragante (fragrant) ‖ FAM chiflado, da (crazy).

balneotherapy [ˈbælniɔˈθerəpi] *n* balneoterapia *f.*

baloney [bəˈləuni] *n* US FAM camelo *m.*

balsa [ˈbɔːlsə] *n* balsa *f* (tree, wood, raft).

balsam [ˈbɔːlsəm] *n* bálsamo *m* (plant, tree, medicine) ‖ CHEM oleorresina *f* ‖ FIG bálsamo *m* || — *balsam apple* balsamina *f* || *balsam fir* balsamero *m* || *balsam poplar* álamo balsámico.

balsamic [bɔːl'sæmik] *adj* balsámico, ca.

Baltic ['bɔːltik] *adj* báltico, ca; *Baltic Sea* mar Báltico.
◆ *n* GEOGR Báltico *m.*

baluster ['bæləstə*] *n* balaustre *m.*
◆ *pl* barandilla *f sing* (handrail).

balustrade [ˌbæləs'treid] *n* balaustrada *f*, barandilla *f* (row of balusters).

bamboo [bæm'buː] *n* BOT bambú *m.*

bamboozle [bæm'buːzl] *vt* engañar, embaucar, engatusar (to trick).

ban [bæn] *n* prohibición *f*, interdicción *f* || JUR bando *m* (proclamation) || REL interdicto *m*; *papal ban* interdicto papal || (ant) maldición *f* (curse) || *to put a ban on* prohibir.
◆ *pl* amonestaciones *f* (banns).

ban [bæn] *vt* prohibir; *to ban nuclear weapons* prohibir las armas nucleares || rechazar (to reject); *public opinion bans drug addiction* la opinión pública rechaza la toxicomanía || poner fuera de la ley (to make illegal); *to ban war* poner la guerra fuera de la ley || SP suspender (a player) || — *he was banned from driving for three months* le quitaron el carnet de conducir durante tres meses || *to be banned by society* estar excluido de la sociedad.

banal [bə'nɑːl] *adj* banal, trivial.

banality [bə'næliti] *n* banalidad *f*, trivialidad *f.*

banana [bə'nɑːnə] *n* plátano *m*, banana *f* [AMER banano *m*] (fruit) || plátano *m*, banano *m* (tree) || FAM *banana republic* república *m* bananera.

band [bænd] *n* banda *f* (group); *a rebel band* una banda de rebeldes; *band of birds* banda de pájaros || pandilla *f*, grupo *m*; *a band of friends* una pandilla de amigos || MUS banda *f*; *military band* banda militar | orquesta *f*; *jazz band* orquesta de jazz || banda *f* (of material, colour); *a dress with a red band around the waist* un vestido con una banda roja en la cintura || cinta *f* (ribbon); *the band of a hat* la cinta de un sombrero || tira *f* (thin strip); *band of paper* tira de papel || venda *f* (bandage) || faja *f* (girdle) || brazalete *m* (armband) || vitola *f*, faja *f* (of cigar) || faja *f* (around newspaper) || lomera *f* (in bookbinding) || MIN capa *f*, estrato *m* || faja *f* (of territory) || haz *m* (of light) || TECH cinta *f*, correa *f* (driving belt) | fleje *m* (round cart wheel) || zuncho *m*, abrazadera *f* (of a gun) || PHYS & RAD banda *f*; *frequency band* banda de frecuencia || — *band brake* freno *m* de cinta || *band conveyor* cinta transportadora || *band saw* sierra *f* de cinta || *brake band* cinta de freno || *elastic band* goma *f* || *one-man band* hombre *m* orquesta.
◆ *pl* alzacuello *m sing.*

band [bænd] *vt* atar (to tie) || vendar (to bandage) || fajar (to put a girdle on) || poner bandas en, rayar (to stripe) || FIG *to band together* unir.
◆ *vi* *to band together* unirse, juntarse.

bandage ['bændidʒ] *n* venda *f* (for blindfolding) || MED venda *f*, vendaje *m.*

bandage ['bændidʒ] *vt* vendar.

Band-Aid ['bænd eid] *n* tirita *f.*

bandanna; bandana [bæn'dɑːnə] *n* pañuelo *m.*

B & B [ˌbiːn'biː] *abbr of* *[bed and breakfast]* pensión que ofrece habitación y desayuno.

bandbox ['bændbɔks] *n* sombrerera *f* || FIG *to look as if one had just stepped out of a bandbox* ir de punta en blanco.

banderole; banderol ['bændərəul] *n* banderola *f.*

bandit ['bændit] *n* bandido *m* || FIG *one-armed bandit* máquina *f* tragaperras.

banditry [-ri] *n* bandidaje *m*, bandolerismo *m.*

bandmaster ['bændˌmɑːstə*] *n* MUS director *m* de una banda.

bandolier; bandoleer [ˌbændə'liə*] *n* bandolera *f* (for carrying rifle) || cartuchera *f*, canana *f* (for cartridges).

bandsman ['bændzmæn] *n* MUS músico *m.*
— OBSERV El plural de esta palabra es *bandsmen.*

bandstand ['bændstænd] *n* quiosco *m* de música.

bandwagon ['bændˌwægən] *n* carro *m* de la banda de música || FIG partido político que triunfa || FIG *to jump on the bandwagon* arrimarse al sol que más calienta (to side with the strongest), seguir la corriente (to follow the crowd).

bandy ['bændi] *adj* patizambo, ba; con las piernas arqueadas (bowlegged).

bandy ['bændi] *vt* pasarse, tirarse (a ball) || FIG juguetear con (to play about with) | intercambiar (words, insults) | repetir (to repeat) || *to bandy about* o *around* difundir (rumours or false ideas).

bandy-legged [-legd] *adj* patizambo, ba; con las piernas arqueadas.

bane [bein] *n* perdición *f*, ruina *f* (ruin, woe, curse); *drink will be the bane of him* la bebida será su perdición || plaga *f* (pernicious element) || veneno *m* (poison) || *it has been the bane of my life* me ha amargado la vida.

baneful ['beinful] *adj* nocivo, va (noxious) || nocivo, va; funesto, ta; pernicioso, sa (harmful).

bang [bæŋ] *n* flequillo *m* (fringe) || golpe *m* (blow); *a bang on the head* un golpe en la cabeza || ruido *m* (noise) || estampido *m*, detonación *f* (of firearm) || explosión *f* (explosion) || energías *f pl*, vitalidad *f* (energy); *he's got no bang left in him* no le quedan energías || BOT cáñamo *m* (bhang) || — FIG & FAM *bang goes* adiós a || AVIAT *supersonic bang* estampido supersónico || *to fall to the floor with a bang* caer ruidosamente al suelo || *to give three bangs on the door* dar tres golpes en la puerta || *to go off with a bang* dar un estallido (fireworks), ser un éxito (to be a success); *the party went off with a bang* la fiesta fue un éxito || *to shut sth. with a bang* cerrar algo de golpe || *to shut the door with a bang* dar un portazo.
◆ *adv* FAM justo; *to arrive bang on time* llegar justo a la hora; *to hit the target bang in the middle* dar justo en el centro de la diana || — FAM *bang in the middle of the war* justo en plena guerra | *bang on* acertado.
◆ *interj* ¡cataplum! (when sth. falls) || ¡pum! (of a shot); *bang, bang! you're dead* ¡pum, pum! muerto || ¡zas! (of a blow).

bang [bæŋ] *vt* golpear, dar un golpe, dar golpes (to hit); *to bang s.o. on the head* golpear a alguien en la cabeza || golpear; *I banged his head on a stone* le golpeé la cabeza contra una piedra || golpearse en, darse un golpe en; *to fall and bang one's head* caer y golpearse en la cabeza || golpear, dar golpes en; *stop banging the desk* deja de dar golpes en la mesa || golpear con, dar golpes con; *the child was banging a ruler on the desk* el niño estaba golpeando la mesa con una regla, el niño estaba dando golpes en la mesa con una regla || tocar (to beat a drum) || aporrear (to play piano, drum, etc. badly) || sacudir (a carpet) || — *to bang about* maltratar; *don't bang the radio about* no maltrates la radio || *to bang a nail in* poner un clavo en, clavar (to nail), remachar un clavo (to drive home) || *to bang down* tirar; *he banged the book down on the table* tiró el libro contra la mesa; poner bruscamente (to put roughly), colgar de un golpe (telephone) || *to bang one's fist on the table* dar un puñetazo en la mesa || *to bang one's hair* dejarse flequillo || *to bang sth. shut* cerrar algo de golpe || *to bang the door* dar un portazo || *to bang up* estropear.
◆ *vi* golpear, dar golpes; *to bang at the door* dar golpes en la puerta, golpear la puerta; *the door was banging all night* la puerta estuvo dando golpes toda la noche || dar un golpe, golpear; *the falling chair banged against the wall* al caer la silla dio un golpe contra la pared || chocar (to bump) || explotar (to explode) || estallar (a balloon) || — *to bang about* armar jaleo (to make noise) || *to bang away* aporrear; *he is banging away on the piano* está aporreando el piano; retumbar incesantemente (guns) || *to bang shut* cerrarse de un golpe.
— OBSERV El verbo *to bang* implica una acción hecha con violencia y ruido: *to bang the lid down on the saucepan* tapar la cacerola bruscamente.

banger ['bæŋgə*] *n* petardo *m* (of fireworks) || FAM salchicha *f* (sausage).

Bangkok ['bæŋkɔk, bɔŋ'kɔk] *pr n* GEOGR Bangkok.

Bangladesh [ˌbæŋglə'deʃ] *pr n* GEOGR Bangla Desh *m.*

bangle ['bæŋgl] *n* ajorca *f*, brazalete *m.*

Bangui [bɔŋ'giː] *pr n* GEOGR Bangui.

banish ['bæniʃ] *vt* desterrar; *to banish s.o. from a place* desterrar a alguien de un sitio; *to banish fear, worries* desterrar el miedo, las preocupaciones.

banishment [-mənt] *n* destierro *m.*

banister ['bænistə*] *n* balaustre *m* (upright support) || barandilla *f* (handrail).
◆ *pl* barandilla *f sing*, pasamanos *m sing.*

banjo ['bændʒəu] *n* MUS banjo *m.*
— OBSERV El plural de la palabra inglesa es *banjos* o *banjoes.*

Banjul [bæn'dʒuːl] *pr n* GEOGR Banjul.

bank [bænk] *n* COMM banco *m* (banking establishment); *bank clerk* empleado de banco || banca *f* (in gambling); *to break the bank* hacer saltar la banca || orilla *f*, ribera *f* (of driver); *on the banks of* a orillas de, en la ribera de || dique *m* (artificial) || loma *f* (raised ground) || pendiente *f* (slope) || terraplén *m*, talud *m* (along road, railway line, etc.) || peralte *m* (in sharp bend) || fila *f*, hilera *f* (row) || banco *m*, bajo *m*, bajío *m* (underwater elevation) || grupo *m* (of clouds) || montón *m* (of snow) || MIN boca *f* de pozo || MUS teclado *m* (of organ) || teclado *m* (of typewriter) || ELECTR batería *f* || US banda *f* (in billiards) | escora *f*, inclinación *f* lateral (of an aeroplane) || (ant) banco *m* (in galleys) | hilera *f* (of oars) || — *blood bank* banco de sangre || COMM *farmer's issuing bank* banco de emisión | *joint-stock bank* banco por acciones | *lending bank*, US *loans bank* banco de préstamos | mortgage bank banco hipotecario | *savings bank* caja *f* de ahorros || *World Bank* Banco Mundial.
◆ *pl* banca *f sing* (banking industry).
— OBSERV At present, the word *banca* or *casa de banca* is rarely used to mean a *banking establishment*, the usual term being *banco*, but, when referring to the banking profession or to all the banks as a whole, *banca* is commonly employed: *la nacionalización de la banca, la jornada hace jornada intensiva.*

bank [bæŋk] *vt* depositar *or* ingresar en el banco (to deposit) || amontonar (earth) || peraltar (a sharp bend) || encauzar (river) || formar hileras de (to line) || TECH cubrir (fire) | juntar en batería (cells) || ladear (a plane) || US *to bank a ball* jugar por banda.
◆ *vi* tener una cuenta (*with* en) || tener como banquero a || dedicarse a la banca || ser banquero (in gambling) || amontonarse (to pile up) || inclinarse lateralmente al virar (aero-

planes) || — *to bank on* contar con || *to bank up* amontonarse.

bank account [-əˌkaunt] *n* cuenta *f* bancaria, cuenta *f* corriente.

bank balance [-ˌbæləns] *n* saldo *m* bancario.

bank bill [-bil] *n* letra *f* de cambio (bill of exchange) || US billete *m* de banco (bank note).

bankbook [-buk] *n* libreta *f* de depósitos || cartilla *f* (of savings banks).

bank credit [-ˌkredit] *n* crédito *m* bancario.

bank draft [-drɑːft] *n* letra *f* bancaria.

banker [-ə*] *n* banquero *m*.

bank holiday [-'hɔlədei] *n* día *m* festivo || US período *m* en que cierran los bancos por orden del gobierno.

— OBSERV En Inglaterra hay varios *bank holidays*: el lunes de Pascua, el lunes de Pentecostés, el primer lunes de septiembre y el día 26 de diciembre.

banking ['bæŋkiŋ] *n* banca *f* (business) || AVIAT inclinación *f* lateral || — *banking account* cuenta bancaria || *banking house* casa *f* de banca.

bank note ['bæŋknəut] *n* billete *m* de banco.

bank of issue ['bæŋkəv'iʃu] *n* banco *m* emisor.

bank rate ['bæŋkreit] *n* tipo *m* de descuento bancario.

bankrupt ['bæŋkrəpt] *adj* quebrado, da; en quiebra (company) || insolvente || arruinado, da (ruined) || FIG falto de, carente de (lacking) || *to go* o *to become bankrupt* quebrar, declararse en quiebra.

◆ *n* quebrado *m* || — *bankrupt's certificate* concordato *m* || *bankrupt's estate* masa *f* de la quiebra || MED *mental bankrupt* demente *m* || *to adjudge* o *adjudicate s.o. bankrupt* declarar en quiebra a alguien.

bankrupt ['bæŋkrəpt] *vt* hacer quebrar (company) || arruinar (to ruin).

bankruptcy ['bæŋkrəptsi] *n* insolvencia *f* (insolvency) || quiebra *f* (of a company) || bancarrota *f* (usually fraudulent) || ruina *f* (ruin) || FIG falta *f*, carencia *f* (lack) | quiebra *f* (failure).

bank statement ['bæŋkˌsteitmənt] *n* extracto *m* de cuenta.

banner ['bænə*] *n* bandera *f* (flag) || REL pendón *m*, estandarte *m* || pancarta *f* (in demonstrations) || *banner headlines* grandes titulares *m*.

◆ *adj* US sobresaliente, excepcional.

banns [bænz] *pl n* amonestaciones *f*, proclamas *f*; *to call* o *to publish* o *to ask* o *to put up the banns* correr las amonestaciones.

banquet ['bæŋkwit] *n* banquete *m*.

banquet ['bæŋkwit] *vt/vi* banquetear.

banquette [bæŋ'ket] *n* banqueta *f* (railway, fortification) || US acera *f* (pavement).

banshee [bæn'ʃi] *n* hada *f* maligna que anuncia la muerte (in Ireland and Scotland).

bantam ['bæntəm] *n* gallo *m* or gallina *f* bántam (domestic fowl) || FIG gallito *m* (small, aggressive person).

bantamweight [-weit] *n* peso *m* gallo (boxer).

banter ['bæntə*] *n* broma *f*, chanza *f*, guasa *f*.

banter ['bæntə*] *vt* burlarse de, chancearse de, guasearse de.

◆ *vi* bromear.

bantling ['bæntliŋ] *n* niño *m*, crío *m*.

baobab ['beiəubæb] *n* BOT baobab (tree).

baptism ['bæptizəm] *n* bautismo *m* (sacrament) || bautizo *m* (christening) || MIL *baptism of fire* bautismo de fuego.

baptismal [bæp'tizməl] *adj* bautismal || — *baptismal certificate* fe *f* de bautismo || *baptismal font* pila *f* del bautismo || *baptismal name* nombre *m* de pila.

Baptist ['bæptist] *n* bautista *m* & *f*, baptista *m* & *f* || *Saint John the Baptist* San Juan Bautista, el Bautista.

baptistery ['bæptistəri]; **baptistry** ['bæptistri] *n* bautisterio *m*, baptisterio *m*.

baptize [bæp'taiz] *vt/vi* bautizar.

bar [bɑː*] *n* barra *f*; *metal bar* barra de metal || barrote *m* (of prison); *behind bars* entre barrotes || barra *f* (of gold, silver) || pastilla *f* (of soap) || barra *f* (of chocolate) || bocado *m*, barra *f* (of horse's bit) || barra *f* (of medal) || franja *f* (of light, colour) || barra *f* (in ballet) || barra *f* (counter) || bar *m* (drinking room) || barra *f* (for the public in an assembly) || TECH palanca *f*, barra *f* (lever) || tranca *f* (of door) || MIL galón *m* (chevron) || MAR barra *f* (of sand) || MUS barra *f* (bar line) | compás *m* (measure) || PHYS bar *m* | baria *f* (barye) || JUR desestimación *f* (of a claim) | tribunal *m* (court); *to summon the prisoner to the bar* hacer comparecer al prisionero ante el tribunal || barra *f* (dock) | colegio *m* de abogados (body of lawyers) | abogacía *f* (profession); *to be called to the bar* ser admitido al ejercicio de la abogacía || HERALD barra *f* || FIG obstáculo *m*, barrera *f* (obstacle) | tribunal *m*; *to be judged at the bar of public opinion* ser juzgado por el tribunal de la opinión pública || — *colour bar* segregación *f* racial || SP *horizontal bar* barra fija | *parallel bars* barras paralelas || *the prisoner at the bar* el acusado.

bar [bɑː*] *prep* excepto, salvo (except) || *bar none* sin excepción.

bar [bɑː*] *vt* atrancar, poner una tranca a; *to bar the door* atrancar la puerta || poner barrotes a (a window) || excluir; *to bar foreigners from important posts* excluir a los extranjeros de los puestos importantes; *barring the possibility of rain* excluyendo la posibilidad de lluvia || impedir (to prevent) || prohibir (to prohibit) || cortar, interceptar (a road) || JUR desestimar || MUS acompasar.

Barabbas [bə'ræbəs] *pr n* Barrabás.

barb [bɑːb] *n* lengüeta *f* (of arrow, fishhook, etc.) || barbilla *f* (of fish) || barba *f* (of feather) || caballo *m* árabe (horse) || FIG dardo *m*, flecha *f* (malicious remark).

barb [bɑːb] *vt* poner lengüetas en (arrow, etc.).

Barbados [bɑː'beidəuz] *pr n* GEOGR Barbados.

Barbara ['bɑːbərə] *pr n* Bárbara *f*.

barbarian [bɑː'bɛəriən] *adj/n* bárbaro, ra.

barbaric [bɑː'bærik] *adj* barbárico, ca; bárbaro, ra.

barbarism ['bɑːbərizəm] *n* GRAMM barbarismo *m* || barbarie *f* (condition).

barbarity [bɑː'bæriti] *n* barbarie *f* (barbarism) || barbaridad *f* (cruelty).

barbarize ['bɑːbəraiz] *vt* barbarizar (language) || volver bárbaro, embrutecer.

◆ *vi* caer en la barbarie || emplear barbarismos (speaking).

barbarous ['bɑːbərəs] *adj* bárbaro, ra (uncivilized, cruel, uncouth) || lleno de barbarismos (language).

Barbary ['bɑːbəri] *pr n* HIST Berbería *f* || ZOOL *Barbary ape* macaco *m*.

barbate ['bɑːbeit] *adj* BOT barbado, da.

barbecue ['bɑːbikjuː] *n* barbacoa *f*.

barbecue ['bɑːbikjuː] *vt* asar a la parrilla.

barbed ['bɑːbd] *adj* con lengüeta (arrow, etc.) || FIG mordaz (word).

barbed wire [-'waiə*] *n* alambre *m* de espino *or* de púas || *barbed-wire entanglement* alambrada *f*.

barbel ['bɑːbel] *n* barbilla *f* (barb of fish) || ZOOL barbo *m*.

barbell ['bɑːəl] *n* barra *f* con pesas.

barber ['bɑːbə*] *n* peluquero *m*, barbero *m* || *barber's* peluquería *f*, barbería *f*.

barbershop [-ʃɔp] *n* peluquería *f*, barbería *f*.

barbette [bɑː'bet] *n* MIL barbeta *f* (of fortress, warship), .

barbican ['bɑːbikən] *n* MIL barbacana *f*.

barbiturate [bɑː'bitjurit] *n* CHEM barbitúrico, *m*.

barbituric [ˌbɑːbi'tjuərik] *adj* barbitúrico, ca.

barbwire ['bɑːbwaiə*] *n* US alambre *m* de espino *or* de púas.

barcarole; barcarolle ['bɑːkərəul] *n* MUS barcarola *f*.

Barcelona [ˌbɑːsi'ləunə] *pr n* GEOGR Barcelona.

bar code ['bɑː kəud] *n* INFORM código *m* de barras.

bard [bɑːd] *n* bardo *m*, vate *m* (poet) || barda *f* (of a horse) || CULIN albardilla *f*.

bard [bɑːd] *vt* bardar (horse) || CULIN emborrizar.

bare [bɛə*] *adj* desnudo, da (naked); *bare from the waist up* desnudo de cintura para arriba || descubierto, ta (head) || descalzo, za (foot) || descubierto, ta (uncovered) || pelado, da; raso, sa (landscape) || raído, da; gastado, da (worn) || vacío, a (empty); *bare cupboard* armario vacío || escaso, sa; exiguo, gua (scant); *bare majority* escasa mayoría || puro, ra (truth) || simple (simple) || escueto, ta; conciso, sa (style) || desnudo, da (walls, trees, wire) || con pocos muebles (room) || desenvainado, da (sword) || — *a bare chance* una remota posibilidad || *bare of* desprovisto de || *the bare essentials* lo imprescindible || *to earn a bare living* ganar lo justo para vivir || *to lay bare* revelar, descubrir (secret), poner al descubierto (surface) || *to sleep on the bare ground* dormir en el mismo suelo || *with one's bare hands* con sus propias manos.

bare [bɛə*] *vt* desnudar || descubrir (to uncover) || desenvainar (sword) || revelar (feelings, etc.) || *to bare one's head* descubrirse.

bareback [-bæk] *adj/adv* a pelo; *to learn bareback riding* aprender a montar a pelo.

barefaced [-feist] *adj* descarado, da (shameless) || lampiño, ña (without beard) || sin máscara (unmasked).

barefoot [-fut] *adj/adv* descalzo, za.

bareheaded [-'hedid] *adj/adv* descubierto, ta; con la cabeza descubierta.

barely [-li] *adv* apenas (hardly); *I barely know him* le conozco apenas || escasamente (insufficiently); *a barely furnished room* una habitación escasamente amueblada.

bareness [-nis] *n* desnudez *f* || lo escueto (of style).

bargain ['bɑːgin] *n* trato *m* (agreement) || negocio *m* (deal) || ganga *f* (advantageous purchase) || — *at a bargain price* a precio de saldo || *bargain counter* o *basement* sección *f* de oportunidades || *bargain day* día *m* de saldos || *bargain driver* regateador, ra || *bargain price* precio irrisorio || *bargain sale* saldos *m pl*, venta *f* de saldos || *into the bargain* además, por añadidura || *it's a bargain!* ¡trato hecho! || *to drive a hard bargain* imponer duras condiciones, pedir mucho || *to get the best of the bargain* salir ganando || *to make* o *to strike* o *to drive a bargain* cerrar un trato || *to make the best of a bad bargain* poner a mal tiempo buena cara.

bargain ['bɑːgin] *vt* ofrecer (to offer to exchange); *he bargained his life in return for his son's safety* ofreció su vida a cambio de la seguridad de su hijo || regatear (to haggle over) || trocar (to barter) || *to bargain away* malbaratar.
◆ *vi* negociar; *to bargain with s.o. for sth.* negociar algo con alguien || regatear (to haggle) || *to bargain for* o *on* esperar (to expect), contar con (to count on).

bargaining [-iŋ] *n* negociación *f* || regateo *m* (haggling) || *collective bargaining* negociaciones colectivas, contrato colectivo.

barge [bɑːdʒ] *n* barcaza *f*, gabarra *f* (for river transport) || falúa *f* (of naval officers, royalty) || SP carga *f* (in football); *fair barge* carga legal.

barge [bɑːdʒ] *vi* *to barge about* moverse torpemente, dar tumbos (to move clumsily) || *to barge in* entrometerse (to interfere) || *to barge in on s.o.* importunar *or* molestar a alguien || *to barge into s.o.* tropezar con alguien || *to barge into the room* irrumpir en la habitación.
◆ *vt* transportar en barcazas || empujar (to push) || SP cargar (in football) || *to barge one's way through the crowd* abrirse paso entre la multitud a empujones.

bargee [bɑːdʒiː] *n* gabarrero *m*, barquero *m* || FAM *to swear like a bargee* jurar como un carretero.

bargeman ['bɑːdʒmən] *n* US ⟶ **bargee.**

barge pole ['bɑːdʒpəul] *n* bichero *m* || FIG *I wouldn't touch it with a barge pole* no lo cogería ni con pinzas (unpleasant object), no quiero saber nada de eso (unpleasant matter).

barhop ['bɑːr,hɔp] *vi* US *to go barhopping* ir de copeo.

barilla [bə'riljə] *n* BOT barrilla *f*.

barite ['bærait] *n* CHEM baritina *f*.

baritone ['bæritəun] *n* MUS barítono *m*.

barium ['bɛəriəm] *n* CHEM bario *m*.

bark [bɑːk] *n* corteza *f* (of tree, of bush) || ladrido *m* (of dog) || estampido *m* (of cannon, pistol) || tos *f* fuerte, tos *f* perruna (cough) | TECH casca *f* (for tanning) || MAR bricbarca *f* (barque) || — FIG *his bark is worse than his bite* perro ladrador poco mordedor || MED *Peruvian bark* quina *f*.

bark [bɑːk] *vt* descortezar (a tree) || despellejar, desollar (to graze) || curtir (to tan) || FIG vociferar, gritar; *to bark an order* gritar una orden.
◆ *vi* ladrar (*at* a) (dogs) || FIG rugir (people, cannon) || FAM toser (to cough) || FAM *to bark up the wrong tree* equivocarse.

barkeeper ['bɑː,kiːpə*] *n* tabernero *m*.

barkentine ['bɑːkəntain] *n* MAR goleta *f*.

barker ['bɑːkə*] *n* pregonero *m* (in fairgrounds, etc.) || FIG gritón, ona (shouter) || máquina *f* para descortezar (for barking trees) || pistola *f* (pistol) || cañón *m* (cannon).

barley ['bɑːli] *n* cebada *f* (cereal); *pearl, peeled barley* cebada perlada, mondada.

barleycorn [-kɔːn] *n* grano *m* de cebada.

barley field [-fiːld] *n* cebadal *m*.

barley sugar [-ʃugə*] *n* azúcar *m* cande.

barley water [-,wɔːtə*] *n* hordiate *m*.

barm [bɑːm] *n* levadura *f* de cerveza.

barmaid ['bɑːmeid] *n* camarera *f* [AMER moza].

barman ['bɑːmən] *n* camarero *m* [AMER mozo].
— OBSERV El plural de esta palabra es *barmen*.

barmy ['bɑːmi] *adj* espumoso, sa (frothy) || FAM chiflado, da; chalado, da (stupid).

barn [bɑːn] *n* granero *m* (for storing grain) || US establo *m* (for cows) | cuadra *f* (for horses) || cobertizo *m* (for vehicles) || PHYS barnio *m*, barn *m* || FIG caserón *m* (big, bare house) || US *barn dance* baile *m* popular que tiene lugar en un granero | *streetcar barn* cochera *f*.

Barnabas ['bɑːnəbəs]; **Barnaby** ['bɑːnəbi] *pr n* Bernabé *m*.

Barnabite ['bɑːnəbait] *n* bernabita *m* (monk).

barnacle ['bɑːnəkl] *n* ZOOL percebe *m* (crustacean) | barnacla *m* (arctic goose) || FAM lapa *f*.
◆ *pl* acial *m sing* (to restrain horse).

barn owl ['bɑːnaul] *n* ZOOL lechuza *f*.

barnstorm ['bɑːnstɔːm] *vi* US recorrer el campo representando comedias (actors) | recorrer el campo pronunciando discursos políticos, para una campaña electoral (politicians).

barnyard ['bɑːnjɑːd] *n* corral *m* || *barnyard fowl* aves *f pl* de corral.

barograph ['bærəgrɑːf] *n* barógrafo *m*.

barometer [bə'rɔmitə*] *n* barómetro *m*; *aneroid, cistern, mercury, recording barometer* barómetro aneroide, de cubeta, de mercurio, registrador.

barometric [,bærə'metrik]; **barometrical** [-əl] *adj* barométrico, ca.

baron ['bærən] *n* barón *m* (nobleman) || doble solomillo *m* (joint of meat) || FIG magnate *m* (magnate); *oil baron* magnate del petróleo.
— OBSERV Los barones ingleses tienen derecho al título de *Lord*, los barones extranjeros al de *Baron*.

baronaje ['bærənidʒ] *n* baronía *f* (class, domain, rank) || lista *f* de lores (book).

baroness ['bærənis] *n* baronesa *f*.

baronet ['bærənit] *n* baronet *m*.

baronial [bə'rəunjəl] *adj* de barón *m* || FIG señorial.

barony ['bærəni] *n* baronía *f*.

baroque [bə'rɔk] *adj* barroco, ca.
◆ *n* barroco *m*.

baroque pearl [-,pəːl] *n* barrueco *m*, berrueco *m* (irregularly shaped pearl).

baroscope ['bærəskəup] *n* PHYS baroscopio *m*.

barque [bɑːk] *n* MAR bricbarca *f* || POET barca *f*.

barquentine ['bɑːkəntiːn] *n* goleta *f*.

barrack ['bærək] *vt* acuartelar (soldiers) || abuchear (to jeer).

barracking [-iŋ] *n* MIL acuartelamiento *m* || abucheo *m* (jeer).

barrack room ['bærəkrum] *n* dormitorio *m* de tropa || *barrack-room joke* chiste *m* verde.

barracks ['bærəks] *pl n* cuartel *m sing* || FIG caserón *m sing* (large, drab house) || US *barracks bag* mochila *f*.

barrack square ['bærək'skwɛə*] *n* MIL plaza *f* de armas.

barracuda [,bærə'kuːdə] *n* barracuda *f* (fish).

barrage ['bærɑːʒ] *n* presa *f* (dam) || barrera *f* de fuego (of shellfire); *creeping barrage* barrera de fuego móvil || barrera *f* (of balloons) || FIG bombardeo *m*, andanada *f* (of questions).

barrage ['bærɑːʒ] *vt* bombardear (to bombard).

barrator; barrater ['bærətə*] *n* JUR pleitista *m*, picapleitos *m inv* || MAR persona *f* culpable de baratería.

barratry ['bærətri] *n* JUR propensión *f* a ocasionar pleitos (incitement of litigations) | baratería *f* || MAR baratería *f* (of the captain).

barred [bɑːd] *adj* listado, da; rayado, da (striped) || atrancado, da (door) || ⟶ **bar.**

barrel ['bærəl] *n* tonel *m*, cuba *f*, barril *m* (of wine, etc.) || barril *m* (of herrings) || cañón *m* (of firearm, feather) || tronco *m* (of quadruped) || depósito *m* (of pen) || cubo *m*, tambor *m* (of watch) || caja *f* (of drum) || TECH tambor *m* || — ANAT *barrel of the ear* caja del tímpano || FAM *to be over a barrel* estar con el agua al cuello | *to scrape the bottom of the barrel* valerse del último recurso.

barrel ['bærəl] *vt* embarrilar, entonelar, poner en barriles (to put in barrels).
◆ *vi* FAM correr mucho.

barrel organ [-,ɔːgən] *n* MUS organillo *m*.

barrel roll [-,rəul] *n* AVIAT tonel (flying stunt).

barrel vault [-,vɔːlt] *n* ARCH bóveda *f* de cañón.

barren ['bærən] *adj* estéril (sterile) || árido, da; yermo, ma; estéril (land) || FIG infructuoso, sa; inútil (fruitless, vain) | vacío, a; estéril (mind, ideas) | seco, ca (style) || *barren of* desprovisto de, sin, falto de.
◆ *n* tierra *f* yerma.

barrenness [-nis] *n* esterilidad *f* (sterility) || aridez *f*, esterilidad *f* (of land).

barrette [bæ'ret] *n* pasador *m* (hair slide).

barricade [,bæri'keid] *n* barricada *f*.

barricade [,bæri'keid] *vt* levantar barricadas en (a street) || FIG *to barricade o.s.* parapetarse.

barrier ['bæriə*] *n* barrera *f* || FIG barrera *f*; *customs barriers* barreras arancelarias || *sonic* o *sound barrier* barrera del sonido.

barrier reef [-,riːf] *n* banco *m or* barrera *f* de coral || *the great Barrier Reef* la gran Barrera.

barring ['bɑːriŋ] *prep* excepto, salvo; *barring death* salvo la muerte.

barrister ['bæristə*]; **barrister-at-law** [-ət'lɔː] *n* abogado *m* que puede defender causas en los tribunales superiores británicos.

barroom ['bɑːrum] *n* bar *m*.

barrow ['bærəu] *n* carretilla *f* (wheelbarrow) || carro *m*, carreta *f* (handcart) || túmulo *m* (grave mound) || GEOGR colina *f* || *barrow boy* vendedor *m* ambulante de fruta.

barstool ['bɑːstul] *n* taburete *m* de bar.

bartender ['bɑː,tendə*] *n* camarero *m* de bar, «barman» *m*.

barter ['bɑːtə*] *n* trueque *m*, permuta *f*.

barter ['bɑːtə*] *vi* trocar; *to barter for furs with spirits* trocar licores por pieles.
◆ *vt* trocar (to trade).

Bartholomew [bɑː'θɔləmjuː] *pr n* Bartolomé *m*.

barycentre; US **barycenter** [,bæri,sentə*] *n* baricentro *m*.

barye ['bæri] *n* PHYS baria *f* (unit of pressure).

barysphere ['bæri,sfiːə*] *n* barisfera *f*.

baryta [bæ'riːtə] *n* CHEM barita *f*.

barytes [bæ'raitiːz] *n* MIN baritina *f*.

barytone ['bæritəun] *n* barítono *m*.

basal ['beisl] *adj* fundamental, básico, ca (essential) || MED basal (metabolism).

basalt ['bæsɔːlt] *n* basalto *m*.

basaltic [bə'sɔːltik] *adj* basáltico, ca.

basan ['bæsən] *n* badana *f*.

bascule ['bæskjuːl] *n* TECH báscula *f* || *bascule bridge* puente basculante *or* levadizo.

base [beis] *n* base *f* (lowest part, foundation, stand, etc.) || raíz *f* (of word) || pie *m* (of mountain) || MATH & CHEM base *f* || MIL base *f*; *naval, airforce base* base naval, aérea || ARCH basa *f* (of column) || SP base *f* || FIG base *f* || — *a drink with a rum base* una bebida a base de ron || *base line* línea *f* de saque (in tennis) || *off base* equivocado, da (mistaken); desprevenido, da (unawares), de improviso (unexpectedly) || FAM *to get to first base* vencer la primera dificultad.

◆ *adj* despreciable, bajo, ja | degradante (degrading) || bajo, ja; de baja ley (metals) || bajo, ja; *base Latin* bajo latín || de base, básico, ca (basic) || MUS bajo, ja (bass).

base [beis] *vt* basar, fundar, fundamentar (*on* en) (arguments, etc.) || estacionar (troops).

baseball [-bɔːl] *n* béisbol *m*.

baseboard [-bɔːd] *n* US zócalo *m*.

baseborn [-bɔːn] *adj* de baja estirpe, de humilde cuna (humble) || bastardo, da (illegitimate).

base camp [-kæmp] *n* MIL campamento *m* base.

Basel ['bɑːzɔl] *pr n* GEOGR Basilea.

baseless ['beislis] *adj* infundado, da; que carece de base *or* de fundamento (groundless).

basement ['beismənt] *n* ARCH basamento *m* (substructure) || sótano *m* (cellar).

baseness ['beisnis] *n* bajeza *f*, vileza *f* (vileness) || ilegitimidad *f* (illegitimacy).

bash [bæʃ] *n* FAM golpetazo *m*, golpazo *m* (blow) || bollo *m* (dent) || FIG intento *m*, tentativa *f* (attempt) || — FIG & FAM *to have a bash* intentarlo | *to have a bash at doing sth.* intentar hacer algo.

bash [bæʃ] *vt* FAM asestar un golpe a (to hit) || — *to bash one's head on a wall* darse con la cabeza en la pared || FAM *to bash up* dar un golpe a (to hit).
◆ *vi* FAM *to bash into s.o.* darse un porrazo contra uno, estrellarse contra uno.

bashful [-ful] *adj* tímido, da; vergonzoso, sa (shy).

bashing [-iŋ] *n* FAM paliza *f*, tunda *f*.

basic ['beisik] *adj* básico, ca; *basic industries* industrias básicas | básico, ca; fundamental, esencial (fundamental) || básico, ca (metals) || elemental; *basic Spanish* español elemental || CHEM & GEOL básico, ca.
◆ *pl n* lo esencial.

basic; Basic ['beisik] *n* INFORM basic *m*.

BASIC ['beisik] *abbr of [Beginners All-purpose Symbolic Instruction Code]* lenguaje BASIC.

basically [-əli] *adv* esencialmente, fundamentalmente.

basicity [bei'sisiti] *n* CHEM basicidad *f*.

basidiomycete [bæˌsidiɔ'maisiːt] *n* basidiomiceto *m* (fungus).

basidium [bæ'sidiɔm] *n* basidio *m* (fungus).
— OBSERV El plural de *basidium* es *basidia*.

basil [bæzl] *n* BOT albahaca *f* (planta).

Basil [bæzl] *pr n* Basilio *m*.

basilar [bə'zilə*]; **basilary** [-ri] *adj* ANAT basilar.

basilic [bə'zilik] *adj* ANAT basílico, ca (vein).

basilica [bə'zilikə] *n* basílica *f* (church).

basilisk ['bæzilisk] *n* basilisco *m* (legendary animal, lizard).

basin ['beisn] *n* palangana *f*, jofaina *f* (washbowl) || lavabo *m* (washbasin) || barreño *m* (for washing up) || cuenco *m* (dish) || taza *f* (of fountain) || dársena *f* (in port) || platillo *m* (of scales) || GEOGR cuenca *f* (containing river, lake) | depresión *f* (depression).

basinet ['bæsinet] *n* bacinete *m* (helmet).

basinful ['beisnful] *n* FAM *to have had a basinful* estar harto.

basis ['beisis] *n* base *f* || — *on a weekly, monthly basis* cada semana, mes || *on the basis of* teniendo como base, si tomamos como base, sobre la base de.
— OBSERV El plural de *basis* es *bases*.

bask [bɑːsk] *vi* tomar el sol (to sunbathe) || dejarse acariciar (to be caressed); *to bask in the soft breeze* dejarse acariciar por la suave brisa || FIG gozar, disfrutar (*in* de); *to bask in the king's favour* gozar del favor del rey || *to bask in the sun* tomar el sol.

basket ['bɑːskit] *n* cesto *m*, cesta *f* || canasta *f* (with two handles) || cesta *f* (for shopping) || barquilla *f* (in balloons) || canasta *f*, cesta *f* (in basketball) || SP *to score a basket* encestar.

basketball [-bɔːl] *n* SP baloncesto *m* [AMER basketball *m*] (game) | balón *m* de baloncesto, balón (ball).

basket-handle [-ˌhændl] *adj* ARCH *basket-handle arch* arco *m* rebajado *or* carpanel *or* apainelado.

basket lunch [-lʌntʃ] *n* US merienda *f*.

basketry ['bɑːskətri] *n* cestería *f*.

basketwork ['bɑːskitwɔːk] *n* cestería *f*.

Basle [bɑːl] *pr n* GEOGR Basilea.

basque [bæsk] *n* jubón *m*.

Basque [bæsk] *pr n* GEOGR vasco, ca || vasco *m*, vascuence *m* (language).
◆ *adj* vasco, ca || — *Basque country* País Vasco [parte francesa] || *Basque provinces* Provincias Vascongadas (in Spain).

bas-relief ['bæsriˌliːf] *n* ARCH bajorrelieve *m*, bajo relieve *m*.

bass [bæs] *n* ZOOL perca *f* (freshwater fish) | róbalo *m*, lubina *f* (marine fish) || BOT tilo *m*.

bass [beis] *n* MUS bajo *m* (part, singer) | contrabajo *m*, violón *m* (instrument).
◆ *adj* MUS bajo, ja || — MUS *bass clef* clave *f* de fa | *bass drum* bombo *m* | *bass fiddle* contrabajo *m* | *bass horn* tuba *f* | *double bass* violón *m*, contrabajo *m*.

basset ['bæsit] *n* GEOL afloramiento *m* (of stratum) || perro *m* basset (dog).

basset ['bæsit] *vi* GEOL aflorar.

basso ['bæsəu] *n* MUS bajo *m*.

bassoon [bə'suːn] *n* MUS fagot *m* || MUS *double bassoon* contrafagot *m*.

bassoonist [-ist] *n* MUS bajonista *m*, fagotista *m*.

bast [bæst] *n* BOT líber *m*.

bastard ['bæstəd] *n* bastardo, da || POP cabrón *m*, hijo *m* de perra.
◆ *adj* bastardo, da (illegitimate) || FIG falso, sa; espurio, ria (not genuine) | degenerado, da; corrompido, da (degenerate) || híbrido, da (hybrid) || TECH bastardo, da; *bastard file* lima bastarda; *bastard sugar* azúcar bastarda || *bastard title* anteportada *f*, portadilla *f*.

bastardize ['bæstədaiz] *vt* declarar bastardo *or* ilegítimo || FIG degradar, corromper (to debase).
◆ *vi* FIG degenerar.

bastardy ['bæstədi] *n* bastardía *f*.

baste [beist] *vt* CULIN rociar (a joint) || US hilvanar (in sewing) || FAM zurrar, apalear (to beat).

bastinado [ˌbæsti'neidəu] *n* tunda *f* de palos, zurra *f* (beating).

basting ['beistiŋ] *n* US hilván *m*, hilvanado *m* (tacking) | hilo *m* de hilvanar (thread) || zurra *f*, paliza *f* (beating).

bastion ['bæstiən] *n* MIL & FIG baluarte *m*, bastión *m*.

bat [bæt] *n* ZOOL murciélago *m* || SP bate *m* (in cricket, baseball) | raqueta *f* (in table tennis) | turno *m* (turn to bat) || golpe *m* (blow) || pala *f*, paleta *f* (of washerwoman) || FAM juerga *f* (spree); *to go on a bat* ir de juerga | ritmo *m*, paso *m*, velocidad *f* (pace) || — *at a rare bat* a toda velocidad || FIG *off one's own bat* por su cuenta | *right off the bat* inmediatamente (immediately), sin más deliberación (without thinking) | *to be as blind as a bat* no ver tres en un burro, ser más ciego que un topo | *to have bats in the belfry* estar mal de la azotea.

bat [bæt] *vi* batear (in cricket, baseball) || FIG *to go to bat for s.o.* acudir en ayuda de alguien, respaldar a alguien.
◆ *vt* golpear (to hit) || — FIG *nobody batted an eyelid* nadie pestañeó, nadie se inmutó | *to bat an idea around* o *back and forth* debatir una idea | *to bat down s.o.'s arguments* echar por tierra los argumentos de uno || *to bat one's eyelashes* parpadear || *to bat the ball out of the cricket ground* mandar la pelota fuera del campo || FIG *without batting an eye* o *an eyelid* sin pestañear, sin inmutarse.

batata [bə'tɑːtə] *n* BOT batata *f*.

Batavian [bə'teiviən] *adj/n* bátavo, va.

batch [bætʃ] *n* hornada *f* (of loaves, cakes) || partida *f*, lote *m*, serie *f*, remesa *f* (of goods) || montón *m* (of letters) || MIL partida *f* (of soldiers) || tanda *f*, grupo *m* (of people) || INFORM *batch processing* procesamiento *m* por lotes *or* batch.

bate [beit] *n* solución *f* alcalina.

bate [beit] *vt* disminuir, rebajar (to reduce) || *with bated breath* en voz baja.

bath [bɑːθ] *n* baño *m*; *to have* o *to take a bath* tomar un baño || bañera *f* (bathtub) || CHEM & PHOT *m* || US cuarto *m* de baño (bathroom).

bath [bɑːθ] *pl* piscina *f sing* (swimming pool) || casa *f* de baños (for bathing) || balneario *m sing* (medicinal).
◆ *adj* de baño; *bath towel* toalla de baño; *bath mat* alfombra de baño; *bath salts* sales de baño.

bath [bɑːθ] *vt* bañar, dar un baño a.
◆ *vi* bañarse, tomar un baño.

Bath chair [-tʃɛə*] *n* silla *f* de ruedas.

bathe [beið] *n* baño *m* (in river, sea, etc.).

bathe [beið] *vt* bañar (to wash) || MED lavar (a wound) | bañarse (one's eyes) || bañar; *the lake bathed the foot of the mountain* el lago bañaba el pie de la montaña || bañar (with light) || *face bathed in tears* cara bañada en lágrimas.
◆ *vi* bañarse (in river, sea, etc.); *to go bathing* ir a bañarse || FIG bañarse.

bather ['beiðə*] *n* bañista *m* & *f*.

bathetic [bə'θetik] *adj* ridículo, la; que pasa de lo sublime a lo ridículo *or* trivial.

bathhouse ['bɑːθhaus] *n* US caseta *f* (on the beach) | casa *f* de baños (public baths).

bathing ['beiðiŋ] *n* baños *m pl*; *sea bathing* baños de mar || *no bathing* prohibido bañarse.

bathing beauty [-'bjuːti] *n* belleza *f* de la playa.

bathing cap [-kæp] *n* gorro *m* de baño.

bathing costume [-ˌkɔstjuːm] *n* traje *m* de baño, bañador *m*.

bathing suit [-sjuːt] *n* bañador *m*, traje *m* de baño.

bathing trunks [-trʌŋks] *pl n* bañador *m sing*, calzón *m sing* de baño (for men).

bathos ['beiθɔs] *n* paso *m* de lo sublime a lo ridículo *or* trivial (in literature) || trivialidad *f* (triteness) || sensiblería *f* (excessive sentimentality).

bathrobe ['bɑːθrəub] *n* albornoz *m*.

bathroom ['bɑːθrum] *n* cuarto *m* de baño.

bathtub ['bɑːθtʌb] *n* bañera *f*, baño *m*.

bathymeter [bæ'θimitər] *n* batímetro *m*.

bathyscaphe ['bæθiskæf] *n* batiscafo *m*.

bathysphere ['bæθisfiə*] *n* batisfera *f*.

batik [bə'tiːk] *n* batik *m*.

batiste [bæ'tiːst] *n* batista *f* (material).

batman ['bætmən] *n* MIL ordenanza *m*.

— OBSERV El plural de esta palabra es *batmen*.

baton ['bætən] *n* porra *f* (of a policeman) || MUS batuta *f* || bastón *m* de mando (symbol of office) || SP testigo *m* (in relay races).

batrachian [bə'treikjən] *adj* ZOOL batracio, cia.
◆ *n* ZOOL batracio *m*.

bats [bæts] *adj* FAM chiflado, da.

batsman [bætsmən] *n* SP bateador *m* || oficial *m* que dirige los aterrizajes [en portaaviones].
— OBSERV El plural de esta palabra es *batsmen*.

battalion [bə'tæljən] *n* MIL batallón *m*.
◆ *pl* FIG batallón *m sing*, ejército *m sing*; *battalions of ants* un ejército de hormigas.

batten ['bætn] *n* listón *m* (strip of wood) || varal *m* (of loom) || varal *m* (in a theatre).

batten ['bætn] *vt* listonar, reforzar con listones (to strengthen with battens) || MAR *to batten down the hatches* fijar con listones los encerados de escotilla.
◆ *vi* cebarse (*on* de) (to glut o.s.) || FIG enriquecerse, prosperar (*on* a costa de) (to another's detriment); *to batten on the State* enriquecerse a costa del Estado | deleitarse, refocilarse (to delight in) | agarrarse a (an argument).

batter ['bætə*] *n* bateador *m* (in cricket, baseball) || pasta *f*, albardilla *f* (in cooking) || PRINT defecto *m* (defect).

batter ['bætə*] *vt* apalear, moler a palos (people) || azotar; *the giant waves battered the ship* las gigantescas olas azotaban el barco || estropear (to ruin); *a battered old hat* un viejo sombrero estropeado || abollar (to dent); *a battered car* un coche abollado || magullar (to bruise) || MIL cañonear, destruir a cañonazos (with cannons) || ARCH dar inclinación a (a wall) || vapulear, criticar violentamente (to criticize) || — *to batter about* maltratar || *to batter s.o. to death* matar a uno a palos || *to batter sth. down* derribar algo, echar algo abajo || *to batter the door in* derribar la puerta, echar la puerta abajo.
◆ *vi* chocar, golpearse (*on* o *against* contra) (to beat, to pound) || ARCH inclinarse (a wall) || *to batter at the door* golpear la puerta.

battering [-riŋ] *n* MIL cañoneo *m*, destrucción *f* a cañonazos.

battering ram [-riŋræm] *n* ariete *m*.

battery ['bætəri] *n* batería *f* (of kitchen utensils) || batería *f* (of hens) || serie *f*, grupo *m*, juego *m* (series set) || JUR agresión *f* || MUS batería *f* (percussion section) || MIL & MAR batería *f* (of artillery, guns) || ELECTR batería *f* (set of cells); *car battery* batería de coche | pila *f* (of transistor radio, etc.) || SP el lanzador y el bateador (in baseball) || — MAR *battery deck* batería || *battery hen* gallina *f* de batería de cría || *storage battery* acumulador *m*, batería *f*.

batting ['bætiŋ] *n* guata *f* (cotton fibre) || SP bateo *m*, acción *f* de batear (cricket, baseball).

battle ['bætl] *n* batalla *f*, combate *m*; *to fight a battle* librar una batalla || FIG lucha *f* || — *battle array* o *formation* orden *m* de combate || FIG *battle royal* batalla campal || *line of battle* frente *m* de batalla || *pitched battle* batalla campal || FIG *that's half the battle* ya hay medio camino andado || *to do battle* librar batalla || FIG *to do battle for* luchar por | *to fight a losing battle* luchar por una causa perdida || *to give battle* dar la batalla || *to join battle* trabar batalla || *to offer battle* presentar batalla.

battle ['bætl] *vt* combatir, luchar contra || *to battle one's way through the crowd* abrirse camino entre la multitud.
◆ *vi* combatir, luchar (*against* contra; *for* por) || FIG luchar; *to battle for one's rights* luchar por sus derechos.

battle-axe; US **battle-ax** [-æks] *n* hacha *f* de armas (weapon) || FIG arpía *f*.

battle cruiser [-,kru:zə*] *n* MAR crucero *m*.

battle cry [-krai] *n* MIL grito *m* de guerra || FIG lema *m* (slogan).

battledore [-dɔ:*] *n* raqueta *f* (racket) || pala *f*, paleta *f* (for washing clothes) || pala *f* (for placing loaves).

battle dress [-dres] *n* MIL uniforme *m* de campaña.

battlefield [-fi:ld] *n* MIL campo *m* de batalla.

battlement [-mnt] *n* ARCH almena *f*.

battleship [-ʃip] *n* acorazado *m*.

battue [bæ'tu:] *n* batida *f* (hunting) || FIG matanza *f* (mass killing).

batty ['bæti] *adj* FAM chalado, da (crazy).

bauble ['bɔ:bl] *n* chuchería *f*, baratija *f* (worthless object) || cetro *m* de bufón (of a jester) || juguete *m* (toy).

baulk [bɔ:k] *n/vt* → **balk.**

bauxite ['bɔ:ksait] *n* bauxita *f*.

Bavaria [bə'vɛəriə] *pr n* GEOGR Baviera *f*.

Bavarian [-n] *adj/n* Bávaro, ra.

bawd [bɔ:d] *n* patrona *f* de burdel | alcahueta *f* (go-between).

bawdy [-i] *adj* obsceno, na; indecente, verde || *bawdy house* lupanar *m*.

bawl [bɔ:l] *vi* gritar, chillar (to shout) || berrear (to bellow) || *to bawl at s.o.* gritarle a uno.
◆ *vt* gritar, vociferar || — *to bawl out* gritar, vociferar; *to bawl out s.o.'s name* vociferar el nombre de uno || FAM *to bawl s.o. out* echar una bronca a uno.

bay [bei] *n* GEOGR bahía *f*; *bay of Pigs* bahía de Cochinos | golfo *m* (large); *bay of Biscay* golfo de Vizcaya | abra *f* (small) | abra *f*, entrada *f* de un llano en una cordillera (opening between mountains) || bayo *m* (colour) || caballo *m* bayo (horse) || crujía *f* (division of a building) || nave *f* (of factory) || pajar *m* (in a barn) || tramo *m* (of bridge) || vano *m*, hueco *m* (window) || ladrido *m*, aullido *m* (barking, howling) || BOT laurel *m* (laurel) || — *at bay* acorralado, da (an animal) || *bomb bay* compartimiento *m* de bombas || *to bring a wild boar to bay* acorralar a un jabalí || *to keep* o *to hold the enemy at bay* mantener a raya al enemigo.
◆ *pl* corona *f sing* de laurel (crown) || FIG laureles *m* (glory) || *to carry off the bays* ganar laureles.
◆ *adj* bayo, ya.

bay [bei] *vi* ladrar (to bark) || aullar (to howl).
◆ *vt* ladrar a; *to bay the moon* ladrar a la luna || acorralar (to corner).

bayadere ['baiə,di:ə*] *n* MIL bayadera *f*.

bayonet ['beiənit] *n* MIL bayoneta *f*; *to fix bayonets* armar *or* calar la bayoneta; *bayonet charge* carga a la bayoneta || TECH bayoneta *f*.

bayonet ['beiənit] *vt* MIL pasar a la bayoneta.

Bayonne [bæ'jɔ:n] *pr n* GEOGR Bayona.

bayou ['bæju:] *n* US brazo *m* pantanoso [de un río].

bay window ['bei'windəu] *n* ventana *f* saledíza || FAM barriga *f* (potbelly).

bazaar [bə'zɑ:*] *n* bazar *m* (Oriental market) || venta *f* benéfica (for charity).

bazan ['beizən] *n* badana *f*.

bazooka [bə'zu:kə] *n* bazooka *m*, bazuca *m*.

BBC *abbr of [British Broadcasting Corporation]* corporación nacional británica de radiodifusión.

BC *abbr of [before Christ]* A. de C., antes de Cristo.

be* [bi:] *vi*

1. CASES WHERE *to be* IS TRANSLATED BY *ser* **2.** TRANSLATED BY *estar* **3.** VERBS WHICH MAY REPLACE *ser* AND *estar* **4.** *to be* IN THE PASSIVE VOICE **5.** *to be* WITH A GERUND **6.** OTHER TRANSLATIONS **7.** IMPERSONAL *to be* **8.** *to be* AS A COMPOUND VERB **9.** *to be* IN ELLIPTICAL CONSTRUCTIONS **10.** EXPRESSIONS WITH *to be*.

1. *To be* IS TRANSLATED BY *ser*

a) when followed by a noun, a pronoun, a numeral, a clause or an infinitive; *he is a doctor* es médico; *the prettiest of the girls is Catherine* la más guapa de las chicas es Catalina; *that is nothing* eso no es nada; *it was you who did it* eres tú quien lo hizo; *we were four* eramos cuatro; *the treasure is what interests him* el tesoro es lo que le interesa; *his ambition is to write an opera* su ambición es escribir una ópera.

b) when followed by an adjective which indicates an essential or inherent characteristic of the subject; *ice is cold* el hielo es frío; *this child is naughty* este niño es malo; *the Mediterranean is blue* el Mediterráneo es azul; *he is rich, obstinate* es rico, obstinado; *he is happy* es feliz.

c) in certain cases when used as an auxiliary verb in the passive voice (see no. 4 below).

d) when used with certain adjectives such as *feliz, infeliz, cierto, indudable, notorio, evidente, frecuente, posible, imposible, probable, improbable, necesario.*

e) when the complement indicates possession, authorship, provenance, composition, cause or purpose; *this watch is Raymond's* este reloj es de Ramón; *it's a Gainsborough* es de Gainsborough; *Barry is from London* Barry es de Londres; *this table is mahogany* esta mesa es de caoba; *it was because of his brother that he was arrested* fue a causa de su hermano que le detuvieron; *this polish is for black shoes* este betún es para zapatos negros.

2. *To be* IS TRANSLATED BY *estar*

a) when used with an adjective or a phrase which indicates an accidental or temporary state; *my tea is cold* mi té está frío; *the child is unhappy when his mother is not there* el niño está triste cuando no está su madre; *the sky was overcast when the storm broke* el cielo estaba encapotado cuando estalló la tormenta; *my uncle is ill* mi tío está enfermo; *how are you?* ¿cómo estás?; *Mary is very pretty today* María está muy guapa hoy; *the soup is too salty* la sopa está demasiado salada; *yesterday you were in a bad mood* ayer estabas de mal humor.

b) to express position in space or time: *he is in the garden* está en el jardín; *Paris is in France* París está en Francia; *we are in summer* estamos en verano.

c) in certain cases when used as an auxiliary verb in the passive voice (see no. 4 below).

d) when used with certain adjectives such as *contento, descontento, satisfecho, insatisfecho, solo, enfermo.*

3. VERBS WHICH MAY REPLACE *ser* AND *estar*

Ser and *estar* may occasionally be replaced by several semi-auxiliary verbs:

a) by *resultar* or *quedar* when the predicate indicates the consequence of a previous action or event; *he was injured in an accident* resultó herido en un accidente; *he was transformed by his journey* quedó transformado por su viaje.

b) by *ir*; *he is always well dressed* siempre va bien vestido; *andar*; *he is always in a bad mood* anda siempre de mal humor; *encontrarse* or *hallarse*; *we were in Madrid when it happened* nos encontrábamos en Madrid cuando ocurrió; *llegar*; *he is always on time* siempre llega a la hora.

c) by *seguir* or *continuar* to indicate a continued state; *he is still ill* sigue enfermo; *he is still at university* continúa en la universidad.

4. *To be* AS AN AUXILIARY IN THE PASSIVE VOICE
a) ser is used as the auxiliary verb in Spanish if the agent, whether expressed or not, is active; *he was arrested by the police* fue arrestado por la policía; *to be loved is every woman's ideal* ser amada es el ideal de toda mujer.
b) estar is used as the auxiliary verb to emphasize the result of an action rather than the action itself; *Spain is separated from France by the Pyrenees* España está separada de Francia por los Pirineos.
c) in Spanish the use of the passive form is often avoided, being replaced by the active form if the agent is expressed or by the reflexive form if the agent is not expressed; *he was knocked down by a car* le atropelló un coche; *English is spoken the world over* se habla inglés en el mundo entero.
5. *To be* WITH A GERUND
To be with a gerund is translated:
a) in most cases by *estar* with the gerund of the accompanying verb; *he is always smoking* siempre está fumando; *they are eating* están comiendo.
b) by the present or future indicative of the accompanying verb when the idea expressed is one of action in the near future; *he is leaving for Madrid tomorrow* se marcha a Madrid mañana.
6. OTHER TRANSLATIONS OF *to be*
a) to be, when followed by certain adjectives, and when the subject is a person or an animal, is often translated by *tener* with the corresponding noun; *he is hot, cold, hungry, thirsty, ashamed, sleepy, in a hurry* tiene calor, frío, hambre, sed, vergüenza, sueño, prisa; *my hands are cold* tengo las manos frías; *to be right* tener razón; *how old are you?* ¿cuántos años tienes?; *I am twenty years old* tengo veinte años.
b) with adjectives expressing emotion caused by a certain event *to be* is translated by *quedarse; I was flabbergasted* me quedé boquiabierto; *he was utterly astonished* se quedó extrañadísimo; *he was very disappointed* se quedó muy desilusionado.
7. IMPERSONAL *to be*
a) in the expression *there is* (there are, there were, etc.) *to be* is translated by *haber; there were not many cars on the road* no había muchos coches en la carretera; *there is no bread* no hay pan.
b) when followed by an adverb or adverbial phrase of time or place, *to be* is translated by *ser* if the subject is impersonal; *do you know where he lives? I think it's here* ¿sabes dónde vive? creo que es aquí; *it is late* es tarde; *it will be in summer* será en verano; *it is one o'clock* es la una; *it was five o'clock* eran las cinco.
c) when used with an adjective in an impersonal expression *to be* is translated by *ser; it is important that I see him* es importante que le vea; *it is useless going now* es inútil ir ahora (notice, however, that with the adjective *claro* the verb *estar* must be used: *it is obvious that he is drunk* está claro que está borracho).
d) other impersonal expressions; *as though it were nothing at all* como quien no quiere la cosa; *he did it as though it were nothing at all* lo hizo como quien no quiere la cosa || *it is time to* ya es hora de || *it's about time!* ¡ya era hora!
8. *To be* AS A COMPOUND VERB
To be after estar después de; *you are after me in the queue* usted está después de mí en la cola | perseguir (to chase); *the hunters were after a fox* los cazadores perseguían un zorro | estar buscando; *what are you after there?* ¿qué estás buscando allí?; *I'm after a job* estoy buscando trabajo || ***to be at*** estar haciendo; *what are you at?* ¿qué estás haciendo? || — *they have been at it a long time* ya llevan mucho tiempo con ello || *while we are at it* de paso, ya que estamos || ***to be away*** estar fuera, estar ausente; *he has been away the whole week* ha estado fuera toda la semana || — *to be away on business* estar en viaje de negocios || *to be well away* estar bebido (to be drunk), estar completamente ensimismado (to be deeply engrossed), estar profundamente dormido (to be asleep) || ***to be before*** estar antes que *or* de; *you are before me* Vd. está antes que yo *or* antes de mí || ***to be for*** ser para; *is this tea for me?* ¿este té es para mí? | servir *or* ser para (to be used for); *this is for cutting your nails* esto sirve para cortarse las uñas | estar por, ser partidario de; *I'm for leaving it until tomorrow* yo estoy por dejarlo hasta mañana; *what team are you for?* ¿por qué equipo estás? || ***to be from*** ser de || ***to be in*** estar, estar en casa (at home); *is Fred in?* ¿está Federico en casa?, ¿está Federico? | estar (at the office) | estar en la cárcel (to be in prison) | estar en el poder; *the Liberals are in* los liberales están en el poder | estar de moda; *trousers are in this year* este año están de moda los pantalones | estar recogido; *the potatoes are in* las patatas están recogidas | haber llegado; *the train is in* ha llegado el tren | batear (in cricket and baseball) || ***to be in for*** ir a; *it looks like we are in for rain* parece que va a llover | tomar parte en, participar en (a competition), ser candidato a (a post), presentarse a (an exam) || ***to be off*** irse; *I'm off* me voy; *I think it's time we were off* creo que ya es hora que nos vayamos *or* de irnos; *I'm off to Madrid this weekend* me voy a Madrid este fin de semana | despegar (an aircraft) | acabar de tomar la salida (in sports); *they're off!* ¡acaban de tomar la salida! | estar fuera (absent) || ***to be on*** poner (film); *what film is on?* ¿qué película ponen? | dar; *the show is now on in Madrid* ahora dan el espectáculo en Madrid | estar en escena (actor) || ***to be out*** estar fuera, haber salido, no estar en casa; *Mrs Smith is out* la Señora Smith ha salido | estar de viaje (travelling) | pasar fuera; *to be out a lot* pasar mucho tiempo fuera; salir; *I was out with some friends yesterday* salí ayer con unos amigos | estar fuera, estar libre (prisoner) | haber salido, haberse publicado; *the book is out* ha salido el libro | haber salido (sun), estar abierto (flower), haber salido del cascarón (bird) | estar sin conocimiento; *he was out for seven seconds* estuvo sin conocimiento durante siete segundos | haberse apagado; *my cigarette is out* se ha apagado mi cigarrillo; estar apagado; *the fire is out* el fuego está apagado | acabarse, terminarse; *before the month is out* antes de que se acabe el mes | haberse agotado; *my patience is out* se me ha agotado la paciencia | haber pasado de moda, no estar ya de moda; *the miniskirt is out* ya no está de moda la minifalda | haberse descubierto; *the secret is out* el secreto se ha descubierto | estar fuera del poder; *now that my party is out* ahora que mi partido está fuera del poder | quedar descartado (possibility), estar eliminado (player), estar fuera del juego (ball), estar fuera de combate (boxer), estar desenvainado (sword) | estar equivocado (to be mistaken); *you are out in your accounts* está equivocado en sus cuentas | faltar (to have too little); *I am five pounds out* me faltan cinco libras | adelantar (to be fast); *his watch is ten minutes out* su reloj adelanta diez minutos | atrasar (to be slow); *his watch is two minutes out* su reloj atrasa dos minutos | haber vencido (lease) | haber sido presentada en sociedad (young girl) || ***to be over*** haberse terminado *or* acabado; *the film is over* la película se ha acabado | quedar; *is there any soup over?* ¿queda algo de sopa?|| ***to be to*** tener que, deber (to have to); *you are to go immediately* tienes que ir inmediatamente | deber (to intend to); *she was to stay two weeks* debía quedarse dos semanas | poder ser (to be possible); *it was not to be denied* no podía ser negado | ir a, deber (to be going to); *he was to die a week later* iba a morir una semana más tarde || *to be up* haberse levantado (out of bed); *is he up yet?* ¿ya se ha levantado? | estar procesado, da (for trial); *he is up for armed robbery* está procesado por robo a mano armada | acabarse; *our time is up* se nos acabó el tiempo ⟶ **up**.
9. *To be* IN ELLIPTICAL CONSTRUCTIONS
In such cases *to be* is often not translated into Spanish; *are you happy? I am* ¿estás contento? sí; *are you ready? no, I'm not* ¿estás listo? no; *he's back is he?* está de vuelta ¿ah sí?.
10. EXPRESSIONS WITH *to be*
As it were digamos, por decirlo así (so to speak) || *as things are* tal y como están las cosas || *be that as it may* sea lo que fuere || *father to be* futuro padre || *God is love* Dios es amor || *here I am and here I'll stay* aquí estoy y aquí me quedo || *how much is it?* ¿cuánto es?, ¿cuánto vale? || *if I were you* si yo fuera Vd., yo en su lugar || *I think, therefore I am* pienso, luego existo || *it's four months since I saw her* hace cuatro meses que no la veo || *it's not that...* no es que... || *it's the 15th of August* estamos a quince de agosto, es el quince de agosto || *leave me* o *let me be* déjame estar, déjame en paz || *let it be!* ¡déjalo! || *not to be missed* que no se debe perder || *not to be o.s.* encontrarse raro || *potatoes are ten pence* las patatas están a diez peniques *or* cuestan diez peniques || *so be it* así sea || *to be about to do* estar a punto de hacer || *to be a long time doing sth.* tardar mucho en hacer algo || *to be a mother to s.o.* ser una verdadera madre para uno || *to be had, to be taken in* dejarse engañar || *to be or not to be* ser o no ser || *to be sure* ¡claro está! (interjection), estar seguro (to be certain) || FIG & FAM *to be with it* estar al corriente *or* al tanto *or* al día (person), estar a la moda *or* de moda (clothes) || *to be with s.o. on sth.* estar de acuerdo con alguien acerca de algo || *we have been in this country (for) two months* llevamos dos meses en este país, hace dos meses que estamos aquí || *were it not for* de no ser por || *what is it to be?* ¿qué va a ser? (in bar) || *what is it to you?* ¿qué te importa? || *what is the date today?* ¿a cuántos estamos hoy? || *you are working enough as it is* ya trabajas bastante.
— OBSERV Ver la conjugación de este verbo en el compendio de gramática.
— OBSERV Pret ***was, were***; pp ***been***.

beach [biːtʃ] *n* playa *f*; *on the beach* en la playa || *beach umbrella* quitasol *m*, parasol *m*.

beach [biːtʃ] *vt/vi* varar.

beachcomber [-ˌkəumə*] *n* raquero *m* (man) || ola *f* (wave) || FIG inútil *m* (good-for-nothing).

beachhead [-hed] *n* cabeza *f* de playa.

beacon [ˈbiːkən] *n* almenara *f* (fire) || faro *m* (lighthouse) || MAR & AVIAT baliza *f* || FIG faro *m*, guía *m* || *aerial beacon* aerofaro *m*.

beacon [ˈbiːkən] *vt* MAR & AVIAT balizar || FIG guiar.

bead [biːd] *n* cuenta *f* (for rosary, necklace); *to thread beads* ensartar cuentas || abalorio *m* (of glass) || gota *f* (drop); *a bead of sweat* una gota de sudor || punto *m* de mira (sight of gun) || burbuja *f* (bubble) || talón *m* (of tyre) || ARCH junquillo *m*, astrágalo *m* (astragal) || CHEM perla *f* (in analysis) || *to draw a bead on* apuntar a.
◆ *pl* rosario *m sing* (rosary) || collar *m sing* (necklace) || — *string of beads* collar || *to tell one's beads* rezar el rosario, pasar las cuentas del rosario.

beading [-iŋ] *n* ARCH astrágalo *m*, junquillo *m* || cuentas *f pl*, abalorios *m pl* (beads).

beadle [ˈbiːdl] *n* pertiguero *m*, macero *m* (in church) || bedel *m* (in university) || alguacil *m* (in law courts).

beadledom [-dəm] *n* papeleo *m*.

beady [-i] *adj* de forma de abalorio || *beady eyes* ojos pequeños, redondos y brillantes.

beagle [ˈbiːgl] *n* beagle *m* (dog).

beak [biːk] *n* pico *m* (of bird) || nariz *f* ganchuda (hooked nose) || pitorro *m* (spout) || promontorio *m* (promontory) ‖ MAR espolón *m* (in galleys) ‖ punta *f* (of anvil) ‖ JUR juez *m* de paz (justice of the peace) | magistrado *m* (magistrate) ‖ MUS boquilla *f*.

beaker ['bi:kə*] *n* cubilete *m*, copa *f* (drinking vessel) ‖ jarra *f* (tumbler in plastic, pottery, etc.) ‖ CHEM cubeta *f* de precipitación.

beakiron ['bi:kaiən] *n* bigornia *f* (anvil).

be-all ['bi:ɔ:l] *n the be-all and end-all* la única razón de la existencia de uno, lo único que importa; *money must not be our be-all and end-all* el dinero no debe ser la única razón de nuestra existencia *or* lo único que nos importe.

beam [bi:m] *n* ARCH viga *f* (for supporting roof, etc.) ‖ rayo *m* (of light) ‖ destello *m* (gleam) ‖ sonrisa *f* radiante (broad smile) ‖ TECH plegador *m* (in loom) | astil *m* (of balance) | balancín *m* (of engine) | lanza *f* (of carriage) | cama *f* (of plough) ‖ MAR bao *m* (timber joining two sides of ship) | manga *f* (breadth) ‖ PHYS haz *m* (parallel rays); *electron beam* haz electrónico | onda *f* dirigida (radio signal) ‖ — FAM *broad in the beam* ancho de caderas ‖ MAR *on the port beam* a babor ‖ FAM *to be off the beam* estar equivocado (wrong) ‖ *to fly o to ride the beam* seguir el haz radioeléctrico.

beam [bi:m] *vi* irradiar ‖ sonreír (to smile) ‖ rebosar (*with* de) (satisfaction, health).
◆ *vt* difundir, emitir (a broadcast) ‖ irradiar (rays, warmth) ‖ emitir (light) ‖ transmitir (message).

beam compass [-'kʌmpəs] *n* compás *m* de vara.

beam-ends [-'endz] *pl n* MAR cabezas *f* de los baos ‖ — MAR *on her beam-ends* escorado ‖ FIG FAM *to be on one's beam-ends* no tener ni un céntimo (to have no money).

beaming ['bi:miŋ] *adj* radiante.

bean [bi:n] *n* BOT judía *f*, alubia *f*, habichuela *f* [AMER frijol *m*, fríjol *m*, poroto *m*] (seed) | haba *f* (broad bean) | grano *m* (of coffee, etc.) ‖ US FAM chola *f*, cabeza *f* ‖ — BOT *French beans* judías *or* habichuelas verdes | *kidney beans* frijoles *m pl* ‖ FAM *not to be worth a bean* no valer un comino | *not to know beans about* no saber ni jota de | *old bean* viejo (friend) ‖ BOT *stick bean* judía verde | FAM *to be full of beans* rebosar de vitalidad | *to be without a bean* no tener un cuarto | *to spill the beans* descubrir el pastel.

beanfeast [-fi:st]; **beano** ['bi:nəu] *n* FAM comilona *f* (big meal) | juerga *f* (binge).

bean sprout ['bi:n spraut]; **bean shoot** ['bi:n ʃu:t] *n* brote *m* de soja.

bear [bɛə*] *n* ZOOL oso, osa; *black, brown, white bear* oso negro, pardo, blanco ‖ FIG oso *m* ‖ bajista *m* (in stock exchange) ‖ — ZOOL *bear cub, young bear* osezno *m* ‖ ASTR *Great, Little Bear* Osa Mayor, Menor ‖ FAM *to be like a bear with a sore head* estar de un humor de perros.

bear* [bɛə*] *vt* soportar (to support); *will it bear the weight?* ¿soportará el peso? ‖ llevar (to carry); *they bore the chest on their shoulders* llevaron el cofre a hombros; *the letter bears his signature* la carta lleva su firma ‖ tener (a name, title, reputation, relation, expression, aspect, meaning, price) ‖ aguantar, soportar (to tolerate); *he can't bear the pain* no puede soportar el dolor; *I can't bear him* no puedo aguantarle ‖ admitir (to admit); *it bears several interpretations* admite varias interpretaciones; *it doesn't bear comparison* no admite comparación ‖ merecer; *to bear mentioning* merecer ser mencionado ‖ ser apropiado para (to be suitable for); *his joke doesn't bear repetition* su chiste no es apropiado para ser repetido ‖ ejercer (power, pressure) ‖ pagar, correr con; *to bear the cost of* pagar los gastos de ‖ dar a luz, tener (to give birth to); *she has borne a girl* ha dado a luz a una niña ‖ dar (to give); *she bore him a son* le dio un hijo; *to bear fruit* dar fruto ‖ resistir; *his alibi doesn't bear close examination* su coartada no resiste un examen a fondo ‖ profesar, tener; *the love she bore him* el amor que le profesaba ‖ — *can you bear me to touch it?* ¿me dejas tocarlo? ‖ *to bear a grudge against s.o.* guardar rencor a alguien ‖ *to bear a hand* echar una mano ‖ *to bear a part in* compartir ‖ *to bear a part o a role in sth.* desempeñar un papel en algo ‖ *to bear a person company* acompañar a una persona, hacer compañía a una persona ‖ *to bear arms* tener armas (to possess), llevar armas (to carry) ‖ *to bear in mind* tener presente, recordar, tener en cuenta ‖ *to bear interest* producir *or* devengar interés ‖ *to bear o.s. well* portarse *or* comportarse bien ‖ *to bear reference to* relacionarse con ‖ *to bear resemblance to* parecerse a ‖ *to bear the responsibility for* ser responsable de.
◆ *vi* torcer (to turn); *the road bears to the right* la carretera tuerce a la derecha ‖ producir (to produce); *the tree bears well* el árbol produce mucho ‖ dirigirse hacia; *the ship bore east* el barco se dirigía hacia el este ‖ *to bear hard o heavily on s.o.* pesar mucho sobre alguien.
◆ *phr v* ***to bear away*** llevarse; *she bore the prize away* se llevó el premio | arribar (a ship) ‖ ***to bear down*** vencer (enemy, opposition) | abatirse (a bird) | navegar con el viento (to sail with the wind) ‖ — *to bear down on* pesar sobre (to weigh on), acercarse a, dirigirse hacia (to draw near) ‖ ***to bear off*** llevarse (to carry off) | MAR alejarse ‖ ***to bear on*** referirse a ‖ ***to bear out*** confirmar, corroborar (to confirm) ‖ ***to bear up*** sostener, ayudar (to support) ‖ — *to bear up against* resistir, aguantar ‖ ***to bear with*** tener paciencia con.

— OBSERV *To bear* va seguido por el infinitivo o por el gerundio.

— OBSERV El pretérito de *bear* es ***bore.*** El participio pasivo es ***borne*** en el sentido de *llevado* y ***born*** cuando significa *nacido.*

bearable ['bɛərəbl] *adj* soportable, llevadero, ra (life) ‖ soportable, aguantable (person, work).

beard [biəd] *n* barba *f*, barbas *f pl* (of people, animals); *to have a beard* llevar *or* gastar barba ‖ BOT arista *f*, barba *f* (awn) ‖ lengüeta *f* (of an arrow) ‖ barba *f* (of a pen).

beard [biəd] *vt* desafiar, retar (to defy).

bearded [-id] *adj* con barba, barbado, da; barbudo, da (fam) (person) ‖ BOT aristado, da (wheat).

beardless [-lis] *adj* barbilampiño, imberbe.

bearer ['bɛərə*] *n* soporte *m* (support) ‖ porteador *m* (carrier) ‖ portador, ra (of message) ‖ portador *m* (of cheque) ‖ poseedor, ra (of passport) ‖ — *bearer bond* título *m* al portador ‖ *bearer cheque* cheque *m* al portador ‖ *mace bearer* macero *m* ‖ *stretcher bearer* camillero *m* ‖ *this tree is a poor bearer* este árbol no da mucho fruto.

bear garden ['bɛəga:dn] *n* FIG casa *f* de locos (noisy place).

bear hug ['bɛə hʌg] *n* abrazo *m* muy fuerte.

bearing ['bɛəriŋ] *n* transporte *m* (transportation) ‖ porte *m*; *a man of noble bearing* un hombre de noble porte; *majestic bearing* porte majestuoso ‖ conducta *f* (behaviour); *his courageous bearing in the battle* su valiente conducta en la batalla ‖ importancia *f*, alcance *m* (importance); *he didn't realize the bearing of her words* no se dio cuenta del alcance de sus palabras ‖ relación *f*, conexión *f* (*on* con) (relevance) ‖ producción *f* ‖ ARCH soporte *m* (support) ‖ TECH cojinete *m*; *ball, needle, roller, thrust bearing* cojinete de bolas, de agujas, de rodillos, de empuje ‖ MED alumbramiento *m*, parto *m* ‖ — *beyond all bearing* insoportable, inaguantable, intolerable ‖ MAR *magnetic bearing* acimut magnético ‖ ARCH *to take its bearing on sth.* apoyarse en algo ‖ FIG *to have no bearing on the matter* no tener nada que ver con el asunto.
◆ *pl* blasón *m sing* (coat of arms) ‖ aspectos *m* (of a question) ‖ — FIG *to get o to find one's bearings* orientarse ‖ MAR *to give one's bearings* dar su posición ‖ FAM *to lose one's bearings* desorientarse ‖ *to take one's bearings* tomar marcaciones, marcarse (in a ship), orientarse (to find one's bearings).
◆ *adj* que produce; *interest bearing* que produce interés.

— OBSERV Compound adjectives formed by adding *-bearing* to a noun may often be rendered in Spanish by the suffix *ífero, ra*: *fruit-bearing* fructífero, ra; *coal-bearing* carbonífero, ra.

bearish ['bɛəriʃ] *adj* FIG huraño, ña (person) ‖ *bearish tendency* tendencia a la baja (in stock exchange).

bearskin ['bɛəskin] *n* piel *f* de oso (fur, rug) ‖ gorro *m* [de piel de oso] (cap).

beast [bi:st] *n* bestia *f* ‖ FIG bestia *f*, bruto *m*, animal *m* ‖ — *beast of burden* bestia de carga ‖ FAM *it's a beast of a day, of a job* es un día, un trabajo espantoso ‖ *wild beast* fiera *f*.
◆ *pl* reses *f*, ganado *m sing* (livestock) ‖ *the King of the beasts* el rey de los animales.

beastliness [-linis] *n* bestialidad *f*.

beastly ['bi:stli] *adj* bestial ‖ FAM asqueroso, sa; repugnante (awful) | maldito, ta; *where's that beastly hat?* ¿dónde está el maldito sombrero? ‖ FAM *beastly weather* tiempo de perros.
◆ *adv* FAM terriblemente; *beastly difficult* terriblemente difícil ‖ *it is beastly hot* hace un calor bestial.

beat [bi:t] *n* latido *m* (of heart, pulse) ‖ pulsación *f* (pulsation) ‖ martilleo *m* (hammering); *the beat of the rain on the roof* el martilleo de la lluvia en el tejado ‖ batir *m*; *the beat of the waves against the rocks* el batir de las olas contra las rocas ‖ sonido *m*, ruido *m* (sound, noise) ‖ redoble *m* (of drums) ‖ ritmo *m* (of verse) ‖ ritmo *m* (of song); *this song has a good beat* esta canción tiene mucho ritmo ‖ ronda *f* (round of duty); *a policeman's beat* la ronda de un policía ‖ competencia *f* (sphere of action); *that is not my beat* eso no es de mi competencia ‖ noticia *f* sensacional que se tiene en exclusiva (scoop) ‖ batida *f* (in hunting) ‖ MUS tiempo *m*; *the third beat of the bar* el tercer tiempo del compás | ritmo *m or* compás *m* marcado por el director de orquesta ‖ — *off beat* excéntrico, ca (eccentric); fuera de tiempo (out of time), sin ritmo (music), fuera de lo común *or* de lo corriente (unusual) ‖ *the beat of the birds' wings* el aleteo de los pájaros.
◆ *adj* → **beaten** ‖ FAM derrengado, da (tired) ‖ — *he has me beat* aquí me ha cogido ‖ *the beat generation* la generación perdida.

beat* [bi:t] *vt* pegar (to spank) ‖ golpear (to hit); *they beat him senseless* le golpearon hasta dejarle inconsciente ‖ dar golpes en, golpear (to pound); *to beat the door, the table* dar golpes en la puerta, en la mesa ‖ abrirse; *to beat a path through the jungle, the crowd* abrirse paso en la jungla, entre la multitud ‖ batir, golpear; *the waves beat the cliffs* las olas batían los acantilados ‖ sacudir (carpet, cushions, etc.) ‖ batir, vencer (to defeat); *the enemy was beaten all along the line* el enemigo fue batido en toda la línea ‖ batir (in cooking) ‖ llegar antes que; *he beat me to the door* llegó a la puerta antes que yo ‖ batir (the wings) ‖ batir (in hunting) ‖ tocar (the drum) ‖ marcar, llevar (rhythm, time); *to beat time* marcar el compás ‖ meter en la cabeza; *he tried to beat some sense into him* intentó meterle un poco de sentido común en la cabeza ‖ dejar perplejo (to baffle) ‖ TECH batir (metals) ‖ SP ganar; *he beat me by five seconds* me ganó por cinco segundos | vencer; *do you think Germany will beat France?* ¿crees que Alemania vencerá a Francia? | batir; *to beat the record* batir el récord || pisar (the ground) || recorrer, batir (the countryside) || — *beat it!* ¡lárgate! || FAM *it beats me* no lo entiendo || *that beats all!* ¡eso es el colmo! || *to beat a nail into* poner un clavo en || *to beat a retreat* batirse en retirada || *to beat black and blue* dar una paliza soberana || FIG *to beat one's brains* devanar los sesos || FAM *to beat s.o. to it* ganarle a uno por la mano || US *to beat the band* a más no poder || *to beat the breast* golpearse el pecho, darse golpes de pecho || *to beat to death* matar a palos.

◆ *vi* latir (the heart) || tener pulsaciones (pulse) || batir, golpear; *the rain beat against the window panes* la lluvia golpeaba contra los cristales || dar golpes (*on* en) (a door) || dar una batida (in hunting) || resonar, redoblar (drums).

◆ *phr v* ***to beat about*** barloventar (ship) || — *to beat about the bush* andarse con rodeos || ***to beat against*** estrellarse contra || ***to beat back*** hacer retroceder, rechazar (to repel) || ***to beat down*** derribar (door, etc.) | superar (to overcome) | vencer (opponent) | regatear (to haggle); *to beat down the price of* regatear el precio de | conseguir que (el vendedor) baje el precio || caer de plomo (sun) || AGR acamar || ***to beat in*** derribar (door, etc.) || ***to beat off*** rechazar (to repel) || dejar atrás (in racing) || ***to beat out*** abrir (path) | martillear (metals) | marcar (rythm) || ***to beat up*** batir (in cooking) | dar una paliza (to thrash).

— OBSERV Pret ***beat***; pp ***beaten, beat***.

beaten [biːtn] *adj* trillado, da; *a beaten track* un camino trillado || MIL vencido, da; batido, da || batido, da; martillado, da (metals) || agotado, da (worn-out, exhausted) || FIG *off the beaten track* aislado, da; retirado, da (isolated), que se sale de lo común; *his ideas are off the beaten track* sus ideas se salen de lo común.

beater [ˈbiːtə*] *n* batidora *f* (in cooking) || ojeador *m*, batidor *m* (in hunting) || sacudidor *m* (duster).

beatific [ˌbiːəˈtifik] *adj* beatífico, ca.

beatification [biːˌætifiˈkeiʃən] *n* beatificación *f*.

beatify [biːˈætifai] *vt* beatificar.

beating [ˈbiːtiŋ] *n* paliza *f* (thrashing); *he took a beating* recibió una paliza || derrota *f* (defeat); *to take a beating* sufrir una derrota || latido *m* (of the heart) || pulsación *f* (pulsation) || ojeo *m*, batida *f* (in hunting) || — *beating of wings* aleteo *m* || *beating up* paliza *f*.

beatitude [biˈætitjuːd] *n* beatitud *f* || REL bienaventuranza *f*.

beatnik [ˈbiːtnik] *n* «beatnik» *m* & *f*.

Beatrice [ˈbiətris]; **Beatrix** [ˈbiətriks] *pr n* Beatriz *f*.

beau [bəu] *n* galán *m* (gallant) || novio *m* (sweetheart) || pretendiente *m* (suitor) || lechuguino *m*, pisaverde *m* (dandy).

◆ *adj* *beau geste* buen detalle *m* || *beau ideal* tipo *m* ideal.

— OBSERV El plural de *beau* es *beaux* o *beaus*.

beauteous [ˈbjuːtjəs] *adj* bello, lla; hermoso, sa.

beautician [bjuːˈtiʃən] *n* especialista *m* & *f* de un instituto de belleza.

beautiful [ˈbjuːtəful] *adj* bello, lla; hermoso, sa; *a beautiful painting, poem* un hermoso cuadro, un bello poema || hermoso, sa (child, animal) || guapa, guapísima (woman); *there were some beautiful girls at the party* había unas chicas guapísimas en la fiesta || precioso, sa; *a beautiful dress* un traje precioso; *a beautiful face* una cara preciosa || magnífico, ca; *it was a beautiful meal* fue una comida magnífica.

◆ *n* *the beautiful* lo bello, lo hermoso, la belleza.

— OBSERV In a literary context a woman may be described as *bella* or *hermosa* in Spanish. *Guapa*, on the other hand, is used in everyday spoken Spanish.

beautify [ˈbjuːtifai] *vt* embellecer.

◆ *vi* embellecerse.

beauty [ˈbjuːti] *n* belleza *f*, hermosura *f* (quality) || belleza *f* (beautiful person or thing); *she is a beauty* es una belleza || — *Beauty and the Beast* la Bella y la Bestia || *beauty contest* concurso *m* de belleza || *beauty cream* crema *f* de belleza || FIG *beauty is but skin-deep* las apariencias engañan || *beauty is in the eye of the beholder* la belleza es subjetiva || *beauty treatment* tratamiento *m* de belleza || FAM *she* o *it is a real beauty* es una preciosidad || *Sleeping Beauty* la Bella durmiente del bosque || FAM *that was a beauty!* ¡qué golpe más bueno! || FIG *the beauty of it is that...* lo bueno es que...

beauty parlour; US **beauty parlor** [-ˌpɑːlə*] *n* salón *m* de belleza, instituto *m* de belleza.

beauty sleep [-sliːp] *n* primer sueño *m*.

beauty spot [-spɔt] *n* lunar *m* (on face) || sitio *m* pintoresco (place).

beaver [ˈbiːvə*] *n* ZOOL castor *m* (animal, fur) || babera *f* (of helmet).

bebop [ˈbiːbɔp] *n* MUS «be-bop» *m*.

becalm [biˈkaːm] *vt* calmar, sosegar || MAR detener por falta de viento (a sailing boat) || *to be becalmed* estar encalmado.

became [biːˈkeim] *pret* → **become**.

because [biˈkɔz] *conj* porque; *he can't come because he is very busy* no puede venir porque está muy ocupado || — *because of* a causa de; *he can't come because of the transport strike* no puede venir a causa de la huelga de transportes || *the more powerful because* tanto más potente cuanto que.

beccafico [ˌbekəˈfikəu] *n* ZOOL becafigo *m* (bird).

béchamel [ˈbeʃɔmel] *n* besamel *f*, bechamel *f* (white sauce).

beck [bek] *n* arroyo *m*, riachuelo *m* (brook) || FAM *to be at s.o.'s beck and call* estar al servicio de uno, estar a la disposición de uno.

becket [ˈbekit] *n* MAR vinatera *f* (for ropes).

beckiron [ˈbekaiən] *n* bigornia *f* (anvil).

beckon [ˈbekən] *vt* hacer señas (to motion); *he beckoned him to approach* le hizo señas para que se acercase || FIG atraer, llamar (to entice); *the prospect of becoming rich beckoned him* la perspectiva de enriquecerse le atraía.

◆ *vi* hacer señas (*to* a).

becloud [biˈklaud] *vt* FIG oscurecer (to darken).

become* [biˈkʌm] *vi* volverse; *she has become much nicer since she got married* se ha vuelto mucho más simpática desde que se casó || hacerse (on one's own merits); *to become a doctor* hacerse médico; *to become famous* hacerse famoso || ponerse; *to become sad* ponerse triste; *to become fat* ponerse gordo || llegar a, llegar a ser (to get to be); *despite his low birth he became president* pese a su humilde origen llegó a ser presidente || quedarse; *to become deaf, blind* quedarse sordo, ciego || llegar a ser; *his daughter became his only consolation* su hija llegó a ser su único consuelo || cumplir; *he'll become 21 next week* cumplirá 21 años la semana que viene | convertirse en, transformarse en; *he became another man* se convirtió en otro hombre; *tadpoles become frogs* los renacuajos se transforman en ranas || — *to become king* subir al trono || *to become known* empezar a ser conocido || *to become of* ser de; *what has become of your friend?* ¿qué ha sido de tu amigo?; *I wonder what has become of them* no sé qué habrá sido de ellos.

◆ *vt* sentar bien, favorecer; *that dress really becomes her* ese vestido le sienta muy bien || ser propio de, convenir a; *such language does not become a young lady* ese lenguaje no es propio de una señorita.

— OBSERV Pret ***became***; pp ***become***.

— OBSERV *Volverse* generally indicates a permanent state; *ponerse* a temporary state; *llegar a* a transformation which implies an effort; *quedarse* an involuntary transformation.

— OBSERV *To become* followed by an adjective may often be rendered in Spanish by a verb alone: *to become rich* enriquecerse; *to become old* envejecerse; *to become thin* adelgazar.

becoming [-iŋ] *adj* favorecedor, ra (attractive) || apropiado, da (proper); *becoming to the occasion* apropiado para el caso.

◆ *n* PHIL devenir *m*.

bed [bed] *n* cama *f*; *I can't sleep in this bed* no puedo dormir en esta cama; *a hospital with five hundred beds* un hospital con quinientas camas || lecho *m* (for animals) || colchón *m* (mattress) || macizo *m*, cuadro *m*, arriate *m* (of flowers); *a bed of roses* un macizo de rosas || lecho *m*, fondo *m*, cauce *m* (of river) || fondo *m* (of sea) || banco *m*; *oyster bed* banco de ostras; *coral bed* banco de coral || firme *m* (of road, railway) || capa *f* (of plaster) || GEOL capa *f*, yacimiento *m*, estrato *m* (stratum) || PRINT pletina *f* (of press) || TECH bancada *f* (of machine) | base *f*, apoyo *m* (support) | lecho *m*; *pig bed* lecho de colada || MIL armón *m* (of gun carriage) || MAR basada *f* (cradle) | cama *f* (of ship's bottom in the mud) || — *bed and board* pensión completa || *bed and breakfast* cama y desayuno || *child of second bed* hijo *m* del segundo matrimonio || *death bed* lecho de muerte || *double bed* cama de matrimonio || *separation from bed and board* separación *f* matrimonial || *single bed* cama individual || *to be brought to bed of a boy* dar a luz a un niño || FIG *to be on a bed of roses* estar en un lecho de rosas || *to get out of bed on the wrong side* levantarse con el pie izquierdo || *to give s.o. a bed for the night* alojar *or* hospedar a alguien una noche || *to go to bed* acostarse || *to make the beds* hacer las camas || *to put s.o. to bed* acostar a alguien || *to stay in bed* guardar la cama (because of an illness) || *to take to one's bed* meterse en la cama, guardar cama || *twin beds* camas separadas *or* gemelas.

bed [bed] *vt* alojar, dar cama a; *he was unable to bed all the guests* no pudo alojar a todos los invitados || fijar, asentar, colocar (to fix) || — *to bed down* acostar, meter en la cama || *to bed out* plantar en un macizo (flowers).

◆ *vi* *to bed down* acostarse.

bedaub [biˈdɔːb] *vt* embadurnar (with paint, etc.).

bedazzle [biˈdæzl] *vt* deslumbrar.

bedbug [ˈbedbʌg] *n* chinche *f* (insect).

bedchamber [ˈbedˌtʃeimbə*] *n* alcoba *f*, dormitorio *m*.

bedclothes [ˈbedkləuðz] *pl n* ropa *f sing* de cama.

bedcover [ˈbedˌkʌvə*] *n* colcha *f*, cubrecama *m*.

bedding [ˈbediŋ] *n* ropa *f* de cama (bedclothes) || cama *f*, lecho *m* (for animals) || ARCH asiento *m*, fundamento *m* || GEOL estratificación *f*.

bedeck [biˈdek] *vt* adornar, engalanar.

bedevil [biˈdevl] *vt* endemoniar (to beset with devils) || molestar, importunar (to pester); *to bedevil s.o. with questions* importunar con preguntas a alguien || agravar, empeorar (to aggravate) || estropear (to spoil) || complicar (to make more complex).

bedevilment [-mənt] *n* molestia *f* (vexation) || posesión *f* diabólica (possession by a devil).

bedew [bi'dju:] *vt* humedecer, bañar.

bedfellow ['bed,feləu] *n* compañero *m or* compañera *f* de cama.

bedgown ['bedgaun] *n* camisón *m*, camisa *f* de dormir.

bedhead ['dhed] *n* cabecera *f.*

bedim [bi'dim] *vt* nublar, oscurecer (to cloud) || amortiguar (the light).

bedizen [bi'daizn] *vt* engalanar (to overadorn).

bed jacket ['bed,dʒækit] *n* mañanita *f.*

bedlam ['bedləm] *n* algarabía *f*, alboroto *m* (uproar, confusion) || casa *f* de locos (madhouse).

bed linen ['bed,linən] *n* ropa *f* blanca.

Bedouin ['beduin] *adj/n* beduino, na.

bedpan ['bedpæn] *n* cuña *f*, orinal *m* de cama || calentador *m* de cama (to warm the bed).

bedplate ['bedpleit] *n* bancada *f*, placa *f* de asiento.

bedpost ['bedpəust] *n* columna *f or* pilar *m* de la cama || FIG *between you and me and the bedpost* dicho sea entre nosotros.

bedraggled [bi'drægld] *adj* manchado de barro (stained) || FIG en ruinas; *bedraggled buildings* edificios en ruinas.

bedrid ['bedrid]; **bedridden** ['bedridn] *adj* postrado en cama.

bedrock ['bedrɔk] *n* GEOL roca *f* de fondo, roca *f* firme || FIG base *f* (basis) | fondo *m* de la cuestión; *to get down to bedrock* ir al fondo de la cuestión.

bedroom ['bedrum] *n* dormitorio *m*, alcoba *f*, cuarto *m* (de dormir), habitación *f* [AMER recámara *f*]; *John is working in his bedroom* Juan está trabajando en su cuarto || — *bedroom farce* vodevil *m*, comedia ligera || *bedroom slipper* zapatilla *f.*

bedside ['bedsaid] *adj* de noche; *bedside table, lamp* mesilla, lámpara de noche || de cabecera; *bedside book* libro de cabecera || MED *bedside manner* comportamiento *m* con un enfermo.
◆ *n* cabecera *f*; *she was at his bedside when he died* estaba en su cabecera cuando murió.

bed-sit ['bedsit] *n* FAM estudio *m.*

bed-sitter ['bed,sitə*]; **bed-sitting-room** ['bed'-sitiŋrum] *n* estudio *m*, apartamento *m* (one-room apartment) || salón *m* con cama (in a flat).

bedsore ['bedsɔ:*] *n* MED escara *f*, llaga *f*, úlcera *f.*

bedspread ['bedspred] *n* colcha *f*, cubrecama *m.*

bedstead ['bedsted] *n* marco *m or* armazón *m* de la cama, cuja *f.*

bedtime ['bedtaim] *n* hora *f* de acostarse.

bed warmer ['bed,wɔ:mə*] *n* (ant) calentador *m* de cama.

bed-wetting ['bed,wetiŋ] *n* enuresis *f inv.*

bee [bi:] *n* abeja *f* (insect) || MAR violín *m* (of bowsprit) || US reunión *f*, tertulia *f* (social gathering) | concurso *m* (contest) || — FIG *busy as a bee* muy ocupado || *carpenter bee* abeja carpintera || *queen bee* abeja maesa *or* maestra *or* reina || FIG *to have a bee in one's bonnet* estar obsesionado (to have an obsesion), estar mal de la cabeza (to be mad) || *worker bee* abeja obrera *or* neutra.

Beeb [bi:b] *n* FAM BBC *f.*

beech [bi:tʃ] *n* BOT haya *f* (tree) || BOT *beech grove* hayal *m.*

beech mast ['bi:tʃma:st] *n* BOT hayucos *m pl.*

beechnut ['bi:tʃnʌt] *n* BOT hayuco *m.*

beech tree ['bi:tʃtri:] *n* BOT haya *f.*

bee-eater ['bi:,i:tə*] *n* ZOOL abejaruco *m* (bird).

beef [bi:f] *n* carne *f* de vaca, vaca *f* (meat) || ganado *m* vacuno (cattle) || FAM fuerza *f* muscular, músculos *m pl* (strength) | corpulencia *f*, carnes *f pl* (fat) || US FAM queja *f* (complaint) || — *chilled beef* carne de vaca refrigerada || *roast beef* rosbif *m* || *salt beef* carne de vaca salada.
— OBSERV El plural de *beef* puede ser *beeves* o *beefs*, este último sobre todo en Estados Unidos.

beef [bi:f] *vi* US quejarse.

beef up [bi:fʌp] *vt* reforzar.

beefeater ['bi:f,i:tə*] *n* alabardero *m* de la Torre de Londres.

beefsteak ['bi:f'steik] *n* bistec *m* [AMER bife *m*].

beef tea ['bi:f'ti:] *n* concentrado *m* de carne.

beefy ['bi:fi] *adj* fornido, da; fuerte.

bee glue ['bi:,glu:] *n* propóleos *m.*

beehive ['bi:haiv] *n* colmena *f.*

Beirut [bei'ru:t] *pr n* GEOGR Beirut.

beekeeper ['bi:,ki:pə*] *n* apicultor, ra.

beekeeping ['bi:,ki:piŋ] *n* apicultura *f.*

beeline ['bi:lain] *n* línea *f* recta || *to make a beeline for sth.* ir derecho hacia algo.

Beelzebub [bi'elzibʌb] *pr n* Belcebú *m.*

been [bi:n] *pp* ⟶ **be.**

beep [bi:p] *n* pito *m*, pitido *m.*

beep [bi:p] *vt/vi* pitar, dar pitidos.

beer [biə*] *n* cerveza *f*; *dark, light beer* cerveza negra, dorada || — *draught beer* cerveza de barril || FIG *it's not all beer and skittles* no todo es coser y cantar | *life is not all beer and skittles* la vida no es un lecho de rosas | *to think no small beer of o.s.* creerse alguien.

beer glass [-gla:s] *n* jarra *f* de cerveza, bock *m.*

beerhouse [-haus] *n* cervecería *f.*

beery ['biəri] *adj* que huele a cerveza (smelling of beer) || — *beery voice* voz aguardentosa || *it was a beery affair* allí se bebió mucho.

beestings ['bi:stiŋz] *pl n* calostro *m* de la vaca.

beeswax ['bi:zwæks] *n* cera *f* de abejas.

beeswing ['bi:zwiŋ] *n* capa *f* de tártaro [en el vino añejo].

beet [bi:t] *n* remolacha *f*; *sugar beet* remolacha azucarera.
◆ *adj* remolachero, ra (industry).

beetle ['bi:tl] *n* escarabajo *m* (insect) || mano *f* (of a mortar) || mazo *m* (mallet) || TECH batán *m* (cloth-beating machine) | martinete *m* (tool for crushing) | pisón *m* (for paving) || FIG & FAM *to be blind as a beetle* no ver tres en un burro.

beetle ['bi:tl] *vt* golpear (to beat) || aplastar con pisón.
◆ *vi* sobresalir amenazadoramente (to jut out); *the beetling crags* los peñascos que sobresalen amenazadoramente.

beetle-browed [-braud] *adj* cejijunto, ta (having bushy eyebrows) || ceñudo, da (frowning).

beetle-crusher [-,krʌʃə*] *n* FAM zapato *m*, bota *f* (boot).

beetroot ['bi:tru:t] *n* remolacha *f.*

beet sugar ['bi:tʃugə*] *n* azúcar *m* de remolacha.

befall* [bi'fɔ:l] *vt* acontecer a; *all the misfortunes which befell the family* todas las desgracias que acontecieron a la familia.
◆ *vi* acontecer (to happen).
— OBSERV Pret ***befell***; pp ***befallen***.
— OBSERV Este verbo se usa únicamente en tercera persona.

befallen [bi'fɔ:lən] *pp* ⟶ **befall.**

befell [bi'fel] *pret* ⟶ **befall.**

befit [bi'fit] *vt* convenir a, corresponder a; *he should behave as befits a man of his age* debería comportarse como corresponde a un hombre de su edad.

befitting [-iŋ] *adj* propio, pia; conveniente.

befog [bi'fɔg] *vt* envolver en niebla; *the town was befogged* la ciudad estaba envuelta en niebla || FIG nublar, oscurecer; *smoke befogged the room* el humo nublaba la habitación; *the drink befogged his senses* la bebida nublaba sus sentidos | confundir (to confuse).

befool [bi'fu:l] *vt* engañar (to deceive).

before [bi'fɔ:*] *adv* antes (earlier); *two weeks before* dos semanas antes; *I will give it to you tomorrow, not before* te lo daré mañana, no antes; *why didn't you tell me before?* ¿por qué no me lo dijiste antes? || anterior, antes; *the night before* la noche anterior, la noche antes || anterior; *the page before* la página anterior || delante, por delante; *there were trees before and behind* había árboles delante y detrás *or* por delante y por detrás || ya (already); *have you been to England before?* ¿ha estado usted ya en Inglaterra?; *we have tried that before* ya lo hemos intentado || — *a short time before, not long before* poco antes || *as never before* como nunca || *before long* dentro de poco || *have you seen him before?* ¿le ha visto usted alguna vez? | *I have never seen him before* no le he visto nunca | *I have seen him before somewhere* le he visto en alguna parte || *long before, a long time before* mucho antes || *the one before* el anterior, la anterior || *to go on before* adelantarse.
◆ *prep* delante de; *to stand before the fire* estar de pie delante del fuego; *to tell s.o. off before the whole class* regañarle a uno delante de toda la clase || antes de (with an idea of order); *the last street before the traffic lights* la última calle antes de los semáforos; *the day before the wedding* el día antes de la boda || ante; *before God and men* ante Dios y ante los hombres; *to appear before the judge* comparecer ante el juez; *he had a brilliant future before him* un brillante futuro se abría ante él || antes que; *he arrived before me* llegó antes que yo; *I would choose this coat before any other* escogería este abrigo antes que cualquier otro || — *before all else* ante todo (above all), antes que nada (first of all) || *before Christ* antes de Jesucristo || *before speaking* antes de hablar || *income before tax* renta *f* antes de deducir los impuestos || *ladies before gentlemen* las señoras primero || *the day before yesterday* antes de ayer || *the motion before the House* la moción presentada ante las Cortes *or* sometida a las Cortes (in Parliament) || *the question before us* el asunto que tenemos que discutir || *the work I have before me* el trabajo que tengo por delante || *to have before one* tener ante los ojos || *to put love before honour* anteponer el amor al honor.
◆ *conj* antes de que (followed by the subjunctive); *before anybody notices* antes de que nadie se dé cuenta || antes de (followed by an infinitive); *before I go out I must write to my parents* antes de salir tengo que escribir a mis padres || FAM *before you know where you are* antes de que te des cuenta.
— OBSERV *Antes de* may only be used to translate the conjunction *before* when the subject of the two clauses is the same: *before we go we must call John* antes de salir tenemos que llamar a Juan; but *before we go I must tell you something* antes de que salgamos tengo que decirte algo.

beforehand [bi'fɔ:hænd] *adv* antes; *to come an hour beforehand* venir una hora antes; *you should have told me beforehand* me lo deberías haber dicho antes || de antemano, con anticipación; *to make preparations beforehand* hacer preparativos de antemano | por adelantado; *to* *ask to be paid beforehand* pedir ser pagado por adelantado ‖ ya (already).

befoul [bi'faul] *vt* ensuciar (to make dirty) ‖ FIG manchar.

befriend [bi'frend] *vt* ofrecer amistad a (to offer friendship to) ‖ ayudar (to help).

befuddled [bi'fʌdld] *adj* atontado, da [por la bebida] ‖ perplejo, ja; atónito, ta (perplexed).

beg [beg] *vi* mendigar (to ask for charity); *he begged from door to door* mendigaba de puerta en puerta ‖ pedir limosna (to ask for alms) ‖ rogar; *make less noise, I beg of you* les ruego que no hagan tanto ruido ‖ pedir (animals) ‖ — *I beg to differ* siento disentir ‖ *I beg to inform you that...* tengo el honor de informarles de que... ‖ *I beg to remind you that...* ruego que me permita recordarle que... ‖ FIG *it's going begging* nadie lo quiere aceptar, comprar, etc. ‖ *to beg for mercy* implorar compasión ‖ *to beg off* disculparse ‖ *to beg off the afternoon* pedir la tarde libre.

◆ *vt* mendigar; *she begged a meal* mendigó una comida ‖ pedir (to ask for); *they begged forgiveness* pidieron perdón ‖ rogar, suplicar (to entreat); *she begged him not to do it* le rogó que no lo hiciese; *I beg you!* ¡se lo suplico! ‖ — *begging the question* petición *f* de principio ‖ *I beg your pardon!* dispénseme, usted perdone, discúlpeme (excuse me) ‖ *I beg you pardon?* ¿cómo? [*Amer* ¿mande?] (what did you say?) ‖ *to beg s.o. off from a duty* pedir que dispensen a alguien de una obligación ‖ *to beg the question* incurrir en una petición de principio.

began [bi'gæn] *pret* ⟶ **begin.**

beget* [bi'get] *vt* engendrar, procrear (children) ‖ FIG engendrar (consequences) ‖ REL *the Only Begotten of the Father* el Unigénito del Padre.

— OBSERV Pret ***begot, begat*** (ant): pp ***begotten***.

beggar ['begə*] *n* mendigo, ga; pordiosero, ra (one who begs) ‖ FAM tío, tía; *the silly beggar!* ¡qué tío más tonto! ‖ — *beggars can't be choosers* a caballo regalado no le mires el diente ‖ *beggar's opera* ópera *f* de cuatro peniques ‖ *poor beggar!* ¡pobre diablo! ‖ *you little beggar!* ¡sinvergüenza!

beggar ['begə*] *vt* arruinar, empobrecer (to impoverish) ‖ *to beggar description* superar toda descripción.

beggarly [-li] *adj* miserable, pobre (miserable) ‖ mezquino, na (mean) ‖ *beggarly wage* sueldo *m* de hambre.

beggar-my-neighbour; US **beggar-my-neighbor** [-mi'neibə*] *n* juego *m* de naipes infantil parecido a la guerrilla.

beggary [-ri] *n* mendicidad *f* ‖ miseria *f* (extreme poverty) ‖ mendigos *m pl* (beggars).

begin* [bi'gin] *vt/vi* empezar, comenzar; *begin when you are ready* empiecen Uds. cuando estén listos; *when the world began* cuando comenzó el mundo; *to begin a letter* empezar una carta ‖ — *beginning from Monday* a partir del lunes ‖ *not to begin to* distar mucho de, estar muy lejos de; *he does not begin to meet the requirements* está muy lejos de satisfacer los requisitos; no encontrar palabras para; *I can't even begin to thank you for your hospitality* no encuentro palabras para agradecerle su hospitalidad ‖ *to begin at the beginning* empezar por el principio ‖ *to begin by doing sth.* empezar por hacer algo *or* haciendo algo ‖ *to begin on sth.* emprender algo ‖ *to begin talks* entablar negociaciones ‖ *to begin to do sth.* o *doing sth.* empezar a hacer algo ‖ *to begin with* para empezar, en primer lugar (first of all), empezar con (to start with).

— OBSERV *To begin* va seguido por el infinitivo o por el gerundio.

— OBSERV Pret ***began***; pp ***begun***.

beginner [bi'ginə*] *n* principiante, ta ‖ iniciador, ra.

beginning [bi'giniŋ] *n* principio *m*, comienzo *m*; *the beginning of the end* el principio del fin; *the beginning of the world, of the book* el principio del mundo, del libro ‖ origen *m*, causa *f* (cause); *nobody knew what the beginning of the feud was* nadie sabía cuál era el origen de la enemistad ‖ orígenes *m pl* (origins); *the political beginning of a country* los orígenes políticos de un país ‖ principios *m pl*; *at the beginning of the month, of the year* a principios de mes, de año ‖ — *beginning with* a partir de ‖ *from beginning to end* desde el principio hasta el final ‖ *in the beginning* al principio ‖ *to make a beginning* empezar.

begone! [bi'gɔn] *interj* (ant) ¡retiraos!, ¡fuera de aquí!

begonia [bi'gəunjə] *n* BOT begonia *f*.

begoniaceae [bigəun'jəsii] *pl n* BOT begoniáceas *f*.

begot [bi'gɔt] *pret* ⟶ **beget.**

begotten [bi'gɔtn] *pp* ⟶ **beget.**

begrime [bi'graim] *vt* tiznar, ennegrecer, ensuciar (to blacken); *the begrimed faces of the miners* las caras tiznadas de los mineros.

begrudge [bi'grʌdʒ] *vt* regatear, escatimar (to quibble over); *the government does not begrudge the money it spends on education* el gobierno no regatea el dinero que gasta en la educación ‖ doler (a uno); *he begrudges spending money on repairs* le duele gastar dinero en reparaciones ‖ envidiar (to envy); *to begrudge s.o. his* o *her good fortune* envidiarle a alguien su buena suerte.

— OBSERV The idea of reluctance given by the verb *to begrudge* may often be rendered in Spanish by the adverbial phrases *a disgusto, de mala gana* (reluctantly): *to begrudge giving, doing sth.* dar, hacer algo a disgusto.

begrudgingly [-iŋli] *adv* a disgusto, de mala gana, a regañadientes.

beguile [bi'gail] *vt* engañar (to deceive); *he realized he had been beguiled* se dio cuenta de que le habían engañado ‖ seducir (to seduce); *beguiled by vague promises* seducido por vagas promesas ‖ entretener (one's leisure) ‖ aliviar (to relieve); *to beguile the tedium of a long voyage* aliviar el tedio de un largo viaje ‖ — *to beguile s.o. into doing sth.* inducir a alguien a hacer algo ‖ *to beguile s.o. out of sth.* robar algo a alguien engañándole (to steal sth. from s.o.) ‖ *to beguile the time doing sth.* entretenerse haciendo algo.

Beguine ['begi:n] *n* REL beguina *f*.

begum ['beigəm] *n* begum *f*.

begun [bi'gʌn] *pp* ⟶ **begin.**

behalf [bi'hɑ:f] *n* *on behalf of* en nombre de; *I thank you on behalf of my country* les doy las gracias en nombre de mi país; en nombre de, de parte de; *they asked me to thank you on their behalf* me pidieron que les diese las gracias en su nombre *or* de su parte; de parte de; *he went to see the boss on my behalf* fue de mi parte a ver al jefe; por; *don't worry yourself on my behalf* no te preocupes por mí; en favor de, por; *to plead on s.o.'s behalf* abogar por alguien, hablar en favor de alguien; para; *a collection on behalf of old people* una colecta para los ancianos ‖ *on behalf of my colleagues and myself* en nombre de mis colegas y en el mío propio.

behave [bi'heiv] *vi* comportarse, portarse, conducirse (to conduct o.s.); *to behave badly* comportarse mal ‖ portarse *or* comportarse bien; *tell the children to behave* di a los niños que se porten bien ‖ funcionar (a machine) ‖ — *behave yourself!* ¡pórtate bien! ‖ *that is no way to behave* no es manera de portarse ‖ *to behave towards* tratar.

behaviour; US **behavior** [bi'heivjə*] *n* conducta *f*, comportamiento *m* (conduct) ‖ TECH funcionamiento *m* (of a machine) ‖ comportamiento *m*; *the behaviour of steel under pressure* el comportamiento del acero bajo presión ‖ *to be on one's best behaviour* portarse de la mejor manera posible.

behaviourism; US **behaviorism** [-rizəm] *n* behaviorismo *m*.

behead [bi'hed] *vt* decapitar, degollar, descabezar.

beheld [bi'held] *pret/pp* ⟶ **behold.**

behest [bi'hest] *n* mandato *m* (command); *at divine behest* por mandato divino ‖ petición *f*, requerimiento *m* (request); *he did it at his friends' behest* lo hizo a petición de sus amigos.

behind [bi'haind] *adv* detrás, atrás; *there are two cars behind* hay dos coches detrás; *is there anything behind?* ¿hay algo atrás? ‖ detrás; *they approached me from behind* se acercaron a mí por detrás ‖ por detrás (around the back) ‖ de atrás; *the one behind* el de atrás ‖ — *the holidays already seem a long way behind* las vacaciones parecen muy lejanas ‖ *to attack s.o. from behind* atacar a alguien por la espalda ‖ *to be behind* estar atrasado (a clock), ir con *or* llevar retraso (train, etc.); *the train was an hour behind* el tren iba con *or* llevaba una hora de retraso; estar retrasado *or* atrasado; *to be behind in one's studies, with one's rent* estar atrasado en los estudios, en el pago del alquiler ‖ *to be behind with one's work* tener trabajo atrasado ‖ *to fall* o *to lag behind* quedarse atrás ‖ *to follow close behind* seguir muy de cerca ‖ *to leave behind* dejar; *we can't leave the dog behind* no podemos dejar el perro; dejar atrás (in a race, etc.); *they left him a long way behind* le dejaron muy atrás; olvidarse, dejarse (to forget) ‖ *to look behind* mirar (hacia) atrás ‖ *to stay* o *to remain behind* quedarse; *only a small group stayed behind* sólo un pequeño grupo se quedó; quedar (to be left).

◆ *prep* detrás de; *behind the house* detrás de la casa; *I would like to know what is behind all that* me gustaría saber qué hay detrás de todo eso ‖ por debajo de (below); *our sales are far behind those of last year* nuestras ventas están muy por debajo de las del año pasado ‖ tras, detrás de; *he left a good memory behind him* dejó un buen recuerdo tras él; *the storm left a trail of destruction behind it* la tormenta dejó un rastro de destrucción tras ella ‖ — *behind one's back* por detrás de uno, a espaldas de uno ‖ *behind the scenes* entre bastidores ‖ *to be behind schedule* llevar retraso (train, boat, etc.), estar atrasado (with one's work) ‖ *to be behind s.o.* apoyarle a uno (to support s.o.), estár más atrasado que uno; *this country is far behind its neighbours* este país está mucho más atrasado que sus vecinos; *she is rather behind the rest of the class* está bastante más atrasada que el resto de la clase ‖ *to look behind one* volver la cabeza, mirar hacia atrás ‖ *to put one's worries behind one* relegar sus preocupaciones al olvido, dejar de lado sus preocupaciones.

◆ *n* trasero *m* (buttocks) ‖ *to fall on one's behind* caerse sentado.

behindhand [-hænd] *adv/adj* retrasado, da; atrasado, da; *to be behindhand with the rent* estar retrasado en el pago del alquiler.

behold* [bi'həuld] *vt* (ant) percibir, advertir (to see) ‖ considerar, ver (to envisage) ‖ *behold!* ¡mirad!

— OBSERV Pret y pp ***beheld***.

beholden [bi'həuldən] *adj* agradecido, da (grateful); *I am very beholden to you* le estoy muy agradecido.

beholder [bi'həuldə*] *n* espectador, ra.

behove [biˈhəuv]; *US* **behoove** [biˈhuːv] *v impers* incumbir (to be necessary for); *it behoves the scientist to work objectively* incumbe al científico trabajar objetivamente ‖ corresponder (to befit); *he plays as behoves the son of a great pianist* toca como corresponde al hijo de un gran pianista; *it ill behoves him to criticize* no le corresponde criticar.
◆ *vi* ser propio (to be fitting) ‖ ser menester (to be necessary).

beige [beiʒ] *adj* beige, de color beige.
◆ *n* beige *m*.

being [ˈbiːiŋ] *n* ser *m*; *human being* ser humano ‖ existencia *f*, ser *m* (existence); *the mother who gave me my being* la madre que me dio el ser ‖ esencia *f* (essence) ‖ REL & PHIL ser *m*; *the Supreme Being* el Ser Supremo ‖ — *in being* existente ‖ *to bring into being* realizar (a plan), engendrar (to beget), crear (to create) ‖ *to come into being* nacer, aparecer.
◆ *adj for the time being* por el momento, de momento.
◆ *conj being as, being that* puesto que, ya que.

Beirut [beiˈruːt] *pr n* GEOGR Beirut.

bejesus [biˈdʒiːzəs] *interj* FAM ¡vaya por Dios! ‖ FAM *to kick the bejesus out of s.o.* molerle a palos a uno.

bejewel [biˈdʒuːəl] *vt* enjoyar, alhajar.

bel [bel] *n* PHYS bel *m*, belio *m*.

belabour; *US* **belabor** [biˈleibə*] *vt* (ant) azotar, apalear (to beat) ‖ extenderse sobre (a subject).

belated [biˈleitid] *adj* tardío, a; demorado, da; *belated congratulation* felicitación tardía ‖ atrasado, da (out of date) ‖ retrasado, da (delayed).

belaud [biˈlɔːd] *vt* alabar, ensalzar.

belay [biˈlei] *n* asidero *m* (hold in mountaineering).

belay [biˈlei] *vt* MAR amarrar (to secure) ‖ asegurar (in mountaineering).
◆ *vi* amarrarse (cables) ‖ FIG *belay!* ¡basta ya!

belaying pin [-iŋpin] *n* MAR cabilla *f*.

belch [beltʃ] *n* eructo *m*, regüeldo *m* (burp).

belch [beltʃ] *vt* FIG arrojar, vomitar; *to belch fire* arrojar fuego.
◆ *vi* eructar (to burp).

beleaguer [biˈliːgə*] *vt* sitiar, asediar, cercar.

belemnite [ˈbeləmnait] *n* belemnita *f* (fossil).

belfry [ˈbelfri] *n* campanario *m*.

Belgian [ˈbeldʒən] *adj/n* belga.

Belgium [ˈbeldʒəm] *pr n* GEOGR Bélgica *f*.

Belgrade [belˈgreid] *pr n* GEOGR Belgrado.

belie [biˈlai] *vt* desmentir, contradecir (to contradict); *to belie a proverb* desmentir un refrán ‖ contrastar con (to contrast with); *his hard eyes belied his delicate features* sus ojos fríos contrastaban con sus delicadas facciones ‖ defraudar (to disappoint); *to belie one's expectations* defraudar sus esperanzas.
— OBSERV El gerundio de este verbo es ***belying***.

belief [biˈliːf] *n* creencia *f*; *my political, religious beliefs* mis creencias políticas, religiosas; *belief in God* creencia en Dios ‖ REL fe *f* (faith); *the war of belief against unbelief* la guerra de la fe contra la incredulidad ‖ confianza *f* (confidence); *he has no belief in doctors* no tiene confianza en los médicos ‖ crédito *m*; *unworthy of belief* que no merece crédito ‖ — *beyond belief* increíble ‖ *in the firm belief that...* en la firme creencia de que... ‖ *it is common belief that...* es la creencia popular que... ‖ *it is my belief that...* estoy convencido de que... ‖ *to the best of my belief* a mi entender, que yo sepa.

believable [biˈliːvəbl] *adj* creíble, verosímil; *a believable explanation* una explicación verosímil.

believe [biˈliːv] *vi* creer; *to believe in God* creer en Dios ‖ ser partidario de (to be in favour of); *I don't believe in smoking* no soy partidario del tabaco ‖ — *I believe not* creo que no ‖ *I believe so* creo que sí ‖ *to make believe* fingir.
◆ *vt* creer; *I believe you* te creo; *I believe it is going to rain* creo que va a llover ‖ — *believe it or not* por extraño que parezca ‖ *believe me!* ¡créeme! ‖ *don't you believe it!* ¡no te lo creas! ‖ *he is believed to be in London* se cree *or* se supone que está en Londres ‖ *to believe one's ears, one's eyes* dar crédito a sus oídos, a sus ojos.

believer [-ə*] *n* creyente *m* & *f* ‖ partidario, ria; *a firm believer in corporal punishment* un firme partidario del castigo corporal.

Belisarius [beliˈsɛəriəs] *pr n* Belisario *m*.

Belisha beacon [bəˈliːʃəˈbiːkən] *n* poste *m* luminoso.

belittle [biˈlitl] *vt* empequeñecer, hacer parecer más pequeño; *the new tower belittles the surrounding houses* la nueva torre hace parecer más pequeñas las casas de alrededor ‖ minimizar; *to belittle one's efforts* minimizar los esfuerzos de uno ‖ despreciar, hacer poco caso de; *don't belittle his advice* no desprecies su consejo ‖ *to belittle o.s.* rebajarse, quitarse importancia, darse poca importancia.

Belize [beˈliːz] *pr n* GEOGR Belice *m*.

bell [bel] *n* campana *f*; *church bell* campana de la iglesia ‖ campanilla *f* (handbell) ‖ timbre *m*; *he rang the bell and entered* tocó el timbre y entró ‖ cencerro *m* (of animals) ‖ cascabel *m* (of collar, toys, etc.) ‖ timbre *m* (of bicycle, alarm clock, etc.) ‖ bramido *m* (of stag) ‖ MUS pabellón *m* (of an instrument) ‖ BOT campanilla *f* (of flower) ‖ MAR campanada *f* ‖ — *diving bell* campana de buzo ‖ FIG *it doesn't ring a bell with me* no me suena ‖ *passing bell* campana que toca a muerto ‖ FIG *sound as a bell* más sano que una manzana (healthy), muy seguro (very safe) | *that rings a bell* eso me suena ‖ *to set all the bells ringing, to ring all the bells full peal* echar las campanas al vuelo.

bell [bel] *vi* acampanarse (to become bell-shaped) ‖ bramar (a stag) ‖ tocar el timbre (to ring).
◆ *vt* poner un cencerro a (animals) ‖ poner un cascabel a (cats) ‖ acampanar (to make bell-shaped) ‖ FIG *to bell the cat* poner el cascabel al gato.

belladonna [ˌbeləˈdɔnə] *n* BOT belladona *f*.

bell-bottomed [ˈbelbɔtəmd] *adj* acampanado, da.

bellboy [ˈbelbɔi] *n* botones *m inv* (at the hotel).

bell buoy [ˈbelbɔi] *n* boya *f* de campana.

belle [bel] *n* beldad *f*, belleza *f* (beautiful woman) ‖ *the belle of the ball* la reina del baile.

belles lettres [ˈbelˈletr] *pl n* bellas letras *f*.

bellflower [ˈbelˌflauə*] *n* BOT campanilla *f*.

bell gable [ˈbelgeibl] *n* ARCH espadaña *f*.

bell glass [ˈbelglɑːs] *n* ⟶ **bell jar**.

bellhop [ˈbelhɔp] *n* *US* botones *m inv* (bellboy).

bellicose [ˈbelikəus] *adj* belicoso, sa; agresivo, va (aggressive) ‖ guerrero, ra (warlike).

bellicosity [ˌbeliˈkɔsiti] *n* belicosidad *f*.

belligerence [biˈlidʒərəns]; **belligerency** [biˈlidʒərənsi] *n* agresividad *f* ‖ beligerancia *f*.

belligerent [biˈlidʒərənt] *adj* beligerante (at war) ‖ agresivo, va (aggressive).
◆ *n* beligerante *m* & *f*.

bell jar [ˈbeldʒɑː*] *n* campana *f*, fanal *m* (to protect objects) ‖ campana *f* (to protect food) ‖ CHEM campana *f* de cristal.

bellow [ˈbeləu] *n* bramido *m*, mugido *m* (of animals) ‖ bramido *m*, rugido *m* (of guns, men in anger) ‖ bramido *m* (of tempest) ‖ fragor *m* (of thunder).

bellow [ˈbeləu] *vi* bramar (a bull, a cow) ‖ FIG bramar, rugir, vociferar.
◆ *vt* cantar a voz en cuello (a song).

bellows [-z] *pl n* fuelle *m sing* (of a camera, etc.) ‖ MUS fuelles *m* ‖ *a pair of bellows* un fuelle.

bellpull [ˈbelpul] *n* tirador *m*.

bell push [ˈbel puʃ] *n* botón *m* del timbre.

bell ringer [ˈbelˌriŋə*] *n* campanero *m* ‖ FIG éxito *m*.

bell-shaped [ˈbelʃeipt] *adj* acampanado, da.

bell tent [ˈbeltent] *n* pabellón *m*, tienda *f* de campaña cónica.

bell tower [ˈbelˌtauə*] *n* campanario *m*.

bellwether [ˈbelˌweðə*] *n* manso *m* (sheep) ‖ FIG cabecilla *m*, jefe *m* (leader).

belly [ˈbeli] *n* vientre *m*, barriga *f* (fam), tripa *f* (fam) (of person) ‖ panza *f* (of animals, things); *the belly of an aeroplane* la panza de un avión ‖ MAR seno *m* (of sail) ‖ MUS tabla *f* de armonía (of an instrument).
— OBSERV Excepto para los animales, la palabra *belly* se emplea poco en inglés con el sentido de vientre. Se le prefiere *stomach*, o incluso *tummy*, que pertenece al lenguaje infantil.

belly [ˈbeli] *vt* hinchar (to make swell out).
◆ *vi* hincharse (to swell out) ‖ pandearse (a wall).

bellyache [-eik] *n* FAM dolor *m* de tripa *or* de barriga *or* de vientre.

bellyache [-eik] *vi* FAM quejarse.

bellyband [-bænd] *n* barriguera *f* (of horses) ‖ faja *f* (for babies).

belly button [-ˌbʌtn] *n* FAM ombligo *m* (navel).

belly dancer [-ˌdɑːnsə*] *n* bailarina *f* que baila la danza del vientre.

bellyflop [-flɔp] *n* panzada *f*, panzazo *m*; *the diving champion did a bellyflop* el campeón de salto dio un panzazo ‖ *bellyflop landing* aterrizaje *m* sobre la panza.

bellyflop [-flɔp] *vi* dar un panzazo ‖ aterrizar sobre la panza (aircraft).

bellyful [-ful] *n* FIG & FAM panzada *f*; *I have had a bellyful of studying* me he dado una panzada de estudiar.

belly landing [-lændiŋ] *n* aterrizaje *m* sobre la panza (aircraft) ‖ *to make a belly landing* aterrizar sobre la panza.

belly laugh [-lɑːf] *n* FAM carcajada *f*; *he gave a belly laugh* soltó una carcajada.

belong [biˈlɔŋ] *vi* pertenecer a, ser de; *this money belongs to him* este dinero le pertenece, este dinero es suyo ‖ ser miembro de (to a party, a society, etc.) ‖ ser socio; *do you belong to that country club?* ¿eres socio de ese club de campo? ‖ ser de (to be native, resident); *he belongs here* es de aquí ‖ deber estar; *this dictionary belongs in every office* este diccionario debe estar en todas las oficinas; *books placed where they don't belong* libros colocados donde no deben estar ‖ incumbir a, competir a (to be incumbent upon) ‖ ser propio de, corresponder a; *such amusements do not belong to his age* tales diversiones no son propias de su edad ‖ ir bien; *cheese belongs with lettuce* el queso va bien con la lechuga ‖ ir, hacer juego; *this hat doesn't belong with your coat* este sombrero no va con tu abrigo; *stockings that don't belong* medias que no hacen juego ‖ estar en su ambiente; *you can live in Paris but you'll never be-*

long there puedes vivir en París, pero nunca estarás en tu ambiente.

belongings [-iŋz] *pl n* cosas *f*, pertenencias *f*, bártulos *m*, efectos *m* personales.

beloved [bi'lʌvd] *adj* querido, da; amado, da.
◆ *n* amado, da.

below [bi'ləu] *adv* abajo; *below there are people waiting* abajo hay gente esperando ‖ de abajo; *the neighbours below* los vecinos de abajo ‖ por debajo; *the underground runs below* el metro pasa por debajo ‖ más abajo; *five houses below on the right* cinco casas más abajo a la derecha; *the passage quoted below* el pasaje citado más abajo ‖ *here below* aquí abajo (on earth).
◆ *prep* debajo de; *my mother-in-law lives below us* mi suegra vive debajo de nosotros ‖ por debajo de; *below the knee* por debajo de la rodilla; *below sea level* por debajo del nivel del mar; *below the average* por debajo de la media ‖ inferior a; *temperatures below normal* temperaturas inferiores a lo normal ‖ — *below cost* a un precio inferior al de coste ‖ *below zero* bajo cero ‖ *it is below me to answer* no me rebajo a contestar.

belowdecks [-deks] *adv* MAR bajo cubierta ‖ MAR *to go belowdecks* bajar.

Belshazzar [bel'ʃæzə*] *pr n* Baltasar *m*.

belt [belt] *n* cinturón *m*; *a leather belt* un cinturón de cuero ‖ bandolera *f* (shoulder belt) ‖ cinto *m* (for carrying weapons) ‖ zona *f* (area); *cotton belt* zona algodonera ‖ cinturón *m* (of mountains) ‖ TECH correa *f*, cinta *f* ‖ MED faja *f* ‖ SP cinturón *m*; *black belt* cinturón negro ‖ FAM golpe *m* (blow) ‖ — *blow below the belt* golpe bajo ‖ TECH *continuous* o *endless belt* correa sin fin | *conveyor belt* cinta transportadora | *drive* o *driving belt* correa de transmisión ‖ *life belt* cinturón salvavidas ‖ *loading belt* cinta *f* (of machine gun) ‖ *seat* o *safety belt* cinturón de seguridad ‖ FIG *to have sth. under one's belt* tener algo en su haber, tener algo terminado | *to tighten one's belt* apretarse el cinturón.

belt [belt] *vt* ceñir; *a dress belted with a golden chain* un traje ceñido con una cadena dorada ‖ rodear (to surround); *a house belted by trees* una casa rodeada de árboles ‖ pegar con una correa (to thrash) ‖ pegar (to hit) ‖ *to belt out* cantar a voz en grito (to sing out).
◆ *vi* FAM *to belt along* ir a todo gas | *to belt past* pasar zumbando | *to belt out* salir pitando ‖ *to belt up* cerrar el pico, callarse.

belt highway [-'haiwei] *n* US carretera *f* de circunvalación (ring road).

belting [-iŋ] *n* TECH correas *f pl* de transmisión | transmisión *f*. ‖ FAM tunda *f*, zurra *f*, paliza *f* (beating).

belt line [-lain] *n* línea *f* de circunvalación.

belvedere ['belvidiə*] *n* belvedere *m*, mirador *m*.

belying [-iŋ] *pres part* ⟶ **belie.**

bemire [bi'maiə*] *vt* encenagar.

bemoan [bi'məun] *vt* lamentar, llorar (sth.) ‖ llorar (s.o.).

bemused [bi'mju:zd] *adj* abstraído, da; absorto, ta (plunged in thought) ‖ perplejo, ja (perplexed).

Ben [ben] *pr n* Benjamín *m* (diminutivo de «Benjamin»).

bench [bentʃ] *n* banco *m*; *she sat on a bench in the park* se sentó en un banco en el parque ‖ banco *m* (work table); *carpenter's bench* banco de carpintero ‖ JUR estrado *m* (judge's seat) | tribunal *m* (court); *the opinion of the bench* la opinión del tribunal ‖ escaño *m* (in Parliament) ‖ desnivel *m* (shelf of ground) ‖ plataforma *f* (at a dog show) ‖ — *testing bench* banco de pruebas ‖ JUR *the Bench* la magistratura | *to be appointed* o *raised to the bench* ser nombrado juez | *to be on the bench* ser magistrado, ser juez | *to bring before the bench* llevar a los tribunales.

bench [bentʃ] *vt* exhibir (a dog) ‖ US SP expulsar del campo (punishment) | retirar del juego (to rest).

bencher [-ə*] *n* decano *m* del Colegio de Abogados.

bench mark [-ma:k] *n* cota *f* de referencia (in topography) ‖ punto *m* de referencia.

bend [bend] *n* curva *f* (curve); *a bend in the road* una curva en la carretera ‖ vuelta *f*, recodo *m* (turn) ‖ meandro *m*, curva *f* (of river) ‖ recodo *m*, ángulo *m* (of pipe, path) ‖ inclinación *f* (of the body) ‖ ANAT sangría *f*, sangradura *f* (of elbow) ‖ combadura *f* (sag) ‖ MAR nudo *m* (knot) ‖ HERALD banda *f* ‖ — *hairpin bend* curva muy cerrada ‖ *sharp bend* curva cerrada ‖ FIG *to go round the bend* volverse loco.
◆ *pl* enfermedad *f sing* de los buzos.

bend* [bend] *vt* curvar, doblar; *it is not easy to bend a bar of iron* no es fácil curvar una barra de hierro; *pain prevents him from bending his back* el dolor le impide doblar la espalda ‖ doblar (on posting magazines, photographs, etc.); *do not bend* no doblar ‖ inclinar (one's head) ‖ encorvar (one's back) ‖ combar (to cause to sag) ‖ doblar (one's knee) ‖ armar (a bow) ‖ FIG dirigir (one's steps, one's eyes, military forces) | desviar (conversation) | dirigir, concentrar; *to bend all one's efforts to a task* dirigir todos sus esfuerzos hacia una tarea; *he couldn't bend his mind to his studies* no podía concentrar la mente en sus estudios ‖ MAR envergar (sail) ‖ — *on bended knee* arrodillado, da; de rodillas ‖ *to bend a key out of shape* doblar *or* torcer una llave ‖ *to bend back* doblar hacia atrás (an object), reflejar (light) ‖ *to bend down* inclinar ‖ *to bend s.o.'s will, to bend s.o. to one's will* someter a alguien, someter a alguien a la voluntad de uno; *he bent her to his will* la sometió a su voluntad ‖ *to bend straight* enderezar ‖ FIG *to bend the rules* hacer una excepción.
◆ *vi* curvarse, doblarse; *the iron bar bent under the weight* la barra de hierro se curvó bajo el peso ‖ encorvarse (a person) ‖ combarse (to sag) ‖ desviarse, torcer (to change direction); *the road bends to the right* la carretera se desvía a la derecha ‖ inclinarse, agacharse (to stoop); *I bent to pick up the book* me incliné para recoger el libro ‖ someterse; *to bend to s.o.'s will* someterse a la voluntad de uno ‖ — *to bend back* inclinarse hacia atrás ‖ *to bend down* inclinarse ‖ FIG *to bend over backwards for s.o.* hacer lo imposible por complacer a alguien.
— OBSERV Pret ***bent***; pp ***bent, bended*** *(ant)*.

bender [-ə*] *n* FAM juerga *f*; *to go on a bender* irse de juerga.

beneath [bi'ni:θ] *adv* debajo; *an awning with tables and chairs beneath* un toldo con mesas y sillas debajo ‖ abajo; *the sky above and the earth beneath* el cielo arriba y la tierra abajo; *the mountains and the little towns beneath* las montañas y los pueblecitos abajo.
◆ *prep* bajo; *the trees bent beneath the weight* los árboles se doblaban bajo el peso ‖ debajo de; *beneath his coat* debajo de su abrigo ‖ — FIG *it's beneath you to lie* mentir es indigno de ti ‖ *to be far beneath s.o.* ser muy inferior a alguien ‖ *to marry beneath o.s.* casarse con alguien de categoría *or* de clase inferior ‖ *you are beneath contempt* ni siquiera eres digno de desprecio.

benedicite [,beni'daisiti] *n* REL benedícite *m*.

Benedict ['benidikt] *pr n* Benito *m* ‖ Benedicto *m* (popes).

benedictine [,beni'diktin] *n* benedictino *m* (liqueur).

Benedictine [,beni'diktin] *adj/n* REL benedictino, na.

benediction [,beni'dikʃən] *n* bendición *f*; *the Pope's benediction* la bendición papal *or* del Papa.

benedictory [,beni'diktəri] *adj* bendecidor, ra.

benefaction [,beni'fækʃən] *n* beneficio *m*, favor *m* (contribution) ‖ obra *f* de beneficencia (act of charity) ‖ donación *f* (charitable donation).

benefactor ['benifæktə*] *n* benefactor *m*, bienhechor *m*.

benefactress ['benifæktris] *n* benefactora *f*, bienhechora *f*.

benefice ['benifis] *n* REL beneficio *m*.

beneficence [bi'nefisəns] *n* beneficencia *f*.

beneficent [bi'nefisənt] *adj* benéfico, ca (influence) ‖ benefactor, ra (person).

beneficial [,beni'fiʃəl] *adj* beneficioso, sa; provechoso, sa (advantageous) ‖ benéfico, ca; *beneficial rain* lluvia benéfica ‖ JUR usufructuario, ria.

beneficiary [,beni'fiʃəri] *n* beneficiario, ria; *contingent beneficiary* beneficiario condicional *or* eventual ‖ REL beneficiado *m*.

benefit ['benifit] *n* beneficio *m*, provecho *m*; *to derive benefit from* sacar beneficio de ‖ ganancia *f* (gain) ‖ ventaja *f* (advantage) ‖ bien *m*; *I did it for your benefit* lo hice por tu bien ‖ subsidio *m* (allowance); *family, old age, unemployment benefit* subsidio familiar, de vejez, de paro ‖ función *f* benéfica (performance) ‖ — *benefit match* partido *m* de homenaje (upon the retirement of a player), partido *m* benéfico (for charity purposes) ‖ JUR *benefit of clergy* fuero eclesiástico ‖ *benefit of the doubt* beneficio de la duda ‖ US *benefit society* mutualidad *f* ‖ *for the benefit of* en beneficio de, en provecho de; *performance for the benefit of the poor* función en beneficio de los pobres; en honor de; *she put on a new hat for his benefit* se puso un nuevo sombrero en su honor ‖ *let me add for your benefit that...* añadiré para su gobierno que... ‖ *marriage without benefit of clergy* matrimonio que no ha sido sancionado por la Iglesia ‖ *to be of benefit for* ser provechoso *or* de provecho para ‖ *under the benefit of inventory* a beneficio de inventario ‖ *without benefit of* sin la ayuda de.

benefit ['benifit] *vt* beneficiar; *to benefit humanity* beneficiar al género humano.
◆ *vi* beneficiar, beneficiarse; *to benefit from* o *by a law* beneficiarse de una ley; *to benefit from the help of* beneficiar de la ayuda de ‖ sacar provecho, aprovecharse; *she benefited by his advice* sacó provecho de su consejo.

Benelux ['benilʌks] *pr n* Benelux *m*.

benevolence [bi'nevələns] *n* benevolencia *f* (kindheartedness) ‖ generosidad *f* (generosity).

benevolent [bi'nevələnt] *adj* benévolo, la ‖ caritativo, va (charitable) ‖ de beneficencia (society).

Bengal [beŋ'gɔ:l] *pr n* GEOGR Bengala *m* ‖ *Bengal light* luz *f* de Bengala, bengala *f*.

Bengali [beŋ'gɔ:li] *adj* bengalí.
◆ *n* bengalí *m* & *f* (people) ‖ bengalí *m* (language).

bengaline ['beŋgəli:n] *n* bengalina *f* (material).

benighted [bi'naitid] *adj* anochecido, da; sorprendido por la noche ‖ FIG ignorante (mind).

benign [bi'nain] *adj* benigno, na ‖ favorable.

benignant [bi'nignənt] *adj* benigno, na ‖ favorable.

benignity [bi'nigniti] *n* benignidad *f* ‖ bondad *f*.

benjamin ['bendʒəmin] *n* benjuí *m.*

Benjamin ['bendʒəmin] *pr n* Benjamin *m.*

Benjamite ['bendʒəmait] *adj/n* benjamita.

bent [bent] *pret/pp* → **bend.**
◆ *adj* curvado, da; torcido, da; doblado, da || FIG decidido, da; empeñado, da; *he is bent on succeeding* está decidido a *or* empeñado en triunfar | inclinado, da (disposed) || — *to be bent on mischief* abrigar malas intenciones || *with eyes bent on* con los ojos fijos en.
◆ *n* inclinación *f* (*for, towards* a, hacia); *he followed his bent* obró de acuerdo con sus inclinaciones || facilidad *f*; *to have a bent for languages* tener facilidad para los idiomas || curvatura *f* (curve) || *to the top of one's bent* hasta el máximo.

bentonite ['bentənait] *n* GEOL bentonita *f.*

benumb [bi'nʌm] *vt* entumecer; *benumbed by the cold* entumecido por el frío || FIG embotar, entorpecer (mind) | dejar paralizado (shock).

benzamide [benzə'maid] *n* CHEM benzamida *f.*

benzedrine ['benzədrin] *n* MED bencedrina *f.*

benzene ['benzi:n] *n* CHEM benceno *m.*

benzilic [ben'zilik] *adj* bencílico, ca.

benzine ['benzi:n] *n* CHEM bencina *f.*

benzoate ['benzəueit] *n* CHEM benzoato *m.*

benzoic [ben'zəuik] *adj* CHEM benzoico, ca.

benzoin ['benzəuin] *n* CHEM benzoína *f* || BOT & CHEM benjuí *m.*

benzol ['benzɔl] *n* CHEM benzol *m.*

bequeath [bi'kwi:ð] *vt* legar (to will).

bequest [bi'kwest] *n* legado *m.*

berate [bi'reit] *vt* regañar, reñir (to scold).

Berber ['bə:bə*] *adj/n* beréber, berebere, berberisco, ca.

bereave* [bi'ri:v] *vt* privar; *the war had bereft him of all hope* la guerra le había privado de toda esperanza; *an accident had bereft him of his father* un accidente le había privado de su padre || despojar; *he was bereft of his possessions* fue despojado de sus bienes || — *his bereaved wife* su desconsolada esposa || *the bereaved* su desconsolada familia.
— OBSERV El verbo *to bereave* tiene dos pretéritos y dos participios pasivos: uno regular, *bereaved*, y otro irregular, *bereft*. El primero se emplea generalmente como participio pasivo y adjetivo con el sentido de *desconsolado*, y el segundo se utiliza como pretérito y participio pasivo cuando significa *privado* o *despojado*.

bereavement [-mənt] *n* pérdida *f* (of a relative) || duelo *m*, luto *m* (mourning); *owing to a recent bereavement* por reciente luto || aflicción *f* (sorrow).

bereft [bi'reft] *pret/pp* → **bereave.**

beret ['berei] *n* boina *f.*

bergamot ['bə:gəmɔt] *n* bergamota *f* (fruit, perfume) || *bergamot tree* bergamoto *m.*

beriberi ['beri'beri] *n* MED beriberi *m.*

berk [bə:k] *n* POP idiota *m* & *f.*

berkelium ['bə:kliəm] *n* berkelio *m.*

Berlin [bə:'lin] *pr n* GEOGR Berlín.

berlin [bə:'lin]; **berline** [bə:'li:n] *n* berlina *f.*

Berliner [bə:'linə*] *n* berlinés, esa.

berm [bə:m] *n* berma *f* (of a fortification).

Bermuda [bə'mju:də] *pr n* GEOGR islas *f pl* Bermudas, Bermudas *f pl.*

Bermuda grass [-grɑ:s] *n* BOT grama *f.*

Bermuda shorts [-'ʃɔ:ts] *pl n* pantalones *m* bermudas, bermudas *m.*

Bern; Berne [bə:n] *pr n* GEOGR Berna.

Bernadette ['bə:nə'det] *pr n* Bernarda *f.*

Bernard ['bə:nəd] *pr n* Bernardo *m.*

Bernardine ['bə:nədin] *adj/n* REL Bernardo, da.

Bernese [bə:'ni:z] *adj/n* Bernés, esa.

berry ['beri] *n* BOT baya *f* || grano *m* (of coffee, of wheat) || hueva *f* (of fish and crustacean).

berry ['beri] *vi* dar fruto.

berserk ['bə:sə:k] *adj* enloquecido, da || *to go berserk* volverse loco.

berth [bə:θ] *n* litera *f* (in trains) || MAR litera *f* (bunk) | camarote *m* (cabin) | atracadero *m*, amarradero *m* (at a dock) || empleo *m*, puesto *m* (job) || FIG *to give s.o. a wide berth* evitar a alguien.

berth [bə:θ] *vt* MAR atracar, amarrar (to moor) | dar camarote a (to furnish with a berth) || dar una litera a (in train).

Bertha ['bə:θə] *pr n* Berta *f.*

beryl ['beril] *n* MIN berilo *m.*

beryllium [be'riljəm] *n* CHEM berilio *m.*

besant ['besənt] *n* bezante *m*, besante *m.*

beseech* [bi'si:tʃ] *vt* implorar, suplicar; *I beseech you for pardon* le suplico que me perdone.
— OBSERV Pret/pp ***besought, beseeched.***

beseeching [-iŋ] *adj* suplicante, implorante.

beseem [bi'si:m] *v impers* (ant) convenir, ser conveniente.

beset* [bi'set] *vt* rodear (to surround); *the problem is beset with difficulties* el problema está rodeado de dificultades || llenar (*with* de) (to stud) || asaltar (to assail); *to be beset by doubts* estar asaltado por las dudas || acosar, perseguir (to pursue) || sitiar, cercar (to besiege) || obstruir (a road) || engaştar (to enchase).
— OBSERV Pret/pp ***beset.***

besetting [-iŋ] *adj* dominante, principal (principal) || obsesionante (temptation).

beside [bi'said] *prep* al lado de, junto a; *he sat beside me* se sentó junto a mí || cerca de (near) || al lado de, comparado con; *his efforts look feeble beside yours* sus esfuerzos parecen débiles comparados con los tuyos || además de (in addition to) || fuera de (aside from) || — *to be beside the point* no tener nada que ver, no venir al caso || *to be beside o.s.* estar fuera de sí.

besides [-z] *adv* además; *the play is excellent, and besides the tickets cost little* la obra es excelente y además las entradas cuestan poco || también (also).
◆ *prep* además de (in addition to); *besides being dear, it is badly made* además de ser caro, está mal hecho || menos, excepto (except); *no one besides you* nadie excepto tú.

besiege [bi'si:dʒ] *vt* MIL sitiar, asediar || FIG asediar, acosar.

besieger [-ə*] *n* sitiador, ra.

besmear [bi'smiə*] *vt* embadurnar, untar (to smear).

besmirch [bi'smə:tʃ] *vt* manchar, ensuciar || FIG manchar, mancillar.

besom ['bi:zəm] *n* escoba *f.*

besought [bi'sɔ:t] *pret* & *p p* → **beseech.**

besotted [bi'sɔtid] *adj* *to be besotted with s.o.* perder la cabeza por alguien || *to be besotted with drink* estar atontado por la bebida.

bespatter [bi'spætə*] *vt* salpicar (*with* de).

bespeak* [bi'spi:k] *vt* apalabrar (to hire, to engage) || dirigir la palabra a (to speak) || demostrar, indicar (to indicate) || encargar (a meal) || reservar (a room).
— OBSERV Pret ***bespoke***; pp ***bespoken, bespoke.***

bespectacled [bi'spektəkld] *adj* que lleva gafas, con gafas.

bespoke [bi'spəuk] *pret/p p* → **bespeak.**
◆ *adj* hecho a la medida (clothing) || que confecciona a la medida (tailor).

bespoken [bi'spəukən] *pp* → **bespeak.**

besprinkle [bi'spriŋkl] *vt* salpicar (*with* de) (a liquid) || espolvorear (*with* de) (a powder).

Bess [bes]; **Bessie; Bessy** [-i] *pr n* Isabelita *f* (diminutivo de «Elizabeth»).

best [best] *adj* (el) mejor, (la) mejor; *this colour is best for you* este color es el mejor para ti; *the best teacher of this subject* el mejor profesor de esta asignatura || — *best man* amigo *m* del novio que hace las veces de padrino en una boda || *best seller* éxito *m* de librería, «best seller» *m* (book); *this novel is the best seller of the week* esta novela es el éxito de librería de la semana || *best seller list* lista *f* de éxitos || *in the best condition for* en las mejores condiciones para || *the best one* el mejor, la mejor; *this is the best one* éste es el mejor || *the best part of* la mayor parte de || *to know what is best for s.o.* saber lo que más le conviene a uno.
◆ *adv* mejor; *the engine runs best at night* el motor funciona mejor por la noche || más; *the best looking girl* la chica más guapa || — *as best he could* lo mejor que pudo || *honey is what bears like best* la miel es lo que más gusta a los osos *or* lo que prefieren los osos || *to come off best* salir ganando || *you had best go* es mejor que te vayas, más vale que te vayas.
◆ *n* lo mejor; *I want the best for you* quiero lo mejor para ti || el mejor, la mejor; *she is the best of women* es la mejor de las mujeres || — *all the best* felicidades *f pl* (congratulations), que le vaya bien (good luck) || *at best* a lo más, en el mejor de los casos || *at one's best* en plena forma, como nunca || *even the best of us* todo el mundo || *I did it for the best* lo hice con la mejor intención || *it's all for the best* es mejor así, más vale que sea así || *it's the best there is* es lo mejor que hay || *Sunday best* traje *m* de los domingos, trapitos *m pl* de cristianar || *the best of it* lo mejor del caso || *to be dressed in one's best* estar de punta en blanco || *to be the best of friends* ser excelentes amigos, ser los mejores amigos del mundo || *to do one's best* hacer todo lo posible (to do one's utmost), hacer lo mejor posible (to do as well as one can) || *to do sth. to the best of one's ability* hacer algo lo mejor posible || *to get the best of it* salir ganando || *to get the best of s.o.* vencer *or* derrotar a alguien || *to get the best out of* sacar todo lo posible de || *to look one's best* estar muy bien, tener muy buen aspecto || *to make the best of* sacar el mejor partido de || *to make the best of it* conformarse || *to the best of my knowledge o of my recollection* que yo sepa, que yo recuerde || *with the best (of them)* como el que más; *he can sing with the best* canta como el que más.

best [best] *vt* vencer, ganar; *she can best him at swimming* le gana nadando.

bestial ['bestjəl] *adj* bestial.

bestiality [,besti'æliti] *n* bestialidad *f.*

bestiary ['bestiəri] *n* bestiario *m.*

bestir [bi'stə:*] *vt* *to bestir o.s.* moverse.

bestow [bi'stəu] *vt* conceder, otorgar; *to bestow a medal on s.o.* conceder una medalla a alguien || conferir (a title) || dar (to give) || dedicar (thought, time) || colocar (to place) || hacer; *to bestow a compliment on s.o.* hacer un cumplido a alguien.

bestowal [bi'stəuəl] *n* concesión *f*, otorgamiento *m.*

bestraddle [bi'strædl] *vt* → **bestride.**

bestrew* [bi'stru:] *vt* sembrar, cubrir; *bestrew with leaves* sembrado de hojas || desparramar, esparcir (to scatter).
— OBSERV Pret ***bestrewed***; pp ***bestrewed, bestrewn.***

bestrewn [-n] *pp* → **bestrew.**

bestridden [biˈstridn] *pp* → **bestride.**

bestride* [biˈstraid] *vt* montar, cabalgar (a horse) ‖ estar sentado a horcajadas en (a chair) ‖ salvar, franquear (a stream).
— OBSERV Pret ***bestrode***; pp ***bestridden***.

bestrode [biˈstrəud] *pret* → **bestride.**

bet [bet] *n* apuesta *f*, puesta *f*, postura *f* ‖ — *to lay* o *to make a bet* hacer una apuesta ‖ *to lay* o *to make a bet on* apostar a ‖ FIG *your best bet is to go at once* lo mejor que puedes hacer es irte en seguida.

bet* [bet] *vt* apostar (*on* a); *to bet two pounds on a horse* apostar dos libras a un caballo; *I bet you two shillings that* te apuesto dos chelines a que ‖ poner (to put) ‖ — *I bet you can't!* ¿a que no puedes? ‖ *you bet we had a good time!* ¡te aseguro que lo pasamos muy bien! ‖ *you bet!*, *you bet your life!* ¡ya lo creo!
◆ *vi* apostar.
— OBSERV Pret y pp ***bet, betted***.

beta [ˈbiːtə] *n* beta *f* ‖ — PHYS *beta particle* partícula *f* beta | *beta ray* rayo *m* beta.

beta-blocker [-blɔkə*] *n* MED betabloqueante *m*.

betake* [biˈteik] *vt* (ant) *to betake o.s. to* ir a (to go), entregarse a; *to betake o.s. to drink* entregarse a la bebida.
— OBSERV Pret ***betook***; pp ***betaken***.

betaken [-ən] *pp* → **betake.**

betatron [ˈbiːtəˌtrɔn] *n* PHYS betatrón *m*.

betel [ˈbiːtəl] *n* BOT betel *m*.

betel nut [-nʌt] *n* BOT areca *f* (fruit).

bête noire [ˈbeitˈnwɑː*] *n* pesadilla *f* (pet aversion).

bethel [ˈbeθəl] *n* templo *m* no conformista ‖ US capilla *f* para marinos.

bethink* [biˈθiŋk] *vt* *to bethink o.s. of* acordarse de, recordar (to remember), pensar en (to think).
— OBSERV Pret y pp ***bethought***.

Bethlehem [ˈbeθlihem] *pr n* GEOGR Belén.

bethought [biˈθɔːt] *pret/pp* → **bethink.**

betide [biˈtaid] *vt/vi* (ant) acontecer, ocurrir (to happen) ‖ *woe betide you!* ¡maldito sea!, ¡maldito seas!
— OBSERV Este verbo se emplea sólo en tercera persona del singular del presente de subjuntivo.

betimes [biˈtaimz] *adv* (ant) al alba, temprano (early) ‖ a tiempo (in good time).

betoken [biˈtəukən] *vt* acusar, denotar, revelar (to be sign of) ‖ presagiar, anunciar (to foreshow).

betook [biˈtuk] *pret* → **betake.**

betray [biˈtrei] *vt* traicionar; *to betray one's country* traicionar a su país ‖ entregar; *to betray s.o. to the enemy* entregar a alguien al enemigo ‖ revelar (to reveal); *to betray a secret* revelar un secreto ‖ demostrar, dar muestras de; *he betrayed little intelligence* demostró poca inteligencia ‖ engañar (a woman) ‖ defraudar (hope, trust).

betrayal [-əl] *n* traición *f* (treason) ‖ revelación *f* (of ignorance, etc.) ‖ engaño *m* (of a woman).

betroth [biˈtrəuð] *vt* prometer en matrimonio ‖ *to be betrothed* desposarse.

betrothal [-əl] *n* esponsales *m pl*, desposorios *m pl*.

betrothed [biˈtrəuðd] *adj/n* prometido, da ‖ *the betrothed* los prometidos.
— OBSERV Las palabras *betrothal* y *betrothed* son más corrientes en Estados Unidos que en Gran Bretaña donde se prefiere usar *engagement* y *engaged*.

better [ˈbetə*] *adj* mejor; *he is better today* está mejor hoy; *this book is better than the other one* este libro es mejor que el otro ‖ mayor; *the better part of the day* la mayor parte del día ‖ — FAM *better half* media naranja, cara mitad (one's wife) | *that's better* eso está mejor, eso va mejor | *that's better!* ¡eso es! ‖ *they have seen better days* han conocido días mejores ‖ *to be better than one's word* cumplir su promesa con creces ‖ *to be no better than* no ser más que; *he is no better than a beggar* no es más que un mendigo ‖ *to get better* mejorar ‖ *to go one better* hacer mejor todavía ‖ *to make sth. better* mejorar algo.
◆ *adv* mejor ‖ — *all the better, so much the better* mejor, tanto mejor ‖ *better and better* cada vez mejor; *he sings better and better* canta cada vez mejor; cada día más; *to like s.o. better and better* apreciar a alguien cada día más ‖ *better late than never* más vale tarde que nunca ‖ *better off* más rico ‖ *better than a pound* más de una libra ‖ *much better* mucho mejor ‖ *the sooner the better* cuanto antes mejor ‖ *to be all the better for* haber mejorado mucho a causa de ‖ FAM *to be better off* estar mejor de dinero (economically), encontrarse mejor (happier) ‖ *to know better; to know better than to* saber que no se debe; *I know better than to play with fire* sé que no se debe jugar con fuego; guardarse de; *he knew better than to believe them* se guardó de creerlos ‖ *to like better* preferir ‖ *to think all the better of s.o. for* estimar todavía más a alguien por ‖ *to think better of it* cambiar de opinión ‖ *you had better* es mejor que, más vale que; *you had better go* es mejor que te vayas, más vale que te vayas.
◆ *n* el mejor, la mejor; *the better of the two* el mejor de los dos ‖ superior *m*; *you must respect your betters* debes respetar a tus superiores ‖ — *a change for the better* una mejora ‖ *for better o worse* para lo bueno y para lo malo, en la suerte y en la desgracia ‖ *for the better* para mejorar ‖ *to get the better of s.o.* vencer a alguien (to defeat), engañar a alguien (to cheat).

better [ˈbetə*] *vt* mejorar (to improve); *to better housing conditions* mejorar las condiciones de alojamiento ‖ superar (to surpass); *he bettered his record by five seconds* superó su marca en cinco segundos ‖ *to better o.s.* mejorar, mejorar de posición.
◆ *vi* mejorar (to improve).

better [ˈbetə*] *n* apostante *m* & *f*.

betterment [ˈbetəmənt] *n* mejora *f*, mejoría *f*, mejoramiento *m* (improvement) ‖ JUR plusvalía *f*.

betting shop [ˈbetiŋʃɔp] *n* agencia *f* de apuestas hípicas.

bettor [ˈbetə*] *n* apostante *m* & *f*.

between [biˈtwiːn] *prep* entre; *the house is between two oaks* la casa está entre dos robles; *between sixty and seventy* entre sesenta y setenta; *they arrived between two and three* llegaron entre las dos y las tres; *the difference between a mule and a horse* la diferencia entre una mula y un caballo; *we did it between the three of us* lo hicimos entre los tres ‖ — MAR *between decks* entrecubierta *f* ‖ *between now and then* de aquí a entonces ‖ *between September and November* de septiembre a noviembre ‖ *between you and me, between ourselves* entre tú y yo, entre nosotros ‖ *closed between 1 and 3* cerrado de 1 a 3 ‖ *in between* entre ‖ *to divide* o *to share between* dividir *or* repartir entre.
◆ *adv* en medio, por medio, entremedias ‖ — *far between* a grandes intervalos ‖ *in between* mientras tanto (meanwhile), en medio ‖ *to come between* interponerse.

betweentimes [-taimz]; **betweenwhiles** [-wailz] *adv* de vez en cuando (at intervals) ‖ en el intervalo, (en el) entretanto (meanwhile).

betwixt [biˈtwikst] *prep* entre.
◆ *adv* en medio (between) ‖ — *betwixt and between* ni una cosa ni otra; *it's betwixt and between* no es ni una cosa ni otra ‖ *the truth lies betwixt and between* hay parte de verdad en ambos casos.

bevatron [ˈbevətrən] *n* PHYS bevatrón *m*.

bevel [ˈbevəl] *n* MATH ángulo oblicuo (angle) ‖ bisel *m* (surface) ‖ — *bevel edge* chaflán *m* ‖ *bevel gear* engranaje cónico ‖ *bevel square* falsa escuadra.

bevel [ˈbevəl] *vt* biselar.

bevelled [-d] *adj* biselado, da.

bevelling [-iŋ] *n* biselado *m*.

beverage [ˈbevəridʒ] *n* bebida *f*.

bevy [ˈbevi] *n* grupo *m* (women) ‖ bandada *f* (birds) ‖ manada *f* (deer, etc.).

bewail [biˈweil] *vt* lamentar, llorar.
◆ *vi* lamentarse.

beware [biˈwɛə*] *vi* tener cuidado; *beware of the dog* tenga cuidado con el perro ‖ *beware!* ¡atención!, ¡cuidado!

bewilder [biˈwildə*] *vt* desconcertar, desorientar, dejar perplejo (to perplex).

bewildering [-riŋ] *adj* desconcertante.

bewilderment [-mənt] *n* desconcierto *m*, perplejidad *f*.

bewitch [biˈwitʃ] *vt* embrujar, hechizar ‖ FIG encantar, fascinar, hechizar (to fascinate).

bewitching [-inŋ] *adj* fascinante.

bey [bei] *n* bey *m*.

beyond [biˈjɔnd] *adv* más allá, más lejos; *the river and the mountains beyond* el río y más allá las montañas; *let us go beyond* vayámonos más lejos.
◆ *prep* más allá de; *we went beyond the river* fuimos más allá del río; *beyond his hopes* más allá de sus esperanzas ‖ fuera de; *beyond his reach* fuera de su alcance; *beyond his plans* fuera de sus planes; *beyond logic* fuera de la lógica ‖ además de (besides); *beyond your regular work, you must type* además de tu trabajo normal tienes que escribir a máquina ‖ pasado, da; *beyond a certain date* pasada cierta fecha; *beyond twelve o'clock* pasadas las doce ‖ más de; *nothing beyond what I already knew* nada más de lo que yo ya sabía; *he is beyond sixty* tiene más de sesenta años ‖ — *beyond bearing* intolerable ‖ *beyond belief* increíble; increíblemente ‖ *beyond description* indescriptible ‖ *beyond doubt* indudable, fuera de duda; indudablemente ‖ *beyond help* irremediable (incurable), perdido, da (lost) ‖ *beyond measure* inmenso; inmensamente ‖ *beyond praise* por encima de todo elogio ‖ *beyond question* incuestionable; incuestionablemente ‖ *beyond the seas* allende los mares ‖ *it is beyond me* eso está fuera de mi alcance (incomprehensible), es superior a mis fuerzas (difficult to do) ‖ *to be living beyond one's means* vivir por encima de sus posibilidades ‖ *to go beyond one's duties* no caer dentro de las atribuciones de alguien.

beyond [biˈjɔnd] *n* *the beyond* el más allá.

Beyrouth [beiˈruːt] *pr n* GEOGR Beirut.

bezant [ˈbezənt] *n* bezante *m*, besante *m*.

bezel [ˈbezl] *n* faceta *f* (of cut gem) ‖ engaste *m* (holding a gem) ‖ bisel *m* (in tools).

bezoar [ˈbezɔə*] *n* bezar *m*, bezaar *m*.

bhang [bæŋ] *n* BOT cáñamo *m* (hemp) | mariguana *f*, marijuana *f*, marihuana *f*.

biacid [baiˈæsid] *adj* CHEM biácido, da (diacid).

biannual [ˌbaiˈænjuəl] *adj* semestral.

bias [ˈbaiəs] *n* tendencia *f*; *strong liberal bias* fuerte tendencia liberal ‖ prejuicio *m*, prevención *f* (prejudice); *you judge her with bias* le juzgas con prejuicio ‖ inclinación *f* (*towards* hacia,

por) ‖ SP descentramiento *m* (of the bowl) ‖ bies *m* (in sewing) ‖ ELECTR voltaje *m* de polarización ‖ — *cut on the bias* cortado al sesgo *or* al bies ‖ *vocational bias* deformación *f* profesional.
◆ *adj* al bies (in sewing).

bias [ˈbaiəs] *vt* influir en, influenciar ‖ — *to be biased* ser parcial ‖ *to be biased against* tener prejuicio en contra de ‖ *to be biased in favour of* ser partidario de.
— OBSERV En pretérito y participio pasado se puede emplear tanto *biassed* como *biased*.

biaxial [baiˈæksjəl]; **biaxal** [baiˈæksəl] *adj* biaxial.

bib [bib] *n* babero *m* (for children) ‖ peto *m* (of apron, of overalls) ‖ FAM *in one's best bib and tucker* vestido de punta en blanco.

bibasic [baiˈbeisik] *adj* CHEM bibásico, ca (dibasic).

bibber [ˈbibə*] *n* FAM bebedor *m*.

bibcock [ˈbibkɔk] *n* grifo *m*.

bibelot [ˈbiːbələu] *n* bibelot *m*.

Bible [ˈbaibl] *pr n* Biblia *f*; *the Holy Bible* la Santa Biblia ‖ *bible paper* papel biblia.

biblical [ˈbiblikəl] *adj* bíblico, ca.

bibliographer [ˌbibliˈɔgrəfə*] *n* bibliógrafo, fa.

bibliographic [ˌbibliəˈgræfik]; **bibliographical** [ˌbibliəˈgræfikəl] *adj* bibliográfico, ca.

bibliography [ˌbibliˈɔgrəfi] *n* bibliografía *f*.

bibliomanía [ˌbibliəuˈmeinjə] *n* bibliomanía *f* (excesive love of books).

bibliophile [ˈbibliəufail] *n* bibliófilo, la.

bibulous [ˌbibjuləs] *adj* bebedor, ra (person) ‖ absorbente (paper).

bicameral [ˈbaiˈkæmərəl] *adj* bicameral.

bicarbide [baiˈkɑːbaid] *n* CHEM bicarburo *m*.

bicarbonate [baiˈkɑːbənit] *n* CHEM bicarbonato *m*; *bicarbonate of soda* bicarbonato de sosa; *sodium bicarbonate* bicarbonato sódico.

bice [bais] *n* azul *m* de cobalto.

bicentenary [ˌbisenˈtiːnəri] *n* bicentenario *m*.

bicentennial [ˌbaisenˈtenjəl] *adj* que ocurre cada doscientos años.
◆ *n* bicentenario, *m*.

bicephalous [baiˈsefələs] *adj* bicéfalo, la.

biceps [ˈbaiseps] *n* ANAT bíceps *m*.

bichloride [ˈbaiˈklɔːraid] *n* CHEM bicloruro *m*.

bichromate [ˈbaiˈkrəumit] *n* CHEM bicromato *m*.

bicipital [baiˈsipitəl] *adj* bicipital.

bicker [ˈbikə*] *n* disputa *f*, pendencia *f*.

bicker [ˈbikə*] *vi* discutir, reñir (persons) ‖ murmurar (stream) ‖ vacilar (light).

bickiron [ˈbikaiən] *n* bigornia *f* (anvil).

bicolour; *US* **bicolor** [ˈbaikʌlə*] *adj* bicolor.

biconcave [baiˈkɔnkeiv] *adj* bicóncavo, va.

biconvex [baiˈkɔnveks] *adj* biconvexo, xa.

bicycle [ˈbaisikl] *n* bicicleta *f*; *to go by bicycle* ir en bicicleta; *he doesn't know how to ride a bicycle* no sabe montar en bicicleta.

bicycle [ˈbaisikl] *vi* ir en bicicleta; montar en bicicleta.

bicyclist [ˈbaisiklist] *n* ciclista *m* & *f*.

bid [bid] *n* oferta *f* (offer) ‖ puja *f*, postura *f* (at an auction sale) ‖ declaración *f* (in bridge) ‖ intento *m*, tentativa *f*; *he failed in his bid for liberty* fracasó en su intento por conseguir la libertad ‖ *US* FAM invitación *f* (to become a member) ‖ — *higher bid* sobrepuja *f* ‖ *to make a bid* pujar (in an auction), declarar (to make a contract in bridge), cumplir el contrato (to score in bridge) ‖ *to make a bid for* intentar conseguir.

bid* [bid] *vt* mandar, ordenar (to command); *she bade him work* le ordenó que trabajase ‖ rogar, pedir; *I bid you be silent* le ruego que guarde silencio ‖ invitar; *to bid s.o. to dinner* invitar a alguien a cenar ‖ dar; *to bid s.o. welcome* dar la bienvenida a alguien ‖ decir (good-bye) ‖ ofrecer, pujar, licitar (at an auction sale); *to bid fifty pounds for* ofrecer cincuenta libras por ‖ declarar (in bridge) ‖ — *to bid defiance to* desafiar a ‖ *to bid farewell to* despedirse de, decir adiós a ‖ *to bid s.o. up to twenty pounds* obligar a alguien a hacer una postura de veinte libras.
◆ *vi* pujar, hacer una oferta (*for* por) (at an auction sale) ‖ declarar (in bridge) ‖ — *the expedition bade fair to be successful* parecía que la expedición iba a ser un éxito ‖ *to bid over s.o.* ofrecer más que alguien ‖ *to bid up* pujar.
— OBSERV Pret ***bade*** o ***bid***; pp ***bidden*** o ***bid***. *Bade* y *bidden* se emplean en todos los sentidos, excepto en los que se refieren a una subasta y a juegos de cartas en cuyos casos sólo se utiliza *bid*.
— OBSERV En la forma activa *to bid* va seguido por el infinitivo sin *to*: *I bid him sit down* y en la forma pasiva por el infinitivo con *to*: *he was bidden to sit down*.

biddable [-əabl] *adj* dócil, sumiso, sa.

bidden [ˈbidn] *pp* → **bid.**

bidder [ˈbidə*] *n* licitador *m*, postor *m* (at an auction sale); *the highest bidder* el mejor postor ‖ declarante *m* & *f* (at bridge).

bidding [ˈbidiŋ] *n* orden *f* (command); *to do s.o.'s bidding* cumplir la orden de alguien ‖ ofertas *f pl*, licitación *f*, puja *f* (at an auction sale) ‖ subasta *f* (in bridge).

bide* [baid] *vt* *to bide one's time* esperar el momento oportuno.
— OBSERV Pret ***bode***; pp ***bided***.

bidet [ˈbiːdei] *n* bidé *m*.

biennial [baiˈeniəl] *adj* bienal.
◆ *n* bienal *f* (exhibition).

biennium [baiˈeniəm] *n* bienio *m*.
— OBSERV El plural de *biennium* es *biennia*.

bier [biə*] *n* andas *f pl* (for coffin) ‖ féretro *m* (coffin).

bifacial [baiˈfeiʃəl] *adj* bifacial.

biff [bif] *n* FAM tortazo *m* (cuff).

biff [bif] *vt* FAM pegar un tortazo a.

bifid [ˈbaiˌfid] *adj* bífido, da.

bifocal [ˈbaiˈfəukəl] *adj* bifocal.
◆ *pl n* lentes *f* bifocales.

bifurcate [ˈbaifəːkeit] *vi* bifurcarse.
◆ *vt* dividir en dos.

bifurcation [ˌbaifəːˈkeiʃən] *n* bifurcación *f*.

big [big] *adj* grande (large); *a big book* un libro grande ‖ mayor; *a big girl* una chica mayor; *his big sister* su hermana mayor ‖ grande (importante); *to do big things* hacer grandes cosas ‖ fuerte (voice) ‖ — FAM *big bug* o *boy* o *daddy* o *fish* o *name* o *gun* o *noise* o *shot* o *wheel* pez gordo ‖ *big cat* felino *m* de gran tamaño ‖ FAM *big deal!* ¡pues qué bien!, ¡vaya cosa! ‖ *big hand* minutero *m* ‖ TECH *big end* cabeza *f* de biela ‖ *big finger* dedo *m* pulgar ‖ *big game* caza *f* mayor ‖ *big hand* minutero ‖ *big heart* gran corazón *m* ‖ *big money* mucho dinero *m* ‖ *big sounding* altisonante ‖ *big talk* fanfarronadas *f pl* ‖ *big toe* dedo gordo del pie ‖ BOT *big tree* secoya *f* ‖ *big with child* embarazada, encinta (woman) ‖ *big with consequences* de consecuencias graves ‖ *big with young* preñada (animals) ‖ *the Big Four* los cuatro Grandes ‖ FAM *to live in a big way* vivir a todo tren | *too big for one's boots*, *US* *to big for one's breeches* o *pants* creído, da; engreído, da | *to think o.s. big* dárselas de listo ‖ *you are a big liar!* ¡menudo embustero eres!, ¡eres un embustero de tomo y lomo!
◆ *adv* FAM *to go over big* tener un éxito enorme ‖ *to talk big* fanfarronear.

— OBSERV The adjective *grande* in Spanish is apocopated before a singular noun: *a large house* una gran casa *or* una casa grande.

bigamist [ˈbigəmist] *n* bígamo, ma.

bigamous [ˈbigəməs] *adj* bígamo, ma.

bigamy [ˈbigəmi] *n* bigamia *f*.

bigaroon [ˌbigəˈruːn]; **bigarreau** [ˈbigərəu] *n* BOT cereza *f* gordal *or* garrafal.

big-bellied [ˈbigˈbelid] *adj* FAM barrigón, ona; tripudo, da | embarazada (pregnant).

big-boned [ˈbigˈbəund] *adj* FAM huesudo, da.

Big Dipper [ˈbigˈdipə*] *n* ASTR Osa *f* Mayor.

big-eared [ˈbigiəd] *adj* orejudo, da.

bigheaded [ˈbigˈhedid] *adj* FAM engreído, da.

bighearted [ˈbigˈhɑːtid] *adj* generoso, sa.

bighorn [ˈbighɔːn] *n* ZOOL carnero *m* de las Montañas Rocosas.

bight [bait] *n* entrante *m* (bend in a coast, in a river) ‖ ensenada *f*, cala *f* (small bay) ‖ MAR seno *m* (of a rope).

big mouth [ˈbigmauθ] *n* FAM bocazas *m* & *f* *inv*.

big-mouthed [ˈbigmauðd] *adj* FAM hablador, ra.

bignoniaceae [bigˈnəunjəsiːi] *pl n* BOT bignoniáceas *f*.

bigot [ˈbigət] *n* fanático, ca.

bigoted [-id] *adj* fanático, ca; intolerante.

bigotry [-ri] *n* fanatismo *m*, intolerancia *f*.

big-time [ˈbigtaim] *adj* influyente.

big top [ˈbigˈtɔp] *n* tienda *f* principal [*AMER* carpa *f* principal] (of a circus).

bigwig [ˈbigwig] *n* FAM pez *m* *or* pájaro *m* gordo.

bike [baik] *n* FAM bici *f* (bicycle).

bike [baik] *vi* ir en bicicleta; montar en bicicleta.

bikini [biˈkiːni] *n* bikini *m* (bathing suit).

bilabial [baiˈleibjəl] *adj* bilabial.
◆ *n* bilabial *f*.

bilabiate [baiˈleibjeit] *adj* BOT bilabiado, da.

bilateral [baiˈlætərəl] *adj* bilateral.

bilberry [ˈbilbəri] *n* BOT arándano *m*.

bile [bail] *n* MED bilis *f inv* ‖ FIG bilis *f inv* ‖ — ANAT *bile duct* conducto *m* biliar ‖ MED *bile stone* cálculo *m* biliar.

bilge [bildʒ] *n* MAR sentina *f* (inner hull) | pantoque *m* (outer hull) | agua *f* de sentina (water) ‖ barriga *f* (of barrel) ‖ FAM idioteces *f pl* ‖ MAR *bilge keel* quilla *f* de balance.

bilge [bildʒ] *vt* MAR desfondar.
◆ *vi* MAR hacer agua.

bilharzia [bilˈhɑːziə]; **bilharziasis** [ˌbilhɑːˈzaiəsis]; **bilharziosis** [ˌbilhɑːziˈəusis] *n* MED bilharciasis *f*, bilarciasis *f*.

biliary [ˈbiljəri] *adj* biliar, biliario, ria; de la bilis.

bilingual [baiˈliŋgwəl] *adj* bilingüe.

bilingualism [-izəm] *n* bilingüismo *m*.

bilious [ˈbiljəs] *adj* MED bilioso, sa ‖ FIG malhumorado, da ‖ MED *bilious attack* trastorno *m* biliar.

biliousness [-nis] *n* MED crisis *f* hepática, trastorno *m* biliar.

bilk [bilk] *vt* engañar, defraudar, estafar (to swindle) ‖ escapársele [a uno] (to evade); *he bilked us* se nos escapó.

bill [bil] *n* factura *f* (invoice); *electricity bill* factura de la electricidad ‖ cuenta *f* (in restaurants, in shops, etc.) ‖ minuta *f* (law and other professions) ‖ programa *f* (in theatres) ‖ hoja *f* (advertising leaflet) ‖ lista *f* (list) ‖ cartel *m* (poster) ‖ JUR proyecto *m* de ley; *to pass a bill* adoptar un proyecto de ley ‖ COMM efecto *m*, letra *f*; *to protest a bill* protestar una letra | bono *m* (bond) || pico *m* (of bird) || promontorio *m* (promontory) || MAR uña *f* (of anchor) || *US* billete *m* de banco (bank note) || — *bill broker* agente *m* de cambio y bolsa || JUR *bill of appeal* demanda *f* de apelación || *bill of costs* relación *f or* estado *m* de gastos || *bill of credit* carta *f* de crédito || *bill of exchange* letra *f* de cambio || *bill of fare* menú *m* || MAR *bill of health* patente *f* de sanidad | *bill of landing* conocimiento *m* de embarque || TUR *bill of rights* carta *f or* declaración *f* de derechos || *bill of sale* contrato *m or* escritura *f* de venta || *post* o *stick no bills* prohibido fijar carteles || FIG *to fill the bill* servir, valer (object), satisfacer los requisitos (person), mantenerse en el cartel (play) || FAM *to foot the bill* cascar, pagar || *to ahead* o *to top the bill* encabezar el reparto (an artist).

bill [bil] *vt* facturar || extender *or* pasar la factura; *you may bill me at the end of the month* puede pasarme la factura a final de mes || anunciar (to advertise).
◆ *vi* juntar los picos (birds) || FAM *to bill and coo* estar como dos tórtolos.

Bill [bil] *pr n* Guillermo *m* (diminutivo de «William»).

billboard ['bilbɔːd] *n* *US* cartelera *f*.

billet ['bilit] *n* leño *m* (for firewood) || ARCH moldura *f* || TECH palanquilla *f* || HERALD billete *m* || MIL alojamiento *m*, acantonamiento *m* (assigned quarters) | boleta *f* de alojamiento (official order) || FAM colocación *f*, puesto *m* (job).

billet ['bilit] *vt* alojar, acantonar.

billet-doux ['bilei'duː] *n* esquela *f* amorosa, carta *f* amorosa.
— OBSERV El plural de *billet-doux* es *billets-doux*.

billfold ['bilfəuld] *n* *US* cartera *f*, billetero *m*.

billhook ['bilhuk] *n* podadera *f*.

billiard ['biljəd] *adj* de billar; *billiard ball, cue, table* bola, taco, mesa de billar || *billiard cloth* tapete *m*, paño *m*.

billiard player [-ˌpleiə*] *n* jugador *m* de billar, billarista *m*.

billiards ['biljədz] *n* billar *m*.

billing ['biliŋ] *n* facturación *f* (of invoices) || orden *m* de importancia (spectacles) || *top billing* estrellato *m*.

billingsgate ['biliŋzgit] *n* FAM lenguaje *m* grosero.

billion ['biljən] *n* billón *m*, millón *m* de millones (in Great Britain) || *US* mil millones.

billionth ['biljənθ] *adj/n* billonésimo, ma (in Great Britain) || *US* mil millonésimo, ma.

billow ['biləu] *n* ola *f* (of water) || FIG oleada *f*; *billows of people* oleadas de gente.

billow ['biləu] *vi* ondular (to undulate) || hincharse, inflarse (to swell).

billowy [-i] *adj* ondulante (undulating) || agitado, da; encrespado, da; *the billowy sea* el mar agitado || hinchado, da; inflado, da (swollen).

billposter ['bilˌpəustə*]; **billsticker** ['bilˌstikə*] *n* cartelero *m*.

billy ['bili] *n* *US* porra *f* (policeman's truncheon).

Billy ['bili] *pr n* Guillermo *m* [diminutivo de *William*].

billycan [-kæn] *n* cazo *m*.

billycock [-kɔk] *n* FAM hongo *m* (hat).

billy goat [-gəut] *n* macho *m* cabrío || *billy-goat beard* perilla *f*, pera *f*.

billy-oh [-əu] *adv* *it's raining like billy-oh* llueve a cántaros || *they fought like billy-oh* lucharon encarnizadamente.

bilobate [bai'ləubeit]; **bilobed** [bai'ləubd] *adj* BOT bilobulado, da.

bilocular [bai'lɔkjulə*]; **biloculate** [bai'lɔkjulit] *adj* BOT bilocular.

biltong ['biltɔŋ] *n* cecina *f*.

bimanal ['baimənəl]; **bimanous** ['baimənəs] *adj* bímano, na.

bimane ['baimein] *n* bímano, na.

bimbo ['bimbəu] *n* POP mujer *f* joven, guapa y poco inteligente.

bimetallic ['baime'tælik] *adj* bimetálico, ca.

bimetallism [bai'metəlizəm] *n* bimetalismo *m*.

bimetalist [bai'metəlist] *adj/n* bimetalista.

bimonthly ['bai'mʌnθli] *adj* bimestral (every two months) || bimensual (twice a month).
◆ *n* publicación *f* bimestral *or* bimensual.
◆ *adv* bimestralmente (every two months) || bimensualmente (twice a month).

bin [bin] *n* cajón *m*, arca *f* || compartimiento *m* (storage compartment) || recipiente *m* (recipient) || carbonera *f* (for coal) || botellero *m* (for wine) || cubo *m* de basura (dustbin) || papelera *f* (for waste paper).

binary ['bainəri] *adj* binario, ria || INFORM binario, ria; *binary element* elemento *m* binario.

bind [baind] *n* lazo *m* (tie) || TECH atasco *m* || FAM lata *f*; *this job is a real bind* este trabajo es una verdadera lata | pesado, da (boring person) || *US* FIG & FAM *to be in a bind* estar metido en un lío.

bind* [baind] *vt* atar, liar (to tie up); *to bind a package with string* atar un paquete con una cuerda || atar (hands, legs) || agavillar (corn) || rematar (to edge) || ribetear (to trim) || encuadernar (pages, fascicles) || obligar (to place under obligation); *to bind s.o. to pay a debt* obligar a alguien a pagar una deuda || ligar (to cause to adhere) || endurecer (to make hard) || ceñir (to encircle) || apretar (the clothes) || vincular; *a treaty binds your country to ours* un tratado vincula su país con el nuestro || unir (to unite) || ratificar (a bargain, a treaty) || recogerse (one's hair) || MED estreñir (to constipate) | vendar (to bandage) || hacer (an insurance) || — *to bind off* menguar; *to bind off three stitches* menguar tres puntos || *to bind o.s. to* comprometerse a || JUR *to bind over* obligar legalmente a || *to bind s.o. as an apprentice to* poner a alguien de aprendiz en casa de || *to bind s.o. down to* obligar a alguien a || MED *to bind up* vendar.
◆ *vi* endurecerse (to grow stiff, hard) || fraguar (cement) || TECH unirse, trabarse (to stick together) | atascarse (to jam) || tener fuerza obligatoria.
— OBSERV Pret y pp ***bound***.

binder [-ə*] *n* encuadernador *m* (of books) || AGR agavilladora *f* || carpeta *f* (for papers) || cubierta *f* (for magazines) || MED faja *f* (strip of material) || ARCH tirante *m* (tie beam) || CHEM aglutinante *m*.

binding [-iŋ] *n* atadura *f* (fastening) || encuadernación *f* (book cover) || ribete *m* (edging); *blanket binding* ribete de la manta || galón *m* (of seam, of hem) || SP ataduras *f pl* (of skis).
◆ *adj* que hay que cumplir, que compromete; *binding promise* promesa que hay que cumplir || obligatorio, ria (*on, upon* para); *decision binding on all parties* decisión obligatoria para todas las partes || astringente, que estriñe (astringent) || *binding energy* energía *f* de unión *or* de enlace.

bindweed ['baindwiːd] *n* BOT correhuela *f*, enredadera *f*.

binge [bindʒ] *n* FAM borrachera *f* || *to go on a binge* o *to have a binge* ir de juerga, ir de parranda.

bingo ['biŋgəu] *n* bingo *m* (game).

bin-liner ['bin lɑinə*] *n* bolsa *f* de la basura.

binnacle ['binəkl] *n* MAR bitácora *f*.

binocular [bi'nɔkjulə*] *adj* binocular.

binoculars [-z] *pl n* prismáticos *m*, gemelos *m*.

binomial [bai'nəumjəl] *n* MATH binomio *m*.
◆ *adj* binomio, mia.

biochemical ['baiəu'kemikəl] *adj* bioquímico, ca.

biochemist ['baiəu'kemist] *n* bioquímico, ca.

biochemistry [-ri] *n* bioquímica *f*.

biodegradable ['baiəudi'greidəbl] *adj* biodegradable.

biogenesis ['baiəu'dʒenisis] *n* biogénesis *f*.

biogenetic [ˌbaiəudʒə'netik]; **biogenetical** [-əl] *adj* biogenético, ca.

biographer [bai'ɔgrəfə*] *n* biógrafo, fa.

biographic [ˌbaiəu'græfik]; **biographical** [-əl] *adj* biográfico, ca.

biography [bai'ɔgrəfi] *n* biografía *f*.

biologic [ˌbaiəu'lɔdʒik]; **biological** [-əl] *adj* biológico, ca; *biological warfare* guerra biológica.

biologist [ˌbai'ɔlədʒist] *n* biólogo *m*.

biology [ˌbai'ɔlədʒi] *n* biología *f*.

biomechanics ['baiɔmi'kæniks] *n* biomecánica *f*.

biophysics [ˌbaiəu'fiziks] *n* biofísica *f*.

biopsy ['baiəpsi] *n* MED biopsia *f*.

biosphere ['baiəsfiə*] *n* biosfera *f*.

biosynthesis [ˌbaiəu'sinθəsis] *n* biosíntesis *f*.

biotherapy [ˌbaiəu'θerəpi] *n* MED bioterapia *f*.

biotite ['baiətait] *n* MIN biotita *f*.

bipartisan [bai'pɑːtizən] *adj* *US* de dos partidos políticos.

bipartite [bai'pɑːtait] *adj* bipartido, da (having two parts) || bipartito, ta (of two parties); *bipartite agreement* acuerdo bipartito.

bipartition [ˌbaipɑː'tiʃən] *n* bipartición *f*.

biped ['baiped] *adj* bípedo, da.
◆ *n* bípedo *m*.

biplane ['baiplein] *n* AVIAT biplano *m*.

bipolar [bai'pəulə*] *adj* bipolar.

bipolarity [ˌbaipəu'læriti] *n* bipolaridad *f*.

biquadratic [ˌbaikwɔ'drætik] *adj* bicuadrado, da.

birch [bəːtʃ] *n* abedul *m* (tree, wood) || *birch* o *birch rod* vara *f* (de abedul) (for flogging).

birch [bəːtʃ] *vt* azotar (to flog).

birchen ['bəːtʃən] *adj* de abedul.

bird [bəːd] *n* ZOOL ave *f*, pájaro *m* (see OBSERV) || caza *f* de pluma (game) || SP volante *m* (badminton) || FAM individuo *m*, tipo *m* (man) | niña *f*, chica *f* (girl) | novia *f*, amiga *f* (girlfriend) || — FIG *a bird in the hand is worth two in the bush* más vale pájaro en mano que ciento volando | *a little bird told me* me lo dijo un pajarito, me lo ha dicho el pajarito verde || *US* *bird dog* perro *m* de caza || FIG *bird of ill omen* pájaro de mal agüero || *bird of paradise* ave del Paraíso || *bird of passage* ave de paso (animal, person) || *bird of peace* paloma *f* de la paz || *bird of prey* ave de presa *or* de rapiña || *bird shot* perdigones *m pl* || *bird's nest* nido *m* de pájaro || *bird's nest soup* sopa *f* de nido de golondrina || FIG *birds of a feather* lobos *m pl* de la misma camada | *birds of a feather flock together* Dios los cría y ellos se juntan | *early bird* madrugador, ra || *migratory bird* ave de paso || *night bird* ave nocturna (animal, person) || FIG *not to eat enough to feed a bird* comer como un pajarito | *the bird has flown* el pájaro voló | *the early bird catches the worm* al que madruga, Dios le ayuda | *to get the bird* ser abucheado (artist, speaker) | *to give s.o. the bird* abuchear a al-

guien (artist, speaker) | *to kill two birds with one stone* matar dos pájaros de un tiro.
— OBSERV *Pájaro* is applied to small birds whereas *ave* is used for larger ones.

birdbath [-bɑːθ] *n* pila *f* para pájaros.

birdbrain [-brein] *n* FAM majadero, ra; mentecato, ta.

birdcage [-keidʒ] *n* jaula *f* || pajarera *f* (large).

birdcall [-kɔːl] *n* canto *m* del pájaro (sound of a bird) || reclamo *m* (for attracting birds).

birdie [-i] *n* pajarito *m*.

birdlime [-laim] *n* liga *f*.

birdseed [-siːd] *n* BOT alpiste *m*.

bird's-eye [-zˌai] *n* ojo *m* de perdiz || *bird's-eye view* vista panorámica.

bird's-nest [-znest] *vi* sacar los pájaros del nido.

birefringence [ˌbairiˈfrindʒəns] *n* PHYS birrefringencia *f*.

bireme [ˈbairiːm] *n* MAR birreme *f*.

biretta [biˈretə] *n* REL birrete *m*, birreta *f*.

Birmingham [ˈbiðːmiŋm] *pr n* GEOGR Birmingham.

biro [ˈbaiərəu] *n* bolígrafo *m*.

birth [bəːθ] *n* nacimiento *m*; *the birth of his first child* el nacimiento de su primer hijo || MED parto *m*; *a difficult birth* un parto difícil || FIG nacimiento *m*, comienzo *m*; *birth of a nation* nacimiento de una nación | origen *m* (origin) | linaje *m*, cuna *f*, origen *m*; *of noble birth* de noble linaje || — *a person of birth* una persona bien nacida || *birth certificate* partida *f* de nacimiento || *birth control* control *m* de la natalidad, regulación *f* de nacimientos, limitación *f* de la natalidad || *by* o *from birth* de nacimiento || *to give birth to* dar a luz (to a child), dar origen a (to cause).

birthday [ˈbəːθdei] *n* cumpleaños *m*; *birthday party* fiesta de cumpleaños || fecha *f* de nacimiento (day of birth) || — *birthday honours* honores que se otorgan con motivo del cumpleaños del rey || FIG & FAM *to be in one's birthday suit* estar como Dios le trajo al mundo.

birthmark [ˈbəːθmɑːk] *n* marca *f* or mancha *f* de nacimiento.

birthplace [ˈbəːθpleis] *n* lugar *m* de nacimiento.

birthrate [ˈbəːθreit] *n* natalidad *f*, índice *m* de natalidad.

birthright [ˈbəːθrait] *n* derechos *m pl* de nacimiento || derechos *m pl* de primogenitura || FIG patrimonio *m*.

birthstone [ˈbəːθstəun] *n* piedra *f* preciosa que corresponde al mes de nacimiento.

bis [bis] *adv* MUS bis.

Biscay [ˈbiskei] *pr n* GEOGR Vizcaya *f* || *Bay of Biscay* mar Cantábrico, golfo *m* de Vizcaya.

biscuit [ˈbiskit] *n* galleta *f* || US bollo *m* (bun) || bizcocho *m*, biscuit *m* (pottery) || beige *m* (colour) || FAM *that takes the biscuit!* ¡eso es el colmo!

bisect [baiˈsekt] *vt* MATH bisecar (angles) || dividir en dos partes.
◆ *vi* bifurcarse (to fork).

bisecting [-iŋ] *adj* bisector, bisectriz.

bisection [baiˈsekʃən] *n* MATH bisección *f* || división *f* en dos partes.

bisector [baiˈsektə*]; **bisectrix** [baiˈsektriks] *n* MATH bisectriz *f*.

bisexual [baiˈsekjual] *adj* bisexual.

bishop [ˈbiʃəp] *n* REL obispo *m* || alfil *m* (in chess) || bebida *f* caliente a base de vino de Oporto (drink) || BOT *bishop's weed* biznaga *f*.

bishopric [-rik] *n* obispado *m*.

bisk [bisk] *n* CULIN sopa *f* de mariscos.

bismuth [ˈbizməθ] *n* bismuto *m*.

bison [ˈbaisn] *n* ZOOL bisonte *m*.

bisque [bisk] *n* sopa *f* de mariscos (soup) || US helado *m* de avellana (ice cream) || bizcocho *m*, biscuit *m* (pottery) || SP ventaja *f*.

Bissau [biˈsau] *pr n* GEOGR Bissau.

bissextile [biˈsekstail] *adj* bisiesto.
◆ *n* año *m* bisiesto (leap year).

bister [ˈbistə*] *n* US bistre *m* (colour).

bistort [ˈbistɔːt] *n* BOT bistorta *f*.

bistoury [ˈbisturi] *n* MED bisturí *m* (scalpel).

bistre [ˈbistə*] *n* bistre *m* (colour).

bistro [ˈbiːstrəu] *n* pequeño restaurante *m* or bar *m*.

bisulcate [baiˈsʌlkeit] *adj* ZOOL bisulco, ca.

bisulfate; bisulphate [baiˈsʌlfeit] *n* CHEM bisulfato *m*.

bisulfide; bisulphide [baiˈsʌlfaid] *n* CHEM bisulfuro *m*.

bisulfite; bisulphite [baiˈsʌlfait] *n* CHEM bisulfito *m*.

bit [bit] *n* trozo *m*, pedazo *m* (small piece); *a bit of bread* un trozo de pan || poco *m* (small amount); *a bit of milk* un poco de leche || poco *m*, rato *m* (short time); *wait a bit* espera un poco || parte *f* (part); *one of the best bits of the play* una de las mejores partes de la obra || bocado *m* (of the bridle) || TECH boca *f*, filo *m* (in tools) | broca *f*, taladro *m* (of the brace) | paletón *m* (of a key) || INFORM bit *m* || — *a bit* un poco; *he is a bit older than I* es un poco mayor que yo || FAM *a bit much* demasiado || *a bit of advice* un consejo || *a bit of garden* un jardincito || *a bit of luck* una suerte (stroke of luck), un poco de suerte (a little luck) || *a bit of news* una noticia || *a good bit* bastante || *bit actor* actor secundario || *bit brace* berbiquí *m* || *bit by bit* poco a poco || *bit part* papel secundario || FAM *bits and pieces* chismes *m pl*, bártulos *m pl* || *I have got a bit of a headache* tengo un ligero dolor de cabeza || *it's not a bit of use* no sirve absolutamente para nada || *it was a bit of a surprise* fue una gran sorpresa || *not a bit* no hay de qué; *thank you! not a bit* ¡gracias! no hay de qué; en absoluto; *are you tired? not a bit* ¿estás cansado? en absoluto || *quite a bit* bastante || *threepenny bit* moneda *f* de tres peniques || *to be a bit of* ser un poco; *he's a bit of an artist* es un poco artista | *to be a bit of all right* estar muy bien || *to be every bit a man* ser un hombre por los cuatro costados || *to blow to bits* hacer añicos, hacer saltar en pedazos || *to do one's bit* hacer *or* poner de su parte || FIG *to give s.o. a bit of one's mind* decirle a uno cuatro verdades | *to go to bits* venirse abajo || *to smash to bits* romper en pedazos, hacer añicos || FIG *to take the bit in one's teeth* desbocarse || US *two bits* veinticinco centavos.

bit [bit] *pret/pp* ⟶ **bite.**

bitch [bitʃ] *n* hembra *f* (female) || perra *f* (dog) | loba *f* (wolf) || FAM bruja *f* (bad tempered woman) | zorra *f* (prostitute) | US FAM queja *f* (complaint) || FAM *son of a bitch* hijo *m* de perra.

bitch [bitʃ] *vi* US FAM quejarse, protestar.

bitchy [ˈbitʃi] *adj* POP malévolo, la (malicious) || rencoroso, sa (spiteful) || *she's really bitchy* es una bruja.

bite [bait] *n* mordisco *m*, dentellada *f* (act) || mordedura *f* (wound) || piscolabis *m*, bocado *m*, refrigerio *m* (a snack) || bocado *m* (mouthful); *give me a bite of your cake* dame un bocado de tu pastel || picadura *f* (of insect, of snake) || dolor *m* agudo (sharp pain) || FIG mordacidad *f*; *his criticism lacks bite* su crítica carece de mordacidad || adherencia *f* (tyres) || TECH agarre *m* (grip) || PRINT lardón *m* || mordida *f*, picada *f* (in fishing) || — *I haven't had a bite all day* no he probado bocado en todo el día (nothing to eat), no han picado en todo el día (in fishing) || FIG & FAM *to put the bite on s.o.* pedir dinero prestado a alguien.

bite* [bait] *vt* morder; *the dog will bite you* el perro te morderá || picar (insect, snake, fish) || penetrar (to pierce) || cortar; *the wind bit her face* el viento le cortaba la cara || quemar; *frost bit the flowers* la helada quemó las flores || picar (pepper) || engañar (to deceive) || TECH agarrarse, agarrar (to grip) | corroer, atacar (to corrode) | morder (file) || MAR agarrar, morder (the anchor) || — FIG *bitten with* poseído de | *once bitten twice shy* gato escaldado del agua fría huye || *to bite off* arrancar con los dientes || FIG *to bite off more than one can chew* abarcar demasiado | *to bite one's lips* o *tongue* morderse los labios *or* la lengua || *to bite one's nails* morderse las uñas || FIG & FAM *to bite s.o.'s head off* echarle una bronca a alguien | *to bite the dust* morder el polvo | *to get bitten* dejarse engañar, picar | *what's biting you?* ¿qué mosca te ha picado?
◆ *vi* morder; *be careful, the dog bites* ten cuidado, el perro muerde || picar (fish, snake, insect) || cortar (cold, wind) || FIG picar (to yield to a lure) || TECH corroer, atacar | agarrar (on a road) || *to bite at* atacar, intentar morder (a dog).
— OBSERV Prep ***bit***; pp ***bitten, bit***.

biter [-ə*] *n* *the biter bit* el cazador cazado.

Bithynia [biˈθiniə] *pr n* Bitinia *f*.

biting [ˈbaitiŋ] *adj* cortante, penetrante (cold) || FIG mordaz, cáustico, ca; sarcástico, ca (words, etc.).

bitt [bit] *n* MAR bita *f*, noray *m* (bollard).

bitten [ˈbitn] *pp* ⟶ **bite.**

bitter [ˈbitə*] *adj* amargo, ga; *bitter almonds* almendras amargas || ácido, da; agrio, gria; *a very bitter lemon* un limón muy ácido || penetrante, cortante, glacial; *bitter cold* frío penetrante || glacial, riguroso, sa; *bitter weather* tiempo glacial || FIG amargo, ga (experience, disappointment, words, person) | acerbo, ba (critic) | encarnizado, da; enconado, da (fight) | profundo, da (contempt) | implacable (enemy, hatred) || — *bitter apple* coloquíntida *f* || *bitter orange* naranja *f* de Sevilla, naranja agria || *to the bitter end* hasta el final.
◆ *n* cerveza *f* amarga (beer).
◆ *pl* bitter *m sing* (drink).

bitterly [-li] *adv* amargamente || FIG con amargura || *it's bitterly cold* hace un frío glacial.

bittern [ˈbitəːn] *n* ZOOL avetoro *m*.

bitterness [ˈbitənis] *n* amargura *f* || acidez *f*, amargor *m* (of lemon) || crudeza *f*, rigor *m* (of winter) || FIG encono *m*, enconamiento *m*, encarnizamiento *m* (of fight) | mordacidad *f*, lo punzante (of words).

bittersweet [ˈbitəswiːt] *adj* agridulce.

bitty [ˈbiti] *adj* FAM fragmentario, ria; poco coherente.

bitumen [ˈbitjumin] *n* betún *m*.

bituminous [biˈtjuːminəs] *adj* bituminoso, sa.

bivalence [baiˈveiləns] *n* CHEM bivalencia *f*.

bivalent [baiˈveilənt] *adj* CHEM bivalente.

bivalve [ˈbaivælv] *adj* bivalvo, va.
◆ *n* bivalvo *m*.

bivouac [ˈbivuæk] *n* vivaque *m*, vivac *m*.

bivouac [ˈbivuæk] *vi* vivaquear.
— OBSERV Pret y pp ***bivouacked***.

biweekly [ˈbaiˈwiːkli] *adj* bisemanal (twice a week) || quincenal (every two weeks).
◆ *adv* dos veces por semana (twice a week) || cada quincena (every two weeks).
◆ *n* publicación *f* bisemanal (twice a week) || publicación *f* quincenal (every two weeks).

biyearly ['baiˈjəːli] *adj* semestral.

biz [biz] *n* FAM negocio *m*, negocios *m pl*.

bizarre [biˈzɑː*] *adj* extraño, ña; curioso, sa (strange) || estrafalario, ria (eccentric).
— OBSERV The word *bizarro* exist in Spanish but means *brave, generous, dashing*.

BL *abbr of [Bachelor of Law(s)* licenciado, da en Derecho.

blab [blæb] *n* FAM chismoso, sa; cotilla *m* & *f* (person) | chisme *m* (gossip).

blab [blæb] *vi* FAM chismorrear, cotillear (to talk indiscretely) | ir con el soplo, ir con el cuento (to inform) | descubrir el pastel (to spill the beans) | no parar de hablar (to chatter).
◆ *vt* FAM revelar, contar (to reveal).

black [blæk] *adj* negro, gra (colour, race) || ennegrecido, da; *black with age* ennegrecido por el tiempo || FIG negro, gra; aciago, ga; funesto, ta; *it was a black year* fue un año aciago | negro, gra; *he has a black future* le espera un negro porvenir | ruin, perverso, sa (wicked); *a black deed* una acción ruin | de estraperlo; *black petrol* gasolina de estraperlo | boicoteado, da; *black goods* productos boicoteados || — FIG *as black as coal* negro como el carbón *or* el tizón | *as black as pitch* negro como el carbón; oscuro como boca de lobo || *black amber* azabache *m* || FIG *black and blue* lleno de cardenales || *black and white* por escrito; *put in down in black and white* ponlo por escrito; en blanco y negro (photography, art, etc.) || *black art* o *black magic* magia negra || *black bear* oso negro || SP *black belt* cinturón negro || *black book* lista negra; *to be in one's black book* estar en la lista negra de uno || AVIAT *black box* caja negra, registrador *m* de vuelo || *black bread* pan negro || HIST *black cap* birrete *m* que usaban los jueces británicos en el momento de pronunciar la sentencia de muerte || *black coffee* café solo || GEOGR *black country* región *f* de los Midlands [en Inglaterra] || BOT *black currant* grosella negra || HIST *Black Death* peste negra || *black economy* economía *f* sumergida || *black eye* ojo morado *or* en compota *or* a la funerala || *black flag* pabellón *m* pirata || GEOGR *Black Forest* Selva Negra || REL *Black Friar* fraile dominico || *black hole* calabozo *m* || *black ice* hielo *m* en el pavimento || *black lead* grafito *m* || PRINT *black letter* letra gótica || *black man* negro *m* || *Black Maria* coche *m* celular (prison van) || FIG *black mark* mala nota || *black mass* misa negra || REL *Black Monk* monje benedictino || *black pepper* pimienta negra || HIST *Black Prince* Príncipe Negro || *Black Power* poder *m* negro (movement) || *black pudding* morcilla *f* || *Black Rod* funcionario *m* de la Cámara de los Lores que mantiene el orden || GEOGR *Black Sea* Mar Negro || FIG *black sheep* oveja negra, garbanzo negro || ZOOL *black snake* culebra inofensiva americana || FIG *black spot* mancha *f* (of one's record) || *black tie* corbata negra de lazo (tie), traje *m* de etiqueta (dinner jacket) || *black-tie dinner* cena de etiqueta || MED *black vomit* vómito negro || FIG *black with rage* rojo de ira || *black woman* negra *f* || FIG *to be in a black mood* estar de mal humor | *to declare sth. black* boicotear algo | *to give a black look* mirar con mala cara.
◆ *n* negro *m* (colour) || negro, gra (person) || luto *m* (mourning); *she was in black* o *wearing black* estaba de luto || FIG *in the black* con saldo positivo (bank account).

black [blæk] *vt* ennegrecer (to make black) || embetunar, limpiar (to polish) || — *to black out* apagar las luces de; *to black out a house* apagar las luces de una casa; tapar (to cover), censurar (to censor) || FAM *to black s.o.'s eye* ponerle a uno el ojo a la funerala || *we were blacked out last night* nos quedamos sin luz anoche.
◆ *vi* ennegrecer || *to black out* perder el conocimiento (to go unconscious).

blackball [-bɔːl] *n* bola *f* negra (ballot).

blackball [-bɔːl] *vt* echar bola negra.

blackbeetle [-ˈbiːtl] *n* cucaracha *f*.

blackberry [-bəri] *n* BOT zarzamora *f*.

blackbird [-bəːd] *n* mirlo *m* (bird).

blackboard [-bɔːd] *n* pizarra *f*, encerado *m*.

black-coated [-ˌkəutid] *adj* *black-coated workers* oficinistas *m pl*.

blackdamp [-dæmp] *n* MIN mofeta *f*.

blacken [-ən] *vi* ennegrecer, ennegrecerse.
◆ *vt* ennegrecer (to make black) || FIG denigrar (to defame) | manchar (one's reputation).

black-eyed [-ˈaid] *adj* de ojos negros.

blackface [-feis] *n* PRINT negrita *f* || maquillaje *m* del actor que interpreta el personaje de un negro.

blackfellow [-feləu] *n* aborigen *m* australiano.

blackguard [ˈblægɑːd] *n* sinvergüenza *m* & *f*, canalla *m*.

blackguard [ˈblægɑːd] *vt* vilipendiar.

blackhead [ˈblækhed] *n* MED espinilla *f*.

blacking [ˈblækiŋ] *n* betún *m* (for shoes).

blackish [ˈblækiʃ] *adj* negruzco, ca.

blackjack [ˈblækdʒæk] *n* pabellón *m* pirata (pirate flag) || veintiuna *f* (card game) || porra *f*, cachiporra *f* (truncheon).

blackjack [ˈblækdʒæk] *vt* aporrear.

blackleg [ˈblækleg] *n* tahúr *m* (swindler) || esquirol *m* (strikebreaker).

blackleg [ˈblækleg] *vt/vi* romper [una huelga].

blacklist [ˈblæklist] *n* lista *f* negra.

blacklist [ˈblæklist] *vt* poner en la lista negra.

blackmail [ˈblækmeil] *n* chantaje *m*.

blackmail [ˈblækmeil] *vt* hacer chantaje, chantajear.

blackmailer [ˈblækmeilə*] *n* chantajista *m* & *f*.

black market [ˈblækˈmɑːkit] *n* mercado *m* negro, estraperlo *m*.

blackmarketeer [-iə*] *n* estraperlista *m* & *f*.

blackness [ˈblæknis] *n* negrura *f* || oscuridad *f* (darkness).

blackout [ˈblækaut] *n* apagón *m* (of lights) || pérdida *f* del conocimiento (of consciousness) || censura *f*.

Blackshirt [ˈblækʃəːt] *n* HIST camisa negra *m*.

blacksmith [ˈblæksmiθ] *n* herrero *m* || *blacksmith's workshop* herrería *f*.

blackthorn [ˈblækθɔːn] *n* BOT endrino *m* || porra *f*, bastón *m* (cudgel).

bladder [ˈblædə*] *n* ANAT vejiga *f* || cámara *f* de aire (of a ball, tyre) || BOT vesícula *f* (in seaweeds) || — MED *bladder worm* cisticerco *m* || *gall bladder* vesícula biliar.

blade [bleid] *n* hoja *f* (of knife, sword, saw, etc.) || hoja *f*, cuchilla *f* (of razor) || cuchilla *f* (of ice skate, etc.) || aspa *f* (of a mill) || BOT brizna *f* (of grass) | limbo *m* (of leaf) || espada *f* (sword) || pala *f* (of an oar) || TECH paleta *f*, pala *f* (fan, propeller) | álabe *m*, paleta *f* (of paddle wheel) | rasqueta *f* (of windscreen or windshield wiper) | cuchilla *f* (of guillotine) | cuchilla *f*, hoja *f* (of machine) || AGR pala *f* (of hoe) || ANAT paletilla *f* || FAM galán *m* (dashing young man) || — FAM *jolly* o *gay old blade* jaranero *m* || *razor blade* cuchilla *or* hoja de afeitar.

blamable; blameable [ˈbleiməbl] *adj* censurable || culpable (guilty).

blame [bleim] *n* culpa *f* (responsibility); *the blame is mine* la culpa es mía || censura *f*, reproche *m* (censure) || — *to bear the blame* tener la culpa || *to lay* o *to put the blame for sth. on* o *upon* echar la culpa de algo a.

blame [bleim] *vt* culpar, echar la culpa; *they blamed him for the crime, they blamed the crime on him* le culparon del crimen, le echaron la culpa del crimen || censurar (to reproach) || — *to be to blame* ser el culpable *or* el responsable, tener la culpa; *he is to blame for the accident* él es el culpable del accidente || *you have only yourself to blame* la culpa es suya.

blameless [-lis] *adj* inocente (innocent) || libre de culpa (free from fault) || irreprochable, intachable (irreproachable).

blameworthy [ˈbleimˌwəːði] *adj* censurable, culpable; *his conduct is blameworthy* su conducta es censurable.

blanch [blɑːntʃ] *vt* blanquear (to make white) || pelar (to peel) || escaldar (to boil) || blanquear, blanquecer (metals).
◆ *vi* palidecer (to grow pale).

blancmange [bləˈmɔnʒ] *n* manjar *m* blanco.

bland [blænd] *adj* templado, da; suave (climate) || afable, suave, amable (manners, person) || suave, poco fuerte (diet).

blandish [-iʃ] *vt* lisonjear, halagar (to coax).
◆ *vi* valerse de halagos.

blandishment [-iʃmənt] *n* halago *m*, zalamería *f*, lisonja *f*.

blank [blæŋk] *adj* en blanco; *leave a blank space* deja un espacio en blanco || liso, sa; sin adornos (wall) || falso, sa (door, window) || mudo, da (map) || FIG sin expresión (look) | vacío, a (empty); *a blank life* una vida vacía; *blank mind* mente vacía | absoluto, ta (impossibility) | profundo, da (despair) | tajante, categórico, ca (definite); *blank denial* denegación categórica | desconcertado, da; perplejo, ja (confused) || — MIL *blank cartridge* cartucho *m* de fogueo || *blank cheque* cheque *m* en blanco (cheque), carta blanca (permission) || PRINT *blank page* guarda *f* || *blank verse* verso blanco *or* suelto.
◆ *n* blanco *m*, hueco *m*, espacio *m* en blanco (in document, etc.); *to leave blanks* dejar espacios en blanco || vacío *m*, laguna *f*; *that is a blank in American history* eso es una laguna en la historia americana || laguna *f* (in one's education) || PRINT puntos *m pl* suspensivos, guión *m* [para sustituir una palabra malsonante] || MIL cartucho *m* de fogueo | blanco *m* (target) || número *m* no premiado (lottery ticket) || papeleta *f* en blanco (ballot) || US impreso *m*, formulario *m* (form) || TECH cospel *m* (coin) | llave *f* ciega (key) || — *double blank* blanca doble (in dominoes) || *in blank* en blanco || FIG *my mind was a complete blank* me falló la memoria | *to draw a blank* llevarse un chasco.

blank [blæŋk] *vt* tachar, borrar (to erase) || US SP impedir que el equipo contrario marque un tanto || *to blank off* tapar.

blanket [-it] *n* manta *f* [AMER frazada *f*] (bed cover, covering for animals, cloak); *electric blanket* manta eléctrica || FIG capa *f*, manto *m*; *a white blanket of snow* una blanca capa de nieve | manto *m*; *the blanket of the night* el manto de la noche || — *blanket bath* lavado *m* de un enfermo en su cama || FIG *security blanket* medidas *f pl* de seguridad || FIG & FAM *to throw a wet blanket over* echar un jarro de agua fría a | *wet blanket* aguafiestas *m* & *f*.
◆ *adj* general || FIG *blanket insurance policy* póliza *f* a todo riesgo.

blanket [-it] *vt* tapar con una manta (to cover up) || envolver (to wrap up) || cubrir con una capa *or* manto; *the city was blanketed in snow* la ciudad estaba cubierta con un manto de nieve || acallar (rumours, questions) || tapar (scandal) || amortiguar (noise) || RAD interferir (radio transmissions) || MAR robar *or* quitar el viento || US cubrir (to apply to).

blankety [-ti]; **blanky** [-i] *adj* FAM maldito, ta.

blankly ['blæŋkli] *adv* con la mirada vacía (without expression) || completamente (utterly) || tajantemente, categóricamente.

blare [blɛə*] *n* trompetazo *m* (of trumpet) || estruendo *m* (loud sound).

blare [blɛə*] *vi* sonar, resonar; *the trumpets blared* las trompetas sonaron || berrear (to blast) || *to blare out* sonar a todo volumen.
◆ *vt* pregonar, proclamar, anunciar a gritos; *the loudspeakers blared the news* los altavoces anunciaron a gritos la noticia.

blarney ['blɑːni] *n* FAM coba *f.*

blarney ['blɑːni] *vt/vi* FAM dar coba.

blasé ['blɑːzei] *adj* hastiado, da; de vuelta de todo.

blaspheme [blæs'fiːm] *vt/vi* blasfemar.

blasphemer [-ə*] *n* blasfemador, ra; blasfemo, ma.

blasphemous ['blæsfiməs] *adj* blasfemador, ra; blasfematorio, ria; blasfemo, ma.

blasphemy ['blæsfimi] *n* blasfemia *f.*

blast [blɑːst] *n* ráfaga *f* (gust); *a blast of air* una ráfaga de aire || TECH inyección *f* de aire | explosión *f* (explosion) | chorro *m* (of air through a jet) | onda *f* de choque (of an explosion) || MUS toque *m* (of a trumpet) || soplo *m* (of bellows) || MIN barreno *m* (amount of dynamite) || AGR añublo *m,* tizón *m* || FIG explosión *f,* estallido *m* (of anger) || — *at full blast* a toda marcha || *blast furnace* alto horno *m* || *blast on the whistle* pitido *m,* silbido *m* || *blast wave* onda de choque || FIG & FAM *to have a blast* pasarlo bomba.

blast [blɑːst] *vt* volar (to blow up); *to blast a rock* volar una roca || abrir, perforar [con barrenos]; *to blast a tunnel* abrir un túnel con barrenos || explotar (to explode) || marchitar (a plant) || derribar (by lightning) || FIG acabar con (hopes) | criticar (to criticize) | manchar (one's reputation) || — FAM *blast you!* ¡maldito sea! || MIL *to blast one's way through* abrirse camino por medio de bombas.
◆ *vi* seguir disparando (with firearms) || FIG & FAM salir pitando || *to blast off* despegar.

blasted [-id] *adj* maldito, ta; condenado, da (damnable).

blastema [blæs'tiːmə] *n* BIOL blastema *m.*

blast-hole ['blɑːst,həul] *n* barreno *m.*

blasting ['blɑːstiŋ] *n* voladura *f* (explosión) || — *blasting cap* detonador *m* || *blasting charge* carga explosiva.

blastoderm ['blæstəudəːm] *n* BIOL blastodermo *m.*

blast-off ['blɑːstɔf] *n* despegue *m* (of missiles).

blastomere ['blæstəmiə*] *n* BIOL blastómero *m.*

blastomycetes ['blæstə,mai'siːtiːz] *pl n* blastomicetos *m* (fungi).

blastomycosis ['blæstəmai'kəusis] *n* MED blastomicosis *f.*

blastula ['blæstjulə] *n* BIOL blástula *f.*

blatancy ['bleitənsi] *n* descaro *m; the blatancy of his words* el descaro de sus palabras || aspecto *m* chillón *or* llamativo || evidencia *f* (obviousness).

blatant ['bleitənt] *adj* evidente, patente (very obvious); *a blatant lie* una mentira patente || estridente, vocinglero, ra (voices) || chillón, ona (colour) || llamativo, va (clothes) || descarado, da (brazen).

blather ['blæðə*] *n* tonterías *f pl.*

blather ['blæðə*] *vi* decir tonterías.

blaze [bleiz] *n* llamarada *f* (burst of flame) || fuego *m* (fire) || resplandor *m* (of sun, of diamonds, etc.); *the blaze of the spotlights* el resplandor de los focos || arranque *m,* rapto *m; in a blaze of anger* en un arranque de ira || estrella *f,* mancha *f* blanca en la frente (in animals) || señal *f,* marca *f* (on a tree) || — FAM *go to blazes!* ¡vete a la porra!, ¡vete al diablo! | *like blazes* como un rayo (like lightning), como un demonio (like mad) || *to be in a blaze* estar en llamas || FAM *to run like blazes* correr como un descosido | *what the blazes...?* ¿qué demonios...?

blaze [bleiz] *vi* arder; *the forest was blazing* el bosque estaba ardiendo || resplandecer, brillar (to shine brightly); *the city was blazing with light* la ciudad resplandecía de luz || — *to blaze away* seguir disparando || *to blaze down on* caer de plano en || *to blaze past* pasar como un rayo || *to blaze up* encenderse (sth.), ponerse furioso (s.o.) || *to blaze with anger* echar chispas (to be furious).
◆ *vt* proclamar (to proclaim) || publicar *or* gritar a los cuatro vientos (to spread news) || señalar, marcar (a tree) || *to blaze a trail* abrir un camino.

blazer ['bleizə*] *n* chaqueta *f* de sport.

blazon ['bleizn] *n* blasón *m* (coat of arms, shield) || FIG ostentación *f.*

blazon ['bleizn] *vt* blasonar || FIG publicar *or* gritar a los cuatro vientos (to blaze).

bleach [bliːtʃ] *n* decolorante *m* (chemical) || lejía *f; put some bleach in the wash* pon un poco de lejía en la colada || blanqueo *m* (whitening).

bleach [bliːtʃ] *vt* blanquear (to whiten) || descolorar (to decolorize) || decolorar (the hair).
◆ *vi* blanquear.

bleacher [-ə*] *n* blanqueador (worker).
◆ *pl* US graderío *m sing,* gradas *f* (seats).

bleaching powder [-iŋ,paudə*] *n* polvo *m* de blanquear.

bleak [bliːk] *adj* desolado, da; pelado, da (countryside) || desapacible (weather) || frío, a (wind) | triste (cheerless); *a bleak smile* una sonrisa triste || frío, a (lacking in kindliness); *a bleak reception* una fría acogida | poco prometedor, ra (outlook).

bleak [bliːk] *n* breca *f,* albur *m* (fish).

blear [bliə*] *vt* nublar (eyes) || difuminar (outline).

bleary [-ri] *adj* nublado, da (eyes) || borroso, sa; impreciso, sa (outline) || agotado, da (worn-out).

bleary-eyed [-aid] *adj* con la vista nublada (because of lack of sleep).

bleat [bliːt] *n* balido *m* (of sheep, etc.) || FIG & FAM gemido *m.*

bleat [bliːt] *vi* balar (sheep) || FIG & FAM gimotear, gemir (to speak plaintively).
◆ *vt* decir con voz quejumbrosa.

bleb [bleb] *n* ampolla *f* (blister) || burbuja *f* (bubble).

bled [bled] *prep & pp* ⟶ **bleed.**

bleed* [bliːd] *vi* sangrar || exudar (plants) || PRINT refilar demasiado || desteñirse (material) || FIG sufrir (to suffer); *her heart bleeds for the misfortunes of mankind* su corazón sufre por las desgracias de la humanidad || dar su vida, derramar su sangre (*for* por) || salirse (water, gas) || FAM escupir (to pay) || — *my nose is bleeding* estoy sangrando *or* echo sangre por la nariz || FAM *to bleed like a pig* echar sangre como un cochino *or* un toro || *to bleed to death* morir desangrado.
◆ *vt* sangrar, sacar sangre a (to draw blood from) || BOT sangrar (plants) || FAM sacar dinero (to extort money from) || PRINT refilar demasiado || — FAM *to bleed o.s. white* sacrificarse | *to bleed s.o. white* o *dry* sacar a uno hasta el último céntimo, esquilmarle a uno, chuparle la sangre a uno.
— OBSERV Pret y pp ***bled.***

bleeder [-ə*] *n* MED hemofílico, ca.
◆ *adj* TECH de purga.

bleeding [-iŋ] *adj* sangrante, sangriento, ta || POP pijotero, ra (damned).
◆ *n* MED sangría *f* || salida *f* (of water, of gas) || sangría *f* (of plants) || TECH purga *f.*

bleep [bliːp] *n* bip *m,* pitido *m.*

bleep [bliːp] *vi* emitir pitidos *or* una señal sonora.
◆ *vt* llamar con un busca (a doctor, etc.).

bleeper ['bliːpə*] *n* busca *m,* avisador *m* (pocket device).

blemish ['blemiʃ] *n* defecto *m,* imperfección *f* || mancha *f,* tacha *f* (moral defect); *without blemish* sin tacha.

blemish ['blemiʃ] *vt* manchar, mancillar (reputation, etc.) || estropear, echar a perder (to spoil).

blench [blentʃ] *vi* retroceder, echarse atrás (to recoil) || pestañear; *without blenching* sin pestañear.

blend [blend] *n* mezcla *f* combinación *f* || mezcla *f* (of tea, of tobacco, etc.).

blend [blend] *vt* mezclar, combinar || casar, armonizar (colours) || armonizar (styles, etc.).
◆ *vi* mezclarse, combinarse || casarse, armonizarse (colours) || *to blend in* mezclarse con, combinarse con.
— OBSERV Aunque este verbo sea regular se emplea a veces la forma *blent* en los tiempos pasados.

blende [blend] *n* MIN blenda *f.*

blender ['blendə*] *n* licuadora *f.*

blending [-iŋ] *n* mezcla *f,* combinación *f.*

blennorrhagia [,blenə'reidʒə] *n* MED blenorragia *f.*

blennorrhoea [,blenə'riːə] *n* MED blenorrea *f.*

bless [bles] *vt* bendecir; *God bless you!* ¡Dios le bendiga! || — *bless you!* ¡Jesús, María y José! (to s.o. who sneezes) || *God bless me!* o *God bless my soul!* ¡Dios mío! || *I'll be blessed if I know* que me maten si lo sé || *to bless o.s.* santiguarse.
— OBSERV Aunque este verbo sea regular se emplea a veces la forma *blest* en los tiempos pasados.
— OBSERV See OBSERV at BENDECIR.

blessed ['blesid]; **blest** [blest] *adj* bendito, ta || santo, ta; *the blessed martyrs* los santos mártires || beato, ta (beatified in Roman Catholicism) || bienaventurado, da; *blessed are the poor in spirit* bienaventurados sean los pobres de espíritu || feliz; *of blessed memory* de feliz memoria || dotado, da; *blessed with an easygoing nature* dotado de un natural apacible || FAM maldito, ta; *that blessed boy!* ¡ese maldito niño! || — *blessed be Thy Name* bendito sea tu Nombre || *blessed event* feliz acontecimiento *m* || *Blessed Sacrament* Santísimo Sacramento || FAM *every blessed day* todos los días | *not a blessed one* ni uno, ni una || FIG *not to know a blessed thing about* no saber maldita cosa de || *the Blessed Virgin* la Santa Virgen || FAM *the whole blessed day* todo el santo día.
— OBSERV See OBSERV at BENDITO.

blessedness ['blesidnis] *n* bienaventuranza *f,* beatitud *f* || FIG felicidad *f.*

blessing ['blesiŋ] *n* bendición *f; to give the blessing* echar *or* dar la bendición || beneficio *m,* ventaja *f* (advantage); *the blessings of civilization* las ventajas de la civilización || — FIG *it's a blessing in disguise* no hay mal que por bien no venga || *to count one's blessings* dar gracias a

Dios, sentirse afortunado || FAM *what a blessing!* ¡qué suerte!

blest [blest] *adj pret y pp* → **blessed.**

blew [blu:] *pret* → **blow.**

blight [blait] *n* AGR roya *f* (rust) | añublo *m*, tizón *m* (mildew) || FIG plaga *f.*

blight [blait] *vt* AGR producir la roya *or* el añublo *or* el tizón || marchitar (to wither) || FIG destrozar, destruir, arruinar (to spoil) | frustrar (to frustrate); *to blight s.o.'s hopes* frustrar las esperanzas de alguien.

blighter ['blaitə*] *n* FAM sinvergüenza *m*, canalla *m* (rogue) | tipo *m*, tío *m* (fellow).

Blighty ['blaiti] *n* MIL & FAM Inglaterra *f.*

blimey ['blaimi] *interj* FAM ¡caray!, ¡leñe!

blimp [blimp] *n* dirigible *m* no rígido || FIG patriotero *m* (jingoist).

blind [blaind] *adj* ciego, ga; *blind from birth* ciego de nacimiento || ARCH falso, sa (window, door) | ciego, ga (wall) || escondido, da (hidden); *a blind crossroad* un cruce escondido || FIG ciego, ga || — *a blind man* un ciego || *a blind woman* una ciega || *blind alley* callejón *m* sin salida || *blind curve* o *corner* curva *f* sin visibilidad || FAM *blind date* cita *f* concertada con alguien a quien no se conoce || *blind flying* vuelo *m* sin visibilidad || *blind gut* intestino ciego || *blind in one eye* tuerto, ta || *blind landing* aterrizaje *m* sin visibilidad *or* a ciegas || *blind letter* carta *f* cuya dirección es ilegible || *blind search* registro *m* a ciegas || ANAT *blind spot* punto ciego del ojo || FAM *blind to the world* borracho como una cuba || FIG *blind with anger* ciego de ira | *in blind man's holiday* al anochecer, entre dos luces || FAM *not to take a blind bit of notice* no hacer el menor caso, no prestar la más mínima atención || *the blind* los ciegos || FIG *it is the blind leading the blind* están tan ciegos uno como otro | *the blind side of s.o.* el punto flaco de uno | *this job is a blind alley* este trabajo no tiene porvenir | *to apply the blind eye of sth.* hacer la vista gorda a una cosa | *to be blind to* no ver (not to see), hacer la vista gorda a (to be unwilling to see) || FAM *to drink o.s. blind* coger una buena trompa || *to go blind* quedarse ciego || FIG & FAM *to turn a blind eye* hacer la vista gorda.

◆ *n* persiana *f*; *Venetian blind* persiana veneciana || toldo *m* (awning) || FIG pretexto (a cover-up); *it was only a blind* no era más que un pretexto | máscara *f* (mask) || MIL blinda *f* || US escondrijo *m* (a hide) | anteojera *f* (of harness) || FIG *to act as a blind for* servir de pantalla a.

◆ *adv* a ciegas; *to go at a thing blind* lanzarse a ciegas a algo || — FAM *to be blind drunk* estar como una cuba, estar morado *or* ciego || *to fly blind* volar sin visibilidad *or* a ciegas.

blind [blaind] *vt* cegar, dejar ciego (to deprive of sight) || FIG deslumbrar (to dazzle) | cegar; *blinded by passion* cegado por la pasión || *he was blinded in the war* se quedó ciego durante la guerra.

◆ *vi* AUT *to blind along* correr a toda velocidad.

blindage ['blaindidʒ] *n* MIL blindaje *m.*

blinder ['blaində*] *n* US anteojera *f.*

blindfold ['blaindfəuld] *n* venda *f.*

◆ *adj/adv* con los ojos vendados.

blindfold ['blaindfəuld] *vt* vendar los ojos.

blinding ['blaindiŋ] *adj* cegador, ra || FIG deslumbrante, cegador, ra.

◆ *n* relleno *m* (filling in of cracks) || gravilla *f* (material) || FIG deslumbramiento *m.*

blindly ['blaindli] *adv* a ciegas, ciegamente.

blindman's buff ['blaindmænz'bʌf] *n* gallina *f* ciega (game).

blindness ['blaindnis] *n* MED ceguera *f*, ceguedad *f* || FIG obcecación *f*, ceguera *f.*

blindworm ['blaindwə:m] *n* ZOOL lución *m.*

blink [bliŋk] *n* parpadeo *m* (of the eyes) || destello *m* (gleam) || *on the blink* averiado, da; estropeado, da.

blink [bliŋk] *vi* parpadear, pestañear (eyes) || destellar (to glimmer) || parpadear (light) || mirar con asombro (in surprise) || — *blinking lights* luces *f* intermitentes || FIG *to blink at a fault* pasar por alto una falta, hacer caso omiso de una falta.

◆ *vt* guiñar (to wink the eyes) || FIG eludir; *to blink the question* eludir la cuestión | negarse a ver (facts) || FIG *to blink an eye* hacer la vista gorda.

blinker [-ə*] *n* anteojera *f* (for horses) || AUT intermitente *m*, luz *f* intermitente || AVIAT faro *m* intermitente || POP ojo *m* (eye).

blinkered [-d] *adj* FIG estrecho, cha de miras.

blinking [-iŋ] *adj* FAM maldito, ta; condenado, da.

blip [blip] *n* punto *m* luminoso (on radar screen), top *m* de eco (of a radar).

bliss [blis] *n* beatitud *f*, dicha *f*, felicidad *f* || FIG *it was bliss!* ¡fue maravilloso!

blissful [-ful] *adj* feliz, dichoso, sa || maravilloso, sa.

blister ['blistə*] *n* MED ampolla *f* (in the skin) || burbuja *f* (in a surface) || vejiga *f* (in a film of paint) || ZOOL *blister beetle* cantárida *f.*

blister ['blistə*] *vt* MED producir ampollas en, levantar ampollas en || FIG criticar, censurar.

◆ *vi* MED cubrirse de ampollas, formarse ampollas.

blistering [-riŋ] *adj* abrasador, ra (sun) || mordaz (letter) || candente (issue).

blithe [blaið] *adj* alegre.

blithering ['bliðəriŋ] *adj* *a blithering idiot* un tonto perdido *or* de capirote.

blithesome ['blaiðsəm] *adj* alegre.

blitz [blits] *n* bombardeo *m* aéreo (air attack) || ataque *m* por sorpresa (sudden attack).

blitz [blits] *vt* bombardear.

blitzkrieg [-kri:g] *n* guerra *f* relámpago.

blizzard ['blizəd] *n* ventisca *f.*

bloat [bləut] *vt* hinchar, inflar (to swell) || ahumar (fish) || FIG envanecer (to make vain) || FIG *bloated with pride* hinchado de orgullo.

◆ *vi* hincharse, inflarse, abotagarse, abotargarse.

bloater [-ə*] *n* arenque *m* ahumado.

blob [blɔb] *n* gota *f* (drop) || borrón *m* (of ink) || mancha *f* (of colour) || SP *to score a blob* no marcar ningún punto *or* tanto.

bloc [blɔk] *n* bloque *m* (in politics).

block [blɔk] *n* bloque *m* (large piece); *a block of marble* un bloque de mármol || zoquete *m*, taco *m* (of wood) || tajo *m* (butcher's, executioner's) || horma *f* (wooden mould) || fraustina *f* (of a milliner) || pella *f* (of butter) || polea *f* (pulley) || MAR motón *m* || zapata *f* (of brake) || calzo *m* (wedge) || cubo *m* (toy) || PRINT cliché *m*, clisé *m* || ARCH bloque *m* (for building) || adoquín *m* (for paving) || bloque *m or* edificio *m* comercial (building with shops, offices, etc.) || manzana *f* [AMER cuadra *f*] (city block) || bloque *m* (of cylinder) || embotellamiento *m*, atasco *m* (traffic) || plataforma *f* (for auction) || cepo *m* (of anvil) || taco *m* (of calendar) || SP bloqueo *m* (of a player) || obstrucción *f* (obstruction) || obstáculo *m*, estorbo *m* (obstacle) || grupo *m*; *a block of seats* un grupo de asientos || ramal *m*, tramo *m* (railway line) || tren *m* (train) || COMM serie *f* de acciones (group of shares) || FAM chola *f* (head) | zoquete *m* (idiot) || — *block and tackle* aparejo *m* de poleas || *block capitals* versalitas *f pl*, mayúsculas *f pl* || *block chain* cadena articulada || *block diagram* bloque diagrama || *block letters* letras *f pl* de molde || *block of flats* bloque *m* de viviendas, casa *f* de vecindad *or* de alquiler || INFORM *block operation* operaciones *f pl* de bloque || *block printing* estampado *m* con molde || *block system* bloqueo automático || *block tin* estaño *m* en lingotes *or* en galápagos || *block vote* voto *m* por cabeza de delegación || *note block* bloc *m* || *to go to the block* ir al cadalso || *to put on the block* vender en subasta.

block [blɔk] *vt* obstruir (to cause obstruction) || obstaculizar, estorbar (to put obstacles) || bloquear (in Parliament, in finances) || cerrar; *to block the way* cerrar el paso || dar forma a [un sombrero] (to shape a hat) || bloquear (wheel) || estampar (in bookbinding) || calzar (a wheel) || SP bloquear (a ball) | obstaculizar (a player) || — *«road blocked»* «calle cortada» || *to block in* o *out* bosquejar, esbozar (to sketch) || *to block off* cortar (road) || *to block up* obstruir (to obstruct), calzar (to wedge), tapar (hole, window, etc.).

◆ *vi* obstruirse (to become blocked).

blockade [blɔ'keid] *n* bloqueo *m*; *to raise a blockade* levantar un bloqueo; *to run a blockade* romper un bloqueo.

blockade [blɔ'keid] *vt* bloquear.

blockade-runner [-'rʌnə*] *n* persona *f or* barco *m* que intenta romper un bloqueo.

blockage ['blɔkidʒ] *n* bloqueo *m* || obstrucción *f.*

blockbuster ['blɔkbʌstə*] *n* bomba *f* de demolición || FIG bombazo *m.*

blockhead ['blɔkhed] *n* FAM alcornoque *m*, zoquete *m*, tarugo *m*, mentecato, ta.

blockhouse ['blɔkhaus] *n* MIL blocao *m.*

bloke [bləuk] *n* FAM tipo *m*, individuo *m*, tío *m.*

blond [blɔnd] *adj/n* rubio *m.*

blonde [blɔnd] *adj/n* rubia *f.*

blood [blʌd] *n* BIOL sangre *f* || FIG sangre *f* (character) | sangre *f*, familia *f* (family) | parentesco *m* (kinship) | sangre *f*, raza *f* (race) | petimetre *m*, currutaco *m* (dandy) || — FIG *bad blood* odio *m* (hatred), rabia *f* (anger) || *blood bank* banco *m* de sangre || *blood brother* hermano *m* carnal || *blood cell* glóbulo *m* || *blood clot* coágulo *m* || *blood count* recuento *m* de glóbulos sanguíneos || *blood donor* donante *m* & *f* de sangre || *blood feud* enemistad *f* mortal || *blood group* grupo sanguíneo || *blood horse* pura sangre *m* || *blood money* precio *m* de la sangre || *blood orange* sanguina *f*, naranja *f* de sangre || *blood plasma* plasma sanguíneo || *blood platelet* plaqueta *f* de sangre || *blood poisoning* envenenamiento *m* de la sangre || *blood pressure* tensión *f* arterial || *blood pudding* morcilla *f* || *blood relation* o *relative* pariente consanguíneo, parienta consanguínea || *blood relationship* consanguinidad *f* || *blood sausage* morcilla *f* || *blood serum* suero sanguíneo || *blood sports* deportes *m pl* cruentos || MED *blood sugar* glicemia *f*, glucemia *f* || *blood test* análisis *m* de sangre || *blood transfusion* transfusión *f* de sangre || *blood type* grupo sanguíneo || *blood vessel* vaso sanguíneo || FIG *blue blood* sangre azul || *high blood pressure* hipertensión *f* || FIG *his blood ran cold* se le heló la sangre | *in cold blood* a sangre fría | *it is o it runs in his blood* lo lleva en la sangre | *new* o *fresh blood* savia *f* nueva | *of the blood royal* de sangre real | *the call of blood* la voz de la sangre | *to be bathed in blood* estar bañado en sangre || *to be gushing blood* estar chorreando sangre || FIG *to have blood on one's hands* tener las manos manchadas de sangre || FIG & FAM *to have got s.o. in one's blood* llevar *or* tener a alguien en la sangre, llevar a alguien en la masa de la sangre | *to have no blood in one's veins* no tener sangre en las venas, tener sangre de horchata | *to* *have one's blood up* estar de un humor de perros || FIG *to infuse new blood in an undertaking* infundir nueva savia en una empresa | *to make one's blood boil* freírle *or* quemarle la sangre a uno | *to make s.o.'s blood run cold* helarle la sangre a uno || *to shed blood* derramar sangre || *to sweat blood* sudar sangre || *whole blood* de pura sangre || *with blood and iron* a sangre y fuego || *without shedding of blood* sin efusión de sangre.

blood [blʌd] *vt* MED sangrar (to bleed) || encarnar, iniciar [a perros de caza haciendo que prueben sangre de una presa] || FIG acostumbrar.

bloodbath [-bɑːθ] *n* matanza *f*, carnicería *f*.

bloodcurdling [ˈblʌdˌkəːdliŋ] *adj* espeluznante, que hiela la sangre.

blooded [blʌdid] *adj* de pura sangre || *cold blooded* de sangre fría.

bloodguilty [ˈblʌdˌgilti] *adj* culpable de derramamiento de sangre.

bloodhound [ˈblʌdhaund] *n* sabueso *m* || FIG sabueso *m*, policía *m*.

bloodily [ˈblʌdili] *adv* sangrientamente, sanguinariamente (in a bloody manner) || cruelmente (cruelly).

bloodiness [ˈblʌdinis] *n* ensangrentamiento *m* (state of being bloody) || crueldad *f* (cruelty).

bloodless [ˈblʌdlis] *adj* incruento, ta; sin efusión de sangre (without bloodshed) || exangüe (without blood) || anémico, ca (anaemic) || insensible, frío, a (lacking emotion) || cruel || FAM que tiene sangre de horchata, débil (having little energy).

bloodletting [ˈblʌdˌletiŋ] *n* sangría *f*.

bloodred [ˈblʌdˈred] *adj* de color rojo sangre.

bloodroot [ˈblʌdrut] *n* BOT sanguinaria *f*.

bloodshed [ˈblʌdʃed] *n* matanza *f* (slaughter) || derramamiento *m or* efusión *f* de sangre (shedding of blood).

bloodshot [ˈblʌdʃɔt] *adj* sanguinolento, ta; inyectado de sangre (eyes).

bloodstain [ˈblʌdstein] *n* mancha *f* de sangre.

bloodstock [ˈblʌdstɔk] *n* caballos *m pl* de pura sangre.

bloodstone [ˈblʌdstəun] *n* sanguinaria *f* (semiprecious stone).

bloodstream [ˈblʌdstriːm] *n* sangre *f*; *to inject sth. in the bloodstream* inyectar algo en la sangre.

bloodsucker [ˈblʌdˌsʌkə*] *n* sanguijuela *f* (animal, person).

bloodthirsty [ˈblʌdˌθəːsti] *adj* sediento *or* ávido de sangre, sanguinario, ria.

bloody [ˈblʌdi] *adj* sangriento, ta; *a bloody battle* una batalla sangrienta || manchado de sangre; ensangrentado, da; *your shirt is bloody* tu camisa está manchada de sangre || sanguinolento, ta; *a bloody boil* un furúnculo sanguinolento || sanguinario, ria (murderous); *a bloody tyrant* un tirano sanguinario || POP condenado, da; puñetero, ra; *that bloody dog!* ¡ese condenado perro!

◆ *adv* POP sumamente, terriblemente || POP *not bloody likely* ni hablar.

bloody [ˈblʌdi] *vt* manchar de sangre, ensangrentar.

bloody-minded [-ˈmaindid] *adj* POP desagradable (unpleasant) | que tiene mal genio (bad-tempered) | malintencionado, da (wicked).

bloody-mindedness [-ˈmaindidnis] *n* POP mal genio *m* (bad temper) | mala intención *f*, mala idea *f* (wickedness).

bloom [bluːm] *n* florecimiento *m* (state of flowering) || floración *f* (period of flowering) || flor *f* (blossom); *in bloom* en flor || color *m* encendido, rubor *m* (on the cheek) || vello *m*, pelusa *f* (in fruit) || brillo *m* (of new coin) || TECH desbaste *m*, «bloom» *m* || aroma *m* (of wine) || — *a flower in its first bloom* una flor recién abierta || *beauty that has lost its bloom* belleza que ha perdido su lozanía || *in full bloom* en flor, florecido, da || FIG *in the full bloom of her beauty* en la plenitud de su belleza | *in the very bloom of one's youth, of life* en la misma flor de la juventud, de la vida || *to burst into bloom* florecer || *to take the bloom off* quitar la frescura a.

bloom [bluːm] *vi* florecer (to blossom) || FIG florecer | resplandecer (to look radiant) | convertirse (*into* en) (to become).

bloomer [-ə*] *n* FAM metedura *f* de pata || FAM *to make a bloomer* meter la pata.

bloomers [-əz] *n* pantalones *m pl* bombachos, pololos *m pl*.

blooming [-iŋ] *adj* floreciente (blossoming) || radiante de salud, resplandeciente (radiant with health) || POP pijotero, ra; pajolero, ra (bloody).

blooper [ˈbluːpə*] *n* US FAM metedura *f* de pata.

blossom [ˈblɔsəm] *n* flor *f* (flower) || *in blossom* en flor.

blossom [ˈblɔsəm] *vi* florecer || — *to blossom into* llegar a ser, convertirse en || *to blossom out* abrirse (flower), alcanzar su plenitud (person).

blot [blɔt] *n* borrón *m*, mancha *f* (of ink) || FIG mancha *f* (on s.o.'s honour) || monstruosidad *f* (eyesore) || FIG *these big buildings are a blot on the landscape* estos grandes edificios afean el paisaje.

blot [blɔt] *vt* emborronar, manchar de tinta (with ink) || secar (with blotting paper) || manchar, ensuciar (to stain) || — *to blot one's record* manchar su hoja de servicio || *to blot out* tachar (to erase), borrar (memories), ocultar (to hide from view), suprimir, liquidar (to kill).

◆ *vi* emborronarse, mancharse de tinta (to become blotted) || hacer borrones (to make blots) || correrse (the ink).

blotch [blɔtʃ] *n* mancha *f* (of ink, of colour) || pústula *f* (pimple) || rojez *f*, mancha *f* (in the skin).

blotch [blɔtʃ] *vt* manchar (to cover with blotches) || cubrir de pústulas (to cover with pimples) || enrojecer (the skin).

blotched [-t]; **blotchy** [-i] *adj* cubierto de manchas (stained) || enrojecido, da (the skin).

blotter [ˈblɔtə*] *n* secante *m*, papel *m* secante (blotting paper) || US registro *m* (record book).

blotting paper [ˈblɔtiŋˌpeipə*] *n* papel *m* secante.

blouse [blauz] *n* blusa *f* (woman's shirt) || MIL guerrera *f* || MAR marinera *f* || *sailor blouse* blusón *m* (for women).

blouson [ˈbloohzonˌ ˈblowzon] *n* cazadora *f* holgada.

blow [bləu] *n* soplo *m*, soplido *m* (blast of air) || ráfaga *f* de viento (strong gust of wind) || golpe *m* (stroke, shock); *to deal* o *to strike s.o. a blow* dar *or* asestar un golpe a alguien || SP golpe *m* (punch) || FIG golpe *m*; *he suffered a severe blow when his mother died* sufrió un golpe duro con la muerte de su madre || POP información *f* secreta || — *at one blow* de un golpe || MUS *blow at* o *on one's trumpet* trompetazo *m* || *blow patch* parche *m* || *give your nose a good blow* suénate bien las narices || FIG *to aim a blow at s.o.'s authority* hacer mella en la autoridad de alguien || *to come to blows* llegar *or* venir a las manos || *to exchange blows* pegarse || *to feel the blow* acusar el golpe || FIG *to go for a blow* ir a dar una vuelta || *to miss one's blow* errar el golpe || FIG *to soften the blow* amortiguar el golpe | *without striking a blow* sin mover un dedo.

— OBSERV When *blow with* is followed by the name of an instrument or weapon, it is generally translated by the noun with the suffix *-ada* if the instrument is pointed: *a blow with a knife* una cuchillada; *a blow with a dagger* una puñalada, etc. or with the suffix *-azo* if the instrument is blunt: *a blow with a hammer* un martillazo; *a blow with a fist* un puñetazo; *a blow with the hand* un manotazo; *a blow with a cane* un bastonazo, etc. There are of course exceptions, like *a blow with a stone* una pedrada.

blow* [bləu] *vi* soplar (wind, mouth) || soplarse; *to blow on one's fingers to warm them* soplarse los dedos para calentárselos || jadear, resollar (to be out of breath) || volar; *to blow out of the window* volar por la ventana || sonar (to sound); *the whistle blew* el silbato sonó || resoplar, expulsar aire (whales) || bufar (horses, bulls) || reventar (tyres) || fundirse (a fuse) || FAM chivarse, soplonear (to denounce) | alardear, fanfarronear (to boast) | irse, largarse (to go) || — FAM *it's blowing great guns* hace un viento que arranca las chimeneas || *to be blowing* hacer viento || *to be blown* estar sin aliento || *to blow on an instrument* tocar un instrumento || *to blow open, shut* abrirse, cerrarse de golpe || FIG *to blow upon s.o.'s reputation* empañar la reputación de alguien || *to puff and blow* jadear (person), resoplar (horse).

◆ *vt* llevar (the wind); *to blow a ship ashore* llevar un barco hacia la costa || soplar, aventar; *to blow the fire* soplar el fuego || soplar (a whistle) || echar (air, smoke) || sonarse (the nose) || soplar (the glass) || reventar (a tyre) || MUS tocar; *to blow the trumpet* tocar la trompeta | dar aire a (an organ) || azotar; *the wind blows the trees* el viento azota los árboles || dejar sin aliento (to put out of breath) || poner huevos en (flies) || fundir (fuse) || vaciar; *to blow a boiler* vaciar una caldera || TECH inyectar (air) || FAM convidar a (to invite) | regalar con (to offer a gift) | malgastar (to waste) | maldecir (to curse) | perder (an opportunity) || — POP *blow the expense!* o *expense be blowed!* ¡al cuerno el gasto! | *I'll be blowed if...!* ¡que me aspen si...! || *to blow bubbles* hacer pompas (with soap), hacer globos (with bubble gum), hacer burbujas (in a liquid) || FIG *to blow hot and cold* jugar con dos barajas (to play a double game), cambiar de opinión cada dos por tres (to hesitate) | *to blow one's lid* o *one's top* salir de sus casillas || FIG & FAM *to blow one's own trumpet* o *horn* echarse flores, darse bombo || *to blow s.o. a kiss* enviar un beso a alguien || AUT *to blow the horn* tocar el claxon || FIG *to know which way the wind blows* saber de qué lado sopla el viento || FAM *well, I'm blowed!* ¡caramba! | *what good wins blows you here?* ¿qué te trae por aquí?

◆ *phr v* *to blow about* dispersar (to scatter) | revolotear (leaves) || *to blow away* arrastrar, llevarse (the wind) | soplar en (dust, etc.) | disipar (fog) || *to blow down* derribar || *to blow in* derribar (door, windowpane) | FAM disipar (one's money), entrar de sopetón (to come in), visitar de paso (to call on) || — *to blow in at* entrar por || *to blow off* quitar (to remove) | volar (to destroy) | vaciar (boiler) | salir volando (a hat) | salirse, escaparse (the steam) | *to blow off about* lamentarse de | FIG *to blow off steam* desfogarse | US FAM *to blow the lid off* descubrir el pastel || *to blow on* denunciar || *to blow out* apagar, soplar (to extinguish) | apagarse (to become extinguished) | hinchar (cheeks) | reventar, estallar (tyre) | fundirse (fuse) | TECH vaciar (boiler) || *to blow over* derribar (tree) | encamar, tumbar (crops) | calmarse (a storm) | olvidarse (scandal) || *to blow up* inflar, hinchar (to inflate) | volar (to destroy) | ampliar (photograph) | explotar (to explode) | reventar (to burst) | soplar, aventar (fire) | FAM dar un bocinazo a (to rebuke), salir de sus casillas (to

lose one's temper) | *it's blowing up for rain* este viento anuncia lluvia | FIG *to be blown up with conceit* estar henchido de orgullo.
— OBSERV Pret ***blew***; pp ***blown***.

blow-by-blow [-bɑi-] *adj* FIG con puntos y comas, pormenorizado, da.

blow-dry [-drɑi] *n* secado *m* con secador de mano (of hair).

blower [-ə*] *n* soplador *m* [de vidrio] (glass worker) || fuelle *m* (bellows) || escape *m* de gas (in a coal mine) || cortina *f*, pantalla *f* (of chimney) || FAM teléfono *m*.

blowfly [-flai] *n* ZOOL moscarda *f*, mosca *f* azul de la carne.

blowgun [-gʌn] *n* cerbatana *f* || pistola *f* (for painting).

blowhole [-həul] *n* ventilador *m* (in tunnel) || sopladura *f*, venteadura *f* (flaw in a metal casting) || respiradero *m* (in ice) || orificio *m* nasal (of whales).

blowing [-iŋ] *n* sopladura *f* (of glass) || soplo *m*, soplido *m* (of wind) || silbido *m* (wind noise).

blowlamp [-læmp] *n* lámpara *f* de soldar, soplete *m*.

blown [bləun] *pp* ⟶ **blow.**
◆ *adj* jadeante, sin aliento (breathless) || hinchado, da; lleno de gases (the stomach) || estropeado, da (food) || *blown glass* vidrio soplado.

blowoff [ˈbləuɔf] *n* tubo *m* de extracción (for blowing off stream, water, etc.) || escape *m*, salida *f* (expelling of air, of water, etc.) || explosión *f* (outburst) || *blowoff valve* válvula *f* de escape.

blowout [ˈbləuaut] *n* reventón *m*, pinchazo *m* (in a tyre) || fusión *f* (of a fuse) || escape *m*, salida *f* (of gas, of steam) || FAM *to have a good blowout* darse un banquetazo.

blowpipe [ˈbləupaip] *n* soplete *m* (for producing high intensity heat); *oxyhydrogen blowpipe* soplete oxhídrico || cerbatana *f* (blowgun) || caña *f* de soplador (blowtube) || MED sonda *f*.

blowtorch [ˈbləutɔːtʃ] *n* US ⟶ **blowlamp.**

blowtube [ˈbləutjuːb] *n* caña *f* de soplador (in glassworking) || cerbatana *f* (blowgun).

blowup [ˈbləuʌp] *n* ampliación *f* (of photograph) || explosión *f* || FIG estallido *m* (of anger) | escándalo *m* | riña *f*, agarrada *f* (quarrel).

blowy [bləui] *adj* ventoso, sa.

blowzy [ˈbləuzi] *adj* desastrado, da; desaliñado, da (untidy) || coloradote, ta (ruddy).

blub [blʌb] *vi* FAM lloriquear.

blubber [-ə*] *n* grasa *f* de ballena (whale fat) || lloriqueo *m*, gimoteo *m* (weeping) || FAM medusa *f* (jellyfish) || *blubber lip* bezo *m*.

blubber [-ə*] *vi* lloriquear, gimotear.
◆ *vt* *to blubber out sth.* decir algo entre llantos.

bludgeon [ˈblʌdʒən] *n* maza *f*, clava *f*, cachiporra *f*.

bludgeon [ˈblʌdʒən] *vt* aporrear, apalear (to hit) || *to bludgeon s.o. into doing sth.* obligar a alguien a hacer algo.

blue [bluː] *adj* azul (colour) || amoratado, da (body); *face blue with cold* cara amoratada de frío || deprimente (depressing) || triste, melancólico, ca (melancholy) || FIG azul (blood) || MED azul; *blue disease* enfermedad azul || conservador, ra (tory) || — MED *blue baby* bebé *m* cianótico || *blue blood* sangre *f* azul || *blue book* libro *m* azul, publicación *f* oficial (government report), guía *f* de personas eminentes (register) || *blue cheese* queso *m* de tipo Roquefort *or* de pasta verde || US FIG *blue chip* valor *m* de primera clase || *blue devils* melancolía *f* || FAM *blue funk* miedo *m* cerval || *blue jeans* pantalones vaqueros || *blue joke* chiste *m* verde || *blue law* ley inspirada en los puritanos || *blue lead* galena *f* || *blue mould* moho *m* || FIG *blue ribbon* galardón máximo, primer premio || FAM *blue rum* matarratas *m inv* || *blue streak* rayo *m*, relámpago *m* || ZOOL *blue tit* alionín *m* || FIG *I've told you till I'm blue in the face* me canso de repetírselo | *once in a blue moon* de Pascuas a Ramos, de higos a brevas | *to feel blue* sentirse deprimido || *to look blue* estar triste || FAM *to talk blue* decir verdulerías | *to tell blue stories* contar chistes verdes | *to turn the air blue* jurar como un carretero.
◆ *n* azul *m* (colour); *light, dark blue* azul claro, oscuro || añil *m*, azulete *m* (in laundering) || FIG conservador, ra (tory) || mar *m* (sea) | cielo *m* (sky) || — *cobalt, deep, pale, navy, Prussian, sky, ultramarine blue* azul cobalto, oscuro, claro, marino, de Prusia, celeste, de ultramar || FIG *out of the blue* como llovido del cielo, de repente.

blue [bluː] *vt* azular || dar azulete a (in laundering) || pavonar (steel) || FAM despilfarrar (money).
◆ *vi* amoratarse (the skin) || azularse (to become blue).

Bluebeard [-biəd] *pr n* Barba Azul.

bluebell [-bel] *n* BOT campanilla *f*, campánula *f* (flower).

blueberry [-beri] *n* BOT arándano *m*.

bluebird [-bəːd] *n* ZOOL azulejo *m*.

blue-black [-blæk] *adj* azul muy oscuro (dark blue), negro azulado *or* con reflejos azules (black).

bluebottle [-bɔtl] *n* ZOOL moscarda *f*, mosca *f* azul || BOT azulejo *m*.

blue-collar [-ˈkɔlə*] *adj* obrero.

blue-eyed [-aid] *adj* de ojos azules || FIG *blue-eyed boy* ojo derecho, preferido *m*.

blueing [-iŋ] *n* azulado *m*, azuleo *m* || US añil *m* (bluing).

bluejack [-dʒæk] *n* vitriolo *m* azul.

bluejacket [-ˌdʒækit] *n* marinero *m*.

bluenose [-nəuz] *n* US puritano, na.

blue-pencil [-ˈpensl] *vt* tachar, censurar (to obliterate) || corregir (to correct).

bluepoint [-pɔint] *n* US ZOOL ostra *f* (oyster).

blueprint [-print] *n* cianotipo *m* (photographic reproduction) || proyecto *m* original (plan).

blues [-z] *n* «blues», estilo *m* de jazz || FAM melancolía *f*, nostalgia *f*, morriña *f*, tristeza *f*.

bluestocking [-ˌstɔkiŋ] *n* literata *f*, marisabidilla *f*, cultalatiniparla *f*.

bluestone [-stəun] *n* CHEM sulfato *m* de cobre.

bluff [blʌf] *n* fanfarronada *f*, farol *m* (act of bluffing) || farol *m* (in pocker) | farolero, ra; fanfarrón, ona (bluffer) || acantilado *m* (cliff) || *to call s.o.'s bluff* hacer que alguien ponga las cartas boca arriba.
◆ *adj* brusco, ca (frank) || cortado a pico, escarpado, da (cliff) || abultado, da (prow).

bluff [blʌf] *vi* tirarse un farol, farolear, fanfarronear.
◆ *vt* engañar (to deceive) || *to bluff s.o. into thinking that* hacer creer a uno que.

bluing [ˈbluːiŋ] *n* US añil *m*, azulete *m*.

bluish [ˈbluːiʃ] *adj* azulado, da; azulino, na; azulenco, ca; azuloso, sa.

blunder [ˈblʌndə*] *n* pifia *f*, metedura *f* de pata, patinazo *m*.

blunder [ˈblʌndə*] *vi* cometer un error, pifiar, meter la pata (fam) (to make a mistake); *I blundered in telling him to go* cometí un error diciéndole que se fuese || — *to blunder against* o *into* tropezar contra || *to blunder one's way along* avanzar a ciegas || *to blunder upon sth.* tropezar con algo.
◆ *vt* *to blunder away* dejar escapar, perder (an opportunity) || *to blunder out* dejar escapar (a secret).

blunderbuss [ˈblʌndəbʌs] *n* trabuco *m* naranjero.

blundering [ˈblʌndəriŋ] *adj* torpe, descuidado, da.

blunt [blʌnt] *adj* embotado, da; desafilado, da (edge, knife) || despuntado, da (pencil) || MATH obtuso, sa (angle) || FIG embotado, da (mind) | franco, ca (straightforward) | terminante, categórico, ca; *a blunt answer* una contestación categórica | brusco, ca (person) || *blunt instrument* instrumento *m* contundente.

blunt [blʌnt] *vt* embotar, desafilar (edge, knife) || despuntar (pencil) || FIG embotar; *life had blunded his feelings* la vida había embotado sus sentimientos.

bluntly [-li] *adv* francamente, sin rodeos.

bluntness [-nis] *n* embotadura *f*, embotamiento *m* (of edge, of knife) || despuntadura *f*, despunte *m* (of pencil) || FIG franqueza *f* | brusquedad *f*.

blur [bləː*] *n* mancha *f* (stain) || vaho *m* (of breath) || aspecto *m* borroso || FIG *to cast a blur on s.o.'s name* empañar la reputación de alguien.

blur [bləː*] *vt* empañar, enturbiar (to smear); *the rain blurs the window panes* la lluvia empaña los cristales || enturbiar (sight) || desdibujar, difuminar; *the fog blurs the outline of the hills* la niebla desdibuja el contorno de las colinas || manchar de tinta, emborronar (to stain) || *to blur out* borrar, ocultar.
◆ *vi* empañarse (to smear) || desdibujarse, difuminarse (sight).

blurb [bləːb] *n* propaganda *f*.

blurred [bləːrd]; **blurry** [ˈbləːri] *adj* empañado, da (glass) || borroso, sa (photograph, etc.); *blurred letters* letras borrosas || confuso, sa; borroso, sa; vago, ga; *blurred memories* recuerdos confusos || *eyes blurred with tears* ojos empañados en lágrimas.

blurt [bləːt] *vt* *to blurt out* dejar escapar (a word, a secret), contar de buenas a primeras (a story), decir bruscamente.

blush [blʌʃ] *n* sonrojo *m*, rubor *m* (of cheeks) || arrebol *m* (red glow) || color *m* de rosa (rosy glow) || encarnado *m* (of flowers) || vistazo *m*, ojeada *f* (look) || *at the first blush* a primera vista.

blush [blʌʃ] *vi* ruborizarse, sonrojarse, ponerse colorado (a person); *to blush for shame* ruborizarse de vergüenza || enrojecer, ponerse rojo *or* colorado (to become red) || arrebolarse (sky) || — *I blush for you* me das vergüenza || *I blush to say that* me da vergüenza *or* me avergüenza decir que || *to blush to the roots of one's hair* ponerse como un pavo, ponerse rojo como una amapola.

blusher [-ə*] *n* colorete *m*.

blushing [-iŋ] *adj* ruborizado, da || tímido, da (bashful).
◆ *n* rubor *m*, sonrojo *m* (blush).

bluster [ˈblʌstə*] *n* estruendo *m* (of storm) || FIG fanfarronada *f*, bravatas *f pl* (swaggering talk) || ruido *m*, estruendo *m* (noise).

bluster [ˈblʌstə*] *vi* bramar (sea) || bramar, soplar con fuerza (wind) || FIG echar bravatas, fanfarronear (to swagger) | vociferar (*against* contra).
◆ *vt* *to bluster out* soltar, proferir (insults, threats).

blustering [-riŋ] *adj* violento, ta (wind) || furioso, sa (sea) || FIG fanfarrón, ona.

Blvd *abbr of* *[boulevard]* Blvr, bulevar.

BM *abbr of* *[British Museum]* British Museum [biblioteca y gran museo londinense].

boa ['bəuə] *n* boa *f* (snake) || boa *m* (fur).

boar [bɔ:*] *n* verraco *m* (hog) || — *wild boar* jabalí *m* || *young wild boar* jabato *m*.

board [bɔ:d] *n* madero *m* (long piece of sawn timber) || tabla *f* (plank) || tablero *m*; *drawing board* tablero de dibujo || tablero *m*, cuadro *m* (control panel) || mesa *f* (table); *ironing board* mesa de planchar || tablón *m* [de anuncios] (for notices) || cartón *m*; *corrugated board* cartón ondulado || cartoné *m* (in bookbinding) || tablero *m* (for chess) || MAR bordo *m*; *on board the ship* a bordo del barco || bordada *f*; *to make a board* dar una bordada || junta *f*, consejo *m* (authoritative body); *board of directors* junta directiva, consejo de administración || comisión *f* (committee) || pensión *f*; *full board* pensión completa || — *above board* en regla; *his papers were above board* sus papeles estaban en regla; franco, ca; sincero, ra (sincere) || *board and lodging* casa y comida || *board of examiners* tribunal *m* de exámenes || *board room* sala *f* del consejo || COMM *Board of Trade* Ministerio *m* de Comercio (US cámara *f* de Comercio) || *board of trustees* junta directiva || COMM *free on board* franco a bordo || FIG *to go by the board* irse al traste, frustrarse; *his plans went by the board because he had no money* sus planes se fueron al traste porque no tenía dinero || MAR *to go on board* subir a bordo || FIG *to let go by the board* abandonar; *he let his plan to visit Egypt go by the board* abandonó el proyecto de visitar Egipto | *to sweep the board* limpiar la mesa (in gambling), llevarse todas las medallas; *Spain swept the board in the championship* España se llevó todas las medallas en el campeonato; llevarse todos los puestos (in an election) | *to throw over board* tirar *or* echar *or* arrojar por la borda.
◆ *pl* tablas *f* (theatre); *to tread the boards* pisar las tablas || — *in boards* en cartoné (books) || *to be on the boards* pisar las tablas (theatre).

board [bɔ:d] *vt* alojar, hospedar (to lodge) || embarcarse en, embarcar en (ship, plane); *we boarded the Queen Mary* embarcamos en el Queen Mary || subir a (train, bus); *we boarded the train as it was moving off* subimos al tren cuando ya estaba en marcha || MAR abordar || entarimar, entablar (floor) || encartonar (book) || *to board up* tapar (window, door), vallar (field).
◆ *vi* alojarse, hospedarse (*with* en casa de) || estar interno; *to board at the school* ser interno en el colegio.

boarder [-ə*] *n* huésped *m* & *f* (in a boardinghouse) || interno, na (at school).

board game ['bɔ:d geim] *n* juego *m* de tablero.

boarding [-iŋ] *n* entablado *m*, entarimado *m* (of floor) || encartonado *m* (of books) || pensión *f* || AVIAT & MAR embarque *m*.

boarding card [-kɑ:d] *n* tarjeta *f* de embarque.

boardinghouse [-iŋhaus] *n* pensión *f*, casa *f* de huéspedes.

boarding school [-iŋ-sku:l] *n* internado *m*.

boardwalk [-wɔ:k] *n* US paseo *m* construido con tablas a lo largo de una playa.

boast [bəust] *n* jactancia *f*, alarde *m*, presunción *f* || *to be the boast of* ser el orgullo de.

boast [bəust] *vi* jactarse, alardear, presumir (*of, about* de); *he boasts that he can do it* se jacta de que puede hacerlo || *that's nothing to boast of* no hay por qué vanagloriarse.
◆ *vt* presumir de, alardear de; *Germany can boast excellent roads* Alemania puede presumir de excelentes carreteras || tener, vanagloriarse de tener; *he boasts two cars and a helicopter* tiene dos coches y un helicóptero.

boaster [-ə*] *n* jactancioso, sa; presumido, da.

boastful [-ful] *adj* jactancioso, sa; presumido, da.

boasting [-iŋ] *n* jactancia *f*, vanagloria *f*.

boat [bəut] *n* MAR barco *m* (any ship) | buque *m*, navío *m* (large) | barca *f*, bote *m* (small vessel) || salsera *f* (for gravy) || — *boat race* regata *f* || *boat train* tren *m* que enlaza con un barco || *by boat* en barco || *cargo boat* buque de carga, carguero *m* || REL *incense boat* naveta *f* || *merchant boat* barco mercante || *pilot boat* barco del práctico || *pleasure boat* barco de recreo || *sailing boat* barco de vela, velero *m* || FIG *to be in the same boat* remar en la misma galera, estar en el mismo caso | *to burn one's boats* quemar las naves | *to miss the boat* perder el tren, perder una oportunidad | *to rock the boat* causar perturbaciones.

boat [bəut] *vt* transportar en barco.
◆ *vi* dar un paseo en barco.

boater [-ə*] *n* canotié *m*, canotier *m*, sombrero *m* de paja.

boathook [-huk] *n* bichero *m*.

boathouse [-haus] *n* cobertizo *m*.

boating [-iŋ] *n* paseo *m* en barco || transporte *m* en barco, navegación *f* en barco.

boatload [-ləud] *n* barcada *f*.

boatman [-mən] *n* barquero *m*.
— OBSERV El plural de esta palabra es *boatmen*.

boatswain ['bəusn] *n* MAR contramaestre *m* || — *boatswain's chair* guindola *f* || *boatswain's mate* segundo contramaestre.

boatyard ['bəutjɑ:d] *n* MAR astillero *m*.

bob [bɔb] *n* movimiento *m* brusco, sacudida *f* (movement) || reverencia *f* (bow) || corcho *m*, flotador *m* (for fishing) || rizo *m* (curl) || pelo *m* corto (haircut) || peluca *f* (wig) || cola *f* cortada (of horse) || borla *f* (of ribbons, etc.) || pendiente *m* (of the ear) || FAM chelín *m* (shilling) || TECH volante *m* (of machine) | lenteja *f* (of pendulum) | plomo *m* (of plumb line) || SP bobsleigh *m* || FAM *a bob a nob* un chelín por barba.

bob [bɔb] *vi* agitarse, menearse || balancearse (in the air, in the water); *the boat is bobbing on the water* el barco se balancea en el agua || hacer una reverencia (to curtsy); *he bobbed to the Queen* hizo una reverencia ante la Reina || — *to bob down* agacharse; *he bobbed down to avoid the blow* se agachó para evitar el golpe || *to bob for apples* intentar coger manzanas con la boca || *to bob in* entrar [un momento] || *to bob up* salir a la superficie (sth. in the water), surgir, presentarse; *the same problem bobbed up again* el mismo problema surgió otra vez.
◆ *vt* mover, menear || cortar [el pelo de una mujer o el rabo de un animal] (to cut) || — *he bobbed his head up and down* subía y bajaba la cabeza.

Bob [bɔb] *pr n* Roberto *m* (diminutivo de «Robert»).

bobber [-ə*] *n* US corcho *m*, flotador *m* (cork float).

bobbery ['bɔbəri] *n* FAM jaleo *m*, alboroto *m* (hubbub).

bobbin ['bɔbin] *n* bobina *f*, carrete *m* (in spinning machine) || canilla *f* (in sewing machine) || bolillo *m* (for making lace) || *bobbin lace* encaje *m* de bolillos.

bobble ['bɔbl] *n* borla *f*.

bobby ['bɔbi] *n* FAM poli *m*.

Bobby ['bɔbi] *pr n* Roberto *m* (diminutivo de «Robert»).

bobby pin [-pin] *n* US pasador *m*.

bobby socks; bobby sox ['bɔbisɔks] *pl n* US medias *f* cortas, calcetines *m*.

bobby-soxer [-ə*] *n* jovencita *f*, tobillera *f*.

bobsled ['bɔbsled]; **bobsleigh** ['bɔbslei] *n* SP bobsleigh *m*.

bobsleigh ['bɔ:slei] *vi* SP correr en bobsleigh.

bobstay ['bɔbstei] *n* MAR barbiquejo *m* de bauprés.

bobtail ['bɔbteil] *adj* rabicorto, ta.
◆ *n* cola *f* cortada (tail) || rabicorto, ta (horse).

bode [bəud] *vt/vi* presagiar; *it bodes no good* no presagia nada bueno || *to bode well, ill* ser de buen, mal agüero.

bodeful [-ful] *adj* ominoso, sa.

bodice ['bɔdis] *n* cuerpo *m* (of a dress) || corpiño *m* (sleeveless waist).

bodiless ['bɔdilis] *adj* sin cuerpo; *a bodiless head* una cabeza sin cuerpo || incorpóreo, a; *a bodiless form walked through the wall* una forma incorpórea atravesó la pared.

bodily ['ɔdili] *adj* corporal, físico, ca; *he was charged with having bodily harm to his wife* fue acusado de haber causado daños corporales a su mujer; *bodily and mental diseases* enfermedades físicas y mentales.
◆ *adv* en conjunto, en masa, en pleno; *the teaching staff resigned bodily* el cuerpo docente dimitió en pleno || en persona (in person).

boding [bəudiŋ] *n* presentimiento *m*.
◆ *adj* ominoso, sa.

bodkin ['bɔdkin] *n* punzón *m* (for making holes) || pasacintas *m inv* (for ribbon) || PRINT punta *f*.

body ['bɔdi] *n* cuerpo *m* (of man or animal); *the human body* el cuerpo humano || cadáver *m*, cuerpo *m* (corpse); *there were five thousand bodies on the battlefield* había cinco mil cadáveres en el campo de batalla; *the victim's body was found in the kitchen* el cuerpo de la víctima fue encontrado en la cocina || tronco *m* (trunk) || cuerpo *m* (of a dress) || CHEM & PHYS cuerpo *m* || MATH sólido *m* || organismo *m*; *a body such as the League of Nations* un organismo como la Sociedad de Naciones || cuerpo *m*, gremio *m* (corporation) || MIL cuerpo *m* || cuerpo *m* (profession); *the body of lawyers* el cuerpo de abogados || cuerpo *m* (of a book) || recopilación *f*; *body of laws* recopilación de leyes || cuerpo *m* (of wine, sauce, paint, etc.) || masa *f* (mass); *a body of water* una masa de agua || masa *f* (of clay) || conjunto *m*, grupo *m* (group) || número *m*; *a large body of people* un gran número de personas || parte *f* principal (main part); *the body of the speech* la parte principal del discurso || tronco *m* (of a tree) || ASTR cuerpo *m*; *heavenly body* cuerpo celeste || PRINT cuerpo *m* [de letra] || TECH bastidor *m* (frame) | vientre *m* (of blast furnace) || AUT carrocería *f*, caja *f* || MAR casco *m* || AVIAT fuselaje *m* || ARCH cuerpo *m* (of a building) | nave *f* (of a church) || MUS caja *f* || FAM individuo *m*, persona *f* (person) || — *body corporate* corporación *f*, persona jurídica || *body odour* olor *m* corporal || *body snatcher* ladrón *m* de cadáveres || *constituent body* cuerpo electoral || *he earns enough money to keep body and soul together* gana lo justo para vivir || *in a body* en masa, en pleno, todos juntos || *learned body* docta asamblea || *legislative body* cuerpo *or* órgano legislativo || *public body* organismo público || *the main body of* la mayor parte de; *the main body of the citizens* la mayor parte de los ciudadanos; el grueso de (the army) || ANAT *yellow body* cuerpo amarillo.

body ['bɔdi] *vt* dar cuerpo a || representar, encarnar, simbolizar.

body-builder [-,bildə*] *n* AUT carrocero *m* || aparato *m* para desarrollar los músculos.

body building [-ˌbildiŋ] *n* SP culturismo *m.*

bodyguard [-gɑːd] *n* guardaespaldas *m inv* (of a person) ‖ guardia *m* de corps (of sovereign).

body stocking [-ˌstɔkiŋ] *n* malla *f.*

bodywork [-wəːk] *n* AUT carrocería *f.*

Boeotia [biˈəuʃjə] *pr n* Beocia *f.*

Boer [ˈbəuə*] *adj/n* bóer.

boffin [ˈbɔfin] *n* FAM científico, ca.

bog [bɔg] *n* ciénaga *f,* pantano *m* ‖ POP cagadero *m.*

bog [ˈbɔg] *vt* *to bog down* atascar (a car, etc.); *the rain bogged the car down in the mud* la lluvia atascó el coche en el barro; obstaculizar; *petty arguments bogged down the progress of the conference* discusiones nimias obstaculizaron el progreso de la conferencia ‖ *to get bogged down* atascarse.

bogey; bogy [ˈbəugi] *n* espectro *m,* fantasma *m; the bogey of war hung over Europe* el espectro de la guerra se cernía sobre Europa ‖ trasgo *m* (evil goblin) ‖ carretón *m,* bogie *m* (of train) ‖ SP recorrido *m* normal (golf) ‖ FIG pesadilla *f* (bugbear).

bogeyman [-mæn] *n* FAM coco *m.*

boggle [ˈbɔgl] *vi* sobresaltarse ‖ FAM *the mind boggles!* quedarse de piedra *or* patidifuso ‖ *to boggle at* vacilar ante (to hesitate).

boggy [ˈbɔgi] *adj* pantanoso, sa.

bogie [ˈbəugi] *n* carretón *m,* bogie *m* (of a wagon).

Bogotá [ˌbɔgəuˈtɑː] *pr n* GEOGR Bogotá.

bogus [bəugəs] *adj* falso, sa (false) ‖ fingido, da; simulado, da (sham) ‖ — *bogus company* compañía fantasma ‖ *bogus transactions* transacciones dudosas.

bogy [ˈbəugi] *n* ⟶ **bogey.**

bohea [bəuˈhiː] *n* té *m* de calidad inferior.

Bohemia [bəuˈhimjə] *pr n* GEOGR Bohemia *f.*

Bohemian [-n] *adj/n* bohemio, mia.

bohemianism [-nizəm] *n* bohemia *f* (Bohemian life).

boil [bɔil] *n* MED furúnculo *m,* divieso *m* ‖ punto *m* de ebullición (boiling point); *to bring to the boil* calentar hasta el punto de ebullición ‖ remolino *m* (in a stream) ‖ — *to be on the boil* estar hirviendo ‖ *to come to the boil* empezar a hervir.

boil [bɔil] *vi* hervir (a liquid) ‖ cocer (to cook) ‖ FIG bullir (to seethe) ‖ — *to boil dry* o *away* consumirse (water), pegarse (vegetables, etc.) ‖ *to boil down* reducirse; *the problem boils down to this* el problema se reduce a esto ‖ *to boil over* salirse; *the milk has boiled over* la leche se ha salido ‖ *to boil with rage* estar furioso, estar (uno) que rabia ‖ FIG *to keep the pot boiling* ganarse el cocido, calentar el puchero (to earn a living).

◆ *vt* cocer (to cook) ‖ hervir (to heat to the boiling point) ‖ pasar por agua (eggs) ‖ *to boil down* reducir ‖ *to boil up* hervir.

boiled [bɔild] *adj* hervido, da ‖ pasado por agua (egg) ‖ almidonado, da (shirt) ‖ US FAM borracho, cha (drunk).

boiler [ˈbɔilə*] *n* caldera *f* ‖ FAM pollo *m* demasiado viejo para asarse ‖ — TECH *boiler house* sala *f* de calderas ‖ *boiler room* sala *f* de calderas (in a boat) ‖ *boiler suit* mono *m* (for workers).

boilermaker [-ˌmeikə*] *n* calderero *m.*

boiling [ˈbɔiliŋ] *adj* hirviendo, hirviente; *boiling water* agua hirviendo ‖ *it's boiling hot* hace un calor espantoso (weather), está ardiendo (object, food).

◆ *n* ebullición *f; boiling point* punto de ebullición.

boisterous [ˈbɔistərəs] *adj* bullicioso, sa; alborotador, ra (persons) ‖ tumultuoso, sa (crowd) ‖ exuberante (character) ‖ revoltoso, sa (children) ‖ furioso, sa; agitado, da (sea) ‖ borrascoso, sa; violento, ta (wind) ‖ tempestuoso, sa (weather) ‖ estrepitoso, sa (laugh).

bold [bəuld] *adj* intrépido, da; valiente (fearless); *his bold actions won him the Military Cross* sus valientes hazañas le valieron la Cruz Militar ‖ audaz; *a bold piece of architecture* una audaz obra arquitectónica ‖ marcado, da; pronunciado, da (marked); *bold features* rasgos marcados ‖ acentuado, da (relief) ‖ fuerte, vigoroso, sa (style) ‖ atrevido, da; audaz; *a bold look* una mirada atrevida; *bold ideas* ideas atrevidas ‖ descarado, da (shameless) ‖ resuelto, ta (resolute) ‖ escarpado, da (steep) ‖ — PRINT *bold type* negrita *f* ‖ *to make bold to* atreverse a, permitirse.

boldface [-feis] *n* PRINT negrita *f.*

bold-faced [-feist] *adj* descarado, da; atrevido, da ‖ PRINT *bold-faced type* negrita *f.*

boldness [-nis] *n* audacia *f,* valor *m,* osadía *f* (courage) ‖ descaro *m* (shamelessness) ‖ fuerza *f,* vigor *m* (of style) ‖ lo escarpado (steepness).

bole [bəul] *n* tronco *m* (of a tree) ‖ bolo *m* (clay); *Armenian bole* bolo arménico ‖ alacena *f* (cupboard).

bolero [bəˈlεərəu] *n* bolero *m* (dance and jacket).

boletus [bəuˈliːtəs] *n* BOT boleto *m* (fungus).

bolide [ˈbəlid] *n* bólido *m.*

bolivar [bɔˈliːvə*] *n* bolívar *m* (monetary unit).

Bolivia [bəˈliviə] *pr n* GEOGR Bolivia *f.*

Bolivian [-n] *adj/n* boliviano, na.

boll [bəul] *n* BOT cápsula *f.*

bollard [ˈbɔləd] *n* noray *m* (on quayside) ‖ poste *m,* mojón *m* (for closing roads to traffic) ‖ luz *f* que señala un cruce (in a junction).

bollocks [ˈbɔləks] *pl n* POP cojones *m pl* (balls) ‖ chorradas *f,* gilipolleces *f* (nonsense).

◆ *interj* ¡cojone!

Bologna [bəˈləunjə] *pr n* GEOGR Bolonia *f.*

Bolognan [-n]; **Bolognian** [-n]; **Bolognese** [ˈbɔlənjiːz] *adj/n* boloñés, esa.

bolometer [bəuˈlɔmitə*] *n* PHYS bolómetro *m.*

Bolshevik [ˈbɔlʃivik] *adj/n* bolchevique.

— OBSERV El plural es *Bolsheviks* o *Bolsheviki.*

Bolshevism [ˈbɔlʃivizəm] *n* bolchevismo *m,* bolcheviquismo *m.*

Bolshevist [bɔlʃivist] *adj/n* bolchevista.

bolster [ˈbəulstə*] *n* cabezal *m,* travesaño *m* (pillow) ‖ ARCH collarín *m* (of a column) ‖ TECH apoyo *m,* soporte *m* (support).

bolster [ˈbəulstə*] *vt* *to bolster up* sostener, apoyar (to support), reforzar (to strengthen), rellenar (to pad), animar, entonar; *her presence bolstered him up* su presencia le animaba.

bolt [bəult] *n* cerrojo *m* (heavy bolt) ‖ pestillo *m* (small bolt) ‖ cerrojo *m* (of rifle) ‖ pestillo *m* (of lock) ‖ TECH perno *m,* tornillo *m* ‖ cuadrillo *m,* saeta *f* (of crossbow) ‖ rayo *m* (of lightning) ‖ pieza *f* (of cloth) ‖ rollo *m* (of paper) ‖ desbocamiento *m* (of a horse) ‖ huida *f,* fuga *f* (flight) ‖ — FIG *as a bolt from the blue* como una bomba; *the news came as a bolt from the blue* la noticia cayó como una bomba | *bolt from the blue* acontecimiento imprevisto ‖ TECH *key bolt* clavija *f* ‖ FIG *to have shot one's last bolt* haber quemado su último cartucho | *to make a bolt for it* escaparse | *to make a bolt for sth.* lanzarse hacia algo.

◆ *adv* *bolt upright* rígido, da; derecho, cha.

bolt [bəult] *vt* cerrar con cerrojo *or* pestillo, echar el cerrojo a; *he bolted the door* cerró la puerta con pestillo ‖ TECH empernar, sujetar con pernos *or* tornillos ‖ FAM engullir (to eat quickly) ‖ cerner (flour) ‖ US abandonar (a party) ‖ — *to bolt out* decir a boca de jarro ‖ *to bolt s.o. in* encerrar a alguien echando el cerrojo ‖ *to bolt s.o. out* dejar a alguien fuera echando el cerrojo.

◆ *vi* largarse, irse (to escape) ‖ desbocarse (horse) ‖ US retirarse (to withdraw).

bolter [-ə*] *n* caballo *m* desbocado (horse) ‖ cedazo *m* (sieve) ‖ US disidente *m* & *f.*

boltrope [ˈbəultrəup] *n* MAR relinga *f.*

bolus [ˈbəuləs] *n* bolo *m* (pill) ‖ *alimentary bolus* bolo alimenticio.

bomb [bɔm] *n* bomba *f; atomic bomb* bomba atómica; *hydrogen bomb* bomba de hidrógeno ‖ — *bomb bay* compartimiento *m* de bombas (in a plane) ‖ *bomb crater* hoyo producido por una bomba, embudo *m* de granada ‖ *bomb disposal squad* brigada *f* de artificieros ‖ *bomb release* lanzamiento *m* de bombas ‖ *bomb release mechanism* dispositivo *m* lanzabombas ‖ *bomb shelter* refugio antiaéreo ‖ *bomb thrower* lanzabombas *m inv* ‖ MED *cobalt bomb* bomba de cobalto ‖ *smoke bomb* bomba de humo ‖ *stink bomb* bomba fétida ‖ *time bomb* bomba de efecto retardado ‖ FIG *to drop* o *to burst like a bomb* caer como una bomba ‖ *volcanic bomb* bomba volcánica.

bomb [bɔm] *vt/vi* bombardear ‖ *to bomb out* destruir con bombas.

bombard [ˈbɔmbɑːd] *n* MIL bombarda *f* (gun).

bombard [bɔmˈbɑːd] *vt* bombardear (with guns or shells) ‖ FIG bombardear, acosar; *the press reporters bombarded him with questions* los periodistas le bombardearon a preguntas *or* le acosaron con preguntas ‖ PHYS bombardear.

bombardier [ˌbɔmbəˈdiə*] *n* bombardero *m.*

bombardment [bɔmˈbɑːdmənt] *n* MIL & PHYS bombardeo *m.*

bombardon [bɔmˈbɑːdən] *n* MUS bombarda *f,* bombardón *m.*

bombasine [ˈbɔmbəziːn] *n* bombasí *m* (material).

bombast [ˈbɔmbæst] *n* ampulosidad *f,* prosopopeya *f,* rimbombancia *f.*

bombastic [bɔmˈbæstik] *adj* ampuloso, sa; rimbombante.

bomber [ˈbɔmə*] *n* bombardero *m.*

bombing [ˈbɔmiŋ] *n* bombardeo *m.*

bombproof [ˈbɔm-pruːf] *adj* a prueba de bombas.

bombshell [ˈbɔmʃəl] *n* MIL obús *m,* granada *f* ‖ FIG & FAM bomba *f; to drop* o *to burst like a bombshell* caer como una bomba | sensación *f; Sophia, latest Hollywood bombshell* Sofía, la última sensación de Hollywood.

bombsight [ˈbɔmsait] *n* visor *m* de bombardeo.

bomb-site [ˈbɔmsait] *n* MIL objetivo *m.*

bombyx [ˈbɔmbiks] *n* bómbice *m,* bómbix *m* (silkworm).

bona fide [-ˈfaidi] *adj* de buena fe, serio, ria (offer) ‖ auténtico, ca (traveller).

bonanza [bəuˈnænzə] *n* bonanza *f* (rich deposit of ore) ‖ FIG mina *f* (de oro) (source of wealth).

Bonaventura [bɔnəvenˈtjuːrə] *pr n* Buenaventura *m.*

bonbon [ˈbɔnbɔn] *n* caramelo *m.*

bond [bɔnd] *n* lazo *m,* vínculo *m; bonds of friendship* lazos de amistad ‖ bono *m; Treasury*

bonds bonos del Tesoro; *bond issue* emisión de bonos || JUR obligación *f* | título *m* (security) || fianza *f* (bail) || COMM depósito *m* || CHEM enlace *m* (of atoms, of ions, etc.) || ARCH aparejo *m* (of bricks); *English bond* aparejo inglés || ELECTR conexión *f* || US seguro *m* de fianza, garantía *f* || — *to be in bond* estar en depósito, estar depositado || *to take out of bond* sacar de la aduana.
◆ *pl* cadenas *f* (shackles) || FIG cautiverio *m sing*; *to be in bonds* estar en cautiverio.
◆ *adj* esclavo, va.

bond [bɔnd] *vt* ARCH aparejar || depositar (in customs) || hipotecar (to mortgage) || garantizar (a debt, etc.) || unir (to bind).

bondage [-idʒ] *n* esclavitud *f*.

bonded [-id] *adj* depositado, da; en depósito (goods) || garantizado, da (debt) || *bonded warehouse* almacén *m* de depósito.

bonderizing ['bɔndəraiziŋ] *n* TECH bonderización *f* (protection against corrosion).

bondholder ['bɔnd,həuldə*] *n* obligacionista *m* & *f*.

bondmaid ['bɔndmeid] *n* esclava *f*.

bondman ['bɔndmən] *n* esclavo *m*, siervo *m*.
— OBSERV El plural de *bondman* es *bondmen*.

bondsman ['bɔndzmən] *n* fiador *m* || esclavo *m*, siervo *m* (bondman).
— OBSERV El plural de *bondsman* es *bondsmen*.

bondstone ['bɔndstəun] *n* ARCH perpiaño *m*.

bone [bəun] *n* hueso *m* (of body) || ballena *f* (of corset, etc.) || barba *f* (of whale) || espina *f*, raspa *f* (of fish) || hueso *m* (of fruits) || hueso *m* (substance); *buttons made of bone* botones de hueso || — FIG *as dry as a bone* o *bone dry* más seco que una pasa | *bone of contention* manzana *f* de la discordia | *bred in the bone* en la masa de la sangre | *funny bone* hueso de la alegría *or* de la suegra | *to break every bone in s.o.'s body* no dejarle a uno un hueso sano | *to have a bone to pick with s.o.* tener que ajustarle las cuentas a uno.
◆ *pl* huesos *m*, restos *m* (remains) || cuerpo *m sing*; *my old bones* mi pobre cuerpo || MUS tarreñas *f* || FAM dados *m* (dice) || — FIG *he won't make old bones* no llegará a hacer huesos viejos | *to be a bag of bones* estar en los huesos | *to feel it in one's bones* tener el presentimiento de ello | *to make no bones about doing sth.* no vacilar en hacer algo | *to make no bones about it* no andarse con rodeos || *wet to the bones* calado hasta los huesos.

bone [bəun] *vt* deshuesar (meat) || quitar el hueso (of fruits) || quitar las espinas *or* las raspas a (fish) || emballenar, poner ballenas (a corset) || FAM birlar (to steal) || US FAM *to bone up* empollar (to study).

bone black [-blæk] *n* carbón *m* animal.

bone china [-'tʃainə] *n* porcelana *f* blanca y translúcida.

boned [-d]; **boneless** [-lis] *adj* sin huesos, deshuesado, da (meat, fruit) || sin espinas, sin raspas (fish).

bone-dry [-'drai] *adj* completamente seco || sediento, ta (thirsty).

bonehead [-hed] *n* FAM tonto, ta; majadero, ra.

bone-idle [-'aidl] *adj* vago, ga.

boneless [-lis] *adj* → **boned.**

bone meal [-mi:l] *n* harina *f* de huesos.

boner [-ə*] *n* US FAM metedura *f* de pata, pifia *f*, plancha *f* || US FAM *to pull a boner* meter la pata, tirarse una plancha.

bonesetter [-,setə*] *n* ensalmador *m*.

bone shaker [-ʃeikə*] *n* FAM cacharro *m* (car).

bonfire ['bɔn,faiə*] *n* hoguera *f* || *bonfire night* noche *f* de las hogueras (on 5th of November).

bongo drum ['bɔŋgəu-drʌm] *n* MUS bongó *m*.

bonhomie ['bɔnɔmi:] *n* afabilidad *f*, bondad *f*.

boniness ['bəuninis] *n* delgadez *f*, demacración *f*.

bon mot [bɔ̃'məu] *n* ocurrencia *f*, agudeza *f*.

Bonn [bɔn] *pr n* GEOGR Bona.

bonnet ['bɔnit] *n* gorro *m*, gorra *f* (for children) || gorra *f* escocesa (for men) || toca *f* (for women) || capó *m* (of cars) || campana *f* (of fireplace) || MAR boneta *f* || TECH sombrerete *m* (of valve).

bonny ['bɔni] *adj* hermoso, sa (babies) || lindo, da; majo, ja; *a bonny lass* una chica muy maja.

bonus ['bəunəs] *n* prima *f*, gratificación *f* (gratuity) || beneficio *m* (earned on production) || dividendo *m* extraordinario (stocks and shares) || beneficio *m* (paid to insurance policy holders) || *cost of living bonus* plus *m* de carestía de vida.

bony ['bəuni] *adj* huesudo, da (with prominent bones) || esquelético, ca (thin) || lleno de huesos (meat) || lleno de espinas (fish) || de hueso (of bone) || óseo, a (like bone).

bonze [bɔnz] *n* bonzo *m*.

boo [bu:] *n* abucheo *m*, pateo *m* || — FIG *he wouldn't say boo to a goose* es de lo más tímido que hay | *not to say boo* no decir ni pío.

boo [bu:] *vt/vi* abuchear, patear.

boob [bu:b] *n* FAM bobo, ba (fool) | teta *f* (breast).

booby ['bu:bi] *n* bobo, ba || último, ma (in a competition).

booby prize [-praiz] *n* premio *m* al peor *or* al último.

booby trap [-træp] *n* trampa *f* || MIL trampa *f* explosiva.

boogie ['bu:gi] *vi* FAM mover el esqueleto.

book [buk] *n* libro *m* (printed work, literary composition, of bible, etc.); *bound book* libro encuadernado *or* empastado; *reference book* libro de consulta; *sacred books* libros sagrados || talonario *m* (of cheques, coupons) || carnet *m* (of stamps, of tickets) || registro *m* (of bets) || carterilla *f* (of matches) || cartilla *f* (of savings) || — *account book* libro de contabilidad || *address book* libro de señas *or* de direcciones || *by the book* según las reglas || *book of Common Prayer* libro de oraciones || *book of Hours* libro de horas || *book of knight-errantry* libro de caballerías || *book review* reseña *f* de libros || *complaints book* libro de reclamaciones || *counterfoil book* (libro) talonario || *exercise book* cuaderno *m* || *in one's book* según el parecer de uno || COMM *letter book* libro copiador || *minute book* libro de actas || *music book* libro de música || FIG *to be in s.o.'s bad books* estar en la lista negra de alguien | *to be in s.o.'s good books* estar en buenos términos con alguien || US *pocket book* libro de bolsillo (paperback) || *record book* libro borrador || *ship's book* libro *or* registro de a bordo || *text book* libro de texto || *the Good Book* la Biblia || *the Great Book of the Public Debt* el Gran Libro | *to burn one's books* o *to throw one's books away* ahorcar los libros || FIG *to bring s.o. to book* pedir cuentas a alguien | *to go by the book* seguir las reglas || *to make a book* registrar las apuestas || FIG *to read s.o. like a book* leer los pensamientos de alguien | *to suit s.o.'s book* convenirle a uno | *to take a leaf out of s.o.'s book* tomar ejemplo de alguien || *to talk like a book* hablar como un libro.
◆ *pl* libros *m*, cuentas *f*, contabilidad *f sing* (accounting) || — *one for the books* hecho *m* memorable || *on the books* registrado en los libros || COMM *to keep the books* llevar los libros *or* las cuentas.

book [buk] *vt/vi* reservar, hacer la reserva de (theatre, hotel, travel, etc.) || contratar (speakers, performers, etc.) || anotar, registrar, asentar (to record in a book) || fichar (suspect) || — *to be booked up* estar completo, no haber localidades (theatre, etc.), tener compromisos (a person) || *to book in* registrarse (at a hotel).

bookable [-əbl] *adj* que se puede reservar (ticket).

bookbinder [-,baində*] *n* encuadernador *m*.

bookbinding [-,baindiŋ] *n* encuadernación *f*.

bookcase [-keis] *n* biblioteca *f*, estantería *f* para libros.

book club [-klʌb] *n* círculo *m* de lectores.

bookend [-end] *n* sujetalibros *m inv*.

bookie [-i] *n* FAM corredor *m* de apuestas.

booking [-iŋ] *n* reserva *f* [*AMER* reservación *f*] (of seats, etc.) || contratación *f* (of artists).

booking clerk [-klɑ:k] *n* taquillero, ra de estación.

booking office [-iŋ,ɔfis] *n* taquilla *f*, despacho *m* de billetes.

bookish [-iʃ] *adj* libresco, ca (style) || pedante; *a bookish writer* un escritor pedante || aficionado a la lectura (fond of reading) || estudioso, sa (fond of studying) || FIG enteradillo, lla (know-all).

book jacket [-,dʒækət] *n* sobrecubierta *f*.

bookkeeper [-,ki:pə*] *n* tenedor *m* de libros, contable *m* & *f*.

bookkeeping [-,ki:piŋ] *n* teneduría *f* de libros, contabilidad *f*.

book learning [-,lə:niŋ] *n* conocimientos *m pl* librescos.

booklet [-lit] *n* folleto *m*.

booklover [-,lʌvə*] *n* bibliófilo, la.

bookmaker [-,meikə*] *n* corredor *m* de apuestas, «bookmaker» *m* (in races) || encuadernador, ra (of books).

bookmark [-mɑ:k] *n* señal *f*, registro *m*.

bookmobile [-məu,bil] *n* biblioteca *f* ambulante.

bookplate [-pleit] *n* ex libris *m* (label).

bookrest [-rest] *n* atril *m* (support).

bookseller [-,selə*] *n* librero, ra.

bookshelf [-ʃelf] *n* estante *m*.
◆ *pl* estantería *f sing*.

bookshop [-ʃɔp] *n* librería *f*.

bookstall [-stɔ:l]; **bookstand** [-stænd] *n* quiosco *m*, puesto *m* de libros (open-air stand) || caseta *f* (in book exhibitions) || quiosco *m*, puesto *m* de periódicos (newsstand).

bookstore [-stɔ:*] *n* US librería *f*.

book value [-,vælju:] *n* valor *m* contable.

bookworm [-wə:m] *n* polilla *f* que roe los libros (larva) || FIG ratón *m* de biblioteca (person).

boom [bu:m] *n* estampido *m* (explosion) || tronido *m* (of cannon) || mugido *m* (of a bittern) || bramido *m* (of waves) || retumbo *m* (of thunder) || auge *m*, «boom» *m* (sudden increase) || MAR botalón *m*, botavara *f* (to stretch the sail foot) | palo *m* de carga (for lifting) | cadena *f* de troncos, barrera *f* de un puerto (floating barrier) || aguilón *m*, brazo *m*, pluma *f* (of crane) || CINEM & RAD jirafa *f* || — CINEM *boom operator* jirafista *m* || *boom years* años *m pl* de prosperidad || *population boom* explosión demográfica.

boom [bu:m] *vi* retumbar (thunder) || tronar (cannon) || resonar (large bell, etc.) || zumbar

(to buzz) || mugir (a bittern) || prosperar, estar en auge (to be prosperous or in demand).
◆ *vt* hacer prosperar (to promote) || hacer tronar (the cannon).

boomerang ['buːməræŋ] *n* bumerang *m* || FIG acción *f* contraproducente.

boomerang ['buːməræŋ] *vi* ser contraproducente.

booming ['buːmiŋ] *adj* que truena (cannon, etc.) || resonante (voice) || en auge (industry, etc.) || próspero, ra (years).

boomtown ['buːmtaun] *n* US ciudad *f* de crecimiento rápido.

boon [buːn] *n* bendición *f* (blessing) || favor *m* (favour).
◆ *adj* alegre (gay).

boor [buə*] *n* patán *m* (peasant, uncouth man).

boorish [-riʃ] *adj* tosco, ca (uncouth).

boost [buːst] *n* empujón *m* hacia arriba || FIG estímulo *m* (incentive) || *to give s.o. a boost* aupar a uno (to lift up), estimular a uno (to encourage), lanzar a uno (to make famous).

boost [buːst] *vt* levantar (to hoist) || impulsar (to thrust) || elevar, aumentar (to increase) || promover, fomentar (to promote) || ayudar (to help) || levantar (spirits) || ELECTR elevar (el voltaje) (in a battery).

booster [-ə*] *n* ELECTR elevador *m* de voltaje || TECH motor *m* auxiliar de propulsión (engine) | aumentador *m* de presión (for increasing pressure) || MED *booster injection* o *shot* revacunación *f*.

booster pump [-əˌpʌmp] *n* bomba *f* para aumentar la presión.

booster rocket [-əˌrɔkit] *n* cohete *m* acelerador.

boot [buːt] *n* bota *f* (footwear) || maleta *f*, maletero *m*, portaequipajes *m inv* (in a car) || MUS tubo *m* de enchufe (of an organ) || caña *f* (of stocking) || calceta *f* (torture device) || FAM puntapié *m*, patada *f* (kick) | despido *m* (dismissal) || US FAM recluta *m* (marine recruit) || — FIG & FAM *I'd bet my boots that* me juego la cabeza a que | *I wouldn't like to be in his boots* no me gustaría estar en su pellejo | *like old boots* estupendamente | *the boot is on the other foot* ha dado la vuelta a la tortilla | *to be too big for one's boots* ser un engreído | *to boot* además, por añadidura | *to die with one's boots on* morir con las botas puestas | *to get the boot* ser puesto de patitas en la calle | *to give the boot* poner de patitas en la calle | *to have one's heart in one's boots* estar con *or* tener el alma en un hilo | *to lick s.o.'s boots* hacer la pelotilla a alguien | *to wipe one's boots on s.o.* tratar con la punta del pie a uno || *you can bet your boots that* puedes estar seguro de que.

boot [buːt] *vt* dar una patada a (to kick) || calzar a (to supply o to put boots on) || — FIG & FAM *to boot it* ir a pie | *to boot s.o. out* poner a alguien de patitas en la calle.

bootblack [-blæk] *n* US limpiabotas *m inv* [AMER lustrabotas *m inv*].

bootee ['buːti] *n* patín *m*, calzado *m* de punto para niños (for babies) || bota *f*, botín *m*, botina *f* (for ladies).

Boötes [bəu'əutiːz] *pl n* ASTR Boyero.

booth [buːð] *n* puesto *m* (in a market) || cabina *f* (to isolate); *telephone booth* cabina telefónica.

bootjack ['buːtdʒæk] *n* sacabotas *m inv*, tirabotas *m inv*.

bootlace ['buːtleis] *n* cordón *m*.

bootleg ['buːtleg] *n* caña *f* (de bota).
◆ *adj* US FAM de contrabando; *bootleg liquor* licor de contrabando.

bootleg ['buːtleg] *vt* US FAM pasar de contrabando (to smuggle) | hacer *or* vender ilegalmente (to make or to sell illegally).

bootlegger [-ə*] *n* US contrabandista *m* de licores.

bootlegging [-ŋ] *n* US contrabando *m* de licores.

bootless ['buːtlis] *adj* inútil, vano, na.

bootlick ['buːtlik] *vt/vi* FAM hacer la pelotilla (to flatter).

boots [buːts] *n* limpiabotas *m inv* [AMER lustrabotas *m inv*] (shoeshine boy) || botones *m inv* (bellboy).

bootstrap ['buːt-stræp] *n* oreja *f*.

boot tree ['buːt-triː] *n* horma *f*.

booty ['buːti] *n* botín *m* (spoils).

booze [buːz] *n* FAM bebida *f* alcohólica | borrachera *f* (drunkenness) || — FAM *to be on the booze* estar de copeo | *to go on the booze* ir de copeo (to go drinking), empezar a beber (to take to drink).

booze [buːz] *vi* FAM beber [bebidas alcohólicas] || FAM *to be boozed up* estar borracho.

boozer [-ə*] *n* FAM borracho *m* | tasca *f* (bar).

boozy ['buːzi] *adj* FAM borracho, cha (person) | en que se bebe mucho (party).

bop [bɔp] *n* MUS be-bop *m*.

bop [bɔp] *vt* golpear.

bo-peep [bəu'piːp] *n* FAM *to play bo-peep* jugar (con un niño) tapándose la cara y descubriéndola de repente.

boracic [bə'ræsik] *adj* CHEM bórico, ca.

boracite ['bɔrəsait] *n* MIN boracita *f*.

borage ['bɔridʒ] *n* BOT borraja *f*.

borate ['bɔːreit] *n* CHEM borato *m*.

borax ['bɔːræks] *n* CHEM bórax *m*.

bordeaux [bɔː'dəu] *adj* burdeos.
◆ *n* burdeos *m* (wine, colour).

Bordeaux [bɔː'dəu] *pr n* GEOGR Burdeos.

border ['bɔːdə*] *n* borde *m*, margen *m* (edge) || orilla *f* (of river, of sea, etc.) || ribete *m* (stripe); *the border of a handkerchief* el ribete de un pañuelo || frontera *f*; *to cross the Spanish border* cruzar la frontera española || arriate *m* (of plants) || THEATR bambalina *f* || *border areas* zonas fronterizas.

border ['bɔːdə*] *vt* bordear || ribetear (in sewing).
◆ *vi* *to border on* lindar con; *Iowa borders on Missouri* Iowa linda con el Misuri; rayar en; *his remarks bordered upon rudeness* sus observaciones rayaron en la grosería.

borderland [-lænd] *n* zona *f* fronteriza || FIG límites *m pl* (limits) | margen *m* (fringe area) | zona *f* imprecisa (vague zone).

border line [-lain] *n* frontera *f*.

borderline [-lain] *adj* fronterizo, za; limítrofe || FIG dudoso, sa; *borderline case* caso dudoso.

bordure ['bɔːdjuə*] *n* HERALD bordura *f*.

bore [bɔː*] *n* taladro *m* (deep hole) || alma *f*, ánima *f* (interior tube of a gun) || calibre *m* (calibre) || FAM pelmazo, za; pesado, da (annoying person) | tostón *m*, lata *f*, rollo *m* (dull person or thing) || MAR subida *f* de la marea.

bore [bɔː*] *vt* taladrar, perforar, horadar || barrenar (with a drill) || perforar (a tunnel) || FAM aburrir (to weary) | fastidiar, dar la lata, dar el rollo *or* el tostón (to annoy) || — FAM *to be bored stiff* o *to tears* aburrirse como una ostra || *to be bored with* estar harto de || *to bore one's way through the crowd* abrirse paso entre la multitud.
◆ *vi* taladrar, perforar, horadar.

bore [bɔː*] *pret* → **bear.**

Boreas ['bɔriæs] *n* Bóreas *m* (north wind).

boredom ['bɔːdəm] *n* aburrimiento *m* || fastidio *m* (nuisance).

borer ['bɔːrə*] *n* taladrador, ra; perforador, ra (person) || taladro *m*, barrena *f* (tool) || taladradora *f*, perforadora *f* (machine) || ZOOL barrenillo *m*.

boric ['bɔːrik] *adj* CHEM bórico, ca.

boring ['bɔːriŋ] *adj* aburrido, da; pesado, da.
◆ *n* taladro *m* (hole) || taladrado *m*, perforación *f* (process) || perforación *f* (of a tunnel).

born [bɔːn] *pp/adj* → **bear** || nacido, da; *born under a lucky star* nacido con buena estrella || nato, ta; *a born poet* un poeta nato || de nacimiento; *a born fool* tonto de nacimiento; *Spanish-born* español de nacimiento || — *her first, latest born* su primero, su último hijo || *he was born in 1928* nació en 1928 || *in all my born days* desde que nací, en toda mi vida || *to be born* nacer || *to be born again* volver a nacer || FIG *to be born of* ser engendrado por, ser el fruto de.

borne [bɔːn] *pp* → **bear.**

Borneo ['bɔːniəu] *pr n* GEOGR Borneo.

boron ['bɔːrɔn] *n* CHEM boro *m*.

borough ['bʌrə] *n* villa *f*, ciudad *f* (town) || barrio *m*, distrito *m* (urban constituency) || municipio *m* (municipality).

Borromean [bɔrə'miən] *adj* *Borromean Islands* islas Borromeas.

borrow ['bɔrəu] *vt* pedir *or* tomar prestado; *to borrow a book from s.o.* pedir a alguien un libro prestado || FIG apropiarse; *to borrow s.o.'s ideas* apropiarse las ideas de alguien | tomar (to quote); *to borrow a phrase from an author* tomar una frase de un autor.
◆ *vi* tomar a préstamo.

borrower [-ə*] *n* prestatario, ria || FIG sablista *m* & *f* (cadger).

borrowing [-iŋ] *n* el tomar prestado; *the borrowing of valuables is not advisable* el tomar prestado objetos valiosos no es recomendable || préstamo *m* (borrowed thing) || FIG adopción *f*.

borstal ['bɔːstl] *n* correccional *m* de menores.

bort [bɔːt] *n* diamante *m* negro, «bort» *m* (poor quality diamond).

bosh [bɔʃ] *n* necedades *f pl* || TECH etalaje *m* (of furnace).

bosket ['bɔskit] *n* bosquecillo *m* (grove) || matorral *m* (thicket).

Bosnia ['bɔzniə] *pr n* GEOGR Bosnia *f*.

Bosnian [-n] *adj/n* bosnio, nia; bosniaco, ca.

bosom ['buzəm] *n* pecho *m* (breast) || pechos *m pl*, senos *m pl* (woman's breasts) || pechera *f* (of a dress) || seno *m*; *she put the letter in her bosom* guardó la carta en el seno || FIG seno *m*; *in the bosom of the Church* en el seno de la Iglesia.
◆ *adj* íntimo, ma; entrañable; *a bosom friend* un amigo íntimo.

bosom ['buzəm] *vt* guardar.

Bosphorus ['bɔsfərəs]; **Bosporus** ['bɔspərəs] *pr n* GEOGR Bósforo *m*.

boss [bɔs] *n* patrón, ona (employer) || jefe, fa (person in charge) || bulto *m*, protuberancia *f* (protuberance) || bollo *m*, chichón *m* (bump) || joroba *f*, giba *f*, corcova *f* (hunchback) | (ant) ombligo *m* (of a shield) || ARCH crucería *f* (of a vault), almohadilla *f* (ornamentation) || repujado *m* (on leather, on silver) || copa *f* (of a bridle) || US jefe *m* (in a party organization) | cacique *m* (with dictatorial authority) || *to be one's own boss* ser uno su propio jefe.

boss [bɔs] *vt* dirigir (to manage) || ARCH almohadillar | repujar (leather, silver) || *to boss about* o *around* marimandonear, mangonear.

bossage [ˈbɔsidʒ] *n* ARCH almohadillado *m* || repujado *m* (leather, silver).

boss-eyed [bɔsˈaid] *adj* FAM bizco, ca.

bossiness [ˈbɔsinis] *n* carácter *m* mandón.

bossy [ˈbɔsi] *adj* FAM mandón, ona.

boston [ˈbɔstən] *n* bostón *m* (game, walz).

bosun [ˈbəusn] *n* MAR contramaestre *m* (boatswain).

bot; bott [bɔt] *n* larva *f* del moscardón, rezno *m* (parasitic larva of the botfly).

botanic [bəˈtænik]; **botanical** [-əl] *adj* botánico, ca; *botanical garden* jardín botánico.

botanist [ˈbɔtenist] *n* botánico, ca; botanista.

botanize [ˈbɔtənaiz] *vi* herborizar.

botany [ˈbɔtəni] *n* botánica *f*.

botany wool [-wul] *n* lana *f* merina.

botch [bɔtʃ] *n* chapucería *f*, chapuza *f*.

botch [bɔtʃ] *vt* chapucear || *to botch it* meter la pata, cometer una pifia || *to botch up* chapucear.

botfly [ˈbɔtflai] *n* moscardón *m*.

both [bəuθ] *adj/pron* ambos, ambas, los dos, las dos; *both girls are pretty* ambas *or* las dos chicas son guapas; *both are pretty* ambas *or* las dos son guapas || — *both expensive and ugly* caro y feo a la vez || *both of them* ellos dos, los dos, ambos || *both of us* nosotros dos || *both of you* vosotros dos || *both she and her mother are pretty* tanto su madre como ella son guapas.
◆ *adv* al mismo tiempo, a la vez.

bother [ˈbɔðə*] *n* preocupación *f* (worry) || molestia *f* (disturbance) || lata *f*, fastidio *m* (nuisance) || — *bother!* ¡caramba!, ¡caray! || *I am giving you a lot of bother* te estoy dando la lata, te estoy fastidiando *or* molestando.

bother [ˈbɔðə*] *vt* preocupar (to worry); *don't bother your head about it* no te preocupes por eso || molestar (to disturb) || dar la lata, fastidiar (to be a nuisance).
◆ *vi* preocuparse (to worry) || *to bother about* o *with* tomarse la molestia de, molestarse por (to take the trouble), preocuparse de *or* por (to worry).

bothersome [-səm] *adj* fastidioso, sa; molesto, ta.

Botswana [bɔˈtswaːnə bɔtˈswaːnə] *pr n* GEOGR Botsuana.

bottle [ˈbɔtl] *n* botella *f*; *a bottle of wine* una botella de vino || biberón *m* (for babies); *brought up on the bottle* criado con biberón || bombona *f* (for butane) || — FIG *to hit* o *to take to* o *to go on the bottle* darse a la bebida | *to sit over the bottle with s.o.* beber una botella entre dos || *to speak over a bottle* hablar tomando una copa.

bottle [ˈbɔtl] *vt* embotellar; *to bottle wine* embotellar vino || enfrascar, envasar (to preserve) || — FIG & FAM *to bottle out* rajarse, dar marcha atrás || *to bottle up* contener, reprimir (feelings, etc.).

bottle bank [-bæŋk] *n* contenedor *m* de botellas para reciclaje.

bottlebrush [-brʌʃ] *n* escobilla *f*, limpiabotellas *m inv*.

bottle drainer [-ˌdreinə*] *n* escurrebotellas *m*.

bottle-fed [-fed] *adj* criado con biberón.

bottleneck [-nek] *n* cuello *m* (de la botella) || FIG estrangulamiento *m* (narrowing) | embotellamiento *m*, atasco *m* (obstruction) | obstáculo *m* (obstacle) | callejón *m* sin salida (dead end).

bottle party [-ˌpaːti] *n* asalto *m*, reunión *f* de amigos en la que cada uno lleva la bebida.

bottler [-ə*] *n* embotellador, ra.

bottle rack [-ræk] *n* botellero *m*, portabotellas *m inv*.

bottling [-iŋ] *n* embotellado *m*, embotellamiento *m* (of wine, etc.).

bottling machine [-iŋməˈʃiːn] *n* embotelladora *f*.

bottom [ˈbɔtəm] *adj* más bajo; *bottom price* precio más bajo || último, ma; *bottom dollar* último dólar || del fondo (at the end) || fundamental, esencial (essential) || FIG *to bet one's bottom dollar* apostar la cabeza, apostar hasta el último céntimo.
◆ *n* fondo *m*; *the bottom of a box, of a valley* el fondo de una caja, de un valle || asiento *m* (seat of a chair, etc.) || culo *m* (of a bottle) || fondo *m* (of a cask) || trasero *m* (buttocks) || fondo *m* (of sea, of river, etc.) || pie *m* (of mountain, of page, etc.) || fondo *m* (far end); *the bottom of a corridor, of a street* el fondo de un pasillo, de una calle || final *m* (inferior level); *to be at the bottom of the class* estar al final de la clase || MAR obra *f* viva (of ship) || bajo *m* (of a dress) || bajos *m pl* (of trousers) || pantalón *m* (of pyjamas) || vega *f* (low-lying land) || FIG origen *m*, causa *f* (cause); *he was at the bottom of* fue la causa de | base *f*, fundamento *m* (basis) | meollo *m*, fondo *m*; *the bottom of the matter* el meollo del asunto | fondo *m*; *to get to the bottom of a mystery* llegar al fondo de un misterio || — *at bottom* o *at the bottom* en el fondo; *he was at bottom modest* en el fondo era modesto || *bottom up* boca abajo || FAM *bottoms up!* ¡apurar las copas! || FIG *from the bottom up* desde el principio (from the beginning) || MAR *to go to the bottom* irse a pique, irse al fondo || *to knock the bottom out of an argument* echar por tierra un argumento || MAR *to send to the bottom* echar a pique, hundir (a ship) || *to touch bottom* tocar fondo || *to work one's way up from the bottom* empezar desde el principio (career, enterprise, etc.) || *who is at the bottom of the scheme?* ¿quién está detrás de todo esto?

bottom [ˈbɔtəm] *vi* tocar fondo (a submarine) || ECON *to bottom out* tocar fondo (recession, unemployement, etc.).
◆ *vt* poner fondo a (a chair, an armchair, etc.) || FIG basar, fundamentar (to base) || llegar al fondo de (a case) || MAR hacer tocar fondo a.

bottom drawer [-ˈdrɔː*] *n* ajuar *m*.

bottom gear [-ˈgiə*] *n* primera *f* (of a car).

bottomless [-lis] *adj* insondable, sin fondo (pit, etc.) || inescrutable, insondable (mystery) || infundado, da (accusation) || FIG *the bottomless pit* el infierno.

bottom line [-lain] *n* resultado *m* final.

bottommost [-məust] *adj* último, ma; *on the bottommost shelf* en el último estante || insondable, inescrutable (mystery, etc.).

bottomry [-ri] *n* MAR contrato *m* a la gruesa.

bottomry [-ri] *vt* MAR dar en prenda [un barco].

botulism [ˈbɔtjuilizəm] *n* MED botulismo *m*.

boudoir [ˈbuːdwaː*] *n* «boudoir» *m*, tocador *m*, gabinete *m*.

bougainvillea [ˌbuːgənˈviljə] *n* BOT buganvilla *f*.

bough [bau] *n* rama *f* (of a tree).

bought [bɔːt] *pret/pp* → **buy.**

bougie [ˈbuːʒiː] *n* MED sonda *f* || vela *f* (candle).

bouillabaisse [ˈbujəbes] *n* bullabesa *f*, sopa *f* de pescado.

bouillon [ˈbuːjɔ̃ː] *n* caldo *m*.

boulder [ˈbəuldə*] *n* canto *m* rodado.

boulder clay [-klei] *n* depósito *m* errático.

boulevard [ˈbuːlvaː*] *n* bulevar *m*.

boulter [ˈbəultə*] *n* palangre *m* (fishing line).

bounce [bauns] *n* bote *m* (of a ball) || salto *m* (jump) || vitalidad *f* || fanfarronería *f* (boastfulness).

bounce [bauns] *vt* hacer botar (a ball) || US FAM botar, poner de patitas en la calle.
◆ *vi* saltar (to jump) || botar, rebotar (a ball) || jactarse, alardear (to boast) || ser rechazado (a cheque) || — FIG *to bounce back* recuperarse | *to bounce back on* repercutir en contra de || *to bounce into* irrumpir en.

bouncer [-ə*] *n* persona *f* encargada de echar a los alborotadores de un club nocturno.

bouncing [-iŋ] *adj* fuerte, robusto, ta (strong).

bouncy [ˈbaunsi] *adj* que bota mucho (ball) || activo, va; vital (person).

bound [baund] *pret/pp* → **bind.**

bound [baund] *adj* destinado, da; *the Greek civilization was bound to disappear* la civilización griega estaba destinada a desaparecer || FIG obligado, da; ligado, da; *she is bound by her word to fulfil what she promised* está obligada por su palabra a cumplir lo que prometió | vinculado, da; ligado, da; *bound by ties of friendship* vinculado por lazos de amistad || encuadernado, da (a book) || US determinado, da; decidido, da; *she is bound to get up whatever the doctor says* está decidida a levantarse diga lo que diga el médico || — *bound hand and foot* atado de pies y manos || *bound up in* absorbido por; *he is bound up in his work* está absorbido por su trabajo || *bound up with* muy relacionado con, estrechamente ligado a; *the welfare of the citizen is bound up with the welfare of the nation* el bienestar del ciudadano está muy relacionado con el bienestar de la nación || *I'm bound to say, to admit that...* debo decir, admitir que... || *it's bound to happen* sucederá seguramente || *she is bound to come* seguramente vendrá || *to be bound for* dirigirse a, ir con destino a.
◆ *n* salto *m* (jump) || bote *m*, rebote *m* (of a ball, etc.) || límite *m*, frontera *f* (boundary).
◆ *pl* límites *m*; *beyond the bounds of decency* más allá de los límites de la decencia || *to be out of bounds* estar en zona prohibida.

bound [baund] *vi* saltar (to jump) || botar (a ball, etc.) || moverse dando saltos *or* botes; *boulders were bounding down the hillside* los cantos rodados bajaban dando botes por la ladera.
◆ *vt* señalar los límites de || confinar con, lindar con (to border on) || *to be bounded by* lindar con.

boundary [-əri] *n* límite *m*, frontera *f* (real or imaginary) || SP jugada *f* que consiste en lanzar la pelota fuera de los límites marcando cuatro o seis puntos (cricket) || *boundary stone* mojón *m*, hito *m*.

bounder [-ə*] *n* grosero *m*, hortera *m*.

boundless [-lis] *adj* ilimitado, da; sin límites.

bounteous [ˈbauntiəs]; **bountiful** [ˈbauntiful] *adj* generoso, sa; *a bounteous gift* un regalo generoso || abundante; *a bounteous crop* una cosecha abundante.

bountied [ˈbauntid] *adj* favorecido, da.

bountiful [ˈbauntiful] *adj* → **bounteous.**

bounty [ˈbaunti] *n* generosidad *f*, liberalidad *f* (generosity) || regalo *m* (gift) || subsidio *m* (subsidy) || prima *f*, gratificación *f* (premium).

bouquet [buˈkei] *n* ramo *m* (of flowers) || aroma *m*, buque *m* (of wine) || CULIN *bouquet garni* ramito *m* de hierbas aromáticas.

bourbon [ˈbəːbən] *n* whisky *m* americano [de maíz y centeno].

Bourbon [ˈbuəbən] *n pr* Borbón.
◆ *adj* borbónico, ca; *Bourbon nose* nariz borbónica.

bourdon [ˈbuədn] *n* MUS bordón *m*.

bourgeois [ˈbuəʒwɑː] *adj/n* burgués, esa.

bourgeoisie [ˌbuəʒwɑːˈziː] *n* burguesía *f*.

bout [baut] *n* combate *m*, encuentro *m*; *a wrestling bout* un combate de lucha libre ‖ asalto *m* (in boxing) ‖ ataque *m* (of illness) ‖ rato *m* (period of time) ‖ turno *m*, tanda *f* (of work).

boutonniere [buːtɔnˈjɛə] *n* *US* flor *f* en el ojal.

bovidae [ˈbəuvidei] *pl n* bóvidos *m*.

bovine [ˈbəuvain] *adj* bovino, na; vacuno, na ‖ FIG *bovine face* cara bovina.
◆ *n* bovino *m*.

bow [bau] *n* MAR proa *f* ‖ saludo *m* (with the head) ‖ reverencia *f*; *he answered with a light bow* contestó con una ligera reverencia ‖ inclinación *f* (bending).

bow [bau] *vt* inclinar, doblar (head or body); *he bowed his head* inclinó la cabeza ‖ doblar (knee) ‖ someter (a will) ‖ — *to bow down* doblegar (to bend), agobiar (to overburden) ‖ *to bow one's appreciation* demostrar su satisfacción con una inclinación de cabeza ‖ *to bow s.o. in, out* recibir, despedir a alguien con una reverencia.
◆ *vi* someterse a; *to bow to the inevitable* someterse a lo inevitable ‖ inclinarse ‖ — *bowing acquaintance* conocido *m* (person), amistad *f* superficial (friendship) ‖ *to bow and scrape* hacer zalemas ‖ *to bow out* retirarse.

bow [bəu] *n* arco *m* (for shooting arrows) ‖ arco *m* (of a violin) ‖ movimiento *m* del arco del violín ‖ arco *m* iris (rainbow) ‖ lazo *m* (in shoelace, ribbon, etc.) ‖ FIG *to draw the long bow* exagerar.

bow [bəu] *vt* arquear, doblar; *the wind bowed the tree* el viento dobló el árbol ‖ MUS tocar (violin).
◆ *vi* arquearse, combarse; *the wall bows inward* la pared se comba hacia dentro.

bow compass [-ˈkʌmpəs] *n* bigotera *f*.

bowdlerize [ˈbaudləraiz] *vt* expurgar.

bowed [baud] *adj* cabizbajo, ja (with grief) ‖ encorvado, da (with age).
— OBSERV Este adjetivo con frecuencia va seguido de la preposición *down* sin que ésta altere su significado.

bowel [ˈbauəl] *n* intestino *m* (intestine) ‖ *bowel movement* evacuación *f* intestinal.
◆ *pl* entrañas *f* (entrails) ‖ FIG entrañas *f*; *the bowels of the earth* las entrañas de la tierra.

bower [ˈbauə*] *n* casita *f* rústica (small house) ‖ cenador *m*, emparrado *m* (leafy shelter) ‖ MAR ancla *f* de leva.

bowerbird [-bəːd] *n* ave *f* del Paraíso.

bowery [ˈbauəri] *n* plantación *f* holandesa en Estados Unidos ‖ *the Bowery* distrito *m* de la parte baja de Manhattan donde viven personas sin hogar.

bowie knife [ˈbəuinaif] *n* cuchillo *m* de monte ‖ machete *m* (of the *US* army).

bowing [ˈbauiŋ] *n* reverencia *f*.

bowl [bəul] *n* tazón *m* (large cup) ‖ cuenco *m* (large hollow dish); *she gave me a bowl of rice* me dio un cuenco de arroz ‖ palangana *f*, jofaina *f* (for washing) ‖ cazoleta *f* (of a pipe) ‖ paleta *f* (of a spoon) ‖ escudilla *f* (hollow dish for eating) ‖ pila *f* (of a fountain) ‖ taza *f* (of a toilet) ‖ platillo *m* (of a beggar) ‖ globo *m* (of a lamp) ‖ GEOGR cuenca *f* (of a river) ‖ bola *f* (ball in bowling) ‖ *US* anfiteatro *m* (amphitheatre) ‖ estadio *m* (stadium) ‖ — *salad bowl* ensaladera *f* ‖ *sugar bowl* azucarero *m*.
◆ *pl* bolos *m*, bochas *f*; *to play bowls* jugar a las bochas.

bowl [bəul] *vt* hacer rodar (a hoop, a barrel, etc.) ‖ lanzar, tirar (cricket ball, bowls, etc.).
◆ *vi* jugar a los bolos *or* a las bochas (bowls, bowling) ‖ — *to bowl along* deslizarse; *the car bowls along the road* el coche se desliza por la carretera ‖ *to bowl over* derribar (to knock over), desconcertar (to surprise) ‖ *to bowl s.o. out* eliminar, poner fuera de juego (cricket).

bowlegged [ˈbəuˈlegd] *adj* con las piernas arqueadas, patizambo, ba; estevado, da.

bowler [ˈbəulə*] *n* sombrero *m* hongo, bombín *m* (hat) ‖ SP lanzador *m*, jugador *m* que lanza la pelota (in cricket) ‖ jugador *m* de bolos.

bowline [ˈbəulin] *n* MAR bolina *f* (of a sail); *on a bowline* de bolina ‖ nudo *m* marinero (knot).

bowling [ˈbəuliŋ] *n* bolos *m pl* (game) ‖ lanzamiento *m* (of cricket ball).

bowling alley [-æli] *n* bolera *f*.

bowling green [-griːn] *n* campo *m* de bolos.

bowman [ˈbəumən] *n* arquero *m*.
— OBSERV El plural de *bowman* es *bowmen*.

bow saw [ˈbəusɔː] *n* sierra *f* de arco.

bowshot [ˈbəuʃɔt] *n* tiro *m* de flecha ‖ *at a bowshot* a tiro de ballesta.

bowsprit [ˈbɔusprit] *n* MAR bauprés *m*.

bowstring [ˈbɔustriŋ] *n* cuerda *f* del arco.

bow tie [ˈbəuˈtai] *n* corbata *f* de lazo.

bow window [ˈbəuˈwindəu] *n* mirador *m*.

bow-wow [ˈbauwau] *n* guau guau *m* (dog in children's language) ‖ guau *m* (bark).

box [bɔks] *n* caja *f*; *a box of chocolates* una caja de bombones ‖ arca *f*, arcón *m*, cofre *m* (large wooden case) ‖ estuche *m* (casket) ‖ palco *m* (in a theatre) ‖ compartimiento *m* (of train, etc.) ‖ «box» *m*, departamento *m* de una cuadra (of stable) ‖ pescante *m* (coach box) ‖ caseta *f*, garita *f* (of sentry) ‖ apartado *m* de correos [*AMER* casilla *f*] (post office) ‖ corte *m*, incisión *f* (in a tree) ‖ bofetón *m* (blow on the ear) ‖ cama *f* (of cart) ‖ BOT boj *m* ‖ TECH caja *f* de chumacera ‖ PRINT cajetín *m* ‖ recuadro *m* (on a newspaper) ‖ SP boxeo *m* (boxing) ‖ puesto *m* donde se sitúa el bateador *or* el lanzador (baseball) ‖ plinto *m* (in gymnastics) ‖ — *christmas box* aguinaldo *m* ‖ FIG *in the wrong box* en difícil postura ‖ *jury box* tribuna *f or* banco *m* del jurado ‖ FIG *to put in the box* meter en la hucha, ahorrar ‖ *witness box* barra *f* de los testigos.

box [bɔks] *vt* embalar, encajonar ‖ PRINT encerrar en un recuadro ‖ — *to box in* encastrar (a sink, a bath), enclaustrar; *to feel boxed in* sentirse enclaustrado ‖ *to box off* cerrar *or* separar con muros (area) ‖ *to box s.o.'s ears* abofetear a alguien ‖ *to box the compass* cuartear la aguja (to turn the ship round), cambiar completamente (to change), volver al punto de partida (to come back to the starting point) ‖ *to box up* encerrar.
◆ *vi* boxear.

box calf [-kɑːf] *n* «boxcalf» *m*, becerro *m* curtido (tanned calfskin).

boxcar [-kɑː*] *n* *US* furgón *m*.

boxer [-ə*] *n* SP boxeador *m* ‖ bóxer *m* (dog).

boxfish [-fiʃ] *n* cofre *m*.

box girder [-ˌgəːdə*] *n* viga *f* tubular *or* de caja.

boxhaul [-hɔːl] *vt* virar en redondo (a ship).

boxing [-iŋ] *n* SP boxeo *m* ‖ embalaje *m*, envase *m* (packing).

Boxing Day [-iŋdei] *n* día *m* laborable después de Navidad en que se suelen dar los aguinaldos.

boxing gloves [-iŋglʌvz] *pl n* guantes *m* de boxeo.

box junction [-dʒʌŋkʃən] *n* área *f* de bloqueo de cruce.

box kite [-kait] *n* cometa *f*.

box number [-ˌnʌmbə*] *n* número *m* de apartado de correos.

box office [-ˌɔfis] *n* taquilla *f* [*AMER* boletería *f*].

box-office [-ˌɔfis] *adj* taquillero, ra; *a good box-office film* una película taquillera.

boxroom [ˈbɔksruːm] *n* trastero *m*.

box spanner [-ˈspænə*] *n* llave *f* de tubo.

box spring [-spriŋ] *n* colchón *m* de muelles.

box stall [-stɔːl] *n* «box» *m*, departamento *m* de una cuadra (for animals in a stable).

boxwood [-wud] *n* boj *m*.

boy [bɔi] *n* niño *m*, chico *m*, muchacho *m* (young man) ‖ hijo *m*, chico *m*, niño *m* (son) ‖ MAR grumete *m* ‖ sirviente *m* indígena, boy *m* (in colonies) ‖ *oh, boy!* ¡vaya!

boyar [bɔiə*] *n* boyardo *m*.

boycott [ˈbɔikət] *n* boicot *m*, boicoteo *m*.

boycott [ˈbɔikət] *vt* boicotear.

boyfriend [ˈbɔifrend] *n* novio *m* (fiancé) ‖ amigo *m* (friend).

boyhood [ˈbɔihud] *n* infancia *f*, niñez *f*.

boyish [ˈbɔiiʃ] *adj* infantil (immature) ‖ de muchacho (tastes, manners, etc.).

boy scout [ˈbɔiˈskaut] *n* explorador *m*.

BR *abbr of* [*British Rail*] compañía de ferrocarriles británicos.

bra [brɑː] *n* sostén *m* (for women).

Brabant [brəˈbænt] *pr n* GEOGR Brabante *m*.

brace [breis] *n* abrazadera *f* (for clasping) ‖ berbiquí *m* (of drill) ‖ par *m* (of pistols, of partridge, etc.); *a brace of cats* un par de gatos ‖ puntal *m* (prop) ‖ PRINT llave *f* ‖ aparato (for teeth) ‖ MED braguero *m* (truss) ‖ aparato *m* ortopédico (orthopedic device) ‖ MUS corchete *m* ‖ ARCH riostra *f*; tirante *m* ‖ MAR braza *f*.
◆ *pl* tirantes *m* (of trousers).

brace [breis] *vt* atar, ligar (with a rope) ‖ ARCH reforzar (to strengthen) ‖ apuntalar (to prop) ‖ tensar (to tighten) ‖ PRINT poner una llave a ‖ MAR bracear (a sail, a rope, oar, etc.) ‖ — *to brace o.s. for sth.* prepararse para algo ‖ *to brace s.o. up* fortalecer a alguien.
◆ *vi* *to brace up* cobrar ánimo.

bracelet [ˈbreislit] *n* pulsera *f*, brazalete *m*.
◆ *pl* FAM esposas *f* (handcuffs).

bracer [ˈbreisə*] *n* estimulante *m*, tónico *m* (tonic); *the news was a bracer for him* la noticia fue un estimulante para él ‖ muñequera *f* (wristband).

brachial [ˈbreikjəl] *adj* braquial.

brachiopod [ˈbrækiəpɔd] *n* ZOOL braquiópodo *m*.

brachycephalic [ˌbrækikeˈfælik] *adj* braquicéfalo, la.

brachyuran [brækˈjuːrən] *n* braquiuro *m*.
— OBSERV El plural de la palabra inglesa es *brachyura*.

bracken [ˈbrækən] *n* BOT helecho *m*.

bracket [ˈbrækit] *n* brazo *m* (of a lamp) ‖ soporte *m* (support) ‖ PRINT paréntesis *m* ‖ llave *f* (brace) ‖ ARCH ménsula *f* (of a roof, of a balcony, etc.) ‖ repisa *f* (on a wall) ‖ grupo *m*, categoría *f* (category of taxpayers).

bracket [ˈbrækit] *vt* poner entre paréntesis ‖ agrupar (to group together) ‖ relacionar (to associate) ‖ sujetar (a shelf on the wall) ‖ MIL precisar [el blanco].

brackish [ˈbrækiʃ] *adj* salobre (water).

bract [brækt] *n* BOT bráctea *f*.

brad [bræd] *n* puntilla *f* (short nail).

bradawl [ˈbrædɔːl] *n* lezna *f*, punzón *m*.

bradypepsia [brædiˈpepsiə] *n* MED bradipepsia *f*.

brae [brei] *n* ladera *f*, pendiente *f* (in Scotland).

brag [bræg] *n* jactancia *f*, alarde *m* (boast).

brag [bræg] *vt/vi* jactarse, alardear.

braggart [ˈbrægət] *n* fanfarrón, ona; jactancioso, sa.

Brahma [ˈbrɑːmə] *pr n* Brahma *m*.

Brahman [ˈbrɑːmən] *n* brahmán *m*.

Brahmanic [brɑːˈmænik]; **Brahmanical** [-əl] *adj* brahmánico, ca.

Brahmin [ˈbrɑːmin] *n* brahmán *m*, brahmín *m*.

Brahminic [brɑːˈminik]; **Brahminical** [-əl] *adj* brahmánico, ca.

braid [breid] *n* trenza *f* (of hair) || galón *m* (of uniform, of blazer, etc.).

braid [breid] *vt* trenzar (hair) || galonear (uniform, blazer, etc.).

brail [breil] *n* MAR candaliza *f*.

brail [breil] *vt* MAR cargar [las velas].

Braille [breil] *n* Braille *m* (writing for the blind).

brain [brein] *n* ANAT cerebro *m* || — FIG *brain drain* fuga *f* de cerebros || *to have sth. on the brain* tener algo metido en la cabeza.
◆ *pl* FIG inteligencia *f sing*, seso *m sing* || CULIN sesos *m* || — *to blow one's brains out* levantarse *or* saltarse la tapa de los sesos || FIG & FAM *to pick s.o.'s brains* consultar con alguien, pedir la opinión de alguien || *to rack* o *to cudgel* o *to beat one's brains* calentarse *or* estrujarse *or* devanarse los sesos | *to turn s.o.'s brains* volverle a uno loco.

brain [brein] *vt* FAM romper la crisma.

braincase [-keis] *n* caja *f* del cráneo.

brainchild [-tʃaild] *n* invento *m*, idea *f* (genial).

brain death [-deθ] *n* MED muerte *f* cerebral.

brain fever [-ˌfiːvə*] *n* MED encefalitis *f*.

brainless [-lis] *adj* tonto, ta; memo, ma; mentecato, ta (silly) || insensato, ta (thoughtless).

brainpan [-pæn] *n* cráneo *m*.

brainpower [-ˌpauə*] *n* capacidad *f* intelectual.

brainsick [-sik] *adj* trastornado mentalmente.

brainstorm [-stɔːm] *n* ataque *m* de locura || FAM inspiración *f*, idea *f* genial.

brainstorming [-iŋ] *n* reunión *f* creativa.

brainteaser [-tiːzə*] *n* rompecabezas *m inv*, acertijo *m*.

brain trust [-trʌst] *n* grupo *m* de expertos, cerebros *m pl*.

brain tumour [-ˌtjumə*]; **brain tumor** [-ˌtjumə] *n* tumor *m* cerebral.

brainwash [-wɔʃ] *vt* FIG lavar el cerebro.

brainwashing [-ˌwɔʃiŋ] *n* FIG lavado *m* del cerebro.

brain wave [-weiv] *n* inspiración *f*, idea *f* genial || MED onda *f* telepática.

brain work [-wəːk] *n* trabajo *m* intelectual.

brainy [ˈbreini] *adj* FAM inteligente, listo, ta.

braise [breiz] *vt* cocer a fuego lento.

brake [breik] *n* freno *m*; *foot brake* freno de pedal; *drum, disc, power-assisted brake* freno de tambor, de disco, asistido; *front, back brake* freno delantero, trasero; *to apply the brake* poner el freno; *to release the brake* soltar el freno || FIG freno *m* || furgoneta *f* (car) || matorral *m*, maleza *f* (thicket) || BOT helecho *m* (bracken) || AGR agramadera *f* (for beating hemp) | grada *f*, rastra *f* (harrow) || *brake horsepower* potencia *f* al freno.

brake [breik] *vt* frenar (to slow down) || agramar (hemp).
◆ *vi* frenar.

brake band [-bænd] *n* cinta *f* del freno.

brake blocks [-blɔks] *pl n* zapatas *f* del freno.

brake drum [-drʌm] *n* tambor *m* del freno.

brake lining [-ˌlainiŋ] *n* guarnición *f* del freno.

brakeman [-mən] *n* guardafrenos *m inv*.
— OBSERV El plural de *brakeman* es *brakemen*.

brake shoe [-ʃuː] *n* TECH zapata *f*.

braking [-iŋ] *n* frenaje *m*, frenado *m*.

bramble [ˈbræmbl] *n* BOT zarza *f*, zarzamora *f*.

brambleberry [-ˌberi] *n* BOT zarzamora *f*.

brambling [ˈbræmbliŋ] *n* pinzón *m* (bird).

brambly [ˈbræmbli] *adj* zarzoso, sa.

bran [bræn] *n* salvado *m*, afrecho *m*.

branch [brɑːntʃ] *n* rama *f* (of a tree) || brazo *m* (of candlestick, horns, etc.) || brazo *m* (of a river) || FIG rama *f* (of a family) || ramo *m*, rama *f* (a part of science, etc.) || ramificación *f* (subdivision) || ramal *m* (railways) || COMM sucursal *f* || TECH derivación *f*.

branch [brɑːntʃ] *vi* echar ramas (trees) || ramificarse (to subdivide) || bifurcarse (to bifurcate) || — *to branch away* bifurcarse || *to branch from* derivarse de || *to branch off* bifurcarse || FIG *to branch off into* extender sus actividades a || *to branch out* bifurcarse.

branchia [ˈbræŋkiə] *n* branquia *f*.
— OBSERV El plural de *branchia* es *branchiae*.

branchial [-l] *adj* branquial.

branching [ˈbrɑːntʃiŋ] *n* bifurcación *f*, derivación *f*.

branchiopodes [ˈbræŋkiəˌpɔdz] *pl n* ZOOL branquiópodos *m*.

branch line [ˈbrɑːntʃ-lain] *n* ramal *m* (of railway).

branch office [ˈbrɑːntʃˌɔfis] *n* sucursal *f*.

brand [brænd] *n* hierro *m* (on cattle, on prisoners, etc.) || marca *f* (trademark) || tea *f*, tizón *m* (charred wood) || BOT roya *f*, tizón *m* (plant disease) || FIG estigma *m* (stigma) || POET acero *m*, espada *f* (sword).

brand [brænd] *vt* marcar con hierro candente, herrar (cattle, prisoners, etc.) || marcar, poner marca de fábrica en || FIG tildar de; *to brand a man a liar* tildar a un hombre de mentiroso | estigmatizar | grabar (in mind) | motejar (to nickname).

Brandenburg [ˈbrændənbəːg] *pr n* Brandeburgo *m*, Brandenburgo *m*.

branding [ˈbrændiŋ] *n* herradero *m*.

branding iron [ˈbrændiŋˌaiən] *n* hierro *m* de marcar (to brand cattle, etc.).

brandish [ˈbrændiʃ] *vt* blandir, esgrimir.

brandling [ˈbrændliŋ] *n* lombriz *f* para cebo.

brand name [ˈbrændneim] *n* marca *f* de fábrica.

brand-new [ˈbrænd-ˈnjuː] *adj* completamente nuevo, flamante.

brandy [ˈbrændi] *n* coñac *m*, brandy *m* (spirit) || aguardiente *m* (liquor); *cherry brandy* aguardiente de cerezas.

brant [brænt] *n* barnacla *m* (wild goose).

brash [bræʃ] *adj* descarado, da; insolente (impudent) || temerario, ria (daring).
◆ *n* escombros *m pl* (of rocks, etc.).

Brasilia [brəˈziljə] *pr n* GEOGR Brasilia.

brass [brɑːs] *n* latón *m*, cobre *m* amarillo (alloy of copper and zinc) || FIG descaro *m*, desfachatez *f* (impudence) || FIG & FAM dinero *m*, parné *m*, pasta *f* [AMER plata *f*] (money) || MUS cobres *m pl* (instruments) || — FAM *the brass* el alto mando | *to be as bold as brass* tener mucha cara | *to get down to brass tacks* ir al grano | *top brass* peces gordos.

brassard [ˈbræsɑːd] *n* brazalete *m*, brazal *m*.

brass band [ˈbrɑːsˈbænd] *n* MUS banda *f*.

brass hat [ˈbrɑːsˈhæt] *n* MIL & FAM oficial *m* de Estado Mayor.

brassie [ˈbrɑːsi] *n* palo *m* de golf.

brassière [ˈbræsiə*] *n* sostén *m*.

brass knuckles [ˈbrɑːsˈnʌklz] *pl n* manopla *f sing*.

brasswork [ˈbrɑːswəːk] *n* objetos *m pl* de latón *or* de cobre amarillo || trabajo *m* del cobre amarillo.

brassy [ˈbrɑːsi] *adj* de latón || de color de cobre || metálico, ca (metallic) || estridente (harsh) || FIG descarado, da (impudent).

brat [bræt] *n* FAM mocoso, sa (bad-mannered child).
◆ *n* palo *m* de golf.

Bratislava [brɑːtisˈlɑːvə] *pr n* GEOGR Bratislava.

brattice [ˈbrætis] *n* tabique *m* de ventilación || parapeto *m* de madera en una fortaleza.

brattle [ˈbrætəl] *vi* traquetear.

bravado [brəˈvɑːdəu] *n* baladronada *f*, bravata *f* (boast) || *piece of bravado* baladronada, bravata.
— OBSERV El plural de *bravado* es *bravadoes* o *bravados*.

brave [breiv] *adj* valeroso, sa; valiente (courageous) || espléndido, da (splendid) || FIG *to put a brave face on sth.* poner a mal tiempo buena cara.
◆ *n* valiente *m* || US guerrero *m* indio.

brave [breiv] *vt* hacer frente a, arrostrar, afrontar (to face) || desafiar (to defy); *to brave death* desafiar la muerte || *to brave it out* aguantar hasta el final.

bravery [-ri] *n* valor *m*, valentía *f* || esplendor *m* (fine appearance).

bravo [ˈbrɑːˈvəu] *interj* ¡bravo!

bravura [brəˈvuərə] *n* arrojo *m*, bravura *f* (show of daring) || MUS ejecución *f* brillante.

brawl [brɔːl] *n* pendencia *f*, reyerta *f* (fight).

brawl [brɔːl] *vi* pelearse (to fight).

brawler [-ə*] *n* alborotador, ra; pendenciero, ra.

brawn [brɔːn] *n* fuerza *f* muscular (muscular strength) || músculo *m* (in arm, in leg) || carne *f* de cerdo adobada (pickled pork) || queso *m* de cerdo (headcheese).

brawny [ˈbrɔːni] *adj* musculoso, sa.

bray [brei] *n* rebuzno *m* (of an ass) || FIG sonido *m* ronco (of trumpets, etc.).

bray [brei] *vi* rebuznar (an ass) || *to bray out* sonar roncamente (trumpets, etc.).

brayer [-ə*] *n* PRINT rodillo *m*.

braze [breiz] *vt* soldar (copper and zinc, zinc and silver, etc.) || broncear (to decorate with brass).

brazen [ˈbreizn] *adj* de latón || bronceado, da (of a hars yellow colour) || bronco, ca (harsh and loud) || FIG descarado, da (shameless).

brazen [ˈbreizn] *vt* *to brazen it out* aguantar una dificultad con descaro.

brazenfaced [breiznfeist] *adj* descarado, da.

brazier [ˈbreizjə*] *n* brasero *m* (for heating) || latonero *m* (brassworker) || *perfume brazier* pebetero *m*.

Brazil [brəˈzil] *pr n* GEOGR Brasil *m*.

brazil [brəˈzil] *n* palo *m* del Brasil, palo *m* brasil, brasil *m* (brazilwood) || tinte *m* de color rojo extraído del palo del Brasil (red dye).

brazilette [brəziˈlet] *n* BOT brasilete *m*.

Brazilian [brəˈziljən] *adj/n* brasileño, ña; brasilero, ra.

Brazil nut [brəˈzilˈnʌt] *n* BOT nuez *f* del Brasil.

brazilwood [brəˈzilˈwud] *n* palo *m* del Brasil, palo *m* brasil, brasil *m*.

brazing [ˈbreiziŋ] *n* soldadura *f*.

Brazzaville [ˈbræzəvil] *pr n* GEOGR Brazzaville.

breach [briːtʃ] *n* brecha *f* (in a wall, etc.) || incumplimiento *m*; *breach of contract* incumplimiento de contrato; *breach of promise* incumplimiento de una promesa || violación *f*, infracción *f*, contravención *f*; *breach of the law* violación de la ley || rompimiento *m* (of waves) || ruptura *f* (break in friendly relations) || desgarramiento *m* (of material) || — *breach of faith* abuso *m* de confianza || *breach of the peace* perturbación *f* del orden público || *breach of trust* abuso *m* de confianza || FIG *to stand in the breach* estar en la brecha | *to step into the breach* acudir en sustitución | *to throw o.s. into the breach* echarse al ruedo.

breach [briːtʃ] *vt* abrir una brecha en (to break through) || violar, infringir, contravenir, quebrantar (a law) || violar (a contract).

bread [bred] *n* pan *m*; *piece of bread* pedazo de pan; *bread and butter* pan con mantequilla || FIG pan *m* (living); *to earn one's bread* ganarse el pan || FAM pasta *f*, parné *m* [AMER plata *f*] (money) || — *brown bread* pan bazo, pan moreno || *communion bread* pan bendito || *fine wheaten bread* pan de flor || FIG *for a crust of bread* por un mendrugo de pan || *fresh bread* pan tierno || *homemade bread* pan casero || FIG *man does not live on bread alone* no sólo de pan vive el hombre || *milk bread* pan de Viena || *our daily bread* el pan nuestro de cada día || *ration bread* pan de munición || *rye bread* pan de centeno || *sliced bread* pan de molde, pan francés || *stale bread* pan duro || *to be on bread and water* estar a pan y agua || FIG *to cast one's bread upon the waters* hacer el bien sin mirar a quien | *to know which side one's bread is buttered on* saber lo que más le conviene a uno | *to take the bread out of s.o.'s mouth* quitarle a uno el pan de la boca || *unleavened bread* pan ácimo || *white bread* pan blanco, pan candeal || *wholemeal bread* pan integral.

bread-and-butter [-əndˌbʌtə*] *adj* corriente (commonplace) || juvenil (youthful) || de agradecimiento (letter).

breadbasket [-ˌbɑːskət] *n* panera *f*, cesto *m* para el pan || FIG granero *m* || FAM barriga *f* (stomach).

bread bin [-bin] *n* panera *f*.

breadboard [-bɔːd] *n* tabla *f* para cortar el pan || TECH tablero *m* de circuitos.

breadcrumb [-krʌm] *n* migaja *f* de pan.
◆ *pl* pan *m sing* rallado || CULIN *in breadcrumbs* empanado, da.

breaded [-id] *adj* CULIN rebozado, da en pan rallado; empanado, da.

breadfruit [-fruːt] *n* fruto *m* del árbol del pan || *breadfruit tree* árbol *m* del pan.

breadline [-lain] *n* US cola *f* para recibir alimentos gratuitamente.

breadstuff [-stʌf] *n* harina *f* (flour) || cereales *m pl* (grain).

breadth [-θ] *n* anchura *f*, ancho *m* (width) || amplitud *f* (extent) || FIG largueza *f*, generosidad *f*.

breadthways [-weiz]; **breadthwise** [-waiz] *adv* a lo ancho.

breadwinner [-ˌwinə*] *n* sostén *m* de la familia.

break [breik] *n* rotura *f*, ruptura *f* (rupture) || abertura *f*, grieta *f* (breach) || interrupción *f*, pausa *f*, descanso *m* (pause) || recreo *m* (in schools, etc.) || tacada *f* (in billiards) || break *m* (car) || FIG claro *m* (in the clouds) | amanecer *m*, alba *f*; *at break of day* al amanecer, al romper el alba || huida *f*, fuga *f*, evasión *f* (from prison) | golpe *m* de suerte (piece of good luck) | ruptura *f* (between friends, family, etc.) | comienzo *m*, principio *m* (beginning) | espacio *m* (blank space) | gallo *m* (in the voice) | cambio *m*, alteración *f*; *a break in the weather* un cambio de tiempo || FIG & FAM oportunidad *f* (opportunity) || cesura *f* (in poetry) || COMM baja *f* (of the stock market) || ELECTR corte *m*, interrupción *f*; *a break in a wiring circuit* un corte en el circuito eléctrico || SP cambio *m* de dirección (of ball) | internada *f* (of player with the ball) | separación *f* (of boxers) || — *bad* o *unlucky break* mala suerte || *lucky break* golpe *m* de suerte || *without a break* sin parar.

break* [breik] *vt* romper, quebrar; *to break a chair* romper una silla || destrozar (to shatter) || amortiguar; *the hedge broke the force of the wind* el seto amortiguó la fuerza del viento || romper; *to break silence, an appointment* romper el silencio, un compromiso; *to break a strike* romper una huelga || quebrantar, violar; *to break the law* quebrantar la ley || degradar (to demote a soldier) || violar, romper; *to break a contract* violar un contrato || faltar a (one's word) || descubrir la clave de, descifrar (a code) || resolver (a case, a mystery) || moderar (strength, speed) || batir; *to break a record* batir un récord || abrir; *to break a path* abrir un camino || deshacer; *to break a set of books* deshacer una colección de libros || destrozar (morally) || arruinar (to reduce to poverty); *this venture will either make you or break you* esta empresa te hará rico o te arruinará || sofocar; *to break a rebellion* sofocar una rebelión || dar; *he broke the news* dio la noticia || domar; *to break a horse* domar un caballo || interrumpir, cortar (to interrupt) || alterar; *to break the peace* alterar el orden || empezar (to begin) || cambiar (a bank note) || — FIG *to break a lance with* batirse con || *to break asunder* dividir en dos || *to break bounds* entrar en zona prohibida || *to break camp* levantar el campo || *to break cover* salir al descubierto || *to break ground* abrir la tierra (the earth), empezar a construir (to begin to build), abrir un nuevo camino (to break fresh ground) || *to break jail* escaparse de la cárcel || *to break one's back* deslomarse || *to break one's fast* romper el ayuno || *to break one's health* quebrantar la salud || FIG *to break one's neck* romperse la crisma (after a fall), deslomarse (working), matarse (to obtain sth.) | *to break s.o.'s neck* partir la cara a uno (to beat s.o. up) || *to break open* abrir forzando (to force open) || *to break o.s. of a habit* quitarse una costumbre || MIL *to break ranks* romper filas || FIG *to break s.o.'s heart* partirle el corazón a uno || FIG *to break the back of a task* haber hecho la mayor parte del trabajo || *to break the bank* hacer saltar la banca (in gambling) || FIG *to break the ice* romper el hielo; *he broke the ice by telling a joke* rompió el hielo contando un chiste || *to break to pieces* hacer pedazos.
◆ *vi* romperse; *the glass fell off the table and broke* el vaso se cayó de la mesa y se rompió || FIG estallar; *the storm broke* la tormenta estalló | terminarse (to come to an end); *the bad weather broke* el mal tiempo se terminó | interrumpirse (to stop) | quebrantarse, resentirse; *his health broke under the strain* su salud se resintió por el esfuerzo | cambiar, mudar; *John's voice is breaking* la voz de Juan está cambiando | bajar; *the stock market broke* la bolsa bajó | arruinarse (to go bankrupt) || dispersarse (troops, clouds, crowd) || romper (waves) || romper, apuntar, rayar (the day) || brotar (plants) || reventarse (an abcess) || divulgarse, propalarse (news, scandal) || SP desviarse (a ball) | separarse (in boxing, dancing); *the referee told them to break* el árbitro les ordenó que se separaran || *to break open* abrirse de par en par (a door).
◆ *phr v* ***to break away*** separarse (to withdraw) | escaparse (to escape) || ***to break down*** derribar (to knock down); *the mob broke down the barricades* la multitud derribó las barricadas | acabar con; *to break down the enemy resistance* acabar con la resistencia enemiga | desglosar (expenses) | hundirse (a bridge) | FIG derrumbarse (morally), debilitarse; *his health broke down* su salud se debilitó; averiarse (car machine) || ***to break in*** intervenir; *to break in on a conversation* intervenir en una conversación | irrumpir (to burst in) | escalar, forzar (burglars) || ***to break into*** escalar, forzar; *the burglars broke into the house* los ladrones escalaron la casa | ponerse a; *to break into song* ponerse a cantar || ***to break off*** romper; *they broke off the engagement* rompieron el compromiso | cortar; *break a few branches off the tree* corta unas cuantas ramas del árbol | interrumpirse (talks) | pararse, detenerse; *he broke off in the middle of the speech* se detuvo en medio del discurso | reñir, terminar (to end a relationship) | desprenderse (to become detached) | *to break it off* reñir || ***to break out*** escaparse (to escape) | salirle a uno; *to break out in spots* salirle a uno manchas | estallar (war, epidemic) || ***to break through*** romper, atravesar, abrirse paso por; *the crowd broke through the police cordon* la muchedumbre rompió el cordón de policía | atravesar; *the sun broke through the heavy mist* el sol atravesó la densa niebla || ***to break up*** romper; *to break up a box* romper una caja | desglosar, separar (words) | desguazar (car, ship) | mullir (soil) | disolver (crowd) | acabar con (to put an end to) | levantar (meeting, etc.) | separarse (husband and wife, partners, etc.) | acabar (to finish); *school breaks up tomorrow* el colegio acaba mañana | terminarse (strike) | disolverse; *the mob broke up* la multitud se disolvió | reñir, terminar (to end a relationship) || ***to break with*** romper con; *to break with the family* romper con la familia | violar, quebrantar (a convention).
— OBSERV Pret ***broke***; pp ***broken***.

breakable [ˈbreikəbl] *adj* quebradizo, za; frágil.

breakage [ˈbreikidʒ] *n* rotura *f* (breaking) || objetos *m pl* rotos (broken things) || indemnización *f* por objetos rotos (allowance).

breakaway [ˈbreikəˌwei] *adj* disidente.
◆ *n* escapada *f* || ruptura *f*.

breakaxe; *US* **breakax** [ˈbreikˌæks] *n* quebracho *m* (hardwood).

break dancing [breikˌdɑːnsiŋ] *n* break dance *m*.

breakdown [ˈbreikdaun] *n* MED depresión *f* nerviosa || avería *f* (of a car, a machine) || CHEM descomposición *f*, análisis *m* || análisis *m* (division into categories) || desglose *m*; *breakdown of expenses* desglose de los gastos || ruptura *f* (of talks, etc.) || interrupción *f* (suspension) || fracaso *m* (failure) || — *breakdown gang* equipo *m* de arreglo de averías || *breakdown lorry* grúa *f*, camión *m* grúa.

breaker [ˈbreikə*] *n* MAR cachón *m*, ola *f* grande || TECH trituradora *f* || ELECTR interruptor *m* automático.

breakfast [ˈbrekfəst] *n* desayuno *m*.

breakfast [ˈbrekfəst] *vi* desayunar.

break-in [ˈbreikin] *n* allanamiento *m*.

breaking ['breikiŋ] *n* rotura *f* || interrupción *f* || — *breaking and entering* allanamiento *m* de morada || *breaking point* punto *m* de ruptura; extremo *m*.

breakneck ['breiknek] *adj* suicida; *breakneck speed* velocidad suicida.

breakthrough ['breik,θru:] *n* ruptura *f* || MIL ruptura *f* (of a front) | penetration *f* || progreso *m*, adelanto *m*, avance *m*; *the discovery of penicillin was a significant breakthrough* el descubrimiento de la penicilina ha sido un gran adelanto.

breakup ['breikʌp] *n* desintegración *f*, desmembramiento *m*; *the breakup of an empire* el desmembramiento de un imperio || división *f* (of a state, etc.) || ruptura *f* (of talks) || deshielo *m* (thaw) || separación *f* (of partners, of husband and wife, etc.) || dispersión *f* (of a crowd).

breakwater ['brek,wɔ:tə*] *n* rompeolas *m inv*.

bream [bri:m] *n* brema *f* (fish).

breast [brest] *n* pecho *m* (of a person) || seno *m*, pecho *m* (of a woman) || pechuga *f* (of a bird) || peto *m* (of armour) || reja *f* (of a plough) || corazón *m*; *in the depths of my breast* en lo más profundo de mi corazón || FIG repecho *m*; *the breast of a hill* el repecho de una colina | antepecho *m*; *the chimney breast* el antepecho de la chimenea || — *to beat one's breast* darse golpes en el pecho || FIG *to make a clean breast of (it)* confesar.

breast [brest] *vt* hacer frente a, arrostrar, enfrentarse a (to brave).

breastbone [-bəun] *n* ANAT esternón *m*.

breast-feed [-fi:d] *vt* amamantar, dar el pecho a.

breast-feeding [-, fi:diŋ] *n* amamantamiento *m*.

breastpin [-pin] *n* alfiler *m* de corbata || US broche *m* (brooch).

breastplate [-pleit] *n* peto *m* (of armour) || petral *m* (of harness).

breaststroke [-strəuk] *n* SP braza *f* de pecho.

breast wall [-wɔ:l] *n* muro *m* de contención (retaining wall) || MIL parapeto *m*.

breastwork [-wə:k] *n* MIL parapeto *m*.

breath [breθ] *n* aliento *m*; *his breath smelled of whisky* su aliento olía a whisky || respiración *f* (breathing); *to hold one's breath* contener la respiración || FIG soplo *m*; *there was not a breath of air* no había un soplo de aire || hálito *m* (of animals) || FIG fragancia *f*; *the breath of spring* la fragancia de la primavera | vida *f*, aliento *m* (life) | pausa *f*, respiro *m* (breather) | rumor *m*; *a breath of scandal* un rumor de escándalo || espiración *f* de aire (in phonetics) || — FIG *a breath of air* un aire renovador | *below one's breath* en voz baja | *in the next breath* inmediatamente después | *in the same breath* en el mismo momento, al mismo tiempo || *out of breath* sin aliento || *to be short of breath* perder fácilmente el aliento || *to catch one's breath* quedarse sin respiración (from surprise, etc.), recobrar el aliento (to get one's breath back) || *to draw breath* respirar || *to draw a deep breath* respirar a fondo || *to draw one's last breath* exhalar el último suspiro || *to gasp for breath* jadear, respirar con dificultad || *to get one's breath back* recobrar la respiración *or* el aliento || *to get out of breath* quedarse sin aliento || *to go out for a breath of air* salir a tomar el aire || FIG *to save one's breath* ahorrar palabras | *to take one's breath away* dejar sin respiración | *to waste one's breath* hablar *or* gastar saliva en balde.

breathable ['bri:ðəbl] *adj* respirable.

breathalyser ['breθəlaizə*] *n* alcoholómetro *m*.

breathe [bri:ð] *vi* respirar || FIG vivir, respirar (to live) || — FIG *to breath again* respirar | *to breathe down one's neck* atosigar (to harass), pisar los talones (to follow) || *to breathe in* aspirar || *to breathe out* espirar.
◆ *vt* aspirar; *to breathe in gulps of fresh air* aspirar grandes bocanadas de aire fresco || FIG respirar; *her look breathed innocence* su aspecto respiraba inocencia || FIG susurrar (to whisper) || — FIG *not to breathe a word of* no decir una palabra de, no decir nada de || *to breathe air into* inflar soplando || *to breathe a sigh* dar un suspiro || FIG *to breathe new life into* dar nueva vida a || *to breathe one's last breath* exhalar el último suspiro || *to breathe out* exhalar.

breather [-ə*] *n* FAM descanso *m*, pausa *f*, respiro *m* (short break); *ten-minute breather* descanso *or* pausa de diez minutos, diez minutos de respiro.

breathing [-iŋ] *n* respiración *f* || GRAMM espíritu *m* (in Greek) || *breathing space* o *spell* descanso *m*, pausa *f*, respiro *m* (rest).

breathless ['breθlis] *adj* jadeante, sin aliento (gasping for breath) || sin vida (lifeless) || FIG intenso, sa; *breathless silence* silencio intenso | sin resuello (astonished) | sin viento, sin aire (stifling).

breathtaking ['breθ,teikiŋ] *adj* punzante, que corta la respiración; *a breathtaking pain* un dolor punzante || FIG asombroso, sa (astonishing); *a breathtaking experience* una experiencia asombrosa | emocionante (thrilling) | impresionante, imponente; *a breathtaking view* una vista impresionante.

breath test [-test] *n* prueba *f* del alcohol.

breathy ['breθi] *adj* velado, da (voice).

bred [bred] *pret/pp* ⟶ **breed.**

breech [bri:tʃ] *n* recámara *f* (of a firearm) || trasero *m* (buttocks).
◆ *pl* pantalones *m* (trousers) || pantalones *m* de montar (knee-length trousers) || — *breeches buoy* salvavidas *m* en forma de pantalón || FIG *to wear the breeches* llevar los pantalones.

breechblock ['bri:tʃblɔk] *n* obturador *m* (in gun).

breeching ['bri:tʃiŋ] *n* retranca *f* (or harness).

breech-loading ['bri:tʃ,ləudiŋ] *adj* de retrocarga (arm).

breed [bri:d] *n* raza *f* (of animals) || BOT variedad *f* (of plants).

breed* [bri:d] *vt* criar (to produce, to raise) || FIG engendrar, producir; *familiarity breeds contempt* la familiaridad produce el menosprecio || criar (to bring up); *country bred* criado en el campo || educar; *well bred* bien educado.
◆ *vi* reproducirse || criarse.
— OBSERV Pret y pp *bred*.

breeder [-ə*] *n* criador, ra (of animals) || ganadero, ra (of cattle) || reproductor, ra (breeding animal).

breeder reactor ['bri:də*-ri'æktə*] *n* TECH reactor generador *m*.

breeding [bri:diŋ] *n* cría *f* (of plants or animals) || FIG clase *f* (background) | educación *f*; *to lack breeding* carecer de educación || — *breeding animal* reproductor, ra || *breeding place* criadero *m* || *breeding season* época *f* de la reproducción.

breeze [bri:z] *n* brisa *f* (gentle wind) || MAR viento *m*; *stiff breeze* viento fuerte || FIG cosa *f* fácil || carbonilla *f* (coke).

breeze [bri:z] *vi* *to breeze in, out* entrar, salir despreocupadamente || *to breeze through* pasar fácilmente (an examination), leer por encima (to read) || *to breeze to* lograr fácilmente.

breeze-block [-blɔk] *n* bloque *m* de coque.

breeziness [-inis] *n* FIG alegría *f*, despreocupación *f*.

breezy [-i] *adj* ventoso, sa; *a breezy afternoon* una tarde ventosa || FIG despreocupado, da; alegre (brisk, cheerful) || *it is breezy* hace viento, hace aire.

Bremen ['breimən] *pr n* GEOGR Brema, Bremen.

Bren gun ['brengʌn] *n* MIL fusil *m* ametrallador.

brer [brə:*] *n* hermano *m* (in fables).

brethren ['breðrin] *pl n* REL hermanos *m*.

Breton ['bretən] *adj/n* bretón, ona.

breve [bri:v] *n* MUS breve *f* || GRAMM breve *f* (short vowel, syllable) || REL breve *m* (pope's letter).

brevet ['brevit] *adj* MIL honorario, ria.
◆ *n* MIL graduación *f* honoraria.

breviary ['bri:vjəri] *n* REL breviario *m*.

brevier [brə'viə*] *n* PRINT breviario *m* (old size of type).

brevity ['breviti] *n* brevedad *f*.

brew [bru:] *n* infusión *f*.

brew [bru:] *vt* fabricar, hacer, elaborar (beer) || preparar, hacer (tea) || FIG fomentar (to stir up) | tramar (to plot).
◆ *vi* fabricar *or* elaborar cerveza || fermentar (to ferment) || reposar; *let the tea brew a few minutes* deja que el té repose unos minutos || FIG prepararse, amenazar; *a storm is brewing* se prepara una tormenta || FAM *to brew up* hacer *or* preparar el té.

brewer [-ə*] *n* cervecero *m* || *brewer's yeast* levadura *f*.

brewery ['bruəri] *n* fábrica *f* de cerveza, cervecería *f*.

brewing [bruiŋ] *n* elaboración *f* *or* fabricación *f* de la cerveza.

briar; brier ['braiə*] *n* BOT zarza *f* (prickly bush) | brezo *m* (used for pipes) || pipa *f* de madera de brezo (pipe) || *briar rose* gavanza *f*.

bribe [braib] *n* soborno *m* || *to take bribes* dejarse sobornar.

bribe [braib] *vt/vi* sobornar.

bribery ['braibəri] *n* soborno *m*.

bric-a-brac ['brikəbræk] *n* baratijas *f pl* (small cheap articles) || curiosidades *f pl* (curiosities).

brick [brik] *n* ladrillo *m*; *brick kiln* horno de ladrillos || tarugo *m*, taco *m* (for children) || lingote *m* (of gold) || bloque *m* (ice cream) || color *m* ladrillo || FIG & FAM buen chico *m* (affable person) || — *hollow, mock, solid brick* ladrillo hueco, visto, macizo || FIG & FAM *to come down on s.o. like a ton of bricks* echarle una bronca a alguien | *to drop a brick* meter la pata, cometer una pifia.

brick [brik] *vt* enladrillar || *to brick up* o *in* tapiar con ladrillos.

brickbat ['brikbæt] *n* trozo *m* de ladrillo || FIG palabra *f* hiriente, pulla *f*.

bricklayer ['brik,leiə*] *n* enladrillador *m*, albañil *m*.

brick partition ['brikpɑ:'tiʃən] *n* tabique *m* de panderete.

brickwork ['brikwə:k] *n* enladrillado *m*, ladrillos *m pl*.

brickworks [-s] *n* ladrillar *m*, fábrica *f* de ladrillos.

brickyard ['brikjɑ:d] *n* almacén *m* *or* fábrica *f*.

bridal ['braidl] *adj* nupcial; *bridal suite* suite nupcial; *bridal bed* tálamo nupcial.
◆ *n* boda *f*.

bride [braid] *n* novia *f* || desposada *f*, novia *f* (after wedding) || *the bride and groom* los novios.

bridegroom [-gru:m] *n* novio *m* ‖ desposado *m*, novio *m* (after wedding).

bridesmaid [-zmeid] *n* dama *f* de honor.

bridge [bridʒ] *n* puente *m*; *stone bridge* puente de piedra ‖ MAR puente *m* ‖ puente *m* (of spectacles) ‖ caballete *m* (of nose) ‖ puente *m* (in dentistry) ‖ puente *m*, caballete *m* (of violin) ‖ ELECTR puente; *Wheatstone bridge* puente de Wheatstone ‖ bridge *m* (card game) ‖ — *boat* o *pontoon bridge* puente de barcas *or* de pontones ‖ *counterpoise bridge* puente de báscula ‖ FIG *golden bridge* puente de plata | *I'll cross that bridge when I come to it* me ocuparé de ello cuando tenga que hacerlo | *much water has flowed under the bridge since then* ha llovido mucho desde entonces ‖ *railway bridge* puente ferroviario ‖ *skew bridge* puente en esviaje ‖ *suspension bridge* puente colgante ‖ *to throw a bridge over* tender un puente sobre.

bridge [bridʒ] *vt* tender un puente sobre (a river) ‖ FIG recorrer (distance) ‖ FIG *to bridge the gap* llenar un vacío, colmar la laguna.

bridgehead [-hed] *n* MIL cabeza *f* de puente.

Bridget ['bridʒit] *pr n* Brígida *f*.

Bridgetown ['bridʒtaun] *pr n* GEOGR Bridgetown.

bridgework ['bridʒwə:k] *n* construcción *f* de puentes ‖ puente *m* (for teeth).

bridging loan ['bridʒiŋ ləun] *n* ECON préstamo *m* de empalme.

bridle ['braidl] *n* brida *f* (of the harness) ‖ frenillo *m* (of tongue) ‖ FIG freno *m* (restraining influence) ‖ TECH tirante *m* ‖ MAR poa *f*.

bridle ['braidl] *vt* embridar, poner la brida a ‖ FIG reprimir, refrenar (emotions, etc.).
◆ *vi* FIG picarse (to take offence).

bridle path [-pɑ:θ] *n* camino *m* de herradura.

bridoon [bri'du:n] *n* MIL bridón *m*.

brief [bri:f] *adj* breve; *a brief remark* una breve observación | conciso, sa (concise) ‖ muy corto, ta; *a brief bathing suit* un bañador muy corto.
◆ *n* informe *m* (report) ‖ sumario *m*, resumen *m* (summary) ‖ REL breve *m* ‖ JUR expediente *m* ‖ MIL instrucciones *f pl* ‖ — *in brief* en pocas palabras, en resumen ‖ JUR *to hold no brief for* no abogar por.
◆ *pl* calzoncillos *m* (underpants), bragas *f* (knickers).

brief [bri:f] *vt* informar (to inform); *he briefed me about the latest developments* me informó sobre los últimos acontecimientos ‖ dar instrucciones a; *to brief a lawyer* dar instrucciones a un abogado ‖ resumir (to sum up).

briefcase [-keis] *n* cartera *f* [AMER portafolio *m*].

briefing [-iŋ] *n* sesión *f* de información ‖ instrucciones *f pl*.

briefly [-li] *adv* brevemente.

briefness [-nis] *n* brevedad *f*, concisión *f*.

brier ['braiə*] *n* ⟶ **briar.**

brig [brig] *n* MAR bergantín *m* ‖ US FAM calabozo *m* (prison).

brigade [bri'geid] *n* MIL brigada *f* ‖ FIG *one of the old brigade* un veterano.

brigade [bri'geid] *vt* MIL formar una brigada con.

brigadier [,brigə'diə*] *n* general *m* de brigada.

brigand ['brigənd] *n* bandido *m*, bandolero *m*.

brigandage [-idʒ] *n* bandolerismo *m*, bandidaje *m*.

brigantine ['brigəntain] *n* MAR bergantín *m*.

bright [brait] *adj* vivo, va; *bright colour* color vivo ‖ claro, ra; *a bright day* un día claro ‖ de sol (sunny) ‖ resplandeciente, brillante (sun) ‖ brillante (light, surface) ‖ FIG vivo, va; alegre (cheerful) | despierto, ta; listo, ta (clever) | radiante (smile, beauty) | prometedor, ra; *a bright future* un futuro prometedor | luminoso, sa (idea) ‖ — *bright and early* muy de mañana ‖ *bright interval* clara *f*, claro *m* (weather) ‖ FIG *bright spark* listillo *m* | *to look on the bright side of things* mirar el lado bueno de las cosas | *you're a bright one!* ¡te has lucido!
◆ *adv* brillantemente.

brighten ['braitn] *vt* aclarar (to make lighter) ‖ pulir (to polish) ‖ *to brighten up* hacer más alegre (house, etc.), alegrar, animar (person).
◆ *vi* aclararse, despejarse; *then the weather brightened up* luego se aclaró el tiempo ‖ FIG animarse, alegrarse (to cheer up) | iluminarse (face).

brightly ['braitli] *adv* brillantemente ‖ FIG alegremente (happily) | ingeniosamente (wittily).

brightness ['braitnis] *n* claridad *f*; *the brightness of dawn* la claridad del amanecer ‖ brillo *m*, resplandor *m* (of sun) ‖ luminosidad *f*, intensidad *f* luminosa (luminosity) ‖ FIG inteligencia *f*, viveza *f* (cleverness).

Bright's disease ['braits-di'zi:z] *n* MED mal *m* de Bright, nefritis *f*.

brill [bril] *n* ZOOL rodaballo *m* (fish).

brilliance ['briljəns]; **brilliancy** [-i] *n* brillantez *f*, brillo *m* ‖ FIG brillantez *f*.

brilliant ['briljənt] *adj* brillante (very bright) ‖ FIG brillante; *a brilliant painter, performance* un pintor, una interpretación brillante | genial, luminoso, sa (idea) | clamoroso, sa (success).
◆ *n* brillante *m* (diamond).

brillantine [,briljən'ti:n] *n* brillantina *f*.

Brillo pad ['briləu ,pæd] *n* estropajo *m* jabonoso de aluminio.

brim [brim] *vi* borde *m* (of cup, of bowl, etc.) ‖ ala *f* (of hat) ‖ *full to the brim* lleno hasta los topes.

brim [brim] *vi* estar lleno hasta los topes ‖ FIG rebosar; *to brim over with happiness* rebosar de alegría ‖ — *broad-brimmed hat* sombrero *m* de ala ancha ‖ *to be brimming with* estar rebosante de.
◆ *vt* llenar hasta el borde *or* hasta los topes.

brimful [-ful]; **brimming** [-iŋ] *adj* lleno hasta el borde ‖ FIG rebosante; *brimful of ideas* rebosante de ideas.

brimmer [-ə*] *n* copa *f* llena hasta el borde.

brimming [-iŋ] *adj* ⟶ **brimful.**

brimstone [-stəun] *n* MIN azufre *m* ‖ FIG fuego *m* del infierno.

brindle ['brindl] *adj* abigarrado, da; berrendo, da.
◆ *n* animal abigarrado *or* berrendo.

brine [brain] *n* salmuera *f* ‖ POET piélago *m* mar *f* (sea).

bring* [briŋ] *vt* traer; *to bring news* traer noticias; *bring her home* tráela a casa; *to bring bad luck* traer mala suerte ‖ llevar, conducir (to take); *he was brought before the magistrate* le llevaron ante el magistrado ‖ FIG persuadir, convencer; *try to bring him to accept* trata de persuadirle para que acepte | llevar; *to bring negotiations to a successful conclusion* llevar las negociaciones a un feliz desenlace; *the series of catastrophes brought him to the brink of despair* la serie de catástrofes le llevó al borde de la desesperación ‖ JUR intentar; *to bring an action* intentar una acción judicial | hacer, formular; *to bring a complaint* hacer una reclamación ‖ introducir; *to bring somebody into the conversation* introducir a alguien en la conversación ‖ dar; *the picture will bring at least 100 pounds* el cuadro dará 100 libras como mínimo ‖ — *to bring near* acercar ‖ *to bring suit* entablar un pleito ‖ *to bring support* prestar ayuda.
◆ *phr v* ***to bring about*** ocasionar, provocar, causar; *to bring about an accident* causar un accidente | efectuar; *to bring about a change* efectuar un cambio | MAR hacer virar (a ship) ‖ ***to bring along*** traer; *may I bring my friend along?* ¿puedo traer a mi amigo? ‖ ***to bring away*** llevarse; *to bring away a prize* llevarse un premio ‖ ***to bring back*** volver a traer (to bring again) | devolver (to return); *to bring back a book* devolver un libro | traer; *he brought back news of the defeat* trajo noticias de la derrota | recordar; *it brings back my childhood* me recuerda mi infancia ‖ ***to bring before*** someter a; *to bring a matter before Parliament* someter una cuestión al Parlamento ‖ ***to bring down*** bajar; *bring a chair down from the bedroom* baja una silla del dormitorio | derribar (horseman, dictator, house, aeroplane) | hacer bajar; *to bring down prices, the temperature* hacer bajar los precios, la temperatura | MATH bajar ‖ — *to bring down the house* hacer que el teatro se venga abajo con los aplausos ‖ ***to bring forth*** dar a luz (a child) | producir (fruit) ‖ ***to bring forward*** acercar (to move nearer) | traer; *bring forward the prisoner* que traigan al preso | presentar; *to bring forward a subject for discussion* presentar un tema para la discusión | plantear (a question) | adelantar (a date) | *brought forward* suma y sigue ‖ ***to bring in*** traer; *to bring in some wood for the fire* traer madera para el fuego | presentar (an argument, a bill) | introducir (the fashion, a topic, a quotation) | hacer entrar, hacer pasar (to show in) | recoger (harvest) | COMM rendir, dar, producir; *an investment that brings in 6%* una inversión que rinde el seis por ciento | JUR pronunciar; *to bring in a verdict of guilty* pronunciar un veredicto de culpabilidad | atraer (crowds) ‖ ***to bring into*** comprometer | *to bring into play* poner en juego | *to bring into the world* traer al mundo ‖ ***to bring off*** lograr, conseguir; *to bring off a master coup* lograr un golpe maestro ‖ rescatar (to rescue) | conducir al éxito (to make a success) ‖ ***to bring on*** causar, provocar; *to bring on a fainting attack* causar un desmayo | conducir a (to lead) ‖ ***to bring out*** sacar; *to bring sth. out of one's pocket* sacar algo del bolsillo | publicar, sacar a luz; *to bring a new atlas out* publicar un nuevo atlas | poner en escena (theatre) | hacer resaltar; *to bring out the differences between two points of view* hacer resaltar las diferencias entre dos puntos de vista | poner de manifiesto, sacar a relucir; *his teacher brought out his self-confidence, his gift for languages* el profesor puso de manifiesto su confianza en sí mismo, su don de lenguas | ayudar a tener confianza en sí mismo (to build up s.o.'s self-confidence) | presentar en sociedad (a debutante) ‖ ***to bring round*** o ***around*** traer; *can she bring her brother round?* ¿puede traer a su hermano? | convencer, persuadir; *I shall bring him round* yo le convenceré | reanimar, hacer volver en sí; *he brought her round after she had fainted* le reanimó después del desmayo | llevar; *to bring the conversation round to a subject* llevar la conversación hacia un tema ‖ ***to bring through*** mantener vivo (to keep alive) | salvar (to save) ‖ — *to bring a patient through* operar un éxito a un paciente ‖ ***to bring to*** reanimar (after fainting) | parar, detener (to stop) ‖ — *to bring a smile to one's lips* hacer sonreír a alguien | *to bring one's mind to bear on a problem* examinar un problema | *to bring o.s. to* resignarse a | *to bring sth. to s.o.'s knowledge* poner algo en conocimiento de alguien | *to bring to bear* concentrar (attention), hacer; *to bring pressure to bear on s.o.* hacer presión sobre alguien | *to bring to book* pedir cuentas a | *to bring to light* revelar, sacar a luz | *to bring to mind* recordar | *to bring to ruin* arruinar | *to bring to task* llamar a capítulo, reprender ‖ ***to bring together*** reunir

(to put together) | reconciliar (enemies) || *to bring under* someter || *to bring up* subir (sth. from downstairs) | acercar (to move nearer) | educar, criar; *a well brought-up child* un niño bien educado | sacar a colación (a topic) | plantear, poner sobre el tapete (a question) | devolver (to vomit) | parar (to stop) || — *to bring up a matter before s.o.* someter algo a la atención de alguien || *to bring up the rear* cerrar la marcha; cubrir la retaguardia (soldiers) || *to bring upon o.s.* buscarse (misfortune).
— OBSERV Pret y pp ***brought***.

brink [briŋk] *n* borde *m* (edge) || orilla *f* (of a river) || FIG *on the brink of* al borde de; *on the brink of disaster* al borde del desastre; a punto de; *on the brink of collapse* a punto de hundirse.

brinkmanship [-manʃip] *n* política *f* arriesgada *or* en la cuerda floja.

briny ['braini] *adj* salado, da; salobre.
◆ *n* mar *m*.

brio ['briəu] *n* brío *m*.

briquette; briquet [bri'ket] *n* briqueta *f* (coal).

brisk [brisk] *adj* lleno de vida (lively) || enérgico, ca; vigoroso, sa (energetic) || fresco, ca (breeze) || activo, va (trade) || — *at a brisk pace* con paso ligero || *to take a brisk walk* dar un paseo rápido.

brisk [brisk] *vt* animar, avivar.
◆ *vi* animarse, avivarse.

brisket ['briskit] *n* CULIN falda *f* (of beef, etc.).

briskness ['brisknis] *n* ligereza *f* (of step) || energía *f* || vivacidad *f* || actividad *f* (of trade).

brisque [brisk] *n* brisca *f*.

bristle ['brisl] *n* cerda *f*.

bristle ['brisl] *vi* erizarse, ponerse de punta || — FIG *bristling with rage* congestionado de rabia | *to bristle with* estar erizado *or* lleno de; *bristling with difficulties* erizado de dificultades.
◆ *vt* erizar, poner de punta.

bristly ['brisli] *adj* erizado, da || cerdoso, sa || *to have a bristly chin* tener la barba crecida.

Bristol board ['bristl-bɔːd] *n* bristol *m*, cartulina *f*.

Britain ['britn] *pr n* GEOGR Gran Bretaña *f* || *battle of Britain* batalla de Inglaterra.

Britannia [bri'tænjə] *pr n* Britania *f*.

Britannic [bri'tænik] *adj* británico, ca; *Her o His Britannic Majesty* Su Majestad Británica.

Briticism ['britisizəm] *n* anglicismo *m*, palabra *f or* expresión *f* típicamente inglesa.

British ['britiʃ] *adj* británico, ca.
◆ *pl prn* británicos *m*.

British Columbia [-kə'lʌmbiə] *pr n* GEOGR Colombia *f* Británica.

Britisher [-ə*] *n* natural *m* de Gran Bretaña.

British Guiana [-gai'ænə] *pr n* GEOGR Guayana *f* Británica, Guyana *f*.

British Isles [-ails] *pl prn* GEOGR islas *f* Británicas.

Briton ['britn] *n* HIST britano, na || británico, ca.

Brittany ['britəni] *pr n* GEOGR Bretaña *f*.

brittle ['britl] *adj* quebradizo, za; frágil || FIG susceptible (person).

broach [brəutʃ] *n* brocheta *f*, espetón *f* (spit) || TECH punzón *m* (punch) | broca *f*, mecha *f* (of a drill) | escariador *m*, mandril *m* (to enlarge a hole) | lezna *f* (in shoemaking) || ARCH aguja *f* (of spire) || broche *m* (brooch).

broach [brəutʃ] *vt* poner en la brocheta, espetar (to put on a spit) || espitar (a barrel, a cask) || FIG empezar, abrir (to begin) | sacar a colación; *to broach the subject* sacar el tema a colación.

broad [brɔːd] *adj* ancho, cha (wide); *a broad avenue* una ancha avenida || extenso, sa; amplio, plia; *a broad stretch of water* una superficie de agua extensa || FIG claro, ra; *a broad hint* una insinuación clara | amplio, plia; *in a broad sense* en sentido amplio | general (term) | atrevido, da; verde (joke, story) | general; *a broad outline* un esquema general | principal, esencial (essential) | comprensivo, va; liberal, tolerante | abierto, ta (smile) || GRAMM abierto, ta (vowel) || — FIG *broad accent* acento cerrado || *in broad daylight* en pleno día || *on broad lines* en grandes líneas, en líneas generales || FIG *to be as broad as it is long* dar igual, dar lo mismo.
◆ *n* anchura *f* (width) || US FAM gachí *f* (woman).

broad bean [-biːn] *n* haba *f*.

broadcast ['brɔːdkɑːst] *n* RAD emisión *f* || *repeat broadcast* reposición *f*.

broadcast* ['brɔːdkɑːst] *vt* emitir, radiar (by radio) || transmitir (by television) || AGR sembrar al voleo || FIG propalar, difundir; *to broadcast a rumour, a piece of news* propalar un rumor, difundir una noticia.
— OBSERV Pret y pp ***broadcast***.

broadcaster [-ə*] *n* locutor, ra (announcer).

broadcasting [-iŋ] *n* radiodifusión *f* (by radio) || transmisión *f*, difusión *f* (by television) || — *broadcasting program* programa *m* de radiodifusión || *broadcasting station* emisora *f*.

broadcloth ['brɔːdklɔθ] *n* paño *m* fino || popelín *m*, popelina *f* (poplin).

broaden ['brɔːdn] *vt* ensanchar || FIG ampliar; *to broaden one's outlook* ampliar las perspectivas.
◆ *vi* ensancharse || FIG ampliarse || *to broaden out* ensancharse.

broad jump ['brɔːd-dʒʌmp] *n* US SP salto *m* de longitud.

broadly ['brɔːdli] *adv* en general, en términos generales; *broadly speaking* hablando en general.

broadly-based [-beist] *adj* de base amplia.

broad-minded ['brɔːd'maindid] *adj* tolerante, liberal, de miras amplias, comprensivo, va.

broadness ['brɔːdnis] *n* anchura *f* (width) || FIG grosería *f* (vulgarity) || *the broadness of his speech* su acento cerrado.

broad-shouldered ['brɔːd'ʃəuldəd] *adj* ancho de espaldas.

broadside ['brɔːdsaid] *n* MAR costado *m* (side of a ship); *broadside on* de costado | batería *f* del costado (guns) | andanada *f* (shots) || FIG retahíla *f*, andanada *f*, sarta *f*; *a broadside of insults* una retahíla de insultos.
◆ *adv* MAR de costado.

broadsword ['brɔːdsɔːd] *n* sable *m*.

broadways ['brɔːdweiz]; **broadwise** [-waiz] *adv* a lo ancho.

brocade [brə'keid] *n* brocado *m*.

brocade [brə'keid] *vt* decorar con brocados.

brocatelle [brɔkə'tel] *n* brocatel *m* (fabric).

broccoli ['brɔkəli] *n* BOT brécol *m*, bróculi *m*.

brochette [brɔ'ʃet] *n* brocheta *f*, pincho *m* (skewer) || CULIN pincho *m*; *to eat brochettes* comer pinchos.

brochure ['brəuʃjuə] *n* folleto *m*.

brock [brɔk] *n* ZOOL tejón *m* (badger).

brocket [-it] *n* ZOOL cervato *m*.

brogue [brəug] *n* zapato *m* grueso (shoe) || acento *m* regional [sobre todo irlandés].

broil [brɔil] *n* carne *f* asada a la parrilla (meat) || FIG pelea *f* (quarrel).

broil [brɔil] *vt* asar (a la parrilla) || FIG asar.
◆ *vi* asarse || FIG asarse | pelearse (to quarrel).

broiler [-ə*] *n* parrilla *f* (grill) || pollo *m* tomatero (para asar) (chicken).

broke [brəuk] *pret* —> **break.**
◆ *adj* FIG & FAM bollado, da; pelado, da; sin blanca (penniless); *to go broke* quedarse sin blanca || FAM *to go for broke* ir a por todas, arriesgar el todo por el todo.

broken ['brəukən] *pp* —> **break.**
◆ *adj* roto, ta || fracturado, da (bones) || interrumpido, da (sleep) || accidentado, da; desigual (ground) || accidentado, da; quebrado, da (relief) || incierto, ta; variable (weather) || violado, da; quebrantado, da (promise, oath, law) || MATH quebrado, da; *broken line* línea quebrada || FIG deshecho, cha; destrozado, da; *a broken man* un hombre destrozado | abatido, da (tone) | quebrado, da (voice) | arruinado, da; quebrantado, da; estragado, da (health) | chapurreado, da (language); *to speak broken English* hablar un inglés chapurreado | arruinado, da (bankrupt).

broken-down [-'daun] *adj* roto, ta; estropeado, da; *a broken-down old car* un viejo coche estropeado || FIG destrozado, da; deshecho, cha (person).

brokenhearted [-'hɑːtid] *adj* con el corazón destrozado.

broken home [-həum] *n* hogar *m* de padres separados.

brokenly [-li] *adv* con la voz quebrada, con palabras entrecortadas.

broken-winded [-'windid] *adj* jadeante || corto de resuello (horse).

broker ['brəukə*] *n* COMM corredor *m*, agente *m* de Bolsa (stockbroker) | agente *m* comercial, corredor *m* (of a company) || *insurance broker* agente *m* de seguros.

brokerage ['brəukəridʒ]; **broking** ['brəukiŋ] *n* COMM corretaje *m*, correduría *f*.

brolly ['brɔli] *n* FAM paraguas *m inv*.

bromate ['brəumeit] *n* CHEM bromato *m*.

bromic ['brəumik] *adj* CHEM brómico, ca.

bromide ['brəumaid] *n* CHEM bromuro *m* || FIG & FAM pelmazo, za (boring person) | trivialidad *f* (trite saying).

bromine ['brəumiːn] *n* CHEM bromo *m*.

bronchia ['brɔŋkiə] *pl n* ANAT bronquios *m*.

bronchial ['brɔŋkjəl] *adj* ANAT bronquial || *bronchial tube* bronquio *m*.

bronchioles ['brɔŋkiəulz] *pl n* ANAT bronquiolos *m*.

bronchiopneumonia ['brɔŋkjəunju'məunjə] *n* MED bronconeumonía *f*.

bronchitic [brɔŋ'kitik] *adj* MED bronquítico, ca.

bronchitis [brɔŋ'kaitis] *n* MED bronquitis *f*.

broncho ['brɔŋkəu] *n* US —> **bronco.**

bronchopneumonia [-nju'məunjə] *n* MED bronconeumonía *f*.

bronchoscope [-skəup] *n* MED broncoscopio *m*.

bronchus ['brɔŋkəs] *n* ANAT bronquio *m*.
— OBSERV El plural de *bronchus* es *bronchi*.

bronco; broncho ['brɔŋkəu] *n* US mustango *m*, potro *m* cerril.

broncobuster ['brɔŋkəuˌbʌstə*] *n* US domador *m* de potros cerriles.

bronze [brɔnz] *n* bronce *m* (alloy) || objeto *m* de bronce || color *m* de bronce.

bronze [brɔnz] *vt* broncear.
◆ *vi* broncearse.

bronzed [-d] *adj* bronceado, da.

bronzesmith [-smiθ] *n* broncista *m*.

brooch [brəutʃ] *n* broche *m*.

brood [bru:d] *n* cría *f*, nidada *f* (of birds) ‖ FIG progenie *f*, prole *f* (children) ‖ — *brood hen* gallina clueca ‖ *brood mare* yegua *f* de vientre.

brood [bru:d] *vt* empollar.
◆ *vi* empollar ‖ — FIG *to brood on* o *over* rumiar, dar vueltas a; *to brood over a problem* darle vueltas a un problema | *to brood over* cernerse sobre (to hang over).

brooder [-ə*] *n* gallina *f* clueca (hen) ‖ incubadora *f*, pollera *f* (for raising young fowl).

broody [-i] *adj* clueca; *broody hen* gallina clueca ‖ FIG melancólico, ca (moody) | pensativo, va (pensive).

brook [bruk] *n* arroyo *m*.

brook [bruk] *vt* soportar, aguantar.

brooklet ['bruklit] *n* arroyuelo *m*.

broom [bru:m] *n* escoba *f* (for sweeping) ‖ BOT retama *f*, hiniesta *f* ‖ FIG *a new broom sweeps clean* las nuevas personas siempre hacen reformas.

broom [bru:m] *vt* barrer.

broomstick [-stik] *n* palo *m* de escoba ‖ escoba *f* (of a witch).

broth [brɔθ] *n* caldo *m*.

brothel ['brɔθl] *n* burdel *m*, lupanar *m*.

brother ['brʌðə*] *n* hermano *m*; *older, younger brother* hermano mayor, menor; *the oldest brother* el hermano mayor ‖ colega *m* & *f* (colleague) ‖ camarada *m* & *f* (comrade) ‖ cofrade *m* (in brotherhood) ‖ compañero *m*, amigo *m* (friend) ‖ REL hermano *m*; *lay brother* hermano lego ‖ — *brothers and sisters* hermanos ‖ *full brother* hermano carnal ‖ *half brother* medio hermano.

brotherhood [-hud] *n* fraternidad *f*, hermandad *f* (condition of being a brother) ‖ cofradía *f*, hermandad *f* (religious group) ‖ gremio *m*; *the literary brotherhood* el gremio de los literatos.

brother-in-law ['brʌðərinlɔ:] *n* cuñado *m*, hermano *m* político.
— OBSERV El plural es *brothers-in-law*.

brotherly ['brʌðəli] *adj* fraternal, fraterno, na.
◆ *adv* fraternalmente.

brougham ['bruəm] *n* berlina *f* (car).

brought [brɔ:t] *pret/pp* ⟶ **bring**.

brow [brau] *n* frente *f* (forehead) ‖ ceja *f* (eyebrow) ‖ cima *f*, cumbre *f* (of a hill) ‖ FIG cara *f*, semblante *m* ‖ *to knit one's brows* fruncir el ceño.

browbeat ['braubi:t] *vt* intimidar (to bully) ‖ *to browbeat into* obligar a.

brown [braun] *n* marrón *m*, castaño *m*.
◆ *adj* marrón; *brown shoes* zapatos marrones ‖ castaño, ña (hair) ‖ moreno, na (by the sun) ‖ pardo, da (bear) ‖ moreno, na (bread, sugar) ‖ — *as brown as a berry* muy moreno [por el sol] ‖ *brown paper* papel *m* de estraza ‖ *brown race* raza cobriza ‖ *brown study* ensimismamiento *m* (mental abstraction).

brown [braun] *vt* CULIN dorar ‖ broncear, tostar, poner moreno (by the sun) ‖ — FIG & FAM *to be browned off with* estar hasta las narices de ‖ *to brown s.o. off* fastidiar a alguien.
◆ *vi* CULIN dorarse ‖ broncearse, tostarse, ponerse moreno (in the sun).

brown-coal [-'kəul] *n* MIN lignito *m*.

Brownian [-iən] *adj* PHYS browniano (movement).

brownie [-i] *n* duende *m* (goblin) ‖ US bizcocho *m* de chocolate y nueces.

Brownie; Brownie Guide [-gaid] *n* niña *f* exploradora (junior girl guide).

browning [-iŋ] *n* browning *m* (gun) ‖ colorante *m*.

brownish [-iʃ] *adj* pardusco, ca.

brownout [-aut] *n* US apagón *m* (of lights).

brown stone [-stəun] *n* US piedra *f* arenisca de color pardo.

browse [brauz] *n* ramoneo *m* ‖ FIG vistazo *m*, ojeada *f*; *to have a quick browse* echar un vistazo rápido.

browse [brauz] *vt/vi* ramonear (leaves) ‖ pacer (grass) ‖ — FIG *I am just browsing* estoy mirando (en una tienda, etc.) | *to browse through a book* hojear un libro.

brucellosis [,bru:sə'ləusis] *n* MED brucelosis *f*.

Bruges [bru:z] *pr n* GEOGR Brujas.

Bruin ['bruin] *pr n* oso *m* (name used in fairy tales).

bruise [bru:z] *n* magulladura *f*, contusión *f*, cardenal *m* (on the body) ‖ daño *m*, machucadura *f* (in fruit) ‖ FIG herida *f* (wound).

bruise [bru:z] *vt* magullar, contusionar (the body); *to have a bruised arm* tener el brazo magullado ‖ dañar, machucar (fruit) ‖ majar, machacar (to crush) ‖ abollar (metal) ‖ FIG herir (feelings).
◆ *vi* magullarse ‖ dañarse, machacarse (fruits) ‖ abollarse (metal) ‖ FIG sentirse herido (feelings) ‖ *he bruises easily* le salen cardenales con facilidad.

bruiser [-ə*] *n* FAM matón *m* (aggressive man) | boxeador *m* (professional boxer).

bruit [bru:t] *n* rumour *m*.

bruit [bru:t] *vt* difundir, divulgar (a rumour).

brunch ['brʌntʃ] *n* US FAM desayuno *m* tardío (late morning meal).

brunette [bru:'net] *n* morena *f*.

brunt [brʌnt] *n* lo más fuerte, lo más recio; *to bear the brunt of an attack* aguantar lo más recio de un ataque ‖ la mayor parte (of the work).

brush [brʌʃ] *n* cepillo *m*, escobón *m* (floor brush) ‖ cepillo *m* (for clothes, shoes, teeth, hair, etc.) ‖ brocha *f* (for painting walls) ‖ pincel *m* (artist's) ‖ bruza *f* (for horses) ‖ escobilla *f*, limpiabotellas *m inv* (for bottles) ‖ cepillado *m* (brushing) ‖ maleza *f*, broza *f* (undergrowth) ‖ leña *f* (twigs) ‖ ELECTR escobilla *f* ‖ PHYS haz *m* de rayos ‖ FIG cola *f* muy poblada, hopo *m* (of squirrel, of fox, etc.) | escaramuza *f* (skirmish) ‖ — *shaving brush* brocha de afeitar ‖ FIG *to have a brush with the law* tener un roce con la policía.

brush [brʌʃ] *vt* cepillar; *to brush the floor* cepillar el suelo ‖ pintar con brocha (walls) ‖ pintar con pincel (painting) ‖ frotar, restregar (to rub hard) ‖ TECH cardar (wool) ‖ rozar; *to brush the wall with one's sleeve* rozar la pared con la manga ‖ FIG *to brush one's way through a crowd* abrirse paso entre la multitud.
◆ *vi* cepillar ‖ *to brush against* o *by* o *past* pasar rozando, rozar al pasar.
◆ *phr v* **to brush aside** dejar de lado ‖ **to brush away** quitar (dust) ‖ **to brush down** cepillar | almohazar (a horse) ‖ **to brush off** quitar (dust) | quitarse de encima (to get rid of) | despedir bruscamente (to dismiss) ‖ **to brush over** aplicar [una ligera capa de pintura] ‖ FIG **to brush up** refrescar; *to brush up one's French* refrescar sus conocimientos de francés | pulir (to polish up) | *to brush up against* rozar.

brushing [-iŋ] *n* cepillado *m*.

brush-off [-ɔf] *n* despedida *f* brusca.

brushstroke [-strəuk] *n* brochazo *m* (with a large brush) ‖ pincelada *f* (with an artist's brush).

brushup [-ʌp] *n* FIG *to give one's French a brushup* refrescar sus conocimientos de francés | *to have a wash and brushup* arreglarse.

brushwood [-wud] *n* maleza *f*, broza *f* (undergrowth) ‖ leña *f* (chopped off tree branches).

brushwork [-wə:k] *n* pintura *f* (painting) ‖ técnica *f* (technique) ‖ pincelada *f*; *Renoir's brushwork* la pincelada de Renoir.

brusque [brusk] *adj* brusco, ca; áspero, ra.

brusqueness [-nis]; **brusquerie** [-əri] *n* brusquedad *f*.

Brussels ['brʌslz] *pr n* GEOGR Bruselas ‖ *Brussels sprouts* coles *f pl* de Bruselas.

brutal ['bru:tl] *adj* brutal (violent) ‖ cruel; *a brutal punishment* un castigo cruel ‖ FIG *the brutal truth* la verdad cruda.

brutality [bru:'tæliti] *n* brutalidad *f* (violence) ‖ crueldad *f* (cruelty).

brutalization [brutəlai'zeiʃən] *n* embrutecimiento *m*.

brutalize ['bru:təlaiz] *vt* embrutecer (to make brutal) ‖ tratar brutalmente (to treat brutally).
◆ *vi* embrutecerse.

brute [bru:t] *adj* bruto, ta; *a brute beast* una bestia bruta ‖ brutal; *brute instincts* instintos brutales ‖ *by brute force* a viva fuerza.
◆ *n* bruto *m*, bestia *f* (animal) ‖ FIG bestia *f* (brutal person) ‖ — FIG *a brute of a job* un trabajo horrible ‖ FAM *you brute!* ¡bestia!

brutish [-iʃ] *adj* bestial (savage) ‖ bruto, ta (stupid) ‖ brutal.

brutishness [-iʃnis] *n* brutalidad *f* (violence) ‖ bestialidad *f* (savagery, stupidity).

bryology [brai'ɔlədʒi] *n* BOT briología *f*.

bryony ['braiəni] *n* BOT brionia *f*.

bryophyte ['braiəfait] *n* BOT briofita *f*.

bryozoan; bryozoon [,braiə'zəuən] *n* ZOOL briozoario *m*, briozoo *m*.
— OBSERV Los plurales de *bryozoan* y *bryozoon* son *bryozoans* y *briozoa*.

BSI *abbr of* *[British Standards Institution]* asociación británica de normalización.

bubble ['bʌbl] *n* burbuja *f* ‖ pompa *f* de jabón; *to blow bubbles* hacer pompas de jabón ‖ burbujeo *m* (bubbling) ‖ TECH sopladura *f* ‖ FIG estafa *f* (swindle) | cosa *f* efímera (sth. short-lived) | ilusión *f* (fantasy) ‖ — *bubble bath* producto *m* para baño de espuma ‖ *bubble gum* chicle *m* de globo ‖ *bubble point* punto *m* de ebullición ‖ *soap bubble* pompa de jabón ‖ FIG *to prick s.o.'s bubble* desengañar a uno.

bubble ['bʌbl] *vi* burbujear ‖ borbotear (when heated); *the water in the pan is beginning to bubble* el agua de la cacerola empieza a borbotear ‖ eructar (to belch, a baby) ‖ — FIG *to bubble over with joy* rebosar de alegría | *to bubble with laughter* reventar de risa.
◆ *vt* hacer borbotear.

bubble and squeak [-ənd'skwi:k] *n* CULIN carne *f* picada frita con patatas y coles.

bubble car [-ka:*] *n* FAM huevo *m* [coche].

bubble chamber [-'tʃeimbə*] *n* PHYS cámara *f* de burbujas.

bubbly ['bʌbli] *adj* burbujeante, con burbujas ‖ efervescente, espumoso, sa (drinks).
◆ *n* FAM champaña *f*, champán *m*.

bubi ['bu:bi] *n* bubi *m* (of Fernando Poo).

bubo ['bu:bəu] *n* MED bubón *m*, buba *f*.
— OBSERV El plural de la palabra inglesa es *buboes*.

bubonic [bju:'bɔnik] *adj* MED bubónico, ca.

buccal ['bʌkəl] *adj* ANAT bucal.

buccaneer [,bʌkə'niə*] *n* bucanero *m*.

buccaneer [,bʌkə'niə*] *vi* piratear.

buccinator ['bʌksineitə*] *n* ANAT buccinador *m*.

Bucephalus [bju'sefələs] *pr n* Bucéfalo *m*.

Bucharest [ˌbjuːkə'rest] *pr n* GEOGR Bucarest.

buck [bʌk] *n* ZOOL macho *m* (of certain animals) | gamo *m*, ciervo *m* (male deer) | macho *m* cabrío (goat) | conejo *m* macho (rabbit) | liebre *f* macho (hare) || ficha *f* (in poker) || brinco *m* (of a horse) || SP potro *m* (in gymnasium) | carga *f* (in american football) || petimetre *m* (dandy) || US FAM dólar *m* | joven *m* indio | burro *m* (sawhorse) || FAM *to make a fast buck* hacer dinero rápidamente | *to pass the buck to s.o.* echarle el muerto a uno.
◆ *adj* macho (male) || raso (soldier).

buck [bʌk] *vt* US FAM resistir porfiadamente a | cargar (in American football) || — *to buck off* desmontar, derribar (its rider) || *to buck up* animar.
◆ *vi* corcovear (a horse) || dar sacudidas (a car, a machine, etc.) || FIG empeñarse || — *to buck up* animarse (to cheer up), darse prisa (to hurry).

bucket [-it] *n* cubo *m*; *a bucket of water* un cubo de agua || TECH cangilón *m* (of waterwheel) | paleta *f* (of turbine) | cuchara *f* (of dredge) || — FAM *it's raining buckets* está lloviendo a cántaros | *to kick the bucket* estirar la pata, hincar el pico.

bucket [-it] *vt* sacar (con cubo).
◆ *vi* apresurarse (to hurry).

bucketful [-itful] *n* cubo *m* || FIG *by the bucketful* en grandes cantidades.

bucket seat [-itˌsiːt] *n* asiento *m* de coche deportivo.

buckeye [-ai] *n* US BOT castaño *m* de Indias.

buckle [-l] *n* hebilla *f* (of shoes, etc.) || pandeo *m* (of wall) || alabeo *m* (of wheel).

buckle [-l] *vt* abrochar (to fasten); *to buckle up one's shoes* abrocharse los zapatos || torcer, combar, pandear (to bend sharply) || alabear (a wheel) || doblar (the knees) || *to buckle on one's sword* ceñirse la espada.
◆ *vi* pandearse, combarse, torcerse; *to buckle under impact* torcerse con un choque || alabearse (wheel) || doblarse (knees) || FIG FAM *to buckle down to* dedicarse con empeño a.

buckler [-lə*] *n* HIST rodela *f*, escudo *m* (shield) || FIG escudo *m*, defensa *f*.

buckling [-liŋ] *n* pandeo *m*.

buck private [-'praivit] *n* US FAM recluta *m*, soldado *m* raso.

buckram [-rəm] *n* bucarán *m* (cloth).

buckshee [-'ʃiː] *adj* FAM gratuito, ta.
◆ *adv* FAM de balde.

buckshot [-ʃɔt] *n* posta *f* zorrera.

buckskin [-skin] *n* ante *m* (the skin of a buck).

buckthorn [-θɔːn] *n* BOT espino *m* cerval.

bucktooth [-'tuːθ] *n* diente *m* saliente.

buckwheat [-wiːt] *n* BOT alforfón *m*, trigo *m* sarraceno.

bucolic [bju'kɔlik] *adj* bucólico, ca.
◆ *n* bucólica *f* (pastoral poem).

bud [bʌd] *n* BOT brote *m* yema *f* (shoot) | capullo *m* (halp-opened flower); *in bud* en capullo || AGR escudete *m* || FIG *to nip in the bud* cortar de raíz.

bud [bʌd] *vt* AGR injertar de escudete || echar (leaves) || *to bud horns* salirle (a un animal) los cuernos.
◆ *vi* BOT brotar, echar brotes || FIG florecer.

Budapest ['bjuːdə'pest] *pr n* GEOGR Budapest.

Buddha ['budə*] *pr n* REL Buda *m*.

Buddhism ['budizəm] *pr n* REL budismo *m*.

Buddhist ['budist] *adj/n* REL budista.

budding ['bʌdiŋ] *adj* FIG en ciernes; *a budding poet* un poeta en ciernes.

buddle ['bʌdl] *n* MIN artesa *f*, lavadero *m*.

buddle ['bʌdl] *vt* MIN lavar.

buddy ['bʌdi] *n* US FAM compañero *m*, camarada *m*, amigote *m*, amigo *m*.

budge [bʌdʒ] *vt* mover (to move) || FIG hacer ceder (to make yield).
◆ *vi* moverse (to move) || FIG ceder (to yield).

budgerigar [-ərigaː*] *n* periquito *m* (bird).

budget ['bʌdʒit] *n* presupuesto *m* || — *budget account* cuenta *f* presupuestaria || *budget reform* reforma presupuestaria || *the Budget* el presupuesto del Estado || FAM *to be on a tight budget* tener que limitar los gastos.

budget ['bʌdʒit] *vt/vi* presupuestar, hacer un presupuesto; *to budget for a new hospital* hacer un presupuesto para un nuevo hospital.

budgetary [-əri] *adj* presupuestario, ria.

budgie ['bʌdʒi] *n* FAM periquito *m*.

Buenos Aires ['bwenəs'aiəriz] *pr n* Buenos Aires.

buff [bʌf] *adj* de color de ante, amarillo, lla.
◆ *n* piel *f* de búfalo (buffalo skin) || color *m* de ante, amarillo *m* || pulidor *m* (polishing device) || rueda *f* pulidora (polishing wheel) || US FAM entusiasta *m* & *f* || FIG *in the buff* en cueros (naked).

buff [bʌf] *vt* dar brillo a; *to buff the floor* dar brillo al suelo || pulir, pulimentar (to smooth) || teñir de color ante *or* amarillo (to dye) || aterciopelar (to give a velvety surface).

buffalo ['bʌfələu] *n* ZOOL búfalo *m* || piel *f* de búfalo || *buffalo robe* piel *f* de búfalo [empleada como manta, alfombra, etc.].
— OBSERV El plural de la palabra *buffalo* es *buffalo, buffaloes* y *buffalos*.

buffalo ['bʌfələu] *vt* US FAM engañar, embaucar (to bamboozle) | confundir (to baffle).

buffer ['bʌfə*] *n* amortiguador *m* (deadening device) || tope *m* (of railway wagons) || parachoques *m inv* (of cars) || INFORM buffer *m*, memoria *f* intermedia || CHEM regulador *m* || — *buffer state* estado *m* tapón || *buffer stop* tope *m* || FAM *old buffer* carca *m*.

buffet ['bʌfit] *n* aparador *m* (sideboard) || alacena *f* (for display) || cantina *f*, fonda *f* (in a railway station) | bar *m* (refreshment bar) || golpe *m* (blow) || bofetada *f* (with the hand) || FIG golpe *m* de mala suerte || — *buffet car* coche *m* bar (in train) || *buffet lunch* o *cold buffet* buffet *m*, comida fría en la cual cada uno se sirve || *buffet supper* cena fría.

buffet ['bʌfit] *vt* golpear (to strike) || abofetear (to slap) || zarandear (to knock about); *ship buffeted about by the wind and the waves* barco zarandeado por el viento y las olas.

buffoon [bə'fuːn] *n* bufón *m*, payaso *m*.

buffoonery [-əri] *n* bufonada *f*, payasada *f*.

bug [bʌg] *n* bicho *m* (insect) || chinche *f* (bedbug) || FAM microbio *m* (bacterium) | fallo *m* [AMER falla *f*] (default) | micrófono *m* oculto | afición *f*, vicio *m*; *to catch the smoking bug* coger el vicio de fumar | molestia *f* (nuisance) || INFORM bicho *m*, bug *m* || FAM *big bug* pez gordo.

bug [bʌg] *vt* FAM ocultar un micrófono en (a room) | escuchar por medio de un micrófono oculto | fastidiar, molestar; *it bugs me not having any money* me molesta no tener dinero || — *bugging device* micrófono oculto || FAM *what's bugging you?* ¿qué te preocupa?

bugaboo ['bʌgəbuː]; **bugbear** ['bʌgbɛə*] *n* pesadilla *f* (worry) || espantajo *m* (object of horror) || coco *m* (bogeyman).

bug-eyed ['bʌgaid] *adj* FAM de ojos saltones.

bugger ['bʌgə*] *n* sodomita *m* || POP tío *m*, sujeto *m* (person) | cabrón *m* (contemptible person) || POP *his son is a little bugger* su hijo es un sinvergüenza.

bugger [bʌgə*'ɔf] *vt* JUR sodomizar, cometer sodomía con.
◆ *vi* POP *to be buggered* estar hecho polvo.
◆ *ph v* POP ***to bugger about*** o ***around*** entretenerse, perder el tiempo | ***to bugger off*** largarse.

buggery ['bʌgəri] *n* sodomía *f*.

buggy ['bʌgi] *n* calesa *f*, «buggy» *m* (light carriage) || cochecillo *m* de niño (pram).

bugle ['bjuːgl] *n* MUS bugle *m* || abalorio *m* (ornament).

bugloss ['bjuːglɔs] *n* BOT buglosa *f*, lengua *f* de buey.

bugs [bʌgz] *adj* US FAM loco, ca; chalado, da (crazy).

buhl [buːl] *n* taracea *f*, marquetería *f*.

build [bild] *n* tipo *m*, figura *f* (physique) || estructura *f*, forma *f* (shape).

build* [bild] *vt* construir; *to build a ship* construir un barco || construir, edificar (a building) || hacer (a nest) || preparar (a fire) || FIG trazar, formar, hacer (plans) | basar, fundamentar (to establish) || FAM *I'm not built that way* no soy así.
◆ *vi* ser constructor || construirse (a house).
◆ *phr v* ***to build in*** empotrar; *to build in a cupboard* empotrar un armario | incorporar || FIG ***to build on*** basar, fundamentar; *to build one's argument on solid facts* basar un argumento en hechos concretos | contar con (promises, hopes, etc.) || ***to build up*** urbanizar, edificar en; *the area is completely built up* la zona está completamente urbanizada | montar, armar (from parts) | elaborar; *to build up a theory* elaborar una teoría | FAM reunir, hacer; *to build up a collection* hacer una colección | crear; *to build up the image of a product* crear la imagen de un producto | aumentar; *to build up sales* aumentar las ventas | fortalecer; *to build up one's health* fortalecer la salud | entonar, animar; *to build s.o. up* entonar a alguien | hacerse; *to build up a clientèle* hacerse una clientela; *to build up a mental picture of sth.* hacerse una idea de algo; *to build up a reputation for o.s.* hacerse una buena reputación | SP *to build up a lead* tomar la delantera.
— OBSERV Pret y pp ***built***.

builder ['bildə*] *n* constructor *m* || ARCH contratista *m* (contractor) | maestro *m* de obras (master builder) || FIG fundador *m* (of an empire, etc.).

building ['bildiŋ] *n* edificio *m*, construcción *f* (house, factory, etc.) || construcción *f* (work of constructing) || *public building* edificio público.

building lease [-liːs] *n* arriendo *m* enfitéutico.

building site [-sait]; **building lot** [-lɔt] *n* solar *m* (for sale, etc.) || obra *f* (under construction).

building society [-səˌsaiəti] *n* sociedad *f* de préstamo inmobiliario.

building trade [-treid] *n* construcción *f*.

buildup ['bildəp] *n* FIG aumento *m*; *a gradual buildup in the traffic* un aumento gradual de la circulación | concentración *f* (of forces) | propaganda *f*; *the film has had big buildup* se ha hecho mucha propaganda sobre esta película || elaboración *f* (development) || enredo *m* (in a drama).

built [bilt] *pret/pp* —→ **build**.

built-in [-'in] *adj* empotrado, da; *a built-in bookcase* una biblioteca empotrada || incorporado, da; *built-in aerial* antena incorporada.

built-up [-'ʌp] *adj* urbanizado, da; *built-up area* zona urbanizada.

bulb [bʌlb] *n* BOT bulbo *m* || ANAT bulbo *m* (enlargement) | bulbo *m* raquídeo (medulla oblongata) || cubeta *f* (of thermometer) || bombilla *f* (lamp).

bulbous ['bʌlbəs] *adj* bulboso, sa.

Bulgaria [bʌl'gɛəriə] *pr n* GEOGR Bulgaria *f*.

Bulgarian [-n] *adj/n* búlgaro, ra.

bulge [bəldʒ] *n* protuberancia *f* || pandeo *m* (in a wall) || FIG alza *f*; *bulge in the birthrate* alza en el índice de natalidad.

bulge [bʌldʒ] *vi* pandearse (to warp) || hincharse (to swell) || sobresalir (to project) || estar abultado (to be bulky).
◆ *vt* pandear (a wall) || abultar (to bulk).

bulging [-iŋ] *adj* abultado, da || hinchado, da (swollen) || pandeado, da (a wall) || *bulging eyes* ojos saltones.
◆ *n* abultamiento *m* || pandeo *m* (of a wall).

bulgy [-i] *adj* protuberante || abultado, da.

bulimia ['bjulimiə] *n* MED bulimia *f*.

bulk [bʌlk] *n* masa *f* (mass) || grosor *m*, espesor *m* (thickness) || volumen *m*, magnitud *f* (volume) || corpulencia *f* (corpulence) || la mayor parte *f*, la mayoría *f*; *the bulk of them are on holiday* la mayoría de ellos están de vacaciones || MAR carga *f* || — *in bulk* a granel, suelto, ta (not packaged) || MAR *to break bulk* desestibar.

bulk [bʌlk] *vt* amontonar (to pile up) || hinchar (to swell) || rellenar; *to bulk out a journal with advertisements* rellenar una revista con anuncios.
◆ *vi* abultar (to occupy space) || aumentar (to increase) || FIG *to bulk large* ser importante.

bulkhead [-hed] *n* MAR mamparo *m* (upright partition).

bulkiness [-inis] *n* volumen *m*, magnitud *f*.

bulky [-i] *adj* voluminoso, sa; abultado, da || pesado, da; de difícil manejo (difficult to handle).

Bull [bul] *n* ASTR Tauro *m*.

bull [bul] *adj* macho; *bull elephant, whale* elefante, ballena macho || grande (big) || en alza, que sube (values) || ECON *bull market* mercado *m* alcista || FIG *bull neck* cuello *m* de toro (short neck).
◆ *n* ZOOL toro *m*; *fighting bull* toro de lidia | macho *m* (of the elephant, whale, seal, etc.) || FIG & FAM bola *f*, trola *f* (lie) | tonterías *f pl*, sandeces *f pl*; *that article is a load of bull* ese artículo es una sarta de tonterías | toro *m* (strong man) || COMM alcista *m* || REL bula *f*; *Golden Bull* bula de oro || — FIG & FAM *to shoot the bull* charlar; *we spent the afternoon shooting the bull* hemos pasado la tarde charlando; decir ton… rías (to talk nonsense) | *to take the bull by* … *horns* coger al toro por los cuernos.

bull [bul] *vt* COMM hacer subir el valor … jugar al alza con (stocks) || COMM *to bull* … *market* jugar al alza.
◆ *vi* COMM subir (stocks).

bulla ['bulə] *n* bula *f* (Roman ornament).

bulldog [-dɔg] *n* «buldog» *m*, dogo *m* || F… bedel *m* (usher) || — POP *bulldog clip* clip *m* … pinza || FIG *bulldog edition* edición *f* de provi… cia (of a newspaper) || FIG & FAM *the bulla*… *breed* los ingleses [como hombres valientes…

bulldog [-dɔg] *vt* US derribar (un anim… agarrándolo por los cuernos.

bulldoze [-dəuz] *vt* mover (la tierra) con u… excavadora || FIG intimidar (to bully) || FIG *bulldoze one's way into* forzar la entrada … (a room), abrirse paso a codazos entre … crowd), meterse en (conversation).

bulldozer [-,dəuzə*] *n* «bulldozer» *m*, excavadora *f*.

bullet ['bulit] *n* bala *f*.

bulletin ['bulitin] *n* boletín *m* || MIL parte *m*, comunicado *m* || — US *bulletin board* tablón *m* de anuncios || *news bulletin* boletín informativo.

bulletproof ['bulitpru:f] *adj* a prueba de balas.

bullet wound ['bulitwu:nd] *n* balazo *m*.

bullfight ['bulfait] *n* corrida *f* [de toros].

bullfighter [-ə*] *n* torero *m*.

bullfighting [-iŋ] *n* tauromaquia *f* (art) || toros *m pl*; *I like bullfighting* me gustan los toros.

bullfinch ['bulfintʃ] *n* ZOOL piñonero *m*, pinzón *m* real.

bullfrog ['bulfrɔg] *n* ZOOL rana *f* mugidora.

bullhead ['bulhed] *n* ZOOL siluro *m* (fish).

bullheaded [-id] *adj* obstinado, da; terco, ca (obstinate) || impetuoso, sa (impetuous).

bullhorn ['bulhɔ:n] *n* US megáfono *m*.

bullion ['buljən] *n* oro *m or* plata *f* en lingotes *or* barras || entorchado *m* (fringe).

bullish ['buliʃ] *adj* COMM alcista, en alza || lleno, na de optimismo.

bullock ['bulək] *n* buey *m*, toro *m* castrado.

bullpen ['bulpen] *n* toril *m*.

bullring ['bulriŋ] *n* plaza *f* de toros (the whole stadium) || ruedo *m* (the central part).

bull session ['bul,seʃən] *n* US tertulia *f* (informal discussion).

bull's-eye ['bulzai] *n* blanco *m*, diana *f*; *to hit the bull's-eye, to score a bull's-eye* dar en el blanco || acierto *m*, tiro *m* que da en el blanco (shot) || FIG acierto *m* (remark) || caramelo *m* redondo y duro (sweet) || MAR ojo *m* de buey, portilla *f* (porthole) | guardacabo (thimble) || cristal *m* abombado (windowpane) || — *bull's-eye lens* lente abombada || ARCH *bull's-eye window* ojo de buey.

bullshit [bulʃit] *n* POP porquería *f* | jilipolladas *f pl* (nonsense).

bullterrier [bul'teriə*] *n* bulterrier *m* (dog).

bully ['buli] *n* peleón *m* (fighter) || SP saque *m* (in hockey) || carne *f* de vaca en conserva (beef).
◆ *adj* FAM formidable.
◆ *interj* *bully for you!* ¡qué bien!, ¡bravo!

bully ['buli] *vt* intimidar (to intimidate) || tiranizar (to tyrannize) || *to bully s.o. into doing sth.* forzar a alguien a que haga algo.
◆ *vi* fanfarronear.

bully beef [-'bi:f] *n* carne *f* de vaca en conserva.

bully-off [-ɔf] *n* SP saque *m*.

bumble ['bʌmbl] *vi* FAM fallar (to miss) | hablar a tropezones (to speak) | andar a tropezones (to walk) | dar traqueteos (a car) || zumbar (insects).
◆ *vt* → **bungle.**

bumblebee ['bʌmblbi:] *n* ZOOL abejorro *m*.

bumbling ['bʌmbliŋ] *adj* FAM torpe.

bumboat ['bʌmbəut] *n* barco *m* de aprovisionamiento.

bumf *n* FAM papeleo *m*.

bummer ['bʌmə*] *n* FAM sablista *m* & *f*, gorrón, ona.

bump [bʌmp] *n* choque *m*, topetón *m* (blow) || porrazo *m*, golpazo *m* (forceful blow) || sacudida *f* (jolt) || porrazo *m*, batacazo *m* (on falling) || chichón *m*, hinchazón *f* (swelling) || protuberancia *f*, bulto *m*, bollo *m* (lump) || choque *m* (in bumping race) || bache *m* (in the road).

bump [bʌmp] *vt* golpear, dar un golpe; *to bump one's head* darse un golpe en la cabeza || mantear (to toss s.o. up and down) || chocar contra (in boat racing) || TECH enderezar (metal) || — FIG *to bump off* cargarse (to kill) | *to bump one's head against the wall* dar con la cabeza contra la pared || FAM *to bump up* subir, aumentar (prices, production).
◆ *vi* darse un golpe, chocar; *to bump into* o *against the wall* darse un golpe contra la pared || — *fancy bumping into you!* ¡qué casualidad encontrarle aquí! || *to bump along* avanzar dando tumbos || FIG *to bump into* tropezar con (to meet).

bumper [-ə*] *adj* abundante; *bumper harvest* cosecha abundante || — *bumper cars* coches *m pl* que chocan || *bumper Christmas issue* edición *f* especial de Navidad || *bumper guard* tope *m*.
◆ *n* parachoques *m inv* (of a car) || (ant) vaso *m* lleno hasta el borde (of ale, etc.) || *bumper to bumper* en caravana (of traffic).

bumping post [-iŋ,pəust] *n* tope *m*.

bumpkin [-kin] *n* paleto *m*, cateto *m*, patán *m*.

bumptious [-ʃəs] *adj* presuntuoso, sa; engreído, da.

bumpy [-i] *adj* desigual, lleno de baches; *bumpy road* carretera llena de baches || zarandeado, da; *a bumpy journey* un viaje zarandeado.

bun [bʌn] *n* bollo *m* (cake) || moño *m* (chignon).

bunch [bʌntʃ] *n* ramo *m*, ramillete *m*; *a bunch of flowers* un ramo de flores || puñado *m* (handful) || manojo *m*; *six pencils tied in a bunch* seis lápices atados en un manojo || mechón *m* (of hair) || racimo *m* (of grapes, of bananas) || ristra *f* (of onions) || FAM grupo *m*, montón *m* …).

…ntʃ] *vt* atar en un manojo (to put …) || agrupar, juntar; *to bunch all the* … *t the end of the sentence* agrupar to… …jetivos al final de la frase || fruncir …
… *unch together* juntarse, agruparse.

…ndl] *n* bulto *m*, fardo *m*, lío *m*; *a* … *ld clothes* un bulto de ropa vieja …, haz *m*; *a bundle of firewood* un haz … millete *m* (of flowers) || — *bundle of* … *m* de papeles || FIG *to be a bundle* …r un manojo de nervios || FAM *to* … *dle with s.o.* pelearse con alguien.

…ndl] *vt* poner desordenadamente … *bundle off* despachar | *to bundle s.o.* …*t* poner a alguien de patitas en la … *dle up* atar en un bulto, liar; *to bun*… *old clothes* atar ropa vieja en un …

… *n* tapón *m*, bitoque *m* (of barrel).

Bully - peleón
intimidar
forzar a alguien que
haga algo
reñidor
agresivo
tiranizar

bung [bʌŋ] *vt* taponar [con bitoque] || FAM largar, arrojar; *bung that knife over here* lárgame ese cuchillo | poner (to put) || *to bung up* atascar, obturar, atorar (to clog up); *the carburettor is bunged up* el carburador está atascado; magullar (to bruise).

bungalow ['bʌŋgələu] *n* «bungalow» *m*, chalé *m*.

bunghole ['bʌŋhəul] *n* piquera *f*, boca *f* de tonel.

bungle ['bʌŋgl] *vt* chapucear; *to bungle a piece of work* chapucear un trabajo || FAM *to bungle it* desperdiciar una oportunidad (to miss one's chance), fastidiarlo (to mess it up).
◆ *vi* chapucear.

bungler [-ə*] *n* chapucero, ra.

bungling [-iŋ] *adj* chapucero, ra || torpe (clumsy).
◆ *n* torpeza *f*.

bunion ['bʌnjən] *n* juanete *m* (on the bit toe).

bunk [bʌŋk] *n* litera *f* (bed) || FAM tonterías *f pl* (nonsense) || *to do a bunk* tomar las de Villadiego (to run away).

bunk [bʌŋk] *vi* US acostarse | poner pies en polvorosa (to flee) || *to bunk down* dormir.

bunker [-ə*] *n* arcón *m* (large bin) || carbonera *f* (for fuel) || MAR pañol *m* del carbón || SP obstáculo *m* artificial, bunker *m* (golf) || MIL refugio *m* subterráneo | casamata *f*, bunquer *m*, bunker *m*.

bunker [-ə*] *vt* meter en la carbonera (fuel) || MAR abastecer de combustible (to fuel) || SP meter en un bunker (a ball) || FIG *to be bunkered* estar en un atolladero.
◆ *vi* MAR abastecerse de combustible, repóstar.

bunkhouse ['bʌŋkhaus] *n* barracón *m*.

bunkum ['bʌŋkəm] *m* tonterías *f pl* (bunk).

bunny ['bʌni] *n* conejito *m* (rabbit).

bunt [bʌnt] *n* seno *m* (of a net) || SP golpe *m* ligero [dado a la pelota] (baseball) || BOT tizón *m*, añublo *m*.

bunt [bʌnt] *vt/vi* golpear ligeramente [la pelota] (in baseball).

bunting [-iŋ] *n* ZOOL verderón *m* | estameña *f* (fabric) || MAR empavesado *m*, banderas *f pl*.

buntline [-lain] *n* MAR briol *m*.

buoy [bɔi] *n* MAR boya *f*; *light buoy* boya luminosa.

buoy [bɔi] *vt* mantener a flote (to keep afloat) || balizar, señalar con boyas (to mark with buoys) || FIG apoyar, sostener (to support) | alentar; *to buoy up s.o.'s hopes* alentar las esperanzas de uno.

buoyancy ['bɔiənsi] *n* flotabilidad *f*, facultad *f* de flotar || PHYS empuje *m* [de un fluido] || AVIAT fuerza *f* de sustentación || COMM firmeza *f* (of stock exchange) | estabilidad *f* (of prices) || FIG optimismo *m*.

buoyant ['bɔiənt] *adj* flotante, boyante (able to float) || FIG optimista (cheerful) || COMM sostenido, da (stock exchange).

bur [bəː*] *n* ⟶ **burr.**

burble ['bəːbl] *n* borboteo *m* (of water).

burble ['bəːbl] *vi* borbotar, borbollar (water) || FIG hacer gorgoritos (baby) | murmurar (brook) | hervir (with anger) || *to burble with laughter* reír ahogadamente.

burbot ['bəːbət] *n* ZOOL lota *f* (fish).

burden ['bəːdn] *n* carga *f* (load); *beast of burden* animal de carga || FIG carga *f*, gravamen *m* (moral) | peso *m*; *the burden of years* el peso de los años | carga *f*; *to be a burden to s.o.* ser una carga para alguien || MAR arqueo *m* || MUS estribillo *m* (refrain) | tema *m or* idea *f* central (of poem, of speech, etc.) || responsabilidad *f*; *the white man's burden* la responsabilidad de los blancos || JUR *burden of proof* carga de la prueba.

burden ['bəːden] *vt* cargar (to load) || FIG cargar; *I don't want to burden you with my problems* no te quiero cargar con mis problemas | gravar; *to burden the people with taxes* gravar a la población con impuestos | agobiar; *burdened with pain* agobiado de dolor.

burdensome [-səm] *adj* FIG pesado, da (heavy); *burdensome responsibility* responsabilidad pesada || oneroso, sa; gravoso, sa (expenses, etc.).

burdock ['bəːdɔk] *n* BOT bardana *f*.

bureau ['bjərəu] *n* escritorio *m*, mesa *f* (writing desk) || agencia *f*, oficina *f*; *employment bureau* agencia de colocaciones || mesa *f* (of a meeting) || US cómoda *f* (chest of drawers) | departamento *m* [del Estado].

bureaucracy [bjuə'rɔkrəsi] *n* burocracia *f*.

bureaucrat ['bjuərəu͵kræt] *n* burócrata *m* & *f*.

bureaucratic [͵bjuərəu'krætik] *adj* burocrático, ca.

burette; US **buret** [bjuə'ret] *n* CHEM bureta *f* (graduated glass tube).

burg [bəːg] *n* HIST burgo *m*.

burgee ['bəːdʒiː] *n* MAR gallardete *m*.

burgeon ['bəːdʒən] *n* BOT brote *m*, retoño *m*.

burgeon ['bəːdʒən] *vi* BOT brotar, retoñar || FIG desarrollarse.

burger ['bəːgə*] *n* FAM hamburguesa *f*.

burgess ['bəːdʒis] *n* ciudadano, na (citizen) || diputado *m* (Member of Parliament).

burgh ['bʌrə] *n* burgo *m*, villa *f* (in Scotland).

burgher ['bəːgə*] *n* burgués, esa; ciudadano, na.

burglar ['bəːglə*] *n* ladrón, ona.

burglar alarm [-ə'lɑːm] *n* alarma *f* antirrobo.

burglarize ['bəːgləraiz] *vi/vi* US robar con allanamiento de morada *or* con fractura.

burglary ['bəːgləri] *n* robo *m* con allanamiento de morada, robo *m* con fractura.

burgle ['bəːgl] *vt/vi* robar (con allanamiento de morada *or* con fractura).

burgomaster ['bəːgə͵mɑːstə*] *n* burgomaestre *m*.

Burgundian [bəː'gʌndjən] *adj/n* borgoñón, ona.

Burgundy ['bəːgəndi] *pr n* Borgoña *f*.

burial ['beriəl] *n* entierro *m*.

burial ground [-graund] *n* cementerio *m*, camposanto *m*.

burin ['bjuərin] *n* TECH buril *m*.

burk [bəːk] *n* POP berzotas *m* & *f inv*.

burl [bəːl] *n* mota *f* (in wool, thread or cloth) || US nudo *m* (in wood).

burl [bəːl] *vt* desmotar (cloth).

burlap ['bəːlæp] *n* arpillera *f*.

burlesque [bəː'lesk] *adj* burlesco, ca.
◆ *n* género *m* burlesco || parodia *f* || US espectáculo *m* de variedades.

burlesque [bəː'lesk] *vt* parodiar.

burly ['bəːli] *adj* fuerte, fornido, da.

Burma ['bəːmə] *pr n* GEOGR Birmania *f*.

Burmese [bəː'miːz] *adj/n* birmano, na.

burn [bəːn] *n* quemadura *f* (damage, injury) || arroyo *m* (brook).

burn* [bəːn] *vt* quemar; *to burn coal* quemar carbón; *he burnt his hand with acid* se quemó la mano con ácido || tostar (almonds) || funcionar con (to run on); *engine which burns diesel oil* motor que funciona con gasoil || gastar, consumir; *an appliance which burns a lot of electricity* un aparato que consume mucha electricidad || cocer (bricks) || calcinar (to calcine) || fundir (metals) || MED cauterizar, quemar (to cauterize) || FAM derrochar, tirar (money) | enfurecer, encolerizar (to anger) | engañar (to trick) || — *to be burned to death* morir quemado || FIG *to burn a hole in one's pocket* quemarle a uno en el bolsillo (money) || *to burn a hole in paper* hacer un agujero en el papel quemándolo || *to burn a house to the ground* incendiar completamente una casa || FIG *to burn one's bridges* o *one's ships* quemar las naves | *to burn the midnight oil* quemarse las pestañas || *to burn to ashes* reducir a cenizas || *to have a burnt taste* saber a quemado.
◆ *vi* arder; *the fire is burning brightly* el fuego está ardiendo vivamente || quemarse, arder; *the house is burning* la casa está ardiendo || quemarse; *if you sit in the sun you will burn* si te sientas al sol te quemarás || estar encendido; *the light is burning* la lámpara está encendida || BOT abrasarse, quemarse (plants) || escocer (a sore) || FIG arder; *to burn with rage* arder de ira || CULIN quemarse, pegarse || quemarse (in games) || — FIG *to burn to* o *to burn with desire for* desear ardientemente | *to burn with impatience* consumirse de impaciencia.
◆ *phr v* ***to burn away*** consumirse || ***to burn down*** incendiar (to set fire to) | incendiarse || ***to burn in*** marcar a fuego || ***to burn into*** quemar (acid) | FIG grabar en || ***to burn off*** quemar || ***to burn out*** quemar | consumirse | extinguirse, apagarse (light, fire) | fundirse (bulb, fuse) | hacer salir por medio del fuego || ***to burn up*** consumir completamente | consumirse completamente | abrasar (to scorch) | enfurecer (to make angry) | enfurecerse (to become angry).
— OBSERV Pret y pp ***burnt, burned***.

burner [-ə*] *n* quemador *m*; *gas burner* quemador de gas || mechero *m*; *Bunsen burner* mechero Bunsen.

burnet [-it] *n* BOT pimpinela *f*.

burning [-iŋ] *adj* ardiente, abrasador, ra; *beneath a burning sun* bajo un sol abrasador || FIG ardiente; *to have a burning desire to do sth.* tener un deseo ardiente de hacer algo || — FIG *a burning question* una cuestión candente || *it's burning hot* está que quema (food), hace un calor abrasador (weather).
◆ *n* quemadura *f* (burn, sunburn) || ardor *m* (in the mouth, etc.) || incendio *m* (fire) || abrasamiento *m*, quemadura *f* (of plants) || cocción *f* (of bricks) || combustión *f*.

burning bush [-iŋ'buʃ] *n* BOT bonetero *m* (wahoo) || REL zarza *f* ardiente.

burning glass [-iŋ'glɑːs] *n* espejo *m* ustorio (mirror that concentrates the sun's rays).

burnish [-iʃ] *n* bruñido *m*, pulido *m*, brillo *m*.

burnish [-iʃ] *vt* bruñir, pulir.

burnous [bəː'nuːs] *n* albornoz *m*.

burnt [bəːnt] *pret/pp* ⟶ **burn.**

burnt offering [-ɔfəriŋ] *n* REL holocausto *m* (sacrifice).

burnt-out [-'aut] *adj* apagado, da || consumido, da.

burp [bəːp] *n* eructo *m*.

burp [bəːp] *vt* US hacer eructar (a child).
◆ *vi* eructar.

burr; bur [bəː*] *n* BOT cubierta *f* espinosa | erizo *m* (of chestnut) || pronunciación *f* gutural de la *r* || acento *m* rústico *or* basto || zumbido *m* (sound) || torno *m*, fresa *f* (dentistry) || TECH rebaba *f* (roughness) | arandela *f* (washer) | piedra *f* amoladera (whetstone) || halo *m* luminoso (round the moon, etc.) || BOT nudo *m* (on wood) || US FAM lapa *f*, persona *f* pegajosa.

burr [bəː*] *vi* pronunciar guturalmente la *r* || zumbar (to make a humming sound).

burrow ['bʌrəu] *n* madriguera *f* (animal's hole) || conejera *f* (rabbit's hole) || FIG escondrijo *m*.

burrow ['bʌrəu] *vt* excavar, cavar || *to burrow one's way into* cavar la tierra para entrar en.
◆ *vi* hacer una madriguera (animals) || esconderse (people) || FIG *to burrow into an affair* ahondar en un asunto.

bursa ['bə:sə] *n* ANAT bolsa *f*, saco *m*.

bursar ['bə:sə*] *n* tesorero, ra (of a college) || becario, ria (holder of a scholarship).

bursary [-ri] *n* tesorería *f* (accounts office) || beca *f* (scholarship).

burst [bə:st] *n* estallido *m*, explosión *f* || reventón *m* (of a tyre) || MIL ráfaga *f* (of fire) || — FIG *burst of activity* explosión *f* de actividad | *burst of anger* arranque *m* de cólera | *burst of applause* salva *f* de aplausos | *burst of laughter* carcajada *f* | *burst of speed* sprint *m* (in sport), carrera *f* (running faster), aceleración *f* (of a car).

burst* [bə:st] *vi* estallar, reventar, explotar; *the pipe has burst* la cañería ha reventado || romperse (dam) || reventar, abrirse (bud) || estallar; *to burst into flames* estallar en llamas || irrumpir (into a room) || FIG desencadenarse (storm) | brillar repentinamente (sun) | prorrumpir, deshacerse; *to burst into tears* deshacerse en lágrimas | reventar; *to burst with laughter* reventar de risa; *to burst with impatience* reventar de impaciencia | rebosar; *he is bursting with health* rebosa de salud || — FIG *to be bursting to do sth.* reventar por hacer algo | *to be full to bursting* estar lleno a reventar, estar reventando | *to burst forth* brotar (from the ground), salir a chorro (to spurt out), abrirse (flowers) | *to burst into song* romper a cantar | *to burst into view* aparecer repentinamente | *to burst open* abrirse violentamente | *to burst out* salir corriendo (of a room), gritar (to shout) | *to burst out laughing* echarse a reír, prorrumpir en carcajadas || *to burst with* reventar de (laughter, eating), rebosar de (emotion, etc.).
◆ *vt* reventar, explotar; *to burst a balloon with a pin* reventar un globo con un alfiler || — *the river will burst its banks* el río se va a salir de madre || *to burst open the door* abrir la puerta de golpe.
— OBSERV Pret y pp ***burst***.

bursting [-iŋ] *adj* muy lleno, na; a rebosar || FAM *bursting at the seams* hasta los topes, a rebosar.

burton ['bə:tn] *n* TECH aparejo *m*, polipasto *m* || FIG & FAM *to go for a burton* fastidiarse.

bury ['beri] *vt* enterrar; *the dog is burying a bone* el perro está enterrando un hueso || sepultar, enterrar (a body) || FIG esconder, ocultar; *he buried his face in his hands* escondió la cara entre las manos || — FIG *buried memories* recuerdos sepultados | *to be buried in thought* estar ensimismado, estar absorto en sus pensamientos || *to bury at sea* dar sepultura en el mar || FIG *to bury one's head in the sand* esconder la cabeza debajo del ala | *to bury o.s. in a book* enfrascarse en la lectura | *to bury o.s. in the country* enterrarse en el campo | *to bury the hatchet* enterrar el hacha de la guerra.

burying beetle ['beriiŋ,bi:tl] *n* ZOOL enterrador *m*.

bus [bʌs] *n* autobús *m* || INFORM bus *m* || — *bus conductor* cobrador, ra || *bus line* línea *f* de autobuses || FIG *to miss the bus* perder la ocasión *or* la oportunidad.

bus [bʌs] *vi* ir en autobús.
◆ *vt* llevar en autobús.

busboy [-bɔi] *n* US mozo *m*, ayudante *m* de camarero (in a restaurant).

busby ['bʌzbi] *n* MIL gorro *m* alto de piel negra.

bush [buʃ] *n* arbusto *m*, matorral *m* (shrub) || breña *f* (rough country) || monte *m* (in Australia) || HIST ramo *m* de hiedra [que indica la venta de vino] || TECH cojinete *m* (bearing) | forro *m* (lining) || FIG & FAM *to beat about the bush* andarse con rodeos.

bush [buʃ] *vi* crecer espesamente.
◆ *vt* poner arbustos en || TECH forrar.

bush baby [-,beibi] *n* ZOOL lemúrido *m*.

bushed [buʃt] *adj* cubierto de malezas || FAM agotado, da; hecho polvo (exhausted).

bushel ['buʃl] *n* medida *f* de áridos.
— OBSERV En Inglaterra esta medida equivale a 36,367 litros y en Estados Unidos a 35,237 litros.

bushhammer ['buʃ,hæmə*] *n* escoda *f*.

bushiness ['buʃinis] *n* espesor *m* (of foliage).

bushing [buʃiŋ] *n* TECH cojinete *m* (bearing) | forro *m* (lining).

bushman ['buʃmən] *n* campesino *m* australiano.

Bushman ['buʃmən] *adj/n* bosquimano, na.

bushranger ['buʃ,reindʒə*] *n* HIST bandido *m*.

bush telegraph ['buʃ,teligrɑ:f] *n* FIG radio *f* macuto.

bushwhacker ['buʃwækə*] *n* montonero *m*, guerrillero *m*.

bushy ['buʃi] *adj* breñoso, sa (ground) || parecido a un arbusto (plant) || tupido, da; espeso, sa; *a bushy moustache* bigotes espesos.

busily ['bizili] *adv* afanosamente.

business ['biznis] *n* negocios *m pl*; *in the business world* en el mundo de los negocios || negocio *m*, comercio *m*, empresa *f*; *to run a television repair business* llevar un negocio de reparaciones de televisores || empleo *m*, ocupación *f*, oficio *m* (occupation) || profesión *f* (profession) || asunto *m*, cuestión *f*; *as regards the business of the broken window* en cuanto al asunto de la ventana rota || asunto *m* (personal); *that is your business* eso es asunto tuyo || — *big business* grandes negocios || *business as usual* continúa la venta en el interior || *business before pleasure* primero es la obligación que la devoción || *business card* tarjeta *f* comercial || *business college* escuela *f* de comercio || *business connections* relaciones *f* de negocio || *business cycle* ciclo *m* comercial || *business deal* trato *m* comercial || *business district* zona *f* comercial || *business hours* horas *f* de trabajo || *business is business* los negocios son los negocios || *business letterhead* membrete *m* || *business machines* máquinas *f* de oficina || *business of the day* orden *m* del día || *business premises* local *m sing* comercial || *business reply envelope* sobre *m* con franqueo concertado || *business school* escuela *f* de comercio || *business suit* traje *m* de calle || *business trip* viaje *m* de negocios || *good business!* ¡perfecto!, ¡bien hecho! || *it's my business* eso es cosa mía || *it's my business to do it* me corresponde hacerlo || *it's no business of mine* no tengo nada que ver con eso, no es asunto mío || *it's none of your business* no es asunto tuyo, a ti qué te importa || *I will make it my business to* me encargaré de || *to be in a place on business* estar en un sitio por razones profesionales || *to be sick of the whole business* estar harto del asunto || *to do business with* comerciar con || FIG *to get down to business* ir al grano || FIG & FAM *to give one the business* darle una zurra a uno (to beat), despachar *or* pasaportar a uno (to kill) || *to go about one's business* ocuparse de sus asuntos || *to have no business to do sth.* no tener derecho de hacer algo, no tener por qué hacer algo || *to make it one's business to do sth.* proponerse hacer algo || FAM *to mean business* hablar *or* actuar en serio | *to mind one's own business* no meterse donde no le llaman, ocuparse de sus propios asuntos | *to send s.o. about his business* mandarle a uno a paseo || *to set up in business as a butcher* montar un negocio de carnicería || FAM *what a business!* ¡qué lío!

businesslike [-laik] *adj* serio, ria; formal (seriousminded) || práctico, ca; eficaz (practical-minded) || metódico, ca; ordenado, da (methodical).

businessman [-mən] *n* hombre *m* de negocios.
— OBSERV El plural de *businessman* es *businessmen*.

businesswoman [-'wumən] *n* mujer *f* de negocios.
— OBSERV El plural es *businesswomen*.

busker ['bʌskə*] *n* músico *m* ambulante.

buskin ['bʌskin] *n* borceguí *m* (half boot) || coturno *m* (worn by greek actors).

busman ['bʌsmən] *n* conductor *m* de autobús (driver) || cobrador *m* de autobús (conductor) || FIG *busman's holiday* día *m* de fiesta que uno pasa trabajando.
— OBSERV El plural de *busman* es *busmen*.

bus stop ['bʌs-stɔp] *n* parada *f* de autobús.

bust [bʌst] *n* busto *m* (sculpture) || busto *m*, pecho *m* [de mujer] || FAM reventón *m* (burst) | juerga *f* (spree); *he went on a bust* fue de juerga | fracaso *m* (failure) | quiebra *f* (bankruptcy) || *bust measurement* perímetro torácico.
◆ *adj* FAM destrozado, da; hecho polvo (broken) | reventado, da (burst) | en bancarrota; arruinado, da (bankrupt) || FAM *to go bust* quebrar.

bust [bʌst] *vt* FAM destrozar, hacer polvo (to break) || COMM llevar a la quiebra || domar (a horse) || FAM dar un puñetazo a.
◆ *vi* FAM hacerse polvo | reventar (laughing) | fracasar (to fail) || COMM quebrar.

bustard ['bʌstəd] *n* ZOOL avutarda *f* (bird).

bustle ['bʌsl] *n* bullicio *m*, agitación *f*, animación *f*; *the bustle of the market place* la animación del mercado || HIST polisón *m* (of a skirt).

bustle ['bʌsl] *vi* ir y venir, apresurarse, ajetrearse.
◆ *vt* apresurar.

bustling [-iŋ] *adj* bullicioso, sa (place) || activo, va (person).

bust-up ['bʌst ʌp] *n* FAM pelea *f*.

busy ['bizi] *adj* ocupado, da; atareado, da; *she was busy sewing* estaba ocupada cosiendo; *I had a very busy day* tuve un día muy ocupado || concurrido, da; bullicioso, sa; *a busy street* una calle muy concurrida || ocupado, da (telephone line) || — FIG *busy as a bee* muy ocupado || *busy hours* horas *f* punta || US *busy signal* señal *f* de comunicando | *it is busy* está comunicando (telephone) || *to get busy* ponerse a trabajar || *to keep busy* estar ocupado (o.s.), ocupar (s.o.).

busy ['bizi] *vt* ocupar || *to busy o.s. about the house* ocuparse en las tareas domésticas.

busybody [-,bɔdi] *n* entrometido, da.

but [bʌt] *conj* pero, mas; *the work is hard, but you are well paid* el trabajo es duro, pero te pagan bien || sino (with «not»); *he is not poor, but rich* no es pobre sino rico || sino que (with «not» and a verb); *he told her not to stay, but to go to the cinema* le dijo que no se quedase sino que fuese al cine || sin (without); *I can't speak to him but I get annoyed* no puedo hablar con él sin enfadarme || sin que; *he never speaks but she contradicts him* nunca habla sin que ella le contradiga || que; *I don't doubt but he will answer* no dudo que conteste || al menos; *you can but try it* al menos puede probarlo.
◆ *adv* no más que, nada más que, solamente, sólo, no... sino; *she is but a child* no es

(nada) más que una niña, no es sino una niña; *you have but to tell me* no tienes más que decírmelo, sólo tienes que decírmelo; *it is nothing but meanness* no es (nada) más que mezquindad, no es sino mezquindad; *I saw her but a moment ago* sólo hace un momento que la vi, la vi hace nada más que un momento || *had I but known* si lo hubiera sabido.
◆ *prep* excepto, salvo, menos; *any day but Thursday suits me* me conviene cualquier día excepto los jueves; *all but they o but them* todos salvo ellos || sino; *what could I do but say yes?* ¿qué podía hacer sino decir que sí? || — *all but* casi, medio (almost); *he was all but dead with fatigue* estaba medio muerto de cansancio || *but for* sin, a no ser por (without); *you couldn't have done it but for him* no hubiera podido hacerlo sin él || *last but one* penúltimo, ma || *the last but two* el segundo antes del último, el antepenúltimo.
◆ *n* pero *m* || *there are no buts about it* no hay pero que valga.

butadiene [ˌbjutəˈdiːn] *n* CHEM butadieno *m*.

butane [ˈbjutein] *n* CHEM butano *m* || *butane gas* gas *m* butano.

butch [butʃ] *adj* POP marimacho, machorra (woman) | macho, machote (man).

butcher [ˈbutʃə*] *n* carnicero, ra || FIG & FAM carnicero, ra (bad surgeon) | sanguinario, ria (cruel person) || *butcher's* carnicería *f*.

butcher [ˈbutʃə*] *vt* matar (animals) || FIG hacer una carnicería con (to kill cruelty) | destrozar (a piece of work).

butcher-bird [-bəːd] *n* alcaudón *m*.

butcher's broom [ˈbutʃəːzˈbruːm] *n* BOT brusco *m*.

butchery [ˈbutʃəri] *n* carnicería *f* || FIG carnicería *f*, matanza *f*.

butler [ˈbʌtlə*] *n* mayordomo *m*.

butt [bʌt] *n* extremo *m* (end) || culata *f*; *rifle butt* culata de fusil || tonel *m*, pipa *f* (barrel) || aljibe *m* (for rainwater) || pie *m*, base *f* (of a plant) || tocón *m* (of a tree) || colilla *f* (of cigarette) || pez *m* plano (flatfish) || blanco *m* (target) || FIG blanco *m*; *to be the butt of other people's jokes* ser el blanco de las bromas de otros || topetazo *m*, cabezazo *m* (blow) || cuero *m* curtido del lomo (leather) || US FAM trasero *m* (buttocks).
◆ *pl* campo *m sing* de tiro al blanco.

butt [bʌt] *vt* topar (a ram) || dar un golpe con la cabeza (a person) || ensamblar, empalmar, unir a tope (to join).
◆ *vi* dar topetazos (a ram) || dar golpes con la cabeza || golpearse (to bump) || FIG *to butt in* meterse en (a conversation).

butter [ˈbʌtə*] *n* mantequilla *f*; *fresh, salted, melted, browned butter* mantequilla fresca, salada, derretida, requemada || — *butter dish* mantequera *f* || *butter knife* cuchillo *m* para la mantequilla || FIG *butter wouldn't melt in his mouth* es una mosquita muerta.

butter [ˈbʌtə*] *vt* untar con mantequilla (to spread with butter) || guisar con mantequilla (to cook with butter) || FIG *to butter up* hacer la pelotilla a (to flatter).

butter bean [-biːn] *n* BOT judía *f*.

buttercup [-kʌp] *n* BOT ranúnculo *m*, botón *m* de oro.

butterfat [-fæt] *n* grasa *f* de la leche.

butterfingers [-ˌfiŋgəz] *n* torpe *m* & *f*, manazas *m* & *f* || *to be a butterfingers* tener manos de trapo.

butterfly [-flai] *n* mariposa *f* || SP braza *f* mariposa (in swimming) || FIG mariposón, ona || FIG *to have butterflies in one's stomach* tener un cosquilleo en el estómago.

butterfly nut [-flaiˌnʌt] *n* TECH tuerca *f* de mariposa.

butterfly valve [-flaiˌvælv] *n* TECH válvula *f* de mariposa.

butteris [-is] *n* pujavante *m*.

buttermilk [-milk] *n* suero *m* (de la leche).

butterscotch [-skɔtʃ] *n* caramelo *m* de azúcar con mantequilla.

buttery [ˈbʌtəri] *adj* mantecoso, sa || FIG & FAM pelotillero, ra (adulator).
◆ *n* despensa *f* (storeroom).

butt hinge [ˈbʌtˌhindʒ] *n* bisagra *f*.

butt joint [ˈbʌtˌdʒɔint] *n* TECH junta *f* a tope.

buttock [ˈbʌtək] *n* nalga *f*.
◆ *pl* FAM trasero *m sing* (of a person) || grupa *f sing* (of a horse).

button [ˈbʌtn] *n* botón *m*; *coat button* botón de abrigo || botón *m*, pulsador *m* (on machine, on bell, etc.); *to press the button* pulsar el botón || tirador *m* (of a door) || BOT botón *m*, yema *f*, capullo *m* (bud) || SP botón *m*, zapata *f* (in fencing) || US insignia *f*, distintivo *m* (badge) || — FAM *on the button* perfecto, ta (perfect), en punto (right on time) | *to be a button short* ser duro de entendederas.
◆ *pl* botones *m sing* (hotel errand boy).

button [ˈbʌtn] *vt* abrochar, abotonar; *to button up one's overcoat* abrocharse el abrigo || poner botones en || FIG & FAM *button your lip!* ¡cósete la boca!
◆ *vi* abrocharse (to fasten) || tener botones || FIG & FAM *to button up* coserse la boca.

buttonhole [-həul] *n* ojal *m* (stitched slit) || presilla *f* (loop) || flor *m* que se lleva en el ojal (flower) || *buttonhole stitch* punto *m* de ojal.

buttonhole [-həul] *vt* hacer ojales en (to make buttonholes in) || FIG enganchar (to detain).

buttonhook [-huk] *n* abrochador *m*.

buttress [ˈbʌtris] *n* ARCH contrafuerte *m* || GEOGR estribación *f* || FIG apoyo *m*, sostén *m*.

buttress [ˈbʌtris] *vt* ARCH apuntalar, reforzar || FIG apoyar, reforzar; *to buttress up one's theory with statistics* apoyar una teoría con estadísticas.

buttstock [ˈbʌtstɔk] *n* culata *f* (of firearm).

butt weld [ˈbʌtweld] *n* TECH soldadura *f* a tope.

butty [ˈbʌti] *n* FAM bocadillo *m*, sandwich *m*.

butyl [ˈbjutil] *n* CHEM butilo *m*.

butylene [-iːn] *n* CHEM butileno *m*.

butyric [bjuˈtirik] *adj* CHEM butírico, ca.

buxom [ˈbʌksəm] *adj* metida en carnes (woman) || rollizo, za (baby).

buy [bai] *n* compra *f* (purchase) || *good buy* ganga *f*, buena compra (bargain).

buy* [bai] *vt* comprar (to purchase); *I bought a house* compré una casa || sobornar, comprar (to bribe); *he cannot be bought* no se le puede sobornar || — FIG & FAM *I'll buy it* me doy por vencido, me rindo (I give in) | *they'll never buy it* no se lo tragarán, no cuajará || *to buy back* volver a comprar || *to buy off* librarse de alguien comprándole || MIL *to buy o.s. out* redimirse (del servicio militar) pagando || *to buy out* comprar la parte de (a partner, etc.) || *to buy over* sobornar || *to buy up* comprar (grandes cantidades de), acaparar.
◆ *vi* comprar || *to buy into* comprar acciones de (a company).
— OBSERV Pret y pp ***bought***.

buyer [-ə*] *n* comprador, ra || COMM *head buyer* jefe *m* de compras.

buyer's market [baiəːzˈmɑːkit] *n* mercado *m* favorable al comprador.

buy-out [-aut] *n* COMM compra *f*; *management buy-out* compra *f* de una empresa por parte de sus ejecutivos.

buzz [bʌz] *n* zumbido *m* (of bees, etc.) || cuchicheo *m* (whispering) || murmullo *m*; *buzz of conversation* murmullo de voces || FAM telefonazo *m* (call).

buzz [bʌz] *vt* murmurar al oído de (to whisper) || pasar rozando to (to fly low and fast over) || FAM llamar, dar un telefonazo a.
◆ *vi* zumbar (to make a humming sound) || murmurar, cuchichear (to murmur) || FIG circular; *the rumour buzzed round the village* el rumor circuló por todo el pueblo || — *the hall buzzed with anticipation* se oyó el murmullo de expectación en la sala || *to buzz about o around* zascandilear || FIG & FAM *to buzz off* largarse.

buzzard [ˈbʌzəd] *n* ZOOL águila *f* ratonera (hawk) | buitre *m* (vulture).

buzzer [ˈbʌzə*] *n* zumbador *m*.

buzzing [ˈbʌziŋ] *n* zumbido *m*.

buzz saw [ˈbʌz-sɔː] *n* TECH sierra *f* circular.

buzzword [ˈbʌzwəːd] *n* FAM palabra *f* pegadiza.

by [bai] *prep* por; *painted by a famous artist* pintado por un artista famoso; *to go by the quickest road* ir por el camino más rápido; *to win by five minutes* ganar por cinco minutos; *by rail* por ferrocarril; *to travel by sea* viajar por mar o vía marítima; *to take s.o. by the hand* coger a uno por la mano; *to swear by God* jurar por Dios; *panel of wood sixty inches by twenty* panel de madera de sesenta pulgadas por veinte; *to be paid by the hour* estar pagado por horas || MATH por (multiplicación); *to multiply four by nine* multiplicar cuatro por nueve | entre; *to divide ten by five* dividir diez entre cinco || al lado de, junto a, cerca de (beside, near); *to sit by the fire* sentarse junto al fuego; *I walked by the house this morning* pasé al lado de la casa esta mañana || según, de acuerdo con (according to); *to go by the rules* actuar según las reglas || de (at); *by night* de noche || de (origin); *Spanish by blood* de sangre española || de (from); *two children by a previous wife* dos niños de una esposa anterior || para (not later than); *we must be there by three o'clock* tendremos que estar allí para las tres; *by then* para entonces || antes de; *by the end of the century* antes de fines de siglo || con; *what do you mean by that?* ¿qué quiere decir con eso? || en (in); *to go by car, by boat* ir en coche, en barco || a (on); *to travel by horse* ir a caballo | a (indicating progression); *little by little* poco a poco; *day by day* día a día; *to go forward by small steps, by leaps and bounds* avanzar a pequeños pasos, a pasos agigantados || a, por (indicating quantity); *they died by the thousand* murieron a millares; *by hundreds* por centenares || — *by appearances* por las apariencias || *by chance* por casualidad || *by far* con mucho || *by heart* de memoria || *by lamplight* a la luz de la lámpara || *by me, by you, by him* a mi lado, a tu lado, a su lado || *by means of* mediante, por medio de || *by now* ya || *by o.s.* solo, la || *by studying you can pass your exam* estudiando puedes aprobar el examen || *by the dozen* por docenas || *by the light of* a la luz de || *by the by* por cierto, a propósito (incidentally), de paso (in passing) || *made by hand* hecho a mano || *north by east* norte cuarta al nordeste || *side by side* lado a lado || *to be known by the name of* ser conocido por or con el nombre de || *to cut production by a quarter* reducir la producción en una cuarta parte.
◆ *adv* al lado, cerca, delante; *he walked by without greeting us* pasó delante sin saludarnos || a un lado, aparte; *to put some money by* poner dinero a un lado || — *by and by* luego, más tarde || *by and large* en general || *close by* muy cerca || *gone by* pasado, da; *in years gone by* en años pasados.

by-by; bye-bye [ˈbaibai] *interj* FAM adiós, hasta luego.

bye [bai] *n* SP carrera *f* hecha sin haber golpeado la pelota (cricket) | hoyo *m* que queda sin ser jugado (golf) | jugador que queda de non.

by-election; bye-election [ˈbaiiˌlekʃən] *n* elección *f* parcial.

byelaw [ˈbailɔː] *n* —› **bylaw.**

bygone [ˈbaigɔn] *adj* pasado, da; del pasado. ◆ *n* cosa *f* pasada ‖ *let bygones be bygones* olvidemos lo pasado; lo pasado, pasado está.

bylaw; byelaw [ˈbailɔː] *n* ordenanza *f* municipal (of a local authority) ‖ estatuto *m* (statute) ‖ reglamento *m* (regulations).

byname [ˈbaiˌneim] *n* apodo *m* (nickname).

bypass [ˈbaipɑːs] *n* carretera *f* de circunvalación ‖ TECH tubo *m* de desviación ‖ ELECTR derivación *f* ‖ MED *bypass operation* bypass *m*.

bypass [ˈbaipɑːs] *vt* desviar; *to bypass the traffic* desviar el tráfico ‖ evitar (to avoid).

bypath [ˈbaipɑːθ] *n* camino *m*, vereda *f*.

byplay [ˈbaiplei] *n* THEATR juego *m* escénico secundario | aparte *m* (in conversation).

by-product [ˈbaiˌprɔdʌkt] *n* subproducto *m*, derivado *m* ‖ FIG consecuencia *f*.

byre [baiə*] *n* establo *m*, vaquería *f*.

byroad [ˈbairəud] *n* carretera *f* secundaria.

Byronic [baiˈrɔnik] *adj* byroniano, na.

bystander [ˈbaiˌstændə*] *n* espectador, ra; mirón, ona; curioso, sa (onlooker) ‖ persona *f* presente ‖ *several innocent bystanders were injured* varios inocentes fueron heridos.

bystreet [ˈbaistriːt] *n* callejuela *f*, calle *f* lateral *or* secundaria.

byte [bait] *n* INFORM byte *m*.

byway [ˈbaiwei] *n* camino *m* apartado.

byword [ˈbaiwəːd] *n* comidilla *f*; *he is the byword of the village* es la comidilla del pueblo ‖ dicho *m* (familiar saying) ‖ refrán *m*, proverbio *m* (proverb) ‖ prototipo *m* (type).

Byzantine [biˈzæntain] *adj/n* bizantino, na.

Byzantium [biˈzæntiəm] *pr n* HIST Bizancio.

C

c [siː] C *f* (letter).

C [siː] *n* MUS do *m*.

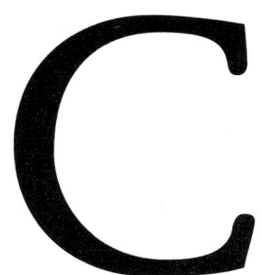

cab [kæb] *n* taxi *m* || cabina *f* (cabin of truck, of locomotive, etc.) || cabriolé *m* (horse-drawn carriage).

cabal [kəˈbæl] *n* cábala *f* (plot) || camarilla *f*, grupo *m* de conspiradores (association of persons) || HIST gabinete *m* secreto de ministros que gobernó Inglaterra bajo Carlos II.

cabal [kəˈbæl] *vi* conspirar, intrigar.

cabala [kəˈbɑlə] *n* REL cábala *f*.

cabalistic [ˌkæbəˈlistik] *adj* cabalístico, ca.

cabaret [ˈkæbərei] *n* cabaret *m* (establishment) || atracciones *f pl*, espectáculo *m* (entertainment).

cabbage [ˈkæbidʒ] *n* col *f*, berza *f* || *cabbage white* mariposa *f* de la col.

cabbage palm [-pɑːm]; **tree** [-triː] *n* BOT palma *f* real, palmito *m*.

cabby [ˈkæbi] *n* FAM taxista *m* & *f* || cocher *m* (of a carriage).

cabdriver [ˈkæbˌdraivə*] *n* US taxista *m* & *f*.

cabin [ˈkæbin] *n* cabaña *f*, choza *f* (small house) || MAR camarote *m* || cabina *f* (of plane, etc.).

cabin boy [-bɔi] *n* MAR camarero *m* de a bordo (servant) | grumete *m* (sailor).

cabin class [-klɑːs] *n* MAR segunda *f* clase.

cabin cruiser [-ˌkruːzə*] *n* MAR yate *m* de recreo.

cabinet [ˈkæbinit] *n* armario *m* (cupboard) || bargueño *m* (piece of furniture with drawers) || vitrina *f* (for display) || caja *f* (of a radio) || gabinete *m*, consejo *m* de ministros (ministers) || *cabinet council* consejo *m* de ministros || *medicine cabinet* botiquín *m*.

cabinetmaker [-ˌmeikə*] *n* ebanista *m*.

cabinetmaking [-ˌmeikiŋ] *n* ebanistería *f*.

cable [ˈkeibl] *n* cable *m* (rope) || cablegrama *m*, telegrama *m* (message) || *overhead cable* línea eléctrica aérea.

cable [ˈkeibl] *vt/vi* cablegrafiar, telegrafiar.

cable address [-əˈdres] *n* dirección *f* telegráfica.

cable car [-kɑː*] *n* teleférico *m* (telpher) || funicular *m* (cable railway).

cablegram [-græm] *n* cablegrama *m*, telegrama *m*.

cable length [-leŋθ] *n* MAR cable *m*.

cable railway [-ˈreilwei] *n* funicular *m*.

cable ship [-ʃip] *n* MAR cablero *m*.

cablet [-it] *n* MAR cabo *m* pequeño.

cable tape [-teip] *n* ELECTR cinta *f* aisladora.

cabman [ˈkæbmən] *n* taxista *m* & *f* || cochero *m* (of a carriage).
— OBSERV El plural de *cabman* es *cabmen*.

cabochon [ˈkæbəʃən] *n* cabujón *m* (gem).

caboodle [kəˈbuːdl] *n* FAM *the whole caboodle* toda la pesca.

caboose [kəˈbuːs] *n* MAR cocina *f* || US furgón *m* de cola (of a train) | cabaña *f* (cabin).

cabotage [ˈkæbətɑːʒ] *n* AVIAT cabotaje *m*.

cab rank [ˈkæb-ræŋk] *n* parada *f* de taxis.

cabriole [ˈkæbriɔul] *n* pata *f* encorvada de los muebles estilo reina Ana y Chippendale.

cabriolet [ˌkæbriəˈlei] *n* cabriolé *m*.

cab stand [kæbstænd] *n* parada *f* de taxis.

cacao [kəˈkɑːəu] *n* BOT cacao *m* || — BOT *cacao bean* cacao *m* || *cacao butter* manteca *f* de cacao.

cachalot [ˈkæʃəlɔt] *n* ZOOL cachalote *m*.

cache [kæʃ] *n* escondite *m*, escondrijo *m* (hiding place) || reserva *f* escondida (of food, etc.).

cache [kæʃ] *vt* esconder, poner en un escondrijo.

cachectic [kəˈkektik] *adj* MED caquéctico, ca.

cachet [ˈkæʃei] *n* MED sello *m*, cápsula *f* (capsule) || FIG sello *m*; *a work which bears the cachet of genius* una obra que lleva el sello del genio.

cachexia [kəˈkeksiə]; **cachexy** [kəˈkeksy] *n* MED caquexia *f*.

cachinnate [ˈkækineit] *vi* (ant) reír a carcajadas.

cachou [ˈkæʃuː] *n* cachú *m*.

cacique [kæˈsiːk] *n* cacique *m*.

cackle [ˈkækl] *n* cacareo *m* (of hen) || FIG & FAM risa *f* aguda (raucous laugh) | cháchara *f* (idle talk) || FIG & FAM *cut the cackle* corta y navega, corta el rollo.

cackle [ˈkækl] *vi* cacarear (hen) || FIG & FAM chacharear (to talk) | reírse agudamente (to laugh).

cacochymy [ˈkækəuˌkimi] *n* cacoquimia *f*.

cacodylate [kækəˈdileit] *n* CHEM cacodilato *m*.

cacophonous [kæˈkɔfənəs] *adj* cacofónico, ca.

cacophony [kæˈkɔfəni] *n* cacofonía *f*.

cactaceous [kækˈteiʃəs] *adj* BOT cactáceo, a; cácteo, a.

cactus [ˈkæktəs] *n* BOT cactus *m*, cacto *m*.
— OBSERV El plural de *cactus* es *cacti*.

cad [kæd] *n* sinvergüenza *m*.

CAD *abbr of [computer-aided design]* CAD, diseño asistido por ordenador.

cadastral [kəˈdæstrəl] *adj* catastral.

cadastre [kəˈdæstə*] *n* JUR catastro *m*.

cadaver [kəˈdeivə*] *n* cadáver *m*.

cadaveric [kəˈdævərik]; **cadaverous** [kəˈdævərəs] *adj* cadavérico, ca.

caddie [ˈkædi] *n* SP «caddy» *m*, persona *f* que lleva los palos (golf) | carrito *m* (trolley).

caddis fly [ˈkædisflai] *n* ZOOL frígano *m*.

caddish [ˈkædiʃ] *adj* desvergonzado, da (behaviour, etc.) || *caddish trick* canallada *f*, granujada *f*.

caddy [ˈkædi] *n* SP «caddy» *m*, persona *f* que lleva los palos (golf) | carrito *m* (trolley) || caja *f* para el té.

cade [keid] *n* BOT enebro *m* (juniper).

cadence [ˈkeidəns] *n* cadencia *f*, ritmo *m* (of sound, of voice) || MUS cadencia *f*.

cadency [-i] *n* cadencia *f* (cadence) || descendencia *f* de la rama menor (in a family).

cadenza [kəˈdenzə] *n* MUS cadencia *f*.

cadet [kəˈdet] *n* MIL cadete *m* || hijo *m* menor (youngest son).

cadge [kædʒ] *vt/vi* gorronear (to sponge) || *to cadge money off s.o.* darle un sablazo a uno.

cadger [-ə*] *n* gorrón, ona; sablista *m* & *f*.

cadi [ˈkɑːdi] *n* cadí *m* (judge).

Cádiz [kəˈdiz, US ˈkædiz] *pr n* GEOGR Cádiz.

cadmic [ˈkædmik] *adj* CHEM cádmico, ca.

cadmium [ˈkædmiəm] *adj* CHEM cadmio *m*.

cadre [ˈkɑːdə*, US ˈkædri] *n* cuadro *m*.

caduceus [kəˈdjuːsjəs] *n* MYTH caduceo *m*.

caducity [kəˈdjuːsiti] *n* caducidad *f*.

caducous [kəˈdjukəs] *adj* caduco, ca.

caecal [ˈsiːkl] *n* ANAT cecal.

caecum [ˈsiːkəm] *n* ANAT ciego *m*, intestino *m* ciego.

Caesar [ˈsiːzə*] *pr n* HIST César *m* || *render therefore unto Caesar the things which are Caesar's and unto God the things which are God's* hay que dar a Dios lo que es de Dios y al César lo que es del César.

Caesarean; Caesarian [siˈzɛərjən] *adj* cesariano, na; cesáreo, a || MED *Caesarean section* o *operation* cesárea *f*, operación cesárea.
◆ *n* MED cesárea *f*, operación *f* cesárea.

caesium [ˈsiːzjəm] *n* cesio *m* (metal).

caesura [siːˈzjuərə] *n* cesura *f* (pause).
— OBSERV El plural es *caesuras* o *caesurae*.

CAF; C and F; c & f *abbr of [cost and freight]* CAF, c y f, coste y flete.

café [ˈkæfei, ˈkæfi] *n* café *m*, restaurante *m* || café *m* (for drinks) || cafetería *f*.

café society [-səˈsaiəti] *n* US gente *f* famosa que frecuenta los cafés de moda.

cafeteria [kæfiˈtiəriə] *n* restaurante *m* de autoservicio.

caffeine [ˈkæfiːn] *n* cafeína *f*.

caftan [ˈkæftən] *n* caftán *m*.

cage [keidʒ] *n* jaula *f* (for keeping birds, animals, etc.) || SP portería *f* (goal) | canasta *f* (in basketball) | campo *m* de entrenamiento (baseball) || *lift cage* jaula de ascensor.

cage [keidʒ] *vt* enjaular || SP encestar (to basket).

cagey; cagy [ˈkeidʒi] *adj* FAM cauteloso, sa; reservado, da.

cahoots [kəˈhuːts] *pl n* FAM *in cahoots with* conchabado con.

CAI *abbr of [computer-aided instruction]* enseñanza asistida por ordenador.

Caiaphas [ˈkaiəfæs] *pr n* Caifás *m*.

caiman [ˈkeimən] *n* ZOOL caimán *m*.

Cain [kein] *pr n* Caín *m* || FIG *to raise Cain* armar jaleo.

caique [kaiˈiːk] *n* MAR caique *m*, esquife *m*.

cairn [kɛən] *n* montón *m* de piedras [como señal] || ZOOL tipo *m* peludo de terrier (dog).

Cairo ['kaiərəu, *US* 'kɛərəu] *pr n* GEOGR El Cairo *m*.

caisson [kə'su:n] *n* TECH cajón *m*, campana *f* | compuerta *f* de dique (used as gate) || MIL cajón *m* de municiones || MED *caisson disease* enfermedad *f* de los buzos.

cajole [kə'dʒəul] *vt* engatusar || *to cajole s.o. into doing sth.* conseguir que uno haga algo engatusándole.

cajolery [-ri] *n* engatusamiento *m*.

cake [keik] *n* bizcocho *m* (without filling) || tarta *f* (with filling) || pastel *m* (individual); *half a dozen cream cakes* media docena de pasteles de nata || pasta *f* (small) || pastilla *f*; *cake of soap* pastilla de jabón || — *Christmas cake* tarta de Navidad || *fish cake* croqueta *f* de pescado || *fruit cake* bizcocho con frutas secas, «cake» *m* || FIG & FAM *to be a piece of cake* ser pan comido, estar tirado | *to sell like hot cakes* venderse como rosquillas | *to take the cake* llevarse la palma, ser el colmo || *wedding cake* tarta nupcial || FIG & FAM *you can't have your cake and eat it* no se puede estar en misa y repicando.

cake [keik] *vi* endurecerse, apelmazarse.

calabash ['kæləbæʃ] *n* BOT calabaza *f*.

calaboose [kælə'bu:s] *n* *US* FAM calabozo *m*.

Calabrian [kə'læbriən] *adj/n* calabrés, esa.

calamar ['kæləmɑ:]; **calamary** ['kæləməri] *n* ZOOL calamar *m*.

calamine ['kæləmain] *n* CHEM calamina *f*.

calamitous [kə'læmitəs] *adj* calamitoso, sa.

calamity [kə'læmiti] *n* calamidad *f*, desgracia *f*.

calandra lark [kə'lændrə'lɑ:k] *n* ZOOL calandria *f*.

calash [kə'læʃ] *n* calesa *f*.

calcaneum [kæl'keiniəm] *n* calcáneo *m*, calcañar *m*.

calcareous, calcarious [kæl'kɛəriəs] *adj* calcáreo, a.

calceolaria [ˌkælsiə'lɛəriə] *n* BOT calceolaria *f*.

calceolate ['kælsjəleit] *adj* BOT calceolado, da.

calces ['kælsi:z] *pl n* ⟶ **calx.**

Calchas ['kælkæs] *pr n* Calcas *m*.

calcic ['kælsik] *adj* CHEM cálcico, ca.

calciferol [kæl'sifərol] *n* CHEM calciferol *m*.

calciferous [kæl'sifərəs] *adj* calcífero, ra.

calcification [ˌkælsifi'keiʃən] *n* calcificación *f*.

calcify ['kælsifai] *vt* calcificar.

◆ *vi* calcificarse.

calcimine ['kælsimain] *n* encalado *m* (whitewash).

calcimine ['kælsimain] *vt* encalar, blanquear.

calcination [ˌkælsi'neiʃən] *n* calcinación *f*.

calcine ['kælsain] *vt* calcinar.

◆ *vi* calcinarse.

calcite ['kælsait] *n* MIN calcita *f*.

calcium ['kælsiəm] *n* CHEM calcio *m* || *calcium oxide* óxido cálcico.

calcspar ['kælkspɑ:*] *n* MIN calcita *f*, carbonato *m* de calcio.

calculable ['kælkjuləbl] *adj* calculable.

calculate ['kælkjuleit] *vt* calcular; *to calculate the area of a circle* calcular el área de un círculo || FIG calcular, suponer (to figure out) | hacer a propósito (para), hacer con el fin (de), calcular; *a promise calculated to win votes* una promesa hecha con el fin de ganar votos.

◆ *vi* hacer cálculos, calcular || FIG contar, confiar; *we are calculating on having good weather* contamos con *or* confiamos en tener buen tiempo.

calculated [-id] *adj* FIG intencional, calculado, da; deliberado, da.

calculating [-iŋ] *adj* de calcular, calculador, ra || FIG calculador, ra; *to be cool and calculating* ser frío y calculador.

calculating machine [-iŋ-mə'ʃi:n] *n* máquina *f* de calcular, calculadora *f*, calculador *m*.

calculation [ˌkælkju'leiʃən] *n* cálculo *m* || FIG cálculo *m*.

calculator ['kælkjuleitə*] *n* calculador *m* (s.o. who calculates) || calculista *m* & *f* (of a project) || tablas *f pl* (set of tables) || calculadora *f*, calculador *m* (machine).

calculous ['kælkjuləs] *adj* MED calculoso, sa.

calculus ['kælkjuləs] *n* MED cálculo *m* || MATH cálculo *m*; *differential, integral calculus* cálculo diferencial, integral.

— OBSERV El plural es *calculi* o *calculuses*.

caldron ['kɔ:ldrən] *n* caldero *m* (cauldron).

calèche [kəlɛʃ] *n* calesa *f*.

Caledonia [kæli'dounjə] *pr n* Caledonia *f* || *New Caledonia* Nueva Caledonia.

calefaction [ˌkæli'fækʃən] *n* calefacción *f*.

calendar ['kælində*] *n* calendario *m* || JUR lista *f*, registro *m* (list) || orden *m* del día (agenda) || santoral *m* (of saints) || — *calendar month* mes *m* civil || *calendar year* año *m* civil.

calendar ['kælində*] *vt* poner en un calendario *or* en una lista || clasificar (documents).

calender ['kælində*] *n* TECH calandria *f*.

calender ['kælində*] *vt* TECH calandrar.

calends ['kælindz] *pl n* calendas *f*.

calendula [kə'lendjulə] *n* BOT caléndula *f*.

calenture ['kæləntjuə*] *n* MED fiebre *f* tropical.

calf [kɑ:f] *n* ANAT pantorrilla *f* || becerro, rra; ternero, ra (young cow) || cría *f* (young elephant, whale, seal, etc.) || becerro *m*, piel *f* de becerro (leather) || masa *f* de hielo || — *in calf* preñada (pregnant) || *the golden calf* el becerro de oro || FIG & FAM *to kill the fatted calf* echar la casa por la ventana [para celebrar la llegada de una persona].

— OBSERV El plural de *calf* es *calves*.

calf bone [-bəun] *n* ANAT peroné *m*.

calf love [-lʌv] *n* amor *m* de jóvenes.

calfskin [-skin] *n* becerro *m*, piel *f* de becerro.

caliber ['kælibə*] *n* *US* ⟶ **calibre.**

calibrate ['kælibreit] *vt* calibrar (guns, cylinders) || graduar (thermometer).

calibration [ˌkæli'breiʃən] *n* calibración *f*, calibrado *m* || graduación *f*.

calibre ['kælibə*] *n* calibre *m* || FIG calibre *m*, capacidad *f* (of a person).

calices ['kæləˌsiz] *pl n* ⟶ **calix.**

caliche [ka'li:tʃi] *n* MIN caliche *m*, nitrato *m* sódico.

calico ['kælikəu] *n* calicó *m*, percal *m*.

California [ˌkæli'fɔ:njə] *pr n* GEOGR California *f*.

Californian [-n] *adj/n* californiano, na.

californium [-niəm] *n* CHEM californio *m*.

caliginous [kə'lidʒinəs] *adj* caliginoso, sa.

caliper ['kælipə*]; **calipers** [-z] *pl n* TECH compás *m sing* de calibre, calibrador *m sing*; *vernier caliper* calibrador micrométrico.

caliph ['kælif] *n* califa *m*.

caliphate [-eit] *n* califato *m*.

calix ['kæliks] *n* copa *f* || REL cáliz *m*.

— OBSERV El plural de *calix* es *calices*.

calk [kɔ:lk] *n* ramplón *m* (in horseshoe).

calk [kɔ:lk] *vt* herrar (shoes) || herrar a ramplón (horseshoe) || *US* MAR calafatear (to caulk).

calkin ['kælkin] *n* clavo *m* (of shoe) || ramplón *m* (of horseshoe).

calking [ˌkɔ:lkiŋ] *n* *US* MAR calafateo *m*.

call [kɔ:l] *n* llamada *f*, llamamiento *m* [AMER llamado *m*]; *to come at s.o.'s call* acudir a la llamada de alguien || llamada *f*, grito *m*; *a call for help* un grito de socorro || llamada *f*; *a telephone call* una llamada telefónica || visita *f* corta (visit to a house, etc.); *to pay* o *to make a call on s.o.* hacer una visita corta a alguien || canto *m* (of a bird) || reclamo *m* (instrument imitating the cry of an animal) || MIL llamamiento *m* (of an annual contingent) | toque *m* (music) || FIG llamada *f*; *call to the priesthood* llamada al sacerdocio; *the call of the sea* la llamada del mar || demanda *f* (claim on time, money) || MAR & AVIAT escala *f*; *port of call* puerto de escala || JUR citación *f*, convocación *f* || COMM demanda *f*, pedido *m* (demand) | opción *f* de compra (in stock market) | solicitación *f* de fondos || acción *f* de igualar y de hacer enseñar las cartas (in poker) || anuncio *m*, declaración *f* (in bridge) || FIG motivo *m*; *there's no call for you to be upset* no hay motivo para que te molestes || — *a call to order* una llamada al orden || *curtain call* llamada a escena || *on call* de guardia (a doctor, etc.), disponible (available), pagadero a la vista (money) || *reverse-charge call* conferencia *f* a cobro revertido (telephone call) || *the actor got several calls* el actor tuvo que salir a saludar varias veces || *to give s.o. a call* llamar a alguien || FIG *to have a close call* librarse por los pelos || *trunk* o *long-distance call* conferencia *f* (interurbana) || *within call* al alcance de la voz.

call [kɔ:l] *vt* llamar; *to call somebody in a loud voice* llamar a alguien a voces || convocar (to summon); *to call a meeting* convocar a una reunión || llamar, despertar (to awaken) || telefonear a, llamar a (to phone) || llamar; *he was called to the priesthood* fue llamado al sacerdocio || llamar, poner (to give a Christian name to) || llamar, decir (to give a nickname to) || llamar; *I call it a swindle* lo llamo una estafa || calcular (to estimate); *I'd call it a good 20 miles* lo calcularía en unas 20 millas largas || reclamar (to attract animals) || JUR convocar, citar (a witness) || COMM pedir el reembolso de (a loan) || hacer enseñar las cartas (in poker) || declarar, anunciar (in bridge) || — *Manchester has called you* lo han llamado de Manchester || *to be called* llamarse; *I am called González* me llamo González || *to be called to the bar* ser recibido de abogado || SP *to call a game* dar por concluido un partido (baseball) || *to call a strike* declarar una huelga || INFORM *to call data* llamar datos || FIG *to call it a day* dar por acabado el día, dejarlo || *to call o.s.* llamarse || FIG *to call s.o. names* poner verde a alguien || *to call s.o.'s attention to* llamar la atención de alguien sobre || *to call the roll* pasar lista || *to call to account* pedir cuentas || *to call to mind* traer a la memoria, recordar || *to call to order* llamar al orden || MIL *to call to the colours* llamar a filas.

◆ *vi* llamar, gritar, dar voces | cantar (bird) || llamar, hacer una llamada (to telephone) || hacer una visita (to pay a visit) || pasar; *I only called to see how you were* pasé sólo para saber cómo estabas; *to call at the butcher's* pasar por la carnicería || hacer escala; *to call at a port* hacer escala en un puerto || parar; *the train calls at every station* el tren para en todas las estaciones || reclamarse (birds) || declarar (in bridge) || — *this is Charles calling, is John in?* soy Carlos, ¿está Juan? || *this is Radio X calling* aquí Radio X || *who is calling?* ¿de parte de quién?

◆ *phr v* *to call after* llamar a || *to call again* venir de nuevo || *to call aside* llamar aparte || *to call at* pasar por, hacer una visita a (to visit) | MAR hacer escala en || *to call away* llamar (to another place) | distraer (s.o.'s attention) || *to call back* volver a llamar (by telephone) | recordar (to remember) | hacer volver; *she called back her son* hizo volver a su hijo | volver (to come back) | *to call back an ambassador* retirar a un embajador || *to call down* hacer bajar | invocar | US regañar, reprender (to scold) || *to call for* llamar a; *to call loudly for s.o.* llamar a alguien a gritos | pedir (to ask for) | ir a buscar, ir a recoger (to fetch) | exigir, pedir (attention, measures, volunteers, etc.) | *to call for help* pedir auxilio *or* socorro || *to call forth* sacar (to draw out) | inspirar, provocar (admiration) | hacer surgir (memories) | suscitar, provocar (protestation) || *to call in* retirar (de la circulación); *to call in old coinage* retirar moneda antigua de la circulación | hacer pasar (to let in) | llamar a; *to call in the fire brigade* llamar a los bomberos | COMM exigir el pago de (debts, etc.) | entrar (to come in) | *to call in question* poner en tela de juicio || *to call off* cancelar, anular (to cancel) | dar por terminado (to put an end to) | llamar (dogs) || *to call on* visitar (to visit) | dar *or* ceder la palabra a; *I call on the next speaker* doy la palabra al siguiente orador | acudir a, recurrir a (for help) | censurar por (to blame) | invocar, apelar a (to invoke) || *to call out* hacer salir; *I don't want to call the doctor out at this time of night* no quiero hacer salir al médico a estas horas de la noche | gritar (to shout) | llamar a la huelga (workers) | desafiar, retar (to challenge) | hacer intervenir (to summon for emergency service) | *to call out for sth.* reclamar algo con insistencia || *to call over* llamar || *to call together* convocar || *to call up* llamar (by telephone, by radio) | MIL llamar a filas | hacer subir (to tell to come up) | hacer surgir (memories) || *to call upon* invocar (God's name) | recurrir a, acudir a (s.o.'s generosity) | dar *or* ceder la palabra (speaker) | *to call upon s.o. to do sth.* pedir a alguien que haga algo.

calla ['kælə] *n* BOT cala *f* || *calla lily* lirio *m* de agua.

call-board [-bɔːd] *n* THEATR tablón *m* de anuncios [para los ensayos de los artistas].

call box [-bɔks] *n* cabina *f* telefónica.

callboy [-bɔi] *n* THEATR traspunte *m* || botones *m inv* (bellboy).

caller [-ə*] *n* persona *f* que llama, el que llama (person making a telephone call) || visita *f* (visitor) || cliente, ta (at a shop).

call girl [-gəːl] *n* FAM prostituta *f*.

call house [-haus] *n* casa *f* de citas.

calligrapher [kə'ligrəfə*] *n* calígrafo, fa.

calligraphic [ˌkæli'græfik] *adj* caligráfico, ca.

calligraphy [kə'ligrəfi] *n* caligrafía *f*.

calling ['kɔːliŋ] *n* llamamiento *m*, llamada *f* [*AMER* llamado *m*] (call) || profesión *f* (occupation) || vocación *f* (spiritual summons) || REL llamada *f* || visita *f*; *calling card, hours* tarjeta, horas de visita || celo *m* (of female cat).

Calliope [kə'laiəpi] *pr n* MYTH Caliope *f*.

calliper ['kælipə*] *n*; **callipers** [-z] *pl n* TECH compás *m sing* de calibre, calibrador *m sing*; *vernier calliper* calibrador micrométrico || MED aparato *m* ortopédico || *slide calliper* pie *m* de rey, compás de corredera.

calliper gauge [-geidʒ] *n* calibrador *m* de mordazas.

callisthenics [ˌkælis'θeniks] *n* calistenia *f*.

call loan ['kɔːl-ləun]; **call money** ['kɔːl'mʌni] *n* COMM dinero *m* pagadero a la vista.

callosity [kæ'lɔsiti] *n* callosidad *f* || FIG insensibilidad *f*.

callous ['kæləs] *adj* calloso, sa (skin) || FIG insensible, duro, ra.

◆ *n* callo *m* (callus).
— OBSERV El plural de *callous* es *callouses* y *calli*.

callousness [-nəs] *n* insensibilidad *f*, dureza *f* (of person).

callow ['kæləu] *adj* inexperto, ta; inmaduro, ra (lacking experience) || implume (young birds).

call sign ['kɔːlsain] *n* RAD sintonía *f*, indicativo *m*.

call-up ['kɔːlʌp] *n* MIL llamada *f* a filas.

callus ['kæləs] *n* callo *m*.
— OBSERV El plural de *callus* es *calluses* o *calli*.

calm [kɑːm] *adj* sosegado, da; tranquilo, la (person) || calmoso, sa (weather) || tranquilo, la (sea).
◆ *n* calma *f*, tranquilidad *f*, sosiego *m* || MAR *dead calm* calma chicha.

calm [kɑːm] *vt* calmar, sosegar, tranquilizar.
◆ *vi* calmarse, sosegarse, tranquilizarse || calmarse (wind, temper).
— OBSERV El verbo *to calm* va seguido frecuentemente por *down*, sin cambiar por ello su sentido: *the sea was calming down* el mar se calmaba.

calmative ['kælmətiv] *adj* calmante.
◆ *n* calmante *m*.

calmly ['kɑːmli] *adv* con calma, tranquilamente.

calmness ['kɑːmnis] *n* calma *f*, tranquilidad *f*.

calomel ['kæləməl] *n* MED calomel *m*, calomelanos *m pl*.

caloric [kə'lɔrik] *adj* PHYS calórico, ca; térmico, ca.
◆ *n* PHYS calórico *m*.

calorie ['kæləri] *n* BIOL & PHYS caloría *f*; *large calorie* caloría grande; *small calorie* pequeña caloría; *gramme calorie* caloría gramo.

calorific [ˌkælə'rifik] *adj* calorífico, ca; *calorific value* o *power* potencia calorífica.

calorimeter [ˌkælə'rimitə*] *n* PHYS calorímetro *m*.

calorimetric [kælə'rimitrik]; **calorimetrical** [ˌkæləri'metrikəl] *adj* PHYS calorimétrico, ca.

calory ['kæləri] *n* BIOL & PHYS caloría *f* (calorie).

calotte [kə'lɔt] *n* solideo *m* (of a priest).

caltrop ['kæltrəp] *n* MIL & BOT abrojo *m*.

calumet ['kæljumet] *n* «calumet» *m*, pipa *f* de la paz.

calumniate [kə'lʌmnieit] *vt* calumniar.

calumniator [kə'lʌmnieitə*] *n* calumniador, ra.

calumniatory [kə'lʌmni'eitəri]; **calumnious** [kə'lʌmniəs] *adj* calumnioso, sa.

calumny ['kæləmni] *n* calumnia *f*.

calvary ['kælvəri] *n* FIG calvario *m*.

Calvary ['kælvəri] *n* calvario *m*.

calve [kɑːv] *vi* parir (cow) || desprenderse (mass of ice).
◆ *vt* parir (a calf).

calves [-z] *pl n* ⟶ **calf.**

Calvin ['kælvin] *pr n* HIST Calvino.

Calvinism [-izəm] *n* REL calvinismo *m*.

Calvinist [-ist] *adj/n* REL calvinista.

Calvinistic [ˌkælvi'nistik] *adj* REL calvinista.

calx [kælks] *n* TECH residuos *m pl or* escorias *f pl* de la calcinación.
— OBSERV El plural de *calx* es *calces* o *calxes*.

calyces ['kælisiːz] *pl n* ⟶ **calyx.**

calypso [kə'lipsəu] *n* MUS calipso *m* (dance).

Calypso [kə'lipsəu] *pr n* MYTH Calipso *f* (nymph).

calyx ['keiliks] *n* BOT cáliz *m* || ANAT cáliz *m* (of the kidney) || TECH corona *f* dentada.
— OBSERV El plural de esta palabra es *calyces* o *calyxes*.

cam [kæm] *n* TECH leva *f*.

CAM *abbr of [computer-aided manufacturing]* CAM, fabricación asistida por ordenador.

camaraderie [ˌkæmə'rɑːdəri] *n* compañerismo *m*, camaradería *f*.

camarilla [ˌkæmə'rilə] *n* camarilla *f*.

camaron [ˌkæmə'rɔn] *n* ZOOL camarón *m* [de agua dulce].

camber ['kæmbə*] *n* comba *f*, combadura *f* || curvatura *f*, peralte *m* (of road) || AUT inclinación *f* (of wheels) || torsión *f*, alabeo *m* (of beams).

camber ['kæmbə*] *vt* combar, arquear.
◆ *vi* combarse, arquearse.

cambist ['kæmbist] *n* cambista *m*.

Cambodia [kæm'bəudjə] *pr n* GEOGR Camboya *f*.

Cambodian [-n] *adj/n* camboyano, na.

cambrel ['kæmbrəl] *n* garabato *m* (butcher's hook).

Cambrian ['kæmbriən] *adj* cambriano, na (Welsh) || GEOL cámbrico, ca.

cambric ['keimbrik] *n* cambray *m*, batista *f*.

Cambridge ['keimbridʒ] *pr n* GEOGR Cambridge.

came [keim] *n* TECH barra *f* de plomo [en una vidriera o ventana].

came [keim] *pret* ⟶ **come.**

camel ['kæməl] *n* ZOOL MAR camello *m*.

cameleer [ˌkæmi'liə*] *n* camellero *m*.

camel hairz; camel's hair ['kæməlz-hɛə*] *n* pelo *m* de camello (fabric).

camellia; camelia [kə'miːljə] *n* BOT camelia *f*.

cameo ['kæmiəu] *n* camafeo *m*.

camera ['kæmərə] *n* PHOT máquina *f* fotográfica || cámara *f* (cinema or television) || JUR cámara *f* del juez || — PHOT *camera obscura* cámara oscura || *camera stand* trípode *m* || JUR *in camera* a puerta cerrada.

cameraman [-mən] *n* cámara *m*, cameraman *m*, operador *m* de cine *or* de televisión.

Cameroons ['kæməruːnz] *pl prn* GEOGR Camerún *m sing* (former protectorate).

Cameroon; Cameroun ['kaeməruːn] *pr n* Camerún *m* (republic).

Camilla; Camille [kə'milə] *pr n* Camila *f*.

Camillus [kə'miləs] *pr n* Camilo *m*.

camisole ['kæmisəul] *n* cubrecorsé *m*.

camomile ['kæməmail] *n* BOT camomila *f*, manzanilla *f* || *camomille tea* manzanilla *f*.

camouflage ['kæmuflɑːʒ] *n* MIL camuflaje *m* || FIG enmascaramiento *m*, disimulación *f*.

camouflage ['kæmuflɑːʒ] *vt* MIL camuflar || FIG enmascarar, disimular (to disguise).

camp [kæmp] *n* campo *m*; *concentration camp* campo de concentración || campamento *m* (military, for holidays) || FIG campo *m*, grupo *m*; *the existentialist camp* el campo existencialista | MIL vida *f* militar || — *holiday camp* campamento *or* colonia *f* de vacaciones || *internment camp* campo de internamiento || *labour camp* colonia penitenciaria || *summer camp* campamento de verano (in tents), colonia *f* de verano (in houses) || *work camp* campo de trabajo || *to break* o *to strike camp* levantar el campo || *to pitch camp* instalar el campo, acampar.

camp [kæmp] *vt* acampar (soldiers) ‖ alojar.
◆ *vi* acampar ‖ — *to camp out* vivir en tiendas de campaña ‖ *to camp out at s.o. else's house* alojarse temporalmente en casa de otro.

camp [kæmp] *adj* afectado, da; amanerado, da (affected) ‖ afeminado, da (effeminate).
◆ *n* afectación *f* ‖ afeminación *f*.

campaign [kæm'pein] *n* campaña *f*; *military, advertising campaign* campaña militar, publicitaria; *election campaign* campaña electoral.

campaign [kæm'pein] *vi* hacer (una) campaña ‖ luchar (to fight).

campaigner [-ə*] *n* FIG paladín *m* ‖ MIL *old campaigner* veterano *m*.

campanile [,kæmpə'ni:li] *n* ARCH campanil *m*, campanario *m*.

campanology [,kæmpə'nɔlədʒi] *n* campanología *f*.

campanula [kəm'pænjulə] *n* BOT campánula *f*, farolillo *m*.

campanulaceae [kəm,pænju'leisii] *pl n* BOT campanuláceas *f*.

campanulate [kəm'pænjuleit] *adj* campaniforme, acampanado, da.

camp bed ['kæmp-bed] *n* catre *m* de tijera.

camp chair ['kæmptʃɛə*] *n* silla *f* de tijera.

campeachy wood [kæm'pi:tʃi-wud] *n* palo *m* (de) campeche.

camper ['kæmpə*] *n* SP campista *m* & *f* (person) ‖ caravana *f* (vehicle).

campfire ['kæmp'faiə*] *n* fuego *m* de campamento.

campfire girl [-gə:l] *n* US muchacha *f* exploradora.

camp follower ['kæmp'fɔləuə*] *n* cantinera *f*.

campground ['kæmp,graund] *n* US camping *m*.

camphor ['kæmfə*] *n* alcanfor *m*.

camphorate [-reit] *vt* alcanforar.

camp hospital ['kæmp'hɔspitəl] *n* MIL hospital *m* de sangre.

camping ['kæmpiŋ] *n* camping *m*; *to go camping* ir de camping ‖ — *camping chair* silla *f* de tijera ‖ *camping ground* o *site* camping *m*.

camp meeting ['kæmp'mi:tiŋ] *n* US REL concentración *f* religiosa al aire libre.

camporee [kæmpə'ri] *n* reunión *f* de exploradores.

campsite ['kæmpsait] *n* camping *m*, sitio *m* donde se acampa ‖ campamento *m* (for boy scouts).

campus ['kæmpɔs] *n* recinto *m* universitario, ciudad *f* universitaria, campus *m*.

camshaft ['kæm,ʃɑ:ft] *n* TECH árbol *m* de levas.

can [kæn] *n* lata *f*; *a can of beer* una lata de cerveza ‖ bote *m*, lata *f* (tin); *can of peaches* bote de melocotones ‖ bidón *m*; *a gallon can of oil* un bidón de aceite de un galón ‖ US lata *f* (flat tin); *can of sardines* lata de sardinas ‖ US FAM chirona *f* (jail) | retrete *m* (toilet) | carga *f* de profundidad (depth charge) ‖ FIG & FAM *to carry the can* pagar el pato.

can* [kæn] *v aux* poder (to be able to); *can you come to dinner tomorrow?* ¿puedes venir a cenar mañana? ‖ poder (to be allowed to); *you can go now* te puedes marchar ‖ saber; *she can speak French* sabe hablar francés ‖ ser capaz de, poder; *I cannot do that type of work* no soy capaz de hacer esa clase de trabajo ‖ — *can you hear me?* ¿me oyes? ‖ *I can't see him* no lo veo ‖ *I could have smacked his face* no le di una torta de milagro, casi le doy una torta ‖ *ugly as could be* de lo más feo.
◆ *vt* enlatar, envasar, conservar en lata (to preserve in a can) ‖ FAM echar del colegio (to expel) | despedir (from a job) | grabar (records, tapes) ‖ FAM *can it!* ¡basta!
— OBSERV El verbo auxiliar *can* es defectivo y sólo se conjuga en presente, pretérito y condicional. El infinitivo y los participios no existen y se sustituyen por *to be able to*. La forma negativa es *cannot* o *can't*; el pretérito y el condicional son *could*.

Canada ['kænədə] *pr n* GEOGR Canadá *m*.

Canadian [kə'neidjən] *adj/n* canadiense.

canal [kə'næl] *n* canal *m* (for navigation) ‖ canal *m*, acequia *f* (for irrigation) ‖ ANAT canal *m*, conducto *m* ‖ ARCH mediacaña *f*, estría *f* ‖ — ANAT *alimentary canal* tubo digestivo ‖ *canal rays* rayos *m* canales.

canalization [,kænəlai'zeiʃən] *n* canalización *f*.

canalize ['kænəlaiz] *vt* canalizar.

canapé ['kænəpei] *n* CULIN canapé *m*.

canard [kæ'nɑ:d] *n* bulo *m* (false piece of news).

Canarian [kæ'nɛərjən] *adj/n* canario, ria.

canary [kə'nɛəri] *n* canario *m* (bird) ‖ amarillo *m* canario (colour) ‖ vino *m* de Canarias.

canary grass [-grɑ:s] *n* alpiste *m*.

Canary Islands [-,ailəndz] *pl prn* GEOGR islas Canarias *f*, Canarias *f*.

canary seed [-si:d] *n* alpiste *m*.

canasta [kə'næstə] *n* canasta *f* (card game).

Canberra ['kænbərə, -brə] *pr n* GEOGR Canberra.

cancan ['kænkæn] *n* cancán *m* (dance).

cancel ['kænsəl] *n* cancelación *f*, anulación *f* ‖ INFORM *cancel key* tecla *f* de anulación.

cancel ['kænsəl] *vt* cancelar (a decree, a contract, etc.); *to cancel a contract* cancelar un contrato ‖ anular, invalidar; *to cancel a cheque* anular un cheque ‖ anular; *to cancel an order, a telephone call, an invitation* anular un pedido, una llamada telefónica, una invitación ‖ tachar, suprimir, borrar (to delete, to cross out); *to cancel a name from a list* borrar un nombre de una lista ‖ matar (postage stamp) ‖ MATH eliminar ‖ contrarrestar (to balance); *the profits cancel the losses* los beneficios contrarrestan las pérdidas.
◆ *vi* MATH *to cancel out* anularse.

cancellate ['kænsəleit]; **cancellated** [-id] *adj* BIOL reticular, reticulado, da.

cancellation ['kænsə'leiʃən] *n* JUR cancelación *f*, anulación *f* ‖ matado *m* (on a stamp) ‖ supresión *f* (deletion).

canceller ['kænsələ] *n* matasellos *m inv*.

cancellous ['kænsələs] *adj* esponjoso, sa (bone).

cancer ['kænsə*] *n* MED cáncer *m*.

Cancer ['kænsə*] *n* ASTR Cáncer *m*.

cancerigenic; cancerogenic [,kænsərə'dʒenik] *adj* MED cancerígeno, na.

cancerologist ['kænsə'rɔlədʒist] *n* cancerólogo *m*.

cancerous ['kænsərəs] *adj* MED canceroso, sa.

cancroid ['kæŋ,krɔid] *adj* MED cancroideo, a.
◆ *n* MED cancroide *m*.

candela [kæn'di:lə] *n* ELECTR candela *f* (unit).

candelabra [,kændi'lɑ:brə] *n* candelabro *m*.

candelabrum [-m] *n* candelabro *m*.
— OBSERV El plural es *candelabra* o *candelabrums*.

candescence [kæn'desns] *n* candencia *f*.

candescent [kæn'desnt] *adj* candente.

candid ['kændid] *adj* sincero, ra; franco, ca (frank) ‖ imparcial, justo, ta ‖ *candid camera* cámara indiscreta.
— OBSERV The Spanish word *cándido* means *naïve*.

candidate [-eit] *n* candidato, ta; *candidate for a post* candidato a *or* para un puesto ‖ opositor, ra (in a competitive examination).

candidature [-itʃə*] *n* candidatura *f*.

candidness ['kændidnis] *n* franqueza *f*, sinceridad *f*.

candied ['kændid] *adj* escarchado, da (cooked in sugar) ‖ cande, candi (sugar).

candle ['kændl] *n* vela *f* (of tallow, of wax) ‖ cirio *m* (in a church) ‖ candela *f* (unit of intensity) ‖ — FIG *he is not fit to hold a candle to him* no le llega a la suela del zapato | *the game is not worth the candle* la cosa no vale la pena | *to burn the candle at both ends* hacer de la noche día.

candle ['kændl] *vt* mirar al trasluz.

candleberry [-,beri] *n* BOT árbol *m* de la cera.

candleholder [-,həuldə*] *n* candelero *m*.

candlelight [-lait] *n* luz *f* de una vela; *by candlelight* a la luz de una vela ‖ FIG atardecer *m*, crepúsculo *m*.

candlelit [-lit] *adj* alumbrado, da con velas.

Candlemas ['kændlməs] *n* REL Candelaria *f*.

candlepower ['kændl,pauə*] *n* candela *f*, bujía *f* (unit).

candlestick ['kændlstik] *n* candelero *m*, palmatoria *f* ‖ cirial *m* (in a church).

candlewick ['kaendlwik] *n* pábilo *m*, mecha *f* de la vela ‖ tela *f* de algodón afelpada (fabric).

candour; US **candor** ['kændə*] *n* sinceridad *f*, franqueza *f* (frankness) ‖ imparcialidad *f*, justicia *f*.
— OBSERV The Spanish words *candor* and *candidez* mean *naïveté*.

candy ['kændi] *n* azúcar *m* cande ‖ US caramelo *m* (sweet), bombón *m* (made of chocolate).

candy ['kændi] *vt* escarchar (fruit, etc.) ‖ cristalizar (sugar).
◆ *vi* escarcharse (fruit) ‖ cristalizarse (sugar).

candy floss [-flɔs] *n* algodón *m* (spun sugar).

candy store [-stɔ:*] *n* confitería *f*.

candytuft [-tʌft] *n* BOT carraspique *m*.

cane [kein] *n* caña *f*; *sugar cane* caña de azúcar ‖ bastón *m* (thin walking stick) ‖ mimbre *m*; *cane furniture* muebles de mimbre ‖ palmeta *f*, vara *f* (instrument of punishment) ‖ — *cane seat* asiento *m* de mimbre *or* de rejilla ‖ *cane sugar* azúcar *m* de caña.

cane [kein] *vt* poner un asiento de mimbre a (a chair) ‖ castigar con la palmeta *or* las varas (to punish).

canebrake ['keinbreik] *n* US cañaveral *m*.

canicular [kə'nikjələ*] *adj* canicular.

canidae ['kænidei] *pl n* ZOOL cánidos *m*.

canine ['keinain] *adj* canino, na ‖ *canine tooth* canino *m*, colmillo *m*, diente canino.
◆ *n* diente *m* canino, colmillo *m*, canino *m* (tooth) ‖ US perro *m*, can *m* (dog).

caning ['keiniŋ] *n* castigo *m* con la palmeta *or* las varas.

canister ['kænistə*] *n* bote *m*, lata *f* (can) ‖ MIL bote *m* de metralla ‖ REL hostiario *m*.

canker ['kæŋkə*] *n* MED úlcera *f* en la boca ‖ VET cancro *m*, llaga *f* gangrenosa ‖ BOT cancro *m* (in fruit trees) ‖ FIG cáncer *m* ‖ MED *canker rash* escarlatina *f*.

canker ['kæŋkə*] *vt* MED ulcerar, gangrenar ‖ FIG corromper.
◆ *vi* MED ulcerarse, gangrenarse ‖ FIG corromperse.

cankerous [-rəs] *adj* gangrenoso, sa; ulceroso, sa.

cankerworm ['kæŋkəˌwəːm] *n* ZOOL gusano *m* [que se come las hojas].

canna ['kænə] *n* BOT cañacoro *m*.

cannabis [-bis] *n* cáñamo *m* de la India (hemp).

canned [kænd] *adj* enlatado, da; en lata, en bote, en conserva; *canned goods* productos enlatados || FAM grabado, da; *canned music* música grabada; *canned speech* discurso grabado | estereotipado, da (stereotyped) | expulsado, da (expelled) | despedido, da (from a job) | borracho, cha; trompa (drunk).

cannel ['kænl]; **cannel coal** [-kəul] *n* MIN carbón *m* bituminoso.

cannelons ['kænəlˌɔns]; **canneloni** [ˌkænə'louni] *pl n* canelones *m*.

canner ['kænə*] *n* conservero, ra.

cannery ['kænəri] *n* fábrica *f* de conservas.

cannibal ['kænibəl] *adj/n* caníbal.

cannibalism [-izəm] *n* canibalismo *m*.

cannibalistic [ˌkænibə'listik] *adj* caníbal.

cannibalize ['kænibəlaiz] *vt* recuperar las piezas aprovechables de [un coche, etc.].

canniness ['kæninis] *n* astucia *f*.

canning ['kæniŋ] *n* enlatado *m* || *canning industry* industria conservera.

cannon ['kænən] *n* MIL cañón *m* (gun) | artillería *f* || carambola *f* (in billiards) || tija *f* (of a key) || cañón *m* (of a horse's bit).
— OBSERV El plural de *cannon* cuando significa *cañón* (pieza de artillería) es generalmente *cannon*. En los demás sentidos es *cannons*.

cannon ['kænən] *vi* hacer carambola (in billiards) || — *to cannon into* o *against* chocar contra || *to cannon off* rebotar contra.
◆ *vt* cañonear.

cannonade [ˌkænə'neid] *n* cañoneo *m*.

cannonade [ˌkænə'neid] *vt/vi* bombardear, cañonear.

cannonball ['kænənbɔːl] *n* HIST bala *f* de cañón || servicio *m* fuerte (tennis).

cannon bone ['kænənbəun] *n* ZOOL caña *f*.

cannon fodder ['kænənˌfɔdə*] *n* FIG carne *f* de cañón.

cannonry ['kænənri] *n* fuego *m* de artillería.

cannon-shot ['kænɛnʃɔt] *n* cañonazo *m* (shot) || bala *f* de cañón (cannonball) || alcance *m* de un cañón (range).

cannot ['kænɔt] ⟶ **can.**

cannula ['kænjələ] *n* MED cánula *f*.
— OBSERV El plural de *cannula* es *cannulae*.

canny ['kæni] *adj* astuto, ta (shrewd) || prudente, cauto, ta (cautious).

canoe [kə'nuː] *n* canoa *f* || SP piragua *f* || FIG FAM *to paddle one's own canoe* arreglárselas solo.

canoe [kə'nuː] *vi* ir en canoa.

canoeing [-iŋ] *n* SP piragüismo *m*.

canoeist [-ist] *n* SP piragüista *m* & *f*.

canon ['kænən] *n* REL canon *m* (church rule, books regarded as a holy unit, part of the mass) | canónigo *m* (member of the chapter) || FIG canon *m*, norma *f*, regla *f* (principle) || catálogo *m* (catalogue) || MUS canon *m* || PRINT doble canon *m* || REL *canon law* derecho canónico.

cañon ['kænjən] *n* cañón *m* (canyon).

canoness ['kænənis] *n* REL canonesa *f*.

canonical [kə'nɔnikəl] *adj* REL canónico, ca || FIG ortodoxo, xa (authorized) || REL *canonical dress* hábitos *m pl* sacerdotales.

canonicals [-z] *pl n* REL hábitos *m* sacerdotales.

canonist ['kænənist] *n* canonista *m*.

canonization [ˌkænənai'zeiʃən] *n* canonización *f*.

canonize ['kənaiz] *vt* REL canonizar.

canonry ['kænənri] *n* REL canonjía *f*.

canoodle [kæ'nuːdl] *vi* FAM besuquearse.

cap opener ['kænoupnə*] *n* abrelatas *m inv*.

canopy ['kænəpi] *n* toldo *m* (awning) || dosel *m*, baldaquín *m*, baldaquino *m* (over a bed) || dosel *m* (over a throne) || ARCH doselete *m* (over niche, etc.) || REL dosel *m* (fixed) | palio *m* (portable) || FIG bóveda *f*; *canopy of heaven* bóveda celeste || AVIAT casquete *m* (of parachute) || AVIAT *ejectable canopy* cubierta *f* de cristal eyectable.

canopy ['kænəpi] *vt* endoselar.

canorous [kə'nɔrəs] *adj* canoro, ra.

cant [kænt] *adj* trivial, vulgar (trite) || insincero, ra; hipócrita (insincere) || de jerga, esotérico, ca (used by particular group) || sesgado, da (on the bias) || ARCH achaflanado, da.
◆ *n* hipocresías *f pl* (insincere talk) || tópicos *m pl*, trivialidades *f pl* (trivial statements) || gazmoñería *f* (insincere piety) || jerga *f*, argot *m* (jargon) || germanía *f* (slang of thieves, etc.) || TECH esquina *f*, chaflán *m* (of a building) | inclinación *f* (slope) | bisel *m* (bevelled edge).

cant [kænt] *vt* inclinar (to tilt) || biselar (to bevel) || poner en ángulo (to set at an angle) || volcar (to overturn) || ARCH chaflanar.
◆ *vi* inclinarse (to slant) || MAR escorar || decir hipocresías (to speak insincerely).

cantabile [kæn'tɑːbili] *adj* MUS cantábile.
◆ *n* MUS cantable *m*.

Cantabrian [kæn'teibriən] *adj* GEOGR Cantábrico, ca || — *Cantabrian Mountains* Cordillera Cantábrica.
◆ *adj/n* cántabro, bra.

Cantabrigian [ˌkæntə'bridʒiən] *adj* de Cambridge.
◆ *n* estudiante *or* licenciado de la Universidad de Cambridge (student) || nativo de Cambridge (native).

cantaloup; cantaloupe ['kæntəluːp] *n* melón *m* cantalupo, cantalupo *m*.

cantankerous [kæn'tæŋkərəs] *n* arisco, ca; intratable (ill-natured) || malhumorado, da (bad-tempered) || irritable || pendenciero, ra (quarrelsome).

cantata [kæn'tɑːtə] *n* cantata *f*.

canteen [kæn'tiːn] *n* cantina *f* (restaurant) || MIL cantina *f* (shop, kit) | cantimplora *f* (bottle) || — *canteen cup* taza metálica || *canteen of cutlery* juego *m* de cubiertos.

canter ['kæntə*] *n* medio galope *m* || FIG & FAM *to win in a canter* ganar cómodamente.

canter ['kæntə*] *vi* ir a medio galope.

Canterbury ['kæntəbəri] *pr n* GEOGR Cantorbery || BOT *Canterbury bell* campánula *f*, farolillo *m*.

cantharides [kæn'θæridiːz] *pl n* MED cantárida *f sing* (pharmaceutical preparation).

cantharis ['kænθəris] *n* ZOOL cantárida *f*.
— OBSERV El plural de *cantharis* es *cantharides*.

cant hook ['kænt-huk] *n* TECH gancho *m* maderero.

canticle ['kæntikl] *n* REL cántico *m*.
◆ *pl* REL Cantar *m sing* de los Cantares.

cantilena [ˌkæntil'einə] *n* cantilena *f*.

cantilever ['kæntiliːvə*] *adj* TECH voladizo, za; en voladizo, (de) cantilever; *cantilever bridge* puente de cantilever | voladizo, za; en voladizo (roof) || *cantilever spring* ballesta *f* cantilever.
◆ *n* TECH viga *f* voladiza || ARCH ménsula *f*.

cantle ['kæntl] *n* arzón *m* trasero (of a saddle) || rodaja *f*, raja *f* (slice) || trozo *m* (piece).

canto ['kæntəu] *n* canto *m* (division of a poem).

canton ['kæntɔn] *n* cantón *m* (of Switzerland, etc.) || HERALD cantón *m*.

canton ['kæntɔn] *vt* dividir en cantones.

canton [kən'tuːn] *vt* MIL acantonar, acuartelar (to quarter).

cantonal ['kæntənl] *adj* cantonal.

cantonment [kæn'tuːnmənt] *n* MIL acantonamiento *m*, acuartelamiento *m* (of troops) | cuartel *m*, campamento *m* (temporary quarters).

cantor ['kæntɔː*] *n* REL chantre *m*.

canvas ['kænvəs] *n* lona *f* (fabric) || toldo *m* (awning) || tienda *f* de campaña [AMER carpa *f*] (tent) || cañamazo *m* (for embroidery) || FIG circo *m* || ARTS lienzo *m* || MAR velamen *m*, velas *f pl* (sails) || — *canvas chair* silla *f* de tijera || *canvas shoes* zapatos *m* de lona || *on the canvas* en la lona, derribado, da || *under canvas* bajo lona (in tents), con velamen desplegado (ship).

canvass ['kænvəs] *n* campaña *f* en busca de votos *or* de pedidos (soliciting for votes or orders) || sondeo *m* (of public opinion).

canvass ['kænvəs] *vt* solicitar votos de (from potential supporters) || solicitar (votes) || COMM buscar pedidos de (from potential clients) | buscar clientes en (a town) || sondear (public opinion) || proponer (an idea) || discutir a fondo (a subject) || US hacer el escrutinio (election returns).
◆ *vi* hacer una campaña electoral (*for* a favor de) || solicitar votos (*for* a favor de) || COMM buscar clientes.

canvasser [-ə*] *n* agente *m* electoral || COMM corredor *m* || US escrutador *m*.

canvassing [-iŋ] *n* campaña *f* electoral.

canyon ['kænjən] *n* cañón *m*.

canzonet [ˌkænzə'net] *n* MUS cantinela *f*, cancioncilla *f*.

caoutchouc ['kautʃuk] *n* caucho *m*.

cap [kæp] *n* gorra *f*; *peaked cap* gorra de visera || gorro *m*; *military, swimming* o *bathing cap* gorro militar, de baño || cofia *f* (of waitress, of maid) || birrete *m* (of judge, of professor) || REL birrete *m*, bonete *m* (of priest) | capelo *m* (of cardinal) | solideo *m* (of Pope) | toca *f* (of nun) | tapa *f* (cover) || cápsula *f*, chapa *f* (of a bottle) || capuchón *m* (of pen) || sombrerete *m* (of mushroom) || puntera *f* (of shoe) || GEOGR casquete *m*; *polar cap* casquete polar || TECH cofia *f* (of a fuse) | caja *f* protectora (of magnetic needle) | guardapolvo *m*, tapa *f* (of watch) || MAR tamborete *m* || SP gorra *f* entregada a cada jugador seleccionado | jugador *m* seleccionado (player) || pistón *m*, fulminante *m* (for children); *cap gun* pistola de fulminantes || ARCH capitel *m* (of column) || — *cap and bells* gorro *m* de campanillas || *cap and gown* toga *f* y bonete || FIG *cap in hand* con el sombrero en la mano, humildemente || *cap of liberty* o *Phrygian cap* gorro frigio || SP *he's got three hundred caps* ha sido seleccionado trescientas veces || FIG *if the cap fits, wear it* aplíquese el cuento; el que se pica, ajos come | *to put on one's thinking cap* reflexionar | *to set one's cap at* poner sus miras en (girl, woman).

cap [kæp] *vt* poner una gorra a (s.o.) || poner cápsula *or* chapa a (a bottle) || poner tapa a (a vessel) || TECH cebar (a fuse) || FIG coronar; *mountain capped with snow* montaña coronada de nieve | poner remate a (job) | superar (to do better than) || SP seleccionar (a player) || conceder un título universitario a (in Scottish university) || — FIG *that caps all!* ¡es el colmo! | *to cap it all* para colmo.

CAP *abbr of [Common Agricultural Policy]* PAC, Política Agrícola Común.

capability ['keipə'biliti] *n* capacidad *f*, competencia *f*, aptitud *f* (of s.o.) || posibilidad *f* (of sth.).

capable ['keipəbl] *adj* capaz; *are you capable of mending the radio?* ¿es usted capaz de arreglar la radio? || capaz, competente; *he's a very capable person* es una persona muy competente || susceptible; *apartment capable of being converted into offices* piso susceptible de ser transformado en oficinas.

capably [-i] *adv* capazmente, de manera competente.

capacious [kə'peiʃəs] *adj* espacioso, sa; amplio, plia (room) || grande (vessel) || holgado, da (clothes).

capacitance [kə'pæsitəns] *n* ELECTR capacitancia *f*.

capacitate [kə'pæsiteit] *vt* JUR capacitar, habilitar (to empower).

capacitor [kə'pæsitə] *n* ELECTR condensador *m*.

capacity [kə'pæsiti] *n* capacidad *f*, cabida *f*; *capacity of a vessel* capacidad de un recipiente || FIG capacidad *f*; *no capacity for concentration* ninguna capacidad de concentración; *work capacity* capacidad de trabajo | calidad *f*; *in his capacity as chairman* en su calidad de presidente || JUR & ELECTR capacidad *f* || AUT cilindrada *f* || — THEATR *capacity house* lleno *m* total || *this room has a sitting capacity of thirty* esta habitación tiene capacidad para treinta personas || *to fill to capacity* llenar completamente || *to work to capacity* producir a pleno rendimiento (factory).

cap-a-pie [,kæpə'pi] *adv* HIST de pies a cabeza (entirely).

caparison [kə'pærisn] *n* caparazón *m* (for horse) || galas *f pl* (ceremonial dress).

caparison [kə'pærisn] *vt* engualdrapar (a horse) || engalanar (s.o.).

cape [keip] *n* esclavina *f* (short cloak) || capa *f* (cloak) || chubasquero *m* (for sailors) || impermeable *m* de hule (for cyclists) || GEOGR cabo *m*, promontorio *m*.

Cape Dutch ['keip-dʌtʃ] *n* Afrikaans *m* (language).

Cape Horn ['keip-hɔ:n] *pr n* GEOGR Cabo *m* de Hornos.

capeline ['kæpə,lin] *n* capellina *f* (hat, bandage).

Cape of Good Hope ['keipəv-gud-həup] *pr n* GEOGR Cabo *m* de Buena Esperanza.

caper ['keipə*] *n* BOT alcaparro *m* (shrub) | alcaparra *f* (bud) || cabriola *f* (jump) || FIG travesura *f* (prank, antic) || — FIG *he's up to his usual capers* está haciendo una de las suyas || *to cut capers* hacer cabriolas (to caper), hacer el loco (to play the fool).

caper ['keipə*] *vi* hacer cabriolas (animals) || corretear, brincar (children).

capercaillie ['kæpə:'keilji] *n* ZOOL urogallo *m*.

Capernaum [kə'pə:njəm] *pr n* HIST Cafarnaum.

Capetian [kə'pi:ʃən] *adj* HIST de los Capetos.
◆ *pr n* HIST Capeto *m*.

Cape Town; Capetown ['keiptaun] *pr n* GEOGR Ciudad *f* del Cabo, El Cabo.

Cape Verde Islands ['keip'və:d,ailəndz] *pl prn* GEOGR islas *f* de Cabo Verde.

capillarity [,kæpi'læriti] *n* capilaridad *f*.

capillary [kə'piləri] *adj* capilar; *capillary tube* tubo capilar.
◆ *n* ANAT capilar *m*, vaso *m* capilar.

capital ['kæpital] *adj* capital; *capital punishment* pena capital || primordial, capital; *of capital importance* de capital importancia || COMM de capital; *capital reserves* reservas de capital || FAM excelente, estupendo, da; magnífico, ca; *a capital entertainment* un espectáculo magnífico || GRAMM mayúscula (letter); *in capitals* en mayúsculas || — *capital assets* activo fijo || *capital city* capital *f* || *capital expenditure* inversión *f* de capital || *capital gains* ganancias *f pl* sobre el capital || — *capital gains tax* impuesto *m* sobre las plusvalías, impuesto *m* sobre las ganancias del capital || *capital goods* bienes *m* de equipo || *capital levy* impuesto *m* sobre el capital || *capital ship* acorazado *m* (battleship) || *capital sin* pecado *m* capital *or* mortal || *capital stock* capital social || *capital transfer tax* impuesto *m* sobre las transferencias de capital.
◆ *n* capital *f* (chief city) || GRAMM mayúscula *f* (letter) || COMM capital *m* || ARCH capitel *m* (of column) || — *capital and labour* capital y trabajo || PRINT *small capitals* versalitas *f* || FIG *to make capital out of* sacar provecho de, aprovechar || COMM *working capital* fondo *m* de operaciones.
— OBSERV En el sentido comercial la palabra inglesa *capital* es invariable: *investment of capital* inversión de capitales.

capitalism [-izəm] *n* capitalismo *m*.

capitalist [-ist] *adj/n* capitalista.

capitalistic [,kæpitə'listik] *adj* capitalista.

capitalization [,kæpitəlai'zeiʃən] *n* capitalización *f*.

capitalize [kæ'pitəlaiz] *vt* COMM capitalizar || escribir *or* imprimir con mayúsculas.
◆ *vi* *to capitalize on* sacar provecho de, aprovechar.

capitation [,kæpi'teiʃən] *n* capitación *f*.

Capitol ['kæpitəl] *pr n* Capitolio *m*.

capitular [kə'pitjulə*] *adj* capitular.
◆ *n* REL capitular *m* (member of a chapter).
◆ *pl* HIST capitulares *f*.

capitulary [-ri] *adj/n* ⟶ **capitular.**

capitulate [kə'pitjuleit] *vi* capitular; *to capitulate to the enemy* capitular ante el enemigo.

capitulation [kə,pitju'leiʃən] *n* capitulación *f*.

capitulum [kə'pitjuləm] *n* BOT & ANAT capítulo *m*.
— OBSERV El plural de *capitulum* es *capitula*.

capon ['keipən] *n* capón *m* (castrated cock).

capotasto [,kæpəu'tæstəu] *n* MUS cejilla *f*, ceja *f*.

capote [kə'pəut] *n* capote *m* (a cloak with a hood).

cappuccino [,kæpə'tʃi:nəu] *n* capuchino *m*.

capriccio [kə'pritʃiəu] *n* capricho *m*.

caprice [kə'pri:s] *n* capricho *m*, antojo *m* (whim) || MUS capricho *m*.

capricious [kə'priʃəs] *adj* caprichoso, sa.

Capricorn ['kæprikɔ:n] *pr n* ASTR Capricornio *m*.

caprification [kæprifi'keiʃən] *n* cabrahigadura *f*.

caprifig ['kæprifig] *n* BOT cabrahigo *m*.

capriole ['kæpriəul] *n* cabriola *f*.

capsicum ['kæpsikəm] *n* pimieto *m*, chile *m*.

capsize [kæp'saiz] *vt* MAR hacer zozobrar (a boat) || (hacer) volcar (to turn over).

capstan ['kæpstən] *n* MAR cabrestante *m*.

capstan lathe [-'leið] *n* TECH torno *m* revólver.

capstone ['kæpstəun] *n* ARCH albardilla *f* || FIG coronamiento *m*.

capsular ['kæpsjulə*] *adj* capsular.

capsule ['kæpsju:l] *n* ANAT, BIOL & BOT cápsula *f* || cápsula *f* (of medicine, of spacecraft, metal top).

captain ['kæptin] *n* capitán *m*; *captain of a ship, of a team* capitán de un barco, de un equipo.

captain ['kæptin] *vt* capitanear.

captaincy [-si] *n* capitanía *f* || *Captaincy General* capitanía general (of a viceroyship).

caption ['kæpʃən] *n* encabezamiento *m*, título *m* (of a chapter, of an article) || pie *m*, leyenda *f* (of illustration, of cartoon) || CINEM subtítulo *m* || JUR indicación *f* de origen (part of a document) | detención *f* (legal arrest).

caption ['kæpʃən] *vt* titular (a chapter, an article) || poner pie a (an illustration, a cartoon).

captious ['kæpʃəs] *adj* capcioso, sa; insidioso, sa; *a captious question* una pregunta capciosa || criticón, ona; reparón, ona (critical).

captiousness [-nis] *n* capciosidad *f* (trickiness) || espíritu *m* crítico (critical mind).

captivate ['kæptiveit] *vt* encantar, cautivar, fascinar.

captivating [-iŋ] *adj* cautivador, ra; fascinador, ra; fascinante, encantador, ra.

captivation [kæpti'veiʃən] *n* fascinación *f*, encanto *m* (fascination).

captivator ['kæptiveitə*] *n* cautivador, ra; fascinador, ra.

captive ['kæptiv] *adj/n* cautivo, va (imprisoned) || FIG cautivado, da; fascinado, da || — *captive balloon* globo cautivo || *to hold captive* mantener cautivo (a prisoner), cautivar, fascinar (to fascinate).

captivity [kæp'tiviti] *n* cautividad *f*, cautiverio *m*.

captor ['kæptə*] *n* apresador, ra; capturador, ra.

capture ['kæptʃə*] *n* captura *f*, apresamiento *m* || MIL toma *f* (taking); *the capture of a town* la toma de una ciudad || preso, sa (person captured) || presa *f*, botín *m* (thing captured).

capture ['kæptʃə*] *vt* capturar, apresar (to take prisoner) || MIL tomar (a place) || FIG atraer, captar (s.o.'s attention, etc.) | acaparar; *to capture a market* acaparar un mercado | captarse, ganarse; *to capture s.o.'s friendship* captarse la amistad de alguien | captar; *the painter captured her expression very well* el pintor captó muy bien su expresión | comer (in chess).

capuchin ['kæpuʃin] *n* capuchón *m*.

Capuchin ['kæpjuʃin] *n* REL capuchino *m* (monk).

capuchin monkey [-mʌŋki] *n* ZOOL mono *m* capuchino, capuchino *m*.

capybara [kæpi'bærə] *n* ZOOL capibara *m*, carpincho *m* (rodent).

car [kɑ:*] *n* coche *m*, automóvil *m* [*AMER* carro *m*]; *to travel by car* viajar en coche || coche *m*, vagón *m* (of a train) || tranvía *m* (tramcar) || jaula *f*, cabina *f* (of lift) || cabina *f* (of cable, of car, etc.) || barquilla *f* (of balloon) || — *car ferry* transbordador *m* para coches || *car park* aparcamiento *m* || *car wash* lavado *m* de coches || *dining car* coche restaurante, coche comedor || *racing car* coche de carreras || *sleeping car* coche cama.

carabao [kærə'bau] *n* ZOOL carabao *m*.

caracara [,kærə'kærə] *n* ZOOL caracará *m*.

Caracas [kə'rækəs] *pr n* GEOGR Caracas.

caracole ['kærəkəul] *n* caracoleo *m*.

caracole ['kærəkəul] *vi* caracolear, hacer caracolas.

caracul ['kærəku:l] *n* caracul *m* (astrakhan).

carafe [kə'ræf] *n* garrafa *f*.

caramel ['kærəmel] *n* caramelo *m* (sweet) || pastilla *f* de leche y azúcar || azúcar *m* quemado (sugar) || color *m* de caramelo (colour).

caramelize [-aiz] *vt* caramelizar.

carapace ['kærəpeis] *n* ZOOL caparazón *m*.

carat ['kærət] *n* quilate *m*; *18 carat gold* oro de 18 quilates.

caravan ['kærəvæn] *n* caravana *f* (of travellers) || carromato *m* (gipsy waggon) || remolque *m*, caravana *f* (towed by a car) || *caravan site* camping *m* para caravanas.

caravaneer [-iə*] *n* caravanero *m*.

caravansary [,kærə'vænsəri]; **caravanserai** [,kærə'vænsərai] *n* caravanseray *m*, caravasar *m*, caravanserrallo *m*.

caravel ['kærəvel] *n* MAR carabela *f*.

caraway ['kærəwei] *n* BOT alcaravea *f* || *caraway seed* carvi *m*.

carbide ['kɑːbaid] *n* CHEM carburo *m*.

carbine ['kɑːbain] *n* carabina *f*.

carbohydrate ['kɑːbəu'haidreit] *n* CHEM carbohidrato *m*, hidrato *m* de carbono.

carbolic [kɑː'bɔlik] *adj* CHEM fénico, ca.

carbon ['kɑːbən] *n* CHEM carbono *m*; *carbon cycle* ciclo de carbono || ELECTR carbón *m* (in batteries, in arc lamps, etc.) || papel *m* carbón (carbon paper) || *carbon dioxide* bióxido *m* or dióxido *m* de carbono, anhídrido *m* carbónico || *carbon monoxide* monóxido *m* de carbono.

carbonaceous [,kɑːbə'neiʃəs] *adj* carbonoso, sa.

carbonado [,kɑːbə'neidəu] *n* MIN carbonado *m*, diamante *m* negro || carbonada *f* (meat, fish).

— OBSERV El plural de la palabra inglesa es *carbonadoes* o *carbonados*.

Carbonaro [kɑːbə'nɑːrəu] *n* HIST carbonario *m*.

— OBSERV El plural de *Carbonaro* es *Carbonari*.

carbonate ['kɑːbənit] *n* CHEM carbonato *m*.

carbonate ['kɑːbəneit] *vt* CHEM carbonatar.

carbonation [kɑːbə'neiʃən] *n* CHEM carbonatación *f*.

carbon copy ['kɑːbən'kɔpi] *n* copia *f* hecha con papel carbón || FIG *he is a carbon copy of his father* es calcado a su padre.

carbonic [kɑː'bɔnik] *adj* CHEM carbónico, ca || CHEM *carbonic-acid gas* anhídrido carbónico.

carboniferous [,kɑːbə'nifərəs] *adj* carbonífero, ra.

◆ *n* GEOL período *m* carbonífero.

carbonization [,kɑːbənai'zeiʃən] *n* carbonización *f*.

carbonize ['kɑːbənaiz] *vt* carbonizar.

◆ *vi* carbonizarse.

carbon paper ['kɑːbən,peipə*] *n* papel *m* carbón.

car boot sale *n* venta *f* de particular a particular de artículos de segunda mano.

carborundum [,kɑːbə'rʌndəm] *n* carborundo *m*.

carboy ['kɑːbɔi] *n* bombona *f*.

carbuncle ['kɑːbʌŋkl] *n* carbúnculo *m* (semiprecious stone) || MED carbunço *m*, carbunclo *m*.

carburant ['kɑːbjurənt] *n* carburante *m*.

carburate ['kɑːbjureit] *vt* carburar.

carburation [,kɑːbju'reiʃən] *n* carburación *f*.

carburet ['kɑːbjuret] *vt* carburar, combinar con carbono.

carburetter; carburettor ['kɑːbjuretə*] *n* TECH carburador *m*.

carburetting ['kɑːbjuretiŋ] *n* CHEM carburación *f*.

carburization [,kɑːbjurai'zeiʃən] *n* carburación (in metallurgy).

carburize ['kɑːbju,raiz] *vt* CHEM carburar.

carcass ['kɑːkəs] *n* res *f* muerta (dead animal) || res *f* abierta en canal (in butchery) || esqueleto *m*, armazón *m* (of a ship, of a building) || armadura *f* (of tyre) || FAM cuerpo *m* (human body) || FAM *to save one's carcass* salvar el pellejo.

carcinogen ['kɑːsinədʒən] *n* MED agente *m* cancerígeno *or* carcinógeno.

carcinoma [,kɑːsi'nəumə] *n* MED carcinoma *m*.

— OBSERV El plural es *carcinomas* or *carcinomata*.

carcinomatous [-təs] *adj* MED carcinomatoso, sa.

card [kɑːd] *n* tarjeta *f*; *visiting card* tarjeta de visita || tarjeta *f* postal, postal *f* (postcard) || carta *f*, naipe *m* (playing card); *to cut, to deal, to shuffle the cards* cortar, repartir, barajar las cartas || ficha *f* (in a file) || carnet *m*; *member's card* carnet de miembro || cartulina *f* (thin cardboard) || TECH carda *f* (for carding textiles) || (ant) gracioso, sa (comic person) || — *card game* juego *m* de cartas || *card index* o *catalogue* fichero *m* || *card table* mesa *f* de juego || *card trick* truco *m* de cartas || *Christmas card* tarjeta de Navidad, crismas *m* || *credit card* tarjeta de crédito || *face* o *court card* figura *f* || *punch card* tarjeta perforada || FAM *queer card* bicho raro || *to get one's cards* ser despedido || FIG *to have a card up one's sleeve* traer algo en la manga | *to play one's last card* jugarse la última carta | *to speak by the card* hablar con seguridad || *wedding card* participación *f* de boda.

◆ *pl* cartas *f*, naipes *m*; *to play cards* jugar a las cartas; *game of cards* partida de cartas || FIG *like a house of cards* como un castillo de naipes || *pack of cards* baraja *f* || FIG *to be on the cards* estar previsto | *to hold all the cards* tener todos los triunfos en la mano | *to lay one's cards on the table* poner las cartas boca arriba | *to play one's cards right* actuar adecuadamente.

card [kɑːd] *vt* TECH cardar (textiles) || poner en una tarjeta.

cardamom ['kɑːdəməm] *n* BOT cardamomo *m*.

cardan ['kɑːdæn] *adj* TECH de cardán; *cardan joint* junta de cardán || *cardan shaft* eje *m* con junta de cardán.

cardboard ['kɑːdbɔːd] *n* cartón *m*; *cardboard box* caja de cartón || *cardboard binding* encuadernación *f* en pasta.

card-carrying [kɑːd'kæriiŋ] *adj* afiliado, da (of party).

card case ['kɑːdkeis] *n* tarjetero *m*.

carder ['kɑːdə*] *n* TECH cardadora *f*, carda *f* (machine) | cardador, ra (person).

cardia ['kɑːdiə] *n* ANAT cardias *m* (in the stomach).

cardiac ['kɑːdiæk] *adj/n* cardiaco, ca; cardíaco, ca; *cardiac muscle* músculo cardíaco; *cardiac arrest* paro cardíaco.

Cardiff ['kɑːdif] *pr n* GEOGR Cardiff.

cardigan ['kɑːdigən] *n* chaqueta *f* de punto, rebeca *f*.

cardinal ['kɑːdinl] *adj* cardinal || esencial, fundamental, principal (of fundamental importance) || purpúreo, a (deep red) || ZOOL purpúreo, a || — *cardinal number* número *m* cardinal || *cardinal point* punto *m* cardinal || *cardinal sins* pecados *m* capitales || *cardinal virtues* virtudes *f* cardinales.

◆ *n* REL cardenal *m* || ZOOL cardenal *m* (bird) || púrpura *f* (colour) || MATH cardinal *m*, número *m* cardinal.

cardinalate [-eit]; **cardinalship** [-ʃip] *n* REL cardenalato *m*.

carding ['kɑːdiŋ] *n* TECH cardadura *f*, carda *f* || *carding machine* cardadora *f*, carda *f*.

cardiogram ['kɑːdiɔgræm] *n* MED cardiograma *m*.

cardiograph ['kɑːdiɔgrɑːf] *n* MED cardiógrafo *m*.

cardiographic [,kɑːdiə'græfik] *adj* MED cardiográfico, ca.

cardiography [kɑːdi'ɔgrəfi] *n* MED cardiografía *f*.

cardiologist [kɑːdi'ɔlədʒist] *n* MED cardiólogo, ga.

cardiology [kɑːdi'ɔlədʒi] *n* MED cardiología *f*.

carditis [kɑː'daitis] *n* MED carditis *f*.

cardoon [kɑː'duːn] *n* BOT cardo *m*.

cardsharp ['kɑːdʃɑːp]; **cardsharper** [-ə*] *n* fullero, ra.

care [kɛə*] *n* cuidado *m*, atención *f*; *to do sth. with great care* hacer algo con mucho cuidado || cuidado *m*; *to be in s.o.'s care* estar al cuidado de alguien || asistencia *f*; *medical care* asistencia médica || inquietud *f*, preocupación *f*; *not to have a care in the world* no tener ninguna preocupación en la vida || cargo *m*; *this matter is in his care* este asunto está a su cargo || — *care of (c/o)* para entregar a (on a letter); *Sr. X, c/o Sr. Y* Sr. Y, para entregar al Sr. X || *handle with care* frágil (on a parcel) || FIG *I'll take care of him!* ¡ya me encargaré yo de él! || *it can take care of itself* eso se resolverá por sí mismo || *take care!* ¡ojo!, ¡cuidado! || *the cares of State* las responsabilidades del gobierno || *to be in the care of a good doctor* atenderle a uno un buen médico || *to take care* tener cuidado || *to take care not to* guardarse de || *to take care of* cuidar de (a person), guardar (an object), ocuparse de (a matter) || *to take care of o.s.* cuidarse || *with care!* ¡cuidado!

care [kɛə*] *vt* preocuparse por; *to care what people say* preocuparse por el qué dirán || *I don't care what happens* no me importa lo que pase.

◆ *vi* importarle a uno; *I don't care a damn* o *tuppence* no me importa un bledo *or* un comino || — *for all I care you can go ahead* por mí lo puedes hacer || *I couldn't care less!* ¡me trae completamente sin cuidado!, ¡me importa un pepino! || *I don't care either way* me da completamente igual || FAM *I don't care if I do* no me disgustaría || *the trouble is he just doesn't care* el problema es que le trae sin cuidado || *to care about* interesarse por, tener interés en || *to care for* cuidar de (to look after); *the nurse-maid cares for the children* la niñera cuida de los niños; *a well cared-for lawn* un césped bien cuidado; gustarle a uno (to like); *I do not care for ice cream* no me gusta el helado; querer (to love); *he cares for her a lot* la quiere mucho; apetecerle a uno, querer; *would you care for an ice cream?* ¿te apetece un helado?, ¿quieres un helado? || *to care to* querer; *would you care to try it on?* ¿quiere usted probárselo? || FAM *what do I care?* ¿y a mí qué me importa? || *would you care to give me your address?* ¿tiene usted inconveniente en darme su dirección?

careen [kə'riːn] *n* MAR carena *f*, carenadura *f*.

careen [kə'riːn] *vt* MAR inclinar, volcar (to turn a ship on its side) | carenar (to clean, to repair).

◆ *vi* MAR dar de banda.

careenage [-idʒ] *n* carenero *m* (place) || gastos *m pl* de carena (expenses) || carena *f*, carenadura *f* (careen).

career [kə'riə*] *adj* de carrera; *career diplomat* diplomático de carrera.

◆ *n* carrera *f* (swift movement); *in full career* en plena carrera || carrera *f*; *to choose a career* escoger una carrera || profesión *f* (profession) || curso *m* (of life) || carrera *f* (of stars).

career [kə'riə*] *vi* correr a toda velocidad.

careerist [kə'riərist] *n* arribista *m* & *f*.

carefree ['kɛəfriː] *adj* despreocupado, da.

careful ['kɛəful] *adj* cuidadoso, sa; cauteloso, sa; prudente (cautious) ‖ cuidadoso, sa; esmerado, da (painstaking) ‖ acicalado, da; esmerado, da (appearance) ‖ cuidado, da; esmerado, da (piece of work) ‖ atento, ta; *careful of the rights of others* atento a los derechos de los demás ‖ — *be careful!* ¡ten cuidado! ‖ *be careful what you do* ten cuidado con lo que haces ‖ *careful!* ¡cuidado!, ¡ojo! ‖ *careful with one's money* económico, ca ‖ *to be careful* tener cuidado (*of* con) ‖ *to be careful to* tener cuidado en.

carefully [-i] *adv* con cuidado, cuidadosamente.

carefulness [-nis] *n* cuidado *m*, esmero *m* (attention to details) ‖ prudencia *f*, cautela *f* (cautiousness).

careless ['kɛəlis] *adj* descuidado, da; negligente (negligent) ‖ despreocupado, da (carefree) ‖ irreflexivo, va; imprudente (thoughtless) ‖ desaliñado, da; descuidado, da (clothes, appearance) ‖ hecho a la ligera *or* sin cuidado; *a careless piece of work* un trabajo hecho a la ligera.

carelessness [-nis] *n* descuido *m*, negligencia *f* (negligence) ‖ desaliño *m* (of clothes, of appearance) ‖ despreocupación *f*, indiferencia *f* (indifference) ‖ *through sheer carelessness* por simple descuido.

caress [kə'res] *n* caricia *f*.

caress [kə'res] *vt* acariciar.

caressing [-iŋ] *adj* acariciador, ra; acariciante.

caret ['kærət] *n* PRINT signo *m* de intercalación.

caretaker ['kɛəˌteikə*] *n* vigilante *m*, guarda *m* ‖ portero, ra (of a block of flats) ‖ FIG *caretaker government* gobierno *m* provisional.

careworn ['kɛəwɔːn] *adj* agobiado por las inquietudes.

carfare ['kɑːfɛə*] *n* US precio *m* del trayecto (public transport) | cambio *m* (money).

cargo ['kɑːgəu] *n* MAR carga *f*, cargamento *m*; *mixed* o *general cargo* carga mixta ‖ MAR *cargo boat* buque *m* de carga, carguero *m*.
— OBSERV El plural de *cargo* es *cargoes* o *cargos*.

car-hire firm ['kɑːhaiəˌfəːm] *n* compañía *f* de coches de alquiler.

carhop ['kɑːhɔp] *n* US camarero, ra [en un restaurante donde se sirve a los clientes en su coche].

Carib ['kærib] *n* Caribe *m* & *f*.

Cariban [-ən] *n* caribe *m* (language).

Caribbean [ˌkæri'biən] *adj* caribe ‖ — GEOGR *Caribbean Islands* islas *f* del Caribe, Antillas *f* | *Caribbean Sea* mar *m* Caribe.

caribou ['kæribuː] *n* ZOOL caribú *m*.

caricatural [ˌkærikə'tjuərəl] *adj* caricaturesco, ca; caricatural.

caricature [ˌkærikə'tjuə*] *n* caricatura *f*.

caricature [ˌkærikə'tjuə*] *vt* caricaturizar.

caricaturist [ˌkærikə'tjuərist] *n* caricaturista *m* & *f*.

caries ['kɛəriiːz] *inv n* MED caries *f*.

carillon ['kæriljən] *n* carillón *m* (bells and sound).

carillon ['kæriljən] *vi* repicar, repiquetear.

caring *adj* solícito, ta; atento, ta ‖ *caring professions* enfermería *f* y asistencia *f* social.

cariole ['kæriəul] *n* US ⟶ **carriole.**

carious ['kɛəriəs] *adj* MED cariado, da.

carking ['kɑːkiŋ] *adj* atormentador, ra (burdensome).

Carlism ['kɑːlizəm] *pr n* carlismo *m*.

Carlist ['kɑːlist] *adj/n* carlista; *Carlist Wars* guerras carlistas.

carload ['kɑːləud] *n* US carga *f* de un carro (load of a freight car) | carga *f* mínima que se beneficia de una tarifa reducida (minimum weight).

Carlovingian [ˌkɑːləu'vindʒiən] *adj/n* carlovingio, gia; carolingio, gia.

carmagnole ['kɑːmənjəul] *n* carmañola *f*.

Carmel ['kɑːməl] *pr n* Carmelo *m* (in Palestine).

Carmelite ['kɑːmilait] *adj/n* REL carmelita.

carminative ['kɑːminətiv] *adj* MED carminativo, va.
◆ *n* MED carminativo, va.

carmine ['kɑːmain] *adj* carmín *inv*.
◆ *n* carmín *m*.

carnage ['kɑːnidʒ] *n* carnicería *f*, matanza *f* (great bloodshed).

carnal ['kɑːnl] *adj* carnal ‖ *carnal knowledge* ayuntamiento *m* carnal.

carnality [kɑː'næliti] *n* sensualidad *f*.

carnation [kɑː'neiʃən] *n* BOT clavel *m* (flower).

carnelian [kə'niːljən] *n* MIN cornalina *f*.

carnival ['kɑːnivəl] *n* carnaval *m* ‖ US feria *f*, verbena *f* (travelling amusements).

carnivore ['kɑːnivɔː*] *n* carnívoro, ra.

carnivorous [kɑːnivərəs] *adj* carnívoro, ra.

carob ['kærəb] *n* BOT algarrobo *m* (tree) ‖ BOT *carob bean* algarroba *f* (fruit).

carol ['kærəl] *n* villancico *m* (Christmas hymn) ‖ canto *m* (of birds).

carol ['kærəl] *vi* cantar villancicos ‖ cantar (birds).
◆ *vt* cantar.

Caroline ['kærəlain] *adj* HIST carolino, na ‖ GEOGR *Caroline Islands* islas Carolinas.

Carolingian [ˌkærə'lindʒjən] *adj/n* HIST carolingio, gia; carlovingio, gia.

carom ['kærəm] *n* US carambola *f* (in billiards).

carotene ['kærətiːn] *n* CHEM caroteno *m*.

carotid [kə'rɔtid] *adj* ANAT carótida (artery).
◆ *n* ANAT carótida *f*.

carotin ['kærətin] *n* CHEM caroteno *m*.

carousal [kə'rauzəl]; **carouse** [kə'rauz] *n* juerga *f*, jarana *f*.

carouse [kə'rauz] *vi* estar de juerga *or* de jarana, correrse una juerga, juerguearse.

carousel [ˌkæruː'zəl] *n* ⟶ **carrousel.**

carouser [kə'rauzə*] *n* juerguista *m* & *f*.

carp [kɑːp] *n* ZOOL carpa *f* (fish).

carp [kɑːp] *vi* quejarse (to complain) ‖ *to carp at* criticar.

carpal ['kɑːpəl] *adj* ANAT carpiano, na.
◆ *n* ANAT carpo *m* (bone).

Carpathian Mountains [kɑː'peiθjən'mauntinz] *pl prn* GEOGR Cárpatos *m*.

carpel ['kɑːpel] *n* BOT carpelo *m*.

carpenter ['kɑːpintə*] *n* carpintero *m* ‖ — ZOOL *carpenter ant, bee, moth* hormiga, abeja, polilla carpintera ‖ *carpenter's horse* caballete *m*.

carpentry ['kɑːpintri] *n* carpintería *f*.

carpet ['kɑːpit] *n* alfombra *f* ‖ moqueta *f* (fitted) ‖ — *carpet beetle* insecto *m* que ataca las alfombras ‖ *carpet slippers* zapatillas *f* ‖ *carpet sweeper* escoba mecánica ‖ FIG *to be on the carpet* estar sobre el tapete (to be under discussion), estar recibiendo una regañina *or* un rapapolvo (to be reprimanded) | *to roll out the red carpet for s.o.* recibir a alguien con todos los honores.

carpet ['kɑːpit] *vt* alfombrar ‖ poner moqueta en (fitted carpet) ‖ FIG echar un rapapolvo a (to scold).

carpetbag ['kɑːpitbæg] *n* HIST bolsa *f* de viaje [hecha de tejido de alfombra].

carpetbagger ['kɑːpitˌbægə*] *n* US HIST politicastro *m* del norte de Estados Unidos que intentaba triunfar en el Sur (politician) ‖ aventurero *m*, estafador *m* (adventurer).

carpeting ['kɑːpitiŋ] *n* alfombrado *m* (carpets) ‖ moqueta *f* (fitted) ‖ tejido *m* para alfombras (carpet fabric).

carpi ['kɑːpai] *pl n* ⟶ **carpus.**

carping ['kɑːpiŋ] *adj* criticón, ona.

carpological [kɑːpə'lɔdʒikəl] *adj* BOT carpológico, ca.

carpology [kɑː'pɔlədʒi] *n* BOT carpología *f*.

carport ['kɑːpɔːt] *n* cobertizo *m* para guardar el coche.

carpus ['kɑːpəs] *n* ANAT carpo *m*.
— OBSERV El plural de *carpus* es *carpi*.

carriage ['kæridʒ] *n* carruaje *m*, coche *m*; *carriage and pair* coche de dos caballos ‖ carroza *f*; *the Queen's carriage* la carroza de la Reina ‖ vagón *m*, coche *m* (railway) ‖ andares *m pl*, manera *f* de andar, porte *m* (manner of holding o.s.) ‖ comportamiento *m*, conducta *f* (behaviour) ‖ manejo *m*, dirección *f* (of a business) ‖ transporte *m*, porte *m* (of goods) ‖ MIL cureña *f* (of gun) ‖ carro *m* (of typewriter, etc.) ‖ — *carriage builder* carrocero *m* ‖ *carriage entrance* entrada *f* de carruajes, puerta cochera ‖ COMM *carriage free, carriage paid* franco de porte, porte pagado ‖ INFORM *carriage return* retorno *m* de carro.

carriageway ['kæridʒwei] *n* AUT calzada *f* ‖ *dual carriageway* carretera *f* de doble calzada.

carrier ['kæriə*] *n* transportista *m* (person) ‖ empresa *f* de transportes (company) ‖ mensajero, ra (messenger) ‖ portaequipajes *m inv* (on a bicycle) ‖ AVIAT transportista *m* ‖ MED portador, ra (of a disease) ‖ MIL portaaviones *m inv* (aircraft carrier) ‖ — *carrier bag* bolsa *f* ‖ *carrier pigeon* paloma mensajera ‖ RAD *carrier wave* onda portadora.

carriole ['kæriəul] *n* carruaje *m* ligero para una persona.

carrion ['kæriən] *n* carroña *f* ‖ ZOOL *carrion crow* corneja *f* (bird).

carrot ['kærət] *n* BOT zanahoria *f*.

carrotene; carrotin [-iːn] *n* CHEM caroteno *m*.

carroty [-i] *adj* color *m* zanahoria; *a carroty dress* un traje color zanahoria ‖ rojo, ja; rojizo, za (hair) ‖ pelirrojo, ja (red-haired).

carrousel; carousel [ˌkæruː'zel] *n* carrusel *m* ‖ tiovivo *m*, caballitos *m pl* (merry-go-round) ‖ torneo *m*, carrusel *m* (tournament).

carry ['kæri] *n* alcance *m* (of a weapon) ‖ transporte *m* entre dos vías navegables (portage) ‖ SP trayecto *m* (of a golf ball).

carry ['kæri] *vt* llevar (to convey); *to carry a parcel under one's arm* llevar un paquete bajo el brazo ‖ traer (to bring) ‖ llevar, transportar (a load); *a lorry carrying logs* un camión que transporta troncos; *a car which carries five persons* un coche que lleva cinco personas ‖ llevar, conducir (a liquid); *these pipes carry oil* estas tuberías llevan petróleo ‖ llevar, tener consigo (on one's person); *I never carry my passport* nunca llevo el pasaporte ‖ sostener (to support); *flyover carried on concrete piles* paso elevado sostenido por pilotes de hormigón ‖ prolongar, extender (to prolong); *the wall is carried to the end of the street* el muro se extiende hasta el final de la calle ‖ tener (on a list) ‖ FIG tener, gozar (to enjoy); *he carries no authority* no tiene ninguna autoridad | llevar consigo, entrañar, implicar (to be accompanied by); *a job which carries great responsibility* un cargo que lleva consigo mucha responsabilidad | acarrear (to give rise to); *an act which will carry serious consequences* una acción que acarreará serias consecuencias | tener (meaning) | retener (in the mind) | sufrir, aguantar, soportar (grief, etc.) || hacer aprobar (to get the approval of) || aprobar (to approve); *carried unanimously* aprobado por unanimidad || llevar; *a number which carries a prize* un número que lleva premio || ganar (to win); *her husband carried the election* su marido ganó las elecciones || salvar (an obstacle) || ganarse, captarse (to capture); *an outstanding performance which carried the audience* una interpretación extraordinaria que se captó al público | llevar (to hold); *she carries her head well* lleva la cabeza con garbo || COMM tener en existencia (to have in stock) | producir (interest, crop) || MIL conquistar, tomar (a position) | ganar (a war) || MAR llevar puesto (sail) || rastrear, seguir (hunting) || MATH llevarse (in addition); *two down, carry one* pongo dos y me llevo uno || US cantar afinado (a tune) || — *to carry a child* estar embarazada || *to carry all before one* ir arrollándolo todo, tener un éxito arrollador || *to carry a person with one* convencer a alguien || *to carry conviction* ser convincente || *to carry insurance* estar asegurado || FIG *to carry one's head high* llevar la cabeza alta || *to carry o.s.* portarse, conducirse || *to carry o.s. well* andar con garbo || FIG *to carry sth. too far* llevar algo demasiado lejos || FIG & FAM *to carry the can* pagar el pato || FIG *to carry the day* triunfar, salir bien | *to have had as much as one can carry* haber bebido todo lo que se puede beber.

◆ *vi* alcanzar, llegar, tener al alcance; *this rifle carries half a mile* este fusil tiene un alcance de media milla || llegar, oírse; *a sound which carries a long way* un sonido que llega muy lejos *or* que se oye desde muy lejos || tener efecto (to be effective) || ser aprobado (a law, a project, etc.).

◆ *phr v* ***to carry about*** llevar consigo (to have on one) | llevar de un lado para otro || ***to carry along*** arrastrar; *he was carried along with the wreckage of his boat* fue arrastrado con los restos del barco | llevar || ***to carry away*** llevarse (sth.) | entusiasmar, exaltar (emotionally); *don't get carried away* no te exaltes | arrebatar (passion) | arrancar, arrebatar; *the masts were carried away by the storm* los mástiles fueron arrancados por la tormenta || ***to carry back*** devolver (to return) | recordar (to remind) || ***to carry down*** bajar || ***to carry forward*** pasar a la página *or* a la columna siguiente (bookkeeping) || — *carried forward* suma y sigue || ***to carry into*** llevar || — *to carry into effect* llevar a cabo, realizar || ***to carry off*** llevarse (to take away); *to carry off a prize, a prisoner* llevarse un premio, a un preso | ganar (an election) | matar (to cause the death of) | realizar, llevar a cabo (a plan) | salir airoso de, salir bien de (difficult situation) || ***to carry on*** seguir, continuar (to continue) | mantener (to hold); *to carry on a conversation* mantener una conversación | ejercer (a profession) | dirigir, llevar adelante (a business) | insistir (to insist) | reñir, discutir (to argue) | hacer una escena (to make a scene) | comportarse (to behave) | FAM tener una aventura || — *carry on!* ¡siga! || *to carry on somehow* ir tirando || FAM *you do carry on!* ¡dale que dale! || ***to carry out*** realizar, llevar a cabo (a plan) | hacer, llevar a cabo (repairs, test) | cumplir (a promise, a threat) || ***to carry over*** llevar a la columna *or* a la página siguiente (bookkeeping) | conservarse (to survive); *customs which have carried over from the last century* costumbres que se han conservado desde el siglo pasado | llevar al otro lado (to transfer) | guardar (to hold over) | convencer (a person) || ***to carry through*** llevar a cabo (a course of action) | ayudar (a salir de un mal paso) (s.o.) || ***to carry up*** subir.

carryall ['kæriɔːl] *n* bolsa *f* (bag) || US carruaje *m* cubierto y tirado por un solo caballo.

carrycot ['kærikɔt] *n* cuna *f* portátil.

carry-on ['kæri'ɔn] *n* FAM lío *m*, jaleo *m* (fuss) | pelea *f* (quarrel).

carry-over ['kæri'əuvə*] *n* COMM suma *f or* saldo *m* anterior (in bookkeeping) || remanente *m* (remainder).

carsick ['kɑːsik] *adj* mareado, da || *I get carsick* me mareo en coche.

cart [kɑːt] *n* carro *m* (drawn by horses) || carreta *f* (drawn by oxen) || carretilla *f*, carro *m* de mano (handcart) || carromato *m* (covered) || cochecito *m*, carrito *m* (child's) || mesa *f* de ruedas, carrito *m* (trolley for tea, etc.) || carrito *m* (supermarket trolley) || — *cart horse* caballo *m* de tiro || *cart rut* o *track* carril *m*, rodada *f* || FIG *to be on the cart* estar en un aprieto | *to put the cart before the horse* empezar la casa por el tejado.

cart [kɑːt] *vt* acarrear, carretear (to convey by cart) || FIG & FAM llevar; *the demonstrators were carted off to the police station* los manifestantes fueron llevados a la comisaría || FAM *to cart about* llevar.

cartage ['kɑːtidʒ] *n* acarreo *m*, porte *m*.

carte [kɑːt] *n* cuarta *f* (fencing) || — *a la carte* a la carta (in restaurant) || FIG *carte blanche* carta blanca.

cartel [kɑː'tel] *n* COMM cártel *m*.

carter ['kɑːtə*] *n* carretero *m* (cart driver) || transportista *m* (carrier).

Cartesian [kɑː'tiːzjən] *adj/n* cartesiano, na.

Carthage [ˌkɑːθidʒ] *pr n* HIST Cartago.

Carthaginian ['kɑːθə'dʒiniən] *adj/n* HIST cartaginés, esa; cartaginense || *Carthaginian wars* Guerras Púnicas.

Carthusian [kɑː'θjuːzjən] *adj/n* REL cartujo *m*.

cartilage ['kɑːtilidʒ] *n* ANAT cartílago *m*.

cartilaginoid [ˌkɑːti'lædʒinɔid] *adj* cartilaginoso, sa; cartilagíneo, a.

cartilaginous [ˌkɑːti'lædʒinəs] *adj* cartilaginoso, sa.

cartload ['kɑːtləud] *adj* carretada *f*; *by cartloads* a carretadas.

cartogram ['kɑːtəgræm] *n* cartograma *m*.

cartographer [kɑː'tɔgrəfə*] *n* cartógrafo, fa.

cartography [kɑː'tɔgrəfi] *n* cartografía *f*.

cartomancy ['kɑːtəumænsi] *n* cartomancia *f*, cartomancía *f*.

carton ['kɑːtən] *n* caja *f* de cartón (cardboard box) || cartón *m* (of cigarettes) || diana *f* (of a target).

cartoon [kɑː'tuːn] *n* caricatura *f* (caricature) || chiste *m* (illustrated joke) || ARTS cartón *m* (preliminary sketch) || tira *f* humorística, historieta *f* (comic strip) || dibujos *m pl* animados (film).

cartoonist [-ist] *n* caricaturista *m* & *f* (caricaturist) || humorista *m* & *f*, dibujante *m* & *f* (s.o. who draws cartoons) || realizador *m* de dibujos animados (of films).

cartouche [kɑː'tuːʃ] *n* ARCH tarjeta *f*.

cartridge ['kɑːtridʒ] *n* cartucho *m* (in firearms); *blank cartridge* cartucho sin bala *or* de fogueo || PHOT cartucho *m* || recambio *m* (for pen) || — *cartridge belt* cartuchera *f*, canana *f* (round the waist), cinta *f* (of a machinegun) || *cartridge clip* cargador *m*, peine *m* (holder for cartridges), *cartridge pen* bolígrafo *m* de recambio.

cartulary ['kɑːtjuləri] *n* cartulario *m*.

cartwheel ['kɑːtwiːl] *n* rueda *f* de carro (wheel of a cart) || FIG voltereta *f* lateral [sobre pies y manos] (somersault) || FAM moneda *f* de un dólar.

cartwright ['kɑːtrait] *n* carretero *m*.

caruncle ['kærəŋkl] *n* ZOOL & BOT carúncula *f* (excrescence, outgrowth).

carve [kɑːv] *vt/vi* cortar (to cut) || tallar, esculpir, cincelar (in stone, in wood) || grabar (on a tree) || CULIN trinchar (meat); *to carve the chicken* trinchar el pollo || — FIG *to carve one's way through* abrirse camino entre || *to carve out* tallar, esculpir; *to carve out a sculpture* tallar una escultura; labrar, hacer (by effort); *to carve out a future* labrarse un porvenir; separar (to separate from), adueñarse de (to take over) || *to carve up* dividir (to divide), cortar (to cut up), acuchillar (to stab).

◆ *vi* esculpir || CULIN trinchar carne.

carvel ['kɑːvəl] *n* MAR carabela *f*.

carver ['kɑːvə*] *n* escultor, ra; tallista, *m* & *f* (person who carves) || CULIN cuchillo *m* de trinchar, trinchante *m* (knife).

◆ *pl* CULIN cubierto *m sing* de trinchar.

carving ['kɑːviŋ] *n* talla *f*, escultura *f* (sculpture) || CULIN arte *m* cisoria (ability of carving) || *carving knife* cuchillo *m* de trinchar, trinchante *m*.

caryatid [ˌkæri'ætid] *n* cariátide *f*.

— OBSERV El plural de *caryatid* es *caryatids* o *caryatides*.

caryopsis [ˌkæri'ɔpsis] *m* BOT cariópside *f*.

cascade [kæs'keid] *adj* escalonado, da; en cascada.

◆ *n* cascada *f*, salto *m* de agua || FIG chorro *m*, torrente *m*.

cascade [kæs'keid] *vi* caer en forma de cascada.

cascarilla [ˌkæskə'rilə] *n* cascarillo *m* (tree).

case [keis] *n* caja *f* (box and its contents) || estuche *m* (rigid; for spectacles, instruments, scissors, knives, etc.) || funda *f* (soft; for pistol, guitar, etc.) || maleta *f* (suitcase) || caja *f* (of watch) || MUS caja *f* (of piano) || TECH camisa *f* || vitrina *f* (showcase) || bastidor *m*, marco *m* (of a door, of a window) || pasta *f* (bookbinding) || PRINT caja *f* (where type is kept); *lower, upper case* caja baja, alta || caso *m*; *in that case* en ese caso; *in most cases* en la mayoría de los casos; *that is not my case* ése no es mi caso || asunto *m*, caso *m*; *the police is working on a drug-smuggling case* la policía está investigando en un asunto de contrabando de drogas || MED caso *m*; *a case of tonsillitis* un caso de amigdalitis || motivo *m* (motive) || FAM caso *m* (strange person) || JUR causa *f*, pleito *m*, proceso *m* || GRAMM caso *m* || — *as the case may be* según el caso || MED *case history* historial clínico, historia clínica || *case law* precedentes *m pl*, jurisprudencia *f* || *case of conscience* caso de conciencia || *he is a case!* ¡es un caso! || *if such is the case* si ése es el caso || *in any case* en todo caso, en cualquier caso, de todas formas || *in case* en caso de que, por si acaso || *in case of* en caso de || *in no case* de ningún modo || *in such a case* en un caso así, en tal caso || *in the case of* en cuanto a, en lo que se refiere a || *it's not a case of* no se trata de || *it's not the case* ése no es el caso || *just in case* por si acaso, por si las moscas || *that alters the case* eso cambia la cosa || *that being the case* si ése es el caso || JUR *the case for the defence* la defensa | *the case for the prosecution* la acusación || *the case in point* el asunto de que se trata || JUR *to bring a case against* poner un pleito a | *to get up a case* instruir un caso || FIG *to have a good* o *a strong case* tener argumentos fuertes *or* convincentes | *to make out one's case* demostrar su punto de vista | *to put forward a good case* presentar argumentos convincentes | *to put* o *to state one's case* presentar sus argumentos, exponer su caso || JUR *to rest one's case* terminar su alegato | *to state the case* exponer los hechos.

case [keis] *vt* embalar, encajonar || poner en un estuche || enfundar (to sheathe) || TECH revestir || *US* FAM *to case the joint* reconocer el terreno.

casebook [-buk] *n* JUR repertorio *m* de jurisprudencia || MED registro *m* que contiene las historias clínicas de los enfermos.

case harden [-hɑːdn] *vt* TECH cementar || FIG insensibilizar, endurecer.

casein ['keisiːin] *n* CHEM caseína *f*.

casemate ['keismeit] *n* MIL casamata *f*.

casement ['keismənt] *n* marco *m* (of a window) || ventana *f* de bisagras (hinged window).

caseous ['keisjəs] *adj* caseoso, sa.

casette [ka'set] *n* ⟶ **cassette.**

casework ['keiswəːk] *n* estudio *m* de los antecedentes personales *or* familiares.

caseworker [-ə*] *n* asistente *m* social, asistenta *f* social.

cash [kæʃ] *n* dinero *m* contante *or* efectivo, metálico, *m* (ready money); *to convert into cash* convertir en dinero efectivo || COMM pago *m* al contado; *cash price* precio *m* al contado | caja *f* || — COMM *cash account* cuenta *f* de caja | *cash book* libro *m* de caja | *cash crop* cultivo *m* comercial | *cash discount* descuento *m* por pago al contado | *cash down* al contado | *cash flow* «cash flow» *m* corriente *f* en efectivo, movimientos *m pl* de efectivos | *cash in hand* o *on hand* efectivo *m* en caja, metálico *m or* líquido *m* disponible | *cash on delivery* envío *m or* entrega *f* contra reembolso | *cash payment* pago *m* al contado | *cash prize* premio *m* en metálico | *cash register* caja registradora | *cash sale* venta *f* al contado | *cash value* valor efectivo | *for cash* al contado | *hard cash* dinero contante y sonante | *in cash* en metálico | *petty cash* dinero para gastos menores || FAM *to be out of cash* estar sin una gorda, estar sin blanca || *to pay cash for sth.* pagar algo al contado.

cash [kæʃ] *vt* cobrar en efectivo || cobrar, hacer efectivo (a cheque) || FIG *to cash in on* sacar provecho de.

cash-and-carry [-ænd-'kæri] *adj* *cash-and-carry system* sistema *m* de pago al contado sin entrega a domicilio.

cashbox [-bɔks] *n* caja *f*.

cashdesk [-desk] *n* caja *f*.

cash dispenser [-dis'pensə*] *n* cajero *m* automático.

cashew [kæ'ʃuː] *n* BOT anacardo *m* || *cashew nut* anacardo *m*.

cashier [kæ'ʃiə*] *n* cajero, ra.

cashier [kæ'ʃiə*] *vt* destituir (to dismiss) || despedir (to fire) || MIL dar de baja || FIG eliminar.

cashmere [kæʃmiə*] *n* cachemira *f* (fabric).

Cashmere [kæʃmiə*] *pr n* GEOGR Cachemira *f*.

cashoo [kæ'ʃu] *n* cato *m*.

cashpoint ['kæʃpɔint] *n* cajero *m* automático.

casing ['keisiŋ] *n* cubierta *f*, envoltura *f* (for wrapping) || funda *f* || estuche *m* (case) || bastidor *m*, marco *m* (of a door, of a window) || revoque *m* (of a wall) || cubierta *f* (of a tyre) || MIN encofrado *m*, entibación *f* || camisa *f* (of a cylinder) || revestimiento *m* (of boilers, etc.) || jareta *f* (in sewing).

casino [kə'siːnəu] *n* casino *m*.

cask [kɑːsk] *n* barril *m*, tonel *m*.

cask [kɑːsk] *vt* entonelar, embarrilar.

casket [-it] *n* cofre *m*, joyero *m* (for holding jewels, etc.) || urna *f* (for the ashes of a cremated person) || *US* ataúd *m* (coffin).

Caspian Sea ['kæpiən'siː] *pr n* GEOGR mar *m* Caspio.

casque [kæsk] *n* HIST yelmo *m* (helmet).

Cassandra [kə'sændrə] *pr n* Casandra *f*.

cassation [kæ'seiʃən] *n* JUR casación *f*.

cassava [kə'sɑːvə] *n* BOT mandioca *f*, yuca *f* (plant) || mandioca *f* (flour) || cazabe *m* (bread).

casserole ['kæsərəul] *n* cacerola *f* (container) || CULIN cazuela *f* (cooker food).

cassette; casette [kə'set] *n* PHOT cartucho *m* || «cassette» *f* (tape recording).

cassette deck [-dek] *n* platina *f*.

cassette player [-pleiə*] *n* casete *m*.

cassette recorder [-ri'kɔːdə*] *n* casete *m*.

cassia ['kæsiə] *n* BOT casia *f*.

Cassiopeia [ˌkæsiə'piːə] *pr n* MYTH & ASTR Casiopea *f*.

cassiterite [kə'sitərait] *n* MIN casiterita *f*.

Cassius ['kæsiəs] *pr n* Casio *m*.

cassock ['kæsək] *n* sotana *f*.

cassowary ['kæsəwɛəri] *n* casuario *m* (bird).

cast [kɑːst] *n* lanzamiento *m* (throw) || distancia *f*, alcance *m* (range) || apariencia *f*, aspecto *m* (appearance) || matiz *m*, tinte *m*, toque *m* (of colour) || naturaleza *f*, carácter *m* (kind) || disposición *f* (of mind) || tirada *f*, jugada *f* (of dice) || número *m* que sale al tirar los dados (number thrown) || caída *f* (of drapery) || cálculo *m* (calculation) || THEATR & CINEM reparto *m* || TECH molde *m*, forma *f* (where metal is poured) | pieza *f* fundida (moulded product) || MATH suma *f* (addition) || ZOOL regurgitación *f* (made by birds of prey) | piel *f* (of reptile) || MED ligero estrabismo *m* (slight squint) | escayola *f* (for immobilizing a broken limb) || — *cast of features* facciones *f pl* || *cast of mind* mentalidad *f*, temperamento *m*.

cast* [kɑːst] *vt* tirar, arrojar, lanzar (to throw) || tirar (dice) || proyectar (shadow) || cambiar, mudar; *the snake casts its skin* la serpiente cambia la piel || emitir (a vote); *not many votes were cast in his favour* no fueron emitidos muchos votos a favor suyo || dar; *I cast my vote for you* le doy mi voto || descartarse de (cards) || echar (a book); *to cast a glance* echar una ojeada || echar (the blame on s.o.) || sumar (to add up) || calcular || vaciar (molten metal, plaster) || fundir (metals) || arrojar, echar (in fishing); *he cast the line into the water* arrojó el sedal al agua || parir antes de tiempo (cow) || THEATR hacer el reparto de; *to cast a play* hacer el reparto de una obra | adjudicar el papel de, dar el papel de, asignar el papel de (to assign); *he was casted as Othello* le fue asignado el papel de Otelo || hacer (a horoscope) || PRINT estereotipar || MAR hacer virar (a boat) || combar, alabear (a beam, etc.) || — *the die is cast* la suerte está echada || MAR *to cast anchor* echar el ancla, anclar, fondear || *to cast an eye at sth.* echar una mirada *or* un vistazo *or* una ojeada a algo || *to cast a shoe* desherrarse (a horse) || *to cast a spell on* hechizar || *to cast doubt upon* poner en duda || *to cast feathers* pelechaz || *to cast into prison* meter en la cárcel || FIG *to cast light on* aclarar, arrojar luz sobre || *to cast loose* soltar || *to cast lots for* sortear, echar a suertes || *to cast one's cares upon* hacer partícipe de sus preocupaciones || *to cast one's eyes on s.o.* mirar a alguien || FIG *to cast one's mind back* volver la vista atrás, rememorar || *to cast the evil eye on* hechizar, aojar.

◆ *vi* volver, virar (to tack) || echar el sedal (fishing) || echar los dados (to throw dice) || vomitar, devolver (to vomit) || combarse, alabearse (a beam) || MATH sumar (to add up) || *to cast loose* soltar las amarras.

◆ *phr v* *to cast about for* buscar (to look for) || *to cast aside* o *away* desechar, descartar (to discard) | abandonar (to abandon) | *to be cast away* naufragar || *to cast down* bajar; *to cast one's eyes down* bajar los ojos | desanimar, abatir (to depress) | derribar || *to cast forth* despedir || *to cast off* abandonar (to abandon) | deshacerse de (a burden) | desechar (old clothes) | cerrar (in knitting) | desamarrar, soltar (a ship) || *to cast on* echar los puntos (in knitting) || *to cast out* echar, arrojar (to expel) | *to cast out devils* exorcizar a los demonios || *to cast up* vomitar (to vomit) | levantar; *to cast one's eyes up* levantar los ojos | sumar (an account).

— OBSERV Pret y pp ***cast***.

castanet [ˌkæstə'net] *n* MUS castañuela *f*.

castaway ['kɑːstəwei] *adj/n* náufrago, ga (shipwrecked) || paria (outcast).

caste [kɑːst] *n* casta *f* || FIG *to lose caste* perder categoría.

castellated ['kæsteleitid] *adj* almenado, da (with battlements) || encastillado, da (like a castle).

caster ['kɑːstə*] *n* TECH vaciador *m* || ⟶ **castor.**

castigate ['kæstigeit] *vt* reprobar, censurar (to rebuke) || castigar (to punish).

castigation [ˌkæsti'geiʃən] *n* castigo *m* (punishment) || reprobación *f*, censura *f* (rebuke).

Castile [kæs'tiːl] *pr m* GEOGR Castilla *f*.

Castilian [kæs'tiliən] *adj/n* castellano, na (people) || castellano *m* (language).

casting ['kɑːstiɛ] *n* pieza *f* fundida || TECH vaciado *m*, colada *f*; *casting bed* lecho de colada || THEATR reparto *m* || piel *f* (of a reptile) || plumas *f pl* (of a bird).

casting net [-net] *n* MAR esparavel *m*.

casting vote [-'vəut] *n* voto *m* de calidad.

cast iron [kɑːst'aiən] *n* hierro *m* colado, arrabio *m*, fundición *f*.

cast-iron [kɑːst'aiən] *adj* FIG inquebrantable, férreo, a (will) | irrefutable (argument) | irrebatible.

castle ['kɑːsl] *n* castillo *m* || torre *f* (in chess) || — FIG *an Englishman's home is his castle* cada uno es rey en su casa | *castles in Spain* o *in the air* castillos en el aire.

castle ['kɑːsl] *vt/vi* enrocar (chess).

cast-on ['kɑːst'of] *adj* desechado, da; de desecho.

castoff ['kɑːstɔf] *n* persona *f or* cosa *f* desechada, desecho *m*.

castor ['kɑːstə*] *n* salero *m* (salt container) || pimentero *m* (pepper container) || azucarero *m* (sugar container) || ruedecilla *f* (wheel) || MED castóreo *m* (substance) || PRINT fundidora *f* || ZOOL castor *m* || castor *m* (hat).

◆ *pl* angarillas *f*, convoy *m sing* (cruet stand).

Castor ['kɑːstə*] *pr n* Cástor *m*.

castoreum [kɑː'stɔːriəm] *n* castóreo *m*.

castor oil ['kɑːstər'ɔil] *n* aceite *m* de ricino.

castrate [kæs'treit] *vt* castrar.

castration [kæs'treiʃən] *n* castración *f*.

casual ['kæʒjuəl] *adj* casual, fortuito, ta; *a casual meeting* un encuentro casual || informal (without formality) || al azar; *to go for a casual stroll* dar un paseo al azar || ocasional, temporero, ra; *casual labour* trabajo ocasional || despreocupado, da (carefree) || desenfadado, da (answer) || hecho de paso (in passing); *a casual suggestion* una sugerencia hecha de paso || sin trascendencia; *casual remark* observación sin trascendencia || — *casual conversation* conversación *f* en que se habla de todo un poco || *casual glance* ojeada *f* || *casual wear* ropa *f* de sport || *casual worker* temporero *m* || *to try to be casual* intentar hacer como si nada *or* no dar importancia a la cosa.

casually [-i] *adv* de paso, sin darle importancia (to say) || de sport (to dress).

casualty [-ti] *n* accidente *m* || víctima *f*; *there were three casualties in the accident* hubo tres víctimas en el accidente || MIL baja *f*; *there were no casualties in the battle* no hubo bajas en la batalla || *casualty department* servicio *m* de urgencias.

casuist ['kæzjuist] *n* casuista *m* & *f*.

casuistic [,kæzju'istik]; **casuistical** [-əl] *adj* casuístico, ca.

casuistry ['kæzjuistri] *n* casuística *f*.

cat [kæt] *n* ZOOL gato, ta | felino, na (feline) || piel *f* de gato (fur) || FIG arpía *f*, pécora *f* (bad woman) || MAR gata *f* || azote *m* (whip) || — FIG *a cat in mittens catches no mice* gato con guantes no caza ratones || *Angora cat* gato de Angora || *cat burglar* ladrón, ona || *cat flap* portilla *f* para el gato || FIG *he thinks he's the cat's whiskers* se cree el rey del mambo | *there's no room to swing a cat* no cabe un alfiler | *to be like a cat on hot bricks* estar sobre ascuas | *to bell the cat* ponerle el cascabel al gato | *to lead a cat-and-dog existence* o *to get along like cats and dogs* llevarse como perros y gatos | *to let the cat out of the bag* descubrir el pastel, irse de la lengua | *to rain cats and dogs* llover a cántaros, caer chuzos de punta | *to see which way the cat jumps* ver de qué lado sopla el viento | *to set the cat among the pigeons* meter el lobo en el redil | *when candles are away all cats are grey* de noche todos los gatos son pardos | *when the cat's away the mice will play* cuando el gato no está, bailan los ratones.

cat [kæt] *vt* MAR izar (the anchor).

catabolic [,kætə'bɔlik] *adj* catabólico, ca.

catabolism [kə'tæbəlizəm] *n* catabolismo *m* (destructive metabolism).

catachresis [,kætə'kri:sis] *n* catacresis *f*.
— OBSERV El plural de *catachresis* es *catachreses*.

cataclysm ['kætəklizəm] *n* cataclismo *m*.

cataclysmic [kætə'klizmik] *adj* catastrófico, ca.

catacomb ['kætəku:m] *n* catacumba *f*.

catafalque ['kætəfælk] *n* catafalco *m*.

Catalan ['kætələn] *adj/n* catalán, ana || catalán *m* (language).

catalepsy ['kætəlepsi] *n* MED catalepsia *f*.

cataleptic [,kætə'leptik] *adj/n* MED cataléptico, ca.

catalogue; US **catalog** ['kætəlɔg] *n* catálogo *m*.

catalogue ['kætəlɔg] *vt* catalogar.

Catalonia [,kætə'ləunjə] *pr n* GEOGR Cataluña *f*.

Catalonian [-n] *adj/n* catalán, ana.

catalyse ['kætəlaiz] *vt* CHEM catalizar.

catalysis ['kə'tælisis] *n* CHEM catálisis *f*.

catalyst [kætəlist] *n* CHEM catalizador *m*.

catalytic [,kætə'litik] *adj* CHEM catalítico, ca; catalizador, ra || AUT *catalytic converter* catalizador *m*.

catalyze ['kætəlaiz] *vt* US catalizar.

catamaran [,kætəmə'ræn] *n* MAR catamarán *m*.

cat-a-mountain [,kætə'mauntin] *n* ZOOL gato *m* montés (wildcat) | leopardo *m*.

cat-and-mouse ['kætən'maus] *adj* *to play a cat-and-mouse game with s.o.* jugar al ratón y al gato con uno.

cataplasm ['kætəplæzəm] *n* MED cataplasma *f*.

catapult ['kætəpʌlt] *n* catapulta *f* || tirador *m*, tiragomas *m inv* (toy).

catapult ['kætəpʌlt] *vt* catapultar.

cataract ['kætərækt] *n* catarata *f*.

catarrh [kə'tɑ:*] *n* MED catarro *m*.

catastrophe [kə'tæstrəfi] *n* catástrofe *f*.

catastrophic [,kætə'strɔfik] *adj* catastrófico, ca.

catbird ['kætbə:d] *n* tordo *m* cantor de América y de Australia (bird).

catboat ['kætbəut] *n* MAR laúd *m*.

catcall ['kætkɔ:l] *n* pitido *m*, silbido *m*.

catcall ['kætkɔ:l] *vt/vi* pitar, silbar.

catch [kætʃ] *n* cogida *f* (the act of catching) || pesca *f* presa *f* captura *f* (in fishing) || pestillo *m* (bolt) || cerradura *f* (of a small box) || hebijón *m* (of a buckle) || MUS canon *m* (popular round) || fragmento *m* (fragment) || juego *m* de pelota (ball game) || FIG truco *m*, trampa *f* (trick) | pega *f* (in a question) || SP parada *f* (of the ball) || — *catch 22* círculo *m* vicioso || *safety catch* fiador *m* || FIG *the catch is that* la pega es que | *to be a good catch* ser un buen partido (man or woman) || *to play catch* jugar a la pelota || *with a catch in one's voice* con la voz entrecortada.

catch* [kætʃ] *vt* coger, agarrar (to seize) || coger, atrapar, prender (to capture) || coger, tomar (the train, the bus) || alcanzar, dar; *the stone caught him on the head* la piedra le alcanzó en la cabeza || coger, sorprender; *to catch s.o. in the act* coger a alguien in fraganti || SP coger (the ball) || coger, contraer (a disease) || FIG contagiarse; *she caught his enthusiasm* se le contagió su entusiasmo || FAM coger, oír; *to catch s.o.'s name* oír el nombre de alguien | coger, entender; *I did not catch the joke* no he cogido el chiste || llamar, captar (attention) || captar, coger; *the painter has caught her expression* el pintor ha sabido captar su expresión || adquirir, coger (a habit, an accent) || engancharse; *he caught his jumper on a nail* se enganchó el jersey en un clavo || coger; *he caught his finger in the door* se cogió el dedo en la puerta || darse; *I caught my knee on that table* di con la rodilla contra esa mesa || recibir (a blow, a shot) || — *I only just caught the bus* por poco pierdía el autobús || *to catch a glimpse of* vislumbrar || *to catch a likeness* coger el parecido || *to catch fire* incendiarse (to burst into flames), encenderse, prenderse (to start burning) || *to catch hold of* agarrarse a || *to catch it* ganarse una paliza (a beating), ganarse una bronca (a reprimand) || *to catch one's breath* quedarse sin respiración (from surprise, etc.), recobrar el aliento (to get one's breath back) || *to catch o.s.* darse cuenta (to realize), contenerse || FAM *to catch s.o. a blow* pegarle un golpe a uno | *to catch s.o. red-handed* coger a alguien con las manos en la masa || *you'll never catch me doing that* nunca me verás a mí hacer eso, nunca me cogerás en ésa || *you will catch it!* ¡te la vas a ganar!
◆ *vi* engancharse (*on* en); *her sleeve caught on a nail* se le enganchó la manga en un clavo || quebrarse (the voice) || prenderse, encenderse (to take fire) || SP jugar de «catcher» (in baseball).
◆ *phr v* *to catch at* tratar de coger || *to catch in* coger con || *to catch on* comprender (to understand) | caer en la cuenta, darse cuenta (to become aware) | coger el truco (to get the knack) | hacerse muy popular (to become popular) || *to catch out* sorprender, coger; *to catch s.o. out in a lie* coger a alguien mintiendo | SP eliminar || *to catch up* alcanzar; *you go ahead and I'll catch you up* id por delante que yo os alcanzaré | enredarse (to become entangled) | poner al día; *I have to catch up with* o *I have to catch up on my work* tengo que poner al día todo el trabajo | ponerse al corriente *or* al día; *to catch up on* o *with the news* ponerse al corriente de las noticias | adquirir, coger (a habit, an accent) | interrumpir (to interrupt).
— OBSERV In certain Latin American countries the word *coger* is not in decent use and is usually replaced by *tomar* or *agarrar*.
— OBSERV pret y pp ***caught***.

catch-as-catch-can [-əz,kætʃkæn] *adj* US hecho de cualquier manera.
◆ *n* SP lucha *f* libre.

catcher [-ə*] *n* SP «catcher» *m*, receptor *m*, jugador *m* que para la pelota (baseball).

catching [-iŋ] *adj* contagioso, sa || FIG pegadizo, za (song, music) | que se pega (habit).

catchment [-mənt] *n* captación *f* || *catchment area* zona *f* de captación (of school, hospital).

catchpenny [-peni] *adj* de pacotilla (of low quality) || facilón, ona; *catchpenny jokes* chistes facilones.

catchphrase [-freiz] *n* lema *m*, «slogan» *m* || estribillo *m* (pet phrase).

catchword [-wə:d] *n* lema *m*, «slogan» *m* || PRINT reclamo *m* || THEATR pie *m* || estribillo *m* (pet word).

catchy [-i] *adj* pegadizo, za; *a catchy melody* una melodía pegadiza || insidioso, sa; capcioso, sa (question).

catechesis [,kæti'kisis] *n* catequesis *f*.
— OBSERV El plural de *catechesis* es *catecheses*.

catechism ['kætikizəm] *n* catecismo *m*.

catechist ['kætikist] *n* catequista *m* & *f*.

catechization [,kætikai'zeiʃən] *n* catequización *f* || FIG interrogatorio *m*.

catechize ['kætikaiz] *vt* catequizar, enseñar el catecismo || FIG preguntar (to question).

catechizer [-ə*] *n* catequizador, ra.

catechu ['kætitʃu:] *n* cato *m*.

catechumen [,kæti'kju:men] *n* catecúmeno, na.

categoric [,kæti'gɔrik]; **categorical** [-əl] *adj* categórico, ca; rotundo, da; terminante; *a categorical denial* una negación rotunda || PHIL *categorical imperative* imperativo categórico.

categorize ['kætigəraiz] *vt* clasificar [por categorías].

category ['kætigəri] *n* categoría *f*.

catena [kə'ti:nə] *n* cadena *f* (connected series).
— OBSERV El plural de *catena* es *catenae* o *catenas*.

catenary [kə'ti:nəri] *adj* catenario, ria || *catenary bridge* puente *m* colgante.
◆ *n* catenaria *f*.

catenate ['kætineit] *vt* encadenar, enlazar, concadenar.

cater ['keitə*] *vi* proveer *or* abastecer de comida (*for* a) || *to cater for all tastes* atender a todos los gustos.

catercorner ['kætə,kɔ:nə*]; **cater-cornered** [-d] *adj* diagonal.
◆ *adv* diagonalmente, en diagonal.

caterer ['keitərə*] *n* proveedor, ra; abastecedor, ra [de comidas de encargo].

catering ['keitəri:ŋ] *n* abastecimiento *m* (de comidas de encargo) || AVIAT mayordomía *f*.

caterpillar ['kætəpilə*] *n* ZOOL oruga *f* || TECH oruga *f* || — *caterpillar tractor* tractor *m* oruga || *caterpillar tread* oruga *f*.

caterwaul ['kætəwɔ:l] *n* maullido *m*.

caterwaul ['kætəwɔ:l] *vi* maullar || pelearse (to quarrel like cats) || FIG berrear, chillar (like cats).

catfish ['kætfiʃ] *n* ZOOL siluro *m*, bagro *m* (fish).

— OBSERV El plural de *catfish* es *catfishes* o *catfish*.

catgut ['kætgʌt] *n* cuerda *f* de tripa (for violin, for tennis racket) ‖ MED catgut *m*.

Catharine ['kæθərin] *pr n* Catalina *f*.

catharsis [kə'θɑːsis] *n* MED purga *f*, catarsis *f* ‖ PHIL catarsis *f*.
— OBSERV El plural de la palabra inglesa es *catharses*.

cathartic [kə'θɑːtik] *adj* catártico, ca; purgativo, va ‖ PHIL catártico, ca.
◆ *n* MED purgante *m*.

cathead ['kæthed] *n* MAR serviola *f*, pescante *m*.

cathedra [kə'θiːdrə] *n* *to speak ex cathedra* hablar ex cátedra.

cathedral [kə'θiːdrəl] *adj* catedral, catedralicio, cia ‖ *cathedral city* ciudad *f* episcopal.
◆ *n* catedral *f*.

Catherine ['kæθrin] *pr n* Catalina *f*.

Catherine wheel [-wiːl] *n* rosetón *m* (window) ‖ girándula *f*, rueda *f* (firework) ‖ voltereta *f* lateral (cartwheel) ‖ TECH rueda *f* catalina.

catheter ['kæθitə*] *n* MED catéter *m*.

cathetometer [,kæθi'tɔmitə*] *n* catetómetro *m*.

cathode ['kæθəud] *n* ELECTR cátodo *m* ‖ — PHYS *cathode ray* rayo catódico | *cathode-ray tube* tubo *m* de rayos catódicos.

cathodic [kə'θɔdik] *adj* catódico, ca.

Catholic ['kæθəlik] *adj* REL católico, ca ‖ FIG universal | liberal ‖ — FIG *a person of catholic tastes* una persona a quien le gusta todo ‖ *Roman Catholic Church* Iglesia Católica Romana.
◆ *n* católico, ca.

Catholicism [kə'θɔlisizəm] *n* REL catolicismo *m*.

catholicity [,kæθəu'lisiti] *n* universalidad *f* ‖ liberalidad *f* ‖ REL catolicidad *f*, catolicismo *m*.

catholicize [kə'θɔlisaiz] *vt* catolizar.

cation ['kætaiən] *n* PHYS catión *m*.

catkin ['kætkin] *n* BOT candelilla *f*, amento *m*.

cat-lick ['kætlik] *n* FAM lavado *m* rápido, lavoteo *m*.

catlike ['kætlaik] *adj* gatuno, na; felino, na.

catmint ['kætmint] *n* BOT nébeda *f*.

catnap ['kætnæp] *n* siesta *f* corta.

catnip ['kætnip] *n* US BOT nébeda *f*.

Cato ['keitəu] *pr n* Catón *m*.

cat-o'-nine-tails ['kætə'nain-teilz] *n* gato *m* de nueve colas (whip).

catoptrics [kə'tɔptriks] *n* catóptrica *f*.

cat's cradle ['kæts,kreidl] *n* juego *m* de la cuna.

cat's eye ['kæts'ai] *n* MIN ojo *m* de gato.
◆ *pl* catafaros *m* [por la carretera].

cat's paw ['kæts-pɔː] *n* MAR ahorcaperro *m* (knot) | ventolina *f* (breeze) ‖ FIG & FAM pelele *m*, instrumento *m* (dupe).

catsup ['kætsəp] *n* salsa *f* de tomate (ketchup).

cattail ['kæt,teil] *n* BOT anea *f*, espadaña *f*.

cattish ['kætiʃ] *adj* malévolo, la; malicioso, sa.

cattle ['kætl] *n* ganado *m* [vacuno] ‖ — *cattle bell* esquilón *m* ‖ *cattle crossing* paso *m* de ganado (on roads) ‖ *cattle lifter* ladrón *m* de ganado, cuatrero, ra ‖ *cattle pass* paso *m* de ganado ‖ *cattle plague* peste bovina ‖ *cattle raising* ganadería *f* ‖ *cattle ranch* ganadería *f* [AMER hacienda *f*, estancia *f*] ‖ US *cattler rustler* ladrón *m* de ganado, cuatrero, ra ‖ *cattle show* feria *f* de ganado ‖ *cattle truck* camión *m* de ganado (lorry), vagón *m* de ganado (on a train).

cattleman ['kætlmən] *n* ganadero *m*.
— OBSERV El plural de esta palabra es *cattlemen*.

catty ['kæti] *adj* gatuno, na; felino, na ‖ FIG malicioso, sa.

Catullus [kə'tʌləs] *pr n* Cátulo *m*.

catwalk ['kætwɔːk] *n* pasarela *f* (footway) ‖ CINEM batería *f* de focos ‖ THEATR puente *m* de trabajo.

Caucasian [kɔː'keizjən] *adj/n* caucásico, ca; caucasiano, na.

Caucasus ['kɔːkəsəs] *pr n* GEOGR Cáucaso *m* (mountains) | Caucasia *f* (country).

caucus ['kɔːkəs] *n* US reunión *f* electoral, reunión *f* de dirigentes (of a party) ‖ comité *m*.

caucus ['kɔːkəs] *vi* US celebrar una reunión electoral, reunir a los dirigentes.

caudal ['kɔːdl] *adj* caudal.

caudate ['kɔːdeit] *adj* caudado, da.

Caudine ['kɔːdain] *adj* HIST *Caudine Forks* Horcas Caudinas.

caught [kɔːt] *pret/pp* → **catch.**

caul [kɔːl] *n* ANAT redaño *m* (part of the peritoneum) | amnios *m* (enclosing the foetus).

cauldron ['kɔːldrən] *n* caldera *f*, caldero *m*.

caulescent [kɔː'lesnt] *adj* BOT caulescente.

cauliflower ['kɔliflauə*] *n* BOT coliflor *f*.

caulk [kɔːlk] *vt* calafatear.

caulking [-iŋ] *n* calafateo *m*.

causal ['kɔːzəl] *adj* causal.

causality [kɔː'zæliti] *n* causalidad *f*.

causation [kɔː'zeiʃən] *n* causalidad *f*.

causative ['kɔːzətiv] *adj* causativo, va.

cause [kɔːz] *n* causa *f*, motivo *m*, razón *f* (motive) ‖ causante *m* & *f*, causa *f*; *they were the cause of the accident* ellos fueron los causantes del accidente ‖ causa *f* (matter of interest and concern); *to fight for a just cause* luchar por una causa justa ‖ JUR causa *f*, pleito *m* (lawsuit) ‖ — *cause célèbre* proceso *m* célebre ‖ *common cause* causa común ‖ *in the cause of* por ‖ *to plead a cause* defender una causa.

cause [kɔːz] *vt* causar; *to cause damage* causar perjuicio ‖ causar, provocar; *to cause an accident* causar un accidente ‖ *to cause s.o. to do sth.* hacer que alguien haga algo, obligar a alguien a hacer algo.

causeless [-lis] *adj* sin causa, sin motivo.

causerie ['kəuzəriː] *n* charla *f* (chat) ‖ artículo *m* breve (short article).

causeway ['kɔːzwei] *n* carretera *f* elevada (raised roadway) ‖ terraplén *m* (embankment).

caustic ['kɔːstik] *adj* CHEM cáustico, ca ‖ FIG cáustico, ca; mordaz (sharply biting) ‖ — *caustic lime* cal viva ‖ *caustic soda* sosa cáustica.
◆ *n* PHYS cáustico *m*.

causticity [kɔːs'tisiti] *n* FIG causticidad *f*, mordacidad *f*.

cauterization [,kɔːtərai'zeiʃən] *n* cauterización *f*.

cauterize ['kɔːtəraiz] *vt* cauterizar.

cautery ['kɔːtəri] *n* cauterio *m* (instrument) ‖ cauterización *f*.

caution ['kɔːʃən] *n* cautela *f*, prudencia *f*, cuidado *m* (wariness) ‖ advertencia *f* (warning) ‖ US fianza *f*, garantía *f* (money deposit) | persona *f* que da una fianza, fiador, ra ‖ — *caution!* ¡cuidado!, ¡atención! ‖ *caution money* fianza *f*, garantía *f* ‖ FAM *he's a caution!* ¡es un caso!

caution ['kɔːʃən] *vt* amonestar (to reprimand) ‖ advertir, avisar (to warn).

cautionary ['kɔːʃnəri] *adj* admonitorio, ria ‖ aleccionador, ra; *cautionary tales* cuentos aleccionadores ‖ preventivo, va (preventive).

cautious ['kɔːʃəs] *adj* cauteloso, sa; precavido, da; cauto, ta; prudente.

cautiousness [-nis] *n* cautela *f*, prudencia *f*, precaución *f*.

cavalcade [,kævəl'keid] *n* cabalgata *f* ‖ FIG desfile *m* (parade).

cavalier [,kævə'liə*] *adj* arrogante (haughty) ‖ desenvuelto, ta (carefree).
◆ *n* jinete *m* (horseman) ‖ HIST caballero *m* (knight) | monárquico *m* partidario de Carlos I de Inglaterra ‖ galán *m*, acompañante *m* (partner).

cavalry ['kævəlri] *n* MIL caballería *f*.

cavalryman [-mən] *n* MIL soldado *m* de caballería.
— OBSERV El plural de *cavalryman* es *cavalrymen*.

cavatina [,kævə'tiːnə] *n* MUS cavatina *f*.

cave [keiv] *n* cueva *f* (natural) ‖ caverna *f* (manmade).

cave [keiv] *vt* cavar (earth).
◆ *vi* *to cave in* derrumbarse, hundirse.

caveat ['keiviæt] *n* JUR aviso *m* de aplazamiento de un proceso ‖ advertencia *f* (warning); *to enter a caveat* hacer una advertencia.

cave dweller ['keiv,dwelə*] *n* troglodita *m* & *f*, cavernícola *m* & *f*.

cave-in ['keivin] *n* derrumbamiento *m* ‖ socavón *m* (in the street).

caveman ['keivmən] *n* hombre *m* de las cavernas (prehistoric human being) ‖ FIG bruto *m*.
— OBSERV El plural de *caveman* es *cavemen*.

cave painting ['keiv, peintiŋ] *n* ARTS pintura *f* rupestre.

cavern ['kævən] *n* caverna *f*, cueva *f* (cave).

cavernous [-əs] *adj* cavernoso, sa.

cavetto [kə'vetəu] *n* ARCH caveto *m*, mediacaña *f*.

caviar; caviare ['kæviɑː*] *n* caviar *m*.

cavil ['kævil] *n* reparo *m*, pero *m*.

cavil ['kævil] *vi* poner reparos *or* peros (*at*, *about* a) ‖ criticar.

cavitation [kævi'teiʃən] *n* MAR & AVIAT cavitación *f*.

cavity ['kæviti] *n* cavidad *f*, hueco *m* ‖ caries *f inv* (in a tooth).

cavort [kə'vɔːt] *vi* corvetear ‖ FIG retozar, juguetear (to romp) | divertirse.

cavy ['keivi] *n* ZOOL cobayo *m*, conejillo *m* de Indias.

caw [kɔː] *n* graznido *m* (of crow, etc.).

caw [kɔː] *vi* graznar.

cay [kei] *n* cayo *m* (of rock) ‖ banco *m* (of sand).

Cayenne [kei'ɛn] *pr n* GEOGR Cayena.

cayenne pepper ['keien'pepə*] *n* pimienta *f* sacada del chile.

cayman ['keimən] *n* ZOOL caimán *m*.

CB *abbr of [Citizen's Band Radio]* CB, banda ciudadana.

CBS *abbr of [Columbian Broadcasting System]* CBS, cadena de radiotelevisión norteamericana.

CD *abbr of [compact disc]* CD, disco compacto.

CDI *abbr of [compact disc interactive]* disco compacto interactivo.

CD-ROM [,siːdiː'rəm] *abbr of [compact disc read only memory]* CD-ROM, disco compacto de memoria de solo lectura.

CDV *abbr of* *[compact disc video]* videodisco copacto.

cease [si:s] *n* *without cease* sin cesar, incesantemente.

cease [si:s] *vt* cesar, suspender (to interrupt) ‖ cesar (to stop) ‖ poner fin a (to bring to an end) ‖ *to cease firing* cesar el fuego.
◆ *vi* cesar, dejar (*from, to* de).

cease-fire [-'faiə*] *n* MIL alto *m* el fuego.

ceaseless [-lis] *adj* incesante, continuo, nua.

ceasing [-iŋ] *n* cese *m*, cesación *f*, cesamiento *m*.

cecal ['si:kl] *adj* ANAT cecal.

Cecil ['sesl] *pr n* Cecilia *f*.

Cecily ['sisili] *pr n* Cecilia *f*.

cecum ['si:kəm] *n* ANAT intestino *m* ciego, ciego *m*.
— OBSERV El plural de *cecum* es *ceca*.

cedar [θi:də*] *n* BOT cedro *m* (tree).

cede [si:d] *vt* ceder.

cedilla [si'dilə] *n* cedilla *f*.

ceiba ['seibə] *n* BOT ceiba *f*.

ceibo ['seibəu] *n* BOT ceibo *m*.

ceil [si:l] *vt* revestir el techo de.

ceiling ['si:liŋ] *n* techo *m* ‖ AVIAT altura *f* máxima, techo *m* ‖ FIG tope *m*, límite *m*, máximo *m* (upper limit); *ceiling price* precio tope ‖ FAM *to hit the ceiling* subirse por las paredes (with anger).

celadon ['selədən] *n* verdeceledón *m* (colour).

celandine ['seləndain] *n* BOT celidonia *f*.

celebrant ['selibrənt] *n* celebrante *m*.

celebrate ['selibreit] *vt* celebrar (a religious ceremony); *to celebrate a wedding* celebrar una boda ‖ celebrar, festejar; *to celebrate a birthday* celebrar un cumpleaños ‖ celebrar, alabar (to praise).
◆ *vi* celebrar (to say mass) ‖ divertirse, pasarlo bien (to amuse o.s.).

celebrated [-id] *adj* famoso, sa; célebre (*for* por).

celebration [,seli'breiʃən] *n* celebración *f* ‖ conmemoración *f* (of an event) ‖ fiesta *f* (party) ‖ festividades *pl* (festivities).

celebratory [,seli'brəitəri] *adj* de celebración.

celebrity [si'lebriti] *n* celebridad *f*, fama *f* (fame) ‖ celebridad *f* (famous person).

celeriac [si'leriæk] *n* BOT apio *m* nabo.

celerity [si'leriti] *n* celeridad *f*.

celery ['seləri] *n* BOT apio *m*.

celeste [si'lest] *adj* celeste.
◆ *n* celeste *m*.

celestial [si'lestjəl] *adj* celestial (divine) ‖ celeste, astronómico, ca (pertaining to the sky) ‖ — *Celestial Empire* Celeste Imperio ‖ *celestial equator* ecuador *m* celeste ‖ *celestial navigation* navegación astronómica ‖ *celestial sphere* esfera *f* celeste.

celiac ['si:ljæk] *adj* ⟶ **coeliac.**

celibacy ['selibəsi] *n* celibato *m*, soltería *f*.

celibate ['selibit] *adj/n* c'elibe, soltero, ra.

cell [sel] *n* celda *f* (in prisons, in monasteries, etc.) ‖ célula *f* (political group) ‖ BIOL célula *f* ‖ ZOOL celdilla *f* (of bees) | ventosa *f* (of octopus) ‖ ELECTR pila *f*; *dry cell* pila seca ‖ INFORM celda *f*, célula *f* ‖ — BIOL *cell division* mitosis *f*, división *f* celular ‖ *photoelectric cell* célula fotoeléctrica.

cellar ['selə*] *n* sótano *m* ‖ bodega *f* (for wines).

cellarage [-ridʒ] *n* almacenaje *m* (storage, price) ‖ bodega *f* (cellar).

cellarer [-rə*] *n* cillerero *m* (in a monastery).

cellaret [,selə'ret] *n* fresquera *f* (for bottles).

cellist ['tʃelist] *n* MUS violoncelista *m* & *f*.

cello; 'cello ['tʃeləu] *n* MUS violoncelo *m*.

cellophane ['seləfein] *n* celofán *m*.

cellular ['seljulə*] *adj* celular.

cellule ['selju:l] *n* BIOL célula *f*.

cellulitis [,selju'laitis] *n* MED celulitis *f*.

celluloid ['seljulɔid] *n* celuloide *m*.

cellulose ['seljuləus] *n* CHEM celulosa *f*.
◆ *adj* celulósico, ca.

Celsius ['selsiəs] *adj* de Celsius; *Celsius scale* escala de Celsius *or* centígrada.

celt [selt] *n* hacha *f* prehistórica.

Celt [kelt] *n* HIST celta *m* & *f*.

Celtiberia [,kelti'biərjə] *pr n* Celtiberia *f*.

Celtic ['keltik] *adj* céltico, ca, celta.
◆ *n* celta *m* (language).

Celtologist [kel'tɔlədʒist] *n* celtista *m* & *f*.

cement [si'ment] *n* cemento *m* ‖ cola *f*, pegamento *m* (glue) ‖ MED cemento *m* (for filling teeth).

cement [si'ment] *vt* cementar, unir con cemento (to join with cement) ‖ revestir de cemento (to cover with cement) ‖ FIG cimentar, fortalecer; *to cement a friendship* cimentar una amistad.

cementation [,si:men'teiʃən] *n* TECH cementación *f* ‖ FIG consolidación *f*, cimentación *f*, fortalecimiento *m*.

cement mixer [s'iment ,miksə*] *n* hormigonera *f*.

cemetery ['semitri] *n* cementerio *m*.

cenobite ['si:nəbait] *n* cenobita *m* & *f*.

cenobitic [sinə'bitik]; **cenobitical** [-əl] *adj* cenobítico; ca; cenobial.

cenotaph ['senəta:f] *n* cenotafio *m*.

Cenozoic ['si:nə'zəuik] *adj* GEOL cenozoico, ca.

cense [sens] *vt* incensar.

censer [-ə*] *n* incensario *m*.

censor [-ə*] *n* censor *m*.

censor [-ə*] *vt* censurar ‖ tachar (to delete).

censorious [sen'sɔ:riəs] *adj* censurador, ra; reprobador, ra.

censorship ['sensəʃip] *n* censura *f*.

censurable ['senʃərəbl] *adj* censurable.

censure ['senʃə*] *n* censura *f*.

censure ['senʃə*] *vt* censurar.

census ['sensəs] *n* censo *m*, empadronamiento *m* ‖ — *census taker* empadronador *m* ‖ *to take a census of* empadronar, levantar el censo de.

cent [sent] *n* centavo *m* (coin) ‖ COMM ciento *m* (percentage); *ten per cent* diez por ciento ‖ FAM *I haven't got a cent* no tengo un céntimo *or* un centavo.

cental ['sentl] *n* quintal *m*.

centaur ['sentɔ:*] *n* MYTH centauro *m*.

centaury [-ri] *n* BOT centaura *f*, centaurea *f*.

centenarian [,senti'nɛəriən] *adj/n* centenario, ria.

centenary [sen'ti:nəri] *adj* centenario, ria.
◆ *n* centenario *m*.

centennial [cen'teniəl] *adj* centenario, ria.
◆ *n* centenario *m*.

center ['sentə*] *n* US ⟶ **centre.**

centerboard [-bɔ:d] *n* US MAR orza *f* de deriva.

centering [-iŋ] *n* US centrado *m*.

centerpiece [-pi:s] *n* US centro *m* de mesa.

centesimal [sen'tesiməl] *adj* centesimal.
◆ *n* centésimo *m*.

centiare ['sentia:r] *n* centiárea *f*.

centigrade ['sentigreid] *adj* centígrado, da; *centigrade scale* escala centígrada; *20 degrees centigrade* 20 grados centígrados.

centigramme; *US* **centigram** ['sentigræm] *n* centigramo *m*.

centilitre; *US* **centiliter** ['senti,litə*] *n* centilitro *m*.

centime ['sa:nti:m] *n* céntimo *m*.

centimetre; *US* **centimeter** ['senti,mi:tə*] *n* centímetro *m* ‖ *centimetre-gram-second system* sistema *m* cegesimal.

centipede ['sentipi:d] *n* ZOOL ciempiés *m inv*.

centner ['sentnə*] *n* quintal *m* métrico.

central ['sentrəl] *adj* central ‖ céntrico, ca; *I live in a central district* vivo en un barrio céntrico ‖ — *central bank* banco *m* central ‖ INFORM *central computer* ordenador *m* central ‖ *central government* gobierno *m* central ‖ *central heating* calefacción *f* central ‖ *central locking* cierre *m* centralizado ‖ INFORM *central memory* memoria *m* central ‖ *central nervous system* sistema nervioso central ‖ *central reservation* mediana *f* (on a motorway) ‖ *central standard time* hora *f* legal correspondiente al meridiano 90° W ‖ *to take a central position on a problem* tomar una postura intermedia en un problema.
◆ *n* central *f* telefónica ‖ telefonista *m* & *f* (operator).

Central African Republic [-'æfrikən ri'pʌblik] *pr n* GEOGR República centroafricana.

Central America [-ə'merikə] *pr n* GEOGR América *f* Central, Centroamérica *f*.

Central American [-ə'merikən] *adj/n* centroamericano, na.

Central European [-,juərə'pi:ən] *adj/n* centroeuropeo, a.

centralism ['sentrəlizəm] *n* centralismo *m*.

centrality [sen'træliti] *n* posición *f* central.

centralization [,sentrəlai'zeiʃən] *n* centralización *f*.

centralize ['sentrəlaiz] *vt* centralizar.

centralizing [-iŋ] *adj* centralizador, ra.
◆ *n* centralización *f*.

centre; *US* **center** ['sentə*] *n* centro *m*; *the centre of the circle* el centro del círculo; *city centre* centro de la ciudad ‖ eje *m* (axis) ‖ alma *f* (of cable) ‖ ARCH cimbra *f* ‖ SP centro *m* ‖ ANAT centro *m* ‖ — TECH *centre bit* o *drill* broca *f* de centrar | *centre distance* distancia *f* entre ejes ‖ SP *centre forward* delantero *m* centro | *centre half* medio *m* centro ‖ *centre of attention* centro *m* de atención ‖ *centre of gravity* centro de gravedad ‖ *community centre* centro social ‖ US *railroad center* centro ferroviario ‖ *the motor centre* el centro motor.

centre ['sentə*] *vt* centrar (to place in the middle, to find the centre) ‖ concentrar, centrar; *to centre one's efforts on doing sth.* concentrar sus esfuerzos en hacer algo ‖ SP centrar (the ball).
◆ *vi* concentrarse, centrarse (*at, around, in, on, upon* en) (to concentrate) ‖ centrarse (*on* sobre); *the conversation centred on tennis* la conversación se centró sobre el tenis.

centreboard [-bɔ:d] *n* MAR orza *f* de deriva.

centrepiece [-pi:s] *n* centro *m* de mesa.

centric ['sentrik]; **centrical** [-əl] *adj* céntrico, ca; central.

centrifugal [sen'trifjugəl] *adj* centrífugo, ga; *centrifugal, force pump* bomba, fuerza centrífuga ‖ centrifugador, ra; *centrifugal machine* máquina centrifugadora.

centrifuge ['sentrifju:ʒ] *n* TECH centrifugadora *f*.

centrifuge ['sentrifju:ʒ] *vt* centrifugar.

centring ['sentəriŋ] *n* centrado *m*.

centripetal [sen'tripitl] *adj* centrípeto, ta; *centripetal acceleration, force* aceleración, fuerza centrípeta.

centrist ['sentrist] *n* centrista *m* & *f*.

centrosome ['sentrəˌsəum] *n* BIOL centrosoma *m*.

centrosphere ['sentrəsfiə*] *n* centro *m* de la Tierra || BIOL centrosfera *f*.

centuple ['sentjupl] *adj* céntuplo, pla.
◆ *n* céntuplo *m*.

centuple ['sentjupl]; **centuplicate** [sen'tju:plikeit] *vt* centuplicar.

centuplicate [sen'tju:pliket] *n* céntuplo *m*.
◆ *adj* céntuplo, pla.

centuries-old ['sentʃurizˌəuld] *adj* secular.

centurion [sen'tjuəriən] *n* HIST centurión *m*.

century ['sentʃuri] *n* siglo *m*; *the 17th century* el siglo XVII || siglo *m*, centuria *f*; *it happened two centuries ago* sucedió hace dos siglos || HIST centuria *f* (in the Roman army) || BOT *Century plant* pita *f*, agave *m*.

CEO *abbr of [Chief Executive Officer]* director general (United States).

cephalalgia [sefə'lældʒə] *n* MED cefalalgia *f*.

cephalic [ke'fælik] *adj* cefálico, ca.

cephalopod ['sefələpɔd] *n* ZOOL cefalópodo *m*.
◆ *adj* cefalópodo, da.

cephalothorax ['sefələ'θɔ:ræks] *n* cefalotórax *m*.

ceraceous [si'reiʃəs] *adj* ceroso, sa (waxy).

ceramic [si'ræmik] *adj* cerámico, ca.

ceramics [-s] *n* cerámica *f*.

ceramist ['seramist] *n* ceramista *m* & *f* (potter).

cerastes [si'ræsti:z] *n* ZOOL cerasta *f*, cerastes *m* (horned viper).

cerate ['siərit] *n* cerato *m*.

ceratin ['kerətin] *n* queratina *f*.

Cerberus ['sə:bərəs] *pr n* MYTH Cerbero *m*, Cancerbero *m*.

cercopithecus [ˌsə:kəupi'θikəs] *n* cercopiteco *m*.

cereal ['siəriəl] *adj* cereal; *cereal plant* planta cereal || *cereal production* producción cerealista *or* de cereales.
◆ *n* cereal *m*.

cerebellum [ˌseri'beləm] *n* ANAT cerebelo *m*.
— OBSERV El plural es *cerebellums* o *cerebella*.

cerebral ['seribrəl] *adj* cerebral || MED *cerebral palsy* parálisis *f* cerebral.

cerebrate ['seribreit] *vi* pensar.

cerebration [ˌseri'breiʃən] *n* actividad *f* mental, función *f* cerebral.

cerebrospinal [ˌseribrəu'spainl] *adj* cerebroespinal || MED *cerebrospinal fluid* líquido cefalorraquídeo | *cerebrospinal meningitis* meningitis *f* cerebroespinal.

cerebrum ['seribrəm] *n* ANAT cerebro *m*.
— OBSERV El plural es *cerebrums* o *cerebra*.

cerecloth ['siəklɔθ]; **cerement** ['siəmənt] *n* mortaja *f* encerada.

ceremonial [ˌseri'məunjəl] *adj* ceremonial || de gala; *ceremonial uniform* uniforme de gala.
◆ *n* ceremonial *m*.

ceremonious [seri'məunjəs] *adj* ceremonioso, sa.

ceremony ['seriməni] *n* ceremonia *f*; *a religious ceremony* una ceremonia religiosa || — *master of ceremonies* maestro de ceremonias (at a formal event), presentador *m* (of a show) || *to stand on ceremony* andarse con ceremonias *or* cumplidos || *without ceremony* sin ceremonias, sin cumplidos.

cereus ['siəriəs] *n* BOT cirio *m*.

cerin ['siərin] *n* cerina *f*.

cerise [sə'ri:z] *adj* de color cereza.
◆ *n* color *m* cereza.

cerite ['siərait] *n* MIN cerita *f*.

cerium ['siəriəm] *n* CHEM cerio *m*.

ceroplastics ['siərəuplɑ:stiks] *n* ceroplástica *f*.

cert [sə:t] *n* FAM *it's a cert!* ¡eso está hecho!, ¡es cosa segura!

certain ['sə:tn] *adj* seguro, ra; cierto, ta; *I am certain that it is not true* estoy seguro de que no es verdad; *it is certain that* es cierto que || cierto, ta; un tal, una tal; *a certain Mrs. Brown* una tal señora Brown || cierto, ta; *a certain resistance* cierta resistencia; *a certain day* cierto día || — *be certain to do that* no dejes de hacerlo || *for certain* seguro, con toda seguridad || *he is certain to be there* es seguro que estará || *I'll make certain* lo averiguaré, lo comprobaré || *to a certain extent* hasta cierto punto || *to make certain of* asegurarse de.

certainly [-li] *adv* desde luego, naturalmente, por supuesto (of course) || naturalmente, con mucho gusto; *certainly, sir!* ¡con mucho gusto, señor! || seguro, sin falta; *I shall certainly do that* lo haré seguro *or* sin falta || — *certainly not!* ¡de ninguna manera!, ¡por supuesto que no!, ¡ni hablar! || *he certainly can run fast* ése sí que corre rápido.

certainty [-ti] *n* certeza *f*, certidumbre *f* || seguridad *f*; *there is no certainty about him coming tomorrow* no hay seguridad de que venga mañana || — *for a certainty* con toda seguridad, a ciencia cierta || *it's a certainty* es cosa segura || *with certainty* a ciencia cierta.

certifiable ['sə:ti'faiəbl] *adj* certificable (capable of being certified) || loco, ca; demente (mad).

certificate [sə'tifikit] *n* certificado *m* (attesting some fact) || diploma *m*, título *m* (academic, etc.) || — *birth certificate* partida *f* de nacimiento || *certificate of baptism* partida *f or* fe *f* de bautismo || *death certificate* partida *f* de defunción || *marriage certificate* certificado *m* de matrimonio, partida *f* de matrimonio.

certificate [sə'tifikeit] *vt* dar un certificado a (to grant a certificate to) || dar un título *or* un diploma a (an academic title).

certification [ˌsə:tifi'keiʃən] *n* certificación *f* || certificado *m*.

certifier ['sə:tifaiə*] *n* certificador *m*.

certify ['sə:tifai] *vt* certificar, atestiguar (to attest) || declarar loco || *certified copy* copia legalizada.

certitude ['sə:titju:d] *n* certeza *f*, certidumbre *f*.

cerulean [si'ru:ljən] *adj* cerúleo, a.
◆ *n* azul *m* celeste (colour).

cerumen [si'ru:mən] *n* cerumen *m* (of ears).

ceruse ['siəru:s] *n* cerusa *f*, albayalde *m*.

cerussite ['siərəsait] *n* MIN cerusita *f*.

Cervantine [sə'vænˌtain] *adj* cervantesco, ca; cervantino, na.

Cervantist [sə'vænˌtist] *n* cervantista *m* & *f*.

cervical ['sə:vikəl] *adj* cervical.

cervical smear [-smiə] *n* frotis *m*.

cervid ['sə:vid] *n* cérvido *m*.
— OBSERV El plural de *cervid* es *cervidae*.

cervine ['sə:vain] *adj* ZOOL cervino, na; cerval.

cervix ['sə:viks] *n* ANAT cerviz *f* (back part of the neck) | cuello *m* del útero (neck of the uterus).
— OBSERV El plural de *cervix* es *cervices* o *cervixes*.

cesium ['siziəm] *n* CHEM cesio *m*.

cessation [se'seiʃən] *n* cese *m*, cesación *f*, cesamiento *m*.

cession ['seʃən] *n* cesión *f*.

cessionary ['seʃənəri] *n* cesionario, ria.

cesspit ['sespit] *n* pozo *m* negro.

cesspool ['sespu:l] *n* pozo *m* negro || FIG sentina *f*.

cestode ['sestəud] *n* ZOOL cestodo *m*.

cetacean [si'teiʃjən] *n* ZOOL cetáceo *m*.

cetonia [se'təunjə] *n* ZOOL cetonia *f*.

Ceylon [si'lɔn] *pr n* GEOGR Ceilán.

Ceylonese [silɔ'ni:z] *adj/n* ceilanés, esa.

chaconne [ʃə'kɔn] *n* MUS chacona *f*.

chafe [tʃeif] *n* rozadura *f* || irritación *f* (irritation) || desgaste *m* (wear caused by rubbing).

chafe [tʃeif] *vt* irritar (to irritate) || desgastar (to wear) || rozar (to rub) || excoriar || frotar (for warmth) || FIG irritar, enfadar (to annoy).
◆ *vi* rozarse; *the cars chafed against each other* los coches se rozaron || desgastarse (to become worn by rubbing) || FIG irritarse, enfadarse (*at* por, a causa de, debido a).

chafer [-ə*] *n* ZOOL abejorro *m*.

chaff [tʃɑ:f] *n* ahechaduras *f pl*, barcia *f* (of wheat) || granzas *f pl* (of other grain) || paja *f* cortada (for animal fodder) || FIG paja *f*, broza *f* (useless writing, talk, etc.) | broma *f* chanza *f* (banter) || FIG *to separate the chaff from the grain* separar la cizaña del buen grano.

chaff [tʃɑ:f] *vt* cortar (hay or straw) || FIG tomar el pelo a (to tease).

chaffer ['tʃɑ:fə*] *n* bromista *m* & *f* (teaser) || regateo *m* (of price).

chaffer ['tʃɑ:fə*] *vi* regatear (to bargain).
◆ *vt* intercambiar (words).

chaffinch ['tʃæfintʃ] *n* ZOOL pinzón *m*.

chafing dish ['tʃeifiŋˌdiʃ] *n* calientaplatos *m inv*.

chagrin ['ʃægrin] *n* disgusto *m*, contrariedad *f* (grief) || desilusión *f*, desengaño *m* (disappointment) || mortificación *f* (mortification).

chagrin ['ʃægrin] *vt* contrariar, disgustar (to grieve) || desilusionar, decepcionar (to dissappoint) || mortificar (to mortify).

chain [tʃein] *n* cadena *f*; *the links of the chain were very strong* los eslabones de la cadena eran muy sólidos; *a chain of hotels* una cadena de hoteles || sucesión *f*, cadena *f* (of facts) || — *chain armour* cota *f* de malla || *chain bridge* puente *m* colgante || *chain coupling* cadena de enganche (for linking rail cars) || *chain gang* cadena (de presidiarios), cuerda *f* de presos || *chain letter* carta *f* que forma parte de una cadena || US *chain lightning* relámpagos *m pl* en zigzag || *chain lock* cadena antirrobo || *chain mail* cota *f* de mallas (armour) || *chain of mountains* cordillera *f*, cadena *f* de montañas || *chain of office* collar *m* de mando (of mayor, high dignitary) || *chain pump* noria *f* de cangilones || CHEM *chain reaction* reacción *f* en cadena || *chain saw* sierra *f* de cadena, tronzadora *f* || MIL *chain shot* bala *f* de cadena || FAM *chain smoker* fumador *m* que enciende un cigarrillo con otro || *chain stitch* punto *m* de cadeneta, cadeneta *f* || *chain store* sucursal *f* [de una cadena de establecimientos] || *chain wheel* plato *m* (de bicicleta), rueda dentada de cadena || *driving chain* cadena de transmisión || *land chain, measuring chain* cadena de agrimensor || *safety chain* cadena de seguridad.
◆ *pl* cadenas *f* (prisoner's fetters).

chain [tʃein] *vt* encadenar.

chain-react [-ri'ækt] *vi* tener reacción en cadena.

chain-smoke [-sməuk] *vi* encender un cigarrillo con otro, fumar pitillo tras pitillo.

chair [tʃεə*] *n* silla *f* (seat); *cane chair* silla de rejilla; *folding chair* silla de tijera *or* plegable; *swivel chair* silla giratoria || cátedra *f* (in a university) || presidencia *f*; *to appeal to the chair* apelar a la presidencia || sillón *m* (of chairman) || presidente *m* (chairman); *to address the chair* dirigirse al presidente || silla *f* eléctrica (electric chair) || TECH cojinete *m* de riel || coche *m* salón (railway carriage) || silla *f* de la reina (child's game) || — *gestatorial chair* silla gestatoria (of the Pope) || *please, take a chair* siéntese por favor || *sedan chair* silla de manos || *to be in the chair* o *to occupy the chair* ocupar la presidencia, presidir || *to leave the chair* levantar la sesión || *to take the chair* tomar la presidencia, presidir || *wing chair* sillón *m* de orejas.

chair [tʃεə*] *vt* llevar a hombros (to shoulder) || llevar en triunfo (to carry in triumph) || presidir (a meeting).

chair car [-kɑ:*] *n* US coche *m* salón (rail car).

chair lift [-lift] *n* telesilla *m* (for skiers).

chairman [-mən] *n* presidente *m*.
— OBSERV El plural de esta palabra es *chairmen*.

chairmanship [-mənʃip] *n* presidencia *f*.

chair rail [-reil] *n* guardasilla *f*.

chairwoman [-ˌwumən] *n* presidenta *f*.
— OBSERV El plural de *chairwoman* es *chairwomen*.

chaise [ʃeiz] *n* tilburi *m* (carriage) || *chaise longue* tumbona *f* (long chair).

chalaza [kə'leizə] *n* BIOL & BOT chalaza *f*.

chalcedony [kæl'sedəni] *n* MIN calcedonia *f*.

chalcography [kæl'kɔgrəfi] *n* calcografía *f*.

chalcopyrite [ˌkælkə'pairait] *n* MIN calcopirita *f*.

Chaldaic [kæl'deik] *adj* caldaico, ca.

Chaldea; Chaldaea [kæl'di:ə] *pr n* Caldea *f*.

Chaldean [-n] *adj/n* caldeo, a.

chalet ['ʃælei] *n* chalet *m*, chalé *m*.

chalice ['tʃælis] *n* REL cáliz *m*.

chalk [tʃɔ:k] *adj* cretáceo, a; *chalk hills* colinas cretáceas || hecho con tiza, a tiza; *a chalk drawing* un dibujo a tiza.
◆ *n* GEOL creta *f* || tiza *f* (for writing on black-boards, etc.) || — FAM *not by a long chalk* ni mucho menos | *to be as different as chalk from cheese* parecerse como el día a la noche, parecerse como un huevo a una manzana.

chalk [tʃɔ:k] *vt* escribir *or* marcar con tiza || poner tiza a (billiard cue) || — *to chalk out* trazar (to sketch out a plan, etc.) || *to chalk up* apuntar (on a board), apuntarse; *to chalk up a victory* apuntarse una victoria.

chalkiness [-inis] *n* naturaleza *f* cretácea.

chalk pit [-pit] *n* cantera *m* de creta.

chalkstone [-stəun] *n* MED concreción *f* cálcica.

chalky ['tʃɔ:ki] *adj* cretáceo, a; gredoso, sa || calcáreo, a (water).

challenge ['tʃælindʒ] *n* desafío *m*, reto *m* || MIL quién vive *m*, alto *m* (of sentry) || FIG estímulo *m*, incentivo *m* (stimulus) | tentativa *f* [para conquistar algo] (attempt) || JUR recusación *f* || SP «challenge» *m* || — *to issue a challenge to s.o.* desafiar a alguien || *to take up the challenge* aceptar el desafío *or* el reto.

challenge ['tʃælindʒ] *vt* desafiar, retar (to a duel, to a game, etc.) || poner en duda, poner en tela de juicio; *to challenge a statement* poner en duda una declaración || requerir; *this matter challenges attention* este asunto requiere atención || poner a prueba (to test) || FIG estimular (to stimulate) || JUR recusar || MIL dar el quién vive a || US impugnar (a vote) || — *to challenge s.o. to do sth.* desafiar a alquien a que haga algo || *to challenge the speaker* hacer objeciones *or* pedir aclaraciones al orador.

challenger [-ə*] *n* retador *m*, desafiador *m* (to a duel, etc.) || SP «challenger» *m*, aspirante *m* (a un título).

challenging [-iŋ] *adj* desafiante || estimulante (work) || provocativo, va (smile).

chalybeate [kə'libiit] *adj* ferruginoso, sa; *chalybeate water* agua ferruginosa.

chalybite ['kælibait] *n* MIN siderita *f*.

chamber ['tʃeimbə*] *n* cámara *f*, aposento *m* (private room) || cámara *f* (legislative or judicial body) || TECH recámara *f* (of a gun) | cámara *f* (of a motor, sluice, furnace) || — *chamber music* música *f* de cámara || *chamber of commerce* cámara de comercio || *chamber orchesta* orquesta *f* de cámara || *chamber of Deputies* cámara de diputados || *chamber pot* orinal *m* || *compression chamber* cámara de compresión || *funeral chamber* cámara mortuoria || *gas chamber* cámara de gas || *upper, lower chamber* cámara alta, baja.
◆ *pl* JUR despacho *m sing*, bufete *m sing* (of a lawyer).

chamberlain ['tʃeimbəlin] *n* chambelán *m*.

chambermaid ['tʃeimbəmeid] *n* doncella *f*, camarera *f*.

chameleon [kə'mi:ljən] *n* ZOOL camaleón *m* || FIG camaleón *m* (person).

chameleonic [ˌkəmi:lj'ɔnik] *adj* FIG inconstante, que cambia mucho de opinión.

chamfer ['tʃæmfə*] *n* bisel *m*, chaflán *m*.

chamfer ['tʃæmfə*] *vt* biselar, chaflanar, achaflanar.

chammy ['ʃæmi] *n* FAM gamuza *f*.

chamois ['ʃæmwɑ:] *n* ZOOL gamuza *f* || *chamois leather* gamuza *f*.
— OBSERV La pronunciación de *chamois* en la expresión *chamois leather* es ['ʃæmi]. El plural de esta palabra es *chamois* o *chamoix*.

chamomile ['kæməmail] *n* BOT manzanilla *f*, camomila *f*.

champ [tʃæmp] *n* FAM campeón *m*.

champ [tʃæmp] *vt/vi* mascar haciendo ruido; *he champed his food* mascaba la comida haciendo ruido || mordiscar, mordisquear (to bite on) || FIG *to champ at the bit* tascar el freno (to show impatience).

champagne [ʃæm'pein] *n* champán *m*, champaña *m*.

champion ['tʃæmpjən] *adj* campeón, ona; *a champion team* un equipo campeón || FAM de primera, estupendo, da; *that's champion!* ¡eso es de primera!
◆ *n* campeón, ona; *a tennis champion* un campeón de tenis || FIG paladín *m*, defensor *m*, adalid *m*; *champion of liberty* paladín de la libertad.

champion ['tʃæmpjən] *vt* defender, hacerse el paladín de, hacerse el campeón de, ser el adalid de.

championship [-ʃip] *n* campeonato *m*; *league championship* campeonato de liga || FIG defensa *f*; *the championship of a cause* la defensa de una causa.

chance [tʃɑ:ns] *adj* casual, fortuito, ta; *a chance meeting* un encuentro casual.
◆ *n* casualidad *f*, azar *m*; *I found it by chance* lo encontré por casualidad || casualidad *f*; *have you a car by any chance?* ¿tiene un coche por casualidad? || azar *m*; *game of chance* juego de azar || destino *m*, fortuna *f*; *chance was against me* la suerte me fue contraria || oportunidad *f*, ocasión *f*; *it was a chance to see the queen* fue una oportunidad de ver a la reina || posibilidad *f*, probabilidad *f* [AMER chance *f*]; *he has no chance of escaping* no tiene ninguna posibilidad de escapar; *the chances are that we are going* la probabilidad es que vayamos || riesgo *m*; *it's chance I have to take* es un riesgo que tengo que correr || — *by sheer chance* por mera casualidad || *it's a long chance* es poco probable || *on the chance that* con la esperanza de que || *on the off chance* en el caso de que, si por casualidad || *to give s.o. a chance* darle a alguien una oportunidad || *to leave it to chance dejarlo al azar* || *to stand a chance* tener probabilidades *or* posibilidades || *to take a chance* correr un riesgo, arriesgarse || *to take no chances* no arriesgarse || *to take one's chance* arriesgarse, tentar la suerte.

chance ['tʃɑ:ns] *vt* arriesgar || probar; *to chance one's luck* probar fortuna || *to chance it* arriesgarse || *to chance one's arm* jugarse el todo por el todo.
◆ *vi* acaecer, suceder; *it chanced that* sucedió que || tener la suerte *or* la oportunidad de || — *he chanced to see me* me vio por casualidad || *to chance upon* tropezar con, encontrar por casualidad; *I chanced upon a friend* tropecé con un amigo.

chancel ['tʃɑ:nsəl] *n* presbiterio *m*, antealtar *m*.

chancellery ['tʃɑ:nsələri] *n* cancillería *f*.

chancellor ['tʃɑ:nsələ*] *n* canciller *m* (of a state, of an embassy) || rector *m* (of a university) || US JUR magistrado *m* || — *chancellor of the Exchequer* ministro *m* de Hacienda || *Lord Chancellor* presidente *m* de la Cámara de los Lores.

chancellory [-ri] *n* cancillería *f*.

chancery ['tʃɑ:nsəri] *n* cancillería *f* (office of a chancellor or of public records) || US juzgado *m*.

Chancery ['tʃɑ:nsəri] *n* JUR tribunal *m* de justicia, chancillería *f*.

chancre ['ʃæŋkə*] *n* MED chancro *m*.

chancy ['tʃɑ:nsi] *adj* arriesgado, da (risky) || incierto, ta (uncertain).

chandelier [ˌʃændi'liə*] *n* araña *f* (of lights).

chandler ['tʃɑ:ndlə*] *n* (ant) cerero, ra; velero, ra (person who sells candles) || proveedor *m* (supplier) || droguista *m* (who sells paint, etc.).

chandlery [-ri] *n* cerería *f* || droguería *f*.

change [tʃeindʒ] *n* cambio *m* (of opinion, position, state, government, etc.); *change of address* cambio de domicilio; *change in the weather* cambio de tiempo || cambio *m*, trueque *m* (exchange for) || cambio *m*, vuelta *f* (money returned); *he kept the change* se quedó con la vuelta || cambio *m* (money changed) || calderilla *f*, suelto *m* (small coins) || cambio *m*, transbordo *m* (of trains) || relevo *m*, cambio *m* (of horses) || muda *f*, cambio *m* (of skin, of clothes) || — *change of heart* cambio de opinión *or* de parecer || *change of life* menopausia *f* || *change of scene* cambio escénico, mutación *f* || *for a change* para variar || *it's a change for the better* es un cambio beneficioso || *no change given* se ruega moneda fraccionaria || *on Change* que trabaja en la Bolsa || FIG *to get no change out of s.o.* no sacarle nada a uno || *to ring the changes* tocar las variaciones de un carillón (campanology), decir *or* hacer una cosa de varias maneras, agotar todas las formas posibles.

change [tʃeindʒ] *vt* cambiar; *to change a wheel* cambiar una rueda; *they have changed the timetable* han cambiado el horario || cambiar, mudar (clothes, nappies, sheets, skin, etc.) || cambiar de; *to change the subject* cambiar de tema; *to change one's shoes* cambiar de zapatos || cambiar, trocar (one thing for another) || — *all change!* ¡bájense por favor! || *to change books, habits* cambiar de libros, de costumbres

|| *to change gear* cambiar de velocidad || *to change hands* cambiar de manos *or* de mano; *this car has changed hands many times* este coche ha cambiado de mano muchas veces || MUS *to change key* cambiar de tono || *to change money* cambiar dinero || *to change one's clothes* cambiarse de ropa || *to change one's mind* cambiar de idea || *to change step* cambiar el paso || *to change the guard* relevar la guardia || *to get changed* cambiarse.

◆ *vi* cambiar; *he has changed a lot* ha cambiado mucho || cambiarse, mudarse (clothes) || transbordar, hacer transbordo; *when I came by train I had to change twice* cuando vine en tren tuve que hacer transbordo dos veces || transformarse, convertirse (to become); *the snow is changing into water* la nieve se está transformando en agua || FIG *to change with the wind* cambiar más que una veleta.

◆ *phr v* ***to change about*** cambiar de dirección || ***to change around*** cambiar de arriba abajo || ***to change down*** o ***up*** cambiar a una velocidad inferior *or* superior (gears) || ***to change over*** cambiar; *we changed over to the decimal system* cambiamos al sistema métrico decimal.

changeability [ˌtʃeindʒəˈbiliti] *n* variabilidad *f.*

changeable [ˈtʃeindʒəbl] *adj* variable (weather, character, etc.) || cambiable (which can be changed) || cambiadizo, za (inconsistent).

changeful [ˈtʃeindʒful] *adj* variable, cambiante.

changeless [ˈtʃeindʒlis] *adj* invariable, inmutable.

changeling [ˈtʃeindʒliŋ] *n* niño *m* cambiado por otro.

changeover [ˈtʃeindzˌəuvə*] *n* cambio *m.*

changing [ˈtʃeindʒiŋ] *adj* que cambia, cambiante.

◆ *n* cambio *m; the changing of a wheel* el cambio de una rueda.

changing room [-ruːm] *n* vestuario *m.*

channel [ˈtʃænl] *n* canal *m* (course for running water) || cauce *m* (the deepest part of a river) || FIG vía *f,* conducto *m; legislation must go through the usual channels* las leyes deben seguir las vías usuales || canal (commercial) || canal *m,* cadena *f; television channel* canal de televisión || ranura *f* (groove) || INFORM canal *m,* vía *f* || — GEOGR *Channel Islands* islas Anglonormandas | *English Channel* o *The Channel* el Canal de la Mancha || *irrigation channel* acequia *f,* canal *m* de riego.

channel [ˈtʃænl] *vt* construir canales en, canalizar (to make channels) || canalizar, encauzar; *to channel water* canalizar agua || formar barrancos en (to make ravines) || FIG encauzar, canalizar (ideas, etc.).

Channel tunnel [-ˌtʌnəl] *n* túnel *m* del Canal de la Mancha.

chanson [ʃanˈsɔn] *n* MUS canción *f* || *chanson de Geste* cantar *m* de gesta.

chant [tʃɑːnt] *n* MUS REL cántico *m* (psalm) || MUS canción *f,* canto *m* (song) || melopea *f* (rythmic repetitive singing) || FIG sonsonete *m,* cantinela *f* (singsong) || *Gregorian chant* canto gregoriano.

chant [tʃɑːnt] *vt* cantar (to sing) || FIG salmodiar, cantar con monotonía (to sing monotonously).

◆ *vi* salmodiar (psalms).

chanter [-ə*] *n* cantor, ra (singer) || REL chantre *m* (of a choir) || MUS caramillo *m* (of bagpipes).

chanterelle [ˌtʃæntəˈrel] *n* BOT mízcalo *m* (fungus).

chantry [ˈtʃɑːntri] *n* REL capellanía *f* (endowment) || capilla *f or* altar *m* para decir misas por el fundador (chapel or altar).

chanty [ˈtʃɑːnti] *n* MAR saloma *f.*

chaos [ˈkeiɔs] *n* caos *m.*

chaotic [keiˈɔtik] *adj* caótico, ca.

chap [tʃæp] *n* FAM tipo *m,* tío *m* || grieta *f* (crack in the skin) || ANAT mandíbula *f* (jaw) | mejilla *f* (cheek) || quijada *f* (of animals) || TECH mordaza *f* (of a vice) || — *be a good chap and do it* sé buen chico y hazlo || *listen, old chap* escucha, hombre || *poor chap* pobre hombre *m,* pobrecillo *m.*

chap [tʃæp] *vt* agrietar.

◆ *vi* agrietarse.

chaparral [ˌtʃæpəˈræl] *n* chaparral *m.*

chapbook [ˈtʃæpbuk] *n* (ant) libro *m* de coplas vendido por las calles.

chape [tʃeip] *n* contera *f,* regatón *m* (of scabbard).

chapel [ˈtʃæpəl] *n* REL capilla *f* (small church, part of church containing an altar) || servicio *m* religioso; *tomorrow chapel will be at nine o'clock* mañana el servicio religioso será a las nueve || templo *m* (nonconformists' place of worship) || gremio *m* (de impresores) (association of printers) || — *chapel master* maestro *m* de capilla || *chapel of ease* capilla sufragánea || *funeral chapel* capilla ardiente.

chaperon; chaperone [ˈʃæpərəun] *n* carabina *f* señora *f* de compañía.

chaperon; chaperone [ˈʃæpərəun] *vt* hacer de carabina con, acompañar [a una señorita].

chapfallen [ˈtʃæpˌfɔːlən] *adj* abatido, da; deprimido, da; alicaído, da.

chaplain [ˈtʃæplin] *n* REL capellán *m.*

chaplaincy [-si] *n* REL capellanía *f.*

chaplet [ˈtʃæplit] *n* guirnalda *f* (of flowers or jewels) || sarta *f* de cuentas (string of beads) || REL rosario *m* (part of rosary) || ARCH moldura *f* de cuentas || FIG sarta *f,* rosario *m,* retahíla *f* (series).

chapman [ˈtʃæpmən] *n* vendedor *m* ambulante.

— OBSERV El plural de *chapman* es *chapmen.*

chapped [tʃæpt] *adj* agrietado, da (skin, hands); cortado, da (lips).

chaps [tʃæps] *pl n* zajones *m,* zahones *m* (leggings).

chapter [ˈtʃæptə*] *n* capítulo *m; a chapter of a book* un capítulo de un libro; *with his death ended a chapter of history* con su muerte se termina un capítulo de la historia || REL cabildo *m* (of canons) || — *chapter house* sala *f* capitular || *chapter of accidents* serie *f* de accidentes *or* desgracias || *to give chapter and verse for sth.* indicar algo con pelos y señales || *to quote chapter and verse* citar literalmente.

chapter [ˈtʃæptə*] *vt* dividir en capítulos.

char [tʃɑː*] *n* asistenta *f* (charwoman) || carbón *m* de leña (charcoal) || FAM té *m* (tea) || umbra *f* (fish).

char [tʃɑː*] *vt* carbonizar (to reduce to carbon) || chamuscar (to scorch).

◆ *vi* carbonizarse || chamuscarse (to be scorched) || trabajar de asistenta (a charwoman).

charabanc [ˈʃærəbæŋ] *n* autocar *m.*

character [ˈkæriktə*] *adj* de carácter; *character actor* actor de carácter.

◆ *n* carácter *m; they have very strong characters* tienen caracteres muy fuertes || personaje *m; the leading character of this play* el personaje principal de esta obra; *a well-known public character* un personaje muy conocido || papel (role); *in the character of* en el papel de || FIG & FAM tipo *m,* individuo *m; he's and odd character!* ¡es un tipo raro! || reputación *f; he is a bad character* tiene mala reputación || PRINT carácter *m,* tipo *m* (symbol, letter) || INFORM carácter *m* || — *character disorder* inadaptación *f* social || *character disorder* inadaptación *f* social || *character reference* informe *m* || *in character of* en calidad de || *main* o *chief character* protagonista *m* & *f* || *to be in character with* ser característico de || *to be out of character with* no ser nada característico de.

characteristic [-ˈristik] *adj* característico, ca.

◆ *n* característica *f.*

characterization [-raiˈzeiʃən] *n* caracterización *f.*

characterize [-raiz] *vt* caracterizar; *his big nose characterizes him* su gran nariz le caracteriza || describir (to portray); *he characterized his brother very well* describió muy bien a su hermano.

characterless [-lis] *adj* sin carácter, sin personalidad.

charade [ʃəˈrɑːd] *n* charada *f* || FIG charada *f.*

charcoal [ˈtʃɑːkəul] *n* carbón *m* vegetal, carbón *m* de leña (carbón) || ARTS carboncillo *m* || *charcoal drawing* dibujo *m* al carbón, carboncillo *m.*

charge [ˈtʃɑːdʒ] *n* cargo *m* (responsability, safekeeping); *take charge of the administration* hazte cargo de la administración || cargo *m* (post) || tarea *f,* trabajo *m* (task) || carga *f,* peso *m* (load); *my brother is a charge on me* mi hermano es una carga para mí || carga *f* (of battery, furnace, firearm) || MIN barreno *m* (explosive) || MIL carga *f* (attack); *to return to the charge* volver a la carga || JUR cargo *m,* acusación *f* (legal accusation) | extracto *m* de los debates (of judge to jury) || embestida *f* (of bull) || carga *f* (sports) || ELECTR carga *f* || precio *m* (price) || blasón *m* (heraldry) || — *at my own charge* a expensas mías, a mi costa || COMM *charge account* cuenta *f* a cargo || *in charge* encargado, da (in command), detenido, da (under arrest) || *in charge of* encargado, da; *he is in charge of the class* está encargado de la clase; al cargo de, al cuidado de (under the supervision of) || *the person in charge* el encargado || *to bring charges against* formular acusaciones contra || *to lay sth. to a person's charge* culpar a alguien de algo || *to make a charge for* facturar a || *to reverse the charges* poner una conferencia a cobro revertido || *to take charge of* encargarse de, hacerse cargo de (responsability), tomar el mando de (direction).

charge [ˈtʃɑːdʒ] *vt* acusar; *they charged him with murder* le acusaron de asesinato || ordenar; *he charged her to be careful* le ordenó que tuviera cuidado || exhortar; *the bishop charged the priests to give it careful consideration* el obispo exhortó a los sacerdotes a que examinaran detenidamente la cuestión || encargar (to entrust) || cargar; *they charged him with presents for the family* le cargaron de regalos para la familia || cobrar; *they charged me 10 pounds* me cobraron 10 libras || cargar; *charge it to my account* cárguemelo en mi cuenta || cargar; *the lorry was charged with wooden planks* el camión estaba cargado con tablas de madera; *to charge a battery, a furnace* cargar una batería, un horno; *to charge a gun* cargar un arma; *the clouds were charged with electricity* las nubes estaban cargadas de electricidad || atacar, cargar (to attack) || cargar (sports) || embestir (a bull) || blasonar (heraldry).

◆ *vi* cargar (soldiers, etc.) || cobrar; *he charges for his services* cobra por sus servicios || cargar (sports) || embestir (a bull) || — FAM *to charge in* irrumpir (en) | *to charge off* salir corriendo.

chargeable [-dʒəbl] *adj* acusable (liable to be accused) || *chargeable to the customer* a cargo del cliente.

chargé d'affaires [ʃɑːʒeidæ'fɛə*] *n* encargado *m* de negocios.

chargehand ['tʃɑːdʒhænd] *n* capataz *m*.

charge nurse ['tʃɑːdʒ nəːs] *n* enfermero, ra jefe.

charger ['tʃɑːdʒə*] *n* ELECTR & MIL cargador *m* ‖ POET corcel *m* (horse).

charge sheet ['tʃɑːdʒ ʃiːt] *n* hoja *f* de denuncia.

charily ['tʃɛərili] *adv* cautelosamente (warily) ‖ parcamente (sparingly).

chariness ['tʃɛərinis] *n* cautela *f* (caution) ‖ parsimonia *f* (parsimony).

chariot ['tʃæriət] *n* carro *m*.

charioteer [,tʃæriə'tiə*] *n* auriga *m*.

charism [kærizəm]; **charisma** [kə'rizmə] *n* carisma *m*.
— OBSERV El plural de *charisma* es *charismata*.

charismatic [,kæriz'mætik] *adj* carismático, ca.

charitable ['tʃæritəbl] *adj* caritativo, va; *he is very charitable towards the poor* es muy caritativo con los pobres ‖ tolerante (tolerant) ‖ comprensivo, va (understanding) ‖ *charitable society* institución benéfica.

charity ['tʃæriti] *n* caridad *f*; *to live on charity* vivir de la caridad ‖ institución *f* benéfica (charitable society) ‖ caridad *f*, limosna *f* (alms) ‖ comprensión *f* (tolerance) ‖ benevolencia *f*, indulgencia *f* ‖ — *charity bazaar* venta benéfica ‖ FIG *charity begins at home* la caridad bien entendida empieza por uno mismo ‖ *charity child* inclusero *m*, hospiciano *m* ‖ REL *sister of charity* hermana *f* de la Caridad ‖ *to be out of charity with* no ser muy caritativo con.

charivari [ʃɑːri'vɑːri] *n* alboroto *m*, guirigay *m* (noise) ‖ cencerrada *f* (mock serenade).

charlady ['tʃɑː'leidi] *n* asistenta *f*.

charlatan ['ʃɑːlətən] *n* charlatán, ana.

charlatanism ['ʃɑːlətənizəm] *n* charlatanismo *m*.

Charlemagne ['ʃɑːlə'mein] *pr n* Carlomagno *m*.

Charles [tʃɑːlz] *n pr* Carlos *m* ‖ ASTR *Charles's Wain* Carro *m* Mayor, Osa *f* Mayor.

charleston ['tʃɑːlstən] *n* charlestón *m* (dance).

charley horse ['tʃɑːlihɔːs] *n* US FAM calambre *m*.

charlock ['tʃɑːlɔk] *n* BOT mostaza *f* silvestre.

Charlotte ['ʃɑːlət] *pr n* Carlota *f*.

charm [tʃɑːm] *n* encanto *m* (attraction) ‖ atractivo *m* (appeal) ‖ hechizo *m* (magic spell) ‖ amuleto *m* (amulet) ‖ dije *m* (trinket) ‖ — *charm bracelet* pulsera *f* de dijes ‖ FIG & FAM *like a charm* a las mil maravillas, perfectamente; *my ruse worked like a charm* mi truco resultó perfectamente ‖ *to be under s.o.'s charm* estar bajo el encanto de alguien ‖ *to fall a victim to s.o.'s charms* sucumbir ante los encantos de alguien ‖ *to turn on the charm* deshacerse en cumplidos.

charm [tʃɑːm] *vt* encantar (to delight); *I was charmed by her kindness* estaba encantado con su amabilidad ‖ hechizar, encantar (snakes) ‖ — *to charm away* hacer desaparecer como por ensalmo; *my troubles were charmed away* mis dificultades desaparecieron como por ensalmo ‖ *to lead a charmed life* ser muy afortunado *or* tener mucha suerte en la vida.

charmer [-ə*] *n* persona *f* encantadora (delightful person) ‖ encantador *m* (of snakes).

charming [-iŋ] *adj* encantador, ra.

charnel house ['tʃɑːnəlhaus] *n* osario *m*.

charred [tʃɑːd] *adj* carbonizado, da (reduced to carbon) ‖ chamuscado, da (scorched).

chart [tʃɑːt] *n* MAR carta *f* de marear *or* marina ‖ mapa *m* (map) ‖ tabla *f* (table) ‖ gráfico *m* (graph) ‖ MUS *the charts* la lista de éxitos.

chart [tʃɑːt] *vt* poner en una carta marina ‖ trazar; *to chart a course* trazar un derrotero.

charter [-ə*] *n* carta *f* (official document granting rights) ‖ estatutos *m pl* (of a society) ‖ fletamento *m*, fletamiento *m* (boat, aeroplane) ‖ alquiler *m* (bus, train) ‖ — *charter flight* vuelo *m* «charter» *or* fletado ‖ *charter member* socio fundador.

charter [-ə*] *vt* conceder carta a (to grant a charter) ‖ fletar (ship, plane) ‖ alquilar (bus, train).

chartered accountant ['tʃɑːtədə'kauntənt] *n* perito *m* contable, perito *m* mercantil.

charterer ['tʃɑːtərə*] *n* fletador *m*.

charterhouse ['tʃɑːtəːhaus] *n* cartuja *f*.

charter party [tʃɑːtə,pɑːti] *n* contrato *m* de flete.

chartreuse [ʃɑː'trəːz] *n* cartuja *f* (monastery) ‖ «chartreuse» *m* (liqueur) ‖ color *m* amarillo verdoso.

charwoman ['tʃɑː,wumən] *n* asistenta *f*.
— OBSERV El plural de *charwoman* es *charwomen*.

chary ['tʃɛəri] *adj* cauto, ta; cauteloso, sa (wary) ‖ parco, ca (sparing); *he is chary in his praise* es parco en alabanzas ‖ avaro, ra (stingy) ‖ tímido, da (shy).

Charybdis [kə'ribdis] *pr n* FIG *to be between Scylla and Charybdis* estar entre Escila y Caribdis.

chase [tʃeis] *n* persecución *f*, caza *f* (pursuit) ‖ caza *f* (hunting) ‖ caña *f* (of gun) ‖ ranura *f* (groove) ‖ TECH canal *m* (in wall) ‖ MAR caza *f* ‖ PRINT rama *f* ‖ *to give chase to* dar caza a.

chase [tʃeis] *vt* perseguir (to run after) ‖ cazar (to hunt) ‖ FIG dar caza a, cazar (a girl) ‖ TECH cincelar (to ornament silver, etc.) | acanalar (to groove) | engastar (jewel) | repujar (to emboss) | aterrajar, filetear, roscar (a screw) ‖ FAM *go chase yourself!* ¡vete al diablo!
◆ *vi* ir corriendo (to hurry).
◆ *phr v* **to chase after** ir detrás de, perseguir a; *Andrew was chasing after Christine* Andrés iba detrás de Cristina ‖ **to chase away** ahuyentar ‖ **to chase from** echar *or* expulsar de ‖ **to chase off** ahuyentar ‖ **to chase out** echar fuera, expulsar ‖ **to chase up** investigar, buscar.

chaser [-ə*] *n* TECH cincel *m* (chisel) ‖ cazador, ra (hunter) ‖ perseguidor, ra (pursuer) ‖ US caza *m* (plane) ‖ grabador, ra (engraver) ‖ TECH roscador *m*, terraja *f* ‖ bebida *f* ligera tomada después de otra más fuerte.

chasm ['kæzəm] *n* sima *f*, abismo *m* (cleft) ‖ FIG abismo *m*.

chassis ['ʃæsi] *n* AUT chasis *m*, bastidor *m* ‖ US FAM cuerpo *m* (body).

chaste [tʃeist] *adj* casto, ta (virtuous) ‖ sobrio, bria; escueto, ta (style).

chasten ['tʃeisn] *vt* limar, pulir, depurar (style) ‖ castigar (to punish) ‖ corregir (to correct) ‖ escarmentar (to teach a lesson).

chasteness ['tʃeistnis] *n* castidad *f*.

chastise [tʃæs'taiz] *vt* castigar.

chastisement ['tʃæstizmənt] *n* castigo *m*.

chastity ['tʃæstiti] *n* castidad *f*; *chastity belt* cinturón de castidad ‖ pureza *f* (of style).

chasuble ['tʃæzjubl] *n* REL casulla *f*.

chat [tʃæt] *n* charla *f*, palique *m* (talk) ‖ *to have a chat about sth.* hablar de algo.

chat [tʃæt] *vi* charlar, estar de palique.
◆ *ph v* FAM *to chat up* ligar con.

château ['ʃætəu] *n* castillo *m*.
— OBSERV El plural es *châteaus* o *châteaux*.

chat show ['tʃæt ʃəu] *n* magazín *m* (on television).

chattel ['tʃætl] *n* JUR bien *m* mueble ‖ *chattel mortgage* hipoteca *f* sobre bienes muebles.

chatter ['tʃætə*] *n* charla *f*, palique *m*, cháchara *f* (talk) ‖ chillido *m* (of apes) ‖ gorjeo *m*, piada *f* (of birds) ‖ murmullo *m* (murmur) ‖ castañeteo *m* (of teeth) ‖ picado *m* (of engine) ‖ ruido *m* (noise).

chatter ['tʃætə*] *vi* parlotear, estar de cháchara, charlar (to chat) ‖ hablar por los codos (to be talkative) ‖ chillar (apes) ‖ piar (birds) ‖ castañetear (teeth) ‖ picar (an engine) ‖ hacer ruido (tool).

chatterbox [-bɔks]; **chatterer** [-rə*] *n* parlanchín, ina; charlatán, ana.

chattiness ['tʃætinis] *n* charloteo *m*; *his chattiness annoyed me* su charloteo me molestaba.

chatty ['tʃæti] *adj* hablador, ra; parlanchín, ina (person) ‖ familiar (informal) ‖ *chatty letter* carta llena de noticias.

chauffeur ['ʃəufə*] *n* chófer *m* [AMER chofer], conductor, ra.

chauffeur ['ʃəufə*] *vt* conducir.

chauvinism ['ʃəuvinizəm] *n* chauvinismo *m*, patriotería *f*.

chauvinist ['ʃəuvinist] *adj/n* chauvinista, patriotero, ra.

chauvinistic [ʃəuvi'nistik] *adj* chauvinista, patriotero, ra.

chaw [tʃɔː] *vt* US masticar ‖ US FAM *to chaw s.o. up* poner a uno verde, poner a uno como chupa de dómine.

chayote [tʃa'jəuti] *n* BOT chayote *m*.

cheap [tʃiːp] *adj* barato, ta (price) ‖ de precio reducido, económico, ca (reduced ticket) ‖ fácil; *a cheap victory* una victoria fácil ‖ bajo, ja; vil (mean) ‖ FIG malo, la; de poca calidad, barato, ta; charro, rra (tawdry) ‖ — *cheap and nasty* malo y barato ‖ *cheap money* préstamo obtenido a bajo interés ‖ *cheap sterling* libra *f* esterlina vendida a bajo precio ‖ *dirt cheap* baratísimo, ma ‖ *on the cheap* a bajo precio, barato ‖ FIG *that's pretty cheap* eso es vergonzoso | *to feel cheap* tener vergüenza ‖ *to hold life cheap* tener en poco la vida ‖ *to make cheaper* abaratar ‖ *to make o.s. cheap* subestimarse, rebajarse ‖ *to turn out cheap* salir barato.
◆ *adv* barato; *he got it very cheap* lo obtuvo muy barato.

cheapen ['tʃiːpən] *vt* rebajar el precio, abaratar (to lower the price) ‖ degradar (to degrade) ‖ FIG *to cheapen o.s.* rebajarse.
◆ *vi* bajar de precio, abaratarse.

cheap-jack ['tʃiːpdʒæk] *n* buhonero *m* (hawker).

cheaply ['tʃiːpli] *adv* barato, a bajo precio.

cheapness ['tʃiːpnis] *n* baratura *f*, lo barato ‖ FIG poca calidad *f* (low quality) ‖ bajeza *f* (lowness).

cheapskate ['tʃiːpskeit] *adj* US FAM tacaño, ña; agarrado, da.

cheat [tʃiːt] *n* tramposo, sa; fullero, ra (in games) ‖ estafador, ra; timador, ra (swindler) ‖ timo *m*, estafa *f* (swindle) ‖ trampa *f* (trick).

cheat [tʃiːt] *vt* estafar, timar (to swindle) ‖ engañar, burlarse de (to deceive) ‖ escapar de, burlar a; *he cheated death on a number of occasions* escapó de la muerte en numerosas ocasiones ‖ *to cheat s.o. out of sth.* estafar algo a alguien.
◆ *vi* hacer trampas (in games) ‖ copiar (in exams).

cheater [-ə*] *n* estafador, ra; timador, ra (swindler) ‖ tramposo, sa; fullero, ra (in games).

cheating [-iŋ] *adj* tramposo, sa (deceiving) ‖ fraudulento, ta (swindling).
◆ *n* trampa *f* (trickery) ‖ timo *m*, estafa *f* (swindle).

check [tʃek] *n* detención *f*, parada *f* (stop) ‖ restricción *f*, freno *m* (restrain) ‖ comprobación *f*, inspección *f* (control) ‖ repaso *m*, examen *m*, inspección *f* (test) ‖ ficha *f* (counter) ‖ MIL revés *m*, contratiempo *m* (reverse) ‖ pérdida *f* de la pista (in hunting) ‖ jaque *m* (chess) ‖ cuadros *m pl* (pattern) ‖ cuadro *m* (each square of the pattern) ‖ tela *f* de cuadros (cloth) ‖ TECH tope *m* ‖ *US* grieta *f* (crack) | marca *f*, señal *f* (mark of approval) | inspector, ra (inspector) | cuenta *f* (bill in a restaurant) | talón *m* (deposit receipt) | cheque *m* (cheque) ⟶ **cheque** ‖ — *to keep a check on* controlar ‖ *to keep* o *to hold in check* contener (to restrain), mantener a raya (a person).
◆ *adj* de control; *check list* lista de control ‖ *check suit* traje de cuadros.
◆ *interj* ¡jaque! (in chess) ‖ *US* ¡bien! (right!).

check [tʃek] *vt* parar, detener; *he checked his horse and dismounted* paró el caballo y bajó; *the window ledge checked his fall* el antepecho de la ventana detuvo su caída ‖ obstaculizar (to hinder) ‖ reprimir, refrenar, contener (to restrain) ‖ inspeccionar, examinar (to examine) ‖ comprobar, averiguar (facts) ‖ poner contraseña a (to mark) ‖ cuadricular (to square) ‖ dar jaque a (chess) ‖ MIL censurar, reprender (to rebuke) ‖ *US* depositar (to deposit) | facturar (to forward luggage) ‖ *to check sth. against sth. else* cotejar *or* comprobar una cosa con otra.
◆ *vi* detenerse, pararse (to stop) ‖ dar jaque (in chess) ‖ perder la pista (in hunting) ‖ concordar (to agree) ‖ comprobar, averiguar (to make sure) ‖ *US* rajarse, agrietarse (to crack).
◆ *phr v* ***to check in*** registrarse (at a hotel) ‖ ***to check off*** marcar (to mark) | contar uno por uno (to count individually) ‖ eliminar (to eliminate) ‖ ***to check on*** comprobar, averiguar (to verify) | inspeccionar ‖ ***to check out*** averiguar, comprobar | sacar prestado (books) | retirar sacar; *he went to the bank to check out some money* fue al banco a sacar dinero | pagar la cuenta y marcharse (from a hotel) ‖ ***to check up*** averiguar, comprobar ‖ ***to check with*** cotejar con, comparar con (to compare), consultar (a person).

checkbook [-buk] *n* *US* talonario *m* de cheques, chequera *f*.

checked [-t] *adj* a cuadros.

checker [-ə*] *n* *US* ficha *f* (in draughts) ‖ cuadro *m* (square) ‖ cuadros *m pl* (pattern).

checker [-ə*] *vt* marcar con cuadros.

checkerboard [-əˌbɔːd] *n* *US* tablero *m* de damas *or* de ajedrez.

checkered [ˈtʃekəd] *adj* a cuadros (cloth) ‖ FIG con altibajos (uneven) | variado, da (varied).

checkers [ˈtʃekəz] *n* *US* damas *f pl* (game).

checking account [ˈtʃekiŋəˌkaunt] *n* *US* cuenta *f* corriente.

checkmate [ˈtʃekˈmeit] *n* jaque *m* y mate (in chess) ‖ FIG fracaso *m* (failure).

checkmate [ˈtʃekˈmeit] *vt* dar jaque y mate (in chess) ‖ FIG ganarle a uno por la mano (to beat) | frustrar (s.o.'s plans) ‖ FIG *to be checkmated* estar en un callejón sin salida.

checkoff [ˈtʃekɔːf] *n* *US* deducción *f* de cierta cantidad del sueldo para pagar la cuota sindical.

checkout [ˈtʃekaut] *n* caja *f* (in self-service shop).

checkpoint [ˈtʃekpɔint] *n* control *m*.

checkrein [ˈtʃekrein] *n* falsa *f* rienda.

checkroom [ˈtʃekruːm] *n* *US* guardarropa *m* (cloakroom) ‖ consigna *f* (left-luggage office).

checkup [ˈtʃekʌp] *n* chequeo *m*, reconocimiento *m* médico general (physical examination) ‖ comprobación *f* (verification) ‖ revisión *f*, examen *m*.

Cheddar [ˈtʃedə*] *n* queso *m* de Cheddar.

cheek [tʃiːk] *n* carrillo *m* (side wall of mouth) ‖ mejilla *f* (the flesh on the cheekbone) ‖ ARCH jamba *f* ‖ FAM caradura *f* (impudence); *to have the cheek of the devil* tener una caradura de mil diablos ‖ — ZOOL *cheek pouch* abazón *m* ‖ *cheek to cheek* con las caras juntas (together), como los dos dedos de una mano (very friendly) ‖ FIG *to go cheek by jowl* ir codo con codo | *to turn the other cheek* poner la otra mejilla ‖ FAM *what a cheek!* ¡qué caradura!
◆ *pl* TECH mordaza *f sing* (of a vice).

cheek [tʃiːk] *vt* FAM tener caradura con, insolentarse con.

cheekbone [ˈtʃiːkbəun] *n* ANAT pómulo *m*.

cheekily [ˈtʃiːkili] *adv* descaradamente, con caradura.

cheekiness [ˈtʃiːkinis] *n* FAM caradura *f*, frescura *f*.

cheeky [ˈtʃiːki] *adj* FAM descarado, da; fresco, ca; caradura.

cheep [tʃiːp] *n* gorjeo *m*, piada *f*.

cheep [tʃiːp] *vi* piar, gorjear (birds).

cheer [tʃiə*] *n* viva *m*, vítor *m* (shout of joy) ‖ consuelo *m* (comfort) ‖ comida *f* (food) ‖ humor *m*, estado *m* de ánimo (mood) ‖ ánimo *m*, regocijo *m* (joy) ‖ — *cheers!* ¡salud! (drinking) ‖ *loud cheers* nutridos aplausos, ovación cerrada ‖ *to be of good cheer* sentirse animoso ‖ *to give three cheers* dar tres hurras ‖ *to make good cheer* comer como un rey.

cheer [tʃiə*] *vt* vitorear, aclamar, ovacionar (to shout with joy) ‖ alegrar, animar (to gladden) ‖ reconfortar (to comfort) ‖ — *to cheer on* animar (fans) ‖ *to cheer up* animar, alentar (morally).
◆ *vi* alegrarse, animarse (to brighten up) ‖ *cheer up!* ¡ánimo!, ¡anímese!

cheerful [ˈtʃiəful] *adj* alegre, animado, da (joyful) ‖ alentador, ra; prometedor, ra (encouraging).

cheerfulness [-nis] *n* alegría *f*.

cheeriness [ˈtʃiərinis] *n* alegría *f*.

cheering [ˈtʃiəriŋ] *adj* esperanzador, ra; alentador, ra; prometedor, ra (encouraging).
◆ *n* ovaciones *f pl*, aplausos *m pl*, vítores *m pl*.

cheerio [ˈtʃiəriˈəu] *interj* FAM ¡adiós!, ¡chao! (at parting) | ¡salud! (drinking).

cheerleader [ˈtʃiəliːdə*] *n* *US* persona *f* que inicia los vivas en un partido (in football, etc.).

cheerless [ˈtʃiəlis] *adj* melancólico, ca; triste.

cheery [ˈtʃiəri] *adj* alegre, animado, da.

cheerystone [-stəun] *n* ZOOL almeja *f* redonda ‖ hueso *m* de cereza (bone) ‖ FIG *it's not worth a cherrystone* no vale un pepino.

cheese [tʃiːz] *n* queso *m*; *grated cheese* queso rallado ‖ — *US* FAM *big cheese* pez gordo (important person) ‖ *cheese cutter* cuchillo *m* para cortar queso ‖ *cheese rennet* cuajaleche *m* ‖ *cheese straws* palitos *m* de queso (cocktail biscuits) ‖ *Dutch cheese* queso de bola ‖ FIG & FAM *hard cheese* mala potra, mala suerte.

cheeseboard [-bɔːd] *n* tabla *f* de quesos.

cheeseburger [-bəːgə*] *n* hamburguesa *f* de queso.

cheesecake [-keik] *n* pastel *m* de queso ‖ FAM fotos *f pl* sugestivas.

cheesecloth [-klɔθ] *n* estopilla *f*.

cheeseparing [ˈtʃiːzˌpɛəriŋ] *adj* tacaño, ña; avaro, ra (mean).
◆ *n* tacañería *f*, avaricia *f* (miserliness) ‖ *cheeseparing economy* economías *f pl* de chicha y nabo.

cheesy [ˈtʃiːzi] *adj* que sabe a queso (tasting of cheese) ‖ caseoso, sa (resembling cheese).

cheetah [ˈtʃiːtə] *n* ZOOL onza *f*, leopardo *m* cazador.

chef [ʃef] *n* jefe *m* de cocina.

chef-d'oeuvre [ʃeiˈdəːvr] *n* obra *f* maestra.
— OBSERV El plural de *chef-d'oeuvre* es *chefs-d'oeuvre*.

chela [ˈkiːlə] *n* ZOOL pinza *f* ‖ REL novicio *m* budista.
— OBSERV El plural de *chela*, cuando significa *pinza*, es *chelae*.

chelonian [keˈləuniən] *n* ZOOL quelonio *m*.

chemical [ˈkemikəl] *adj* químico, ca; ***chemical symbol*** símbolo químico; ***chemical engineer*** ingeniero químico; *chemical warfare* guerra química; *chemical weapons* armas químicas.
◆ *n* sustancia *f* química, producto *m* químico.

chemin de fer [ʃəˌmɛ̃ndəˈfɛə*] *n* ferrocarril *m* (card game).

chemise [ʃəˈmiːz] *n* camisa *f* (for women).

chemist [ˈkemist] *n* químico, ca (in chemistry) ‖ farmacéutico, ca (in pharmacy) ‖ *chemist's* farmacia *f*; *all-night chemist's* farmacia de guardia.

chemistry [-ri] *n* química *f*.

chemotherapy [ˌkeməuˈθerəpi] *n* quimioterapia *f*.

chenille [ʃəˈniːl] *n* felpilla *f* (textile) ‖ *US* tela *f* de algodón afelpada (candlewick).

chenopodiaceae [ˌkiːnəpəudiˈeisii] *pl n* BOT quenopodiáceas *f*.

cheque; *US* **check** [tʃek] *n* cheque *m*; *to write a cheque* o *to make out a cheque for a thousand pounds* extender un cheque de mil libras; *to cash a cheque* cobrar un cheque ‖ — *bearer cheque* cheque al portador ‖ *blank cheque* cheque *m* en blanco (cheque), carta blanca (permission) ‖ *cheque to order* o *order cheque* cheque nominativo *or* nominal ‖ *cheque without cover* o *dud cheque* (fam) o *cheque that bounces* (fam) cheque sin fondos ‖ *crossed cheque* cheque cruzado ‖ *open cheque* cheque al portador ‖ *to pay by cheque* pagar con cheque ‖ *traveller's cheque* cheque de viaje.

chequebook [ˈtʃekbuk] *n* talonario *m* de cheques, chequera *f*.

cheque card [ˈtʃek kɑːd] *n* tarjeta *f* de identificación bancaria.

chequer [ˈtʃekə*] *n* cuadro *m* (square) ‖ cuadros *m pl* (pattern).

chequer [ˈtʃekə*] *vt* marcar con cuadros.

chequerboard [-bɔːd] *n* tablero *m* de damas *or* de ajedrez.

chequered [-d] *adj* a cuadros (cloth) ‖ FIG con altibajos (uneven) | variado, da (varied).

chequers [-z] *pl n* *US* damas *f pl*.

cherimoya [tʃeriˈmɔiə] *n* BOT chirimoyo *m* (árbol) ‖ *cherimoya fruit* chirimoya *f*.

cherish [ˈtʃeriʃ] *vt* querer, amar (to love) ‖ FIG abrigar (hopes, fears, etc.) | cuidar (to take care of).

cheroot [ʃəˈruːt] *n* puro *m* cortado en ambos extremos.

cherry [ˈtʃeri] *adj* de color cereza (colour).
◆ *n* BOT cerezo *m* (tree) | cereza *f* (fruit); *cherry brandy* aguardiente de cereza ‖ rojo *m* cereza (colour) ‖ — BOT *cherry laurel* lauroceraso *m* | *cherry wood* madera *f* de cerezo.

chert ['tʃə:t] *n* MIN sílex *m*, pedernal *m*.

cherub ['tʃerəb] *n* querubín *m*.
— OBSERV El plural es *cherubs* o *cherubim*.

chervil ['tʃə:vil] *n* BOT perifollo *m*.

Cheshire cat ['tʃeʃə kæt] *n* gato *m* de Cheshire || *Cheshire cat grin* sonrisa *f* de oreja a oreja.

chess [tʃes] *n* ajedrez *m*.

chessboard ['tʃesbɔ:d] *n* tablero *m* de ajedrez.

chessel ['tʃesəl] *n* encella *f* (for cheese).

chessman ['tʃesmæn] *n* pieza *f* de ajedrez.
— OBSERV El plural de *chessman* es *chessmen*.

chess player ['tʃespleiə*] *n* ajedrecista *m* & *f*.

chest [tʃest] *n* ANAT pecho *m* || caja *f* (for tea, for opium) || cofre *m* (coffer) || FIG dinero *m*, fondos *m pl* (funds) || — *chest cavity* cavidad torácica || *chest of drawers* cómoda *f* || *chest protector* pechera *f* || *chest voice* voz *f* de bajo || FIG & FAM *to get it off one's chest* desahogarse, echarlo fuera | *to throw out one's chest* sacar el pecho.

chesterfield ['tʃestəfi:ld] *n* sofá *m* (settee) || abrigo *m* elegante (overcoat).

chestnut ['tʃesnʌt] *n* BOT castaño *m* (tree) | castaña *f* (fruit) | castaño *m* de Indias (horse chestnut) || castaño *m*, marrón *m* (colour) || FAM chiste *m* viejo || alazán *m* (horse) || VET espejuelo *m* (callus) || FIG *to pull s.o.'s chesnusts out of the fire* sacar a uno las castañas del fuego.
◆ *adj* castaño, ña; marrón (colour) || alazán, ana (horse).

chesty ['tʃesti] *adj* FAM ancho de pecho || FIG & FAM delicado de los bronquios | presumido, da; postinero, ra (boasting) || *chesty cough* tos *f* de pecho.

cheval-de-frise [ʃə'vældə'fri:z] *n* caballo *m* de frisa.
— OBSERV El plural es *chevaux-de-frise*.

cheval glass [ʃə'vælglɑ:s] *n* espejo *m* de cuerpo entero.

chevalier [ˌʃevə'liə*] *n* caballero *m*.

cheviot ['tʃeviət] *n* cordero *m* de Cheviot (animal) || cheviot *m* (fabric).

chevron ['ʃevrən] *n* HERALD cheurón *m* || MIL galón *m*.

chew [tʃu:] *n* masticación *f* (mastication) || mascada *f* de tabaco (tobacco).

chew [tʃu:] *vt* masticar, mascar || mascar (tobacco) || morder (one's nails) || — FIG & FAM *to chew one's ear off* dar la lata | *to chew one's nails* morderse los puños | *to chew out* echar una bronca | *to chew the fat* o *the rag* estar de palique | *to chew sth. over* rumiar algo | *to chew the cud* rumiar | *to chew up* estropear (sth.), echar una bronca (to a person).
◆ *vi* mascar tabaco || mascar, masticar.

chewing [-iŋ] *n* masticación *f*, mascadura *f* || *chewing gum* chicle *m*.

chewy [-wi] *adj* FAM correoso, sa.

chi [kai] *n* ji *f* (Greek letter).

chiaroscuro [kiˌɑ:rəs'kuərəu] *n* claroscuro *m*.

chiasma [kai'æzmə] *n* ANAT quiasma *m*.
— OBSERV El plural es *chiasmata* o *chiasmas*.

Chibcha ['tʃibtʃə] *n* chibcha *m* & *f*.

chibouque; chibouk [tʃi'bu:k] *n* chibuquí *m* (pipe).

chic [ʃi:k] *adj* elegante, distinguido, da; de buen gusto.
◆ *n* elegancia *f*, distinción *f*, «chic» *m*.

chicane [ʃi'kein] *n* triquiñuela *f* (trickery) || fallo *m* (cards) || argucia *f*, trapacería *f* (legal trick) || través *m* (car racing).

chicane [ʃi'kein] *vt* engañar con triquiñuelas (to trick) || embrollar, enredar (to quibble).
◆ *vi* hacer triquiñuelas [AMER chicanear].

chicanery [-ri] *n* argucia *f*, trapacería *f*.

Chicano [ʃi'kɑ:nəu] *adj/n* chicano, na.

chichi ['ʃi:ʃi:] *adj* cursi.

chichimec ['tʃitʃimek]; **chichimeca** [ˌtʃitʃi'mekɔ]; **chichimeco** [-'mekəu] *n* chichimeco, ca.

chichimecan [ˌtʃitʃi'mekən] *adj* chichimeco, ca.

chick [tʃik] *n* polluelo *m* (chicken) || US FAM chavala *f* (girl).

chickadee ['tʃikədi:] *n* paro *m* (bird).

chicken ['tʃikin] *n* pollo *m* (bird) || FAM gallina *m* (coward) | chavala *f* (young girl) || — FIG & FAM *don't count your chickens before they're hatched* no hay que vender la piel del oso antes de haberlo matado, eso es el cuento de la lechera | *it's a chicken and egg situation* ¿qué es or fue primero, el huevo o la gallina? || FIG & FAM *to be chicken* ser un gallina | *to be no spring chicken* no haber nacido ayer | *to go to bed with the chickens* acostarse con las gallinas.

chicken ['tʃikin] *vi* FAM *to chicken out* rajarse.

chicken farmer [-ˌfɑ:mə*] *n* avicultor, ra.

chicken farming [-ˌfɑ:miŋ] *n* avicultura *f*.

chicken feed [-fi:d] *n* alimento *m* para las gallinas (food for hens) || FIG & FAM muy poco dinero, una miseria (money).

chickenhearted [-ˌhɑ:tid] *adj* FIG gallina, cobarde (cowardly).

chicken pox [-pɔks] *n* MED varicela *f*.

chicken run [-rʌn] *n* gallinero *m*.

chick-pea ['tʃikpi:] *n* garbanzo *m*.

chickweed ['tʃikwi:d] *n* BOT pamplina *f*.

chicle ['tʃikəl] *n* chicle *m*, gomorresina *f*.

chicory ['tʃikəri] *n* achicoria *f* (in coffee) || escarola *f* (in salads).

chid [tʃid] *pret/pp* —> **chide.**

chide* [tʃaid] *vt/vi* reprender, regañar.
— OBSERV Pret ***chid, chided***; pp ***chid, chidden, chided***.

chidden ['tʃidən] *pp* —> **chide.**

chief [tʃi:f] *n* jefe *m* & *f* (leader, head) | jefe *m*, cacique *m* (of tribe) || HERALD jefe *m* (upper part of a shield) || — *chief executive* jefe del ejecutivo || *chief inspector* inspector, ra jefe || MIL *chief of staff* jefe del estado mayor || *in chief* en jefe.
◆ *adj* principal; *the chief export is oil* la exportación principal es el petróleo.

chiefly [-li] *adv* principalmente, sobre todo.

chieftain ['tʃi:ftən] *n* cacique *m*, jefe *m* (of a clan).

chieftaincy [-si]; **chieftainship** [-ʃip] *n* jefatura *f*.

chiffon ['ʃifɔn] *n* gasa *f* (material).

chiffonier [ʃifə'niə*] *n* cómoda *f* estrecha y alta, «chiffonier» *m* (chest of drawers).

chigger ['tʃigə*] *n* ZOOL nigua *f*.

chignon ['ʃi:njɔ̃] *n* moño *m* (hair).

chigoe ['tʃigəu] *n* ZOOL nigua *f*.

chilblain ['tʃilblein] *n* MED sabañón *m*.

child [tʃaild] *n* niño, ña (young boy or girl); *child prodigy* niño prodigio || hijo, ja (son or daughter); *adopter, legitimate, natural child* hijo adoptivo, legítimo, natural; *foster child* hijo de leche || discípulo, la; hijo, ja; *child of the devil* hijo del diablo || FIG producto *m*, hijo *m*, hija *f*; *child of his imagination* producto de su imaginación || — *child benefit* subsidio semanal que el gobierno británico paga por cada hijo || *child care* puericultura *f* || *child care centre* guardería *f* infantil || *child labour* trabajo *m* de menores, explotación *f* de menores || FIG *child's play* juego *m* de niños || *child welfare* protección *f* de la infancia || *with child* embarazada, encinta, en estado.
— OBSERV El plural de *child* es *children*.

childbearing [-ˌbɛəriŋ] *n* maternidad *f* || *childbearing woman* mujer fecunda.

childbed [-bed] *n* sobreparto *m* || *woman in childbed* mujer de parto.

childbirth [-bə:θ] *n* parto *m*, alumbramiento *m* || *to die in childbirth* morir de sobreparto.

Childermas ['tʃildəmæs] *n* día *m* de los Inocentes.

childhood ['tʃaildhud] *n* niñez *f*, infancia *f* || — *early childhood* primera infancia || FIG *second childhood* segunda infancia.

childish ['tʃaildiʃ] *adj* infantil, pueril || *don't be childish!* ¡no seas niño!

childishness [tʃaildiʃnis] *n* puerilidad *f*, infantilismo *m*, niñería *f*.

childless ['tʃaildlis] *adj* sin hijos.

childlike ['tʃaildlaik] *adj* infantil, de niño || FIG inocente, ingenuo, nua.

childminder ['tʃaildˌmaində*] *n* persona *f* que cuida niños en su casa.

children ['tʃildrən] *pl n* —> **child.**

children's home [-z həum] *n* asilo *m* infantil.

Chile ['tʃili] *pr n* GEOGR Chile *m*.

Chilean [-ən] *adj/n* chileno, na.

chili ['tʃili] *n* BOT chile *m*.

chill [tʃil] *adj* helador, ra; helado, da; *a chill wind* un viento helador || FIG frío, a (recepción, etc.).
◆ *n* frío *m* (of temperature) || MED tiritona *f*, escalofrío *m* (shiver) || FIG frialdad *f* || TECH lingotera *f* || — *chills and fever* fiebre *f* intermitente | *there was a chill in the air* hacía fresquito (weather), había un ambiente frío (atmosphere) || FIG *to cast a chill over one's spirits* caerle a uno como un jarro de agua fría || *to catch a chill* enfriarse, coger frío || *to take the chill off* entibiar, templar.

chill [tʃil] *vt* enfriar (to make cold) || refrigerar (meat) || TECH templar (metal).
◆ *vi* enfriarse (to become cold) || tiritar, tener escalofríos (to shiver) || TECH endurecerse al temple.

chiller [-ə*] *n* historia *f* espeluznante.

chilli ['tʃili] *n* BOT chile *m*.

chilliness [-nis] *n* frío *m* || FIG frialdad *f*.

chilling ['tʃiliŋ] *n* refrigeración *f* (of meat).
◆ *adj* espeluznante.

chilly ['tʃili] *adj* fresco, ca; *a chilly morning* una mañana fresca || frío, a; *his attitude was rather chilly* su actitud fue bastante fría || friolero, ra (sensitive to cold).

chimaera [kai'mi:rə] *n* —> **chimera.**

chime [tʃaim] *n* carillón *m* (bells, sound) || MUS vibráfono *m*.
◆ *pl* carillón *m sing*.

chime [tʃaim] *vt* tocar (to ring) | dar; *the clock chimed six o'clock* el reloj dio las seis.
◆ *vi* sonar, repicar || — *to chime in* intervenir en la conversación; *he chimed in with a stupid remark* intervino en la conversación soltando una tontería || FIG & FAM *to chime in with* estar de acuerdo con (to agree with), concordar con (to fit in with).

chimera [kai'miərə] *n* MYTH quimera *f* || FIG quimera *f* (foolish idea).

chimere [tʃi'miə*] *n* REL especie de sobrepelliz *f* (bishop's robe).

chimeric [kai'merik]; **chimerical** [kai'merikəl] *adj* quimérico, ca.

chimney ['tʃimni] *n* chimenea *f* (of a house, train, mountain, etc.) || chimenea *f* volcánica (in a volcano) || tubo *m* de cristal del quinqué (of a lamp) || — *chimney corner* espacio *m* junto a la chimenea || *chimney flue* cañón *m* de chimenea || *chimney pot* cañón *m* de chimenea || *chimney stack* fuste *m* de la chimenea || *chimney sweep* deshollinador *m*, limpiachimeneas *m inv* || *chimney sweep's brush* deshollinador *m* || *sitting in the chimney corner* sentado al amor de la lumbre || FIG *to smoke like a chimney* fumar como una chimenea.

chimneypiece [-pi:s] *n* manto *m* de chimenea.

chimp [tʃimp] *n* FAM chimpancé *m*.

chimpanzee [ˌtʃimpən'zi] *n* ZOOL chimpancé *m*.

chin [tʃin] *n* barbilla *f*, mentón *m* || — *chin strap* barboquejo *m* || *double chin* papada *f* || FIG *keep your chin up!* ¡ánimo!, ¡anímese! | *to keep one's chin up* no desanimarse || US FAM *to take it on the chin* mantenerse firme || FAM *up to the chin* o *chin deep* hasta el cuello.

china ['tʃainə] *adj* de loza, de porcelana || *china closet* chinero *m* (a piece of furniture).
◆ *n* china *f* (ceramic) || porcelana *f* (porcelain) || loza *f* (crockery) || *china clay* caolín *m*.

China ['tʃainə] *pr n* GEOGR China *f*.

chinaberry ['tʃainəˌberi] *n* BOT jaboncillo *m*.

Chinaman ['tʃainəmən] *n* chino *m*.
— OBSERV El plural de *Chinaman* es *Chinamen*.

Chinatown ['tʃainətaun] *n* US barrio *m* chino.

chinaware ['tʃainəwɛə*] *n* china *f* (ceramic).

chinch bug ['tʃintʃbʌg] *n* ZOOL chinche *f*.

chinchilla [tʃin'tʃilə] *n* chinchilla *f* (animal and fur).

chin-chin ['tʃin'tʃin] *interj* ¡salud!

chincough ['tʃinkɔf] *n* MED tos ferina *f*.

chine [tʃain] *n* lomo *m* (meat) || GEOL cresta *f*, cumbre *f* (ridge) | barranco *m* (gully).

chine [tʃain] *vt* deslomar.

Chinese ['tiʃai'ni:z] *adj* chino, na.
◆ *n* chino, na (native of China) || chino *m* (language) || — *chinese lantern* farolillo *m* de papel || *Chinese puzzle* rompecabezas *m inv* chino.

chink [tʃiŋk] *n* raja *f*, grieta *f* (fissure) || resquicio *m* (crack) || sonido *m* metálico, tintineo *m* (light sound) || FAM chino, na (Chinese) | pasta *f*, moni *m* [AMER plata *f*] (money) || FIG *a chink in s.o.'s armour* el punto flaco de alguien.

chink [tʃiŋk] *vt* hacer sonar, hacer tintinear || FAM *to chink glasses* chocar las copas, brindar.
◆ *vi* sonar, tintinear.

chinless ['tʃinləs] *adj* FAM acoquinado, da, pusilánime.

chinook [tʃi'nuk] *n* viento *m* cálido de las montañas Rocosas, Oregón y Washington.

chintz [tʃints] *n* zaraza *f* (cloth).

chintzy [-i] *adj* US de oropel.

chin-wag ['tʃinwæg] *n* FAM palique *m*.

chin-wag ['tʃinwæg] *vi* FAM parlotear, estar de cháchara *or* de palique.

chip [tʃip] *n* pedacito *m*, trocito *m* (piece of glass, etc.) || viruta *f* (of metal, of wood) || astilla *f* (splinter) || lasca *f* (of a stone) || muesca *f* (mark made by chipping) || mella *f* (on china); *there is a chip on the rim of this cup* hay una desportilladura en el borde de esta taza || ficha *f* (gambling) || CULIN patata *f* frita || INFORM pastilla *f*, chip *m* || — *chip ax* hachuela *f* || *chip basket* cestito *m* || INFORM *chip card* tarjeta *f* de memoria, tarjeta *f* con chip, tarjeta chip || *chip shot* chip *m* (golf) || FAM *he has had his chips* está perdido || FIG *(he is) a chip off the old block* de tal palo, tal astilla || US FAM *in the chips* forrado de dinero || FAM *the chips are down* la suerte está echada || FIG *to have a chip on one's shoulder* guardar un resentimiento.

chip [tʃip] *vt* astillar (to splinter) || mellar (a knife) || desportillar (a plate) || cepillar (with a plane) || cascar (an egg) || trabajar con el escoplo (with a chisel) || cortar (potatoes) || FAM tomar el pelo a (to pull one's leg) || SP picar (a ball).
◆ *vi* astillarse || desportillarse (plate); *this china chips easily* esta porcelana se desportilla fácilmente || mellarse (a knife) || cascarse (an egg) || hacer un «chip» (in golf) || FAM *to chip in* decir (to say), apostar (to bet), compartir los gastos (to share expenses), poner (to contribute).

chipboard ['tʃipbɔ:d] *n* cartón *m* (cardboard) || madera *f* aglomerada (wood).

chipmunk ['tʃipmʌnk] *n* ZOOL ardilla *f* listada.

chipped beef ['tʃipt'bi:f] *n* US carne *f* ahumada de vaca cortada en lonchas finas.

chipper ['tʃipə*] *adj* US FAM alegre, jovial, animado, da.

chippings ['tʃipiŋz] *pl n* lascas *f pl*.

chip shop ['tʃip ʃəp] *n* tienda *f* de pescado frito y patatas fritas.

chi-rho ['kai'rəu] *n* REL monograma *m* de Cristo.

chiromancy ['kaiərəmænsi] *n* quiromancia *f*.

chiropodist [[ki'rɔpədist] *n* MED pedicuro, ra; callista *m* & *f*.

chiropody [ki'rɔpədi] *n* MED quiropodia *f*.

chiropractic ['kairəˌpræktik] *n* quiropráctica *f*.

chiropractor ['kairəˌpræktə*] *n* quiropráctico, ca.

chiropter ['kaiərɔptə*] *n* ZOOL quiróptero *m*.

chiropteran [kairɔptəren] *adj* quiróptero, ra.
◆ *n* quiróptero *m*.
— OBSERV El plural de *chiropteran* es *chiroptera*.

chirp [tʃə:p]; **chirrup** ['tʃirəp] *n* gorjeo *m* (of birds) || canto *m*, chirrido *m* (of crickets).

chirp [tʃə:p]; **chirrup** ['tʃirəp] *vt/vi* gorjear (birds) || cantar, chirriar (crickets).

chirpiness [-inis] *n* FAM alegría *f*, animación *f*.

chirpy [-i] *adj* FAM alegre, animado, da.

chirr [tʃə:*] *n* chirrido *m* (of crickets, etc.).

chirr [tʃə:*] *vi* chirriar.

chirrup ['tʃirəp] *n/vt/vi* ⟶ **chirp.**

chisel ['tʃizl] *n* TECH cincel *m*, escoplo *m* (tool) | cortafrío *m* (cold chisel) || FIG estafa *f*, timo *m*.

chisel ['tʃizl] *vt* TECH cincelar (to tool) | escoplear (to mortice) || FIG & FAM estafar, timar.

chiselled; chiseled [-d] *adj* cincelado, da || FIG cincelado, da; *chiselled features* rostro cincelado.

chiseller [-ə*] *n* TECH cincelador *m* || FIG & FAM estafador *m*, timador *m*.

chit [tʃit] *n* chica *f*, muchacha *f* (girl) || niño *m* (boy) || nota *f*, tarjeta *f* (note) || vale *m*, cuenta *f*, nota *f* (of a sun owed).

chitchat ['tʃittʃæt] *n* cháchara *f*, palique *m* (gossip).

chitin ['kaitin] *n* quitina *f*.

chitinous [-əs] *adj* quitinoso, sa.

chitterlings ['tʃitəliŋʒ] *pl n* mondongo *m sing* frito *or* cocido.

chitty ['tʃiti] *n* FAM nota *f*.

chivalrous ['ʃivəlrəs] *adj* caballeroso, sa.

chivalry ['ʃivəlri] *n* caballerosidad *f* (conventions) || caballería *f* (order).

chive [tʃaiv] *n* BOT cebolleta *f*.

chivy; chivvy ['tʃivi] *vt* perseguir (to chase) || *to chivi s.o. about* no dejar a alguien en paz.

chlamys ['klæmis] *n* clámide *f*.

Chloe ['kləui] *pr n* Cloe *f*.

chloral ['klɔ:rəl] *n* CHEM cloral *m* || CHEM *chloral hydrate* hidrato *m* de cloral.

chlorate ['klɔ:rit] *n* CHEM clorato *m*.

chloric ['klɔ:rik] *adj* CHEM clórico, ca.

chloride ['klɔ:raid] *n* CHEM cloruro *m*; *chloride of lime* cloruro de cal.

chlorinate ['klɔ:rineit] *vt* CHEM tratar con cloro.

chlorine ['klɔ:ri:n] *n* CHEM cloro *m*.

chloroform ['klɔrəfɔ:m] *n* CHEM cloroformo *m*.

chloroform ['klɔrəfɔ:m] *vt* cloroformizar.

chloromycetin [ˌklɔ:rəumai'si:tin] *n* MED cloromicetina *f*.

chlorophyll, chlorophyl ['klɔrəfil] *n* clorofila *f*.

chlorophyllian [ˌklɔrə'filiən] *adj* clorofílico, ca; *chlorophyllian function* función clorofílica.

chlorophyllous [ˌklɔrə'filəs] *adj* clorofílico, ca.

chloroplast ['klɔrəplæst] *n* BOT cloroplasto *m*.

chlorosis [klə'rəusis] *n* MED BOT clorosis *f*.

chlorotic [klə'rɔtik] *adj* clorótico, ca.

chock [tʃɔk] *n* calzo *m*, cuña *f* (wedge).

chock [tʃɔk] *vt* calzar (to wedge) || *to chock up* llenar hasta el máximo *or* hasta los topes.

chockablock ['tʃɔkəblɔk] *adj* hasta los topes, atestado, da; de bote en bote.

chock-full ['tʃɔk'ful] *adj* hasta los topes, atestado, da; de bote en bote.

chocolate ['tʃɔkəlit] *adj* de chocolate (made of chocolate) || de color chocolate || US *chocolate candy* bombón *m*.
◆ *n* chocolate *m*; *drinking chocolate* chocolate a la taza; *plain chocolate* chocolate para crudo || bombón *m*, chocolatina *f* (sweet) || — *bar of chocolate* tableta *f or* barra *f* de chocolate || *chocolate factory* chocolatería *f* || *chocolate pot* chocolatera *f* || *chocolate shop* chocolatería *f*.

choice [tʃɔis] *adj* escogido, da; selecto, ta || de primera calidad (wine, etc.).
◆ *n* elección *f*, selección *f* (act of choosing) || opción *f* (right to choose) || preferencia *f*, elección *f* (sth. chosen) || surtido *m* (variety) || FAM flor *f* y nata, crema *f* (best) || — *by choice* por gusto || *of one's choice* elegido, da; de su elección || *to have no choice* no tener alternativa || *to have no choice but to* no tener más remedio que || *to have plenty of choice* tener donde escoger || *to make* o *to take one's choice* escoger, elegir.

choiceness [-nis] *n* lo escogido, calidad *f*.

choir ['kwaiə*] *n* MUS coro *m*, coral *f* || ARCH coro *m*.

choir ['kwaiə*] *vt/vi* MUS cantar a coro; *to choir a hymn* cantar un himno a coro.

choirboy [-bɔi] *n* MUS REL niño *m* de coro.

choirmaster [-ˌma:stə*] *n* director *m* de coro (of a choral society) || REL maestro *m* de capilla.

choke [tʃəuk] *n* TECH obturador *m* (valve) || ELECTR bobina *f* de reactancia || AUT estrangulador *m* || MED ahogo *m*, sofocamiento *m* || obstrucción *f* || pelusa *f* (of artichokes).

choke [tʃəuk] *vt* estrangular (to strangle) || asfixiar, ahogar (to asphyxiate) || apagar, sofocar, extinguir (fire) || obstruir, atascar; *weeds were choking the river* las hierbas obstruían el río || ahogar (voice) || TECH obturar || — *to choke back* o *down* contener, reprimir, sofocar (feelings) || *to choke down sobs* ahogar el llanto || *to choke s.o. off* callar *or* silenciar a uno (to sil-

ence), fastidiar (to annoy) || *to choke up* obstruir, atascar.
◆ *vi* asfixiarse, ahogarse (to suffocate) || obstruirse, atascarse (to get blocked up) || FIG quedarse sin respiración (with emotion) || atragantarse (*on* con); *to choke on a fishbone* atragantarse con una espina || — *to choke up* atascarse, obstruirse || *to choke with laughter* reír ahogadamente.

chokebore [-bɔː*] *n* estrangulamiento *m* (of a sporting gun).

chokecherry [-,tʃeri] *n* BOT cereza *f* silvestre (fruit) | cerezo *m* silvestre (tree).

choke coil [-kɔil] *n* ELECTR bobina *f* de reactancia.

choked ['tʃəukt] *adj* ahogado, da (voice) || FAM disgustado, da (person).

chokedamp [-dæmp] *n* mofeta *f* (gas).

choker ['tʃəukə*] *n* TECH obturador *m* || AUT estrangulador *m* || estola *f* (narrow fur piece) || gargantilla *f* (necklace) || cuello *m* alto (collar).

choky ['tʃəuki] *adj* ahogado, da; *a choky voice* una voz ahogada || sofocante, asfixiante; *choky atmosphere* atmósfera sofocante.

choledoc ['kɔlidɔd] *adj* ANAT colédoco.
◆ *n* ANAT colédoco *m*.

choler ['kɔlə*] *n* (ant) cólera *f* || (ant) MED bilis *f*.

cholera ['kɔlərə] *n* MED cólera *m*; *cholera morbus* cólera morbo.

choleric ['kɔlərik] *adj* colérico, ca || MED colérico, ca.

cholesterine [kə'lestəriːn] *n* colesterina *f*.

cholesterol [kə'lestərɔl] *n* colesterol *m*.

choose* [tʃuːz] *vt* escoger, elegir (to select) || — REL *the chosen ones* los elegidos || *the Chosen People* el Pueblo Elegido.
◆ *vi* escoger, elegir (to make a choice) || querer (to like); *as you choose* como quiera || preferir (to prefer) || decidir (to decide) || — *he cannot choose but* no tiene más remedio que, no tiene otra alternativa que || *there is nothing to choose between them* son iguales, vale tanto el uno como el otro || *to choose to do sth.* optar por hacer algo, decidirse por hacer algo || *to pick and choose* ser muy exigente.
— OBSERV pret ***chose***; pp ***chosen***.

choosing [-iŋ] *n* elección *f*, selección *f*.

choosy; choosey [-i] *adj* FAM quisquilloso, sa; exigente; difícil (fussy).

chop [tʃɔp] *n* golpe *m*, tajo *m* (a cut) || hachazo *m*, tajo *m* (with an axe) || chuleta *f* (meat) || chapoteo *m* (of the sea) || COMM sello *m* (seal) | marca *f* (brand) | licencia *f* || FIG & FAM *to get the chop* ser despedido.
◆ *pl* FAM morros *m* (mouth) | quijada *f sing* (jaws of an animal) || — *chops and changes* cambios *m pl* || *to lick one's chops* relamerse.

chop [tʃɔp] *vt* cortar; *to chop wood* cortar leña || CULIN picar (to mince) || cortar, tajar (to cut up) || tronchar; *to chop a branch off a tree* tronchar una rama de un árbol || SP dar efecto a, cortar; *to chop the ball* dar efecto a la pelota || MED cortar || FIG cortar (one's words) || — *to chop down* disminuir || FIG *to chop logic* discutir || *to chop off s.o.'s head* cortar la cabeza a alguien, degollar a alguien || *to chop trees down* talar *or* cortar árboles || *to chop up* cortar en trozos (to cut in pieces), picar (meat).
◆ *vi* MAR saltar (the wind) | chapotear (the sea) || — *to chop at* hacer cortes en || *to chop and change* cambiar (de opinión) || *to chop back* dar media vuelta || FAM *to chop in* intervenir, meter baza.

chop-chop ['tʃɔp'tʃɔp] *interj* FAM ¡de prisa!, ¡rápido! (quickly) || ¡en seguida! (at once).

chopine ['tʃɔpin] *n* chapín *m* (shoe).

chopper [['tʃɔpə*] *n* hacha *f* (axe) || cuchilla *f*, tajadera *f* (of butcher) || FAM helicóptero *m* || AGR cortarraíces *m inv*, cortadora *f* de raíces.

chopping ['tʃɔpiŋ] *n* corte *m* (of wood) || picadura *f* (of tobacco, etc.) || — FAM *chopping and changing* fluctuaciones *f pl* cambios *m pl* frecuentes || *chopping block, chopping board* tajo *m* || *chopping knife* tajadera *f*, cuchilla *f*.

choppy ['tʃɔpi] *adj* picado, da (sea) || variable (wind) || FIG inconexo, xa (ideas) | cortado, da (style).

chopstick ['tʃɔpstik] *n* palillo *m* (eating utensil).

choral ['kɔːrəl] *adj* MUS coral || *choral society* orfeón *m*.

choral; chorale [kɔ'rɑːl] *n* MUS coral *f*.

chord [kɔːd] *n* MUS acorde *m* (combination of notes) | cuerda *f* (string) || FIG fibra *f*; *to touch the right chord* tocar la fibra sensible || MATH cuerda *f* (on an are) || AVIAT profundidad *f* del ala || ANAT cuerda *f*; *vocal chords* cuerdas vocales || solera *f* (of a beam) || MUS *broken* o *spread chord* arpegio *m* || *to strike a chord (with s.o.)* tocar la fibra sensible (de alguien).

chordate ['kɔːdit] *adj* ZOOL cordado, da.
◆ *n* cordado *m*.

chore [tʃɔː*] *n* faena *f*, quehacer *m*; *household chores* faenas de la casa || tarea *f* penosa (hard task) || trabajo *m* rutinario (routine task).

chorea [kɔ'riə] *n* MED corea *f*, baile *m* de San Vito.

choreographer [,kɔri'əgrəfə*] *n* coreógrafo *m*.

choreographic [,kɔriə'græfik] *adj* coreográfico, ca.

choreography [,kɔri'ɔgrəfi] *n* coreografía *f*.

choriamb ['kɔriæmb] *n* coriambo *m*.

chorioid ['kɔːrɔid] *adj/n* ⟶ **choroid.**

chorion ['kɔːriən] *n* ANAT corión *m*.

chorister ['kɔristə*] *n* corista *m* (choir singer) || US director *m* de un coro.

chorography [kɔ'rɔgræfi] *n* corografía *f*.

choroid; chorioid ['kɔːrɔid] *adj* coroideo, a.
◆ *n* coroides *f inv*.

chortle ['tʃɔːtl] *n* risa *f* ahogada.

chortle ['tʃɔːtl] *vi* reír entre dientes, reír ahogadamente || *«not I», he chortled* yo no, dijo riéndose.

chorus ['kɔːrəs] *n* MUS coro *m* || conjunto *m* (of chorus girls) || estribillo *m* (of a song) || — *chorus girl* corista *f* || FIG *chorus of protests* coro de protestas || *in chorus* en coro.

chorus ['kɔːrəs] *vt* cantar *or* decir en coro.
◆ *vi* cantar *or* hablar en coro.

chose [tʃəuz] *pret* ⟶ **choose.**

chosen [-n] *pp* ⟶ **choose.**

chough [tʃʌf] *n* ZOOL chova *f* (bird).

chouse [tʃaus] *vt* estafar, timar (to swindle); *to chouse sth. out of s.o.* estafar algo a alguien.

choux pastry ['ʃuː peistri] *n* pasta *f* brisé.

chow [tʃau] *n* perro *m* chino || US FAM jamancia *f*, manduca *f*, comida *f* (food).

chowder ['tʃaudə*] *n* US CULIN sopa *f* de pescado.

chrematistic [,kremə'tistik] *adj* crematístico, ca.

chrematistics [-s] *n* crematística *f*.

chrestomathy [kres'tɔməθi] *n* crestomatía *f*.

chrism ['krizəm] *n* REL crisma *m*.

chrismal ['krizməl] *n* REL capillo *m* de cristianar.

Christ [kraist] *pr n* REL Cristo *m* || — *Jesus Christ* Jesucristo || *the Christ child* el Niño Jesús.
◆ *interj* FAM ¡por Dios!

christen ['krisn] *vt* REL bautizar || bautizar, llamar; *they christened him David* lo llamaron David || FIG bautizar (a ship, a building, etc.).

Christendom ['krisndəm] *n* cristiandad *f*.

christening ['krisniŋ] *n* bautismo *m*, bautizo *m*.
◆ *adj* bautismal.

Christian ['kristjən] *adj/n* REL cristiano, na || — REL *Christian Brothers* Hermanos de la Doctrina Cristiana | *Christian era* era cristiana || *Christian name* nombre *m* de pila.

christiania [,kristi'ɑːnjə] *n* cristianía *m* (in skiing).

Christianity [,kristi'æniti] *n* REL cristianismo *m* (religión) | cristiandad *f* (Christendom).

Christianization [,kristjənai'zeiʃən] *n* cristianización *f*.

Christianize ['kristijənaiz] *vt* cristianizar.

Christine ['kristiːn] *pr n* Cristina *f*.

Christlike ['kraistlaik] *adj* como Cristo.

Christliness ['kraistlinis] *n* espíritu *m* cristiano.

Christmas ['krisməs] *n* Navidad *f* || — *at Christmas* por Navidades || *Christmas box* aguinaldo *m* || *Christmas cake* tarta *f* de Navidad || *Christmas card* tarjeta *f* de Navidad, christmas *m inv*, crismas *m inv* || *Christmas carol* villancico *m* || *Christmas Day* día *m* de Navidad || *Christmas Eve* Nochebuena *f*, Noche Buena || *Christmas pudding* pastel *m* de Navidad || *Christmas rose* eléboro negro || *Christmas stocking* zapatos *m pl* de Reyes || *Christmas time* Navidades *f pl* || *Christmas tree* árbol *m* de Navidad (tree; part of oil well) || *Father Christmas* Papá Noel *m* || *Merry Christmas* ¡Felices Pascuas!

Christmassy ['krisməsi] *adj* FAM navideño, ña.

Christmastide ['krisməstaid] *n* Pascuas *f pl* Navidades *f pl*.

Christopher ['kristəfə*] *pr n* Cristóbal *m*.

christ's-thorn ['kraistsθɔːn] *n* BOT espina *f* santa.

christy ['kristi] *n* cristianía *m* (in skiing).

chromate ['krəumit] *n* CHEM cromato *m*.

chromatic [krə'mætik] *adj* cromático, ca || — MED *chromatic aberration* aberración cromática || *chromatic printing* impresión *f* en color || *chromatic scale* escala cromática.

chromaticism [krə'mætisizəm] *n* MUS cromatismo *m*.

chromatin ['krəumətin] *n* BIOL cromatina *f*.

chromatism ['krəumətizəm] *n* cromatismo *m*.

chrome [krəum] *n* cromo *m* || — *chrome green* verde *m* de cromo || *chrome red* rojo *m* de cromo || *chrome steel* acero *m* al cromo.

chromic [-ik] *adj* crómico, ca.

chromium ['krəumjəm] *n* CHEM cromo *m*.

chromium-plating [-'pleitiŋ] *n* TECH cromado *m*.

chromolithograph ['krĵməu'liθəgrɑːf] *n* cromolitografía *f*.

chromosome ['krəuməsəum] *n* BIOL cromosoma *m*.

chromosphere ['krəuməsfiə*] *n* ASTR cromosfera *f*.

chronic ['krɔːnik] *adj* crónico, ca (deep-seated) || FIG empedernido, da; *a chronic gambler* un jugador empedernido || FAM terrible, fatal (very bad); *the actor gave a chronic performance* el actor tuvo una actuación terrible.

chronicity [krɔ'nisiti] *n* cronicidad *f*.

chronicle ['krɔnikl] *n* crónica *f*.

chronicle ['krɔnikl] *vt* hacer la crónica de.

chronicler [-ə*] *n* cronista *m* & *f*.

chronograph ['krɔnəgrɑːf] *n* cronógrafo *m*.

chronographer [-ə*] *n* cronógrafo *m*.

chronologer [krə'nɔlədzə*] *n* cronólogo *m*.

chronological [ˌkrɔnə'lɔdʒikəl] *adj* cronológico, ca.

chronologist [krə'nɔlədʒist] *n* cronologista *m* cronólogo *m*.

chronology [krə'nɔlədʒi] *n* cronología *f*.

chronometer [krə'nɔmitə*] *n* cronómetro *m*.

chronometric [ˌkrɔnə'metrik]; **chronometrical** [-əl] *adj* cronométrico, ca.

chronometry [krə'nɔmitri] *n* cronometría *f*.

chrysalid ['krisəlid] *n* ZOOL crisálida *f*.

chrysalis ['krisəlis] *n* ZOOL crisálida *f*.
— OBSERV El plural es *chrysalises* o *chrysalides*.

chrysanthemum [kri'sænθəməm] *n* crisantemo *m*.

chub [tʃʌb] *n* ZOOL cacho *m* (fish).

chubby ['tʃʌbi] *adj* gordinflón, ona; rechoncho, cha (body) ‖ mofletudo, da (face).

chubby-cheeked [-tʃiːkt] *adj* mofletudo, da.

chuck [tʃʌk] *n* CULIN paletilla *f* (of meat) ‖ calzo *m* (chock) ‖ TECH mandril *m* ‖ mamola *f* (tap under the chin) ‖ FAM tiro *m* (throw) ‖ cloqueo *m* (of hens, etc.) ‖ chasquido *m* (of the tongue) ‖ SP disco *m* (in ice hockey) ‖ US FAM jamancia *f*, comida *f* (food) ‖ FAM *to give s.o. the chuck* echar a alguien, poner a alguien de patitas en la calle.

chuck [tʃʌk] *vt* golpear en la barbilla, hacer la mamola a (tap under the chin) ‖ FAM tirar, arrojar, echar (to throw) | abandonar, dejar (to give up) ‖ TECH sujetar con el mandril ‖ — FAM *chuck it!* ¡basta! | *to chuck away* tirar (to throw away), despilfarrar (money), desperdiciar, perder (a chance) | *to chuck out* tirar (things), poner de patitas en la calle, echar (people) | *to chuck up* mandar a paseo (to give up).

chucker-out ['tʃʌkər'aut] *n* FAM matón *m* [encargado de echar a los alborotadores de un club].
— OBSERV El plural de *chucker-out* es *chuckers-out*.

chuckhole ['tʃʌkˌhəul] *n* bache *m*.

chuckle ['tʃʌkl] *n* risa *f* ahogada, risita *f* ‖ *to have a good chuckle over sth.* reírse mucho de algo.

chuckle ['tʃʌkl] *vi* reír entre dientes (to laugh) ‖ cloquear (a hen) ‖ *to chuckle at* o *over* reírse de.

chucklehead [-hed] *n* FAM alcornoque *m*, zoquete *m* (blockhead).

chuck wagon ['tʃʌkˌwægən] *n* US FAM carromato *m* con provisiones.

chufa ['tʃufə] *n* BOT chufa *f* (earth almond).

chuffed [tʃʌft] *adj* FAM contento, ta.

chug [tʃʌg] *n* resoplido *m* (of steam engine) ‖ traqueteo *m* (of an internal combustion engine).

chug [tʃʌg] *vi* resoplar (a steam engine) ‖ traquetear (an internal combustion engine).

chukkar; chukker ['tʃʌkə*] *n* SP período *m* de juego (in polo).

chum [tʃʌm] *n* FAM compinche *m*, compañero *m* ‖ *to be great chums* ser buenos compañeros *or* muy amigos.

chum [tʃʌm] *vi* FAM ser muy amigos ‖ — FAM *to chum up* hacerse amigos | *to chum up with s.o.* hacerse amigo de alguien.

chummy [-i] *adj* FAM amistoso, sa (friendly) ‖ — FAM *to be chummy* ser muy amigos | *to be chummy with s.o.* ser muy amigo de alguien.

chump [tʃʌmp] *n* cadera *f* (meat) ‖ tarugo *m* (of wood) ‖ FAM majadero, ra (silly person) | azotea *f*, chaveta *f* (head); *to be off one's chump* estar mal de la azotea.

chump chop [-tʃɔp] *n* chuleta *f*.

chunk [tʃʌŋk] *n* pedazo *m* (of bread, etc.) ‖ tarugo *m* (of wood) ‖ cantidad *f* grande (large amount) ‖ parte *f* (part).

chunky [-i] *adj* fornido, da (person) ‖ grueso y pesado (things).

church [tʃəːtʃ] *n* REL iglesia *f* (catholic) | templo *m*, iglesia *f* (protestant) | oficio *m* religioso (service) | misa *f* (mass); *after church* después de la misa ‖ — REL *Church of England* iglesia anglicana | *Church of Jesus Christ of Latter-day Saints* iglesia de los mormones | *Mother Church* la Santa Madre Iglesia.
◆ *adj* de la iglesia; *the church roof* el tejado de la iglesia ‖ eclesiástico, ca; *the Church authorities* las autoridades eclesiásticas ‖ — *church militant* iglesia militante ‖ *church music* música sacra ‖ *church service* oficio religioso ‖ FIG *poor as a church mouse* más pobre que las ratas.

church [tʃəːtʃ] *vt* REL purificar.

churchgoer [-gəuə*] *n* REL practicante *m* & *f*, persona *f* que va a misa.

churchgoing [-ˌgəuiŋ] *n* REL práctica *f*.
◆ *adj* practicante.

churching [-iŋ] *n* REL ceremonia *f* de purificación.

churchman ['tʃəːtʃmən] *n* REL clérigo *m*, eclesiástico *m*, sacerdote *m* (of roman catholic church) | pastor *m* (of protestant church) | anglicano *m*.
— OBSERV El plural de *churchman* es *churchmen*.

churchwarden ['tʃəːtʃwɔːdn] *n* REL mayordomo *m* ‖ pipa *f* larga.

churchwoman ['tʃəːtʃˌwumən] *n* anglicana *f*.
— OBSERV El plural es *churchwomen*.

churchy ['tʃəːtʃi] *adj* FAM beato, ta.

churchyard ['tʃəːtʃjɑːd] *n* cementerio *m*, campo *m* santo (cemetery) ‖ patio *m* de la iglesia (yard).

churl [tʃəːl] *n* patán *m*, palurdo *m* (boor) ‖ FAM refunfuñón *m* (grouser) | tacaño *m* (niggard).

churlish ['tʃəːliʃ] *adj* grosero, ra (boorish) ‖ FAM refunfuñón, ona (grumpy) | tacaño, ña (miserly).

churlishness ['tʃəːliʃnis] *n* patanería *f* ‖ FAM malhumor *m* (peevishness) | tacañería *f* (stinginess).

churn [tʃəːn] *n* mantequera *f* (for making butter) ‖ lechera *f* (milk container).

churn [tʃəːn] *vt* batir (milk) ‖ hacer (butter) ‖ remover, agitar; *the propeller churned the water* la hélice agitaba el agua ‖ — *to churn out* producir en profusión ‖ *to churn up* remover, revolver; *the plough churned up the earth* el arado removía la tierra.
◆ *vi* agitarse, revolverse; *the sea churned all round us* el mar se agitaba a nuestro alrededor ‖ CULIN hacer mantequilla (to make butter).

churrigueresque ['tʃurigɛə'resk] *adj* ARTS churrigueresco, ca.

chute [ʃuːt] *n* salto *m* de agua (waterfall) ‖ conducto *m* (pipe) ‖ tolva *f* (hopper) ‖ rampa *f* (ramp) ‖ tobogán *m* (in swimming pool) ‖ FAM paracaídas *m inv* (parachute).

chutney ['tʃʌtni] *n* salsa *f* picante.

chyle [kail] *n* quilo *m*.

chyme [kaim] *n* BIOL quimo *m*.

CIA *abbr of [Central Intelligence Agency]* CIA, servicio de inteligencia norteamericano.

ciao! [tʃau] *interj* ¡chao!

ciborium [si'bɔːriəm] *n* REL copón *m* (for host) ‖ ciborio *m* (altar canopy).
— OBSERV El plural de *ciborium* es *ciboria*.

cicada [si'kɑːdə] *n* ZOOL cigarra *f*.

cicatrice ['sikətris] *n* cicatriz *f*.

cicatricle [si'kætrikəl] *n* cicatriz *f* (cicatrice) ‖ cicatrícula *f* (in bird and reptile eggs).

cicatrix ['sikətriks] *n* cicatriz *f*.
— OBSERV El plural de *cicatrix* es *cicatrices* o *cicatrixes*.

cicatrization [ˌsikətri'zeiʃən] *n* cicatrización *f*.

cicatrizant ['sikətraizənt] *n* MED cicatrizante *m*.

cicatrize ['sikətraiz] *vt* MED cicatrizar.
◆ *vi* MED cicatrizarse, cicatrizar.

cicatrizing [-iŋ] *adj* MED cicatrizante.

cicely ['sisili] *n* BOT perifollo *m*.

Cicero ['sisərəu] *pr n* Cicerón *m*.

cicerone [ˌtʃitʃə'rəuni] *n* cicerone *m*.
— OBSERV El plural de *cicerone* es *ciceroni* o *cicerones*.

Ciceronian [ˌsisə'rəunjən] *adj* ciceroniano, na.

cicindela [sisin'delə] *n* ZOOL cicindela *f*.

cider ['saidə*] *n* sidra *f* ‖ US zumo *m* de manzana (apple juice) ‖ — *cider house* fábrica *f* de sidra, sidrería *f* ‖ *cider press* lagar *m* ‖ US *hard cider* sidra.

CIF ['siː-ai-ef] *abbr of cost, insurance and freight* CIF, coste, seguro y flete.

cigar [si'gɑː*] *n* cigarro *m* puro, puro *m* ‖ — *cigar band* vitola *f* ‖ *cigar case* cigarrera *f*, petaca *f* ‖ *cigar cutter* cortapuros *m inv* ‖ *cigar holder* boquilla *f* ‖ *cigar maker* cigarrera *f* ‖ *cigar shop* o *store* estanco *m*, expendeduría *f* de tabaco [AMER cigarrería *f*].

cigarette [ˌsigə'ret] *n* cigarrillo *m*, pitillo *m* (fam) ‖ — *cigarette case* pitillera *f* ‖ *cigarette end* colilla *f* ‖ *cigarette holder* boquilla *f* ‖ *cigarette lighter* encendedor *m*, mechero *m* ‖ *cigarette paper* papel *m* de fumar.

cigarillo [ˌsigɑ'riləu] *n* purito *m* [de señoritas].

cilia ['siliə] *pl n* cilios *m*.

ciliary ['siliəri] *adj* ANAT ciliar.

ciliate ['silieit] *adj* ciliado, da.
◆ *n* ciliado *m*.

cilice ['silis] *n* cilicio *m*.

cilium ['siliəm] *n* cilio *m*.
— OBSERV El plural de *cilium* es *cilia*.

cinch [sintʃ] *n* cincha *f* (of saddle) ‖ FIG & FAM apretón *m* (grip) | control *m*, dominio *m* ‖ FAM *it's a cinch* está tirado (easy), es cosa segura (sure).

cinch [sintʃ] *vt* cinchar (a saddle) ‖ FIG & FAM asegurar (to assure).

cinchona [siŋ'kəunə] *n* BOT quino *m* ‖ *cinchona bark* quina *f*.

cincture ['siŋktʃə*] *n* (ant) cinto *m* ‖ ARCH filete *m*.

cinder ['sində*] *n* carbonilla *f* (of burnt coal) ‖ escoria *f* (slag from a furnace) ‖ *cinder track* pista *f* de ceniza.
◆ *pl* cenizas *f* volcánicas (from a volcano) ‖ ceniza *f sing*, cenizas *f* (residue of burnt coal).

Cinderella [ˌsində'relə] *pr n* Cenicienta *f*.

cindery ['sindəri] *adj* ceniciento, ta.

cinecamera ['siniˌkæmərə] *n* tomavistas *m inv*, cámara *f* cinematográfica.

cinema ['sinəmə] *n* cine *m*; *continuous performance cinema* cine de sesión continua; *silent cinema* cine mudo; *talking cinema* cine sonoro.

cinemagoer [-gəuə*] *n* aficionado *m* al cine.

Cinemascope ['sinəməˌskəup] *n* cinemascope *m*.

cinematic [ˌsinə'mætik] *adj* cinemático, ca.

cinematics [-s] *n* cinemática *f* (kinematics).

cinematograph [ˌsinəˈmætəgrɑːf] *n* cinematógrafo *m*.

cinematographer [sinəməˈtɔgrəfə*] *n* cámara *m*, operador *m*, cameraman *m*.
— OBSERV *Cameraman* is an Anglicism which, though frequently used, is better replaced by *operador* or *cámara*.

cinematographic [ˌsinəmætəˈgræfik] *adj* cinematográfico, ca.

cinematography [ˌsinəməˈtɔgrəfi] *n* cinematografía *f*.

cinerama [ˌsinəˈrɑːmə] *n* cinerama *m*.

cineraria [ˌsinəˈrɛəriə] *n* BOT cineraria *f*.

cinerarium [ˌsinəˈrɛəriəm] *n* nicho *m* para urnas cinerarias.
— OBSERV El plural de *cinerarium* es *cineraria*.

cinerary [ˈsinərəri] *adj* cinerario, ria; *cinerary urn* urna cineraria.

cinerator [ˈsinəreitə*] *n* US horno *m* crematorio.

cinereous [siˈniəriəs] *adj* cinéreo, a; ceniciento, ta.

Cingalese; Cinghalese [ˌsiŋgəˈliːz] *adj/n* cingalés, esa.

cinnabar [ˈsinəbɑ*] *n* MIN cinabrio *m*.

cinnamic [siˈnæmik] *adj* CHEM cinámico, ca.

cinnamon [ˈsinəmən] *n* BOT cinamomo *m*, canelo *m* || canela *f* (spice).

cinqfoil [ˈsiŋkfɔil] *n* BOT cincoenrama *f*.

cinque [siŋk] *n* cinco *m*.

cinquefoil [ˈsiŋkfɔil] *n* BOT cincoenrama *f*.

cipher; cypher [ˈsaifə*] *n* MATH cero *m* (zero) || cifra *f*, número *m* (numeral) || clave *f*, código *m*, cifra *f* (code); *cipher message* mensaje en clave || cifra *f*, monograma *m* (monogram) || zumbido *m* (of an organ) || FIG *he is a mere cipher* es un cero a la izquierda.

cipher [ˈsaifə*] *vt* cifrar (to put in ciphers) || MATH calcular || poner en clave (using a code).
◆ *vi* MATH cifrar, calcular || zumbar (an organ note).

cipolin [ˈsipəlin] *n* cipolino *m*.

cippus [ˈsipəs] *n* cipo *m* (memorial stone).
— OBSERV El plural de esta palabra es *cippi*.

circa [ˈsəːkə] *prep* hacia; *circa 1920* hacia 1920.

circle [ˈsəːkl] *n* círculo *m*, corro *m*, rueda *f*; *to stand in circle* hacer un corro || MATH círculo *m* || FAM circunferencia *f* (circumference) || FIG círculo *m*; *circle of friends* círculo de amigos || ojera *f* (round the eyes) || THEATR piso *m* principal || ASTR órbita *f* (orbit) | halo *m* (of the moon) | revolución *f*, vuelta *f* || GEOGR círculo *m*; *polar circle* círculo polar || AVIAT diámetro *m* (of the propeller) || línea *f* de circunvalación (in the underground) || — *Antarctic, Arctic Circle* Círculo Polar Antártico, Ártico || MAR *azimuth circle* círculo acimutal || *family circle* círculo familiar || MATH *great, small circle* círculo máximo, menor || *in a circle* en círculo || *to be in a vicious circle* estar en un círculo vicioso || *to come full circle* volver al punto de partida (in arguments) || *to go round in circles* tomar el camino más largo (to take the longest road), dar vueltas (to walk round and round), estar en un círculo vicioso (in arguments) || FIG *to square the circle* encontrar la cuadratura del círculo || AUT *turning circle* radio *m* de giro || THEATR *upper circle* segundo piso.
◆ *pl* círculos *m*, medios *m*, esferas *f*; *in high circles* en las altas esferas; *from well-informed circles* de círculos bien informados.

circle [ˈsəːkl] *vt* rodear, cercar (to put a circle round) || dar la vuelta a (to go round) || ceñir, rodear, circundar (to surround) || dar vueltas *or* girar alrededor de (to move around).
◆ *vi* girar, dar vueltas; *the planes circle overhead* los aviones dan vueltas en el aire || *to circle round* circular (news, object).

circlet [ˈsəːklit] *n* círculo *m* pequeño || venda *f* (band) || anillo *m* (ring).

circuit [ˈsəːkit] *n* circuito *m* (route) || gira *f* (journey) || perímetro *m* (perimeter) || recorrido *m* (course) || rodeo *m* (long way round); *to make a wide circuit* dar un gran rodeo || ELECTR circuito *m* || JUR distrito *m*, jurisdicción *f* || cadena *f* (of cinemas, of theatres) || SP circuito *m*, recorrido *m* || ASTR revolución *f*, vuelta *f* || FIG serie *f* (of acts) || — ELECTR *circuit breaker* cortacircuitos *m inv* || JUR *circuit court* tribunal *m* de distrito || US *circuit rider* predicador *m* ambulante || ELECTR *short circuit* cortocircuito *m*.

circuit [ˈsəːkit] *vt* dar la vuelta a.

circuitous [səːˈkjuitəs] *adj* indirecto, ta.

circuitry [ˈsəːkitri] *n* circuitería *f*.

circular [ˈsəːkjulə*] *adj* circular; *circular motion* movimiento circular || de circunvalación (railway) || FIG indirecto, ta || — *circular letter* circular *f* || MATH *circular measure* medición *f* del círculo || *circular saw* sierra *f* circular || *circular tour* circuito *m*.
◆ *n* circular *f* (letter).

circularize [ˈsəːkjuləraiz] *vt* mandar circulares a || anunciar por circulares.

circulate [ˈsəːkjuleit] *vt* circular; *to circulate an order* circular una orden || hacer circular, divulgar (news) || hacer circular (a letter, a paper, etc.).
◆ *vi* circular.

circulating [-iŋ] *adj* circulante; *circulating library* biblioteca circulante || COMM *circulating capital* capital *m* disponible *or* circulante.

circulation [ˌsəːkjuˈleiʃən] *n* circulación *f* || difusión *f* (of news) || tirada *f* (of a newspaper) || — *blood circulation* circulación de la sangre || COMM *notes in circulation* billetes *m* en circulación || *to put into circulation* poner en circulación || *to withdraw from circulation* retirar de la circulación.

circulatory [ˌsəːkuˈleitəri] *adj* circulatorio, ria; *circulatory system* aparato circulatorio.

circumambient [ˌsəːkəmˈæmbiənt] *adj* ambiente circundante.

circumambulate [ˌsəːkəmˈæmbjuleit] *vt* dar la vuelta a.
◆ *vi* andar de un lado para otro || FIG andar con rodeos.

circumbendibus [ˌsəːkəmˈbendibəs] *n* FAM circunloquios *m pl*, rodeos *m pl*.

circumbscribed [-d] *adj* circunscrito, ta; circunscripto, ta.

circumcise [ˈsəːkəmsaiz] *vt* circuncidar.

circumcised [-d] *adj* circunciso, sa.

circumcision [ˌsəːkəmˈsiʒən] *n* circuncisión *f*.

circumference [səːˈkʌmfərəns] *n* circunferencia *f*.

circumflex [ˈsəːkəmfleks] *adj* circunflejo.
◆ *n* circunflejo *m*, acento *m* circunflejo.

circumflex [ˈsəːkəmfleks] *vt* poner acento circunflejo en.

circumfuse [ˌsəːkəmˈfjuːz] *vt* echar, difundir (to spread) || derramar (a liquid) || rodear (to surround) || *circumfused with light* bañado de luz.

circumjacent [ˌsəːkəmˈdʒeisənt] *adj* circunyacente.

circumlocution [ˌsəːkəmləˈkjuːʃən] *n* circunlocución *f*, circunloquio *m*.

circumnavigate [ˌsəːkəmˈnævigeit] *vt* circunnavegar.

circumnavigation [ˈsəːkəmnæviˈgeiʃən] *n* circunnavegación *f*.

circumpolar [ˈsəːkəmˈpəulə*] *adj* ASTR circumpolar.

circumscribe [ˈsəːkəmskraib] *vt* circunscribir || limitar (powers).

circumscription [ˌsəːkəmˈskripʃən] *n* circunscripción *f* || límite *m* || contorno *m* (outline) || inscripción *f* circular (of a coin).

circumspect [ˈsəːkəmspekt] *adj* circunspecto, ta.

circumspection [ˈsəːkəmˈpekʃən] *n* circunspección *f* (caution).

circumstance [ˈsəːkəmstəns] *n* circunstancia *f* (essential fact); *in* o *under the circumstances* en estas circunstancias || detalle *m* (detail) || ceremonia *f* (stiff ceremonial).
◆ *pl* posición *f sing*, situación *f sing* (material welfare) || — JUR *extenuating circumstances* circunstancias atenuantes || *in bad circumstances* apurado, da; en un apuro || *in easy circumstances* acomodado, da || *narrow circumstances* mal paso *m* || *under no circumstances* en ningún concepto.

circumstantial [ˌsəːkəmˈstænʃəl] *adj* circunstancial (incidental) || circunstanciado, da (detailed) || JUR indirecto, ta (evidence).

circumstantiality [ˈsəːkəmˌstænʃiˈæliti] *n* acumulación *f* de detalles || detalle *m* (detail).

circumstantiate [ˌsəːkəmˈstænʃjeit] *vt* corroborar, confirmar.

circumvallate [ˌsəːkəmˈvælit] *vt* circunvalar.

circumvallation [-væˈleiʃən] *n* circunvalación *f*.

circumvent [ˌsəːkəmˈvent] *vt* embaucar, engañar (to baffle) || burlar, circunvenir (the law) || rodear, evitar (to avoid) || MIL rodear.

circumvolution [ˌsəːkəmvəˈljuːʃən] *n* circunvolución *f* (turn).

circus [ˈsəːkəs] *n* circo *m* (entertainment) || plaza *f* circular, glorieta *f* (road junction) || HIST circo *m* (roman arena) || AVIAT escuadrilla *f*.
◆ *adj* circense.

cirque [səːk] *n* GEOL circo *m*.

cirrhosis [siˈrəusis] *n* MED cirrosis *f*.

cirrhotic [siˈrəutik] *adj* MED cirroso, sa.

cirriped [ˈsiriped] *n* ZOOL cirrípedo *m*.

cirrocumulus [ˈsirəuˈkjuːmjuləs] *n* cirrocúmulo *m*.
— OBSERV El plural de *cirrocumulus* es *cirrocumuli*.

cirrostratus [sirəuˈstrɑːtəs] *n* cirroestrato *m*.
— OBSERV El plural de *cirrostratus* es *cirrostrati*.

cirrous [ˈsirəs] *adj* BOT & ZOOL cirroso, sa.

cirrus [ˈsirəs] *n* cirro *m* (cloud) || BOT & ZOOL cirro *m* (tendril feeler).
— OBSERV El plural de *cirrus* es *cirri*.

cisalpine [sisˈælpain] *adj* cisalpino, na.

cissie; cissy [ˈsisi] *n* ⟶ **sissy**.

cissoid [ˈsisɔid] *n* MATH cisoide *f*.

cist [sist] *n* cista *f*.

Cistercian [sisˈtəːʃən] *adj* cisterciense || *Cisternian Order* Orden *f* del Císter, Císter *m*, Cistel *m*.
◆ *n* cisterciense *m* & *f*.

cistern [ˈsistən] *n* cisterna *f*, aljibe *m* (for rainwater) || tanque *m*, depósito *m* (at the top of a house) || cisterna *f*, cisternilla *f* (in a water closet) || cubeta *f* (of a barometer).

cistus [ˈsistəs] *n* BOT cisto *m*.

citadel [ˈsitədl] *n* ciudadela *f* || FIG baluarte *m*, ciudadela *f* (stronghold).

citation [saiˈteiʃən] *n* cita *f*, citación *f* (quotation) || JUR citación *f* || MIL mención *f*, citación *f*.

cite [sait] *vt* citar ‖ MIL mencionar, citar ‖ JUR citar.

cithara ['siθərə] *n* MUS cítara *f*.

citify ['sitifai] *vt* urbanizar.

citizen ['sitizn] *n* ciudadano, na; habitante (inhabitant) ‖ súbdito, ta; ciudadano, na (of a country) ‖ ciudadano, na (of a town) ‖ paisano *m* (civilian).

citizenry [-ri] *n* ciudadanos *m pl*.

citizenship [-ʃip] *n* ciudadanía *f*.

citrate ['sitrit] *n* CHEM citrato *m*.

citric ['sitrik] *adj* cítrico, ca; *citric acid* ácido cítrico.

citron ['sitrən] *n* cidra *f* (fruit) ‖ cidro *m* (tree).

citronella ['sitrə'nelə] *n* BOT citronela *f*.

citrus ['sitrəs] *n* BOT fruta *f* agria *or* cítrica.
◆ *pl* agrios *m*, cítricos *m*.
— OBSERV El plural de *citrus* es *citrus* o *citruses*.

city ['siti] *n* ciudad *f* ‖ — *city block* manzana *f* [AMER cuadra *f*] ‖ *City Council* ayuntamiento *m*, concejo *m* municipal ‖ *city edition* edición *f* local (of a newspaper) ‖ *city editor* redactor *m* financiero (of financial section of a newspaper), redactor *m* local (in United States) ‖ *city father* concejal *m* ‖ *city hall* ayuntamiento *m* (building), municipalidad *f*, municipio *m* ‖ US *city manager* administrador *m* municipal ‖ *city planning* urbanización *f* ‖ FAM *city slicker* capitalino, na ‖ *garden city* ciudad *f* jardín ‖ *the City* centro financiero de Londres ‖ *the Eternal City* la Ciudad Eterna.
◆ *adj* de la ciudad, municipal ‖ COMM financiero, ra.
— OBSERV Generalmente la palabra *city* se aplica a una ciudad de mayor amplitud que la que designa *town*.

cityscape [-skeip] *n* paisaje *m* urbano.

city-state [-steit] *n* ciudad *f* estado.

civet ['sivit] *n* ZOOL civeta *f* ‖ algalia *f* (used in perfume) ‖ *civet cat* gato *m* de Algalia, civeta *f*.

civic ['sivik] *adj* cívico, ca; *civic rights* derechos cívicos ‖ municipal; *civic authorities* autoridades municipales ‖ *civic centre* parte *f* de la ciudad donde están los edificios públicos.

civics [-s] *n* educación *f* cívica.

civil ['sivl] *adj* civil; *civil war, marriage* guerra, matrimonio civil ‖ JUR civil; *civil law* derecho civil ‖ educado, da; urbano, na (well-bred) ‖ cortés (polite) ‖ pasivo, va (defence) ‖ civil, paisano, na (not military) ‖ laico, ca (lay) ‖ — *civil death* muerte *f* civil ‖ *civil disobedience* resistencia pasiva ‖ *civil engineer* ingeniero *m* civil ‖ *civil engineering* ingeniería *f* civil ‖ *civil liberties* libertades *f pl* civiles ‖ *civil list* presupuesto *m* de la casa real aprobado por el Parlamento ‖ JUR *civil procedure* procedimiento *m* civil ‖ *civil rights* derechos *m* civiles ‖ *civil servant* funcionario, ria ‖ *civil service* administración *f* pública ‖ *civil year* año *m* civil.

civilian [si'viljən] *adj* civil, de paisano; *civilian clothes* traje de paisano.
◆ *n* civil *m*, paisano *m*.

civility [si'viliti] *n* urbanidad *f*, civilidad *f*, cortesía *f* (politeness).

civilization [ˌsivilai'zeiʃən] *n* civilización *f*.

civilize ['sivilaiz] *vt* civilizar.
◆ *vi* civilizarse.

civilly ['sivili] *adv* cortésmente.

civism ['sivizəm] *n* civismo *m*.

civvies ['siviz] *pl n* FAM traje *m sing* de paisano ‖ *in civvies* de paisano, vestido de paisano.

clack [klæk] *n* ruido *m* seco (sound) ‖ castañeteo *m* (of teeth) ‖ FAM charla *f* (chat) ‖ TECH *clack valve* chapaleta *f*.

clack [klæk] *vi* hacer un ruido seco (to make a sound) ‖ FAM charlar (to chatter) ‖ castañetear (teeth) ‖ cloquear (hen).

clad *adj* vestido, da (*in* de); *clad in velvet* vestido de terciopelo.
— OBSERV La palabra inglesa *clad* es el pretérito y el participio pasivo arcaicos de *to clothe*.

clad [klæd] *vt* revestir.

cladding ['klædiŋ] *n* TECH revestimiento *m*.

claim [kleim] *n* demanda *f*, petición *f* (the demanding of sth.) ‖ derecho *m* (right); *to have a claim on s.o., on sth.* tener derecho sobre alguien, a algo ‖ JUR demanda *f*; *to put in a claim* presentar una demanda ‖ reclamación *f*, reivindicación *f* (of a right to a possession) ‖ pretensi'on *f* (to a title) ‖ demanda *f* (insurance) ‖ declaración *f*, afirmación *f* (statement) ‖ propiedad *f* (land) ‖ US MIN concesión *f* ‖ — *claim agent* agente *m* de reclamaciones ‖ *claim check* comprobante *m* ‖ *claim form* solicitud *f* de prestaciones ‖ *to assert one's claim to* hacer valer su derecho a ‖ *to have a claim against* tener motivo para reclamar contra ‖ *to have a claim on s.o.'s attention* merecer la atención de alguien ‖ *to lay claim to* reclamar como propio.

claim [kleim] *vt* exigir, pedir; *to claim a thousand pounds damage* exigir mil libras por daños y perjuicios ‖ reclamar, reivindicar; *to claim a right* reclamar un derecho ‖ declarar, afirmar, pretender (to assert) ‖ necesitar, requerir (to need) ‖ *to claim s.o.'s attention* requerir la atención de alguien.

claimable ['kleiməbəl] *adj* reclamable.

claimant ['kleimənt] *n* JUR demandante *m* & *f* ‖ pretendiente *m*; *the claimant to the throne* el pretendiente al trono ‖ JUR *rightful claimant* derecho-habiente *m*.

claimless ['kleimlis] *adj* JUR sin derecho.

clairvoyance [klɛə'vɔiəns] *n* clarividencia *f*.

clairvoyant [klɛə'vɔiənt] *adj/n* clarividente.

clam [klæm] *n* ZOOL almeja *f* ‖ grapa *f* (clamp) ‖ FAM *to shut up like a clam* callarse como un muerto.

clam [klæm] *vi* pescar almejas ‖ FAM *to clam up* callarse como un muerto.

clamant ['kleimənt] *adj* estrepitoso, sa (noisy) ‖ urgente, acuciante, apremiante (demanding attention).

clambake ['klæmbeik] *n* US reunión *f* donde se guisan almejas y otros alimentos al aire libre (social gathering) ‖ US FAM mitin *m* (political rally).

clamber ['klæmbə*] *n* subida *f* a gatas.

clamber ['klæmbə*] *vi* gatear, subir gateando.

clammy ['klæmi] *adj* frío y húmedo (damp) ‖ pegajoso, sa (sticky).

clamor ['klæmə*] *n* US → **clamour.**

clamorous ['klæmərəs] *adj* clamoroso, sa; vociferante (vociferous) ‖ ruidoso, sa (noisy) ‖ FIG acuciante, apremiante, urgente (clamant).

clamorously [-li] *adv* a voces.

clamour; (US clamor) ['klæmə*] *n* clamor *m* (noise) ‖ vociferaciones *f pl*, clamor *m* (outcry) ‖ reclamación *f*, reivindicación *f* (claim).

clamour; (US clamor) ['klæmə*] *vi* clamar, vociferar (to make an outcry) ‖ hacer ruido (to make noise) ‖ *to clamour for sth.* pedir algo a voces.

clamp [klæmp] *n* TECH abrazadera *f* (brace) | grapa *f* (for fastening) | cárcel *f* (in carpentry) | tornillo *m* (of a bench) | borne *m* (in electricity) ‖ montón *m* (pile).

clamp [klæmp] *vt* TECH sujetar con abrazadera *or* grapa ‖ amontonar (to pile up) ‖ sujetar (to grasp).
◆ *vi* andar con paso lento ‖ — FIG *to clamp down on* suprimir (to wipe out), reprimir ‖ FAM *to clamp down on s.o.* apretarle los tornillos a uno.

clamp-down ['klæmpdaun] *n* represión *f*, restricción *f* repentina.

clan [klæn] *n* clan *m* (a social group, a large family) ‖ tribu *f* (tribe) ‖ facción *f* (clique).

clandestine [klæn'destin] *adj* clandestino, na.

clang [klæŋ] *n* sonido *m or* ruido *m* metálico.

clang [klæŋ] *vt* hacer sonar.
◆ *vi* sonar ‖ tener un sonido metálico.

clanger [-ə*] *n* FAM plancha *f*, metedura *f* de pata ‖ FAM *to drop a clanger* meter la pata, tirarse una plancha.

clangorous ['klæŋgərəs] *adj* resonante, sonoro, ra; estrepitoso, sa.

clangour; (US clangor) ['klæŋgə*] *n* sonido *m* metálico ‖ estrépito *m*, estruendo *m* (noise).

clank [klæŋk] *n* ruido *m* metálico.

clank [klæŋk] *vt* hacer sonar.
◆ *vi* sonar ‖ hacer un ruido metálico.

clannish ['klæniʃ] *adj* que tiene espíritu de clan ‖ exclusivista (cliquish).

clannishness [-nis] *n* espíritu *m* de clan ‖ exclusivismo *m*.

clansman ['klænzmən] *n* miembro *m* de clan.
— OBSERV El plural de esta palabra es *clansmen*.

clap [klæp] *n* ruido *m* seco, estampido *m* (sharp noise) ‖ palmada *f* (with hands) ‖ FAM purgaciones *f pl* (blennorrhagia) ‖ *a clap of thunder* un trueno.

clap [klæp] *vt* aplaudir (to applaud) ‖ FAM poner (to put) ‖ — *to clap in jail* meter en la cárcel ‖ *to clap one's eyes on* ver ‖ *to clap one's hands* dar palmadas en la espalda ‖ *to clap on the brakes* frenar en seco ‖ *to clap shut* cerrar de golpe.
◆ *vi* aplaudir (to applaud) ‖ dar palmadas (for rhythm).

clapboard [-bɔːd] *n* US ARCH chilla *f*, tablilla *f*.

clapboard [-bɔːd] *vt* US ARCH revestir con chillas *or* tablillas.

clapped out ['klæpt aut] *adj* FAM destartalado, da.

clapper [-ə*] *n* badajo *m* (of a bell) ‖ tarabilla *f* (of a mill) ‖ chapaleta *f* (of a pump) ‖ carraca *f* (rattle) ‖ — *clapper boards* claqueta *f sing* ‖ *clapper boy* claquetista *m* ‖ FAM *to run like the clappers* correr como un loco.

clapping [-iŋ] *n* aplausos *m pl* ‖ palmadas *f pl*.

claptrap ['klæptræp] *n* FAM charlatanería *f* (insincere talk) | perorata *f* (pretentious talk) | música *f* celestial (nonsense).
◆ *adj* vacío, a; huero, ra.

claque [klæk] *n* THEATR claque *f*.

Clare [klɛə] *n* REL clarisa *f*.

claret ['klærət] *adj* clarete (wine) ‖ burdeos (colour).
◆ *n* clarete *m* (wine).

clarification [ˌklærifi'keiʃən] *n* clarificación *f* (of liquid, etc.) ‖ aclaración *f*, clarificación *f* (of situation).

clarifier ['klærifaiə*] *n* clarificador *m* (for wine) ‖ clarificadora *f* (for sugar).

clarify ['klærifai] *vt* clarificar (a liquid) ‖ aclarar, clarificar; *the teacher clarified the matter* el profesor aclaró la cuestión.

◆ *vi* aclararse, clarificarse.

clarinet [ˌklæri'net] *n* MUS clarinete *m*.

clarinettist; (US clarinetist) [-ist] *n* clarinetista *m* & *f*, clarinete *m*.

clarion ['klæriən] *adj* claro y potente, sonoro, ra.
◆ *n* MUS clarín *m* (musical instrument, organ stop) || HIST corneta *f* (war trumpet).

clarity ['klæriti] *n* claridad *f*.

clash [klæʃ] *n* ruido *m* metálico (as of cymbals) || estruendo *m*, estrépito *m* (noise) || ruido *m*, choque *m* (of weapons) || choque *m*, encuentro *m* (between forces, persons) || desacuerdo *m*, conflicto *m* (between opinions, interests, etc.) || disparidad *f*, contraste *m* (of colours) || coincidencia *f* (of dates) || — *timetable clash* incompatibilidad *f* de horario || *verbal clash* choque verbal.

clash ['klæʃ] *vt* golpear; *to clash cymbals* golpear los platillos || hacer sonar (bells) || hacer chocar.
◆ *vi* sonar; *the cymbals clashed* los platillos sonaron || chocar, encontrarse (forces) || chocar (to collide) || estar en desacuerdo, chocar (opinions, interests, etc.) || coincidir (dates); *his party clashed with my theatre engagement* su fiesta coincidió con mi cita para ir al teatro || matarse, desentonar; *these colours clash* estos colores se matan.

clasp [klɑːsp] *n* cierre *m* (fastening device) || broche *m* (of belt, book, etc.) || apretón *m* (of hands) || MIL pasador *m* || — *clasp knife* navaja *f* de muelle || *hair clasp* pasador *m* para el pelo.

clasp [klɑːsp] *vt* abrazar (to embrace) || agarrar (to grasp) || abrochar (to fasten) || estrechar, apretar (hand).
◆ *vi the two hands clasped in token of agreement* las dos manos se estrecharon en señal de acuerdo.

class [klɑːs] *n* clase *f*; *working class* clase obrera *or* trabajadora || clase *f* (on a train, ship, plane); *first class* primera clase || clase *f* (group of students); *a class of twenty-five students* una clase de veinticinco estudiantes || clase *f* (lesson); *evening class* clase nocturna || clase *f* (excellence); *she has real class* tiene mucha clase || clase *f*, calidad *f* (quality); *grapes of the first class* uvas de primera calidad || BIOL clase *f* || categoría *f*, clase *f* (kind) || US promoción *f*; *1972 class* promoción de 1972 || — *class struggle* o *warfare* lucha *f* de clases || *first class degree* sobresaliente *m* || *governing, lower, middle, upper class* clase dirigente, baja, media, alta || *in a class apart, in a class by itself* sin par, sin igual || *in a class of his* o *her own* único, ca; incomparable || US *senior class* curso *m* superior.

class [klɑːs] *vt* clasificar.

class-conscious [-'kɔnʃəs] *adj* que tiene conciencia de clase.

class-consciousness [-'kɔnʃəsnis] *n* conciencia *f* de clase.

classic ['klæsik] *adj* clásico, ca.
◆ *n* clásico *m* (writer, literary work) || estudiante *m* & *f* de lengua y literatura clásicas (student).

classical [-əl] *adj* clásico, ca; *classical music* música clásica || — *classical architecture* arquitectura neoclásica (of the eighteenth century), arquitectura renacentista (of the Renaissance) || *classical Latin* latín clásico || *classical scholar* erudito *m* en lenguas clásicas.

classicism ['klæsisizəm] *n* clasicismo *m* || humanismo *m*.

classicist ['klæsisist] *n* clasicista *m* & *f* || humanista *m* & *f*.

classics ['klæsiks] *pl n* lenguas *f* clásicas (Greek and Latin) || clásicos *m*, autores *m* clásicos; *the classics of English literature* los clásicos de la literatura inglesa || obras *f* clásicas, clásicos *m* (literary works).

classifiable ['klæsifaiəbl] *adj* clasificable.

classification [ˌklæsifi'keiʃən] *n* clasificación *f*.

classified ['klæsifaid] *adj* clasificado, da || — *classified advertisements* anuncios *m pl* por palabras [clasificados por secciones] || *classified information* información *f* de difusión secreta *or* reservada.

classifier ['klæsifaiə*] *n* clasificador, ra (person) || MIN clasificador *m* (machine).

classify ['klæsifai] *vt* clasificar (*in, into, under* en).

classless ['klɑːsləs] *adj* sin clases (society).

classmate ['klɑːsmeit] *n* compañero *m* de clase, compañera *f* de clase.

classroom ['klɑːsrum] *n* clase *f*, aula *f* (in school) || aula *f* (in university).

classy ['klɑːsi] *adj* FAM elegante, con clase.

clastic ['klæstik] *adj* GEOL clástico, ca.

clatter ['klætə*] *n* estrépito *m*; *the dishes fell down with a great clatter* los platos se cayeron con gran estrépito || choque *m* (of several things striking) || trápala *f*, chacoloteo *m* (of hooves) || triquitraque *m* (of train) || guirigay *m*, algarabía *f* (confused chatter).

clatter ['klætə*] *vt* hacer sonar con estrépito || chocar.
◆ *vi* sonar con estrépito || FAM charlar (to talk) || chacolotear (hooves) || *to clatter down the stairs* bajar las escaleras estrepitosamente.

Claud; Claude [klɔːd] *pr n* Claudio *m*.

clause [klɔːz] *n* cláusula *f*; *a clause in the will* una cláusula en el testamento || GRAMM oración *f*, cláusula *f* || — *additional clause* cláusula adicional || *escape clause* cláusula de excepción || *most-favoured-nation clause* cláusula del país más favorecido.

claustral [klɔːstrəl] *adj* claustral.

claustrophobia [ˌklɔːstrə'fəubjə] *n* claustrofobia *f*.

clavecin ['klævisin] *n* MUS clavecín *m*.

clavichord ['klævikɔːd] *n* MUS clavicordio *m*.

clavicle ['klævikl] *n* ANAT clavícula *f*.

clavicymbal [ˌklævi'simbəl] *n* MUS clavicímbalo *m*.

clavier [klə'viə*] *n* teclado *m*.

claw [klɔː] *n* ZOOL garra *f* (hooked nail of bird, animal) | uña *f* (of cat) | garra *f*, zarpa *f* (clawed foot) | pinza *f* (of crab, etc.) || TECH garfio *m* (claw-shaped implement) || FAM garra *f*, mano *f* (hand) || — *claw bar* pata *f* de cabra, sacaclavos *m inv* || *claw coupling* acoplamiento dentado || *claw hammer* martillo *m* de orejas | FAM *to show one's claws* enseñar las uñas.

claw [klɔː] *vt* arañar (to scratch) || desgarrar (to tear) || agarrar (to clutch) || FAM rascar || *to claw back* recuperar (money).
◆ *vi* arañar (to scratch at) || dar zarpazos (to make grasping motions) || agarrarse (to grasp at) || MAR *to claw off* barloventear.

clawed [-d] *adj* con zarpas (having claws) || arañado, da (scratched) || TECH dentado, da.

clay [klei] *n* arcilla *f* || FIG barro *m* || *clay pit* gredal *m*.

clayey [-i]; **clayish** [-iʃ] *adj* arcilloso, sa.

claymore ['kleimɔː*] *n* claymore *f* (Scottish sword).

clean [kliːn] *adj* limpio, pia; *a very clean little boy* un niño muy limpio; *clean shirt* camisa limpia; *clean cut* corte limpio || puro, ra; limpio, pia (pure) || puro, ra; limpio, pia (food, person) || bien proporcionado, da; *a car with clean lines* un coche con líneas bien proporcionadas || fino, na (ankle) || hábil, diestro, tra (deft) || despejado, da (unobstructed) || en blanco (paper) || SP limpio, pia; *clean player, jump* jugador, salto limpio || FIG vacío, a; limpio, pia; *his pockets were clean* tenía los bolsillos vacíos | limpio, pia (broke) | sin mancha, sin tacha (irreproachable); *to lead a clean life* llevar una vida sin tacha | decente || — FIG *clean as a new pin* limpio como una patena *or* como los chorros del oro *or* como un espejo || *clean bill of health* patente de sanidad limpia || *clean police record, clean sheet* registro de antecedentes penales limpio || FIG & FAM *to come clean about sth.* confesar algo || *to make a clean copy of* poner en limpio.
◆ *adv* completamente, por completo; *I clean forgot* se me ha olvidado completamente || limpiamente || — FAM *clean broke* pelado, da; limpio, pia || FIG *to get clean away* desaparecer sin dejar rastro.
◆ *n* limpiado *m*, limpiada *f*; *I'm going to give it a clean* le voy a dar un limpiado.

clean [kliːn] *vt* limpiar; *to clean the windows* limpiar las ventanas || pelar (vegetales) || MIN limpiar; *to clean gold* limpiar oro || limpiar en seco (to dry-clean) || — *to clean down* limpiar || *to clean off* quitar || *to clean one's nails* limpiarse las uñas || *to clean one's teeth* lavarse los dientes || *to clean o.s. up* lavarse, asearse || *to clean out* vaciar (to empty), limpiar (to make clean) || FIG & FAM *to clean s.o. out* limpiar *or* desplumar a alguien || *to clean up* ordenar (to tidy up), ganarse (a fortune), limpiar a fondo (to make neat), acabar con (to finish with), lavarse, asearse (to wash) | *to clean up a town* limpiar una ciudad de sitios indeseables.
◆ *vi* hacer la limpieza || *to clean up* hacer la limpieza (to tidy), ganarse una fortuna.

clean-cut [-'kʌt] *adj* bien cortado, da || claro, ra || FAM bien hecho, cha (figure) | perfilado, da (features) | sano, na (wholesome).

cleaner [-ə*] *n* limpiador, ra (person) || asistenta *f* (charwoman) || producto *m* para la limpieza (product) || aparato *m* de limpieza (device).
◆ *pl vacuum cleaner* aspiradora *f* || tinte *m sing*, tintorería *f sing*.

cleanhanded [-'hændid] *adj* FIG con las manos limpias.

cleaning ['kliːniŋ] *n* limpieza *f*; *dry cleaning* limpieza en seco || — *cleaning fluid* quitamanchas *m inv* || *cleaning rag* trapo *m* de la limpieza.

clean-limbed [kliːn'limbd] *adj* de miembros bien formados.

cleanliness ['klenlinis] *n* limpieza *f*.

cleanly [kliːnli] *adv* limpiamente.

cleanly ['klenli] *adj* limpio, pia.

cleanness ['kliːnnis] *n* limpieza *f*.

clean-out ['kliːnaut] *n* limpiado *m*.

cleanse [klenz] *vt* purificar, limpiar (from sin) || limpiar; *to cleanse the wound* limpiar la herida || curar, limpiar (of leprosy).

cleanser [-ə*] *n* producto *m* para la limpieza.

clean-shaven ['kliːn'ʃeivn] *adj* bien afeitado, da || lampiño, ña (smooth-faced).

cleansing ['klensiŋ] *n* purificación *f* (purification) || limpieza *f* (of a wound) || curación *f* (of a leper).
◆ *adj* limpiador, ra || *cleansing cream* o *milk* desmaquillador *m*.

cleanup ['kliːn'ʌp] *n* limpieza *f* (cleaning) || eliminación *f*.

clear [kliə*] *adj* claro, ra; *clear view, voice* vista, voz clara; *clear statement* declaración clara; *clear handwriting* letra clara || claro, ra; transparente (a liquid) || claro, ra; evidente; *a clear proof* una prueba clara || claro, ra; neto, ta; *a clear majority* una clara mayoría || tranquilo, la; *clear conscience* conciencia tranquila || libre (of sorrow, care, debts, obstacles, etc.)

|| libre; *the way is clear* el camino está libre || despejado, da; *clear sky* cielo despejado || terso, sa; *clear complexion* cutis terso || completo, ta; entero, ra; *six clear months* seis meses enteros || COMM neto, ta; líquido, da || SP sin faltas (round) || — *all clear!* ¡no hay peligro! || FIG *as clear as crystal* o *as day* más claro que el agua | *as clear as mud* nada claro || *clear of* libre de || *clear profit* beneficio neto || *he was perfectly clear about it* lo dijo muy claramente || *I'm not very clear on the matter* no tengo una idea muy clara del asunto || *is that clear?* ¿está claro? || *I want to make it clear that...* quiero dejar claro *or* bien sentado que... || *the all clear (signal)* la señal de fin de alarma || FIG *the coast is clear* no hay moros en la costa (there is no one about), pasó el peligro (the danger has passed) || *to be clear of debts* no tener deudas, estar libre de deudas || *to get sth. clear* dejar algo bien sentado || *to make o.s. clear* explicarse claramente *or* con claridad.

◆ *adv* claramente || MAR a la altura (*of* de) || — *I can hear you loud and clear* le oigo claramente *or* muy bien || *to get clear away* desaparecer sin dejar rastro || *to jump clear, to crawl clear* quitarse de en medio de un salto *or* a gatas || *to keep clear of* evitar || *to shine clear* brillar con claridad || *to speak loud and clear* hablar alto y claro || *to stand clear of* mantenerse a distancia de, apartarse de || *to steer clear of* evitar.

◆ *n* claro *m*, espacio *m* libre || *to be in the clear* estar fuera de peligro (out of danger), estar libre de deudas (of debts), estar *or* quedar fuera de toda sospecha (from suspicion).

clear [kliə*] *vt* limpiar; *to clear a street of snow* limpiar la calle de nieve || despejar (of obstruction) || dispersar (a crowd) || aclarar (to make clear) || quitar (to remove) || AGR rozar (a field) || clarificar (wine) || JUR probar *or* demostrar la inocencia de; *the evidence cleared him* las pruebas demostraron su inocencia | acreditar, habilitar, capacitar (by security) || saltar (to jump) || salvar (an obstacle) || ganar, sacar [beneficio] (net profit) || pagar, liquidar, saldar (a debt) || satisfacer (a mortgage) || quitar; *to clear the table* quitar la mesa || aclararse (the throat) || evacuar, aliviar (the bowels) || MED depurar, limpiar (blood) || pasar sin rozar; *the lorry cleared the bridge* el camión pasó sin rozar el puente || abrir; *to clear the way* abrir el camino || descargar (to unload) || evacuar, desalojar; *to clear the court* evacuar la sala || liquidar (to sell off unwanted stocks) || aprobar; *the boss cleared their proposals* el jefe aprobó sus propuestas || FIG aclarar (a question) | limpiar (of suspicion, blame, etc.) | descargar, aliviar (one's conscience) || MAR sacar de la aduana (goods), salir de (the harbour) || autorizar (an aircraft to take off, etc.) || COMM compensar (a cheque) || SP despejar (the ball in football) || desatorar (a pipe) || — MIL *to clear the decks for action* tocar zafarrancho de combate || *to clear sth. with s.o.* proponer algo a alguien || *to clear the air* aclarar las cosas || FAM *to clear the ground* despejar el terreno.

◆ *vi* aclararse (to become clear) || volverse más claro (to become clearer) || derretirse (snow) || despejarse (weather, sky) || MAR zarpar || SP despejar (in football) || dispersarse (the crowd) || desaparecer (a symptom) || venderse (goods).

◆ *phr v* **to clear away** quitar (to take away) | disiparse (fog, clouds) | largarse, irse (to go) || **to clear off** irse, largarse (to go away) | liquidar (debts, goods) || **to clear out** limpiar (to clean) | vaciar (to empty) | COMM liquidar | echar (s.o.) | irse, largarse (to go away) || — *to clear out of the way* quitar de en medio || **to clear through** pasar por | ser aprobado por || **to clear up** limpiar (to clean) | ordenar (to tidy up) | aclarar; *to clear up a problem* aclarar un problema | resolver, disipar (doubt) | aclararse, despejarse (weather) | despejarse (the sky) | terminar, comerse (food).

clearance ['kliərəns] *n* espacio *m* libre (between two objects) || altura *f* libre, margen *m* de altura (of a bridge) || gálibo *m* (of a wagon) || despeje *m* (removal of obstructions) || MAR despacho *m* de aduanas (by the customs) | certificado *m* de aduana (clearance papers) || acreditación *f*, habilitación *f* (by security) || COMM compensación *f* (of a cheque) | liquidación *f* (of goods) || holgura *f* (between two parts in machinery) || SP despeje *m* (in football) || distancia *f* al suelo (of vehicles) || permiso *m* (permission) || AGR desmonte *m*, roza *f* || — *clearance sale* liquidación *f* || *slum clearance* supresión *f* del chabolismo.

clear-cut ['kliə'kʌt] *adj* bien definido, da || claro, ra.

clear-eyed ['kliə'raid] *adj* de ojos claros || FIG clarividente, perspicaz.

clearheaded ['kliə'hedid] *adj* lúcido, da || perspicaz.

clearing ['kliəriŋ] *n* aclaramiento *m* (the making clear) || claro *m*; *a clearing in a wood* un claro en un bosque || clara *f*, escampada *f* (of the weather) || COMM compensación *f* (of a cheque) | liquidación *f* (of account) || recogida *f* (of the letter box) || despeje *m* (removal of obstructions) || CULIN clarificación *f* (of a líquid) || AGR roza *f*, desmonte *m* || MED evacuación *f*, alivio *m* (of the bowels) || MAR despacho *m* de aduanas.

clearing bank [-bæŋk] *n* COMM banco *m* de compensación.

clearinghouse [-haus] *n* COMM cámara *f* de compensación || agencia *f* distribuidora (of news).

clearing-up [-ʌp] *n* limpieza *f* (cleaning) || ordenamiento *m* (tidying up) || *I'll help you with the clearing up* te ayudaré a recoger.

clearly ['kliəli] *adv* claramente || evidentemente, con toda evidencia.

clearness ['kliənis] *n* claridad *f*.

clear-sighted ['kliə'saitid] *adj* clarividente, perspicaz.

clearout [-aut] *n* FAM limpieza *f*.

clearway ['kliəwei] *n* carretera *f* en la que no se puede aparcar.

cleat [kli:t] *n* TECH abrazadera *f* (to secure a rope, etc.) || MAR cornamusa *f* || clavo *m* (of shoes).

cleavage ['kli:vidʒ] *n* hendidura *f* (splitting) || BIOL división *f* (of a cell) || CHEM desdoblamiento *m* (of molecules) || MIN crucero *m* || división *f* (of opinion, etc.) || escote *m* (in dress) || canal *f* (in body).

cleave* [kli:v] *vt* hender, partir (to split) || FIG cortar, surcar; *the ship cleft the waves* el barco cortaba las olas | separar (to separate) | abrirse (camino); *he cleft his way through the jungle* se abrió camino a través de la jungla.

◆ *vi* partirse, henderse (to split) || (ant) pegarse, adherirse (to adhere) | ser fiel (*to* a) (to be faithful).

— OBSERV El verbo *to cleave* tiene tres pretéritos *(clove, cleaved* y *cleft)* y tres participios pasivos *(cloven, cleaved* y *cleft)*, excepto cuando significa *pegarse, adherirse* y *ser fiel*, en cuyo caso el pasado y el participio pasivo son regulares (*cleaved*).

cleaver [kli:və*] *n* cuchilla *f* (of a butcher).

clef [klef] *n* MUS clave *f*.

cleft [kleft] *adj* hendido, da; partido, da (split) || dividido, da (divided) || MED *cleft palate* fisura palatina.

◆ *pret/pp* ⟶ **cleave.**

◆ *n* grieta *f*, hendidura *f* (a split).

cleft stick [-stik] *n* dilema *m*; *he was caught in a cleft stick* estaba en un dilema.

clematis ['klemətis] *n* BOT clemátide *f*.

clemency ['klemənsi] *n* clemencia *f*.

clement ['klemənt] *adj* clemente.

Clement ['klemənt] *pr n* Clemente *m*.

Clementine [-ain] *pr n* Clementina *f*.

clench [klentʃ] *n* apretón *m* (a pressing) || agarrón *m* (grip).

clench [klentʃ] *vt* apretar, presionar (to press) || apretar (one's fists, teeth) || remachar (rivet, nail) || sujetar, agarrar (to grip).

clencher [-ə*] *n* ⟶ **clincher.**

Cleopatra [kliə'pætrə] *pr n* Cleopatra *f*.

clepsydra ['klepsidrə] *n* clepsidra *f* (water clock).

— OBSERV El plural de *clepsydra* es *clepsydrae* o *clepsydras*.

clerestory ['kliəstəri] *n* ARCH triforio *m* (church window).

clergy ['klə:dʒi] *n* REL clero *m*.

clergyman [-mən] *n* REL clérigo *m*, sacerdote *m* (priest) | «clergyman» *m*, pastor *m* protestante (protestant).

— OBSERV El plural de esta palabra es *clergymen*.

cleric ['klerik] *n* REL (ant) clérigo *m*.

clerical [-əl] *adj* clerical (of the clergy) || de oficina, oficinesco, ca (of the work of a clerk) || — *clerical error* error *m* de copia || *clerical work* trabajo *m* de oficina || *clerical worker* oficinista *m* & *f*.

◆ *n* clerical *m* (clericalist) || clérigo *m* (priest).

clericalism [-əlizəm] *n* clericalismo *m*.

clerisy ['klerisi] *n* intelectualidad *f*.

clerk [klɑ:k] *n* oficinista *m* & *f*, empleado, da *m* de oficina (office worker) || empleado, da (of a bank) || recepcionista *m* & *f* (at a hotel) || funcionario, ria (in a ministry, council, etc.) || (ant) clérigo *m* (clergyman) || sacristán *m* (in a parish) || JUR pasante *m* (of an attorney) || SP juez *m* (in horse racing) || US dependiente, ta (shop assistant) || — *clerk of the works* maestro *m* de obras || JUR *clerk of the court* escribano *m* forense || *town clerk* secretario *m* del ayuntamiento.

clerkship [-ʃip] *n* oficio *m or* ocupación *f or* empleo *m* de oficinista || JUR pasantía *f* (of an attorney's clerk) | escribanía *f* (of a clerk of the court).

clever ['klevə*] *adj* listo, ta; inteligente (intelligent) || hábil (skilful); *he's very clever with his hands* es muy hábil con sus manos || ingenioso, sa (ingenious); *that's clever!* ¡qué ingenioso! || astuto, ta (cunning).

cleverness [-nis] *n* inteligencia *f*, listeza *f* (intelligence) || habilidad *f* (skill) || ingenio *m*.

clew [klu:] *n* ovillo *m* (of thread) || MAR puño *m* de escota (lower corner of a sail) | anillo *m* del puño de escota (loop) || indicio *m*, pista *f* (clue) || *clew line* chafaldete *m*.

◆ *pl* cabuyeras *f* (of hammock).

clew [klu:] *vt* hacer un ovillo, enrollar (thread) || FIG dar una pista, dar un indicio || MAR *to clew up* cargar (a sail).

cliché ['kli:ʃei] *n* PRINT cliché *m*, clisé *m* || FIG tópico *m*, lugar *m* común, frase *f* estereotipada.

click [klik] *n* chasquido *m* || taconeo *m* (of heels) || tecleo *m* (of typewriter) || TECH trinquete *m* || *click!* ¡clic!

click [klik] *vt* chascar, chasquear (the tongue, etc.) || *to clik one's heels* taconear (repeatedly), dar un taconazo (a soldier).

◆ *vi* chascar, chasquear (to make a clicking sound) || FIG & FAM gustarse, llevarse bien; *the two clicked immediately* los dos se gustaron en seguida | tener éxito (to be a success) || FIG FAM *I didn't understand and suddenly it clicked* no lo entendía y de pronto caí en lo que significaba.

client ['klaiənt] *n* cliente *m* & *f*.

clientele [ˌkliːɑːn'tel] *n* clientela *f*, clientes *m pl*.

cliff [klif] *n* acantilado *m* (on coast) || SP escalamiento *m* de peñascos (in mountaineering).

cliff dweller [-dwelə*] *n* US troglodita *m* & *f*.

cliff-hanger [-ˌhæŋgə*] *n* FAM situación *f* de suspense.

cliff-hanging [-hæŋiŋ] *adj* tenso, sa; de tensión (moment) || emocionante, de suspense (film, etc.).

cliffy ['klifi] *adj* escarpado, da.

climacteric [klai'mæktərik] *adj* climatérico, ca || FIG crítico, ca.
◆ *n* MED climaterio *m* || FIG momento *m* crítico.

climacterium [klaimæk'tiriəm] *n* MED climaterio *m*.

climactic [klai'mæktik] *adj* culminante.

climate ['klaimit] *n* clima *m* (weather condition) || región *f*, país *m* (region) || FIG atmósfera *f*, ambiente *m* (atmosphere).

climatic [klai'mætik] *adj* climático, ca.

climatological [ˌklaimətə'lɔdʒikəl] *adj* climatológico, ca.

climatology [ˌklaimə'tɔlədʒi] *n* climatología *f*.

climax ['klaimæks] *n* punto *m* culminante (culmination) || clímax *m* (ascending scale) || clímax *m* (of a play).

climax ['klaimæks] *vt* llevar al punto culminante.
◆ *vi* llegar al punto culminante.

climb [klaim] *n* subida *f*, escalada *f*, ascensión *f* (of a mountain) || AVIAT subida *f* (of an aircraft) || FIG ascenso *m*.

climb [klaim] *vt* subir, escalar (mountain) || subir (hill, stairs) || subir a, trepar a; *the boys are climbing the trees* los niños están subiendo a los árboles.
◆ *vi* subir (road, aeroplane) || subir, elevarse; *the mercury in the thermometer is climbing* el mercurio del termómetro está subiendo || trepar (plants) || escalar, hacer alpinismo (mountaineering) || ASTR ascender, subir (sun) || FIG subir, ascender (in social rank, in power, etc.) || — *to climb down* bajar (to go down), volverse atrás (to abandon an attitude, opinion, etc.) || *to climb out* salir trepando (of a hole), bajar (of a vehicle) || *to climb over* salvar trepando || *to climb up* subir trepando, trepar por.

climb-down [daun] *n* FAM vuelta atrás *f* (in negotiations, etc.).

climber [-ə*] *n* trepador, ra; escalador, ra (person who climbs) || alpinista *m* & *f*, montañero, ra (mountaineer) || escalador, ra (in cycling) || FIG arribista *m* || BOT enredadera *f*, planta *f* trepadora || ZOOL trepadora *f*.

climbing [-iŋ] *adj* trepador, ra || —. *climbing frame* pórtico *m* de escalada || *climbing irons* trepadoras *f pl*, garfios *m pl* para trepar || ZOOL *climbing perch* perca trepadora || *climbing rope* cuerda *f* de nudos para trepar.
◆ *n* escalada *f*, alpinismo *m*, montañismo *m* || FIG arribismo *m*.

clime [klaim] *n* región *f* || clima *m* (climate).

clinch [klintʃ] *n* SP cuerpo a cuerpo *m* || MAR entalingadura *f* || remache *m* (of nail, rivet) || fin *m*, término *m*, conclusión *f*, cierre *m* (of a deal, etc.) || FAM abrazo *m* apasionado (embrace).

clinch [klintʃ] *vt* cerrar; *to clinch a deal* cerrar un trato || remachar (rivet, nail) || apretar (teeth, fists) || afianzar (to secure) || FIG resolver definitivamente (to solve) | remachar (argument) | confirmar (suspicions) | ganarse (a post, title, etc.) || MAR entalingar || FIG *that clinches it!* ¡no hay más que hablar!
◆ *vi* SP luchar cuerpo a cuerpo || FAM abrazarse estrechamente (to embrace).

clincher; clencher [-ə*] *n* argumento *m* decisivo (argument that settles a dispute) || remachador *m* (riveter) || clavo *m* remachado (nail) || MAR entalingadura *f*.

cling* [kliŋ] *vi* *to cling to* agarrarse; *the child clung to its mother* el niño se agarró a su madre; ceñirse a, ir ceñido a; *the boat clung to the coastline* el barco iba ceñido a la costa; pegarse a (clothes), aferrarse a; *to cling to the past, to a hope* aferrarse al pasado, a una esperanza; colgar; *the village clung to the mountain side* el pueblo colgaba en la ladera de la montaña; apegarse a (a friend, habit, etc.), persistir en (to persist in) || *to cling to one another* abrazarse fuertemente *or* estrechamente.
— OBSERV Pret & pp ***clung***.

clinger [-ə*] *n* FAM lapa *f*.

clingfilm [-film] *n* hoja *f* protectora transparente, film *m* transparente (for foodstuff).

clinging [-iŋ] *adj* ceñido, da; ajustado, da (dress) || pegajoso, sa; tenaz (odour) || pegajoso, sa (person).

clingstone [-stəun] *n* BOT pavía *f*, albérchigo *m* (peach).

clinic ['klinik] *n* MED dispensario *m*, ambulatorio *m* (part of hospital, place for free medical assistance) || clínica *f* (medical instruction, private place of consultation).

clinical [-əl] *adj* clínico, ca || *clinical thermometer* termómetro clínico.

clink [kliŋk] *n* FAM chirona *f*, cárcel *f* (prison); *in the clink* en chirona || tintín *m*, sonido *m* metálico, tintineo *m* (sound) || choque *m* (of glasses).

clink [kliŋk] *vt* hacer tintinear || chocar; *to clink glasses with* chocar copas con.
◆ *vi* tintinear.

clinker [-ə*] *n* TECH escoria *f* de hierro, cagafierro *m* (of iron) | escoria *f* de hulla (of coal) | ladrillo *m* vitrificado *or* holandés (brick) || FAM persona *f or* cosa *f* estupenda.

clinker-built [-ə*ˌbilt] *adj* MAR de tingladillo.

clinkstone [-stəun] *n* fonolita *f*.

clinometer [klai'nɔmitə*] *n* clinómetro *m*.

clip [klip] *n* clip *m*, sujetapapeles *m inv* (for fastening things together) || broche *m* (brooch) || pinza *f* (for hair rollers) || horquilla *f*, clip *m* (for hair) || prendedor *m*, sujetador *m* (of a pen, biro) || cargador *m* (of cartridges) || esquileo *m* (action of clipping) || vellón *m* (quantity of wool clipped from a sheep) || tijeretada *f* (with scissors) || lana *f* esquilada en una temporada (season's yield of wool) || recorte *m* (a cutting) || TECH collar *m*, abrazadera *f* || fragmento *m* (of film) || FAM bofetada *f*, torta *f* (a cuff with the hand) || SP zancadilla *f* (in American football) || — US *clip joint* bar *or* cabaret sumamente caro | *to go at a fair clip* ir a buen paso.

clip [klip] *vt* sujetar (to fasten together) || esquilar (animals) || recortar (to trim) || desbarbar (coins) || FAM abofetear (to cuff) || cortar (hair, wings) || picar (tickets) || SP poner la zancadilla a, zancadillear (in American football) || — *clipped form* forma abreviada || *to clip one's words* comerse las palabras || FIG *to clip s.o.'s wings* cortarle las alas a alguien || *to clip sth. on to* prender algo en.
◆ *vi* US FAM *to clip along* ir a buen paso.

clipboard [-bɔːd] *n* carpeta *f* de pinza.

clip-on [-ɔn] *adj* de clip, que se sujeta con un clip.

clipper ['klipə*] *n* esquilador *m* (of sheep) || MAR & AVIAT clíper *m* (ship and plane).
◆ *pl* esquiladora *f sing* (for animals) || maquinilla *f sing* para cortar el pelo (for people) | tijeras *f* de podar (for hedges) || *nail clippers* cortaúñas *m inv*.

clippie ['klipi] *n* FAM cobradora *f* (in the bus).

clipping ['klipiŋ] *n* esquileo *m* (of sheep) || recorte *m* (of metal, material) || corte *m* (of hair) || recorte *m* (of newspaper) || *hedge clippings* ramas cortadas.
◆ *adj* cortante (cutting) || rápido, da (swift) || FAM estupendo, da.

clique [kliːk] *n* pandilla *f*, camarilla *f*.

cliquey [-i]; **cliquish** [-iʃ]; **cliquy** [-i] *adj* exclusivista.

clitoris ['klitəris] *n* ANAT clítoris *m*.

cloaca [kləu'eikə] *n* cloaca *f*.

cloak [kləuk] *n* capa *f* (sleeveless outer garment) || MIL capote *m* || FIG manto *m*; *cloak of snow* manto de nieve || — FIG *a cloak of mystery* un velo de misterio | *under the cloak of* al amparo de; *under the cloak of religion they committed many atrocities* al amparo de la religión cometieron muchas atrocidades; so capa de, con el pretexto de (under a pretext).

cloak [kləuk] *vt* encubrir, disimular (to hide); *to cloak one's disapproval with a smile* disimular su desaprobación con una sonrisa || cubrir, encapotar; *the hills were cloaked with mist* la niebla cubría las colinas.

cloak-and-dagger [-ən'dægə*] *adj* de capa y espada; *cloak-and-dagger story* novela de capa y espada || de espionaje (of spies) || *the cloak-and-dagger boys* el servicio secreto.

cloakroom ['kləukrum] *n* guardarropa *m* (in a theatre, etc.) || servicios *m pl* (lavatory) || consigna *f*, depósito *m* de equipajes (for deposit of luggage).

clobber ['klɔbə*] *n* FAM pingos *m pl*, trapos *m pl* (clothes) | trastos *m pl* (personal effects).

clobber ['klɔbə*] *vt* FAM dar una paliza (to beat).

cloche [klɔʃ] *n* campana *f* de cristal (to protect plants) || sombrero *m* de mujer de forma acampanada (bell-shaped hat).

clock [klɔk] *n* reloj *m* (timepiece) || cronómetro *m* (chronometer) || TECH contador *m* (instrument connected to a machine) | reloj *m* de fichar, reloj *m* registrador (time clock) | velocímetro *m* (speedometer) | cuentakilómetros *m inv* (milometer) | taxímetro *m* (taximeter) || FAM molinillo *m* (of dandelion) | jeta *f* (face) || dibujo *m* lateral (of socks or stockings) || INFORM reloj *m* || — *against the clock* contra reloj || *alarm clock* despertador *m*, reloj despertador || *around the clock* durante 24 horas || *cuckoo clock* reloj de cuco || *electric clock* reloj eléctrico || *to put a clock on* cronometrar || *to put the clocks back* atrasar los relojes || FIG *to set* o *to turn the clock back* volver el reloj atrás || *to sleep the clock round* dormir doce horas seguidas.

clock [klɔk] *vt* cronometrar, tomar el tiempo de (with a stopwatch) || registrar (with a speedometer) || FAM *to clock up* apuntarse (a victory).
◆ *vi* *to clock in* o *on* fichar, picar (in factory), llegar al trabajo (to arrive at work) || *to clock out* o *off* fichar la salida.

clockdial [-daiəl]; **clockface** [-feis] *n* esfera *f* del reloj.

clocklike [-laik] *adj* puntual como un reloj.

clockmaker [-ˌmeikə*] *n* relojero *m*.

clockwise [-waiz] *adv* en el sentido de las agujas del reloj.

clockwork [-wəːk] *adj* de cuerda; *a clockwork car* un cochecito de cuerda || puntual.

◆ *n* maquinaria *f* de reloj (mechanism of a clock) ‖ mecanismo *m* de relojería; *machinery driven by clockwork* maquinaria movida por un mecanismo de relojería ‖ mecanismo *m* (of a toy) ‖ FIG *like clockwork* como un reloj, con precisión.

clod [klɔd] *n* AGR terrón *m* (of earth) | tierra *f* (soil) ‖ CULIN aguja *f* (of beef) ‖ FAM patán *m*, paleto *m*.

clod crusher [-ˌkrʌʃə*] *n* AGR desterronadora *f*.

cloddish [-iʃ] *adj* FAM memo, ma; tonto, ta; paleto, ta.

clodhopper [ˈklɔdˌhɔpə*] *n* patán *m*, paleto *m*, destripaterrones *m inv* (country lout).
◆ *pl* FAM zapatos *m*, zapatones *m* (big heavy shoes).

Clodowig [ˈklɔdɔvig] *pr n* Clodoveo *m*.

clog [klɔg] *n* zueco *m* (wooden shoe) ‖ traba *f* (fetter for animals) ‖ FIG traba *f*.

clog [klɔg] *vt* atascar, obstruir, atorar; *leaves clogged the drain* las hojas atascaban el desagüe ‖ embarrar (with mud) ‖ llenar, cubrir; *wet clay clogged our shoes* la arcilla húmeda nos cubría los zapatos ‖ entorpecer (to hinder movement) ‖ estorbar, obstaculizar (to be an encumbrance to) ‖ trabar (animals).
◆ *vi* atascarse, obstruirse, atorarse (to become blocked up) ‖ espesarse (to become thick).

clogging [-iŋ] *n* atasco *m*, atoramiento *m*.

cloisonné [klwæzɔˈnei] *adj* tabicado, da.
◆ *n* esmalte *m* tabicado.

cloister [ˈklɔistə*] *n* ARCH claustro *m* (covered walk) ‖ REL monasterio *m*, convento *m*, claustro *m* (monastery, convent) ‖ *the cloister* la clausura, la vida conventual *or* monástica, el claustro (monastic life).

cloister [ˈklɔistə*] *vt* enclaustrar (to confine in a convent, etc.) ‖ FIG encerrar, aislar (to isolate).

cloistered [-d] *adj* enclaustrado, da (isolated from the outside world) ‖ monástico, ca; conventual (monastic) ‖ — FIG *cloistered life* vida *f* de ermitaño ‖ *cloistered walk* arcadas *f pl*.

cloistral [ˈklɔistrəl] *adj* claustral.

clone [kləun] *n* clon *m*.

close [kləus] *adj* cercano, na; *close relative* pariente cercano ‖ íntimo, ma; *close friend* amigo íntimo ‖ unido, da; *I am close to my brother* estoy muy unido a mi hermano ‖ cercano, na (near) ‖ cerrado, da (shut) ‖ minucioso, sa; detallado, da; detenido, da; profundo, da; *close examination* examen minucioso ‖ fiel, exacto, ta; *close translation* traducción fiel ‖ preciso, sa (argument) ‖ mal ventilado, da (room) ‖ cargado, da (air) ‖ a cerrado (smell) ‖ sofocante, bochornoso, sa (weather) ‖ GRAMM cerrado, da; *close vowels* vocales cerradas ‖ COMM restringido, da (credit) | justo, ta (price) ‖ estrecho, cha; *a close watch* una estrecha vigilancia ‖ secreto, ta (secretive) ‖ cerrado, da; poco accesible (society) ‖ estrecho, cha (contact) ‖ cerrado, da; reservado, da (character) ‖ profundo, da (silence) ‖ oculto, ta (hidden) ‖ prohibido, da (forbidden) ‖ ajustado, da; ceñido, da (clothes) ‖ compacto, ta (compact) ‖ apretado, da (writing) ‖ tupido, da; *close texture* tejido tupido ‖ recio, cia (rain) ‖ parecido, da; *a texture close to that of wool* una contextura parecida a la de la lana ‖ reñido, da; *close game* partido reñido ‖ igualado, da; reñido, da; *the voting was very close* la votación estaba muy igualada ‖ cerrado, da (chess) ‖ FAM tacaño, ña: agarrado, da (stingy) ‖ — *a close resemblance* un gran parecido ‖ *at close quarters, at close range* de cerca ‖ MIL *close column* columna cerrada ‖ *close combat* combate *m* cuerpo a cuerpo ‖ *close quarters* lugar estrecho ‖ *close season* veda *f* (for hunting and fishing), temporada *f* de descanso (in sports) ‖ *close shave* afeitado muy apurado ‖ *close time* veda *f* ‖ FAM *it was a close shave* ha faltado el canto de un duro ‖ *to pay close attention* prestar mucha atención.
◆ *n* recinto *m* (enclosed place) ‖ calle *f* (street).
◆ *adv* cerca (near) ‖ completamente; *the door was shut close* la puerta estaba completamente cerrada ‖ — *according to the people close to the Prime Minister* según personas allegadas al Primer Ministro ‖ *close at hand* a mano ‖ *close by* muy cerca ‖ *close on nine o'clock* casi las nueve ‖ *close to* cerca de, junto a; *my house is close to the river* mi casa está cerca del río; casi (almost) ‖ *close together* muy juntos ‖ *they finished the race very close* terminaron la carrera casi a la vez ‖ *to be close on sixty* rondar *or* pisar los sesenta ‖ *to come close* acercarse ‖ *to cut one's hair close* cortar el pelo al rape ‖ *to fit close* estar apretado *or* ajustado ‖ *to get close to* acercarse a ‖ *to keep close* mantenerse oculto ‖ *to keep close to the text* ajustarse al texto ‖ *to run s.o. close, to run s.o. close second* seguir a alguien muy de cerca.

close [kləuz] *n* final *m*, fin *m* (an end) ‖ MIL & SP cuerpo *m* a cuerpo ‖ MUS cadencia *f* (cadence) ‖ — *at the close of the day* al caer el día ‖ *to bring sth. to a close* terminar algo ‖ *to come to a close* terminar.

close [kləuz] *vt* cerrar; *to close the door* cerrar la puerta ‖ tapar (a hole, view) ‖ acabar, terminar (to finish) ‖ COMM saldar (an account) | cerrar (a deal) | cerrar, liquidar (a bank account) ‖ clausurar (a meeting, ceremony, etc.) ‖ cerrar (a list, a vote) ‖ cerrar, clausurar (a debate) ‖ acortar (a distance) ‖ MIL cerrar (ranks) ‖ ELECTR cerrar (circuit).
◆ *vi* cerrarse (to shut) ‖ acabarse, terminarse (to come to an end) ‖ acercarse (to draw near) ‖ estar de acuerdo (to agree) ‖ llegar a las manos (to grapple) ‖ MIL cerrar filas (ranks).
◆ *phr v* ***to close about*** rodear ‖ ***to close down*** cerrar [definitivamente]; *to close down through lack of money* cerrar por falta de dinero | cerrar, cerrar la emisión (a radio station, etc.) ‖ ***to close in*** rodear (to surround) | acercarse (to draw near) | encerrar (to shut in) | acortarse; *the days are closing in* los días se están acortando | caer, cerrarse; *the night was closing in* la noche caía *or* se cerraba ‖ — *to close in on* o *upon s.o.* envolver a alguien, rodear *or* cercar a alguien ‖ *to close off* cerrar ‖ *to close on* alcanzar ‖ US ***to close out*** liquidar ‖ ***to close round*** rodear ‖ ***to close up*** cerrar (to shut) | cerrar (a shop) ‖ cerrarse (flowers, ranks) | taparse (aperture) | arrimarse más, juntarse más (to crowd together) | cicatrizarse (a wound) | callarse (to fall silent).

close-cropped [-ˌkrɔpt] *adj* rapado, da; al rape.

closed [kləuzd] *adj* cerrado, da (shut, inaccessible) ‖ cerrado, da (road) ‖ concluido, da; acabado, da (finished) ‖ exclusivo, va; reservado, da (reserved) ‖ vedado, da (hunting) ‖ cerrado, da (vowel) ‖ de miras estrechas, cerrado, da (mind) ‖ cerrado, da (society, etc.) ‖ — *closed chapter* asunto concluido ‖ *closed circuit* circuito cerrado ‖ US *closed primary* votación *f* preliminar ‖ *closed season* veda *f* ‖ JUR *closed session* sesión *f* a puerta cerrada ‖ *closed shop* establecimiento *m* que contrata solamente a miembros sindicados.

closed-door [-ˈdɔː*] *adj* a puerta cerrada.

closed-end [-ˈend] *adj* COMM de capital limitado.

closedown [ˈkləuzdaun] *n* cierre *m* (radio, television) ‖ cierre *m* (of a factory) ‖ caída *f* (of night).

closefisted [ˈkləusˈfistid] *adj* FAM tacaño, ña; agarrado, da (stingy).

close-fitting [ˈkləusˈfitiŋ] *adj* ajustado, da; ceñido, da.

close-grained [ˈkləusˈgreind] *adj* tupido, da (fibre) ‖ MIN de grano fino.

close-hauled [ˈkləusˈhɔːld] *adj* MAR de bolina.

close-knit [ˈkləusˈnit] *adj* unido, da (family, etc.).

close-lipped [ˈkləuslipt] *adj* callado, da; reservado, da (not talking much).

closely [ˈkləusli] *adv* cerca, de cerca (near) ‖ atentamente (carefully) ‖ estrechamente; *closely connected with* estrechamente relacionado con ‖ densamente (built, populated, etc.) ‖ apretadamente (writing) ‖ exactamente, fielmente (a translation) ‖ — *closely contested* muy reñido ‖ *closely packed* muy apretados unos contra otros (objects) ‖ *you resemble David very closely* te pareces mucho a David.

closeness [ˈkləusnis] *n* cercanía *f*, proximidad *f* (nearness) ‖ intimidad *f* (intimacy) ‖ minuciosidad *f*, detalle *m* (thoroughness) ‖ fidelidad *f* (of a translation) ‖ tacañería *f* (meanness) ‖ exactitud *f* (of a resemblance) ‖ mala ventilación *f* (stuffiness) ‖ bochorno *m*, pesadez *f* (of weather) ‖ GRAMM cerrazón *f* (of vowels) ‖ inaccesibilidad *f* (of a society, club, etc.) ‖ lo reñido (of competition, voting) ‖ lo compacto, compacidad *f* (compactness) ‖ densidad *f* (density) ‖ lo tupido (of a texture) ‖ carácter *m* poco comunicativo (of a person).

closeout [ˈkləuzaut] *n* liquidación *f* (of stock).

close-set [ˈkləusˈset] *adj* junto, ta (eyes, etc.).

close-shaven [ˈkləusˌʃeivən] *adj* bien afeitado.

closet [ˈklɔzit] *n* US armario *m*, ropero *m* (for clothes) ‖ retrete *m*, water *m* (water closet) ‖ gabinete *m* (private room) ‖ — *closet drama* teatro (para ser) leído ‖ FAM *closet strategist* estratega *m* de café.

closet [ˈklɔzit] *vt* encerrar ‖ *to closet o.s. with* encerrarse con.

close-up [ˈkləusʌp] *n* primer plano *m* (in photography, cinema).

closing [ˈkləuziŋ] *adj* final, último, ma ‖ COMM de cierre (prices) ‖ *closing time* hora *f* de cerrar *or* de cierre.
◆ *n* cierre *m* ‖ conclusión *f* (concluding portion) ‖ COMM cierre *m* (inventory) | liquidación *f* (account).

closure [ˈkləuʒə*] *n* fin *m* (end) ‖ cierre *m* (closing) ‖ conclusión *f* (conclusion) ‖ clausura *f* (in Parliament) ‖ cierre *m* (of T.V., etc.).

clot [klɔt] *n* grumo *m* (of a liquid) ‖ coágulo *m* (of blood) ‖ FAM bobo, ba; tonto, ta.

clot [klɔt] *vt* coagular, cuajar.

cloth [klɔθ] *n* tela *f*, paño *m* (fabric) ‖ trapo *m* (rag) ‖ mantel *m* (tablecloth) ‖ THEATR telón *m* ‖ MAR vela *f* ‖ FIG clero *m* (the clerical profession) ‖ — *American cloth* hule *m* ‖ *bound in cloth* encuadernado en tela ‖ *cloth of gold* tisú *m* de oro ‖ *to lay the cloth* poner la mesa.
◆ *adj* de tela.
— OBSERV El plural de esta palabra es *cloths*.

clothe* [kləuð] *vt* vestir (*in, with, as* de) ‖ FIG revestir, cubrir (to cover).
— OBSERV Pret & p p ***clothed, clad*** (ant).

clothes [-z] *pl n* ropa *f sing* (bedclothes, laundry) ‖ vestidos *m*, ropa *f sing* (garments) ‖ — *clothes bag* bolsa *f* de la ropa sucia ‖ *clothes basket* cesta *f* de la ropa sucia (of clothes to be washed), canasta *f* de la plancha (of clothes waiting to be ironed) ‖ *clothes brush* cepillo *m* de la ropa ‖ *clothes hanger* percha *f* ‖ ZOOL *clothes moth* polilla *f* ‖ *clothes peg* pinza *f* ‖ *clothes tree* perchero *m*, percha *f* ‖ *in plain clothes* de paisano ‖ *suit of clothes* traje *m*.

clotheshorse [-zhɔːs] *n* tendedero *m* (for airing).

clothesline [-zlain] *n* cuerda *f* para tender la ropa, tendedero *m*.

clothespin [-zpin] *n* US pinza *f*.

clothespole [-zpəul] *n* palo *m* del tendedero.

clothier ['kləuðiə*] *n* fabricante *m* & *f* de paños (person who makes cloth) || pañero, ra (person who sells cloth) || sastre *m* (tailor) || *clothier's shop* pañería *f* (for cloth), sastrería *f* (for clothes).

Clothilda [kləu'ðildə*] *pr n* Clotilde *f*.

clothing ['kləuðiŋ] *n* vestir *m* (act) || ropa *f* (clothes) || — *article of clothing* prenda *f* de vestir || *clothing trade* industria *f* de la confección.

Clotilda [kləu'tildə] *pr n* Clotilde *f*.

clotted cream ['klɔtid kriːm] *n* nata *f* muy espesa [típica de Devonshire].

cloture ['kləu'tʃə*] *n* US clausura *f*.

cloud [klaud] *n* nube *f* (in the sky, a liquid, a precious stone) || vaho *m* (in a mirror) || nube *f* (of dust, smoke, locusts) || capa *f* (of gas) || FIG sombra *f* de tristeza, nube *f* | nube *f* (crowd) || — *cloud chamber* cámara *f* de niebla || FIG *every cloud has a silver lining* no hay mal que por bien no venga | *on cloud seven* en el séptimo cielo | *passing cloud* nube de verano | *to have one's head in the clouds* estar en las nubes | *under a cloud* bajo sospecha (under suspicion), deprimido, da (depressed) | *under the cloud of night* amparado por la noche | *up in the clouds* en las nubes.

cloud [klaud] *vt* nublar; *smoke clouded the room* el humo nublaba la habitación || ensombrecer, nublar (to darken) || empañar (glass) || vetear (wood) || FIG oscurecer, obcecar, obnubilar (s.o.'s mind) | empañar, manchar (s.o.'s reputation) | entristecer (s.o.'s face).
◆ *vi* nublarse (to become cloudy) || ensombrecerse (to darken) || enturbiarse (liquid) || empañarse (glass) || FIG obnubilarse, obcecarse (mind) | empañarse, mancharse (reputation) | entristecerse (face).

cloudburst [-bəːst] *n* chaparrón *m* (heavy shower).

cloud-capped ['-kæpt] *adj* coronado de nubes.

cloudiness ['klaudinis] *n* nubosidad *f*, nebulosidad *f* || lo turbio (of liquid) || FIG tristeza *f* (of s.o.'s face) | lo oscuro, nebulosidad *f* (of style).

cloudland ['klaudlænd] *n* FIG mundo *m* imaginario.

cloudless ['klaudlis] *adj* despejado, da; sin nubes.

cloudlet ['klaudlit] *n* nube *f* pequeña.

cloudy ['klaudi] *adj* nuboso, sa (resembling clouds) || nublado, da; encapotado, da; *cloudier sky* cielo más nublado; *it is cloudy today* hoy está nublado || empañado, da; *cloudy glass* cristal empañado || turbio, bia (liquid) || FIG vago, ga; nebuloso, sa; *cloudy ideas* ideas vagas | triste (person).

clough [klʌf] *n* barranco *m* (ravine).

clout [klaut] *n* FAM tortazo *m* (blow) || pieza *f* (for patching) || blanco *m* (target) || tiro *m* que da en el blanco (hit) || chapa *f* (shoes) || FIG influencia *f* || FIG *ne'er cast a clout till May is out* hasta el cuarenta de mayo no te quites el sayo.

clout [klaut] *vt* FAM abofetear, pegar un tortazo (to slap) || remendar (to patch).

clove [kləuv] *n* BOT clavo *m* (spice) | clavero *m* (tree) || diente *m* (of garlic) || *clove hitch* ballestrinque *m* (knot).

clove [kləuv] *pret* → **cleave.**

cloven [-ən] *pp* → **cleave.**
◆ *adj* hendido, da; *cloven hoof* pezuña hendida || FAM *to show the cloven hoof* enseñar la oreja.

cloven-hoofed [-huːft] *adj* de pezuña hendida.

clover ['kləuvə*] *n* BOT trébol *m* || FAM *to be in clover* vivir a cuerpo de rey.

cloverleaf [-liːf] *n* TECH cruce *m* en trébol || BOT hoja *f* de trébol.
— OBSERV El plural de esta palabra es *cloverleaves*.

Clovis ['kləuvis] *pr n* Clodoveo *m*.

clown [klaun] *n* payaso *m*, clown *m* (in circus) || FIG patán *m* (boor) || villano *m* (peasant).

clown [klaun] *vi* ser un payaso (to be a clown) || hacer el payaso (to make people laugh).

clownery [-əri] *n* payasadas *f pl*.

clownish [-iʃ] *adj* bufón, ona (comical) || patán, grosero, ra (boorish) || torpe (clumsy).

cloy [klɔi] *vt/vi* empalagar || FIG hartar, saciar.

cloying [-iŋ] *adj* empalagoso, sa.

club [klʌb] *n* garrote *m*, cachiporra *f* (stout stick) || SP palo *m* (golf, hockey) || asociación *f* (association) || club *m* (circle) || casino *m* (for gaming) || cotización *f* (subscription) || — *club sandwich* sandwich *m* vegetal con pollo y bacon || *club soda* agua *f* de Seltz || *club steak* filete *m* de solomillo || FIG & FAM *to be in the club* estar preñada (pregnant).
◆ *pl* bastos *m* (in Spanish cards) || trébol *m sing* (in standard pack).

club [klʌb] *vt* dar garrotazos a, aporrear, dar cachiporrazos a (to beat) || reunir (persons, resources).
◆ *vi* reunirse || — *to club together* reunirse; *they clubbed together to buy a present* se reunieron para comprar un regalo || *to club with* asociarse con, aliarse a.

clubfoot ['fut] *n* pie *m* zopo.
— OBSERV El plural de esta palabra es *clubfeet*.

clubhaul [-'hɔːl] *vt* MAR virar sobre el ancla.

clubhouse [-'haus] *n* sede *f* de un club, club *m*.

clubman [-mən] *n* miembro *m* or socio *m* de un club (member) || US aficionado *m* a la vida de club (who spends much time in clubs).
— OBSERV El plural de *clubman* es *clubmen*.

clubroom [-rum] *n* sala *f* de reunión de un club.

cluck [klʌk] *n* cloqueo *m* (of hens) || FIG & FAM mentecato, ta (simpleton).

cluck [klʌk] *vi* cloquear (hens) || chascar (with the tongue) || FAM parlotear (a person).

clue [kluː] *n* pista *f* (lead for police, etc.) || indicio *m* (isolated piece of evidence) || clave *f* (key to problem, mystery, etc.) || indicación *f* (in crossword) || *I haven't a clue* no tengo ni idea, no tengo la menor idea.

clued-up ['kluːd ʌp] *adj* FAM que está al tanto, bien informado, da.

clueless ['klulis] *adj* desorientado, da; despistado, da.

clump [klʌmp] *n* grupo *m* (of trees) || macizo *m*, mata *f* (of flowers) || terrón *m* (of earth) || FAM pisada *f* fuerte (sound) | tortazo *m* (blow).

clump [klʌmp] *vt* agrupar.
◆ *vi* agruparse (to form clumps) || FAM andar con pisadas fuertes (to tramp).

clumpish [-iʃ] *adj* torpe.

clumsiness ['klʌmzinis] *n* torpeza *f* (awkwardness) || desmaña *f* (unskilfulness) || FIG falta *f* de delicadeza *or* de tacto (lack of tact) | chabacanería *f* (lack of refinement) || pesadez *f* (of objects).

clumsy ['klʌmzi] *adj* torpe (awkward) || desmañado, da (unskilful) || FIG chabacano, na (without refinement) | indelicado, da; sin tacto (tactless) || pesado, da (object).

clung [klʌŋ] *pret* & *pp* → **cling.**

Cluniac ['kluːniæk] *adj* REL cluniacense.
◆ *n* REL cluniacense *m*.

cluster ['klʌstə*] *n* grupo *m* (of people, trees, houses) || racimo *m* (of fruits); *a cluster of grapes* un racimo de uvas || ASTR enjambre *m* (of stars) || macizo *m*, mata *f* (of shrubs) || enjambre *m* (of bees) || hato *m*, manada *f* (of cattle).

cluster ['klʌstə*] *vi* arracimarse, apiñarse, agruparse (people) || BOT arracimarse (plants).

clutch [klʌtʃ] *n* agarrón *m* (grip) || AUT embrague *m* | pedal *m* del embrague, embrague *m* (clutch pedal) || TECH cuchara *f* (of a crane) || nidada *f* (of eggs) || garra *f* (of animals) || SP llave *f*, presa *f* (in wrestling) || POP garra *f* (hand) || — AUT *clutch disc* disco *m* de embrague | *clutch pedal* pedal del embrague, embrague | *plate clutch* embrague de discos | *to disengage the clutch* desembragar | *to engage* o *to let in* o *to throw in the clutch* embragar | FIG *to fall into s.o.'s clutches* caer en las garras de alguien.

clutch [klʌtʃ] *vt* agarrar, asir || AUT embragar || — FIG *to clutch s.o. into one's arms* estrechar a alguien entre sus brazos | *to clutch to one's breast* estrechar contra su corazón *or* su pecho.
◆ *vi* agarrarse || — *to clutch at* agarrarse a, agarrar || FIG *to clutch at a hope* aferrarse a una esperanza | *to clutch at straws* agarrarse a un clavo ardiendo.

clutch bag [-bæg] *n* bolso *m* de mano.

clutter ['klʌtə*] *n* FAM desorden *m*, confusión *f* (untidy mess) || montón *m* (of things).

clutter ['klʌtə*] *vt* desordenar (to make untidy) || *to clutter up* llenar, atestar; *the table was cluttered up with books* la mesa estaba llena de libros.
◆ *vi* desordenar las cosas || ajetrearse (to bustle).

clyster ['klistə*] *n* MED clister *m*, clistel *m*.

Co. *abbr of [company]* Cía., compañía.

coach [kəutʃ] *n* coche *m* (carriage) || carroza *f* (ceremonial carriage) || diligencia *f* (stagecoach) || AUT autocar *m* || vagón *m*, coche *m* (of a train) || professor *m* particular (tutor) || SP entrenador, ra || — *coach box* pescante *m* || *coach house* cochera *f*, cobertizo *m* || *coach station* terminal *f* de autocares.

coach [kəutʃ] *vt* dar clases particulares, preparar intensamente [para un examen]; *he coaches me in Spanish* me da clases particulares de español || SP entrenar, preparar (to train).
◆ *vi* dar clases particulares || viajar en diligencia *or* en coche.

coachbuilder [-ˌbildə*] *n* carrocero *m*.

coaching [-iŋ] *n* clases *f pl* particulares || preparación *f* (for an examination) || SP entrenamiento *m*, preparación *f* (training).

coachman ['kəutʃmən] *n* cochero *m*.
— OBSERV El plural de *coachman* es *coachmen*.

coachwork ['kəutʃwəːk] *n* AUT carrocería *f*.

coaction [kəu'ækʃən] *n* coacción *f* (coercion) || acción *f* conjunta (joint action).

coadjutant [kəu'ædʒutənt] *adj* coadyuvante.
◆ *n* ayudante *m* & *f*, auxiliar *m* & *f*.

coadjutor [kəu'ædʒutə*] *n* REL coadjutor *m*, coadyutor *m*.

coagulant [kəu'ægjulənt] *n* coagulante *m*.

coagulate [kəu'ægjuleit] *vt* coagular (to cause to congeal) || CHEM precipitar.

◆ *vi* coagularse (to congeal).

coagulation [kəu,ægju'leiʃən] *n* coagulación *f.*

coagulum [kəu'ægjuləm] *n* coágulo *m.*
— OBSERV El plural de *coagulum* es *coagula.*

coal [kəul] *n* GEOL carbón *m,* hulla *f; coal mine* mina de carbón || — *anthracite coal* antracita *f* || MAR *coal bunker* carbonera *f* || *coal cellar* carbonera *f* || *coal cutter* rozadora *f,* máquina rozadora || *coal dust* carbón en polvo, polvo *m* de carbón, cisco *m* || *coal face* frente *m* de arranque del carbón || *coal gas* gas *m* de alumbrado, gas *m* de hulla || *coal measures* rocas carboníferas || *coal merchant* carbonero *m* || *coal miner* minero *m* de carbón || *coal mining* explotación hullera || US *coal oil* petróleo *m* (petroleum), queroseno *m* (kerosene) || *coal scuttle* cubo *m* para el carbón || *coal tar* alquitrán *m* de hulla || *live coal* ascua *f,* brasa *f* || FIG *to blow the coals* echar leña al fuego, avivar la llama | *to carry coals to Newscastle* ir a vendimiar y llevarse de postre uvas, echar agua en el mar || FIG & FAM *to rake* o *to haul over the coals* echar un rapapolvo *or* una bronca.

coal [kəul] *vt* proveer de carbón (a ship, etc.).
◆ *vi* proveerse de carbón.

coal-black [-'blæk] *adj* negro como el carbón *or* como un tizón.

coalesce [,kəuə'les] *vi* fundirse (to merge) || unirse (to unite in coalition) || MED soldarse.

coalescence [-ns] *n* unión *f* (coalition) || fusión *f* (merger) || MED soldadura *f.*

coalfield ['kəulfi:ld] *n* yacimiento *m* de carbón (deposit) || mina *f* de carbón (mine) || cuenca *f* carbonífera (region).

coalheaver ['kəul,hi:və*] *n* carbonero *m.*

coalition [,kəuə'liʃən] *n* coalición *f.*

coalitionist [-ist] *n* coalicionista *m* & *f.*

coalman ['kəulmæn] *n* carbonero *m.*
— OBSERV El plural de esta palabra es *coalmen.*

coalming ['kəumiŋ] *n* MAR brazola *f.*

coalmouse ['kəulmaus] *n* paro *m* carbonero (bird).
— OBSERV El plural de esta palabra es *coalmice.*

coalpit ['kəulpit] *n* mina *f* de carbón.

coarse [kɔ:s] *adj* tosco, ca; basto, ta; burdo, da; *coarse stockings* medias bastas || basto, ta (badly made) || grosero, ra; basto, ta; *coarse person* persona basta; *coarse joke* chiste grosero || áspero, ra (hands, skin) || agudo, da; estridente (noise, voice) || de grano grueso (sugar) || grueso, sa (flour, sand, etc.) || — *coarse file* lima *f* de desbastar || *coarse grinding* esmerilado basto.

coarse fishing [-,fiʃiŋ] *n* pesca *f* de fondo.

coarse-grained [-greind] *adj* de grano grueso || FIG basto, ta; grosero, ra.

coarse-minded [-maindid] *adj* grosero, ra; basto, ta.

coarsen ['kɔ:sn] *vt* volver grosero, embrutecer (a person) || volverse basto (thing) || curtir (skin).
◆ *vi* volverse grosero, embrutecerse (person) || volver basto (things) || curtirse (skin).

coarseness [-is] *n* tosquedad *f,* basteza *f* (poor quality) || ordinariez *f,* grosería *f* (rudeness) || indecencia *f,* basteza *f,* grosería *f* (of a joke) || aspereza *f* (of hands, skin).

coast [kəust] *n* costa *f* (seashore) || costa *f,* litoral *m* (coastline) || deslizamiento *m* (freewheeling) || US cuesta *f,* pendiente *f* (slope) || FIG *the coast is clear* no hay moros en la costa (there is no one about), pasó el peligro (the danger has passed).

coast [kəust] *vt* MAR hacer cabotaje en (from port to port) | bordear la costa de, costear; *we coasted Spain* bordeamos la costa de España.
◆ *vi* MAR hacer cabotaje | bordear la costa, costear (to follow the coast) || deslizarse cuesta abajo [sin pedalear o sin motor] (to freewheel).

coastal [-əl] *adj* costero, ra; costanero, ra || *coastal trading* o *traffic* cabotaje *m.*

coaster [-ə*] *n* MAR barco *m* de cabotaje || tabla *f* para el queso (cheeseboard) || carrito *m* (for drinks) || montaña *f* rusa (big dipper) || US salvamantel *m* (mat).

coastguard [-gɑ:d] *n* MAR guardacostas *m inv* || *coastguard cutter* o *vessel* guardacostas.

coasting [-iŋ] *adj* MAR de cabotaje || *coasting trade* cabotaje *m.*

coastline [-lain] *n* litoral *m,* costa *f.*

coastwards [-wədz] *adv* hacia la costa.

coastwise [-waiz] *adv* a lo largo de la costa, bordeando la costa.

coat [kəut] *n* abrigo *m* (overcoat) || chaqueta *f,* americana *f* [AMER saco *m*] (man's jacket) || lana *f* (of sheep) || pelo *m* (of horse, dog, etc.) || MIL capote *m* || mano *f,* capa *f; a coat of paint* una mano de pintura || BOT binza *f,* tela *f* (of an onion) | piel *f* (of fruits) || ANAT membrana *f* || FIG capa *f,* manto *m* || — *coat armour,* US *coat armor* escudos *m pl* de armas || *coat hanger* percha *f* || *coat of arms* escudo *m* de armas || *coat of mail* cota *f* de malla || FIG *to cut one's coat according to one's cloth* vivir según las posibilidades de uno, gobernar su casa según su bolsa, saber adaptarse a las circunstancias | *to dust one's coat* sacudir el polvo a uno | *to turn one's coat* cambiar de camisa, chaquetear, volver (la) casaca || *to wear the king's coat* servir al rey (as a soldier) || *white coat* bata *f* (of a doctor, chemist, etc.).

coat [kəut] *vt* cubrir, revestir (*with* de) (to cover) || dar una mano *or* capa de pintura (with paint) || CULIN rebozar (meat, fish, etc.) | bañar (*with* en) (with a liquid) || ELECTR forrar.

coated [-id] *adj* cuché (paper) || MED sucio, cia; saburroso, sa (tongue).
◆ *pp* → **coat.**

coatee [kəuti] *n* chaquetilla *f* corta || MIL guerrera *f.*

coati [kəu'ɑ:ti] *n* ZOOL coatí *m.*

coating ['kəutiŋ] *n* capa *f,* mano *f* (of paint, etc.) || rebozado *m,* rebozo *m* (of meat, fish, etc.) || baño *m* (with a liquid) || paño *m* de abrigo (cloth).

coattail ['kəutteil] *n* faldón *m* (of a coat).

coauthor ['kəu'ɔ:θə*] *n* coautor, ra.

coax [kəuks] *vt* engatusar, persuadir con halagos (to persuade); *to coax s.o. into doing sth.* engatusar a alguien para que haga algo || lograr con paciencia (to obtain) || — *to coax s.o. along* engatusar a uno || *to coax sth. out of s.o.* sonsacarle algo a alguien halagándolo *or* engatusándolo.

coaxial ['kəu'æksjəl]; **coaxal** [kəu'æksəl] *adj* coaxial; *coaxial cable* cable coaxial.

coaxing ['kəuksiŋ] *adj* zalamero, ra; adulador, ra (flattering) || engatusador, ra (wheedling).
◆ *n* halagos *m pl,* zalamerías *f pl* (flattery) || engatusamiento *m* (wheedling).

cob [kɔb] *n* ZOOL cisne *m* (swan) | jaca *f* (horse) || avellana *f* (nut) || mazorca *f* (maize) || pan *m* redondo (loaf) || trozo *m* redondo de carbón (coal) || ARCH adobe *m.*

cobalt [kəubɔ:lt] *n* CHEM cobalto *m* || — *cobalt blue* azul *m* cobalto || *cobalt bomb* bomba *f* de cobalto.

cobble ['kɔbl] *n* adoquín *m* (square stone) || guijarro *m* (round stone).

cobble ['kɔbl] *vt* adoquinar (to pave with square stones) || empedrar con guijarros (with round stones) || remendar (to mend) || FAM *to cobble together* chapucear (to mend).

cobbler [-ə*] *n* zapatero *m,* zapatero *m* remendón (shoemender) || US tarta *f* de fruta | bebida *f* helada de vino, azúcar y limón.

cobblestone ['kɔblstəun] *n* adoquín *m* (square stone) || guijarro *m* (round stone).

cobnut ['kɔbnʌt] *n* BOT avellana *f.*

COBOL ['kəubɔl] *n* INFORM COBOL *m.*

COBOL *abbr of [Common Business-Oriented Language]* lenguaje COBOL.

cobra ['kəubrə] *n* ZOOL cobra *f* (snake).

cobweb ['kɔbweb] *n* telaraña *f* || FIG red *f,* tejido *m.*

coca ['kəukə] *n* BOT coca *f* || coca *f* (drink).

Coca-cola ['kəukə'kəulə] *n* Coca-cola *f,* coca *f.*

cocaine [kə'kein] *n* CHEM cocaína *f* || — *cocaine addict* cocainómano, na || *cocaine addiction* cocainomanía *f.*

coccus ['kɔkəs] *n* MED coco *m.*
— OBSERV El plural de *coccus* es *cocci.*

coccygeal [kɔk'sidʒiəl] *adj* coccígeo, a.

coccyx ['kɔksiks] *n* ANAT cóccix *m,* coxis *m.*
— OBSERV El plural de *coccyx* es *coccyges* o *coccyxes.*

Cochin-China ['kɔtʃin'tʃainə] *pr n* GEOGR Cochinchina *f.*

cochineal ['kɔtʃini:l] *n* cochinilla *f* (dye, insect).

cochlea ['kɔkliə] *n* ANAT caracol *m* óseo, cóclea *f.*
— OBSERV El plural de *cochlea* es *cochleae.*

cochlear [-*] *adj* coclear.

cock [kɔk] *n* gallo *m* (the male of the fowl) || macho *m* (male bird); *cock sparrow* gorrión macho || veleta *f* (weathercock) || aguja *f,* fiel *m* (of balance) || estilo *m* (of sundial) || grifo *m* (tap) || percutor *m* (of a gun) || inclinación *f* (tilting) || pico *m* (of a cocked hat) || montón *m* de heno (of hay) || POP polla *f* (male organ) || FAM amigo *m* (mate) || — *at full cock* amartillado, da (firearms) || *cock of the eye* guiñada *f,* mirada *f* || *cock of the rock* gallo de roca || FIG FAM *cock of the walk* gallito *m* del lugar || *cock of the wood* gallo de monte *or* silvestre, urogallo *m* || FIG *cock sparrow* gallito *m* || *fighting cock* gallo de pelea || FAM *old cock!* ¡viejales! || *the cock of his nose* su nariz respingona.

cock [kɔk] *vt* erguir, levantar; *the dog cocked its ears* el perro levantó las orejas || ladear (to tilt a hat) || montar, amartillar (a gun) || amontonar (hay) || — *to cock a snook* hacer burla con la mano || *to cock one's eye at* dirigir una mirada a (s.o.), echar un vistazo a (sth.) || FIG *to cock the ears* aguzar el oído || POP *to cock up sth.* hacer un lío de algo.
◆ *vi* erguirse, levantarse (to lift) || FIG gallear (to show off).

cockade [kɔ'keid] *n* escarapela *f.*

cock-a-doodle-doo ['kɔkədu:dl'du:] *n* quiquiriquí *m.*

cock-a-hoop ['kɔkə'hu:p] *adj* jubiloso, sa; rebosante de alegría || *to be cock-a-hoop* brillarle a uno los ojos de alegría.
◆ *adv* alegremente, jubilosamente.

Cockaigne [kɔ'kein] *n* tierra *f* de Jauja.

cock-a-leekie ['kɔkə'li:ki] *n* CULIN caldo *m* de pollo y puerros.

cock-and-bull story ['kɔkən'bul'stɔ:ri] *n* FAM cuento *m* chino, patraña *f,* camelo *m.*

cockatoo [,kɔkə'tu:] *n* ZOOL cacatúa *f* (parrot).

cockatrice ['kɔkətrais] *n* MYTH basilisco *m.*

cockboat ['kɔkbəut] *n* MAR bote *m*.

cockchafer ['kɔk,tʃeifə*] *n* ZOOL abejorro *m*.

cockcrow ['kɔkkrəu] *n* canto *m* del gallo || FIG amanecer *m*, alba *f* (dawn) || *at cockcrow* al amanecer, al cantar del gallo, al despuntar el alba.

cocked ['kɔkt] *adj cocked hat* sombrero de tres picos || FIG FAM *to knock into a cocked hat* dar *or* pegar una paliza (to beat completely), dar ciento y raya a (to be superior), destruir totalmente (to ruin).

cocker ['kɔkə*] *n* cocker *m* (dog) || gallero *m* (breeder of gamecocks) || *cocker spaniel* cocker *m*.

cockerel [-rəl] *n* ZOOL pollo *m*, gallo *m* joven.

cockeyed ['kɔkaid] *adj* FAM bizco, ca (cross-eyed) | torcido, da (awry) | disparatado, da (absurd) | trompa *inv* (drunk).

cockfight; **cockfighting** ['kɔkfait]; [-iŋ] *n* pelea *f* de gallos.

cockhorse ['kɔk'hɔ:s] *n* caballo *m* de juguete.
◆ *adv* a horcajadas (riding).

cockiness ['kɔkinis] *n* descaro *m*, caradura *f*, frescura *f* (cheek) || presunción *f*, engreimiento *m* (cocksureness).

cockish ['kɔkiʃ] *adj* FAM engreído, da.

cockle ['kɔkl] *n* ZOOL berberecho *m* | concha *f* de berberecho (shell) || BOT neguilla *f* || arruga *f* (wrinkle) || MAR cascarón *m* de nuez || estufa *f* (stove) || FIG *the cockles of the heart* las entretelas del corazón.

cockle ['kɔkl] *vt* arrugar.
◆ *vi* arrugarse.

cockleboat [-bəut] *n* MAR cascarón *m* de nuez.

cockleshell ['kɔklʃəl] *n* concha *f* de berberecho (shell) || cascarón *m* de nuez (small boat).

cockloft ['kɔklɔft] *n* desván *m* (garret).

cockney ['kɔkni] *n* lenguaje *m or* acento *m* característico de los barrios bajos de Londres || habitante *m* & *f* de los barrios bajos de Londres || londinense *m* que habla con acento chabacano.

cockpit ['kɔkpit] *n* AVIAT cabina *f* del piloto, carlinga *f* || MAR caseta *f* del timón || reñidero *m* [AMER cancha *f*] (for cockfights) || campo *m* de batalla (battleground) || FIG palestra *f*, arena *f*.

cockroach ['kɔkrəutʃ] *n* ZOOL cucaracha *f*.

cockscomb ['kɔkskəum] *n* cresta *f* de gallo.

cockshut ['kɔkʃʌt] *n* crepúsculo *m*.

cockspur ['kɔkspə:*] *n* ZOOL espolón *m*.

cocksure ['k'ɔkʃuə*] *adj* FAM engreído, da; presumido, da (self-confident) | completamente seguro, ra (absolutely sure).

cocktail ['kɔkteil] *n* cóctel *m*, cocktail *m* (drink, appetizer, etc.) || caballo *m* de raza cruzada y de cola recortada (horse) || — *cocktail cabinet* mueble bar || *cocktail dress* vestido *m* de cóctel || *m* || *cocktail party* cóctel *m*, cocktail *m* || *cocktail shaker* coctelera *f* || *cocktail snacks* tapas *f pl* || *cocktail stick* palillo *m* de cóctel.

cockup ['kɔkʌp] *n* PRINT inicial *f*.

cocky ['kɔki] *adj* FAM engreído, da; presumido, da (cocksure) | fresco, ca; descarado, da (pert).

coco ['kəukəu] *n* BOT coco *m* (fruit) | cocotero *m*, coco *m* (tree) || FAM chola *f* (head).

cocoa ['kəukəu] *n* cacao *m* (drink, powder) || — *cocoa bean* grano *m* de cacao || *cocoa butter* manteca *f* de cacao.

coconut; **cocoanut** ['kəukənʌt] *n* BOT coco *m* (fruit) || — BOT *coconut* o *cocoanut grove* cocotal *m* | *coconut* o *cocoanut palm* cocotero *m*, coco *m*.

cocoon [kə'ku:n] *n* capullo *m* (of silkworm, etc.).

cod [kɔd] *n* ZOOL bacalao *m* (fish).

coda ['kəudə] *n* MUS coda *f*.

coddle ['kɔdl] *vt* mimar (to pamper) || US cocer a fuego lento (to cook slowly).

code [kəud] *n* JUR código *m* || clave *f*, cifra *f* (system of signals) || FIG código *m* (of concepts) || — *area code, code number* prefijo *m* (telephone) || *code of honour* código del honor || *code of practice* código *m* deontológico || *code word* palabra *f* en clave || *highway code* código de la circulación || *Morse code* alfabeto *m* Morse.

code [kəud] *vt* cifrar, poner en clave || INFORM codificar.

codefendant ['kəudi'fendənt] *n* JUR coacusado, da.

codeine ['kəudi:n] *n* MED codeína *f*.

coder ['kəudə*] *n* INFORM codificador *m*.

codex ['kəudeks] *n* códice *m*.
— OBSERV El plural de *codex* es *codices*.

codfish ['kɔd,fiʃ] *n* ZOOL bacalao *m* (fish).

codger ['kɔdʒə*] *n* FAM vejete *m* (old man).

codicil ['kɔdisil] *n* codicilo *m*.

codification [,kɔdifi'keiʃən] *n* codificación *f*.

codifier [kɔdi'faiə*] *n* codificador, ra.

codify ['kɔdifai] *vt* JUR codificar || poner en clave (to code).

coding ['kəudiŋ] *n* INFORM codificación *f*.

codling ['kɔdliŋ] *n* bacalao *m* pequeño (fish).

cod-liver oil ['kɔdlivər'ɔil] *n* aceite *m* de hígado de bacalao.

co-driver ['kəu,draivə*] *n* copiloto *m*.

codswallop ['kɔdzwɔləp] *n* FAM tonterías *f pl*, paparruchas *f pl*.

co-ed; **coed** ['kəu'ed] *n* US FAM alumna *f* de un colegio mixto.

coeducation ['kəu,edju'keiʃən] *n* coeducación *f*, enseñanza *f* mixta.

coeducational [-l] *adj* coeducacional, mixto, ta.

coefficient [,kəui'fiʃənt] *n* coeficiente *m*.

coelacanth ['si:ləkænθ] *n* ZOOL celacanto *m*.

coelenterate [si:'lentəreit] *n* ZOOL celentéreo *m*.

coeliac; **celiac** ['si:liæk] *adj* ANAT celíaco, ca; celiaco, ca || MED *coeliac disease* celíaca *f*.

coendou [kəu'endu:] *n* ZOOL coendú *m*.

coenobite ['si:nəbait] *n* REL cenobita *m* & *f*.

coenobitic [,si:nə'bitik]; **coenobitical** [-əl] *adj* cenobítico, ca; cenobial.

coequal [kəu'i:kwəl] *adj/n* igual [a otro].

coerce [kəu'ə:s] *vt* JUR & PHYS coercer || forzar, obligar, coaccionar (*into* a) (to force).

coercible [kəu'ə:sibl] *adj* JUR & PHYS coercible.

coercion [kəu'əʃəm] *n* JUR & PHYS coerción *f* || coacción *f* (by force).

coercive [kəu'ə:siv] *adj* coactivo, va (compelling) || JUR & PHYS coercitivo, va.

coetaneous [,kəui:'teiniəs] *adj* coetáneo, a.

coeternal [,kəui:'tə:nl] *adj* coeterno, na.

coeval [kəu'i:vəl] *adj/n* coetáneo, a.

coexist ['kəuig'zist] *vi* coexistir, convivir.

coexistence [-əns] *n* coexistencia *f*, convivencia *f*.

coexistent ['kəuig'zistənt] *adj* coexistente.

coffee ['kɔfi] *n* café *m* (bean and drink); *black, white coffee* café solo, con leche || BOT café *m*, cafeto *m* (plant) || — *coffee bar* café *m* || *coffee bean* grano *m* de café || *coffee break* descanso *m* para tomar café || *coffee cup* taza *f* de café || *coffee grounds* poso *m sing*, zurrapa *f sing* || *coffee grower* o *planter* cafetalero *m*, cafetero *m* || *coffee mill* molinillo *m* de café || *coffee plantation* plantación *f* de café, cafetal *m* || *coffee roaster* tostador *m* de café || *coffee shop* café *m* || *coffee spoon* cucharilla *f* de café || *coffee table* mesita *f* baja || *coffee tree* cafeto *m* || *roasted coffee* café torrefacto.
◆ *adj* cafetalero, ra; cafetero, ra; de café; *coffee production* producción cafetalera || color café, de color café (coffee-coloured); *a coffee dress* un traje color café.

coffeehouse [-haus] *n* café *m*.

coffee morning [-,mɔ:niŋ] *n* reunión *f* benéfica que tiene lugar por la mañana.

coffeepot [-pɔt] *n* cafetera *f*.

coffeeroom [-rum] *n* café *m*.

coffee-table book [-teiblbuk] *n* libro *m* lujoso, ilustrado, para adornar.

coffer ['kɔfə*] *n* caja *f*, arca *f* (for storing money) || ARCH artesón *m*.
◆ *pl* fondos *m* (funds).

coffer ['kɔfə*] *vt* ARCH artesonar || atesorar (money).

cofferdam [-dæm] *n* ataguía *f* (dam) || MAR compartimiento *m* estanco.

coffin ['kɔfin] *n* ataúd *m*, féretro *m* (for funerals) || cavidad *f* del casco (of hoof) || PRINT carro *m* (of a machine) || — *coffin bone* bolillo *m* (of horse) || FAM *coffin nail* pitillo *m* (cigarette).

cog [kɔg] *n* TECH diente *m* (of wheel, gear) | rueda *f* dentada (wheel) | espiga *f* (in carpentry) || FIG eslabón *m*, pieza *f* (person); *a cog in the machine* pequeña pieza del engranaje.

cog [kɔg] *vt* hacer trampas con (to cheat) || cargar (a die) || TECH endentar, poner dientes a | ensamblar con espigas (in carpentry).
◆ *vi* TECH engranarse || hacer trampa.

cogency ['kəudʒənsi] *n* fuerza *f*, poder *m* (of an argument) || JUR lo bien fundado, legitimidad *f*.

cogent ['kəudʒənt] *adj* fuerte, convincente, poderoso, sa.

cogged ['kɔgd] *adj* TECH dentado, da (wheel) || cargado, da; falso, sa (dice).

cogitable ['kɔdʒi'təbl] *adj* concebible.

cogitate ['kɔdʒiteit] *vt/vi* reflexionar, meditar, cavilar, cogitar.

cogitation [,kɔdʒi'teiʃən] *n* reflexión *f*, meditación *f*, cogitación *f*.

cognac ['kɔnjæk] *n* coñac *m* (brandy).

cognate ['kɔgneit] *adj* JUR cognado, da || GRAMM afín || similar (alike).
◆ *n* JUR cognado *m* || GRAMM palabra *f* afín.

cognation [kɔg'neiʃən] *n* JUR cognación *f*.

cognition [kɔg'niʃən] *n* percepción *f* || PHIL cognición *f*.

cognitive ['kɔgnitiv] *adj* PHIL cognoscitivo, va.

cognizable ['kɔgnizəbl] *adj* cognoscible || JUR enjuiciable.

cognizance ['kɔgnizəns] *n* conocimiento *m* (knowledge) || JUR competencia *f*, incumbencia *f* || HERALD emblema *m* || — *beyond one's cognizance* fuera de la competencia de uno || *to have cognizance of* tener conocimiento de || *to take cognizance of* tener en cuenta || *within my cognizance* de mi incumbencia, de mi competencia.

cognizant ['kɔgnizɔnt] *adj* conocedor, ra; sabedor, ra || JUR competente (*of* para) || *to be cognizant of* saber.

cognize [kɔg'naiz] *vt* conocer.

cognomen [kɔg'nəumen] *n* cognomen *m* (in ancient Rome) || apodo *m* (nickname) || apellido *m* (surname).

— OBSERV El plural de *cognomen* es *cognomens* o *cognomina*.

cognoscible [kɔg'nɔsibl] *adj* cognoscible.

cogwheel ['kɔgwi:l] *n* rueda *f* dentada.

cohabit [kəu'hæbit] *vi* cohabitar, vivir juntos.

cohabitation [,kəuhæbi'teiʃən] *n* cohabitación *f*.

coheir ['kəu'εə*] *n* coheredero *m*.

coheiress ['kəu'εəris] *n* coheredera *f*.

cohere [kəu'hiə*] *vi* adherirse, pegarse (to stick together) || FIG ser coherente (style, planning, etc.).

coherence [kəu'hiərəns]; **coherency** [-i] *n* coherencia *f*, adherencia *f*, cohesión *f* || FIG coherencia *f*.

coherent [kəu'hiərənt] *adj* coherente.

coherer [kəu'hiərə*] *n* RAD cohesor *m*.

cohesion [kəu'hi:ʒən] *n* cohesión *f*.

cohesive [kəu'hi:siv] *adj* cohesivo, va.

cohesiveness [-nis] *n* cohesión *f*.

cohibit [kəu'hibit] *vt* cohibir.

cohort ['kəuhɔ:t] *n* cohorte *f*.

coif [kɔif] *n* cofia *f* (cap) || JUR birrete *m* || MIL cofia *f* || BOT cofia *f*.

coiffure [kwɑ:'fjuə] *n* peinado *m*.

coign [kɔin] *n* pico *m*, parte *f* saliente || *coign of vantage* posición ventajosa.

coil [kɔil] *n* rizo *m* (of hair) || rollo *m* (of rope) || MAR aduja *f* || ELECTR carrete *m*, bobina *f* (in electromagnetics) || anillo *m* (of snake) || espiral *f* (of smoke) || vuelta *f* (a single turn) || serpentín *m* (of pipe) || *coil spring* muelle *m* en espiral.

coil [kɔil] *vt* enrollar, arrollar || MAR adujar || ELECTR embobinar, enrollar.
◆ *vi* enrollarse, arrollarse (to wind itself up) || enroscarse (a snake) || serpentear (a river, etc.) || *to coil up* hacerse un ovillo.

coin [kɔin] *n* moneda *f* || — FIG *to pay s.o. in his* o *her own coin* pagar a alguien con la misma moneda || *to toss a coin* echar una moneda al aire, echar a cara o cruz.

coin [kɔin] *vt* acuñar (coins) || FIG inventar (tales) | acuñar, inventar, crear (words, expressions) || FIG & FAM amasar, amontonar (money) || — FAM *to coin a phrase* para ser original (ironically) || FIG *to coin money* amasar una fortuna.

coinage ['kɔinidʒ] *n* acuñación *f* (making of coins) || moneda *f* (money) || sistema *m* monetario (monetary system) || FIG invención *f* (of tales, words, sentences, etc.).

coin-box ['kɔinbɔks] *n* teléfono *m* público (automático) de monedas.

coincide [,kənin'said] *vi* coincidir.

coincidence [kəu'insidəns] *n* coincidencia *f* || casualidad *f* (chance).

coincident [kəu'insidənt] *adj* coincidente.

coincidental [kəu,insi'dentl] *adj* coincidente (coinciding) || casual (chance).

coiner [kɔinə*] *n* acuñador *m* (who makes coins) || falsificador *m* de moneda (counterfeiter) || FIG inventor, ra; creador, ra (of words, etc.).

coin-operated ['kɔin,ɔpəreitid] *adj* que funciona con monedas.

coir ['kɔiə*] *n* bonote *m*, fibra *f* de coco.

coition [kəu'iʃən]; **coitus** ['kəuitəs] *n* coito *m*.

coke [kəuk] *n* cok *m*, coque *m* (coal) || FAM Coca *f* (Coca-cola) | cocaína *f* (cocaine).

coke [kəuk] *vt* convertir en cok, coquizar, coquificar.
◆ *vi* convertirse en cok.

cokernut ['kəukənʌt] *n* coco *m* (coconut).

cola ['kəulə] *n* BOT cola *f*.

colander ['kʌləndə*] *n* colador *m*.

colander ['kʌləndə*] *vt* colar.

colchicum ['kɔltʃikəm] *n* BOT cólquico *m*.

Colchis ['kɔlkis] *pr n* GEOGR Cólquida *f*.

colcothar ['kɔlkəθɑ:*] *n* colcótar *m*.

cold [kəuld] *adj* frío, a; *a cold day* un día frío; *a cold meal* una comida fría || frigorífico, ca (room, store) || FAM frío, a; muerto, ta (dead) || FIG frío, a; indiferente (without enthusiasm) | frío, a (frigid) | frío, a; poco amistoso, sa; *a cold reception* un recibimiento frío | frío, a; desapasionado, da; objetivo, va (calm, objective) | deprimente (dispiriting) | frío, a (far from the thing sought) | viejo, ja (news) | sin conocimiento, inconsciente, fuera de combate; *to knock s.o. cold* dejar a alguien fuera de combate || ARTS frío, a (colours) || SP débil, vago, ga (scent) || — *as cold as ice* más frío que el hielo, helado, da || *cold chisel* cortafrío *m* || *cold comfort* poco consuelo || *cold cream* «cold cream» *m*, crema *f* para el cutis || *cold cuts* fiambres variados || FAM *cold feet* mieditis *f* | *cold fish* persona pesada || *cold forging* forjado en frío || *cold frame* cajonera *f* (for plants) || *cold front* frente frío (in meteorology) || *cold meat* fiambres *m pl* (food), fiambre *m* (corpse) || *cold pack* compresa fría || *cold riveting* remachado en frío || FAM *cold shoulder* frialdad *f* || *cold snap* ola *f* de frío || *cold sore* herpes *m* labial || *cold spell* ola *f* de frío || *cold steel* arma blanca || *cold storage* conservación *f* en cámara frigorífica || *cold sweat* sudor frío || FIG *cold war* guerra fría || *cold wave* ola *f* de frío || FIG *in cold blood* a sangre fría || *it's bitterly cold* hace un frío que pela *or* un frío de perros || *to be cold* hacer frío (weather); *it's very cold today* hoy hace mucho frío; tener frío (persons), estar frío (things) || *to be very cold* hacer mucho frío (weather), tener mucho frío (persons), estar muy frío (things) || *to get cold* enfriarse (things), refrescar, empezar a hacer frío (weather) || FIG & FAM *to give s.o. the cold shoulder* tratar a alguien con frialdad | *to have* o *get cold feet* estar *or* ponerse nervioso, tener *or* coger mieditis || FIG *to have s.o. cold* tener a alguien en el bolsillo | *to leave s.o. cold* dejar a uno frío | *to make s.o.'s blood run cold* hacer que a alguien se le hiele la sangre | *to put into cold storage* echar en el olvido, dejar en suspenso.
◆ *adv* de repente, en seco (suddenly) || de plano, llanamente (plainly) || perfectamente (perfectly).
◆ *n* frío *m* (low temperature) || MED constipado *m*, resfriado *m*, catarro *m* || — *to catch cold* coger frío || MED *to catch a cold* resfriarse, acatarrarse, coger un resfriado | *to have a cold* estar constipado *or* resfriado *or* acatarrado || FIG *to leave s.o. out in the cold* dejar a alguien al margen *or* en la estacada.

cold-blooded ['kəuld'blʌdid] *adj* FIG insensible (insensitive) | cruel, despiadado, da (callous) || ZOOL de sangre fría.

cold-bloodedness [-nis] *n* sangre *f* fría.

cold-draw* ['kəuld,drɔ:] *vt* estirar en frío.
— OBSERV Pret ***cold-drew***; pp ***cold-drawn***.

cold-drawn [-n] *pp* → **cold-draw.**

cold-drew ['kəuld,dru:] *pret* → **cold-draw.**

coldhearted ['kəuld'hɑ:tid] *adj* insensible, frío de corazón.

coldish ['kəuldiʃ] *adj* fresquito, ta.

coldness ['kəuldnis] *n* frialdad *f* || frío *m*, temperatura *f* fría (cold) || FIG frialdad *f*.

cold-press ['kəuld'pres] *vt* prensar en frío.

cold-setting ['kəuld'setiŋ] *n* fraguado *m* en frío.

cold-short ['kəuld'ʃɔ:t] *adj* quebradizo, za (metal).

cold-shoulder ['kəuld'ʃəuldə*] *vt* tratar con frialdad (to treat with coldness) || volver la espalda a (to rebuff).

cole [kəul] *n* BOT colza *f* (rape).

colegatee [kəulegə'ti:] *n* colegatario, ria.

coleopteron [,kɔli'ɔptərən] *n* ZOOL coleóptero *m*.
— OBSERV El plural de *coleopteron* es *coleoptera*.

coleslaw ['kəulslɔ:] *n* ensalada *f* de col.

colewort ['kəulwə:t] *n* BOT col *f*.

colic ['kɔlik] *n* MED cólico *m*; *hepatic, nephritic colic* cólico hepático, nefrítico || MED *lead* o *painter's colic* cólico saturnino.
◆ *adj* cólico, ca.

colicky [-i] *adj* que tiene *or* causa cólico.

Coliseum [,kɔli'siəm] *pr n* Coliseo *m*.

colitis [kɔ'laitis] *n* MED colitis *f*.

collaborate [kə'læbəreit] *vi* colaborar.

collaboration [kə,læbə'reiʃən] *n* colaboración *f* || colaboracionismo *m* (in politics).

collaborator [kə'læbəreitə*] *n* colaborador, ra (in a work, etc.) || colaboracionista *m* & *f* (in politics).

collage [kɔ'lɑ:ʒ] *n* ARTS collage *m*.

collapse [kə'læps] *n* derrumbamiento *m*, desplome *m* (a falling down) || MED colapso *m* || FIG fracaso *m* (failure) | ruina *f* (financial ruin) | hundimiento *m*, derrumbamiento *m* (of business, government) | caída *f* vertical (of prices) || TECH pandeo *m* (of a beam).

collapse [kə'læps] *vt* derrumbar, echar abajo (to cause to collapse) || plegar; *to collapse a tent* plegar una tienda de campaña.
◆ *vi* derrumbarse, desplomarse, caerse (to fall down) || desinflarse (balloon) || MED tener *or* sufrir un colapso || plegarse (to fold) || FIG fracasar (to fail) | arruinarse (to go bankrupt) | derrumbarse, hundirse, venirse abajo (a business, a government) | bajar verticalmente (prices) || TECH pandearse (beam) | alabearse (wheel).

collapsible [-əbl] *adj* plegable.

collar ['kɔlə*] *n* cuello (of a shirt, dress, etc.) || collar *m* (of animals) || collera *f* (of a harness) || TECH collarín *m*, abrazadera *f* || collar *m* (of an order) || CULIN carne *f* atada para guisar || BOT cuello *m* || — ARCH *collar beam* falso tirante || *stiff collar* cuello duro || FAM *to get hot under the collar* acalorarse (to get angry).

collar ['kɔlə*] *vt* agarrar *or* coger por el cuello (to seize) || acollarar, poner collar a (to put a collar on) || FIG coger, capturar (to capture) || FAM acorralar (to stop and talk to) | mangar (to appropriate) || CULIN atar (fish, meat) || TECH poner abrazadera a.

collarbone ['kɔləbəun] *n* ANAT clavícula *f*.

collaret; collarette [,kɔlə'ret] *n* cuello *m* de encaje.

collate [kɔ'leit] *n* confrontar, cotejar (to compare) || ordenar (pages, illustrations) || verificar, comprobar (to verify) || REL colacionar, conferir (an ecclesiastical benefice) || JUR colacionar.

collateral [kɔ'lætərəl] *adj* paralelo, la; *collateral arguments* argumentos paralelos || colateral (accompanying, secondary) || JUR auxiliar, adicional || COMM subsidiario, ria; *collateral security* garantía subsidiaria || colateral (a relative).
◆ *n* colateral *m* & *f* (relative) || COMM garantía *f* subsidiaria.

collation [kɔ'leiʃən] *n* cotejo *m*, comparación *f*, confrontación *f* (of texts) || REL colación *f* (of a benefice) || (ant) colación *f* (snack) || JUR *collation of property* colación de bienes.

collator [kɔ'leitə*] *n* REL colador *m*.

colleague ['kɔli:g] *n* colega *m* & *f*.

collect [kə'lekt] *adj/adv* US a cobro revertido (telephone call, telegram, etc.).

collect ['kɔləkt] *n* REL colecta *f*.

collect [kə'lekt] *vt* coleccionar (to gather as a hobby) ‖ reunir, juntar (to gather together) ‖ reunir (to gather people together) ‖ recaudar (taxes, money for charity) ‖ allegar (funds) ‖ cobrar (rents, bills, etc.) ‖ recoger (to gather in, to pick up); *the teacher collected the examination papers* el profesor recogió los exámenes; *I'm going to collect my skirt from the cleaners* voy a recoger la falda a la tintorería ‖ amontonar (wealth) ‖ poner en orden (one's thoughts) ‖ inferir, deducir (to deduce) ‖ — *to collect o.s.* recobrar el dominio de sí mismo ‖ *to collect up* recoger (to pick up).
◆ *vi* congregarse, reunirse (people) ‖ acumularse, amontonarse (things) ‖ cobrar (rent, bill, etc.) ‖ REL hacer una colecta (to take up a collection) ‖ ser coleccionista (to be a collector) ‖ *to collect on delivery* contra reembolso (cash on delivery).

collectable [-əbl] *adj* cobrable.

collected [kə'lektid] *adj* FIG sosegado, da (calm) | recogido, da (pensive) ‖ —> **collect** ‖ — *collected short stories* colección *f* de novelas cortas ‖ *collected works* obras completas.

collection [kə'lekʃən] *n* colección *f* (pictures, fashion, stamps, models, etc.) ‖ colecta *f*, cuestación *f* (money for charity) ‖ grupo *m*, reunión *f* (of people) ‖ reunión *f* (of things) ‖ montón *m* (mass) ‖ cobro *m* (of rent, bill, etc.) ‖ recaudación *f* (of taxes) ‖ recogida *f* (of post, eggs) ‖ REL colecta *f* (in church).
◆ *pl* examen *m sing* final.

collective [kə'lektiv] *adj* colectivo, va ‖ — *collective agreement* convenio colectivo ‖ *collective bargaining* negociaciones colectivas, contrato colectivo ‖ *collective farm* granja colectiva ‖ GRAMM *collective noun* nombre *or* sustantivo colectivo, colectivo *m* ‖ *collective security* garantía colectiva.
◆ *n* colectividad *f*.
— OBSERV Los nombres colectivos van seguidos de un verbo en singular cuando predomina el concepto de unidad y de un verbo en plural cuando prevalece el concepto de pluralidad: *is the family at home?* ¿está la familia en casa?; *the family were stricken with grief* todos los miembros de la familia se afligieron.

collectivism [-izəm] *n* colectivismo *m*.

collectivist [-ist] *adj/n* colectivista.

collectivity [,kəlek'tiviti] *n* colectividad *f*.

collectivization [kə,lektivi'zeiʃən] *n* colectivización *f*.

collectivize [kə'lektivaiz] *vt* colectivizar.

collector [kə'lektə*] *n* recaudador, ra (of taxes) ‖ empleado *m* que recoge los billetes (of tickets) ‖ cobrador *m* (of rents, bills, etc.) ‖ coleccionista *m* & *f* (of stamps, coins, etc.) ‖ TECH colector *m*.

college ['kɔlidʒ] *n* colegio *m*; *the college of barristers, doctors* el colegio de abogados, de médicos; *Eton college* colegio de Eton ‖ colegio *m* mayor (as in Oxford, Cambridge, etc.) ‖ facultad *f* (part of the university) ‖ escuela *f* (technical) ‖ MUS conservatorio *m* ‖ US universidad *f* autónoma ‖ — *College of Cardinals, Sacred College* colegio de cardenales *or* cardenalicio ‖ *electoral college* colegio electoral.

collegial [kə'li:dʒjəl] *adj* colegial ‖ US universitario, ria.

collegian [kə'li:dʒjən] *n* estudiante *m* & *f* (at university) ‖ colegiado, da (of a college of doctors, etc.).

collegiate [kə'li:dʒiit] *adj* colegiado, da; *collegiate member* miembro colegiado ‖ colegial (relating to a college) ‖ superior (school) ‖ US universitario, ria ‖ *collegiate church* colegiata *f*, iglesia *f* colegial, colegial *f*.

collet ['kɔlit] *n* TECH collar *m* ‖ engaste *m* (for gems).

collide [kə'laid] *vi* chocar (*with* con, contra) ‖ FIG chocar, estar en conflicto.

collie ['kɔli] *n* perro *m* pastor escocés.

collier ['kɔliə*] *n* minero *m* (coal miner) ‖ MAR barco *m* carbonero.

colliery ['kɔljəri] *n* mina *f* de carbón.

colligate ['kɔligeit] *vt* relacionar (to relate) ‖ unir (to bind).

collimation [,kɔli'meiʃən] *n* PHYS colimación *f*.

collimator ['kɔlimeitə*] *n* PHYS colimador *m*.

collision [kə'liʒən] *n* colisión *f*, choque *m*; *there was a collision between a bus and a lorry* hubo un choque entre un autobús y un camión ‖ FIG choque *m*, conflicto *m* (of ideas).

collocate ['kɔləkəit] *vt* colocar, ordenar, disponer.

collocation [,kɔlə'keiʃən] *n* colocación *f*, ordenación *f*, disposición *f*.

collodion [kə'ləudjən] *n* CHEM colodión *m*.

collogue [kɔ'ləug] *vi* tener una entrevista privada.

colloid ['kɔlɔid] *adj* CHEM coloide.
◆ *n* CHEM coloide *m*.

colloidal [kɔ'lɔidəl] *adj* CHEM coloidal.

collop ['kɔləp] *n* filete *m* (slice of meat).

colloquial [kə'ləukwiəl] *adj* familiar.

colloquialism [-izəm] *n* expresión *f* familiar ‖ lengua *f* familiar.

colloquist ['kɔləkwist] *n* participante *m* & *f* en un coloquio, interlocutor, ra.

colloquy ['kɔləkwi] *n* coloquio *m*.

collude [kə'lu:d] *vi* estar de connivencia.

collusion [kə'lu:ʒən] *n* JUR colusión *f* ‖ *to enter into collusion with* estar de connivencia con.

collusive [kə'lu:siv] *adj* JUR colusorio, ria.

collyrium [kɔ'liriəm] *n* MED colirio *m*.
— OBSERV El plural es *collyria* o *collyriums*.

collywobbles ['kɔli,wɔblz] *pl n* FAM ruidos *m* de tripas, borborigmos *m* ‖ FAM *it gives me the collywobbles* me pone los pelos de punta.

Cologne [kə'ləun] *pr n* GEOGR Colonia *f*.

Colombia [kə'lɔmbiə] *pr n* GEOGR Colombia *f*.

Colombian [-n] *adj/n* colombiano, na.

Colombo [kə'lʌmbəu] *pr n* GEOGR Colombo.

colon ['kəulən] *n* ANAT colon *m* ‖ PRINT dos puntos (:).

colón [kɔ'lɔn] *n* colón *m* (Costa Rican money).

colonel ['kə:nl] *n* MIL coronel *m*.

colonial [kə'ləunjəl] *adj* colonial; *colonial period* época colonial ‖ colonizador, ra (power).
◆ *n* colono *m* (inhabitant of a colony).

colonialism [-izəm] *n* colonialismo *m*.

colonialist [-ist] *adj/n* colonialista.

colonist ['kɔlənist] *n* colonizador, ra (person who colonizes) ‖ colono *m* (inhabitant of a colony).

colonization [,kɔlənai'zeiʃən] *n* colonización *f*.

colonize ['kɔlənaiz] *vt* colonizar.
◆ *vi* establecer una colonia (to found a colony) ‖ establecerse en una colonia (to settle in a colony).

colonizer [-ə*] *n* colonizador, ra.

colonnade [,kɔlə'neid] *n* ARCH columnata *f*.

colony ['kɔləni] *n* colonia *f*.

colophon ['kɔləfən] *n* colofón *m*.

colophony ['kɔlə,fəuni] *n* CHEM colofonía *f*.

color ['kʌlə*] *n* US —> **colour.**

color ['kʌlə*] *vt/vi* US —> **colour.**

colorable ['kʌlərəbl] *n* US —> **colourable.**

Colorado [,kɔlə'rɑ:dəu] *pr n* GEOGR Colorado *m* ‖ ZOOL *Colorado beetle* escarabajo *m* de la patata.

colorant ['kʌlərənt] *n* US colorante *m*.

coloration [,kʌlə'reiʃən] *n* US coloración *f* | colorido *m*.

color-bearer ['kʌlə,bɛərə*] *n* US MIL abanderado *m*.

color-blind ['kʌləblaind] *adj* US daltoniano, na.

color-blindness [-nis] *n* US daltonismo *m*.

colorcast ['kʌləkɑ:st] *n* US televisión *f* en color.

colorcast ['kʌləkɑ:st] *vt/vi* US televisar en color.

colored ['kʌləd] *adj* US —> **coloured.**

colorful ['kʌləful] *adj* US —> **colourful.**

colorimeter [,kʌlə'rimitə*] *n* colorímetro *m*.

coloring ['kʌləriŋ] *n* US —> **colouring.**

colorist ['kʌlərist] *n* US colorista *m* & *f*.

colorless ['kʌləlis] *adj* US —> **colourless.**

colossal [kə'lɔsl] *adj* colosal (huge).

Colossians [kɔ'lɔʃənz] *pl n* REL colosenses *m*; *Epistle to the Colossians* Epístola a los colosenses.

colossus [kə'lɔsəs] *n* coloso *m* ‖ *the Colossus of Rhodes* el Coloso de Rodas.
— OBSERV El plural de *colossus* es *colossi* o *colossuses*.

colostrum [kə'lɔstrəm] *n* calostro *m*, colostro *m*.

colour; US **color** ['kʌlə*] *n* color *m*; *this dress is a nice colour* este vestido tiene un color bonito; *complementary colours* colores complementarios; *what colour is it?* ¿de qué color es? ‖ color *m*, tez *f* (complexion) ‖ color *m*, tinte *m* (dye) ‖ color *m* (racial complexion); *a man of colour* un hombre de color ‖ ARTS colorido *m*, tonos *m pl* (effect of colours) ‖ MUS calidad *f* de tono ‖ ambiente *m*, color *m* (in literature); *local colour* color local ‖ color *m*, opinión *f*, tendencia *f* (of a newspaper) ‖ PRINT color *m* ‖ — *colour bar* barrera *f* racial ‖ *colour box* caja *f* de pinturas ‖ US *colour line* barrera *f* racial ‖ *colour photography* fotocromía *f*, fotografía *f* en colores ‖ INFORM *colour monitor* monitor *m* en color ‖ PRINT *colour printing* cromolitografía *f* ‖ *colour scheme* combinación *f* de colores ‖ *colour television* televisión *f* en color ‖ *fast colour* color sólido ‖ *high colour* color subido ‖ *in colour* en colores ‖ *in full colour* a todo color ‖ FAM *let's see the colour of your money!* ¡a ver la pasta! ‖ *off colour* descolorido, da (colourless), indispuesto, ta (sick), verde (joke) ‖ *that skirt is green in colour* esa falda es de color verde ‖ FIG *to change colour* mudar de color ‖ FIG *to lend* o *to give colour to sth.* dar una apariencia de verdad a algo, hacer que algo parezca verosímil ‖ *to lose colour* palidecer ‖ FIG *to take all the colour out of sth.* quitarle toda la gracia a algo | *under colour of* con el pretexto de, so pretexto de, so color de.
◆ *pl* MIL ceremonia *f sing* de izar *or* de arriar la bandera ‖ MAR pabellón *m sing*, colores *m* (flag) ‖ MIL colores *m*, bandera *f sing* ‖ distintivo *m sing*, colores *m* (of athletic team) ‖ — MIL *to call to the colours* llamar a filas ‖ *to come through with flying colours* salir airoso ‖ MIL *to hoist the colours* izar la bandera | *to join the colours* alistarse en el ejército ‖ FIG *to nail one's colours to the mast* mantenerse firme | *to paint in dark colours* pintar con negros colores | *to put false*

colours upon presentar bajo un falso color || MIL *to serve with the colours* servir en el ejército || FIG *to show one's true colours* quitarse la máscara | *to stick to one's colours* mantenerse fiel a sus principios || MIL *with flying colours* con banderas desplegadas || MIL *with the colours* en filas.

colour; *US* **color** ['kʌlə*] *vt* colorear, colorar (to impart colour to) || teñir (to dye) || pintar (to paint) || FIG adornar, embellecer, colorear, amenizar (a description, report, one's style) | alterar, desvirtuar (feelings, opinions, views) || FAM curar, quemar, ennegrecer (a pipe).
◆ *vi* colorearse || cambiar de color || sonrojarse, ruborizarse, ponerse colorado (to blush).

colourable; *US* **colorable** [-rəbl] *adj* verosímil (plausible) || engañoso, sa (deceptive) || JUR *colourable imitation* imitación fraudulenta.

colourant [-rənt] *n* colorante *m*.

colouration ['kʌlə'reiʃən] *n* coloración *f* || colorido *m* (colour).

colour-bearer ['kʌlə,bεərə*] *n* MIL abanderado *m*.

colour-blind ['kʌləblaind] *adj* daltoniano, na.

colour-blindness [-nis] *n* daltonismo *m*.

coloured; *US* **colored** ['kʌləd] *adj* de color, coloreado, da (having colour) || de color (of race) || FIG tendencioso, sa (biased) || FIG *highly coloured narrative* relato lleno de colorido.

colourful; *US* **colorful** ['kʌləful] *adj* lleno de color (full of colour) || animado, da (lively, interesting) || pintoresco, ca (person, character).

colouring; *US* **coloring** ['kʌləriŋ] *n* coloración *f* || color *m*, colorido *m* (colour) || ARTS colorido *m* || colorido *m* (of skin) || colorante *m* (colouring matter) || FIG alteración *f* (of facts) | apariencia *f* (aspect) || *colouring book* libro *m* para colorear.
◆ *adj* colorante.

colourist ['kʌlərist] *n* colorista *m* & *f*.

colourless; *US* **colorless** ['kʌləlis] *adj* incoloro, ra; sin color (without colour) || descolorido, da; sin color (having lost its colour) || FIG soso, sa (dull).

colt [kəult] *n* ZOOL potro *m* (young horse) || FIG joven *m* inexperto, pipiolo *m*, novato *m* (young and inexperienced person) | juvenil *m* (young cricketer) || MIL colt *m* (revolver) || MAR azote *m*.

colter [-ə*] *n* US cuchilla *f* [del arado].

coltish [-iʃ] *adj* FIG novato, ta; inexperto, ta (young) | juguetón, ona (frisky).

coltsfoot [-sfut] *n* BOT tusilago *m*.
— OBSERV El plural de *coltsfoot* es *coltsfoots*.

columbarium [,kɔləm'bεəriəm] *n* columbario *m* || palomar *m* (dovecot).
— OBSERV El plural de *columbarium* es *columbaria*.

Columbia [kə'lʌmbiə] *pr n* GEOGR Columbia *f*, Colombia *f*; *British Columbia* Colombia Británica.

Columbian [-n] *adj* colombino, na.

columbine ['kɔləmbain] *n* BOT aguileña *f*.
◆ *adj* columbino, na.

Columbus [kə'lʌmbəs] *pr n* Colón || — *Christopher Columbus* Cristóbal Colón || *Columbus Day* día *f* de la Raza *or* de la Hispanidad.

column ['kɔləm] *n* ARCH columna *f*; *Corinthian column* columna corintia || columna *f* (of a newspaper, book) || MIL columna *f*; *in columns of three* en columnas de a tres || — FIG *fifth column* quinta columna || TECH *fractionating column* columna de fraccionamiento || ARCH *rostral column* columna rostrada *or* rostral || ANAT *spinal column* columna vertebral || AUT *steering column* columna de dirección.

columnar [kə'lʌmnə*] *adj* de forma de columna.

columnist ['kɔləmnist] *n* US columnista *m* & *f*, periodista *m* & *f* (journalist).

colza ['kɔlzə] *n* BOT colza *f*.

coma ['kəumə] *n* MED coma *m* || ASTR cabellera *f* (of a Comet); *coma Berenices* Cabellera de Berenice || BOT coma *f* (of leaves or hairs) || coma *f* (imperfection in lens) || MED *in a coma* en estado comatoso.
— OBSERV El plural de la palabra inglesa *coma* es *comae*.

Comanche [kə'mæntʃi] *adj/n* comanche (Indian).

comate ['kɔmeit] *adj* cabelludo, da.
◆ *n* compañero, ra.

comatose ['kəumətəus] *adj* MED comatoso, sa.

comb [kəum] *n* peine *m* || peineta *f* (ornamental) || TECH carda *f* (for wool) || almohaza *f* (currycomb) || cresta *f* (crest of a bird, wave of mountain) || panal *m* (honeycomb) || MIL cimera *f* (of helmet) || ELECTR escobilla *f* || — FAM *to cut s.o.'s comb* bajarle los humos a alguien || *to give one's hair a comb* peinarse.

comb [kəum] *vt* peinar (to arrange hair) || cardar (wool) || almohazar (a horse) || registrar a fondo (to search) || — *to comb one's hair* peinarse || *to comb out* limpiar (to clean out), desenmarañar (hair).
◆ *vi* romperse, romper (the waves).

combat ['kɔbət] *n* combate *m* || — *combat mission, post, zone* misión, puesto, zona de combate || US MIL *combat team* equipo *m* de combate.

combat ['kɔmbət] *vt* combatir, luchar contra.
◆ *vi* combatir, luchar.

combatant ['kɔmbətənt] *adj/n* combatiente.

combative ['kɔbətiv] *adj* combativo, va.

combe [ku:m] *n* valle *m* estrecho.

comber ['kəumə*] *n* cardador, ra (person who combs wool) || TECH máquina *f* cardadora || ola *f* grande y encrespada (wave).

combination [,kɔmbi'neiʃən] *n* combinación *f* (act of combining) | asociación *f* (of persons) || combinación *f* (underwear) || MATH & CHEM combinación *f* || FIG cúmulo *m*, conjunto *m* (of circumstances) || *combination lock* cerradura *f* de combinación.

combinatorial [,kɔmbinə'tɔrjəl] *adj* MATH combinatorio, ria; *combinatorial analysis* análisis combinatorio.

combine ['kɔmbain] *n* asociación *f* (of people) || COMM cártel *m* || AGR segadora trilladora *f*, cosechadora *f* || — *combine harvester* cosechadora *f*, segadora trilladora *f* || COMM *horizontal combine* consorcio *m*.

combine ['kɔm'bain] *vt* unir, fusionar; *he has combined his business with his brother's* ha unido su negocio con el de su hermano || combinar; *he combined business with pleasure* combinó el negocio con la diversión || CHEM combinar.
◆ *vi* unirse, asociarse, fusionarse; *the two businesses have combined* los dos negocios se han unido || CHEM combinarse || JUR sindicarse || FIG ligarse, unirse (*against* contra).

combined [-d] *adj* MIL combinado, da (operation) || unido, da (*with* a) || *combined set* microteléfono *m*, pesa *f* (telephone).

combing ['kəumiŋ] *n* peinada *f* (of hair) || TECH peinado *m*, cardadura *f*.
◆ *pl* peinaduras *f*.

combo ['kɔmbəu] *n* FAM conjunto *m* de jazz.

comb-out ['kəumaut] *n* FAM *to give a place a comb-out* registrar un lugar a fondo.

combustible [kəm'bʌstəbl] *adj* combustible || FIG ardiente.
◆ *n* combustible *m*.

combustion [kəm'bʌstʃən] *n* combustión *f* || — *combustion chamber* cámara *f* de combustión || *combustion engine* motor *m* de combustión.

combustor [kəm'bʌstə*] *n* cámara *f* de combustión (of gas turbine, jet engine).

come* [kʌm] *vi* venir; *he came to the party* vino a la fiesta; *take life as it comes* toma la vida como viene; *spring comes after winter* la primavera viene después del invierno || llegar; *the water comes up to my chin* el agua me llega a la barbilla || hacer, recorrer (a distance); *he has come ten miles* ha recorrido diez millas || pasar; *he came through the wood* pasó por el bosque || recaer; *the title came to the younger son* el título recayó en el hijo más pequeño || venir, proceder; *he comes from a wealthy family* procede de una familia rica || producirse, surgir; *a misunderstanding came between us* se produjo un malentendido entre nosotros || salir, resultar; *good wines come expensive* los vinos buenos salen caros; *nothing came of it* no resultó nada de ello || ocurrir, suceder, pasar (to happen); *you know what comes of drinking too much* ya sabes lo que sucede por beber mucho; *a change has come over his life* ha ocurrido un cambio en su vida || existir, hacerse; *it comes in two sizes* se hace en dos tamaños || POP correrse (to have an orgasm) || — FAM *come again?* ¿cómo? || *come, come!* ¡vamos! || *come here!* ¡ven!, ¡ven aquí! || *come now!* ¡vamos! || *come summer and I will see him again* el próximo verano lo volveré a ver || *come what may* pase lo que pase || *coming!* ¡voy! || *don't come the young innocent* no te hagas el inocente || FIG *easy come, easy go* del mismo modo que viene se va || *first come, first served* el que se adelanta nunca pierde || *he had it coming* tuvo *or* recibió su merecido || *how come?* ¿cómo es eso? || *I could see it coming* lo veía venir || *I don't know whether I'm coming or going* ya no sé ni lo que hago || *it came as a great surprise to us* fue una gran sorpresa para nosotros || *it comes to this* en resumen || *it will be a year come Monday* hará un año el próximo lunes || *time to come* tiempos futuros || *to come a cropper* darse un batacazo || *to come again* venir de nuevo, volver || *to come and go* ir y venir || *to come apart* desprenderse (to come off), ser desmontable (able to be dismantled), estropearse; *this chair is coming apart* esta silla se está estropeando || *to come asunder* deshacerse || *to come between* interponerse entre || *to come clean* confesarlo todo || *to come easy to* costar poco esfuerzo, ser fácil para || *to come from* venir de || *to come loose* soltarse, desatarse || *to come near* acercarse a (s.o.), estar a punto de *or* a dos dedos de, faltar poco para; *I came near fainting* estuve a punto de desmayarme || *to come next* seguir || *to come of age* alcanzar la mayoría de edad || *to come short of* no llegar a, no alcanzar || *to come to power, to the throne* subir al poder, al trono || *to come to the wrong person* acudir a la persona menos indicada || *to come to think of it* pensándolo bien || *to come undone* o *unstuck* deshacerse || *what do you come here for?* ¿a qué vienes?, ¿qué vienes a hacer aquí?
◆ *phr v* *to come about* suceder, ocurrir; *how did this accident come about?* ¿cómo sucedió este accidente? | MAR virar (ship) | cambiar (wind) || *to come across* encontrarse con, tropezar con (person) | encontrar (thing) | US FAM apoquinar (to fork out) | hacer lo que se pide (to do as one is told) | ser comprendido (to be understood) | ser apreciado (to be appreciated) || *to come after* venir detrás de | venir en busca de || *to come along* ir, andar | venir también || — *come along!* ¡venga! || *to come around* o *round*, US *to come around* venir; *he came round to see us* vino a vernos | volver en sí; *he came round one hour after the accident* volvió en sí una hora después del accidente | restablecerse (from an illness) | cambiar de dirección | MAR

virar (a ship) | ceder (to yield) | hacer una visita (to visit) || — *he came round to my point of view* me dio la razón, se dejó convencer, aceptó mi punto de vista || ***to come at*** encontrar, llegar a (to reach); *I came at the solution* encontré la solución | atacar (to attack) || ***to come away*** desprenderse (to become detached) || salir, irse (to leave) || ***to come back*** volver (to return) | volver en sí (to regain consciousness) | venir *or* volver a la memoria; *the name has just come back to me* el nombre me acaba de venir a la memoria | replicar (to answer) | desquitarse (to get even) || — *to come back with* contestar diciendo || ***to come before*** llegar antes | ser sometido a | anteceder | JUR comparecer ante (the court) || ***to come by*** conseguir, lograr, obtener (to obtain) | pasar por [un sitio]; *he came by this morning* pasó por aquí esta mañana || ***to come down*** bajar; *he came down the stairs* bajó las escaleras | desplomarse, derrumbarse (building, etc.) | caerse (to fall) | llegar (to reach) | venir a menos (to lose status) || — *all these houses are coming down* se van a derribar estas casas | *to come down on* echarse encima; *the authorities came down on him* las autoridades se le echaron encima | *to come down to* llegar a *or* hasta (to reach), reducirse a (to amount to) | *to come down with* caer enfermo con || ***to come for*** venir a buscar; *he came for a paper* vino a buscar un periódico || ***to come forth*** aparecer || ***to come forward*** presentarse | avanzar | responder a la llamada || ***to come in*** entrar (to enter); *that is where you come in* ahí es donde tú entras | llegar; *he came in first in the hundred metres* llegó el primero en los cien metros | ponerse de moda (to become fashionable) | empezar (season) | estar (to be) | sacar, ganar (to get) | subir (tide) | ser presentado (an invoice) | ser cobrado (a sum) | llegar al poder (a party) | llegar a ser (to become) || — *come in* ¡pase!, ¡adelante! | FAM *to come in for* recibir (scolding, praise) | *to come in handy* o *useful* resultar útil || ***to come into*** entrar en (a room, etc.); *to come into play* entrar en juego | llegar a (power) | participar en (to take part) | recibir (inheritance) | heredar (to inherit) | entrar en posesión de (to acquire) || — *to come into one's own* hacer valer sus méritos | *to come into sight* aparecer | *to come into the world* venir al mundo | *to come into trouble* meterse en un lío || ***to come off*** caerse (to fall off) | desprenderse (page, wheel) | salir (stain) | quitarse (to be removed) | salir; *it came off all right* salió bien | ser un éxito, salir bien (to be a success) | tener lugar; *the wedding comes off next week* la boda tendrá lugar la semana que viene || — *come off it!* ¡vamos, anda! || ***to come on*** avanzar (to advance) | encontrar (to find) | progresar, mejorar (to make progress) | llegar (season, storm) | caer (night) | ser discutido (question) | THEATR salir a escena (actor) | ser representado, representarse (play) || — *come on!* ¡vamos!, ¡venga! | FAM *I have two parties coming on* tengo dos fiestas en perspectiva | *it came on to rain* empezó a llover || ***to come out*** salir; *he came out of the house* salió de la casa | declararse; *they came out on strike* se declararon en huelga | salir; *ten photographs came out* salieron diez fotografías; *you have come out well* has salido bien | salir, publicarse; *the magazine comes out monthly* la revista se publica mensualmente | ser presentada (en sociedad); *she came out at eighteen* fue presentada en sociedad a los dieciocho años | BOT crecer, salir | MED salir; *I came out in spots* me salieron granos | THEATR empezar, salir | salir, descubrirse (truth) | salir, quitarse (stain) | *to come badly out of* salir mal parado de || — *to come out with* publicar (news), revelar (to reveal), saltar con, salir con (a remark, idea, etc.), soltar (a curse) || ***to come over*** venir; *he is coming over next summer* vendrá el verano que viene | pasar (to happen); *I don't know what came over me* no sé lo que me pasó | sobrevenir, invadir; *a great sadness came over them* les invadió una gran tristeza | ponerse; *he came over all funny* se puso muy raro | llegar; *his voice came over clearly* su voz llegó con claridad | ser comprendido (to be understood) | ser apreciado (to be appreciated) || — *to come over to* pasarse a (s.o.'s side), dejarse convencer por (an opinion) || ***to come through*** calar; *the rain comes through my coat* el agua me cala el abrigo | pasar por (sufferings) | sobrellevar, vencer (difficulties) | salir; *he came through the accident unhurt* salió ileso del accidente | pasar [sin detenerse] (train) | concretarse (to materialize) || ***to come to*** llegar a; *how did you come to do that?* ¿cómo llegaste a hacer eso?; *to come to an end* llegar a su término | pasar (to happen) | ir a ver (s.o.) | ceder, dejarse convencer (to yield) | ascender; *what does the bill come to?* ¿a cuánto asciende la cuenta? | volver en sí; *he came to* volvió en sí | venir a la mente, ocurrírsele [a uno] (an idea) || — *to come to a point* acabar en punta | *to come to blows* llegar a las manos | *to come to light* salir a luz || ***to come together*** reunirse, juntarse (to join) | venir juntos || ***to come under*** venir bajo | caer bajo (s.o.'s influence) | entrar en (a heading) || — *to come under s.o.'s notice* llegar al conocimiento de uno || ***to come up*** subir; *he came up the stairs* subió las escaleras | brotar, salir (plants) | salir (fashion) | JUR comparecer | surgir; *the matter came up at the last meeting* el asunto surgió en la última reunión || — *to come up against* tropezarse con | *to come up to* ascender a (a degree), satisfacer (expectations), estar a la altura de (s.o., a task), acercarse a (to approach), llegar a *or* hasta (to reach) | *to come up with* alcanzar (to overtake), proponer, sugerir (to suggest) || ***to come upon*** tropezar con, encontrar a (s.o.) | encontrar (sth.) | descubrir (a secret) | caer encima de, precipitarse contra (the enemy) | reclamar (to ask) || — *it came upon me that...* se me ocurrió que... || ***to come within*** entrar en || — *to come within s.o.'s jurisdiction* competer a, ser de la incumbencia *or* de la competencia de.

— OBSERV Pret ***came***; pp ***come***.

come-at-able [kʌm'ætəbl] *adj* accesible.

comeback ['kʌmbæk] *n* reaparición *f* (return) || vuelta *f* || réplica *f* (retort) || *to make a comeback* volver a escena, reaparecer (actors, etc.).

comedian [kə'mi:diən] *n* comediante *m*, actor *m*, cómico *m* (infr) (in theatre) | cómico *m* (in variety) || autor *m* cómico (writer) || FIG cómico *m*.

comedienne [kə,medi'en] *n* comedianta *f*, actriz *f*, cómica *f* (infr) (in theatre) || cómica *f* (in variety).

comedo ['kɔmi:dəu] *n* MED comedón *m*.

— OBSERV El plural de *comedo* es *comedones* o *comedos*.

comedown ['kʌmdaun] *n* humillación *f* || decadencia *f*, bajón *m* (loss of status) || desilusión (disappointment) || revés *m* (setback).

comedy ['kɔmidi] *n* comedia *f* || — *comedy of character* comedia de carácter *or* de figurón || *comedy of intrigue* comedia de enredo || *comedy of manners* comedia de costumbres || *comedy of situation* comedia de enredo || *light comedy* comedia ligera || *musical comedy* comedia musical.

come-hither ['kʌmhiðə*] *adj* seductor, ra; sugestivo, va.

comeliness ['kʌmlinis] *n* atractivo *m*, encanto *m*.

comely ['kʌmli] *adj* atractivo, va.

come-on ['kʌmɔn] *n* llamada *f* (inviting gesture) || US incentivo *m*, atractivo *m*, aliciente *m*.

comer ['kʌmə*] *n* el que llega, la que llega || US FAM promesa *f*, persona *f* que promete || — *all comers* todos los que vengan || *the first comer* el primer llegado *or* venido, el que llega primero || *to challenge all comers* desafiar a todos.

comestible [kə'mestibl] *adj* comestible.

comestibles [-z] *pl n* comestibles *m*.

comet ['kɔmit] *n* cometa *m*.

comeuppance [kʌ'mʌpəns] *n* US castigo *m* (merecido), merecido *m*.

comfit ['kʌmfit] *n* dulce *m*, confite *m*.

comfort ['kʌmfət] *n* FIG consuelo *m* (consolation) | alivio *m* (relief) || bienestar *m*, «confort» *m* (well being) || comodidad *f*; *this house has many comforts* esta casa tiene muchas comodidades || — US *comfort station* servicios *m pl* (lavatory) || *to live in comfort* vivir cómodamente.

comfort ['kʌmfət] *vt* consolar (to solace) || aliviar (to be a relief) || animar, confortar (to hearten).

comfortable [-əbl] *adj* cómodo, da; confortable; *is your bed comfortable?* ¿es cómoda su cama? || cómodo, da; *to make o.s. comfortable* ponerse cómodo || agradable; *a comfortable atmosphere* un ambiente agradable || decente, bueno, na; *a comfortable income* ingresos decentes || suficiente (sufficient) || holgado, da (living) || tranquilo, la (unworried).

comfortableness [-nis] *n* comodidad *f*.

comfortably [-i] *adv* confortablemente, cómodamente || fácilmente (easily) || *to be comfortably off* vivir con holgura *or* con desahogo.

comforter ['kʌmfətə*] *n* consolador, ra (one who comforts) || chupete *m* (for babies) || bufanda *f* (scarf) || US edredón *m* (eiderdown) || REL *the Comforter* el Espíritu Santo.

comforting ['kʌmfətiŋ] *adj* consolador, ra; reconfortante, alentador, ra.

comfortless ['kʌmfətlis] *adj* incómodo, da (lacking comfort) || abandonado, da; desamparado, da.

comfort-loving ['kʌmfət,lʌviŋ] *adj* comodón, ona.

comfy ['kʌmfi] *adj* FAM cómodo, da.

comic ['kɔmik] *adj* cómico, ca || — *comic book* Tebeo *m* || *comic opera* ópera bufa || *comic strip* tira cómica, historieta *f*.

◆ *n* cómico, ca (comedian) || Tebeo *m* (magazine) || — FIG *he is a comic!* ¡es un cómico! || *the comic of life* el lado cómico de la vida.

comical ['kɔmikəl] *adj* cómico, ca; divertido, da; gracioso, sa.

comicality [kɔmi'kæliti]; **comicalness** ['kɔmikəlnis] *n* comicidad *f*, lo cómico.

coming ['kʌmiŋ] *adj* próximo, ma; venidero, ra; que viene; *the coming year* el año próximo || FIG prometedor, ra; *a coming actor* un actor prometedor.

◆ *n* venida *f*, llegada *f* || REL advenimiento *m* || — *coming away* salida *f* || *coming back* vuelta *f* || *coming on* principio *m* || *coming out* salida *f*; presentación *f* en sociedad (of a débutante) || *comings and goings* idas *f* y venidas || *coming up* ascensión *f*, llegada *f*, acercamiento *m*.

comitia [kɔ'miʃiə] *pl n* HIST comicios *m*.

comity ['kɔmiti] *n* cortesía *f* || *comity of nations* acuerdo *m* entre naciones.

comma ['kɔma] *n* GRAMM coma *f* || MUS coma *f* || MED vírgula *f*, vibrión *m* del cólera || — *in inverted commas* entre comillas || *inverted commas* comillas *f pl*; *to open, to close the inverted commas* abrir, cerrar las comillas.

command [kə'mɑ:nd] *n* orden *f*, mandato *m* (order) || mando *m* (authority) || dominio *m*; *command of a language* dominio de una lengua; *command over o.s.* dominio de sí mismo || MIL mando *m*; *command word* voz de mando; *command post* puesto de mando | unidad *f* militar;

defence command unidad militar de defensa | comandancia *f* (zone) | dominio *m*; *the guns had command over the valley* las armas tenían dominio sobre el valle ‖ — *at* o *by s.o.'s command* por orden de alguien ‖ *high command* alto mando ‖ *his command was the fifth artillery division* estaba al mando de la quinta división de artillería, mandaba la quinta división de artillería ‖ *in command of* al mando de ‖ *money at one's command* dinero *m* disponible ‖ *to be at s.o.'s command* estar a las órdenes de alguien, estar a la disposición de alguien ‖ *to be in command of* estar al mando de, mandar (person), dominar (pass, fort) ‖ *to have at one's command, to have a command of* dominar (languages) ‖ *to take command* tomar el mando ‖ *under the command of* bajo el mando de.

command [kəˈmɑːnd] *vt* mandar (to control) ‖ dominar; *to command one's temper* dominar el mal genio; *the house commands the whole bay* la casa domina toda la bahía; *to command the market* dominar el mercado ‖ mandar, ordenar; *he commanded them to leave* les ordenó que se marcharan; *to command sth. to be done* ordenar que se haga algo ‖ merecer (to deserve) ‖ disponer de, poseer (to have at one's disposal) ‖ exigir (a good salary) ‖ tener (view) ‖ llamar, atraer, captar (attention) ‖ infundir (respect) ‖ suscitar (admiration) ‖ venderse a (to be sold) ‖ *yours to command!* ¡a sus órdenes!
◆ *vi* mandar.

commandant [ˌkɔmənˈdænt] *n* MIL comandante *m*.

commandeer [ˌkɔmənˈdiə*] *vt* expropiar, requisar [para uso militar] ‖ reclutar por fuerza (men) ‖ FAM apoderarse de.

commander [kəˈmɑːndə*] *n* MIL comandante *m* ‖ MAR capitán *m* de fragata ‖ jefe *m* (leader) ‖ comendador *m* (in knighthood) ‖ *commander in chief* comandante en jefe.
— OBSERV El plural de la expresión *commander in chief* es *commanders in chief*.

commandership [-ʃip] *n* mando *m* (command) ‖ comandancia *f* (position) ‖ MAR cargo *m* de capitán de fragata.

commandery [-ri] *n* encomienda *f*.

commanding [kəˈmɑːndiŋ] *adj* dominante (dominating) ‖ imponente (demanding respect) ‖ dominante; *a commanding position* una posición dominante ‖ MIL que está al mando ‖ MIL *commanding officer* jefe *m*, comandante *m*.

commandment [kəˈmɑːndmənt] *n* REL mandamiento *m*; *the Ten Commandments* los diez mandamientos.

command module [kəˈmɑːndˌmɔdjul] *n* módulo *m* de mando (space).

commando [kəˈmɑːndəu] *n* MIL comando *m*.
— OBSERV El plural de commando es *commandos* o *commandoes*.

command performance [kəˈmɑːnd pəˌfɔːməns] *n* representación *f* teatral dada a petición del jefe del Estado.

commeasurable [kəˈmeʒərəbl] *adj* proporcionado, da.

commemorate [kəˈmeməreit] *vt* conmemorar.

commemoration [kəˌmeməˈreiʃən] *n* conmemoración *f*.

commemorative [kəˈmemərətiv] *adj* conmemorativo, va.

commence [kəˈmens] *vt/vi* comenzar, empezar.

commencement [-mənt] *n* comienzo *m*, principio *m* (beginning) ‖ US ceremonia *f* de entrega de diplomas (university).

commend [kəˈmend] *vt* encomendar, confiar (to entrust); *to commend one's soul to God* encomendar su alma a Dios ‖ recomendar (to recommend) ‖ alabar (to praise); *to commend s.o. for his* o *o her bravery* alabar a alguien por su valentía ‖ aprobar (to approve) ‖ — (ant) *commend me for him* salúdele de mi parte ‖ *to commend itself to* gustar a.

commendable [kəˈmendəbl] *adj* recomendable ‖ digno de elogio (praiseworthy).

commendably [-i] *adv* de un modo digno de elogio.

commendam [kəˈmendəm] *n* REL encomienda *f*.

commendation [ˌkɔmenˈdeiʃən] *n* alabanza *f*, encomio *m*, elogio *m* (praise) ‖ recomendación *f* (recommendation).

commendatory [kɔˈmendətəri] *adj* REL comendatario ‖ elogioso, sa (laudatory).

commensal [kəˈmensəl] *n* comensal *m*.

commensurability [kəˌmenʃərəˈbiliti] *n* conmensurabilidad *f*.

commensurable [kəˈmenʃərəbl] *adj* conmensurable ‖ proporcionado, da.

commensurate [kəˈmenʃərit] *adj* proporcionado, da.

comment [ˈkɔment] *n* comentario *m* (explanatory note) ‖ observación *f* (remark) ‖ *no comment* sin comentarios.

comment [ˈkɔment] *vi* comentar, hacer comentarios *or* observaciones (*on, upon* sobre) ‖ criticar (to criticize).

commentary [ˈkɔməntəri] *n* comentario *m* ‖ observación *f* (remark) ‖ RAD *running commentary* reportaje *m* en directo.

commentate [ˈkɔmenˌteit] *vt* comentar ‖ narrar [las incidencias de] (a match, show, etc.).

commentator [ˈkɔmenteitə*] *n* comentarista *m* & *f* (who analyzes) ‖ locutor, ra (who reports).

commerce [ˈkɔməːs] *n* comercio *m* (trade) ‖ comercio *m*, ayuntamiento *m* (sexual intercourse).

commercial [kəˈməːʃəl] *adj* comercial; *commercial treaty* tratado comercial; *commercial street* calle comercial ‖ mercantil; *commercial law* derecho mercantil ‖ — *commercial agency* agencia *f* comercial ‖ *commercial bank* banco *m* comercial ‖ *commercial college* escuela *f* de comercio ‖ *commercial television* televisión *f* comercial ‖ *commercial vehicle* vehículo *m* comercial, utilitario *m* ‖ *commercial traveller* viajante *m* de comercio ‖ *commercial value* valor *m* comercial.
◆ *n* RAD anuncio *m* (advertisement) | programa *m* publicitario (publicity programme) ‖ viajante *m* de comercio (commercial traveller).

commercialism [-izəm] *n* mercantilismo *m*.

commercialization [kəˌməːʃəlaiˈzeiʃən] *n* comercialización *f*.

commercialize [kəˈməːʃəlaiz] *vt* comercializar.

commie [ˈkɔmi] *n* POP rojo, ja; comunista *m* & *f*.

comminate [ˈkɔmineit] *vt* conminar.

commination [ˌkɔmiˈneiʃən] *n* conminación *f*.

comminatory [ˈkɔminətəri] *adj* conminatorio, ria.

commingle [kɔˈmiŋgl] *vt* mezclar.
◆ *vi* mezclarse.

comminute [ˈkɔminjuːt] *vt* triturar, pulverizar (to crush) ‖ JUR parcelar (property) ‖ *comminated fracture* fractura conminuta.

comminution [kɔmiˈnjuːʃən] *n* trituración *f*, pulverización *f* (crushing) ‖ JUR parcelación *f* (of property).

commiserable [kəˈmizərəbl] *adj* lastimoso, sa; que da lástima.

commiserate [kəˈmizəreit] *vi* compadecerse (*with* de).
◆ *vt* compadecer.

commiseration [kəˌmizəˈreiʃən] *n* conmiseración *f*, compasión *f*, lástima *f*.

commissar [ˌkɔmiˈsɑː*] *n* comisario *m* (in the USSR).

commissariat [ˌkɔmiˈsɛəriət] *n* comisaría *f* (government department) ‖ MIL intendencia *f*.

commissary [ˈkɔmisəri] *n* comisario *m* (representative commissar) ‖ REL comisario *m* ‖ comisario *m* (senior police officer) ‖ US economato *m* (government store).

commission [kəˈmiʃən] *n* nombramiento *m* (to a post, a task, etc.) ‖ comisión *f*; *a commission of nine per cent* una comisión del nueve por ciento; *the commission to investigate the disaster* la comisión para investigar el desastre ‖ cometido *m* (assignment) ‖ encargo *m* (charge) ‖ misión *f* (mission) ‖ perpetración *f*, ejecución *f* (of a crime) ‖ delegación *f* (of authority) ‖ MIL despacho *m* de oficial (certificate) | grado *m* de oficial (rank) ‖ — *commission agent* comisionista *m* ‖ *commission merchant* comisionista *m* ‖ US *commission plan* gobierno *m* municipal que ejerce funciones legislativas y ejecutivas ‖ *done on commission* hecho por encargo ‖ *in commission* en servicio activo ‖ *on commission* como comisionista ‖ *out of commission* inservible (thing), fuera de servicio (person) ‖ MAR *to put a ship in, out of commission* armar, desarmar un barco ‖ *to work on a commission basis* trabajar a comisión.

commission [kəˈmiʃən] *vt* comisionar (to give a commission) ‖ encargar (to order); *to commission a portrait* encargar un retrato ‖ poner en servicio (a ship) ‖ MIL nombrar (an officer) ‖ MIL *commissioned officer* oficial *m*.

commissionaire [kəˌmiʃəˈnqnə*] *n* portero *m* (doorkeeper) ‖ recadero *m* (messenger).

commissioner [kəˈmiʃənə*] *n* comisionado *m*, miembro *m* de una comisión (member of commission) ‖ comisario *m*; *High Commissioner* Alto Comisario.

commissure [ˈkɔmisjuə*] *n* comisura *f*.

commit [kəˈmit] *vt* confiar (to entrust) ‖ cometer (a crime) ‖ cometer, hacer (error) ‖ comprometer; *committed literature* literatura comprometida ‖ entregar (to the flames, to the waves) ‖ encarcelar (to prison) ‖ encerrar, internar (a madman) ‖ JUR someter a una comisión ‖ encomendar (one's soul to God) ‖ — *to commit for trial* citar ante los tribunales ‖ *to commit o.s.* comprometerse ‖ *to commit sth. to paper* o *to writing* consignar algo por escrito ‖ *to commit to memory* aprender de memoria.

commitment [-mənt]; **committal** [-mitl] *n* compromiso *m* (pledge) ‖ cometido *m* (assignment) ‖ JUR encarcelamiento *m* (to prison) | auto *m* de prisión (order) ‖ internamiento *m*, reclusión *f* (of a madman) ‖ devolución *f* a una comisión (of a bill) ‖ presentación *f* (of a project) ‖ ejecución *f* (of a crime) ‖ COMM compromiso *m* ‖ entierro *m* (burial) ‖ inmersión *f* (in water).

committee [kəˈmiti] *n* comité *m*, comisión *f* (body of people); *committee of experts* comisión de expertos ‖ JUR curador *m* ‖ — *committee of honour* comité de honor ‖ *committee of the whole (house)* pleno *m* ‖ *committee of ways and means* comisión del presupuesto ‖ *joint committee* comisión conjunta *or* paritaria ‖ *management committee* consejo *m* de administración ‖ *standing committee* comisión permanente ‖ *to sit on a committee* ser miembro de una comisión.

committeeman [-mən] *n* miembro *m* de un comité *or* de una comisión.
— OBSERV El plural de esta palabra es *committeemen*.

commix [kə'miks] *vt* mezclar.
◆ *vi* mezclarse.

commode [kə'məud] *n* cómoda *f* (chest of drawers) || silla *f* con orinal, silla *f* retrete.

commodious [kə'məudjəs] *adj* espacioso, sa.

commodity [kə'mɔditi] *n* mercancía *f* [AMER mercadería], artículo *m*, producto *m* || *commodity agreement* acuerdo *m* comercial.

commodore ['kɔmədɔː*] *n* MAR comodoro *m*.

common ['kɔmən] *adj* común; *common staircase* escalera común || público, ca; común; *common opinion* opinión pública || ordinario, ria; vulgar; *common manners* modales ordinarios || MATH común; *common factor* factor común; *common multiple* común múltiplo || normal, usual; *it is common to dine at eight o'clock* es usual cenar a las ocho || común, corriente (frequent) || GRAMM común; *common gender, noun* género, nombre común || MIL raso (soldier) || municipal (council) || consuetudinario, ria (law) || — *common as dirt* de lo más ordinario || MÚS *common chord* acorde *m* simple || *common carrier* empresa pública de transporte || *common cold* constipado *m*, catarro *m* || *common council* ayuntamiento *m*, concejo *m* municipal || *common councilman* concejal *m* || *common crier* pregonero *m* || MATH *common denominator* común denominador *m* | *common divisor* divisor *m* común || US *common fraction* fracción ordinaria || *common ground* tema *m* de interés mutuo || *common informer* confidente *m* de la policía || *common herd* vulgo *m*, masa *f* || *common man* hombre medio, hombre *m* de la calle || *Common Market* Mercado *m* Común || FIG *common or garden* ordinario, ria || REL *Common Prayer* liturgia anglicana || JUR *common property* bienes *m pl* que pertenecen a la colectividad || *common room* sala *f* común | *common sense* buen sentido *m*, sentido *m* común || COMM *common stock* acciones ordinarias | MUS *common time* compás *m* de cuatro por cuatro || *common touch* contacto *m* con el pueblo || *common year* año *m* común || *in common* en común || *in common use* de uso corriente || *in common with* de acuerdo con || *it is common knowledge that...* es del dominio público que... (a piece of news), todo el mundo sabe que... (everybody knows that...) || *of a common accord* de común acuerdo || *the common people* el pueblo || *the common run of humanity* el común de los mortales.
◆ *n* ejido *m*, terreno *m* comunal (area of land) || — REL *common of martyrs* común de mártires || *common of pasturage* derecho *m* de pasto || *out of the common* fuera de lo corriente.
◆ *pl* pueblo *m sing* (common people) || Cámara *f sing* de los Comunes (of parliament) || refectorio *m sing* (in a college) || víveres *m* (food) || — *on short commons* a media ración || *the House of Commons* la Cámara de los Comunes.

commonage [-idʒ] *n* JUR pasto *m* libre (land) | derecho *m* de pasto (right) || comunidad *f* || pueblo *m* (commonalty).

commonalty [-əlti] *n* vulgo *m* (people not of the upper classes) || pueblo *m* (people in general) || comunidad *f* || JUR corporación *f*.

commoner [-ə*] *n* plebeyo, ya (not a peer) || estudiante sin beca (in Oxford University) || miembro *m* de la Cámara de los Comunes (in Parliament).

common-law [-lɔː] *adj* de hecho; *common-law marriage* matrimonio de hecho.

commonly [-li] *adj* comúnmente, generalmente (usually) || de un modo común *or* vulgar.

commonness [-nis] *n* frecuencia *f* (of an event) || vulgaridad *f* (of a person).

commonplace [-pleis] *adj* común, vulgar || *commonplace book* libro *m* de citas.
◆ *n* tópico *m*, lugar *m* común.

commons [-z] *pl n* ⟶ **common.**
— OBSERV Aunque esta palabra sea plural se construye con el singular.

commonsense [-sens] *adj* lógico, ca.

commonweal [-wiːl] *n* (ant) bien *m* público | estado *m*.

commonwealth [-welθ] *n* república *f*, democracia *f* || estado *m* (state) || bien *m* público (commonweal).

Commonwealth [-welθ] *pr n* «Commonwealth» *f*, Comunidad *f* de Naciones.

commotion [kə'məuʃən] *n* disturbio *m*, agitación *f* (disturbance) || alboroto *m* (noisy disturbance) || conmoción *f* (mental turmoil).

communal ['kɔmjunəl] *adj* comunal.

communalism [-izəm] *n* JUR descentralización *f* del poder, regionalización *f*.

commune ['kɔmjuːn] *n* municipio *m* (administrative unit) || *the Commune* la Comuna (in Paris).

commune [kɔ'mjuːn] *vi* comunicarse (to communicate) || REL comulgar (to receive communion).

communicability [kə,mjuːnikə'biliti] *n* comunicabilidad *f*.

communicable [kə'mjuːnikəbl] *adj* comunicable || contagioso, sa (disease).

communicant [kə'mjuːnikənt] *n* comunicante *m* & *f* (person who communicates information) || REL comulgante *m* & *f* (who receives communion).

communicate [kə'mjuːnikeit] *vt* comunicar (information, feelings, etc.) || contagiar (a disease).
◆ *vi* REL comulgar || comunicarse; *the rooms communicate* las habitaciones se comunican || INFORM *to communicate (with)* dialogar.

communication [kə,mjuːni'keiʃən] *n* comunicación *f*; *radio communication* comunicación por radio; *road communication* comunicación por carretera || comunicado *m*, comunicación *f*; *an official communication* un comunicado oficial.
◆ *pl* comunicaciones || — INFORM *communications link* o *protocol* protocolo *m* de comunicación || *communications satellite* satélite *m* de telecomunicaciones.

communication cord [-kɔːd] *n* palanca *f or* anilla *f* de emergencia (in trains).

communicative [kə'mjuːnikətiv] *adj* comunicativo, va; expansivo, va.

communion [kə'mjuːnjən] *n* comunión *f*.

communiqué [kə'mjuːnikei] *n* comunicado *m* oficial.

communism ['kɔmjunizəm] *n* comunismo *m*.

communist ['kɔmjunist] *adj/n* comunista.

community [kə'mjuːniti] *n* comunidad *f*; *community of goods* comunidad de bienes; *community of interest* comunidad de intereses || vecindario *m* (local inhabitants) || colectividad *f*, sociedad *f* (people in general) || FIG comunidad *f* (of ideas) || — *community centre* centro *m* social | US *community chest* fondo *m* para beneficencia pública || *community home* hogar *m or* centro *m* de custodia para menores || *community property* comunidad de bienes; bienes *m* municipales.

communization [kɔmjunai'zeiʃən] *n* comunización *f*.

communize ['kəmjuːnaiz] *vt* convertir en propiedad comunal; *the king communized the church lands* el rey convirtió las tierras de la iglesia en propiedad comunal || hacer comunista (people, countries).

commutability [kə,mjuːtə'biliti] *n* JUR conmutabilidad *f*.

commutable [kə'mjuːtəbl] *adj* JUR conmutable.

commutate ['kɔmjuteit] *vt* ELECTR conmutar.

commutation [,kɔmju'teiʃən] *n* JUR conmutación *f* || ELECTR conmutación *f*, cambio *m* de dirección de la corriente || conmutación *f* (of payment) || US *commutation ticket* abono *m*.

commutative [kə'mjuːtətiv] *adj* conmutativo, va.

commutator ['kɔmjuteitə*] *n* conmutador *m*.

commute [kə'mjuːt] *vt* JUR & ELECTR conmutar.
◆ *vi* viajar; *he commutes daily between Windsor and London* viaja diariamente de Windsor a Londres.

commuter [-ə*] *n* viajero, ra [que hace diariamente el mismo trayecto y tiene un abono].

comose ['kəuməus] *adj* BOT cabelludo, da.

compact [kəm'pækt] *adj* compacto, ta; *a compact mass* una masa compacta || recogido, da; *a compact house* un casa recogida || conciso, sa; *a compact book* un libro conciso || denso, sa (dense) || *compact of* compuesto de.

compact ['kɔmpækt] *n* pacto *m*, convenio *m* (agreement) || coche *m* no muy grande || — *general compact* común acuerdo *m* || *powder compact* polvera *f*.

compact [kəm'pækt] *vt* condensar || apretar, comprimir || componer.

compact disc ['kɔmpækt disk] *n* disco *m* compacto, compact disc || *compact disc player* reproductor *m* de compact disc, compact disc *m*.

companion [kəm'pænjən] *n* compañero, ra; *a travelling companion* un compañero de viaje || acompañante *m* & *f*; *companion wanted for elderly lady* se requiere acompañante para señora mayor || caballero *m* de grado inferior (in knighthood) || — MAR *companion hatch* cubierta *f* de escotilla | *companion hatchway* escotilla *f* | *companion ladder* escala *f* de toldilla.

companionable [-əbl] *adj* sociable.

companionship [-ʃip] *n* compañerismo *m* (fellowship) || compañeros *m pl* (companions).

companionway [-wei] *n* MAR escalera *f* de toldilla.

company ['kʌmpəni] *n* COMM compañía; *he owns an insurance company* es propietario de una compañía de seguros | empresa *f*; *building company* empresa constructora || compañía *f*; *her mother was good company for me* su madre me hizo mucha compañía || compañías *f pl*; *he keeps bad company* tiene malas compañías || compañero, ra (companion) || compañerismo *m* (companionship) || invitado, da; *I have company for lunch* tengo invitados para almorzar || visita *f* (visitors) || MAR tripulación *f* (crew) || MIL THEATR compañía *f* || — *better alone than in bad company* más vale estar solo que mal acompañado || *company manners* buenos modales || *company union* sindicato *m* libre [de una empresa] || *in company* en compañía || *joint-stock company* sociedad anónima || *limited-liability company* sociedad (de responsabilidad) limitada || *present company excepted* mejorando lo presente || *to bear company* acompañar || *to be expecting company* estar esperando visita || *to keep company with* asociarse con (to associate), salir con (lovers) || *to keep s.o. company* hacer compañía a alguien || *to part company* separarse; *the two travellers parted company* los dos viajeros se separaron; terminar (to end a friendship) || *touring company* compañía teatral que se dedica a hacer giras || *two's company, three's a crowd* ni amor ni señoría quieren compañía.

comparable ['kɔpərəbl] *adj* comparable.

comparative [kəm'pærətiv] *adj* comparativo, va || relativo, va; *her party was a comparative success* su fiesta fue un éxito relativo || comparado, da; *comparative studies* estudios comparados || GRAMM *comparative degree* grado comparativo.
◆ *n* GRAMM comparativo *m*.

comparatively [-li] *adv* en comparación, comparativamente || relativamente.

comparator [kɔm'pærətə*] *n* PHYS comparador *m*.

compare [kəm'pɛə*] *n* comparación *f* || *beyond compare, past compare* sin comparación, sin par.

compare [kəm'pɛə*] *vt* comparar; *to compare a film with a play* comparar una película con una obra de teatro; *to compare notes* comparar apuntes || GRAMM formar el comparativo de || — *as compared with* comparado con || *they are not to be compared* no se pueden comparar.
◆ *vi* poderse comparar || *to compare favourably with* no ser inferior a.

comparison [kəm'pærisn] *n* comparación *f*; *beyond comparison* sin comparación; *it bears no comparison with the other* no admite comparación con el otro || — *in comparison with* o *to* en comparación con, comparado con || — *in* o *by comparison* en comparación.

compartment [kəm'pɑːtmənt] *n* compartimiento *m*, departamento *m* (in a railway carriage) || MAR compartimiento *m*; *watertight compartment* compartimiento estanco || sección *f* (in parliamentary business) || departamento *m*, sección *f* (department).

compartmentalize; compartmentalise [ˌkɔmpɑːt'mentlaiz] *vt* compartimentar.

compass ['kʌmpəs] *n* brújula *f* (for determining direction) || MAR & AVIAT compás *m*, brújula *f*, aguja *f* || compás *m* (for making circles) || círculo *m* (circle) || límites *m pl* (limits) || espacio *m* (space) || alcance *m* (range) || extensión *f* (extent) || MUS extensión *f* (of the voice) || — *compass bearing* rumbo *m* || *compass card* rosa náutica, rosa *f* de los vientos || TECH *compass plane* cepillo redondo || *compass rose* rosa *f* de los vientos || *compass saw* sierra *f* de contornar || *pair of compasses* compás *m* || *points of the compass* puntos *m* de la brújula.

compass ['kʌmpəs] *vt* dar la vuelta a (to go round) || rodear (to surround) || comprender, captar (to grasp mentally) || urdir, tramar (to plot) || lograr, conseguir (to obtain).

compassion [kəm'pæʃən] *n* compasión *f* || *to move s.o. to compassion* mover a uno a compasión.

compassionate [-it] *adj* compasivo, va (sympathetic, understanding).

compatibility [kəm,pætə'biliti] *n* compatibilidad *f* || INFORM compatibilidad *f*.

compatible [kəm'pætəbl] *adj* compatible || INFORM compatible.

compatriot [kəm'pætriət] *n* compatriota *m* & *f*.

compeer [kɔm'piə*] *n* igual *m* (equal) || compañero, ra (companion).

compel [kəm'pel] *vt* compeler, obligar (to oblige) || imponer; *his honesty compels respect* su honradez impone respeto.

compellation [kɔmpə'leiʃən] *n* tratamiento *m* || nombre *m* (name).

compelling [kəm'peliŋ] *adj* apremiante (urgent) || obligatorio, ria (compulsory) || irresistible (driving) || fuerte (personality) || *compelling urge* necesidad *f* urgente.

compendious [kəm'pendiəs] *adj* compendioso, sa; conciso, sa.

compendium [kəm'pəndiəm] *n* compendio *m*.
— OBSERV El plural de *compendium* es *compendiums* o *compendia*.

compensate ['kɔmpenseit] *vt* indemnizar (to repay) || PHYS compensar || compensar (to make up for).
◆ *vi to compensate for* compensar.

compensating [-iŋ] *adj* TECH *compensating gear* engranaje *m* diferencial || *compensating pendulum* péndulo compensador.

compensation [ˌkɔmpen'seiʃən] *n* compensación *f* (the act of compensating) || indemnización *f* (indemnity) || remuneración *f* || recompensa *f* (reward) || TECH & PHYS compensación *f* || *compensation balance* balanza *f* de compensación.

compensative [kəm'pensətiv] *adj* compensativo, va; compensador, ra.

compensator ['kɔmpenseitə*] *n* compensador *m*.

compensatory [kəm'pensətəri] *adj* compensatorio, ria || — *compensatory damages* indemnización *f sing* por daños y perjuicios || *compensatory lengthening* alargamiento compensatorio (of vowels).

compère ['kɔmpɛə*] *n* presentador *m*.

compère ['kɔmpɛə*] *vt/vi* presentar.

compete [kəm'piːt] *vi* competir.

competence ['kɔmpitəns] *n* competencia *f*, aptitud *f* (sufficient ability) || sueldo *m* suficiente para vivir (modest income) || JUR competencia *f*.

competent ['kɔmpitənt] *adj* competente, apto, ta; capaz (having necessary qualities) || adecuado, da (suitable) || JUR competente.

competition [ˌkɔmpi'tiʃən] *n* competición *f*; *an athletic competition* una competición atlética || COMM competencia *f* || oposición *f* (examination for certain posts) || concurso *m* (contest).

competitive [kəm'petitiv] *adj* de competencia (spirit) || de libre competencia (market) || — *competitive examination* oposición *f* || *competitive price* precio competitivo.

competitor [kəm'petitə*] *n* competidor, ra; rival *m* & *f* || COMM competidor *m* || opositor, ra (for certain posts) || concursante *m* & *f* (in a contest).

compilation [ˌkɔpi'leiʃən] *n* compilación *f* || INFORM compilación *f*.

compile [kəm'pail] *vt* compilar || INFORM compilar.

compiler [-ə*] *n* compilador, ra || INFORM compilador m.

complacence [kəm'pleisəns]; **complacency** [kəm'pleisənsi] *n* satisfacción *f* de sí mismo.

complacent [kəm'pleisnt] *adj* satisfecho de sí mismo.

complain [kəm'plein] *vi* quejarse, lamentarse (*of, about* de; *that* de que) || JUR presentar una demanda.

complainant [kəm'pleinənt] *n* JUR demandante *m* & *f*, querellante *m* & *f*.

complaint [kəm'pleint] *n* queja *f* (expression of dissatisfaction); *he made a complaint to the police* presentó una queja a la policía || reclamación *f* (about quality of service, etc.) || enfermedad *f*; *he suffers from a stomach complaint* tiene una enfermedad del estómago || JUR demanda *f*; *he lodged a complaint* entabló una demanda || US JUR acusación *f*.

complaisance [kəm'pleizəns] *n* complacencia *f*, amabilidad *f*.

complaisant [kəm'pleizənt] *adj* complaciente, amable.

complement ['kɔplimənt] *n* complemento *m*; *wine is the complement to a good dinner* el vino es el complemento de una buena comida || MIL efectivo *m* || GRAMM complemento *m* || MAR dotación *f* || MATH complemento *m* || MED *complement fixation* fijación *f* del complemento || *a full complement of* un juego *m or* conjunto *m* completo de (of things), un número *m* completo de (of people).

complement ['kɔmpliment] *vt* complementar.

complemental [ˌkɔmpli'mentl] *adj* complementario, ria.

complementary [ˌkɔmpli'mentəri] *adj* complementario, ria; *complementary angles, colours* ángulos, colores complementarios.

complete [kəm'pliːt] *adj* completo, ta; *the complete works of Shakespeare* las obras completas de Shakespeare; *a complete stranger* un completo desconocido || acabado, da; concluido, da; terminado, da; *his work is complete* su trabajo está concluido || total; *a complete surprise* una sorpresa total || consumado, da (consummate) || perfecto, ta.

complete [kəm'plit] *vt* completar; *he wants two more volumes to complete the set* le faltan dos volúmenes para completar su colección || terminar, acabar, concluir (to finish) || completar, complementar; *travel completes an education* el viajar complementa la educación || llenar; *to complete a form* llenar un formulario.

completion [kəm'pliːʃən] *n* terminación *f*, conclusión *f* || realización *f* (execution).

complex ['kɔmpleks] *adj* complejo, ja (not simple); *a complex idea* una idea compleja || complejo, ja; complicado, da (having many parts); *complex machinery* maquinaria complicada || CHEM complejo, ja || — MATH *complex fraction* fracción compuesta | *complex number* número complejo || GRAMM *complex sentence* oración compuesta.
◆ *n* complejo *m*; *an industrial complex* un complejo industrial || complejo *m* (in psychology).

complexion [kəm'plekʃən] *n* cutis *m*, tez *f* || FIG aspecto *m*, cariz *m*; *matters took on a new complexion* los asuntos tomaron un nuevo cariz.

complexioned [-d] *adj* de tez, de cutis; *fair complexioned* de tez clara.

complexity [kəm'pleksiti] *n* complejidad *f*.

compliance [kəm'plaiəns] *n* obediencia *f* (submission) || conformidad *f* (aquiescement) || *in compliance with* de acuerdo con.

compliant [kəm'plaiənt] *adj* acomodaticio, cia (accommodating) || dócil, sumiso, sa (obedient).

complicate ['kɔmplikeit] *adj* complicado, da; complejo, ja.

complicate ['kɔmplikeit] *vt* complicar.
◆ *vi* complicarse.

complicated [-id] *adj* complicado, da; complejo, ja.

complication [ˌkɔmpli'keiʃən] *n* complicación *f*.

complicity [kəmp'plisiti] *n* complicidad *f*.

compliment ['kɔmplimənt] *n* cumplido *m* (expression of praise); *he paid compliments* hizo cumplidos || atención *f* (kind attention) || detalle *m* (kind gesture) || piropo *m* (amorous flattery).
◆ *pl* saludos *m*; *pay my compliments to your wife* mis saludos a su mujer | enhorabuena *f sing*; *my compliments to the chef* mi enhorabuena al cocinero || — *compliments of the season* felices Pascuas || *compliments slip* tarjeta *f* comercial || *with the publisher's compliments* obsequio *m sing* de la editorial.

compliment ['kɔmplimənt] *vt* cumplimentar, felicitar || alabar (to praise) || requebrar, piropear (a woman).

complimentary [ˌkɔmpli'mentəri] *adj* elogioso, sa; halagador, ra (eulogistic) || — *complimentary copy* obsequio *m* del autor || *complimentary ticket* billete *m or* entrada *f* de favor.

compline; complin ['kɔmplin] *n* REL completas *f pl* (last service of the day).

complot ['kɔmplɔt] *n* complot *m*, conspiración *f*.

comply [kəm'plai] *vi* acceder, conformarse (with wishes) || obedecer (to obey) || *to comply with* cumplir con (the rules), acatar (the law).

component [kəm'pəunənt] *adj* componente, constituyente.
◆ *n* componente *m* || INFORM componente *m*.

comport [kəm'pɔːt] *vt/vi* concordar || *to comport o.s.* portarse, conducirse, comportarse.

comportment [-mənt] *n* comportamiento *m*, conducta *f*.

compose [kəm'pəuz] *vt* componer || calmar, sosegar (to make calm) || *to compose o.s.* calmarse, sosegarse.
◆ *vi* componer.

composed [-d] *adj* tranquilo, la; sereno, na.

composedness [-dnis] *n* tranquilidad *f*, serenidad *f*, calma *f*.

composer [-ə*] *n* MUS compositor, ra.

composing [-iŋ] *adj* de composición || — *composing machine* máquina *f* de componer || PRINT *composing stick* componedor *m*.
◆ *n* composición *f*.

compositae [kɔm'pɔsitiː] *pl n* BOT compuestas *f*.

composite ['kɔpəzit] *adj* compuesto, ta; *composite number* número compuesto || BOT compuesto, ta || ARCH compuesto, ta.
◆ *n* BOT compuesta *f* || CHEM compuesto *m* || ARCH orden *m* compuesto.

composition [ˌkɔmpə'ziʃən] *n* composición *f* || redacción *f*, composición *f* (an essay) || ejercicio *m* (exercise) || MATH composición *f* de fuerzas || COMM transacción *f*, acuerdo *m*.

compositor [kəm'pɔzitə*] *n* PRINT cajista *m*.

compos mentis ['kɔmpɔs'mentis] *adj* en su sano juicio.

compost ['kɔmpɔst] *n* abono *m*, estiércol *m* vegetal.

compost ['kɔmpɔst] *vt* abonar (to fertilize) || convertir en abono.

composure [kəm'pəuʒə*] *n* calma *f*, serenidad *f*, compostura *f*.

compote ['kɔmpɔt] *n* CULIN compota *f*.

compound ['kɔmpaund] *adj* compuesto, ta || — *compound circuit* circuito combinado || ZOOL *compound eye* ojo compuesto || MATH *compound fraction* fracción compuesta || MED *compound fracture* fractura complicada || COMM *compound interest* interés compuesto || BOT *compound leaf* hoja digitada || *compound lens* lente compuesta || MATH *compound number* número compuesto || GRAMM *compound sentence* oración compuesta.
◆ *n* compuesto *m* || recinto *m* cercado (enclosed land) || palabra *f* compuesta (word).

compound [kɔm'paund] *vt* componer (to make by combining) || combinar, mezclar (to combine) || arreglar (to arrange) || agravar (an error) || COMM liquidar (una deuda) pagando sólo una parte | calcular [interés compuesto].
◆ *vi* arreglarse, llegar a un acuerdo (to compromise) || combinarse, mezclarse (to combine).

comprehend [ˌkɔmpri'hend] *vt* comprender.

comprehensibility [ˌkɔmpriˌhensə'biliti] *n* comprensibilidad *f*.

comprehensible [ˌkɔmpri'hensəbl] *adj* comprensible.

comprehension [ˌkɔmpri'henʃən] *n* comprensión *f*.

comprehensive [ˌkɔmpri'hensiv] *adj* amplio, plia; de gran amplitud, extenso, sa; *politics is a comprehensive term* el término política es muy amplio || de conjunto, general, global (survey, view) || comprensivo, va; *a comprehensive mind* una mente comprensiva || a todo riesgo (insurance) || — *comprehensive charge* precio *m* todo incluido || US *comprehensive examination* reválida *f* || *comprehensive school* instituto *m* de segunda enseñanza.

comprehensiveness [-nis] *n* comprensión *f* || amplitud *f*, gran extensión *f*.

compress ['kɔmpres] *n* MED compresa *f* || TECH prensa *f* para comprimir el algodón en balas.

compress [kɔm'pres] *vt* comprimir (to reduce by pressure) || FIG condensar (to condense).

compressed [-t] *adj* comprimido, da (pressed together) || FIG condensado, da (condensed) || — *compressed air* aire comprimido || *compressed air brake* freno neumático.

compressibility [kəmˌpresi'biliti] *n* compresibilidad *f* (capacity to be compressed).

compressible [kəm'presəbl] *adj* compresible, comprimible.

compression [kəm'preʃən] *n* compresión *f*; *compression chamber* cámara de compresión.

compressor [kəm'presə*] *n* compresor *m*.

comprise; US comprize [kəm'praiz] *vt* comprender (to include) || constar de (to consist of).

compromise ['kɔmprəmaiz] *n* compromiso *m*, acomodo *m*, arreglo *m*; *we shall have to come to a compromise over this point* tendremos que llegar a un arreglo sobre este punto || término *m* medio; *a compromise between two different opinions* un término medio entre dos opiniones distintas || *to be a compromise to* comprometer.

compromise ['kɔmprəmaiz] *vi* llegar a un arreglo (to agree); *if you disagree with me, we shall have to compromise* si no estás de acuerdo conmigo, tendremos que llegar a un arreglo || transigir (to yield); *I am willing to compromise over the price* estoy dispuesto a transigir sobre el precio.
◆ *vt* comprometer (to endanger) || arreglar (a quarrel, etc.).

compromising [-iŋ] *adj* comprometedor, ra.

comptometer [kɔmp'tɔmitə*] *n* TECH máquina *f* de calcular.

comptroller [kən'trəulə*] *n* (ant) administrador *m* || COMM interventor *m*.

compulsion [kɔm'pʌlʃən] *n* obligación *f*, fuerza *f*; *he did it under compulsion* lo hizo por obligación *or* a la fuerza || coacción *f* (coercion) || impulso *m* (impulse) || *to be under compulsion to do sth.* estar obligado a hacer algo.

compulsive [kɔm'pʌlsiv] *adj* obligatorio, ria (obligatory) || coercitivo, va (coercive) || incorregible, empedernido, da; *a compulsive gambler* un jugador empedernido.

compulsorily [kəm'pʌlsərili] *adv* obligatoriamente.

compulsory [kəm'pʌlsəri] *adj* obligatorio, ria (obligatory) || coercitivo, va (coercive) || *compulsory purchase* compra *f* forzosa.

compunction [kəm'pʌŋkʃən] *n* REL compunción *f* || remordimiento *m* (pricking of conscience) || *without compunction* sin escrúpulo.

compunctious [kəm'pʌŋkʃəs] *adj* compungido, da.

computable [kəm'pjuːtəbl] *adj* computable, calculable.

computation [ˌkɔmpjuː'teiʃən] *n* cómputo *m*, cálculo *m*.

compute [kɔm'pjuːt] *vt* computar, calcular.

computer [-ə*] *n* computador *m*, computadora *f*, ordenador *m*, calculador *m*, calculadora *f* || — *computer centre* centro *m* de cálculo || *computer dating* citas *f pl* por ordenador || *computer expert* o *specialist* informático, ca || *computer games* juegos *m pl* de ordenador || *computer language* lenguaje *m* de máquina || *computer science* informática *f*.

computer-aided [-ˌeidid]**; computer-assisted** [-əˌsistid] *adj* INFORM asistido, da por ordenador || — *computer-aided design* diseño *m* asistido por ordenador || *computer-aided drawing* dibujo *m* asistido por ordenador || *computer-aided instruction* enseñanza *f* asistida por ordenador.

computerize [-əraiz] *vt* tratar (data) || informatizar || *to be computerized* tener computadoras.

computing [-iŋ] *n* informática *f* || — *computing power* potencia *f* de cálculo || *he's in computing* trabaja de informático.

comrade ['kɔmrid] *n* camarada *m* & *f*.

comrade-in-arms [-in'ɑːmz] *n* compañero *m* de armas.

comradeship [-ʃip] *n* camaradería *f*.

con [kɔn] *n* contra *m*; *pros and cons* los pros y los contras || — FAM *con game* estafa *f* | *con man* estafador *m*.

con; US conn [kɔn] *vt* MAR gobernar.

con [kɔn] *vt* aprender de memoria, memorizar (to learn by heart) || estudiar; *to con a lesson* estudiar una lección || FAM estafar, timar; *he conned me out of five pounds* me estafó cinco libras || FAM *to con s.o. into doing sth.* persuadir a alguien para que haga algo.

conation [kəu'neiʃən] *n* PHIL volición *f*.

conative ['kəunətiv] *adj* PHIL volitivo, va.

concatenate [kɔn'kætineit] *adj* concatenado, da; concadenado, da.

concatenation [kɔnˌkæti'neiʃən] *n* concatenación *f*, encadenamiento *m*, serie *f*.

concave ['kɔnkeiv] *adj* cóncavo, va.
◆ *n* concavidad *f*.

concavity [kɔn'kæviti] *n* concavidad *f*.

concavo-concave [kɔn'keivəu'kɔnkeiv] *adj* PHYS bicóncavo, va.

concavo-convex [kɔn'keivəu'kɔnveks] *adj* PHYS cóncavoconvexo, xa.

conceal [kən'siːl] *vt* ocultar || JUR encubrir.

concealment [-mənt] *n* ocultación *f* || JUR encubrimiento *m* || escondite *m* (hiding place).

concede [kən'siːd] *vt* reconocer, admitir (to admit) || conceder, otorgar (to grant) || *to concede the game, to concede victory* darse por vencido.
◆ *vi* ceder, hacer una concesión.

conceit [kən'siːt] *n* presunción *f*, vanidad *f*, engreimiento *m* (pride) || agudeza *f*, dicho *m* ingenioso, concepto *m* (literary) || noción *f*, concepto *m* (notion).

conceited [kən'siːtid] *adj* engreído, da; presumido, da; vanidoso, sa.

conceitedness [-nis] *n* presunción *f*, vanidad *f*, engreimiento *m*.

conceivable [kən'siːvəbl] *adj* concebible, imaginable.

conceive [kən'siːv] *vt* concebir; *to conceive an idea* concebir una idea || BIOL concebir.
◆ *vi* concebir || *to conceive of* concebir, imaginarse.

concenter [kɔn'sentə*] *vt/vi* US → **concentre.**

concentrate ['kɔnsəntreit] *vt* concentrar (troops) ‖ concentrar (attention) ‖ enfocar, concentrar (rays).
◆ *vi* concentrarse; *we must concentrate on our work* debemos concentrarnos en nuestro trabajo ‖ concentrarse (troops).

concentrate ['kɔnsəntreit] *n* concentrado *m*.

concentration [,kɔnsən'treiʃən] *n* concentración *f* ‖ *concentration camp* campo *m* de concentración.

concentre; US **concenter** [kɔn'sentə*] *vt* concentrar, hacer converger *or* convergir.
◆ *vi* concentrarse, converger, convergir.

concentric [kɔn'sentrik]; **concentrical** [-l] *adj* concéntrico, ca.

concentricity [kɔnsen'trisiti] *n* concentricidad *f*.

concept ['kɔnsept] *n* concepto *m*.

conception [kən'sepʃən] *n* concepción *f* (of child, idea) ‖ idea *f*; *he has no conception of the work involved* no tiene ni idea del trabajo que eso supone.

conceptional [-əl] *adj* concepcional.

conceptism ['kənseptizəm] *n* conceptismo *m*.

conceptive [kən'septiv] *adj* conceptivo, va.

conceptual [kən'septjuəl] *adj* conceptual.

conceptualism [-izəm] *n* PHIL conceptualismo *m*.

conceptualist [-ist] *n* PHIL conceptualista *m* & *f*.

concern [kən'sə:n] *n* asunto *m*, cosa *f*; *it's no concern of yours* no es asunto tuyo ‖ intereses *m pl*; *he has a concern in the industry* tiene intereses en la industria ‖ empresa *f* (business) ‖ preocupación *f*, inquietud *f* (worry); *he regarded his sick mother with concern* miró a su madre enferma con inquietud ‖ conexión *f*, relación *f*; *it has no concern with them* no tiene relación con ellos ‖ — *a matter of some concern to us* un asunto que nos interesa *or* que nos preocupa mucho ‖ *of concern* de interés ‖ *of what concern is it to you?* ¿a Ud. qué le importa?
◆ *pl* asuntos *m* (private affairs).

concern [kən'sə:n] *vt* tratar de (to have as a subject); *this book concerns fencing* este libro trata de esgrima ‖ meterse; *don't concern yourself with politics* no te metas en la política ‖ complicar, implicar; *he was concerned in a scuffle* fue complicado en una pelea ‖ afectar, atañer, concernir (to affect); *it concerns him only indirectly* le afecta sólo indirectamente ‖ estar relacionado con, relacionarse con, referirse a (to be related to) ‖ preocupar (to worry); *your behaviour concerns me deeply* tu comportamiento me preocupa mucho ‖ — *as concerns* respecto de, respecto a, refiriéndose a ‖ *as far as I am concerned* por lo que a mí se refiere ‖ *to whom it may concern* a quien corresponda.

concerned [-d] *adj* preocupado, da; inquieto, ta (worried); *he had a concerned face* tenía cara preocupada; *she was concerned to know* estaba preocupada por saber ‖ *those concerned* los interesados.

concerning [-iŋ] *prep* con respecto a, acerca de, concerniente a, refiriéndose a, referente a.

concert ['kɔnsət] *n* concierto *m*, acuerdo *m* (agreement); *to work in concert with* obrar de concierto *or* de común acuerdo con ‖ concierto *m* (musical performance) ‖ — MUS *concert grand* piano *m* de cola | *concert pitch* diapasón *m* normal.

concert [kən'sə:t] *vt* concertar.
◆ *vi* obrar de concierto.

concerted [-id] *adj* concertado, da.

concertgoer ['kɔnsət,gəuə*] *n* aficionado *m* a los conciertos, melómano, na.

concertina [,kɔnsə'ti:nə] *n* MUS concertina *f*.

concertina [,kɔnsə'ti:nə] *vi* arrugarse (on impact).

concertmaster ['kɔnsət,mɑ:stə*] *n* US MUS concertino *m*.

concerto [kən'tʃə:təu] *n* MUS concierto *m*.
— OBSERV El plural de *concerto* es *concerti* o *concertos*.

concession [kən'seʃən] *n* concesión *f*.

concessionaire; concessionnaire [kən'seʃə'nεə*] *n* concesionario, ria.

concessionary [kən'seʃənəri] *adj* del concesionario (rights) ‖ concesionario, ria.

concessive [kən'sesiv] *adj* concesivo, va.

conch [kɔŋk] *n* ZOOL caracol *m* marino (sea snail) ‖ concha *f* (shell) ‖ ARCH bóveda *f* de concha ‖ ANAT concha *f*.

concha ['kɔŋkə] *n* ANAT concha *f*.
— OBSERV El plural de *concha* es *conchae*.

conchiferous [kɔn'kifərəs] *adj* conchífero, ra.

conchoid ['kɔŋkɔid] *n* MATH concoide *f*.

conchoidal [kɔŋ,kɔidəl] *adj* concoideo, a.

concierge [,kɔ̃:nsi'εəʒ] *n* portero, ra.

conciliar [kɔn'siliə*] *adj* conciliar.

conciliate [kən'silieit] *vt* conciliar.

conciliation [kən,sili'eiʃən] *n* conciliación *f*; *conciliation board* tribunal de conciliación laboral; *conciliation court* tribunal de conciliación ‖ reconciliación *f* (reconcilement).

conciliator [kən'silieitə*] *n* conciliador, ra.

conciliatory [kən'siliətəri] *adj* conciliatorio, ria; conciliador, ra.

concise [kən'sais] *adj* conciso, sa.

conciseness [kən'saisnis]; **concision** [kən'siʒən] *n* concisión *f*.

conclave ['kɔnkleiv] *n* cónclave *m*.

conclude [kən'klu:d] *vt* concluir, acabar (to end) ‖ firmar, concertar (a treaty, etc.) ‖ concluir (to deduce).
◆ *vi* concluirse, terminarse (to come to an end) ‖ concluir, terminar; *he concluded by saying* terminó diciendo ‖ decidir (to decide).

conclusion [kən'klu:ʒən] *n* conclusión *f* (finish, deduction) ‖ firma *f* (of a treaty) ‖ — *in conclusion* en conclusión ‖ *to jump to conclusions* sacar conclusiones precipitadas.

conclusive [kən'klu:siv] *adj* conclusivo, va; concluyente ‖ *conclusive evidence* pruebas definitivas.

concoct [kən'kɔkt] *vt* CULIN confeccionar (to mix) ‖ FIG urdir, fraguar, maquinar (to plot) | inventar.

concoction [kən'kɔkʃən] *n* mezcla *f* (mixture) ‖ brebaje *m* (brew) ‖ FIG maquinación *f* (of a plot) | fabricación *f* (of lies) | invento *m* (lie).

concomitance [kən'kɔmitəns]; **concomitancy** [-i] *n* concomitancia *f*.

concomitant [kən'kɔmitənt] *adj* concomitante.
◆ *n* cosa *f* que acompaña otra.

concord ['kɔŋkɔ:d] *n* concordia *f* (state of agreement) ‖ MUS acorde *m* ‖ GRAMM concordancia *f*.

concordance [kən'kɔ:dəns] *n* concordancia *f* (agreement) ‖ concordancias *f pl* (index).

concordant [kən'kɔ:dənt] *adj* concordante, concorde ‖ MUS armonioso, sa.

concordat [kɔn'kɔ:dæt] *n* REL concordato *m*.

concourse ['kɔŋkɔ:s] *n* concurrencia *f* (coming together) ‖ confluencia *f* (of rivers) ‖ US encrucijada *f* (in a park) | vestíbulo *m* (in railway station).

concrete ['kɔnkri:t] *n* hormigón *m* [AMER concreto *m*] (for building); *concrete steel, reinforced concrete* hormigón armado.
◆ *adj* concreto, ta (not abstract) ‖ TECH de hormigón (made of concrete) ‖ *concrete mixer* hormigonera *f*.

concrete ['kɔnkri:t] *vt* cubrir con hormigón (to cover) ‖ solidificar (to harden).

concretion [kən'kri:ʃən] *n* concreción *f* ‖ MED cálculo *m*.

concubinage [kɔn'kju:binidʒ] *n* concubinato *m*.

concubine ['kɔŋkjubain] *n* concubina *f*.

concupiscence [kən'kju:pisəns] *n* concupiscencia *f*.

concupiscent [kən'kju:pisənt] *adj* concupiscente.

concur [kən'kə:*] *vi* estar de acuerdo (to agree) ‖ concurrir, coincidir (to coincide) ‖ — *to concur in* convenir en ‖ *to concur with* estar de acuerdo con.

concurrence [kən'kʌrəns]; **concurrency** [-i] *n* concurrencia *f* ‖ coincidencia *f* (coincidence) ‖ acuerdo *m* (agreement).

concurrent [kən'kʌrənt] *adj* concurrente (coinciding) ‖ JUR común; *concurrent powers* poderes comunes | opuesto, ta (rights).

concuss [kən'kʌs] *vt* MED conmocionar ‖ MED *to be concussed* sufrir una conmoción cerebral.

concussion [kən'kʌʃən] *n* MED conmoción *f* cerebral.

condemn [kən'dem] *vt* condenar (to censure, to punish); *the papers condemned the strike* los periódicos condenaron la huelga; *he was condemned to death* le condenaron a muerte ‖ declarar en ruina; *the house was condemned* la casa fue declarada en ruina ‖ confiscar (smuggling).

condemnable [-nəbl] *adj* condenable, censurable.

condemnation [,kɔndem'neiʃən] *n* condenación *f* (judgment) ‖ condena *f* (punishment) ‖ FIG condena *f*.

condemnatory [kən'demnətəri] *adj* condenatorio, ria.

condemned [kən'demd] *adj* condenado, da ‖ *condemned cell* celda *f* de los condenados a muerte.

condensability [kən,densə'biliti] *n* condensabilidad *f*.

condensable [kən'densəbl] *adj* condensable.

condensation [,kɔden'seiʃən] *n* condensación *f* (action) ‖ vaho *m* (vapour) ‖ resumen *m* (of a document or speech) ‖ *condensation trail* estela *f* de condensación.

condense [kən'dens] *vt* PHYS condensar ‖ condensar, resumir (document, speech, etc.) ‖ *condensed milk* leche condensada.
◆ *vi* condensarse.

condenser [kən'densə*] *n* condensador *m*.

condescend [,kɔndi'send] *vi* condescender, dignarse; *the king condescended to receive his subjects* el rey condescendió a recibir a sus súbditos; *he condescended to say hello* se dignó saludar.

condescending [,kɔndi'sendiŋ] *adj* condescendiente.

condescension [,kɔndi'senʃən] *n* condescendencia *f*.

condign [kən'dain] *adj* merecido, da; *condign punishment* castigo merecido.

condiment ['kɔndimənt] *n* condimento *m*.

condisciple ['kɔndi'saipl] *n* condiscípulo, la.

condition [kən'diʃən] *n* condición *f* (stipulation); *the conditions of the contract* las condiciones del contrato; *I shall do it on one condition* lo

haré con una condición || condición *f* (social status); *people of every condition* gente de toda condición || estado *m* (state); *in a liquid condition* en estado líquido; *a bicycle in good condition* una bicicleta en buen estado || condiciones *f pl*; *to be in no condition to do sth.* no estar en condiciones de hacer algo; *this merchandise arrived in bad condition* estas mercancías llegaron en malas condiciones || estado *m* de salud; *his condition is very grave* su estado de salud es muy grave || oración *f* condicional || — *on condition that...* a condición de que... || *out of condition* en malas condiciones físicas || *under any condition* de ningún modo || *we try to keep in condition* intentamos mantenernos en forma.
◆ *pl* condiciones *f* (terms) || circunstancias *f* (circumstances) || — *weather conditions permitting* si el tiempo no lo impide || *working conditions* condiciones de trabajo.

condition [kən'diʃən] *vt* condicionar; *supply is conditioned by demand* la oferta está condicionada por la demanda || poner en condiciones, preparar; *to condition a horse for a race* poner en condiciones a un caballo para una carrera || acondicionar (a place, a substance, the air); *to condition a room for a dance* acondicionar un salón para un baile.

conditional [kən'diʃənl] *adj* condicional || GRAMM potencial, condicional (mood) | condicional; *conditional clause* oración condicional || *to be conditional on* depender de.
◆ *n* GRAMM potencial *m*, condicional *m* | oración *f* condicional.

conditioned [kən'diʃənd] *adj* condicionado, da; *conditioned reflexes* reflejos condicionados || acondicionado, da (place, substance, air).

conditioner [kən'diʃənə*] *n* acondicionador *m* || *air conditioner* acondicionador *m* de aire.

conditioning [kən'diʃəniŋ] *n* condicionamiento *m* || acondicionamiento *m* (of place, substance, air) || *air conditioning* aire acondicionado.

condo ['kɔndəʊ] *n* US FAM condominio *m*.

condole [kən'dəul] *vi* condolerse, compadecer (to commiserate); *to condole with s.o.* condolerse de *or* compadecer a alguien || dar el pésame.

condolence [kən'dəuləns] *n* condolencia *f* || — *please accept my condolences* le acompaño en el sentimiento || *to express* o *to send one's condolences for* dar el pésame por.

condom ['kɔndɔm] *n* condón *m* (contraceptive).

condominium ['kɔndə'miniəm] *n* condominio *m*.

condonation [,kɔndəu'neiʃən] *n* condonación *f*, perdón *m*.

condone [kən'dəun] *vt* condonar, perdonar (to forgive) || permitir que continúe (what ought to be stopped).

condor ['kɔndɔ*] *n* cóndor *m* (bird, coin).

conduce [kən'dju:s] *vi* conducir; *to conduce to a result* conducir a un resultado.

conducive [kən'dju:siv] *adj* conducente; *measures conducive to a solution* medidas conducentes a una solución || conveniente; *exercise is conducive to good health* el ejercicio es conveniente para la buena salud || propicio, cia (helpful).

conduct ['kɔndʌkt] *n* conducta *f*, comportamiento *m* (behaviour) || dirección *f*, conducción *f* (direction).

conduct [kən'dʌkt] *vt* conducir, llevar; *he conducted me to my room* me condujo a mi habitación || dirigir; *he conducted his business from his home* dirigía su negocio en su casa; *he conducted the orchestra at that concert* dirigió la orquesta en ese concierto || conducir; *steel conducts electricity* el acero conduce la electricidad || — *conducted tour* visita acompañada || *to conduct o.s.* comportarse, conducirse.
◆ *vi* dirigir una orquesta || conducir (a way) || ELECTR ser conductor.

conductance [-əns] *n* ELECTR conductancia *f*.

conductibility [kən,dʌktə'biliti] *n* conductibilidad *f*.

conduction [kən'dʌkʃən] *n* conducción *f*.

conductive [kən'dʌktiv] *adj* conductivo, va; conductor, ra.

conductivity [,kɔndʌk'tiviti] *n* conductividad *f*.

conductor [kən'dʌtə*] *n* guía *m* (guide) || director *m* (of orchestra, choir) || cobrador *m* (of a bus) || PHYS conductor *m* || US revisor *m* (of trains) || *lightning conductor* pararrayos *m inv*.

conductress [kən'dʌktris] *n* cobradora *f* (of a bus) || directora *f*.

conduit ['kɔndit] *n* conducto *m* || ELECTR tubo *m*.

condyle ['kɔndil] *n* ANAT cóndilo *m*.

condyloid ['kɔndilɔid] *adj* BOT condiloideo, a.

condyloma [kɔndi'ləumə] *n* MED condiloma *m*.
— OBSERV El plural de *condyloma* es *condylomata*.

cone [kəun] *n* MATH cono *m* || BOT piña *f* || cucurucho *m*; *ice-cream cone* cucurucho de helado || TECH *cone gear* engranaje cónico.

cone-shaped [-ʃeipt] *adj* cónico, ca; coniforme.

coney; cony ['kəuni] *n* ZOOL conejo *m* (rabbit) || piel *f* de conejo (rabbit fur).

confab ['kɔnfæb] *n* FAM cháchara *f*, palique *m*.

confab ['kɔnfæb] *vi* FAM charlotear, estar de cháchara *or* de palique.

confabulate [kən'fæbjuleit] *vi* charlar.

confabulation [kən'fæbju'leiʃən] *n* charla *f*.

confect ['kɔnfekt] *vt* confeccionar, preparar (to prepare) || forjar (to invent lies).

confection [kən'fekʃən] *n* CULIN dulce *m*, confite *m* || COMM confección *f* (of clothes) || mixtura *f*, confección *f* (compound of drugs).

confectioner [-ə*] *n* confitero, ra || repostero, ra (pastrycook) || US *confectioner's sugar* azúcar glaseado.

confectionery [kən'fekʃnəri] *n* confitería *f* (shop, trade) || dulces *m pl* (sweets) || repostería *f* (cake shop).

confederacy [kən'fedərəsi] *n* confederación *f*.

confederal [kən'fedərəl] *adj* confederal.

confederate [kən'fedərit] *adj* confederado, da.
◆ *n* cómplice *m* (an accomplice) || confederado, da (ally).

confederate [kən'fedəreit] *vi* confederarse.
◆ *vt* confederar.

confederation [kən,fedə'reiʃən] *n* confederación *f*.

confederative [kən'fedərətiv] *adj* confederativo, va.

confer [kən'fə*] *vi* consultar; *to confer with s.o.* consultar con alguien || conferenciar (to hold a conference).
◆ *vt* conferir, otorgar (*on* a).

conference ['kɔnfərəns] *n* consulta *f* (consultation) || conferencia *f*, congreso *m* (meeting) || entrevista *f*, reunión *f* (talks) || US federación *f* deportiva (sporting league).

conferment [kən'fə:mənt] *n* concesión *f*.

confess [kən'fes] *vt* confesar; *we must confess our sins* debemos confesar nuestros pecados; *Father Smith confessed me* el padre Smith me confesó.
◆ *vi* confesarse (a sinner) || confesar (a confessor) || *to confess a crime* confesar un crimen.

confessed [-d] *adj* declarado, da || confesado, da.

confession [kən'feʃən] *n* confesión *f* || tumba *f* (tomb) || — *confession of faith* profesión *f* de fe || *on their own confession* según propia confesión || *the seal of confession* el secreto de confesión || *to go to confession* confesarse || *to hear confession* confesar || *to make a full confession* confesar de plano.

confessional [kən'feʃənl] *adj* confesional.
◆ *n* confesionario *m*, confesonario *m* (where confession is heard) || confesión *f* (practice).

confessor [kən'fesə*] *n* confesor *m* || director *m* espiritual (spiritual adviser).

confetti [kən'feti] *n* confetti *m pl*, papelillos *m pl*.

confidant [,ɔnfi'dænt] *n* confidente *m*.

confidante [,kɔnfi'dænt] *n* confidente *f* || THEATR confidenta *f*.

confide [kən'faid] *vt* confiar.
◆ *vi to confide in* fiarse de (to trust), confiarse a (to share secrets).

confidence ['kɔfidəns] *n* confianza *f* (trust) || confidencia *f* (secret) || confianza *f*, seguridad *f* en sí mismo || — *confidence man* estafador *m* || *confidence trick* estafa *f*, fraude *m* || *in confidence* en confianza || *to betray s.o.'s confidence* defraudar la confianza de alguien || *to take s.o. into one's confidence* depositar su confianza en alguien.

confident ['kɔnfidənt] *adj* seguro, ra; convencido, da (certain) || seguro de sí mismo (self-assured) || presuntuoso, sa (presumptuous) || — *he is confident of the future* tiene fe en el futuro || *he said it in a confident tone* lo dijo en un tono seguro.
◆ *n* confidente *m* & *f*.

confidential [,kɔnfi'denʃəl] *adj* confidencial || de confianza; *a confidential secretary* una secretaria de confianza || íntimo, ma (friend).

confiding [kən'faidiŋ] *adj* confiado, da.

configurate [kən,figju'reit] *vt* configurar, dar forma.

configuration [kən,figju'reiʃən] *n* configuración *f* || INFORM *configuration; system configuration* configuración del sistema.

configure [kən'figjuə*] *vt* configurar, dar forma || INFORM configurar.

confine ['kɔnfain] *n* confín *m*, límite *m*.

confine [kən'fain] *vt* confinar (to isolate, to imprison) || limitar (to restrict); *confine your remarks to the main issue* limite usted sus observaciones al tema en cuestión || — *he was confined to his bed* tenía que guardar cama || *to be confined* estar de parto (a woman) || *to confine o.s. to* limitarse a.
◆ *vi* ser fronterizos, estar contiguos.

confinement [-mənt] *n* confinamiento *m* (state of being confined) || limitación *f*, límite *m* (restriction) || obligación *f* de guardar cama (to bed) || parto *m* (childbirth) || prisión *f* (prison).

confirm [kən'fə:m] *vt* confirmar || ratificar; *to confirm a treaty* ratificar un tratado || REL confirmar.

confirmand [kɔnfə'mænd] *n* REL confirmando, da.

confirmation [,kɔnfə'meiʃən] *n* confirmación *f* || ratificación *f* (of treaty) || REL confirmación *f*.

confirmatory [kən'fə:mətəri] *adj* confirmativo, va; confirmatorio, ria.

confirmed [kən'fəːmd] *adj* confirmado, da ‖ empedernido, da; *a confirmed bachelor* un solterón empedernido ‖ crónico, ca (illness).

confiscate ['kɔnfiskeit] *vt* confiscar, incautarse de.

confiscation [ˌkɔnfis'keiʃən] *n* confiscación *f*, incautación *f*.

confiscator ['kɔnfiskeitə*] *n* confiscador, ra.

confiscatory [kən'fiskətəri] *adj* de confiscación.

confiteor [kɔn'fitiɔː*] *n* REL confíteor *m*.

conflagration ['kɔnflə'greiʃən] *n* conflagración *f* (war) ‖ incendio *m* (fire).

conflation [kən'fleiʃən] *n* combinación *f* de dos textos.

conflict ['kɔnflikt] *n* conflicto *m*; *conflict of interest* conflicto de intereses.

conflict ['kɔnflikt] *vi* luchar (to struggle, to contend) ‖ chocar (to clash).

conflicting [-iŋ] *adj* contrario, ria; contrapuesto, ta.

confluence ['kɔnfluəns] *n* confluencia *f*.

confluent ['kɔnfluənt] *adj* confluente.
◆ *n* confluente *m*, tributario *m* (river).

conflux ['kɔnflʌks] *n* confluencia *f*.

conform [kən'fɔːm] *vi* conformarse ‖ someterse; *you must conform to discipline* tienes que someterte a la disciplina ‖ ajustarse; *to conform to the regulations* ajustarse a las reglas.
◆ *vt* conformar ‖ ajustar (to adapt).

conformability [kənˌfɔːmə'biliti] *n* conformidad *f*.

conformable [kən'fɔːməbl] *adj* conforme; *conformable to* conforme con.

conformation [ˌkɔnfɔː'meiʃən] *n* conformación *f* ‖ ajuste *m*, amoldamiento *m*, adaptación *f*.

conformism [kən'fɔːmizəm] *n* conformismo *m*.

conformist [kən'fɔːmist] *n* conformista *m* & *f*.

conformity [kən'fɔːmiti] *n* conformidad *f* ‖ *in conformity with* conforme a *or* con.

confound [kən'faund] *vt* confundir (to confuse) ‖ frustrar (to foil) ‖ desconcertar (to disconcert) ‖ maldecir (to damn) ‖ — FAM *confound him!* ¡maldito sea! | *confound it* ¡caray!

confounded [-id] *adj* FAM maldito, ta; condenado, da | desconcertado, da.

confraternity [ˌkɔnfrə'təːniti] *n* hermandad *f*, confraternidad *f*.

confront [kən'frʌnt] *vt* hacer frente a; *a robber confronted me* un ladrón me hizo frente ‖ enfrentar, confrontar (to bring face to face) ‖ presentarse; *many difficulties confronted us* se nos presentaban muchas dificultades ‖ confrontar (to compare).

confrontation [kənfrʌn'teiʃən] *n* confrontación *f*.

Confucius [kən'fjuːʃjəs] *pr n* Confucio *m*.

confuse [kən'fjuːz] *vt* confundir (to mix up, to perplex) ‖ desconcertar (to disconcert) ‖ — *to confuse the issue* complicar las cosas ‖ *to get confused* hacerse un lío.

confusing [-iŋ] *adj* confuso, sa (confused) ‖ desconcertante.

confusion [kən'fjuːʒən] *n* confusión *f*, desorden *m* ‖ confusión *f*, desconcierto *m* (bewilderment) ‖ confusión *f* (embarrassment) ‖ — *a sea of confusion* un mar de confusiones ‖ *to be in confusion* estar en desorden (untidy), estar confuso, sa (embarrassed).

confutation [ˌkɔnfjuː'teiʃən] *n* refutación *f*.

confute [kən'fjuːt] *vt* refutar, confutar.

congeal [kən'dʒiːl] *vi* congelarse (to freeze) ‖ coagularse (to coagulate) ‖ FIG petrificarse, anquilosarse.
◆ *vt* congelar (to freeze) ‖ coagular (to coagulate).

congealment [-mənt]; **congelation** [ˌkɔndʒi'leiʃən] *n* congelación *f* (a freezing) ‖ coagulación *f* (coagulation).

congener ['kɔndʒinə*] *n* congénere *m* & *f*.

congenerous [kən'dʒenərəs] *adj* congénere.

congenial [kən'dʒiːnjəl] *adj* agradable (agreeable) ‖ apropiado, da; conveniente (suitable) ‖ similar (kindred) ‖ compatible.

congenital [kən'dʒenitl] *adj* congénito, ta.

conger ['kɔŋgə*]; **conger eel** [-iːl] *n* ZOOL congrio *m*.

congeries [kɔn'dʒiəriːz] *inv n* montón *m*.

congest [kən'dʒest] *vt* congestionar.
◆ *vi* congestionarse.

congested [-id] *adj* congestionado, da ‖ BOT apiñado, da ‖ superpoblado, da (overpopulated).

congestion [kən'dʒestʃən] *n* congestión *f* ‖ superpoblación *f* (overpopulation).

conglobate ['kɔngləubeit] *vt* conglobar.

conglomerate [kən'glɔmərit] *adj* conglomerado, da.
◆ *n* GEOL conglomerado *m* ‖ conglomeración *f*.

conglomerate [kən'glɔməreit] *vt* conglomerar.
◆ *vi* conglomerarse.

conglomeration [kənˌglɔmə'reiʃən] *n* conglomeración *f* ‖ FAM montón *m* (of things).

conglutinate [kən'gluːtineit] *vt* conglutinar.
◆ *vi* conglutinarse.

conglutination [kəngluːti'neiʃən] *n* conglutinación *f*.

Congo ['kɔŋgəu] *pr n* GEOGR Congo *m*.

Congolese [ˌkɔŋgəu'liz] *adj/n* congolés, esa; congoleño, ña.

congratulate [kən'grætjuleit] *vt* felicitar, dar la enhorabuena, congratular; *I congratulated him on the birth of his daughter* le felicité por el nacimiento de su hija ‖ *to congratulate o.s.* congratularse.

congratulation [kənˌgrætju'leiʃən] *n* congratulación *f*, felicitación *f*; *I send you my sincerest congratulations* reciba Ud. mis más sinceras congratulaciones ‖ *congratulations!* ¡enhorabuena!, ¡felicidades!, ¡muchas felicidades!

congratulatory [kən'grætjulətəri] *adj* congratulatorio, ria; de felicitación.

congregate ['kɔngrigeit] *vi* congregarse.
◆ *vt* congregar.

congregation [ˌkɔŋgri'geiʃən] *n* congregación *f* ‖ REL feligreses *m pl*, fieles *m pl* (of a parish) | congregación *f* (of monks, nuns, etc.).

congregational [-əl] *adj* de la congregación ‖ *the Congregational Church* la Iglesia Congregacionalista.

Congregationalism [ˌkɔŋgri'geiʃnəlizəm] *n* REL congregacionalismo *m*.

congress ['kɔŋgres] *n* congreso *m* (formal meeting) ‖ congreso *m*; *the US Congress* el Congreso de los Estados Unidos.

congressional [kɔŋ'greʃənl] *adj* del congreso.

congressman ['kɔŋgresmən] *n* miembro *m* del Congreso de los Estados Unidos ‖ congresista *m* (of a meeting).
— OBSERV El plural de *congressman* es *congressmen*.

congruence ['kɔŋgruəns]; **congruency** [-i] *n* congruencia *f*.

congruent ['kɔŋgruənt] *adj* congruente.

congruity [kɔŋ'gruːiti] *n* congruencia *f*.

congruous ['kɔŋgruəs] *adj* congruo, grua; congruente.

conic ['kɔnik] *adj* cónico, ca.
◆ *n* geometría *f* cónica.

conical [-əl] *adj* cónico, ca.

conidium [kəu'nidjəm] *n* BOT conidio *m*.
— OBSERV El plural de *conidium* es *conidia*.

conifer ['kəunifə*] *n* BOT conífera *f*.

coniferous [kəu'nifərəs] *adj* BOT conífero, ra.

coniform ['kəunifɔːm] *adj* BOT coniforme; cónico, ca.

conium [kəu'naiəm] *n* BOT cicuta *f* (hemlock).

conjectural [kən'dʒektʃərəl] *adj* conjetural.

conjecture [kən'dʒektʃə] *n* conjetura *f*.

conjecture [kən'dʒektʃə] *vt* conjeturar.
◆ *vi* hacer conjeturas.

conjoin [kən'dʒɔin] *vt* unir.
◆ *vi* unirse.

conjoint ['kɔndʒɔint] *adj* conjunto, ta; *conjoint efforts* esfuerzos conjuntos.

conjugable ['kɔdʒugəbl] *adj* conjugable.

conjugal ['kɔndʒugəl] *adj* conyugal.

conjugate ['kɔndʒugit] *adj* enlazado, da (joined together) ‖ conjugado, da; *conjugate points* puntos conjugados ‖ GRAMM congénere (word).

conjugate ['kɔndʒugeit] *vt* conjugar.
◆ *vi* conjugarse (a verb, etc.).

conjugation [ˌkɔndʒu'geiʃən] *n* conjugación *f*.

conjunct [kən'dʒʌŋkt] *adj* conjunto, ta; unido, da.

conjuction [kən'dʒʌŋkʃən] *n* conjunción *f* ‖ *in conjunction with* conjuntamente con.

conjunctiva [ˌkɔndʒʌŋk'taivə] *n* ANAT conjuntiva *f*.
— OBSERV El plural de la palabra inglesa es *conjunctivae* o *conjunctivas*.

conjuctive [kən'dʒʌŋktiv] *adj* ANAT conjuntivo, va; *conjunctive tissue* tejido conjuntivo ‖ GRAMM conjuntivo, va.
◆ *n* conjunción *f*.

conjunctivitis [kənˌdʒʌŋkti'vaitis] *n* MED conjuntivitis *f*.

conjuncture [kən'dʒʌŋktʃə*] *n* coyuntura *f*.

conjuration [ˌkɔndʒuə'reiʃən] *n* REL conjuro *m*.

conjure [kən'dʒuə*] *vt* suplicar.

conjure ['kʌndʒə*] *vt* conjurar (to invoke a spirit) ‖ hacer aparecer (by sleight of hand); *to conjure a rabbit from a hat* hacer aparecer un conejo de un sombrero ‖ *to conjure up* evocar.
◆ *vi* hacer juegos de manos.

conjurer; conjuror [-rə*] *n* prestidigitador *m*.

conk [kɔŋk] *n* FAM napia *f* (nose) | coco *m* (head).

conk [kɔŋk] *vt* FAM golpear [en la cabeza].
◆ *vi* FAM *to conk out* fastidiarse, estropearse.

conker [-ə*] *n* BOT castaño *m* de Indias.

conn [kɔn] *vt* MAR gobernar.

connate ['kɔneit] *adj* innato, ta; congénito, ta (inborn) ‖ similar (alike).

connatural [kə'nætʃərəl] *adj* connatural, innato, ta; congénito, ta (innate) ‖ similar (alike).

connect [kə'nekt] *vt* conectar (to join together) ‖ relacionar (to relate) ‖ poner [en comunicación] (*with* con) (on the phone) ‖ ELECTR conectar, enchufar (to plug in).
◆ *vi* juntarse, unirse (to join) ‖ empalmar, enlazar (trains) ‖ cambiar a (to change train) ‖ ELECTR conectarse ‖ *to connect with* ponerse en

relación con (people), comunicarse con (a room), relacionarse con (to be related to).

connected [-id] *adj* conectado, da (joined together) || relacionado, da (associated) || empalmado, da (two wagons) || coherente (coherent) || emparentado, da (related) || enchufado, da (plugged in).

connecter [-ə*] *n* conectador *m* || empalme *m* (joint).

Connecticut [kə'netikət] *pr n* GEOGR Connecticut.

connecting [-iŋ] *adj* *connecting gear* embrague *m* || *connecting link* eslabón *m*, lazo *m*, vínculo *m*, nexo *m* || *connecting rod* biela *f*.

connection; connexion [kə'nekʃən] *n* ELECTR & TECH conexión *f* | empalme *m*, unión *f* || empalme *m*, enlace *m* (of trains, buses, etc.) || unión *f* (joint) || FIG pariente *m* (relative) | relación *f* (between persons); *to have good connections* tener buenas relaciones || respecto *m*; *in this connection* a este respecto; *in connection with* con respecto a.

connective [kə'nektiv] *adj* conectivo, va || *connective tissue* tejido conjuntivo.
◆ *n* GRAMM conjunción *f*.

connector [kə'nektə*] *n* conectador *m* || empalme *m* (joint).

connexion [kə'nekʃən] *n* → **connection.**

conning ['kɔniŋ] *adj* MAR *conning tower* torre *f* de mando (of a ship), torrecilla *f* (of a submarine).

conniption [kə'nipʃən] *n* US FAM rabieta *f*.

connivance; connivence [kə'naivəns] *n* connivencia *f*.

connive [kə'naiv] *vi* confabularse; *he connived with Andrew to rob the bank* se confabuló con Andrés para robar el banco || *to connive at* hacer la vista gorda a.

connoisseur [,kɔnə'sə:*] *n* conocedor, ra; experto, ta; perito, ta.

connotation [,kɔnəu'teiʃən] *n* connotación *f*.

connote [kə'nəut] *vt* connotar || implicar, traer consigo (to imply).

connubial [kə'nju:bjəl] *adj* connubial, conyugal.

conoid ['kəunɔid] *n* MATH conoide *m*.
◆ *adj* MATH conoidal, conoideo, a.

conquer ['kɔŋkə*] *vt* conquistar || vencer; *to conquer a habit* vencer un hábito.
◆ *vi* triunfar, vencer.

conquering [-riŋ] *adj* victorioso, sa.

conqueror [-rə*] *n* conquistador; *William the Conqueror* Guillermo el Conquistador || vencedor, ra; triunfador, ra.

conquest ['kɔŋkwest] *n* conquista *f*.

conquistador [kəŋ'kistadɔ:*] *n* conquistador *m*.
— OBSERV El plural en inglés es *conquistadores* o *conquistadors*.

Conrad ['kɔnræd] *pr n* Conrado *m*.

Cons. *abbr of [Conservative]* conservador, ra | *abbr of [Constitution]* constitución.

consanguineous [,kɔnsæŋ'gwiniəs] *adj* consanguíneo, a (related by blood).

consanguinity [,kɔnsæŋ'gwiniti] *n* consanguinidad *f*.

conscience ['kɔnʃəns] *n* conciencia *f*; *to have a clear conscience* tener la conciencia tranquila *or* limpia || — *case of conscience* caso *m* de conciencia || *conscience money* dinero *m* que se da para descargar la conciencia || *for conscience's sake* en descargo de conciencia || *guilty conscience* conciencia sucia || *in all conscience* en conciencia || *matter of conscience* caso *m* de conciencia || *to have a guilty conscience* remorderle a uno la conciencia || *to have sth. on one's conscience* tener un peso en la conciencia.

conscienceless [-lis] *adj* sin escrúpulo, sin conciencia.

conscience-stricken [-,strikən] *adj* contrito, ta; arrepentido, da.

conscientious [,kɔnʃi'enʃəs] *adj* concienzudo, da || *conscientious objector* objetor *m* de conciencia.

conscientiousness [-nis] *n* escrupulosidad *f*.

conscious ['kɔnʃəs] *adj* consciente || — *to become conscious* volver en sí || *to become conscious of* darse cuenta de || *to be conscious* tener conocimiento || *to be conscious of* tener conciencia de, saber.

consciousness [-nis] *n* conciencia *f* || MED conocimiento *m*; *he lost consciousness* perdió el conocimiento.

conscript ['kɔnskript] *n* MIL recluta *m*.
◆ *adj* alistado, da || *conscript father* padre conscripto.

conscript [kən'skript] *vt* MIL reclutar, alistar.

conscription [kən'skripʃən] *n* MIL reclutamiento *m*.

consecrate ['kɔnsikreit] *vt* consagrar.

consecration [,kɔnsigreiʃən] *n* consagración *f*.

consecrator ['kɔnsikreitə*] *n* consagrante *m*.

consecratory ['kɔnsikreitəri] *adj* consagrante.

consecution [,kɔnsi'kju:ʃən] *n* ilación *f* (logical sequence) || sucesión *f*.

consecutive [kən'sekjutiv] *adj* consecutivo, va || sucesivo, va; consecutivo, va (following in regular order).

consensual [kən'sensjuəl] *adj* consensual.

consensus [kən'sensəs] *n* consenso *m*; *consensus of opinion* consenso general.

consent [kən'sent] *n* consentimiento *m* || — *by common consent* de mutuo acuerdo, de común acuerdo || *silence gives consent* quien calla otorga.

consent [kən'sent] *vi* consentir; *to consent to* consentir en.

consentient [kən'sentʃənt] *adj* acorde, unánime || que consiente.

consequence ['kɔnsikwəns] *n* consecuencia *f* || — *in consequence* por consiguiente || *in consequence of* a consecuencia de, como resultado de || *of no consequence* sin importancia || *persons of consequence* personas *f* importantes || *to take the consequences* aceptar las consecuencias.

consequent ['kɔnsikwənt] *n* consecuencia *f* || GRAMM & MATH consecuente *m*.
◆ *adj* consiguiente || *consequent on* o *upon* consecutivo a.

consequential ['kɔnsi'kwenʃəl] *adj* consecuente || suficiente (self-important) || *consequential damages* daños indirectos.

consequently ['kɔnsikwəntli] *adv* consecuentemente, en consecuencia, por lo tanto, por consiguiente.

conservancy [kən'sə:vənsi] *n* conservación *f*, preservación *f* (of natural resources) || comisión *f* portuaria.

conservation [,kɔnsə:'veiʃən] *n* conservación *f* || conservación *f*, preservación *f* (of natural resources).

conservatism [kən'sə:vətizəm] *n* conservadurismo *m* [*AMER* conservatismo *m*].

conservative [kən'sə:vətiv] *adj* conservador, ra || por lo bajo, moderado, da; *conservative estimate* cálculo moderado || prudente; *a conservative investment* una inversión prudente || *conservative party* partido conservador.
◆ *n* conservador, ra (person) || producto *m* para la conservación (preservative).

conservatoire [kən'sə:vətwa:*] *n* MUS conservatorio *m*.

conservator [kən'sə:vətə*] *n* conservador *m*.

conservatory [kən'sə:vətri] *n* invernadero *m* (for plants) || MUS conservatorio *m* (conservatoire).

conserve [kən'sə:v] *n* conserva *f*.

conserve [kən'sə:v] *vt* conservar.

consider [kən'sidə*] *vt* considerar || darse cuenta de (to realize) || examinar (to study) || pensar (en) (to think) || tener en cuenta (to take into account) || — *all things considered* considerándolo bien || *consider yourself lucky* date por satisfecho.

considerable [kən'sidərəbl] *adj* considerable || importante, considerable (amount).

considerably [-i] *adv* considerablemente.

considerate [kən'sidərit] *adj* considerado, da; atento, ta.

considerately [-li] *adv* con consideración.

consideration [kən,sidə'reiʃən] *n* consideración *f* || retribución *f* (payment) || — *after due consideration* después de un detenido examen de la cuestión || *a little consideration costs you nothing* un poco de consideración no te cuesta nada || *for a consideration* por una gratificación || *he shows consideration for others* trata a los demás con consideración || *in consideration of his age* en consideración a su edad || *on no consideration will I do it* no lo haré bajo ningún concepto || *out of consideration for s.o.* por consideración a alguien || *to take into consideration* tomar en consideración || *the question under consideration* la cuestión que se está estudiando *or* examinando || *to act without due consideration* actuar sin reflexionar || *to give consideration to* considerar.

considered [kən'sidəd] *adj* considerado, da.

considering [kən'sidəriŋ] *prep* teniendo en cuenta, considerando (in view of).
◆ *adv* después de todo; *it's not too bad, considering* después de todo, no está mal.

consign [kən'sain] *vt* consignar || COMM consignar || enviar (to send) || confiar (to entrust).

consignatary [kən'signətəri] *n* consignatario, ria.

consignee [,kɔnsai'ni] *n* COMM consignatario *m*.

consignment [kən'sainmənt] *n* COMM consignación *f* (deposit) | envío *m*, expedición *f* (of goods) || *on consignment* en consignación, en depósito.

consigner; consignor [kən'sainə*] *n* consignador *m*.

consist [kən'sist] *vi* consistir, radicar (to lie essentially); *its advantage consists in its simplicity* su ventaja consiste en su simplicidad || componerse, constar (to be composed of); *the human body consists of many parts* el cuerpo humano se compone de muchas partes.

consistency [kən'sistənsi] *n* consistencia *f* (of density) || firmeza *f* (of behaviour); *his behaviour lacks consistency* su conducta carece de firmeza || conformidad *f*, acuerdo *m* (agreement); *consistency between versions* conformidad entre las versiones || coherencia *f* (coherence).

consistent [kən'sistənt] *adj* de acuerdo, consecuente; *his conduct is not consistent with his promises* su conducta no está de acuerdo con sus promesas; *his behaviour is not consistent with his teaching* su comportamiento no es consecuente con sus enseñanzas || firme (going on without change); *a consistent advocate of peace* un firme defensor de la paz || coherente (coherent).

consistorial [ˌkɔnsis'tɔːriəl] *adj* REL consistorial.

consistory [kən'sistəri] *n* REL consistorio *m.*

consolable [kən'səuləbl] *adj* consolable.

consolation [ˌkɔnsə'leiʃən] *n* consuelo *m* ‖ *consolation prize* premio *m* de consolación.

consolatory [kən'sɔlətəri] *adj* consolador, ra.

console [kən'səul] *vt* consolar.

console ['kɔsəul] *n* ménsula *f,* soporte *m* (shelf support) ‖ consola *f* (table) ‖ MUS consola *f* (of organ) ‖ mesa *f* de control (in theatre, in television studio) ‖ mueble *m* para aparato de radio *or* televisión (cabinet for radio or television) ‖ TECH & INFORM pupitre *m,* consola *f* ‖ — INFORM *console operator* operador, ra de consola ‖ *console table* consola *f.*

consoler [kən'səulə*] *n* consolador, ra.

consolidate [kən'sɔlideit] *vt* consolidar, reforzar (to strengthen) ‖ comprimir (to compress) ‖ consolidar (debts).
◆ *vi* comprimirse (to become compressed) ‖ COMM fusionarse (to merge) ‖ consolidarse (to become strengthened).

consolidation [kənˌsɔli'deiʃən] *n* consolidación *f* ‖ COMM fusión *f* (merger) | consolidación *f* (of debts).

consoling [kən'səuliŋ] *adj* consolador, ra.

consols [kən'sɔlz] *pl n* fondos *m* consolidados.

consommé [kən'sɔmei] *n* consomé *m,* caldo *m.*

consonance ['kɔnsənəns] *n* consonancia *f* (in music, in poetry) ‖ PHYS resonancia *f.*

consonant ['kɔnsənənt] *adj* de acuerdo, conforme (consistent); *behaviour consonant with principles* conducta de acuerdo con *or* conforme a unos principios ‖ consonante (in music, poetry, grammar) ‖ PHYS resonante.
◆ *n* GRAMM consonante *f.*

consonantal [ˌkɔnsə'næntl] *adj* GRAMM consonántico, ca.

consort ['kɔnsɔːt] *n* consorte *m* & *f* (of reigning monarch) ‖ MAR escolta *f* ‖ asociación *f* ‖ *in consort with* de acuerdo con.

consort [kən'sɔːt] *vi* asociarse (*with* con) (to associate) ‖ estar de acuerdo, concordar (to be in accord).

consortium [kən'sɔːtjəm] *n* consorcio *m.*
— OBSERV El plural es *consortia* o *consortiums.*

conspectus [kən'spektəs] *n* estudio *m* general (comprehensive survey) ‖ sinopsis *f,* cuadro *m* sinóptico (synopsis).

conspicuous [kən'spikjuəs] *adj* visible; *a conspicuous landmark* un punto de referencia visible ‖ llamativo, va (attracting attention); *a conspicuous tie* una corbata llamativa ‖ notable, insigne (remarkable); *conspicuous gallantry* notable galantería ‖ manifiesto, ta; patente (obvious); *a conspicuous violation* una violación manifiesta ‖ — *to be conspicuous by one's absence* brillar por su ausencia ‖ *to make o.s. conspicuous* llamar la atención ‖ *to play a conspicuous part* desempeñar un papel importante.

conspicuousness [-nis] *n* evidencia *f* ‖ lo llamativo.

conspiracy [kən'spirəsi] *n* conspiración *f.*

conspirator [kən'spirətə*] *n* conspirador, ra.

conspire [kən'spaiə*] *vi* conspirar.
◆ *vt* urdir, maquinar (a plot).

constable ['kʌnstəbl] *n* policía *m,* guardia *m* (policeman) ‖ (ant) condestable *m* ‖ administrador *m* de un castillo real.

constabulary [kən'stæbjuləri] *n* policía *f*; *the mounted constabulary* la policía montada.
◆ *adj* de policía, policial.

Constance ['kɔnstəns] *pr n* Constanza ‖ GEOGR *Constance Lake* lago *m* Constanza.

constancy ['kɔnstənsi] *n* constancia *f* (steadfastness) ‖ fidelidad *f,* lealtad *f* (loyalty) ‖ fortaleza *f* (endurance) ‖ invariabilidad *f* (stability).

constant ['kɔnstənt] *adj* constante (unceasing, stable) ‖ leal, fiel (loyal).
◆ *n* MATH & PHYS constante *f.*

Constantine ['kɔnstəntain] *pr n* Constantino *m.*

Constantinople [ˌkɔnstænti'nəupl] *pr n* GEOGR Constantinopla.

constellate ['kɔnstəleit] *vpr* tachonar, sembrar (to stud) ‖ agrupar (to group) ‖ constelar (to spangle).
◆ *vi* agruparse ‖ ASTR formar una constelación.

constellation ['kɔnstə'leiʃən] *n* constelación *f.*

consternate ['kɔnstəneit] *vt* consternar ‖ *to be consternated* consternarse.

consternation [ˌkɔnstə'neiʃən] *n* consternación *f.*

constipate ['kɔnstipeit] *vt* estreñir.

constipation [ˌkɔnsti'peiʃən] *n* estreñimiento *m.*

constituency [kən'stitjuənsi] *n* distrito *m* electoral, circunscripción *f* (area) ‖ colegio *m* electoral, electorado *m* (body of voters).

constituent [kən'stitjuənt] *n* componente *m* (component) ‖ votante, elector, ra (votes) ‖ JUR poderdante *m.*
◆ *adj* constitutivo, va; constituyente (component) ‖ electoral (having power to elect) ‖ constituyente (modifying a constitution); *constituent assembly* asamblea constituyente.

constitute ['kɔnstitjuːt] *vt* constituir (to set up, to make up) ‖ nombrar (to appoint).

constitution [ˌkɔnsti'tjuːʃən] *n* constitución *f* (setting up, physical condition, principles) ‖ estatutos *m pl* (statutes).

constitutional [ˌkɔnsti'tjuːʃənl] *adj* constitucional ‖ *constitutional law* derecho político.
◆ *n* paseo *m* higiénico.

constitutionalism [ˌkɔnsti'tjuːʃnəlizəm] *n* constitucionalismo *m.*

constitutionalist [kɔnst'itjuːʃnəlist] *n* especialista *m* en derecho político (student of constitutionalism) ‖ partidario *m* del constitucionalismo, constitucionalista *m* & *f* (supporter of constitutionalism).

constitutionality [ˌkɔnstitjuːʃə'næliti] *n* constitucionalidad *f.*

constitutionalize [ˌkɔnsti'tjuːʃnəlaiz] *vt* constitucionalizar.

constitutionally [ˌkɔnsti'tjuːʃnəli] *adv* JUR constitucionalmente ‖ físicamente.

constitutive ['kɔnstitjuːtiv] *adj* constitutivo, va.

constrain [kən'strein] *vt* constreñir, obligar, forzar (to compel) ‖ encerrar (to confine) ‖ incomodar, violentar (to embarrass).

constrained [-d] *adj* incómodo, da; violento, ta (embarrassed) ‖ forzado, da; obligado, da (compelled) ‖ encerrado, da (confined) ‖ *constrained smile* risa forzada.

constraint [kən'streint] *n* coacción *f,* imperativo *m,* fuerza *f* (compulsion) ‖ turbación *f,* confusión *f,* molestia *f* (sense of embarrassment) ‖ encierro *m* (restriction of liberty) ‖ represión *f* (of feelings).

constrict [kən'strikt] *vt* estrechar (to make narrower) ‖ oprimir (to compress) ‖ estrangular (a vein).

constricted [-id] *adj* estrecho, cha; limitado, da; *constricted outlook* visión estrecha.

constriction [kən'strikʃən] *n* constricción *f* ‖ estrangulamiento *m* (of a vein).

constrictive [kən'striktiv] *adj* constrictivo, va.

constrictor [kən'striktə*] *n* ANAT músculo *m* constrictor, constrictor *m* ‖ ZOOL constrictor *m,* boa *f* constrictor.

constringent [kən'strindʒənt] *adj* constringente.

construable [kən'struːəbl] *adj* analizable (able to be analysed) ‖ interpretable (interpretable) ‖ explicable (explicable).

construct [kən'strʌkt] *vt* construir.

construction [kən'strʌkʃən] *n* construcción *f* ‖ composición *f* escultórica (sculpture) ‖ estructura *f* (structure) ‖ — *to put a good, a bad construction on s.o.'s words* interpretar bien, mal las palabras de alguien ‖ *under construction* en construcción.

constructional [-l] *adj* de la construcción ‖ estructural.

constructionist [-ist] *n* US persona *f* que interpreta la ley a su manera.

constructive [kən'strʌktiv] *adj* constructivo, va ‖ JUR por deducción, implícito, ta.

constructiveness [-nis] *n* carácter *m* constructivo.

constructor [kən'strʌktə*] *n* constructor *m.*

construe [kən'struː] *vt* GRAMM construir (to combine in syntax) ‖ analizar (a sentence) ‖ traducir literalmente (to translate) ‖ interpretar (to interpret).
◆ *vi* GRAMM tener construcción gramatical ‖ *not to construe* estar mal construido, da.

consubstantial [ˌkɔnsəb'stænʃəl] *adj* REL consubstancial.

consubstantiate [ˌkɔnsəb'stænʃieit] *vt* REL unir en una sola y misma substancia.

consubstantiation ['kɔnsəbˌstænʃi'eiʃən] *n* REL consubstanciación *f.*

consuetude ['kɔnswitjuːd] *n* costumbre *f.*

consuetudinary [ˌkɔnswi'tjuːdinəri] *adj* consuetudinario, ria.
◆ *pl n* devocionario *m sing* (book).

consul ['kɔnsəl] *n* cónsul *m.*

consular ['kɔnsjulə*] *adj* consular.

consulate ['kɔnsjulit] *n* consulado *m.*

consulship ['kɔnsəlʃip] *n* consulado *m.*

consult [kən'sʌlt] *vt/vi* consultar.

consultancy [kən'sʌltənsi] *n* consultoría *f.*

consultant [kən'sʌltənt] *n* JUR asesor *m* jurídico ‖ MED especialista *m* (doctor) ‖ TECH consejero *m* técnico ‖ *engineering consultant* ingeniero consultor.

consultation [ˌkɔnsəl'teiʃən] *n* consulta *f.*

consultative [kən'sʌltətiv] *adj* consultivo, va.

consulting [kən'sʌltiŋ] *adj* consultor, ra ‖ — *consulting hours* horas *f* de consulta ‖ *consulting office* o *room* consultorio *m,* consulta *f.*

consultor [kən'sʌltə*] *n* consultor *m.*

consumable [kən'sjuːməbl] *adj* COMM consumible, de consumo.
◆ *n* artículo *m* de consumo.

consume [kən'sjuːm] *vt* COMM consumir ‖ comerse (to eat) ‖ beberse (to drink) ‖ consumir (fire) ‖ tomar (time) ‖ *to be consumed with envy* estar muerto de envidia *or* carcomido por la envidia.

consumer [-ə*] *n* consumidor, ra ‖ — *consumer durables* bienes *m* de consumo duraderos ‖ *consumer goods* bienes *m* de consumo ‖ *consumer society* sociedad *f* de consumo ‖ *consumer tax* impuesto *m* de consumo.

consumerism [kən'sjuːmərizm] *n* protección *m* de los consumidores.

consummate [kʌn'sʌmit] *adj* consumado, da; *consummate liar* mentiroso consumado.

consummate ['kɔnsəmeit] *vt* consumar || satisfacer (a wish).

consummation [,kɔnsə'meiʃən] *n* consumación *f* (act of completing) || culminación *f* (fulfilment); *the consummation of a life's work* la culminación del trabajo de una vida.

consumption [kən'sʌmpʃən] *n* consumo *m* (in economy) || destrucción *f* (destruction); *the consumption of the forest by the flames* la destrucción del bosque por el fuego || consumo *m*, consumición *f* (act of consuming) || FAM tisis *f*, consunción *f* (tuberculosis) || *consumption tax* impuesto *m* de consumo.

consumptive [kən'sʌmptiv] *adj* destructivo, va (destructive) || FAM tísico, ca (tuberculous).
◆ *n* FAM tísico, ca.

contact ['kɔntækt] *n* contacto *m* || — *to be in contact with* estar en contacto con || ELECTR *to break contact* interrumpir el contacto || *to come into contact with* tocar (to touch), chocar con (to clash), entrar en contacto con (to deal with), encontrar (to meet) || *to get into contact with* ponerse en contacto con || *to have contacts* tener relaciones || *to lose contact with s.o.* perder el contacto con alguien || *to make contact with s.o.* lograr ponerse en contacto con alguien, lograr localizar a alguien.
◆ *adj* de contacto; *contact lens* lente de contacto || — ELECTR *contact breaker* interruptor *m* || *contact flying* vuelo *m* con visibilidad || *we were the contact men of the firm* éramos los representantes de la empresa.

contact ['kəntækt] *vt* ponerse en contacto con.

contactor [-ə*] *n* ELECTR interruptor *m* automático.

contagion [kən'teidʒən] *n* contagio *m*, contaminación *f*.

contagious [kən'teidʒəs] *adj* contagioso, sa.

contagiousness [-nis] *n* contagiosidad *f*.

contagium [kən'teidʒiəm] *n* virus *m*.
— OBSERV El plural de *contagium* es *contagia*.

contain [kən'tein] *vt* contener (to enclose, to include) || contener (to restrain); *she couldn't contain her laughter* no pudo contener la risa || MATH ser divisible por || *to contain o.s.* contenerse.

container [-ə*] *n* recipiente *m* (receptacle) || contenedor *m* (for transporting goods) || envase *m* (package).

containerize [-əraiz] *vt* poner en contenedores.

containment [kən'teinmənt] *n* contención *f*.

contaminant [kən'tæminənt] *n* contaminador *m*, contaminante *m*.

contaminate [kən'tæmineit] *vt* contaminar (disease, environment) || contaminar, corromper (morally).

contamination [kən,tæmi'neiʃən] *n* contaminación *f*, contagio *m* (of a disease) || contaminación *f* (of environment) || corrupción *f*, contaminación *f* (corruption).

contemn [kən'tem] *vt* desdeñar, despreciar.

contemplate ['kɔntempleit] *vt* contemplar (to look attentively) || considerar, examinar (to consider) || contar con, prever (to expect) || estar pensando en (to be considering).
◆ *vi* reflexionar.

contemplation [,kɔntem'pleiʃən] *n* contemplación *f* (act of looking) || contemplación *f*, meditación *f* || consideración *f*, examen *m* (study) || proyecto *m*, perspectiva *f* (plan); *no changes are in contemplation* no hay cambios en perspectiva.

contemplative ['kɔntempleitiv] *adj/n* contemplativo, va.

contemplator ['kɔntempleitə*] *n* contemplador, ra.

contemporaneity [kən,tempərə'ni:iti] *n* contemporaneidad *f*.

contemporaneous [kən,tempə'reinjəs] *adj* contemporáneo, a.

contemporary [kən'tempərəri] *adj/n* contemporáneo, a.

contemporize [kən'tempəraiz] *vt* volver contemporáneo.

contempt [kən'tempt] *n* desprecio *m*, desdén *m* || — *contempt of court* desacato *m* a los tribunales || *to hold in contempt* despreciar.

contemptibility [kən,temptə'biliti] *n* bajeza *f*.

contemptible [kən'temptəbl] *adj* despreciable, desdeñable.

contemptuous [kən'temptjuəs] *adj* despreciativo, va; desdeñoso, sa; despectivo, va (gesture) || desdeñoso, sa (person).

contend [kən'tend] *vi* contender, luchar (to struggle) || disputar (to argue) || competir (to compete).
◆ *vt* afirmar, sostener; *he contended that he was right* afirmó que tenía razón || disputar (to argue).

contender [-ə*] *n* competidor, ra; contendiente *m* & *f* (rival).

contending [-iŋ] *adj* en conflicto; opuesto, ta; *contending passions* pasiones en conflicto || litigante; *contending parties* partes litigantes.

content [kən'tent] *vt* contentar || *to content o.s. with* contentarse con.

content [kən'tent] *adj* contento, ta || *to rest content* conformarse, darse por contento.

content [kən'tent] *n* contento *m* || voto *m* a favor (vote) || — *not content* voto en contra || *to one's heart's content* hasta quedarse satisfecho.

content ['kɔntent] *n* contenido *m* (substance contained) || capacidad *f* (capacity) || índice *m* de materias (index) || contenido *m* (of speech, argument, book) || significado *m* (significance) || contenido *m*, proporción *f*; *gold content* contenido en oro, proporción en oro.

contented [kən'tentid] *adj* contento, ta.

contention [kən'tenʃən] *n* contienda *f* (struggle) || controversia *f*, discusión *f* (controversy) || opinión *f* (opinion) || *to be in contention for sth.* competir por algo.

contentious [kən'tenʃəs] *adj* peleón, ona; pendenciero, ra; belicoso, sa (people) || discutible (issue) || JUR contencioso, sa.

contentiousness [-nis] *n* carácter *m* pendenciero.

contentment [kən'tentmənt] *n* contento *m*.

conterminous [kɔn'tə:minəs] *adj* limítrofe.

contest ['kɔntest] *n* competición *f*, prueba *f* (competition) || concurso *m*; *beauty contest* concurso de belleza || lucha *f*, contienda *f* (struggle) || controversia *f*, discusión *f* (controversy) || *beyond contest* impugnable, incontestable.

contest [kən'test] *vt* impugnar, rebatir (to question) || disputar (to dispute) || presentarse como candidato a (election, seat in Parliament).
◆ *vi* luchar, contender.

contestable [kən'testəbl] *adj* discutible.

contestant [kən'testənt] *n* contrincante *m* (in a match, fight) || candidato, ta (in election, etc.) || concursante *m* & *f*.

contestation [kɔntes'teiʃən] *n* controversia *f*, disputa *f* (controversy) || impugnación *f* (a questioning).

context ['kɔntekst] *n* contexto *m*.

contextual [kɔn'tekstjuəl] *adj* según el contexto (depending on the context) || del contexto.

contexture [kɔn'tekstjə*] *n* contextura *f*.

contiguity [,kɔnti'gju:iti] *n* contigüidad *f*.

contiguous [kən'tigjuəs] *adj* contiguo, gua.

continence ['kɔntinəns] *n* continencia *f*.

continent ['kɔntinənt] *adj* continente.
◆ *n* continente *m* || *the Continent* el continente europeo.

continental [,kɔnti'nentl] *adj* continental || de Europa continental || — *continental climate* clima *m* continental || *continental drift* deriva *f* de los continentes || *continental shelf* plataforma *f* continental.
◆ *n* habitante *m* del continente europeo.

continental quilt [-kwilt] *n* edredón *m* nórdico.

contingency [kən'tindʒənsi] *n* contingencia *f*, eventualidad *f* (possibility) || acontecimiento *m* fortuito (event) || PHYL contingencia *f*.
◆ *pl* gastos *m* accesorios (expenses).

contingent [kən'tindʒənt] *adj* contingente, eventual (liable to happen) || aleatorio, ria (aleatory) || derivado, da (incidental); *risks contingent to mining* riesgos derivados de la minería || supeditado, da; subordinado, da (dependent) || accidental, fortuito, ta (accidental) || contingente (in logic) || *contingent on* o *upon* dependiente de.
◆ *n* MIL contingente *m* (of troops) || representación *f*; *the Spanish contingent at the Olympics* la representación española en los Juegos Olímpicos || contingencia *f* (which may or may not happen).

continual [kən'tinjuəl] *adj* continuo, nua.

continuance [kən'tinjuəns] *n* permanencia *f* (in office, place) || duración *f* (duration) || continuación *f* || perpetuación *f* (of species) || JUR aplazamiento *m*.

continuant [kən'tinjuənt] *n* GRAMM consonante.
◆ *adj* GRAMM continuo, nua (consonant).

continuation [kən,tinju'eiʃən] *n* continuación *f*.

continuative [kən'tinjuətiv] *adj* continuativo, va.

continuator [kən'tinjueitə*] *n* continuador, ra.

continue [kən'tinju:] *vt* continuar (to go on with, to resume, to prolong) || seguir, continuar; *to continue working* seguir trabajando || mantener (to prolong the employment of s.o.) || prolongar (to lengthen) || JUR aplazar.
◆ *vi* continuar || seguir, continuar; *he continues to be chairman* sigue en la presidencia || prolongarse (to extend) || *to be continued* continuará.

continuity ['kɔnti'nju:iti] *n* continuidad *f* || guión *m* (cinema, radio) || intervalo *m* hablado *or* musical (between two programs) || MATH continuidad *f* || *continuity girl* secretaria *f* de rodaje.

continuous [kən'tinjuəs] *adj* continuo, nua || *continuous assessment* evaluación *f* continua.

continuum [kən'tinjuəm] *n* MATH cantidad *f* *or* serie *f* continua.
— OBSERV El plural es *continua* o *continuums*.

contort [kən'tɔ:t] *vt* retorcer, torcer.

contortion [kən'tɔ:ʃən] *n* contorsión *f* (a twisting) || FIG deformación *f*; *contortion of the truth* deformación de la verdad.

contortionist [kən'tɔ:ʃənist] *n* contorsionista *m* & *f*.

contour ['kɔntuə*] *n* contorno *m* (outline) || curva *f* de nivel (of map) || — *contour line* curva de nivel || *contour map* mapa topográfico.

contour ['kɔntuə*] *vt* levantar curvas de nivel en (to mark with contours) || trazar (una carretera) siguiendo las curvas de nivel || contornear, perfilar.

contraband ['kɔntrəbænd] *n* contrabando *m* || *contraband of war* contrabando de guerra.
◆ *adj* de contrabando.

contrabandist ['kɔntrəbændist] *n* contrabandista *m* & *f*.

contrabass ['kɔntrə'beis] *n* MUS contrabajo *m* (instrument).

contrabassist [-ist] *n* contrabajo *m* (musician).

contrabassoon ['kɔntrəbə'suːn] *n* MUS contrafagot *m* (instrument).

contraception [,kɔntrə'sepʃən] *n* contracepción *f*.

contraceptive [,kɔntrə'septiv] *adj* anticonceptivo, va; contraceptivo, va || *contraceptive pill* píldora *f* anticonceptiva.
◆ *n* contraceptivo *m*.

contract ['kɔntrækt] *n* contrato *m*; *contract of purchase and sale* contrato de compraventa || contrato *m* (in bridge) || contrata *f* (of public works).

contract [kən'trækt] *vt* contraer (debts) || contratar (to make a contract) || coger (a chill, a cold) || fruncir (eyebrow) || contraer (to shrink, to shorten) || contraer (muscles).
◆ *vi* contraerse (to shrink) || hacer un contrato (to enter into a contract).

contractile [kən'træktail] *adj* contráctil.

contractility [,kɔntræk'tiliti] *n* contractilidad *f*.

contracting [kən'træktiŋ] *adj* contratante; *contracting party* parte contratante.
◆ *n* contratación *f* (engagement).

contraction [kən'trækʃən] *n* MED contracción *f* || GRAMM contracción *f*.

contractive [kən'træktiv] *adj* contractivo, va.

contractor [kən'træktə*] *n* contratista *m* (person or firm undertaking work) || ANAT músculo *m* que se contrae.

contractual [kən'træktjuəl] *adj* contractual.

contradict [,kɔntrə'dikt] *vt* contradecir || *to contradict o.s.* contradecirse.

contradiction [,kɔntrə'dikʃən] *n* contradicción *f* || *to be a contradiction in terms* ser contradictorio.

contradictious [,kəntrə'dikʃəs] *adj* contradictorio, ria (contrary) || contradictor, ra (person).

contradictorily [,kɔntrə'diktərili] *adv* contradictoriamente.

contradictoriness [,kɔntrə'diktərinis] *n* contradicción *f*, carácter *m* contradictorio.

contradictory [,kɔntrə'diktəri] *adj* contradictorio, ria.
◆ *n* contradictoria *f* (in logic).

contradistinction [,kɔntrədis'tiŋkʃən] *n* oposición *f*, contraste *m*.

contradistinguish [,kɔntrədis'tiŋgwiʃ] *vt* diferenciar, contrastar.

contrail ['kɔntreil] *n* estela *f*.

contraindicate [,kɔntrə'indikeit] *vt* contraindicar.

contraindication [,kɔntrəindi'keiʃən] *n* contraindicación *f*.

contraindicative [,kɔntrəin'dikətiv] *adj* contraindicante.

contralto [kən'træltəu] *n* contralto *m*.
◆ *adj* de contralto.

contraposition [,kɔntrəpə'ʒiʃən] *n* contraposición *f*.

contraption [kən'træpʃən] *n* artefacto *m*, aparato *m*, artilugio *m* (contrivance) || FAM chisme *m* (thing).

contrapuntal [,kɔntrə'pʌntl] *adj* MUS de contrapunto.

contrapuntist ['kɔntrəpʌntist] *n* contrapuntista *m*.

contrariety [,kɔntrə'raiəti] *n* oposición *f* || inconsistencia *f* (inconsistency).

contrarily ['kɔntrərili] *adv* contrariamente.

contrariness ['kɔntrərinis] *n* espíritu *m* de contradicción || oposición *f*.

contrariwise ['kɔntrəriwaiz] *adv* al contrario (on the contrary) || en sentido opuesto (the opposite way) || viceversa.

contrary ['kɔntrəri] *adj* contrario, ria (opposed) || que siempre está llevando la contraria; *he was a very contrary child* era un niño que siempre estaba llevando la contraria || *don't be so contrary!* ¡no me lleves la contraria!
◆ *n* lo contrario || — *on the contrary* al contrario, por el contrario || *quite the contrary!* ¡todo lo contrario! || *to the contrary* en contra; *I have nothing to say to the contrary* no tengo nada que decir en contra.
◆ *pl* TECH impurezas *f*, cuerpos *m* extraños.
◆ *adv* contrariamente; *contrary to public opinion* contrariamente a lo que la opinión pública cree.

contrast ['kɔntrɑːst] *n* contraste *m*; *in contrast* por contraste || *to be a contrast to* contrastar con.

contrast [kən'trɑːst] *vt* contrastar, hacer contrastar.
◆ *vi* contrastar.

contrasting [kən'trɑːstiŋ] *adj* contrastante.

contravene [,kɔntrə'viːn] *vt* JUR contravenir (to infringe) || ir en contra de (to go against) || negar (to deny) || oponerse a (to oppose).

contravener [-ə*] *n* JUR contraventor, ra.

contravening [-iŋ] *adj* JUR contraventor, ra.

contravention [,kɔntrə'venʃən] *n* JUR contravención *f*.

contredanse ['kɔ̃ntrədɑns] *n* contradanza *f*.

contretemps ['kɔ̃ntrətɑːŋ] *n* contratiempo *m*.

contribute [kən'tribjuːt] *vt* contribuir (con) (to donate) || escribir (newspaper articles) || aportar (to provide information, etc.).
◆ *vi* contribuir || colaborar (to a newspaper).

contribution [,kɔntri'bjuːʃən] *n* contribución *f* || artículo *m*, colaboración *f* (to a newspaper) || intervención *f* (in discussion) || aportación *f* (of funds, information, etc.) || *to lay under contribution* hacer contribuir.

contributive [kən'tribjutiv] *adj* contributivo, va; contribuyente.

contributor [kən'tribjutə*] *n* contribuyente *m* & *f* || colaborador, ra (of a newspaper, etc.).

contributory [-ri] *adj* contribuyente, cooperante || — *contributory negligence* responsabilidad *f* de la víctima en un accidente || *contributory pension* pensión *f* de retiro.
◆ *n* accionista *m* que en caso de liquidación de una sociedad debe contribuir al pago de las deudas.

contrite ['kɔntrait] *adj* contrito, ta.

contrition [kən'triʃən] *n* contrición *f*.

contrivable [kən'traivəbl] *adj* realizable, factible (feasible) || imaginable (imaginable).

contrivance [kən'traivəns] *n* invención *f* (invention) || artefacto *m*, aparato *m* (mechanical appliance) || ingenio *m* (resourcefulness); *it required considerable contrivance to get us there in time* necesitamos mucho ingenio para llegar allí a tiempo || invento *m*, invención *f*; *his excuse was a mere contrivance* su excusa era una pura invención.

contrive [kən'traiv] *vt* inventar, idear; *he contrived a means of getting out of classes* ideó una estratagema para no ir a clase; *he contrived a new kind of tool* inventó un nuevo tipo de herramienta || conseguir (to manage); *he contrived to raise his family on very little money* consiguió sacar adelante a su familia con muy poco dinero.

contrived [-d] *adj* artificial.

contriver [-ə*] *n* autor, ra.

control [kən'trəul] *n* control *m* (direction, restraint, regulation) || autoridad *f* (authority) || control *m*, dominación *f* (power) || control *m*, comprobación *f*, verificación *f* || control *m* (checkpoint in rally, etc.) || testigo *m* (standard of comparison) || espíritu *m* que controla al médium || — *birth control* regulación *f* de nacimientos, limitación *f* de la natalidad, control de natalidad || *control board* tablero *m* de mando || *control column* palanca *f* de mando || *control desk* pupitre *m*, consola *f* || INFORM *control drive* armario *m* de control *or* de mando | *control key* tecla *f* de control || *control knob* botón *m* (de mando) || *control panel* tablero *m* de instrumentos || *control point* punto *m* de control || *control room* sala *f* de control || *control tower* torre *f* de control || INFORM *control unit* unidad *f* de control || *dual control* doble mando *m* || *remote control* mando *m* a distancia || *the epidemic is beyond our control* la epidemia está fuera de nuestro control || *to be in control* tener el mando || *to be out of control* estar fuera de control || *to be under control* estar bajo control || *to get under control* conseguir dominar || *to lose control of* perder el control de || *to lose control of o.s.* perder el control de sí mismo.
◆ *pl* mandos *m* (of aircraft, vehicle).

control [kən'trəul] *vt* controlar (to restrain, to regulate); *control your temper* controla el mal humor || tener autoridad sobre *or* bajo su mando; *he controls two thousand men* tiene autoridad sobre dos mil hombres || controlar (to direct); *he controls the steel industry* controla la industria del acero || verificar, comprobar, controlar (to verify) || manejar (vehicle) || TECH regular, controlar (to regulate) | poner en marcha, accionar (to work).

controllable [-əbl] *adj* controlable.

controlled [-d] *adj* controlado, da || dirigido, da (economy).

controller [-ə*] *n* director *m* (director) || COMM interventor *m* || inspector *m* (inspector) || control *m* (controlling device) || ELECTR combinador *m* || AVIAT controlador *m*; *air traffic controller* controlador del tráfico aéreo || INFORM controlador *m*.

controlling [-iŋ] *adj* predominante; *controlling interest* interés predominante || dirigente (governing) || determinante (decisive).

controversial [,kɔntrə'vəːʃəl] *adj* polémico, ca; controvertible, discutible (disputable) || discutidor, ra; polémico, ca (person).

controversy ['kɔntrəvəːsi] *n* controversia *f*, polémica *f*, discusión *f* || *beyond* o *without controversy* incuestionable, incontrovertible.

controvert ['kɔntrəvəːt] *vt* controvertir, discutir, debatir (to discuss) || contradecir (to deny).

controvertible [-əbl] *adj* controvertible.

contumacious [,kɔntyu,meiʃəs] *adj* contumaz.

contumacy ['kɔntjuməsi] *n* contumacia *f*.

contumelious [,kɔntju'miːljəs] *adj* afrentoso, sa; ofensivo, va.

contumely ['kɔntjuːmli] *n* contumelia *f*, ofensa *f*, afrenta *f*.

contuse [kən'tju:z] *vt* contusionar.

contusion [kən'tju:ʒən] *n* contusión *f.*

conundrum [kə'nʌndrəm] *n* adivinanza *f* (riddle) ‖ enigma *m* (problem).

conurbation [,kɔnə:'beiʃən] *n* conurbación *f.*

convalesce [,kɔnvə'les] *vi* convalecer.

convalescence [,kɔnvə'lesns] *n* convalecencia *f.*

convalescent [,kɔnvə'lesnt] *adj* convaleciente ‖ *convalescent home* casa *f* de convalecencia, clínica *f* de reposo.
◆ *n* convaleciente *m* & *f.*

convection [kən'vekʃən] *n* PHYS convección *f.*

convector [kən'vektə*] *n* estufa *f* de convección.

convene [kən'vi:n] *vt* convocar (to call together) ‖ citar (to summon).
◆ *vi* reunirse.

convenience [kən'vi:njəns] *n* conveniencia *f*; *marriage of convenience* matrimonio de conveniencia ‖ ventaja *f* (advantage); *living near one's work is a great convenience* vivir cerca de donde uno trabaja es una gran ventaja ‖ comodidad *f*, confort *m* (comfort) ‖ dispositivo *m* útil (useful device) ‖ — *at your convenience* cuando guste, cuando le sea posible ‖ *at your earliest convenience* tan pronto como le sea posible ‖ *it is a great convenience* es muy cómodo ‖ *to make a convenience of s.o.* abusar de alguien ‖ *to suit one's convenience* convenirle a uno.
◆ *pl* servicios *m* (toilets).

convenience foods [-,fu:dz] *pl n* alimentos *m* congelados *or* enlatados, platos *m* preparados.

convenient [kən'vi:njənt] *adj* cómodo, da (handy) ‖ conveniente (suitable) ‖ práctico, ca (tool) ‖ oportuno, na (time) ‖ bien situado, da (place) ‖ *if it is convenient for you* si le conviene.

convent ['kɔnvənt] *n* convento *m.*

convention [kən'venʃən] *n* convenio *m* (agreement between nations) ‖ convención *f* (usage) ‖ congreso *m*, asamblea *f* (conference).
◆ *pl* conveniencias *f* (polite practices) ‖ convencionalismo *m sing* (conventionalism).

conventional [-əl] *adj* convencional (deriving from convention, not original) ‖ clásico, ca (traditional); *conventional weapons* armas clásicas.

conventionalist [-əlist] *n* convencionalista *m* & *f.*

conventionality [kən,venʃə'næliti] *n* convencionalismo *m.*

conventionalize [kən'venʃənəlaiz] *vt* hacer convencional (to make conventional) ‖ ARTS estilizar (to stylize).

conventual [kən'ventjuəl] *adj* conventual.
◆ *n* REL miembro *m* de un convento.

converge [kən'və:dʒ] *vi* converger, convergir (*on, upon, in* en).
◆ *vt* hacer converger *or* convergir.

convergence [kən'və:dʒəns] *n* convergencia *f.*

convergent [kən'və:dʒənt]; **converging** [kən'və:dʒiŋ] *adj* convergente.

conversable [kən'və:səbl] *adj* sociable, tratable (sociable) ‖ conversador, ra (fond of conversation) ‖ a propósito para la conversación.

conversance [kən'və:səns]; **conversancy** [-i] *n* familiaridad *f* ‖ conocimiento *m* (acquaintance through study).

conversant [kən'və:sənt] *adj* versado, da; entendido, da (informed about); *conversant with the matter* versado en la materia ‖ familiarizado, da; conocedor, ra (well acquainted) ‖ *to become conversant with* familiarizarse con.

conversation [,kɔnvə'seiʃən] *n* conversación *f* [AMER plática *f*]; *to make conversation* dar conversación ‖ JUR trato *m* carnal ‖ — *conversation piece* tema *m* de conversación (something that arouses conversation), interior *m*, escena *f* de interior (genre painting) ‖ *criminal conversation* adulterio *m.*
◆ *pl* conversaciones *f.*

conversational [-l] *adj* locuaz, hablador, ra (person) ‖ familiar, de la conversación (tone) ‖ INFORM conversacional; *conversational terminal* terminal *m* conversacional.

conversationalist [-list] *n* conversador, ra; hablador, ra.

converse ['kɔnvə:s] *n* proposición *f* recíproca (in logic) ‖ lo opuesto, lo contrario (opposite) ‖ MATH recíproca *f.*
◆ *adj* opuesto, ta; contrario, ria.

converse [kən'və:s] *vi* conversar, hablar [AMER platicar].

conversely [kən'və:sli] *adv* a la inversa.

conversion [kən'və:ʃən] *n* conversión *f*, transformación *f* (from one state to another) ‖ JUR apropiación *f* ilícita (of property) ‖ SP transformación *f* ‖ REL, COMM & MATH conversión *f.*

convert [kən'və:t] *vt* convertir, transformar (to change, to transform) ‖ REL, COMM & MATH convertir ‖ SP transformar (a try in rugby) ‖ JUR apropiarse ilícitamente.
◆ *vi* convertirse ‖ SP transformar un ensayo.

convert ['kɔnvə:t] *n* converso, sa.

converter [kən'və:tə*] *n* TECH convertidor *m* ‖ ELECTR transformador *m.*

convertibility [kən,və:tə'biliti] *n* convertibilidad *f.*

convertible [kən'və:təbl] *adj* convertible (able to be converted) ‖ transformable ‖ COMM convertible ‖ GRAMM intercambiable (interchangeable) ‖ descapotable (car).
◆ *n* descapotable *m* (car).

convex ['kɔn'veks] *adj* convexo, xa.

convexity [kɔn'veksiti] *n* convexidad *f.*

convexo-convex [kɔn'veksəu'kɔnveks] *adj* biconvexo, xa.

convey [kən'vei] *vt* transportar, llevar (to carry) ‖ transmitir (to transmit, to pass on) ‖ sugerir, dar a entender; *what does his speech convey to you?* ¿qué te sugiere su discurso? ‖ expresar, dar (meaning) ‖ JUR hacer cesión de, transferir.

conveyable [kən'veiəbl] *adj* transportable (transportable) ‖ comunicable (communicable) ‖ transmisible (transmissible) ‖ conductible (current) ‖ JUR transferible, transmisible.

conveyance [kən'veiəns] *n* transporte *m* (means and act of conveyance) ‖ transmisión *f* (transmission) ‖ JUR traspaso *m* ‖ escritura *f* de traspaso (deed).

conveyancer [-ə*] *n* JUR notario *m* que hace escrituras de traspaso.

conveyancing [-iŋ] *n* redacción *f* de una escritura de traspaso.

conveyer; conveyor [kən'veiə*] *n* transportador *m* ‖ cinta *f* transportadora ‖ conductor *m* ‖ JUR cedente *m* ‖ *conveyor belt* cinta transportadora.

convict ['kɔnvikt] *n* presidiario, ria (criminal serving a sentence) ‖ convicto, ta (one convicted of crime).

convict [kən'vikt] *vt* declarar culpable, condenar (to prove guilty) ‖ hacer admitir (of an error, etc.) ‖ traicionar (to betray) ‖ condenar (to condemn).

conviction [kən'vikʃən] *n* JUR condena *f*, sentencia *f* ‖ declaración *f* de culpabilidad ‖ convicción *f* (strong belief) ‖ *to carry conviction* ser convincente.

convince [kən'vins] *vt* convencer.

convincible [kən'vinsəbl] *adj* que se deja convencer.

convincing [kən'vinsiŋ] *adj* convincente.

convivial [kən'viviəl] *adj* amigo de la buena mesa ‖ alegre, sociable, jovial, festivo, va (person) ‖ alegre (occasion, atmosphere).

convocation [,kɔnvəu'keiʃən] *n* convocación *f* (calling together) ‖ asamblea *f*, junta *f* (academic, legislative, etc.) ‖ REL sínodo *m.*

convoke [kən'vəuk] *vt* convocar.

convolute ['kɔnvəlu:t] *adj* retorcido, da; enroscado, da (coiled, rolled on itself) ‖ ZOOL enrollado, da.
◆ *n* enroscadura *f* (a coil).

convolute ['kɔnvəlu:t] *vi* enrollarse.
◆ *vt* enrollar.

convoluted ['kɔnvəlu:tid] *adj* retorcido, da; sinuoso, sa (twisted) ‖ complicado, da; intrincado, da (complicated).

convolution [,kɔnvə'lu:ʃən] *n* circunvolución *f.*

convolve [kən'vɔlv] *vt* arrollar, enrollar.
◆ *vi* arrollarse, enrollarse.

convolvulaceae [kənvɔlvju'leiʃii] *pl n* BOT convolvuláceas *f.*

convolvulus [kən'vɔlvjuləs] *n* BOT enredadera *f.*
— OBSERV El plural de *convolvulus* es *convolvuluses* o *convolvuli.*

convoy ['kɔnvɔi] *n* convoy *m* ‖ escolta *f* (escort) ‖ *under* o *in convoy* en convoy.

convoy ['kɔnvɔi] *vt* escoltar.

convoyer [-ə*] *n* escolta *f* (boat).

convulse [kən'vʌls] *vt* convulsionar (to throw into convulsions) ‖ hacer dislocarse de risa (to make laugh) ‖ — *to be convulsed with anger, fear* descomponerse de ira, de miedo ‖ *to be convulsed with laughter* dislocarse de risa ‖ *to be convulsed with pain* contorsionarse de dolor.

convulsion [kən'vʌlʃən] *n* convulsión *f* (involuntary spasm) ‖ conmoción *f* (earthquake, etc.).
◆ *pl* conmociones *f* (political, social upheaval) ‖ carcajadas *f* (uncontrollable laughter).

convulsive [kən'vʌlsiv] *adj* convulsivo, va.

cony ['kəuni] *n* piel *f* de conejo ‖ conejo *m* (rabbit).

coo [ku:] *n* arrullo *m.*
◆ *interj* ¡toma!, ¡anda!, ¡vaya!

coo [ku:] *vi* arrullar (pigeons, lovers) ‖ hacer gorgoritos (babies).

cooing [-iŋ] *n* arrullos *m pl.*

cook [kuk] *n* cocinero, ra ‖ FIG *too many cooks spoil the broth* muchas manos en un plato hacen mucho garabato.

cook [kuk] *vt* guisar, cocinar ‖ asar (to roast) ‖ FAM falsificar (the accounts) ‖ urdir, maquinar (a plot) ‖ — FAM *he is cooked* está aviado, está perdido ‖ *to cook a meal* hacer *or* preparar una comida ‖ *to cook lunch* hacer la comida ‖ FAM *to cook up* inventar; *to cook up an excuse* inventar una excusa; preparar, tramar; *he is cooking something up* está tramando algo.
◆ *vi* cocinar, guisar; *I like cooking* me gusta cocinar ‖ guisarse (food) ‖ ser cocinero, ra ‖ FAM *what's cooking?* ¿qué sucede?, ¿qué ocurre?

cookbook [-buk] *n* US libro *m* de cocina.

cooker ['kukə*] *n* cocina *f* (stove) ‖ olla *f*; *a pressure cooker* una olla de presión, una olla exprés ‖ fruta *f* para cocer (fruit to be eaten cooked) ‖ verdura *f* que cuece fácilmente.

cookery ['kukəri] *n* arte *m* culinario, cocina *f*.

cookery book [-buk] *n* libro *m* de cocina.

cookhouse ['kukhaus] *n* cocina *f* [de un barco].

cookie ['kuki] *n* US galleta *f* || US FAM tipo *m* (fellow) | guapa *f* (girl).

cooking ['kukiŋ] *n* cocción *f* (act) || cocina *f*; *French cooking* cocina francesa || *to do the cooking* guisar.
◆ *adj* de cocina || para cocer (fruit).

cooky ['kuki] *n* → **cookie** || FAM cocinero, ra (cook).

cool [ku:l] *adj* fresco, ca (refreshingly cold, chilly); *it is cool* hace fresco || tranquilo, la (calm) || frío, a (unenthusiastic); *to be cool towards s.o.* ser frío con alguien || insolente; fresco, ca (impudent) || sereno, na; frío, a (in a crisis) || frío, a (colours) || fresco, ca (garments) || FAM fenómeno, na (excellent) || — FAM *as cool as a cucumber* más fresco que una lechuga | *it costs a cool ten thousand* cuesta la friolera de diez mil || FIG *keep cool, play it cool* no te pongas nervioso, tómatelo con calma || *keep in a cool place* conservar en un lugar fresco || FAM *to be a cool hand* o *a cool one* ser un fresco || *to go* o *to get cool* enfriarse (a liquid), refrescarse (a person) || *to leave to get cool* dejar enfriarse.
◆ *n* frescor *m*, fresco *m* (fresh air) || *in the cool* al fresco.

cool [ku:l] *vt* enfriar || refrigerar (to refrigerate) || FIG calmar || FAM *cool it!* ¡calma!
◆ *vi* enfriarse || refrescarse (weather) || FIG calmarse || — *to cool down* enfriarse (machines), calmarse (persons), enfriarse (feelings) || *to cool off* enfriarse (enthusiasm), calmarse (persons).

coolant ['ku:lənt] *n* líquido *m* refrigerante.

cooler ['ku:lə*] *n* enfriador *m* || refrigerador *m* (refrigerator) || FAM bebida *f* refrescante, refresco *m* (drink) | sombra *f*, chirona *f* (prison).

cool-headed ['ku:l'hedid] *adj* sereno, na.

coolie; cooly ['ku:li] *n* coolí *m*, culi *m*.

cooling ['ku:liŋ] *adj* refrescante || TECH refrigerante, refrigerador, ra; de refrigeración; *cooling system* sistema de refrigeración; *cooling tower* torre *f* de enfriamiento *or* de refrigeración.
◆ *n* refrigeración *f*.

cooling-off period [-ɔf,piəriəd] *n* ECON tregua *f* (break) | período *m* reflexión (to cancel a contract).

coolish ['ku:liʃ] *adj* fresquito, ta.

coolly ['ku:li] *adv* fríamente || tranquilamente (calmly) || FAM con frescura, con descaro.

coolness ['ku:lnis] *n* frescor *m*, fresco *m* (quality of being cool) || frialdad *f* (lack of enthusiasm) || serenidad *f*, calma *f*, frialdad *f* (self-assurance) || sangre *f* fría (composure) || frescura *f* (boldness).

coombe [ku:m] *n* valle *m* estrecho.

coon [ku:n] *n* US ZOOL mapache *m* || FAM negro *m*.

coop [ku:p] *n* gallinero *m* (for poultry) || caseta *f* (cabin) || FIG & FAM cárcel *f*, chirona *f* || FIG *to fly the coop* fugarse, escaparse.

coop [ku:p] *vt* encerrar || FIG & FAM *to coop up* encerrar, enjaular (to confine).

co-op; US **coop** ['kəuɔp] *n* FAM cooperativa *f* || *co-op apartment* copropiedad *f*.

cooper ['ku:pə*] *n* tonelero *m* || fabricante *m* de vinos (wine merchant).

cooper ['ku:pə*] *vt* fabricar *or* reparar (toneles o barriles) || embarrilar (to put into casks).

cooperage ['ku:pəridʒ] *n* tonelería *f*.

cooperate [kəu'ɔpəreit] *vi* cooperar.

cooperation [kəu,ɔpə'reiʃən] *n* cooperación *f*.

cooperative [kəu'ɔpərətiv] *adj* cooperativo, va || servicial, dispuesto a ayudar (helpful).
◆ *n* cooperativa *f*.

cooperator [kəu'ɔpəreitə*] *n* cooperador, ra.

coopery ['ku:pəri] *n* tonelería *f*.

co-opt [kəu'ɔpt] *vt* cooptar, elegir por votación colectiva.

co-option [kəu'ɔpʃən] *n* cooptación *f*, elección *f* por votación colectiva.

coordinate [kəu'ɔ:dinit] *adj* igual, semejante (equal) || coordinado, da (coordinated) || — *coordinate geometry* geometría analítica || *coordinate paper* papel cuadriculado.
◆ *n* MATH coordenada *f* || igual *m* & *f*, semejante *m* & *f*.
◆ *pl* prendas *f* sueltas que se pueden combinar.

coordinate [kəu'ɔ:dineit] *vt* coordinar.
◆ *vi* coordinarse.

coordinating [kəu'ɔ:dineitiŋ] *adj* coordinador, ra, coordinante; *coordinating conjunction* conjunción *f* coordinante.

coordination [kəu,ɔ:di'neiʃən] *n* coordinación *f*.

coordinative [kəu'ɔ:dinətiv] *adj* coordinativo, va.

coordinator [kəu'ɔ:dineitə*] *n* coordinador, ra.

coot [ku:t] *n* fúlica *f* (bird) || FAM memo, ma (idiot).

cootie ['ku:ti] *n* US FAM piojo *m*.

cop [kɔp] *n* FAM poli *m* (copper) || canilla *f* (of yarn) || *cops and robbers* justicias y ladrones (game).

cop [kɔp] *vt* FAM cargarse; *he copped 20 years* se cargó 20 años | pillar, pescar, coger (to seize) || — FAM *he was* o *he got copped by the police* le pilló la policía | *to cop it* ganársela, pagarla; *now you'll cop it* ahora te la vas a ganar.
◆ *vi* FAM *to cop out* escaquearse, rajarse.

copaiba [kɔ'paibə] *n* BOT copaiba *f*.

copal ['kəupəl] *n* copal *m*.

coparcenary ['kəu'pɑ:sinəri] *n* participación *f* en una herencia || copropiedad *f*.

coparcener ['kəu'pɑ:sinə*] *n* coheredero, ra.

copartner ['kəu'pɑ:tnə*] *n* copartícipe *m*, consocio *m*.

copartnership [-ʃip] *n* asociación *f* || coparticipación *f*.

cope [kəup] *n* REL capa *f* pluvial (cape) || ARCH albardilla *f* (coping) || FIG bóveda *f* (of heaven).

cope [kəup] *vt* REL poner la capa pluvial || poner albardilla (a wall) || poner una bóveda (to vault).
◆ *vi* FAM arreglárselas; *don't worry, I can cope* no te preocupes, ya me las arreglaré | dar abasto; *I have so many things to do that I can't cope* tengo tantas cosas que hacer que no puedo dar abasto || *to cope with a situation* hacer frente a *or* enfrentarse con una situación || *we can't cope with the children* no podemos con los niños.

copeck ['kəupek] *n* copec *m*, kopeck *m*.

Copernicus [kəu'pə:nikəs] *pr n* Copérnico *m*.

copestone ['kəupstəun] *n* piedra *f* de albardilla *or* de remate || FIG remate *m*.

copier ['kɔpiə*] *n* imitador, ra (imitator) || copista *m* (copyist) || multicopista *f* (machine).

copilot ['kəu'pailət] *n* AVIAT copiloto *m*.

coping ['kəupiŋ] *n* albardilla *f* || *coping stone* piedra *f* de albardilla *or* de remate || FIG remate *m*.

copious ['kəupjəs] *adj* copioso, sa; abundante (plentiful) || prolífico, ca (an author) || rico, ca (language) || prolijo, ja (style).

copiousness [-nis] *n* abundancia *f*, profusión *f*, copiosidad *f*.

coplanar [,kəu'pleinə*] *adj* MATH *coplanar forces* fuerzas coplanarias.

cop-out ['kɔpɑut] *n* FAM escaqueo *m*.

copper ['kɔpə*] *n* cobre *m* (metallic element) || FAM perra *f* (small coin) | penique *m* (penny) | calderilla *f*, dinero *m* suelto (small change) || caldera *f* (boiler) || FAM poli *m* (policeman).
◆ *adj* de cobre (made of copper) || cobrizo, za (copper-coloured) || — *copper pyrites* calcopirita *f* || *copper sulphate* sulfato *m* de cobre.

copper ['kɔpə*] *vt* cubrir *or* revestir con cobre.

copperas ['kɔpərəs] *n* caparrosa *f* verde.

copperbottomed ['kɔpə,bɔtəmd] *adj* con fondo de cobre.

copper-coloured; US **copper-colored** ['kɔpə,kʌləd] *adj* cobrizo, za.

copperplate ['kɔpəpleit] *n* lámina *f* de cobre (plate of copper for engraving) || grabado *m* en cobre (impression) || letra *f* caligrafiada (handwriting).

coppersmith ['kɔpəsmiθ] *n* calderero *m* en cobre.

coppery ['kɔpəri] *adj* cobrizo, za.

coppice ['kɔpis] *n* soto *m*, bosquecillo *m*.

copra ['kɔprə] *n* BOT copra *f*.

coprocessor ['kəuprəusesə*] *n* INFORM coprocesador *m*.

coprolite ['kɔprəlait] *n* GEOL coprolito *m*.

coprology [kə'prɔlədʒi] *n* escatología *f*.

copse [kɔps] *n* soto *m*, bosquecillo *m*.

Copt [kɔpt] *n* copto, ta.

Coptic ['kɔptik] *adj* copto, ta.
◆ *n* copto *m* (language).

copula ['kɔpjulə] *n* cópula *f*.

copulate ['kɔpjuleit] *vi* copular.

copulation [,kɔpju'leiʃən] *n* cópula *f*.

copulative ['kɔpjulətiv] *adj* copulativo, va || *copulative verb* verbo copulativo.
◆ *n* cópula *f*, palabra *f* copulativa.

copy ['kɔpi] *n* copia *f* (reproduction, duplicate) || original *m*, manuscrito *m*, texto *m* (of an article) || ejemplar *m* (of book) || número *m*, ejemplar *m* (of paper) || modelo *m* (pattern) || asunto *m*; *the case made good copy for the reporters* el proceso fue un buen asunto para los reporteros || — *carbon copy* papel *m* carbón || JUR *certified copy* copia legalizada || *fair copy* copia en limpio || *rough copy* borrador *m* || *to make a fair copy of* pasar en limpio.

copy ['kɔpi] *vt/vi* copiar || copiar, imitar.

copybook ['kɔpibuk] *n* cuaderno *m* de caligrafía *or* de ejercicios || COMM libro *m* copiador || — FIG *copybook maxims* tópicos *m*, lugares *m* comunes | *to blot one's copybook* manchar su reputación.

copycat ['kɔpikæt] *n* FAM copión, ona; mono *m* de imitación.

copydesk ['kɔpidesk] *n* mesa *f* del redactor.

copy-edit ['kɔpi,edit] *vt* corregir [el manuscrito].

copy editor ['kɔpi,editə*] *n* corrector *m* de manuscritos || redactor *m* jefe (of a newspaper).

copyholder ['kɔpi,həuldə*] *n* PRINT atendedor, ra.

copying ink ['kɔpiiŋ,iŋk] *n* PRINT tinta *f* de copiar.

copyist ['kɔpiist] *n* copista *m*.

copyreader ['kɔpi,ri:də*] *n* corrector *m* de manuscritos.

copyright ['kɔpirait] *n* «copyright» *m*, propiedad *f* literaria || derechos *m pl* de autor (roy-

alties) || *copyright reserved* reservado el derecho de reproducción.
◆ *adj* protegido por la propiedad literaria.

copyright ['kɔpirait] *vt* registrar (una publicación) en el registro de la propiedad literaria.

copy typist ['kɔpi,taipist] *n* mecanógrafo, fa.

copywriter ['kɔpi'raitə*] *n* redactor *m* de textos publicitarios.

coquet; coquette [kɔ'ket] *vi* coquetear (to flirt) || FIG acariciar (to toy with); *to coquet with a suggestion* acariciar una sugerencia.

coquetry ['kɔkitri] *n* coquetería *f.*

coquette [kɔ'ket] *n* coqueta *f.*

coquettish [kɔ'ketiʃ] *adj* coqueto, ta; coquetón, ona.

cor! [kɔ:*] *interj* POP ¡diablos!

coracle ['xkɔrəkl] *n* barquilla *f* de cuero *or* de hule.

coral ['kɔrəl] *n* coral *m.*
◆ *adj* de coral, coralino, na || — *coral reef* arrecife *m* de coral || ZOOL *coral snake* coral *f,* coralillo *m.*

coralliferous [kɔrə'lifərəs] *adj* coralífero, ra.

coralline ['kɔrəlain] *n* coralina *f.*
◆ *adj* coralino, na.

corallite ['kɔrəlait] *n* coral *m* fósil (fossil coral) || mármol *m* coralino.

coralloid ['kɔrəlɔid] *adj* coralino, na.

cor anglais ['kɔ:rɑŋ'glei] *n* MUS corno *m* inglés.

corbel ['kɔ:bəl] *n* ARCH ménsula *f.*

corbel ['kɔ:bəl] *vt* ARCH poner ménsulas.
◆ *vi* formar un voladizo.

corbelling [-iŋ] *n* saledizo *m.*

corbie ['kɔ:bi] *n* cuervo *m* (bird) || *corbie gable* hastial escalonado.

cord [kɔ:d] *n* cuerda *f* (string, rope) || cordón *m* (of habit) || canutillo *m* (on textiles) || pana *f* (corduroy) || cordón *m* (insulated wire) || FIG lazo *m,* vínculo *m* || — ANAT *spinal cord* médula *f* espinal | *umbilical cord* cordón *m* umbilical.
◆ *pl* pantalón *m sing* de pana (trousers) || ANAT *vocal cords* cuerdas *f* vocales.

cord [kɔ:d] *vt* atar con cuerda.

cordage ['kɔ:didʒ] *n* cordaje *m* (ropes) || MAR jarcias *f pl.*

cordate ['kɔ:deit] *adj* en forma de corazón.

corded ['kɔ:did] *adj* atado con cuerdas (fastened) || perlado, da; «perlé» (cotton) || de canutillo (fabric).

cordial ['kɔ:djəl] *adj* cordial.
◆ *n* cordial *m.*

cordiality [,kɔ:di'æliti] *n* cordialidad *f.*

cordillera [,kɔ:di'ljɛərə] *n* cordillera *f.*

cordless ['kɔ:dləs] *adj* inalámbrico, ca (electrical appliance, telephone).

córdoba ['kɔ:dəbə] *n* córdoba *m* (monetary unit of Nicaragua).

Córdoba ['kɔ:dəbə] *pr n* Córdoba (in Argentina).

cordon ['kɔ:dn] *n* cordón *m* || *cordon bleu* cocinero *m* de primera clase (cook).

cordon ['kɔ:dn] *vt* *to cordon off* acordonar.

Cordova ['kɔ:dəvə] *pr n* GEOGR Córdoba (Spanish town).

Cordovan [-n] *adj* cordobés, esa || de cuero cordobés (made of leather).
◆ *n* cuero *m* cordobés, cordobán *m* (leather) || cordobés, esa (from Cordova).

corduroy ['kɔ:dərɔi] *n* pana *f.*
◆ *pl* pantalones *m* de pana (trousers).
◆ *adj* de pana || US *corduroy road* camino *m* de troncos.

cordwood ['kɔ:dwud] *n* haz *m* de leña || leña *f.*

core [kɔ:*] *n* BOT corazón *m* (of fruit) || corazón *m* (of timber) || FIG corazón *m,* núcleo *m,* centro *m* (innermost part) | núcleo *m,* foco *m* (of resistance, etc.) | esencia *f* (essence or gist) || MED clavo *m* (of a boil) | foco *m* (of infection) || GEOL núcleo *m* | testigo *m* (drilling) || ELECTR núcleo *m* || alma *f* (of ropes, cables) || — FIG *rotten to the core* podrido hasta la médula | *Spaniard to the core* español hasta los huesos, español hasta la médula.

core [kɔ:*] *vt* quitar el corazón de.

coreligionary ['kəuri'lidʒənəri]; **coreligionist** ['kəuri'lidʒənist] *n* correligionario, ria.

corer ['kɔ:rə*] *n* despepitadora *f,* deshuesadora *f.*

corespondent ['kəuris,pɔndənt] *n* cómplice *m* del demandado (in divorce).

corf [kɔ:f] *n* MIN vagoneta *f* || cesta *f* (in fishing).

corgi ['kɔ:gi] *n* ZOOL perro *m* galés.

coriaceous [,kɔri'eiʃəs] *adj* coriáceo, a.

coriander [,kɔri'ændə*] *n* BOT coriandro *m,* cilantro *m,* culantro *m.*

corindon [kə'rindən] *n* corindón *m.*

Corinth ['kɔrinθ] *pr n* GEOGR Corinto.

Corinthian [kə'rinθiən] *adj/n* corintio, tia.

corium ['kɔ:riəm] *n* ANAT dermis *f,* piel *f.*
— OBSERV El plural de *corium* es *coria.*

cork [kɔ:k] *n* BOT corcho *m* || corcho *m,* tapón *m* (stopper) || corcho *m,* flotador *m* (for fishing) || — *cork jacket* chaleco *m* salvavidas || BOT *cork oak* alcornoque *m* || BOT *cork tree* alcornoque *m* || *to draw the cork of a bottle* descorchar una botella.

cork [kɔ:k] *vt* poner el tapón, taponar (to stop a bottle) || tiznar con corcho quemado (to blacken).

corkage ['kɔ:kidʒ] *n* derecho *m* que se paga en un restaurante por el descorche de una botella que no es de la casa.

corked [kɔ:kt] *adj* que sabe a corcho (wine) || con tapón, taponado, da (bottle) || tiznado con corcho quemado (face).

corker ['kɔ:kə*] *n* FAM bola *f,* mentira *f* (lie) | tipo *m* formidable | cosa *f* formidable | argumento *m* irrefutable || máquina *f* de taponar.

corking ['kɔ:kiŋ] *adj* FAM estupendo, da; formidable.

corklike ['kɔ:klaik] *adj* corchoso, sa.

corkscrew ['kɔ:kskru:] *n* sacacorchos *m inv.*
◆ *adj* de caracol; *a corkskrew staircase* una escalera de caracol || en espiral (curl).

corkscrew ['kɔ:kskru:] *vi/vt* girar en espiral (to curl) || serpentear (a path, river, etc.).

cork-tipped ['kɔ:ktipt] *adj* con boquilla *or* filtro de corcho.

corkwood ['kɔ:kwud] *n* BOT balsa *f.*

corky ['kɔ:ki] *adj* de corcho, acorchado, da (like cork) || BOT suberoso, sa || FIG caprichoso, sa.

corm [kɔ:m] *n* BOT bulbo *m.*

cormorant ['kɔ:mərənt] *n* ZOOL cormorán *m,* mergo *m,* cuervo *m* marino.

corn [kɔ:n] *n* US maíz *m* (maize) || grano *m* (grain of pepper, etc.) || trigo *m* (wheat) || avena *f* (oats) || granos *m pl,* cereales *m pl* (cereals) || MED callo *m* || FAM chiste *m* malo (bad joke) || US FAM whisky *m* de maíz (drink) || *corn on the cob* maíz en la mazorca.

corn [kɔ:n] *vt* salar.

cornaceae [kɔ:'neisii] *pl n* BOT córneas *f.*

corn bread ['kɔ:nbred] *n* US borona *f,* pan *m* de maíz.

corn cake ['kɔ:nkeik] *n* borona *f.*

corn chandler ['kɔ:n,tʃɑ:ndlə*] *n* triguero *m.*

corncob ['kɔ:nkɔb] *n* mazorca *f* (central part of an ear of maize) || pipa *f* hecha de mazorca (pipe).

corn cockle ['kɔ:n,kɔkl] *n* neguilla *f,* neguillón *m.*

corncrake ['kɔ:nkreik] *n* ZOOL rey *m* de codornices (bird).

corncrib ['kɔ:nkrib] *n* granero *m.*

corn cutter ['kɔ:n,kʌtə*] *n* cortacallos *m inv.*

cornea ['kɔ:niə] *n* córnea *f.*

corned beef ['kɔ:nd'bi:f] *n* carne *f* en conserva *or* en lata.

cornel ['kɔ:nl] *n* BOT cornejo *m.*

cornelian [kɔ:'ni:ljən] *n* cornalina *f.*

corneous ['kɔ:niəs] *adj* córneo, a; calloso, sa.

corner ['kɔ:nə*] *n* esquina *f* (outside angle); *the corner house* la casa de la esquina; *the corner shop* la tienda *f* de la esquina || rincón *m* (inside angle) || pico *m* (of a table, etc.) || curva *f* (bend, curve) || FIG rincón *m,* parte *f* (region) || cantonera *f* (for protecting photographs, edges, etc.) || SP córner *m,* saque *m* de esquina (in football) || rabillo *m* (of the eye) || comisura *f* (of mouth) || monopolio *m* (in commerce) || — *corner piece* rinconera *f* || *done in a corner* hecho a escondidas || *in the chimney corner* al amor de la lumbre || *it's round the corner* está a la vuelta de la esquina || *out of the corner of one's eye* con el rabillo del ojo || FIG *to be in a tight corner* estar en un apuro *or* en un aprieto || FIG *to cut corners* tomar atajos (to shorten the distance), economizar esfuerzos *or* dinero || *to drive s.o. into a corner* arrinconar, acorralar || FIG *to go to the four corners of the earth* ir a las cinco partes del mundo | *to rub the corners off s.o.* pulir a alguien || *to turn the corner* doblar la esquina (of a street), salir del apuro *or* del mal paso.

corner ['kɔ:nə*] *vt* poner cantoneras (to provide a book with corners) || poner en una esquina (to set in a corner) || acorralar, arrinconar (to drive someone into a corner) || monopolizar, acaparar; *to corner the market* acaparar el mercado || abordar (to accost) || FIG poner en un apuro *or* en un aprieto.
◆ *vi* hacer esquina (a house) || doblar una esquina || tomar una curva (a car).

cornered [-d] *adj* esquinado, da; angulado, da; que tiene ángulos || FIG en un apuro, en un aprieto (in trouble) || arrinconado, da; acorralado, da || — *a three-cornered hat* un sombrero de tres picos || *four-cornered competition* competición entre cuatro participantes.

corner kick ['kɔ:nə*kik] *n* SP córner *m,* saque *m* de esquina.

cornerstone ['kɔ:nəstəun] *n* ARCH piedra *f* angular.

cornerways ['kɔ:nəweiz] *adv* diagonalmente.

cornerwise ['kɔ:nəwaiz] *adv* diagonalmente.

cornet ['kɔ:nit] *n* MUS corneta *f* || cucurucho *m* (paper, ice cream, etc.) || MAR insignia *f,* corneta *f* (flag) || toca *f* (of nun).

cornetist; cornettist ['kɔ:nitist] *n* corneta *m.*

cornfield ['kɔ:nfi:ld] *n* trigal *m,* campo *m* de trigo (of wheat) || US maizal *m,* campo *m* de maíz.

cornflakes ['kɔ:nfleiks] *pl n* copos *m* de maíz.

cornflour ['kɔ:nflauə*] *n* harina *f* de maíz.

cornflower ['kɔ:nflauə*] *n* BOT aciano *m.*

corn husk ['kɔ:nhʌsk] *n* US vaina *f.*

cornice ['kɔ:nis] *n* ARCH cornisa *f.*

Cornish ['kɔ:niʃ] *adj* de Cornualles.
◆ *n* idioma *m* de Cornualles.

corn liquor ['kɔ:n,likə*] *n* US whisky *m* de maíz.

cornmeal ['kɔːnmiːl] *n* harina *f* de maíz.

corn pone ['kɔːnpəun] *n* US borona *f*, pan *m* de maíz.

corn silk ['kɔːnsilk] *n* barbas *f pl* de maíz.

cornstalk ['kɔːnstɔːk] *n* BOT tallo *m* del maíz.

cornstarch ['kɔːnstɑːtʃ] *n* US maicena *f*.

corn sugar ['kɔːnʃugə*] *n* US azúcar *m* de almidón de maíz.

corn syrup ['kɔːn,sirəp] *n* US glucosa *f*.

cornucopia [,kɔːnju'kəupjə] *n* cornucopia *f*, cuerno *m* de la abundancia.

Cornwall ['kɔːnwəl] *n* Cornualles *m*.

corn whiskey ['kɔːn'wiski] *n* US whisky *m* de maíz.

corny ['kɔːni] *adj* productor de trigo (of wheat) || US productor de maíz || FAM viejo, ja (old) | rancio, cia; trillado, da; sobado, da (stale) | malo, la (bad); *a corny joke* un chiste malo || MED calloso, sa.

corolla [kə'rɔlə] *n* BOT corola *f*.

corollary [kə'rɔləri] *n* MATH corolario *m* || FIG consecuencia *f*, corolario *m*.
◆ *adj* consecuente.

corona [kə'rəunə] *n* corona *f*.
— OBSERV El plural de *corona* en inglés es *coronae*.

coronal ['kɔrənəl] *n* guirnalda *f* (wreath) || cerco *m* (of gold, stones, etc.).

coronary ['kɔrənəri] *adj* coronario, ria (like a crown) || ANAT coronario, ria; *coronary artery* arteria coronaria; *coronary thrombosis* trombosis coronaria.

coronation ['kɔrə'neiʃən] *n* coronación *f*.

coroner ['kɔrənə*] *n* oficial *m* de justicia de la Corona que investiga los casos de muerte violenta o accidentes [especie de juez de primera instancia].

coronet ['kɔrənit] *n* corona *f* (of nobility) || tortillo *m* (of a baron) || diadema *f* (decorative headdress for ladies) || ZOOL corona *f* del casco.

corozo [kə'rəuzə] *n* BOT corozo *m*, corojo *m*.

Corp. *abbr of [corporation]* sociedad anónima.

corpora ['kɔpərə] *pl n* —› **corpus.**

corporal ['kɔːpərəl] *adj* corporal; *corporal punishment* castigo corporal.
◆ *n* REL corporal *m* || MIL cabo *m*; *corporal of the guard* cabo de guardia.

corporality [,kɔːpə'ræliti] *n* corporalidad *f*.

corporate ['kɔːpərit] *adj* corporativo, va (of a corporation) || colectivo, va || combinado, da; *corporate efforts* esfuerzos combinados || JUR constituido, da (body) | constituido en sociedad (business) | municipal (land, office) || — *corporate name* nombre *m* social || *corporate town* municipalidad *f* || *status of body corporate* personalidad jurídica.

corporation [,kɔːpə'reiʃən] *n* corporación *f* || sociedad *f* anónima || FAM panza *f*, barriga *f* (abdomen) || *municipal corporation* ayuntamiento *m*.

corporative ['kɔːpərətiv] *adj* corporativo, va.

corporativism [-izəm] *n* corporativismo *m*.

corporeal [kɔ'pɔːriəl] *adj* corpóreo, a || JUR material.

corporeality [kɔːpɔːri'æliti]; **corporeity** ['kɔːpə'riiti] *n* corporeidad *f*, materialidad *f*.

corposant ['kɔːpəznt] *n* fuego *m* de San Telmo.

corps [kɔː] *inv n* MIL cuerpo *m* || — *corps de ballet* cuerpo de ballet || *corps diplomatique* cuerpo diplomático || *medical corps* cuerpo de sanidad || *Service Corps* cuerpo de intendencia.

corpse [kɔːps] *n* cadáver *m*.

corpsman [kɔːmən] *n* US MIL miembro *m* del cuerpo de sanidad | ambulanciero *m*.
— OBSERV El plural de *corpsman* es *corpsmen*.

corpulence ['kɔːpjuləns]; **corpulency** [-i] *n* corpulencia *f*.

corpulent ['kɔːpjulənt] *adj* corpulento, ta.

corpus ['kɔːpəs] *n* ; **corpora** ['kɔpərə] *pl n* cuerpo *m sing*, recopilación *f sing* || capital *m sing* || — ANAT *corpus callosum* cuerpo calloso || *Corpus Christi* Corpus Cristi *m sing* || *corpus delicti* cuerpo del delito.
— OBSERV El plural de *corpus* es *corpora*.

corpuscle; corpusale ['kɔːpʌsl] *n* ANAT corpúsculo *m*, glóbulo *m*; *red corpuscles* glóbulos rojos || PHYS corpúsculo *m* (atom, etc.).

corpuscular [kɔː'pʌsjulə*] *adj* corpuscular; *corpuscular theory* teoría corpuscular.

corpuscule ['kɔːpʌsl] *n* —› **corpuscle.**

corral [kɔː'rɑːl] *n* corral *m*.

corral [kɔː'rɑːl] *vt* encorralar, acorralar (animals) || cercar con (wagons) || FAM hacerse con (to lay hold of).

correct [kə'rekt] *adj* correcto, ta (behaviour, person) || exacto, ta (accurate) || bueno, na (taste) || justo, ta (right) || — *am I correct in telling that...?* ¿no es cierto que...? || *they are perfectly correct* tienen toda la razón.

correct [kə'rekt] *vt* corregir.

correction [kə'rekʃən] *n* corrección *f* || — *house of correction* reformatorio *m*, correccional *m* || *under correction* salvo error u omisión.

correctional [kə'rekʃənl] *adj* correccional.

correctitude [kə'rektitjuːd] *n* corrección *f*.

corrective [kə'rektiv] *adj* correctivo, va || *corrective glasses* gafas correctoras.
◆ *n* correctivo *m*.

correctness [kə'rektnis] *n* corrección *f* (of behaviour, of style) || rectitud *f* (of judgment) || exactitud *f* (accuracy).

corrector [kə'rektə*] *n* corrector *m*.

correlate ['kɔrileit] *n* correlativo *m*.

correlate ['kɔrileit] *vt* poner en correlación, correlacionar.
◆ *vi* tener correlación, estar en correlación.

correlation [,kɔri'leiʃən] *n* correlación *f*.

correlative [kɔ'relətiv] *adj* correlativo, va.
◆ *n* correlativo *m*.

correspond [,kɔris'pɔnd] *vi* corresponder.

correspondence [,kɔris'pɔndəns] *adj* correspondencia *f* || — *correspondence course* curso *m* por correspondencia || *correspondence school* escuela *f* por correspondencia.

correspondency [-i] *n* correspondencia *f*.

correspondent [,kɔris'pɔndənt] *n* corresponsal *m* & *f* (of a newspaper, a firm).
◆ *adj* correspondiente.

corresponding [,kɔris'pɔndiŋ] *adj* correspondiente || *corresponding member* miembro *m* correspondiente.

corrida [kɔ'riːdə] *n* corrida *f* (bullfight).

corridor ['kɔridɔː*] *n* pasillo *m*, corredor *m* || GEOGR corredor *m*.

corrie ['kɔri] *n* GEOGR circo *m*.

corrigenda [,kɔri'dʒendə] *pl n* erratas *f*; fe *f sing* de erratas.

corrigendum ['kɔri'dʒendəm] *n* errata *f*.
— OBSERV El plural es *corrigenda*.

corrigible ['kɔridʒəbl] *adj* corregible, enmendable.

corroborant [kə'rɔbərənt] *adj* corroborante.
◆ *n* MED tónico *m*, corroborante *m*.

corroborate [kə'rɔbəreit] *vt* corroborar.

corroboration [kə,rɔbə'reiʃən] *n* corroboración *f*.

corroborative [kə'rɔbərətiv] *adj* corroborativo, va.

corroborator [kə'rɔbəreitə*] *n* testigo *m*.

corroboratory [kə'rɔbərətəri] *adj* US corroborativo, va.

corrode [kə'rəud] *vt* corroer.
◆ *vi* corroerse.

corrodible [kə'rəudibl] *adj* corrosible.

corrosion [kə'rəuʒən] *n* corrosión *f*.

corrosive [kə'rəusiv] *adj* corrosivo, va.
◆ *n* corrosivo *m*.

corrosiveness [-nis] *n* corrosividad *f*.

corrugate ['kɔrugeit] *vt* ondular (cardboard, iron) || estriar (glass) || gofrar, estampar (paper).

corrugation [,kɔru'geiʃən] *n* estrías *f pl* || ondulado *m* (of cardboard, iron) || gofrado *m* (of paper).

corrupt [kə'rʌpt] *adj* corrompido, da; corrupto, ta || estragado, da (taste) || corrompido, da; pervertido, da (perverted) || venal (open to bribery) || *corrupt practices* corrupción *f sing*.

corrupt [kə'rʌpt] *vt* corromper || sobornar (to bribe) || alterar (a text).
◆ *vi* corromperse.

corruptibility [kə,rʌptə'biliti] *n* corruptibilidad *f*.

corruptible [kə'rʌptəbl] *adj* corruptible.

corrupting [kə'rʌptiŋ] *adj* corruptor, ra.

corruption [kə'rʌpʃən] *n* corrupción *f*.

corruptive [kə'rʌptiv] *adj* corruptivo, va.

corruptness [kə'rʌptnis] *n* venalidad *f*, corruptela *f*, corrupción *f*.

corsage [kɔː'sɑːʒ] *n* cuerpo *m* (of a dress) || ramillete *m* (flowers).

corsair ['kɔːsɛə*] *n* corsario *m*.

corselet; corslet ['kɔːslit] *n* coselete *m* (armour) || faja *f* (undergarment) || ZOOL coselete *m*.

corset ['kɔːsit] *n* corsé *m* (for women) || MED corsé *m* ortopédico.

corsetière [,kɔːsə'tjɛə*] *n* corsetera *f*.

Corsica ['kɔːsikə] *pr n* GEOGR Córcega *f*.

Corsican [-n] *adj/n* corso, sa.

corslet ['kɔːslit] *n* —› **corselet.**

cortège [kɔːteiʒ] *n* cortejo *m*, séquito *m*, comitiva *f*.

Cortes ['kɔːtes] *pl n* Cortes *f* (Spanish Parliament).

cortex ['kɔːteks] *n* ANAT & BOT corteza *f*.
— OBSERV El plural es *cortices* o *cortexes*.

cortical ['kɔːtikəl] *adj* ANAT cortical.

cortisone ['kɔːtizəun] *n* MED cortisona *f*.

corundum [kə'rʌndəm] *n* MED corindón *m*.

Corunna [kɔ'rʌnə] *pr n* GEOGR La Coruña.

coruscate ['kɔrəskeit] *vi* centellear, brillar || FIG brillar.

coruscation [,kɔrəs'keiʃən] *n* brillo *m*, centelleo *m* (brilliance) || FIG destello *m* (of wit).

corvette; US **corvet** [kɔː'vet] *n* MAR corbeta *f*.

corvina [kɔː'vinə] *n* ZOOL corvina *f* (fish).

corymb ['kɔrimb] *n* BOT corimbo *m*.

coryphaeus [,kɔri'fiːəs] *n* corifeo *m*.
— OBSERV El plural de *coryphaeus* es *coryphaei*.

coryphée [,kɔri'fei] *n* primer bailarín *m*, primera bailarina *f*.

coryza [kə'raizə] *n* MED coriza *f*, catarro *m* nasal.

cos [kɔs] *n* lechuga *f* romana.

cosecant ['kəu'siːkənt] *n* MATH cosecante *f*.

cosh [kɔʃ] *n* porra *f*, cachiporra *f*.

cosh [kɔʃ] *vt* dar un porrazo a.
cosher ['kɔʃə*] *vt* mimar.
cosignatory ['kəu'signətəri] *n* cosignatario, ria.
cosily; cozily ['kəuzili] *adv* confortablemente, cómodamente (comfortably) || cariñosamente (affectionately).
cosine ['kəusain] *n* MATH coseno *m*.
cosiness; coziness ['kəuzinis] *n* comodidad *f*.
cosmetic [kɔz'metik] *adj* cosmético, ca.
◆ *n* cosmético *m*.
cosmetician [kɔzmə'tiʃən] *n* vendedor *m* de productos de belleza.
cosmetic surgery [kɔz'metik'sə:dʒəri] *n* cirugía *f* estética.
cosmic ['kɔzmik] *adj* cósmico, ca; *cosmic rays* rayos cósmicos; *cosmic dust* polvo cósmico; *cosmic radiation* radiación cósmica.
cosmogonic [,kɔzmə'gɔnik] *adj* cosmogónico, ca.
cosmogony [kɔz'mɔgəni] *n* cosmogonía *f*.
cosmographer [kɔz'mɔgrəfə*] *n* cosmógrafo *m*.
cosmographic [,kɔzmə'græfik] *adj* cosmográfico, ca.
cosmography [kɔz'mɔgrəfi] *n* cosmografía *f*.
cosmological [,kɔzmə'lɔdʒikəl] *adj* cosmológico, ca.
cosmology [kɔz'mɔlədʒi] *n* cosmología *f*.
cosmonaut ['kɔzmənɔ:t] *n* cosmonauta *m*.
cosmopolitan [,kɔzmə'pɔlitən] *adj/n* cosmopolita.
cosmopolite [kɔz'mɔpəlait] *n* cosmopolita *m* & *f*.
cosmorama [,kɔzmə'rɑ:mə] *n* cosmorama *m*.
cosmos ['kɔzmɔs] *n* cosmos *m*.
Cossack ['kɔsæk] *adj/n* Cosaco, ca.
cosset ['kɔsit] *n* US animal *m* favorito.
cost [kɔst] *n* costo *m*, coste *m*; *cost price* precio de coste || precio *m* (price) || gastos *m pl* (expenses); *cost free* sin gastos || — *at any cost* cueste lo que cueste, a toda costa || FIG *at great cost* tras grandes esfuerzos || *at small cost* a buen precio || *at the cost of* a costa de || *cost of living* coste de vida || *cost-of-living allowance, cost-of-living bonus* plus *m* de carestía de vida || *he'll do it whatever the cost* lo hará cueste lo que cueste || *to count the cost* considerar los riesgos || *to one's cost* a expensas de uno; *I learnt it to my cost* lo supe a mis expensas.
◆ *pl* JUR costas *f* || *at all costs* cueste lo que cueste, a toda costa.
cost* [kɔst] *vt* calcular el coste de.
◆ *vi* costar; *it cost 1 000 pesetas* costó 1 000 pesetas || valer, costar; *how much does this cost?* ¿cuánto vale esto? || FIG costar; *his foolishness cost him his life* su insensatez le costó la vida || *cost what it may* cueste lo que cueste.
— OBSERV Pret y pp ***cost***.
cost accountant [-ə,kauntənt] *n* contable *m* & *f* de costes.
cost accounting [-ə'kauntiŋ] *n* contabilidad *f* de costes.
costal ['kɔstl] *adj* costal (relating to ribs).
co-star ['kəustɑ:] *n* cada uno de los actores principales en una película.
Costa Rica ['kɔstə'rikə] *pr n* GEOGR Costa Rica *f*.
Costa Rican [-n] *adj/n* costarriqueño, ña; costarricense.
cost-effective ['kɔst i,fektiv] *adj* rentable.
coster ['kɔstə*]; **costermonger** [-,mʌŋgə*] *n* vendedor *m* ambulante.
costing ['kɔstiŋ] *n* cálculo *m* del coste || fijación *f* del precio.
costive ['kɔstiv] *adj* estreñido, da (constipated) || FIG & FAM tacaño, ña (stingy).
costiveness [-nis] *n* estreñimiento *m* || FIG & FAM tacañería *f* (stinginess).
costless ['kɔstlis] *adj* gratis.
costliness ['kɔstlinis] *n* alto precio *m*, precio *m* elevado, lo caro || FIG suntuosidad *f*.
costly ['kɔstli] *adj* caro, ra; costoso, sa || US FIG suntuoso, sa.
cost-plus ['kɔst'plʌs] *n* precio *m* de coste más el beneficio.
costume ['kɔstju:m] *n* traje *m* (style of clothing, etc.); *local costume* traje típico de la región, traje regional || disfraz *m* (disguise); *costume ball* baile de disfraces || traje *m* sastre (lady's suit) || traje *m* de baño (bathing suit) || — *costume jewellery* bisutería *f*, joyas *f pl* de fantasía || *costume piece* obra *f* de teatro de época.
◆ *pl* THEATR vestuario *m sing*.
costume ['kɔstju:m] *vt* vestir (to dress) || disfrazar (to disguise).
costumier [kɔs'tju:miə*]; US **costumer** *n* THEATR encargado *m* del vestuario.
cosy; cozy ['kəuzi] *adj* confortable, cómodo, da (comfortable); *it is very cosy here* aquí se está muy confortable || cariñoso, sa; agradable (people) || íntimo, ma; acogedor, ra (place) || *to play it cosy* obrar con cautela.
◆ *n* cubretetera *m* (tea cosy).
cot [kɔt] *n* cuna *f* (children's bed) || US cama *f* de campaña, catre *m* (camp bed) || hamaca *f* (hammock) || cabaña *f* (shelter) || dedil *m* (fingerstall).
cotangent ['kəu'tændʒənt] *n* MATH cotangente *f*.
cot death syndrome ['kɔt deθ ,sindrəm] *n* MED síndrome *m* de muerte súbita infantil.
cote [kəut] *n* palomar *m* (dovecote) || redil *m* (sheepcot).
co-tenant ['kəu'tenənt] *n* coinquilino, na.
coterie ['kəutəri] *n* tertulia *f*, peña *f* (people meeting regularly) || círculo *m* (literary) || camarilla *f* (clique).
cothurnus [kə'θə:nəs] *n* coturno *m* (buskin).
— OBSERV El plural de *cothurnus* es *cothurni*.
cotillion [kə'tiljən] *n* cotillón *m* (ball).
cotta ['kɔtə] *n* sobrepelliz *f*.
cottage ['kɔtidʒ] *n* casa *f* de campo (country house) || chalet *m*, chalé *m* (villa) || choza *f* (farm labourer's dwelling).
cottage cheese [-'tʃi:z] *n* requesón *m*.
cottage industry [-'indʌstri] *n* industria *f* casera.
cottage loaf [-'ləuf] *n* pan *m* casero.
cottage pie [-pai] *n* CULIN pastel *m* de patatas relleno de carne picada.
cottager ['kɔtidʒə*] *n* labrador *m* || inquilino *m* de una casa de campo.
cotter ['kɔtə*] *n* TECH chaveta *f* || *cotter pin* pasador *m* de chaveta.
cotton ['kɔtn] *n* algodón *m*; *printed cotton* algodón estampado; *absorbent cotton* algodón hidrófilo || algodonero *m* (plant).
◆ *adj* de algodón, algodonero, ra; *cotton industry* industria algodonera.
cotton ['kɔtn] *vi* *to cotton on* o *up to* atraer (to attract), coger cariño a (s.o.), comprender, captar (a meaning), aficionarse a (to take a liking).
cotton batting [-'bætiŋ] *n* algodón *m* en rama.
cotton belt [-belt] *n* US zona *f* algodonera.
cotton candy [-'kændi] *n* algodón *m* (sweet).
cotton gin [-dʒin] *n* desmotadora *f*.
cotton plant [-plɑ:nt] *n* algodonero *m*.
cotton plantation [-plɑ:n,teiʃən] *n* algodonal *m*, plantación *f* de algodón.
cotton print [-print] *n* estampado *m* de algodón.
cottonseed [-si:d] *n* semilla *f* de algodón.
cottontail [-teil] *n* ZOOL conejo *m* de rabo blanco.
cotton thistle [-,θisl] *n* BOT cardo *m* borriquero.
cotton waste [-weist] *n* borra *f* de algodón.
cottonwood [-wud] *n* BOT álamo *m* de Virginia.
cotton wool [-wul] *n* algodón *m* en rama, guata *f* || MED algodón *m* hidrófilo || FIG *he was brought up in cotton wool* fue criado entre algodones.
cotyledon [,kɔti'li:dən] *n* BOT cotiledón *m*.
couch [kautʃ] *n* sofá *m* (a sofa) || lecho *m*, cama *f* (bed) || capa *f* de cebada (in brewing) || guarida *f* (animal's lair) || *couch grass* grama *f*.
couch [kautʃ] *vt* expresar (to express) || poner en ristre (a lance) || acostar (in bed) || redactar (in writing) || FIG disimular, encubrir || *to couch o.s.* acostarse.
◆ *vi* tumbarse (to lay o.s. down) || emboscarse (to hide) || acostarse (to have sexual intercourse) || recogerse (an animal) || *to couch down* agacharse.
couchant ['kautʃənt] *adj* HERALD acostado, da.
couchette [ku:'ʃet] *n* litera *f* (on train).
cougar ['ku:gə*] *n* ZOOL puma *m*.
cough [kɔf] *n* tos *f*; *to have a cough* tener tos; *cough drop* pastilla para la tos; *cough mixture* o *syrup* jarabe *m* para la tos.
cough [kɔf] *vi* toser.
◆ *vt* *to cough out* escupir al toser, expectorar || *to cough up* escupir (to spit), expectorar (to expectorate), escupir, cascar (to pay).
could [kud] *pret* ⟶ **can.**
couldn't ['kudənt] contracción de «could not».
coulee ['ku:li] *n* GEOL corriente *f* or torrente *m* de lava || barranco *m* (ravine).
coulisse [ku:'lis] *n* THEATR bastidor || bolsín *m* (stock exchange) || corredera *f* (groove, slot).
coulomb ['ku:lɔm] *n* ELECTR culombio *m* (unit of electric charge).
coulter ['kəultə*] *n* cuchilla *f* [del arado].
council ['kaunsl] *n* consejo *m* (advisory assembly); *council of ministers* consejo de ministros || ayuntamiento *m* (of towns and cities) || REL concilio *m* || — *city* o *town council* concejo *m* municipal, ayuntamiento *m* || *council house* vivienda protegida || *council of war* consejo de guerra.
councillor; US **councilor** ['kaunsilə*] *n* concejal *m* || REL conciliar *m*.
councilman ['kaunsəlmən] *n* concejal *m*.
— OBSERV El plural de *councilman* es *councilmen*.
counsel ['kaunsəl] *n* consejo *m* (advice) || abogado *m* (lawyer) || abogados *m pl* (lawyers) || asesor *m* jurídico (legal adviser) || — *counsel for the defence* abogado defensor || *counsel for the prosecution* fiscal *m* || *counsel of perfection* consejo *m* imposible de seguir || *to be counsel for* defender a, abogar por || *to keep one's own counsel* guardar un secreto, callarse || *to take counsel with* pedir consejo a, consultar a.
counsel ['kaunsəl] *vt* aconsejar.
◆ *vi* pedir consejo, consultar.

counselling; US **counseling** [-iŋ] *n* asesoramiento *m*.

counsellor; US **counselor** ['kaunsələ*] *n* consejero *m* (of an embassy) ‖ asesor *m*, consejero *m* (adviser) ‖ US abogado *m* (lawyer).

counsellor-at-law [-ætlɔː] *n* asesor *m* jurídico.

— OBSERV El plural es *counsellors-at-law*.

count [kaunt] *n* cuenta *f*, cálculo *m* (a calculation) ‖ total *m*, suma *f* (sum) ‖ recuento *m* (recount) ‖ escrutinio *m* (of votes) ‖ conde *m* (a noble) ‖ JUR cargo *m* ‖ SP cuenta *f* (in boxing) ‖ — *out of the count* fuera de combate ‖ *to keep count of* llevar la cuenta de ‖ *to lose count of* perder la cuenta de.

count [kaunt] *vt* contar; *count the mistakes* cuenta los errores ‖ contar hasta; *I counted ten* conté hasta diez ‖ contar, tener *or* tomar en cuenta (to include); *not counting* sin contar ‖ considerar (to consider) ‖ calcular (to calculate).

◆ *vi* contar; *to count on one's fingers* contar con los dedos de la mano; *that doesn't count* eso no cuenta ‖ ser, haber (to number) ‖ *counting from tomorrow* a partir de mañana.

◆ *phr v* ***to count against*** ir en contra de ‖ ***to count down*** contar hacia atrás ‖ ***to count for*** valer por ‖ ***to count in*** incluir ‖ ***to count off*** separar ‖ ***to count on*** contar con; *to count on winning* contar con la victoria ‖ ***to count out*** ir contando (to reckon up), declarar fuera de combate (in boxing), no contar con (not to count on), eliminar (to eliminate); *to count out the House* aplazar la sesión [porque no hay quórum] ‖ ***to count up*** contar; *to count up to* ascender a, sumar.

countable [-əbl] *adj* contable, que se puede contar.

countdown ['kauntdaun] *n* cuenta *f* atrás, cuenta *f* hacia atrás.

countenance ['kauntinəns] *n* semblante *m*, cara *f*, expresión *f*; *sad countenance* cara triste; *to change countenance* cambiar de cara ‖ — *to be out of countenance* estar turbado *or* desconcertado ‖ *to give countenance to* apoyar ‖ *to keep one's countenance* no perder la serenidad *or* la seriedad ‖ *to lend countenance to* apoyar ‖ *to lose countenance* turbarse ‖ *to put s.o. out of countenance* desconcertar a uno.

countenance ['kauntinəns] *vt* apoyar (to support) ‖ aprobar (to approve).

counter ['kauntə*] *adj* contrario, ria; opuesto, ta.

◆ *adv* en dirección contraria ‖ *to go* o *run counter to* oponerse a, ir en contra de.

◆ *n* pecho *m* (of a horse) ‖ MAR bovedilla *f* ‖ mostrador *m* (shops) ‖ ficha *f* (in games, for telephones) ‖ contra *f* (in boxing, fencing) ‖ ventanilla *f* (in banks) ‖ contrafuerte *m* (in shoes) ‖ computadora *f* (a computer) ‖ contador *m*; *Geiger counter* contador Geiger ‖ MUS contrapunto *m* (counterpoint) ‖ — *over the counter* al contado ‖ *under the counter* bajo mano.

counter ['kauntə*] *vi* contraatacar (to answer an attack) ‖ pelear a la contra (in boxing).

◆ *vt* contestar a; *to counter a threat* contestar a una amenaza ‖ oponerse a (to oppose) ‖ contrariar, ir en contra de (schemes, plans) ‖ parar (to parry in fencing).

counteraccusation ['kauntərˌækju'zeiʃən] *n* contraacusación *f*.

counteract [ˌkauntə'rækt] *vt* contrarrestar (to neutralize) ‖ frustrar, contrariar (to frustrate); *I counteracted his plans* frustré sus planes ‖ oponerse a (to act in opposition to); *I counteracted his instructions* me opuse a sus instrucciones.

counteraction [ˌkauntə'rækʃən] *n* oposición *f* ‖ neutralización *f*.

counteractive [ˌkauntə'ræktiv] *adj* contrario, ria.

conterattack ['kauntərəˌtæk] *n* contraataque *m*.

counterattack ['kauntərə'tæk] *vt/vi* contraatacar.

counter attraction ['kauntərə'trækʃən] *n* atracción *f* contraria.

counterbalance ['kauntəˌbæləns] *n* contrapeso *m* ‖ compensación *f*.

counterbalance ['kauntə'bæləns] *vt/vi* contrapesar, contrabalancear ‖ compensar.

counterblast ['kauntəblɑːst] *n* réplica *f* (retort) ‖ contraataque *m*.

counterblow ['kauntəˌbləu] *n* contragolpe *m*.

counterbrace ['kauntəbreis] *vt* ARCH afirmar con riostras.

counterchange [kauntə'tʃeindʒ] *vt* intercambiar, cambiar.

countercharge ['kauntətʃɑːdʒ] *vt* JUR reconvención *f* ‖ MIL contraataque *m*.

countercharge ['kauntətʃɑːdʒ] *vt* JUR reconvenir ‖ MIL contraatacar.

countercheck ['kauntətʃek] *n* fuerza *f* antagonista *or* contraria ‖ obstáculo *m*, impedimento *m*, traba *f* (obstacle) ‖ segundo control *m*, comprobación *f* de una verificación (a checking of a check).

countercheck ['kauntətʃek] *vt* contrarrestar (to counter) ‖ comprobar por segunda vez (to verify).

counterclaim ['kauntəkleim] *n* JUR contradenuncia *f*, reconvención *f*.

counterclaim ['kauntəkleim] *vt* reconvenir.

counterclockwise ['kauntə'klɔkwaiz] *adj/adv* en sentido opuesto a las agujas del reloj.

countercurrent ['kauntəˌkʌrənt] *n* contracorriente *f*.

counter-demonstration ['kauntəˌdeməns'treiʃən] *n* contramanifestación *f*.

counterespionage ['kauntə'respiənɑːʒ] *n* contraespionaje *m*.

counterfeit ['kauntəfit] *adj* falsificado, da (falsified) ‖ simulado, da; fingido, da (feigned).

◆ *n* falsificación *f*, imitación *f* ‖ moneda *f* falsa.

counterfeit ['kauntəfit] *vt* falsificar (to falsify) ‖ simular, fingir (to feign).

counterfeiter ['kauntəˌfitə*] *n* falsificador *m* (of money) ‖ simulador *m*.

counterfoil ['kauntəfɔil] *n* talón *m*, matriz *f* (of a cheque, etc.) ‖ *counterfoil book* talonario *m*.

counterfort ['kauntəfɔːt] *n* contrafuerte *m*.

counterfugue ['kauntəfjuːg] *n* MUS contrafuga *f*.

counterinquiry ['kauntərin'kwaiəri] *n* nueva información *f*, nueva investigación *f*.

counterinsurance ['kauntərin'ʃuərəns] *n* contraseguro *m*.

counterintelligence ['kauntərin'telidʒərins] *n* contraespionaje *m*.

counterirritant [kauntər'iritənt] *n* revulsivo *m*.

counterman ['kauntəmən] *n* dependiente *m*.

— OBSERV El plural de *counterman* es *countermen*.

countermand [ˌkauntə'mɑːnd] *n* contraorden *m*.

countermand [ˌkauntə'mɑːnd] *vt* anular, revocar (a command) ‖ COMM anular (an order).

countermarch ['kauntəmɑːtʃ] *n* contramarcha *f*.

countermarch ['kauntəmɑːtʃ] *vi* contramarchar.

countermark ['kauntəmɑːk] *n* contramarca *f*, contraseña *f*.

countermeasure ['kauntəˌmeʒə*] *n* contramedida *f*.

countermine ['kauntəmain] *n* MIL contramina *f* ‖ FIG contramaniobra *f* (counterplot).

countermine ['kauntəmain] *vt* MIL contraminar ‖ FIG frustrar (to thwart).

countermove ['kauntəmuːv] *n* contraataque *m*.

countermure ['kauntəmjuə*] *n* contramuralla *f*, contramuro *m*.

counteroffensive ['kauntərə'fensiv] *n* MIL contraofensiva *f*.

counterorder ['kauntərˌɔːdə*] *n* contraorden *f*.

counterpane ['kauntəpein] *n* cubrecama *m*, colcha *f* (bedspread).

counterpart ['kauntəpɑːt] *n* colega *m* & *f* (colleague); *the American ambassador met his Russian counterpart* el embajador americano se entrevistó con su colega ruso ‖ sosia *m*, doble *m* (double) ‖ réplica *f* (replica) ‖ FIG complemento *m* (complement) ‖ MUS contrapaso *m* ‖ duplicado *m*, doble *m* (copy) ‖ pareja *f* (of ornament, picture) ‖ JUR contrapartida *f*.

counterplan ['kauntəplæn] *n* contraproyecto *m*.

counterplea ['kauntəpliː] *n* JUR contrarréplica *f*.

counterplot ['kauntəplɔt] *n* contramaniobra *f*.

counterplot ['kauntəplɔt] *vi* preparar una contramaniobra.

counterpoint ['kauntəpɔint] *n* MUS contrapunto *m*.

counterpoise ['kauntəpɔiz] *n* contrapeso *m*.

counterpoise ['kauntəpɔiz] *vt* contrapesar, hacer contrapeso a ‖ FIG contrapesar, compensar.

counterproductive ['kauntəprə'dʌktiv] *adj* contraproducente.

counterproject ['kauntəˌprɔdʒekt] *n* contraproyecto *m*.

counterproof ['kauntəpruːf] *n* contraprueba *f*.

counterproposal ['kauntəprə'pəuzəl] *n* contrapropuesta *f*.

counterpunch ['kauntəpʌntʃ] *n* contragolpe *m*.

Counter-Reformation ['kauntərefə'meiʃən] *n* Contrarreforma *f*.

counterrevolution ['kauntərevə'luːʃən] *n* contrarrevolución *f*.

counterrevolutionary [-əri] *adj/n* contrarrevolucionario, ria.

countersank ['kauntəsæŋk] *pret* → **countersink.**

counterscarp ['kauntəskɑːp] *n* contraescarpa *f*.

counterseal ['kauntəsiːl] *n* contrasello *m*.

counterseal ['kauntəsiːl] *vt* contrasellar.

countershaft ['kauntəʃɑːft] *n* eje *m* secundario, transmisión *f* intermedia.

countersign ['kauntəsain] *n* MIL contraseña *f*, consigna *f* (password) ‖ contrafirma *f*, refrendata *f*.

countersign ['kauntəsain] *vt* contrafirmar, refrendar ‖ ratificar.

countersignature ['kauntə'signitʃə*] *n* contrafirma *f*, refrendata *f*.

countersink ['kauntəsiŋk] *n* avellanador *m*, broca *f* (tool) ‖ agujero *m* avellanado (hole).

countersink* ['kauntəsiŋk] *vt* TECH avellanar.

— OBSERV Pret ***countersank***; pp ***countersunk***.

counterstatement ['kauntə,steitmənt] *n* contradeclaración *f*.

counterstroke ['kauntəstrəuk] *n* contragolpe *m*.

countersunk ['kauntəsʌŋk] *pp* ⟶ **countersink.**

countertenor ['kauntə'tenə*] *n* MUS contralto *m*.

counterterm ['kauntətə:m] *n* GRAMM antónimo *m*.

countervail ['kauntəveil] *vt* compensar || contrarrestar.

◆ *vi* *to countervail against* prevalecer contra.

counterweigh ['kauntəwei] *vt* contrapesar, hacer contrapeso a || sopesar, pesar (to think over).

◆ *vi* servir de contrapeso.

counterweight ['kauntəweit] *n* contrapeso *m*.

counterweight ['kauntəweit] *vt* poner contrapeso a.

counterword ['kauntəwə:d] *n* palabra *f* de significado poco preciso.

countess ['kauntis] *n* condesa *f*.

counting ['kauntiŋ] *n* cuenta *f* (count).

countinghouse [-haus] *n* oficina *f* de contabilidad.

countless ['kauntlis] *adj* incontable, innumerable, sin número.

countrified ['kʌntrifaid] *adj* rústico, ca || provinciano, na.

country ['kʌntri] *n* país *m* (region, land, polictal state, people of a country) || campo *m* (as opposed to town); *to live in the country* vivir en el campo || — *cattle country* país ganadero || *mother country* madre *f* patria || *to appeal* o *to go to the country* convocar elecciones generales.

◆ *adj* del campo.

country-and-western [-ənd,westən] *n* US música *f* country.

country club [-klʌb] *n* club *m* de campo.

country cousin [-'kʌzn] *n* provinciano, na.

country-dance [-'dɑ:ns] *n* baile *m* regional.

country estate [-is'teit] *n* finca *f* [AMER hacienda *f*, estancia *f*].

countryfolk [-fəuk] *n* gente *f* del campo, campesinos *m pl*.

country house [-'haus] *n* casa *f* de campo (house in the country) || casa *f* solariega (of a nobleman).

countryman [-mən] *n* campesino *m* (who lives in the country) || compatriota *m* (a compatriot) || habitante *m* (of a specified district).

— OBSERV El plural de *countryman* es *countrymen*.

country people [-,pi:pl] *pl n* campesinos *m*, gente *f sing* del campo.

countryroad [-'rəud] *n* camino *m* vecinal.

countryseat [-'si:t] *n* finca *f*.

countryside [-said] *n* campo *m* (rural area, inhabitants) || paisaje *m* (landscape).

countrywoman [-,wumən] *n* campesina *f* (who lives in the country) || compatriota *f* (a compatriot) || habitante *f* (of a specified district).

— OBSERV El plural de *countrywoman* es *countrywomen*.

countship ['kauntʃip] *n* condado *m*.

county ['kaunti] *n* condado *m* || — *county borough* ciudad *f* de más de 50 000 habitantes || *county council* ayuntamiento *m* (organization), municipio *m* (territory) || *county court* juzgado *m* municipal || US *county seat* capital *f* de un condado || *county town* capital *f* de un condado.

coup [ku:] *n* golpe *m* || — *coup de grâce* golpe de gracia || *coup d'état* golpe de estado || *coup de théâtre* sorpresa *f*, lance imprevisto.

coupé ['ku:pei] *n* cupé *m*.

couple ['kʌpl] *n* par *m* (pair) || pareja *f* (married or engaged pair, partners in a dance) || PHYS par *m* | enganche *m* (a coupler) || yunta *f* (of oxen) || pareja *f* de perros de caza (two hounds) || traílla *f* doble (leash) || *I have a couple of things to do* tengo un par de cosas que hacer.

couple ['kʌpl] *vt* emparejar (to pair) || enganchar (wagons) || asociar (to associate) || ELECTR conectar, acoplar || TECH acoplar | empalmar (two cables).

◆ *vi* aparearse (animals) || emparejarse (to join in pairs) || conectarse (radio) || copular (to copulate).

coupler ['kʌplə*] *n* aparato *m* de conexión (in radio) || enganche *m* (of wagons) || ELECTR acoplamiento *m* | empalme *m*.

couplet ['kʌplit] *n* pareado *m* (verse).

coupling ['kʌpliŋ] *n* conexión *f* (action of connecting) || enganche *m* (wagons, cars) || empalme *m* || acoplamiento *m* || asociación *f* (ideas) || cópula *f* (sexual intercourse).

coupon ['ku:pɔn] *n* cupón *m* || boleto *m* (in football pools) || *coupon bond* vale *m*.

courage ['kʌridʒ] *n* valor *m*, valentía *f* || — *courage!* ¡ánimo! || *take courage!* ¡anímate! || *to have the courage of one's convictions* ser consecuente con sus principios || *to lose courage* desanimarse || *to pluck up courage, to screw up one's courage* armarse de valor || *to take courage* cobrar ánimo || *to take one's courage in both hands* hacer de tripas corazón.

courageous [kə'reidʒəs] *adj* valiente, valeroso, sa.

courgette [kuə'ʒet] *n* BOT calabacín *m*.

courier ['kʌriə*] *n* guía *m* & *f* (a guide) || mensajero *m*, correo *m* (letter carrier) || correo *m* (diplomatic).

course [kɔ:s] *n* curso *m* (progress in space or time); *the course of life* el curso de la vida; *the course of the river* el curso del río || ASTR curso *m*, trayectoria *f* (of the Sun, Moon) || recorrido *m*, trayectoria *f* (of a bullet) || recorrido *m* (of a piston) || dirección *f*, rumbo *m*, ruta *f* (direction); *change course and head for London* cambia de dirección y dirígete a Londres || dirección *f* (of a lode) || curso *m* (development); *the course of events* el curso de los acontecimientos || camino *m*, vía *f* (way, means); *several courses are open to us* varios caminos se abren ante nosotros || línea *f*; *course of action, of conduct* línea de acción, de conducta || curso *m* (series of lessons) || carrera *f* (university career) || programa *m* (of education) || ciclo *m*; *a course of lectures* un ciclo de conferencias || plato *m* (any of the parts of a meal) || servicio *m* (sitting) || pista *f* (track) || hipódromo *m* (racecourse) || campo *m* (for golf) || MED curso *m* (of a disease) | serie *f* (of injections) | reglas *f pl* (periods) | tratamiento *m*; *to put s.o. on a course of medicine* recetar a uno un tratamiento médico || ARCH hilada *f* || AGR rotación *f* de cultivos || COMM corriente *f* | cotización *f* (of exchange) || MAR vela *f* baja (sail) | rumbo *m* (way); *to change one's course* cambiar de rumbo || galería *f* (in a mine) || — *as a matter of course* naturalmente || *by course of law* según las leyes || *close course* circuito cerrado || *first course* entrada *f*, principio *m* (of a meal) || *in course of* en curso de || *in due course* a su debido tiempo || *in the course of* en el transcurso de, durante || *in the ordinary course of events* normalmente, lógicamente || *last course* postre *m* || *main course* plato fuerte || *of course* claro, por supuesto, desde luego || *that's a matter of course* esto cae de su peso || *to be off course* perder el rumbo || *to be on course* seguir el rumbo || *to hold one's course* seguir el camino trazado || *to set course for* poner *or* hacer rumbo a || *to take a middle course* tirar por la calle de en medio, evitar los extremos || *to take one's own course* seguir su camino || *to take* o *to run its course* seguir su curso.

course [kɔ:s] *vt* cazar (to hunt) || hacer correr (to race).

◆ *vi* correr (blood, liquid).

courser [-ə*] *n* corcel *m* (horse) || ZOOL corredora *f* (bird).

courseware *n* INFORM programa *or* software *m* didáctico.

coursing [-iŋ] *n* cacería *f*.

court [kɔ:t] *n* patio *m* (courtyard) || callejón *m* sin salida (alley) || plaza *f* (of a church) || sala *f* (big room) || corte *f* (of royalty) || palacio *m* (palace) || JUR audiencia *f* (audience); *open court* audiencia pública | tribunal *m*; *High Court* Tribunal Supremo || comisión *f*; *court of inquiry* comisión de investigación || corte *m* (wooing); *to pay court to s.o.* hacer la corte a alguien || SP cancha *f* || — *court of last resort* tribunal de última instancia || *court of law* juzgado *m* || *court order* orden *f* judicial || *juvenile court* tribunal de menores || *to bring* o *to take to court* llevar a los tribunales || *to fall out of court with* perder el favor de || *to go to court* acudir a los tribunales || *to rule out of court* desestimar [una demanda] || *to settle a case out of court* llegar a un arreglo amistoso.

court [kɔ:t] *vt* cortejar, hacer la corte a (to woo) || buscar, solicitar (to look for) || incitar a; *to court s.o. into doing sth.* incitar a uno a que haga algo || exponerse a, ir al encuentro de (disappointment, failure) || pedir, solicitar; *to court inquiry* solicitar una investigación.

◆ *vi* ser novios, estar en relaciones (two people) || tener novio, tener novia; *is she courting?* ¿tiene novio?

court card [-kɑ:d] *n* figura *f*.

court day [-dei] *n* día *m* hábil.

courteous ['kə:tjəs] *adj* cortés, atento, ta.

courteousness [-nis] *n* cortesía *f*.

courtesan [,kɔ:ti'zæn] *n* cortesana *f* (prostitute).

courtesy ['kə:tisi] *n* cortesía *f* || *to exchange courtesies* intercambiar cumplidos || *by courtesy of* por gentileza de, gracias a.

court hand ['kɔ:t'hænd] *n* letra *f* gótica.

courthouse ['kɔ:thaus] *n* Palacio *m* de Justicia.

courtier ['kɔ:tjə*] *n* cortesano *m*.

courtliness ['kɔ:tlinis] *n* cortesía *f* || distinción *f*, elegancia *f*.

courtly ['kɔ:tli] *adj* cortés || distinguido, da; elegante.

court-martial ['kɔ:t'mɑ:ʃəl] *n* consejo *m* de guerra, tribunal *m* militar.

— OBSERV El plural es *courts-martial* o *court-martials*.

court-martial ['kɔ:t'mɑ:ʃəl] *vt* juzgar en consejo de guerra.

Court of Appeals ['kɔ:təvə'pi:lz] *n* tribunal *m* de apelación.

courtroom ['kɔ:tru:m] *n* sala *f* de un tribunal.

courtship ['kɔ:tʃip] *n* cortejo *m* (action of courting) || noviazgo *m* (engagement).

courtshoe ['kɔ:tʃu:] *n* escarpín *m*.

courtyard ['kɔ:tjɑ:d] *n* patio *m*.

couscous ['kuskus] *n* cuscús *m*.

cousin ['kʌzn] *n* primo, ma; *first cousin* primo hermano *or* carnal || *first cousin once removed* sobrino segundo (one's first cousin's child), tío segundo (one's parent's firts cousin).

cousin-german [-'dʒə:mən] *n* primo *m* hermano, prima *f* hermana; primo *m* carnal, prima *f* carnal.
— OBSERV El plural es *cousins-german.*

cousinhood [-hud] ; **cousinship** [-ʃip] *n* primazgo *m*, parentesco *m* de primo.

couture [ku'tjuə*] *n* alta costura *f.*

couturier [ku:'tu:riei] *n* modisto *m*, modista *f.*

cove [kəuv] *n* cala *f*, ensenada *f* (bay) ‖ ARCH bovedilla *f* ‖ cueva *f* (cave) ‖ FAM tío *m*, sujeto *m* (guy).

cove [kəuv] *vi* ARCH abovedarse.

coven ['kʌvn] *n* aquelarre *m.*

covenant ['kʌvənənt] *n* convenio *m* (agreement) ‖ pacto *m*; *covenant of the League of Nations* pacto de la Sociedad de Naciones ‖ contrato *m* (contract) ‖ REL alianza *f.*

covenant ['kʌvənənt] *vt* concertar.
◆ *vi* convenir ‖ pactar.

Coventry ['kɔvəntri] *pr n* GEOGR Coventry ‖ FIG & FAM *to send s.o. to Coventry* hacer el vacío a alguien.

cover ['kʌvə*] *n* cubierta *f* (in general) ‖ tapa *f* (a lid) ‖ tapa *f* (binding of a book) ‖ forro *m* (protection of books) ‖ portada *f* (of magazine) ‖ funda *f* (a fitted covering) ‖ cubierta *f* (of a tyre) ‖ envoltura *f* (of a parcel) ‖ refugio *m* (a concealing shelter) ‖ cobertura *f*, fondos *m pl* (money to meet liabilities) ‖ tapete *m* (of a table) ‖ cobertor *m*, colcha *f* (on bed) ‖ cubierto *m* (table service) ‖ sobre *m* (envelope) ‖ faja *f*, banda *f* (of newspaper) ‖ pretexto *m*, excusa *f* (pretence) ‖ protección *f*, amparo *m* (protection) ‖ — *from cover to cover* de cabo a rabo ‖ *to break cover* salir al descubierto ‖ *to take cover* ponerse a cubierto ‖ *under cover* al abrigo; bajo techo, a cubierto ‖ *under registered cover* certificado, da ‖ *under separate cover* por separado ‖ *under (the) cover of* al amparo de ‖ *under the same cover* adjunto, ta.
◆ *pl* ropa *f sing* de cama (bedclothes).

cover ['kʌvə*] *vt* tapar (to put a cover on) ‖ cubrir; *the field was covered with snow* el campo estaba cubierto de nieve ‖ cubrirse (the head) ‖ cubrir, proteger (to protect) ‖ cubrir, defender (to defend) ‖ apuntar (to aim a gun) ‖ MIL cubrir ‖ ocupar una extensión de (to occupy) ‖ cubrir (a bet) ‖ encuadernar (to bind a book) ‖ forrar (to protect a book) ‖ cubrir (to include in an insurance policy) ‖ asegurar (to insure) ‖ cubrir (to defray costs) ‖ estar encargado de, ocuparse de (to be responsible for); *he covers the north of the country* está encargado del norte del país ‖ SP cubrir ‖ abarcar, cubrir (to embrace) ‖ cubrir, recorrer (a distance) ‖ dominar, cubrir (a landscape) ‖ informar sobre (to report) ‖ cubrir (animals) ‖ empollar (to hatch) ‖ — *to cover o.s. with glory* cubrirse de gloria ‖ *to cover up* cubrir completamente (to cover thoroughly), encubrir (offence), copar (gambling), disimular, ocultar (to conceal) ‖ *to cover with honours* cubrir de honores.
◆ *vi* cubrir ‖ *to cover up for* encubrir.

coverage ['kʌvəridʒ] *n* alcance *m* (reach) ‖ circulación *f* (of a newspaper) ‖ reportaje *m* (report) ‖ respaldo *m* (of money) ‖ fondos *m pl* (of a cheque) ‖ extensión *f*, riesgos *m pl* cubiertos (of an insurance) ‖ FIG protección *f*, amparo *m.*

coveralls ['kʌvərɔ:lz] *n* bata *f* (coat) ‖ mono *m* (overalls).

cover charge ['kʌvətʃɑ:dʒ] *n* precio *m* del cubierto.

covered waggon; *US* **covered wagon** ['kʌvəd'wægən] *n* carromato *m.*

covered way ['kʌvəd'wei] *n* MIL camino *m* cubierto, corredor *m.*

cover girl ['kʌvəgə:l] *n* modelo *f* fotográfica.

covering ['kʌvəriŋ] *n* cubierta *f*, envoltura *f* (wrapping) ‖ abrigo *m* (dress, etc.) ‖ — *a covering of snow* una capa de nieve ‖ *covering action* acción *f* de cobertura ‖ *covering fire* fuego *m* de protección ‖ *covering letter* carta explicatoria.

coverlet ['kʌvəlit] *n* colcha *f*, cubrecama *m* (bedspread) ‖ cubrepiés *m inv* (counterpane).

covert ['kʌvət] *n* matorral *m* (thicket) ‖ refugio *m*, abrigo *m* (shelter).
◆ *pl* plumas *f.*
◆ *adj* furtivo, va; *covert glance* mirada furtiva ‖ secreto, ta (secret) ‖ cubierto, ta; abrigado, da (sheltered).

coverture ['kʌvətjuə*] *n* envoltura *f* (of a package) ‖ refugio *m*, abrigo *m* (refuge) ‖ escondrijo *m* (concealment) ‖ JUR estado *m* legal de una mujer casada.

cover-up ['kʌvərʌp] *n* FAM coartada *f* (alibi) ‖ encubrimiento *m* (concealment).

cover version ['kʌvə,və:ʃən] *n* versión *f* (of a song).

covet ['kʌvit] *vt* codiciar.

covetous ['kʌvitəs] *adj* codicioso, sa; ávido, da.

covetousness [-nis] *n* codicia *f*, avidez *f.*

covey ['kʌvi] *n* nidada *f* (brood) ‖ bandada *f* (flock) ‖ FIG grupo *m.*

covings ['kəuviŋz] *pl n* ARCH dovelas *f.*

cow [kau] *n* ZOOL vaca *f* (of ox family); *milch cow* vaca lechera ‖ hembra *f* (of other animals); *cow seal* foca hembra ‖ *cow elephant* elefanta *f* ‖ — FIG *the time of the lean cows* la época de las vacas flacas | *to wait till the cows come home* esperar sentado, esperar hasta que las ranas críen pelos.

cow [kau] *vt* acobardar, intimidar.

coward [-əd] *n* cobarde *m* & *f.*

cowardice [-ədis] *n* cobardía *f.*

cowardliness [-ədlinis] *n* cobardía *f.*

cowardly [-ədli] *adj* cobarde.
◆ *adv* cobardemente.

cowbell [-bel] *n* cencerro *m.*

cowboy [-bɔi] *n* vaquero *m.*

cowcatcher [-,kætʃə*] *n* *US* rastrillo *m* delantero, quitapiedras *m inv.*

cower [-ə*] *vi* acobardarse, encogerse (from fear) ‖ agacharse (to crouch).

cowfish [-fiʃ] *n* ZOOL manatí *m* (sea cow).

cowgirl [-gə:l] *n* vaquera *f.*

cowhand [-hænd] *n* *US* vaquero *m.*

cowherd [-hə:d] *n* vaquero *m.*

cowhide [-haid] *n* cuero *m* ‖ látigo *m* de cuero (whip).

cowl [kaul] *n* REL capucha *f* ‖ capirote *m* (of penitent) ‖ sombrerete *m* de chimenea ‖ capó *m* (of a car) ‖ capota *f* (of plane).

cowlick ['kaulik] *n* remolino *m*, mechón *m* (of hair).

cowling ['kauliŋ] *n* capota *f* (of plane).

cowman ['kaumən] *n* vaquero *m* (cowherd) ‖ *US* ganadero *m* (cattle owner).
— OBSERV El plural de *cowman* es *cowmen.*

co-worker ['kəu'wə:kə*] *n* colaborador, ra.

cowpox ['kaupɔks] *n* VET vacuna *f.*

cowpuncher ['kau,pʌntʃə*] *n* *US* vaquero *m.*

cowrie; **cowry** ['kauri] *n* ZOOL cauri *m.*
— OBSERV El plural de estas palabras es *cowries.*

cowshed ['kauʃed] *n* establo *m.*

cowslip ['kauslip] *n* BOT prímula *f.*

cox [kɔks] *n* SP timonel *m.*

cox [kɔks] *vt* SP gobernar.
◆ *vi* SP hacer de timonel.

coxa ['kɔksə] *n* ANAT & ZOOL cadera *f* (hip).
— OBSERV El plural de *coxa* es *coxae.*

coxalgia [kɔks'ældʒjə] *n* MED coxalgia *f.*

coxcomb ['kɔkskəum] *n* fatuo, tua.

coxswain ['kɔksn, 'kɔkswein] *n* timonel *m* (helmsman) ‖ patrón *m* (person in charge of a boat).

coy [kɔi] *adj* tímido, da (shy) ‖ remilgado, da (demure) ‖ *coy of speech* parco en palabras.

coyly [-li] *adv* tímidamente.

coyness [-nis] *n* timidez *f* ‖ afectación *f.*

coyote [kɔi'əut] *n* ZOOL coyote *m.*

coypu ['kɔipu:] *n* ZOOL coipo *m*, coipu *m.*

cozily ['kəuzili] *adv* ⟶ **cosily.**

coziness ['kəuzinis] *n* ⟶ **cosiness.**

cozy ['kəuzi] *adj/n* ⟶ **cosy.**

CP *abbr of [Communist Party]* PC, Partido Comunista.

CPI *abbr of [Consumer Price Index]* IPC, índice de precios al consumo.

CPU *abbr of [central processing unit]* CPU, unidad central de proceso.

crab [kræb] *n* ZOOL cangrejo *m* (crustacean) ‖ ASTR Cáncer *m* ‖ TECH torno *m* ‖ AVIAT deriva *f* ‖ ladilla *f* (insect) ‖ FIG gruñón *m* (grumbly) ‖ SP FAM *to catch a crab* dar un falso golpe de remo.

crab [kræb] *vt* AVIAT hacer ir a la deriva ‖ FIG criticar (to find fault with) | estropear (to frustrate).
◆ *vi* AVIAT ir a la deriva ‖ pescar cangrejos (to catch crabs) ‖ FIG refunfuñar, quejarse.

crab apple [-,æpl] *n* BOT manzana *f* silvestre.

crabbed ['kræbid] *adj* malhumorado, da (morose) ‖ enrevesado, da (intricate).

crabber ['kræbə*] *n* cangrejero, ra (person) ‖ barca *f* para pescar cangrejos (boat) ‖ FIG gruñón *m.*

crabbiness ['kræbinis] *n* malhumor *m*, mal genio *m.*

crabby ['kræbi] *adj* malhumorado, da; gruñón, ona (grumbly) ‖ hosco, ca (peevish).

crab louse ['kræblaus] *n* ZOOL ladilla *f.*

crack [kræk] *n* restallido *m*, chasquido *m*, traquido *m*; *the crack of a whip* el chasquido de un látigo ‖ crujido *m* (of branches, etc.) ‖ detonación *f* (of a firearm) ‖ golpe *m* (blow) ‖ raja *f*, resquebrajadura *f* (split); *a cup with a crack* una taza con una raja ‖ grieta *f*, hendidura *f* (in the ground, in walls) ‖ abertura *f* (opening) ‖ rendija *f* (slit); *the light came in through a crack in the door* la luz entraba por una rendija en la puerta ‖ FAM murmuración *f*, chismorreo *m*, habladuría *f* (gossip) | chiste *m* (joke) | favorito *m* (favourite) ‖ campeón *m*, as *m* (star) | tipo *m* curioso (strange person) ‖ gallo *m* (in the voice) ‖ momento *m*, instante *m* (trice); *in a crack* en un momento ‖ FAM robo *m* con fractura ‖ *US* FAM pulla *f*, chacota *f* (gibe) | intento *m* (attempt) ‖ — *at the crack of dawn* al amanecer, al romper el alba ‖ *crack of doom* día *m* del Juicio Final ‖ *nasty crack* observación malintencionada, broma pesada ‖ *to have a crack at* intentar ‖ *to take a crack at* dar un golpe a, pegar a (to strike), intentar (to try).
◆ *adj* de primera (excellent).

crack [kræk] *vt* restallar, chasquear; *to crack a whip* restallar un látigo ‖ golpear, pegar (to hit) ‖ chasquear (the fingers) ‖ crujir (the knuckles) ‖ cascar (to break a nut) ‖ romper, partir (to break) ‖ agrietar, hender (the earth) ‖ rajar, resquebrajar (glass, stone) ‖ agrietar, cuartear (a wall) ‖ astillar (a bone) ‖ agrietar (the skin) ‖ cascar (the voice) ‖ FAM forzar (a safe) ‖ CHEM craquear, fraccionar (oil) ‖ FIG arruinar, echar abajo (s.o.'s credit) ‖ perturbar, trastornar (the calm) | hacer (pun) | contar (to tell a joke) | gastar (to play a joke) | derribar, vencer (an

obstacle) | encontrar la solución a, resolver (a difficulty) | explicar (a mystery) | descifrar (a code) | abrir, destapar (a bottle) || — *he isn't as good as he is cracked up to be* no es tan bueno como lo pintan *or* como dicen || *to crack up* destrozar (to break), alabar, ensalzar (to praise).
◆ *vi* agrietarse, resquebrajarse (to split) || restallar, chasquear (a whip) || reventar (to burst) || crujir (the knuckles) || romperse, partirse, abrirse (to break) || rajarse, resquebrajarse (glass, stone) || agrietarse, cuartearse (a wall) || astillarse (a bone) || agrietarse (the skin) || detonar (a rifle) || fraccionarse (petroil, oil) || cascarse, quebrarse (voice) || mudar (boy's voice) || FIG ceder, rendirse, darse por vencido (to give in) | fallar (to fail) | perder el control de sí mismo (to lose control) | volverse loco (to go crazy) | arruinarse, venirse abajo, hundirse (to break down) | charlar (to chatter) | bromear, decir bromas (to joke) || — FIG *at a cracking pace* a todo correr || *to crack down on* tomar medidas enérgicas contra || *to crack on sail* avanzar a toda vela, desplegar todas las velas || *to crack up* destrozarse, hacerse pedazos (to fall into pieces), volverse loco, ca (to break down mentally), venirse abajo, agotarse (to break down physically), estrellarse (a plane), quebrar (economy), darse autobombo, darse pisto (to boast), reírse a carcajadas (to laugh) || *to get cracking* darse prisa, apresurarse (to hurry), empezar (to start).

crackbrain [-brein] *n* FAM chiflado, da; loco, ca.

crackbrained [-breind] *adj* FAM chiflado, da; loco, ca.

crackdown [-daun] *n* medidas *f pl* enérgicas.

cracked [krækt] *adj* agrietado, da (split) || resquebrajado, da; rajado, da (glass, stone) || cuarteado, da; agrietado, da (wall) || FAM chiflado, da (crazy) | desafinado, da (tuneless) | cascado, da (old man's voice).

cracker ['krækə*] *n* galleta *f* (biscuit) || buscapiés *m inv* (firework) || sorpresa *f*; *to pull a Christmas cracker* abrir una sorpresa.
◆ *pl* papillotes *m* (hair curlers).

crackerjack [-dʒæk] *adj* FAM magnífico, ca; maravilloso, sa; de primera.
◆ *n* FAM maravilla *f* (first-rate thing) | campeón *m*, as *m* (skilful person).

crackers ['krækəz] *adj* FAM loco, ca; chiflado, da.

cracking ['krækiŋ] *n* cracking *m*, craqueo *m* (of oil).
◆ *adj* FIG & FAM extraordinario, ria | muy rápido, da; *a cracking pace* un paso muy rápido.

crackle ['krækl] *n* crepitación *f*, chisporroteo *m* (of fire, of wood) || crujido *m* (of leaves) || grieteado *m* (in glassware) || ruido *m* parásito, fritura *f* (on the telephone).

crackle ['krækl] *vi* crepitar, chisporrotear (fire) || crujir (leaves, etc.) || agrietarse (glaze).
◆ *vt* estrujar, hacer crujir (papers, etc.).

crackling [-iŋ] *n* crepitación *f*, chisporroteo *m* (of fire, of wood) || crujido *m* (of leaves) || grieteado *m* (in glassware) || ruido *m* parásito, fritura *f* (on the telephone).
◆ *pl* chicharrones *m* (roasted pork skin).

crackly [-i] *adj* crepitante, chisporroteante (fire) || quebradizo, za (fragile).

cracknel ['kræknəl] *n* galleta f (biscuit).
◆ *pl* US torreznos *m* (small pieces of fat), chicharrones (cracklings).

crackpot ['krækpɔt] *adj/n* FAM chiflado, da; chalado, da.

cracksman ['kræksmən] *n* FAM atracador *m*.
— OBSERV El plural de *cracksman* es *cracksmen*.

crack-up ['krækʌp] *n* FAM caída *f* (of a plane) | choque *m* (collision) | depresión *f* nerviosa (mental breakdown) | colapso *m* (physical breakdown) | quiebra *f* (of a firm).

cracky ['kræki] *adj* agrietado, da (full of cracks) || resquebrajadizo, za (liable to crack) || FAM chiflado, da (crazy) || *by cracky!* ¡córcholis!

Cracow ['krækəu] *pr n* GEOGR Cracovia *f*.

cradle ['kreidl] *n* cuna *f*; *a baby in its cradle* un niño en su cuna; *the cradle of civilization* la cuna de la civilización || soporte *m*, horquilla *f* (for phone) || MAR basada *f*, cuna *f* de botadura (support for ships under construction) | boya *f* pantalón (lifesaving device) || MIN criba *f* || MED arco *m* | entablillado *m* (for fractures) || soporte *m* (of a plane) || AGR armazón *f* de la guadaña (for scythe) || andamio *m* volante (used by house painters, etc.) || rascador *m* dentado (engraving tool) || *cradle car* vagoneta *f* basculante.

cradle ['kreidl] *vt* acostar, poner en la cuna (to put a baby in a cradle) || acunar, mecer (to hold a baby) || AGR segar || MIN lavar, pasar por la criba || FIG *cradled in luxury* criado en buenos pañales.

cradlesong [-sɔŋ] *n* canción *f* de cuna, nana *f*.

craft [krɑːft] *n* arte *m* (a trade requiring skill, or that skill) || gremio *m* (a guild) || trabajo *m* manual, oficio *m* (trade) || astucia *f*, habilidad *f*, maña *f* (cunning) || embarcación *f*, navío *m* (boat) || aparato *m*, avión *m* (aircraft) || — *craft union* gremio *m*, corporación *f* || *the Craft* la masonería.
— OBSERV El plural de *craft* cuando significa *embarcación* o *avión* es *craft*.

craftily [-ili] *adv* astutamente.

craftiness [-inis] *n* astucia *f*, maña *f*, habilidad *f*.

craftsman ['krɑːftsmən] *n* artesano *m* (artisan) || artista *m* (an artist in his or her trade) || FIG artífice *m*, realizador *m*.
— OBSERV El plural de craftsman es *craftsmen*.

craftsmanship [-ʃip] *n* artesanía *f* || oficio *m* (of writer) || habilidad *f*, destreza *f* (skill) || ejecución *f*, realización *f* (execution).

crafty ['krɑːfti] *adj* astuto, ta; hábil, mañoso, sa.

crag [kræg] *n* despeñadero *m* (steep, rugged cliff) || risco *m* (projecting rock).

cragged ['krægid] *adj* peñascoso, sa; rocoso, sa; escarpado, da.

craggedness [-nis]; **cragginess** ['kræginis] *n* rocosidad *f*, carácter *m* escarpado.

craggy ['krægi] *adj* peñascoso, sa; escarpado, da; rocoso, sa.

crake [kreik] *n* ZOOL rascón *m*, rey *m* de codornices.

cram [kræm] *n* apretura *f* (of people) || FAM estudio *m* de última hora | bola *f*, mentira *f* (lie).

cram [kræm] *vt* abarrotar, atiborrar, atestar (to fill very full) || meter a la fuerza (to force sth. in) || meter (in the pocket) || cebar (fowl) || hartar (to stuff) || US atiborrarse de (to eat sth. greedily) || FAM llenar (one's memory) | dar clases intensivas a (to teach intensively).
◆ *vi* atiborrarse, atracarse (with food) || FAM empollar (before an exam) | bromear (to joke).

crambo ['kræmbəu] *n* juego *m* consistente en rimar palabras.
— OBSERV El plural de *crambo* es *cramboes*.

crammer ['kræmə*] *n* empollón, ona (student).

cramp [kræmp] *n* pinza *f* de unión (metal wall support) || grapa *f* (staple) || cárcel *f* (clamp) || FIG obstáculo *m*, traba *f* || MED calambre *m* (contraction of muscles) || FIG *under the cramp of* atenazado por.
◆ *pl* MED retortijones *m* (intestinal pain).

cramp [kræmp] *vt* poner trabas a, obstaculizar (to hinder) || dar calambre a (a muscle) || apretar (to secure with a cramp) || poner grapas a (papers) || girar, dar vueltas a (a wheel) || FIG & FAM *to cramp s.o.'s style* cohibir a alguien, cortar las alas de alguien.
◆ *vi* tener un calambre.

cramped [-t] *adj* apiñado, da; *we are cramped in this room* estamos apiñados en esta habitación || exiguo, gua (place) || apretado, da (writing) || molesto, ta; violento, ta (awkward) || *in cramped circumstances* en la estrechez.

cramp iron ['kræmpˌaiən] *n* grapa *f*.

crampon ['kræmpən] *n* garfio *m* (grappling hook) || SP crampón *m* (in climbing).

cranberry ['krænbəri] *n* BOT arándano *m*.

crane [krein] *n* ZOOL grulla *f* (bird) || grúa *f* (machine for raising and lowering weights); *bridge, gantry crane* grúa de puente, de pórtico || jirafa *f* (for camera) || MAR pescante *m* (davit) || sifón *m* (siphon) || — *crane boom* aguilón *m* de grúa || *crane driver* conductor *m* de grúa, gruista *m* || ZOOL *crane fly* típula *f*.

crane [krein] *vt* estirar (the neck) || TECH levantar con grúa.
◆ *vi* estirar el cuello.

craneman ['kreinmən] *n* conductor *m* de grúa, gruista *m*.
— OBSERV El plural de esta palabra es *cranemen*.

cranesbill ['kreinzbil] *n* BOT geranio *m*.

cranial ['kreinjəl] *adj* craneal, craneano, na.

craniology ['kreiniˈɔlədʒi] *n* craneología *f*.

cranium ['kreinjəm] *n* cráneo *m*.
— OBSERV El plural de *cranium* es *crania* o *craniums*.

crank [kræŋk] *n* TECH manivela *f* (handle) | cigüeñal *m* (crankshaft) || chiflado, da (fool) || excéntrico, ca (an excentric person) || chifladura *f* (craziness) || manía *f*, capricho *m* (whim) || extravagancia *f*.
◆ *adj* estropeado, da.

crank [kræŋk] *vt* arrancar (un coche) con la manivela || poner una manivela a (to provide with a crank) || acodar (to square).
◆ *vi* arrancar con la manivela.

crankcase [-keis] *n* TECH cárter *m*.

crankily ['kræŋkili] *adv* de mala manera || caprichosamente.

crankiness ['kræŋkinis] *n* irritabilidad *f*, mal humor *m* (irritability) || excentricidad *f* (excentricity) || capricho *m*, manía *f* (whim) || chifladura *f* (craziness) || mal funcionamiento *m* (of machines).

crankpin ['kræŋpin] *n* muñón *f* del cigüeñal.

crankshaft ['kræŋʃɑːft] *n* cigüeñal *m*; *crankshaft gear* piñón del cigüeñal.

cranky ['kræŋki] *adj* irritable (irritable) || chiflado, da (crazy) || excéntrico, ca (eccentric) || caprichoso, sa (capricious) || estropeado, da; descompuesto, ta (machines).

crannied ['krænid] *adj* agrietado, da.

cranny ['kræni] *n* grieta *f*.

crap [kræp] *n* US juego *m* de dados || POP porquería *f* (rubbish) | disparate *m* (nonsense) | trola *f* (lie) | mierda *f* (excrement).

crap [kræp] *vi* tirar los dados || POP cagar (to defecate).

crape [kreip] *n* crespón *m*.

crappy ['kræpi] *adj* POP de mierda.

craps [kræps] *pl n* US dados *m*; *to shoot craps* jugar a los dados, tirar los dados.

crapulence ['kræpjuləns] *n* crápula *f* (debauchery) || embriaguez *f* (drunkenness).

crapulent ['kræpjulənt]; **crapulous** ['kræpjuləs] *adj* crapuloso, sa (debauched) || borracho, cha (drunk).

crash [kræʃ] *n* estrépito *m* (loud noise) || estallido *m*, estampido *m* (of a gun) || choque *m* (collision) || accidente *m* (of railway, car) || caída *f*, accidente *m* (of aircraft) || quiebra *f* (of a business) || tela *f* para toallas.
◆ *adj* intensivo, va (course) || rápido, da (dive, diet) || de emergencia, forzoso, sa (landing) || protector, ra (helmet).

crash [kræʃ] *vi* retumbar (to make a violent noise); *the thunder crashed* el trueno retumbó || estallar (to explode) || dar un estallido (to detonate) || chocar (to collide) || estrellarse, caer (aeroplane); *to crash into a hill* estrellarse contra una colina || quebrar (business) || fracasar (to fail) || romperse, hacerse pedazos (to break) || tener un accidente (to have an accident) || derrumbarse (to fall in) || — *to crash about* o *around* andar de un lado a otro armando mucho ruido || *to crash down* caer con gran estrépito || *to crash into* irrumpir; *he crashed into the room* irrumpió en la habitación; estrellarse contra, chocar contra; *the car crashed into the tree* el coche chocó contra el árbol.
◆ *vt* estrellar || — *to crash a party* colarse en una fiesta || *to crash one's way through* abrirse camino arrollándolo todo.

crash barrier [-ˌbæriə*] *n* barrera *f* protectora.

crash-dive [-daiv] *vi* MAR sumergirse rápidamente.

crashing [-iŋ] *adj* FAM arrollador, ra (success) || completo, ta (utter) | impresionante (stunning).

crash-land [-lænd] *vi* AVIAT hacer un aterrizaje forzoso *or* de emergencia.

crasis ['kreisis] *n* GRAMM crasis *f inv*.
— OBSERV El plural de *crasis* es *crases*.

crass [kræs] *adj* craso, sa (ignorance) || obtuso, sa; estúpido, da (person) || burdo, da; tosco, ca (coarse) || grueso, sa (thick).

crassness ['kræsnis] *n* enormidad *f* (of an error) || tosquedad *f*, grosería *f* (coarseness) || estupidez *f* (stupidity).

crate [kreit] *n* cajón *m*, embalaje *m* || FAM cacharro *m* (car).

crater ['kreitə*] *n* cráter *m*.

cravat [krə'væt] *n* corbata *f* (tie) || pañuelo *m* (scarf).

crave [kreiv] *vt* desear ardientemente, ansiar, anhelar (to desire strongly) || implorar, suplicar (to beg) || reclamar, solicitar (attention).
◆ *vi* *to crave after* o *for* desear ardientemente, ansiar, anhelar, consumirse por.

craven ['kreivən] *adj* cobarde, timorato, ta.
◆ *n* cobarde *m* & *f*.

craving ['kreiviŋ] *n* deseo *m* ardiente, ansia *f*, anhelo *m* (*for* de) || antojo *m* (in pregnancy).
◆ *adj* voraz, insaciable (appetite) || intenso, sa; ardiente (desire) || tiránico, ca (need).

craw [krɔː] *n* buche *m* (of a bird) || FIG & FAM *it sticks in my craw* no me lo trago.

crawfish ['krɔːfiʃ] *n* ZOOL cangrejo *m* de río (freshwater crustacean) | langosta *f* (spiny lobster).

crawl [krɔːl] *n* arrastramiento *m*, deslizamiento *m* (of a snake) || criadero *m* (enclosure for fish) || marcha *f* lenta (slow movement) || SP «crawl» *m* (swimming) || *at a crawl* a paso lento.

crawl [krɔːl] *vi* andar a cuatro patas, andar a gatas, gatear (to move on hands and knees) || andar a paso de tortuga, avanzar lentamente (to move slowly) || deslizarse, reptar (a snake) | arrastrarse; *he crawled to the hole* se arrastró hasta el agujero || trepar (plants) || sentir un hormigueo (the flesh); *I crawl all over* siento un hormigueo por todo el cuerpo || SP nadar el «crawl» || circular lentamente en busca de clientes (a taxi) || FIG arrastrarse a los pies de, humillarse ante; *I crawled to him* me arrastré a sus pies || — FIG & FAM *it makes my skin crawl* me pone los pelos de punta || *to crawl along* avanzar paso a paso || *to crawl by* pasar lentamente || *to crawl under* meterse debajo de || *to crawl with* estar lleno de, hervir de (to be full), sentir un hormigueo a causa de (to creep).

crawler [-ə*] *n* oruga *f* (of a tractor) || tractor *m* oruga (tractor) || reptil *m* | FIG persona *f* rastrera.

crawly [-i] *adj* FAM espeluznante, horripilante.

crayfish ['kreifiʃ] *n* ZOOL cangrejo *m* de río (freshwater crustacean) | langosta *f* (spiny lobster).

crayon ['kreiən] *n* carboncillo *m* (charcoal) || pastel *m*, lápiz *m* de pastel || dibujo *m* al pastel (drawing) || ELECTR carbón *m* || FIG esbozo *m*, bosquejo *m*.

crayon ['kreiən] *vt* dibujar al pastel *or* con carboncillo || FIG esbozar, bosquejar.

craze [kreiz] *n* manía *f* (fad) || capricho *m* (whim) || moda *f* (fashion) || chifladura *f*, locura *f* (exaggerated enthusiasm).

craze [kreiz] *vt* enloquecer.
◆ *vi* cuartearse, agrietarse.

crazed [-d] *adj* loco, ca; *half crazed* medio loco || agrietado, da (pottery).

crazily [-ili] *adv* locamente.

craziness [-inis] *n* locura *f* (madness).

crazy ['kreizi] *adj* loco, ca (foolish, insane) || disparatado, da; loco, ca (idea) || en ruina (unsound) || desvencijado, da (furniture) || de baldosas irregulares (paving) || — FAM *to be crazy about s.o.* estar loco por alguien || *to be crazy with joy* estar loco de alegría || *to drive* o *to send s.o. crazy* volver loco a alguien || *to go crazy* volverse loco || *to run like crazy* correr como un loco.

crazy bone [-bəun] *n* US hueso *m* de la alegría (funny bone).

crazy quilt [-kwilt] *n* centón *m*, colcha *f* hecha con retales de distintos colores y tamaños || FIG lío *m* (jumble).

creak [kriːk] *n* crujido *m* (of floorboards) || chirrido *m* (of door hinges).

creak [kriːk] *vi* crujir (floor) || chirriar (hinges).

creaky ['kriːki] *adj* chirriante (door hinges) || que cruje (floorboards) || FIG poco seguro, ra.

cream [kriːm] *n* nata *f*, crema *f* (of milk) || nata *f* (in confectionery); *whipped cream* nata batida || crema *f* (soup) || CHEM crema *f* || crema *f* (cosmetics) || FIG crema *f* (best part of anything) || crema *f* (liqueur) || — FIG *the cream of the crop* la flor y nata, la crema | *the cream of the joke* lo más gracioso del caso.
◆ *adj* crema, color crema.

cream [kriːm] *vt* batir (to beat) || descremar, desnatar (to skim cream from milk) || poner crema (in tea, coffee, on one's face) || FIG *to cream off* seleccionar (best talents).
◆ *vi* formar nata (milk) || hacer espuma (to foam).

cream cheese [-'tʃiːz] *n* queso *m* de nata.

creamer [-ə*] *n* desnatadora *f*.

creamery [-əri] *n* lechería *f* (where milk is sold) || mantequería *f* (for cheese, butter and cream).

cream of tartar [-əv'tɑːtə*] *n* crémor *m* tartárico.

cream tea *n* té *m* servido con bollos, mantequilla, mermelada y nata.

creamy ['kriːmi] *adj* cremoso, sa.

crease [kriːs] *n* doblez *m*, pliegue *m* (fold) || arruga *f* (wrinkle) || raya *f* (of trousers) || SP línea *f* de la puerta | línea *f* del bateador (in cricket).

crease [kriːs] *vt* doblar, plegar (to fold) || arrugar (to wrinkle) || hacer la raya de (one's trousers).
◆ *vi* arrugarse (to wrinkle) || doblarse, plegarse (to fold).

creaseless [-lis] *adj* inarrugable.

creasy [-i] *adj* arrugado, da.

create [kri'eit] *vt* crear.
◆ *vi* FAM protestar, armar jaleo (to protest).

creation [kri'eiʃən] *n* creación *f* || FAM alboroto *m*, jaleo *m* (fuss).

creative [kri'eitiv] *adj* creador, ra.

creativeness [-nis] *n* creatividad *f*, facultad *f* creadora, inventiva *f*.

creativity [ˌkriei'tiviti] *n* facultad *f* creadora, inventiva *f*, creatividad *f*.

creator [kri'eitə*] *n* creador, ra.

creature ['kriːtʃə*] *n* criatura *f* (a living human or animal) || animal *m*, bicho *m* (animal) || FIG fruto *m*, obra *f*, producto *m*, creación *f*; *a creature of the imagination* una obra de la imaginación | instrumento *m*, juguete *m* (a servile tool of s.o. else) || — *creature comforts* comodidades *f* materiales || *poor creature!* ¡pobrecito!, ¡pobrecita!

crèche [kreiʃ] *n* guardería *f* (nursery) || nacimiento *m* (a model of the Nativity).

credence ['kriːdəns] *n* creencia *f* (belief) || crédito *m* (credit); *I gave credence to him* le di crédito || *letters of credence* cartas *f* credenciales.

credential [kri'denʃəl] *adj* credencial.

credentials [kri'dənʃəlz] *pl n* credenciales *f*.

credibility [ˌkredi'biliti] *n* credibilidad *f*, verosimilitud *f*.

credible ['kredəbl] *adj* creíble, verosímil.

credit ['kredit] *n* crédito *m*; *I have credit at the butcher's* tengo crédito en la carnicería || COMM haber *m*; *on the credit side* en el haber; *credit and debit* debe y haber | crédito *m* || honor *m*, prestigio *m* (good name); *he is a credit to the school* hace honor a la escuela || influencia *f* (influence) || fe *f*, creencia *f*, crédito *m* (belief) || US asignatura *f* (to get a degree) || — *credit balance* saldo acreedor || *credit card* tarjeta *f* de crédito || *credit facilities* facilidades *f pl* de crédito || *credit line* nota *f* que indica la procedencia de lo mencionado || *credit note* nota *f* de crédito || *credit rating* solvabilidad *f* || *credit squeeze* restricciones *f pl* de crédito || *credit union* banco *m* de crédito || *credit where it's due* el honor a quien le corresponda || *in credit* con saldo positivo || *it does him credit* le honra, dice mucho a su favor || *on credit* a crédito, a plazos [AMER a cuotas] (terms) || *to buy on credit* comprar a crédito, comprar a plazos || *to come out of sth. with credit* salir bien de algo || *to gain credit* confirmarse || *to give credit* dar crédito || *to give credit to* dar crédito a || *to give s.o. credit for sth.* atribuir *or* reconocer a alguien el mérito de algo || *to his credit* en su haber, a su favor || *to lend credit to* acreditar || *to pass with credit* sacar un notable || *to take credit for* atribuirse el mérito de || *we do not give credit* no se fía (shop) || *with credit* muy decentemente, muy bien.
◆ *pl* ficha *f sing* técnica (of a film) || *tax credits* deducciones tributarias.

credit ['kredit] *vt* creer, dar crédito a (to believe) ‖ FIG atribuir, reconocer; *he is credited with great intelligence* se le atribuye una gran inteligencia ‖ ingresar, abonar en cuenta (to enter money in an account) ‖ poner en el haber (to enter on the credit side of a balance sheet).

creditable [-əbl] *adj* digno de elogio, encomiable, loable (praiseworthy) ‖ digno de crédito (believable) ‖ de buena reputación (of good repute).

creditably [-əbli] *adv* de forma encomiable ‖ honrosamente.

creditor [-ə*] *n* acreedor, ra.

credo ['kri:dəu] *n* credo *m*.

credulity [kri'dju:liti] *n* credulidad *f*.

credulous ['kredjuləs] *adj* crédulo, la.

creed [kri:d] *n* credo *m*.

creek [kri:k] *n* cala *f* (small bay) ‖ US riachuelo *m* (small arm of a river) ‖ FAM *up the creek* en un aprieto.

creel [kri:l] *n* nasa *f* (angler's basket).

creep [kri:p] *n* arrastramiento *m*, deslizamiento *m* (act or pace of creeping) ‖ GEOL deslizamiento *m* ‖ hormigueo *m* (in the skin) ‖ FAM pelotillero, ra (toady) | desgraciado, da (unpleasant person).
◆ *pl* FAM carne *f sing* de gallina (gooseflesh); *to give s.o. the creeps* poner a alguien la carne de gallina | pavor *m*, miedo *m* (fear).

creep* [kri:p] *vi* arrastrarse, deslizarse, reptar (to move with body prone to the floor) ‖ gatear, andar a gatas (babies on their hands and knees) ‖ deslizarse (to move stealthily) ‖ ir muy despacio (to go slowly) ‖ deslizarse (an error) ‖ trepar (plants) ‖ FAM ponérsele a uno la carne de gallina; *my flesh crept* se me puso la carne de gallina ‖ FIG arrastrarse a los pies de, humillarse ante (to humble o.s.) ‖ sentir hormigueo (to tingle) ‖ — *to creep about on tiptoe* ir de puntillas ‖ *to creep by* pasar lentamente ‖ *to creep in, out* entrar, salir silenciosamente ‖ *to creep to s.o.* hacer la pelotilla *or* dar la coba a uno ‖ *to creep up on s.o.* acercarse sigilosamente a uno.
— OBSERV Pret y pp *crept*.

creeper [-ə*] *n* BOT enredadera *f* ‖ trepador *m* (for climbing) ‖ ZOOL ave *f* trepadora (bird) ‖ MAR rezón *m* ‖ US pelele *m* (for baby).
◆ *pl* US tacos *m* (for boots).

creeping [-iŋ] *adj* MED progresivo, va ‖ MIL móvil (barrage).
◆ *n* ⟶ **creep**.

creepy [-i] *adj* espeluznante, horripilante.

creepy-crawly ['kri:pi'krɔ:li] *n* bicho *m*.

creese [kri:s] *n* puñal *m* malayo, cris *m*.

cremate [kri'meit] *vt* incinerar.

cremation [kri'meiʃən] *n* cremación *f*, incineración *f* (of the dead).

cremator [kri'meitə*] *n* horno *m* crematorio (place of cremation) ‖ incinerador *m* (person).

crematorium [,kremə'tɔ:riəm] *n* crematorio *m*, horno *m* crematorio.
— OBSERV El plural de *crematorium* es *crematoria* o *crematoriums*.

crematory ['kremətəri] *n* crematorio *m*, horno *m* crematorio.
◆ *adj* crematorio, ria.

crenate ['kri:neit] *adj* BOT dentado, da.

crenellate; crenelate ['krenileit] *vt* almenar.

crenellation; crenelation [,kreni'leiʃən] *n* almenaje *m*, almenas *f pl*.

Creole ['kri:əul] *adj/n* criollo, lla.

creosol ['kriəsɔl] *n* CHEM creosol *m*, aceite *m* de creosota.

creosote ['kriəsəut] *n* CHEM creosota *f*.

creosote ['kriəsəut] *vt* creosotar.

creosoting [-iŋ] *n* TECH creosotado *m*.

crêpe; crepe [kreip] *n* crespón *m* (fabric) ‖ crepé *m* (rubber).

crepitant ['krepitənt] *adj* crepitante.

crepitate ['krepiteit] *vt* crepitar (to crackle) ‖ crujir (joints).

crepitation [krepi'teiʃən] *n* crepitación *f*.

crept [krept] *pret/pp* ⟶ **creep**.

crepuscular [kri'pəskjulə*] *adj* crepuscular.

crescendo [kri'ʃendəu] *adj/adv* MUS crescendo.
◆ *n* MUS crescendo *m*.

crescent ['kresnt] *n* luna *f* creciente (the waxing moon) ‖ medialuna *f* (any half-moon shape) ‖ media luna *f* (emblem).
◆ *adj* creciente.

cresol ['krisɔl] *n* CHEM cresol *m*.

cress [kres] *n* BOT berro *m*.

crest [krest] *n* cresta *f* (on the head of animals) ‖ cimera *f* (on helmet) ‖ penacho *m* (plume of helmet) ‖ cresta *f* (top of wave) ‖ cima *f*, cumbre *f*, cresta *f* (of hill) ‖ copa *f* (of tree) ‖ crines *f pl* (a mane) ‖ ARCH caballete *m*, cumbrera *f* ‖ HERALD timbre *m*.

crest [krest] *vt* coronar (a wall) ‖ poner un penacho a ‖ ARCH poner un caballete a ‖ FIG subir hasta la cima *or* cumbre de (a hill, etc.).
◆ *vi* encresparse (wave).

crested lark [-id'lɑ:k] *n* ZOOL cogujada *f*.

crestfallen [-,fɔ:lən] *adj* alicaído, da; cabizbajo, ja.

cretaceous [kri'teiʃəs] *adj* gredoso, sa; cretáceo, a.

Cretaceous [kri'teiʃəs] *adj* cretáceo, a.
◆ *n* cretáceo *m*.

Cretan ['kri:tən] *adj/n* cretense.

Crete [kri:t] *pr n* GEOGR Creta *f*.

cretin ['kretin] *n* cretino, na.

cretinism ['kretinizəm] *n* cretinismo *m*.

cretinous ['kretinəs] *adj* cretino, na.

cretonne [kre'tɔn] *n* cretona *f* (material).

crevasse [kri'væs] *n* GEOL grieta *f*.

crevice ['krevis] *n* grieta *f*.

crew [kru:] *n* tripulación *f* (of ship, aircraft) ‖ MIL dotación *f* (of tank, gun) ‖ equipo *m* (body of men working together) ‖ banda *f*, cuadrilla *f* (a mob) ‖ *ground crew* personal *m* de tierra.

crew [kru:] *pret* ⟶ **crow**.

crew cut [-kʌt] *n* pelo *m* cortado al cepillo (very short hairstyle).

crewel ['kru:il] *n* estambre *m*.

crew-necked ['kru:nekt] *adj* de cuello redondo (jumper, etc.).

crib [krib] *n* pesebre *m* (rack) ‖ cuadra *f* (stable) ‖ US cuna *f* (cot) ‖ belén *m*, nacimiento *m* (crèche) ‖ traducción *f* literal de una obra clásica para uso en los colegios ‖ FAM plagio *m* (a plagiarism) | chuleta *f* (in exam) | caja *f* de caudales (in banks) ‖ nasa *f* (trap for fish) ‖ FAM cuadra *f* (room) | casucha *f* (house) ‖ ARCH encofrado *m* ‖ MIN entibación *f* (framework of a mine shaft) ‖ puntales *m pl* (heavy timber supports) ‖ US arca *f* (bin for grain).

crib [krib] *vt* FAM copiar (to copy unfairly) | plagiar (to plagiarize) ‖ MIN entibar (to line with timber) ‖ ARCH poner encofrado a ‖ almacenar (grains) ‖ encerrar, confinar (to lock in) ‖ FAM birlar, robar (to steal).
◆ *vi* FAM usar chuletas (a student) ‖ plagiar (to plagiarize).

cribwork [-wə:k] *n* entibación *f*, encofrado *m*.

crick [krik] *n* calambre *m* (cramp) ‖ tortícolis *m* & *f* (in the neck) ‖ lumbago *m* (in the back).

crick [krik] *vt* dar tortícolis (in the neck) ‖ dar lumbago (in the back) ‖ dar un calambre.

cricket ['krikit] *n* ZOOL grillo *m* ‖ SP criquet *m*, cricket *m* ‖ FIG *it's not cricket!* ¡esto no es jugar limpio!

cricketer [-ə*] *n* jugador *m* de cricket.

cricoid ['kraikɔid] *adj* ANAT cricoides.
◆ *n* ANAT cricoides *m inv*.

crier ['kraiə*] *n* pregonero *m*; *town crier* pregonero público.

crikey! ['kraiki] *interj* FAM ¡mecachis!

crime [kraim] *n* crimen *m* (a violation of the law); *crime wave* ola de crímenes ‖ criminalidad *f*; *an increase in crime* un aumento de la criminalidad.

Crimea [krai'miə] *pr n* GEOGR Crimea *f*.

criminal ['kriminl] *adj/n* criminal; *a criminal action* una acción criminal; *to arrest a criminal* detener a un criminal ‖ — *criminal law* derecho *m* penal ‖ *criminal lawyer* penalista *m* & *f*, criminalista *m* & *f* ‖ *criminal record* antecedentes *m pl* penales.

criminalist [-əlist] *n* criminalista *m* & *f*.

criminality [,krimi'næliti] *n* criminalidad *f*.

criminate ['krimineit] *vt* incriminar ‖ condenar.

crimination [,krimi'neiʃən] *n* incriminación *f*.

criminative ['kriminətiv]; **criminatory** ['kriminətəri] *adj* acusatorio, ria.

criminological [,kriminɔ'lɔdʒikəl] *adj* criminológico, ca.

criminilogist [,krimi'nɔlədʒist] *n* criminologista *m* & *f*, criminalista *m* & *f*.

criminology [,krimi'nɔlədʒi] *n* criminología *f*.

crimmer ['krimə*] *n* variedad *f* de caracul.

crimp [krimp] *n* rizos *m pl* (in hair) ‖ ondulación *f* (corrugation) ‖ reclutador, ra (of soldiers, etc.) ‖ US FAM obstáculo *m*, traba *f*.

crimp [krimp] *vt* ondular (to wave) ‖ rizar (to curl) ‖ fruncir, plisar (cloth) ‖ encañonar (linen) ‖ estrechar (a tube) ‖ acanalar (to make flutings in) ‖ acuchillar (to gash newly killed fish) ‖ dar forma (to mould) ‖ MIL reclutar ‖ US estorbar, obstaculizar, poner trabas a.

crimson ['krimzn] *adj* carmesí ‖ *to turn crimson* enrojecer, ponerse rojo (sky), ponerse colorado, sonrojarse (s.o.).
◆ *n* carmesí *m*.

crimson ['krimzn] *vt* teñir de carmesí.
◆ *vi* sonrojarse, ponerse colorado (to blush).

cringe [krindʒ] *vi* encogerse, acobardarse (to shrink) ‖ agacharse (to cower) ‖ humillarse, rebajarse (to lower o.s.).

cringing [-iŋ] *adj* servil ‖ rastrero, ra (abject).

cringle ['kriŋgl] *n* MAR garrucho *m*.

crinkle ['kriŋkl] *n* arruga *f* (wrinkle) ‖ ondulado *m* ‖ rizado *m* (of hair) ‖ frunce *m*, pliegue *m* (pleat) ‖ crujido *m* (crisp sound).

crinkle ['kriŋkl] *vi* arrugarse (to wrinkle) ‖ rizarse (to ridge) ‖ ondularse (to ripple) ‖ crujir (to rustle) ‖ crepitar (the fire, etc.).
◆ *vt* arrugar (to wrinkle) ‖ ondular (to wave) ‖ rizar (hair).

crinkly [-i] *adj* arrugado, da (wrinkled) ‖ ondulado, da (wavy) ‖ rizado, da (hair) ‖ crujiente (leaves, silk, etc.).

crinoid ['krainɔid] *n* ZOOL crinoideo *m*.

crinoline ['krinəli:n] *n* miriñaque *m* (a hopped petticoat) ‖ crinolina *f* (fabric of horsehair).

cripes [kraips] *interj* FAM ¡caramba!

cripple ['kripl] *adj/n* tullido, da; lisiado, da.

cripple ['kripl] *vt* lisiar, tullir (a person) || estropear (a ship, etc.) || FIG paralizar.

crippling [-iŋ] *adj* abrumador, ra; demoledor, ra.

crisis ['kraisis] *n* crisis *f inv*; *cabinet crisis* crisis ministerial || *to draw to a crisis* llegar al punto crucial *or* crítico.

— OBSERV El plural de la palabra inglesa es *crises*.

crisp [krisp] *adj* fresco, ca; *crisp lettuce* lechuga fresca || vivificante (air) || directo, ta; vigoroso, sa; *a crisp style* un estilo directo || curruscante (bread, biscuit) || decidido, da; resuelto, ta (resolute) || crujiente (snow) || claro, ra; preciso, sa (analysis) || animado, da (dialogue) || tajante (tone).

◆ *n* patata *f* frita a la inglesa.

crisp [krisp] *vt* encrespar, rizar (cloth, hair) || volver curruscante (bread, etc.).

◆ *vi* encresparse, rizarse (hair) || ponerse curruscante (bread, etc.).

crispation [kris'peiʃən] *n* crispamiento *m* (of the skin) || rizado *m* (curling).

crisper ['krispə*] *n* tenacillas *f pl* de rizar, rizador *m* para el pelo.

crispness ['krispnis] *n* encrespado *m*, rizado *m* (of hair) || frío *m* vivificante (air) || crujido *m* (of snow) || consistencia *f* curruscante (of bread, etc.) || claridad *f* (of style, music, etc.) || FIG vivacidad *f*.

crispy ['krispi] *adj* ⟶ **crisp**.

crisscross ['kriskrɔs] *n* entrecruzamiento *m* || cruz *f* (signature) || FIG enredo *m*, enmarañamiento *m*.

◆ *adj* entrecruzado, da.

crisscross ['kriskrɔs] *vt* entrecruzar.

◆ *vi* entrecruzarse.

criterion [krai'tiəriən] *n* criterio *m*.

— OBSERV El plural de *criterion* es *criteria*.

critic ['kritik] *n* crítico *m* (reviewer) || criticón, ona (faultfinder).

critical ['kritikəl] *adj* exigente, criticón, ona (demanding) || crítico, ca; *critical faculty* sentido crítico; *critical point* punto crítico || PHYS & MATH crítico, ca || *to be critical of* criticar.

critically ['kritikli] *adv* críticamente, gravemente || *to be critically ill* estar en estado crítico.

criticaster ['kriti,kæstə*] *n* criticastro *m*.

criticism ['kritisizəm] *n* crítica *f*.

criticize ['kritisaiz] *vt/vi* criticar.

criticizer [-ə*] *n* criticón, ona.

critique [kri'ti:k] *n* crítica *f*.

croak [krəuk] *n* croar *m*, canto *m* (of frog) || graznido *m* (of raven) || gruñido *m* (of people).

croak [krəuk] *vi* croar, cantar (frog) || graznar (raven) || FIG gruñir, refunfuñar (to complain) | augurar desgracias (to predict evil) || FAM reventar, palmar (to die).

◆ *vt* decir refunfuñando (to grumble) || FIG pronosticar, presagiar (to forebode) || FAM apiolar, liquidar (to kill).

Croat [krəuət] *adj/n* croata.

Croatian [krəu'eiʃjən] *adj/n* croata.

crochet ['krəuʃei] *n* ganchillo *m*, «croché» *m*.

crochet ['krəuʃei] *vt* hacer a ganchillo.

◆ *vi* hacer ganchillo.

crock [krɔk] *n* cántaro *m* (earthenware pot) || FAM carcamal *m* (worn-out person) | cacharro *m* (worn-out thing) | jamelgo *m* (nag).

crock [krɔk] *vt* lisiar.

◆ *vi* lisiarse.

crockery ['krɔkəri] *n* loza *f*.

crocket ['krɔkit] *n* ARCH follaje *m*.

crocodile ['krɔkədail] *n* ZOOL cocodrilo *m* || FIG fila *f* de a dos (double file) || FIG *to shed crocodile tears* llorar lágrimas de cocodrilo.

crocodilians [krɔkə'diliəns] *pl n* cocodriloideos *m*.

crocus ['krəukəs] *n* BOT azafrán *m*.

— OBSERV El plural de *crocus* es *crocuses* o *croci*.

Croesus ['kri:səs] *pr n* Creso *m*.

croft [krɔft] *n* huerta *f* arrendada (small rented holding) || huerto *m* (adjoining a cottage).

crofter ['krɔftə*] *n* colono *m*.

croissant ['krwɑ:sɑ:ŋ] *n* cruasán *m*.

cromlech ['krɔmlek] *n* crómlech *m*.

crone [krəun] *n* FAM arpía *f*, bruja *f*.

crony ['krəuni] *n* FAM amigote *m* (chum).

crook [kruk] *n* cayado *m* (for shepherds) || báculo *m* (of a bishop) || gancho *m* (a hook) || recodo *m* (of a path, river, etc.) || ángulo *m*, curva *f*, codo *m* (of anything hooked) || corva *f* (of leg) || pliegue *m* (of elbow) || FAM ladrón *m*, timador *m* (swindler).

crook [kruk] *vt* encorvar, doblar (to bend) || enganchar (to grasp with a hook) || FAM estafar, timar (to swindler) || FAM *to crook the elbow* empinar el codo.

◆ *vi* encorvarse, doblarse.

crooked [-id] *adj* torcido, da; doblado, da (twisted) || retorcido, da (wood) || curvo, va; curvado, da (bent) || encorvado, da (bent with age) || tortuoso, sa; sinuoso, sa (path) || zambo, ba (leg) || corvo, va; ganchudo, da (nose) || FIG tortuoso, sa (means) | poco limpio, pia (person, practice).

crookedness [-nis] *n* sinuosidad *f* (of a path) || FIG falta *f* de honradez.

croon [kru:n] *n* tarareo *m*, canturreo *m*.

croon [kru:n] *vt* tararear, cantar a media voz, canturrear.

crooner [-ə*] *n* cantante *m* melódico.

crop [krɔp] *n* cosecha *f* (harvest) || cultivo *m* (cultivated produce); *crop rotation* rotación de cultivos || buche *m* (gullet of bird) || fusta *f* (hunting whip) || mango *m*, empuñadura *f* (handle of whip) || corte *m* de pelo (haircut) || pelo *m* muy corto (style); *she wears her hair in a crop* lleva el pelo muy corto || cuero *m* (a hide) || espaldilla *f* (meat) || FIG montón *m*; *a crop of difficulties* un montón de dificultades | cosecha *f* (collection) || — *crop year* campaña *f* agrícola || *in crop* cultivado, da || *out of crop* sin cultivo || *to have a fine crop of hair* tener una buena mata de pelo.

crop [krɔp] *vt* cortar muy corto (hair) || cortar (the grass) || recortar (to cut off ends) || podar (shrubs, etc.) || desmochar (branches) || desorejar, cortar las puntas de las orejas a (to clip ears) || cortar la cola de (to cut the tail) || cosechar (to harvest) || cultivar (to cultivate) || plantar, sembrar (to plant with); *to crop a field with clover* plantar un campo de trébol || tundir (textiles).

◆ *vi* rendir (land) || pacer (sheep) || — *to crop out* o *up* aflorar || FIG *to crop up* surgir, aparecer.

crop-eared [-iəd] *adj* con las orejas cortadas.

cropper ['krɔpə*] *n* tundidora *f* (textiles) || cortacéspedes *m inv* (for grass) || cultivador *m*, agricultor *m* (one who cultivates) || segador *m* (harvestman) || FAM *to come a cropper* darse un batacazo (to fall), ser cateado; *I came a cropper in history* me catearon en historia.

croquet ['krəukei] *n* SP croquet *m*.

croquette [krɔ'ket] *n* croqueta *f*.

crosier ['krəuʒə*] *n* báculo *m*.

cross [krɔs] *m* cruz *f* || cruce *m* (of streets) || cruce *m* (of phone lines, etc.) || golpe *m* cruzado (in boxing) || cruce *m* (between breeds) || trazo *m* horizontal (as on the letter «t») || FIG mezcla *f* (mixing) | cruz *f*, prueba *f* (burden) || FAM estafa *f*, timo *m* (swindle) || — *on the cross* sesgado, da; al bies (woodwork, textiles), fraudulentamente || *Red Cross* Cruz Roja || FIG *to be a cross between* ser una mezcla de | *to bear one's cross* llevar su cruz || *to make the sign of the cross* hacer la señal de la cruz, santiguarse || *to take the Cross* ir a una cruzada.

◆ *adj* cruzado, da; transversal (transverse) || cruzado, da (breed) || contrario, ria; opuesto, ta (contrary) || enfadado, da (angry); *he is cross with me* está enfadado conmigo || — FAM *as cross as two sticks* de un humor de perros || *to get cross* enfadarse.

cross [krɔs] *vt* cruzar (to place crosswise, to mark a cheque, to interbreed) || cruzar (the arms, legs) || atravesar, cruzar (to go across); *to cross the road* cruzar la calle; *bridge crossing the river* puente que atraviesa el río || cruzarse con (a person) || contrariar (to oppose) || frustrar (to thwart, to frustrate) || marcar con una cruz (to mark with a cross) || REL hacer la señal de la cruz a || poner un trazo horizontal a (a letter) || montar a horcajadas sobre (a horse, a saddle) || — *to cross off* o *out* tachar || *to cross one's arms* cruzarse de brazos || *to cross one's mind* ocurrírsele a alguien, pasar por la mente; *suddenly an idea crossed my mind* de pronto se me ocurrió una idea || *to cross o.s.* santiguarse || *to cross over* atravesar || *to cross s.o.'s palm with silver* llenar las manos de alguien de monedas de plata || *to cross swords with* cruzar la espada con (to fight), medir las armas con, habérselas con (to argue) || *to cross the border* pasar *or* cruzar *or* atravesar la frontera.

◆ *vi* cruzarse (roads, letters, breeds, etc.) || pasar, cruzar, atravesar (to go over).

crossbar [-bɑ*] *n* travesaño *m* || tranca *f* (of the door) || barra *f* (on bicycle) || larguero *m* (of the goal) || PRINT crucero *m*.

crossbeam [-bi:m] *n* viga *f* transversal.

crossbearer [-,bɛərə*] *n* REL crucero *m*.

crossbench [-bentʃ] *n* escaño *m* de los diputados independientes en el Parlamento británico.

crossbow [-bəu] *n* ballesta *f*.

crossbred [-bred] *pret & pp* ⟶ **crossbreed.**

◆ *adj* cruzado, da; híbrido, da.

crossbreed [-bri:d] *n* híbrido *m*.

crossbreed* [-bri:d] *vt* cruzar.

— OBSERV Pret y pp ***crossbred***.

crossbreeding [-,bri:diŋ] *n* cruce *m*.

cross-Channel [-,tʃænl] *adj* que hace la travesía del Canal de la Mancha (boat).

cross-check [-tʃek] *vi/vt* comprobar otra vez.

cross-country [-'kʌntri] *adj* a campo traviesa || *cross-country race* «cross-country» *m*, «cross» *m*, carrera *f* a campo traviesa *or* a campo través.

crosscurrent [-'kʌrənt] *n* contracorriente *f*.

crosscut [-kʌt] *n* corte *m* transversal (a diagonal cut) || atajo *m* (path running crosswise) || MIN crucero *m*.

crosscut [-kʌt] *vt* cortar transversalmente.

cross-examination [-ig,zæmi'neiʃən] *n* interrogatorio *m* hecho para comprobar lo declarado anteriormente.

cross-examine [-ig'zæmin] *vt* interrogar [para comprobar lo declarado anteriormente].

cross-eyed [-aid] *adj* bizco, ca.

cross-fertilization [-,fə:tilai'zeiʃən] *n* fecundación *f* cruzada.

cross-fertilize [-'fə:tilaiz] *vt* fecundar por fecundación cruzada.

cross fire [-faiə*] *n* fuego *m* cruzado || FIG *exposed to cross fire* cogido entre dos fuegos.

cross-grained [-greind] *adj* de fibras irregulares *or* cruzadas (wood) || FIG intratable (people) | intrincado, da; enmarañado, da (problem, etc.).

cross hairs [-hɛəz] *pl n* retículo *m sing*, retícula *f sing*.

crosshatch [-hætʃ] *vt* sombrear.

crosshead [-hed] *n* TECH cruceta *f* || subtítulo *m* (in a newspaper).

crossing [-iŋ] *n* travesía *f* (sea voyage) || cruce *m* (intersection) || paso *m* de peatones, cruce *m* (for crossing roads) || paso *m* a nivel (rail) || paso *m* (for crossing rivers) || cruce *m*, cruzamiento *m* (of races) || *crossing gate* barrera *f* de paso a nivel.

crossing out [-iŋˌaut] *n* tachadura *f*.

crossing-over [-iŋˌəuvə*] *n* entrecruzamiento *m*.

cross-legged [-legd] *adj* con las piernas cruzadas.

cross-linkage [-'liŋkidʒ] *n* CHEM eslabón *m*.

crossly [-li] *adv* con enfado, malhumoradamente.

crossover [-'əuvə*] *n* paso *m*.

crosspatch [-pætʃ] *n* FAM gruñón, ona.

crosspiece [-pi:s] *n* travesaño *m*.

cross-purposes [-'pə:pəsiz] *pl n* fines *m* opuestos, objetivos *m* opuestos || *we are (talking) at cross-purposes* hay un malentendido.

cross-question [-'kwestʃən] *n* pregunta *f* hecha para comprobar declaraciones anteriores.

cross-question [-'kwestʃən] *vt* interrogar [para comprobar declaraciones anteriores].

cross-refer [-ri'fə*] *vt* remitir a.
◆ *vi* hacer una remisión.

cross-reference [-'refrəns] *n* referencia *f*, remisión *f*.

crossroad [-rəud] *n* cruce *m* (road crossing another).
◆ *pl* cruce *m sing* || FIG encrucijada *f sing*; *at the crossroads* en la encrucijada.

cross ruling [-'ru:liŋ] *n* cuadrícula *f*.

cross section [-'sekʃən] *n* sección *f or* corte *m* transversal (a transverse section) || MATH sección *f* recta || FIG muestra *f* representativa (a representative sample).

cross stitch [-stitʃ] *n* punto *m* de cruz.

cross talk [-tɔ:k] *n* réplicas *f pl* ocurrentes || cruce *m* de líneas (of phone) || RAD interferencia *f*.

crosstie [-tai] *n* US traviesa *f*.

crosstrees [-tri:z] *pl n* MAR crucetas *f*.

crosswalk [-ˌwɔ:k] *n* cruce *m*, paso *m* de peatones.

crossway [-ˌwei] *n* encrucijada *f*.

crosswind [-wind] *n* viento *m* de costado.

crosswise [-waiz] *adv* en forma de cruz (in the form of a cross) || transversalmente.

crossword [-wə:d] *n* crucigrama *m*.

crotch [krɔtʃ] *n* horquilla *f* (of a tree) || cruz *f*, entrepierna *f*, entrepiernas *f pl* (of a person).

crotchet ['krɔtʃit] *n* MUS negra *f* || FIG idea *f* fija, manía *f*, capricho *m*.

crotchety ['krɔtʃiti] *adj* de mal genio, arisco, ca (surly) || fantasioso, sa; caprichoso, sa; excéntrico, ca (eccentric).

Croton bug [-bʌg] *n* ZOOL cucaracha *f*.

crouch [krautʃ] *vi* estar en cuclillas *or* agachado (to be squatting) || agacharse, ponerse en cuclillas (to squat) || encogerse (before springing) || FIG rebajarse || *to crouch down* agacharse, ponerse en cuclillas.

croup [kru:p] *n* MED garrotillo *m*, crup *m*.

croup; croupe [kru:p] *n* grupa *f* (of a horse).

croupier ['kru:piə*] *n* «croupier» *m*.

crouton [kru'tɔn] *n* cuscurro *m*, cuscurrón *m*.

crow [krəu] *n* ZOOL cuervo *m* (bird) || quiquiriquí *m*, cacareo *m* (call of a cock) || balbuceo *m* (of a baby) || TECH palanca *f* || — FIG *as the crow flies* a vuelo de pájaro, en línea recta || US FAM *to eat crow* reconocer su error.

crow* [krəu] *vi* cantar, cacarear (a cock) || balbucear (baby) || gritar con entusiasmo || — *to crow over* pavonearse *or* jactarse de || *to crow over s.o.* salir triunfante de alguien.
— OBSERV Pret ***crew, crowed***; pp ***crowed***.

crowbar ['krəubɑ*] *n* palanca *f*.

crowd [kraud] *n* multitud *f*, muchedumbre *f* (many people) || pandilla *f*, grupo *m* (a clique) || público *m*, espectadores *m pl* (spectators) || vulgo *m* (common people) || FIG & FAM montón *m*, gran cantidad *f* (heap); *a crowd of things* un montón de cosas || THEATR comparsas *m pl* || CINEM extras *m pl* || — *in a crowd* en tropel, todos juntos || *there was quite a crowd* había un gran gentío *or* mucha gente || *to follow the crowd* dejarse llevar por los demás.

crowd [kraud] *vt* atestar, llenar (to fill space) || amontonar, apiñar, reunir (to collect) || empujar (to push) || apresurar (to hurry) || apremiar (to put under pressure) || *to crowd (on) sail* hacer fuerza de vela.
◆ *vi* amontonarse, apiñarse (to throng) || reunirse, congregarse (to assemble).
◆ *phr v* *to crowd around* o *together* agolparse, amontonarse, apiñarse || ***to crowd down*** bajar en tropel || ***to crowd in*** entrar en tropel || ***to crowd out*** salir en tropel; *they crowded out of the house* salieron de la casa en tropel; dejar fuera, excluir; *your report was crowded out* su informe fue dejado fuera [del periódico] || — *he was crowded out of the race* en la carrera le estorbaron el paso || ***to crowd round*** apiñarse en torno (de).

crowded [-id] *adj* lleno, na; atestado, da || muy concurrido, con mucho público (spectacle) || — *crowded together* apretados unos contra otros || *the theater was crowded* el teatro estaba atestado de gente, había mucha gente en el teatro.

crowfoot ['krəufut] *n* BOT ranúnculo *m* || MAR cabuyera *f* || MIL abrojo *m*.
— OBSERV El plural de *crowfoot* es *crowfeet* excepto en el sentido botánico, para el cual se usa *crowfoots*.

crown [kraun] *n* corona *f* || ARCH coronamiento *m*, remate *m* || parte *f* central (of a road) || copa *f* (of a hat) || cumbre *f*, cima *f* (of a hill) || copete *m*, cresta *f* (of a bird) || caballete *m* (of a roof) || coronilla *f* (of the head) || corona *f* (coin); *half a crown* media corona || ANAT corona *f* (of a tooth) || copa *f* (of a tree) || mesa *f* (of an anvil) || FIG coronación *f*, coronamiento *m*, remate *m* (of life's work) || cápsula *f* (of a bottle) || parte *f* superior (of a bell) || clave *f* (of a vault) || MAR diamante *m* (of the anchor) || — MIN *crown block* caballete *m* portapoleas || *crown cap, crown cork* cápsula *f* || *Crown colony* colonia *f* de la Corona || JUR *Crown court* tribunal *m* de la Corona || *crown glass* crownglass *m* || *Crown jewels* joyas *f* reales *or* de la Corona || *Crown land* patrimonio *m* de la Corona || *Crown law* derecho *m* penal || *crown lens* lente convexa || *Crown prince* príncipe heredero || TECH *crown wheel* corona dentada || *the Crown* la Corona.

crown [kraun] *vt* coronar (a monarch, a building); *crowned head* testa coronada || FIG coronar, completar, rematar (to complete) || poner una corona a (a tooth) || coronar (in draughts) || FIG coronar, recompensar, galardonar (to reward) || dar forma convexa, bombear (a road) || FAM dar un golpe en la cabeza a (to hit on the head) || *to crown it all* para rematarlo todo.

crowning [-iŋ] *adj* supremo, ma.
◆ *n* coronación *f*.

crow's-foot ['krəuzfut] *n* pata *f* de gallo (of the eyes) || MIL abrojo *m* (caltrop).
— OBSERV El plural de esta palabra es *crow's-feet*.

crow's nest ['krəuznest] *n* torre *f* de vigía, atalaya *f*.

crozier ['krəuʒə*] *n* REL báculo *m*.

crucial ['kru:ʃəl] *adj* crucial, decisivo, va; crítico, ca; *crucial problems* problemas cruciales || ANAT en forma de cruz, crucial.

cruciate ['kru:ʃieit] *adj* BOT cruciforme || ZOOL cruzado, da.

crucible ['kru:sibl] *n* crisol *m* || FIG crisol *m* || *crucible steel* acero *m* de crisol.

crucifer ['kru:sifə*] *n* REL cruciferario *m* || BOT crucífera *f*.

cruciferae [kru'sifəri] *pl n* BOT crucíferas *f*.

cruciferous [kru:'sifərəs] *adj* crucífero, ra.

crucified ['kru:sifaid] *adj* crucificado, da.

crucifix ['kru:sifiks] *n* REL crucifijo *m*.

crucifixion [ˌkru:si'fikʃən] *n* crucifixión *f*.

cruciform ['kru:sifɔ:m] *adj* cruciforme.

crucify ['kru:sifai] *vt* crucificar (to put to death on a cross) || FIG mortificar (to mortify) | martirizar (to torment).

crude [kru:d] *adj* crudo, da (raw) || bruto, ta (steel, etc.) || sin refinar, crudo, da; bruto, ta (oil, petrol) || crudo, da; vivo, va (light) || crudo, da; brutal (reality, statement) || basto, ta; ordinario, ria (vulgar) || tosco, ca; mal acabado, da; *crude furniture* muebles toscos || verde (fruit) || MED latente (disease) | sin asimilar (undigested).
◆ *n* crudo *m*, petróleo *m* crudo *or* sin refinar.

crudeness [-nis]; **crudity** [-iti] *n* crudeza *f* (rawness) || ordinariez *f* (vulgarity) || tosquedad *f* (coarseness).

cruel [kruəl] *adj* cruel.

cruelly [-i] *adv* cruelmente.

cruelty ['kruəlti] *n* crueldad *f* || *society for the prevention of cruelty to animals* sociedad protectora de animales.

cruet ['kru:it] *n* vinagreras *f pl*, angarillas *f pl* (for oil and vinegar) || REL vinajera *f*.

cruise [kru:z] *n* MAR crucero *m*.

cruise [kru:z] *vi* MAR hacer un crucero (to make a sea voyage) | patrullar (to be in search of enemy ships) || ir a una velocidad de crucero (at cruising speed) || circular lentamente (to drive slowly) || FIG andar, ir.

cruise missile [-ˌmisɑil] *n* MIL mísil *m* teledirigido.

cruiser [kru:zə*] *n* MAR crucero *m* (warship) | barco *m* para cruceros (passenger boat).

cruiserweight [-weit] *n* semipesado *m* (in boxing).

cruising [kru:ziŋ] *adj* de crucero || *cruising speed* velocidad *f* de crucero (of aircraft), velocidad económica (of cars).
◆ *n* crucero *f*.

crumb [krʌm] *n* migaja *f*, trozo *m*, pedazo *m* (a fragment) || miga *f* (the inside of a loaf of bread).

crumb [krʌm] *vt* empanar (to coat with bread) || desmigar, desmigajar (to break into crumbs).

crumble ['krumbl] *vt* desmenuzar (to break into small pieces) || desmigar, desmigajar (bread).
◆ *vi* derrumbarse (to fall) || deshacerse (to fall to pieces) || desmigajarse, desmigarse

(bread) || desmoronarse (walls) || FIG pulverizarse.

crumbly ['krʌmbli] *adj* desmenuzable || desmoronadizo, za (a wall, house, etc.).

crumby ['krʌmi] *adj* empanado, da (covered with crumbs) || blando, da (soft).

crummy ['krʌmi] *adj* FAM que no vale nada, malísimo, ma (bad) | de mala muerte (place).

crump [krʌmp] *n* golpe *m* fuerte (hard hit) || explosión *f* (of bombs).

crumpet ['krʌmpt] *n* bollo *m* blando || FIG & FAM cholla *f*, cabeza *f* (head) || FIG & FAM *to be off one's crumpets* estar chiflado.

crumple ['krʌmpl] *n* arruga *f*.

crumple ['krʌmpl] *vt* arrugar.
◆ *vi* arrugarse || *to crumple up* desplomarse (to fall), aplastarse (to be squashed).

crunch [krʌntʃ] *n* crujido *m* (noise) || mascadura *f* (action) || FIG momento *m* decisivo.

crunch [krʌntʃ]; **scrunch** *vt* masticar [haciendo ruido] (to crush with the teeth) || triturar (to grind) || hacer crujir; *to crunch one's way through snow* hacer crujir la nieve a su paso.
◆ *vi* crujir.

crunchy [krʌntʃi] *adj* que cruje, crujiente.

cruor ['kru:ɔ:*] *n* MED crúor *m*.

crupper ['krʌpə*] *n* baticola *f* (of harness) || grupa *f* (of a horse); *on the crupper* a la grupa.

crural ['kruərəl] *adj* ANAT crural, femoral.

crusade [kru:'seid] *n* cruzada *f* (war) || FIG campaña *f*, cruzada *f*; *crusade against drink* campaña contra el alcohol.

crusade [kru:'seid] *vi* hacer una cruzada; *el Cid crusaded against the Moors* el Cid hizo una cruzada contra los moros || FIG hacer una campaña *or* una cruzada; *they crusade against drink* hacen una campaña contra la bebida.

crusader [-ə*] *n* cruzado *m*.

crush [krʌʃ] *n* aglomeración *f*, multitud *f* (crowd); *there was a great crush in the train* había una gran aglomeración en el tren || aplastamiento *m* (squashing) || apretón *m* (squeeze) || choque *m*, colisión *f* (collision) || pasaje *m* estrecho (fenced passage for sheep) || — *I hate the crush of public transport* odio los apretones de los transportes públicos || FAM *I have a crush on her* estoy loco perdido por ella || *orange crush* naranjada *f*.

crush [krʌʃ] *vt* aplastar (to squash, to spoil by pressure) || arrugar, aplastar (to crease) || estrujar (paper) || machacar, triturar (to reduce to powder, to small pieces) || exprimir, prensar (grapes) || apiñar (people) || FIG aplastar (to subdue, to silence) | apretar (to hug violently) | aplastar, reprimir (a revolt) | abrumar (to overwhelm) || — *crushed rock* o *stone* grava *f* || *to crush one's way through the crowd* abrirse paso con dificultad entre la muchedumbre.
◆ *vi* amontonarse, apretujarse; *hundreds crushed into the small room* cientos de personas se amontonaban en la pequeña habitación || aplastarse (to squash).

crusher [-ə*] *n* FIG argumento *m* aplastante, respuesta *f* contundente || TECH trituradora *f*.

crush hat [-'hæt] *n* clac *m*.

crushing [-iŋ] *adj* aplastante (argument, defeat, etc.) || abrumador, ra (overwhelming).
◆ *n* trituración *f*.

crust [krʌst] *n* corteza *f* (of a loaf) || mendrugo *m* (dry piece of bread) || CULIN pasta *f*, pastel *m* (of a pie) || GEOL corteza *f*; *crust of the Earth* corteza terrestre || BOT corteza *f* || MED postilla *f*, costra *f* || poso *m*, depósito *m* (in wine bottle or barrel) || capa *f* dura (of snow, ice, etc.) || ZOOL caparazón *m* || FIG máscara *f* (outer appearance) || US FAM caradura *f*, frescura *f* (cheek) || FIG *the upper crust* la flor y nata.

crust [krʌst] *vt* encostrar, formar una costra en || MED formar una postilla en.
◆ *vi* encostrarse, formarse una costra || MED formarse una postilla.

crustacean [krʌs'teiʃjən] *adj* crustáceo, a.
◆ *n* crustáceo *m*.

crustily ['krʌstili] *adv* bruscamente.

crustiness ['krʌstinis] *n* brusquedad *f*, malhumor *m* || dureza *f* (of bread).

crusty ['krʌsti] *adj* crujiente || de corteza dura (bread) || FAM brusco, ca; desabrido, da; malhumorado, da.

crutch [krʌtʃ] *n* MED muleta *f* (support) || cruz *f*, entrepierna *f*, entrepiernas *f pl* (crotch) || ARCH puntal *m* || MAR candelero *m* || soporte *m* (for motorcycles) || FIG apoyo *m*, soporte *m*.

crux [krʌks] *n* quid *m* (of a matter) || punto *m* crucial || lo esencial || enigma *m* (literary problem).
— OBSERV El plural de *crux* es *cruxes* o *cruces*.

cruzeiro [kru'zeirəu] *n* cruceiro *m*, cruzeiro *m* (Brazilian coin).

cry [krai] *n* grito *m* (shout); *to utter* o *to give a cry* dar un grito || pregón *m* (of a street vendor, etc.) || lloro *m*, llanto *m* (weeping) || — *to be a far cry from* mediar un gran abismo entre; *virtue is a far cry from vice* media un gran abismo entre la virtud y el vicio || *to be in full cry after* estar persiguiendo || *to have a good cry* llorar a lágrima viva.

cry [krai] *vt* gritar (to shout) || pregonar (to call out wares, news, etc.) || llorar (to weep).
◆ *vi* gritar (to call out in pain, anger, etc.) || llorar (to weep); *he cried for joy* lloraba de alegría || aullar (animals).
◆ *phr v* ***to cry down*** despreciar (to belittle) | desacreditar (to disparage) | hacer callar por medio de gritos || ***to cry for*** pedir; *to cry for mercy* pedir merced | requerir, necesitar (to need) || ***to cry off*** romper, deshacer; *to cry off a deal* romper un trato | rajarse; *at the last moment he cried off* en el último momento se rajó || ***to cry out*** clamar, exclamar || — *to cry out against* clamar contra | *to cry out for sth.* pedir algo a gritos || ***to cry over*** lamentarse de || ***to cry to*** clamar; *to cry to heaven* clamar al cielo || ***to cry up*** exaltar, enaltecer, glorificar.

crybaby ['krai,beibi] *n* llorón, ona.

crying ['kraiiŋ] *adj* llorón, ona || FIG escandaloso, sa; que clama al cielo; *a crying injustice* una injusticia que clama al cielo.
◆ *n* grito *m* (shout) || lloro *m*, llanto *m* (weeping) || pregón *m* (of a street vendor, etc.).

cryogen ['kraiədʒən] *n* criógeno *m*.

cryolite ['kraiəlait] *n* criolita *f*.

cryometry [krai'ɔmitri]; **cryoscopy** [krai'ɔskəpi] *n* crioscopia *f*.

crypt [kript] *n* cripta *f* (cell or cavity) || ANAT cripta, folículo *m*.

cryptic ['kriptik] *adj* secreto, ta; oculto, ta (secret, hidden) || enigmático, ca (enigmatic).

cryptically ['kriptikəli] *adv* a medias palabras (to speak).

cryptogam ['kriptəugæm] *n* BOT criptógama *f*.

cryptogram ['kriptəugræm] *n* criptograma *m*.

cryptographer [krip'tɔgrəfə*] *n* criptógrafo, fa.

cryptographic [kriptə'græfik] *adj* criptográfico, ca.

cryptography [krip'tɔgrəfi] *n* criptografía *f*.

crystal ['kristl] *adj* de cristal (of crystal) || cristalino, na (very clear) || — *crystal ball* bola *f* de cristal || *crystal detector* detector *m* de galena || *crystal gazer* pitonisa *f*.
◆ *n* cristal *m*.

crystalline ['kristəlain] *adj* de cristal (of or like crystal) || cristalino, na (extremely clear) || *crystalline lens* cristalino *m* (of the eye).

crystallization [,kristəlai'zeiʃən] *n* cristalización *f*.

crystallize ['kristəlaiz] *vt* cristalizar.
◆ *vi* cristalizarse.

crystallized [-d] *adj* cristalizado, da || escarchado, da (fruta).

crystallizer [-ə*] *n* cristalizador *m*.

crystallographic [kristələ'græfik] *adj* cristalográfico, ca.

crystallography [kristə'lɔgrəfi] *n* cristalografía *f*.

crystalloid ['kristəlɔid] *adj* cristaloide.
◆ *n* cristaloide *m*.

crystalloidal [,kristə'lɔidəl] *adj* cristaloideo, a.

CS gas ['si: es,gæs] *n* gas *m* lacrimógeno.

cub [kʌb] *n* cachorro *m* (of lion, bear, tiger, wolf) || cría *f* (of other animals) || novato, ta; *cub reporter* periodista novato || niño *m* explorador (boy scout).

cub [kʌb] *vt/vi* parir.

Cuba ['kju:bə] *pr n* GEOGR Cuba.

cubage ['kju:bidʒ] *n* cubicación *f*.

Cuban ['kju:bən] *adj/n* cubano, na.

cubature ['kju:bətjuə*] *n* cubicación *f*.

cubbyhole ['kʌbihəul] *n* armario *m* pequeño (small cupboard) || habitación *f* pequeña, chiribitil *m* (workroom).

cube [kju:b] *n* MATH cubo *m* || — MATH *cube root* raíz cúbica || *sugar cube* terrón *m* de azúcar.

cube [kju:b] *vt* MATH elevar al cubo, cubicar || cortar en forma de cubo (to cut into cubes).

cubic ['kju:bik] *adj* cúbico, ca; *cubic equation* ecuación cúbica.

cubicle [-l] *n* cubículo *m* || caseta *f* (changing room) || camarilla *f* (in a dormitory).

cubiform ['kju:bifɔ:m] *adj* de forma cúbica.

cubism ['kju:bizəm] *n* cubismo *m*.

cubist ['kju:bist] *adj/n* cubista.

cubit ['kju:bit] *n* codo *m* (measure).

cubital [-l] *adj* cubital.

cubitus [-əs] *n* MED cúbito *m*.

cuboid ['kju:bɔid] *adj* de forma cúbica.
◆ *n* ANAT cuboides *m inv* (bone).

cuckold ['kʌkəuld] *n* cornudo *m* (husband).

cuckold ['kʌkəuld] *vt* poner los cuernos a.

cuckoo ['kuku:] *n* cuco *m*, cuclillo *m* (bird) || cucú *m* (song) || *cuckoo clock* reloj *m* de cuco.
◆ *adj* FAM mentecato, ta; majadero, ra (silly).

cuckoopint ['kuku:pint] *n* BOT aro *m*.

cucumber ['kju:kʌmbə*] *n* BOT pepino *m* || US *cucumber tree* magnolio *m*, magnolia *f*.

cucurbit [kju:'kə:bit] *n* BOT cucúrbita *f*.

cud [kʌd] *n* bolo *m* alimenticio (of ruminants) || *to chew the cud* rumiar (animals, people).

cuddle ['kʌdl] *n* abrazo *m*.

cuddle ['kʌdl] *vt* abrazar.
◆ *vi* abrazarse || *to cuddle up* acurrucarse; *to cuddle up to s.o.* acurrucarse contra alguien.

cuddlesome [-səm]; **cuddly** ['kʌdli] *adj* mimoso, sa; cariñoso, sa.

cuddly [-i] *adj* mimoso, sa (person) || *cuddly toy* muñeco *m* de peluche.

cuddy ['kʌdi] *n* camarote *m* pequeño (in a ship) ‖ alacena *f* (closet) ‖ armario *m* (cupboard) ‖ FAM borrico *m*.

cudgel ['kʌdʒəl] *n* garrote *m* (big stick) ‖ porra *f* (weapon) ‖ FIG *to take up the cudgels for* sacar la cara por, salir en defensa de.

cudgel ['kʌdʒəl] *vt* dar garrotazos a (with a big stick) ‖ golpear con la porra a, aporrear (with a weapon) ‖ FIG *to cudgel one's brains* devanarse los sesos.

cue [kjuː] *n* THEATR & MUS entrada *f*, pie *m* ‖ señal *f*, seña *f* (signal) ‖ indicación *f* convenida; *don't do anything until he has given you the cue* no hagas nada antes de que te haya dado la indicación convenida ‖ norma *f*, ejemplo *m*; *New York takes its cue from Paris fashions* Nueva York sigue las normas de la moda de París ‖ humor *m* (temper) ‖ taco *m* (in billiards) ‖ US → **queue** ‖ *cue ball* bola blanca (in billiards) ‖ *on cue* a tiempo.

cue [kjuː] *vt* trenzar (to braid) ‖ indicar (to indicate).
◆ *vi* US hacer cola.

cuff [kʌf] *n* puño *m* (of sleeves) ‖ vuelta *f* (of trousers) ‖ bofetada *f* (blow) ‖ — FAM *off the cuff* espontáneo, a (adjetivo); de improviso (adverbio) | *on the cuff* a plazos.
◆ *pl* esposas *f* (handcuffs).

cuff [kʌf] *vt* abofetear (to slap) ‖ poner puños a (sleeves) ‖ esposar (to handcuff).

cuff links [-liŋks] *pl n* gemelos *m*.

Cufic ['kjufik] *adj* cúfico, ca.

cuirass [kwi'ræs] *n* coraza *f* (armour) ‖ ZOOL coraza *f*, caparazón *m*.

cuirassier [ˌkwirə'siə*] *n* coracero *m*.

cuisine [kwi'ziːn] *n* cocina *f* (cooking).

cul-de-sac ['kuldə'sæk] *n* callejón *m* sin salida ‖ ANAT conducto *m* con un solo orificio.

culinary ['kʌlinəri] *adj* culinario, ria.

cull [kʌl] *n* desecho *m*.

cull [kʌl] *vt* entresacar, escoger (to select) ‖ coger (flowers).

cullender ['kʌlində*] *n* colador *m*, escurridor *m* (colander).

cullet ['kʌlit] *n* desperdicios *m pl* de vidrio.

culm [kʌlm] *n* BOT caña *f*, tallo *m* ‖ cisco *m* (coal dust) ‖ antracita *f* (anthracite).

culminant ['kʌlminənt] *adj* culminante.

culminate ['kʌlmineit] *vi* culminar (*in* en, con).
◆ *vt* hacer culminar, llevar a su culminación.

culmination [ˌkʌlmi'neiʃən] *n* culminación *f*.

culottes [kjuː'lɔts] *pl n* falda *f sing* pantalón.

culpability [ˌkʌlpə'biliti] *n* culpabilidad *f*.

culpable ['kʌlpəbl] *adj* culpable.

culprit ['kʌlprit] *n* culpable *m* & *f* (guilty person) ‖ JUR acusado, da (accused).

cult [kʌlt] *n* culto *m* (*of* a) (religious worship) ‖ culto *m* (*of* a) (admiration) ‖ *personality cult* culto de la personalidad.

cultivable ['kʌltivəbl]; **cultivatable** ['kʌltiveitəbl] *adj* cultivable.

cultivate ['kʌltiveit] *vt* cultivar; *to cultivate land, friendship, an art* cultivar la tierra, la amistad, un arte ‖ criar (oysters, silkworms, etc.).

cultivated [-id] *adj* AGR cultivado, da ‖ culto, ta (person).

cultivation [ˌkʌlti'veiʃən] *n* AGR cultivo *m* ‖ cultura *f* (of a person) ‖ cría *f* (of oysters, etc.).

cultivator ['kʌltiveitə*] *n* cultivador *m* ‖ criador, ra (of oysters, silkworms, etc.).

cultural ['kʌltʃərəl] *adj* cultural ‖ *Cultural Revolution* Revolución *f* cultural.

culture ['kʌltʃə*] *n* cultura *f*; *popular, physical culture* cultura popular, física ‖ cultivo *m* (development by study) ‖ cultivo *m* (of soil, plants) ‖ cría *f* (of oysters, silkworms, etc.) ‖ BIOL cultivo *m*; *culture medium* caldo de cultivo.

cultured [-d] *adj* AGR cultivado, da ‖ culto, ta (person) ‖ *cultured pearl* perla cultivada, perla *f* de cultivo.

culture shock [-ʃɔk] *n* choque *m* cultural.

culture-vulture [-ˌvʌltʃə*] *n* intelectualoide *m* & *f*.

culver ['kʌlvə*] *n* paloma *f* torcaz *or* zurita (dove).

culverin ['kʌlvərin] *n* MIL culebrina *f*.

culvert ['kʌlvət] *n* alcantarilla *f* (sewer) ‖ ELECTR conducto *m* subterráneo.

cumber ['kʌmbə*] *vt* estorbar, molestar.

cumbersome ['kʌmbəsəm]; **cumbrous** ['kʌmbrəs] *adj* molesto, ta; incómodo, da (annoying) ‖ pesado, da (heavy) ‖ de mucho bulto, voluminoso, sa (big).

cumin; cummin ['kʌmin] *n* BOT comino *m*.

cummerbund ['kʌməbʌnd] *n* faja *f*.

cumulate ['kjuːmjuleit] *vt* acumular, amontonar.
◆ *vi* acumularse, amontonarse.

cumulation [ˌkjuːmju'leiʃən] *n* acumulación *f*, amontonamiento *m*.

cumulative ['kjuːmjulətiv] *adj* acumulativo, va ‖ plural (voting) ‖ acumulado, da (condemnation, interest) ‖ — JUR *cumulative evidence* pruebas acumuladas ‖ *cumulative preference shares* acciones *f* preferentes acumulativas.

cumulocirrus ['kjuːmjuləu'sirəs] *n* cirrocúmulo *m* (cloud).

cumulonimbus ['kjuːmjuləu'nimbəs] *n* cumulonimbo *m* (cloud).

cumulostratus ['kjuːmjuləu'streitəs] *n* estratocúmulo *m* (cloud).

cumulous ['kjuːmjuləs] *adj* en forma de cúmulo ‖ compuesto de cúmulos.

cumulus ['kjuːmjuləs] *n* cúmulo *m* (cloud) ‖ cúmulo *m*, acumulación *f* (a great quantity).
— OBSERV El plural de *cumulus* es *cumuli*.

cuneate ['kjuːniit] *adj* cuneiforme (wedge-shaped).

cuneiform ['kjuːniifɔːm] *adj* cuneiforme (writing) ‖ *cuneiform bone* hueso *m* cuneiforme, cuña *f*.
◆ *n* escritura *f* cuneiforme.

cunning ['kʌniŋ] *adj* astuto, ta (clever) ‖ ingenioso, sa; hábil, mañoso, sa (skilful) ‖ astuto, ta; taimado, da (sly) ‖ US mono, na; lindo, da (sweet, charming).
◆ *n* astucia *f* (slyness) ‖ ingenio *m*, ingeniosidad *f*, habilidad *f*, maña *f* (skill) ‖ agudeza *f*, sutileza *f* (keenness).

cunt [kʌnt] *n* POP coño *m*.

cup [kʌp] *n* taza *f* (bowl-shaped vessel); *cup of tea* taza de té ‖ copa *f* (trophy) ‖ REL cáliz *m* ‖ cubilete *m*, vaso *m* metálico (metal cup) ‖ cap *m* (drink) ‖ BOT cáliz *m* (of a flower) ‖ ANAT cavidad *f* (of bones) ‖ MED ventosa *f* (glass bowl) ‖ cangilón *m* (of water wheel) ‖ FIG cáliz *m* (of sorrow, bitterness, etc.) | copa *f* (of pleasures) ‖ cazuela *f*, copa *f* (of bikini, bra) ‖ hoyo *m* (hollow) ‖ — FAM *in one's cups* trompa, curda (drunk) | *it is not my cup of tea* no me gusta mayormente.

cup [kʌp] *vt* ahuecar (the hands) ‖ MED aplicar ventosas a ‖ *to cup one's hands to one's mouth* hacer bocina con las manos (to shout).

cupbearer ['kʌpˌbɛərə*] *n* copero *m*.

cupboard ['kʌbəd] *n* aparador *m* (sideboard) ‖ alacena *f* (built in) ‖ armario *m* (wardrobe) ‖ FIG & FAM *cupboard love* amor interesado.

cupel ['kjuːpəl] *n* copela *f*.

cupellation [-eiʃən] *n* copelación *f*.

cupful ['kʌpful] *n* taza *f* (contents of a cup).

cup holder ['kʌpˌhəuldə*] *n* SP campeón, ona.

Cupid ['kjuːpid] *n* Cupido *m*; *Cupid's bow* arco de Cupido.

cupidity [kjuː'piditi] *n* codicia *f*.

cupola ['kjuːpələ] *n* ARCH cúpula *f* (rounded roof) | linterna *f* (dome-shaped superstructure) ‖ MAR & MIL cúpula *f* ‖ TECH cubilote *m*.

cupped [kʌpt] *adj* en forma de bocina (the hands).

cupping ['kʌpiŋ] *n* MED aplicación *f* de ventosas.

cupreous ['kjuːpriəs] *adj* cuproso, sa.

cupressaceae [kjuːprə'sæsii] *pl n* BOT cupresáceas *f*.

cupric ['kjuːprik] *adj* cúprico, ca.

cupriferous [kjuː'prifərəs] *adj* cuprífero, ra.

cuprite ['kjuːprait] *n* MIN cuprita *f*.

cupronickel [ˌkjuːprə'nikəl] *n* cuproníquel *m*.

cuprous ['kjuːprəs] *adj* cuproso, sa.

cup-tie ['kʌptai] *n* SP partido *m* para ganar la copa.

cupule ['kjuːpjul] *n* BOT cúpula *f*.

cur [kəː*] *n* perro *m* que no es de raza (dog) ‖ FAM perro *m*, canalla *m* (person) ‖ FAM *mangy cur* perro sarnoso.

curability [ˌkjuərə'biliti] *n* curabilidad *f*.

curable ['kjuərəbl] *adj* curable.

curaçao ['kjuərə'səu] *n* curasao *m* (liqueur).

Curaçao [ˌkjuərə'səu] *pr n* Curazao.

curacy ['kjuərəsi] *n* REL coadjutoría *f*.

curare; curari [kju'rɑːri] *n* curare *m* (poison).

curassow ['kjuərəsəu] *n* ZOOL guaco *m* (bird).

curate ['kjuərit] *n* REL coadjutor *m*.

curative ['kjuərətiv] *adj* curativo, va.
◆ *n* remedio *m*.

curator [kjuə'reitə*] *n* conservador, ra (of a museum, art gallery, etc.) ‖ JUR curador *m*, tutor *m* ‖ miembro *m* del cuerpo administrativo de la universidad.

curb [kəːb] *n* barbada *f* (of harness) ‖ bordillo *m* (kerb) ‖ brocal *m* (of well) ‖ barandilla *f* (protective barrier) ‖ FIG restricción *f*, freno *m* (a restraint); *I put a curb on his abuses* puse freno a sus abusos | estorbo *m* (obstacle) ‖ US COMM bolsín *m* ‖ — *curb bit* freno *m*, bocado *m* ‖ ARCH *curb roof* tejado abuhardillado.

curb [kəːb] *vt* poner la barbada a (a horse) ‖ poner bordillo a (a pavement) ‖ FIG contener, reprimir, refrenar (to restrain).

curbstone ['kəːbstəun] *n* piedra *f* del bordillo.

curculio [kək'juːljəu] *n* ZOOL gorgojo *m*.

curd [kəːd] *n* cuajada *f*, requesón *m*.

curdle ['kəːdl] *vt* cuajar.
◆ *vi* cuajarse, coagularse (to form into curds) ‖ FAM *it made my blood curdle* se me heló la sangre en las venas.

curdy ['kəːdi] *adj* cuajado, da; coagulado, da.

cure [kjuə*] *n* cura *f* (course of treatment) ‖ remedio *m* (remedy) ‖ curación *f*, cura *f* (successful treatment) ‖ REL cura *f*; *cure of souls* cura de almas ‖ cura *f* (of food, by smoking) ‖ salazón *f* (by salting) ‖ curtido *m* (of leather).

cure [kjuə*] *vt* curar (to restore to health) ‖ remediar (to remedy) ‖ curar (by smoking) ‖ salar (by salting) ‖ vulcanizar (rubber) ‖ curtir (leather) ‖ FIG remediar, poner remedio a.
◆ *vi* curarse.

cure-all [-ɔːl] *n* panacea *f*, curalotodo *m*.

cureless [-lis] *adj* incurable.

curettage [kju'retidʒ] *n* MED raspado *m*, legrado *m*.

curette [kjuə'ret] *n* MED raspador *m*, cureta *f*, legra *f*.

curette [kjuə'ret] *vt* MED hacer un raspado a, raspar.

curfew ['kə:fju:] *n* toque *m* de queda (signal) || queda *f* (time).

curia ['kjuəriə] *n* REL curia *f* || *Curia (Romana)* Curia Romana.

— OBSERV El plural de *curia* es *curiae*.

curial [-l] *adj* curial.

curie ['kjuəri] *n* PHYS curie *m* (unit of measurement).

curietherapy [-'θerəpi] *n* MED curieterapia *f*.

curio ['kjuəriəu] *n* curiosidad *f*, fruslería *f*.

curiosity [,kjuəri'ɔsiti] *n* curiosidad *f* (inquisitiveness, strangeness) || curiosidad *f*, objeto *m* curioso (curious object) || — FIG *curiosity killed the cat* por la boca muere el pez || *curiosity shop* tienda *f* de antigüedades.

curious ['kjuəriəs] *adj* curioso, sa (inquisitive) || curioso, sa; extraño, ña (odd) || *I am curious of* tengo curiosidad por.

curiously [-li] *adv* curiosamente || *curiously enough* aunque parezca extraño, por muy curioso que parezca.

curium ['kjuəriəm] *n* PHYS curio *m* (radioactive element).

curl [kə:l] *n* rizo *m*, bucle *m* (of hair) || espiral *m*, voluta *f* (of smoke) || encrespamiento *m* (of waves) || veta *f* redondeada (in wood grain) || sinuosidad *f*, zigzag *m*, serpenteo *m* (sinuousness) || torcedura *f* (twisting) || BOT zarcillo *m* || FIG *with a curl of the lip* con una mueca de desprecio.

curl [kə:l] *vt* rizar (the hair) || arrollar (paper) || — *to curl o.s. up* acurrucarse, hacerse un ovillo || *to curl the lip* hacer una mueca de desprecio.

◆ *vi* rizarse (hair) || arrollarse (to roll up) || abarquillarse (to wrinkle) || encresparse (waves) || hacer espirales *or* volutas (smoke) || zigzaguear, serpentear (a path, etc.).

curler [-ə*] *n* rulo *m*, bigudí *m* (hair roller) || ola *f* al romper (wave) || SP jugador, ra (de curling).

◆ *pl* tenacillas *f* de rizar (curling iron).

curlew ['kə:lju:] *n* zarapito *m* (bird).

curlicue ['kə:likju:] *n* floritura *f*, floreo *m*, adorno *m* (in handwriting).

curliness ['kə:linis] *n* rizado *m*, ensortijamiento *m*.

curling ['kə:liŋ] *n* rizado *m* (of hair) || SP «curling» *m* || — *curling iron* tenacillas *f pl* de rizar || *curling paper* papillote *m* || *curling pin* bigudí *m*.

curlpaper ['kə:l,peipə*] *n* papillote *m*.

curly ['kə:li] *adj* rizado, da (hair) || en espiral (in spiral) || sinuoso, sa (winding).

curmudgeon [kə:'mʌdʒən] *n* cascarrabias *m* & *f inv* persona *f* de mal genio *or* de malas pulgas.

currant ['kʌrənt] *n* BOT grosella *f* (berry) || pasa *f* (dried grape) || *black currant* grosella negra (fruit), grosellero negro (bush).

currency ['kʌrənsi] *n* moneda *f* [en circulación] (money); *currency convertibility* convertibilidad de la moneda || dinero *m* en circulación || uso *m* corriente (general use); *it had a certain currency* tuvo un uso bastante corriente || extensión *f* (general acceptance) || temporada *f* (time during which a thing is current) || — *currency allocation* cupo *m* de divisas que se permite sacar de un país || *floating currency* moneda flotante || *foreign currency* divisa *f*, moneda extranjera || *to gain currency* llegar a ser creído.

current ['kʌrənt] *adj* corriente (in general use) || general (prevalent); *current opinion* la opinión general || actual (of the present time); *the current crisis* la crisis actual || admitido, da; aceptado, da (accepted) || en curso; *current year* año en curso || último, ma (magazine); *current issue* último número || corriente (expenses) || abierto, ta (credit, etc.) || de curso legal (money) || — COMM *current account* cuenta corriente || *current affairs* acontecimientos *m pl* de actualidad || *current assets* activo *m* disponible || ELECTR *current breaker* interruptor eléctrico | *current density* densidad *f* de corriente || *current liabilities* pasivo *m* exigible || *current meter* hidrómetro *m* || *current rate of exchange* cambio *m* del día.

◆ *n* corriente *f* (of air, water) || curso *m* de agua (stream) || ELECTR corriente *f*; *alternating, direct current* corriente alterna, continua || marcha *f*, curso *m* (of events).

currently ['kʌrəntli] *adv* corrientemente (generally) || actualmente (at present).

curricle ['kʌrikl] *n* coche *m* de dos caballos.

curricular [kə'rikjulə*] *adj* del plan de estudios.

curriculum [kə'rikjuləm] *n* plan *m* de estudios, programa *m* de estudios || *curriculum vitae* curriculum vitae *m*, historial *m* profesional.

— OBSERV El plural de la palabra *curriculum* es *curricula* o *curriculums*.

currier ['kʌriə*] *n* zurrador *m*, adobador *m*.

currish ['kəriʃ] *adj* arisco, ca; huraño, ña (surly).

curry ['kʌri] *n* «curry» *m*, cari *m* (spice).

curry ['kʌri] *vt* guisar con «curry» (to cook with curry) || almohazar (a horse) || zurrar, adobar (leather) || — *to curry favour* buscar favores || *to curry favour with s.o.* buscar el favor de alguien.

◆ *vi* guisar con «curry».

currycomb [-kəum] *n* almohaza *f*.

curse [kə:s] *n* maldición *f*; *under a curse* bajo una maldición || blasfemia *f* (oath) || palabrota *f* (rude word) || reniego *m*, voto *m* (imprecation) || REL excomunión *f*, anatema *m* || FIG calamidad *f*, maldición *f* (bane) || *a curse on him!* ¡maldito sea!

curse [kə:s] *vt* maldecir (to utter a curse on s.o.) || afligir (to afflict) || REL excomulgar, anatematizar || *curse him!* ¡maldito sea!

◆ *vi* blasfemar (to blaspheme) || decir palabrotas (to say rude words).

cursed ['kə:sid]; **curst** [kə:st] *adj* maldito, ta (under a curse) || FAM maldito, ta (blasted).

cursing ['kə:siŋ] *adj* maldiciente || blasfemador, ra || palabrotero, ra.

◆ *n* maldición *f* || blasfemias *f pl* (oaths) || palabrotas *f pl* (rude words).

cursive ['kə:siv] *adj* cursivo, va; bastardilla.

◆ *n* letra *f* cursiva, cursiva *f*, letra *f* bastardilla, bastardilla *f*.

cursor ['kə:sə*] *n* cursor *m*.

cursoriness [-rinis] *n* rapidez *f*, superficialidad *f*.

cursory [-ri] *adj* precipitado, da; rápido, da; superficial; *cursory reading* lectura rápida.

curst [kə:st] *adj* → **cursed.**

curt [kə:t] *adj* breve, conciso, sa (short in speech) || lacónico, ca (laconic) || brusco, ca; seco, ca (blunt).

curtail [kə:'teil] *vt* abreviar, acortar (to curt short) || reducir (to reduce, to cut down).

curtailment [-mənt] *n* acortamiento *m*, abreviación *f* || reducción *f* (of expenses, credits).

curtain ['kə:tn] *n* cortina *f* (for windows, of rain, fire, etc.); *to draw the curtain* correr la cortina; *to draw back the curtain* descorrer la cortina || THEATR telón *m*; *to lower the curtain* bajar el telón | subida *f or* bajada *f* del telón (raising or lowering of the curtain) || MIL cortina *f* (of ramparts) || FIG cortina *f*, velo *m* (veil) || — *blind curtain* persiana *f* || THEATR *curtain call* llamada *f* a escena [para saludar] | *curtain raiser* sainete *m* (short play), introducción *f* (introduction) | *curtain wall* paneles *m pl* | *front curtain* telón *m* de boca || FIG *iron curtain* telón *m* de acero || *net* o *lace curtain* visillo *m* || THEATR *safety curtain* telón metálico | *the curtain falls* baja el telón | *the curtain rises* sube el telón.

◆ *pl* FAM final *m sing*, fin *m sing* (the end, death).

curtain ['kə:tn] *vt* poner cortinas en || FIG encubrir, tapar || *to curtain off* separar con cortina.

curtly ['kə:tli] *adv* secamente, bruscamente || brevemente, de manera concisa || lacónicamente.

curtness ['kə:tnis] *n* sequedad *f*, brusquedad *f* || concisión *f*, brevedad *f* (conciseness) || laconismo *m*.

curtsy; curtsey ['kə:tsi] *n* reverencia *f*; *to drop a curtsy* hacer una reverencia.

curtsy; curtsey ['kə:tsi] *vi* hacer una reverencia.

curule ['kjuəru:l] *adj* curul.

curvaceous [kə:'veiʃəs] *adj* curvilíneo, a.

curvature ['kə:vətʃə*] *n* curvatura *f* (curve) || esfericidad *f* (of the Earth) || encorvamiento *m*; *curvature of the spine* encorvamiento de la columna vertebral || MAR cimbra *f*.

curve [kə:v] *n* curva *f* || curva *f*, vuelta *f* (of a road) || pistola *f* (of draftsman).

curve [kə:v] *vt* doblar, encorvar.

◆ *vi* doblarse, encorvarse (to take the shape of a curve) || torcerse, hacer una curva (a road).

curved [kə:vd] *adj* curvo, va; *curved line* línea curva || doblado, da; encorvado, da.

curvet [kə:'vet] *n* corveta *f* (of a horse).

curvet [kə:'vet] *vi* hacer corvetas, corvetear (a horse) || FIG retozar, juguetear.

curvilinear [,kə:vi'liniə*]; **curvilineal** [,kə:vi'liniəl] *adj* curvilíneo, a.

curving ['kə:viŋ] *adj* que hace una curva || que se dobla.

◆ *n* curva *f*.

curvometer [kə:'vɔmitə*] *n* curvímetro *m*.

curvy ['kə:vi] *adj* curvilíneo, a.

cusec ['kjusek] *n* pie *m* cúbico por segundo (of the flow of a fluid).

cushat ['kʌʃət] *n* paloma *f* torcaz *or* zurita (dove).

cushion ['kuʃən] *n* cojín *m*, almohadón *m* (for sitting on, etc.) || banda *f* (of billiard table) || acerico *m*, almohadilla *f* (for pins) || VET ranilla *f* (of horse's hoof) | cuarto trasero *m* (buttocks of animal) || TECH colchón *m*; *air cushion* colchón de aire || almohadilla *f* (for office stamp) || FIG amortiguador *m*, colchón *m*; *the grass acted as a cushion to his fall* la hierba hizo de amortiguador en su caída || FAM rosca *f* (of fat).

cushion ['kuʃən] *vt* poner almohadones *or* cojines en || poner en un cojín (to seat) || rellenar (a seat, etc.) || almohadillar, acolchar (to pad) || FIG amortiguar (to absorb shock) | proteger (to shield from) | sofocar (to suppress) | mimar (to cosset) || recostar (to lean as on a cushion) || dejar (la bola) pegada a la banda (billiards).

cushy ['kuʃi] *adj* FIG & FAM fácil, cómodo, da || — *cushy life* vida tranquila *or* facilona || *cushy number* o *job* chollo *m*, momio *m*, ganga *f*.

cusp [kʌsp] *n* cúspide *f* (apex) || MATH vértice *m* || ARCH vértice *m* || cuerno *m* (of the Moon).

cuspid ['kʌspid] *n* diente *m* canino, colmillo *m*.

cuspidal ['kʌspidəl] *adj* puntiagudo, da.

cuspidor ['kʌspidɔ:*] *n* US escupidera *f.*

cuss [kʌs] *n* FAM maldición *f* (curse) | individuo *m*, tipo *m*, tío *m* (fellow) | palabrota *f* (rude word).

cuss [kʌs] *vt/vi* FAM maldecir ‖ decir palabrotas (to say rude words).

cussed ['kʌsid] *adj* FAM terco, ca; cabezón, ona (stubborn) | maldito, ta (cursed).

cussedness [-nis] *n* espíritu *m* de contradicción ‖ terquedad *f*, obstinación *f* (stubbornness).

custard ['kʌstəd] *n* CULIN natillas *f pl* ‖ — *caramel custard* flan *m* ‖ *custard apple* chirimoya *f*, anona *f* (fruit), chirimoyo *m*, anona *f* (tree).

custodial [kʌs'təudjəl] *adj* de la custodia (of custody) ‖ del guardián (of custodian).

◆ *n* REL custodia *f.*

custodian [kʌs'təudjən] *n* guardián, ana; custodio *m* ‖ portero, ra (of a building) ‖ conservador, ra (of a museum).

custody ['kʌstədi] *n* custodia *f*, guardia *f* ‖ prisión *f*, detención *f* (prison) ‖ — *in custody* bajo custodia, custodiado, da; detenido, da ‖ *remanded in custody* mantenido bajo custodia ‖ *to give into custody* entregar a la policía ‖ *to take s.o. into custody* detener a uno.

custom ['kʌstəm] *n* costumbre *f* (habit); *as is the custom* según costumbre; *ill custom* mala costumbre ‖ clientela *f* (customers) ‖ JUR derecho *m* consuetudinario.

◆ *pl* derechos *m* de aduana, aranceles *m*, derechos *m* arancelarios (duty) | aduana *f sing*; *customs officer* agente de aduana; *to go through (the) customs* pasar la aduana.

◆ *adj* aduanero, ra; de aduana ‖ US hecho de encargo, a la medida (made-to-order) ‖ que trabaja por encargo (dealer in made-to-order goods).

customariness ['kʌstəmərinis] *n* costumbre *f.*

customary ['kʌstəməri] *adj* acostumbrado, da; de costumbre, habitual ‖ JUR consuetudinario, ria ‖ *it is customary to* es costumbre.

custom-built ['kʌstəm'bilt] *adj* hecho de encargo, a la medida.

customer ['kʌstəmə*] *n* cliente *m* & *f* (purchaser); *to attract customers* atraer a clientes ‖ FAM individuo *m*, tipo *m*, tío *m*; *an awkward customer* un tipo difícil.

custom-free ['kʌstəmfri:] *adj* exento de aranceles, libre de derechos arancelarios.

customhouse ['kʌstəmhaus]; **customs-house** ['kʌstəmzhaus] *n* aduana *f* ‖ — *customhouse broker* agente *m* de aduana ‖ *customhouse officer* aduanero, ra, vista *m* de aduana.

customize, customise ['kʌstəmaiz] *vt* US hacer de encargo *or* a la medida.

custom-made ['kʌstəm'meid] *adj* hecho de encargo, a la medida.

customs ['kʌstəmz] *pl n* ⟶ **custom.**

Customs and Excise [-ənd ek,saiz] *pl n* departamento *m* de administración de aranceles aduaneros.

customshouse [-haus] *n* ⟶ **customhouse.**

customs union [-ju:njən] *n* unión aduanera.

custom-tailor ['kʌstəm,teilə*] *n* US sastre *m* a la medida.

cut [kʌt] *adj* cortado, da; *cut flowers* flores cortadas; *a well cut suit* un traje bien cortado ‖ castrado (castrated) ‖ reducido, da; *cut prices* precios reducidos ‖ tallado, da (glass, diamond) ‖ picado, da (tobacco).

◆ *n* corte *m* (incision) ‖ muesca *f* (notch) ‖ herida *f* (gash) ‖ corte *m*, cortadura *f* (small wound) ‖ tajo *m*, chirlo *m* (on the face) ‖ filo *m*, corte *m* (cutting edge) ‖ reducción *f* (in prices, wages, etc.) ‖ corte *m* (in an article, a play) ‖ corte *m*, interrupción *f* (on TV, films, radio) ‖ recorte *m* (clipping) ‖ golpe *m* (thrashing stroke) ‖ latigazo *m* (with a whip) ‖ cuchillada *f* (with a knife) ‖ FAM parte *f*; *his cut was 10 %* su parte era el 10 % ‖ corte *m* (of electricity) ‖ trozo *m*, corte *m* (piece of meat) ‖ tajada *f* (slice) ‖ rebanada *f* (of bread) ‖ corte *m* (of hair, clothes) ‖ MED incisión *f*, corte *m* ‖ SP corte *m* ‖ zanja *f* (railway cutting) ‖ corte *m* (of a pack of cards) ‖ GEOGR entrada *f* ‖ FIG & FAM corte *m* (verbal attack) | golpe *m* (misfortune) ‖ PRINT grabado *m* ‖ grabado *m* en madera (woodcut) ‖ talla *f* (of jewels) ‖ FAM ausencia *f* (from school) ‖ TECH pasada *f* (of a machine tool) ‖ — *cold cuts* fiambres *m* ‖ FIG & FAM *cut of one's jib* semblante *m*, aspecto *m* ‖ *short cut* atajo *m* ‖ *sword cut* estocada *f* ‖ FIG *the cut and thrust* la lucha (the struggle) | *there is no short cut to fame* no se consigue fácilmente la gloria | *to be a cut above the rest* ser superior a los demás, estar por encima de los demás ‖ *whose cut is it?* ¿quién corta? (in cards).

cut* [kʌt] *vt* cortar (to make an incision, to wound, to sever, to separate into pieces, slices, to halve a pack of cards) ‖ segar (to reap) ‖ talar (trees) ‖ cortar; *to cut the lawn* cortar el césped ‖ cortar (clothes, in tailoring) ‖ acortar (to make smaller or shorter) ‖ cruzar (to intersect) ‖ bajar, reducir; *to cut the price of meat by 2 %* reducir el precio de la carne un 2 por ciento ‖ cortar, romper (connections) ‖ cortar, parar (an engine) ‖ cortar (communications) ‖ reducir, acortar, abreviar (a speech, visit, etc.) ‖ repartir, dividir (benefits, booty) ‖ cortar, hacer cortes en; *to cut a film* hacer cortes en una película ‖ excavar, abrir (trench, canal) ‖ abrir (an opening) ‖ FIG herir, lastimar (to hurt one's feelings) | dejarse de, acabar con; *cut the clowning!* ¡déjese de payasadas! ‖ penetrar (the cold) ‖ FAM faltar a, fumarse (classes, lectures) ‖ cortar (alcohol, wine) ‖ disolver (grease) ‖ diluir (a liquid) ‖ picar (tobacco) ‖ castrar (to castrate) ‖ echar, salir (teeth); *he cut his teeth* echó los dientes, le salieron los dientes ‖ ARTS grabar, tallar, esculpir ‖ hacer; *to cut a notch* hacer una muesca ‖ tallar (stones) ‖ tallar, labrar (diamond) ‖ aterrajar, roscar (screw) ‖ MAR soltar, largar (one's moorings) ‖ SP cortar, dar efecto a (a ball) ‖ grabar (a record) ‖ MED abrir (an abscess) ‖ desglosar (a film) ‖ — *to cut a corner* coger una curva en diagonal ‖ FIG *to cut a dash* ser elegante (to be smart), darse pisto (to make a display of o.s.), causar sensación (to cause sensation), hacer buen papel (to do well) ‖ *to cut adrift* desatar ‖ FIG *to cut a fine figure* causar buena impresión (to give a good impression), tener buen tipo (appearance), ser elegante (smartness) ‖ *to cut a long story short* en pocas palabras, para abreviar ‖ *to cut asunder* separar ‖ *to cut capers* hacer cabriolas (to caper), hacer el loco (to play the fool) ‖ FIG *to cut corners* tomar atajos (to shorten the distance), economizar esfuerzos *or* dinero ‖ *to cut it fine* calcular muy justo ‖ *to cut loose* soltar; *to cut a rope loose* soltar una cuerda; soltar las amarras (boat), liberarse (to free o.s. from domination), pasárselo en grande (to enjoy o.s.), soltarse el pelo (to drop all restraint) ‖ FIG *to cut no ice* no convencer; no tener importancia | *to cut one's coat according to one's cloth* gobernar su boca según su bolsa | *to cut one's losses* abandonar algo muy costoso ‖ *to cut one's nails* cortarse las uñas ‖ FIG *to cut one's throat* arruinarse ‖ *to cut one's way through* abrirse paso entre ‖ *to cut open* abrir con un corte ‖ FIG *to cut short* cortar en seco (discussion) | *to cut s.o. dead* negar el saludo a uno, pasar cerca de uno sin saludarle | *to cut s.o. short* interrumpir bruscamente *or* cortar en seco a uno (to interrupt), dejarle cortado a uno (to silence) ‖ *to cut the prices* vender a precio reducido ‖ *to cut the thread of the argument* cortar el hilo del discurso ‖ *to cut to pieces* hacer pedazos *or* trizas | FIG *to cut to the bone* reducir a lo mínimo | *to cut to the heart* o *to the quick* herir en lo vivo (to hurt s.o.'s feelings) ‖ *to have one's hair cut* cortarse el pelo.

◆ *vi* cortar; *this knife cuts badly* este cuchillo corta mal ‖ cortar; *we cut through the forest* cortamos por el bosque ‖ cortarse; *this stone cuts easily* esta piedra se corta con facilidad ‖ cruzarse (two roads) ‖ cortar, penetrar (the cold) ‖ cortar (at cards) | — CINEM *cut!* ¡corten! ‖ FIG *to cut and run* salir pitando (to go), levar anclas (a ship) | *to cut both ways* ser un arma de dos filos ‖ *to cut loose* escaparse ‖ *to cut to the left* doblar a la izquierda ‖ *to cut through s.o.'s coat* atravesar el abrigo de alguien ‖ *to cut through the air* hendir el aire.

◆ *phr v* ***to cut across*** cortar completamente | cortar por; *to cut across the town* cortar por la ciudad | FIG ir en contra de; *this cuts across all my principles* esto va en contra de todos mis principios ‖ — *to cut across a field* pasar a campo traviesa ‖ ***to cut along*** irse deprisa ‖ ***to cut away*** cortar | FAM salir pitando (to run away) ‖ ***to cut back*** acortar (to make shorter) | podar (to trim) | CINEM retroceder | reducir, disminuir (expenses) | volver (to come back) ‖ ***to cut down*** cortar (trees) | acortar (to shorten) | AGR segar (corn) | reducir (expenses) | cortar, hacer cortes en (a speech) ‖ — *to cut down on smoking* fumar menos (to smoke less), gastar menos en cigarrillos ‖ ***to cut in*** interrumpir (to interrupt) | colarse (to push in) | insertar (to insert) | meterse en la conversación | AUT cerrar el paso, cerrarse | conectar (an engine) | sacar a bailar a la pareja de otra persona (in dancing) ‖ — *to cut in and out* colarse ‖ *to cut in on* hacer partícipe en (benefits), incluir en (to include), interrumpir (a conversation), entrar en (card game) | FIG *to cut s.o. in on a deal* meterle a uno en un asunto ‖ ***to cut into*** acortar, reducir (to shorten) | cortar (cake) | mermar (savings) ‖ ***to cut off*** cortar | llevarse; *death cut him off in his prime* la muerte se lo llevó en la flor de la edad | separar (to separate) | aislar; *we were cut off by the flood* estuvimos aislados por la inundación | amputar (to amputate) † tapar (the view) | cortar, parar (an engine) | pararse, dejar de funcionar (a car, etc.) | cortar (telephone, current) | desheredar (to disinherit) | MIL cortar la retirada a | romper (negotiations) | cortar el camino a (to bar s.o.'s way) | marcharse, irse (to go) ‖ ***to cut out*** recortar; *to cut a photo out of a paper* recortar una foto en un periódico | cortar (a garment) | hacer, cavar (a hole) | suplantar (to supplant) | omitir, excluir (to omit) | eliminar (to eliminate) | suprimir (to suppress) | dejar de; *to cut out smoking* dejar de fumar | dejarse de; *cut out the nonsense* déjate de tonterías | pararse (engine) | US separar (of the herd) ‖ — FAM *cut it out!* ¡basta ya! | *to be cut out for* o *to* estar hecho para; *he is not cut out to be a farmer* no está hecho para ser agricultor ‖ ***to cut up*** cortar en pedazos (to cut into pieces) | cortar, trinchar (meat in slices), picar (in small pieces) | cortar (paper, wood) | destrozar (to destroy) | FIG poner por los suelos (to criticize harshly) | apenar (to distress) | alardear (to boast) | dejar carriles en (a road) | US hacer tonterías (to play the fool).

— OBSERV Pret y pp *cut*.

cut-and-dried [-ən'draid] *adj* previsto [hasta el más mínimo detalle].

cutaneous [kju:'teinjəs] *adj* cutáneo, a.

cutaway ['kʌtəwei] *n* corte *m*, sección *f* (of a machine).

cutback ['kʌtbæk] *n* reducción *f* ‖ restricción *f* ‖ resumen *m* de lo anterior (of a serialized story).

cute [kju:t] *adj* US listo, ta; astuto, ta (sharp-witted) ‖ mono, na; lindo, da (attractive).

cuteness [-nis] *n* astucia *f* (cleverness) ‖ US monería *f* [AMER lindura *f*]

cut glass ['kʌt'glɑ:s] *n* cristal *m* tallado.

cuticle ['kju:tikl] *n* cutícula *f*.

cutis ['kju:tis] *n* ANAT cutis *m*.
— OBSERV El plural de la palabra inglesa *cutis* es *cutes* o *cutises*.

cutlass ['kʌtləs] *n* MIL alfanje *m* ‖ US machete *m*.

cutler ['kʌtlə*] *n* cuchillero *m*.

cutlery [-ri] *n* cubiertos *m pl*, cubertería *f* (used at table) ‖ objetos *m pl* cortantes (razors, shears, etc.) ‖ cuchillería *f* (the trade of a cutler).

cutlet ['kʌtlit] *n* chuleta *f* (chop) ‖ croqueta *f* (of chopped meat or fish).

cutoff ['kʌtɔf] *n* corte *m*, cese *m* ‖ US brazo *m* muerto (of a river) | atajo *m* (short cut) ‖ TECH obturador *m* (of a cylinder) ‖ cierre *m* de admisión.

cutoff point *n* punto *m* límite, tope *m*.

cutout ['kʌtaut] *n* recorte *m*, figura *f* recortada (design made by cutting) ‖ recortable *m*, dibujo *m* para recortar (design prepared for cutting) ‖ TECH válvula *f* de escape | escape *m* libre ‖ ELECTR cortacircuitos *m inv*, interruptor *m* | fusible *m*, plomo *m* (fuse).

cut-price ['kʌtprais] *adj* a precio reducido.

cutpurse ['kʌtpə:s] *n* carterista *m* & *f*, ratero, ra.

cut-rate ['kʌtreit] *adj* rebajado, da.

cutter ['kʌtə*] *n* cortador, ra (person who cuts) ‖ cantero *m*, tallista *m* & *f* (of stone) ‖ tallista *m* & *f* (of precious stones) ‖ desglosador, ra (of film) ‖ TECH cizalla *f* (wire cutter) ‖ MAR cúter *m* (single-masted boat) | patrullero *m*, guardacostas *m inv* (coastguard boat) ‖ incisivo *m* (tooth) ‖ US trineo *m* (sledge) ‖ *coastguard* o *revenue cutter* guardacostas *m inv*.

cutthroat ['kʌtθrəut] *adj* sanguinario, ria (murderous) ‖ implacable; *cutthroat competition* una rivalidad implacable ‖ a tres (card games).
◆ *n* asesino, na (murderer) ‖ navaja *f* barbera (razor).

cutting ['kʌtiŋ] *adj* cortante (sharp); *cutting edge* filo cortante ‖ cortante (wind) ‖ penetrante (rain) ‖ mordaz, incisivo, va; hiriente (remarks, etc.).
◆ *n* corte *m* ‖ BOT tala *f* (of trees) | poda *f* (of rose trees) | esqueje *m* (slip) ‖ talla *f* (of a diamond) ‖ corte *m* (of a garment) ‖ recorte *m* (piece cut off) ‖ retal *m* (of cloth) ‖ recorte *m* (from a newspaper) ‖ zanja *f* (for road, railway) ‖ abertura *f* (of a channel) ‖ paso *m* (in a wood) ‖ reducción *f* (of prices, wages) ‖ desglose *m* (of a film) ‖ *cutting iron* cortafrío *m*.

cuttle ['kʌtl] *n* ZOOL jibia *f*.

cuttlebone [-bəun] *n* ZOOL jibión *m*.

cuttlefish [-fiʃ] *n* ZOOL jibia *f*.

cutty ['kʌti] *adj* corto, ta.

cutwater ['kʌt,wɔ:tə*] *n* MAR tajamar *m*, roda *f*, espolón *m* ‖ tajamar *m* (of a bridge).

cutwork ['kʌtwə:k] *n* calado *m* (in lace).

cutworm ['kʌtwə:m] *n* US ZOOL oruga *f*.

CV *abbr of [curriculum vitae]* CV, curriculum vitae.

cyanidation [saiənai'deiʃən]; **cyaniding** ['saiənaidiŋ] *n* cianuración *f*.

cyanide ['saiənaid] *n* CHEM cianuro *m* ‖ *cyanide process* cianuración *f*.

cyanite ['saiənait] *n* MIN cianita *f*.

cyanogen [sai'ænədʒin] *n* CHEM cianógeno *m*.

cyanosis [saiə'nəusis] *n* MED cianosis *f*.

cyanotype [sai'ænətaip] *n* cianotipo *m* (blueprint).

Cybele ['sibəli:] *pr n* Cibeles *f*.

cybernetics [,saibə:'netiks] *n* cibernética *f*.

cyclamen ['sikləmən] *n* ciclamen *m*, ciclamino *m*.

cycle ['saikl] *n* ciclo *m*; *life cycle* ciclo de la vida ‖ ASTR órbita *f* ‖ bicicleta *f* (bicycle) ‖ *cycle race* carrera *f* ciclista.

cycle ['saikl] *vi* pasar por un ciclo (to move in cycles) ‖ ir en bicicleta; *I cycled home last night* anoche fui a casa en bicicleta ‖ montar en bicicleta (to ride a bicycle).

cyclic ['saiklik]; **cyclical** [-əl] *adj* cíclico, ca.

cycling ['saikliŋ] *n* ciclismo *m*.
◆ *adj* ciclista; *cycling race* carrera ciclista ‖ en bicicleta (tour).

cyclist ['saiklist] *n* ciclista *m* & *f*.

cyclo-cross ['saikləkrɔs] *n* SP ciclocrós *m*.

cycloid ['saiklɔid] *n* MATH cicloide *f*.

cycloidal [sai'klɔidl] *adj* cicloidal, cicloideo, a.

cyclometer [sai'klɔmitə*] *n* contador *m* kilométrico de bicicleta.

cyclonal ['saiklənəl] *adj* ciclonal, ciclónico, ca.

cyclone ['saikləun] *n* ciclón *m* ‖ US *cyclone cellar* refugio *m* anticiclones.

cyclonic [sai'klɔnik] *adj* ciclónico, ca.

cyclopean [sai'kləupjən] *adj* ciclópeo, a.

Cyclops ['saiklɔps] *n* MYTH Cíclope *m*.
— OBSERV El plural de *Cyclops* es *Cyclopes*.

cyclorama [,saiklə'rɑ:mə] *n* ciclorama *m*.

cyclostomes ['saikləstəumz]; **cyclostomi** ['saikləstəumi] *pl n* ZOOL ciclóstomos *m*.

cyclostyle ['saikləstail] *n* ciclostilo *m*.

cyclothymia [,saiklə'θaimiə] *n* MED ciclotimia *f*.

cyclotron ['saiklətrɔn] *n* ciclotrón *m*.

cygnet ['signit] *n* ZOOL pollo *m* de cisne.

Cygnus ['signəs] *n* ASTR Cisne *m*.

cylinder ['silində*] *n* cilindro *m* ‖ — *cylinder block* bloque *m* de cilindros ‖ *cylinder capacity* o *charge* cilindrada *f* ‖ *cylinder head* culata *f* de cilindro ‖ *cylinder press* rotativa *f*.

cylindric [si'lindrik]; **cylindrical** [-əl] *adj* cilíndrico, ca.

cyma ['saimə] *n* ARCH gola *f*, cimacio *m*.

cymbal ['simbəl] *n* MUS címbalo *m*, platillo *m*.

cyme [saim] *n* BOT cima *f*.

cynegetic ['saini'dʒetik] *adj* cinegético, ca.

cynegetics [-s] *n* cinegética *f*.

cynic ['sinik] *adj/n* cínico, ca ‖ —→ **cynical.**

cynical ['sinikəl]; **cynic** ['sinik] *adj* cínico, ca ‖ escéptico, ca; desengañado, da (disillusioned) ‖ sarcástico, ca (sarcastic) ‖ burlón, ona; despreciativo, va (sneering).

cynically [-i] *adj* cínicamente ‖ escépticamente ‖ burlonamente, despreciativamente.

cynicism ['sinisizəm] *n* cinismo *m* ‖ escepticismo *m*, desengaño *m* (disillusion) ‖ burla *f*, desprecio *m* ‖ carácter *m* sarcástico.

cynocephalus [,sainəu'sefələs] *n* cinocéfalo *m* (monkey).

cynosure ['sinəzjuə*] *n* centro *m* de atracción ‖ ASTR Osa Menor *f* ‖ *cynosure of every eye* blanco *m* de las miradas.

cypher ['saifə*] *n* —→ **cipher.**

cyphosis [sai'fəusis] *n* cifosis *f*.

cypress ['saipris] *n* BOT ciprés *m* (tree).

cyprinid ['siprənid] *n* ZOOL ciprino *m*.

Cypriot; Cypriote ['sipriət] *adj/n* chipriota.

Cyprus ['saiprəs] *pr n* GEOGR Chipre.

Cyrenaica [,saiərə'neiikə] *pr n* Cirenaica *f*.

cyrenian [sai'ri:njən] *adj/n* cirineo, a.

Cyril ['siril] *pr n* Cirilo *m*.

Cyrillic [si'rilik] *adj* cirílico, ca.

cyst [sist] *n* quiste *m* (growth) ‖ vesícula *f* (bladder).

cystic ['sistik] *adj* enquistado, da; quístico, ca (like a cyst) ‖ ANAT cístico, ca ‖ MED *cystic fibrosis* fibrosis *f inv* quística.

cysticercus [sisti'sə:kəs] *n* ZOOL cisticerco *m* (tapeworm larva).
— OBSERV El plural de *cysticercus* es *cysticerci*.

cystitis [sis'taitis] *n* MED cistitis *f*.

cystotomy [sis'tɔtəmi] *n* cistotomía *f*.

cytisus ['sitisəs] *n* BOT citiso *m*, codeso *m*.

cytology [sai'tɔlɔdʒi] *n* citología *f*.

cytoplasm ['saitəuplæzəm] *n* BIOL citoplasma *m*.

czar [zɑ:*] *n* zar *m*.

czardas ['tʃɑr,dæʃ] *n* czarda *f* (dance).

czarevitch ['zɑ:rivitʃ] *n* zarevitz *m*.

czarina [zɑ:'ri:nə] *n* zarina *f*.

czarism ['zɑ:rizəm] *n* zarismo *m*.

Czech [tʃek] *adj/n* checo, ca.

Czechoslovak ['tʃekə'sləuvæk] *adj/n* checoslovaco, ca.

Czechoslovakia ['tʃekəslə'vækiə] *pr n* GEOGR Checoslovaquia *f*.

Czechoslovakian [-n] *adj/n* checoslovaco, ca.

D

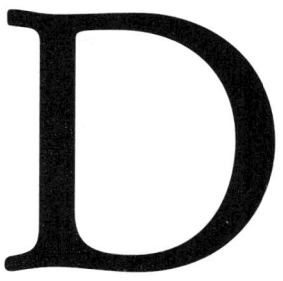

d [di:] *n* d *f* (letter) || MUS re *m* || signo *m* que representa un penique antiguo (English old penny) || *D day* día *m* D.

— OBSERV La *d* que representa el penique antiguo es una abreviatura de la palabra latina *denarius*.

dab [dæb] *adj* FAM *to be a dab hand at* ser un hacha en.

◆ *adv* US FAM *right dab in the middle* justo en el centro, en pleno centro.

◆ *n* FAM hacha *m* (expert) || golpe *m* ligero (a light blow or stroke) || toque *m*; *a dab of paint* un toque de pintura || pizca *f*, poquito *m* (bit) || mancha *f* (of mud) || platija *f*, gallo *m* (fish).

◆ *pl* huellas *f* digitales *or* dactilares.

dab [dæb] *vt* golpear ligeramente (to strike) || dar unos toques de; *to dab paint on the wall* dar unos toques de pintura en la pared || *to dab a stain with a sponge* quitar una mancha con una esponja.

dabber [-ə*] *n*, tampón *m* (for inking).

dabble ['dæbl] *vt* salpicar (to splash) || rociar (to sprinkle) || mojar (to wet).

◆ *vi* chapotear (in water) || FIG interesarse superficialmente (*in, at* en, por) (to do sth. superficially) | meterse; *to dabble in politics* meterse en política.

dabbler [-ə*] *n* diletante *m*.

dabchick ['dæbtʃik] *n* somorgujo *m* (bird).

dabster ['dæbstə*] *n* FAM diletante *m* (dabbler) | hacha *m* (dab).

Dacca ['dækə] *pr n* GEOGR Dacca.

dace [deis] *n* albur *m* (fish).

dachshund ['dækshund] *n* perro *m* salchicha.

Dacian ['deisjən] *adj/n* dacio, cia.

dactyl ['dæktil] *n* dáctilo *m* (in poetry).

dad [dæd] *n* papá *m*.

Dada ['dɑ:dɑ:]; **Dadaism** [-zəm] *n* dadaísmo *m*.

Dadaist ['dɑ:dɑ:ist] *adj/n* dadaísta.

daddy ['dædi] *n* FAM papá *m*, papaíto *m*.

daddy longlegs [-'lɔŋlegz] *n* ZOOL típula *f* (crane fly) || *US* ZOOL segador *m* (arachnid).

dado ['deidəu] *n* ARCH dado *m* (of a pedestal) | rodapié *m*, friso *m* (of a wall).

daedal ['di:dəl]; **daedalian** [-iən] *adj* ingenioso, sa; habilidoso, sa (skilful) || complejo, ja (intricate).

Daedalus ['di:dələs] *pr n* MYTH Dédalo *m*.

daemon ['di:mən] *n* ⟶ **demon.**

daffodil ['dæfədil] *n* BOT narciso *m*.

daffy ['dæfi] *adj* *US* FAM chalado, da; chiflado, da.

daft [dɑ:ft] *adj* FAM tonto, ta || *to go daft over* chiflarse por.

daftness [-nis] *n* FAM chifladura *f*.

dagger ['dægə*] *n* daga *f*, puñal *m* (weapon) || PRINT obelisco *m* || — FIG *to be at daggers drawn* estar a matar | *to look daggers at s.o.* fulminar a alguien con la mirada.

dago ['deigəu] *n* término despectivo aplicado a españoles, portugueses e italianos.

daguerreotype [də'gerəutaip] *n* daguerrotipo *m*.

dahlia ['deiljə] *n* BOT dalia *f* (plant, flower).

Dahoman [də'həumən] *adj/n* dahomeyano, na.

Dahomey [də'həumi] *pr n* GEOGR Dahomey *m*.

daily ['deili] *adj* diario, ria; cotidiano, na || — FAM *daily dozen* ejercicios *m pl* matinales || REL *our daily bread* el pan nuestro de cada día.

◆ *adv* diariamente, a diario, cada día.

◆ *n* diario *m* (newspaper) || asistenta *f* (charwoman).

daintily ['deintili] *adv* delicadamente || elegantemente || de una manera refinada, finamente.

daintiness ['deintinis] *n* delicadeza *f* (delicacy) || elegancia *f* || remilgos *m pl* (squeamishness).

dainty ['deinti] *n* bocado *m* exquisito.

◆ *adj* delicado, da; fino, na (taste) || exquisito, ta; delicado, da (food) || delicado, da; difícil (fussy) || elegante, primoroso, sa (delicately pretty) || precioso, sa (lovely) || remilgado, da (affected).

dairy ['dɛəri] *n* vaquería *f* (part of a farm) || lechería *f* (where milk, cheese and butter are sold) || — *dairy cattle* vacas lecheras || *dairy farm* granja *f* de vacas || *dairy products* productos lácteos.

dairymaid [-meid] *n* lechera *f*.

dairyman [-mən] *n* lechero *m*.

— OBSERV El plural de *dairyman* es *dairymen*.

dais ['deiis] *n* tarima *f*, estrado *m*.

daisy ['deizi] *n* margarita *f* (flower) || FIG perla *f*, joya *f* (pearl) || — SP *daisy cutter* pelota *f* rasante || FIG & FAM *to push up daisies* criar malvas (to be dead).

daisywheel [-wi:l] *adj* INFORM de margarita; *daisywheel printer* impresora de margarita.

Dakar ['dækɑ:*] *pr n* GEOGR Dakar.

Dalai Lama ['dælai'lɑ:mə] *pr n* REL Dalai Lama *m*.

dale [deil] *n* valle *m*.

Dalesman ['deilzmən] *n* habitante de una región con valles, situada en el norte de Inglaterra y llamada «the Dales».

— OBSERV El plural de esta palabra es *Dalesmen*.

Dallas ['dæləs] *pr n* GEOGR Dallas.

dalliance ['dæliəns] *n* flirteo *m*, coqueteo *m* (flirting) || frivolidad *f* (trifling).

dally ['dæli] *vi* flirtear, coquetear (amorously) || remolonear (to loiter) || perder el tiempo (to waste time) || juguetear (to play) || entretenerse (with an idea) || FIG burlarse, reírse (*with* de) | tomar a la ligera (to take lightly).

◆ *vt* *to dally the time away* perder el tiempo.

Dalmatia [dæl'meiʃjə] *pr n* GEOGR Dalmacia *f*.

Dalmatian [-n] *adj* dálmata (from Dalmatia).

◆ *n* dálmata *m* & *f* (person) || dálmata *m* (dog).

dalmatic [dæl'mætik] *n* dalmática *f*.

daltonian [dɔl'təuniən] *adj/n* daltoniano, na.

daltonism ['dɔltənizəm] *n* MED daltonismo *m*.

dam [dæm] *n* dique *m* (barrier across a water flow) || presa *f*, embalse *m* (a reservoir of water) || madre *f* (female parent of animals).

dam [dæm] *vt* embalsar, represar (water) || construir un dique en (a river) || construir una presa sobre (a lake, etc.) || FIG *to dam up* poner un dique a, contener.

damage ['dæmidʒ] *n* daño *m*; *the damage caused by hail* el daño causado por el granizo || FIG perjuicio *m* || FIG & FAM *what's the damage?* ¿cuánto le debo?

◆ *pl* JUR daños *m* y perjuicios.

damage ['dæmidʒ] *vt* dañar (to harm) || estropear (to spoil) || FIG perjudicar.

◆ *vi* dañarse.

damageable [-əbl] *adj* que se puede dañar.

damaging [-iŋ] *adj* perjudicial.

Damascene ['dæməsi:n] *adj* damasceno, na; damasquino, na || *Damascene work* damasquinado *m*.

◆ *n* damasceno, na.

damascene ['dæməsi:n] *vt* damasquinar.

Damascus [də'mɑ:skəs] *pr n* GEOGR Damasco || REL *road to Damascus* camino *m* de Damasco.

damask ['dæməsk] *adj* adamascado, da; damascado, da; damasquino, na (linen) || de color *m* rosa de Damasco || damasquino, na (metal).

◆ *n* damasco *m* (linen) || acero *m* damasquino *or* de Damasco || damasquinado *m* (Damascene work).

damask ['dæməsk]; **damaskeen** [-:n] *vt* damasquinar (to damascene) || adamascar (to weave patterns into a fabric).

dame [deim] *n* dama *f* || *US* FAM mujer *f* (woman) || FAM *an old dame* una señora de edad.

— OBSERV El título de *dame* se concede a las mujeres que tienen ciertas condecoraciones.

dammit! ['dæmit] *interj* FAM ¡córcholis!, ¡mecachis!

damn [dæm] *n* FAM *I don't give* o *I don't care a damn* no me importa un comino, me trae sin cuidado | *it's not worth a damn* no vale un comino.

◆ *adj* FAM maldito, ta; *that damn car* ese maldito coche.

◆ *adv* FAM muy; *it's damn good* está muy bien.

damn [dæm] *vt* condenar (to condemn) || maldecir (to curse) || FIG echar a perder || — FAM *damn!, damn it!* ¡córcholis!, ¡mecachis! | *I'll be damned if I know* no tengo la menor idea de eso | *it is as near to lying as damn is to swearing*

si no es una mentira se le parece mucho | *well, I'm damned!* ¡mecachis!
◆ *vi* soltar tacos (to swear).

damnable ['dæmnəbl] *adj* condenable (deserving condemnation) || detestable (detestable) || molesto, ta; fastidioso, sa (annoying).

damnation [dæm'neiʃən] *n* REL condenación *f* || FIG crítica *f* mordaz, vapuleo *m* (of a play, un author, etc.).
◆ *interj* ¡maldición!

damnatory ['dæmnətəri] *adj* condenatorio, ria || FIG abrumador, ra; irrecusable (evidence).

damned [dæmd] *adj* condenado, da (doomed) || condenado, da; réprobo, ba (condemned to eternal punishment) || FAM maldito, ta; *that damned boy* ¡ese maldito niño! | tremendo, da; *a damned lie* una mentira tremenda || *to do one's damnedest* hacer lo humanamente posible.
◆ *n* REL *the damned* los réprobos, los condenados.
◆ *adv* sumamente || *it's damned cold!* ¡hace un frío horrible *or* terrible!

damnify ['dæmnifai] *vt* damnificar, perjudicar.

damning ['dæmiŋ] *adj* irrecusable (proof) || mortal (sin).

Damocles ['dæməkli:z] *pr n* Damocles; *Damocles' sword* espada de Damocles.

damp [dæmp] *adj* húmedo, da.
◆ *n* humedad *f* (moisture) || MIN mofeta *f* (in general) | grisú *m* (firedamp) || FIG desánimo *m*, desaliento *m* (depression) || *damp course* aislante hidrófugo (in a wall).

damp [dæmp]; **dampen** [dæmpən] *vt* humedecer (to moisten) || mojar (to wet) || PHYS amortiguar || MUS amortiguar, apagar || FIG desanimar, desalentar, descorazonar (to discourage) | cortar (the appetite) | disminuir (ardour, zeal) || — *to damp down* sofocar, apagar (a fire) || FIG *to damp s.o.'s spirits* desanimar *or* desalentar a alguien.
◆ *vi* humedecerse (to moisten) || mojarse (to get wet) || amortiguarse (waves, sounds, etc.) || AGR *to damp off* pudrir por exceso de humedad.

dampener [-ənə*] *n* amortiguador *m*.

damper ['dæmpə*] *n* MUS sordina *f*, apagador *m* || humedecedor *m*, humectador *m* (for moistening stamps, envelopes, etc.) || regulador *m* de tiro (for chimney) || TECH registro *m* || PHYS amortiguador *m* || FAM aguafiestas *m inv* (person) | chasco *m* (disappointment) || FIG *to put a damper on* apagar (the enthusiasm), caer como un jarro de agua fría en (a gathering), frenar (the economy).

damping ['dæmpiŋ] *n* humedecimiento *m* || PHYS amortiguación *f*, amortiguamiento *m*.

dampish ['dæmpiʃ] *adj* algo húmedo, ligeramente húmedo.

dampness ['dæmpnis] *n* humedad *f*.

damsel ['dæmzəl] *n* damisela *f*.

damson ['dæmzən] *n* BOT ciruela *f* damascena (fruit) | ciruelo *m* damasceno (tree).

Danaids [dæ'neiidz] *pr n* MYTH Danaides *f*.

dance [dɑ:ns] *n* baile *m* || danza *f* (ritual or tribal); *sword dance* danza de las espadas || — *dance band* orquesta *f* de baile || *dance floor* pista *f* de baile || *dance hall* sala *f* de baile || *dance music* música *f* de baile || *dance of death* danza de la muerte || MED *St Vitus's dance* baile de San Vito || FIG *to lead s.o. a dance* traerle a uno al retortero.

dance [dɑ:ns] *vi/vt* bailar || FIG saltar, bailar, danzar || — *shall we dance?* ¿bailas?, ¿quieres bailar? || *to dance on points* bailar de puntas || FIG *to dance to another tune* mudar de tono.

dancer [-ə*] *n* bailarín, ina (professional dancer) || bailaor, ra (of flamenco) || persona *f* que baila.

dancing [-iŋ] *adj* de baile; *dancing partner* pareja de baile || *dancing girl* corista *f*.
◆ *n* baile *m*.

dandelion ['dændilaiən] *n* BOT diente *m* de león.

dander ['dændə*] *n* caspa *f* (dandruff) || US FAM malhumor *m* (temper) | rabia *f* (anger) || — US FAM *to get one's dander up* salir de sus casillas | *to get s.o.'s dander up* sacar a alguien de sus casillas.

dandify ['dændifai] *vt* acicalar, poner de tiros largos.

dandle ['dændl] *vt* hacer saltar sobre las rodillas (a child) || mimar (to caress).

dandruff ['dændrʌf] *n* caspa *f* (in hair).

dandy ['dændi] *n* dandi *m*, dandy *m*, petimetre *m* (man) || MAR balandra *f* || carro *m* del lechero (cart).
◆ *adj* US excelente (very good) | muy elegante (smart).

dandyish ['dændiiʃ] *adj* elegantón, ona.

Dane [dein] *n* danés, esa || ZOOL *great dane* perro danés.

danger ['deindʒə*] *n* peligro *m* || — *danger* peligro de muerte (sign) || *danger list* estado *m* crítico; *to be on a danger list* estar en estado crítico || *danger money* prima *f* or plus *m* de peligrosidad || *danger signal* señal *f* de peligro || *danger zone* área de peligro *or* peligrosa || *in danger of* en peligro de || *no danger of* no hay peligro de || *to be out of danger* estar fuera de peligro.

dangerous ['deindʒərəs] *adj* peligroso, sa.

dangle ['dæŋgl] *vt* balancear en el aire (to swing) || colgar, dejar colgado (to hang) || FIG hacer brillar, dejar entrever (to let see).
◆ *vi* balancearse (to swing) || colgar (to hang) || — FIG *to dangle after* ir tras de | *to keep s.o. dangling* tener a alguien pendiente.

Danish ['deiniʃ] *n* danés *m* (language).
◆ *adj* danés, esa || *Danish pastry* brioche *m* danés, bollo *m* con pasas.

dank [dæŋk] *adj* malsano y húmedo (damp) || que huele a humedad (which smells damp).

dankness [-nis] *n* humedad *f* || olor *m* a humedad.

danse macabre ['dɑ:nsmækɑ:br] *n* danza *f* macabra.

Dantean [dæn'ti:ən]; **Dantesque** [dæn'tesk] *adj* dantesco, ca.

Danube ['dænju:b] *pr n* GEOGR Danubio *m*.

dap [dæp] *n* rebote *m* (of a ball) || muesca *f* (in wood).

dap [dæp] *vt* hacer rebotar (a ball) || hacer muescas en (wood).
◆ *vi* rebotar (ball, stone) || zambullirse (bird).

Daphne [dæfni] *pr n* Dafne *f*.

Daphnis ['dæfnis] *pr n* Dafnis *m*.

dapper ['dæpə*] *adj* atildado, da; apuesto, ta (spruce) || vivo, va (active).

dapple ['dæpl] *n* moteado *m*.

dapple ['dæpl] *vt* motear.
◆ *vi* motearse (skin) || aborregarse (sky).

dappled [-d] *adj* moteado, da (horse).

dapple-grey ['dæpl'grei] *adj* tordo, da (horse).

Dardanelles [,dɑ:də'nelz] *pl prn* GEOGR Dardanelos *m*.

dare [dɛə*] *n* desafío *m*, reto *m* (challenge); *to take a dare* aceptar un reto.

dare [dɛə*] *vt* desafiar; *to dare s.o. to do sth.* desafiar a alguien a hacer algo || desafiar, arrostrar (to face) || atreverse a; *how dare you say that?* ¿cómo se atreve a decir eso? || *I dare say* a mi parecer (in my opinion), quizás, tal vez (perhaps).
◆ *vi* atreverse, osar.
— OBSERV Además del pretérito regular *dared*, el verbo *to dare* tiene una forma antigua, *durst*.

daredevil [-,devl] *adj/n* temerario, ria; atrevido, da.

daredevilry [-ri]; US **daredeviltry** [-tri] *n* temeridad *f*, audacia *f*, atrevimiento *m*.

daresay ['dɛə'sei] *vt/vi* US *I daresay* a mi parecer; quizás.

daring ['dɛəriŋ] *adj* atrevido, da; osado, da.
◆ *n* atrevimiento *m*, osadía *f*.

Darius [də'raiəs] *pr n* Darío *m*.

dark [dɑ:k] *adj* oscuro, ra; obscuro, ra; *dark room* habitación oscura; *dark green* verde oscuro || moreno, na (hair, complexion) || negro, gra (race) || FIG amenazador, ra (threatening) | triste, sombrío, a; *the dark days of winter* los tristes días de invierno | sombrío, a; negro, gra (the future) | oculto, ta; *dark practices* actividades ocultas | enigmático, ca; misterioso, sa (mysterious) | tenebroso, sa (designs) | oscuro, ra; obscuro, ra (a prophecy) | ignorante || FAM siniestro, tra; *he is a dark one* es un tipo siniestro || — *Dark Ages* Edad *f* de las tinieblas, primeros años de la Edad Media || *dark glasses* gafas *f pl* oscuras || FIG *keep it dark!* ¡no digas nada! || *the Dark Continent* el Continente Negro || FIG *to be a dark horse* no ser favorito, ser un «outsider» (horse), tenérselo bien callado (person) || *to become o to get o to grow dark* anochecer, hacerse de noche (at nightfall), oscurecerse (room, etc.).
◆ *n* oscuridad *f*, obscuridad *f* (absence of light) || noche *f* (night) || sombra *f* (in painting) || — *after dark* después del anochecer || *at dark* al anochecer, al caer la noche || FIG *leap in the dark* salto *m* en el vacío || *to be in the dark* estar a oscuras || *to be left in the dark* quedarse a oscuras || FIG *to keep s.o. in the dark* ocultarle algo a uno.

darken ['dɑ:kən] *vt* oscurecer || poner moreno (the complexion) || FIG entristecer (to sadden) | ensombrecer (the future) | nublar, oscurecer (s.o.'s mind) || FAM *not to darken s.o.'s door* no poner los pies en casa de alguien.
◆ *vi* oscurecerse || ponerse moreno (complexion) || FIG ponerse negro *or* sombrío (future) | oscurecerse, nublarse (mind).

darkie ['dɑ:ki] *n* FAM negro, gra.

darkish ['dɑ:kiʃ] *adj* que tira a oscuro || que tira a moreno (hair) || US FAM negro, gra (person).

darkle ['dɑ:kəl] *vi* oscurecerse (to darken) || ocultarse (to hide).

darkling [dɑ:kliŋ] *adj* oscuro, ra.
◆ *adv* a oscuras.

darkly ['dɑ:kli] *adv* tristemente (gloomily) || misteriosamente (mysteriously).

darkness ['dɑ:knis] *n* oscuridad *f* || — *Prince of Darkness* Ángel *m* de las tinieblas || *to be in darkness* estar a oscuras || *to cast s.o. into outer darkness* condenar a uno a las penas del infierno.

darkroom ['dɑ:krum] *n* PHOT cámara *f* oscura.

darling ['dɑ:liŋ] *adj/n* querido, da; *my darling David* mi querido David || — *a darling little house* una monada *or* una preciosidad de casa || *he is a darling* es un encanto || *mother's darling, spoilt darling* niño mimado || *yes, darling* sí, querido; sí, querida.

darn [dɑ:n] *adj* FAM maldito, ta; *that darn car* ¡ese maldito coche!
◆ *adv* muy, sumamente.

◆ *n* zurcido *m* (mended hole) || FAM comino *m*; *I don't give a darn* me importa un comino.
◆ *interj* FAM *darn it!* ¡córcholis!, ¡mecachis!

darn [dɑːn] *vt* zurcir (to mend) || ⟶ **damn.**

darned [-d] *adj* zurcido, da (mended) || FAM maldito, ta (damned).

darnel ['dɑːnl] *n* BOT cizaña *f*.

darner ['dɑːnə*] *n* huevo *m* de madera para zurcir (ball) || aguja *f* de zurcir (needle) || zurcidor, ra (person).

darning [dɑːniŋ] *n* zurcido *m* || *darning needle* aguja *f* de zurcir.

dart [dɑːt] *n* dardo *m* (pointed missile) || movimiento *m* rápido (swift movement) || punzada *f* (of pain) || pinza *f* (in dressmaking) || SP lanzamiento *m* || lengua *f*, résped *m*, réspede *m* (of snake) || aguijón *m* (of insects) || *to make a dart for the door* precipitarse hacia la puerta.
◆ *pl* dardos *m* (game).

dart [dɑːt] *vt* lanzar.
◆ *vi* precipitarse (*for* hacia) || FIG *to dart away* salir como una flecha, salir disparado.

dartboard [-bɔːd] *n* blanco *m* (target).

dartre ['dɑːtə*] *n* MED herpes *m pl* & *f pl*.

dartrous ['dɑːtrəs] *adj* MED herpético, ca.

Darwinian [dɑː'winiən] *adj* darwiniano, na.

Darwinism ['dɑːwinizəm] *n* darvinismo *m*.

dash [dæʃ] *n* choque *m*; *the dash of oars striking the water* el choque de los remos con el agua || romper *m* (breaking); *the dash of the waves on the rocks* el romper de las olas contra las rocas || carrera *f* (rush) || raya *f* (in telegraphy) || PRINT guión *m* (small) | raya *f* (large) || CULIN poco *m*, gotas *f pl* (of brandy, etc.); *tea with a dash of milk* té con un poco de leche | pizca *f*, poco *m* (of garlic, vanilla) | chorrito *m* (of vinegar) || SP carrera *f* corta de velocidad (sprint) || plumada *f*, trazo *m* (with a pen) || pincelada *f*, toque *m* (of an artist) || brochazo *m* (of a decorator) || AUT salpicadero *m* (instrument panel) | guardabarros *m inv* (mudguard) || FIG garbo *m* (grace) | brío *m* (verve) | empuje *m*, dinamismo *m*, energía *f* (drive) || — *a dash of colour* una nota de color || *at a dash* de un golpe || FIG *to cut a dash* ser elegante (to be smart), darse pisto (to make a display of o.s.), causar sensación (to cause sensation), hacer buen papel (to do well) || *to make a dash at* lanzarse sobre (the enemy) || *to make a dash for* precipitarse hacia; *to make a dash for the exit* precipitarse hacia la salida || *to make a dash for it* huir precipitadamente; *the thieves made a dash for it* los ladrones huyeron precipitadamente || *you'll have to make a dash for it* tendréis que correr.
◆ *interj* ¡demonios!

dash [dæʃ] *vt* estrellar, romper (to shatter) || chocar (to knock) || tirar, lanzar, arrojar (to throw violently) || salpicar (*with* de) (to splash) || CULIN sazonar (with spices) | mezclar, cortar (with water) || realzar (with colour) || FIG defraudar (hopes) | desanimar (to dishearten) || — *to dash sth. to pieces* hacer algo pedazos || *to dash to the ground* tirar al suelo (objects), echar por tierra (argument).
◆ *vi* ir de prisa (people and vehicles) || precipitarse (to rush) || chocar (*into* contra).
◆ *phr v* ***to dash against*** estrellarse contra, romperse contra; *the waves dashed against the cliff* las olas se rompían contra el acantilado | lanzar contra || ***to dash along*** ir corriendo || ***to dash at*** lanzarse sobre || ***to dash away*** irse corriendo | quitar rápidamente (to remove) || ***to dash by*** o ***past*** pasar corriendo; *the thief dashed past* el ladrón pasó corriendo || ***to dash down*** tirar al suelo (to throw on the floor) | anotar (to write down) || ***to dash in*** entrar precipitadamente || ***to dash off*** escribir deprisa; *he dashed off a letter* escribió una carta deprisa | hacer muy deprisa; *he dashed off his homework* hizo sus deberes muy deprisa | irse corriendo; *he dashed off* se fue corriendo || ***to dash out*** salir precipitadamente || ***to dash up*** llegar corriendo; *the boy dashed up to the door* el niño llegó corriendo a la puerta | subir corriendo; *to dash up the stairs* subir las escaleras corriendo.

dashboard [-bɔːd] *n* salpicadero *m* (instrument panel) || US guardabarros *m inv* (mudguard).

dasher [dæʃə*] *n* batidor *m*, paleta *f* (in a churn) || FAM presuntuoso, sa; farolero, ra || US AUT guardabarros *m inv*.

dashing ['dæʃiŋ] *adj* fogoso, sa (horse) || garboso, sa; gallardo, da (debonair) || elegante, apuesto, ta (elegant) || dinámico, ca; enérgico, ca (spirited) || presuntuoso, sa (showy).

dastard ['dæstəd] *n* cobarde *m* (coward).

dastardly [-li] *adj* cobarde (cowardly) || ruin, vil (crime).

DAT *abbr of* *[Digital audio tape]* cinta de audio digital.

data ['deitə] *pl n* ⟶ **datum** || datos *m*; *we need more data* necesitamos más datos || INFORM dato *m* || — INFORM *data bank* banco *m* de datos | *data carrier* soporte *m* de datos | *data entry* o *input* entrada *f* de datos | *data flow* flujo *m* de datos | *data handling capacity* capacidad *f* de proceso *or* de tratamiento | *data medium* soporte *m* de datos | *data processing* informática *f* (science), proceso *m or* procesamiento *m* de datos, tratamiento *m* de la información *or* de datos; *data processing system* sistema *m* de proceso de datos.

date [deit] *n* fecha *f*; *what is today's date?* ¿cuál es la fecha de hoy?; *to put the date on a letter* poner la fecha en una carta || época *f*; *of medieval date* de época medieval || COMM plazo *m* || BOT dátil *m* (fuit) | datilero *m* (tree) || cita *f*; *to have a date* tener una cita || US novio *m*, novia *f*; amigo, ga || — *at an early date* en fecha próxima || *date of birth* fecha *f* de nacimiento || *final* o *closing date* fecha tope || *on a fixed date* a fecha fija || *out of date* anticuado, da; pasado de moda (old fashioned) || *to be up to date* ser moderno (modern), estar al día (facts, etc.) || *to be up to date in one's work* estar al día en el trabajo, tener el trabajo al día || *to be up to date on the news* estar al corriente de las noticias || *to bring s.o. up to date* poner a alguien al corriente | *to bring sth. up to date* poner algo al día || *to date, up to date* hasta la fecha || *to make a date* citarse, darse cita || *to make a date with* citar, dar cita || *who is your date?* ¿con quién sales?

date [deit] *vt* datar, fechar (to write a date on, to assign a date to) || dar cita, citar (to make an appointment with) || salir con; *she has been dating him for a long time* sale con él desde hace mucho tiempo || *to date back* antedatar.
◆ *vi* datar; *a friendship dating from before the war* una amistad que data de antes de la guerra || poner la fecha || quedar anticuado (to become old-fashioned) || *to date back to* remontarse a.

dated ['deitid] *adj* fechado, da (bearing a date) || anticuado, da (old-fashioned).

dateless ['deitlis] *adj* sin fecha (undated) || inmemorial (very ancient) || eterno, na (everlasting).

dateline ['deitlain] *n* fecha *f* (in a letter, etc.).

date line ['deitlain] *n* meridiano *m* de cambio de fecha.

date palm ['deitpɑːm] *n* BOT palmera *f* datilera.

date stamp ['deitstæmp] *n* fechador *m*.

dation ['deiʃən] *n* JUR dación *f*.

dative ['deitiv] *adj* GRAMM dativo, va || JUR dativo, va; *tutor dative* tutor dativo.
◆ *n* GRAMM dativo *m*; *in the dative* en dativo.

datum ['deitəm] *n* dato *m* (known fact) || — *datum line* línea *f* de referencia || *datum point* punto *m* de referencia.
— OBSERV El plural de la palabra *datum* es *data*.

daub [dɔːb] *n* revestimiento *m* (coating) || mancha *f* (smear) || pintarrajo *m*, mamarracho *m* (unskilfully painted picture).

daub [dɔːb] *vt* revestir (con) (to coat) || embadurnar (to smear) || pintarrajear (to paint unskifully).
◆ *vi* pintarrajear.

dauber [-ə*]; **daubster** ['dɔːbstə*] *n* embadurnador, ra (who smears) || pintamonas *m* & *f inv* (poor painter).

dauby [-i] *adj* pegajoso, sa (sticky) || embadurnado, da (smeared) || pintarrajeado, da (poorly painted).

daughter ['dɔːtə*] *n* hija *f*.

daughter-in-law ['dɔːtərinlɔ] *n* nuera *f*, hija *f* política.
— OBSERV El plural es *daughters-in-law*.

daughterly ['dɔːtəli] *adj* filial.

daunt [dɔːnt] *vt* intimidar (to intimidate) || desanimar, desalentar (to dishearten).

daunting [-iŋ] *adj* desalentador, ra.

dauntless [-lis] *adj* intrépido, da.

dauphin ['dɔːfin] *n* delfín *m*.

dauphine ['dɔːfiːn]; **dauphiness** [-is] *n* delfina *f*.

davenport ['dævnpɔːt] *n* escritorio *m* pequeño (small writing desk) || US sofá cama *m*.

davit ['dævit] *n* MAR pescante *m*.

Davy Jone's locker ['deivi'dʒəunz'lɔkə*] *n* FIG fondo *m* del mar [en cuanto hace de tumba].

Davy lamp ['deivilæmp] *n* MIN lámpara *f* de seguridad.

daw [dɔː] *n* ZOOL chova *f* (bird).

dawdle ['dɔːdl] *vt* *to dawdle away* malgastar (time).
◆ *vi* holgazanear (to loiter) || andar despacio (to walk slowly) || perder el tiempo (to waste time).

dawdler [-ə*] *n* holgazán, ana (lazy person) || persona *f* que anda despacio, rezagado, da (slow walker).

dawn [dɔːn] *n* alba *m*, aurora *f*, amanecer *m* (daybreak) || FIG alborear *m*, albores *m pl*; *the dawn of civilization* los albores de la civilización || — *at dawn* al alba || *dawn breaks* raya el alba || *dawn chorus* canto *m* de los pájaros al amanecer || *to work from dawn to dusk* trabajar de sol a sol.

dawn [dɔːn] *vi* amanecer, alborear (to begin to grow light) || FIG esbozarse (a smile) || — FIG *a new era has dawned* ha nacido una nueva era | *then it dawned on me* entonces caí en la cuenta.

day [dei] *n* día *m*; *all day* todo el día; *every day* todos los días; *the day we were maried* el dia en que nos casamos; *a few days after I met him* a los pocos días de conocerle, pocos días después de conocerle; *it's not his day today* hoy no es su día || jornada *f* (of work); *a six hour day* una jornada de seis horas || fiesta *f*; *Labour Day* Fiesta del Trabajo || época *f*; *the best singer of his day* el mejor cantante de su época || tiempo *m* (time) || — *all day long* durante todo el día, todo el santo día || *another day, some other day* otro día | *any day* cualquier día || *at the close of the day* al caer el día || *by day* de día || *by the day* al día; a jornal (to work) || *day after day, day in day out* día tras día || *day and night*

día y noche || *day by day* día a día || *day off* día libre, día de descanso || *day of obligation* día de precepto || *day of reckoning* día de ajustar cuentas (for settling accounts), día del Juicio Final (Last Judgment) || *every other day* cada dos días, un día sí y otro no || *from day to day* de día en día (gradually), al día; *to live from day to day* vivir al día || *from one day to the next* de un día al otro || *from this day onward* de hoy en adelante || *good day!* ¡buenos días! || REL *holy day* fiesta *f* || *in his day* en sus tiempos || *in this day and age* en estos días, en la actualidad || FIG *it's all in a day's work* son gajes del oficio || *it was a black day for the country* fue un día aciago para el país || *it was broad day* era muy de día || *Mother's Day* día de la madre || *one day, one fine day* un día, un buen día || *some day* algún día || *the day after* al día siguiente || *the day after tomorrow* pasado mañana || *the day before* el día anterior || *the day before his death* la víspera de su muerte || *the day before yesterday* anteayer, antes de ayer || *the next day* al día siguiente, el día siguiente || *the next day but one* dos días después, a los dos días || *the other day* el otro día || *this day* hoy || *this day week* dentro de ocho días || *this very day* hoy mismo || *to a day* exactamente || FIG *to call it a day* dar por acabado el día, dejarlo || *to have had one's day* estar fuera de uso; haber pasado de moda || FIG *to know the time of day* saber cuántas son cinco | *tomorrow is another day* mañana será otro día | *to save for a rainy day* ahorrar para los momentos difíciles || *to take a day off* coger un día libre *or* un día de descanso || *to win the day* llevarse la palma, triunfar || *twice a day* dos veces al *or* por día || *working day* día laborable (weekday), jornada *f* (number of hours).
◆ *pl* días *m*; *her dancing days are over* sus días de bailarina se han acabado; *to the end of his days* hasta el fin de sus días || *days of grace* plazo *m* de respiro || *in the days of* en los días de || *it's early days yet* todavía es pronto || *one of these days* un día de éstos, uno de estos días || *these days* hoy en día || *to have seen better days* haber conocido días mejores.

daybed [-bed] *n* meridiana *f*.

daybook [-buk] *n* diario *m*.

day boy [-bɔi] *n* externo *m* (pupil).

daybreak [-breik] *n* amanecer *m*, alba *f*.

daydream [-driːm] *n* ensueño *m* (reverie) || ilusión *f* (a wish or plan not likely to be realized).

daydream [-driːm] *vi* soñar despierto.

daydreamer [-ˌdriːmə*] *n* soñador, ra.

day girl [-gəːl] *n* externa *f* (pupil).

day labourer; *US* **day laborer** [-ˈleibərə*] *n* jornalero *m*, peón *m*.

daylight [-lait] *n* luz *f* del día || luz *f* (open space) || amanecer *m*, alba *f* (dawn) || — *by daylight* de día (by day), a la luz del día (by the light of day) || *in broad daylight* en pleno día || *in daylight* a la luz del día || US *to burn daylight* perder el tiempo || FIG *to let daylight into s.o.* pegar un tiro a alguien | *to let in some daylight on a subject* aclarar un asunto | *to scare the (living) daylights out of s.o.* pegar un susto de muerte a alguien | *to see daylight* ver claro, llegar a comprender (to understand), ver la luz del día (to be published), ver el final de un trabajo (to conclude) | *to throw daylight on* aclarar (to clarify), sacar a luz (to disclose).

daylight robbery [-ˈrɔbəri] *n* FIG robo *m*, robo *m* a mano armada.

daylight-saving time [-laitˌseiviŋˈtaim] *n* hora *f* de verano.

daylong [-lɔŋ] *adj* que dura todo el día.
◆ *adv* todo el día.

day nursery [-ˈnəːsəri] *n* guardería *f* infantil.

day-old [-əuld] *adj* de un día; *a day-old baby* un niño de un día.

day return [-riˈtəːn] *n* billete *m* de ida y vuelta [en el mismo día].

days [deiz] *adv* de día.

day school [ˈdeiskuːl] *n* externado *m*, colegio *m* sin internado.

day shift [ˈdeiʃift] *n* turno *m* de día.

dayspring [ˈdeispriŋ] *n* aurora *f*, alba *f*.

daystar [ˈdeistɑː*] *n* lucero *m* del alba (Venus) || Sol *m* (the Sun).

daytime [ˈdeitaim] *n* día *m*; *in the daytime* de día.

day-to-day [ˈdeitəˈdei] *adj* cotidiano, na; *day-to-day life* vida cotidiana.

day trip [ˈdeitrip] *n* excursión *f* de un solo día.

daywork [ˈdeiwəːk] *n* trabajo *m* a jornal || trabajo *m* hecho en un día.

daze [deiz] *n* aturdimiento *m*; *to come out of one's daze* salir del aturdimiento || atolondramiento *m* (bewilderment) || deslumbramiento *m* (dazzle) || *in a daze* aturdido, da.

daze [deiz] *vt* aturdir (to stun) || atolondrar, atontar (to bewilder) || deslumbrar (to dazzle).

dazedly [-dli] *adv* con su aire atolondrado *or* atontado.

dazzle [ˈdæzl] *n* deslumbramiento *m* || resplandor *m* (brightness) || FIG deslumbramiento *m*.

dazzle [ˈdæzl] *vt/vi* deslumbrar; *dazzled by the headlights* deslumbrado por los faros || FIG deslumbrar; *the conjuror dazzled his audience* el prestidigitador deslumbró al público.

dazzling [-iŋ] *adj* deslumbrante, deslumbrador, ra; *a dazzling success* un éxito deslumbrante.
◆ *n* deslumbramiento *m*.

DDT [ˈdiːdiːˈtiː] *abbr of [dichlorodiphenyltrichloroethane]* DDT (insecticida).

deacon [ˈdiːkən] *n* diácono *m*.

deaconate [ˈdiːkənit] *n* diaconado *m*.

deaconess [ˈdiːkənis] *n* diaconisa *f*.

deaconry [ˈdiːkənri] *n* diaconato *m*, diaconado *m*.

deaconship [ˈdiːkənʃip] *n* diaconato *m*, diaconado *m*.

deactivate [diːˈæktiveit] *vt* desactivar.

dead [ded] *adj* muerto, ta; *to be dead* estar muerto; *dead city* ciudad muerta; *dead language* lengua muerta; *dead weight* peso muerto || difunto, ta; *the dead king* el difunto rey || absoluto, ta; *dead cert* certeza absoluta; *dead secret* secreto absoluto || absoluto, ta; completo, ta (silence, quietness) || insensible; *dead to remorse* insensible a los remordimientos || apagado, da (fire, colour, volcano, oven) || marchito, ta; seco, ca (leaf) || mate (gold) || sin vida (picture) || sordo, da (voice, ache, etc.); *dead sound* sonido sordo || estancado, da (water) || agotado, da (well, mine) || descargado, da (battery) || gastado, da (used); *dead matches* cerillas gastadas || anticuado, da (obsolete) || inerte; *dead matter* materia inerte || adormecido, da; entumecido, da (limb) || AGR improductivo, va; estéril (soil) || ARCH ciego, ga (arch, window) || FAM muerto, ta (very tired) || SP fuera de juego (ball) || ELECTR sin corriente, desconectado, da || inmóvil (part of machine) || COMM estancado, da (business) | ficticio, cia (account) | irrecuperable, incobrable (loan) | completo, ta; total (loss) | muerto, ta; improductivo, va (money) || JUR en desuso (law) | muerto, ta (letter) || — *dead and gone, dead and buried, dead as a doornail, dead as a mutton* muerto y bien muerto || FIG *dead duck* fracaso *m* seguro || *dead hours* horas muertas || *dead letters* cartas desechadas || *dead loss* pérdida *f* total (of money), nulidad *f*, birria *f* (things); *the film is a dead loss* la película es una birria; inútil *m* & *f*, nulidad *f* (person) || *dead man* muerto *m* || *dead march* marcha *f* fúnebre || FIG *dead men* cascos *m pl* de botella | *dead men tell no tales* los muertos no hablan || *dead shot* tiro certero (which hits the target), tirador certero (person) || *dead silence* silencio sepulcral *or* completo || FIG *dead spit* vivo retrato || *dead stop* parada *f* en seco || FAM *dead to the world* borracho perdido (drunk), como un leño (asleep) || *dead water* aguas muertas *or* mansas *or* estancadas || *dead woman* muerta *f* || FAM *drop dead!* ¡vete al cuerno! || *he has been dead 2 years* hace dos años que se murió || *I wouldn't be seen dead there* allí no se me ha perdido nada || *more dead than alive* más muerto que vivo || *on a dead level* a nivel, de nivel || FAM *over my dead body!* ¡ni hablar! || *the dead calm* o *still* la calma chicha || *the dead hours of night* la quietud de la noche || *the wire has gone dead* la línea está cortada || FAM *to be a dead ringer for s.o.* ser calcado a alguien || *to drop down dead* caerse muerto || *to fall dead* caer muerto; amainar (the wind) || *to give s.o. up for dead* dar por muerto a uno || *to go dead* dormirse, entumecerse (a limb), dejar de funcionar, cortarse (radio, phone, etc.) || *to strike* o *to kill s.o. (stone) dead* matar a uno || *wanted dead or alive* se busca vivo o muerto.
◆ *adv* FAM completamente (completely); *dead sure* completamente seguro || muy; *dead slow* muy lento || justo; *dead in the centre* justo en medio; *dead on time* justo a tiempo || — *dead tired* muerto de cansancio || *to be dead set against* estar resueltamente opuesto a || *to be dead set on sth.* estar empeñado en algo || *to stop dead* pararse en seco.
◆ *n* *in the dead of night* en plena noche || *in the dead of winter* en pleno invierno, en lo más recio del invierno || *the dead* los muertos || *the dead of night* el silencio de la noche || *to rise from the dead* resucitar de entre los muertos.

dead beat [ˈdedˈbiːt] *adj* FAM muerto, ta; rendido, da (exhausted).

deadbeat [ˈdedbiːt] *adj* TECH aperiódico, ca.
◆ *n* FIG & FAM gorrón, ona; aprovechado, da.

dead centre; *US* **dead center** [ˈdedˈsentə*] *n* TECH punto *m* muerto.

dead-drunk [ˈdedˈdrʌŋk] *adj* borracho perdido.

deaden [ˈdedn] *vt* amortiguar; *to deaden a sound, a blow* amortiguar un sonido, un golpe || calmar, aliviar; *to deaden pain* calmar el dolor || embotar (feeling) || insonorizar (a wall, etc.) || volver mate (gold) || disminuir (vitality).
◆ *vi* amortiguarse (sound, blow) || desbravarse (wine) || embotarse (sensibility) || disminuir (vitality).

dead end [ˈdedˈend] *n* callejón *m* sin salida (street with no exit, situation without solution).

dead-end [ˈdedˈend] *adj* sin salida (street) || barriobajero, ra (of the slums) || *dead-end job* trabajo *m* sin porvenir.

deadening [ˈdedniŋ] *adj* aislante (for walls, etc.).

deadeye [ˈdedai] *n* MAR vigota *f*.

deadfall [ˈdedfɔːl] *n* trampa *f*.

deadhead [ˈdedhed] *n* persona *f* que tiene pase (for the cinema, theatre, etc.).

dead heat [ˈdedˈhiːt] *n* empate *m*.

deadline [ˈdedlain] *n* fecha *f* tope, plazo *m*, límite *m*; *the deadline for the construction* la fecha tope para la construcción || US línea *f* vedada (of a prison) || *to meet one's deadline* respetar el plazo fijado.

dead load [ˈdedˈləud] *n* peso *m* muerto.

deadlock ['dedlɔk] *n* punto *m* muerto || TECH cerradura *f* con pestillo de golpe.

deadlock ['dedlɔk] *vt* llevar a un punto muerto.
◆ *vi* llegar a un punto muerto.

deadly ['dedli] *adj* mortal; *a deadly wound* una herida mortal; *deadly sin* pecado mortal; *deadly enemy* enemigo mortal || a muerte (fight) || absoluto, ta; *with deadly skill* con destreza absoluta || JUR abrumador, ra (evidence) || devastador, ra (critics) || nocivo, va; pernicioso, sa (habit, effect, etc.) || certero, ra (shot) || cadavérico, ca (pallor) || FAM fatal, terrible (very bad).
◆ *adv* extremadamente, terriblemente; *deadly boring* extremadamente aburrido.

deadly nightshade [-'naitʃeid] *n* belladona *f*, belladama *f*.

deadness ['dednis] *n* falta *f* de vida || color *m* mate (of gold) || COMM estancamiento *m* || entumecimiento *m* (of limb) || CULIN desbravación *f* (of wine).

deadpan ['dedpæn] *adj* FAM inexpresivo, va.

dead reckoning ['ded'rekniŋ] *n* AVIAT & MAR estima *f*.

Dead Sea ['ded'si:] *pr n* GEOGR mar *m* Muerto.

deadweight ['dedweit] *n* peso *m* muerto (weight of an inert mass) || MAR carga *f* máxima, peso *m* muerto || FIG lastre *m*, carga *f* (burden).

deadwood ['dedwud] *n* rama *f* muerta (dead branch) || persona *f or* cosa *f* inútil (useless person *or* thing) || mercancía *f* inservible || MAR durmientes *m pl*.

deaf [def] *adj* sordo, da; *he went deaf* se quedó sordo || FIG sordo, da || — *deaf and dumb* sordomudo, da || FAM *to be as deaf as a post* estar más sordo que una tapia || FIG *to turn a deaf ear* hacerse el sordo, no prestar oídos.
◆ *n the deaf* los sordos.

deaf-aid [-eid] *n* aparato *m* para sordos.

deaf-and-dumb [-ən'dʌm] *adj* sordomudo, da || *deaf-and-dumb alphabet* alfabeto *m* de los sordomudos.

deafen ['defn] *vt* ensordecer (to make deaf) || amortiguar (a sound) || ARCH insonorizar.

deafening [-iŋ] *adj* ensordecedor, ra.

deaf-mute ['def'mju:t] *adj/n* sordomudo, da.

deafness ['defnis] *n* sordera *f*.

deal [di:l] *n* reparto *m* (of cards) || vez *f*, turno *m* (a turn to distribute cards) || transacción *f*, negocio *m*, trato *m* (business transaction) || trato *m*, tratamiento *m* (treatment); *raw deal* trato injusto || convenio *m*, arreglo *m* (agreement) || cantidad *f* (large amount) || tablón *m*, madero *m* (board of wood) || pino *m*, abeto *m* (wood) || — *a good deal, a great deal* mucho, una gran cantidad || *it's a deal!* ¡trato hecho! || *square deal* trato equitativo *or* justo, justicia *f* || *to make a great deal of* dar importancia a (sth.), tener en mucho a (s.o.) || *your deal* tu vez, te toca.

deal [di:l*] *vt* repartir, distribuir (to distribute) || dar, repartir, distribuir (cards) || asestar, dar; *to deal s.o. a blow* asestarle un golpe a alguien.
◆ *vi* dar *or* repartir *or* distribuir las cartas.
◆ *phr v to deal by* comportarse *or* portarse con || *to deal in* comerciar en || *to deal out* repartir, distribuir || *to deal with* tratar con; *I deal with large business organizations* trato con grandes empresas || tratar a; *to deal justly with s.o.* tratar con justicia a alguien | comportarse *or* portarse con (to behave) | enfrentarse con (to meet a situation) | resolver (a difficulty) | tratar de *or* sobre (a subject) | ocuparse de, encargarse de; *I'll deal with him* yo me encargaré de él | castigar; *the murderer will be dealt with* el asesino será castigado | hacer sus compras en (one's regular tradesman).
— OBSERV Pret y pp ***dealt***.

dealer [-ə*] *n* negociante *m* & *f*, comerciante *m* & *f* (merchant) || mano *f* (in cards).

dealing [-iŋ] *n* trato *m* (treatment) || comportamiento *m*, conducta *f* (behaviour) || COMM comercio *m*.
◆ *pl* relaciones *f*, trato *m sing* || transacciones *f*.

dealt [delt] *pret/pp* → **deal.**

dean [di:n] *n* REL deán *m* || decano *m* (in university) || US decano *m* (senior member).

deanery ['di:nəri] *n* REL deanato *m*, deanazgo *m* (the office of dean) | residencia *f* del deán (residence) || decanato *m* (of university).

deanship ['di:nʃip] *n* REL deanato *m*, deanazgo *m* || decanato *m* (of university).

dear [diə*] *adj* querido, da; *dear Patrick* querido Patricio || costoso, sa; caro, ra (costly) || caro, ra; carero, ra (charging high prices) || sincero, ra; profundo, da (sincere) || FIG costoso, sa; *a dear victory* una victoria costosa || — *dear Madam* estimada Señora || *dear me!, oh dear!* ¡Dios mío! || *dear Sir* muy señor mío || *he is dear to me* le quiero mucho, le tengo mucho cariño || *it is dear to me* le tengo mucho cariño (jewel), lo aprecio mucho (place, idea) || *my dear George* querido Jorge || FAM *to run for dear life* correr desesperadamente.
◆ *adv* caro (dearly); *it will cost you dear* te va a costar caro || *to hold dear* querer (s.o.), apreciar.
◆ *n* querido, da; *my dear* querido mío || — *an old dear* una viejecita encantadora || *be a dear!* ¡sé bueno! || *he is such a dear* es un encanto.

dearest [-ist] *n* querido, da.

dearly [-li] *adv* cariñosamente (very affectionately) || caro; *it will cost you dearly* te va a costar caro || — *the peace we so dearly seek* la paz que tanto deseamos || *to love s.o. dearly* querer muchísimo a uno || *we would dearly love to know* nos encantaría saber.

dearness [-nis] *n* COMM carestía *f*, lo caro (of life, etc.) || afecto *m*, cariño *m* (love).

dearth [də:θ] *n* escasez *f*, carestía *f*.

deary ['diəri] *n* FAM querido, da.

death [deθ] *n* muerte *f*; *to die a violent death* morir de muerte violenta || defunción *f*, fallecimiento *m*; *to notify a death* notificar una defunción || FIG fin *m*, muerte *f*; *the death of all hopes* el fin de todas las esperanzas || — *a living death* una vida horrible || *Black Death* peste negra || *death to traitors!* ¡mueran los traidores! || *pale as death* pálido como un muerto || *proof of death* acta *f* de defunción || FAM *sick to death* hasta la coronilla || *to be at death's doors* estar a las puertas de la muerte || *to be death to* ser muy peligroso || FIG *to be the death of one* matarle a uno || *to be working o.s. to death* matarse trabajando || FAM *to catch one's death of cold* agarrar un constipado de campeonato | *to death* muerto de; *bored to death* muerto de aburrimiento || *to do to death* matar, dar muerte || *to hold on like grim death* agarrarse fuertemente (to hold on tightly), resistir firmemente (to resist) || *to put to death* matar, dar muerte (to kill), ejecutar, ajusticiar (to execute) || *to the death* hasta la muerte || *to work one's employees to death* matar a sus empleados trabajando || *wounded to the death* herido de muerte.
◆ *pl* necrología *f sing* (in newspaper).

deathbed [-bed] *n* lecho *m* de muerte || FAM *deathbed repentance* arrepentimiento *f* de última hora.

death bell [-bel] *n* tañido *m* fúnebre, toque *m* a muerto.

deathblow [-bləu] *n* golpe *m* mortal.

death certificate [-sə'tifikit] *n* certificado *m* de defunción, partida *f* de defunción.

death-dealing [-di:liŋ] *adj* mortífero, ra.

death duty [-,dju:ti] *n* derechos *m pl* de sucesión, impuesto *m* sobre sucesiones.

death house [-haus] *n* pabellón *m* de los condenados a muerte || *to be in the death house* estar en capilla.

death knell [-nel] *n* toque *m* a muerto || FIG golpe *m* de gracia.

deathless [-lis] *adv* inmortal.

deathlike [-laik] *adj* cadavérico, ca (face) || sepulcral (silence) || como muerto, inmóvil (person) || *to look deathlike* tener cara de muerto.

deathly [-li] *adj* mortal, de muerte, mortífero, ra (illness, wound, etc.) || sepulcral (silence) || cadavérico, ca (face).
◆ *adv* mortalmente || *deathly pale* más pálido que un muerto, pálido como un muerto.

death mask [-ma:sk] *n* mascarilla *f*.

death penalty [-,penəlti] *n* pena *f* de muerte.

death rate [-reit] *n* mortalidad *f*, índice *m* de mortalidad.

death rattle [-rætl] *n* estertor *m* de la muerte.

death roll [-rəul] *n* lista *f* de víctimas (list of dead persons) || número *m* de muertos; *the death roll stands at 87* el número de muertos asciende a 87 || MIL lista *f* de bajas.

death row [-rəu] *n* US galería *f* de los condenados a muerte.

death's-head [-shed] *n* calavera *f* (skull) || ZOOL mariposa *f* de la muerte.

death tax [-tæks] *n* derechos *m pl* de sucesión, impuesto *m* sobre sucesiones.

death toll [-təul] *n* número *m* de víctimas.

deathtrap [-træp] *n* lugar *m* peligroso (unsafe place).

death warrant [-,wɔrənt] *n* sentencia *f* de muerte.

deathwatch [-wɔtʃ] *n* velatorio *m* (watch over a dead person) || guardia *f* de un condenado a muerte || ZOOL *deathwatch beetle* reloj *m* de la muerte.

deb [deb] *n* FAM debutante *f*.

debacle; débacle [dei'ba:kl] *n* desastre *m* (collapse, disaster) || MIL derrota *f* || deshielo *m* (breaking-up of ice).

debar [di'ba:*] *vt* excluir (*from* de) || prohibir; *to debar s.o. from doing sth.* prohibir a alguien que haga algo || privar de (a right) || impedir (to prevent).

debase [di'beis] *vt* alterar (coinage) || desvalorizar (to devalue) || FIG degradar, rebajar.

debasement [-mənt] *n* alteración *f* (coinage) || FIG degradación *f*.

debatable [di'beitəbl] *adj* discutible (questionable) || en litigio; *debatable territory* territorio en litigio.

debate [di'beit] *n* discusión *f*, debate *m* (discusion) || controversia *f* (controversy) || — *open to debate* discutible || *the problem under debate* el problema que se está discutiendo.

debate [di'beit] *vt* discutir, debatir (a question) || controvertir, discutir (a statement) || considerar (to consider).
◆ *vi* discutir (*with* con).

debater [-ə*] *n* persona *f* que toma parte en una discusión *or* un debate || polemista *m* & *f*.

debating [-iŋ] *adj* controvertido, da; *debating point* punto controvertido || *debating society* asociación *f* que organiza debates.

debauch [di'bɔ:tʃ] *vt* corromper, pervertir ‖ seducir (a woman).
◆ *vi* pervertirse.

debauchee [ˌdebɔ:'tʃi:] *n* libertino, na.

debauchery [di'bɔ:tʃəri] *n* libertinaje *m*, disolución *f* (dissipation) ‖ corrupción *f*, perversión *f*; *debauchery of youth* corrupción de menores.

debenture [di'bentʃə*] *n* COMM obligación *f*.

debilitate [di'biliteit] *vt* debilitar.

debilitation [dibili'teiʃən] *n* debilitación *f*.

debility [di'biliti] *n* debilidad *f*.

debit ['debit] *n* débito *m* (entry of money owed) ‖ debe *m*, pasivo *m* (left-hand side of an account) ‖ — *debit balance* saldo *m* deudor ‖ *debit entry* débito ‖ *debit note* nota *f* de cargo.

debit ['debit] *vt* cargar en cuenta.

debonair; US **debonaire** [ˌdebə'nɛə*] *adj* jovial, alegre (cheerful) ‖ cortés, afable (polite) | agraciado, da (graceful) ‖ gallardo, da; garboso, sa (charming, elegant).

debouch [di'bautʃ] *vi* salir (to emerge) ‖ desembocar (river, street).

debouchment [-mənt] *n* salida *f* (emergence) ‖ desembocadura *f* (of a river, of a street).

debride [di'braid] *vt* MED desbridar.

debrief [di:'bri:f] *vt* interrogar.

debris ['debri:] *n* escombros *m pl* (broken remains) ‖ GEOL detritos *m pl*.

debt [det] *n* deuda *f*; *in debt to* en deuda con; *out of debt* libre de deudas; *public* o *national debt* deuda pública; *I was deeply in debt* tenía muchas deudas; *floating debt* deuda flotante; *consolidated* o *funded debts* deudas consolidadas ‖ — *bad debt* deuda incobrable *or* morosa ‖ *debt collector* cobrador, ra de deudas ‖ *debt of honour* deuda de honor ‖ *to be in s.o.'s debt* estar en deuda con uno ‖ *to run into debt* contraer deudas.

debtor ['detə*] *n* deudor, ra (person owing money) ‖ COMM debe *m* (in bookkeeping).

debunk [di:'bʌŋk] *vt* FAM desenmascarar (to unmask) | desacreditar, desprestigiar (to discredit).

début; US **debut** ['deibju:] *n* debut *m*, presentación *f* (first appearance) ‖ presentación *f* en sociedad, puesta *f* de largo (of girls) ‖ *to make one's début* ponerse de largo, ser presentada en sociedad (girl), hacer sus primeras armas (in a job), debutar (in the theatre).

débutante; US **debutante** ['debjuta:nt] *n* joven *f* que hace su presentación en sociedad, «debutante» *f*.

decade ['dekeid] *n* decenio *m* (ten years) ‖ década *f* (ten days) ‖ decena *f* (of a rosary).

decadence ['dekədəns] *n* decadencia *f*.

decadent ['dekədənt] *adj/n* decadente ‖ ARTS *the Decadents* los decadentes.

decaffeinate [di:'kæfi:neit]; **decaffeinize** [di:'kæfi:naiz] *vt* descafeinar.

decagon ['dekəgən] *n* MATH decágono *m*.

decagonal [de'kægənal] *adj* decagonal.

decagram; **decagramme** ['dekəgræm] *n* decagramo *m*.

decahedron [dekə'hi:drən] *n* MATH decaedro *m*.

decalcification [di:ˌkælsifi'keiʃən] *n* descalcificación *f*.

decalcify [di:'kælsifai] *vt* descalcificar ‖ *to become decalcified* descalcificarse.

decalcomania [diˌkælkə'meiniə] *n* calcomanía *f*.

decalitre; US **decaliter** ['dekəˌli:tə*] *n* decalitro *m* (measure of capacity).

Decalogue; US **decalog** ['dekəlɔg] *n* REL Decálogo *m*.

decametre; US **decameter** ['dekəˌmi:tə*] *n* decámetro *m*.

decamp [di'kæmp] *vi* FAM largarse, pirarse (to go away) ‖ MIL decampar, levantar el campo.

decant [di'kænt] *vt* decantar.

decantation [ˌdi:kæn'teiʃən] *n* decantación *f*.

decanter [di'kæntə*] *n* garrafa *f* ‖ TECH decantador *m*.

decanting [di'kæntiŋ] *n* decantación *f*.

decapitate [di'kæpiteit] *vt* decapitar (to behead).

decapitation [diˌkæpi'teiʃən] *n* decapitación *f*.

decapod ['dekəpɔd] *n* ZOOL decápodo *m*.

decarbonate [di:'ka:bəneit] *vt* CHEM descarbonatar.

decarbonization [di:'ka:bənai'zeiʃən] *n* TECH descarburación *f*.

decarbonize [di:'ka:bənaiz] *vt* descarburar.

decarbonizer [-ə*] *n* TECH descarburante *m*.

decarbonizing [-iŋ] *adj* TECH descarburante.
◆ *n* TECH descarburación *f*.

decarburization [di:ˌka:bjuərai'zeiʃən] *n* TECH descarburación *f*.

decarburize [di:'ka:bjuəraiz] *vt* TECH descarburar.

decarburizer [-ə*] *n* TECH descarburante *m*.

decarburizing [-iŋ] *adj* TECH descarburante.
◆ *n* TECH descarburación *f*.

decastere ['dekəsti:ə*] *n* diez estéreos *m pl*.

decasyllabic ['dekəsi'læbik]; **decasyllable** ['dekəsiləbl] *adj* decasílabo, ba.
◆ *n* decasílabo *m*.

decathlon [de'kæθlɔn] *n* SP decatlón *m*.

decay [di'kei] *n* caries *f* (of a tooth) ‖ descomposición *f* (descomposition) ‖ PHYS desintegración *f* progresiva (of radioactive materials) ‖ decadencia *f* (of morals, culture, country, etc.) ‖ ruina *f*, deterioro *m* (of buildings) ‖ debilitamiento *m* (of health, sight) ‖ disminución *f* (of sounds, etc.) ‖ marchitamiento *m* (of plants) ‖ putrefacción *f* (rotting) ‖ *to fall into decay* caer en ruinas.

decay [di'kei] *vi* cariarse (tooth) ‖ descomponerse (to descompose) ‖ PHYS desintegrarse (radioactive materials) ‖ decaer (morals, culture, country, etc.) ‖ deteriorarse (to deteriorate) ‖ caerse, caer en ruinas (buildings) ‖ debilitarse (health, sight) ‖ disminuir (sounds, etc.) ‖ marchitarse (plants) ‖ pudrirse (to rot) ‖ marchitarse (beauty) ‖ FIG desvanecerse (hope) | desaparecer (friendships).
◆ *vt* pudrir; *water decays wood* el agua pudre la madera ‖ cariar (tooth).

decease [di'si:s] *n* fallecimiento *m*, defunción *f*.

decease [di'si:s] *vi* morir, fallecer.

deceased [-t] *adj/n* difunto, ta.

deceit [di:si:t] *n* engaño *m* (cheating) ‖ decepción *f* (disappointment) ‖ fraude *m* (fraud) ‖ mentira *f* (lying) ‖ superchería *f* (crick).

deceitful [-ful] *adj* engañoso, sa (deceiving) ‖ fraudulento, ta (fraudulent) ‖ mentiroso, sa (lying) ‖ falso, sa (two-faced).

deceitfulness [-fulnis] *n* lo engañoso *m* ‖ falsedad *f*.

deceive [di'si:v] *vt* engañar ‖ defraudar (hopes) ‖ — *in my memory does not deceive me* si la memoria no me falla, si mal no recuerdo ‖ *to deceive o.s.* engañarse.

deceiver [-ə*] *n* embustero, ra.

deceiving [-iŋ] *adj* decepcionante, desilusionante (disappointing) ‖ engañoso, sa (deceptive).
◆ *n* deception *f*.

decelerate [di:'seləreit] *vt* aminorar *or* disminuir la velocidad de.
◆ *vi* ir más despacio, decelerar.

deceleration [di:ˌselə'reiʃən] *n* deceleración *f*, disminución *f* de la velocidad.

December [di'sembə*] *n* diciembre *m*; *December 25* o *25th* el 25 de diciembre.

decemvir [di'emvə*] *n* decenviro *m*.

decency ['di:snsi] *n* decencia *f*, decoro *m* ‖ decoro *m* (in language, behaviour, etc.).

decennary [di'senəri] *adj* decenal.
◆ *n* decenio *m*, decenario *m*.

decennial [di'senjəl] *adj* decenal.
◆ *n* décimo aniversario *m*.

decent ['di:snt] *adj* decente, decoroso, sa (observing propriety) ‖ razonable, decente (satisfactory); *decent wages* un sueldo decente ‖ FAM bueno, na; formal; *a decent chap* un buen chico | amable, simpático, ca; *to be decent to s.o.* ser amable con alguien | visible, presentable (not naked).

decentralization [di:ˌsentrəlai'zeiʃən] *n* descentralización *f*.

decentralize [di:'sentrəlaiz] *vt* descentralizar.

decentralizing [-iŋ] *adj* descentralizador, ra.

decentre [di:'sentə*] *vt* PHYS descentrar.

deception [di'sepʃən] *n* engaño *m*.

deceptive [di'septiv] *adj* engañoso, sa.

deceptiveness [-nis] *n* apariencia *f* engañosa.

dechristianization [di:ˌkristjənai'zeiʃən] *n* descristianización *f*.

dechristianize [di:'kristjənaiz] *vt* descristianizar.

decibel ['desibel] *n* PHYS decibel *m*, decibelio *m*.

decide [di'said] *vt* decidir ‖ resolver (a conflict).
◆ *vi* decidir ‖ *to decide on* o *upon* decidir (sth. being done), determinar, fijar (a line of action), optar por (to choose).

decided [-id] *adj* decidido, da; resuelto, ta; determinado, da (determined) ‖ marcado, da (difference) ‖ determinado, da; claro, ra (opinion) ‖ indudable (undeniable) ‖ categórico, ca; tajante (refusal).

decidedly [-li] *adv* decididamente, sin duda.

decidedness [di'saididnis] *n* determinación *f*.

deciding [di'saidiŋ] *adj* decisivo, va ‖ *deciding vote* voto *m* decisivo.

decidua [di'sidjuə] *n* ANAT membrana *f* caduca.
— OBSERV El plural de *decidua* es *deciduae*.

deciduous [di'sidjuəs] *adj* caduco, ca (leaf) ‖ de hoja caduca (tree) ‖ FIG efímero, ra.

decigram, decigramme ['desigræm] *n* decigramo *m*.

decilitre; US **deciliter** ['desiˌli:tə*] *n* decilitro *m*.

decimal ['desiməl] *adj* decimal ‖ — *decimal fraction* fracción *f* decimal ‖ *decimal point* coma *f* (of decimal fraction) ‖ *decimal system* sistema decimal.
◆ *n* MATH decimal *m*; *decimal place* lugar *m* del decimal.

decimalize ['desiməlaiz] *vt* aplicar el sistema decimal a.

decimate ['desimeit] *vt* diezmar.

decimation [ˌdesiˈmeiʃən] *n* acción *f* de diezmar.

decimetre; *US* **decimeter** [ˈdesiˌmiːtə*] *n* decímetro *m*.

decipher [diˈsaifə*] *n* descifrado *m*.

decipher [diˈsaifə*] *vt* descifrar.

decipherable [diˈsaifərəbl] *adj* descifrable.

decipherer [diˈsaifərə*] *n* descifrador, ra.

deciphering [-iŋ] *adj* descifrador, ra.
◆ *n* desciframiento *m*, descifrado *m*.

decision [diˈsiʒən] *n* decisión *f*; *the decision is final* la decisión es definitiva; *to make o to take a decision* tomar una decisión ‖ resolución *f*, determinación (resoluteness) ‖ JUR fallo *m*.

decisive [diˈsaisiv] *adj* decisivo, va; *decisive proof* prueba decisiva ‖ concluyente; *a decisive experiment* una experiencia concluyente ‖ tajante (tone) ‖ decidido, da (manner).

deck [dek] *n* MAR cubierta *f* (of ship) ‖ piso *m* (of bus) ‖ baraja *f* (pack of cards) ‖ FAM suelo *m* ‖ TECH tablero *m*, piso *m* (of bridge) | techo *m* (of wagon) ‖ — MAR *below decks* en la bodega (of a ship) | *between decks* entrepuente *m*, entrecubierta *f* ‖ FAM *hit the deck!* ¡cuerpo a tierra! ‖ *on deck* en cubierta ‖ *to clear the decks* tocar zafarrancho de combate.

deck [dek] *vt* adornar, engalanar (to trim) ‖ MAR poner cubierta a ‖ FAM *to deck o.s. out* ponerse de tiros largos *or* de punta en blanco.

deck chair [-tʃɛə*] *n* tumbona *f*.

decker [-ə*] *n* *single-decker* autobús *m* de un piso (bus), barco *m* de una cubierta (boat).

deckhand [-hænd] *n* marinero *m* de cubierta.

deckhouse [-haus] *n* MAR camareta *f* alta.

deckle edge [ˈdekledʒ] *n* barbas *f pl* (of paper).

declaim [diˈkleim] *vt/vi* declamar.

declamation [ˌdekləˈmeiʃən] *n* declamación *f*.

declamatory [diˈklæmətəri] *adj* declamatorio, ria.

declaimer [diˈkleimə*] *n* declamador, ra.

declarant [diˈklærənt] *n* JUR declarante *m* & *f*.

declaration [ˌdekləˈreiʃən] *n* declaración *f*; *declaration of war* declaración de guerra; *customs declaration* declaración de aduana; *to make a declaration to the police* hacer una declaración a la policía ‖ proclamación *f*; *declaration of the poll* proclamación de los resultados ‖ INFORM declaración *f* ‖ — *declaration of bankruptcy* declaración de quiebra ‖ *Declaration of Human Rights* Declaración de los Derechos Humanos; *Declaration of the Rights of Man* Declaración de los Derechos del Hombre ‖ *declaration of love* declaración de amor.

declaratory [diˈklærətəri] *adj* declaratorio, ria.

declare [diˈklɛə*] *vt* declarar; *to declare war on a country* declarar la guerra a un país; *have you anything to declare?* ¿tiene usted algo que declarar? ‖ proclamar; *to declare s.o. the winner* proclamar a alguien ganador; *to declare one's innocence* proclamar la inocencia de uno ‖ cantar, acusar (in card games) ‖ declarar (in bridge) ‖ — *to declare off* abandonar ‖ *to declare o.s.* declararse; confesar; *I declare myself completely at a loss* confieso que estoy completamente perdido.
◆ *vi* declarar (in cricket) ‖ *to declare against, for* pronunciarse *or* declararse en contra, a favor ‖ *well I declare!* ¡vaya por Dios!

declared [-d] *adj* declarado, da; *declared profits* beneficios declarados ‖ declarado, da; manifiesto, ta (opinion).

declaredly [diˈklɛəridli] *adv* abiertamente, declaradamente.

declassify [diːˈklæsifai] *vt* levantar el secreto oficial de (documents).

declension [diˈklənʃən] *n* GRAMM declinación *f* ‖ desviación *f* (from a definite direction) ‖ inclinación *f*, declive *m* (slope) ‖ decadencia *f* (decline).

declinable [diˈklainəbl] *adj* declinable.

declination [ˌdekliˈneiʃən] *n* negativa *f* (refusal) ‖ PHYS & ASTR declinación *f* ‖ declive *m* (slope) ‖ decadencia *f* (decline).

decline [diˈklain] *n* disminución *f* (decrease) ‖ decaimiento *m* (decay) ‖ decadencia *f*, ocaso *m*; *the decline of the Roman Empire* la decadencia del Imperio Romano ‖ ocaso *m* (of life) ‖ baja *f* (in price or number) ‖ declive *m* (downward slope) ‖ caída *f*, ocaso *m* (of the day) ‖ ocaso *m* (of the sun) ‖ MED enfermedad *f* de postración ‖ negativa *f* (refusal) ‖ *to be on the decline* debilitarse; *his health is on the decline* su salud se está debilitando; disminuir; *the crime rate is on the decline* la criminalidad está disminuyendo; estar en decadencia.

decline [diˈklain] *vt* rehusar, rechazar (an offer, etc.) ‖ negarse (*to* a) (to do sth.) ‖ inclinar (to incline) ‖ GRAMM declinar.
◆ *vi* rehusar, negarse (to refuse) ‖ decaer (to decay) ‖ decaer, debilitarse (strength) ‖ disminuir (to diminish) ‖ bajar (prices) ‖ inclinarse (to slope down) ‖ declinar (the sun, the day) ‖ MED debilitarse.

declining [-iŋ] *adj* declinante ‖ *in his declining years* en sus últimos años, en el ocaso de su vida.

declivity [diˈkliviti] *n* declive *m*.

declutch [diːklʌtʃ] *vi* AUT desembragar.

declutching [-iŋ] *n* AUT desembrague *m*.

decoct [diˈkɔkt] *vt* extraer por medio de la decocción.

decoction [diˈkɔkʃən] *n* decocción *f* (decocting) ‖ extracto *m* (extract).

decode [ˈdiːˈkəud] *vt* descifrar ‖ INFORM decodificar.

decoder [-ə*] *n* descifrador, ra (person) ‖ decodificador *m* (machine) ‖ INFORM decodificador *m*.

decoding [-iŋ] *n* desciframiento *m*, descifrado *m* ‖ INFORM decodificación *f*.

decoke [ˈdiːˈkəuk] *vt* descarburar (un motor).

décolletage [ˈdeikɔlˈtɑːʒ] *n* escote *m*.

décolleté [ˈdeikɔlˈtei] *adj* escotado, da.
◆ *n* escote *m*.

decolonization [diːˌkɔlənaiˈzeiʃən] *n* descolonización *f*.

decolonize [diːˈkɔlənaiz] *vt* descolonizar.

decolourize; *US* **decolorize** [diːˈkɔləraiz] *vt* descolorir, descolorar.

decompensation [diːˌkɔmpənˈseiʃən] *n* descompensación *f*.

decomposable [ˌdiːkəmˈpəuzəbl] *adj* descomponible.

decompose [ˌdiːkəmˈpəuz] *vt* descomponer (to break up into parts) ‖ pudrir, descomponer (to break up into parts) ‖ pudrir, descomponer, corromper (to cause to rot) ‖ CHEM descomponer ‖ FIG analizar, descomponer.
◆ *vi* descomponerse (to break up into parts) ‖ pudrirse, descomponerse, corromperse (to rot).

decomposition [ˌdiːkɔmpəˈziʃən] *n* descomposición *f* (into parts) ‖ descomposición *f*, putrefacción *f* (rotting).

decompound [ˌdiːkəmˈpaund] *vt* descomponer.

decompress [ˌdiːkəmˈpres] *vt* descomprimir.

decompression [ˌdiːkəmˈpreʃən] *n* descompresión *f*; *decompression chamber* cámara de descompresión.

decompressor [ˌdiːkəmˈpresə*] *n* descompresor *m*.

decongestion [ˌdiːkənˈdʒestʃən] *n* descongestión *f*.

deconsecrate [diːˈkɔnsikreit] *vt* secularizar (a church).

decontaminate [ˈdikənˈtæmineit] *vt* descontaminar, desinfectar.

decontamination [ˌdikəntæmiˈneiʃən] *n* descontaminación *f*, desinfección *f*.

decontrol [ˈdiːkɔnˈtrəul] *vt* liberalizar.

décor; *US* **decor** [ˈdeikɔː*] *n* THEATR decorado *m* ‖ decoración *f* (decoration).

decorate [ˈdekəreit] *vt* decorar, adornar (to adorn) ‖ pintar (to paint) ‖ empapelar (to paper) ‖ condecorar (with a medal).

decoration [ˈdekəˈreiʃən] *n* decoración *f* (décor) ‖ adorno *m* (sth. decorative) ‖ condecoración *f* (medal, ribbon, etc.).

decorative [ˈdekərətiv] *adj* decorativo, va (ornamental) ‖ *decorative arts* artes decorativas.

decorator [ˈdekəreitə*] *n* decorador, ra (who plans interior design) ‖ pintor *m* (painter) ‖ empapelador *m* (paperhanger).

decorous [ˈdekərəs] *adj* decoroso, sa.

decorticate [diːˈkɔːtikeit] *vt* descortezar (trees) ‖ pelar, descascarar, quitar la cáscara a (to peel) ‖ descascarillar (rice).

decortication [ˈdiːkɔːtiˈkeiʃən] *n* descortezamiento *m* (of trees) ‖ descascaramiento *m*, peladura *f* (peeling) ‖ descascarillamiento *m* (of rice).

decorum [diˈkɔːrəm] *n* decoro *m*.

decoy [diˈkɔi] *n* señuelo *m* (artificial bird to lure game) ‖ cimbel *m* (real bird to lure game) ‖ cebo *m* (bait) ‖ FIG gancho *m*, señuelo *m* (person used as bait).

decoy [diˈkɔi] *vt* atraer con señuelo (an animal) ‖ FIG atraer | seducir (a woman).

decrease [ˈdiːkriːs] *n* disminución *f*; *decrease in value* disminución de valor ‖ *to be on the decrease* ir disminuyendo.

decrease [diːˈkriːs] *vt* disminuir (to diminish) ‖ menguar (in knitting).
◆ *vi* disminuir.

decreasing [-iŋ] *adj* decreciente, menguante.

decree [diˈkriː] *n* decreto *m* (of a ruling body or authority); *to issue a decree* promulgar un decreto ‖ JUR sentencia *f* ‖ — JUR *decree absolute* sentencia *f* definitiva de divorcio | *decree nisi* sentencia provisional de divorcio.

decree [diˈkriː] *vt* decretar (to appoint or order by decree) ‖ pronunciar (a penalty).
◆ *vi* promulgar un decreto.

decree-law [-lɔː] *n* JUR decreto ley *m*.

decrement [ˈdekrimənt] *n* MATH & ELECTR decremento *m* ‖ disminución *f* (decrease).

decrepit [diˈkrepit] *adj* decrépito, ta.

decrepitate [diˈkrepiteit] *vi* decrepitar, crepitar.

decrepitude [diˈkrepitjuːd] *n* decrepitud *f*.

decrescendo [ˌdiːkriˈʃendəu] *adj/adv* MUS decrescendo.
◆ *n* MUS decrescendo *m*.

decrescent [diˈkresənt] *adj* decreciente, menguante.

decretal [diˈkriːtəl] *n* REL decretal *f*.

decretist [diˈkriːtist] *n* canonista *m*.

decry [diˈkrai] *vt* censurar, criticar (to censure) ‖ COMM depreciar, desvalorizar (money).

decubitus [di'kju:bitəs] *n* MED decúbito *m*; *supine, prone decubitus* decúbito supino, prono.

decuple ['dekjupl] *adj* décuplo, pla.
◆ *n* décuplo *m*.

decuple ['dekjupl] *vt* decuplar, decuplicar.
◆ *vi* decuplarse, decuplicarse.

decurrent [di'kʌrənt] *adj* BOT decurrente.

dedicate ['dedikeit] *vt* dedicar (a book, one's life) || dedicar, consagrar (a church) || US inaugurar || *to dedicate o.s. to* dedicarse a.

dedicated *adj* entregado, da || INFORM dedicado, da.

dedication [,dedi'keiʃən] *n* dedicación *f* (devotion, act of dedicating) || dedicatoria *f* (inscription).

dedicatory ['dedikətəri] *adj* dedicatorio, ria.

deduce [di'dju:s] *vt* deducir (to infer).

deducible [-əbl] *adj* deducible.

deduct [di'dʌkt] *vt* deducir, restar, descontar.

deductible [-əbl] *adj* deducible.

deduction [di'dʌkʃn] *n* deducción *f*, descuento *m*, rebaja *f* (a subtracting, the amount deducted) || conclusión *f*, deducción *f* (conclusion).

deductive [di'dʌktiv] *adj* deductivo, va.

deed [di:d] *n* acto *m*, acción *f* (any act) || hecho *m* (sth. done) || hazaña *f*, proeza *f* (outstanding feat) || ejecución *f*, realización *f* (fulfilment) || JUR escritura *f* || — *in deed* de hecho || *in word and deed* de palabra y obra || *to change one's name by deed poll* cambiar su apellido por escritura legal.

deem [di:m] *vt* considerar, juzgar, creer || *to deem highly of s.o.* tener muy buena opinión de alguien.

deep [di:p] *adj* profundo, da; hondo, da; *deep well* pozo profundo; *deep sight* suspiro hondo || de profundidad; *a well twenty feet deep* un pozo de veinte pies de profundidad || de fondo; *a cupboard a metre deep* un armario de un metro de fondo || de ancho; *a wall twenty feet deep* una pared de veinte pies de ancho || ancho, cha (wide) || hundido, da (eyes) || profundo, da (sleep, wound, wrinkle) || metido, da; hundido, da; *with his hands deep in his pockets* con las manos hundidas en los bolsillos || FIG cargado, da; lleno, na; *deep in debt* cargado de deudas | absorto, ta (in thought, meditation) | a fondo, profundo, da; *deep study* estudio a fondo | riguroso, sa (mourning) | profundo, da (despair, feelings, learning, character); *deep sorrow* tristeza profunda | profundo, da; grave (voice, sound) | grande (disgrace, shame, interest, secrets) | profundo, da; completo, ta (mystery, silence) || oscuro, ra (night) | poco claro, oscuro, ra (scheme) | espeso, sa (shadow) | grave (sin) | difícil de entender (conduct) | astuto, ta (shrewd) || subido, da; oscuro, ra (colours) || MUS grave (sound) || — *deep drinker* gran bebedor || *to be thrown in at the deep end* tener que empezar por lo más difícil || FIG & FAM *to go off the deep end* perder los estribos (to lose one's control), obrar con precipitación (to act rashly).
◆ *adv* profundamente; *to dig deep* cavar profundamente; *to sleep deep* dormir profundamente || — *deep down* o *inside en el fondo* || *deep in his heart* en lo más profundo de su corazón || *deep into the night* hasta muy entrada la noche || *deep-lying cause* causa profunda, causa principal || *the difference runs deep* hay una gran diferencia || *to be deep in love* estar profundamente enamorado || *to drink deep* beber mucho [de una vez] || *to form up four deep* formarse de cuatro en fondo || *to play deep* jugar fuerte.
◆ *n* piélago *m* (sea) || abismo *m* (abyss) || profundidad *f* || *in the deep of winter* muy entrado el invierno, en pleno invierno.

deep-chested [-'tʃestid] *adj* ancho de pecho.

deep-dyed [-'daid] *adj* US completamente teñido || US FAM redomado, da; completo, ta (total).

deepen [-ən] *vt* hacer más profundo, ahondar (a hole, etc.) || intensificar (colour, emotion) || MUS hacer más grave (sound) || FIG profundizar.
◆ *vi* hacerse más hondo or profundo || intensificarse (colour, emotion) || aumentar (to increase).

deepfreeze [-'fri:z] *n* congelador *m* (freezer) || congelación *f* (freezing) || FIG *in deepfreeze* archivado, da (project).

deepfreeze [-'fri:z] *vt* congelar.

deep-fry [-frɑi] *vt* freír en abundante aceite.

deep-laid [-leid] *adj* muy bien preparado (plan).

deeply [-li] *adv* profundamente, hondamente || intensamente; *deeply coloured* intensamente coloreado || profundamente, muy; *deeply offended* profundamente ofendido || *to breathe deeply* respirar hondo, respirar a pleno pulmón.

deepness [-nis] *n* profundidad *f*, hondura *f*.

deep-rooted [-'ru:tid] *adj* profundamente arraigado.

deep-sea [-'si] *adj* de alta mar || *deep-sea fishing* pesca *f* de altura.

deep-seated [-'si:tid] *adj* profundamente arraigado, da || de origen profundo (earthquake, etc.) || de origen interno (illness, etc.).

deep-set [-set] *adj* hundido, da (eyes) || profundamente arraigado, da (deep-rooted).

deep water [-'wɔ:tə*] *n* dificultad *f*, apuro *m*, aprieto *m* || FIG *to get into deep water* meterse en dificultades.

deepwater [-'wɔ:tə*] *adj* profundo, da (deep) || de alta mar, de altura (fishing, navigation).

deer [diə*] *inv n* ZOOL ciervo *m*, venado *m*.

deerhound [-haund] *n* galgo *m* para cazar ciervos.

deerskin [-skin] *n* gamuza *f*.

deerstalker [-,stɔ:kə*] *n* cazador *m* (de venado) al acecho (hunter) || gorro *m* de cazador de ciervos (cap).

deerstalking [-'stɔ:kiŋ] *n* caza *f* de venado al acecho.

de-escalate [di:'eskəleit] *vt* desescalar.

de-escalation [,di:eskə'leiʃən] *n* desescalada *f*.

deface [di'feis] *vt* desfigurar (to spoil appearance) || mutilar (a statue) || estropear, deteriorar (a wall, a door) || desgarrar (a poster) || matar (a stamp) || borrar (an inscription).

defacement [-mənt] *n* desfiguración *f* (spoiling of appearance) || mutilación *f* (of statue) || deterioro *m* (of wall, door) || desgarramiento *m* (of poster) || matado *m* (of stamp) || borradura *f* (erasure).

de facto [di:'fæktəu] *adj/adv* de hecho, de facto.

defalcate ['di:fælkeit] *vi* desfalcar, malversar fondos.

defalcation [,di:fæl'keiʃən] *n* desfalco *m*, malversación *f* de fondos.

defalcator [,di:fælkeitə*] *n* malversador, ra; desfalcador, ra.

defamation [,defə'meiʃən] *n* difamación *f*.

defamatory [di'fæmətəri] *adj* difamatorio, ria; difamante.

defame [di'feim] *vt* difamar.

defamer [-ə*] *n* difamador, ra.

default [di'fɔ:lt] *n* JUR contumacia *f*, rebeldía *f*; *judgment by default* sentencia en rebeldía || descuido *m*, negligencia *f* (of duty) || SP incomparecencia *f* || falta *f*, ausencia *f* (absence) || incumplimiento *m*, falta *f* de pago (of debt) || — *in default of* a falta de, en ausencia de || JUR *in default whereof* en cuyo defecto || SP *to win by default* ganar por incomparecencia del adversario.

default [di'fɔ:lt] *vt* JUR condenar en rebeldía || dejar de pagar (a debt, etc.) || SP dejar de presentarse a, perder por incomparecencia (a contest).
◆ *vi* JUR estar en rebeldía || dejar de cumplir el pago, faltar a sus compromisos (to fail to pay a debt) || SP dejar de presentarse, perder por incomparecencia.

defaulter [-ə*] *n* JUR contumaz *m* & *f*, rebelde *m* & *f* (absentee) | delincuente *m* (offender) || COMM moroso, sa (s.o. who fails to pay his debts) || desfalcador, ra; malversador, ra (embezzler) || MIL rebelde *m*.

defeasance [di'fi:zəns] *n* JUR anulación *f* || JUR *defeasance clause* cláusula resolutoria.

defeasible [di'fi:zəbl] *adj* JUR anulable.

defeat [di'fi:t] *n* MIL derrota *f* || fracaso *m* (failure) || JUR anulación *f*.

defeat [di'fi:t] *vt* vencer, derrotar || derrotar (the government) || hacer fracasar, desbaratar (projects) || JUR anular || — *to defeat s.o. in his* o *her hopes* defraudar las esperanzas de alguien || *to defeat s.o. in his* o *her plans* desbaratar los planes de alguien.

defeatism [di'fi:tizəm] *n* derrotismo *m*.

defeatist [di'fi:tist] *adj/n* derrotista.

defeature [di'fi:tʃə*] *vt* desfigurar.

defecación [,di:fi'keiʃən] *n* defecación *f*.

defecate [di:fikeit] *vt/vi* defecar.

defect [di'fekt] *n* defecto *m*.

defect [di'fekt] *vi* desertar; *to defect from a political party* desertar de un partido político || *to defect to a country* huir a un país.

defection [di'fekʃən] *n* deserción *f*, defección *f*.

defective [di'fektiv] *adj* defectuoso, sa (having faults) || incompleto, ta (incomplete) || GRAMM defectivo, va; *defective verb* verbo defectivo || anormal (abnormal).
◆ *n* persona *f* anormal (abnormal person) || GRAMM verbo *m* defectivo.

defectiveness [-nis] *n* defectuosidad *f*, imperfección *f*.

defector [di'fektə*] *n* tránsfuga *m* & *f*, trásfuga *m* & *f*, desertor, ra.

defence; US defense [di'fens] *n* defensa *f*; *defence of a town, of an idea* defensa de una ciudad, de una idea || JUR defensa *f*; *to call upon the defence to speak* conceder la palabra a la defensa || SP defensa *f* (defenders) || — JUR *Counsel for the defence* abogado defensor || *in the defence of* en defensa de || *passive defence* defensa pasiva || *to come out in s.o.'s defence* salir en defensa de alguien.
◆ *pl* MIL defensas *f*.

defenceless [-lis] *adj* indefenso, sa.

defend [di'fend] *vt* defender (*against* contra; *from* de); *to defend a country, an idea* defender un país, una idea || *to defend o.s.* defenderse.

defendant [di'fendənt] *adj/n* JUR demandado, da (in civil case) || acusado, da (in criminal case).

defender [di'fendə*] *n* defensor, ra || SP defensa *m* || *defensor of the Faith* defensor de la fe.
◆ *pl* SP defensa *f sing*.

defending [di'fendiŋ] *adj* defensor, ra ‖ *defending champion* campeón *m* titular.

defenestration [di,fenə:'streiʃən] *n* defenestración *f.*

defense [di'fens] *n* US ⟶ **defence.**

defenseless [-lis] *adj* US indefenso, sa.

defensible [di'fensəbl] *adj* defendible (easily defended) ‖ justificable (justifiable).

defensive [di'fensiv] *adj* defensivo, va.
◆ *n* defensiva *f* ‖ *on the defensive* a la defensiva.

defer [di'fə:*] *vt* diferir, aplazar (to postpone) ‖ MIL dar una prórroga a ‖ delegar (an affair, function, etc.) ‖ someter (to submit).
◆ *vi* deferir, remitirse (*to* a) ‖ tardar; *without deferring any longer* sin tardar más.

deference ['defərəns] *n* deferencia *f* ‖ — *in deference to, out of deference to* por respeto a, por deferencia a ‖ *with all due deference to you* con perdón de usted.

deferent ['defərənt] *adj* ANAT deferente.

deferential ['defə'renʃəl] *adj* deferente, respetuoso, sa.

deferment [di'fə:mənt] *n* aplazamiento *m* ‖ MIL prórroga *f.*

deferrable [di'fə:rəbl] *adj* diferible, aplazable.
◆ *n* US MIL persona *f* con derecho a prórroga.

deferred [di'fə:d] *adj* diferido, da; aplazado, da ‖ COMM diferido, da ‖ MIL que beneficia de una prórroga ‖ *deferred annuity* renta vitalicia de pago diferido.

defiance [di'faiəns] *n* desafío *m*, reto *m* ‖ — *in defiance of* con desprecio de ‖ *to bid defiance to* desafiar a ‖ *to set s.o. at defiance* desafiar a alguien.

defiant [di'faiənt] *adj* provocativo, va; provocador, ra; desafiante (challenging) ‖ de desafío, desafiante, retador, ra (tone).

defiantly [-li] *adv* con tono *or* aire retador.

deficiency [di'fiʃənsi] *n* deficiencia *f* ‖ COMM déficit *m* (of budget) | descubierto *m* (of account) ‖ — MED *deficiency disease* enfermedad *f* por carencia | *mental deficiency* debilidad *f* mental.

deficient [di'fiʃənt] *adj* deficiente ‖ MED atrasado, da ‖ *to be deficient in* carecer de.
◆ *n* MED atrasado *m* mental.

deficit ['defisit] *n* COMM déficit *m* (of balance) | descubierto *m* (of account).

defier [di'faiə*] *n* desafiador, ra; retador, ra.

defilade [,defi'leid] *n* MIL desenfilada *f.*

defilade [,defi'leid] *vt* MIL desenfilar.

defile ['di:fail] *n* desfiladero *m* (gully).

defile ['difail] *vi* MIL desfilar.

defile [di'fail] *vt* ensuciar, manchar (to soil) ‖ profanar (to desecrate) ‖ desflorar, deshonrar, violar (a woman) ‖ deshonrar, mancillar (reputation).

defilement [di'failmənt] *n* mancha *f*, ensuciamiento *m* (soiling) ‖ profanación *f* (desecration) ‖ mancha *f*, mancilla *f* (of the reputation, etc.) ‖ deshonra *f*, desfloración *f* (of a woman).

definable [di'fainəbl] *adj* definible.

define [di'fain] *vt* definir (to give a definition of) ‖ caracterizar, definir (to characterize) ‖ formular, definir (to formulate) ‖ precisar, definir (to outline the function of) ‖ determinar, definir; *to define the limits of a field* determinar los límites de un campo.

definite ['definit] *adj* definido, da; determinado, da (limiting) ‖ claro, ra (clear) ‖ claro, ra; preciso, sa; categórico, ca (answer) ‖ preciso, sa (needs) ‖ determinado, da (date) ‖ definitivo, va (final) ‖ GRAMM definido, da; determinado, da; *definite article* artículo definido ‖ limitado, da (powers) ‖ seguro, ra (certain) ‖ — *it's definite that...* no hay duda que... ‖ *to arrange a definite date* fijar una fecha determinada.

definitely [-li] *adv* claramente ‖ categóricamente, rotundamente (categorically) ‖ sin duda alguna, seguramente (without doubt) ‖ de modo definitivo, definitivamente ‖ — *he is definitely mad* está completamente loco ‖ *they are definitely not coming* es completamente seguro que no vienen.
◆ *interj* ¡desde luego!, ¡por supuesto!

definition [,defi'niʃən] *n* definición *f* ‖ TECH definición *f* (telescope, television) ‖ PHOT claridad *f*, nitidez *f* ‖ limitación *f* (of powers) ‖ *by definition* por definición.

definitive [di'finitiv] *adj* definitivo, va.

deflagrate ['defləgreit] *vt* hacer deflagar.
◆ *vi* deflagar.

deflagration [,deflə'greiʃən] *n* deflagración *f.*

deflagrator ['deflagreitə*] *n* deflagrador *m.*

deflate [di'fleit] *vt* deshinchar, desinflar (ball, tyre) ‖ COMM provocar la deflación de ‖ FIG rebajar (vanity, pride) | reducir (hopes).
◆ *vi* desinflarse, deshincharse.

deflation [di'fleiʃən] *n* desinflado *m*, desinflamiento *m* ‖ COMM deflación *f.*

deflationary [di'fleitʃənəri] *adj* deflacionista.

deflator [di'fleitə*] *n* índice *m* de deflación.

deflect [di'flekt] *vt* desviar ‖ AUT hacer girar (wheels).
◆ *vi* desviarse.

deflection [di'flekʃən] *n* desviación *f* (of stream, light, compass) ‖ AUT giro *m.*

deflector [di'flektə*] *n* deflector *m.*

defloration [,di:flɔ:'reiʃən] *n* desfloración *f*, desfloramiento *m.*

deflower [di:'flauə*] *vt* desflorar.

defoliate [di:'fəulieit] *vt* deshojar.
◆ *vi* deshojarse.

defoliation [di:fəuli'eiʃən] *n* defoliación *f.*

deforcement [di'fɔ:smənt] *n* JUR detentación *f*, usurpación *f.*

deforciant [di'fɔ:ʃənt] *n* JUR detentador, ra.

deforest [di'fɔrist] *vt* despoblar de árboles, desmontar, talar.

deforestation [difɔris'teiʃən] *n* despoblación *f* forestal, desmonte *m*, tala *f.*

deform [di'fɔ:m] *vt* deformar (body, thing) ‖ desfigurar, afear (person).
◆ *vi* deformarse ‖ desfigurarse.

deformation [,difɔ'meiʃən] *n* deformación *f* (of body, thing) ‖ desfiguración *f* (of people).

deformed [di'fɔ:md] *adj* deformado, da (changed in form) ‖ deforme (misshappen) ‖ disforme (ugly).

deformity [di'fɔ:miti] *n* deformidad *f.*

defraud [di'frɔ:d] *vt* defraudar, estafar ‖ FIG perjudicar.

defraudation [,difrɔ'deiʃən] *n* defraudación *f.*

defrauder [di'frɔ:də*] *n* defraudador, ra; estafador, ra.

defray [di'frei] *vt* costear, pagar, sufragar.

defrayal [-əl] ; **defrayment** [-mənt] *n* pago *m.*

defrock ['di'frɔk] *vt* obligar a colgar los hábitos.

defrost [di'frɔst] *vt* deshelar ‖ descongelar (fridge).

defrosting [-iŋ] *n* descongelación *f.*

deft [deft] *adj* hábil, diestro, tra (skilful).

deftly [-li] *adv* con destreza, con habilidad.

deftness [-nis] *n* destreza *f*, habilidad *f.*

defunct [di'fʌŋkt] *adj/n* difunto, ta (dead) ‖ FIG que ya no existe (extinct).

defuse [di'fju:z] *vt* ELECTR desactivar ‖ FIG calmar, sacar la tensión.

defy [di'fai] *vt* desafiar, retar (to challenge) ‖ resistir a (to resist) ‖ *it defies description* es imposible describirlo.

degauss ['di'gaus] *vt* MAR desimantar, desimanar.

degeneracy [di'dʒenərəsi] *n* degeneración *f.*

degenerate [di'dʒenərit] *adj/n* degenerado, da.

degenerate [di'dʒenəreit] *vi* degenerar (*into* en).

degeneration [di,dʒenə'reiʃən] *n* degeneración *f.*

degenerative [di'dʒenərətiv] *adj* degenerativo, va; degenerante.

deglutition [,diglu:'tiʃən] *n* deglución *f.*

degradation [,degrə'deiʃən] *n* degradación *f.*

degrade [di'greid] *vt* degradar (to lower in rank, to humiliate) ‖ degradar, envilecer (to debase morally) ‖ rebajar (the quality) ‖ GEOL desgastar ‖ PHYS degradar.
◆ *vi* degenerar (race, etc.) ‖ GEOL desgastarse.

degrading [-iŋ] *adj* degradante; *degrading conduct* conducta degradante.

degrease ['di'gri:s] *vt* desengrasar.

degree [di'gri:] *n* grado *m* (step) ‖ grado *m*, punto *m* (pitch) ‖ categoría *f*, rango *m*; *of low degree* de baja categoría ‖ grado *m* (of relationship) ‖ título *m* (of university) ‖ GRAMM, MATH, GEOGR & PHYS grado *m*; *to stand at fifteen degrees* marcar quince grados ‖ grada *f* (of the altar) ‖ — *bachelor's degree* licenciatura *f* ‖ *by degrees* gradualmente, progresivamente, poco a poco ‖ *doctor's degree* doctorado *m* ‖ JUR *first-degree murder* asesinato *m* ‖ *honorary degree* doctorado *m* «honoris causa» ‖ JUR *second-degree murder* homicidio *m* por imprudencia ‖ MED *third-degree burns* quemaduras *f pl* de tercer grado ‖ *to a certain degree, to some degree, in some degree* hasta cierto punto ‖ *to a degree* sumamente ‖ JUR *to give s.o. the third degree* sacudir a uno ‖ *to take a degree in* licenciarse en ‖ *to the highest degree* en sumo grado.

degression [di'greʃən] *n* disminución *f.*

degressive [di'gresiv] *adj* decreciente.

degust [di'gʌst] *vt* probar (to taste).

dehisce [di'his] *vi* BOT abrirse.

dehiscent [di'hisnt] *adj* BOT dehiscente.

dehorn [di:'hɔ:n] *vt* descornar (an animal).

dehumanization [di:'hju:mənai'zeiʃən] *n* deshumanización *f.*

dehumanize [di:'hju:mənaiz] *vt* deshumanizar.

dehumidify [di:hju'midifai] *vt* deshumedecer.

dehydrate [di:'haidreit] *vt* deshidratar.

dehydration [di:hai'dreiʃən] *n* deshidratación *f.*

dehydrogenate [di:hai'drɔdʒeneit] *vt* deshidrogenar.

dehydrogenation [di:haidrɔdʒə'neiʃən] *n* deshidrogenación *f.*

dehydrogenize [di:hai'drɔdʒenaiz] *vt* deshidrogenar.

dehypnotize ['di:'hipnətaiz] *vt* deshipnotizar.

deice ['di:'ais] *vt* descongelar, deshelar.

deicer [-ə*] *n* descongelador *m* ‖ AVIAT dispositivo *m* antihielo.

deicide ['di:isaid] *n* deicidio *m* (killing of a god) ‖ deicida *m* & *f* (killer of a god).

deicing ['di:'aisiŋ] *n* descongelación *f.*

deification [ˌdi:ifi'keiʃən] *n* deificación *f.*

deify ['di:ifai] *vt* divinizar, deificar.

deign [dein] *vt* dignarse a; *to deign a reply* dignarse a dar una respuesta.
◆ *vi* dignarse (*to* a).

deism ['di:izəm] *n* REL deísmo *m.*

deist ['di:ist] *n* REL deísta *m* & *f.*

deistic [di:'istik] *adj* deísta.

deity ['di:iti] *n* deidad *f,* divinidad *f* (divine nature) ‖ deidad *f,* dios *m,* diosa *f* (god) ‖ *the Deity* Dios *m.*

deject [di'dʒekt] *vt* descorazonar, desanimar, desalentar.

dejecta [di'dʒektə] *pl n* excrementos *m,* deyecciones *f* ‖ GEOGR deyecciones *f.*

dejected [di'dʒektid] *adj* descorazonado, da; desanimado, da; desalentado, da.

dejection [di'dʒekʃən] *n* desaliento *m,* abatimiento *m* (low spirits) ‖ MED deyección *f.*

delate [di'leit] *vt* denunciar, delatar.

delation [di'leiʃən] *n* denuncia *f,* delación *f.*

delator [di'leitə*] *n* delator, ra.

Delaware ['deləwεə*] *pr n* GEOGR Delaware.

delay [di'lei] *n* retraso *m,* dilación *f* ‖ demora *f* (wait) ‖ — *to take no delay in* no demorarse en ‖ *without delay* sin dilación, sin demora, en seguida.

delay [di'lei] *vt* retrasar (to make late) ‖ aplazar, demorar (to postpone) ‖ estorbar (to hinder) ‖ entretener (to hold up).
◆ *vi* tardar ‖ *don't delay!* ¡no te entretengas!

delayed action [di'leid'ækʃən] *n* efecto *m* retardado; *delayed-action bomb* bomba de efecto retardado.

delaying [di'leiiŋ] *adj* dilatorio, ria; *delaying tactics* tácticas dilatorias.

dele ['di:li] *n* PRINT dele *m,* deleátur *m.*

dele ['di:li] *vt* suprimir, tachar (to delete).

delectable [di'lektəbl] *adj* deleitable, delicioso, sa.

delectation [di:lek'teiʃən] *n* delectación *f,* deleite *m.*

delegacy ['deligəsi] *n* delegación *f.*

delegate ['deligit] *n* delegado, da ‖ US diputado, da (in the Chamber of Representatives).

delegate ['deligeit] *vt* delegar; *to delegate one's powers to s.o.* delegar sus poderes a *or* en alguien.

delegation [deli'geiʃən] *n* delegación *f* (act, body).

delegatory [deli'geitəri] *adj* delegatorio, ria.

delete [di'li:t] *vt* tachar, suprimir ‖ INFORM suprimir ‖ INFORM *delete key* tecla *f* de borrado.

deleterious [ˌdeli'tiːəriəs] *adj* deletéreo, a (physically harmful) ‖ perjudicial (morally harmful).

deletion [di'li:ʃən] *n* tachadura *f,* supresión *f.*

delft [delft]; **delftware** [-wεə*] *n* cerámica *f* de Delft.

deliberate [di'libərit] *adj* deliberado, da (intentional) ‖ prudente (cautious) ‖ premeditado, da (premeditated) ‖ lento, ta; pausado, da (unhurried).

deliberate [di'libəreit] *vt* reflexionar, meditar.
◆ *vi* reflexionar (to ponder) ‖ deliberar (*on* sobre); *the judges deliberated behind closed doors* los jueces deliberaron a puerta cerrada.

deliberately [di'libəritli] *adv* a propósito, deliberadamente (voluntarily) ‖ prudentemente (circumspectly) ‖ lentamente, pausadamente (slowly).

deliberation [diˌlibə'reiʃən] *n* deliberación *f,* discusión *f* (debate) ‖ reflexión *f* ‖ lentitud *f* (slowness) ‖ *after due deliberation* después de pensarlo bien.

deliberative [di'libərətiv] *adj* deliberativo, va; deliberante; *deliberative assembly* asamblea deliberante.

delible ['delibl] *adj* deleble.

delicacy ['delikəsi] *n* delicadeza *f,* fragilidad *f* (fragility) ‖ delicadeza *f* (elegance, consideration, sensitivity, tenuousness, skill) ‖ manjar *m* exquisito (choise food) ‖ MED debilidad *f* ‖ TECH sensibilidad *f* (of compass).

delicate ['delikit] *adj* delicado, da (needing great skill or tact) ‖ delicado, da; frágil (fragile) ‖ delicado, da; primoroso, sa (work) ‖ suave (colours) ‖ sutil (subtle); *a delicate hint* una indirecta sutil; *a delicate distinction* una distinción sutil ‖ fino, na; *a delicate sense of smell* un olfato muy fino ‖ delicado, da; escrupuloso, sa (scrupulous) ‖ delicado, da; fino, na (taste) ‖ ligero, ra (touch) ‖ delicado, da; suave (odour) ‖ refinado, da; *a delicate upbringing* una educación refinada ‖ exquisito, ta (food) ‖ delicado, da (tactful, considerate) ‖ MED delicado, da; frágil (health) ‖ TECH sensible (compass).

delicatessen [ˌdelikə'tesn] *n* tienda *f* de platos preparados (shop) ‖ platos *m pl* preparados.

delicious [di'liʃəs] *adj* delicioso, sa; exquisito, ta.

delict [di'likt] *n* JUR delito *m; in flagrant delict* en flagrante delito.

delight [di'lait] *n* deleite *m,* delicia *f* ‖ encanto *m; one of the delights of England* uno de los encantos de Inglaterra ‖ — *much to my delight* con gran regocijo mío ‖ *the poem is sheer delight* el poema es una verdadera maravilla ‖ *to take delight in sth., in doing sth.* deleitarse con algo, en hacer algo.

delight [dilait] *vt* deleitar; *music delights the ear* la música deleita el oído ‖ encantar; *to be delighted with sth.* estar encantado con algo; *I am delighted to meet you* estoy encantado de conocerle.
◆ *vi* deleitarse ‖ — *to delight in doing sth.* deleitarse en hacer algo ‖ *to delight in sth.* deleitarse con algo.

delightful [-ful] *adj* delicioso, sa; encantador, ra.

delightfulness [-fulnis] *n* encanto *m.*

Delilah [di'lailə] *pr n* Dalila *f.*

delimit [di'limit]; **delimitate** [-eit] *vt* delimitar.

delimitation [diˌlimi'teiʃən] *n* delimitación *f.*

delineate [di'linieit] *vt* delinear, trazar (to outline) ‖ bosquejar, esbozar (to sketch) ‖ delimitar (to delimit) ‖ FIG describir, pintar (to describe).

delineation [diˌlini'eiʃən] *n* delineación *f* (outlining) ‖ dibujo *m* (drawing) ‖ boceto *m,* bosquejo *m* (sketch) ‖ FIG descripción *f.*

delineator [di'linieitə*] *n* dibujante *m* & *f.*

delinquency [di'liŋkwənsi] *n* JUR delincuencia *f; juvenile delinquency* delincuencia juvenil ‖ delito *m* (fault) ‖ culpa *f* (guilt).

delinquent [di'liŋkwənt] *adj/n* delincuente ‖ *juvenile delinquent* delincuente juvenil, joven delincuente.

deliquesce [ˌdeli'kwes] *vi* licuarse.

deliquescence [ˌdeli'kwesns] *n* delicuescencia *f.*

delirious [di'liriəs] *adj* delirante ‖ *to be delirious* delirar.

delirium [di'liriəm] *n* MED & FIG delirio *m* ‖ MED *delirium tremens* delirium tremens *m.*

— OBSERV El plural de la palabra inglesa es *deliriums* o *deliria.*

deliver [di'livə*] *vt* repartir, entregar (goods) ‖ entregar (to hand over) ‖ repartir (mail) ‖ dar (a message) ‖ expresar, formular (an opinion) ‖ pronunciar (a speech) ‖ dar (a lecture) ‖ rendir (accounts) ‖ lanzar (the ball) ‖ pegar, dar, asestar (a blow) ‖ MED asistir para dar a luz (a woman) ‖ liberar (to free) ‖ JUR pronunciar ‖ MIL iniciar (a attack) ‖ librar (a battle) ‖ lanzar (a missile) ‖ — REL *deliver us from evil* líbranos del mal ‖ *stand and deliver!* ¡la bolsa o la vida! ‖ *the doctor delivered her of her child* el médico le asistió en el nacimiento de su hijo ‖ *to be delivered of a child* dar a luz a un niño ‖ *to deliver o.s. of* expresar (an opinion) ‖ *to deliver o.s. over* o *up to justice* entregarse a la justicia ‖ *to deliver over* o *up* entregar ‖ FIG *to deliver the goods* cumplir su parte, cumplir lo convenido ‖ COMM «we deliver» entrega *f* a domicilio.

deliverance [di'livərəns] *n* liberación *f* (a rescuing or being rescued) ‖ declaración *f* (opinion) ‖ JUR fallo *m,* veredicto *m.*

deliverer [di'livərə*] *n* libertador, ra; liberador, ra ‖ COMM repartidor, ra.

delivery [di'livəri] *n* entrega *f* (of a parcel, shop orders) ‖ reparto *m* (of mail) ‖ distribución *f* (distribution) ‖ expedición *f* (of goods) ‖ pronunciación *f* (of a speech, lecture, etc.) ‖ manera *f* de expresarse (manner of speaking) ‖ liberación *f* (saving) ‖ MED parto *m,* alumbramiento *m* ‖ SP lanzamiento *m* (in cricket, baseball, etc.) ‖ JUR cesión *f* ‖ TECH caudal *m* (of water) ‖ — *delivery boy* recadero *m,* chico *m* de los recados ‖ *delivery note* nota *f* de entrega ‖ MED *delivery room* sala *f* de partos ‖ *delivery service* servicio *m* a domicilio ‖ *delivery van* furgoneta *f* de reparto ‖ US *General Delivery* lista *f* de Correos [*AMER* poste restante] ‖ *to take delivery of* recibir.

deliveryman [-mən] *n* repartidor *m.*

— OBSERV El plural de *deliveryman* es *deliverymen.*

dell [del] *n* pequeño valle *m* (small valley).

delouse ['di:laus] *vt* despiojar, espulgar.

Delphi ['delfai] *pr n* GEOGR Delfos.

delphinium [del'finiəm] *n* BOT espuela *f* de caballero.

delta ['deltə] *n* delta *f* (Greek letter) ‖ delta *m* (of a river) ‖ AVIAT *delta-winged* con alas en forma de delta.

deltaic [del'teiik] *adj* deltaico, ca.

deltoid ['deltɔid] *adj* deltoideo, a; deltoides.
◆ *n* ANAT deltoides *m inv.*

delude [di'lu:d] *vt* engañar ‖ *to delude o.s. with false hopes* forjarse ilusiones.

deluge ['delju:dʒ] *n* inundación *f* (flood) ‖ diluvio *m* (heavy fall of rain) ‖ FIG avalancha *f,* alud *m* (of people, letters, etc.).

deluge ['delju:dʒ] *vt* inundar ‖ FIG abrumar (with requests) ‖ inundar de ‖ — FIG *deluged with tears* bañado en lágrimas ‖ *to be deluged with presents* lloverle a uno los regalos.

delusion [di'lu:ʒən] *n* engaño *m,* error *m* ‖ ilusión *f* ‖ MED alucinación *f* ‖ — *delusions of grandeur* megalomanía *f,* delirio *m* de grandezas ‖ *to labour under a delusion* estar equivocado *or* engañado.

delusive [di'lu:siv] *adj* engañoso, sa (deceiving) ‖ ilusorio, ria (illusory).

de luxe [də'lʌks] *adj* de lujo.

delve [delv] *vi* AGR cavar ‖ bajar, inclinarse (a road, etc.) ‖ FIG *to delve into* ahondar (a problem), hurgar en (one's pocket, a drawer).
◆ *vt* AGR cavar ‖ FIG explorar.

demagnetization ['di:'mægnitai'zeiʃən] *n* desmagnetización *f,* desimantación *f,* desimanación *f.*

demagnetize [diː'mægnitaiz] *vt* desmagnetizar, desimantar, desimanar.

demagog ['deməgɔg] *n* US demagogo *m*.

demagogic [demə'gɔgik]; **demagogical** [-əl] *adj* demagógico, ca.

demagogue ['deməgɔg] *n* demagogo *m*.

demagogy ['deməgɔgi] *n* demagogia *f*.

demand [di'mɑːnd] *n* petición *f*, solicitud *f* (request) ‖ reclamación *f* (for payment) ‖ exigencia *f* (urgent claim) ‖ COMM demanda *f*; *a big demand for cotton dresses* una gran demanda de vestidos de algodón ‖ — *by popular demand* a petición del público ‖ *he has many demands on his time* sus asuntos le tienen muy ocupado ‖ *in demand* muy solicitado ‖ *it makes great demands on my strength* requiere muchos esfuerzos ‖ *on demand* a petición ‖ *the pressing demands for housing* la urgente necesidad de viviendas.

demand [di'mɑːnd] *vt* exigir (to ask for emphatically) ‖ requerir (to require); *the matter demands careful consideration* la cuestión requiere un examen detenido ‖ reclamar; *he demanded his rights* reclamó sus derechos ‖ *he demanded to see it* insistió en verlo.

demandant [-ənt] *n* JUR demandante *m* & *f*.

demand bill [-bil] *n* COMM letra *f* a la vista.

demand deposit [-di'pɔzit] *n* COMM depósito *m* a la vista.

demand draft [-drɑːft] *n* COMM letra *f* a la vista.

demanding [-iŋ] *adj* exigente (person) ‖ absorbente (absorbing) ‖ agotador, ra (exhausting).

demand loan [-ləun] *n* COMM préstamo *m* reembolsable a petición.

demarcate ['diːmɑːkeit] *vt* demarcar.

demarcation [ˌdiːmɑː'keiʃən] *n* demarcación *f* ‖ — *demarcation dispute* conflicto *m* de competencias [entre miembros de sindicatos] ‖ *demarcation line* línea *f* de demarcación.

démarche ['deimɑːʃ] *n* gestión *f*, diligencia *f*.

dematerialization ['diːməˌtiəriəlai'zeiʃən] *n* desmaterialización *f*.

dematerialize ['diːmə'tiəriəlaiz] *vt* hacer *or* volver inmaterial.
◆ *vi* hacerse *or* volverse inmaterial.

demean [di'miːn] *vt* rebajar ‖ *to demean o.s.* rebajarse (to lower o.s.).

demeanour; US **demeanor** [-ə*] *n* conducta *f*, comportamiento *m* (behaviour) ‖ porte *m* (bearing).

dement [di'ment] *n* US MED demente *m* & *f*, loco, ca.

dement [di'ment] *vt* MED volver loco a.

demented [-id] *adj* MED demente, loco, ca.

dementedly [-idli] *adj* como un loco.

dementia [di'menʃiə] *n* MED demencia *f* ‖ MED *dementia praecox*, US *dementia precox* demencia precoz.

demerara [ˌdemə'rɛərə] *n* azúcar *m* terciado.

demerit [diː'merit] *n* demérito *m*, desmerecimiento *m* (fault).

demesne [di'mein] *n* propiedad *f* (estate) ‖ casa *f* y tierras solariegas (of a lord) ‖ JUR plena propiedad *f* ‖ FIG esfera *f* (of activity).

demigod ['demigɔd] *n* semidiós *m*.

demijohn ['demidʒɔn] *n* damajuana *f*.

demilitarization ['diːˌmilitərai'zeiʃən] *n* desmilitarización *f*.

demilitarize ['diː'militəraiz] *vt* desmilitarizar.

demimonde ['demi'mɔ̃ːnd] *n* mujeres *f pl* de vida alegre.

demineralize [diː'minərəlaiz] *vt* desmineralizar.

demise [di'maiz] *n* defunción *f*, fallecimiento *m* (death) ‖ JUR cesión *f* | transmisión *f* (transfer of sovereignty).

demise [di'maiz] *vt* JUR legar (by will or lease) | transmitir (to transfer).
◆ *vi* JUR transmitirse por herencia ‖ morir (to die).

demisemiquaver ['demisemiˌkweivə*] *n* fusa *f*.

demission [di'miʃən] *n* dimisión *f*.

demist [diː'mist] *vt* eliminar el vaho de.

demister [diː'mistə*] *n* dispositivo *m* antivaho.

demit [di'mit] *vi* dimitir.
◆ *vt* dimitir de.

demitasse ['demiˌtæs] *n* US taza *f* de café.

Demiurge ['diːmiəːdʒ] *n* demiurgo *m*.

demo ['deməu] *n* FAM mani *f*, manifestación *f*.

demob ['diːmɔb] *n* FAM soldado *m* desmovilizado.

demob [diː'mɔb] *vt* FAM desmovilizar.

demobilization [ˌdiməubilai'zeiʃən] *n* desmovilización *f*.

demobilize [diː'məubilaiz] *vt* desmovilizar.

democracy [diː'mɔkrəsi] *n* democracia *f*.

democrat ['deməkræt] *n* demócrata *m* & *f* ‖ *Christian Democrat* democratacristiano, na.

democratic [ˌdemə'krætik] *adj* democrático, ca ‖ — *Christian Democratic* democratacristiano, na ‖ *democratic party* partido demócrata.

democratization [di'mɔkrətai'zeiʃən] *n* democratización *f*.

democratize [di'mɔkrətaiz] *vt* democratizar.
◆ *vi* democratizarse.

Democritus [di'mɔkritəs] *pr n* Demócrito *m*.

démodé [ˌdeiməu'dei] *adj* pasado de moda.

demographer [diː'mɔgrəfə*] *n* demógrafo *m*.

demographic [ˌdiːməgræfik] *adj* demográfico, ca.

demography [di'mɔgrəfi] *n* demografía *f*.

demoiselle [ˌdəmwa'zɛl] *n* ZOOL libélula *f* (dragonfly) ‖ damisela *f* (damsel).

demolish [di'mɔliʃ] *vt* echar abajo, derribar, demoler (a building) ‖ destruir (to raze) ‖ FIG destruir, echar abajo *or* por tierra (an argument) ‖ FAM zamparse (to eat).

demolisher [-ə*] *n* demoledor, ra.

demolition [ˌdemə'liʃən] *n* demolición *f*, derribo *m* (of a building) ‖ destrucción *f*.

demon; daemon ['diːmən] *n* demonio *m* ‖ espíritu *m* (spirit) ‖ demonio *m*, diablo *m*; *this child is a demon* este niño es un demonio ‖ demonio *m*; *driven by a demon of avarice* impulsado por el demonio de la avaricia ‖ FIG hacha *m* (ace) ‖ FIG *to be a demon for work* ser una fiera para el trabajo.

demonetize [diː'mʌnitaiz] *vt* desmonetizar.

demoniac [di'məuniæk] *adj* endemoniado, da; demoniaco, ca (possessed by a demon) ‖ demoniaco, ca; diabólico, ca (fiendish).
◆ *n* demoniaco, ca; endemoniado, da.

demoniacal [ˌdiːməu'naiəkəl]; **demonic** [diː'mɔnik] *adj* demoniaco, ca; diabólico, ca.

demonism ['diːmənizəm] *n* creencia *f* en los demonios.

demonstrability [ˌdemənstrə'biliti] *n* posibilidad *f* de ser demostrado.

demonstrable ['demənstrəbl] *adj* demostrable.

demonstrate ['demənstreit] *vt* demostrar, probar (to prove) ‖ demostrar (to make clear) ‖ mostrar, hacer la demostración de (the working of a machine, etc.) ‖ MATH demostrar ‖ FIG manifestar.
◆ *vi* manifestarse, hacer una manifestación (to show public simpathy, to protest) ‖ MIL hacer una demostración.

demonstration [ˌdeməns'treiʃən] *n* manifestación *f* (expression of public feeling for or against sth.) ‖ demostración *f*, prueba *f*; *demonstration of affection* demostración de cariño; *fruit falling offers a demostration of gravity* la caída de la fruta es una demostración de la fuerza de gravedad; *to give a demonstration of how a piece of equipment works* hacer una demostración de cómo funciona un aparato ‖ MIL demostración *f*.

demonstrative [di'mɔnstrətiv] *adj* GRAM demostrativo, va; *demonstrative adjectives* adjetivos demostrativos ‖ convincente (convincing) ‖ demostrativo, va; expansivo, va (person).
◆ *n* GRAMM demostrativo *m*.

demonstrator ['demənstreitə*] *n* demostrador, ra ‖ manifestante *m* & *f* (participant in a public protest meeting) ‖ auxiliar *m* & *f* (in a laboratory).

demoralization [diˌmɔrəlaizeiʃən] *n* desmoralización *f*.

demoralize [di'mɔrəlaiz] *vt* desmoralizar.

demoralizer [-ə*] *n* desmoralizador, ra.

demoralizing [-iŋ] *adj* desmoralizador, ra; desmoralizante.

Demosthenes [di'mɔsθəniːz] *pr n* Demóstenes *m*.

demote [di'məut] *vt* degradar.

demotic [di'mɔtik] *adj* popular (popular) ‖ demótico, ca (of ancient Egyptian writing).

demotion [di'məuʃən] *n* degradación *f*.

demotivate [diː'məutiveit] *vt* desmotivar, desanimar.

demount [di'maunt] *vt* desmontar, desarmar.

demulcent [di'mʌlsənt] *adj* MED emoliente.
◆ *n* MED emoliente *m*.

demur [di'məː*] *n* objeción *f* ‖ vacilación *f* (hesitation).

demur [di'məː*] *vi* hacer objeciones (to object) ‖ vacilar (to hesitate).

demure [di'mjuə*] *adj* comedido, da (sober) ‖ recatado, da (modest) ‖ remilgado, da (affectedly modest) ‖ gazmoño, ña (prudish).

demurely [-li] *adv* recatadamente (modestly) ‖ con gazmoñería.

demureness [-nis] *n* recato *m* (of a girl, dress, etc.) ‖ gazmoñería *f* (prudery).

demurrage [di'mʌridʒ] *n* MAR sobrestadía *f* ‖ almacenaje *m* (storage free) ‖ cantidad *f* cobrada por el Banco de Inglaterra por lingote depositado.

demurrer [di'məːrə*] *n* JUR excepción *f* perentoria.

demystify [diː'mistifɑi] *vt* desmitificar.

den [den] *n* guarida *f* (animal's lair) ‖ guarida *f* (gang hideout); *den of thieves* guarida de ladrones ‖ cuchitril *m* (dirty little room) ‖ antro *m*; *den of vice* antro de perversión ‖ US estudio *m* (small room).

denarius [di'nɛəriəs] *n* denario *m*.
— OBSERV El plural de *denarius* es *denarii*.

denary ['diːnəri] *adj* denario, ria; decimal.

denationalization [diːˌnæʃnəlai'zeiʃən] *n* desnacionalización *f*.

denationalize [diː'næʃnəlaiz] *vt* desnacionalizar.

denaturalization [diːˌnætʃrəlai'zeiʃən] *n* desnaturalización *f*.

denaturalize [di:'nætʃrəlaiz] *vt* desnaturalizar.

denaturation [di:ˌneitʃəreiʃən] *n* CHEM desnaturalización *f*.

denature [di:ˌneitʃə*] *vt* desnaturalizar ‖ *denatured alcohol* alcohol desnaturalizado.

dendrite ['dendrait] *n* dendrita *f*.

dene [di:n] *n* duna *f* (dune) ‖ pequeño valle *m*, vallejo *m* (valley).

denegation [ˌdi:ni'geiʃən] *n* denegación *f*.

dengue ['deŋgi] *n* MED dengue *m*.

deniable [di'naiəbl] *adj* negable.

denial [di'naiəl] *n* negación *f* (an assertion that sth. is not true, disavowal) ‖ negativa *f* (refusal) ‖ rechazamiento *m* (rejection) ‖ mentís *m* (to a statement) ‖ abnegación *f* (self-denial) ‖ JUR *denial of justice* denegación *f* de justicia.

denicotinize [di'nikətinaiz] *vt* desnicotinizar.

denier [di'naiə*] *n* negador, ra.

denier ['deniei] *n* denier *m* (of stockings).

denigrate ['denigreit] *vt* denigrar.

denigration [ˌdeni'greiʃən] *n* denigración *f*.

denigrator ['denigreitə*] *n* denigrante *m* & *f*, denigrador, ra.

denigratory [ˌdeni'greitəri] *adj* denigrante, denigrador, ra.

denim ['denim] *n* mahón *m* (cotton fabric).
◆ *pl* pantalones *m* vaqueros (jeans) ‖ mono *m sing* (overall).

denitration [ˌdi:nai'treiʃən]; **denitrification** ['di:ˌnaitrifi'keiʃən] *n* desnitrificación *f*.

denitrify [di:'naitrifai] *vt* desnitrificar.

denizen ['denizn] *n* ciudadano, na; habitante *m* & *f* (people) ‖ habitante *m* & *f*; *the lion is a denizen of the jungle* el león es un habitante de la selva ‖ JUR residente *m* extranjero ‖ GRAMM palabra *f* extranjera naturalizada ‖ BOT planta *f* aclimatada ‖ ZOOL animal *m* aclimatado.

Denmark ['denmɑ:k] *pr n* GEOGR Dinamarca *f*.

denominate [di'nɔmineit] *vt* denominar.

denomination [diˌnɔmi'neiʃən] *n* denominación *f* ‖ unidad *f* (of weight, measure) ‖ secta *f*, confesión *f*; *Baptist denomination* secta baptista ‖ valor *m* (of coins) ‖ clase *f*, tipo *m* (kind).

denominational [diˌnɔmi'neiʃənl] *adj* REL sectario, ria (sectarian) ‖ religioso, sa; confesional (education).

denominative [di'nɔminətiv] *adj* denominativo, va.

denominator [di'nɔmineitə*] *n* MATH denominador *m*; *the least* o *the lowest common denominator* el mínimo común denominador.

denotation [ˌdi:nəu'teiʃən] *n* indicación *f* ‖ designación *f* (name) ‖ señal *f*, indicio *m* (sign) ‖ significado *m* (meaning) ‖ extensión *f* (of a word).

denotative [di'nəutətiv] *adj* revelador, ra (*of* de).

denote [di'nəut] *vt* denotar (to mark) ‖ indicar (to indicate) ‖ significar (to stand for).

dénoument; *US* **denouement** [dei'nu:mɑ:ŋ] *n* desenlace *m* (of a play or story) ‖ FIG desenlace *m*.

denounce [di'nauns] *vt* denunciar (a thief, a treaty) ‖ FIG alzarse contra (an abuse) | censurar (to criticize).

denouncement [-mənt] *n* ⟶ **denunciation.**

denouncer [-ə*] *n* denunciante *m* & *f*, denunciador, ra.

dense [dens] *adj* denso, sa (thick, packed together) ‖ FAM torpe (person) | craso, sa (ignorance) ‖ PHYS denso, sa (body, metal) | opaco, ca (negative).

densely [-li] *adv* densamente ‖ *densely ignorant* de una ignorancia supina *or* crasa.

denseness ['densnis] *n* ⟶ **density.**

densify ['densifai] *vt* densificar.

densimeter [den'simetə*] *n* PHYS densímetro *m*.

density ['densiti] *n* densidad *f* (thickness) ‖ FAM torpeza *f* (slowness) ‖ PHYS densidad *f* ‖ INFORM *double density* doble densidad (diskette).

dent [dent] *n* bollo *m*, abolladura *f* (hollow) ‖ mella *f* (in blade).

dent [dent] *vt* abollar (surface) ‖ mellar (blade).
◆ *vi* abollarse (surface) ‖ mellarse (blade).

dental ['dentl] *adj* dental; *dental floss* hilo *or* seda dental; *dental prothesis* prótesis dental ‖ GRAMM dental ‖ MED *dental surgeon* odontólogo *m*.
◆ *n* GRAMM dental *f*.

dentate ['denteit] *adj* BOT dentado, da; *dentate leaf* hoja dentada ‖ dentado, da (notched).

dentation [den'teiʃən] *n* borde *m* dentado.

dented ['dentid] *adj* abollado, da (surface) ‖ mellado, da (blade).

denticle ['dentikl] *n* ARCH dentículo *m* ‖ dientecillo *m* (small tooth).

denticulate [den'tikjələt]; **denticulated** [den'tikjəleitid] *adj* denticulado, da.

denticulation [ˌdentikjə'leiʃən] *n* borde *m* dentado.

dentifrice ['dentrifris] *n* dentífrico *m*.

dentil ['dentil] *n* ARCH dentículo *m*.

dentine; *US* **dentin** ['denti:n] *n* ANAT dentina *f*, esmalte *m* de los dientes.

dentist ['dentist] *n* MED dentista *m* & *f* ‖ *to go to the dentist's* ir al dentista.

dentistry [-ri] *n* odontología *f*.

dentition [den'tiʃən] *n* dentición *f*.

denture ['dentʃə*] *n* dentadura *f* postiza.

denudation ['di:nju:'deiʃən] *n* GEOL denudación *f*.

denude [di'nju:d] *vt* desnudar (to make naked) ‖ descarnar (bone) ‖ descortezar (a tree) ‖ GEOL denudar ‖ FIG despojar (to strip).

denunciation [diˌnʌnsi'eiʃən]; **denouncement** [di'naunsmənt] *n* denuncia *f* (of a thief) ‖ denuncia *f*, anulación *f*, ruptura *f* (of a treaty) ‖ FIG condena *f* (of an abuse) | censura *f* (criticism).

denunciative [di'nʌnsiətiv] *adj* denunciador, ra.

denunciator [di'nʌnsieitə*] *n* denunciador, ra; denunciante *m* & *f*.

deny [di'nai] *vt* negar (to dispute); *I don't deny it* no lo niego ‖ desmentir (to give the lie to) ‖ repudiar (s.o., faith) ‖ rechazar (charge) ‖ denegar, rechazar (request) ‖ negar (to refuse) ‖ — *to be denied to* ser negado a ‖ *to deny o.s. sth.* privarse de algo ‖ *to deny the door to s.o.* cerrar la puerta a alguien.

deodorant [di:'əudərənt] *adj* desodorante.
◆ *n* desodorante *m*.

deodorize [di:'əudəraiz] *vt* desodorizar.

deontology [ˌdi:ɔn'tɔlədʒi] *n* deontología *f*.

deoxidation [di:ˌɔksi'deiʃən]; **deoxidization** [di:ˌɔksidai'zeiʃən] *n* CHEM desoxidación *f*.

deoxidize [di:'ɔksidaiz] *vt* CHEM desoxidar.

deoxidizer [-ə*] *n* CHEM desoxidante *m*.

deoxidizing [-iŋ] *adj* desoxidante.

deoxygenate [di:'ɔksidʒəneit] *vt* CHEM desoxigenar.

deoxyribonucleic [di:'ɔksi'raibəu'nju:kliik] *adj* CHEM desoxirribonucleico, ca (acid).

depart [di'pɑ:t] *vi* marcharse, irse (to go away) ‖ salir (to get off or out) ‖ apartarse, salirse (*from* de) (to deviate) ‖ morir (to die).
◆ *vt* *to depart this life* pasar a mejor vida.

departed [-id] *adj* pasado, da (bygone) ‖ difunto, ta; *my departed husband* mi difunto marido.
◆ *n* *the departed* el difunto, la difunta, los difuntos.

department [di'pɑ:tmənt] *n* departamento *m*, sección *f* (in a store) ‖ sección *f* (in a college, university) ‖ servicio *m*; *the accounting department* el servicio de contabilidad ‖ ramo *m* (branch) ‖ negociado *m* (in a ministry) ‖ departamento *m* (administrative district in France) ‖ FIG esfera *f* (sphere of activity) ‖ *US* departamento *m*, ministerio *m*; *Department of State* departamento de Estado, Ministerio de Asuntos Exteriores; *Department of Labor, of the Interior, of the Navy* Ministerio de Trabajo, de Gobernación [AMER del Interior], de Marina.

departmental [ˌdi:pɑ:t'mentl] *adj* departamental ‖ *departmental head* jefe *m* de servicio.

department store [di:'pɑ:tməntˌstɔ:*] *n* gran almacén *m*.

departure [di'pɑ:tʃə*] *n* marcha *f*, partida *f* (a going away) ‖ salida *f*; *the departure of the train is at nine o'clock* la salida del tren es a las nueve ‖ desviación *f* (deviation) ‖ FIG orientación *f*; *to make a new departure in physics* dar una nueva orientación a la física ‖ MAR diferencia *f* de longitud contada desde el punto de partida ‖ *to take one's departure* marcharse, irse.

departure lounge [-laundʒ] *n* sala *f* de embarque.

depauperate [di:'pɔ:pəreit] *vt* empobrecer, depauperar.

depauperation [di:ˌpɔ:pə'reiʃən] *n* empobrecimiento *m*, depauperación *f* (impoverishment) ‖ MED depauperación *f*.

depend [di'pend] *vi* depender; *it depends on whether you are in a hurry or not* depende de si tienes prisa o no; *I depend upon my father* dependo de mi padre ‖ contar con; *we are depending on you!* ¡contamos contigo! ‖ fiarse de; *you can never depend on what he says* no se puede uno fiar nunca de lo que dice ‖ JUR estar pendiente (suit) ‖ — *that depends* eso depende, según ‖ *to depend on one's work for one's living* vivir de su trabajo ‖ *to depend on o.s.* bastarse a sí mismo ‖ *you may depend on it* puede estar seguro.

dependability [diˌpendə'biliti] *n* formalidad *f*, seriedad *f* (of s.o.) ‖ seguridad *f* (of a machine).

dependable [di'pendəbl] *adj* fiable, seguro, ra; formal (trustworthy) ‖ seguro, ra (things).

dependance [di'pendəns] *n* *US* ⟶ **dependence.**

dependant [di'pendənt] *n* persona *f* a cargo.
◆ *pl* servidumbre *f sing* (servants).

dependence [di'pendəns]; *US* **dependance** *n* dependencia *f*; *the dependence of one person on another* la dependencia de una persona de otra ‖ dependencia *f* (*upon* de), subordinación *f* (*upon* de), subordinación *f* (*upon* a) (subordination) ‖ confianza *f* (*on, upon* en) (trust).

dependency [-i] *n* dependencia *f*.

dependent [di'pendənt] *adj* dependiente (*on* de) (persons, lands) ‖ subordinado, da (*on* a) (subordinate) ‖ GRAMM subordinado, da; *dependent clause* oración subordinada ‖ *to be dependent on* depender de.
◆ *n* persona *f* a cargo.

depersonalization [di,pə:snəlai'zeiʃən] *n* despersonalización *f.*

depersonalize [di'pə:snəlaiz] *vt* despersonalizar.

dephase [di:'feiz] *vt* ELECTR defasar.

dephasing [-iŋ] *n* defasaje *m.*

dephosphorize [di:,fɔsfəraiz] *vt* desfosforar.

depict [di'pikt] *vt* ARTS pintar, representar || FIG describir, pintar (to describe).

depiction [di'pikʃən] *n* ARTS pintura *f* || descripción *f,* pintura *f* (description).

depilate ['depileit] *vt* depilar.

depilation [,depi'leiʃən] *n* depilación *f.*

depilatory [di'pilətəri] *adj* depilatorio, ria.
◆ *n* depilatorio *m.*

deplenish [di'pleniʃ] *vt* vaciar || COMM desproveer.

deplete [di'pli:t] *vt* agotar (to exhaust provisions, ammunition) || reducir (to reduce) || MIL desguarnecer (a garrison) || MED descongestionar.

depletion [di'pli:ʃən] *n* agotamiento *m* (exhaustion of provisions, ammunition, etc.) || disminución *f,* reducción *f* (lessening) || MED descongestión *f.*

deplorable [di'plɔ:rəbl] *adj* deplorable, lamentable.

deplore [di'plɔ:*] *vt* deplorar, lamentar || *it is to be deplored* es de lamentar, es deplorable.

deploy [di'plɔi] *vt* MIL & FIG desplegar.
◆ *vi* MIL desplegarse.

deployment [-mənt] *n* MIL despliegue *m.*

deplume [di:'plu:m] *vt* desplumar (to pluck) || FIG despojar.

depolarization ['di:,pəulərai'zeiʃən] *n* PHYS despolarización *f.*

depolarize [di:'pəuləraiz] *vt* PHYS despolarizar.

depolarizer [-ə*] *n* PHYS despolarizador *m.*

depone [di'pəun] *vi* JUR deponer.

deponent [di'pəunənt] *adj* GRAMM deponente.
◆ *n* GRAMM verbo *m* deponente || deponente *m* & *f,* declarante *m* & *f* (witness).

depopulate [di:'pɔpjuleit] *vt* despoblar.
◆ *vi* despoblarse.

depopulation [di:,pɔpju'leiʃən] *n* despoblación *f.*

deport [di'pɔ:t] *vt* JUR expulsar (an alien) | deportar (a convict) || *to deport o.s.* comportarse, portarse.

deportation [,di:pɔ'teiʃən] *n* JUR expulsión *f* (of an alien) | deportación *f* (of a convict).

deportee [,di:pɔ:'ti] *n* JUR deportado, da.

deportment [di'pɔ:tmənt] *n* porte *m* (bearing) || conducta *f,* comportamiento *m* (behaviour).

deposal [di'pəuzəl] *n* deposición *f,* destronamiento *m* (of a king) || destitución *f* (from office).

depose [di'pəuz] *vt* deponer, destronar (to dethrone) || destituir (to remove from office) || JUR deponer, declarar.
◆ *vi* JUR deponer, declarar.

deposit [di'pɔzit] *n* depósito *m* (in a bank) || poso *m,* sedimento *m,* depósito *m* (sediment) || depósito *m* (in electrolysis) || MIN yacimiento *m* || señal *f* (pledge); *to leave ten pounds deposit on a refrigerator* dejar una señal de diez libras para un refrigerador || entrada *f; to put a deposit on a flat* dar una entrada para un piso.

deposit [di'pɔzit] *vt* depositar (to put sth. down) || depositar, sedimentar (to leave a layer or coating of) || depositar (money in bank) || ingresar (money in one's account) || dar de señal (to pledge) || dar una entrada de, hacer un desembolso inicial de (when buying houses, cars, etc.) || poner (eggs).

deposit account [-ə,kaunt] *n* cuenta *f* de depósitos a plazo.

depositary [di'pɔzitəri] *n* depositario, ria (person) || depositaría *f* (storehouse).

deposition [,depə'ziʃən] *n* deposición *f,* destronamiento *m* (of a king) || destitución *f* (from office) || JUR deposición *f,* declaración *f* || depósito *m* (deposit) || REL descendimiento *m* (of Christ).

depositor [di'pɔzitə*] *n* depositador, ra; depositante *m* & *f* || cuentacorrentista *m* & *f* (person who holds an account).

depository [-ri] *n* depositario, ria (person) || depositaría *f* (storehouse).

depot ['depəu] *n* almacén *m* (storehouse) || MIL depósito *m* || cochera *f,* depósito *m* (for buses) || US estación *f* (station).

deprave [di'preiv] *vt* depravar, pervertir.

depraver [-ə*] *n* depravador, ra.

depravity [di'præviti] *n* depravación *f* (perversion).

deprecate ['deprikeit] *vt* desaprobar.

deprecation [,depri'keiʃən] *n* desaprobación *f* (disapproval) || deprecación *f* (prayer).

deprecative [,depri'keitiv]; **deprecatory** ['deprikətəri] *adj* de desaprobación (disapproving); *a deprecative murmur* un murmullo de desaprobación || tímido, da (smile).

depreciate [di'pri:ʃieit] *vt* depreciar (money) || abaratar (goods) || despreciar, menospreciar (to belittle).
◆ *vi* depreciarse (money) || bajar (in price).

depreciation [di,pri:ʃi'eiʃən] *n* depreciación *f* (of money) || abaratamiento *m* (of goods) || FIG desprecio *m.*

depreciator [di'pri:ʃieitə*] *n* depreciador, ra.

depreciative [di'pri:ʃieitiv]; **depreciatory** [di'pri:ʃjətəri] *adj* depreciador, ra (lessening in value) || peyorativo, va; despectivo, va (pejorative).

depredate ['deprideit] *vt* depredar.

depredation [,depri'deiʃən] *n* depredación *f.*
◆ *pl* estragos *m* (ravages).

depredator ['deprideitə*] *n* depredador *m.*

depress [di'pres] *vt* deprimir (to dispirit) || debilitar (to weaken) || bajar (to lower) || disminuir (to lessen) || presionar, apretar (to push down) || AUT pisar (the pedal) || MATH reducir (an equation) || COMM reducir (trade) | deprimir (economy) || hacer bajar (prices).

depressant [-ənt] *adj* MED calmante, sedante.
◆ *n* MED calmante *m,* sedante *m.*

depressed [-t] *adj* deprimido, da; desanimado, da (miserable) || necesitado, da (needy); *depressed areas* áreas necesitadas || COMM de depresión (period) | deprimido, da (economy).

depressing [-iŋ] *adj* deprimente.

depression [di'preʃən] *n* GEOGR & MED depresión *f* || depresión *f,* crisis *f* económica (slump) || FIG abatimiento *m,* depresión *f* (dejection).

depressive [di'presiv] *adj* deprimente, depresivo, va (depressing) || propenso a la depresión (easily depressed).

depressor [di'presə*] *n* ANAT depresor *m* || ELECTR elevador *m* de voltaje.

depressurization ['di:,preʃərai'zeiʃən] *n* descompresión *f.*

depressurize ['di:'preʃəraiz] *vt* descomprimir.

deprival [di'praivəl] *n* privación *f.*

deprivation [,depri'veiʃən] *n* privación *f* || pérdida *f* (loss) || JUR *deprivation of office* suspensión *f* de empleo.

deprive [di'praiv] *vt* privar; *to deprive s.o. of food* privar a alguien de alimento || JUR destituir (to remove from office) || *to deprive o.s.* privarse.

deprived [-d] *adj* desheredado, da; *the deprived ones of the world* los desheredados de la fortuna || *deprived child* niño desgraciado.

de profundis [deiprəu'fʌndis] *n* REL de profundis *m.*

depth [depθ] *n* profundidad *f; the depth of the ocean* la profundidad del océano; *depth of field* profundidad de campo; *depth of feeling* profundidad de sentimiento || lo más profundo, lo más hondo; *in the depth of his heart* en lo más profundo de su corazón || intensidad *f* (of colour) || corazón *m; the depth of the forest* el corazón del bosque || MUS gravedad *f* || — *in depth* a fondo; *to study a matter in depth* estudiar una cuestión a fondo; en profundidad (defence) || *in the depth of winter* en pleno invierno, en lo más crudo del invierno || *the lake is ten feet in depth* el lago tiene una profundidad de diez pies || *to be out of one's depth* perder pie (in water), estar perdido, no entender nada (not to understand) || *to get out of one's depth* perder pie (in water), meterse en honduras.
◆ *pl* abismo *m sing* || *in the depths of despair* completamente desesperado.

depth charge [-tʃɑ:dʒ] *n* carga *f* de profundidad.

depth gauge [-geidʒ] *n* sonda *f.*

depurate ['depjuəreit] *vt* depurar.
◆ *vi* depurarse.

depuration [,depjuə'reiʃən] *n* depuración *f.*

depurative ['depjuərətiv] *adj* MED depurativo, va || depuratorio, ria (cleansing).
◆ *n* MED depurativo *m.*

depurator ['depjuəreitə*] *n* depurador *m.*

deputation [,depju'teiʃən] *n* delegación *f.*

depute [di'pju:t] *vt* delegar.

deputize ['depjutaiz] *vt* delegar.
◆ *vi* sustituir (*for* a).

deputy ['depjuti] *n* delegado *m* (member of a deputation) || suplente *m,* sustituto *m* (substitute) || diputado *m* (member of a legislative body); *Chamber of Deputies* Cámara de Diputados || — *Deputy Chairman* vicepresidente *m* || *Deputy Director General* Director General Adjunto || *deputy head* subdirector, ra || *deputy judge* juez suplente *or* adjunto || *deputy mayor* teniente *m* de alcalde.

deracinate [di'ræsineit] *vt* desarraigar.

derail [di'reil] *vt* hacer descarrilar.
◆ *vi* descarrilar.

derailment [-mənt] *n* descarrilamiento *m.*

derange [di'reindʒ] *vt* trastornar el juicio a, enloquecer (to make insane) || desarreglar (to throw into confusion) || estropear (to cause to go out of order) || perturbar, molestar (to annoy).

deranged [-d] *adj* loco, ca.

derangement [-mənt] *n* MED trastorno *m* mental || desorden *m,* desarreglo *m* (disorder).

derat [di:'ræt] *vt* desratizar.

derate [di:'reit] *vt* desgravar, reducir los impuestos sobre.

deratization [di:,rætai'zeiʃən] *n* desratización *f.*

derby ['dɑ:bi] *n* US hongo *m* (hat).

Derby ['dɑ:bi] *pr n* GEOGR Derby || derby *m* (horse race).

deregulate [di:'regjuleit] *vt* desregular.

deregulation [di:ˌregju'leiʃən] *n* desregulación *f.*

derelict ['derilikt] *adj* abandonado, da.
◆ *n* MAR derrelicto *m*, pecio *m* ‖ FIG deshecho *m* (worthless thing or person).

dereliction [ˌderi'likʃən] *n* abandono *m* (abandonment) ‖ descuido *m*, negligencia *f* (of duty) ‖ MAR retirada *f* (of the sea).

deride [di'raid] *vt* mofarse de, burlarse de.

derision [di'riʒən] *n* mofa *f* ‖ irrisión *f* (laughing-stock) ‖ *to hold s.o. in derision* mofarse de uno, hacer mofa de uno.

derisive [di'raisiv]; **derisory** [di'raisəri] *adj* burlón, ona; mofador, ra (mocking) ‖ irrisorio, ria (petty, ridiculous).

derivation [ˌderi'veiʃən] *n* derivación *f.*

derivative [di'rivətiv] *adj* derivado, da.
◆ *n* CHEM & GRAMM derivado *m* ‖ MATH derivada *f* (differential coefficient).

derive [di'raiv] *vt* derivar ‖ sacar (profit, ideas, etc.).
◆ *vi* derivar, derivarse (to be derived) ‖ provenir, proceder; *his money derives from the savings he made in Germany* su dinero procede de lo que ahorró en Alemania.

derm [də:m]; **derma** [-ə] *n* ANAT dermis *f.*

dermal [-əl] *adj* ANAT dérmico, ca.

dermatitis [ˌdə:mə'taitis] *n* MED dermatitis *f*, dermitis *f.*

dermatologist [ˌdə:mə'tɔlədʒist] *n* dermatólogo *m.*

dermatology [ˌde:mɔ'tɔlədʒi] *n* dermatología *f.*

dermatosis [ˌdə:mə'təusis] *n* MED dermatosis *f.*
— OBSERV El plural de *dermatosis* es *dermatoses.*

dermic ['də:mik] *adj* ANAT dérmico, ca.

dermis ['də:mis] *n* ANAT dermis *f.*

dermoskeleton [ˌdə:mə'skelitn] *n* ANAT dermatoesqueleto *m.*

derogate ['derəgeit] *vi to derogate from* atentar contra, ir en contra de (rights, liberty), ir contra (one's dignity), rebajarse de (one's rank).

derogation [ˌderə'geiʃən] *n* menosprecio *m* (contempt) ‖ derogación *f* [de una ley] (of a law) ‖ *to the derogation of* en detrimento de.

derogatory [di'rɔgətəri] *adj* despectivo, va (disparaging) ‖ JUR derogatorio, ria ‖ FIG *derogatory to* que va en contra de (s.o.'s dignity), indigno de (s.o.'s rank).

derrick ['derik] *n* grúa *f* (crane) ‖ torre *f* de perforación, «derrick» *m* (of an oil well).

derring-do ['deriŋ'du:] *n* valor *m* ‖ *deeds of derring-do* hazañas *f pl.*

derv [də:v] *n* diesel *m*, gasolina *f* diesel.

dervish ['də:viʃ] *n* REL derviche *m.*

DES *abbr of [Department of Education and Science]* Ministerio británico de educación y ciencia.

desalinate [di:sælineit] *vt* desalar, desalinizar.

desalination [ˌdi:sæli'neiʃən] *n* desalación *f*, desalinización *f.*

descale ['di:'skeil] *vt* desincrustar.

descaling [-iŋ] *n* desincrustación *f.*

descant ['deskænt] *n* MUS contrapunto *m* ‖ FIG *a descant on religion* una larga conferencia sobre religión.

descant ['deskænt] *vi* MUS cantar en contrapunto ‖ FIG disertar largamente (to discourse at large).

descend [di'send] *vi* descender, bajar (to come or to go down) ‖ ASTR ponerse (the sun) ‖ — *to descend from* descender de ‖ *to descend on* o *upon* caer sobre ‖ *to descend to* rebajarse a (to lower o.s. to), pasar a (a property).
◆ *vt* descender, bajar; *to descend the stairs* bajar la escalera.

descendant; descendent [di'sendənt] *n* descendiente *m* & *f.*

descended [di'sendid] *adj to be descended from* descender de ‖ *well descended* de buena familia.

descendible [di'sendibl] *adj* JUR transmisible (property).

descending [di'sendiŋ] *adj* descendiente, descendente ‖ *in descending order* de mayor a menor, en orden decreciente.

descent [di'sent] *n* descenso *m*, bajada *f* (a going down) ‖ declive *m*, pendiente *m* (slope) ‖ descenso *m* (a way down) ‖ descendencia *f* (lineage) ‖ SP descenso *m* ‖ incursión *f* (raid) ‖ JUR transmisión *f* ‖ REL descendimiento *m*; *Descent from the Cross* Descendimiento de la Cruz ‖ FIG decadencia *f* (decline).

describable [dis'kraibəbl] *adj* describible, descriptible.

describe [dis'kraib] *vt* describir ‖ calificar; *to describe o.s. as intelligent* calificar a uno de inteligente ‖ trazar (a geometrical figure) ‖ *to describe o.s. as an actor* presentarse como actor.

description [dis'kripʃən] *n* descripción *f* (account, explanation); *it answers your description* corresponde a su descripción ‖ clase *f*, tipo *m* (kind, sort); *toys of every description* juguetes de todas clases.

descriptive [dis'kriptiv] *adj* descriptivo, va; *descriptive geometry, anatomy* geometría, anatomía descriptiva ‖ GRAMM calificativo, va (adjective).

descry [dis'krai] *vt* divisar, columbrar (to see) ‖ descubrir (to discover).

desecrate ['desikreit] *vt* REL profanar.

desecration [ˌdesi'kreiʃən] *n* REL profanación *f.*

desecrator ['desikreitə*] *n* REL profanador, ra.

desegregate ['di:'segrigeit] *vt* suprimir la segregación racial en.

desegregation [ˌdi:səgri'geiʃən] *n* supresión *f* de la segregación racial.

deselect [ˌdi:si'lekt] *vt* rechazar como candidato, ta (an existing MP).

desensitization [ˌdi:sensiti'zeiʃən] *n* insensibilización *f.*

desensitize ['di:'sensitaiz] *vt* insensibilizar.

desert ['dezət] *adj* desierto, ta; desértico, ca; *desert island* isla desierta.
◆ *n* desierto *m.*

desert [di'zə:t] *vt* abandonar; *his courage deserted him* su valor le abandonó ‖ MIL desertar de.
◆ *vi* MIL desertar; *to desert from the army* desertar del ejército.

deserter [-ə*] *n* desertor *m.*

desertion [di'zə:ʃən] *n* MIL deserción *f* ‖ abandono *m* (abandon).

deserts [dzə:tz] *pl n to get one's deserts* tener *or* llevarse su merecido.

deserve [di'zə:v] *vt* merecer; *he deserves punishing* merece castigo; *he deserves to win* merece ganar ‖ ser digno de; *to deserve praise* ser digno de elogios ‖ *you'll get what you deserve* tendrás *or* te llevarás tu merecido.
◆ *vi to deserve well of* merecer el reconocimiento de ‖ *to deserve well of one's country* hacerse digno de la patria.

deserved [-d] *adj* merecido, da.

derserving [-iŋ] *adj* digno, na; *he is deserving of our esteem* es digno de nuestro aprecio ‖ meritorio, ria (action) ‖ de mérito (person).

déshabillé; US **deshabille** [ˌdeizæ'bi:ei] *n* ⟶ **dishabille.**

desiccant ['desikənt] *adj* desecativo, va.
◆ *n* desecativo *m.*

desiccate ['desikeit] *vt* desecar.
◆ *vi* desecarse.

desiccation [ˌdesi'keiʃən] *n* desecación *f.*

desiccative [de'sikətiv] *adj* desecativo, va.
◆ *n* desecativo *m.*

desiccator ['desikeitə*] *n* desecador *m.*

desiderative [di'zidərətiv] *adj* GRAMM desiderativo, va.

desideratum [di'zidə'reıtəm] *n* desiderátum *m.*
— OBSERV El plural de *desideratum* es *desiderata.*

design [di'zain] *n* dibujo *m* (pattern, drawing) ‖ bosquejo *m* (in painting) ‖ boceto *m* (in sculpture) ‖ estilo *m*, diseño *m* (style) ‖ ARCH plano *m* ‖ propósito *m*, intención *f* (intention) ‖ mala intención *f* (bad intention) ‖ proyecto *m* (scheme) ‖ — *by design* intencionalmente, a propósito ‖ *to have designs on sth.* haber puesto sus miras en.

design [di'zain] *vt* diseñar (to prepare plans or sketches for) ‖ dibujar (to draw) ‖ ARTS esbozar ‖ inventar (to invent) ‖ crear (to create) ‖ concebir; *a well designed building* un edificio bien concebido ‖ planear, proyectar (to intend) ‖ imaginar (to contrive) ‖ destinar (to destine).
◆ *vi* hacer diseños *or* dibujos.

designate ['dezignit] *adj* designado, da ‖ nombrado, da (appointed).

designate ['dezigneit] *vt* designar (to name for a duty) ‖ nombrar (to appoint); *to designate s.o. for a post* nombrar a alguien para un puesto ‖ señalar (to point out) ‖ denominar (to name).

designation [ˌdezig'neiʃən] *n* designación *f* ‖ nombramiento *m* (appointment) ‖ denominación *f* (naming).

designedly [di'zainidli] *adv* a propósito.

designer [di'zainə*] *n* diseñador, ra ‖ delineante *m* (draughtsman) ‖ FIG autor, ra ‖ — *dress designer* modista *m* ‖ THEATR *stage designer* escenógrafo *m.*

designing [di'zainiŋ] *n* diseño *m* (of a machine) ‖ creación *f* (of a dress).
◆ *adj* intrigante ‖ *a designing old man* un viejo intrigante.

desilver [di:'silvə*]; **desilverize** [di:'silvəraiz] *vt* desplatar.

desinence ['desinəns] *n* GRAMM desinencia *f.*

densinential ['desinənʃəl] *adj* GRAMM desinencial.

desiderability [diˌzaiərə'biliti] *n* lo atractivo, lo apetecible ‖ conveniencia *f* (advisability); *the desirability of a reform* la conveniencia de una reforma ‖ atractivo *m* (of a woman).

desirable [di:'zaiərəbl] *adj* deseable ‖ conveniente, deseable (proper); *I don't think it desirable to go* no creo que sea conveniente ir ‖ atractivo, va (attractive).

desire [di'zaiə*] *n* deseo *m*; *all his desires have been met* todos sus deseos han sido satisfechos ‖ petición *f* (request) ‖ deseo *m*, instinto *m* sexual (sexual).

desire [di'zaiə*] *vt* desear ‖ rogar, pedir; *I desire you to come at three o'clock* le ruego que venga a las tres ‖ querer (to want) ‖ — *it is to be desired that...* es deseable que... ‖ *it leaves much to be desired* deja mucho que desear.

desirous [di'zaiərəs] *adj* deseoso, sa || *to be desirous of* o *to* desear.

desist [di'zist] *vi* desistir (*from* de) || *to desist from smoking* dejar de fumar.

desistance [di'zistəns] *n* desistimiento *m*.

desk [desk] *n* pupitre *m* (at school) || mesa *f* de despacho, despacho *m*, escritorio *m* (in an office) || COMM caja *f* || REL atril *m* (lectern) || US redacción *f* (editorial department of a newspaper).

desk clerk [-klɑːk] *n* US recepcionista *m* & *f* de hotel.

desktop publishing ['desktɔp,pʌbliʃiŋ] *n* INFORM autoedición, microedición.

desman ['desmən] *n* ZOOL desmán *m*, ratón *m* almizclero.

desolate ['desəlit] *adj* solitario, ria (lonely) || deshabitado, da (uninhabited) || asolado, da; desolado, da (waste) || desierto, ta (deserted) || afligido, da; desconsolado, da (disconsolate).

desolate ['desəleit] *vt* asolar, arrasar (to lay waste); *the town was desolated by an earthquake* la ciudad fue asolada por un terremoto || despoblar (to depopulate) || abandonar (to forsake) || afligir, desconsolar (to distress).

desolating [-iŋ] *adj* desolador, ra.

desolation [,desə'leiʃən] *n* asolamiento *m* (destruction) || desolación *f* (barren state) || aflicción *f*, desconsuelo *m* (grief) || desierto *m* (desert) || soledad *f* (loneliness).

desoxyribonucleic [de'sɔksi'raibəun'juːkliik] *adj* CHEM desoxirribonucleico, ca (acid).

despair [dis'pɛə*] *n* desesperación *f*; *to be the despair of* ser la desesperación de || *to be in despair* estar desesperado.

despair [dis'pɛə*] *vi* desesperar, desesperarse; *I despair at not hearing from him* me desespero por no recibir noticias suyas || *her life is despaired of* se ha perdido toda esperanza de salvarle la vida.

despairing [-riŋ] *adj* desesperado, da.

despatch [dis'pætʃ] *n/vt* —> **dispatch.**

despatcher [-ə*] *n* expedidor, ra.

desperado [despə'rɑːdəu] *n* forajido *m*, bandido *m*.

— OBSERV El plural es *desperadoes* o *desperados*.

desperate ['despərit] *adj* desesperado, da || apremiante (urgency, need) || capaz de cualquier cosa (ruthless) || encarnizado, da (conflict) || enérgico, ca (resistance) || muy grave, mortal (wound, illness) || muy grave, desesperado, da (situation) || heroico, ca (remedy) || — *desperate ills call for desperate measures* a grandes males grandes remedios || *I am desperate for* necesito con gran urgencia || *they are getting desperate* empiezan a desesperarse.

desperately [-li] *adv* desesperadamente || encarnizadamente (to fight) || locamente; *desperately in love* locamente enamorado || — *desperately ill* gravemente enfermo, enfermo de gravedad || *he was desperately afraid* tenía muchísimo miedo, tenía un miedo espantoso.

desperation [,despə'reiʃən] *n* desesperación *f* || *in desperation* a la desesperada; *they operated on him in desperation* le operaron a la desesperada; desesperado, da (in despair).

despicable [dis'pikəbl] *adj* despreciable, desdeñable.

despise [dis'paiz] *vt* despreciar, menospreciar, desdeñar.

despite [dis'pait] *prep* a pesar de; *despite what he says* a pesar de lo que dice.
◆ *n* despecho *m* (offended pride) || odio *m* (hatred) || *in despite of* a pesar de.

despoil [dis'pɔil] *vt* despojar; *to despoil s.o. of sth.* despojar a alguien de algo || saquear (to plunder).

despoiler [-ə*] *n* expoliador, ra.

despoilment [-mənt]; **despoliation** [,dispəuli'eiʃən] *n* expoliación *f* (spoliation) || saqueo *m* (plundering).

despondence [dis'pɔndəns]; **despondency** [-i] *n* desánimo *m*, desaliento *m*, descorazonamiento *m*.

despondent [dis'pɔndənt] *adj* desanimado, da; desalentado, da; descorazonado, da (disheartened) || pesimista (pessimistic).

despot ['despɔt] *n* déspota *m*; *Nero was a cruel despot* Nerón fue un déspota cruel; *the child is a real despot* el niño es un verdadero déspota.

despotic [des'pɔtik] *adj* despótico, ca; *a despotic government, husband* un gobierno, un marido despótico.

despotism ['despətizəm] *n* despotismo *m*; *enlightened despotism* el despotismo ilustrado.

despumate ['despjumeit] *vt* espumar.

desquamate ['deskwəmeit] *vi* MED descamarse.

desquamation [,deskwə'meiʃən] *n* MED descamación *f*.

dessert [di'zəːt] *n* postre *m*; *what is there for dessert?* ¿qué hay de postre?

dessertspoon [-spuːn] *n* cuchara *f* de postre.

dessert wine [-wɑin] *n* vino *m* dulce.

destabilize, destabilise [diː'steibəlaiz] *vt* desestabilizar.

destination [,desti'neiʃən] *n* destino *m*; *the destination of a ship* el destino de un barco; *to arrive at* o *to reach one's destination* llegar a destino.

destine ['destin] *vt* destinar (*for, to* a) || — MAR *to be destined for* salir con destino a || *to be destined to be Prime Minister* estar llamado a ser Primer Ministro || *to be destined to fail* estar condenado al fracaso.

destiny ['destini] *n* destino *m*.

destitute ['destitjuːt] *adj* indigente, desvalido, da; necesitado, da || — *destitute of* desprovisto de || *the destitute* los indigentes, los desvalidos, los necesitados || *to be destitute* estar en la miseria.

destitution [,desti'tjuːʃən] *n* indigencia *f*, miseria *f*, desvalimiento *m* (poverty) || falta *f*, carencia *f* (lack) || destitution *f* (deprivation of office).

destroy [dis'trɔi] *vt* destruir (to demolish) || matar (to kill) || matar, sacrificar (horse, etc.) || aniquilar (to annihilate) || FIG destruir (reputation, etc.) | anular (influence, etc.).

destroyer [-ə*] *n* MAR destructor *m*.

destructible [dis'trʌktəbl] *adj* destructible.

destruction [dis'trʌkʃən] *n* destrucción *f* (demolition) || FIG ruina *f*, perdición *f*; *to rush to one's destruction* correr a la ruina.

destructive [dis'trʌktiv] *adj* destructivo, va; destructor, ra || destrozón, ona (child) || dañino, na (animal) || *destructive of* o *to* perjudicial para.

destructiveness [-nis] *n* destructividad *f* (tendency) || poder *m* destructivo *or* de destrucción (power).

destructor [dis'trʌktə*] *n* incinerador *m* *or* quemadero *m* de basuras.

desuetude [di'sjuitjuːd] *n* desuso *m*; *to fall into desuetude* caer en desuso.

desultory ['desəltəri] *adj* inconexo, xa (disconnected) || poco metódico, ca (work, person, etc.) || sin orden ni concierto (conversation).

detach [di'tætʃ] *vt* separar (*from* de) (to separate) || MIL destacar.

detachable [-əbl] *adj* separable || postizo, za (collar) || amovible, desmontable (parts of machine).

detached [-t] *adj* independiente (independent); *detached house* casa independiente || suelto, ta; *detached extracts* trozos sueltos || separado, da (separate) || objetivo, va (objective) || indiferente, despreocupado, da (unworried) || desenvuelto, ta (manners) || MIL destacado, da || — *to become detached* separarse || *to live detached from the world* vivir aislado del mundo.

detachment [-mənt] *n* separación *f* (separation) || MIL destacamento *m* || objetividad *f* (objectivity) || despreocupación *f*, despego *m*, indiferencia *f* (indifference) || MED desprendimiento *m* (of retina) || desenganche *m* (of trains).

detail ['diːteil] *n* detalle *m*, pormenor *m*; *in full detail* con todo detalle, con todos los pormenores || ARTS detalle *m* || MIL destacamento *m* || — *to go into detail* entrar en detalles || *to tell sth. in detail* contar algo detalladamente *or* con todo detalle.

detail ['diːteil] *vt* detallar, pormenorizar (to relate in detail) || enumerar (to itemize) || MIL destacar (*for, to* para).

detailed [-d] *adj* detallado, da (picture, story); pormenorizado, da (list).

detain [di'tein] *vt* retener (to keep) || JUR detener || — *he was detained at the meeting* se entretuvo en la reunión || *to be detained by snow* retrasarse a causa de la nieve.

detainee [,diːtei'niː] *n* detenido, da; preso, sa.

detainer [di'teinə*] *n* JUR toma *f* de posesión (of property) | orden *f* de detención (of incarceration) | detención *f* (of an object).

detect [di'tekt] *vt* advertir (to note) || percibir (to perceive) || descubrir (to discover) || TECH detectar; *to detect enemy aircraft* detectar aviones enemigos.

detectable [-əbl] *adj* perceptible.

detecting [-iŋ] *adj* detector, ra.

detection [di'tekʃən] *n* descubrimiento *m* || detección *f*; *mine detection* detección de minas.

detective [di'tektiv] *n* detective *m*.

detective story [-,stɔːri] *n* novela *f* policíaca.

detector [di'tektə*] *n* detector *m*; *lie detector* detector de mentiras; *mine detector* detector de minas || descubridor *m*.

detent [di'tent] *n* TECH escape *m* (of a watch) | trinquete *m* (of a machine).

détente [deitɑnt] *n* relajación *f* de la tensión [entre países].

detention [di'tenʃən] *n* detención *f*, arresto *m* || MIL arresto *m* || — *detention barracks* calabozo *m sing* || *detention centre* centro *m* de detención para menores.

deter [di'təː*] *vt* disuadir (to dissuade); *he deterred me from doing it* me disuadió de hacerlo || desanimar (to dishearten); *don't let the rain deter you* que no te desanime la lluvia || *your threats will not deter me* no me asustarás *or* no me harás desistir con amenazas.

deterge [di'təːdʒ] *vt* deterger.

detergent [-ənt] *adj* detergente.
◆ *n* detergente *m*.

deteriorate [di'tiəriəreit] *vt* empeorar (to make worse) || deteriorar (to wear out) || depreciar, desvalorizar (to lower the value of).
◆ *vi* empeorar (to become worse); *the situation is deteriorating* la situación está empeorando || deteriorarse (to wear out) || degenerar (race).

deterioration [diˌtiəriəˈreiʃən] *n* empeoramiento *m* (worsening) || deterioro *m* (wearing out) || degeneración *f* (of race) || decadencia *f* (decline).

determent [diˈtəːmənt] *n* disuasión *f* || *for the determent of* para disuadir a, para asustar a.

determinable [diˈtəːminəbl] *adj* determinable.

determinant [diˈtəːminənt] *adj* determinante.
◆ *n* MATH determinante *m* || factor *m or* elemento determinante (determining factor).

determinate [diˈtəːminit] *adj* determinado, da.

determination [diˌtəːmiˈneiʃən] *n* determinación *f*, resolución *f*, decisión *f* (firmness of purpose) || determinación *f*, decisión *f* (decision) || fijación *f* (of a date, etc.) || JUR resolución *f*, fallo *m* (decision) | fijación *f* (of penalty) | rescisión *f*, anulación *f* (of a contract) || determinación *f* (determining) || *in his determination to win* estando resuelto a ganar.

determinative [diˈtəːminətiv] *adj* determinante || GRAMM determinativo, va; *determinative adjective* adjetivo determinativo.
◆ *n* GRAMM determinativo *m*.

determine [diˈtəːmin] *vt* determinar (to fix); *to determine the causes of an accident* determinar las causas de un accidente; *that determined me to try* eso me determinó a intentar || causar, provocar (to cause) || resolver (to settle) || fijar, determinar (date) || definir, determinar (limits) || decidir (to decide); *to determine to do sth.* decidir hacer algo || JUR rescindir, anular (a contract) || *to be determined by* depender de; *his answer will be determined by what happens today* su respuesta depende de lo que pase hoy.
◆ *vi* JUR expirar || *to determine on* decidirse por.

determined [-d] *adj* decidido, da; resuelto, ta; *a determined person* una persona decidida || determinado, da (date, price) || *to be determined to do sth.* estar decidido *or* resuelto a hacer algo.

determining [-iŋ] *adj* decisivo, va; determinante.

determinism [diˈtəːminizəm] *n* PHIL determinismo *m*.

determinist [diˈtəːminist] *adj/n* PHIL determinista *m* & *f*.

deterministic [diˌtəːmiˈnistik] *adj* determinista.

deterrence [diˈterəns] *n* disuasión *f*.

deterrent [diˈtərənt] *adj* disuasivo, va.
◆ *n* freno *m* (obstacle) || fuerza *f* de disuasión, fuerza *f* disuasoria (armaments) || *to act as a deterrent to* disuadir.

detersion [diˈtəːʃən] *n* detersión *f*.

detersive [diˈtəːsiv] *adj* detergente, detersivo, va.
◆ *n* detergente *m*.

detest [diˈtest] *vt* detestar, odiar; *to detest a person, a travelling* detestar a una persona, los viajes.

detestable [diˈtestəbl] *adj* detestable, odioso, sa.

detestation [ˌdiːtesˈteiʃən] *n* odio *m*, aborrecimiento *m* || *to hold in detestation* odiar, aborrecer.

dethrone [diˈθrəun] *vt* destronar.

dethronement [-mənt] *n* destronamiento *m*.

detonate [ˈdetəneit] *vi* detonar.
◆ *vt* hacer detonar.

detonating [-iŋ] *adj* detonante || *detonating fuse* detonador *m*, fulminante *m*.

detonation [ˌdetəˈneiʃən] *n* detonación *f*.

detonator [ˌdetəneitə*] *n* detonador *m*, fulminante *m*.

detour [ˈdiːtuə*] *n* desvío *m*, desviación *f* (deviation) || vuelta *f*, rodeo *m* (to avoid some obstacle); *he made a detour* dio un rodeo.

detoxicate [diːˈtɔksikeit]; **detoxify** [diːˈtɔksifai] *vt* desintoxicar.

detract [diˈtrækt] *vi* *to detract from* quitar; *to detract from s.o.'s merit* quitarle mérito a alguien; empañar, deslucir (s.o.'s reputation).
◆ *vt* disminuir, reducir (to reduce) || quitar (to take away) || denigrar (to disparage).

detraction [diˈtrækʃən] *n* denigración *f*.

detractor [diˈtræktə*] *n* detractor, ra.

detrain [diːˌtrein] *vi* bajarse del tren.
◆ *vt* desembarcar de un tren (troops, etc.).

detriment [ˈdetrimənt] *n* detrimento *m*, perjuicio *m*; *to the detriment of* en detrimento de; *without detriment to* sin causar detrimento *or* perjuicio a.

detrimental [ˌdetriˈmentl] *adj* perjudicial (*to* a, para).

detritus [diˈtraitəs] *n* GEOL detrito *m*.

detruncate [diːˈtrʌŋkeit] *vt* truncar.

deuce [djuːs] *n* dos *m* (cards, dice) || cuarenta iguales *m pl* (in tennis) || FIG demonio *m*, diablo *m*; *what the deuce is that?* ¿qué diablos es esto?, ¿qué demonios es esto? || — FAM *a deuce of a noise* un ruido tremendo, un ruido de mil demonios | *to play the deuce with* estropear (sth.), arruinar (s.o.'s health).
◆ *interj* ¡diablos!

deuced [-t] *adj* FAM de mil demonios, tremendo, da (tremendous) | maldito, ta (damned).
◆ *adv* FAM terriblemente, sumamente (very).

deuterium [djuːˈtiəriəm] *n* CHEM deuterio *m*.

deuteron [ˈdjuːtərɔn] *n* PHYS deuterón *m*.

Deuteronomy [ˌdjuːtəˈrɔnəmi] *pr n* REL Deuteronomio *m*.

devaluate [diːˈvæljueit] *vt* devaluar, desvalorizar.

devaluation [ˌdiːvæljuˈeiʃən] *n* devaluación *f*, desvalorización *f*.

devalue [ˈdiːˈvæljuː] *vt* devaluar, desvalorizar.

devastate [ˈdevəsteit] *vt* devastar, asolar (to ravage) || FIG *I was devastated* me quedé anonadado.

devastating [-iŋ] *adj* devastador, ra || arrollador, ra; *the devastating force of the wind* la fuerza arrolladora del viento || entristecedor, ra; desconsolador, ra; *devastating news* noticias entristecedoras || aplastante, abrumador, ra (argument).

devastation [ˌdevəsˈteiʃən] *n* devastación *f*.

devastator [ˈdevəsteitə*] *n* devastador, ra.

develop [diˈveləp] *vt* desarrollar (to expand); *to develop one's body, industry* desarrollar el cuerpo, la industria || hacer desarrollar; *the rain and sun develop the seed* la lluvia y el sol hacen desarrollar la semilla || echar (to begin to have) || aprovechar (resources) || urbanizar (land) || explotar (a business, mine, etc.) || fomentar (to promote) || perfeccionar (process) || realizar (a new technique) || empezar a tener (difficulties) || adquirir, tomar, coger (taste, hatred) || contraer, coger (to catch an illness) || incubar; *I think my child is developing measles* creo que mi hijo está incubando el sarampión || contraer (a habit) || mostrar (a talent) || manifestar (a tendency) || MIL desplegar (troops) || PHOT revelar || MATH desarrollar || MUS desarrollar || — *he developed a pain in his leg this morning* le empezó a doler la pierna esta mañana || *to develop a speed of...* desarrollar una velocidad de...
◆ *vi* desarrollarse (mind, body, species, to expand, etc.); *this country's industry has developed a lot* la industria de este país se ha desarrollado mucho || producirse (to arise) || aparecer (to appear); *a cloud has developed* ha aparecido una nube || aumentar, crecer (interest, hatred, taste, etc.) || ir; *how is the work developing?* ¿cómo va el trabajo?

developer [-ə*] *n* PHOT revelador *m*.

developing [-iŋ] *adj* en (vías de) desarrollo; *developing countries* países en vías de desarrollo.
◆ *n* desarrollo *m*.

development [-mənt] *n* desarrollo *m* (expansion, evolution); *the development of a plant, of an industry* el desarrollo de una planta, de una industria; *child at the most rapid stage of development* niño en pleno desarrollo || evolución *f*; *the development of the situation* la evolución de la situación || tendencia *f* (tendency) || acontecimiento *m*, hecho *m* (event) || cambio *m* (change) || explotación *f*, aprovechamiento *m* (of resources) || urbanización *f* (of towns, cities) || fomento *m* (promotion) || progreso *m* (progress) || PHOT revelado *m* || MIL despliegue *m* (of troops) || MUS & MATH desarrollo *m* || — *any developments?* ¿hay algo nuevo? || *development area* polo *m* de desarrollo || *development plan* plan *m* de desarrollo || *his works represent a new development in literature* sus obras señalan una nueva tendencia en literatura || *new developments in medecine enable us to cure tuberculosis* los últimos descubrimientos de la medicina nos permiten curar la tuberculosis.

developmental [diˌveləpˈmentl] *adj* de desarrollo (project, etc.) || para el desarrollo (aid, etc.) || experimental || del desarrollo (disease).

deviant [ˈdiːviənt] *adj* pervertido, da (sex) || extravagante (behaviour).
◆ *n* invertido *m* sexual, pervertido, da || extravagante *m* & *f*.

deviate [ˈdiːvieit] *n* US invertido *m* sexual || extravagante *m* & *f*.

deviate [ˈdiːvieit] *vi* desviarse.
◆ *vt* desviar.

deviation [ˌdiːviˈeiʃən] *n* desviación *f*; *deviation of light, of a magnetic needle* desviación de la luz, de la aguja imantada || alejamiento *m* (from de truth) || MATH desviación *f* || inversión *f* (sexual).

deviationism [ˌdiːviˈeiʃənizəm] *n* desviacionismo *m*.

deviationist [ˈdiːviˈeiʃənist] *n* desviacionista *m* & *f*.

device [diˈvais] *n* FIG ardid *m*, estratagema *f* (scheme) || dispositivo *m*, aparato *m* (mechanical contrivance) || mecanismo *m* || ingenio *m*, artefacto *m*; *nuclear device* ingenio nuclear || HERALD emblema *m* | lema *m* (motto) || FAM *to leave s.o. to his own devices* dejar a uno que se las arregle solo.

devil [ˈdevl] *n* diablo *m*, demonio *m* (evil spirit) || FIG diablo *m* || aprendiz *m*; *printer's devil* aprendiz de imprenta || secretario *m* (lawyer's) || negro *m* (writer's) || — FIG *a devil of a problem* un problema dificilísimo *or* diabólico *or* de todos los diablos | *a devil of a mess* un lío tremendo | *a devil of a noise* un ruido de mil demonios, un ruido infernal | *a poor devil* un pobre diablo | *a she-devil* una arpía | *better the devil we know (than the devil we don't know)* más vale malo conocido que bueno por conocer | *between the devil and the deep blue sea* entre la espada y la pared | *devil a one!* ¡ni uno! || FAM *devil's bones* dados *m* | *devil's books* cartas *f*, naipes *m* || FIG *go to the devil!* ¡vete al diablo! | *it's the devil* es dificilísimo | *he is a bit of a devil* es un conquistador (a man), es un diablillo (child) | *how the devil?* ¿cómo demonios?, ¿cómo diablos? | *like the devil* como llevado por el diablo (to go), muchísimo (to work, to study) | *little devil* demonio, diablillo | *talk of the devil!* hablando del rey de Roma por la puerta asoma || *the Devil* el Diablo, el Demonio || FIG *the devil!* ¡qué diablos! | *the devil finds work for idle hands* cuando el diablo no tiene nada que hacer con el rabo mata moscas | *the devil is not so black as he is painted* el diablo no es tan feo como lo pintan || *the devil on two sticks* el diablo cojuelo || FIG *the devil's advocate* el abogado del diablo || FAM *the devil take it!* ¡al diablo! | *there'll be the devil to pay!* ¡la vamos a pagar! || FIG *to be a real devil* ser el mismísimo demonio | *to be possessed of the devil* tener el diablo en el cuerpo, ser de la piel del diablo, estar poseído por el demonio | *to do it for the devil of it* hacerlo porque le da a uno la gana | *to give the devil his due* ser justo | *to play the devil with* arruinar, estropear | *to raise de devil* armarla, armar un escándalo | *to run like the devil* correr como un descosido | *to send to the devil* enviar al diablo, mandar a paseo | *to work like the devil* trabajar como un negro | *we had the devil of a job (to)* nos costó muchísimo trabajo | *what the devil...?* ¿qué diablos...?, ¿qué demonios...?

devil ['devil] *vt* CULIN sazonar con mucho picante || US molestar, fastidiar (to annoy).
◆ *vi* trabajar de aprendiz *or* de secretario *or* de negro.

devilfish [-fiʃ] *n* ZOOL pulpo *m* (octopus) | mantarraya *f* (ray).

devilish [-iʃ] *adj* diabólico, ca.
◆ *adv* sumamente, terriblemente.

devilishly [-iʃli] *adv* REL diabólicamente || FAM terriblemente, sumamente.

devilism [-izəm] *n* satanismo *m*.

devil-may-care [-mei'kɛə*] *adj* despreocupado, da (carefree) || temerario, ria (rash).

devilment [-mənt] *n* diablura *f* (mischief) || maldad *f* (wickedness) || FIG *to be full of devilment* tener el diablo en el cuerpo, ser de la piel del diablo.

devilry [-ri]; **deviltry** [-tri] *n* diablura *f* (mischief) || maldad *f* (wickedness) || magia *f* negra (black magic) || osadía *f*, atrevimiento *m* (daring).

devious ['di:vjəs] *adj* sinuoso, sa; tortuoso, sa (road) || tortuoso, sa (person) || poco limpio, pia (means).

deviousness [-nis] *n* tortuosidad *f*.

devisable [di'vaizəbl] *adj* concebible, imaginable.

devise [di'vais] *n* JUR disposiciones *f pl* testamentarias (clause) | legado *m* (gift).

devise [di'vaiz] *vt* concebir, idear, imaginar (a plan, etc.) || inventar (to invent) || tramar, maquinar (to plot) || JUR legar.

devisee [,devi'zi:] *n* JUR legatario, ria.

deviser [di'vaizə*] *n* inventor, ra; autor, ra.

devisor [,devi'zɔ:*] *n* JUR testador, ra.

devitalize [di:'vaitəlaiz] *vt* debilitar || desvitalizar (a tooth).

devitrification [di:,vitrifi'keiʃən] *n* desvitrificación *f*.

devitrify [di:'vitrifai] *vt* desvitrificar.

devoid [di'vɔid] *adj* *devoid of* desprovisto de, sin || *devoid of cares* libre de cuidados.

devolution ['di:və'lu:ʃən] *n* JUR transmisión *f* (inheritance) || BIOL degeneración *f* || delegación *f* (of powers).

devolve [di'vɔlv] *vt* transmitir || delegar (powers).
◆ *vi* recaer (*on, to, upon* sobre); *the responsibility devolved upon his successor* la responsabilidad recayó sobre su sucesor || incumbir, corresponder (*upon* a) (to be incumbent upon).

Devonian [de'vəunjən] *adj* devoniano, na; devónico, ca || *the Devonian* el devónico, el devoniano.

devote [di'vəut] *vt* dedicar; *to devote one's life to helping the poor* dedicar su vida a ayudar a los pobres || — *to be devoted to s.o.* querer mucho a uno || *to devote o.s. to* dedicarse a.

devoted [-id] *adj* leal, fiel (loyal) || devoto, ta (devout) || dedicado, da (dedicated).

devotedly [-idli] *adv* con devoción.

devotee [,devəu'ti] partidario, ria; devoto, ta (supporter) || devoto, ta (devout person).

devotion [di'vəuʃən] *n* devoción *f*, afecto *m* (affection) || lealtad *f* (loyalty) || dedicación *f* (to studies, etc.) || afición *f* (addiction) || devoción *f*, piedad *f*, fervor *m* (devoutness).
◆ *pl* REL oraciones *f* || *book of devotions* devocionario *m*.

devotional [-l] *adj* piadoso, sa; devoto, ta (attitude, soul) || piadoso, sa (articles).

devour [di'vauə*] *vt* devorar || FIG devorar; *he devoured the book in one evening* devoró el libro en una noche; *the flames devoured the building* las llamas devoraron el edificio || *to be devoured with envy* morirse de envidia, carcomerse de envidia.

devourning [-riŋ] *adj* devorador, ra.

devouringly [-riŋli] *adj* ávidamente.

devout [di'vaut] *adj* devoto, ta (very religious) || sincero, ra (earnest).

devoutly [-li] *adv* con devoción.

devoutness [-nis] *n* devoción *f*.

dew [dju:] *n* rocío *m* (morning damp) || FIG flor *f* (of youth) | gotas *f pl* (drops).

dew [dju:] *vi* rociar.
◆ *vt* bañar de rocío.

dewberry [-beri] *n* BOT zarzamora *f*.

dewclaw [-klɔ:] *n* garra *f* (of dogs, etc.).

dewdrop [-drɔp] *n* gota *f* de rocío.

dewfall [-fɔ:l] *n* relente *m* (evening dew) || caída *f* del rocío.

dewlap [-læp] *n* papada *f* (of animals).

dew point [-pɔint] *n* punto *m* de condensación.

dewy ['dju:i] *adj* rociado, da; cubierto de rocío || húmedo, da (wet) || FIG puro, ra; virginal.

dewy-eyed [-aid] *adj* ingenuo, nua.

dexter ['dekstə*] *adj* a mano derecha || HERALD diestro, tra.

dexterity [deks'teriti] *n* destreza *f*, habilidad *f*.

dextrin ['dekstrin] *n* CHEM dextrina *f*.

dextrorotary [,dekstrəu'rəutəri] *adj* US PHYS dextrógiro, ra.

dextrorotatory [,dekstrəu'rəutətəri] *adj* PHYS dextrógiro, ra.

dextrorse [deks'trɔ:s] *adj* dextrorso, sa.

dextrose ['dekstrəus] *n* dextrosa *f*.

dextrous ['dekstrəs] *adj* diestro, tra; hábil.

dey [dei] *n* dey *m* (prince of Algiers).

diabetes [,daiə'bi:ti:z] *n* MED diabetes *f*.

diabetic [,daiə'betik] *adj/n* MED diabético, ca.

diabolic ['daiə'bɔlik]; **diabolical** [-əl] *adj* diabólico, ca.

diabolism [dai'æbəlizəm] *n* brujería *f* (sorcery) || magia *f* negra (black magic) || satanismo *m*.

diabolo [di'ɑ:bələu] *n* diábolo *m* (toy).

diacid [dai'asid] *adj* CHEM biácido, da.

diaconal [dai'ækənl] *adj* REL diaconal.

diaconate [dai'ækənit] *n* REL diaconato *m*, diaconado *m*.

diacritic [,daiə'kritik] *adj* diacrítico, ca.
◆ *n* signo *m* diacrítico.

diacritical [-əl] *adj* diacrítico, ca.

diad ['daiæd] *n* pareja *f* (couple).

diadem ['daiədem] *n* diadema *f*.

diaeresis [dai'iərisis] *n* GRAMM diéresis *f*.
— OBSERV El plural de *diaeresis* es *diaereses*.

diagnose ['daiəgnəuz] *vt* MED diagnosticar.
◆ *vi* MED hacer un diagnóstico.

diagnosis [,daiəg'nəusis] *n* MED diagnóstico *m* (of disease) | diagnosis *f inv* (science).
— OBSERV El plural de la palabra inglesa es *diagnoses*.

diagnostic [,daiəg'nɔstik] *adj* MED diagnóstico, ca.
◆ *n* MED síntoma *m* (symptom) | diagnosis *f inv* (science) || diagnóstico *m* (statement).

diagonal [dai'ægənəl] *adj* diagonal.
◆ *n* diagonal *f*.

diagonally [-i] *adv* en diagonal, diagonalmente.

diagram ['daiəgræm] *n* diagrama *m* (to explain a phenomenon) || gráfico *m* (chart) || esquema *m* (sketch) || MATH figura *f*.

diagrammatic [,daiəgrə'mætik] *adj* esquemático, ca.

dial ['daiəl] *n* esfera *f* (of a clock) || esfera *f*, dial *m* (of radio) || botón *m* selector || cuadrante *m* (of a sundial) || reloj *m* de sol (sundial) || disco *m* (of a telephone) || limbo *m* (of measuring instruments) || FAM cara *f*, jeta *f* (face).

dial ['daiəl] *vt* marcar (un número) || sintonizar (the radio).
◆ *vi* marcar (un número).

dialect ['daiəlekt] *n* dialecto *m*.

dialectal [,daiə'lektl] *adj* dialectal.

dialectic [,daiə'lektik] *adj* PHIL dialéctico, ca.
◆ *n* PHIL dialéctica *f*.

dialectical [-əl] *adj* PHIL dialéctico, ca.

dialectician [,daiə'lek'tiʃən] *n* PHIL dialéctico, ca.

dialectics [,daiə'lektiks] *n* dialéctica *f*.

dialectology [,daiəlek'tɔlədʒi] *n* dialectología *f*.

dialling code ['dɑiəliŋkəud] *n* prefijo *m* telefónico.

dialling tone ['daiəliŋ-təun] *n* señal *f* para marcar (of telephone).

dialog ['daiəlɔg] *n* US diálogo *m*.

dialogist [dai'ælədʒist] *n* dialoguista *m* & *f* (dialogue writer) || interlocutor, ra (speaker).

dialogue ['daiəlɔg] *n* diálogo *m* || *dialogue writer* dialoguista *m* & *f*.

dialogue ['daiəlɔg]; **dialogize** ['daiəlɔgaiz] *vi* dialogar.

dial tone ['daiəl-təun] *n* US señal *f* para marcar (of telephone).

dialysis [dai'ælisis] *n* CHEM diálisis *f*.

dialyze ['daiəlaiz] *vt* CHEM dializar.

diamagnetism ['daiə'mægnitizəm] *n* ELECTR diamagnetismo *m*.

diamanté [diə'mæntei] *adj* adornado, da con pedrería falsa y lentejuelas.

diamantiferous [daiəmən'tifərəs] *adj* diamantífero, ra.

diameter [dai'æmitə*] *n* MATH diámetro *m*.

diametral [dai'æmitrəl]; **diametric** [,daiə'metrik]; **diametrical** [-əl] *adj* MATH diametral.

diametrically [-əli] *adv* diametralmente.

diamond ['daiəmənd] *n* diamante *m* (stone); *rough diamond* diamante en bruto || oro *m* (in

Spanish cards), diamante *m* (in standard cards) || MATH rombo *m* || cortavidrios *m inv* (glass cutter) || aguja *f*, diamante *m* (of record players) || US SP campo *m* de béisbol || PRINT tipo *m* muy pequeño.
◆ *adj* diamantado, da (like a diamond) || diamantífero, ra (containing diamond); *diamond field* región diamantífera || de diamante (made of diamond) || MATH rombal || diamantino, na (sparkling) || *diamond wedding* bodas *f pl* de diamante.

diamond ['daiəmənd] *vt* adornar con diamantes.

diamond-bearing [-ˌbɛəriŋ] *adj* diamantífero, ra.

diamond cutter ['kʌtə*] *n* diamantista *m*.

diamond-shaped [-ʃeipt] *adj* romboidal.

diamond-yielding [-ˌjiːldiŋ] *adv* diamantífero, ra.

diapason [ˌdaiə'peisn] *n* MUS diapasón *m* (of an organ, of pitch, tuning fork) | crescendo *m* armonioso (of a choir) | armonía *f* (harmony).

diaper ['daiəpə*] *n* ARCH motivo *m* romboidal *or* geométrico || tela *f* bordada *or* adamascada (linen) || MED paño *m* higiénico (sanitary towel) || US pañal *m* (for babies) || US *diaper rash* sarpullido *m* (inflammation).

diaper ['daiəpə*] *vt* US poner el pañal a (a baby).

diaphaneity [ˌdaiəfə'niiti]; **diaphanousness** [dai'æfənəsnis] *n* diafanidad *f*.

diaphanous [dai'æfənəs] *adj* diáfano, na (filmy).

diaphragm ['daiəfræm] *n* diafragma *m*.

diaphragmatic ['daiəfræg'mætik] *adj* diafragmático, ca.

diarchy ['daiɑːki] *n* diarquía *f*.

diarist ['daiərist] *n* diarista *m* & *f*.

diarrhea; diarrhoea [ˌdaiə'riə] *n* MED diarrea *f*.

diary ['daiəri] *n* diario *m* (of personal experiences) || agenda *f* (for appointments, etc.).

Diaspora [dai'æspərə] *n* diáspora *f*.

diastase ['daiəsteis] *n* BIOL diastasa *f*.

diastole [dai'æstəli] *n* ANAT & GRAMM diástole *f*.

diastolic [daiə'stɔlik] *adj* ANAT diastólico, ca.

diathermy ['daiəˌθəːmi] *n* MED diatermia *f*.

diathesis [dai'æθəsis] *n* diátesis *f*.
— OBSERV El plural de *diathesis* es *diatheses*.

diatomic [ˌdaiə'tɔmik] *adj* CHEM diatómico, ca (with two atoms) | bivalente (bivalent).

diatonic ['daiə'tɔnik] *adj* MUS diatónico, ca; *diatonic scale* escala diatónica.

diatribe ['daiətraib] *n* diatriba *f*; *to pronounce a diatribe* lanzar una diatriba.

diazo [dai'æzəu] *adj* CHEM diazoico, ca; *diazo compounds* compuestos diazoicos.

dibasic [dai'beisik] *adj* CHEM dibásico, ca.

dibber ['dibə*]; **dibble** ['dibl] *n* plantador *m*, almocafre *m*.

dibble ['dibl] *vi* plantar con plantador *or* almocafre.

dibs [dibz] *pl n* tabas *f* (game) || FAM parné *m sing* (money).

dice [dais] *pl n* dados *m* || — *dice box* cubilete *m* de dados || FAM *no dice* no hay nada que hacer, ni hablar || *to load the dice* cargar los dados.

dice [dais] *vi* jugar a los dados || FIG *to dice with death* jugar con la muerte.
◆ *vt* cortar en cuadritos || *to dice away a fortune* perder una fortuna jugando a los dados.

dicey ['daisi] *adj* peligroso, sa (dangerous) || incierto, ta; dudoso, sa (uncertain).

dichloride [dai'klɔːraid] *n* CHEM bicloruro *m*.

dichotomize [dai'kɔtəmaiz] *vt* dividir en dos.
◆ *vi* dividirse en dos || formar una dicotomía *f*.

dichotomy [dai'kɔtəmi] *n* dicotomía *f*.

dichroism ['daikrəuizəm] *n* dicroísmo *m*.

dichromate ['dai'krəumeit] *n* CHEM bicromato *m*.

dichromatic ['daikrə'mætik] *adj* dicromático, ca.

dichromatism [dai'krəumætizəm] *n* dicromatismo *m*.

dick [dik] *n* POP polla *f* (penis) || US POP sabueso *m*, detective *m*.

Dick [dik] *pr n* FAM Ricardo *m* (diminutivo de «Richard»).

dickens ['dikinz] *n* FAM diablo *m* || *what the dickens...?* ¿qué diablos...?, ¿qué demonios...?

dicker ['dikə*] *n* COMM decena *f* || US regateo *m* (bargaining).

dicker ['dikə*] *vi* US regatear (to bargain).

dicky; dickey ['diki] *n* pechera *f* postiza (on shirt) || babero *m* (bib, pinafore) || AUT spider *m* || ZOOL burrito *m* (ass) | pajarito *m* (bird).
◆ *adj* FAM debilucho, cha (person) | defectuoso, sa (thing).

dicotyledon ['daiˌkɔti'liːdən] *n* BOT dicotiledónea *f*.

dicotyledoneae [daiˌkɔtili'dəuniːi] *pl n* BOT dicotiledóneas *f*.

dictaphone ['diktəfəun] *n* dictáfono *m*.

dictate ['dikteit] *n* mandato *m*, orden *f* (authoritative command) || dictado *m*; *the dictates of conscience* los dictados de la conciencia.

dictate [dik'teit] *vt* dictar (to say aloud) || mandar, ordenar (to order) || FIG inspirar, dictar || *to dictate terms* imponer condiciones.
◆ *vi* mandar || dictar (to a secretary) || *I won't be dictated to* a mí no me manda nadie.

dictation [dik'teiʃən] *n* dictado *m*; *to take dictation* escribir al dictado; *musical dictation* dictado musical || mandato *m*, orden *f* (dictate).

dictator [dik'teitə*] *n* dictador *m*.

dictatorial [ˌdiktə'tɔːriəl] *adj* dictatorial; *dictatorial powers* poderes dictatoriales.

dictatorship [dik'teitəːʃip] *n* dictadura *f*; *dictatorship of the proletariat* dictadura del proletariado.

diction ['dikʃən] *n* dicción *f* (enunciation) || estilo *m*, lenguaje *m* (choice of words).

dictionary ['dikʃənəri] *n* diccionario *m* || FIG *walking* o *living dictionary* enciclopedia *f* ambulante.

dictum ['diktəm] *n* máxima *f*, sentencia *f* (maxim) || dicho *m* (saying) || afirmación *f*, declaración *f* (statement) || JUR dictamen *m*.
— OBSERV El plural de *dictum* es *dicta* o *dictus*.

did [did] *pret* ⟶ **do**.

didactic [di'dæktik] *adj* didáctico, ca.

didacticism [di'dæktisizəm] *n* didáctica *f*.

didactics [di'dæktiks] *n* didáctica *f*.

didapper ['daidæpə*] *n* somorgujo *m* (bird).

diddle ['didl] *vt* FAM timar, estafar (to swindle); *she diddled me out of one hundred pounds* me timó cien libras || US FAM menear (to move) || US *to diddle away* perder (time).

diddler [-ə*] *n* FAM timador, ra; estafador, ra.

didn't ['didnt] *n* contraction of did not.

dido ['daidəu] *n* US FAM travesura *f* (prank).
— OBSERV El plural es *didoes* o *didos*.

die [dai] *n* dado *m* (cube used in playing dice) || ARCH dado *m* (pedestal) || CULIN cuadrito *m* || TECH matriz *f* (for shaping) | troquel *m* (for minting) | hilera *f* (for drawing wire) | terraja *f* (for screwing) | punzón *m* (for hand punching) || — FIG *as straight as a die* más derecho que una vela (not bent), de una perfecta honradez (honest) | *the die is cast* la suerte está echada.
— OBSERV El plural de *die*, cuando significa «dado para jugar» o «cuadrito» es *dice*. En los demás casos es regular (*dies*).

die [dai] *vi* morir, morirse; *he died of cancer* murió de cáncer; *he died a hero* murió como un héroe; *the word died on his lips* la palabra murió en sus labios || extinguirse (light) || desaparecer (to disappear) || calarse, pararse (motor) || — *his secret died with him* se llevó su secreto a la tumba || *I am dying!* ¡me muero! || *I nearly died of shame!* ¡me morí de vergüenza! || *never say die!* no hay que darse por vencido, mientras hay vida hay esperanza || *old habits die hard* genio y figura hasta la sepultura || *to be dying for* morirse por || *to be dying to do sth.* morirse por hacer algo || *to die a violent death* morir de muerte violenta || *to die away* desvanecerse (sound), difuminarse (colour), amainar (wind), desmayarse (to faint) || *to die down* apagarse (a fire), desvanecerse (sound), amainar (wind), decaer (conversation), disminuir (agitation) || *to die hard* tardar en desaparecer || *to die in one's bed* morir en la cama || *to die like flies* caer como chinches *or* como moscas || *to die of laughter* o *laughing* morirse de risa || *to die off* desaparecer, ir desapareciendo, extinguirse, ir extinguiéndose (race, family), marchitarse (leaves) || *to die out* desaparecer; apagarse (fire) || *to die suddenly* morir de repente || *to die with one's boots on* morir con las botas puestas || *to do or die* vencer o morir.

die-cast [-kɑːst] *vt* TECH fundir a presión, troquelar.

die-casting [-ˌkɑːstiŋ] *n* TECH (pieza), *f* fundida a presión *or* troquelada.

diehard ['daihɑːd] *adj/n* intransigente.

dielectric [ˌdaii'lektrik] *adj* ELECTR dieléctrico, ca.
◆ *n* ELECTR dieléctrico *m*.

dieresis [dai'iərisis] *n* US GRAMM diéresis *f*.
— OBSERV El plural de *dieresis* es *diereses*.

diesel ['diːzəl] *adj* TECH diesel; *diesel engine* motor diesel || *diesel oil* o *fuel* gasoil *m*, gas-oil *m*, aceite pesado.
◆ *m* diesel.

diesinker ['daisiŋkə*] *n* TECH grabador *m* de troqueles.

diesis ['daiisis] *n* PRINT signo *m* de referencia || MUS sostenido *m*, diesi *f*.
— OBSERV El plural de *diesis* es *dieses*.

diestock ['daistɔk] *n* TECH terraja *f*.

diet ['daiət] *n* alimentación *f* (daily fare) || régimen *m*, dieta *f* (prescribed course of food); *to be on a diet* estar a régimen; *to put on a diet* poner a régimen || dieta *f* (for convalescents, sick people).

diet ['daiət] *vt* poner a régimen *or* a dieta.
◆ *vi* estar a régimen *or* a dieta.

Diet ['daiət] *n* dieta *f* (assembly).

dietary ['daiətəri] *adj* dietético, ca; *dietary fibre* fibra dietética.
◆ *n* alimentación *f*, régimen *m* alimenticio (in hospital, prison).

dieter ['dɑiətə*] *n* persona *f* a régimen.

dietetic [ˌdaii'tetik] *adj* dietético, ca.

dietetics [-s] *n* MED dietética *f*.

dietician; US dietitian [ˌdaii'tiʃən] *n* MED bromatólogo *m*, médico *m* dietético.

differ ['difə*] *vi* ser distinto, ser diferente (to be unlike); *their jobs differ* sus trabajos son distintos || no están de acuerdo (to disagree); *they differ on this point* no estar de acuerdo en este punto || — *I beg to differ* siento disentir *or* no estar de acuerdo || *they differ widely in their* *tastes* tienen gustos completamente distintos, sus gustos difieren completamente.

difference ['difrəns] *n* diferencia *f*; *a difference between two figures* una diferencia entre dos cifras; *the difference in age* la diferencia de edad || discrepancia *f*, desacuerdo *m* (disagreement) || HERALD lambel *m* || — *difference of opinions* contraste *m* de pareceres (in Parliament) || *it makes a great difference* no es lo mismo, es muy diferente || *it makes no difference* da lo mismo, da igual || *it makes no difference to me* me da igual, me da lo mismo || *to make a difference between two things* diferenciar dos cosas, hacer una distinción entre dos cosas || *to pay the difference* pagar la diferencia || *to split the difference* partir la diferencia || *what difference does it make?* ¿qué más da?

different ['difrənt] *adj* diferente, distinto, ta (*from* de).

differential [ˌdifə'renʃəl] *adj* diferencial; *differential calculus, equation* cálculo, ecuación diferencial.
◆ *n* TECH diferencial *f* (of a car) || MATH diferencial || US tarifa *f* diferencial (in transport, cost).

differentiate [ˌdifə'renʃieit] *vt* diferenciar, distinguir.
◆ *vi* diferenciarse (to become differentiated) || distinguir; *to differentiate between two things* distinguir entre dos cosas.

differentiation [ˌdifərenʃi'eiʃən] *n* diferenciación *f*.

differing ['difəriŋ] *adj* discordante (discrepant) || diferente (unlike).

difficult ['difikəlt] *adj* difícil || *you are making life difficult for me* me haces la vida imposible.

difficulty [-i] *n* dificultad *f*; *I overcame a difficulty* vencí una dificultad; *he makes difficulties* crea dificultades || — *financial difficulties* apuros *m* económicos, problemas financieros || *he is having difficulties with his son* tiene problemas con su hijo || *I find difficulty in talking* tengo dificultad en hablar || *ship in difficulties* barco *m* en peligro || *the difficulty is to...* lo difícil es... || *to be in difficulties* estar en un apuro *or* en un aprieto || *to get into difficulties* meterse en un lío (to get into trouble), verse en un apuro (to be in trouble) || *to get out of one's difficulties* salir de apuro || *we have no difficulty in getting spare parts* no nos es difícil encontrar piezas de recambio || *with difficulty* difícilmente, con dificultad.

diffidence ['difidəns] *n* timidez *f*, falta *f* de confianza en sí mismo.

diffident ['difidənt] *adj* tímido, da; que no tiene confianza en sí mismo.

diffidently [-li] *adv* con timidez, tímidamente.

diffract [di'frækt] *vt* PHYS difractar.

diffraction [di'frækʃən] *n* PHYS difracción *f*.

diffractive [di'fræktiv] *adj* PHYS difrangente.

diffuse [di'fjuːs] *adj* difuso, sa.

diffuse [di'fjuːz] *vt* difundir; *to diffuse light* difundir luz || desprender (heat).
◆ *vi* difundirse; *perspiration diffuses through pores* la transpiración se difunde por los poros.

diffused [-d] *adj* difuso, sa.

diffuser [-ə*] *n* TECH difusor *m*.

diffusible [di'fjuːzəbl] *adj* difusible.

diffusion [di'fjuːʒən] *n* difusión *f*.

diffusive [di'fjuːsiv] *adj* difuso, sa.

diffusor [di'fjuzə*] *n* TECH difusor *m*.

dig [dig] *n* golpe *m*; *a dig in the ribs* un golpe en las costillas || empujón *m* (push) || codazo *m* (with the elbow) || FIG pinchazo *m*, pulla *f* (sarcastic remark) || excavation *f*; *an archeological dig* una excavación arqueológica || US FAM empollón *m* (at school) || FIG *to have a dig at s.o.* meterse con alguien.
◆ *pl* FAM pensión *f sing* (boardinghouse) | alojamiento *m sing* (lodgings).

dig [dig] *vt* cavar (to break the ground) || excavar (to excavate) || hacer (a hole) || escarbar (animals) || extraer, sacar (coal) || hincar, clavar; *to dig spurs into a horse* hincar las espuelas en un caballo || FAM gustar; *do you dig electronic music?* ¿te gusta la música electrónica? | comprender, captar (to understand) || — *to dig in* enterrar (manure), clavar (nails, claws, etc.) || *to dig into* hundir, clavar || *to dig one's heels in* mantenerse en sus trece || *to dig o.s. in* atrincherarse (soldier) || *to dig out* excavar (hole), sacar, extraer (buried object), sacar (to bring out), encontrar (to find) || *to dig s.o. with one's elbow* dar codazos a uno || *to dig up* desenterrar (buried object), arrancar, desarraigar (plant), roturar (land), levantar (street), descubrir (to discover).
◆ *vi* cavar || FAM alojarse (to lodge) || — US FAM *to dig at* o *into* empollar (to study hard) || *to dig deeper into a subject* ahondar en un tema, profundizar un tema || *to dig for gold* buscar oro || FAM *to dig in* atacar (to start eating) || *to dig into* investigar || FAM *to dig into a cake* hincarle el diente a un pastel || *to dig into one's pocket* hurgar en el bolsillo.
— OBSERV Pret y pp ***dug***.

digest ['daidʒest] *n* resumen *m* || JUR digesto *m*.

digest ['daidʒest] *vt* digerir; *to digest food* digerir la comida || resumir (to summarize) || ordenar (to arrange) || FIG asimilar; *have you digested everything that is important in the book?* ¿ha asimilado todo lo importante del libro? | tragarse, digerir (to stomach).
◆ *vi* digerirse; *this food digests very well* esta comida se digiere muy bien || digerir la comida.

digestibility [di'dʒestəbiliti] *n* digestibilidad *f*.

digestible [di'dʒestəbl] *adj* digerible, digestible.

digestion [di'dʒestʃən] *n* digestión *f* || FIG asimilación *f*.

digestive [di'dʒestiv] *adj* digestivo, va; *digestive system* aparato digestivo || *digestive biscuit* galleta *f* digestiva *or* integral.
◆ *n* digestivo *m*.

digger ['digə*] *n* cavador *m* (s.o. who digs) || excavador, ra (on archaeological site) || excavadora *f* (machine) || minero *m* (gold miner) || AGR plantador *m* (dibble) | roturador *m* (grubber) || FAM australiano *m*.

digging ['digiŋ] *n* AGR cava *f*.
◆ *pl* mina *f sing* (mine) || excavaciones *f* (archaeological) || FAM pensión *f sing* (boardinghouse) | alojamiento *m sing* (lodgings).

digit ['didʒit] *n* dedo *m* (finger, toe) || MATH dígito *m*.

digital ['didʒitl] *adj* digital || INFORM digital || — *digital audio tape* cinta de audio digital || INFORM *digital computer* ordenador *m* digital | *digital keyboard* teclado *m* numérico.
◆ *n* MUS tecla *f*.

digitalin [ˌdidʒi'teilin] *n* MED digitalina *f*.

digitalis [ˌdidʒi'teilis] *n* BOT digital *f* || MED digitalina *f*.

digitalization [diˌdʒitəlaiseiʃn] *n* INFORM digitalización *f*.

digitate ['didʒitit]; **digitated** ['didʒiteitid] *adj* ZOOL & BOT digitado, da.

digitiform ['didʒitifɔːm] *adj* digitiforme.

digitigrade ['didʒitigreid] *adj* ZOOL digitígrado, da.
◆ *n* ZOOL digitigrado *m*.

digitize; digitise ['didʒitaiz] *vt* INFORM digitalizar.

digitizer [-ə*] *n* INFORM digitalizador *m*.

diglot ['daiglɔt] *adj* US bilingüe.
◆ *n* US edición *f* bilingüe.

dignified ['dignifaid] *adj* solemne (solemn); *to speak in a dignified tone* hablar con tono solemne || digno, na; decoroso, sa (act).

dignify ['dignifai] *vt* dignificar || realzar (to give distinction) || FAM dar un nombre rimbombante a.

dignifying [-iŋ] *adj* dignificante, honroso, sa.

dignitary ['dignitəri] *n* REL dignatario *m*.

dignity ['digniti] *n* dignidad *f* || — *it is beneath your dignity to accept* no puede dignarse a aceptar || *to stand on one's dignity* hacerse respetar.

digress [dai'gres] *vi* desviarse, apartarse (to deviate); *he digressed from the main subject* se apartó del tema principal || hacer una digresión (to divagate).

digression [dai'greʃən] *n* digresión *f*.

dihedral [dai'hiːdrəl] *adj* MAT diedro.
◆ *n* MATH diedro *m*.

dihedron [dai'hiːdrən] *n* MATH diedro *m*.

dike; dyke [daik] *n* dique *m* (protective bank) || arroyo *m* (waterway) || tapia *f* (wall) || zanja *f* (ditch) || terraplén *m* (causeway) || MIN dique *m* || FIG dique *m*, barrera *f* (obstacle).

dike [daik] *vt* proteger con un dique || retener con diques.

diktat ['diktæt] *n* imposición *f*.

dilacerate [di'læsəreit] *vt* dilacerar, desgarrar.

dilaceration [diˌlæsə'reiʃən] *n* dilaceración *f*, desgarramiento *m*.

dilapidated [-id] *adj* derruido, da (building) || desvencijado, da (car) || muy estropeado (clothes).

dilapidation [diˌlæpi'deiʃən] *n* estado *m* ruinoso (disrepair) || JUR deterioro *m* || GEOL desprendimiento *m*.

dilatability [daiˌleitə'biliti] *n* dilatabilidad *f*.

dilatable [dai'leitəbl] *adj* dilatable.

dilatation [ˌdailei'teiʃən] *n* dilatación *f*.

dilate [dai'leit] *vt* dilatar.
◆ *vi* dilatarse (to swell) || FIG dilatarse; *to dilate upon a subject* dilatarse sobre un tema.

dilation [dai'leiʃən] *n* dilatación *f*.

dilative [dai'leitiv] *adj* dilatador, ra.

dilator [dai'leitə*] *n* dilatador *m*.

dilatoriness ['dilətərinis] *n* tardanza *f*, demora *f*, dilación *f*.

dilatory ['dilətəri] *adj* JUR dilatorio, ria || lento, ta (people).

dilemma [di'lemə] *n* dilema *m*.

dilettante [ˌdili'tænti] *n* diletante *m* & *f*.
— OBSERV El plural de la palabra inglesa es *dilettanti* o *dilettantes*.

diligence ['diliʒɑːns] *n* diligencia *f* (coach).

diligence ['dilidʒəns] *n* diligencia *f* (care).

diligent ['dilidʒənt] *adj* diligente.

dill [dil] *n* BOT eneldo *m*.

dilly-dally ['dilidæli] *vi* vacilar, titubear (to hesitate) || perder el tiempo (to waste time).

diluent ['diljuənt] *adj* diluyente, diluente, disolvente.
◆ *n* disolvente *m*.

dilute [dai'ljuːt] *adj* diluido, da (liquid) || suavizado, da; diluido, da (colour) || FIG suavizado, da; atenuado, da.

dilute [dai'ljuːt] *vt* diluir (liquid) || suavizar, diluir (colours) || FIG atenuar, suavizar.
◆ *vi* diluirse || FIG atenuarse, suavizarse.

dilution [dai'lu:ʃən] *n* dilución *f*.

diluvial [dai'lu:vjəl]; **diluvian** [dai'lu:vjən] *adj* diluvial; *diluvial sediments* sedimentos diluviales || diluviano, na; *diluvian rain* lluvia diluviana.

diluvium [dai'lu:vjəm] *n* GEOL diluvial *m*.
— OBSERV El plural de *diluvium* es *diluviums* o *diluvia*.

dim [dim] *adj* oscuro, ra (not bright, dark) || débil, pálido, da; *the dim light of a candle* la luz pálida de una vela || lejano, na; *dim memory* recuerdo lejano || borroso, sa (vague, blurred); *the dim outline of a mountain* la silueta borrosa de una montaña || apagado, da; sin brillo (colour) || sordo, da; apagado, da (sound) || turbio, bia; *his sight is dim* tiene la vista turbia || FIG sombrío, a (view) || FAM tonto, ta; torpe || — *to grow dim* oscurecerse (light), nublarse (sight), borrarse, difuminarse (outline, memory) || *to take a dim view of sth.* ver algo con malos ojos.
◆ *n* AUT luz *f* de cruce (dipped headlights).

dim [dim] *vt* bajar (light) || oscurecer (room) || borrar, difuminar (outline) || nublar (sight) || empañar, nublar; *tears dimmed her eyes* las lágrimas le empañaban los ojos || apagar (colour) || amortiguar, apagar (sound) || FIG borrar, difuminar (memory) | empañar (s.o.'s glory) || AUT *to dim one's lights* poner luz de cruce, bajar los faros.
◆ *vi* oscurecerse (light) || apagarse (colour) || borrarse, difuminarse (outline) || amortiguarse, apagarse (sound) || nublarse (sight) || FIG borrarse, difuminarse (memory) | desvanecerse (beauty) | empañarse (s.o.'s glory).

dime [daim] *n* US moneda *f* de 10 centavos || — US *dime novel* novelucha *f*, novela barata | *dime store* almacén *m* donde se venden artículos baratos | *they were a dime a dozen* los había a porrillo.

dimension [di'menʃən] *n* dimensión *f*; *overall* o *external dimensions* dimensiones exteriores.

dimensional [di'menʃənl] *adj* dimensional.

diminish [di'miniʃ] *vt/vi* disminuir.

diminished [di'miniʃt] *adj* disminuido, da || JUR *diminished responsibility* responsabilidad *f* atenuada.

diminishing [di'miniʃiŋ] *adj* decreciente, menguante || ECON *diminishing returns* rendimientos *m pl* decrecientes.

diminuendo [di,minju'endəu] *adv* MUS diminuendo.
◆ *n* MUS diminuendo *m*.

diminutive [di'minjutiv] *adj* diminuto, ta (very small) || GRAMM diminutivo, va.
◆ *n* GRAMM diminutivo *m*.

dimissory [di'misəri] *adj* de dimisión || *dimissory letters* dimisorias *f pl*.

dimity ['dimiti] *n* bombasí *m* (fabric).

dimly ['dimli] *adv* poco; *dimly lit* poco iluminado || vagamente, de una manera confusa (to remember) || vagamente, indistintamente (to see).

dimmer ['dimə*] *n* ELECTR regulador *m* de voltaje.
◆ *pl* AUT luces *f* de estacionamiento *or* de cruce.

dimness ['dimnis] *n* lo apagado (of colours) || palidez *f* (of light) || lo oscuro, oscuridad *f* (of a room) || debilidad *f* (of sight) || lo borroso (of outline, memory).

dimorphic [dai'mɔ:fik] *adj* dimorfo, fa.

dimorphous [dai'mɔ:fəs] *adj* dimorfo, fa.

dimple ['dimpl] *n* hoyuelo *m* (on cheek).

dimple ['dimpl] *vt* formar hoyuelos en (the cheeks) || rizar (water).
◆ *vi* tener hoyuelos (to show dimples) || rizarse (water).

dimwit ['dimwit] *n* FAM tonto, ta.

dim-witted ['dim'witid] *adj* FAM tonto, ta.

din [din] *n* jaleo *m*, estrépito *m*; *to kick up a din* armar jaleo, formar un estrépito || clamoreo *m*, alboroto *m* (of a crowd).

din [din] *vt* meter en la cabeza; *to din Spanish verbs into a pupil* meterle los verbos españoles en la cabeza a un alumno || machacar con (to repeat insistently); *to did sth. into s.o.'s ears* machacar los oídos de uno con algo || *the noise dinned my ears* el ruido me ensordecía.
◆ *vi* armar jaleo || hacer mucho ruido.

dinar ['di:nɑ:*] *n* dinar *m* (coin).

dine [dain] *vi* cenar || — *to dine in* cenar en casa || *to dine on* o *off sth.* cenar algo || *to dine out* cenar fuera.
◆ *vt* dar de cenar; *we dined them well* les dimos bien de cenar || ser capaz para, tener cabida para (to have room for); *the table dines ten* la mesa tiene cabida para diez personas.

diner ['dainə*] *n* comensal *m* & *f* || US coche *m* restaurante (in a train) | restaurante *m* barato (cheap restaurant).

dinette [dai'net] *n* US comedor *m* pequeño.

ding [diŋ] *vi* sonar.
◆ *vt* repetir insistentemente, machacar con.

ding dong ['diŋ'dɔŋ] *n* tintineo *m* (of a hand bell) || talán talán *m* (of a big bell).
◆ *adj* reñido, da (battle).

dinghy ['diŋgi] *n* MAR bote *m* (small boat) || bote *m* neumático (inflatable boat).

dinginess ['dindʒinis] *n* sordidez *f* (of city, house) || color *m* apagado, lo deslustrado (of curtains) || lo sucio (of furniture, clothes, etc.).

dingle ['diŋgl] *n* GEOGR valle *m* arbolado.

dingo ['diŋgəu] *n* dingo *m* (dog).

dingy ['dindʒi] *adj* sórdido, da (dirty looking) || deslustrado, da (dull) || sucio, cia (dirty).

dining car [-kɑ:*] *n* coche *m* restaurante, coche *m* comedor.

dining hall [-hɔ:l] *n* refectorio *m*.

dining room [-rum] *n* comedor *m*.

dinky ['diŋki] *adj* FAM mono, na; bonito, ta; lindo, da (pretty) || US FAM diminuto, ta (small).

dinner ['dinə*] *n* cena *f* (in the evening) || comida *f* (at midday) || banquete *m* (formal) || servicio *m*, turno *m* (in trains) || — *dinner hour, dinner time* la hora de cenar *or* de comer || *dinner jacket, dinner coat* esmoquin *m*, smoking *m* || *dinner pail* fiambrera *f* || *dinner party* cena *f* || *dinner service, dinner set* vajilla *f* || *dinner table* mesa *f* de comedor || *dinner waggon* carrito *m* || *to go out to dinner* cenar fuera || *to have dinner* cenar (in the evening), comer (at midday).

dinosaur ['dainəsɔ:*] *n* dinosaurio *m*.

dint [dint] *n* bollo *m*, abolladura *f* || *by dint of* a fuerza de.

dint [dint] *vt* bollar, abollar.

diocesan [dai'ɔsisən] *adj/n* diocesano, na.

diocese ['daiəsis] *n* diócesis *f*, diócesi *f*.

diode ['daiəud] *n* diodo *m*.

Dionysia [,daiə'niziə] *pl n* Dionisiacas *f*.

Dionisyac [,daiə'nisiæk]; **Dionysian** [,daiə'nisiən] *adj* dionisiaco, ca; dionisíaco, ca.

Dionysus; Dionysos [,daiə'naisəs] *pr n* MYTH Dioniso *m*, Dionisos *m*.

diopter; dioptre [dai'ɔptə*] *n* PHYS dioptría *f*.

dioptric [dai'ɔptrik]; **dioptrical** [-əl] *adj* PHYS dióptrico, ca.

dioptrics [-s] *n* PHYS dióptrica *f*.

diorite ['daiərait] *n* MIN diorita *f*.

dioxide [dai'ɔksaid] *n* CHEM bióxido *m*.

dip [dip] *n* inmersión *f* (of sth. in water) || baño *m*, chapuzón *m* (a quick swim); *to have a dip* darse un chapuzón || depresión *f* (of ground, road, horizon) || baño *m* (liquid) || picado *m* (of a plane) || vela *f* de sebo (candle) || GEOL buzamiento *m* || declive *m*, pendiente *f* (downward slope) || inclinación *f* (inclination) || inclinación *f* de la aguja magnética (of compass) || baja *f*, bajada *f* (of prices, etc.) || MAR calado *m* (of a ship) || CULIN salsa *f*.

dip [dip] *vt* mojar, bañar (into a liquid) || sumergir (to immerse) || dar un baño, dar un chapuzón, zambullir (s.o.) || mojar (pen) || meter (one's hand, face, etc.) || sacar (to scoop) || inclinar (the scale) || MAR inclinar (la bandera) en señal de saludo (flag) || TECH tratar por inmersión *or* con un baño | teñir (to dye) || — FIG & FAM *to dip one's fingers into* entrometerse en || AUT *to dip one's lights* poner luz de cruce, bajar los faros.
◆ *vi* sumergirse (to plunge) || darse un baño, darse un chapuzón, zambullirse (to have a swim) || meter la mano (to put a hand into); *he dipped into the drawer* metió la mano en el cajón || descender; *the sun dipped behind the hill* el sol descendió por detrás de la colina || bajar en picado (aeroplane) || bajar (ground, road) || bajar (prices) || inclinarse (scale) || GEOL buzar || FIG hojear (to browse through); *I dipped into the dictionary* hojeé el diccionario | meterse (to meddle); *to dip into politics* meterse en política || — FIG *to dip into one's capital* echar mano a su dinero | *to dip into the future* prever el futuro.

dip circle [-'sə:kl] *n* aguja *f* de inclinación.

diphase ['daifeiz] *adj* difásico, ca.

diphteria [dif'θiəriə] *n* MED difteria *f*.

diphtheric [dif'θerik]; **diftheritic** [,difθə'ritik] *adj* MED diftérico, ca.

diphthong ['difθɔŋ] *n* GRAMM diptongo *m*.

diphthongize ['difθɔŋgaiz] *vt* GRAMM diptongar.
◆ *vi* GRAMM diptongarse.

diplodocus [di'plɔdəkəs] *n* ZOOL diplodoco *m*.

diploma [di'pləumə] *n* diploma *m*.

diplomacy [di'pləuməsi] *n* diplomacia *f* || FIG diplomacia *f*.

diplomat ['dipləmæt] *n* diplomático *m*.

diplomatic [,diplə'mætik] *adj* diplomático, ca || — *diplomatic bag* US *diplomatic corps*, valija diplomática || *diplomatic corps* cuerpo diplomático || *diplomatic immunity* inmunidad diplomática.

diplomatics [-s] *n* diplomática *f*.

diplomatist [di'pləumətist] *n* diplomático *m*.

dip needle ['dip'ni:dl] *n* aguja *f* de inclinación.

dipolar [dai'pəulə*] *adj* PHYS bipolar.

dipper ['dipə*] *n* somorgujo *m* (bird) || CULIN cucharón *m* (for table) | cazo *m*, cacillo *m* (for kitchen) || TECH cuchara *f* (of excavator) | conmutador *m* de luces de cruce (in cars) | pinzas *f pl* (in photography) || — US *big dipper* montaña rusa | *the Great* o *Big Dipper* la Osa Mayor (in astronomy) | *the Little Dipper* la Osa Menor.

dipsomania ['dipsəu'meinjə] *n* dipsomanía *f*.

dipsomaniac ['dipsəu'meinjæk] *adj/n* dipsómano, na.

dipstick ['dipstik] *n* varilla *f* graduada, indicador *m* de nivel.

dipteral ['diptərəl] *adj* ARCH díptero, ra; *a dipteral temple* un templo díptero.

dipteran ['diptərən] *n* ZOOL díptero *m*.
◆ *n* díptero *m*.

dipteron ['diptə'rɔn] *n* ZOOL díptero *m*.

— OBSERV El plural de la palabra inglesa es *diptera.*

dipterous ['diptərəs] *adj* ZOOL díptero, ra.

diptych ['diptik] *n* díptico *m.*

dire ['daiə*] *adj* horrible, terrible, espantoso, sa (dreadful) || extremo, ma (extreme); *dire measures* medidas extremas || *to be in dire need of* necesitar urgentemente.

direct [di'rekt, dai'rekt] *adj* directo, ta (straight) || franco, ca (frank) || tajante (blunt) || directo, ta (immediate); *the direct causes of his illness* las causas directas de su enfermedad; *the direct results of the catastrophe* las consecuencias directas de la catástrofe || directo, ta (descent, taxation) || textual, literal (quotation) || GRAMM directo, ta; *direct object* complemento directo; *direct speech* discurso directo || ELECTR continuo, nua; *direct current* corriente continua || — INFORM *direct access* acceso *m* directo || *direct action* acción *f* directa || *direct debit* domiciliación *f* bancaria || US *direct discourse* estilo directo || *the direct opposite of sth.* exactamente lo contrario de algo.
◆ *adv* directamente; *the train goes direct to London* el tren va directamente a Londres.

direct [di'rekt, dai'rekt] *vt* dirigir (letter, instrument, steps, film, orchestra, company, etc.) || mandar, ordenar; *he directed me to draw up detailed plans* me mandó elaborar planes detallados || indicar; *can you direct me to the station?* ¿me puede indicar dónde está la estación? || — *to direct one's attention to* fijar la atención en || *to direct one's gaze towards* dirigir la mirada hacia || *to direct s.o.'s attention to sth.* señalar algo a la atención de uno, llamar la atención de alguien sobre algo.
◆ *vi* dirigir.

direction [di'rekʃən, dai'rekʃən] *n* dirección *f*; *they entrusted him with the direction of the work* le confiaron la dirección de la obra; *we are going in the same direction* vamos en la misma dirección || dirección *f* (of film, company, etc.) || — CINEM *executive direction* dirección general de producción || *in the direction of* en dirección a.
◆ *pl* instrucciones *f* || *directions for use* instrucciones para el uso, modo *m* de empleo.

directional [-l] *adj* direccional, orientable.

direction finder [-,faində*] *n* radiogoniómetro *m.*

direction indicator [-,indikeitə*] *n* AUT intermitente *m.*

directive [di'rektiv, dai'rektiv] *adj* directivo, va.
◆ *n* orden *f*, instrucción *f* (order).
◆ *pl* directrices *f*, directivas *f*; *I have given them perfectly clear directives* les he dado directrices perfectamente claras.

directly [di'rektli, dai'rektli] *adv* directamente (in a direct manner) || inmediatamente, en seguida (immediately); *he came in directly* entró en seguida || exactamente, justo; *he lives directly opposite the church* vive exactamente en frente de la iglesia.
◆ *conj* en cuanto (as soon as).

directness [di'rektnis, dai'rektnis] *n* franqueza *f.*

director [di'rektə*, dai'rektə*] *n* director *m* || — *board of directors* consejo *m* de administración, junta directiva || *director general* director general || *direction of production* director de producción || *film director* director de cine || *managing director* director gerente || *spiritual director* director espiritual.

directorate [di'rektərit, dai'rektərit] *n* cargo *m* de director, dirección *f* (post) || consejo *m* de administración, junta *f* directiva (board of directors).

directorial [,direk'tɔːriəl, dairek'tɔːriəl] *adj* directoral; *directorial powers* poderes directorales || directivo, va.

directorship [di'rektəʃip, dai'rektəʃip] *n* cargo *m* de director, dirección *f.*

directory [di'rektəri, dai'rektəri] *n* guía *f* telefónica (telephone) || directorio *m* (book of directions) || libro *m* de instrucciones (set of rules) || consejo *m* de administración, junta *f* directiva (directorate) || INFORM directorio *m* || *directory enquiries* servicio *m* de información telefónica.
◆ *adj* directorio, ria.

Directory [di'rektəri, dai'rektəri] *n* HIST directorio *m.*

direct primary [di'rekt'praiməri] *n* US elección *f* preliminar en la que el candidato es designado directamente por el pueblo.

directress [di'rektris, dai'rektris] *n* directora *f.*

directrix [di'rektriks, dai'rektriks] *n* directriz *f.*
— OBSERV El plural de *directrix* es *directrices* o *directrixes.*

dirge [dəːdʒ] *n* canto *m* fúnebre (funeral hymn) || endecha *f* (lament).

dirigible ['diridʒəbl] *adj* ANAT dirigible.
◆ *n* AVIAT dirigible *m.*

diriment ['diriment] *adj* JUR dirimente; *diriment impediment* impedimento dirimente.

dirk [dəːk] *n* puñal *m.*

dirk [dəːk] *vt* apuñalar.

dirt [dəːt] *n* suciedad *f* (dirtiness) || mugre *f* (filth) || porquería *f* (soiling matter) || basura *f* (litter) || barro *m* (mud) || excremento *m* (of animals) || porquerías *f pl* (obscenities); *to talk dirt* decir porquerías || cochinada *f* (dirty trick) || TECH tierra *f* aurífera || US tierra *f* (earth) || — FIG *to do dirt to s.o.* hacer una cochinada a alguien | *to eat dirt* tragar quina | *to throw dirt at s.o.* poner a alguien como un trapo | *to treat s.o. like dirt* tratar a alguien como a una zapatilla.

dirt-cheap ['dəːt'tʃiːp] *adj* FAM baratísimo, ma; tirado, da.

dirt farmer ['dəːt'fɑːmə*] *n* US FAM cultivador *m.*

dirtiness ['dəːtinis] *n* suciedad *f* || porquería *f* (obscenity) || FIG bajeza *f* (meanness).

dirt track ['dəːt-træk] *n* pista *f* de ceniza (for motorcycle racing).

dirty ['dəːti] *adj* sucio, cia (unclean); *a dirty handkerchief* un pañuelo sucio || lleno de barro (muddy) || FAM malísimo, ma; de perros (weather); *a dirty night* una noche de perros || FIG sucio, cia; *dirty business* negocios sucios; *a dirty mind* una mente sucia | sucio, cia; *dirty grey* gris sucio | lascivo, va (look) || FAM verde (obscene); *a dirty joke* un chiste verde; *a dirty old man* un viejo verde | grosero, ra; obsceno, na (language) || — *dirty trick* mala pasada, mala jugada || FIG *don't wash your dirty linen in public* los trapos sucios se lavan en casa || FIG & FAM *to do the dirty on s.o., to play a dirty trick on s.o.* jugar una mala pasada a uno, hacer una mala jugada *or* una cochinada a uno.

dirty ['dəːti] *vt* ensuciar || embarrar, enlodar (to muddy) || FIG manchar (to stain).
◆ *vi* ensuciarse || FIG mancharse.

disability [,disə'biliti] *n* MED incapacidad *f* física *or* mental || JUR incapacidad *f* || desventaja *f* (disadvantage).

disable [dis'eibl] *vt* incapacitar (*from* para) (to incapacitate legally) || dejar imposibilitado (to incapacitate physically) || lisiar (to cripple) || dejar mentalmente incapacitado (to incapacitate mentally) || poner fuera de uso, volver inservible (to render useless) || impedir (to prevent).

disabled [-d] *adj* inválido, da; imposibilitado, da || JUR incapacitado, da || *the disabled* los inválidos.

disablement [-mənt] *n* incapacidad *f.*

disabuse [,disə'bjuːz] *vt* desengañar.

disaccord [,disə'kɔːd] *n* desacuerdo *m.*

disadvantage [,dsəd'vɑːntidʒ] *n* desventaja *f*, inconveniente *m* || — *to be at disadvantage* estar en situación desventajosa || *to the disadvantage of* en perjuicio de, en detrimento de.

disadvantage [,disəd'vɑːntidʒ] *vt* perjudicar.

disadvantageous [,disædvɑːn'teidʒəs] *adj* desventajoso, sa.

disaffected [-id] *adj* desafecto, ta.

disaffection [,disə'fekʃən] *n* desafección *f*, desafecto *m* || descontento *m* (discontent).

disaffirm [,disə'fəːm] *vt* desmentir (to contradict) || JUR casar, anular (a sentence) | denunciar (a contract).

disagree [,disə'griː] *vi* no estar de acuerdo, estar en desacuerdo (to differ) || discrepar; *their testimonies disagree* sus testimonios discrepan || no aprobar, no estar de acuerdo; *I disagree with your policy* no apruebo su política || no convenir, sentar mal (to be unsuitable); *the climate disagrees with him* el clima no le conviene || sentar mal (to upset the digestion) || reñir (to quarrel).

disagreeable [,disə'griəbl] *adj* desagradable (unpleasant) || desagradable, antipático, ca (ill-natured).

disagreement [,disə'griːmənt] *n* desacuerdo *m* (lack of agreement) || disconformidad *f*; *there is a disagreement between their versions* hay disconformidad entre sus versiones || riña *f*, altercado *m* (squabble).

disallow ['disə'lau] *vt* rechazar (to refuse to admit) || anular (in sport) || prohibir (to forbid).

disannul [,disə'nʌl] *vt* anular (to annul).

disappear [,disə'piə*] *vi* desaparecer.

disappearance [,disə'piərəns] *n* desaparición *f.*

disappoint [,disə'pɔint] *vt* decepcionar, desilusionar; *the film disappointed me* la película me ha decepcionado || defraudar, decepcionar; *her son disappointed her* su hijo le ha defraudado || faltar a su palabra (to break a promise); *you promised to come but you disappointed me* prometiste venir pero faltaste a tu palabra.

disappointed [-id] *adj* decepcionado, da; desilusionado, da; defraudado, da || desengañado, da (love) || — *I was disappointed by his performance* me decepcionó su actuación || *to be disappointed in love* sufrir un desengaño amoroso *or* desengaños amorosos.

disappointing [-iŋ] *adj* decepcionante.

disappointment [-mənt] *n* decepción *f*, desilusión *f* || disgusto *m* (displeasure) || — *disappointment in love* desengaño amoroso || *to be a disappointment to s.o.* decepcionar a alguien.

disapprobation [,disæprəu'beiʃən] *n* desaprobación *f* (disapproval).

disapprobatory [,disəprəu'beitəri] *adj* desaprobador, ra; desaprobatorio, ria.

disapproval [,disə'pruːvəl] *n* desaprobación *f.*

disapprove ['disə'pruːv] *vt* desaprobar.
◆ *vi* no gustarle a uno (people); *I disapprove of him* no me gusta || desaprobar; *he disapproved of my conduct* desaprobó mi comportamiento || estar en contra; *to disapprove of sth. being done* estar en contra de que se haga algo.

disapproving [-iŋ] *adj* desaprobador, ra.

disapprovingly [-iŋli] *adv* con desaprobación.

disarm [dis'ɑːm] *vt* desarmar.
◆ *vi* desarmar, deponer las armas.

disarmament [dis'ɑːməmənt] *n* desarme *m*.

disarming [dis'ɑːmiŋ] *adj* que desarma.
◆ *n* desarme *m*.

disarrange ['disə'reindʒ] *vt* desordenar, desarreglar (to untidy) || desbaratar (plans).

disarrangement [-mənt] *n* desorden *m*, desarreglo *m* (disorder) || desbaratamiento *m* (of plans).

disarray ['disə'rei] *n* desorden *m* (lack of order); *a room in disarray* una habitación en desorden || desaliño *m* (of dress) || *to flee in disarray* huir a la desbandada.

disarray ['disə'rei] *vt* hacer huir (the enemy) || desarreglar, desordenar (to untidy) || desarreglar (s.o.'s dress).

disarticulate ['disɑː'tikjuleit] *vt* desarticular.
◆ *vi* desarticularse.

disarticulation [ˌdisɑːˌtikju'leiʃən] *n* desarticulación *f*.

disassemble [ˌdisə'sembl] *vt* desmontar, desarmar.

disassembly [-i] *n* desmontaje *m*, desarme *m*.

disassociate [ˌdisə'səuʃieit] *vt/vi* ⟶ **dissociate.**

disaster [di'zɑːstə*] *n* desastre *m* (catastrophe) || FIG desastre *m* (complete failure); *the dance was a disaster* el baile fue un desastre || *to court disaster* correr al desastre.

disastrous [di'zɑːstrəs] *adj* desastroso, sa.

disavow ['disə'vau] *vt* renegar de (one's faith, one's family, friends) || negarse a aceptar la responsabilidad de (an action) || desaprobar (to disapprove).

disavowal [-əl] *n* negación *f* || desaprobación *f*.

disband [dis'bænd] *vt* disolver (an organization) || dispensar (people) || licenciar (troops).
◆ *vi* disolverse || dispersarse.

disbandment [-mənt] *n* disolución *f* (of an organization) || dispersión *f* (of people) || licenciamiento *m* (of troops).

disbar [dis'bɑː*] *vt* JUR expulsar del colegio de abogados.

disbarment [-mənt] *n* JUR expulsión *f* del colegio de abogados.

disbelief ['disbi'liːf] *n* incredulidad *f*.

disbelieve ['disbi'liːv] *vt* no creer.
◆ *vi* no creer || ser incrédulo.

disbeliever [-ə*] *n* descreído, da; incrédulo, la.

disbranch [dis'brɑːntʃ] *vt* podar.

disbud [dis'bʌd] *vt* desyemar (plants) || descornar (cattle).

disburden [dis'bəːdn] *vt* descargar || FIG *to disburden o.s.* desahogarse, aliviarse.

disburse [dis'bəːs] *vt* desembolsar.

disbursement [dis'bəːsmənt] *n* desembolso *m*.

disc [disk] *n* ⟶ **disk.**

discalceate [dis'kælsiit]; **discalced** [dis'kælst] *adj* REL descalzo, za.

discard ['diskɑːd] *n* descarte *m* (in card games) || desecho *m* (sth. rejected).

discard [dis'kɑːd] *vt* descartarse de, descartar (cards) || desechar, descartar (to cast aside) || desechar; *to discard an old suit* desechar un traje viejo || tirar (to throw away) || FIG renunciar a (to abandon).
◆ *vi* descartarse.

discern [di'səːn] *vt* discernir, distinguir; *to discern good from evil* discernir el bien del mal || percibir (to perceive).

discernible [di'səːnibl] *adj* distinguible, discernible || perceptible.

discerning [di'səːniŋ] *adj* perspicaz.

discernment [di'səːnmənt] *n* discernimiento *m*, perspicacia *f* (discrimination) || criterio *m*, discernimiento *m*; *to act with discernment* actuar con discernimiento.

discharge ['dis'tʃɑːdʒ] *n* descarga *f*; *the discharge of the ship* la descarga del barco || descarga *f*, disparo *m*; *he heard the discharge of a gun* oyó la descarga de una escopeta || disparo *m* (of arrows) || escape *m* (of gases) || JUR liberación *f* (of a prisoner) | rehabilitación *f* (of a bankrupt) | absolución *f* (of the accused in court) || MIL licencia *f* absoluta || descargo *m*, exoneración *f* (of taxes, etc.) || descargo *m*, pago *m* (of a debt) || recibo *m* (certificate of payment) || cumplimiento *m*, ejercicio *m*, desempeño *m*; *in the discharge of his duties* en el ejercicio de sus funciones || cumplimiento *m* (of a vow) || MED supuración *f* | pus *m* (pus) | alta *f* (from hospital) || ELECTR & PHYS descarga *f* || decoloración *f* (process of removing dye) || decolorante *m* (chemical for removing dye) || destitución *f* (from a post) || despido *m* (of a worker) || — *discharge tube* tubo luminoso || *discharge valve* válvula *f* de escape || *to the discharge of* en descargo de.

discharge [dis'tʃɑːdʒ] *vt* descargar; *to discharge a cargo* descargar un cargamento || verter; *the factory discharges waste into the river* la fábrica vierte los residuos en el río || saldar (a debt) || disparar, descargar (a gun) || disparar (arrows) || lanzar (a bomb) || despedir (a worker) || JUR absolver (the accused) | liberar, poner en libertad (a prisoner) | rehabilitar (a bankrupt) || dar de alta, dar el alta (patient) || MIL dar de baja (disabled soldier) | licenciar (soldiers) || desempeñar; *to discharge one's duties* desempeñar sus funciones || cumplir con, cumplir; *to discharge one's duty* cumplir con su deber || eximir, descargar (to free from an obligation) || arrojar, echar (pus) || perder (its colour) || desprender (gas) || ELECTR & PHYS descargar || *to discharge s.o. from doing sth.* dispensar a alguien de hacer algo.
◆ *vi* descargar (a ship) || supurar (to suppurate) || descargarse, dispararse (a gun) || ELECTR & PHYS descargarse || verter; *the sewers discharge in the river* las cloacas vierten en el río || descargar (river) || desteñirse, correrse (colour).

discharger [-ə*] *n* descargador *m*.

disciple [di'saipl] *n* discípulo, la.

disciplinant ['disiplinənt] *n* disciplinante *m* & *f* (in holy week).

disciplinarian [ˌdisipli'nɛəriən] *adj* disciplinario, ria.
◆ *n* ordenancista *m* & *f*, partidario *m* de una disciplina rigurosa.

disciplinary ['disiplinəri] *adj* disciplinario, ria; *disciplinary batallion* batallón disciplinario.

discipline ['disiplin] *n* disciplina *f*.

discipline ['disiplin] *vt* disciplinar (to submit to discipline) || castigar (to punish).

disc jockey ['diskˌdʒɔki] *n* locutor *m* que presenta discos en la radio, «disc jockey» *m* || pinchadiscos *m inv*, «disc jockey» *m* (in a discotheque).

disclaim [dis'kleim] *vt* rechazar (authority, responsibility) || JUR renunciar a (a legal claim) || *I disclaim any part in the murder* niego rotundamente haber tomado parte en el asesinato.
◆ *vi* renunciar.

disclaimer [-ə*] *n* JUR renuncia *f* (of a right) || denegacion *f* (denial) || rectificación *f*; *he sent a disclaimer to the newspaper* envió una rectificación al periódico.

disclose [dis'kləuz] *vt* revelar (to reveal); *to disclose a secret* revelar un secreto.

disclosure [dis'kləuzə*] *n* revelación *f* (of a secret) || descubrimiento *m* (of hidden objects).

disco ['diskəu] *n* disco *f*, discoteca *f*.

disco ['diskəu] *vi* FAM ir de disco, ir a la disco (to go to a disco) || bailar música disco (to dance).

discobolus [dis'kɔbələs] *n* discóbolo *m*.

discography [dis'kɔgrəfi] *n* catálogo *m* de discos.

discoid ['diskɔid]; **discoidal** [dis'kɔidəl] *adj* discoidal, discoideo, a.

discolour; *US* **discolor** [dis'kʌlə*] *vt* descolorar, desteñir; *the sun discolours the curtains* el sol descolora las cortinas || manchar, desteñir en (to stain); *the red shirt has discoloured the sheets* la camisa roja ha desteñido en las sábanas.

discolouration; *US* **discoloration** [disˌkʌlə'reiʃən] *n* descoloración *f*, descoloramiento *m*.

discomfit [dis'kʌmfit] *vt* desconcertar.

discomfiture [dis'kʌmfitʃə*] *n* desconcierto *m*.

discomfort [dis'kʌmfət] *n* molestia *f* (physical pain) || malestar *m* (feeling of uneasiness) || incomodidad *f* (lack of comfort) || preocupación *f* (worry) || aflicción *f*, pesar *m* (sorrow).

discomfort [dis'kʌmfət] *vt* molestar (to cause uneasiness) || preocupar (to worry) || afligir (to sadden).

discommode [ˌdiskə'məud] *vt* incomodar, molestar.

discompose [ˌdiskəm'pəuz] *vt* perturbar, turbar (s.o.) || descomponer (s.o.'s countenance).

discomposure [ˌdiskəm'pəuʒə*] *n* desconcierto *m* (of a person) || alteración *f* (of the face).

disconcert [ˌdiskən'səːt] *vt* desconcertar (to confuse) || perturbar, trastornar; *this disconcerts my plans* esto trastorna mis planes.

disconcerting [-iŋ] *adj* desconcertante.

disconcertment [-mənt] *n* desconcierto *m* (confusion) || trastorno *m*, perturbación *f* (upsetting).

disconnect ['diskə'nekt] *vt* ELECTR desconectar || desarticular (two parts) || separar (one part from another) || desenganchar (wagons).

disconnected [-id] *adj* desconectado, da; *a disconnected television* una televisión desconectada || sin conexión, sin relación; *disconnected events* sucesos sin conexión || deshilvanado, da; inconexo, xa (speech, style).

disconnection; **disconnexion** [diskə'nekʃən] *n* desconexión *f* || desarticulación *f* (of two parts) || separación *f* || FIG *f* de conexión, incoherencia *f*.

disconsolate [dis'kɔnsəlit] *adj* desconsolado, da.

disconsolation [disˌkɔnsə'leiʃən] *n* desconsuelo *m*.

discontent ['diskən'tənt] *vt* descontentar.

discontented [-id] *adj* descontento, ta.

discontentedness [-idnis]; **discontentment** [-mənt] *n* descontento *m*.

discontinuance [ˌdiskən'tinjuəns] *n* cesación *f*, interrupción *f* || JUR suspensión *f* (of a suit) | sobreseimiento *m* (of a case).

discontinuation [ˌdiskənˌtinju'eiʃən] *n* cesación *f*, interrupción *f*, discontinuación *f*.

discontinue ['diskən'tinjuː] *vt* discontinuar, interrumpir (to stop) || **suspender** (one's sub-

scription) || JUR sobreseer (a case) || *to discontinue doing sth.* dejar de hacer algo.
◆ *vi* cesar, interrumpirse, suspenderse.

discontinuity ['dis,kɔnti'njuiti] *n* discontinuidad *f* (lack of continuity) || interrupción *f* || falta *f* de ilación; *discontinuity of ideas* falta de ilación en las ideas.

discontinuous ['diskən'tinjuəs] *adj* discontinuo, nua || interrumpido, da.

discophile ['diskəfaie] *n* discófilo, la.

discord ['diskɔ:d] *n* discordia *f*, disensión *f* (disagreement); *to sow discord* sembrar la discordia || MUS disonancia *f*.

discord ['diskɔ:d] *vi* discrepar, discordar.

discordance [dis'kɔ:dəns]; **discordancy** [-i] *n* discordancia *f*; *discordance between the statements and the facts* discordancia entre los dichos y los hechos || discordia *f*, disensión *f* (disagreement) || MUS discordancia *f*, disonancia *f*.

discordant [dis'kɔ:dənt] *adj* discordante (opinions, notes) || discorde, en desacuerdo (people) || MUS discorde || *discordant with* opuesto a, en desacuerdo con.

discotheque ['diskəutek] *n* discoteca *f*.

discount ['diskaunt] *n* descuento *m*; *to give a discount to* conceder un descuento a; *bank discount* descuento bancario || — *at a discount* a precio reducido, con descuento (goods), por debajo de la par (shares) || FIG *politeness is at a discount* ya no se cotiza la cortesía.

discount ['dis'kaunt] *vt* descontar (in finance) || rebajar, disminuir (to reduce) || no hacer caso de (to disregard); *you must discount half of what he says* no debes hacer caso de la mitad de lo que dice || dejar de lado (to leave out) || contar con (to anticipate); *we had already discounted this loss* ya habíamos contado con esa pérdida.
◆ *vi* descontar letras de cambio.

discountable [-əbl] *adj* COMM descontable.

discountenance [dis'kauntinəns] *vt* estar en contra de (to be against) || desaprobar (to disapprove of) || desconcertar, turbar (to abash).

discount house ['diskaunt-haus] *n* tienda *f* que vende artículos a precio reducido.

discount rate ['diskaunt-reit] *n* tipo *m* de descuento.

discount store ['diskaunt stɔ:] *n* tienda *f* de rebajas.

discourage [dis'kʌridʒ] *vt* desanimar, desalentar, descorazonar; *this hard work discourages them* este duro trabajo les desanima || no fomentar; *inflation discourages saving* la inflación no fomenta el ahorro || *to discourage from* recomendar que no (to advise against); *the police discourage people from driving too fast* la policía recomienda a la gente que no conduzca muy de prisa; hacer desistir de, disuadir (to dissuade from); *the sight of the enemy discouraged them from attacking* la vista del enemigo les hizo desistir de atacar.

discouragement [-mənt] *n* desánimo *m*, desaliento *m*, desmoralización *f*. || desaprobación *f*.

discouraging [-iŋ] *adj* desalentador, ra; descorazonador, ra; desmoralizador, ra.

discourse [dis'kɔ:s] *n* discurso *m* (speech) || conversación *f* [AMER plática *f*] || disertación *f* (dissertation) || tratado *m*, discurso *m* (treatise).

discourse [dis'kɔ:s] *vi* disertar (*upon* sobre) || conversar [AMER platicar] (to talk).

discourteous [dis'kə:tjəs] *adj* descortés.

discourtesy [dis'kə:tisi] *n* descortesía *f*.

discover [dis'kʌvə*] *vt* descubrir; *to discover a new antibiotic* descubrir un nuevo antibiótico || darse cuenta de (to realize).

discoverer [-rə*] *n* descubridor, ra.

discovery [dis'kʌvəri] *n* descubrimiento *m* || *the age of discovery* la época de los descubrimientos.

discredit [dis'kredit] *n* descrédito *m* (loss of reputation) || duda *f* (disbelief); *to throw discredit upon a statement* poner una declaracion en duda || — *to be a discredit to* deshonrar a || *to be to the discredit of* ir en descrédito de || *to bring discredit on o.s., to fall into discredit* desacreditarse || *to cast* o *to throw discredit on s.o.* desacreditar a uno.

discredit [dis'kredit] *vt* desacreditar (to destroy s.o.'s trustworthiness) || poner en duda, dudar de, no dar crédito a (to refuse to believe); *to discredit s.o.'s evidence* poner en duda el testimonio de alguien || deshonrar (to dishonour).

discreditable [dis'kreditəbl] *adj* indigno, na; *conduct discreditable to a doctor* conducta indigna de un médico || vergonzoso, sa (shameful) || *her performance was far from discreditable* su actuación, fue bastante buena.

discredited [dis'kreditid] *adj* desacreditado, da.

discreet [dis'kri:t] *adj* discreto, ta || circunspecto, ta.

discrepancy [dis'krepənsi] *n* discrepancia *f*; *there is a discrepancy between the two versions* hay discrepancia entre las dos versiones || diferencia *f* (between numbers).

discrepant [dis'krepənt] *adj* discrepante (*with, from* de) || diferente.

discrete [dis'kri:t] *adj* MATH & MED discreto, ta || PHIL abstracto, ta || distinto, ta (separate) || INFORM *discrete transistor* transistor *m* discreto.
— OBSERV No se confunda esta palabra con *discreet*.

discreteness [-nis] *n* distinción *f*.

discretion [dis'kreʃən] *n* discreción *f* (prudence) || circunspección *f* || juicio *m*, razón *f* (judgment) || — *age of discretion* edad *f* del juicio, uso *m* de razón || *at discretion* a discreción || *at the discretion of* a juicio de || *at your discretion* como usted guste, a su gusto || *to use one's own discretion* hacer lo que a uno le parezca.

discretionary [dis'kreʃnəri] *adj* discrecional; *discretionary power* poder discrecional.

discriminant [dis'kriminənt] *n* MATH discriminante *m* (mathematical expression).

discriminate [dis'krimineit] *vt* discriminar, distinguir; *to discriminate good from bad* discriminar lo bueno de lo malo || distinguir; *his height discriminates him from his friends* su estatura le distingue de sus amigos.
◆ *vi* discriminar, distinguir; *to discriminate between good and bad* discriminar entre lo bueno y lo malo || — *to discriminate against* discriminar, hacer discriminaciones en contra de || *to discriminate in favour of* hacer discriminaciones en favor de.

discriminating [-iŋ]; **discriminative** [-nətiv] *adj* juicioso, sa (people) || discriminatorio, ria (laws, tariff, etc.) || muy bueno (taste) || distintivo, va (sign) || fino, na; muy bueno (ear).

discrimination [dis,krimi'neiʃən] *n* discriminación *f*, distinción *f* || discriminación *f*; *racial discrimination* discriminación racial || discernimiento *m* (discernment) || buen gusto *m* (good taste).

discriminative [dis'kriminətiv] *adj* ⟶ **discriminating.**

discriminatory [dis'kriminətəri] *adj* discriminatorio, ria.

discrown [dis'kraun] *vt* descoronar (a king).

discursive [dis'kə:siv] *adj* divagador, ra (rambling) || deshilvanado, da (speech) || discursivo, va (proceeding by reasoning); *discursive method* método discursivo.

discus ['diskəs] *n* SP disco *m*; *throwing the discus* lanzamiento del disco || SP *discus thrower* lanzador *m* de disco.
— OBSERV El plural de *discus* es *discuses* o *disci*.

discuss [dis'kʌs] *vt* discutir (to exchange ideas about, to debate) || hablar de (to talk about).

discussion [dis'kʌʃən] *n* discusión *f*; *subject for discussion* tema de discusión || — *to be under discussion* estar en discusión, estar siendo discutido || *to come up for discussion* ser sometido a discusión.

disdain [dis'dein] *n* desdén *m*, desprecio *m*.

disdain [dis'dein] *vt* desdeñar, despreciar (to have contempt for) || no dignarse; *to disdain to answer* no dignarse a contestar.

disdainful [-ful] *adj* desdeñoso, sa; despectivo, va (expressing disdain) || desdeñoso, sa (aloof).

disease [di'zi:z] *n* enfermedad *f*; *occupational disease* enfermedad profesional; *contagious disease* enfermedad contagiosa || FIG mal *m*, enfermedad *f*.

diseased [-d] *adj* enfermo, ma.

disembark ['disim'ba:k] *vt/vi* desembarcar.

disembarkation [,disemba:'keiʃən]; **disembarkment** [,disem'ba:kmənt] *n* desembarco *m* (of people) || desembarque *m* (of goods).

disembarrass ['disim'bærəs] *vt* desembarazar.

disembodied ['disim'bɔdid] *adj* incorpóreo, a.

disembody ['disim'bɔdi] *vt* separar del cuerpo.

disembogue [,disim'beug] *vt* verter.
◆ *vi* desembocar, desaguar.

disembowel [,disim'bauəl] *vt* desentrañar, destripar.

disembowelment [-mənt] *n* desentrañamiento *m*, destripamiento *m*.

disembroil [,disim'brɔil] *vt* desenmarañar, desembrollar.

disenchant ['disin'tʃa:nt] *vt* desencantar, desilusionar.

disenchantment [-mənt] *n* desencanto *m*, desilusión *f*.

disencumber ['disinkʌmbə*] *vt* desembarazar, librar.

disendow ['disin'dau] *vt* privar de una dotación (a church).

disengage [,disin'geidʒ] *vt* desenganchar (to uncouple, to unhook) || soltar (to detach) || liberar (to free) || desengranar (gears) || MIL retirar (troops) || AUT *to disengage the clutch* desembragar.
◆ *vi* desengancharse || soltarse || liberarse || MIL retirarse.

disengaged [-d] *adj* libre (free) || suelto, ta (loose) || desenganchado, da || AUT desembragado, da (clutch).

disengagement [-mənt] *n* retirada *f* (in fencing) || MIL retirada *f* de las tropas || liberación *f* || AUT desembrague *m* || ruptura *f* de compromiso matrimonial.

disentail ['disin'teil] *vt* liberar, desamortizar (property).

disentailment [-mənt] *n* desamortización *f* (of property).

disentangle ['disin'tæŋgl] *vt* desenredar, desenmarañar (to unravel); *to disentangle one's hair* desenredar el pelo || desenmarañar, de-

senredar, poner en claro (an intrigue) || descubrir (a puzzle).
◆ *vi* desenredarse, desenmarañarse.

disentanglement [ˌdisinˈtæŋglmənt] *n* desenmarañamiento *m*, desenredo *m* || FIG solución *f*.

disentomb [ˌdisinˈtuːmb] *vt* desenterrar.

disequilibrium [ˈdisekwiˈlibriəm] *n* desequilibrio *m*.

disestablish [ˈdisisˈtæbliʃ] *vt* separar (la Iglesia) del Estado.

disestablishment [ˌdisisˈtæbliʃmənt] *n* separación *f* (de la Iglesia) del Estado.

disesteem [ˈdisisˈtiːm] *n* poco aprecio *m* || descrédito *m* (discredit).

disesteem [ˈdisisˈtiːm] *vt* desestimar, despreciar.

disfavour; *US* **disfavor** [ˈdisˈfeivə*] *n* desgracia *f* || desaprobación *f* (disapproval) || desventaja *f* (disadvantage) || *to fall into disfavour* caer en desgracia (people), caer en desuso (word, custom).

disfavour; *US* **disfavor** [disˈfeivə*] *vt* desfavorecer || desaprobar (to disapprove).

disfigure [disˈfigə*] *vt* desfigurar || afear (to spoil); *pylons which disfigure the landscape* postes que afean el paisaje.

disfigurement [disˈfigəmənt] *n* desfiguración *f* || afeamiento *m* (spoiling).

disfranchise; disenfranchise [ˈdisˈfræntʃaiz] *vt* privar de los derechos civiles *or* del derecho de votación.

disgorge [disˈgɔːdʒ] *vt* devolver, vomitar (to vomit) || verter, descargar (a river) || devolver (to give back) || desembuchar (birds).

disgrace [disˈgreis] *n* deshonra *f* (loss of honour) || ignominia *f* (ignominy) || vergüenza *f* (cause of shame) || desgracia *f* (disfavour) || — *this room is a disgrace* esta habitación es una vergüenza || *to be in disgrace* haber caído en desgracia (person), estar castigado (child) || *to bring disgrace on* deshonrar || *to fall into disgrace* caer en desgracia.

disgrace [disˈgreis] *vt* deshonrar (to bring shame upon); *to disgrace one's family* deshonrar a la familia || *he was disgraced for his behaviour* su comportamiento le hizo caer en desgracia.

disgraceful [-ful] *adj* vergonzoso, sa (shameful) || deshonroso, sa (dishonourable); *disgraceful act* acto deshonroso || *disgraceful!* ¡qué vergüenza!

disgracefulness [-fulnis] *n* lo vergonzoso.

disgruntled [disˈgrʌntld] *adj* contrariado, da; descontento, ta (*at* de) || disgustado, da (*with* con).

disguisable [disˈgaizəbl] *adj* FIG disimulable.

disguise [disˈgaiz] *n* disfraz *m* || FIG disfraz *m* || *in disguise* disfrazado, da.

disguise [disˈgaiz] *vt* disfrazar || FIG disimular (to hide) | disfrazar; *to disguise the voice* disfrazar la voz || *to disguise o.s. as* disfrazarse de.

disgust [disˈgʌst] *n* repugnancia *f*, asco *m* || *to fill with disgust* repugnar, dar asco.

disgust [disˈgʌst] *vt* repugnar, dar asco a (to fill with loathing) || indignar (to make indignant).

disgusted [-id] *adj* asqueado, da.

disgusting [-iŋ] *adj* repugnante, asqueroso, sa.

disgustingly [-iŋli] *adv* de una manera asquerosa, asquerosamente || *he is disgustingly mean* es de una tacañería que da asco.

dish [diʃ] *n* plato *m* (eating vessel) || fuente *f* (serving vessel) || plato *m* (food) || PHOT cubeta *f* || — FAM *reading is not my dish* no me gusta mayormente leer | *she is quite a dish* es un bombón.
◆ *pl* platos *m*; *to wash the dishes* fregar los platos.

dish [diʃ] *vt* dar forma cóncava *or* convexa a (to shape) || ahuecar (to hollow) || servir (food) || arruinar (chances) || FAM vencer (to outmanoeuvre) || — FAM *to dish out* dar (news), dar, asestar (blows), infligir (a punishment), pagar (to pay), gastar (to spend) || *to dish up* servir (food), sacar, presentar; *to dish up the same arguments time and again* sacar siempre los mismos argumentos.

dishabille [ˌdisæˈbiːl]; **déshabillé;** *US* **deshabille** [ˌdeizæˈbiːei] *n* traje *m* de casa, bata *f*; *to be in dishabille* estar en traje de casa.

dish aerial [ˈdiʃɛəriəl] *n* antena *f* parabólica.

disharmonious [ˌdishɑːˈməuniəs] *adj* disonante (sounds) || discorde, discordante (opinions).

disharmonize [disˈhɑːmənaiz] *vt* desarmonizar.

disharmony [ˈdisˈhɑːməni] *n* falta *f* de armonía || MUS disonancia *f*.

dishcloth [ˈdiʃklɔθ] *n* bayeta *f*, trapo *m* de fregar.

dishearten [disˈhɑːtn] *vt* descorazonar, desanimar, desalentar.

disheartening [-iŋ] *adj* desalentador, ra; descorazonador, ra.

dishevel [diˈʃəvəl] *vt* despeinar (one's hair) | desaliñar, desarreglar (clothes).

dishevelled; *US* **disheveled** [-d] *adj* despeinado, da (hair) || desaliñado, da; desarreglado, da (clothes).

dishevelment [-mənt] *n* desorden *m* (of hair) || desaliño *m* (of clothes).

dishful [ˈdiʃful] *n* plato *m*.

dishonest [disˈɔnist] *adj* poco íntegro, gra; poco honrado, da (people) || fraudulento, ta (dealings).

dishonesty [disˈɔnisti] *n* falta *f* de honradez (lack of honesty) || fraude *m* (fraud).

dishonour; *US* **dishonor** [disˈɔnə*] *n* deshonra *f*, deshonor *m* || falta *f* de pago, rechazo *m* (of a bill, etc.).

dishonour; *US* **dishonor** [disˈɔnə*] *vt* deshonrar (to bring shame on); *to dishonour a woman* deshonrar a una mujer || faltar a; *to dishonour one's word* faltar a su palabra || rechazar, negarse a pagar (a cheque).

dishonourable; *US* **dishonorable** [disˈɔnərəbl] *adj* deshonroso, sa.

dishouse [disˈhauz] *vt* expulsar.

dishpan [ˈdiʃpæn] *n* *US* barreño *m*.

dishrack [ˈdiʃræk] *n* escurreplatos *m inv*.

dish towel [ˈdiʃˌtauəl] *US* trapo *m or* paño *m* de cocina.

dishwarmer [ˈdiʃˌwɔːmə*] *n* calientaplatos *m inv*.

dishwasher [ˈdiʃˌwɔʃə*] *n* lavaplatos *m* & *f inv* (person) || máquina *f* lavaplatos, lavaplatos *m inv*, lavavajillas *m inv* (machine).

dishwater [ˈdiʃˌwɔːtə*] *n* agua *f* de fregar platos || FAM agua *f* sucia (weak tea or coffee).

dishy [ˈdiʃi] *adj* FAM guapo, pa; atractivo, va.

disillusion [ˌdisiˈluːʒən] *vt* desilusionar; *to be disillusioned with* quedar desilusionado con *or* de.

disillusionment [-mənt] *n* desilusión *f*.

disincentive [ˌdisinˈsentiv] *n* freno *m*.

disinclination [ˌdisinkliˈneiʃən] *n* aversión *f*, poca inclinación *f*.

disincline [ˈdisinˈklain] *vt* quitar las ganas de || *to be disinclined to* estar poco dispuesto a, tener pocas ganas de.

disinfect [ˌdisinˈfekt] *vt* desinfectar.

disinfectant [ˌdisinˈfektənt] *n* desinfectante *m*.
◆ *adj* desinfectante.

disinfection [ˌdisinˈfekʃən] *n* desinfección *f*.

disinfest [ˌdisinˈfest] *vt* desinfestar.

disinfestation [ˌdisinfesˈteiʃən] *n* *rat disinfestation* desratización *f*.

disinflationary [ˌdisinˈfleiʃənəri] *adj* desinflacionista, deflacionista.

disinformation [disˌinfəˈmeiʃən] *n* desinformación *f*.

disingenuous [ˌdisinˈdʒenjuəs] *adj* insincero, ra; falso, sa; disimulado, da.

disinherit [ˈdisinˈherit] *vt* desheredar.

disinheritance [ˌdisinˈheritəns]; **disinheriting** [ˈdisinˈheritiŋ] *n* desheredamiento *m*, desheredación *f*.

disintegrate [disˈintigreit] *vt* desintegrar, disgregar.
◆ *vi* desintegrarse, disgregarse.

disintegration [disˌintiˈgreiʃən] *n* desintegración *f*; *atomic disintegration* desintegración atómica.

disinter [ˈdisinˈtəː*] *vt* desenterrar.

disinterest [disˈintrist] *n* desinterés *m*.

disinterested [disˈintristid] *adj* desinteresado, da (without vested interest) || imparcial (unbiased) || indiferente.

disinterment [ˌdisinˈtəːmənt] *n* desenterramiento *m*, exhumación *f*.

disinvestment [ˌdisinˈvestmənt] *n* ECON cese *m* de las inversiones, desinversión *f*.

disjoin [disˈdʒɔin] *vt* separar, desunir.
◆ *vi* separarse, desunirse.

disjoint [disˈdʒɔint] *vt* desarticular || trinchar (a fowl).

disjointed [-id] *adj* sin conexión, inconexo, xa (incoherent) || desarticulado, da || desunido, da (disunited).

disjunction [disˈdʒʌŋkʃən] *n* separación *f* || GRAMM & PHIL disyunción *f*.

disjunctive [disˈdʒʌŋktiv] *adj* GRAMM & PHIL disyuntivo, va.
◆ *n* GRAMM conjunción *f* disyuntiva || PHIL proposición *f* disyuntiva.

disk; disc [disk] *n* disco *m*; *Newton's disk* disco de Newton || ANAT disco *m* (of bone) || SP disco *m*; *disk thrower* lanzador de disco || TECH disco *m* (of brake) | disco *m* (of plough) || disco *m* (record) || INFORM disco *m*; *disk unit* unidad de disco || — *parking disk* disco de control || INFORM *start-up disk* disco de arranque.

disk drive [-draiv] *n* INFORM disquetera *f*.

diskette [disˈket] *n* INFORM disquete *m*, disco *m* flexible || *diskette drive* lectora *f* de discos.

dislikable [disˈlaikəbl] *adj* antipático, ca; odioso, sa.

dislike [disˈlaik] *n* aversión *f*, antipatía *f* (*for, of* a) || *to take a dislike to s.o.* cogerle antipatía a uno.

dislike [disˈlaik] *vt* tener antipatía a, no gustarle a uno, tener aversión a; *he dislikes me* me tiene antipatía, no le gusto, me tiene aversión || no gustarle a uno; *I dislike music* no me gusta la música || *I don't dislike him* no me disgusta, no le encuentro antipático.

— OBSERV El verbo *dislike* se construye siempre con el gerundio: *I dislike working* no me gusta trabajar.

dislocate [ˈdisləukeit] *vt* dislocar (to put out of joint) || desarreglar, trastornar (plans) || *to* *dislocate one's jaw, one's shoulder* desencajarse la mandíbula, dislocarse el hombro.

dislocation [ˌdisləuˈkeiʃən] *n* dislocación *f*, desarticulación *f* (putting out of joint) ‖ trastorno *m*, desarreglo *m* (of plans) ‖ dislocación *f* (of a bone) ‖ desencajamiento *m* (of jaw).

dislodge [disˈlɔdʒ] *vt* desalojar (to oust); *to dislodge the enemy from the fort* desalojar al enemigo del fuerte ‖ sacar (to remove) ‖ desalojar, hacer salir (an animal).

dislodgement [-mənt]; **dislodging** [-iŋ] *n* desalojamiento *m*.

disloyal [ˈdisˈlɔiəl] *adj* desleal; *disloyal to his brother* desleal con su hermano.

disloyalty [-ti] *n* deslealtad *f*.

dismal [ˈdizməl] *adj* deprimente, triste; *dismal landscape* paisaje triste ‖ triste, sombrío, a (face) ‖ tenebroso, sa (dark) ‖ deprimido, da (depressed) ‖ lúgubre, triste (voice) ‖ catastrófico, ca (failure) ‖ lamentable (very bad) ‖ FAM *the dismals* nostalgia *f*, morriña *f*.

dismantle [disˈmæntl] *vt* desmantelar ‖ desarmar, desmontar; *to dismantle a watch* desarmar un reloj.

dismantlement [-mənt]; **dismantling** [-iŋ] *n* desarme *m*, desmontaje *m* (of machine) ‖ desmantelamiento *m* (of a place).

dismast [ˈdisˈmɑːst] *vt* MAR desarbolar.

dismasting [-iŋ] *n* MAR desarboladura *f*.

dismay [disˈmei] *n* consternación *f*; *to look in dismay* mirar con consternación ‖ desaliento *m* (discouragement) ‖ espanto *m* (fright) ‖ *to fill s.o. with dismay* consternarle a uno.

dismay [disˈmei] *vt* consternar ‖ espantar (to frighten) ‖ desalentar (to discourage).

dismember [disˈmembə*] *vt* desmembrar; *to dismember an empire* desmembrar un imperio.

dismemberment [-mənt] *n* desmembramiento *m*.

dismiss [disˈmis] *vt* despedir; *after supper, he dismissed the servant and went to bed* después de cenar, despidió al criado y fue a acostarse; *he was dismissed from his job* le despidieron de su trabajo ‖ destituir (high officials) ‖ MIL licenciar (to discharge) ‖ dar permiso para retirarse (to send away) ‖ disolver (an assembly) ‖ alejar (to discard mentally); *dismiss those sad thoughts* aleja esos tristes pensamientos ‖ descartar (an idea) ‖ despachar, acabar con (to treat briefly); *he dismissed the subject in a few words* despachó el asunto en pocas palabras ‖ JUR desestimar (a claim) | absolver (the accused) ‖ MIL *dismiss!* ¡rompan filas!

◆ *vi* MIL romper filas.

dismissal [disˈmisəl] *n* despido *m* (of servants, of employees) ‖ destitución *f* (of high officials) ‖ disolución *f* (of an assembly) ‖ abandono *m* (of an idea, a thought, etc.) ‖ JUR rechazamiento *m*, desestimación *f* ‖ MIL licenciamiento *m*.

dismissive [disˈmisiv] *adj* desdeñoso, sa.

dismount [ˈdisˈmaunt] *vi* apearse, bajarse, desmontarse (from a horse, etc.).

◆ *v tr* desmontar ‖ TECH desarmar, desmontar ‖ desengastar (a jewel).

disobedience [ˌdisəˈbiːdjəns] *n* desobediencia *f*.

disobedient [ˌdisəˈbiːdjənt] *adj* desobediente.

disobey [ˈdisəˈbei] *vt/vi* desobedecer.

disoblige [ˈdisəˈblaidʒ] *vt* contrariar, disgustar (to displease) ‖ no hacer un favor a, no complacer (not to oblige).

disobliging [-iŋ] *adj* poco servicial, poco complaciente (not obliging) ‖ desagradable, molesto, ta (unpleasant).

disorder [disˈɔːdə*] *n* desorden *m* (untidiness, state of confusion) ‖ desorden *m*, disturbio *m* (riot) ‖ trastorno *m* (ailment); *nervous disorders* trastornos nerviosos.

disorder [disˈɔːdə*] *vt* desordenar (to disarrange) ‖ trastornar (to upset the health of).

disorderliness [-linis] *n* desorden *m*.

disorderly [-li] *adj* desordenado, da; desarreglado, da (room, etc.) ‖ desordenado, da (person) ‖ alborotado, da (debate, meeting) ‖ escandaloso, sa (scandalous) ‖ desarreglado, da (life) ‖ — *disorderly conduct* conducta escandalosa (behaviour), alteración *f* del orden público ‖ FIG *disorderly house* casa *f* de lenocinio (brothel), casa *f* de juego (gambling house).

disorganization [disˌɔːgənaiˈzeiʃən] *n* desorganización *f*.

disorganize [disˈɔːgənaiz] *vt* desorganizar.

disorganized; disorganised [-d] *adj* desorganizado, da.

disorient [disˈɔːrient]; **disorientate** [-eit] *vt* desorientar ‖ ARCH orientar mal (a church).

disorientation [disɔːrienˈteiʃən] *n* desorientación *f*.

disown [disˈəun] *vt* no reconocer como suyo (one's offspring) ‖ repudiar (to repudiate) ‖ negar (to deny) ‖ no reconocer (one's signature) ‖ desautorizar (an agent).

disparage [disˈpæridʒ] *vt* menospreciar, despreciar (to belittle) ‖ denigrar (to speak badly of) ‖ desacreditar (to discredit).

disparagement [-mənt] *n* descrédito *m* (discredit) ‖ denigración *f* (detraction) ‖ menosprecio *m* (underestimation) ‖ *I haven't written it in disparagement of him* no lo he escrito para desprestigiarle.

disparager [-ə*] *n* detractor, ra.

disparaging [-iŋ] *adj* despectivo, va; menospreciativo, va (word, look) ‖ denigrante (speech).

disparagingly [-iŋli] *adv* con desprecio, despectivamente.

disparate [ˈdispərit] *adj* dispar.

disparity [disˈpæriti] *n* disparidad *f*.

dispassionate [disˈpæʃnit] *adj* desapasionado, da (without emotion) ‖ imparcial (unbiased).

dispatch; despatch [disˈpætʃ] *n* expedición *f*, despacho *m* (of letter, message) ‖ envío *m* (of messenger) ‖ expedición *f*, envío *m* (of parcels) ‖ despacho *m* (official report) ‖ MIL parte *m* ‖ COMM servicio *m* de expedición ‖ ejecución *f* (a putting to death) ‖ despacho *m* (of business, duty) ‖ diligencia *f* (promptitude).

dispatch; despatch [disˈpætʃ] *vt* expedir, remitir (a letter, parcels) ‖ enviar (messenger) ‖ matar, despachar (to kill) ‖ despachar (meal, work, business, etc.).

dispatch boat [-bəut] *n* MAR aviso *m*.

dispatch box [-bɔks] *n* caja *f* or estuche *m* portadocumentos.

dispatcher [disˈpætʃə*] *n* expedidor, ra.

dispatch rider [disˈpætʃˌraidə*] *n* correo *m* or mensajero *m* militar.

dispel [disˈpel] *vt* disipar.

dispensable [disˈpensəbl] *adj* prescindible, innecesario, ria (not necessary) ‖ REL dispensable.

dispensary [disˈpensəri] *n* dispensario *m* (hospital) ‖ farmacia *f* (laboratory).

dispensation [ˌdispenˈseiʃən] *n* dispensa *f*, exención *f* (exemption from a rule, law, etc.) ‖ decreto *m* divino, designio *m* divino (fate ordained by providence) ‖ distribución *f*, reparto *m* (of rewards, alms) ‖ JUR administración *f* ‖ ley *f*; *the Mosaic dispensation* la Ley mosaica.

dispense [disˈpens] *vt* distribuir, repartir (to distribute) ‖ preparar (drugs) ‖ administrar (justice) ‖ aplicar (laws, rules) ‖ administrar (sacrament) ‖ eximir, dispensar (to exempt).

◆ *vi* dar dispensa ‖ *to dispense with* prescindir de.

dispenser [-ə*] *n* distribuidor, ra (s.o. who distributes) ‖ dispensador, ra (of favours) ‖ farmacéutico, ca (chemist) ‖ administrador, ra (of justice) ‖ distribuidor *m* automático (machine).

dispensing chemist [disˈpensiŋ ˌkemist] *n* farmacéutico, ca.

dispersal [disˈpəːsəl] *n* dispersión *f*.

disperse [disˈpəːs] *vt* dispersar; *the wind dispersed the clouds* el viento dispersó las nubes; *the police dispersed the demonstrators* la policía dispersó a los manifestantes ‖ situar, apostar (to put in position); *to disperse troops along the road* apostar tropas a lo largo de la carretera ‖ dipersar, diseminar (news) ‖ PHYS dispersar (light).

◆ *vi* dispersarse ‖ *we dispersed to our homes* nos fuimos cada uno a nuestra casa.

dispersed [-t] *adj* disperso, sa.

dispersion [disˈpəːʃən] *n* dispersión *f*.

dispersive [disˈpəːsiv] *adj* dispersivo, va.

dispirit [diˈspirit] *vt* desalentar, desanimar.

dispirited [-id] *adj* desalentado, da; desanimado, da.

dispiriting [-iŋ] *adj* desalentador, ra; deprimente.

dispiteous [disˈpitiəs] *adj* despiadado, da.

displace [disˈpleis] *vt* desplazar, cambiar de lugar, trasladar (to remove from its usual place) ‖ destituir (to remove from office) ‖ quitar el puesto a (to oust) ‖ sustituir, reemplazar (to substitute) ‖ desplazar (to take the place of); *a ship displaces water* un barco desplaza agua ‖ CHEM & PHYS desplazar ‖ *displaced person* persona desplazada, expatriado, da.

displacement [-mənt] *n* desplazamiento *m*, traslado *m*, cambio *m* de sitio (move) ‖ destitución *f* (from office) ‖ sustitución *f*, reemplazo *m* (substitution) ‖ MAR, CHEM & PHYS desplazamiento *m*.

display [disˈplei] *n* exhibición *f* (a showing); *on display* en exhibición ‖ exposición *f* (a show) ‖ alarde *m* (of emotion) ‖ despliegue *m* (of energy) ‖ demostración *f* (demonstration) ‖ MIL desfile *m*, parada *f* ‖ pompa *f*; *a parade with great display* un desfile con mucha pompa ‖ TECH representación *f* visual (data processing) ‖ INFORM visualización *f*, presentación *f* ‖ — *display artist* escaparatista *m* & *f* ‖ INFORM *display board* tablero *m* | *display screen* pantalla *f* de visualización ‖ *display window* escaparate *m* [AMER vidriera *f*].

display [disˈplei] *vt* exhibir, exponer (to show); *shops display their goods in the windows* las tiendas exhiben sus artículos en los escaparates ‖ demostrar, mostrar; *he displays great intelligence* muestra una gran inteligencia ‖ desplegar (energy) ‖ lucir; *he displayed a new tie* lucía una nueva corbatá ‖ INFORM visualizar, mostrar en pantalla.

displease [disˈpliːz] *vt/vi* disgustar, desagradar, molestar.

displeased [-d] *adj* disgustado, da; molesto, ta; *displeased at* disgustado con.

displeasing [-iŋ] *adj* desagradable.

displeasure [disˈpleʒə*] *n* disgusto *m*, desagrado *m*; *to show displeasure* mostrar desagrado; *to my great displeasure* con gran disgusto mío ‖ *to incur s.o.'s displeasure* enojar or disgustar a alguien.

disport [dis'pɔːt] *vt* *to disport o.s.* entretenerse (to amuse o.s.).

disposable [dis'pəuzəbl] *adj* disponible (available) ‖ para tirar; *disposable wrapping* envase para tirar.

disposal [dis'pəuzəl] *n* arreglo *m*, colocación *f*, disposición *f* (arrangement) ‖ destrucción *f*, eliminación *f*; *disposal of refuse* destrucción de las basuras ‖ neutralización *f* (of bombs) ‖ evacuación *f*; *sewage disposal* evacuación de las aguas residuales ‖ resolución *f* (of question, difficulty) ‖ COMM venta *f* (sale) ‖ traspaso *m* (of property) ‖ — *at the disposal of* a la disposición de ‖ *at your disposal* a la disposición de usted, a su disposición ‖ *to have at one's disposal* tener a su disposición, disponer de.

dispose [dis'pəuz] *vt* disponer, colocar (to place) ‖ inclinar, disponer (to incline) ‖ mover (to move) ‖ determinar, disponer (to determine).
◆ *vi* disponer; *man proposes, God disposes* el hombre propone y Dios dispone ‖ *to dispose of* tirar (to throw away), disponer de (to have at one's disposal), echar por tierra (arguments), deshacerse de (to get rid of), traspasar (to transfer), vender (to sell), despachar (a matter), poner fin a (to stop), resolver (to settle), despachar, liquidar (to kill), consumir, comer (to eat), apabullar (an interlocutor), emplear, ocupar (one's time).

disposed [-d] *adj* dispuesto, ta ‖ *to be well disposed to* o *towards s.o.* estar bien dispuesto, ta hacia alguien.

disposition [,dispə'ziʃən] *n* disposición *f*; *at the disposition of* a la disposición de ‖ disposición *f*, colocación *f* (arrangement) ‖ traspaso *m* (transfer of property) ‖ disposición *f*, carácter *m* (nature) ‖ predisposición *f* (tendency) ‖ propensión *f* (inclination) ‖ designio *m* (dispensation) ‖ preparativo *m*, disposición *f* (plan) ‖ — JUR *disposition inter vivos* donación *f* entre vivos | *dispositions of a will* disposiciones testamentarias.

dispossess ['dispə'zes] *vt* desposeer ‖ JUR desahuciar (to expropriate) ‖ *to dispossess o.s. of* desposeerse de, desprenderse de.

dispossession [,dispə'zeʃən] *n* desposeimiento *m* ‖ JUR desahucio *m* (expropiation).

dispraise [dispraise] *n* crítica *f* (blame) ‖ desprecio *m* (contempt).

dispraise [dis'preiz] *vt* criticar (to blame) ‖ despreciar (to contempt).

disproof ['dis'pruːf] *n* refutación *f*.

disproportion ['disprə'pɔːʃən] *n* desproporción *f*.

disproportional [-l]; **disproportionate** [-it]; **disproportioned** [-d] *adj* desproporcionado, da.

disprovable [dis'pruːvəbl] *adj* refutable.

disprove ['dis'pruːv] *vt* refutar.

disputable [dis'pjuːtəbl] *adj* discutible, controvertible, disputable.

disputant [dis'pjuːtənt] *n* discutidor, ra; controversista *m* & *f*.

disputation [,dispju'teiʃən] *n* controversia *f* ‖ discusión *f*, debate *m* (discussion).

disputatious [,dispju'teiʃəs] *adj* disputador, ra ‖ disputable, discutible, controvertible.

dispute [dis'pjuːt] *n* disputa *f* (quarrel) ‖ controversia *f* (controversy) ‖ discusión *f*, debate *m* ‖ JUR litigio *m*; *under dispute* en litigio ‖ — *beyond dispute* indiscutible, incontrovertible ‖ *in dispute* en debate ‖ *labour dispute* conflicto *m* laboral ‖ *territory in dispute* territorio *m* en litigio.

dispute [dis'pjuːt] *vi* discutir (*about, over* de, sobre) ‖ disputarse (to quarrel).
◆ *vt* poner en duda (to question the truth of) ‖ discutir (an order, a question) ‖ disputar (to fight for); *to dispute a prize* disputar un premio ‖ *a much disputed question* un asunto muy controvertido.

disputer [-ə*] *n* disputador, ra.

disqualification [dis,kwɔlifi'keiʃən] *n* incapacidad *f*, inhabilitación *f* (incapacity) ‖ SP descalificación *f* (of a competitor) | desclasificación *f* (of a team).

disqualify [dis'kwɔlifai] *vt* incapacitar, inhabilitar (to render unfit, to take legal right from) ‖ SP descalificar (a competitor) | desclasificar (a team) ‖ *I was disqualified from driving for a year* me retiraron el carnet de conducir por un año.

disquiet [dis'kwaiət] *n* preocupación *f*, inquietud *f*, intranquilidad *f*.
◆ *adj* preocupado, da; inquieto, ta; intranquilo, la.

disquiet [dis'kwaiət] *vt* preocupar, inquietar, intranquilizar.

disquieting [-iŋ] *adj* preocupante, inquietante.

disquietude [dis'kwaiitjuːd] *n* preocupación *f*, inquietud *f* (worry) ‖ agitación *f* ‖ malestar *m* (uneasiness).

disquisition [,diskwi'ziʃən] *n* disquisición *f*.

disrate [dis'reit] *vt* MAR degradar.

disregard ['disri'gɑːd] *n* indiferencia *f* ‖ despreocupación *f*, descuido *m* (neglect) ‖ JUR violación *f*, desacato *m* (of the law) ‖ *with disregard for his own life* con desprecio de su vida.

disregard ['disri'gɑːd] *vt* no hacer caso de, desatender, hacer caso omiso de; *to disregard s.o.'s advice* no hacer caso de los consejos de uno ‖ despreocuparse de, descuidar (to neglect) ‖ JUR violar, desacatar (the law).

disregardful [-ful] *adj* que no hace caso de (of s.o.'s advice) ‖ negligente (neglectful) ‖ despreocupado, da (careless) ‖ poco respetuoso, sa (of the law).

disrelish [dis'reliʃ] *n* repugnancia *f*, aversión *f*.

disrepair ['disri'pɛə*] *n* mal estado *m*, desarreglo *m* ‖ *to fall into disrepair* descomponerse, deteriorarse (machinery), caer en ruina (house).

disreputable [dis'repjutəbl] *adj* de mala reputación *or* fama (not respectable) ‖ vergonzoso, sa (shameful) ‖ lamentable (shabby).

disrepute ['disri'pjuːt] *n* mala reputación *f*, desprestigio *m*, descrédito *m* ‖ — *to bring into disrepute* desprestigiar, desacreditar ‖ *to fall into disrepute* desprestigiarse, desacreditarse.

disrespect ['disris'pekt] *n* falta *f* de respeto ‖ *he meant no disrespect* no quería ofenderle.

disrespect [,disris'pekt] *vt* faltar el respeto a.

disrespectful [-ful] *adj* irrespetuoso, sa.

disrobe ['dis'rəub] *vi* desvestirse, desnudarse.
◆ *vt* desvestir, desnudar.

disroot [dis'ruːt] *vt* arrancar de raíz, desarraigar.

disrupt [dis'rʌpt] *vt* trastornar, alterar (to upset) ‖ romper (to break up) ‖ interrumpir; *to disrupt the traffic* interrumpir el tráfico ‖ desbaratar, trastornar (plans) ‖ desorganizar (to disorganize).

disruption [dis'rʌpʃən] *n* ruptura *f* ‖ interrupción *f* ‖ desbaratamiento *m*, trastorno *m* (of plans) ‖ desorganización *f*.

disruptive [dis'rʌptiv] *adj* ELECTR disruptivo, va ‖ que trastorna *or* desorganiza ‖ perjudicial (harmful).

disruptor [dis'rʌptə*] *n* disruptor *m*.

dissatisfaction ['dis,sætis'fækʃən] *n* descontento *m*, insatisfacción *f* (*at, with* de, con).

dissatisfied ['dis'sætisfaid] *adj* descontento, ta; insatisfecho, cha.

dissatisfy ['dis'sætisfai] *vt* no satisfacer (to fail to satisfy) ‖ disgustar, descontentar, desagradar (to make discontented).

dissect [di'sekt] *vt* disecar (to cut open for examination) ‖ abrir (to open up) ‖ FIG examinar detenidamente (to examine in detail) ‖ *dissecting room* sala *f* de disección.

dissection [di'sekʃən] *n* disección *f*, disecación *f* (act of dissecting) ‖ examen *m* detenido (close examination).

dissector [di'sektə*] *n* disecador, ra; disector, ra (person) ‖ escalpelo *m* (instrument).

disseise; disseize [dis'siːz] *vt* JUR desposeer.

disseisin;; disseizin [dis'siːzin] *n* JUR desposesión *f or* desposeimiento *m* ilegal.

dissemble [di'sembl] *vt* ocultar, disimular ‖ simular, fingir (a virtue, etc.).
◆ *vi* disimular.

dissembler [di'semblə*] *n* disimulador, ra.

disseminate [di'semineit] *vt* diseminar (to scatter) ‖ difundir, propagar (beliefs, propaganda, etc.).
◆ *vi* diseminarse ‖ difundirse, propagarse.

dissemination [di,semi'neiʃən] *n* diseminación *f* (a spreading) ‖ difusión *f*, propagación *f* (of beliefs, propaganda).

disseminator [di'semineitə*] *n* difusor, ra; propagador, ra.

dissension [di'senʃən] *n* disensión *f* ‖ *to sow dissension* sembrar la discordia.

dissent [di'sent] *n* disensión *f* ‖ disidencia *f* ‖ disentimiento *m* (disagreement).

dissent [di'sent] *vi* disentir (*from* de) (not to agree with) ‖ disidir (to refuse to accept a doctrine).

dissenter [di'sentə*] *n* disidente *m* & *f*.

dissenting [di'sentiŋ] *adj* disidente.

dissert [di'səːt]; **dissertate** ['disəteit] *vi* disertar (*on* de).

dissertation [,disə'teiʃən] *n* disertación *f* ‖ informe *m* (treatise) ‖ tesis *f* (for a doctorate).

dissertator ['disəteitə*] *n* disertador, ra; disertante *m* & *f*.

disserve [dis'səːv] *vt* perjudicar.

disservice [-is] *n* perjuicio *m* ‖ *to do s.o. a disservice* perjudicar a alguien.

dissever [dis'sevə*] *vt* separar, desunir.
◆ *vi* separarse, desunirse.

dissidence ['disidəns] *n* disidencia *f* ‖ disentimiento *m*, desacuerdo *m* (disagreement).

dissident ['disidənt] *adj/n* disidente.

dissimilar ['di'similə*] *adj* distinto, ta; desigual, diferente, desemejante (*to* de).

dissimilarity [,disimi'læriti] *n* disimilitud *f*, desemejanza *f*, desigualdad *f*, diferencia *f*.

dissimilate [di'simileit] *vt* desasimilar ‖ disimilar (in phonetics).

dissimilation ['disimi'leiʃən] *n* disimilación *f* (in phonetics) ‖ desasimilación *f* (catabolism).

dissimulate [di'simjuleit] *vt/vi* disimular.

dissimulation [di,simju'leiʃən] *n* disimulo *m*, disimulación *f*.

dissimulator [di'simjuleitə*] *n* disimulador, ra.

dissipate ['disipeit] *vt* disipar (clouds, doubts) ‖ dispersar (efforts) ‖ disipar, derrochar (one's resources) ‖ dispersar (a crowd).
◆ *vi* disiparse ‖ dispersarse.

dissipated [-id] *adj* disipado, da ‖ disoluto, ta; *dissipated life* vida disoluta.

dissipation [ˌdisiˈpeiʃən] *adj* disipación *f* || dispersión *f* (of efforts) || disipación *f*, derroche *m* (of resources) || disolución *f* (debauchery).

dissociable [diˈsəuʃjəbl] *adj* disociable.

dissociate [diˈsəuʃieit]; **disassociate** [ˌdisəˈsəuʃieit] *vt* disociar || *to dissociate o.s. from* desolidarizarse de, disociarse de.
◆ *vi* disociarse.

dissociation [diˌsəusiˈeiʃən] *n* disociación *f*.

dissolubility [diˌsɔljuˈbiliti] *n* disolubilidad *f*.

dissoluble [diˈsɔljubl] *adj* disoluble.

dissolute [ˈdisəluːt] *adj* disoluto, ta.

dissoluteness [-nis] *n* disolución *f*.

dissolution [ˌdisəˈluːʃən] *n* disolución *f* (of meeting, society, marriage) || disolución *f* (melting) || rescisión *f* (of a contract).

dissolvable [diˈzɔlvəbl] *adj* soluble || JUR disoluble.

dissolve [diˈzɔlv] *vt* disolver || disipar (illusions) || descomponer, desintegrar (to disintegrate) || JUR rescindir (a contract) | disolver (a society) || FIG dispersar, desvanecer (clouds) | dispersar (crowd).
◆ *vi* disolverse || descomponerse, desintegrarse || FIG deshacerse; *she dissolved into tears* se deshizo en lágrimas || CINEM fundirse (to fade into another picture).

dissolve [diˈzɔlv] *n* CINEM fundido *m*.

dissolved [-d] *adj* disuelto, ta.

dissolvent [diˈzɔlvənt] *adj* disolvente.
◆ *n* disolvente *m*.

dissonance [ˈdisənəns] *n* MUS disonancia *f* || FIG desacuerdo *m*, disentimiento *m*.

dissonant [ˈdisənənt] *adj* disonante, discordante (discordant) || FIG en desacuerdo (*from*, *to* con).

dissuade [diˈsweid] *vt* disuadir (*from* de) || desconsejar (to advise against).

dissuasion [diˈsweiʒən] *n* disuasión *f*.

dissuasive [diˈsweisiv] *adj* disuasivo, va.

dissyllabic [ˈdisiˈlæbik] *adj* ⟶ **disyllabic.**

dissyllabe [diˈsiləbl] *n* ⟶ **disyllable.**

dissymmetric [ˈdisiˈmetrik]; **dissymmetrical** [-əl] *adj* disimétrico, ca.

dissymmetry [ˈdiˈsimitri] *n* disimetría *f*.

distaff [ˈdistɑːf] *n* rueca *f*.
◆ *adj* *the distaff side of a family* la rama femenina de una familia.

distance [ˈdistəns] *n* distancia *f* (an interval in space); *at a distance of two kilometers* a dos kilómetros de distancia || lejanía *f* (remoter part of a view) || FIG distancia *f* (reserve, aloofness) || MUS intervalo *m* || — *at* o *from a distance* de lejos || *at a distance of ten years* después de diez años || *at a respectable distance* a respetable *or* respetuosa distancia || *in the distance* en la lejanía, a lo lejos || *long-distance aeroplane* avión *m* de larga distancia || SP *long-distance race* carrera *f* de fondo | *middle-distance runner* corredor *m* de medio fondo || *to cut down* o *to reduce the distance* acortar las distancias || *to keep at a distance* mantener *or* tener a distancia || *to keep one's distance* guardar la distancia (of vehicles in a convoy), guardar las distancias (to remain aloof) || *town within walking distance* ciudad adonde se puede ir andando || *within speaking distance* al alcance de la voz.

distance [ˈdistəns] *vt* alejar (to maintain at a distance) || distanciar (to outdistance).

distant [ˈdistənt] *adj* distante, lejano, na (far away) || lejano, na (remote in time, far removed in relationship, likeness, etc.); *a distant cousin* un primo lejano; *a distant resemblance* un lejano parecido || FIG distante || *ten miles distant* a diez millas.

distantly [-li] *adv* de lejos || FIG con frialdad || *to be distantly related* ser parientes lejanos.

distaste [ˈdisˈteist] *n* aversión *f* (*for* por, a).

distasteful [disˈteistful] *adj* desagradable.

distemper [disˈtempə*] *n* moquillo *m* (dog's disease) || malestar *m* (uneasiness) || malhumor *m*, mal genio *m* (bad temper) || temple *m* (paint) || pintura *f* al temple (method of painting) || JUR desorden *m* (turnmoil).

distemper [disˈtempə*] *vt* pintar al temple (to paint) || poner de malhumor (to anger).

distend [disˈtend] *vt* distender || hinchar (to swell) || dilatar (to dilate).
◆ *vi* distenderse || hincharse.

distensible [disˈtensəbl] *adj* extensible || dilatable, hinchable.

distension; *US* **distention** [disˈtenʃən] *n* distensión *f* || hinchazón *f* (swelling) || dilatación *f* (dilatation).

distich [ˈdistik] *n* POET dístico *m*.

distil; **distill** [disˈtil] *vt/vi* destilar.

distillate [ˈdistilit] *n* destilado *m*.

distillation [ˌdistiˈleiʃən] *n* destilación *f*.

distiller [disˈtilə*] *n* destilador *m* (person, still).

distillery [disˈtiləri] *n* destilería *f*.

distinct [disˈtiŋkt] *adj* distinto, ta (*from* de) (different) || claro, ra (clear) || marcado, da; señalado, da; bien determinado, da (marked, definite); *distinct tendency* tendencia bien determinada || *as distinct from* a diferencia de.

distinction [disˈtiŋkʃən] *n* distinción *f* || — *in distinction from* o *to* a distinción de || *of distinction* distinguido, da; *a man of distinction* un hombre distinguido; notable, eminente, distinguido, da; *a writer of distinction* un escritor notable || *to draw* o *make a distinction between* hacer una distinción entre || *to gain distinction* distinguirse || *with distinction* con sobresaliente (qualification).

distinctive [disˈtiŋktiv] *adj* distintivo, va || *distinctive to* característico de.

distinctness [disˈtiŋktnis] *n* claridad *f* || diferencia *f*.

distinguish [disˈtiŋgwiʃ] *vt/vi* distinguir; *to distinguish one thing from another* distinguir una cosa de otra || *to distinguish o.s.* distinguirse.

distinguishable [-əbl] *adj* distinguible.

distinguished [-t] *adj* distinguido, da (elegant) || eminente, distinguido, da; notable; *a distinguished writer* un escritor eminente.

distort [disˈtɔːt] *vt* retorcer, torcer, deformar (to twist out of shape) || FIG desvirtuar; *to distort the meaning of a text* desvirtuar el sentido de un texto.

distortion [disˈtɔːʃən] *n* deformación *f*, torcimiento *m* (twisting) || PHOT & PHYS distorsión *f* || FIG desnaturalización *f*, deformación *f*, desvirtuación *f*.

distract [disˈtrækt] *vt* distraer (to divert the attention of) || distraer, apartar (attention) || aturdir, confundir (to confuse) || enloquecer (to drive mad) || *to distract the enemy* distraer al enemigo.

distracted [-id] *adj* distraído, da.

distraction [disˈtrækʃən] *n* distracción *f* (being distracted) || aturdimiento *m*, confusión *f* (bewilderment) || locura *f* (frenzy) || distracción *f*, entretenimiento *m*, diversión *f* (amusement) || *to drive to distraction* volver loco.

distrain [disˈtrein] *vi* JUR embargar.

distrainee [ˌdistreiˈniː] *n* JUR embargado, da.

distrainer; **distrainor** [ˌdistreiˈnə*] *n* JUR embargador, ra.

distraint [disˈtreint] *n* JUR embargo *m*.

distrait [disˈtrei] *adj* distraído, da.

distraught [disˈtrɔːt] *adj* loco, ca; enloquecido, da || muy turbado, da (upset).

distress [disˈtres] *n* aflicción *f*, desolación *f* || congoja *f*, angustia *f* (anguish) || miseria *f* || (poverty) || peligro *m*, apuro *m* (danger or difficulty); *ship in distress* barco en peligro || MED agotamiento *m* || JUR embargo *m* || — MAR *distress signal* señal *f* de socorro || FIG *to be in distress* estar en un apuro.

distress [disˈtres] *vt* afligir, desolar (to afflict) || angustiar (to anguish) || MED agotar || JUR embargar.

distressed [-t] *adj* afligido, da (afflicted) || angustiado, da (anguished) || en la miseria (poor) || en peligro (in danger) || MED agotado, da.

distressing [-iŋ] *adj* angustioso, sa (grievous).

distribute [disˈtribjut] *vt* distribuir, repartir; *to distribute money among the poor* distribuir dinero entre los pobres || clasificar (statistical information) || COMM & PRINT distribuir.

distributed *adj* distribuido, da; repartido, da || INFORM *distributed data processing* o *computing* informática *f* distribuida.

distributing [-iŋ] *adj* distribuidor, ra.

distribution [ˌdistriˈbjuːʃən] *n* distribución *f*, reparto *m* || clasificación *f* (in statistics) || COMM & PRINT distribución *f*.

distributive [disˈtribjutiv] *adj* distributivo, va.
◆ *n* GRAMM adjetivo *m* distributivo.

distributor [disˈtribjutə*] *n* distribuidor, ra || AUT distribuidor *m*, delco *m*.

district [ˈdistrikt] *n* región *f* (region) || barrio *m* (of a town) || distrito *m* (political or geographical division) || — *US district attorney* fiscal *m* de un distrito judicial || *district council* ayuntamiento *m* de distrito *or* de barrio | *US district court* tribunal *m* federal | *district manager* representante *m* regional || *district nurse* enfermero, ra de zona [que visita a domicilio] || *federal, postal district* distrito federal, postal || *university district* distrito universitario.

distrophia [disˈtrəufiə]; **dystrophy** [ˈdistrəfi] *n* MED distrofia *f*.

distrust [disˈtrʌst] *n* desconfianza *f*, recelo *m* (mistrust) || sospechas *f pl* (suspicion).

distrust [disˈtrʌst] *vt* desconfiar de || sospechar.

distrustful [-ful] *adj* desconfiado, da; receloso, sa (distrusting) || sospechoso, sa (suspicious).

distrustfully [-fuli] *adv* con recelo, desconfiadamente.

disturb [disˈtəːb] *vt* molestar (to bother); *don't disturb yourself* no se moleste || mover, agitar (to agitate) || preocupar (to worry) || desordenar (to move out of order) || perturbar, alterar (the peace) || trastornar (s.o.'s mind) || perturbar, alterar (plans) || PHYS perturbar || *do not disturb* se ruega no molestar.

disturbance [disˈtəːbəns] *n* alboroto *m* (row) || disturbio *m* (public disorder) || preocupación *f* (worry) || molestia *f* (trouble) || perturbación *f* (atmospheric, magnetic, etc.) || trastorno *m* (of the mind) || — *disturbance in the night* escándalo nocturno || *disturbance of the peace* alteración *f* del orden público.

disturbed [disˈtəːbd] *adj* preocupado, da (worried) || trastornado, da (unbalanced).

disturbing [disˈtəːbiŋ] *adj* perturbador, ra || molesto, ta (annoying) || preocupante (worrying).

disunion [ˈdisˈjuːnjən] *n* desunión *f*.

disunite [ˈdisjuːˈnait] *vt* desunir.
◆ *vi* desunirse.

disunity [disˈjuːniti] *n* desunión *f*.

disuse [dis'ju:s] *n* desuso *m*; *to fall into disuse* caer en desuso ‖ abandono *m*.

disuse [dis'ju:z] *vt* dejar de usar.

disyllabic; dissyllabic [disi'læbik] *adj* bisilábico, ca; disilábico, ca; bisílabo, ba; disílabo, ba.

disyllable; dissyllable [di'siləbl] *n* bisílabo *m*, bisilábico *m*, disílabo *m*, disilábico *m*.

ditch [ditʃ] *n* zanja *f* (trench) ‖ canal *m* (for drainage) ‖ acequia *f* (for irrigation) ‖ cuneta *f* (at the side of a road) ‖ foso *m* (surrounding a castle) ‖ SP foso *m* ‖ — FIG & FAM *the Ditch* el Canal de la Mancha | *to the last ditch* hasta el final.

ditch [ditʃ] *vi* abrir zanjas (to make ditches) ‖ hacer acequias (for irrigation) ‖ AUT volcar en la cuneta (a car) ‖ hacer un amaraje forzoso (a plane).
◆ *vt* hacer zanjas *or* acequias en ‖ AUT hacer volcar en la cuneta (to overturn) ‖ FAM abandonar (to abandon) | tirar, deshacerse de (to get rid of).

ditcher [-ə*] *n* peón *m* caminero.

dither ['diðə*] *n* *to be in a dither, to be all of a dither* estar muy excitado, estar muy nervioso (in an excited condition), estar temblando (trembling).

dither ['diðə*] *vi* estar nervioso (to be excited) ‖ temblar (to tremble).

dithery [-ri] *adj* nervioso, sa.

dithyramb ['diθiræmb] *n* ditirambo *m*.

dithyrambic [diθi'ræmbik] *adj* ditirámbico, ca.
◆ *n* ditirambo *m*.

dittany ['ditəni] *n* BOT díctamo *m*.

ditto ['ditəu] *n* comillas *f pl* (mark used to indicate repetition) ‖ ídem *m* ‖ duplicado *m* (duplicate).
◆ *adv* ídem, del mismo modo.

ditto machine [-mə'ʃi:n] *n* multicopista *f*.

ditty ['diti] *n* cancioncilla *f* ‖ FIG cantinela *f*.

ditty bag [-bæg] *n* MAR bolsa.

diuresis [,daijuə'ri:sis] *n* MED diuresis *f*.
— OBSERV El plural de la palabra inglesa es *diureses*.

diuretic [,daijuə'retik] *adj* MED diurético, ca.
◆ *n* MED diurético *m*.

diurnal [dai'ə:nl] *adj* diurno, na.
◆ *n* REL diurno *m* (book).

diuturnity [daiə'tə:niti] *n* diuturnidad *f*.

diva ['di:və] *n* diva *f* (singer).

divagate ['daivəgeit] *vi* divagar.

divagation [,daivə'geiʃən] *n* divagación *f*.

divalent ['dai,veilənt] *adj* bivalente.

divan [di'væn] *n* diván *m* (council, sofa, poetry) ‖ fumadero *m* (smoking room).

divaricate [dai'værikeit] *vi* bifurcarse (to fork).

divarication [dai'væri'keiʃən] *n* bifurcación *f* ‖ FIG divergencia *f*.

dive [daiv] *n* zambullida *f* (a diving into water) ‖ salto *m* [AMER clavado *m*] (in competitions) ‖ inmersión *f*, sumersión *f* (of a submarine) ‖ picado *m*, descenso *m* en picado (of aircraft, birds) ‖ estirada *f* (of a goalkeeper) ‖ FAM tasca *f* (bar) ‖ FIG & FAM *to make a dive into* meterse en.

dive* [daiv] *vi* saltar (into water with controlled grace) ‖ tirarse de cabeza, zambullirse de cabeza (into water head first) ‖ bucear (underwater) ‖ sumergirse (a submarine) ‖ bajar en picado (planes) ‖ zambullirse (birds) ‖ hacer una estirada, tirarse (a goalkeeper) ‖ meterse; *he dived under the table* se metió debajo de la mesa ‖ FIG lanzarse, meterse (into an affair, etc.) ‖ — *to dive into* meterse en ‖ *to dive into one's pocket* meterse la mano en el bolsillo.
— OBSERV Pret ***dived, dove***; pp ***dived***.

dive-bomb [-bɔm] *vt* bombardear en picado.

dive bomber [-,bɔmə*] *n* avión *m* de bombardeo en picado.

dive-bombing [-,bɔmiŋ] *n* bombardeo *m* en picado.

diver [-ə*] *n* buzo *m* ‖ SP saltador, ra ‖ ZOOL somorgujo *m* ‖ *pearl diver* pescador *m* de perla.

diverge [dai'və:dʒ] *vi* bifurcarse, separarse, divergir (to go in branching directions) ‖ FIG apartarse (to turn aside); *to diverge from the truth* apartarse de la verdad | salirse (from the normal).
◆ *vt* desviar.

divergence [dai'və:dʒəns] *n* divergencia *f*.

divergent [daivə:dʒənt] *adj* divergente.

divers ['daivəz] *adj* varios, rias; diversos, sas (several).

diverse [dai'və:s] *adj* diverso, sa; distinto, ta; diferente (different) ‖ diverso, sa; variado, da (varied).

diversification [dai,və:sifi'keiʃən] *n* diversificación *f*, variación *f*.

diversiform [dai'və:sifɔ:m] *adj* diversiforme.

diversify [dai'və:sifai] *vt* diversificar.

diversion [dai'və:ʃən] *n* desviación *f* (of river, road, etc.) ‖ diversión *f* (mental distraction) ‖ MIL diversión *f*.

diversionary [dai'və:ʃənəri] *adj* MIL de diversión.

diversity [dai'və:siti] *n* diversidad *f*.

divert [dai'və:t] *vt* desviar; *to divert an aeroplane* desviar un avión ‖ distraer; *to divert s.o.'s attention* distraer la atención de alguien ‖ divertir (to amuse) ‖ *to divert o.s.* divertirse.

diverting [dai'və:tiŋ] *adj* divertido, da.

divertissement [di'və:tismənt] *n* diversión *f* (entertainment) ‖ MUS divertimento *m* (piece of light instrumental music) | intermedio *m* (short interlude between the acts of a play).

divest [dai'vest] *vt* desposeer (of possessions) ‖ despojar (of honours) ‖ quitar (clothing) ‖ *to divest o.s. of one's rights* renunciar a sus derechos.

divestiture [-itʃə*]; **divestment** [-mənt] *n* desposeimiento *m* (of possessions) ‖ despojo *m* (of honours).

dividable [di'vaidəbl] *adj* divisible.

divide [di'vaid] *vt* dividir; *to divide into five groups* dividir en cinco grupos ‖ MATH dividir ‖ *to divide the House* hacer que la Cámara vote ‖ *to divide up* dividir.
◆ *vi* dividirse ‖ votar; *the House divided* el Parlamento votó ‖ — *divide and conquer* divide y vencerás ‖ MATH *to divide into* estar contenido en; *5 divides into 20 four times* cinco está contenido cuatro veces en veinte.

divide [di'vaid] *n* US línea *f* divisoria de las aguas (watershed).

divided [-id] *adj* dividido, da.

dividend ['dividend] *n* MATH & COMM dividendo *m* ‖ — COMM *accrued, interim dividend* dividendo acumulado, provisional ‖ *to pay dividends* proporcionar dividendos.

divider [di'vaidə*] *n* divisor, ra.
◆ *pl* compás *m sing* de punta fija *or* seca.

dividing [di'vaidiŋ] *adj* divisor, ra; divisorio, ria ‖ *dividing line* línea *f* divisoria.

divi-divi ['divi'divi] *n* BOT dividivi *m*.

divination [,divi'neʃən] *n* adivinación *f*.

divinatory ['divi,neitəri] *adj* divinatorio, ria.

divine [di'vain] *n* teólogo *m* (theologian) ‖ eclesiástico *m* (clergyman).
◆ *adj* divino, na; *divine punishment* castigo divino ‖ FIG divino, na.

divine [di'vain] *vt/vi* adivinar.

diviner [-ə*] *n* adivinador, ra; adivino, na.

diving ['daiviŋ] *n* SP salto *m* [AMER clavado *m*] (in competitions) ‖ buceo *m* (underwater) ‖ AVIAT picado *m*.

diving bell [-bel] *n* campana *f* de buzo.

diving board [-bɔ:d] *n* trampolín *m*.

diving suit [-sju:t] *n* escafandra *f*.

divining [di'vainiŋ] *adj* adivinatorio, ria ‖ *divining rod* varilla *f* de zahorí.

divinity [di'viniti] *n* divinidad *f* (quality of being divine) ‖ teologia *f*.

divisibility [di,vizi'biliti] *n* divisibilidad *f*.

divisible [di'vizəbl] *adj* divisible.

division [di'viʒən] *n* división *f* ‖ distribución *f*, reparto *m* (distribution) ‖ separación *f*, división *f* (partition) ‖ sección *f*, ramo *m* (section) ‖ MATH & MIL división *f* ‖ votación *f* (in Parliament); *division lobby* zona de votación; *to insist on a division* exigir una votación ‖ graduación *f* (of a thermometer, etc.) ‖ FIG división *f*, desunión *f*, discordia *f* (discord) | división *f*, discrepancia *f* (of opinions) ‖ — MATH *division sign* signo *m* de dividir ‖ *to come to a division* votar (to vote), someterse a votación (a bill).

divisional [di'viʒənl] *adj* divisionario, ria; divisional ‖ *divisional coin* moneda fraccionaria.

divisive [di'vaisiv] *adj* que causa división *or* discordia.

divisor [di'vaiʒə*] *n* MATH divisor *m*.

divorce [di'vɔ:s] *n* divorcio *m*; *to sue for a divorce* pedir el divorcio ‖ FIG divorcio *m* ‖ *to get a divorce from* divorciarse de.

divorce [di'vɔ:s] *vt* divorciarse de; *he divorced her* se divorció de ella ‖ divorciar; *the judge divorced them* el juez les divorció.

divorcee [di,vɔ:'si:] *n* divorciado, da.

divot ['divət] *n* tepe *m*, gallón *m* (in golf).

divulgation [,daivʌl'geiʃən] *n* divulgación *f*.

divulge [dai'vʌldʒ] *vt* divulgar.

divulgement [-mənt]; **divulgence** [dai'vʌldʒəns] *n* divulgación *f*.

divulger [-ə*] *n* divulgador, ra.

divulsion [dai'vʌlʃən] *n* MED divulsión *f*.

dixie; dixy ['diksi] *n* marmita *f*, olla *f*.

dizziness ['dizinis] *n* mareo *m*, vértigo *m*.

dizzy ['dizi] *adj* mareado, da; atacado de vértigo (feeling dizziness) ‖ vertiginoso, sa (heights, speed) ‖ US FAM bobo, ba; alelado, da (stupid) ‖ *to feel dizzy* estar mareado, tener vértigo.

Djibouti [dʒi'bu:ti] *pr n* GEOGR Yibuti.

Djibouti City [-'siti] *pr n* GEOGR Yibuti.

DNA [di:'en'ei] *abbr of [deoxyribonucleic acid]* ADN, ácido desoxirribonucleico.

do [dəu] *n* MUS do *m*.

do [du:] *n* FAM fiesta *f* (party) | ceremonia *f* | estafa *f*, timo *m* (swindle) | lío *m* (trouble) ‖ — *the do's and do nots of society* las reglas que hay que respetar en la sociedad ‖ FAM *that's not fair do's!* ¡es injusto!

do* [du:] *vt* hacer (to carry out an action); *what is he doing now?* ¿qué está haciendo ahora? ‖ dedicarse a (to have an occupation); *he does painting* se dedica a la pintura ‖ ocuparse de (to deal with); *to do the suburbs* ocuparse de los suburbios ‖ cumplir con, hacer (to fulfil); *to do one's duty* cumplir con su deber ‖ hacer (to cover a distance); *he did Madrid to Paris in twenty hours* hizo Madrid París en veinte horas; *my car does a hundred miles an* *hour* mi coche hace cien millas por hora || recorrer (to tour); *we are doing Italy this year* vamos a recorrer Italia este año || visitar (to visit) || hacer (to render); *to do s.o. a favour* hacer un favor a alguien || venir bien, convenir (to serve); *this hotel will do us* este hotel nos vendrá bien || hacer (a part) || hacer de (to play the part of); *who's doing Orpheus in the film?* ¿quién hace de Orfeo en la película? || representar (to present a play) || traducir (to translate); *to do Milton into Spanish* traducir Milton al castellano || vender, hacer (to sell); *we do you this article at ten pounds* le vendemos este artículo por diez libras || trabajar (to work) || estudiar; *I am doing medicine* estoy estudiando medicina || FAM timar, estafar (to swindle); *you've been done* te han timado | coger (to catch); *the police did him for speeding* la policía le cogió por exceso de velocidad || entrar a robar en; *the burglars did my house last night* los ladrones entraron a robar en mi casa anoche || cumplir (a sentence) || tratar; *he did me well* me trató bien || peinar (hair) || lavar (teeth) || hacer, afeitar (beard) || arreglar (nails) || fregar (the dishes) || limpiar (a room) || resolver (a problem) || hacer (to cook); *a steak well done* un filete muy hecho || dárselas de (to feign) || — *do what she would, she couldn't* por más que hizo no lo consiguió || *I've done it!* ¡lo conseguí! || FAM *nothing doing!* ¡ni hablar! || *now you've done it!* ¡buena la has hecho! || *to be done* estar agotado (tired), estar hecho, estar terminado (finished) || *to do battle* luchar, librar batalla || *to do duty as* servir de || *to do harm* hacer daño (to hurt), perjudicar (to prejudice) || *to do justice* hacer justicia || *to do one credit* decir mucho en su favor || *to do one good* hacer bien a uno, sentarle bien a uno || *to do one's best* hacer todo lo posible (to do one's utmost), hacer lo mejor posible (to do as well as one can) || *to do one's bit* hacer *or* poner de su parte || *to do one's hair* peinarse || *to do one's nails* arreglarse las uñas || *to do one's shoes* limpiarse los zapatos || *to do one's teeth* lavarse los dientes || *to do o.s. well* darse buena vida (to live well), no privarse de nada (to lack nothing) || *to do right by s.o.* tratar bien a alguien || FAM *to do s.o. out of sth.* birlar algo a alguien || *to do the honours of* hacer los honores de || FAM *to do the trick* servir [para el caso], resolver el problema || FAM *to do time* estar en prisión || *to do to death* matar || *to do wonders* hacer maravillas || *to have one's hair done* arreglarse el pelo || *what can I do about it?* ¿qué quiere que le haga? || *what can I do for you?* ¿en qué puedo servirle? || *what else can be done?* ¿qué más se puede hacer? || *what's done is done* a lo hecho, pecho.

◆ *vi* hacer; *do as I did* haz como hice yo || irle a alguien (to make progress); *how is she doing?* ¿qué tal le va? || estar, sentise, irle a uno (to feel) || valer (to be suitable); *this book will not do* este libro no vale || ocurrir, pasar; *what's doing here?* ¿qué pasa aquí? || — *do well and dread no shame* haz bien y no mires a quién || *he did right* hizo bien || *how do you do?* encantado, da; mucho gusto (when introduced), ¿cómo está usted? (how are you?) || *it doesn't do to* no conviene || *that will do* ya está bien || *that will never do* eso no puede ser || *to do or die* vencer o morir || *to do well* ir bien (business), ir por buen camino, medrar (person), estar recuperándose (invalid), darse bien (plant), salir bien; *he did well in his exam* salió bien del examen; hacer bien; *he would do well to see the dentist* haría bien en ir al dentista || *to do well by* portarse bien con || *to make do with* arreglárselas con.

◆ *v aux* (en interrogaciones); *do you speak Spanish?* ¿habla usted español? || (en negaciones); *I do not speak English* no hablo inglés; *do not lie* no mientas || (con una inversión); *never did I say anything of the sort* nunca dije tal cosa || (para dar mayor énfasis al imperativo); *do tell me* dímelo, por favor || (para acentuar el significado del verbo); *I do love Mary* quiero a María de verdad; *do come and see me* no deje de venir a verme; *he did transmit your request to her* seguramente le transmitió tu petición.

◆ *v substitute* hacer; *I'll tell him don't* se lo voy a decir no lo haga; *he painted these flowers much better than she could have done* él pintó estas flores mucho mejor que ella hubiera podido hacerlo || (para evitar la repetición del verbo); *sing as I do* canta como yo; *do yo sing? yes, I do* ¿cantas? sí; *do you play piano? no, I don't* ¿sabes tocar el piano? no; *he dances well, so does she* él baila bien, ella también || — *he doesn't live here, does he?* no vive aquí, ¿verdad? || *he writes well, doesn't he?* escribe bien, ¿verdad? || *please do* por supuesto, naturalmente, por favor.

◆ ***to do again*** volver a hacer, hacer otra vez, hacer de nuevo || ***to do away with*** suprimir (s.o., sth.) | abolir (a custom) || ***to do by*** tratar || ***to do down*** timar || ***to do for*** llevar a casa a (to work in s.o.'s house) | servir de (to serve as) | FAM matar, cargarse (to kill) | hundir (to ruin) | FAM *we're done for!* ¡estamos perdidos! || FAM ***to do in*** cargarse a (to kill) | agotar, derengar (to exhaust); *to do out* arreglar (to tidy) | decorar (to decorate) | vestir (to dress) | FAM robar (to steal) || ***to do over*** volver a hacer (to do again) | revisar (to revise) | retocar (a painting) | cubrir (*with* con) || ***to do up*** atarse (shoelaces) | abrocharse (belt, buttons) | envolver (to wrap up) | poner pañales a (a baby) | cerrar (a letter) | arreglar (an old garment) | renovar (to renovate) | arreglar, ordenar (to arrange) | preparar, guisar (food) | FAM reventar, derrengar (to exhaust) || — *to do up one's face* maquillarse, pintarse || ***to do with*** hacer con; *what did you do with my hat?* ¿qué has hecho con mi sombrero? | aguantar (to tolerate); *I can't do with him* no le puedo aguantar | conformarse con; *I do with very little food* me conformo con muy poca comida | tener que ver con; *I have nothing to do with this matter* no tengo nada que ver con este asunto | estar relacionado con (to be related to) || — *I could do with a cup of tea* no me vendría mal *or* me gustaría tomarme una taza de té || *to have done with* haber acabado con || ***to do without*** prescindir de, arreglárselas sin || — *I can do without your remarks* puede ahorrarse sus comentarios.

— OBSERV Pret ***did***; pp ***done***.

doable ['du:əbl] *adj* factible, realizable.

dobbin ['dɔbin] *n* caballo *m* de tiro || US FAM jamelgo *m*.

Doberman pinscher [,dəubəmən 'pintʃə*] *n* ZOOL doberman *m*.

doc [dɔk] *n* FAM galeno *m*, doctor *m*.

docent [dəu'sent] *n* US profesor *m* auxiliar.

docile ['dəusail] *adj* dócil.

docility [dəu'siliti] *n* docilidad *f*.

dock [dɔk] *n* maslo *m* (of an animal's tail) || muñón *m* de la cola (stump) || baticola *f* (crupper of saddle) || banquillo *m* de los acusados (in courtroom) || dársena *f* (for boats) || muelle *m* (platform) || andén *m* (of railway) || US malecón *m* (pier) || — *dry dock* dique seco || *floating dock* dique *m* flotante || AUT *in dock* averiado (car) || *loading dock* embarcadero *m*.

◆ *pl* puerto *m sing*.

dock [dɔk] *vt* cortar (to cut) || descolar, cortar la cola a (to shorten the tail of) || acortar, reducir (to shorten) || deducir, descontar (*off* de) (to deduct a sum of money) || multar (to fine) || hacer entrar en dársena (to bring a ship into the dock).

◆ *vi* atracar al muelle (ship) || llegar (to arrive) || acoplarse (spacecraft).

dockage [-idʒ] *n* MAR muellaje *m*, derechos *m pl* por atracar || reducción *f*.

docker ['dɔkə*]; **dockhand** ['dɔkhænd] *n* cargador *m or* descargador *m* de muelle, cargador *m or* descargador *m* de puerto, «docker» *m*, estibador *m*.

docket ['dɔkit] *n* rótulo *m*, etiqueta *f* (label) || lista *f* (list) || certificado *m* de aduana (custom warrant) || US orden *m* del día, agenda *f* || JUR registro *m* de sumarios de causas.

docket ['dɔkit] *vt* rotular, poner un rótulo en (to label) || registrar (to register).

dockhand ['dɔk,hænd] *n* ⟶ **docker.**

docking ['dɔkiŋ] *n* MAR atracamiento *m* || acoplamiento *m* (spacecraft).

docklands ['dɔkləndz] *pl n* zona *f* portuaria *or* del puerto.

dockyard ['dɔkjɑ:d] *n* astillero *m* (shipbuilder's yard) || arsenal *m* (naval yard).

doctor ['dɔktə*] *n* médico, ca (person qualified in medicine); *family doctor* médico de cabecera || doctor, ra (university title); *Doctor of Laws, of Science* doctor en derecho, en ciencias || REL doctor *m*; *doctor of the Church* doctor de la Iglesia || — *honorary doctor* doctor honoris causa || *to be under the doctor's care* seguir un tratamiento médico || *woman doctor* médica *f*.

doctor ['dɔktə*] *vt* atender, asistir (to administer medical attention to) || adulterar (food, text) || falsificar, amañar (accounts) || apañar, arreglar (to patch up) || conceder el título de doctor (in university) || POP capar (to castrate).

◆ *vi* ser médico (to be a doctor) || tomar medicinas (a patient).

doctoral [-rəl] *adj* doctoral.

doctorate [-rit] *n* doctorado *m* || *to take one's doctorate* presentar la tesis de doctorado.

doctrinaire [dɔktri'nɛə*] *adj/n* doctrinario, ria.

doctrinal [dɔk'trainəl] *adj* doctrinal.

doctrine ['dɔktrin] *n* doctrina *f*; *Aristotelian, Buddhist doctrine* doctrina aristotélica, budista || *it is a matter of doctrine that...* es teoría corriente que...

docudrama ['dɔkju,drɑ:mə] *n* docudrama *m*.

document ['dɔkjumənt] *n* documento *m* || JUR escritura *f*; *legal document* escritura pública.

document ['dɔkjumənt] *vt* documentar || probar con documentos.

document case [-keis] *n* portadocumentos *m inv*, cartera *f* [AMER portafolio *m*].

documentary [dɔkju'mentəri] *adj* documental; *documentary proof* prueba documental || *documentary film* documental *m*.

◆ *n* documental *m* (film).

documentation [dɔkjumen'teiʃən] *n* documentación *f*.

dodder ['dɔdə*] *n* BOT cuscuta *f*.

dodder ['dɔdə*] *vi* temblequear (to tremble) || tambalearse, andar con paso inseguro (to totter) || AUT *to dodder along* ir tranquilamente.

dodderer [-ə*] *n* FAM *an old dodderer* un viejo chocho.

doddering [-riŋ]; **doddery** [-ri] *adj* chocho, cha.

doddle ['dodə] *n* FAM *it's a doddle* está chupado, es pan comido.

dodecagon [dəu'dekəgən] *n* MATH dodecágono *m*.

dodecagonal [dəude'kægənəl] *adj* MATH dodecágono, na.

dodecahedron ['dəudikə'hedrən] *n* MATH dodecaedro *m*.

dodecaphonic ['dəudekə'fɔnik] *adj* MUS dodecafónico, ca.

dodecasyllabic ['dəudekəsi'læbik] *adj* dodecasílabo, ba.

dodge [dɔdʒ] *n* regate *m* (quick evasive movement) || truco *m* (trick); *he is up to all the dodges* conoce todos los trucos || esquiva *f*, finta *f* (of a boxer) || sistema *m*, truco *m* (trick).

dodge [dɔdʒ] *vi* echarse a un lado, hurtar el cuerpo, esquivarse (to move to one side); *he dodged when I tried to hit him* se echó a un lado cuando intenté pegarle || esconderse, echarse (*behind* detrás) (to hide) || andar con rodeos (in speech) || SP hacer un regate, regatear (in football, etc.) | hacer una finta (in boxing) || *to dodge about* andarse con rodeos.
◆ *vt* eludir; *to dodge a question* eludir una pregunta || zafarse; *he dodged military service* se zafó del servicio militar || esquivar (a blow, etc.) || regatear (in football, etc.) || evitar (to avoid); *to dodge the traffic* evitar el tráfico || despistar, dar esquinazo a (a pursuer) || mover, desplazar (to move) || FAM fumarse (to skive); *to dodge a class* fumarse una clase || *to dodge it* escurrir el bulto.

dodgems ['dɔdʒəms] *pl n* coches *m* que chocan.

dodger ['dɔdʒə*] *n* tramposo, sa (tricky person) || tunante, ta; marrullero, ra (shifty rascal) || MIL emboscado *m* || US octavilla *f* (handbill).

dodgy ['dɔdʒi] *adj* astuto, ta; marrullero, ra.

dodo ['dəudəu] *n* FIG *as old as a dodo* más viejo que la nana, un vejestorio.
— OBSERV El plural es *dodoes* o *dodos*.

doe [dəu] *n* coneja *f* (female rabbit) || liebre *f* (female hare) || gama *f* (female deer).

doer ['du:ə*] *n* persona *f* activa || autor, ra (*of* de).

does [dʌz] *3rd pers sing pres* ⟶ **do.**

doeskin ['dəuskin] *n* ante *m* (deer skin).

doesn't [dʌznt] contraction of «does not».

doff [dɔf] *vt* quitarse (to take off) || librarse de (to get rid of).

dog [dɔg] *n* perro *m* (animal) || macho *m* (of fox, jackal, wolf) || TECH cabezal *m* (mechanical gripping device) | grapa *f* (iron bar for joining timbers together) || ASTR can *m*; *Great Dog, Little* o *Lesser Dog* Can Mayor, Can Menor || FAM perro *m* (person) | desastre *m*, fracaso *m* (of a play) | — FIG *beware of the dog* cuidado con el perro || FIG *dead dog* persona *f* que ha venido a menos || FAM *dirty dog* canalla *m*, tío cochino || *dog collar* collar *m* de perro || *dog fox* zorro *m* || *dog show* exposición canina || FIG *dog tired* rendido, da || *dog wolf* lobo *m* || FIG *every dog has his day* a cada cerdo le llega su San Martín || *hot dog* perro caliente || *it's a dog's life* es una vida de perros || FAM *lucky dog* tío *m* con suerte || *Newfoundland dog* perro de Terranova || FIG *not to have a dog's chance* no tener la menor probabilidad || *pedigree dog* perro de casta || *stray dog* perro sin dueño || FIG & FAM *the dog in the manger* el perro del hortelano (que ni come ni deja comer) || FIG & FAM *to be as sick as a dog* estar más malo que los perros | *to be top dog* ser el gallito del lugar (to rule the roost), ser el mejor (to be first) | *to die a dog's death* morir como un perro | *to lead a dog's life* llevar una vida de perros || US FAM *to put on the dog* darse pisto || FIG *to treat s.o. like a dog* tratar a alguien como a un perro || US FIG *to work like a dog* trabajar como un condenado.
◆ *pl* morillos *m* (pair of supports for logs in an open hearth) || — FIG *barking dogs don't bite* perro ladrador poco mordedor | *dead dogs don't bite* muerto el perro se acabó la rabia | *let sleeping dogs lie* más vale no meneallo || FAM *the dogs* carrera *f sing* de galgos || FIG & FAM *to go to the dogs* ir a la ruina (business), malearse (person).

dog [dɔg] *vt* seguir; *to dog s.o.'s footsteps* seguir los pasos de alguien || perseguir (to pursue).

dogaressa [,dɔgə'resə] *n* dogaresa *f*.

dogberry ['dɔgberi] *n* BOT fruto *m* del cornejo || *dogberry tree* cornejo *m*.

dog biscuit ['dɔg'biskit] *n* galleta *f* de perro.

dogcart ['dɔgkɑ:t] *n* coche *m* de dos ruedas.

dogcatcher ['dɔg,kætʃə*] *n* perrero *m*.

dog days ['dɔgdeiz] *pl n* canícula *f sing* (summer).

doge [dəudʒ] *n* dux *m* (in Venice).

dog-ear ['dɔgiə*] *n* esquina *f* doblada de una página.

dog-eared [-d] *adj* sobado, da (book).

dog-eat-dog ['dɔg i:t dɔg] *adj* FAM implacable, despiadado, da.

dog-end ['dɔgend] *n* POP colilla *f*.

dogfight ['dɔgfait] *n* pelea *f* entre perros || combate *m* aéreo || FAM trifulca *f* (brawl).

dogfish ['dɔgfiʃ] *n* cazón *m*, lija *f* (fish).

dog food ['dɔgfu:d] *n* comida *f* para perros.

dogged ['dɔgid] *adj* obstinado, da; tenaz.

doggedness [-nis] *n* obstinación *f*, tenacidad *f*.

doggerel ['dɔgərəl] *n* aleluyas *f pl* (bad verse).

doggie ['dɔgi] *n* perrito *m*.

doggie bag [-bæg] *n* FAM bolsa *f* para las sobras (provided by a restaurant).

doggish ['dɔgiʃ] *adj* que se parece a un perro, perruno, na; de perros || FIG arisco, ca (surly) || US FAM aparatoso, sa (showy).

doggo ['dɔgəu] *adj* FAM *to lie doggo* estar escondido.

doggone ['dɔggɔn] *adj* US FAM maldito, ta.
◆ *interj* US FAM ¡caray!

doggy ['dɔgi] *n* perrito *m*.
◆ *adj* perruno, na; de perros (dog-like) || FIG arisco, ca (surly) || aficionado a los perros (fond of dogs) || US aparatoso, sa (showy) || — *there is a doggy smell* huele a perros || *to swim doggy paddle* nadar como un perro.

doghouse ['dɔghaus] *n* US perrera *f* (kennel) || FIG *to be in the doghouse* haber caído en desgracia.

dog Latin ['dɔg'lætin] *n* latín *m* macarrónico.

dogma ['dɔgmə] *n* dogma *m*.
— OBSERV El plural de la palabra inglesa es *dogmas* o *dogmata*.

dogmatic [dɔg'mætik] *adj* dogmático, ca.

dogmatics [dɔg'mætiks] *n* dogmática *f*.

dogmatism ['dɔgmətizəm] *n* dogmatismo *m*.

dogmatist ['dɔgmətist] *n* dogmatista *m* (believer in dogmatism) || dogmatizador, ra; dogmatizante *m* & *f* (who states categorically).

dogmatize ['dɔgmətaiz] *vt/vi* dogmatizar.

do-gooder ['du:'gudə*] *n* persona *f* bien intencionada, bienhechor, ra.

dog rose ['dɔgrəuz] *n* BOT escaramujo *m*, rosal *m* silvestre.

dog's age ['dɔgzeidʒ] *n* US FIG & FAM siglos *m pl*, miles *m pl* de años (a long time).

dogsbody ['dɔgsbɔdi] *n* FAM burro *m* de carga (drudge).

dogsled ['dɔgsled] *n* trineo *m* tirado por perros.

Dog Star ['dɔgstɑ:*] *n* ASTR Sirio *m*.

dog tag ['dɔgtæg] *n* US placa *f* de identificación.

dog-tired ['dɔg'taiəd] *adj* FAM rendido, da.

dogvane ['dɔgvein] *n* MAR cataviento *m*.

dogwatch ['dɔgwɔtʃ] *n* MAR guardia *f* de 4 a 6 y de 6 a 8 de la tarde.

dogwood ['dɔgwud] *n* BOT cornejo *m*.

doily ['dɔili] *n* tapete *m*.

doing ['du:iŋ] *n* obra *f*; *it is not of my doing* no es obra mía.
◆ *pl* actuación *f sing* (behaviour) || actividades *f* (activities) || acontecimientos *m* (happenings, events) || fiestas *f* (social events) || chisme *m sing*, cachivache *m sing* (thing).

doit [dɔit] *n* ochavo *m* (old coin) || FAM *I don't care a doit for it* me importa un bledo.

do-it-yourself ['du:itjɔ:'self] *adj* que uno hace o construye uno mismo || hágalo usted mismo (book titles) || *a do-it-yourself man* un hombre mañoso.

doldrums ['dɔldrəmz] *pl n* MAR zona *f sing* de las calmas, calmas *f* ecuatoriales || FIG *to be in the doldrums* estar deprimido (person), estar parado (business), estar estancado (economy), estar en calma (stock exchange).

dole [dəul] *n* subsidio *m* de paro (unemployment pay) || distribución *f*, reparto *m* (distribution) || parte *f* (share) || limosna *f* (alms) || *to be on the dole* estar acogido al paro, estar parado.

dole [dəul] *vt* *to dole out* repartir [parcamente].

doleful [-ful] *adj* triste (appearance, news) || triste, afligido, da (person) || lastimero, ra; quejumbroso, sa (cry) || lúgubre (dreary).

dolefulness [-nis] *n* tristeza *f*, melancolía *f*.

dolichocephalic ['dɔlikəuke'fælik] *adj* ANAT dolicocéfalo, la.

dolichocephalism [,dɔlikəu'kefəlizəm] ; **dolichocephaly** ['dɔlikəu'kefəli] *n* dolicocefalia *f*.

doll [dɔl] *n* muñeca *f* (toy, girl).

doll [dɔl] *vt* FAM *to doll o.s. up* emperejilarse, empingorotarse | *to doll up* emperejilar, empingorotar.

dollar ['dɔlə*] *n* dólar *m* || US *dollar diplomacy* diplomacia *f* del dólar.

dolled up ['dɔldʌp] *adj* FAM emperejilado, da; empingorotado, da.

dollhouse ['dɔlhaus] *n* US casa *f* de muñecas.

dollop ['dɔləp] *n* FAM masa *f*.

doll's house ['dɔlzhaus] *n* US casa *f* de muñecas.

dolly ['dɔli] *n* muñeca *f* (doll) || batidor *m* (for thumping clothes) || carretilla *f* de ruedas (wheeled trolley) || CINEM travelín *m*, plataforma *f* rodante.

dolly bird [-bə:d] *n* FAM niña *f* mona.

dolman ['dɔlmən] *n* dormán *m* (jacket) || *dolman sleeve* manga japonesa.

dolmen ['dɔlmən] *n* dolmen *m*.

Dolomites ['dɔləmaits] *pl prn* GEOGR Dolomitas *f*.

dolomitic ['dɔlə'mitik] *adj* GEOGR dolomítico, ca.

dolor ['dəulər] *n* US dolor *m*.

dolorous ['dɔlərəs] *adj* doloroso, sa.

dolose [də'ləus] *adj* JUR doloso, sa (fraudulent).

dolour ['dəulə*] *n* dolor *m*.

dolphin ['dɔlfin] *n* ZOOL delfín *m* (mammal) | dorado *m* (fish).

dolt [dəult] *n* idiota *m* & *f*, bobo, ba.

doltish ['dəultiʃ] *adj* idiota, bobo, ba.

domain [də'mein] *n* dominio *m* (territory under one ruler) || finca *f* (estate) || FIG campo *m*, ámbito *m*, esfera *f* (field of activity).

dome [dəum] *n* ARCH cúpula *f*, domo *m* || FIG bóveda *f* | cumbre *f* redondeada (of a hill) || US FAM chola *f* (head).

dome [dəum] *vt* cubrir con una cúpula (to cover) || dar forma de cúpula a (to shape).

domestic [də'mestik] *adj* doméstico, ca; *domestic service* servicio doméstico || hogareño, ña; casero, ra (home-loving) || doméstico, ca; de uso doméstico (appliance) || nacional, in-

terior (trade, market, flight, etc.) || ZOOL doméstico, ca; *domestic animal* animal doméstico || — *domestic appliance* electrodoméstico *m* || *domestic arts* artes domésticas || INFORM *domestic automation* o *home system* automatización *f* doméstica || *domestic help* doméstico, ca || *domestic life* vida *f* de familia || *domestic quarrels* riñas *f* conyugales (between married people), luchas intestinas (in politics) || *domestic science* economía doméstica.
◆ *n* doméstico, ca (servant).

domesticable [də'mestikəbl] *adj* domesticable.

domesticate [də'mestikeit] *vt* domesticar (animals) || civilizar (savages) || aclimatar (plants) || volver casero (person) || *domesticated woman* mujer de su casa.
◆ *vi* volverse casero.

domestication [də,mesti'keiʃən] *n* domesticación *f* (of animals) || civilización *f* (of savages) || aclimatación *f* (of plants) || carácter *m* casero (of people).

domesticity [,dəumes'tisiti] *n* domesticidad *f* (of animals) || vida *f* casera.
◆ *pl* asuntos *m* domésticos.

domicile ['dɔmisail] *n* domicilio *m*.

domicile ['dɔmisail] *vt* domiciliar.
◆ *vi* domiciliarse, tener domicilio.

domiciliary [,dɔmis'iljəri] *adj* domiciliario, ria.

domiciliation [dɔmisili'eiʃən] *n* domiciliación *f*.

dominance ['dɔminəns]; **dominancy** [-si] *n* dominación *f* || predominio *m* (predominance).

dominant ['dɔminənt] *adj* dominante || *to be dominant over* dominar.
◆ *n* MUS & BIOL dominante *f*.

dominate ['dɔmineit] *vt/vi* dominar.

dominating [-iŋ] *adj* dominador, ra; dominante.

domination [,dɔmi'neiʃən] *n* dominación *f*.
◆ *pl* REL dominaciones *f* (dominions).

domineer [,dɔmi'niə*] *vt* *to domineer over* dominar tiránicamente a, tiranizar a.

domineering [-iŋ] *adj* dominante, autoritario, ria.

Dominic ['dɔminik] *pr n* Domingo *m*.

Dominica [,dɔmi'niːkə] *pr n* GEOGR Dominica *f*.

dominical [də'minikəl] *adj* dominical.

Dominican [də'minikən] *adj/n* dominicano, na (of Dominican Republic) || REL dominico, ca; dominicano, na.

Dominican Republic [-ri'pʌblik] *pr n* GEOGR República *f* Dominicana.

dominion [də'minjən] *n* dominio *m*.
◆ *pl* REL dominaciones *f*.

domino ['dɔminəu] *n* dominó *m* (game, dress); *to play dominoes* jugar a los dominós.
— OBSERV El plural de la palabra inglesa es *dominoes* o *dominos*.

don [dɔn] *n* catedrático *m* (university teacher) || don *m* (Spanish and Italian title) || hidalgo *m* (nobleman) || FAM as *m*, hacha *m* (*at* en) (ace).

don [dɔn] *vt* ponerse (a garment) || vestirse de (a certain colour or material).

donate [dəu'neit] *vt* donar, hacer donación de; *he donated 15 000 pesetas* donó 15 000 pesetas; *he donated his house* hizo donación de su casa || dar, donar (blood).

donating [-iŋ] *adj* donante.

donation [dəu'neiʃən] *n* JUR donación *f*; *donation inter vivos* donación entre vivos || donativo *m* (gift, contribution).

donative ['dəunətiv] *n* donativo *m*.

donator [dəu'neitə*] *n* donatario, ria.

done [dʌn] *pp* → **do** || **terminado, da (finished)** || **hecho, cha (cooked)** || **gastado, da (worn-out)** || **rendido, da; agotado, da (tired)** || — *done!* ¡trato hecho! || *done to a turn* en su punto (meat) || *done with* acabado, da || *it is not done* esto no se hace || *it is not done to* no es elegante, es de mal gusto || *leave it like that and have done with it* déjalo así y ya está || *to have done with* haber acabado con || *well done* muy hecho, cha (meat) || *well done!* ¡muy bien!

donjon ['dɔndʒən] *n* calabozo *m*, mazmorra *f* (prison) || torre *f* del homenaje (keep of a castle).

donkey ['dɔŋki] *n* burro *m*, asno *m* || FAM burro, rra; bruto, ta | FAM *donkey's years* siglos *m pl*, miles de años *m pl*.

donkey engine [-'endʒin] *n* motor *m* auxiliar || locomotora *f* pequeña.

donkey jacket [-,dʒækit] *n* chaqueta *f* gruesa de obrero.

donnish ['dɔniʃ] *adj* pedante || profesoral.

donor ['dəunə*] *n* donante *m* & *f*; *blood donor* donante de sangre || JUR donatario, ria.

don't [dəunt] (contraction of «do not»).

donzel ['dɔnzl] *n* (ant) doncel *m* (pageboy).

doodad ['duːdæd] *n* US FAM chisme *m*, cosa *f*.

doodle ['duːdl] *n* garabatos *m pl* (writing) || dibujitos *m pl* (drawing).

doodle ['duːdl] *vi* garabatear, hacer garabatos (in writing) || pintarrajear (in drawing).

doodlebug ['duːdlbʌg] *n* bomba *f* teledirigida (flying bomb) || US varilla *f* de zahorí.

doom [duːm] *n* destino *m* [funesto] (calamitous fate) || perdición *f* (ruin) || muerte *f* (death) || REL juicio *m* final || JUR juicio *m*.

doom [duːm] *vt* REL & JUR condenar (*to* a) || predestinar (to predestine) || *doomed to failure* condenado al fracaso.

doomsday ['duːmzdei] *n* REL día *m* del juicio final || FAM *till doomsday* hasta el juicio final.

door [dɔː*] *n* puerta *f*; *revolving door* puerta giratoria || — FIG *at death's door* a las puertas de la muerte || *automatic door* puerta automática || *back door* puerta trasera || *behind closed doors* a puerta cerrada || *door-to-door salesman* vendedor *m* a domicilio || *from door to door* de puerta en puerta || *front door* puerta de entrada || *glass door* puerta de cristal, puerta vidriera || *hidden door* puerta excusada *or* falsa || *next door* en la casa de al lado || *out of doors* al aire libre (in the open air), fuera (outside) || *secret door* puerta secreta || *sliding door* puerta de corredera || FIG *there's the door!* ¡ahí tienes la puerta! | *this is next door to* esto raya en || *to break the door open* echar la puerta abajo || FIG *to close the door upon* cerrar la puerta a | *to find all doors closed* encontrar todas las puertas cerradas | *to have an open door* tener puerta abierta | *to knock the door down* echar la puerta abajo | *to lay a charge at the door of* echar la culpa a | *to leave a door open* dejar una puerta abierta | *to lie at s.o.'s door* recaer sobre alguien | *to open the door to* abrir la puerta a | *to show s.o. the door* enseñar la puerta a uno || *to show s.o. to the door* acompañar a alguien hasta la puerta || *to slam the door* dar un portazo || FIG *to slam the door in s.o.'s face* dar a uno con la puerta en las narices | *when one door closes another always opens* cuando una puerta se cierra, cien se abren || *within doors* en casa.

doorbell ['dɔːbel] *n* timbre *m* (de la puerta).

doorcase ['dɔːkeis] *n* marco *m* de la puerta.

doorframe ['dɔːfreim] *n* marco *m* de la puerta.

door-handle ['dɔː,hændl] *n* manilla *f*, tirador *m* (door lever).

doorhead ['dɔːhed] *n* dintel *m*.

doorjamb ['dɔːdʒæm] *n* jamba *f* de la puerta.

doorkeeper ['dɔːkiːpə*] *n* portero *m* (of a hotel) || conserje *m* (of public building) || REL ostiario *m*.

doorknob ['dɔːnɔb] *n* pomo *m* de la puerta.

doorknocker ['dɔː,nɔkə*] *n* picaporte *m*, aldaba *f*, llamador *m*.

doorman ['dɔːmən] *n* portero *m*.
— OBSERV El plural de esta palabra es *doormen*.

doormat ['dɔːmæt] *n* felpudo *m*, estera *f*.

doornail ['dɔːneil] *n* clavo *m* de puerta || — FIG *dead as a doornail* muerto y bien muerto | *deaf as a doornail* más sordo que una tapia.

doorplate ['dɔːpleit] *n* placa *f* [que se pone en la puerta].

doorpost ['dɔːpəust] *n* jamba *f* de puerta.

doorstep ['dɔːstep] *n* umbral *m* (threshold) || peldaño *m* (step).

doorstepping [-iŋ] *n* FAM fisgoneo *m* periodístico.
◆ *adj* FAM fisgón, ona; entrometido, da (journalist).

doorstop ['dɔːstɔp] *n* tope *m* de puerta (wooden strip) || retenedor *m* (to hold a door open).

doorway ['dɔːwei] *n* portal *m* || FIG puerta *f*.

dooryard ['dɔːjaːd] *n* US patio *m*.

dope [dəup] *n* FAM droga *f* (narcotic) | información *f*, informes *m pl* (information) | idiota *m* & *f* (idiot) || barniz *m* (varnish) || lubricante *m* (lubricant).

dope [dəup] *vt* drogar || SP dopar || US FAM *to dope out* sacar (to deduce).

dope fiend [-fiːnd] *n* US FAM toxicómano, na.

dopey ['dəupi] *adj* tonto, ta (stupid) || atontado, da (fuddled).

doping ['dəupiŋ] *n* SP doping *m*, drogado *m*.

dor [dɔː*] *n* ZOOL escarabajo *m* pelotero (dung beetle) | abejorro *m* (flying beetle).

dorado [də'raːdəu] *n* ZOOL dorado *m* (fish).

Dorian ['dɔːriən] *adj/n* dorio, ria.

Doric ['dɔrik] *adj* dórico, ca; *Doric order* orden dórico.
◆ *n* dórico *m* (Greek dialect).

dormancy ['dɔːmənsi] *n* letargo *m* (of animals) || sueño *m* (sleep) || inactividad *f*.

dormant *adj* inactivo, va; *to lie dormant* estar inactivo || letárgico, ca (animals) || inactivo, va (volcano) || latente (latent) || JUR caído en desuso (a title) | inaplicado, da (a law).

dormer ['dɔːmə*] *n* buhardilla *f*.

dormitory ['dɔːmitri] *n* dormitorio *m*.

Dormobile ['dɔːməbiːl] *n* caravana *f* (small caravan) (registered trademark).

dormouse ['dɔːmaus] *n* lirón *m* (animal).
— OBSERV El plural de esta palabra es *dormice*.

dorsal ['dɔːsəl] *adj* ANAT dorsal.

dory ['dɔːri] *n* pez *m* de san Pedro (fish) || US bote *m* (fishing boat).

dosage ['dəusidʒ] *n* dosificación *f* (determination) || dosis *f inv* (amount) || administración *f* de un medicamento (giving) || FIG dosis *f inv*.

dose [dəus] *n* dosis *f inv* (amount of medicine) || FIG dosis *f inv*.

dose [dəus] *vt* dosificar (to determine the dose of) || administrar un medicamento a, medicinar || alcoholizar (wine) || *to dose o.s. with* seguir un tratamiento a base de.

dosing ['dəusiŋ] *n* dosificación *f*.

doss [dɔs] *n* FAM piltra *f*, catre *m* (bed).

doss [dɔs] *vi* FAM dormir ‖ FAM *to doss down* dormir.

dossal ['dɔsəl] *n* dosel *m*.

dosser ['dɔsə*] *n* FAM vagabundo, da.

doss house ['dɔshaus] *n* FAM fonducha *f*, posada *f* del peine, pensión *f* de mala muerte.

dossier ['dɔsiei] *n* expediente *m*.

dot [dɔt] *n* punto *m* (point) ‖ FAM chaval *m* (boy) ‖ — FAM *off one's dot* loco, ca ‖ *on the dot* puntualmente; *to arrive on the dot* llegar puntualmente; en punto; *it's two o'clock on the dot* son las dos en punto; a toca teja; *to pay on the dot* pagar a toca teja ‖ *three dots* puntos suspensivos.

dot [dɔt] *vt* poner el punto a (to put a dot on) ‖ puntear (a line) ‖ salpicar (to scatter) ‖ MUS puntear ‖ — *dotted line* línea *f* de puntos, punteado *m* ‖ FAM *I dotted him one* le di un porrazo ‖ FIG *to dot one's i's and cross one's t's* poner los puntos sobre las íes.

DOT *abbr of [Department of Transportation]* ministerio de transportes norteamericano.

dotage ['dəutidʒ] *n* chochez *f* ‖ *to be in one's dotage* estar chocho, cha.

dotal ['dəutəl] *adj* dotal.

dotard ['dəutəd] *n* viejo *m* chocho, vieja *f* chocha.

dotation [dəu'teiʃən] *n* dotación *f*.

dote [dəut] *vi* chochear (an old person) ‖ *to dote on* adorar, estar chocho por.

doting [-iŋ] *adj* chocho, cha.

dotmatrix printer ['dɔtmeitriks,printə*] *n* INFORM impresora *f* matricial de puntos.

dotty ['dɔti] *adj* FAM chiflado, da; chalado, da (daft) ‖ punteado, da (with dots).

double ['dʌbl] *adj* doble ‖ en dos ejemplares (in duplicate) ‖ doblado, da (folded) ‖ repetido, da (repeated) ‖ para dos personas (room) ‖ FIG doble; *to lead a double life* llevar una doble vida; *double meaning* doble sentido ‖ — *I am double your age* soy dos veces mayor que tú ‖ *to be in double figures* ser de dos cifras (number) ‖ *your income is double what it was last year* sus ingresos son dos veces lo que eran el año pasado *or* el doble de lo que eran el año pasado.
◆ *adv* doble; *to see double* ver doble ‖ — *double as long as* dos veces más largo que ‖ *double or nothing, double or quits* doble o nada ‖ *to pay double* pagar el doble ‖ *to ride double* montar dos en un caballo ‖ *to sleep double* dormir dos en una cama.
◆ *n* doble *m* (quantity, actor) ‖ MIL paso *m* ligero ‖ — FAM *at the double* corriendo | *on the double* con toda rapidez.
◆ *pl* doble *m sing*; *men's, ladies, mixed doubles* doble caballeros, damas, mixto.

double ['dʌbl] *vt* doblar, duplicar (in quantity, size, weight) ‖ redoblar (efforts) ‖ doblar (to fold) ‖ cerrar (the fist) ‖ THEATR doblar ‖ doblar (in bridge) ‖ *to double back* o *up* doblar (to fold).
◆ *vi* duplicarse, doblarse (to become double) ‖ doblarse (to fold up) ‖ servir al mismo tiempo de (to serve as) ‖ correr a paso ligero (to run) ‖ — *to double back* volver sobre sus pasos (person), dar un rodeo (river) ‖ CINEM *to double for* doblar a ‖ *to double round* dar la vuelta por ‖ *to double up* doblarse (from pain), compartir una habitación (to share a room), compartir una cama (to share a bed) ‖ FIG & FAM *to double up with laughter* mondarse *or* partirse de risa.

double-acting [-'æktiŋ] *adj* de doble efecto.

double agent [-'eidʒnt] *n* agente *m* & *f* doble.

double bar [-'bɑː*] *n* MUS barras *f pl*.

double-barrelled [-'bærəld] *adj* de dos cañones (gun) ‖ FAM compuesto, ta (surname) ‖ FIG de doble efecto.

double bass [-'beis] *n* MUS contrabajo *m*, violón *m*.

double bassoon [-bə'suːn] *n* MUS contrafagot *m*.

double bed [-'bed] *n* cama *f* de matrimonio, cama *f* camera, cama *f* doble.

double-bedded [-'bedid] *adj* con dos camas.

double bill [-'bil] *n* CINEM programa *m* doble.

double boiler [-'bɔilə*] *n* baño *m* maría.

double-bottomed [-,bɔtəmd] *adj* de doble fondo.

double-breasted [-'brestid] *adj* cruzado, da (coat).

double-check [-'tʃek] *vt* comprobar dos veces.

double chin [-'tʃin] *n* papada *f*.

double cream [-'kriːm] *n* CULIN crema *f* de leche muy espesa.

double-cross [-'krɔs] *n* traición *f*.

double-cross [-'krɔs] *vt* traicionar.

double dagger [-'dægə*] *n* PRINT obelisco *m* doble, signo *m* de referencia.

double-dealer [-'diːlə*] *n* embustero *m* (cheat) ‖ traidor *m* (traitor).

double-dealing [-diːliŋ] *n* doblez *m*, duplicidad *f*.

double-decker [-'dekə*] **; two-decker** *n* autobús *m* de dos pisos ‖ MAR barco *m* de dos cubiertas ‖ *US* sandwich *m or* emparedado *m* doble.

double declutch [-'diːklʌt] *vi* AUT hacer doble desembrague.

double Dutch [-dʌtʃ] *n* FAM chino *m* (gibberish); *to talk double Dutch* hablar chino.

double-edged [-'edʒd] *adj* de dos filos.

double-entendre ['duːblaːn'tɑːndr] *n* expresión *f* con doble sentido.

double entry ['dʌbl'entri] *n* COMM partida *f* doble ‖ *double-entry bookkeeping* contabilidad *f* por partida doble.

double-faced ['dʌbl'feist] *adj* de dos caras ‖ FIG doble.

double fault ['dʌbl'fɔːlt] *n* doble falta *f* (in lawn tennis).

double feature ['dʌbl'fiːtʃə*] *n* programa *m* doble, dos películas *f pl*.

double glazing ['dʌbl'gleiziŋ] *n* doble acristalamiento.

double-headed ['dʌbl'hedid] *adj* bicéfalo, la.

double-jointed ['dʌbl'dʒɔintid] *adj* con articulaciones dobles.

double-lock ['dʌbl'lɔk] *vt* cerrar con dos vueltas.

double-park ['dʌble'pɑːk] *vt/vi* aparcar en doble fila.

double pneumonia ['dʌbl nju'məunjə] *n* MED neumonía *f* doble.

double-quick ['dʌbl'kwik] *adj* ligero (step).
◆ *adv* a paso ligero.

double sided ['dʌbl'saidid] INFORM doble cara *f* (diskette).

double-spaced ['dʌbl'speist] *adj* con doble espacio (in typewriting).

doubled standards ['dʌbl'stændədz] *pl n* criterios *m pl* distintos ‖ *to apply double standards* no medir con el mismo rasero.

doublet ['dʌblit] *n* jubón *m* (garment) ‖ doblete *m* (jewel, linguistics) ‖ PHYS objetivo *m* doble.

double take ['dʌbl'teik] *n* reacción *f* retardada ‖ *to do a double take* tardar en reaccionar.

double-talk ['dʌbltɔːk] *n* palabras *f pl* con doble sentido.

double-talk ['dʌbltɔːk] *vi* hablar con segundas.

double time ['dʌbl'taim] *n* paso *m* ligero.

doubleton ['dʌbltən] *n* dos cartas del mismo palo, doblete *m*.

doubloon [dʌb'luːn] *n* doblón *m* (coin).

doubly ['dʌbli] *adv* doblemente; *doubly magnanimous* doblemente magnánimo ‖ por duplicado (in duplicate).

doubt [daut] *n* duda *f* (*about, as, to* de); *to call in doubt* poner en duda ‖ — *beyond doubt* fuera de duda ‖ *in doubt* dudoso, sa ‖ *make no doubt about it* puede estar seguro de ello ‖ *no doubt* sin duda ‖ *there is no doubt about it* no cabe la menor duda ‖ *there is no doubt that...* no cabe duda de que... ‖ *to be in doubt about, to have one's doubts about* tener sus dudas acerca de ‖ *to clear up s.o.'s doubts* sacar de dudas a uno ‖ *to put in a doubt* hacer dudar (to give doubt to), poner en duda (to question) ‖ *to shed one's doubts* salir de dudas ‖ *when in doubt, don't; when in doubt, abstain* en la duda abstente ‖ *without a* o *any doubt* sin duda alguna ‖ *without the shadow of a doubt* sin sombra de duda ‖ *without the slightest doubt* sin la menor duda.

doubt [daut] *vt* dudar; *I doubt it* lo dudo ‖ dudar de, poner en tela de juicio (to question) ‖ desconfiar (to distrust).
◆ *vi* dudar (*about, of* de) ‖ *I doubt whether he'll come* no sé si vendrá, no estoy seguro de que venga, dudo que venga.

doubter [-ə*] *n* escéptico, ca.

doubtful [-ful] *adj* dudoso, sa; poco seguro, ra; *the results are doubtful* los resultados son dudosos ‖ indeciso, sa (irresolute) ‖ dudoso, sa; sospechoso, sa (character, place, society) ‖ dudoso, sa (taste) ‖ vago, ga (vague) ‖ — *to be doubtful of* o *about* dudar de ‖ *we were still doubtful about speaking to her* no nos decidíamos todavía a hablarle.

doubting Thomas ['dautiŋ'tɔməs] *n* FIG incrédulo, la.

doubtless ['dautlis] *adv* sin duda, indudablemente.

douceur [duː'səː*] *n* propina *f* (gratuity) ‖ guante *m*, mamelas *f pl* (bribe).

douche [duːʃ] *n* ducha *f* (jet of water) ‖ irrigador *m* (instrument used) ‖ MED irrigación *f*.

douche [duːʃ] *vt* irrigar.
◆ *vi* irrigarse.

doucine [duː'siːn] *n* ARCH cimacio *m*.

dough [dəu] *n* masa *f*, pasta *f* ‖ *US* FAM pasta *f* [*AMER* plata *f*] (money).

doughboy [-bɔi] *n* *US* MIL soldado *m* de infantería.

doughnut [-nʌt] *n* rosquilla *f*, buñuelo *m*.

doughty ['dauti] *adj* valiente.

doughy ['dpui] *adj* pastoso, sa.

dour [duə*] *adj* austero, ra (sullen) ‖ severo, ra (severe) ‖ terco, ca; obstinado, da (obstinate).

Douro ['duərəu] *pr n* GEOGR Duero *m*.

douse; dowse [daus] *vt* mojar (to soak or to put in water) ‖ MAR arriar (sails) ‖ FAM apagar (to extinguish).

dove [dʌv] *n* ZOOL paloma *f* ‖ FIG & FAM *my dove* mi cielo, mi amor.

dove [dəuv] *pret* → **dive.**

dovecot; dovecote ['dʌvkɔt] *n* palomar *m*.

dovetail ['dʌvteil] *n* TECH cola *f* de milano.

dovetail ['dʌvteil] *vt* ensamblar a cola de milano (in carpentry) || FIG enlazar, unir (to link) || encajar (to fit).
◆ *vi* FIG enlazar (to be linked) | encajar (to fit).

dowager ['dauədʒə*] *n* viuda *f* que goza de una pensión *or* viudedad *or* del título de su marido || FAM señora *f* mayor || *queen dowager* reina viuda.

dowdiness ['daudinis] *n* desaliño *m* (slovenliness) || falta *f* de elegancia.

dowdy ['daudi] *adj* desaliñado, da (slovenly) || poco elegante (not smart).

dowel ['dauəl] *n* clavija *f*.

dowel ['dauəl] *vt* sujetar con una clavija, enclavijar.

dower ['dauər] *n* viudedad *f* (property retained by a widow) || dote *f* (dowry) || don *m* (natural gift).

down [daun] *n* plumón *m* (on birds) || vello *m* (any fine hair growth) || pelusa *f* (fuzz, on fruit) || loma *f* (treeless upland) || US duna *f* (dune) || US SP «down» *m* || — *his ups and downs* sus más y sus menos, sus altibajos || FIG & FAM *to have a down on s.o.* tenerle manía a uno, tenerle tirria a uno.
◆ *adj* descendente; *a down current* una corriente descendente || bajo, ja; *the river is down* el río está bajo; *prices are down now* los precios están bajos ahora || deprimido, da (depressed) || agotado, da (tired) || COMM al contado, inicial (payment) || SP fuera de juego | fuera de combate (in boxing) || desinflado, da (tyre) || *down train* tren que sale de la capital, tren descendente.
◆ *adv* hacia abajo; *they rolled the ball down* hicieron rodar la pelota hacia abajo || en el suelo; *to hit a man when he is down* pegar a un hombre cuando está en el suelo || por escrito; *to take s.o.'s name down* poner el nombre de alguien por escrito || COMM al contado (to pay) || FAM *down and out* sin una perra, sin un cuarto (broke), fuera de combate (in boxing) || *down below* abajo || *down, boy!* ¡quieto! (to a dog) || *down here* por aquí || *down to* hasta; *down to date* hasta la fecha || *down to where?* ¿hasta dónde? || *down under* en Australia, en Nueva Zelanda, en las antípodas || *¡down with the king!* ¡abajo el rey! || *face down* boca abajo || *further down* más abajo || *he is twenty francs down* le faltan veinte francos || *the curtains are down* se han bajado las cortinas || *the team was three down* el equipo iba perdiendo por tres puntos || *the wind is down* ha amainado el viento || FIG *to be down* haber acabado el curso (a student) || FAM *to be down on s.o.* tenerle manía *or* tirria a alguien || *to be down with* estar con; *he is down with flu* está con gripe || *to come down in the world* venir a menos || *to copy down* copiar || *to fall down* caerse || *to take o to write down* apuntar || *two down, one to go* dos fuera, uno me queda || *up and down* de arriba abajo.
◆ *prep* abajo; *it is down the street a little* está un poco más abajo de la calle || — *down the centuries* a través de los siglos || *down the road* más abajo || *to go down the river* ir río abajo || *to go down the street* bajar la calle || *to run down the street* bajar la calle corriendo.
— OBSERV Existen muchos casos en los cuales el adverbio *down* modifica el sentido del verbo que le antecede *(to go down, to let down, to pull down, etc.)* y no puede traducirse separadamente. Es imprescindible por consiguiente consultar el verbo correspondiente donde las distintas acepciones están tratadas con todo detalle (ver «to pull down» en el artículo dedicado a «pull»).

down [daun] *vt* tirar al suelo; *to down s.o.* tirar a alguien al suelo || derribar (a plane) || vaciar de un trago (a drink) || tragar (food) || *to down tools* declararse en huelga.

down-and-out ['daunənd'aut] *adj* pobre, pobrísimo, ma; sin un céntimo.
◆ *n* pobre *m* & *f*.

down-at-heel ['daunəthi:l] *adj* desaliñado, da (slovenly) || gastado, da; destaconado, da (shoes) || FAM pelado, da; sin un cuarto (penniless).

downbeat ['daunbi:t] *adj* FAM pesimista, deprimido, da (depressed) | relajado, da; tranquilo, la (relaxed).

downcast ['daunkɑ:st] *adj* abatido, da (depressed) || bajo, ja (directed downwards); *downcast eyes* ojos bajos.
◆ *n* MIN pozo *m* de ventilación.

downer ['daunə*] *n* FAM tranquilizante *m* (drug) | muermo (person, experience).

downfall ['daunfɔ:l] *n* chaparrón *m* (a fall of rain) || caída *f* (of snow) || caída *f* (a fall from greatness); *the down fall of an empire, of a ministry* la caída de un imperio, de un ministerio || perdición *f* (cause of ruin); *drink will be his downfall* la bebida será su perdición || ruina *f* || US trampa *f* (trap).

downgrade ['daungreid] *n* bajada *f*, descenso *m* || FIG *to be on the downgrade* ir cuesta abajo, estar en decadencia.

downgrade ['daungreid] *vt* degradar.

downhaul ['daunhɔ:l] *n* MAR candaliza *f*.

downhearted ['daun'hɑ:tid] *adj* descorazonado, da; abatido, da || *to make downhearted* descorazonar, desanimar.

downhill ['daunhil] *adj* en pendiente || SP *downhill race* carrera *f* de descenso (ski).
◆ *adv* cuesta abajo || *to go downhill* bajar, ir cuesta abajo (road, car), ir cuesta abajo, estar en decadencia (person).
◆ *n* bajada *f*, pendiente *f*, declive *m*.

downloading *n* INFORM telecarga *f*.

downpour ['daunpɔ:] *n* aguacero *m*, chaparrón *m*.

downright ['daunrait] *adj* categórico, ca (straightforward) || sincero, ra; franco, ca (sincere) || patente, evidente, manifiesto, ta; *a downright lie* una mentira patente || verdadero, ra; *a downright swindle* un verdadero timo || *downright fool* tonto rematado.
◆ *adv* categóricamente, rotundamente; *he refused downright* se negó rotundamente || realmente, verdaderamente (positively) || completamente.

downside ['daunsaid] *n* bajada *f*, bajón *m* (of share prices, etc.).

Down's syndrome ['daunz,sindrəum] *n* MED síndrome *m* de Down.

downstage ['daunsteidʒ] *adj/adv* THEATR en *or* hacia la parte delantera del escenario.
◆ *n* THEATR proscenio *m*.

downstair ['daun'stɛə*]; **downstairs** [-z] *adj* de abajo.
◆ *adv* abajo || *to go o to come downstairs* bajar la escalera.
◆ *n* US planta *f* baja (ground floor).

downstream ['daunstri:m] *adj/adv* río abajo.

downstroke ['daunstrəuk] *n* palo *m* (of a letter) || TECH carrera *f* descendente (of a piston).

downthrow ['daunθrəu] *n* GEOL corrimiento *m*.

downtime ['dauntaim] *n* ECON tiempo *m* improductivo *or* de inactividad.

down-to-earth ['dauntu'ə:θ] *adj* prosaico, ca.

downtown ['dauntaun] *adv* US al *or* en el centro de la ciudad.
◆ *adj* céntrico, ca; del centro de la ciudad.
◆ *n* US centro *m*.

downtrodden ['daun,trɔdn] *adj* pisoteado, da; *downtrodden grass* hierba pisoteada || FIG oprimido, da (oppressed).

downturn ['dauntə:n] *n* vuelta *f* hacia abajo || COMM baja *f*.

downward ['daunwəd] *adj* descendente (road, movement) || ulterior (time) || COMM a la baja (tendency).
◆ *adv* hacia abajo.

downwards [-z] *adv* hacia abajo || *from the fourteenth century downwards* desde el siglo XIV.

downwind ['daunwind] *adj/adv* a favor del viento, con el viento (in the same direction as the wind).

downy ['dauni] *adj* velloso, sa || suave (soft).

dowry ['dauəri] *n* dote *f* (of a girl) || FIG don *m*, dote *m* (talent).

dowse [dauz] *vi* buscar agua con una varilla de zahorí.
◆ *vt* mojar (to soak or to put in water) || MAR arriar (sails) || FAM apagar to extinguish.

dowser [-ə*] *n* zahorí, *m*.

doxy ['dɔksi] *n* POP ramera *f*, zorra *f* (whore) | querida *f* (mistress).

doyen ['dɔiən] *n* decano *m*.

doze [dəuz] *n* cabeza *f*; *to have a doze after cunch* echar una cabezada después del almuerzo.

doze [dəuz] *vi* dormitar || *to doze off* dormirse, echar una cabezada.

dozen ['dʌzn] *n* docena *f* (twelve); *a dozen eggs* una docena de huevos || — FIG *a dozen words* unas cuantas palabras | *baker's dozen* docena *f* del fraile || *by the dozen* por docenas, a docenas (goods), a docenas (in great quantity).
◆ *pl* docenas *f*, miles *m*; *dozens of times* miles de veces || FIG *in dozens* a docenas.
— OBSERV La palabra *dozen* es invariable cuando va seguida por un sustantivo y precedida por una cifra o su equivalente: *three dozen eggs* tres docenas de huevos; *how many dozen?* ¿cuántas docenas?

dozy ['dəuzi] *adj* soñoliento, ta; medio dormido, da.

drab [dræb] *adj* pardo, da (colour) || FIG monótono, na; gris; *a drab existence* una vida gris.
◆ *n* pardo *m* (colour) || sayal *m* (cloth) || FIG lo gris, monotonía *f* || marrana *f*, mujer *f* sucia (slut) || mujer *f* perdida (prostitute).

drabble ['dræbl] *vt* manchar de barro.
◆ *vi* chapotear (through the mud) || mancharse de barro (to get stained).

drachm [dræm]; **drachma** ['drækmə] *n* dracma *f*.
— OBSERV El plural de las palabras inglesas *drachm* y *drachma* es *drachmas*, *drachmae* o *drachmai*.

Draconian [drei'kəunjən]; **Draconic** [drei'kɔunik] *adj* draconiano, na.

draff [dræf] *n* heces *f pl*, poso *m* (dregs) || aguas *f pl* sucias (slops) || residuo *m* de la cebada utilizado en la fabricación de la cerveza (in brewery) || FIG heces *f pl*.

draft [drɑ:ft] *n* borrador *m* (in writing) || boceto *m*, esbozo *m* (in drawing) || bosquejo *m* (a rough plan of work) || redacción *f*, versión *f*; *first draft of a novel* primera redacción de una novela || JUR minuta *f* (of an act) | proyecto *m* (of an agreement) || COMM libramiento *m* (payment from an account) | letra *f* de cambio, giro *m* (bill) || MIL quinta *f* (conscription) | destacamento *m* (of troops) || forma *f* acampanada (of a mould) || trazo *m* (in masonry) || US corriente *f* (of air) | tiro *m* (of a chimney) | trago *m* (of liquid) | calado *m* (of a boat) || — *draft bill* anteproyecto *m* de ley || *draft horse*

caballo *m* de tiro || *on draft* de barril, a presión (beer).
◆ *pl* juego *m sing* de damas.

draft [drɑ:ft] *vt* hacer un proyecto de (to sketch) || hacer un borrador de (in writing) || redactar (to draw up); *to draft a text* redactar un texto || esbozar (in drawing) || ARCH trazar una línea en (in masonry) || MIL destacar (troops) | llamar a filas, reclutar (conscript).

draftee [drɑ:fti:] *n* US MIL quinto *m*, recluta *m*.

draftsman ['drɑ:ftsmən] *n* delineante *m*, dibujante *m* (designer) || pieza *f*, dama *f* (in draugths) || JUR redactor *m* de proyectos de ley.
— OBSERV El plural de esta palabra es *draftsmen*.

draftsmanship [-ʃip] *n* dibujo *m* lineal.

drafty ['drɑ:fti] *adj* que tiene corrientes de aire.

drag [dræg] *n* arrastre *m* (towing) || AGR grada *f*, rastro *m*, rastra *f* || rastra *f* (device for searching the river bed) || estorbo *m* (sth. or s.o. which hinders); *to be a drag on* ser un estorbo para || FAM calada *f*, chupada *f* (a draw on a cigarette) || AVIAT resistencia *f* aerodinámica || TECH galga *f* (brake) || THEATR disfraz *m* de mujer || FAM cuña *f*, enchufe *m* (influence) | calle *f* (street) | carrera *f* de velocidad (race) | guateque *m*, fiesta *f* (party) | rollo *m*, pesado *m* (boring person) | lata *f* (bother) || — MAR *drag anchor* ancla *f* flotante || *in drag* disfrazado de mujer || FAM *what a drag!* ¡qué lata!

drag [dræg] *vt* arrastrar (to haul or pull); *to drag a table* arrastrar una mesa; *to drag one's feet* arrastrar los pies || dragar, rastrear (river, lake, etc.) || AGR rastrillar || TECH engalgar, calzar (a wheel) || FAM dar la lata, dar el rollo (to bore) || FIG distraer, entretener (from one's work) || — *to drag along* arrastrar || FIG *to drag down* hundir; *to drag s.o. down* hundir a alguien || *to drag in* hacer entrar a la fuerza (sth., s.o.), traer por los cabellos (a subject) || *to drag on* arrastrar, llevar (one's life), alargar (a speech) || *to drag out* sacar; *to drag s.o. out of bed* sacar a alguien de la cama; dar largas a (an affair), arrastrar, llevar (one's life) || MAR *to drag the anchor* garrar || *to drag up* sacar (sth., s.o.), sacar a colación (an old story), dejar que se críe solo (a child).
◆ *vi* arrastrarse || rezagarse (to lag behind) || AGR rastrillar || hacerse largo; *this film is beginning to drag* esta película empieza a hacerse larga || MAR garrar (an anchor) || *to drag on* no acabar nunca, ser interminable, ir para largo.

dragging ['drægiŋ] *n* dragado *m*.

draggle ['drægl] *vt* manchar de barro.
◆ *vi* mancharse de barro || rezagarse (to lag behind).

draggletail ['drægltei1] *n* mujer *f* desarreglada (slut).

drag link ['drægliŋk] *n* barra *f* de acoplamiento.

dragnet ['drægnet] *n* red *f* barredera.

dragoman ['drægəumən] *n* dragomán *m*.

dragon ['drægən] *n* dragón *m* (mythical animal) || FIG arpía *f*, fiera *f* (fierce woman) || ZOOL *flying dragon* dragón *m* (reptile).

dragonfly [-flai] *n* ZOOL libélula *f*.

dragon tree [-tri:] *n* BOT drago *m*.

dragoon [drə'gu:n] *n* MIL dragón *m*.

dragoon [drə'gu:n] *vt* tiranizar || forzar, obligar (*into* a) (to bully s.o. into a course of action).

dragrope ['drægrəup] *n* cable *m* de arrastre (a towing rope) || freno *m* (for an aerostat).

dragster ['drægstə*] *n* coche *m* de carreras trucado.

drain [drein] *n* tubo *m* de desagüe, desaguadero *m* (pipe for carrying away water) || canal *m* de drenaje (for draining off water) || boca *f* de alcantarilla, sumidero *m* (inlet to a sewer) || MED tubo *m* de drenaje || TECH purga *f* || FIG sangría *f* (of money) | pérdida *f*, disminución *f* (of strength) || — FIG *brain drain* fuga *f* de cerebros || FAM *to throw money down the drain* tirar el dinero por la ventana.
◆ *pl* alcantarillado *m sing* (sewage system).

drain [drein] *vt* desaguar (to conduct water away from) || AGR avenar || secar (linen) || escurrir (bottles, etc.) || apurar, vaciar (to empty by drinking) || MED drenar (an abscess) || desecar (a marsh) || desaguar (mine) || TECH purgar (a cylinder, a machine) | vaciar (boilers) | descebar (a pump) || FIG agotar (resources, strength) || FAM *to drain s.o. dry* esquilmarle a uno.
◆ *vi* escurrirse (bottles, etc.) || desaguar (river).

drainage [-idʒ] *n* desagüe *m* || AGR avenamiento *m* || desecación *f* (of a marsh) || alcantarillado *m* (sewage system) || — GEOGR *drainage basin* cuenca hidrográfica || MED *drainage tube* tubo *m* de drenaje.

drainer [-ə*] *n* escurridero *m* || escurreplatos *m inv* (for dishes) || AGR avenador *m*.

draining [-iŋ] *n* desagüe *m* || AGR avenamiento *m* || desecación *f* (of a marsh).

draining board [-iŋbɔ:d] *n* escurridero *m*.

drainpipe ['dreinpaip] *n* tubo *m* de desagüe || FAM *drainpipe trousers* pantalones muy estrechos.

drake [dreik] *n* ZOOL pato *m* || mosca *f* (in fishing).

Dralon ['dreiln] *n* dralón *m* (registered trademark).

dram [dræm] *n* dracma *f* (weight) || FAM copita *f* (of alcoholic drink); *a dram of whisky* una copita de whisky | pizca *f* (bit).

drama ['drɑ:mə] *n* drama *m*; *lyric drama* drama lírico || FIG drama *m*.

dramatic [drə'mætik]; **dramatical** [-əl] *adj* dramático, ca; impresionante.

dramatically [-li] *adv* dramáticamente, impresionantemente.

dramatics [-s] *n* THEATR teatro *m* || FIG teatro *m* (dramatic behaviour).

dramatist ['dræmətist] *n* THEATR dramaturgo, ga.

dramatization; dramatisation [ˌdræmətai'zeiʃən] *n* dramatización *f*.

dramatize ['dræmətaiz] *vt* adaptar al teatro (to adapt a novel for a play) || FIG dramatizar.
◆ *vi* adaptarse al teatro.

dramaturge ['dræmətə:dʒ]; **dramaturgist** [-ist] *n* dramaturgo, ga.

dramaturgy ['dræməˌtə:dʒi] *n* dramaturgia *f*.

drank [dræŋk] *pret* → **drink.**

drape [dreip] *n* caída *f* (the manner of hanging); *the drape of a dress* la caída de un traje || colgadura *f* (hanging) || US cortina *f* (curtain).

drape [dreip] *vt* adornar con colgaduras, tapizar (to decorate) || cubrir; *walls draped with flags* muros cubiertos de banderas || drapear (a cloth) || ARTS disponer los ropajes || FAM *to drape o.s. in one's dignity* encasillarse en su dignidad.

draper ['dreiə*] *n* pañero, ra.

drapery ['dreipəri] *n* pañería *f* (draper's shop) || telas *f pl* (fabrics) || colgaduras *f pl*, tapices *m pl* (hangings) || ARTS ropaje *m* (of a statue) || drapeado *m* (artistic arrangement of clothing).

drastic ['dræstik] *adj* drástico, ca (measures, action, etc.) || importante (reduction) || MED drástico, ca.

drastically [-əli] *adv* de una manera drástica.

drat [dræt] *interj* FAM ¡caramba!

draught [drɑ:ft] *n* rastreo *m* (the act of dragging with a net) || redada *f* (amount of fish in a net) || tracción *f* (pulling of a vehicle) || sorbo *m*, trago *m* (act of drinking); *at a draught* de un trago || corriente *f* (current of air) || aire *m*; *to make draught with a fan* hacer aire con un abanico || tiro *m* (of a chimney) || MAR calado *m* || bosquejo *m* (a rough plan of work) || trazo *m* (in masonry) || dama *f*, pieza *f* (a piece in the game of draughts) || MED poción *f* || FIG & FAM *to feel a draught* sufrir las consecuencias.
◆ *pl* juego *m sing* de damas.
◆ *adj* de tiro (animals); *draught horse* caballo de tiro || de barril, a presión (drawn from a barrel); *draught beer* cerveza de barril.

draught [drɑ:ft] *vt* → **draft.**

draughtboard [-bɔ:d] *n* tablero *m* de damas.

draughtsman [-smən] *n* → **draftsman.**
— OBSERV El plural de esta palabra es *draughtsmen*.

draughtsmanship [-smənʃip] *n* dibujo *m* lineal.

draughty ['drɑ:fti] *adj* que tiene corrientes de aire.

Dravidian [drə'vidiən] *n* drávida *m* & *f*.

draw [drɔ:] *n* SP empate *m* (game or match that ends without a winner) || tablas *f pl* (in chess) || chupada *f*, calada *f* (smoking) || sorteo *m* (of lots) || lotería *f* (lottery) || tracción *f*, tiro *m* (of a horse, a vehicle) || tiro *m* (of a chimney) || CULIN infusión *f* || COMM artículo *m* de reclamo || obra *f* taquillera (play) || FAM atracción *f* (thing that attracts) || artilugios *m pl* para conseguir confidencias || TECH estirado *m* || US parte *f* movible de un puente levadizo (of a drawbridge) || — *draw works* torno *m* (in oil wells) || *quick on the draw* rápido en sacar la pistola.

draw* [drɔ:] *vt* tirar de; *to draw a cart* tirar de un carro || atraer (to attract); *to draw s.o.'s eye* atraer la mirada de alguien || FIG atraer (public) || extraer (to pull out, to extract) || limpiar, destripar; *to draw fish* limpiar el pescado || destripar, vaciar (fowl) || dibujar (to make a picture); *to draw in ink, in pencil, freehand, from nature, by gouache* dibujar con *or* a pluma, con *or* a lápiz, a mano alzada, del natural, a la aguada || trazar (a line) || levantar, hacer, trazar (a map) || trazar (to delineate in words); *the book's characters are well drawn* los personajes del libro están bien trazados || sacar; *to draw water from a well* sacar agua de un pozo; *to draw a nail* sacar un clavo; *to draw a tooth* sacar una muela; *to draw conclusions* sacar conclusiones; *to draw a confession from s.o.* sacar una confesión a alguien; *to draw profit from* sacar provecho de; *to draw money from a bank account* sacar dinero de una cuenta bancaria || formular, decir (an opinion, etc.) || hacer (comparisons) || JUR redactar (a document) || aspirar (to inhale) || tomar (breath) || estirar (to stretch) || alargar (a speech) || hacer madurar; *to draw an abscess* hacer madurar un absceso || acarrear, traer consigo (to entail) || llevar, incitar; *to draw s.o. into doing sth.* llevar a alguien a que haga algo || recibir, cobrar (to earn); *he draws a very high salary* recibe un salario muy elevado || librar, extender (a cheque) || girar, librar (a bill) || ganar, llevarse (a prize) || sortear (lots) || MAR calar, tener un calado de (a ship) || rastrear, batir (woods, etc.) || hinchar (to swell) || correr (to close curtains, a bolt) || descorrer (to open curtains, a bolt) || bajar (the blinds) || quitar (to take away) || desenfundar, sacar (pistol, knife) || desenvainar, sacar (sword) || tensar (a bow) || robar (a card from the pack) || arrastrar, hacer echar (trumps) || levantar (a drawbridge) || TECH estirar (a wire) | vaciar (a casting) | extraer, sacar (coal) || AUT remolcar, tirar de (a car) || hacer hablar; *to try to draw s.o.* intentar hacer hablar a alguien || fruncir, arrugar (the face) || MIL provocar (enemy fire) || — FIG *his face was drawn* tenía la cara cansada || *to draw a blank* llevarse un chasco || *to draw a distinction* o *a line between* distinguir entre, hacer una distinción entre || *to draw a game with* empatar con || *to draw attention* llamar *or* atraer la atención || *to draw blood* hacer sangrar || *to draw lots* sortear; *to draw lots for a bottle of wine* sortear una botella de vino; echar a suertes; *they drew lots to see who would go* echaron a suertes a ver quién iría || *to draw one's hand across one's forehead* pasarse la mano por la frente || *to draw s.o. from* apartar a alguien de || *to draw s.o. into conversation* entablar conversación con alguien || *to draw straws* echar pajas || *to draw tight* apretarse (the belt) || *to feel drawn to* sentirse atraído por.

◆ *vi* tirar (horse) || dibujar (pictures) || sortear (lots) || tirar (a chimney) || reposar (tea) || sacar el arma (the pistol) || SP empatar || hacer tablas (in chess) || dirigirse (*towards* hacia) || THEATR ser taquillero (a play) || — *to draw ahead* destacarse (a runner) || *to draw alongside* ponerse de costado || *to draw near to* acercarse a.

◆ *phr v* ***to draw apart*** separar | separarse || ***to draw aside*** apartar (sth.) | llamar aparte (s.o.) | descorrer (curtain) | apartarse || ***to draw asunder*** separar || ***to draw away*** llevarse | apartar (s.o. from sth.) | alejarse; *the car drew away* el coche se alejó | destacarse; *the favourite drew away from the rest of the runners* el favorito se destacó del resto de los corredores || ***to draw back*** retirar | descorrer (curtains) | retroceder (to move back) | FIG retirar (one's word), volverse atrás, echarse para atrás (to back down) || ***to draw down*** bajar (the blinds) || ***to draw forth*** hacer salir (s.o.) | sacar (sth.) | provocar (to provoke) | hacer saltar (tears) || ***to draw in*** tirar hacia dentro (s.o., sth.) | retraer (claws) | tirar de (reins) | aspirar (air) | entrar (to enter) | entrar en la estación (trains) | aparcar (a car) | acortarse, hacerse más cortos (days) | FIG comprometer || ***to draw off*** quitarse (one's shoes) | retirar (troops) | sacar (wine) | MED sacar (blood) | desviar, apartar (the attention) || ***to draw on*** ponerse (clothing) | incitar (to induce) | recurrir a; *to draw on one's imagination* recurrir a la imaginación | inspirarse en (to get one's ideas from) | ocasionar, causar (to cause) | pasar; *time draws on* el tiempo pasa | acercarse; *evening was drawing on* la noche se acercaba || ***to draw out*** sacar (sth.) | sacar, arrancar (a nail) | alargar, estirar (to stretch) | TECH estirar (a wire) | ARTS trazar (patterns, plan) | COMM sacar (money) | redactar (a document) | salir de la estación (trains) | FIG hacer durar, dar largas a (an affair), alargar, hacer durar (speech) | FAM hacer hablar, desatar la lengua (s.o.) || ***to draw to*** correr (curtains) || — *to draw to an end* llegar a su fin || ***to draw together*** juntar (two things) | unir (people) | unirse | reunirse || ***to draw up*** subir (a blind) | subirse, remangarse (sleeves, etc.) | acercar; *draw up a chair and sit down* acerca una silla y siéntate | redactar (a document) | preparar (the budget) | hacer (an account) | elaborar (a plan) | trazar (an itinerary) | MIL ordenar para el combate | TECH apretar (a nut) | sacar del agua (a boat) | acercarse (to get close) | pararse (to stop); *to draw up short* pararse en seco || — *to draw o.s. up* enderezarse (to straighten o.s.), incorporarse (in bed), erguirse (with pride) | *to draw up with s.o.* alcanzar a alguien || FIG ***to draw upon*** hacer uso de, valerse de.

— OBSERV Pret ***drew***; pp ***drawn***.

drawback ['drɔːbæk] *n* inconveniente *m* (*to* de) (shortcoming) || desventaja *f* (disadvantage) || COMM «drawback» *m*, reintegro *m* de los derechos de aduana pagados por las materias primas que sirvieron para productos de exportación, prima *f* a la exportación.

drawbar ['drɔːbɑː*] *n* barra *f* de tracción.

drawbench ['drɔːbentʃ] *n* TECH hilera *f*.

drawbridge ['drɔːbridʒ] *n* puente *m* levadizo.

drawee [drɔː'iː] *n* COMM girado *m*, librado *m*.

drawer ['drɔːə*] *n* dibujante *m* & *f* (artist) || cajón *m* (of table, sideboard, etc.) || COMM girador *m*, librador *m*.

◆ *pl* FAM calzoncillos *m* (underpants) || bragas *f* (knickers).

drawing ['drɔːiŋ] *n* dibujo *m* (picture, action); *charcoal, pencil, ink, freehand drawing* dibujo al carbón, a lápiz, a pluma, a mano alzada || extracción *f* (extraction) || TECH vaciado *m* (of casting) | estirado *m* (of wire) | extracción *f* (of coal) || COMM giro *m*; *drawing rights* derechos de giro || US sorteo *m* || — *drawing from nature* o *life* dibujo del natural || *mechanical drawing* dibujo industrial.

drawing account [-əˌkaunt] *n* US cuenta *f* de depósito a la vista.

drawing board [-bɔːd] *n* tablero *m* de dibujo || FIG *back to the drawing board* vuelta *f* a empezar.

drawing card [-kɑːd] *n* FAM atracción *f*.

drawing knife [-naif] *n* TECH plana *f*.

drawing mill [-mil] *n* trefilería *f*, fábrica *f* de alambre.

drawing paper [-ˌpeipə*] *n* papel *m* de dibujo.

drawing pen [-pen] *n* tiralíneas *m inv*.

drawing pin [-pin] *n* chincheta *f*, chinche *f*.

drawing room [-rum] *n* salón *m* (sitting room) || recepción *f* (formal reception).

drawing up [-ʌp] *n* redacción *f* || elaboración *f* (of a plan) || preparación *f* (of the budget).

drawknife ['drɔːnaif] *n* TECH plana *f*.

drawl [drɔːl] *n* voz *f* cansina.

drawl [drɔːl] *vi* hablar lenta y cansinamente, hablar con una voz cansina.

◆ *vt* arrastrar; *to drawl the words* arrastrar las palabras || decir con una voz cansina.

drawn [drɔːn] *pp* → **draw** || *drawn butter* mantequilla derretida.

drawn-out [-aut] *adj* FIG prolongado, da; interminable.

drawnwork [-wəːk] *n* calado *m*.

drawplate ['drɔːpleit] *n* TECH hilera *f*.

draw poker ['drɔː'pəukə*] *n* póker *m* cerrado.

drawshave ['drɔːʃeiv] *n* TECH plana *f*.

drawstring ['drɔːstriŋ] *n* cordón *m*, cinta *f* [que se pasa por una jareta].

dray [drei] *n* narria *f* (cart).

dray horse ['dreihɔːs] *n* caballo *m* de tiro.

drayman ['dreimən] *n* transportista *m*.

— OBSERV El plural de *drayman* es *draymen*.

dread [dred] *n* pavor *m*, terror *m* (great fear) || aprensión *f* (apprehension) || — *in dread of* con el temor de || *to be in dread of* tener temor *or* pavor a.

◆ *adj* espantoso, sa (dreadful).

dread [dred] *vt* temer, tener temor *or* pavor a || — *he dreads flying* le horroriza ir en avión || *to dread to think* no atreverse a pensar.

dreadful [-ful] *adj* espantoso, sa (fearful) || FIG horrible; *I've heard dreadful things about him* he oído cosas terribles acerca de él | malísimo, ma; fatal (very bad) || — FIG *how dreadful!* ¡qué horror! | *I feel dreadful about it* me da vergüenza.

dreadfully [-fuli] *adv* terriblemente; *dreadfully ugly* terriblemente feo || fatal (very badly) || *I'm dreadfully sorry* lo siento en el alma || *I was dreadfully frightened* tuve *or* pasé un miedo espantoso.

dreadlocks [-lɔks] *pl n* peinado *m* rafta.

dreadnought ['drednɔːt] *n* MAR acorazado *m*.

dream [driːm] *n* sueño *m* (when sleeping); *the dream came true* el sueño se volvió realidad || ensueño *m* (when awake) || FIG sueño *m*, ilusión *f* || — *bad dream* pesadilla *f* || *life's dream* sueño dorado || FIG *my greatest dream is to be a millionaire* el sueño de mi vida es ser millonario | *she was wearing a dream of a hat* llevaba un sueño de sombrero *or* un sombrero precioso || *sweet dreams!* ¡que sueñes con los angelitos! || *to be in a dream* estar soñando || *to see sth. in a dream* ver algo en sueños.

dream* [driːm] *vt/vi* soñar (*about, of* con) || FIG soñar; *to dream of wealth* soñar con riquezas | pensar; *to dream of one's youth* pensar en su juventud | imaginarse (to fancy) || — *I would not dream of doing it* no se me ocurriría hacerlo, no lo haría ni soñando || *to dream away* pasar soñando (one's time) || *to dream up* idear, inventar.

— OBSERV Pret y pp ***dreamed, dreamt***.

dreamer [-ə*] *n* soñador, ra.

dreamily ['driːmili] *adv* como si estuviera soñando.

dreamland ['driːmlænd] *n* país *m* de los sueños || mundo *m* de ensueño (lovely place).

dreamless ['driːmlis] *adj* sin sueños || sin ilusiones.

dreamlike ['driːmlaik] *adj* de ensueño.

dreamt [dremt] *pret/pp* → **dream.**

dreamworld ['driːmwəld] *n* mundo *m* de ensueño.

dreamy ['driːmi] *adj* soñador, ra (people) || vago, ga (vague) || de ensueño (delightful) || lleno de sueños (sleep) || *isn't it dreamy!* ¡qué preciosidad!

dreariness ['driərinis] *n* monotonía *f*, tristeza *f* (of life, etc.) || insipidez *f*, falta *f* de interés (of a book).

dreary ['driəri] *adj* monótono, na; triste (life, countryside) || insípido, da; sin interés (book) || aburrido, da (boring).

dredge [dredʒ] *n* draga *f*.

dredge [dredʒ] *vt* dragar (to clear a harbour, river) || espolvorear (to sprinkle) || FIG *to dredge up* sacar a luz.

◆ *vi* dragar (to use a dredge).

dredger [-ə*] *n* draga *f* (dredge) || espolvoreador *m* (for sprinkling flour, sugar, etc.).

dredging [-iŋ] *n* dragado *m* || *dredging machine* draga *f*.

dreg [dreg] *n* rastro *m*, resto *m* (small amount).

◆ *pl* poso *m sing*, heces *f* (of liquids) || FIG hez *f sing*; *the dregs of society* la hez de la sociedad; *he drained the cup to the dregs* apuró la copa hasta las heces.

drench [drentʃ] *n* VET pócima *f*, poción *f* || chaparrón *m*, aguacero *m* (of rain).

drench [drentʃ] *vt* empapar, calar (to soak) || VET administrar una pócima a || — *drenched in blood* bañado en sangre || *to be drenched to the skin* estar calado hasta los huesos.

dress [dres] *n* vestimenta *f* (attire) || ropa *f* (clothing) || vestido *m*, traje *m* (woman's frock) || traje *m*; *court dress* traje de corte || — *evening dress* traje de etiqueta (for men), traje de noche (for women) || *full dress* traje de etiqueta (for men), traje de noche (for women), uniforme de gala (for military men) || *morning dress* traje de calle (man), traje de casa (woman) || *wedding dress* traje de novia.

dress [dres] *vt* vestir (to put clothes on, to wear clothes); *to be dressed in silk* estar vestido *or* ir vestido de seda || decorar, arreglar (show windows) || adornar (to decorate) || peinar, arreglar (hair) || MIL alinear (troops) || MED vendar (a wound) || almohazar (a horse) || AGR abonar (soil) | cultivar (garden) | podar (fruit tree) || TECH adobar, curtir (skins) | labrar (stone) | aderezar, aprestar (cloth) | preparar (cotton, wool) | desbastar (timber) | cepillar (wood) || CULIN aderezar (food) | aliñar (salad) || MAR empavesar (a ship) || — FAM *dressed to kill* de tiros largos, de punta en blanco | *to be dressed up to the nines* estar de punta en blanco | *to dress down* echar un rapapolvo (to scold), pegar una paliza (to thrash) || *to dress one's hair* peinarse || *to dress out* ataviar || *to dress up* vestir, poner de tiros largos || *to dress up as* disfrazar de || *to get dressed* vestirse, arreglarse.
◆ *vi* vestirse, vestir; *to dress with taste* vestirse con gusto || vestirse (on a ceremonial occasion) || MIL alinearse || — *to dress up* vestirse, ponerse de tiros largos || *to dress up as* disfrazarse de.

dressage ['dresɑːʒ] *n* doma *f* clásica (of a horse).

dress ball [-bɔːl] *n* baile *m* de etiqueta.

dress circle [-'səːkl] *n* THEATR piso *m* principal.

dress coat [-'kəut] *n* frac *m*.

dress designer [-diˌzainə*] *n* modelista *m* & *f*.

dresser ['dresə*] *n* aparador *m* (cupboard) || THEATR camarero, ra (person who helps an actor) || MED ayudante *m* (surgeon's assistant) || MIN punterola *f* || TECH adobador *m* (of skins) || US tocador *m*, coqueta *f* (dressing table).

dressing ['dresiŋ] *n* vestir *m*, vestirse *m* (act) || ropa *f* (clothes) || MED vendaje *m* (for an injury) || CULIN aliño *m* (for food, salad, etc.) || AGR abono *m* (fertilizer) || MAR empavesado *m* || MIL formación *f* (of troops) || TECH adobo *m*, curtido *m* (of skins) | labrado *m* (of stone) | aderezo *m*, apresto *m* (of cloth) | preparación *f* (of cotton, wool) | desbaste *m* (of timber) | cepilladura *f* (of wood).

dressing case [-keis] *n* neceser *m*.

dressing down [-'daun] *n* FAM rapapolvo *m* (talking-to); *to give s.o. a dressing down* echar un rapapolvo a alguien | paliza *f* (thrashing).

dressing gown [-gaun] *n* bata *f*.

dressing room [-rum] *n* tocador *m*, cuarto *m* de vestir (in a house) || THEATR camerino *m*, camarín *m*.

dressing station [-ˌsteiʃən] *n* MIL puesto *m* de socorro.

dressing table [-ˌteibl] *n* tocador *m*, coqueta *f*.

dressmaker ['dresˌmeikə*] *n* modista *m* & *f*.

dressmaking ['dresˌmeikiŋ] *n* costura *f*.

dress rehearsal ['dresri'həːsəl] *n* ensayo *m* general.

dress shield ['dresʃiːld] *n* sobaquera *f*.

dress shirt ['dresʃəːt] *n* camisa *f* de frac.

dress suit ['dressjuːt] *n* traje *m* de etiqueta.

dress uniform ['dres'juːnifɔːm] *n* MIL uniforme *m* de gala.

dressy ['dresi] *adj* elegante || *a dressy gown* un traje de vestir.

drew [druː] *pret* → **draw.**

dribble ['dribl] *n* goteo *m* (of a liquid) || SP regate *m*, drible *m*, finta *f* || llovizna *f* (rain).

dribble ['dribl] *vi* babear (babies) || gotear (to trickle) || SP driblar, regatear.
◆ *vt* derramar *or* dejar caer gota a gota (to cause to flow in a trickle) || SP driblar con, regatear con.

driblet; dribblet ['driblit] *n* pequeña cantidad *f* || *by* o *in driblets* poco a poco.

dribs [dribz] *pl n* *in dribs and drabs* poco a poco, en pequeñas cantidades.

dried [draid] *adj* seco, ca || seco, ca; paso, sa (fruit).

drier; dryer ['draiə*] *n* secador *m* (device) || secadora *f* (machine for drying clothes) || tendedero *m* (rack for drying clothes) || TECH secadero *m* || secante *m* (for painting).

drift [drift] *n* arrastramiento *m*, arrastre *m* (process of being driven by the wind) || MAR & AVIAT deriva *f* || ventisquero *m* (of snow) || nube *f* (of dust) || ráfaga *f* (of rain) || montón *m* (of sand, etc.) || desplazamiento *m*, movimiento *m* (of people) || significado *m* (meaning) || propósito *m*, objetivo *m* (purpose) || curso *m* (of affairs) || tendencia *f* (trend) || MIL desviación *f* (of a shell or projectile) || ARCH empuje *m* horizontal (of an arch) || GEOL terrenos *m pl* de acarreo (debris accumulated by water) | derrubios *m pl* depositados por los glaciares (debris accumulated by ice) | deriva *f* (of continents) || MAR corriente *f* oceánica (current) | velocidad *f* (speed of a current) | dirección *f* (course of a current) || TECH punzón *m* | botador *m* de roblones (for rivets) || — MAR *drift anchor* ancla *f* flotante || *drift angle* ángulo *m* de deriva || *drift sand* arena movediza || *I get the drift of it* lo entiendo || *the drift from the land* el éxodo rural, el abandono del campo.

drift [drift] *vi* ser arrastrado por la corriente (to be carried by a current of water or wind) || derivar, ir a la deriva (to be carried off course) || amontonarse (sand, snow) || FIG ir a la deriva, vivir sin rumbo (to live without aim) | encaminarse, tender (questions, events) || — *to drift along* vagar || *to drift around* pasearse || *to drift in* llegar || *to drift off* dormirse lentamente || *to drift with the current* dejarse llevar por la corriente || *to let things drift* dejarse llevar por los acontecimientos.
◆ *vt* empujar, llevar (to carry along) || empujar (clouds) || amontonar (sand, snow) || acarrear (downstream) || conducir en armadía (wood) || TECH escariar.

drifter [-ə*] *n* trainera *f* (fishing boat) || FIG vagabundo *m* (aimless person).

drift net [-net] *n* MAR traína *f*, red *f* barredera.

driftpin ['driftpin] *n* mandril *m*.

driftwood ['driftwud] *n* madera *f* flotante.

drill [dril] *n* instrucción *f* (training, instruction) || ejercicios *m pl* (series of exercises) || TECH taladro *m*, broca *f*, barrena *f* (tool for boring holes) | berbiquí *m* (brace) | taladradora *f* (machine) | fresa *f* (of a dentist) || MIN barrena *f* | perforadora *f*, trépano *m* (in oil prospecting) || AGR surco *m* (furrow) | hilera *f* (row of seeds or plants) | sembradora *f* (machine for sowing) || dril *m* (cotton fabric) || dril *m* (monkey) || FAM manera *f*; *what is the drill for doing this?* ¿cuál es la manera de hacer esto? || — *drill chuck* portabroca *f* || *drill press* perforadora *f*.

drill [dril] *vt* MIL enseñar la instrucción a, ejercitar || enseñar por medio de ejercicios o repeticiones (to teach) || FIG entrenar (to train) || TECH taladrar (to bore holes in) | perforar (a well) | sondear, perforar (looking for oil, etc.) | hacer (a hole) || AGR sembrar en hileras (to sow).
◆ *vi* hacer un agujero || TECH perforar || MIL hacer la instrucción || hacer ejercicios (to do exercises) || FIG entrenarse (to train).

drilling ['driliŋ] *n* perforación *f* (boring) || MIL instrucción *f*.

drily; dryly ['draili] *adv* secamente || con guasa, con un tono guasón; *to answer drily* contestar con un tono guasón.

drink [driŋk] *n* bebida *f* (liquid to be consumed) || copa *f* (alcoholic liquid); *to stand s.o. a drink* convidar a alguien a una copa; *I took a drink* tomé una copa || algo de beber; *would you like a drink?* ¿quieres algo de beber? || vaso *m* (of water, milk) || bebida *f* (excessive drinking); *drink will be the death of you* la bebida será tu perdición || FIG mar *m* (sea) || — *after-dinner drink* licor *m*, copa *f* || *long drink* bebida larga || *soft drink* bebida no alcohólica *or* sin alcohol || *strong drink* bebida alcohólica || *to have a drink* tomar algo || *to take to drink* darse a la bebida.

drink* [driŋk] *vt/vi* beber (beer, water, etc.); *to drink from the bottle* beber de la botella || absorber (plants) || beber (to be an habitual drinker) || tomar; *would you like something to drink?* ¿quieres tomar algo?; *I never drink tea* nunca tomo té; *to drink the waters* tomar las aguas || FIG beberse; *to drink one's wages* beberse todo lo que se gana || brindar por (to toast) || — FIG *to drink away* beberse (one's fortune), ahogar (one's sorrows) || *to drink down* beber de un trago || *to drink hard* beber mucho || FIG *to drink in* beber, beberse || FIG & FAM *to drink like a fish* beber como una esponja *or* como un cosaco || *to drink off* beber de un trago || *to drink o.s. into debt* beberse la fortuna || *to drink s.o. under the table* aguantar más bebiendo que otro || *to drink to* brindar por, beber a la salud de || *to drink up* bebérselo todo; terminar de beber.
— OBSERV Pret ***drank***, pp ***drunk***.

drinkable ['driŋkəbl] *adj* potable, bebible.
◆ *pl n* FAM bebida *f sing*.

drink-driving [dr'iŋdraiviŋ] *n* delito *m* por conducir en estado de embriaguez.

drinker ['driŋkə*] *n* bebedor, ra.

drinking ['driŋkiŋ] *n* beber *m* (act); *excessive drinking can have bad consequences* el beber en exceso puede tener malas consecuencias || FIG bebida *f*; *to take to drinking* darse a la bebida.

drinking bout [-baut] *n* juerga *f*, orgía *f*, borrachera *f*.

drinking fountain [-fauntin] *n* fuente *f* de agua potable.

drinking song [-sɔŋ] *n* canción *f* báquica.

drinking trough [-trɔf] *n* bebedero *m*, abrevadero *m* (water trough).

drinking-up time [-ʌpˌtaim] *n* hora *f* de acabarse las bebidas y marcharse (en un pub).

drinking water [-ˌwɔːtə*] *n* agua *f* potable.

drip [drip] *n* goteo *m* (a falling in drops) || gota *f* (drop) || ARCH goterón *m* || FAM tonto *m*, mentecato *m* (simpleton) | pelma *m*, pesado *m* (bore).

drip [drip] *vi* gotear (to fall in drops) || chorrear (to be soaked).
◆ *vt* dejar caer gota a gota.

drip-dry ['drip'drai] *adj* que seca rápidamente y no necesita planchado.

drip-feed ['dripˌfiːd] *vt* alimentar con gota a gota *or* suero.

dripping ['dripiŋ] *n* goteo *m* (act) || gotas *f pl* (drops) || CULIN grasa *f*, pringue *f* (from meat).
◆ *adj* que gotea || — *dripping with perspiration* bañado en sudor || *to be dripping wet* estar calado hasta los huesos.

dripping pan [-pæn] *n* CULIN grasera *f*.

dripping tube [-tjuːb] *n* cuentagotas *m inv*.

dripstone ['dripstəun] *n* ARCH goterón *m*.

drive [draiv] *n* vuelta *f* en coche, paseo *m* en coche (short ride) || excursión *f* (round trip) ||

viaje *m* (journey) || trayecto *m*; *it's an hour's drive* es un trayecto de una hora || ojeo *m*, batida *f* (in hunting) || conducción *f* del ganado (of cattle) || MIL ofensiva *f* (major offensive) || FIG vigor *m*, energía *f*, empuje *m* (energy) | expansión *f* (of a nation) | campaña *f* (campaign) | apremio *m* (pressure) | instinto *m*, impulso *m*; *the sex drive* el instinto sexual || SP «drive» *m*, pelota *f* rasante (in tennis) | «drive» *m* (in golf) || AUT tracción *f*; *front-wheel drive* tracción delantera | conducción *f* [AMER manejo *m*]; *right-hand drive* conducción a la derecha || TECH transmisión *f* | propulsión *f* || camino *m* de entrada (private road, parking space in front of a garage) || calle *f* (road) || camino *m* (through a forest) || flotación *f* (floating of logs) || armadía *f* (floating logs) || torneo *m* (of bridge, etc.) || — AUT *direct drive* directa *f* | *drive belt, gear, shaft* correa *f*, engranaje *m*, eje *m* de transmisión | *to go for a drive* ir a dar una vuelta en coche.

drive* [draiv] *vt* conducir [AMER manejar] (to control a vehicle) || llevar (to convey in a vehicle) || recorrer (a distance) || llevar (wind, water) || guiar, llevar, conducir (cattle) || empujar (to push forward) || arrojar; *the sea drove the ship on to the rocks* el mar arrojó el barco contra las rocas || echar (to force a person to leave); *to drive s.o. from o out of the house* echar a alguien de la casa || asestar (a blow) || lanzar (a projectile) || COMM tratar (business) | cerrar; *to drive a bargain* cerrar un trato | ejercer (a trade) || SP mandar (a ball) || ojear, batir (in hunting) || FIG hacer trabajar mucho (to make work hard) | conducir, llevar; *to drive s.o. to despair* llevar a alguien a la desesperación | empujar; *his bad luck drove him to drink* su mala suerte le empujó a la bebida | forzar, obligar (to compel) | aplazar (to postpone) || TECH abrir, perforar; *to drive a tunnel* abrir un túnel | construir (to build a railway, road, etc.) | hacer funcionar, poner en movimiento, accionar (a machine) | clavar (a nail) | apretar (a nut) | hacer (a hole) | hincar; *to drive a stake into the ground* hincar una estaca en el suelo | meter, hacer entrar, introducir (to put in) || — *to drive an idea out of s.o.'s mind* sacarle a uno una idea de la cabeza || FIG *to drive a point home* remachar el clavo || *to drive a way through* abrirse paso por || *to drive into a corner* acorralar || *to drive s.o. mad* volverle a uno loco || *to drive s.o. wild* sacarle a uno de sus casillas || *to drive sth. into s.o.'s head* meterle a uno algo en la cabeza || SP *to drive the ball* jugar una pelota rasante (in tennis).

◆ *vi* ir en coche (to travel by car); *to drive to a place* ir en coche a un sitio || conducir [AMER manejar]; *can you drive?* ¿sabes conducir? || golpear, azotar; *the snow was driving against the windows* la nieve azotaba los cristales || TECH entrar (a nail) || MAR derivar || SP dar el «drive» (golf) | jugar una pelota rasante (tennis).

◆ *phr v* *to drive at* insinuar, querer decir (to mean) | pretender (to aim at) | consagrarse intensamente a (a work) | dirigirse hacia (in a car) || — *to let drive at* asestar un golpe a || ***to drive away*** alejar, apartar (s.o., sth.) | irse (en coche) || ***to drive back*** hacer retroceder | acompañar en coche; *I'll drive you back to your house* te acompañaré en coche a tu casa | volver *or* regresar en coche (to return by car) || ***to drive by*** pasar (por) || ***to drive in*** entrar (by car) | clavar (nail, dagger) || ***to drive into*** atropellar (s.o.) | chocar contra (a tree, etc.) | entrar en (a garage) || ***to drive off*** alejar, apartar | irse en coche || ***to drive on*** seguir su camino || ***to drive out*** echar | hacer salir (to oblige to come out) | sacar (a nail) | salir en coche || ***to drive over*** atropellar; *to drive over a dog* atropellar un perro | ir en coche (to go by car) || ***to drive through*** pasar (por) || ***to drive up*** acercarse (to approach) | llegar (to arrive).

— OBSERV Pret ***drove***; pp ***driven***.

drive-in-cinema ['draivin'sinəmə] *n* cine *m* donde se ven las películas desde el coche.

drive-in bank ['draivin'bæŋk] *n* banco *m* donde se atiende a los clientes sin que bajen de su coche.

drive-in restaurant ['draivin'restərɔ̃ŋ] *n* restaurante *m* donde sirven a los clientes sin que bajen del coche.

drivel ['drivəl] *n* tonterías *f pl*; *to talk drivel* decir tonterías.

drivel ['drivl] *vi* babear (to slaver) || FAM decir tonterías || *to drivel away* malgastar (time).

driven ['drivn] *pp* —→ **drive.**

driver ['draivə*] *n* conductor, ra; chófer *m* (person who drives a car, bus) || camionero *m* (of lorries) || maquinista *m* (of trains) || taxista *m* & *f* (of taxi) || corredor *m*, piloto *m* (of racing car) || cochero *m* (of coach) || TECH rueda *f* motriz || *driver's licence* permiso *m* de conducir *or* de conducción, carnet *m* de conducir.

driveway ['draivwei] *n* camino *m* de entrada (leading to the street) || camino *m* (way) || calle *f* (street).

driveway ['draivwei] *n* camino *m* de entrada (leading to the street) || camino *m* (way) || calle *f* (street).

driving [draiviŋ] *n* conducción *f* [AMER manejo *m*]; *driving lesson* lección de conducción || TECH transmisión *f*; *driving belt* correa de transmisión || — FIG *driving force* fuerza *f* motriz || *driving instructor* profesor, ra de autoescuela || *driving licence* permiso *m* de conducción *or* de conducir, carnet *m* de conducir || *driving mirror* retrovisor *m* || *driving school* autoescuela *f* || *driving test* examen *m* para sacar el carnet de conducir || *driving wheel* rueda motriz.

◆ *adj* torrencial (rain).

drizzle ['drizl] *n* llovizna *f*.

drizzle ['drizl] *vi* lloviznar.

droit [drɔit] *n* JUR derecho *m* (right).

droll [drəul] *adj* divertido, da (amusing) || extraño, ña; raro, ra (odd).

drollery ['drəuləri] *n* gracia *f* (act, quality, remark).

dromedary ['drʌmədəri] *n* ZOOL dromedario *m*.

drone [drəun] *n* ZOOL zángano *m* (male bee) || AVIAT avión *m* teledirigido || MUS roncón *m* (pipe of a bagpipe) | gaita *f* (bagpipe) || zumbido *m* (noise made by bees, aircraft, machinery, etc.) || murmullo *m* (of people, voices, etc.) || FAM zángano *m*, holgazán *m*, vago *m* (loafer) || MUS *drone bass* bajo continuo.

drone [drəun] *vt* murmurar, ronronear || *to drone away* malgastar (time).

◆ *vi* murmurar (people) || zumbar (bees, machinery, etc.) || FAM holgazanear || *to drone on* hablar monótonamente.

drool [dru:l] *n* tonterías *f pl*.

◆ *vi* babear || FIG *to drool over* caérsele a uno la baba por.

droop [dru:p] *n* inclinación *f* (of head) || caída *f* (of eyelids) || encorvamiento *m* (of shoulders) || caída *f* (of branches, trees) || FIG languidez *f*.

droop [dru:p] *vi* inclinarse (to hang down) || caerse (eyelids) || estar encorvado (people) || marchitarse (flowers) || FIG debilitarse (to lose strength) | desanimarse (to become dispirited) | decaer (to decline).

◆ *vt* inclinar (head) || bajar (eyelids) || encorvar (shoulders).

drooping [-iŋ] *adj* inclinado, da (head) || bajado, da (eyes) || caído, da (shoulders) || gacho, cha; caído, da (ears) || marchito, ta (flower) || FIG lánguido, da | abatido, da.

drop [drɔp] *n* gota *f* (of blood, rain, sweat, water) || colgante *m* (of chandelier) || pendiente *m* [AMER arete *m*] (earring) || colgante *m*, dije *m* (of necklace) || pastilla *f* (sweet) || gota *f*, pizca *f* (a bit) || FAM gota *f*, poquito *m* (small amount of drink) | gota *f* (small amount of rain) || caída *f* (fall) || bajada *f* (in pressure, voltage, etc.) || baja *f* (in prices) || descenso *m*, baja *f* (in temperature) || disminución *f* (in values, sales, etc.) || pendiente *f*, bajada *f* (slope); *there is a drop from the hill to the valley* hay una pendiente de la colina al valle || desnivel *m* (sudden descent, difference in level) || precipicio *m* (abyss) || altura *f* (the height of fall) || MED gota *f*; *drop by drop* gota a gota || THEATR telón *m* (curtain) || trampa *f* (of gallows) | caída *f* (of a person being hung) || descenso *m* (of a parachute) || lanzamiento *m* (of sth. by parachute) || MIL aprovisionamiento *m* aéreo || TECH escudo *m* (of a lock) || SP botepronto *m* (kick) || — FIG *a drop in the ocean* o *in a bucket* una gota de agua en el mar | *at the drop of a hat* en seguida (at once), con cualquier pretexto (on the least pretext) | *to get* o *to have the drop on* llevar la delantera a | *to have had a drop too much* haber bebido más de la cuenta | *to take a drop* tomar una gota *or* un trago.

drop [drɔp] *vt* dejar caer (to let fall); *I dropped the handkerchief* dejé caer el pañuelo || soltar (to let go off); *he dropped the hot plate* soltó el plato hirviendo || echar gota a gota (a liquid) || derramar (tears) || dejar escapar [un punto] (to miss a stitch in knitting) || echar (a letter) || derribar (to knock down) || FIG dejar de (to give up a habit); *I have to drop smoking* tengo que dejar de fumar | dejar (conversation, friend, work) | interrumpir (to break off a conversation) | renunciar a (an idea) | echar, expulsar (to throw out) || soltar (to say); *to drop a coarse word* soltar un taco || dejar; *I'll drop you at the station* te dejaré en la estación || lanzar [en paracaídas] (to land by parachute) || bajar (eyes, voice, prices, hem); *they dropped their eyes* bajaron la mirada || THEATR bajar (the curtain) || ZOOL parir (to give birth to) || MATH trazar, tirar (to draw a line) || MIL lanzar (bombs) || perder (points, games) || SP marcar, meter (to score a goal) | dar al botepronto a (a ball) || FIG comerse (not to pronounce in speech) | no usar, omitir; *cases in which the article is dropped* casos en que el artículo no se usa || despegarse de (to leave behind, to advance ahead of) || FAM perder (money) | cargarse (to kill) || MAR echar (anchor) || AUT rebajar (the chassis) || — US FAM *to drop a brick* meter la pata, cometer una pifia || *to drop a curtsey* hacer una reverencia || *to drop a hint* tirar *or* soltar una indirecta || *to drop a line* o *a card* poner unas líneas *or* una postal a alguien.

◆ *vi* caerse, caer (to fall); *he dropped dead* se cayó muerto || dejarse caer (to flop down) || caerse de cansancio, desplomarse (from exhaustion) || gotear (to drip) || bajar (temperature, prices, voice, etc.) || disminuir, bajar (value, sales, etc.) || amainar (wind) || bajar, descender (ground) || acabarse, terminarse (conversation) | escaparse (remark) || — *to drop around* o *by* o *over* pasar || *to drop asleep* quedarse dormido || *to drop away* irse uno tras otro (persons), disminuir (to diminish), quedarse atrás (a runner) || *to drop behind* quedarse atrás || *to drop in on s.o.* pasar por casa de alguien || *to drop into the habit of* coger la costumbre de || *to drop off* caer (leaves), disminuir (to diminish), caerse, desprenderse (part), dormirse (to fall asleep), morir (to die) | FIG *to drop on* reñir (to scold) || *to drop on one's knees* caer de rodillas || *to drop out* dejar caer (sth.), omitir (a syllabe, a name, etc.), abandonar, retirarse (of a contest), desaparecer (letter), irse; *it has dropped out of my mind* se me ha ido de la cabeza ‖ *to drop to the rear* quedarse atrás, dejarse adelantar.

drop curtain ['drɔp,kəːtn] *n* THEATR telón *m*.

drop-forge ['drɔp'fɔːdʒ] *vt* forjar a martillo.

drop hammer ['drɔp,hæmə*] *n* martillo *m* pilón.

dropkick ['drɔpkik] *n* botepronto *m*.

drop leaf ['drɔpliːf] *n* ala *f* abatible (of a table).

droplet ['drɔplit] *n* gotita *f*.

droplight ['drɔplait] *n* ELECTR lámpara *f* transportable.

dropout ['drɔpaut] *n* abandono *m* ‖ US estudiante que abandona la universidad antes de graduarse | marginado, da (hippies, etc.).

dropper ['drɔpə*] *n* MED cuentagotas *m inv*.

dropping ['drɔpiŋ] *n* caída *f* (fall) ‖ MED descendimiento *m* (of womb) ‖ parto *m* (of an animal).
◆ *pl* gotas *f* (drops) ‖ migas *f* (of food, etc.) ‖ excrementos *m* (of animals), cagadas *f* (of birds, mice, etc.), cagarrutas *f* (of sheep, goats, etc.), cagajones *m* (of horses, donkeys, etc.).
◆ *adj* goteante, chorreante (dripping).

drop press ['drɔppres] *n* martillo *m* pilón (drop hammer).

drop shot ['drɔpʃɔt] *n* SP dejada *f* (in tennis).

dropsical ['drɔpsikəl] *adj* MED hidrópico, ca ‖ FIG hinchado, da.

dropsy ['drɔpsi] *n* MED hidropesía *f*.

dross [drɔs] *n* TECH escoria *f*.

drought [draut]; **drouth** [drauθ] *n* sequía *f*.

drove [drəuv] *n* manada *f* (herd of cattle) ‖ cincel *m* (chisel).
◆ *pl* FIG manadas *f*; *in droves* a manadas.

drove [drəuv] *pret* ⟶ **drive.**

drover [-ə*] *n* boyero *m*, vaquero *m*.

drown [draun] *vi* ahogarse.
◆ *vt* ahogar (to kill by suffocation) ‖ anegar (to flood) ‖ FIG anegar, bañar; *eyes drowned in tears* ojos anegados en lágrimas | ahogar; *words drowned by applause* palabras ahogadas por los aplausos ‖ — FIG *to drown one's sorrows* ahogar sus penas ‖ *to drow o.s.* ahogarse ‖ FIG *we were drowned in letters* fuimos inundados de cartas.

drowse [drauz] *vi* estar medio dormido, da; estar adormecido, da ‖ *to drowse off* adormecerse.
◆ *vt* adormecer ‖ *to drowse away one's time* pasar el tiempo dormitando.

drowsiness [-inis] *n* somnolencia *f*, modorra *f* ‖ FIG apatía *f*.

drowsy [-i] *adj* soñoliento, ta (sleepy) ‖ soporífero, ra (lulling) ‖ FIG apático, ca (apathetic).

drub [drʌb] *vt* apalear (to cudgel) ‖ pegar una paliza (to trash) ‖ FIG derrotar, pegar una paliza (fam) (to defeat overwhelmingly) ‖ *to drub sth. into s.o.* meter algo en la cabeza de alguien.

drubbing [-iŋ] *n* paliza *f* (beating) ‖ FIG derrota *f*, paliza *f* (fam) (defeat).

drudge [drʌdʒ] *n* FAM esclavo *m* [del hogar o del trabajo].

drudge [drʌdʒ] *vi* apencar, currelar (to work).

drudgery ['drʌdʒəri] *n* trabajo *m* pesado.
— OBSERV Esta palabra nunca va precedida por el artículo indefinido *a*.

drug [drʌg] *n* medicamento *m*, medicina *f* (medicament) ‖ droga *f* (narcotic) ‖ FIG *drug on the market* artículo *m* imposible de vender.

drug [drʌg] *vt* drogar (s.o.) ‖ echar una droga en (a drink) ‖ — FIG *to be drugged with* estar harto de ‖ *to drug o.s.* drogarse.

drug abuse [-ə,bjuːs] *n* consumo *m* abusivo de drogas.

drug addict [-ædikt] *n* toxicómano, na; drogadicto, ta.

drug addiction [-ə,dikʃən] *n* toxicomanía *f*.

druggist ['drʌgist] *n* farmacéutico, ca.

drugstore ['drʌgstɔː*] *n* US farmacia *f* (a chemist's) | «drugstore» *m*, almacén *m* donde se venden productos farmacéuticos, comestibles, tabacos, periódicos, etc.

druid ['druːid] *n* druida *m*.

drum [drʌm] *n* MUS tambor *m* ‖ bidón *m* (metal container) ‖ ANAT tímpano *m* ‖ TECH tambor *m* (cylinder) | tambor *m*, cilindro *m* (of a revolver) | bobina *f*, carrete *m* (in electricity) ‖ ARCH tambor *m* ‖ tamborileo *m*, repiqueteo *m* (sound) ‖ — MUS *bass drum* bombo *m* ‖ MIL *drum major* tambor mayor ‖ *drum roll* redoble *m* de tambor ‖ FIG *to beat the drum for* dar bombo a.
◆ *pl* batería *f sing* (in an orchestra).

drum [drʌm] *vt/vi* MUS tocar el tambor ‖ FIG tamborilear con; *to drum one's fingers* tamborilear con los dedos ‖ — FIG *to drum out* expulsar | *to drum sth. into s.o.'s ears* machacar los oídos de alguien con algo | *to drum sth. into s.o.'s head* meterle a alguien algo en la cabeza | *to drum up* conseguir (support, trade).

drumbeat ['drʌmbiːt] *n* MUS toque *m* del tambor.

drumfire ['drʌm,faiə*] *n* MIL fuego *m* graneado.

drumhead ['drʌmhed] *n* MUS piel *f*, parche *m* [del tambor] ‖ *drumhead court-martial* consejo *m* de guerra sumarísimo.

drummer ['drʌmə*] *n* MUS tambor *m* (in a band) | batería *m* (in a group) ‖ US viajante *m* de comercio.

drumming ['drʌmiŋ] *n* tamborileo *m*.

drumstick ['drʌmstik] *n* palillo *m* de tambor (for drum) ‖ muslo *m* de ave (of birds) ‖ FAM zanca *f* (leg).

drunk [drʌŋk] *pp/adj* ⟶ **drink** ‖ borracho, cha (through drinking) ‖ FIG ebrio, a; *drunk with happiness* ebrio de alegría ‖ — *drunk and disorderly* que se comporta escandalosamente a causa de la embriaguez (person), escandaloso, sa a causa de la embriaguez (conduct) ‖ FAM *to be as drunk as a lord* estar borracho como una cuba ‖ *to be drunk on brandy* haberse emborrachado con coñac, estar borracho de coñac ‖ *to get drunk* emborracharse.
◆ *n* borracho, cha (drunk person) ‖ US juerga *f*; *to go on a drunk* irse de juerga.

drunkard [-əd] *n* borracho, cha.

drunken [-ən] *adj* borracho, cha; *a drunken man* un hombre borracho ‖ de borrachos (of drunkards) ‖ de embriaguez; *drunken state* estado de embriaguez.

drunkenness [-ənnis] *n* embriaguez *f*, borrachera *f*.

drupe [druːp] *n* BOT drupa *f*.

druse [druːz] *n* MIN drusa *f*.

dry [drai] *adj* seco, ca (not wet; arid, etc.) ‖ firme: *dry land* tierra firme ‖ para áridos (measure) ‖ seco, ca; desecado, da (leaf, wood) ‖ seca (a cow) ‖ seco, ca (wine, bread) ‖ FIG sin inspiración, acabado, da: *a dry poet* un poeta sin inspiración | aburrido, da (boring): *this book is very dry* este libro es muy aburrido | agudo, da (wit, etc.) | sediento, ta; seco, ca (thirsty) | árido, da (a subject) | simple (simple): *dry facts* hechos simples | seco, ca (answer, character, style) ‖ ELECTR seco, ca: *dry battery* o *cell* pila seca ‖ COMM líquido, da (money) ‖ de práctica (shooting) ‖ US prohibicionista (country) ‖ — *dry fly* mosca *f* flotante [para pescar] ‖ US *dry goods* mercería *f* ‖ CHEM *dry ice* nieve carbónica ‖ US *dry law* ley seca ‖ *dry nurse* ama seca ‖ *I am dry* tengo sed ‖ FAM *not to be dry behind the ears yet* tener la leche en los labios ‖ *to go dry* secarse ‖ *to run dry* secarse, agotarse.
◆ *n* US FAM prohibicionista *m* & *f*.

dry [drai] *vt* secar ‖ secar, agotar (a well) ‖ CULIN desuerar (butter) | poner a secar (fruit) ‖ *to dry up* secar completamente.
◆ *vi* secarse ‖ secarse, agotarse (to run dry) ‖ *to dry up* secarse completamente (to become dry), callarse (to be quiet); *dry up!* ¡cállate!

dryad ['draiəd] *n* MYTH dríada *f*, dríade *f*.

dryasdust ['draiəz,dʌst] *adj* aburrídisimo, ma.

dry-clean ['drai'kliːn] *vt* limpiar en seco.

dry cleaner [-ə*] *n* tintorero, ra ‖ *dry cleaner's* tintorería *f*, tinte *m*.

dry cleaning [-iŋ] *n* limpieza *f* en seco.

dryer [draiə*] *n* ⟶ **drier.**

dry-eyed ['drai'aid] *adj* sin lágrimas.

dry farm ['drai'fɑːm] *n* finca *f* de secano.

dry farming [-iŋ] *n* cultivo *m* de secano.

dry ginger ['drɑi,dʒindʒə*] *n* ginger-ale *m* seco.

dryly ['draili] *adv* ⟶ **drily.**

dryness [drainis] *n* sequedad *f*.

dry point ['draipɔint] *n* punta *f* seca (needle for engraving) ‖ grabado *m* con punta seca (engraving).

dry rot ['drai'rɔt] *n* putrefacción *f* de la madera ‖ FIG putrefacción *f*, desintegración *f*.

dry run ['drɑirʌn] *n* ensayo *m*.

dry-salt ['drai'sɔːlt] *vt* salar (meat).

dry-shod ['drai'ʃɔd] *adj/adv* a pie enjuto.

dry-stone wall ['drɑistəun,wɔːl] *n* pared *f* or muro *m* de piedra (without cement).

dry wash ['drai'wɔʃ] *n* ropa *f* lavada pero no planchada.

DTI *abbr of [Department of Trade and Industry]* ministerio británico de industria y comercio.

dual ['djuəl] *adj* doble; *dual citizenship* doble nacionalidad; *dual ignition* encendido doble; *dual personality* doble personalidad ‖ GRAMM dual.
◆ *n* GRAMM dual *m*.

dual control [-kən'trəul] *n* doble mando *m* (in a car).

dualism ['djuəlizəm] *n* dualismo *m*.

dualist ['djuəlist] *n* dualista *m* & *f*.

dualistic [,djuə'listik] *adj* dualista.

duality [dju'æliti] *n* dualidad *f*.

dual-purpose ['djuəl'pəːpəs] *adj* de dos usos.

dub [dʌb] *vt* armar [caballero] (to knight) ‖ apodar (to nickname) ‖ doblar (film) ‖ volver a grabar (to rerecord) ‖ adobar (skins).

dubbed [dʌbd] *adj* doblado, da (voice, film).

dubbin ['dʌbiŋ] *n* adobo *m* ‖ cera *f* (for boots).

dubbing ['dʌbiŋ] *n* adobo *m* (dubbin) ‖ doblaje *m* (of a film).

dubiety [dju'baiəti] *n* incertidumbre *f*.

dubious ['djuːbjəs] *adj* dudoso, sa; poco seguro, ra; *dubious result* resultado dudoso ‖ ambiguo, gua; equívoco, ca (not clear) ‖ indeciso, sa (irresolute) ‖ discutible, controvertible (questionable) ‖ sospechoso, sa (shady) ‖ — *to be dubious about* tener dudas sobre ‖ *to be dubious of* dudar de.

dubiously [-li] *adv* dudosamente, con duda ‖ de una manera sospechosa.

dubiousness [-nis] *n* incertidumbre *f*, duda *f* (uncertainty) || lo ambiguo, lo equívoco (of a compliment).

dubitable ['dju:bitəbl] *adj* dudoso, sa.

dubitative ['dju:bitətiv] *adj* dubitativo, va.

Dublin ['dʌblin] *pr n* GEOGR Dublín.

ducal ['dju:kəl] *adj* ducal.

ducat ['dʌkət] *n* ducado *m* (coin).

duchess ['dʌtʃis] *n* duquesa *f*; *Her Grace The Duchess* la señora duquesa.

duchy ['dʌtʃi] *n* ducado *m* (territory).

duck [dʌk] *n* pato *m* (drake); *wild duck* pato salvaje || pata *f* (female duck) || CULIN pato *m* || SP cero *m* (in cricket) | esquiva *f* (in boxing) || AUT camión *m* anfibio || dril *m* (cloth) || zambullida *f*, chapuzón *m* (in water) || agachada *f* (preventive move) || FIG & FAM pichoncito *m*, cariño *m* || — FIG *in two shakes of a duck's tail* en un periquete, en un santiamén | *lame duck* incapaz *m* & *f* (ineffectual person), cosa inútil (useless thing), persona *f* incapacitada (physically handicapped person), especulador *m* insolvente (insolvent speculator) || US FAM *lame duck* cesante *m*, funcionario *m* cesante (official), diputado *m* no reelegido (congressman) || *the words glanced off him like water off a duck's back* oía las palabras como quien oye llover || *to take to sth. like a duck to water* adaptarse fácilmente a algo, hallarse en su elemento con algo.
◆ *pl* pantalones *m* de dril || — FAM *fine weather for the ducks* tiempo lluvioso || *to play ducks and drakes* hacer pijotas *or* cabrillas en el agua || FIG *to play ducks and drakes with one's money* despilfarrar el dinero.

duck [dʌk] *vt* agachar (to lower suddenly) || FAM fumarse; *to duck a class* fumarse una clase || zambullir (in water) || esquivar (a blow) || FIG eludir (a problem).
◆ *vi* agacharse (to bob down suddenly) || zambullirse (in water) || — *to duck out* desaparecer || *to duck out on* eludir.

duckbill ['dʌkbil] *n* monotrema *m*, ornitorrinco *m* (animal).

duckboard ['dʌkbɔ:d] *n* enrejado *m* de madera.

ducker [dʌkə*] *n* somorgujo *m* (bird).

duck-footed ['dʌkfutid] *adj* palmípedo, da.

ducking ['dʌkiŋ] *n* zambullida *f*, chapuzón *m* || *ducking stool* silla *f* en que se zambullía a los condenados a modo de castigo.

duckling ['dʌkliŋ] *n* ZOOL patito *m* || *the ugly duckling* el patito feo.

duckweed ['dʌkwi:d] *n* lenteja *f* de agua.

ducky ['dʌki] *adj* mono, na; precioso, sa.
◆ *n* querido, da; cariño *m*.

duct [dʌkt] *n* conducto *m* (of gas) || ELECTR tubo *m* || ANAT canal *m*, conducto *m*; *tear duct* canal *or* conducto lagrimal || ANAT *auditory duct* conducto auditivo.

ductile ['dʌktail] *adj* dúctil.

ductility [dʌk'tiliti] *n* ductilidad *f*.

ductless ['dʌktlis] *adj* ANAT endocrino, na; de secreción interna; *ductless glands* glándulas endocrinas.

dud [dʌd] *adj* falso, sa (false); *a dud note* un billete falso || sin fondos (a cheque) || incapaz (a person) || inútil (useless) || defectuoso, sa (faulty) || COMM *dud stock* mercancía *f* invendible.
◆ *n* MIL proyectil *m* que no estalla (shell) || COMM mercancía *f* invendible || FAM desastre *m*, calamidad *f*; *a dud at mathematics* un desastre en matemáticas || *to be a dud* ser falso (coin).
◆ *pl* FAM trapos *m*, ropa *f sing* (clothes).

dude [dju:d] *n* US petimetre *m* || US *dude ranch* rancho *m* para turistas.

dudgeon ['dʌdʒən] *n* cólera *f*, ira *f* (anger) || *in high dudgeon* muy enojado, da; iracundo, da.

due [dju:] *adj* COMM pagadero, ra (payable) || debido, da; *with due care* con el debido cuidado; *in due time* a su debido tiempo || — COMM *debts due by us* deudas nuestras | *debts due to us* créditos *m pl* a nuestro favor | *due bill* reconocimiento *m* de deuda | *due date* vencimiento *m* || *due to* debido a || COMM *falling due* vencimiento *m* || *he is due to arrive next month* debe llegar el mes que viene || *to be due to* deberse a; *it's due to your negligence* se debe a su negligencia || *to be due to s.o.* corresponder a (to fall to) || COMM *to fall* o *to become due* vencer || *train due at four o'clock* tren que debe llegar a las cuatro.
◆ *n* merecido *m* (that which s.o. deserves); *he got his due* se llevó su merecido; *to give s.o. his due* dar a alguien su merecido || COMM deuda *f*; *to pay one's dues* pagar sus deudas || FIG *we must give him his due* hay que ser justo con él.
◆ *pl* derechos *m*; *harbour dues* derechos de fondeo *or* anclaje || cuota *f sing* (for the rights of membership).
◆ *adv* MAR derecho hacia; *due north* derecho hacia el norte.

duel ['djuəl] *n* duelo *m*; *to fight a duel* batirse en duelo; *it was a duel to the death* fue un duelo a muerte.

duel ['djuəl] *vi* batirse en duelo.

duellist; US **duelist** [-ist] *n* duelista *m*.

duenna [dju'enə] *n* (ant) dueña *f*.

Duero ['dweirɔ] *pr n* GEOGR Duero *m*.

duet [dju'et] *n* MUS dúo *m*.

duettist [dju'etist] *n* MUS duetista *m* & *f*.

duff [dʌf] *n* CULIN budín *m*, pudín *m* || cisco *m* (coal) || US humus *m*, mantillo *m*.
◆ *adj* FAM sin valor.

duff [dʌf] *vt* falsificar (to fake) || FAM *to duff up* dar una paliza.

duffel ['dʌfəl] *n* muletón *m* (cloth) || US ropa *f* para cambiarse.

duffel bag [-bæg] *n* bolsa *f* de lona.

duffel coat [-kəut] *n* trenca *f* (overcoat).

duffer ['dʌfə*] *n* FAM zoquete *m* (stupid person) | desastre *m*, calamidad *f* (incompetent person) || vendedor *m* ambulante, buhonero *m* (peddler).

duffle ['dʌfəl] *n* muletón *m*.

duffle coat [-kəut] *n* trenca *f* (overcoat).

dug [dʌg] *n* teta *f* (of animal) || ubre *f* (of cow).

dug [dʌg] *pret/pp* → **dig**.

dugout ['dʌgaut] *n* MAR piragua *f* || MIL refugio *m* subterráneo, trinchera *f* (shelter) || FAM militarote *m*.

duke [dju:k] *n* duque *m*; *His Grace The Duke* el señor duque.
◆ *pl* FAM puños *m* (fists).

dukedom ['dju:kdəm] *n* ducado *m* (title).

dulcet ['dʌlsit] *adj* dulce, suave.

dulcify ['dʌlsifai] *vt* dulcificar.

dulcimer ['dʌlsimə*] *n* MUS dulcimer *m*.

Dulcinea [ˌdʌlsi'niə] *n* Dulcinea *f*.

dulia [dju:'laiə] *n* REL dulia *f*.

dull [dʌl] *adj* lerdo, da; torpe (obtuse) || lento, ta; tardo, da (slow) || monótono, na; insulso, sa (drab) || sin sabor, insulso, sa (flat) || sin relieve (lacklustre) || sin vida (lifeless) || pesado, da (tedious) || soso, sa (uninteresting) || apagado, da (colours) || mate (surface) || pálido, da (light) || sordo, da (pain, sounds) || embotado, da (sense) || flojo, ja; *trade is dull* los negocios están flojos || muerto, ta (season, etc.) || gris, desapacible (weather) || triste (cheerless) || deprimido, da (depressed) || taciturno, na; sombrío, a (sullen) || oscuro, ra (dark) || embotado, da (blunt) || *to have a dull sense of hearing* ser duro de oído.

dull [dʌl] *vt* aliviar (to lessen pain) || oscurecer (to darken) || enfriar (emotions) || embotar (senses) || entorpecer (mind) || apagar (colours) || deslustrar, volver mate (surface) || amortiguar, apagar (sounds) || embotar (a knife) || debilitar (attention) || entristecer (to sadden).
◆ *vi* aliviarse (pain) || oscurecerse (to become dark) || enfriarse (emotions) | embotarse (senses) || entorpecerse (mind) || embotarse (a knife) || debilitarse (attention) || entristecerse (to become sad) || volverse mate (surface) || apagarse (colours) || amortiguarse, apagarse (sounds).

dullard ['dʌləd] *n* FAM lelo, la; burro, rra.

dullish ['dʌliʃ] *adj* torpe, de cortos alcances (person) || pesado, da (tedious) || con poco brillo (colour) || apagado, da; sordo, da (sound).

dullness ['dʌlnis] *n* torpeza *f* (stupidity) || monotonía *f*, insulsez *f* (drabness) || insipidez *f*, lo soso (flatness) || tristeza *f* (sadness) || pesadez *f* (tediousness) || falta *f* de vida (lifelessness) || lo apagado (of colours) || falta *f* de brillo (of surface) || flojedad *f* (of trade) || embotamiento *m* (of senses) || TECH embotamiento *m* (bluntness) || *dullness of hearing* dureza *f* de oído.

dully [dʌli] *adv* lentamente (slowly) || torpemente (stupidly) || sordamente || de una manera aburrida.

duly ['dju:li] *adv* debidamente (properly) || a su debido tiempo (on time) || COMM *I duly received your favour of* acuso recibo de su atenta del.

Duma ['du:mə] *n* HIST Duma *f*.

dumb [dʌm] *adj* mudo, da (not speaking); *born dumb* mudo de nacimiento || FIG mudo, da (*with* de) || FAM estúpido, da; tonto, ta (stupid) || — *dumb animal* animal *m* || *dumb motions* señas *f* || *dumb show* pantomima *f* || *the dumb* los mudos || *to strike s.o. dumb* dejar a alguien sin habla *or* mudo.

dumbbell [-bel] *n* SP pesa *f* || US FAM bobo, ba.

dumbfound; dumfound [dʌm'faund] *vt* dejar sin habla, enmudecer || *to be dumbfounded* quedarse sin habla *or* pasmado.

dumbly [dʌmli] *adv* sin decir nada || en silencio || FAM estúpidamente.

dumbness [dʌmnis] *n* MED mudez *f* || FIG mutismo *m* || FAM estupidez *f*.

dumbstruck ['dʌmstrʌk] *adj* mudo, da; sin habla.

dumbwaiter ['dʌm'weitə*] *n* carrito *m* (trolley) || US montaplatos *m inv* (lift).

dumdum ['dʌmdʌm] *n* dum-dum *f* (bullet).

dumfound [dʌm'faund] *vt* → **dumbfound**.

dummy ['dʌmi] *n* objeto *m* ficticio (display article) || maniquí *m* (of tailor) || títere *m*, muñeco *m* (puppet) || chupete *m* (for babies) || muerto *m* (in cards) || PRINT maqueta *f* || FIG testaferro *m* (cover) | FAM tonto, ta; bobo, ba || SP *to sell the dummy* hacer una finta de pase, fintar (in rugby).
◆ *adj* falso, sa; ficticio, cia.

dummy ['dʌmi] *vi* SP fintar (in rugby).

dump [dʌmp] *n* vertedero *m* (scrap heap) || FIG & FAM tugurio *m* (hovel) | poblacho *m* (village) || MIL depósito *m* || — *dump lorry* o *truck* volquete *m* || INFORM *dump memory* análisis *m* de memoria || FIG *to be down in the dumps* tener murria *or* ideas negras.

dump [dʌmp] *vt* descargar, verter [algo de un camión, tren, etc.] (to unload) || tirar (to throw down, to throw away) || deshacerse de (to get rid of) || COMM inundar el mercado con || expulsar a un país extranjero (immigrants).
dumper truck ['dʌmpətrʌk] *n* volquete *m*.
dumping [-iŋ] *n* descarga *f* || dumping *m*, venta *f* de un producto en el extranjero a un precio inferior al aplicado en el interior || INFORM vaciado *m* (memory) || — *no dumping* prohibido tirar basura || *nuclear dumping* vertido *m* de desechos radioactivos.
dumpish [-iʃ] *adj* FAM desalentado, da; que tiene ideas negras *or* murria.
dumpling [-liŋ] *n* CULIN budín *m* relleno de carne *or* fruta | masa *f* hervida.
dumpy [dʌmpi] *adj* FAM regordete, ta.
dun [dʌn] *adj* pardo, da.
◆ *n* color *m* pardo || caballo *m* pardo (horse) || COMM petición *f* de reembolso (demand) | acreedor *m* insistente (insistent creditor).
dun [dʌn] *vt* COMM apremiar (a debtor).
dunce [dʌns] *n* FAM burro *m* || FAM *dunce's cap* US *dunce cap*, orejas *f pl* de burro.
dunderhead ['dʌndəhed] *n* idiota *m* & *f*, burro, rra.
dune [dju:n] *n* duna *f*.
dung [dʌŋ] *n* excrementos *m pl* (of animals) || boñiga *f* (of cow) || cagajón *m* (of horse) || AGR estiércol *m* (manure).
dungarees [,dʌŋgə'ri:z] *pl n* mono *m sing* (overall).
dung beetle ['dʌŋ,bi:tl] *n* ZOOL escarabajo *m* pelotero.
dungeon ['dʌndʒən] *n* calabozo *m*, mazmorra *f* (prison) || torre *f* del homenaje (keep).
dunghill ['dʌŋhil] *n* estercolero *m*.
dunk [dʌŋk] *vt* mojar, remojar.
◆ *vi* tirarse al agua.
dunnage ['dʌnidʒ] *n* maderos *m pl* de estibar.
duo ['dju:əu] *n* dúo *m*.
duodecimal [,djuəu'desimal] *adj* MATH duodecimal.
duodecimo [,djuəu'desiməu] *adj* en dozavo (book).
duodenal [,djuə'di:nl] *adj* ANAT duodenal || MED *duodenal ulcer* úlcera *f* del duodeno.
duodenum [,djuəu'di:nəm] *n* ANAT duodeno *m*.
— OBSERV El plural es *duodenums* o *duodena*.
duologue ['djuəlɔg] *n* diálogo *m*.
dupe [dju:p] *n* FAM primo, ma.
dupe [dju:p] *vt* embaucar, engañar (to cheat) || timar (to swindle).
duper [-ə*] *n* embaucador, ra; engañador, ra (cheater) || timador, ra (swindler).
duplex [dju:pleks] *adj* TECH dúplex; *duplex line* o *link* enlace dúplex || doble (double).
◆ *n* dúplex *m*.
duplex ['dju:pleks] *vt* ELECTR establecer un enlace dúplex en.
duplexer [-ə*] *n* dispositivo *m* para enlace dúplex.
duplicate ['dju:plikit] *adj* duplicado, da || de recambio, de repuesto (parts).
◆ *n* doble *m*, copia *f*, duplicado *m* (copy) || *in duplicate* por duplicado.
duplicate ['dju:plikeit] *vt* duplicar; *to duplicate a document, the locks on a door* duplicar un documento, las cerraduras de una puerta || multicopiar, hacer *or* tirar con multicopista, reproducir.
duplicating [-iŋ] *n* duplicación *f* || tirada *f* con multicopista, reproducción *f* con multicopista || *duplicating machine* multicopista *f*.
◆ *adj* duplicador, ra.
duplication [,dju:pli'keiʃən] *n* duplicación *f* || reproducción *f* || duplicado *m*, copia *f* (copy).
duplicator ['dju:plikeitə*] *n* multicopista *f* [AMER miméografo *m*].
duplicity [dju'plisiti] *n* doblez *f*, duplicidad *f*.
durability [,djuərə'biliti] *n* durabilidad *f*, duración *f*, lo duradero.
durable ['djuərəbl] *adj* duradero, ra || *durable goods* productos no perecederos.
duralumin [djuə'ræljumin]; **duraluminium** [djuər,ælju'minjəm] *n* CHEM duraluminio *m*.
dura mater ['djuərə'meitə*] *n* ANAT duramáter *f*, duramadre *f*.
duramen [djuə'reimen] *n* BOT duramen *m*.
durance ['djuərəns] *n* JUR detención *f*, prisión *f*.
duration [djuə'reiʃən] *n* duración *f* || FAM *for the duration* mientras dure la guerra.
Dürer ['djuərə*] *pr n* Durero.
duress [djuə'res] *n* JUR coacción *f*, coerción *f* (compulsion); *under duress* bajo coacción | prisión *f* (imprisonment).
Durex ['dju:reks] *n* condón *m* (registered trademark).
during ['djuəriŋ] *prep* durante.
durst [də:st] *pret* —> **dare.**
dusk [dʌsk] *n* crepúsculo *m* (twilight) || oscuridad *f* (gloom) || *at dusk* al atardecer, al anochecer.
◆ *adj* oscuro, ra.
duskiness ['dʌskinis] *n* oscuridad *f* || color *m* moreno (of complexion).
dusky ['dʌski] *adj* oscuro, ra (gloomy) || moreno, na (complexion).
dust [dʌst] *n* polvo *m*; *covered with dust* cubierto de polvo || cenizas *f pl* (remains of dead person) || BOT polen *m* || — FIG *to bite the dust* morder el polvo | *to let the dust settle* esperar que se calme la borrasca | *to lick the dust* morder el polvo || *to make* o *to raise a dust* levantar una polvareda || FIG *to raise* o *to kick up a dust* armar un escándalo | *to throw dust in s.o.'s eyes* engañar a alguien con falsas apariencias.
dust [dʌst] *vt* limpiar el polvo de, quitar el polvo a (to clean dust off) || espolvorear (to powder) || FIG & FAM *to dust s.o.'s jacket* o *s.o.'s coat* sacudirle el polvo a uno.
◆ *vi* limpiar el polvo || US FAM *to dust out* poner pies en polvorosa.
dustbin ['dʌstbin] *n* cubo *m* de la basura.
dust bowl ['dʌstbəul] *n* terreno *m* pelado por la erosión.
dust cart [-kɑ:t] *n* camión *m* de la basura.
dustcloth [-klɔθ] *n* US trapo *m* (duster) || funda *f* (cover).
dust cloud [-klaud] *n* polvareda *f*, nube *m* de polvo.
dustcoat [-,kəut] *n* guardapolvo *m*.
dust cover [-'kʌvə*] *n* sobrecubierta *f* (of books) || funda *f*, guardapolvo *m* (of furniture).
dust devil [-,devl] *n* tormenta *f* de polvo.
duster ['dʌstə*] *n* trapo *m* (cloth) || plumero *m* (with feathers) || borrador *m* (for blackboard) || US guardapolvo *m* (overalls) | pulverizador *m* (spray).
dustiness ['dʌstinis] *n* lo polvoriento.
dusting ['dʌstiŋ] *n* limpieza *f* (cleaning) || FAM paliza *f* (thrashing) || espolvoreo *m* (light sprinkling) || capa *f* de polvo.
dust jacket ['dʌst,dʒækit] *n* sobrecubierta *f* (of a book).
dustman ['dʌstmən] *n* basurero *m*.
— OBSERV El plural es *dustmen*.
dustpan ['dʌstpæn] *n* recogedor *m*.
dust sheet ['dʌstʃi:t] *n* funda *f*, guardapolvo *m*.
dust shot ['dʌstʃɔt] *n* MIL mostacilla *f*.
dust storm ['dʌststɔ:m] *n* tormenta *f* de polvo.
dustup ['dʌstʌp] *n* FAM riña *f*, pelea *f*.
dusty ['dʌsti] *adj* polvoriento, ta (powdery) || cubierto de polvo (covered with dust) || ceniciento, ta (dust-coloured) || vago, ga (answer) || FAM *it's not so dusty* no está nada mal.
Dutch [dʌtʃ] *adj* holandés, esa.
◆ *n* holandés *m* (language) || — FIG *Dutch courage* valentía *f* que da la bebida | *to beat the Dutch* ser extraordinario | *to go Dutch* pagar cada uno lo suyo, pagar a escote.
◆ *pl* holandeses *m*.
Dutch elm disease ['dʌtʃ elm di,zi:z] *n* BOT enfermedad *f* del olmo holandés.
Dutchman [-mən] *n* holandés *m* || — MUS *flying Dutchman* buque *m* fantasma || FIG & FAM *if that picture is genuine I'm a Dutchman* que me corten la mano si este cuadro es auténtico.
— OBSERV El plural de esta palabra es *Dutchmen*.
Dutchwoman [-,wumən] *n* holandesa *f*.
— OBSERV El plural de esta palabra es *Dutchwomen*.
duteous ['dju:tjəs] *adj* deferente (respectful) || obediente.
dutiable ['dju:tjəbl] *adj* JUR sujeto a derechos arancelarios *or* de aduana.
dutiful ['dju:tiful] *adj* obediente, sumiso, sa (obedient) || deferente (respectful) || servicial (obliging).
dutifully [-i] *adv* con deferencia *or* sumisión.
duty ['dju:ti] *n* deber *m*, obligación *f*; *to do one's duty* cumplir con su obligación; *to fail in one's duty* faltar a su deber || TECH rendimiento *m* || impuesto *m* (tax) || derechos *m pl* arancelarios, derechos *m pl* de aduana, aranceles *m pl* (at customs) || función *f*; *to fulfil one's duties* desempeñar sus funciones || — *as in duty bound* como es debido || *for duty's sake, from a sense of duty* por cumplido, para cumplir || *in duty to* en consideración a || *in the line of duty* en cumplimiento de los deberes de uno || *I shall make it my duty to* me encargaré de || *on duty* de servicio || *to be off duty* estar libre, no estar de servicio || MIL *to be on sentry duty* estar de guardia || *to be s.o.'s duty to* incumbirle a uno, corresponderle a uno || *to do duty for s.o.* sustituir a alguien || *to do duty for sth.* servir de algo, hacer las veces de algo || *to do one's duty by* o *to s.o.* cumplir con alguien || *to pay a duty call* hacer una visita de cumplido || *to pay one's duty to* saludar respetuosamente a || *to take up one's duties* tomar posesión de un empleo *or* cargo, entrar en funciones.
duty-free ['dju:ti'fri:] *adj* libre *or* exento de derechos de aduana, en franquicia aduanera || *duty-free shop* tienda *f* libre de impuestos.
duty officer ['dju:ti,ɔfisə*] *n* persona *f* de guardia.
duty-paid ['dju:ti'peid] *adj/adv* con los derechos arancelarios pagados.
duumvir [dju'ʌmvə*] *n* duumviro *m*.
duvet ['dju:vei] *n* edredón *m* nórdico.
DVLC *abbr of [Driver and Vehicle Licensing Centre]* centro británico de licencias para vehículos y conductores.
dwarf [dwɔ:f] *adj/n* enano, na.
dwarf [dwɔ:f] *vt* achicar, empequeñecer (to make seem small) || impedir que crezca (to prevent from growing).
dwarfish ['dwɔ:fiʃ] *adj* enano, na.
dwarfishness [,dwɔ:fiʃnis] *n* MED enanismo *m* || tamaño *m* diminuto, pequeñez *f*.

dwarfism ['dwɔːfizəm] *n* MED enanismo *m*.

dwell [dwel] *n* TECH parada *f* momentánea.

dwell* [dwel] *vi* morar, vivir (to live) || *to dwell on* extenderse en, hablar extensamente de (a subject), insistir en, hacer hincapié en (to emphasize), acentuar (a syllable), fijarse en (gaze), detenerse en (a thought).
— OBSERV Pret y pp ***dwelt***.

dweller ['dwelə*] *n* habitante *m* & *f* (*in, on* de).

dwelling ['dweliŋ] *n* morada *f*, vivienda *f* || FIG insistencia *f*.

dwelling house [-haus] *n* casa *f* particular.

dwelt [dwelt] *pret/pp* —→ **dwell.**

dwindle ['dwindl] *vi* menguar, disminuir || *to dwindle to nothing* quedar reducido a nada.

dwindling [-iŋ] *adj* decreciente, menguante.

dyad ['daiæd] *n* pareja *f* (couple).

dyarchy ['daiɑːki] *n* diarquía *f*.

dye [dai] *n* tinte *m* (colouring matter) || color *m*, tono *m* (colour) || — *fast dye* color sólido || FIG *of the deepest dye* de la peor catadura.

dye [dai] *vt* teñir || *to have a coat dyed black* mandar teñir un abrigo de negro.
— OBSERV El gerundio de este verbo es *dyeing*. No se confunda con *dying*, gerundio del verbo *to die* (morir).

dyeing [-iŋ] *n* tinte *m*.

dyer [-ə*] *n* tintorero, ra.

dyer's-weed ['daiəzwiːd] *n* BOT gualda *f*.

dyestuff ['daistʌf] *n* tinte *m*, materia *f* colorante.

dyewood ['daiwud] *n* madera *f* tintórea.

dying ['daiiŋ] *adj* moribundo, da (about to die) || FIG mortecino, na (waning, failing) | en vías de desaparición (about to disappear) | — *dying words* últimas palabras || FAM *I'm dying to see you* me muero de ganas de verte.

dyke [daik] *n* —→ **dike.**

dynamic [dai'næmik] *adj* dinámico, ca.

dynamics [dai'næmiks] *n* PHYS dinámica *f*.

dynamism ['dainəmizəm] *n* dinamismo *m*.

dynamist ['dainəmist] *n* dinamista *m* & *f*.

dynamite ['dainəmait] *n* dinamita *f* || FIG *this story is dynamite* esta historia es explosiva.

dynamite ['dainəmait] *vt* dinamitar, volar con dinamita.

dynamiter [-ə*] *n* dinamitero, ra.

dynamiting [-iŋ] *n* voladura *f* con dinamita.

dynamo ['dainəməu] *n* dinamo *f*, dínamo *f*.

dynamoelectric [ˌdainəməui'lektrik]; **dynamoelectrical** [-əl] *adj* dinamoeléctrico, ca.

dynamometer [ˌdainə'mɔmitə*] *n* dinamómetro *m*.

dynastic [di'næstik]; **dynastical** [-əl] *adj* dinástico, ca.

dynasty ['dinəsti] *n* dinastía *f*.

dyne [dain] *n* PHYS dina *f*.

dysenteric [ˌdisn'terik] *adj* MED disentérico, ca.

dysentery ['disəntri] *n* MED disenter'ia *f*.

dyslexia [dis'leksiə] *n* MED dislexia *f*.

dyslexic [dis'leksik] *adj* MED disléxico, ca.

dyslogistic [ˌdislɔ'dʒistik] *adj* peyorativo, va; despectivo, va.

dyspepsia [dis'pepsiə]; **dyspepsy** [dis'pepsi] *n* MED dispepsia *f*.

dyspeptic [dis'peptik] *adj/n* MED dispéptico, ca.

dysphasia [dis'feiʒjə] *n* MED disfasia *f*.

dyspnoea; *US* **dyspnea** [dis'pniə] *n* disnea *f*.

dysuric [dis'juərik] *adj* MED disúrico, ca.

E

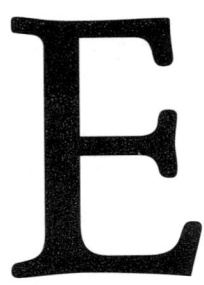

e [iː] *n* e *f* (letter) || MUS mi *m*; *E major, minor, flat, sharp* mi mayor, menor, bemol, sostenido.

each [iːtʃ] *n* cada; *each child had a book* cada niño tenía un libro || *each and every man* todos los hombres sin excepción.

◆ *pron* cada uno, cada una; *one of each* uno de cada uno; *he gave us a pound each* nos dio una libra a cada uno; *they are two pesetas each* valen dos pesetas cada uno || — *each for himself* cada cual por su cuenta || *to each his own* a cada cual lo suyo || *two bottles each* dos botellas por persona.

each other [-ˈʌðə*] *pron* uno a otro, una a otra, unos a otros, unas a otras, el uno al otro, etc.; *the two of them help each other a lot* los dos se ayudan mucho uno a otro; *John and David complain of each other* Juan y David se quejan el uno del otro *or* uno de otro.

— OBSERV *Each other* sólo debe emplearse cuando se trata de dos personas. Si hay una más, ha de decirse *one another*.

— OBSERV The reciprocal sense of *each other* is often conveyed in Spanish by a simple reflexive verb: *they greeted each other* se saludaron. This may, however, result in ambiguity in Spanish between the reciprocal and the reflexive meanings: *se hirieron* can mean «they hurt each other» or «they hurt themselves». In this case «they hurt each other» would be better translated by *se hirieron uno a otro*.

— OBSERV The appropriate preposition must be inserted as follows: *they laughed at each other* se han reído uno de otro.

— OBSERV Two alternative translations expressing the idea of reciprocal action are *mutuamente* and *recíprocamente*: *they envy each other* se envidian mutuamente.

eager [ˈiːgə*] *adj* grande; *eager hopes* grandes esperanzas; *eager appetite* gran apetito || ávido, da; ansioso, sa (hungry); *eager for riches, for fame, for knowledge* ávido de riquezas, de fama, de saber || apasionado, da; *an eager student* un estudiante apasionado || deseoso, sa; *eager to start* deseoso de empezar; *eager to please* deseoso de contentar a la gente *or* de gustar || apremiante, vehemente, vivo, va; ardiente; *eager desire* deseo ardiente || — *an eager glance* una mirada de deseo (desirous), una mirada entusiasta (excited) || *an eager public* un público anhelante || *don't be so eager!* ¡ten paciencia! || *eager cold* frío agudo *or* penetrante || *to be eager for* ansiar, anhelar, tener gran deseo de || *to be eager to do sth.* anhelar *or* ansiar hacer algo, desear vivamente hacer algo || *to be in eager pursuit of* perseguir ansiosamente.

◆ *n* US MAR macareo *m*, barra *f*.

eagerly [-li] *adv* ávidamente (to eat, to read, etc.) || ansiosamente (to desire) || atentamente (to listen) || impacientemente (impatiently).

eagerness [-nis] *n* impaciencia *f* (impatience) || ansia *f*, anhelo *m*; *his eagerness to succeed, to learn* su ansia de tener éxito, de aprender.

eagle [ˈiːgl] *n* ZOOL águila *f* (bird); *golden eagle* águila real *or* caudal || águila *f* (emblem) || ASTR águila *f* (constellation) || SP hoyo *m* conseguido en dos golpes menos que la media (in golf) || — *the Black Eagle of Prussia* el águila negra de Prusia || *the Imperial Eagle* el águila imperial.

eagle eye [-ˈai] *n* FIG ojo *m* de lince.

eagle-eyed [-aid] *adj* *to be eagle-eyed* tener ojos de lince.

eagle owl [-aul] *n* búho *m* real (bird).

eagle ray [-rei] *n* águila *f* de mar (fish).

eaglet [ˈiːglit] *n* aguilucho *m* (young eagle).

eagre [ˈeigə*] *n* MAR macareo *m*, barra *f*.

ear [iə*] *n* ANAT oreja *f* (outer part); *to have big ears* tener grandes orejas; *pricked, drooping ears* orejas tiesas, gachas | oído *m*; *inner, middle ear* oído interno, medio || oído *m* (sense); *to have a good ear* tener buen oído || espiga *f* (of corn) || oreja *f*, asa *f* (of vase, etc.) || — MUS *by ear* de oído || FIG *it goes in at one ear and out at the other* por un oído le entra y por otro le sale | *my ears are burning* me están pitando *or* silbando los oídos || TAUR *to cut an ear, two ears* cortar una oreja, dos orejas || FIG *to fall down about one's ears* venirse abajo (plans) | *to fall on deaf ears* caer en saco roto | *to give* o *to lend an ear to* prestar oído *or* oídos a || FAM *to give s.o. a thick ear, to clip s.o.'s ear* darle una torta a uno || *to have no ear for music* tener mal oído || *to have sharp ears* tener el oído fino || FIG *to have the ear of* gozar de la confianza de, tener influencia con, hacerse escuchar por | *to keep* o *to have one's ear to the ground* mantenerse alerta, mantenerse al corriente | *to listen with half an ear* escuchar a medias | *to open one's ears* abrir los oídos | *to play by ear* tocar de oído | *to play it by ear* improvisar sobre la marcha | *to prick up one's ears* aguzar el oído | *to set people by the ears* sembrar la discordia entre la gente | *to turn a deaf ear* no prestar oídos, hacerse el sordo, hacer oídos de mercader | *up to the ears in debt* abrumado de deudas, empeñado hasta la camisa | *walls have ears* las paredes oyen.

earache [ˈiəreik] *n* dolor *m* de oídos.

eardrop [ˈiədrɔp] *n* pendiente *m*, arete *m* (earring).

eardrum [ˈiədrʌm] *n* ANAT tímpano *m*.

earflap [ˈiəflæp] *n* orejera *f* (of hat) || ANAT pabellón *m* de la oreja.

earing [ˈiəriŋ] *n* MAR empuñidura *f*.

earl [əːl] *n* conde *m*.

earlap [ˈiəlæp] *n* ANAT pabellón *m* de la oreja.

earldom [əːldəm] *n* condado *m*.

earlier [ˈəːliə*] *adv* más temprano || anterior || *earlier on* antes.

earlobe [ˈiələub] *n* ANAT lóbulo *m*.

early [ˈəːli] *adj* temprano, na; *at an early age* a temprana edad; *early vegetables* verduras tempranas || primero, ra (first); *the early stages* las primeras etapas; *an early model of a car* uno de los primeros modelos de un coche; *the early poets* los primeros poetas; *early youth* primera juventud || rápido, da; pronto, ta (quick); *an early reply* una contestación rápida || temprano, na; prematuro, ra; precoz (premature); *his early death* su muerte prematura; *an early summer* un verano precoz || próximo, ma (imminent); *at an early date* en fecha próxima || matutino, na (of the early morning); *the early silence* el silencio matutino || primitivo, va; *early art* arte primitivo || — *at an early date* en fecha próxima, muy pronto (soon), muy pronto (in the past) || *at the earliest* como muy pronto || *at the earliest possible moment* lo más pronto posible || *at your earliest convenience* con la mayor brevedad || *earliest youth* tierna *or* primera infancia (infancy) || *early closing day* día en que las tiendas cierran por la tarde || *early education* primera enseñanza || *early life* juventud *f*, años *f pl* juveniles (youth); *in my early life* en mi juventud || *early retirement* jubilación *f* anticipada || *early riser* madrugador, ra || CINEM *early show* primera función || MIL *early warning system* sistema *m* de alarma rápida || *in the early afternoon* al principio de la tarde || *in the early morning* de madrugada, muy de mañana || *the earliest times* los tiempos más remotos || *the early ages* los primeros días *or* tiempos || *the early morning* la madrugada || *to be early days yet* ser todavía demasiado pronto || *to have an early dinner* cenar temprano || *to keep early hours* levantarse y acostarse temprano || *we are in our early thirties* tenemos poco más de treinta años.

◆ *adv* temprano; *to get up, to arrive early* levantarse, llegar temprano; *it was early in the morning* fue por la mañana temprano || al principio de, a principios de (at the beginning of); *early (on) in the winter* a principios del invierno; *early in one's life, one's career* al principio de su vida, de su carrera; *early on the list* al principio de la lista || antes (before); *he let me off five minutes early* dejó que me fuese cinco minutos antes || pronto; *man learnt to use tools early on* el hombre aprendió pronto a emplear las herramientas || con tiempo, con mucha anticipación, con mucha antelación (in advance); *to book one's tickets early* comprar las entradas con tiempo || — *as early as possible* lo más pronto posible, cuanto antes || *as early as the tenth century* ya en el siglo X (diez) || *bright and early* muy temprano || *earlier on* antes || *early enough* a tiempo (in time), bastante temprano || *to die early* morir joven *or* prematuramente.

early bird [-bəd] *n* FIG madrugador, ra (early riser) | persona *f* que llega temprano || FIG *the early bird catches the worm* al que madruga, Dios le ayuda.

Early Bird [-bəːd] *n* Pájaro *m* del Alba (satellite).

earmark [ˈiəmɑːk] *n* señal *f* en la oreja (of livestock) || FIG marca *f* distintiva, característica *f*, señal *f*.

earmark [ˈiəmɑːk] *vt* poner una señal en la oreja (livestock) || dejar una señal en || reservar, poner aparte (*for* para) (to put aside) || destinar (*for* a) (to destine) || consignar, asignar (credits).

earn [əːn] *vt* ganar; *I earn twenty pounds a week* gano veinte libras por semana || merecer, merecerse, hacerse acreedor a, ganarse (to deserve); *he had earned a rest* había merecido un

descanso || valer; *the theft earned him three months in gaol* el robo le valió tres meses de cárcel || obtener, conseguir (to obtain) || COMM devengar; *shares which earn interest* acciones que devengan interés || *to earn one's living* ganarse la vida.
◆ *vi* trabajar, ganarse la vida; *her sons are all earning now* sus hijos ya trabajan todos || COMM devengar interés (shares).

earner ['ɔːnə*] *n* persona *f* que gana dinero.

earnest ['əːnist] *n* prenda *f*, señal *f* (token); *an earnest of his good intentions* una prenda de sus buenas intenciones || arras *f pl*, fianza *f* (deposit to confirm a contract) || *in earnest* en serio; *to be in earnest* hablar en serio; sinceramente (sincerely).
◆ *adj* sincero, ra (sincere); *an earnest appeal* una llamada sincera || aplicado, da (hard-working) || serio, ria (serious); *life is earnest* la vida es seria || ardiente (eager).

earnestness [-nis] *n* seriedad *f* (seriousness) || sinceridad *f* (sincerity) || ardor *m* (of pleadings).

earning power ['əːniŋ,pauə*] *n* rentabilidad *f*.

earnings ['əːniŋz] *pl n* ingresos *m* (income) || sueldo *m sing* (salary) || ganancias *f*, beneficios *m*, utilidades *f* (profits).

earnings-related [-ri,leitid] *adj* de acuerdo con los ingresos (pension, benefit).

earphone ['iəfəun] *n* auricular *m* [*AMER* audífono *m*].

earpick ['iəpik] *n* escarbaorejas *m inv*, mondaoídos *m inv*.

earpiece ['iəpiːs] *n* auricular *m* (of a telephone).

earplug ['iəplʌg] *n* tapón *m* para los oídos.

earring ['iəriŋ] *n* pendiente *m* [*AMER* arete *m*].

earshell [iəʃel] *n* ZOOL oreja *f* de mar.

earshot ['iəʃɔt] *n* alcance *m* del oído; *within earshot* al alcance del oído; *out of earshot* fuera del alcance del oído.

ear-splitting ['iəsplitiŋ] *adj* ensordecedor, ra (deafening) || estridente (strident).

earth [əːθ] *n* tierra *f* (planet); *the Earth is divided into continents* la Tierra está dividida en continentes || tierra *f* (soil, solid surface of planet) || guarida *f*, madriguera *f* (of fox, badger) || ELECTR cable *m* de toma de tierra || AGR tierra *f* || — FIG *down to earth* prosaico, ca || *on earth* en el mundo (in the world), diablo, demonios; *who on the earth is it?* ¿quién diablo es?; *where on earth have you been?* ¿dónde demonios has estado? || REL *on Earth as it is in Heaven* así en la Tierra como en el Cielo || FIG *to come back* o *down to earth* bajar de las nubes, volver a la realidad || FAM *to cost the earth* costar un potosí *or* un ojo de la cara || FIG *to move heaven and earth* mover cielo y tierra | *to promise the earth* prometer el oro y el moro || *to run to earth* cazar (un animal) hasta que se meta en su guarida (an animal), encontrar *or* descubrir por fin (a person, information, etc.).

earth [əːθ] *vt* acollar (to heap soil on or round) || ELECTR conectar a tierra.

earth almond [-,ɑːmənd] *n* BOT chufa *f*.

earthborn [-bɔːn] *adj* mortal (mortal) || humano, na (human).

earthbound [-baund] *adj* terrestre || FIG prosaico, ca.

earthen ['əːθən] *adj* de barro (pottery, etc.) || de tierra (walls, dams, etc.).

earthenware [-wɛə*] *n* alfarería *f*, objetos *m pl* de barro || *glazed earthenware* loza *f*.
◆ *adj* de barro.

earthlight ['əːθlait] *n* luz *f* cenicienta (of the moon).

earthliness ['əːθlinis] *n* lo terrenal || mundanalidad *f* (worldliness).

earthling ['əːθliŋ] *n* terrícola *m* & *f* (an inhabitant of the earth) || criatura *f* humana (a mortal human) || persona *f* mundana (worldly-minded person).

earthly ['əːθli] *adj* terrenal, terreno, na; *earthly passions* pasiones terrenas || mundanal (not spiritual) || — *earthly paradise* paraíso *m* terrenal || FAM *to be of no earthly use* no servir absolutamente para nada | *to see no earthly reason* no ver ninguna razón | *you haven't an earthly* no tienes ninguna posibilidad de salir bien.

earthmover ['əːθ,muːvə*] *n* excavadora *f*.

earthnut ['əːθnʌt] *n* cacahuete *m*, maní *m* (peanut) || chufa *f* (earth almond) || trufa *f* (truffle).

earthquake ['əːθkweik] *n* terremoto *m*, temblor *m* de tierra (tremor) || FIG convulsión *f*, conmoción *f* (upheaval).

earthshattering ['əːθ,ʃætəriŋ] *adj* FIG extraordinario, ria.

earthshine ['əːθʃain] *n* luz *f* cenicienta.

earthward ['əːθwəd]; **earthwards** [-z] *adv* hacia la tierra.

earthwork ['əːθwəːk] *n* terraplén *m* (bank of earth) || movimiento *m* de tierras (in construction work).

earthworm ['əːθwəːm] *n* gusano *m*, lombriz *f*.

earthy ['əːθi] *adj* terroso, sa (like earth) || FIG grosero, ra; tosco, ca (bawdy, gross) | terrenal, mundano, na (worldly).

ear trumpet ['iə,trʌmpit] *n* trompetilla *f* acústica.

earwax ['iəwæks] *n* cerumen *m*.

earwig ['əwig] *n* tijereta *m* (insect).

ease [iːz] *n* facilidad *f*; *he lifted the load with great ease* levantó la carga con mucha facilidad || facilidad *f*, soltura *f*; *she speaks with ease* habla con soltura || tranquilidad *f*, seguridad *f* (tranquillity); *a kind of ease came over him* le entró una especie de tranquilidad || naturalidad *f* (naturalness); *his ease of manner* la naturalidad de su comportamiento || alivio *m* (from pain) || comodidad *f* (comfort) || — *at ease* a gusto, cómodo, da; a sus anchas (relaxed), en posición de descanso (soldiers) || *ease of mind* tranquilidad *f* || *ill at ease* molesto, ta (uncomfortable); inquieto, ta; intranquilo, la (anxious) || *put yourself at ease* póngase cómodo || MIL *stand at ease!* en su lugar, ¡descanso! || *to live a life of ease* llevar una vida cómoda (comfortably), vivir con desahogo (to be well-off) || *to take one's ease* descansar || *with ease* fácilmente.

ease [iːz] *vt* aliviar, mitigar (pain) || facilitar (to make easy) || aflojar (a screw, bolt, pressure) || tranquilizar (one's mind) || aligerar (weight) || suavizar, mitigar (to soften) || relajar (tension) || mover (poner, etc.) con cuidado; *to ease a cupboard away from the wall* apartar un armario de la pared con cuidado || MAR arriar, largar || *to ease o.s. of a burden* quitarse un peso de encima.
◆ *vi* relajarse (tensions) || aliviarse (pain) || amainar (wind) || disminuir (rain) || *to ease off* o *up* bajar (to go down); *the fever has eased up* la fiebre ha bajado; *sales have eased off* las ventas han bajado; trabajar menos (to work less), descansar (person), volverse menos tenso (a situation).
— OBSERV En inglés las preposiciones *off* y *up* se añaden a menudo al verbo *to ease* sin que cambie por eso su sentido inicial.

easeful [-ful] *adj* tranquilo, la.

easel ['iːzl] *n* caballete *m* (of a painter).

easement ['iːzmənt] *n* JUR servidumbre *f*.

easily ['iːzili] *adv* fácilmente, con facilidad (without difficulty) || fácilmente; *it could easily happen* podría ocurrir fácilmente || con tranquilidad, con calma; *to take things easily* tomarse las cosas con calma || fácilmente, con mucho (by far); *this one is easily the best* éste es fácilmente el mejor || bien; *the motor runs easily* el motor funciona bien || muy; *easily breakable* muy frágil || — *easily operated* de fácil manejo || *it could easily be* podría ser así || *more easily said than done* más fácil decirlo que hacerlo.

easiness ['iːzinis] *n* facilidad *f* || comodidad *f* (comfort) || tranquilidad *f* (tranquillity) || soltura *f* (of action) || COMM flojedad *f* (of market).

east [iːst] *adj* del este; *east wind* viento del este || Oriental, del Este; *east Africa* África Oriental; *East Germany* Alemania Oriental; *east coast* costa oriental || que da al este (a window, a door, etc.) || este; *the east wing of the house* el ala este de la casa.
◆ *adv* hacia el este; *to travel east* viajar hacia el este || al este; *my house lies east of London* mi casa está al este de Londres || — *my window looks east* mi ventana da al este || *the wind blows east* hay viento del este.
◆ *n* este *m* (cardinal point) || este *m*, parte *f* oriental (of a country or region); *I live in the East of England* vivo en el este de Inglaterra || Oriente *m* (Orient); *Near East* Próximo *or* Cercano Oriente; *Middle East* Oriente Medio; *Far East* Lejano *or* Extremo Oriente || levante *m* (direction of the rising sun, eastern mediterranean countries) || — *east by north* este cuarta al nordeste || *east by south* este cuarta al sudeste || US *the East* estados situados en el nordeste de EE.UU.

eastbound ['iːstbaund] *adj* dirección este, con rumbo al este.

East End [-'end] *pr n* la parte más oriental de Londres [donde están los muelles].

Easter ['iːstə*] *n* Pascua *f* de Resurrección, Pascua *f* Florida || Semana *f* Santa (period); *are you going away at Easter?* ¿vas de vacaciones en Semana Santa?
◆ *adj* de Pascua de Resurrección (service, etc.) || de Semana Santa (festivities) || — *Easter Day* o *Sunday* Domingo *m* de Resurrección || *Easter egg* huevo *m* de Pascua || *Easter Saturday* Sábado *m* de Gloria, Sábado Santo || *Easter week* Semana Santa.

Easter Island [-'ɑilənd] *pr n* GEOGR isla *f* de Pascua.

easterly ['iːstəli] *adj* del este (wind) || este (dirección).
◆ *adv* hacia el este (toward the east) || del este (from the east).
◆ *n* viento *m* del este.

eastern [iːstən] *adj* oriental, este; *the eastern part of the house* la parte este de la casa || del este; *the eastern provinces* las provincias del este || hacia el este (motion) || oriental (oriental) || — *Eastern bloc countries* países *m pl* del bloque del Este || *the eastern hemisphere* el hemisferio oriental.

Eastern Church [-tʃəːtʃ] *n* REL Iglesia *f* Oriental.

Easterner ['iːstənə*] *n* US habitante *m* de la parte nordeste de los EE. UU.

easternmost ['iːstənməust] *adj* más oriental.

Eastern time ['iːstəntaim]; **Eastern standard time** ['iːstən'stændəd,taim] *n* hora *f* del meridiano 75 al oeste de Greenwich [tiene cinco horas de retraso con relación a la hora de Greenwich].

Eastertide ['iːstətaid] *n* REL tiempo *m* pascual.

East Indian [iːst'indjən] *adj* de las Indias Orientales.

East Indies [iːst'indiz] *pl prn* GEOGR Indias *f* Orientales.

easting ['iːstiŋ] *n* MAR marcha *f* hacia el este.

east-northeast ['iːstnɔːθ'iːst] *n* estenordeste *m*.

East Pakistan ['iːst‚pɑːkis'tɑːn] *pr n* GEOGR Pakistán *m* Oriental.

east-southeast ['iːstsauθ'iːst] *n* estesudeste *m*.

eastward ['iːstwəd] *adj/adv* hacia el este.

eastwards [-z] *adv* hacia el este.

easy ['iːzi] *adj* fácil; *an easy problem to solve* un problema fácil de resolver; *easy style* estilo fácil; *an easy opponent* un adversario fácil; *an easy woman* una mujer fácil ‖ tranquilo, la (conscience, mind) ‖ natural, afable (manner) ‖ suelto, ta (not awkward) ‖ flexible, tolerante (tractable) ‖ pausado, da (pace) ‖ suave (gentle) ‖ leve (punishment) ‖ flojo, ja (loose) ‖ cómodo, da; desahogado, da (life) ‖ cómodo, da (person) ‖ fácil de engañar (gullible) ‖ laxo, xa (morals, virtue) ‖ COMM abundante (plentiful) | con poca demanda (trade) | flojo, ja (market) | bajo, ja (interest rate) ‖ FAM agradable ‖ — *an easy* un buen, unos buenos; *it cost him an easy million* le costó un buen millón ‖ *by easy payments, on easy terms* con facilidades de pago ‖ *easy come, easy go* lo que el agua trae, el agua lleva ‖ *easy to get on with* muy amable ‖ *easy to run* de fácil manejo ‖ *he is an easy person to live with* es fácil vivir con él ‖ *he is easy* le da igual *or* lo mismo ‖ *it is only too easy to yield to temptation* es muy fácil caer en la tentación ‖ *to be an easy fit* estarle cómodo a uno ‖ FAM *to be as easy as pie* o *as falling off a log* o *as shelling peas* o *a ABC* o *as winking* o *as can be* o *as anything* estar tirado, ser muy fácil ‖ FIG *to be on easy street* llevar una vida acomodada ‖ *to feel easy in one's mind* estar tranquilo ‖ COMM *to get easier* bajar (prices).
◆ *adv* FAM fácilmente (easily) ‖ — *easier said than done* más fácil es decirlo que hacerlo ‖ *easy does it!* ¡cuidado!, ¡despacito! ‖ *to go easy with* o *on* tener cuidado con, no gastar demasiado (not to waste), ser benévolo con (to be kind to), tener cuidado con (to be careful with) ‖ MIL *to stand easy* quedarse en posición de descanso | *to take it easy* descansar (to rest), ir despacio (to go slowly), tomárselo con calma, no preocuparse (not to worry); *take it easy!* ¡tómatelo con calma!; no ponerse nervioso (to remain calm), ir con cuidado (carefully), perder el tiempo (to idle).
◆ *n* descanso *m*.

easy chair [-tʃɛə*] *n* butacón *m*, sillón *m*.

easy game [-'geim] *n* FIG presa *f* fácil.

easygoing [-gəuiŋ] *adj* tolerante (tolerant) ‖ despacioso, sa; lento, ta (slow) ‖ indolente, descuidado, da (careless) ‖ de trato fácil (good-natured).

easy mark [-'mɑːk] *n* US FIG presa *f* fácil.

easy money [-'mʌni] *n* dinero *m* fácilmente ganado.

eat* [iːt] *vt* comer; *he ate an apple* comió una manzana; *horses eat oats* los caballos comen cebada ‖ FIG tragar, consumir; *this old car eats oil* este viejo coche traga aceite | corroer (to corrode); *acid eats metals* el ácido corroe los metales ‖ — FIG *to be eaten up with envy* consumirse de envidia | *to be hungry enough to eat a horse* tener un hambre canina ‖ *to eat away* corroer (to corrode), desgastar (to wear away), devorar ‖ *to eat breakfast* tomar el desayuno, desayunar ‖ FIG *to eat crow* o *humble pie* reconocer su error ‖ *to eat dinner* tomar la cena, cenar ‖ FIG *to eat like a horse* comer como un sabañón *or* como un regimiento ‖ *to eat lunch* tomar el almuerzo, almorzar ‖ *to eat off* devorar ‖ *to eat one's fill* comer bien ‖ FIG *to eat one's heart out* consumirse (de dolor) ‖ *to eat one's words* tragarse las palabras ‖ *to eat out* roer ‖ FIG *to eat s.o. out of house and home* dejar a alguien sin un céntimo [por haber comido mucho] ‖ *to eat s.o.'s head off* comerse vivo a alguien ‖ *to eat up* comerse; *he ate it all up* se lo comió todo; devorar; *the car ate up the kilometres* el coche devoraba los kilómetros ‖ FIG *what's eating you?* ¿qué mosca te ha picado? (why are you angry?), ¿qué te está carcomiendo? (what is troubling you?).
◆ *vi* comer; *they are eating* están comiendo ‖ comerse (to be eaten) ‖ ser sabroso; *this meat eats well* esta carne es muy sabrosa ‖ — *to eat into* corroer (metal, etc.), mermar (one's savings), desgastar (to wear away) ‖ *to eat through* corroer (to corrode) ‖ FIG *to have s.o. eating out of one's hand* tener dominado a alguien.
— OBSERV Pret ***ate***; pp ***eaten***.

eatable [-əbl] *adj* comible, comestible.
◆ *pl* comestibles *m*.

eaten *pp* ⟶ **eat.**

eater [-ə*] *n* comedor, ra (person who eats) ‖ fruta *f* de mesa (fruit) ‖ — *he is a big eater* es un comilón ‖ *he is a slow eater* come lentamente.

eating [-iŋ] *n* el comer, acción *f* de comer ‖ comida *f* (food) ‖ — *eating apple* manzana *f* para comer cruda ‖ *eating house* restaurante *m* ‖ *to be good eating* ser sabroso, sa.

eats [-s] *pl n* comestibles *m*, comida *f sing* (things to eat).

eau de Cologne ['əudəkə'ləun] *n* agua *f* de colonia, colonia *f*.

eaves [iːvz] *pl n* ARCH alero *m sing* ‖ ARCH *eaves trough* canalón *m*.

eavesdrop [-drɔp] *vi* escuchar indiscretamente.

eavesdropper [-drɔpə*] *n* indiscreto, ta; persona *f* que escucha indiscretamente.

ebb [eb] *n* MAR menguante *m*, reflujo *m* ‖ FIG caída *f*, decadencia *f* ‖ — FIG *at a low ebb* en el punto más bajo de ‖ *ebb tide* marea *f* menguante (of the sea), decadencia *f* (decline) ‖ *the ebb and flow* el flujo y reflujo (of tide), los altibajos *m pl* (ups and downs) ‖ FIG *to be at a low ebb* estar decaído | *to be on the ebb* ir disminuyendo.

ebb [eb] *vi* MAR bajar, menguar (tide) ‖ FIG decaer, disminuir.

ebenaceae [‚ebə'neisiːi] *pl n* BOT ebenáceas *f*.

ebon ['ebən] *adj* de ébano.

ebonite [-ait] *n* ebonita *f* (rubber).

ebony ['ebəni] *n* BOT ébano *m* (tree, wood).
◆ *adj* de ébano (made of ebony) ‖ color de ébano (colour).

Ebro ['iːbrəu] *pr n* GEOGR Ebro *m* (river).

ebullience [i'bʌljəns]; **ebulliency** [-i] *n* ebullición *f* ‖ FIG exaltación *f*, entusiasmo *m*, exuberancia *f*.

ebullient [i'bʌljənt] *adj* FIG exaltado, da; entusiasta, exuberante.

ebullition [ebə'liʃən] *n* ebullición *f* (boiling) ‖ FIG arranque *m*, arrebato *m* (outburst).

eburnean [i'bəːniən] *adj* ebúrneo, a.

EC *abbr of [European Community]* CE, Comunidad Europea.

ecce homo ['eksi'həuməu] *n* eccehomo *m*, ecce homo *m*.

eccentric [ik'sentrik] *adj* excéntrico, ca; *eccentric circles* círculos excéntricos; *eccentric behaviour* comportamiento excéntrico.
◆ *n* excéntrico, ca (person) ‖ TECH excéntrica *f*.

eccentricity [eksen'trisiti] *n* excentricidad *f*.

ecchymosis [eki'məusis] *n* MED equimosis *f*.

Ecclesiastes [i‚kliːzi'æstiːz] *n* REL Eclesiastés *m*.

ecclesiastic [i‚kliːzi'æstik] *n* REL eclesiástico *m*.
◆ *adj* eclesiástico, ca.

ecclesiastical [-əl] *adj* REL eclesiástico, ca.

Ecclesiasticus [i‚kliː'æstikəs] *n* REL eclesiástico *m*.

echelon ['eʃəlɔn] *n* MIL escalón *m* ‖ grado *m* (grade) ‖ nivel *m* (level).

echelon ['eʃəlɔn] *vt* escalonar.

echinite ['ekinait] *n* erizo *m* de mar fósil.

echinoderm [e'kainəu‚dəːm] *n* equinodermo *m*.

echinoid [e'kainɔid] *n* equinoideo *m*, erizo *m* de mar.

echinus [e'kainəs] *n* ZOOL equino *m*, erizo *m* de mar ‖ ARCH equino *m*.
— OBSERV El plural de *echinus* es *echini*.

echo ['ekəu] *n* eco *m* ‖ FIG eco *m*, resonancia *f* (sympathetic reaction) ‖ repetición *f*; *his latest book is an echo of his previous one* su último libro es una repetición del anterior ‖ — *echo chamber* cámara *f* de resonancia ‖ *echo sounder* sonda acústica ‖ *to cheer to the echo* ovacionar.
— OBSERV El plural de *echo* es *echoes*.

echo ['ekəu] *vi* resonar, hacer eco ‖ — *echoed wave* onda reflejada ‖ *the footsteps echoed in the room* se oía el eco de los pasos en la habitación.
◆ *vt* repetir; *the mountains echoed back his shout* las montañas repitieron su grito ‖ imitar (to imitate) ‖ adherirse a, hacerse eco de (to second).

éclair ['eiklɛə*] *n* relámpago *m* (cake).

eclampsia [i'klæmpsiə] *n* MED eclampsia *f*.

éclat ['eiklɑː] *n* brillo *m* ‖ éxito *m* clamoroso (great success).

eclectic [ek'lektik] *adj/n* ecléctico, ca.

eclecticism [ek'lektisizəm] *n* eclecticismo *m*.

eclipse [i'klips] *n* ASTR eclipse *m* ‖ FIG eclipse *m*.

eclipse [i'klips] *vt* ASTR eclipsar ‖ FIG eclipsar, deslucir (to outshine).

ecliptic [i'kliptik] *n* ASTR eclíptica *f*.
◆ *adj* eclíptico, ca.

eclogue ['eklɔg] *n* égloga *f* (poem).

ECM *abbr of [European Common Market]* MCE, Mercado Común Europeo.

ecological [‚ekə'lɔdʒikəl] *adj* ecológico, ca.

ecologist [iː'kɔlədʒist] *n* ecólogo *m*.

ecology [iː'kɔledʒi] *n* ecología *f*.

econometrics [iː‚kɔnə'metriks] *n* econometría *f*.

economic [iː‚kə'nɔmik] *adj* económico, ca; *economic crisis* crisis económica; *European Economic Community* Comunidad Económica Europea.

economical [-əl] *adj* económico, ca; *an economical car* un coche económico; *an economical person* una persona económica.

economics [-s] *n* economía *f*, economía *f* política (science); *to study economics* estudiar economía ‖ rentabilidad *f*; *the economics of advertising* la rentabilidad de la publicidad ‖ *School of Economics* Escuela *f* de Ciencias Económicas.

economist [i'kɔnəmist] *n* economista *m* & *f* ‖ FAM persona *f* ahorrativa.

economize [i'kɔnəmaiz] *vt/vi* economizar (*on* en).

economy [i'kɔnəmi] *n* economía *f*; *capitalist, planned economy* economía capitalista, planificada ‖ economía *f*, ahorro *m* (saving); *for economy's sake* por ahorro ‖ — *economy class* clase económica *or* turista || *economy drive* reajuste *m* económico || *to practise economy* economizar.

economy-sized [-,saizd] *adj* tamaño *m* familiar *or* económico.

ecosystem ['ekəusistəm] *n* ecosistema *m*.

écru; US ecru ['eikru:] *adj* crudo, da (colour).

ECSC *abbr of [European Coal & Steel Community]* CECA, Comunidad Europea del Carbón y el Acero.

ecstasize ['ekstəsaiz] *vt* extasiar.
◆ *vi* extasiarse.

ecstasy ['ekstəsi] *n* éxtasis *f*; *to go into ecstasy* caer en éxtasis || arrebato *m*; *in an ecstasy of love* en un arrebato de amor || *to go into ecstasies over* extasiarse ante.

ecstatic [eks'tætik] *adj* extático, ca.

ecstatically [-əli] *adv* con éxtasis.

ectoderm ['ektəudə:m] *n* BIOL ectodermo *m*.

ectoparasite ['ektəu'pærəsait] *n* ectoparásito *m*.

ectoplasm ['ektəuplæzəm] *n* ectoplasma *m*.

ECU *abbr of [European Currency Unit]* ECU, unidad monetaria europea.

Ecuador ['ekwə'dɔ:] *pr n* GEOGR Ecuador *m*.
— OBSERV The official name of this country is *El Ecuador*.

Ecuadoran [-rən]; **Ecuadorean; Ecuadorian** [-riən] *adj/n* ecuatoriano, na.

ecumene ['i:kjumi:n] *n* ecumene *m*.

ecumenical [,i:kju'menikəl] *adj* ecuménico, ca.

ecumenicalism [-izəm] *n* ecumenismo *m*.

eczema ['eksimə] *n* MED eczema *m*.

eczematous [ek'semətəs] *adj* MED eczematoso, sa.

edacious [i'deiʃəs] *adj* voraz, devorador, ra.

edacity [i'dæsiti] *n* voracidad *f*.

eddy ['edi] *n* remolino *m* (whirling movement) || contracorriente *f* (countercurrent) || *eddy current* corriente parásita, corriente *f* de Foucault.

eddy ['edi] *vi* arremolinarse, formar remolinos.

edelweiss ['eidlvais] *n* BOT edelweiss *m*.

edema [i'di:mə] *n* MED edema *m*.

edematous [i'demətəs] *adj* MED edematoso, sa.

Eden ['i:dn] *n* Edén *m* (garden).

Edenic [i'denik] *adj* edénico, ca.

edentate [i'denteit] *adj* desdentado, da.
◆ *n* ZOOL desdentado *m*.

edge [edʒ] *n* borde *m*; *the edge of a cliff, of a table* el borde de un acantilado, de una mesa; *he was on the edge of disaster* estaba al borde del desastre || orilla *f*, borde *m* (of water); *at the edge of the pond* a orillas *or* en la orilla del estanque || canto *m* (vertical part); *the top of the table is red and the edge yellow* la parte superior de la mesa es roja y el canto amarillo || filo *m*, corte *m* (of cutting tools) || margen *m* (of page) || límite *m*, linde *m* (limit) || extremidad *f* (outside part, farthest part) || borde *m* (border) || cresta *f* (of a mountain) || línea *f* saliente (of nose) || labio *m* (of a wound) || limbo *m* (of sun, moon) || arista *f*; *a cube has twelve edges* un cubo tiene doce aristas || ángulo *m* (angle) || canto *m* (of a coin, book) || FIG ventaja *f*; *to have the edge on s.o.* llevar ventaja a alguien || afueras *f sing* (of town) || — *a knife with a sharp* o *keen edge* un cuchillo bien afilado || *blunt edge* canto *m* (of a knife) || *cutting edge* corte *m*, filo *m* || FIG *his nerves are on edge* tiene los nervios de punta || AVIAC *leading edge* borde *m* de ataque || *milled edge* cordoncillo *m* || FIG *not to put too fine an edge on it* hablando en plata || *to be on edge* estar de canto (to be edgeways), tener los nervios de punta (to be nervous) || FIG *to give s.o. the sharp edge of one's tongue* echarle una bronca a alguien || *to put an edge on a blade* afilar una hoja || FIG *to set one's nerves on edge* ponerle a uno los nervios de punta | *to set one's teeth on edge* darle dentera a uno || *to stand a board on edge* poner una tabla de canto || *to take the edge off* embotar (to blunt), acallar (one's appetite), embotar (one's feelings), quitarle fuerza a (an argument) || *words with an edge to them* palabras *f* mordaces.

edge [edʒ] *vt* bordear; *trees edged the lake* unos árboles bordeaban el lago || afilar (to sharpen) || ribetear (in sewing) || mover *or* meter *or* acercar, (etc.) poco a poco *or* con cuidado; *they edged the piano back to the wall* acercaron el piano a la pared con cuidado || — FIG *to edge on* incitar | *to edge one's way through* abrirse paso poco a poco | *to edge o.s. in* introducirse poco a poco | *to edge out* eliminar poco a poco, conseguir eliminar.
◆ *vi* andar de lado (to move sideways) || avanzar con cautela (to move carefully); *he edged along the top of the wall* avanzaba con cautela por el muro || — *to edge away* alejarse poco a poco || *to edge in* abrirse paso poco a poco, conseguir meterse || *to edge up* trepar lentamente *or* con cuidado (to climb) || *to edge up to s.o.* acercarse cautelosamente a alguien.

edgebone ['edʒbəun] *n* cadera *f* (aitchbone).

edged [edʒd] *adj* cortante (blade) || ribeteado, da (in sewing).

edgeless [edʒlis] *adj* embotado, da (blunt).

edge tool ['edʒtu:l] *n* herramienta *f* cortante.

edgeways ['edʒweiz]; **edgewise** ['edʒwaiz] *adv* de lado, de costado (sideways) || de canto (on end) || FIG *not to be able to get a word in edgeways* no poder meter baza.

edging [edʒiŋ] *n* orla *f*, ribete *m* (in sewing) || borde *m* (of path).

edgy [edʒi] *adj* afilado, da || FIG nervioso, sa.

edible ['edibl] *adj* comestible (eatable).
◆ *pl n* comestibles *m*.

edict ['i:dikt] *n* edicto *m*.

edification [,edifi'keiʃən] *n* edificación *f*.

edificatory ['edifi,keitəri] *adj* edificante.

edifice ['edifis] *n* edificio *m* [imponente] || FIG estructura *f*, edificio *m* (of ideas, science, etc.).

edify ['edifai] *vt* edificar; *to edify by one's example* edificar con el ejemplo.

edifying [-iŋ] *adj* edificante.

edile ['i:dail] *n* edil *m* (Roman magistrate).

Edinburgh ['edinbərə] *pr n* GEOGR Edimburgo *m*.

edit ['edit] *vt* preparar para la imprenta (to prepare for printing) || redactar (to prepare articles) || dirigir (to direct a newspaper) || corregir (to correct) || montar (film) || adaptar (to adapt) || quitar, suprimir (to cut out) | *to edit out* quitar, suprimir, cortar (to cut out).

editing [-iŋ] *n* redacción *f* (writing) || dirección *f* (of newspaper) || corrección *f*, revisión *f* (correction) || montaje *m* (of film) || INFORM edición *f*.

edition [i'diʃən] *n* edición *f*; *first edition* primera edición; *paperback edition* edición en rústica || tirada *f*; *an edition of 50 000* una tirada de 50 000 || FIG versión *f*; *he is a smaller edition of his brother* es una versión de su hermano en más pequeño.

editio princeps [i'diʃiəu'prinseps] *n* edición *f* príncipe.
— OBSERV El plural de *editio princeps* es *editiones principes*.

editor ['editə*] *n* redactor *m* jefe (head of editorial staff) || director *m*; *editor of a dictionary* director de un diccionario || INFORM editor *m* || *editor's note* nota *f* de la redacción.

editorial [,edi'tɔ:riəl] *adj* editorial || de la dirección || — *editorial staff* redacción *f* || US *editorial writer* editorialista *m* & *f*.
◆ *n* editorial *m*, artículo *m* de fondo (article).

editorialist [,edi'tɔ:riəlist] *n* editorialista *m* & *f*.

editor in chief ['editərin'tʃi:f] *n* redactor *m* jefe, jefe *m* de redacción.

editorship ['editəʃip] *n* dirección *f*; *under the editorship of* bajo la dirección de || redacción *f* (in a publishing house) || cargo *m* de redactor jefe (of a newspaper).

educable ['edjukəbl] *adj* educable.

educate ['edjukeit] *vt* educar; *he was educated in France* fue educado en Francia || dar carrera de; *they educated their son for the law* dieron a su hijo la carrera de derecho || instruir; *to educate s.o. in elementary psychology* instruir a alguien en psicología elemental || educar (one's palate, etc.) || amaestrar (an animal).

educated [-id] *adj* cultivado, da; culto, ta; *he seems very educated* parece muy culto || instruido, da; *educated in the art of* instruido en el arte de || culto, ta; *educated speech* lenguaje culto || bien educado, da (well-bred) || amaestrado, da (animal).

education [,edju'keiʃən] *n* enseñanza *f* (schooling, teaching); *primary, secondary education* primera, segunda enseñanza || educación *f* (upbringing); *hunting was part of his education* la caza formaba parte de su educación || formación *f*; *they gave me a good education at that school* recibí una buena formación en esa escuela || instrucción *f* (in specific field); *education in the art of* instrucción en el arte de || cultura *f* (culture) || amaestramiento *m* (of animals) || — *further education* estudios universitarios, enseñanza superior || *Ministry of Education* Ministerio *m* de Educación || *physical education* educación física || *to have a classical education* haber hecho estudios clásicos.

educational [,edu'keiʃənl] *adj* educativo, va; *new educational methods* nuevos métodos educativos; *an educational film* una película educativa || docente (teaching); *educational centre* centro docente.

educationalist [,edju'keiʃnəlist]; **educationist** [,edju'keiʃənist] *n* especialista *m* en pedagogía.

educative ['edjukətiv] *adj* educativo, va.

educator ['edjukeitə*] *n* educador, ra || especialista *m* & *f* en pedagogía (educationist).

educe [i'dju:s] *vt* deducir, sacar.

educt ['i:dʌkt] *n* CHEM producto *m* de descomposición || FIG deducción *f*.

eduction [i'dʌkʃən] *n* TECH evacuación *f*, descarga *f* | escape *m* (of steam) || FIG deducción *f*.

edulcorate [i'dʌlkəreit] *vt* edulcorar, endulzar.

Edward ['edwəd] *pr n* Eduardo *m*.

Edwardian [ed'wɔ:djən] *adj* eduardiano, na.

EEC *abbr of [European Economic Community]* CEE, Comunidad Económica Europea.

eel [i:l] *n* ZOOL anguila *f* (fish).

eelworm ['i:lwə:m] *n* ZOOL anguílula *f*.

e'en [i:n] *adv* → **even.**

e'er [ɛə*] *adv* → **ever.**

eerie; eery ['iəri] *adj* misterioso, sa (mysterious) || horripilante (frightening) || extraño, ña (strange).

efface [i'feis] *vt* borrar (to rub out) || FIG borrar; *to efface a memory* borrar un recuerdo | eclipsar (to outshine) || *to efface o.s.* conseguir pasar desapercibido.

effacement [-mənt] *n* borradura *f* || FIG desaparición *f*.

effect [i'fekt] *n* efecto *m*; *cause and effect* causa y efecto; *his words had no effect on her* sus palabras no le hicieron ningún efecto; *of no effect* sin efecto; *the Compton effect* el efecto Compton || efecto *m*, resultado *m*, consecuencia *f* (result) || impresión *f*, efecto *m*; *clothes which create an effect of youthfulness* ropa que da la impresión de juventud || fin *m*, propósito *m*, intención *f* (purpose); *to speak to that effect* hablar con esa intención || sentido *m*, tenor *m* (sense) || — *for effect* para causar efecto, para impresionar || *in effect* en efecto, en realidad (in fact), vigente (a law) || *or words to that effect* o algo por el estilo || *side effect* efecto secundario || *striving after effect* efectismo *m* || *to be in effect* estar vigente (a law) || *to bring* o *to put into effect* poner en vigor (a law), aplicar, empezar a aplicar (a rule) || *to carry into effect* llevar a cabo, realizar, ejecutar || *to create a good, a bad effect* ser de buen, de mal efecto || *to give effect to* hacer efectivo || *to go into effect* entrar en vigor || *to have no effect* no dar resultado || *to have the desired effect* producir el efecto deseado || *to no effect* en vano, inútilmente, sin resultado || *to take effect* surtir efecto (medicine, etc.), entrar en vigor, tener efecto (law, timetable, etc.) || *to the effect that...* con el propósito de... (with the intention of), en el sentido de que... (in order that), especificando que... (specifying that) || *to the same effect, to that effect* por el estilo, en el mismo sentido || *to this effect* con este fin || *with effect from* con efecto a partir de, que surte efecto a partir de.
◆ *pl* efectos *m*; *special effects* efectos especiales; *sound effects* efectos sonoros; *personal effects* efectos personales || *no effects* sin fondos (on a cheque).

effect [i'fekt] *vt* efectuar, realizar, llevar a cabo; *the crossing was effected without difficulty* la travesía se realizó sin dificultad || hacer (saving).

effective [i'fektiv] *adj* eficaz; *those pills are very effective* esas píldoras son muy eficaces || efectivo, va; real; *effective power* potencia efectiva || impresionante (striking) || vigente, en vigor, en vigencia (in force); *the rules effective at the present time* las normas vigentes en la actualidad || MIL disponible; *effective troops* tropas disponibles || — TECH *effective capacity, force* capacidad *f*, fuerza *f* útil || *to become effective* entrar en vigor (law), (empezar a) aplicarse (measures).

effectively [-li] *adv* eficazmente (efficiently) || de hecho, en efecto (in fact).
◆ *pl n* efectivos *m*.

effectiveness [-nis] *n* eficacia *f* (efficiency) || efecto *m* (effect) || vigencia *f* (of a law).

effectual [i'fektʃual] *adj* eficaz || válido, da (valid).

effectuate [i'fektjueit] *vt* efectuar, realizar, ejecutar.

effeminacy [i'feminəsi] *n* afeminación *f*, afeminamiento *m*.

effeminate [i'feminit] *adj* afeminado, da.
◆ *n* afeminado, da.

efferent ['efərənt] *adj* eferente; *efferent blood vessels* vasos eferentes.

effervesce [,efə'ves] *vi* estar *or* entrar en efervescencia (to fizz) | ser efervescente (to be effervescent) || FIG hervir, bullir (in anger) || FIG *to effervesce with joy* rebosar de alegría.

effervescence [-ns]; **effervescency** [-nsi] *n* efervescencia *f*.

effervescent [efə'vesnt] *adj* efervescente.

effete [e'fiːt] *adj* agotado, da (land) || ineficaz, estéril, vano, na (ineffective) || gastado, da (wornout) || agotado, da (exhausted) || degenerado, da (degenerate) || decandente (decadent).

efficacious [,efi'keiʃəs] *adj* eficaz.

efficaciousness [-nis]; **efficacy** ['efikəsi] *n* eficacia *f*.

efficiency [i'fiʃənsi] *n* eficacia *f*, eficiencia *f*; *he works with great efficiency* trabaja con mucha eficacia || rendimiento *m*; *the efficiency of a machine* el rendimiento de una máquina.

efficient [i'fiʃənt] *adj* eficaz, eficiente; *an efficient secretary* una secretaria eficaz || eficaz (effective) || de buen rendimiento (machine) || *efficient cause* causa *f* eficiente.

effigy ['efidʒi] *n* efigie *f*; *to burn s.o. in effigy* quemar a alguien en efigie.

effloresce [,eflɔː'res] *vi* BOT florecer (to blossom).

efflorescence [-ns] *n* CHEM eflorescencia *f* || BOT florecimiento *m*.

efflorescent [-nt] *adj* CHEM eflorescente || BOT floreciente.

effluence ['efluəns] *n* emanación *f*.

effluent ['efluənt] *n* chorro *m*.

effluvium [e'fluːvjəm] *n* efluvio *m*.
— OBSERV El plural de *effluvium* es *effluvia* o *effluviums*.

efflux ['eflʌks] *n* flujo *m* (of liquid) || escape *m* (of gas) || transcurso *m* (of time).

effort ['efət] *n* esfuerzo *m*; *to make an effort to* hacer un esfuerzo para; *I spared no effort* no escatimé esfuerzos; *without effort* sin esfuerzo; *wasted efforts* esfuerzos vanos || FAM obra *f*; *have you seen his last effort?* ¿has visto su última obra? | tentativa *f* (attempt) || PHYS fuerza *f* efectiva || *to be worth the effort* valer la pena.

effortless [-lis] *adj* fácil, sin ningún esfuerzo.

effraction [i'frækʃən] *n* efracción *f*.

effrontery [i'frʌntəri] *n* descaro *m*, desfachatez *f*, desvergüenza *f*, caradura *f*, frescura *f*.

effulgence [e'fʌldʒəns] *n* refulgencia *f*, resplandor *m*.

effulgent [e'fʌldʒənt] *adj* refulgente, resplandeciente.

effuse [e'fjuːz] *vt* verter, derramar (to pour out) || difundir (to spread).
◆ *vi* derramarse.

effusion [i'fjuːʒən] *n* efusión *f* (shedding) || FIG efusión *f*, desahogo *m*, expansión *f* (of emotion) || MED derrame *m* || CHEM efusión *f*.

effusive [i'fjuːsiv] *adj* efusivo, va.

effusiveness [-nis] *n* carácter *m* efusivo.

EFL *abbr of* *[English as a foreign langugage]* inglés como idioma extranjero.

EFTA *abbr of* *[European Free Trade Association]* AELC, asociación europea de libre comercio.

e. g. ['iː'dʒiː] *abbr of* v. g., verbi gratia, verbigracia.

egalitarian [i,gæli'tɛəriən] *adj/n* igualitario, ria.

Egeria [i'dʒiəriə] *pr n* Egeria *f*.

egg [eg] *n* huevo *m*; *fried egg* huevo frito || FAM bomba *f* (bomb) || — FIG & FAM *a bad egg* una mala persona | *a good egg* una buena persona | *as sure as eggs* tan cierto como que dos y dos son cuatro || *bad egg* huevo podrido || *boiled egg* huevo pasado por agua || *darning egg* huevo de zurcir || *Easter egg* huevo de Pascuas || *hard-boiled egg* huevo duro || *in the egg* en embrión || *new-laid egg* huevo fresco || *poached egg* huevo escalfado || *scrambled eggs* huevos revueltos || *soft-boiled egg* huevo pasado por agua || *to boil an egg* pasar un huevo por agua || FIG *to kill the goose that lays the golden egg* matar la gallina de los huevos de oro || *to lay an egg* poner un huevo || FIG *to put all one's eggs in one basket* jugárselo todo a una carta | *to tread on eggs* andar *or* ir pisando huevos.

egg [eg] *vt* *to egg on* incitar.

eggbeater ['eg,biːtə] *n* US batidor *m* de huevos.

egg cell ['egsel] *n* MED óvulo *m*.

eggcup ['egkʌp] *n* huevera *f*.

egg flip ['egflip] *n* «flip» *m*, ponche *m* de huevo.

egghead ['eghed] *n* FAM intelectual *m* | científico *m*.

eggnog ['egnɔg] *n* «flip» *m*, ponche *m* de huevo.

eggplant ['egplɑːnt] *n* BOT berenjena *f*.

egg-shaped ['egʃeipt] *adj* oviforme, ovoide.

eggshell ['egʃel] *n* cascarón *m* de huevo.
◆ *adj* frágil.

egg timer ['eg,taimə*] *n* reloj *m* de arena (for cooking).

egg-whisk ['egwisk] *n* batidor *m* de huevos.

egg white ['egwait] *n* clara *f* de huevo.

egis ['iːdʒis] *n* —→ **aegis.**

eglantine ['egləntain] *n* BOT escaramujo *m*.

ego ['egəu] *n* PHIL ego *m*, yo *m* || FAM amor *m* propio (self-esteem) | egoísmo *m* (selfishness) || FAM *he's always on an ego trip* tiene un ego descomunal.

egocentric [,egəu'sentrik]; **egocentrical** [-əl] *adj/n* egocéntrico, ca.

egocentrism ['egəu'sentrizəm] *n* egocentrismo *m*.

egoism ['egəuizəm] *n* egoísmo *m*.

egoist ['egəuist] *n* egoísta *m* & *f* (selfish person) || egoísta *m* & *f*.

egoistic [,egəu'istik]; **egoistical** [-əl] *adj* egoísta.

egotism ['egəutizəm] *n* egoísmo *m* (selfishness) || egotismo *m* (self-importance).

egotist ['egəutist] *n* egotista *m* & *f* (self-important person).

egotistic [,egəu'tistik]; **egotistical** [-əl] *adj* egoísta (selfish) || egotista (self-important).

egregious [i'griːdʒəs] *adj* notorio, ria (flagrant) || atroz (atrocious) || extraordinario, ria (extraordinary) || enorme (error).

egregiousness [-nis] *n* notoriedad *f* (notoriety) || atrocidad *f* (atrocity) || enormidad *f* (of an error).

egress ['iːgres]; **egression** [i'greʃən] *n* salida *f* (exit) || ASTR emersión *f*.

egret ['iːgret] *n* ZOOL garceta *f* (bird).

Egypt ['iːdʒipt] *pr n* GEOGR Egipto *m*.

Egyptian [i'dʒipʃən] *adj/n* egipcio, cia.

Egyptologist ['iːdʒip'tɔlədʒist] *n* egiptólogo, ga.

Egyptology ['iːdʒip'tɔlədʒi] *n* egiptología *f*.

eh! [ei] *interj* ¡eh!

eider ['aidə*] *n* eider *m*, pato *m* de flojel (bird).

eiderdown ['aidədaun] *n* edredón *m*.

eight [eit] *adj* ocho.
◆ *n* ocho *m*; *the eight of clubs* el ocho de trébol || ocho *f pl* (time); *I'll come at eight* vendré a las ocho; *five past eight* las ocho y cinco || SP equipo *m* de ocho (team) || ocho *m* (boat) || carrera *f* para ocho (race) || — *a boy of eight* un niño de ocho años || FIG *to have had one over the eight* llevar una copa de más.

eight ball [-bɔːl] *n* US SP bola *f* negra (in pool) || FIG & FAM *to be behind the eight ball* estar en un apuro.

eighteen ['ei'tiːn] *adj* dieciocho, diez y ocho.
◆ *n* dieciocho *m*, diez y ocho *m*.

eighteenth [ˈeiˈtiːnθ] *adj* decimoctavo, va (ordinal) || dieciochavo, va (partitive); *eighteenth part* dieciochava parte || *the eighteenth century* el siglo XVIII [dieciocho].
◆ *n* decimoctavo, va; diez y ocho *m* & *f*, dieciocho *m* & *f* (in a series) || dieciochavo *m*, dieciochava *f* parte (fraction) || diez y ocho, dieciocho; *John XVIII* (the eighteenth) Juan XVIII [diez y ocho] || dieciocho *m*, día *m* dieciocho (date); *the eighteenth of January* el dieciocho de enero.

eightfold [ˈeitfəuld] *adj* multiplicado por ocho.
◆ *adv* ocho veces.

eighth [eitθ] *adj* octavo, va.
◆ *adv* en octavo lugar || *to come eight* salir el octavo (in a competition).
◆ *n* octavo, va (in a series) || octavo *m*, octava parte *f* (fraction) || ocho *m*, día *m* ocho (date); *he is coming on the eighth* viene el día ocho || octavo; *Henry VIII* (the eighth) Enrique VIII [octavo] || MUS octava *f*.

eighth note [-nəut] *n* US MUS corchea *f*.

eight hundred [ˈeitˈhʌndrəd] *adj* ochocientos, tas.
◆ *n* ochocientos *m*.

eight hundredth [-θ] *adj/n* octingentésimo, ma.

eightieth [ˈeitiiθ] *adj* octogésimo, ma.
◆ *n* octogésimo, ma; ochenta *m* & *f* (in eightieth position) || octogésimo *m*, octogésima parte *f* (fraction).
— OBSERV When the word *eightieth* means «in eightieth position» it is more often translated by *ochenta* than by *octogésimo*.

eighty [ˈeiti] *adj* ochenta.
◆ *n* ochenta *m*.
◆ *pl* años *m* ochenta; *in the eighties* en los años ochenta || *she is in her eighties* tiene unos ochenta años.

eikon [ˈaikən] *n* icono *m* (ikon).

einsteinium [ˈainstainjəm] *n* CHEM einstenio *m*.

Eire [ˈɛərə] *pr n* GEOGR Eire *m*.

either [ˈaiðə*, US, ˈiːðə*] *adj* cada, ambos (both); *there were cars parked on either side of the street* había coches aparcados a cada lado *or* en ambos lados de la calle || cualquiera de los dos; *either of the tables will do* cualquiera de las dos mesas valdrá || ninguno de los dos (with negation); *I can't find either book* no encuentro ninguno de los dos libros || *either way* de cualquier modo.
◆ *pron* cualquiera de los dos, uno u otro; *you can use either of them* te puedes servir de cualquiera de los dos || ninguno de los dos, ni uno ni otro (with negation); *I didn't see either of them* no vi ni a uno ni a otro || *either of us* cualquiera de nosotros.
◆ *adv* tampoco; *I don't like him or his family or his friends either* no me gusta él, ni su familia, ni sus amigos tampoco; *I can't find my pencil either* no encuentro mi lápiz tampoco.
◆ *conj either... or* o... o; *either he goes or I go* o se va él o me voy yo.

ejaculate [iˈdʒækjuleit] *vt* exclamar, proferir de repente (to exclaim) || lanzar (a cry) || eyacular (semen).

ejaculation [iˌdʒækjuˈleiʃən] *n* exclamación *f* (exclamation) || jaculatoria *f* (prayer) || eyaculación *f* (of semen).

ejaculatory [iˈdʒæljulətəri] *adj* exclamatorio, ria || jaculatorio, ria (prayer).

eject [idˈʒeikt] *vt* expulsar (flames, cartridge, etc.) || expulsar, echar; *they ejected the demonstrators* expulsaron a los manifestantes || desahuciar (a tenant) || expulsar (from a party, a job, etc.) || eyectar, expeler (from a plane, etc.).

ejecta [iˈdʒektə] *pl n* deyecciones *f* (of volcano) || materias *f* expulsadas.

ejection [iˈdʒekʃən] *n* expulsión *f* || desahucio *m* (of a tenant) || *ejection seat* asiento *m* eyectable *or* lanzable.

ejectment [iˈdʒektmənt] *n* expulsión *f* || desahucio *m* (of tenants).

ejector [iˈdʒektə*] *n* eyector *m* (of firearm) || *ejector seat* asiento *m* eyectable *or* lanzable.

eke [iːk] *vt* escatimar, hacer durar (to make last); *to eke out the provisions* escatimar los víveres || suplir las deficiencias de, complementar (one's salary, etc.) || *to eke out a livelihood* ganarse la vida a duras penas.

el [el] *n* US ferrocarril *m* elevado.

elaborate [iˈlæbərit] *adj* complicado, da (complicated) || detallado, da (detailed) || trabajado, da (style, artistic works) || primoroso, sa (decoration) || rebuscado, da (affected) || de muchos platos (meal).

elaborate [iˈlæbəreit] *vt* elaborar (to produce) || elaborar; *to elaborate a plan* elaborar un proyecto || ampliar, desarrollar (to enlarge upon, to develop).
◆ *vi* explicarse (to explain o.s.) || explicarse con muchos detalles (in great detail) || — *to elaborate on* explicar con más detalles || *to refuse to elaborate* negarse a dar más detalles.

elaborately [iˈlæbəritli] *adv* con cuidado, cuidadosamente (carefully) || de modo complicado, complicadamente || con detalles, detalladamente.

elaborateness [iˈlæbəritnis] *n* esmero *m*, cuidado *m* (care) || complejidad *f* (of a mechanism).

elaboration [iˈlæbəˈreiʃən] *n* explicación *f* (of texts, etc.) || elaboración *f* (of a plan) || complicación *f*.

eland [ˈiːlənd] *n* ZOOL alce *m* africano.

élan vital [eiˈlɑːŋviːˈtæl] *n* impulso *m*, elan *m* vital (vital force).

elapse [iˈlæps] *vi* pasar, transcurrir (time).

elastic [iˈlæstik] *adj* elástico, ca; *gases are very elastic* los gases son muy elásticos || FIG elástico, ca; flexible; *an elastic plan* un proyecto elástico || — *elastic band* goma (elástica) || *elastic limit* límite *m* de elasticidad, límite elástico.
◆ *n* elástico *m*.

elasticated [iˈlæstikeitid] *adj* elástico, ca, con elásticos.

elasticity [ˌelæsˈtisiti] *n* elasticidad *f* || FIG elasticidad *f*, flexibilidad *f*.

elate [iˈleit] *vt* regocijar; *she was elated at her triumph* su triunfo le regocijó.

elated [-id] *adj* de regocijo, de alegría (cry, etc.).

elaterid [iˈlætərid] *adj* ZOOL elatérido, da.

elation [iˈleiʃən] *n* regocijo *m*, júbilo *m*.

Elba [ˈelbə] *pr n* GEOGR Elba *f* (island).

Elbe [ˈelbə] *pr n* GEOGR Elba *m* (river).

elbow [ˈelbəu] *n* codo *m* (of arm) || codillo *m* (of animals) || recodo *m* (bend in road) || codo *m* (in pipe) || — FAM *at one's elbow* al alcance de la mano || *out at elbows* raído, da (clothes); desharrapado, da (person) || FIG *to bend* o *to crook* o *to lift the elbow* empinar el codo (to drink) | *to be up to the elbows in work* estar agobiado de trabajo || *to lean one's elbows on* apoyar los codos en, acodarse en || FIG *to rub elbows with* codearse con.

elbow [ˈelbəu] *vt* dar un codazo a; *he elbowed him in the stomach* le dio un codazo en el estómago || empujar con el codo (to push) || apartar con el codo (to push aside) || *to elbow one's way through the crowd* abrirse paso a codazos entre la muchedumbre.
◆ *vi* abrirse paso a codazos || formar un codo *or* recodo.

elbow grease [-griːs] *n* FIG fuerza *f* de puños, energía *f*.

elbowroom [-rum] *n* FIG sitio *m*, espacio *m* (space) | libertad *f* de acción, campo *m* libre (freedom to act).

elder [ˈeldə*] *adj* mayor; *his elder daughter* su hija mayor || *Pliny the Elder* Plinio el Viejo.
◆ *n* mayor *m*; *respect for one's elders* respeto a los mayores || anciano *m* (of a village, tribe, etc.) || REL anciano *m* || BOT saúco *m* (tree) || *he is two years my elder* es dos años mayor que yo.

elderberry [ˈeldəˌberi] *n* BOT baya *f* del saúco (fruit) | saúco *m* (tree).

elderly [ˈeldəli] *adj* mayor de edad || — *elderly people* la gente mayor || *to be getting elderly* ir para viejo.

eldest [ˈeldist] *adj* mayor; *John is the eldest of the children* Juan es el mayor de los niños.

El Dorado [ˌeldəˈrɑːdəu] *pr n* Eldorado *m*.

Eleanor [ˈelinə*] *pr n* Leonor *f*.

elecampane [ˌelikæmˈpein] *n* BOT helenio *m*.

elect [iˈlekt] *adj* elegido, da (chosen) || electo, ta; *the President-elect* el Presidente electo.
◆ *pl n the elect* los elegidos *m*.

elect [iˈlekt] *vt* elegir; *to elect a chairman* elegir a un presidente; *he elected to leave* eligió marcharse.
◆ *vi* elegir.

election [iˈlekʃən] *n* elección *f* || — *election campaign* campaña *f* electoral || *election returns* resultados *m pl* electorales || *election time* período *m* electoral || *general election* elecciones generales || *local elections* elecciones *f pl* municipales || *to call* o *to hold an election* convocar elecciones || *to stand for an election* presentar su candidatura, presentarse a una elección.

electioneer [iˈlekʃəˈniə*] *vi* hacer campaña electoral.

electioneering [-riŋ] *n* campaña *f* electoral (campaign) || maniobras *f pl* electorales (election rigging).

elective [iˈlektiv] *adj* electivo, va; *an elective post* un puesto electivo || electoral; *an elective system, body* un sistema, un cuerpo electoral || US facultativo, va (study) || *elective affinity* afinidad electiva.
◆ *n* US asignatura *f* facultativa.

elector [iˈlektə*] *n* elector, ra || HIST elector *m*.

electoral [iˈlektərəl] *adj* electoral || — US *electoral college* colegio *m* electoral || *electoral roll* censo *m* electoral.

electorate [iˈlektərit] *n* electorado *m* || distrito *m* electoral (district).

Electra [iˈlektrə] *pr n* Electra *f*.

electress [iˈlektris] *n* electriz *f*.

electric [iˈlektrik] *adj* eléctrico, ca; *electric guitar* guitarra eléctrica || FIG cargado de electricidad, muy tenso, sa (atmosphere) || — *electric appliances* aparatos eléctricos || *electric blanket* manta eléctrica || *electric blue* azul eléctrico || *electric chair* silla eléctrica || *electric cooker* cocina eléctrica || *electric current* corriente *f* eléctrica || *electric eye* célula fotoeléctrica || *electric fire* estufa *f* eléctrica || *electric fixtures* instalación eléctrica || *electric generator* electrógeno *m* || *electric heating* calefacción eléctrica || *electric light* luz eléctrica || *electric lighting* alumbrado eléctrico || *electric motor* motor eléctrico, electromotor *m* || *electric pump* electrobomba *f* || *electric ray* torpedo *m* (fish) || *electric razor* o *shaver* maquinilla de afeitar eléctrica || *electric shock* electrochoque *m* || *electric tape* cinta aisladora || *electric welding* soldadura eléctrica || *electric wiring* instalación eléctrica.

electrical [-əl] *adj* eléctrico, ca ‖ FIG cargado de electricidad, muy tenso, sa (atmosphere) ‖ — *electrical engineer* ingeniero electrotécnico ‖ *electrical engineering* electrotecnia *f*, ingeniería eléctrica ‖ *electrical household appliances* aparatos electrodomésticos ‖ *electrical supplies* material eléctrico.

electrically [-əli] *adv* por electricidad.

electrician [ilek'triʃən] *n* electricista *m* & *f*.

electricity [ilek'trisiti] *n* electricidad *f*; *static electricity* electricidad estática.

electrics [i'lektriks] *pl n* instalación *f* eléctrica.

electrification [i'lektrifi'keiʃən] *n* electrificación *f*.

electrify [i'lektrifai] *vt* electrificar (railway, industry, etc.) ‖ electrizar (to produce electricity in) ‖ FIG electrizar.

electrifying [i'lektrifaiiŋ] *adj* FIG electrizante.

electrize [i'lektraiz] *vt* electrizar.

electroacoustics [i'lektrəuə'ku:stiks] *n* PHYS electroacústica *f*.

electroanalysis [i'lektrəuə'næləsis] *n* CHEM electroanálisis *m*.

electrocardiogram [i'lektrəu'kɑ:djəugræm] *n* MED electrocardiograma *m*.

electrocardiograph [i'lektrəu'kɑ:djəugrɑ:f] *n* MED electrocardiógrafo *m*.

electrocardiography [i'lektrəu,kɑ:di'ɔgrəfi] *n* MED electrocardiografía *f*.

electrocautery [i'lektrəu'kɔ:təri] *n* MED electrocauterio *m*.

electrochemical [i'lektrəu'kemikəl] *adj* electroquímico, ca.

electrochemistry [i'lektrəu'kemistri] *n* electroquímica *f*.

electrocoagulation [i'lektrəukəu,ægju'leiʃən] *n* MED electrocoagulación *f*.

electrocute [i'lektrəkju:t] *vt* electrocutar.

electrocution [i,lektrə'kju:ʃən] *n* electrocución *f*.

electrode [i'lektrəud] *n* PHYS electrodo *m*.

electrodynamic [i'lektrəudai'næmik] *adj* electrodinámico, ca.

electrodynamics [-s] *n* electrodinámica *f*.

electrodynamometer [i'lektrəu,dainə'mɔmitə] *n* electrodinamómetro *m*.

electroencephalogram [i'lektrəuen'sefələugræm] *n* MED electroencefalograma *m*.

electroencephalograph [i'lektrəuen'sefələugrɑ:f] *n* MED electroencefalógrafo *m*.

electroencephalography [i'lektrəu,en,sefə'lɔgrəfi] *n* MED electroencefalografía *f*.

electrokinetics [i'lektrəukai'netiks] *n* electrocinética *f*.

electrolier [i,lektrə'li:ə*] *n* araña *f* (chandelier).

electrolysis [ilek'trɔlisis] *n* CHEM electrólisis *f*.

electrolyte [i'lektrəulait] *n* CHEM electrólito *m*.

electrolytic [i'lektrə'litik] *adj* CHEM electrolítico, ca.

electrolyze [i'lektrəulaiz] *vt* electrolizar.

electromagnet [i'lektrəu'mægnit] *n* PHYS electroimán *m*.

electromagnetic [i'lektrəu'mægnetik] *adj* electromagnético, ca; *electromagnetic wave* onda electromagnética.

electromagnetism [i'lektrəu'mægnitizəm] *n* PHYS electromagnetismo *m*.

electromechanical [i'lektrəumi'kænikəl] *adj* electromecánico, ca.

electromechanics [i'lektrəumi'kæniks] *n* electromecánica *f*.

electrometallurgy [i'lektrəume'tælədʒi] *n* electrometalurgia *f*.

electrometer [ilek'trɔmitə] *n* electrómetro *m*.

electrometry [ilek'trɔmitri] *n* PHYS electrometría *f*.

electromotive [i'lektrəuməutiv] *adj* electromotor, ra ‖ *electromotive force* fuerza electromotriz.

electromotor [i'lektrəu'məutə*] *n* electromotor *m*.

electron [i'lektrɔn] *n* PHYS electrón *m* ‖ *electron beam, microscope, tube, bombardment* haz, microscopio, tubo, bombardeo electrónico.

electronegative [i'lektrəu'negətiv] *adj* PHYS electronegativo, va.

electronic [ilek'trɔnik] *adj* electrónico, ca ‖ *electronic mail* correo *m* electrónico.

electronics [-s] *n* electrónica *f*.

electron volt [i'lektrɔnvɔlt] *n* PHYS electronvoltio *m*.

electropathy [ilek'trɔpəθi] *n* electroterapia *f*.

electrophone [i'lektrəfəun] *n* electrófono *m*.

electrophorus [ilek'trɔfərəs] *n* PHYS electróforo *m*.

— OBSERV El plural es *electrophori*.

electroplate [i'lektrəupleit] *vt* galvanizar.

electroplating [-iŋ] *n* galvanoplastia *f*.

electropositive [i'lektrəu'pɔzətiv] *adj* electropositivo, va.

electroscope [i'lektrəskəup] *n* PHYS electroscopio *m*.

electroshock [i'lektrəu,ʃɔk] *n* MED electrochoque *m*.

electrostatic [i'lektrəu'stætik] *adj* electrostático, ca.

electrostatics [-s] *n* electrostática *f*.

electrotechnical [i'lektrəu'teknikəl] *adj* electrotécnico, ca.

electrotechnics [i'lektrəu'tekniks] *n* electrotecnia *f*.

electrotherapy [i'lektrəu'θerəpi] *n* MED electroterapia *f*.

electrothermic [i'lektrəu'θə:mik] *adj* PHYS electrotérmico, ca.

electrothermy [i'lektrəu,θə:mi] *n* PHYS electrotermia *f*.

electrotype [i'lektrəutaip] *n* galvano *m*.

electrotype [i'lektrəutaip] *vt* galvanotipar.

electrotyping [-iŋ] *n* galvanotipia *f*.

electuary [i'lektjuəri] *n* MED electuario *m*.

eleemosynary [elii:'mɔsinəri] *adj* limosnero, ra; caritativo, va (charitable) ‖ de caridad ‖ que vive de limosnas.

elegance ['eligəns] *n* elegancia *f*.

elegant ['eligənt] *adj* elegante ‖ elegante, refinado, da (refined).

elegiac ['eli'dʒaiək]; **elegiacal** [-əl] *adj* elegiaco, ca; elegiaco, ca ‖ *elegiac couplet* dístico elegíaco.

elegize ['elidʒaiz] *vt* escribir una elegía a.

elegy ['elidʒi] *n* elegía *f* (poem).

element ['elimənt] *n* elemento *m* (part of a whole) ‖ parte *f*; *there is an element of truth in what he said* hay una parte de verdad en lo que dijo ‖ factor *m*, parte *f*; *the personal element* el factor personal ‖ BIOL, CHEM, PHYS, REL & ELECTR elemento *m* ‖ FIG *to be in one's element* estar en su elemento.

◆ *pl* elementos *m* (rudiments); *elements of mathematics* elementos de matemáticas ‖ elementos *m* (of nature); *the four elements* los cuatro elementos.

elemental [,eli'mentl] *adj* elemental (elementary) ‖ de los elementos (of the elements) ‖ CHEM elemental.

elementary [,eli'mentəri] *adj* elemental, fundamental (basic) ‖ CHEM elemental ‖ US *elementary school* escuela primaria.

elephant ['elifənt] *n* ZOOL elefante *m* ‖ — *cow elephant* elefanta *f* ‖ *elephant seal* elefante marino ‖ *young elephant* elefantillo *m*.

elephantiasic [,elifən'taiəsik] *adj* MED elefantiásico, ca; elefanciaco, ca; elefancíaco, ca.

elephantiasis [,elifən'taiəsis] *n* MED elefantiasis *f*, elefancia *f*.

elephantine [,eli'fæntain] *adj* FIG colosal, enorme (big) | torpe (awkward) | pesado, da; *elephantine wit* humor pesado.

elevate ['eliveit] *vt* elevar (to raise) ‖ elevar (style, dignity, temperature) ‖ aumentar (price) ‖ alzar, levantar (eyes, voice) ‖ ascender (rank of a person) ‖ levantar (one's mind) ‖ regocijar (to elate) ‖ REL elevar, alzar (the host) ‖ MIL elevar (a gun) ‖ *to elevate s.o.'s hopes* alimentar las esperanzas de uno.

elevated [-id] *adj* elevado, da ‖ aéreo, a (railway) ‖ elevado, da (road) ‖ FAM alegre (gay).

◆ *n* US metro *m* aéreo.

elevation [,eli'veiʃən] *n* elevación *f* (action, angle, hill) ‖ ascenso *m* (of a person) ‖ altitud *f*, altura *f* (of a plane) ‖ GEOGR elevación *f* ‖ ARCH alzado *m* (plan) ‖ REL *the Elevation* la Elevación.

elevator ['eliveitə*] *n* elevador *m* (a machine for raising things) ‖ timón *m* de profundidad (of aeroplane) ‖ ANAT elevador *m* (muscle) ‖ US ascensor *m* [AMER elevador *m*] (lift for people) | montacargas (goods lift) | silo *m* con elevador (a grain storage building).

eleven [i'levn] *adj* once.

◆ *n* once *m* (number) ‖ once *f pl* (time); *he arrived at eleven* llegó a las once ‖ SP once *m*, equipo *m* (team); *the Madrid eleven* el once madrileño.

eleven-plus [-plʌs] *n* ingreso *m*, examen *m* de ingreso.

— OBSERV El *eleven-plus* es un examen que hacen los niños al final de la primera enseñanza para saber en qué escuela secundaria pueden ingresar.

elevens [i'levnz]; **elevenses** [i'levnziz] *pl n* comida *f sing* ligera, once *f pl*.

eleventh [i'levənθ] *adj* onceavo, va; undécimo, ma; onceno, na ‖ FIG *at the eleventh hour* en el último momento.

◆ *n* undécimo, ma; onceno, na; *the eleventh on the list* el undécimo en la lista ‖ onzavo *m*, undécima parte *f* (fraction) ‖ once *m*, día *m* once (date); *on the eleventh of August* el once de agosto ‖ once *m*; *Pius XI* (the eleventh) Pío XI [once].

elf [elf] *n* duende *m*.

— OBSERV El plural de *elf* es *elves*.

elfin ['elfin] *adj* de los duendes (of elves) ‖ mágico, ca.

◆ *n* duendecillo *m*.

elfish ['elfiʃ]; **elvish** ['elviʃ] *adj* de los duendes (of elves) ‖ mágico, ca ‖ FIG travieso, sa (mischievous) | pequeño, ña (small).

elicit [i'lisit] *vt* sacar (the truth) ‖ provocar (to cause) ‖ obtener (to obtain).

elide [i'laid] *vt* elidir (in speech) ‖ suprimir (to strike out).

eligibility [,elidʒə'biliti] *n* eligibilidad *f*.

eligible ['elidʒəbl] *adj* elegible (by votation) ‖ adecuado, da (suitable) ‖ deseable (desirable)

|| atractivo, va (attractive) || — *an eligible young man* un buen partido || *to be eligible for a pension* tener derecho a una pensión.

eliminate [i'limineit] *vt* eliminar.

elimination [i,limi'neiʃən] *n* eliminación *f*.

eliminative [i'liminətiv] *adj* eliminador, ra.

eliminator [i'limineitə*] *n* eliminador, ra.

eliminatory [i'liminətəri] *adj* eliminatorio, ria || SP *eliminatory heat* o *round* eliminatoria *f*.

elinvar ['elinvɑ:] *n* elinvar *m* (of nickel and chrome).

Elisha [i'laiʃə] *pr n* Eliseo *m*.

elision [i'liʒən] *n* elisión *f*.

élite; *US* **elite** [ei'li:t] *n* élite *f*, lo más selecto, minoría *f* selecta.

elitist [ei'li:tist] *adj* elitista.

elixir [i'liksə*] *n* elixir *m*.

Elizabeth [i'lizəbəθ] *pr n* Isabel *f*.

Elizabethan [i'lizə'bi:θən] *adj* elisabetiano, na; isabelino, na (of Elisabeth I of England).

elk [elk] *n* ZOOL alce *m* || *US* wapití *m*.

ell [el] *n* ana *f* (former measure).

ellipse [i'lips] *n* MATH elipse *f*.

ellipsis [-is] *n* GRAMM elipsis *f*.
— OBSERV El plural de la palabra inglesa es *ellipses*.

ellipsoid [i'lipsɔid] *n* MATH elipsoide *m*.

ellipsoidal [,elip'sɔidl] *adj* elipsoidal.

elliptic [i'liptik]; **elliptical** [-əl] *adj* elíptico, ca.

elm [elm] *n* olmo *m* (tree).

elocution [,elə'kju:ʃən] *n* elocución *f* (manner) || declamación *f* (art).

elocutionary ['elə'kju:ʃnəri] *adj* declamatorio, ria.

elocutionist ['elə'kju:ʃnist] *n* profesor *m* de elocución || declamador, ra.

elongate ['i:lɔŋgeit] *vt* extender, alargar.

elongation ['i:lɔŋ'geiʃən] *n* elongación *f* || alargamiento *m* (extension).

elope [i'ləup] *vi* fugarse [con un amante] || fugarse para contraer matrimonio.

elopement [-mənt] *n* fuga *f*.

eloquence ['eləkwəns] *n* elocuencia *f*.

eloquent ['eləkwənt] *adj* elocuente.

El Salvador [,el,sælvə'dɔ:*] *pr n* GEOGR El Salvador *m*.

else [els] *adj/adv* otro, otra; *have you anything else to do?* ¿tienes otra cosa que hacer?; *anyone else would have failed* cualquier otro hubiera fracasado; *anything else is unworkable* cualquier otra cosa es irrealizable || más; *nothing else* nada más; *no one* o *nobody else* nadie más; *who else?* ¿quién más?; *what else?* ¿qué más?; *anything else, sir?* ¿algo más, señor?; *I could not do else than laugh* no pude hacer más que reírme || — *all else, everything else* todo lo demás || *anyone* o *anybody else* cualquier otra persona, cualquier otro, cualquier otra || *anywhere else* en cualquier otro sitio, en cualquier otra parte (position); *if it had been anywhere else* si hubiera sido en cualquier otro sitio; a cualquier otro sitio, a cualquier otra parte (motion); *take me anywhere else but there* llévame a cualquier otro sitio menos allí; ningún otro sitio (after negative); *he can't be anywhere else* no puede estar en ningún otro sitio || *everyone else* todos los demás || *everywhere else* en todas partes (position), a todas partes (motion) || *how else?* ¿de qué otra manera? || *little else remains to be done* fuera de esto queda muy poco por hacer || *much else* todavía mucho; *much else remains to be done* queda todavía mucho por hacer || *no one else could have done it but him* nadie más que él hubiera podido hacerlo || *nowhere else* en ningún otro sitio, en ninguna otra parte (position), a ningún otro sitio, a ninguna otra parte (motion) || *or else* si no; *telephone him tomorrow or else it will be too late* llámale mañana si no será demasiado tarde; *do as I say or else...* haz lo que yo digo si no... || *say anything else except that* di lo que quieras menos eso, di cualquier cosa menos eso || *someone else, somebody else* otro, otra; *you are taking me for s.o. else* me está tomando por otro || *something else* otra cosa; *let us speak of something else* vamos a hablar de otra cosa; algo más, otra cosa; *I have something else to tell you* tengo algo más que decirle || *they didn't see anyone else* no vieron a nadie más, no vieron a ninguna otra persona || *when else?* ¿en qué otro momento? || *where else?* ¿en qué otro sitio? (position), ¿a qué otro sitio? (motion).

elsewhere ['els'wɛə*] *adj* en otro sitio, en otra parte (at another place) || a otro sitio, a otra parte (to another place).

elucidate [i'lu:sideit] *vt* dilucidar, aclarar, poner en claro.

elucidation [i'lu:si'deiʃən] *n* aclaración *f*, elucidación *f*, dilucidación *f*.

elucidator [i'lu:sideitə*] *n* dilucidador, ra.

elucidatory [i,lu:si'deitəri] *adj* aclaratorio, ria.

elude [i'lu:d] *vt* eludir (a question) || esquivar, evitar (a blow) || despistarse de (one's pursuer) || escapar de (to escape) || zafarse de (an obligation) || burlar (the law) || — *the answer eluded me* no pude encontrar la solución || *their names elude me* se me han ido de la memoria sus nombres.

eludible [-ibl] *adj* evitable, eludible.

elusion [i'lu:ʒən] *n* escapatoria *f*, evasión *f*.

elusive [i'lu:siv] *adj* evasivo, va (evasive) || escurridizo, za (slippery) || difícil de conseguir.

elusiveness [-nis] *n* carácter *m* evasivo.

elusory [i'lu:səri] *adj* evasivo, va.

elver ['elvə*] *n* ZOOL angula *f*.

elves [elvz] *pl n* —> **elf.**

elvish ['elviʃ] *adj* —> **elfish.**

Elysian [i'liziən] *adj* MYTH Elíseo, a; *Elysian Fields* Campos Elíseos.

Elysium [i'liziəm] *pr n* Elíseo *m*.

elytron ['elitrɔn] *n* ZOOL élitro *m*.
— OBSERV El plural de *elytron* es *elytra*.

elytrum ['elitrəm] *n* ZOOL élitro *m*.
— OBSERV El plural de *elytrum* es *elytra*.

elzevir ['elziviə] *n* PRINT elzevir *m*, elzevirio *m*.

em [em] *n* eme *f* (letter) || PRINT cuadratín *m*.

emaciate [i'meiʃieit] *vt* adelgazar (person) || demacrar (face) || AGR empobrecer (soil).

emaciated [-id] *adj* demacrado, da (face).

emaciation [i'meisi'eiʃən] *n* demacración *f* (of face) || adelgazamiento *m* (of a person).

emanate ['eməneit] *vi* proceder, emanar.

emanation [,emə'neiʃən] *n* emanación *f*.

emancipate [i,mænsipeit] *vt* emancipar.

emancipation [i,mænsi'peiʃən] *n* emancipación *f*.

emancipator [i'mænsipeitə*] *n* emancipador, ra.

emancipatory [i'mænsi,peitəri] *adj* emancipador, ra.

emarginate [i'mɑ:dʒinit] *adj* emarginado, da.

emasculate [i'mæskjuleit] *vt* castrar, emascular || FIG mutilar.

emasculation [i,mæskju'leiʃən] *n* castración *f*, emasculación *f* || FIG mutilación *f*.

embalm [im'bɑ:m] *vt* embalsamar (a corpse, to perfume) || FIG conservar.

embalmer [-ə*] *n* embalsamador, ra.

embalmment [-mənt] *n* embalsamamiento *m*.

embank [im'bænk] *vt* construir un muro de contención, terraplenar (a roadway) || encauzar con diques, poner diques a (a river).

embarcation [,embɑ:'keiʃən] *n* —> **embarkation.**

embargo [em'bɑ:gəu] *n* prohibición *f* || MAR JUR embargo *m* || — *to be under an embargo* estar prohibido || *to put an embargo on* prohibir.
— OBSERV El plural de la palabra inglesa es *embargoes*.

embargo [em'bɑ:gəu] *vt* MAR & JUR embargar || prohibir (to forbid).

embark [im'bɑ:k] *vt* embarcar.
◆ *vi* embarcarse (*for* con rumbo a; *on* en) || FIG *to embark on* emprender (to start).

embarkation; embarcation [,embɑ:'keiʃən] *n* embarco *m* (of people) || embarque *m* (of goods) || *embarkation card* tarjeta *f* de embarque.

embarkment [-mənt] *n* terraplenado *m* (action) || terraplén *m* (bearing road, railway) || muro *m* de contención, terraplén *m* (wall) || dique *m* (of a river).

embarrass [im'bærəs] *vt* desconcertar, turbar, embarazar (to disconcert) || poner en un aprieto (to put in a tight spot) || molestar, estorbar, embarazar (to hinder) || complicar, dificultar (to complicate) || — *to be embarrassed* pasar vergüenza, sentirse molesto, estar violento || *to be financially embarrassed* estar mal de dinero, tener apuros económicos.

embarrassing [-iŋ] *adj* violento, ta; molesto, ta; embarazoso, sa.

embarrassment [-mənt] *n* desconcierto *m*, confusión *f*, turbación *f* (confusion) || vergüenza *f* (shame) || molestia *f* (trouble) || estorbo *m* (nuisance) || *financial embarrassment* apuros *m pl* de dinero, dificultades económicas, apuros económicos.

embassy ['embəsi] *n* embajada *f*.

embattle [im'bætl] *vt* MIL formar en orden de batalla || ARCH almenar (walls) | fortificar (a castle).

embay [im'bei] *vt* MAR abrigar en una ensenada || FIG rodear.

embed [im'bed] *vt* empotrar || clavar, hincar (weapon, etc.) || FIG meter, fijar (in mind).

embellish [im'beliʃ] *vt* embellecer (to beautify) || adornar (to adorn).

embellishment [-mənt] *n* embellecimiento *m* || adorno *m* (adornment).

ember ['embə*] *n* ascua *f*, rescoldo *m*.

Ember days [-deiz] *pl n* REL témporas *f*.

embers ['embəz] *pl n* ascuas *f*.

embezzle [im'bezl] *vt* malversar, desfalcar.

embezzlement [-mənt] *n* malversación *f*, desfalco *m*.

embezzler [-ə*] *n* malversador, ra; desfalcador, ra.

embitter [im'bitə*] *vt* FIG envenenar (a quarrel) | agriar, amargar (a person).

embittered [-d] *adj* amargado, da (bitter) || resentido, da; rencoroso, sa (resentful).

emblaze [im'bleiz] *vt* iluminar (to light up) || encender (to kindle) || engalanar (to adorn).

emblazon [im'bleizən] *vt* HERALD blasonar || FIG ensalzar, alabar (to extol).

emblazoned [-d] *adj* engalanado, da (decorated) || exhibido, da (displayed).

emblazonry [-ri] *n* HERALD blasón *m* || FIG adorno *m* brillante.

emblem ['embləm] *n* símbolo *m*, emblema *m* (symbol) || HERALD divisa *f*, emblema *m*.

emblematic [ˌembli'mætik] ; **emblematical** [-əl] *adj* simbólico, ca; emblemático, ca.

emblements ['emblmənts] *pl n* JUR frutos *m* de la tierra.

embodiment [im'bɔdimənt] *n* personificación *f*, encarnación *f*; *he is the very embodiment of vice* es la misma personificación del vicio || incorporación *f*.

embody [im'bɔdi] *vt* personificar, encarnar (to be the concrete expression of) || materializar, dar cuerpo a (to give clear form to) || incluir (to include) || expresar (an idea).

embog [im'bɔg] *vt* atascar.

embolden [im'bəuldən] *vt* dar ánimo a, alentar, envalentonar.

embole ['embəli] *n* embolia *f*.

embolism ['embəlizəm] *n* MED embolia *f*.

emboly ['embəli] *n* embolia *f*.

embosom [im'buzəm] *vt* abrazar, apretar contra sí (to embrace) || rodear, cercar, encerrar (to enclose).

emboss [im'bɔs] *vt* grabar en relieve || gofrar (paper) || repujar (leather, silver).

embossment [-mənt] *n* gofrado *m* (of paper) || grabado *m* en relieve (engraving) || repujado *m* (of leather, silver).

embouchure [ˌɔmbu'ʃuə*] *n* desembocadura *f* (of a river) || MUS embocadura *f*.

embowel [im'bauəl] *vt* sacar las tripas, destripar.

embower [im'bauə*] *vt* enramar, esconder entre las ramas.

embrace [im'breis] *n* abrazo *m*.

embrace [im'breis] *vt* abrazar (to hug) || aprovecharse de, aprovechar (to seize); *to embrace an opportunity* aprovechar una oportunidad || abarcar, contener, incluir (to encompass); *«democracy» embraces many concepts* la palabra «democracia» abarca muchos conceptos || aceptar (an offer) || adoptar, abrazar (a doctrine, a conduct) || dedicarse a (a profession).
◆ *vi* abrazarse; *they embraced* se abrazaron.

embranchment [im'brɑːntʃmənt] *n* ramificación *f*, bifurcación *f* || brazo *m* (of a river).

embrasure [im'breiʒə*] *n* ARCH alféizar *m* (of a window) || MIL tronera *f*, cañonera *f* (loophole).

embrocate ['embrəukeit] *vt* MED dar fricciones.

embrocation [ˌembrəu'keiʃən] *n* embrollo *m*.

embroglio [em'brəuljəu] *n* embrollo *m*.

embroider [im'brɔidə*] *vt* bordar; *embroidered by hand* bordado a mano || FIG adornar, embellecer (a story, etc.).
◆ *vi* bordar.

embroiderer [-rə*] *n* bordador, ra.

embroideress [-ris] *n* bordadora *f*.

embroidery [-ri] *n* bordado *m* || FIG adorno *m* (of a story, etc.).

embroil [im'brɔil] *vt* embrollar, enredar (to entangle) || enredar, envolver (to involve) || sembrar la discordia entre (to set at odds).

embroilment [-mənt] *n* embrollo *m*, enredo *m*.

embrown [im'braun] *vt* oscurecer.

embryo ['embriəu] *n* embrión *m* || FIG embrión *m*, germen *m*; *in embryo* en embrión.
◆ *adj* embrionario, ria.

embryologic [ˌembrieu'lɔdʒik] ; **embryological** [-əl] *adj* embriológico, ca.

embryologist [ˌembri'ɔlədʒist] *n* embriólogo *m*.

embryology [ˌembri'ɔlədʒi] *n* embriología *f*.

embryonic [ˌembri'ɔnik] *adj* embrionario, ria.

emcee ['emsiː] *n* US maestro *m* de ceremonias (at a formal event), presentador *m* (of a show).

emend [i'mend] ; **emendate** [-eit] *vt* enmendar.

emendation [ˌiːmen'deiʃən] *n* enmienda *f*.

emendatory [i'mendətəri] *adj* de enmienda.

emerald ['emərəld] *n* esmeralda *f* (stone) || color *m* esmeralda (colour).
◆ *adj* esmeralda *inv* (colour) || *the Esmerald Isle* la verde Erín (Ireland).

emerge [i'məːdʒ] *vi* salir, emerger (to rise from a fluid) || surgir, salir (to come out) || sacarse (to be brought out by investigation) || JUR deducirse || aparecer, surgir (to be discovered) || *it emerges that...* resulta que...

emergence [i'məːdʒəns] *n* salida *f*, emergencia *f* (the act of emerging) || BOT excrecencia *f*.

emergency [i'məːdʒənsi] *n* emergencia *f* (unexpected event) || situación *f* crítica, crisis *f* (crisis) || MED urgencia *f* || necesidad *f* urgente (need) || — *case of emergency* caso *m* de emergencia *or* de urgencia || *emergency services* servicios *m pl* de urgencia || *emergency stop* parada *f* de emergencia || *in an emergency* en caso de emergencia || *national emergency* crisis *f* nacional || *state of emergency* estado *m* de emergencia; estado de excepción (for political reasons) || *to provide for emergencies* prevenirse contra toda eventualidad || *to rise to the emergency* mostrarse a la altura de las circunstancias.
◆ *adj* de emergencia; *emergency exit* salida de emergencia || de urgencia (measure) || forzoso, sa (forced); *emergency landing* aterrizaje forzoso || de seguridad; *emergency brake* freno de seguridad || de alarma (bell) || provisional (bridge, dwelling) || extraordinario, ria.

emergent [i'məːdʒənt] *adj* emergente (emerging) || inesperado, da (unexpected) || joven (nation).

emeritus [i'meritəs] *adj* honorario, ria; emérito, ta.

emersion [i'məːʃən] *n* ASTR emersión *f*, reaparición *f*.

emery ['eməri] *n* MIN esmeril *m* || — *emery board* lima *f* de uñas || *emery cloth* tela *f* de esmeril || *emery paper* papel *m* esmerilado *or* de lija, lija *f*.

emetic [i'metik] *adj* emético, ca; vomitivo, va.
◆ *n* emético *m*, vomitivo *m*.

emigrant ['emigrənt] *adj/n* emigrante.

emigrate ['emigreit] *vi* emigrar.

emigration [ˌemi'greiʃən] *n* emigración *f*.

emigratory ['emigrətəri] *adj* emigratorio, ria.

émigré ['emigrei] *n* emigrado, da.

eminence ['eminəns] *n* eminencia *f* || — FIG *grey eminence* eminencia gris || REL *His Eminence* Su Eminencia.

éminence grise ['eiminɑːns'griːz] *n* eminencia *f* gris.

eminent ['eminənt] *adj* eminente.

eminently [-li] *adv* eminentemente, sumamente.

emir [e'miə*] *n* emir *m*.

emirate [e'miərit] *n* emirato *m*.

emissary ['emisəri] *n* emisario, ria.

emission [i'miʃən] *n* emisión *f*.

emissive [i'misiv] *adj* emisivo, va; de emisión.

emit [i'mit] *vt* emitir (a sound, light, money) || emitir, expresar (opinion, etc.) || desprender (heat) || despedir, desprender (an odour) || echar, arrojar (smoke) || dar (a cry).

emitter [-ə*] *n* RAD emisora *f*.

Emmanuel [i'mænjuəl] *pr n* Manuel *m*.

emmetrope ['emətrəup] *n* emétrope *m* & *f*.

emmetropia [ˌem'ətrəupjə] *n* MED emetropía *f*.

emmetropic [ˌemə'trɔpik] *adj* MED emétrope.

emollient [i'mɔliənt] *adj* emoliente.
◆ *n* emoliente *m*.

emolument [i'mɔljumənt] *n* emolumento *m*.

emote [i'məut] *vi* manifestar emoción || US FAM comportarse de forma demasiado teatral.

emotion [i'məuʃən] *n* emoción *f*.

emotional [i'məuʃənl] *adj* emocional (relating to the emotions, appealing to the emotions) || emotivo, va; conmovedor, ra; *an emotional farewell* una despedida conmovedora || emotivo, va; *an emotional person* una persona emotiva.

emotionalism [i'məuʃnəlizəm] *n* emotividad *f*, sentimentalismo *m*.

emotionality [iˌməuʃə'næliti] *n* emotividad *f*, emocionabilidad *f*, sensibilidad *m*.

emotionally [i'məuʃənəli] *adv* con emoción.

emotive [i'məutiv] *adj* emotivo, va.

emotiveness [-nis] ; **emotivity** [iməu'tiviti] *n* emotividad *f*.

empale [im'peil] *vt* ⟶ **impale.**

empanel [im'pænl] *vt* JUR seleccionar (to select) | inscribir (to list).

empathy ['empəθi] *n* empatía *f*.

empennage [im'penidʒ] *n* AVIAT planos *m pl* de estabilización, estabilizador *m*, empenaje *m* || aleta *f* (of a bomb) || plumas *f pl* (of an arrow).

emperor ['empərə*] *n* emperador *m* || ZOOL pavón *m* (butterfly).

emperorship [-ʃip] *n* imperio *m*.

emphasis ['emfəsis] *n* GRAMM acento *m*, acentuación *f* (stress) || FIG acento *m*, énfasis *m* (to call special attention) | importancia *f* | insistencia *f* (insistence) || *to lay emphasis on a fact, on a word* subrayar un hecho, una palabra, hacer hincapié en un hecho, en una palabra.
— OBSERV El plural de *emphasis* es *emphases*.

emphasize ['emfəsaiz] *vt* GRAMM acentuar, poner el acento en || FIG subrayar, recalcar, hacer hincapié en, poner de relieve, acentuar [*AMER* enfatizar].

emphatic [im'fætik] *adj* enfático, ca (adding emphasis) || enérgico, ca (strongly marked) || GRAMM acentuado, da (stressed) || decidido, da (resolute) || categórico, ca (categorical); *I was most emphatic* fui muy categórico.

emphatically [-əli] *adv* enérgicamente, categóricamente || enfáticamente.

emphysema [ˌemfi'siːmə] *n* MED enfisema *m*.

emphysematous [ˌemfi'semətəs] *adj* MED enfisematoso, sa.

emphyteusis [ˌemfi'tjuːsis] *n* JUR enfiteusis *f* (lease).

emphyteuta [ˌemfi'tjuːtə] *n* JUR enfiteuta *m* & *f*.

emphyteutic [ˌemfi'tjuːtik] *adj* JUR enfitéutico, ca.

empire ['empaiə*] *n* imperio *m* || — *the Empire* el Sacro Imperio Romano Germánico (Holy Roman Empire), el Imperio [de Napoleón] (of Napoleon), el Imperio Británico (British Empire) || *the Empire State* el estado de Nueva York.
◆ *adj* imperio (style).

empire-building [-ˌbildiŋ] *adj* expansionista.

empiric [emˈpirik] *adj/n* empírico, ca.

empirical [-əl] *adj* empírico, ca.

empiricism [emˈpirisizəm] *n* empirismo *m*.

empiricist [emˈpirisist] *n* empírico, ca.

emplacement [imˈpleismənt] *n* emplazamiento *m*.

employ [imˈplɔi] *n* empleo *m* || — *in s.o.'s employ* empleado por alguien, al servicio de alguien || *they are in my employ* son empleados míos.

employ [imˈplɔi] *vt* emplear.

employable [-əbl] *adj* utilizable, empleable.

employé [ɔmˈplɔiei] *n* empleado, da.

employee [ˌemploiˈiː] *n* empleado, da.

employer [ˌemplɔiə*] *n* empresario, ria; empleador, ra (who employs people); *employer's union* sindicato de empresarios || usuario, ria (user).
◆ *adj* empresarial, de empresarios.

employment [imˈplɔimənt] *n* empleo *m*; *full employment* pleno empleo || trabajo *m* (work) || ocupación *f* (occupation) || uso *m* (use) || — *employment agency* agencia *f* de colocaciones || *employment contract* contrato *m* de trabajo || *employment exchange* o *bureau* bolsa *f* de trabajo || *employment legislation* legislación *f* laboral || *employment offered* puesto *m* vacante || *employment office* oficina *f* de empleo || *employment wanted* solicitan trabajo || *to be in employment* tener trabajo || *to give employment to* emplear a || *to look for employment* buscar empleo *or* trabajo.

empoison [imˈpɔizn] *vt* envenenar.

emporium [emˈpɔːriəm] *n* emporio *m* (a big market) || (ant) emporio *m*, almacén *m* (a store).
— OBSERV El plural es *emporiums* o *emporia*.

empower [imˈpauə*] *vt* facultar, autorizar, habilitar.

empress [ˈempris] *n* emperatriz *f*.

emptiness [ˈemptinis] *n* vacío *m* || FIG vaciedad *f*, vacuidad *f* (of a person, words, etc.).

empty [ˈempti] *adj* vacío, a (with nothing in it) || vacío, a; desocupado, da (a house) || desierto, ta (place) || vacante (an employment) || vacío, ca (words, etc.) || sin sentido (meaningless) || FAM vacío, ca; hambriento, ta (hungry) || AGR vacía *f* (not pregnant) || *empty of* sin, desprovisto de.
◆ *n* envase *m* vacío, recipiente *m* vacío || *returnable empties* cascos *m* *or* envases *m* en depósito.

empty [ˈempti] *vt* vaciar, dejar vacío (to make empty) || vaciar (the contents) || despojar, quitar (of meaning).
◆ *vi* vaciarse (to become empty) || quedarse vacío (a car) || quedar desocupado (a flat) || quedarse vacante (an employment) || desaguar, desembocar (a river).

empty-handed [-ˈhændid] *adj* con las manos vacías.

empty-headed [-ˈhedid] *adj* casquivano, na; sin nada en la cabeza.

empurple [imˈpəːpl] *vt* enrojecer.

empyreal [ˌempaiˈriːəl] *n* ·empíreo, a.

Empyrean [ˌempaiˈriːən] *n* empíreo *m*.

EMS *abbr of [European Monetary System]* SME, Sistema Monetario Europeo.

emu [ˈiːmjuː] *n* emú *m* (bird).

emulate [ˈemjuleit] *vt* emular || INFORM emular.

emulation [ˌemjuˈleiʃən] *n* emulación *f* || INFORM emulación *f* || *in emulation of each other* a cual mejor, a cual más.

emulative [ˈemjulətiv] *adj* emulador, ra.

emulator [ˈemjuleitə*] *n* emulador, ra; émulo, la || INFORM emulador *m*.

emulous [ˈemjuləs] *adj* émulo, la || *to be emulous of honours* ambicionar honores.

emulsifier [iˈmʌlsifaiə*] *n* emulsor *m*.

emulsify [iˈmʌlsifai] *vt* emulsionar.

emulsion [iˈmʌlʃən] *n* emulsión *f*.

emulsive [iˈmʌlsiv] *adj* emulsivo, va.

en [en] *n* PRINT cuadratín *m* || ene *f* (letter).

enable [iˈneibl] *vt* permitir (to permit) || JUR permitir, autorizar, capacitar, habilitar.

enact [iˈnækt] *vt* JUR promulgar (a law) | dar fuerza de ley a (a bill) | decretar (to decree) || representar (to act, to represent) || hacer, efectuar (to do).
◆ *vi* actuar.

enactment [-mənt] *n* promulgación *f* (of a law) || estatuto *m* (statute) || decreto *m* (decree).

enamel [iˈnæməl] *n* esmalte *m* || *enamel paint* esmalte *m*.

enamel [iˈnæməl] *vt* esmaltar.

enamelled [-d] *adj* esmaltado, da.

enameller [-ə*] *n* esmaltador *m*.

enamelling [-iŋ] *n* esmaltado *m*.

enamelware [-ˌwɛə] *n* utensilios *m pl* de hierro esmaltado.

enamour; *US* **enamor** [iˈnæmə*] *vt* enamorar (to inspire love) || FIG cautivar, seducir.

enamoured; *US* **enamored** [-d] *adj* enamorado, da; *she was enamoured of me* estaba enamorada de mí || aficionado, da (of a thing); *she was enamoured of* era muy aficionada a || aferrado, da (of an idea).

en bloc [ɑːˈblɔk] *adj* en bloque.

encaenia [enˈsiːnjə] *n* conmemoración *f*.

encaged [inˈkeidʒd] *adj* enjaulado, da.

encamp [inˈkæmp] *vi* MIL acamparse.
◆ *vt* MIL acampar.

encampment [-mənt] *n* MIL campamento *m*.

encapsulate [enˈkæpsjuleit] *vt* FIG encerrar.

encase; incase [inˈkeis] *vt* encajonar (in a box) || encerrar (to enclose) || cubrir (to cover).

encash [inˈkæʃ] *vt* hacer efectivo, cobrar.

encashment [-mənt] *n* cobro *m*.

encaustic [enˈkɔːstik] *n* encausto *m*.
◆ *adj* encáustico, ca.

enceinte [ɑːˈsɛ̃ːnt] *n* recinto *m* (fortress).

encephalic [ˌenkəˈfælik] *adj* ANAT encefálico, ca.

encephalitis [ˌenkefəˈlaitis] *n* MED encefalitis *f*.

encephalogram [enˈsefələugræm] *n* MED encefalograma *m*.

encephalograph [enˈsefələugrɑːf] *n* MED electroencefalógrafo *m* (apparatus) | encefalograma *m* (result).

encephalography [ˌensefəˈlɔgrəfi] *n* MED encefalografía *f*.

encephalomyelitis [enˈsefələuˌmaiəˈlaitis] *n* encefalomielitis *f*.

encephalon [enˈsefələn] *n* ANAT encéfalo *m*.
— OBSERV El plural de *encephalon* es *encephala*.

enchain [inˈtʃein] *vt* encadenar.

enchainment [-mənt] *n* encadenamiento *m*.

enchant [inˈtʃɑːnt] *vt* encantar.

enchanter [-ə*] *n* hechicero *m* (sorcerer) || encanto *m*, hechizo *m* (s.o. who fascinates).

enchanting [-iŋ] *adj* encantador, ra.

enchantment [-mənt] *n* encanto *m* (charm) || encantamiento *m*, hechizo *m* (of a sorcerer).

enchantress [-ris] *n* hechicera *f* (sorceress) || encanto *m*, hechicera *f* (s.o. who fascinates).

enchase [inˈtʃeis] *vt* engastar, engarzar (to set a gem) || incrustar (to inlay) || grabar (to engrave) || embutir (to emboss) || repujar (leather).

encina [inˈsiːnə] *n* BOT encina *f*.

encircle [inˈsəːkl] *vt* rodear, cercar || ceñir (to fasten round) || MIL envolver.

encirclement [-mənt] *n* circunvalación *f* (a surrounding) || MIL envolvimiento *m* (of troops) | cerco *m* (of a town).

encircling [inˈsəːkliŋ] *adj* que circunvala || MIL envolvente.

enclasp [inˈklɑːsp] *vt* abrazar.

enclave [ˈenkleiv] *n* enclave *m*.

enclisis [ˈenkləsis] *n* GRAMM énclisis *f*.

enclitic [inˈklitik] *adj* GRAMM enclítico, ca.
◆ *n* GRAMM enclítica *f*.

enclose; inclose [inˈkləuz] *vt* encerrar (to shut in) || rodear, cercar (to surround) || adjuntar, remitir adjunto (to include in a letter); *the enclosed letter* la carta adjunta; *enclosed herewith* encontrará adjunto || encerrar, incluir, abarcar (to contain) || REL enclaustrar || *I enclose herewith* remito adjunto.

enclosure; inclosure [inˈkləuʒə*] *n* encierro *m* (act of shutting in) || cerco *m*, cercado *m* (fence) || recinto *m* (space included within certain limits) || REL enclaustramiento *m* || carta *f* adjunta, documento *m* adjunto *or* anexo (in a letter).

encomiast [enˈkəumiæst] *n* encomiasta *m* & *f*, panegirista *m* & *f*.

encomiastical [-əl] *adj* encomiástico, ca; laudatorio, ria; panegírico, ca.

encomium [enˈkəumjəm] *n* encomio *m*, elogio *m*.
— OBSERV El plural es *encomiums* o *encomia*.

encompass [inˈkʌmpəs] *vt* abarcar (to include) || cercar, rodear (to surround) || envolver (to envelop) || llevar a cabo (to accomplish).

encore [ɔŋˈkɔː*] *interj* ¡otra vez!, ¡otra!, ¡bis!, ¡que se repita!
◆ *n* repetición *f* || *to give an encore* repetir *or* bisar a petición del público.

encore [ɔŋˈkɔː*] *vt* pedir la repetición a *or* de (to call for an encore) || repetir, bisar (to repeat).

encounter [inˈkauntə*] *n* encuentro *m*.

encounter [inˈkauntə*] *vt* encontrarse con, encontrar, tropezar con (to meet by chance) || encontrar, tropezar con, enfrentarse a (to face a difficulty) || MIL enfrentarse con.

encourage [inˈkʌridʒ] *vt* animar, alentar (to help by sympathetic interest); *the spectators encouraged the players* los espectadores alentaron a los jugadores; *I encouraged him to do it* le animé para que lo hiciese || incitar; *he was encouraged to steal* le incitaron a robar || estimular, fomentar (to promote, to stimulate); *to encourage industry* estimular la industria || fortalecer (to strengthen a belief).

encouragement [-mənt] *n* ánimo *m*, aliento *m* (courage) || incitación *f* (incitement) || estímulo *m*, fomento *m* (promotion, stimulation of industry, etc.) || incentivo *m* (incentive) || *to give encouragement* dar ánimo *or* ánimos a.

encouraging [-iŋ] *adj* alentador, ra; *encouraging results* resultados alentadores || prometedor, ra; halagüeño, ña (promising); *encouraging prospects* perspectivas halagüeñas || que da ánimos; *to be an encouraging person* ser una persona que da ánimos.

encouragingly [-iŋli] *adv* en tono alentador.

encroach [inˈkrəutʃ]; **entrench** [inˈtrentʃ] *vi* *to encroach on* usurpar (s.o.'s rights), meterse en, inmiscuirse en (to intrude on); *he encroached on my affairs* se metía en mis asuntos; abusar de (to abuse); *to encroach on s.o.'s good nature* abusar de la amabilidad de alguien; quitar; *to encroach on s.o.'s time* quitar tiempo a alguien; invadir (to invade).

encroachment [-mənt]; **entrenchment** [-mənt] *n* usurpación *f* (appropriation) ‖ abuso *m* (abuse) ‖ intrusión *f* ‖ invasión *f*.

encrust [in'krʌst] *vt* incrustar; *encrusted with* incrustado de.
◆ *vi* incrustarse, cubrirse de costra.

encumber [in'kʌmbə*] *vt* estorbar (to hamper) ‖ cargar; *encumbered with parcels* cargado de paquetes ‖ sobrecargar (the market) ‖ llenar; *encumbered with footnotes* lleno de notas ‖ obstruir (to block) ‖ gravar (with taxes, etc.).

encumbrance [in'kʌmbrəns] *n* estorbo *m*, obstáculo *m* (hindrance) ‖ JUR carga *f*, gravamen *m*; *free from encumbrances* libre de gravámenes ‖ *without encumbrance* sin familia.

encyclic [en'siklik]; **encyclical** [-kəl] *adj* REL *encyclical letter* encíclica *f*.
◆ *n* REL encíclica *f*.

encyclopedia; encyclopaedia [en'saikləu'pi:djə] *n* enciclopedia *f*.

encyclopedic; encyclopaedic [en,saikləu'pi:dik]; **encyclopedical; encyclopaedical** [-əl] *adj* enciclopédico, ca.

encyclopedism [en,saikləu'pi:dizəm] *n* enciclopedismo *m* ‖ conocimientos *m pl* enciclopédicos (knowledge).

encyclopedist; encyclopaedist [en,saikləu'pi:dist] *n* enciclopedista *m* & *f*.

encyst [in'sist] *vt* MED enquistar.
◆ *vi* MED enquistarse.

encystment [-mənt]; **encystation** [insis'teiʃən] *n* MED enquistamiento *m*.

end [end] *adj* final; *the end result* el resultado final; *end product* producto final.
◆ *n* fin *m*, final *m* (finish); *until the end* hasta el final ‖ fin *m*; *the end of a reel* el fin de un carrete ‖ extremo *m*; *the other end of the street* el otro extremo de la calle ‖ parte *f*; *the fashionable end of town* la parte elegante de la ciudad ‖ extremo *m*, límite *m* (limit) ‖ pedazo *m*, trozo *m*, resto *m* (remant) ‖ cabo *m* (tail end); *a candle end* un cabo de vela ‖ punta *f* (point) ‖ PHIL fin *m*, causa *f* final ‖ pie *m* (of a perpendicular) ‖ colilla *f* (of a cigarette) ‖ término *m* (termination) ‖ muerte *f*, fin *m* (death); *a tragic end* un trágico fin ‖ destrucción *f* (destruction) ‖ propósito *m*, fin *m*, objetivo *m* (aim); *she achieved her ends* consiguió sus fines; *to what end?* ¿con qué propósito? ‖ método *m* (means) ‖ SP lado *m* ‖ — FAM *and that's the end of it* y sanseacabó ‖ *at the end of the day* al final ‖ *at the end of the year* al final del año, a fines de año ‖ *at the end of two years* después de dos años, al cabo de dos años ‖ *end on* de frente ‖ *end to end* unidos por los extremos (next to), uno tras otro (one behind the other) ‖ *for days on end* día tras día ‖ *from end to end* de un extremo a otro, desde el principio hasta el final ‖ FAM *he is no end of a fellow* es un chico estupendo ‖ *I did it in the end* acabé haciéndolo *or* por hacerlo ‖ *in the end* al final, al fin ‖ *it did me no end of good* me hizo un bien inmenso ‖ *latter end of s.o.'s life* los últimos años de uno ‖ *no end of* muchísimos, muchísimas ‖ *on end* erizado, de punta (hair), derecho, de pie (upright), incesantemente, sin parar (nonstop), seguido, da (consecutive) ‖ *that's the end of the money* se acabó el dinero ‖ *that will be the end of him* esto acabará con él ‖ *the end justifies the means* el fin justifica los medios ‖ *the end of the world* el fin del mundo ‖ *there is an end to everything* principio y fin quieren las cosas ‖ *to be an end in itself* ser un fin *or* objetivo por sí mismo ‖ *to be at an end* estar acabado (finished), tocar a su fin (finishing) ‖ *to be at one's wit's end* no saber qué hacer ‖ *to bring to an end* llevar a su fin, terminar ‖ *to come to an end* llegar a su fin, terminarse ‖ *to gain one's ends* lograr sus propósitos ‖ FIG *to get hold of the wrong end of the stick* tomar el rábano por las hojas ‖ FIG & FAM *to go off the deep end* perder los estribos (to lose one's control), obrar con precipitación (to act rashly) ‖ FIG *to keep one's end up* hacer bien lo que a uno le corresponde ‖ *to make an end of* acabar con ‖ FIG *to make an end of s.o.* enviar a alguien a paseo | *to make ends meet* o *to make both ends meet* hacer equilibrios para vivir | *to meet one's end* encontrar la muerte ‖ *to no end* en vano, inútilmente ‖ *to put an end to* poner fin a ‖ *to reach its end* tocar a su fin ‖ *to stand on end* ponerse de punta (hair) ‖ *to start at the wrong end* empezar por el final ‖ *to the end that...* para que..., a fin de que..., con el objeto de que... ‖ FIG *to think no end of s.o.* tener muy buen concepto de uno ‖ *to this end* con este fin, para este fin ‖ *we are at the end of our patience* se nos ha agotado la paciencia ‖ *you'll never hear the end of it* no te dejarán olvidarlo nunca.

end [end] *vt* acabar, terminar, finalizar, poner fin a (to finish) ‖ acabar con (abuses, etc.) ‖ terminar (one's days) ‖ FAM *to end it all* acabar con la vida.
◆ *vi* terminarse, acabarse (to terminate) ‖ terminar sus días (to die) ‖ acabar, terminar; *he ended by eating* acabó comiendo ‖ — *to end in* terminar en ‖ *to end off* acabar; *to end off a story* acabar una historia; terminarse; *the path ends off abruptly* el sendero se termina de repente ‖ *to end up* acabar, terminar (to finish), ir a parar; *the car ended up in my garden* el coche fue a parar a mi jardín.

end-all [-ɔ:l] *n* objetivo *m* final ‖ *the be-all and the end-all* la única razón de la existencia de uno, lo único que importa; *money must not be our be-all and end-all* el dinero no debe ser la única razón de nuestra existencia *or* lo único que nos importe.

endamage [in'dæmidʒ] *vt* dañar, perjudicar.

endanger [in'deindʒə*] *vt* poner en peligro.

endangered [-d] *adj* en peligro ‖ *endangered species* especie *f sing* en peligro de extinción.

endear [in'diə*] *vt* hacer querer (*to* por) ‖ *to endear o.s. to* hacerse querer, granjearse las simpatías de; *he endeared himself to his friends* se hizo querer por sus amigos.

endearing [-riŋ] *adj* simpático, ca; atractivo, va (attractive) ‖ encantador, ra (charming).

endearment [-mənt] *n* palabra *f or* frase *f* cariñosa (word or phrase which expresses affection) ‖ caricia *f* (caress) ‖ cariño *m*, afecto *m*, encariñamiento *m* (affection).

endeavour; US **endeavor** [in'devə*] *n* esfuerzo *m*, empeño *m* (effort) ‖ tentativa *f*, intento *m* (attempt) ‖ *to use very endeavour to* no regatear esfuerzos para.

endeavour; US **endeavor** [in'devə*] *vi* esforzarse (*to* por), intentar, procurar.

endemic [en'demik] *adj* endémico, ca.
◆ *n* endemia *f*.

end-grain ['end'grein] *adj/adv* a contrahílo.

ending ['endiŋ] *n* fin *m*, final *m* ‖ final *m*, desenlace *m*; *the book has a happy ending* el libro tiene un desenlace feliz ‖ GRAMM desinencia *f*, terminación *f*.

endive ['endiv] *n* BOT endibia *f*.

endleaf ['endli:f] *n* guarda *f* (of a book).

endless ['endlis] *adj* interminable, inacabable ‖ infinito, ta ‖ TECH sin fin.

endmost ['endməust] *adj* más remoto, último, ma.

endocardial [endəu'kɑ:djəl] *adj* endocardiaco, ca.

endocarditis [endəukɑ:'daitis] *n* MED endocarditis *f*.

endocardium [,endəu'kɑ:djəm] *n* ANAT endocardio *m*.
— OBSERV El plural de *endocardium* es *endocardia*.

endocarp ['endəukɑ:p] *n* ANAT endocarpio *m*.

endocranium [,endəu'kreinjəm] *n* ANAT endocráneo *m*.
— OBSERV El plural de *endocranium* es *endocrania*.

endocrine ['endəukrain] *adj* ANAT endocrino, na.
◆ *n* ANAT glándula *f* endocrina.

endocrinal [,endəu'krainəl]; **endocrinic** [,endɔ'krinik]; **endocrinous** [end'dɔkrinəs] *adj* endocrino, na.

endocrinologist [,endəukri'nɔlədʒist] *n* endocrinólogo, ga.

endocrinology [,endəukri'nɔlədʒi] *n* MED endocrinología *f*.

endoderm ['endəudə:m] *n* endodermo *m*.

endodermis [,endəu'də:mis] *n* endodermis *f*.

endogamy [en'dɔgəmi] *n* endogamia *f*.

endogenous [en'dɔdʒənəs] *adj* endógeno, na.

endoparasite ['endəu'pærəsait] *n* ZOOL endoparásito *m*.

endoparasitic ['endəu,pærə'sitik] *adj* endoparásito, ta.

endoplasm ['endəuplæzəm] *n* endoplasma *m*.

endorse; indorse [in'dɔ:s] *vt* COMM endosar (a cheque) | avalar (a bill) ‖ aprobar (to approve) ‖ aceptar (to accept) ‖ apoyar, respaldar (to support) ‖ confirmar (to confirm) ‖ escribir los detalles de una sanción en (a driving licence, etc.) ‖ visar (a passport) ‖ *to endorse over* transferir.

endorsee [,endɔ:'si:] *n* endosatario, ria.

endorsement [in'dɔ:smənt] *n* COMM endoso *m* (of a cheque) | aval *m*, respaldo *m* (guarantee) ‖ aprobación *f* (approval) ‖ apoyo *m*, respaldo *m* (support).

endorser [in'dɔ:sə*] *n* endosador, ra; endosante *m* & *f*.

endoscope ['endəuskəup] *n* MED endoscopio *m*.

endoscopy [en'dɔskəpi] *n* MED endoscopia *f*.

endoskeleton ['endəu'skelitən] *n* ANAT endoesqueleto *m*.

endosmometer [,endɔz'mɔmitə*] *n* endosmómetro *m*.

endosmosis [,endɔz'məusis] *n* CHEM endósmosis *f*.

endosmotic ['endɔz'mɔtik] *adj* CHEM endosmótico, ca.

endosperm ['endəuspə:m] *n* BOT endosperma *m*.

endothelium [,endəu'θi:ljəm] *n* ANAT endotelio *m*.
— OBSERV El plural de *endothelium* es *entothelia*.

endothermal [,endəu'θə:məl]; **endothermic** [,endəu'θə:mik] *adj* endotérmico, ca.

endotoxin [,endəu'tɔksin] *n* BIOL endotoxina *f*.

endow [in'dau] *vt* dotar ‖ hacer una donación a (to a hospital) ‖ FIG dotar; *endowed with intelligence* dotado de inteligencia.

endowment [-mənt] *n* donación *f* (act of endowing, money given) ‖ fundación *f*, creación *f* (foundation) ‖ FIG don *m*, dote *f* (natural gift).

endpaper ['end,peipə*] *n* guarda *f* (of a book).

end product ['end,prɔdʌkt] *n* producto *m* final.

endue; indue [in'dju:] *vt* dotar (with virtues) || ponerse (a garment) || poner (with a garment) || investir (with an office).

endurable [in'djuərəbl] *adj* soportable, tolerable, aguantable (bearable).

endurance [in'djuərəns] *n* aguante *m*, resistencia *f* (capacity to put up with pain) || AVIAT autonomía *f* de vuelo || duración *f* (duration) || — *beyond* o *past endurance* inaguantable, insoportable || *endurance race* carrera *f* de resistencia || *endurance test* prueba *f* de resistencia.

endure [in'djuə*] *vt* aguantar, soportar, sobrellevar (to suffer patiently) || tolerar (to tolerate).
◆ *vi* aguantarse (to remain set in purpose) || durar, perdurar (to last for a long time).

enduring [-riŋ] *adj* perdurable, duradero, ra (lasting) || resistente (resistant) || paciente, sufrido, da (patient).

endways ['endweiz]; **endwise** [-waiz] *adv* de pie (upright) || de canto (edgewise) || unidos por los extremos (next to) || uno tras otro (one behind the other) || longitudinalmente (lengthwise).

enema ['enimə] *n* MED enema *m*, lavativa *f*.
— OBSERV El plural de *enema* es *enemas* o *enemata*.

enemy ['enimi] *adj* enemigo, ga.
◆ *n* enemigo, ga || — *to go over to the enemy* pasarse al enemigo || *to make enemies* hacerse enemigos.

energetic [,enə'dʒetik] *adj* enérgico, ca (forceful) || PHYS energético, ca.

energetics [-s] *n* energética *f*.

energize ['enədʒaiz] *vt* vigorizar, dar energía a, dar vigor a (to give energy to) || ELECTR excitar (an electromagnet) | imanar (a coil) || FIG activar, estimular.
◆ *vi* obrar con energía *or* con vigor || FIG activarse.

energumen [,enə:'gju:mən] *n* energúmeno, na || FIG fanático, ca.

energy ['enədʒi] *n* energía *f*; *atomic energy* energía atómica; *a person with lots of energy* una persona que tiene mucha energía.

energy-saving [-,seiviŋ] *adj* que ahorra energía.

enervate ['enə:vit] *adj* deprimido, da; decaído, da (depressed) || debilitado, da (weakened) || falto de vigor (lacking vitality).

enervate ['enə:veit] *vt* debilitar (to weaken) || deprimir (to depress).

enervating [-iŋ] *adj* enervador, ra; enervante || deprimente (depressing).

enervation [,enə:'veiʃən] *n* debilitación *f* (weakening) || depresión *f* (depression).

enfeeble [in'fi:bl] *vt* debilitar (to weaken).

enfeeblement [-mənt] *n* debilitación *f*, debilitamiento *m*.

enfeoff [in'fef] *vt* enfeudar.

enfeoffment [-mənt] *n* enfeudación *f*, enfeudamiento *m* (investing with a fief) || acta *f* de enfeudación (document).

enfetter [in'fetə*] *vt* poner los grilletes a || FIG encadenar.

enfilade [,enfi'leid] *n* MIL enfilada *f*.

enfilade [,enfi'leid] *vt* MIL batir por el flanco *or* en enfilada, enfilar || *enfilading fire* tiro *m* de enfilada.

enfold [in'fəuld] *vt* envolver (to wrap up) || estrechar; *to enfold in an embrace* estrechar en un abrazo || rodear (to surround).

enforce [in'fɔ:s] *vt* imponer; *to enforce obedience* imponer la obediencia || insistir en (to insist) || dar fuerza a reforzar (to give strenght) || hacer valer (claims) || forzar (one's way) || hacer respetar (rights) || poner en vigor (to put into effect) || hacer cumplir; *the purpose of the police is to enforce the law* la policía tiene que hacer cumplir la ley.

enforceable [in'fɔ:sibl] *adj* ejecutorio, ria (contract) || aplicable (law).

enforced [in'fɔ:st] *adj* forzado, da || inevitable.

enforcement [in'fɔ:smənt] *n* JUR entrada *f* en vigor (putting into effect) | aplicación *f* (of the law) || coacción *f* (coerción).

enframe [in'freim] *vt* encuadrar.

enfranchise [in'fræntʃaiz] *vt* conceder derechos políticos (to a person, etc.) || conceder derechos municipales (to a town) || conceder el derecho de votar (to give the right to vote) || libertar, liberar (to free) || FIG liberar, emancipar.

enfranchisement [in'fræntʃizmənt] *n* liberación *f* (form slavery) || concesión *f* de derechos políticos (to a person, etc.) || concesión *f* de derechos municipales (to a town) || concesión *f* del derecho de votar || FIG liberación *f*, emancipación *f*.

engage [in'geidʒ] *vt/vi* comprometer, empeñar (one's honour) || empeñar, dar (one's word) || comprometerse; *he engaged to do it* se comprometió a hacerlo || prometer en matrimonio (one's daughter) || contratar (a worker) || ajustar, apalabrar, tomar a su servicio (a servant) || reservar (theatre seats, room, etc.) || alquilar (a taxi) || ocupar (telephone); *to engage the line for twenty minutes* ocupar la línea durante veinte minutos || ocupar (to keep busy) || llamar (s.o.'s attention) || requerir (efforts) || atraer, granjearse (s.o.'s affection) || entablar con; *to engage s.o. in conversation* entablar conversación con alguien || MIL librar, entablar, trabar (a battle) | entablar un combate con; *to engage the enemy* entablar un combate con el enemigo | emplear, utilizar (troops) | reclutar (soldiers) || TECH meter, poner; *he engaged the first gear* metió la primera velocidad | embragar (the clutch) | engranar (gear wheel) | hacer funcionar (a machine) || — *to be engaged in conversation* estar hablando || *to be engaged in the textile business* trabajar en la industria textil || *to be engaged in war* participar en la guerra (to take part), estar en guerra (to be fighting) || *to engage for* prometer || *to engage in battle* entablar un combate || *to engage in conversation with s.o.* entablar conversación con alguien || *to engage in politics* meterse en política || *to engage o.s. to do sth.* comprometerse a hacer algo.

engaged [-d] *adj* prometido, da (pledged to marry) || ocupado, da (busy, not free) || comprometido, da; *I am engaged tomorrow* estoy comprometido para mañana || MIL combatiente (fighting) || contratado, da (a worker) || ajustado, da; apalabrado, da (a servant) || TECH metido, da (gear) | embragado, da (clutch) | engranado, da (gear wheel) || ARCH empotrado, da (column) || — *engaged tone* señal *f* de comunicando (telephone) || *the engaged couple* los novios || *to be engaged* estar comunicando (telephone) || *we've been engaged for five years* somos novios desde hace cinco años.

engagement [-mənt] *n* compromiso *m*; *to carry out one's engagements* cumplir con sus compromisos || compromiso *m*; *social engagements* compromisos sociales; *I have a prior engagement* ya tengo un compromiso || cita *f* (appointment) || contratación *f*, contrata *f* (of workers) || ajuste *m*, apalabramiento *m* (of servants) || colocación *f*, empleo *m*, puesto *m* (job) || petición *f* de mano (betrothal) || noviazgo *m*; *we had a very long engagement* tuvimos un noviazgo muy largo || MIL combate *m* (battle) || SP encuentro *m* (match) || TECH engranaje *m* (of gear wheels) | embrague *m* (of a car) || *engagement ring* sortija *f* de pedida.

engaging [-iŋ] *adj* simpático, ca; atractivo, va.

engarland [in'gɑ:lənd] *vt* adornar con guirnaldas.

engender [in'dʒendə*] *vt* engendrar (a child) || FIG engendrar, causar.

engine ['endʒin] *n* motor *m*; *internal-combustion engine* motor de combustión interna; *jet engine* motor de reacción || máquina *f* (machine) || artefacto *m*, ingenio *m*, máquina *f* (of warfare) || locomotora *f* (locomotive); *steam engine* locomotora de vapor || FIG medio *m* (means) || — *engine block* bloque *m* del motor || *engine driver* maquinista *m* || *engine nacelle* bloque *m* del motor (of aircraft) || *engine room* sala *f* de máquinas || *engine shed* depósito *m* de locomotoras.

engineer [,endʒi'niə*] *n* ingeniero *m*; *consulting, mining, sound, army, chemical engineer* ingeniero consultor, de minas, del sonido, militar, químico || mecánico *m* (workman) || MIL ingeniero *m* militar (officer) | soldado *m* del Cuerpo de Ingenieros (soldier) || FIG autor *m* || US maquinista *m* (of railways) || *civil engineer* ingeniero civil, ingeniero de Caminos, Canales y Puertos.

engineer [,endʒi'niə*] *vt* construir (roads, bridges, etc.) || FIG & FAM lograr (to achieve) | idear (to conceive) | maquinar (a plot).

engineering [-riŋ] *n* ingeniería *f*; *civil engineering* ingeniería civil || técnica *f*; *hydraulic engineering* técnica hidráulica || FIG maniobras *f pl*, maquinaciones *f pl*.

enginery ['endʒinəri] *n* maquinaria *f*, máquinas *f pl* || FIG maniobras *f pl*, maquinaciones *f pl*.

engird [in'gə:d] *vt* ceñir.

England ['iŋglənd] *pr n* GEOGR Inglaterra *f*.

English ['iŋgliʃ] *adj* inglés, esa || — *English Channel* Canal *m* de la Mancha || BOT *English daisy* margarita *f* || MUS *English horn* corno *m* inglés.
◆ *n* inglés *m* (language); *I study English* estudio inglés || — *the English* los ingleses || *to speak the King's English* o *the Queen's English* hablar un inglés correcto || *what is the English for «mesa»?* ¿cómo se dice mesa en inglés?

English ['iŋgliʃ] *vt* traducir al inglés.

Englishman ['iŋgliʃmən] *n* inglés *m*.
— OBSERV El plural es *Englishmen*.

Englishwoman ['iŋgliʃ,wumən] *n* inglesa *f*.
— OBSERV El plural es *Englishwomen*.

englut [in'glʌt] *vt* engullir, tragar.

engorge [in'gɔ:dʒ] *vt* devorar (to devour) || MED congestionar | obstruir.
◆ *vi* tragar.

engorgement [-mənt] *n* MED congestión *f* | obstrucción *f*.

engraft [in'grɑ:ft] *vt* injertar (to graft in) || FIG inculcar (principles, habits, etc.).

engrailed [in'greild] *adj* HERALD angrelado, da.

engrain [in'grein] *vt* inculcar (habits, tastes, etc.) || teñir (to dye).

engrave [in'greiv] *vt* grabar; *to engrave with a burin* grabar al buril || FIG grabar, imprimir.

engraver [-ə*] *n* grabador, ra.

engraving [-iŋ] *n* grabado *m*; *stipple engraving* grabado punteado; *intaglio engraving* grabado en hueco.

engross [in'grəus] *vt* absorber (s.o.'s attention) || acaparar, monopolizar (conversation, products, etc.) || copiar, pasar a limpio (to make a fair copy of).

engrossing [-iŋ] *adj* absorbente.

engrossment [-mənt] *n* absorción *f* (of attention) || redacción *f* de una copia (of documents) || monopolio *m*, acaparamiento *m* (of products, etc.).

engulf [in'gʌlf] *vt* sepultar, tragarse; *the river engulfed the island* el río se tragó la isla || sumergir, hundir (to sink) || rodear (to surround completely).

enhance [in'hɑːns] *vt* acrecentar, aumentar, intensificar || incrementar, aumentar (prices, etc.) || realzar, dar realce a (beauty, etc.).

enhancement [-mənt] *n* acrecentamiento *m*, aumento *m* || incremento *m*, aumento *m* (of prices) || realce *m* (of beauty).

enigma [i'nigmə] *n* enigma *m*.
— OBSERV El plural es *enigmas* o *enigmata*.

enigmatic [ˌenig'mætik]; **enigmatical** [-əl] *adj* enigmático, ca.

enjambment; enjambement [in'dʒæmmənt] *n* encabalgamiento *m* (in poetry).

enjoin [in'dʒɔin] *vt* imponer; *to enjoin obedience* imponer obediencia || ordenar (to command) || JUR prohibir (to forbid).

enjoy [in'dʒɔi] *vt* disfrutar de, gozar de (to delight in); *to enjoy life* disfrutar de la vida || disfrutar de, gozar de (to have the use of) || divertirse en, pasarlo bien en; *did you enjoy the party?* ¿lo pasaste bien en la fiesta? || gustar; *did you enjoy the book?* ¿te gustó el libro?; *he enjoys writing* le gusta escribir || — *enjoy your meal!* ¡que aproveche! || *enjoy yourself!* ¡que lo pase bien!, ¡que se divierta! || *to enjoy o.s.* divertirse, pasarlo bien.

enjoyable [in'dʒɔiəbl] *adj* agradable (pleasant) || divertido, da (amusing).

enjoyment [in'dʒɔimənt] *n* placer *m*, fruición *f*; *with real enjoyment* con verdadero placer || diversión *f* (sth. enjoyed) || uso *m* (the use of sth.) || disfrute *m* (possession).

enkindle [in'kindl] *vt* encender (to light up) || FIG atizar, avivar (passions) | acalorar, encender, inflamar (to inflame).

enlace [in'leis] *vt* entrelazar (to entwine) || rodear (to encircle).

enlacement [-mənt] *n* entrelazamiento *m*.

enlarge [in'lɑːdʒ] *vt* ampliar, agrandar (to make bigger) || ensanchar (a town) || extender, ampliar (to expand); *to enlarge the field of one's activities* extender el campo de su actividad || ampliar (an organization) || PHOT ampliar || desarrollar (intelligence) || PHYS & MED dilatar || US poner en libertad (to free).
◆ *vi* agrandarse, ampliarse (to become bigger) || ensancharse (a town) || PHOT ampliarse || *to enlarge on* o *upon* extenderse sobre, tratar detalladamente, hablar extensamente sobre.

enlargement [-mənt] *n* aumento *m* (development) || apéndice *m* (to a book) || PHOT ampliación *f* || extensión *f* (extension) || ensanche *m*, ensanchamiento *m* (of a town, etc.) || ampliación *f* (of an organization); *the enlargement of the Common Market* la ampliación del Mercado Común || ampliación *f* (of a shop) || aumento *m* (of s.o.'s fortune) || explicación *f* detallada (of a subject) || PHYS & MED dilatación *f* || liberación *f* (from prison).

enlarger [-ə*] *n* PHOT ampliadora *f*.

enlighten [in'laitn] *vt* aclarar, dar aclaraciones sobre (a problem) || informar, instruir (to give information to s.o.) || iluminar, ilustrar (mind).

enlightened [in'laitnd] *adj* culto, ta || bien informado, da (well informed) || ilustrado, da (despot).

enlightening [in'laitniŋ] *adj* informativo, va || instructivo, va.

enlightenment [in'laitnmənt] *n* aclaración *f* (an enlightening) || ilustración *f* (illustration) || *the Age of Enlightenment* el Siglo Ilustrado *or* de la Ilustración, el Siglo de las Luces.

enlist [in'list] *vt* MIL reclutar, alistar (to recruit) || FIG conseguir, lograr, obtener (help, support) | reclutar (helpers).
◆ *vi* MIL alistarse || *to enlist before the usual age* alistarse voluntario.

enlisted man [-id,mən] *n* US soldado *m* de tropa.
— OBSERV El plural es *enlisted men*.

enlistment [-mənt] *n* MIL alistamiento *m*, reclutamiento *m* || FIG reclutamiento *m*.

enliven [in'laivn] *vt* animar, avivar (to give animation) || alegrar, animar (to make gayer) || estimular, animar (business).

en masse [ɑːŋ'mæs] *adv* en masa.

enmesh [in'meʃ] *vt* enredar, coger en una red.

enmity ['enmiti] *n* enemistad *f*.

ennoble [i'nəubl] *vt* ennoblecer.

ennoblement [-mənt] *n* ennoblecimiento *m*.

ennobling [i'nəubliŋ] *n* ennoblecimiento *m*.

ennui [ɑː'nwiː] *n* aburrimiento *m* (boredom).

enology [iː'nɔlədʒi] *n* enología *f*.

enormity [i'nɔːmiti] *n* atrocidad *f*, monstruosidad *f* (a shocking crime or error) || enormidad *f* (huge size).

enormous [i'nɔːməs] *adj* enorme (in amount, degree, size) || monstruoso, sa; atroz (crime, error).

enough [i'nʌf] *adj* bastante, suficiente; *it's enough to* hay bastante para; *he has enough money to buy it* tiene bastante dinero para comprarlo.
◆ *adv* suficientemente, bastante; *he is tall enough to* es bastante alto para || bastante (quite, fairly); *she looks well enough* tiene bastante buena cara || US FAM muy; *he was happy enough to meet you* estaba muy contento de verte || — *it's good enough* está bien || *oddly* o *strangely enough* por extraño que parezca || *sure enough* más que seguro, sin duda alguna || *well enough* bastante bien.
◆ *interj* ¡basta! || *enough of your nonsense!* ¡basta de tonterías!
◆ *n* lo bastante, lo suficiente; *he has enough to live on* tiene lo suficiente para vivir || — *enough and to spare* de sobra || *enough is enough* basta y sobra || *it is enough for me to know that...* me basta saber que... || *that's enough* ya está bien, con eso basta || *there's more than enough for all of us* hay más que bastante para todos nosotros || *we have had enough of her* estamos hartos de ella.

enounce [i'nauns] *vt* proclamar (to proclaim) || enunciar (to state) || pronunciar (to pronounce).

enouncement [-mənt] *n* declaración *f* || enunciación *f*.

enplane [in'plein] *vi* subirse a un avión, tomar el avión.

enquire [in'kwaiə*] *vt/vi* ⟶ **inquire.**

enquiry [in'kwaiəri] *n* ⟶ **inquiry.**

enrage [in'reidz] *vt* enfurecer, poner furioso (to make furiously angry) || enloquecer; *enraged by thirst* enloquecido por la sed.

enrapture [in'ræptʃə*] *vt* arrebatar, extasiar, embelesar.

enrich [in'ritʃ] *vt* enriquecer || fertilizar, abonar (soil) || FIG enriquecer || *to enrich o.s.* enriquecerse.

enrichment [in'ritʃmənt] *n* enriquecimiento *m* || fertilización *f*, abono *m* (of soil).

enrobe [in'rəub] *vt* vestir.

enrol; enroll [in'rəul] *vt* inscribir, apuntar en la lista (to include in a list) || registrar (to enter in a register) || matricular (a student) || MIL alistar.
◆ *vi* inscribirse (in a list) || matricularse (to join an establishment) || MIL alistarse.

enrolment; enrollment [-mənt] *n* alistamiento *m* (in the forces) || matriculación *f* (in university) || inscripción *f* (in a list) || registro *m* (in a register).

enroot [in'ruːt] *vt* arraigar.

en route [ɑː'ruːt] *adv* en el camino || *to be en route for* ir camino de, ir en dirección de.

ens [enz] *n* PHIL ente *m*.
— OBSERV El plural de *ens* es *entia*.

ensanguine [inθæŋgwin] *vt* ensangrentar.

ensconce [in'skɔns] *vt* esconder, ocultar (to conceal) || *to be ensconced in* estar cómodamente instalado en, estar arrellanado en.

ensemble [ɑːn'sɑːmbl] *n* conjunto *m* || MUS conjunto *m* | orquesta *f* de cámara || THEATR compañía *f* || conjunto *m* (dress).

enshrine [in'ʃrain] *vt* REL poner en un relicario || encerrar (to enclose) || FIG conservar religiosamente (to put in an honoured place).

enshroud [in'ʃraud] *vt* envolver || disimular.

ensign ['ensain] *n* enseña *f*, pabellón *m* (flag) || abanderado *m* (standard bearer) || insignia *f*, distintivo *m* (badge) || US MAR alférez *m*.

ensilage ['ensilidʒ] *n* ensilaje *m*, ensilado *m*.

ensilage ['ensilidʒ]; **ensile** ['ensail] *vt* ensilar.

enslave [in'sleiv] *vt* esclavizar.

enslavement [-mənt] *n* esclavitud *f*.

enslaver [-ə*] *n* esclavista *m* & *f*.

ensnare [in'snɛə*] *vt* coger en una trampa.

ensphere [in'sfiə*] *vt* abarcar.

ensue [in'sjuː] *vi* resultar (to result) || seguirse, seguir (to follow) || originarse (to be caused).

ensuing [-iŋ] *adj* consiguiente, resultante || siguiente (year).

ensure [in'ʃuə*] *vt* asegurar.

enswathe [in'sweið] *vt* envolver || fajar, poner pañales (a baby).

entablature [en'tæblətʃə*] *n* ARCH entablamento *m*.

entail [in'teil] *n* JUR vínculo *m* (link).

entail [in'teil] *vt* traer consigo, acarrear, ocasionar (to bring as a consequence) || suponer, implicar (to involve) || JUR vincular.

entailment [-mənt] *n* JUR vinculación *f*.

entangle [in'tæŋgl] *vt* enredar, enmarañar; *to entangle a ball of wool* enredar un ovillo de lana; *he got entangled in the rope* se enredó en la cuerda || complicar, enredar, liar (to involve in difficulties) || FIG *to get entangled* meterse en un lío.

entanglement [-mənt] *n* enredo *m*, embrollo *m* (an entangling or being entangled) || MIL alambrada *f* || FIG lío *m*; *to keep out of the entanglement* no meterse en el lío | lío *m* (love affair).

entasis ['entəsis] *n* ARCH éntasis *f*.

entelechy [en'teləki] *n* entelequia *f*.

entente [ɑːn'tɑːnt] *n* convenio *m*, alianza *f*, acuerdo *m* || HIST *Entente Cordiale* Entente *f* Cordial.

enter ['entə*] *vt* entrar en; *to enter a room* entrar en una habitación; *to enter the age of space travel* entrar en la era de los vuelos espaciales || penetrar en, entrar en (to penetrate into) || pasarse por; *it never entered my head* nunca se me pasó por la cabeza || meterse en; *to enter politics* meterse en política || entrar en, tomar parte en, participar en (a conversation, competition, plot, etc.) || entrar en, ingresar en; *to*

enter a firm entrar en una empresa || hacerse miembro de (to join) || abrazar (a profession) || inscribir; *to enter a car for a race* inscribir un coche para una carrera || inscribir, apuntar (in a list) || registar (to record) || matricular (a child in a school) || matricularse en; *to enter one's name for the summer school* matricularse en los cursos de verano || presentar (a request, claim, etc.) || formular, elevar; *she entered a protest* elevó una protesta || JUR entablar, intentar (an action), interponer (an appeal), depositar, registrar en el depósito legal (a book), declarar (a cargo) || MIL alistarse en || declarar (for customs) || — FAM *to enter an appearance* hacer acto de presencia || *to enter religion* abrazar el estado religioso.
◆ *vi* entrar (to go or to come in) || THEATR entrar en *or* salir a escena.
◆ *phr v* ***to enter for*** tomar parte en, participar en (race) | presentarse como candidato a (post) || ***to enter into*** empezar (to start upon) | entablar, iniciar (negotiations) | tomar parte en, participar en (a conversation) | establecer (relations) | concertar (agreement) | celebrar (contract) | cerrar (bargain) | contraer (obligation) | comprender (a joke) | entrar en, meterse en; *to enter into details* entrar en detalles | compartir (feelings) | entrar en; *this never entered into the plans* esto nunca entró en los planes || ***to enter up*** registrar (in accounts) || ***to enter upon*** o *on* comenzar, emprender, empezar (to begin) | tomar posesión de (a property).

enteralgia [ˌentər'ældʒiə] *n* MED enteralgia *f.*

enteric [en'terik] *adj* MED entérico, ca; intestinal || *enteric fever* fiebre entérica *or* tifoidea.

enteritis [ˌentə'raitis] *n* MED enteritis *f.*

enterprise ['entəpraiz] *n* empresa *f*; *a business enterprise* una empresa comercial; *a dangerous enterprise* una empresa peligrosa || iniciativa *f* (personal characteristic); *spirit of enterprise* espíritu de iniciativa || carácter *m* emprendedor || *private enterprise* sector privado, empresa privada.

enterprise zone [-zəun] *n* zona *f* industrial.

enterprising [-iŋ] *adj* emprendedor, ra || lleno de iniciativa || decidido, da (resolute).

entertain [ˌentə'tein] *vt* recibir (to receive as a guest) || entretener, divertir (to amuse) || mantener (conversation, relations) || albergar, abrigar (to have in one's mind); *to entertain the hope that...* abrigar la esperanza de que... || *considerar* (to consider) || *to entertain friends to dinner* invitar a unos amigos a cenar.
◆ *vi* recibir invitados.

entertainer [-ə*] *n* artista *m* & *f* (in show business) || animador, ra (amusing person) || anfitrión, ona (host, hostess).

entertaining [-iŋ] *adj* entretenido, da; divertido, da.

entertainment [-mənt] *n* entretenimiento *m*, diversión *f*, distracción *f* (amusement) || espectáculo *m* (public performance) || hospitalidad *f*, recibimiento *m* (hospitality) || recepción *f* (reception) || — *entertainment allowance* gastos *m pl* de representación || *entertainment tax* impuesto aplicado a los espectáculos.

enthral; enthrall [in'θrɔːl] *vt* cautivar.

enthraling; enthralling [-iŋ] *adj* cautivador, ra.

enthralment; enthrallment [-mənt] *n* encanto *m*, embeleso *m*.

enthrone [in'θrəun] *vt* entronizar.

enthronement [-mənt] *n* entronización *f.*

enthuse [in'θjuːz] *vi* entusiasmarse; *to enthuse over sth.* entusiasmarse por algo.

enthusiasm [in'θjuːziæzəm] *n* entusiasmo *m*.

enthusiast [in'θjuːziæst] *n* entusiasta *m* & *f.*

enthusiastic [in'θjuːzi'æstik] *adj* entusiástico, ca (praise, etc.) || entusiasta (person) || *to be enthusiastic about* o *to become enthusiastic over* entusiasmarse por.

entia ['enʃiə] *pl n* ⟶ **ens.**

entice [in'tais] *vt* seducir (to seduce) || atraer (to attract) || convencer; *to entice s.o. away from his duty* convencer a uno para que abandone su obligación.

enticement [-mənt] *n* atractivo *m* (attraction) || seducción *f* (seduction) || tentación *f.*

enticing [-iŋ] *adj* atractivo, va; seductor, ra || tentador, ra.

entire [in'taiə*] *adj* entero, ra; completo, ta; *the entire fleet* la flota entera || total, todo, da; entero, ra; *the entire population* toda la población || intacto, ta; *the stocks are still entire* las existencias están aún intactas || BOT entero, ra || entero, ra (a horse).
◆ *n* semental *m* (horse) || FIG totalidad *f.*

entirely [in'taiəli] *adv* completamente, totalmente, enteramente (wholly) || únicamente (solely).

entirety [in'taiərəti] *n* totalidad *f*; *the country in its entirety* el país en su totalidad.

entitle [in'taitl] *vt* dar derecho a (to empower); *this ticket entitles you to a seat* este billete le da derecho a sentarse || titular, dar el título de (to give a title to) || *to be entitled* tener derecho; *you are entitled to think what you want* tienes derecho a pensar lo que quieras; titularse (a book, a film, etc.).

entitlement [-mənt] *n* derecho *m*.

entity ['entiti] *n* PHIL entidad *f* || *legal entity* persona jurídica.

entomb [in'tuːm] *vt* enterrar, sepultar.

entomological [-əl] *adj* entomológico, ca.

entomologist [ˌentə'mɔlədʒist] *n* entomólogo *m*.

entomology [ˌentə'mɔlədʒi] *n* entomología *f.*

entomophagous [ˌentə'mɔfəgəs] *adj* ZOOL entomófago, ga.

entomophily [ˌentə'mɔfili] *n* entomofilia *f.*

entourage [ˌɔntu'rɑːʒ] *n* séquito *m* (retinue) || allegados *m pl* (people who are close to) || ambiente *m*, entorno *m* (surroundings).

entozoan [ˌentə'zəuən] *n* ZOOL entozoario *m*.

entr'acte ['ɔntrækt] *n* entracto *m*.

entrails ['entreilz] *pl n* entrañas *f.*

entrain [in'trein] *vt* poner en un tren (troops).
◆ *vi* tomar el tren (troops).

entrance ['entrəns] *n* entrada *f* || admisión *f*, ingreso *m*; *entrance examination* examen de ingreso || bocacalle *f* (to a street) || THEATR salida *f* a escena || — *entrance hall* vestíbulo *m*, entrada *f* || *no entrance* prohibida la entrada || *tradesmen's entrance* entrada de servicio || *to pay one's entrance fee* pagar los derechos de entrada *or* de admisión.

entrance [in'trɑːns] *vt* arrebatar, extasiar (to overcome with joy) || poner en trance (to put into a trance).

entrancement [-mənt] *n* arrebato *m*, éxtasis *m* || trance *m*.

entrancing [-iŋ] *adj* encantador, ra; fascinante.

entrant ['entrənt] *n* participante *m* & *f* (candidate) || principiante *m* & *f* (beginner) || persona *f* que entra; *late entrants are a nuisance in a theatre* las personas que entran tarde en un teatro molestan mucho.

entrap [in'træp] *vt* coger en una trampa.

entreat [in'triːt] *vt* suplicar, implorar, rogar.

entreaty [in'triːti] *n* súplica *f*, ruego *m*.

entrechat [ɑntrə'ʃɑː] *n* trenzado *m* (dance).

entrée; US entree ['ɔntrei] *n* entrada *f* || CULIN entrada *f*, principio *m* || US plato *m* fuerte (main course).

entrench; intrench [in'trentʃ] *vt* atrincherar || *the enemy entrenched themselves on the hill* el enemigo se atrincheró en la colina.
◆ *vi* atrincherarse || ⟶ **encroach.**

entrenchment [-mənt] *n* atrincheramiento *m* || ⟶ **encroachment.**

entrepôt ['ɔntrəpəu] *n* centro *m* comercial de importación y distribución || almacén *m* (storehouse).

entrepreneur [ˌɔntrəprə'nəː*] *n* empresario *m* (man who runs a business) || intermediario *m* (middleman) || contratista *m* (of works).

entresol ['ɔntrəsɔl] *n* entresuelo *m*.

entrust [in'trʌst] *vt* confiar (to commit) || encargar (*with* de) (s.o.).

entry ['entri] *n* entrada *f* (entrance) || acceso *m* (access) || vestíbulo *m*, recibidor *m*, entrada *f* (hall) || pasadizo *m* (a narrow lane leading to a building) || bocacalle *f* (to a street) || entrada *f*, artículo *m* (in a book, etc.) || ingreso *m* (into profession, etc.) || SP participante *m* & *f* (entrant) | lista *f* de participantes (list) || COMM partida *f* (item); *double-entry, single-entry bookkeeping* contabilidad por partida doble, simple || — INFORM *entry data* datos *m* de entrada || *entry fee* entrada *f* || *entry form* solicitud *f* de inscripción || *no entry* dirección prohibida (streets), prohibida la entrada (on a door) || *forcible entry* violación *f* de domicilio, allanamiento *m* de morada || *to force an entry* allanar la morada.

entryway [-wei] *n* US entrada *f.*

entwine [in'twain] *vt* entrelazar (to plait) || enroscar (to twist around).
◆ *vi* entrelazarse || enroscarse.

entwist [in'twist] *vt* enroscar.

enucleate [i'njuːkliit] *adj* sin núcleo.

enucleate [i'njuːklieit] *vt* deshuesar, desosar (to extract the stone from a fruit, etc.) || BIOL extraer el núcleo de || MED extirpar, enuclear (a tumour) || FIG explicar, aclarar, esclarecer.

enucleation [i'njuːkli'eiʃən] *n* BIOL extracción *f* del núcleo || MED extirpación *f* de un tumor, enucleación *f* || FIG aclaración *f*, esclarecimiento *m* (of a problem).

enumerate [i'njuːməreit] *vt* enumerar.

enumeration [iˌnjuːmə'reiʃən] *n* enumeración *f.*

enumerative [i'njuːmərətiv] *adj* enumerativo, va.

enunciate [i'nʌnsieit] *vt* enunciar (a principle) || formular, enunciar (to state) || pronunciar, articular (sounds, syllables, etc.) || proclamar (to proclaim).
◆ *vi* articular (to articulate).

enunciation [iˌnʌnsi'eiʃən] *n* enunciado *m*, enunciación *f* (of a principle) || pronunciación *f*, articulación *f* (of sounds, syllables) || proclamación *f*, declaración *f.*

enunciative [i'nʌnʃjətiv] *adj* enunciativo, va.

enunciator [i'nʌnsieitə*] *n* persona *f* que enuncia *or* declara algo.

envelop [in'veləp] *vt* envolver.

envelop; envelope ['envələup] *n* sobre *m* (for letters) || funda *f* (cover) || envoltura *f*, cubierta *f* (of an airship) || ANAT & BOT túnica *f* || MATH envolvente *f.*

enveloping [in'veləpiŋ] *adj* envolvente.

envelopment [in'veləpmənt] *n* envoltura *f* (wrapper) || envolvimiento *m* (wrapping up).

envenom [in'venəm] *vt* envenenar, emponzoñar.

enviable ['enviəbl] *adj* envidiable.

envious ['enviəs] *adj* envidioso, sa || — *it made him envious of their riches* le dio envidia de su riqueza || *to be envious of* tener envidia de, envidiar a (s.o.).

environ [in'vaiərən] *vt* rodear.

environment [in'vaiərənmənt] *n* medio ambiente *m*, entorno *m*; *pollution of the environment* contaminación del medio ambiente || ambiente *m* (surroundings) || INFORM entorno *m*.

environmental [in,vaiərən'mentəl] *adj* ambiental.

environmentalist [-ist] *n* persona *f* preocupada por el medio ambiente, ecologista *m* & *f*.

environs [in'vaiərənz] *pl n* alrededores *m*, cercanías *f*.

envisage [in'vizidʒ] *vt* imaginarse, concebir, pensar en (to have a mental picture of) || pensar, creer; *I do not envisage arriving before ten o'clock* no pienso llegar antes de las diez || proyectar, tener la intención de; *I envisage going to France* proyecto irme a Francia || enfocar, ver (to look at); *I had not envisaged the matter in that light* no había enfocado la cuestión de esta manera || pretender llegar a; *I don't envisage an agreement* no pretendo llegar a un acuerdo || prever (to foresee).

envision [in'viʒən] *vt* US imaginar.

envoy ['envɔi] *n* enviado *m*, mensajero *m* (s.o. sent on a mission) || *envoy extraordinary* enviado extraordinario.

envy ['envi] *n* envidia *f*; *he could not hide his envy* no podía ocultar su envidia || cosa *f* envidiada (sth. desired) || *she was the envy of the other girls* las otras chicas la envidiaban.

envy ['envi] *vt* envidiar, tener envidia de; *I don't envy you* no te envidio.
◆ *vi* tener envidia.

enwrap [in'ræp] *vt* envolver (to envelop) || FIG absorber (to engross).

enwreathe [in'ri:ð] *vt* adornar con guirnaldas.

enzootic [,enzəu'ɔtik] *n* enzootia *f*.

enzyme ['enzaim] *n* enzima *f*.

eocene ['i:əusi:n] *adj* GEOL eoceno.
◆ *n* eoceno *m*.

eolith ['i:əuliθ] *n* eolito *m*.

EPA [Environmental Protection Agency] agencia norteamericana para la protección del medio ambiente.

eparch ['epɑ:k] *n* eparca *m*.

epaulet; epaulette ['epəulet] *n* MIL charretera *f*.

épée ['eipei] *n* espada *f*.

epeira [e'pairə] *n* ZOOL epeira *f*.

epenthesis [e'penθisis] *n* GRAMM epéntesis *f*.

epergne [i'pə:n] *n* centro *m* de mesa.

ephebe [i'fib]; **ephebus** [-əs] *n* efebo *m*.
— OBSERV El plural de *ephebus* es *ephebi*.

ephedrine ['efidrin] *n* efedrina *f*.

ephemera [i'femərə] *n* ZOOL efímera *f*, cachipolla *f* || cosa *f* efímera.
— OBSERV El plural de la palabra *ephemera* es *ephemerae* o *ephemeras*, pero es preferible emplear este último.

ephemeral [i'femərəl] *adj* efímero, ra.

ephemeris [i'femərıs] *n* efemérides *f pl*.
— OBSERV El plural de *ephemeris* es *ephemerides*.

ephemeron [i'femərɔn] *n* ZOOL efímera *f*, cachipolla *f*.
— OBSERV El plural es *ephemera* o *ephemerons*.

Ephesus ['efisəs] *pr n* GEOGR Éfeso.

epiblast ['epiblæst] *n* BIOL epiblasto *m*.

epic ['epik] *n* poema *f* épico, épica *f*, epopeya *f*.
◆ *adj* épico, ca || FIG épico, ca.

epicarp ['epikɑ:p] *n* BOT epicarpio *m*.

epicene ['episi:n] *adj* GRAMM epiceno || hermafrodita.
◆ *n* hermafrodita.

epicentre; US **epicenter** ['epi,sentə*] *n* epicentro *m*.

epicure ['epikjuə*] *n* epicúreo, a (pleasure seeker) || gastrónomo, ma; sibarita *m* & *f* (gastronome).

Epicurean [,epikjuə'ri:ən] *adj/n* epicúreo, a.

epicureanism [-izəm]; **epicurism** ['epikjuərizəm] *n* epicureísmo *m*.

Epicurus [,epi'kjuərəs] *pr n* Epicuro *m*.

epicycle ['episaikl] *n* epiciclo *m*.

epicyclic [,epi'saiklik] *adj* epicíclico, ca.

epicycloid [,epi'saiklɔid] *n* MATH epicicloide *f*.

epidemic [,epi'demik] *n* MED epidemia *f* || FIG ola *f*.
◆ *adj* epidémico, ca.

epidemical [-əl] *adj* epidémico, ca.

epidermal [,epi'də:məl]; **epidermic** [,epi'də:mik] *adj* epidérmico, ca.

epidermis [,epi'də:mis] *n* epidermis *f*.
— OBSERV El plural de la palabra inglesa es *epidermes*.

epididymis [,epi'didəmis] *n* ANAT epidídimo *m*.

epigastric [,epi'gæstrik] *adj* ANAT epigástrico, ca.

epigastrium [,epi'gæstriəm] *n* ANAT epigastrio *m*.
— OBSERV El plural de *epigastrium* es *epigastria*.

epigeal [,epi'dʒiəl]; **epigean** [,epi'dʒiən] *adj* BOT & ZOOL epigeo, a.

epigenesis [,epi'dʒenisis] *n* epigénesis *f*.

epigenetic [,epidʒə'netik] *adj* epigenético, ca.

epigeous [,epi'dʒiəs] *adj* epigeo, a.

epiglottis [,epi'glɔtis] *n* epiglotis *f*.

epigone ['epigəun] *n* epígono *m*.

epigram ['epigræm] *n* epigrama *m*.

epigrammatic [,epigrə'mætik]; **epigrammatical** [-əl] *adj* epigramático, ca.

epigrammatist [,epi'græmətist] *n* epigramista *m*, epigramatista *m*.

epigraph ['epigrɑ:f] *n* epígrafe *m*.

epigraphic [,epi'græfik]; **epigraphical** [-əl] *adj* epigráfico, ca.

epigraphist [e'pigrəfist] *n* epigrafista *m* & *f*.

epigraphy [e'pigrəfi] *n* epigrafía *f*.

epilepsy ['epilepsi] *n* epilepsia *f*.

epileptic [,epi'leptik] *adj/n* MED epiléptico, ca.

epilogue; US **epilog** ['epilɔg] *n* epílogo *m*.

Epiphany [i'pifəni] *n* REL Epifanía *f*.

epiphenomenon ['epifi'nɔminən] *n* epifenómeno *m*.
— OBSERV El plural de *epiphenomenon* es *epiphenomena*.

epiphysis [i'pifəsis] *n* ANAT epífisis *f*.
— OBSERV El plural de *epiphysis* es *epiphyses*.

epiphyte ['epifait] *n* BOT epifita *f*.

epiphytic [,epi'fitik]; **epiphytical** [-əl] *adj* BOT epifito, ta.

episcopacy [i'piskəpəsi] *n* REL episcopado *m*.

episcopal [i'piskəpəl] *adj* REL episcopal.

episcopalian [i,piskə'peiljən] *adj/n* REL episcopalista.

episcopate [i'piskəupit] *n* REL episcopado *m*.

episode ['episəud] *n* episodio *m*.

episodic [,epi'sɔdik]; **episodical** [-əl] *adj* episódico, ca.

episternum [,epis'tə:nəm] *n* ANAT episternón *m*.
— OBSERV El plural de *episternum* es *episterna*.

epistle [i'pisl] *n* epístola *f*.

Epistle [i'pisl] *n* REL epístola *f*.

epistolary [i'pistələri] *adj* epistolar.
◆ *n* epistolario *m*.

epistyle ['epistail] *n* ARCH arquitrabe *m*.

epitaph ['epitɑ:f] *n* epitafio *m*.

epithalamial [,epiθə'leimjəl]; **epithalamic** [,epiθə'læmik] *adj* epitalámico, ca.

epithalamion [,epiθə'leimjən] *n* epitalamio *m*.
— OBSERV El plural de *epithalamion* es *epithalamia*.

epithalamium [,epiθə'leimjən] *n* epitalamio *m*.
— OBSERV El plural es *epithalamiums* o *epithalamia*.

epithelial [,epi'θi:ljəl] *adj* epitelial.

epithelioma [,epi,θi:li'əumə] *n* MED epitelioma *m*.

epithelium ['epi'θi:ljəm] *n* ANAT epitelio *m*.
— OBSERV El plural es *epitheliums* o *epithelia*.

epithet ['epiθet] *n* epíteto *m*.

epitome [i'pitəmi] *n* epítome *m*, resumen *m*, compendio *m* (summary) || FIG personificación *f*.

epitomize [i'pitəmaiz] *vt* resumir, compendiar || FIG ser la personificación de.

epizootic [,epizəu'ɔtik] *n* epizootia *f*.

epizooty [,epizəu'ɔti] *n* epizootia *f*.

epoch ['i:pɔk] *n* época *f*; *to mark an epoch* hacer época.

epoch-making [-,meikiŋ] *adj* que hace época.

epode ['epəud] *n* POET epodo *m*.

eponym ['epəunim] *n* epónimo *m*.

eponymic [,epə'nimik]; **eponymous** [i'pɔniməs] *adj* epónimo, ma.

epopee ['epəpi:]; **epopoeia** [,epə'piə] *n* epopeya *f*.

epos ['epɔs] *n* epopeya *f*.

epsilon [ep'sailən] *n* épsilon *f*.

Epsom ['epsəm] *pr n* GEOGR Epsom || CHEM *Epsom salts* sulfato *m* de magnesio, sal *f* de la Higuera.

equability [,ekwə'biliti] *n* ecuanimidad *f* (composure) || uniformidad *f*, igualdad *f*.

equable ['ekwəbl] *adj* regular, uniforme; *an equable climate* un clima regular || ecuánime (calm); *equable disposition* temperamento ecuánime.

equal ['i:kwəl] *adj* igual; *she is equal to you* ella es igual que tú; *equal in value* de igual valor || igualado, da; *an equal match* un partido igualado || igual, mismo, ma; *you have equal rights* tienes los mismos derechos || equitativo, va (treatment) || regular, uniforme (uniform) || — *all things being equal* si todo sigue igual || *equal distance* equidistancia *f* || SP *equal on points* empatados || *equal opportunities* igualdad *f* de oportunidades || *equal pay* igualdad *f* de salario || *equal rights* igualdad *f* de derechos || *equal sign* signo *m* de igualdad || *equal to* igual que; *her share is equal to his* su parte es igual que la de él; equivalente a (equivalent to) || *on equal terms* en un plano de igualdad || *other things being equal* si todo sigue igual, en igualdad de condiciones || *to be equal to* tener fuerzas *or* ánimo para (a task), estar a la altura de (a situation) || *to feel equal to a task* sentirse con

fuerzas para hacer un trabajo || *with equal ease* con la misma facilidad, con igual facilidad.
◆ *n* igual *m* & *f* || *to treat s.o. as an equal* tratar a uno de igual a igual.

equal ['i:kwəl] *vt* igualar, ser igual a (to be or become equal to) || igualar (to come up to the standard of) || ser igual a, ser; *three and five equals eight* tres más cinco son ocho.

equalitarian [ik,wɔli'tɛərjən] *adj* igualitario, ria.

equality [i:'kwɔliti] *n* igualdad *f* || *to be on an equality with* estar en un pie de igualdad con.

equalization [,i:kwəlai'zeiʃən] *n* igualación *f*, igualamiento *m* || SP empate *m* || compensación *f*; *equalization fund* fondo de compensación.

equalize ['i:kwəlaiz] *vt/vi* igualar || SP empatar, igualar.

equalizer [-ə*] *n* SP tanto *m* del empate || ELECTR compensador *m*.

equally ['i:kwəli] *adv* igualmente (to the same degree) || equitativamente (equitably) || *equally matched* de igual fuerza.

equanimity [,ekwə'nimiti] *n* ecuanimidad *f*.

equate [i'kweit] *vt* MATH poner en ecuación || FIG igualar, equiparar (to regard as equal) | comparar (to compare).

equation [i'kweiʒən] *n* MATH ecuación *f*; *quadratic equation* ecuación de segundo grado || CHEM ecuación *f* química || MATH *simple equation* ecuación de primer grado.

equator [ik'weitə*] *n* ecuador *m*.

equatorial ['ekwə'tɔ:riəl] *adj* ecuatorial.
◆ *n* ecuatorial *m*.

Equatorial Guinea [-'gini] *pr n* GEOGR Guinea Ecuatorial.

equerry ['ekwəri] *n* caballerizo *m* de la casa real.

equestrian [i'kwestriən] *adj* ecuestre.
◆ *n* caballista *m*, jinete *m*.

equestrienne [i,kwestri'en] *n* amazona *f*, caballista *f* (woman who rides on horseback).

equiangular ['i:kwi'æŋgjulə*] *adj* MATH equiángulo, la.

equidistance ['i:kwi'distəns] *n* equidistancia *f*.

equidistant ['i:kwi'distənt] *adj* equidistante.

equilateral ['i:kwi'lætərəl] *adj* equilátero, ra.
◆ *n* MATH lado *m* equilátero (side) | figura *f* equilátera (figure).

equilibrant [i'kwilibrənt] *n* TECH fuerza *f* equilibrante.

equilibrate [i'kwilibreit] *vt* equilibrar.
◆ *vi* mantenerse en equilibrio, estar en equilibrio.

equilibrist [i:'kwilibrist] *n* equilibrista *m* & *f*.

equilibrium [,i:kwi'libriəm] *n* equilibrio *m*.
— OBSERV El plural es *equilibriums* o *equilibria*.

equimolecular [,ikwiməu'lekjulə*] *adj* CHEM equimolecular.

equine ['ekwain] *adj* equino, na.
◆ *n* caballo *m*.

equinoctial ['i:kwi'nɔkʃəl] *adj* equinoccial || *equinoctial circle* o *line* línea *f* equinoccial.

equinox ['i:kwinɔks] *n* equinoccio *m*.

equip [i'kwip] *vt* equipar, proveer.

equipage ['ekwipidʒ] *n* equipo *m* (materials for an expedition) || carruaje *m*, carroza *f* (carriage).

equipment [i'kwipmənt] *n* equipo *m* || herramientas *f pl* (tools) || FIG aptitud *f*, dotes *f pl* || material *m* móvil (railways).

equipoise ['ekwipɔiz] *n* contrapeso *m* (counterweight) || equilibrio *m* (the state of equilibrium).

equipollence [,ik:kwi'pɔləns] *n* equivalencia *f*.

equipollent [,i:kwi'pɔlənt] *adj* equivalente *m*.

equiponderant [,i:kwi'pɔndərənt] *adj* del mismo peso.

equiponderate [,i:kwi'pɔndəreit] *vt* hacer del mismo peso (to make equal in weight) || contrapesar (to counterbalance).
◆ *vi* equiponderar.

equitable ['ekwitəbl] *adj* justo, ta; equitativo, va.

equitation ['ekwi'teiʃən] *n* equitación *f*.

equity ['ekwiti] *n* equidad *f*, justicia *f* (justice) || US valor *m* de una propiedad después de haber deducido la cantidad en que está hipotecada || — *equity capital* capital *m* en acciones ordinarias || *equity of a statute* espíritu *m* de una ley || *equity of redemption* derecho *m* de redimir una hipoteca || *equity securities* acciones *f* ordinarias.
◆ *pl* acciones.

equivalence [i'kwivələns]; **equivalency** [-i] *n* equivalencia *f*.

equivalent [i'kwivələnt] *adj* equivalente || *to be equivalent to* equivaler a, ser equivalente a.
◆ *n* equivalente *m*.

equivocal [i'kwivəkəl] *adj* equívoco, ca (ambiguous) || dudoso, sa (suspect, doubtful).

equivocally [-i] *adv* equívocamente.

equivocate [i'kwivəkeit] *vi* usar equívocos, dar una respuesta ambigua.

equivocation [i'kwivə'keiʃən] *n* ambigüedad *f*.

equivocator [i'kwivəkeitə*] *n* persona *f* que se vale siempre de equívocos.

equivoque ['ekwivəuk] *n* equívoco *m* (quibble).

er [ə:] onomatopoeia em, mm.

era ['iərə] *n* era *f*; *the Christian era* la era cristiana; *the atomic era* la era atómica || *to mark an era* hacer época.

eradiate [i'reidieit] *vt* irradiar.

eradiation [i'reidi'eiʃən] *n* irradiación *f*.

eradicable [i'rædikəbl] *adj* desarraigable || FIG extirpable, erradicable.

eradicate [i'rædikeit] *vt* AGR desarraigar (plants) || FIG erradicar, extirpar (habits, etc.).

eradication [i'rædi'keiʃən] *n* AGR desarraigo *m* || FIG erradicación *f*, extirpación *f*.

eradicator [i'rædikeitə*] *n* extirpador *m* || borratintas *m inv* (ink remover).

erasable [i'reizəbl] *adj* borrable.

erase [i'reiz] *vt* borrar || INFORM borrar.

eraser [i'reizə*] *n* borrador *m*, goma *f* de borrar (a rubber for pencil) || borrador *m* (a cloth pad for rubbing chalk) || raspador *m* (knife).

erasing head [i'reiziŋ'hed] *n* cabeza *f* supresora (of tape recorder) || INFORM cabeza *f* de borrado.

Erasmian [i'ræzmiən] *adj/n* erasmista.

Erasmus [i'ræzməs] *pr n* Erasmo *m*.

erasure [i'reiʒə*] *n* borradura *f* || raspadura *f*.

erbium ['ə:bjəm] *n* CHEM erbio *m*.

ere [ɛə*] *prep* (ant) antes de.
◆ *conj* (ant) antes de que.

erect [i'rekt] *adj* erguido, da; *to stand erect* estar erguido || erizado, da; de punta (hair, etc.) || derecho, cha; de pie (upright) || vertical.

erect [i'rekt] *vt* levantar, erigir; *to erect a monument* levantar un monumento; *to erect a barrier between two people* levantar una barrera entre dos personas || levantar (to set upright) || montar, armar (to assemble) || MATH trazar, levantar; *to erect a perpendicular* trazar una perpendicular || establecer (to establish) || erigir (a principle).
◆ *vi* erguirse.

erectile [-ail] *adj* eréctil.

erection [i'rekʃən] *n* erección *f* || erección *f*, construcción *f* (of a building) || constitución *f*, establecimiento *m* (of a court) || TECH montaje *m* (of a machine) || construcción *f*, edificio *m* (building).

erector [i'rektə*] *n* erector *m* || TECH montador *m*.

eremite ['erimait] *n* eremita *m*, ermitaño *m*.

eremitic [,eri'mitik]; **eremitical** [-əl] *adj* eremítico, ca.

erethism ['erəθizəm] *n* MED eretismo *m*.

erewhile [ɛə'wail] *adv* hace poco.

erg [ə:g] *n* PHYS ergio *m*, erg *m*.

ergonomics [,ə:gə'nɔmiks] *n* ergonomía *f*.

ergosterol [ə:'gɔstərɔl] *n* ergosterol *m*.

ergot ['ə:gət] *n* cornezuelo *m* (of rye).

ergotism [-izəm] *n* ergotismo *m*.

ergotize [-aiz] *vt* AGR atacar del cornezuelo || *ergotized corn* trigo atacado del cornezuelo.
◆ *vi* ergotizar.

Erin ['iərin] *pr n* (ant) GEOGR Erín *f*, Irlanda *f*.

eristic [e'ristik] *adj* polémico, ca.

Eritrea [,eri'treiə] *pr n* GEOGR Eritrea *f*.

ermine ['ə:min] *n* armiño *m* (animal and fur) || HERALD armiño *m*.

Ernest ['ə:nist] *pr n* Ernesto *m*.

erode [i'rəud] *vt* corroer, desgastar; *acid erodes metal* el ácido corroe los metales || erosionar (to wear away).
◆ *vi* corroerse, desgastarse || erosionarse.

erogenous [i'rɔdʒənəs] *adj* erógeno, na.

Eros ['erəs] *pr n* MYTH Eros *m*.

erosion [i'rəuʒən] *n* erosión *f* (of rocks, etc.) | corrosión *f*, desgaste *m* (of metals).

erosive [i'rəusiv] *adj* erosivo, va.

erotic [i'rɔtik] *adj* erótico, ca.
◆ *n* poema *m* erótico.

erotica [i'rɔtikə] *n* literatura *f* erótica.

erotically [i'rɔtikəli] *adv* eróticamente.

eroticism [e'rɔtisizəm]; **erotism** ['erətizəm] *n* erotismo *m*.

erotomania [i,rɔtə'meinjə] *n* MED erotomanía *f*.

erotomaniac [i,rɔtə'meinjæk] *n* erotómano, na.

err [ə:*] *vi* errar, equivocarse (to make a mistake) || *she does not err on the side of modesty* no peca de modesta.

errand ['erənd] *n* recado *m*; *to run an errand* hacer un recado || — *errand boy* recadero *m* || *to be on an errand* estar haciendo un recado || *to go on an errand* hacer un recado || *what errand brings you here?* ¿qué le trae por aquí?

errant ['erənt] *adj* errante, que yerra (erring or straying) || errante (wandering) || *errant knight* caballero *m* andante.

errantry [-ri] *n* caballería *f* andante || vida *f* errante.

errata [e'rɑ:tə] *pl n* fe *f sing* de erratas.

erratic [i'rætik] *adj* irregular; *erratic attendance* asistencia irregular || irregular, desigual; *his writings are brilliant but erratic* sus escritos son muy buenos pero desiguales || excéntrico, ca; extravagante, original (eccentric) || voluble (changing) || GEOL & MED errático, ca.
◆ *n* GEOL canto *m* rodado.

erratically [-əli] *adv* de manera irregular.

erratum [e'rɑ:təm] *n* errata *f*.
— OBSERV El plural de la palabra inglesa es *errata*.

erroneous [i'rəunjəs] *adj* erróneo, a; equivocado, da.

error ['erə*] *n* error *m*, equivocación *f* (mistake); *to fall into error* caer en un error, cometer una equivocación || extravío *m*, yerro *m* (wrongdoing) || SP error *m* (in baseball) || MATH error *m* || INFORM error *m* || *errors and omissions excepted* salvo error u omisión || *in error* por error.

ersatz ['ɛəzæts] *adj* sucedáneo, a.
◆ *n* sucedáneo *m*.

Erse [ə:s] *adj* gaélico, ca.
◆ *n* gaélico *m* (language).

erstwhile ['ə:stwail] *adv* antiguamente.
◆ *adj* antiguo, gua.

erubescent [,eru'besns] *adj* ruboroso, sa.

eruct [i'rʌkt]; **eructate** [-eit] *vt* arrojar (to spew out); *a volcano eructs molten lava* el volcán arroja lava fundida.
◆ *vi* eructar (to belch).

eructation [,i:rʌk'teiʃən] *n* eructo *m* (belch).

erudite ['erudait] *adj/n* erudito, ta.

erudition [,eru'diʃən] *n* erudición *f*.

erupt [i'rʌpt] *vt* arrojar (volcano, geyser, etc.).
◆ *vi* estar *or* entrar en erupción (volcano) || brotar, surgir (geyser) || estallar (to burst out) || MED hacer erupción (on the skin) | salir (teeth, etc.) || FIG *to erupt into a house* irrumpir en una casa.

eruption [i'rʌpʃən] *n* erupción *f* (of a volcano) || brote *m*, surgimiento *m* (of a geyser) || estallido *m*, explosión *f* (of violence) || arrebato *m* (of passion, etc.) || MED erupción *f*.

eruptive [i'rʌptiv] *adj* eruptivo, va.

erysipelas [,eri'sipiləs] *n* MED erisipela *f*.

erythema [,iri'θi:mə] *n* MED ericema *m*.

erythroblast [i'riθəblæst] *n* BIOL eritroblasto *m*.

erythrocyte [i'riθrəsait] *n* BIOL eritrocito *m*.

ESA *abbr of [European Space Agency]* AEE, agencia espacial europea.

escalade [,eskə'leid] *n* MIL escalada *f* || FIG escalada *f*.

escalade [,eskə'leid] *vt* escalar.

escalate ['eskəleit] *vt* agravar, intensificar (war) || subir (prices).
◆ *vi* agravarse, intensificarse (war) || *to escalate into* desembocar en (a problem, etc.).

escalation ['eskə'leiʃən] *n* agravación *f*, agravamiento *m*, intensificación *f*, escalada *f* (of war) || FIG subida *f* (of prices) | escalada *f*.

escalator ['eskəleitə*] *n* escalera *f* mecánica, escalera *f* automática || *escalator clause* cláusula *f* en un contrato que permite variar las condiciones de éste de acuerdo con un índice económico.

escalop; escallop [is'kɔləp] *n* ZOOL venera *f*.

escapade [,eskə'peid] *n* aventura *f*.

escape [is'keip] *n* escapatoria *f*, fuga *f* (flight) || escape *m* (of gas, steam) || salida *f* (of liquid) || escapatoria *f* (loophole, way out) || evasión *f* (from worries, responsibilities, etc.) || — JUR *escape clause* cláusula de excepción || AVIAT *escape hatch* escotilla *f* de salvamento || *escape pipe* tubo *m* de escape || *escape route* vía *f* de escape || *fire escape* escalera *f* de incendios || *to have a narrow escape* escaparse por los pelos *or* por un pelo || *to make one's escape* escapar.

escape [is'keip] *vt* escaparse; *a cry of pain escaped him* se le escapó un grito de dolor || escapar de, librarse de (punishment, death, etc.) || evadir, rehuir (to avoid) || eludir, evitar (to elude) || — *his name escapes me* no me sale su nombre, su nombre se me ha ido de la memoria || *it would not have escaped the notice of anyone* no se le habría escapado a nadie || *we just escaped being caught* por poco nos cogieron.
◆ *vi* escaparse, escapar, fugarse (to get free) || librarse, salvarse (to avoid an accident, etc.) || salirse, escaparse (to leak) || evadirse (to escape from one's troubles).

escapee [,eskei'pi:] *n* fugitivo, va; evadido, da.

escapement [is'keipmənt] *n* TECH escape *m*.

escapeway [is'keipwei] *n* salida *f* de socorro.

escapism [is'keipizəm] *n* FIG evasión *f*.

escapist [is'keipist] *adj* de evasión.

escapologist [,eskei'pɔlədʒist] *n* rey *m* de la evasión.

escarp [is'kɑ:p]; **escarpment** [-mənt] *n* escarpadura *f*, escarpa *f* (steep slope) || escarpa *f* (of a fortress).

escarp [is'kɑ:p] *vt* escarpar.

escarpment [-mənt] *n* ⟶ **escarp.**

eschalot ['eʃəlɔt] *n* BOT ascalonia *f*, chalote *m*.

eschar ['eskɑ:*] *n* MED escara *f*.

eschatological [,eskətɔ'lɔdʒikəl] *adj* escatológico, ca.

eschatology [,eskə'tɔlədʒi] *n* escatología *f*.

escheat [is'tʃi:t] *n* JUR reversión *f* de bienes al señor feudal *or* a la corona *or* al Estado || tierras *f pl* entregadas al señor feudal *or* a la corona *or* al Estado.

escheat [is'tʃi:t] *vt/vi* revertir tierras al señor feudal *or* a la corona *or* al Estado.

eschew [is'tʃu:] *vt* evitar, abstenerse de.

eschewal [-əl] *n* abstención *f*.

escort ['eskɔ:t] *n* escolta *f* (to give protection or guard or out of courtesy) || séquito *m*, acompañamiento *m* (suite) || MAR escolta *f* | buque escolta *m* (ship) || acompañante *m* (a male companion) || — *escort agency* agencia *f* de señoritas de compañía || *under escort* bajo escolta.

escort [is'kɔ:t] *vt* escoltar (to accompany as an escort) || acompañar (to accompany as a courtesy).

escritoire [,eskri'twɑ:*] *n* escritorio *m*.

escrow ['eskrəu] *n* plica *f* || *in escrow* en depósito.

escudo [es'ku:dəu] *n* escudo *m* (Portuguese and Chilean monetary unit).

esculent ['eskjulənt] *adj* comestible (eatable).

escutcheon [is'kʌtʃən]; **scutcheon** *n* escudo *m* de armas (shield) || MAR espejo *m* de popa, escudo *m* || escudo *m*, escudete *m* (plate round a lock) || FIG *a blot on one's escutcheon* una mancha en su hoja de servicio.

Eskimo ['eskiməu] *adj/n* esquimal || *Eskimo dog* perro *m* esquimal.
— OBSERV El plural es *Eskimos* o *Eskimo*.

esophagus [i:'sɔfəgəs] *n* ANAT esófago *m*.
— OBSERV El plural de *esophagus* es *esophagi*.

esoteric [,esəu'terik] *adj* esotérico, ca (doctrine, literature) || confidencial (plan).

esoterism [,esəu'terizəm] *n* esoterismo *m*.

espadrille [,espə'dril] *n* alpargata *f*.

espagnolette [es'pænjə'let] *n* falleba *f*.

espalier [is'pæljə*] *n* árbol *m* en espaldera || espaldera *f* (for fruit tree) || emparrado *m* (trellis).

esparto [es'pɑ:təu] *n* BOT esparto *m*.

especial [is'peʃəl] *adj* especial, particular; *of especial importance* de importancia especial || excepcional (exceptional) || *in especial* en especial, en particular (in particular), especialmente (especially).

especially [-i] *adv* especialmente, particularmente || sobre todo (mainly).

Esperanto [,espə'ræntəu] *n* esperanto *m*.

espial [is'paiəl] *n* espionaje *m* (espionage) || observación *f* (observation) || descubrimiento *m*, revelación *f*.

espionage [,espiə'nɑ:ʒ] *n* espionaje *m*.

esplanade [,esplə'neid] *n* explanada *f* || paseo *m* marítimo (on the seafront).

espousal [is'pauzəl] *n* adopción *f* (of a doctrine) || adhesión *f* (*of* a) *f* (of a cause).

espouse [is'pauz] *vt* casarse con, desposar (to marry) || casar (to give in marriage) || FIG adherirse a, abrazar (a cause) | adoptar (an idea).

espresso [es'presəu] *n* café *m* exprés.

esprit de corps ['espri:də'kɔ:*] *n* sentido *m* de solidaridad.

espy [is'pai] *vt* percibir, divisar, columbrar.

Esquimau ['eskiməu] *adj/n* esquimal.

Esquire [is'kwaiə*] *n* señor Don; *John Bull Esq (Esquire)* Sr. D. (señor don), John Bull.
— OBSERV El título *esquire* se emplea en lugar de *Mister (Mr)* y siempre se pone detrás del nombre y apellido.

essay ['esei] *n* redacción *f*, composición *f* (in schools) || ensayo *m* (erudite work) || tentativa *f*, intento *m* (attempt) || prueba *f* (of a rejected design for a stamp or for paper money).

essay ['esei] *vt* probar, someter a prueba (to test) || intentar, probar, ensayar (to attempt).
◆ *vi* intentar, hacer un intento.

essayist [-ist] *n* ensayista *m* & *f*.

esse ['esi] *n* PHIL existencia *f* (actual existence) | esencia *f* (essential being).

essence ['esns] *n* esencia *f* || esencia *f*, perfume *m* (concentrated extract) || extracto *m* (extract) || fondo *m*; *the essence of the matter* el fondo de la cuestión || *in essence* esencialmente.

essential [i'senʃəl] *adj* esencial, imprescindible, necesario, ria (necessary) || fundamental; *an essential difference* una diferencia fundamental || innato, ta; *his essential selfishness* su egoísmo innato || *essential oil* aceite *m* esencial.
◆ *n* lo esencial (sth. basic or fundamental).
◆ *pl* elementos *m* esenciales || *to stick to essentials* ir al grano.

essentially [-i] *adv* fundamentalmente, básicamente.

establish [is'tæbliʃ] *vt* establecer, fundar; *to establish a university* fundar una universidad || establecer, constituir (a government) || establecer; *to establish law and order* establecer la ley y el orden; *to establish communication* establecer comunicación || sentar, establecer; *to establish a precedent* sentar un precedente || comprobar (to verify) || hacer constar (one's rights) || establecer, probar, demostrar (a fact, one's innocence) || entablar (relations) || hacer oficial, reconocer (to make into the official national Church) || demostrar, probar (to prove) || instalar; *her father established them in a house* su padre los instaló en una casa || *to establish o.s.* establecerse (to set o.s. up), crearse una reputación (to make a reputation), arraigar (sth.).

established [-t] *adj* establecido, da || arraigado, da; *an established custom* una costumbre arraigada || de plantilla (staff) || oficial, de Estado (Church) || de buena reputación, de buena fama (highly reputed) || sabido, da; conocido, da (fact) || constituido, da (authorities).

establishment [-mənt] *n* establecimiento *m* (a being established) || servidumbre *f* (the servants of a household) || personal *m* (staff) || establecimiento *m*, fundación *f*, institución *f* (foundation) || establecimiento *m* (place of business) || fijación *f* (of a residence) || demostración *f* || comprobación *f* (of facts) || MIL fuerzas *f pl*, efectivos *m pl* (troops) || *to be on the establishment* formar parte del personal, estar en plantilla.

Establishment [-mənt] *n* clase *f* dirigente (ruling class) || iglesia *f or* religión *f* oficial *or* del Estado (official national Church).

estate [is'teit] *n* propiedad *f* (property) || finca *f* [*AMER* hacienda *f* estancia *f*] (land) || urbanización *f* (a tract of land developed for residential purposes) || fortuna *f* (fortune) || herencia *f* (inheritance) || estado *m* (a class in society); *third estate* estado llano || JUR balance *m* (of a bankrupt) | testamentaria *f* (of a dead person) || — *real estate* bienes *m pl* raíces || *the fourth estate* la prensa || *to come to man's estate* llegar a la edad viril || *to leave a large estate* dejar una gran fortuna.

estate agency [-,eidʒənsi] *n* agencia *f* inmobiliaria.

estate agent [-,eidʒənt] *n* COMM agente *m* inmobiliario || administrador *m* (manager of an estate).

estate car [-kɑː*] *n* furgoneta *f*, break *m*.

estate duty [-,djuːti] *n* impuesto *m* de sucesión.

esteem [is'tiːm] *n* estima *f*, estimación *f*, aprecio *m* || *I hold him in high esteem* le tengo en gran estima, le estimo en mucho, le aprecio mucho.

esteem [is'tiːm] *vt* estimar, apreciar (to have a high opinion of) || considerar, estimar (to regard); *to esteem it a privilege* considerarlo un privilegio || *to esteem o.s. lucky* considerarse afortunado.

ester ['estə*] *n* CHEM éster *m*.

esterification [es,terifi'keiʃən] *n* CHEM esterificación *f* (of an acid).

esterify [es'terifai] *vt* esterificar.
◆ *vi* esterificarse.

esthete ['iːsθiːt] *n* esteta *m* & *f*.

esthetic [iːs'θetik] *adj* estético, ca.

estimable ['estiməbl] *adj* estimable.

estimate ['estimit] *n* estimación *f*, apreciación *f*, cálculo *m* aproximado (a judgment of size, number, quantity, value, etc.) || presupuesto *m* (a statement of the cost of a piece of work) || — *at a rough estimate* haciendo un cálculo aproximado || *estimate of quantities and costs* presupuesto aproximado.
◆ *pl* presupuesto *m sing*.

estimate [,estimeit] *vt* estimar, apreciar, calcular aproximadamente || FIG estimar, juzgar (to gauge).
◆ *vi* *to estimate for* hacer un presupuesto de.

estimation [·esti'meiʃən] *n* juicio *m*, parecer *m*, opinión *f*; *in my estimation* a mi juicio, a mi parecer, en mi opinión || estima *f*, aprecio *m* (esteem) || estimación *f* (estimate).

estimative ['estimətiv] *adj* estimatorio, ria.

estimator ['estimeitə*] *n* tasador *m*, estimador *m*.

estival [iːs,taivəl] *adj* estival.

estivate ['iːstiveit] *vi* pasar el verano en estado de letargo.

Estonia [e'stəunjə] *pr n* GEOGR Estonia.

estop [is'tɔp] *vt* JUR desestimar una demanda [por imposibilidad legal de admitir una afirmación o alegación contraria a lo que se ha afirmado anteriormente].

estoppel [-əl] *n* JUR desestimación *f* de una demanda [por afirmar algo que contradice lo dicho anteriormente].

estovers [is'təuvəz] *pl n* JUR derecho *m sing* de hacer leña | pensión *f sing* alimenticia (to a wife divorced from her husband).

estrange [is'treindʒ] *vt* alejar, separar || hacer perder el afecto *or* el cariño (from a person) || hacer perder la afición a (from a thing) || *to become estranged from* enajenarse la amistad de, alejarse de.

estrangement [-mənt] *n* alejamiento *m*, separación *f* || pérdida *f* del afecto (loss of affection) || desavenencia *f* (discord).

estreat [i'striːt] *n* JUR extracto *m* de las minutas de un tribunal.

estrogen ['iːstrədʒin] *n* estrógeno *m*.

estrum ['iːstrəm]; **estrus** ['iːstrəs] *n* US celo *m*, estro *m* || FIG estro *m*.

estuarial [,estju'ɛərjəl]; **estuarine** ['estjuərain] *adj* del estuario.

estuary ['estjuəri] *n* estuario *m*.

esurience [i'sjuəriəns]; **esuriency** [-i] *n* voracidad *f*.

esurient [i'sjuəriənt] *adj* voraz, ávido de comida, hambriento, ta.

eta ['iːtə] *n* eta *f* (Greek letter).

et cetera [it'setrə] *adv* etcétera, etc.

etceteras [-z] *pl n* cosas *f*.

etch [etʃ] *vt* grabar al agua fuerte.

etcher [etʃə*] *n* acuafortista *m* & *f*, aguafuertista *m* & *f*.

etching ['etʃiŋ] *n* grabado *m* al agua fuerte, aguafuerte *m*.

eternal [i'təːnl] *adj* eterno, na (lasting for ever) || incesante, eterno, na; *stop this eternal arguing!* ¡para esta incesante discusión! || — *the Eternal City* la Ciudad Eterna || *the Eternal Father* el Padre Eterno.

eternity [i'təːniti] *n* eternidad *f*.

eternity ring [-riŋ] *n* alianza *f* de diamantes.

eternize [iː'təːnaiz] *vt* perpetuar, eternizar.

ethane ['eθein] *n* CHEM etano *m*.

ethanol ['eθənɔl] *n* alcohol *m* etílico.

ether ['iːθə*] *n* éter *m*. || *ether addict* eterómano, na.

ethereal [i'θiəriəl] *adj* etéreo, a; *the ethereal vault* la bóveda etérea.

etherify ['iːθerifai] *vt* convertir en éter, eterificar.

etherize ['iːθəraiz] *vt* eterizar, anestesiar con éter.

ethic ['eθik] *adj* ético, ca.
◆ *n* PHIL ética *f* || ética *f*, moralidad *f*.

ethical [-əl] *adj* ético, ca || honrado, da (honourable) || moral.

ethics [-s] *n* PHIL ética *f* || ética *f*, moralidad *f*.

Ethiopia [iːθi'əupjə] *pr n* GEOGR Etiopía *f*.

Ethiopian [-n] *adj/n* etíope.

ethmoid ['eθmɔid] *adj* ANAT etmoides.
◆ *n* ANAT etmoides *m*.

ethmoidal [eθ'mɔidəl] *adj* etmoides, etmoidal.

ethnarch ['eθnɑːk] *n* etnarca *m*.

ethnic ['eθnik]; **ethnical** [-əl] *adj* étnico, ca; *ethnic minority* minoría étnica.

ethnographer [eθ'nɔgrəfə] *n* etnógrafo *m*.

ethnographic [,eθnəu'græfik]; **ethnographical** [-əl] *adj* etnográfico, ca.

ethnography [eθ'nɔgrəfi] *n* etnografía *f*.

ethnologic [,eθnəu'lɔdʒik]; **ethnological** [-əl] *adj* etnológico, ca.

ethnologist [eθ'nɔlədʒist] *n* etnólogo *m*.

ethnology [eθ'nɔlədʒi] *n* etnología *f*.

ethnos ['eθnɔs] *n* etnia *f*.

ethos ['iːθɔs] *n* genio *m*, carácter *m* distintivo (of a group of people).

ethyl ['eθil] *n* CHEM etilo *m* || *ethyl alcohol* alcohol etílico.

ethylene ['eθiliːn] *n* CHEM etileno *m*.

etiolate ['iːtiəuleit] *vt* descolorar (the skin) || BOT ajar, marchitar (plants).

etiolation [,iːtiəu'leiʃən] *n* marchitamiento *m*, ajamiento *m* (of plants) || descoloración *f*, palidez *f* (of skin) || debilitamiento *m*, debilitación *f* (weakening).

etiological [,iːtiə'lɔdʒikəl] *adj* etiológico, ca.

etiology [,iːti'ɔlədʒi] *n* etiología *f*.

etiquette ['etiket] *n* etiqueta *f*, ceremonial *m*, protocolo *m* (in polite society) || buenos modales *m pl* (decorum) || normas *f pl* profesionales, ética *f* profesional (of professional conduct) || protocolo *m*; *court etiquette* el protocolo de la corte || *it is not etiquette to* no está bien.

Etruscan [i'trʌskən] *adj/n* etrusco, ca.

étude ['eitjuːd] *n* MUS estudio *m*.

etymological [,etimə'lɔdʒikəl] *adj* etimológico, ca.

etymologist [,eti'mɔlədʒist] *n* etimólogo, ga; etimologista *m* & *f*.

etymologize [,eti'mɔlədʒaiz] *vt* buscar la etimología de.
◆ *vi* estudiar etimología.

etymology [,eti'mɔlədʒi] *n* etimología *f*.

etymon ['etimɔn] *n* raíz *f* (of a word).
— OBSERV El plural es *etymons* o *etyma*.

eucalyptol [,juːkə'liptəl] *n* eucaliptol *m*.

eucalyptus [,juːkə'liptəs] *n* BOT eucalipto *m*.
— OBSERV El plural es *eucalypti* o *eucalyptuses*.

Eucharist ['juːkərist] *n* REL Eucaristía *f*.

Eucharistic [,juːkə'ristik]; **Eucharistical** [-əl] *adj* eucarístico, ca.

euchre; *US* **eucher** ['juːkə*] *n* juego *m* de cartas.

euchre; *US* **eucher** ['juːkə*] *vt* derrotar.

Euclid ['juːklid] *pr n* Euclides; *Euclid's postulate* el postulado de Euclides.

Euclidean [juː'klidiən] *adj* euclidiano, na.

eudaemonism; **eudemonism** [juː'diːmənizəm] *n* eudemonismo *m*.

eugenic [juː'dʒenik] *adj* eugenésico, ca.

eugenics [-s] *n* eugenesia *f*.

eulogia [juː'ləudʒjə] *n* REL eulogia *f*.

eulogist ['juːlədʒist] *n* elogiador, ra; panegirista *m* & *f*; encomiador, ra.

eulogistic [,juːlə'dʒistik] *adj* laudatorio, ria; elogiador, ra; encomiástico, ca.

eulogize ['juːlədʒaiz] *vt* elogiar, encomiar, loar.

eulogy ['juːlədʒi] *n* elogio *m*, encomio *m* (high praise) || panegírico *m* (speech, statement).

eunuch ['juːnək] *n* eunuco *m*.

euonymus [ju'ɔniməs] *n* BOT bonetero *m*.

eupatorium [juːpə'tɔːrjəm] *n* BOT eupatorio *m*.

eupeptic [juː'peptik] *adj* eupéptico, ca.

euphemism ['juːfimizəm] *n* eufemismo *m*.

euphemistic ['juːfi'mistik] *adj* eufemístico, ca.

euphemize ['juːfimaiz] *vt* expresar por medio de eufemismos.
◆ *vi* usar eufemismos.

euphonic [juː'fɔnik]; **euphonious** [juː'fəunjəs] *adj* eufónico, ca.

euphony ['juːfəni] *n* eufonía *f*.

euphorbia [juː'fɔːbjə] *n* BOT euforbio *m*.

euphorbium [juː'fɔːbjəm] *n* euforbio *m*.

euphoria [juː'fɔːriə] *n* euforia *f*.

euphoric [juː'fɔːrik] *adj* eufórico, ca.

Euphrates [juː'freitiːz] *pr n* GEOGR Eufrates.

euphuism ['ju:fju:izəm] *n* eufuismo *m.*

euphuist [ˌju:fju:ist] *adj/n* eufuista.

euphuistic ['ju:fju:'istik] *adj* eufuístico, ca ‖ FIG ampuloso, sa; rimbombante.

Eurasia [juə'reiʒjə] *pr n* GEOGR Eurasia *f.*

Eurasian [-n] *adj/n* eurasiático, ca.

eureka! [juə'ri:kə] *interj* ¡eureka!

eurhythmic [ju:'riðmik]; **eurhythmical** [-ikəl] *adj* eurítmico, ca.

eurhythmics [-s] *n* euritmia *f.*

Euripides [juə'ripidi:z] *pr n* Eurípides *m.*

Eurocrat ['juərəukræt] *n* FAM eurócrata *m* & *f.*

Eurodollar [ˌjuərəu'dɔlə*] *n* eurodólar *m.*

Europe ['juərəp] *pr n* GEOGR Europa *f.*

European [ˌjuərə'pi:ən] *adj/n* europeo, a ‖ — *European Economic Community* Comunidad *f* Económica Europea.

Europeanization [ˌjuərəˌpiənai'zeiʃən] *n* europeización.

Europeanize [ˌjuərə'piənaiz] *vt* europeizar.

europium [ju'rəupjəm] *n* CHEM europio *m.*

Eurovision ['juərəˌviʒən] *n* eurovisión *f.*

eurythmy [ju:'riðmi] *n* euritmia *f.*

Euskarian [ju:s'kεəriən] *adj/n* éuscaro, ra.

eustachian tube [ju:s'teiʃjən'tju:b] *n* ANAT trompa *f* de Eustaquio.

Eustachius [ju:s'teikjəs] *pr n* Eustaquio *m.*

euthanasia [ˌju:θə'neizjə] *n* eutanasia *f.*

evacuant [i'vækjuənt] *n* MED evacuativo, va; evacuatorio, ria; evacuante.

◆ *n* MED evacuativo *m*, evacuante *m.*

evacuate [i'vækjueit] *vt* evacuar (a dangerous place) ‖ hacer salir; *to evacuate air from a cylinder* hacer salir el aire de un cilindro ‖ evacuar (from the body) ‖ desocupar, vaciar (a house) ‖ PHYS hacer el vacío en.

evacuation [i·vækju'eiʃən] *n* evacuación *f* ‖ escape *m* (of a gas) ‖ deposición *f* (from the body).

evacuee [iˌvækju:'i:] *n* evacuado, da.

evadable [i'veidəbl] *adj* evitable, eludible.

evade [i'veid] *vt* evadir, eludir, evitar, esquivar (to avoid) ‖ escaparse de (to escape) ‖ sustraerse a (taxes).

◆ *vi* usar evasivas.

evaginate [i'vædʒineit] *vt* volver de dentro afuera, volver al revés (a tubular organ).

evaluate [i'væljueit] *vt* valuar, valorar, valorizar, evaluar (to determine the monetary value of) ‖ calcular, estimar (to estimate) ‖ evaluar (to weigh up) ‖ juzgar (to judge) ‖ interpretar (to interpret) ‖ MATH hallar el valor numérico de.

evaluation [iˌvælju'eiʃən] *n* evaluación *f*, valoración *f*, valuación *f* ‖ evaluación *f* ‖ cálculo *m* (estimation) ‖ interpretación *f.*

evanesce ['i:və'nes] *vi* desvanecerse, esfumarse, desaparecer (to vanish).

evanescence [-ns] *n* desvanecimiento *m*, evanescencia *f*, desaparición *f.*

evanescent [-nt] *adj* evanescente, efímero, ra.

evangelic ['i:væn'dʒelik]; **evangelical** [-l] *adj* evangélico, ca ‖ *Evangelical Church* Iglesia Evangélica.

evangelism [i'vændʒilizəm] *n* propagación *f* del Evangelio, evangelización *f* (effort to spread the gospel) ‖ evangelismo *m* (Evangelical Church doctrines).

evangelist [i'vændʒilist] *adj/n* evangelista, evangelizador, ra ‖ *Saint John the Evangelist* San Juan Evangelista.

evangelistic [iˌvændʒilistik] *adj* evangélico, ca.

evangelization [iˌvændʒelai'zeiʃən] *n* evangelización *f.*

evangelize [i'vændʒilaiz] *vt* evangelizar.

evaporable [i'væpərəbl] *adj* evaporable.

evaporate [i'væpəreit] *vt* evaporar ‖ deshidratar (milk, vegetables, etc.) ‖ *to evaporate down* reducir por evaporación.

◆ *vi* evaporarse ‖ FIG desvanecerse, evaporarse.

evaporation [i·væpə'reiʃən] *n* evaporación *f* ‖ deshidratación *f* por evaporación (of milk, of vegetables, etc.).

evaporator [i'væpəreitə*] *n* evaporador *m.*

evasion [i'veiʒən] *n* evasión *f*, escapatoria *f* (the act of evading the law, a danger, etc.) ‖ evasión *f*, fuga *f* (flight) ‖ evasión *f*, evasiva *f* (avoidance of a question, of the truth) ‖ evasión *f* (of taxes).

evasive [i'veisiv] *adj* evasivo, va.

evasiveness [-nis] *n* calidad *f* de evasivo.

Eve [i:v] *pr n* Eva *f.*

eve [i:v] *n* víspera *f*; *on the eve of his departure* en la víspera de su partida ‖ REL vigilia *f* ‖ crepúsculo *m* (dusk) ‖ — *Christmas Eve* Nochebuena *f* ‖ *New Year's Eve* Noche *f* Vieja ‖ FIG *on the eve of* en vísperas de.

evection [i'vekʃən] *n* ASTR evección *f.*

even ['i:vən] *adj* regular, uniforme, constante (uniform) ‖ suave (smooth) ‖ llano, na (level) ‖ liso, sa (flat) ‖ ecuánime (calm) ‖ imperturbable (not easily ruffled) ‖ tranquilo, la; sereno, na; apacible (placid) ‖ equitativo, va; justo, ta (fair) ‖ a nivel (at the same level) ‖ igual, semejante, idéntico, ca (equal) ‖ par (number) ‖ exacto, ta; *an even ten seconds* diez segundos exactos ‖ redondo, da (sum of money) ‖ — *even with* al mismo nivel que, al nivel de ‖ FIG *I'll get even with you yet!* ¡me las pagarás! ‖ *of even date* del actual ‖ SP *to become even* empatar, igualar ‖ *to be even with s.o.* estar en paz con alguien ‖ *to break even* quedar igual (gambling), cubrir los gastos ‖ *to get even* desquitarse ‖ *to make even* allanar, alisar ‖ *to stand an even chance* tener tantas posibilidades de éxito como de fracaso ‖ *to stay even* cubrir los gastos.

◆ *adv* siquiera; *he didn't even answer three of the questions* ni siquiera contestó a tres preguntas ‖ incluso, hasta, aun; *even if, even now* incluso si, incluso ahora; *even John would have done it* incluso Juan lo hubiera hecho; *she wears a coat even when it is hot* lleva abrigo incluso cuando hace calor ‖ aún, todavía; *it is even colder than yesterday* hace aún más frío que ayer ‖ incluso (indeed) ‖ — *even as* en cuanto; *even as he opened the door* en cuanto abrió la puerta; del mismo modo que (as) ‖ *even if* o *even though* aunque, aun cuando ‖ *even so* aun así.

even ['i:vən] *vt* nivelar, igualar, allanar (ground) ‖ igualar (to make equal) ‖ — *to even out* repartir en partes iguales (amount) ‖ *to even up* igualar (score), balancear (finance).

◆ *vi* nivelarse ‖ — *to even out* igualarse (prices), allanarse (ground) ‖ *to even up* emparejarse, nivelarse ‖ *to even up on s.o.* desquitarse con uno.

evenhanded [-'hændid] *adj* imparcial.

evening ['i:vniŋ] *n* tarde *f*; *yesterday evening* ayer por la tarde; *in the evening* por la tarde ‖ anochecer *m*, noche *f* (between sunset and bedtime) ‖ FIG ocaso *m* (of a man's life, of a civilization, etc.) ‖ velada *f*; *musical evening* velada musical ‖ — *evening class* clase nocturna ‖ *evening dress* traje *m* de etiqueta (for men), traje *m* de noche (for women) ‖ *evening gown* traje *m* de noche ‖ *evening paper* periódico *m* de la tarde ‖ THEATR *evening performance* función *f* de noche ‖ *evening star* estrella *f* vespertina, lucero *m* de la tarde ‖ *evening was coming on* estaba anocheciendo ‖ *good evening!* ¡buenas tardes! (early), ¡buenas noches! (at sunset).

evenly [i:vənli] *adv* uniformemente ‖ imparcialmente, equitativamente (fairly).

even-minded ['i:vən-maindid] *adj* ecuánime.

evenness ['i:vənnis] *n* igualdad *f* ‖ lo liso (smoothness) ‖ calma *f*, serenidad *f*, ecuanimidad *f* (of mind) ‖ uniformidad *f*, regularidad *f* (of temperature, of speed, etc.) ‖ imparcialidad *f* (of treatment) ‖ ecuanimidad *f*, justicia *f* (fairness).

evensong ['i:vənsɔŋ] *n* REL vísperas *f pl.*

event [i'vent] *n* suceso *m*, acontecimiento *m* (an occurrence) ‖ acontecimiento *m*; *going to the opera is quite an event for us* ir a la ópera es un gran acontecimiento para nosotros ‖ consecuencia *f*, resultado *m* (outcome) ‖ caso *m*; *in the event of raining* en caso de que llueva ‖ número *m* (in a programme) ‖ encuentro *m* (in boxing, etc.) ‖ SP prueba *f* (separate item in a programme of games) ‖ — *at all events, in any event* en todo caso, pase lo que pase ‖ *current events* actualidades *f* ‖ *in the normal course of events* si todo sigue bien ‖ *the event will show* ya veremos lo que pasa ‖ *to be expecting a happy event* estar esperando un feliz acontecimiento.

event [i'vent] *vi* SP participar en concursos hípicos (horse, rider).

even-tempered ['i:vən-tempəd] *adj* ecuánime, sereno, na.

eventful [i'ventful] *adj* lleno de acontecimientos, agitado, da (full of interesting events) ‖ memorable; *on that evenful morning* en aquella memorable mañana.

eventide ['i:vəntaid] *n* anochecer *m*, noche *f.*

eventide home [-həum] *n* residencia *f* de ancianos.

eventing [i'ventiŋ] *n* participación *f* en concursos hípicos (horse, rider).

eventless [i'ventlis] *adv* sin incidentes.

eventual [i'ventʃuəl] *adj* final (ultimate) ‖ posible, eventual (contingent).

eventuality [iˌventju'æliti] *n* eventualidad *f*, caso *m*; *in all eventualities* en cualquier caso.

eventually [i'ventʃuəli] *adv* finalmente, en definitiva, al fin y al cabo; *he will do it eventually* finalmente lo hará ‖ con el tiempo (in the long run).

eventuate [i'ventjueit] *vi* resultar (to come as a result) ‖ acabarse, terminarse (*in* por) (to finish) ‖ US acontecer, suceder (to happen).

ever ['evə*] *adv* siempre (always); *he came late, as ever* vino tarde, como siempre ‖ nunca, jamás; *no man has ever doubted my word* nunca ha dudado nadie de mi palabra ‖ nunca; *they hardly ever go to the cinema* casi nunca van al cine; *better than ever* mejor que nunca; *it is hotter than ever* hace más calor que nunca ‖ alguna vez; *have they ever met?* ¿se han visto alguna vez? ‖ — *as soon as ever I can* en cuanto pueda ‖ FAM *did you ever?* ¿habrase visto? ‖ *did you ever buy it?* ¿lo compraste por fin? ‖ *ever after, ever since* desde entonces (since then), desde (que) (after) ‖ *ever and anon* de vez en cuando ‖ *ever so* muy; *I am ever so happy* estoy muy contento ‖ *ever so little* muy poco ‖ *ever so much* mucho, muchísimo; *I thank you ever so much* se lo agradezco mucho ‖ FAM *ever such* muy; *she's ever such a nice girl* es una chica muy simpática ‖ *for ever* para siempre ‖ *for ever and a day, for ever and ever* para *or* por siempre jamás ‖ *if he ever comes back* si se le ocurre volver, si vuelve alguna vez ‖ *it is ever so hot* hace un calor terrible ‖ *not ever* nunca jamás ‖ *the coldest day ever* el día más frío que he conocido ‖ *what ever did she say?* ¿qué demonios dijo? ‖

what ever's the matter with you? ¿qué demonios te pasa? || *worst ever* sin precedente, único || *yours ever* cordialmente suyo (letter).

everchanging [-'tʃeindiʒiŋ] *adj* cambiadizo, za.

Everest (Mount) ['evərist] *pr n* GEOGR monte Everest.

everglade ['evəgleid] *n* US terreno *m* pantanoso cubierto de hierbas altas.

evergreen ['evəgri:n] *adj* de hoja perenne || FIG imperecedero, ra; vivo, va; *evergreen memories* recuerdos imperecederos.
◆ *n* árbol *m or* planta *f* de hoja perenne.

everlasting [,evə'lɑ:stiŋ] *adj* eterno, na; perpetuo, tua; sin fin (eternal) || interminable, eterno, na (never ceasing) || BOT *everlasting flower* siempreviva *f*.
◆ *n* eternidad *f* || ser *m* eterno (God) || BOT siempreviva *f*.

evermore ['evə'mɔ:*] *adv* eternamente, siempre || *for evermore* por *or* para siempre jamás.

evert [i'və:t] *vt* volver de dentro afuera.

every ['evri] *adj* todo, da; *have every confidence in him* ten toda confianza en él; *you have every reason to fear him* tiene toda la razón en temerle || todo, da; todos los, todas las, cada; *every man knows it* todos los hombres lo saben || todos los, todas las; *every day* todos los días; *she was given every chance to* se le dieron todas las posibilidades para || cada; *every other day, every two days* cada dos días || — *every bit a man* todo un hombre, un hombre por los cuatro costados || *every man for himself* ¡sálvese quien pueda! || *every man jack of them* todos sin excepción || *every now and again, every now and then* de vez en cuando || *every once in a while* alguna que otra vez || *every one* cada uno, cada cual (each), todos, todas; *every one of them* todos ellos || *every other Saturday* un sábado sí y otro no, cada dos sábados || *every so often* alguna que otra vez || *every time* siempre, cada vez; *you win every time* ganas siempre || *every way* en todos los aspectos || *every which way* por todas partes || *he is every bit as pleased as you are* está igual de contento que tú, está tan contento como tú || *he is every inch a patriot* es patriota hasta la médula *or* de pies a cabeza || *to give every assistance* ayudar en todo lo posible.

everybody ['evribɔdi] *pron* todo el mundo, todos, das.

everyday ['evridei] *adj* diario; ria; de todos los días || rutinario, ria (routine) || corriente (usual) || — *an everyday event* un suceso cotidiano *or* corriente || *for everyday use* de uso diario.

Everyman ['evrimæn] *n* hombre *m* de la calle, ciudadano *m* medio.

everyone ['evriwʌn] *pron* todo el mundo, todos, das.

everything ['evriθiŋ] *pron* todo; *I like everything* me gusta todo.

everywhere ['evriwɛə*] *adv* por *or* en todas partes (in every place, every position); *everywhere in England* en todas partes de Inglaterra || a todas partes, por todas partes (to every place, every motion); *he wants to go everywhere* quiere ir a todas partes || dondequiera que (wherever); *everywhere he goes* dondequiera que vaya || totalmente; *his evidence is everywhere coherent* su declaración es totalmente coherente.

evict [i'vikt] *vt* desahuciar, desalojar, expulsar (from a house) || excluir.

eviction [i'vikʃən] *n* desahucio *m*.

evidence ['evidəns] *n* evidencia *f* || indicio *m*, prueba *f* (sign) || hechos *m pl*, datos *m pl* (facts) || JUR prueba *f* (proof) | testimonio *m*, declaración *f* de un testigo (information given by a witness) | testigo *m* & *f* (witness); *evidence for the defence, for the prosecution* testigo de descargo, de cargo || justificante *m*, comprobante *m* (of indebtedness) || — *in evidence* manifiesto, ta; evidente || *to call s.o. in evidence* llamar a alguien como testigo || *to give evidence* declarar como testigo, prestar declaración || *to show evidence of* presentar señales de || FIG *to turn Queen's evidence* delatar a un cómplice.

evidence ['evidəns] *vt* evidenciar, probar, manifestar, demostrar (to show up) || JUR declarar (a witness) | justificar (to show proofs).

evident ['evidənt] *adj* evidente, patente, manifiesto, ta.

evidential [,evi'denʃəl] *adj* JUR probatorio, ria.

evidently ['evidəntli] *adv* por supuesto, desde luego, naturalmente, manifiestamente, evidentemente.

evil ['i:vl] *adj* malo, la; perverso, sa; depravado, da (immoral) || malo, la; malvado, da; perverso, sa (wicked) || malo, la; funesto, ta; nefasto, ta (baleful) || malo, la; nocivo, va (harmful) || aciago, ga (unlucky) || horrible (smell) || maligno, na; *evil spirit* espíritu maligno.
◆ *n* mal *m* (what is morally wrong) || desgracia *f* (what is materially harmful) || *evil eye* mal de ojo, aojamiento *m*.
— OBSERV Los comparativos y superlativos de *evil* son *worse* y *worst* aunque también se emplean *more evil* y *most evil*.

evildoer [-'du:ə*] *n* malhechor, ra; malvado, da.

evil-eyed [-'aid] *adj* que echa mal de ojo.

evil-looking [-'lukiŋ] *adj* de aspecto siniestro.

evil-minded [-'maindid] *adj* malpensado, da (salacious) || malintencionado, da (malevolent) || malvado, da; malo, la (malicious).

evil-smelling [-'smeliŋ] *adj* maloliente, fétido, da.

evil-tongued [-tʌŋd] *adj* que habla mal de la gente, de mala lengua.

evince [i'vins] *vt* mostrar, manifestar (a desire) || dar pruebas *or* muestras de, revelar (a quality).

eviscerate [i'visəreit] *vt* destripar (to disembowel) || FIG debilitar, quitar la sustancia a.

evocable [i'vəukəbl] *adj* evocable.

evocation [,evəu'keiʃən] *n* evocación *f*.

evocative [i'vɔkətiv] *adj* evocador, ra.

evocatory [i'vɔkətəri] *adj* evocador, ra; evocatorio, ria.

evoke [i'vəuk] *vt* provocar, producir; *his words evoked laughter* sus palabras provocaron la risa | evocar (to bring to mind) || llamar (spirits).

evolute ['i:vəlu:t] *n* evoluta *f* (curve).

evolution [,i:və'lu:ʃən] *n* evolución *f* || PHYS desprendimiento *m* (of gas, etc.) || MATH extracción *f* de raíces | evolución *f* (of a curve) || FIG desarrollo *m*.

evolutionary [,i:və'lu:ʃnəri] *adj* evolutivo, va.

evolutionism [,i:və'lu:ʃənizəm] *n* evolucionismo *m*.

evolutionist [,i:və'lu:ʃənist] *n* evolucionista *m* & *f*.

evolve [i'vɔlv] *vi* evolucionar || desarrollarse (to develop) || MATH extraer raíces.
◆ *vt* desarrollar (to develop) || PHYS desprender, despedir (gas, heat) || FIG desarrollar (an argument) | sacar (a conclusion).

evolvement [-mənt] *n* desarrollo *m* (development) || MATH extracción *f* de raíces || desprendimiento *m* (of gas, of heat) || deducción *f* (of a conclusion).

evulsion [i'vʌlʃən] *n* MED extracción *f*.

ewe [ju:] *n* ZOOL oveja *f*.

ewer ['ju:ə*] *n* jarra *f*, aguamanil *m*.

ex [eks] *prep* sin (without) || fuera de (out) || — *ex dividend* sin cupón || *ex dock* en el muelle || *ex factory* en fábrica, franco en fábrica || *ex store price* precio *m* en almacén || *ex tax value* precio *m* sin impuestos || *ex works price* precio *m* en fábrica.

ex- [eks] *pref* ex; *ex-minister* ex ministro; *ex-servicemen* ex combatientes || antiguo, gua; *an ex-pupil* un antiguo alumno.

exacerbate [eks'æsə:beit] *vt* exacerbar.

exacerbation [eks,æsə'beiʃən] *n* exacerbación *f*.

exact [ig'zækt] *adj* exacto, ta || *to be exact* para ser exacto, ta; más concretamente.

exact [ig'zækt] *vt* exigir (*of, from* a) (to demand) || lograr por la fuerza (money).

exactable [-əbl] *adj* exigible.

exacting [-iŋ] *adj* exigente (person) || severo, ra; riguroso, sa (conditions) || duro, ra (work) || agotador, ra (exhausting).

exaction [ig'zækʃən] *n* exacción *f*; *exation of taxes* exacción de impuestos.

exactitude [ig'zæktitju:d] *n* exactitud *f*.

exactly [ig'zæktli] *adv* exactamente (precisely); *to reveal exactly what one is thinking* revelar exactamente lo que uno está pensando || precisamente; *he was not exactly pleased* no estaba precisamente contento || exactamente, en punto (in time).

exactness [ig'zæktnis] *n* exactitud *f*.

exaggerate [ig'zædʒəreit] *vt* exagerar.

exaggerated [-id] *adj* exagerado, da.

exaggeration [ig,zædʒə'reiʃən] *n* exageración *f*.

exalt [ig'zɔ:lt] *vt* exaltar, elevar (to raise up) || exaltar, arrebatar (to elate) || ensalzar, exaltar (to praise) || intensificar, avivar (colours).

exaltation [,egzɔ:l'teiʃən] *n* exaltación *f* || *exaltation of the Holy Cross* exaltación de la Santa Cruz.

exalted [ig'zɔ:ltid] *adj* exaltado, da || elevado, da (style) || eminente (person) || muy favorable (an opinion, etc.).

exam [ig'zæm] *n* FAM examen *m*; *to pass an exam* aprobar un examen.

examination [ig,zæmi'neiʃən] *n* examen *m*; *to sit* o *to take* o *to do* o *to go in for an examination* hacer *or* sufrir un examen, presentarse a un examen; *qualifying examination* || examen eliminatorio || examen *m* (of a matter) || MED reconocimiento *m* || JUR instrucción *f*, sumario *m* (of a case) | interrogatorio *m* (of a defendant) | inspección *f*, registro *m* (of customs) | investigación *f* (inquiry) | revisión *f* (of accounts) || — *entrance examination* examen de ingreso || *examination paper* preguntas *f pl* del examen (questions), respuestas *f pl* del examen (answers) || *to take an examination in history* examinarse de historia || *under examination* sometido a examen, que se está examinando.

examine [ig'zæmin] *vt* examinar (sth.) || examinar a, someter a un examen (a student) || JUR instruir (a case) | interrogar a (a defendant) | hacer declarar a (a witness) | revisar (accounts) | investigar (to inquire) | registrar (customs) || MED reconocer, hacer un reconocimiento médico a.
◆ *vi* interrogar (to question).

examinee [ig,zæmi'ni:] *n* examinado, da; candidato, ta.

examiner [ig'zæminə*] *n* examinador, ra.

examining magistrate [ig'zæminiŋ'mædʒistreit] *n* JUR juez *m* de instrucción.

example [ig'zɑ:mpl] *n* ejemplo *m*; *after* o *following the example of* siguiendo el ejemplo de, a ejemplo de; *beyond example* sin ejemplo ‖ ejemplar *m* (copy) ‖ MATH problema *m* ‖ — *for example* por ejemplo ‖ *for example's sake* para ejemplo, como ejemplo ‖ *to follow s.o.'s example* tomar ejemplo de uno ‖ *to hold s.o. up as an example* citar a uno como ejemplo ‖ *to make an example of s.o.* dar a alguien un castigo ejemplar ‖ *to set an example* dar ejemplo ‖ *to take as an example* tomar por *or* como ejemplo ‖ FIG *without example* sin ejemplo, sin precedente.

exanimate [ig'zænimit] *adj* MED exánime, inanimado, da ‖ FIG sin vida, poco animado.

exanthem [ig'zænθəm]; **exanthema** ['egzæn'θi:mə] *n* MED exantema *m*.
— OBSERV El plural es *exanthemas* o *exanthemata*.

exarch ['eksɑ:k] *n* exarca *m*.

exasperate [ig'zɑ:spəreit] *vt* exasperar (to irritate) ‖ exacerbar (to exacerbate) ‖ *to get exasperated* exasperarse.

exasperating [-iŋ] *adj* exasperante ‖ irritante.

exasperation [igzɑ:spə'reiʃən] *n* exasperación *f*.

ex cathedra ['ekskə'θi:drə] *adj/adv* ex cátedra.

excavate ['ekskəveit] *vt* excavar.

excavation [ˌekskə'veiʃən] *n* excavación *f* (digging).

excavator ['ekskəveitə*] *n* TECH excavadora *f* (machine) | excavador *m* (person).

exceed [ik'si:d] *vt* exceder (quantity); *income exceeds expenditure by a hundred pounds* los ingresos exceden los gastos en cien libras ‖ superar (hopes) ‖ rebasar, sobrepasar (a limit) ‖ excederse en; *he exceeded his duty* se excedió en sus funciones.

exceeding [-iŋ] *adj* excesivo, va.

exceeding [-iŋli] *adv* sumamente, extremadamente.

excel [ik'sel] *vt* superar.
◆ *vi* sobresalir.

excellence ['eksələns] *n* excelencia *f*.

Excellency [-i] *n* excelencia *f*; *His Excellency* Su Excelencia.

excellent ['eksələnt] *adj* excelente.

excelsior [ek'selsiɔ:*] *n* US virutas *f pl* que se emplean para rellenar.

except [ik'sept] *prep* excepto, salvo, exceptuando a, con excepción de ‖ — *except for* excepto ‖ *except that* excepto que, sólo que, salvo que.

except [ik'sept] *vt* excluir, exceptuar ‖ JUR recusar (a witness).
◆ *vi* *to except against* hacer objeciones a.

excepted [-id] *adj* con *or* a excepción de; *Tim excepted, everyone left* se fueron todos a excepción de Tim.

excepting [-iŋ] *prep* excepto, exceptuando a, salvo, con excepción de.

exception [ik'sepʃən] *n* exclusión *f* (exclusion) ‖ excepción *f* (something excepted); *to be an exception to the rule* ser una excepción a la regla; *the exception proves the rule* la excepción confirma la regla ‖ JUR recusación *f* (of a witness) ‖ objeción *f* (objection) ‖ — *by way of an exception* por excepción, a título excepcional ‖ *to make an exception* hacer una excepción ‖ *to take exception to* ofenderse por, molestarse por (to resent), objetar (to object) ‖ *without exception* sin excepción ‖ *with the exception of* con *or* a excepción de.

exceptionable [ik'sepʃnəbl] *adj* recusable (witness) ‖ reprochable, censurable (open to objection).

exceptional [ik'sepʃənl] *adj* excepcional.

exceptionally [ik'sepʃənli] *adv* excepcionalmente.

excerpt ['eksə:pt] *n* extracto *m*.

excerption [ek'sə:pʃən] *n* extracto *m*.

excess [ik'ses] *n* exceso *m* ‖ COMM excedente *m* (surplus) ‖ FIG exceso *m* ‖ — *in excess* en exceso ‖ *in excess of* superior a ‖ *to excess* en *or* con exceso; *to eat to excess* comer con exceso.
◆ *adj* excedente ‖ — *excess luggage* exceso de equipaje ‖ *excess weight* exceso de peso.

excessive [ik'sesiv] *adj* excesivo, va.

excess-profits tax [-'prɔfittæks] *n* impuestos *m pl* sobre beneficios excesivos.

exchange [iks'tʃeindʒ] *n* cambio *m* (change) ‖ intercambio *m* (interchange); *exchange of students* intercambio de estudiantes ‖ cambio *m* (of foreing currency) ‖ canje *m* (of prisoners) ‖ Bolsa *f* (stocks, shares, etc.); *exchange quotation* cotización de la Bolsa ‖ central *f* telefónica (for telephones) ‖ lonja *f* (of commodities) ‖ — *bill of exchange* letra *f* de cambio ‖ *exchange broker* cambista *m* ‖ *exchange control* control *m* de divisas ‖ *exchange of views* cambio de impresiones ‖ *exchange premium* agio *m* ‖ *foreign exchange* divisas *f pl* ‖ *in exchange for* a cambio de ‖ *rate of exchange* tipo *m* de cambio ‖ *Stock Exchange* bolsa *f* de valores ‖ *the Labour exchange* la bolsa *f* del trabajo.

exchange [iks'tʃeindʒ] *vt* cambiar (to change); *to exchange an old car for a new one* cambiar un coche viejo por uno nuevo ‖ canjear (prisoners) ‖ intercambiar (to interchange) ‖ cambiar (foreign currency) ‖ cambiar; *to exchange views with* cambiar impresiones con ‖ hacerse (courtesies) ‖ cruzar; *to exchange words* cruzar palabras ‖ darse, propinarse (blows) ‖ — *they exchanged glances* cruzaron una mirada, sus miradas se cruzaron ‖ *to exchange for* cambiarse por ‖ *to exchange greetings* saludarse, cambiar saludos ‖ *to exchange greetings with* saludar a ‖ *to exchange signs* hacerse señas.

exchangeable [-əbl] *adj* cambiable ‖ canjeable ‖ intercambiable.

exchequer [iks'tʃekə*] *n* hacienda *f* (finances) ‖ Tesoro *m* público, fisco *m*, erario *m* (treasury) ‖ JUR tribunal *m* (court) ‖ — *Chancellor of the Exchequer* Ministro *m* de Hacienda ‖ *Exchequer bonds* bonos *m pl* del Tesoro.

excipient [ik'sipiənt] *n* MED excipiente *m*.

excise [ek'saiz] *n* impuestos *m pl* sobre el consumo, impuestos *m pl* indirectos (tax) ‖ patente *f* (licence).

excise [ek'saiz] *vt* gravar con unos impuestos (to tax) ‖ extirpar (to cut out) ‖ suprimir (to omit) ‖ MED sajar.

exciseman [-mən] *n* recaudador *m* de impuestos.
— OBSERV El plural de *exciseman* es *excisemen*.

excision [ek'siʒən] *n* MED extirpación *f*, excisión *f* (removal) | incisión *f* (incision) ‖ FIG corte *m* (cut out) | supresión *f*.

excitability [ikˌsaitə'biliti] *n* excitabilidad *f*.

excitable [ik'saitəbl] *adj* excitable ‖ FIG nervioso, sa (nervous) | emocionable (emotional).

excitant ['eksitənt] *n* excitante *m*.

excitation [ˌeksi'teiʃən] *n* excitación *f* ‖ FIG nerviosismo *m* | emoción *f*.

excitative [ek'saitətiv] *adj* excitante.

excitatory [ek'saitətəri] *adj* excitante.

excite [ik'sait] *vt* emocionar; *the news has excited me* la noticia me ha emocionado ‖ entusiasmar; *I'm excited with my new car* estoy entusiasmado con mi coche nuevo ‖ excitar (to stimulate) ‖ incitar (to urge) ‖ poner nervioso (to irritate) ‖ provocar (admiration, jealousy, etc.) ‖ despertar (one's imagination) ‖ excitar (a crowd) ‖ ELECTR excitar; *to excite a dynamo* excitar una dinamo.

excited [id] *adj* entusiasmado, da (enthused) ‖ emocionado, da (deeply moved) ‖ excitado, da (agitated) ‖ nervioso, sa (nervous) ‖ ELECTR excitado, da ‖ — *don't get excited* no te excites ‖ *to get excited* emocionarse (to be deeply moved), entusiasmarse (to enthuse), alborotarse, agitarse (the crowd), acalorarse (a discussion).

excitedly [-idli] *adv* con entusiasmo.

excitement [-mənt] *n* excitación *f* ‖ entusiasmo *m* (enthusiasm) ‖ emoción *f*; *the news caused great excitement* la noticia causó gran emoción ‖ alboroto *m* (disturbance) ‖ agitación *f* (agitation).

exciter [ik'saitə*] *n* PHYS excitador *m*.

exciting [ik'saitiŋ] *adj* apasionante; *an exciting life* una vida apasionante ‖ excitante ‖ emocionante; *how exciting!* ¡qué emocionante!

exclaim [iks'kleim] *vi* exclamar ‖ *to exclaim against* o *at* o *upon* clamar en contra.
◆ *vt* gritar.

exclamation [ˌeksklə'meiʃən] *n* exclamación *f* ‖ GRAMM *exclamation mark*, US *exclamation point* signo *m* de admiración.

exclamative [ˌeksklə'meitiv] *adj* exclamativo, va.

exclamatory [eks'klæmətəri] *adj* exclamatorio, ria.

exclave ['ekskleiv] *n* parte *f* de un Estado situada fuera de sus fronteras.

exclude [iks'klu:d] *vt* excluir (to leave out); *to exclude all possibility of doubt* excluir cualquier posibilidad de duda ‖ no admitir (not to admit).

excluding [-iŋ] *prep* excepto, con exclusión de, exceptuando a.

exclusion [iks'klu:ʒən] *n* exclusión *f*; *to the exclusion of* con exclusión de.

exclusive [iks'klu:siv] *adj* exclusivo, va (sole); *exclusive model* modelo exclusivo; *exclusive selling rights* derechos exclusivos de venta ‖ selecto, ta (select); *exclusive neighbourhood* vecindad selecta ‖ cerrado, da; *exclusive society* sociedad cerrada ‖ exclusivista (policy) ‖ — *exclusive interview* entrevista en exclusiva ‖ *exclusive rights* exclusividad *f* ‖ *mutually exclusive possibilities* posibilidades que se excluyen ‖ *to have exclusive rights to* tener la exclusiva de.
◆ *n* exclusiva *f*, exclusividad *f*.
◆ *adv* exclusive (not counting the first and last mentioned) ‖ *exclusive of* excluyendo, sin tener en cuenta.

exclusively [iks'klu:sivli] *adv* exclusivamente, en exclusiva.

exclusiveness [iks'klu:sivnis] *n* exclusividad *f*.

exclusivity [eksklu:'siviti] *n* exclusividad *f*, exclusiva *f*.

excogitate [eks'kɔdʒiteit] *vt* inventar, imaginar (to contrive) ‖ maquinar, tramar (to plot).

excogitation [eks·kɔdʒi'teiʃən] *n* invención *f*.

excommunicant ['ekskə'mju:nikənt] *n* excomulgado, da.

excommunicate [ˌekskə'mju:nikeit] *adj/n* REL excomulgado, da.

excommunicate [ˌekskəˈmjuːnikeit] *vt* REL excomulgar.

excommunication [ˈekskəˌmjuːniˈkeiʃən] *n* excomunión *f*.

ex-convict [ˈeksˈkɔnvikt] *n* ex presidiario *m*.

excoriate [eksˈkɔːrieit] *vt* excoriar.

excoriation [eksˌkɔːriˈeiʃən] *n* excoriación *f*.

excrement [ˈekskrimənt] *n* excremento *m*.

excremental [ˌekskriˈmentl] *adj* excrementicio, cia.

excrescence [iksˈkresns]; **excrescency** [-i] *n* excrecencia *f*, excrescencia *f*.

excrescent [iksˈkresnt] *adj* saliente (forming excrescence) || superfluo, flua (superfluous).

excreta [eksˈkriːtə] *pl n* excrementos *m*.

excrete [eksˈkriːt] *vi* excretar.

excretion [eksˈkriːʃən] *n* excreción *f*.

excretory [eksˈkriːtəri] *adj* excretorio, ria; excretor, ra.
◆ *n* órgano *m* excretorio.

excruciate [iksˈkruʃieit] *vt* torturar, atormentar.

excruciating [-iŋ] *adj* intolerable, insoportable (hard to bear) || atroz, insoportable (pain).

excruciatingly [-iŋli] *adv* atrozmente || FAM *it is excruciatingly funny* es para morirse de risa.

excruciation [iksˌkruʃiˈeiʃən] *n* suplicio *m*, tortura *f*, tormento *m*.

exculpate [ˈekskʌlpeit] *vt* disculpar || *to exculpate o.s. from* disculparse de.

exculpation [ˌekskʌlˈpeiʃən] *n* disculpa *f*.

exculpatory [eksˈkʌlpətəri] *adj* justificante, justificativo, va || de disculpa (letter).

excurrent [eksˈkʌrənt] *adj* que brota, que mana (blood) || de salida.

excursion [iksˈkəːʃən] *n* excursión *f* (trip) || MIL incursión *f*, correría *f* || ASTR desviación *f* || FIG digresión *f* (in speech) || — *excursion train* tren *m* de recreo || *excursion trip* viaje *m* de recreo.

excursionist [-ist] *n* excursionista *m* & *f*.

excursive [eksˈkəːsiv] *adj* digresivo, va (speech, etc.) || inclinado a la digresión (people) || errabundo, da (imagination) || superficial (reading) || de recreo (trip).

excursus [eksˈkəːsəs] *n* apéndice *m* (in a book) || digresión *f* (in a literary work).
— OBSERV El plural es *excursuses* o *excursus*.

excusable [iksˈkjuːzəbl] *adj* excusable, disculpable, perdonable.

excuse [iksˈkjuːs] *n* excusa *f*, disculpa *f*; *to make excuses* dar excusas; *to admit of no excuse* no tener disculpa; *to make sth. one's excuse* dar algo como excusa || razón *f*, justificación *f* (reason) || pretexto *m* (pretext).

excuse [iksˈkjuːz] *vt* excusar, disculpar, perdonar; *nothing can excuse such carelessness* nada puede excusar tal descuido || dispensar de, eximir de (a duty); *you are excused work today* está dispensado de trabajar hoy; *the teacher excused him from coming to school* el profesor le dispensó de venir al colegio || perdonar; *to excuse s.o. sth.* perdonar algo a alguien || — *excuse me!* ¡perdón!, ¡discúlpeme!, ¡perdone Ud! || *excuse my saying so* perdone mi atrevimiento || *may I be excused for a moment* ¿puedo salir un momento? || *to excuse o.s.* pedir permiso (before leaving) || *to excuse o.s. for* disculparse de, excusarse de.

ex-directory [ˌeks diˈrektəri] *adj* no incluido, da en la guía telefónica (person, telephone number).

exeat [ˈeksiæt] *n* permiso *m* de salida (in colleges) || REL exeat *m*, permiso *m*, licencia *f*.

execrable [ˈeksikrəbl] *adj* execrable, abominable, odioso, sa; detestable.

execrate [ˈeksikreit] *vt* execrar, abominar, odiar (to abhor) || maldecir (to curse).
◆ *vi* proferir maldiciones (to curse).

execration [ˌeksiˈkreiʃən] *n* odio *m*, execración *f*, abominación *f* || maldición *f* (curse).

executable [ˈeksikjuːtəbl] *adj* ejecutable.

executant [igˈzekjutənt] *n* ejecutante *m* & *f*.

execute [ˈeksikjuːt] *vt* ejecutar, cumplir; *to execute an order* ejecutar una orden || ejecutar; *to execute a dance* ejecutar un baile; *to execute a prisoner* ejecutar a un prisionero; *to execute a will* ejecutar un testamento || realizar, llevar a cabo, ejecutar, hacer (to carry out) || desempeñar, llevar a cabo; *to execute the duties of director* desempeñar las funciones de director || servir, despachar (a trade order) || hacer (a banker's order) || firmar (a treaty, a contract) || JUR legalizar (a document).

execution [ˌeksiˈkjuːʃən] *n* ejecución *f* (of a criminal) || cumplimiento *m*, ejecución *f* (of orders) || realización *f*, ejecución *f* (carrying out) || desempeño *m* (of one's duty) || MUS ejecución *f* || JUR legalización *f* (of a document) || firma *f* (of a treaty, of a contract) || ejecución *f* (of a judgment) || ejecución *f* de embargo (distress) || INFORM ejecución *f* || *writ of execution* ejecutoria *f*.

executioner [ˌeksiˈkjuːʃnə*] *n* verdugo *m*.

executive [igˈzekjutiv] *adj* ejecutivo, va (government, power) || de ejecución (ability) || ejecutivo, va; dirigente (function) || — *executive board* consejo *m* de dirección || US *Executive Mansion* la Casa Blanca (in Washington), el Palacio del Gobernador (in a State capital) || *executive officer* segundo comandante *m* || *executive secretary* secretario ejecutivo.
◆ *n* poder *m* ejecutivo (branch of government) || ejecutivo *m* (businessman).

executor [igˈzekjutə*] *n* ejecutor, ra || JUR albacea *m*, ejecutor *m* testamentario.

executorship [-ʃip] *n* ejecutoría *f*.

executory [igˈzekjutəri] *adj* JUR ejecutorio, ria || ejecutivo, va || US administrativo, va.

executrix [igˈzekjutriks] *n* albacea *f*, ejecutora *f* testamentaria.
— OBSERV El plural es *executrices* o *executrixes*.

exegesis [eksiˈdʒiːsis] *n* exégesis *f*.
— OBSERV El plural de la palabra inglesa es *exegeses*.

exegete [ˈeksidʒiːt] *n* exegeta *m*.

exegetic [ˌeksiˈdʒetik]; **exegetical** [-əl] *adj* exegético, ca.

exegetics [-s] *pl n* teología *f sing* exegética, exégesis *f*.

exemplar [igˈzemplə*] *n* ejemplo *m*, modelo *m* (a model) || ejemplar *m* (a copy).

exemplariness [igˈzemplərinis]; **exemplarity** [ˌegzemˈplæriti] *n* ejemplaridad *f*.

exemplary [igˈzempləri] *adj* ejemplar; *an exemplary husband* un marido ejemplar; *an exemplary punishment* un castigo ejemplar || típico, ca (typical).

exemplification [igˌzemplifiˈkeiʃən] *n* ejemplificación *f*, demostración *f* por el ejemplo (an exemplifying) || ejemplo *m* (an example) || JUR copia *f* legalizada.

exemplify [igˈzemplifai] *vt* demostrar con ejemplos, ilustrar con ejemplos || servir de ejemplo para, ilustrar || JUR hacer una copia legalizada de.

exempt [igˈzempt] *adj* exento, ta; libre; eximido, da; dispensado, da (*from* de).

exempt [igˈzempt] *vt* eximir, dispensar (*from* de).

exemption [igˈzempʃən] *n* exención *f* || franquicia *f* (from custom duties).

exequatur [ˌeksiˈkweitə*] *n* exequatur *m inv*.

exequies [ˈeksikwiz] *pl n* exequias *f*.

exercise [ˈeksəsaiz] *n* ejercicio *m*; *in the exercise of my duties* en el ejercicio de mis funciones; *breathing exercises* ejercicios respiratorios || — *exercise book* cuaderno *m* || *exercise yard* patio *m* || *practical exercises* clases prácticas || *to take exercise* hacer ejercicio.

exercise [ˈeksəsaiz] *vt* ejercer (rights, duties, authority, influence, profession) || usar de, proceder con (patience) || entrenar (to train an animal, a team) || hacer ejercicios con (one's body) || sacar de paseo (a dog) || ejercitar; *to exercise charity* ejercitar la caridad; *to exercise children in mathematics* ejercitar a los niños en las matemáticas || preocupar; *this problem has exercised the best brains in the country* este problema ha preocupado a los cerebros más insignes del país || MIL instruir a || — *to exercise care* tener cuidado || *to exercise o.s.* ejercitarse.
◆ *vi* entrenarse (to take physical exercise) || ejercitarse || MIL hacer la instrucción.

exercitation [egˌzəːsiˈteiʃən] *n* ejercicio *m*.

exergue [ekˈsəːg] *n* exergo *m*.

exert [igˈzəːt] *vt* ejercer || *to exert o.s.* esforzarse, hacer esfuerzos.

exertion [igˈzəːʃən] *n* esfuerzo *m* [excesivo] (effort) || ejercicio *m* (of authority) || empleo *m* (of strenght).

exeunt [ˈeksiʌnt] *vi* THEATR salen, se van (the actors).

exfoliate [eksˈfəulieit] *vt* exfoliar.

exfoliation [eksˌfəuliˈeiʃən] *n* exfoliación *f*.

ex gratia [eks ˈgreiʃə] *adj* sin obligación legal (payment, grant).

exhalation [ˌekshəˈleiʃən] *n* exhalación *f*.

exhale [eksˈheil] *vt/vi* exhalar || despedir (gas, smell).

exhaust [igˈzɔːst] *n* escape *m* (the expulsion of steam or gases) || gas *m* de escape (gases or steam expelled) || tubo *m* de escape (pipe).

exhaust [igˈzɔːst] *vt* agotar; *he exhausted my patience* me agotó la paciencia; *they exhausted the ammunition* agotaron las municiones; *to exhaust a topic of conversation* agotar un tema de conversación; *I am exhausted* estoy agotado || vaciar (to empty a container) || extraer (to remove a liquid, a gas) || empobrecer (soil).

exhausted [-id] *adj* exhausto, ta; agotado, da (worn-out).

exhaustible [-ibl] *adj* agotable.

exhausting [-iŋ] *adj* agotador, ra.

exhaustion [igˈzɔːstʃən] *n* agotamiento *m*.

exhaustive [igˈzɔːstiv] *adj* exhaustivo, va; completo, ta.

exhibit [igˈzibit] *n* objeto *m* expuesto || JUR documento *m* || US exposición *f* || *on exhibit* expuesto, ta.

exhibit [igˈzibit] *vt* mostrar, dar muestras de (to display); *to exhibit symptoms of hysteria* mostrar síntomas de histeria || presentar (documents, passport, ticket) || mostrar al público (theater, sports) || exponer (paintings, sculpture, object for sale).
◆ *vi* exponer, hacer una exposición.

exhibition [ˌeksiˈbiʃən] *n* exposición *f* (a display or art) || beca *f* (scholarship) || presentación *f* (of documents, of tickets, etc.) || FIG ostentación *f*, alarde *m* | demostración *f*, manifestación *f* || — *Ideal Home Exhibition* Salón *m* de Artes Domésticas || *to make an exhibition of o.s.* ponerse en ridículo, hacer el ridículo.

exhibitioner [ˌeksiˈbiʃnə*] *n* becario, ria.

exhibitionism [,eksi'biʃnizəm] *n* exhibicionista *m* & *f.*

exhibitor [ig'zibitə*] *n* expositor, ra || US CINEM exhibidor *m.*

exhilarate [ig'ziləreit] *vt* alegrar, animar, levantar el ánimo, regocijar.

exhilarating [-iŋ] *adj* estimulante, tónico, ca.

exhilaration [ig·zilə'reiʃən] *n* alegría *f,* regocijo *m* (high spirits) || efecto *m* estimulante.

exhilarative [ig'zilərətiv] *adj* estimulante, tónico, ca; vivificante.

exhort [ig'zɔ:t] *vt* exhortar || recomendar (action, measures).

exhortation [,egzɔ:'teiʃən] *n* exhortación *f.*

exhortative [ig'zɔ:tətiv] *adj* exhortativo, va.

exhortatory [ig'zɔ:tətəri] *adj* exhortatorio, ria.

exhumation [,ekshju:'meiʃən] *n* exhumación *f.*

exhume [eks'hju:m] *vt* exhumar || FIG desenterrar.

exigence ['eksidʒəns]; **exigency** [-i] *n* exigencia *f* (need) || caso *m* de emergencia (emergency).

exigent ['eksidʒənt] *adj* exigente (exacting) || urgente (urgent).

exigible ['eksidʒibl] *adj* exigible (*against, from* a).

exiguity [,eksi'gju:iti] *n* exigüidad *f.*

exiguous [eg'zigjuəs] *adj* exiguo, gua.

exile ['eksail] *n* exilio *m* (banishment from one's country, voluntary living outside one's country); *government in exile* gobierno en el exilio || exiliado, da; exilado, da (person) || cautiverio *m* (of Jews) || *to go into exile* exiliarse, exilarse.

exile ['eksail] *vt* exiliar, exilar.

exist [ig'zist] *vi* existir; *do angels exist?* ¿existen los ángeles?; *after we have ceased to exist* después de que hayamos dejado de existir || subsistir, vivir; *how do you manage to exist on such little money?* ¿cómo te las arreglas para subsistir con tan poco dinero?

existence [ig'zistəns] *n* existencia *f* || PHIL ser *m,* entidad *f* || — *to have been in existence for ten years* existir desde hace diez años || *to come into existence* nacer, empezar a existir.

existent [ig'zistənt] *adj* existente (that exists) || actual, presente (present).

existential [,egzis'tenʃəl] *adj* existencial.

existentialism [-izəm] *n* existencialismo *m.*

existentialist [-ist] *adj/n* existencialista.

existing [ig'zistiŋ] *adj* existente.

exit ['eksit] *n* salida *f* (a way out); *emergency exit* salida de emergencia || mutis *m* (an actor's leaving of the stage) || FAM fin *m* (death) || — INFORM *exit data* datos *m pl* de salida || *exit visa* visado *m* de salida.

exit ['eksit] *vi* THEATR hacer mutis || morir (to die).

ex libris [eks'laibris] *n* ex libris (bookplate).

exocarp ['eksəuka:p] *n* BOT epicarpio *m.*

exocrine ['eksəukrin] *adj* exocrino, na.

exodus ['eksədəs] *n* éxodo *m*; *rural exodus* éxodo rural.

ex officio [,eksə'fiʃiəu] *adv/adj* *to act ex officio* actuar de oficio || *member ex officio* miembro de oficio, miembro de derecho.

exogamic [,eksəu'gæmik]; **exogamous** [,eksəugæməs] *adj* exógamo, ma.

exogamy [ek'sɔgəmi] *n* exogamia.

exogenous [ek'sɔdʒinəs] *adj* exógeno, na.

exonerate [ig'zɔnəreit] *vt* exonerar de, dispensar de, eximir de (a burden, an obligation) || disculpar (to exculpate).

exoneration [ig,zɔnə'reiʃən] *n* exoneración *f,* dispensa *f* (freeing) || disculpa *f* (exculpation).

exophthalmus; exophthalmos [,eksɔf'θælməs] *n* MED exoftalmía *f.*

exorbitance [ig'zɔ:bitəns]; **exorbitancy** [-i] *n* carácter *m* desorbitado, exorbitancia *f.*

exorbitant [ig'zɔ:bitənt] *adj* exorbitante, desorbitado, da; excesivo, va; desmesurado, da.

exorcise ['eksɔ:saiz] *vt* exorcizar, conjurar.

exorciser [-ə*] *n* exorcista *m.*

exorcism ['eksɔ:sizəm] *n* exorcismo *m.*

exorcist ['eksɔ:sist] *n* exorcista *m.*

exorcize ['eksɔ:saiz] *vt* exorcizar, conjurar.

exordial [ek'sɔ:djəl] *adj* introductorio, ria.

exordium [ek'sɔ:djəm] *n* exordio *m.*
— OBSERV El plural de *exordium* es *exordiums* o *exordia.*

exoskeleton [eksos'skelitn] *n* dermatoesqueleto *m.*

exosmosis [eksɔs'məusis] *n* exósmosis *f.*

exoteric [,eksəu'terik] *adj* exotérico, ca.

exothermic [,eksəu'θə:mik] *adj* exotérmico, ca.

exotic [ig'zɔtik] *adj* exótico, ca.
◆ *n* planta *f* exótica || palabra *f* exótica.

exosticism [ig'zɔtisizəm]; **exotism** [ig'zɔtizəm] *n* exotismo *m.*

expand [iks'pænd] *vt* dilatar (to make larger); *heat expands metals* el calor dilata los metales || desarrollar (to cause to increase); *to expand trade* desarrollar el comercio || ensanchar, extender, ampliar (to enlarge) || ampliar; *the pocket dictionary was expanded* el diccionario de bolsillo fue ampliado || desarrollar (a topic, a formula, an algebraic expression) || extender, abrir, desplegar (wings).
◆ *vi* dilatarse (to become larger); *metals expand when they are heated* los metales se dilatan cuando se les calienta || extenderse (to extend) || ensancharse (to broaden); *the river expands and forms a lake* el río se ensancha y forma un lago || desarrollarse; *Japanese trade expanded after the war* el comercio japonés se desarrolló después de la guerra || volverse expansivo (to become affable); *he is expanding lately* se está volviendo expansivo últimamente || abrirse (flowers) || *to expand on* o *upon* extenderse sobre, tratar detalladamente.

expandability [ikspændə'biliti] *n* expansibilidad *f.*

expandable [iks'pændəbl] *adj* expansible, dilatable || extensible.

expanded [iks'pændid] *adj* INFORM expandido, da; *expanded keyboard* teclado expandido; *expanded memory* memoria expandida.

expanse [iks'pæns] *n* extensión *f* (extent) || expansión *f* || envergadura *f* (of wings).

expansibility [iks,pænsə'biliti] *n* expansibilidad *f.*

expansible [iks'p, aensəbl] *adj* extensible || PHYS expansible, dilatable.

expansile [iks'pænsail] *adj* expansible.

expansion [iks'pænʃən] *n* expansión *f,* dilatación *f* (of gas) || dilatación *f* (of metals) || ampliación *f* (of a subject) || extensión *f* (extent) || ensanche *m* (of a town) || MATH desarrollo *m* || expansión *f,* desarrollo *m* (of trade).

expansionism [-izəm] *n* expansionismo *m.*

expansionist [-ist] *adj/n* expansionista.

expansive [iks'p, aensiv] *adj* expansivo, va; comunicativo, va (people) || extenso, sa; amplio, plia (broad, wide) || expansivo, va (tending to expand); *the expansive energy of steam* la energía expansiva del vapor || dilatable (metals).

expansiveness [-nis] *n* FIG expansibilidad *f,* carácter *m* expansivo || PHYS expansibilidad *f,* dilatabilidad *f.*

ex parte ['eks'pa:ti] *adj* unilateral, de una de las partes.

expatiate [eks'peiʃieit] *vi* extenderse.

expatiation [eks·peiiʃi'eiʃən] *n* disertación *f.*

expatriate [eks'pætriit] *adj/n* expatriado, da.

expatriate [eks'pætrieit] *vt* desterrar, expatriar || *to expatriate o.s.* expatriarse.
◆ *vi* expatriarse.

expatriation [eks,pĭri'eiʃən] *n* expatriación *f.*

expect [iks'pekt] *vt* suponer (to think likely); *I expect the train will be late* supongo que el tren llegará con retraso; *I expect so* así supongo || esperar (to anticipate the coming of); *we're all expecting you* todos te esperamos; *he's expecting the bill any day* espera la cuenta un día de estos || esperar (to hope for); *you can't expect any money* no esperes ningún dinero || esperar, contar con (to require sth. of s.o.); *a speech will be expected of you* se espera que haga usted un discurso; *you are expected to work late if need be* esperamos que se quede trabajando si es necesario || *I expected as much* ya me lo esperaba.
◆ *vi* FAM *to be expecting* estar esperando (to be pregnant).

expectancy [iks'pektənsi] *n* expectación *f,* expectativa *f* (state of expectation) || esperanza *f*; *life expectancy* esperanza de vida.

expectant [iks'pektənt] *adj* expectante || candidato, ta (to a job) || ilusionado, da (hopeful) || *expectant mother* mujer embarazada, futura madre.

expectantly [-li] *adv* con expectación.

expectation [,ekspek'teiʃən] *n* esperanza *f* (hope); *we work in the expectation of being paid* trabajamos con la esperanza de que nos paguen; *it is beyond our expectations* supera nuestras esperanzas || previsión *f* (anticipation); *contrary to all expectations* en contra de todas las previsiones || expectativa *f*; *to live in expectation* vivir a la expectativa || perspectiva *f*; *happiness in expectation* felicidad en perspectiva || — *a man of great expectations* un futuro heredero || *contrary to expectations* contrariamente a lo esperado || *expectation of life* esperanza *f* de vida, vida media || *in expectation of* en expectación de, en espera de || *to come up to s.o.'s expectations* estar a la altura de las esperanzas de uno, colmar las esperanzas de uno || *to fall short of s.o.'s expectations* defraudar las esperanzas de uno || *to live up to one's expectations* estar a la altura de lo que uno esperaba || *to succeed beyond one's expectations* tener más éxito de lo previsto.

expectorant [eks'pektərənt] *adj* expectorante.
◆ *n* expectorante *m.*

expectorate [eks'pektəreit] *vt/vi* escupir, expectorar (to spit).

expectoration [eks,pektə'reiʃən] *n* expectoración *f.*

expedience [iks'pi:djəns]; **expediency** [-i] *n* conveniencia *f,* oportunidad *f* || *on grounds of expediency* por conveniencia propia.

expedient [iks'pi:djənt] *adj* conveniente, oportuno, na.
◆ *n* expediente *m,* recurso *m.*

expedite ['ekspidait] *vt* acelerar (to hasten) || dar curso a (petition, legal matter) || despachar, expedir (business, task) || facilitar (progress).

expedition [,ekspi'diʃən] *n* expedición *f*; *rescue expedition* expedición de salvamento.

expeditionary [-əri] *adj* expedicionario, ria; *expeditionary force* cuerpo expedicionario.

expeditious [ˌekspiˈdiʃəs] *adj* expeditivo, va; expedito, ta.

expel [iksˈpel] *vt* expulsar (person) ‖ expulsar, arrojar, expeler; *to expel smoke through the mouth* expulsar humo por la boca.

expellant; expellent [iksˈpelənt] *adj* expelente.

expend [iksˈpend] *vt* gastar (to spend) ‖ emplear (time) ‖ agotar (to use up completely) ‖ dedicar, consagrar (efforts) ‖ poner (care).

expendable [iksˈpendəbl] *adj* prescindible (people) ‖ gastable (things).

expenditure [iksˈpenditʃə*] *n* gasto *m*, desembolso *m* (of money) ‖ gasto *m*, empleo *m* (of time) ‖ gasto *m* (of energy).

expense [iksˈpens] *n* gasto *m*; *overhead expenses* gastos generales ‖ JUR costa *f*; *legal expenses* costas judiciales ‖ — *all expenses paid* con todos los gastos pagados ‖ *at great expense* con mucho gasto ‖ *at my expense* a costa mía, a mi costa ‖ *at the expense of* a costa *or* a expensas de ‖ *expense account* cuenta *f* de gastos de representación ‖ *incidental expenses* gastos imprevistos ‖ *regardless of expense* sin escatimar gastos ‖ *to go to any expense* hacer todo lo posible ‖ *to go to expense* meterse en gastos ‖ *to go to the expense of* meterse en gastos para ‖ *to meet expenses* hacer frente a los gastos ‖ *to put to expense* obligar a gastar mucho dinero ‖ *to spare no expense* no escatimar gastos.

expensive [-iv] *adj* caro, ra; costoso, sa.

experience [iksˈpiəriəns] *n* experiencia *f*; *to know from one's own experience* saber por experiencia propia ‖ *it hasn't happened in my experience* nunca me ocurrió tal cosa.

experience [iksˈpiəriəns] *vt* experimentar; *I experienced great joy* experimenté gran placer ‖ sufrir (a loss) ‖ tener (difficulties) ‖ saber por experiencia (to know from experience).

experienced [-t] *adj* experimentado, da (with experience) ‖ experto, ta (expert).

experiential [ekspiəˈrienʃəl] *adj* experimental, empírico, ca.

experiment [iksˈperimənt] *n* experimento *m*; *a chemistry experiment* un experimento químico ‖ — *as an experiment* como experimento ‖ *experiment station* estación experimental.

experiment [iksˈperimənt] *vi* hacer experimentos, experimentar.

experimental [eksˌperiˈmentl] *adj* experimental.

experimentalist [eksˈperiˈmentəlist] *n* experimentador, ra.

experimentation [iksˌperimenˈteiʃən] *n* experimentación *f*.

experimenter [iksˈperimentə*] *n* experimentador, ra.

expert [ˈekspəːt] *adj* experto, ta (skilful) ‖ JUR pericial (provided by an expert).

◆ *n* experto, ta; perito, ta ‖ — *according to expert opinion* a juicio de peritos ‖ *to be an expert in the matter* o *on the subject* ser experto en la materia ‖ *with the eye of an expert* con ojos de perito.

expertise [ˌekspəːˈtiːz] *n* pericia *f*, habilidad *f* (skilfulness) ‖ competencia *f* (competence).

expert system [ˈekspəːtˈsistim] *n* INFORM sistema *m* experto.

expiable [ˈekspiəbl] *adj* expiable.

expiate [ˈekspieit] *vt* expiar.

expiation [ˌekspiˈeiʃən] *n* expiación *f*.

expiatory [ˈekspiətəri] *adj* expiatorio, ria.

expiration [ˌekspaiəˈreiʃən] *n* expiración *f*, terminación *f* (a coming to an end) ‖ espiración *f* (a breathing out) ‖ expiración *f* (death) ‖ COMM vencimiento *m* (of a bill, etc.).

expire [ikspaiə*] *vt* espirar, expeler (air, etc.).

◆ *vi* expirar, terminar (to come to an end) ‖ expirar (to die) ‖ COMM expirar, vencer ‖ caducar (to become void).

expiry [iksˈpaiəri] *n* expiración *f*, terminación *f* (ending) ‖ COMM vencimiento *m*.

explain [iksˈplein] *vt* explicar; *explain to me how it happened* explícame cómo ha ocurrido ‖ exponer; *to explain one's thought* exponer su pensamiento ‖ — *to be explained* explicarse ‖ *to explain away* justificar ‖ *to explain o.s.* explicarse; *explain yourself!* ¡explíquese usted!

◆ *vi* dar explicaciones.

explainable [-əbl] *adj* explicable.

explanation [ˌekspləˈneiʃən] *n* explicación *f* ‖ aclaración *f* (of an obscure point) ‖ FIG *to come to an explanation with s.o.* tener una explicación con alguien.

explanatory [iksˈplænətəri] *adj* explicativo, va ‖ aclaratorio, ria (clarifying).

expletive [eksˈpliːtiv] *adj* GRAMM expletivo, va.

◆ *n* GRAMM voz *f* expletiva (used to pad out a sentence) ‖ taco *m* (an oath).

explicable [ˈeksplikəbl] *adj* explicable.

explicate [ˈeksplikeit] *vt* explicar (a text) ‖ aclarar (an obscure point) ‖ exponer (to expound).

explication [ˌekspliˈkeiʃən] *n* explicación *f* ‖ exposición *f* (detailed account).

explicative [eksˈplikətiv]; **explicatory** [eksˈplikətəri] *adj* explicativo, va.

explicit [iksˈplisit] *adj* explícito, ta.

explicitness [-nis] *n* claridad *f*, precisión *f*.

explode [iksˈpləud] *vt* hacer explotar, estallar (to cause to burst) ‖ refutar (a myth, a theory) ‖ desmentir (rumours) ‖ *exploded view* vista esquemática.

◆ *vi* explotar, estallar ‖ FIG explotar, reventar (with anger, etc.) ‖ FIG *to explode with laughter* prorrumpir en risa.

exploit [ˈeksplɔit] *n* hazaña *f*, proeza *f*.

exploit [eksˈplɔit] *vt* explotar.

exploitable [iksˈplɔitəbl] *adj* explotable.

exploitation [ˌeksplɔiˈteiʃən] *n* explotación *f*.

exploitative [eksˈplɔitətiv] *adj* explotador, ra.

exploiter [iksˈplɔitə*] *n* explotador *m*.

exploration [ˌeksplɔːˈreiʃən] *n* exploración *f*; *underwater exploration* exploración submarina.

explorative [eksˈplɔːrətiv]; **exploratory** [eksˈplɔːrətəri] *adj* exploratorio, ria.

explore [iksˈplɔː*] *vt* explorar ‖ FIG explorar, sondear.

◆ *vi* *to explore for oil* explorar el terreno en busca de petróleo.

explorer [-rə*] *n* explorador, ra (person) ‖ MED sonda *f*.

explosion [iksˈpləuʒən] *n* explosión *f*; *the explosion of a bomb* la explosión de una bomba ‖ — *explosion engine* motor *m* de explosión ‖ *population explosion* explosión demográfica.

explosive [iksˈpləusiv] *adj* explosivo, va.

◆ *n* explosivo *m* ‖ explosiva *f* (consonant).

explosiveness [-nis] *n* carácter *m* explosivo.

expo [ˈekspəu] *n* expo *f*, exposición *f*.

exponent [eksˈpəunənt] *n* intérprete *m* & *f*; *an exponent of the Bible* un intérprete de la Biblia; *an exponent of Bach's music* un intérprete de la música de Bach ‖ defensor, ra; *an exponent of aid to underveloped countries* un defensor de la ayuda a los países subdesarrollados ‖ experto, ta; perito, ta; *an exponent of the art of engraving* un experto en el arte de grabar ‖ FIG exponente *m* & *f*; *the leading exponent of this art* el máximo exponente de este arte ‖ MATH exponente *m* (index).

exponential [ekspəuˈnenʃəl] *adj* MATH exponencial *m*.

export [ˈekspɔːt] *adj* exportador, ra ‖ de exportación; *export duty* derechos de exportación.

◆ *n* exportación *f* (trade, act) ‖ artículo *m* de exportación (commodity).

export [eksˈpɔːt] *vt* exportar; *to export oranges from Spain* exportar naranjas de España.

exportable [-əbl] *adj* exportable.

exportation [ˌekspɔːˈteiʃən] *n* exportación *f*.

exporter [eksˈpɔːtə*] *n* exportador, ra.

exporting [-iŋ] *n* exportación *f*.

◆ *adj* de exportación, exportador, ra.

expose [iksˈpəuz] *vt* exponer (to leave uncovered, unprotected); *to expose one's head to the sun* exponer la cabeza al sol; *to expose the soldiers to unnecessary risks* exponer a los soldados a peligros innecesarios ‖ descubrir, exponer (to leave open to attack); *to expose one's flank to the enemy* descubrir el flanco al enemigo ‖ descubrir (a plot, an impostor, a crime) ‖ COMM exponer (goods) ‖ revelar (to reveal) ‖ REL exponer ‖ exponer (to display) ‖ demostrar, revelar, poner al descubierto (to uncover) ‖ *to be exposed* estar orientado; *the house is exposed to the south* la casa está orientada al sur; estar poco protegido; *the house on the hill is very exposed* la casa de la colina está muy poco protegida.

exposé [eksˈpəuzei] *n* exposición *f* (of a theme) ‖ desenmascaramiento *m* (an exposure to sth. shameful) ‖ revelación *f*.

exposed [iksˈpəuzd] *adj* expuesto, ta ‖ descubierto, ta.

exposition [ˌekspəuˈziʃən] *n* exposición *f* (to a danger, of goods, of facts, etc.) ‖ introducción *f* ‖ comentario *m* (of a literary work) ‖ MUS, PHOT & REL exposición *f* ‖ abandono *m* (of a child) ‖ exposición *f* (exhibition).

expositive [eksˈpɔzitiv]; **expository** [eksˈpɔzitəri] *adj* expositivo, va; descriptivo, va.

expositor [eksˈpɔzitə*] *n* expositor, ra ‖ comentador, ra (commentator).

ex post facto [ekspəustˈfæktə] *adj* JUR con efecto retroactivo.

expostulate [iksˈpɔstjuleit] *vi* reconvenir, amonestar (*with* a) ‖ protestar.

expostulation [iksˌpɔstjuˈleiʃən] *n* amonestación *f*, reconvención *f* (reproach) ‖ protesta *f*.

exposure [iksˈpəuʒə*] *n* exposición *f* (to light, cold, heat, etc.) ‖ PHOT fotografía *f* (a piece of a film); *to make an exposure* sacar una fotografía ‖ exposición *f* (an exposing of a piece of film); *time of exposure* tiempo de exposición ‖ denuncia *f* (a denouncing) ‖ orientación *f*, situación *f* (aspect of a house) ‖ abandono *m* (of a child) ‖ FIG revelación *f* (of a secret) ‖ descubrimiento *m* (of a criminal) ‖ PHOT *exposure meter* exposímetro *m*, fotómetro *m*.

expound [iksˈpaund] *vt* comentar, explicar (to interpret) ‖ exponer (to state with great detail).

express [iksˈpres] *adj* expreso, sa (explicit, special); *express order* orden expresa; *he left with the express intention of calling* salió con la expresa intención de llamar ‖ rápido, da (service) ‖ urgente (fast); *an express letter* una carta urgente; *express post* correo urgente ‖ exacto, ta (image) ‖ expreso (train) ‖ de tiro rápido (rifle).

◆ *n* expreso *m* (train) || correo *m* urgente || US servicio *m* de urgencia (a fast delivery service).
◆ *adv* por correo urgente (by post) || por tren expreso (by express train).

express [iks'pres] *vt* expresar; *to express an opinion* expresar una opinión; *his work expresses his attitude to life* su obra expresa su actitud ante la vida || MATH expresar || exprimir (to press) || US enviar por expreso || *to express o.s.* expresarse.

expressible [iks'presəbl] *adj* posible de expresar (which can be stated) || exprimible (which can be pressed).

expression [iks'preʃən] *n* expresión *f* || *as an expression of thanks* en señal de agradecimiento || *beyond expression* más de lo que uno se puede figurar.

expressionism [-izəm] *n* expresionismo *m*.

expressionist [-ist] *adj/n* expresionista.

expressionless [-lis] *adj* inexpresivo, va || sin significado.

expressive [iks'presiv] *adj* expresivo, va || *expressive of* que expresa, que denota.

expressiveness [-nis] *n* expresividad *f*.

expressly [iks'presli] *adv* expresamente.

expressman [-mən] *n* empleado del servicio de urgencia.
— OBSERV El plural de *expressman* es *expressmen*.

expressway [iks'preswei] *n* US autopista *f* (road).

expropriate [eks'prəuprieit] *vt* expropiar || FIG desposeer (*from* de).

expropriation [eks,prəupri'eiʃən] *n* expropiación *f* || FIG desposeimiento *m*.

expropriator [eks'prəuprieitə*] *n* expropiador, ra.

expulsion [iks'pʌlʃən] *n* expulsión *f*.

expulsive [iks'pʌlsiv] *adj* expulsivo, va.

expunction [iks'pʌŋkʃən] *n* borradura *f*, tachadura *f* (erasure) || supresión *f*.

expunge [eks'pʌndʒ] *vt* borrar, tachar (to erase) || suprimir (to suppress).

expurgate ['ekspə:geit] *vt* expurgar.

expurgation [,ekspə:'geiʃən] *n* expurgación *f*.

expurgatory [eks'pə:gətəri] *adj* expurgatorio, ria.

exquisite ['ekskwizit] *adj* exquisito, ta || perfecto, ta (perfect) || delicado, da; fino, na (delicate) || MED intenso, sa (pain).
◆ *n* petimetre *m*, figurín *m*.

exquisiteness [-nis] *n* exquisitez *f* || perfección *f* || delicadeza *f* (refinement) || MED intensidad *f*.

exsanguine [eks'sæŋgwin] *adj* exangüe (bloodless) || anémico, ca (anaemic).

exscind [ek'sind] *vt* cortar, escindir.

exsert [ek'sə:t] *vt* proyectar, sacar.

exsertion [-ʃən] *n* proyección *f*.

ex-serviceman [eks'sə:vismən] *n* excombatiente *m*.
— OBSERV El plural es *ex-servicemen*.

exsiccate ['eksikeit] *vt* desecar, secar.

exsiccation [,eksi'keiʃən] *n* desecación *f*.

exsiccator ['eksikeitə*] *n* secante *m*.

extant [eks'tænt] *adj* existente.

extemporarily [iks'tempərərili] *adv* US improvisadamente.

extemporary [iks'tempərəri] *adj* improvisado, da.

extempore [eks'tempəri] *adj* improvisado, da.
◆ *adv* improvisadamente, de improviso || *to speak extempore* improvisar un discurso.

extemporization [eks,tempərai'zeiʃən] *n* improvisación *f*.

extemporize [iks'tempəraiz] *vt/vi* improvisar.

extend [iks'tend] *vt* prolongar (to lengthen); *to extend a holiday, a road* prolongar unas vacaciones, una calle || ampliar (to widen); *to extend the meaning of a word* ampliar el significado de una palabra || extender, ensanchar (to enlarge) || estirar (one's body) || MIL desplegar (troops) || aumentar (to increase) || extender, alargar (to hold out); *to extend the arm horizontally* extender el brazo horizontalmente || tender (the hand) || ofrecer (aid) || dar (welcome) || enviar (an invitation) || JUR evaluar (to assess) | embargar (to seize) || prorrogar (time limit); *to extend a note* prorrogar un pagaré || conceder; *to extend credits to s.o.* conceder créditos a alguien || llevar a la página siguiente (in bookkeeping) || desarrollar (to write out in full) || exigir el máximo esfuerzo a (to tax the strength of) || extender (one's influence, knowledge) || manifestar (sympathy) || — *to extend an invitation to* invitar a || *to extend o.s.* esforzarse, hacer esfuerzos || *to extend shorthand* transcribir taquigrafía.
◆ *vi* extenderse || prolongarse || llegar, alcanzar (to reach) || *to extend over* abarcar.

extended [-id] *adj* prolongado, da (lengthened) || extendido, da (stretched out, widespread) || alargado, da (the arm) || tendido, da (the hand) || aumentado, da (increased) || prorrogado, da (a period) || ampliado, da (enlarged in scope, etc.) || intenso, sa (an effort) || INFORM extendido, da (memory, etc.) || MIL desplegado, da (formation) | abierto, ta (order).

extended-play record [-plei'rekɔ:d] *n* maxi-single *m*.

extendible [-ibl]; **extendable** [-əbl] *adj* extensible.

extensibility [iks,tensə'biliti] *n* extensibilidad *f*.

extensible [iks'tensəbl] *adj* extensible, extensivo, va.

extensile [eks'tensai] *adj* extensible.

extension [iks'tenʃən] *n* extensión *f* (an extending or being extended) || prolongación *f* (addition); *a canal extension* la prolongación de un canal || anexo *m*; *the hotel extension* el anexo del hotel || aumento *m* (increase) || prórroga *f* (of time) || extensión *f* (phone); *put me through to extention 333* póngame con la extensión 333 || TECH larguero *m* (of table) || PHYS, MED, PHIL & GRAMM extensión *f* || vulgarización *f*, divulgación *f*, extensión *f*; *extension programme* programa de divulgación || — *by extension* por extensión || *extension ladder* escalera *f* extensible || *extension spring* muelle *m* de tracción || *extension table* mesa *f* con largueros *or* extensible.

extensive [iks'tensiv] *adj* extenso, sa (vast) || extensivo, va (farming).

extensor [iks'tensə*] *n* músculo *m* extensor.

extent [iks'tent] *n* extensión *f* (length, area) || punto *m* (degree); *to what extent is our country industrialized?* ¿hasta qué punto esta industrializado nuestro país? || alcance *m* (scope) || JUR embargo *m* || — *credit to the extent of forty pounds* crédito hasta la cantidad de cuarenta libras || *I would not go to that extent* no iría tan lejos || *the extend of the damage* la importancia de los daños || *to a certain extent* hasta cierto punto || *to a great* o *large extent* en gran parte || *to a lesser extent* en menor grado || *to such an extent* hasta tal punto || *to that extent* hasta este punto || *to the extent of* hasta el punto de || *to the full extent* en toda su extensión || *to the full extent of his power* hasta el máximo de su capacidad || *within the extent of his jurisdiction* dentro de los límites de su jurisdicción.

extenuate [eks'tenjueit] *vt* atenuar, disminuir.

extenuating [-iŋ] *adj* JUR atenuante; *extenuating circumstances* circunstancias atenuantes.

extenuation [eks,tenju'eiʃən] *n* atenuación *f*.

extenuative [eks'tenjuətiv]; **extenuatory** [eks'tenjuətəri] *adj* US atenuante.

exterior [eks'tiəriə*] *adj* exterior (outer) || MATH externo, na (angle).
◆ *n* exterior *m* (outside) || aspecto *m* (appearance).
◆ *pl* CINEM exteriores *m*.

exteriority [eks,tiəri'ɔriti] *n* exterioridad *f*.

exteriorization [eksti:əriərai'zeiʃən] *n* exteriorización *f*.

exteriorize [eks'tiəriəraiz] *vt* exteriorizar.

exterminate [iks'tə:mineit] *vt* exterminar.

exterminating [-iŋ] *adj* exterminador, ra.

extermination [iks,tə:mi'neiʃən] *n* exterminio *m*, exterminación *f*.

exterminator [iks'tə:mineitə*] *n* exterminador, ra.

extern [eks'tə:n] *n* US médico *m* externo (doctor) | externo, na (pupil).

external [eks'tə:nl] *adj* externo, na (medicine, angle); *for external use only* sólo para uso externo; *external angle* ángulo externo || exterior (situated on the outside); *external walls* murallas exteriores || exterior (foreign); *external events* asuntos exteriores || exterior (of what lies outside the mind); *external reality* realidad exterior.
◆ *n* aspecto *m* exterior, apariencia *f*.

externalization [eks,tə:nəlai'zeiʃən] *n* exteriorización *f*.

externalize [eks'tə:nəlaiz] *vt* exteriorizar.

externally [eks'tə:nəli] *adv* exteriormente.

exterritorial ['eks,teri'tɔ:riəl] *adj* extraterritorial.

exterritoriality ['eks,teri,tɔ'riæliti] *n* extraterritorialidad *f*.

extinct [iks'tiŋkt] *adj* extinto, ta; extinguido, da (race) || extinguido, da; apagado, da (fire, volcano) || *to become extinct* extinguirse.

extinction [iks'tiŋkʃən] *n* extinción *f*.

extinguish [iks'tiŋgwiʃ] *vt* extinguir (to put out) || apagar (a light, a fire, etc.) || eclipsar (to outshine completely) || extinguir, amortizar (a debt) || extinguir (to put an end to) || reducir al silencio a (to silence) || JUR abolir || FIG destruir (hope) | extinguir (family, race) | suprimir, destruir (to eliminate).

extinguishable [-əbl] *adj* extinguible.

extinguisher [-ə*] *n* extintor *m* (for putting out a fire) || apagador *m* (for putting out candles) || apagador *m* (s.o. who extinguishes).

extirpate ['ekstə:peit] *vt* extirpar.

extirpation [,ekstə:'peiʃən] *n* extirpación *f*.

extirpator ['ekstə:peitə*] *n* extirpador *m*.

extol; US **extoll** [iks'təul] *vt* ensalzar, alabar (s.o.) || encomiar, alabar (sth.).

extolling [-iŋ]; **extolment** [-mənt] *n* ensalzamiento *m*, alabanza *f*, encomio *m*, elogio *m*.

extort [iks'tɔ:t] *vt* arrancar, sacar de mala manera *or* por la fuerza (signature, promise, confession, etc.); *to extort sth. out of s.o.* sacar algo de alguien por la fuerza.

extortion [iks'tɔ:ʃən] *n* extorsión *f*, exacción *f*, concusión *f*.

extortionate [iks'tɔ:ʃnit] *adj* exorbitante, excesivo, va; desorbitado, da (price).

extortioner [iks'tɔ:ʃnə*]; **extortionist** [-ist] *n* concusionario, ria.

extra ['kstrə] *pref* extra [con el sentido de «fuera de»].

extra ['ekstrə] *adj* extra (of superior quality) || de más, de sobra; *we have two extra beds* tenemos dos camas de más || adicional, suplementario, ria (additional) || extraordinario, ria (dish) || suplementario, ria (servant) || no incluido, aparte; *singing lessons are extra* las clases de canto no están incluidas *or* son aparte || de recambio, de repuesto (part) || — *extra charge* recargo *m* || *extra fare* suplemento *m* || *extra luggage* exceso *m* de equipaje || *extra pay* paga extraordinaria || *extra postage* sobretasa *f* || SP *extra time* prórroga *f* || *extra weight* sobrecarga *f* || *extra work* horas extraordinarias.
◆ *n* recargo *m* (extra charge) || suplemento *m*, extra *m*; *to pay for the extras* pagar los suplementos || CINEM extra *m* & *f* || criado *m* suplementario (servant) || edición *f* especial (newspaper) || US repuesto *m*, recambio *m* (spare part).
◆ *adv* extraordinariamente; *extra difficult* extraordinariamente difícil || *extra good quality* de calidad extraordinaria *or* superior.

extract ['ekstrækt] *n* extracto *m*, trozo *m* (of a book) || extracto *m*, concentrado *m* (of meat, etc.) || CHEM extracto *m* || *extract from police records* certificado *m* de penales.

extract [iks'trækt] *vt* extraer, sacar; *to extract a tooth* extraer una muela; *oil is extracted from olives* el aceite se extrae de las aceitunas || sacar (passages from books, sounds) || sacar (to obtain); *did you manage to extract any information from him?* ¿conseguiste sacarle alguna información? || MATH & CHEM extraer.

extractable [iks'træktəbl]; **extractible** [iks'træktəbl] *adj* extraíble.

extraction [iks'trækʃən] *n* extracción *f* (extracting) || origen *m* (descent); *Welsh by extraction* galés de origen || *of low extraction* de baja extracción.

extractive [iks'træktiv] *adj* extractivo, va.

extractor [iks'træktə*] *n* extractor *m* (of a gun) || tenazas *f pl*, alicates *m pl* (of dentist) || *extractor fan* extractor.

extracurricular ['ekstrəkə'rikjulə] *adj* fuera del programa de estudios || extraescolar (out-of-school).

extraditable ['ekstrədaitəbl] *adj* sujeto a extradición.

extradite ['ekstrədait] *vt* conceder la extradición de, entregar (to hand over) || obtener la extradición de (to obtain).

extradition [ˌekstrə'diʃən] *n* extradición *f*.

extrados [eks'treidɔs] *n* extradós *m*, trasdós *m*.

extrajudicial ['ekstrədʒu:'diʃəl] *adj* extrajudicial.

extralegal [ekstrə'li:gəl] *adj* extralegal.

extramarital ['ekstrə'mæritəl] *adj* extramatrimonial, fuera del matrimonio.

extramural ['ekstrə'mjuərəl] *adj* situado extramuros (outside the walls) || para estudiantes libres; *extramural course* curso para estudiantes libres || de carácter privado (activities) || *extramural lecturer* profesor encargado de cursos dados fuera de la universidad.

extraneous [eks'treinjəs] *adj* extraño, ña; externo, na (coming from outside); *extraneous influences* influencias externas || ajeno a la cuestión (not belonging to the matter); *extraneous details* detalles ajenos a la cuestión.

extraordinary [iks'trɔ:dnri] *adj* extraordinario, ria; *ambassador extraordinary* embajador extraordinario; *extraordinary powers* poderes extraordinarios || extraordinario, ria (remarkable) || raro, ra (odd) || sorprendente (astonishing).

extrapolate [eks'træpəuleit] *vt* extrapolar.

extrapolation [eksˌtræpəu'leiʃən] *n* MATH extrapolación *f*.

extrasensory ['ekstrə'sənsəri] *adj* extrasensible.

extrasensory [ˌekstrə'sensəri] *adj* extrasensorial; *extrasensory perception* percepción extrasensorial.

extraterrestrial ['ekstrəti'restrjəl] *adj* extraterrestre.

extraterritorial ['ekstrəˌteri'tɔ:riəl] *adj* extraterritorial.

extrauterine [ekstrə'ju:tərain] *adj* extrauterino, na.

extravagance [iks'trævigəns]; **extravagancy** [-i] *n* despilfarro *m*, derroche *m* (of spending) || prodigalidad *f* (prodigality) || extravagancia *f* (eccentricity).

extravagancy [-i] *n* ⟶ **extravagance.**

extravagant [iks'trævigənt] *adj* despilfarrador, ra; derrochador, ra (wasteful) || pródigo, ga (lavish) || dispendioso, sa; de lujo; *extravagant tastes* gustos dispendiosos || extravagante; *extravagant language* lenguaje extravagante; *extravagant ideas* ideas extravagantes || exorbitante, desorbitado, da (price) || excesivo, va (praise).

extravaganza [eksˌtrævə'gænzə] *n* THEATR farsa *f* || MUS fantasía *f* || extravagancia *f* (in behaviour, in speech) || historia *f* extravagante.

extravasate [eks'trævəseit] *vt* extravasar.
◆ *vi* extravasarse.

extreme [iks'tri:m] *adj* extremo, ma; *extreme cold* frío extremo; *extreme right wing in politics* extrema derecha en política || excepcional, extremo, ma; *an extreme case* un caso excepcional || *extreme in one's views* de opiniones extremas.
◆ *n* extremo *m*; *he is worried to the extreme that he doesn't eat* está preocupado hasta el extremo de no comer || MATH extremo *m* || — FIG *extremes meet* los extremos se tocan || *in the extreme* extremadamente, en extremo, en sumo grado || *to carry to extremes* llevar al extremo || *to go from one extreme to the other* pasar de un extremo a otro || *to go to extremes* llegar a extremos.

extremely [-li] *adv* extremadamente, sumamente.

Extreme Unction ['ekstri:m'ʌŋkʃən] *n* REL extremaunción *f*.

extremism [iks'tri:mizəm] *n* extremismo *m*.

extremist [iks'trimist] *adj/n* extremista.

extremity [iks'tremiti] *n* extremidad *f* (the very end) || situación *f* extrema (dangerous situation) || necesidad *f* extrema, apuro *m* (necessity); *in this extremity* en semejante apuro || extremo *m*; *in the extremity of his endurance* al extremo de su resistencia || — *to be at the last extremity* estar en las últimas || *to be driven to extremity* estar en un gran apuro.
◆ *pl* extremidades *f* (furthest ends, feet and hands) || medidas *f* extremas (extreme measures).

extricable ['ekstrikəbl] *adj* solucionable.

extricate ['ekstrikeit] *vt* librar, sacar (from a difficulty) || desenredar (to disentangle) || liberar, desprender (a gas, heat) || *to extricate o.s. from* conseguir salir de.

extrication [ˌekstri'keiʃən] *n* liberación *f*.

extrinsic [eks'trinsik] *adj* extrínseco, ca.

extrorse ['extrɔ:s] *adj* BOT extrorso, sa.

extroversion [ˌekstrəu'və:ʃən] *n* extroversión *f*.

extrovert ['ekstrəuvə:t] *n* extrovertido, da.

extroverted [-id] *adj* extrovertido, da.

extrude [eks'tru:d] *vt* TECH estirar (metal) || expulsar (to force out).
◆ *vi* sobresalir.

extrusion [eks'tru:ʒən] *n* extrusión *f*, estirado *m* (of metal) || expulsión *f*.

exuberance [ig'zju:bərəns] *n* exuberancia *f*.

exuberant [ig'zju:bərənt] *adj* exuberante.

exudation [eksju:'deiʃən] *n* exudación *f*.

exude [ig'zju:d] *vt/vi* exudar, rezumar.

exult [ig'zʌlt] *vi* exultar, alegrarse mucho, regocijarse || *to exult over* triunfar sobre.

exultant [ig'zʌltənt] *adj* exultante, regocijado, da; jubiloso, sa.

exultation [ˌegzʌl'teiʃən] *n* exultación *f*, júbilo *m*, regocijo *m*.

exutory [eg'zju:təri] *n* MED exutorio *m*.

exuviae [ig'zju:vii:] *pl n* camisa *f sing*, piel *f sing* (of animals).

exuviate [ig'zju:vieit] *vt* echar.

exuviation [igˌzju:vi'eiʃən] *n* muda *f* de la piel.

ex-voto ['eks'vəutəu] *n* exvoto *m*.

eyas ['aiəs] *n* ZOOL halcón *m* niego.

eye [ai] *n* ojo *m*; *big eyes* ojos grandes || ojo *m* (of a needle) || hembra *f* de corchete (of a hook) || ojo *m* (in the handle of a tool) || ojete *m* (of a boot) || lazada *f* (of thread) || BOT yema *f*, botón *m* || ojo *m* (of bread, cheese, hurricane) || MIL diana *f* (on a target) || FIG vista *f*, visión *f*, ojo *m* (view); *he has good eyes* tiene buena vista | mirada *f* (look); *to follow with one's eyes* seguir con la mirada || ocelo *m*, ojo *m* (of a peacock's tail) || — *almond eyes* ojos achinados *or* rasgados || FIG *an eye for an eye* ojo por ojo || *as far as the eye can see* hasta donde alcanza la vista || *before my very eyes* delante de mis propios ojos (before s.o.), a ojos vistas (rapidly) || FIG & FAM *black eye* ojo a la funerala, ojo en compota | *bulging* o *protruding eye* ojo de besugo, ojo saltón || *by eye* a ojo || *electric eye* ojo eléctrico || *evil eye* mal *m* de ojo, aojamiento *m* || *eye bank* banco *m* de ojos || *eye contact* contacto *m* ocular || *eye patch* parche *m* || MIL *eyes right!* ¡vista a la derecha! || *glass eye* ojo de cristal || FIG & FAM *his eyes are bigger than his belly* llena antes los ojos que la barriga *or* que la tripa || *his eyes filled with tears* se le arrasaron los ojos en lágrimas || MAR *in the eye of the wind* contra el viento || FIG *in the eyes of* a los ojos de | *in the mind's eye* en la imaginación | *in the twinkling of an eye* en un abrir y cerrar de ojos | *it hits you in the eye* salta a la vista || FAM *it's all my eye!* ¡es puro camelo! | *keep your eyes peeled!* ¡ojo alerta! || RAD *magic eye* ojo mágico || FAM *my eye!* ¡por Dios! (astonishment), ¡ni hablar! (contradiction) || FIG *no eye like the eye of the master* el ojo del amo engorda al caballo | *not to believe one's eyes* no dar crédito a sus ojos || *not to take one's eyes off* no quitar los ojos de encima, no quitar ojo a || *pleasing to the eye* agradable a la vista || FAM *private eye* detective *m* || *saucy eyes* ojos pícaros || *slant eyes* ojos oblicuos || *sunken eyes* ojos hundidos || *tears came to his eyes* se le humedecieron los ojos || *there is more to this than meets the eye* esto tiene su intríngulis, no es tan sencillo como parecía || FIG *to be all eyes* ser todo ojos | *to be in the public eye* estar a la vista | *to be the apple of one's eye* ser la niña de los ojos de alguien || FAM *to be up to one's eyes in work* estar hasta aquí de trabajo | *to black s.o.'s eye* poner a uno un ojo a la funerala | *to bring s.o. into the public eye* dar a conocer a alguien al público | *to catch one's eye* llamar la atención a uno | *to close* o *to shut one's eyes* cerrar los ojos | *to cock one's eyes at* dirigir una mirada a (s.o.), echar un vistazo a (sth.) | *to cry one's eyes out* llorar a lágrima viva | *to fix one's eyes upon* clavar los ojos *or* la mirada en || FAM *to give s.o. a black eye* poner a uno un ojo a la funerala || FIG *to give s.o. the glad eye, to make sheep's eyes at s.o.* echar miradas cariñosas *or* miraditas a alguien, mirar con ternura a alguien | *to have a good* o *a sure* o *an accurate eye* tener buen ojo *or* ojo clínico *or* ojo de buen cubero | *to have an eye for* tener buen ojo para (to have a due sense of) | *to have an eye to* tener en cuenta | *to have eyes like a hawk* tener ojos de lince | *to have one's eyes about one* andar con cien ojos || SP *to have one's eyes on* tener el ojo acostumbrado || FIG *to have one's eyes on* echar el ojo a, tener los ojos puestos en (to watch with interest), vigilar, no perder de vista (to keep under observation) | *to have one's eyes on everything* estar en todo | *to keep an eye on* estar pendiente de, echar una mirada a; *keep an eye on the time or we will be late* estate pendiente de la hora o llegaremos tarde; no perder de vista, vigilar (to keep under observation), no quitar los ojos de encima (to watch with interest) | *to keep one's eyes open* abrir el ojo, andar ojo alerta | *to leap to the eye* saltar a los ojos | *to look a fool in s.o.'s eyes* pasar a los ojos de uno como un tonto | *to look at out of the corner of one's eye* mirar con el rabillo del ojo || *to look into s.o.'s eyes* o *face* mirar a *or* en los ojos || FIG *to make eyes at* echar miraditas a (a girl) | *to make s.o.'s eyes open* asombrar a alguien | *to open s.o.'s eyes* abrir los ojos a alguien | *to put the evil eye on* echar mal de ojo a || *to roll one's eyes* poner los ojos en blanco || *to rub one's eyes* restregarse los ojos || FIG *to run one's eye over* echar un vistazo a, recorrer con la vista | *to see eye to eye with* ver con los mismos ojos que, estar de acuerdo con | *to see with half an eye* ver a primera vista || *to set eyes on* (alcanzar a) ver || FIG *to sèt one's eye on* poner el ojo *or* los ojos en | *to sleep with one eye open* dormir con los ojos abiertos | *to the eye* por encima, a primera vista | *to turn a blind eye* cerrar los ojos, hacer la vista gorda | *to view with a jaundiced eye* mirar con ojos envidiosos | *under one's very eyes* delante de los propios ojos de uno | *with an eye to* con miras a | *with one's eyes open, closed* con los ojos abiertos, cerrados | *with the naked eye* a simple vista | *you can see it with half an eye* salta a los ojos.

eye [ai] *vt* mirar; *to eye from head to foot* mirar de pies a cabeza || FAM *to eye up* echar miraditas.

eyeball ['aibɔːl] *n* ANAT globo *m* del ojo.

eyebath ['aibɑːθ] *n* lavaojos *m inv*, ojera *f*.

eyebolt ['aibəult] *n* TECH armella *f*, cáncamo *m*.

eyebrow ['aibrau] *n* ANAT ceja *f* || *to raise one's eyebrows* arquear las cejas (showing surprise, disbelief).

eye-catcher ['aikætʃə*] *n* cosa *f* que llama la atención.

eye-catching ['aikætʃiŋ] *adj* llamativo, va.

eyecup ['aikʌp] *n* US lavaojos *m inv*, ojera *f*.

eyed [aid] *adj* de ojos; *black-eyed* de ojos negros.

eyedropper ['aidrɔpə*] *n* cuentagotas *m inv*.

eyeflap ['aiflæp] *n* anteojera *f*.

eyeful ['aiful] *n* FAM vistazo *m*; *to get an eyeful of* echar un vistazo a.

eyeglass ['aiglɑːs] *n* monóculo *m* (monocle) || lente *m* & *f* (of an optical instrument) || lavaojos *m inv*, ojera *f* (eyebath).

eyehole ['aihəul] *n* mirilla *f* (in a door) || agujero *m* (a hole) || ANAT órbita *f or* cuenca *f* del ojo.

eyelash ['ailæʃ] *n* pestaña *f*.

eyeless ['ailis] *adj* ciego, ga.

eyelet ['ailit] *n* ojete *m*.

eyelid ['ailid] *n* ANAT párpado *m* || FIG & FAM *to hang on by one's eyelids* estar pendiente de un hilo.

eyeliner ['ilainə*] *n* eyeliner *m*.

eye-opener ['ai'əupnə*] *n* sorpresa *f*.

eyepiece ['aipiːs] *n* ocular *m*.

eyeshade ['aiʃeid] *n* visera *f*.

eyeshadow ['ai'ʃædəu] *n* sombreador *m* (cosmetic).

eyeshot ['aiʃɔt] *n* vista *f*, alcance *m* de la vista.

eyesight ['aisait] *n* vista *f*.

eyesore ['aisɔː*] *n* algo que ofende la vista, monstruosidad *f*.

eyespot ['aispɔt] *n* ZOOL mancha *f* ocular.

eyestalk ['aistɔːk] *n* ZOOL pedúnculo *m*.

eyestrain ['aistrein] *n* vista *f* cansada || *to get eyestrain* tener la vista cansada.

eyetooth ['aituːθ] *n* colmillo *m* || FIG *he would give his eyetooth to go with her* daría un ojo de la cara por acompañarla.

eyewash ['aiwɔʃ] *n* colirio *m* (lotion for the eyes) || FIG tonterías *f pl*, disparates *m pl* (nonsense); *that's all eyewash* eso son disparates | música *f* celestial (drivel).

eyewater ['ai,wɔːtə*] *n* MED humor *m* ácueo.

eyewitness ['ai'witnis] *n* testigo *m* ocular.

eyot [eit] *n* GEOGR islote *m*, isla *f* pequeña.

eyrie ['aiəri] *n* aguilera *f*.

F

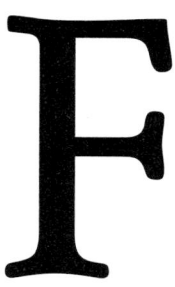

f [ef] *n* F *f* (letter) || MUS Fa *m*; *F clef* clave de fa.

fa [fɑ:] *n* MUS Fa *m* (fixed fa) | Subdominante *f* (movable).

fab [fæb] *adj* FAM estupendo, da; fabuloso, sa; macanudo, da (marvellous).

Fabian ['feibjən] *adj* contemporizador, ra || *Fabian Society* Sociedad Fabiana.

fable ['feibl] *n* fábula *f*; *the fables of La Fontaine* las fábulas de La Fontaine || FIG fábula *f*, mentira *f*, cuento *m* (falsehood) | mito *m*, fábula *f*, leyenda *f* (myth).

fable ['feibl] *vi* escribir fábulas || FIG contar fábulas *or* cuentos || *it is fabled that* se cuenta que, según la leyenda.

fabled [-d] *adj* legendario, ria (legendary) || FIG fabuloso, sa (fictious, fabulous).

fabric ['fæbrik] *n* tejido *m*, tela *f* (material) || estructura *f* (structure) || textura *f* (texture) || fábrica *f*, edificio *m* (building) || REL fábrica *f* || FIG índole *f* (kind); *people of all fabric* gente de toda índole.

fabricate ['fæbrikeit] *vt* fabricar (to construct, to manufacture) || labrar; *to fabricate steel into plates* labrar acero en chapas || FIG forjar, inventar; *to fabricate a story* forjar una historia | falsificar (evidence, documents, etc.).

fabrication [,fæbri'keiʃən] *n* fabricación *f* (construction, manufacture) || FIG mentira *f*, cuento *m*, invención *f* (lie); *the whole thing is a fabrication* todo es un cuento | falsificación *f* (of evidence).

fabricator ['fæbrikeitə*] *n* fabricante *m* || FIG mentiroso, sa; embustero, ra (liar).

fabulist ['fæbjulist] *n* fabulista *m* & *f* || FIG cuentista *m* & *f* (liar).

fabulous ['fæbjuləs] *adj* fabuloso, sa || FAM estupendo, da; fabuloso, sa; macanudo, da (marvellous).

façade [fə'sɑ:d] *n* fachada *f* || FIG fachada *f* (appearance); *the country's prosperity was nothing but a façade* la prosperidad del país era pura fachada.

face [feis] *n* cara *f*, rostro *m*; *a pretty face* una cara bonita || cara *f*, semblante *m* (countenance); *a sad face* una cara triste || FIG aspecto *m* (aspect) | cariz *m*; *the situation has taken on another face* la situación ha tomado otro cariz || mueca *f*, gesto *m* (grimace) || careta *f* (mask) || cara *f*, cara *f* dura, caradura *f*, descaro *m*, desfachatez *f* (cheek, nerve) || superficie *f* (surface) || superficie *f*, faz *f* (of the Earth) || lado *m*, cara *f* (side) || parte *f* delantera (front) || ARCH fachada *f*, frente *m* (façade) || cara *f* (of cards, coins, cliff) || esfera *f* (of clock) || recto *m* (of a sheet of paper) || derecho *m* (of cloth) || haz *f* (of leaf) || paramento *m* (of wall) || TECH cotillo *m* (of hammer) | mesa *f*, plana *f* (of an anvil) || MIN frente *m* de ataque || PRINT ojo *m* || — FAM *a face like a wet weekend* cara de viernes *or* de Cuaresma || *face down* boca abajo || *face massage* masaje *m* facial || MIL *face to* frente a, enfrente de || *face to face* cara a cara || *face up* boca arriba || FAM *I didn't do it for your pretty face* no lo hice por tu bella *or* por tu linda cara || *in the face of* frente a, ante (in the presence of), a pesar de (despite) || *I said it in his face* se lo dije en la cara || FIG *it's staring you in the face* lo tiene ante las narices (a thing), salta a la vista (a solution) | *on the face of it* o *of things* a primera vista || *the Holy Face* la Santa Faz || FIG *to do sth. until one is blue in the face* hartarse de hacer algo || *to fall flat on one's face* caerse de bruces || FIG *to fly in the face of* burlarse de (convention), hacer caso omiso de (s.o.'s rights) | *to have a face as long as a poker* tener cara de alma en pena || *to keep a straight* o *a firm face* mantenerse impávido || *to laugh in s.o.'s face* reírse en la cara de uno || *to look square in the face* mirar en los ojos, mirar fijamente || FIG *to lose face* perder prestigio, quedar mal || *to make* o *to pull a wry face* torcer el gesto || *to make* o *to pull faces* hacer muecas || *to pull a face like* poner cara de || FIG *to pull* o *to wear a long face* poner cara larga | *to put a good face on it* ponerle buena cara | *to put on a face of importance* dárselas de persona importante | *to put on a face to suit the occasion* poner cara de circunstancias | *to save face* salvar las apariencias || *to see from the look on one's face that* poder ver en la cara de alguien que || *to set face for home* dirigirse a casa || FIG *to set one's face against sth.* negarse a, oponerse firmemente a || *to show one's face* dejarse ver, aparecer || FAM *to slam the door in s.o.'s face* darle a uno con la puerta en las narices | *to slap s.o.'s face* abofetear a alguien, darle un tortazo a alguien | *to smash s.o.'s face in* romper la cara a uno || FIG *to stare death in the face* ver la muerte de cerca || *to tell s.o. to his face that* decirle a uno en la cara que | FIG *to throw sth. in s.o.'s face* echarle algo en cara a alguien || *to turn red in the face* ponerse colorado (with shame), ponerse rojo (with anger) || *unfriendly face* cara de pocos amigos || *wry face* mueca.

face [feis] *vt* mirar hacia, dar a, estar orientado hacia; *our house faces the park* nuestra casa da al parque || estar enfrente de (to be opposite) || mirar hacia (to look towards) || volver la cara hacia, mirar hacia (to turn towards); *he faced the orchestra* volvió la cara hacia la orquesta || enfrentarse con, arrostrar; *to face great danger* enfrentarse con grandes peligros; *to face the facts* enfrentarse con los hechos || hacer frente a, afrontar (a problem) || arrostrar, hacer frente a (the consequences) || enfrentarse a *or* con, hacer frente a (the enemy, a person) || hacer frente a (to stand up to) || soportar, aguantar (to stand); *I don't think I can face another week here* creo que no podré soportar otra semana aquí || presentarse ante; *he won't dare face her now* ahora no se atreverá a presentarse ante ella || volver, poner boca arriba, enseñar (cards) || forrar (in sewing) || TECH revestir (to put a new surface on) | alisar (to smoothe) || CULIN poner una capa de (caramel) || — *facing each other* uno enfrente del otro, uno frente al otro || *facing east* con orientación al este || *let's face it* hay que reconocerlo, reconozcámoslo || *the problem that faces me* el problema que se me plantea || *to be faced with a difficulty* enfrentarse con una dificultad || MIL *to face about* mandar dar media vuelta || *to face it out* mantenerse firme || *to face s.o. with* confrontar *or* carear a alguien con || *to face the music* afrontar las consecuencias || *to face the wall* ponerse de cara a la pared.

◆ *vi* dar a, mirar hacia; *my bedroom faces north* mi cuarto da al norte || volverse (to turn) || — MIL *about face!* ¡media vuelta! | *left face!* ¡media vuelta a la izquierda! || *to face about* dar media vuelta (person, soldier) || *to face on to* mirar hacia, dar a || *to face up to* enfrentarse con (danger, etc.), hacer frente a (to stand up to s.o.), soportar (to put up with) .

face ache [-eik] *n* MED neuralgia *f* facial.

face card [-kɑ:d] *n* figura *f* (in card games).

facecloth [-klɔθ] *n* guante *m*, manopla *f*, pañito *m* [para lavarse la cara] || sudario *m* (for a corpse).

face cream [-kri:m] *n* crema *f* de belleza.

face flannel [-flænl] *n* guante *m*, manopla *f*, pañito *m* [para lavarse la cara].

face-harden [-hɑ:dn] *vt* TECH cementar (metals).

faceless [-lis] *adj* sin cara || anónimo, ma.

face-lifting [-,liftiŋ] *n* MED operación *f* facial de estética, estiramiento *m* de la piel || FIG lavado *m*; *this building needs a face-lifting* este edificio necesita un lavado.

face-pack [-pæk] *n* mascarilla *f* facial.

face powder [-'paudə*] *n* polvos *m pl* para la cara.

facer [-ə*] *n* FAM bofetada *f* (blow) | lío *m*, engorro *m* (difficulty) | revés *m* (setback).

face-saving [-'seiviŋ] *adj* para salvar las apariencias.

facet ['fæsit] *n* faceta *f* (of gem, bone, eye; aspect).

facet ['fæsit] *vt* labrar en facetas (gems).

faceted [-id] *adj* labrado en facetas, con facetas.

facetiae [fə'si:ʃii:] *pl n* gracias *f*, agudezas *f* (witticisms) || libros *m* humorísticos (books).

facetious [fə'si:ʃəs] *adj* chistoso, sa; gracioso, sa; jocoso, sa.

facetiousness [-nis] *n* gracia *f*, jocosidad *f*.

face-to-face ['feistə'feis] *adv* cara a cara; *to come face-to-face with s.o.* encontrarse cara a cara con alguien.

face value [feis'vælju:] *n* valor *m* nominal (of bill, etc.) || valor *m* facial (of stamps, etc.) || *to take sth. at face value* creer algo a pie juntillas.

facia ['feiʃə] *n* letrero *m* (of a shop) || tablero *m* de mandos, salpicadero *m* (of a car).

facial ['feiʃəl] *adj* facial.

◆ *n* masaje *m* facial (massage).

facies ['feiʃii:z] *inv n* MED facies *m*.

facile ['fæsail] *adj* fácil (easy); *a facile victory* una victoria fácil || fácil; *a man with a facile tongue, pen* un hombre de palabra, de pluma fácil || vivo, va (mind) || acomodaticio, cia (easy-going) || superficial.

facilitate [fə'siliteit] *vt* facilitar; *to facilitate s.o. in sth* facilitar algo a alguien.

facility [fə'siliti] *n* facilidad *f*; *to have a facility for maths* tener facilidad para las matemáticas; *a task of incredible facility* una tarea de una facilidad increíble.
◆ *pl* facilidades *f*; *credit facilities* facilidades de crédito ‖ instalaciones *f*; *sports facilities* instalaciones deportivas ‖ *transportation facilities* medios *m* de comunicación.

facing ['feisiŋ] *n* revestimiento *m* (of a wall) ‖ guarnición *f* (decorative trimming).
◆ *pl* vueltas *f* (of a uniform).
◆ *adj* de enfrente; *on the facing wall* en la pared de enfrente.

facsimile [fæk'simili] *n* facsímil *m*, facsímile *m*.

facsimile transmission [-trænz'miʃən] *n* INFORM telecopia *f*.

fact [fækt] *n* hecho *m*; *the fact is that* el hecho es que; *it is a fact that* es un hecho que ‖ realidad *f*; *to distinguish fact from fiction* distinguir la realidad de la ficción ‖ — *accomplished fact* hecho consumado ‖ *as a matter of fact* en realidad ‖ *for a fact* seguro, con toda seguridad ‖ *in fact, in point of fact* en realidad ‖ *it's a matter of fact* es una realidad, es un hecho, es cosa probada ‖ *the fact of the matter is that* la verdad es que ‖ *the fact remains that* a pesar de todo ‖ *to know for a fact that* saber a ciencia cierta que.
◆ *pl* datos *m* (information) ‖ — *hard facts* las duras realidades de la vida ‖ FAM *the facts of life* las cosas de la vida ‖ *to stick to the facts* atenerse a los hechos.

fact-finding [-,faindiŋ] *adj* de investigación, de indagación.

faction ['fækʃən] *n* facción *f*.

factious ['fækʃəs] *adj* faccioso, sa.

factitious [fæk'tiʃəs] *adj* facticio, cia; artificial.

factor ['fæktə*] *n* factor *m*, elemento *m*; *the factors contributing to his success* los factores que contribuyen a su éxito ‖ MATH factor *m* ‖ BIOL factor *m*; *rhesus factor* factor rhesus ‖ COMM agente *m* de venta ‖ AGR administrador *m* de fincas (in Scotland) ‖ — *factor of safety* coeficiente *m* de seguridad ‖ MATH *highest common factor* máximo común divisor.

factorage [-ridʒ] *n* COMM corretaje *m*, factoría *f* (business) | comisión *f* (charges).

factorial [fæktɔ:riəl] *n* MATH factorial *f*.

factorize ['fæktəraiz] *vt* MATH descomponer en factores.

factory ['fæktəri] *n* fábrica *f*.

factory farming [-,fa:miŋ] *n* cría *f* intensiva de aves.

factory ship [-ʃip] *n* buque *m* factoría.

factotum [fæk'təutəm] *n* factótum *m*.

fact sheet ['fæktʃi:t] *n* hoja *f* informativa.

factual ['fæktʃuəl] *adj* objetivo, va (objective) ‖ basado en hechos (based on facts) ‖ real.

factuality [,fæktʃu'æləti]; **factualness** ['fæktʃuəlnəs] *n* objetividad *f*.

facula ['fækjulə] *n* ASTR fácula *f*.
— OBSERV El plural de la palabra inglesa es *faculae*.

facultative ['fækəltətiv] *adj* facultativo, va (optional) ‖ eventual.

faculty ['fækəlti] *n* facultad *f*; *the faculty of speech* la facultad de hablar ‖ facilidad *f* (*for* para), don *m* (*for* de) (gift); *he has a faculty for languages* tiene facilidad para los idiomas ‖ facultad *f* (in a university); *faculty of Law* facultad de Derecho ‖ profesorado *m*, cuerpo *m* docente, facultad *f* (teaching body) ‖ cuerpo *m* facultativo (physicians) ‖ facultad *f* (authorization).
◆ *pl* facultades *f*; *in possession of all his faculties* en posesión de todas sus facultades.

fad [fæd] *n* manía *f*, capricho *m* (whim) ‖ novedad *f*, moda *f*; *the latest fad* la última novedad.

faddish [-iʃ]; **faddist** [-ist]; **faddy** [-i] *adj* maniático, ca; caprichoso, sa (whimsical) ‖ aficionado a seguir la moda.

fade [feid] *vi* desteñirse (colours when washed) ‖ descolorarse, decolorarse (to lose colour) ‖ marchitarse (flowers) ‖ apagarse (light) ‖ desvanecerse (sound) ‖ FIG desvanecerse (pictures, memories, etc.); *my memory of those days has almost completely faded* el recuerdo de aquellos días se ha desvanecido casi totalmente | desaparecer gradualmente (to disappear gradually) | decaer (interest) | desaparecer (to vanish) | fundirse; *to fade into the distance* fundirse en la distancia ‖ — *to fade away* desvanecerse (to disappear), consumirse (to waste away) ‖ *to fade in* aparecer progresivamente (picture), subir progresivamente (sound) ‖ *to fade out* desaparecer progresivamente (picture), desvanecerse (sound).
◆ *vt* descolorar, decolorar (to discolour) ‖ desteñir (colours when washed) ‖ marchitar (flowers) ‖ — *to fade in* hacer aparecer progresivamente (picture) ‖ *to fade out* hacer desaparecer progresivamente (picture).

faded [-id] *adj* descolorido, da (dress) ‖ marchito, ta (plants).

fade-in [-in] *n* CINEM fundido *m*.

fadeless [-lis] *adj* inmarchitable, inmarcesible (plant) ‖ que no se destiñe (dress).

fade-out [-aut] *n* CINEM fundido *m*.

fading [-iŋ] *n* RAD desvanecimiento *m* de la señal, «fading» *m* ‖ CINEM *fading in, fading out* fundido *m*.

faecal ['fi:kəl] *adj* fecal.

faeces ['fi:si:z] *pl n* excrementos *m*, heces *f*.

faff [fæf] *vi* FAM no hacer nada en particular, hacer esto y lo otro; *she faffed about* o *around all day long* no hizo nada en particular en todo el día.

faery ['feiəri] *adj* de hada, de hadas ‖ FIG encantador, ra (charming) ‖ — *fairy footsteps* pasos ligeros ‖ *fairy godmother* hada madrina.
◆ *n* mundo *m* or país *m* de las hadas.

fag [fæg] *n* faena *f*, trabajo *m* penoso (tiresome job) ‖ cansancio *m* (weariness) ‖ alumno *m* que sirve a otro mayor (in school) ‖ FAM pitillo *m* (cigarette) ‖ US POP marica *m* (homosexual) ‖ *what a fag* ¡vaya faena!

fag [fæg] *vi* trabajar como un negro (to work hard) ‖ *to fag for s.o.* servir a uno (in school).
◆ *vt* cansar, fatigar (to tire) ‖ *to be fagged out* estar rendido, estar molido.

fag end [-'end] *n* sobras *f pl*, desperdicios *m pl* (leftovers) ‖ pestañas *f pl* (of cloth) ‖ FAM colilla *f* (of cigarette).

faggot; fagot ['fægət] *n* haz *m* de leña (sticks) ‖ haz *m* de barras de hierro (metal bars) ‖ haz *m*, manojo *m* (bundle) ‖ US POP marica *m* (homosexual).

faggot; fagot ['fægət] *vt* hacer manojos or haces de ‖ adornar con vainicas (in sewing).

faggoting; fagoting [-iŋ] *n* vainicas *f pl* (in sewing).

fah [fa:] *n* MUS fa *m*.

Fahrenheit thermometer ['færənhait-θə'mɔmitə*] *n* termómetro *m* de Fahrenheit.

faience [fai'ɑns] *n* loza *f* fina.

fail [feil] *n* falta *f*; *without fail* sin falta ‖ suspenso *m* (in exams).

fail [feil] *vi* fallar; *the electricity often fails in winter* la electricidad falla muchas veces en invierno; *the engine failed* el motor falló; *when all else failed he had to ask for help* cuando le falló todo tuvo que pedir ayuda ‖ dejar; *I shall not fail to tell him* no dejaré de decírselo; *don't fail to...* no deje de... (see OBSERV) ‖ fracasar, fallar (to be unsuccessful); *the experiment failed* el experimento fracasó; *the attack failed* el ataque fracasó; *his business failed* su negocio fracasó ‖ frustrarse (hopes) ‖ no conseguir, no lograr (not to succeed) ‖ fallar (to get worse); *his sight is failing* le está fallando la vista ‖ faltar; *to fail in one's duty* faltar a su deber ‖ acabarse; *when the food supplies failed* cuando se acabaron los víveres ‖ ser suspendido (in exams) ‖ decaer, debilitarse (to weaken) ‖ COMM quebrar ‖ — *a failed musician* un músico fracasado ‖ *I failed in maths* me suspendieron en matemáticas ‖ *I fail to see why* no veo por qué ‖ *I have an idea that cannot fail* tengo una idea que no puede fallar ‖ *to fail by few votes* perder por pocos votos.
◆ *vt* suspender (a pupil); *they failed me* me suspendieron ‖ no aprobar (an exam) ‖ fallar; *he failed me at the last minute* me falló en el último momento; *my strength is failing me* me están fallando las fuerzas; *his memory often fails him* su memoria le falla a menudo ‖ faltar; *words fail me to describe it* me faltan palabras para describirlo.
— OBSERV *To fail to do sth.* may often be translated into Spanish by a simple negative: *he failed to come* no vino; *he failed to answer the invitation* no contestó a la invitación.

failing [-iŋ] *n* defecto *m* (defect) ‖ falta *f* (fault) ‖ punto *f* flaco, flaqueza *f*, debilidad *f* (weakness) ‖ fracaso *m* (failure) ‖ COMM quiebra *f*.
◆ *prep* a falta de; *failing wine we all drank water* a falta de vino todos bebimos agua ‖ *failing that* de no ser posible.

faille [feil] *n* falla *f* (material).

fail-safe ['feil seif] *adj* de seguridad garantizada ‖ *fail-safe device* mecanismo *m* de seguridad.

failure ['feiljə*] *n* fracaso *m*; *the failure of the plan, of the experiment* el fracaso del proyecto, del experimento; *the play was a failure* la obra fue un fracaso; *as a doctor he is a failure* como médico es un fracaso; *his failure to make himself understood* su fracaso en hacerse comprender ‖ fallo *m* (omission, fault); *his failure to keep his promise* su fallo en cumplir su promesa ‖ fallo *m*; *engine failure* fallo en el motor ‖ avería *f* (breakdown) ‖ corte *m*, interrupción *f* (of electricity) ‖ incumplimiento *m*; *failure to pay the rent* incumplimiento en el pago del alquiler; *failure to comply with the rules* incumplimiento de las reglas ‖ suspenso *m* (in an examination) ‖ fracasado, da (person who has failed) ‖ COMM quiebra *f* (bankruptcy) ‖ MED ataque *m* ‖ — *failure to pay* falta *f* de pago ‖ *his failure to appear caused a scandal* el hecho de que no se presentase causó un escándalo ‖ *power failure* corte de corriente or de luz.

fain [fein] *adj* dispuesto, ta (willing) ‖ contento, ta (happy) ‖ forzado, da (compelled).
◆ *adv* de buena gana (willingly).

faint [-t] *adj* mareado, da; a punto de desmayarse (about to collapse); *to feel faint* estar mareado ‖ débil (weak) ‖ ligero, ra (slight); *a faint resemblance* un ligero parecido ‖ timorato, ta; temeroso, sa (timid) ‖ pálido, da; apagado, da (colour) ‖ casi imperceptible (trace) ‖ vago, ga; ligero, ra (idea) ‖ borroso, sa; indistinto, ta; *the faint outline* la silueta borrosa ‖ tenue (thin) ‖ — *not to have the faintest idea* no tener la más mínima idea ‖ *to be faint with hunger* estar muerto de hambre.
◆ *n* desmayo *m*, desfallecimiento *m* (swoon) ‖ — *to be in a faint* estar desmayado ‖ *to fall into a faint* desmayarse.

faint [feint] *vi* desmayarse, perder el conocimiento (to swoon) ‖ (ant) debilitarse (to weaken) || *to be fainting with hunger* morirse de hambre.

fainthearted [-'hɑːtid] *adj* pusilánime, medroso, sa; cobarde.

faintly ['feintli] *adv* ligeramente (slightly) || débilmente (weakly).

faintness ['feintnis] *n* debilidad *f* (weakness) || desmayo *m* (swoon) || tenuidad *f* (thinness) || palidez *f* (of a colour) || falta *f* de claridad (of an inscription).

faints; feints [feints] *pl n* alcohol *m sing* de cabeza [que se recoge en la primera y la última fase de la destilación del whisky].

fair [fɛə*] *adj* bello, lla; hermoso, sa; *a fair maiden* una hermosa doncella || rubio, bia (hair) || blanco, ca; claro, ra (complexion) || justo, ta; equitativo, va (just) || imparcial (impartial) || honrado, da; íntegro, gra (honest) || amable; *fair words* palabras amables || bueno, na (reputation) || favorable, prometedor, ra; esperanzador, ra (prospects) || favorable, bueno, na (wind) || bueno, na (weather) || razonable (price) || mediano, na; regular (middling) || acertado, da; atinado, da (comment) || limpio, pia; *fair play* juego limpio || leal, franco, ca (competition) || en limpio (copy) || bueno, na; *a fair amount of money* una buena cantidad de dinero || — *as is only fair* como es debido *or* justo || *but to be fair* pero en honor a la verdad || *fair defeat* derrota justa || FAM *fair enough!* ¡vale!, ¡muy bien! || *fair example* buen ejemplo || *fair to middling* mediano, bastante bueno || *in a fair fight* en buena lid || *it's not fair!* ¡no hay derecho! || *it's not fair on the students* es injusto para los estudiantes || *the fair sex* el bello sexo || *to be fair* hacer buen tiempo (weather) || *to be fair and square* ser honrado a carta cabal || *to be in a fair way to* estar en buen camino de || *to give s.o. a fair hearing* escuchar a uno imparcialmente || *to give s.o. fair warning* avisar a uno || *to have a fair chance of winning* tener bastantes posibilidades de ganar || *to have more than one's fair share* tener más de lo que le corresponde a uno.
◆ *adv* exactamente, justo; *it hit him fair between the eyes* le dio justo entre los ojos || amablemente (kindly) || cortésmente (politely); *to speak s.o. fair* hablar a alguien cortésmente || honradamente (honestly) || bastante, mucho (enough) || bien, correctamente (well) || en limpio (copy) || francamente (squarely) || — *to bid fair to* tener posibilidades *or* probabilidades de || *to play fair* jugar limpio.

fair [fɛə*] *n* verbena *f* (sideshows and amusements) || feria *f* (exhibition, market); *agricultural, livestock fair* feria del campo, de ganado; *trade fair* feria de muestras || *fun fair* parque *m* de atracciones.

fair copy [-'kɔpi] *n* copia *f* en limpio (of a draft, etc.) || *to make a fair copy of* poner en limpio.

fair game [-geim] *n* caza *f* legal (in hunting) || FIG presa *f* fácil; *to be fair game for pickpockets* ser presa fácil para los rateros | hazmerreír *m* (target for ridicule) || FIG *this girl is fair game* esta chica no es terreno vedado.

fairgoer [-'gəuə*] *n* feriante *m* & *f*.

fairground [-'graund] *n* parque *m* de atracciones (fun fair) || real *m* (for exhibitions and amusements) || feria *f* (for trade exhibitions).

fair-haired [-hɛəd] *adj* rubio, bia || FAM preferido, da; mimado, da; *fair-haired boy* niño mimado.

fairing ['fɛəriŋ] *n* carena *f* (aerodynamic structure).

fairish ['fɛəriʃ] *adj* FAM regular.

fairleader ['fɛə'liːdə*] *n* MAR guía *f*.

fairly ['fɛəːli] *adj* con justicia, equitativamente, imparcialmente (in an equitable manner) || honradamente (honestly) || bastante; *he plays fairly well* juega bastante bien || realmente (positively) || completamente (completely) || claramente (clearly).

fair-minded ['fɛə'maindid] *adj* imparcial, justo, ta; equitativo, va.

fairness ['fɛənis] *n* hermosura *f*, belleza *f* (beauty) || blancura *f* (of complexion) || color *m* rubio (of hair) || franqueza *f*, imparcialidad *f*, equidad *f* (justice) || claridad *f* (of weather) || lo limpio (of a copy) || *in all fairness to* para ser justo con.

fair-spoken ['fɛə'spəukən] *adj* bien hablado, da.

fair-trade ['fɛə'treid] *adj* US *fair-trade agreement* acuerdo por el cual se compromete a no vender un producto por debajo del precio fijado por el fabricante.

fairway ['fɛəwei] *n* MAR canalizo *m* || calle *f* (in golf).

fair-weather ['fɛə,weðə*] *adj* FIG *fair-weather friend* amigo *m* no dispuesto a prestar ayuda en la desgracia.

fairy ['fɛəri] *n* hada *f* (supernatural being) || US POP marica *m* (effeminate man).
◆ *adj* de hada, de hadas || FIG encantador, ra (charming) || — *fairy footsteps* pasos ligeros || *fairy godmother* hada madrina.

fairy lamps [-,læmps] *pl n* bombillas *f* de colores (for decoration).

fairyland [-lænd] *n* país *m* de las hadas || FIG lugar *m* de ensueño.

fairy lights [-,laits] *pl n* bombillas *f* de colores (for decoration).

fairy ring [-riŋ] *n* anillo *m* mágico (of a fairy) || círculo *m* oscuro de hierba (of grass).

fairy tale [-teil] *n* cuento *m* de hadas (story) || FIG cuento *m* (lie).

fait accompli ['feitækɔm'pliː] *n* hecho *m* consumado.

faith [feiθ] *n* confianza *f* (trust) || fe *f*; *religious faith* fe religiosa; *profession of faith* profesión de fe || — *in bad, in good faith* de mala, de buena fe || *in faith* en verdad || *political faith* doctrina política, credo político || *to accept* o *to take sth. on faith* creer algo || *to break faith with s.o.* faltar a la palabra dada a alguien || *to have blind faith in* tener una fe ciega en || *to have faith* o *to place one's faith in s.o., to pin one's faith on s.o.* fiarse de alguien, tener confianza *or* fe en alguien || *to have faith, to place one's faith in sth.* o *to pin one's faith on* o *to sth.* contar con algo, confiar en algo || *to keep faith with s.o.* cumplir con la palabra dada a alguien || *to plight one's faith* empeñar su palabra || (ant) *upon my faith* a fe mía || *what faith do you belong to?* ¿qué religión tiene?

faith cure [-kjuə*] *n* curación *f* por la fe.

faithful [-ful] *adj* fiel; *faithful to one's oath* fiel a su juramento; *faithful to one's friends* fiel a *or* con *or* para con sus amigos; *a faithful report of the events* un relato fiel de los acontecimientos || exacto, ta (accurate) || fidedigno, na (credible) || digno de confianza (trustworthy) || *the faithful* los fieles.

faithfully [-fuli] *adv* fielmente || fielmente, lealmente || con exactitud, fielmente (accurately) || *yours faithfully, G. Brown* le saluda atentamente, G. Brown.

faithfulness [-fulnis] *n* fidelidad *f*; *faithfulness between husband and wife* fidelidad conyugal || lealtad *f*, fidelidad *f* (loyalty) || exactitud *f* (accuracy).

faithless ['feiθlis] *adj* desleal (disloyal) || infiel; *a faithless wife* una mujer infiel || pérfido, da; traidor, ra (treacherous) || poco seguro, ra (unreliable) || inexacto, ta (inaccurate) || REL infiel, descreído, da.

faithlessness [-nis] *n* infidelidad *f* || deslealtad *f* || perfidia *f* || inexactitud *f* (inaccuracy) || REL descreimiento *m*.

fake [feik] *n* falsificación *f* || impostor, ra; *don't trust him, he is a fake* no te fíes de él, es un impostor || tongo *m* (in sports, etc.); *the fight was a fake* el combate era tongo || MAR aduja *f* (of a rope) || *this is not the genuine painting, it is a fake* este cuadro no es auténtico, es falso.
◆ *adj* falso, sa; *fake diamonds* diamantes falsos || falsificado, da (counterfeit) || fingido, da; *a fake friendship* una amistad fingida.

fake [feik] *vt/vi* falsificar (to counterfeit) || fingir, simular; *a faked reaction* una reacción fingida || adulterar (a text) || amañar (to rig a fight) || MAR adujar (a rope) || SP fintar || *to fake up* fabricar (to contrive), inventar (an excuse), falsificar (to counterfeit).

faker [-ə*] *n* impostor, ra || estafador, ra (swindler) || falsificador, ra (counterfeiter).

faking ['feikiŋ] *n* falsificación *f*; *the faking of a signature* la falsificación de una firma.

fakir ['feikiə*] *n* fakir *m*, faquir *m*.

Falange ['fælændʒ] *n* Falange *f*.

Falangist [fə'lændʒist] *adj/n* falangista.

falchion ['fɔːltʃən] *n* alfanje *m*, cimitarra *f* (sword).

falcon ['fɔːlkən] *n* halcón *m*.

falconer [-ə*] *n* halconero *m*, cetrero *m*.

falconet ['fɔːlkənet] *n* ZOOL halcón *m* de pequeño tamaño.

falconry ['fɔːlkənri] *n* cetrería *f*, halconería *f*.

faldstool ['fɔːldstuːl] *n* facistol *m*, atril *m*.

Falkland Isles ['fɔːklənd-ailz] *pl prn* GEOGR islas *f* Malvinas.

fall [fɔːl] *n* caída *f*; *he died from a fall* se murió de una caída || caída *f* (of leaves) || caída *f*, derrumbamiento *m*; *the fall of the Roman Empire* la caída del Imperio Romano || caída *f* (of a stronghold) || derrumbamiento *m* (of earth, of rocks, etc.) || caída *f* (of a skirt, etc.) || baja *f*, disminución *f* (of price, demand, temperature) || declive *m*, pendiente *f* (slope) || bajada *f* (of a theatre curtain) || FIG caída *f* (from virtue); *the fall of Adam* la caída de Adán | caída *f* (of day) | final *m* (of year, etc.) || aparejo *m* (hoisting tackle) || tira *f* (of hoisting tackle) || SP caída *f* (in wrestling) || MAR reflujo *m* (of the tide) || camada *f* (of animals) || US otoño *m* (autumn) || — *fall of snow* capa *f* de nieve (layer); *a six-inch fall of snow* una capa de nieve de seis pulgadas; nevada *f*, caída de nieve; *a heavy fall of snow* una fuerte nevada || *free fall* caída libre (of parachutist) || *in the fall of the year* a fines de año || FIG *to head* o *to ride for a fall* ir a la ruina, correr hacia un peligro.
◆ *pl* cascada *f sing*, salto *m sing* (of water) || *Niagara Falls* las cataratas del Niágara.
◆ *adj* US otoñal, del otoño.

fall* [fɔːl] *vi* caer (by force of gravity) || caer, caerse; *he fell from the horse* se cayó del caballo || bajar, descender (prices, demand) || bajar (temperature, fever, floodwater, tide, voice) || caer (skirt, curtains) || caerse, derrumbarse, desplomarse (a building) || bajar (to slope) || desembocar, ir a dar; *the Ebro falls into the Mediterranean* el Ebro desemboca en el Mediterráneo || caer (a soldier, a stronghold, a government) || amainar (the wind) || caer (night, silence, event, date) || decaer (conversation) || corresponder, tocar (privilege, task); *it fell to him to do it* le tocó a él hacerlo || tocar, caer; *the prize fell to my uncle* el premio le tocó a mi tío || caer (under s.o.'s influence, etc.); *to fall under s.o.'s power* caer bajo el dominio de alguien || recaer (accent) || dividirse; *to fall into three categories* dividirse en tres categorías || entrar; *these considerations fall under another category* estas consideraciones entran en otra categoría || decaer (to decay) || pecar, caer (to sin) || quedarse, volverse; *to fall dumb* quedarse mudo || quebrar (to go bankrupt) || dar (a shot, an arrow) || nacer (animals) || — *his face fell* puso cara larga || *his glance fell* bajó los ojos || *night was falling* anochecía || *to fall across* dar con || *to fall apart* caerse a pedazos || *to fall a prey to* caer en manos de (to fall into the hands of), ser víctima de (to be the victim of) || *to fall asleep* dormirse, quedarse dormido || FIG *to fall by the cannon* morir de un cañonazo || *to fall due* vencer (payment) || *to fall flat* fracasar (to fail), no hacer ninguna gracia (joke) || *to fall foul of* chocar con || REL *to fall from grace* perder la gracia || *to fall from one's lips* salir de la boca de uno || *to fall ill* caer enfermo || *to fall in love with* enamorarse de || *to fall in price* bajar de precio || *to fall into disrepair* deteriorarse || *to fall into disuse* caer en desuso || *to fall into line with* conformarse con (s.o.'s ideas), conformarse con las ideas de (s.o.) || *to fall into temptation* caer en la tentación || *to fall into the habit of* coger el hábito de, acostumbrarse a || *to fall short of* ser insuficiente para (to be insufficient), no alcanzar (not to reach) || *to fall short of the target* no alcanzar el blanco, no dar en el blanco (a shot) || *to fall to pieces* hacerse pedazos (to break up), caerse a pedazos (house, person), hundirse (business) || *to fall under s.o.'s competence* caer dentro de la competencia de alguien, ser de la competencia de alguien || *to fall under suspicion* hacerse sospechoso || *to fall within one's province* ser de la incumbencia de uno, incumbirle a uno || *to let fall* dejar escapar (words, secret) || FIG *you fell wide of the target* no acertaste.

◆ *phr v* FAM ***to fall about*** troncharse, partirse; *to fall about laughing* troncharse *or* partirse de risa || ***to fall away*** desaparecer (to disappear) | desprenderse (stage of rocket, loose rocks, etc.) | descender, inclinarse (to slope downwards) | hundirse (ground) | REL apostatar | MED adelgazar || — *to fall away from* abandonar || ***to fall back*** caerse de espaldas | retroceder, retirarse (to recede) | MIL replegarse || — *to fall back on* echar mano a *or* de, recurrir a; *he fell back on his savings* echó mano a sus ahorros, recurrió a sus ahorros | *to fall back on one's word* desdecirse || ***to fall behind*** retrasarse (to be behind schedule) | quedarse atrás (to be left behind) || ***to fall down*** caer | caer *or* caerse al suelo (on the ground) | postrarse, prosternarse (to prostrate o.s.) | derrumbarse (house) | ser suspendido, suspenderle a uno; *he fell down in maths* le suspendieron en matemáticas, fue suspendido en matemáticas | fallar; *to fall down on the job* fallar en el trabajo | fracasar (plan) | — *to fall down a precipice* caer en un precipicio || FAM ***to fall for*** chiflarse por, volverse loco por (to fall in love) | — *to fall for a trick* caer en la trampa | FAM *to fall for it* tragárselo (to believe), picar (to take the bait) || ***to fall in*** caerse, desplomarse (roof, walls) | hundirse (cheeks) | COMM vencer (term) | JUR expirar (lease) || MIL formar filas | — MIL *fall in!* ¡a formar1 | *to fall in with* encontrarse con (to meet), estar de acuerdo con (to agree with), aceptar (a proposal), acceder a (a request), adherirse a (an opinion) || ***to fall off*** caer | caer de, caerse de (to drop from); *a tile fell off the roof* una teja se cayó del tejado | desprenderse (to come off); *the door handle fell off* se desprendió el picaporte | caerse; *his bicycle hit a stone and he fell off* su bicicleta dio con una piedra y se cayó | bajar, disminuir (to decrease); *the demand has fallen off* la demanda ha bajado | decaer; *the tourist trade has fallen off* la industria turística ha decaído | enfriarse (zeal, interest) | empeorar (to get worse) || MAR abatir || ***to fall on*** o ***upon*** caer en (date, etc.); *his birthday falls on Saturday* su cumpleaños cae en sábado | caer sobre (enemy, food) | caer en (accent) | tocar a, corresponder a; *it fell upon me to invite him to lunch* me tocó a mí invitarle a comer | — *to fall on one's back* caerse *or* caer de espaldas || ***to fall out*** caerse (of the window, etc.) | reñir (to quarrel); *I have fallen out with him* he reñido con él | salir, resultar; *things fell out well* salieron bien las cosas | MIL romper filas; *fall out!* ¡rompan filas! | — *to fall out of the habit of* perder la costumbre de || ***to fall over*** caerse || tropezar con (an obstacle) || — *to fall over each other for sth.* disputarse algo | *to fall over o.s.* desvivirse || ***to fall through*** venirse abajo, fracasar (project, etc.) || ***to fall to*** ponerse a, empezar a (to begin) | ponerse a trabajar (to start working) | empezar a comer (to start eating) | cerrarse (to close by itself) | tocar a, corresponder a (to be the duty of) | — *to fall to one's lot* caerle en suerte a uno.

— OBSERV Pret ***fell***; pp ***fallen***.

fallacious [fəˈleiʃəs] *adj* falaz (misleading) || erróneo, a (erroneous).

fallacy [ˈfæləsi] *n* falacia *f*, sofisma *m* || idea *f* falsa *or* errónea (mistaken idea) || engaño *m* (deception).

fal-lal [ˈfælˈlæl] *n* faralá *m*.

fallback [ˈfɔːlbæk] *n* retirada *f*.

fallen [ˈfɔːlən] *pp* ⟶ **fall.**

◆ *adj* caído, da || FIG perdido, da || *the fallen* los caídos.

fall guy [ˈfɔːlgai] *n* US FAM cabeza *f* de turco (scapegoat).

fallibility [ˈfæliˈbiliti] *n* falibilidad *f*.

fallible [ˈfæləbl] *adj* falible.

falling [fɔːliŋ] *n* caída *f*.

falling away [-ˈəwei] *n* MED adelgazamiento *m* || REL apostasía *f* || FIG abandono *m* (of supporters).

falling back [-bæk] *n* MIL repliegue *m*, retirada *f*.

falling in [-in] *n* derrumbamiento *m*, hundimiento *m* (of a building) || MIL formación *f* || JUR expiración *f* || COMM vencimiento *m* (of a debt).

falling off [-ɔf] *n* COMM baja *f* (of prices) || disminución *f* (lessening) || empeoramiento *m* (worsening) || FIG defección *f*.

falling out [-aut] *n* caída *f* (of hair) || FIG enfado *m*, desacuerdo *m*.

falling sickness [-ˈsiknis] *n* MED epilepsia *f*.

falling star [-staː*] *n* estrella *f* fugaz.

Fallopian [fəˈləupiən] *adj* ANAT *Fallopian tube* trompa *f* de Falopio.

fallout [ˈfɔːlaut] *n* lluvia *f* radiactiva || *fallout shelter* refugio atómico.

fallow [ˈfæləu] *adj* AGR en barbecho; *to lie fallow* estar en barbecho || FIG inculto, ta || leonado, da (colour).

◆ *n* barbecho *m*.

fallow [ˈfæləu] *vt* AGR barbechar.

fallow deer [-diə*] *n* ZOOL gamo *m*.

false [fɔːls] *adj* falso, sa; *false accusation* acusación falsa || erróneo, a; falso, sa; *a false conclusion* una conclusión errónea || mal entendido, da; *false pride* orgullo mal entendido || postizo, za; *false teeth* dientes postizos || falso, sa (disloyal, fake); *a false friend* un falso amigo; *a false door* una puerta falsa || MUS falso, sa; desafinado, da (note) || falso, sa; forzado, da (not natural) || ANAT falso, sa; *false ribs* costillas falsas || BOT falso, sa; *false acacia* acacia falsa || — *false alarm* falsa alarma || *false bottom* doble fondo *m* || *false ceiling* cielo raso || US *false face* máscara *f* || *false imprisonment* detención ilegal || JUR *false pretences* estafa *f* || SP *false start* salida nula || *false step* paso *m* en falso || *false to the core* más falso que Judas || *to bear false witness* jurar en falso || *to sail under false colours* navegar bajo pabellón falso (a ship), atribuirse una personalidad falsa (people) || *to take a false step* dar un paso en falso.

◆ *adv* hipócritamente; *to act false* actuar hipócritamente || *to play s.o. false* traicionar a uno.

falsehearted [fɔːlsˈhɑːtid] *adj* pérfido, da; traicionero, ra.

falsehood [ˈfɔːlshud] *n* falsedad *f* (falseness) || mentira *f* (lie) || *to distinguish truth from falsehood* distinguir lo falso de lo verdadero.

falsely [fɔːlsli] *adv* falsamente, con falsedad || mal; *to interpret sth. falsely* interpretar algo mal.

falseness [ˈfɔːlsnis] *n* inexactitud *f*, falsedad *f* (lack of accuracy) || infidelidad *f* (of a lover, etc.) || perfidia *f* (wickedness) || falsedad *f* (duplicity).

falsetto [fɔːlˈsetəu] *n* MUS falsete *m*.

◆ *adj* de falsete (voice).

◆ *adv* *in falsetto* con voz de falsete.

falsies [ˈfɔlsiz] *pl n* rellenos *m* (brassière).

falsification [ˈfɔːlsifiˈkeiʃən] *n* falsificación *f* (of documents) || adulteración *f* (of wine, etc.).

falsify [ˈfɔːlsifai] *vt* falsificar (documents) || desvirtuar (to distort) || adulterar (liquor, wine) || desmentir, refutar (to prove to be false) || frustrar (hopes, etc.).

falsity [ˈfɔːlsiti] *n* falsedad *f*.

faltboat [ˈfɔːltbəut] *n* bote *m* plegable.

falter [ˈfɔːltə*] *vi* titubear, vacilar (in walking) || titubear (in speech) || quebrarse, desfallecer (voice) || vacilar (in actions) || FIG fallar; *his resolution faltered* le falló la determinación || *with faltering voice* con voz titubeante (hesitant), con voz quebrada (through emotion).

◆ *vt* decir balbuceando || *to falter out* balbucir (an excuse, etc.).

faltering [-riŋ] *adj* vacilante, titubeante.

falteringly [-riŋli] *adv* con voz titubeante (hesitantly) || con voz quebrada (from emotion) || con paso vacilante (walking).

fame [feim] *n* fama *f*, reputación *f*; *ill fame* mala fama || — *Sheffield, of stainless steel fame* Sheffield, ciudad famosa por su acero inoxidable || *to find fame* conseguir la fama, triunfar || *to rise to fame* hacerse el famoso.

famed [-d] *adj* afamado, da; famoso, sa || *she is not as beautiful as she is famed to be* no es tan hermosa como dicen.

familial [fəˈmiljəl] *adj* familiar, de familia.

familiar [fəˈmiljə*] *adj* familiar, conocido, da; *a familiar voice* una voz familiar || de todos los días (often repeated); *a familiar story* un cuento de todos los días || familiar (colloquial); *a familiar expression* una expresión familiar || íntimo, ma (friend) || — *at times his answers are too familiar* a veces contesta con demasiada confianza || *I am familiar with that* eso me es familiar, estoy familiarizado con eso, conozco bien eso || *it's the familiar story* es lo de siempre || *that sounds familiar* eso me suena || *to be on familiar terms with s.o.* tener confianza con alguien || *to get too familiar with s.o.* tomarse demasiadas confianzas con uno || *to make o.s. familiar with* familiarizarse con.

◆ *n* amigo *m* íntimo, familiar *m* (close friend) || demonio *m* familiar (spirit) || REL familiar *m*.

familiarity [fəˌmiliˈæriti] *n* familiaridad *f* (*with* con), conocimiento *m* (*with* de) || familiaridad *f*, confianza *f* (absence of formality).

◆ *pl* familiaridades *f*, confianzas *f*.

familiarize [fəˈmiljəraiz] *vt* acostumbrar, familiarizar, habituar; *to familiarize s.o. with the procedure* acostumbrar a uno al sistema || *to familiarize o.s. with* familiarizarse con.

family [ˈfæmili] *n* familia *f* || BOT, ZOOL & GRAMM familia *f* || — *his integrity runs in the fa-*

mily su integridad le viene de familia || REL *the Holy Family* la Sagrada Familia || FAM *to be in the family way* estar en estado interesante || *to be one of the family* ser como de la familia || *to have a big family* tener muchos hijos *or* mucha familia || *with one's family* en familia.
◆ *adj* familiar, de familia; *family resemblance* o *likeness* parecido de familia; *family allowance* subsidio familiar || — *family doctor* médico *m* de cabecera *or* de familia || *family man* padre *m* de familia (with a family), hombre casero (devoted to his home) || US *family name* apellido *m* (surname) || *family planning* planificación *f* familiar || *family room* cuarto *m* de estar || *family skeleton* vergüenza *f* de la familia, secreto *m* de familia || *family tree* árbol genealógico.

famine ['fæmin] *n* escasez *f* (shortage of food) || hambre *f*, inanición *f* (starvation); *to die of famine* morir de inanición || escasez *f*, carestía *f* (scarcity); *coal famine* escasez de carbón.

famish ['fæmiʃ] *vt* (ant) hacer morir de hambre, hacer padecer hambre.
◆ *vi* (ant) morirse de hambre, padecer hambre.

famished [-t] *adj* famélico, ca; muerto de hambre || FIG *to be famished* estar muerto de hambre.

famous ['feiməs] *adj* famoso, sa; célebre (renowned) || FIG & FAM fabuloso, sa; excelente, magnífico, ca; *a famous idea* una idea excelente.

famously [-li] *adv* FIG & FAM estupendamente, a las mil maravillas; *she sings famously* canta a las mil maravillas.

famulus ['fæmjuləs] *n* ayudante *m* de un mago *or* alquimista (of a sorcerer) || fámulo *m* (of a scholar).
— OBSERV El plural de *famulus* es *famuli*.

fan [fæn] *n* abanico *m*; *she hid her face behind her fan* ocultó su rostro tras el abanico || TECH ventilador *m* (mechanically operated) | paleta *f* (blade of a propeller) || AGR bieldo *m*, aventadora *f* (for winnowing) || aficionado, da; entusiasta *m* & *f*; admirador, ra (devotee) || admirador, ra (of a pop star) || SP hincha *m* & *f* || — *fan club* club *m* de admiradores || *fan heater* convector *m*, estufa *f* de aire || *fan mail* correspondencia *f* de los admiradores.

fan [fæn] *vt* abanicar (a person) || agitar (the air) || acariciar; *the breeze fanned her face* la brisa le acariciaba el rostro || avivar (with a bellows); *he took the bellows and fanned the fire* cogió el fuelle y avivó el fuego || soplar sobre (to blow on) || AGR aventar (to winnow) || abrir en abanico (cards, etc.) || TECH ventilar || FIG avivar (passion, etc.) | excitar (curiosity, etc.) || *to fan o.s.* abanicarse.
◆ *vi* abrirse en abanico; *the soldiers fanned out* los soldados se abrieron en abanico.

fanatic [fə'nætik] *adj/n* fanático, ca.

fanatical [-əl] *adj* fanático, ca.

fanaticism [fə'nætisizəm] *n* fanatismo *m*.

fanaticize [fə'nætisaiz] *vt* fanatizar.
◆ *vi* volverse fanático.

fan belt ['fænbelt] *n* AUT correa *f* del ventilador.

fancied ['fænsid] *adj* favorito, ta; preferido, da; *his fancied pupil did badly in the test* su alumno preferido hizo mal el examen || imaginario, ria; *fancied illness* enfermedad imaginaria.

fancier ['fænsiə*] *n* aficionado, da || soñador, ra (imaginer).

fanciful ['fænsiful] *adj* imaginario, ria; fantástico, ca (unreal) || extravagante (odd); *a fanciful hairstyle* un peinado extravagante || imaginativo, va; fantasioso, sa (imaginative) || caprichoso, sa (whimsical).

fancy ['fænsi] *n* fantasía *f*, imaginación *f* (imaginative faculty) || capricho *m*, antojo *m* (whim) || idea *f* || ilusión *f*, quimera *f* (delusion) || afición *f*, gusto *m*; *to take a fancy to music, to tennis* tomar afición a la música, al tenis || gusto *m* (taste); *a person of delicate fancy* una persona de gusto delicado || — *it is my fancy* o *I have a fancy that they are lovers* tengo la impresión de que son amantes || *the fancy took me to learn Chinese* se me antojó aprender chino || *to take a fancy to s.o.* tomar cariño a alguien || *to take a fancy to sth.* encapricharse por algo || *to take* o *to catch s.o.'s fancy* gustarle a uno || *what takes your fancy most?* ¿qué es lo que más te apetece?
◆ *adj* de adorno (ornamental) || de fantasía, de imitación (goods); *fancy jewels* joyas de fantasía || de lujo; *fancy shop* tienda de lujo || exorbitante, excesivo, va; *a fancy price* un precio exorbitante || elegante (elegant) || estrafalario, ria (extravagant) || US selecto, ta; fino, na (foodstuffs).

fancy ['fensi] *vt* imaginarse, imaginar (to imagine); *I can't fancy him doing that* no me lo puedo imaginar haciendo eso || suponer, creer (to suppose, to believe); *I fancy he is annoyed* supongo que se ha enfadado || tener la impresión de que, parecerle a uno (to suspect); *I fancy you are hiding sth.* tengo la impresión de que me ocultas algo, me parece que me ocultas algo || gustar; *I don't fancy the idea* no me gusta la idea; *Peter fancies Mary* a Pedro le gusta María || apetecer; *she fancies that dress* le apetece ese vestido || — *fancy!, fancy that!, just fancy!* ¡imagínate!, ¡imagínese!, ¡fíjate!, ¡fíjese!, ¡vaya! || *fancy her becoming a nun!* ¡parece mentira que se haya metido a monja! || *to fancy o.s.* ser un creído || *to fancy o.s. as* presumir de, dárselas de || *to fancy o.s. sth.* creerse *or* imaginarse algo; *she fancies herself a film star* se cree una estrella de cine.

fancy diving [-'daiviŋ] *n* saltos *m pl* acrobáticos.

fancy dress [-dres] *n* disfraz *m* || — *fancy-dress ball* baile *m* de disfraces || *in fancy dress* disfrazado, da.

fancy-free [-fri:] *adj* sin compromiso (not committed in love) || despreocupado, da (carefree).

fancy goods [-gudz] *pl n* objetos *m or* artículos *m* de fantasía.

fancy man [-mən] *n* FAM chulo *m* (pimp) | amante *m*, querido *m* (lover).

fancy woman [-'wumən] *n* FAM amante *f*, querida *f* (mistress) | mujer *f* de vida alegre (prostitute).

fancywork [-wək] *n* labor *f* (in sewing).

fandango [fæn'dæŋgəu] *n* MUS fandango *m*.

fanfare ['fænfɛə*] *n* fanfarria *f* (of trumpets, etc.).

fanfaronade [ˌfænfærə'nɑ:d] *n* fanfarronada *f*, baladronada *f*.

fang [fæŋ] *n* colmillo *m* (of tiger, of wolf, etc.) || diente *m* (of snake) || espiga *f* (of a tool) || raíz *m* (of a tooth).

fanged [-d] *adj* con colmillos.

fanlight ['fænlait] *n* ARCH montante *m* de abanico.

fanner ['fænə*] *n* AGR aventadora *f*.

fanon ['fænən] *n* REL manípulo *m*.

fan palm ['fæn-pɑ:m] *n* BOT miraguano *m*.

fantail ['fænteil] *n* cola *f* en forma de abanico (tail) || paloma *f* colipava (pigeon) || papamoscas *m inv* (flycatcher) || TECH cola *f* de milano.

fantasia [fæn'teizjə] *n* MUS fantasía *f*.

fantasize ['fætəsaiz] *vt/vi* fantasear.

fantast ['fæntæst] *n* soñador, ra.

fantastic; phantasy [fæn'tæstik] *adj* fantástico, ca; imaginario, ria (unreal) || fantástico, ca; extraño, ña (quaint).

fantasy ['fæntəsi] *n* imaginación *f*, fantasía *f* (imagination) || fantasía *f* (sth. imagined) || capricho *m* (whim) || ensueño *m* (daydream) || MUS fantasía *f*.

fan tracery ['fæntreisəri] *n* ARCH nervios *m pl* en abanico.

fan vaulting ['fænvɔ:ltiŋ] *n* ARCH bóveda *f* de abanico.

FAO *abbr of [Food and Agriculture Organization]* FAO, Organización de las Naciones Unidas para la Agricultura y la Alimentación.

far [fɑ:*] *adv* lejos; *is it far?* ¿está lejos? || mucho; *far better* mucho mejor; *far beyond* mucho más allá de; *far more* mucho más || muy; *far distant* muy distante || — *as far as* hasta; *we went as far as Guadalajara* fuimos hasta Guadalajara; que; *as far as I know, as far as I can tell* que yo sepa; por lo que; *as far as I can judge* por lo que puedo juzgar; *as far as I am concerned* por lo que a mí se refiere || FIG *as far as possible* en lo posible, en la medida de lo posible || *as far back as we can recall* hasta donde alcanza la memoria || *by far* con mucho; *he's by far the best* es con mucho el mejor || FIG *far and away* con mucho; *she is far and away the prettiest* es con mucho la más guapa || *far and near, far and wide* por todas partes || *far away* lejos || *far away from* lejos de || *far from* lejos de || FIG *far be it from to criticize* no tengo la menor intención de criticar || *far from* lejos de || *far from it* ni mucho menos || *to be far gone* estar pasado (food), estar bebido (to be drunk), estar muy mal (to be ill) || *to be far gone in* estar muy metido en (to be deeply involved in) || *to be too far gone* estar demasiado avanzado (disease, illness, etc.) || *far into the night* hasta muy avanzada la noche, hasta muy tarde (very late) || *far off* lejos (distant), a lo lejos (in the distance) || *far too much* demasiado || *from far off* desde lejos, de lejos || *having reached this far* a estas alturas || *how far can he be trusted?* ¿hasta qué punto se puede uno fiar de él? || *how far have you got?* ¿hasta dónde *or* hasta qué punto han llegado? || *how far is it to Madrid?* ¿cuánto hay de aquí a Madrid? || *in so far as* en la medida en que || FIG *she's not far off sixty* tiene casi sesenta años | *she wasn't far from tears* estaba al borde de las lágrimas, estaba a punto de llorar || *so far* tan lejos; *I didn't know he travelled so far* no sabía que había viajado tan lejos; hasta ahora; *so far so good* hasta ahora todo va bien; hasta aquí *or* allí (up to here or there) || *so far this month* en lo que va de mes || FIG *that's as far as I'll go* de allí no paso | *that's going too far!* ¡esto es demasiado!, ¡es el colmo! || *thus far* hasta ahora (until now), hasta aquí *or* allí (up to here or there) || *to carry far* oírse de lejos (voice, etc.) || FIG *to carry sth. too far* llevar algo demasiado lejos *or* al extremo || *to go far* llegar lejos; *this boy will go far* este muchacho llegará lejos; tener valor, servir para mucho; *money doesn't go far these days* actualmente el dinero tiene poco valor; cundir (mucho); *this box of soap goes far* este paquete de jabón cunde mucho; ir lejos, exagerar (to exaggerate); *that's going a bit far* eso es ir un poco lejos || *to go far into the desert* adentrarse mucho en el desierto || FIG *to go far towards* contribuir mucho a | *to go so far as to say, as to call, etc.* llegar a decir, a llamar, etc. | *to go too far* ir demasiado lejos, pasarse de la raya | *to push s.o. too far* sacarle a uno de sus casillas | *you weren't far out* casi aciertas.
◆ *adj* lejano, na; distante, remoto, ta (distant) || largo, ga (long); *a far journey* un viaje largo || otro, otra; opuesto, ta (other, opposite); *at the far end* en el otro extremo; *on the far bank* en la orilla opuesta.

farad ['færəd] *n* ELECTR faradio *m*, farad *m*.

faraday ['færədi] *n* ELECTR & CHEM faraday *m*.

faradic [,færə'dik] *adj* ELECTR farádico, ca.

faraway ['fɑːrəwei] *adj* remoto, ta; lejano, na; *faraway parts of the world* las zonas lejanas de la Tierra || FIG ausente, perdido, da; *he has a faraway look in his eyes* tiene la mirada perdida.

farce [fɑːs] *n* THEATR farsa *f* || FIG farsa *f*; *the trial was a farce* el proceso fue una farsa || CULIN relleno *m*.

farce [fɑːs] *vt* CULIN rellenar || FIG rellenar.

farceur [fɑː'səː*] *n* bromista *m* (joker) || farsante *m* (actor).

farcical ['fɑːsikəl] *adj* absurdo, da; ridículo, la; grotesco, ca; *farcical situation* situación ridícula || divertido, da (funny).

farcicality [-iti] *n* ridiculez *f*.

farcy ['fɑːsi] *n* VET muermo *m*.

fare [fɛə*] *n* precio *m* del billete *or* del recorrido *or* del viaje, tarifa *f* (in public transport) || billete *m* (ticket) || pasaje *m* (in a boat) || pasajero, ra; viajero, ra (passenger) || viajero, ra (in a bus) || cliente *m* & *f* (in a taxi) || comida *f* (food) || — *excess fare* suplemento *m* || *fares please!* ¡billetes por favor! || *how much is the fare to Madrid?* ¿cuánto es el billete para Madrid?, ¿cuánto cuesta el viaje a Madrid? || *minimum fare* bajada *f* de bandera (in a taxi).

fare [fɛə*] *vi* viajar (to travel) || irle a uno; *how did you fare in London?* ¿cómo te ha ido en Londres?, ¿qué tal te fue en Londres? || comer (to eat) || — *to fare alike* correr la misma suerte || *to fare forth* irse, ponerse en camino || *to fare well* irle bien a uno (to do well), comer bien (to eat well).

Far East ['fɑː'iːst] *pr n* GEOGR Extremo Oriente *m*, Lejano Oriente *m*.

fare stage ['fɛə* steidʒ] *n* sección (of bus).

farewell ['fɛə'wel] *interj* ¡adiós!, ¡vaya con Dios!

◆ *n* adiós *m*; *to say farewell* decir adiós || *to bid farewell to, to take one's farewell of* despedirse de.

◆ *adj* de despedida; *a farewell party* una fiesta de despedida.

farfetched ['fɑː'fetʃt] *adj* inverosímil (not plausible) || exagerado, da (exaggerated) || rebuscado, da (complicated) || traído por los cabellos (forced).

far-flung ['fɑː'flʌŋ] *adj* extenso, sa (of huge extent) || remoto, ta (remote).

farina [fə'rainə] *n* harina *f* (flour) || fécula *f* (of potatoes) || almidón *m* (starch).

farinaceous [,færi'neiʃəs] *adj* farináceo, a.

farinose ['færinəus] *adj* harinoso, sa || BOT farináceo, a.

farm [fɑːm] *n* granja *f*, finca *f* [AMER hacienda *f*] (for cultivation or animal breeding) || criadero *m* (of oysters, fish, mink, etc.).

◆ *adj* agrícola, del campo; *farm labour* trabajo agrícola; *farm products* productos agrícolas.

farm [fɑːm] *vt* cultivar, labrar (to till) || *to farm out* arrendar (to let), mandar hacer fuera [de una fábrica u oficina] (work).

◆ *vi* cultivar la tierra (to till) || ser agricultor (to be a farmer).

farmer [-ə*] *n* agricultor *m*, cultivador *m* || granjero, ra [AMER hacendado *m*] (farm owner) || campesino, na (peasant).

farmhand ['fɑːmhænd] *n* mozo *m* de labranza, peón *m*, trabajador *m* agrícola *or* del campo.

farmhouse ['fɑːmhaus] *n* granja *f*, finca *f*, alquería *f* [AMER hacienda *f*].

farming ['fɑːmiŋ] *n* labranza *f*, cultivo *m* (till) || agricultura *f* (agriculture) || cría *f* (of animals).

◆ *adj* agrícola; *farming country* país agrícola; *farming year* campaña agrícola.

farm labourer; US **farm laborer** ['fɑːmleibərə*] *n* trabajador *m* agrícola *or* del campo, peón *m*.

farmland ['fɑːmlænd] *n* tierras *f pl* de labrantío.

farmstead ['fɑːmsted] *n* granja *f*, finca *f*.

farmyard ['fɑːmjɑːd] *n* corral *m*.

far-off ['fɑːrɔf] *adj* remoto, ta (in time and space).

farrago [fə'rɑːgəu] *n* fárrago *m*.

— OBSERV El plural de la palabra inglesa es *farragoes*.

far-reaching ['fɑːriːtʃiŋ] *adj* de mucho alcance, trascendental; *far-reaching consequences* consecuencias trascendentales.

farrier ['færiə*] *n* herrador *m* (smith) || veterinario *m* (veterinary).

farrow ['fɑrəu] *n* lechigada *f* de cerdos (litter of pigs) || parto *m* (giving birth to pigs).

farrow ['færəu] *vt/vi* parir (a sow).

farseeing ['fɑː'siːiŋ] *adj* prudente, precavido, da; previsor, ra; *farseeing measures* medidas prudentes || perspicaz (perspicacious).

farsighted ['fɑːsaitid] *adj* MED hipermétrope || perspicaz, clarividente (having foresight) || prudente, precavido, da (cautious).

farsightedly [-li] *adv* con perspicacia, con clarividencia.

farsightedness [-nis] *n* perspicacia *f*, clarividencia *f* (foresight) || prudencia *f* (cautiousness) || MED hipermetropía *f*.

fart [fɑːt] *n* POP pedo *m*.

fart [fɑːt] *vi* POP peerse, echarse un pedo.

farther ['fɑːθə*] *adj* más lejano, na (in space or time).

◆ *adv* más lejos (in space) || más adelante (in time) || más (to a greater degree); *farther on* más adelante || además (moreover) || *to get farther and farther away from* alejarse cada vez más de.

— OBSERV *Farther* es el comparativo de *far*.

farthermost [-məust] *adj* más lejano, na.

farthest ['fɑːðist] *adj* más lejano, na (most distant) || más largo, ga (longest).

◆ *adv* más lejos.

— OBSERV *Farthest* es el superlativo de *far*.

farthing ['fɑːðiŋ] *n* cuarto *m* de penique (old coin) || FAM bledo *m*, comino *m*; *I don't care a farthing* me importa un bledo || FAM *that's not worth a brass farthing* no vale un real *or* un comino.

farthingale [-geil] *n* verdugado *m*, guardainfante *m*, miriñaque *m* (type of petticoat).

fascia ['feiʃə] *n* faja *f* (band) || MED venda *f*, vendaje *m* || ASTR banda *f* or anillo *m* que rodea un planeta || ARCH faja *f* || AUT salpicadero *m*, tablero *m* de mandos (dashboard).

fasciate ['fæʃiit] *adj* MED vendado, da || ZOOL rayado, da; listado, da (striped).

fascicle ['fæsikl] *n* fascículo *m* (of fibres, of nerves) || BOT fascículo *m* || ramo *m* (of flowers) || fascículo *m* (of a publication).

fascicule ['fæsikjuːl]; **fasciculus** [-əs] *n* fascículo *m* (of a book) || ANAT fascículo *m*.

— OBSERV El plural de *fasciculus* es *fasciculi*.

fascinate ['fæsineit] *vt* fascinar.

fascinating [-iŋ] *adj* fascinante, fascinador, ra.

fascination [,fæsi'neiʃən] *n* fascinación *f*, hechizo *m* (fascinating) || encanto *m*, atractivo *m* (charm).

fascine [fæ'siːn] *n* MIL fajina *f*.

Fascism ['fæʃizəm] *n* fascismo *m*.

Fascist ['fæʃist] *adj/n* fascista.

Fascistic [fæ'ʃistik] *adj* fascista.

fashion ['fæʃən] *n* manera *f*, modo *m*; *that is his fashion of doing things* es su modo de hacer las cosas || moda *f* (of dresses, of suits); *what will the fashion be this year?* ¿cuál será la moda de este año? || elegancia *f*, distinción *f* (elegance) || costumbre *f* (custom) || — *after a fashion* en cierto modo (in a manner), más o menos (somehow), hasta cierto punto (to some extent) || *after the fashion of* a imitación de, a la manera de || FAM *all the fashion* muy de moda || *fashion magazine* revista *f* de modas || *in fashion* de moda || *in one's own fashion* a su estilo || *in the Paris fashion* a la moda de París || *in the Spanish fashion* a la española || *it is not her fashion to act like that* no acostumbra obrar así || *out of fashion* pasado de moda || *to be in fashion* estar de moda, estilarse || *to come into fashion* ponerse de moda || *to dress in the latest fashion* vestirse a la última moda || *to go out of fashion* dictar la moda || *to speak a language after a fashion* chapurrear un idioma || *woman of fashion* mujer elegante *or* distinguida.

fashion ['fæʃən] *vt* moldear (to mould) || hacer; *to fashion a whistle from a piece of wood* hacer un silbato con un trozo de madera || labrar (to work) || forjar (to forge) || formar (to shape) || adaptar, ajustar (to fit).

fashionable [-əbl] *adj* de moda; *a fashionable dress, painter* un traje, un pintor de moda; *it's fashionable to go to Saint Tropez* está de moda ir a Saint Tropez || elegante; *fashionable summer resort* lugar elegante de verano.

◆ *n* persona *f* elegante.

fashionably [-əbli] *adv* a la moda, elegantemente.

fashion model [-'mɔdl] *n* modelo *m* & *f*.

fashion parade [pə'reid]; **fashion show** [-ʃəu] *n* desfile *m* de modas *or* de modelos, presentación *f* de modelos.

fashion plate [-pleit] *n* figurín *m* (picture) || FIG figurín *m* | mujer *f* esclava de la moda (woman).

fashion show [-ʃəu] *n* → **fashion parade**.

fast [fɑːst] *adj* rápido, da; veloz; *fast runner* corredor veloz || rápido, da; *a fast road* una carretera rápida; *fast train* tren rápido || ligero, ra; ágil; *fast steed* corcel ligero || adelantado, da (a watch); *your watch is ten minutes fast* su reloj está diez minutos adelantado || sólido, da; inalterable; *fast colours* colores sólidos || indeleble (indelible) || resistente a; *acid-fast* resistente a los ácidos || atascado, da (in mud) || fiel, constante, seguro, ra; *a fast friend* un amigo fiel || cerrado, da (closed) || encajado, da; atrancado, da (door, drawer) || seguro, ra; firme, estable (fixed, securely) || ajetreado, da (active); *to live a fast life* llevar una vida ajetreada || disoluto, ta (dissolute) || PHOT rápido, da || SP seco y firme (pitch) || — *fast money* dinero que se gana rápidamente || FIG *fast woman* mujer fresca || *to make fast* sujetar (to fix), atar (to tie), amarrar (a boat) || FIG & FAM *to pull a fast one on s.o.* jugar una mala jugada *or* pasada a alguien.

◆ *adv* rápidamente, de prisa; *don't speak so fast* no hables tan rápidamente || firmemente (firmly, securely) || profundamente, completamente (thoroughly) || (ant) cerca (near) || — *hold fast!* ¡agarraos! (hold tight), ¡para! (stop), ¡alto! (halt) || *not so fast!* ¡un momento!, ¡más despacio! || *to be fast asleep* estar profundamente dormido || *to be stuck fast* estar completamente atascado (in mud), estar completamente encajado (a door, etc.) || *to hold fast* no deshacerse (a knot, etc.), agarrarse bien (a person) || FIG *to hold fast to* mantenerse firme en (an argument) | *to play fast and loose with*

jugar con (s.o.'s affections, s.o.) || *to rain fast* llover a cántaros || *to run fast* correr rápidamente (s.o.), adelantar (a watch) || *to stand fast* mantenerse firme (to be firm).
◆ *n* ayuno *m*; *fast day* día de ayuno; *to break one's fast* romper el ayuno || MAR amarra *f* (rope).

fast [gfɑːst] *vi* ayunar.

fastback [-bæk] *n* AUT coche *m* de forma aerodinámica.

fasten ['fɑːsen] *vt* sujetar (to attach); *he fastened two sheets of paper with a clip* sujetó dos hojas de papel con un clip || fijar (to fix) || pegar (with paste) || abrochar; *she fastens her dress at the back* se abrocha el vestido por detrás || atar (parcels, bundles, shoelaces) || amarrar (a boat) || cerrar (to shut) || encerrar (to enclose) || FIG fijar, clavar (one's eyes) | atribuir (responsibility) | echar, achacar; *to fasten the blame on s.o.* echar la culpa a alguien.
◆ *vi* agarrarse, sujetarse; *I fastened on to the handrail* me agarré al pasamano || fijarse (one's attention, one's eyes, etc.) || cerrarse (door, window, box, etc.) || abrocharse (garment) | *to fasten on to an idea* aferrarse a una idea || *to fasten on to a pretext* valerse de un pretexto || *to fasten on to s.o.* pegarse a uno (to stick to), fijarse en uno (to stare at).

fastener [-ə*] *n* cierre *m* (of a box, of a window) || corchete *m* (of a dress) || cremallera *f* (zip) || cerrojo *m* (of a door) || clip *m*, sujetador *m*, sujetapapeles *m inv* (for papers).

fastening [-iŋ] *n* fijación *f* || abrochamiento *m* (of a garment) || cierre *m* (of a box, of a window) || corchete *m* (of a dress) || cremallera *f* (zip) || cerrojo *m* (of a door) || clip *m*, sujetador *m*, sujetapapeles *m inv* (for papers).
◆ *pl* TECH piezas *f* de unión.

fast food *n* comida *f* rápida (snack) || hamburguesería *f*, fast-food *m* (restaurant).

fastidious [fəs'tidiəs] *adj* melindroso, sa; delicado, da (about food, about lodgings, etc.) || quisquilloso, sa; *the boss is very fastidious when he checks the reports* el jefe es muy quisquilloso cuando revisa los informes || exigente (demanding).
— OBSERV La palabra *fastidioso* corresponde a *tedious, annoying* o *irksome*.

fastidiousness [-nis] *n* melindre *m*, delicadeza *f* excesiva.

fastness ['fɑːstnis] *n* firmeza *f* (firmness) || solidez *f* (of dyes) || rapidez *f* (speed) || fortaleza *f* (stronghold) || adelanto *m* (of a watch) || constancia *f* (of friendship).

fat [fæt] *adj* grueso, sa; gordo, da; obeso, sa (persons) || que tiene mucha grasa (meat) || grasiento, ta (greasy) || fértil, feraz (land) || cebado, da (animal for slaughter) || FAM lucrativo, va (job, position, etc.) || FIG muy hermoso, sa (bank account) | repleto, ta (purse) | grande, pingüe; *a fat profit* un gran beneficio | torpe (dull) || — FIG & FAM *a fat chance he has!* ¡ni soñarlo! | *a fat lot I care!* ¡me importa un pepino! | *a fat lot of good* o *use that was* pues sí que ha valido de mucho | *a fat lot of work you have done this morning!* ¡pues sí que has hecho mucho trabajo esta mañana! || *to grow fat* engordar.
◆ *n* grasa *f*, carnes *f pl* (of a fat person) || gordo *m*, grasa *f*; *this meat has a lot of fat* esta carne tiene mucho gordo || CULIN manteca *f* de cerdo (lard) || sebo *m*, grasa *f* (grease) || CHEM grasa *f* || — FIG & FAM *the fat is in the fire* se va a armar la gorda | *to chew the fat* estar de palique | *to live on the fat of the land* vivir a cuerpo de rey.

fat [fæt] *vt/vi* —→ **fatten.**

fatal ['feitl] *adj* mortal (accident) || fatal, funesto, ta (very serious); *his death had fatal consequences* su muerte tuvo consecuencias funestas || fatídico, ca; *the fatal day arrived for David to take a decision* llegó para David el día fatídico de tomar una decisión || *the fatal sisters* las Parcas.

fatalism ['feitəlizəm] *n* fatalismo *m*.

fatalist ['feitəlist] *n* fatalista *m* & *f*.

fatalistic [,feitə'listik] *adj* fatalista.

fatality [fə'tæliti] *n* calamidad *f*, desgracia *f*; *floods, earthquakes and other fatalities* inundaciones, terremotos y otras calamidades || muerte *f* (death) || muerto, ta; víctima *f* (in accidents, wars, etc.) || fatalidad *f*; *the fatality that marked his family* la fatalidad que pesó sobre su familia.

fatally ['feitəli] *adv* fatalmente (by destiny) || mortalmente (mortally).

fate [feit] *n* destino *m*, suerte *f*; *fate stepped in and prevented our meeting* el destino se interpuso e impidió nuestro encuentro || muerte *f* (death); *on the 12th of May he met his fate* el 12 de mayo encontró la muerte || *we cannot tell what fate has in store for us* no podemos saber lo que la suerte nos va a deparar.

fate [feit] *vt* predestinar || condenar; *fated to fail* condenado al fracaso || *it is fated that* está escrito que, es inevitable que.

fateful ['feitful] *adj* profético, ca || decisivo, va (decisive) || fatal (inevitable) || fatídico, ca.

Fates [feits] *pl prn* MYTH Parcas *f*.

fathead ['fæthed] *n* FAM imbécil *m* & *f*, tonto, ta.

father ['fɑːðə*] *n* padre *m* || REL padre *m*; *Father Bartolomé de las Casas* el Padre Bartolomé de las Casas || padre *m* de familia (civil status) || — FIG *a miserly father makes a lavish son* a padre ganador, hijo gastador || *conscript father* padre conscripto || *Father Christmas* Papá Noel || *father confessor* padre espiritual || *foster father* padre nutricio || *from father to son* de padres a hijos || *God the Father* Dios Padre || *Heavenly Father* Padre Eterno || FIG *like father like son* de tal palo, tal astilla || *Our Father* Padre Nuestro *m*, Padrenuestro *m* (prayer) || *the Holy Father* el Santo Padre, el Padre Santo (the pope) || *the Fathers of the Christian Church* los (Santos) Padres de la Iglesia || FIG *to be a father to* ser un padre para | *to be the father of* ser el autor de (bill, resolution, etc.).

father ['fɑːðə*] *vt* engendrar (to create) || FIG ser el autor de (to be the author of) | patrocinar (to support) | ser el padre de; *he is the father of modern astronomy* es el padre de la astronomía moderna | atribuir (to attribute).

fatherhood [-hud] *n* paternidad *f*.

father-in-law [-riŋlɔː] *n* suegro *m*, padre *m* político.

fatherland [-lænd] *n* patria *f*, madre *f* patria.

fatherless [-lis] *adj* huérfano de padre (orphan) || sin padre (bastard).

fatherly [-li] *adj* paternal, paterno, na; de padre (of the father); *fatherly duties* deberes paternos || paternal; *in a fatherly tone* con un tono paternal.
◆ *adv* paternalmente.

fathom ['fæðəm] *n* MAR braza *f* (measure, depth) || MAR *fathom line* sonda *f*.

fathom ['fæðəm] *vt* sondar, sondear (water depth) || FIG comprender, entender; *I can't fathom this theory* no puedo comprender esta teoría | desentrañar (to unravel a mystery) | penetrar en (to penetrate).

fathomless [-lis] *adj* insondable; *fathomless pit* pozo insondable || FIG insondable; *fathomless mysteries* misterios insondables | impenetrable.

fatidical [fə'tidicəl] *adj* fatídico, ca.

fatigue [fə'tiːg] *n* cansancio *m*, fatiga *f* (weariness) || fatiga *f* (of metals) || MIL fajina *f*, faena *f* || — MIL *fatigue dress* traje *m* de fajina | *fatigue party, fatigue detail* destacamento *m* de fajina.
◆ *pl* MIL traje *m* de fajina.

fatigue [fə'tiːg] *vt* fatigar, cansar (to tire out).

fatiguing [-iŋ] *adj* fatigoso, sa; agotador, ra.

fatless ['fætləs] *adj* sin grasa (food).

fatling ['fætliŋ] *n* cebón *m*.

fatness ['fætnis] *n* gordura *f* (of a person) || FIG fertilidad *f*, feracidad *f* (of land).

fatten ['fætn] ; **fat** [fæt] *vt* cebar, engordar (an animal) || enriquecer, abonar, fertilizar (soil) || FAM engordar (a person) || *to fatten up* cebar, engordar (an animal), engordar (a person).
◆ *vi* engordar (to grow fat).

fattening [-iŋ] *adj* que engorda.
◆ *n* engorde *m*, ceba *f* || *fattening animals* animales *m pl* de engorde.

fattish ['fætiʃ] *adj* FAM regordete, ta; gordinflón, ona.

fatty ['fæti] *adj* ANAT adiposo, sa (tissue, degeneration) || graso, sa; *fatty acid* ácido graso.
◆ *n* FAM gordinflón, ona (person).

fatuitous [fə'tjuitəs] *adj* fatuo, tua; necio, cia.

fatuity [fə'tjuːiti] *n* fatuidad *f*, necedad *f*.

fatuous ['fætjuəs] *adj* fatuo, tua; necio, cia.

fatuousness [-nis] *n* fatuidad *f*.

faucal [ixfɔːkəl] *adj* gutural.

fauces ['fɔːsiːz] *pl n* ANAT fauces *f*.

faucet ['fɔːsit] *n* US grifo *m* (tap) | espita *f* (of a barrel).

faugh [fɔː] *interj* ¡fu!

fault [fɔːlt] *n* culpa *f*; *it is your fault* es tu culpa, es culpa tuya; *whose fault is it?* ¿quién tiene la culpa? || defecto *m*, imperfección *f*; *she loves me in spite of all my faults* me quiere a pesar de todos mis defectos || defecto *m* (of material, of metals, etc.) || GEOL falla *f* || SP falta *f* (in tennis) || error *m*, falta *f*; *an essay with numerous faults of syntax* una redacción con muchos errores de sintaxis || pérdida *f* del rastro (in hunting) || TECH avería *f* (breakdown) || (ant) falta *f*, carencia *f* (lack) || — *John was at fault in the accident* Juan tuvo la culpa del accidente || *to a fault* excesivamente || *to catch s.o. in fault* coger a uno en falta || *to find fault with s.o., sth.* criticar a alguien, algo || *your memory is at fault* usted recuerda mal || *you were at fault in not warning me* hizo mal en no avisarme.

fault [fɔːlt] *vt* criticar; *you can't fault him in matters of grammar* no le puedes criticar en cuestiones de gramática || GEOL provocar una falla en.
◆ *vi* GEOL tener una falla.

faultfinder [-,faində*] *n* criticón, ona.

faultfinding [-,faindiŋ] *n* crítica *f* || *faultfinding is his favourite pastime* su afición favorita es criticar.
◆ *adj* criticón, ona.

faultiness ['fɔːltinis] *n* imperfección *f*.

faultless ['fɔːltlis] *adj* intachable, perfecto, ta (irreproachable) || perfecto, ta; sin defecto; *a faultless diamond* un diamante sin defecto.

faulty ['fɔːlti] *adj* malo, la; *faulty excuse* excusa mala || erróneo, a (mistaken) || defectuoso, sa (machine) || imperfecto, ta.

faun [fɔːn] *n* MYTH fauno *m*.

fauna ['fɔːnə] *n* ZOOL fauna *f*.
— OBSERV El plural de la palabra inglesa es *faunas* o *faunae*.

Faust [faust] *pr n* Fausto *m*.

fauvism ['fəuvizəm] *n* fauvismo *m* (a movement in painting).

faux-bourdon ['fəubuː'doŋ] *n* MUS fabordón *m*.

faux pas ['fəu'pɑː] *n* metedura *f* de pata (social blunder).

favor ['feivə*] *n/vt* US → **favour.**

favorable ['feivərəbl] *adj* US → **favourable.**

favored ['feivərəd] *adj* US → **favoured.**

favorite ['feivərit] *adj/n* US → **favourite.**

favorite son [-sʌn] *n* US hijo *m* predilecto (famous man) | candidato *m* predilecto.

favoritism [-izəm] *n* US → **favouritism.**

favour; US **favor** ['feivə*] *n* favor *m; to do s.o. a favour* hacerle a alguien un favor; *to ask a favour of* pedir un favor a || favoritismo *m* (partiality) || favor *m* (advantage); *two points in our favour* dos puntos a nuestro favor || COMM carta *f*, atenta *f; your favour of the third inst.* su atenta del tres del corriente || favor *m; to seek the favour of the king* buscar el favor del rey || obsequio *m* (gift); *party favours* obsequios dados en una fiesta || permiso *m* (permission); *by your favour* con su permiso || favor *m* (ribbon) || favor *m* (of a woman) || — *to be in favour* estar de moda (to be fashionable), ser apreciado (to be popular) || *to be in favour of s.o., of sth.* estar a favor de alguien, de algo || *to be in favour with s.o., in s.o.'s favour* gozar del favor *or* de la protección de alguien || *to be out of favour* no estar de moda (unfashionable), dejar de ser apreciado (to be no longer popular) || *to be out of favour with s.o.* haber perdido el favor de alguien, haber caído en desgracia con alguien || *to fall out of favour with s.o.* perder el favor de alguien, caer en desgracia con alguien || *to find favour in s.o.'s eyes, to find favour with s.o.* ganarse el favor de alguien, gustarle a uno || *to look on s.o.* o *on sth. with favour* mirar a alguien, algo con buenos ojos || *under favour of the night* al amparo de la noche || *with favour* favorablemente (favourably).

favour ['feivə*] *vt* favorecer; *fortune favours the brave* la fortuna favorece a los valientes; *this reform favours injustice* esta reforma favorece las injusticias || favorecer; *blue favours you* el azul te favorece || estar a favor de (to approve); *the senator favours his appointment* el senador está a favor de su nombramiento || apoyar (to support) || preferir (to prefer) || ser favorable a (to be favourable) || obsequiar (to give a present) || dotar (with intelligence, etc.) || parecerse a (to resemble); *she favours her mother* se parece a su madre || — *most favoured nation clause* cláusula *f* de la nación más favorecida || *to favour s.o. with a visit* honrar a alguien con una visita.

favourable; US **favorable** ['feivərəbl] *adj* favorable || favorable, propicio, cia (conditions).

favoured; US **favored** ['feivəd] *adj* favorecido, da || predilecto, ta; preferido, da; favorito, ta (favourite).

favourite; US **favorite** ['feivərit] *adj* favorito, ta; preferido, da; predilecto, ta.
◆ *n* favorito, ta || favorito *m*, valido *m*, privado *m* (of a king, etc.) || querida *f* (mistress) || SP favorito, ta.

favouritism; US **favoritism** [-izəm] *n* favoritismo *m*.

favus ['feivəs] *n* MED favo *m*.

fawn [fɔːn] *n* ZOOL cervato *m*.
◆ *adj* color de gamuza.

fawn [fɔːn] *vi* hacer fiestas (a dog) || parir (to give birth to a fawn) || *to fawn on* o *upon* adular.

fawning [-iŋ] *adj* adulador, ra; servil.
◆ *n* adulación *f*, servilismo *m*.

fax [fɔks] *n* fax *m* || *to send a fax* enviar un fax || *to send by fax* enviar por fax.

fay [fei] *n* hada *f*.

faze [feiz] *vt* US desconcertar.

FCO *abbr of [Foreign and Commonwealth Office]* ministerio británico de asuntos exteriores y de la Commonwealth.

fealty [iafːəlti] *n* lealtad *f*, fidelidad *f*.

fear [fiə*] *n* miedo *m*, temor *m; fear of God* temor de *or* a Dios || — *for fear of* por miedo de (with verb), por miedo a (with noun) || *for fear that* por miedo de que *or* a que || FAM *no fear!* ¡ni hablar! || *there is no fear of failure* no hay ningún riesgo de fracaso || *to be in fear of* tener miedo a || *to go in fear of one's life* temer por su vida || FIG & FAM *to put the fear of God into s.o.* dar un susto mortal a uno.

fear [fiə*] *vt* temer, tener miedo de *or* a (see OBSERV); *I fear there may be a war* temo que haya una guerra || *to be feared* de temer; *he is to be feared* es de temer.
◆ *vi* temer, tener miedo || — *never fear!* ¡no temas!, ¡no hay cuidado! || *to fear for* temer por; *I fear for his sanity* temo por su salud mental.

— OBSERV The construction *tener miedo de* usually precedes a verbal complement and *tener miedo a* a noun: *tener miedo de morir* to be afraid to die; *tener miedo a la muerte* to fear death. This rule, however, is not strict and is sometimes disregarded in practice.

fearful ['fiəful] *adj* espantoso, sa; horrible; *the railway accident was fearful* el accidente de ferrocarril fue espantoso || temeroso, sa (frightened) || FAM tremendo, da; espantoso, sa; *what a fearful mess!* ¡qué lío más espantoso! || — *fearful of* temeroso de || *to be fearful of* temer || *to be fearful of doing sth.* temer hacer algo.

fearfully [-i] *adv* FAM terriblemente, tremendamente, horriblemente; *it was a fearfully hot day* era un día terriblemente caluroso || con miedo, con temor.

fearless [fiəlis] *adj* audaz, bravo, va; valiente, intrépido, da.

fearlessly [-li] *adv* audazmente, intrépidamente.

fearlessness [-nis] *n* intrepidez *f*, audacia *f*.

fearsome ['fiəsəm] *adj* temible, espantoso, sa (frightful) || temeroso, sa (frightened) || timorato, ta (timid).

feasibility [ˌfiːʒə'biliti] *n* viabilidad *f*.

feasible ['fiːzəbl] *adj* factible, hacedero, ra; viable, posible || verosímil, posible, plausible; *his story sounds feasible* su historia parece verosímil.

feast [fiːst] *n* fiesta *f* religiosa || banquete *m* (meal) || FAM comilona *f* (huge meal) || — *immovable, movable feast* fiesta fija, movible *or* móvil || FIG *to be a feast for the eyes* regalar la vista, ser un regalo para los ojos.

feast [fiːst] *vt* agasajar, festejar || FIG *feast your eyes on that* regálate la vista con eso.
◆ *vi* deleitarse, regalarse; *he feasted himself on chocolates* se regaló con bombones || banquetear (to eat a rich meal).

feast day [-dei] *n* día *m* festivo *or* de fiesta, fiesta *f*.

feat [fiːt] *n* proeza *f*, hazaña *f* (deed); *a remarkable feat* una gran hazaña || prueba *f; a feat of endurance* una prueba de resistencia || *feat of arms* hecho *m* de armas.

feather ['feðə*] *n* pluma *f* || plumas *f pl* (of an arrow) || TECH barbilla *f*, lengüeta *f* (for a grove) | pestaña *f*, reborde *m* (flange) | defecto *m*, jardín *m* (flaw of a gem) || — FIG *birds of a feather* lobos *m pl* de la misma camada | *birds of a feather flock together* Dios les cría y ellos se juntan || *feather bed* colchón *m* de plumas || *feather duster* plumero *m* || *feather pillow* almohada *f* de plumas || *that's a feather in your cap* es un tanto que te apuntas | *to be in fine feather* estar en forma | *to be in high feather* estar de muy buen humor | *to show the white feather* ser un gallina, mostrarse cobarde (to exhibit cowardice) | *you could have knocked me down with a feather* casi me caigo de espaldas.
◆ *pl* plumas *f*, plumaje *m sing* (plumage).

feather ['feðə*] *vt* emplumar (an arrow) || adornar *or* ribetear con plumas (to decorate with feathers) || TECH machihembrar (to join two pieces) || alzar (oars in rowing) || AVIAT poner en bandera (a propeller in aircraft) || FIG *to feather one's nest* hacer su agosto.
◆ *vi* cubrirse de plumas (a bird) || ondular (to move like feathers).

featherbed [-bed] *vt* FIG obligar (a los empresarios) a emplear más trabajadores de los que necesitan | favorecer, subvencionar; *the government featherbeds the miners* el gobierno favorece a los mineros.

featherbedding [-bediŋ] *n* US disminución *f* de las horas de trabajo por obrero para evitar el paro | obligación *f* de emplear un cupo de trabajadores superior al necesario.

featherbed rule [-bedruːl] *n* US medida *f* que adoptan los sindicatos para obligar a los empresarios a emplear más trabajadores de los necesarios.

featherbrain [-brein] *n* FAM cabeza *f* de chorlito.

featherbrained [-breind] *adj* FAM estúpido, da; necio, cia; *featherbrained idea* idea necia | casquivano, na (person) || FAM *featherbrained idiot* tonto perdido.

feathered ['feðəd] *adj* emplumado, da (adornment, arrow) || con plumas (hat) || AVIAT en bandera (propeller) || alzado, da (oars) || FIG alado, da (winged) | veloz, ligero, ra (swift) || *feathered game* caza *f* de pluma.

featheredge ['feðəredʒ] *n* borde *m* delgado (very thin edge) || bisel *m* (bevelled edge).

featherhead ['feðəhed] *n* FAM cabeza *f* de chorlito.

feathering ['feðəriŋ] *n* plumaje *m* (of birds) || plumas *f pl* (of an arrow).

featherstitch ['feðəstitʃ] *n* punto *m* de espina.

featherweight ['fəðəweit] *n* peso *m* pluma (boxing) || cosa *f* muy ligera || SP *a featherweight fight* un combate de pesos pluma.
◆ *adj* de peso pluma (boxing) || muy ligero, ra (very light) || FIG de poco peso, de poca entidad.

feathery ['feðəri] *adj* plumoso, sa || ligero como una pluma (light); *feathery snow* nieve ligera como una pluma || cubierto de plumas (covered with feathers) || de plumas, con plumas (hat).

feature ['fiːtʃə*] *n* característica *f* (characteristic) || rasgo *m* (of a face) || figura *f* (shape) || artículo *m* principal, crónica *f* especial (in a newspaper) || CINEM película *f* principal, película *f* de largo metraje; *what feature is showing?* ¿cuál es la película principal? || *main feature* película principal (film), atracción *f* principal.
◆ *pl* rostro *m sing*, semblante *m sing* (face) || facciones *f*, rasgos *m; he has hard features* tiene facciones duras.

feature ['fiːtʃə*] *vt* presentar (film, actor) || representar (to represent) || describir; *the book features the life of a monk on an island* el libro describe la vida de un fraile en una isla || caracterizar (to be a striking feature of) || presentar (news, article) || imaginarse (to imagine); *I can't feature that* no puedo imaginarme eso || destacar, poner de relieve (to emphasize) || *this film features Charlie Chaplin* en esta película trabaja *or* actúa como protagonista Charlie Chaplin.
◆ *vi* figurar, constar (to appear, to figure).

featured [-d] *adj* destacado, da; puesto de relieve (emphasized) || principal (actor, etc.) || *he is fine-featured* tiene rasgos finos.

feature film [-film] *n* película *f* principal.

feature-length [-leŋθ] *adj* de largo metraje (film) || largo, ga; extenso, sa (article).

featureless [-lis] *adj* sin rasgos distintivos || monótono, na (monotonous).

febrifuge ['febrifju:dʒ] *adj* MED febrífugo, ga.
◆ *n* MED febrífugo *m*.

febrile ['fi:brail] *adj* febril.

February ['februəri] *n* febrero *m*; *it happened on the 27th of February* ocurrió el 27 de febrero.

fecal ['fi:kəl] *adj* US fecal (faecal).

feces ['fi:si:z] *pl n* US excrementos *m*, heces *f*.

feckless ['feklis] *adj* débil (weak) || incapaz (helpless) || ineficaz (inefficient) || inútil (useless) || irreflexivo, va (irresponsible).

feculence ['fekjuləns] *n* feculencia *f*.

feculent ['fekjulənt] *adj* feculento, ta (foul with impurities) || sucio, cia (filthy).

fecund ['fi:kənd] *adj* fecundo, da.

fecundate ['fi:kəndeit] *vt* fecundar (to make fruitful or prolific) || fertilizar (the land) || fecundar (a flower).

fecundation [,fi:kən'deiʃən] *n* fecundación *f*.

fecundity [fi'kʌnditi] *n* fecundidad *f*.

fed [fed] *pret/pp* → **feed.**

federal ['fedərəl] *adj/n* federal.

federalism ['fedərəlizm] *n* federalismo *m*.

federalist ['fedərəlist] *adj/n* federalista.

federate ['fedərit] *adj* federado, da.
◆ *n* federado *m*.

federate ['fedəreit] *vt* federar.
◆ *vi* federarse.

federation [,fedə'reiʃən] *n* federación *f*.

federative ['fedərətiv] *adj* federativo, va.

fed up ['fedʌp] *adj* FAM harto, ta; hasta la coronilla.

fee [fi:] *n* honorarios *m pl*, emolumentos *m pl* (of a professional, doctor, lawyer, etc.) || derechos *m pl* de matrícula, matrícula *f* (at a university) || cuota *f* (to a club) || gratification *f* (gratuity) || HIST feudo *m* (in medieval times) || JUR hacienda *f*, patrimonio *m* (in a will) || — *entrance fee* entrada *f* || *retaining fee* anticipo *m* || *school fees* precio *m* de la escolaridad [y de la pensión en el caso de un internado] || *to hold in fee* poseer (to own) || *to pay one's school fees* pagar el colegio.

fee [fi:] *vt* contratar (to hire) || pagar los honorarios a (to pay).

feeble ['fi:bl] *adj* débil (weak) || de poco peso, poco convincente; *a feeble argument* un argumento poco convincente || tenue; *a feeble light* una luz tenue.

feebleminded [-'maindid] *adj* débil mental (mentally deficient) || tonto, ta (silly) || irresoluto, ta (irresolute).

feebleness ['fi:blnis] *n* debilidad *f*.

feed [fi:d] *n* pienso *m* (food for cattle) || forraje *m* (fodder) || comida *f* (food for babies) || FAM comilona *f*; *we had a nice feed last night* tuvimos una buena comilona anoche || TECH alimentación *f* (act of feeding a machine); *injection feed* alimentación por inyección; *feed pump* bomba de alimentación | mineral *m* bruto (of blast furnace) | avance *m* (of machine tool) | alimentador *m* (feeder) || *to be off one's feed* haber perdido el apetito.

feed* [fi:d] *vt* dar de comer a (to give food to); *she fed us well* nos dio bien de comer; *to feed the chickens* dar de comer a las gallinas; *she feeds her children a lot of fruit* les da de comer mucha fruta a los niños || alimentar; *he has twelve children to feed* tiene doce hijos que alimentar; *rice does not feed one properly* el arroz no alimenta mucho || nutrir, alimentar (to nourish) || dar de mamar, amamantar (to suckle) || dar el biberón a (a baby with a bottle) || FIG alimentar; *to feed coal into a fire* alimentar un fuego con carbón; *to feed one's mind* alimentar el espíritu; *this river feeds the reservoir* este río alimenta el depósito | avivar (one's anger) | dar (hopes) | acrecentar (to heighten) | alimentar (one's vanity) | mantener (to maintain) | suministrar (to supply); *this pipeline feeds gas to the northern cities* este gasoducto suministra gas a las ciudades del norte | suministrar, abastecer (water) | suministrar electricidad a; *this generator feeds the whole city* este generador suministra electricidad a la ciudad entera || TECH alimentar (a blast furnace) | introducir (pieces into a machine) | desplazar, hacer avanzar (machine tools) | alimentar; *to feed information into a computer* alimentar una computadora con datos || THEATR dar la réplica a (an actor) || SP pasar (the ball) || — FAM *to be fed up with* estar harto de, estar hasta la coronilla de || *to feed back* realimentar || *to feed up* sobrealimentar (person), cebar, engordar (animals).
◆ *vi* comer (to eat) || AGR pacer, pastar (to graze) || — *to feed back* proceder (news, etc.), pitar (a microphone) || *to feed off* vivir de (at the expense of); *to feed off the State* vivir del Estado || *to feed on* alimentarse con (to live on).
— OBSERV Pret y pp *fed*.

feedback ['fi:dbæk] *n* ELECTR realimentación *f* || reacción *f* || reaprovechamiento *m* (of information).

feed bag ['fi:dbæg] *n* US morral (nose bag) || US FIG & FAM *to put on the feed bag* jalar, llenar la tripa.

feeder ['fi:də*] *n* alimentador *m* (of a machine) || canal *m* alimentador (of lake, of reservoir) || río *m* tributario, afluente *m* (tributary) || ramal *m* (of railway) || carretera *f* secundaria (road) || ELECTR cable *m* alimentador || SP lanzador *m* || biberón *m* (feeding bottle) || babero *m* (child's bib) || animal *m* de engorde (fattening animal) || alimentador *m* (of cattle) || — FAM *he's a prodigious feeder* come como una lima || *this plant is a large feeder* esta planta requiere mucho abono.

feeding ['fi:diŋ] *n* comida *f*; *the feeding of the lions takes place at 8 o'clock* la comida de los leones tiene lugar a las ocho || alimentación *f* (of domestic animals) || TECH alimentación *f* (of machine) | avance *m* (of machine tool) || INFORM *feeding device* dispositivo *m* de alimentación || *feeding time* la hora de la comida.

feeding bottle [-,bɔtl] *n* biberón *m*.

feeding trough [-trɔf] *n* comedero *m*.

feed pipe ['fi:dpaip] *n* tubo *m* de alimentación.

feed rack ['fi:dræk] *n* comedero *m*, pesebre *m* (for animals) || TECH cremallera *f* de avance.

feedstuff ['fi:dstʌf] *n* alimentos *m pl* para el ganado.

feel [fi:l] *n* tacto *m*; *soft to the feel* suave al tacto || sensación *f* (sensation) || atmósfera *f*; *the empty room had a strange feel about it* había una atmósfera extraña en la habitación vacía || sentido *m*; *to have a feel for colours* tener sentido de los colores || disposición *f*, aptitudes *f pl*; *to have a feel for the piano* tener disposición para tocar el piano || — *to get the feel of sth.* coger le el truco a algo (to acquire the knack), acostumbrarse a algo (to get used to) || *to have a feel vocar* || *to have a sticky feel* ser pegajoso al tacto || *to recognize sth. by its feel* reconocer algo al tacto.

feel* [fi:l] *vt* tocar; *go and feel the water* ve a tocar el agua || mirar; *feel how soft it is* mira lo blando que es || sentir; *I can't feel the heat* no siento el calor || sentir, tener, experimentar; *I don't feel much pity for him* no tengo mucha compasión por él || sentir [los efectos de]; *the whole country felt the earthquake* el país entero sintió el terremoto || sentir; *to feel the presence of s.o.* sentir la presencia de alguien || tener el presentimiento de que, sentir; *she felt things were about to go wrong* tuvo el presentimiento de que las cosas iban a tomar mal cariz || parecerle (a uno), tener la impresión de que, creer que; *I feel you are right* me parece que tienes razón || darse cuenta de (to realize); *you must feel your position* debe darse cuenta de su situación || tomar (pulse) || MIL tantear, sondear (the enemy, the ground) || POP sobar, magrear (to caress) || — *I feel a song coming on* me apetece mucho cantar || *I have felt the cold this winter* he pasado frío este invierno || *to feel interest in* tener interés por || *to feel one's way* ir a tientas (to grope), andar con pies de plomo (to act cautiously), tantear el terreno (to explore) || FIG *to feel (quite) o.s.* encontrarse bien || *to feel out* sondear || *to feel s.o.'s vengeance* sufrir la venganza de alguien || *to feel strongly that* estar convencido de que || *to feel the heat* ser sensible al calor, no aguantar el calor.
◆ *vi* sentir || ser [al tacto]; *it feels smooth* es liso || estar; *its feels cold* está frío || parecer; *the room feels damp* el cuarto parece húmedo || encontrarse, sentirse, estar; *I feel tired* me encuentro cansado; *how do you feel?* ¿cómo se encuentra?; *to feel all the better for it* sentirse mejor || tener; *I feel cold, hot, hungry, sleepy* tengo frío, calor, hambre, sueño || hacer; *it feels cold today* hace frío hoy || pensar (to think); *how do you feel about it?* ¿qué piensas de esto? || — *how does it feel to...?* ¿qué impresión hace...? || *if you feel like it* si te parece, si te apetece || *it feels like rain* parece que va a llover || *to feel about in* ir a tientas por || *to feel as if* tener la impresión de que, parecerle (a uno) que; *I feel as if you don't like me* me parece que no me quieres || *to feel bad about* sentir (to regret) || *to feel certain* o *sure that* estar seguro de que || *to feel for s.o.* sentirlo por alguien, compadecer a alguien || *tho geel for sth.* buscar algo a tientas || *to feel for the enemy* buscar al enemigo || *to feel in (one's pockets)* registrar (los bolsillos) || *to feel like* apetecer; *do you feel like a beer?* ¿te apetece una cerveza?; tener ganas de; *I feel like going to the pictures* tengo ganas de ir al cine; parecer; *it feels like wool* parece lana || FIG *to feel like death* encontrarse fatal || *to feel sorry for s.o.* compadecer a alguien || *to feel sorry for sth.* sentir algo (to regret) || *to feel strongly about* tener ideas muy fijas sobre || *to feel strongly for* tener sentimientos muy profundos por || *to feel up to* sentirse capaz de [hacer algo] || *we feel with you* o *for you in your loss* le acompañamos en el sentimiento.
— OBSERV Pret y pp *felt*.

feeler [-ə*] *n* bigotes *m pl* (cat's whiskers) || cuerno *m* (of a snail) || antena *f* (of insects) || tentáculo *m* (of octopus, etc.) || TECH calibrador *m* (gauge) || FIG *to put out a feeler* lanzar una sonda, efectuar un sondeo.

feeling [-iŋ] *n* sentimiento *m*; *feelings of gratitude* sentimientos de gratitud || sensación *f*; *feeling of weightlessness* sensación de ingravidez || impresión *f*, presentimiento *m*; *I have the feeling that this will fail* tengo la impresión de que eso va a fracasar || opinión *f*, parecer *m*, sentir *m* (opinion); *my feeling is that* mi parecer es que || sensibilidad *f*; *I have no feeling in my leg* no tengo sensibilidad en la pierna; *to play the piano with feeling* tocar el piano con sensibilidad || sentido *m*; *she has a feeling for music* tiene el sentido de la música || amor *m*; *a feeling for his homeland* amor a su patria || ternura *f* (tenderness) || emoción *f* (emotion); *to speak*

with feeling hablar con emoción || compasión *f; feeling for the suffering of others* compasión por el sufrimiento de los demás || sentimientos *m pl; during the crisis feeling ran high* durante la crisis los sentimientos estaban exacerbados || tacto *m* (sense of touch) || — *a man of feeling* un hombre sensible || *bad feeling* resentimiento *m sing* || *good feeling* buenos sentimientos || *hard feelings* resentimiento || *ill feeling* malos sentimientos || *to have a feeling for nature* ser sensible a la naturaleza || *to have kind feelings for* tener sentimientos amistosos por || *to have no feelings* no tener sensibilidad, ser insensible || *to hurt s.o.'s feelings* herir los sentimientos de alguien || *to relieve one's feelings* desahogarse.
◆ *adj* sensible; *a feeling heart* un corazón sensible || muy sentido, da (grief).

feelingly [-iŋli] *adv* con emoción; *to speak feelingly* hablar con emoción || con sensibilidad; *to sing feelingly* cantar con sensibilidad.

feet [fiːt] *pl n* ⟶ **foot.**

feign [fein] *vt* fingir, aparentar, simular; *to feign indifference* fingir indiferencia || fingir, fingirse; *to feign illness* fingir estar enfermo, fingirse enfermo; *to feign sleep* fingirse dormido || inventar (an excuse).
◆ *vi* fingir.

feigned [-d] *adj* fingido, da; simulado, da; *feigned joy* alegría fingida || ficticio, cia || falso, sa (false).

feint [feint] *n* SP finta *f* | amago *m*, finta *f* (in fencing) || MIL maniobra *f* fingida || amago *m* (mock attack) || *to make a feint of working* fingir estar trabajando.

feint [feint] *vi* SP fintar, hacer una finta.

feints [feints] *pl n* ⟶ **faints.**

feisty ['faisti] *adj* US FAM vivo, va (spirited) | susceptible, irritable (touchy).

feldspar ['feldspɑː*]; **feldspath** ['feldspɑθ] *n* MIN feldespato *m*.

felicitate [fi'lisiteit] *vt* congratular, felicitar || (ant) alegrar.

felicitation [fi,lisi'teiʃən] *n* congratulación *f*, felicitación *f*, enhorabuena *f*.

felicitous [fi'lisitəs] *adj* oportuno, na; afortunado, da; feliz (well chosen).

felicity [fi'lisiti] *n* felicidad *f* (happiness) || idea *f* feliz (idea) || expresión *f* feliz (expression) || *to express o.s. with felicity* expresarse bien.

felid ['fiːlid] *n* ZOOL félido *m*.

felidae ['fiːlidei] *pl n* ZOOL félidos *m*.

feline ['fiːlain] *adj* ZOOL & FIG felino, na.
◆ *n* ZOOL felino *m*.

fell [fel] *n* páramo *m* (moor) || colina *f* rocosa (hill) || piel *f*, pellejo *m* (skin of animal) || corte *m*, tala *f*, árboles *m pl* cortados en una temporada.
◆ *adj* POET cruel, feroz (cruel) || funesto, ta (deadly) || *in one feel swoop* de un golpe.

fell [fel] *vt* talar, cortar (trees) || derribar (to knock down) || sobrecargar (in sewing).

fell [fel] *pret/pp* ⟶ **fall.**

feller [felə*] *n* leñador *m*, talador *m* || US FAM individuo *m*, tipo *m*, tío *m* (fellow) | muchacho *m* (boy).

felling ['feliŋ] *n* tala *f*, corte *m* (of trees).

fellow ['feləu] *n* chico *m* (boy); *a nice fellow* un chico simpático || hombre *m* (man) || persona *f* (person) || compañero *m*, camarada *m*, amigo *m* (companion) || pareja *f* (mate, counterpart) || colega *m* (colleague) || FAM individuo *m*, tipo *m*, tío *m*; *he is an odd fellow* es un tío extraño | uno *m*; *a fellow has to rest from time to time* uno tiene que descansar de vez en cuando || igual *m*, par *m* (peer); *it has no fellow* no tiene igual, no tiene par || becario *m* (university researcher) || miembro *m* del consejo de gobierno de una facultad || socio *m*, miembro *m* (of society) || — *he is a poor fellow* es un pobre diablo || *my dear fellow!* ¡hombre! || *old fellow* viejo amigo || *poor little fellow!* ¡pobrecito!, ¡pobrecillo! || *young fellow* joven *m*.
◆ *pl* compañeros *m*, amigos *m* (friends).
◆ *adj* *fellow being* semejante *m*, prójimo *m* || *fellow boarder* comensal *m* || *fellow candidate* candidato *m* del mismo partido que otro | *fellow citizens* conciudadanos *m* || *fellow countrymen* compatriotas *m* || *fellow creature* prójimo *m* || *fellow feeling* simpatía *f*, compañerismo *m* || *fellow member* consocio *m* || *fellow men* prójimos *m* || *fellow musician, doctor, etc.* colega *m* (de un músico, doctor, etc.) || *fellow partner* asociado *m* || *fellow passenger* compañero *m* de viaje || *fellow student* compañero *m*, condiscípulo *m* || *fellow sufferer* compañero *m* de fatigas || *fellow traveller* compañero *m* de viaje (on a trip), simpatizante *m* (in politics) || *fellow worker* compañero *m* de trabajo, colega *m*.

fellowman [-mən] *n* semejante *m*, prójimo *m*.
— OBSERV El plural de *fellowman* es *fellowmen*.

fellowship [-ʃip] *n* comunidad *f*; *Christian fellowship* comunidad cristiana || compañerismo *m*, camaradería *f* (companionship) || fraternidad *f*, solidaridad *f* (solidarity) || comunión *f*; *intellectual fellowship* comunión de ideas || comunidad *f* (of interests) || asociación *f* (association) || compañía *f*, grupo *m* (group) || asociación *f*, sociedad *f* (organized association) || beca *f* (scholarship) || título *m* de miembro *or* socio (position) || dignidad *f* de miembro del consejo de gobierno de una facultad.

felo-de-se ['fiːləudiː'siː] *n* JUR suicida *m* & *f* (who has committed suicide) || suicidio *m* (suicide).
— OBSERV El plural es *felones-de-se* o *felos-de-se*.

felon ['felən] *n* JUR criminal *m* || MED panadizo *m*, uñero *m* (infection).
◆ *adj* malvado, da (wicked) || criminal.

felonious [fi'ləunjəs] *adj* JUR criminal, delictivo, va; delictuoso, sa || malvado, da (wicked).

felonry ['felənri] *n* JUR criminales *m pl*.

felony ['feləni] *n* JUR crimen *m*, delito *m* grave.

felspar ['felspɑː*] *n* MIN feldespato *m*.

felt [felt] *n* fieltro *m* || *roofing felt* cartón *m* embreado de techumbres.
◆ *adj* de fieltro; *a felt hat* un sombrero de fieltro.

felt [felt] *vt* enfurtir, convertir en fieltro (to make into felt) || cubrir con fieltro (to cover) || poner fieltro debajo de (a carpet).
◆ *vi* ponerse como el fieltro (garments).

felt [felt] *pret/pp* ⟶ **feel.**

felting [-iŋ] *n* enfurtido *m* (process) || fieltro *m* (felt).

felucca [fe'lʌkə] *n* MAR falucho *m*.

female ['fiːmeil] *adj* hembra; *a female rhinoceros* un rinoceronte hembra || femenino, na; *the female sex* el sexo femenino || de mujer, femenino, na; *a female voice* una voz de mujer || de las mujeres; *female education* educación de las mujeres || TECH hembra; *female screw* tornillo hembra || BOT femenino, na || *female friend, cousin* amiga *f*, prima *f*.
◆ *n* hembra *f*; *the female of the species* la hembra de la especie || mujer *f* (woman) || chica *f* (girl) || TECH hembra *f* || POP hembra *f*.

feme [fiːm] *n* JUR mujer *f*; *feme sole* mujer soltera *or* viuda; *feme covert* mujer casada.

feminine ['feminin] *adj* femenino, na; *feminine fashion* moda femenina || afeminado, da (effeminate) || GRAMM femenino, na.
◆ *n* GRAMM femenino *m*.

femininity [femi'niniti] *n* feminidad *f* (womanliness) || mujeres *f* (womankind).

feminism ['feminizəm] *n* feminismo *m*.

feminist ['feminist] *adj/n* feminista.

feminization [,feminai'zeiʃən] *n* afeminación *f*.

feminize ['feminaiz] *vt* afeminar.
◆ *vi* afeminarse.

femme fatale ['fæmfæ'tɑːl] *n* vampiresa *f*.

femoral ['femərəl] *adj* femoral.

femur ['fiːmə*] *n* ANAT fémur *m*.
— OBSERV El plural de la palabra inglesa es *femurs* o *femora*.

fen [fen] *n* pantano *m*.

fence [fens] *n* cerca *f*, cercado *m*, valla *f*, vallado *m*; *a fence around a garden* una valla alrededor de un jardín || empalizada *f* (wooden fence) || SP valla *f* (in show jumping) | esgrima *f* (fencing) || encubridor, ra [de objetos robados] (receiver) || sitio *m* donde se ocultan objetos robados (receiving place) || guarda *f* (of a lock) || TECH guía *f* (of saw, of plane) || FIG barrera *f* (barrier) || — FIG *to come down on the right side of the fence* ponerse del lado del que gana | *to sit on the fence* nadar entre dos aguas (not to commit o.s.),ver los toros desde la barrera (to wait).

fence [fens] *vi* SP practicar la esgrima; *he fences for a hobby* practica la esgrima como pasatiempo | saltar (to jump) | luchar; *in the final France will fence against Sweden* en la final Francia luchará contra Suecia || FIG contestar con evasivas (to answer evasively) || traficar con objetos robados.
◆ *vt* cercar, vallar; *his land is fenced with barbed wire* su terreno está cercado con alambre de púas || encerrar (animals) || FIG proteger || — *to fence in* cercar (land), encerrar (animals), arrinconar, acorralar (to corner), limitar (to limit) || *to fence off* separar con una cerca (to separate two parts), aislar (to isolate), interceptar (road, street, etc.) || *to fence out* excluir.

fenceless [-lis] *adj* sin cercar, sin valla || FIG indefenso, sa.

fencer ['fensə*] *n* SP esgrimidor, ra (in fencing) || caballo *m* de saltos (in steeplechasing).

fence season ['fenssiːzn] *n* tiempo *m* de veda (in hunting).

fencing ['fensiŋ] *n* SP esgrima *f* || vallado *m*, cercado *m* (fences) || material *m* para construir cercas o vallas (material) || tráfico *m* con objetos robados || — *fencing bout* encuentro *m* de esgrima || *fencing foil* florete *m* || *fencing master* maestro *m* de armas *or* de esgrima.

fend [fend] *vt* defender || *to fend off* desviar (a blow), repeler, rechazar (an attack).
◆ *vi* *to fend for* mantener; *three children to fend for* tres hijos que mantener || *to fend for o.s.* arreglárselas, valerse por sí mismo.

fender ['fendə*] *n* pantalla *f* (of fire) || MAR defensa *f* (on a boat) || quitapiedras *m inv*, salvavidas *m inv* (of locomotive) || US parachoques *m inv* (bumper) | guardabarros *m inv* (mudguard).

fenestrate [fi'nestreit] *adj* fenestrado, da.

fenestration [,fenis'treiʃən] *n* ARCH ventanaje *m* || MED fenestración *f*.

fen fire ['fen'aiə*] *n* fuego *m* fatuo.

Fenian ['fiːnjən] *n* HIST feniano *m*.

fennec ['fenik] *n* zorro *m* del Sáhara.

fennel ['fenl] *n* BOT hinojo *m*.

feoff [fef] *n* feudo *m*.

feoff [fef] *vt* enfeudar.

feoffee [fe'fi:] *n* feudatario, ria.

feoffer [fefə:*] *n* persona *f* que enfeuda.

feoffment ['fefmənt] *n* feudo *m*, enfeudación *f*.

feracious [fə'reiʃəs] *adj* feraz, fértil.

feral ['fiərəl] *adj* salvaje (wild) || feroz, feral (fierce) || fúnebre (gloomy).

Ferdinand ['fə:dinənd] *pr n* Fernando *m*.

feretory ['feritəri] *n* REL relicario *m*.

feria ['fiəriə] *n* REL feria *f*.

— OBSERV El plural de la palabra inglesa es *feriae*.

ferial ['fiəriəl] *adj* REL ferial.

ferine ['fiərain] *adj* salvaje, ferino, na.

fermata ['fə:ma:tə] *n* MUS calderón *m*.

ferment ['fə:ment] *n* fermento *m* (fermenting agent) || fermentación *f* (fermentation) || FIG agitación *f* (commotion).

ferment ['fə:ment] *vt* fermentar, hacer fermentar (to cause fermentation) || FIG agitar (to stir up).

◆ *vi* fermentar (to undergo fermentation) || FIG fermentar; *social discontent was fermenting* el descontento social estaba fermentando.

fermentable [-əbl] *adj* fermentable.

fermentation [,fə:menteiʃən] *n* fermentación *f* || FIG agitación *f*.

fermium ['fɛəmjəm] *n* CHEM fermio *m*.

fern [fə:n] *n* BOT helecho *m*.

fernery [-əri] *n* BOT helechal *m*.

ferny* [-i] *adj* cubierto de helechos.

ferocious [fə'rəuʃəs] *adj* feroz, fiero, ra (animal); *a ferocious lion* un león fiero || feroz (person, look) || FIG violento, ta; *a ferocious attack* un ataque violento.

ferociousness [-nis] *n* ferocidad *f*, crueldad *f*.

ferocity [fə'rɔsiti] *n* ferocidad *f*.

ferrate ['fereit] *n* CHEM ferrato *m*.

ferreous ['feriəs] *adj* CHEM ferroso, sa.

ferret ['ferit] *n* hurón *m* (animal).

ferret ['ferit] *vt* cazar con hurones || *to ferret out* conseguir descubrir (a secret), conseguir encontrar (a person).

◆ *vi* huronear, cazar con hurones || FIG registrar, hurgar; *he ferreted (about) in the drawer for the letter* registró el cajón para encontrar la carta | huronear (to pry).

ferric ['ferik] *adj* férrico, ca.

ferricyanide [feri'saiənaid] *n* CHEM ferricianuro *m*.

ferriferous [fe'rifərəs] *adj* ferrífero, ra.

Ferris wheel ['feriswi:l] *n* noria *f* (in amusement parks).

ferrite ['ferait] *n* CHEM ferrito *m* (salt) || MIN ferrita *f* (ore).

ferroconcrete ['ferəu'kɔŋkri:t] *n* hormigón *m* armado.

ferrocyanide [ferəu'saiənaid] *n* CHEM ferrocianuro *m*.

ferromagnetic ['ferəumæg'netik] *adj* ferromagnético, ca.

ferromanganese ['ferəu'mæŋgə'ni:z] *n* ferromanganeso *m*.

ferronickel ['ferau'nikl] *n* ferroníquel *m*.

ferroprusiate ['ferəu'prʌʃiit] *n* ferroprusiato *m*.

ferrous ['ferəs] *adj* ferroso, sa.

ferruginous [fe'ru:dʒinəs] *adj* ferruginoso, sa (containing iron) || aherrumbrado, da (rust-coloured).

ferrule ['feru:l] *n* contera *f*, regatón *m* (tip of umbrella, stick, etc.) || abrazadera *f*, virola *f* (metal ring on tool, pole, etc.).

ferry ['feri] *n* transbordador *m* (boat) || embarcadero *m* (place).

ferry ['feri] *vt* transportar (to transport) || cruzar (a river, etc.) || entregar (avión, coche, barco) conduciéndolo de la fábrica al comprador (to deliver) || transportar por avión (to transport by air) || *to ferry across* transportar *or* llevar por barco.

ferryboat [-bəut] *n* transbordador *m*.

ferry bridge [-bridʒ] *n* puente *m* transbordador.

ferrying [-iŋ] *n* transbordo *m* || transporte *m* en barco.

ferryman [-mən] *n* barquero *m*.

— OBSERV El plural de *ferryman* es *ferrymen*.

fertile ['fə:tail] *adj* fértil, feraz (soil) || BIOL fecundo, da || FIG abonado, da; *fertile ground for communism* campo abonado para el comunismo | fecundo, da; fértil; *fertile imagination* imaginación fecunda.

fertility [fə:'tiliti] *n* fertilidad *f*, feracidad *f* (of soil) || BIOL fecundidad *f*.

fertilizable ['fə:tilaizəbl] *adj* fertilizable.

fertilization [,fə:tilai'zeiʃən] *n* fertilización *f* (of soil) || BIOL fecundación *f*.

fertilize ['fə:tilaiz] *vt* abonar, fertilizar (soil) || BIOL fecundar.

fertilizer [-ə*] *n* abono *m*, fertilizante *m*; *nitrate fertilizers* abonos nitrogenados.

fertilizing [-iŋ] *n* fertilización *f*.

◆ *adj* fertilizante.

ferula ['ferjulə] *n* BOT férula *f* || férula *f*, palmeta *f* (ferule) || (ant) cetro *m*.

ferule ['feru:l] *n* férula *f*, palmeta *f* (kind of cane).

fervency ['fə:vənsi] *n* fervor *m*.

fervent ['fə:vənt] *adj* ferviente, fervoroso, sa; ardiente.

fervid ['fə:vid] *adj* ferviente, fervoroso, sa.

fervour; *US* **fervor** ['fə:və*] *n* fervor *m*, ardor *m*; *he spoke with fervour of his leader* habló con fervor de su jefe || fervor *m*; *the fervour of his faith* el fervor de su fe || calor *m* intenso (heat).

fescue ['feskju:] *n* puntero *m* (teacher's pointer).

fess; **fesse** [fes] *n* HERALD faja *f*.

festal ['festl] *adj* festivo, va (day) || de fiesta (garments, etc.).

fester ['festə*] *vi* MED supurar, enconarse (to produce pus) || pudrirse (to putrefy) || FIG enconarse (to become bitter).

◆ *vt* FIG alimentar, nutrir (hatred) | envenenar, emponzoñar (to embitter) || MED enconar.

festival ['festəvəl] *n* fiesta *f* (celebration); *Church festivals* fiestas religiosas || festival *m*; *song festival* festival de la canción.

◆ *adj* de fiesta || de festival.

festive ['festiv] *adj* festivo, va; alegre (gay); *to be in a festive mood* estar de un humor festivo || de fiestas; *festive season* temporada de fiestas.

festivity [fes'tiviti] *n* festividad *f*, fiesta *f* (celebration) || regocijo *m* (gaiety).

festoon [fes'tu:n] *n* festón *m* (in sewing) || guirnalda *f* (garland) || ARCH festón *m*.

festoon [fes'tu:n] *vt* festonear.

festooned [fe'stu:nd] *adj* festoneado, da.

festoonry [-ri] *n* decoración *f* con guirnaldas *or* festones || festoneado *m* (in sewing).

fetal ['fi:tl] *adj* BIOL fetal.

fetation [fi:'teiʃən] *n* BIOL gestación *f*, desarrollo *m* del feto.

fetch [fetʃ] *n* estratagema *f* (trick) || aparición *f* (of a living person).

fetch [fetʃ] *vt* buscar; *go and fetch the doctor* ve a buscar al médico || traer (to bring) || ir a buscar, ir por; *fetch water from the river* ve a buscar agua al río || alcanzar (to reach); *to fetch a very high price* alcanzar un precio muy elevado || asestar, pegar (a blow) || hacer brotar; *a blow which fetched blood* un golpe que hizo brotar la sangre || atraer; *he was fetched by the idea of the voyage* le atraía la idea del viaje || dar; *to fetch a sigh* dar un suspiro || — *fetch it here!* ¡tráelo! || *how much did it fetch?* ¿por cuánto se vendió? || *to fetch one's breath* tomar aliento || *to fetch tears to one's eyes* hacerle subir a uno las lágrimas a los ojos || *you fetched me all this way for nothing* me has hecho venir desde tan lejos *or* me fuiste a buscar tan lejos para nada.

◆ *vi* MAR navegar || — *fetch and carry!* ¡busca! (to a dog) || *to fetch and carry for* hacer los recados de (to do minor tasks).

◆ *phr v* ***to fetch about*** dar bordadas (a sailing boat) || ***to fetch away*** llevarse | MAR desamarrarse || ***to fetch back*** traer; *fetch some wine back with you* trae vino cuando vuelvas | decir *or* hacer que vuelva (a person) || ***to fetch down*** bajar; *fetch me down the dictionary* bájame el diccionario | derribar (to shoot down game) || ***to fetch in*** traer para dentro || hacer entrar (a person) | recoger (washing) || ***to fetch out*** sacar (sth.) | quitar (a stain) | hacer salir (s.o.) || ***to fetch through*** alcanzar el puerto (a boat) | superar las dificultades (to overcome difficulties) || ***to fetch up*** subir; *fetch me up a towel* súbeme una toalla | vomitar (to vomit) | ir a parar (*in* a) (to end up) | MAR llegar (to arrive) | pararse (to stop) | *US* criar, educar (children).

fetching [-iŋ] *adj* atractivo, va.

fête; *US* **fete** [feit] *n* fiesta *f* (festival) || santo *m* (saint's day).

fête [feit] *vt* festejar.

feticide ['fi:təsaid] *n* feticidio *m*.

fetid ['fetid] *adj* fétido, da; hediondo, da.

fetidity [-iti]; **fetidness** [-nis] *n* fetidez *f*, hediondez *f*.

fetish ['fi:tiʃ] *n* fetiche *m* (idol) || FIG culto *m*; *to make a fetish of the past* tener un culto por el pasado | obsesión *f*.

fetishism [-izəm] *n* fetichismo *m*.

fetishist [-ist] *n* fetichista *m* & *f*.

fetishistic [-istik] *adj* fetichista.

fetlock ['fetlɔk]; *US* **fetterlock** ['fetəlɔk] *n* espolón *m* (projection) || cerneja *f* (tuft of hair) || *fetlock joint* menudillo *m* (of horse).

fetor ['fi:tə*] *n* hedor *m*, hediondez *f*.

fetter ['fetə*] *n* traba *f* (of animal).

◆ *pl* grilletes *m*, grillos *m* (of prisoners, of slaves, etc.) || FIG trabas *f*; *the fetters placed on world trade* las trabas puestas al comercio internacional || *to be in fetters* estar encadenado.

fetter ['fetə*] *vt* encadenar, poner grillos a, engrillar (people) || trabar (animals) || FIG poner trabas a (to hinder).

fetterlock [-lɔk] *n* → **fetlock.**

fettle ['fetl] *n* condición *f*, estado *m*, forma *f* (persons, horses, etc.) || revestimiento *m* del horno de pudelación || *in fine fettle* en buenas condiciones (fit), de buen humor (in good mood).

fettle ['fetl] *vt* arreglar (to put in order) || limpiar (to clean) || desbarbar (moulded ware) || revestir (a furnace).

fetus ['fi:təs] *n* feto *m*.

— OBSERV El plural de *fetus* es *fetuses*.

feud [fju:d] *n* HIST feudo *m* (estate); *land in feud* tierra en feudo || enemistad *f* hereditaria, odio *m* hereditario (enmity) || — *at feud with* peleado a muerte con || *family feuds* disensiones *f* familiares (inveterate strife between families).

feud [fju:d] *vi* pelear, luchar.

feudal ['fju:dl] *adj* feudal; *feudal lord* señor feudal.

feudalism ['fju:dəlizəm] *n* feudalismo *m*.

feudality [fju:'dæliti] *n* feudalidad *f* (state) ‖ feudo *m* (feud).

feudalize ['fju:dəlaiz] *vt* enfeudar.

feudatory ['fju:dətəri] *adj/n* feudatario, ria.

feudist ['fju:dist] *n* camorrista *m* & *f* (participant in a quarrel).

fever ['fi:və*] *n* MED fiebre *f*, calentura *f*; *he has a high fever, he is running a high fever* tiene mucha fiebre | fiebre *f*; *typhoid, algid, yellow, intermittent fever* fiebre tifoidea, álgida, amarilla, intermitente ‖ FIG fiebre *f*; *election fever* fiebre electoral | agitación *f* ‖ — *fever pitch* punto *m* culminante (emotion, tension, etc.) ‖ *milk fever* fiebre láctea ‖ *scarlet fever* escarlatina *f* ‖ *to be in a fever* tener fiebre.

fever ['fi:və*] *vt* MED dar fiebre a ‖ FIG apasionar, inflamar, enardecer.

feverfew ['fi:vəˌfju:] *n* BOT matricaria *f*.

feverish ['fi:vəriʃ] *adj* febril, calenturiento, ta ‖ FIG febril.

feverishness [-nis] *n* febrilidad *f*.

feverous ['fi:vərəs] *adj* febril.

few [fju:] *adj* poco, ca (not many); *few people came* vino poca gente; *there are few books on the subject* hay pocos libros sobre este tema ‖ raro, ra; poco numeroso, sa (rare); *such occasions are few* tales ocasiones son raras ‖ — *a few* algunos, algunas, unos (cuantos), unas (cuantas), unos pocos, unas pocas; *give me a few cigarettes* dame algunos cigarrillos ‖ *a few hundred pounds* unos centenares de libras ‖ *a good few, some few, quite a few* muchos, muchas, bastantes; *he has quite a few friends* tiene bastantes amigos ‖ *during the last few days* estos últimos días ‖ *every few days* cada dos o tres días ‖ *few and far between* raro, ra; escaso, sa; contadísimo, ma ‖ *in the next few days* dentro de unos días ‖ *not a few* no pocos, no pocas, muchos, muchas, bastantes ‖ *one of the few people who* uno de los pocos que ‖ *the buses run every few minutes* los autobuses pasan cada dos o tres minutos ‖ *with few exceptions* con pocas excepciones.
◆ *n* minoría *f*; *laws made for the few* leyes hechas para una minoría ‖ pocos, cas; *few of them can read and write* pocos saben leer y escribir; *there are very few of us who can remember him* somos muy pocos en acordarnos de él ‖ — *a few* algunos, algunas, unos cuantos, unas cuantas, unos pocos, unas pocas; *only a few understood him* sólo le entendieron algunos ‖ *a few of* algunos de; *a few of us remained* algunos de nosotros nos quedamos ‖ *a good few, some few, quite a few* un buen número, muchos, muchas, bastantes; *a good few of his friends* muchos de sus amigos ‖ *a privileged few* una minoría privilegiada ‖ *many are called but few are chosen* muchos son los llamados, pocos los escogidos ‖ *not a few* muchos, muchas ‖ *the happy few* los privilegiados.

fewer [-ə*] *comp adj* menos; *there were fewer people than I expected* había menos gente de lo que esperaba; *he has fewer friends than I* tiene menos amigos que yo; *no fewer than* no menos de ‖ — *the fewer the better* cuantos menos mejor ‖ *to become fewer* ser cada vez menos numeroso.

fewest [-ist] *superl adj* menos; *I have fewer books than you but she has the fewest* yo tengo menos libros que tú, pero ella es la que menos tiene.

fey [fei] *adj* medio loco, ca (slightly mad) ‖ destinado a morir (destined to die) ‖ vidente (clairvoyant).

fez [fez] *n* fez *m*, gorro *m* (felt cap).
— OBSERV El plural de la palabra inglesa es *fezzes*.

fiancé [fi'ɑnsei] *n* novio *m*, prometido *m*.

fiancée [fi'ɑnsei] *n* novia *f*, prometida *f*.

fiasco [fi'æskəu] *n* fiasco *m*, fracaso *m*.
— OBSERV El plural de la palabra inglesa es *fiascoes* o *fiascos*.

fiat ['faiæt] *n* fíat *m*, autorización *f*.
◆ *adj* fiduciario, ria (money).

fiat ['faiæt] *vt* autorizar.

fib [fib] *n* FAM mentirijilla *f*, bola *f* (lie); *to tell a fib* decir una mentirijilla.

fib [fib] *vi* decir una mentirijilla *or* mentirijillas, mentir.

fibber [-ə*] *n* FAM mentirosillo, lla; mentiroso, sa.

fibre; *US* **fiber** ['faibə*] *n* fibra *f*; *vegetable fibre* fibra vegetal; *man-made* o *artificial fibre* fibras artificiales ‖ FIG carácter *m* ‖ — *fibre optics* fibra óptica ‖ *staple fibre* fibrana *f* ‖ *textile fibre* fibra textil.

fibreboard; *US* **fiberboard** [-bɔ:d] *n* panel *m* de fibras de madera.

fibreglass; *US* **fiberglass** [-glɑ:s] *n* fibra *f* de vidrio.

fibril ['faibril]; **fibrilla** [-ə] *n* fibrilla *f*.
— OBSERV El plural de *fibrilla* es *fibrillae*.

fibrillation [faibri'leiʃən] *n* MED fibrilación *f*.

fibrin ['faibrin] *n* fibrina *f*.

fibrinogen [fai'brinədʒin] *n* fibrinógeno *m*.

fibrocement ['faibrəˌsi'ment] *n* fibrocemento *m*.

fibroid ['faibrɔid] *adj* fibroso, sa.
◆ *n* MED fibroma *m*.

fibroma [fai'brəumə] *n* MED fibroma *m*.
— OBSERV El plural de la palabra inglesa es *fibromata* o *fibromas*.

fibrositis [ˌfaibrə'saitəs] *n* MED fibrositis *f inv*.

fibrous ['faibrəs] *adj* fibroso, sa.

fibula ['fibjulə] *n* ANAT peroné *m* (bone) ‖ fíbula *f* (brooch).
— OBSERV El plural de la palabra inglesa es *fibulae* o *fibulas*.

fibular [-ə*] *adj* ANAT del peroné, peroneo, a; fibular.

fichu ['fi:ʃu:] *n* pañuelo *m* (scarf).

fickle ['fikl] *adj* inconstante, veleidoso, sa; voluble.

fickleness [-nis] *n* inconstancia *f*, veleidad *f*, volubilidad *f*.

fictile ['fiktil] *adj* figulino, na.

fiction ['fikʃən] *n* ficción *f* ‖ novela *f*, novelística *f*, género *m* novelístico (literature) ‖ — *fact and fiction* la realidad y la ficción ‖ JUR *legal fiction* ficción de derecho *or* legal ‖ *that's all fiction* aquello es pura imaginación.

fictional ['fikʃənl] *adj* novelesco, ca (literature) ‖ ficticio, cia (not restricted to fact).

fictionalize ['fikʃnəlaiz] *vt* novelar, novelizar.

fictitious [fik'tiʃəs] *adj* ficticio, cia; *fictitious name* nombre ficticio ‖ imaginario, ria (imaginary) ‖ fingido, da (feigned); *fictitious emotion* emoción fingida.

fictitiousness [fik'tiʃəsnis] *n* lo ficticio, carácter *m* ficticio.

fictive ['fiktiv] *adj* ficticio, cia ‖ imaginario, ria (imaginary) ‖ fingido, da (feigned).

fid [fid] *n* MAR pasador *m* (to separate rope strands) | cuña *f* del mastelero (mast support) ‖ cuña *f* (wedge).

fiddle ['fidl] *n* MUS violín *m* (instrument) | violinista *m* (musician) ‖ MAR tabla *f* de mal tiempo ‖ FAM trampa *f*, superchería *f* (trick) ‖ — FIG & FAM *face as long as a fiddle* cara larga | *fit as a fiddle* más sano que una manzana, en plena forma ‖ *tax fiddle* evasión *f* fiscal ‖ FIG *to play second fiddle* desempeñar un papel secundario.

fiddle ['fidl] *vi* FAM tocar el violín ‖ juguetear, enredar; *stop fiddling with that pencil* deja de juguetear con ese lápiz ‖ *to fiddle about* perder el tiempo.
◆ *vt* tocar (a tune) ‖ FAM camelar, embaucar; *they fiddled him into buying it* le camelaron para que lo comprase | amañar (to falsify); *to fiddle the accounts* amañar las cuentas | agenciarse (a job) ‖ *to fiddle one's time away* perder el tiempo.

fiddlededee! ['fidldi'di:] *interj* ¡pamplinas!, ¡tonterías!, ¡bobadas!

fiddle-faddle ['fidlˌfædl] *n* tonterías *f pl*, necedades *f pl*, bobadas *f pl*.

fiddle-faddle ['fidlˌfædl] *vi* perder el tiempo.

fiddler ['fidlə*] *n* violinista *m* (musician) ‖ FAM tramposo *m* (trickster).

fiddler crab [-kræb] *n* barrilete *m*.

fiddlestick ['fidlstik] *n* MUS arco *m* de violín.
◆ *pl* FAM tonterías *f* ‖ *fiddlesticks!* ¡tonterías!, ¡bobadas!, ¡pamplinas!

fiddling [ˌfidliŋ] *adj* trivial, insignificante, fútil.

fiddly ['fidli] *adj* FAM dificultoso, sa; complicado, da (to handle).

fidelity [fi'deliti] *n* fidelidad *f* ‖ RAD *high fidelity* alta fidelidad.

fidget ['fidʒit] *n* agitación *f* nerviosa ‖ fuguillas *m inv*, persona *f* que no para de moverse ‖ FAM *to have the fidgets* no poder estarse quieto.

fidget ['fidʒit] *vi* moverse; *stop fidgeting* deja de moverte ‖ impacientarse, ponerse nervioso ‖ — *to fidget about* no poder estarse quieto ‖ *to fidget with* juguetear *or* enredar con.
◆ *vt* ponerse nervioso.

fidgety ['fidʒiti] *adj* nervioso, sa; impaciente, febril (nervous) ‖ agitado, da; que no deja de moverse, que no puede estarse quieto (restless).

fiducial [fi'dju:ʃjəl] *adj* *fiducial line* fiducial *f*.

fiduciary [fi'dju:ʃjəri] *adj* COMM fiduciario, ria.
◆ *n* fiduciario *m*.

fie! [fai] *interj* (ant) ¡qué vergüenza!

fief [fi:f] *n* HIST feudo *m* (property).

field [fi:ld] *n* campo *m*; *a field of maize* un campo de maíz; *a playing field* un campo de deportes ‖ extensión *f* (of ice, of water) ‖ campo *m* (of snow) ‖ MIL, HERALD & PHYS campo *m*; *field of battle* campo de batalla; *magnetic, electric, acoustic field* campo magnético, eléctrico, acústico ‖ MIN yacimiento *m*; *oil field* yacimiento petrolífero ‖ FIG campo *m*, sector *m*, esfera *f*; *the field of medicine* el campo de la medicina; *field of activity* campo de actividad | terreno *m*; *it's not my field* ése no es mi terreno | campo *m* (background) ‖ SP participantes *m pl* (in a contest) | competidores *m pl* (in a race) | jugadores *m pl* (players) | equipo *m* (team) | todos los competidores salvo el favorito ‖ — *field of vision* campo visual ‖ MIL *in the field* en campaña ‖ *landing field* campo de aterrizaje ‖ MED *operative field* campo operatorio ‖ FIG *to have a clear field* tener campo libre ‖ MIL *to hold the field* no ceder terreno ‖ FIG *to leave the field open* o *clear* dejar el campo libre ‖ MIL *to take the field* entrar en campaña ‖ FIG *to take the field* salir a la palestra ‖ *to work in the field* trabajar en el terreno (researchers, etc.).

field [fi:ld] *vi* SP parar y devolver la pelota (in cricket and baseball).
◆ *vt* SP parar y devolver (the ball) || presentar (a team).

field army [-'ɑ:mi] *n* MIL ejército *m* de operaciones.

field artillery [-ɑ:'tiləri] *n* MIL artillería *f* de campaña.

field book [-buk] *n* MIL libreta *f* de campo.

field day [-dei] *n* MIL día *m* de maniobras || día *m* en el campo (for scientific study) || US reunión *f* de atletismo | fiesta *f* al aire libre | gran día *m* (great day); *they had a field day* fue un gran día para ellos.

fielder [-ə*] *n* SP jugador *m* del equipo que no batea (in cricket and baseball).

field event [-i'vent] *n* SP competición *f* atlética [salto y lanzamiento].

fieldfare [-fɛə*] *n* zorzal *m* (bird).

field glasses [-glɑ:siz] *pl n* gemelos *m* [de campaña].

field gun [-gʌn] *n* MIL cañón *m* de campaña.

field hockey [-'hɔki] *n* US SP hockey *m* sobre hierba.

field hospital [-'hɔspitl] *n* MIL hospital *m* de campaña, hospital *m* de sangre.

field kitchen [-'kitʃin] *n* MIL cocina *f* de campaña.

field magnet [-'mægnit] *n* PHYS electroimán *m* del campo || *field-magnet coil* bobina *f* de inducción.

field marshal [-'mɑ:ʃəl] *n* MIL mariscal *m* de campo.

field mouse [-maus] *n* ratón *m* campesino.
— OBSERV El plural de *field mouse* es *field mice*.

field officer [-'ɔfisə*] *n* MIL jefe *m*, oficial *m* superior.

field of honour [-əvɔnə*] *n* campo *m* del honor (for duel) || campo *m* de batalla (battlefield).

field of view [-əvvju:] *n* campo *m* visual.

fieldsman [-zmən] *n* SP jugador *m* del equipo que no batea (in cricket and baseball).
— OBSERV El plural de *fieldsman* es *fieldsmen*.

field sports [-spɔ:ts] *pl n* deportes *m* al aire libre.

field winding [-,waindiŋ] *n* arrollamiento *m* *or* devanado *m* inductor.

fieldwork [-wə:k] *n* trabajo *m* en el terreno (on the spot).
◆ *pl* MIL obras *f* de campaña.

fiend [fi:nd] *n* demonio *m*, diablo *m* (devil, demon) || desalmado, da; malvado, da (cruel person) || US FAM fanático, ca (fanatic) || — *dope fiend* toxicómano, na || *fresh-air fiend* enamorado del aire libre || *to be a fiend for* ser una fiera para.

fiendish [-iʃ] *adj* diabólico, ca; demoniaco, ca; *to take a fiendish delight in* experimentar un placer diabólico en.

fierce [fiəs] *adj* feroz, fiero, ra (animal) || cruel, violento, ta (person) || horroroso, sa (weather) || intenso, sa (heat) || fortísimo, ma; *the wind was fierce* hacía un viento fortísimo || ardiente, furioso, sa (desire) || violento, ta (envy, hatred) || furioso, sa (attack) || encarnizado, da (battle, struggle) || feroz (look) || acérrimo, ma; fanático, ca (supporter).

fierceness [-nis] *n* ferocidad *f*, fiereza *f* (of animal) || crueldad *f* (of a person) || violencia *f* (violence) || ardor *m* (ardour) || lo horroroso (of weather) || intensidad *f* (intensity) || encarnizamiento *m* (of battle).

fieriness ['faiərinis] *n* ardor *m* (of sun, passion) || pasión *f*, acaloramiento *m*, apasionamiento *m* (of speech) || lo picante (of food) || fogosidad *f* (of a horse).

fiery ['faiəri] *adj* llameante (flaming) || ardiente (burning) || apasionado, da (passionate) || fogoso, sa (temper) || brioso, sa; fogoso, sa (horse) || acalorado, da (speech) || encendido, da (eyes, colour) || rojo, ja (hair) || fuerte, picante (taste) || abrasador, ra (sun) || inflamable (gas) || con grisú (mine) || *a fiery sunset* un ocaso arrebolado.

fiesta ['fiestə] *n* fiesta *f*.

FIFA *abbr of [Fédération Internationale de Football Association]* FIFA, Federación Internacional de Fútbol Asociación.

fife [faif] *n* MUS pífano *m* (instrument).

fifteen ['fif'ti:n] *adj* quince; *she is fifteen years old* tiene quince años de edad.
◆ *n* quince *m*.

fifteenth [-θ] *adj* decimoquinto, ta.
◆ *n* decimoquinto, ta || quinzavo *m*, quinzava parte *f* (fraction) || quince *m*, día *m* quince; *we shall go on the fifteenth of March* iremos el día quince de marzo || quince; *Louis XV (the fifteenth)* Luis XV [quince].

fifth [fifθ] *adj* quinto, ta; *the fifth door* la quinta puerta.
◆ *n* quinto, ta || quinto *m*, quinta parte *f* (fraction) || cinco *m*, día *m* cinco; *today is the fifth of June* hoy es el día cinco *or* el cinco de junio || quinto, ta; *Henry V (the fifth)* Enrique V [quinto] || MUS quinta *f*.

fifth column [-'kɔləm] *n* quinta columna *f*.

fifth columnist [-'kɔləmnist] *n* quintacolumnista *m*.

fifthly ['fifθli] *adv* en quinto lugar.

fiftieth ['fiftiəθ] *adj* quincuagésimo, ma.
◆ *n* quincuagésimo, ma || quincuagésimo *m*, quincuagésima parte *f* (fraction).

fifty ['fifti] *adj/n* cincuenta.
◆ *pl* años *m* cincuenta (sixth decade of a century) || *she is in her fifties* tiene unos cincuenta años.
— OBSERV *Fifty-first, fifty-second*, etc., are translated by *quincuagésimo primero, quincuagésimo segundo*, etc.

fifty-fifty [-'fifti] *adv* FAM a medias; *let's go fifty-fifty* vayamos a medias.

fiftyish [-tiʃ] *adj* cincuentón, ona.

fig [fig] *n* BOT higo *m* (fruit) | higuera *f* (tree) || FAM bledo *m*, comino *m*, higo *m*, pepino *m*; *I don't care a fig* me importa un bledo *or* un comino, no se me da un higo | atavío *m* (dress) | forma *f* (condition) || — FAM *a fig for it!* ¡me importa un pepino! || *fig leaf* hoja *f* de higuera (of tree), hoja *f* de parra (of statue).

fight [fait] *n* lucha *f*, pelea *f*; *street fights* luchas callejeras; *a fight to the death* una lucha a muerte || disputa *f* (argument) || MIL batalla *f*, combate *m* (battle) || SP combate *m* (in boxing) || combatividad *f* (fighting spirit); *to show fight* mostrar combatividad || ánimo *m* (courage) || FIG lucha *f*; *the fight for life* la lucha por la vida || — *in fair fight* en buena lid || *there was no fight left in him* ya no tenía ánimo para luchar || *to have a fight* pelearse || *to pick a fight with s.o.* provocar a alguien, meterse con uno || *to put up a good fight* defenderse bien.

fight* [fait] *vt* pelearse con, pelear con, luchar con (a person) || luchar contra, combatir; *to fight disease, vandalism* luchar contra la enfermedad, contra el vandalismo || combatir (fire) || luchar contra (in a war) || discutir, impugnar (a point) || — *to fight a battle* librar una batalla, librar combate || *to fight a bull* torear *or* lidiar un toro || *to fight a duel* batirse en duelo || *to fight a war* hacer una guerra || *to fight a war against a country* hacer la guerra a un país || *to fight cocks* echar los gallos a pelear || *to fight one's way* luchar por abrirse camino || *to fight one's way out* abrirse camino luchando || *to fight the good fight* combatir por una causa justa.
◆ *vi* luchar, combatir; *to fight against* o *with the enemy* luchar *or* combatir contra el enemigo || pelear; *I saw two men fighting* vi a dos hombres que estaban peleando || SP boxear, combatir (in boxing), luchar, combatir (in wrestling) || FIG luchar || FAM reñir (to quarrel) || — *to fight fair* luchar limpiamente || *to fight for* luchar *or* combatir por || *to fight like a tiger* o *a wildcat* luchar como un gato panza arriba || *to fight shy of* evitar || *to fight through difficulties* superar *or* vencer dificultades || *to fight to a finish* luchar hasta el final.
◆ *phr v* ***to fight back*** rechazar (the enemy, an attack) | contener, retener (tears, laughter) | reprimir (emotions) | defenderse, resistir || ***to fight down*** reprimir || ***to fight off*** luchar contra (disease, sleep) | rechazar (an attack) || ***to fight out*** aguantar (to endure) || — *to fight it out* luchar hasta resolverlo, luchar hasta llegar a una decisión.
— OBSERV Pret y pp ***fought.***.

fighter [-ə*] *n* MIL combatiente *m*, guerrero *m* (soldier) || AVIAT avión *m* de caza, caza *m* || FIG luchador, ra; persona combativa || SP púgil *m*.

fighter bomber [-'bɔmə*] *n* cazabombardero *m*.

fighter plane [-plein] *n* AVIAT avión *m* de caza, caza *m*.

fighting ['faitiŋ] *adj* combatiente || *fighting spirit* combatividad *f*.
◆ *n* lucha *f*, pelea *f* || MIL & SP combate *m*.

fighting chance [-tʃɑ:ns] *n* mucha posibilidad *f* de tener éxito (if great efforts are made).

fighting cock [-kɔk] *n* gallo *m* de pelea.

figment ['figmənt] *n* ficción *f*, invención *f* || *a figment of one's imagination* un producto de su imaginación.

figpecker ['figpekə*] *n* papafigo *m*, papahigo *m* (bird).

figurant ['figjurənt] *n* figurante *m*.

figurante ['figju'rɑ[zs[zz :nt] *n* figurante *f*.

figuration [,figju'reiʃən] *n* figuración *f* (action) || forma *f*, configuración *f* (shape) || perfil *m*, contorno *m*, silueta *f* (outline).

figurative ['figjurətiv] *adj* figurado, da; *figurative language* lenguaje figurado || figurativo, va (art) || metafórico, ca (style).

figure ['figə*] *n* cifra *f*, número *m*, guarismo *m* (number) || cifra *f*; *the production figures are low* las cifras de producción son bajas || COMM precio *m* (price) || suma *f*, cantidad *f* (sum) || figura *f*, estatua *f* (statue) || figura *f*; *geometric figures* figuras geométricas || dibujo *m* (sketch) || ilustración *f* (illustration in book) || figura *f*, personaje *m* (person); *important historic figure* importante figura histórica || tipo *m*, figura *f*; *she has a lovely figure* tiene un tipo estupendo || línea *f*; *to keep one's figure* guardar la línea || forma *f*, silueta *f*; *a figure loomed up out of the mist* una silueta apareció en la niebla || figura *f* (in dancing, in skating) || GRAMM & MUS figura *f* || — *a fine figure of a woman* una mujer bien hecha *or* que tiene buen tipo || *central figure* figura central (in a drama) || *figure of speech* tropo *m*, figura *f* retórica (rethoric), manera *f* de hablar || SP *figure skating* patinaje artístico || *in round figures* en números redondos || *in single, double figures* en números de una, de dos cifras || *to be good at figures* dársele bien los números a uno; *I'm very good at figures* se me dan muy bien los números || *to cut a (brilliant) figure* hacer un buen papel || *to have a good figure* tener buena presencia || *to put a figure on sth.* poner precio a algo.

figure ['figə*] *vt* representar (to portray) || imaginar, representarse (to picture mentally)

|| estampar (materials) || MATH poner en cifras || FAM imaginarse, suponer, figurarse (to consider); *I figure it will take twenty years* me imagino que tardará veinte años || — *figured language* lenguaje figurado || *to figure out* comprender (to understand), explicarse; *I can't figure out why it doesn't work* no me explico por qué no marcha; calcular (to calculate), resolver (a problem), descifrar (writing).
◆ *vi* hacer cálculos (to calculate) || figurar; *to figure briefly in history* figurar brevemente en la historia; *his name figured on the guest list* su nombre figuraba en la lista de invitados || US FAM ser probable || — THEATR *to figure as* hacer el papel de || *to figure on* contar con (to count on), tener la intención de (to plan) || *to figure out at* sumar, ascender a (to amount to).

figured bass [-dbæs] *n* MUS bajo *m* cifrado.

figurehead [-hed] *n* MAR mascarón *m* de proa || FIG testaferro *m*.

figurine ['figjuri:n] *n* figurilla *f*, estatuilla *f*.

Fiji [ʒfi:'dʒi:] *pr n* Fiyi.

filagree ['filəgri:] *n/vt* ⟶ **filigree.**

filament ['filəmənt] *n* filamento *m*.

filament lamp [-læmp] *n* lámpara *f* incandescente.

filamentous [,filə'mentəs] *adj* filamentoso, sa.

filar ['failə] *adj* *filar microscope* microscopio *m* de ocular reticulado.

filaria [fi'lɛərjə] *n* MED filaria *f*.
— OBSERV El plural de la palabra inglesa *filaria* es *filariae*.

filariasis [filə'raiəsis]; **filariosis** [filə'raiəsis] *n* MED filariosis *f*, filariasis *f*.

filature ['filətʃə*] *n* hilandería *f*, fábrica *f* de hilados (place) || devanadera *f* (reel) || devanado *m* (reeling).

filbert ['filbə:t] *n* avellana *f* (nut) || avellano *m* (bush).

filch [filtʃ] *vt* hurtar, robar.

filcher [-ə*] *n* ratero, ra.

file [fail] *n* lima *f* (tool); *dead-smooth file* lima sorda || ficha *f*; *personal file* ficha personal || carpeta *f* (folder) || fichero *m* (container for cards) || archivador *m*, archivo *m* (container for documents) || archivo *m* (archive); *police files* archivos de la policía || expediente *m* (dossier) || fila *f* (line) || INFORM fichero *m* || MIL fila *f*; *in file* en fila || — *card-index file* fichero *m* || INFORM *file allocation* asignación *f* de fichero | *file creation* creación *f* de fichero | *file editor* editor *m* de fichero | *file management* gestión *f* or de ficheros || *Indian file* fila india || *in single file* en fila de a uno || *to be on file* estar archivado || *to close the file on a case* dar carpetazo a un asunto, dar por terminado un asunto || *to take one's place in the file* ponerse en cola.

file [fail] *vt* limar; *to file one's nails* limarse las uñas || archivar, clasificar (a card, a document) || INFORM archivar || JUR presentar (a petition); *to file a petition for divorce* presentar una demanda de divorcio.
◆ *vi* marchar en fila || — US *to file for a pension* hacer una petición de *or* solicitar una pensión || *to file in, out* entrar, salir en fila *or* uno tras otro || *to file past* desfilar ante.

file card [-ka:d] *n* ficha *f*.

filer ['failə*] *n* TECH limador *m* || archivero, ra (filing clerk).

filet [fi'lei] *n* encaje *m* (lace) || CULIN filete *m*.

filial ['filjəl] *adj* filial.

filiation [,fili'eiʃən] *n* JUR filiación *f* (father-son relationship) || filiación *f*; *to determine the filiation of a language* determinar la filiación de una lengua.

filibuster ['filibʌstə*] *n* filibustero *m* (pirate) || US obstruccionista *m* (person who delays proceedings) | obstruccionismo *m* (use of delaying tactics).

filibuster ['filibʌstə*] *vi* ser un filibustero || US practicar el obstruccionismo.
◆ *vt* US obstruir (the passage of a bill, etc.).

filibusterer [-rə*] *n* US obstruccionista *m*.

filibustering [-riŋ] *n* filibusterismo *m* || US obstruccionismo *m*.

filiform ['filifɔ:m] *adj* filiforme.

filigree ['filigri:]; **filagree** ['filəgri:qb] *n* filigrana *f*.

filigree ['filigri:]; **filagree** ['filəgri:qb] *vt* afiligranar.

filing ['failiŋ] *n* limadura *f* (action of filing metals, etc.) || colocación *f* en un archivo *or* en un fichero || clasificación *f*; *the filing of papers* la clasificación de papeles || INFORM clasificación *f*.
◆ *pl* limaduras *f*; *iron filings* limaduras de hierro.

filing cabinet [-'kæbinit] *n* archivo *m*, fichero *m*.

filing card [-ka:d] *n* ficha *f*.

filing clerk [kla:k] *n* archivero, ra; archivista *m* & *f*.

Filipino [fili'pi:nəu] *adj/n* filipino, na.

fill [fil] *n* hartura *f*, hartazgo *m* || pipa *f* (of tobacco) || terraplén *m* (embankment) || — *to eat one's fill* hartarse de comer (very much), comer lo suficiente *or* bien (just enough) || *to have had one's fill of sth.* estar harto de algo || *to take a fill of tobacco* cargar la pipa.

fill [fil] *vt* llenar; *he filled my glass* me llenó el vaso; *smoke filled the room* el humo llenaba el cuarto || ocupar (space, post) || cubrir (a vacancy) || ocupar, llenar (time) || llenar (food) || empastar (a tooth) || cargar (to load) || tapar, rellenar, llenar (a crack, a hole) || CULIN rellenar || chapar (with gold) || hinchar; *the wind filled the sails* el viento hinchaba las velas || inflar (a tyre) || cumplir con, satisfacer (requirements) || FIG llenar; *to fill s.o. with rage, with confusion* llenar a uno de ira, de confusión || US despachar (an order) | extender, hacer (prescription) || — *fill her up!* ¡llénelo! (petrol tank) || *the thoughts which filled his mind* las ideas que le llenaban la cabeza || *to be filled to capacity* estar completamente lleno || *to fill one's part well* desempeñar bien su papel.
◆ *vi* llenarse.
◆ *phr v* ***to fill in*** terraplenar, rellenar (a hole in the ground) | rellenar, llenar (a form) | poner (the date in a form) | extender (a cheque) | completar (an outline) || — *to be filling in time* pasar el rato (use) | *to fill in for somebody* reemplazar a alguien | *to fill s.o. in* poner a alguien al corriente || ***to fill out*** rellenar (a form, an essay, a speech) | hinchar (a balloon) | hincharse (sails in the wind) | llenarse (cheeks) | engordar (to grow fatter) || ***to fill up*** llenar; *fill my glass up, please* lléname el vaso, por favor | llenarse; *the tank filled up with water* el depósito se llenó de agua | rellenar, llenar (a form) | hartar, llenar; *the meal filled me up* la comida me llenó || — *to fill up with fuel* repostar a tope (a plane, a boat).

filler [-ə*] *n* relleno *m* (to increase weight or bulk) || tripa *f* (of a cigar) || masilla *f* (to fill in cracks) || artículo *m* (de relleno) (in newspaper, etc.).

filler cap [-kæp] *n* tapón *m* de depósito de gasolina.

fillet ['filit] *n* CULIN filete *m* (of meat, of fish) || cinta *f* (band) || ARCH & PRINT filete *m*.

fillet ['filit] *vt* recoger con una cinta (hair) || CULIN cortar en filetes || filetear (to adorn with a fillet).

filling [,filiŋ] *n* relleno *m* || terraplenado *m* (of a ditch) || empaste *m* (of a tooth) || trama *f* (of a material).
◆ *adj* que llena mucho (food).

filling station [-'steiʃən] *n* estación *f* de servicio.

fillip ['filip] *n* capirotazo *m* (flick of the finger) || papirotazo *m* (quick blow) || FIG estímulo *m* (stimulus).

fillip ['filip] *vt* dar un capirotazo a (to flick) || dar un papirotazo a (to strike) || FIG estimular (to stimulate).

fillister ['filistə*] *n* guillame *m* (plane).

fill-up ['filʌp] *n* relleno *m*.

filly ['fili] *n* potra *f* (young mare) || FIG muchacha *f* (girl).

film [film] *n* película *f*, capa *f* (thin layer) || PHOT película *f* || CINEM película *f*, filme *m*; *to shoot a film* rodar una película; *to make a film* hacer una película || cine *m*, cinema *m*; *film fan* aficionado al cine; *film producer* productor de cine || nube *f* (in the eye) || FIG velo *m* (of smoke, of mist, etc.) || — *film industry* industria cinematográfica || *film library* cinemateca *f*, filmoteca *f* || PHOT *roll of film* carrete *m*, rollo *m* || CINEM *silent film* película muda.

film [film] *vt* CINEM rodar, filmar (a scene, a story) | filmar (people, events); *to film a sunset* filmar una puesta de sol | hacer una versión cinematográfica de (a book) || cubrir con una película *or* capa (to coat with a layer).
◆ *vi* rodar || *to film over* cubrirse con una película *or* capa.

filmgoer [-gəuə*] *n* aficionado *m* al cine.

filminess [-inis] *n* diafanidad *f*, transparencia *f* (transparency).

filming [-iŋ] *n* filmación *f*, rodaje *m*.

film star [-sta:*] *n* astro *m* de cine (man) || estrella *f* de cine (woman).

filmstrip [-strip] *n* película *f* [para ilustrar una conferencia *or* una lección].

film studio [-'stju:diəu] *n* estudio *m* (de cine).

filmy ['filmi] *adj* diáfano, na; transparente (transparent) || nublado, da (misty).

Filofax ['failəufæks] *n* agenda *f* de hojas intercambiables (registered trademark).

filter ['filtə*] *n* filtro *m*; *air filter* filtro de aire; *oil, petrol filter* filtro de aceite, de gasolina || PHYS & PHOT filtro *m* || *filter paper* papel *m* de filtro.

filter ['filtə*] *vt* filtrar.
◆ *vi* filtrarse; *to filter through a paper* filtrarse a través de *or* por un papel || — FIG *to filter into* infiltrarse en || *to filter through* o *out* llegar a saberse, filtrarse.

filtering [-riŋ] *n* filtración *f*.
◆ *adj* filtrante.

filter tip ['filtətip] *n* boquilla *f* con filtro (tip) || cigarrillo *m* con filtro (cigarette).

filter-tipped ['filtətipt] *adj* con filtro, emboquillado, da.

filth [filθ] *n* suciedad *f*, porquería *f*, inmundicia *f* (dirt) || FIG obscenidades *f pl*, porquerías *f pl* (bad language, bad thoughts).

filthiness [-inis] *n* suciedad *f* (dirtiness) || FIG obscenidad *f*.

filthy [-i] *adj* asqueroso, sa; mugriento, ta; inmundo, da (very dirty) || obsceno, na; asqueroso, sa (obscene) || FIG de perros (weather, temper) || — FIG *filthy lucre* vil metal *m* (money) | *filthy rich* asquerosamente rico.

filtrate ['filtrit] *n* líquido *m* filtrado.

filtrate ['filtreit] *vt* filtrar.
◆ *vi* filtrarse (to filter) || FIG filtrarse; *revolutionary elements have filtrated into the country* ele-

mentos revolucionarios se han filtrado en el país.

filtration [fil'treiʃən] *n* filtración *f* || *filtration plant* planta *f* depuradora.

fin [fin] *n* aleta *f* (of fish) || rebaba *f* (of metal casting) || AVIAT plano *m* de deriva || AUT aleta *f* || US FAM mano *m* (hand) | billete *m* de cinco dólares (bill).

fin [fin] *vt* TECH proveer de aletas.
◆ *vi* aletear.

finagle [fi'neigl] *vt* US conseguir con artimañas.
◆ *vi* US trampear.

final ['fainl] *adj* último, ma; final; *final performance* última representación; *final chapter* último capítulo || decisivo, va; terminante, definitivo, va (decisive) || último, ma (ultimate); *that is my final word* es mi última palabra || GRAMM final; *final conjunction* conjunción final || — *and that's final* y sanseacabó || PHIL *final cause* causa *f* final || COMM *final demand* último aviso *m* de pago.
◆ *n* final *f* (deciding race, game); *the cup final* la final de copa || última tirada *f* (of a newspaper) || MUS nota *f* final || COMM *final demand* último aviso *m* de pago.
◆ *pl* exámenes *m* finales (examinations).

finale [fi'nɑːli] *n* MUS final *m* || THEATR escena *f* final || FIG final *m* (end).

finalism ['fainəlizəm] *n* PHIL finalismo *m*.

finalist ['fainəlist] *n* SP finalista *m* & *f*.

finality [fai'næliti] *n* determinación *f* (determination) || carácter *m* definitivo (decisiveness) || irrevocabilidad *f* || PHIL finalidad *f* || *he said it with finality* lo dijo de modo terminante.

finalize ['fainəlaiz] *vt* finalizar (to complete) || aprobar de modo definitivo (to give final approval).

finally ['fainəli] *adv* finalmente, por último; *finally, I should like to add* finalmente, quisiera añadir || por fin; *so you finally came!* ¡por fin has llegado! || definitivamente (once and for all).

finance [fai'næns] *n* finanzas *f pl* || — *finance bill* ley presupuestaria || *finance company* compañía financiera || *Minister of Finance* Ministro *m* de Hacienda [AMER Ministro *m* de Finanzas].
◆ *pl* fondos *m* (resources).

finance [fai'næns] *vt* financiar.

financial [fai'nænʃəl] *adj* financiero, ra || económico, ca; *financial year* año *or* ejercicio económico || *financial statement* estado financiero.

financier [fai'nænsiə*] *n* financiero *m*.

financing [fai'nænsiŋ] *n* financiación *f*, financiamiento *m*.

finback ['fin,bæk] *n* rorcual *m* (whale).

finch [fintʃ] *n* pinzón *m* (bird).

find [faind] *n* hallazgo *m*, descubrimiento *m*.

find* [faind] *vt* encontrar, hallar; *I found that money I lost* he encontrado el dinero que perdí || encontrar; *to find one's way* encontrar el camino; *how do you find the wine?* ¿cómo encuentras el vino?; *to find sth. easy* encontrar algo fácil; *to find s.o. boring* encontrar aburrido a alguien || proporcionar, facilitar (to provide); *the employer finds them accommodation* el empresario les proporciona alojamiento || JUR declarar; *the jury found him guilty* el jurado lo declaró culpable | pronunciar (sentence) || FIG sorprender; *I found him looking through the keyhole* le sorprendí mirando por la cerradura || comprobar; *it has been found that it was not true* se ha comprobado que no era verdad || — *all found* con comida y alojamiento, todo incluido (salary) || *I find the job dull* el trabajo me resulta pesado || *if you can find time* si tienes tiempo || *leave everything as you find it* deja todo como lo has encontrado || *the arrow found its mark* la flecha dio en el blanco || *the statement found its way to the newspapers* la declaración llegó hasta los periódicos || *to be found* encontrarse || *to find fault with* criticar || *to find favour with s.o.* caerle en gracia a uno || *to find it in one's heart to* ser capaz de || *to find o.s.* encontrarse a sí mismo (to discover one's possibilities), encontrarse (to feel); *how do you find yourself?* ¿cómo te encuentras?; verse; *to find o.s. obliged to* verse obligado a; encontrar; *did you find yourself a flat?* ¿encontraste piso? || *to find s.o. out* sorprender a alguien (to catch s.o.), descubrir a alguien (to discover) || *to find sth. out* averiguar algo, enterarse de algo (to check up on), descubrir algo, enterarse de algo (to discover) || *to find the courage to* tener el valor de || *to try to find* buscar || *we found it impossible* nos fue imposible, lo encontramos imposible.
◆ *vi* JUR fallar; *how did the jury find?* ¿cómo falló el jurado?; *to find for* fallar en favor de || — *seek and ye shall find* busca y hallarás || *to find out about* averiguar, enterarse de.
— OBSERV Pret y pp ***found***.

finder [-ə*] *n* descubridor, ra; hallador, ra || inventor, ra; descubridor, ra (inventor) || PHOT visor *m* (of a camera) || anteojo *m* buscador (of telescope).

finding [-iŋ] *n* descubrimiento *m* (discovery) || JUR fallo *m*, decisión *f*.
◆ *pl* hallazgos *m*; *to exhibit the findings of an archaeological expedition* exponer los hallazgos de una expedición arqueológica || resultados; *to publish the findings of one's research* publicar los resultados de su investigación || conclusiones *f* (conclusions) || herramientas *f* (tools).

fine [fain] *adj* excelente; *a fine performance* una excelente representación || hermoso, sa (beautiful) || elegante (smart); *fine clothes* ropa elegante || admirable, excelente (person) || agradable (pleasant); *a fine feeling* una sensación agradable || magnífico, ca; bueno, na; *a fine future* un magnífico porvenir || refinado, da; fino, na (refined); *fine taste* gusto refinado || primoroso, sa; *fine hand* letra primorosa || bueno, na (good); *fine weather* buen tiempo || fino, na; delicado, da; *a fine lace* un encaje fino || fino, na; *fine sand* arena fina || agudo, da; fino, na (sharp); *a fine point* una punta fina; *a fine sense of justice* un agudo sentido de la justicia || ligero, ra; sutil (slight); *a fine distinction* una ligera diferencia || puro, ra; fino, na (metals); *fine gold* oro puro || FAM menudo, da; *that's a fine mess we're in!* ¡en menudo lío estamos metidos!; *a fine friend you are!* ¡menudo amigo eres tú! || — *fine fellow* buen mozo || *fine sentiments* buenos sentimientos || *gold eighteen carats fine* oro de dieciocho quilates || *is it fine out?* ¿hace buen tiempo? || *one of these fine days* un día de éstos || *that's fine!* ¡muy bien!, ¡estupendo! || *to make a fine job of sth.* hacer un buen trabajo con algo.
◆ *adv* en trozos pequeños; *she chopped garlic fine* cortó el ajo en trozos pequeños || fino; *to grind coffee fine* moler fino el café || mucho; *that would suit me fine* esto me convendría mucho || muy bien (well) || — FIG *to cut it fine* llegar justo a tiempo (to arrive just in time), calcular muy justo || *to cut one's profits too fine* reducir demasiado sus beneficios || *to feel fine* sentirse bien.
◆ *n* multa *f* (as a punishment); *a heavy fine* una multa de mucha cuantía || *in fine* en resumidas cuentas.

fine [fain] *vt* multar, poner una multa a (to punish) || purificar (to purify) || refinar (to refine) || *to fine down* afinar; *to fine down the lines of a car* afinar la línea de un coche; afilar (a pencil), purificar (to purify), refinar (to refine).
◆ *vi* purificarse || afinarse (to become slimmer).

fine arts [-ɑːts] *pl n* bellas artes *f*.

fine-draw [-drɔː] *vt* zurcir (torn materials) || estirar (wire) || FIG sutilizar.

fine-drawn [-drɔːn] *adj* fino, na (features) || invisible (mend) || estirado, da (wire) || sutil (subtle).

fine-grained [-greind] *adj* de grano fino.

finely ['fainli] *adv* hermosamente (beautifully) || finito (thinly) || finamente (delicately).

fineness [-nis] *n* finura *f*, fineza *f*, delicadeza *f* (delicacy) || finura *f*, tenuidad *f* (thinness) || elegancia *f* (elegance) || belleza *f* (beauty) || excelencia *f* (excellence) || agudeza *f* (sharpness) || pureza *f* (purity) || ley (of metals).

finery [-əri] *n* refinería *f* (refinery) || galas *f pl*; *to dress up in all one's finery* vestirse con sus mejores galas.

finespun [-s'pʌn] *adj* fino, na; hilado muy fino (silk, etc.) || sutil (subtle).

finesse [fi'nes] *n* fineza *f*, delicadeza *f* (delicacy) || estratagema *f*, treta *f* (strategy) || diplomacia *f*, tacto *m* (diplomacy) || astucia *f* (cunning) || discernimiento *m* (subtlety of judgment) || impase *m*, impás *m* (in bridge).

finesse [fi'nes] *vi* hacer el impase (bridge).
◆ *vt* conseguir por artimañas; *to finesse one's way into a position* conseguir un puesto por artimañas.

fine-tooth comb ['faintuːθ'kəum]; **fine-toothed comb** ['faintuːθt'kəum] *n* peine *m* espeso || *to go through a room with a fine-tooth comb* registrar un cuarto a fondo.

fine-tune ['faintʃuːn] *vt* hacer una puesta a punto, ajustar.

finger ['fiŋgə*] *n* dedo *m* (of hand, of glove); *little, middle, ring, index finger* dedo meñique, del corazón, anular, índice || dedo *m* (measure); *two fingers of whisky* dos dedos de whisky || TECH trinquete *m* || — FIG *his fingers are all thumbs* es muy desmañado | *I can't quite put my finger on it* no veo lo que puede ser | *let's keep our fingers crossed!* ¡ojalá salga todo bien! | *to burn one's fingers* cogerse los dedos || FIG & FAM *to have a finger in every pie* estar metido en todo, meter las manos en todo | *to have had a finger in the pie* haber metido las manos *or* estar pringado en el asunto | *to have green fingers* tener habilidad para la jardinería | *to lay a finger on s.o.* alzar la mano a alguien | *to lift a finger* mover un dedo | *to put one's finger on* señalar (to indicate), dar informaciones sobre (to inform on), denunciar, delatar (to denounce) | *to put one's finger on it* dar en el clavo (to guess right) | *to put one's finger on the sore spot* poner el dedo en la llaga | *to slip through one's fingers* escapársele a uno de las manos | *to snap one's fingers at s.o.* burlarse de alguien | *to twist s.o. round one's little finger* manejar a uno a su antojo.

finger ['fiŋgə*] *vt* tocar (to touch) || MUS tocar, tañer, pulsar (a stringed instrument) | teclear (a tune on the piano) | marcar la digitación en (written music) || FAM robar (to steal).

finger biscuit [-'biskit] *n* CULIN lengua *f* de gato.

fingerboard [-bɔːd] *n* MUS diapasón *m* (of a stringed instrument) | teclado *m* (of a piano).

finger bowl [-bəul] *n* enjuague *m*.

fingerbreadth [-bredθ] *n* dedo *m* (dimension).

fingered [-d] *adj* con dedos || BOT & MUS digitado, da.

fingering [-riŋ] *n* manoseo *m* (action of touching) || MUS digitación *f*.

fingerling [-liŋ] *n* ZOOL salmoncillo *m* (young salmon) || US pececillo *m* (small fish).

fingermark [-maːk] *n* dedada *f*.

fingernail [-neil] *n* uña *f*.

finger plate [-pleit] *n* chapa *f* de protección (of doors).

finger post [-pəust] *n* poste *m* indicador.

fingerprint [-print] *n* huella *f* dactilar *or* digital; *to take s.o.'s fingerprints* tomar las huellas dactilares *or* digitales a alguien.

fingerprint [-print] *vt* tomar las huellas dactilares *or* digitales a.

fingerstall [-stɔːl] *n* dedil *m* (protective covering of rubber, etc.).

fingertip [-tip] *n* punta *f or* yema *f* de los dedos || dedil *m* (protection) || — FIG *to have sth. at one's fingertips* saber algo al dedillo | *to one's fingertips* de pies a cabeza (completely).

finial ['fainiəl] *n* florón *m*.

finickiness ['finiknis] *n* melindre *m*, remilgo *m*.

finicky ['finiki] *adj* melindroso, sa; remilgado, da; afectado, da.

finish ['finiʃ] *n* fin *m*, final *m*, conclusión *f* (end) || acabado *m* (of a surface); *a gloss finish* un acabado brillante || perfección *f* || SP llegada *f* (in a race) || ARTS última mano *f* || buenos modales *m pl* (social polish) || — *that was the finish of him* aquello fue su ruina || *to be in at the finish* presenciar el final || *to fight to the finish* luchar hasta el final.

finish ['finiʃ] *vt* terminar, acabar; *to finish a book, a story* terminar un libro, un relato || llegar al final de (a journey) || acabar con; *the fever almost finished him* la fiebre casi acabó con él || dar el último toque *or* los últimos toques *or* la última mano a, rematar (to add the finishing touch) || TECH acabar || — *to finish off* rematar (to complete, to kill) || *to finish up* acabar, terminar.
◆ *vi* acabar, terminar; *how does the play finish?* ¿cómo acaba la obra?; *he finished by saying* terminó diciendo..., terminó por decir... || SP llegar; *he finished second* llegó el segundo || — *to finish with* acabar con || *to finish with one's boyfriend* reñir con *or* acabar con el novio || FIG & FAM *wait till I've finished with him!* ¡ya verás cómo le dejo!

finished [-t] *adj* acabado, da; terminado, da; *is the job finished?* ¿está terminado el trabajo? || FIG consumado, da; excelente (perfect); *a finished speaker* un orador excelente || TECH acabado, da || agotado, da; rendido, da (tired) || *he is finished as a politician* está acabado como político.

finisher [-ə*] *n* SP participante *m* que llega a la meta || TECH máquina *f* acabadora (machine) | acabador, ra (person) || FAM golpe *m* de gracia (final blow).

finishing [-iŋ] *adj* último, ma; *finishing touch* último toque, última mano || — SP *finishing line* línea *f* de llegada; meta *f* || *finishing school* escuela *f* privada de educación social para señoritas.
◆ *n* acabado *m*.

finite ['fainait] *adj* MATH & PHIL finito, ta || GRAMM conjugado, da (form of verb).

fink [fiŋk] *n* US FAM esquirol *m*, rompehuelgas *m inv* (strikebreaker).

Finland ['finlənd] *pr n* GEOGR Finlandia *f*.

Finn [fin] *n* finlandés, esa.

finnan haddie [ˌfinən'hædi]; **finnan haddock** [-'hædək] *n* bacalao *m* ahumado.

finned [find] *adj* con aletas.

Finnic ['finik] *adj* finés, esa; finlandés, esa.
◆ *n* finés *m* (language).

finnicking [-iŋ] *adj* melindroso, sa; remilgado, da; afectado, da.

finnicky [-i] *adj* melindroso, sa; remilgado, da; afectado, da.

Finnish ['finiʃ] *adj* finlandés, esa.
◆ *n* finlandés *m* (language).

fiord [fjɔːd] *n* fiordo *m*.

fir [fəː*] *n* abeto *m*.

fire ['faiə*] *n* fuego *m*; *to light a wood fire* encender un fuego de leña; *to put out the fire* apagar el fuego || incendio *m*; *the factory was destroyed by fire* la fábrica fue destruida por un incendio; *forest fire* incendio forestal || estufa *f*; *electric, gas fire* estufa eléctrica, de gas || MIL fuego *m*; *artillery fire* fuego de artillería; *to come under the enemy's fire* caer bajo el fuego del enemigo || FIG fuego *m*, ardor *m* (passion) || — FIG *a rapid fire of questions* una serie de preguntas | *between two fires* entre dos fuegos | *fire and brimstone* fuegos *m pl* del infierno || MIL *fire at will* fuego a discreción || *Greek fire* fuego griego || MIL *heavy, running fire* fuego nutrido, graneado || CULIN *on a slow fire* a fuego lento || FIG *there is no smoke without fire* cuando el río suena, agua lleva | *to add fuel to the fire* echar leña al fuego || *to be on fire* estar ardiendo || *to be under fire* estar bajo el fuego del enemigo (troops), estar sometido a críticas, ser atacado (under criticism) || *to catch* o *to take fire* prenderse, encenderse (to start burning), incendiarse (to burst into flames) || FIG *to go through fire and water* afrontar toda clase de peligros || *to miss fire* fallar || *to open fire* romper el fuego || FIG *to play with fire* jugar con fuego || *to set sth. on fire, to set fire to sth.* prenderle fuego a algo || FIG *to set the world on fire* cubrirse de gloria || *to sit by the fire* estar sentado al amor de la lumbre, estar sentado al lado de la chimenea || *trial by fire* prueba del fuego.
◆ *interj* MIL ¡fuego! (order) || ¡fuego! (call for help).

fire [faiə*] *vt* disparar (a gun, a bullet) || tirar; *to fire a salute* tirar una salva || lanzar (rocket, torpedo, etc.) || explotar (a mine) || prender (a fuse) || AUT encender || incendiar, prender fuego a (to set fire to) || lanzar, arrojar (to throw) || FIG soltar (remark, insults, etc.); *to fire a question at s.o.* soltar una pregunta a alguien | inflamar (passion) | infundir; *to fire s.o. with enthusiasm* infundir entusiasmo a alguien | enardecer; *his speech fired the crowd* su discurso enardeció a la multitud | echar (to dismiss) || cocer (bricks, pottery) || cargar, alimentar (to supply with fuel) || calentar (oven) || secar al fuego (to dry) || — *to fire off* disparar (a shot), soltar (a question, etc.) || *to fire questions at s.o.* bombardear a alguien con preguntas || *to fire up* calentar (oven), cargar, alimentar (to supply with fuel).
◆ *vi* encenderse || hacer fuego, disparar; *to fire at s.o.* hacer fuego contra alguien || dispararse (a gun) || explotar (explosives) || encenderse; *one of the cylinders is not firing* uno de los cilindros no se enciende || funcionar (to run, to work) || — MIL *fire at will!* ¡fuego a discreción! || FIG *fire away!* ¡adelante! || *to fire on* hacer fuego sobre *or* contra || US *to fire up* enfurecerse.

fire alarm [-əˌlɑːm] *n* alarma *f* de incendios.

firearm [-ɑːm] *n* arma *f* de fuego.

fireball [-bɔːl] *n* bola *f* de fuego || bólido *m* (meteor).

fireboat [-bəut] *n* barco *m* bomba.

fire bomb [-bɔm] *n* bomba *f* incendiaria.

firebox [-bɔks] *n* fogón *m*.

firebrand [-brænd] *n* tea *f* (burning wood) || botafuego *m* (lighted torch) || FIG agitador *m* (agitator).

firebreak [-breik] *n* cortafuego *m*.

firebrick [-brik] *n* ladrillo *m* refractario.

fire brigade [-brigeid] *n* bomberos *m pl*, cuerpo *m* de bomberos.

firebug [bʌg] *n* US FAM incendiario, ria; pirómano, na.

fireclay [-klei] *n* arcilla *f* refractaria.

fire control [-kənˌtrəul] *n* MIL dirección *f or* conducción *f* de tiro || extinción *m* de incendios.

firecracker [-'krækə*] *n* US petardo *m*.

fire curtain [-'kəːtn] *n* cortina *f* de fuego.

firedamp [-dæmp] *n* grisú *m* (in mines).

fire department [-di'pɑːtmənt] *n* US bomberos *m pl*, cuerpo *m* de bomberos.

firedog [-dɔg] *n* morillo *m*.

fire door [-dɔː*] *n* puerta *f* cortafuegos.

fire drill [-dril] *n* simulacro *m* de incendio [para enseñar a la gente cómo puede escapar en caso de incendio].

fire-eater [-ˌiːtə*] *n* tragafuegos *m inv* (in a circus) || FIG matamoros *m* (aggressive person).

fire engine [-ˌendʒin] *n* coche *m* de bomberos.

fire escape [-isˌkeip] *n* escalera *f* de incendios *or* de emergencia (in buildings).

fire extinguisher [-iksˌtiŋgwiʃə*] *n* extintor *m* de incendios.

fire fighter [-faitə*] *n* bombero *f* (fireman).

firefly [-flai] *n* luciérnaga (beetle).

fireguard [-gɑːd] *n* pantalla *f* (of a fireplace) || cortafuego *m* (firebreak).

firehouse [-haus] *n* US parque *m* de bomberos.

fire hydrant [-'haidrənt] *n* boca *f* de incendio.

fire insurance [-inˌʃuərəns] *n* seguro *m* contra incendios.

fire irons [-ˌaiənz] *pl n* útiles *m* de chimenea.

firelight [-lait] *n* luz *f* del hogar, lumbre *f*.

fire-lighter [-ˌlaitə*] *n* astillas *f pl* para encender el fuego.

firelock [-lɔk] *n* trabuco *m* de pedernal.

fireman [-mən] *n* bombero *m* (member of a fire brigade) || fogonero *m* (of locomotive, etc.).
— OBSERV El plural de esta palabra es *firemen*.

fire opal [-əupəl] *n* MIN girasol *m*.

fire pan [-pæn] *n* brasero *m*.

fireplace [-pleis] *n* chimenea *f*.

fireplug [-plʌg] *n* boca *f* de incendio.

firepower [-ˌpauə*] *n* MIL potencia *f* de fuego.

fireproof [-pruːf] *adj* ininflamable, incombustible, ignífugo, ga || refractario, ria (brick, clay, etc.).

fireproof [-pruːf] *vt* hacer ininflamable *or* ignífugo, ignifugar.

fire-raiser [-reizə*] *n* incendiario, ria.

fire-raising [-'reiziŋ] *n* incendio *m* premeditado.

fire screen [-skriːn] *n* pantalla *f*.

fire service [-ˌsəːvis] *n* cuerpo *m* de bomberos.

fire ship [-ʃip] *n* brulote *m*.

fireside [-said] *n* hogar *m* || *to sit down by the fireside* sentarse al amor de la lumbre, sentarse al lado de la chimenea.
◆ *adj* al amor de la lumbre || US sin protocolo, familiar (informal).

fire station [-'steiʃən] *n* parque *m* de bomberos.

firestone [-stəun] *n* pedernal *m* (flint) || piedra *f* refractaria.

firetrap [-træp] *n* edificio *m* con salidas de emergencia insuficientes en caso de incendio.

fire wall [-wɔːl] *n* cortafuego *m*.

fire warden [-'wɔːdn] *n* US funcionario *m* encargado de la protección contra incendios.

firewater [-ˌwɔːtə*] *n* FAM aguardiente *m*, matarratas *m inv*.

firewood [-wud] *n* leña *f*.

firework [-wəːk] *n* fuego *m* de artificio. ◆ *pl* fuegos *m* artificiales (display) ‖ FIG *then the fireworks started* entonces se armó la gorda.

firing ['faiəriŋ] *n* disparos *m pl*; *firing could be heard* podían oírse disparos ‖ combustible *m* (fuel) ‖ carga *f*, alimentación *f* (of furnace) ‖ cocción *f* (of pottery) ‖ AUT encendido *m* ‖ VET cauterización *f* ‖ FIG despido *m*, expulsión *f* (dismissal) ‖ *the firing of the ships' cannons* el cañoneo de los barcos.

firing line [-lain] *n* línea *f* de fuego.

firing party [-ˌpaːti] *n* US pelotón *m* de ejecución.

firing pin [-pin] *n* percutor *m*, percusor *m*.

firing squad [-skwɔd] *n* pelotón *m* de ejecución ‖ US piquete *m* de salvas (who fires a salute).

firm [fəːm] *adj* firme, sólido, da; *firm foundation* base sólida ‖ firme; *firm decision* decisión firme ‖ estable (stable) ‖ estable, firme (prices) ‖ COMM en firme; *firm offer, order* oferta, pedido en firme | firme (shares) ‖ *to rule a country with a firm hand* gobernar un país con mano dura. ◆ *adv* firme; *to stand firm* mantenerse firme ‖ *to hold firm to* agarrarse bien a (an object), mantenerse firme en (one's opinions). ◆ *n* empresa *f*, firma *f* (company) ‖ razón *f* social (name).

firm [fəːm] *vt* asegurar, afianzar (to make secure) ‖ concretar (to settle) ‖ reforzar (to strenghen) ‖ *to firm up a deal* concretar un negocio ‖ *to firm up one's muscles* reafirmar *or* endurecer los músculos. ◆ *vi* mejorar (to improve) ‖ *to firm up* endurecerse (músculos).

firmament ['fəːməmənt] *n* firmamento *m*.

firmer chisel ['fəːmə*'tʃizl] *n* formón *m*.

firmly ['fəːmli] *adv* firmemente, sólidamente ‖ firmemente; *I firmly believe that* creo firmemente que.

firmness ['fəːmnis] *n* firmeza *f* (stability) ‖ FIG firmeza *f* (resolution, strength); *firmness in one's convictions, of character* firmeza de convicciones, de carácter.

firn ['fəːn] *n* nevero *m*.

first [fəːst] *adj* primero, ra (see OBSERV); *the first three months* los tres primeros meses; *first row* primera fila; *the first man* el primer hombre; *first secretary* primer secretario ‖ básico, ca; fundamental (basic); *first principles* principios básicos ‖ elemental, rudimentario, ria (elementary) ‖ más mínimo, ma; *he hasn't the first idea about drawing* no tiene la más mínima idea del dibujo ‖ — *at first hand* de primera mano ‖ *at first sight* a primera vista ‖ PHIL & REL *first cause* causa primera ‖ *first edition* primera edición, edición príncipe (of a book), primera edición (of a newspaper) ‖ AUT *first gear* primera *f*, primera velocidad; *to put a car in first gear* poner un coche en primera ‖ GRAMM *first person* primera persona ‖ *first things first* lo primero es lo primero ‖ *First World War* Primera Guerra Mundial ‖ *in the first place* en primer lugar ‖ *I shall do it first thing tomorrow* es lo primero que haré mañana ‖ *not to know the first thing about* no tener la más mínima idea de ‖ *the first house but one* la segunda casa. ◆ *adv* por primera vez; *we first went there last year* fuimos allí por primera vez el año pasado ‖ en primer lugar, primero (firstly) ‖ antes, primero; *you must finish your work first* tienes que acabar el trabajo antes ‖ — *first and foremost* antes que nada, ante todo ‖ *first and last* en todos los aspectos ‖ *first come, first served* el que se adelanta nunca pierde ‖ *first of all* en primer lugar, ante todo ‖ *first or last* tarde o temprano ‖ *head first* de cabeza ‖ *I would die first!* ¡antes morir! ‖ *ladies first* las señoras primero ‖ *to come first* llegar primero (in a race), ser lo primero; *my family comes first* mi familia es lo primero ‖ FIG *to get in first* adelantarse a los demás ‖ *to go first* ir *or* entrar el primero (to be the first), viajar en primera (to travel first-class) ‖ *to say first one thing, then another* decir primero una cosa, luego otra ‖ *to travel first* viajar en primera clase ‖ *women and children first* las mujeres y los niños primero ‖ *you go first* Ud. primero. ◆ *n* primero, ra; *the first of the speakers* el primero de los oradores; *Isabel I (the first)* Isabel I [primera] ‖ sobresaliente *m* (degree); *to get a first* sacar sobresaliente ‖ día *m* uno, uno *m*, primero *m* (date); *the first of January* el día uno de enero ‖ AUT primera *f* (gear) ‖ — *at first* al principio ‖ *from first to last* desde el principio hasta el final ‖ *from the first* desde el principio ‖ *that's the first I've heard about it* es la primera noticia que tengo ‖ *the first to arrive* el primero (*or* los primeros) en llegar ‖ *to be the first to* ser el primero en. ◆ *pl* artículos *m* de primera calidad.
— OBSERV The adjective *primero* is apocopated to *primer* when preceeding a masculine noun: *the first day* el primer día.

first aid [-eid] *n* MED primeros auxilios *m pl* (emergency treatment).

first-aid kit [-eidkit] *n* botiquín *m* de urgencia.

first-aid post [-eidpəust] *n* casa *f* de socorro.

first base [beis] *n* US SP primera base *f* (in baseball) ‖ US *to get to first base* hacer algún progreso, haber dado el primer paso.

firstborn [-bɔːn] *adj/n* mayor, primogénito, ta.

first-class [-klaːs] *adj* de primera clase; *first-class ticket* billete de primera clase ‖ de primera calidad, de primera categoría (of the best quality); *a first-class film* una película de primera calidad ‖ sobresaliente (examination marks). ◆ *adv* en primera; *to travel first-class* viajar en primera.

first-cousin [-'kʌzn] *n* primo hermano *or* carnal ‖ *first cousin once removed* sobrino segundo (one's first cousin's child), tío segundo (one's parent's first cousin).

first day [-dei] *n* US día *m* de emisión (of a stamp) | domingo *m* (used by Quakers).

first-day-cover [-dei'kʌvə*] *n* sobre *m* del día de emisión de un sello.

first floor [flɔː*] *n* primer piso *m* ‖ US planta *f* baja.

firstfruits [-fruːts] *pl n* frutas *f* tempranas ‖ FIG primeros frutos *m*.

firsthand [-hænd] *adv/adj* de primera mano ‖ *at firsthand* directamente.

First Lady [-'leidi] *n* Primera Dama *f*.

first lieutenant [-lef'tenənt] *n* US teniente *m*.

firstling [-liŋ] *n* primogénito *m* (of animals) ‖ FIG primeros frutos *m pl*.

firstly [-li] *adv* en primer lugar, primero.

first mate [-meit] *n* MAR segundo oficial *m*.

first mortgage [-'mɔːgidʒ] *n* primera hipoteca *f*.

first name [-neim] *n* nombre *m* de pila, nombre *m*.

first night [-nait] *n* noche *f* de estreno, estreno *m*.

first nighter [-'naitə*] *n* persona *f* que asiste a todos los estrenos.

first offender [-ə'fendə*] *n* JUR persona *f* que comete un delito por primera vez.

first officer [-'ɔfisə*] *n* MAR primer piloto *m*.

first papers [-'peipəz] *pl n* US solicitud *f sing* de naturalización.

first-past-the-post [-paːst ðə pəust] *adj* por mayoría simple (electoral system).

first quarter [-'kwɔːtə*] *n* cuarto *m* creciente (of the moon).

first-rate [-reit] *adj* de primera clase *or* calidad *or* categoría (finest quality). ◆ *adv* muy bien.

first refusal [-ri'fjuːzəl] *n* COMM primera opción *f* de compra.

first sergeant [-'saːdʒənt] *n* US sargento *m*.

first water [-'wɔːtə*] *n* primera calidad *f* (of diamond) ‖ FIG primera categoría *f*.

firth [-fəːθ] *n* estuario *m*, brazo *m* de mar.

fisc [fisk] *n* fisco *m*, tesoro *m* público, erario *m*.

fiscal ['fiskəl] *adj* fiscal ‖ *fiscal year* año *or* ejercicio económico. ◆ *n* fiscal *m*.

fish [fiʃ] *n* pez *m* (in water) ‖ pescado *m* (food) ‖ refuerzo *m* (for building) ‖ MAR jimelga *f* ‖ eclisa *f*, mordaza *f* (fishplate) ‖ FIG & FAM tipo *m*, tío *m* (fellow) ‖ ASTR Piscis *m pl* ‖ — FIG *a different kettle of fish* harina de otro costal ‖ *fish and chips* pescado frito con patatas fritas ‖ *flying fish* pez volador ‖ *freshwater fish* pez de agua dulce ‖ FIG *he's a queer fish* es un tipo extraño | *neither fish nor fowl* ni chicha ni limonada, ni carne ni pescado | *poor fish* pobre hombre | *there are lots more fish in the sea* no es la única persona en el mundo | *to be like a fish in water* estar como pez en el agua | *to drink like a fish* beber como una esponja | *to feed the fishes* ahogarse (to drown) | *to feel like a fish out of water* sentirse como gallo en corral ajeno *or* como pez fuera del agua | *to have other fish to fry* tener algo mejor que hacer ‖ *salt-water fish* pez de agua salada.

fish [fiʃ] *vi* pescar (to go fishing) ‖ FIG buscar; *to fish for compliments* buscar elogios; *to fish in one's pocket* buscar en el bolsillo ‖ — FIG *to fish in troubled waters* pescar en río revuelto ‖ *to go fishing* ir de pesca. ◆ *vt* pescar en; *to fish a river* pescar en un río ‖ pescar (fish, pearls) ‖ FIG sacar; *to fish a coin out of one's pocket* sacar una moneda del bolsillo ‖ TECH unir con eclisas (rails, etc.) ‖ — *to fish out a river* vaciar de peces un río ‖ FAM *to fish secrets out of s.o.* sonsacar a alguien.

fish ball [-bɔːl] *n* croqueta *f* de pescado.

fish bone [-bəun] *n* espina *f*.

fishbowl [-bəul] *n* pecera *f*.

fish breeding [-'briːdiŋ] *n* piscicultura *f*.

fish cake [-keik] *n* croqueta *f* de pescado.

fish carver [-'kaːvə*] *n* cuchillo *m* para el pescado.

fisher [-ə*] *n* pescador *m* (man) ‖ barco *m* pesquero (boat) ‖ ZOOL marta *f* de América (marten).

fisherman ['fiʃəːmən] *n* pescador *m* (person) ‖ barco *m* pesquero (boat).
— OBSERV El plural es *fishermen*.

fisherwoman ['fiʃəːwumən] *n* pescadora *f*.
— OBSERV El plural es *fisherwomen*.

fishery ['fiʃəri] *n* pesquería *f*, industria *f* pesquera, pesca *f* (industry) ‖ pesquería *f* (fishing area) ‖ criadero *m* de peces (place where fish are bred) ‖ derecho *m* de pesca (right).

fish farm ['fiʃfaːm] *n* piscifactoría *f*.

fish finger [fiʃfiŋgə*] *n* CULIN filete *m* de pescado empanado.

fish flour [fiʃflauə*] *n* harina *f* de pescado.

fish glue ['fiʃ-glu:] *n* cola *f* de pescado.

fish hatchery ['fiʃhætʃəri] *n* vivero *m or* criadero *m* de peces.

fish hawk ['fiʃhɔ:k] *n* ZOOL pigargo *m*.

fishhook ['fiʃhuk] *n* anzuelo *m*.

fishing ['fiʃiŋ] *n* pesca *f*.

fishing boat [-bəut] *n* barco *m* de pesca *or* pesquero.

fishing ground [-graund] *n* pesquería *f*, zona *f* de pesca.

fishing line [-lain] *n* sedal *m*.

fishing net [-net] *n* red *f* de pesca.

fishing rod [-rɔd] *n* caña *f* de pescar.

fishing tackle [-'tækl] *n* aparejo *m* de pescar.

fish joint [fiʃdʒɔint] *n* junta *f* de eclisa (railway).

fish kettle [fiʃketl] *n* besuguera *f*.

fishline ['fiʃlain] *n* US sedal *m*.

fish market [fiʃmɑ:kit] *n* mercado *m* de pescado.

fish meal ['fiʃmi:l] *n* harina *f* de pescado.

fishmonger ['fiʃmʌŋgə*] *n* pescadero *m* || *fishmonger's shop, fishmonger's* pescadería *f*.

fishnet ['fiʃnet] *n* malla *f* (fabric) || *fishnet stockings, tights* medias *f pl* leotardos *m pl* de malla.

fishplate ['fiʃpleit] *n* eclisa *f*, mordaza *f* (of a railway line).

fish pole ['fiʃpəul] *n* US caña *f* de pescar.

fishpond ['fiʃpɔnd] *n* vivero *m*, criadero *m* (for breeding) || estanque *m* con peces (in a garden) || FAM mar *m* (sea).

fish slice ['fiʃslais] *n* pala *f* para freír pescado.

fish story ['fiʃstɔ:ri] *n* FAM cuento *m* inverosímil, historia *f* increíble.

fishtail ['fiʃteil] *vi* AVIAT colear.

fish trap ['fiʃtræp] *n* nasa *f*.

fishwife ['fiʃwaif] *n* pescadera *f* || FIG & FAM verdulera *f*, mujer *f* malhablada.
— OBSERV El plural de esta palabra es *fishwives*.

fishworm ['fiʃwə:m] *n* gusano *m*.

fishy ['fiʃi] *adj* a pescado; *a fishy smell* un olor a pescado || rico en peces, abundante en peces (rich in fish) || sin brillo (eyes) || FAM sospechoso, sa (suspicious) | poco claro, ra; turbio, bia (not clear) || — FIG *there's sth. fishy going on* hay gato encerrado | *to smell fishy* oler mal, oler a chamusquina || *to taste fishy* saber a pescado.

fissile ['fisail] *adj* fisible, físil, escindible, fisionable.

fission ['fiʃən] *n* PHYS fisión *f*, escisión *f* (of nucleus) || fisión *f*, escisión *f* (splitting of cell).

fissionable ['fiʃnəbl] *adj* fisionable, fisible.

fissure ['fiʃə*] *n* grieta *f*, hendidura *f*, fisura *f* (a cleft or split); *the earthquake opened up fissures in the rocks* el terremoto abrió grietas en las rocas || ANAT fisura *f*.

fissure ['fiʃə*] *vt* rajar, agrietar, hender, cuartear.
◆ *vi* cuartearse, agrietarse, rajarse, henderse.

fist [fist] *n* puño *m* || FIG letra *f* (writing) || FAM mano *f* (hand) || — *to clench one's fists* apretar los puños || *to shake one's fist at* amenazar con el puño || *to strike s.o. with one's fist* dar un puñetazo *or* puñetazos a alguien.

fist [fist] *vt* dar puñetazos a (to hit) || asir (to grasp).

fistic ['fistik] *adj* pugilístico, ca.

fisticuffs ['fistikʌf] *pl n* pelea *f sing* a puñetazos (fight) || puñetazos *m* (blows).

fistula ['fistjulə] *n* MED fístula *f*.
— OBSERV El plural de la palabra inglesa es *fistulas* o *fistulae*.

fistular [-ə*]; **fistulous** [-əs] *adj* fistular, fistuloso, sa.

fit [fit] *adj* conveniente, apropiado, da; *do what you think fit* haz lo que te parezca conveniente || apto, ta, capaz (competent); *he isn't fit to do the job* no es apto para hacer el trabajo, no es capaz de hacer el trabajo || capacitado, da (qualified) || apropiado, da; adecuado, da (suitable); *I need a dress fit for a wedding* necesito un traje apropiado para una boda || justo, ta (just) || digno, na (worthy); *he is not fit to live* no es digno de vivir || sano, na; bien de salud, en buen estado físico (healthy); *to be very fit* estar muy bien de salud || SP en forma (in good form); *the captain is not fit today* el capitán no está en forma hoy || — *fit for a king* digno de un rey || US *he is fit to be tied* está que echa chispas || *I'm not fit to be seen right now* no estoy visible de momento || *it is not fit to be seen* no es digno de verse (film, etc.) || *that's all he is fit for* no sirve para otra cosa, no sirve para más || *the meat is not fit to eat* la carne no se puede comer || *this car is not fit for the road* este coche no está en buenas condiciones || *this dress is not fit to wear* no me puedo poner este vestido || *to be as fit as a fiddle* estar más sano que una manzana, estar en plena forma || *to be fit to drop* estar a punto de caerse de agotamiento || *to get fit* entrenarse (to train), reponerse, recuperarse (from an illness) || *to keep fit* mantenerse en forma || *to see fit* juzgar conveniente || *to think fit to* estimar conveniente.
◆ *adv* *to cry fit to break one's heart* llorar a lágrima viva || *to laugh fit to burst* partirse *or* desternillarse de risa || *to run fit to collapse* correr como un descosido.
◆ *n* arrebato *m* (short spell); *he had a fit of anger* le dio un arrebato de cólera || ataque *m* (outburst); *he went into a fit of laughter* le dio un ataque de risa || MED ataque *m*, acceso *m*; *a fit of madness* un ataque de locura || — *a fit of energy* un arranque de energía || *by fits and starts* a trompicones, a rachas || *fainting fit* síncope *m* || *to be a good fit* estar bien ajustado, tener buen corte (clothes), encajar bien (machine part) || FIG *to be in fits (of laughter)* morirse de risa || *to have* o *to throw a fit* darle a uno un ataque; *he had a fit* le dio un ataque.

fit [fit] *vt* capacitar (to qualify); *his experience fits him for the job* su experiencia lo capacita para el trabajo || cuadrar con, corresponder a, responder a, estar de acuerdo con (to tally with); *he fits the description* responde a la descripción || adaptar, adecuar, ajustar (to adapt); *to fit a policy to a new situation* adaptar una política a una nueva situación || preparar (to prepare) || sentar bien a, ir bien a; *his coat fits him well* el abrigo le sienta bien || hacer juego con (a colour scheme) || tomar medidas a (to measure); *to fit s.o. for a suit* tomar medidas a alguien para un traje || probar (to try on); *to fit a suit on s.o.* probarle un traje a alguien || entallar (to tailor a dress) || encontrar sitio para, meter (to find room for); *I can't fit this cupboard anywhere* no puedo meter este armario en ninguna parte || encajar; *to fit one part into another* encajar una pieza en otra || unir (to join together) || entrar en; *the key doesn't fit the lock* la llave no entra en la cerradura || colocar (to put); *I'm going to fit it on the wall* lo voy a colocar en la pared; *to fit a new window* colocar una nueva ventana || poner (a carpet); *they fitted my carpet yesterday* me pusieron la moqueta ayer || equipar con, proveer de (to supply with); *to fit new headlamps to a car* equipar un coche con nuevos faros || introducir (to introduce) || incluir (to include) || — *a meal to fit the occasion* una comida apropiada para la ocasión || *to fit in* intercalar, meter; *to fit in an extra commercial between programmes* intercalar otro anuncio entre los programas; tener tiempo para; *can we fit in one more game before dinner?* ¿tenemos tiempo para jugar otro partido antes de cenar?; meter, encajar; *to fit a television in between two cupboards* encajar un televisor entre dos armarios; atender (a customer); *we could fit you in at five o'clock* le podríamos atender a las cinco || *to fit out* equipar (to equip), armar (a ship) || *to fit up* equipar || *to make the punishment fit the crime* adaptar el castigo al crimen.
◆ *vi* encajar; *pieces that fit together* piezas que encajan una con otra || caber; *the cupboard doesn't fit in the car* el armario no cabe en el coche || sentar (clothes); *how does the suit fit?* ¿cómo te sienta el traje?; *it fits you very well* le sienta muy bien || adaptarse, ajustarse (to adjust o.s.) || corresponder, estar de acuerdo, cuadrar (facts, figures, etc.) || — FIG *if the cap fits, wear it* aplíquese el cuento; el que se pica, ajos come | *it all fits now!* ¡ahora está todo claro!, ¡ya lo veo todo claro! | *to fit in with* cuadrar con (things), congeniar con, llevarse bien con; *he doesn't fit in with my friends* no congenia con mis amigos || *to fit a T* sentar como anillo al dedo (clothes), encajar perfectamente (into a space).

fitch [fitʃ]; **fitchet** [et]; **fitchew** [-tʃu:] *n* ZOOL turón *m* (polecat) | mofeta *f* (skunk).

fitful ['fitful] *adj* MED espasmódico, ca || cambiadizo, za (changeable) || caprichoso, sa (capricious) || irregular.

fitfully [-i] *adv* a rachas.

fitment ['fitmənt] *n* mueble *m* (piece of furniture).
◆ *pl* mobiliario *m sing* (fittings).

fitness ['fitnis] *n* conveniencia *f*, oportunidad *f* (suitability) || salud *f* (health) || aptitud *f* (aptitude).

fitted ['fitid] *adj* apto, ta; capacitado, da (qualified, suited); *to be fitted for sth.* estar capacitado para algo, ser apto para algo || entallado, da; ceñido, da (tailored) || hecho a la medida (made-to-measure) || empotrado, da (cupboard).

fitter ['fitə*] *n* ajustador *m* (mechanic) || probador, ra (in tailoring).

fitting ['fitiŋ] *adj* oportuno, na; apropiado, da (just); *a fitting remark* una observación apropiada || propio, pia; justo, ta; *it is fitting that he be elected president* es justo que sea elegido presidente || digno, na (worthy) || — *a badly fitting suit* un traje que sienta mal || *it is not fitting that* no está bien que.
◆ *n* ajuste *m* (of two pieces) || colocación *f*, instalación *f* (of a machine, etc.) || mueble *m* (piece of furniture) || prueba *f* (of clothes) || medida *f* (size) || horma *f* (width of shoe).
◆ *pl* mobiliario *m sing*, muebles *m* (furniture) || accesorios *m* (accessories) || — *bathroom fittings* aparatos sanitarios || *electrical fittings* accesorios eléctricos.

five [faiv] *adj* cinco || — *five hundred* quinientos *m* (number), quinientos, tas (adjective); *five hundred apples* quinientas manzanas || *five hundredth* quingentésimo, ma.
◆ *n* cinco *m* (number, card, figure) || SP equipo *m* de cinco jugadores || US FAM billete *m* de cinco dólares || — *five o'clock* las cinco || FIG *five o'clock shadow* sombra *f* de barba || *ten past five* las cinco y diez.

five-and-ten ['faivəntən] *n* US tienda *f* donde todo vale cinco *or* diez centavos.

five-day week ['faivdei'wi:k] *n* semana *f* de cinco días laborables.

fivefold ['faivfəuld] *adj* multiplicado por cinco, quíntuplo, pla || *to increase fivefold* multiplicar por cinco, quintuplicar.

fiver ['faivə*] *n* FAM billete *m* de cinco libras (note) || SP jugada *f* que vale cinco puntos || US FAM billete *m* de cinco dólares (bill).

fives ['faivz] *n* SP juego *m* inglés de pelota parecido al frontón.

five-star [faivsta:*] *adj* de cinco estrellas; *a five-star hotel* un hotel de cinco estrellas.

five-year ['faivjə:] *adj* quinquenal; *five-year plan* plan quinquenal.

fix [fiks] *n* aprieto *m*, apuro *m* (difficult situation) || MAR & AVIAT situación *f*, posición *f*, localización *f* || — *to be in a bad* o *in a tight fix* estar en un apuro *or* en un aprieto, estar con el agua al cuello || MAR & AVIAT *to get a fix on* localizar || FIG & FAM *to have a fix* tomar una dosis de droga.

fix [fiks] *vt* fijar, asegurar, sujetar (to secure) || ajustar (to fasten firmly) || fijar, decidir; *nothing has been fixed yet* no se ha decidido nada todavía || fijar, determinar, establecer (prices) || fijar, señalar (date) || precisar, determinar (a position) || fijar (attention) || clavar, fijar (eyes) || poner (hopes) || grabar (in one's memory) || echar; *to fix the blame on s.o.* echar la culpa a alguien || arreglar, componer (to mend) || FAM arreglar, amañar; *they fixed the race* arreglaron la carrera | untar la mano, sobornar (to bribe); *they fixed him so he would not talk* le untaron la mano para que no hablase || CHEM fijar (to make solid) || PHOT fijar (a negative) || MIL calar (bayonet) | acampar (to set up camp) || US arreglar (hair, nails) | preparar, servir, dar (food, drink); *she fixed me a drink* me sirvió una copa; *I'm fixing your breakfast* te estoy preparando el desayuno | resolver || — *how are we fixed for time?* ¿cómo andamos de tiempo? || FAM *I'll fix him* ya le arreglaré las cuentas, yo me encargo de él || *it's all fixed* ya está todo arreglado || SP & FAM *it was fixed* hubo tongo || FAM *that ought to fix him* con esto tendría que callarse || *to fix o.s. up* arreglarse || *to fix up* proveer, proporcionar; *they fixed him up with everything he needed* le proveyeron *or* le proporcionaron todo lo que necesitaba; organizar (to arrange); *they fixed up a return match* organizaron un partido de vuelta; conseguir una cita (to arrange an interview), instalar (to set up); *he fixed up a darkroom* instaló un cuarto oscuro; colocar (to place); *the cupboard was fixed up in the corner* se colocó el armario en la esquina; acondicionar; *he fixed up the room as a workshop* acondicionó la habitación para taller; arreglar, componer (to mend), curar (to cure), arreglarse, ponerse de acuerdo; *fix it up with him* ponte de acuerdo *or* arréglate con él.
◆ *vi* fijarse || *to fix on* o *upon* decidirse por, escoger (to choose).

fixate ['fikseit] *vt* US fijar.
◆ *vi* US concentrarse, fijar la mirada, fijarse (*on, upon* en).

fixation [fik'seiʃən] *n* fijación *f*.

fixative ['fiksətiv] *n* fijador *m* (for hair, for photos, etc.).
◆ *adj* fijador, ra.

fixed [fikst] *adj* fijo, ja; *a fixed seat* una silla fija; *a fixed income* una renta fija; *fixed salary* sueldo fijo || CHEM fijo, ja (nonvolatile); *a fixed acid* un ácido fijo || FAM amañado, da; arreglado, da; *a fixed election* una elección arreglada || — *fixed bayonet* bayoneta calada || *fixed idea* idea fija || INFORM *fixed point* coma *f* fija || US *to be well fixed* estar acomodado.

fixer ['fiksə*] *n* PHOT fijador *m* || US sobornador *m* (briber).

fixing ['fiksiŋ] *n* fijación *f* || PHOT fijado *m*, fijación *f*.
◆ *pl* guarnición *f sing* (of a dish) || accesorios *m pl* (accesories).

fixity ['fiksiti] *n* fijeza *f* || estabilidad *f*, fijeza *f* (stability).

fixture ['fikstʃə*] *n* instalación *f* fija (sth. permanent) || aparato *m*, dispositivo *m* (device) || accesorio *m* (accesory) || artefacto *m* (contrivance) || SP fecha *f* fijada (date) | encuentro *m*, partido *m* (match) || FIG & FAM *he is a fixture here* parece que siempre ha estado aquí.

fizz [fiz] *n* burbujeo *m* (sparkle) || efervescencia *f* (effervescence) || FAM gaseosa *f*, bebida *f* gaseosa (effervescent drink) | champaña *f*, champán *m* (champagne) || ruido *m* sibilante (hissing).

fizz [fiz] *vi* burbujear (effervescent liquid) || hacer un ruido sibilante.

fizzle ['fizl] *n* FAM fracaso *m*, fallo *m* (failure).

fizzle ['fizl] *vi* burbujear (effervescent liquid) || hacer un ruido sibilante || FIG & FAM *to fizzle out* fallar, fracasar.

fizzy ['fizi] *adj* efervescente, gaseoso, sa (mineral water, etc.) || espumoso, sa (wine).

fjord [fjɔ:d] *n* fiordo *m*.

flab [flæb] *n* FAM grasa *f*, michelín *m*.

flabbergast ['flæbəgɑ:st] *vt* pasmar, asombrar; *I was flabbergasted by his success* su éxito me dejó pasmado, me quedé pasmado ante su éxito.

flabbiness ['flæbinis] *n* blandura *f*, flaccidez *f*, flacidez *f* (of muscles) || flaccidez *f*, flacidez *f* (of flesh).

flabby ['flæbi] *adj* fláccido, da; fofo, fa; flojo, ja (skin, muscles, etc.) || FIG soso, sa (style) | blandengue (lacking character) | debilucho, cha (weak).

flabellum [flə,beləm] *n* flabelo *m*.
— OBSERV El plural de *flabellum* es *flabella*.

flaccid ['flæksid] *adj* fláccido, da; flácido, da.

flaccidity [flæk'siditi] *n* flaccidez *f*, flacidez *f*.

flag [flæg] *n* bandera *f*, pabellón *m* (banner); *the French flag* la bandera francesa; *the regiment's flag* la bandera del regimiento || banderín *m* (pennant) || banderín *m* (in sports) || banderita *f* (charity) || bandera *f* (in a taxi) || pluma *f* secundaria (of birds) || BOT lirio *m* || baldosa *f*, losa *f* (paving stone) || rabo *m* (of a hunting dog) || — *answering flag* bandera de inteligencia || *flag at half-mast* bandera a media asta || *flag of truce* bandera de parlamento *or* de paz || *quarantine flag* bandera amarilla || *to deck a building with flags* engalanar un edificio con banderas || *to dip the flag* arriar (la) bandera || *to hoist the flag* izar la bandera || FIG *to keep the flag flying* mantener alto el pabellón | *to show the flag* hacer acto de presencia (to make an appearance) || *to strike the flag* arriar (la) bandera || *to take the pledge of allegiance to the flag* jurar la bandera || *white flag* bandera blanca.

flag [flæg] *vt* embaldosar, enlosar (to pave) || hacer señales con banderas a (to signal) || transmitir por señales (a message) || *to flag down* detener haciendo señales.
◆ *vi* colgar (to hang) || flaquear (to weaken) || decaer (interest, enthusiasm) || languidecer (conversation) || marchitarse (plants).

Flag Day [-dei] *n* día *m* de la banderita || US catorce *m* de junio.

flagellant ['flædʒilənt] *adj/n* flagelante.

flagellatae [flædʒe'leiti:i] *pl n* BIOL flagelados *m*.

flagellate ['flædʒeleit] *vt* flagelar, azotar.

flagellation [,flædʒe'leiʃən] *n* flagelación *f*.

flagellator ['flædʒeleitə*] *n* flagelador, ra.

flagellum [flə'dʒeləm] *n* BIOL flagelo *m*.
— OBSERV El plural de *flagellum* es *flagella* o *flagellums*.

flageolet [,flædʒəu'let] *n* MUS chirimía *f*.

flagging [flægiŋ] *adj* flojo, ja; desmadejado, da.
◆ *n* embaldosado *m*, enlosado *m* (paving stones).

flagitious [flə'dʒiʃəs] *adj* malvado, da (wicked) || infame (vile).

flagman ['flægmən] *n* guardavía *m*.
— OBSERV El plural de esta palabra es *flagmen*.

flag officer ['flæg,ɔfisə*] *n* oficial *m* general de Marina [almirante, vicealmirante o contralmirante].

flagon ['flægən] *n* jarra *f* (with a handle) || REL vinajera *f* || botella *f* (de dos litros) (large bottle).

flagpole ['flægpəul] *n* asta *f* de bandera.

flagrancy ['fleigrənsi] *n* flagrancia *f*, lo escandaloso.

flagrant ['fleigrənt] *adj* flagrante (conspicuous) || escandaloso, sa; descarado, da (scandalous).

flagrante delicto [flæ'græntidi'liktə] *n* JUR flagrante delito *m*.

flagship ['flægʃip] *n* MAR buque *m* insignia *or* almirante.

flagstaff ['flægstɑ:f] *n* asta *f* de bandera.

flag station ['flæg'steiʃən] *n* apeadero *m* (railway).

flagstone ['flægstəun] *n* bladosa *f*, losa *f*.

flail [fleil] *n* AGR mayal *m*, desgranador *m*.

flail [fleil] *vt* desgranar (to thresh) || azotar (to thrash) || sacudir (to beat) || agitar (to wave).
◆ *vi* agitarse (to wave about).

flair [flɛə*] *n* instinto *m* (instinct) || don *m*; *he has a flair for saying the wrong thing* tiene el don de decir lo que no debe; *he has a flair for languages* tiene don de lenguas || talento *m*; *he has a flair for acting* tiene talento de actor || *to have a flair for bargains* tener buena vista *or* buen olfato para las gangas.

flak [flæk] *n* MIL fuego *m* antiaéreo | artillería *f* antiaérea (guns).

flake [fleik] *n* copo *m* (thin fragment); *flake of snow* copo de nieve || escama *f* (of mica) || desconchón *m* (thin scale); *flake of paint* desconchón de pintura || trozo *m*, pedazo *m*; *flakes of fish* pedazos de pescado || chispa *f* (of fire) || copo *m* (of cereal) || cañizo *m* (for drying fish) || — *flake pastry* hojaldre *m* || *soap flakes* jabón *m sing* en escamas, escamas de jabón.

flake [fleik] *vt* desconchar; *to flake paint off a wall* desconchar la pintura de una pared || cubrir de copos (to cover with flakes) || FAM *to be flaked out* estar agotado *or* rendido.
◆ *vi* desconcharse, desprenderse (to come away in pieces) || caer en copos (to fall like snow) || FAM *to flake out* caer rendido.

flake white [-wait] *n* albayalde *m*.

flaky ['fleiki] *adj* escamoso, sa || CULIN hojaldrado, da || *flaky pastry* hojaldre *m*.

flambé ['flɑmbei] *adj* CULIN flameado, da; *flambé bananas* plátanos flameados.

flambeau ['flæmbəu] *n* hachón *m*, antorcha *f*.
— OBSERV El plural es *flambeaux* o *flambeaus*.

flamboyance [flæm'bɔiəns] *n* extravagancia *f*.

flamboyant [flæm'bɔiənt] *adj* llamativo, va; vistoso, sa (clothes, etc.) || extravagante (ostentatious) || flameante (flame-like) || rimbombante, florido, da (style) || ARCH flamígero, ra; florido, da (Gothic style).
◆ *n* BOT framboyán *m*.

flame [fleim] *n* llama *f* (burning gas) || llamarada *f* (a sudden blaze) || destello *m*, reflejo *m* (of a diamond) || brillo *m* (of a colour) || FIG llama *f* (of passion) || FAM amor *m* (boy or girl-

friend); *and old flame of mine* un antiguo amor mío || FIG *the flame of youth* el ardor juvenil.
◆ *pl* fuego *m sing*; *the flames of sunset* el fuego del ocaso || — *in flames* en llamas || *to burst into flames* incendiar (house), empezar a arder (papers, etc.) || *to commit a manuscript to the flames* entregar un manuscrito a las llamas || *to commit s.o. to the flames* condenar a alguien a la hoguera || *to go up in flames* arder.

flame [fleim] *vt* MED flamear (to sterilize) || CULIN flamear.
◆ *vi* arder, llamear (to burn) || brillar (to shine) || encenderse (face) || *to flame up* inflamarse (people); *he flamed up with passion* se inflamó de pasión; arder, inflamarse (objects).

flamenco [flə'meŋkəu] *n* flamenco *m*.
◆ *adj* flamenco, ca; *flamenco guitar* guitarra flamenca || *flamenco song* cante flamenco.

flameout ['fleimaut] *n* AVIAT avería *f* en el sistema de combustión (jet engines).

flameproof ['fleimpru:f] *adj* ininflamable, a prueba de fuego.

flamethrower ['fleimθrəuə*] *n* MIL lanzallamas *m inv* (weapon).

flaming ['fleimiŋ] *adj* llameante (in flames) || abrasador, ra (very hot) || FIG ardiente, apasionado, da (passionate) || FAM maldito, ta.
◆ *n* flameado *m*.

flamingo [flə'miŋgəu] *n* flamenco *m* (bird).
— OBSERV El plural es *flamingos* o *flamingoes*.

flammable ['flæməbl] *adj* inflamable.

flan [flæn] *n* tarta *f* de frutas (fruit tart) || flan *m* (baker custard).

Flanders ['flɑ:ndəz] *pr n* GEOGR Flandes *m*.

flange [flændʒ] *n* pestaña *f*, reborde *m* (projecting rim) || pestaña *f*, ceja *f* (of a wheel) || collarín *m* (of a pipe) || base *f* (of a rail).

flange [flændʒ] *vt* rebordear.

flanger [-ə*] *n* TECH rebordeador *m*.

flank [flæŋk] *n* ijada *f*, ijar *m* (of an animal) || costado *m* (of a person) || MIL flanco *m*; *they attacked on the right flank* atacaron por el flanco derecho || ladera *f*, falda *f* (of a hill) || lado *m* (side).

flank [flæŋk] *vt* bordear; *the trees flanked the road* los árboles bordeaban el camino || lindar con (to adjoin) || MIL flanquear || *flanked by mountains* flanqueado por montañas.

flannel ['flænl] *n* franela *f* (material) || pañito *m* para lavarse la cara, guante *m*, manopla *f* (for washing) || trapo *m* (duster) || FAM coba *f* (flattery).
◆ *pl* pantalones *m* de franela (trousers) || ropa *f sing* interior de franela (underwear).
◆ *adj* de franela.

flannel ['flænl] *vt* frotar con un pañito || FAM dar coba a (to flatter).

flannelette [flænl'et] *n* franela *f* de algodón.

flap [flæp] *n* solapa *f* (of envelopes, book cover, etc.) || carterita *f* (of pocket) || faldón *m* (of coat) || ala *f* (of hat) || oreja *f* (of shoe) || ala *f* abatible (of table) || trampa *f* (of counter) || chasquido *m* (noise) || gualdrapazo *m* (movement of sail) || aleteo *m* (of wings, etc.) || aletazo *m* (stroke of the wing) || bofetada *f* (slap) || FAM confusión *f* (loss of self-confidence) | jaleo *m* (fuss) | crisis *f* || AVIAT alerón *m*, «flap» *m* (of aircraft) || MED colgajo *m* (piece of skin) || ANAT lóbulo *m* (of the ear) || — FAM *there was a big flap about it* se armó un lío *or* un jaleo | *to get into a flap* ponerse nervioso.

flap [flæp] *vt* batir (wings) || agitar (arms) || sacudir (to shake) || dar una bofetada a (to slap).
◆ *vi* aletear (wings) || restallar, chasquear (flag) || gualdrapear (sail) || FAM ponerse nervioso.

flapdoodle [-,du:dl] *n* FAM tonterías *f pl*, bobadas *f pl* (nonsense).

flapjack [-dʒæk] *n* torta *f* (cake) || polvera *f* [plana y redonda] (powder compact).

flapper [-ŋ*] *n* batidor *m* (thing that flaps) || matamoscas *m inv* (fly swatter) || polluelo *m* (young duck or partridge) || ZOOL aleta *f* [ancha] (large flipper) | cola *f* (tail of crustacean) || joven *f* emancipada de los años veinte.

flapping [-iŋ] *n* aleteo *m* (of wings) || ondeo *m* (of flag) || gualdrapazo *m* (of sail).

flare [flɛə*] *n* fulgor *m* (shine) || llamarada *f* (blaze) || MIL & MAR & AVIAT cohete *m* de señales, bengala *f* (signal) || ensanchamiento *m* (widening) || vuelo *m*; *the skirt needs more flare* la falda necesita más vuelo || PHOT mancha *f* luminosa || FIG arrebato *m* (of anger) || *a skirt with a flare* una falda acampanada || *solar flare* erupción *f* solar.
◆ *pl* pantalones *m* acampanados.

flare [flɛə*] *vt* hacer llamear (to cause to emit flames) || ensanchar (to make wider) || acampanar (trousers, skirt).
◆ *vi* llamear (fire, flames) || acampanarse (clothes) || ensancharse (to get wider) || resplandecer (light) || *to flare up* llamear (flames, light), encolerizarse, ponerse furioso (in anger), estallar (to break out), declararse (epidemic).

flareback [-bæk] *n* llamarada *f* (in a furnace).

flare path [-pɑ:θ] *n* AVIAT pista *f* iluminada con balizas.

flare-up [-ʌp] *n* llamarada *f* (flames) || FIG arrebato *m* de cólera (anger) | pelea *f*, riña *f* (quarrel) | estallido *m* (of a revolution) | declaración *f* (of an epidemic).

flaring [-iŋ] *adj* resplandeciente (light) || llamativo, va (colour) || acampanado, da (skirt).

flash [flæʃ] *adj* FAM chillón, ona; llamativo, va (gaudy) | elegante (elegant) | chulo, la (vulgarly pretentious) || *flash language* germanía *f*.
◆ *n* destello *m* (sudden burst of light) || centelleo *m* (sparkle, glitter) || PHOT flash *m*, luz *f* relámpago || fogonazo *m* (flame of gun) || instante *m*, momento *m* (short space of time); *in a flash* en un momento || FIG resquicio *m*; *a flash of hope* un resquicio de esperanza | rasgo *m* (sudden manifestation); *a flash of genious* o *of wit* un rasgo de ingenio | ráfaga *f*; *a flash of inspiration* una ráfaga de inspiración | ostentación *f* || noticia *f* de última hora, flash *m* (on radio, on television, etc.) || — FIG *a flash in the pan* una llamarada, una cosa que no dura || *a flash of lightning* un relámpago || FIG *like* o *as a flash* como un relámpago.

flash [flæʃ] *vt* despedir, lanzar (to emit light) || transmitir (to transmit a message) || esgrimir (a sword, a knife) || dirigir; *flash the torch this way* dirige la linterna por aquí || encender (to light); *flash the torch on* enciende la linterna || reflejar (to reflect) || FIG echar (a smile) | lanzar (a glance) | enseñar con ostentación; *he flashed a wad of banknotes at me* me enseñó con ostentación un fajo de billetes || TECH chapar (to coat) | laminar (glass) || — *he flashed the light in my eyes* me deslumbró con la linterna || *to flash about* o *around* hacer ostentación de; *he always flashes his money around* siempre hace ostentación de su dinero.
◆ *vi* echar destellos, destellar (to emit momentary light) || centellear (a light, stars, a jewel, etc.) || brillar (to shine); *his knife flashed in the sun* su cuchillo brilló al sol || — FIG *an idea flased across* o *through my mind* se me ocurrió una idea, una idea me pasó por la cabeza | *his eyes flashed with anger* echaba chispas || CINEM *to flash back* retroceder || FIG *to flash past, across, etc.* pasar, cruzar, etc. como un rayo.

flashback [-bæk] *n* escena *f* retrospectiva (cinema, novel, etc.) || retroceso *m* de la llama (in a furnace).

flashboard [-bɔ:d] *n* alza *f* móvil (of a dam).

flashbulb [-bʌlb] *n* PHOT flash *m*, bombilla *f* de magnesio.

flash card [-kɑ:d] *n* lámina *f* ilustrativa (teaching aid).

flasher [-ə*] *n* luz *f* intermitente.

flash flood [-flʌd] *n* US riada *f*.

flashgun [-gʌn] *n* PHOT disparador *m* de flash.

flashily [ili] *adv* ostentosamente.

flashiness [-inis] *n* ostentación *f* || color *m or* aspecto *m* llamativo (of clothes).

flashing [-iŋ] *adj* intermitente (light) || brillante (eyes).

flash lamp [-læmp] *n* linterna *f* (torch) || PHOT flash *m*, luz *f* relámpago, lámpara *f* relámpago.

flashlight [-'lait] *n* linterna *f* (torch) || PHOT flash *m*, luz *f* relámpago || MAR luz *f* intermitente (of a lighthouse).

flashover [-'əuvə*] *n* ELECTR descarga *f*.

flash point [-pɔint] *n* punto *m* de inflamación.

flashy [-i] *adj* chillón, ona; llamativo, va (showy) || ostentoso, sa (ostentatious) || de relumbrón (jewel).

flask [flɑ:sk] *n* CHEM matraz *m* || frasco *m* (pocket container) || termo *m* (thermos) || polvorín *m* (for powder) || caja *f* de moldear (in foundries).

flat [flæt] *adj* llano, na (level); *flat countryside* paisaje llano || plano, na (object, surface) || uniforme, liso, sa (uniform) || suave (curve) || chato, ta (nose) || plano, na (foot) || arrasado, da (after a bombing) || horizontal (horizontal) || tendido, da (taut) || mate (without gloss) || sin relieve (picture) || FIG categórico, ca; rotundo, da; terminante (outright); *a flat refusal* una negativa rotunda | soso, sa; insípido, da (style, taste, etc.) | monótono, na (monotonous); *flat existence* vida monótona | aburrido, da; pesado, da (boring) | deprimido, da (depressed) || COMM inactivo, va (market) | uniforme (price) | fijo, ja (rate) | sin intereses (shares) || MUS bemol; *C flat* do bemol | desafinado, da (below correct pitch) | sordo, da; apagado, da (sound) || AUT desinflado, da (tyre) | descargado, da (battery) || SP sin obstáculos (horse racing) | liso, sa; *100 metres flat* 100 metros lisos || MAR en calma (sea) || — *bombed flat* arrasado por las bombas || FAM *flat as a pancake* completamente llano, na; liso como la palma de la mano (ground), totalmente liso (uniform), aplastado, da (crushed) || *flat beer* cerveza muerta *or* que ha perdido el gas || *flat joke* chiste malo *or* grosero || *in ten seconds flat* en diez segundos justos || FIG *that's flat!* ¡es mi última palabra! | *to feel flat* no estar en forma, estar abatido *or* deprimido | *to fall flat* fracasar (to fail), no hacer ninguna gracia (joke) || *to fall flat on one's back* caer *or* caerse de espaldas || *to fall flat on one's face* caer *or* caerse de bruces || *to lay flat* arrasar; *to lay a town flat* arrasar una ciudad; extender; *to lay sth. flat on the table* extender algo sobre la mesa.
◆ *adv* completamente (absolutely) || terminantemente, categóricamente, rotundamente; *he told me flat I could not go* me dijo categóricamente que yo no podía ir || — FAM *to be flat broke* estar sin blanca, no tener un céntimo | *to go flat out* ir a todo gas, ir a toda mecha | *to go flat out for* hacer todo lo posible para conseguir || MUS *to play* o *to sing flat* desafinar || *to turn sth. down flat* rechazar algo de plano.
◆ *n* superficie *f* plana (surface) || plano *m* (of a sword) || palma *f* (of hand) || llano *m* (flat

land) || THEATR trasto *m*, decorado *m* móvil (portable scenery) || piso *m* (set of rooms) || apartamento *m* (small dwelling) || MUS bemol *m* || pinchazo *m* (flat tyre) || batea *f* (flatcar) || MAR chata *f*, chalana *f* (boat) | bajo *m*, bajío *m* (shallow) || MUS *sharps and flats* teclas negras (of a piano), sostenidos y bemoles (in written music).

flatboat [-bəut] *n* chalana *f*, chata *f* (boat).

flatcar [-kɑ:*] *n* batea *f* (railway carriage).

flat-chested [-,tʃestid] *adj* lisa, sin pecho (a woman).

flatfish [-fiʃ] *n* platija *f* (fish).

flatfoot [-fut] *n* pie *m* plano || FAM poli *m* (policeman).

flat-footed [-'futid] *adj* de pies planos (having flat feet) || FAM patoso, sa (clumsy) || US FAM resuelto, ta (determined).

flatiron [-,aiən] *n* plancha *f* (for pressing).

flatlet [-let] *n* piso *m* pequeño.

flatly [-li] *adv* categóricamente, terminantemente, rotundamente (categorically) || completamente (absolutely).

flatmate [-meit] *n* compañero, ra de piso.

flatness [-nis] *n* llanura *f*, lo llano (of land) || lisura *f* (smoothness) || insipidez *f* (of taste) || FIG monotonía *f* (monotonoy).

flat-nosed [-nəuzd] *adj* chato, ta.

flat racing [-,reisiŋ] *n* SP carrera *f* plana.

flat spin [-spin] *n* AVIAT barrena *f* plana.

flatten ['flætn] *vt* aplastar (to crush) || aplanar, allanar (to make flat) || alisar (to smooth) || CULIN & FIG volver soso *or* insípido || MUS bemolar || volver mate (colours, painting) || FIG derribar (to knock down) | aplastar (to defeat) || *to flatten o.s. against the ground* pegarse al suelo.
◆ *vi* aplanarse, allanarse || CULIN & FIG volverse soso *or* insípido || perder el gas (beer, etc.) || AVIAT *to flatten out* enderezarse.

flatter ['flætə*] *vt* adular, halagar, lisonjear (to praise); *to flatter the ladies* adular a las mujeres || halagar (to gratify the vanity); *he was flattered by the invitation* se sintió halagado con la invitación || favorecer (to make look more handsome); *the dress, the hairstyle flatters you* el vestido, el peinado te favorece; *the portrait flatters you* estás favorecido en el retrato || — *to flatter o.s.* congratularse, jactarse (*on,* de; *that* de que) (to be pleased), presumir (to show off) || *to flatter o.s. with hopes* abrigar esperanzas.

flatterer [-rə*] *n* adulador, ra; lisonjero, ra.

flattering [-riŋ] *adj* favorecedor, ra; que favorece; *a flattering dress* un vestido favorecedor || adulador, ra; lisonjero, ra; halagador, ra (person) || halagüeño, ña; lisonjero, ra (words).

flatteringly [-riŋli] *adv* con palabras lisonjeras.

flattery [-ri] *n* halago *m*, adulación *f*, lisonja *f*; *flattery will get you nowhere* la adulación no te llevará a ninguna parte || halagos *m pl*, adulaciones *f pl*, lisonjas *f pl* (words) || *a piece of flattery* un halago, una lisonja.

flattop ['flætɔp] *n* US MAR portaaviones *m inv*.

flatulence ['flætjuləns] *n* flatulencia *f* || FIG pomposidad *f*, ampulosidad *f* (of style) | engreimiento *m* (conceit).

flatulent ['flætjulənt] *adj* MED flatulento, ta || FIG ampuloso, sa; pomposo, sa (pretentious) | engreído, da; hinchado, da (person).

flatus ['fleitəs] *n* flato *m*.

flatware ['flætwɛə] *n* platos *m pl* y cubiertos.

flatways ['flætweiz]; **flatwise** ['flætwaiz] *adv* horizontalmente, de plano.

flatworm ['flætwə:m] *n* platelminto *m*.

flaunt [flɔ:nt] *n* ostentación *f*, alarde *m*.

flaunt [flɔ:nt] *vt* ostentar, hacer alarde de (to display proudly); *he flaunts his riches* hace alarde de su riqueza || US burlarse de (to flout).
◆ *vi* ondear (a flag, etc.) || pavonearse (to show off).

flautist ['flɔ:tist] *n* flautista *m* & *f*.

flavescent [flə'vesənt] *adj* amarillento, ta.

flavour; US **flavor** ['fleivə*] *n* sabor *m*, gusto *m* (taste); *an orange flavour* un sabor a naranja; *a pleasant flavour* un sabor agradable || aroma *m* || condimento *m* (flavouring) || FIG sabor *m*; *a poem with a classical flavour* un poema de sabor clásico.

flavour; US **flavor** ['fleivə] *vt* condimentar, sazonar || FIG *to flavour a novel with mystery* darle un tinte de misterio a una novela.

flavouring; US **flavoring** [-riŋ] *n* condimento *m*.

flavourless; US **flavorless** [-lis] *adj* insípido, da, soso, sa.

flaw [flɔ:] *n* grieta *f* (crack or gap) || defecto *m*, desperfecto *m*, imperfección *f* (a blemish, a defect) || jardín *m* (in a gem) || defecto *m*, pelo *m*, quebraza *f* (in metal) || fallo *m* (error, weakness); *this was the only flaw in his argument* era el único fallo en su argumento || borrasca *f* (squall).

flaw [flɔ:] *vt* estropear (to spoil) || agrietar (to crack) || *I flawed his argument on two points* encontré dos fallos en su argumento.
◆ *vi* agrietarse || estropearse.

flawed [-d] *adj* defectuoso, sa; imperfecto, ta.

flawless [lis] *adj* sin defecto, perfecto, ta.

flax [flæks] *n* BOT lino *m*.

flaxen [-ən] *adj* de lino || rubio, bia (blond).

flaxseed ['flæksi:d] *n* linaza *f*.

flay [flei] *vt* desollar (an animal) || FIG despellejar, desollar (to criticize harshly) | desollar (to charge extortionately).

flayer [-ə*] *n* desollador, ra.

flea [fli:] *n* ZOOL pulga *f* || *to send s.o. away* o *off with a flea in his ear* echar a alguien con cajas destempladas, mandar a alguien con viento fresco.

fleabite ['fli:bait] *n* picadura *f* de pulga (the bite of a flea) || FIG cosa *f* sin importancia.

flea-bitten [,fli:'bitn] *adj* picado de pulgas || infestado de pulgas (flea-infested) || moteado, da (horse) || FAM miserable.

fleam [fli:m] *n* VET fleme *m*.

flea market [fli:'mɑ:kit] *n* rastro *m*, mercado *m* de objetos de segunda mano.

flea pit ['fli:pit] *n* FAM cine *m* de baja categoría.

flèche [fleiʃ] *n* ARCH aguja *f*.

fleck [flek] *n* mota *f*, pinta *f* (small mark, speck) || mancha *f* (patch of light, of colour) || peca *f* (freckle) || partícula *f* (of dust).

fleck [flek] *vt* motear || salpicar (with paint).

flection ['flekʃən] *n* flexión *f* (a bending) || curvatura *f* (a bent part) || GRAMM flexión *f*, inflexión *f*.

fled [fled] *pret/pp* → **flee.**

fledge [fledʒ] *vi* emplumecer.
◆ *vt* emplumar (to provide with feathers) || criar (to bring up a bird).

fledged [-d] *adj* plumado, da || *fully-fledged* con todas sus plumas (birds) || desarrollado, da (fully grown) || FIG con todas las de la ley, hecho y derecho (doctor, lawyer, man, etc.) || *full-fledged member* miembro *m* de pleno derecho.

fledgling; **fledgeling** [-liŋ] *n* pájaro *m* volatón, pajarito *m* (bird) || FIG novato *m* (novice) || crío *m* (youngster) || *fledgling poet* poeta *m* en ciernes.

flee* [fli:] *vt* huir de (to run away from) || evitar (to shun); *to flee temptation* evitar la tentación.
◆ *vi* huir (to run away) || refugiarse (*to* en) || FIG desvanecerse; *night had fled* la noche se había desvanecido.
— OBSERV Pret y pp ***fled***.

fleece [fli:s] *n* lana *f* (wool) || piel *f* (animal skin with wool) || vellón *m* (sheared wool) || muletón *m* (for lining) || FIG capa *f* (of snow, of clouds, etc.) || — *the Golden Fleece* el Vellocino de Oro || *the Order of the Golden Fleece* la Orden del Toisón de Oro.

fleece [fli:s] *vt* esquilar (sheep) || FIG desplumar, pelar (to rob).

fleecy [-i] *adj* lanoso, sa; lanudo, da (covered with wool) || aborregado, da (sky) || encrespado, da (sea) || en copos (snow).

fleet [fli:t] *n* flota *f*; *fishing air fleet* flota pesquera, aérea || armada *f* (national navy) || escuadra (of cars).
◆ *adj* veloz (swift) || fugaz (transient) || *fleet of foot* veloz, rápido, da.

fleet-footed [-,futid] *adj* veloz, rápido, da.

fleeting [-iŋ] *adj* fugaz, efímero, ra (ephemeral) || breve (very short).

Fleming ['flemiŋ] *n* flamenco, ca.

Flemish ['flemiʃ] *adj* flamenco, ca || *Flemish bond* aparejo flamenco.
◆ *n* flamenco *m* (languaje).

flench [flentʃ]; **flense** [flenz] *vt* despellejar (whale, seal).

flesh [fleʃ] *n* carne *f* (of man, of animals) || pulga *f* (of fruit) || FIG carne *f* (sensual nature of man); *sins of the flesh* pecados de la carne | género *m* humano (mankind) || color *m* carne (colour) || — FIG *flesh and blood* la naturaleza humana, el hombre || *in the flesh, in flesh and blood* en carne y hueso, en persona (in person) | *one's own flesh and blood* los de su propia sangre | *to make s.o.'s flesh creep* o *crawl* ponerle a uno la carne de gallina | *to put on flesh* echar carnes.

flesh [fleʃ] *vt* encarnar (hunting dogs) || cebar, engordar (to fatten animals) || descarnar (to remove flesh) || clavar (a sword) || FIG *to flesh out* desarrollar (argument).

flesh-coloured; US **flesh-colored** [-,kʌləd] *adj* de color carne.

flesh-eating [-,i:tiŋ] *adj* carnívoro, ra.

flesh fly [-flai] *n* ZOOL moscón *m*.

fleshings ['fleʃiŋz] *pl n* THEATR mallas *f* de color carne || piltrafas *f* (scraps of flesh).

fleshless ['fleʃlis] *adj* descarnado, da.

fleshliness ['fleʃlinis] *n* apetitos *m pl* carnales.

fleshly ['fleʃli] *adj* carnal || sensual.

fleshpots ['fleʃpɔts] *pl n* lujo *m sing* (luxury) || FIG lugares *m* de perdición.

flesh wound ['fleʃwu:nd] *n* MED herida *f* superficial.

fleshy ['fleʃi] *adj* gordo, da (people) || carnoso, sa (limb, fruit).

fletch ['fletʃ] *vt* emplumar.

fleur-de-lis; **fleur-de-lys** ['flə:də'li:s] *n* HERALD flor *f* de lis.
— OBSERV El plural de estas palabras es *fleurs-de-lis* y *fleurs-de-lys*.

fleuron ['flə:rən] *n* florón *m*.

flew [flu:] *pret* → **fly.**

flews [flu:z] *pl n* belfos *m*, morros *m* (of dogs).

flex [fleks] *n* ELECTR flexible *m*.

flex [fleks] *vt* doblar.
◆ *vi* doblarse.

flexibility [ˌfleksəˈbiliti] *n* flexibilidad *f.*

flexible [ˈfleksəbl] *adj* flexible (easily bent, pliable) ‖ FIG elástico, ca; flexible (able to be modified); *a very flexible plan* un plan muy elástico ‖ flexible, adaptable (responsive to changing conditions) ‖ flexible (character).

flexion [ˈflekʃən] *n* → **flection.**

flexitime [ˈfleksitaim] *n* horario *m* flexible.

flexor [ˈfleksə*] *n* músculo *m* flexor, flexor *m.*

flexure [ˈflekʃə*] *n* flexión *f* (action of being flexed) ‖ curva *f* (bend, curve) ‖ GEOL pliegue *m.*

flibbertigibbet [ˈflibətiˈdʒibit] *n* casquivano, na (irresponsible person) ‖ chismoso, sa (gossip).

flick [flik] *n* golpecito *m* (light stroke) ‖ latigazo *m* suave (with a whip) ‖ capirotazo *m* (of the fingers) ‖ pasada *f* (of a duster) ‖ toque *m* (with a paintbrush) ‖ movimiento *m* rápido (of the wrist) ‖ chasquido *m* (sound) ‖ FAM película *f,* filme *m* ‖ — *a flick of the whip* un latigazo ‖ FAM *the flicks* el cine.

flick [flik] *vt* chasquear (a whip, one's fingers) ‖ tirar (a coin, a pellet, etc.) ‖ dar un golpecito a (to strike) ‖ dar un capirotazo a (s.o.'s ear) ‖ — *to flick through* hojear ‖ *to flick one's tail* dar un coletazo ‖ *to flick sth. away* o *off* quitar algo con un capirotazo *or* un golpecito.
◆ *vi* moverse (to move).

flicker [-ə*] *n* parpadeo *m* (of light, eyelids) ‖ llama *f* vacilante (flame) ‖ FIG resquicio *m*; *a flicker of hope* un resquicio de esperanza ‖ — *a flicker of fear* un estremecimiento ‖ FIG *not a flicker of life* ni la menor señal de vida.

flicker [-ə*] *vi* vacilar (flames) ‖ parpadear (light) ‖ temblar (leaves) ‖ aletear (birds) ‖ ondear (flag) ‖ danzar (shadows) ‖ oscilar (a needle) ‖ FIG *his life is flickering out* su vida se está apagando.

flick-knife [-naif] *n* navaja *f* automática.

flier; flyer [ˈflaiə*] *n* aviador, ra (aviator) ‖ volatinero, ra (acrobat) ‖ FIG bólido *m* (a fast vehicle, a horse, etc.) | expreso *m* (train) ‖ aleta *f* (of spinning machine) ‖ US prospecto *m* (handbill) | operación *f or* inversión *f* arriesgada (reckless gamble).
◆ *pl* escalones *m,* peldaños *m* (steps).

flight [flait] *n* vuelo *m* (act or mode of flying, a journey by air) ‖ recorrido *m,* trayectoria *f* (distance flown by aeroplane, by a bird, etc.) | trayectoria *f* (of bullet) ‖ bandada *f* (group of birds) ‖ escuadrilla *f* (group of aircraft) ‖ descarga *f* (of arrows) ‖ SP línea *f* de obstáculos (set of hurdles) | cucharilla *f* (fishing) | flecha *f* ligera (light arrow) ‖ vuelo *m* (of imagination) ‖ rasgo *m* (of wit) ‖ huida *f,* fuga *f* (act of fleeing) ‖ — AVIAT *blind flight* vuelo sin visibilidad | *flight crew* tripulación *f* | *flight deck* cubierta *f* de aterrizaje (aircraft carriers), cabina *f* de piloto (of an aircraft) | *flight engineer* mecánico *m* de a bordo | *flight formation* formación *f* de vuelo | *flight leader* o *commander* jefe *m* de patrulla ‖ *flight of capital* evasión *f or* fuga *f* de capitales ‖ *flight of fancy* ilusión *f* ‖ *flight of steps* tramo *m* de escalera (staircase), escalinata *f* (outside steps) ‖ AVIAT *flight path* trayectoria de vuelo | *flight recorder* registrador *m* de vuelo | *in flight* en vuelo; *to refuel in flight* repostar en vuelo; durante el vuelo; *drinks served in flight* bebidas servidas durante el vuelo; huyendo (fleeing) | *orbital flight* vuelo orbital | *reconnaissance flight* vuelo de reconocimiento ‖ *to put to flight* poner en fuga (the enemy), ahuyentar (to scare away) ‖ *to take flight* alzar el vuelo ‖ *to take to flight* darse a la fuga.
◆ *pl* ZOOL remeras *f* (of a bird) ‖ *she lives two flights up* vive dos pisos más arriba.

flight [flait] *vi* volar en bandadas (birds).
◆ *vt* cazar al vuelo.

flightless [-lis] *adj* incapacitado para volar.

flighty [-i] *adj* frívolo, la; ligero, ra (frivolous) ‖ caprichoso, sa (capricious) ‖ inconstante (changeable) ‖ casquivano, na (irresponsible).

flimflam [ˈflim-flæm] *n* FAM fruslería *f,* tontería *f* ‖ US engaño *m* (deception).

flimsiness [ˈflimzinis] *n* debilidad *f,* endeblez *f* (weakness) ‖ fragilidad *f* ‖ ligereza *f* (of cloth) ‖ finura *f* (of paper).

flimsy [ˈflimzi] *adj* débil, endeble (weak) ‖ frágil (fragile) ‖ ligero, ra (cloth) ‖ fino, na (paper) ‖ insustancial (lacking substance) ‖ FIG flojo, ja; *a flimsy excuse* una excusa floja.
◆ *n* papel *m* cebolla (transfer paper) ‖ FAM billete *m* de banco, pápiro *m* (banknote).
◆ *pl* copias *f* hechas en papel cebolla.

flinch [flintʃ] *n* mueca *f* de dolor *or* de desagrado ‖ *to bear pain without a flinch* soportar el dolor sin pestañear.

flinch [flintʃ] *vi* retroceder (to draw back) ‖ echarse atrás, acobardarse; *to flinch from an unpleasant duty* echarse atrás ante un trabajo desagradable ‖ vacilar (to hesitate) ‖ inmutarse, pestañear; *to bear pain without flinching* soportar el dolor sin inmutarse ‖ encogerse; *he flinched under the lash of the whip* se encogió bajo el latigazo; *his face flinched* se le encogió la cara.

flinders [ˈflindəz] *pl n* astillas *f pl; to break into flinders* hacerse astillas.

fling [fliŋ] *n* lanzamiento *m* (a throw) ‖ baile *m* escocés (dance) ‖ FIG pulla *f* (sarcastic attack) ‖ FAM juerga *f* (a wild time) ‖ — FAM *to go on* o *to have a fling* echar una cana al aire | *to have a fling at* probar, intentar; *have a fling at opening this door* prueba tú a ver si abres esta puerta | *to have one's fling* correrla | *youth will have its fling* hay que aceptar los excesos de la juventud.

fling* [fliŋ] *vt* arrojar, lanzar, tirar (to hurl, to throw); *he flung a stone at me* me tiró una piedra ‖ echar (to move violently); *he flung his arms around her neck* le echó los brazos al cuello ‖ precipitar, lanzar (to send into attack) ‖ soltar (abuse, etc.) ‖ sumir; *the news flung the crowd into confusion* la noticia sumió a la multitud en la confusión ‖ — *he flung the door in my face* me dio con la puerta en las narices ‖ *he flung the door open* abrió la puerta de golpe ‖ *he flung the door shut* cerró la puerta de golpe ‖ *to fling o.s.* lanzarse, tirarse, arrojarse ‖ *to fling o.s. into a chair* dejarse caer en una silla ‖ *to fling s.o. into jail* meter a uno en la cárcel, encarcelar a uno.
◆ *vi* precipitarse, lanzarse (to dash).
◆ *phr v* *to fling about* esparcir (objects) | agitar (arms, etc.) | despilfarrar (money) ‖ ***to fling aside*** tirar (to throw away) | dejar de lado; *he flung aside the advice of his friends* dejó de lado los consejos de sus amigos ‖ ***to fling away*** tirar (to throw) | desperdiciar (an opportunity) ‖ ***to fling back*** devolver (ball) | echar hacia atrás (the head) | rechazar (the enemy) ‖ ***to fling down*** tirar al suelo | derribar (a building) ‖ ***to fling off*** quitarse rápidamente (clothes) | salir disparado (to go out) ‖ ***to fling out*** cocear (horses) | soltar (a remark) | abrir (one's arms) | FAM poner de patitas en la calle (to kick s.o. out) | salir disparado; *he flung out of the room* salió disparado de la habitación ‖ FAM ***to fling up*** abandonar (one's job, etc.).
— OBSERV Pret y pp ***flung***.

flint [flint] *n* pedernal *m* (rock) ‖ hacha *f* de sílex (prehistoric tool) ‖ piedra *f,* pedernal *m* (anything hard); *a heart of flint* un corazón de piedra ‖ piedra *f* de chispa, pedernal *m* (for striking fire, for guns) ‖ piedra *f* de mechero (of cigarette lighter) ‖ FIG & FAM *to skin a flint* ser tacaño.

flint glass [-glɑːs] *n* flint-glass *m,* flintglas *m* (heavy brilliant glass).

flintlock [-lɔk] *n* fusil *m* de chispa (gun) ‖ llave *f* de chispa (gunlock).

flinty [-i] *adj* de pedernal ‖ FIG de piedra (heart).

flip [flip] *n* capirotazo *m* (flick of the fingers) ‖ golpe *m* (quick blow) ‖ vuelo *m* (short plane flight) ‖ flip *m* (drink) ‖ *with a flip of its tail* de *or* con un coletazo.

flip [flip] *vt* dar un capirotazo a (to flick) ‖ echar (algo) al aire (con los dedos) (to toss with the fingers) ‖ quitarse de un manotazo; *he flipped an insect from his face* se quitó de un manotazo el insecto que tenía en la cara ‖ — *he flipped the book shut* cerró el libro de golpe ‖ *to flip a coin* echar a cara o cruz (to toss up) ‖ FAM *to flip one's lid* volverse loco.

flip-flop [-flɔp] *n* chancleta *f* (sandal) ‖ SP voltereta *f* hacia atrás ‖ INFORM báscula *f* biestable, flip-flop.

flippancy [ˈflipənsi] *n* ligereza *f* (lack of seriousness) ‖ impertinencia *f* (flippant remark).

flippant [ˈflipənt] *adj* ligero, ra; frívolo, la (frivolous) ‖ irrespetuoso, sa; impertinente (lacking respect).

flipper [ˈflipə*] *n* aleta *f* (of whale, of seal) ‖ FAM garra *f,* mano *f* (hand).
◆ *pl* aletas *f* (of a swimmer).

flipping *adj* FAM maldito, ta.

flip side *n* cara *f* B (of record).

flirt [fləːt] *n* mariposón *m* (man) ‖ coqueta *f* (girl) ‖ meneo *m* (quick movement).

flirt [fləːt] *vt* agitar (fan, bird's tail, etc.).
◆ *vi* flirtear, coquetear (to play at courtship) ‖ — FIG *to flirt with a dangerous situation* jugar con una situación peligrosa | *to flirt with an idea* acariciar una idea.

flirtation [fləːˈteiʃən] *n* coqueteo *m,* flirteo *m.*

flirtatious [fləːˈteiʃəs] *adj* coqueto, ta (glance, woman) ‖ mariposón (man).

flit [flit] *n* revoloteo *m* (of birds) ‖ mudanza *f* secreta (act of moving out secretly) ‖ *to do a moonlight flit* mudarse a escondidas, irse a la chita callando (to move out secretly), desaparecer de la noche a la mañana (to disappear overnight).

flit [flit] *vi* revolotear (to make short flights) ‖ mudarse a escondidas (to move out secretly) ‖ — FIG *an idea flitted through his mind* le pasó una idea por la cabeza ‖ *to flit about* ir y venir sin ruido.

flitch [flitʃ] *n* costero *m* (of tree trunk) ‖ — *flitch beam* viga *f* de tablones adosados ‖ *flitch of bacon* lonja *f* de tocino.

flitter [ˈflitə*] *vi* revolotear.

flittermouse [-maus] *n* murciélago *m* (bat).

flivver [ˈflivə*] *n* US FAM cacharro *m* (cheap old car of plane).

float [fləut] *n* flotador *m* (for aircraft, fishing nets, carburettor, cistern, life raft) ‖ corcho *m* (on a fishing line) ‖ balsa *f* (raft) ‖ ZOOL vejiga *f* natatoria (of fish) ‖ masa *f* flotante (of weeds, ice, etc.) ‖ carroza *f* (for carnivals, for displays) ‖ llana *f* (trowel for smoothing).
◆ *pl* THEATR candilejas *f.*

float [fləut] *vi* flotar; *to float on the water, through the air* flotar en el agua, en el aire ‖ ondear, flotar (flag in the wind) ‖ FIG flotar; *ideas floated through his mind* las ideas flotaban en su mente | vagar (to wander aimlessly) | correr (rumours) ‖ COMM flotar (a currency) ‖ — *it floated to the surface* salió a la superficie ‖ FIG *to float along with the stream* dejarse llevar por la corriente | *to float on air* estar eufórico ‖ *to float*

on one's back flotar boca arriba, hacer el muerto || *to float to the surface* salir a la superficie.
◆ *vt* hacer flotar (to support) || poner a flote (to set afloat) || inundar (to flood) || lanzar (a company, a business) || hacer correr (rumours, ideas) || COMM hacer flotar (a currency) | emitir (shares, loan) || allanar (to smooth).

floatable ['fləutəbl] *adj* flotable.

floatage; flotage ['fləutidʒ] *n* flotación *f* (act of floating) || flotabilidad *f* (ability to float) || obra *f* muerta (part of a boat over waterline) || tonelaje *m* a flote, arqueo *m* (tonnage) || pecios *m pl* (flotsam).

floatation; flotation [fləu'teiʃən] *n* flotación *f* || COMM emisión *f* (of loan) | lanzamiento *m* (of a firm).

floater ['fləutə*] *n* flotador *m* (thing that floats) || COMM título *m* (security) || FAM persona *f* que cambia a menudo de domicilio o de empleo || US persona *f* que vota en más de un colegio electoral.

float-feed ['fləutfi:d] *n* AUT alimentación *f* por flotador.

floating ['fləutiŋ] *adj* flotante (that floats, not fixed in place, variable) || MED & ANAT & TECH flotante; *floating kidney* riñón flotante; *floating ribs* costillas flotantes; *floating axle* eje flotante || COMM circulante; *floating capital* capital circulante | flotante; *floating debt, currency* deuda, moneda flotante || — *floating bridge* pontón *m* flotante, puente *m* de pontones (pontoon bridge), puente *m* de balsas (of rafts), pontón *m* (moveable part of bridge), transbordador *m* (ferry) || *floating dock* dique *m* flotante || *floating island* isla *f* flotante (floating mass of earth), natillas *f pl* con merengue *or* crema batida (dessert) || *floating light* buque *m* faro (lightship), boya luminosa (light buoy) || INFORM *floating point* coma *f* flotante || *floating vote* o *votes* votos indecisos.
◆ *n* flotación *f* (of currency).

floatplane ['fləutplein] *n* hidroavión *m*.

floatstone ['fləutstəun] *n* MIN ópalo *m* capaz de flotar.

float valve ['fləutvælv] *n* TECH válvula *f* de flotador.

floc [flɔk] *n* CHEM flóculo *m*.

floccose ['flɔkəus] *adj* BOT velludo, da.

flocculate ['flɔkjulit] *adj* CHEM floculado, da.

flocculate ['flɔkjuleit] *vi* CHEM flocular.

floccule ['flɔkju:l] *n* CHEM flóculo *m*.

flocculent ['flɔkjulɛt] *adj* lanudo, da (woolly) || CHEM floculento, ta || BOT velludo, da.

flocculus ['flɔkjuləs] *n* mechón *m*, copo *m* (tuft) || CHEM & ASTR flóculo *m*.
— OBSERV El plural de *flocculus* es *flocculi*.

floccus ['flɔkəs] *n* mechón *m*, copo *m* (tuft).
— OBSERV El plural de *floccus* es *flocci*.

flock [flɔk] *n* bandada *f* (of birds) || rebaño *m* (of goats, of sheep) || muchedumbre *f*, tropel *m*, multitud *f* (of people) || REL grey *f*, rebaño *m* (of Christ) | feligresía *f*, feligreses *m pl* (parishioners) || mechón *m* (tuft) || borra *f* (filling for cushions, etc.) || — *flocks and herds* ganado *m* lanar y vacuno || *to come in flocks* venir en tropel.

flock [flɔk] *vi* congregarse, reunirse (to gather) || venir en tropel (to come in great numbers) || — *to flock in* entrar en tropel || *to flock together* congregarse, reunirse.
◆ *vt* US rellenar con borra.

flock paper [-peipə*] *n* papel *m* aterciopelado.

floe [fləu] *n* témpano *m* de hielo.

flog [flɔg] *vt* azotar (to beat) || FAM hacer trabajar demasiado (to drive too hard); *don't flog the engine so hard* no hagas trabajar tanto el motor | vender (to sell) || — FIG *to flog a dead horse* azotar el aire || *to flog to death* malar a latigazos (a person), machacar los oídos con (a theory, etc.).

flogging [iŋ] *n* paliza *f*, azotaina *f* (beating) || flagelación *f* (punishment).

flood [flʌd] *n* inundación *f* (of water) || FIG flujo *m*, torrente *m* (of words) | raudales *m pl* (of light) | torrente *m* (of tears) || pleamar *f* (high tide) || REL diluvio *m* || — *in flood* crecido, da; *the river is in flood* el río está crecido || FIG *to weep floods of tears* llorar a lágrima viva.

flood [flʌd] *vt* inundar (to cover with water) || AGR anegar (a meadow) | irrigar (to irrigate) || hacer crecer *or* desbordar (a river) || FIG inundar; *the country was flooded with foreigners* el país estaba inundado de extranjeros.
◆ *vi* crecer (to rise) || desbordar (to overflow) || — *to flood in* entrar a raudales, entrar en tropel (people), llegar a montones (letters, etc.) || *to flood out* salir a raudales, salir en tropel.

flood control [-kən'trəul] *n* medidas *f pl* defensivas contra las inundaciones.

floodgate [-geit] *n* esclusa *f*, compuerta *f*.

flooding [-iŋ] *n* inundación *f*.

floodlight [-lait] *n* foco *m*.

floodlight [-lait] *vt* iluminar con focos.

floodlighting [-'laitiŋ] *n* iluminación *f* con focos.

floodmark [-mɑ:k] *n* nivel *m* de la marea alta.

flood tide [-taid] *n* pleamar *f*, marea *f* creciente.

floor [flɔ:*] *n* suelo *m*, piso *m* (of buildings); *he was sitting on the floor* estaba sentado en el suelo || tablero *m*, piso *m* (of a bridge) || piso *m* (storey) || fondo *m* (of sea) || pista *f* (of a dance hall) || nivel *m* mínimo (of prices) || hemiciclo *m* (for debates) || delegados *m pl*, congresistas *m pl* (in a meeting); *to invite questions from the floor* invitar a los delegados a que hagan preguntas || MAR varenga *f* || — *first floor* primer piso (in England), planta baja (in the United States) || *ground floor* planta baja || *second floor* segundo piso (in England), primer piso (in the United States) || *to give the floor* dar *or* conceder la palabra || *to have the floor* tener la palabra || *top floor* ático *m*, piso *m* alto || *to take the floor* hacer uso de la palabra, tomar la palabra (to speak), salir a bailar (to dance) || FIG & FAM *to wipe the floor with s.o.* pegar una paliza a alguien (to defeat).

floor [flɔ:*] *vt* solar (a room) || echar al suelo (to knock down) || FIG apabullar (to silence).

floorage ['flɔ:ridʒ] *n* suelo *m*, espacio *m*.

floorboard ['flɔ:bɔ:d] *n* tabla *f* del suelo (plank covering floor) || AUT piso *m*, suelo *m*.

floorcloth [-klɔθ] *n* trapo *m*, bayeta *f* [para fregar el suelo] || linóleo *m* (linoleum).

floorer [-rə*] *n* solador *m* (workman) || FAM pregunta *f* desconcertante (puzzling question) | golpe *m* (blow).

flooring [-riŋ] *n* solado *m* || entarimado *m* (floorboards) || suelo *m* (floor) || revestimiento *m* para el suelo (material).

floor lamp [-læmp] *n* lámpara *f* de pie.

floor leader [-'li:də*] *n* US jefe *m* de partido.

floor plan [-plæn] *n* planta *f* de piso.

floor polish [-'pɔliʃ] *n* cera *f* para el suelo.

floor show [-ʃəu] *n* atracciones *f pl* [en la pista de baile].

floor waiter [-weitə*] *n* camarero *m* de piso (in a hotel).

floorwalker [-wɔ:kə*] *n* US jefe *f* de sección *or* de departamento (in a shop).

floozy ['flu:zi] *n* US FAM mujer *f* de vida airada.

flop [flɔp] *n* FAM fracaso *m* (failure) || sonido *m* sordo (sound).

flop [flɔp] *vi* dejarse caer pesadamente, desplomarse; *he flopped down in his bed* se dejó caer pesadamente en la cama || agitarse (a fish) || dar aletazos, aletear (birds) || FAM fracasar (to be a failure).
◆ *vt* dejar caer pesadamente.

flophouse [-haus] *n* US FAM posada *f or* pensión *f* de mala muerte (doss house).

floppy [-i] *adj*. flojo, ja; blando, da (not rigid) || colgante (hanging).

floppy disk [-disk] *n* INFORM disco *m* flexible *or* blando, disquete *m*, floppy *m*.

flora [flɔ:rə] *n* BOT flora *f*.
— OBSERV El plural de la palabra inglesa es *florae* o *floras*.

floral [-l] *adj* floral.

Florence ['flɔrəns] *pr n* GEOGR Florencia.

Florentine ['flɔrəntain] *adj/n* florentino, na.

florescence [flɔ:'resns] *n* BOT florescencia *f*.

florescent [flɔ:'resnt] *adj* en flor.

floret ['flɔ:rit] *n* BOT flósculo *m*.

floriated ['fɔ:rieitid] *adj* floreado, da.

floriculture ['flɔ:rikʌltʃə*] *n* floricultura *f*.

florid ['flɔrid] *adj* florido, da; *florid style* estilo florido || rojo, ja; colorado, da (face).

Florida ['flɔridə] *pr n* GEOGR Florida.

floridity [flɔ'riditi] *n* floridez *f* || rubicundez *f* (of face).

florilegium [,flɔri'li:dʒjəm] *n* florilegio *m*.
— OBSERV El plural de *florilegium* es *florilegia*.

florin ['flɔrin] *n* moneda *f* de dos chelines, florín *m* (in Great Britain) || florín *m* (in the Netherlands).

florist ['flɔrist] *n* florista *m* & *f* (who sells flowers) || *florist's, florist's shop* florería *f*.

floss [flɔs] *n* seda *f* floja (silk) || BOT seda *f* vegetal || borra *f* (of cocoon).

floss silk [-'silk] *n* seda *f* floja.

flossy ['flɔsi] *adj* sedoso, sa || FAM elegante (smart).

flotage ['fləutidʒ] *n* ⟶ **floatage.**

flotation [fləu'teiʃən] *n* ⟶ **floatation.**

flotilla [fləu'tilə] *n* MAR flotilla *f*.

flotsam ['flɔtsəm]; **flotsam and jetsam** [-'dʒetsəm] *n* pecios *m pl* (wreckage of a ship) || fruslerías *f pl* (objects of little value) || FIG vagabundos *m pl* (drifters).

flounce [flauns] *n* volante *m* (in sewing) || movimiento *m* brusco (movement).

flounce [flauns] *vt* adornar con volantes.
◆ *vi* moverse bruscamente, forcejear || *to flounce out* salir enfadado.

flounder ['flaundə*] *n* platija *f* (fish).

flounder ['flaundə*] *vi* andar con dificultad (in mud, in water, etc.) || forcejear (to struggle) || enredarse, no saber qué decir (in speaking).

flour ['flauə*] *n* harina *f* || *pure wheaten flour* flor *f* de harina, harina de flor.

flour ['flauə*] *vt* enharinar (to put flour in or on) || moler (grain).

flourish ['flʌriʃ] *n* ostentación *f* (ostentation) || movimiento *m*, ademán *m* (gesture) || molinete *m*, floreo *m* (in fencing) || MUS floreo *m* || rúbrica *f* (on signature) || rasgo *m*, floreo *m* (in writing) || toque *m* de trompeta (fanfare) || prosperidad *f* (prosperity).

flourish ['flʌriʃ] *vi* florecer, prosperar (to thrive) || crecer (plants) || usar de floreos (in writing, in speaking, etc.) || jactarse (to boast).

◆ *vt* agitar (to wave) ‖ esgrimir, blandir (to brandish) ‖ adornar (to ornament) ‖ hacer alarde de (to display ostentatiously).

flourishing [-iŋ] *adj* floreciente, próspero, ra.

flour mill ['flauəmil] *n* molino *m* harinero.

floury ['flauəri] *adj* harinoso, sa (like or of flour) ‖ enharinado, da (covered with flour).

flout [flaut] *vt* burlarse de, reírse de.
◆ *vi* *to flout at* burlarse de, reírse de.

flow [fləu] *n* flujo *m* (action of flowing) ‖ caudal *m* (volume of liquid) ‖ chorro *m* (jet); *flow of water from a tap* chorro de agua del grifo ‖ corriente *f* (current) ‖ circulación *f* (circulation of blood) ‖ caída *f* (of drapery, etc.) ‖ FIG flujo *m* (of words) | torrente *m* (of tears) | afluencia *f*, flujo *m* (of goods, etc.) | flujo *m*, derrame *m* (of blood) | paso *m* (passing) | curso *m* (course) ‖ subida *f*, flujo *m* (of tide) ‖ fluidez *f* (flowing quality) ‖ movimiento *m* (movement) ‖ INFORM flujo *m* (of information) ‖ COMM movimiento *m* (of capital).

flow [fləu] *vi* fluir (liquid) ‖ circular (blood in the body) ‖ derramarse, correr (blood from the body) ‖ manar, correr (blood of a wound) ‖ fluir, correr (river) ‖ subir, crecer (tide) ‖ correr (tears) ‖ FIG correr (to be plentiful); *champagne flowed* el champán corrió ‖ ondear (in the wind) ‖ *to flow past* pasar (delante de).
◆ *phr v* *to flow away* irse ‖ ***to flow back*** refluir ‖ ***to flow from*** salir de | provenir de, proceder de; *wisdom flows from experience* la sabiduría proviene de la experiencia ‖ ***to flow in*** entrar a raudales ‖ ***to flow into*** desembocar en (river) ‖ ***to flow out*** salir a raudales ‖ ***to flow over*** desbordarse (river) | rebosar (vessel) | ***to flow together*** confluir (rivers) ‖ ***to flow with*** abundar en.

flowchart ['fləutʃɑ:t]; **flow diagram** ['fləu-diagræm] *n* organigrama *m*, diagrama *m*, gráfico *m* ‖ INFORM organigrama *m*, ordinograma *m*.

flower ['flauə*] *n* BOT flor *f*; *to grow flowers* cultivar flores ‖ FIG flor *f*; *in the flower of youth* en la flor de la juventud | flor *f* y nata, crema *f* (the best part); *the flower of the nation's youth* la flor y nata de los jóvenes del país ‖ — *artificial flower* flor artificial ‖ *flower bed* arriate *m*, cuadro *m* ‖ *flower girl* florista *f* ‖ *flower grower* floricultor, ra ‖ *flower growing* floricultura *f* ‖ *flower piece* ramillete *m* (a flower arrangement), cuadro *m* de flores (painting of flowers) ‖ *flower shop* tienda *f* de flores, florería *f* ‖ *flower show* exposición *f* de flores ‖ *flower vase* florero *m* ‖ *plant in flower* planta en flor.
◆ *pl* flor *f sing* (del vino, del azufre) ‖ *no flowers by request* no se admiten flores ni coronas.

flower ['flauə*] *vi* florecer.
◆ *vt* adornar con flores ‖ AGR hacer florecer.

flower-de-luce [-də'lu:s] *n* HERALD flor *f* de lis.

floweret ['flauərit] *n* BOT flósculo *m* (floret) ‖ florecita *f* (small flower).

floweriness ['flauərinis] *n* floridez *f*.

flowering ['flauəriŋ] *n* floración *f*, florecimiento *m*.
◆ *adj* floreciente.

flowerpot ['flauəpɔt] *n* maceta *f*, tiesto *m*.

flowery ['flauəri] *adj* florido, da; *a flowery garden* un jardín florido ‖ FIG florido, da (style, language).

flowing [ˌfləuiŋ] *adj* fluido, da (style) ‖ fluente, fluyente (stream) ‖ largo, ga (beard) ‖ suelto, ta (hair) ‖ ascendente (tide) ‖ de mucho vuelo (dress).
◆ *n* flujo *m*.

flown [fləun] *pp* ⟶ **fly** ‖ exaltado, da (exalted) ‖ (ant) hinchado, da.

flow sheet [ˌfləuʃi:t] *n* gráfico *m*, diagrama *m* (in factory, in workshop, etc.).

flu [flu:] *n* MED gripe *f*.

fluctuate ['flʌktjueit] *vi* fluctuar, variar, oscilar; *the price fluctuates between nine and ten pounds* el precio fluctúa entre nueve y diez libras ‖ subir y bajar (waves).
◆ *vt* hacer fluctuar.

fluctuating [-iŋ] *adj* fluctuante.

fluctuation [ˌflʌktju'eiʃən] *n* fluctuación *f*, variación *f*, oscilación *f*; *market fluctuations* fluctuaciones del mercado.

flue [flu:] *n* MAR trasmallo *m* (fishing net) ‖ pelusa *f*, borra *f* (fluff) ‖ chimenea *f* (chimney) ‖ TECH conducto *m* de humos, humero *m* (chimney pipe) | conducto *m* (for air conditioning) | tubo *m* (pipe) ‖ MUS boca *f* (of an organ).

fluency ['fluənsi] *n* facilidad *f*, soltura *f*, fluidez *f* (of speech) ‖ dominio *m*; *her fluency in English* su dominio del inglés.

fluent ['fluənt] *adj* bueno, na; *he speaks fluent Spanish* habla un español bueno ‖ fluido, da (in writing) ‖ — *he is fluent in English* domina el inglés, habla el inglés con soltura ‖ *to be a fluent speaker* hablar con soltura.

fluently [-li] *adv* de corrido, con soltura (in speaking); *he speaks Spanish fluently* habla español con soltura ‖ con fluidez (in writing).

flue pipe ['flu:paip] *n* MUS cañón *m* (of an organ).

flue stop ['flu:stɔp] *n* MUS flautado *m* (of an organ).

fluff [flʌf] *n* pelusa *f* (soft mass) ‖ pelotillas *f pl* de polvo (dust) ‖ THEATR pifia *f* ‖ FAM *a bit of fluff* un bombón, una chica mona.

fluff [flʌf] *vt* mullir (pillow, soil, etc.) ‖ esponjar (wool, cotton) ‖ FAM decir mal, equivocarse en (su papel) (in theatre) | errar (a shot) ‖ TECH afelpar, apomazar (leather) ‖ — FAM *to fluff one's entrance* salir al escenario a destiempo (an actor) | *to fluff one's exam* ser cateado *or* suspendido en un examen.
◆ *vi* esponjarse (wool, cotton).

fluffiness [-inis] *n* esponjosidad *f*.

fluffy [-i] *adj* que tiene pelusa (cloth) ‖ cubierto de plumón (chicken, etc.) ‖ velloso, sa (downy) ‖ esponjado, da (hair) ‖ vaporoso, sa (dress) ‖ mullido, da (pillow, soil, etc.) ‖ aborregado, da (clouds).

fluid ['fluid] *n* fluido *m* ‖ — *fluid drive* transmisión hidráulica ‖ *fluid mechanics* mecánica *f* de los fluidos ‖ *fluid ounce* onza *f* líquida.
◆ *adj* fluido, da ‖ inestable (not settled) ‖ FIG cambiadizo, za; variable; *his opinions are fluid* sus opiniones son cambiadizas | flexible (plan).

fluidify [ˌfluid:fai] *vt* fluidificar.

fluidity [flu'iditi] *n* fluidez *f* ‖ FIG inestabilidad *f* | variabilidad *f* (of opinions).

fluke [flu:k] *n* MAR uña *f* (of anchor, of harpoon, etc.) ‖ lengüeta *f* (of arrow) ‖ aleta *f* (of whale) ‖ ZOOL trematodo *m* (worm) | platija *f* (flatfish) ‖ FAM chiripa *f* (stroke of luck in billiards) | *to win by a fluke* ganar por *or* de chiripa.

fluke [flu:k] *vt* ganar por chiripa.
◆ *vi* tener chiripa (to be lucky) ‖ ganar por chiripa (in billiards).

fluky [-i] *adj* de suerte (lucky) ‖ variable (breeze).

flume ['flu:m] *n* saetín *m* (of mill) ‖ resbaladero *m* (for timber) ‖ US cañada *f* (gorge).

flummery ['flʌməri] *n* pamplinas *f pl* (nonsense) ‖ camelo *m* (flattery) ‖ flan *m* [dulce hecho esencialmente con harina, leche, huevos].

flummox ['flʌməks] *vt* FAM despistar, desconcertar (to confuse).

flump [flʌmp] *vt* *to flump sth. down* dejar caer algo [ruidosamente].
◆ *vi* *to flump about* andar con paso pesado ‖ *to flump down* desplomarse.

flung [flʌŋ] *pret/pp* ⟶ **fling.**

flunk [flʌŋk] *vt* US FAM ser suspendido *or* cateado en; *to flunk an exam* ser suspendido en un examen | suspender, catear; *they flunked me in Chinese* me suspendieron en chino ‖ US FAM *to flunk s.o. out of college* echar a alguien del instituto.
◆ *vi* US FAM ser suspendido *or* cateado (to fail) | abandonar (to give up).

flunk [flʌŋk] *n* US FAM suspenso *m* (failure).

flunkey; US **flunky** ['flʌŋki] *n* lacayo *m* (liveried servant) ‖ FAM pelotillero *m*, lacayo *m* (toady).

fluor ['flu:ɔ:*] *n* CHEM fluorita *f*.

fluoresce [fluə'res] *vi* ser fluorescente.

fluorescence [fluə'resns] *n* fluorescencia *f*.

fluorescent [fluə'resnt] *adj* fluorescente; *fluorescent lamp* lámpara fluorescente.

fluoridation [ˌfluərai'deiʃən] *n* fluoración *f*.

fluoride ['fluəraid] *n* CHEM fluoruro *m*.

fluorine ['fluəri:n] *n* MIN flúor *m*.

fluorite ['fluərait] *n* MIN fluorita *f*, espato *m* flúor.

fluorspar ['fluəspɑ:*] *n* CHEM espato *m* flúor.

flurry ['flʌri] *n* ráfaga *f* (of wind) ‖ borrasca *f*, nevisca *f*, nevada *f* (of snow) ‖ chubasco *m*, chaparrón *m* (of rain) ‖ convulsión *f* (spasm) ‖ agitación *f*, nerviosismo *m* (excitement) ‖ frenesí *m*; *a flurry of activity* un frenesí de actividad ‖ — *a flurry of alarm* un gran pánico ‖ *the death flurry* los últimos estertores ‖ *to be in a flurry* estar nervioso *or* aturrullado.

flurry ['flʌri] *vt* poner nervioso (to fluster).

flush [flʌʃ] *n* sofoco *m* (fever, illness) ‖ rubor *m*, sonrojo *m* (embarrassment) ‖ arrebol *m* (of sky) ‖ transporte *m*, arrebato *m* (of joy) ‖ brote *m* (of vegetation) ‖ resplandor *m* (of youth, colour, light) ‖ vuelo *m* repentino (of birds) ‖ alud *m*, lluvia *f*, gran cantidad *f* (of money, etc.) ‖ gran limpieza *f* con agua (cleansing) ‖ cisterna *f*, descarga *f* de agua (in a lavatory) ‖ flux *m* (in poker) ‖ — *hot flush* sofoco de calor ‖ *in the flush of victory* en medio de la euforia de la victoria ‖ FIG *not to be in the first flush of youth* no estar en su primera juventud ‖ *royal, straight flush* escalera *f* real, de color ‖ *these words brought a flush to his face* estas palabras le hicieron ruborizarse ‖ FIG *to be in the full flush of health* estar rebosante de salud.
◆ *adj* a nivel; *flush with* a nivel con ‖ empotrado, da; encajado, da; *the wardrobe is flush with the wall* el armario está empotrado en la pared ‖ embutido, da (screw) ‖ próximo a desbordarse, crecido, da (a stream) ‖ abundante, copioso, sa (abundant) ‖ lozano, na (full of vigour) ‖ ruboroso, sa (face) ‖ FAM adinerado, da (rich) | liberal (lavish).
◆ *adv* a nivel, al mismo nivel ‖ en pleno, na; *flush in the face* en plena cara.

flush [flʌʃ] *vi* ruborizarse, sonrojarse, ponerse colorado (to blush) ‖ subir; *the blood flushed into his face* le subió la sangre a la cara ‖ arrebolarse (the sky) ‖ resplandecer (colour, light) ‖ brotar (to flow suddenly) ‖ emprender el vuelo (birds) ‖ BOT echar renuevos *or* brotes ‖ MED tener sofocos ‖ — *to flush with anger* ponerse rojo de ira ‖ *to flush over* desbordarse, salirse de madre (river) ‖ *to flush up* ruborizarse, ponerse colorado ‖ FAM *to flush up to the ears* subírsele a uno el pavo.
◆ *vt* limpiar (con agua), baldear; *to flush the floor with a bucket of water* limpiar el suelo con

un cubo de agua || inundar (a meadow) || rebosar; *flushed with pride* rebosante de orgullo || levantar (game) || nivelar (to make level) || ruborizar, sonrojar (to blush) || BOT hacer crecer (plants) || *to flush the toilet* tirar de la cadena.

fluster ['flʌstə*] *n* agitación *f*, nerviosismo *m*.

fluster ['flʌstə*] *vt* poner nervioso || *to get flustered* ponerse nervioso.
◆ *vi* ponerse nervioso.

flute [fluːt] *n* MUS flauta *f*; *transverse* o *German flute* flauta travesera | flautado *m* (of organ) || acanaladura *f* (groove) || estría *f* (of glass) || cañón *m*, encañonado *m* (of ruffle) || cañón *m*, pliegue *m* (of cloth) || ARCH acanaladura *f*, estría *f* (of column).

flute [fluːt] *vi* MUS tocar la flauta || FIG hablar, cantar con voz aflautada.
◆ *vt* decir con voz aflautada (to say) || MUS tocar con la flauta || acanalar (to make grooves) || estriar (glass) || encañonar (cloth) || ARCH acanalar, estriar.

flute player ['fluːtpleiə*] *n* flautista *m* & *f*.

fluting ['fluːtiŋ] *n* acanaladuras *f pl* (grooves) || encañonado *m* (of ruffle) || acanaladura *f*, estriado *m* (of column) || *fluting iron* plancha *f* de encañonar (for pressing ruffles).

flutist ['fluːtist] *n* flautista *m* & *f*.

flutter ['flʌtə*] *n* ondulación *f* (of curtains, of flag) || aleteo *m* (of wing) || parpadeo *m* (of eyelids) || FIG agitación *f* (excitement) | alboroto *m* (confusion) | emoción (emotion) || MED palpitación *f* (of heart) | pulsación *f* irregular (of pulse) || FAM impresión *f*; *his speech made quite a flutter* su discurso causó gran impresión | apuesta *f* baja (bet) | especulación *f* de poca importancia (speculation) || AVIAT trepidación *f*, vibración *f* || TECH oscilación *f* del sonido (on a recording) || — FIG *her heart was in a flutter* le latía el corazón | *to be all in a flutter* estar muy nervioso | *to cause a flutter in the dovecotes* sembrar el alboroto, armar un escándalo || FIG *to be in a flutter of excitement* estar excitado *or* emocionado | *to put s.o. in a flutter* poner nervioso a alguien.

flutter ['flʌtə*] *vi* revolotear (birds, leaves, etc.) || batir (wings of a bird) || ondear, ondular (curtain, flag) || palpitar (heart) || latir irregularmente (pulse) || — FIG & FAM *his mother is always fluttering round him* su madre está siempre detrás de él | *to flutter about* o *around* dar vueltas || *to flutter down* caer revoloteando || *to make s.o.'s heart flutter* hacerle latir el corazón a uno.
◆ *vt* agitar (to flap) || batir (wings) || FIG poner nervioso.

fluvial ['fluːvjəl] *adj* fluvial.

flux [flʌks] *n* flujo *m* (flow) || MAR flujo *m* || FIG torrente *m* (of words) | afluencia *f* (of people, of ideas, etc.) | cambios *m pl* frecuentes (changes) || PHYS & CHEM flujo *m*; *magnetic flux* flujo magnético || TECH fundente *m* (for metals) | castina *f* (for minerals) | desoxidante *m* (for deoxidizing) || *to be in a state of flux* estar siempre cambiando.

flux [flʌks] *vt* añadir un fundente a (for fusion) || fundir (to melt).
◆ *vi* fundirse.

fluxion ['flʌkʃən] *n* MED fluxión *f* || flujo *m* || MATH diferencial *f*.

fly [flai] *n* vuelo *m* (flight) || mosca *f* (insect, bait); *fly rod* caña de mosca || pata *f* (on dresses) || tejadillo *m* (entrance of a tent) || alero *m* (outer canvas of a tent) || extremo *m* de la bandera (edge of a flag) || envergadura *f* (span) || guarda *f* (of book) || simón *m*, coche *m* de punto (carriage) || TECH volante *m* (flywheel) || US bragueta *f* (of trousers) || — FIG & FAM *he's the only fly in the ointment* es la única pega || US FIG & FAM *to be on the fly* ajetrearse || FIG & FAM *to catch flies* cazar *or* papar moscas (to daydream) || *to catch on the fly* coger al vuelo (a ball) || FIG & FAM *to put a fly in the ointment* poner trabas *or* pegas || *to rise to* o *to take the fly* picar (fish), picar el anzuelo (to fall into the trap), tragárselo (to believe); *I don't rise to that fly* eso no me lo trago.
◆ *pl* bragueta *f sing* (of trousers) || telares *m* (theatrical) | FIG & FAM *there are no flies on him* no se chupa el dedo, no tiene ni pizca de tonto | *to die* o *to fall* o *to go down like flies* caer como moscas || FIG *you catch more flies with honey than with vinegar* más moscas se cogen con miel que con hiel.
◆ *adj* FAM ladino, na; astuto, ta (sly).

fly* [flai] *vi* volar (bird, aeroplane) || ir en avión (to go by plane); *to fly to Paris* ir a París en avión || saltar (sparks, cork, etc.) || flotar (flag, hair) || FAM irse volando *or* corriendo, irse de prisa (to hurry); *I must fly now* tengo que irme corriendo ahora || FIG huir, escapar (to escape) | pasar *or* irse volando (time) | correr (gossip) | alzarse (to rise) || — FIG & FAM *his watch has flown* su reloj ha desaparecido | *insults were flying thick and fast* llovían los insultos | *the bird has flown* el pájaro voló || *to fly asunder* hacerse pedazos || *to fly at* cazar con halcón (hawking), lanzarse sobre (to attack), arremeter contra uno (shouting) || *to fly for one's life* huir para salvar la vida || FIG *to fly from s.o.'s mouth* salir de la boca de uno (words) || FIG & FAM *to fly high* picar alto || FIG *to fly in the face of* burlarse de (convention), hacer caso omiso de (s.o.'s rights) | *to fly into a temper* ponerse furioso || FIG & FAM *to fly off the handle* salir *or* salirse de sus casillas || FIG *to fly open* abrirse de un golpe | *to fly to pieces* hacerse pedazos | *to fly to s.o.* ir a ponerse bajo la protección de alguien | *to fly to s.o.'s assistance* correr en ayuda *or* en auxilio de uno | *to fly to the head* subirse a la cabeza (success) | *to let fly* disparar (weapon), soltar (insults), salir de sus casillas (with anger), empezar a repartir golpes (to start hitting out) | *to let fly at s.o.* arremeter contra uno (shouting), asestarle un golpe a uno (to hit out at), disparar contra alguien (with a firearm) | *to make the money fly* gastar mucho dinero, despilfarrar el dinero || FIG & FAM *to send s.o. flying* tirarle a uno al suelo | *to send sth. flying* echar algo a rodar | *to send sth. flying at s.o.* tirarle algo a alguien | *to send the enemy flying* hacer huir al enemigo.
◆ *vt* echar a volar; *to fly a kite* echar a volar una cometa || pilotar (an aeroplane) || izar (to hoist); *to fly a flag* izar una bandera || enarbolar; *the ship flies the British flag* este barco enarbola la bandera británica || atravesar *or* cruzar en avión; *to fly the Atlantic* cruzar el Atlántico en avión || transportar *or* llevar en avión; *they flew their troops into France* llevaron sus tropas a Francia en avión || mandar, enviar (a man or rocket into space) || recorrer en avión; *to fly five thousand miles in a month* recorrer cinco mil millas en avión en un mes || soltar (a hawk) | cazar (game) || evitar (to avoid) || huir de (a country).
◆ *phr v* *to fly about* revolotear (birds) || *to fly along* ir volando | *to fly away* emprender el vuelo || *to fly back* volver rápidamente (to hurry back) | volver en avión (by plane) | volver (bird) || *to fly by* pasar volando (to hurry by) | pasar cerca de *or* al lado de; *the aeroplane flew by the Statue of Liberty* el avión pasó cerca de la estatua de la Libertad | FIG pasar volando (time) || *to fly off* emprender el vuelo (birds) || irse rápidamente (people) | saltar (buttons) | desprenderse (to break off) || *to fly out* salir (birds) | irse en avión (by plane) | salir rápidamente (to hurry out) || — FIG & FAM *to fly out at s.o.* arremeter contra alguien || *to fly over* volar sobre, sobrevolar || *to fly past* desfilar (planes in formation) || *to fly up* subir volando || — *to fly up the stairs* subir corriendo la escalera.
— OBSERV Pret ***flew***; pp ***flown***.

fly agaric [-'ægərik] *n* BOT amanita *f* (mushroom).

flyaway [-əˌwei] *adj* suelto, ta (clothing) || FIG casquivano, na; frívolo, la (people) | descabellado, da (ideas) || listo para el vuelo (aircraft).

fly ball [-bɔːl] *n* US pelota *f* bateada al aire (in baseball).

flybelt [-belt] *n* área *f* plagada de moscas tsetsé.

flyblow [-bləu] *n* cresa *f*.

flyblown [-bləun] *adj* lleno de cresas (meat) || FIG cochambroso, sa (dirty); *a flyblown hotel* un hotel cochambroso | mancillado, da (reputation).

fly-by-night [-bəˌnait] *adj* poco de fiar, poco seguro, ra (unrealiable) || efímero, ra (transitory).
◆ *n* persona *f* poco de fiar || FAM noctámbulo *m*, ave *f* nocturna (night rambler).

flycatcher [-ˌkætʃə*] *n* ZOOL papamoscas *m inv*.

flyer [-ə*] *n* ⟶ **flier.**

fly-fishing [-ˌfiʃiŋ] *n* pesca *f* con moscas.

flying [-iŋ] *adj* volador, ra; *a flying machine* un aparato volador || volante (able to fly) || ondeante, flameante (flag) || rápido, da; muy breve; *a flying visit* una visita rápida || volante; *a flying bridge* un puente volante; *a flying squad* un equipo volante || de vuelo; *a flying suit* un traje de vuelo || de aviación; *flying club* club de aviación || — *flying fortress* fortaleza *f* volante || *flying scaffold* andamio suspendido || MIL *flying squadron* escuadra ligera || *flying time* horas *f pl* de vuelo (flying hours), duración *f* del vuelo (duration of flight).
◆ *n* vuelo *m* (flight) || aviación *f* || pilotaje *m* (pilotage) || suelta *f* (of hawk, etc.) || — AVIAT *blind flying* vuelo sin visibilidad || *trick flying* acrobacia aérea.

flying boat [-bəut] *n* hidroavión *m*.

flying bomb [-bɔm] *n* MIL bomba *f* volante.

flying buttress [-bʌtris] *n* ARCH arbotante *m*.

flying colours; US **flying colors** [-'kʌləz] *pl n* FIG éxito *m* rotundo || FIG *to come off with flying colours* salir airoso.

flying doctor [-dɔktə*] *n* médico, ca rural aerotransportado, da (in Australia).

Flying Dutchman [-'dʌtʃmən] *n* buque *m* fantasma (ghost ship).

flying field [-fiːld] *n* campo *m* de aviación.

flying fish [-fiʃ] *n* ZOOL pez *m* volador.

flying jib [-dʒib] *n* MAR petifoque *m*.

flying picket [-ˌpikit] *n* piquete *m* de huelga que actúa por todo el país.

flying saucer [-ˌsɔːsə*] *n* platillo *m* volante.

flying squirrel [-'skwirəl] *n* ZOOL ardilla *f* volante.

flying start [-stɑːt] *n* SP salida *f* lanzada || FIG principio *m* feliz (good beginning) || FIG *to get off to a flying start* empezar muy bien.

flyleaf ['flaiˌliːf] *n* guarda *f* (of book).

flyover ['flaiˌəuvə*] *n* paso *m* elevado (motorway) || US desfile *m* de aviones (flypast).

flypaper ['flaiˌpeipə*] *n* papel *m* matamoscas.

flypast ['flaiˌpɑːst] *n* desfile *m* de aviones.

fly sheet ['flaiˌʃiːt] *n* hoja *f* suelta (loose sheet) || prospecto *m* (handbill).

flyspeck ['flaiˌspek] *n* cagadita *f* de mosca (fly excrement) || mancha *f* (dirty mark).

flyswatter ['flaiˌswɔtə*] *n* matamoscas *m inv*.

flytrap ['flaiˌtræp] *n* BOT atrapamoscas *m inv*.

flyweight ['flai,weit] *n* SP peso *m* mosca.

flywheel [-wi:l] *n* TECH volante *m*.

FM *abbr of [frequency modulation]* FM, frecuencia modulada.

foal [fəul] *n* ZOOL potro *m*, potra *f*.

foal [fəul] *vt/vi* parir.

foam [fəum] *n* espuma *f*.

foam [fəum] *vi* espumar, hacer espuma (liquid) || hacer espuma (sea) || echar espumarajos, espumajear (animal) || FIG *to foam with rage* o *at the mouth* echar espumarajos de cólera, espumajear de ira.

foaminess [-inis] *n* espumosidad *f*.

foaming [-iŋ] *adj* espumoso, sa; encrespado, da (sea) || FIG furioso, sa (angry).

foam rubber [-'rʌbə*] *n* goma *f* espuma, gomespuma *f*.

foamy [-i] *adj* espumoso, sa.

fob [fɔb] *n* faltriquera *f*, bolsillo *m* del reloj (for watch) || US leontina *f* (watch chain).

fob [fɔb] *vt* *to fob s.o. off* engañar a alguien (to fool s.o.) || *to fob sth. off* hacer pasar algo por || *to fob sth. off on s.o.* colar algo a alguien.

f.o.b. ['efəu'bi:] *free on board* franco a bordo.

fob chain ['fɔbtʃein] *n* leontina *f* (watch chain).

focal ['fəukəl] *adj* focal; *focal length* distancia focal.

focalization [fəukəlai'zeiʃən] *n* PHYS enfoque *m* | focalización *f* (in electronics) || MED localización *f*.

focalize ['fəukəlaiz] *vt* PHYS enfocar | focalizar (in electronics) || MED localizar (an infection).

◆ *vi* MED localizarse.

fo'c'sle ['fəuksl] *n* MAR castillo *m* de proa (forecastle).

focus ['fəukəs] *n* PHYS & MATH foco *m* || distancia *f* focal (focal distance) || epicentro *m* (in seismology) || FIG foco *m*, centro *m*; *the focus of Greek civilization* el foco de la civilización griega || MED foco *m* (of a disorder) || — *depth of focus* profundidad *f* de foco || *fixed focus* foco fijo || *in focus* enfocado, da || *out of focus* fuera de foco, desenfocado, da || FIG *the world in focus, focus on the world* panorama *m* del mundo, ojeada *f* al mundo || *to bring into focus* enfocar.

— OBSERV El plural de *focus* es *foci* o *focuses*.

focus ['fəukəs] *vt* hacer converger (light) || enfocar; *to focus the binoculars on a point* enfocar los prismáticos en un punto || ajustar; *to focus a microscope* ajustar un microscopio || FIG fijar, concentrar; *to focus one's attention on a problem* fijar su atención en un problema || *all eyes were focused on her* todos los ojos estaban clavados en ella.

◆ *vi* converger (light) || FIG fijarse, centrarse; *to focus on a problem* centrarse en un problema | enfocar; *we must focus on the racial problem from a humanitarian point of view* tenemos que enfocar el problema racial desde un punto de vista humanitario.

focusing [-iŋ] *n* convergencia *f* (of light) || enfoque *m* (of microscope, of camera, etc.).

fodder ['fɔdə*] *n* forraje *m*, pienso *m*; *green, mixed fodder* forraje verde, mixto.

foe [fəu] *n* enemigo *m*.

foehn [fə:n] *n* viento *m* caliente y muy seco (föhn).

foetal [fi:tl] *adj* fetal; *foetal life* vida fetal.

foetation [fi:'teiʃən] *n* BIOL gestación *f*, desarrollo *m* del feto.

foeticide ['fi:təsaid] *n* feticidio *m*.

foetus ['fi:təs] *n* feto *m*.

fog [fɔg] *n* niebla *f*, bruma *f* || PHOT velo *m* || AGR hierba *f* de segundo corte || FIG & FAM *to be in a fog* estar en un mar de confusiones, no saber a qué atenerse.

fog [fɔg] *vt* envolver en niebla || empañar (to mist up) || velar (in photography) || confundir, ofuscar (to confuse) || oscurecer (to obscure).

◆ *vi* *to fog up* empañarse (to mist up), velarse (in photography), ofuscarse (a person), nublarse, oscurecerse (landscape).

fog bank [-bæŋk] *n* niebla *f* espesa.

fogbound [-baund] *adj* inmovilizado por la niebla.

fogey ['fəugi] *n* ⟶ **fogy.**

fogginess ['fɔginis] *n* nebulosidad *f* (of the atmosphere) || niebla *f*; *the fogginess of the morning prevented me from going out* la niebla que había por la mañana me impidió salir.

foggy ['fɔgi] *adj* brumoso, sa; nebuloso, sa; de niebla; *a foggy day* un día brumoso || velado, da (in photography) || FIG vago, ga; *I have a foggy impression of Barcelona* tengo una vaga idea de lo que es Barcelona || FIG & FAM *I haven't the foggiest idea!* ¡no tengo la más mínima idea!

foghorn ['fɔghɔ:n] *n* MAR sirena *f* de niebla || FIG & FAM *a foghorn voice* una voz ronca.

fog lamp ['fɔglæmp]; **fog light** ['fɔglait] *n* faro *m* antiniebla.

fogy; foggy ['fəugi] *n* FAM *old fogy* vejestorio *m*, carcamal *m* (very old person) || FAM *to be (a bit of) an old fogy* estar chapado a la antigua.

föhn [fə:n] *n* viento *m* caliente y muy seco.

foible ['fɔibl] *n* punto *m* flaco, debilidad *f* (mild failing) || extravagancia *f* (odd feature) || manía *f* (fad); *this is a foible of his* es una manía suya || parte *f* de la hoja de la espada situada entre la mitad y la punta (in fencing).

foil [fɔil] *n* hoja *f* fina de metal (thin sheet of metal) || azogue *m* (in mirrors) || laminilla *f* de metal pulido (in jewelry) || oropel *m* (of copper) || pan *m* (of gold) || ARCH lóbulo *m* || FIG contraste *m* || rastro *m*, huella *f* (trail) || florete *m* (in fencing) || fracaso *m* (failure) || FIG *to serve as a foil to* hacer resaltar, realzar.

foil [fɔil] *vt* chapar (to plate) || azogar (a mirror) || aniquilar, frustrar (efforts) || hacer fracasar (scheme) || desbaratar *or* hacer fracasar los planes de; *the police foiled the robber* la policía desbarató los planes del ladrón || ARCH adornar con lóbulos || FIG realzar, hacer resaltar (to enhance).

foil paper [-'peipə*] *n* papel *m* de aluminio *or* de estaño.

foilsman [-zmən] *n* floretista *m*.

— OBSERV El plural de esta palabra es *foilsmen*.

foist [fɔist] *vt* FAM colar; *to foist a bad coin on s.o.* colar una moneda falsa a alguien | meter; *to foist s.o. into a deal* meter a alguien en un asunto | endosar; *to foist a job on s.o.* endosar un trabajo a alguien || imputar, atribuir; *to foist a book on an author* imputar un libro a un autor || *to foist o.s. on s.o.* imponerse a alguien.

fold [fəuld] *n* redil *m*, aprisco *m* (for sheep) || rebaño *m* (flock); *a fold of sheep* un rebaño de corderos || REL grey *f*, rebaño *m* (religious community) | redil *m*; *to bring back a lost sheep to the fold* hacer volver al redil a una oveja descarriada || pliegue *m*, doblez *f* (crease in clothes or in paper) || arruga *f* (wrinkle) || GEOL & ANAT pliegue *m*.

fold [fəuld] *vt* acorralar, encerrar, meter en un aprisco (sheep) || doblar, plegar; *to fold a blanket* doblar una manta || cruzar; *to fold one's hands* cruzar las manos || plegar, recoger (wings) || envolver (to wrap, to surround) || — *to fold back* volver (collar) || *to fold one's arms* cruzarse de brazos || *to fold s.o. in one's arms* abrazar a alguien, estrechar a alguien entre los brazos || *to fold up* plegar (umbrella), envolver (to wrap up), doblar, plegar (clothes, blanket, chairs, etc.), cerrar (case, deal), liquidar (business).

◆ *vi* doblarse, plegarse || FIG fracasar (to fail) || *to fold up* doblarse, plegarse (to bend), fracasar (to fail), quebrar (to go bankrupt), liquidarse (to close down).

foldaway [-ə,wei] *adj* plegable.

foldboat [-bəut] *n* bote *m* plegable.

folder [-ə*] *n* carpeta *f*, subcarpeta *f* (for documents) || folleto *m*, prospecto *m*, desplegable *m* (leaflet) || TECH máquina *f* plegadora, plegadora *f*.

folderol ['fɔldə'rɔl] *n* US trasto *m*, cachivache *m* (unnecessary object) | tonterías *f pl* (nonsense).

folding ['fəuldiŋ] *adj* plegable; *folding table* mesa plegable || de tijera, plegable (bed, chair) || de fuelle (camera, door) || — *folding machine* máquina plegadora, plegadora *f* || *folding screen* biombo *m* || *folding seat* traspuntín *m*, trasportín *m*, traspontín *m*, asiento *m* plegable.

◆ *n* GEOL plegamiento *m*.

foliaceous [,fəuli'eiʃəs] *adj* BOT foliáceo, a.

foliage ['fəuliidʒ] *n* follaje *m* (leaves).

foliate ['fəuliit] *adj* BOT foliado, da.

foliate ['fəulieit] *vt* foliar (to number pages) || ARCH adornar con lóbulos || azogar (a mirror) || batir (metal).

◆ *vi* BOT echar hojas || hojear (metal).

foliation [,fəuli'eiʃən] *n* BOT foliación *f* || foliación *f* (of pages) || TECH chapado *m* (plating) | azogado *m* (of mirror) | laminado *m* (lamination) || ARCH adorno *m* con lóbulos (ornamentation with foils) | follaje *m* (leaflike decoration) || GEOL estructura *f* laminar.

folio ['fəuliəu] *n* PRINT folio *m* (leaf); *in folio* en folio || infolio *m*, libro *m* en folio (book) || hoja *f* de un libro de contabilidad que contiene el debe y el haber || JUR unidad *f* de medida para evaluar la extensión de un documento [72 ó 90 palabras en Inglaterra, 100 en Estados Unidos].

◆ *adj* PRINT en folio.

folio ['fəuliəu] *vt* foliar, paginar.

foliole ['fəuliəl] *n* BOT foliolo *m*.

folk [fəuk] *n* gente *f*; *I don't mix with that kind of folk* no me mezclo con esta clase de gente || pueblo *m*; *the British folk* el pueblo británico || — *common folk* pueblo *m* || *country folk* campesinos *m pl*.

◆ *pl* FAM familia *f sing* (family) | amigos *m* (friends) || FAM *the old folks at home* los viejos, los padres.

◆ *adj* popular; *folk art* arte popular.

folk dance [-dɑ:ns] *n* baile *m* tradicional *or* folklórico.

folklore [-lɔ:*] *n* folklore *m*.

folkloric [-,lɔ:rik] *adj* folklórico, ca.

folklorist [-,lɔ:rist] *n* folklorista *m* & *f*.

folk music [-mjusik] *n* música *f* popular.

folk singer [-,siŋgə*] *n* cantante *m* & *f*, de canciones populares.

folk song [-sɔŋ] *n* canción *f* popular.

folksy [-si] *adj* US popular | campechano, na (very sociable).

folk tale [-teil] *n* cuento *m* popular.

folkways [-weiz] *pl n* costumbres *f*.

follicle ['fɔlikl] *n* folículo *m*.

follicular [fɔ'likjulə*] *adj* folicular.

folliculitis [fɔlikju'laitis] *n* MED foliculitis *f*.

follies ['fɔliz] *pl n* THEATR revista *f sing*.

follow ['fɔləu] *n* carambola *f* corrida (in billiards) || continuación *f*.

follow ['fɔləu] *vt* seguir; *Wednesday follows Tuesday* el miércoles sigue al martes; *he was followed by his mother* iba seguido por su madre; *to follow a car* seguir un coche; *to follow fashion* seguir la moda; *he spoke so fast that I couldn't follow him* hablaba tan rápidamente que no podía seguirle; *the boat follows the coast* el barco sigue la costa; *he followed my advice* siguió mi consejo; *he followed his father's example* siguió el ejemplo de su padre; *he follows his son's studies* sigue los estudios de su hijo || perseguir (to pursue); *to follow the enemy* perseguir al enemigo || dedicarse a (to dedicate o.s. to) || ejercer (to practise a profession); *he follows the medical profession* ejerce la medicina || — *do you follow rugby?* ¿te interesa el rugby? || *following* a consecuencia de, como consecuencia de; *following the decision taken by the Board* a consecuencia de la decisión tomada por el Consejo || *it follows that* de ello resulta *or* se deriva que || *to follow a person out* entrar detrás de una persona || *to follow suit* servir, jugar del mismo palo (in cards), seguir el ejemplo (to follow the example set).
◆ *vi* seguir; *a long silence followed* un largo silencio siguió || resultar, derivarse (to result) || — *I answered as follows* contesté lo siguiente || *that doesn't follow* no es lógico || *the requirements are as follows* los requisitos son los siguientes.
◆ *phr v* **to follow on** seguir (in the same direction) | reemplazar, sustituir; *he followed on from his father as director* sustituyó a su padre como director | jugar un segundo turno justo después del primero [el mismo equipo] (in cricket) || — *to follow on behind* venir *or* ir detrás | *to follow on from* ser la consecuencia lógica de || **to follow out** seguir hasta el final | llevar a cabo (a plan) || **to follow through** llevar a cabo | SP seguir el golpe || **to follow up** seguir de cerca (s.o.) | perseguir (to pursue) | seguir (a clue, a case) | sacar provecho de (a success) | investigar sobre, profundizar, obtener más detalles sobre (to seek further details) | dar más detalles sobre (to give further details) | reforzar (to consolidate) | hacer seguir; *we followed up the bombardment with an attack* hicimos seguir el bombardeo por un ataque.

follower [-ə*] *n* seguidor, ra; partidario, ria (supporter) || secuaz *m* (of a gangster) || partidario, ria (of a party) || admirador, ra (admirer) || discípulo *m* (disciple) || aficionado, da (of a sport) || TECH pieza *f* movida por otra || *followers of fashion* los que siguen la moda.
◆ *pl* séquito *m sing* (of a king).

following [-iŋ] *adj* siguiente; *the following day* el día siguiente || MAR *following wind* viento *m* en popa.
◆ *n* partidarios *m pl*, seguidores *m pl*; *the statesman has quite a following* el hombre de Estado tiene muchos partidarios || discípulos *m pl* (disciples) || secuaces *m pl* (of a gangster) || séquito *m* (of king) || *the following* lo siguiente.

follow-my-leader [-mi'li:də*]; **follow-the-leader** [-ðə'li:də*] *n* juego *m* que consiste en hacer lo que otro manda.

follow-through [-'θru:] *n* SP continuación *f* del movimiento.

follow-up [-'ʌp] *n* continuación *f*; *this record is the follow-up to his last success* este disco es la continuación de su último éxito || consecuencia *f* (consequence); *as a follow-up to his latest hit, he is now playing in Hamlet* a consecuencia de su último éxito, ahora está trabajando en Hamlet || COMM carta *f* de insistencia, recordatorio *m* || MED tratamiento *m* complementario.
◆ *adj* complementario, ria; *follow-up research* investigaciones complementarias || COMM de insistencia (letter).

folly ['fɔli] *n* locura *f*, desatino *m*, disparate *m* (foolish act or idea).

foment [fəu'ment] *vt* fomentar; *to foment a rebelion* fomentar una rebelión || MED fomentar, aplicar fomentos *or* paños calientes a.

fomentation [,fəumen'teiʃən] *n* instigación *f*, fomento *m*; *the fomentation of discord* la instigación a la discordia, el fomento de la discordia || MED fomento *m*, paño *m* caliente (compress).

fomenter [fəu'mentə*] *n* promotor, ra; fomentador, ra; *fomenter of troubles* promotor de disturbios.

fond [fɔnd] *adj* cariñoso, sa; afectuoso, sa (affectionate) || indulgente; *spoiled by a fond father* mimado por un padre indulgente || inocente (naïve) || — *he had fond hopes of* abrigaba *or* acariciaba esperanzas de || *I have fond memories of* recuerdo con cariño || *to become fond of s.o.* tomar cariño a alguien || *to become fond of sth.* aficionarse a algo || *to be fond of s.o.* tenerle cariño a alguien; querer a alguien; *he is fond of his children* quiere a sus hijos; gustarle alguien a uno; *I am fond of brunettes* me gustan las morenas; apreciar (to appreciate); *he is very fond of sweets* le gustan mucho los caramelos; ser aficionado a algo; *he is very fond of hunting* es muy aficionado a la caza.

fondant ['fɔndənt] *n* pasta *f* de azúcar.

fondle ['fɔndl] *vt* acariciar (to caress) || mimar; *the mother was fondling her child* la madre estaba mimando a su hijo.

fondly ['fɔndli] *adv* con cariño, cariñosamente; *he looked fondly at her* le miró con cariño || inocentemente; *he fondly imagined that* se imaginaba inocentemente que.

fondness ['fɔndnis] *n* cariño *m*, afecto *m* (affection) || indulgencia *f* (indulgence) || afición *f*; *his fondness of hunting* su afición a la caza.

fondue [,f˜ɔdu:] *n* CULIN plato *m* a base de queso derretido o carne frita.

font [fɔnt] *n* REL pila *f* | PRINT fundición *f*, casta *f* || FIG fuente *f* (source) | manantial *m*, fuente *f* (spring).

fontanel, fontanelle [fɔntə'nel] *n* ANAT fontanela *f*.

food [fu:d] *n* alimento *m*; *food for animals* alimento para el ganado || comida *f*; *food and drink* comida y bebida || comestibles *m pl*; *food shop* tienda de comestibles || suministro *m* (supply) || FIG alimento *m*; *mental food* alimento para el espíritu || — *food allowance* dietas *f pl* || *food chain* cadena *f* trófica *or* alimentaria || *food mixer* batidora *f* eléctrica || MED *food poisoning* intoxicación alimenticia || *food safe* fresquera *f* || *food value* valor nutritivo || *the food is good and cheap here* aquí se come bien y barato || FAM *to be off one's food* no tener apetito, no tener ganas de comer || FIG *to give food for thought* dar materia en que pensar || *to give s.o. food* dar de comer a alguien.

foodstuff [-stʌf] *n* producto *m* alimenticio.

fool [fu:l] *n* tonto, ta; imbécil *m* & *f* (stupid) || bufón *m* (jester) || — *any fool could do it* cualquier tonto lo haría, es pan comido || *don't be a fool!* ¡no seas tonto! || FAM *I am nobody's fool* a mí no me la dan, a mí no me toman el pelo || *more fool you* allá tú, peor para ti; *more fool you if anything happens* peor para ti si pasa algo || FAM *silly fool* pedazo de tonto || FIG *there's no fool like an old fool* a la vejez, viruelas || *to act o to play the fool* hacer el tonto || *to be a born fool* ser tonto de nacimiento, ser más tonto que una mata de habas || *to make a fool of o.s.* ridiculizarse, hacer el ridículo || *to make a fool of s.o.* ridiculizar a alguien, poner a alguien en ridículo.
◆ *adj* US tonto, ta; *to be fool enough to* ser bastante tonto como para.

fool [fu:l] *vt* engañar (to deceive) || tomar el pelo a (to pull s.o.'s leg) || estafar; *to fool s.o. out of his money* estafarle a alguien el dinero || dejar perplejo, ja; confundir (to leave puzzled) || — *they fooled me into doing it* me convencieron de que lo tenía que hacer, me embaucaron de tal manera que lo hice || *to fool away* malgastar (time), despilfarrar, malgastar (money).
◆ *vi* bromear (to joke, to kid); *he's only fooling* sólo está bromeando || hacer el tonto (to play the fool) || — *stop fooling!* ¡déjate de tonterías! || *to fool about* o *around* juguetear; *stop fooling around with that gun* deja de juguetear con esta escopeta; perder el tiempo en tonterías (to waste time), hacer el tonto (to play the fool).

foolery ['fu:ləri] *n* tontería *f* || *stop that foolery!* ¡déjate de tonterías!

foolhardiness ['fu:l,hɑ:dinis] *n* temeridad *f*.

foolhardy ['fu:l,hɑ:di] *adj* temerario, ria.

fooling ['fu:liŋ] *n* broma *f* (joking) || engaño *m* (deception) || *no fooling* sin broma, en serio.

foolish ['fu:liʃ] *adj* insensato, ta (unwise) || tonto, ta; necio, cia; estúpido, da (silly) || descabellado, da; *a foolish suggestion* una sugerencia descabellada || ridículo, la (ridiculous) || — *I felt very foolish* me sentí muy ridículo || *that was foolish of you* eso fue una tontería por tu parte || *to make s.o. look foolish* ridiculizar a uno || *you foolish thing!* ¡qué tonto eres!

foolishness [-nis] *n* insensatez *f* || tontería *f*, necedad *f*, insensatez *f* (silly thing) || locura *f*, disparate *m* (folly) || ridiculez *f* (ridiculousness).

foolproof ['fu:l,pru:f] *adj* infalible (plan, scheme) || a toda prueba, que no se puede estropear (device).

foolscap ['fu:lzkæp] *n* pliego *m* de varios tamaños [12 × 15 pulgadas, 13, 5 × 17 pulgadas y 13 × 8 pulgadas].

fool's cap; foolscap ['fu:lzkæp] *n* gorro *m* de bufón (jester's cap) || orejas *f pl* de burro (dunce's cap).

fool's errand ['fu:lz'erənd] *n* empresa *f* descabellada; *to go on a fool's errand* lanzarse en una empresa descabellada || *to send on a fool's errand* mandar hacer algo inútil.

fool's gold ['fu:lz'gəuld] *n* pirita *f* [de hierro o de cobre].

fool's paradise ['fu:lz'pærədaiz] *n* *to live in a fool's paradise* vivir entre nubes, no tener la cabeza sobre los hombros.

fool's parsley ['fu:lz'pɑ:sli] *n* BOT cicuta *f* menor.

foot [fut] *n* ANAT pie *m* || pata *f* (of dog, etc.) || pie *m* (of stocking, mountain, wall, verse) || pie *m*, pies *m pl* (of bed); *at the foot of the bed* al pie de la cama || paso *m* (step); *to walk with a light foot* andar con paso ligero || pata *f* (of piece of furniture) || pie *m*, parte *f* inferior (of a page) || final *m* (of list, etc.) || pie *m* (base) || arranque *m*, pie *m* (of stairs) || pie *m* (measure); *running foot* pie lineal || pie *m*, parte *f* opuesta a la cabecera (of a table) || MIL infantería *f* || PRINT pie *m* || MAR pujamen *m* (of a sail) || TECH pie *m* prensatelas (of a sewing machine) | zapata *f* (of a rail) || — *bound hand and foot* atado de pies y manos || *by foot* a pie, andando || MIL *foot soldier* soldado *m* de a pie, infante *m* || *from head to foot* de pies a cabeza, de arriba abajo || *hind foot* pata trasera || *my hind foot!, my foot!* ¡narices! || *on foot* a pie, andando (walking), en marcha (under way), en vivo (cattle) || *swift* o *fleet of foot* rápido (animal), veloz, rápido, da (people) || FIG *to catch on the wrong foot* coger desprevenido || *to change foot* cambiar el paso || FIG *to get one's foot in the door* introducirse | *to have a foot in both camps* jugar con dos barajas | *to have one foot in the grave* estar con un pie en el sepulcro | *to put one's best foot forward* o *foremost* esmerarse | *to put one's foot down* pisar el acelerador (in a car), dar prueba de autoridad (to be firm) | *to put one's foot in it* meter la pata || *to set foot on* pisar; *to set foot on an island* pisar una isla || FIG *to start off on the right foot* entrar con buen pie || *under foot* bajo los pies, debajo de los pies (beneath one's feet) || US *his toys are always getting underfoot* sus juguetes estorban siempre el paso || *to trample underfoot* pisotear.

◆ *pl* residuos *m* (dregs) || — *at one's feet* a los pies de uno || FIG *feet of clay* pies de arcilla || *on one's feet* de pie (standing) | *to be back on one's feet* haberse recuperado (person), haber salido a flote (enterprise, etc.), haberse restablecido (economy) || *to be on one's feet all day long* estar trajinando todo el día || FIG *to be swept off one's feet* volverse loco | *to carry off one's feet* arrebatar || *to drag one's feet* arrastrar los pies (in walking), hacerse el remolón (to stall, to delay) || FIG *to find one's feet* acostumbrarse (to accustom o.s.),saber desenvolverse (to manage well) | *to get back on one's feet* restablecerse (person, economy), salir a flote (enterprise, etc.) | *to get cold feet* tener miedo || *to get* o *to be under one's feet* estar por medio || FIG *to have one's feet on the ground* tener los pies en la tierra || *to jump to one's feet* levantarse de un salto || FIG *to keep one's feet* mantenerse firme || *to knock s.o. off his feet* tirar a alguien al suelo (by hitting), tirar de espaldas (by surprise) || *to land* o *to fall on one's feet* caer de pie || FAM *to put one's feet up* repantigarse || *to rise to one's feet* levantarse, ponerse de pie || FIG *to set* o *to put s.o. on his feet* lanzar a alguien (to put in a good position), hacer levantar cabeza (to help out of difficulty) | *to set sth. back on its feet* restablecer algo | *to stand on one's own two feet* valerse por sí mismo, volar con sus propias alas || *to stay off one's feet* no andar mucho | *to take the load* o *weight off one's feet* descansar | *to think on one's feet* pensar rápidamente.

— OBSERV El plural de *foot* es *feet*, excepto cuando significa *residuos* en cuyo caso es *foots*.

foot [fut] *vt* hacer el pie de (stocking) || pisar (to tread) || sufragar, costear, pagar (expenses) || sumar (to add up) || FAM *to foot it* ir andando *or* a pie (to walk), bailar (to dance).

◆ *vi* avanzar (to proceed) || *to foot up to* alcanzar.

footage [-idʒ] *n* longitud *f* en pies (length) || metraje *m* (of film).

foot-and-mouth-disease [-ænd'mauθdi'zi:z] *n* VET fiebre *f* aftosa.

football [-bɔ:l] *n* SP fútbol *m*, balompié *m* || balón *m*, pelota *f* (ball) || — *football field* campo *m* de fútbol [AMER cancha *f* de fútbol] || *football player* futbolista *m*, jugador *m* de fútbol || *football pools* quinielas *f* || *football tournament* torneo futbolístico || *table football* futbolín *m*.

footballer [-bɔ:lə*] *n* SP futbolista *m*.

footbath [-bɑ:θ] *n* baño *m* de pies || MED pediluvio *m*, baño *m* de pies.

footboard [-bɔ:d] *n* tabla *f* donde están los pedales (in a car) || tabla *f* del pescante (in a carriage) || pie *m*, pies *m pl* (of bed) || estribo *m* (running board of car).

footboy [-bɔi] *n* lacayo *m*, criado *m*.

foot brake [-breik] *n* freno *m* de pedal.

footbridge [-bridʒ] *n* pasarela *f*, puente *f* para peatones.

foot-candle [-ˌkændl] *n* PHYS candela *f* por pie cuadrado.

footcloth [-klɔθ] *n* gualdrapa *f* (of horse) || alfombra *f* (carpet).

footed [-id] *adj* con pie; *a footed fruit bowl* un frutero con pie || con patas; *a footed bed* una cama con patas || *four-footed* con cuatro patas.

footer [-ə*] *n* cosa *f or* persona *f* que mide cierto número de pies || SP fútbol *m*, balompié *m* || *my yatch is a sixty footer* mi yate mide sesenta pies de longitud *or* tiene sesenta pies de largo.

footfall [-fɔ:l] *n* paso *m*, pisada *f*.

foot fault [-fɔ:lt] *n* SP falta *f* de pie (tennis).

footgear [-giə*] *n* calzado *m*.

foothill [-hil] *n* colina *f* al pie de una montaña.

◆ *pl* estribaciones *f* (of a mountain).

foothold [-ˌhəuld] *n* punto *m* de apoyo para el pie || FIG posición *f*; *to gain a foothold in the international market* tomar posición en el mercado internacional || — FIG *the rumour had gained a foothold* el rumor había llegado a ser creído || *to lose one's foothold* perder pie.

footing [-iŋ] *n* pie *m*, equilibrio *m*; *to loose one's footing* perder pie *or* el equilibrio || FIG base *m* (basis) | pie *m*; *on an equal footing* en un pie de igualdad | condición *f* (standing) | posición *f* || colocación *f* del pie (of stocking) || colocación *f* de los pies (in dancing, in fencing) || MATH suma *f* || ARCH zapata *f* (of building) | zócalo *m* (of column) || — *on a war footing* en pie de guerra || FIG *to be on a friendly footing with* tener relaciones amistosas con | *to be on a good footing with* estar en buenos términos con | *to gain a footing* conseguir establecerse || *to miss one's footing* poner el pie en falso.

footle [-l] *vt/vi* FAM hacer el tonto || — FAM *to footle around* o *about* perder el tiempo en tonterías | *to footle one's time away* perder el tiempo.

footless [-lis] *adj* sin pies || FIG sin fundamento.

footlights [-laits] *pl n* candilejas *f* (of stage) || FIG teatro *m* (the acting profession).

footling [-liŋ] *adj* FAM fútil (trivial).

footloose [-lu:s] *adj* libre || *footloose and fancy free* libre como el aire.

footman [-mən] *n* lacayo *m*, criado *m*.

— OBSERV El plural de esta palabra es *footmen*.

footmark [-mɑ:k] *n* huella *f*, pisada *f*.

footnote [-nəut] *n* nota *f* (al pie de la página).

footpace [-peis] *n* paso *m* (speed).

footpad [-pæd] *n* bandolero *m*, salteador *m* de caminos.

footpath [-pɑ:θ] *n* senda *f*, sendero *m*, camino *m* (in woods, in fields) || acera *f* (pavement).

footplate [-pleit] *n* plataforma *f* (of railway engine).

foot-pound [-paund] *n* PHYS pie *m* libra (unit of energy).

footprint [-print] *n* huella *f*, pisada *f*.

footrace [-reis] *n* SP carrera *f* pedestre.

footrail [-ˌreil] *n* rodapié *m*.

footrest [-rest] *n* reposapiés *m inv* || estribo *m* (of motorcycle).

footrope [-rəup] *n* MAR marchapié *m*.

foot rule [-ru:l] *n* regla *f* de un pie (ruler).

footscraper [-ˌskreipə*] *n* limpiabarros *m inv*.

footsie [-si] *n* FAM *to play footsie with* dar con el pie a.

footslog [-slɔg] *vi* andar.

foot soldier [-'səuldʒə*] *n* MIL soldado *m* de infantería *or* de a pie, infante *m*.

footsore [-sɔ:*] *adj* con los pies cansados *or* doloridos.

footstalk [-stɔ:k] *n* BOT pedúnculo *m*, pecíolo *m* || pedúnculo *m* (of barnacle).

footstep [-step] *n* paso *m*, pisada *f* || FIG *to follow in s.o.'s footsteps* seguir los pasos de alguien.

footstock [-stɔk] *n* contrapunta *f* (of a lathe).

footstone [-stəun] *n* ARCH primera piedra *f* || lápida *f* [al pie de un sepulcro].

footstool [-stu:l] *n* escabel *m*, taburete *m*.

foot warmer [-ˌwɔ:mə*] *n* calientapiés *m inv*.

footway [-wei] *n* acera *f* (pavement) || sendero *m*, senda *f*, camino *m* (pathway).

footwear [-wɛə*] *n* calzado *m*.

footwork [-wə:k] *n* SP juego *m* de piernas.

footworn [-wɔ:n] *adj* trillado, da; *a footworn path* un camino trillado || desgastado, da (stairs) || con los pies cansados (person).

foozle ['fu:zl] *vt* FAM errar (blow).

fop [fɔp] *n* petimetre *m*, pisaverde *m*, currutaco *m*.

foppery ['fɔpəri]; **foppishness** ['fɔpiʃnis] *n* afectación *f* || fatuidad *f*, presunción *f* (vanity).

foppish ['fɔpiʃ] *adj* afectado, da || presumido, da; fatuo, tua (conceited).

foppishness [-nis] *n* ⟶ **foppery**.

for [fɔ:*]

A. PREPOSITION **1.** TRANSLATED BY *para* **2.** TRANSLATED BY *por* **3.** TRANSLATED BY *de* **4.** TRANSLATED BY OTHER PREPOSITIONS **5.** LOCUTIONS **B.** CONJUNCTION

A. PREPOSITION

1. TRANSLATED BY «para» to express «with the purpose of»; *a book for studying* un libro para estudiar; «destined to»; *a gift for his mother* un regalo para su madre; «in the direction of»; *I am leaving for London me marcho a Londres;* «considering the usual nature of»; *that was a clever remark for John* aquella era una observación inteligente para Juan; *you are small for your age* eres bajo para la edad que tienes; «at» (of time); *I have got an engagement for 10 o'clock* tengo una cita para las diez; «during»; *we have work for two years* tenemos trabajo para dos años.

2. TRANSLATED BY «por» to express «on behalf of»; *I'll sign for you* firmaré por ti; «in exchange of»; *sold for 10 pounds* vendido por diez libras; *blow for blow* golpe por golpe; «because of»; *for this reason* por esta razón; *he was punished for his crime* fue castigado por su crimen; *famous for his heroic deeds* famoso por sus hazañas; «for the benefit of»; *I did it for you* lo hice por ti; «in spite of»; *for all his studying he will never know anithing* por mucho que estudie no sabrá nunca nada; «compared with»; *for every adult there were ten children* por cada adulto había diez niños.

3. TRANSLATED BY «de» to express «as the effect of»; *she shouted for joy* gritó de alegría; «representing»; *A for Andrew* A de Andrés; «to the amount of»; *a bill for 5 pounds* una cuenta de cinco libras; «to have»; *eager for news* ávido de noticias; «to»; *the train for Paris* el tren de París.

4. TRANSLATED BY other prepositions. Desde hace (in indefinite time); *I have been in Manchester for three months* estoy en Manchester desde hace tres meses || durante (in definite time); *he worked for eight hours* trabajó durante ocho horas || antes de (before); *he won't be back for a week* no volverá antes de una semana || en honor de (in honour of); *a banquet for the mayor* un banquete en honor del alcalde || a favor de, en favor de (in favour of); *he was for a negotiated peace* estaba a favor de una paz negociada; *campaign for women's lib* campaña a favor de la liberación de la mujer || a, para con (towards); *affection for children* cariño a los niños; *respect for his parents* respeto para con sus padres || en lugar de, en vez de, como (in place of); *he used a cup for a soup bowl* utilizó una taza en vez de un plato sopero || como (as); *I want you for my wife* te quiero como mu-

jer || para que (in order that); *I have brought this for you to see* he traído esto para que lo veas || contra (against); *campaign for pollution control* campaña contra la contaminación || en cuanto a (as regards).
5. LOCUTIONS *as for* en cuanto a || *for all that* a pesar de todo eso, con todo y con eso || *for ever* para siempre (eternally), siempre (always) || *for ever and ever* para siempre jamás || *for him to fall now would be fatal* caerse ahora sería fatal para él, sería fatal que se cayera ahora || *for o.s.* solo, la; *I can do it for myself* lo puedo hacer solo || *for sale* en venta || *for that to be possible* para que eso sea posible || *for the time being* de momento, por ahora || *I for one* yo personalmente || FAM *I'm all for it* me parece muy bien || *I'm for Madrid* voy a Madrid || *it is best for you to go* más vale que te vayas || *it is for you to* a ti te toca || *it is time for lunch* es la hora de comer || *I travelled for miles and miles* recorrí muchas millas || *I want to see it for myself* quiero verlo yo mismo || FAM *now we are (in) for it!* ¡ahora se va a armar! || *oh, for...!* ¡ojalá!; *oh, for a fine day!* ¡ojalá hiciese un buen día!; ¡quién tuviera...!; *oh, for an ice cream!* ¡quién tuviera un helado! || *speaking for myself* hablando en mi nombre *ir* en nombre propio || *there is nothing for it but to* no hay más remedio que || *to come for* venir a por *or* a buscar || *to go for* ir a por *or* a buscar || *to go for a walk* (ir a) dar un paseo || FAM *to go for s.o.* gustarle a uno alguien; *I really go for him* me gusta mucho || *to leave s.o. for dead* dejar a uno por muerto || *to make a name for o.s.* hacerse un nombre || *to write for the papers* escribir para *or* en los periódicos || *were it not for that* si no hubiera sido por eso, de no haber sido por eso (in the past tense), de no ser por eso, si no fuera por eso (in the present) || *what for?* ¿para qué? (with what aim), ¿por qué? (why) || *what is the French for «spoon»?* ¿cómo se dice «cuchara» en francés? || *what is this for?* ¿para qué sirve esto? || *where are you going for your holiday?* ¿adónde vas de vacaciones?
B. CONJUNCTION ya que, pues, puesto que (because, seeing that).
— OBSERV *For* when used in an expression of duration of time in the future is either not translated in Spanish or translated by *por* or *para*: *I am going to Pamplona for two weeks* voy a pamplona dos semanas, voy a Pamplona por *or* para dos semanas.

forage ['fɔridʒ] *n* forraje *m*.

forage ['fɔridʒ] *vi* forrajear, buscar el forraje (to collect forage) || FIG hurgar (to search) || FIG *to forage for* buscar hurgando.
◆ *vt* forrajear (hay, etc.) || dar forraje a (animals) || FIG saquear (to plunder).

forage plant [-plænt] *n* AGR planta *f* forrajera.

forager ['fɔridʒə*] *n* MIL forrajeador *m*.

forasmuch as [fərəz'mʌtʃæz] *conj* puesto que, ya que.

foray ['fɔrei] *n* correría *f*, incursión *f* (raid) || saqueo *m* (pillage).

foray ['fɔrei] *vi* hacer una incursión *or* una correría.
◆ *vt* saquear (to plunder).

forbad [fə'bæd] *pret* → **forbid.**

forbade [fə'bæd] *pret* → **forbid.**

forbear ['fɔ:bɛə*] *n* antepasado *m*.

forbear ['fɔ:bɛə*] *vi* contenerse (to refrain) || abstenerse; *to forbear from drinking* abstenerse de beber || *to forbear with* soportar con paciencia.
◆ *vt* abstenerse de.
— OBSERV Pret ***forbore***; pp ***forborne***.

forbearance [fɔ:bɛərəns] *n* indulgencia *f* (tolerance) || paciencia *f* (patience) || dominio *m* sobre sí mismo (self-control) || abstención *f*.

forbearing [fɔ:'bɛəriŋ] *adj* indulgente || paciente.

forbid* [fə'bid] *vt* prohibir; *I forbid you to leave the house* te prohibo que salgas de casa, te prohibo salir de casa; *to forbid sth. to s.o.* prohibir algo a alguien || FIG impedir (to prevent) || — *God* o *Heaven forbid!* ¡Dios no lo quiera! || *smoking strictly forbidden* prohibido fumar || *to forbid s.o. the house* negarse a recibir a alguien.
— OBSERV Pret ***forbad, forbade***; pp ***forbidden***.

forbiddance [fə'bidəns] *n* prohibición *f*.

forbidden [fə'bidn] *pp* → **forbid.**

forbidding [fə'bidiŋ] *adj* impresionante, imponente; *a forbidding task* una tarea impresionante || severo, ra (stern) || inhóspito, ta; *a forbidding country* un país inhóspito || odioso, sa (repellent) || amenazador, ra (threatening); *a forbidding sky* un cielo amenazador || terrible (terrifying).

forbore [fɔ:'bɔ:*] *pret* → **forbear.**

forborne [fɔ:'bɔ:n] *pp* → **forbear.**

force [fɔ:s] *n* fuerza *f*; *we had to use force to restrain him* tuvimos que emplear la fuerza para contenerle; *to resort to force* recurrir a la fuerza; *the force of an argument* la fuerza de un argumento; *force of character* fuerza de carácter || contingente *m* (contingent) || PHYS fuerza *f*; *centrifugal, inertial force* fuerza centrífuga, de inercia || policía *f*, fuerza *f* pública (police) || MIL cuerpo *m*; *expeditionary force* cuerpo expedicionario || — *brute force* fuerza bruta || *by force* a la fuerza, por fuerza || *by force of* a fuerza de || *by force of circumstances* debido a las circunstancias || *by force of habit* por costumbre, por la fuerza de la costumbre || *by sheer force* a viva fuerza || *in force* en vigor, vigente || *in (full) force* en masa || *labour force* mano *f* de obra || *sales force* vendedores *m pl* || *to be in force* estar en vigor, estar vigente, regir || *to come into force* entrar en vigor || *to join forces* unirse || *to put into force* poner en vigor, hacer entrar en vigor, aplicar || *to yield to force* rendirse a la fuerza.
◆ *pl* MIL fuerzas *f*; *armed forces* fuerzas armadas; *land forces* fuerzas terrestres.

force [fɔ:s] *vt* forzar, obligar; *to force s.o. to do sth.* o *into doing sth.* obligar a alguien a que haga algo || forzar (a door, a lock, a key) || meter a la fuerza; *to force a coin into a slot* meter a la fuerza la moneda en una ranura || AGR forzar, activar la maduración de || MIL tomar por asalto, forzar (to take) || GRAMM forzar (meaning) || forzar, violar (a woman) || TECH inyectar (air) || — *to be forced to* verse obligado a, estar forzado a || *to force a smile* sonreír de dientes afuera, sonreír forzadamente || *to force one's way* abrirse paso; *to force one's way through the crowd* abrirse paso entre la muchedumbre; entrar por (la) fuerza; *to force one's way into a house* entrar por la fuerza en una casa || *to force s.o. into doing sth.* hacer un esfuerzo por hacer algo, esforzarse por hacer algo || *to force s.o. into* hacer entrar por la fuerza a alguien en || *to force s.o. into a corner* o *against a wall* arrinconar a uno || FIG *to force s.o.'s hand* forzarle la mano a alguien || *to force the pace* forzar *or* apresurar *or* apretar el paso.
◆ *phr v* *to force away* obligar a alejarse || *to force back* hacer retroceder (the enemy) | contener, reprimir (tears) || *to force down* obligar a bajar (to push down) | tragar por la fuerza (to swallow unwillingly) | hacer tragar (to force to swallow) | cerrar por la fuerza (a lid, etc.) | obligar a aterrizar (a plane) | hacer bajar (prices) | inyectar (air) || *to force from* arrancar || *to force in* conseguir hacer entrar, hacer entrar *or* introducir por la fuerza || *to force off* quitar por la fuerza, conseguir despegar (sth. which is stuck) | hacer salir de; *to force a lorry off the road* hacer salir un camión de la carretera || *to force out* obligar a salir, hacer salir por la fuerza | arrancar (to pull out) | eliminar [a un jugador] (in baseball) | pronunciar con dificultad (words) | sacar (the truth) || — *to force out a few words of congratulation* pronunciar unas palabras de felicitación de boca para fuera | *to force the truth out of s.o.* obligar *or* forzar a uno a decir la verdad || *to force through* conseguir hacer entrar || *to force up* obligar a subir, hacer subir por la fuerza | hacer subir (prices) || *to force upon* imponer; *he tries to force his ideas upon me* intenta imponerme sus ideas | obligar a aceptar *or* tomar; *he forced a drink upon me* me obligó a tomar una copa.

forced [-t] *adj* forzado, da; *forced smile* sonrisa forzada || TECH a presión (feed) || — *forced labour* trabajo obligatorio || AVIAT *forced landing* aterrizaje forzoso || *forced march* marcha forzada.

force-feed ['fɔ:s fi:d] *vt* alimentar a la fuerza.

forceful [-ful] *adj* fuerte; *a forceful personality* una personalidad fuerte || contundente (convincing); *a forceful speech* un discurso contundente || enérgico, ca; vigoroso, sa (energetic).

forcefulness [-fulnis] *n* fuerza *f*, energía *f*.

force majeure [fɔ:smæ'ʒə*] *n* fuerza *f* mayor.

forcemeat ['fɔ:smi:t] *n* picadillo *m* de relleno, relleno *m*.

forceps ['fɔ:seps] *inv n* MED fórceps *m* (in obstetrics) | gatillo *m*, tenazas *f pl* (in dentistry).

force pump ['fɔ:spʌmp] *n* TECH bomba *f* impelente.

forcible ['fa:sabl] *adj* contundente; *a forcible argument* un argumento contundente || fuerte, enérgico, ca (style) || a la fuerza, por fuerza (by force) || — JUR *forcible detainer* posesión ilegal obtenida por la violencia | *forcible entry* violación *f* de domicilio, allanamiento *m* de morada.

forcibly [-i] *adv* por la fuerza (by force) || enérgicamente (energetically).

ford [fɔ:d] *n* vado *m*.

ford [fɔ:d] *vt* vadear.

fordable ['fɔ:dəbl] *adj* vadeable.

fore [fɔ:*] *adj* delantero, ra; *the fore legs* las patas delanteras || anterior, delantero, ra; *the fore part* la parte anterior || MAR de proa.
◆ *adv* delante, en la parte delantera.
◆ *prep* ante.
◆ *n* MAR proa *f*, parte *f* delantera || — *at the fore* en el palo de trinquete (in ships), en la cabeza (in a leading position) || FIG *to be to the fore* ocupar un lugar preeminente | *to come to the fore* empezar a destacar *or* a ser conocido || MIL *to the fore!* ¡adelante!
◆ *interj* ¡cuidado! (in golf).

fore and aft [-ænd'a:ft] *adv* MAR de proa a popa.

fore-and-aft [-ænda:ft] *adj* longitudinal || de proa a popa.

fore and after [-ænda:ftə*] *n* MAR goleta *f*, barco *m* de velas áuricas || bicornio *m* (hat).

fore-and-aft rig [-ænda:ftrig] *n* MAR aparejo *m* de velas áuricas.

fore-and-aft sail [-ænda:ftseil] *n* MAR vela *f* áurica.

forearm [-r'a:m] *n* ANAT antebrazo *m*.

forearm [-r'a:m] *vt* prevenir.

forebear [-'bɛə*] *n* antepasado *m*.

forebode [-'bəud] *vt* anunciar, presagiar; *a policy that forebodes disaster* una política que anuncia un desastre || presentir, tener el presentimiento de (to have a presentiment).

foreboding [-'bəudiŋ] *n* presentimiento *m* || presagio *m* (sign of things to come).

forebrain [-brein] *n* ANAT cerebro *m* anterior.

forecast [-k':st:] *n* previsión *f*, pronóstico *m* ‖ pronóstico *m* (in racing) ‖ *weather forecast* parte meteorológico (weather report), previsión meteorológica (predicting weather).

forecast [-kɑ:st] *vt* pronosticar.

forecaster [-ˌkɑ:stə*] *n* pronosticador, ra.

forecastle ['fəuksl] *n* MAR castillo *m* de proa.

foreclose [fɔ:'kləuz] *vt* excluir (to preclude) ‖ JUR privar del derecho de redimir una hipoteca.
◆ *vi* JUR ejecutar una hipoteca.

foreclosure [fɔ:k'ləuʒə*] *n* exclusión *f* ‖ JUR ejecución *f* de una hipoteca.

forecourt ['fɔ:kɔ:t] *n* antepatio *m* (of a building) ‖ SP parte *f* del campo cercana a la red (tennis, badminton).

foredoom [fɔ:'du:m] *n* destino *m*.

foredoom [fɔ:θdu:m] *vt* condenar de antemano; *an attempt that was foredoomed to failure* un intento que estaba condenado de antemano al fracaso ‖ (ant) predeterminar, predestinar.

fore edge ['fɔ:redʒ] *n* canal *f* (of book).

forefather ['fɔ:':ðə*] *n* antepasado *m*.

forefinger ['fɔ:ˌfɑðə*] *n* índice *m*, dedo *m* índice.

forefoot ['fɔ:fut] *n* pata *f* delantera (of an animal) ‖ MAR pie *m* de la roda.

forefront ['fɔ:frʌnt] *n* primer plano *m*, vanguardia *f* ‖ MIL primera fila *f*, vanguardia *f*, frente *m* ‖ — *this question is still in the forefront* esta cuestión sigue en primer plano ‖ *to come to the forefront* empezar a destacar.

foregather [fɔ:'gæðə*] *vi* reunirse.

forego* [fɔ:'gəu] *vt* renunciar a, privarse de (to forgo) ‖ preceder, anteceder (to precede).
— OBSERV Pret *forewent*; pp *foregone*.

foregoing [fɔ:'gəuiŋ] *adj* anteriormente mencionado, da (above) ‖ precedente, anterior (preceeding).
◆ *n* lo anteriormente dicho.

foregone [fɔ:'gɔn] *adj* conocido de antemano (conclusion, etc.) ‖ inevitable (determined) ‖ previsto, ta (anticipated) ‖ pasado, da (previous).
◆ *pp* ⟶ **forego.**

foreground ['fɔ:graund] *n* primer plano *m*, primer término *m* ‖ FIG primer plano *m*.

forehand ['fɔ:hænd] *adj* previo, via (prior) ‖ *forehand stroke* golpe derecho *or* directo (in tennis).
◆ *n* golpe *m* derecho *or* directo (in tennis) ‖ cuarto *m* delantero (of a horse).

forehanded [-id] *adj* US precavido, da; prudente (prudent) | acomodado, da (well-off) | derecho, cha; directo, ta (stroke in tennis).

forehead ['fɔ:hed] *n* ANAT frente *f* ‖ parte *f* delantera (front part).

foreign ['fɔrin] *adj* extranjero, ra; *foreign languages* lenguas extranjeras ‖ exterior; *foreign trade* comercio exterior ‖ ajeno, na; *this behaviour is foreign to his nature* este comportamiento es ajeno a su naturaleza ‖ — *foreign affairs* asuntos exteriores [AMER relaciones exteriores] ‖ *foreign aid* ayuda *f* exterior ‖ *foreign body* cuerpo extraño ‖ *foreign correspondent* corresponsal en el extranjero ‖ *foreign currency* o *exchange* divisas *f pl* ‖ *foreign debt* deuda externa *or* exterior ‖ *foreign legion* legión extranjera ‖ *foreign money order* giro *m* internacional ‖ *Foreign Office* Ministerio de Asuntos Exteriores [AMER Ministerio de Relaciones Exteriores] ‖ *foreign parts* el extranjero ‖ *Foreign Secretary, Foreign Minister* ministro *m* de Asuntos Exteriores [AMER ministro *m* de Relaciones Exteriores] ‖ *foreign travel* viajes *m pl* al *or* en el extranjero.

foreigner ['fɔrinə*] *n* extranjero, ra (from another country) ‖ forastero, ra (from another region).

forejudge [fɔ:'dʒʌdʒ] *vt* prejuzgar.

foreknow* [fɔ:'nəu] *vt* saber de antemano.
— OBSERV Pret *foreknew*; pp *foreknown*.

foreknowledge ['fɔ:'nɔlidʒ] *n* presciencia *f*.

foreland ['fɔ:lənd] *n* promontorio *m*, cabo *m*.

foreleg ['fɔ:leg] *n* pata *f* delantera (of a dog) ‖ brazo *m* (of a horse).

forelock ['fɔ:lɔk] *n* copete *m*, mechón *m* de pelo (hair) ‖ TECH clavija *f* (fastening device) ‖ *to take time by the forelock* coger la ocasión por los pelos.

foreman ['fɔ:mən] *n* capataz *m* (in a factory) ‖ mayoral *m* (in a farm) ‖ ARCH capataz *m*, maestro *m* de obras, aparejador *m* ‖ PRINT regente *m* ‖ JUR presidente *m* del jurado.
— OBSERV El plural es *foremen*.

foremast ['fɔ:mɑ:st] *n* MAR palo *m* de trinquete.

forementioned [fɔ:'menʃənd] *adj* anteriormente mencionado, da.

foresmost ['fɔ:məust] *adj* primero, ra; *one of the foremost producers of cotton* uno de los primeros productores de algodón ‖ *to be first and foremost* ser el primero de todos.
◆ *adv* *first and foremost* ante todo, antes que nada.

forename ['fɔ:neim] *n* nombre *m* [de pila].

forenamed [-d] *adj* anteriormente mencionado, da.

forenoon [ˌfɔ:nu:n] *n* mañana *f*.
◆ *adj* matutino, na; matinal.

forensic [fə'rensik] *adj* JUR forense; *forensic surgeon* médico forense; *forensic medicine* medicina forense | del foro; *forensic eloquence* elocuencia del foro.

foreordain [ˌfɔ:rɔ:'dein] *vt* predestinar, predeterminar.

foreordination [ˌfɔ:rɔ:də'neiʃən] *n* predestinación *f*, predeterminación *f*.

forepart ['fɔ:pɑ:t] *n* parte *f* delantera ‖ principio *m* (beginning).

forepeak ['fɔ:pi:k] *n* MAR bodega *f* de proa.

forequarter ['fɔ:ˌkwɔ:tə*] *n* cuarto *m* delantero [de la res].

forereach [fɔ:'ri:tʃ] *vt* MAR adelantar, pasar (to overtake).
◆ *vi* MAR ganar terreno.

forerun [fɔ:'rʌn] *vt* preceder.

forerunner [-ə*] *n* precursor, ra ‖ predecesor, ra (predecessor) ‖ anunciador, ra (herald) ‖ presagio *m* (omen) ‖ antepasado *m* (forebear) ‖ *the Forerunner* el Precursor de Cristo.

foresaid ['fɔ:sed] *adj* anteriormente mencionado, da; susodicho, cha.

foresail ['fɔ:seil] *n* MAR trinquete *m*.

foresaw [fɔ:'sɔ:] *pret* ⟶ **foresee.**

foresee [fɔ:'si:] *vt* prever; *he had foreseen the problem* había previsto el problema.
— OBSERV Pret *foresaw*; pp *foreseen*.

foreseeable [-əbl] *adj* previsible ‖ — *for the foreseeable future* por mucho tiempo ‖ *in the foreseeable future* en un futuro inmediato.

foreseen [fɔ:'si:n] *pp* ⟶ **foresee.**

foreshadow [fɔ:'ʃædəu] *vt* presagiar (to presage) ‖ prefigurar (to prefigure).

foresheet ['fɔ:ʃi:t] *n* MAR escota *f* del trinquete.
◆ *pl* MAR parte *f sing* delantera de un barco.

foreshore ['fɔ:ʃɔ:] *n* playa *f* [entre los límites de pleamar y bajamar].

foreshorten [fɔ:'ʃɔ:tən] *vt* ARTS escorzar.

foreshortening [-iŋ] *n* escorzo *m*.

foreshow [fɔ:'ʃəu] *vt* presagiar.

foreside ['fɔ:said] *n* parte *f* anterior.

foresight ['fɔ:sait] *n* previsión *f* ‖ punto *m* de mira (of a rifle) ‖ *to have foresight* ser previsor *or* precavido.

foresighted [-id] *adj* previsor, ra (farsighted) ‖ precavido, da (cautious).

foreskin ['fɔ:skin] *n* ANAT prepucio *m*.

forest ['fɔrist] *n* selva *f*; *the virgin forest* la selva virgen ‖ bosque *m* (wood) ‖ FIG intrincamiento *m*; *a forest of masts in a harbour* un intrincamiento de palos en un puerto ‖ — US FIG *he can't see the forest for the trees* los árboles impiden ver el bosque ‖ *State forests* patrimonio *m sing* forestal del Estado.
◆ *adj* selvático, ca; de la selva; *forest animals* animales de la selva ‖ forestal; *forest botany, fire* botánica, incendio forestal.

forest ['fɔrist] *vt* poblar de árboles.

forestage ['fɔ:steidʒ] *n* proscenio *m* (in a theatre).

forestal ['fɔ:ristəl] *adj* forestal; *forestal resources* recursos forestales.

forestall [fɔ:'stɔ:l] *vt* adelantarse a, anticiparse a (people) ‖ anticiparse a (circumstances) ‖ COMM acaparar, monopolizar (a market).

forestation ['fɔris'teiʃən] *n* plantación *f* de bosques ‖ repoblación *f* forestal (reafforestation).

forestay ['fɔ:stei] *n* MAR estay *m* del trinquete.

forester ['fɔristə*] *n* guardabosque *m* (officer in charge of a forest) ‖ silvicultor *m* (forestry expert) ‖ habitante *m* de un bosque (who lives in a forest) ‖ ZOOL canguro *m* gigante.

forest ranger ['fɔ:rist'reindʒə*] *n* US guardabosque *m*, guarda *m* forestal.

forestry ['fɔristri] *n* bosques *m pl* (woods) ‖ silvicultura *f* ‖ — *Forestry Commission* Administración *f* de montes ‖ *forestry expert* silvicultor *m*.

foretaste ['fɔ:teist] *n* anticipación *f*.

foretaste [fɔ:'teist] *vt* conocer *or* probar de antemano.

foretell* [fɔ:'tel] *vt* predecir, pronosticar (to predict) ‖ presagiar (to forebode).
— OBSERV Pret y pp *foretold*.

forethought ['fɔ:θɔ:t] *n* prudencia *f*, previsión *f* (prudence) ‖ premeditación *f*; *crime of forethought* crimen con premeditación.
◆ *adj* premeditado, da.

foretoken [fɔ:'təukən] *n* presagio *m*, signo *m* precursor.

foretold [fɔ:'təuld] *pret/pp* ⟶ **foretell.**

foretooth ['fɔ:tu:θ] *n* ANAT incisivo *m*, diente *m* incisivo.
— OBSERV El plural de *foretooth* es *foreteeth*.

foretop ['fɔ:tɔp] *n* MAR cofa *f* del trinquete.

fore-topgallant mast ['fɔ:təpgæləntmɑ:st] *n* MAR mastelerillo *m* de juanete de proa.

fore-topgallant sail ['fɔ:təpˌgæləntseil] *n* MAR juanete *m* de proa.

fore-topmast ['fɔ:tɔp'mɑ:st] *n* MAR mastelero *m* de velacho.

fore-topsail ['fɔ:tɔpseil] *n* MAR velacho *m*.

for ever; US **forever** [fə'revə*] *adv* para siempre; *he is gone for ever* se ha ido para siempre ‖ FIG siempre; *he is for ever complaining* siempre se está quejando ‖ *for ever and ever* para siempre jamás.

forevermore [fə'revə'mɔ:*] *adv* (ant) para siempre jamás.

forewarn [fɔ:'wɔ:n] *vt* prevenir, avisar, advertir (to warn) ‖ *forewarned is forearmed* hombre prevenido vale por dos.

forewent [ˈfɔːwent] *pret* ⟶ **forego.**

forewoman [ˈfɔːˌwumən] *n* JUR presidente *f* del jurado || encargada *f* (of a workshop, etc.).
— OBSERV El plural de esta palabra es *forewomen*.

foreword [ˈfɔːwəːd] *n* prólogo *m*, prefacio *m*.

foreyard [ˈfɔːjɑːd] *n* MAR verga *f* del trinquete.

forfeit [ˈfɔːfit] *n* multa *f* (fine) || prenda *f* (in a game) || JUR pérdida *f* de un derecho (loss of a right) || FIG pérdida *f* (loss) | castigo *m* (punishment).
◆ *pl* juego *m sing* de prendas.
◆ *adj* confiscado, da (confiscated) || perdido, da.

forfeit [ˈfɔːfit] *vt* JUR perder (a right) | comisar, decomisar, confiscar (a property) || perder (to lose).

forfeiture [ˈfɔːfitʃə*] *n* pérdida *f* (of licence, of right) || confiscación *f* (of property).

forgather [ˈfɔːgæðə*] *vi* reunirse.

forgave [fəˈgeiv] *pret* ⟶ **forgive.**

forge [fɔːdʒ] *n* TECH fragua *f* (furnace) | herrería *f*, forja *f*, fundición *f* (ironworks).

forge [fɔːdʒ] *vt* fraguar, forjar (metal) || falsificar (to counterfeit); *to forge a signature* falsificar una firma || FIG fraguar, forjar (project, friendship, etc.).
◆ *vi* avanzar (to move forward) || — *to forge ahead* hacer grandes progresos (to make progress), avanzar [rápidamente] (to move forward) || *to forge ahead of s.o.* adelantar a alguien.

forger [-ə*] *n* herrero *m*, forjador *m* (metal worker) || falsificador *m* (counterfeiter).

forgery [-əri] *n* falsificación *f* (counterfeiting) || documento *m or* billete *m* falsificado, moneda *f* falsificada (sth. forged).

forget* [fəˈget] *vt* olvidar, olvidarse de; *I forgot my watch* me olvidé del reloj, olvidé el reloj || dejar (to leave); *I forgot it in the train* lo dejé en el tren || no fijarse en; *I forgot the time* no me fijé en la hora || olvidar; *try to forget it* intenta olvidarlo || — *and don't you forget it!* ¡que no se te olvide! || *forget it!* ¡deja! (don't bother), ¡de nada! (reply to «thank you»), ¡no importa! (it doesn't matter), ¡no se preocupe! (don't worry) || *never to be forgotten* inolvidable || *to forget o.s.* olvidarse de uno mismo (to act unselfishly), propasarse (to behave thoughtlessly); *he forgot himself and hit her* se propasó y le pegó || *to forget to do sth.* olvidarse de hacer algo, olvidársele a uno hacer algo; *I forgot to ring you up* se me olvidó llamarte por teléfono.
◆ *vi* tener poca memoria (to have a bad memory) || olvidar; *I went away to forget* me marché para olvidar || — *I forget right now* no me acuerdo ahora mismo || *let's forget about it* olvidémoslo || *she had to bring me a book but she forgot* tenía que traerme un libro pero se le olvidó.
— OBSERV Pret *forgot*; pp *forgotten*.

forgetful [-ful] *adj* olvidadizo, za; desmemoriado, da; que tiene muy mala memoria (apt to forget) || descuidado, da (negligent) || — *forgetful of his pain* olvidando su dolor, haciendo caso omiso de su dolor || *she is very forgetful* tiene muy mala memoria.

forgetfulness [-fulnis] *n* falta *f* de memoria (lack of memory) || olvido *m*; *a moment of forgetfulness* un momento de olvido || descuido *m* (negligence) || despiste *m* (absentmindedness).

forget-me-not [fəˈgetminɔt] *n* BOT nomeolvides *f inv*, raspilla *f*, miosota *f*.

forgettable [fəˈgetəbl] *adj* olvidable.

forging [ˈfɔdʒiŋ] *n* forja *f*.

forgivable [fəˈgivəbl] *adj* perdonable.

forgive* [fəˈgiv] *vt* perdonar; *to forgive s.o. for sth.* perdonar algo a alguien; *to forgive s.o. a debt* perdonar una deuda a uno.
— OBSERV Pret *forgave*; pp *forgiven*.

forgiven [-n] *pp* ⟶ **forgive.**

forgiveness [-nis] *n* perdón *m*; *to ask for forgiveness* pedir perdón || remisión *f*, perdón *m* (of sins) || perdón *m* (of a debt) || indulgencia *f* (willingness to forgive).

forgiving [-iŋ] *adj* propenso a perdonar, indulgente, clemente.

forgo* [fɔːˈgəu] *vt* renunciar a, privarse de (to do without) || desperdiciar (an opportunity) || *I cannot forgo mentioning it* no puedo dejar de mencionarlo.
— OBSERV Pret *forwent*; pp *forgone*.

forgone [fɔːˈfɔn] *pp* ⟶ **forgo.**

forgot [fɔːˈgɔt] *pret* ⟶ **forget.**

forgotten [fəˈgɔtn] *pp* ⟶ **forget.**

fork [fɔːk] *n* tenedor *m* (cutlery) || horca *f*, horquilla *f* (for gardening) || horquilla *f* (to support a branch, etc.) || bifurcación *f* (of road) || horcadura *f* (of a tree) || zigzag *m* (of lightning) || horcajo *m*, confluencia *f* (in a river) || TECH horquilla *f* (of bicycle) || ANAT horcajadura *f* (crotch) || MUS diapasón *m* (tuning fork).

fork [fɔːk] *vt* cargar con la horca, coger con la horca (hay, etc.) || atacar al mismo tiempo [dos peones] (in chess) || FAM *to fork out* o *over* o *up* soltar, aflojar (money).
◆ *vi* bifurcarse || FAM *to fork out* o *over* o *up* aflojar *or* soltar la mosca (to pay).

forked [-t] *adj* ahorquillado, da (fork-shaped) || bifurcado, da (roads) || BOT bífido, da || *forked lightning* relámpago en zigzag.

forklift [ˈfɔːklift]; **forklift truck** [-trʌk] *n* TECH carretilla *f* elevadora.

forlorn [fəˈlɔːn] *n* triste, melancólico, ca (sad) || desesperado, da (desperate); *a forlorn cry* un grito desesperado || desolado, da; *a forlorn landscape* un paisaje desolado || abandonado, da (abandoned) || *forlorn hope* empresa desesperada (hopeless undertaking), destacamento *m* de soldados encargados de una misión peligrosa (soldiers).

form [fɔːm] *n* forma *f* (shape, nature); *it was published in book form* se publicó en forma de libro; *form and substance* forma y fondo || figura *f*, cuerpo *m* (figure) || manera *f*, forma *f*; *there are several forms of saying it* hay varias maneras de decirlo || clase *f*, tipo *m*; *two forms of government* dos tipos de gobierno || formulario *m* (document); *application form* formulario de inscripción; *to fill in a form* llenar un formulario || banco *m* (bench) || clase *f* (class) || curso *m* (year, at school); *first form* primer curso || forma *f*; *to be in good form* estar en forma; *to be on the top of one's form* estar en plena forma || GRAMM & PHIL forma *f* || PRINT forma *f*, molde *m* || JUR forma *f* || TECH molde *m*, forma *f* (mould) | encofrado *m*, entibación *f* (for concrete) || cama *f*, madriguera *f* (of hare) || — *bad form* malos modales (bad manners) || *for form, for form's sake* para cumplir, para que no se diga || *form of worship* ritos *m pl* || *good form* buenos modales || *in due form* en debida forma, como es debido || *it is only a form of speech* es un decir || *it's just for form's sake, it's a mere matter of form* es para guardar las formas || *to be off form* no estar en forma, estar en baja forma || *to go through the form of refusing* hacer el paripé de rechazar [algo] || *to take the form of* consistir en (to consist of).
◆ *pl* gradas *f* (rows of seats) || *true to form* como es de esperar.

form [fɔːm] *vt* hacer (to make); *he formed a statue out of a piece of wood* hizo una estatua con un trozo de madera || modelar, moldear; *to form the clay* modelar el barro || formar; *to form a circle* formar un círculo || formar, construir (to put together); *to form a sentence* construir una frase || formar (s.o.'s character) || pronunciar, decir (to pronounce); *difficulty in forming certain words* dificultad en decir ciertas palabras || crear (to create a habit) || adquirir (to acquire a habit) || hacerse, formarse (ideas, opinion) || hacer, concebir, elaborar (a plan) || sacar (conclusion) || constituir, integrar, componer (to constitute) || crear (to set up); *to form a society* crear una sociedad || formar (government, team) || concertar (to conclude); *they decided to form an alliance* decidieron concertar una alianza || GRAMM formar; *how do you form the gerund?* ¿cómo forma Ud. el gerundio? || TECH moldear (to mould) || MIL formar || *to form a queue* ponerse en cola (to make a queue), hacer cola (to queue).
◆ *vi* tomar forma; *an idea is forming in his mind* una idea está tomando forma en su mente || formarse; *clouds began to form* empezaban a formarse nubes || — MIL *form up!* ¡a formar!, ¡formen filas! | *to form up* formar, formarse, formar filas.

formal [ˈfɔːməl] *adj* formal; *he gave his formal consent* dio su acuerdo formal || solemne; *a formal speech* un discurso solemne || formalista (person); *don't be so formal!* ¡no seas tan formalista! || ceremonioso, sa; *he spoke to me in a formal manner* me habló de una manera ceremoniosa || protocolario, ria; *formal terms* términos protocolarios || de cumplido, de cortesía; *we had to make a formal visit* tuvimos que hacer una visita de cumplido || oficial; *a formal invitation* una invitación oficial || de etiqueta (dinner, ball, etc.); *a formal dress* un traje de etiqueta || en debida forma; *a formal receipt* un recibo en debida forma || tradicional (traditional) || muy correcto, ta; *a formal style* un estilo muy correcto || COMM en firme (order) || PHIL esencial | formal.
◆ *n* US traje *m* de etiqueta (dress) | baile *m* de etiqueta.

formaldehyde [fɔˈmældihaid] *n* formaldehído *m*.

formalin; formaline [ˈfɔːməlin] *n* CHEM formalina *f*.

formalism [ˈfɔːməlizəm] *n* formalismo *m*.

formalist [ˈfɔːməlist] *n* formalista *m* & *f*.

formalistic [-ik] *adj* formalista.

formality [fɔːˈmæliti] *n* formalidad *f*, trámite *m* (requirement); *one must go through a lot of formalities to get in* hay que pasar por muchas formalidades para entrar || ceremonia *f* (ceremony) || rigidez *f* (of manner) || — *as a mere formality* para *or* por cumplir.
◆ *pl* ceremonial *m sing* (proper procedure) || *to comply with all the necessary formalities* cumplir con todos los requisitos.

formalize [ˈfɔːməlaiz] *vt* formalizar (to make formal) || dar forma a (to shape).
◆ *vi* ser formalista (to be formal).

formally [ˈfɔːməli] *adv* formalmente || en debida forma, como es debido (in due form) || en cuanto a la forma (with regard to form) || ceremoniosamente (ceremoniously) || oficialmente (officially).

format [ˈfɔːmæt] *n* tamaño *m* (dimension) || PRINT formato *m*, tamaño *m* || INFORM formato || US concepción *f* (of a radio programme).

format [ˈfɔːmæt] *vt* INFORM formatear.

formation [fɔːˈmeiʃən] *n* formación *f*; *geological formation* formación geológica || MIL formación *f*; *close-order formation* formación en orden cerrado; *formation in threes* formación de a tres || FIG formación *f* || MIL *in battle formation* en orden de combate.

formative [ˈfɔːmətiv] *adj* de formación; *formative years* años de formación || formativo, va (which forms); *formative influence* influencia formativa || GRAMM formativo, va.

formatting ['fɔːmætiŋ] *n* INFORM formateado *m*.

former ['fɔːmə*] *adj* anterior (previous); *in a former existence* en una vida anterior || primero, ra (first mentioned) || antiguo, gua; ex; *the former Prime Minister* el antiguo Primer Ministro || pasado, da; antiguo, gua; *in former days* en tiempos pasados || *he is but a shadow of his former self* no es más que una sombra de sí mismo.
◆ *pron* ése, ésa, aquél, aquélla, el primero, la primera.

formerly [-li] *adv* anteriormente (previously) || antiguamente, antes, en tiempos pasados (before, in olden days).

formic ['fɔːmik] *adj* fórmico.

Formica [fɔː'maikə] *n* (trademark), formica *m*.

formicary ['fɔːmikəri] *n* hormiguero *m*.

formication [,fɔːmikeiʃən] *n* MED formicación *f*.

formidable ['fɔːmidəbl] *adj* enorme, formidable (task) || formidable, terrible (adversary) || terrible (look) || FIG impresionante, tremendo, da (impressive).

formless ['fɔːmlis] *adj* sin forma, informe.

form letter [fɔːm'letə*] *n* US circular *f*.

formol ['fɔːmɔl] *n* CHEM formol *m*.

Formosa [fɔː'məusə] *pr n* GEOGR Formosa *f*.

formula ['fɔːmjulə] *n* fórmula *f*; *courtesy formula* fórmula de cortesía || MATH & CHEM fórmula *f* || AUT fórmula *f*; *formula one car* coche de fórmula uno.
— OBSERV El plural de la palabra inglesa es *formulas* o *formulae*.

formulary ['fɔːmjuləri] *n* formulario *m*.

formulate ['fɔrmjuleit] *vt* formular.

formulation [,fɔːmju'leiʃən] *n* formulación *f*.

formulism ['fɔːmjulizəm] *n* formulismo *m*.

fornicate ['fɔːnikeit] *vi* fornicar.

fornicate ['fɔːnikit] *adj* ARCH abovedado, da.

fornication [,fɔːnikeiʃən] *n* fornicación *f*.

fornicator ['fɔːnikeitə*] *n* fornicador, ra.

fornicatress ['fɔːnikətris]; **fornicatrix** [fɔːni'keitriks] *n* fornicadora *f*.

fornix ['fɔːniks] *n* ARCH bóveda *f*.

forsake* [fə'seik] *vt* abandonar, dejar (to abandon); *she forsook her children* abandonó a sus hijos || renunciar a (to give up).
— OBSERV Pret *forsook*; pp *forsaken*.

forsaken [fə'seikən] *pp* ⟶ **forsake.**

forsook [fə'suk] *pret* ⟶ **forsake.**

forsooth [fə'suːθ] *adv* (ant) en verdad.

forspent [fə'spent] *adj* (ant) exhausto, ta.

forswear* [fɔː'swɛə*] *vt* abjurar (de), renunciar solemnemente a || *to forswear o.s.* perjurar, jurar en falso.
— OBSERV Pret *forswore*; pp *forsworn*.

forswore [fɔː'swɔː*] *pret* ⟶ **forswear.**

forsworn [-n] *pp* ⟶ **forswear.**
◆ *adj* perjuro, ra.

forsythia [fɔː'saiθjə] *n* BOT forsythia *f*.

fort [fɔːt] *n* fortaleza *f*, fuerte *m* || FIG *to hold the fort* quedarse vigilando.

forte ['fɔːti] *n* fuerte *m* (talent) || MUS forte *m*.
◆ *adj/adv* MUS forte.

forth [fɔːθ] *adv* en adelante || — *and so forth* y así sucesivamente; *back and forth* de acá para allá (to walk) || para adelante y para atrás (to sway) || *back and forth motion* movimiento de vaivén || *to go back and forth* ir y venir, ir de un sitio para otro || *from that day forth* desde aquel día en adelante || *to come forth* aparecer || *to go forth* irse, ir; *go forth and tell the world* id e instruid a todas las naciones || *to put forth* echar (leaves).

forthcoming [fɔːθ'kʌmiŋ] *adj* próximo, ma; venidero, ra (approaching); *in the forthcoming weeks* en las próximas semanas || próximo, ma; *the forthcoming session* la próxima reunión || abierto, ta; amable; *Andalusians are a very forthcoming people* los andaluces son una gente muy abierta || de próxima publicación (soon to appear) || *the expected aid was not forthcoming* no recibimos la ayuda esperada.

forthright ['fɔːθ'rait] *adj* franco, ca; directo, ta (person) || rotundo, da (refusal).

forthwith ['fɔːθ'wiθ] *adv* en seguida, enseguida, inmediatamente, en el acto (at once).

fortieth ['fɔːtiiθ] *adj* cuadragésimo, ma; cuarentavo, va || cuarenta; *the fortieth chapter* el capítulo cuarenta.
◆ *n* cuarentavo *m*, cuadragésima parte *f* (one of forty parts) || cuadragésimo, ma || *she was the fortieth in the queue* era la cuarenta de la cola.

fortification [,fɔːtifi'keiʃən] *n* MIL fortificación *f* || reforzamiento *m* (of an argument) || fortalecimiento *m* (of a person).

fortifier ['fɔːtifaiə*] *n* fortificante *m* (tonic).

fortify ['fɔːtifai] *vt* MIL fortificar (a town) || fortalecer, fortificar (health) || reforzar; *to fortify a dam, an argument* reforzar una presa, un argumento || fortalecer (to give moral strength) || US enriquecer (foodstuff) | encabezar (wine).
◆ *vi* MIL construir fortificaciones.

fortifying [-iŋ] *adj* fortalecedor, ra.

fortissimo [fɔː'tisiməu] *adj* MUS fortísimo, ma.
◆ *adv* MUS fortísimo.

fortitude ['fɔː'titjuːd] *n* fortaleza *f*, fuerza *f*, entereza *f*.

fortnight ['fɔːtnait] *n* quince días *m pl*, dos semanas *f pl*; *I am going to spend a fortnight in Spain* voy a pasar quince días en España.

fortnightly ['fɔːt,naitli] *adj* quincenal, bisemanal.
◆ *adv* quincenalmente, cada quince días, bisemanalmente.
◆ *n* revista *f* or publicación *f* bisemanal.

FORTRAN *abbr of [Formula Translation] lenguaje FORTRAN.*

fortress ['fɔːtris] *n* fortaleza *f*.

fortuitous [fɔː'tjuitəs] *adj* fortuito, ta; casual.

fortuistoutly [-li] *adv* fortuitamente, por casualidad.

fortuity [foː'tjuiti] *n* casualidad *f*.

fortunate ['fɔːtʃnit] *adj* afortunado, da (lucky); *a fortunate woman* una mujer afortunada || afortunado, da; feliz (favourable) || oportuno, na (opportune); *a fortunate arrival* una llegada oportuna || — *how fortunate!* ¡qué suerte! || *it was fortunate that he was there* fue una suerte que estuviera allí.

fortune ['fɔːtʃən] *n* fortuna *f* (destiny); *the wheel of fortune* la rueda de la fortuna || suerte *f*, fortuna *f* (luck); *stroke of fortune* golpe de suerte || fortuna *f* (wealth); *he went to South America to make his fortune* fue a América del Sur para hacer fortuna || FAM fortuna *f*, dineral *m*; *it cost a fortune* costó un dineral || — FIG *to marry a fortune* casarse con una mujer rica || *to tell one's fortune* decirle a alguien la buenaventura || *to try one's fortune* probar fortuna.

fortune hunter [-'hʌntə*] *n* cazador *m* de dotes (one who marries money) || aventurero *m* (adventurer).

fortune-teller [-'telə*] *n* adivino, na || echadora *f* de buenaventura, pitonisa *f* (palmist).

forty ['fɔːti] *n* cuarenta *m* || — *in the forties* en los años cuarenta || *to be in one's forties* tener unos cuarenta años.
◆ *adj* cuarenta.
— OBSERV *Forty-first, forty-second* etc. are translated by *cuadragésimo primero, cuadragésimo segundo* etc.

forty-niner [-'nainə*] *n* US aventurero *m* que se dirigió hacia California en búsqueda de oro en el año 1849.

forty winks [-wiŋks] *pl n* FAM cabezada *f sing*, siestecita *f sing*, sueñecito *m sing*.

forum ['fɔːrəm] *n* foro *m* || FIG tribuna *f*; *the UN is a forum for world discussions* la ONU es una tribuna para las discusiones internacionales.
— OBSERV El plural de la palabra *forum* es *forums* o *fora*.

forward ['fɔːwəd] *adj* delantero, ra (front); *the forward wheels of a car* las ruedas delanteras de un coche || hacia adelante; *a forward movement* un movimiento hacia adelante || adelantado, da; avanzado, da; *he is forward for his age* está muy adelantado para su edad; *the book is well forward* el libro está muy adelantado || avanzado, da (progressive) || MIL avanzado, da || MAR de la proa || impertinente, descarado, da (overbold); *I found him a little forward* le encontré un poco impertinente || atrevido, da (bold); *he is very forward with the girls* es muy atrevido con las chicas || de avance (gears) || adelantado, da (crop) || SP delantero, ra (line) || COMM para entrega futura (buying, etc.) | en fecha futura (delivery) || SP *forward pass* pase adelantado (in rugby).
◆ *adv* adelante, hacia adelante; *he gave a step forward* dio un paso adelante || hacia adelante; *he ran forward* corrió hacia adelante || en adelante; *from this time forward* desde ahora en adelante || MAR hacia la proa || — *forward!* ¡adelante! || MIL *forward march!* ¡de frente, ar! || *to look forward to* esperar [con ansia] || *we have got forward with our work* hemos adelantado el trabajo.
◆ *n* delantero *m* (in football).
— OBSERV Como este adverbio modifica el sentido de varios verbos: *to bring, to carry, to put*, etc., se ha tratado en el artículo correspondiente a cada uno de ellos.

forward ['fɔːwəd] *vt* expedir, enviar (to send) || FIG patrocinar; *to forward a project* patrocinar un proyecto | promover (to promote) || *please forward* remítase al destinatario *or* a las nuevas señas (in a letter).

forwarder [-ə*] *n* COMM agente *m* de tranporte || FIG promotor, ra.

forwarding [-iŋ] *n* expedición *f* (sending) || transporte *m* || *forwarding address* dirección *f* [donde remitir el correo] || *forwarding agent* agente *m* de tránsito *or* de transporte.

forward-looking [-,luːkiŋ] *adj* previsor, ra (person) || progresista (idea).

forwardness [-nis] *n* precocidad *f* (precociousness, earliness) || adelantamiento *m* (progress) || modernismo *m*, progresismo *m* (progressiveness) || atrevimiento *m*, audacia *f* (boldness) || descaro *m*, desfachatez *f* (pertness).

forwards [-z] *adv* hacia adelante, adelante.

forwent [fɔː'went] *pret* ⟶ **forgo.**

fossa ['fɔːsə] *anat* fosa *f*; *nasal fossae* fosas nasales.
— OBSERV El plural de *fossa* es *fossae*.

fosse [fɔs] *n* foso *m* (ditch).

fossette [fɔ'set] *n* hoyuelo *m*.

fossil ['fɔsl] *n* fósil *m* || FIG & FAM fósil *m*.
◆ *adj* fósil || *fossil fuel* combustible *m* fósil.

fossilization [,fɔsilai'zeiʃən] *n* fosilización *f*.

fossilize [ˈfɔsilaiz] *vi* fosilizarse ‖ FIG volverse anticuado (a person).
◆ *vt* fosilizar.

foster [ˈfɔstə*] *vt* criar (to bring up) ‖ FIG abrigar (ideas, hopes, etc.) | patrocinar (a project) | fomentar, promover (to promote) | favorecer (to favour).

fosterage [-ridʒ] *n* crianza *f* (rearing) ‖ entrega *f* a padres adoptivos ‖ FIG promoción *f*, fomento *m* (promotion).

foster brother [-brʌðə*] *n* hermano *m* de leche.

foster child [-tʃaild] *n* hijo *m* adoptivo, hija *f* adoptiva.

foster daughter [-ˈdɔːtə*] *n* hija *m* adoptiva.

foster father [-ˌfɑːðə*] *n* padre *m* adoptivo.

fostering [-riŋ] *n* promoción *f*, fomento *m*.

fosterling [-liŋ] *n* hijo *m* adoptivo, hija *f* adoptiva.

foster mother [-ˌmʌðə*] *n* madre *f* adoptiva.

foster nurse [-nəːs] *n* nodriza *f*.

foster parent [-ˈpɛərənt] *n* padre *m* adoptivo, madre *f* adoptiva.
◆ *pl* padres *m* adoptivos.

foster sister [-ˌsistə*] *n* hermana *f* de leche.

foster son [-sʌn] *n* hijo *m* adoptivo.

fought [fɔːt] *pret/pp* ⟶ **fight.**

foul [faul] *adj* asqueroso, sa; sucio, cia (dirty) ‖ fétido, da (smell) ‖ viciado, da (air) ‖ sucio, cia (water) ‖ horrible (horrible) ‖ grosero, ra (language) ‖ asqueroso, sa; espantoso, sa (weather) ‖ contrario, ria (wind, tide) ‖ obstruido, da (obstructed) ‖ peligroso, sa (dangerous) ‖ ilícito, ta (fraudulent) ‖ MAR encepado, da (anchor) | enmarañado, da (propeller) | sucio, cia (ship bottom) | malo, la (sea bottom) ‖ atascado, da (gun) ‖ SP sucio, cia; *foul play* jugada sucia | ilícito, ta; *foul blow* golpe ilícito | bateado fuera de los límites (in baseball) ‖ — *by fair means or foul* por las buenas o por las malas ‖ *foul bill of health* patente sucia ‖ *foul trick* mala jugada, jugarreta *f* ‖ *to be in a foul mood* estar de un humor de perros ‖ *to fall* o *to run foul of* chocar con.
◆ *adv to play foul* jugar sucio ‖ *to play s.o. foul* hacerle a uno una jugarreta *or* una mala jugada.
◆ *n* choque *m* (collision) ‖ SP falta *f* (unfair play) | pelota *f* bateada fuera de los límites (in baseball).

foul [faul] *vt* ensuciar (to dirty) ‖ FIG mancillar, manchar (one's reputation) | obstruir, atorar (to obstruct) ‖ atascar (gun, pipe) ‖ enmarañar (to entangle) ‖ chocar con *or* contra (to collide with) ‖ MAR encepar (anchor) | enmarañar (propeller) ‖ SP cometer una falta contra (an opponent) | batear fuera de los límites (in baseball) ‖ FIG *to foul up* hacer fallar.
◆ *vi* ensuciarse (to become dirty) ‖ obstruirse, atorarse (to get obstructed) ‖ atascarse (gun) ‖ MAR enceparse (anchor) | enmarañarse (propeller) ‖ SP cometer una falta.

foulard [fuːˈlɑːd] *n* fular *m* (material) ‖ pañuelo *m* (scarf).

foul ball [ˈfaulbɔːl] *n* SP bola *f* mala (in bowling) | pelota *f* bateada fuera de los límites (in baseball).

foul line [ˈfaullain] *n* SP una de las líneas que delimitan el campo y que no se puede pasar.

foulmouthed [ˈfaulmauðd] *adj* malhablado, da.

foulness [ˈfaulnis] *n* suciedad *f*, asquerosidad *f* (dirtiness) ‖ fetidez *f* (stink) ‖ atoramiento *m* (clogging) ‖ vileza *f*, infamia *f* (of a deed) ‖ grosería *f*, obscenidad *f* (of language).

foul-smelling [ˈfaulˈsmeliŋ] *adj* hediondo, da.

found [faund] *vt* TECH fundir, vaciar (metal) | fundir (glass) ‖ fundar (to establish); *to found a school, a family* fundar una escuela, una familia ‖ ARCH echar los cimientos de (to lay the foundations) | construir; *a building founded on solid rock* un edificio construido sobre roca firme ‖ FIG fundamentar, fundar; *to found one's opinion on* fundamentar su opinión en | basar; *a film founded on facts* una película basada en los hechos.
◆ *vi* fundarse, fundamentarse, basarse.

found [faund] *pret/pp* ⟶ **find.**

foundation [faunˈdeiʃən] *n* fundación *f* (establishment, endowment, institution); *the foundation of a shool, of a city* la fundación de una escuela, de una ciudad ‖ cimientos *m pl*; *to lay the foundations of a building* echar los cimientos de un edificio ‖ firme *m* (roadbed) ‖ FIG fundamento *m*, base *f* (basis, basic principles) ‖ forro *m* (backing of material) ‖ fondo *m* (in embroidery) ‖ maquillaje *m* de fondo (cosmetic) ‖ — *foundation member* miembro fundador ‖ *scholar on the foundation* becario, ria ‖ FIG *to lay the foundations of* sentar las bases de, echar los cimientos de ‖ *to put s.o. on the foundation* concederle a uno una beca ‖ FIG *to shake the very foundations of a theory* quebrantar las bases de una teoría.

foundationer [-ə*] *n* becario, ria.

foundation garment [-ˈgɑːmənt] *n* corsé *m*.

foundation stone [-stəun] *n* primera piedra *f* (of a building) ‖ FIG piedra *f* angular (cornerstone).

founder [ˈfaundə*] *n* fundador, ra ‖ TECH fundidor *m* ‖ VET infosura *f*, aguadura *f* (of horses) ‖ *founder member* miembro *m* fundador (of a club, an organization).

founder [ˈfaundə*] *vi* derrumbarse, hundirse (building) ‖ hundirse, irse a pique (ship) ‖ derrumbarse, desplomarse (to fall) ‖ VET padecer infosura (horse) ‖ atascarse (to get stuck) ‖ FIG hundirse, irse a pique (company) | fracasar (to fail).
◆ *vt* hundir (ship) ‖ VET producir infosura.

foundering [-riŋ] *n* derrumbamiento *m* ‖ MAR hundimiento *m*.

founder's shares [-zˈʃɛə*z] *pl n* partes *f* de fundador.

founding [ˈfaundiŋ] *adj* fundador, ra.

founding father [ˈfaundiŋˈfɑːðə*] *n* fundador *m* (founder) ‖ autor *m* de la constitución norteamericana.

foundling [ˈfaundliŋ] *n* expósito, ta (abandoned child) ‖ inclusero, ra (living in a hospital).

foundling hospital [-ˈhɔspitl] *n* inclusa *f*.

foundress [ˈfaundris] *n* fundadora *f*.

foundry [ˈfaundri] *n* fundición *f*.

fount [faunt] *n* fuente *f* (fountain) ‖ manantial *m* (of a river) ‖ fuente *f*; *a fount of wisdom* una fuente de sabiduría ‖ PRINT fundición *f*, casta *f* (font).

fountain [ˈfauntin] *n* fuente *f* (natural or artificial) ‖ manantial *m* (of a river) ‖ surtidor *m* (water jet) ‖ depósito *m* (for ink, for oil) ‖ FIG fuente *f* (source) ‖ US *soda fountain* bar *m* donde sólo se venden bebidas sin alcohol.

fountainhead [-ˈhed] *n* manantial *m* (of a river) ‖ FIG fuente *f*.

fountain pen [-pen] *n* pluma *f* estilográfica.

four [fɔː*] *adj* cuatro.
◆ *n* cuatro *m* (number, card, figure) ‖ SP equipo *m* de cuatro personas (team) | golpe *m* que da cuatro puntos (in cricket) ‖ — *four o'clock* las cuatro ‖ *four of a kind* un póker *m* (at cards) ‖ *it's five past four* son las cuatro y cinco ‖ *on all fours* a gatas (on hands and knees), análogo, ga (*with* a) (similar).

four-cornered [-ˈkɔːnəd] *adj* cuadrangular.

four-cycle [-ˌsaik] *adj* de cuatro tiempos.

four-dimensional [-dimenʃənl] *adj* cuadridimensional.

four-door [-dɔː*] *adj* de cuatro puertas.

four-engined [-ˈendʒind] *adj* cuadrimotor, cuatrimotor (aeroplane) ‖ *four-engined plane* cuadrimotor *m*, cuatrimotor *m*.

four-eyes [-aiz] *n* FAM cuatro ojos *m*.

four-flush [-flʌʃ] *vi* US FAM tirarse un farol (to bluff).

four-flusher [-ˈflʌʃə*] *n* US FAM farolero, ra (bluffer) | embustero, ra (trickster).

fourfold [-fəuld] *adj* cuádruple.
◆ *adv* cuatro veces.

four-footed [-futid] *adj* cuadrúpedo, da.

four-handed [-ˈhændid] *adj* para cuatro (game) ‖ MUS a cuatro manos ‖ ZOOL cuadrúmano, na.

four hundred [-ˈhʌndred] *adj* cuatrocientos, tas.
◆ *n* cuatrocientos *m*.

four-in-hand [ˈfɔːrinˈhænd] *n* coche *m* tirado por cuatro caballos (vehicle) ‖ corbata *f* de nudo corredizo (tie).

four-leaf clover [ˈfɔːliːfˈkləuvə*] *n* trébol *m* de cuatro hojas.

four-letter word [ˈfɔːˈletə*wəːd] *n* palabrota *f*, taco *m*.

four-month [ˈfɔːmʌnθ] *adj* cuatrimestral.

four-monthly [-li] *adj* cuatrimestral.

four-o'clock [ˈfɔːrəˈklɔk] *n* BOT dondiego *m* de noche.

four-part [ˈfɔːpɑːt] *adj* MUS para cuatro voces.

fourpence [ˈfɔːpəns] *n* cuatro peniques *m pl*.

fourpenny [ˈfɔːpəni] *adj* de cuatro peniques.

four-poster [ˈfɔːˈpəustə] *n* cama *f* con cuatro columnas.

fourscore [ˈfɔːskɔː*] *adj* ochenta.
◆ *n* ochenta *m*.

foursome [ˈfɔːsəm] *n* partido *m* de dos contra dos (in golf) ‖ grupo *m* de cuatro personas.

foursquare [ˈfɔːskwɛə*] *adj* cuadrado, da (square) ‖ sincero, ra; franco, ca (forthright).
◆ *adv* firmemente (firmly) ‖ sinceramente, francamente (sincerely).

four-stroke [fɔːsˈtrəuk] *adj* de cuatro tiempos (engine).

four-syllable [fɔːˈsiləbl] *adj* cuatrisílabo, ba.

fourteen [ˈfɔːˈtiːn] *adj* catorce.
◆ *n* catorce *m*.

fourteenth [-θ] *adj* decimocuarto, ta.
◆ *n* decimocuarto, ta ‖ catorzavo *m*, decimocuarta parte *f* (fraction) ‖ catorce *m*, día *m* catorce; *he came on the fourteenth* vino el catorce ‖ catorce; *Louis XIV (the fourteenth)* Luis XIV [catorce].

fourth [fɔːθ] *adj* cuarto, ta ‖ MATH *fourth dimension* cuarta dimensión.
◆ *n* cuarto, ta ‖ cuarto *m*, cuarta parte *f* (fraction) ‖ cuatro *m*, día *m* cuatro; *the fourth of February* el cuatro de febrero ‖ cuarto; *Henry IV (the fourth)* Enrique IV [cuarto] ‖ cuarta velocidad *f* (gear) ‖ MUS cuarta *f*.
◆ *adv* en cuarto lugar ‖ *to come fourth* salir *or* ser el cuarto (in competition).

fourth estate [-isˈteit] *n* US FAM prensa *f*.

fourthly [-li] *adv* en cuarto lugar.

four-wheel [fɔˈːwiːl] *adj* de cuatro ruedas ‖ *car with four-wheel drive* coche *m* de cuatro ruedas motrices.

fowl [faul] *n* aves *f pl* de corral, ave *f* de corral (poultry) ‖ gallo *m* (cock) ‖ gallina *f* (hen) ‖ pollo *m* (chicken) ‖ pollo *m* (meat) ‖ aves *f pl* (birds).

fowler [-ə*] *n* cazador *m* de aves.

fowling piece ['fauliŋpi:s] *n* escopeta *f*.

fowl pest ['faulpest] *n* VET peste *f* aviar.

fowl plague ['faulpleig] *n* VET peste *f* aviar.

fox [fɔks] *n* ZOOL zorra *f*, zorro *m* || zorro *m* (fur) || FIG zorro *m* (sly person).
— OBSERV The word *zorro* is used when referring to the male fox, whereas *zorra* is used to indicate both the female fox and the species in general.

fox [fɔks] *vt* engañar (to trick, to fool) || dejar perplejo, desconcertar (to baffle) || manchar (to stain) || remendar (shoes).
◆ *vi* mancharse (paper) || fingir (to simulate).

fox brush [-brʌʃ] *n* rabo *m* or cola *f* de zorra.

foxglove [-glʌv] *n* BOT digital *f*, dedalera *f*.

fox hole [-həul] *n* zorrera *f*.

foxhole [-həul] *n* MIL pozo *f* de tirador.

foxhound [-haund] *n* perro *m* raposero.

fox hunt [-hʌnt] *n* caza *f* de zorros.

foxiness [-inis] *n* astucia *f*, zorrería *f* (cunning).

foxtail [-teil] *n* BOT cola *f* de zorra || rabo *m* de zorra, cola *f* de zorra (tail).

fox terrier [-'teriə*] *n* fox terrier *m*, perro *m* raposero (dog).

fox-trot [-trɔt] *n* fox trot *m* (dance) || trote *m* corto (of a horse).

foxy ['fɔksi] *adj* astuto, ta (cunning) || marrón, rojizo, za (colour) || manchado, da; descolorido, da (stained) || agrio, agria (sour).

foyer ['fɔiei] *n* THEATR foyer *m*.

fracas ['frækɑ:] *n* gresca *f*, riña *f*, reyerta *f*.
— OBSERV Mientras en Inglaterra el plural de *fracas* es *fracas*, en Estados Unidos es *fracases*.

fraction ['frækʃən] *n* MATH fracción *f*, quebrado *m*; *continued, decimal, improper, proper fraction* fracción continua, decimal, impropia, propia || fracción *f* (of time) || parte *f*; *a large fraction of the electorate* una gran parte del electorado || pequeña parte *f* (small portion) || REL fracción *f*; *the fraction of the bread* la fracción del pan || CHEM fracción *f* || FIG *a fraction* un poco; *a fraction closer* un poco más cerca.

fraction ['frækʃən] *vt* fraccionar.

fractional [-l] *adj* MATH fraccionario, ria || fraccionario, ria (coin) || ínfimo, ma (very small); *a fractional risk* un riesgo ínfimo || CHEM fraccionado, da; *fractional distillation* destilación fraccionada.

fractionalize ['frækʃnəlaiz] *vt* fraccionar.

fractionate ['frækʃneit] *vt* CHEM fraccionar.

fractionation [frækʃn'eiʃən] *n* CHEM fraccionamiento *m*.

fractious ['frækʃəs] *adj* díscolo, la (ungovernable) || resabiado, da (horse) || caprichoso, sa (temperamental) || quejumbroso, sa (complaining) || malhumorado, da; displicente (peevish).

fracture ['fræktʃə*] *n* GEOL fractura *f* || MED fractura *f*; *comminuted, compound, greenstick fracture* fractura conminuta, complicada, en tallo verde || fractura *f*, rotura *f*, rompimiento *m* (breaking).

fracture ['fræktʃə*] *vt* fracturar; *fractured skull* cráneo fracturado || agrietar (to crack) || FIG quebrantar.
◆ *vi* fracturarse.

fraenum ['fri:nəm] *n* ANAT frenillo *m*.
— OBSERV El plural es *fraena* o *fraenums*.

fragile ['frædʒail] *adj* frágil; *a fragile glass, mechanism* un vaso, un mecanismo frágil || FIG frágil, delicado, da (health).

fragility [frə'dʒiliti] *n* fragilidad *f*.

fragment ['frægmənt] *n* fragmento *m* || *to smash sth. to fragments* hacer algo añicos *or* pedazos.

fragment ['frægmənt] *vt* fragmentar.

fragmental [fræg'mentl]; **fragmentary** ['frægməntəri] *adj* fragmentario, ria.

fragmentation [,frægmen'teiʃən] *n* fragmentación *f*.

fragrance ['freigrəns] *n* fragancia *f*, perfume *m*.

fragrant ['freigrənt] *adj* fragante (sweet-smelling).

frail [freil] *adj* frágil (fragile) || débil (weak) || delicado, da (delicate).
◆ *n* capazo *m*, capacho *m* (for figs or raisins) || US FAM gachí *f* (woman, girl).

frailty ['freilti] *n* fragilidad *f* (fragility) || delicadeza *f* (delicacy) || debilidad *f* (weakness) || FIG flaqueza *f* (moral weakness).

fraise [freiz] *n* TECH avellanador *m*, fresa *f* (drill) || frisa *f* (fortification) || gorguera *f* (ruff).

frame [freim] *n* marco *m* (of picture, door, window) || armazón *f* (of building, of machine, etc.) || cuadro *m* (of bicycle) || entramado *m* (of wall) || armadura *f* (of armchair) || armadura *f* (of bed) || marco *m* (of tennis racket) || armazón *f* (of umbrella) || bastidor *m* (for embroidery) || montura *f* (of spectacles) || estatura *f*, esqueleto *m* (stature) || cuerpo *m* (body) || FIG estructura *f*; *the frame of society* la estructura de la sociedad || AUT chasis *m*, bastidor *m* || AGR cajonera *f*, cama *f* || panal *m* (of beehive) || MAR cuaderna *f* (rib) | cuadernas *f pl* armazón *f* (entire framework) || MIN entibación *f*, entibado *m* || imagen *f* (in filmstrips, in television) || SP jugada *f* (turn) | triángulo *m* (snooker triangle) || FIG *frame of mind* estado *m* de ánimo.

frame [freim] *vt* enmarcar (to enclose); *to frame a photograph* enmarcar una fotografía || encuadrar (image on a screen) || elaborar, concebir (to devise); *to frame a plan* elaborar un plan || hacerse (an opinion) || inventar (a story) || tramar (a plot) || formular, expresar; *to frame a question* formular una cuestión || pronunciar (to pronounce) || hacer la armazón de (to make a frame for) || ensamblar (to put together) || formar (to shape) || adaptar (to adjust) || construir (a structure, a novel) || FAM amañar (an accusation) | incriminar, culpar, amañar las pruebas de tal manera que sea acusada (una persona inocente).
◆ *vi* ir (to develop).

frame house [-haus] *n* casa *f* de madera.

frame of reference [-ɔ'refrəns] *n* MATH sistema *m* de coordenadas || punto *m* de referencia.

framer [-ə*] *n* autor, ra || ARTS montador *m* *or* fabricante *m* de marcos.

frame-up [ʌp] *n* FAM maquinación *f*.

framework [-wə:k] *n* armazón *f* (of buildings, ships, machines) || estructura *f*; *the framework of a novel* la estructura de una novela || — *open framework* entramado *m*, celosía *f* || *within the framework of* en el marco de.

framing ['freimiŋ] *n* marco *m* (of picture) || colocación *f* del marco (action) || armazón *f* (framework) || encofrado *m* (of concrete) || expresión *f*, formulación *f* (of ideas) || elaboración *f* (of plan, constitution) || maquinación *f* (of a plot) || construcción *f* (building) || formación *f* (shaping) || CINEM encuadre *m*.

franc [fræŋk] *n* franco *m* (monetary unit).

France [frɑ:ns] *pr n* GEOGR Francia *f*.

Frances [frɑ:nsis] *pr n* Francisca *f*.

franchise ['fræntʃaiz] *n* derecho *m* de voto (suffrage) || US concesión *f*, licence *f*.

franchise ['fræntʃaiz] *vt* US otorgar la concesión de, dar una licencia para.

Francis ['frɑ:nsis] *pr n* Francisco *m*.

Franciscan [fræn'siskən] *adj/n* franciscano, na.

francium ['frænsi:əm] *n* CHEM francio *m*.

Franco-Belgian ['fræŋkəu'beldʒən] *adj* franco-belga.

Francoist ['fræŋkəuist] *adj/n* franquista.

francophile ['fræŋkəfil] *adj/n* francófilo, la.

francophobe ['fræŋkəfəub] *adj/n* francófobo, ba.

Franco-Spanish ['fræŋkəu'spæniʃ] *adj* francoespañol, la.

frangible ['frændʒibl] *adj* frágil.

frangipane ['frændʒəpein]; **frangipani** [,frændʒə'pɑ:ni] *n* pastel *m* de almendras (dessert).

frank [fræŋk] *adj* franco, ca; sincero, ra (sincere); *frank look* mirada franca || abierto, ta; *a frank face* una cara abierta; *a frank rebellion* una rebelión abierta.
◆ *n* sello *m* que indica la franquicia (mark) || franquicia *f* (right) || carta *f* exenta de franqueo (letter).

frank [fræŋk] *vt* mandar (una carta) exenta de franqueo (to mail) || franquear (to stamp).

Frank [fræŋk] *n* HIST Franco, ca || Francisco *m* (Christian name).

frankfurter ['fræŋkfə:tə*] *n* salchicha *f* de Francfort.

frankincense ['fræŋkin,sens] *n* incienso *m*, olíbano *m* (fragrant gum resin).

franking ['fræŋkiŋ] *n* franqueo *m* (stamping) || *franking machine* máquina franqueadora *or* de franquear.

Frankish ['fræŋkiʃ] *adj* franco, ca.
◆ *n* franco *m* (language).

franklin ['fræŋklin] *n* HIST poseedor *m* de un feudo franco.

frankness ['fræŋknis] *n* franqueza *f*, sinceridad *f*.

frantic ['fræntik] *adj* frenético, ca (frenzied) || loco, ca; *frantic with anger, with joy* loco de ira, de alegría || desesperado, da; *frantic efforts* esfuerzos desesperados || *to drive s.o. frantic* sacarle de quicio a uno, volverle a uno loco.

frantically [-əli] *adv* frenéticamente (in a frenzy) || locamente (madly) || desesperadamente (desperately).

frap [fræp] *vt* MAR apretar (a rope).

frappé [fræ'pei] *adj* granizado, da (drink).
◆ *n* granizado *m*.

frater ['freitə*] *n* HIST & REL refectorio *m* de un monasterio | hermano *m* (brother).

fraternal [frə'tə:nl] *adj* fraternal, fraterno, na; *fraternal love* amor fraterno || US fraterno, na (of a fraternity) || *fraternal twins* gemelos falsos.

fraternity [frə'tə:niti] *n* fraternidad *f* (brotherhood) || REL hermandad *f*, cofradía *f* || asociación *f* (association) || US club *m* de estudiantes.

fraternization [,frætənai'zeiʃən] *n* fraternización *f*.

fraternize ['frætənaiz] *vi* fraternizar, confraternizar.

fratricide ['freitrisaid] *n* fratricida *m* & *f* (murderer) || fratricidio *m* (crime).

fraud [frɔ:d] *n* fraude *m* (criminal deception) || engaño *m*, timo *m*, superchería *f* (sth. done to deceive) || impostor *m* (person).

fraudulence ['frɔ:djuləns] *n* fraudulencia *f*.

fraudulent ['frɛdjulənt] *adj* fraudulento, ta; *fraudulent bankruptcy* quiebra fraudulenta.

fraught [frɔ:t] *adj* *fraught with* lleno de, cargado de.

fray [frei] *n* combate *m* (fight) || refriega *f*, riña *f* (brawl) || parte *f* deshilachada *or* raída (of cloth) || FIG *to enter the fray* salir a la palestra.

fray [frei] *vt* desgastar, raer; *a frayed collar* un cuello raído || escodar (a deer) || FIG *to fray s.o.'s nerves* atacarle los nervios a uno.
◆ *vi* deshilacharse, desgastarse, raerse (clothing, carpet, rope).

frayed [-d] *adj* deshilachado, da; raído, da (cloth).

fraying [-iŋ] *n* fleco *m*, hilacha *f* (frayed edge).

frazzle [ˈfræzl] *n* agotamiento *m* (exhaustion) || hilacha *f* (frayed edge) || *worn to a frazzle* hecho un trapo, completamente agotado.

frazzle [ˌræzl] *vt* desgastar, deshilachar, raer (to fray) || agotar; *frazzled with the heat* agotado por el calor.

freak [friːk] *n* monstruo *m* (monster) || ejemplar *m* anormal (abnormal specimen) || fenómeno *m* (prodigy) || cosa *f* extraña *or* imprevista *or* inesperada; *it was a freak that he passed the exam* fue una cosa extraña que aprobara el examen || capricho *m*; *freaks of fortune* caprichos de la fortuna || FAM tío *m* extraño *or* estrafalario (strange fellow).
◆ *adj* imprevisto, ta; inesperado, da (unexpected) || extraño, ña; estrafalario, ria (strange).

freak [friːk] *vi* FAM *to freak out* hacer el viaje (to take a drug) | dejarse llevar por estímulos visuales o auditivos | bailar como un loco (to dance wildly).
◆ *vt* abigarrar.

freakish [-iʃ] *adj* extraño, ña; estrafalario, ria (eccentric) || monstruoso, sa (monstruous) || anormal (abnormal) || inesperado, da (unexpected) || caprichoso, sa (whimsical).

freaky [ˈfriːki] *adj* extraño, ña; raro, ra (strange) || monstruoso, sa (monstrous) || anormal (abnormal).

freckle [ˈfrekl] *n* peca *f*.

freckle [ˈfrekl] *vt* cubrir de pecas.
◆ *vi* cubrirse de pecas.

freckled [-d]**; freckle-faced** [-feist]**; freckly** [-i] *adj* pecoso, sa; lleno de pecas.

Frederick [ˈfredrik] *pr n* Federico *m*.

free [friː] *adj* libre; *a free people, man* un pueblo, un hombre libre; *the free world* el mundo libre; *when will you be free?* ¿cuándo estarás libre?; *free society* sociedad libre; *free translation* traducción libre || libre, desocupado, da (place); *is the flat still free?* ¿está todavía libre el piso? || libre, independiente (state) || libre (unmarried) || vacante, libre (post) || gratis, gratuito, ta (which cost nothing); *a free ticket* una entrada gratis || libre; *free of debt* libre de deudas || suelto, ta (loose) || desatado, da (untied) || desenvuelto, ta (bearing, manner) || abierto, ta; sincero, ra (sincere) || subido de tono (language) || generoso, sa (generous) || FIG libre; *free road* vía libre || COMM libre (market, competition) | franco, ca (exempt from taxes); *free port* puerto franco | exento de derechos de aduana (goods) | espontáneo, a (offer) || libre (verse) || autorizado, da; permitido, da (authorized) || CHEM & PHYS libre; *free oxygen* oxígeno libre; *free energy* energía libre || — *admission free* entrada libre || FIG *as free as a bird* más libre que un pájaro || *for free* gratis, gratuitamente || *free and easy* despreocupado, da (carefree); poco ceremonioso, sa (unceremonious) || *free city* ciudad *f* libre || *free enterprise* libre empresa *f* || *free gift* prima *f* || TECH *free motion* holgura *f* || *free of charge* sin gastos, gratis || *free of duty* libre *or* exento de derechos de aduana || *free of tax* exento *or* libre de impuestos || *free sample* muestra gratuita || *free speech* libertad *f* de expresión || COMM *post and package free* franco de porte y embalaje || *this place is free from dust* en este sitio no hay polvo || *to be free from* estar libre de (cares, debt, etc.), no tener; *this product is free from defects* este producto no tiene defectos || *to be free of s.o.* haberse librado de alguien || *to be free of speech* hablar muy libremente || *to be free to* ser libre de || FIG *to be free with one's fists* tener las manos largas || *to be free with one's money* no reparar en gastos || *to be very free with criticism* criticar muy libremente, criticar mucho || *to break* o *to get free* liberarse, soltarse || *to feel free to* no tener reparos en || FIG *to have a free hand* o *rein* tener campo libre, tener carta blanca || *to make free with sth.* utilizar algo a su antojo *or* como si fuera cosa propia || *to set free* liberar (a person), libertar (a slave), libertar, poner en libertad, liberar (a prisoner), soltar (a bird, etc.) || *to work free* soltarse (to come loose), deshacerse (knot).
◆ *adv* sin pagar, gratuitamente, gratis; *we got in free* entramos sin pagar || libremente; *bulls running free in the streets* toros que corren libremente por las calles.
— OBSERV Nótese que la palabra *free* se utiliza también como sufijo y significa entonces *sin*: *after ten years of accident-free driving*, después de haber conducido diez años sin accidente.

free [friː] *vt* poner en libertad, soltar, libertar, liberar (a prisoner) || libertar (a slave) || liberar (from domination) || libertar, liberar, librar (from tyranny, etc.) || liberar (from a debt, an obligation) || salvar (to save) || soltar (to let loose) || soltar (something stuck); *he managed to free his hands* logró soltarse las manos || desenredar (to untangle) || desatar, soltar (to untie) || desatascar (to unblock a pipe) || desembarazar, despejar (to clean up) || exentar, eximir (to exempt) || *to free a property from mortgage* levantar la hipoteca.

free alongside ship [-əˈlɔŋˈsaidʃip] *adj* MAR franco en el muelle (goods).

freebie; freebee *n* FAM obsequio *m* comercial (gift).

freeboard [-bɔːd] *n* MAR obra *f* muerta.

freebooter [-ˌbuːtə*] *n* filibustero *m*, pirata *m*.

freeborn [-ˈbɔːn] *adj* nacido libre.

freedman [friːdmæn] *n* liberto *m*.
— OBSERV El plural de esta palabra es *freedmen*.

freedom [-dəm] *n* libertad *f*; *freedom of movement* libertad de movimiento || exención *f*; *freedom from taxation* exención de impuestos || libertad *f* completa; *to give s.o. the freedom of one's flat* dar a alguien libertad completa para utilizar el apartamento que uno tiene || soltura *f* (of manner, of style) || desenvoltura *f* (ease) || COMM entrada *f* libre || — *freedom fighter* luchador, ra por la libertad || *freedom of a city* ciudadanía *f* de honor || *freedom of conscience, of speech* libertad de conciencia, de expresión || *freedom of the individual* libertad individual || *freedom of the press* libertad de prensa || *freedom of the seas* libertad de los mares || *freedom of worship* libertad de cultos.

freedwoman [-ˌdwumən] *n* liberta *f*.
— OBSERV El plural de esta palabra es *freedwomen*.

free fight [-fait] *n* trifulca *f*, refriega *f*.

freefone [-fəun] *n* número *m* gratuito.

free-for-all [-fərˌɔːl] *n* pelea *f*, refriega *f* (brawl).

freehand [-hænd] *n* a pulso; *freehand drawing* dibujo a pulso.

freehanded [-ˈhændid] *adj* generoso, sa (generous).

freehold [-həuld] *n* HIST alodio *m*, feudo *m* franco || propiedad *f* absoluta.
◆ *adj* HIST alodial.

freeholder [-həuldə*] *n* HIST propietario *m* de un alodio || propietario *m* absoluto.

free house [-haus] *n* bar *m* (pub).

free kick [-kik] *n* SP golpe *m* franco.

free labour; US free labor [-ˈleibə*] *n* trabajadores *m pl* no sindicados.

free lance [-ˈlɑːns] *n* personal *f* que trabaja independientemente (who works independently) || persona *f* que no pertenece a ningún partido (in politics) || HIST mercenario *m*.

free-lance [-lɑns] *adj* independiente.

free-lance [-lɑns] *vi* trabajar independientemente.

free list [-list] *n* lista *f* de personas a las que se le envían muestras *or* entradas gratuitas (list of persons) || lista *f* de productos libres de derechos de aduana (list of goods).

free liver [-ˈlivə*] *n* vividor, ra.

freeloader [-ləudə*] *n* US gorrón, ona.

free love [-lʌv] *n* amor *m* libre.

freely [-li] *adv* libremente || liberalmente (generously) || abundantemente (profusely) || francamente, abiertamente (to speak) | sin cumplidos (without ceremony) || voluntariamente (willingly) || gratuitamente, gratis (without paying).

freeman [-mən] *n* ciudadano *m* libre, hombre *m* libre.
— OBSERV El plural de esta palabra es *freemen*.

freemartin [-ˈmɑːtən] *n* ZOOL ternera *f* estéril.

freemason [-ˌmeisən] *n* francmasón *m*, masón *m*.

freemasonry [-ˌmeisənri] *n* francmasonería *f*, masonería *f* || FIG compañerismo *m*.

free on board [-ɔnˈbɔːd] *adj/adv* franco a bordo.

free-range [-reindʒ] *adj* de granja (hens, eggs).

freesia [ˈfriːzə] *n* BOT fresia *f*.

free soil [-sɔil] *n* territorio *m* donde la esclavitud era ilegal.

free-spoken [-ˈspəkən] *adj* franco, ca; sincero, ra.

freestanding [-ˈstændiŋ] *adj* independiente, autoportante.

freestone [-stəun] *n* sillar *m*, piedra *f* de sillería (used in building) || hueso *m* de una fruta que no se adhiere a la carne (stone of a fruit) || fruta *f* cuyo hueso no se adhiere a la carne (fruit).

freestyle [-stail] *n* estilo *m* libre || — *freestyle wrestling* lucha *f* libre || *the 100 metres freestyle* los 100 metros libres.

freethinker [-ˈθiŋkə*] *n* librepensador, ra.

freethinking [-ˈθiŋkiŋ] *n* librepensamiento *m*.

free time [-taim] *n* tiempo *m* libre, momentos *m pl* de ocio.

Freetown [ˈfriːtaun] *pr n* GEOGR Freetown.

free trade [-treid] *n* librecambio *m*, libre cambio *m* [AMER libre comercio *m*]; *free trade area* zona de libre cambio.

free-trade [-treid] *adj* librecambista.

free trader [-ˌtreidə*] *n* librecambista *m* & *f*.

freeway [-ˈwei] *n* US autopista *f* sin peaje.

freewheel [-ˈwiːl] *n* rueda *f* libre.

freewheel [-ˈwiːl] *vi* andar con rueda libre (a bicycle) || ir en punto muerto (car) || US FIG & FAM obrar a su antojo [haciendo caso omiso de toda clase de principios].

freewheeling [-iŋ] *adj* despreocupado, da; libre (carefree).

free will [-wil] *n* libre albedrío *m* ‖ *of one's own free will* por propia voluntad.

freeze [friːz] *n* helada *f*; *crops destroyed by the freeze* cosechas destruidas por la helada ‖ congelación *f*, bloqueo *m* (of prizes, wages, credits).

freeze* [friːz] *vi* helarse, congelarse (from cold) ‖ FIG quedarse inmóvil (to avoid being seen) | quedarse helado *or* paralizado (*with* de) (fear, etc.) ‖ — FIG *to freeze on to* pegarse a ‖ FIG & FAM *to freeze to death* morirse de frío ‖ FIG *to freeze up* quedarse rígido, da ‖ *when the lake freezes over* cuando se hiela el lago.
◆ *vt* helar (to turn to ice) ‖ congelar (to preserve by refrigeration) ‖ refrigerar (to chill) ‖ FIG congelar, bloquear (credits, prices, wages) | bloquear (an account) ‖ FIG *to freeze out* deshacerse de (to get rid of), excluir (to exclude).
◆ *v impers* helar.
— OBSERV Pret *froze*; pp *frozen*.

freeze-dry [-drai] *vt* deshidratar por congelación (food, vaccines).

freeze-frame [-freim] *n* CINEM parada *f or* detención *f* de imagen, imagen *f* congelada.

freeze-frame [-freim] *vt* CINEM congelar imagen.

freezer [-ə*] *n* congelador *m* (for frozen foods) ‖ heladera *f* (for making ice cream).

freezing [ˈfriːziŋ] *adj* glacial; *freezing weather* tiempo glacial ‖ — *freezing mixture* mezcla *f* refrigerante ‖ FIG *it's freezing (cold)* hace un frío espantoso *or* un frío que hiela las piedras.
◆ *n* congelación *f* (of foodstuffs) ‖ COMM congelación *f*, bloqueo *m* (of prices, etc.) ‖ helada *f* (of a river) ‖ *twenty degrees below freezing* veinte grados bajo cero.

freezing point [-pɔint] *n* punto *m* de congelación.

free zone [ˈfriːzəun] *n* US zona *f* franca.

Freiburg [ˈfraibəːg] *pr n* GEOGR Friburgo.

freight [freit] *n* flete *m* (by plane and ship) ‖ mercancías *f pl* (by other means of transport); *freight train* tren de mercancías ‖ carga *f* (load) ‖ transporte *m* (transportation).

freight [freit] *vt* fletar (plane, ship) ‖ cargar (other means of transport) ‖ transportar (to transport).

freightage [-idʒ] *n* flete *m* (by plane and ship) ‖ carga *f* (by other means of transport) ‖ transporte *m*.

freight car [ˈfreitkaː*] *n* US vagón *m* de mercancías.

freight elevator [ˈfreitˈeliveitə*] *n* US montacargas *m inv*.

freighter [ˈfreitə*] *n* buque *m* de carga, carguero *m* (ship) ‖ avión *m* de carga (plane) ‖ transportista *m* (carrier) ‖ fletador *m* (maritime or air shipping agent) ‖ US vagón *m* de mercancías.

French [frentʃ] *adj* francés, esa.
◆ *n* francés *m* (language) ‖ *the French* los franceses.

French bean [-biːn] *n* judía *f or* habichuela *f* verde.

French bread [-bred] *n* barra *f* de pan francés.

French chalk [-tʃɔːk] *n* esteatita *f*, jaboncillo *m* de sastre.

French cuff [-kʌf] *n* puño *m* doble.

French doors [-dɔːz] *pl n* puertaventana *f sing*.

French dressing [-ˈdresiŋ] *n* vinagreta *f*.

French fries [-fraiz] *pl n* US patatas *f* fritas [AMER papas *f* fritas].

French Guiana [-gaiˈænə] *pr n* GEOGR Guyana francesa.

French horn [-hɔːn] *n* MUS trompa *f* de llaves.

Frenchify [ˈfrentʃifai] *vt* afrancesar.

French kiss [-kis] *n* *to give a French kiss* darse la lengua.

French leave [-liːv] *n* *to take French leave* despedirse a la francesa.

French letter [-ˈletə*] *n* POP condón *m*.

Frenchman [-mən] *n* francés *m* ‖ HIST buque *m* francés (ship).
— OBSERV El plural de esta palabra es *Frenchmen*.

French pastry [-ˈpeistri] *n* pequeños pasteles *m pl* rellenos con crema.

French polish [-pɔliʃ] *n* laca *f* (for furniture).

French-polish [-ˈpɔliʃ] *vt* laquear (furniture).

French Riviera (the) [-riviˈɛərə] *pr n* GEOGR la Costa *f* Azul.

French roll [-rəul] *n* panecillo *m*.

French-speaking [-ˌspiːkiŋ] *adj* de habla francesa, francófono, na; *French-speaking countries* países de habla francesa.

French telephone [-ˈtelifəun] *n* microteléfono *m*.

French toast [-təust] *n* torrija *f* (slice of bread dipped in milk and egg).

French window [-ˈwindəu] *n* puertaventana *f*.

Frenchwoman [-ˈwumən] *n* francesa *f*.
— OBSERV El plural de esta palabra es *Frenchwomen*.

Frenchy [ˈfrentʃi] *n* FAM franchute, ta.

frenetic [friˈnetik] *adj* frenético, ca.

frenulum [ˈfriːnələm] *n* ANAT frenillo *m*.
— OBSERV El plural de esta palabra es *frenula*.

frenum [ˈfriːnəm] *n* ANAT frenillo *m*.
— OBSERV El plural de esta palabra es *frena* o *frenums*.

frenzied [ˈfrənzid] *adj* frenético, ca; *frenzied applause* aplausos frenéticos ‖ enloquecido, da; *a frenzied look in his eyes* una mirada enloquecida en sus ojos ‖ de frenesí; *the last frenzied moments before curtain call* los últimos momentos de frenesí antes de que se levante el telón.

frenzy [ˈfrenzi] *n* frenesí *m* (near madness) ‖ arrebato *m*; *a frenzy of rage* un arrebato de cólera ‖ — *a frenzy of joy* una alegría loca ‖ *a frenzy of preparation* preparaciones frenéticas ‖ *a frenzy of work* un trabajo febril ‖ *to drive to frenzy* volver loco, poner frenético.

frequency [ˈfriːkwənsi] *n* frecuencia *f*; *the frequency of his visits* la frecuencia de sus visitas ‖ RAD & PHYS frecuencia *f*; *high, low frequency* frecuencia alta, baja ‖ *frequency modulation* frecuencia modulada, modulación *f* de frecuencia.

frequency meter [-ˈmitə*] *n* frecuencímetro *m*.

frequent [ˈfriːkwent] *adj* frecuente; *frequent visits* visitas frencuentes ‖ corriente; *it is quite a frequent practice* es una costumbre muy corriente ‖ habitual (customer) ‖ asiduo, dua (visitor) ‖ rápido, da (pulse).

frequent [friˈkwent] *vt* frecuentar (to go often to) ‖ REL frecuentar; *to frequent the sacraments* frecuentar los sacramentos.

frequentative [friˈkwentetiv] *adj* GRAMM frecuentativo, va.
◆ *n* verbo *m* frecuentativo, frecuentativo *m*.

frequenter [friˈkwentə*] *n* frecuentador *m*.

frequently [ˈfriːkwently] *adv* a menudo, frecuentemente.

fresco [ˈfreskəu] *n* ARTS fresco *m* ‖ FIG fresco *m*; *a vast historical fresco* un vasto fresco histórico.
— OBSERV El plural de la palabra inglesa es *frescoes* o *frescos*.

fresco [ˈfreskəu] *vt* pintar al fresco.

fresh [freʃ] *adj* fresco, ca; *fresh eggs* huevos frescos; *fresh fruit* fruta fresca ‖ tierno, na; fresco, ca; *fresh bread* pan tierno ‖ puro, ra (air) ‖ dulce (river water) ‖ natural (water from the tap) ‖ fresco, ca (cold, brisk) ‖ FIG fresco, ca; de buen color (complexion) | fresco, ca (not tired); *to feel as fresh as a daisy* sentirse fresco como una rosa | fresco, ca (recent); *fresh news* noticias frescas | nuevo, va; otro, otra (new, another); *a fresh sheet of paper* otra hoja de papel; *to start a fresh life* empezar una vida nueva | fresco, ca; descarado, da (cheeky, impertinent) ‖ — FIG *fresh from* recién salido de (factory, etc.), recién llegado de (country, place) ‖ *in the fresh air* al aire libre ‖ FIG *it is still fresh in my memory* está todavía fresco en mi memoria | *to get fresh with s.o.* ponerse fresco con uno | *to give s.o. fresh courage* dar nuevos ánimos a alguien | *to make a fresh start* empezar de nuevo.
◆ *adv* recientemente (recently) ‖ *we're fresh out of tomatoes* se nos han acabado los tomates.
◆ *n* frescor *m*, fresco *m*; *in the fresh of the morning* en el frescor de la mañana ‖ avenida *f* (caused by rain, by melted snow) ‖ corriente *f* de agua dulce que penetra en el mar.

freshen [ˈfreʃn] *vt* refrescar (to refresh) ‖ desalar (to remove the salt from) ‖ — *that shower has freshened me up* la ducha me ha refrescado ‖ *to freshen o.s. up* refrescarse.
◆ *vi* refrescar (weather, wind) ‖ *to freshen up* refrescarse.

fresher [ˈfreʃə*] *n* estudiante *m* & *f* de primer año (at university).

freshet [ˈfreʃit] *n* avenida *f* (caused by rain, by melted snow) ‖ corriente *f* de agua dulce que penetra en el mar.

freshly [ˈfreʃli] *adv* recién, recientemente; *freshly picked fruit* fruta recién cogida ‖ frescamente.

freshman [ˈfreʃmən] *n* estudiante *m* de primer año.
— OBSERV El plural de esta palabra es *freshmen*.

freshness [ˈfreʃnis] *n* frescura *f* (coolness) ‖ frescura *f* (of bread, of eggs, etc.) ‖ frescura *f*, lozanía *f* (of complexion, of a person) ‖ novedad *f* (novelty) ‖ frescura *f*, descaro *m* (cheek).

freshwater [ˈfreʃˌwɔːtə*] *adj* de agua dulce (fish, etc.) ‖ US de provincia (college, town).

fret [fret] *n* MUS traste *m* (of stringed instrument) ‖ ARCH greca *f* (repeated pattern) ‖ calado *m* (network pattern) ‖ desgaste *m* (wearing away) ‖ parte *f* desgastada (worn spot) ‖ preocupación *f* (worry) ‖ enfado *m* (irritation) ‖ *to be in a fret* estar preocupado.

fret [fret] *vt* ARCH adornar con grecas ‖ desgastar (to wear away) ‖ cavar; *the river fretted a channel through the rock* el río cavó un canal en la roca ‖ agitar, rizar (water) ‖ rozar (to rub) ‖ irritar, molestar (to vex) ‖ preocupar (to worry) ‖ MUS poner trastes a (an instrument).
◆ *vi* preocuparse (to worry); *to fret about one's health* preocuparse por su salud ‖ atormentarse (to torture o.s.) ‖ lamentarse, quejarse (to complain) ‖ irritarse, enojarse (to become vexed) ‖ desgastarse (to wear away) ‖ rizarse (water) ‖ *to fret at s.o.'s nerves* ponerle a uno los nervios de punta.

fretful [-ful] *adj* preocupado, da (worried) ‖ irritable ‖ apenado, da (upset) ‖ descontento, ta (discontented) || molesto, ta (ill at ease) || quejumbroso, sa (complaining).

fretsaw [-sɔː] *n* sierra *f* de calar, segueta *f*.

fretwork [-wəːk] *n* calado *m* (openwork) || grecas *f pl*.

Freudian [ˌfrɔidjən] *adj/n* freudiano, na || *Freudian slip* lapsus *m inv* freudiano.

friability [ˌfraiəˈbiliti] *n* friabilidad *f*.

friable [ˈfraiəbl] *adj* friable.

friar [ˈfraiə*] *n* REL fraile *m*, monje *m*, religioso *m* (brother); *to become a friar* meterse a fraile || fray *m* (in titles) || PRINT fraile *m* || — REL *black friar* dominico *m* | *white friar* carmelita *m*.

friar's balsam [-zˈbɔːlsəm] *n* benjuí *m*, tintura *f* de benjuí.

friary [ˈfraiəri] *n* REL monasterio *m*, convento *m* de monjes | orden *f* de religiosos.

fribble [ˈfribl] *n* frívolo, la (person) || fruslería *f* (trifle).

◆ *adj* frívolo, la.

fribble [ˈfribl] *vi* perder el tiempo en fruslerías.

◆ *vt* malgastar, desperdiciar (time, money).

fricandeau [ˈfrikəndəu] *n* CULIN fricandó *m*.

fricassee [ˌfrikəˈsiː] *n* CULIN estofado *m*.

fricative [ˈfrikətiv] *adj* GRAMM fricativo, va.

◆ *n* fricativa *f*.

friction [ˈfrikʃən] *n* fricción *f* || TECH fricción *f*, rozamiento *m* || FIG fricción *f*, roce *m*, desavenencia *f*.

friction tape [-teip] *n* ELECTR cinta *f* aislante.

Friday [ˈfraidi] *n* viernes *m*; *he will be here on Friday* estará aquí el viernes || *Good Friday* Viernes Santo.

fridge [fridʒ] *n* FAM refrigerador *m*, nevera *f*.

fridge-freezer [-ˈfriːzə*] *n* nevera *f* con congelador.

fried [fraid] *adj* frito, ta; *fried eggs* huevos fritos.

friend [frend] *n* amigo, ga; *he's a friend of mine* es un amigo mío; *lifelong friend* amigo de toda la vida *or* de siempre || FIG amigo, ga; *friends of the poor* amigos de los pobres; *friends of the arts* amigos de las artes || cuáquero, ra (Quaker) || partidario, ria (supporter) || aliado *m* (ally) || — *a doctor friend of mine* un médico amigo mío || FIG *a friend in need is a friend indeed* en la necesidad *or* en el peligro se conoce al amigo || *bosom* o *close friend* amigo íntimo || *friend!* ¡gente de paz! || *my honourable* o *learned friend* mi eminente colega || *to be friends with* ser amigo de || *school friend* compañero *or* compañera de clase || FIG *to have a friend at court* o *friends in high places* tener buenas aldabas *or* enchufe || *to keep friends with* seguir siendo amigo de || *to make friends again* reconciliarse, hacer las paces || *to make friends with* hacerse amigo de, trabar amistad con || *we are the best of friends* somos muy amigos || FIG *you look like you lost your last friend* parece que se te ha muerto la madre.

friendless [-lis] *adj* sin amigos, solo, la.

friendliness [-linis] *n* simpatía *f*, amabilidad *f* (amiability) || bondad *f* (kindness) || amistad *f* (friendship).

friendly [-li] *adj* amable, simpático, ca; *to be friendly with* ser amable con || amistoso, sa; *a friendly smile* una sonrisa amistosa || amigo, ga; *friendly country* país amigo || aliado, da; *friendly forces* fuerzas aliadas || bondadoso, sa; *friendly act* acción bondadosa || favorable; *friendly wind* viento favorable; *official attitude which is friendly to investors* actitud oficial que es favorable a los inversionistas || de amigo; *friendly advice* consejo de amigo || de amigos; *friendly gathering* reunión de amigos || acogedor, ra; *a friendly fire burned in the hearth* un fuego acogedor ardía en el hogar || JUR & SP amistoso, sa || — *to become friendly with* hacerse amigo de || *to be on friendly terms with* estar en buenos términos con.

friendly society [-səˈsaiəti] *n* mutualidad *f*.

friendship [ˈfrendʃip] *n* amistad *f*.

frier [fraiə*] *n* → **fryer.**

Friesian [ˈfriːzjən] *adj/n* frisio, sia.

Friesland [ˈfriːzlənd] *pr n* GEOGR Frisia *f*.

frieze [friːz] *n* ARCH friso *m* || frisa *f* (cloth) || cenefa *f* (of wallpaper).

frigate [ˈfrigit] *n* MAR fragata *f*.

frigate bird [-bəːd] *n* fragata *f*.

fright [frait] *n* susto *m* (sudden shock); *he was seized with fright* le dio un susto || miedo *m* (fear) || FIG espantajo *m* (person); *to look a fright* estar hecho un espantajo | horror *m* (horrible sight) || *to take fright* asustarse (*at* de).

frighten [-n] *vt* asustar; *sudden movements frighten the horse* los movimientos bruscos asustan al caballo || dar un susto (to give a fright) || — *he was frightened at the thought of* le asustaba la idea de || *he was frightened to do it* o *of doing it* le asustaba hacerlo || *to be easily frightened* ser asustadizo || *to be frightened* tener miedo, asustarse || *to be frightened to death* morirse de miedo, estar muerto de miedo || *to frighten away* o *off* espantar, ahuyentar || *to frighten s.o. into doing sth.* conseguir que alguien haga algo amenazándole.

frightening [-niŋ] *adj* espantoso, sa.

frightful [-ful] *adj* espantoso, sa; horrible, horroroso, sa (causing horror, disgust, shock) || FIG tremendo, da; *a frightful thirst* una sed tremenda | espantoso, sa; malísimo, ma; pésimo, ma (very bad).

frightfully [-fuli] *adv* terriblemente || — *she is frightfully pleased* está la mar de contenta, está contentísima *or* muy contenta || *we are frightfully sorry* lo sentimos enormemente *or* en el alma.

frightfulness [-fulnis] *n* horror *m* (horror) || terrorismo *m* (in warfare).

frigid [ˈfridʒid] *adj* glacial, muy frío; *frigid climate* clima muy frío || FIG frío, a; *to be frigid toward s.o.* ser frío con alguien || MED frígido, da.

frigidity [friˈdʒiditi]; **frigidness** [ˈfridʒidnis] *n* frialdad *f* || MED frigidez *f*.

frigid zone [ˈfridʒidzəun] *n* zona *f* glacial.

frigorific [frigəˈrifik] *adj* frigorífico, ca.

frill [fril] *n* encañonado *m* (fluting) || volante *m*, faralá *m* (flared edge) || pechera *f*, chorrera *f* (on shirt front) || gorguera *f* (ruff) || CULIN adorno *m* de papel.

◆ *pl* FIG adornos *m*; *a straightforward story with no frills* una historia sencilla sin adornos | afectación *f sing* (affectation) || collarín *m sing* (of bird).

frill [fril] *vt* encañonar, alechugar (clothes).

◆ *vi* PHOT arrugarse.

frilled [-d] *adj* encañonado, da; alechugado, da (fluted) || con volantes (skirt, dress) || con pechera, con chorrera (shirt) || con collarín (bird) || PHOT arrugado, da.

frillies [ˈfriliz] *pl n* ropa *f sing* interior con perifollos (underwear).

frilly [ˈfrili] *adj* con volantes (dress) || encañonado, da; alechugado, da (fluted) || FIG con muchos adornos.

fringe [frindʒ] *n* franja *f*, fleco *m* (of material); *the fringe of a shawl* el flecho de un chal || flequillo *m* (of hair) || linde *m*, lindero *m* (of a forest) || franja *f*; *a fringe of trees* una franja de árboles || FIG margen *m*; *to live on the fringe of society* vivir al margen de la sociedad | periferia *f*; *to live just on the fringe of London* vivir justo en la periferia de Londres | borde *m* (of a lake, etc.) | pequeña parte *f*; *to touch upon the fringe of a problem* tocar una pequeña parte de un problema || PHYS franja *f*; *interference fringe* franja de interferencia || — FIG *fringe benefits* beneficios complementarios || *fringe groups* grupos marginales.

fringe [frindʒ] *vt* poner una franja a, orlar, franjar, franjear (to put a fringe on) || bordear (to border) || FIG orlar; *fluffy clouds fringed the horizon* nubes aborregadas orlaban el horizonte.

frippery [ˈfripəri] *n* cursilería *f*, afectación *f* (affected elegance).

◆ *pl* perifollos *m* (gaudy ornaments) || baratijas *f* (trashy ornaments).

Frisbee [ˈfrizbi] *n* Frisbee *m* (game) (registered trademark).

Frisian [ˈfriziən] *adj/n* frisio, sia || HIST frisón, ona.

frisk [frisk] *n* brinco *m*, salto *m* (leap) || diversión *f* (gay time) || FAM registro *m*, cacheo *m* (search).

frisk [frisk] *vi* retozar, brincar (to leap about) || juguetear (to play about).

◆ *vt* mover, menear (to shake) || FAM registrar, cachear (to search) | birlar (to steal).

friskily [ˈfriskili] *adv* alegremente (joyfully) || retozando, jugueteando (playfully).

frisky [ˈfriski] *adj* retozón, ona; juguetón, ona (child, dog) || fogoso, sa (horse) || vivo, va (lively).

frit [frit] *n* frita *f* (for making glass and glazes).

frit [frit] *vt* TECH fritar, sintetizar, calcinar.

frith [friθ] *n* estuario *m*, brazo *m* de mar.

fritter [ˈfritə*] *n* CULIN buñuelo *m*, fruta *f* de sartén.

fritter [ˈfritə*] *vt* fragmentar, desmenuzar (to split up) || *to fritter away* malgastar, desperdiciar.

fritting [ˈfritiŋ] *n* TECH fritaje *m*, fritado *m*, calcinación *f*, sinterización *f*.

frivol [ˈfrivəl] *vt* *to frivol away* desperdiciar, malgastar.

◆ *vi* perder el tiempo en frivolidades.

frivolity [friˌvɔliti] *n* frivolidad *f*.

frivolous [ˈfrivələs] *adj* frívolo, la (person) || fútil, de poca entidad, de poco peso; *a frivolous argument* un argumento fútil.

frizz [friz] *n* rizo *m* (curl) || pelo *m* crespo (hair).

frizz [friz] *vt* rizar (hair) || TECH rizar (nap of cloth) || CULIN freír.

◆ *vi* rizarse || CULIN chisporrotear (to sizzle) | quemarse, chamuscarse (to burn).

frizzle [ˈfrizl] *n* rizo *m* (curl) || pelo *m* crespo (hair).

frizzle [ˈfrizl] *vt* rizar (hair) || CULIN freír.

◆ *vi* rizarse (hair) || CULIN chisporrotear (to sizzle) | quemarse, chamuscarse (to burn).

frizzly [ˈfrizli]; **frizzy** [ˈfrizi] *adj* muy rizado, da; crespo, pa (hair).

fro [frəu] *adv* *to go to and fro* ir de un lado para otro, ir y venir.

frock [frɔk] *n* hábito *m* (monk's habit) || bata *f* (for women and workmen) || babero *m* (for children) || jersey *m* de marinero (worn by sailors) || vestido *m* ligero (dress) || FIG & REL *to give up the frock* colgar los hábitos.

frock coat [-ˈkəut] *n* levita *f*.

frog [frɔg] *n* rana *f* (animal) || anillo *m*, anilla *f* (on belt) || alamares *m pl* (fastener) || ranilla *f* (of horse's hoof) || TECH cruce *m* (of rails) | aguja *f* aérea (of trolley wires) || FAM franchute, ta (Frenchman, Frenchwoman) || — *frogs' legs* ancas *f* de rana ‖ FIG *to have a frog in one's throat* tener carraspera.

frogfish [-fiʃ] *n* ZOOL pejesapo *m*.

froggy ['frɔgi] *n* FAM franchute, ta.

frogman [,frɔgmən] *n* hombre *m* rana.
— OBSERV El plural de *frogman* es *frogmen*.
— OBSERV The plural of *hombre rana* is *hombres rana*.

frog-march [,frɔgmɑ:tʃ] *vt* llevar por la fuerza [a alguien sujetándole por las piernas y por los brazos].

frogspawn ['frɔgspɔ:n] *n* huevas *f pl* de rana.

frolic ['frɔlik] *n* jugueteo *m*, juego *m* alegre (playing about) ‖ travesura *f* (mischief) ‖ fiesta *f* (party) ‖ *to have a frolic* divertirse.
◆ *adj* alegre, animado (lively) ‖ juguetón, ona (playful) ‖ travieso, sa (mischievous).

frolic ['frɔlik] *vi* divertirse (to have fun) ‖ retozar (to leap about) ‖ juguetear (to play about) ‖ hacer travesuras (to get up to mischief).

frolicsome [-səm] *adj* retozón, ona; juguetón, ona (children, animals) ‖ travieso, sa (mischievous) ‖ alegre (gay).

from [frɔm] *prep* de; *ten miles from London* a diez millas de Londres; *where are you from?* ¿de dónde eres?; *he jumped from the wall* saltó del muro; *to shelter from* protegerse de; *he suffers from the cold* sufre del frío; *to tremble from fear* temblar de miedo; *to escape from* escapar de; *I received a letter from a friend* recibí una carta de un amigo ‖ desde; *from above* desde arriba; *the view from the window* la vista desde la ventana; *to be sick from childhood* estar enfermo desde su niñez; *from your point of view* desde su punto de vista ‖ a partir de, desde; *from that day* a partir de ese día; *watches from three pounds* relojes a partir de tres libras ‖ con; *fuels made from coal* combustibles hechos con carbón ‖ a; *to steal, to take, to buy sth. from s.o.* robar, quitar, comprar algo a alguien; *I learnt that from reading the papers* me enteré al leer los periódicos; *to write from s.o.'s dictation* escribir al dictado ‖ en; *to drink from a glass* beber en un vaso; *to learn sth. from a book* aprender algo en un libro ‖ de, sacado de (the work of an author, etc.); *a quotation from Shakespeare* una cita de Shakespeare ‖ por; *to speak from one's own experience* hablar por experiencia propia; *to act from conviction* actuar por convicción; *from good motives* por motivos válidos ‖ según, por (according to); *from what he has just said* según lo que acaba de decir; *from what I saw* por lo que he visto ‖ entre (between, among); *chosen from twenty candidates* escogido entre veinte candidatos ‖ de parte de (on behalf of); *tell him that from me* díselo de mi parte; *I have brought it to you from a friend* te lo traigo de parte de un amigo ‖ procedente de, de; *goods from foreign countries* mercancías procedentes de países extranjeros; *the train from Birmingham* el tren procedente de Birmingham ‖ ante (before); *to shrink from a danger* retroceder ante un peligro ‖ — *as from* a partir de ‖ *far from* lejos de; *far from Madrid* lejos de Madrid; *he was far from the best* estaba lejos de ser el mejor ‖ *from afar* desde lejos ‖ *from among* de entre ‖ *from birth* de nacimiento (deaf, blind, etc.) ‖ *from memory* de memoria ‖ *from now on* de ahora en adelante, a partir de ahora ‖ *from... onwards* a partir de ‖ *from the bottom of my heart* de todo corazón ‖ *from... till* desde... hasta ‖ *from... to* de... en; *from bad to worse* de mal en peor; *from house to house* de casa en casa; de... a, desde... hasta; *from six to eight o'clock* de seis a ocho, desde las seis hasta las ocho; entre... y (between) ‖ *he prevented me from doing it* me impidió hacerlo ‖ *judging from* o *to judge from* a juzgar por ‖ *to be away from home* estar fuera, no estar en casa ‖ *to date from* datar de ‖ *to die from* morir de ‖ *to have known s.o. from childhood* conocer a alguien desde niño ‖ *to judge from appearances* juzgar por las apariencias ‖ *to know good from bad* distinguir lo bueno de lo malo ‖ *to paint from nature* pintar del natural ‖ MATH *to substract* o *to take two from four* restar dos de cuatro ‖ *to take away books from a child* quitarle los libros a un niño ‖ *to translate from English* traducir del inglés ‖ *we heard* o *learnt* o *got it from Peter* nos lo dijo Pedro, nos enteramos por Pedro.

frond [frɔnd] *n* BOT fronda *f*.

Fronde [frˉɔd] *pr n* HIST fronda *f*.

fronded ['frɔndid] *adj* BOT frondoso, sa.

frondescence [frɔ'desəns] *n* fronda *f*.

frondose ['frɔndəs] *adj* frondoso, sa (leafy).

front [frʌnt] *n* parte *f* delantera; *the front of the train, of the car, of the chair* la parte delantera del tren, del coche, de la silla ‖ fachada *f* (of building) ‖ escaparate *m* (of a shop) ‖ principio *m*; *front of the queue, of the book* principio de la cola, del libro ‖ cara *f* (face) ‖ frente *f* (forehead) ‖ playa *f* (beach) ‖ paseo *m* a orillas de la playa (sea front) ‖ pechera *f* (of shirt) ‖ frente *m* (meteorology); *cold, warm front* frente frío, cálido ‖ tupé *m* (wig) ‖ FIG frente *m*; *popular front* frente popular | nivel *m*, terreno *m*; *the news on the home front is encouraging* las noticias al nivel nacional son alentadoras | apariencia *f* (outward demeanour) | fachada *f*; *the florist's served as a front for the dope smugglers* el florista sirvió de fachada a los traficantes de droga | cara *f*, caradura *f*, rostro *m* (effrontery) ‖ MIL frente *m*; *battle front* frente de batalla ‖ auditorio *m* (in theatre) ‖ — *at* o *in the front* en el frente (of battle), delante (forward) ‖ *from the front* por delante, de frente; *an attack from the front* un ataque de frente *or* por delante ‖ *front to front* frente a frente ‖ *in front* delante ‖ *in front of* delante de la casa; en frente de (facing, opposite) ‖ *seen from the front* visto de frente ‖ FIG *to change front* mudar de táctica | *to come to the front* empezar a destacar | *to come to the front again* volver sobre el tapete (a question, problem) ‖ *to go in front* ir delante *or* en cabeza ‖ FIG *to put on a bold front* hacer de tripas corazón.
◆ *adj* delantero, ra; *front legs* patas delanteras ‖ principal (door, etc.) ‖ primero, ra (first); *front row* primera fila ‖ GRAMM palatal (letter) ‖ — *front steps* escalinata *f sing* (of important buildings), escaleras *f* de la puerta principal (of a house) ‖ *the front view of the house* la casa vista de frente.

front [frʌnt] *vt* dar a; *the house fronts the lake* la casa da al lago ‖ estar delante de; *a rose garden fronts the house* un jardín de rosas está delante de la casa ‖ poner una fachada a; *to front a house with marble* poner una fachada de mármol a una casa ‖ revocar (to clean a façade) ‖ hacer frente a, afrontar (the enemy, problems, etc.) ‖ carear; *to front two people* carear a dos personas ‖ GRAMM palatalizar.
◆ *vi* dar a; *my bedroom fronts onto the street* mi dormitorio da a la calle ‖ FIG *to front for* servir de fachada a (illegal activities).

frontage [-idʒ] *n* extensión *f* de tierras; *the army won a frontage on the ocean* el ejército conquistó una extensión de tierras a orillas del océano ‖ terreno *m* [entre una casa y la carretera] ‖ fachada *f* (face of building) ‖ orientación *f* (direction faced) ‖ alineación *f* (line).

frontal [-l] *adj* ANAT frontal; *frontal bone* hueso frontal ‖ de frente; *frontal attack, view* ataque, vista de frente ‖ del frente (in meteorology).
◆ *n* frontal *m* (of altar) ‖ fachada *f* (façade) ‖ ANAT frontal *m* (bone).

front bench [-bentʃ] *n* una de las dos filas de escaños ocupados por los ministros del Gobierno y sus equivalentes en la oposición [en la Cámara de Diputados británica].

front bencher [-'bentʃə*] *n* ministro *m* del Gobierno o su equivalente en la oposición.

front door [-dɔ:*] *n* entrada *f or* puerta *f* principal.

front-end [-end] *adj* INFORM frontal; *front-end computer* ordenador frontal.

frontier ['frʌntiə*] *n* frontera *f* ‖ FIG frontera *f* ‖ US zona *f* situada entre regiones colonizadas y las que no han sido todavía exploradas.
◆ *adj* fronterizo, za; *frontier dispute* conflicto fronterizo.

frontiersman [-smən] *n* fronterizo *m* (who lives on a frontier) ‖ US colonizador *m*, pionero *m*.
— OBSERV El plural de esta palabra es *frontiersmen*.

frontispiece ['frʌntispi:s] *n* frontispicio *m*.

frontlet ['frʌntlit] *n* venda *f* (headband) ‖ frente *m* (animal's forehad) ‖ frontal *m* (of an altar).

front line ['frʌntlain] *n* MIL primera línea *f*.

frontline ['frʌntlain] *adj* MIL de la primera línea *f*.

front man ['frʌntmæn] *n* presentador *m* (on television) ‖ portavoz *m* & *f* (of group).

front matter ['frʌnt,mætə*] *n* páginas *f pl* preliminares [de un libro].

fronton ['frɔntɔn] *n* ARCH frontón *m*.

front page ['frʌnt'peidʒ] *n* primera plana *f* (of newspaper) ‖ *front page news* noticia *f* de la primera plana, noticia *f* sensacional.

front room ['frʌntrum] *n* sala *f* de estar.

front-runner ['frʌntʒrʌnə*] *n* favorito, ta (in competition).

frontstall ['frʌntstɔ:l] *n* testera *f* (of a horse's armour).

front-wheel drive ['frʌntwi:l'draiv] *n* tracción *f* delantera.

frost [frɔst] *n* escarcha *f* (frozen dew) ‖ helada *f* (freezing) ‖ FIG frialdad *f* (coldness) | fracaso *m* (failure) ‖ — *ten degrees of frost* diez grados bajo cero ‖ *white frost* escarcha.

frost [frɔst] *vt* cubrir de escarcha (to cover with frost) ‖ helar (to freeze) ‖ quemar (plants) ‖ CULIN escarchar (cakes) ‖ esmerilar (glass) ‖ glasear (metals) ‖ US congelar (vegetables).
◆ *vi* cubrirse de escarcha (windows, etc.) ‖ helarse (to freeze).

frostbite [-bait] *vt* MED congelar ‖ quemar (plants).

frostbitten [-,bitn] *adj* MED congelado, da ‖ quemado, da (plants).

frostiness [-inis] *n* FIG frialdad *f*.

frosting [-iŋ] *n* CULIN azúcar *m* glaseado (mixture) | glaseado *m* (action of icing a cake) ‖ TECH glaseado *m* (of metal) | esmerilado *m* (of glass) ‖ escarcha *f* (for decoration).

frostwork [-wə:k] *n* escarcha *f*.

frosty [i] *adj* muy frío, a (very cold) ‖ de helada; *a frosty day* un día de helada ‖ escarchado, da; cubierto de escarcha (frost-covered) ‖ helado, da (frozen) ‖ canoso, sa (hair) ‖ FIG glacial (reception, etc.) ‖ *it was frosty yesterday* ayer heló.

froth [frɔθ] *n* espuma *f* (foam, bubbles, lather, etc.) ‖ espumarajos *m pl* (from animal's mouth) ‖ FIG palabras *f pl* al aire (trivial words) ‖ FIG & FAM *to be on the froth* echar espumarajos por la boca, espumajear (to be angry).

froth [frɔθ] *vt* batir (to whip up).
◆ *vi* espumar, hacer espuma (to foam) ‖ *to froth at the mouth* echar espumarajos por la boca, espumajear.

frothy ['frɔθi] *adj* espumoso, sa (covered with froth) ‖ vaporoso, sa (fluffy) ‖ FIG vacío, a (words, etc.).

frou-frou ['fru:fru:] *n* frufrú *m* (rustling noise) || faralá *m* (frilly trimming).

froward ['frəuəd] *adj* obstinado, da (stubborn) || rebelde (not easily controlled).

frown [fraun] *n* ceño *m* || *to say sth. with a frown* decir algo frunciendo el entrecejo *or* el ceño.

frown [fraun] *vi* fruncir el ceño *or* el entrecejo || — *to frown at* mirar frunciendo el ceño *or* el entrecejo || FIG *to frown on* o *upon* desaprobar (to disapprove of).

◆ *vt* *to frown s.o. into silence* hacer callar a uno mirándole con severidad.

frowning [-iŋ] *adj* severo, ra; de reprobación (glance) || FIG amenazador, ra (menacing).

frowsty ['frausti] *adj* que huele a cerrado.

frowziness ['frauzinis] *n* descuido *m*, desaliño *m*.

frowzy ['frauzi] *adj* descuidado, da (slovenly) || desaliñado, da (dishevelled) || desordenado, da (disorderly) || despeinado, da (unkempt) || que huele a cerrado (musty) || sucio, cia (dirty).

froze [frəuz] *pret* ⟶ **freeze.**

frozen [-n] *pp* ⟶ **freeze.**

◆ *adj* congelado, da (food, etc.) || helado, da; *children skating on the frozen lake* niños que patinan en el lago helado || FIG congelado, da; bloqueado, da (prices, credits, wages) | bloqueado, da (an account) | paralizado, da (with terror) | frío, a (not moved).

fructiferous [frʌk'tifərəs] *adj* fructífero, ra.

fructification [ˌfrʌktifi'keiʃən] *n* fructificación *f*.

fructify ['frʌktifai] *vi* fructificar, dar fruto (plants) || FIG fructificar, dar fruto.

◆ *vt* fecundar.

fructose ['frʌktəs] *n* CHEM fructosa *f*.

fructuous ['frʌktjuəs] *adj* fructífero, ra; fructuoso, sa.

frugal ['fru:gəl] *adj* frugal; *a frugal meal, life* una comida, una vida frugal || ahorrador, ra; económico, ca (thrifty).

frugality [fru:'gæliti] *n* frugalidad *f*.

frugivorous [fru:'dʒivərəs] *adj* frugívoro, ra.

fruit [fru:t] *n* BOT fruto *m*; *to bear fruit* dar fruto; *dehiscent fruit* fruto dehiscente; *fleshy fruits* frutos carnosos || fruta *f* (for eating); *a diet of salads and fruit* régimen de ensaladas y fruta; *you don't eat enough fruit* no comes bastante fruta; *the apple is a fruit* la manzana es una fruta || FIG fruto *m*; *his efforts finally bore fruit* sus esfuerzos acabaron por dar fruto || US FAM marica *m* (homosexual) || — *candied fruit* fruta escarchada || *dried fruit* fruta seca || *early fruit* fruta temprana || FIG *forbidden fruit* fruta prohibida, fruto prohibido || *fruit bowl* o *dish* frutero *m* || *fruit industry* industria frutera || *fruit tree* árbol *m* frutal || FIG *the fruits of the earth* los frutos de la tierra | *the tree is known by its fruit* por el fruto se conoce el árbol.

— OBSERV *Fruto* is a botanical term, whereas *fruta* is used to denote edible fruits.

fruit [fru:t] *vi* dar fruto.

fruitage [-idʒ] *n* fruto *m*.

fruitcake [-keik] *n* pastel *m* de fruta.

fruiter [-ə*] *n* buque *m* frutero (boat) || árbol *m* frutal (tree) || *this tree is a poor fruiter* este árbol da poco fruto.

fruiterer [-ərə*] *n* frutero, ra (merchant) || *fruiterer's* frutería *f*.

fruitful [-ful] *adj* fructífero, ra; fértil (land, etc.) || productivo, va (productive) || FIG fructuoso, sa; provechoso, sa.

fruitfulness [-fulnis] *n* productividad *f* (productivity) || fertilidad (fertility) || FIG lo fructuoso, lo provechoso.

fruitiness [-tinis] *n* olor *m or* sabor *m* a fruta (smell, taste) || pastosidad *f* (of voice) || FIG & FAM sabor *m* (of a story) | sal *f* (of jokes).

fruition [fru'iʃən] *n* fruición *f*, goce *m* (enjoyment) || fructificación *f* (of plants) || FIG cumplimiento *m*, realización *f* (accomplishment) || — *to bring to fruition* realizar || *to come to fruition* realizarse.

fruit juice ['fru:tdʒu:s] *n* zumo *m* de fruta, jugo *m* de fruta.

fruitless ['fru:tlis] *adj* FIG infructuoso, sa; inútil || BOT estéril.

fruit machine ['fru:tməˈʃi:n] *n* máquina *f* tragaperras.

fruit salad ['fru:tˌsæləd] *n* ensalada *f* de frutas.

fruit salts ['fru:tsɔ:lts] *pl n* sales *f* de frutas.

fruit stand ['fru:tstænd] *n* US frutería *f*.

fruit sugar ['fru:t'ʃugə*] *n* CHEM fructosa *f*.

fruity ['fru:ti] *adj* que huele *or* sabe a fruta, con sabor *or* olor a fruta || FIG pastoso, sa (voice) || FIG & FAM sabroso, sa (story) | picante (jokes).

frumentaceous [ˌfru:mən'teiʃəs] *adj* frumentario, ria; frumenticio, cia.

frumenty ['fru:mənti] *n* papilla *f* de trigo.

frump [frʌmp] *n* birria *f* (*fam*), espantajo *m* (unattractive woman) || persona *f* chapada a la antigua (old-fashioned person) || FAM *old frump* bruja *f*.

frumpish [-iʃ]; **frumpy** [-i] *adj* desaliñado, da (dowdy) || anticuado, da; chapado a la antigua (old-fashioned) || malhumorado, da (ill-tempered).

frustrate [frʌs'treit] *vt* frustrar; *to frustrate a plot* frustrar un complot || echar a perder, impedir; *the high wind frustrated all attempts at rescue* el viento fuerte echó a perder toda alternativa de salvamento || *I feel frustrated* me siento frustrado.

frustration [frʌs'treiʃən] *n* frustración *f* || decepción *f* (disappointment).

frustum ['frʌstəm] *n* MATH tronco *m*.

— OBSERV El plural de esta palabra es *frusta* o *frustums*.

fry [frai] *n* fritada *f*, fritura *f* (fried meal) || asadura *f* frita, despojos *m pl* fritos; *pig's fry* asadura frita de cerdo || US fiesta *f* al aire libre en que se comen manjares fritos.

— OBSERV El plural de *fry* es *fries*.

fry [frai] *pl n* alevines *m* (young fish) || salmoncillos *m* (small salmon) || morralla *f sing*, pescado *m* menudo (small fish) || *small fry* fritura *f sing* (fish), gente *f sing* menuda (children), gente *f sing* de poca monta (people).

fry [frai] *vt* freír || US FAM electrocutar || *fried fish* pescado frito.

◆ *vi* freírse || FIG *to fry in the heat* asarse de calor.

fryer; frier [-ə*] *n* pollo *m* tomatero (chicken) || sartén *f* (pan).

frying [-iŋ] *n* freidura *f*, freimiento *m*.

frying pan [-iŋpæn] *n* sartén *f* || FIG *to jump out of the frying pan into the fire* salir de Guatemala y meterse en Guatepeor, salir de Málaga para entrar en Malagón.

fuchsia ['fju:ʃə] *n* BOT fucsia *f*.

fuchsine; fuchsin ['fu:ksi:n] *n* CHEM fucsina *f*.

fuck [fʌk] *vt/vi* POP joder || — POP *fuck it!* ¡joder! | *fuck off!* ¡vete a la mierda!

fucking [-iŋ] *adj* POP jodido, da || *this fucking car* este coche de mierda.

◆ *adv* POP de puta madre, muy; *it's fucking difficult* es muy difícil.

fucus ['fju:kəs] *n* BOT fuco *m*.

— OBSERV El plural de la palabra *fucus* es *fucuses* o *fuci*.

fuddle ['fʌdl] *n* embriaguez *f*, borrachera *f* (drunken state) || confusión *f* || — *to be in a fuddle* estar bebido || *to go on the fuddle* irse de juerga *or* de jarana.

fuddle ['fʌdl] *vt* emborrachar (to intoxicate) || confundir.

◆ *vi* empinar el codo, ser un borracho.

fuddy-duddy ['fʌdi'dʌdi] *n* FAM carcamal *m*, persona *f* chapada a la antigua (old-fashioned) | quisquilloso, sa (fussy).

fudge [fʌdʒ] *n* dulce *m* de azúcar (sweet) || PRINT última noticia *f* || cuento *m*, mentira *f* (lie) || tonterías *f pl* (nonsense).

◆ *interj* ¡tonterías!

fudge [fʌdʒ] *vi* fallar, faltar (*on* a) (to fail to live up to) || PRINT insertar una noticia de última hora.

◆ *vt* inventar (to invent) || amañar, arreglar (to fiddle) || chapucear (to botch) || PRINT insertar como noticia de última hora || eludir (to dodge).

Fuegian [fju'i:dʒiən] *adj/n* fueguino, na.

fuel [fjuəl] *n* combustible *m* || gasolina *f* (petrol) || carburante *m*; *they have found a new fuel for the motor car* han encontrado un nuevo carburante para el automóvil || FIG pábulo *m*; *to be fuel for* dar pábulo a || FIG *to add fuel to the fire* echar leña al fuego.

fuel [fjuəl] *vi* repostar, repostarse.

◆ *vt* alimentar (a furnace) || abastecer de combustible (ships, rockets, etc.) || echar gasolina a (cars).

fuel oil [-ɔil] *n* fuel *m*, fuel-oil *m*.

fuel pump [-pʌmp] *n* gasolinera *f*, surtidor *m* de gasolina.

fug [fʌg] *n* aire *m* espeso *or* cargado *or* viciado.

fugacious [fju'geiʃəs] *adj* fugaz (fleeting) || BOT caduco, ca (caducous).

fugacity [fju'gæsti] *n* fugacidad *f*.

fuggy ['fʌgi] *adj* cargado, da; espeso, sa (atmosphere) || *it smells fuggy* huele a cerrado.

fugitive ['fju:dʒitiv] *adj* fugitivo, va (running away) || FIG fugitivo, va; efímero, ra; *fugitive happiness* felicidad efímera | pasajero, ra; efímero, ra (changeable) | fugaz; *fugitive memory, moment* recuerdo, momento fugaz | esparcido, da (scattered) || FIG *a colour fugitive to light* un color poco resistente a la luz.

◆ *n* fugitivo, va || refugiado, da.

fugleman ['fju:glmæn] *n* MIL gastador *m* || FIG jefe *m* (leader) | portavoz *m* (spokesman).

— OBSERV El plural de esta palabra es *fuglemen*.

fugue [fju:g] *n* MUS fuga *f* || MED amnesia *f* temporal.

fulcrum ['fʌlkrəm] *n* fulcro *m* || FIG punto *m* de apoyo.

— OBSERV El plural de *fulcrum* es *fulcra* o *fulcrums*.

fulfil; US **fulfill** [ful'fil] *vt* cumplir (a promise, an order, a command) || cumplir con (obligation) || satisfacer (wishes, requirements, hopes) || llevar a cabo (a task, a plan) || desempeñar (a function) || servir (a purpose) || seguir (instructions) || escuchar (prayers) || realizar (ambitions).

fulfilment; US **fulfillment** [-mənt] *n* cumplimiento *m* (of promise, order, obligation, duties) || satisfacción *f* (of wishes, hopes, requirements) || ejecución *f* (of instructions, of a task) || realización *f*; *the fulfilment of a plan* la realización de un proyecto.

fulgent ['fʌldʒənt] *adj* fulgente, fúlgido, da.

fulgurant ['fʌlgjuərənt] *adj* fulgurante.

fulgurate ['fʌlgjuəreit] *vi* fulgurar.

fulgurating [-iŋ] *adj* MED fulgurante.

fulica ['fjuləkə] *n* ZOOL fúlica *f* (coot).

fuliginous [fjuː'lidʒinəs] *adj* fuliginoso, sa.

full [ful] *adj* lleno, na; *a room full of people, of smoke* una sala llena de gente, de humo; *a dictionary full of examples* un diccionario lleno de ejemplos; *the bottle is full* la botella está llena; *to lead a very full life* llevar una vida muy llena ‖ completo, ta; lleno, na (theatre, bus, etc.) ‖ completo, ta; *a full study of the subject* un estudio completo del tema; *a full report* un informe completo; *full payment* pago completo; *in full retreat* en completa derrota ‖ completo, ta; entero, ra (freedom, liberty) ‖ lleno, na (voice, moon, animals with young) ‖ extenso, sa (extensive) ‖ lleno, na; relleno, na (face) ‖ relleno, na (figure) ‖ grueso, sa (lips) ‖ íntegro, gra (text) ‖ sin descuento, íntegro, gra; completo, ta (price, fare) ‖ pleno, na; *in full daylight* en pleno día; *in full development* en pleno desarrollo; *in full possession of one's faculties* con pleno dominio de sus facultades ‖ largo, ga (at least); *it will take us two full hours to do it* tardaremos dos horas largas en hacerlo ‖ entero, ra (whole); *I waited a full hour* esperé una hora entera; *full term of office* mandato entero ‖ holgado, da; amplio, plia (clothes) ‖ de etiqueta (dress) ‖ de gala (uniform) ‖ todo, da; *at full speed* a toda velocidad; *to bear the full brunt of the criticism* soportar todo el peso de la crítica ‖ máximo, ma; *full capacity, potency* capacidad, potencia máxima ‖ mucho, cha; *to have a full flavour* tener mucho sabor ‖ completo, ta (meal) ‖ cargado, da; *I have had a very full day* he tenido un día muy cargado; *a man full of years* un hombre cargado de años ‖ lleno, na; *full of hope* lleno de esperanza ‖ colmado, da (of honours) ‖ carnal; *a full brother* un hermano carnal ‖ exacto, ta; *full measure* medida exacta; *full weight* peso exacto ‖ crecido, da (river, stream) ‖ titular (teacher) ‖ MAR desplegado, da (sails) ‖ GRAMM velar (back) ‖ — JUR *full age* mayoría *f* de edad ‖ MIL *full discharge* licencia absoluta ‖ *full employment* pleno empleo ‖ *full heart* corazón acongojado *or* oprimido (sad) ‖ *full house* no hay localidades (notice outside theatre) ‖ *full member* miembro *m* de pleno derecho ‖ FIG *full of* absorto en (thoughts, etc.) ‖ *full orchestra* orquesta *f* [con todos los instrumentos] ‖ *full powers* plenos poderes ‖ *full session* sesión plenaria, pleno *m* ‖ *full of the brim* o *to overflowing* lleno hasta los topes ‖ *full up* completamente lleno (very full), lleno, na; completo, ta (bus, etc.), lleno, na; harto, ta; ahíto, ta (after a meal) ‖ FAM *I'm full* no puedo más (after eating) ‖ *in full agreement* completamente de acuerdo ‖ *in full colour* a todo color ‖ *in full detail* con todo detalle ‖ *in the full sense of the word* en toda la extensión de la palabra ‖ *to be full of a subject* conocer un tema a fondo ‖ *to be full of o.s.* ser muy creído ‖ *to be full of praise for s.o.* deshacerse en elogios sobre uno ‖ *to fill sth. full* llenar algo hasta los topes ‖ *to make full use of* emplear al máximo ‖ *to take full advantage of* aprovecharse al máximo de ‖ *with full particulars* con todos los detalles.
◆ *adv* justo (rigth); *full in the centre* justo en el medio ‖ por lo menos (at least); *it was full five miles away* estaba por lo menos a cinco millas ‖ completamente (completely) ‖ — *full in the face* en plena cara ‖ *full well* perfectamente, muy bien; *she knew it full well* lo sabía muy bien.
◆ *n* máximo *m* (greatest amount, number, etc.) ‖ totalidad *f* (totality) ‖ — *in full* con todas sus letras (name, address), íntegro, gra (payment, text), íntegramente (to pay) ‖ *the moon is at the full* es luna llena ‖ *to enjoy sth. to the full* disfrutar lo más posible de algo ‖ *to have one's full of sth.* estar harto de algo ‖ *to the full* completamente.

full [ful] *vt* dar amplitud a (a dress) ‖ abatanar (textiles).
◆ *vi* US estar llena (the moon).

fullback [-bæk] *n* SP defensa *m* (in football) | zaguero *m* (in rugby, American football).

full-blooded [-'blʌdid] *adj* de raza, de pura sangre (thoroughbred) ‖ FIG verdadero, ra; cabal; *a full-blooded socialist* un socialista cabal | robusto, ta; vigoroso, sa (vigorous) | apasionado, da (passionate) ‖ MED sanguíneo, a.

full-blown [-'bləun] *adj* abierto, ta (flower) ‖ desarrollado, da (fully grown) ‖ FIG verdadero, ra; *a full-blown scandal* un verdadero escándalo | con todas las de la ley, hecho y derecho (full-fledged).

full-bodied [-'bɔdid] *adj* fuerte (person) ‖ CULIN de mucho cuerpo (wine).

full-bred [-bred] *adj* de raza, de pura sangre ‖ *full-bred horse* caballo *m* de pura sangre, pura sangre *m*.

full-dress [-dres] *adj* de etiqueta (clothes) ‖ de gala (uniform) ‖ de etiqueta, de gala (dinner) ‖ FIG completo, ta ‖ *full-dress rehearsal* ensayo *m* general.

fuller [-ə*] *n* abatanador *m* (of textiles) ‖ tajadera *f* (of blacksmith) ‖ estría *f* (groove) ‖ — *fuller's earth* tierra *f* de batán ‖ *fuller's teasel* o *fuller's thistle* cardencha *f*.

fullface [-feis] *n* PRINT negrita *f*.

full-fashioned [-'fæʃənd] *adj* US menguado, da (stockings, etc.).

full-fledged [-'fledʒd] *adj* con todas sus plumas (birds) ‖ desarrollado, da (fully grown) ‖ FIG con todas las de la ley, hecho y derecho (doctor, lawyer, man, etc.) ‖ *full-fledged member* miembro *m* de pleno derecho.

full-frontal [-'frʌntl] *adj* de un desnudo integral (of nude picture).

full-grown [-'grəun] *adj* crecido, da (tree) ‖ adulto, ta (person).

fullhearted [-'hɑːtid] *adj* completo, ta.

full house [-'haus] *n* full *m* (in card games) ‖ lleno *m* (in theatres, etc.) ‖ no hay localidades (notice outside theatre).

full-length [-leŋθ] *adj* de cuerpo entero (portrait, mirror) ‖ de tamaño normal (of the standard length) ‖ *full-length film* largo metraje.

full-mouthed [-mauðd] *adj* ZOOL que tiene todos sus dientes (cattle) ‖ FAM sonoro, ra (loud).

fullness [-nis] *n* plenitud *f* ‖ amplitud *f* (of skirt) ‖ abundancia *f* (of details) ‖ riqueza *f* (of style) ‖ *in the fullness of time* a su debido tiempo (at the appointed time), con el tiempo (eventually).

full-page [-peidʒ] *adj* de página entera (advertisement, picture, article).

full-scale [-'skeil] *adj* de tamaño natural (drawing) ‖ completo, ta; total.

full-size [-'saiz]; **full-sized** [-'saizd] *adj* de tamaño natural.

full stop [-'stɔp] *n* punto *m* (punctuation mark) ‖ punto *m* final (at the end of text) ‖ FIG *to come to a full stop* pararse.

full-swing [-swiŋ] *adv* en plena actividad.

full tilt [-tilt] *adv* a toda velocidad.

full-time [-'taim] *adj* de jornada completa, de plena dedicación (job, employee, etc.).
◆ *adv to work full-time* hacer la jornada completa.

fully [,fuli] *adv* completamente, enteramente (completely); *I fully agree with you* estoy completamente de acuerdo con Ud. ‖ por lo menos (at least); *fully fifty people* por lo menos cincuenta personas.

fully-fashioned [-'fæʃənd] *adj* menguado, da (stockings, etc.).

fulminant ['fʌlminənt] *adj* MED fulminante.

fulminate ['fʌlmineit] *vi* fulminar, explotar, detonar ‖ FIG *to fulminate against immorality* tronar contra la inmoralidad.
◆ *vt* fulminar (decree, invectives, etc.) ‖ hacer explotar (to make explode).

fulminating [-iŋ] *adj* fulminante; *fulminating powder* pólvora fulminante.

fulmination [,fʌlmi'neiʃən] *n* fulminación *f* ‖ detonación *f* (loud explosion).

fulsome ['fulsəm] *adj* obsequioso, sa; servil (person) ‖ excesivo, va; exagerado, da (compliments) ‖ hipócrita (insincere).

fulsomeness [-nis] *n* hipocresía *f* (lack of sincerity) ‖ servilismo *m*, obsequiosidad *f* (excessive deference).

fulvous ['fʌlvəs] *adj* leonado, da.

fumarole ['fjuːmə,rəul] *n* fumarola *f*.

fumble ['fʌmbl] *n* torpeza *f*.

fumble ['fʌmbl] *vt* toquetear, manosear (to fiddle with) ‖ dejar caer (to drop) ‖ — *to fumble one's way* buscar su camino a tientas ‖ *to fumble the door open* abrir la puerta torpemente.
◆ *vi* hurgar; *to fumble in a drawer, in one's pocket* hurgar en un cajón, en el bolsillo ‖ ir *or* andar a tientas (to feel one's way) ‖ — *to fumble for* buscar (words), buscar a tientas (an object) ‖ *to fumble with* manejar torpemente.

fumbler [-ə*] *n* torpe *m* & *f*.

fume [fjuːm] *n* vapor *m*; *to give off fumes* desprender vapores; *fumes of wine* vapores de vino ‖ gas *m* ‖ FIG & FAM *to be in a fume* estar bufando de cólera.
◆ *pl* humo *m sing* (smoke); *factory fumes* humo de las fábricas.

fume [fjuːm] *vi* humear, echar humo (to give off smoke) ‖ echar *or* emitir vapores (to give off vapour) ‖ desprenderse (smoke, vapour) ‖ FIG bufar de cólera (to be angry).
◆ *vt* ahumar (to expose to fumes).

fumigate ['fjuːmigeit] *vt* fumigar.

fumigation [,fjumi'geiʃən] *n* fumigación *f*.

fumigator ['fjumigeitə*] *n* fumigador *m*.

fumigatory [,fjumi'geitəri] *adj* fumigatorio, ria.

fun [fʌn] *n* alegría *f* (merriment); *full of fun* lleno de alegría ‖ gracia *f*; *to be poor fun* no tener gracia; *I don't see the fun in that* no le veo la gracia ‖ diversión *f* (amusement) ‖ — *all the fun of the fair* todas las atracciones de la feria ‖ *for fun* en broma (jokingly), para reírse (for a laugh) ‖ *for the fun of it* para reírse ‖ *in fun* en broma ‖ FIG & FAM *like fun!* ¡ni hablar! | *this is where the fun starts* ahora nos vamos a divertir ‖ *to be great fun* ser muy divertido ‖ *to have fun* divertirse, pasarlo bien ‖ *to have great fun* divertirse mucho, pasarlo en grande ‖ FAM *to like one's bit of fun* gustarle a uno bromear ‖ *to make fun of, to poke fun at* reírse de ‖ *to spoil the fun* aguar la fiesta ‖ *what fun!* ¡qué divertido!
— OBSERV La palabra *fun* nunca va precedida por el artículo *a*.

fun [fʌn] *vi* US FAM bromear.

funambulist [fju'næmbjulist] *n* funámbulo, la.

Funchal [fun'ʃɑːl] *pr n* GEOGR Funchal.

function ['fʌŋkʃən] *n* función *f* (purpose, duty, role); *to fulfil a function* desempeñar una función ‖ acto *m*, solemnidad *f* (official ceremony) ‖ recepción *f* ‖ REL ceremonia *f* ‖ MATH, GRAMM & CHEM función *f* ‖ ANAT función *f*; *functions of the heart* funciones del corazón ‖ INFORM *function key* tecla *f* de función ‖ *in my function as a magistrate* como magistrado, en mi calidad de magistrado.

function ['fʌŋkʃən] *vi* funcionar.

functional ['fʌŋkʃənl] *adj* funcional; *functional architecture* arquitectura funcional.

functionary ['fʌŋkʃnəri] *n* funcionario, ria.

functioning ['fʌŋkʃəniŋ] *n* funcionamiento *m*.

fund [fʌnd] *n* COMM fondo *m*; *building fund* fondo para la construcción; *International Monetary Fund* Fondo Monetario Internacional ‖ reserva *f* (reserve) ‖ FIG fuente *f* (source); *to have a fund of anecdotes* ser una fuente de anécdotas | fondo *m* (stock); *a fund of wisdom* un fondo de sabiduría.
◆ *pl* fondos *m* (resources); *available funds* fondos disponibles ‖ deuda *f sing* pública (government debt) ‖ fondos *m pl* públicos (public securities).

fund [fʌnd] *vt* consolidar (debt) ‖ colocar (to put in a fund) ‖ invertir (to invest).

fundament ['fʌndəmənt] *n* ano *m* (anus) ‖ trasero *m*, nalgas *f pl* (buttocks) ‖ US fundamento *m*, base *f*.

fundamental [ˌfʌndə'mentl] *adj* fundamental.
◆ *pl n* fundamentos *m*.

fundamentalism [ˌfʌndə'mentəlizm] *n* fundamentalismo *m*.

fundamentalist [ˌfʌndə'mentəlist] *adj* fundamentalista.
◆ *n* fundamentalista *m* & *f*.

fundamentally [-i] *adv* fundamentalmente, esencialmente.

fund-raising ['fʌndˌreiziŋ] *n* recaudación *f* de fondos.
◆ *adj* para recaudar fondos ‖ *fund-raising party* fiesta *f* benéfica.

fundus ['fʌndʌs] *n* ANAT fondo *m*.
— OBSERV El plural de *fundus* es *fundi*.

funeral ['fjuːnərəl] *n* funeral *m*, funerales *m pl*, exequias *f pl* (service) ‖ entierro *m* (burial) ‖ cortejo *m* fúnebre (procession) ‖ — *state funeral* exequias nacionales ‖ FIG & FAM *it's not my funeral* me trae sin cuidado | *that's his funeral* allá él, con su pan se lo coma.
◆ *adj* fúnebre; *funeral chant* canto fúnebre; *funeral procession* cortejo fúnebre; *funeral march* marcha fúnebre ‖ funerario, ria (urn) ‖ — US *funeral home* o *parlor* funeraria *f* ‖ *funeral pyre* hoguera *f* ‖ *funeral service* misa *f* de «corpore insepulto» *or* de cuerpo presente.

funerary ['fjuːnəreri] *adj* funerario, ria; funeral.

funereal [fjuː'niəriəl] *adj* fúnebre (mournful).

fun fair [fʌn'fɛə*] *n* parque *m* de atracciones.

fungi ['fʌŋgai] *pl n* ⟶ **fungus**.

fungible ['fʌndʒibl] *adj* JUR fungible.

fungicide ['fʌndʒisaid] *n* fungicida *m*.

fungosity [fʌŋ'gɔsiti] *n* fungosidad *f*.

fungous ['fʌŋgəs] *adj* fungoso, sa.

fungus ['fʌŋgəs] *n* BOT hongo *m* ‖ MED fungo *m*.
— OBSERV El plural de la palabra *fungus* es *fungi* o *funguses*.

funicular [fjuː'nikjulə*] *adj* funicular ‖ *funicular railway* funicular *m*.
◆ *n* funicular *m*.

funiculus [fjuː'nikjuləs] *n* cordón *m* umbilical.
— OBSERV El plural de la palabra inglesa es *funiculi*.

funk [fʌŋk] *n* FAM canguelo *m*, jindama *f* (state of fright); *to be in a funk* tener canguelo ‖ gallina *m* (coward).

funk [fʌŋk] *vt* FAM tener miedo a *or* de (to fear) | rajarse ante (to shirk).
◆ *vi* FAM tener canguelo | rajarse.

funk hole [-həul] *n* trinchera *f*, refugio *m* subterráneo ‖ FAM refugio *m*.

funky [-i] *adj* FAM cobarde, cagueta (coward).

funnel ['fʌnl] *n* embudo *m* (for pouring liquids) ‖ chimenea *f* (of boat, steam engine) ‖ conducto *m* (of ventilation, etc.) ‖ TECH tolva *f* (hopper).

funnel ['fʌnl] *vt* verter por un embudo ‖ encauzar (to direct).

funnies ['fʌniz] *pl n* US FAM tiras *f* cómicas (cartoon strips).

funnily ['fʌnili] *adv* graciosamente ‖ FAM de una manera muy rara.

funny ['fʌni] *adj* divertido, da; gracioso, sa (amusing) ‖ FAM raro, ra; extraño, ña (strange); *how funny!* ¡qué raro!; *this tea tastes funny* este té tiene un sabor extraño | raro, ra (ill); *I feel a bit funny* me siento algo raro ‖ — *don't get funny with me!* ¡no te hagas el gracioso! ‖ *he's just trying to be funny* se está haciendo el gracioso ‖ FAM *I came over all funny* me sentí muy raro | *I find it funny that...* me parece extraño que... | *it strikes me as funny that...* me resulta raro que... ‖ *it was too funny for words* era de lo más gracioso ‖ FAM *let's have no funny business* no quiero cosas raras | *that's funny!* ¡qué raro! ‖ *the funny part of it* lo gracioso del caso ‖ *the funny thing about it is that...* lo raro *or* lo curioso del caso es que...
◆ *n* MAR esquife *m*.

funny bone [-bəun] *n* hueso *m* de la alegría *or* de la suegra (in the elbow).

funny farm [-fɑːm] *n* US FAM casa *f* de locos, manicomio *m* (mental hospital).

funnyman [-mæn] *n* US cómico *m*.
— OBSERV El plural de esta palabra es *funnymen*.

funny papers [-'peipəz] *pl n* US tiras *f* cómicas.

fun run ['fʌnrʌn] *n* FAM carrera *f* con fines benéficos.

fur [fəː*] *n* pelo *m*, pelaje *m* (of living animal) ‖ piel *f* (pelt) ‖ abrigo *m or* chaqueta *f* de piel *or* de pieles (coat) ‖ sarro *m* (in kettle) ‖ saburra *f*, sarro *m* (on tongue) ‖ caza *f* de pelo (in hunting) ‖ FIG *to make the fur fly* armar la de Dios es Cristo.
◆ *adj* de pieles, de piel; *fur coat* abrigo de pieles.

fur [fəː*] *vt* forrar con pieles (a coat) ‖ depositar sarro en, incrustar (to coat with a deposit) ‖ cubrir de sarro (tongue).
◆ *vi* *to fur up* cubrirse de sarro.

furbelow ['fəːbiləu] *n* faralá *m* (flounce).
◆ *pl* FIG ringorrangos *m* (funny trimmings).

furbish ['fəːbiʃ] *vt* bruñir, acicalar, pulir (to polish) ‖ *to furbish up* renovar, restaurar (to renovate), pulir (to brush up).

furcate ['fəːkeit] *adj* ahorquillado, da (forked) ‖ hendido, da (hoof) ‖ bifurcado, da (road).

furcate ['fəːkeit] *vi* bifurcarse (a road).

furcula ['fəːkjulə] *n* espoleta *f* (wishbone).
— OBSERV El plural de *furcula* es *furculae*.

Furies ['fjuəriz] *pl prn* MYTH Furias *f*.

furious ['fjuəriəs] *adj* furioso, sa; *he got furious* se puso furioso ‖ frenético, ca (frantic) ‖ violento, ta; furioso, sa (violent) ‖ *at a furious pace* a toda velocidad.

furl [fəːl] *n* rollo *m* (of paper, etc.).

furl [fəːl] *vt* MAR aferrar (the sails) ‖ cerrar (a fan, an umbrella) ‖ poner a media asta (flag) ‖ recoger (wings) ‖ arrollar, enrollar (to roll up).
◆ *vi* enrollarse.

furlong ['fəːlɔŋ] *n* estadio *m*, medida *f* de 201 metros.

furlough ['fəːləu] *n* permiso *m*; *to be on furlough* estar de permiso.

furnace ['fəːnis] *n* horno *m*; *blast furnace* alto horno; *open-hearth furnace* horno de hogar abierto; *reverberatory furnace* horno de reverbero; *arc furnace* horno de arco ‖ hogar *m* (of boiler) ‖ estufa *f* (for domestic heating) ‖ FIG horno *m* (hot place).

furnace ['fəːnis] *vt* calentar en un horno.

furnish ['fəːniʃ] *vt* amueblar (a house, room) ‖ suministrar, proporcionar, proveer (to supply); *to furnish the soldiers with food* suministrar comida a los soldados, proveer a los soldados de comida ‖ proporcionar, facilitar (to give) ‖ dar (an opportunity) ‖ equipar (to equip); *to furnish a fortress with guns* equipar una fortaleza con cañones ‖ aducir (proof) ‖ *furnished room* cuarto amueblado.

furnisher [-ə*] *n* proveedor *m* (who supplies) ‖ vendedor *m* de muebles (who sells furniture).

furnishings [-iŋz] *pl n* muebles *m*, mobiliario *m sing* (furniture) ‖ accesorios *m* (accessories) ‖ US artículos *m*, ropa *f sing* (things to wear); *men's furnishings* artículos para caballeros.

furniture ['fəːnitʃə*] *n* muebles *m pl*, mobiliario *m* (of a house) ‖ herraje *m* (of door) ‖ accesorios *m pl* (accessories) ‖ MAR aparejo *m* (of boat) ‖ — *a piece of furniture* un mueble ‖ *furniture van* camión *m* de mudanzas ‖ *furniture warehouse, furniture repository* guardamuebles *m inv* ‖ *set of furniture* muebles *m pl*, mobiliario *m*.

furor ['fjuərɔː*] *n* furor *m*.

furore [fjuə'rɔːri] *n* furor *m* (enthusiasm); *to make* o *to create a furore* hacer furor.

furrier ['fʌriə*] *n* peletero *m* ‖ *furrier's* peletería *f*.

furring ['fəːriŋ] *n* guarnición *f or* forro *m* de piel (trimming, lining) ‖ TECH incrustación *f* (coating) | desincrustación *f* (cleaning) ‖ ARCH revestimiento *m* ‖ sarro *m* (on the tongue).

furrow [ˌʌrəu] *n* AGR surco *m* ‖ arruga *f* (on the face) ‖ ARCH estría *f* ‖ ranura *f* (groove) ‖ surco *m* (of a ship).

furrow ['fʌrəu] *vt* surcar ‖ arrugar (the face).
◆ *vi* arrugarse (one's face).

furry ['fəːri] *adj* peludo, da (hairy) ‖ sarroso, sa (tongue deposit).

further ['fəːðə*] *adj* otro, otra (more distant); *on the further side of the river* al otro lado del río ‖ nuevo, va; otro, otra (new, another); *a further topic of conversation* otro tema de conversación; *until further orders* hasta nueva orden; *until further notice* hasta nuevo aviso ‖ otro, otra; adicional (additional); *further amendment* enmienda adicional ‖ otro, otra; más; *one further question* una pregunta más, otra pregunta ‖ ulterior, posterior (later); *further examination* examen posterior ‖ superior (education) ‖ — *after further consideration* después de examinarlo con más detenimiento ‖ COMM *further to my letter of the 1rst* con relación a mi carta del 1.
◆ *adv* más lejos, más allá; *it is dangerous to go any further* es peligroso ir más lejos ‖ más; *to drive further south* ir más al sur; *further back* más atrás; *further off* más lejos; *further down* más abajo; *further on* o *along* más adelante; *not to kwow any further* no saber nada más ‖ además (moreover); *let us further suppose that...* supongamos además que... ‖ — *how much further?* ¿qué distancia queda? ‖ *this mustn't go any further* esto debe quedar entre nosotros ‖ *to go further into* estudiar más a fondo.

further ['fəːðə*] *vt* favorecer, fomentar; *to further understanding between nations* favorecer la comprensión entre los pueblos.

furtherance [ˈfəːðərəns] *n* adelantamiento *m*, adelanto *m* (advancement) ‖ fomento *m* (promotion) ‖ *in furtherance of* para fomentar, para favorecer.

furthermore [ˈfəːðəˈmɔː*] *adv* además.

furthermost [ˈfəːðəməust] *adj* más lejano, na (most distant).

furthest [ˈfəːðist] *adj* más lejano, na (most distant) ‖ extremo, ma (extreme) ‖ *to push sth. to its furthest limits* llevar algo hasta el último extremo.
◆ *adv* más lejos.

furtive [ˈfəːtiv] *adj* furtivo, va.

furuncle [ˈfjuərʌŋkl] *n* MED furúnculo *m*.

furunculosis [ˌfjurʌŋkjuˈləusis] *n* MED furunculosis *f*.

fury [ˈfjuəri] *n* furia *f*, furor *m* (anger) ‖ furia *f*; *the fury of the wind* la furia del viento ‖ violencia *f* (violence) ‖ FIG furia *f* (angry woman) ‖ — *like fury* furiosamente, con furia ‖ *to be in a fury* estar hecho una furia.

furze [fəːz] *n* BOT aulaga *f*, aliaga *f*.

fusain [ˈfjuːzæn] *n* carboncillo *m* (charcoal) ‖ dibujo *m* al carbón (drawing).

fuscous [ˈfʌskəs] *adj* pardo, da.

fuse [fjuːz] *n* ELECTR fusible *m*, plomo *m* ‖ mecha *f* (piece of cord, etc.); *to light the fuse encender la mecha* ‖ espoleta *f* (detonating device); *the fuse of a grenade* la espoleta de una granada ‖ — *fuse box* caja *f* de fusibles ‖ *fuse wire* hilo *m or* alambre *m* fusible.

fuse [fjuːz] *vt* fundir (to melt) ‖ poner espoleta a (a missile) ‖ FIG fusionar (to join together) ‖ *to fuse the lights* fundir los plomos.
◆ *vi* fundirse (to melt) ‖ fundirse; *the lights have fused* se han fundido los plomos ‖ FIG fusionarse (to merge) ‖ MED soldarse (broken bones).

fusee; fuzee [fjuːˈzi] *n* caracol *m* (of clock) ‖ fósforo *m* grande [que no apaga el viento] (match) ‖ señal *f* luminosa (railway signal) ‖ sobrecaña *f* (of horse).

fuselage [ˈfjuːzilɑːʒ] *n* fuselaje *m* (of aircraft).

fusible [ˈfjuːzəbl] *adj* fusible, fundible.

fusilier; fusileer [ˌfjuːziˈliə*] *n* MIL fusilero *m*.

fusillade [ˈfjuːziˈleid] *n* descarga *f* de fusilería (rapid fire) ‖ tiroteo *m* (repeated fire) ‖ fusilamiento *m* (execution) ‖ FIG lluvia *f* (of questions).

fusillade [ˌfjuːziˈleid] *vt* fusilar (to shoot down) ‖ atacar con una descarga de fusilería (to attack).

fusion [ˈfjuːʒən] *n* fusión *f*; *fusion point* punto de fusión ‖ fusión *f*, fundición *f* (melting of metals) ‖ FIG fusión *f* (union).

fusion bomb [-bɔb] *n* bomba *f* termonuclear.

fuss [fʌs] *n* jaleo *m*, alboroto *m* (commotion); *what is all the fuss about?* ¿por qué tanto jaleo? ‖ quejas *f pl* (complaints); *let's have no more fuss from you* déjate de quejas ‖ lío *m* (trouble) ‖ remilgos *m pl* (affectation); *after a great deal of fuss he accepted* aceptó después de muchos remilgos ‖ cumplidos *m pl* (ceremony) ‖ — *a lot of fuss about nothing* mucho ruido y pocas nueces ‖ *it's not worth the fuss* no vale *or* no merece la pena ‖ *there's no need to make such a fuss* no es para tanto ‖ FAM *to kick up a fuss, to make a great fuss* armar un escándalo ‖ *to make a fuss of s.o.* deshacerse en atenciones con alguien, mimar (to pay too much attention), encomiar (to praise) ‖ *to make too much fuss of s.o.* hacer cumplidos con alguien.

fuss [fʌs] *vi* preocuparse [por pequeñeces] (to worry) ‖ quejarse (to complain) ‖ agitarse (to bustle) ‖ — *to fuss over s.o.* deshacerse en atenciones con uno ‖ *to fuss with* toquetear.
◆ *vt* molestar, fastidiar (to bother).

fussbudget [-ˌbʌdʒit] *n* US FAM → **fusspot.**

fussiness [ˈfʌsinis] *n* agitación *f* ‖ cumplidos *m pl* (ceremony) ‖ afectación *f*, falta *f* de sencillez (lack of simplicity).

fusspot [ˈfʌspɔt] *n* FAM quisquilloso, sa (punctilious) | remilgado, da; melindroso, sa (finicky) | quejica *m* & *f* (who complains) | persona *f* que anda con cumplidos (lacking simplicity).

fussy [ˈfʌsi] *adj* exigente (exacting) ‖ delicado, da; escrupuloso, sa (about food) ‖ quisquilloso, sa (punctilious) ‖ remilgado, da; melindroso, sa (finicky) ‖ que anda con cumplidos (lacking simplicity) ‖ rebuscado, da; recargado, da (overornate) ‖ nervioso, sa (nervous).

fustian [ˈfʌstiən] *n* fustán *m* (cloth) ‖ grandilocuencia *f*, prosopopeya *f* (pomposity).
◆ *adj* de fustán (made of fustian) ‖ ampuloso, sa; grandilocuente (pompous).

fustigate [ˈfʌstigeit] *vt* fustigar.

fusty [ˈfʌsti] *adj* mohoso, sa (musty) ‖ que huele a cerrado (stale-smelling) ‖ anticuado, da; chapado a la antigua (old-fashioned).

futile [ˈfjuːtail] *adj* inútil, vano, na (vain); *a futile attempt* un intento vano ‖ frívolo, la; fútil (frivolous) ‖ pueril (childish).

futility [fjuːˈtiliti] *n* inutilidad *f* (uselessness) ‖ frivolidad *f*, futileza *f*, futilidad *f* (frivolity).

Futon [ˈfutɔn] *n* futón *m* (registered trademark).

futtock [ˈfʌtək] *n* MAR genol *m*.

future [ˈfjuːtʃə*] *adj* futuro, ra; *future events* sucesos futuros; *future wife* futura esposa ‖ venidero, ra; futuro, ra (days, years, etc.) ‖ GRAMM futuro (tense).
◆ *n* futuro *m*, porvenir *m* ‖ GRAMM futuro *m* (tense) ‖ FIG porvenir *m* (situation) ‖ FAM futuro, ra (fiancé) ‖ — GRAMM *future perfect* futuro perfecto *or* anterior ‖ *in (the) future* en lo futuro, en el futuro, en lo sucesivo ‖ *in the near future* en un futuro próximo.
◆ *pl* COMM futuros *m*, entregas *f* a plazo.

futurism [ˈfjuːtʃərizəm] *n* futurismo *m*.

futurist [ˈfjuːtʃərist] *adj/n* futurista.

futuristic [fjuːtʃəˈristik] *adj* futurista.

futurity [fjuːˈtjuəriti] *n* futuro *m* (future) ‖ suceso *m* futuro (future event) ‖ REL vida *f* futura.

fuze [fjuːz] *n* mecha *f* (made of cord, etc.); *to light the fuze* encender la mecha ‖ espoleta *f* (detonating device); *the fuze of a grenade* la espoleta de una granada.

fuze [fjuːz] *vt* poner espoleta a (a missile).

fuzee [fjuːˈzi] *n* → **fusee.**

fuzz [fʌz] *n* pelusa *f* (fluff) ‖ borra *f* (of cotton plant) ‖ vello *m* (on face) ‖ aspecto *m* borroso (blurred effect) ‖ FAM poli *f*, policía *f*.

fuzz [fʌz] *vi* soltar pelusa; *this wool tends to fuzz* esta lana tiene tendencia a soltar pelusa ‖ volverse borroso (to get blurred).
◆ *vt* empañar (to blur).

fuzzy [ˈfʌzi] *adj* rizado, da (very curly) ‖ deshilachado, da (frayed) ‖ velloso, sa (fluffy) ‖ borroso, sa (blurred).

fylfot [ˈfilfɔt] *n* esvástica *f*, cruz *f* gamada.

G

g [dʒiː] *n* g *f* (letter of the alphabet).

G *n* MUS sol *m*.

gab [gæb] *n* FAM palique *m* (chatter) ‖ — FAM *stop your gab* cierra el pico | *to have the gift of the gab* tener mucha labia.

gab [gæb] *vi* FAM estar de palique, charlotear.

gabardine ['gæbədiːn] *n* gabardina *f*.

gabble ['gæbl] *n* FAM farfulla *f*, habla *f* atropellada | charloteo *m* (chatter).

gabble ['gæbl] *vi* FAM farfullar, hablar atropelladamente (to jabber) | charlotear (to chatter).

◆ *vt* FAM decir atropelladamente (to say).

gabby ['gæbi] *n* US FAM charlatán, ana; parlanchín, ina.

gaberdine ['gæbədiːn] *n* gabardina *f*.

gabion ['geibjən] *n* MIL gavión *m*.

gable [geibl] *n* ARCH aguilón *m*, gablete *m* ‖ — *gable end* hastial *m* ‖ *gable roof* tejado *m* de dos aguas.

Gabon ['gæbən] *pr n* GEOGR Gabón *m*.

Gabriel ['geibriəl] *pr n* Gabriel *m*.

Gabriella [geibriələ] *pr n* Gabriela *f*.

gaby ['geibi] *n* FAM mentecato, ta.

gad [gæd] *n* AGR aguijón *m* ‖ barra *f* puntiaguda (bar) ‖ cuña *f* (wedge) ‖ FIG & FAM callejeo *m* (stroll) ‖ *gad!* ¡caramba!, ¡cáspita!

gad [gæd] *vi* *to gad about* callejear, ir de acá para allá (to stroll).

gadabout ['gædəbaut] *n* callejero, ra; trotacalles *m* & *f inv*, azotacalles *m* & *f inv*.

gadfly ['gædflai] *n* ZOOL tábano *m* ‖ FAM persona *f* molesta.

gadget ['gædʒit] *n* artilugio *m*, chisme *m* (article of little importance) ‖ aparato *m*, dispositivo *m* (device).

gadid ['geidid]; **gadoid** ['geidɔid] *adj* gádido, da.

◆ *n* gádido *m*.

Gaditan [gæditən] *adj/n* gaditano, na.

gadolinium [gædə'linjəm] *n* gadolinio *m*.

gadroon [gə'druːn] *n* ARCH moldura *f* ovalada, gallón *m*.

Gael [geil] *n* gaélico, ca.

Gaelic ['geilik] *adj* gaélico, ca.

◆ *n* gaélico *m* (language).

gaff [gæf] *n* arpón *m*, garfio *m* (harpoon) ‖ MAR cangrejo *m* ‖ FAM teatrucho *m* (theatre) ‖ espolón (of fighting cock) ‖ — *gaff sail* vela *f* cangreja ‖ FAM *to blow the gaff* descubrir el pastel | *to stand the gaff* tener aguante.

gaff [gæf] *vt* arponear (fish) ‖ poner un espolón de acero (a fighting cock) ‖ US FAM engañar.

gaffe [gæf] *n* *to make a gaffe* meter la pata, tirarse una plancha.

gaffer ['gæfə*] *n* FAM tío *m* (fellow) | jefe *m* (boss) | capataz *m* (foreman).

gag [gæg] *n* mordaza *f* (to stop s.o. from speaking) ‖ supresión *f* de la libertad de expresión (prevention of freedom of speech) ‖ broma *f* (hoax) ‖ «gag» *m*, chiste *m* (joke) ‖ truco *m* (trick) ‖ clausura *f* de un debate (closure of a debate) ‖ THEATR morcilla *m* (ad lib).

gag [gæg] *vt* amordazar (to prevent from speaking) ‖ dar náuseas a (to nauseate) ‖ clausurar (to close) ‖ obstruir (to obstruct) ‖ FIG hacer callar, amordazar.

◆ *vi* THEATR meter morcilla ‖ tener náuseas (to retch) ‖ bromear (to joke).

gaga ['gɑːgɑː] *adj* FAM chocho, cha ‖ — FAM *to be going gaga* chochear | *to go gaga over* encapricharse por, volverse chocho por.

gage [geidʒ] *n* desafío *m* (challenge) ‖ prenda *f*, garantía *f* (pledge) ‖ → **gauge.**

gage [geidʒ] *vt* dar como garantía, dar en prenda (to pledge) ‖ FIG comprometer ‖ → **gauge.**

gaggle ['gægəl] *n* manada *f* (of geese) ‖ FIG FAM *a gaggle of housewives* un corro de comadres.

gaggle ['gægəl] *vi* graznar (geese).

gaiety ['geiəti] *n* alegría *f* ‖ *gaieties* regocijos *m*, diversiones *f*.

gaily ['geili] *adv* alegremente.

gain [gein] *n* ganancia *f*, beneficio *m* (winnings) ‖ aumento *m* (increase); *gain in weight* aumento de peso ‖ ventaja *f* (advantage) ‖ muesca *f* (notch).

gain [gein] *vt* ganar (to win, to earn) ‖ llegar a, alcanzar, ganar (to reach) ‖ conseguir (to obtain) ‖ recobrar, recuperar (the balance) ‖ adquirir (to acquire) ‖ conquistar (to conquer) ‖ granjearse, captarse (s.o.'s affection, etc.) ‖ adelantar (a clock) ‖ — *to gain ground* ganar terreno ‖ *to gain the upper hand* tomar la ventaja ‖ *to gain time* ganar tiempo ‖ *you have gained weight* has engordado.

◆ *vi* adelantar (a clock) ‖ mejorar (to improve) ‖ ganar; *to gain by the change* ganar con el cambio ‖ aumentar, acrecentar (to increase) ‖ subir (shares) ‖ — *to gain in prestige* ganar prestigio ‖ *to gain in weight* engordar ‖ *to gain on* ganar terreno a.

gainer [-ə*] *n* ganador, ra ‖ *to be the gainer* salir ganando.

gainful ['geinful] *adj* ganancioso, sa; remunerador, ra; lucrativo, va (profitable).

gainsay [gein'sei] *vt* negar; *I don't gainsay it* no lo niego.

gait [geit] *n* andares *m pl*, paso *m*, modo *m* de andar; *with unsteady gait* con paso poco seguro.

gaiter ['geitə*] *n* polaina *f*.

gal [gæl] *n* PHYS gal *m* ‖ FAM chica *f* (girl).

gala ['gɑːlə] *n* gala *f*, fiesta *f* ‖ SP competición *f* ‖ — *gala dress* traje *m* de etiqueta ‖ *gala performance* función *f* de gala.

galactic [gə'læktik] *adj* ASTR galáctico, ca ‖ MED lácteo, a.

galactose [gə'læktəus] *n* CHEM galactosa *f*.

galalith ['gæləliθ] *n* galalita *f*.

galantine ['gæləntiːn] *n* CULIN galantina *f*.

galanty show [gə'læntiʃəu] *n* sombras *f pl* chinescas.

Galápagos Islands [gə'læpəgəs'ailəndz] *pl n* GEOGR islas *f* Galápagos.

galaxy ['gæləksi] *n* ASTR galaxia *f* ‖ FIG constelación *f*, pléyade *f*.

gale [geil] *n* vendaval *m* (strong wind) ‖ tempestad *f* (storm) ‖ FIG *gales of laughter* carcajadas *f*.

galena [gə'liːnə] *n* MIN galena *f*.

Galicia [gə'liʃiə] *pr n* GEOGR Galicia *f* (in Spain) | Galitzia *f* (in Central Europe).

Galician [-n] *adj* gallego, ga; galaico, ca.

◆ *n* gallego, ga (inhabitant of Galicia, Spain) ‖ gallego *m* (language of Galicia, Spain).

Galician [-n] *adj* de Galitzia.

◆ *n* habitante *m* & *f* de Galitzia.

Galilean [gæli'liən] *adj/n* galileo, a.

Galilee ['gælili:] *pr n* GEOGR Galilea *f*.

galipot ['gælipɔt] *n* galipote *m*.

gall [gɔːl] *n* VET matadura *f*, rozadura *f* (injury to a horse's skin) ‖ ANAT vesícula *f* biliar (gallbladder) ‖ bilis *f* (bile) ‖ hiel *f* (of an animal) ‖ BOT agalla *f* (unnatural growth) ‖ FAM descaro *m*, frescura *f*, caradura *f* (cheek) ‖ FIG amargura *f*, hiel *f* (bitterness) | herida *f* en el amor propio (in s.o.'s pride).

gall [gɔːl] *vt* VET hacer una matadura *or* una rozadura, excoriar (to chafe) ‖ FIG molestar (to annoy) | herir en el amor propio (to mortify).

gallant ['gælənt] *adj* valiente, valeroso, sa (courageous) ‖ elegante, garboso, sa (stately in appearance) ‖ atento, ta (attentive) ‖ galante (attentive towards women) ‖ lucido, da (showy) ‖ espléndido, da; noble (steed) ‖ de amor (poem).

◆ *n* elegante *m* (man of fashion) ‖ galán *m* (ladie's man).

gallant ['gælənt] *vt* galantear.

◆ *vi* ser galante.

gallantry ['gæləntri] *n* cortesía *f* (courtesy) ‖ galantería *f* (chivalrous attention, compliment) ‖ valor *m*, valentía *f* (courage) ‖ heroísmo *m* (heroism).

gallbladder ['gɔːl,blædə*] *n* ANAT vesícula *f* biliar.

galleass ['gæliəs] *n* MAR galeaza *f*.

galleon ['gæliən] *n* MAR galeón *m*.

gallery ['gæləri] *n* galería *f* ‖ tribuna *f* (for spectators) ‖ THEATR gallinero *m*, paraíso *m* ‖ museo *m* (museum) ‖ galería *f* (for works of art) ‖ galería *f* (in mining) ‖ MAR galería *f* ‖ FIG *to play to the gallery* actuar para la galería.

galley ['gæli] *n* MAR galera *f* | cocina *f* (kitchen) ‖ PRINT galera *f* (tray for holding composed type) | galerada *f* (galley proof).

◆ *pl* galeras *f*; *to condemn to the galleys* condenar a galeras.

galley proof [-pruːf] *n* PRINT galerada *f*.

galley slave [-sleiv] *n* galeote *m*.

galliard ['gæljəd] *n* gallarda *f* (dance).

galliass ['gæliəs] *n* MAR galeaza *f*.

gallic ['gælik] *adj* CHEM gálico, ca.

Gallic ['gælik] *adj* gálico, ca; galo, la.

Gallicism ['gælisizəm] *n* GRAMM galicismo *m*.

gallicize ['gælisaiz] *vt* afrancesar.
◆ *vi* afrancesarse.

gallimaufry [gæli'mɔ:fri] *n* mescolanza *f*.

gallinaceous [gæli'neiʃəs] *adj* ZOOL gallináceo, a.

galling [gɔ:liŋ] *adj* mortificante, irritante.

gallinule ['gælinju:l] *n* ZOOL polla *f* de agua.

galliot ['gæliət] *n* MAR galeota *f*.

gallipot ['gælipɔt] *n* galipote *m*.

gallium ['gæljəm] *n* CHEM galio *m*.

gallivant [gæli'vænt] *vi* corretear, callejear (to gad about).

gallon ['gælən] *n* galón *m* [medida de líquido equivalente a 4,55 litros en Inglaterra y a 3,79 litros en EE UU].

galloon [gə'lu:n] *n* galón *m* (braid).

gallop ['gæləp] *n* galope *m*; *hand gallop* galope medio *or* sostenido ‖ — *at all gallop* a galope ‖ *at full gallop* a galope tendido ‖ *to go at a gallop* galopar, ir a galope.

gallop ['gæləp] *vi* galopar ‖ FIG & FAM *to gallop through a book* leer un libro por encima.
◆ *vt* hacer galopar.

galloping ['gæləpiŋ] *adj* galopante ‖ MED *galloping consumption* tisis *f* galopante.

Gallo-Roman ['gæləu'rəumən] *adj* galorromano, na.

gallows ['gæləuz] *pl n* cadalso *m sing*, patíbulo *m sing*, horca *f sing* (for those condemned to death) ‖ MIN castillete *m sing* de extracción.

gallowsbird ['gæləuzbə:d] *n* FAM carne *f* de horca.

gallstone ['gɔ:lstəun] *n* MED cálculo *m* biliar.

Gallup poll ['gælʌppəul] *n* sondeo *m* de la opinión pública.

galluses ['gæləsiz] *pl n* FAM tirantes *m*.

galop ['gæləp] *n* galop *m* (dance).

galore [gə'lɔ:*] *adj/adv* en cantidad, en abundancia.

galosh [gə'lɔʃ] *n* chanclo *m*.

galumph [gə'lʌmf] *vi* FAM dar saltos de alegría.

galvanic [gæl'vænik] *adj* PHYS galvánico, ca ‖ FIG forzado, da (smile).

galvanism ['gælvənizəm] *n* PHYS galvanismo *m*.

galvanization [ˌgælvənai'zeiʃən] *n* PHYS galvanización *f*.

galvanize ['gælvənaiz] *vt* PHYS galvanizar ‖ FIG galvanizar.

galvanocautery ['gælvənɔ'kɔ:təri] *n* MED galvanocauterio *m*.

galvanometer [ˌgælvə'nɔmitə*] *n* galvanómetro *m*.

galvanoplastic [gælvənɔ'plæstik] *adj* galvanoplástico, ca.

galvanoplastics [-s]; **galvanoplasty** [-ti] *n* galvanoplastia *f*.

gam [gæm] *n* manada *f* de ballenas ‖ FAM pierna *f* (leg).

gamba ['gæmbə] *n* MUS viola *f* de gamba.

gambado [gæm'beidəu] *n* brinco *m* (of horse) ‖ FIG travesura *f* (a prank).

Gambia ['gæmbiɑ] *pr n* GEOGR Gambia.

gambit ['gæmbit] *n* gambito *m* (in chess) ‖ FIG táctica *f*, estratagema *f*.

gamble ['gæmbl] *n* jugada *f* (game) ‖ empresa *f* arriesgada (risky undertaking).

gamble ['gæmbl] *vt* arriesgar (to risk) ‖ jugar, apostar (to bet) ‖ *to gamble away* perder en el juego.
◆ *vi* jugar (to play for money) ‖ arriesgarse (to take a risk) ‖ FIG *to gamble on* confiar en (que), contar con.

gambler [-ə*] *n* jugador, ra.

gambling [-iŋ] *n* juego *m* ‖ — *gambling den* garito *m* ‖ *gambling game* juego de envite ‖ *gambling house* casa *f* de juego.

gamboge [gæm'bu:ʒ] *n* gutagamba *f*.

gambol ['gæmbəl] *vi* brincar, saltar.

gambrel [gæmbrəl] *n* garabato *m* (butcher's hook) ‖ ZOOL corvejón *m* ‖ ARCH cubierta *f* a la holandesa (roof).

game [geim] *n* juego *m* (for amusement); *game of chance* juego de azar ‖ juego *m*; *Olympic games* juegos olímpicos ‖ deporte *m* (sport) ‖ partido *m* (in football, baseball, basket, tennis, etc.) ‖ juego *m* (in tennis, part of a match) ‖ juego *m* (player's style) ‖ partida *f* (card, chess, etc.); *to have* o *to play a game of billiards* jugar una partida de billar ‖ manga *f* (bridge) ‖ caza *f* (in hunting) ‖ FAM lío *m* (fuss) ‖ FIG juego *m*; *he saw through your game* vio su juego; *to spoil s.o.'s game* estropear el juego de uno ‖ — *big game* caza mayor ‖ FAM *fair game for* buena presa para ‖ *game of forfeits* juego de prendas ‖ INFORM *games program* o *software* programa *m or* software *m* de juegos ‖ US *game warden* guardabosque *m*, guarda *m* de caza ‖ FIG *off one's game* en baja forma | *paying game* empresa lucrativa | *the game is up!* ¡se acabó! ‖ *to beat s.o. at his own game* ganar a alguien en su propio terreno ‖ *to be game* haber ganado ‖ *to be game all* estar empatados ‖ FAM *to be on the game* ser una mujer de vida alegre ‖ FIG *to be on to s.o.'s game* conocer el juego de alguien | *to give the game away* descubrir las cartas | *to have the game in one's hands* tener todas las bazas en la mano | *to make game of* tomar a broma, burlarse de | *to play a double game* hacer doble juego ‖ *to play a good game* jugar bien ‖ FIG *to play s.o.'s game* hacer el juego de alguien, servir los propósitos de uno | *to play the game* jugar limpio, actuar honradamente ‖ FAM *what's your game?* ¿qué haces?
◆ *adj* de caza (of hunting) ‖ valiente (brave) ‖ tullido, da; lisiado, da (a limb) ‖ — *are you game?* ¿te animas? ‖ *to be game for anything* no tener miedo a nada.

game [geim] *vi/vt* jugar.

gamebag [-bæg] *n* morral *m* (of hunter).

game bird [-bə:d] *n* ave *f* de caza.

gamecock [-kɔk] *n* gallo *m* de pelea *or* de riña.

gamekeeper [-ˌki:pə*] *n* guardabosque *m*, guarda *m* de caza, guardamonte *m*.

game licence [-ˌlaisəns] *n* licencia *f* de caza.

gamely [-li] *adv* valientemente, animosamente.

gameness [-nis] *n* valentía *f*, valor *m*.

game preserve [-pri'zə:v]; **game reserve** [-ri'zə:v] *n* coto *m* de caza, vedado *m* de caza.

gamesmanship ['geimzmənʃip] *n* arte *m* de ganar en el juego con métodos poco ortodoxos.

gamesome [-səm] *adj* alegre, retozón, ona.

gamester [-stə*] *n* jugador, ra.

gamete ['gæmi:t] *n* BIOL gameto *m*.

game warden [geim'wɔ:dn] *n* guardabosque *m*, guarda *m* de caza, guardamonte *m*.

gamey ['geimi] *adj* → **gamy.**

gamin ['gæmən] *n* golfillo *m*.

gamine [gæ'mi:n] *n* golfilla *f*.

gaming ['geimiŋ] *n* juego *m*; *gaming house* casa de juego.

gamma ['gæmə] *n* gamma *f* ‖ PHYS *gamma rays* rayos *m pl* gamma.

gammadion [gə'meidi:ən]; **gammation** [gə'meiʃi:ən] *n* cruz *f* gamada.
— OBSERV El plural es *gammadia* y *gammatia*.

gammer ['gæmə*] *n* FAM abuela *f*, tía *f*; *gammer Smith* la tía Smith.

gammon ['gæmən] *n* jamón *m* ahumado (ham) ‖ tocino *m* ahumado (bacon) ‖ FAM mentira *f* (lie).

gammon ['gæmən] *vt* curar [jamón] (ham) ‖ MAR trincar ‖ FAM engañar.
◆ *vi* FAM bromear (to joke) ‖ fingir (to feign).

gammy ['gæmi] *adj* FAM tullido, da; lisiado, da.

gamopetalous [gæmə'petələs] *adj* gamopétalo, la.

gamosepalous [gæmə'sepələs] *adj* gamosépalo, la.

gamp [gæmp] *n* FAM paraguas *m inv*.

gamut ['gæmət] *n* MUS gama *f* ‖ FIG gama *f*, serie *f*.

gamy; gamey ['geimi] *adj* manido, da (meat) ‖ abundante en caza (wood) ‖ valiente (courageous) ‖ US picante, salaz (spicy).

gander ['gændə*] *n* ganso *m* (goose) ‖ FAM mentecato, ta; papanatas *m* & *f inv* (idiot) ‖ US FAM ojeada *f*; *he took a gander at* echó una ojeada a.

gang [gæŋ] *n* cuadrilla *f*, brigada *f*, equipo *m* (of workers) ‖ pandilla *f*, cuadrilla *f* (a band of people who go round together) ‖ banda *f*, gang *m* (of gangsters) ‖ juego *m* (of tools) ‖ MIN ganga *f*.

gang [gæŋ] *vi* ir (in Scottish) ‖ — *to gang up* agruparse ‖ *to gang up on* conspirar contra, confabularse contra, unirse contra (to conspire against), atacar en grupo (to attack in a gang) ‖ *to gang up with* unirse a.

ganger [-ə*] *n* capataz *m*, jefe *m* de equipo.

Ganges ['gændʒi:z] *pr n* GEOGR Ganges *m*.

gang hook ['gæŋhuk] *n* anzuelo *m* múltiple.

gangland ['gæŋlænd] *adj* hampesco, ca; de los bajos fondos.
◆ *n* trampa *f*.

gangling ['gæŋgliŋ] *adj* FAM larguirucho, cha.

ganglion ['gæŋgliən] *n* MED & ANAT ganglio *m* ‖ FIG centro *m*, foco *m* (of activity).
— OBSERV El plural de *ganglion* es *ganglions* o *ganglia*.

gangly ['gæŋgli] *adj* US FAM larguirucho, cha.

gangplank ['gæŋgplænk] *n* MAR plancha *f*.

gangrene ['gæŋgri:n] *n* MED gangrena *f*.

gangrene ['gæŋgri:n] *vi* gangrenarse.
◆ *vt* gangrenar.

gangrenous ['gæŋgrenəs] *adj* MED gangrenoso, sa.

gangster ['gæŋstə*] *n* gángster *m*, pistolero *m*.

gansterism [-rizəm] *n* gangsterismo *m*, bandidaje *m* (organized use of violence).

gangue [gæŋ] *n* MIN ganga *f*.

gangway [-wei] *n* pasillo *m* (passage between rows of seats, etc.) ‖ MAR plancha *f* (gangplank) | portalón *m* (opening) | pasamano *m* (platform between forecastle and quarterdeck) | pasarela *f* (for disembarking) ‖ THEATR pasarela *f* ‖ *gangway!* ¡paso!

gannet ['gænit] *n* ZOOL alcatraz *m* (bird).

gangry [gæntri] *n* caballete *m* (for barrels) ‖ pórtico *m* (for crane) ‖ torre *f* de lanzamiento (of rockets) ‖ *gantry crane* grúa *f* de pórtico.

gaol [dʒeil] *n* cárcel *f*.

gaol [dʒeil] *vt* encarcelar.

gaolbird [-bəːd] *n* presidiario *m* reincidente, preso *m* reincidente.

gaolbreak [-breik] *n* evasión *f*, fuga *f*.

gaoler [-ə*] *n* carcelero *m*.

gap [gæp] *n* portillo *m* (in a wall) || brecha *f*, boquete *m* (breach) || desfiladero *m*, quebrada *f* (between mountains) || hueco *m* (cavity) || resquicio *m* (crack) || espacio *m* (in writing) || vacío *m* (unfilled space) || laguna *f* (in text, s.o.'s education) || intervalo *m* (of time) || claro *m* (in a wood, in traffic) || pausa *f* (pause) || diferencia *f* (difference); *to fill the gap* suprimir la diferencia || desequilibrio *m* (imbalance).

gape [geip] *n* bostezo *m* (yawn) || mirada *f* atónita (look).

gape [geip] *vi* quedarse boquiabierto (to stare in surprise) || abrirse (mucho), estar (muy) abierto (to be wide open) || bostezar (to yawn) || pensar en las musarañas, papar moscas (to let one's mind wander).

gaping [-iŋ] *adj* abierto, ta (open) || boquiabierto, ta (surprised).

garage ['gærɑːdʒ, *US* gə'rɑːʒ] *n* garaje *m* || — *garage attendant* garajista *m* (person in charge) || *garage owner* garajista *m*.

garage ['gærɑːdʒ, *US* gə'rɑːʒ] *vt* dejar en el garaje.

garb [gɑːb] *n* vestido *m*, vestidura *f*.

garb [gɑːb] *vt* vestir.

garbage ['gɑːbidʒ] *n* basura *f* || FIG basura *f* || — *garbage can* cubo *m* de la basura || *garbage collector* o *man* basurero *m* || *garbage disposal* vertedero *m or* colector *m* de basuras || *garbage incinerator* incinerador *m* de basura.

garble ['gɑːbl] *vt* amañar, falsificar (to falsify) || desvirtuar (facts) || truncar (a quotation) || mutilar (a text).

garbled [-d] *adj* confuso, sa (note, message).

garden ['gɑːdn] *n* jardín *m* (of flowers) || huerto *m* (where foodstuffs are grown) || huerta *f*, región *f* fértil, jardín *m* (large fertile region) || jardín *m* (botany) || — *back* o *kitchen garden* huerto || FAM *to lead s.o. up the garden path* engañar *or* embaucar a alguien.
◆ *pl* parque *m sing*, jardines *m* || calle *f sing* (street) || *zoological gardens* parque zoológico.
◆ *adj* de jardín (flowers) || de la huerta, del huerto (vegetables) || de jardinería (tools).

garden ['gɑːdn] *vi* trabajar en un jardín *or* en un huerto.

garden centre [-ˌsentə*] *n* centro *m* de jardinería (shop).

garden city [-'siti] *n* ciudad jardín *f*.

gardenal [-əl] *n* gardenal *m*.

gardener ['gɑːdnə*] *n* jardinero, ra (of flowers) || hortelano, na (of vegetables) || *landscape gardener* jardinero paisajista.

gardenia [gɑː'diːnjə] *n* BOT gardenia *f*.

gardening ['gɑːdniŋ] *n* jardinería *f* (of flowers) || horticultura *f* (of vegetables).

garden party ['gɑːdnˌpɑːti] *n* «garden party» *m*, fiesta *f* al aire libre.

garfish ['gɑːfiʃ] *n* ZOOL aguja *f*.

garganey ['gɑːgəni] *n* zarceta *f* (bird).

Gargantua [gɑː'gæntjuə] *pr n* Gargantúa *m*.

gargantuan [-n] *adj* enorme, tremendo, da.

garget ['gɑːgət] *n* VET mastitis *f*.

gargle ['gɑːgl] *n* MED gargarismo *m* (liquid) | gárgara *f*, gárgaras *f pl*, gargarismo *m* (treatment).

gargle ['gɑːgl] *vi* hacer gárgaras, gargarizar.

gargoyle ['gɑːgɔil] *n* ARCH gárgola *f*.

garish ['gɛəriʃ] *adj* chillón, ona; llamativo, va.

garland ['gɑːlənd] *n* guirnalda *f* (wreath) || antología *f* || MAR eslinga *f*.

garland ['gɑːlənd] *vt* adornar con guirnaldas, enguirnaldar.

garlic ['gɑːlik] *n* BOT ajo *m*.

garment ['gɑːmənt] *n* prenda *f* [de vestir].
◆ *pl* ropa *f sing*.

garner ['gɑːnə*] *n* AGR granero *m* || FIG abundancia *f*.

garner ['gɑːnə*] *vt* AGR guardar en un granero || FIG acumular.

garnet ['gɑːnit] *n* MIN granate *m*.
◆ *adj* granate.

garnish ['gɑːniʃ] *n* aderezo *m*, adorno *m* || CULIN guarnición *f*, aderezo *m*.

garnish ['gɑːniʃ] *vt* aderezar, adornar (to decorate) || CULIN guarnecer, aderezar || JUR embargar (to garnishee) | citar (to summon) | retener (payment).

garnishee [ˌgɑːni'ʃiː] *n* JUR embargado, da.

garnishment ['gɑːniʃmənt] *n* JUR embargo *m* | orden *f* de retención de pagos | citación *f* || embellecimiento *m*, adorno *m* (embellishment) || CULIN guarnición *f*, aderezo *m*.

garniture ['gɑːnitʃə*] *n* aderezo *m* (condiments) || guarnición *f* (additional to main plate).

Garonne [gæ'rɔn] *pr n* GEOGR Garona *m*.

garotte [gə'rɔt] *n* garrote *m*.

garotte [gə'rɔt] *vt* agarrotar (to garrotte).

garotting [-iŋ] *n* garrote *m* (garrotting).

garpike ['gɑːpaik] *n* ZOOL aguja *f* (fish).

garret ['gærət] *n* buhardilla *f* (room), desván *m* (attic, loft).

garrison ['gærisn] *n* MIL guarnición *f*; *to be in garrison in a city* estar de guarnición en una ciudad.

garrison ['gærisn] *vt* guarnecer (a place) || poner en guarnición (troops).

garrotte; *US* **garrote** [gə'rɔt] *n* garrote *m*.

garrotte; *US* **garrote** [gə'rɔt] *vt* agarrotar.

garrotting; *US* **garroting** [-iŋ] *n* garrote *m*.

garrulity [gæ'ruːliti] *n* locuacidad *f*, garrulidad *f*.

garrulous ['gæruləs] *adj* locuaz, parlanchín, ina; gárrulo, la (person) || verboso, sa (style).

garter ['gɑːtə*] *n* liga *f* || *order of the Garter* orden *f* de la Jarretera.

garter ['gɑːtə*] *vt* poner una liga.

garter belt [-belt] *n* *US* liguero *m*, portaligas *m inv*.

garth [gɑːθ] *n* patio *m*.

gas [gæs] *n* gas *m* (substance); *illuminating gas* gas de alumbrado; *laughing, tear gas* gas hilarante, lacrimógeno || FAM parloteo *m*, palique *m* (chatter) || grisú *m* (in mining) || *US* gasolina *f* (petrol) || — *asphyxiating* o *lethal* o *poison gas* gas asfixiante *or* de combate || *by gas* de gas || *coal gas* gas de hulla || *gas burner* mechero *m* de gas || *gas chamber* cámara *f* de gas || *gas cooker* cocina *f* de gas || *gas engine* motor *m* de gas || *gas fire* estufa *f* de gas || *gas fitter* gasista *m*, empleado *m* del gas || *gas furnace* horno *m* de gas || MED *gas gangrene* gangrena gaseosa || *gas lighter* encendedor *m* de gas || *gas lighting* alumbrado *m* de gas || *gas mask* careta *f* antigás || *gas meter* contador *m* de gas || *gas oven* horno *m* de gas || *gas pipe* tubería *f* de gas || *gas pipeline* gasoducto *m* || *gas plant* fábrica *f* de gas || *gas ring* hornillo *m* de gas || *US gas station* surtidor *m* de gasolina, gasolinera *f* || *gas welding* soldadura autógena || *marsh gas* gas de los pantanos || *producer gas* gas pobre || *water gas* gas de agua || *US to step on the gas* pisar el acelerador.

gas [gæs] *vt* asfixiar con gas (to kill by gas) || *to gas up* proveer de gas.
◆ *vi* despedir gas (to give off gas) || FAM camelar (to cheat) | charlotear, estar de palique (to chatter).

gasbag [-bæg] *n* cámara *f* de gas || FAM camelista *m* & *f* (cheater) | parlanchín, ina (chatterbox).

Gascon ['gæskən] *adj/n* gascón, ona.

Gascony ['gæskəni] *pr n* GEOGR Gascuña *f*.

gaseous ['gæsjəs] *adj* gaseoso, sa.

gash [gæʃ] *n* cuchillada *f* (wound).

gash [gæʃ] *vt* acuchillar.

gasholder ['gæsˌhəuldə*] *n* *US* gasómetro *m*.

gashouse ['gæshaus] *n* *US* fábrica *f* de gas.

gasification [ˌgæsifi'keiʃən] *n* gasificación *f*.

gasify ['gæsifai] *vt* gasificar.
◆ *vi* gasificarse.

gas jet ['gæsdʒet] *n* mechero *m* de gas (gas burner) || llama *f* (flame).

gasket ['gæskit] *n* AUT junta *f* de culata.

gaslight ['gæslait] *n* alumbrado *m* de gas, luz *f* de gas || TECH mechero *m* de gas.

gasman ['gæsmæn] *n* gasista *m*, empleado *m* del gas.
— OBSERV El plural de esta palabra es *gasmen*.

gasogene ['gæsədʒiːn] *n* gasógeno *m*.

gasoline; **gasolene** ['gæsəliːn] *n* *US* gasolina *f*.

gasometer [gæ'sɔmitə*] *n* gasómetro *m*.

gasp [gɑːsp] *n* boqueada *f* (before dying) || grito *m* de asombro (of surprise) || jadeo *m* (difficulty in breathing) || *to be at one's last gasp* estar dando las últimas boqueadas, estar en las últimas.

gasp [gɑːsp] *vi* quedar boquiabierto, ta (with surprise) || jadear (to pant) || — *to gasp for air* hacer esfuerzos para respirar || *to make s.o. gasp* dejar boquiabierto a uno.
◆ *vt* *to gasp out* decir con voz entrecortada.

gasper [-ə*] *n* FAM pito *m*, pitillo *m* (cigarette).

gasping [-iŋ] *n* jadeo *m*.

gaspy [gɑːspi] *adj* jadeante.

gassed [gæst] *adj* gaseado, da || FAM borracho, cha.

gassing ['gæsiŋ] *n* asfixia *f* con gas (killing by gas) || gasificación *f* (gasification) || MIL ataque *m* con gas || FAM charloteo *m* (chatter).

gassy ['gæsi] *adj* gaseoso, sa.

gasteropod ['gæstərəpɔd] *n* ZOOL —> **gastropod.**

gastight ['gæstait] *adj* a prueba de gas, hermético, ca.

gastralgia [gæs'trældʒiə] *n* MED gastralgia *f*.

gastric ['gæstrik] *adj* ANAT gástrico, ca; *gastric juice* jugo gástrico.

gastritis [gæs'traitis] *n* MED gastritis *f*.

gastroenteritis ['gæstrɔinteˌraitis] *n* MED gastroenteritis *f*.

gastroenterology ['gæstrɔinte'rɔlədʒi] *n* gastroenterología *f*.

gastronome ['gæstrənəum] *n* gastrónomo, ma.

gastronomic [ˌgæstrə'nɔmik]; **gastronomical** [-əl] *adj* gastronómico, ca.

gastronomist [gæs'trɔnəmist] *n* gastrónomo, ma.

gastronomy [gæs'trɔnəmi] *n* gastronomía *f*.

gastropod ['gæstrəuˌpɔd]; **gasteropod** ['gæstərəpɔd] *n* ZOOL gasterópodo *m*, gastrópodo *m*.

gasworks ['gæswəːks] *n* fábrica *f* de gas.

gat [gæt] *n* *US* FAM revólver *m*.

gate [geit] *n* verja *f* (metal barrier in wall or fence) || puerta *f* (of city, entrance, etc.) || pórtico *m* (of church) || entrada *f* (of a public place, football stadium, etc.) || puerta *f* (at airport) || barrera *f* (of railway crossing) || puerto *m* (of mountains) || compuerta *f* (of sluice) || recaudación *f*, taquilla *f* (number of tickets sold) || US FAM *to give s.o. the gate* poner a uno en la calle.

gate [geit] *vt* castigar sin salir (in school) || poner puerta a.

gateau ['gɑtəʊ] *n* tarta *f* con nata o frutas.

gatecrash [-kræʃ] *vt* FAM colarse en.
◆ *vi* FAM colarse.

gatecrasher [-'kræʃə*] *n* FAM persona *f* que se cuela.

gatehouse [-haus] *n* casa *f* del guarda de un parque (of a park) || caseta *f* del guardabarrera (of railway crossing).

gatekeeper [-,ki:pə*] *n* guardabarrera *m* & *f* (of railway crossing) || portero, ra (doorkeeper).

gateleg table ['geitleg'teibl] *n* mesa *f* plegable, mesa *f* de alas abatibles.

gate money ['geit'mʌni] *n* recaudación *f*, taquilla *f* (admission receipts).

gatepost ['geit'pəust] *n* pilar *m*, poste *m*.

gateway ['geitwei] *n* ⟶ **gate** || FIG puerta *f* (means of approach).

gather ['gæðə*] *n* AGR cosecha *f* || pliegue *m*, frunce *m* (in sewing).

gather ['gæðə*] *vt* recoger (to pick up) || juntar, reunir (to put together) || juntar, unir (to join) || acumular (to collect, to amass) || cosechar (to harvest) || coger (to pick flowers, etc.) || fruncir (to sew, to pucker) || recobrar; *to gather breath* recobrar el aliento || cobrar (strenght, etc.) || deducir (to deduce) || recaudar (money) || SP recoger (the ball) || — FIG *rolling stone gathers no moss* agua pasada no mueve molino || *to gather dirt* ensuciarse || *to gather honey* libar (to bees) || *to gather in* recaudar (taxes) || *to gather one's energies* reunir sus fuerzas || *to gather o.s. together* reponerse || *to gather o.s. up* acurrucarse || *to gather speed* ganar velocidad || *to gather that...* tener entendido que... (to understand), sacar la conclusión de que... (to deduce) || *to gather together* reunir, juntar || *to gather up* recoger.
◆ *vi* acumularse, amontonarse (things) || reunirse, juntarse (persons) || aumentar, incrementar (to increase) || madurar (abscess) || formarse (pus).

gathering [-iŋ] *n* reunión *f*, asamblea *f* || concurrencia *f*, asistentes *m pl* (people present) || recolección *f* (colletion) || cosecha *f* (of fruit) || MED absceso *m* || pliegue *m*, frunce *m* (in sewing).

GATT *abbr of [General Agreement on Tariffs and Trade]* GATT, Acuerdo General sobre Aranceles Aduaneros y Comercio.

gauche [gəuʃ] *adj* torpe, desmañado, da.

gaucherie ['gəuʃəri:] *n* torpeza *f*.

gaucho [gautʃəu] *n* gaucho *m*.
◆ *adj* gauchesco, ca; *gauche life* vida gauchesca.

gaud [gɔ:d] *n* dije *m* (trinket).

gaudy ['gɔ:di] *adj* chillón, ona; llamativo, va.

gauffer ['gɔfə*] *vt* ⟶ **goffer.**

gauge; gage [geidʒ] *n* calibre *m* (calibre) || medida *f* (measure) || muestra *f*, indicación *f* (demonstration); *this work gives us a gauge of his abilities* este trabajo nos da una muestra de sus capacidades || entrevía *f*, ancho *m* (of railway line) || AUT batalla *f* (of wheels) || gramil *m* (in carpentry) || TECH calibrador *m*, galga *f* (for measuring diameter) | indicador *m* (meter) | manómetro *m* (for pressure) || MAR calado *m* (draught) | barlovento *m*; *to have the weather gauge of* estar a barlovento de || — TECH *marking gauge* gramil || FIG *to take the gauge of* determinar, estimar.

gauge; gage [geidʒ] *vt* calibrar (to measure the diameter of) || medir (to measure) || aforar, medir la capacidad de (a cask) || arquear (ships) || calcular (to calculate) || determinar (to assess) || apreciar, estimar (s.o.'s capacities).

gauger [-ə*] *n* aforador *m*.

gauging [-iŋ] *n* aforo *m* (of cask) || medida *f* (measure) || MAR arqueo *m*.

Gaul [gɔ:l] *n* HIST galo, la (people) | Galia *f* (country).

gaunt [gɔ:nt] *adj* demacrado, da (lean) || FIG lúgubre (desolate) | feroz (grim).

gauntlet ['gɔ:ntlit] *n* guantelete *m* (in armour) || guante *m* (glove) || — *to run the gauntlet* correr baquetas (as punishment) || FIG *to run the gauntlet of* estar sometido a | *to take up the guantlet* recoger el guante | *to throw down the gauntlet* arrojar el guante.

gauss [gaus] *n* ELECTR gauss *m*.

gauze [gɔ:z] *n* gasa *f* (of cloth) || tela *f* metálica (of wire) || FIG bruma *f* (thin haze).

gauzy ['gɔ:zi] *adj* diáfano, na.

gave [geiv] *pret* ⟶ **give.**

gavel ['gævl] *n* martillo *m*.

gavial ['geiviəl] *n* ZOOL gavial *m*.

gavotte [gə'vɔt] *n* MUS gavota *f*.

gawk [gɔ:k] *n* bobo, ba.

gawk [gɔ:k] *vi* papar moscas || *to gawk at* mirar tontamente (a).

gawky ['gɔ:ki] *adj* torpe (awkward) || desgarbado, da (ungainly).

gawp [gɔ:p] *vi* papar moscas || *to gawp at* mirar tontamente (a).

gay [gei] *adj* alegre || FAM homosexual (homosexual).

gazabo [gə'zeibəu] *n* FAM tipo *m*, tío *m* (fellow).

gaze [geiz] *n* mirada *f* fija (stare) || contemplación *f* (act).

gaze [geiz] *vi* mirar || — *to gaze at* mirar fijamente; contemplar || *to gaze into space* estar con la mirada perdida.

gazebo [gə'zi:bəu] *n* belvedere *m*.
— OBSERV El plural es *gazebos* o *gazeboes*.

gazelle [gə'zel] *n* ZOOL gacela *f*.

gazette [gə'zet] *n* gaceta *f* || Boletín *m* Oficial (official publication) || *gazette writer* gacetero *m*.

gazette [gə'zet] *vt* publicar en el Boletín Oficial.

gazetteer [,gæzi'tiə*] *n* diccionario *m* geográfico.

gazogene ['gæzədʒi:n] *n* gasógeno *m*.

gazump [gə'zʌmp] *vt* FAM hacer una oferta superior (not to buy a property, because s.o. offers more money).

GB *abbr of [Great Britain]* GB, Gran Bretaña.

GDP *abbr of [gross domestic product]* PIB, producto interior bruto.

gear [giə*] *n* equipo *m* (equipment) || ropa *f* (clothing) || efectos *m pl* personales (personal belongings) || arreos *m pl*, aparejo *m* (of a horse) || herramientas *f pl* (tools) || mecanismo *m* (mechanism) || dispositivo *m* (device) || engranaje *m* (of machinery); *differential gear* engranaje del diferencial; *timing gear* engranaje de distribución || velocidad *f*, cambio *m*, marcha *f* (for a car) || embrague *m* (clutch) || desarrollo *m* (for a bicycle) || MAR aparejo *m* || — *bottom gear* primera velocidad || *gear teeth* engranaje *m sing* (cogs) || *in gear* engranado, da || *in low gear* en primera velocidad || *neutral gear* punto muerto || FIG *out of gear* descompuesto, ta || *reversing gear* marcha *f* atrás || *to change gear* cambiar de velocidad || *top gear* cuarta velocidad || *to put into gear* meter una velocidad, cambiar de velocidad (car), engranar || *to throw into, out of gear* embragar, desembragar.

gear [giə*] *vt* aparejar, poner los arreos a (a horse) || engranar (to put into gear) || adaptar, ajustar (to adapt) || — *to gear down* desmultiplicar || *to gear up* multiplicar.
◆ *vi* engranar.

gearbox [-bɔks] *n* caja *f* de cambios, caja *f* de velocidades.

gear-change lever [-tʃeindʒ'li:və*]; **gear lever** [-,li:və*]; US *n* palanca *f* de cambio de velocidades.

gear differential [giə*,difə'renʃəl] *n* piñón *m* diferencial.

gearing [-iŋ] *n* engranaje *m* (gears, meshing).

gearshift [-ʃift] *n* cambio *m* de velocidades.

gear wheel [-wi:l] *n* piñón *m* (of bicycle) || rueda *f* dentada.

gecko ['gekəu] *n* ZOOL salamanquesa *f*.

gee [dʒi:] *interj* ¡caramba! || *gee up!* ¡arre! (to a horse).

geese [gi:s] *pl n* ⟶ **goose.**

geezer ['gi:zə*] *n* FAM tío *m*, viejo *m*.

Gehenna [gi'henə] *n* gehena *f* (hell).

geisha ['geiʃə] *n* geisha *f* (Japanese woman).

gel [dʒel] *n* CHEM gel *m*.

gel [dʒel] *vi* gelificarse.

gelatin; gelatine [,dʒelə'ti:n] *n* gelatina *f*.

gelatinous [dʒi'lætinəs] *adj* gelatinoso, sa.

geld [geld] *vt* castrar, capar.

gelder [-ə*] *n* capador *m*, castrador *m*.

Gelderland ['geldə,lænd] *pr n* GEOGR Güeldres *f*.

gelding ['geldiŋ] *n* castración *f* (castration) || caballo *m* castrado (horse).

gelid ['dʒelid] *adj* helado, da; gélido, da.

gelignite ['dʒelignait] *n* gelignita *f* (explosive).

gem [dʒem] *n* gema *f*, piedra *f* preciosa (jewel) || FIG alhaja *f*, joya *f* (thing, person) || *a gem of a child* una preciosidad de niño.

gemelli [dʒe'meli] *pl n* ANAT músculos *m* gemelos.

geminate ['dzemineit] *adj* geminado, da; gémino, na.

Gemini ['dʒeminai] *pl n* ASTR Géminis *m*.

gemma ['dʒemə] *n* BOT yema *f*.
— OBSERV El plural de *gemma* es *gemmae*.

gemmate ['dʒemeit] *vi* reproducirse por gemación.

gemmation [dʒe'meiʃən] *n* gemación *f*.

Gemonies ['dʒeməniz] *pl prn* HIST Gemonias *f*.

gemstone ['dʒemstəun] *n* piedra *f* preciosa.

gen [dʒen] *n* FAM información *f* || FAM *to get the gen on* informarse sobre.

gen [dʒen] *vi* FAM *to gen up* informarse.

gendarme ['ʒɑ:ndɑ:m] *n* gendarme *m*.

gendarmerie; gendarmery [,ʒɑ:ndɑ:mə'ri:] *n* gendarmería *f*.

gender ['dʒendə*] *n* GRAMM género *m*; *masculine, feminine, neutral gender* género masculino, femenino, neutro || FAM sexo *m*.

gender ['dʒendə*] *vt* engendrar.

gene [dʒi:n] *n* BIOL gene *m*, gen *m*.

genealogical [,dʒi:njə'lɔdʒikəl] *adj* genealógico, ca; *genealogical tree* árbol genealógico.

genealogist [ˌdʒiːni'ælədʒist] *n* genealogista *m* & *f*.

genealogy [ˌdʒiːni'ælədʒi] *n* genealogía *f*.

genera ['dʒenərə] *pl n* ⟶ **genus.**

general ['dʒenərəl] *adj* general; *as a general rule* por regla general; *in a general way* de modo general; *the general opinion* la opinión general; *general paralysis* parálisis general ‖ *in general* en general, por lo general, generalmente.
◆ *n* MIL & REL general *m* ‖ chica *f* para todo (servant).

General Certificate of Education [-sə'tifikeitov,edjuː'keiʃən] *n* reválida *f*.

General Court [-kɔːt] *n* US Asamblea *f* Legislativa.

general delivery [-di'livəri] *n* US lista *f* de correos.

generalissimo [ˌdʒenərə'lisiməu] *n* MIL generalísimo *m*.

generality [ˌdʒenə'ræliti] *n* generalidad *f*.

generalization [ˌdʒenerəlai'zeiʃən] *n* generalización *f*.

generalize ['dʒenərəlaiz] *vt/vi* generalizar.

general knowledge ['dʒenərəlˌnɔlidʒ] *n* cultura *f* general.

generally ['dʒenərəli] *adj* generalmente, por lo general, en general ‖ *generally speaking* hablando en términos generales.

general meeting [-ˌmiːtiŋ] *n* asamblea *f* general.

general practice ['dʒenərəlˌpræktis] *n* medicina *f* general.

general practitioner ['dʒenərəlpræk'tiʃnə*] *n* médico *m* de medicina general, internista *m*.

general-purpose [-'pəːpəs] *adj* de uso general.

generalship ['dʒenərəlʃip] *n* MIL estrategia *f*, táctica *f* militar (military skill) | generalato *m* (grade of general) ‖ don *m* de mando (leadership).

general staff ['dʒenərəlstɑːf] *n* MIL estado *m* mayor.

general store ['dʒenərəlˌstɔː*] *n* almacén *m*.

general strike ['dʒenərəlˌstraik] *n* huelga *f* general.

generate ['dʒenəreit] *vt* engendrar, generar, producir (to produce) ‖ BIOL procrear, engendrar ‖ MATH & ELECTR generar; *to generate an electric current* generar una corriente eléctrica.

generating [-iŋ] *adj* generador, ra; *generating station* central generadora.

generation [ˌdʒenə'reiʃən] *n* generación *f*; *spontaneous generation* generación espontánea; *the rising generation* la nueva generación ‖ INFORM generación *f* de máquinas ‖ *generation gap* conflicto *m or* barrera *f* generacional.

generative ['dʒenərətiv] *adj* generativo, va.

generator ['dʒenəreitə*] *n* TECH generador *m*.

generatrix ['dʒenəreitriks] *n* MATH generatriz *f*.
— OBSERV El plural de *generatrix* es *generatrices*.

generic [dʒi'nerik]; **generical** [-kəl] *adj* genérico, ca.

generosity [ˌdʒenə'rɔsiti] *n* generosidad *f*.

generous ['dʒenərəs] *adj* generoso, sa (*to* con, para) ‖ AGR fértil, rico, ca (soil) ‖ abundante (copious).

genesis ['dʒenisis] *n* génesis *f*.
— OBSERV El plural de la palabra inglesa es *geneses*.

Genesis ['dʒenisis] *n* REL Génesis *m*.

genet ['dʒenit] *n* ZOOL jineta *f*.

genetic [dʒi'netik] *adj* genético, ca ‖ *genetic engineering* ingeniería *f* genética.

geneticist [dʒi'netisist] *n* genetista *m* & *f*, geneticista *m* & *f*.

genetics [dʒinetiks] *n* genética *f*.

Geneva [dʒi'niːvə] *pr n* GEOGR Ginebra.

Genevan [dʒi'niːvən]; **Genevese** [dʒi'niːviːz] *adj/n* ginebrino, na; ginebrés, esa.

genial ['dʒiːnjəl] *adj* afable, cordial, simpático, ca (people) ‖ suave, clemente (weather) ‖ reconfortante, vivificante (warmth) ‖ genial (talent).

geniality [ˌdʒiːni'æliti] *n* afabilidad *f*, simpatía *f*, cordialidad *f* (of person) ‖ clemencia *f*, suavidad *f* (of climate).

genic ['dʒiːnik] *adj* genético, ca.

genie ['dʒiːni] *n* genio *m* [en los cuentos árabes].
— OBSERV El plural de *genie* es *genies* o *genii*.

genipap ['dʒenipæp] *n* BOT mamón *m*.

genista [dʒxi'nistə] *n* BOT retama *f*.

genital ['dʒenitl] *adj* genital.

genitalia [ˌdʒeni'teiljə]; **genitals** ['dʒenitlz] *pl n* ANAT órganos *m* genitales.

genitive ['dʒenitiv] *n* GRAMM genitivo *m*.

genitourinary ['dʒenitəu'juərinəri] *adj* ANAT genitourinario, ria.

genius ['dʒiːnjəs] *n* genio *m*; *she is a genius* ella es un genio; *the genius of the language* el genio de la lengua ‖ — *he has a genius for making friends* tiene don de gente, tiene un don especial para hacerse amigos ‖ *he has a genius for mathematics* es un genio para las matemáticas.
— OBSERV El plural de *genius* es *geniuses* o *genii*.

Genoa ['dʒenəuə] *pr n* GEOGR Génova.

genocide ['dʒenəusaid] *n* genocidio *m*.

Genoese [ˌdʒenəu'iːz] *adj/n* genovés, esa.

genotype ['dʒiːnətaip] *n* BIOL genotipo *m*.

genre [ʒɑːŋr] *n* género *m*, tipo *m*, clase *f* ‖ ARTS *genre painting* pintura *f* de género.

gent [dʒent] *n* FAM señor *m*, sujeto *m*, individuo *m* (man).
◆ *pl* caballeros *m* (lavatory).

genteel [dʒen'tiːl] *adj* fino, na; distinguido, da; de buen tono (refined) ‖ cursi (excessively refined) ‖ cortés (polite).

gentian ['dʒenʃiən] *n* BOT genciana *f*.

gentile ['dʒentail] *adj* gentil, no judío (not jewish) ‖ gentil (pagan) ‖ GRAMM gentilicio, cia (gentilic).
◆ *n* gentil *m*.

gentilic [dʒen'tilik] *adj* gentilicio, cia; *gentilic noun, adjective* nombre, adjetivo gentilicio.
◆ *n* gentilicio *m*.

gentility [dʒen'tiliti] *n* finura *f*, distinción *f* (refinement) ‖ cursilería *f* (pretentiousness) ‖ cortesía *f* (politeness).

gentle ['dʒentl] *adj* suave (mild) ‖ bondadoso, sa (kind) ‖ amable (friendly) ‖ cortés, fino, na (polite) ‖ moderado, da (moderate) ‖ ligero, ra (light, not violent) ‖ lento, ta (slow) ‖ manso, sa (tame) ‖ de buena familia, bien nacido, da (of good birth) ‖ — *gentle reader* apreciado lector ‖ *of gentle birth* de buena familia, bien nacido, da ‖ *the gentle sex* el sexo débil.

gentlefolk [-fəuk] *n* gente *f* bien nacida.

gentleman ['dʒentlmən] *n* caballero *m*, señor *m* (well-bred man) ‖ señor *m*, caballero *m* (man) ‖ gentilhombre *m* (at court) ‖ — *gentleman in waiting* gentilhombre de cámara ‖ *gentleman of the road* salteador *m* de caminos.
◆ *pl* muy señores míos, muy señores nuestros (in letters) ‖ caballeros *m* (lavatory) ‖ *ladies and gentlemen!* ¡señoras y señores!, ¡señoras y caballeros!
— OBSERV El plural de esta palabra es *gentlemen*.

gentleman-at-arms [-ət'ɑːmz] *n* guardia *m* de corps.
— OBSERV El plural es *gentlemen-at-arms*.

gentleman farmer [-fɑːmə*] *n* terrateniente *m*.
— OBSERV El plural es *gentlemen farmers*.

gentlemanlike [-laik] *adj* caballeroso, sa.

gentlemanly [-li] *adj* caballeroso, sa.

gentleman's agreement; gentlemen's agreement ['dʒentlmænzə'griːmənt] *n* acuerdo *m* entre caballeros.

gentleman's gentleman ['dʒentlmənz'dʒentlmən] *n* ayuda *m* de cámara.

gentleness ['dʒentlinis] *n* amabilidad *f* (kindness) ‖ bondad *f* (goodness) ‖ suavidad *f* (mildness) ‖ mansedumbre *f* (of animals).

gentlewoman ['dʒentlwumən] *n* señora *f*, dama *f*.
— OBSERV El plural de esta palabra es *gentlewomen*.

gently ['dʒentli] *adv* amablemente (kindly) ‖ suavemente (smoothly) ‖ despacio, poco a poco (slowly).

gentry ['dʒentri] *n* pequeña nobleza *f*, alta burguesía *f*, pequeña aristocracia *f* (people of good family) ‖ gente *f* (people).

genuflect ['dʒenjuflekt] *vi* doblar la rodilla, hacer una genuflexión.

genuflection; genuflexion [ˌdʒenju'flekʃən] *n* genuflexión *f*.

genuine ['dʒenjuin] *adj* verdadero, ra (real) ‖ sincero, ra; franco, ca (frank) ‖ auténtico, ca; genuino, na; legítimo, ma (authentic).

genuineness [-nis] *n* autenticidad *f*.

genus ['dʒiːnəs] *n* género *m*.
— OBSERV El plural de *genus* es *genera*.

geocentric [ˌdʒiəu'sentrik]; **geocentrical** [-kəl] *adj* geocéntrico, ca.

geode ['dʒiəud] *n* GEOL geoda *f*.

geodesic [ˌdʒiəu'desik] *adj* geodésico, ca.
◆ *n* MATH geodésica *f*.

geodesy [dʒi'ɔdisi] *n* geodesia *f*.

geodetic [dʒi'ɔdetik] *adj* geodésico, ca.

geodetics [-s] *n* geodésica *f*.

geographer [dʒi'ɔgrəfə*] *n* geógrafo *m*.

geographic [dʒiə'græfik] *adj* geográfico, ca.

geographical [-əl] *adj* geográfico, ca.

geography [dʒi'ɔgrəfi] *n* geografía *f*.

geoid ['dʒiːɔid] *n* geoide *m*.

geologic [dʒiə'lɔdʒik]; **geological** [-əl] *adj* geológico, ca.

geologist [dʒi'ɔlədʒist] *n* geólogo *m*.

geologize [dʒi'ɔlədʒaiz] *vi* estudiar geología.

geology [dʒi'ɔlədʒi] *n* geología *f*.

geomagnetic [ˌdʒiːəumæg'netik] *adj* geomagnético, ca.

geometer [dʒi'ɔmitə*] *n* geómetra *m*.

geometric [dʒiə'metrik] *adj* MATH geométrico, ca; *geometric progression* progresión geométrica; *geometric ratio* razón geométrica; *geometric mean* media geométrica.

geometrical [-əl] *adj* MATH geométrico, ca; *geometrical construction* construcción geométrica.

geometrician [ˌdʒiəumə'triʃən] *n* geómetra *m*.

geometrize [dʒi'ɔmetraiz] *vt* representar geométricamente.

geometry [dʒi'ɔmitri] *n* MATH geometría *f*; *plane, descriptive, solid geometry* geometría plana, descriptiva, del espacio.

geomorphology [,dʒi:əumɔ:'fɔlədʒi] *n* geomorfología *f*.

geophysical ['dʒi:əu'fizikəl] *adj* geofísico, ca.

geophysicist ['dʒi:əu'fizist] *n* geofísico *m*.

geophysics [dʒi:əu'fiziks] *n* geofísica *f*.

geopolitics [dʒi:əu'pɔlitiks] *n* geopolítica *f*.

Geordie ['dʒɔ:di] *n* FAM nativo, va de Tyneside || dialecto de Tyneside.

George [dʒɔ:dʒ] *pr n* Jorge *m*.

Georgetown ['dʒɔ:dʒtaun] *pr n* GEOGR Georgetown.

Georgia ['dʒɔ:dʒjə] *pr n* GEOGR Georgia *f*.

Georgian ['dʒɔ:dʒjən] *adj/n* georgiano, na.

georgic ['dʒɔ:dʒik] *adj* geórgico, ca.
◆ *pl n* geórgicas *f* (poem by Virgil).

geosyncline [,dʒi:əu'sinklain] *n* GEOL geosinclinal *m*.

Gerald ['dʒerəld] ; **Gerard** ['dʒera:d] *pr n* Gerardo *m* (Christian name).

geranium [dʒi'reinjən] *n* BOT geranio *m*.

gerbil; gerbille ['dʒə:bil] *n* ZOOL gerbo *m*, jerbo *m*.

gerfalcon ['dʒə:,fɔ:lkən] *n* XOOL gerifalte *f* (bird).

geriatrician [,dʒeriə'triʃən] *n* MED geriatra *m* & *f*.

geriatrics [,dʒeri'ætriks] *n* MED geriatría *f*.

germ [dʒə:m] *n* BIOL germen *m* || MED bacilo *m* (bacillus) | microbio *m* (of a disease) | bacteria *f* (bacterium) || FIG germen *m* || — *germ carrier* portador *m* de gérmenes || *germ cell* gameto *m* || *germ killer* germicida *m*, microbicida *m*, bactericida *m* || *germ warfare* guerra bacteriológica.

German ['dʒə:mən] *adj* alemán, ana.
◆ *n* alemán, ana (inhabitant of Germany) || alemán *m* (language).

german ['dʒə:mən] *adj* hermano, na (cousin) || carnal (brother) || FIG relacionado, da.

germane [dʒə:'mein] *adj* FIG relacionado, da.

Germania [dʒə:'meinjə] *pr n* Germania *f*.

Germanic [dʒə:'mænik] *adj* germánico, ca.
◆ *n* germánico *m*.

germanium [dʒə:'meinium] *n* CHEM germanio *m*.

German measles ['dʒə:mən'mi:zlz] *n* MED rubéola *f* (infectious disease).

germanophile [dʒə:'mænəfail] *adj/n* germanófilo, la.

germonophobe [dʒə:'mænəfəub] *adj/n* germanófobo, ba.

German shepherd ['dʒə:mən'ʃepəd] *n* US perro *m* pastor alemán (dog).

German silver ['dʒə:mən'silvə*] *n* MIN alpaca *f*, metal *m* blanco, plata *f* alemana.

Germany ['dʒə:məni] *pr n* GEOGR Alemania *f*.

germicidal [,dʒə:mi'saidl] *adj* germicida, microbicida, bactericida.

germicide ['dʒə:misaid] *n* MED germicida *m*, microbicida *m*, bactericida *m*.

germinal ['dʒə:minl] *adj* germinal || FIG embrionario, ria.

germinate ['dʒə:mineit] *vi* germinar.
◆ *vt* hacer germinar.

germination [,dʒə:mi'neiʃən] *n* germinación *f*.

germinative [,dʒə:mi'neitiv] *adj* germinativo, va.

germ-killing ['dʒə:m'kiliŋ] *adj* bactericida.

gerontocracy [,dʒerən'tɔkrəsi] *n* gerontocracia *f*.

gerontology [,dʒerən'tɔlədʒi] *n* MED gerontología *f*.

gerrymander ['dʒerimændə*] *n* división *f* arbitraria de los distritos electorales para ser favorecido en las elecciones.

gerrymander; jerrymander ['dʒerimændə*] *vt* dividir (los distritos electorales) para sacar ventaja en las elecciones.

gerund ['dʒerənd] *n* GRAMM gerundio *m*.

gerundive [dʒi'rʌndiv] *n* GRAMM gerundio *m*.

gesso ['dʒesəu] *n* yeso *m*.

gest [dʒest] *n* gesta *f*.

Gestapo [ges'ta:pəu] *n* Gestapo *f*.

gestate ['dʒesteit] *vt* gestar (to carry) || FIG concebir, gestar (an idea).

gestation [dʒes'teiʃən] *n* gestación *f*.

gestatorial [,dʒestə'tɔ:riəl] *adj* gestatorio, ria; *gestatorial chair* silla gestatoria.

geste [dʒest] *n* *chanson de geste* cantar *f* de gesta.

gesticulate [dʒes'tikjuleit] *vi* gesticular, hacer ademanes.

gesticulation [dʒes,tikju'leiʃən] *n* gesticulación *f*, ademanes *m pl*, movimientos *m pl*.

gesticulative [dʒes,tikju'leitiv] *adj* gesticulador, ra; gestero, ra.

gesture ['dʒestʃə*] *n* gesto *m*, ademán *m*, movimiento *m*; *he always makes a lot of gestures with his hands* siempre hace muchos gestos con las manos || FIG detalle; *what a nice gesture on your part!* ¡qué buen detalle de tu parte! | muestra *f* (token).

gesture ['dʒestʃə*] *vi* gesticular, hacer gestos *or* ademanes.
◆ *vt* expresar con gestos *or* con ademanes.

gesundheit [gə'zunt,hait] *interj* ¡Jesús! (after sneezing).

get* [get] *vt* obtener, tener; *did you get an answer?* ¿tuviste contestación? || recibir; *I got your letter this morning* recibí tu carta esta mañana || recibir, tener; *he got a lovely present* tuvo un regalo precioso || ir a buscar, traer; *would you get me a cup of tea?* ¿quieres traerme una taza de té? || buscar; *go and get a cup of coffee* vete a buscar una taza de café || llamar (to call); *to get the doctor* llamar al médico || comprar (to buy) || encontrar (to find) || llevarse, ganar; *who has got the prize?* ¿quien se llevó el premio? || llevarse; *he got the worst of it* se llevó la peor parte || lograr, conseguir (to obtain) || conseguir, proporcionar (to provide); *I'll get you a pen* te conseguiré una pluma || ganar (to earn); *he gets two thousand pesetas a week* gana dos mil pesetas por semana || dar (to hit); *the bullet got him in the arm* la bala le dio en el brazo || recibir (to suffer); *he got a bump on the head* recibió un porrazo en la cabeza || coger [AMER agarrar] (to catch); *the police got the thief* la policía cogió al ladrón; *she got the measles* cogió el sarampión || coger (to reproduce); *the artist got the expression well* el artista cogió bien la expresión || sacar (to extract); *to get aluminium from bauxite* sacar aluminio de la bauxita || obtener, caerle a uno, echarle a uno; *he got twenty years for murder* le echaron veinte años por asesinato || marcar (points) || sacar (profit) || llevar (to bring); *he got it to my house* lo llevó a mi casa || mandar (to send) || hacer, preparar (to prepare); *I'm going to get breakfast* voy a preparar el desayuno || convencer (to persuade); *can you get him to come?* ¿puedes convencerle de que venga? || conseguir; *we got him to talk on this subject* conseguimos que hablara de este tema || poner; *he gets me angry* me pone furioso || FAM llegar a comprender (to understand); *I don't get it* no llego a comprenderlo | oír (to hear) | matar (to kill) | poner nervioso (to irritate) | conmover (to move) | chiflar; *his paintings get me* sus cuadros me chiflan || hablar con; *he couldn't get you by phone* no pudo hablar con usted por teléfono || RAD captar, sintonizar con || US FAM ver (to see) | poner en un aprieto (to put in a fix) || — *adding two and three you get five* dos y tres son cinco || *can I get you a drink?* ¿quiere tomar algo? || *could you get me Madrid on the phone?* ¿me puede poner con Madrid? || FAM *I'll get you one day!* ¡ya me las pagarás! || *I've got Madrid on the phone* tengo Madrid al teléfono || *she got her man* encontró al hombre de su vida || FAM *that's got me* no tengo ni idea || *to get a bad name* adquirir mala fama || *to get a wife* casarse || *to get going* poner en marcha || FAM *to get in bad* darle a uno fuerte (disease, love) | *to get in hot* tener una bronca || FIG *to get one's back up* picarse (to become annoyed) || US REL *to get religion* convertirse || *to get some sleep* dormir un poco || *to get s.o. on to a subject* conseguir que alguien hable de un tema || *to get sth. by heart* aprender algo de memoria || *to get sth. done* mandar hacer algo (by s.o. else), conseguir hacer *or* terminar algo (o.s.) || *to get things done* conseguir que se hagan las cosas || *to get with child* dejar embarazada || *to have got* tener; *I haven't got any money* no tengo dinero || *to have got to* tener que; *she has got to go there* tiene que ir allí || FAM *what's got you?* ¿qué te pasa?, ¿qué mosca te ha picado? || *what's that got to do with it?* ¿qué tiene eso que ver? || FAM *you'll get it from your father!* ¡tu padre te va a echar una bronca! || *you must get your hair cut* tienes que hacerte cortar el pelo, tienes que cortarte el pelo || FAM *you've got me there* ya me has cogido.
◆ *vi* ponerse (to become); *he got better* se puso mejor || llegar; *I got there at two o'clock* llegué allí a las dos || ir (to go) || FAM irse (to leave) || — FAM *get going!* ¡muévete! || *how far have you got?* ¿hasta dónde has llegado? || FIG *to get above o.s.* subírsele a uno los humos || *to get doing sth.* ponerse a *or* empezar a hacer algo (see OBSERV II) || *to get dressed* vestirse || *to get married* casarse || *to get shaved* afeitarse || FIG *to get somewhere* abrirse camino (to make one's way), progresar (to progress), sacar algo en claro (to clarify sth.) || *to get used to* acostumbrarse a || *to get used to it* acostumbrarse.
◆ *phr v* **to get about** desplazarse; *he couldn't get about because of his broken leg* no podía desplazarse con la pierna rota | difundirse, propalarse; *rumours quickly get about* los rumores se difunden rápidamente | viajar mucho, ir a muchos sitios (to travel) | levantarse y salir (after sickness) || **to get across** atravesar, cruzar; *to get across the road* cruzar la carretera | hacer comprender; *I can't get across to you what I mean* no puedo hacerte comprender lo que quiero decir | ser comprendido (to be understood) | ser apreciado; *the singer got across to the audience* el cantante fue apreciado por el público || **to get after** perseguir; *the police got after the burglars* la policía persiguió a los ladrones || **to get ahead** progresar, salir adelante; *he will get ahead in the company* progresará en la empresa || **to get along** hacer progresos, progresar (to progress) | encontrarse mejor, mejorar; *the patient is getting along* el enfermo está mejorando | ir; *how are you getting along with your work?* ¿cómo le va el trabajo? | llevarse bien; *we get along together* nos llevamos bien | ir tirando; *we are not rich but we get along* no somos ricos pero vamos tirando | arreglárselas; *I'll get along somehow* me las arreglaré de una manera o de otra | marcharse, irse (to leave); *I must be getting along* tengo que marcharme | seguir andando (to go on walking) | hacer venir (to bring s.o.) | llevar; *we got him along to hospital* lo llevamos al hospital || — FAM *get along with you!* ¡déjate de bobadas! | *to get along without* pasar sin, prescindir de | US *to get along with*

sth. seguir, continuar; *get along with your work!* ¡sigue trabajando! || ***to get around*** viajar (to travel) | salir (to go out) | difundirse, propalarse (rumours) | evitar, soslayar (to avoid) | saber manejar (s.o.) || — *to get around to* llegar a || ***to get at*** alcanzar, llegar a (to reach) | entrar en contacto con (to come into contact) | conseguir; *I can't get at my money until the bank opens* no puedo conseguir dinero hasta que abra el banco | estar detrás de (to pester); *my mother is always getting at me* mi madre siempre está detrás mio | reñir (to scold) | meterse con (to tease) | insinuar; *what are you getting at?* ¿qué insinúas? | pretender (to try to obtain) | averiguar, descubrir (the truth) | atacar (to criticize) | estropear (to spoil) | comprar, sobornar (to bribe) || — *to get at the drink* ponerse a beber || ***to get away*** escaparse (to escape) | alejarse; *to get away from the coast* alejarse de la costa | conseguir marcharse (to leave) | irse (to go away) | separar (to separate) | llevar, llevarse (to take away) | quitar; *I got the gun away from him* le quité la pistola | librarse; *he managed to get away from that boring person* consiguió librarse de esa persona pesada | liberar; *to get s.o. away from the hands of the enemy* liberar a alguien de las manos del enemigo | AUT arrancar || — *get away (from here)!* ¡fuera (de aquí)! || *get away with you!* ¡déjate de tonterías! || *to get away with* llevarse (to steal) || *to get away with it* no ser castigado (not to be punished), conseguir hacerlo (to succeed) || *you won't get away with it* ya lo pagarás || ***to get back*** volver a poner (*into* en) | volver, regresar (to return); *he got back home* volvió a su casa | *he didn't get his money back* no le devolvieron el dinero, no recuperó *or* no recobró su dinero | *to get back at* vengarse de, desquitarse con || ***to get behind*** atrasarse; *he got behind in his work* se atrasó en el trabajo | quedarse atrás (to lag behind) | penetrar (to penetrate) | respaldar (to back) | conseguir el apoyo *or* el respaldo de (to get support) || ***to get by*** arreglárselas (to manage); *we are not rich but we get by* no somos ricos pero nos las arreglamos | defenderse; *he can get by in German* se defiende en alemán | burlar la vigilancia de, conseguir pasar inadvertido delante de | conseguir pasar (sth.) || ***to get down*** bajar (to descend) | deprimir (to depress) | desanimar (to discourage) | escribir, poner por escrito (to write) | apuntar; *I'll get your name down on my list* apuntaré su nombre en mi lista | tragarse; *I couldn't get my steak down* no pude tragarme el filete | *to get down on one's knees* arrodillarse | *to get down to* ponerse a; *to get down to work* ponerse a trabajar; abordar (a problem) | *to get down to the facts* ir al grano || ***to get in*** entrar | llegar; *the train got in at ten o'clock* el tren llegó a las diez | montar en (a car) | volver, regresar (to come back) | ser elegido (to be elected) | recibir (to receive) | recoger (crops, etc.) | recaudar (taxes) | cobrar (debts) | decir (word) | asestar (blow) || — FAM *I could hardly get a word in edgeways* no pude meter baza | *to get in the habit of* coger la costumbre de, acostumbrarse a | *to get in with* trabar amistad con || ***to get into*** entrar en (a place) | subir, montarse en (to board); *I got into the train* subí al tren | ponerse (to put on); *he got into his pyjamas* se puso el pijama | meterse en; *he got into bed* se metió en la cama | poner en; *to get the key into the lock* poner la llave en la cerradura || — *I can't get it into your head* no puedo metértelo en la cabeza || *to get into a rage* ponerse furioso || *to get into bad habits* adquirir malas costumbres || *to get into trouble* meterse en un lío || FAM *what's got into you?* ¿qué mosca te ha picado? || ***to get off*** apearse de, bajarse de, bajar de; *I got off the bus* me apeé del autobús; *I got off my horse* me bajé del caballo | escapar; *he got off with a light sentence* escapó con una sentencia poco severa | marcharse (to go away) | arrancar (a car) | salir (train) | despegar (aircraft) | librarse de (a duty) | librarse; *to get off with a fine* librarse con una multa | quitar (a stain) | quitarse (clothes); *she can't get her dress off* no puede quitarse el vestido | despachar (work) | mandar (a letter) | soltar (a remark) | JUR hacer absolver | FAM sacar de apuro (to get s.o. out of a jam) || — FAM *get off!* ¡suelta! || *to get off lightly* salir bien parado || *to get off one's chair* levantarse || *to get off to sleep* dormir, conciliar el sueño || FAM *to get off with* ligar con || FIG *to tell s.o. where to get off* cantarle a uno las verdades del barquero || ***to get on*** subir a, subirse a, montarse en; *I got on the train* subí al tren | ponerse en; *the cat got on my lap* el gato se puso en mi regazo | desenvolverse; *he is getting on well at school* se desenvuelve bien en el colegio | hacer progresos, progresar (to make progress) | medrar (to succeed); *Mary has got on in life* María ha medrado en la vida | llevarse bien; *we get on together* nos llevamos bien | envejecer (to grow old) | hacerse tarde; *what time is it? it's getting on* ¿qué hora es? se está haciendo tarde | ponerse (clothes) | irse (to go); *I must be getting on now* me tengo que ir ahora || — *get on with it* ponte a hacerlo || *he is getting on for sixty* está rondando los sesenta || *how are you getting on?* ¿qué tal está?, ¿cómo le va? || *I can't get on with Latin* no me entra el latín || *it's getting on for six o'clock* son cerca de las seis || *to be always getting on at s.o. to do sth.* estar siempre detrás de uno para que haga algo || *to get on at s.o. about sth.* meterse con alguien acerca de algo || FAM *to get on s.o.'s nerves* crisparle los nervios a uno || *to get on to* localizar; *how did the police get on to that thief?* ¿cómo localizó la policía a ese ladrón?; llegar hasta; *how did we get on to that subject?* ¿cómo hemos llegado a este tema?; descubrir; *to get on to the trick* descubrir el truco; conseguir hablar con (to speak to), encargarse de; *I'll get on to that for you* me encargaré de ello para Ud. || *to get on with one's work* seguir trabajando || ***to get out*** salir (to exit) | escaparse (to escape) | bajarse, bajar (of a train) | sacar (to take out) | quitar (a stain) | publicar, sacar (a book) | resolver (a problem) | pronunciar (words) | sacar (a car, a boat) | hacer (a list) | trazar (plans) | difundirse (news) | hacerse público (secret) | FIG sacar; *what do you get out of this?* ¿qué sacas de esto? || — FAM *get out!* ¡fuera! | *to get out of* librarse de; *he got out of military service* se libró del servicio militar; perder; *you must get out of this bad habit* tienes que perder esta mala costumbre; quitar; *I must gēt you out of this bad habit* tengo que quitarte esta mala costumbre; sacar; *to get a secret, money out of s.o.* sacarle a uno un secreto, dinero; salir; *to get out of trouble* salir de un apuro; sacar; *I got him out of trouble* le saqué de apuro || SP *to get s.o. out* sacar a un bateador del campo (in cricket) || ***to get over*** cruzar; *I got over the river* crucé el río | recorrer (a distance) | pasar por encima; *to get over a fence* pasar por encima de una valla | superar, salvar; *to get over an obstacle* salvar un obstáculo | pasar por alto (to overlook) | vencer (a difficulty) | sobreponerse (to recover from a loss, a grief) | reponerse (an illness, a fright) | perder (a bad habit) | olvidar (to forget) | hacer comprender (to make understood) | ser apreciado (a play, etc.) | acabar con, sacarse de encima; *we must get it over before Friday* tenemos que acabar con esto antes del viernes || — *let's get it over* acabemos de una vez || *they got over with the meeting* acabaron de una vez por todas con la reunión || ***to get round*** dar la vuelta a | soslayar (difficulty, law) | persuadir (to convince) || — *to get round the world* dar la vuelta al mundo || *to get round to* llegar a || ***to get through*** (conseguir) pasar por | acabar con, terminar (to finish) | hacer (to do) | aprobar; *to get through an exam* aprobar un examen | conseguir que apruebe; *he got all his pupils through* consiguió que aprobaran todos sus alumnos | conseguir comunicar; *I got through to Madrid yesterday* conseguí comunicar con Madrid ayer | abrirse paso; *the troops got through to the besieged town* las tropas se abrieron paso hasta la ciudad sitiada | llegar; *at the end the news got through to him* al final le llegó la noticia | meter en la cabeza, hacer comprender (to make understood); *I can't get through to you that smoking is dangerous* no puedo meterte en la cabeza que el tabaco es peligroso | JUR hacer aprobar; ser aprobado (a bill) | FAM gastarse; *I got through a hundred pounds in two days* me gasté cien libras en dos días || — *to get through the day* pasar el día || ***to get to*** llegar a (to succeed in) | aprender a; *to get to do sth.* aprender a hacer algo || — *to get to work* ponerse a trabajar || ***to get together*** reunir | reunirse (to assemble) | ponerse de acuerdo (to agree) || ***to get under*** ponerse debajo de || — *to get under way* ponerse en camino (to set out), avanzar, progresar (to progress), zarpar (ship) || ***to get up*** levantarse; *I got up late this morning* me levanté tarde esta mañana | levantarse, ponerse de pie (to stand up) | levantar; *I have to get my husband up for work* tengo que levantar a mi marido para que vaya a trabajar | subirse, trepar (to climb) | subir; *to get up a slope* subir una cuesta | levantar (to lift) | subir (to take up) | desencadenarse (a storm) | levantarse (wind) | embravecerse (sea) | organizar (a party) | montar (a play) | tramar (a plot) | forjar, fraguar (a story) | preparar (lecture) | estudiar (to make a special study of) | repasar (to learn again) | COMM presentar (goods) | disfrazar (to disguise) | acicalarse (to dress up) || — *to get o.s. up* vestirse de, disfrazarse de; *he got himself up as a sailor* se vistió de marinero; maquillarse (to make up) || *to get up speed* acelerar || *to get up to* llegar a *or* hasta (to reach), hacer (to do) || *to get up to mischief* hacer de las suyas.

— OBSERV El verbo *to get* tiene el pretérito y el participio pasivo irregulares, ***got***. Además de éste, en Estados Unidos se usa también la forma ***gotten*** para el participio pasivo.

— OBSERV Cuando el verbo *to get* va seguido por un gerundio se traduce por *ponerse a* o *empezar a*: *once he gets speaking you can't stop him* cuando se pone a hablar, no hay quien lo pare.

— OBSERV En muchos casos, cuando el verbo *to get* antecede un adjetivo o un participio pasivo, se traduce al castellano por un simple verbo: *to get old* envejecer; *to get drunk* emborracharse; *to get fat* engordar; *to get killed* matarse; *to get one's hands dirty* ensuciarse las manos.

— OBSERV In some Latin-American countries the word *coger* is not in decent use. It is substituted therefore by *agarrar*.

get-at-able [-ætəbl] *adj* accesible.

getaway [-əweil] *n* huida *f*, fuga *f* (escape) || SP salida *f* (start) | escapada *f* (breakaway) || AUT arranque *m*.

Gethsemane [geθ'semənі] *pr n* Getsemaní.

get-together ['get'tə'geðə*] *n* reunión *f* (meeting) || fiesta *f* [sin cumplidos] (informal party).

getup [-ʌp] *n* FAM vestimenta *f*, atavío *m* (a style of dressing) | disfraz *m* (fancy dress) | maquillaje *m* (makeup) || presentación *f* (of a publication) || US energía *f*.

get-up-and-go [-əndgəu] *n* FAM empuje *m*.

get-well card ['getwelkɑ:d] *n* tarjeta *f* enviada a un enfermo deseándole una pronta mejoría.

gewgaw ['gju:gɔ:] *n* chuchería *f*, fruslería *f*.

geyser ['gaizə*] *n* géiser *m* (a hot spring) || calentador *m* de agua (water heater).

Ghana ['gɑ:nə] *pr n* GEOGR Ghana.

Ghanaian [gɑ:'neiən] *adj/n* ghanés, esa.

ghastliness ['gɑːstlinis] *n* aspecto *m* siniestro || palidez *f* cadavérica (pallor).

ghastly ['gɑːstli] *adj* horroroso, sa (gruesome) || cadavérico, ca; *a ghastly pallor* una palidez cadavérica || pálido, da; mortecino, na (light) || FAM espantoso, sa.
◆ *adv* terriblemente, horriblemente.

ghee [giː] *n* mantequilla *f* clarificada de búfalo *or* de vaca.

Ghent [gent] *pr n* GEOGR Gante.

gherkin ['gəːkin] *n* pepinillo *m*.

ghetto ['getəu] *n* judería *f*, ghetto *m* (jewish quarter) || ghetto *m* (where members of a minority live).

ghetto blaster [-ˌblɑːstə*] *n* FAM radio *f* portátil de gran potencia.

ghost [gəust] *n* fantasma *m*, aparecido *m*, espectro *m*; *this castle has ghosts* este castillo tiene fantasmas || imagen *f* fantasmas (in optics) || — *not the ghost of a chance* ni la más remota posibilidad || *the Holy Ghost* el Espíritu Santo || *to give up the ghost* entregar el alma, exhalar el último suspiro.

ghost [gəust] *vt* escribir (un libro) para otro || rondar por (to haunt).
◆ *vi* hacer de negro (to write for another).

ghostly [-li] *adj* fantasmal, espectral (like a ghost) || (ant) espiritual (spiritual).

ghostwrite ['gəustrɑit] *vt* escribir un libro para otro.
◆ *vi* hacer de negro (to write for another).

ghost-writer [-ˌraitə*] *n* negro *m*.

ghoul [guːl] *n* espíritu *m* necrófago (a corpsedevouring spirit) || FAM persona *f* macabra || profanador *m* de cementerios.

ghoulish [-iʃ] *adj* macabro, bra.

giant ['dʒaiənt] *n* gigante *m*.
◆ *adj* gigantesco, ca; gigante.

giantess ['dʒaiəntis] *n* giganta *f*.

gib [dʒib] *n* TECH chaveta *f*.

gibb [dʒib] *vt* MAR ⟶ **jib.**

gibber ['dʒibə*] *vi* farfullar.

gibberish ['dʒibəriʃ] *n* galimatías *m*, jerigonza *f*.

gibbet ['dʒibit] *n* horca *f*.

gibbet ['dʒibit] *vt* ahorcar || FIG poner en la picota.

gibbon ['gibən] *n* gibón *m* (monkey).

gibbosity [gi'bɔsiti] *n* gibosidad *f*.

gibbous ['gibəs] *adj* giboso, sa; gibado, da (humpbacked).

gibe; jibe [dʒaib] *n* mofa *f*, sarcasmo *m*.

gibe [dʒaib] *vt* mofarse de, burlarse de.
◆ *vi* burlarse, mofarse (to scoff).

giblets ['dʒiblets] *pl n* menudillos *m*.

Gibraltar [dʒi'brɔːltə*] *pr n* GEOGR Gibraltar; *the Rock, the Straits of Gibraltar* el peñón, el estrecho de Gibraltar.

Gibraltarian [ˌdʒibrɔːl'tɛəriən] *n* gibraltareño, ña.

gid [gid] *n* VET modorra *f*.

giddiness ['gidinis] *n* mareo *m*, vértigo *m* (dizziness).

giddy ['gidi] *adj* mareado, da (dizzy); *I feel giddy* estoy mareado || que da vértigo, vertiginoso, sa (which produces dizziness) || FIG frívolo, la; ligero, ra; atolondrado (frivolous).

gift [gift] *n* regalo *m*, obsequio *m* (a present) || JUR donación *f*; *deed of gift* donación entre vivos || don *m* (natural talent); *gift of tongues* don de lenguas || dote *f* (of an artist) || REL ofrenda *f* || COMM prima *f* || — FIG *it's a gift!* ¡está tirado!, ¡es muy fácil! | *to be in the gift of* estar en manos de || *to have the gift of the gab* tener mucha labia || *you would not have it as gift* no lo querrías ni regalado.

gift [gift] *vt* dotar (to endow with natural talent) || regalar, obsequiar (to bestow as a gift).

gifted ['giftid] *adj* dotado, da (endowed by nature) || talentudo, da; talentoso, sa (talented).

gift token ['giftˌtəukən]; **gift voucher** ['giftˌvɑutʃə*] *n* vale *m* para comprar un regalo.

gift-wrapped ['giftræpt] *adj* envuelto, ta para regalo.

gig [gig] *n* canoa *f* (a light boat) || arpón *m* (a fish spear) || calesa *f* (a two-wheeled carriage) || US sedal *m* con varios anzuelos (for fishing) | actuación *f* (a performance) | castigo *m* (in school).

gigantic [dʒai'gæntik] *adj* gigantesco, ca.

giggle ['gigl] *n* risita *f* || *the giggles* la risa tonta.

giggle ['gigl] *vi* reírse tontamente.

giggly ['gigli] *adj* propenso a reírse.

gigolo ['ʒigələu] *n* «gigolo» *m*, chulo *m*.

gild [gild] *n* ⟶ **guild.**

gild [gild] *vt* dorar (to make golden) || dar brillo a (to make attractive) || FIG *to gild the pill* dorar la píldora.

gilded [-id]; **gilt** [gilt] dorado, da.

gildhall ['gildhɔːl] *n* ⟶ **guildhall.**

gilder [-ə*] *n* dorador, ra.

gilding ['gildiŋ] *n* dorado *m*, doradura *f* || FIG oropel *m*.

gill [gil] *n*. branquia *f*, agalla *f* (of fish) || papada *f* (of birds, animals) || laminilla *f* (of plants) || barranco *m* (a ravine) || TECH aleta *f* || FIG *to look green about the gills* tener mala cara.

gill [dʒil] *n* medida *f* de líquidos (one quarter of a pint).

gill [gil] *vt* limpiar (to gut a fish) || atrapar por las agallas (to catch by the gills).

gillie ['gili] *n* ayudante *m*.

gillyflower ['dʒiliˌflauə*] *n* (ant) BOT alhelí *m*.

gilt [gilt] *n* dorado *m* (gilding) || FIG oropel *m*, brillo *m* superficial (superficial glitter) || FAM parné *m*, pasta *f*, plata *f* (money) || cerda *f* joven (young sow).
◆ *adj* ⟶ **gilded.**

gilt-edged ['giltedʒd] *adj* con cantos dorados || *gild-edged securities* valores *m pl or* títulos *m pl* de máxima garantía.

gilthead ['gilthed] *n* dorada *f* (fish).

gimbals ['dʒimbəlz] *pl n* MAR suspensión *f sing* de cardán.

gimcrack ['dʒimkræk] *n* baratija *f*, fruslería *f*.
◆ *adj* de lance (furniture) || de bisutería (jewel).

gimlet ['gimlit] *n* TECH barrera *f* de mano.

gimlet ['gimlit] *vt* barrenar.

gimlet eye [-ai] *n* mirada *f* penetrante.

gimmick ['gimik] *n* FAM artefacto *m*, artilugio *m* (a gadget) | truco *m* (trick).

gimp [gimp] *n* galón *m*.

gin [dʒin] *n* ginebra *f* (drink) || «gin rummy» *m* (card game) || cabria *f* (a tripod hoist) || trampa *f* (a snare) || TECH desmotadora *f* (for removing seeds from fibres) || *gin fizz* «gin fizz» *m* (drink).

gin [dʒin] *vt* atrapar (to catch animals) || desmotar (to clean fibres).

ginger ['dʒindʒə*] *n* BOT jengibre *m* || FIG & FAM garra *f*; *a book that lacks ginger* un libro al que le falta garra || color *m* rojizo (reddish-yellow colour).
◆ *adj* rojizo, za.

ginger ['dʒindʒə*] *vt* echar jengibre a (to add ginger to) || FAM animar (to liven up).

ginger ale [-'eil]; **ginger beer** [-'biə*] *n* «ginger ale» *m*, gaseosa *f* de jengibre.

gingerbread [-bred] *n* pan *m* de jengibre || FIG *gingerbread work* decoración recargada y de mal gusto, decoración cursi.

ginger group [-gruːp] *n* grupo *m* de presión.

gingerly [-li] *adj* cauteloso, sa.
◆ *adv* cautelosamente.

ginger nut [-nʌt]; **gingersnap** ['dʒindʒəsˌnæp] *n* galleta *f* de jengibre.

gingery ['dʒindʒəri] *adj* rojizo, za (reddish-yellow coloured) || que sabe a jengibre (having the taste of ginger) || FIG vivo, va (high-spirited) | agudo, da; punzante (remark, etc.) | picante (spicy).

gingham ['giŋəm] *n* guinga *f*, guingán *m* (fabric).

gingival [dʒin'dʒaivəl] *n* MED gingivitis *f*.

ginner ['dʒinə*] *n* desmotador, ra.

gin rummy ['dʒin'rʌmi] *n* «gin rummy» *m*.

ginseng ['dʒinseŋ] *n* BOT gingseng *m*, ginsén *m*.

Gioconda [dʒɔ'kɔndə] *pr n* ARTS Gioconda *f*.

gipsy ['dʒipsi] *adj/n* gitano, na (in Western Europe) || zíngaro, ra (in Central Europe).

gipsy moth [-mɔθ] *n* ZOOL lagarta *f*.

giraffe [dʒi'rɑːf] *n* ZOOL jirafa *f*.

girandole ['dʒirəndəul] *n* candelabro *m* (a candle holder) || pendiente *m* (an earring) || girándula *f* (a rotating water jet of firework).

girasol; girasole ['dʒirəˌsɔl] *n* BOT girasol *m*.

gird* [gəːd] *vt* ceñir (to fasten with a belt); *he girded his sword* ciñó la espada || rodear (to surround) || FIG investir || *to gird o.s. for the battle* prepararse para la lucha.
— OBSERV Pret y pp ***girded, girt.***

girder ['gəːdə*] *n* viga *f*.

girdle ['gəːdl] *n* faja *f* (sash, woman's undergarment) || arista *f* (of a gem) || cinturón *m* (a belt) || FIG cinturón *m*.

girdle ['gəːdl] *vt* ceñir (to bind) || rodear (to encircle).

girl [gəːl] *n* chica *f*, muchacha *f* || niña *f* (small child) || chica *f*, joven *f* (a young unmarried woman) || FAM chica *f* || muchacha *f* (a servant) || novia *f* (a sweetheart) || alumna *f* (of a school) || *girl Friday* secretaria *f* para todo.

girl friend [-frend] *n* novia *f*, amiga *f*, amiguita *f* (of a boy) || amiga *f* (of a girl).

girlhood [-hud] *n* juventud *f*, niñez *f*.

girlie magazine [-limægəˈziːn] *n* FAM revista *f* de destape.

girlish [-liʃ] *adj* de niña (of a girl) || afeminado, da (effeminate).

girl scout [-skaut] *n* exploradora *f*.

giro ['dʒairəu] *n* sistema *m* de transferencia bancaria || *giro cheque* cheque *m* postal de subsidio social (for unemployment).

Gironde [ʒiːr˜ɔd] *pr n* GEOGR Gironda *f*.

Girondist [dʒi'r˜ɔndist] *adj/n* HIST girondino, na.

girt [gəːt] *pret/pp* ⟶ **gird.**

girth [gəːθ] *n* cincha *f* (strap for securing a pack) || circunferencia *f* (circumference) || gordura *f* (stoutness) || dimensiones *f pl* (dimensions).

gist [dʒist] *n* esencia *f*, quid *m*, fondo *m*, lo esencial (heart of the matter) || JUR motivo *m* principal.

give [giv] *n* elasticidad *f*.

give* [giv] *vt* dar; *give me the book* dame el libro; *I give you twenty francs for that* te doy veinte francos por eso; *he gave a start* dio un salto; *they gave a cry of delight* dieron un grito de alegría; *he gave a sigh* dio un suspiro; *she*

gave signs of life dio señales de vida; *I'd give my life for you* daría mi vida por ti; *I would give my eyetooth to go* daría un ojo de la cara por ir; *I give you my word* te doy mi palabra; *I'm going to give a lecture* voy a dar una conferencia; *they will give a show tomorrow* darán una función mañana ‖ regalar, dar (to offer as a present); *I had this book given to me* me dieron este libro ‖ proveer de (to provide with) ‖ pasar, dar (to hand over) ‖ entregar (to deliver) ‖ indicar (pressure, etc.) ‖ hacer (a gesture) ‖ conceder, dar (to grant); *God has given me what I prayed for* Dios me ha concedido lo que le pedí ‖ administrar, dar (the sacraments) ‖ conceder; *I'll give you that* te concedo eso ‖ ceder; *to give ground to the enemy* ceder terreno al enemigo ‖ imponer (to inflict) ‖ dar, poner; *she was given a pretty name* le han puesto un nombre bonito ‖ contagiar; *I gave you a cold* te contagié el resfriado ‖ pronunciar (a speech) ‖ decir, venir con; *don't give me that* no me vengas con eso ‖ comunicar; *please, give us your decision* comuníquenos su decisión, por favor ‖ MED poner (to administer) ‖ JUR pronunciar; *to give a sentence* pronunciar un fallo | condenar a, dar (punishment) ‖ dejar (to leave); *he gave money for the poor when he died* dejó dinero para los pobres cuando murió ‖ dejar (to lend); *give me your watch* déjame el reloj ‖ dedicar (to devote) ‖ poner con (on the phone); *give me the police* póngame con la policía ‖ COMM & BOT dar ‖ brindar por; *I give you the mayor* brindo por el alcalde ‖ — FIG *give him an inch and he'll take a yard* dale la mano y te cogerá el brazo ‖ *give him my compliments* salúdele respetuosamente de mi parte ‖ *give him my love* dale recuerdos ‖ *«give way»* «ceda el paso» ‖ *he was given to believe that...* le hicieron creer que... ‖ *how long do you give your diet?* ¿cuánto tiempo crees que va a durar tu régimen? ‖ FAM *I don't give a damn!* ¡no me importa un bledo!, ¡no me importa un comino! ‖ *I gave fifty pounds for my car* el coche me costó cincuenta libras ‖ FIG *I gave him what for* le di su merecido ‖ FAM *I'll give it to you!* ¡te vas a enterar! | *I'll give you ball if I catch you!* ¡ya te voy a dar yo pelota si te cojo! ‖ *to be much given to* ser muy aficionado a, gustarle mucho a, ser muy dado a ‖ *to give a laugh* soltar la risa ‖ *to give (an account) of* dar cuenta de ‖ *to give a recitation* recitar un poema ‖ *to give a smile to* sonreír a ‖ *to give a thought to* acordarse de, recordar ‖ *to give attention to* prestar atención a ‖ *to give birth to* dar a luz (to a child), dar origen a (to cause) ‖ *to give ear, help to* prestar oídos, ayuda a ‖ FAM *to give it to s.o.* echarle una bronca a alguien (to scold), pegarle una buena paliza a alguien (to beat) ‖ *to give mouth to* expresar ‖ *to give notice of* avisar de ‖ *to give notice to* despedir (an employee), despedirse (one's master), presentar la dimisión (one's employer) ‖ *to give o.s. airs* darse aires ‖ *to give o.s. one hour for* necesitar una hora para | *to give o.s. to* dedicarse a, entregarse a ‖ *to give rise to* causar, ocasionar ‖ *to give s.o. a glance* echarle una mirada a alguien ‖ *to give s.o. a hand* echarle una mano a uno ‖ *to give s.o. a lift* llevar a alguien en coche ‖ *to give s.o. a song* cantar para alguien ‖ *to give s.o. notice* despedir a uno (to dismiss) ‖ *to give s.o. to understand that...* dar a entender a alguien que... ‖ *to give sth. into s.o.'s hands* entregar algo a alguien ‖ *to give sth. to eat* dar algo de comer | *to give two weeks notice* avisar con dos semanas de anticipación ‖ *two and two gives four* dos y dos son cuatro.
◆ *vi* hacer regalos; *he enjoys giving at Christmas* le gusta hacer regalos por Navidades ‖ ceder (to yield to pressure) ‖ dar de sí (to stretch) ‖ — *to feel one's legs give beneath one* flaquearle las piernas a uno ‖ FIG *to give as good as one gets* pagar con la misma moneda ‖ *to give and take* hacer concesiones mutuas ‖ *to give on to* dar a ‖ FAM *what gives?* ¿qué pasa?
◆ *phr v* ***to give away*** distribuir, repartir (to distribute) | regalar (a present) | revelar, descubrir (to discover) | entregar (prizes) | deshacerse de (to ged rid of) ‖ — *to give away the bride* llevar la novia al altar ‖ *to give o.s. away* traicionarse ‖ *to give s.o. away* traicionar *or* denunciar a alguien ‖ FIG *to give the show away* descubrir el pastel, revelar un secreto ‖ ***to give back*** devolver ‖ ***to give forth*** divulgar (news) | emitir (a sound) | despedir (smell, gas, etc.) ‖ ***to give in*** darse por vencido, rendirse (to admit defeat) | ceder (to yield) | dar (one's name) | entregar (to hand in); *to give in a document* entregar un documento | *to give in to* ceder ante ‖ ***to give off*** despedir, emitir ‖ ***to give out*** distribuir, repartir (to distribute) | emitir (to emit) | anunciar (to proclaim) | divulgar (to spread) | agotarse (supplies) | acabarse (strength, patience) | sufrir una avería (engine) ‖ — *to give (s.o.) out to be* hacer pasar por ‖ ***to give over*** entregar (to hand over) | dejar de (to stop); *to give over crying* dejar de llorar ‖ — *give over!* ¡basta ya! (stop it) ‖ *to give o.s. over to* abandonarse a ‖ ***to give up*** dejar, abandonar (to abandon) | renunciar a, dimitir de (one's appointment) | dejar (one's business) | vender (one's property) | darse por vencido, rendirse (to admit defeat) | entregar (to hand over) | dejar por imposible (to renounce an impossible task) | ceder (to yield) | desahuciar (a sick person) | dejar de; *I gave up smoking* dejé de fumar ‖ — *to give it up* darse por vencido ‖ *to give o.s. up* entregarse ‖ *to give o.s. up to* entregarse a (vice), dedicarse a (study) ‖ *to give s.o. up* dejar a alguien, acabar con alguien ‖ *to give s.o. up for lost, for dead* dar a alguien por perdido, por muerto ‖ *to give up one's seat to s.o.* ceder el asiento a alguien ‖ *to give up the crown* renunciar a la corona ‖ *to give up on* dejar por imposible, desistir (to abandon an impossible task).
— OBSERV Pret ***gave***; pp ***given***.

give-and-take ['givən'teik] *n* toma y daca *m*, concesiones *f pl* mutuas.

giveaway ['givəwei] *n* revelación *f* involuntaria (indiscrete disclosure) ‖ FAM examen *m* tirado (easy examination) ‖ ganapierde *m* (in draughts) ‖ US regalo *m*, obsequio *m* (free gift) | FAM concurso *m* radiofónico ‖ *giveaway price* precio de saldo.

given [givn] *pp* ⟶ **give.**
◆ *adj* fijado, da; dado, da (fixed) ‖ dado, da; *he is much given to* es muy dado a; *given my strength* dada mi fuerza ‖ determinado, da (determined); *in a given moment* en un momento determinado ‖ MATH dado, da ‖ — *any given* cualquier; *at any given moment* en cualquier momento ‖ US *given name* nombre *m* de pila ‖ *she is given that way!* ¡ella es así!

giver ['givə*] *n* donador, ra; donante *m* & *f*.

giving ['giviŋ] *n* don *m* (gift) ‖ — *giving away* reparto *m*, distribución *f* (of prizes), denuncia *f* (of s.o.) ‖ *giving back* devolución *f*, restitución *f* ‖ *giving forth* publicación *f* (of news), emisión *f* (of sound) ‖ *giving in* entrega *f* ‖ *giving up* abandono *m*.

gizzard [gizəd] *n* molleja *f* (of a bird) ‖ FIG & FAM *that sticks in my gizzard* no puedo tragar eso.

glabrous ['gleibrəs] *adj* lampiño, ña; glabro, bra (face) ‖ BOT liso, sa.

glacé [glæ'sei] *adj* escarchado, da (covered with sugar) ‖ helado, da (frozen) ‖ glaseado, da (glossy).

glacial ['gleiʃəl] *adj* glacial; *glacial period* período glacial; *glacial zones* zonas glaciales; *glacial wind* viento glacial ‖ glaciar; *glacial deposits* depósitos glaciares.

glaciation [glæsi'eiʃən] *n* glaciación *f*.

glacier ['glæsjə*] *n* GEOL glaciar *m*, ventisquero *m* [AMER helero *m*].

glaciology [glæ'sjɔlədʒi] *n* GEOL glaciología *f*.

glacis ['gleisis] *n* glacis *m*, explanada *f*.
— OBSERV El plural de la palabra inglesa es *glacis* o *glacises*.

glad [glæd] *adj* contento, ta; alegre (pleased) ‖ feliz (happy) ‖ agradable, bueno, na (giving pleasure) ‖ — US *glad hand* saludo afectuoso ‖ *to be glad* alegrarse; *I am glad to see you* me alegro de verte ‖ *to be very glad to help s.o.* tener mucho gusto en ayudar a alguien ‖ FAM *to give s.o. the glad eye* echar miradas cariñosas a alguien.

gladden ['glædn] *vt* alegrar.

glade [gleid] *n* claro *m* (in a wood).

gladiator ['glædieitə*] *n* gladiador *m*.

gladiolus [glædi'əuləs] *n* BOT gladiolo *m*, gladiolo *m* (flower).
— OBSERV El plural de gladiolus es *gladioli, gladiolus* o *gladioluses*.

gladly ['glædli] *adv* alegremente ‖ con mucho gusto (willingly).

gladness ['glædnis] *n* alegría *f*.

gladsome ['glædsəm] *adj* alegre, contento, ta.

Gladstone bag ['glædstənbæg] *n* maletín *m*.

glair [glɛə*] *n* clara *f* de huevo.

glamor ['glæmə*] *n* US encanto *m*, atractivo *m*.

glamorize ['glæməraiz] *vt* adornar ‖ embellecer.

glamorous ['glæmərəs] *adj* encantador, ra; atractivo, va.

glamour ['glæmə*] *n* encanto *m* ‖ *glamour girl* muchacha atractiva, guapa *f*.

glance [glɑːns] *n* mirada *f*, ojeada *f*, vistazo *m* (look) ‖ destello *m* (of light) ‖ MIN mineral *m* lustroso ‖ desviación *f* (deflection) ‖ SP golpe *m* con efecto (in cricket) ‖ — *at a glance* de un vistazo ‖ *at first glance* a primera vista.

glance [glɑːns] *vt* golpear con efecto (in cricket) ‖ *to glance one's eye over* echar una mirada a.
◆ *vi* echar una mirada *or* una ojeada *or* un vistazo (*at* a) (to have a look at) ‖ brillar (to shine) ‖ botar con efecto (to bounce at an angle) ‖ — *to glance aside* apartar la vista ‖ *to glance off* tocar, tratar por encima (a subject), rebotar (a bullet) ‖ *to glance over* mirar por encima, echar un vistazo a ‖ *to glance over a problem* tratar un problema por encima.

glancing [-iŋ] *adj* obliguo, cua ‖ indirecto, ta.

gland [glænd] *n* ANAT & BOT glándula *f*; *lachrymal gland* glándula lagrimal ‖ TECH casquillo *m* (of a stuffing box).

glanders ['glændəz] *pl n* VET muermo *m sing*.

glandular ['glændjulə*] *adj* glandular ‖ MED *glandular fever* mononucleosis *f inv* infecciosa.

glandulous ['glændjuləs] *adj* glanduloso, sa.

glans [glænz] *n* ANAT bálano *m*, glande *m* (of the penis) | glande *m* clitoridiano (of the clitoris).
— OBSERV El plural de *glans* es *glandes*.

glare [glɛə*] *n* luz *f* deslumbrante (strong light) ‖ deslumbramiento *m* (dazzle) ‖ mirada *f* feroz *or* airada (fierce look) ‖ colorido *m* chillón (flashiness) ‖ ostentación *f* (boasting).

glare [glɛə*] *vi* relumbrar, brillar (to shine) ‖ deslumbrar (to dazzle) ‖ mirar airadamente (to stare fiercely) ‖ saltar a la vista (to be too evident).

glaring [-riŋ] *adj* deslumbrante; deslumbrador, ra (dazzling) ‖ resplandeciente, brillante (bright) ‖ chillón, ona (flashy) ‖ evidente, manifiesto, ta (conspicuous) || airado, da; feroz (fierce).

Glasgow ['glɑːzgəu] *pr n* GEOGR Glasgow.

glass [glɑːs] *n* vidrio *m* (substance) || vaso *m* (drinking vessel) || copa *f* (drinking vessel with stem) || espejo *m* (mirror) || cristal *m* (protective covering) || lente *f* (lens) || reloj *m* de arena (hourglass) || cristalería *f* (glassware) || cristal *m* (pane) || cristal *m* (of a picture, watch) || barómetro *m* (barometer) || catalejo *m* (telescope) || invernadero *m* (greenhouse) || escaparate *m* (of a shop).
◆ *pl* gafas *f*, lentes *m* [AMER anteojos *m*, espejuelos *m*] (spectacles) || gemelos *m* (binoculars).

glass bead [-biːd] *n* abalorio *m*.

glassblower [-ˌbləuə*] *n* soplador *m* de vidrio.

glass case [-keis] *n* COMM escaparate *m* || campana *f* de cristal (for protecting).

glass cutter [-ˌkʌtə*] *n* cortavidrio *m*, diamante *m*, grujidor *m* (tool).

glass door [-dɔ*] *n* puerta *f* de cristales.

glass eye [-ai] *n* ojo *m* de cristal.

glass factory [-'fæktəri] *n* cristalería *f*.

glass fibre [-'faibə*] *n* fibra *f* de vidrio, vitrofibra *f*.

glassful [-ful] *n* vaso *m*.

glasshouse [-haus] *n* invernadero *m* (greenhouse) || fábrica *f* de cristal (glassworks) || MIL prisión *f* militar.

glassmaker [-meikə*] *n* vidriero *m*.

glass paper [-ˌpeipə*] *n* papel *m* de lija.

glassware [-wɛə*] *n* cristalería *f*, artículos *m pl* de cristal.

glasswool [-wul] *n* lana *f* de vidrio.

glasswork [-wəːk] *n* cristalería *f* (glassware).
◆ *pl* fábrica *f sing* de vidrio.

glasswort [-wəːt] *n* BOT sosa *f*.

glassy ['glɑːsi] *adj* vidrioso, sa (dull, lifeless) || vítreo, a (like glass) || liso, sa (smooth) || cristalino, na (water).

Glaswegian [glæs'wiːdʒən] *adj* de Glasgow.
◆ *n* persona *f* de Glasgow.

glaucoma [glɔː'kəumə] *n* MED glaucoma *m* (disease of the eye).

glaucous ['glɔːkəs] *adj* glauco, ca.

glaze [gleiz] *n* vidriado *m* (for pottery) || brillo *m* (sheen) || barniz *m* (varnish) || US aguanieve *f* (sleet) | terreno *m* helado (icy ground).

glaze [gleiz] *vt* poner cristales a (a window) || vidriar (pottery) || barnizar (to varnish) || sacar brillo a (to polish) || glasear (cakes, paper) || poner vidrioso (eye) || *to glaze in* poner cristales a.
◆ *vi* ponerse vidrioso.

glazier ['gleizjə*] *n* vidriero *m*.

glazing ['gleiziŋ] *n* barniz *m* (varnish) || barnizado *m* (action of varnishing) || cristales *m pl* (windowpanes) || glaseado *m* (of cakes, paper).

gleam [gliːm] *n* destello *m*, rayo *m* || FIG resquicio *m*; *a gleam of hope* un resquicio de esperanza | punta *f* (of irony) | chispa *f* (of intelligence).

gleam [gliːm] *vi* destellar, brillar.

glean [gliːn] *vt/vi* espigar || FIG recoger, cosechar.
◆ *vi* espigar.

gleaner [-ə*] *n* espigador, ra.

gleaning [-iŋ] *n* espigueo *m* || FIG rebusca *f*.

glebe [gliːb] *n* REL terreno *m* beneficial.

glee [gliː] *n* regocijo *m*, júbilo *m* || MUS canción *f* para tres o más voces sin acompañamiento || MUS *glee club* coral *f*.

gleeful ['gliːful]; **gleesome** [-səum] *adj* regocijado, da; jubiloso, sa; alegre.

gleet [gliːt] *n* MED gota *f* militar.

glen [glen] *n* cañada *f*.

glengarry [glen'gæri] *n* gorro *m* escocés.

glenoid ['gliːnɔid] *adj* ANAT glenoideo, a || ANAT *glenoid cavity* cavidad glenoidea, glena *f*.

glib [glib] *adj* fácil (too pat) || de mucha labia (person) || liso, sa; resbaladizo, za (surface) || *to have a glib tongue* tener la lengua suelta.

glibness [-nis] *n* labia *f*, facundia *f* || soltura *f* (of speech).

glide [glaid] *n* deslizamiento *m* (gentle movement) || AVIAT planeo *m*, vuelo *m* sin motor || MUS ligadura *f* || GRAMM semivocal *f*.

glide [glaid] *vt* hacer deslizar (to make to move gently) || AVIAT hacer planear.
◆ *vi* deslizarse (to move smoothly) || AVIAT planear || *the years glide by* pasan los años.

glider [-ə*] *n* AVIAT planeador *m* || US columpio *m* (swing).

gliding [-iŋ] *n* deslizamiento *m* (gentle movement) || AVIAT planeo *m*, vuelo *m* sin motor (sport of flying in gliders).

glimmer ['glimə*] *n* luz *f* tenue, luz *f* trémula (faint light) || espejeo *m* (of water) || FIG resquicio *m* (of hope) | chispa *f* (of intelligence).

glimmer ['glimə*] *vi* brillar tenuemente || espejear (water).

glimpse [glimps] *n* vislumbre *f*, visión *f* momentánea || *to catch a glimpse of* vislumbrar.

glimpse [glimps] *vt/vi* vislumbrar, entrever || *to glimpse at* echar una ojeada a.

glint [glint] *n* destello *m*, centelleo *m*.

glint [glint] *vi* destellar, centellear.
◆ *vt* reflejar.

glissade [gli'sɑːd] *n* deslizamiento *m*.

glisten ['glisn] *n* brillo *m*, resplandor *m*.

glisten ['glisn] *vi* relucir, brillar || FIG *all that glistens is not gold* no es oro todo lo que reluce.

glitch [glitʃ] *n* FAM avería *f*, fallo *m* (of equipment).

glitter ['glitə*] *n* brillo *m*.

glitter ['glitə*] *vi* relucir, brillar || FIG *all that glitters is not gold* no es oro todo lo que reluce.

glittering ['glitəriŋ] *adj* reluciente, brillante.

glitzy ['glitsi] *adj* FAM deslumbrante.

gloaming ['gləumiŋ] *n* crepúsculo *m*.

gloat [gləut] *vi* recrearse con, refocilarse con.

glob [glɔb] *n* US gota *f* (drop).

global ['gləubəl] *adj* global; *global view* vista global; *global method* método global || esférico, ca (spherical) || mundial (of the world).

globate ['gləubeit] *adj* esférico, ca.

globe [gləub] *n* globo *m*, esfera *f* || esfera *f* terrestre, globo *m* terráqueo (the Earth) || globo *m* (of a lamp).

globefish ['gləubfiʃ] *n* ZOOL orbe *m*.

globe-trotter [-ˌtrɔtə*] *n* trotamundos *m inv*.

globose ['gləubəus] *adj* globoso, sa; globular.

globular ['glɔbjulə*] *adj* globular.

globule ['glɔbjul] *n* glóbulo *m*.

globulin ['glɔbjuːlin] *n* CHEM globulina *f*.

globulous ['glɔbjuləs] *adj* globuloso, sa.

glomerate ['glɔmərət] *adj* aglomerado, da.

glomeration [glɔmə'reiʃən] *n* aglomeración *f*.

gloom [gluːm]; **gloominess** [gluːminis] *n* penumbra *f* (semidarkness) || melancolía *f*, tristeza *f* (melancholy) || pesimismo *m* || *to cast a gloom over* entristecer.

gloom [gluːm] *vi* encapotarse (sky) || entristecerse.

gloominess [gluːminis] *n* → **gloom.**

gloomy ['gluːmi] *adj* oscuro, ra; tenebroso, sa (dark) || melancólico, ca (melancholic) || deprimente (depressing) || pesimista; *to feel gloomy* sentirse pesimista || encapotado, da (sky).

gloria ['glɔːriə] *n* REL gloria *m* || ARTS gloria *f*.

glorification [glɔːrifi'keiʃən] *n* glorificación *f*.

glorified ['glɔrifaid] *adj* con pretensiones de.

glorify ['glɔrifai] *vt* glorificar || alabar (to praise).

gloriole ['glɔːriəul] *n* ARTS halo *m*.

glorious ['glɔːriəs] *adj* glorioso, sa || radiante (day) || espléndido, da; magnífico, ca (wonderful) || colosal, enorme, mayúsculo, la; *glorious mess* lío colosal.

glory ['glɔːri] *n* gloria *f*; *glory be to the Father* gloria al Padre; *these paintings are the glory of the museum* estos cuadros son las glorias del museo; *Cervantes is one of the glories of Spain* Cervantes es una de las glorias de España; *the king in all his glory* el rey en toda su gloria; *the saints who are in glory* los santos que están en la Gloria || gloria *f*, fama *f* (renowm) || ARTS gloria *f* (aureole) || belleza *f* (beauty) || — FAM *glory hole* leonera *f* (room in disorder) || FIG *in one's glory* en la gloria; *he is in his glory* está en la gloria | *to cover o.s. in* o *with glory* cubrirse de gloria | *to go to glory* irse al otro mundo.

glory ['glɔːri] *vi* gloriarse, enorgullecerse (*in* de) (to be proud) || exultar (to exult).

gloss [glɔs] *n* glosa *f* (comment, interpretation, explanation) || glosario *m* (glossary) || glosa *f* (poetical composition) || brillo *m*, lustre *m* (sheen) || FIG oropel *m* || *gloss paint* pintura *f* brillante *or* esmaltada.

gloss [glɔs] *vt* glosar (a text) || desvirtuar, glosar (to misinterpret) || dar brillo a, lustrar (to put a sheen on) || *to gloss over* encubrir (to cover up), disfrazar (to disguise).
◆ *vi* hacer glosas.

glossarist ['glɔsərist]; **glossator** ['glɔsətə*] *n* glosador, ra.

glossary ['glɔsəri] *n* glosario *m*.

glossiness ['glɔsinis] *n* brillo *m*, lustre *m*.

glossy ['glɔsi] *adj* brillante, lustroso, sa || brillante (photograph) || liso, sa (hair) || glaseado, da (paper).
◆ *n* revista *f* impresa en papel glaseado (magazine).

glottal ['glɔtl]; **glottic** ['glɔtik] *adj* glótico, ca (pertaining to the glottis).

glottis ['glɔtis] *n* ANAT glotis *f inv*.

glove [glʌv] *n* guante *m*; *boxing gloves* guantes de boxeo || — *glove box* o *compartment* guantera *f* (in a car) || *glove factory* o *shop* guantería *f* || *glove stretcher* ensanchador *m* de guantes || FIG *to fit like a glove* sentar como anillo al dedo | *to go hand in glove* ser uña y carne | *to take up the glove* recoger el guante | *to throw down the glove* arrojar el guante | *with the gloves off* sin miramientos.

glove ['glʌv] *vt* enguantar.

glover ['glʌvə*] *n* guantero, ra.

glow [gləu] *n* incandescencia *f* (emission of light without smoke or flame) || brillo *m* (of jewel) || resplandor *m* (glaze) || color *m* vivo, luminosidad *f* (bright colour) || arrebol *m* (of sun) || calor *m* (heat) || rubor *m* (in cheeks) || calor *m*, ardor *m* (of feelings).

glow [gləu] *vi* estar al rojo vivo (metal) || brillar (to shine) || rebosar de; *to glow with health* rebosar de salud || estar encendido (to be lit up) || enrojecerse (complexión) || enardecerse, encenderse (with passion).

glower ['glauə*] *n* mirada *f* furiosa.

glower ['glauə*] *vi* lanzar una mirada furiosa.

glowing [gləuiŋ] *adj* incandescente ‖ al rojo vivo (metal, etc.) ‖ rojo, ja (complexion) ‖ encendido, da (cheeks) ‖ vivo, va (fire, colour) ‖ brillante (light) ‖ entusiasta (enthusiastic) ‖ cálido, da (style, terms) ‖ *glowing with health* rebosante de salud.

glowworm ['gləuwə:m] *n* ZOOL luciérnaga *f*, gusano *m* de luz.

gloze [gləuz] *vt* *to gloze over* encubrir.

glucemia [glu'si:mjə] *n* MED glucemia *f*, glicemia *f*.

glucide ['glu:said] *n* CHEM glúcido *m*.

glucinium[glu:'sinjəm] ;**glucinum**['glu:sinəm] *n* CHEM glucinio *m*.

glucometer [glukɔ'mitə*] *n* glucómetro *m*.

glucose ['glu:kəus] *n* CHEM glucosa *f*.

glucoside ['glu:kəsaid] *n* CHEM glucósido *m*.

glue [glu:] *n* pegamento *m*, cola *f*.

glue [glu:] *vt* pegar.
◆ *vi* pegarse.

glue-sniffing [-,snifiŋ] *n* inhalación *f* or esnifada *f* de cola.

gluey ['glu:i] *adj* pegajoso, sa.

glum [glʌm] *adj* sombrío, a; taciturno, na; triste.

glut [glʌt] *n* superabundancia *f*, exceso *m* (of the market) ‖ saciedad *f*, hartazgo *m* (of food).

glut [glʌt] *vt* inundar (the market) ‖ hartar, saciar (to overfeed).

gluteal ['glu:ti:əl] *adj* ANAT glúteo, a.

gluten ['glu:tən] *n* gluten *m*.

gluteus [glu'tiəs] *n* ANAT glúteo *m* (muscle).
— OBSERV El plural de *gluteus* es *glutei*.

glutinous ['glu:tinəs] *adj* glutinoso, sa; pegajoso, sa.

glutton ['glʌtn] *n* glotón, ona (excessive eater) ‖ ZOOL glotón *m* ‖ — *glutton for work* trabajador *m* incansable ‖ *to be a glutton for sth.* ser insaciable de algo.

gluttonous ['glʌtnəs] *adj* glotón, ona.

gluttony ['glʌtni] *n* glotonería *f*, gula *f* ‖ *sin of gluttony* pecado *m* de gula.

glyceride ['glisəraid] *n* CHEM glicérido *m*.

glycerin ['glisərin]; **glycerine** [glisə'ri:n] *n* CHEM glicerina *f*.

glycerol ['glisərɔl] *n* CHEM glicerol *m*.

glycerophosphate ['glisərəu'fɔsfeit] *n* CHEM glicerofosfato *m*.

glycogen ['glikəudʒen] *n* CHEM glicógeno *m*.

glycol ['glaikɔl] *n* CHEM glicol *m*.

glycoside ['glaikəsaid] *n* CHEM glucósido *m*.

glyph [glif] *n* glifo *m*.

glyptic ['gliptik] *n* glíptica *f*.

glyptodon ['gliptədɔn]; **glyptodont** ['gliptədɔnt] *n* gliptodonte *m*.

glyptography [glip'tɔgrəfi] *n* gliptografía *f*.

G-man ['dʒi:mæn] *n* US FAM agente *m* del FBI (Federal Bureau of Investigation).

GMT *abbr of [Greenwich Mean Time]* hora media de Greenwich.

gnarl [nɑ:l] *n* nudo *m* (in wood).

gnarled [-d]; **gnarly** [-i] *adj* nudoso, sa.

gnash [næʃ] *vt* rechinar.

gnashing [-iŋ] *n* rechinamiento *m*.

gnat [næt] *n* ZOOL mosquito *m*.

gnaw* [nɔ:] *vt/vi* roer.
— OBSERV Pret ***gnawed***; pp ***gnawed, gnawn***.

gnawing [-iŋ] *n* roedura *f* ‖ retortijón *m* (of stomach).

gneiss [nais] *n* GEOL gneis *m*.

gnome [nəum] *n* gnomo *m* (small imaginary person) ‖ duende *m* (goblin) ‖ enano *m* (dwarf).

gnomic ['nəumik] *adj* gnómico, ca.

gnomon ['nəumən] *n* gnomon *m*.

gnosis ['nəusis] *n* PHIL gnosis *f*.

gnostic ['nɔstik] *adj/n* PHIL gnóstico, ca.

gnosticism ['nɔstisizəm] *n* PHIL gnosticismo *m*.

GNP *abbr of [gross national product]* PNB, producto nacional bruto.

gnu [nu:] *n* ZOOL ñu *m*.

go [gəu] *n* energía *f* (energy); *to have lots of go* tener mucha energía ‖ — *at one go* en una sola vez ‖ *is it a go?* ¿está resuelto?, ¿estamos de acuerdo? ‖ *it's a go* trato hecho ‖ *it's all the go* está muy en boga ‖ *it's your go* te toca a ti ‖ *no go* inútil ‖ *on the go* ocupado, da (busy) ‖ FAM *the go* la moda ‖ *to have a go at sth.* intentar algo ‖ *to make a go of sth.* tener éxito en algo ‖ *what a pretty go!* ¡vaya desastre!
◆ *adj* listo, ta.

go* [gəu] *vi* ir; *I am going to the cinema* voy al cine; *I must go to Paris* tengo que ir a París; *to go and fetch* ir a buscar; *to go barefoot* ir descalzo; *salary goes by age* el sueldo va según la edad; *the meeting was going very well* la reunión iba muy bien; *to go to school* ir al colegio; *to go to war* ir a la guerra; *how are things going?* ¿cómo van las cosas?; *these colours go very well* estos colores van muy bien ‖ salir (to depart); *the coach goes at seven o'clock* el autocar sale a las siete ‖ irse (to leave); *he went at midnight* se fue a medianoche ‖ irse (to be spent); *all his money goes on wine* se le va el dinero en vino ‖ hacer; *this car goes at 50 miles an hour* este coche hace 50 millas por hora ‖ desaparecer (to disappear); *the pain soon goes* pronto desaparece el dolor ‖ ser suprimido (to be abolished); *Latin is going to go next term* el latín será suprimido el próximo trimestre ‖ llegar (to reach); *the property goes as far as the river* la finca llega hasta el río ‖ funcionar; *this clock does not go* este reloj no funciona; *it goes by electricity* funciona con electricidad ‖ quedarse, volverse (to become); *to go blind* quedarse ciego; *to go mad* volverse loco ‖ ponerse; *he went red* se puso colorado; *it has gone very cold* se ha puesto muy frío ‖ salir, resultar; *all has gone well* todo ha salido bien ‖ sonar (to sound); *the bell goes at three* el timbre suena a las tres ‖ decir (to say); *the story goes that...* la historia dice que... ‖ hacer (to carry out an action); *go like this* haz así ‖ pasar; *it went unobserved* pasó desapercibido ‖ escapar (to escape); *he went unpunished* escapó sin castigo ‖ acudir; *you must go to him to get what you want* tienes que acudir a él para obtener lo que quieres ‖ romperse (to break) ‖ ceder (to give way); *the beam went* cedió la viga ‖ caerse, caer (to fall) ‖ fundirse (a fuse) ‖ gastarse (to wear out); *my shoes have gone* se me han gastado los zapatos ‖ caber (to fit); *it won't go into the box* no cabe en la caja ‖ ponerse, ir (to be placed); *coats go on the peg* los abrigos se ponen en la percha ‖ venderse (to be sold); *it went for fifty pounds* se vendió por cincuenta libras ‖ tener curso legal, valer (currency) ‖ transcurrir, pasar (time) ‖ contribuir (to be a contributing factor); *it all goes to show that...* todo contribuye a demostrar que... ‖ pasar (to be given to) ‖ ser ganado (to be won) ‖ ser; *how does that story go?* ¿cómo es esa historia? ‖ estar disponible (to be available) ‖ valer; *anything goes* todo vale ‖ morir (to die) ‖ — *anything that's going* lo que haya ‖ *as far as that goes* por lo que se refiere a esto ‖ *as things go* según y como van las cosas ahora ‖ *four into twenty goes five* veinte entre cuatro son cinco (in mathematics) ‖ *from the word go* desde el principio, desde que el mundo es mundo ‖ SP *go!* ¡ya! ‖ JUR *going, going, gone!* ¡a la una... a las dos... a las tres! ‖ *he's a good teacher as teachers go* es un buen profesor dentro de lo que cabe ‖ *his sight went* perdió la vista ‖ *how goes it?* ¿cómo va eso?, ¿qué tal? ‖ *it's all right as far as it goes* está bien dentro de lo que cabe ‖ *let's go!* ¡vamos!, ¡vámonos! ‖ *that goes for me to* yo también ‖ *there he goes!* ¡ahí va! ‖ *there is an hour to go before* queda una hora antes ‖ FIG *there you go again!* ¡otra vez con la misma canción! ‖ *the song goes like this* la canción es así ‖ FAM *they have gone and done it!* ¡buena la han hecho! ‖ *to be going sixty* andar por los sesenta ‖ *to be going to* ir a, estar a punto de (to be about to); *I am going to sing* voy a cantar; ir a (to intend to) ‖ *to come and go* ir y venir ‖ *to go bail for* salir fiador por ‖ *to go bang* explotar ‖ *to go far* llegar lejos; *this boy will go far* este muchacho llegará lejos; tener valor, servir para mucho; *money doesn't go far these days* actualmente el dinero tiene poco valor; cundir (mucho); *this box of soap goes far* este paquete de jabón cunde mucho; ir lejos, exagerar (to exaggerate); *that's going a bit far* eso es ir un poco lejos ‖ *to go fifty-fifty* ir a medias ‖ *to go for a walk* (ir a) dar un paseo ‖ *to go hunting* ir de caza ‖ *to go near* acercarse a ‖ *to go on a journey* ir de viaje ‖ *to go on an errand* ir a hacer un recado ‖ *to go on strike* declararse en huelga ‖ *to go shopping* ir de compras ‖ *to go to prove* demostrar ‖ *to go to the trouble of* tomarse la molestia de ‖ *to keep going* mantener; *he managed to keep the firm going* consiguió mantener la empresa; mantener con vida; *the doctors kept him going* los médicos le mantuvieron con vida; hacer funcionar (a machine, a motor, etc.), mantener (to maintain), hacer durar (to make last) ‖ *to let go* soltar (to release), dejar en libertad (to set free), fondear, anclar (to drop anchor) ‖ *to let go off* soltar ‖ *to let o.s. go* dejarse llevar, abandonarse (to lose one's inhibitions), abandonarse, dejarse, descuidarse (to cease to have pride in o.s.) ‖ *to let o.s. go on a subject* dejarse llevar por un tema ‖ *to set going* poner en marcha ‖ *what I say goes* aquí se hace lo que yo digo ‖ MIL *who goes there?* ¿quién va?
◆ *vt* andar, recorrer (to cover); *we have gone five miles* hemos andado cinco millas ‖ apostar, hacer una apuesta de (to bet); *to go 5 000 pesetas* apostar 5 000 pesetas ‖ declarar (in cards) ‖ hacer; *to go a journey* hacer un viaje ‖ ir por (to travel by); *to go to the short way* ir por el camino más corto ‖ dar (to strike); *it has gone six* ya han dado las seis ‖ ofrecer; *I'll go six pounds for the car* ofrezco seis libras por el coche ‖ — *to go it* ir a toda velocidad (to go fast), echar el resto (to work hard), correrla (to live it up) ‖ *to go it alone* obrar por su cuenta ‖ *to go one better on s.o.* superar a alguien.
◆ *phr v* ***to go about*** circular, correr (rumour, story) | ir de un sitio para otro (to circulate) | MAR virar de bordo | hacer; *you're not going about it right* no lo estás haciendo bien | ocuparse de (to be occupied with) | salir; *he goes about a great deal* sale mucho | recorrer; *to go about the country* recorrer el país | emprender (a task) ‖ ***to go after*** perseguir (to chase) | seguir (to follow) | andar tras (to try to obtain) ‖ ***to go against*** ir en contra de ‖ ***to go along*** pasar por (a street) | seguir, continuar (to continue) | estar de acuerdo (to agree) ‖ — *as we go along* sobre la marcha ‖ FAM *go along with you!* ¡qué va! ‖ *to go along with* acompañar a ‖ ***to go around*** dar la vuelta (to make one's way around) | dar un rodeo; *to go ten miles around* dar un rodeo de unas diez millas | girar (to revolve) | circular, correr (rumour, story, etc.) | ir a casa de, ir a ver a; *I'm going around to Barry's* voy a casa de Barry, voy a ver a Barry | ir; *I'm going around to the cafe* voy al café ‖ — *is there enough to go around?* ¿hay para todos? ‖ ***to go at*** atacar, acometer ‖ — FAM *go at it!* ¡venga! ‖ ***to go away*** irse,

marcharse (to leave) | desaparecer (to disappear) || — *to go away with* llevarse || ***to go back*** volver, regresar | retroceder; *to go back two paces* retroceder dos pasos | volver; *to go back to the beginning* volver al principio | remontarse; *to go back to the Flood* remontarse al diluvio || — *to go back on one's steps* desandar lo andado | *to go back on one's word* faltar a su palabra || ***to go before*** preceder, anteceder (to precede) | ir delante de (to proceed in front of) | tener prelación sobre (to be more important) | ser sometido a (to be submitted to) || ***to go below*** bajar (in a boat) || ***to go between*** interponerse *or* mediar entre || ***to go by*** pasar, transcurrir (time) | pasar (to move past) | pasar cerca de; *I went by the directions* seguir las instrucciones || — *to go by appearances* juzgar por las apariencias || *to go by the name of* llamarse || ***to go down*** bajar (to descend) | ponerse (sun) | hundirse (a ship) | amainar (wind) | bajar (temperature, tide) | ser acogido; *his songs went down well* sus canciones fueron bien acogidas | pasar la historia; *Columbus went down as a heroe* Colón pasó a la historia como un héroe | ser vencido (to be defeated) | pasar; *this pill needs water to help it go down* esta píldora necesita agua para pasar | digerirse, pasar (food) | dejar la universidad (to leave a university) | desinflarse (tyre) | disminuir (to disminish) | decaer (to decline) | extenderse (to extend) | estar escrito *or* apuntado (to be written down) || — *to go down before* sucumbir ante || *to go down with* coger, caer enfermo de (an illness) || *to go down with s.o.* gustarle a uno || ***to go for*** ir por, ir a buscar (to fetch) | atacar (to attack) | valer para (to be applicable to) | votar por (to be in favour of) || — FAM *I go for dancing* me gusta mucho bailar | *to go for each other* pelearse || ***to go in*** entrar (to enter) | caber (to fit) | ocultarse (the sun) | ponerse (clothes) | SP entrar (in cricket) || — *to go in for* presentar su candidatura a (an appointment), seguir (a course of lectures), adoptar (a doctrine), comprarse (to buy), dedicarse a (to engage o.s. in), entregarse a (a vice), participar en (to participate in); *to go in for an examination* examinarse || *to go in with* asociarse con || ***to go into*** entrar en (to enter) | dedicarse a (to engage o.s. in) | examinar a fondo, profundizar (a question) || — *to go into a discussion about* entablar una discusión sobre, empezar a discutir sobre || *to go into hysterics* ponerse histérico || *to go into mourning* ponerse de luto || ***to go off*** marcharse, irse (to leave) | dispararse (to fire, of a gun) | explotar (to explode) | sonar (to ring, to sound) | estropearse (to go bad) | FAM dejar de gustarle a uno; *I've gone off cheese* ha dejado de gustarme el queso | THEATR hacer mutis | salir (to turn out); *everything went off well* todo salió bien | dormirse (to go to sleep) | desmayarse (to lose consciousness) | desaparecer (to disappear) | COMM venderse || — *to go off the rails* descarrilar || *to go off with sth.* llevarse algo || ***to go on*** seguir, continuar (to continue); *he went on talking for hours* siguió hablando horas y horas | seguir su camino | avanzar, progresar (to progress) | pasar a (to proceed to); *to go on to the next item* pasar al punto siguiente | partir de, basarse en (to base arguments upon) | THEATR salir a escena | pasar, transcurrir (time) | durar (to last) | estar bien (to fit); *my gloves won't go on* los guantes no me están bien | comportarse (to behave) | ocurrir (to happen) | encenderse (lights) || — *don't go on so!* ¡no insistas! | FAM *go on!* ¡qué va! (with incredulity), ¡vaya! (with surprise), ¡sigue! (carry on!) || *how are you going on?* ¿qué tal estás? || *it's going on for two o'clock* son casi las dos || *to be going on for sixty* andar por los sesenta || *to go on about* hablar constantemente de || *to go on at* regañar, reprender || *what is going on here?* ¿qué pasa aquí? || ***to go out*** salir (to move out of somewhere) | salir (to be published) | apagarse (matches, fire, light) | desaparecer (to disappear) | pasar de moda (to cease to be fashionable) | declararse en huelga, estar en huelga (to strike) | dejar el poder (a politician) | tener un desafío (duel) || — *my heart went out to him* en seguida me resultó simpático, le cogí simpatía en seguida || FAM *out you go!* ¡fuera de aquí! || *to go out to dinner* cenar fuera || ***to go over*** cruzar (to cross) | pasar por encima de; *to go over the wall* pasar por encima del muro | recorrer (a house, the ground) | ir; *to go over to England* ir a Inglaterra | pasarse a (to change one's allegiance to); *to go over to the enemy* pasarse al enemigo | examinar (to investigate in detail) | revisar (to revise) | retocar (a drawing) | repasar (a lesson) | ensayar (to rehearse) | ser acogido (to be received); *the film went over well* la película fue bien acogida | volcar (to overturn) || ***to go round*** dar la vuelta (to make one's way around) | dar un rodeo; *to go ten miles round* dar un rodeo de unas diez millas | girar (to revolve) | circular, correr (rumour, story, etc.) | ir a casa de, ir a ver a; *I'm going round to Barry's* voy a casa de Barry, voy a ver a Barry | ir; *I'm going round to the café* voy al café | *is there enough to go round?* ¿hay para todos? || ***to go through*** atravesar (to pass from one side to the other) | pasar por (window, hole) | examinar a fondo (to examine) | pasar por, sufrir (to undergo) | ser aprobado; *the bill has gone through* el proyecto de ley ha sido aprobado | ejecutar (to perform) | gastar (to spend) | vender (to sell out) || — *to go through with* llevar a cabo || ***to go together*** ir juntos; *they went to the cinema together* fueron al cine juntos | armonizar, ir juntos (colours) | salir juntos, ir juntos (a boy and girl) || ***to go under*** hundirse (to sink) | ponerse (sun) | sucumbir (to succumb) || — FAM *he is going under* está de capa caída | *he is gone under* es un hombre acabado || ***to go up*** subir; *to go up the stairs* subir las escaleras; *the prices are going up* los precios van subiendo | levantarse (to be erected) | ingresar; *to go up to the university* ingresar en la universidad | subir, montarse (in an aeroplane) | explotar (to explode) | ir; *to go up to town* ir a la ciudad | acercarse, dirigirse; *to go up to s.o.* acercarse a alguien || — *to go up a river* ir aguas arriba || *to go up for an exam* examinarse || *to go up in flames* quemarse, arder || ***to go with*** acompañar (to accompany) | hacer juego con, armonizarse con (colours, etc.) | ir con; *red wine goes with cheese* el vino tinto va con el queso | corresponder; *a salary which goes with the job* un sueldo que corresponde al trabajo | FAM tener relaciones con (lovers) | *to go with the times* ser de su tiempo || ***to go without*** pasar sin, prescindir de | arreglárselas (to manage) || — *it goes without saying* ni qué decir tiene (needless to say), eso cae de su peso (it is obvious).

— OBSERV Pret ***went***; pp ***gone***.

goad [gəud] *n* aguijada *f* (stick for driving cattle) || pincho *m* (wooden spike) || FIG aguijón *m*, acicate *m* (incentive).

goad [gəud] *vt* aguijar, aguijonear || pinchar (to prick) || FIG aguijonear, incitar.

go-ahead ['gəuəhəd] *adj* emprendedor, ra || activo, va.

◆ *n* vía *f* libre (signal) || FIG autorización *f*.

goal [gəul] *n* SP gol *m*, tanto *m*; *to score a goal* marcar un gol | portería *f* (structure) || FIG objetivo *m*, meta *f*, fin *m*; *his goal was to be a doctor* su objetivo era ser médico || — SP *goal area* área *f* de gol | *goal average* goal average *m*, cociente *m* de goles.

goalee; goalie [-i] *n* SP FAM portero *m*, guardameta *m*.

goalkeeper [-ˌkiːpə*] *n* SP portero *m*, guardameta *m*.

goal kick [-kik] *n* SP saque *m* de puerta.

goal line [-lain] *n* SP línea *f* de gol (in football) | línea *f* de meta (in rugby).

goalpost [-pəust] *n* SP poste *m*.

goal scorer [-skɔːrə*] *n* SP goleador *m*.

goat [gəut] *n* ZOOL cabra *f* (female) | macho *m* cabrío (male) || ASTR capricornio *m* || US FIG & FAM cabeza *f* de turco (scapegoat) || FIG *to get s.o.'s goat* molestar *or* fastidiar a uno.

goatee [gəu'tiː] *n* barbas *f pl* de chivo, perilla *f*.

goatherd ['gəuthəːd] *n* cabrero *m*, guardacabras *m* & *f inv*.

goatish ['gəutiʃ] *adj* cabruno, na || FIG libidinoso, sa.

goatskin ['gəutskin] *n* piel *f* de cabra.

goatsucker ['gəutˌsʌkə*] *n* chotacabras *m inv*, zumaya *f* (bird).

gob [gɔb] *n* trozo *m* (piece) || FAM boca *f* (mouth) | lapo *m* (spit) | US marinero *m* (sailor) | FAM *gobs of* gran cantidad de.

gobbet ['gɔbit] *n* fragmento *m* de un texto (extract of a text) || FAM bocado *m* (mouthful).

gobble ['gɔbl] *vt* engullir || *to gobble down* o *up* engullir, comer ávidamente.

◆ *vi* comer mucho (to eat) || gluglutear (a turkey).

gobble ['gɔbl] *n* gluglú *m* (of turkey).

gobbledygook; gobbledegook [gɔbldi'guk] *n* US FAM jerga *f* burocrática.

gobbler ['gɔblə*] *n* FAM pavo *m* macho (turkey) | tragón *m*, comilón *m* (eater).

go-between ['gəubi'twiːn] *n* intermediario, ria; mediador, ra (negotiator) || mensajero, ra (messenger) || alcahuete, ta (pimp).

Gobi Desert ['gəubiˌdezət] *pr n* GEOGR desierto de Gobi.

goblet ['gɔblit] *n* copa *f*.

goblin ['gɔblin] *n* duende *m*.

go-by ['gəubai] *n* *to give s.o. the go-by* no hacer caso a alguien || *to give sth. the go-by* hacer caso omiso de algo.

go-cart ['gəukɑːt] *n* coche *m* silla (pushchair) || carrillo *m* de juguete (homemade toy) || carretilla *f* de mano (handcart).

god [gɔd] *n* REL Dios *m*; *it was an act of God* fue obra de Dios || — *Almighty God* Dios Todopoderoso || *by God!* ¡voto a Dios! || *for God's sake!* ¡por Dios!, ¡por amor de Dios! || *God!* ¡Dios mío!, ¡Dios Santo! || *God be praised!, praise be to God!* ¡alabado *or* bendito sea Dios! || *God be* o *God with you!* ¡anda *or* vete *or* vaya con Dios! || *God bless you!* ¡Dios le bendiga! || *God forbid!* ¡no lo permita Dios!, ¡Dios me libre!, ¡no lo quiera Dios! || *God forgive me!* ¡que Dios me perdone! || *God has forsaken him* Dios le ha dejado de su mano || *God helps those who help themselves* a Dios rogando y con el mazo dando || *God help us!* ¡que Dios nos asista *or* nos coja confesados! || *God help you!* ¡Dios le asista *or* le ayude! || *God knows...* Dios es testigo..., sabe Dios... || *God protect you!* ¡Dios le ampare!, ¡que Dios le guarde! || *God repays a hundredfold* Dios da ciento por uno || *God's will be done!* ¡sea lo que Dios quiera! || *God tempers the wind to the shorn lamb* Dios aprieta pero no ahoga || *God the Son, God made Man* Dios Hijo, Dios hecho Hombre || *God willing* Dios mediante, si Dios quiere || *God will provide!* ¡Dios proveerá! || *may God repay you!* ¡Dios se lo pagará!, ¡Dios se lo pague! || *my God!* ¡Dios mío! || *render therefore unto Caesar the things which are Caesar's and unto God things that are God's* hay que dar a Dios lo que es de Dios y al César lo que es del César || *thank God!* ¡gracias a Dios!, ¡a Dios gracias! || *to swear by almighty God* poner a Dios por testigo || *to thank*

God, to give thanks to God dar gracias a Dios || *would to God that...* quiera Dios que...
◆ *pl* THEATR FAM gallinero *m sing*, paraíso *m sing* || dioses *m*; *the gods of Olympus* los dioses del Olimpo.

godchild ['gɔdtʃaild] *n* ahijado, da.
— OBSERV El plural es *godchildren*.

goddam; goddamn ['gɔdæm] *adj* POP maldito, ta; *that goddam car* ese maldito coche.
◆ *adv* POP muy; *it's goddam funny* es muy gracioso.

goddaughter [gɔd,dɔːtə*] *n* ahijada *f*.

goddess ['gɔdes] *n* diosa *f*.

godfather ['gɔd,fɑːðə*] *n* padrino *m* (*to* de).

God-fearing ['gɔd'fiəriŋ] *adj* temeroso de Dios, piadoso, sa.

godforsaken ['gɔdfə,seikn] *adj* dejado de la mano de Dios.

godhead ['gɔdhed] *n* divinidad *f*.

godless ['gɔdlis] *adj* descreído, da; ateo, a.

godlike ['gɔdlaik] *adj* divino, na.

godliness ['gɔdlinis] *n* santidad *f* || devoción *f*, piedad *f* (piousness).

godly ['gɔdli] *adj* santo, ta || devoto, ta; piadoso, sa.

godmother ['gɔd,mʌðə*] *n* madrina *f* (*to* de).

godown ['gəudaun] *n* almacén *m* en ciertos países asiáticos.

godparent ['gɔd,pɛərənt] *n* padrino *m* (godfather) || madrina *f* (godmother).

God's acre ['gɔdz'eikə*] *n* FAM cementerio *m*, camposanto *m*.

godsend ['gɔdsend] *n* don *m* del cielo.

godson ['gɔdsʌn] *n* ahijado *m*.

godspeed ['gɔd'spiːd] *n* buena suerte *f*.

goffer ['gəufə*] *n* TECH gofradora *f* (for paper).

goffer ['gəufə*]**; gauffer** ['gɔfə*] *vt* encañonar (material) || gofrar (paper).

goffering [-iŋ] *n* encañonado *m* (of material) || gofrado *m* (of paper).

go-getter ['gəu'getə*] *n* FAM ambicioso, sa; buscavidas *m* & *f inv*.

goggle ['gɔgl] *vi* tener los ojos desorbitados || *to goggle at* mirar con los ojos desorbitados.

goggle-eyed [-aid] *adj* de ojos saltones.

goggles [-z] *pl n* gafas *f* (of divers, driver, etc.).

Goidelic [gɔi'delik] *adj* gaélico, ca.

going [gəuiŋ] *n* salida *f*, ida *f* || camino *m*; *the going was rough* el camino era accidentado || manera *f* de proceder, conducta *f* (behaviour) || paso *m* (speed) || FIG progreso *m* || — *he has a lot going for him* tiene mucho a su favor || FIG & FAM *that's good going* esto ha salido muy bien.
◆ *adj* que funciona bien; *a going concern* una empresa que funciona bien || existente; *one of the best firms going* una de las mejores empresas existentes || corriente (price).

going-over [-'əuvə*] *n* inspección *f* || FAM paliza *f* (beating).

goings-on ['gəuiŋz'ɔn] *pl n* FAM tejemanejes *m*.

goitre; US **goiter** ['gɔitə*] *n* MED bocio *m*.

go-kart ['gəukɑːt] *n* SP kart *m*.

gold [gəuld] *n* MIN oro *m* (metal) || dorado *m*, oro *m* (colour) || — FIG *all that glitters is not gold* no es oro todo lo que reluce || *beaten gold* oro batido || *dead gold* oro mate || *fine gold* oro de ley || *gold bars* oro en barras || *gold bath* baño *m* de oro || *gold billet* lingote *m* de oro || *gold dust* oro en polvo, polvo *m* de oro || *gold ingot* lingote *m* de oro || *gold leaf, gold foil* oro en hojas, pan *m* de oro || *gold mine* mina *f* de oro (where gold is mined), mina *f* (profitable concern) || *gold plate* vajilla *f* de oro || *gold printing* impresión *f* en oro || *gold reserve* reserva *f* de oro || *gold rush* fiebre *f* del oro || FIG *heart of gold* corazón *m* de oro || FIG *to be worth its weight in gold* valer su peso en oro || *white gold* oro blanco.
◆ *adj* de oro (necklace, etc.); *gold coin* moneda de oro || oro (colour) || oro; *gold standard* patrón oro; *gold value* valor oro.

gold-bearing [-'bɛəriŋ] *adj* aurífero, ra; *gold-bearing land* terreno aurífero.

goldbeater [-'biːtə*] *n* batidor *m* de oro, batihoja *m*.

goldbrick [-brik] *n* FIG & FAM estafa *f*, timo *m* (sham) | oropel *m* (glitter) || US FAM holgazán, ana (shirker) || FIG & FAM *to sell s.o. a goldbrick* vender a alguien gato por liebre, timar a alguien.

goldbrick [-brik] *vi* US FAM holgazanear.
◆ *vt* FIG FAM timar, dar gato por liebre.

Gold Coast [-kəust] *pr n* GEOGR Costa *f* de Oro.

gold digger [-'digə*] *n* buscador *m* de oro (miner) || FAM aventurera *f* (woman).

gold diggings [-'digiŋz] *pl n* placer *m sing* aurífero.

golden [-dən] *adj* dorado, da (colour) || de oro (made of gold) || áureo, a (number) || de oro (rule, wedding) || ZOOL dorado, da; *golden eagle* águila dorada; *golden pheasant* faisán dorado || FIG excelente; *a golden opportunity* una excelente oportunidad | dorado, da (flourishing); *the golden day of boxing* la época dorada del boxeo || rubio, bia (hair) || — FIG *Golden age* Edad *f* de Oro || *golden anniversary* o *wedding* bodas *f pl* de oro || *golden calf* becerro *m* de oro || FIG *golden goose* gallina *f* de los huevos de oro | *golden mean* término medio (moderation) || *golden rule* regla *f* de oro || *golden syrop* melaza *f*.

Golden Fleece ['gəuldən'fliːs] *n* MYTH vellocino *m* de oro || *Order of the Golden Fleece* Orden *f* del Toisón de Oro.

goldenrod ['gəuldən,rɔd] *n* BOT vara *f* de oro *or* de San José.

goldfield ['gəuldfiːld] *n* MIN yacimiento *m* de oro.

gold-fillet ['gəuldfild] *adj* chapado de oro (watch, etc.) || empastado con oro (tooth).

goldfinch ['gəuldfintʃ] *n* jilguero *m* (bird).

goldfish ['gəuldfiʃ] *n* pez *m* de colores (fish).

gold-plated ['gəuldpleitəd] *adj* dorado, da || chapado de oro (watch, etc.).

goldsmith ['gəuldsmiθ] *n* orfebre *m*.

golf [gɔlf] *n* SP golf *m*.

golfball typewriter ['gɔlfbɑːl ,taiprɑitə*] *n* máquina *f* de escribir cabeza esférica.

golf club [-klʌb] *n* palo *m* de golf (implement) || club *m* de golf (association).

golf course [-kɔːs]; **golf links** [liŋks] *n* campo *m* de golf.

golfer ['gɔlfə*] *n* SP golfista *m* & *f*, jugador *m* de golf.

Golgotha ['gɔlgəθə] *pr n* Gólgota *m*.

goliard ['gəuliɑːd] *n* goliardo *m*.

Goliath [gəu'laiəθ] *pr n* Goliath *m*.

golly! ['gɔli] *interj* ¡cáspita!, ¡Dios mío!

gollywog; golliwog [gɔliwɔg] *n* muñeco *m* negro de trapo.

golosh [gə'lɔʃ] *n* chanclo *m* (galosh).

Gomorrah [gə'mɔrə] *pr n* HIST Gomorra.

gonad ['gɔnæd] *n* BIOL gónada *f*.

gondola ['gɔndələ] *n* góndola *f* (Venetian boat) || góndola *f*, barquilla *f* (of an airship, balloon) || US barcaza *f* (barge) | batea *f* (open railway wagon).

gondolier [,gɔndə'liə*] *n* gondolero *m*.

gone [gɔn] *pp* ⟶ **go.**
◆ *adj* pasado, da (past) || dado, da (hour) || JUR adjudicado, da || FAM loco, ca (in love with) | agotado, da (exhausted) | magnífico, ca; espléndido, da (excellent) | acabado, da (worn-out) | muerto, ta; *when I'm gone* cuando me haya muerto || — *gone with child* embarazada || *gone with the wind* lo que el viento se llevó || *the coal is all gone* se acabó el carbón, ya no queda carbón || *to be far gone* estar pasado (food), estar bebido (to be drunk), estar muy mal (to be ill) || *to be far gone in* estar muy metido en (to be deeply involved in) || *to be gone* estar fuera; *I won't be gone five minutes* no estaré fuera más de cinco minutos || FAM *to be gone on* estar loco por || *to be six months gone* estar de seis meses (pregnant) || *to be too far gone* estar demasiado avanzado (disease, illness, etc.).

goner ['gɔnə*] *n* FAM enfermo *m* desahuciado (very sick person) | hombre *m* perdido (ruined man).

gonfalon ['gɔnfələn] *n* gonfalón *m*, estandarte *m*.

gonfalonier [,gɔnfələ'niə*] *n* gonfalonero *m*, abanderado *m* (standard bearer).

gong [gɔŋ] *n* gong *m*.

gongorism ['gɔŋgərizəm] *n* gongorismo *m*.

goniometer [gəuni'ɔmitə*] *n* goniómetro *m*.

goniometry [gəuni'ɔmetri] *n* goniometría *f*.

gonna ['gɔnə] FAM contraction of «going to».

gonococcus [,gɔnə'kɔkəs] *n* gonococo *m*.
— OBSERV El plural de *gonococcus* es *gonococci*.

gonorrhoea; US **gonorrhea** ['gɔnə'riːə] *n* MED gonorrea *f*.

goo [guː] *n* FAM sustancia *f* pegajosa (sticky matter) | sentimentalismo *m* (sentimentalism).

goober ['guːbə*] *n* US cacahuete *m* [AMER maní *m*, cacahuate *m*] (peanut).

good [gud] *adj* bueno, na; *a good person* una buena persona; *good soldier* buen soldado; *milk is good for your health* la leche es buena para la salud; *a good thrashing* una buena paliza; *I had a good night* pasé una buena noche; *he comes from a good family* es de buena familia || amable (kind); *she was very good to me* fue muy amable conmigo; *that is very good of you* es Ud. muy amable || agradable, bueno, na (pleasant) || más de, largo, ga; *he has been here for a good hour* ha estado aquí más de una hora || ventajoso, sa (advantageous) || competente (competent) || útil (useful) || válido, da; *this ticket is not good* este billete no es válido || — *a good deal* mucho, mucha || *a good* o *some* o *quite a few* un buen número, muchos, muchas, bastantes; *a good few of his friends* muchos de sus amigos || *a good many* un buen número, muchos, muchas || *a good sort* una buena persona || *a good turn* un favor || *a good while* un buen rato || *all in good time* todo a su debido tiempo || *as good as* como si, prácticamente; *it's as good as done* es como si estuviera hecho, está prácticamente hecho || *as good as gold* bueno como un ángel || *as good as new* como nuevo || *as good as saying that...* tanto como decir que... || *be good!* ¡sé bueno! || *good!* ¡muy bien! || *good afternoon, good evening* buenas tardes || *good and late* bien tarde || *good and ready* bien preparado | *Good Book* Biblia *f* || *good deal* buen negocio | *good fellow* buen chico || *good for...* bueno para... || *good for a laugh* divertido, da || *good for you!* ¡estupendo! || *Good Friday* Viernes Santo || *Good Lord, heavens, gracious, grief!* ¡madre mía! || *good looks* belleza *f* || *good luck* buena suerte || *good manners* buenos modales || *good money* buena cantidad de dinero || *good morning*

buenos días || *good name* buena reputación || *good night* buenas noches || *good offices* buenos oficios || *good sense* sentido *m* común, buen sentido, sensatez *f*, juicio *m* || *good word* recomendación *f* || *in good spirits* de buen humor || *in good time* a tiempo (in time), a su debido tiempo (at the proper time), rápidamente (quickly) || *it's a good job* menos mal que; *it's a good job he came* menos mal que vino || *please be so good as to...* tenga la bondad de... || *that's a good one!* ¡menuda bola! (that's hard to believe), ¡ésa sí que es buena! (that is good) || *to be as good as one's word* ser hombre de palabra || *to be good at* ser fuerte en, tener capacidad para || *to be good enough for* valer para, convenir a; *do you think this paper is good enough for writing letters on?* ¿cree Ud. que este papel vale para la correspondencia? || FIG *to be good for* valer (to be worth), disponer de (money), durar (to be able to last), estar en condiciones de hacer (to have the necessary energy) || *to be good with children* tener arte para los niños || *to be of good cheer* sentirse animoso || *to be too good to be true* ser demasiado bueno para ser cierto || *to drink more than is good for one* beber más de la cuenta || *to feel good* sentirse bien (in health), estar satisfecho (satisfied) || *to give as good as one gets* pagar con la misma moneda || *to have a good time* pasarlo bien || *to hold good for* valer para || *to make good* prosperar (to prosper), triunfar (to succeed), cubrir (a deficit), compensar, recuperar (expenses, a loss), pagar (to pay), hacer valer (one's rights), reparar (an injustice), cumplir (one's promise), llevar a cabo, realizar (one's purpose), demostrar (a statement), comprobar (accusation) || *to make good a loss to s.o.* indemnizar a alguien por una pérdida || *to make good cheer* comer como un rey || *to put in* o *to say a good word for s.o.* decir unas palabras en favor de alguien || *very good* muy bien || *would you be so good as to...?* ¿sería tan amable de...?
◆ *n* bien *m*; *the powers of good and evil* los poderes del bien y del mal; *he did it for his own good* lo hizo por su propio bien || utilidad *f* (usefulness) || buenos *m pl* (persons) || — *for good* definitivamente, para siempre (for always) || *for good and all* de una vez para siempre || *for the good of* en bien de || *it's no good* de nada sirve || *no good* inútil (useless), sin valor (worthless) || *no good will come of it* nada bueno puede salir de ahí || *the good* lo bueno || *to be no good at* no servir para || *to be up to no good* tener mala idea, estar tramando algo malo || *to come to no good* acabar mal || *to do good* hacer el bien || *to do one good* hacer bien a uno, sentarle bien a uno || *to the good* provechoso, sa (beneficial), de beneficio, a favor de uno (in profit) || *what's the good of running?* ¿de qué sirve correr?
◆ *pl* → **goods**.
◆ *adv* bien || *it has been a good long time* hace mucho tiempo.
— OBSERV El comparativo de *good* es *better* y el superlativo *best*.

good-bye; US **good-by** [gud'bai] *interj* ¡adiós!
◆ *n* adiós *m*, despedida *f* || *to say good-bye to* despedirse de.

good-fellowship [gud,feləuʃip] *n* compañerismo *m*, camaradería *f*.

good-for-nothing ['gudfə,nʌθiŋ] *adj* inútil, que no sirve para nada.
◆ *n* inútil *m* & *f*.

good-hearted [gud'hɑ:tid] *adj* de buen corazón.

good humour; US **good humor** [gud'hju:mə*] *n* buen humor *m*.

good-humoured; US **good-humored** [-d] *adj* de buen humor, jovial || alegre (gay).

goodies ['gudiz] *pl n* US dulces *m*.

good-looking [gud'lukiŋ] *adj* guapo, pa; bien parecido, da.

goodly ['gudli] *adj* grande, considerable (big) || agradable (pleasant) || bien parecido, da (good-looking).

good-natured [gud'neitʃəd] *adj* amable, bondadoso, sa.

good-neighbour; US **good-neighbor** [gud'neibə*] *adj* de buena vecindad; *good-neigbour policy* política de buena vecindad.

goodness ['gudnis] *n* bondad *f* (quality or state of being good) || sustancia *f* (of food) || calidad *f* (quality) || — *for goodness sake!* ¡por Dios! || *Goodness gracious!* ¡Dios mío! || *Goodness knows!* ¡Dios sabe! || *I wish to goodness!* ¡ojalá! || *my goodness* ¡madre mía! ¡Dios mío! || *thank goodness!* ¡gracias a Dios!

goods [gudz] *pl n* → **good** || **bienes** *m* (possessions) || COMM géneros *m*, artículos *m* || mercancías *f* (merchandise); *good train* tren de mercancías || — *by goods* por tren de mercancías || *canned goods* conservas *f* en lata || *consumer goods* bienes *m* de consumo || *goods and chattels* muebles *m* y enseres, efectos *m* personales || *goods wagon* furgón *m* || *to catch with the goods* coger in fraganti *or* con las manos en la masa || *to deliver the goods* repartir las mercancías (merchandise), cumplir sus compromisos (to keep one's promise) || US *to have the goods on s.o.* tener pruebas de culpabilidad contra alguien.

good-tempered ['gud'tempəd] *adj* de buen carácter (not easily angered) || de buen humor (not angry) || amistoso, sa (friendly).

good-time Charlie [gud'taim'tʃɑ:li] *n* vividor *m*.

goodwill ['gud'wil] *n* de buena voluntad *f*; *a goodwill mission* una misión de buena voluntad || clientela *f* (of a business) || buen nombre *m* (reputation).

goody ['gudi] *n* dulce *m*.
◆ *interj* ¡qué bien!

goody-goody ['gudi'gudi] *adj/n* gazmoño, ña; santurrón, ona.
◆ *interj* ¡qué bien!, ¡estupendo!, ¡magnífico!

gooey ['gu:i] *adj* FAM pegajoso, sa (sticky) | sentimental, empalagoso, sa (sentimental).

goof ['gu:f] *n* FAM mentecato, ta (person) || US FAM pifia *f* (a blunder).

goof [gu:f] *vt* US FAM chafallar.
◆ *vi* US FAM cometer una pifia || US FAM *to goof off* hacerse el remolón.

goofy ['gu:fi] *adj* mentecato, ta.

goon ['gu:n] *n* US FAM tonto, ta; mentecato, ta | terrorista *m* pagado.

goose [gu:s] *n* ZOOL ganso *m*, oca *f*, ánsar *m* || FIG ganso, sa; bobo, ba (silly person) || — FIG & FAM *his goose is cooked* está aviado || FIG & FAM *to cook s.o.'s goose* hacerle la pascua a uno | *to kill the goose that lays the golden eggs* matar la gallina de los huevos de oro.
◆ *pl* plancha *f* de sastre (tailor's iron) || *the geese of the Capitol* los gansos del Capitolio.
— OBSERV El plural de *goose* es *geese*.

goose barnacle [-,bɑ:nəkl] *n* ZOOL percebe *m*.

gooseberry ['guzbəri] *n* BOT grosellero *m* espinoso (plant) | grosella *f* espinosa (fruit) || — *gooseberry bush* grosellero espinoso || FAM *he was born under a gooseberry bush* le trajo la cigüeña | *to play gooseberry* hacer de carabina, llevar la cesta.

gooseflesh ['gu:sfleʃ] *n* FIG carne *f* de gallina.

goosefoot ['gu:sfut] *n* BOT pata *f* de gallo.

goose pimples ['gu:s'pimplz] *pl n* FIG carne *f sing* de gallina.

goose step ['gu:sstep] *n* MIL paso *m* de ganso.

goose-step ['gu:sstep] *vi* ir a paso de ganso.

gopher ['gəufə*] *n* ZOOL ardilla *f* terrestre (burrowing rodent).

Gordian ['gɔ:djən] *adj* gordiano (knot).

gore [gɔ:*] *n* sangre *f* coagulada (shed blood) || nesga *f*, cuchillo *m* (in a skirt, dress, etc.) || MAR cuchillo *m*.

gore [gɔ:*] *vt* cornear, dar cornadas (to wound with horns) || acuchillar, poner nesgas en (a dress, etc.) || cortar en triángulo (to cut into a triangular shape).

gorge [gɔ:dʒ] *n* desfiladero *m*, garganta *f* (between hills) || gola *f* (of a fortification) || masa *f* que obstruye (choking mass) || FAM comilona *f* (gluttonous feed) || FIG *to make one's gorge rise* revolverle el estómago a uno.

gorge [gɔ:dʒ] *vt* atiborrar, hartar (to fill with food) || engullir, tragar (to gulp down) || obstruir (to choke) || llenar (to fill up).
◆ *vi* atracarse, hartarse (*on* de).

gorgeous ['gɔ:dʒəs] *adj* magnífico, ca; espléndido, da (magnificent) || FAM bonito, ta (nice).

gorgerin ['gɔ:dʒərin] *n* ARCH collarino *m* (of column).

gorget ['gɔ:dʒit] *n* gola *f*, gorguera *f*, gorjal *m*, colla *f* (piece of harmour) || collar *m* (on the throat of a bird, etc.) || toca *f*, griñón *m* (medieval wimple).

Gorgon ['go:gən] *n* MYTH Gorgona *f*.

gorgonize ['gɔ:gənaiz] *vt* petrificar.

gorilla [gə'rilə] *n* ZOOL gorila *m* (ape).

gormandize ['gɔ:məndaiz] *vi* comer con glotonería.

gormless ['gɔ:mləs] *adj* FAM estúpido, da; bobalicón, ona.

gorse [gɔ:s] *n* GOT tojo *m*, aulaga *f*.

gory ['gɔ:ri] *adj* ensangrentado, da (person) || sangriento, ta (fight).

gosh! [gɔʃ] *interj* ¡cielos! || — *by Gosh!* ¡por Dios! || *good Gosh!* ¡santo Dios! || *my Gosh* ¡Dios mío!

goshawk ['gɔshɔ:k] *n* azor *m*, halcón *m* palumbario (bird).

gosling ['gɔzliŋ] *n* ansarón *m* (bird) || FIG ganso, sa; mentecato, ta.

go-slow [gəu'sləu] *n* tipo *m* de huelga que consiste en trabajar con excesiva meticulosidad y lentitud.

Gospel ['gɔspəl] *n* REL evangelio *m*; *the Gospel according to Saint John* el Evangelio según San Juan || — *gospel book* evangeliario *m* || FIG *this is the gospel truth* esto es el evangelio.

gospeller; US **gospeler** ['gɔspələ*] *n* REL evangelista *m*.

gossamer ['gɔsəmə*] *n* telaraña *f* (spiders thread) || gasa *f* (gauzy material).
◆ *adj* muy fino, na.

gossip ['gɔsip] *n* cotilleo *m*, comadreo *m*, chismorreo *m* (tittle-tattle) || charla *f* (chatter) || cotilla *m* & *f*, chismoso, sa (scandalmonger) || — *gossip column* ecos *m pl* de sociedad || *gossip shop* lugar *m* donde se chismorrea, mentidero *m* || *piece of gossip* chisme *m*.

gossip ['gɔsip] *vi* cotillear, chismorrear, chismear (to talk scandal) || charlar (to chatter).

gossiper [-ə*] *n* cotilla *m* & *f*, chismoso, sa (scandalmonger) || charlatán, ana; hablador, ra (chatterer).

gossiping [-iŋ] *adj* chismoso, sa.
◆ *n* cotilleo *m*, chismorreo *m*, comadreo *m*.

gossipmonger ['gɔsip'mʌŋgə*] *n* cotilla *m* & *f*, chismoso, sa.

gossipy [-i] *adj* cotilla, chismoso, sa (person) || anecdótico, ca; familiar (style).

got [gɔt] *pret/pp* ⟶ **get.**

Goth [gɔθ] *n* godo *m* || FIG vándalo, la.

Gotham ['gɔθəm] *adj* US FAM neoyorquino, na.

◆ *n* Nueva York.

Gothic ['gɔθik] *adj* godo, da (applied to people) || gótico, ca (art, literature, etc.); *gothic language, type* lengua, letra gótica.

◆ *n* lengua *f* gótica (language) || gótico *m*; *flamboyant gothic* gótico flamígero.

gotta ['gɔtə] FAM contraction of «have got to».

gotten ['gɔtn] *pp* US ⟶ **get.**

— OBSERV En inglés el participio pasivo *gotten* no se usa más que en ciertas expresiones como *ill-gotten gains* (bienes adquiridos por medios ilícitos), mientras que se emplea mucho en los Estados Unidos.

gouache [gu'ɑːʃ] *n* ARTS pintura *f* a la aguada, aguada *f.*

gouge [gaudʒ] *n* TECH gubia *f*, escoplo *m or* formón *m* de mediacaña.

gouge [gaudʒ] *vt* escoplear con gubia *or* con formón de mediacaña (to chisel out) || FAM arrancar, sacar; *to gouge out s.o.'s eyes* arrancar los ojos a alguien.

gourd [guəd] *n* calabaza *f.*

gourmand ['guəmənd] *n* goloso, sa; glotón, ona.

gourmet ['guəmei] *n* gastrónomo, ma.

gout [gaut] *n* MED gota *f* || gota *f* (drop).

gouty [-i] *adj* MED gotoso, sa.

govern ['gʌvən] *vt* gobernar, dirigir (to rule); *to govern a country* gobernar un país || dirigir, administrar (affairs) || dominar (to restrain); *to govern one's passions* dominar las pasiones || guiar (to determine); *self-interest governs her actions* el egoísmo guía sus actos || regir (to serve as rule for) || determinar (to determine) || GRAMM regir || regular (to control the speed or power of).

◆ *vi* gobernar || prevalecer, predominar (to prevail).

governable [-əbl] *adj* gobernable || manejable.

governance [-əns] *n* gobierno *m* || autoridad *f* (authority).

governess [-nis] *n* aya *f*, institutriz *f* (of children) || gobernadora *f.*

governing [-iŋ] *adj* gobernante, dirigente; *governing class* clase gobernante || dominante, rector, ra; *governing idea* idea rectora || — *governing body* consejo *m* de administración || *governing hand* mano dura.

government [-mənt] *n* gobierno *m* (of a state); *federal, totalitarian government* gobierno federal, totalitario || dirección *f*, administración *f*, gestión *f* (of a society) || FIG dominio *m* (of passions) || GRAMM régimen *m.*

◆ *adj* del gobierno, del Estado || gubernamental (newspaper, party) || del gobernador (house) || administrativo, va.

governmental [gʌvən'mentl] *adj* gubernamental, gubernativo, va.

governor ['gʌvənə*] *n* gobernador *m*; *governor of the Bank of Spain* gobernador del Banco de España || gobernador *m* (of a town, a province, a colony) || director *m* (of a prison) || administrador *m*, director *m* (of an institution) || FAM jefe *m* (boss) || padre *m*, viejo *m* (father) || TECH regulador *m* || *provincial governor* gobernador civil.

governor-general [-'dʒenərəl] *n* gobernador *m* general.

— OBSERV El plural de la palabra inglesa es *governors-general* o *governor-generals.*

governorship [-ʃip] *n* gobierno *m*; *civil governorship* gobierno civil.

gowk [gauk] *n* cuclillo *m* (bird) || FAM bobo, ba; necio, cia (silly person).

gown [gaun] *n* traje *m* largo (of woman) || toga *f* (of lawyers, academics, etc.) || *dressing gown* bata *f.*

gownsman [-zmən] *n* universitario *m.*

— OBSERV El plural de *gownsman* es *gownsmen.*

GP *abbr of [general practitioner]* médico de medicina general, internista.

grab [græb] *n* cuchara *f* (mechanical device) || asimiento *m* (the act of snatching) || — FAM *to be up for grabs* estar libre || *to make a grab at sth.* intentar agarrar algo.

◆ *adj* tomado al azar (at random) || de sostenimiento (rail in buses, etc.).

grab [græb] *vt* agarrar (to snatch) || asir, coger, agarrar (to take) || pillar; *the police grabbed him before he could escape* la policía le pilló antes de que pudiese escapar || apropiarse (to seize illegally, forcibly) || echar mano a (to lay hands on) || FAM *to grab a bite* tomar un bocado.

◆ *vi to grab at* tratar de coger *or* de agarrarse a.

grace [greis] *n* gracia *f*, elegancia *f*, distinción *f* (charm, elegance) || gracia *f*, garbo *m* (fine bearing) || cortesía *f*, delicadeza *f* (courtesy); *he had the grace to say thank you* tuvo la cortesía de decir gracias || gracia *f*, perdón *m* (forgiveness) || bondad *f*, benevolencia *f*, gracia *f* (kindness) || favor *m* (favour) || REL gracia *f* (god's divine grace); *in a state of grace* en estado de gracia | bendición *f* de la mesa (prayer at meals) || plazo *m*, demora *f* (delay) || — *by the grace of* gracias a || *by the grace of God* por la gracia de Dios || *grace cup* última copa || FIG *her saving grace is her smile* la sonrisa es lo que la salva || *in this year of grace* en este año de gracia || *to fall from grace* caer en desgracia || *to say grace* bendecir la mesa || *with bad grace* de mala gana || *with good grace* de buena gana || *Your Grace* Su Excelencia (a duke), Su Ilustrísima (a bishop), Su Alteza (a prince).

◆ *pl* MYTH gracias; *the Three Graces* las tres Gracias || — *to be in s.o. bad graces* haber caído en desgracia con uno || *to be in s.o. good graces* gozar del favor de alguien || *to get into s.o.'s good graces* congraciarse con uno || *to put on airs and graces* darse aires.

grace [greis] *vt* adornar, embellecer (to adorn) || honrar (to honour).

graceful [-ful] *adj* elegante (elegant) || agraciado, da (nice) || gracioso, sa; lleno de gracia, precioso, sa (attractive, pleasing) || airoso, sa; garboso, sa (a movement) || cortés, delicado, da (polite).

gracefulness [-fulnis] *n* gracia *f.*

graceless [-lis] *adj* falto de gracia, sin gracia (lacking grace); *graceless features* facciones sin gracia || desgarbado, da (gawky) || feo, a (ugly) || descortés (impolite) || REL que no está en estado de gracia.

gracile ['græsil] *adj* grácil.

gracious ['greiʃəs] *adj* gracioso, sa (showing grace) || cortés, afable (courteous) || grato, ta; placentero, ra (pleasant) || amable (kind); *she was very gracious to me* estuvo muy amable conmigo || indulgente (lenient) || REL misericordioso, sa || — *Good gracious!, gracious me!* ¡válgame Dios! || *His o Her Gracious Majesty* Su Graciosa Majestad.

graciousness [-nis] *n* gracia *f* || benevolencia *f*, bondad *f* (kindness) || amabilidad *f* (affability) || REL misericordia *f.*

grackle ['grækl] *n* estornino *m*, quiscal *m* (bird).

gradate [grə'deit] *vt* graduar || degradar (colours).

◆ *vi* graduarse || degradarse (colours).

gradation [grə'deiʃən] *n* gradación *f* || degradación *f* (of colours).

grade [greid] *n* grado *m* (degree in rank, quality, etc.) || clase *f*, categoría *f* (of person or things) || cruce *m* de un pura sangre y otro que no lo es para mejorar la raza (of animals) || US curso *m* (in school) | nota *f* (mark given to a pupil) | pendiente *f* (gradient) | nivel *m* (level) || — US *grade crossing* paso *m* a nivel || *grade school* escuela primaria || FIG *to make the grade* llegar al nivel necesario.

grade [greid] *vt* graduar (to arrange in grades, to gradate) || degradar (colours) || nivelar (road, railway, etc.) || cruzar (animales) para mejorar la raza || clasificar (goods) || US calificar (in school) || *to grade up* cruzar (animales) para mejorar la raza.

gradient ['greidjənt] *n* pendiente *f*, declive *m* (declivity) || cuesta *f* (slope) || índice *m* de aumento *or* de disminución (of temperature, pressure, etc.) || PHYS gradiente *m.*

gradin [greidin]; **gradine** [grədiːn] *n* grada *f.*

gradual ['grædʒuəl] *n adj* gradual, progresivo, va.

◆ *n* REL gradual *m.*

graduate ['grædʒuət] *n* graduado, da; diplomado, da; titulado, da (from university) || CHEM probeta *f* graduada (tube) | frasco *m* graduado (flask).

graduate ['grædjueit] *vt* graduar || degradar (colours) || dar un diploma *or* un título a (a student).

◆ *vi* graduarse, sacar el título, diplomarse (to become a graduate); *to graduate as a doctor of philosophy* graduarse de doctor en filosofía || *to graduate into* convertirse progresivamente en.

graduate school ['grædʒuətskuːl] *n* US escuela *f* para graduados.

graduate student ['grædʒuət'stjuːdənt] *n* estudiante *m* & *f* de una escuela para graduados.

graduation [grædju'eiʃən] *n* graduación *f* || entrega *f* de un título (by the university).

graduator ['grædjueitə*] *n* TECH graduador *m.*

graffito [græ'fiːtəu] *n* pintada *f*, dibujo *m or* inscripción *f* en una pared.

— OBSERV El plural de *graffito* es *graffiti.*

graft [grɑːft] *n* AGR & MED injerto *m* || guante *m*, mamelas *f pl*, soborno *m* (corruption of public officer) || FAM trabajo *m*; *building roads is hard graft* hacer carreteras es un trabajo duro.

graft [grɑːft] *vt* AGR & MED injertar.

◆ *vi* injertarse, unirse [por medio de un injerto] || hacer un injerto (to make a graft) || dar guante, sobornar (to bribe) || FAM trabajar; *he has been grafting all day* ha estado trabajando todo el día.

graftage [-idʒ]; **grafting** [-iŋ] *n* injerto *m*; *shield grafting* injerto de escudete.

grafter [-ə*] *n* injertador *m* (person) || navaja *f or* cuchilla *f* de injertar (tool) || sobornador, ra (briber).

Grail [greil] *n* REL Grial *m*; *the Holy Grail* el Santo Grial.

grain [grein] *n* grano *m* (a cereal seed) || cereales *m* (cereals) || grano *m* (of sand, of salt) || poco *m*, pizca *f*; *not a grain of common sense* ni pizca de buen sentido || grano *m* (the smallest unit of weight) || veta *f* (of stone) || fibra *f*, grano *m* (of wood) || flor *f* (of leather) || PHOT grano *m* || — *against the grain* a contrapelo || FIG *take what he says with a grain of salt* créete la mitad de lo que dice || *that's a grain of comfort* ya es un consuelo || *to saw with the grain* serrar en la dirección de la veta.

grain [grein] *vt* vetear (wood, stone) || granear (stone for lithographic work) || granular (to give a granular surface to).
◆ *vi* volverse granulado, granularse.

grain elevator [-'eliveitə*] *n* silo *m* de cereales con elevador.

grainy [-i] *adj* granular || granado, da (full of grain) || granoso, sa; *grainy leather* cuero granoso || veteado, da (stone, marble).

gram [græm] *n* gramo *m* (unit of mass) || garbanzo *m* (chick-pea) || — *gram atom* átomo-gramo *m* || *gram atomic mass* o *weight* átomo-gramo *m* || *gram molecular mass* o *weight* molécula *f* gramo || *gram molecule* molécula *f* gramo.

grama ['græmə] *n* BOT grama *f.*

graminaceae [,greimi'neisii]; **gramineae** [,greimi'nei] *pl n* BOT gramíneas *f.*

graminaceous [,greimi'neiʃəs]; **gramineous** [grei'miniəs] *adj* BOT gramíneo, a.

gramma ['græmə] *n* BOT grama *f.*

grammar ['græmə*] *n* gramática *f*; *comparative, historical grammar* gramática comparativa, histórica || *grammar school* instituto *m* de segunda enseñanza (in Great Britain), escuela primaria (in United States).

grammarian [grə'mɛəriən] *n* gramático, ca.

grammatical [grə'mætikəl] *adj* gramatical.

gramme [græm] *n* gramo *m.*

gramophone ['græməfəun] *n* gramófono *m* (old style) || tocadiscos *m inv* (record player).

grampus ['græmpəs] *n* ZOOL orca *f.*

gran [græn] *n* abuelita *f.*

granadilla [grænə'dilə] *n* BOT granadilla *f.*

granary ['grænəri] *n* granero *m.*

grand [grænd] *adj* grandioso, sa; magnífico, ca; espléndido, da (splendid); *a grand view* una vista magnífica || importante (distinguished) || grande (great) || principal (staircase) || completo, ta; general (total) || MUS de cola (piano) || FAM fenomenal, grandioso, sa; estupendo, da; *it's been a grand day* ha sido un día fenomenal || — *that would be grand!* ¡sería estupendo!, ¡sería grandioso! || *to have a grand time* pasarlo estupendamente *or* en grande.
◆ *n* piano *m* de cola || FAM mil dólares *m pl.*

grandam ['grændæm] *n* abuelita *f*, abuela *f.*

Grand Canyon (the) [græn'kænjən] *pr n* GEOGR el Gran Cañón.

grandaunt ['grændɑːnt] *n* tía *f* abuela.

grandchild ['grænt∫aild] *n* nieto, ta.

granddad ['grændæd] *n* abuelito *m*, abuelo *m.*

granddaughter ['græn,dɔːtə*] *n* nieta *f.*

grand duchess ['grænd'dʌt∫is] *n* gran duquesa *f.*

grand duke ['grænd'djuːk] *n* gran duque *m.*

grandee [græn'diː] *n* grande *m* (nobleman); *Spanish grandee* grande de España.

grandeur ['grændʒə*] *n* grandiosidad *f* (magnificence); *the grandeur of the spectacle* la grandiosidad del espectáculo || nobleza *f*, grandeza *f* (nobility).

grandfather ['grænd,fɑːðə*] *n* abuelo *m* || *grandfather clock* reloj *m* de caja.

grandiloquence [græn'diləkwəns] *n* grandilocuencia *f.*

grandiloquent [græn'diləkwənt] *adj* grandilocuente, grandilocuo, cua.

grandiose ['grændiəus] *adj* grandioso, sa.

grandiosity [grændi'ɔsiti] *n* grandiosidad *f.*

grand jury [grænd'dʒuəri] *n* US JUR jurado *m* de acusación.

grand lodge [grænd'lɔdʒ] *n* gran oriente *m* (of Freemasons).

grandma ['grænmɑː] *n* abuelita *f*, abuela *f.*

grand mal ['grænd'mæl] *n* MED epilepsia *f.*

grand master [grænd'mɑːstə*] *n* gran maestre *m* (of an order) || gran maestro *m* (in chess).

grandmother ['grænd,mʌðə*] *n* abuela *f.*

grandnephew ['grænd,nevjuː] *n* sobrino *m* nieto.

grandniece ['grænniːs] *n* sobrina *f* nieta.

grand opera [græn'ɔpərə] *n* MUS ópera *f.*

grandpa ['grænpɑː] *n* abuelito *m*, abuelo *m.*

grandparent ['græn,pɛərənt] *n* abuelo, la.
◆ *pl* abuelos *m.*

grand piano [grænpi'ænəu] *n* piano *m* de cola.

grand prix ['grænpriː] *n* SP gran premio *m*, grand prix *m.*

grand prize ['græn,praiz] *n* premio *m* gordo.

grandsire ['græn,saiə*] *n* antepasado *m.*

grand slam ['grænslæm] *n* bola *f* (in bridge) || FIG éxito *m* rotundo.

grandson ['grænsʌn] *n* nieto *m.*

grandstand ['grænstænd] *n* tribuna *f.*

grand total ['gr,təutl] *n* total *m.*

granduncle ['grænd,ʌŋkl] *n* tío *m* abuelo.

grand vizier ['græn,vi'ziə*] *n* gran vizir *m.*

grange [greindʒ] *n* finca *f*, cortijo *m* [AMER hacienda *f*, estancia *f*] (farm) || casa *f* solariega (manor house).

granite ['grænit] *n* granito *m.*
◆ *adj* granítico, ca.

granitic [græ'nitik] *adj* granítico, ca.

granivorous [græ'nivərəs] *adj* granívoro, ra.

granny ['græni] *n* abuelita *f* (grandmother) || FAM comadre *f* || *granny flat* anexo *m* a una vivienda habilitado para un pariente anciano.

grant [grɑːnt] *n* concesión *f*, otorgamiento *m* (the act of granting) || concesión *f* (thing granted) || subvención *f* (money donated) || JUR cesión *f* | donación *f* (gift) || beca *f* (scholarship).

grant [grɑːnt] *vt* conceder, otorgar; *to grant a favour* conceder un favor || admitir; *granted that you are right* admitiendo que tienes razón; *he doesn't grant that he is wrong* no admite estar equivocado || asentir a (a proposition) || donar (to give) || JUR ceder, transferir || — *granted* o *granting that...* dado que... || *to take it for granted that...* dar por supuesto *or* por sentado que... || *to take s.o. for granted* no apreciar lo que vale alguien.

grant-aided [-'eidid] *adj* subvencionado, da.

grantee [grɑːntiː] *n* JUR cesionista *m* & *f* | donante *m* & *f*, donador, ra.

grant-in-aid [grɑːntineid] *n* subvención *f.*

grantor [grɑːn'tɔː*] *n* otorgante *m* || JUR cesionista *m* & *f* | donante *m* & *f*, donador, ra.

granular ['grænjulə*] *adj* granular || MED granulado, da.

granulate ['grænjuleit] *vt* granular.
◆ *vi* granularse.

granulated sugar [-id∫ugə*] *n* azúcar *m* cristalizado.

granulation [,grænjulei∫ən] *n* granulación *f*, granulado *m.*

granule ['grænjuːl] *n* gránulo *m.*

granulous ['grænjuləs] *adj* granuloso, sa.

grape [greip] *n* BOT uva *f* || — *grape harvest* vendimia *f* || *grape juice* mosto *m* (for wine), zumo *m* de uva (drink) || *grape sugar* glucosa *f.*
◆ *pl* VET grapas *f* || FIG *sour grapes!* ¡están verdes!

grapefruit ['greipfruːt] *n* pomelo *m*, toronja *f* (fruit).

grapeshot ['greip∫ɔt] *n* metralla *f.*

grapevine ['greipvain] *n* vid *f* (plant) || parra *f* (in the wall) || FAM rumores *m pl* (gossip) | medio *m* de comunicación *or* de recepción de informaciones || FAM *I heard on the grapevine that...* me he enterado de que...

graph [græf] *n* gráfico *m*, gráfica *f* || *graph paper* papel cuadriculado || INFORM *graph plotter* trazador *m* de gráficos.

graphic ['græfik] *adj* gráfico, ca; *graphic arts* artes gráficas || FIG gráfico, ca || INFORM *graphic data processing* informática *f* gráfica.

graphical [-əl] *adj* gráfico, ca.

graphics ['græfiks] *n* artes *f pl* gráficas || INFORM *graphics software* software *m* gráfico | *graphics terminal* terminal *m* gráfico | *graphics pad* o *tablet* paleta *f* gráfica.

graphite ['græfait] *n* grafito *m.*

graphologist [græ'fɔlədʒist] *n* grafólogo, ga.

graphology [græ'fɔlədʒi] *n* grafología *f.*

grapnel ['græpnəl] *n* rezón *m* (of anchor).

grapple ['græpl] *n* rezón *m* (grapnel) || lucha *f* cuerpo a cuerpo (fight).

grapple ['græpl] *vt* agarrar (to grip) || MAR aferrar con el rezón.
◆ *vi* luchar cuerpo a cuerpo (to fight) || intentar resolver; *to grapple with a problem* intentar resolver un problema || MAR echar el rezón.

grappling iron ['græpliŋ,aiən] *n* MAR rezón *m.*

grasp [grɑːsp] *n* asimiento *m* (grip) || apretón *m* (of hands) || dominio *m*; *a good grasp of grammar* un gran dominio de la gramática || control *m* || alcance *m* (range); *beyond my grasp* fuera de mi alcance || comprensión *f* (understanding) || — *to fall into s.o.'s grasp* caer en manos de alguien || *to have a good grasp of* dominar || *to loose one's grasp* soltar presa || *within one's grasp* al alcance de uno.

grasp [grɑːsp] *vt* agarrar, asir (to seize hold of) || estrechar, apretar (the hand) || sujetar (to hold firmly) || empuñar (weapon) || entender, comprender, captar (to understand) || apoderarse de (power).
◆ *vi* aprovechar; *to grasp at an opportunity* aprovechar una oportunidad || *to grasp at* intentar agarrar (an object).

grasper [-ə*] *n* avaro, ra.

grasping [-iŋ] *adj* avaro, ra; codicioso, sa.

grass [grɑːs] *n* hierba *f*, yerba *f* (green herbage) || pasto *m* (pasture) || césped *m* (lawn); *grass court* terreno de césped || FAM mariguana *f* || — *keep off the grass* prohibido pisar el césped || FIG *there's a snake in the grass* hay gato encerrado (sth.), hay un traidor (s.o.) || *to be at grass* estar pastando || FIG *to hear the grass grow* sentir crecer la hierba | *to let the grass grow under one's feet* perder el tiempo.

grass [grɑːs] *vt* sembrar de hierba (to plant with grass) || US apacentar, pacer (animals).
◆ *vi* cubrirse de hierba.

grasshopper ['grɑːs,hɔpə*] *n* ZOOL saltamontes *m inv* (insect).

grassland ['grɑːslænd] *n* prado *m*, pasto *m*, pastizal *m.*

grass roots ['grɑːsruːts] *n* población *f* rural (rural population) || raíz *f*, fundamento *m*, base *f* (the fundamental part).

grass-roots ['grɑːsruːts] *adj* básico, ca; fundamental || popular || rural.

grass snake ['grɑːs'sneik] *n* ZOOL culebra *f.*

grass widow ['grɑːs'widəu] *n* mujer *f* cuyo marido está ausente || US divorciada *f* | mujer *f* separada de su marido.

grassy ['grɑːsi] *adj* cubierto de hierba, herboso, sa (covered with grass) || herbáceo, a (like grass) || de color verde hierba.

grate [greit] *n* parrilla *f* (of a fireplace) || chimenea *f* (fireplace) || verja *f*, reja *f*, enrejado *m* (of a window) || criba *f*, tamiz *m*, cedazo *m* (sieve).

grate [greit] *vt* poner un enrejado *or* una verja *or* una reja a (to put a grating on) || rallar; *to grate cheese* rallar queso || hacer rechinar; *to grate one's teeth* hacer rechinar los dientes.
◆ *vi* chirriar (to make a harsh sound) || rechinar (the teeth) || *to grate on* crispar, irritar (the nerves), lastimar, herir (the ear).

grateful [-ful] *adj* agradecido, da (feeling thankfulness) || agradable, grato, ta (agreeable) || *to be grateful for* agradecer (por), estar agradecido por.

gratefully [-fuli] *adv* con agradecimiento, con gratitud.

gratefulness [-fulnis] *n* agradecimiento *m*, gratitud *f*.

grater [-ə*] *n* rallador *m*.

graticule ['grætikjuːl] *n* PHYS retícula *f*.

gratification [-grætifi'keiʃən] *n* gratificación *f* (reward) || FIG placer *m*, satisfacción *f*, contento *m*; *to her great gratification* con gran satisfacción suya.

gratifier ['grætifaiə*] *n* gratificador, ra.

gratify ['grætifai] *vt* satisfacer, agradar (to satisfy) || agradar a, dar gusto a (to please) || satisfacer (a whim) || gratificar, dar una gratificación a (to reward) || *to be gratified to* alegrarse de.

gratifying [-iŋ] *adj* satisfactorio, ria; agradable, grato, ta.

gratin ['grætɛ̃ːŋ] *n* CULIN gratén *m*, gratín *m*.

grating ['greitiɛ] *n* verja *f*, enrejado *m*, reja *f* || PHYS retícula *f*.
◆ *adj* áspero, ra (harsh) || chirriante (sound) || rechinante (teeth) || irritante, molesto, ta (irritating).

gratis ['greitis] *adv* gratis.

gratitude ['grætitjuːd] *n* gratitud *f*, agradecimiento, *m* (thankfulness).

gratuitous [grə'tjuːitəs] *adj* gratuito, ta || JUR *gratuitous contract* contrato *m* a título gratuito.

gratuitousness [-nis] *n* gratuidad *f*.

gratuity [grə'tjuːiti] *n* propina *f* (tip) || gratificación *f* (gift of money) || aguinaldo *m* (at Christmas).

gratulatory ['grætjulətəri, US 'grætʃələ,tɔːriː] *adj* de felicitación.

gravamen [grə'veimən] *n* agravio *m* (grievance) || JUR fundamento *m* (of a charge).
— OBSERV El plural de la palabra inglesa *gravamen* es *gravamina* o *gravamens*.

grave [greiv] *adj* serio, ria (warranting anxiety) || solemne (solemn) || importante (important) || severo, ra; oscuro, ra (colour) || grave (critical) || GRAMM grave (accent) || MUS grave, bajo, ja.
◆ *n* sepultura *f*, tumba *f* (tomb) || GRAMM acento *m* grave || — *pauper's grave* fosa *f* común || FIG *to turn in one's grave* retorcerse *or* revolverse en su tumba || *with one foot in the grave* con un pie en el sepulcro.

grave [greiv] *vt* grabar, esculpir, tallar (to carve) || FIG grabar (in one's mind).

graveclothes ['greivkləuðz] *pl n* mortaja *f sing*.

gravedigger ['greiv,digə*] *n* sepulturero *m*, enterrador *m*.

gravel [ixgrævəl] *n* grava *f*, guijo *m* (small stones); *gravel path* camino de grava || MED arenilla *f*.

gravel ['grævəl] *vt* echar una capa de grava a, cubrir con grava || FIG desconcertar.

gravelled ['grævəld] *adj* cubierto, ta de grava, (path, road).

gravelly ['grævəli] *adj* lleno de grava.

gravely ['greivli] *adv* gravemente.

graven ['greivən] *adj* esculpido, da; grabado, da; tallado, da.

graven image [-'imidʒ] *n* ídolo *m*.

gravestone ['greivstəun] *n* lápida *f* sepulcral, lápida *f* mortuoria.

graveyard ['greivjɑːd] *n* cementerio *m*.

gravid ['grævid] *adj* embarazada (a woman) || preñada (an animal) || siniestro, tra (portentous).

gravimetry [grə'vimətri] *n* gravimetría *f*.

graving dock ['greiviŋdɔk] *n* MAR dique *m* de carena.

gravitate ['græviteit] *vi* PHYS gravitar || FIG tender hacia, ser atraído por, dirigirse hacia.

gravitation [grævi'teiʃən] *n* PHYS gravitación *f*; *universal gravitation* gravitación universal || FIG tendencia *f*.

gravitational [-əl] *adj* de gravitación, de gravedad.

gravity ['græviti] *n* gravedad *f* (of an illness, a situation, an accident) || PHYS gravedad *f*; *laws of gravity* leyes de la gravedad; *centre of gravity* centro de gravedad || *specific gravity* peso específico.
◆ *adj* de gravedad.

gravure [grə'vjuə*] *n* fotograbado *m*.

gravy ['greivi] *n* CULIN salsa *f* || US FAM ganga, *f* || *gravy boat* salsera *f* || FIG & FAM *gravy train* chollo *m* (business, job).

gray, graybeard —> **grey, greybeard,** etc.

grayling [-liŋ] *n* tímalo *m* (fish).

graze [greiz] *n* rozadura *f*, roce *m* (rubbing) || pasto *m* (grass) || apacentamiento *m* (pasturing).

graze [greiz] *vt* rozar (to rub gently) || raspar (to scrape) || apacentar (cattle).
◆ *vi* rozar (to rub) || pastar, pacer (to feed).

grazier ['greizjə*] *n* ganadero, ra.

grazing ['greiziŋ] *n* apacentamiento *m*, pastoreo *m* (feeding) || pasto *m* (land).

grease [griːs] *n* grasa *f*.

grease [griːz] *vt* engrasar || TECH engrasar, lubricar, lubrificar || FIG & FAM *to grease the hand* o *palm of* untar la mano a.

grease gun [griːsgʌn] *n* TECH pistola *f* engrasadora, engrasador *m*.

greasepaint ['griːspeint] *n* maquillaje *m*.

grease trap ['griːstræp] *n* TECH sifón *m* colector de grasas.

greasiness ['griːzinis] *n* untuosidad *f*, lo grasiento.

greasy ['griːzi] *adj* grasiento, ta; *greasy food* comida grasienta || resbaladizo, za (slippery) || ensebado (pole) || sucio, cia (wool) || mugriento, ta (filthy) || FIG cobista (flattering).

greasy pole [griːsipəul] *n* cucaña *f*.

great [greit] *adj* grande (big); *we heard a great noise* oímos un gran ruido || grande (high); *the airplane flies at great altitude* el avión vuela a gran altura; *great speed* gran velocidad || grande (large); *a great number of people* un gran número de gente || FIG grande (eminent, splendid); *a great man* un gran hombre; *I gave a great party* di una gran fiesta || mucho, largo (time); *for a great while* durante mucho tiempo || importante (important) || favorito, ta (favourite) || noble (noble) || principal (stairs) || avanzado, da (age) || FAM estupendo, da; espléndido, da; magnífico, ca (excellent) || — *Alexander the Great* Alejandro Magno || *great at* o *on* muy bueno en || *great at* o *for* o *on* aficionado a || *great big* enorme, muy grande || *great with...* lleno de... || *she is a great friend of mine* es muy amiga mía || *to have a great time* pasarlo en grande *or* estupendamente || *to my great surprise* con gran sorpresa mía.
◆ *adv* FAM muy bien, estupendamente.
◆ *n* FIG grande *m*.

great-aunt [-'ɑːnt] *n* tía *f* abuela.

Great Barrier Reef (the) [-'bæriə* riːf] *pr n* GEOGR la Gran Barrera del Coral.

Great Bear [-bɛə*] *n* ASTR Osa *f* Mayor.

Great Britain [-'britn] *pr n* Gran Bretaña *f*.

great circle [-'səːkl] *n* círculo *m* máximo.

greatcoat [-kəut] *n* abrigo *m*, gabán *m*.

Great Dane [-dein] *n* mastín *m* danés (dog).

greater [greitə*] *adj comp* mayor || *Greater London* gran Londres.

Greater Dog ['greitə*,dɔg] *n* ASTR Can *m* Mayor.

greatest [greitist] *adj superl* mayor; *his greatest enemy* su mayor enemigo.

great-grandchild [-ʒgræntʃaild] *n* biznieto, ta; bisnieto, ta.
— OBSERV El plural es *great-grandchildren.*.

great-granddaughter [-'græn,dɔːtə*] *n* biznieta *f*, bisnieta *f*.

great-grandfather [-'græn,fɑːðə*] *n* bisabuelo *m*.

great-grandmother [-'græn,mʌðə*] *n* bisabuela *f*.

great-grandparent [-'grænd,pɛərənt] *n* bisabuelo, la.
◆ *pl* bisabuelos *m*.

great-grandson [-'grænsʌn] *n* biznieto *m*, bisnieto *m*.

great-great-granchild [-greit'græn,tʃaild] *n* tataranieto, ta.
— OBSERV El plural es *great-great-grandchildren.*

great-great-granddaughter [-greit'græn,dɔːtə*] *n* tataranieta *f*.

great-great-grandfather [-greit'græn,fɑːðə*] *n* tatarabuelo *m*.

great-great-grandmother [-greit'græn,mʌðə*] *n* tatarabuela *f*.

great-great-grandparent [-greit'grænd,pɛərənt] *n* tatarabuelo, la.
◆ *pl* tatarabuelos *m*.

great-great-grandson [-greit'grænsʌn] *n* tataranieto *m*.

greathearted [-'hɑːtid] *adj* valiente (brave) || generoso, sa; magnánimo, ma (magnanimous).

greatheartedness [-'hɑːtidnis] *n* valentía *f* (courage) || generosidad *f*, magnanimidad *f* (generosity).

great horned owl [-hɔːndaul] *n* ZOOL búho *m* real.

greatly ['greitli] *adv* enormemente, grandemente, mucho, muy.

great-nephew [greit'nevjuː] *n* sobrino *m* nieto.

greatness ['greitneis] *n* grandeza *f*.

great-niece [greitniːs] *n* sobrina *f* nieta.

great-uncle ['greit'ʌŋkl] *n* tío *m* abuelo.

Great War [-wɔː*] *n* Gran Guerra *f*, Primera Guerra *f* Mundial.

greave [griːv] *n* greba *f* (of an armour).
— OBSERV Esta palabra se usa generalmente en plural.

greaves [griːvz] *pl n* chicharrones *m*.

grebe [griːb] *n* colimbo *m* (bird).

Grecian ['gri:ʃən] *adj* griego, ga || *Grecian nose* nariz *f* griega.
◆ *n* helenista *m & f.*

Greco-Latin ['grekəu'lætin] *adj* grecolatino, na.

Greco-Roman ['grekəu'rəumən] *adj* grecorromano, na.

Greece [gri:s] *pr n* GEOGR Grecia *f.*

greed [gri:d]; **greediness** [-inis] *n* avaricia *f*, codicia *f*, avidez *f* (for wealth) || glotonería *f*, gula *f* (for food).

greedy [-i] *adj* glotón, ona; goloso, sa (gluttonous) || avaro, ra (*for* de) (avaricious, ambitious).

Greek [gri:k] *adj* griego, ga || *Greek fire* fuego griego.
◆ *n* griego, ga (native of Greece) || griego *m* (language) || — *Greek language* griego *m* || FIG & FAM *it's all Greek to me* es griego *or* chino para mí.

Greek Orthodox Church [-'ɔ:θədɔkstʃə:tʃ] *n* REL Iglesia *f* ortodoxa griega.

green [gri:n] *adj* verde (colour) || verde (unripe) || tierno, na (a shoot) || verde; *green wood* leña verde || crudo, da (meat) || sin curar (bacon) || en verde; *green hide* cuero en verde || fresco, ca (fresh) || pálido, da; lívido, da; verde (having a pale complexion) || lozano, na; *green old age* vejez lozana || FIG verde (immature) | novato, ta; inexperimentado, da (inexperienced) | crédulo, la; simplón, ona (gullible) || — *green fodder* forraje *m* verde || FIG *he is green with envy* se lo come la envidia, está verde de envidia.
◆ *n* verde *m* (colour) || verdor *m* (verdure) || césped *m* (lawn) || prado *m* (pasture) || pista *f* (for playing) || campo *m*, «green» *m* (in golf) || terreno *m* comunal, ejido *m* (a stretch of grass for public use).
◆ *pl* verduras *f* (vegetables) || ramas *f* y hojas verdes (for decoration).

green [gri:n] *vt* poner verde.
◆ *vi* volverse verde, verdear.

greenback [-bæk] *n* US FAM pápiro *m* (banknote).

green bean [-bi:n] *n* US judía *f* verde.

greenbelt [-belt] *n* zona *f* verde.

Green Beret [-ˌberei] *n* MIL & FAM comando británico *or* norteamericano.

green card [-kɑ:d] *n* carta *f* verde (car insurance).

greenery [-əri] *n* verdor *m* (verdure) || invernadero *m* (greenhouse).

green-eyed [-aid] *adj* celoso, sa; envidioso, sa (jealous) || de ojos verdes.

greenfinch [-fintʃ] *n* verderón *m* (bird).

greenfly [-flai] *n* ZOOL pulgón *m*.

greengage [-geidʒ] *n* BOT ciruela *f* claudia.

greengrocer [-'grəusə*] *n* verdulero, ra || *greengrocer's* verdulería *f.*

greengrocery [-ˌgrəusəri] *n* verdulería *f.*
◆ *pl* verduras *f* y frutas.

greenhorn [-hɔ:n] *n* simplón, ona (simpleton) || novato, ta; bisoño, ña (new).

greenhouse [-haus] *n* invernadero *m* || *greenhouse effect* efecto *m* invernadero.

greenish [-iʃ] *adj* verdoso, sa.

greenkeeper [-ki:pə*] *n* encargado, da de un campo de golf.

Greenlander [-lænd] *pr n* GEOGR Groenlandia *f.*

Greenlander [-lændə*] *n* groenlandés, esa.

green light [-lait] *n* FAM luz *f* verde (permission).

green manure [-mə'njuə*] *n* abono *m* vegetal.

green meat [-mi:t] *n* herbaje *m*.

greenness [-nis] *n* verdor *m*, lo verde || FIG bisoñería *f*, inexperiencia *f.*

green paper [-ˌpeipə*] *n* libro *m* verde (government paper).

Green Party [-ˌpɑ:ti] *n* partido *m* verde (ecologists).

green pepper [-pepə*] *n* pimiento *m* verde.

greenroom [-rum] *n* THEATR camerino *m* (dressing room).

greensand [-sænd] *n* GEOL arenisca *f* verde.

greensickness [-siknis] *n* MED clorosis *f.*

greenstone [-stəun] *n* diorita *f.*

greenstuff [-stʌf] *n* verduras *f pl* (vegetables).

greensward [-swɔ:d] *n* césped *m*.

green vitriol [-'vitriəl] *n* CHEM caparrosa *f* verde.

Greenwich ['grinidʒ] *n* GEOGR Greenwich || *Greenwich mean time* la hora según el meridiano de Greenwich.

greet [gri:t] *vt* saludar; *he greeted me with a smile* me saludó con una sonrisa || dar la bienvenida, recibir (to salute the arrival of) || FIG acoger || *to greet the eyes* presentarse a la vista.

greeting [-iŋ] *n* saludo *m* (expression of salutation) || recibimiento *m* (welcome) || felicitación *f*; *greetings card* tarjeta de felicitaciones; *greetings telegram* telegrama de felicitaciones.
◆ *pl* recuerdos *m* (in a letter).

gregarious [gri'gɛəriəs] *adj* gregario, ria; *gregarious instinct* instinto gregario || FIG sociable.

grège [greiʒ] *n* seda *f* cruda.

Gregorian [gri'gɔ:riən] *adj* gregoriano, na; *Gregorian chant, calendar* canto, calendario gregoriano.

Gregory ['gregəri] *pr n* Gregorio *m*.

greige [greiʒ] *n* seda *f* cruda.
◆ *adj* crudo, da (colour).

gremial ['gri:miəl] *n* REL gremial *m*.

gremlin ['gremlin] *n* duende *m*.

grenade [gri'neid] *n* MIL granada *f*; *hand grenade* granada de mano.

grenadier [grenə'diə*] *n* MIL granadero *m*.

grenadilla [grenə'dilə] *n* BOT granadilla *f.*

grenadine [ˌgrenə'di:n] *n* granadina *f.*

gressorial [gre'sɔ:rjəl] *adj* ZOOL ambulatorio, ria.

grew [gru:] *pret* → **grow.**

grey [grei] *adj* gris (colour) || rucio, cia (horse) || crudo, da (textiles) || cano, na (hair) || FIG triste, gris (sad) | nublado, da (overcast) | gris; *grey eminence* eminencia gris.
◆ *n* gris *m* (colour) || primeras luces *f pl*; *the first grey of dawn* las primeras luces del amanecer || caballo *m* tordo (horse) || *to turn grey* volverse gris (to become grey), encanecer (hair).

grey [grei] *vt* poner gris.
◆ *vi* volverse gris (to become grey) || encanecer (hair).

grey area [-ɛəriə] *n* aspecto *m* poco claro (of a subject, a situation).

greybeard [-biəd] *n* anciano *m* (old man).

Grey Friar [-'fraiə*] *n* franciscano *m*.

grey-haired [-'hɛəd]; **grey-headed** [-'hedid] *adj* canoso, sa.

greyhound [-haund] *n* galgo *m* (dog).

greying [-iŋ] *adj* canoso, sa.

greyish [-iʃ] *adj* grisáceo, a (grey) || entrecano, na; canoso, sa (hair).

grey matter [-'mætə*] *n* materia *f* gris, sustancia *f* gris.

greyness [-nis] *n* color *m* gris, gris *m*.

grey squirrel [-'skwirəl] *n* ZOOL ardilla *f* gris.

grid [grid] *n* verja *f*, reja *f* (grating) || ELECTR red *f* (network) | rejilla *f* (lattice) || cuadrícula (on a map) || CULIN parrilla *f* (gridiron) || THEATR peine *m*.

griddle ['gridl] *n* plancha *f* (for cooking) || TECH criba *f.*

griddlecake [-keik] *n* hojuela *f*, «crepe» *f.*

gride [graid] *vi* rechinar, chirriar.

gridiron ['gridˌaiən] *n* parrilla *f* (used for broiling) || red *f* (of pipes, etc.) || MAR carenero *m*, varadero *m* || THEATR peine *m* || US campo *m* de fútbol.

grief [gri:f] *n* pena *f*, dolor *m*, pesar *m*, aflicción *f*, congoja *f* || — *good grief!* ¡voto al chápiro verde! || *to bring to grief* apenar a, causar pesar a || *to come to grief* sufrir un accidente; *the car came to grief on the motorway* el coche sufrió un accidente en la autopista; estropearse; *the lamp came to grief* la lámpara se estropeó; fracasar, irse al traste; *my plan came to grief* mi plan fracasó.

grief-stricken [-strikən] *adj* desconsolado, da; apesadumbrado, da.

grievance ['gri:vəns] *n* queja *f* (complaint) || motivo *m* de queja (cause for complaint) || injusticia *f*, agravio *m* (injury).

grieve [gri:v] *vt* afligir, apenar, dar pena; *it grieves me to tell him it* me da pena decírselo || lamentar (to complain) || *to be grieved at* o *by* afligirse con *or* por *or* de.
◆ *vt* afligirse, apenarse || *to grieve about* o *at* o *over* lamentar.

grievous ['gri:vəs] *adj* doloroso, sa; penoso, sa (causing pain, trouble, suffering) || dolorido, da; apenado, da (hurt) || lastimoso, sa (pitiful) || grave (serious) || cruel (loss) || lamentable (error, fault) || intenso, sa (pain) || JUR *grievous bodily harm* lesiones *f pl* corporales graves.

griffin ['grifin] *n* MYTH grifo *m* || US recién llegado *m*.

griffon ['grifən] *n* grifón *m* (dog) || MYTH grifo *m* (griffin).

grifter ['griftə*] *n* US FAM tramposo, sa.

grig [grig] *n* grillo *m* (cricket) || angula *f*, cría *f* de la anguila (small eel) || FIG persona *f* que tiene azogue en las venas.

grill [gril] *n* parrilla *f* (gridiron) || asado *m* a la parrilla || parrillada *f* (a dish of grilled food) || restaurante *m* donde se sirven asados, parrilla *f* || → **grille** || *mixed grill* plato combinado.

grill [gril] *vt* asar a la parrilla (to broil on a gridiron) || torturar con fuego (to torture) || FIG someter a un interrogatorio severo (to interrogate).
◆ *vi* asarse a la parrilla || FIG someterse a un interrogatorio severo.

grillage ['grilidʒ] *n* entramado *m* de madera.

grille [gril] *n* rejilla *f* (of convent parlour) || mirilla *f* con enrejado (of a door) || ventana *f* con reja *or* barrotes (barred window) || reja *f*, verja *f* (protective barrier) || enrejado *m* (for ventilation).

grilled [grild] *adj* asado a la parrilla.

grillroom ['grilrum] *n* parrilla *f*, restaurante *m* donde se sirven asados.

grilse [grils] *n* ZOOL salmón *m* joven que vuelve del mar por primera vez.

grim [grim] *adj* feroz, severo, ra | torvo, va; ceñudo, da (expression) || inflexible, inexorable (unrelenting); *a grim determination* una determinación inflexible || terrible, horrible (threatening, forbidding) || porfiado, da; muy reñido, da (struggle) || solemne (solemn) || frío, a (cheerless) || macabro, bra; lúgubre, siniestro, tra (sinister) || desagradable (disagreeable) || *the grim truth* la pura verdad.

grimace [gri'meis] *n* mueca *f*.

grimace [gri'meis] *vi* hacer muecas.

grimalkin [gri'mælkin] *n* gato *m* viejo (cat) || FIG & FAM bruja *f* (unpleasant woman).

grime [graim] *n* mugre *f*, suciedad *f*.

grime [graim] *vt* ensuciar.

griminess ['graiminis] *n* suciedad *f*, mugre *f*.

grimness ['grimnis] *n* aspecto *m* siniestro *or* lúgubre || inflexibilidad *f* || porfía *f* (of struggle).

grimy ['graimi] *adj* mugriento, ta; sucio, cia.

grin [grin] *n* sonrisa *f* abierta (smile) || risa *f* burlona *or* socarrona (sneer) || mueca *f* (grimace).

grin [grin] *vt* expresar con una sonrisa *or* con una mueca.

◆ *vi* sonreír abiertamente (to smile broadly) || hacer una mueca de dolor (in pain) || reír burlonamente (in scorn) || enseñar los dientes (to bare the teeth) || — FIG *to grin and bear it* poner al mal tiempo buena cara | *to grin like a Cheshire cat* sonreír abiertamente.

grind [graind] *n* trabajo *m or* estudio *m* pesado *or* penoso (hard work) || pendiente *f* muy empinada (steep slope) || ⟶ **grinding** || SP carrera *f* de obstáculos || US FAM empollón, ona (student).

grind* [graind] *vt* moler (to mill) || pulverizar (to pulverize) || triturar (to crash) || picar (meat) || afilar (to sharpen) || esmerilar (valves, diamonds, glass) || hacer rechinar (one's teeth) || tocar (a barrel organ) || agobiar, oprimir (to oppress) || — *to grind down* oprimir, desgastar (to wear away), reducir; *to grind down to dust* reducir a polvo; acabar con; *to grind down the opposition* acabar con la oposición | *to grind out a tune* desgranar una canción (a barrel organ) || FAM *to grind sth. into s.o.'s head* meterle algo en la cabeza a alguien.

◆ *vi* molerse (to mill) || triturarse (to crash) || pulverizarse (to pulverize) || afilarse (to sharpen) || picarse (to meat) || andar con dificultad (to move laboriously) || FAM empollar (to study hard) || trabajar duramente (to work hard) || chirriar (to grate) || *to grind to a halt* pararse lenta y ruidosamente (vehicle).

— OBSERV Pret y pp ***ground***.

grinder ['graində*] *n* afilador *m* (of knives) || afiladora *f* (sharpener) || muela *f* (grindstone) || moledor *m* (for sugar cane) || molinillo *m* (for coffee, pepper) || molino *m* (mill) || trituradora *f* (crusher).

◆ *pl* muelas *f pl* (teeth).

grindery ['graindəri] *n* materiales *m pl* de zapatero *or* de talabartero || taller *m* de afilador (where tools are ground).

grinding ['graindiŋ] *n* afilado *m* (of knives) || molienda *f* (milling) || trituración *f* (crushing) || esmerilado *m* (of valves, glass, etc.) || chirrido *m* (shrill sound) || FIG opresión *f*.

grindstone ['graindstəun] *n* muela *f* (for sharpening) || piedra *f* de amolar (from which stones for grinding are made) || FIG *to keep one's nose to the grindstone* trabajar con ahínco, trabajar sin levantar cabeza.

gringo ['griŋgəu] *n* gringo *m*.

grip [grip] *n* asimiento *m* (tight hold) || mango *m* (of racket, etc.) || asidero *m* (handle) || empuñadura *f* (of weapon) || apretón *m* (of hands) || dominio *m*, poder *m*, control *m* (power) || comprensión *f* (mental grasp) || interés *m*; *the play lost its grip in the third act* la obra perdió su interés en el tercer acto || TECH sujeción *f* || horquilla *f* (for the hair) || dolor *m* agudo (pain) || US maletín *m*, bolsa *f* de viaje || — *to come to grips* luchar a brazo partido, pelear (to fight), enfrentarse; *to come to grips with the situation* enfrentarse con la situación || FIG *to get a grip on o.s.* dominarse, controlarse || *to get to grips with a problem* atacar un problema || FIG *to lose one's grip* perder el control.

grip [grip] *vt* agarrar (to grasp) || empuñar (a weapon) || apretar, estrechar (hands) || captar la atención; *the play gripped the audience* la obra de teatro captó la atención del público || sujetar (to hold).

◆ *vi* agarrarse.

gripe [graip] *n* ⟶ **grasp** & **grip** || retortijón *m* (pain in the bowels) || FAM *he likes a good gripe* le gusta quejarse.

gripe [graip] *vt* ⟶ **grasp** & **grip** || dar retortijones en (in the bowels).

◆ *vi* FAM quejarse (to complain) || sentir retortijones (in the bowels).

griper [-ə*] *n* US FAM gruñón, ona; refunfuñador, ra.

grippe [grip] *n* MED gripe *f*.

gripping ['gripiŋ] *adj* cautivante, fascinante.

grippy ['gripi] *adj* griposo, sa.

gripsack ['gripsæk] *n* US bolsa *f* de viaje, maletín *m* (small bag).

grisaille [gri'zeil] *n* grisalla *f*.

grisly ['grizli] *adj* horroroso, sa; espantoso, sa.

grist [grist] *n* grano *m* para moler (grain for grinding) || malta *f* molida (malt) || molienda *f* (quantity of grain ground at one time) || FIG beneficio *m*, ganancia *f* || US FAM cantidad *f*, montón *m* || — FIG *it's all grist to his mill* saca provecho de todo | *to bring grist to the mill* aportar su granito de arena.

gristle ['grisl] *n* cartílago *m*.

gristly ['grisli] *adj* cartilaginoso, sa.

grit [grit] *n* asperón *m*, gres *m*, arenisca *f* (sandstone) || granos *m pl* de arena (tiny particles of sand) || grano *m* (structure of stone) || FIG valor *m*, valentía *f*, ánimo *m* (courage) | resistencia *f* (tenacity) | entereza *f*, carácter *m* (character) | firmeza *f* (of character).

grit [grit] *vt/vi* rechinar || FIG *to grit one's teeth* rechinar los dientes (to grate), apretar los dientes (in determination).

grits [grits] *pl n* sémola *f sing* || grava *f sing* (for road surfacing) || US maíz *m sing* a medio moler (coarse hominy).

grittiness ['gritinis] *n* FIG valor *m*, valentía *f*, ánimo *m*.

gritty ['griti] *adj* FIG valiente, animoso, sa (plucky) || arenoso, sa (sandy).

grizzle ['grizl] *vt* hacer encanecer.

◆ *vi* encanecer (hair) || quejarse (to complain) || lloriquear, gimotear (to cry).

grizzled [-d] *adj* entrecano, na (hair).

grizzly ['grizli] *adj* entrecano, na (hair) || pardo (bear).

◆ *n* oso *m* pardo (grizzly bear).

groan [grəun] *n* gemido *m*, quejido *m* (moan) || gruñido *m* (of disapproval).

groan [grəun] *vt* decir con voz quejumbrosa.

◆ *vi* gemir, quejarse (to moan) || sufrir (to suffer) || crujir (to creak) || gruñir, refunfuñar (to grumble).

groat [grəut] *n* moneda *f* de cuatro peniques.

groats [grəuts] *pl n* avena *f sing* mondada.

grocer ['grəusə*] *n* tendero, ra [AMER abarrotero, ra; pulpero, ra] || *grocer's* tienda *f* de ultramarinos *or* de comestibles, ultramarinos *m* [AMER tienda *f* de abarrotes, pulpería *f*].

grocery ['grəusəri] *n* tienda *f* de comestibles, *or* de ultramarinos, ultramarinos *m* [AMER tienda *f* de abarrotes, pulpería *f*] (grocer's shop).

◆ *pl* comestibles *m* [AMER abarrotes *m*].

grog [grɔg] *n* grog *m*, ponche *m* (drink).

grogginess ['grɔginis] *n* inseguridad *f*, inestabilidad *f* || atontamiento *m* (of a boxer).

groggy ['grɔgi] *adj* «groggy» (a boxer) || tambaleante (after drinking) || débil (after illness) || inestable, poco seguro (unstable) || con debilidad en las patas delanteras (a horse).

groin [grɔin] *n* ANAT ingle *f* || ARCH arista *f* de bóveda (projecting edge).

◆ *pl* ARCH crucería *f sing*.

groin [grɔin] *vt* ARCH construir con bóveda de crucería.

grommet ['grʌmet] *n* ojal *m*.

groom [grum] *n* novio *m* (bridegroom) || mozo *m* de cuadra (of horses) || ayuda *m* de cámara (in royal palace).

groom [grum] *vt* almohazar (a horse) || preparar (to prepare) || arreglar, acicalar (to make smart).

groomsman [-zmən] *n* padrino *m* de boda.

— OBSERV El plural de *groomsman* es *groomsmen*.

groove [gru:v] *n* ranura *f* (small rut or channel) || garganta *f* (of a rail, pulley or runner) || acanaladura *f* (of a column) || estría *f* (stria) || surco *m* (of record) || rodada *f* (of car) || PRINT cran *m* (of letters) || FIG rutina *f* (routine) || FIG *in the groove* en plena forma (on the top of one's form), de moda (in fashion).

groove [gru:v] *vt* acanalar, hacer ranuras en || rayar, estriar.

grooved [-d] *adj* acanalado, da; estriado, da || rayado, da (a gun).

grooving [-iŋ] *n* ⟶ **groove** || *grooving plane* acanalador *m*.

groovy [-i] *adj* FAM fenómeno, na; estupendo, da (wonderful).

grope [grəup] *vi/vt* andar a tientas || — *to groope for* buscar a tientas || *to grope one's way in* entrar a tientas.

groping ['grəupiŋ] *adj* inseguro, ra.

gropingly [grəupiŋli] *adv* a tientas.

grosbeak ['grəusbi:k] *n* ZOOL piñonero *m* (bird of the finch family).

gross [grəus] *adj* gordo, da; grueso, sa (fat) || grueso, sa (thick) || denso, sa (dense) || grande; *gross negligence* gran negligencia || craso, sa; flagrante (glaring); *gross ignorance* ignorancia crasa || grosero, ra; ordinario, ria (vulgar) || verde, indecente (obscene) || zafio, fia; lerdo, da (rough) || basto, ta; grosero, ra (unrefined); *gross humour* humor grosero || bruto, ta; *gross profit* beneficio bruto; *gross weight* peso bruto || total (overall) || general || insensible || — *gross amount* importe *m* total || *gross national product* producto nacional bruto || *gross ton* tonelada larga.

◆ *n* total *m*, totalidad *f* (totality) || gruesa *f*, doce docenas *f pl* (twelve dozen); *a gross of pencils* una gruesa de lápices || — *by the gross* al por mayor || *in gross, in the gross* en total, en conjunto.

gross [grəus] *vt* US recaudar en bruto.

grossly [-li] *adv* enormemente, excesivamente; *he was grossly over weight* estaba excesivamente gordo.

grossness [-nis] *n* enormidad *f* (of a crime) || grosería *f* (of language) || magnitud *f* (of a body) || espesor *m*, grueso *m* (thickness) || densidad *f*.

grotesque [grəu'tesk] *adj* ARCH grotesco, ca || grotesco, ca (absurd).

◆ *n* obra *f* grotesca (painting, sculpture) || grotesco *m*, grutesco *m* (grotesque style).

grotesquerie; US **grotesquery** [grəu'teskəri] *n* carácter *m* grotesco, lo grotesco.

grotto ['grɔtəu] *n* gruta *f*, cueva *f*.

— OBSERV El plural de esta palabra es *grottoes* o *grottos*.

grotty ['grɔti] *adj* FAM de mala muerte, lamentable.

grouch [grautʃ] *n* cascarrabias *m* & *f inv*, refunfuñón, ona (grumbling person) || mal humor *m*, malhumor *m* (bad humour) || motivo *m* de queja (cause for grumbling) || *to have a grouch against* estar resentido con alguien.

grouch [grautʃ] *vi* refunfuñar (to complain) || estar de mal humor (to be bad-tempered).

grouchy [-i] *adj* malhumorado, da (bad-tempered) || refunfuñón, ona (grumbling).

ground [graund] *n* suelo *m*, tierra *f* (the surface of the earth) || tierra *f* (the upper soil) || terreno *m* (piece of land) || SP campo *m*, terreno *m*; *football ground* campo de fútbol || campo *m* (of a battle) || GEOGR territorio *m*, tierra *f* || FIG terreno *m*, campo *m* (field) | fundamento *m*, base *f* (basis) | motivo *m*, razón *f* (motive) | tema *m* (subject) || ARTS fondo *m* (background); *on a green ground* sobre un fondo verde || fondo *m* (of water, of the sea) || US ELECTR tierra *f*, toma *f* de tierra || — FIG *above ground* en vida, con vida, vivo, va || *breeding ground of vice* terreno abonado para el vicio || *camping ground* camping *m* || FIG *down to the ground* completamente | *from the ground up* completamente || *Holy ground* Tierra Santa || FIG *into the ground* hasta más no poder | *on delicate ground* en situación delicada || *on the ground* sobre el terreno || *piece of ground* terreno *m* || FIG *to be on one's own ground* estar en su propio terreno, estar en su elemento | *to break fresh* o *new ground* abrir un nuevo camino || *to break ground* abrir la tierra (the earth), empezar a construir (to begin to build), abrir un nuevo camino (to break fresh ground) || FIG *to cover the ground* discutir todos los puntos | *to cut the ground from under s.o.'s feet* tomarle la delantera a alguien | *to drop* o *to throw on the ground* dar en tierra con || *to fall to the ground* caer al suelo (to fall), venirse abajo, fracasar (to fail) || *to gain ground* ganar terreno || *to get off the ground* despegar, quitar tierra (a plane), llevarse a cabo, realizarse (to be carried out) || FIG *to give ground* ceder terreno | *to go over the same ground* repetir la misma canción | *to go to ground* esconderse | *to hold one's ground* mantenerse firme | *to keep one's* o *both feet on the ground* tener los pies en la tierra | *to lose ground* perder terreno | *to shift one's ground* cambiar de táctica | *to stand one's ground* mantenerse en sus trece, no ceder | *to suit s.o. down to the ground* venirle al pelo *or* de perilla a uno, convenir mucho a alguien (sth.), sentar a alguien como anillo al dedo (a dress) || MAR *to take the ground* encallar, varar || FIG *to touch ground* tocar tierra | *to workship the ground s.o. walks on* besar la tierra que alguien pisa.
◆ *pl* jardines *m*, jardín *m sing* (enclosed land attached to a house) || poso *m sing* (dregs) || zurrapa *f sing* (coffee sediment) || — FIG *on the grounds of* por motivos de, por razones de, a causa de (because of) | *on the grounds that* porque.

ground [graund] *vt* MAR hacer encallar, varar (a ship) || AVIAT obligar a permanecer en tierra (to confine to the ground) || enseñar los conocimientos básicos a (to teach basic facts) || preparar a fondo de (in painting) || ELECTR conectar con tierra || poner en tierra (to place on the ground) || MIL descansar (arms) || FIG fundar, basar || — FIG *well grounded* bien fundado | *well grounded in* muy versado en, muy entendido en.

ground [graund] *pret/pp* → **grind.**
◆ *adj* a ras de tierra || terrestre || FIG fundamental | básico, ca || — de tierra; *ground crew* o *staff* personal de tierra || ELECTR *ground cable* cable de toma de tierra | *ground connection* toma de tierra.

ground-cherry [-'tʃeri] *n* BOT alquequenje *m*.

ground control [-kən'trəul] *n* control *m* desde tierra.

ground cover [-,kʌvə*] *n* matas *f pl*, arbustos *m pl*.

grounder [-ə*] *n* SP pelota *f* rasa.

ground fire [-faiə*] *n* fuego *m* antiaéreo.

ground floor [-'flɔ:*] *n* planta *f* baja.

groundhog [-'hɔg] *n* marmota *f* (animal).

ground ice [-ais] *n* hielo *m* de fondo.

grounding [-iŋ] *n* *to have a good grounding in* tener una buena base en.

ground lead [-li:d] *n* ELECTR conductor *m* a tierra.

groundless [-lis] *adj* sin fundamento, infundado, da || sin base.

ground level [-'levl] *n* nivel *f* del suelo.

groundling [-liŋ] *n* pez *m* que vive en el fondo del agua || planta *f* rastrera (creeping plant) || THEATR mosquetero *m*.

groundnut [-nʌt] *n* BOT cacahuete *m* [AMER cacahuate *m*, maní *m*] (peanut) | chufa *f* (earth almond).

ground plan [-plæn] *n* ARCH plano *m*, planta *f* || FIG proyecto *m* fundamental.

ground plate [-pleit] *n* US ELECTR placa *f* de conexión a tierra || ARCH durmiente *m*.

ground rent [-rent] *n* alquiler *m* del terreno.

groundsel [-səl] *n* BOT zuzón *m*.

groundsheet [-ʃi:t] *n* tela *f* impermeable.

groundsman [-zmən] *n* encargado *m* de campo (of sports field), jardinero *m* (of park).

ground speed [-spi:d] *n* AVIAT velocidad *f* respecto a la tierra.

ground squirrel [-'skwirəl] *n* ZOOL ardilla *f* terrestre.

ground swell [-'swel] *n* mar *m* de fondo || ola *f* de fondo.

ground wave [-weiv] *n* onda *f* terrestre.

ground wire [-'waiə*] *n* US ELECTR cable *m* de toma de tierra.

groundwork [-wə:k] *n* base *f* (basis); *to do the groundwork for* echar las bases de || plan (of a novel) || fundamento *m* (foundation) || fondo *m* (background).

group [gru:p] *n* grupo *m*, agrupación *f* || ARTS & MUS conjunto *m* || grupo *m* (of figures) || TECH haz *m* (of rails) || — *blood group* grupo sanguíneo || *group insurance* seguro colectivo || *group therapy* terapia *f* de grupo || *pressure group* grupo de presión.

group [gru:p] *vt* agrupar.
◆ *vi* agruparse.

group captain [-'kæptin] *n* AVIAT jefe *f* de escuadrilla.

grouper ['gru:pə*] *n* mero *m* (fish).

groupie ['gru:pi] *n* FAM *m* & *f* de un cantante *or* una estrella *or* un grupo musical.

grouping ['gru:piŋ] *n* agrupación *f*, agrupamiento *m*.

grouse [graus] *n* urogallo *m* (bird) || FAM queja *f* (complain).

grouse [graus] *vi* quejarse (to complain).

grout [graut] *n* ARCH lechada *f*.

grout [graut] *vt* ARCH rellenar con lechada.

grove [grəuv] *n* arboleda *f*, bosquecillo *m* (small group of trees) || *orange grove* naranjal *m*.

grovel ['grɔvl] *vi* arrastrarse (to slide) || FIG humillarse, rebajarse, arrastrarse (to humiliate o.s.) || FIG *to grovel in the dust* morder el polvo.

groveller; groveler [-ə*] *n* persona *f* servil.

grovelling; groveling [-iŋ] *adj* servil, rastrero, ra (servile).

grow* [grəu] *vt* cultivar; *to grow vegetables* cultivar verduras || dejar crecer (to allow to grow); *to grow a beard* dejarse crecer la barba || adquirir; *to grow a habit* adquirir una costumbre || FIG cultivar.
◆ *vi* crecer (to increase in size) || desarrollarse (to develop) || cultivarse, ser cultivado (to be cultivated) || aumentar, crecer, incrementar (to increase) || hacerse, volverse (to become); *to grow bolder* hacerse más atrevido || llegar a (to come to) || ponerse (pale, red, etc.) || — FIG *they don't grow on every tree* no se encuentran a la vuelta de la esquina || *to grow accustomed* acostumbrarse || *to grow better* mejorar || *to grow dark* oscurecer || *to grow old* envejecer || *to grow to do sth.* llegar a hacer algo || *to grow used to* acostumbrarse a || *to grow weary* cansarse.
◆ *phr v* **to grow apart** distanciarse || **to grow from** derivarse de (to derive from) || **to grow into** hacerse, convertirse en, llegar a ser || **to grow on** o **upon** llegar a gustar; *a picture that grows on you* una película que llega a gustar | arraigar (custom) || **to grow out of** quedársele pequeño; *the child has grown out of his jacket* al niño la chaqueta se le ha quedado pequeña | perder (a habit) | derivarse de (to stem from) || — *to grow out of fashion* pasar de moda || **to grow up** crecer mucho (a child) | hacerse mayor (to reach adulthood) | establecerse (to become prevalent) | desarrollarse (to extend) | madurar (in mind) || — *to grow up together* criarse juntos.

— OBSERV Pret ***grew***; pp ***grown***.

grower [-ə*] *n* cultivador, ra (one who grows vegetables) || *this plant is a fast grower* esta planta crece rápidamente.

growing [-iŋ] *n* crecimiento *m* (of a child) || cultivo *m* (of plants) || desarrollo *m* (development).
◆ *adj* creciente (increasing) || que crece, en crecimiento (child) || *growing pains* dolores producidos por el crecimiento (of children).

growl [graul] *n* gruñido *m* (of person, dog) || retumbo *m* (of a gun).

growl [graul] *vt* decir refunfuñando.
◆ *vi* gruñir, refunfuñar (a person) || gruñir (a dog) || retumbar (a gun).

growler [-ə*] *n* simón *m* (four-wheeled cab) || témpano *m* de hielo (small iceberg) || FAM refunfuñador, ra; refunfuñón, ona (grumbler).

growling [-iŋ] *adj* refunfuñador, ra (person) || que retumba (gun).

grown [grəun] *adj* adulto, ta || *grown over with* cubierto de.
◆ *pp* → **grow.**

grown-up [-ʌp] *adj* adulto, ta (adult) || crecido, da (child, plant).
◆ *n* adulto, ta; mayor *m* (person).

growth [grəuθ] *n* crecimiento *m* (increase in size); *growth factor* factor de crecimiento || incremento *m*, aumento *m* (increase) || desarrollo *m* (development); *economic growth* desarrollo económico || cultivo *m* (of plants) || vegetación *f* || MED bulto *m*, excrecencia *f* (tumour) || origen *m* (origin); *of foreign growth* de origen extranjero || — ECON *growth rate* tasa *f or* índice *m* de crecimiento || *to reach full growth* alcanzar su plenitud, alcanzar su pleno desarrollo.

groyne [grɔin] *n* espolón *m*, espigón *m*.

grub [grʌb] *n* ZOOL larva *f*, gusano *m* || FAM comida *f*, manducatoria *f*, jamaica *f* (food) | esclavo *m* del trabajo (drudge) | plumífero *m*, escritorzuelo *m* (hack) || US empollón *m* (at school).

grub [grʌb] *vt* cavar (to dig) || limpiar de hierbas (a land) || FAM dar de comer (to feed) || *to*

grub up o out desenterrar, descubrir (to discover), arrancar, extirpar (to extirpate).
◆ *vi* cavar (to dig) ‖ hozar (a pig) ‖ FIG hurgar (to search laboriously) ‖ FAM pringar, apencar, acurrelar (to work) | empollar (to study) | manducar, jalar, jamar (to eat).

grubber [-ə*] *n* AGR roturadora *f* ‖ FAM gran trabajador *m* (hard-working person) | empollón *m* (at school) | comilón *m* (eater).

grubbiness [-inis] *n* suciedad *f*.

grubby [-i] *adj* sucio, cia (dirty) ‖ agusanado, da (grub-infested).

grubstake [-steik] *n* US subvención *f* or ayuda *f* concedida a un prospector con la condición de que éste reparta lo que encuentre | crédito *m* (credit).

grubstake [-steik] *vt* subvencionar a, ayudar a (a miner) ‖ conceder un crédito a (to give credit to).

grudge [grʌdʒ] *n* rencor *m*, resentimiento *m* ‖ *to bear s.o. a grudge* estar resentido con alguien, guardar rencor a alguien.

grudge [grʌdʒ] *vt* envidiar (to envy) ‖ dar a regañadientes (to give) ‖ ver con malos ojos (to resent).

grudgingly [grʌdʒiŋli] *adv* a regañadientes.

gruel [gruəl] *n* CULIN gachas *f pl*.

gruelling [-iŋ] *adj* penoso, sa; duro, ra (hard) ‖ agotador, ra (exhausting).
◆ *n* prueba *f* dura ‖ paliza *f* (beating).

gruesome ['gru:səm] *adj* espantoso, sa; horrible.

gruff [grʌf] *adj* ronco, ca (harsh) ‖ brusco, ca (blunt).

gruffness [-nis] *n* brusquedad *f*.

grumble ['grʌmbl] *n* queja *f* (complaint) ‖ rugido *m*, retumbo *m* (of a gun, thunder, etc.).

grumble ['grʌmbl] *vt* decir refunfuñando.
◆ *vi* quejarse (*at, about* de) (to complain) ‖ refunfuñar (to moan) ‖ retumbar a lo lejos, rugir (gun, thunder).

grumbler [-ə*] *n* refunfuñador, ra; refunfuñón, ona.

grumbling [-iŋ] *adj* gruñón, ona; refunfuñón, ona.

grume [gru:m] *n* grumo *m*, cuajarón *m*, coágulo *m* (clot of blood).

grummet ['grʌmet] *n* ojal *m*.

grumous ['gru:məs] *adj* grumoso, sa.

grumpiness [grʌmpinis] *n* malhumor *m*, mal genio *m*.

grumpish ['grʌmpiʃ]; **grumpy** ['grʌmpi] *adj* malhumorado, da; gruñón, ona.

grunt [grʌnt] *n* gruñido *m* (sound).

grunt [grʌnt] *vt* decir gruñendo.
◆ *vi* gruñir.

grunter [-ə*] *n* FAM marrano *m* (pig) ‖ FIG refunfuñón, ona (grumbler).

grunting [-iŋ] *adj* gruñidor, ra.

Gruyère ['gru:jɛə*] *n* gruyere *m* (cheese).

gryphon ['grifən] *n* MITH grifo *m*.

G-string ['dʒi:striŋ] *n* FAM taparrabo *m* (garment).

guacamole [gwækə'məuli] *n* guacamol *m*, guacamole *m*.

guaco ['gwɑ:kəu] *n* BOT guaco *m*.

Guadaloupe [gwɑ:də'lu:p] *pr n* GEOGR Guadalupe *f* (island).

guaiacol ['gwaiəkɔl] *n* guayacol *m*.

guaiacum ['gwaiəkəm] *n* BOT guayacán *m* (tree) | guayaco *m* (wood).

guama ['gwɑ:mə] *n* BOT guamo *m*, guama *f* (tree) | guama *f* (fruit).

guanaco [gwə'nɑ:kəu] *n* ZOOL guanaco *m*.

Gaunche ['gwæntʃ] *adj/n* guanche (first inhabitants of the Canary Islands).

guano ['gwɑ:nəu] *n* guano *m* (fertilizer).

guarani [gwɑ:rə'ni:] *adj/n* guaraní.

guarantee [gærən'ti:] *n* garantía *f* (pledge, promise) ‖ COMM garantía *f*; *to give a six-month guarantee* dar una garantía de seis meses | certificado *m* de garantía (certificate) ‖ JUR garantía *f*, fianza *f* (guaranty) | persona *f* garantizada | fiador, ra; garante *m* & *f* (guarantor) ‖ *under guarantee* bajo garantía.

guarantee [gærən'ti:] *vt* garantizar; *to guarantee a clock for a year* garantizar un reloj por un año ‖ garantizar, ser fiador de (to act as a guarantor for) ‖ garantizar, avalar (a bill) ‖ responder de (s.o.'s conduct) ‖ asegurar (to ensure).

guaranteed [-d] *adj* garantizado, da ‖ asegurado, da.

guarantor [gærən'tɔ:*] *n* garante *m* & *f*.

guard [gɑ:d] *n* guardia *f* (a keeping watch, a ceremonial escort, a protective force, body of people set to keep watch) ‖ centinela *m*, guardia *m* (sentry) ‖ guardián *m*, guarda *m* (warder) ‖ jefe *m* de tren (of train) ‖ salvaguardia *f*, protección *f* (safeguard) ‖ guarda *f*, guarnición *f*, guardamano *m* (of a sword) ‖ SP guardia *f* (in boxing, fencing) | defensa *m* (in basketball, American football) ‖ TECH dispositivo *m* protector *or* de seguridad (in machinery) ‖ — MIL *advance guard* avanzada *f* | *changing of the guard* relevo *m* de la guardia ‖ *civil guard* guardia civil ‖ SP *low guard* guardia baja ‖ *new* o *relieving guard, old guard* guardia entrante, saliente ‖ FIG *to be off one's guard* estar descuidado *or* desprevenido ‖ *to be on guard* estar de guardia ‖ FIG *to be on one's guard* estar en guardia ‖ *to catch s.o. off guard* coger a alguien desprevenido ‖ MIL *to change the guard* relevar la guardia | *to come off guard* salir de guardia | *to go on guard* entrar en guardia ‖ *to keep guard over* vigilar | *to mount guard* montar la guardia, hacer guardia ‖ FIG *to put o.s. on guard* ponerse en guardia | *to put s.o. on his guard* poner en guardia a uno ‖ MIL *to stand guard* montar la guardia ‖ *under guard* a buen recaudo.
◆ *pl* guardia *f sing* (royal regiment).

guard [gɑ:d] *vt* vigilar, custodiar; *to guard a prisoner* vigilar a un prisionero ‖ proteger, defender (to defend, to provide with a guard, protective device, etc.) ‖ escoltar (to escort) ‖ guardar; *to guard the gates of the city* guardar las puertas de la ciudad.
◆ *vi* *to guard against* protegerse contra (to take precautions), guardarse; *guard against doing that* guárdate de hacer eso; impedir, evitar (to prevent).

guard boat [-bəut] *n* patrullero *m*, guardacostas *m*.

guard chain [-tʃein] *n* cadena *f* de seguridad.

guard dog [-dɔg] *n* perro *m* guardián.

guarded ['gɑ:did] *adj* precavido, da; cauteloso, sa (cautious) ‖ protegido, da ‖ custodiado, da.

guardedly [-li] *adv* cautelosamente, con cautela.

guardhouse ['gɑ:dhaus]; **guardroom** ['gɑ:drum] *n* prisión *f* militar (for military prisoners) ‖ cuerpo *m* de guardia (for the guard and military police).

guardian ['gɑ:djən] *n* tutor, ra (of an orphan) ‖ guardián *m*, guarda *m* (custodian) ‖ conservador, ra (of a museum) ‖ guardián *m* (superior of a Franciscan convent) ‖ *guardian angel* ángel *m* de la Guarda, ángel custodio.

guardianship [-ʃip] *n* tutela *f* (legal responsibility of guardian) ‖ amparo *m*, protección *f* (protection) ‖ conservación *f* (of a museum).

guard iron ['gɑ:d'aiən] *n* quitapiedras *m inv* (on a train).

guard rail ['gɑ:dreil] *n* barandilla *f* (of staircase) ‖ contracarril *m* (of rails).

guardroom ['gɑ:drum] *n* → **guardhouse.**

guardsman ['gɑ:dzmən] *n* MIL guardia *m*.
— OBSERV El plural de *guardsman* es *guardsmen*.

Guatemala [gwæti'mɑ:lə] *pr n* GEOGR Guatemala *m*.

Guatemalan [-n] *adj/n* guatemalteco, ca.

guava ['gwɑ:və] *n* guayabo *m* (tree) ‖ guayaba *f* (fruit) ‖ — *guava grove* guayabal *m* ‖ *guava jelly* guayaba *f*.

gubernatorial [gu:bənə'tɔriəl] *adj* gubernativo, va ‖ del gobernador ‖ FAM paternal.

gudgeon ['gʌdʒən] *n* gobio *m* (fish) ‖ TECH muñón *m*, gorrón *m* (of an axle) | clavija *f* (peg) ‖ MAR hembra *f* del gorrón, muñonera *f* (of a rudder) ‖ FAM tonto, ta; pánfilo, la (idiot) ‖ AUT *gudgeon pin* eje *m* del pistón.

Guelders ['geldəz] *pr n* GEOGR Güeldres *f*.

guerdon ['gə:dən] *n* galardón *m*, recompensa *f*.

guerilla; guerrilla [gə'rilə] *n* guerrillero *m* ‖ — *guerrilla band* guerrilla *f* (group) ‖ *guerrilla fighter* guerrillero *m* ‖ *guerrilla warfare* guerrilla *f*, guerra *f* de guerrillas.

Guernsey ['gə:nzi] *pr n* GEOGR Guernesey.

guess [ges] *n* cálculo *m* (an estimate) ‖ conjetura *f*, suposición *f* (conjecture); *to make a guess at* hacer suposiciones sobre ‖ acierto *m*; *of easy guess* de fácil acierto ‖ US opinión *f*, parecer *m*; *my guess is that...* mi parecer es que... ‖ — *at a guess* a primera vista ‖ *at a rough guess* a ojo de buen cubero ‖ *I give you three guesses* te doy tres oportunidades para acertar ‖ FAM *it's anybody's guess* no se sabe ‖ *it's my guess that...* a mí me parece que..., yo creo que... ‖ *to have* o *to make a guess* intentar adivinar.

guess [ges] *vt/vi* adivinar; *I will never guess* nunca lo adivinaré ‖ acertar (to conjecture correctly) ‖ suponer (to suppose); *he guessed as much* ya lo suponía; *I guessed her to be younger* suponía que era más joven ‖ US pensar, creer, suponer; *I guess so* así lo creo yo ‖ — *guess who!* ¡adivina quién soy! ‖ *to guess at* intentar adivinar ‖ *to guess right* acertar ‖ *to keep s.o. guessing* mantener a uno a la expectativa *or* en la incertidumbre *or* en suspenso.

guessing game [-ingeim] *n* acertijo *m*, adivinanza *f*.

guesswork [-wə:k] *n* conjetura *f*, conjeturas *f pl*; *it's all guesswork* son puras conjeturas ‖ *by guesswork* a ojo de buen cubero.

guest [gest] *n* invitado, da (who receives hospitality) ‖ huésped, da (at a hotel) ‖ visita *f* (visit) ‖ BIOL parásito *m* ‖ — *be my guest* yo invito ‖ *guest of honour* invitado de honor ‖ *guest room* cuarto *m* de huéspedes ‖ *guest star* estrella *f* invitada ‖ *paying guest* huésped *m* que paga una pensión.

guesthouse [-haus] *n* casa *f* de huéspedes.

guff [gʌf] *n* FAM cuento *m*; *that's a load of guff* todo eso son cuentos.

guffaw [gʌ'fɔ:] *n* carcajada *f*, risotada *f*.

guffaw [gʌ'fɔ:] *vi* reírse a carcajadas.

guggle [gʌgl] *vi* borbotar (water).

Guiana [gai'ænə] *pr n* GEOGR Guayana *f*.

guidance ['gaidəns] *n* conducción *f*, dirección *f*, guía *f* (act of guiding) ‖ consejo *m*, asesoramiento *m* (advice) ‖ gobierno *m* (leadership) ‖ orientación *f*; *vocational guidance* orientación profesional ‖ *I am telling you this for your guidance* le digo esto para su buen gobierno.

guide [gaid] *n* guía *m* & *f* (person who guides) || guía *f* (book of information) || guía *f*, método *m* para principiantes (instructions book) || guía *f* (example) || consejero, ra; guía *m* (adviser, principle governing behaviour); *let conscience be your guide* que la conciencia sea tu consejera || exploradora *f* (girl guide) || TECH guía *f*.

guide [gaid] *vt* guiar; *to guide some tourists* guiar a unos turistas || dirigir; *to guide a boat* dirigir un barco; *to guide s.o. in his studies* dirigir a uno en sus estudios || dirigir, gobernar (to govern) || orientar (to advise) || AVIAT pilotar.
◆ *vi* hacer de guía (to act as a guide).

guidebook [-buk] *n* guía *f* turística.

guide dog [-dɔg] *n* perro *m* lazarillo.

guided missile [-id'misail] *n* proyectil *m* teledirigido.

guide line [-lain] *n* línea *f* directiva, directiva *f*, directriz *f* (directive) || principio *m* (principle) || pauta *f* (model).

guidepost [-pəust] *n* poste *m* indicador.

guide rope [-rəup] *n* cuerda *f* guía (of a balloon).

guidon ['gaidən] *n* MIL guión *m*, banderín *m* (pennant) || portaguión *m* (standard bearer).

guild; gild [gild] *n* gremio *m*, corporación *f* (association) || guilda *f*.

guilder ['gildə*] *n* florín *m*.

guildhall; gildhall ['gild'hɔ:l] *n* lugar *m* de reunión de un gremio || ayuntamiento *m* (town hall).

guile [gail] *n* engaño *m* (trickery) || astucia *f* (wiliness).

guileful ['gailful] *adj* engañoso, sa (who tricks) || astuto, ta (wily).

guileless ['gaillis] *adj* sin engaño (act) || franco, ca; leal (frank) || cándido, da; inocente (naïve).

guillemot ['gilimɔt] *n* pájaro *m* bobo (bird).

guillotine [,gilə'ti:n] *n* guillotina *f* (for beheading people, machine for cutting paper).

guillotine [gilə'ti:n] *vt* guillotinar.

guillotining [-iŋ] *n* guillotinamiento *m*.

guilt [gilt] *n* culpa *f* (the fact of having committed a legal or moral offence) || culpabilidad *f*; *guilt feelings* sentimiento de culpabilidad.

guiltiness [-inis] *n* culpabilidad *f*.

guiltless [-lis] *adj* inocente || FIG ignorante.

guilty [-i] *adj* culpable; *to plead guilty* declararse culpable; *they found him guilty* lo declararon culpable || — *not guilty* soy inocente || *to have a guilty conscience* remorderle a uno la conciencia || *to plead not guilty* declararse inocente || *verdict of guilty* sentencia *f* de culpabilidad.

guinea ['gini] *n* guinea *f* (monetary unit).

Guinea ['gini] *pr n* GEOGR Guinea *f*.

Guinea-Bissau ['ginibi'sau] *pr n* GEOGR Guinea-Bissau.

guinea fowl [-faul]; **guinea hen** [-hen] *n* ZOOL gallina *f* de Guinea, pintada *f*.

Guinean ['giniən] *adj/n* guineo, a.

Guinea pig ['ginipig] *n* ZOOL conejillo *m* de Indias, cobaya *f*, cobayo *m* [AMER cuy *m*] || FIG conejillo *m* de Indias.

guipure [gi'pyr] *n* guipur *m*.

guise [gaiz] *n* modo *m*, guisa *f*; *in this guise* de ese modo || apariencia *f* (outward appearance) || pretexto *m*; *under the guise of* con el pretexto de, so pretexto de.

guitar [gi'tɑ:*] *n* guitarra *f* || *guitar maker, guitar seller* guitarrista *m*.
◆ *adj* de guitarra; *guitar music* música de guitarra.

guitarist [gi'tɑ:rist] *n* guitarrista *m* & *f*.

gulch [gʌlʃ] *n* barranco *m*.

gulden ['guldən] *n* florín *m*.

gules [gju:lz] *n* HERALD gules *m pl*.

gulf [gʌlf] *n* golfo *m* (large bay) || FIG abismo *m* (huge gap) || *the Gulf* el Golfo Pérsico.

Gulf Stream [-stri:m] *pr n* GEOGR Corriente *f* del Golfo.

gulfweed [-wi:d] *n* BOT sargazo *m*.

gull [gʌl] *n* gaviota *f* (bird) || FAM primo, ma; pánfilo, la (a dupe).

gull [gʌl] *vt* pegársela, engañar.

gullet ['gʌlit] *n* ANAT esófago *m* || FAM garganta *f*, gaznate *m* (throat) || canal *m* (channel) || barranco *m*, hondonada *f* (gully).

gullibility [gʌli'biliti] *n* FAM credulidad *f*.

gullible ['gʌləbl] *adj* FAM crédulo, la; bobo, ba.

gully ['gʌli] *n* hondonada *f*, barranco *m* (ravine).

gulp [gʌlp] *n* trago *m* (drink); *at one gulp* de un trago || bocado *m* (food) || FIG nudo *m* en la garganta (of anxiety).

gulp [gʌlp] *vt* tragarse (to swallow) || *to gulp down* reprimir, contener (one's rage, etc.), tragarse, echarse al coleto (a drink).
◆ *vi* tragar, engullir || FIG tener un nudo en la garganta (to be anxious) || *to gulp for breath* respirar hondo.

gum [gʌm] *n* goma *f* (natural substance or sth. similar) || gomero *m*, árbol *m* del que se saca la goma (gum tree) || resina *f* (resin) || caucho *m* (rubber) || chicle *m* (chewing gum) || pegamento *m*, goma *f* (glue to stick) || legaña *f* (of the eyes) || ANAT encía *f* (of mouth) || — FAM *¡by gum!* ¡caray! || *gum arabic* goma arábiga || *gum resin* gomorresina *f* || *gum tree* gomero *m* || FAM *up a gum tree* en un lío.
◆ *pl* US chanclos *m* de goma.

gum [gʌm] *vt* pegar con goma (to stick with gum) || engomar (to smear with gum) || FIG FAM *to gum up* paralizar, parar (to stop), estropear (to spoil).
◆ *vi* exudar goma (to exude gum) || espesarse (to become gummy).

Gumbo ['gʌmbəu] *n* dialecto *m* hablado en Luisiana.

gumboil ['gʌmbɔil] *n* flemón *m*.

gumboot ['gʌmbu:t] *n* bota *f* de agua.

gumdrop ['gʌmdrɔp] *n* US pastilla *f* de goma.

gumma ['gʌmə] *n* MED goma *f*.
— OBSERV El plural de *gumma* es *gummata*.

gummatous ['gʌmətəs] *adj* MED gomoso, sa.

gumminess ['gʌminis] *n* gomosidad *f*, pegajosidad *f*, viscosidad *f*.

gummy ['gʌmi] *adj* gomoso, sa (containing or like gum) || pegajoso, sa (sticky) || viscoso, sa (viscous) || legañoso, sa (eyes) || hinchado, da (ankle).

gumption ['gʌmpʃən] *n* FAM sentido *m* común, seso *m* (common sense) | vigor *m*, brío *m*, energía *f* (drive) | iniciativa *f* (initiative) | gramática *f* parda (skill).

gumshoe ['gʌmʃu:] *n* US zapato *m* de goma | FAM detective.

gun [gʌn] *n* arma *f* (weapon) || revólver *m* (revolver) || pistola *f* (pistol) || fusil *m*; *needle gun* fusil de aguja || escopeta *f* (for hunting); *double-barrelled gun* escopeta de dos cañones || rifle *m* (for big game) || escopeta *f*, carabina *f*; *air gun* escopeta de aire comprimido || ametralladora *f* (machine gun) || cañón *m* (cannon) || disparo *m* (shot) || cañonazo *m* (discharge) || cazador *m*, escopeta *f* (hunter); *a party of six guns* un grupo de seis cazadores || pistolero *m* (killer) || pistola *f* (for painting) || inyector *m* (for lubricating) || — FAM *big gun* pez gordo || *machine gun* ametralladora || *six-gun salute* salva de seis cañonazos || *the guns* la artillería; *antiaircraft guns* artillería antiaérea || *to bring the gun to the shoulder* encararse el fusil, echarse el fusil a la cara || FIG *to go great guns* avanzar a buen paso | *to jump the gun* adelantarse (to act before the proper time) | *to stick to one's guns* mantenerse en sus trece.

gun [gʌn] *vt* disparar a (to shoot) || US FAM acelerar a fondo (a car) || US FAM *to gun down* matar (a tiros).
◆ *vi* FAM acelerar a fondo (car) || ir de caza (to go hunting) || *to gun for* cazar (to hunt), andar a la caza de (to look for), perseguir (to aim at).

gun barrel [-,bærəl] *n* cañón *m* de escopeta.

gunboat [-bəut] *n* MAR cañonero *m*, lancha *f* cañonera.

gun carriage [-,kæridʒ] *n* cureña *f*.

gun case [-keis] *n* funda *f* de escopeta.

guncotton [-,kɔtn] *n* algodón *m* pólvora (cellulose nitrate).

gunge [gʌndʒ] *n* FAM mugre *f*.

gun crew [-kru:] *n* dotación *f* de una batería.

gun deck [-dek] *n* batería *f*, cubierta *f* de batería.

gundog [-dɔg] *n* perro *m* de caza.

gunfight [-,fait] *n* pelea *f* a tiros, tiroteo *m*.

gunfire [-faiə*] *n* fuego *m*, disparo *m* [de escopeta, pistola, fusil, cañón, etc.] || MIL fuego *m* de artillería, cañoneo *m* || tiroteo *m* (shooting).

gunk [gʌŋk] *n* US FAM mugre *f*, porquería *f*.

gun licence [-'laisəns] *n* licencia *f* de armas.

gunlock [-lɔk] *n* llave *f* de fusil.

gunman [-mən] *n* pistolero *m* (gangster).
— OBSERV El plural de *gunman* es *gunmen*.

gunmetal [,metl] *n* bronce *m* de cañón (variety of bronze) || bronce *m* industrial (used for belt buckles, toys, etc.) || gris *m* oscuro (colour).

gunnel ['gʌnl] *n* MAR regala *f*, borda *f*.

gunner ['gʌnə*] *n* MIL artillero, *m* || arponero *m* (harpooner) || cazador *m*, escopeta *f* (hunter).

gunnery ['gʌnəri] *n* artillería *f* (artillery).

gunny [gʌni] *n* yute *m* (jute) || arpillera *f*, tela *f* de saco (coarse cloth).

gunpoint [gʌnpɔint] *n* *at gunpoint* a punta de pistola.

gunport ['gʌnpɔ:t] *n* porta *f*, cañonera *f*.

gunpowder ['gʌn,paudə*] *n* pólvora *f*.

gun room ['gʌnrum] *n* MAR sala *f* de suboficiales || armería *f*, sala *f* de armas (room for sporting guns).

gunrunner ['gʌn,rʌnə*] *n* traficante *m* de armas.

gunrunning [-iŋ] *n* tráfico *m* or contrabando *m* de armas.

gunshot ['gʌnʃɔt] *n* disparo *m* (a shot) || tiro *m*; *out of gunshot* fuera de tiro || cañonazo *m* (of cannon) || *within gunshot* a tiro de fusil.

gun-shy ['gʌnʃai] *adj* asustadizo, za.

gunsmith ['gʌnsmiθ] *n* armero *m* || *gunsmith's shop* armería *f*.

gunstock ['gʌnstɔk] *n* culata *f*.

gunwale ['gʌnl] *n* MAR regala *f*, borda *f*.

gurgitation [gə:dzi'teiʃən] *n* hervor *m*, ebullición *f* (of boiling water) || burbujeo *m* (of cold water).

gurgle ['gə:gl] *n* borboteo *m* (of water) || gorjeo *m* (of a child) || murmullo *m* (of stream).

gurgle ['gə:gl] *vi* borbotear (water) || gorjear (children).

gurnard ['gə:nəd]; **gurnet** ['gə:nit] *n* rubio *m* (fish).

guru ['guru:] *n* REL gurú *m* || FIG líder *m*, guía *m*.

gush [gʌʃ] *n* chorro *m* (outpour) || FIG efusión *f* exagerada *or* excesiva (exaggerated display of feeling) | torrente *m* (of words).

gush [gʌʃ] *vt* derramar || FIG decir con excesiva efusión (to utter too effusively).
◆ *vi* salir a chorros *or* a borbotones, brotar (to flow out) || FIG *to gush over* hablar con excesiva efusión de.

gusher [-ə*] *n* pozo *m* surtidor, pozo *m* brotante [de petróleo] || FIG persona *f* muy efusiva *or* expansiva.

gushing [-iŋ] *adj* que brota, que sale a chorros || FIG efusivo, va; expansivo, va (person).

gusset ['gʌsit] *n* cuchillo *m*, escudete *m* (in sewing) || ARCH cartabón *m*.

gust [gʌst] *n* ráfaga *f*, racha *f* (of wind) || bocanada *f* (of smoke, etc.) || aguacero *m*, chaparrón *m* (of rain) || explosión *f* (of noise) || acceso *m*, arrebato *m*; *a gust of anger* un acceso de cólera.

gustation [gʌs'teiʃən] *n* gustación *f* (act of tasting) || gusto *m* (sense of taste).

gustily ['gʌstili] *adv* en ráfagas || FIG impetuosamente.

gustiness ['gʌstinis] *n* impetuosidad *f*.

gusto ['gʌstəu] *n* placer *m*; *with gusto* con placer || entusiasmo *m*.

gusty ['gʌsti] *adj* que viene en ráfagas; *gusty rain* lluvia que viene en ráfagas || ventoso, sa; borrascoso, sa; *a gusty day* un día ventoso || FIG impetuoso, sa.

gut [gʌt] *n* ANAT intestino *m*, tripa *f* || cuerda *f*, tripa *f* (used in musical instruments) || sedal *m* (for fishing) || paso *m* estrecho (narrow passage of water).
◆ *pl* FAM tripas *f*, barriga *f sing* (entrails) | agallas *f*, energía *f sing*, nervio *m sing* (pluck and determination) | fuerza *f sing* (force).
◆ *adj* fundamental, esencial || FAM visceral; *gut reaction* reacción visceral.

gut [gʌt] *vt* destripar (to remove the entrails) || limpiar (fishes) || vaciar (to empty) || FIG resumir (a book) | extraer lo esencial de || *the fire gutted the house* el fuego no dejó más que las paredes de la casa.

gutta ['gʌtə] *n* ARCH gota.
— OBSERV El plural de *gutta* es *guttas* o *guttae*.

gutta-percha ['gʌtə'pə:tʃə] *n* gutapercha *f*.

gutter ['gʌtə*] *n* canal *m*, canalón *m* (of a roof) || arroyo *m*, cuneta *f* (of street) || cuneta *f* (of roads) || FIG arroyo *m*; *to raise s.o. from the gutter* sacar a alguien del arroyo || espacio *m* en blanco entre los sellos (philately) || ranura *f*, estría *f* (groove, channel).

gutter ['gʌtə*] *vt* poner canalones (in a house) || abrir surcos en (the soil) || acanalar (to groove).
◆ *vi* correr (water) || derretirse (candles) || *to gutter out* apagarse.

gutter press [-pres] *n* prensa *f* sensacionalista.

guttersnipe [-snaip] *n* golfillo *m*, pilluelo, la.

guttural ['gʌtərəl] *adj* gutural.
◆ *n* gutural *f*.

gutturalize ['gʌtərəlaiz] *vt* pronunciar guturalmente.

guv [gʌv] *n* FAM jefe *m*, amo *m*.

guy [gai] *n* FAM tío *m*, tipo *m*, individuo *m*, sujeto *m*, chico *m* (fellow); *a great guy* un tío formidable | mamarracho *m*, adefesio *m* (ridiculous person) || viento *m*, tirante *m* (rope of chain).

guy [gai] *vt* sujetar con viento *or* tirante (to fasten with guys) || remedar a, parodiar a (to parody) || ridiculizar (to ridicule) || tomar el pelo a (to tease).

Guy [gai] *pr n* Guido *m*.

Guyana [gai'ænə] *pr n* GEOGR Guyana *f*.

guzzle ['gʌzl] *vt/vi* FAM soplarse (to drink greedily and rapidly) | engullirse, tragarse, zamparse (to eat greedily and rapidly).

guzzler ['gʌzlə*] *n* FAM bebedor, ra (drunkard) | comilón, ona (glutton).

gybe; jibe [dʒaib] *vt* MAR poner a la capa, poner en facha.
◆ *vi* MAR ponerse a la capa, ponerse en facha.

gym [dʒim] *n* gimnasio *m* (gymnasium) || gimnasia *f* (gymnastics) || *gym shoes* zapatos *m* de tenis *or* de lona.

gymkhana [dʒim'kɑ:nə] *n* gymkhana *f*.

gymnasium [dʒim'neizjəm] *n* SP gimnasio *m* || instituto *m* (school in Germany).
— OBSERV El plural de *gymnasium* es *gymnasia* o *gymnasiums*.

gymnast ['dʒimnæst] *n* gimnasta *m* & *f*.

gymnastic [dʒim'næstik] *adj* gimnástico, ca.

gymnastics [-s] *n* gimnasia *f*.

gymnosperm ['dʒimnə'spə:m] *n* BOT gimnosperma *f* (seed plant).

gymslip ['dʒimslip] *n* túnica *f* de colegio (school uniform).

gynaeceum [gaini'si:əm] *n* gineceo *m*.
— OBSERV El plural de *gynaeceum* es *gynaecea*.

gynaecological; US **gynecological** [gainikə'lɔdʒikəl] *adj* ginecológico, ca.

gynaecologist; US **gynecologist** [gaini'kɔlədʒist] *n* ginecólogo, ga.

gynaecology; US **gynecology** [gaini'kɔlədʒi] *n* ginecología *f*.

gynoecium; US **gynecium** [gaini'si:əm] *n* gineceo *m*.
— OBSERV El plural es *gynoecia* y *gynecia*.

gyp [dʒip] *n* US FAM timo *m* (cheat) | timador, ra (swindler) || criado *m* en la Universidad de Cambridge.

gyp [dʒip] *vt/vi* US FAM timar.

gypseous ['dʒipsiəs] *adj* yesoso, sa.

gypsum ['dʒipsəm] *n* yeso *m* || *gypsum pit* yesera *f*.

gypsum ['dʒipsəm] *vt* enyesar.

gypsy ['dʒipsi] *adj/n* gitano, na (in Western Europe) || zíngaro, ra (in Central Europe).

gypsy moth [-mɔθ] *n* ZOOL lagarta *f*.

gyrate ['dʒaiərit] *vi* girar.

gyration [dʒaiə'reiʃən] *n* giro *m*, vuelta *f*, rotación *f*.

gyratory ['dʒaiərətəri] *adj* giratorio, ria.

gyre ['dʒaiə*] *n* rotación *f*.

gyre ['dʒaiə*] *vi* girar, dar vueltas.

gyrfalcon ['dʒə:,fɔ:lkən] *n* US ZOOL gerifalte *m*.

gyro ['dʒaiərəu] *n* giroscopio *m* (gyroscope) || brújula *f* giroscópica, girocompás *m*.

gyrocompass ['dʒaiərəu,kʌmpəs] *n* brújula *f* giroscópica, girocompás *m*.

gyropilot ['dʒaiərəu'pailət] *n* piloto *m* automático, giropiloto *m*.

gyroplane ['dʒaiərəplein] *n* autogiro *m*.

gyroscope ['gaiərəskəup] *n* giroscopio *m*.

gyrostabilizer [dʒaiərəu'steibilaizə*] *n* estabilizador *m* giroscópico.

gyrostat ['gaiərəustæt] *n* giróstato *m* || estabilizador *m* giroscópico.

H

h [eitʃ] *n* h *f* (letter of alphabet).

habeas corpus ['heibjes'kɔːpəs] *n* JUR hábeas corpus.

— OBSERV El *hábeas corpus* es un principio destinado a evitar que se mantenga a un detenido en prisión preventiva sin que haya un motivo que lo justifique. El *writ of habeas corpus* estipula que los funcionarios que tienen a un detenido bajo su custodia deben llevarle ante los tribunales.

haberdasher ['hæbədæʃə*] *n* mercero, ra (dealer in small articles) ‖ US camisero, ra (shirt dealer) | dueño *m* de una tienda de artículos para caballeros.

haberdashery [-ri] *n* mercería *f* (shop) ‖ artículos *m pl* de mercería (goods) ‖ US camisería *f* (shop) | ropa *f* para caballeros (men's clothing).

habergeon ['hæbədʒən] *n* cota *f* de mallas.

habiliments [hə'bilimәntz] *pl n* ropa *f sing*.

habit ['hæbit] *n* costumbre *f*, hábito *m*; *to fall into the habit of* coger la costumbre de ‖ hábito *m* (monk's or nun's robe); *to take the habit* tomar el hábito ‖ amazona *f*, traje *m* de montar (for riding sidesaddle) ‖ traje *m* (costume, dress) ‖ manera *f* de ser (characteristic condition of mind) ‖ constitución *f* (condition of body) ‖ manera *f* de crecer ‖ — *by* o *from* o *out of habit* por costumbre ‖ *habit of mind* manera *f* de ver las cosas, carácter *m* ‖ *to be in the habit of doing sth.* acostumbrar *or* tener la costumbre de *or* soler hacer algo ‖ *to get into the habit of doing sth.* acostumbrarse a hacer algo ‖ *to get out of the habit of doing sth.* perder la costumbre de hacer algo ‖ *to kick the habit of* quitarse de.

habit ['hæbit] *vt* vestir (to dress).

habitability [hæbitə'biliti] *n* habitabilidad *f*.

habitable ['hæbitəbl] *adj* habitable.

— OBSERV La palabra inglesa *habitable* se aplica sobre todo a las casas, mientras *inhabitable* se emplea particularmente para calificar los países y lugares.

habitant ['hæbitənt] *n* habitante *m* & *f*.

habitant; habitan ['hæbit˜ɔːŋ] *n* canadiense *m* francés.

habitat ['hæbitæt] *n* habitat *m*, hábitat *m*.

habitation [,hæbi'teiʃən] *n* habitación *f* (act of living in a place) ‖ morada *f* (dwelling).

habit-forming ['hæbit,fɔːmiŋ] *adj* que crea hábito.

habitual [hə'bitjuəl] *adj* habitual, acostumbrado, da (usual, accustomed) ‖ inveterado, da; empedernido, da; *a habitual smoker* un fumador empedernido.

habitually [-i] *adv* habitualmente (regularly) ‖ por costumbre (by habit).

habituate [hə'bitjueit] *vt* acostumbrar, habituar (to accustom) ‖ US FAM frecuentar, ir a menudo a (to go frequently).

habitué [hə'bitjuei] *n* cliente *m* habitual (of a restaurant) ‖ asiduo, dua (of a club).

Habsburg [hapsbəːg] *pr n* HIST Habsburgo.

hachure [hæ'ʃuə*] *n* raya *f*.

hachure [hæ'ʃuə*] *vt* señalar *or* sombrear con rayas.

hacienda [,hæsi'endə] *n* hacienda *f*.

hack [hæk] *n* penco *m*, jamelgo *m* (worn-out horse) ‖ caballo *m* de alquiler (horse let out for hire) ‖ caballo *m* de silla (saddle horse) ‖ coche *m* de alquiler (coach) ‖ FAM taxi *m* | taxista *m* (driver) ‖ escritorzuelo *m* (bad writer) ‖ negro *m* (drudge) ‖ comedero *m* (for a hawk's meat) ‖ SP puntapié *m* (kick) ‖ corte *m* (cut) ‖ mella *f* (notch) ‖ hachazo *m*, machetazo *m* (rough cut, sharp blow) ‖ hacha *f*, machete *m* (tool) ‖ MIN pico *m* ‖ tos *f* seca (dry cough) ‖ encella *f* (for drying cheese).

◆ *adj* mercenario, ria (writer, work) ‖ trillado, da (hackneyed) ‖ *hack stand* parada *f*.

hack [hæk] *vt* cortar, acuchillar (to cut) ‖ cortar con hacha *or* con machete ‖ FIG usar a menudo (to employ often) ‖ alquilar (to hire) ‖ SP dar un puntapié a ‖ FAM destrozar ‖ *to hack to pieces* destrozar, hacer trizas, hacer pedazos.

◆ *vi* toser (to cough) ‖ montar a caballo (to ride for pleasure) ‖ — *to hack at* acuchillar (s.o.), hachear (sth.) ‖ *to hack for* ser el negro de (to be a writer's substitute).

hackamore ['hækəmɔ*] *n* US jáquima *f*, cabestro *m* (halter).

hackberry ['hækberi] *n* BOT almez *m* (tree or wood) ‖ almeza *f* (fruit).

hack hammer [hæk'hæmə*] *n* alcotana *f*, martillo *m* para desbastar piedra.

hacking ['hækiŋ] *adj* MED seco, ca (cough).

hackle ['hækl] *n* pluma *f* del cuello (of a cock) ‖ pelo *m* erizado (of a dog) ‖ mosca *f* para pescar (in fishing) ‖ rastrillo *m* (for combing flax).

◆ *pl* collar *m sing* (of birds) ‖ FAM *with one's hackles up* indignado, da; echando chispas.

hackle ['hækl] *vt* rastrillar (the flax) ‖ cortar (to hack) ‖ FAM destrozar, mutilar.

hackman ['hækmən] *n* cochero *m* ‖ FAM taxista *m*.

— OBSERV El plural de esta palabra es *hackmen*.

hackmatack ['hækmətæk] *n* BOT alerce *m*.

hackney ['hækni] *n* caballo *m* de alquiler (hack) ‖ caballo *m* de silla (saddle horse) ‖ coche *m* de alquiler (coach).

◆ *adj* FIG trillado, da.

hackney carriage ['hækni'kæridʒ]; **hackney coach** [-kəutʃ] *n* coche *m* de alquiler.

hackneyed ['hæknid] *adj* trillado, da; *a hackneyed theme* un tema trillado ‖ estereotipado, da; *a hackneyed phrase* una expresión estereotipada.

hacksaw ['hæksɔː] *n* sierra *f* para metales.

hackwork ['hækwəːk] *n* trabajo *m* comercializado.

had [hæd] *pret/pp* ⟶ **have.**

haddock ['hædək] *n* abadejo *m* (fish).

hade [heid] *n* GEOL inclinación *f*, buzamiento *m*.

hade [heid] *vi* GEOL buzar.

Hades [heidiːz] *pr n* Hades *m* (Pluto) ‖ infierno *m* (hell).

Hadrian ['heidriən] *pr n* Adriano *m*.

haematic [hiː'mætik] *adj* hemático, ca.

haematin ['hiːmətin] *n* hematina *f*.

haematite ['hemətait] *n* MIN hematites *f*.

haematocyte ['hemətəu,sait] *n* hematocito *m*.

haematologist [hiːmə'tɔlədʒist] *n* hematólogo *m*.

haematology [hiːmətɔlədʒi] *n* MED hematología *f*.

haematoma ['hiːmətəumə] *n* MED hematoma *m*.

— OBSERV El plural es *haematomas* o *haematomata*.

haematosis [hiːmə'təusis] *n* BIOL hematosis *f*.

haematozoan [hiːmətəu'zəuən]; **haematozoon** [hiːmətəu'zəuɔn] *n* hematozoario *m*.

— OBSERV El plural es *haematozoa*.

haematuria [hiːmə'tjuəriə] *n* MED hematuria *f*.

haemocyte ['hiːməsait] *n* hematocito *m*.

haemoglobin [hiːməu'gləubin] *n* hemoglobina *f*.

haemolysis [hiː'mɔləsis] *n* hemólisis *f*.

haemophilia [hiːməu'filiə] *n* hemofilia *f*.

haemophiliac [-k] *n* hemofílico, ca.

haemoptysis [hiː'məuptisis] *n* MED hemoptisis *f*.

haemorrhage ['hemәridʒ] *n* MED hemorragia *f*.

haemorrhoidal [hemə'rɔidəl] *adj* MED hemorroidal.

haemorrhoids ['hemərɔidz] *pl n* MED hemorroides *f*, almorranas *f*.

haemostatic [hiːmə'stætik] *adj* MED hemostático, ca.

◆ *n* MED hemostático *m*.

haft [hɑːft] *n* mango *m* (of a knife) ‖ puño *m* (of a sword).

haft [hɑːft] *vt* poner mango a (a knife) ‖ poner puño a (a sword).

hag [hæg] *n* bruja *f* (ugly old woman).

haggard ['hægəd] *adj* ojeroso, sa (looking worn out) ‖ macilento, ta (very pale) ‖ extraviado, da (wildeyed) ‖ zahareño, ña (hawk).

◆ *n* halcón *m* zahareño.

haggis ['hægis] *n* plato *m* típico escocés hecho con las asaduras del cordero.

haggish ['hægiʃ] *adj* de bruja.

haggle ['hægl] *n* regateo *m*.

haggle ['hægl] *vi* regatear ‖ *to haggle about* o *over* regatear.

haggler ['hæglə*] *n* regateador, ra.

haggling ['hægliŋ] *n* regateo *m*.

Haghe (The) [heig] *pr n* GEOGR La Haya.

hagiographer [hægi'ɔgrəfə*] *n* hagiógrafo *m*.

hagiography [hægi'ɔgrəfi] *n* hagiografía *f*.

hagiology [hægi'ɔlədʒi] *n* hagiología *f.*

hagridden ['hægrid'n] *adj* atormentado por las pesadillas ‖ FIG obsesionado, da.

ha-ha [hɑːhɑː] *interj* ¡ja, ja, ja!

haick; haik [haik] *n* almalafa *f.*

hail [heil] *n* granizo *m* (frozen raindrops) ‖ FIG lluvia *f*, granizada *f*; *a hail of arrows* una lluvia de flechas ‖ grito *m* (call) ‖ saludo *m* (salute) ‖ *within hail* al alcance de la voz.
◆ *interj* ¡hola! ‖ REL *Hail, Mary, full of grace* Dios te salve, María, llena eres de gracia.

hail [heil] *vt* llamar; *to hail a person* llamar a una persona; *to hail a taxi* llamar un taxi ‖ saludar (to salute) ‖ aclamar (to acclaim) ‖ FIG acoger; *he hailed the news with joy* acogió las noticias con alegría ‖ FIG & FAM lanzar una andanada de (blows, insults).
◆ *vi* granizar ‖ — FIG *to hail down on* llover sobre ‖ *to hail from* proceder de, venir de (to come from), ser de (to be a native of).

hail-fellow; hail-fellow-well-met ['heil,feləu'wel'met] *adj* simpático, ca.

Hail Mary ['heil'mɛəri] *n* REL Avemaría *f.*

hailstone ['heilstəun] *n* granizo *m*, piedra *f.*

hailstorm ['heilstɔːm] *n* granizada *f.*

hair [hɛə*] *n* pelo *m* (of human or animal body) ‖ pelo *m*, cabello *m* (on human head); *to have one's hair cut* cortarse el pelo ‖ crin *f*, cerda *f* (of horse's mane) ‖ cerda *f* (of pig) ‖ BOT pelo *m*, vello *m*, pelusa *f*, pelusilla *f* ‖ — *against the hair* a contrapelo ‖ *head of hair* pelo *m*, cabellera *f* ‖ FAM *keep your hair on!* ¡no te sulfures! | *not to touch a hair on s.o.'s head* no tocarle ni un pelo a alguien | *not to turn a hair* no movérsele a uno un pelo ‖ FIG *to a hair* exactamente ‖ *to comb one's hair* peinarse ‖ *to do one's hair* peinarse, arreglarse el pelo ‖ US FAM *to get in one's hair* ponerle a uno nervioso, atacar los nervios a uno ‖ *to have one's hair done* ir a la peluquería ‖ *to let one's hair down* dejarse el pelo suelto, soltarse el pelo (to undo one's hair), soltarse, el pelo (to be free in behaviour) ‖ *to lose one's hair* caérsele a uno el pelo ‖ FIG *to make s.o.'s hair stand on end* ponerle a uno los pelos de punta ‖ *to put up one's hair* recogerse el pelo ‖ FIG *to split hairs* hilar muy fino | *to tear each other's hair out* tirarse de los pelos (to squabble) | *to tear one's hair* tirarse de los pelos, mesarse los cabellos ‖ *white hair* cana *f*, canas *f pl.*

hairband [-,bænd] *n* cinta *f.*

hairbrained [-'breind] *adj* FIG ligero de cascos, atolondrado, da (harebrained).

hairbreadth [-bredθ]**; hairsbreadth** [-zbredθ] *n* FIG pelo *m* ‖ — FIG *by a hairbreadth* por los pelos, por un pelo; *he escaped by a hairbreadth* se libró por los pelos; por muy poco; *he lost the election by a hairbreadth* perdió las elecciones por muy poco; un pelo; *he didn't depart by a hairbreadth from the instructions* no se apartó un pelo de las instrucciones | *to a hairbreadth* muy; *accurate to a hairbreadth* muy exacto | *within a hairbreadth* a dos dedos, a dos pasos.
◆ *adj* *to have a hairbreadth escape* escapar por los pelos, escapar por el canto de un duro.

hairbrush [-brʌʃ] *n* cepillo *m* [para el pelo].

haircloth [-klɔθ] *n* tela *f* de crin (cloth) ‖ REL cilicio *m* (hair shirt).

hair clip [-klip] *n* horquilla *f.*

haircut [-kʌt] *n* corte *m* de pelo; *to have a haircut* cortarse el pelo.

haircutting [-,kʌtiŋ] *n* corte *m* de pelo (haircut) ‖ peluquería *f.*

hairdo [-duː] *n* peinado *m.*

hairdresser [-,dresə*] *n* peluquero, ra.

hairdresser's [-,dresəːz] *n* peluquería *f.*

hairdressing [-,dresiŋ] *n* peluquería *f* (work of a hairdresser) ‖ peinado *m* (hairdo).

hair dryer [-draiə*] *n* secador *m* [para el pelo].

hair dye [-dai] *n* tinte *m* para el pelo.

hair grip [-grip] *n* horquilla *f.*

hairiness [-inis] *n* pilosidad *f* ‖ abundancia *f* de pelo.

hairless [-lis] *adj* sin pelo (animal) ‖ lampiño, ña (face) ‖ sin pelo, calvo, va (head).

hairline [-lain] *n* nacimiento *m* del pelo (limit of hair growth) ‖ trazo *m* (of a letter) ‖ rayita *f* (thin line).
◆ *adj* muy fino, na; *hairline fracture* hendidura *or* grieta muy fina ‖ FIG muy pequeño, ña; sutil.

hair lock [-lɔk] *n* rizo *m* de pelo.

hairnet [-net] *n* redecilla *f.*

hairpiece [-piːs] *n* postizo *m.*

hairpin [-pin] *n* horquilla *f.*
◆ *adj* *hairpin bend* curva muy cerrada.

hair-raising [-,reiziŋ] *adj* que pone los pelos de punta, espeluznante.

hair-remover [-ri'muːvə*] *n* depilatorio *m.*

hair restorer [-ris'tɔːrə*] *n* tónico *m* capilar.

hairsbreadth [-zbredθ] *adj/n* ⟶ **hairbreadth.**

hair setting [-'setiŋ] *n* marcado *m.*

hair shirt [-'ʃəːt] *n* REL cilicio *m.*

hair slide [-slaid] *n* pasador *m.*

hairsplitting [-,splitiŋ] *n* sutilezas *f pl.*
◆ *adj* sutil (argument) ‖ quisquilloso, sa (person).

hair stroke [-strəuk] *n* perfil *m* (of a letter).

hairstyle [-stail] *n* peinado *m.*

hairstylist [-ist] *n* estilista *m* & *f* (hairdresser).

hairy ['hɛəri] *adj* peludo, da (covered with hair, like hair) ‖ melenudo, da (having more hair than normal) ‖ FIG antiguo, gua (a joke, etc.).

Haiti ['heiti] *pr n* GEOGR Haití *m.*

Haitian ['heiʃjən] *adj/n* haitiano, na.

hake [heik] *n* merluza *f* (fish).

halation [hə'leiʃən] *n* PHOT halo *m.*

halberd ['hælbəːd] *n* alabarda *f.*

halberdier [,hælbə'diə*] *n* alabardero *m.*

halcyon ['hælsiən] *n* alción *m.*
◆ *adj* alciónico; *halcyon days* días alciónicos.

hale [heil] *adj* sano, na; robusto, ta ‖ *to be hale and hearty* estar más sano que una manzana, ser fuerte como un roble.

half [hɑːf] *adj* medio, dia; *half an hour, a half hour* media hora; *two and a half pints* dos pintas y media ‖ mediano, na; *half knowledge of the subject* mediana idea del asunto ‖ a medias; *half owner* propietario a medias ‖ — *half a dozen* media docena ‖ *half..., half* mitad..., mitad; *half man half beast* mitad hombre, mitad animal.
◆ *adv* a medias; *to half do sth.* hacer algo a medias ‖ medio; *half asleep* medio dormido; *half crying* medio llorando ‖ — *half as many, half as much* la mitad ‖ *half as much again* la mitad más ‖ *he is half as big again as his brother* tiene una vez y media la estatura de su hermano ‖ *it isn't half bad* no está nada mal ‖ *it isn't half cold!* ¡hace muchísimo frío! ‖ *not half* no poco, mucho; *you liked it? not half!* ¿te gustó? ¡no poco!; muy; *she's not half pretty* es muy mona ‖ *to be half* estar casi; *I was half sure she'd come* estaba casi seguro de que vendría.
◆ *n* mitad *f*; *half of the time he does nothing* la mitad del tiempo no hace nada ‖ parte *f*; *the larger half* la parte más grande; *a good half* una gran parte ‖ medio *m*; *two and a half* dos y medio ‖ semestre *m* (of school year) ‖ SP medio *m* (player); *left half* medio izquierda | tiempo *m* (division of a match); *the first half* el primer tiempo | campo *m* (of a sports pitch) ‖ media pinta *f*; *a half of bitter* media pinta de cerveza ‖ cuarto *m*; *a half of butter* un cuarto de mantequilla ‖ — FIG *better half* media naranja, cara mitad (wife) | *by half* con mucho; *bigger by half* con mucho más grande ‖ *by halves* a medias ‖ *half and half* mitad y mitad ‖ *half past ten,* US *half after ten* las diez y media ‖ *outward half* billete *m* de ida ‖ *return half* billete *m* de vuelta ‖ *to be too... by half* pasarse de...; *he is too clever by half* se pasa de listo ‖ *to cut in half* o *in halves* cortar por la mitad ‖ *to go halves with* ir a medias con ‖ *too long by half* demasiado largo ‖ *two hours and a half* dos horas y media.
— OBSERV El plural de *half* es *halves.*
— OBSERV Cuando *half* califica un sustantivo, el verbo concuerda con dicho sustantivo: *half the apple is bad, half the apples are bad.* Si *half* se emplea solo y representa una gran cantidad, el verbo puede ir en plural: *half are sold.*

half-a-crown [-ə'kraun] *n* media corona *f* (coin).

half-alive [-ə'laiv] *adj* medio muerto, ta.

half-and-half [-ændhɑːf] *adj* mitad y mitad.
◆ *adv* a medias.

halfback [-bæk] *n* SP medio *m.*

halfback line [-bæklain] *n* SP línea *f* media.

half-baked [-'beikt] *adj* FIG mal concebido, da; apresurado, da (poorly planned) | disparatado, da; tonto, ta (foolish) ‖ CULIN medio cocido, da.

half binding [-,baindiŋ] *n* media pasta *f.*

half blood [-blʌd] *n* mestizo, za.

half-blood [-blʌd] *adj* medio, dia; *half-blood sister* media hermana.

half-board [-bɔːd] *n* media pensión *f.*

half boot [-buːt] *n* bota *f* corta, bota *f* de media caña.

half-bound [-baund] *adj* encuadernado en media pasta.

half-bred [-bred] *adj* mestizo, za.

half-breed [-briːd] *n* mestizo, za.

half brother [,brʌðə*] *n* hermanastro *m*, medio hermano *m.*

half-caste [-kɑːst] *adj/n* mestizo, za.

half-closed [-kləuzd] *adj* entreabierto, ta.

half cock [-kɔk] *n* *at half cock* con el seguro echado (gun) ‖ FIG *to go off at half cock* actuar con precipitación (to act to hastily).

half crown [-'kraun] *n* media corona *f* (two shillings and a half).

half-dead [-ded] *adj* medio muerto, ta.

half-dollar [-'dɔlə*] *n* medio dólar *m.*

half-empty [-'empti] *adj* medio vacío, a.

half fare [-fɛə*] *n* medio billete *m.*

half-full [-ful] *adj* medio lleno, na; a medio llenar.

halfhearted [-'hɑːtid] *adj* que carece de entusiasmo, poco entusiasta.

halfheartedly [-'hɑːtidli] *adv* sin entusiasmo.

half-holiday [-'hɔlədi] *n* medio día *m* festivo.

half hour [-'áuə*] *n* media hora *f*; *to be taken every half-hour* para tomar cada media hora ‖ *the train leaves on the half-hour* el tren sale a la media *or* cada media hora.
◆ *adj* de media hora; *half-hour journey* viaje de media hora.

half-hourly [-'auəli] *adv* cada media hora.
◆ *adj* de cada media hora.

half-length [-leŋθ] *adj* de medio cuerpo (portrait).
◆ *n* SP medio cuerpo *m* ‖ busto *m* (portrait).

half-life [-laif] *n* período *m* (in nuclear reaction).

half-light [-lait] *n* primeras luces *f pl*, amanecer *m* (of the dawn) ‖ media luz *f* (before darkness).
◆ *adj* a media luz.

half-mast [-'mɑ:st] *n* *at half-mast* a media asta.

half measures [-'meʒə:z] *pl n* *to take half measures* tomar medidas poco eficaces, aplicar paños calientes.

half-moon [-'mu:n] *n* ASTR media luna *f* ‖ media luna *f* (of fingernails).

half mourning [-'mɔ:niŋ] *n* medio luto *m* (period) ‖ vestido *m* de medio luto (costume).

half-note [-'nəut] *n* US MUS blanca *f*.

half-opened [-'əupənd] *adj* medio abierto, ta; entreabierto, ta.

half pay [-'pei] *n* media paga *m*, medio sueldo *m*.

halfpenny ['heipni] *n* medio penique *m* (coin).
— OBSERV El plural es *halfpence* o *halfpennies*.

half-price ['hɑ:f'prais] *adv* a mitad de precio.

half relief [-ri'li:f] *n* ARTS medio relieve *m*.

half-seas over [-si:z'əuvə*] *adj* FAM calamocano, na; achispado, da; entre Pinto y Valdemoro.

half sister [-sistə*] *n* hermanastra *f*, media hermana *f*.

half step [-step] *n* US MUS semitono *m*.

half term [-tə:m] *n* vacaciones *f pl* escolares a mitad de trimestre (holiday).

half-timbered [-'timbəd] *adj* con entramado de madera.

half time [-'taim] *n* SP descanso *m*.

half-time [-'taim] *adj* de media jornada (work) ‖ — *the half-time score* el tanteo en el descanso ‖ *to work half-time* trabajar media jornada.

half title [-'taitl] *n* PRINT anteportada *f*, portadilla *f* (of a book).

halftone [-təun] *n* PRINT media tinta *f*, medio tono *m* ‖ MUS semitono *m*.

halftone [-təun] *adj* PRINT a media tinta.

half-truth [-tru:θ] *n* verdad *f* a medias.

half-turn [-tə:n] *n* media vuelta *f*.

halfway [-'wei] *adj* medio, dia; intermedio, dia; *halfway point* punto medio ‖ parcial (partial); *halfway measures* medidas parciales.
◆ *adv* a medio camino, a mitad de camino; *halfway between two points* a medio camino entre dos puntos; *halfway to Paris* a mitad de camino de París ‖ — *halfway up* a media cuesta, en la mitad de la cuesta ‖ *to do halfway* hacer a medias ‖ FIG *to meet s.o. halfway* partir la diferencia con uno (about a price), llegar a un arreglo con uno (arrangement).

half-wit [-wit] *n* tonto, ta; imbécil *m* & *f*.

half-witted [-'witid] *adj* tonto, ta; imbécil.

half-year [-'jə:*] *n* semestre *m*.

half-yearly [-'jə:li] *adj* semestral.
◆ *adv* semestralmente, cada seis meses.

halibut ['hælibət] *n* halibut *m* (fish).

halieutic [,hæli'ju:tik] *adj* haliéutico, ca.

halieutics [-s] *n* haliéutica *f*.

halitosis [hæli'təusis] *n* halitosis *f inv*.

hall [hɔ:l] *n* entrada *f*, vestíbulo *m*, «hall» *m* (entrance room) ‖ sala *f* (in a castle, large building); *concert hall* sala de conciertos ‖ comedor *m* (dining hall in college, etc.) ‖ casa *f* solariega (mansion) ‖ colegio *m* mayor (college) ‖ US pasillo *m*, corredor *m* (corridor) ‖ — *city hall* ayuntamiento *m* (building), municipalidad *f*, municipio *m* ‖ *dance hall* sala *f* de baile ‖ *hall of fame* galería *f* de personajes (memorial) ‖ *hall of residence* residencia *f* universitaria ‖ *Town Hall* ayuntamiento *m*.

hallelujah [,hæli'lu:jə] *n* aleluya *m* o *f*.

halliard ['hæljəd] *n* MAR driza *f*.

hallmark ['hɔ:lmɑ:k] *n* contraste *m* (official stamps of guarantee) ‖ FIG sello *m*; *the hallmark of genius* el sello del genio.

hallo [hə'ləu] *interj* —→ **hullo**.

hallo [hə'ləu] *vi* gritar.

halloo [hə'lu:] *n* grito *m*.
◆ *interj* ¡hala! (in hunting).

halloo [hə'lu:] *vi* gritar (to shout) ‖ llamar (to call).

hallow ['hæləu] *vt* santificar; *hallowed by Thy Name* santificado sea Tu Nombre ‖ FIG venerar, reverenciar.

hallowed ['hæləud] *adj* santo, ta (ground).

Hallowe'en; US **Halloween** ['hæləu'i:n] *n* víspera *f* del Día de Todos los Santos.

hallucinate [hə'lu:sineit] *vt* alucinar.
◆ *vi* alucinarse.

hallucination [hə,lu:si'neiʃən] *n* alucinación *f*.

hallucinatory [hə,lu:si'neiʃən] *adj* alucinante.

hallucinogen [hə'lu:sinədʒen] *n* alucinógeno *m*.

hallux ['hælʌks] *n* ANAT dedo *m* gordo del pie.
— OBSERV El plural de *hallux* es *halluces*.

hallway ['hɔ:lwei] *n* US entrada *f*, vestíbulo *m*, «hall» *m* (entrance room) | pasillo *m*, corredor *m* (connecting passage).

halm [hɑ:m] *n* —→ **haulm**.

halo ['heiləu] *n* ASTR halo *m* ‖ REL aureola *f*, nimbo *m* ‖ FIG halo *m*, aureola *f*.

halo ['heiləu] *vt* ASTR rodear con un halo ‖ REL aureolar, nimbar.

halogen ['hæləudʒən] *n* CHEM halógeno *m*.

halogenous [hə'lɔdʒinəs] *adj* CHEM halógeno, na.

halography [hə'lɔgrəfi] *n* CHEM halografía *f*.

haloid ['hælɔid] *adj* haloideo, a.
◆ *n* haloideo *m*.

halt [hɔ:lt] *adj* (ant) cojo, ja.
◆ *n* alto *m*, parada *f* (temporary stop) ‖ interrupción *f* ‖ parada *f*, apeadero *m* (small railway station) ‖ (ant) cojera *f* (lameness) | lisiados *m pl* (cripples) ‖ — *halt!* ¡alto! ‖ *to bring to a halt* parar, detener ‖ *to call a halt* mandar hacer algo ‖ FIG *to call a halt to* poner coto a ‖ *to come to a halt* pararse.

halt [hɔ:lt] *vt* parar, detener (to stop sth. or s.o.) ‖ interrumpir.
◆ *vi* pararse (to stop) ‖ hacer alto ‖ interrumpirse ‖ cojear (in walking) ‖ FIG *to halt between two opinions* vacilar entre dos opiniones.

halter [-ə*] *n* cabestro *m*, ronzal *m*, jáquima *f* (of a horse) ‖ soga *f*, dogal *m* (for hanging criminals) ‖ US blusa *f* sin espalda (blouse).

halter [-ə*] *vt* poner el ronzal a, encabestrar (a horse) ‖ ahorcar (a criminal) ‖ FIG poner trabas a (to hamper).

halting [-iŋ] *adj* vacilante (marked by hesitation) ‖ cojo, ja; defectuoso, sa (verse).

halve [hɑ:v] *vt* compartir (to share equally) ‖ partir en dos, partir por la mitad (to divide into two portions) ‖ reducir a la mitad (to lessen by half) ‖ TECH machihembrar (in woodwork) ‖ SP empatar.

halves [hɑ:vz] *pl n* —→ **half.**

halyard ['hæljəd] *n* MAR driza *f*.

ham [hæm] *n* jamón *m* (food); *ham sandwich* bocadillo de jamón ‖ ANAT corva *f* (back of the thigh) ‖ — FAM *ham actor* comicastro *m*, mal actor *m* ‖ *radio ham* radioaficionado, da.
◆ *pl* FAM nalgas *f*, trasero *m sing*.

ham [hæm] *vt* FAM exagerar, interpretar de una manera exagerada (a part).

hamadryad [,hæmə'draiəd] *n* ZOOL cinocéfalo *m* (baboon) | cobra *f* real (snake) ‖ MYTH hamadría *f*, hamadríada *f*.

Hamburg ['hæmbə:g] *pr n* GEOL Hamburgo.

hamburger ['hæmbə:gə*] *n* hamburguesa *f*.

hamburg steak [hæmbə:gsteik]; **hamburger steak** ['hæmbəgəsteik] *n* hamburguesa *f*.

ham-fisted ['hæm'fistid] *adj* que tiene manazas ‖ FIG torpe (clumsy).

hamlet ['hæmlit] *n* aldea *f*, caserío *m*.

hammer ['hæmə*] *n* martillo *m* (tool) ‖ macillo *m* (in a piano) ‖ percusor *m* (of a firearm) ‖ martillo *m* (the gavel of a judge, auctioneer) ‖ martinete *m* (drop hammer) ‖ ELECTR vibrador *m* automático (trembler) ‖ ANAT martillo *m* (in the ear) ‖ SP martillo *m*; *throwing the hammer* lanzamiento del martillo ‖ — FIG *between the hammer and the anvil* entre la espada y la pared ‖ *blow of a hammer* martillazo *m* ‖ *the hammer and sickle* la hoz y el martillo ‖ *to come under the hammer* salir a subasta ‖ FIG *to go at it hammer and tongs* luchar con todas sus fuerzas *or* a brazo partido (fighting), echar el resto (working).

hammer ['hæmə*] *vt* martillar, martillear (to hit sth. with a hammer) ‖ batir; *to hammer iron* batir el hierro ‖ clavar (a nail, etc.) ‖ COMM declarar insolvente (on the Stock Exchange) | hacer bajar (prices) ‖ — FIG *to hammer a book, a film* despedazar un libro, una película | *to hammer an opponent* machacar un adversario (in boxing), dar una paliza a un adversario (to beat by a large margin) | *to hammer a point home* insistir *or* hacer hincapié en un punto ‖ *to hammer into shape* forjar a martillo (metals, etc.), poner a punto (a project) ‖ FIG *to hammer one's brains* romperse la cabeza | *to hammer sth. into s.o.* meterle algo en la cabeza a uno.
◆ *vi* martillar.
◆ *phr v* **to hammer at** aporrear (a door) ‖ **to hammer away** trabajar con ahínco (*at* en) | insistir, hacer hincapié (*on* en) ‖ **to hammer down** remachar ‖ **to hammer in** clavar ‖ **to hammer on** aporrear; *to hammer on the door* aporrear la puerta ‖ **to hammer out** extender bajo el martillo (metal, leather, etc.) | inventar (an excuse) | llegar a (an agreement, etc.).

hammerer ['hæmərə*] *n* martillador *m*.

hammerhead [hæməhed] *n* cabeza *f* de martillo (the head of a hammer) ‖ ZOOL pez *m* martillo ‖ US FAM mentecato, ta (blockhead).

hammering [-riŋ] *n* martilleo *m* ‖ MIL machaqueo *m*, martilleo *m*, bombardeo *m* intensivo ‖ FAM paliza *f* (thrashing).

hammerlock [-lɔk] *n* SP llave *f* al brazo (in wrestling).

hammersmith ['hæməsmiθ] *n* martillador *m*.

hammock ['hæmək] *n* hamaca *f* ‖ MAR coy *m*.

hamper ['hæmpə*] *n* cesta *f*, canasta *f* (large basket) ‖ FIG obstáculo *m*, estorbo *m*.

hamper ['hæmpə*] *vt* obstaculizar, estorbar, impedir, poner trabas a.

hamster ['hæmstə*] *n* hámster *m* (rodent).

hamstring ['hæmstriŋ] *n* ANAT tendón *m* de la corva.

hamstring [ˈhæmstriŋ] *vt* cortar el tendón de la corva, desjarretar (to sever the harmstring) || FIG paralizar, incapacitar (to cripple).

hand [hænd] *n* mano *f* (part of the body); *the right hand* la mano derecha || manecilla *f,* mano *f* (of a clock) || aguja *f* (of an instrument) || escritura *f,* letra *f* (writing); *by the same hand* con la misma letra || firma *f* (signature) || aplausos *m pl,* ovación *f* (applause); *the audience gave her a big hand* el público le dio una gran ovación || mano *f* (for marriage); *to give one's hand to* conceder su mano a || autoridad *f* (authority) || palmo *m* (measure) || MAR marinero *m* | tripulante *m* (on board ship) || trabajador *m,* operario *m,* mano *f* (workman) || AGR peón *m* || manojo *m* (of tobacco) || mano *f,* racimo *m* (bunch); *a hand of bananas* un racimo de plátanos || mano *f* (handstone for maize, cocoa, etc.) || mano *f* (a round of cards); *one last hand!* ¡la última mano! || mano *f* (player) || partida *f* (game) || mano *f,* cartas *f pl; I have a good hand* tengo una buena mano || FIG mano *f; two portraits by the same hand* dos retratos por la misma mano; *to have a good hand for painting* tener buena mano para la pintura; *give her a hand* échale una mano || influencia *f* || — FAM *a cool hand* un fresco || *at close hand* muy cerca, a mano || *at first, at second hand* de primera, de segunda mano || *at hand* a mano, muy cerca (within reach), muy cerca (very close in future time), listo, ta (ready) || *by* o *with a masterly hand* con mano maestra || *by hand* a mano; *made by hand* hecho a mano; *written by hand* escrito a mano; con biberón (by feeding from a bottle), en mano; *to deliver sth. by hand* entregar algo en mano; a fuerza de brazos (with the hands) || *by the hand* de la mano || *from hand to hand* de mano en mano || FIG *from hand to mouth* al día; *to live from hand to mouth* vivir al día || FIG *hand and foot* de pies y manos || *hand in hand* de la mano; *to walk hand in hand* pasearse de la mano; cogidos de la mano; *we were sitting hand in hand* estábamos sentados cogidos de la mano; de común acuerdo; *both countries will walk hand in hand* los dos países actuarán de común acuerdo || FIG *hand on heart* poniéndose la mano en el pecho | *hand over fist* rápidamente || *hand to hand* cuerpo a cuerpo || FIG *he can turn his hand to anything* lo mismo sirve para un barrido que para un fregado | *I had no hand in it* no tengo nada que ver con este asunto || *in hand* que se está estudiando *or* discutiendo, que está entre manos; *the matter in hand* el problema que se está estudiando; en la mano; *sword in hand* con la espada en la mano; dominado, da (under control), entre manos (in progress), en reserva (in reserve), en efectivo, disponible; *money in hand* dinero disponible || *in one's own hand* de su puño y letra, de su propia mano || FIG *iron hand in a velvet glove* mano de hierro en guante de seda || *leading hand* mano (in card games) || FIG *not to do a hand's turn* estar mano sobre mano, no dar golpe | *not to lift a hand* no mover un dedo | *on hand* a mano (within reach), en reserva (in reserve), pendiente (unresolved) || *on the left hand* a la izquierda || *on the one hand... on the other* por un lado... por otro, por una parte... por otra || *on the right hand* a la derecha || *out of hand* en seguida (immediately), fuera de control (out of control) || *situation well in hand* situación *f* que se ha conseguido dominar || *sleight of hand* juego *m* de manos || *to ask for the hand of* pedir la mano de (in marriage) || FIG *to bear s.o. a hand* echar una mano a uno | *to be hand in glove together* ser uña y carne (in intimate association), estar conchabados (in close cooperation) || *to be near at hand* estar muy cerca || FIG *to be s.o.'s right hand* ser el brazo derecho de alguien | *to be tied hand and foot* estar atado de pies y manos | *to bite the hand that feeds one* volverse en contra de su bienhechor, ser poco agradecido || *to come to hand* llegar a su destino (a letter) || *to force s.o.'s hand* forzarle la mano a alguien || *to get one's hand in* adquirir práctica || *to get out of hand* desmandarse (persons) || FIG *to get* o *to have the upper hand* llevar ventaja | *to go hand in hand* ir juntos || FAM *to grease s.o.'s hand* untarle la mano a alguien || *to hand* a mano | *to have a free hand* tener campo libre, tener carta blanca || *to have a hand in* intervenir en, tomar parte en, tener participación en || *to have in one's hand* tener en sus manos || FIG *to have s.o. eating out of one's hand* poder manejar a alguien como se quiere || *to have work on hand* tener trabajo entre manos || *to hold out* o *to offer one's hand* tender la mano a || *to keep one's hand in* no perder la práctica (*at* de) || FIG *to know sth. like the back of one's hand* conocer algo como la palma de la mano || *to lend (helping) hand* echar una mano a || *to put into s.o.'s hand* poner en manos de alguien || FIG *to put one's hand down* echarse la mano al bolsillo || *to put one's hand to* emprender || *to raise one's hand against s.o.* alzarle *or* levantarle la mano a alguien || *to rule with a heavy* o *hard hand* gobernar con mano dura || *to set one's hand to* firmar (to sign), emprender (to begin) || FIG *to show one's hand* descubrir su juego, poner las cartas boca arriba | *to stain one's hand with blood* ensangrentarse las manos || *to take a hand in* intervenir en || *to take in hand* ocuparse de, encargarse de || *to take one's life in one's hand* jugarse la vida || *to take s.o.'s hand* coger la mano de alguien || *to throw in one's hand* tirar las cartas (in card games) || *to turn one's hand to* dedicarse a || *to wait on s.o. hand and foot* ser el esclavo de alguien, desvivirse por alguien || *to write a good hand* tener buena letra || *we have five minutes in hand* nos quedan cinco minutos || *with a firm hand* con firmeza || *with a heavy hand* con mano dura || *with high hand* despóticamente || *you couldn't see your hand in front of you* no se veía absolutamente nada, no se veía la mano || *your letter of the 10th is to hand* he recibido su carta del 10.

◆ *pl* MAR tripulación *f sing* || — *all hands on deck!* ¡toda la tripulación a cubierta! || *at the hands of* por (obra de) || FIG *clean hands* manos limpias || COMM *goods left on our hands* mercancías *f pl* que no se han vendido || *hands off!* ¡las manos quietas!, ¡no toquen! || *hands together* con las manos juntas || FIG *hands to the plough!* ¡manos a la obra! || *hands up!* ¡arriba las manos!, ¡manos arriba! (raise both hands), ¡levante la mano! (raise one hand as in a vote) || *in the hands of* en manos de || *into s.o.'s own hands* en propia mano || FIG *lost with all hands* no se salvó nadie || FIG *my hands are tied* tengo las manos atadas, estoy maniatado | *on all hands* o *every hand* por todas partes || *on hands and knees* a gatas, a cuatro patas || *on one's hands* en manos de uno, a cargo de uno || *out of one's hands* fuera de su alcance || *the children are on my hands all day* los niños están conmigo todo el día || FIG *to be clay in the hands of* ser un títere en manos de | *to be free with one's hands* tener las manos largas, ser largo de manos || *to be in good hands* estar en buenas manos || *to change hands* cambiar de manos (sth. carried or held), cambiar de dueño (property, shop, etc.) || *to clap hands* batir palmas || *to come to hands* llegar a las manos || FIG *to dirty* o *to soil one's hands* ensuciarse las manos | *to fall into the hands of* caer en las manos de || *to get sth. off one's hands* deshacerse de algo, quitarse algo de encima || FIG *to grab a chance with both hands* no dejar escapar una oportunidad || FIG *to have one's hands full* estar muy ocupado; *I have my hands full with this new job* estoy muy ocupado con este nuevo trabajo || *to hold hands* ir cogidos de la mano || *to join hands* unirse || *to join hands in marriage* casarse || *to keep one's hands off* no tocar || *to lay hands on* echar mano a (to take), tocar (to touch), ponerle la mano encima a, alzarle la mano a (to injure), imponer las manos a (in blessing, confirming, etc.), encontrar (to find) || *to leave in s.o.'s hands* dejar en manos de uno || *to need hands* estar falto de brazos *or* de mano de obra || *to place o.s. in s.o.'s hands* ponerse en manos de alguien || *to play into s.o.'s hands* hacerle el juego a alguien || *to shake hands* dar la mano, estrechar la mano; *I shook hands with the President* le di la mano al Presidente; *the President shook hands with me* el Presidente me dio la mano; darse la mano; *they shook hands* se dieron la mano || *to take sth. off s.o.'s hands* quitarle a alguien algo || *to take sth. on one's hands* encargarse de algo || *to take the law into one's own hands* tomarse la justicia por su mano || *to talk with one's hands* hablar con las manos || *to throw up one's hands* echarse *or* llevarse las manos a la cabeza || *to tie s.o.'s hands* atar a uno de manos *or* las manos || FIG *to wash one's hands of* lavarse las manos de || *to win hands down* ganar fácilmente || *vote by show of hands* votación *f* a mano alzada.

◆ *adj* de mano; *hand grenade* granada de mano; *hand lugagge* equipaje de mano || hecho a mano (handmade).

hand [hænd] *vt* dar; *he handed her the ticket* le dio el billete || alargar, dar; *will you hand me that book?* ¿quiere alargarme este libro? || ayudar a; *he handed her into the taxi* le ayudó a subir al taxi; *he handed her out of the taxi* le ayudó a salir del taxi || MAR aferrar || FAM *to hand it to s.o.* reconocer algo a alguien; *I've got to hand it to you* tengo que reconocértelo.

◆ *phr v* **to hand about** hacer circular, pasar de mano en mano || **to hand down** transmitir; *songs handed down from generation to generation* canciones transmitidas de generación en generación | ayudar a bajar (from a carriage) | bajar (to pass down) | anunciar (a sentence) || **to hand in** presentar (a resignation, etc.) | entregar (to give) | ayudar a entrar *or* a subir || SP **to hand off** apartar con la mano (in rugby) || **to hand on** transmitir (traditions) | comunicar (news) | pasar, dar (to give) || **to hand out** dar (to give) | aplicar (a punishment, etc.) | distribuir, repartir (to distribute) || **to hand over** entregar | transmitir (one's authority) | ceder (one's property) || **to hand round** pasar de mano en mano, hacer circular.

handbag [-bæg] *n* bolso *m* [AMER saco *m,* cartera *f*].

handball [-bɔːl] *n* SP balonmano *m* (sport) | pelota *f* de balonmano (ball).

handbarrow [-ˈbærəu] *n* carretilla *f* (wheelbarrow) || parihuelas *f pl,* camilla *f,* andas *f pl* (stretcher).

handbell [-bel] *n* campanilla *f.*

handbill [-bil] *n* prospecto *m.*

handbook [-buk] *n* guía *f* (guidebook) || manual *m,* libro *m* de referencias (reference book) || libro *m* de apuntes (book of a bookmaker).

hand brake [-breik] *n* AUT freno *m* de mano.

handcar [-kɑː*] *n* vagoneta *f,* carretilla *f* de servicio, zorrilla *f.*

handcart [-kɑːt] *n* carretilla *f.*

handclasp [-klɑːsp] *n* apretón *m* de manos.

handcraft [-krɑːft] *n* → **handicraft.**

handcuff [-kʌf] *vt* poner las esposas a, esposar.

handcuffs [-kʌfs] *pl n* esposas *f.*

handed [hændid] *adj* de... manos; *white-handed* de manos blancas.

handful [-ful] *n* puñado *m* || FIG puñado *m; a handful of survivors* un puñado de supervivientes || FAM *this child is a real handful* este niño es una verdadera lata *or* un bicho malo.

hand glass [-glɑːs] *n* espejo *m* de mano (mirror) || lupa *f* (magnifying glass) || MAR reloj *m* de arena (a quarter or half-minute sandglass).

handgrip [-grip] *n* mango *m* (of tennis racquet, golf club) || puño *m* (of motorcycle, bicycle) || apretón *m* de manos (handshake) || *to come to handgrips* tener una agarrada, llegar a las manos.

handgun [-gʌn] *n* pistola *f*.

handicap ['hændikæp] *n* desventaja *f*, «handicap» *m* (disadvantage) || FIG obstáculo *m* (hindrance) || SP «handicap» *m*.

handicap ['hændikæp] *vt* perjudicar (to put at a disadvantage) || SP conceder un handicap a || *to be handicapped* estar en situación de inferioridad; tener desventajas; estar desfavorecido, da.

handicapped [-t] *adj* MED subnormal.

handicraft ['hændikrɑːft]; **handcraft** [hændkrɑːft] *n* artesanía *f* (occupation, art) || habilidad *f* manual (manual skill).

handily ['hændili] *adv* diestramente, hábilmente (in a handy way) || convenientemente (conveniently) || a mano (near) || US con facilidad (easily).

handiness ['hændinis] *n* destreza *f*, habilidad *f* (skill) || proximidad *f* (closeness) || conveniencia *f*, comodidad *f* (convenience) || manejabilidad *f*, lo manejable (of a ship, etc.).

handiwork ['hændiwəːk] *n* obra *f*; *this is some of John's handiwork* ésta es obra de Juan || trabajo *m* manual.

handkerchief ['hæŋkətʃif] *n* pañuelo *m*.

handle ['hændl] *n* mango *m* (grip of a tool, weapon, utensil, etc.) || asa *f* (of bag, basket, cup) || puño *m* (of a bicycle, etc.) || pomo *m* (of sword, stick, door knob) || manilla *f*, manija *f*, tirador *m* (door lever) || brazo *m*, palanca *f* (lever) || tirador *m* (of a drawer) || varal *m* (of handcart) || AUT manivela *f* || manubrio *m* (of hurdy-gurdy) || FIG pretexto *m* (pretext) || FAM título *m* (title) || — FIG *to fly off the handle* salir *or* salirse de sus casillas | *to give handle to* dar pie a, dar motivo a.

handle ['hændl] *vt* tocar; *please do not handle the goods* por favor no toque la mercancía || manejar; *he can handle a saw* sabe manejar una sierra || manipular; *to handle heavy pieces* manipular piezas pesadas || dirigir, gobernar; *to handle a boat* dirigir un barco || conducir [AMER manejar] (a car) || controlar, dominar (to control); *the police could not handle the crowd* la policía no podía controlar a la multitud || poder con, tener capacidad para; *the factory cannot handle the increase in demand* la fábrica no puede con el aumento de la demanda || ocuparse de (to deal with) || tratar; *I don't know how to handle this problem* no sé cómo tratar este problema; *she is hard to handle* es difícil de tratar || tratar en, comerciar en (to do business in) || tener; *they don't handle that brand* no tienen esta marca || manejar (business) || SP tocar con la mano (in football) || — *handle with care* frágil (inscription on a parcel) || FIG *to handle with kid gloves* tratar con muchos miramientos *or* con mucho tacto.

◆ *vi* manejarse || ser manejable; *this car handles well* este coche es muy manejable.

handlebar ['hændlbɑː*] *n* manillar *m*, guía *f* (of a bicycle).

— OBSERV Esta palabra se emplea frecuentemente en plural.

handler ['hændlə*] *n* COMM negociante *m*, tratante *m* || SP entrenador, ra.

handless ['hændlis] *adj* manco, ca || FIG torpe (clumsy).

handling ['hændliŋ] *n* manejo *m* (of tools, etc.) || manipulación *f*, manutención *f* (of goods) || conducción *f* [AMER manejo *m*] (of a car) || gobierno *m* (of a ship) || manera *f* de tratar (of a matter) || trato *m* (of a person) || SP toque *m* con la mano || *rough handling* malos tratos.

handmade ['hænd'meid] *adj* hecho a mano.

handmaid ['hændɔeid] *n* criada *f*.

hand-me-down ['hændmiːdaun] *adj* FAM heredado, da; de segunda mano, usado, da.

◆ *pl n* FAM ropa *f sing* heredada *or* de segunda mano *or* usada.

handout ['hændaut] *n* prospecto *m*, folleto *m* (leaflet) || octavilla *f* (political propaganda leaflet) || comunicado *m* de prensa (release) || información *f* || US limosna *f* (given to a tramp).

handpick ['hændpik] *vt* escoger a dedo (people) || escoger con sumo cuidado (things).

handrail ['hændreil] *n* pasamano *m*, barandilla *f*.

handsaw ['hændsɔː] *n* serrucho *m*, sierra *f* de mano.

hands-down ['hændzdaun] *adj* fácil || indisputable, sin lugar a dudas.

handsel ['hændsəl] *n* aguinaldo *m* (New Year's gift) || señal *f* (pledge).

handsel ['hændsəl] *vt* estrenar (to use for the first time) || inaugurar (to inaugurate) || dar un aguinaldo a (s.o.).

handset ['hændset] *n* microteléfono *m*, pesa *f*.

handsewn ['hændsəun] *adj* cosido a mano.

handshake ['hændʃeik] *n* apretón *m* de manos.

hands-off ['hændzɔf] *adj* de no intervención.

hands-on ['hændzɔn] *n* INFORM comando *m* manual.

handsome ['hændsəm] *adj* hermoso, sa; guapo, pa; bello, lla (women) || apuesto, ta; guapo, pa (men) || elegante (smart) || considerable (large); *a handsome prize* un premio considerable || muy bueno, na; *a handsome salary* un salario muy bueno || generoso, sa (generous) || grande; *a country house of handsome proportions* una casa de campo de grandes proporciones || *to do the handsome thing by s.o.* portarse muy bien con alguien.

handsomely [-li] *adv* bien, elegantemente, con elegancia (smartly) || bien, generosamente (generously).

handsomeness [-nis] *n* belleza *f* || generosidad *f*.

handspike ['hændspaik] *n* MAR espeque *m* || palanca *f* (lever).

handspring ['hændspriŋ] *n sp* voltereta *f* sobre las manos, salto *m* mortal.

handstand ['hændstænd] *n* SP pino *m*.

handstone ['hændsəun] *n* mano *f* (for grinding maize, etc.).

hand-to-hand ['hændtu'hænd] *adj* cuerpo a cuerpo.

◆ *adv* cuerpo a cuerpo.

hand-to-mouth ['hændtu'mauθ] *adj* *to lead a hand-to-mouth existence* vivir al día.

handwheel ['hændwiːl] *n* volante *m*.

handwork ['hændwəːk] *n* trabajo *m* hecho a mano.

handwoven ['hænd,wəuvən] *adj* tejido a mano.

handwriting ['hænd,raitiŋ] *n* letra *f* (one person's style); *I recognize your handwriting* conozco su letra || escritura *f* (writing done by hand).

— OBSERV Esta palabra no lleva nunca el artículo *a*.

handwritten ['hænd,ritn] *adj* escrito a mano; *a handwritten letter* una carta escrita a mano.

handy ['hændi] *adj* a mano, cercano, na (close at hand); *the shops are handy* las tiendas están a mano || mañoso, sa (able to do small jobs) || diestro, tra; hábil (dexterous) || práctico, ca; cómodo, da (convenient) || manejable (easily handled) || útil (useful) || *to come in handy* venir bien.

handyman ['hændimæn] *n* factótum *m* (man employed to do many jobs) || hombre *f* mañoso (skilful man).

— OBSERV El plural es *handymen*.

hang ['hæŋ] *n* caída *f* (of garment) || inclinación *f*, declive *m* (slope) || FAM comino *m*, bledo *m*; *I don't give a hang* me importa un bledo || FAM *to get the hang of sth.* cogerle el truco a algo (to get the knack), comprender *or* entender algo (to understand).

hang* ['hæŋ] *vt* colgar (to suspend, to fasten pictures); *to hang sth. on the wall* colgar algo en la pared || adornar (to ornament); *she hung the room with pictures and drapes* adornó el cuarto con cuadros y colgaduras || pegar, poner (wallpaper, posters, etc.) || cubrir (to cover) || ahorcar (to kill by suspending from the neck) || manir (game or meat) || bajar (one's head) || hacer flotar (in the air) || — FAM *hang it!* ¡por Dios! | *hang you!* ¡maldito seas! || *I'll be hanged if...* que me ahorquen si... || *to hang o.s.* ahorcarse.

◆ *vi* colgar (to be suspended); *painting hanging on the wall* cuadro colgado en la pared || caer (garments, curtains) || inclinarse (to lean) || ser ahorcado (a criminal) || flotar (in the air) || estar pendiente (to be pending) || — *to hang by a thread* pender de un hilo || *to hang heavy* transcurrir lentamente (time) || *to leave a question hanging* dejar pendiente una cuestión.

◆ *ph v* FAM ***to hang about*** o ***around*** vagar, haraganear, perder el tiempo (to loiter) | andar rondando por (a place) | andar rondando (s.o.) | esperar (to wait) || ***to hang back*** quedarse atrás (to be reluctant to advance) | vacilar (to hesitate) | hacerse el remolón (to shirk) || ***to hang behind*** rezagarse || ***to hang down*** caer, colgar (hair) | inclinarse (tower) || ***to hang on*** mantenerse firme, resistir, aguantar (to resist) | quedarse, permanecer (to remain) | agarrarse (to hold on) | depender de (to depend upon) | estar pendiente de; *the people hung on his words* la gente estaba pendiente de sus palabras || — FAM *hang on!* ¡espérate! (wait) | *to hang one on* pegar un golpe a | *to hang on to* agarrarse a; pegarse a (to stick to) || ***to hang out*** tender, colgar (to put out washing) | colgar fuera | sacar (the tongue) | izar (a flag or signal) | estar suspendido | FAM vivir (to reside) | US FAM frecuentar (to frequent) || ***to hang over*** estar suspendido sobre | FIG cernerse sobre (to threaten) | US sobrevivir; estar pendiente (problem) || ***to hang together*** ser lógico (argument) | permanecer unidos, ayudarse mutuamente (persons) || ***to hang up*** colgar (to suspend, to end a telephone conversation) | cortar, apagar (TV) | FAM retrasar (to delay) | aplazar (to postpone) || ***to hang upon*** estar pendiente de (one's words).

— OBSERV El verbo *to hang* tiene un pretérito y un participio pasivo irregulares (***hung***) excepto cuando significa *ahorcar* en cuyo caso son regulares (***hanged***).

hangar ['hæŋə*] *n* AVIAT hangar *m* || cobertizo *m* (shed).

hangdog ['hæŋdɔg] *adj* avergonzado, da.

hanger ['hæŋə*] *n* gancho *m* (in general) || percha *f* (clothes hanger) || percha *f*, gancho *m* (for hats) || alzapaño *m* (for curtains) || llares *m pl* (for pots) || puñal *m* (dagger) || verdugo *m* (hangman).

hanger-on ['hæŋər'ɔn] *n* lapa *f*, pegote *m* (person who attaches himself to another) || gorrón, ona; parásito *m* (parasite).

hanging ['hæŋiŋ] *adj* colgante, pendiente (suspended) || colgante (bridge, garden) || patibulario, ria; lúgubre (look) || feroz (judge) || FAM que merece la horca (matter) | *hanging committee* comité *m* que selecciona las obras que se han de exponer.
◆ *n* colgamiento *m* (action of hanging) || horca *f*, ejecución *f* en la horca (of a criminal); *to deserve hanging* merecer la horca || colocación *f* (of bells, wallpaper) || empapelado *m* (of a room).
◆ *pl* colgaduras *f* (curtains).

hang-glider ['hæŋ,glaidə*] *n* SP ala *f* delta.

hang-gliding ['hæŋ,glaidiŋ] *n* SP vuelo *m* libre, ala *f* delta; *to go hang-gliding* hacer ala delta.

hangman ['hæŋmən] *n* verdugo *m*.
— OBSERV El plural de esta palabra es *hangmen*.

hangnail ['hæŋneil] *n* padrastro *m*.

hangout [hæŋaut] *n* FAM lugar *m* de reunión habitual, cuartel *m* general, guarida *f*.

hangover ['hæŋ,əuvə*] *n* FAM resaca *f* (after drinking) || restos *m pl* (remains).

hang-up ['hæŋʌp] *n* FAM complejo *m*, inhibición *f*.

hank [hæŋk] *n* madeja *f* (of wool) || ovillo *m* (of cotton) || MAR anillo *m* de una vela || FIG madeja *f* (of hair).

hanker ['hæŋkə*] *vi* *to hanker for* o *after* anhelar, ansiar.

hankering ['hæŋkəriŋ] *n* anhelo *m* (strong desire) || añoranza *f* (nostalgia).

hankie; hanky ['hæŋki] *n* FAM pañuelo *m*.

hanky-panky ['hæŋki'pæŋki] *n* FAM trucos *m pl* (tricks) | trampa *f* (trickery, deception) | camelo *m* (con).

Hanoi [hæ'nɔi] *pr n* GEOGR Hanoi.

Hansard ['hænsɑːd] *pr n* actas *f pl* oficiales de los debates parlamentarios.

hanse [hæns] *n* hansa *f*.

hanseatic [,hænsi'ætik] *adj* hanseático, ca.

hansom ['hænsəm] *n* cabriolé *m*, coche *m* de dos ruedas tirado por un caballo.

hap [hæp] *n* casualidad *f* (chance) || destino *m*, suerte *f* (fortune).

hap [hæp] *vi* ocurrir por casualidad.

haphazard ['hæp'hæzəd] *adj* fortuito, ta; casual.
◆ *adv* a la buena de Dios.
◆ *n* casualidad.

hapless ['hæplis] *adj* desgraciado, da; desventurado, da.

haplessness [-nis] *n* infortunio *m*, desventura *f*.

ha'p'orth ['heipəθ] *n* FAM medio penique *m*.
— OBSERV Esta palabra es la forma abreviada de *halfpennyworth*.

happen ['hæpən] *vi* suceder, ocurrir, pasar; *how did it happen?* ¿cómo ocurrió?, ¿cómo sucedió?; *it happened in June* pasó en junio; *if an accident happens* si ocurre un accidente || producirse, ocurrir; *the accident happened at 12 o'clock* el accidente se produjo a las 12 || lograr; *how did you happen to find it?* ¿cómo logró encontrarle? || — *don't let this happen again* que eso no vuelva a suceder || *how does it happen that?* ¿cómo puede ser que? || *if you happen to see him* si por casualidad lo ves || *I happened to be out* dio la casualidad de que estaba fuera || *it so happens that...* o *as it happens...* da la casualidad de que... || *to happen on* o *upon* dar con (to find) || *whatever happens, no matter what happens, happen what may* pase lo que pase.

happening [-iŋ] *n* suceso *m*, acontecimiento *m* (event) || «happening» *m* [espectáculo artístico improvisado en el que participa el público].

happily ['hæpili] *adv* felizmente (in a happy way) || afortunadamente (luckily) || *they lived happily ever after* vivieron felices, comieron perdices y a mí no me dieron (in a fairy tale).

happiness ['hæpinis] *n* felicidad *f* || alegría *f* (merriment) || contento *m* (contentment) || propiedad *f* (of a word, sentence).

happy ['hæpi] *adj* feliz; *she was happy with her husband* era feliz con su marido; *he's a happy man* es un hombre feliz; *a happy life* una vida feliz || contento, ta; *he is happy in his work* está contento con su trabajo || alegre; *a happy character* un carácter alegre; *a happy tune* una melodía alegre || FAM alegre (tipsy) | apropiado, da; acertado, da; feliz (appropriate) || — *are you happy with the idea?* ¿te parece bien la idea? || *happy birthday!* ¡felicidades!, ¡feliz cumpleaños! || *happy ending* final *m* feliz, feliz desenlace *m* || *happy hour* happy hour (in bars, pubs) || *I am happy to see you* me alegra verle, me alegro de verle || *I am happy to tell you that...* tengo mucho gusto en decirle que... || *I am very happy for you* me alegro mucho por ti || *to be as happy as a lark* estar más alegre que unas Pascuas.

happy-go-lucky ['hæpigəu'lʌki] *adj* despreocupado, da || *a happy-go-lucky type* un viva la virgen.

Hapsburg ['hæpsbəːg] *pr n* HIST Habsburgo.

hara-kiri ['hærə'kiri] *n* haraquiri *m*.

harangue [hə'ræŋ] *n* arenga *f*.

harangue [hə'ræŋ] *vt* arengar.

Harare [hə'rɑːri] *pr n* GEOGR Harare.

harass ['hærəs] *vt* acosar, hostigar; *to harass s.o. with questions* acosar a alguien a preguntas || agobiar; *he was harassed by the cares of a large family* estaba agobiado por los cuidados de una gran familia || atormentar (to worry) || MIL hostilizar, hostigar || *harassed by doubts* acosado por las dudas.

harassment [-mənt] *n* hostigamiento *m* (pestering) || tormento *m* (worry) || MIL hostigamiento *m*.

harbinger ['hɑːbindʒə*] *n* precursor *m* (person) || presagio *m* (thing).

harbinger ['hɑːbindʒə*] *vt* anunciar, ser el precursor de.

harbour; US harbor ['hɑːbə*] *n* puerto *m* (port) || FIG puerto *m*, refugio *m*.

harbour; US harbor ['hɑːbə*] *vt* encubrir (a criminal) || hospedar (to lodge) || FIG abrigar (hopes) | tener (suspicions) | contener (to contain) || *to harbour a grudge* guardar rencor.
◆ *vi* ponerse a cubierto, refugiarse.

harbourage; US harborage [-ridʒ] *n* refugio *m* || MAR fondeadero *m* (place) | fondeo *m* (act).

harbour master; US harbor master [-,mɑːstə*] *n* capitán *m* de puerto.

hard [hɑːd] *adj* duro, ra; *a hard egg* un huevo duro; *a hard man* un hombre duro; *hard climate* clima duro || resistente (strong) || difícil; *this question is hard to answer* esta pregunta es difícil de contestar || arduo, dua; duro, ra; *a hard work* un trabajo duro || difícil, duro, ra; *a hard life* una vida difícil || malo, la; *hard times* malos tiempos; *hard luck* mala suerte || severo, ra (*on, to, towards* con); *a hard punishment* un castigo severo; *a hard teacher* un profesor severo || fuerte (blow) || riguroso, sa (winter, weather) || innegable, incontestable (undeniable); *hard facts* hechos innegables || alcohólico, ca; *hard drinks* bebidas alcohólicas || agraz, áspero, ra (wine) || fermentado, da; *hard cider* sidra fermentada || de piedra; *a hard heart* un corazón de piedra || duro, ra (voice, words) || difícil (person); *he is hard to get on with* es difícil llevarse bien con él || cruel (fate) || apretado, da (knot) || GRAMM fuerte (consonants *g, c, s*) || penetrante; *a hard look* una mirada penetrante || firme (muscle) || escleroso, sa (tissues) || MIL encarnizado, da; *hard fight* lucha encarnizada || SP reñido, da (match) || COMM sostenido, da (stock market) || — *a hard bargain* un trato poco ventajoso || *a hard drinker* un gran bebedor || *a hard worker* una persona muy trabajadora || *hard and fast* estricto, ta; inflexible (rule) || SP *hard court* pista *f* de tenis de cemento || *hard currency* divisa fuerte || *hard feelings* resentimiento *m sing* || *hard hat* casco protector || *hard left* extrema izquierda || FIG *hard nut to crack* hueso duro de roer || *hard of hearing* duro de oído || *hard right* extrema derecha || *hard sell* publicidad agresiva [hecha por un vendedor] || *hard to deal with* de trato difícil || *hard water* agua gorda *or* dura || *it's hard work for him to...* le cuesta mucho trabajo... || *no hard feelings* olvidémoslo || *on the cold hard ground* en el mismo suelo || *to be as hard as nails* ser muy resistente (to be resistent), tener un corazón de piedra (to be hardhearted) || *to be hard on one's clothes* gastar mucho la ropa || *to have a hard time of it* pasarlo mal || *to make it hard for s.o.* hacerle las cosas difíciles a uno || *what hard luck!* ¡qué mala suerte! || *you are too hard on him* eres demasiado severo con él.
◆ *adv* fuerte; *hit it hard* dale fuerte; *it is raining hard* está lloviendo fuerte || severamente, con severidad (severely) || mucho; *to work hard* trabajar mucho; *to drink hard* beber mucho || — *hard by* muy cerca || *hard come by* difícilmente obtenido || *hard upon* muy de cerca || *to be freezing hard* helar fuerte || *to be hard at it* trabajar mucho *or* con ahínco || *to beg hard for sth.* pedir algo con insistencia || FAM *to be hard up* no tener un céntimo || *to be hard upon s.o.'s heels* ir pisando los talones a alguien || *to die hard* tardar en desaparecer (rumour), tener siete vidas como los gatos (person) || *to follow hard after* seguir de cerca || *to go hard with s.o.* irle mal a alguien || FIG *to hit s.o. hard* ser un golpe duro para alguien || *to hold on hard* agarrarse bien || *to look hard* mirar fijamente.

hardback ['hɑːdbæk] *n* edición *f* encuadernada en cartoné.

hard-bitten ['hɑːd'bitn] *adj* tenaz, duro, ra (enduring).

hard-boiled ['hɑːd'bɔild] *adj* duro, ra (egg) || FIG duro, ra.

hard cash ['hɑːdkæʃ] *n* dinero *m* contante y sonante.

hard-core [hɑːdkɔː*] *adj* incondicional, empedernido, da; endurecido, da.

hard-drawn ['hɑːd'drɔːn] *adj* estirado en frío (metal).

harden ['hɑːdn] *vt* endurecer (to make hard) || MED endurecer (tissues) || FIG endurecer, insensibilizar (one's heart) | acostumbrar, curtir (to inure) || TECH templar (steel) || — *to harden o.s. to the cold* acostumbrarse al frío || *to harden s.o. to war* aguerrir a alguien.
◆ *vi* endurecerse (to become hard) || subir (prices) || acostumbrarse (to accustom o.s.) || endurecerse (to become unfeeling).

hardener [-ə*] *n* sustancia *f* que sirve para endurecer algo.

hardening [-iŋ] *n* endurecimiento *m* || temple *m* (of steel) || FIG endurecimiento *m*.

hard disk ['hɑːddisk] *n* INFORM disco *m* duro.

hard-featured ['hɑːd'fiːtʃəd] *n* de facciones duras.

hardfisted ['hɑːd,fistid] *adj* de manos callosas || FIG mezquino, na; tacaño, ña (mean).

hard-fought ['hɑːdfɔːt] *adj* reñido, da.

hardheaded ['hɑːd'hedid] *adj* realista, práctico, ca || terco, ca; testarudo, da (stubborn).

hardheadedness [-nis] *n* terquedad *f*, testarudez *f* (stubbornness) || realismo *m*.

hardhearted ['hɑːd'hɑːtid] *adj* sin corazón, insensible, duro de corazón.

hardheartedness [-nis] *n* dureza *f* de corazón, falta *f* de sensibilidad.

hard-hitting ['hɑːd'hitiŋ] *adj* duro, ra; crítico, ca.

hardiness ['hɑːdinis] *n* vigor *m*, resistencia *f*, aguante *m* (strength) || FIG osadía *f*, atrevimiento *m*, audacia *f* (boldness).

hard labour; *US* **hard labor** ['hɑːd'leibə*] *n* JUR trabajos *m pl* forzados *or* forzosos.

hard line ['hɑːdlain] *n* línea *f* dura.

hard-line ['hɑːdlain] *adj* firme, intransigente.

hardliner [-ə*] *n* radical *m* & *f*, extremista *m* & *f*.

hardly ['hɑːdli] *adv* apenas, escasamente (scarcely) || duramente (harshly) || severamente (severely) || difícilmente, con dificultad (not easily) || — *hardly anyone* casi nadie || *hardly ever* casi nunca || *he could hardly have said that...* es muy poco probable que haya dicho que... || *it can hardly be doubted that...* no cabe duda que..., es de lo más probable que... || *you need hardly say* huelga decir.
◆ *interj* ¡qué va!

hardmouthed ['hɑːdmauðd] *adj* duro de boca; *hardmouthed horse* caballo duro de boca.

hardness ['hɑːdnis] *n* dureza *f* (quality of not being soft) || dificultad *f* (difficulty) || rigor *m* (of winter) || dureza *f*, gordura *f* (of water) || severidad *f* (severity) || insensibilidad *f* (of heart) || *hardness of hearing* dureza de oído.

hard pressed ['hɑːdprest] *adj* apremiado, da.

hards [hɑːdz] *pl n* desechos *m* de cáñamo *or* de lino.

hard-set ['hɑːdset] *adj* apurado, da (in trouble) || que ha fraguado, endurecido, da (cement) || empollado, da; incubado, da (egg).

hard-shell ['hɑːdʃel] *adj* que tiene un caparazón duro (mollusc) || FIG duro, ra; inflexible.

hardship ['hɑːdʃip] *n* dificultad *f*, apuro *m*; *I have suffered great hardships* he pasado muchos apuros || dificultad *f* (difficulty).

hard shoulder ['hɑːd'ʃəuldə*] *n* arcén *m* (in motorway).

hard-solder ['hɑːd'sɔldə*] *vt* TECH soldar con cobre.

hardtack ['hɑːdtæk] *n* MAR galleta *f*.

hardtop ['hɑːdtɔp] *n* descapotable *m* con capota dura.

hardware ['hɑːdwεə*] *n* ferretería *f*, quincallería *f* (articles of metal) || MIL armas *f pl* || INFORM equipo *m* físico, hardware *m* || — *hardward dealer* ferretero *m*, quincallero *m* || *hardware shop* o *store* ferretería *f*, quincallería *f*.

hardwearing ['hɑːd,wεəriŋ] *adj* resistente (material).

hard-won ['hɑːdwʌn] *adj* ganado a duras penas *or* con mucha dificultad.

hardwood ['hɑːdwud] *n* madera *f* dura.

hard-working ['hɑːd'wəːkiŋ] *adj* trabajador, ra.

hardy ['hɑːdi] *adj* robusto, ta || BOT resistente || FIG atrevido, da; audaz.

hare [hεə*] *n* ZOOL liebre *f* || — FAM *mad as a March hare* loco de atar *or* de remate *or* rematado, más loco que una cabra | *to run with the hare and hunt with the hounds* ponerle una vela a Dios y otra al diablo | *to start a hare* andarse con rodeos.

hare [hεə*] *vi* volar, correr muy de prisa.

hare and hounds [hεə*ændhaundz] *n* ⟶ **paper chase.**

harebell [-bəl] *n* BOT campánula *f*.

harebrained [-breind] *adj* atolondrado, da; ligero de cascos.

harehound [-haund] *n* lebrel *m* (dog).

harelip [-'lip] *n* MED labio *m* leporino.

harem ['hεərəm] *n* harén *m*.

hare's-foot trefoil ['hεəzfut'trefɔil] *n* BOT pie *m* de liebre.

haricot ['hærikəu] *n* BOT judía *f* (bean) || CULIN guiso *m* de cordero con judías (stew).

hark [hɑːk] *vt* (ant) escuchar.
◆ *vi* (ant) escuchar || — FIG *to hark back to* volver a (to go back to), recordar (to remember) || *to hark to* escuchar, prestar oído a.

harken ['hɑːkən] *vt* escuchar.

harl; harle [hɑːl] *n* hebra *f* (of flax, hemp) || mosca *f* (in fishing).

harlequin ['hɑːlikwin] *n* arlequín *m*.
◆ *adj* abigarrado, da.

harlequinade [,hɑːlikwi'neid] *n* arlequinada *f*, payasada *f*.

harlot [hɑːlət] *n* ramera *f* (prostitute).

harlotry [-ri] *n* prostitución *f*.

harm [hɑːm] *n* daño *m*; *the bad weather has done a lot of harm to the crop* el mal tiempo ha hecho mucho daño a la cosecha || perjuicio *m* || — *there is no harm in her* no es una mala mujer || *there is no harm in saying so* no es malo decirlo, no hay ningún mal en decirlo || *to be out of harm's way* estar a salvo || *to do harm to* perjudicar a, hacer mal a || *to keep out of harm's way* mantenerse a salvo.

harm [hɑːm] *vt* dañar, estropear (sth.) || perjudicar (s.o., s.o.'s interest) || hacer daño (to hurt physically).

harmful [-ful] *adj* perjudicial (*to* para) || dañino, na (pest, etc.) || nocivo, va; dañino, na (thing) || pernicioso, sa (person).

harmfulness [-fulnis] *n* maldad *f* (of a person) || lo perjudicial || nocividad *f* (of a thing).

harmless [-lis] *adj* inofensivo, va.

harmlessly [-lisli] *adv* inocentemente.

harmlessness [-lisnis] *n* inocuidad *f* (of a beverage, etc.) || inocencia *f*.

harmonic [hɑː'mɔnik] *adj* PHYS, MUS & MATH armónico, ca.
◆ *n* armónico *m*.

harmonica [hɑː'mɔnikə] *n* MUS armónica *f*.

harmonics [hɑː'mɔnikz] *n* MUS armonía *f*.

harmonious [hɑː'məunjəs] *adj* armonioso, sa || *to live in harmonious peace* vivir en paz y armonía.

harmonist ['hɑːmənist] *n* MUS armonista *m*.

harmonium [hɑː'məunjəm] *n* MUS armonio *m* (reed organ).

harmonization [,hɑːmənai'zeiʃən] *n* MUS armonización *f*.

harmonize ['hɑːmənaiz] *vt/vi* armonizar.

harmony ['hɑːməni] *n* armonía *f*.

harness ['hɑːnis] *n* guarniciones *f pl*, arreos *m pl*, arneses *m pl* (for draught animals) || andadores *m pl* (for children) || HIST arnés *m* || — *harness maker* guarnicionero *m*, talabartero *m* || FIG *to be back in harness* haber reanudado el trabajo | *to die in harness* morir con las botas puestas *or* al pie del cañón | *to get back in harness* reanudar el trabajo.

harness ['hɑːnis] *vt* enjaezar, poner los arreos a (to put a harness on) || enganchar; *to harness a horse to a carriage* enganchar un caballo a un carro || aprovechar (a river, waterfall).

harp [hɑːp] *n* MUS arpa *f*.

harp [hɑːp] *vi* MUS tocar el arpa || — FAM *to be always harping on the same string* estar siempre con la misma cantinela | *to harp on* machacar.

harpist ['hɑːpist] *n* MUS arpista *m* & *f*.

harpoon [hɑː'puːn] *n* arpón *m*.

harpoon [hɑː'puːn] *vt* arponear.

harpsichord ['hɑːpsikɔːd] *n* MUS clavicordio *m*, clave *m*, clavecín *m*.

harpy ['hɑːpi] *n* arpía *f* || FIG arpía *f*.

harquebus ['hɑːkwibəs] *n* arcabuz *m*.

harridan ['hæridən] *n* FIG bruja *f*, arpía *f*.

harrier ['hæriə*] *n* ZOOL especie *f* de halcón (hawk) | perro *m* de caza (hound) || SP corredor *m* de cross-country.

harrow ['hærəu] *n* AGR grada *f*.

harrow ['hærəu] *vt* AGR gradar || FIG destrozar, partir (s.o.'s heart) | atormentar (s.o.).

harrowing [-iŋ] *adj* desgarrador, ra; angustioso, sa.

harry ['hæri] *vt* acosar (to harass) || asolar, arrasar (to ravage).

Harry ['hæri] *pr n* Enrique *m* || FAM *old Harry* Pedro Botero (the Devil) | *to play old Harry with* fastidiar, estropear (to spoil), hacer pasarlas moradas (to pester).

harsh [hɑːʃ] *adj* áspero, ra (to the touch, to the taste) || discordante (sound) || duro, ra; severo, ra (severe) || desabrido, da (character) || violento, ta (contrast) || chillón, ona (colour) || muy duro, ra (words) || áspero, ra (voice).

harshness [-nis] *n* aspereza *f* (to the touch, to the taste) || discordancia *f* (of a sound) || severidad *f* (severity) || desabrimiento *m* (of character).

hart [hɑːt] *n* ZOOL ciervo *m*.

hartshorn [-shɔːn] *n* ZOOL cuerno *m* de ciervo || CHEM amoniaco *m*.

harum-scarum ['hεərəm'skεərəm] *adj* atolondrado, da.
◆ *n* atolondrado, da; cabeza *f* de chorlito.

haruspex [hə'rʌspeks] *n* HIST arúspice *m*.
— OBSERV El plural de *haruspex* es *haruspices*.

harvest ['hɑːvist] *n* cosecha *f*, siega *f* (of cereals) || recolección *f*, cosecha *f* (of vegetables) || vendimia *f* (of grapes) || cosecha *f* (yield of crops); *a good harvest* una buena cosecha || FIG cosecha *f* || *harvest festival* fiesta *f* de la cosecha.

harvest ['hɑːvist] *vt* cosechar, recoger.
◆ *vi* cosechar, hacer la cosecha.

harvest bug [-bʌg] *n* ZOOL ácaro *m*.

harvester [-ə*] *n* segador, ra; cosechador, ra (person) || segadora *f* (machine).

harvester-thresher [-əθreʃə*] *n* segadora trilladora *f* (machine).

harvestman [-mæn] *n* AGR segador *m* || ZOOL segador *m*.
— OBSERV El plural de esta palabra es *harvestmen*.

harvest time [-taim] *n* mies *f*, siega *f*.

has [hæz] *3rd pers sing pres indic* ⟶ **have.**

has-been [-biːn] *n* FAM persona *f* acabada.

hash [hæʃ] *n* CULIN picadillo *m* || FAM estropicio *m* (mess) | mezcolanza *f*, revoltillo *m*, lío *m* (mix-up) || — FAM *to make a hash of* estropear por completo | *to settle s.o.'s hash* ajustarle las cuentas a uno, cargarse a uno.

hash [hæʃ] *vt* CULIN picar || FAM hacer un lío || — US FAM *to hash out* discutir a fondo | *to hash up* embrollar.

hash browns [-braunz] *pl n* US CULIN patatas *f pl* hervidas y después fritas.

hasheesh ['hæfiʃ]; **hashish** ['hæʃiːʃ] *n* hachís *m inv*.

haslet ['heizlit] *n* CULIN asaduras *f pl.*

hasp [hɑːsp] *n* pestillo *m* (of door) || cierre *m* (of padlock) || falleba *f* (of window) || broche *m* (of books) || madeja *f* (of thread).

hassle ['hæsəl] *n* US FAM follón *m*, jaleo *m* (heated discussion) | pelea *f* (squabble).

hassock ['hæsək] *n* cojín *m* (cushion) || mata *f* de hierba (tuft of grass).

haste [heist] *n* prisa *f* || — *in haste* de prisa, apresuradamente || FIG *more haste less speed* vísteme despacio que tengo prisa || *to make haste* darse prisa, apresurarse.

haste [heist] *vi* (ant) apresurarse, darse prisa.

hasten ['heisn] *vt* apresurar, acelerar (sth.) || dar prisa a (s.o.) || *to hasten one's steps* apresurar el paso, apretar el paso.
◆ *vi* apresurarse, darse prisa || — *to hasten away* o *off* o *out* irse precipitadamente || *to hasten back* volver a toda prisa || *to hasten in* entrar a toda prisa || *to hasten up* llegar corriendo.

hastily ['heistili] *adv* de prisa, apresuradamente (quickly) || sin reflexionar, a la ligera (rashly).

hastiness [heistinis] *n* prisa *f*, rapidez *f* || precipitación *f*.

hasty ['heisti] *adj* apresurado, da (rash) || hecho de prisa, precipitado, da (done with haste) || rápido, da (quick) || ligero, ra; irreflexivo, va; *it was a very hasty decision* fue una decisión muy irreflexiva.

hat [hæt] *n* sombrero *m*; *to put one's hat on* ponerse el sombrero; *with one's hat on* con el sombrero puesto *or* en la cabeza || — *bowler hat* sombrero hongo, bombín *m* || *cardinal's hat* capelo cardenalicio || *cocked hat* sombrero de tres picos *or* de candil || *crush hat* sombrero de muelles || *felt hat* sombrero flexible || *hat in hand* humildemente || *hat shop* sombrería *f* || FIG *hats off!* ¡hay que descubrirse! | *I'll eat my hat if...* que me ahorquen si... | *keep it under your hat* no diga nada de eso | *my hat!* ¡naranjas! || *opera hat* sombrero de muelles || *panama hat* jipijapa *m* || *soft hat* sombrero flexible || *straw hat* sombrero de paja || *three-cornered hat* sombrero de tres picos || *to pass the hat* pasar la gorra (to collect) || *top hat* sombrero de copa || FIG *to take one's hat off to* descubrirse ante | *to talk through one's hat* decir tonterías, disparatar, desbarrar (to talk nonsense) | *to throw one's hat in the ring* echarse al ruedo.

hatband [-bænd] *n* cinta *f* del sombrero.

hat block [-blɔk] *n* horma *f*.

hatbox [-bɔks] *n* sombrerera *f*.

hatch [hætʃ] *n* salida *f* del huevo *or* del cascarón || pollada *f* (brood) || ventanilla *f* (for serving) || MAR escotilla *f* | trampa *f* (trapdoor) | compuerta *f* (floodgate) || rayado *m*, sombreado *m* (drawing) || FAM *down the hatch!* ¡salud!

hatch [hætʃ] *vt* incubar, empollar (to incubate) || hacer salir del cascarón (chickens) || rayar, sombrear (to stripe with parallel lines) || FIG maquinar, idear, tramar (a plot).
◆ *vi* salir del cascarón *or* del huevo || FIG madurar.

hatchback [-bæk] *n* portón trasero de un coche (door) || coche con portón trasero (car).

hatchel ['hætʃəl] *n* rastrillo *m*.

hatchery ['hætʃəri] *n* criadero *m*.

hatchet ['hætʃit] *n* hacha *f* || — *hatchet face* rostro afilado || *to bury the hatchet* enterrar el hacha de la guerra, hacer las paces || *to dig up the hatchet* desenterrar el hacha de guerra || FIG & FAM *hatchet job* crítica *f* virulenta (written or spoken).

hatchet-faced [-feist] *adj* de facciones enjutas, de rostro afilado.

hatching ['hætʃiŋ] *n* incubación *f* (of eggs) || salida *f* del cascarón *or* del huevo (of chickens) || PRINT sombreado *m* || FIG maquinación *f*.

hatchment ['hætʃmənt] *n* HERALD escudo *m* que lleva las armas de un caballero fallecido.

hatchway ['hætʃwei] *n* MAR escotilla *f*.

hate [heit] *n* odio *m*; *I could see hate in his eyes* veía odio en su mirada.

hate [heit] *vt* odiar, aborrecer, detestar (to abhor); *I hate her* la odio || FIG odiar, detestar; *he hates to get up early* odia levantarse temprano | sentir, lamentar (to regret); *I should hate to disappoint you* lamentaría decepcionarle || *he hates to be contradicted* no soporta que le contradigan.

hateful [-ful] *adj* odioso, sa; aborrecible.

hatless ['hætlis] *adj* sin sombrero.

hatpin ['hætpin] *n* alfiler *m* de sombrero.

hatrack ['hætræk] *n* percha *f* para sombreros.

hatred ['heitrid] *n* odio *m* (*for* a), aborrecimiento *m* (*for* de) || *out of hatred for* por odio a.

hatter ['hætə*] *n* sombrerero, ra || FAM *to be as mad as a hatter* estar más loco que una cabra.

hat trick ['hættrik] SP triple tanteo *m* (scored by one player).

hauberk ['hɔːbəːk] *n* cota *f* de mallas.

haughtiness ['hɔːtinis] *n* altanería *f*, altivez *f*, arrogancia *f*.

haughty ['hɔːti] *adj* altanero, ra; altivo, va; arrogante.

haul [hɔːl] *n* tirón *m* (heavy pull) || trayecto *m*, recorrido *m* (journey) || redada *f* (in fishing) | botín *m* (loot) || US camionaje *m*, transporte *m*, acarreo *m*.

haul [hɔːl] *vt* arrastrar (to drag) || acarrear (to transport by rail, road) || AUT remolcar (a car) || — *to haul down the flag* arriar bandera (to lower the colours) || *to haul over the coals* echar una bronca *or* un rapapolvo || *to haul up* izar.
◆ *vi* tirar de (to pull) || MAR halar.

haulage [-idʒ] *n* transporte *m*, acarreo *m*, camionaje *m*.

hauler ['hɔːlə*]; **haulier** ['hɔːljə*] *n* transportista *m*.

haulm [hɔːm] *n* BOT rastrojo *m* (after harvesting) | tallo *m* (stalk).

haunch [hɔːntʃ] *n* ANAT cadera *f* || ARCH riñón *m* de una bóveda || CULIN pernil *m* || — ANAT *haunch bone* hueso iliaco || *to sit on one's haunches* ponerse en cuclillas.

haunt [hɔːnt] *n* lugar *m* frecuentado (*of* por), lugar *m* predilecto || guarida *f* (of animals, criminals, etc.).

haunt [hɔːnt] *vt* aparecer en (ghosts) || frecuentar (to frequent) || seguir, perseguir (to follow s.o. around) || perseguir, obsesionar, atormentar (memories) || *to be haunted* estar encantado.

haunting [-iŋ] *adj* obsesionante.

hautbois; hautboy ['əubɔi] *n* MUS oboe *m* || BOT fresón *m* (strawberry).

Havana [hə'vænə] *pr n* GEOGR La Habana (city) || FAM habano *m* (cigar).

Havanan [-n] *adj/n* habanero, ra; habano, na.

have [hæv] *n* rico *m* || timo *m* (swindle) || *the haves and the have-nots* los ricos y los pobres.

have* [hæv] *vt* tener; *they have two cars* tienen dos coches; *I have four brothers* tengo cuatro hermanos; *he has good ideas* tiene buenas ideas; *to have news, talks, a discussion, a quarrel, influenza* tener noticias, conversaciones, una discusión, una riña, gripe || recibir, tener (to receive); *I had a letter from John today* he recibido una carta de Juan esta mañana || llevar, tener; *the coat has no label* el abrigo no lleva etiqueta || permitir; *I won't have it!* ¡no lo permitiré!; *I won't have them do this* no permitiré que hagan eso || decir; *the story has it that...* la historia dice que...; *as Lorca has it* como dice Lorca || tomar; *have a drink* tome una copa; *have another biscuit* tome otra galleta || tomar, coger; *I had my holidays in June* cogí las vacaciones en junio || encontrar (to find); *I have no words to express my desperation* no encuentro palabras para expresar mi desesperación || conseguir, encontrar; *it is to be had at the butcher's* esto se consigue en la carnicería || saber; *I have it by heart* lo sé de memoria || enterarse, saber; *I had it from the baker* me enteré por el panadero || tener conocimientos de; *I have Chinese* tengo conocimientos de chino || dar (to give); *let me have an answer* dame una contestación || hacer; *to have a trip* hacer un viaje || pasar (to spend); *to have a pleasant evening* pasar una noche agradable; *to have a good time* pasarlo bien || mandar; *have him cut the lawn* mándale cortar el césped; *to have a dress made* mandar hacer un traje; *to have sth. done* mandar hacer algo || tener ganado; *now he has the game* ahora tiene ganada la partida || tener agarrado; *his opponent had him by the neck* su adversario le tenía agarrado por el cuello || FAM engañar (to deceive); *I've been had, they had me* me han engañado | entender (to understand); *do you have me?* ¿me entiendes? || — *and what have you* y qué sé yo (and so on) || *as luck would have it he arrived on time* la suerte dispuso que llegara a tiempo || *have it your own way* haga lo que quiera || *he had his leg broken* se rompió la pierna || *he had his wallet stolen* le robaron la cartera || *I had better do it* más vale que lo haga || *I had rather do it* preferiría hacerlo || *I'll have you know* para que sepa usted || *I won't have it!* ¡no me lo creo! || *I would have the government ban alcohol* quisiera que el Gobierno prohibiese el alcohol || *let me have your book* dame tu libro || *now I have you!* ¡ya te tengo! (to catch) || *to have a baby* tener un niño || *to have a bath* darse un baño, bañarse || *to have a cigarette* fumarse un cigarrillo || *to have a game* jugar *or* echar una partida || *to have a haircut* cortarse el pelo || *to have a lesson* dar clase || *to have an operation* operarse, sufrir una operación || *to have a shave* afeitarse || *to have a shower* ducharse || *to have a try* intentar || *to have breakfast* desayunar || *to have dinner* comer || *to have done with* haber acabado con || *to have it* ganar (to win), acertar (to guess), cobrar (to be punished, etc.) || *to have it that* declarar, afirmar (to assert) || *to have lunch* almorzar || *to have sth. to do* tener algo que hacer || *to have to* tener que, deber; *I have to go* tengo que irme || *to have to do with* tener que ver con || *to have trouble with* tener problemas con || *to let s.o. have it* pegarle a alguien, darle (una paliza) a alguien (to hit), decirle a alguien cuatro verdades (to remonstrate) || *to let s.o. have sth.* dejarle algo a alguien || *what would you have me do?* ¿qué quieres que haga? || *will you have...?* ¿quieres...? || *you've got me there* aquí me has cogido.
◆ *v aux* haber; *I have seen* he visto; *I had gone* había ido; *he has been speaking for two hours* está hablando desde hace dos horas; *I have studied here for five months* hace cinco meses que estudio aquí || — *I have a brother* —*so have I* tengo un hermano —yo también || *I haven't seen you for weeks* hace semanas que no te veo, no te he visto desde hace semanas || *it has grown* —*so it has!* ha crecido —¡ya lo creo! || *to have just done* acabar de hacer || *you haven't washed* —*I have!* no te has lavado —sí || *you've been drinking* —*I haven't* has bebido —no.
◆ *phr v* **to have about** llevar (consigo) || **to have against** tener en contra || **to have at** atacar || **to have back** hacer volver (s.o.) || — *you can have it back tomorrow* se lo devolverán mañana

|| *to have down* tener apuntado (written down) | hacer venir, invitar (invited) | derribar (to knock down) || *to have in* dejar *or* dejar pasar (to show in) | tener en casa (guest, workmen) || — *to have it in for s.o.* tenerla tomada con alguien || *to have it in one* ser capaz de (hacer algo) || *to have on* llevar, tener; *to have a coat on* llevar un abrigo | poner en (to bet) || — *to have nothing on* estar desnudo (to be naked), no tener nada sobre (to have no information about), no ser nada comparado con (to be nothing compared to), no tener nada que hacer (to have nothing to do) || FAM *to have s.o. on* tomar el pelo a alguien || *to have sth. on* estar vestido (to be dressed), tener algo sobre (to possess information), tener un compromiso (to have a prior engagement) || *to have out* hacer salir || — *to have a tooth out* arrancarse una muela, sacarse una muela || FAM *to have it out with* poner las cosas en claro con || *to have one's appendix out* operarse de apendicitis || *to have one's tonsils out* operarse de amígdalas || *to have up* hacer venir, invitar (guests) | llevar ante los tribunales (for a crime, etc.) | hacer levantarse (to make get up).

— OBSERV Cuando el verbo *to have* significa *to possess* va seguido muy frecuentemente en el habla corriente por el participio pasivo *got* sin que sea modificado el sentido: *I have got a house* tengo una casa.

— OBSERV El pretérito y el participio pasivo de este verbo son irregulares (***had***) así como la tercera persona del singular del presente de indicativo (***has***).

haven ['heivn] *n* MAR abrigo *m* natural, abra *f* (small natural harbour) || FIG refugio *m* (shelter).

have-not [hævnɔt] *n* pobre *m*.

haven't ['hævnt] contraction of «have not».

haversack ['hævəsæk] *n* mochila *f*.

having ['hæviŋ] *n* posesión *f*.
◆ *pl* haber *m sing*, bienes *m*, fortuna *f sing*.

havoc ['hævək] *n* estragos *m pl*; *to make havoc of, to pay havoc with* hacer estragos en.

haw [hɔ:] *n* ZOOL membrana *f* nictitante || BOT baya *f* del espino (berry) | espino *m* (hawthorn) || vacilación *f* al hablar, carraspeo *m*.
◆ *interj* ¡ria! (to horse).

Hawaii [hɑ:'waii:] *pr n* GEOGR Hawai.

Hawaiian [hɑ:'waiiən] *adj/n* hawaiano, na || MUS *hawaiian guitar* guitarra hawaiana.

haw-haw ['hɔ:hɔ:] *n* risa *f* estúpida, carcajada *f*.

hawk [hɔ:k] *n* halcón *m* (bird) || esparavel *m* (plasterer's) || carraspeo *m* (cough) || FIG buitre *m* || — FIG *hawks and doves* halcones y palomas || *hawk nose* nariz aguileña.

hawk [hɔ:k] *vt* vender de puerta en puerta (to sell from door to door) || pregonar, vender por las calles (to peddle in the streets by shouting) || — *to hawk about* difundir, propalar (news) || *to hawk up* expectorar, arrojar tosiendo (to cough up).
◆ *vi* carraspear (to cough) || ser vendedor ambulante (to be a hawker) || SP cazar con halcón (in hunting).

hawker [-ə*] *n* vendedor ambulante (seller) || cetrero *m*, halconero *m* (falconer).

hawk-eyed [-aid] *adj* con ojos de lince.

hawking [-iŋ] *n* halconería *f* (hunting) || MED carraspeo *m* || venta *f* ambulante.

hawkmoth [-mɔθ] *n* ZOOL esfinge *f*.

hawk-nosed [nəuzd] *adj* de nariz aguileña.

hawse [hɔ:z] *n* MAR escobén *m* (hawsehole).

hawser ['hɔ:zə*] *n* MAR guindaleza *f*.

hawthorn ['ɔ:θɔ:n] *n* BOT espino *m*.

hay [hei] *n* BOT heno *m*; *to make hay* hacer heno || — FIG *make hay while the sun shines* a la ocasión la pintan calva || FAM *to hit the hay* irse al catre, irse a la piltra (to go to bed) || FIG *to make hay of sth.* enredar algo (to mix up), echar algo abajo *or* por tierra (an argument).

hay [hei] *vt* secar [hierba] (to dry grass) || echar forraje a (to feed).
◆ *vi* hacer heno, henificar.

haycock [-kɔk] *n* montón *m* de heno, almiar *m*.

hay fever [-,fi:və*] *n* MED fiebre *f* del heno.

hayfield [-fi:ld] *n* henar *m*.

hayfork [-fɔ:k] *n* AGR bieldo *m*.

hayloft [-lɔft] *n* henil *m*.

haymaking [-'meikiŋ] *n* AGR siega *f* del heno, henificación *f*.

hayrack [-ræk] *n* pesebre *m*.

hayrick [-rik] *n* almiar *m*.

hayseed [-si:d] *n* US FAM paleto *m*, cateto *m*.

haystack [-stæk] *n* almiar *m* || FIG *to look for a needle in a haystack* buscar una aguja en un pajar.

haywire ['-aiə*] *adj* FAM estropeado, da (out of order) | desorganizado, da (mixed-up) | chalado, da; loco, ca (mad) || FAM *to go haywire* estropearse (machine, etc.), desorganizarse (plan, etc.), volverse loco (person).
◆ *n* alambre *m* para atar el heno.

hazard ['hæzəd] *n* peligro *m*, riesgo *m* (risk); *to run the hazard* correr el riesgo || azar *m* (chance) || SP servicio *m* ganador (tennis) | obstáculo *m* (golf) | tronera *f* (billiards) || — *at all hazards* cueste lo que cueste || *at hazard* en juego.

hazard ['hæzəd] *vt* arriesgar, poner en peligro (to endanger) || aventurar (a guess).

hazardous [-əs] *adj* arriesgado, da; peligroso, sa; aventurado, da.

haze [heiz] *n* neblina *f* (of vapour) || FIG confusión *f*, vaguedad *f*.

haze [heiz] *vt* MAR agobiar de faenas || US dar una novatada a (a new student).

hazel ['heizl] *n* BOT avellano *m* (tree).
◆ *adj* de avellano || *hazel eyes* ojos *m* de color de avellana.

hazelnut [-nʌt] *n* avellana *f* (fruit).

haziness ['heizinis] *n* nebulosidad *f* || FIG nebulosidad *f*, vaguedad *f*.

hazy ['heizi] *adj* nebuloso, sa || FIG nebuloso, sa; confuso, sa; vago, ga (vague, obscure) | vago, ga (indefinite) || FAM achispado, da (tipsy) || FIG *I'm hazy about Latin* tengo unos conocimientos muy vagos de latín.

H-bomb ['eitʃbɔm] *n* bomba *f* H_2.

he [hi:] *pron* él; *I don't sing but he does* no canto pero él sí || *he who* el que, quien; *he who believes in God* el que crea en Dios.
◆ *adj* macho; *he-goat* macho cabrío.
◆ *n* macho *m* (animal) || hombre *m*, varón *m* (man).

— OBSERV A diferencia del pronombre *él*, el pronombre inglés *he* sólo se emplea para personas, no para cosas.

head [hed] *n* cabeza *f* (part of body); *my head hurts* me duele la cabeza || cabeza *f* (of procession, axe, etc.); *I was at the head of the list* estaba en cabeza de la lista || jefe *m*, cabeza *m* (chief); *head of the family* cabeza de familia || director, ra (of school, etc.); *he was the head of the organization* era el director de la organización || nacimiento *m*, cabecera *f* (of river) || cabecera *f* (of bed, table) || cabecero *m* (headboard of a bed) || espuma *f* (of beer) || nata *f* (of milk) || MIN frente *m* || cara *f* (of a coin) || punta *f* (of arrow, spear) || cotillo *m* (of hammer) || tapa *f* (of cask) || cabeza *f* (of nail, pin); *nails with larger heads* clavos con la cabeza más grande || puño *m* (of stick) || proa *f* (of ship) || altura *f* de caída (of water) || presión *f* (of steam) || cabeza *f* (of bridge) || parte *f* superior (of column) || GEOGR punta *f* (headland) || cabeza *f*, res *f* (of cattle) || asta *f* (of deer) || cogollo *m* (of cabbage) || copa *f* (of tree) || cabezuela *f* (of flowers) || cabeza *f* (of asparagus, garlic) || espiga *f* (of corn) || culata *f* (of cylinder) || cabeza *f*, persona *f*; *a dollar of a head* un dólar por cabeza || encabezamiento *m* (of a chapter) || título *m* (on a newspaper) || capítulo *m*, sección *f*, rúbrica *f* (section) || punto *m* (point) || principio *m*; *begin at the head of the page* empiece por el principio de la página || MUS parche *m* (of a drum) || cabeza *f* (of a tape recorder); *recording, playback, erasing head* cabeza sonora, auditiva, supresora || cabezal *m* (of a lathe) || MIL ojiva *f*, cabeza *f* (of a missile) || MAR gratil *m* (of sails) || cuerpo *m* (of bell) || facilidad *f*, aptitud *f*, cabeza *f*; *a good head for figures* una gran facilidad para los números || cabeza *f*, inteligencia *f* (intelligence) || punto *m* decisivo *or* crítico, culminación *f*; *things are coming to a head* las cosas llegan a un punto crítico || US FAM retrete *m* || — *at the head of* a la cabeza de || *by a head* por una cabeza || *crowned head* testa coronada || *from head to foot* de pies a cabeza, de arriba abajo || *head boy, girl* delegado *m*, delegada *f* del colegio || *head count* recuento *m* de participantes *or* de asistentes || *head down* con la cabeza baja || *head first* de cabeza || *head of department* jefe de servicio || *head of hair* pelo *m*, cabellera *f* || *head of state* jefe de Estado || *head on* de frente || *head teacher* director, ra (of school) || *heads I win, tails you lose* cara o cruz || *head wind* viento *m* en contra || FIG *he can do it standing on his head* lo puede hacer con los ojos cerrados || *he is a head taller than I* me saca la cabeza || FIG *he is head and shoulders above me* me aventaja en mucho | *I can't make head or tail of this* esto no tiene ni pies ni cabeza (I don't understand) | *Mary is head over heels in love with me* María anda de cabeza por mí, María está locamente enamorada de mí | *not to lift one's head* no levantar cabeza | *on your own head be it* ¡allá tú! | *out of his own head* de su propia cosecha | *over one's head* fuera del alcance de uno (a subject), por encima de uno, sin avisar a uno || *the lettuce is a shilling a head* cada lechuga cuesta un chelín || FIG *they put their heads together* se consultaron entre sí, cambiaron impresiones | *to act* o *to go over s.o.'s head* actuar a espaldas de alguien | *to beat one's head against a brick wall* darse de cabeza contra la pared || *to be at the head of* estar al frente de (troops), encabezar, estar al principio *or* en cabeza de (a list) || FIG *to be hanging over one's head* estar pendiente de un hilo || FAM *to be off* o *out of one's head* estar loco, estar chalado, haber perdido el juicio *or* la cabeza || FIG *to be on s.o.'s head* estar bajo la responsabilidad de uno || FAM *to be weak* o *soft in the head* andar mal de la cabeza, estar mal de la cabeza | *to bite s.o.'s head off* echar una bronca a alguien || FIG *to bother one's head about* preocuparse por | *to bring sth. to a head* llevar algo a un punto decisivo | *to come into one's head* pasarle a uno por la cabeza || *to come to a head* abrirse (abscess), llegar a un punto decisivo || FAM *to eat one's head off* comer como una lima *or* como un sabañón || FIG *to enter s.o.'s head* pasarle a uno por la cabeza | *to gather head* cobrar fuerzas | *to get it into one's head to do...* metérsele a uno en la cabeza hacer... | *to get sth. through s.o.'s head* meter algo en la cabeza de alguien | *to give a horse its head* dar rienda suelta a un caballo | *to give s.o. his head* dejar a alguien obrar a su antojo | *to go head and shoulders into* meterse de cabeza en || *to go head over heels* dar una voltereta (to somersault), caer patas arriba (to fall) || FAM *to go off* o *out of one's head* perder el juicio *or* la cabeza || *to go straight out of s.o.'s head* írsele a uno de la cabeza || FIG *to go to one's head* subírsele a la cabeza | *to hang*

o *to hide one's head* caérsele a uno la cara de vergüenza || *to have a bad head* tener dolor de cabeza || FIG *to have a good head on one's shoulders* ser capaz *or* inteligente | *to have one's head screwed on* tener la cabeza en su sitio | *to hit the nail on the head* dar en el clavo, acertar | *to keep one's head* no perder la cabeza | *to keep one's head above water* mantenerse a flote | *to knock on the head* dar al traste con | *to laugh one's head off* reír a mandíbula batiente | *to lay o to put heads together* colaborar | *to lose one's head* perder la cabeza | *to make head* hacer progresos | *to make heads turn* hacer volver la cabeza, atraer mucho la atención || *to nod one's head* asentir con la cabeza || *to put price on s.o.'s head* poner la cabeza de uno a precio || FIG *to put it into s.o.'s head* metérselo en la cabeza a alguien | *to put out of one's head* quitarse de la cabeza, dejar de pensar en || MATH *to reckon in one's head* calcular mentalmente || *to shake one's head* negar con la cabeza || FIG *to speak over the head of* no ponerse al alcance de || *to stand on one's head* hacer el pino || FIG *to take it into one's head to do sth.* metérsele a uno en la cabeza hacer algo || FIG *to talk one's head off* hablar por los codos | *to talk s.o.'s head off* poner la cabeza bomba a alguien || *to toss for sth. heads or tails* echar algo a cara o cruz || FIG *to turn s.o.'s head* subírsele a la cabeza a uno | *two heads are better than one* cuatro ojos ven más que dos | *use your head* reflexione un poco | *we took it into our heads to...* se nos ocurrió...
◆ *adj* principal || delantero, ra || *head post office* casa *f* de correos.

head [hed] *vt* encabezar; *to head a demonstration* encabezar una manifestación; *his name heads the list* su nombre encabeza la lista; *the date heads the letter* la fecha encabeza la carta || ir en cabeza de (to precede) || estar a la cabeza de; *the girl heads her class at school* la muchacha está a la cabeza de su clase en la escuela || dirigir, estar a la cabeza de (a firm, etc.) || coronar; *the spire heads the tower* la aguja corona la torre || titular (to entitle) || desmochar (to cut the head off); *to head a tree* desmochar un árbol || poner tapa a (a cask) || conducir, llevar; *they headed the herd into a valley* condujeron el ganado a un valle || bordear, dar la vuelta a (a cape, etc.) || SP dar un cabezazo a, cabecear (the ball) | meter de cabeza (a goal) || — *to head back* ojear (game), cortar la retirada a (the enemy) || *to head off* cortar el paso a, interceptar el camino a (s.o.), desviar (a question), disuadir (from doing sth.) || MAR *to head the ship for* hacer rumbo a.
◆ *vi* *to head for* dirigirse hacia (to move forward), hacer rumbo a (a ship) || *to head for ruin* ir a la ruina.

headache [-eik] *n* dolor *m* de cabeza || FIG quebradero *m* de cabeza.

headband [-bænd] *n* cinta *f* (for the hair) || casco *m* (of earphones) || PRINT cabecera *f*.

headbanger [-bæɛə*] *n* FAM fan *m* & *f* de música heavy metal.

headboard [-bɔ:d] *n* cabecero *m* (of a bed).

headcheese [-tʃi:z] *n* US queso *m* de cerdo.

headdress [-dres] *n* tocado *m*.

headed [-id] *adj* con membrete (paper) || BOT repolludo, da (cabbage) || — *black-headed* de pelo negro (person), de cabeza negra (animal) || *two-headed* bicéfalo, la.

header [-ə*] *n* salto *m* de cabeza (dive headfirst) || caída *f* de cabeza (fall) || ARCH tizón *m* || SP cabezazo *m* (in football) || *to take a header* caerse de cabeza.

headfirst [-fə:st] *adv* de cabeza.

headframe [-freim] *n* castillete *m* de extracción (of a mine).

headgear [-giə*] *n* tocado *m* (headdress).

headhunter [-ˌhʌntə*] *n* cazador *m* de cabezas, cazatalentos *m* & *f* (in business).

head-hunting [-ˌhʌntiŋ] *n* caza *f* de talentos (in business).

heading [-iŋ] *n* encabezamiento *m*, título *m* (of a chapter) || membrete *m* (of a letter) || breve introducción *f* (introductory paragraph) || rúbrica *f*, apartado *m* (section) || SP cabezazo *m* || MAR & AVIAT rumbo *m*, orientación *f*.

head lamp [-læmp] *n* AUT faro *m* || farol *m* (of locomotive).

headland [-lænd] *n* GEOGR punta *f*, promontorio *m*, cabo *m*.

headless [-lis] *adj* sin cabeza (body, nail) || ZOOL acéfalo, la || FIG sin cabeza, sin jefe | sin cabeza, tonto, ta (foolish).

headlight [-lait] *n* AUT faro *m* || farol *m* (of locomotive).

headline [-lain] *n* título *m* (in a book) || titular *m* (in a newspaper) || MAR rebenque *m* || — *to hit the headlines* ser pasto de la actualidad || *to make the headlines* estar en primera plana.

headlong [-lɔŋ] *adj* de cabeza (with the head foremost) || precipitado, da (hasty) || impetuoso, sa (impetuous) || escarpado, da (cliffs).
◆ *adv* de cabeza (headfirst) || precipitadamente (hastily).

headman [-'mæn] *n* jefe *m*.
— OBSERV El plural de esta palabra es *headmen*.

headmaster [-'mɑ:stə*] *n* director *m*.

headmistress [-'mistris] *n* directora *f*.

head-on [-'ɔn] *adj/adv* de frente.

headphones [-fəunz] *pl n* auriculares *m* [AMER audífonos *m*].

headpiece [-ˌpi:s] *n* yelmo *m* || PRINT cabecera *f*.

headquarters [-'kwɔ:təz] *pl n* MIL cuartel *m sing* general || oficina *f sing* central (main office) || sede *f sing* (of an organization) || domicilio *m sing* social (of a firm) || FIG centro *m sing* de operaciones, cuartel *m sing* general.

headrest [-rest] *n* cabecero *m*, cabezal *m*.

headroom [-rum] *n* altura *f* libre (under a bridge).

headscarf [-skɑ:f] *n* pañuelo *m* para la cabeza.

headset [-set] *n* auriculares *m pl* [AMER audífonos *m pl*].

headship [-ʃip] *n* dirección *f*.

headshrinker [-ʃriŋkə*] *n* reductor *m* de cabezas || FAM psiquiatra *m*.

headsman [-zmæn] *n* verdugo *m*.
— OBSERV El plural de esta palabra es *headsmen*.

headspring [-spriŋ] *n* fuente *f*, manantial *m* (of a river).

headstall [-stɔ:l] *n* jáquima *f*.

headstand [-stænd] *n* vertical *f*, pino *m* (gymnastics).

head start [-stɑ:t] *n* ventaja *f* (in a competition, a race).

headstock [-stɔk] *n* TECH contrapunta *f*.

headstone [-stəun] *n* lápida *f* mortuoria (tombstone) || ARCH piedra *f* angular.

headstream [-stri:m] *n* arroyo *m* que constituye el nacimiento de un río.

headstrong [-strɔŋ] *adj* voluntario, ria; testarudo, da.

head voice [-vɔis] *n* MUS falsete *m*.

headwaiter [-weitə*] *n* jefe *m* de comedor, «maître» *m*.

headwaters [-'wɔ:təz] *pl n* cabecera *f sing*.

headway [-wei] *n* progreso *m* (progress) || salida *f* (of a ship) || altura *f* libre (headroom) || *to make headway* hacer progresos (to make progress), avanzar (to move forward).

headword [-wə:d] *n* encabezamiento *m*.

headwork [-wə:k] *n* trabajo *m* mental.

heady [-i] *adj* embriagador, ra (intoxicating) || fuerte (wine) || vertiginoso, sa; *the heady heights* las alturas vertiginosas || FIG impetuoso, sa | sensato, ta (judicious).

heal [hi:l] *vt* curar (a disease, a patient) || cicatrizar, curar (a wound) || FIG curar, remediar || FIG *to heal the breach between two people* reconciliar a dos personas.
◆ *vi* cicatrizarse (wounds) || curarse, sanar (people) || FIG remediarse.

heal-all [-ɔ:l] *n* panacea *f*.

healer [-ə*] *n* curador, ra.

healing [-iŋ] *adj* cicatrizante (ointment) || curativo, va (remedy).
◆ *n* curación *f* (of disease) || cicatrización *f* (of wound).

health [helθ] *n* salud *f* || sanidad *f*; *public health* sanidad pública || — *good health!* ¡salud! || *health centre* consultorio *m or* centro *m* médico || *health certificate* certificado médico || *health food* alimentos *m pl* naturales || *health measures* medidas sanitarias || *health officer* inspector *m* de sanidad || *health resort* balneario *m* || *Ministry of Health* Dirección *f* General de Sanidad || *to be in bad, in good health* estar bien, mal de salud || *to drink s.o.'s health* beber a la salud de alguien || *to your health!* ¡a tu salud!

healthful [-ful] *adj* saludable, sano, na.

healthiness [-inis] *n* salubridad *f*.

healthy [-i] *adj* sano, na (in good health) || sano, na; saludable; *a healthy climate* un clima sano || salubre (salubrious) || considerable (part) || favorable (impression) || bueno, na; *healthy appetite* buen apetito || sano, na (sound) || *to have a healthy look* estar rebosante de salud.

heap [hi:p] *n* montón *m*; *a heap of rubbish* un montón de basura; *a heap of troubles* un montón de problemas || — US *a whole heap of* un montón de, montones de || *heaps of* un montón de, montones de || FAM *to be struck all of a heap* quedarse pasmado.

heap [hi:p] *vt* amontonar || colmar, llenar (a dish) || FIG colmar de (praises, etc.) || — *a heaped spoonful* una cucharada colmada || *to heap up* amontonar.

hear [hiə*] *vt* oír; *he heard my voice* oyó mi voz; *he heard me coming* me oyó venir || escuchar; *she refused to hear me* se negó a escucharme || recibir; *I can't hear you now* no puedo recibirle ahora || tomar; *to hear a child's lesson* tomar la lección a un niño || asistir a (lectures) || saber, enterarse de (a piece of news) || JUR ver (a case) | oír (a witness, defendant) || MUS & RAD escuchar || — *I have heard he is ill* me han dicho que está enfermo, he oído decir que está enfermo || US *I hear you talking* estoy completamente de acuerdo con lo que Ud. dice || *to be heard* oírse || *to hear confession* confesar || *to hear Mass* oír misa || *to hear out* escuchar hasta el final.
◆ *vi* oír; *I can hear you, I'm not deaf* le oigo, no estoy sordo || — *hear, hear!* ¡muy bien! || *he won't hear of it* no quiere oír hablar de ello || *let me hear from you* escríbame, déme noticias suyas || *to hear about* oír hablar de (to listen to), saber, enterarse de (to know) || *to hear from* tener noticias de, saber; *I heard from her yesterday* tuve noticias de ella ayer || *to hear of* tener noticias de (to learn of), saber, enterarse de (to be informed of), oír hablar de; *I never heard of such a thing* nunca oí hablar de tal cosa || FAM

you will hear of it! ¡ya verás lo que es bueno!, ¡ya oirás hablar de esto!
— OBSERV Pret y pp ***heard***.

heard [hə:d] *pret/pp* → **hear.**

hearer ['hiərə*] *n* oyente *m* & *f*.
◆ *pl* auditorio *m sing*.

hearing ['hiəriŋ] *n* oído *m* (sense) || audición *f* (act of hearing); *the hearing of a sound* la audición de un sonido || JUR audición *f* (of witnesses) | audiencia *f*, vista *f* (of a case) || MUS audición *f* || — *hard of hearing* duro de oído || *in s.o.'s hearing* en presencia de alguien || *out of hearing* fuera del alcance del oído || *to come to s.o.'s hearing* llegar a oídos de alguien, llegar al conocimiento de uno || *to give s.o. a fair hearing* escuchar a alguien imparcialmente || *to refuse s.o. a hearing* negarse a escuchar a alguien || *within hearing* al alcance del oído.

hearing aid [-eid] *n* aparato *m* para sordos.

hearken ['hɑ:kən] *vi* *to hearken to* escuchar (to listen).

hearsay ['hiəsei] *n* rumor *m* || *to know sth. by hearsay* o *from hearsay* saber algo de oídas.

hearse [hə:s] *n* coche *m* fúnebre.

heart [hɑ:t] *n* ANAT corazón *m*; *heart transplant* transplante de corazón || FIG corazón *m*; *she has a kind heart* tiene buen corazón; *he went off with a heavy heart* se fue con el corazón encogido | fondo *m* (of a matter) | centro *m*, corazón *m* (of a place) | centro *m*, casco *m*, corazón *m* (of a city) | ánimo *m*, corazón *m* (courage) || corazón *m* (of a fruit, etc.) || cogollo *m* (of lettuce) || AGR estado *m* (of the soil) || — *at heart* en el fondo || *by heart* de memoria || FIG *change of heart* cambio *m* de parecer || FAM *dear heart!* ¡amor mío! || *from one's heart* de todo corazón || *from the bottom of my heart* de todo corazón || *have a heart!* ¡ten piedad! || *heart and soul* con toda el alma, en cuerpo y alma || MED *heart attack* ataque *m* al corazón | *heart disease* enfermedad *f* cardiaca *or* del corazón | *heart failure* colapso *m* || *heart of the matter* meollo *m* de la cuestión || *heart of oak* valiente *m* || *heart to heart* franco, ca || *in one's heart* en el fondo (del corazón) || *in one's heart of hearts* en lo más recóndito de su corazón || *in the heart of winter* en pleno invierno || *my heart missed* se me encogió el corazón || *my heart sank* se me cayó el alma a los pies || *not to have the heart to do sth.* no tener corazón *or* valor para hacer algo || *out of heart* desanimado, da; descorazonado, da || *set your heart at rest* no se preocupe, tranquilícese || *to appeal to the heart* hablar al corazón || *to be good at heart* tener buen corazón || *to be in no heart for laughing* no tener ganas de reír || *to break s.o.'s heart* partirle el corazón a uno || *to cry one's heart out* llorar a lágrima viva || *to die of a broken heart* morirse de pena || *to do one's heart good* alegrarle a uno || *to eat one's heart out* consumirse (with grief, remorse, etc.) || *to get straight to the heart of the matter* ir al grano || *to get to the heart of* entrar en el fondo de || *to give one's heart to* dar su corazón a || *to have a change of heart* cambiar de opinión || *to have a heart of gold* tener un corazón que se sale del pecho, tener un corazón de oro || *to have at heart* tomar a pecho || *to have heart trouble* padecer del corazón || *to have no heart* no tener corazón || *to have one's heart in one's boots* estar con *or* tener el alma en un hilo || *to have one's heart in one's mouth* tener el alma en un hilo, tener el corazón en un puño || *to have one's heart in one's work* poner toda su alma en el trabajo || *to have one's heart in the right place* tener buen corazón || *to lose heart* descorazonarse, desanimarse || *to lose one's heart to* enamorarse de, dar su corazón a || *to one's heart delight* o *content* hasta quedarse satisfecho || *to open one's heart to* abrir su pecho a || *to set one's heart on doing* poner todo su afán en hacer || *to take heart* cobrar ánimo || *to take sth. to heart* tomar algo a pecho || *to wear one's heart on one's sleeve* llevar el corazón en la mano || *to win s.o.'s heart* enamorar a alguien || *with all one's heart* con toda su alma (to love), de todo corazón (to say) || *with half a heart* sin entusiasmo || *you're a man after my own heart* eres un hombre de los que me gustan.
◆ *pl* corazones *m* (in cards); *the eight of hearts* el ocho de corazones || copas *f* (in Spanish cards).

heartache [-eik] *n* angustia *f*, pesar *m*, pena *f*, congoja *f*.

heartbeat [-bi:t] *n* latido *m* del corazón.

heartbreak [-breik] *n* congoja *f*, angustia *f*.

heartbreaking [-'breikiŋ] *adj* desgarrador, ra; que parte el corazón.

heartbroken [-ˌbrəukən] *adj* *to be heartbroken* tener el corazón destrozado *or* desgarrado (to be overwhelmed with grief) || *to be heartbroken about sth.* sentir mucho algo, lamentar algo.

heartburn [-bə:n] *n* MED acedía *f*.

heartburning [-bə:niŋ] *n* envidia *f* (jealousy) || rencor *m* (rancour) || descontento *m* (discontent).

hearten ['hɑ:tn] *vt* animar, alentar.

heartfelt ['hɑ:tfelt] *adj* sincero, ra; sentido, da.

hearth [hɑ:θ] *n* hogar *m* || FIG hogar *m*; *without hearth or home* sin casa ni hogar || TECH crisol *m* (of blast furnace) | solera *f* (of reverberatory furnace).

heartland ['hɑ:tlænd] *n* centro *m* (region).

hearthstone [-stəun] *n* piedra *f* de la chimenea || blanco *m* de España (for cleaning) || US hogar *m* (home).

heartily ['hɑ:tili] *adv* cordialmente (warmly) || sinceramente (sincerely) || de buena gana (to eat, to laugh) || completamente (fully); *I heartily agree with you* estoy completamente de acuerdo con Ud.

heartiness ['hɑ:tinis] *n* cordialidad *f* (warmth) || sinceridad *f* (sincerity) || entusiasmo *m* (enthusiasm) || campechanía *f* (friendliness of a person).

heartless ['hɑ:tlis] *adj* despiadado, da; cruel, sin corazón, inhumano, na.

heartlessness ['hɑ:tlisnis] *n* crueldad *f*, inhumanidad *f*, falta *f* de humanidad.

heartrending ['hɑ:t'rendiŋ] *adj* desgarrador, ra; *a heartrending cry* un grito desgarrador || conmovedor, ra (moving).

heart-searching ['hɑ:tˌsə:tʃiŋ] *n* examen *m* de conciencia.

heartsease ['hɑ:tsi:z] *n* BOT trinitaria *f* || FIG sosiego *m*, serenidad *f*.

heartsick ['hɑ:tsik] *adj* desanimado, da || FAM *heartsick lover* enamorado perdido.

heartstrings ['hɑ:tstriŋz] *pl n* *to play on s.o.'s heartstrings* tocarle la fibra sensible a uno.

heart-to-heart ['hɑ:tə'hɑ:t] *adj* franco, ca; sincero, ra (candid) || *to have a heart-to-heart talk with s.o.* tener una conversación íntima con alguien.

heartthrob ['hɑ:tθrɔb] *n* guapetón *m*.

heart-warming ['hɑ:tˌwɔ:miŋ] *adj* reconfortante, alentador, ra.

heart-whole ['hɑ:thəul] *adj* libre (not in love) || sincero, ra (sincere) || que no ha perdido ánimo (undismayed).

heartwood ['hɑ:twud] *n* BOT duramen *m*.

hearty ['gɑ:ti] *adj* cordial (cordial); *a hearty welcome* una cordial bienvenida || sincero, ra (sincere) || campechano, na (good-hearted, cheerful) || robusto, ta; sano, na (strong and healthy) || fuerte, enérgico, ca (vigorous) || abundante (meal) || bueno, na (appetite) || fértil (land) || FAM *to be a hearty eater* tener un buen saque.
◆ *n* MAR compañero *m*.

heat [hi:t] *n* calor *m*; *specific heat* calor específico; *blistering heat* calor abrasador || calefacción *f*; *the heat should be turned off* habría que apagar la calefacción || FIG calor *m*; *in the heat of the battle, of the argument* en el calor de la batalla, de la discusión | pasión *f* (passion) || ZOOL celo *m*; *on heat* en celo || SP eliminatoria *f*, serie *f* || MED mancha *f* roja (on the skin) || — *dead heat* empate *m* || FIG *to get into a heat* acalorarse || *to heat sth. to red heat* calentar algo al rojo, poner algo al rojo || US FAM *to turn the heat on* ejercer una presión sobre.
◆ *adj* de calor; *heat exchanger* cambiador de calor; *heat wave* ola de calor || térmico, ca; *heat energy* energía térmica; *heat engine* motor térmico || — *heat lightning* fucilazo *m*, relámpago *m* de calor || *heat rash* sarpullido *m*.

heat [hi:t] *vt* calentar || FIG acalorar.
◆ *vi* calentarse || FIG acalorarse.

heated [-id] *adj* acalorado, da (argument, etc.) || caliente (air) || *to get heated* acalorarse.

heater [-ə*] *n* calentador *m* (stove, furnace) || radiador *m* (radiator) || ELECTR filamento *m* || US POP revólver *m*, pistola *f* (pistol).

heath [hi:θ] *n* BOT brezo *m* (plant) || brezal *m* (land) || terreno *m* baldío (uncultivated land).

heathen ['hi:ðən] *adj/n* pagano, na || FIG salvaje (ill-mannered person) || *the heathen* los paganos.

heathenish ['hi:ðəniʃ] *adj* pagano, na || FIG bárbaro, ra; salvaje.

heathenism ['hi:ðənizəm] *n* paganismo *m* || FIG barbarie *f*.

heathenize ['hi:ðənaiz] *vt* paganizar.

heather ['hðə*] *n* BOT brezo *m*.

heathery [-ri]; **heathy** ['hi:θi] *adj* cubierto de brezos.

heating ['hi:tiŋ] *adj* de caldeo; *heating surface* superficie de caldeo || calorífico, ca; *heating power* potencia calorífica || calentador, ra (warming).
◆ *n* calefacción *f*; *central heating* calefacción central || calentamiento *m*.

heat-resistant ['hi:tri'zistənt] *adj* resistente al calor, calorífugo, ga.

heat-seeking ['hi:t'si:kiŋ] *adj* MIL atraído, da por el calor (missile).

heatstroke ['hi:tstrəuk] *n* MED insolación *f*.

heave [hi:v] *n* gran esfuerzo *m* [para levantar] (big effort) || tirón *m* (pull) || empujón *m* (push) || movimiento *m*, agitación *f* (of waves) || palpitación *f* (of the breast) || náusea *f* (nausea) || GEOL desplazamiento *m* lateral.
◆ *pl* VET huélfago *m sing*.

heave* [hi:v] *vt* tirar de (to pull) || empujar (to push) || levantar (to lift) || exhalar (a sigh) || arrojar, tirar, lanzar (to throw) || MAR levantar (the anchor) || GEOL desplazar lateralmente.
◆ *vi* subir y bajar (waves) || levantarse (road) || palpitar (breast) || tener náuseas (to retch) || jadear (to pant) || MAR virar || — MAR *to heave at* halar de (a rope) | *to heave back* soltar | *to heave in sight* aparecer | *to heave off* hacerse a la mar | *to heave out* largar las velas | *to heave to* ponerse al pairo, pairar.
— OBSERV Cuando *to heave* significa «levantar, tirar, empujar, etc.», se aplica siempre a objetos pesados e indica la necesidad de un gran esfuerzo.
— OBSERV Cuando tiene un sentido marítimo, *to heave* tiene un pretérito y un participio pasivo irregulares (***hove***).

heaven ['hevn] *n* cielo *m*; *to go to heaven* ir al cielo || FIG gloria *f* (sensation); *this is heaven* esto es (la) gloria | paraíso *m* (place); *this place*

is heaven este sitio es el paraíso || Dios *m; Heaven protect you!* ¡que Dios le guarde! || — *by heaven!* ¡cielos! || *for heaven's sake!* ¡por amor de Dios!, ¡por Dios! || *Heaven forbid!* ¡Dios me *or* te *or* le libre! || *Heaven knows* sabe Dios, Dios es testigo || *thank Heaven!* ¡gracias a Dios! || FIG *to be in the seventh heaven* estar en el séptimo cielo | *to cry out to heaven* clamar al cielo | *to move heaven and earth* mover cielo y tierra.
◆ *pl* cielo *m sing* (sky); *the stars shone in the heavens* las estrellas brillaban en el cielo || *good heavens!* ¡Dios mío!, ¡madre mía!

heavenly [-li] *adj* celestial || FIG divino, na || ASTR celeste; *heavenly body* cuerpo celeste.

heaven-sent [-sent] *adj* FIG llovido del cielo; *a heaven-sent opportunity* una oportunidad llovida del cielo.

heavenward[-wəd]; **heavenwards** [-wədz] *adv* hacia el cielo.

heaver ['hi:və*] *n* cargador *m*, descargador *m*.

heavily ['hevili] *adv* pesadamente (to walk, to fall) || mucho; *to drink heavily* beber mucho; *to lose heavily* perder mucho || profundamente; *to sigh, to sleep heavily* suspirar, dormir profundamente || con dificultad (to breathe, etc.) || *heavily damaged* muy estropeado.

heaviness ['hevinis] *n* pesadez *f* (of the body) || peso *m* (of a burden) || pesadez *f* (of a meal) || peso *m* (of taxes) || — *heaviness in the head* cabeza pesada || *heaviness of heart* tristeza *f*.

heavy ['hevi] *adj* pesado, da; *a heavy suitcase* una maleta pesada; *a heavy metal* un metal pesado || fuerte (rain, emphasis, meal, scent, storm, waves, blow) || grande (expense, loss, defeat) || grueso, sa (line, scar, paper, cloth, cable, sea) || pesado, da (head, eyes) || cargado, da; pesado, da (atmosphere) || pesado, da (weather) || intenso, sa (electric current) || espeso, sa; denso, sa (liquid) || denso, sa (traffic, population) || abundante (harvest) || difícil, malo, la (surface); *it was heavy going* el camino era difícil || encapotado, da (sky) || de peso (important) || duro, ra (strict); *to rule with a heavy hand* gobernar con mano dura || triste (sad) || oprimido, da (heart) || malo, la (humour) || abatido, da; deprimido, da (depressed) || torpe (clumsy) || cansado, da (tired) || profundo, da (sleep, silence, sigh) || grave, grande (responsibility) || difícil, penoso, sa (difficult) || pesado, da (difficult to digest) || pesado, da (tread) || pesado, da; lento, ta (slow) || arcilloso, sa (soil) || pesado, da (road) || empinado, da (gradient) || pesado, da (boring) || corpulento, ta (stout) || THEATR serio, ra (part) || MIL pesado, da; grueso, sa (artillery) | graneado, da (fire) || SP pesado, da (weight) || MED bueno, na (cold) || CHEM pesado, da (hydrogen, oil) || — FIG *a heavy burden* una carga pesada || *an engine which is heavy on petrol* un motor que consume mucha gasolina || *heavy industry* industria pesada || PRINT *heavy type* negrita *f* || *heavy water* agua pesada || *heavy with young* grávida, preñada (animals) || *is it heavy?* ¿pesa mucho? || *the air was heavy with smoke* el aire estaba cargado de humo || *to be a heavy drinker, eater, smoker* beber, comer, fumar mucho || *we've had a heavy day* hemos tenido un día muy cargado.
◆ *adv* → **heavily** || — *time hangs heavy on his hands* se le hace muy largo el tiempo || *to hang heavy* transcurrir muy lentamente (time) || *to lie heavy on one's conscience* pesarle a uno en la conciencia.
◆ *pl n* MIL artillería *f sing* pesada.

heavy-duty [-'dju:ti] *adj* para trabajos duros || para grandes cargas (lifting devices, etc.).

heavy-handed [-'hændid] *adj* severo, ra; autoritario, ria (domineering) || torpe (clumsy).

heavyhearted [-'hɑ:tid] *adj* afligido, da; pesaroso, sa; con el corazón oprimido.

heavyset [-set] *n* US rechoncho, cha (stocky).

heavyweight [-weit] *n* SP peso *m* pesado || SP *light heavyweight* peso semipesado.

hebdomadal [heb'dɔmədl] *adj* semanal, hebdomadario, ria.

hebetate ['hebiteit] *vt* embrutecer.
◆ *vi* embrutecerse.

hebetude ['hebitju:d] *n* embrutecimiento *m*.

Hebraic [hi:'breiik] *adj* hebraico, ca.

hebrew ['hi:bru:] *adj* hebreo, a.
◆ *n* hebreo, a (people) || hebreo *m* (language).

Hebrides ['hebridi:z] *pl prn* GEOGR Hébridas *f*.

hecatomb ['hekətu:m] *n* hecatombe *f*.

heck [hek] *interj* FAM → **hell.**

heckle ['hekl] *n* rastrillo *m*.

heckle ['hekl] *vt* interrumpir (a un orador) haciendo preguntas molestas || rastrillar (flax, hemp).

heckler [-pq*] *n* pesona *f* que interrumpe a un orador haciendo preguntas molestas.

hectare ['hektɑ:*] *n* hectárea *f*.

hectic ['hektik] *adj* agitado, da; ajetreado, da; *a hectic day* un día agitado; *a hectic life* una vida ajetreada || febril; *hectic activity* actividad febril || MED héctico, ca; hético, ca; tísico, ca || FAM *hectic confusion* barullo *m*.
◆ *n* fiebre *f* héctica, tisis *f*.

hectogramme; US **hectogram** ['hektəugræm] *n* hectogramo *m*.

hectolitre; US **hectoliter** ['hektəu,li:tə*] *n* hectolitro *m*.

hectometre; US **hectometer** ['hektəu,mi:tə*] *n* hectómetro *m*.

hector ['hektə*] *n* matamoros *m inv*.

hector ['hektə*] *vt* intimidar (con bravatas).
◆ *vi* echar bravatas.

hectowatt ['hektəuwɔt] *n* ELECTR hectovatio *m*.

heddle ['hedəl] *n* lizo *m* (of a loom).

hedge [hedʒ] *n* seto *m*, seto *m* vivo (of garden, field) || hilera *f*, fila *f* (of police) || FIG barrera *f* (barrier) || *quickset hedge* seto vivo.

hedge [hedʒ] *vt* cercar (to enclose) || FIG proteger, guardar (to protect) | protegerse contra (to protect o.s.) | poner trabas a (to hinder) || compensar (bet) || — *to hedge in* cercar || FIG *to hedge in* o *about with* rodear de || *to hedge off* separar con un seto.
◆ *vi* FIG contestar con evasivas, salir por la tangente (to refuse to commit o.s.) | parapetarse; *to hedge behind the rules* parapetarse detrás de los reglamentos || COMM hacer operaciones de bolsa compensatorias || hacer apuestas compensatorias.

hedgehog [-hɔg] *n* ZOOL erizo *m* || MIL alambrada *f* (barbed wire).

hedgehop [-hɔp] *vi* AVIAT volar bajo *or* en vuelo rasante.

hedgehopping [-'hɔpiŋ] *n* AVIAT vuelo *m* rasante.

hedgerow [-rəu] *n* seto *m*, seto *m* vivo.

hedonism ['hi:dəunizəm] *n* hedonismo *m*.

hedonist ['hi:dəunist] *n* hedonista *m* & *f*.

hedonistic [hidɔ'nistik] *adj* hedonista.

heebie-jeebies [,hibi'dʒibiz] *pl n* US FAM *to have the heebie-jeebies* estar hecho un manojo de nervios.

heed [hi:d] *n* atención *f*; *pay* o *give* o *take heed to what he says* presta atención a lo que dice || cuidado *m* (care); *take heed not to lose it* ten cuidado de no perderlo || — *to take heed of s.o.'s advice* tener en cuenta *or* tomar en consideración los consejos de alguien || *to take no heed of* no hacer caso de, no tener en cuenta.

heed [hi:d] *vt* tener en cuenta, hacer caso de (to take notice) || prestar atención a (to pay attention to).

heedful [-ful] *adj* atento, ta (*of* a) (attentive) || cuidadoso, sa (careful).

heedless [-lis] *adj* desatento, ta (inattentive) || descuidado, da; despreocupado, da (careless) || *to be heedless of advice* hacer caso omiso de los consejos.

heedlessly [-lisli] *adv* a la ligera, con despreocupación.

heedlessness [-lisnis] *n* desatención *f* || descuido *m*, despreocupación *f* (carelessness).

hee-haw ['hi:hɔ:] *n* rebuzno *m* (of an ass) || FIG & FAM carcajada *f* (coarse laugh).

hee-haw ['hi'hɔ:] *vi* rebuznar (an ass) || FIG & FAM reír a carcajadas (to laugh).

heel [hi:l] *n* ANAT talón *m* || talón *m* (of sock, stocking, shoe) || tacón *m* (on sole of shoe); *high heels* tacones altos || FIG talón *m* [parte inferior y trasera de una cosa] | restos *m pl* (remainder) | pico *m* (crust of bread) || MUS talón *m* (of violin bow) || MAR escora *f* (list) | talón *m* (of the keel) || US FIG & FAM sinvergüenza *m* (cad) || — FIG *Achilles' heel* talón de Aquiles | *heels over head, head over heels* patas arriba | *to be at* o *on s.o.'s heels* seguirle a uno de cerca, pisarle los talones a uno || *to be down at heel* tener el tacón gastado (shoe), estar desaliñado, estar mal vestido, estar desharrapado (s.o.) || FIG *to be under the heel of the invader* estar bajo el yugo del invasor | *to bring s.o. to heel* meter a alguien en cintura *or* en vereda, someter a alguien || *to come to heel* acudir [un perro cuando se le llama] || FIG *to cool* o *to kick one's heels* hacer antesala (in a building), estar de plantón (waiting in the street) | *to follow close* o *to tread on s.o.'s heels* pisarle los talones a uno | *to kick up one's heels* echar una cana al aire | *to lay by the heels* pillar, poner en chirona (to put in jail) | *to show a clan pair of heels, to take to one's heels* poner pies en polvorosa | *to turn on one's heel* volver de espaldas, dar media vuelta.

heel [hi:l] *vt* poner tacón a (a shoe) || remendar el talón de (a sock, stocking) || poner espolones a (a cock) || SP talonar (a ball) || MAR inclinar || FIG seguir de cerca, pisarle los talones a.
◆ *vi* seguir de cerca al amo (a dog) || taconear (in dancing) || MAR escorar (to list).

heeled [-d] *adj* de tacón (shoes) || US FAM *well-heeled* de mucho dinero (wealthy).

heeling [-iŋ] *n* SP talonaje *m*.

heelpiece [-pi:s] *n* tacón *m* (heel of a shoe) || talón *m* reforzado (of stocking).

heelpost [-pəust] *n* montante *m* (of a door).

heeltap [-tæp] *n* tapa *f* de tacón (of a shoe) || escurriduras *f pl* (last drops of liquid).

heft [heft] *n* US FAM peso *m* (weight) | mayor parte *f* (bulk).

heft [heft] *vt* levantar (to lift) || sopesar (to test the weight of).

hefty [-i] *adj* pesado, da (heavy) || robusto, ta; fornido, da (robust).

hegemony [hi'geməni] *n* hegemonía *f*.

Hegira ['hedʒirə] *n* hégira *f*, héjira *f*.

he-goat ['hi:'gəut] *n* macho cabrío *m*.

heifer ['hefə*] *n* novilla *f*, vaquilla *f*.

heigh! [hei] *interj* ¡oiga!, ¡oye!, ¡eh! (to s.o.) || ¡ah! (of surprise).

heigh-ho! ['hei'həu] *interj* ¡ay!

height [hait] *n* altura *f*; *the height of a building* la altura de un edificio; *height above sea level* altura sobre el nivel del mar; *to be ten feet in height* tener una altura de diez pies || estatura *f* (of people) || altura *f* (natural elevation) || colina *f*, cerro *m* (hill) || montaña *f*, monte *m* (mountain) || altura *f*, cima *f*, cumbre *f*; *the heights of the Himalayas* las cimas del Himalaya || FIG colmo *m*; *the height of stupidity* el colmo de la tontería | cumbre *f*; *the height of one's career* la cumbre de su carrera | punto *m* culminante, culminación *f*; *it was at its height* estaba en su punto culminante | lo más recio, punto *m* culminante; *at the height of the storm* en lo más recio de la tormenta || — *height sickness* vértigo *m* [AMER soroche *m*, puna *f*] || FIG *in the height of summer* en pleno verano || *it's the height of fashion* es el último grito || *to be afraid of heights* tener vértigo || *what height are you?* ¿cuánto mides?, ¿qué estatura tienes?

heighten [-n] *vt* elevar, levantar, hacer más alto (wall, building) || FIG aumentar (one's enjoyment, etc.) | realzar (to enhance).
◆ *vi* aumentar (to increase) || intensificarse (to become more intense).

heightening [-niŋ] *n* elevación *f* (of a wall, etc.) || aumento *m* (intensificación).

heinous ['heinəs] *adj* atroz, nefando, da (crime).

heir [ɛə*] *n* heredero *m*; *to appoint s.o. as one's heir* instituir heredero *or* por heredero a uno || — JUR *heir apparent* heredero forzoso || *heir at law* heredero legítimo || *heir presumptive* presunto heredero || FIG *the new government was heir to an economic crisis* el nuevo gobierno heredó una crisis económica || *to fall heir to a property* heredar una propiedad.

heirdom [-dəm] *n* JUR herencia *f* (inheritance) || cualidad *f* de heredero (heirship).

heiress [-ris] *n* heredera *f* || FIG soltera *f* rica.

heirloom [-lu:m] *n* reliquia *f or* joya de familia || FIG herencia *f*.

heirship [-ʃip] *n* JUR cualidad *f* de heredero.

Hejira ['hedʒirə] *n* hégira *f*, héjira *f*.

held [held] *pret/pp* → **hold.**

Helen ['helin] *pr n* Helena *f*, Elena *f*.

heliacal [hi'laiəkəl] *adj* ASTR heliaco, ca.

helical ['helikəl] *adj* TECH helicoidal.

helices ['helisi:z] *pl n* → **helix.**

helicoid ['helikɔid] *n* MATH helicoide *m*.
◆ *adj* helicoidal.

helicon ['helikɔn] *n* MUS helicón *m*.

helicopter ['helikɔptə*] *n* helicóptero *m*.

heliocentric [,hi:liəu'sentrik] *adj* ASTR heliocéntrico, ca.

heliochromy [,hi:liəu'krəumi] *n* heliocromía *f* (colour photography).

Heliogabalus [,hi:liəu'gæbələs] *pr n* Heliogábalo *m*.

heliograph ['hi:liəugra:f] *n* heliógrafo *m*.

heliograph ['hi:liəugra:f] *vt* comunicar por heliógrafo (a message).

heliography [hi:li'ɔgrafi] *n* heliografía *f*.

heliogravure ['hi:liəugrə'vjuə*] *n* heliograbado *m*, huecograbado *m* (photoengraving).

heliometer [,hi:li'ɔmitə*] *n* heliómetro *m*.

helioscope [,hi:ljəskəup] *n* helioscopio *m*.

heliotherapy ['hi:liəu'θerəpi] *n* helioterapia *f*.

heliotrope ['heljətrəup] *n* BOT & MIN heliotropo *m*.

heliotropin [hi:'liɔtrəpin] *n* CHEM heliotropina *f*.

heliotypy ['hi:ljətaipi] *n* heliotipia *f* (process).

heliport ['helipɔ:t] *n* helipuerto *m*.

helium ['hi:ljəm] *n* CHEM helio *m* || CHEM *helium nucleus* helión *m*.

helix ['hi:liks] *n* ANAT, MATH & ZOOL hélice *m* || ARCH voluta *f*, espiral *f*.
— OBSERV El plural de la palabra inglesa es *helixes* o *helices*.

hell [hel] *n* infierno *m*; *sinners go to hell* los pecadores van al infierno || FIG garito *m* (gambling house) || — FIG & FAM *a hell of a* estupendo, da; macanudo, da (very good); *it was a hell of a (good) party* ha sido un guateque estupendo; de mil demonios, fatal, malísimo, ma (very bad); *I've had a hell of a day at the office* he pasado un día fatal en la oficina; de mil demonios, infernal; *a hell of a noise* un ruido de mil demonios; excesivo, va; *to pay a hell of a price* pagar un precio excesivo | *a hell of a lot* muchísimo | *as hell* muy; *as fast as hell* muy rápido || FIG *come hell or high water* pase lo que pase, contra viento y marea || FIG & FAM *go to hell* ¡vete al infierno!, ¡vete al diablo! || FIG *it is better to reign in hell than to serve in heaven* más vale ser cabeza de ratón que cola de león | *just for the hell of it* por puro gusto | *like hell* a demonios (to smell), como un negro (to work), como un descosido (to run) | *like hell!* ¡ni hablar! | *oh hell!* ¡demonio!, ¡caramba!, ¡caray! | *the hell of it is that...* lo peor del caso es que... | *the road to hell is paved with good intentions* el camino del infierno está empedrado de buenas intenciones | *till hell freezes over* cuando las ranas críen pelos | *to be hell on* ser malísimo para | *to give s.o. hell* hacerle a uno pasar las negras *or* pasarlas moradas | *to go hell for leather* ir como si se le llevara el diablo | *to go through hell* pasarlas moradas || FIG & FAM *to hell with...!* fuera...! | *to hell with it!* ¡qué diablos! | *to play hell with* estropear, echar a perder (to ruin) | *to raise hell* armar la de Dios es Cristo | *what the hell...!* ¡qué diablos...!, ¡qué demonios...! | *who the hell?* ¿quién diablos?
◆ *interj* ¡demonio!, ¡caramba!

hell-bent [-bent] *adj* US FAM completamente decidido (*on* a).

hellcat [-kæt] *n* arpía *f*, bruja *f*.

hellebore ['helibɔ:*] *n* BOT eléboro *m* || BOT *white hellebore* vedegambre *m*.

Hellene ['heli:n] *n* heleno, na.

Hellenic [he'li:nik] *adj* helénico, ca; heleno, na.

Hellenism ['helinizəm] *n* helenismo *m*.

Hellenist ['helinist] *n* helenista *m* & *f*.

Hellenize ['helinaiz] *vt* helenizar.

hellfire ['hel'faiə*] *n* fuego *m* del infierno.

hellhound ['helhaund] *n* MYTH Cancerbero *m* || FIG monstruo *m*.

hellish ['heliʃ] *adj* infernal, diabólico, ca (infernal) || horrible; *it was a hellish sight* era un espectáculo horrible || — FAM *it was hellish cold* hacía un frío de mil demonios | *it was hellish difficult* era tremendamente difícil.

hellishness [-nis] *n* maldad *f*.

hello! ['he'ləu] *interj* ¡hola! (greeting) || ¡oiga!, ¡oye! (to call attention) || ¡diga! (when answering telephone) || ¡oiga! (when phoning somebody) || ¡vaya! (surprise).

Hell's Angel ['helz'eindʒel] *n* ángel *m* del infierno.

helm [helm] *n* MAR timón *m*; *to be at the helm* llevar el timón || yelmo *m* (helmet) || FIG timón *m*; *to take the helm* empuñar el timón.

helmet ['helmit] *n* casco *m* (of soldier, fireman, etc.) || escafandra *f* (of diver) || careta *f* (of worker) || (ant) yelmo *m*.

helminth ['helminθ] *n* ZOOL helminto *m*.

helminthiasis [helmin'θaiəsis] *n* MED helmintiasis *f*.

helmsman ['helmzmən] *n* timonel *m*, timonero *m*.
— OBSERV El plural de esta palabra es *helmsmen*.

helot ['helət] *n* ilota *m* (Spartan serf).

help [help] *n* ayuda *f*; *to ask for help* pedir ayuda; *to give s.o. some help* prestar ayuda a uno || socorro *m*, auxilio *m* (to s.o. in danger); *to shout for help* pedir socorro a gritos; *to go to s.o.'s help* prestar socorro a alguien || ayuda *f*; *my son is a great help to me* mi hijo es una gran ayuda para mí || remedio *m*; *there's no help for it* no hay más remedio || criado, da (servant) || empleado *m* (employee) || criados *m pl* (servants) || empleados *m pl* (employees); *it's difficult to get help these days* es difícil conseguir empleados en estos tiempos || — *can I be of any help?* ¿le puedo ayudar? || *daily help* asistenta *f* || *help!* ¡socorro! || *home help* trabajadora *f* familiar || *mother's help* chica *f* que cuida a los niños en una familia || *past help* desahuciado, da; perdido, da || *to come to s.o.'s help* acudir en auxilio de uno || *with the help of* con la ayuda de.

help [help] *vt* ayudar; *will you help me with this problem?* ¿me quiere ayudar con este problema? || auxiliar, socorrer (a person in danger) || aliviar (to relieve); *this will help the pain* esto aliviará el dolor || evitar (to avoid); *we cannot help his going if he wants to* no podemos evitar que se vaya si quiere; *things we cannot help* cosas que no podemos evitar || servir (to serve); *to help s.o. to more meat* servir más carne a uno || facilitar (to facilitate) || fomentar (a scheme) || — *I can't help it* no lo puedo remediar || *I can't help wishing I'd known sooner* la verdad es que me hubiera gustado saberlo antes || *I (he, etc.) couldn't help laughing, I (he, etc.) couldn't help but laugh* no pude (pudo, etc.) menos que reír || *it can't be helped* no hay más remedio, no se puede remediar || *I won't be longer than I can help* no tardaré más de lo necesario || *not if I can help it* no si lo puedo evitar || *so help me God!* ¡bien lo sabe Dios! || *that didn't help matters much* eso no sirvió de mucho || *to help along* ayudar (s.o.), fomentar (a scheme) || *to help down* ayudar a bajar || *to help o.s.* servirse; *help yourself to cheese* sírvete queso; mangar (to steal); *to help o.s. to s.o.'s wallet* mangarle la cartera a uno || *to help s.o. off with his coat* ayudar a uno a quitarse el abrigo || *to help s.o. on with his coat* ayudar a uno a ponerse el abrigo || *to help s.o. out* echarle una mano a uno, ayudar a uno (to lend a hand), ayudar a uno a salir (from a place), ayudar a uno a bajar (from a car) || *to help s.o. up* ayudar a uno a levantarse *or* a subir.

helper [-ə*] *n* ayudante *m*, auxiliar *m* & *f*, asistente *m* || colaborador, ra (collaborator).

helpful [-ful] *adj* útil (useful) || provechoso, sa (beneficial) || servicial (obliging) || amable (kind).

helpfulness [-nis] *n* utilidad *f* (usefulness) || amabilidad *f* (kindness).

helping [-iŋ] *adj* *to lend s.o. a helping hand* echarle una mano a alguien || ayuda *f* (help) || ración *f*, porción *f* (portion) || plato *m* (plate) || *would you like a second helping?* ¿quieres repetir?

helpless [-lis] *adj* desamparado, da; desvalido, da (unprotected); *a helpless orphan* un huérfano desamparado || impotente, incapaz (powerless) || incapaz, inútil (incapable); *this boy is completely helpless* este chico es completamente incapaz || impotente, imposibilitado, da (an invalid) || *helpless creature* criatura indefensa.

helplessly [-lisli] *adv* en vano, inútilmente || sin esperanza.

helplessness [-lisnis] *n* desamparo *m* || impotencia *f* (powerlessness) || incapacidad *f* (incapability).

helpline [-lain] *n* servicio *m* telefónico de socorro.

helpmate [-meit]; **helpmeet** [-mi:t] *n* buen compañero *m*, buena compañera *f* (companion) || esposo, sa (spouse).

Helsinki ['helsiŋki] *pr n* GEOGR Helsinki.

helter-skelter ['heltə'skeltə*] *adj* ajetreado, da; *a helter-skelter life* una vida ajetreada || *a helter-skelter flight* una desbandada.
◆ *adv* atropelladamente (to run, etc.) || a la desbandada (to flee) || en desorden (in random order).
◆ *n* tobogán *m* (in a fair) || barullo *m*, ajetreo *m* (confusion); *the helter-skelter of life today* el barullo de la vida actual || desbandada *f* (confused hurry).

helve [helv] *n* mango *m* (handle) || FIG *to throw helve after hatchet* echar la soga tras el caldero.

Helvetia [hel'vi:ʃjə] *pr n* GEOGR Helvecia *f*.

hem [hem] *n* dobladillo *m* (of garment) || FIG orilla *f*, borde *m* (edge).
◆ *interj* ¡ejem!

hem [hem] *vt* hacer un dobladillo en || FIG *to hem in* encerrar, rodear.
◆ *vi* carraspear (to clean one's throat) || FIG *to hem and haw* vacilar al hablar.

he-man ['hi:mæn] *n* FAM machote *m*.
— OBSERV El plural de esta palabra es *he-men*.

hematic [hi:'mætik] *adj* US hemático, ca.

hematin; **hematine** ['hi:mətin] *n* US hematina *f* (haematin).

hematite ['hemɔtait] *n* US MIN hematites *f*.

hematocyte ['həmətəusait] *n* US hematocito *m*.

hematologist [hi:mə'tɔlədʒist] *n* US MED hematólogo *m*.

hematology [hi:mə'tɔlədʒi] *n* US MED hematología *f*.

hematoma ['hi:mətəumə] *n* US hematoma *m*.
— OBSERV El plural de la palabra americana es *hematomas* o *hematomata*.

hematosis [hi:mə'təusis] *n* US BIOL hematosis *f*.

hematozoan; **hematozoon** [hi:mətəu'zəuən] *n* US ZOOL hematozoario *m*.
— OBSERV El plural es *hematozoa*.

hematuria [hi:mə'turjə] *n* US hematuria *f*.

hemeralopia [ˌhemərə'ləupjə] *n* MED nictalopía *f*.

hemicycle ['hemiˌsaikl] *n* hemiciclo *m*.

hemidemisemiquaver ['hemi'demi'semikˌweivə*] *n* MUS semifusa *f*.

hemihedral [ˌhemi'hi:drəl] *adj* hemiedro, dra.

hemiplegia [ˌhemi'pli:dʒə] *n* MED hemiplejía *f*, hemiplejia *f*.

hemiplegic [-ik] *adj/n* hemipléjico, ca.

hemiptera [he'miptərə] *pl n* ZOOL hemípteros *m*.

hemipteran; US **hemipteron** [-n] *n* ZOOL hemíptero *m*.

hemisphere ['hemisfiə*] *n* hemisferio *m* || FIG campo *m*, sector *m* (field).

hemispheric [ˌhmis'ferik]; **hemispherical** [-əl] *adj* hemisférico, ca.

hemistich ['hemistik] *n* POET hemistiquio *m*.

hemline ['hemlain] *n* bajo *m* (of a skirt) || *hemlines have gone up this year* los trajes son más cortos este año.

hemlock ['hemlɔk] *n* BOT cicuta *f*.

hemocyte [hi:məsait] *n* US hematocito *m*.

hemoglobin [hi:məu'gləubin] *n* US hemoglobina *f* (haemoglobin).

hemolysis [hi:'mɔləsis] *n* US hemólisis *f*.

hemophilia [hi:məu'filiə] *n* US hemofilia *f*.

hemophiliac [-k] *n* US hemofílico, ca.

hemophilic [hi:məu'filik] *adj* US hemofílico, ca.

hemoptysis [hi:'məuptisis] *n* US MED hemoptisis *f* (haemoptysis).

hemorrhage ['hemәridʒ] *n* MED hemorragia *f*.

hemorrhagic [-ik] *adj* US MED hemorrágico, ca.

hemorrhoidal [hemərɔidəl] *adj* US MED hemorroidal.

hemorrhoids ['hemərɔidz] *pl n* MED hemorroides *f*, almorranas *f*.

hemostatic [hi:mə'stætik] *adj* MED hemostático, ca.
◆ *n* MED hemostático *m*.

hemp [hemp] *n* cáñamo *m* (plant, fibre) || hachís *m* (hashish) | marihuana *f* (marijuana) || — *field of hemp* cañamar *m* || *Indian hemp* hachís || *Manila hemp* cáñamo de Manila, abacá *m*.

hempseed [-si:d] *n* cañamón *m*.

hemstitch [hemstitʃ] *n* vainica *f* (sewing).

hemstitch [hemstitʃ] *vt* hacer vainica en.

hen [hen] *n* gallina *f* (chicken) || hembra *f* (female bird) || FAM mujer *f* (woman) || — FAM *hen party* reunión *f* de mujeres | *old church hen* rata *f* de sacristía | *old hen* viejarrona *f*.

henbane [-bein] *n* beleño *m* (plant).

hence [hens] *adv* de aquí a (from now); *two years hence* de aquí a dos años || por lo tanto, de aquí (therefore); *hence the evils which plague us* de aquí los males que venimos padeciendo || de aquí (from this place); *three miles hence* a tres millas de aquí || de acá, de este bajo mundo (from this life).
◆ *interj* ¡fuera de aquí!

henceforth [-'fɔ:θ] *adv* de ahora en adelante.

henceforward [-'fɔ:wəd] *adv* de ahora en adelante.

henchman ['hentʃmən] *n* hombre *m* de confianza (trusted underling) || secuaz *m* (follower) || guardaespaldas *m inv* (bodyguard) || US partidario *m* (supporter).
— OBSERV El plural de esta palabra es *henchmen*.

hencoop ['henku:p] *n* gallinero *m*.

hendecagon [hen'dekəgən] *n* endecágono *m*.

hendecasyllabic [hendekәsi'læbik] *adj* endecasílabo, ba.

hendecasyllable ['hendekəˌsiləbl] *n* endecasílabo *m*.

henequen ['henikən] *n* BOT henequén *m*.

henhouse ['hen'haus] *n* gallinero *m*.

henna ['henə] *n* BOT alheña *f*.

hennery ['henəri] *n* corral *f* (poultry yard) || gallinero *m* (henroost) || granja *f* avícola (poultry farm).

henpeck ['henpek] *vt* dominar (one's husband).

henpecked [-t] *adj* dominado por su mujer.

henroost ['henru:st] *n* gallinero *m*.

henry ['henri] *n* ELECTR henrio *m* (unit).

Henry ['henri] *pr n* Enrique *m*.

hep [hep] *adj* US FAM enterado, da (well informed) | moderno, na (modern) | aficionado, da [al jazz].

hepatic [hi'pætik] *adj* hepático, ca.

hepatica [hi'pætikə] *n* BOT hepática *f*.

hepatitis [ˌhepə'taitis] *n* MED hepatitis *f*.

hepcat ['hepkæt] *n* US FAM aficionado *m* a la música de jazz.

hepped up ['heptʌp] *adj* FAM entusiasta.

heptachord ['heptəkɔ:d] *n* MUS heptacordio *m*, heptacordo *m*.

heptagon ['heptəgən] *n* heptágono *m*.

heptagonal ['heptəgən] *adj* heptágono, na; heptagonal.

heptahedron ['heptə'hedrən] *n* MATH heptaedro *m*.

heptameter [hep'tæmitə*] *n* heptámetro *m* (verse).

heptarchy [hep'tɑ:ki] *n* heptarquía *f*.

heptasyllabic ['heptəsi'læbik] *adj* heptasílabo, ba.

heptasyllable ['heptə'silæbl] *n* heptasílabo *m*.

heptathlon [hep'tæθlɔn] *n* SP heptatlón *m*.

her [hə:*] *poss adj* su; *her mouth* su boca; *her ears* sus orejas || de ella (to distinguish «her» from «his»); *is it her book or his?* ¿es el libro de ella o de él?
◆ *pers pron of 3rd pers f sing* la (accusative); *I saw her yesterday* la vi ayer; *he loves her* la quiere || le (dative); *he gave her a pound* le dio una libra; *he hit her* le pegó (see OBSERV) || ella (after a preposition); *it is for her* es para ella || *to her who told you so* a la que se lo dijo.
— OBSERV The English possessive adjective is often translated by the definite article in Spanish: *he bit her hand* le mordió la mano; *she took her gloves from her bag* sacó los guantes del bolso.
— OBSERV When the direct and indirect objects are both pronouns, the dative *le* becomes *se* and is placed before the accusative pronoun: *he gave it to her* se lo dio; *give it to her* dáselo.

Heracles [herəkli:z] *pr n* Heracles *m*.

herald ['herəld] *n* heraldo *m* || FIG precursor *m*, anunciador *m* (forerunner).

herald ['herəld] *vt* anunciar.

heraldic [he'rældik] *adj* heráldico, ca.

heraldry ['herəldri] *n* heráldica *f* (science) || escudos *m pl* de armas (coats of arms) || *book of heraldry* libro *m* de armas, armorial *m*.

herb [hə:b] *n* hierba *f*; *medicinal herbs* hierbas medicinales.
◆ *pl* CULIN finas *f* hierbas.

herbaceous [hə:'beiʃəs] *adj* BOT herbáceo, a.

herbage ['hə:bidʒ] *n* herbaje *m* (herbaceous plants) || JUR herbaje *m*, derecho *m* de pastoreo.

herbal ['hə:bəl] *adj* herbario, ria.
◆ *n* herbario *m* (book).

herbalist ['hə:bəlist] *n* herbolario *m*.

herbarium [hə:'bɛəriəm] *n* herbario *m*.
— OBSERV El plural de *herbarium* es *herbaria* o *herbariums*.

Herbert ['hə:bət] *pr n* Herberto *m*.

herbicide ['hə:bisaid] *n* herbicida *m*.

herbivore [hə:'bivɔ:*] *n* ZOOL herbívoro, ra.

herbivorous [hə:'bivərəs] *adj* ZOOL herbívoro, ra.

herborist ['hə:bərist] *n* herbolario *m*.

herborize ['hə:bəraiz] *vi* herborizar.

Herculean [ˌhə:kju:'liən] *adj* hercúleo, a.

hercules ['hə:kjuli:z] *n* FAM hércules *m* (strong man).

Hercules ['hə:kjuli:z] *pr n* Hércules *m*.

Hercynian [hə:'sinjən] *adj* GEOL herciniano, na.

herd [hə:d] *n* manada *f*, rebaño *m* (of animals) || piara *f* (of pigs) || pastor *m*; vaquero *m* (herdsman) || FIG manada *f*, multitud *f* (of people) || — FIG *the common herd* el vulgo, la masa | *the herd instinct* el instinto gregario.

herd [hə:d] *vt* guardar (to watch) || reunir en manada (to round up) || conducir [en manada] (to drive) || FIG apiñar, agrupar.
◆ *vi to herd into a place* entrar en manada en un sitio || *to herd together* reunirse *or* juntarse en manada (cattle), apiñarse (people) || *to herd with* asociarse a.

herdbook [-buk] *n* libro *m* genealógico de una raza bovina.

herdsman [-zmən] *n* pastor *m* (of sheep) || vaquero *m* (of cattle).
— OBSERV El plural de esta palabra es *herdsmen*.

here [hiə*] *adv* aquí; *here it is* aquí está || aquí, acá; *come here* ven aquí || en este momento, ahora (at this moment) || en ese momento (at that moment) || de aquí; *I prefer this one here* prefiero éste de aquí || — *are they here yet?* ¿han llegado ya? || *here and now* ahora mismo || *here and there* aquí y allá, acá y allá || *here below* aquí abajo || *here goes!* ¡vamos a ver! || *here is, here are* he aquí, aquí está, aquí están || *here is your hat* aquí está su sombrero, aquí tiene usted su sombrero || *here it goes!* ¡ahí va! || *here lies* aquí yace || *here's to friendship!* ¡brindemos por la amistad! || *here she comes* ya viene || *here, there and everywhere* en todas partes || *here we are* aquí estamos (upon arrival), ya está (that's it) || *here you are!* ¡aquí lo tiene! || *in here, please* por aquí, por favor || *look here!* ¡mire!, ¡oiga! || *near here* aquí cerca, por aquí || FIG *that's neither here nor there* eso no tiene nada que ver, eso no viene al caso || FAM *this here book, this book here* este libro || *up to here* hasta aquí.
◆ *interj* ¡presente! (present) || ¡toma!; *here! I don't need this* ¡toma!, no lo necesito || ¡oiga!, ¡oye! (calling attention).

hereabout [-rəˌbaut]; **hereabouts** [-s] *adv* por aquí.

hereafter [-r'ɑ:ftə*] *adv* de ahora en adelante (from now on) || en el futuro (in the future) || en la otra vida (in the after life) || más adelante, a continuación (later in the book).
◆ *n* otra vida *f*, más allá *m* (after life) || porvenir *m*, futuro *m* (future).

hereby [-'bai] *adv* por este medio (by this means) || por la presente (in this document).

hereditary [hi'reditəri] *adj* hereditario, ria.

heredity [hi'rediti] *n* BIOL herencia *f*.

herein ['hiər'in] *adv* en esto (in this) || en ésta (in letters) || aquí mencionado, da (specified) || aquí dentro (inside) || sobre este punto (in this matter) || *the letter enclosed herein* la carta adjunta.

hereinabove ['hiərinəˌbʌv] *adv* más arriba.

hereinafter ['hiərin'ɑ:ftə*] *adv* más adelante, a continuación, más abajo.

hereinbefore ['hiərinbi'fɔ:*] *adv* arriba, más arriba.

hereinbelow ['hiərinbiləu] *adv* más abajo.

hereof [hiər'ɔv] *adv* de esto (of this) || su; *this box and the contents hereof* esta caja y su contenido.

hereon [hiər'ɔn] *adj* sobre esto, acerca de esto.

heresiarch [he'ri:ziɑ:k] *n* heresiarca *m*.

heresy ['herəsi] *n* herejía *f*.

heretic ['herətik] *n* hereje *m* & *f*.
◆ *adj* herético, ca.

heretical [hi'retikəl] *adj* herético, ca.

hereto ['hiə'tu:] *adv* a esto || *affixed* o *annexed hereto* adjunto, ta.

heretofore ['hiətu'fɔ:*] *adv* hasta ahora (until now) || antes (formerly).

hereunder [hiər'ʌndə*] *adv* más abajo, más adelante, a continuación.

hereupon ['hiərə'pɔn] *adv* en seguida (at once) || en esto (thereupon) || sobre esto (upon this) || por consiguiente (consequently).

herewith ['hiə'wið] *adv* adjunto, ta (enclosed).

heritable ['heritəbl] *adj* JUR heredable (property) | apto para heredar (person) || hereditario, ria (disease, etc.).

heritage ['heritidʒ] *n* JUR herencia *f* || FIG patrimonio *m*.

heritor ['heritə*] *n* heredero, ra.

herl [hə:l] *n* mosca *f* (in fishing).

hermaphrodite [hə:'mæfrədait] *adj/n* hermafrodita.

hermaphroditic [hə:ˌmæfrə'ditik]; **hermaphroditical** [-əl] *adj* hermafrodita.

hermaphroditism [-tizəm] *n* hermafroditismo *m*.

hermeneutic [ˌhə:mən'ju:tik]; **hermeneutical** [-əl] *adj* hermenéutico, ca.

Hermes ['hə:mi:z] *pr n* Hermes *m*.

hermetic [hə:'metik]; **hermetical** [-əl] *adj* hermético, ca.

hermetically [-əli] *adv* herméticamente.

hermeticism [hə:'metisizəm]; **hermetism** [hə:'metizəm] *n* hermetismo *m*.

hermit ['hə:mit] *n* ermitaño *m*.

hermitage ['hə:mitidʒ] *n* ermita *f*.

hermit crab ['hə:mit'kræb] *n* ZOOL ermitaño *m*, paguro *m*.

hern [hə:n] *n* ZOOL garza *f* (heron).

hernia ['hə:njə] *n* MED hernia *f*.
— OBSERV El plural de *hernia* es *hernias* o *herniae*.

hero ['hiərəu] *n* héroe *m* (superman, warrior) || héroe *m*, protagonista *m*, personaje *m* principal (in a novel, etc.).
— OBSERV El plural de *hero* es *heroes*.

Herod ['herəd] *pr n* Herodes *m*.

Herodotus [he'rɔdətəs] *pr n* Herodoto *m*, Heródoto *m*.

heroic [hi'rəuik] *adj* heroico, ca || FIG heroico, ca (remedy, decision, verse, etc.) | extremo, ma (measures) | radical (medical treatment).
◆ *n* verso *m* heroico, decasílabo *m*.
◆ *pl* grandilocuencia *f sing*.

heroical [-əl] *adj* → **heroic.**

heroicomic [həˌreuikɔmik] *adj* heroicocómico, ca.

heroin ['herəuin] *n* MED heroína *f*.

heroine ['herəuin] *n* heroína *f* || protagonista *f*, personaje *m* principal (in a novel, etc.).

heroism ['herəuizəm] *n* heroísmo *m*.

heron ['herən] *n* garza *f*, garza *f* real (bird).

hero worship ['hiərəu·wə:ʃip] *n* veneración *f* || culto *m* a los héroes.

hero-worship ['hiərəuˌwə:ʃip] *vt* rendir culto a, venerar.

herpes ['hə:pi:z] *n* MED herpes *m pl* or *f pl*, herpe *m* or *f*.

herpetic [hə:'petik] *adj* MED herpético, ca.

herpetology [ˌhə:pə'tɔlədʒi] *n* herpetología *f*.

herring ['heriŋ] *n* arenque *m* (fish) || — CULIN *red herring* arenque ahumado || FAM *red herring* pretexto *m* para desviar la atención | *to draw a red herring across the track* desviar la atención, despistar.

herringbone [-bəun] *adj* de espiga (cloth, clothes, etc.) || de espinapez (floors and walls) || *herringbone stitch* punto *m* de escapulario.
◆ *n* espiga *f* (in cloth) || espinapez *f* (in floors and walls).

hers [hə:z] *poss pron* suyo, ya; *I didn't know the money was hers* no sabía que el dinero era suyo || el suyo, la suya; *of the two dresses I prefer hers* de los dos vestidos prefiero el suyo || de ella; *it is hers not his* es de ella, no de él || el de ella, la de ella; *this wallet is hers not his* esta cartera es la de ella no la de él || *of hers* suyo, ya; *a friend of hers* un amigo suyo.
— OBSERV When *suyo, suya* which means both *his* and *hers*, might result in ambiguity in Spanish, constructions with *de ella* may be used to avoid confusion.
— OBSERV Téngase en cuenta que el pronombre posesivo *hers* se puede aplicar tanto a un objeto como a varios: *give me hers* dame el suyo, dame los suyos.

herself [hə:'self] *pers pron of 3rd pers f sing* se (reflexive); *she washed herself* se lavó || ella (misma), sí (misma) (after preposition); *she bought it for herself* se lo compró para ella misma || ella misma (emphatic); *she didn't believe it until she had seen it herself* no se lo creía hasta haberlo visto ella misma || en persona (in person) || — *she did it all by herself* lo hizo ella sola || *she is not herself today* no se siente bien hoy.

hertz [hə:ts] *n* PHYS hertz *m*, hertzio *m*, hercio *m*.

hertzian [-iən] *adj* PHYS hertziano, na; *hertzian wave* onda hertziana.

he's [hi:z] contraction of «he is» or «he has».

hesitance ['hezitəns]; **hesitancy** [-i] *n* vacilación *f*, indecisión *f*, irresolución *f*; *he missed the opportunity because of his hesitancy* perdió la oportunidad por culpa de su vacilación.

hesitant ['hezitənt] *adj* vacilante (speech, actions) || vacilante, irresoluto, ta; indeciso, sa (character) || *a baby's first hesitant steps* los primeros pasos titubeantes de un niño.

hesitantly [-li] *adv* con indecisión, con irresolución.

hesitate ['heziteit] *vi* vacilar; *he hesitated to take the first step* vaciló en dar el primer paso; *I hesitate between the green one and the red one* vacilo entre el verde y el rojo; *he didn't hesitate to...* no vaciló en... || no decidirse; *I'm still hesitating about joining the expedition* no me decido todavía a tomar parte en la expedición || vacilar, titubear (when speaking) || — *he hesitates at nothing* no repara en nada, no se arredra por nada || *without hesitating* sin vacilar.

hesitating [-iŋ] *adj* vacilante, indeciso, sa || poco seguro, ra.

hesitatingly [-iŋli] *adv* con indecisión, con irresolución.

hesitation [ˌhezi'teiʃən] *n* vacilación *f*, irresolución *f*, indecisión *f* (indecision) || duda *f* (doubt) || *without further hesitation* sin vacilar más.

Hesperian [hes'piəriən] *adj* occidental.

Hesperides [hes'peridi:z] *pl prn* MYTH Hespérides *f* (nymphs).

hessian ['hesiən] *n* arpillera *f*.

hetaera [hi'tiərə]; **hetaira** [hi'tairə] *n* hetaira *f*, hetera *f*.
— OBSERV El plural de la palabra *hetaera* es *hetaerae* o *hetaeras* y el de la palabra *hetaira* es *hetairai* o *hetairas*.

heteroclite ['hetərəuklait] *adj* heteróclito, ta.

heterodox ['hetərəudɔks] *adj* heterodoxo, xa.

heterodoxy [-i] *n* heterodoxia *f*.

heterodyne ['hetərəudain] *adj* ELECTR heterodino, na.
◆ *n* ELECTR heterodino *m*.

heterogamous [ˌhetə'rɔgəməs] *adj* heterógamo, ma.

heterogamy [ˌhetə'rɔgəmi] *n* heterogamia *f*.

heterogeneity ['hetərəudʒi'ni:iti] *n* heterogeneidad *f*.

heterogeneous ['hetərəu'dʒi:njəs] *adj* heterogéneo, a.

heterogenesis [,hetərəu'dʒenisis] *n* heterogenia *f*.

heteronomy [,hetə'rɔnəmi] *n* heteronomía *f*.

heterosexual ['hetərəu'seksjuəl] *adj/n* heterosexual.

het up ['het,ʌp] *adj* FAM acalorado, da.

heuristic [hjuə'ristik] *adj* heurístico, ca.
◆ *n* heurística *f*.

hevea ['hi:vi:ə] *n* BOT hevea *m*.

hew* [hju:] *vt* cortar (to cut) || talar, cortar (trees) || labrar, tallar (to shape) || — *to hew down* talar || *to hew out* tallar (a statue), excavar (a hole), hacerse (a career).
◆ *vi* dar golpes con el hacha || US conformarse (*to* con).
— OBSERV Pret ***hewed***; pp ***hewed, hewn***.

hewn [hju:n] *pp* ⟶ **hew.**

hex [heks] *n* bruja *f* (witch) || mal *m* de ojo, maleficio *m* (jinx).

hex [heks] *vt* embrujar.

hexachord ['heksəkɔ:d] *n* MUS hexacordo *m*.

hexadecimal ['heksə'desiməl] *adj* INFORM hexadecimal.

hexagon ['heksəgən] *n* hexágono, *m*.

hexagonal [hek'sægənl] *adj* hexagonal.

hexahedral ['heksə'hedrəl] *adj* hexaédrico, ca.

hexahedron ['heksə'hedrən] *n* hexaedro *m*.
— OBSERV El plural de *hexahedron* es *hexahedrons* o *hexahedra*.

hexameter [hek'sæmitə*] *n* hexámetro *m*.

hexametrical [heksə'metrikəl] *adj* hexámetro, tra.

hey! [hei] *interj* ¡eh! ¡oye!, ¡oiga! || *hey presto!* ¡y listo!

heyday ['heidei] *n* auge *m*, apogeo *m*; *the heyday of the Empire* el auge del Imperio || flor *f*; *heyday of youth, of life* flor de la juventud, de la edad.

Hezekiah [,hezi'kaiə] *pr n* Ezequías *m*.

HF *abbr of [high frequency]* HF, alta frecuencia.

hi [hai] *interj* ¡oye! || US FAM ¡hola! (hullo).

hiatus [hai'eitəs] *n* GRAMM hiato *m* || FIG laguna *f* (gap).
— OBSERV El plural de esta palabra es *hiatuses* o *hiatus*.

hibernal [hai'bə:nl] *adj* POET invernal, hibernal.

hibernate ['haibəneit] *vi* hibernar (animals) || invernar (people).

hibernating [-iŋ] *adj* hibernante (animals).

hibernation [,haibə'neiʃən] *n* hibernación *f* (of animals).

Hibernian [hai'bə:njən] *adj/n* POET irlandés, esa.

hibiscus [hi'biskəs] *n* BOT hibisco *m*.

hicatee ['hikəti:] *n* ZOOL hicotea *f* (tortoise).

hiccup; hiccough ['hikʌp] *n* hipo *m* || *to have the hiccups* tener hipo.

hiccup; hiccongh ['hikʌp] *vi* hipar, tener hipo.
◆ *vt* decir (algo) hipando.

hick [hik] *adj/n* US cateto, ta; paleto, ta.

hickory ['hikəri] *n* BOT nogal *m* americano.

hicotee ['hikəti:] *n* ZOOL hicotea *f* (tortoise).

hid [hid] *pret/pp* ⟶ **hide.**

hidalgo [hi'dælgəu] *n* hidalgo *m*.

hidden ['hidn] *pp* ⟶ **hide.**
◆ *adj* escondido, da || FIG oculto, ta; *his words had a hidden meaning* sus palabras tenían un sentido oculto.

hide [haid] *n* puesto *m* (concealed place) || piel *f* (animal skin) || piel *f*, cuero *m* (tanned skin) || FAM pellejo *m* (of a person) || — FAM *to have a thick hide* ser un caradura | *to save one's hide* salvar el pellejo | *to tan s.o.'s hide* dar una paliza *or* zurrar la badana a alguien | *we haven't seen hide nor hair of him* no le hemos visto el pelo.

hide* [haid] *vt* esconder (*from* de); *hidden treasure* tesoro escondido; *where can we hide the presents?* ¿dónde podemos esconder los regalos? || ocultar (*from* a); *to hide sth. from s.o.* ocultar algo a alguien || ocultar, disimular; *to hide one's fears, ones thoughts* ocultar sus temores, sus pensamientos || tapar, ocultar (to cover up); *to hide one's face in one's hands* taparse la cara con las manos, ocultar el rostro entre las manos; *a cloud hid the sun* una nube ocultaba el sol || encubrir; *to hide the truth, a criminal* encubrir la verdad, a un criminal || FAM dar una paliza (to thrash).
◆ *vi* esconderse, ocultarse; *to hide under the bed* esconderse debajo de la cama || FIG ampararse; *he is hiding behind his authority* se ampara en su autoridad || *to hide out* esconderse, estar escondido.
— OBSERV Pret ***hid***; pp ***hidden, hid***.

hide-and-seek ['haid'nsi:k] *n* escondite *m* [AMER escondidas *f pl*]; *to play hide-and-seek* jugar al escondite.

hideaway ['haidə,wəi] *n* escondite *m*, escondrijo *m*.

hidebound ['haidbaund] *adj* de miras estrechas (narrow-minded) || chapado a la antigua (old-fashioned) || conservador, ra (conservative) || estrecho, cha (ideas) || con la piel pegada a los huesos (cattle, etc.).

hideous ['hidiəs] *adj* horroroso, sa; horrible, espantoso, sa (ugly, frightful) || repelente, repugnante (repugnant) || monstruoso, sa (monstrous).

hideousness [-nis] *n* atrocidad *f*, horror *m* (of a crime) || fealdad *f* espantosa (of a person).

hideout ['haidaut] *n* escondite *m*, escondrijo *m*.

hiding ['haidiŋ] *n* ocultación *f*, disimulación *f* (of one's joy, etc.) || JUR encubrimiento *m* (of a criminal) || FAM paliza *f*; *to give s.o. a good hiding* darle a uno una buena paliza || — *to be in hiding* estar escondido || *to come out of hiding* salir de su escondite || *to go into hiding* esconderse.

hiding place [-pleis] *n* escondite *m*.

hie [hai] *vi* POET ir de prisa.

hiemal ['haiəməl] *adj* invernal.

hierarch ['haiərɑ:k] *n* jerarca *m*.

hierarchic [,haiə'rɑ:kik]; **hierarchical** [-əl]; **hierarchal** ['haiərɑ:kəl] *vt* jerárquico, ca.

hierarchize ['hɑ'ərɑ:kaiz] *vt* jerarquizar.

hierarchy ['haiərɑ:ki] *n* jerarquía *f*.

hieratic [,haiə'rætik]; **hieratical** [-əl] *adj* hierático, ca.

hieroglyph [,haiərəuglif] *n* jeroglífico *m*.

hieroglyphic [,haiərəu'glifik] *adj* jeroglífico, ca.
◆ *pl n* jeroglíficos *m*.

Hieronymite [,haiə'rɔnimait] *pr n* REL jerónimo *m*.

Hieronymus [,haiə'rɔniməs] *pr n* Jerónimo *m*.

hierophant ['haiərəufænt] *n* hierofanta *m*, hierofante *m*.

hi-fi ['hai'fai] *n* alta *f* fidelidad.
◆ *adj* de alta fidelidad.
— OBSERV Esta palabra es la abreviatura de *high fidelity*.

higgle ['higl] *vi* regatear.

higgledy-piggledy ['higldi'pigldi] *adv* en desorden, a la buena de Dios.
◆ *adj* desordenado, da (disorderly) || revuelto, ta (in a mess).

high [hai] *adj* alto, ta (building, official, command, collar); *a high hill* una colina alta; *High Commissioner* Alto Comisario || de alto, de altura; *the wall is six feet high* la pared tiene seis pies de alto || alto, ta; elevado, da (price, percentage, wages, temperature, thoughts) || elevado, da (language) || grande (number, speed, altitude, hopes, respect) || fuerte (wind, explosive) || alto, ta; importante (post) || mayor (altar, mass, street) || violento, ta; vehemente (passion) || agudo, da (voice) || alto, ta (musical note) || culminante; *it was the high time of my life* fue el período culminante de mi vida || superior (quality) || pleno, na; *at high noon* en pleno mediodía || crecido, da (river) || brillante (polish, shine) || pasado, da (foodstuffs) || picante (sauce) || manido, da (game) || subido, da (colour) || sumo (pontiff) || altanero, ra (manner) || ELECTR alto, ta (frequency) || PHYS alto, ta (pression) || GRAMM alto, ta; *High German* alto alemán || FAM achispado, da (drunk) || — MAR *a high sea is running* el mar está encrespado || *high and dry* en seco (boat), plantado, da (person) || *high and low* de todas las clases (people) || FIG *high and mighty* engreído, da || *high antiquity* la antigüedad remota || MED *high blood pressure* hipertensión *f* arterial, presión alta || MIL *high command* alto mando || JUR *High Court* Tribunal Supremo || *high day* día *m* de fiesta || SP *high diving* salto *m* de palanca || *highest bid* mejor postura *f* (in auction) || *high fidelity* alta fidelidad || *high hand* despotismo *m* || *high hat* sombrero *m* de copa (top hat) || FAM *high jinks* jolgorio *m*, juerga *f*, jarana *f*; *to be up to high jinks* estar de jarana || SP *high jump* salto *m* de altura || *high living* vida regalada || *high officials* altos funcionarios || FIG *high point* punto *m or* momento *m* culminante || *high priest* sumo sacerdote || *high relief* alto relieve || *high school* instituto *m* de segunda enseñanza || *high sea, high seas* alta mar || *high season* temporada *f* alta || *high society* alta sociedad || *high spirits* alegría *f*, buen humor *m* || *high tea* merienda cena *f* || *high technology* alta tecnología *f*, tecnología punta || MED *high temperature, high fever* fiebre *f* fuerte || FIG *high tide* apogeo *m* (high point) || JUR *high treason* alta traición || *high water* marea alta (sea), crecida *f* (river) || *how high is that wall?* ¿cuál es la altura de esta pared?, ¿cuánto mide esta pared? || *in high places o circles* en las altas esferas || *in the highest sense of the word* en toda la extensión de la palabra || *it is high time that* ya es hora de que; *it's high time you learnt the lesson* ya es hora de que aprendas la lección || *on the high seas* en alta mar || *the Most High* el Altísimo (God) || FIG *to be high* estar drogado || *to be in high spirits* estar de buen humor || *to have a high opinion of s.o.* tener buen concepto de alguien, tener en mucho a alguien || *to have high words with s.o.* tener unas palabras con alguien || *to live the high life* darse la gran vida || *to set a high value on sth.* dar un gran valor a algo || *to speak of s.o. in high terms* hablar en términos elogiosos de alguien, hablar muy bien de alguien || *to the highest degree* hasta el máximo || *we have been friends since we were so high* somos amigos desde niños.
◆ *adv* alto; *to aim high* apuntar alto || alto, a gran altura; *to fly high* volar a gran altura || fuerte; *to blow high* soplar fuerte; *to play o to stake high* jugar fuerte || muy bien; *high paid* muy bien pagado || — *boats cannot sail very high up this river* los barcos no pueden llegar muy arriba en este río || *high above o high over sth.* muy por encima de algo || *how high?* ¿hasta

qué altura? (how far up), ¿cuánto? (price) || FIG *to aim high* picar muy alto | *to climb* o *to rise high* subir muy alto || *to come high on a list* estar al principio de una lista || FIG *to fly high* picar muy alto || *to fly 3 000 metres high* volar a una altura de 3 000 metros || *to go as high as* llegar hasta || *to go back high in the past* volver muy atrás en el pasado || *to run high* ser alto [precios], ser numerosos; *accidents are running high this year* son numerosos los accidentes este año; estar encrespado (the sea), estar crecido (river), estar acalorado (spirits), estar desencadenado (passions) || *to search high and low for sth.* buscar algo por todas partes *or* de arriba abajo || *to sing high* cantar con voz aguda || *words ran high* la discusión fue muy acalorada.
◆ *n* altura *f* || extremo *m*, máximo *m* || zona *f* de alta presión || US FAM récord *m*, alto nivel *m* || US AUT directa *f*, cuarta velocidad *f* || — *from on high* de arriba || *on high* en las alturas, en el cielo.

highball [-bɔːl] *n* US whisky *f* con agua *or* soda y hielo.

highborn [-bɔːn] *adj* linajudo, da; de alta alcurnia.

highboy [-bɔi] *n* cómoda *f* alta.

highbrow [-brau] *adj/n* intelectual.

highchair [-tʃɛə*] *n* silla *f* alta para niño.

high-class [-klɑːs] *adj* de categoría (classy) || de primera clase (first-class).

higher [-ə*] *adj* más alto, más alta (bigger) || mayor (number, speed, altitude) || superior; *higher vertebrate* vertebrado superior; *higher mathematics* matemáticas superiores; *higher education* enseñanza superior.

highest [-əst] *adj* más alto || sumo, ma; supremo, ma (supreme) || mayor, máximo, ma || REL *Glory to God in the highest* Gloria a Dios en las alturas.

highfalutin [-fə'luːtin]; **highfaluting** [-fə'luːtiŋ] *adj* pomposo, sa (pompous) || presumido, da (pretentious).

high-flier [-flaiə*] *n* joven ambicioso, sa.

high-flown [-fləun] *adj* altisonante, rimbombante (words).

high-flying [-,flaiiŋ] *adj* ambicioso, sa (person) || disparatado, da (hopes).

high-frequency ['-friːkwənsi] *adj* ELECTR de alta frecuencia.

high-grade [-'greid] *adj* de calidad superior || *high-grade petrol* gasolina *f* plomo, supercarburante *m*.

highhanded [-'hændid] *adj* arbitrario, ria (arbitrary) || despótico, ca; tiránico, ca (overbearing).

high-hat [-'hæt] *adj* US FAM snob, esnob, presumido, da (stuck-up) | engreído, da (arrogant).
◆ *n* snob *m* & *f*, esnob *m* & *f*.

high-hat [-'hæt] *vt* US FAM desairar, tratar con desprecio.

high-heeled [-hiːld] *adj* de tacón alto (shoes).

highjack [-,dʒæk] *vt* —> **hijack.**

highjacker [-,dʒækə*] *n* —> **hijacker.**

highjacking [-,dʒækiŋ] *n* —> **hijacking.**

highland [-lənd] *adj* montañoso, sa (mountainous) || de las montañas, de las tierras altas (customs, etc.) || montañés, esa (people).
◆ *n* tierras *f pl* altas, región *f* montañosa, montañas *f pl*.

highlander [-'ləndə*] *n* montañés, esa.

highlands [-ləndz] *pl n* montañas *f*, tierras *f* altas, región *f sing* montañosa.

Highlands [-ləndz] *pl prn* GEOGR región *f sing* montañosa de Escocia.

high-level [-'levl] *adj* de alto nivel || INFORM *high-level language* lenguaje *m* de alto nivel.

highlight [-lait] *n* ARTS toque *m* de luz || FIG punto *m or* momento *m* culminante, atracción *f* principal (of a spectacle, etc.) | característica *f* notable, lo saliente (marking feature).

highlight [-lait] *vt* ARTS poner los toques de luz || FIG destacar, subrayar, hacer resaltar.

highly [-li] *adv* muy (very); *highly pleased* muy contento || muy bien; *a highly paid position* un puesto muy bien pagado || sumamente (extremely) || favorablemente (favourably) || — *highly bred* de buena raza (animals) || *highly coloured* subido de color, de color subido || *highly placed* muy bien situado || *highly seasoned* muy picante || *highly strung* tenso, sa (nerves); hipertenso, sa; muy nervioso, sa (person) || *to speak highly of s.o.* hablar muy bien de alguien || *to think highly of s.o.* tener en mucho a alguien.

high-minded [-'maindid] *adj* magnánimo, ma || noble, de sentimientos elevados.

highness [-nis] *n* alteza *f* (prince, princess) || altura *f*, nivel *m* (level) || nobleza *f* de sentimientos (of mind) || *His, Her* o *Your Highness* Su Alteza.

high-octane [-'ɔktein] *adj* de gran índice de octano || *high-octane gasoline* gasolina *f* plomo, supercarburante *m*.

high-pitched [-'pitʃt] *adj* agudo, da (note, voice) || empinado, da (roof) || realzado, da; peraltado, da (arch) || FIG elevado, da.

high-powered [-'pauəd] *adj* de gran potencia || FIG dinámico, ca (person).

high-pressure [-'preʃə*] *adj* de alta presión || FAM enérgico, ca (salesman).

high-pressure [-'preʃə*] *vt* FAM ejercer una presión sobre.

high-priced [-'praist] *adj* muy caro, ra; de alto precio.

high-profile [-'prəufail] *adj* que se hace notar (person).

high-proof [-'pruːf] *adj* con mucho alcohol.

high-ranking [-'ræŋkiŋ] *adj* de alta graduación, superior (official) || de categoría.

high-rise [-raiz] *adj* *high-rise building* edificio de muchos pisos, edificio elevado.

high-risk [-risk] *adj* de alto riesgo, peligroso, sa.

highroad [-rəud] *n* carretera *f* (main road) || FIG camino *m* real (shortest way).

high-sounding [-,saundiŋ] *adj* altisonante.

high-speed [-spiːd] *adj* de gran velocidad, rápido, da || *high-speed steel* acero rápido.

high-spirited [-'spiritid] *adj* animoso, sa (courageous) || alegre (merry) || fogoso, sa (horses).

high-strung [-'strʌŋ] *adj* tenso, sa (nerves) || hipertenso, sa; muy nervioso, sa (person).

hightail [-tail] *vi* US FAM salir pitando.

high-tech; hi-tech [-tek] *adj* de alta tecnología, de tecnología de punta *or* avanzada.

high-tension [-'tenʃən] *adj* ELECTR de alta tensión.

high-test [-'test] *adj* *high-test fuel* supercarburante *m*, gasolina *f* plomo.

high-toned [-'təund] *adj* de mucha categoría || elegante (stylish) || FAM pretencioso, sa.

high-up ['haiʌp] *adj* FAM importante.
◆ *n* FAM persona *f* importante, personalidad *f*.

highway [-wei] *n* carretera *f* || JUR vía *f* pública || US autopista *f* || — *highway code* código *m* de la circulación || *highway robbery* asalto *m*, atraco *m*.

highwayman [-weimən] *n* salteador *m* de caminos.
— OBSERV El plural de esta palabra es *highwaymen*.

high wire [-waiə*] *n* cuerda *f* floja.

hijack; highjack [-,dʒæk] *vt* robar (goods in transit) || asaltar, atracar (people) || forzar, obligar (to oblige) || secuestrar, desviar (aeroplanes).

hijacker; highjacker [-,dʒækə*] *n* asaltador, ra || secuestrador, ra; pirata *m* del aire (of aeroplanes).

hijacking; highjacking [-,dʒækiŋ] *n* asalto *m* || secuestro *m* (of aeroplanes).

hike [haik] *n* excursión *f* a pie || *to go on a hike* hacer una excursión, ir de excursión.

hike [haik] *vi* ir de excursión (to go on a hike) || ir andando, ir a pie (to go walking).
◆ *vt* US aumentar (prices, production) || — FAM *to hike it* ir andando || *to hike up* subirse (one's trousers, etc.).

hiker [-ə*] *n* excursionista *m* & *f*.

hiking [-iŋ] *n* excursionismo *m*.

hilarious [hi'lɛəriəs] *adj* hilarante, divertidísimo, ma (funny) || alegre (merry) || *hilarious laughter* carcajada *f*.

hilarity [hi'læriti] *n* hilaridad *f*.

hill [hil] *n* colina *f*, cerro *m*, otero *m* || cuesta *f* (slope) || montoncillo *m* (small heap) || — FAM *to be over the hill* tener muchos años (to be old) | *to go over the hill* desertar (to desert), largarse (to escape) | *to take to the hills* echarse al monte | *up hill and down dale* por todos los lados.

hillbilly [-bili] *n* serrano, na; montañés, esa.

hillock [-lək] *n* altozano *m*, montecillo *m*.

hillside [-'said] *n* ladera *f*.

hilltop [-'tɔp] *n* cumbre *f* de una colina.

hilly [-i] *adj* montuoso, sa; accidentado, da || con cuestas empinadas (road).

hilt [hilt] *n* puño *m*, empuñadura *f* (of dagger, sword) || FIG *up to the hilt* hasta las cachas, hasta el cuello (to be involved), completamente, totalmente (to prove sth., to commit o.s.).

hilt [hilt] *vt* poner un puño *or* una empuñadura a.

him [him] *pers pron of 3rd pers m sing* lo, le (accusative); *I saw him go* lo vi marcharse (see OBSERV) || le (dative); *give him the book* dale el libro; *who did that to him?* ¿quién le ha hecho esto? (see OBSERV) || él (after a preposition); *it's for him* es para él; *whom shall I give it to? him or her?* ¿a quién se lo doy? ¿a él o a ella? || *to him who* al que.
— OBSERV The Spanish Academy acknowledges the use of *le* instead of *lo* in the accusative case of the third person masculine singular, but esteems it preferable to reserve this pronoun for the dative case. This use of *le* is for more common in Spain than in Latin America.
— OBSERV When the direct and indirect objects are both pronouns the dative *le* becomes *se* and is placed before the accusative pronoun: *he sold it to him* se lo vendió; *give it to him* dárselo.

Himalayas [,himə'leiəz] *pl prn* GEOGR Himalaya *m sing*.

himself [him'self] *pers pron of 3rd pers m sing* se (reflexive); *he has hurt himself* se ha hecho daño || *él* (mismo), sí (mismo); *for himself* para él || él mismo (emphatic); *if he hadn't said so himself* si no lo hubiera dicho él mismo || en persona (in person) || *he did it all by himself* lo hizo él solo.

hind [haind] *adj* trasero, ra (back) || FIG *to talk the hind leg off a donkey* hablar por los codos.
◆ *n* ZOOL cierva *f* (female deer) || gañán *m*, mozo *m* de labranza (farm worker).

— OBSERV El comparativo del adjetivo *hind* es *hinder* y el superlativo *hindmost* o *hindermost*.

hinder [-ə*] *vt* entorpecer, dificultar (to make difficult); *snow hinders the traffic* la nieve entorpece la circulación || poner trabas a, obstaculizar (to obstruct); *the break of the cease-fire hindered negotiations* la ruptura del alto el fuego puso trabas a las negociaciones || estorbar (to get in the way) || impedir (to prevent); *to hinder s.o. from doing sth.* impedir a uno hacer algo, impedir a uno que haga algo.
◆ *vi* ser un estorbo.

hindermost ['haindəməust] *adj* → **hindmost.**

Hindi ['hindi:] *n* hindi *m*.

hindmost ['haindməust]; **hindermost** ['haindəməust] *adj* trasero, ra; posterior (rear) || último, ma (last) || *hindmost part* parte trasera *or* de atrás.

Hindoo ['hin'du:] *adj/n* hindú.

hindquarters ['haind'kwɔ:təz] *pl n* cuartos *m* traseros || FIG & FAM trasero *m sing*.

hindrance ['hindrəns] *n* obstáculo *m*, estorbo *m* (*to* para) || impedimento *m* (prevention).

hindsight ['haindsait] *n* MIL alza *f* (of arms) || FIG percepción *f* restrospectiva.

Hindu ['hin'du:] *adj/n* hindú.

Hinduism ['hinduizəm] *n* hinduismo *m*.

Hindustan [,hindu'stɑ:n] *pr n* GEOGR Indostán *m*.

Hindustani [,hindu'stɑ:ni] *adj* indostanés, esa; indostano, na.
◆ *n* indostano, na; indostanés, esa || indostaní *m* (language).

hinge [hindʒ] *n* TECH bisagra *f*, charnela *f* | bisagra *f*, gozne *m* (of door) || ZOOL charnela *f* (of molluscs) || fijasellos *m inv* (for stamps) || FIG eje *m*, punto *m* esencial.

hinge [hindʒ] *vi* FIG depender; *his career hinges upon this speech* su carrera depende de este discurso || TECH girar (*on* sobre).
◆ *vt* engoznar, poner bisagras.

hinged [-d] *adj* de bisagra.

hinny ['hini] *n* ZOOL burdégano *m*.

hint [hint] *n* indirecta *f*; *I dropped him a hint* le tiré una indirecta; *I think that was a hint for us to leave* creo que eso fue una indirecta para que nos marcháramos || pista *f* (clue); *I can't guess it, give me a hint* no lo puedo adivinar, dame una pista || consejo *m* (piece of advice) || indicación *f*, indicio *m* (indication) || idea *f*; *give me a hint as to how the novel ends* dame una idea de cómo acaba la novela || FIG pizca *f* (trace); *there is not a hint of malice in his words* no hay ni una pizca de malicia en lo que dice | sombra *f*; *there is not a hint of truth in his story* no hay una sombra de verdad en su historia || — *a broad hint* un insinuación muy clara || *to take the hint* darse por aludido (bad sense), aprovechar el consejo (to follow advice) || *to throw out a hint that...* dar a entender que..., insinuar que...

hint [hint] *vt* dar a entender, insinuar.
◆ *vi* soltar indirectas || *to hint at* insinuar; *what are you hinting at?* ¿qué estás insinuando?; aludir a, hacer alusión a; *he hinted at the possibility of* aludió a la posibilidad de.

hinterland ['hintəlænd] *n* interior *m*.

hip [hip] *n* ANAT cadera *f*; *hip joint* articulación de la cadera | perímetro *m* de caderas (measurement) || BOT escaramujo *m* (fruit of rose) || ARCH lima *f* tesa || — *hip bath* baño *m* de asiento || *hip flask* petaca *f* || ARCH *hip roof* tejado *m* de cuatro aguas || FIG *to have s.o. on the hip* tener a uno acorralado || *to sway one's hips* contonearse.
◆ *interj hip! hip! hurrah!* ¡hurra!, ¡viva!

hipbone ['hipbəun] *n* cía *f*, hueso *m* de la cadera.

hip hop ['hiphɔp] *n* música *f* hip-hop.

Hipparchus [hi'pɑ:kəs] *pr n* Hiparco *m*.

hipped [hipt] *adj* de cuatro aguas (roof) || FAM desanimado, da; triste (depressed) | obsesionado, da (*on* por).

hippie; hippy ['hipi] *n* hippie *m* & *f*, hippy *m* & *f*.

hippo ['hipəu] *n* FAM hipopótamo *m*.

hippocampus [,hipəu'kæmpəs] *n* hipocampo *m*, caballo *m* marino.
— OBSERV El plural de *hippocampus* es *hippocampi*.

Hippocrates [hi'pɔkrəti:z] *pr n* Hipócrates *m*.

Hippocratic [,hipəu'krætik] *adj* hipocrático, ca.

hippodrome ['hipədrəum] *n* HIST hipódromo *m*.

hippogriff; hippogryph ['hipəgrif] *n* MYTH hipogrifo *m*.

hippophagous [hi'pɔfəgəs] *adj* hipófago, ga; hipofágico, ca.

hippophagy [hi'pɔfədʒi] *n* hipofagia *f*.

hippopotamus [,hipə'pɔtəməs] *n* ZOOL hipopótamo *m*.
— OBSERV El plural es *hippopotamuses* o *hippopotami*.

hippy ['hipi] *n* → **hippie.**

hipster ['hipstə*] *n* US FAM joven *f* excéntrico | músico *m* de jazz.

hircine ['hə:sain] *adj* cabruno, na (goat-like).

hire ['haiə*] *n* alquiler *m* (of house, etc.) || sueldo *m* (wages) || contratación *f* (engagement) || COMM interés *m* (of capital) || — *for hire* de alquiler (house, televisión, etc.), libre (taxi) || *for hire* se alquila (notice) || *hire purchase* compra *f* a plazos; *to buy sth. on hire purchase* comprar algo a plazos || *on hire* alquilado, da || *to get a television on hire* alquilar una televisión.

hire ['haiə*] *vt* alquilar; *I should like to hire a television* quisiera alquilar una televisión || contratar (a person); *we shall have to hire s.o. to do the job* tendremos que contratar a alguien para que haga el trabajo || *to hire out* alquilar.

hired [-d] *adj* de alquiler (carriage) || MIL mercenario, ria || JUR a sueldo, pagado, da (assassin).

hireling [-liŋ] *n* mercenario *m*.

hirer [-ə*] *n* arrendador, ra.

hirsute ['hə:sju:t] *adj* hirsuto, ta.

his [hiz] *poss adj* su (see OBSERV); *his mouth* su boca; *his ears* sus orejas || de él (to distinguish «his» from «her»); *is it his book or hers?* ¿es el libro de él o de ella?
◆ *poss pron* suyo, suya (see OBSERV); *I didn't know the money was his* no sabía que el dinero era suyo || el suyo, la suya; *of the two suits I prefer his* de los dos trajes prefiero el suyo || de él; *it is his, not hers* es de él, no de ella || el *or* la de él; *this wallet is his* esta cartera es la de él || *of his* suyo, ya; *a friend of his* un amigo suyo.
— OBSERV The English possessive adjective is often translated by the definite article in Spanish: *she bit his hand* le mordió la mano; *with his hands in his pocket* con las manos en el bolsillo.
— OBSERV When *suyo, suya* which means both *his* and *hers*, might result in ambiguity in Spanish, constructions with *de él* may be used to avoid confusion.
— OBSERV Téngase en cuenta que el pronombre posesivo *his* se puede aplicar tanto a un objeto como a varios: *give me his* dame el suyo, dame los suyos.

Hispania [his'pænjə] *pr n* Hispania *f* (Roman name for Iberian Peninsula).

Hispanic [his'pænik] *adj* hispánico, ca.

Hispanicism [his'pænisizəm] *n* hispanismo *m*.

Hispanicist [his'pænisist] *n* hispanista *m* & *f*.

hispanicize [his'pænisaiz]; **hispanize** ['hispənaiz] *vt* hispanizar.

hispanist [hispənist] *n* hispanista *m* & *f*.

Hispano-America [his'pænəuə'merikə] *pr n* GEOGR Hispanoamérica *f*.

Hispano-American [-n] *adj/n* hispanoamericano, na.

Hispano-Arabic [his'pænəu'ærəbik] *adj* hispanoárabe.

Hispano-Jewish [his'pænəu'dʒu:iʃ] *adj* hispanojudío, a.

Hispanophile [his'pænəufail] *n* hispanófilo, la.

Hispanophobe [his'pænəufəub] *n* hispanófobo, ba.

Hispanophobia [hispænəu'fəubjə] *n* hispanofobia *f*.

hispid ['hispid] *adj* híspido, da.

hiss [his] *n* siseo *m* (to call attention) || silbido *m* (of disapproval) || silbido *m* (of air, steam, etc.) || silbido *m* (of snake) || GRAMM letra *f* sibilante.
◆ *pl* silbidos *m*, silba *f sing*, pita *f sing*, abucheo *m sing* (of disapproval).

hiss [his] *vt* silbar || THEATR silbar, pitar, abuchear.
◆ *vi* silbar.

histamine ['histəmi:n] *n* BIOL histamina *f*.

histological [,histə'lɔdʒikəl] *adj* histológico, ca.

histologist [his'tɔlədʒist] *n* histólogo, ga.

histology [his'tɔlədʒi] *n* histología *f*.

historian [his'tɔ:riən] *n* historiador, ra.

historiated [histə'rieitid] *adj* historiado, da (adorned); *historiated letter* letra historiada.

historic [his'tɔrik] *adj* histórico, ca.

historical [-əl] *adj* histórico, ca; *a historical novel* una novela histórica || FAM memorable, histórico, ca (meeting) || GRAMM *historical present* presente histórico.

historicity [histə'risiti] *n* historicidad *f*.

historiographer [his,tɔ:ri'ɔgrəfə*] *n* historiógrafo, fa.

historiography [his,tɔ:ri'ɔgrəfi] *n* historiografía *f*.

history [histəri] *n* historia *f*; *the history of literature, of aviation* la historia de la literatura, de la aviación || — REL *Bible* o *sacred history* Historia Sacra *or* Sagrada || *natural history* historia natural || FIG *that's ancient history* eso es cosa vieja || *that's the way history is written!* ¡así se escribe la historia! || *to go down in history* pasar a la historia || *to know the inner history of an affair* conocer todos los pormenores de un asunto.

histrion ['histriən] *n* histrión *m*.

histrionic [,histri'ɔnik] *adj* histriónico, ca.

histrionics [-s] *pl n* histrionismo *m sing* || FIG comedia *f*, teatro *m* (display of emotion).

hit [hit] *n* golpe *m*; *a hit on the head* un golpe en la cabeza || tiro *m* (in sports); *what a good hit!* ¡qué tiro más bueno! | tiro *m* certero, acierto *m* (when aiming at sth.) || MIL impacto *m* || FIG pulla *f* (sarcastic remark); *to have a hit at s.o.* tirar una pulla a uno | ataque *m* (attack) || éxito *m*, sensación *f* (success, sensation) | acierto *m* (in guessing) || — *direct hit* impacto directo (of bomb, artillery, etc.), acierto, tiro certero || *hit or miss* al azar, a la buena de Dios || *hit parade* lista *f* de éxitos || *hit record* o *song* éxito *m* || *lucky hit* golpe *m* de suerte || FAM *smash hit* exitazo *m* || FIG *that's a hit at you!* ¡esto va por ti! || *the play was a big hit* la obra tuvo mucho éxito ‖ *to be a hit* ser un éxito, tener éxito (to be successful), dar en el blanco (to hit the target) ‖ FIG *to make a hit* ser un éxito (to be a success), acertar (to hit the mark), dar el golpe (to make an impact) | *to make a hit with s.o.* caerle en gracia a uno, caerle simpático a uno ‖ *to score* o *to make a hit* dar en el blanco, acertar; *he made five hits* dio cinco veces en el blanco ‖ FIG *to take a hit at* atacar.

hit* [hit] *vt* pegar a, golpear (to strike); *he hit me, mummy* mamá, me ha pegado; *to hit hard* pegar fuerte ‖ dar en; *to hit the target* dar en el blanco *or* en el objetivo; *he hit the bottle with a stone* dio en la botella con una piedra ‖ dar; *I think I hit him* creo que le he dado; *I've been hit!* ¡me han dado! ‖ herir (to wound) ‖ chocar contra *or* con; *the car hit the wall, a stone* el coche chocó contra el muro, con una piedra ‖ darse; *he hit his head on the lamp* se dio con la cabeza en la lámpara ‖ azotar; *the gales which hit many cities* las tempestades que azotaron muchas ciudades ‖ alcanzar; *he was hit by two shots* fue alcanzado por dos tiros ‖ alcanzar, llegar a (a price, etc.) ‖ sobrecoger; *the panic which hit the population* el pánico que sobrecogió a la población ‖ dar, pegar, asestar (a blow); *she hit him a slap in the face* le dio una bofetada en la cara ‖ dar a; *to hit a nail with a hammer* darle a un clavo con un martillo ‖ FIG atinar con, acertar (to guess) | encontrar, dar con (to find) | afectar; *his company was hard hit by the strike* su compañía fue seriamente afectada por la huelga | herir (one's pride) | tropezar con (difficulties) | ganar (money) | echarse en (bed, floor) ‖ SP marcar; *he hit a six* marcó un seis (in cricket) ‖ US FIG llegar a (to arrive at); *when we hit the motorway* cuando llegamos a la autopista ‖ — FIG & FAM *it hits you in the eye* salta a la vista ‖ *our ship hit stormy weather* nuestro barco fue cogido por una tempestad ‖ FIG *then it hit me that...* de repente caí en la cuenta de que... | *to hit a man when he is down* rematar a un hombre ‖ *to hit below the belt* dar un golpe bajo ‖ *to hit home* dar en el blanco (a blow, an insult) ‖ FIG *to hit it* dar en el clavo | *to hit it off with s.o.* hacer buenas migas con alguien, llevarse bien con alguien | *to hit one's fancy* apetecer a uno ‖ *to hit s.o. back* devolverle a uno los golpes ‖ FIG *to hit s.o. off* remedar *or* imitar a alguien (to imitate), captar el parecido de alguien (to portray well) ‖ FAM *to hit the bottle* darle a la botella, darse a la bebida ‖ *to hit the brake, the accelerator* darle al freno, al acelerador ‖ *to hit the mark* dar en el clavo, acertar ‖ FIG & FAM *to hit the nail on the head* dar en el clavo | *to hit the road* irse, largarse ‖ FAM *to hit the sack* irse al catre ‖ US FIG *to hit the spot* venirle muy bien a uno.

◆ *vi* dar, golpear; *his head hit against the wall* su cabeza dio contra la pared ‖ chocar; *the car hit against the kerb* el coche chocó contra el borde de la acera ‖ US encenderse (cylinders) ‖ — FIG *hit or miss* a la buena de Dios, al azar ‖ MIL *to hit and run* atacar y retirarse ‖ *to hit at, to hit out at* dar *or* asestar un golpe a (one blow), dar golpes a (several times), meterse con, tirar pullas a (to attack verbally) ‖ *to hit back* devolver los golpes ‖ FIG *to hit on* o *upon* dar en (the mark), dar con, encontrar; *to hit on the right word* dar con la palabra adecuada; ocurrírsele (a uno); *he hit on the idea that* o *of* se le ocurrió la idea de que *or* de.

— OBSERV Pret y pp ***hit***.

hit-and-miss ['hitənmis]; **hit-or-miss** ['hitɔːmis] *adj* al azar.

hit-and-run ['hitən'rʌn] *adj* que causa un accidente y se da a la fuga (driver).

hitch [hitʃ] *n* obstáculo *m*, impedimento *m* (hindrance); *this was a serious hitch in the negotiations* esto representaba un grave obstáculo para el buen desarrollo de las negociaciones ‖ dificultad *f*, problema *m*, pega *f* (*fam*); *there shouldn't be any hitch* no tendría que haber ningún problema ‖ tirón *m* (sharp pull) ‖ movimiento *m* brusco (sudden movement) ‖ alto *m or* parada repentina (stop) ‖ cojera *f* (limp) ‖ MAR vuelta *f* de cabo (knot) ‖ US MIL período *m* militar ‖ — *if there is the slightest hitch* si surge la menor dificultad ‖ RAD *technical hitch* incidente técnico ‖ *without a hitch* sin problema alguno, sin ningún tropiezo.

hitch [hitʃ] *vt* atar, amarrar (to tie) ‖ atar; *to hitch a horse to a tree* atar un caballo a un árbol ‖ enganchar; *to hitch horses to a cart* enganchar los caballos al carro; *to hitch a trailer to a car* enganchar un remolque a un coche ‖ uncir (oxen) ‖ MAR amarrar ‖ subirse (one's trousers, socks) ‖ remangarse, arremangarse (one's sleeves) ‖ apretarse (one's belt) ‖ — FAM *to get hitched* casarse ‖ *to hitch a ride* hacerse llevar en coche ‖ *to hitch one's chair to the table* acercar a tirones la silla hacia la mesa.

◆ *vi* andar a trompicones (to walk haltingly) ‖ engancharse; *the trailer hitches on to the car* el remolque se engancha al coche ‖ engancharse (to get caught); *her skirt hitched on a nail* su falda se enganchó en un clavo ‖ hacer autostop (to hitchhike) ‖ FAM llevarse bien (to get on well).

— OBSERV El verbo transitivo *to hitch* se emplea frecuentemente con la proposición *up* sin que cambie el significado.

hitchhike ['hitʃhaik] *vi* hacer autostop.

hitchhiker [-ə*] *n* autostopista *m* & *f*.

hitchhiking [-iŋ]; **hitching** ['hitʃiŋ] *n* autostop *m*.

hither ['hiŋə*] *adv* aquí, acá (here) ‖ *hither and thither* acá y acullá.

◆ *adj* más cercano, na (nearest) ‖ este, esta (this).

hitherto ['hiŋə'tuː] *adv* hasta ahora ‖ hacia acá.

hitherward ['hiðə'wəd] *adv* por aquí, hacia aquí.

hitman ['hitmæn] *n* asesino *m* a sueldo.

hitter ['hitə*] *n* golpeador *m* ‖ *to be a good hitter* pegar fuerte (in boxing), ser un buen bateador (in cricket, etc.).

Hittite ['hitait] *adj/n* hitita.

HIV *abbr of [human immunodeficiency virus]* VIH, virus de inmunodeficiencia humana.

hive [haiv] *n* colmena *f* (for bees) ‖ enjambre *m* (swarm) ‖ FIG *a hive of industry* una colmena humana.

◆ *pl* MED urticaria *f sing*.

hive [haiv] *vt* meter en la colmena, encorchar (bees) ‖ acopiar (honey) ‖ FIG almacenar (goods) | albergar (to lodge).

◆ *vi* vivir en una colmena (bees) ‖ FIG vivir en comunidad (people) ‖ *to hive off* enjambrar.

ho [həu] *interj* ¡eh!, ¡oiga! (to call attention) ‖ MAR *land ho!* ¡tierra a la vista!

hoar [hɔː*] *adj* cano, na (hair) ‖ blanco, ca (frost).

◆ *n* escarcha *f* (hoarfrost).

hoard [hɔːd] *n* tesoro *m*; *a miser's hoard* el tesoro de un avaro ‖ provisión *f*; *a squirrel's hoard of nuts* la provisión de nueces de una ardilla ‖ FIG colección *f*, repertorio *m*; *he has a hoard of anecdotes* tiene un repertorio de anécdotas.

hoard [hɔːd] *vt* acumular, amontonar; *to hoard supplies* acumular provisiones ‖ acaparar (sth. in short supply) ‖ atesorar (money).

hoarder [-ə*] *n* acaparador, ra.

hoarding [-iŋ] *n* acumulación *f*, amontonamiento *m* (of supplies) ‖ atesoramiento *m* (of money) ‖ acaparamiento *m* (of sth. in short supply) ‖ valla *f* (temporary fence) ‖ cartelera *f*, valla *f* publicitaria (billboard).

hoarfrost ['hɔːfrɔst] *n* escarcha *f*.

hoariness ['hɔːrinis] *n* canicie *f* (of hair) ‖ blancura *f* (whiteness).

hoarse [hɔːs] *adj* ronco, ca (husky) ‖ — *to be hoarse* tener la voz ronca ‖ *to shout o.s. hoarse* enronquecer a fuerza de gritar, desgañitarse.

hoarseness [-is] *n* ronquedad *f* (of a sound) ‖ MED ronquera *f* (of voice).

hoary ['hɔːri] *adj* cano, na (hair) ‖ que tiene el pelo cano (person) ‖ FIG viejo, ja (old).

hoax [həuks] *n* broma *f* [de mal gusto] (practical joke) ‖ bola *f* (lie) ‖ mistificación *f* (trick) ‖ engaño *m* (deceptive action) ‖ *to play a hoax on s.o.* engañar a alguien.

hoax [həuks] *vt* gastar una broma (to play a trick on) ‖ engañar (to deceive).

hob [hɔb] *n* repisa *f* (of a chimney) ‖ duende *m* (goblin) ‖ TECH fresa *f* ‖ patín *m* (of a sledge) ‖ — US *to play hob with* causar trastorno a, trastornar (to cause an upset), tomarse libertades con | *to raise hob* armar jaleo.

hobble ['hɔbl] *n* traba *f*, maniota *f* (fetter) ‖ cojera *f* (halting walk) ‖ FIG traba *f*, obstáculo *m* (hindrance).

hobble ['hɔbl] *vt* trabar, manear (to join the legs of an animal) ‖ hacer cojear (to cripple) ‖ FIG poner trabas a, obstaculizar.

◆ *vi* cojear (to limp).

hobbledehoy ['hɔbldi'hɔi] *n* adolescente *m* (youth) ‖ zangolotino *m* (clumsy boy).

hobble skirt ['hɔblskəːt] *n* falda *f* tubo.

hobby ['hɔbi] *n* pasatiempo *m* favorito, afición *f* ‖ ZOOL baharí *m*, tagarote *m* (hawk).

hobbyhorse [-hɔːs] *n* caballito *m* de juguete (a children's wooden horse) ‖ caballo *m* mecedor (a rocking horse) ‖ FIG caballo *m* de batalla (favourite topic) ‖ FIG *to ride one's hobbyhorse* estar siempre con la misma canción.

hobgoblin ['hɔbgɔblin] *n* duende *m* ‖ FIG espantajo *m*.

hobnail ['hɔbneil] *n* clavo *m* ‖ *hobnail boots* botas *f pl* de clavos.

hobnailed [-d] *adj* con clavos.

hobnob ['hɔbnɔb] *vi* codearse (to be on friendly terms); *to hobnob with the rich* codearse con la gente rica ‖ beber (to drink).

hobo ['həubəu] *n* US vagabundo, da (tramp) | temporero *m* (a seasonal migratory worker).

hock [hɔk] *n* corvejón *m*, jarrete *m* (of animal's leg) ‖ vino *m* de Rin ‖ — US FAM *hock shop* Monte *m* de Piedad | *in hock* empeñado, da (in pawn).

hock [hɔk] *vt* desjarretar ‖ US FAM empeñar (to pawn).

hockey ['hɔki] *n* SP hockey *m*; *field hockey* hockey sobre hierba; *ice hockey* hockey sobre hielo; *hockey on skates* hockey sobre ruedas *or* patines.

hocus ['həukəs] *vt* engañar (to deceive) ‖ drogar (to drug s.o.) ‖ echar una droga en (a drink).

hocus-pocus ['həukəs'pəukəs] *n* pasapasa *m* (magic) ‖ FIG trampa *f* (trickery) ‖ camelo *m* (meaningless, distracting talk) ‖ truco *m* (trick).

◆ *interj* abracadabra.

hocus-pocus ['həukəs'pəukəs] *vt* engañar (to trick).

hod [hɔd] *n* cuezo *m* (trough) ‖ capacho *m* (for carrying bricks) ‖ cubo *m* para el carbón (coal scuttle).

hod carrier [-'kæriə*] *n* peón *m* de albañil.

hodgepodge ['hɔdʒpɔdʒ] *n* → **hotchpotch.**

hodman ['hɔdmən] *n* peón *m* de albañil.

— OBSERV El plural de esta palabra es *hodmen*.

hoe [həu] *n* azada *f*, azadón *m*.

hoe [həu] *vt* azadonar (to dig) || sachar (to weed) || FIG *to have a long row to hoe* tener tela para cortar.

hog [hɔg] *n* ZOOL cerdo *m*, puerco *m*, marrano *m* [*AMER* chancho *m*] (pig) || FIG & FAM cerdo *m*, puerco *m*, marrano *m* [*AMER* chancho *m*] (greedy person) || — VET *hog cholera* peste porcina || FIG & FAM *to go the whole hog* llegar hasta el final (to finish what one has started), poner toda la carne en el asador (to commit o.s. entirely).

hog [hɔg] *vt* arquear || FAM acaparar (to keep for o.s.).
◆ *vi* arquearse.

hogback [-bæk] *n* montaña *f* escarpada [*AMER* cuchilla *f*].

hoggish [-iʃ] *adj* glotón, ona (greedy) || guarro, ra (filthy).

hogmanay [-mənei] *n* noche *f* vieja, nochevieja *f* [en Escocia] || aguinaldo *m* (gift).

hogshead [-zhed] *n* pipa *f* (large cask) || medida *f* que equivale aproximadamente a 240 litros.

hog-tie [-tai] *vt* atar las cuatro patas de (an animal) || *US* trabar, poner trabas a (to hamper).

hogwash [-wɔʃ] *n* bazofia *f* (pigswill) || desperdicios *m pl* (leftovers) || *US* tonterías *f pl*, disparates *m pl*.

hoi polloi [hɔi'pɔlɔi] *n* *US* masa *f*, masas *f pl*, populacho *m* (common people).

hoist [hɔist] *n* levantamiento *m* (lifting) || torno *m*, cabria *f* (lifting mechanism) || montacargas *m inv* (lift, elevator) || grúa *f* (crane) || MAR guinda *f* (of mast) | relinga *f* (of sail) || *to give s.o. a hoist* aupar a alguien.

hoist [hɔist] *vt* izar (flag, sails) || levantar (heavy things) || subir; *to hoist the merchandise on to the boat* subir las mercancías al barco || MIN salar (coal, etc.).

hoity-toity ['hɔiti'tɔiti] *adj* FAM presumido, da || FAM *to be hoity-toity* darse pote.
◆ *interj* FAM ¡anda ya!

hold [həuld] *n* asidero *m*; *there were no holds on the rock face* no había asideros en la roca || autoridad *f*, dominio *m* (control authority) || MIL fortificación *f* || prisión *f* (jail) || MUS calderón *m* || MAR bodega *f* (of ship) || SP llave *f*, presa *f* (in wrestling) || — *catch hold!* ¡toma! || *to catch* o *to grab* o *to grasp* o *to lay* o *to seize hold of* coger, agarrar (to catch, to take, to pick up, etc.), agarrarse a (to hang on to) || *to gain a strong hold on, to gain a firm hold over* apoderarse de (to take control of), llegar a dominar (a country) || *to get hold of* coger, agarrar; *wait until I get hold of you* espera a que te coja; encontrar (to find); *this stamp is hard to get hold of* este sello es difícil de encontrar; conseguir (to obtain); *where did you get hold of that?* ¿dónde conseguiste esto?; apoderarse de (secret information, etc.), localizar (to get in touch with); *I'll try to get hold of her* intentaré localizarla || *to get hold of an idea* ocurrírsele a uno una idea || *to get hold on s.o.* dominarse || *to have a firm hold on the situation* dominar la situación || *to have a firm hold on* o *over s.o.* tener ascendiente sobre alguien || *to keep a strong hold on* controlar rigurosamente (prices, spending, etc.) || *to keep hold of* no soltar; *I kept hold of the rope* no solté la cuerda; agarrarse a (a railing), conservar a toda costa (privileges, etc.) || *to lose hold of* soltar || *to lose one's hold on* perder su influencia sobre (to lose one's influence on) || *to relax one's hold* aflojar la mano (to relax one's grip), abrir la mano (to become less strict) || *to take hold* afianzarse || *to take hold of* coger, agarrar (to catch, to pick up, etc.), agarrarse a (to hang on to), apoderarse de (to take control of), dominar (to control).

hold* [həuld] *vt* tener; *he was holding the book in his hand* tenía el libro en la mano || agarrar (to grasp) || sujetar; *you hold the nail, the ladder for me* sujéteme el clavo, la escalera || guardar (to keep) || tener capacidad para, caber; *it holds five people* tiene capacidad para cinco personas, caben cinco personas || mantener; *she held her head above the water* mantuvo la cabeza fuera del agua; *to hold s.o.'s interest* mantener el interés de uno || sostener (to keep from falling); *to hold the roof* sostener el tejado || defender (opinion) || reservar (room, tickets) || ocupar, tener (a post) || desempeñar (a function) || ocupar (territory) || tener (to possess); *to hold funds* tener fondos || poseer (a title, medal, etc.) || considerar; *I don't hold myself responsible* no me considero responsable || tomar; *to hold s.o. to be a fool* tomarle a uno por tonto || mantener, sostener; *he holds that it is possible* mantiene que es posible || creer (to believe) || hacer cumplir; *to hold one to his word* hacer cumplir a uno su palabra || tener; *he holds funny ideas on the subject* tiene extrañas ideas sobre el asunto || contener; *to hold one's breath* contener la respiración || JUR presidir; *a judge holds court* un juez preside el tribunal | detener (to arrest) | retener, tener; *to hold s.o. in the police station* retener a uno en la comisaría | tener (a contract) || celebrar (a meeting, a religious service) || tener (a conversation) || MIL mantenerse en, retener (an occupied position) | defender (one's own ground) || MUS sostener (a note) || SP tener (a record) || — *hold it!* ¡para!, ¡espera! || *hold the line* no cuelgue, no se retire (on the telephone) || *there is no holding him* no hay quien te pare || *to be held* celebrarse, tener lugar (concert, meeting) || *to hold an inquiry* hacer una encuesta || *to hold a parley with s.o.* parlamentar || *to hold hands* ir cogidos de la mano || *to hold one's audience* mantener la atención *or* el interés del público || *to hold o.s. ready for* estar listo *or* preparado para || *to hold o.s. still* quedarse quieto || *to hold o.s. upright* mantenerse derecho || *to hold s.o. hostage* tener a uno como rehén || *to hold s.o. in respect* tener respeto a alguien || *to hold s.o. prisoner* tener preso a alguien || *to hold s.o.'s hand* cogerle la mano a alguien || *to hold s.o. tight in one's arms* estrechar a uno en sus brazos || *to hold sth. cheap* menospreciar algo || *to hold sth. fast* o *tight* sujetar *or* agarrar bien algo || *to hold sth. in mind* recordar algo || *to hold sth. in position* sujetar algo, mantener algo en posición || *to hold the key to the puzzle* tener la clave del enigma || *to hold the road well* tener buena adherencia *or* estabilidad, agarrarse bien (a car) || *what the future holds* lo que nos reserva el futuro.
◆ *vi* mantenerse, sostenerse || agarrarse (to seize) || pegarse (to adhere) || ser válido, valer, seguir siendo válido (to be valid); *my offer still holds* mi oferta es válida todavía || aguantar, resistir; *I don't know if the rope will hold* no sé si la cuerda resistirá || resistir (not to give way) || durar (to last); *my luck cannot hold for ever* mi suerte no puede durar siempre || *to hold good for* valer para.
◆ *phr v* ***to hold back*** reprimir, contener (tears, emotions) | contener (a crowd) | retener (a person) | guardar (to keep in reserve) | ocultar (the truth); *you are not holding anything back from me?* ¿no me estarás ocultando algo? | vacilar (to hesitate) | abstenerse, contenerse (to refrain) || — *to hold back for* reservarse para || *to hold back from doing sth.* guardarse de hacer algo || ***to hold by*** pegarse a (to adhere) | mantenerse fiel a (one's beliefs) | mantenerse fiel a, aferrarse a (one's opinions) || ***to hold down*** sujetar (a person on the ground, etc.) | bajar (to lower) | oprimir (to oppress) || — *to hold down a job* conservar su puesto (to have a job), estar a la altura de su cargo (to be able to keep a job) || ***to hold forth*** perorar (to talk at length) | hablar detenidamente; *to hold forth on a subject* hablar detenidamente de un tema | ofrecer (to offer) || ***to hold in*** refrenar (a horse, one's passions) | contener, reprimir (emotions) || — *to hold o.s. in* contenerse, dominarse || ***to hold off*** sujetar (a dog, a person); *they had to hold him off to avoid a fight* tuvieron que sujetarle para evitar una pelea | rechazar, resistir a (an attack) | mantener a distancia (to keep s.o. away) | contener (a crowd) | aplazar (to postpone) | esperar (to wait) | mantenerse a distancia (to stay away) | vacilar (to hesitate) || — *I hope the storm will hold off* espero que no estalle la tormenta || — *the rain is holding off* hasta ahora no llueve || ***to hold on*** sujetar; *this screw holds the propeller on* este tornillo sujeta la hélice | agarrarse; *hold on tight* agárrate bien; *hold on to my belt* agárrate a mi cinturón | resistir, aguantar; *can you hold on another two days?* ¿puede resistir dos días más? | esperar (to wait) || — *hold on!* ¡no cuelgue!, no se retire (on the telephone) | *hold on a moment* espera un momento | *to hold on to a post* mantenerse en su puesto || ***to hold out*** tender, alargar (one's hand) | ofrecer (to offer) | dar (hopes) | durar (to last) | resistir; *how long can they hold out without food?* ¿cuánto tiempo pueden resistir sin comer?; *to hold out against the enemy* resistir al enemigo || — *to hold out for* insistir en || ***to hold over*** aplazar, diferir (to postpone) | dejar (pendiente); *let's hold this over until the next meeting* dejemos esto hasta la próxima reunión | amenazar con (to threaten) || — *to be held over* quedar pendiente || ***to hold to*** pegarse a (to stick) | aferrarse a (one's opinion) | mantenerse fiel a (a belief) || ***to hold together*** sujetar, unir (various parts); *the two boards are held together by a nail* las dos tablas de madera están unidas por un clavo | mantener unido; *a good leader holds the nation together* un buen dirigente mantiene la nación unida | mantenerse unido (to stick together); *the government held together throughout the crisis* el gobierno se mantuvo unido durante la crisis | poder sostenerse (an alibi) | ser coherente (a story) | ir unido; *drink, poverty, crime, all these hold together* la bebida, la miseria y el crimen, todo va unido || ***to hold up*** sostener, sujetar; *there is nothing holding the wall up* no hay nada que sujete la pared | levantar (to lift up); *hold your hand, your head up* levante la mano, la cabeza | poner; *to hold something up to the light* poner algo a contraluz; *to hold s.o. up as a model* poner a alguien como ejemplo; *to hold s.o. up to ridicule* poner a alguien en ridículo | estorbar, entorpecer; *roadworks hold up the traffic* las obras entorpecen el tráfico | interrumpir (to interrupt) | retrasar (to delay) | suspender; *the trial was held up when the witness did not appear* el juicio fue suspendido al no comparecer el testigo | suspender (payments) | detener; *the train was held up for five minutes* el tren fue detenido durante cinco minutos | asaltar, atracar (to attack, to rob) | mantenerse en pie (to remain standing) | seguir bueno (weather) | durar (good weather) | aguantar, resistir || ***to hold with*** estar con, estar de parte de; *those who hold with me* los que están conmigo *or* de mi parte | estar de acuerdo con (to agree with) | aprobar; *I don't hold with such behaviour* no apruebo esos modales.

— OBSERV Pret y pp ***held***.

holdall [-ɔ:l] *n* bolsa *f* de viaje (bag) || maleta *f* (suitcase).

holdback [-bæk] *n* estorbo *m*, obstáculo *m* (obstacle) || retención *f* (of salary) || seguro *m* (lock).

holder [-ə*] *n* poseedor, ra; *the holder of the winning ticket* el poseedor del billete premiado; *holder of the middleweight title* el poseedor del título de los pesos medios (in boxing) || tenedor *m* (of bonds, etc.); *the holder of a bill of exchange* el tenedor de una letra de cambio || portador *m* (bearer) || arrendatario, ria (tenant) || inquilino, na (of a flat) || titular *m* & *f* (of office, title, passport, etc.) || soporte *m* (support) || asidero *m* (handle) || agarrador *m* (of an iron) || receptáculo *m* (receptacle) || — *cigarette holder* boquilla *f* || *curtain holder* alzapaño *m* || SP *record holder* plusmarquista *m* & *f*, recordman *m*, recordwoman *f*.

— OBSERV Cuando la palabra *holder* se emplea en la formación de compuestos equivale frecuentemente al prefijo español *porta* (penholder *portaplumas*).

holdfast [-fɑːst] *n* TECH grapa *f* || BOT zarcillo *m*.

holding [-iŋ] *n* posesión *f* (possession) || terreno *m*, propiedad *f* (piece of land) || celebración *f* (of a session) || «holding» *m* (financial organization) || SP *holding is forbidden in boxing* en boxeo está prohibido agarrarse.

◆ *pl* COMM valores *m* en cartera (shares, etc. in a company).

holding company [-iŋ'kʌmpəni] *n* COMM «holding» *m*.

holdover [-ˌəuvə*] *n* US vestigio *m* (remnant) | continuación *f* || SP *three and three holdovers from last year's team playing* quedan tres jugadores del equipo del año pasado.

holdup [-ʌp] *n* atraco *m* a mano armada || interrupción *f* (of services) || embotellamiento *m*, atasco *m* (traffic jam) || *holdup man* atracador *m*.

hole [həul] *n* agujero *m*, boquete *m* (small hole, in clothes, etc.); *there's a hole in the bucket* el cubo tiene un agujero; *to cut a hole in the ice* hacer un agujero en el hielo || hoyo *m*; *to dig a hole* cavar un hoyo || cavidad *f* (cavity) || boquete *m*, agujero *m* (in wall) || bache *m* (in roads) || madriguera *f* (of rabbits) || agujero *m*, ratonera *f* (of mice) || FIG poblacho *m* (town) | cuchitril *m* (unpleasant house) | apuro *m*, aprieto *m* (tight spot) || SP hoyo *m* (in golf); *hole in one* hoyo en uno || — FIG *a hole to crawl out of* una escapatoria | *money burns a hole in his pocket* el dinero le quema en el bolsillo | *the journey knocked a big hole in his finances* el viaje mermó considerablemente sus finanzas | *to knock holes in an argument* echar abajo un argumento || *to wear into holes* agujerearse.

hole [həul] *vt* agujerear (to make holes in) || hacer un boquete *or* un agujero en (a wall) || abrir, perforar (a tunnel) || SP meter en el hoyo (a ball).

◆ *vi* SP meter la pelota en el hoyo (in golf) || FIG & FAM *to hole up* esconderse (to hide).

hole-and-corner ['həulənd'kɔːnə*] *adj* clandestino, na; secreto, ta.

holey ['həuli] *adj* agujereado, da.

holiday ['hɔlidei] *n* fiesta *f*, día *m* de fiesta, día *m* festivo; *today is a holiday* hoy es fiesta || vacaciones *f pl*; *two weeks' holiday* dos semanas de vacaciones; *to be on holiday* estar de vacaciones.

◆ *pl* vacaciones *f*; *summer holidays* vacaciones de verano || — *holidays with pay* vacaciones retribuidas *or* pagadas || *where did you spend your summer holidays?* ¿dónde veraneaste?

◆ *adj* de fiesta (atmosphere, clothes) || de veraneo (place) || alegre, festivo (spirit) || *holiday season* época *f* de las vacaciones.

holiday ['hɔlidei] *vi* pasar las vacaciones || veranear (in summer).

holidaying [-iŋ] *n* vacaciones *f pl* || veraneo *m* (in summer).

holidaymaker [-ˌmeikə*] *n* persona *f* que está de vacaciones || veraneante *m* & *f* (in summer).

holiness ['həulinis] *n* santidad *f* || *His Holiness Pope John XXIII* Su Santidad el Papa Juan XXIII.

Holland ['hɔlənd] *pr n* GEOGR Holanda *f*.

Hollander [-ə*] *n* holandés, esa.

hollands [-z] *n* ginebra *f* holandesa.

holler ['hɔlə*] *vt/vi* FAM gritar (to shout).

hollow ['hɔləu] *adj* hueco, ca; *hollow tree* árbol hueco; *hollow sound* sonido hueco || ahuecado, da; cavernoso, sa (voice) || hundido, da; *hollow eyes, cheeks* ojos hundidos, mejillas hundidas || encajonado, da (road) || vacío, a (stomach) || FIG vacío, a; *hollow promises* promesas vacías | falso, sa (friendship) | engañoso, sa (peace) | vano, na (triumph).

◆ *adv* a hueco; *it sounds hollow* suena a hueco || FIG & FAM por completo; *to beat s.o. hollow* derrotar por completo a alguien.

◆ *n* hueco *m*; *in the hollow of one's hand* en el hueco de la mano || hondonada *f*; *a village situated in a hollow* un pueblo situado en una hondonada || agujero *m* (hole) || depresión *f* (depression).

hollow ['hɔləu] *vt* *to hollow out* ahuecar; *to hollow out a tree trunk* ahuecar el tronco de un árbol; abrir, cavar; *to hollow a channel* abrir un surco; cavar (the ground), vaciar (to empty); *to hollow out one half of a coconut shell* vaciar la mitad de un coco; escotar (the neck of a dress).

hollow-eyed [-aid] *adj* de ojos hundidos || ojeroso, sa (from sickness or fatigue).

hollowness [-nis] *n* cavidad *f* (hole) || FIG vaciedad *f* (of words, etc.) | falsedad *f* (of friendship).

hollow ware [-wɛə*] *n* platos *m pl* y recipientes *m pl* hondos.

holly ['hɔli] *n* BOT acebo *m*.

hollyhock [-hɔk] *n* malva *f* loca, malvarrosa *f* (plant, flower).

holm [həum] *n* BOT encina *f* (oak) || isleta *f* (islet) || vega *f* (flat river bank) || BOT *holm oak* encina *f*.

holmium ['həulmjəm] *n* CHEM holmio *m*.

holocaust ['hɔləkɔːst] *n* holocausto *m* (sacrifice) || destrucción *f* por el fuego.

holograph ['hɔləugrɑːf] *adj* olmegrafo, fa.

◆ *n* ológrafo *m*.

holographic [hɔlə'græfik]; **holographical** [-əl] *adj* ológrafo, fa; *holographic will* testamento ológrafo.

holohedral [ˌhɔləu'hiːdrəl] *adj* holoédrico, ca.

holothurian [ˌhɔləu'θjuəriən] *n* ZOOL holoturia *f*.

hols [hɔlz] *pl n* FAM vacaciones *f*.

holster ['həulstə*] *n* pistolera *f*, funda *f* de pistola.

holt [həult] *n* bosquecillo *m* (copse) || colina *f* poblada de árboles, monte *m* (hill).

holus-bolus ['həuləs'bəuləs] *adv* FAM completamente (altogether) | de un trago (to swallow).

holy ['həuli] *adj* santo, ta; *the holy Catholic Church* la santa Iglesia católica; *Holy Sepulcher* Santo Sepulcro; *Holy Week* Semana Santa; *holy war* guerra santa || sagrado, da; *Holy Family* Sagrada Familia || sacro, cra; *the Holy Roman Empire* el Sacro Imperio Romano || bendito, ta (bread, water).

Holly Alliance [-ə'laiəns] *n* HIST Santa Alianza *f*.

Holy Bible [-'baibl] *n* REL Santa Biblia *f*.

Holy City [-'siti] *n* REL Ciudad *f* Santa (Rome, Jerusalem, etc.) || FIG cielo *m* (heaven).

Holy Communion [-kə'mjuːnjən] *n* REL Sagrada Comunión *f*.

holy day [-dei] *n* día *m* de fiesta, fiesta *f*.

Holy Face [-feis] *n* REL Santa Faz *f*.

Holy Father [-'fɑːðə*] *n* REL Padre *m* Santo, Santo Padre *m*.

Holy Ghost [-gəust] *n* REL Espíritu *m* Santo.

Holy Grail [-greil] *n* REL Santo Grial *m*.

Holy Land [-lænd] *n* REL Tierra *f* Santa.

Holy Office [-'ɔfis] *n* Santo Oficio *m*.

holy of holies [-ov'həuliz] *n* sanctasanctórum *m pl*.

holy orders [-'ɔːdəz] *pl n* REL órdenes *f* sagradas || *to take* o *to enter holy orders* ordenarse (to be ordained).

Holy Scripture [-'skriptʃə*] *n* REL Sagrada Escritura *f*.

Holy See [-siː] *n* REL Santa Sede *f*.

Holy Spirit [-'spirit] *n* REL Espíritu *m* Santo.

holystone [-stəun] *n* MAR piedra *f* arenisca que se usa para limpiar la cubierta de un barco.

holystone [-stəun] *vt* MAR limpiar con piedra arenisca.

homage ['hɔmidʒ] *n* homenaje *m*; *to pay* o *to do homage to* rendir homenaje a.

home [həum] *n* casa *f*; *at home* en casa; *to leave home* marcharse a casa || hogar *m*; *home, sweet home* hogar, dulce hogar; *the comforts of home* las comodidades del hogar || domicilio *m*; *the police searched his home* la policía registró su domicilio; *goods delivered to your home* servicio a domicilio || asilo *m*; *old people's home* asilo de ancianos; *children's home* asilo de niños || hogar *m* (institute); *soldier's home* hogar del soldado || FIG morada *f*; *one's last home* su última morada; *my home is in heaven* mi morada está en el cielo | patria *f* (homeland) | patria *f* chica, ciudad *f* natal (home town) | tierra *f*; *Spain, the home of the orange* España, tierra de la naranja | cuna *f*; *the home of fine arts* la cuna de las Bellas Artes || BIOL & ZOOL habitat *m* (habitat) || meta *f* (in games) || — FIG *a home from home* una segunda casa | *an Englishman's home is his castle* cada uno es rey en su casa || *at home and abroad* dentro y fuera del país || *east, west, home's best* no hay nada como la casa de uno || *make yourself at home* está usted en su casa || *maternity home* casa de maternidad || FIG *men make houses, but women make homes* el hombre hace la casa, pero la mujer hace el hogar || MED *rest home* casa de reposo || *there's no place like home* no hay nada como la casa de uno || *to be away from home* estar fuera (de casa) || FIG *to be* o *to feel at home* sentirse a gusto (with s.o.), estar en su elemento (to be in one's element), sentirse como en su casa (in s.o. else's house) || *to give s.o. a home* darle un hogar a alguien || *to have neither house nor home* no tener casa ni hogar, no tener donde caerse muerto || *to make one's home in London* establecerse en Londres || *to make o.s. at home* sentirse como en su casa.

◆ *adj* casero, ra; *home cooking* cocina casera; *home remedy* remedio casero || del hogar, hogareño, ña; *home comforts* las comodidades del hogar || de familia; *home life* vida de familia || doméstico, ca; *my wife looks after home finances* mi mujer se ocupa de la economía doméstica || natal, nativo, va; *home town* ciudad natal || nacional; *home front* frente nacional || interior, nacional; *home affairs* asuntos interiores; *home politics* política interior; *home market* mercado nacional || del país; *home news* noticias del país || metropolitano, na (population) || SP de casa; *the home team* el equipo de casa; *the home ground* el campo de casa | en casa; *to play a home game* jugar un partido en casa | de llegada (straight) || — *home address* domicilio *m*,

dirección privada *or* particular ‖ *home appliances* aparatos electrodomésticos ‖ *home economics* economía doméstica ‖ FIG *home ground* terreno *m* conocido ‖ *home journey* viaje *m* de regreso *or* de vuelta, viaje *m* a casa ‖ *Home Office* Ministerio *m* del Interior ‖ *home port* puerto *m* de origen ‖ *Home Secretary* Ministro *m* del Interior ‖ *mental home* casa de salud *or* de reposo ‖ FAM *to give s.o. a few home truths* cantarle *or* decirle cuatro verdades a uno, cantarle *or* decirle a uno las verdades del barquero.
◆ *adv* a casa (motion); *I'm going home* voy a casa; *I don't like the people he brings home* no me gusta la gente que trae a casa ‖ en casa (at home); *to stay home* quedarse en casa ‖ a fondo; *to drive home* meter a fondo ‖ en el blanco; *to hit home* dar en el blanco ‖ — FIG *it came home to him* se dio perfecta cuenta de ello ‖ *nothing to write home about* nada del otro mundo ‖ *to be home* estar de vuelta (after a journey), estar en casa, estar; *is John home?* ¿está Juan? ‖ FIG *to bring sth. home to s.o.* conseguir que alguien se de perfecta cuenta de algo ‖ *to come home* volver a casa (to one's house), volver a su país (to one's country) ‖ *to drive a nail home* remachar el clavo ‖ FIG *to go home* dar en el blanco (shot), causar impresión (speech, reproach) | *to push one's insults home* poner a alguien de vuelta y media ‖ *to see o to take s.o. home* acompañar a alguien ‖ *to send s.o. home from abroad* repatriar a alguien ‖ *to strike home* dar en el blanco.

home [həum] *vt* dirigir (missiles, etc.).
◆ *vi* volver a casa (pigeons) ‖ *to home in on a target* dirigirse hacia el blanco (missiles, etc.).

home-baked [-'beikt] *adj* casero, ra; hecho en casa (cakes).

home-brewed [-'bru:d] *adj* casero, ra; hecho en casa.

homecoming [-ˌkʌmiŋ] *n* regreso *m*, regreso *m* al hogar.

Home Counties [-ˌkauntiz] *pl n* condados *m pl* que rodean Londres.

home fire [-'faiə] *n* fuego *m* del hogar ‖ FIG *to keep the home fires burning* hacer que todo siga marchando igual.

homegrown [-'grəun] *adj* de cosecha propia (from one's own land) ‖ del país (grown locally).

homeland [-lænd] *n* patria *f*, tierra *f* natal.

homeless [-lis] *adj* sin casa ni hogar ‖ *millions homeless* millones de personas sin hogar.

homelike [-laik] *adj* íntimo, ma; hogareño, ña.

homeliness [-linis] *n* sencillez *f* (simplicity) ‖ intimidad *f* (privacy) ‖ US fealdad *f* (ugliness).

home-loving [-lʌviŋ] *adj* hogareño, ña; casero, ra.

homely [-li] *adj* sencillo, lla; llano, na (simple) ‖ familiar (atmosphere, style) ‖ casero, ra; doméstico, ca (home) ‖ cómodo, da (comfortable) ‖ feúcho, cha (not attractive).

homemade [-'meid] *adj* casero, ra (meals) ‖ hecho en casa, casero, ra; de fabricación casera.

homeopath ['həumjəupæθ] *n* MED homeópata *m*.

homeopathic [ˌhəumjəu'pæθik] *adj* MED homeópata (doctor) | homeopático, ca (medicine).

homeopathy [həumi'ɔpəθi] *n* MED homeopatía *f*.

homeowner ['həumˌəunə*] *n* propietario, ria [de la vivienda en la que vive].

homer ['həumə*] *n* paloma *f* mensajera (pigeon).

Homer ['həumə*] *pr n* Homero *m*.

Homeric [həu'merik]; **Homerical** [-əl] *adj* homérico, ca.

home rule ['həumru:l] *n* autonomía *f*, gobierno *m* autónomo.

home run ['həumrʌn] *n* US SP carretera *f* completa del bateador [AMER jonrón *m*] (in baseball).

homesick ['həumsik] *adj* nostálgico, ca ‖ *to be homesick* tener morriña, sentir nostalgia, añorar.

homesickness [-nis] *n* nostalgia *f*, morriña *f*, añoranza *f*.

homespun ['həumspʌn] *adj* casero, ra; tejido en casa (cloth) ‖ sencillo, lla; llano, na (unsophisticated).
◆ *n* tela *f* tejida en casa (fabric).

homestead ['həumsted] *n* granja *f* [AMER estancia *f*, hacienda *f*] (farm) ‖ US heredad *f*.

home straight ['həumstreit] *n* SP recta *f* final.

homestretch ['həumstretʃ] *n* US SP recta *f* final *or* llegada (of a racecourse).

hometown ['həumtaun] *n* pueblo *m* or ciudad *f* natal (birthplace) ‖ pueblo *m* or ciudad *f* de residencia (town of residence).

homeward ['həumwəd] *adj* de regreso, de vuelta (journey).
◆ *adv* hacia casa (to one's house) ‖ hacia la patria (to one's country) ‖ MAR rumbo a su puerto de origen ‖ *to be homeward bound* volver a casa *or* a su patria.

homewards [-z] *adv* hacia casa (to one's house) ‖ hacia la patria (to one's country).

homework ['həumwə:k] *n* deberes *m pl*.

homicidal [ˌhɔmi'saidl] *adj* homicida.

homicide ['hɔmisaid] *n* homicidio *m* (crime) ‖ homicida *m* & *f* (criminal).

homily ['hɔmili] *n* homilía *f* ‖ FIG sermón *m*, rapapolvo *m*.

homing ['həumiŋ] *adj* TECH *homing head* cabeza buscadora | *homing missile* proyectil *m* con cabeza buscadora ‖ ZOOL *homing pigeon* paloma mensajera (bird).
◆ *n* dirección *f* por radio.

hominy ['hɔmini] *n* US maíz *m* molido.

homocentre ['həuməuˌsentə*] *n* homocentro *m*.

homoeopath ['həumjəupæθ] *n* MED homeópata *m*.

homoeopathic [ˌhəumjəu'pæθik] *adj* MED homeópata (doctor) | homeopático, ca (medicine).

homoeopathy [ˌhəumi'ɔpəθi] *n* MED homeopatía *f*.

homogeneity [ˌhɔməudʒe'ni:iti] *n* homogeneidad *f*.

homogeneous [ˌhɔməu'dʒi:njəs] *adj* homogéneo, a.

homogenization [hɔməuˌdʒənai'zeiʃən] *n* homogeneización *f*.

homogenize [hɔ'mɔdʒənaiz] *vt* homogeneizar.

homograph ['hɔməugrɑ:f] *n* homógrafo *m*.

homographic [ˌhɔməu'græfik] *adj* GRAMM homógrafo, fa.

homography [hɔ'mɔgrəfi] *n* homografía *f*.

homologation [hɔmələ'geiʃən] *n* homologación *f*.

homologize [həu'mɔlədʒaiz] *vi* corresponder (*with* a).
◆ *vt* hacer corresponder.

homologous [hɔ'mɔləgəs] *adj* CHEM & MATH homólogo, ga.

homologue; US **homolog** ['hɔməlɔg] *n* BIOL elemento *m* homólogo.

homology [hɔ'mɔlədʒi] *n* homología *f*.

homonym ['hɔmənim] *n* homónimo *m*.

homonymic [ˌhɔmɔ'nimik]; **homonymous** [hɔ'mɔniməs] *adj* homónimo, ma.

homonymy [hɔ'mɔnimi] *n* homonimia *f*.

homophone ['hɔməufəun] *n* homófono *m*.

homophonic [ˌhɔmə'fɔnik]; **homophonous** [ˌhɔmə'fɔnəs] *adj* homófono, na.

homophony [hɔ'mɔfəni] *n* homofonía *f*.

homosexual ['həuməu'seksjuəl] *adj/n* homosexual.

homosexuality ['həuməuseksju'æliti] *n* homosexualidad *f*.

homothetic [hɔmə'θetik] *adj* MATH homotético, ca.

homunculus [həu'mʌŋkjuləs] *n* homúnculo *m*.

— OBSERV El plural de *homunculus* es *homunculi*.

homy ['həumi] *adj* íntimo, ma.

Honduran [hɔ'djuərən] *adj/n* hondureño, ña.

Honduras [hɔn'djuərəs] *pr n* GEOGR Honduras *f*.

hone [həun] *n* piedra *f* de afilar.

hone [həun] *vt* afilar.

honest ['ɔnist] *adj* honrado, da; recto, ta; *a thoroughly honest person* una persona honrada de los pies a la cabeza; *an honest judge* un juez recto ‖ sincero, ra; franco, ca; *give me your honest opinion* dame tu opinión sincera ‖ honesto, ta (decent, chaste) ‖ razonable (reasonable) ‖ justo, ta; equitativo, va (fair) ‖ — *by honest means* en buena lid ‖ *I didn't do it, honest* no lo he hecho yo, te lo prometo *or* te lo juro ‖ *the honest truth* la pura verdad ‖ *to earn an honest living* ganarse la vida honradamente.

honestly [-li] *adv* honradamente ‖ sinceramente, francamente; *I honestly believed that...* creía sinceramente que... ‖ con toda sinceridad; *honestly, I can assure you* con toda sinceridad te puedo asegurar ‖ — *honestly!* ¡hay que ver! ‖ *honestly?* ¿de verdad? ‖ *honestly speaking* con toda sinceridad.

honesty [-i] *n* honradez *f*, rectitud *f*; *to put honesty above everything* poner la honradez por encima de todo ‖ sinceridad *f* (sincerity) ‖ honestidad *f* (chastity).

honey ['hʌni] *n* miel *f*; *as sweet as honey* tan dulce como la miel ‖ US FAM cielo *m*, mi vida (term of endearment) ‖ — US FAM *hello, honey!* ¡hola, guapa! | *that's a honey of a dress* este traje es precioso ‖ FIG *to be all sugar and honey, to be all honey* ser todo miel.

honey ['hʌni] *vt* endulzar (to sweeten) ‖ FIG halagar (to flatter).

honeybee [-bi:] *n* abeja *f* [doméstica].

honeycomb [-kəum] *n* panal *m* ‖ FIG laberinto *m*; *the old part of the town is a honeycomb of narrow streets* la parte antigua de la ciudad es un laberinto de callejuelas ‖ TECH sopladura *f* (in metal).
◆ *adj* TECH en forma de panal ‖ *honeycomb radiator* radiador *m* de rejilla.

honeycomb [-kəum] *vt* acribillar (to make holes in) ‖ carcomer, roer; *beams honeycombed by woodworm* vigas roídas por la carcoma ‖ FIG *hills honeycombed with caves* colinas llenas de cuevas.

honeydew [-dju:] *n* zumo *m* dulce (of plants) ‖ melón *m* dulce (melon).

honeyed; honied [-d] *adj* endulzado con miel ‖ FIG *honeyed words* palabras melosas.

honeymoon [-mu:n] *n* luna *f* de miel, viaje *m* de novios.

honeymoon [-mu:n] *vi* pasar la luna de miel, hacer su viaje de novios.

honeymooner [-muːnə*] *n* recién casado *m*, recién casada *f*.

honeysuckle [-ˌsʌkl] *n* BOT madreselva *f*.

honied [-d] *adj* ⟶ **honeyed.**

honk [hɔŋk] *n* graznido *m* (of goose) ‖ bocinazo *m* (of car horn).

honk [hɔŋk] *vi* graznar (a goose) ‖ tocar la bocina (with a horn).

honkie-tonk; honky-tonk ['hɔŋkitɔŋk] US FAM garito *m*.

Honolulu [hɔnə'luːluː] *pr n* GEOGR Honolulú.

honor ['ɔnə*] *n/vt* US ⟶ **honour.**

honorable ['ɔnərəbl] *adj* US ⟶ **honourable.**

honorableness [-nis] *n* US ⟶ **honourableness.**

honorarium [ˌɔnə'rɛəriəm] *n* honorarios *m pl*.
— OBSERV El plural de *honorarium* es *honoraria* o *honorariums*.

honorary ['ɔnərəri] *adj* honorario, ria; de honor; *honorary member* miembro honorario ‖ honorífico, ca (duties).

honorific [ˌɔnə'rifik] *adj* honorífico, ca.
◆ *n* tratamiento *m* honorífico.

honour; US **honor** ['ɔnə*] *n* honor *m* (moral integrity, virtue); *a man of honour* un hombre de honor; *his honour is a stake* su honor está en juego; *your presence is an honour for me* su presencia es un honor para mí ‖ honra *f*, honor *m* (in the eyes of others); *to fight to defend one's honour* luchar en defensa de su honra; *to lose one's honour* perder la honra ‖ orgullo *m*, honra *f*; *to be an honour to one's country* ser un orgullo de su país ‖ condecoración *f* (medal, decoration) ‖ Señoría *f* (title); *Your Honour* Su Señoría *f* ‖ — FIG *a prophet is no honour in his own country* nadie es profeta en su tierra ‖ *field of honour* campo *m* del honor ‖ *honour bright!* ¡a fe mía! ‖ FIG *honour to whom honour is due* a tal señor tal honor ‖ *in honour of* en honor de ‖ *Legion of Honour* Legión *f* de Honor ‖ *on my honour!* ¡palabra de honor! ‖ *point of honour* amor propio ‖ FIG *there is honour among thieves* un lobo a otro no se muerden ‖ *to be in honour bound to, to be on one's honour to* estar obligado por el honor a, estar moralmente obligado a ‖ *to deem* o *to consider* o *to regard it an honour to* tener a honra ‖ *to do honour to one's regiment* ser un orgullo para su regimiento ‖ *to do* o *to pay honour to s.o.* rendir honores a alguien ‖ *to have the honour of* tener el honor de ‖ *to swear on one's honour* jurar por su honor ‖ *upon my honour!* ¡por mi honor!, ¡palabra de honor! ‖ *word of honour* palabra *f* de honor.
◆ *pl* honores *m*; *with full military honours* con todos los honores militares ‖ licenciatura *f sing* superior (honours degree) ‖ cartas *f* más altas [de los triunfos] (in cards) ‖ FIG honores *m* de la casa; *let me do the honours* déjame que haga los honores de la casa ‖ — *honours degree* licenciatura *f* superior ‖ *honours list* lista *f* de premios ‖ *honours of war* honores de la guerra ‖ *last honours* honras fúnebres ‖ FIG *to carry off the honours* llevarse la palma ‖ *to pass an examination with honours* sacar un sobresaliente.

honour; US **honor** ['ɔnə*] *vt* honrar; *to honour our God* honrar a Dios; *to honour one's father and mother* honrar padre y madre; *to honour with one's presence* honrar con su presencia ‖ honrar, hacer honor a (to be a credit to); *to honour one's family name* hacer honor a su apellido ‖ honrar, premiar (for one's services) ‖ rendir homenaje (to pay homage) ‖ cumplir con, hacer honor a (one's word) ‖ hacer honor a (one's signature) ‖ satisfacer, honrar, hacer honor a (one's debts) ‖ COMM aceptar (a cheque).

honourable; US **honorable** ['ɔnərəbl] *adj* honorable; *an honourable family* una familia honorable ‖ honrado, da (honest) ‖ honroso, sa (praiseworthy); *honourable actions* acciones honrosas; *honourable feelings* sentimientos honrosos; *an honourable treaty* un tratado honroso ‖ — *honourable mention* mención honorífica ‖ *the Honourable member for* el Ilustre representante de.

honourableness; US **honorableness** [-nis] *n* honorabilidad *f* ‖ honradez *f* (honesty).

honourably; US **honorably** [-i] *adv* honradamente, honorablemente, honrosamente.

hooch [huːtʃ] *n* US FAM aguardiente *m*.

hood [hud] *n* capucha *f* (attached to the collar of a garment) ‖ capirote *m* (pointed hat) ‖ muceta *f* (of academic gown) ‖ capota *f* (of car, pram) ‖ capirote *m* (of falcon) ‖ ARCH campana *f* (of fireplace) | sombrerete *m* (of chimney) ‖ US capó *m* (bonnet of a car) ‖ US FAM rufián *m*, matón *m* (hoodlum) ‖ *Little Red Riding Hood* Caperucita Roja.

hood [hud] *vt* cubrir con una capucha *or* un capirote ‖ encapirotar (a falcon) ‖ poner capota a (a car) ‖ tapar (to cover up).

hooded [-id] *adj* con capota (car, pram) ‖ con capucha (man) ‖ encapirotado, da (falcon) ‖ ZOOL capuchino, na (of two different colours) | moñudo, da (having a crest) ‖ *hooded snake* cobra *f*.

hoodlum [-ləm] *n* matón *m*, rufián *m*.

hoodoo ['huːduː] *n* US FAM vudú *m* (religion) | aojo *m*, mal *m* de ojo (evil spell) | gafe *m* (jinx).

hoodoo ['huːduː] *vt* US FAM echar mal de ojo a, aojar a (to put a curse on) | traer mala suerte (to bring bad luck).

hoodwink ['hudwiŋk] *vt* vendar los ojos a (to blindfold) ‖ engañar (to deceive, to trick).

hooey ['huːi] *n* FAM tonterías *f pl* (nonsense).

hoof [huːf] *n* casco *m*, pezuña *f* ‖ pata *f* (foot) ‖ — *cattle on the hoof* ganado *m* en pie ‖ *cloven hoof* pata hendida.
— OBSERV El plural es *hoofs* o *hooves*.

hoof [huːf] *vt* FAM *to hoof it* ir andando, ir en el coche de San Fernando (to walk), bailar (to dance).

hoofed [huːft] *adj* ungulado, da.

hook [huk] *n* gancho *m*, garfio *m* (for holding, for lifting) ‖ anzuelo *m* (in fishing); *baited hook* anzuelo con cebo ‖ aldabilla *f* (of door, window, etc.) ‖ percha *f* (for hanging clothes) ‖ corchete *m* (on a dress) ‖ garabato *m* (in butcher's shop) ‖ AGR hoz *f* ‖ SP gancho *m* (in boxing) ‖ FIG recodo *m* (of river, road, etc.) | punta *f* (headland) ‖ — FIG *by hook or by crook* por las buenas o por las malas ‖ AGR *manure hook* horca *f* para el estiércol ‖ *meat hook* garabato *m* ‖ *off the hook* descolgado, da (telephone) ‖ US FIG *on one's own hook* por iniciativa propia (without getting advice), solo, la (by o.s.) ‖ FIG & FAM *to get s.o. off the hook* sacar a uno de un apuro | *to sling one's hook* irse con la música a otra parte | *to swallow a story hook, line and sinker* tragarse el anzuelo, creérselo todo ‖ *to take the hook* picar (fish), tragar el anzuelo (person).
◆ *pl* FAM garras *f* (hands) ‖ *hooks and eyes* corchetes *m*.

hook [huk] *vt* enganchar (to fasten); *to hook a trailer to a car* enganchar un remolque a un coche ‖ colgar (to hang up) ‖ atar; *to hook a string round the handle of a door* atar una cuerda al picaporte ‖ pescar, coger (fish) ‖ poner; *to hook the ball to the line* poner el cebo en el anzuelo ‖ encorvar (to curve, to bend) ‖ dar forma de gancho a (to make into the form of a hook) ‖ abrochar (a dress, etc.) ‖ enganchar con el bichero (a boat) ‖ encornar (a bull) ‖ FIG pescar; *to hook a new client* pescar un nuevo cliente ‖ SP talonar (a ball in rugby) | dar un gancho (in boxing) | dar efecto a (the ball in baseball) ‖ US FAM birlar, robar (to steal) ‖ — *her dress got hooked on a nail* su vestido se enganchó en un clavo ‖ *to hook arms* agarrarse del brazo ‖ *to hook a rug* hacer una alfombra de nudo ‖ *to hook in* enganchar (a horse), poner entre corchetes (words), echar el guante a (to catch hold of) ‖ US FIG & FAM *to hook it* pirárselas, largarse ‖ *to hook on* enganchar (to attach), colgar (to hang) ‖ *to hook up* abrochar (to fasten clothes), poner (curtains), enganchar (to attach), conectar (to connect), acoplar (to couple).
◆ *vi* engancharse; *the rope hooked on to the branch* la cuerda se enganchó en la rama ‖ torcer; *the road hooks round to the left* la carretera tuerce a la izquierda ‖ SP dar un gancho (in boxing) ‖ US FIG & FAM largarse, pirárselas (to go) ‖ — *to hook at* dar cornadas, cornear (the bull) ‖ *to hook on to* pegarse a (a person) ‖ *to hook up* abrocharse.

hooka; hookah ['hukə] *n* narguile *m* (Oriental pipe).

hooked [hukt] *adj* ganchudo, da (hook-shaped); *a hooked nose* una nariz ganchuda ‖ — *hooked rug* alfombra de nudo ‖ *hooked on drugs* adicto a las drogas ‖ *to get hooked on* enviciarse en, aficionarse a.

hooker [hukə*] *n* SP talonador *m* (in rugby) ‖ MAR urca *f*.

hookey ['huki] *n* FAM *to play hookey* hacer novillos.

hookup ['hukʌp] *n* red *f* de circuitos (to make a radio, etc.) ‖ conexión *f* (connection) ‖ emisión *f* transmitida a varios países [por Eurovisión o Mundovisión] ‖ FAM alianza *f*.

hookworm ['hukwəːm] *n* ZOOL anquilostoma *m* ‖ MED anquilostomiasis *f* (illness).

hooky ['huki] *n* *to play hooky* hacer novillos.

hooligan ['huːligən] *n* gamberro *m*.

hooliganism [huli'gænizəm] *n* gamberrismo *m*.

hoop [huːp] *n* aro *m* (of skirt, child's toy) ‖ fleje *m* (of barrel) ‖ aro *m* (in crocket) ‖ llanta *f* (of a wheel) ‖ *to trundle a hoop* jugar al aro.

hoop [huːp] *vi* ⟶ **whoop.**
◆ *vt* enarcar (a cask).

hoopla [huːplɑː] *n* juego *m* de aros (at a fair).

hoopoe ['huːpuː] *n* abubilla *f* (bird).

hoopskirt ['huːpˌskəːt] *n* miriñaque *m*.

hooray! [hu'rei] *interj* ¡hurra!

hoosegow ['husgau] *n* US FAM trena *f*, chirona *f* (gaol).

hoot [huːt] *n* ululato *m* (of an owl) ‖ bocinazo *m* (of a car) ‖ toque *m* de sirena (of a boat, factory) ‖ silbato *m* (of a locomotive) ‖ grito *m* (shout) ‖ — *a hoot of laughter* una risotada ‖ FIG *I don't care a hoot o two hoots* no me importa un bledo *or* un pepino *or* un pito ‖ *this is not worth a hoot* esto no vale un pito *or* un comino.

hoot [huːt] *vi* ulular (owl) ‖ silbar (person) ‖ abuchear (to boo) ‖ dar un bocinazo, tocar la bocina (car) ‖ dar un toque de sirena (ship) ‖ pitar (siren) ‖ silbar (a train) ‖ *to hoot with laughter* carcajearse.
◆ *vt* abuchear, pitar, silbar (to boo).

hooter [-ə*] *n* sirena *f* (siren) ‖ bocina *f* (of a car).

hoove [huːv] *n* VET meteorismo *m*.

hoover [-ə*] *n* aspiradora *f*.

hoover [-ə*] *vt* pasar la aspiradora en.

hooves [huːvz] *pl n* ⟶ **hoof.**

hop [hɔp] *n* BOT lúpulo *m* ‖ saltito *m*, salto *m*, brinco *m* (little jump) ‖ salto *m* a la pata coja (on one foot) ‖ vuelo *m* (by plane) ‖ etapa *f* (stage of a journey) ‖ FAM baile *m* (dance) | estupefaciente *m* (narcotic) | trola *f*, cuento *m* (lie) ‖ — SP *hop, step and jump; hop, skin and* *jump* triple salto || FIG & FAM *to catch s.o. on the hop* pillar a alguien con las manos en la masa (to catch s.o. red-handed), coger desprevenido a alguien (to catch s.o. unawares).

hop [hɔp] *vi* saltar, brincar, dar un saltito *or* saltitos || ir a saltitos; *to hop along the street* ir a saltitos por la calle || saltar a la pata coja (on one leg) || saltar; *to hop out of bed* saltar de la cama; *to hop over the fence* saltar la valla || dar *or* pegar un salto; *hop across to the baker's for me* pega un salto a la panadería por mí || FAM bailar (to dance) || — FIG *to hop from one thing to another* pasar de una cosa a la otra || *to hop off* largarse (to go away), bajar de un salto de (a bus, a bicycle, etc.) || *to hop over to* darse una vuelta por, pegar un salto a; *I think I'll hop over to London at the weekend* este fin de semana creo que me daré una vuelta por Londres || *to hop to it* echar manos a la obra.
◆ *vt* saltar (to jump over) || US subir a, coger (a bus, etc.) || — FAM *hop it!* ¡lárgate! || *to hop a train, to hop a ride in a train* subirse en un tren en marcha para no pagar billete || FAM *to hop the twig* estirar la pata (to die) | *to hop up* drogar.

hope [həup] *n* esperanza *f*; *hope is my only consolation* la esperanza es mi único consuelo; *new hopes for peace* nuevas esperanzas de paz; *there is a hope of success* hay esperanza de éxito || posibilidad *f* (chance) || — *as a last hope* como última esperanza || *in the hope of* o *that* con la esperanza de *or* de que || *land of hope* tierra *f* de promisión || *one should never lose hope* la esperanza es lo último que se pierde || FAM *some hopes!* ¡espérate sentado! || *there is no hope for him* no le queda ninguna esperanza || *to be beyond hope* ser un caso desesperado || *to build up hopes* hacerse ilusiones || *to fulfil one's hopes* llenar las esperanzas de uno || *to give hope for* o *that* dar esperanza de *or* de que || *to have high hopes* tener muchas esperanzas || *to have hopes that* tener esperanzas de que || *to have little hope* tener pocas esperanzas || *to live in hope of sth.* tener la esperanza de algo || *to live on hope* vivir de esperanzas || *to place all one's hopes in s.o.* poner todas sus esperanzas en alguien || *we must hope against hope* la esperanza es lo último que se pierde || *whilst there is life, there is hope* mientras hay vida hay esperanza.

hope [həup] *vi* esperar; *I hope so* espero que sí; *I hope not* espero que no || — *I should hope so!* ¡eso espero! || *to hope for* tener esperanzas de; *to be hoping for success* tener esperanzas de éxito; contar con (to count on); *we are hoping for good weather* contamos con el buen tiempo; esperar; *all we can do is to hope for a miracle* todo lo que podemos hacer es esperar un milagro | *to hope in* confiar en.
◆ *vt* esperar; *I hope he will come* espero que vendrá || — *hoping to hear from you* en espera de tus gratas noticias (in letters) || *to hope to God that...* esperar en Dios que...

hope chest [-tʃest] *n* US FAM ajuar *m*.

hopeful [-ful] *adj* esperanzador, ra; alentador, ra; prometedor, ra; *the situation seems hopeful* la situación parece esperanzadora || optimista; *he is in a hopeful mood* está de un humor optimista || confiado, da (confident) || que promete, prometedor, ra (promising) || *to be hopeful that...* tener muchas esperanzas de que...
◆ *n* promesa *f* (person).

hopefully [-fuli] *adv* con optimismo || de un modo alentador *or* prometedor.

hopefulness [-fulnis] *n* optimismo *m* || aspecto *m* alentador *or* prometedor (of a situation).

hopeless [-nis] *adj* desesperado, da (case, state, etc.); *the situation seems hopeless* la situación parece desesperada || imposible; *it's a hopeless job* es un trabajo imposible || MED desahuciado, da (an incurable person) || FAM inútil (useless) | perdido, da; *a hopeless drunkard* un borracho perdido || *to give sth. up as hopeless* dejar algo por imposible.

hopelessly [-lisli] *adv* sin esperanza, con desesperación || desesperadamente (in love) || *to be hopellessly drunk* estar borracho perdido, estar completamente borracho.

hopelessness [-lisnis] *n* desesperación *f* || inutilidad *f* (of an effort) || estado *m* desesperado (of incurable person, a situation).

hophead ['hɔphed] *n* US FAM drogadicto, ta; toxicómano, na.

hop-o'-my-thumb ['hɔpəmi'θʌm] *n* FAM enano, na (midget).

hopped up ['hɔptʌp] *adj* US FAM drogado, da | excitado, da (excited) | arreglado, da (a car engine).

hopper ['hɔpə*] *n* ZOOL insecto *m* saltador || TECH tolva *f* (of mill) | tragante *m* (of furnace) || MAR gánguil *m* (boat) || FAM pulga *f* (flea) || *hopper car* vagón *m* tolva.

hopping ['hɔpiŋ] *adj he is hopping mad* está que bota, está que trina (he is angry).

hopple ['hɔpl] *n* traba *f*, maniota *f* (rope).

hopscotch ['hɔpskɔtʃ] *n* infernáculo *m*, tejo *m* [AMER rayuela *f*] (game).

Horace ['hɔrəs] *pr n* Horacio *m*.

horde [hɔːd] *n* horda *f* || FIG multitud *f*.

horizon [hə'raizn] *n* horizonte *m*; *on the horizon* en el horizonte || FIG horizonte *m*, perspectiva *f*.

horizontal [,hɔri'zɔntl] *adj* horizontal || SP *horizontal bar* barra fija.
◆ *n* horizontal *f* (line).

horizontally [,hɔri'zɔntli] *adv* horizontalmente.

hormonal [hɔː'məunəl] *adj* hormonal.

hormone ['hɔːməun] *n* BIOL hormona *f*.

horn [hɔːn] *n* cuerno *m*, asta *f* (of a bull, deer) || asta *f*, cuerno *m* (substance); *a horn comb* un peine de asta || cuerno *m* (of an insect, snail, the moon) || MUS trompa *f*, cuerno *m* || bocina *f*, claxon *m* (of a car); *to blow the horn* tocar la bocina || calzador *m* (for shoes) || pabellón *m*, bocina *f* (of gramophone, loudspeaker) || brazo *m* (of river) || punta *f* (of anvil) || — MUS *French horn* trompa *f* || FIG *horn of plenty* cuerno de la abundancia, cornucopia *f* || MUS *horn player* trompa *m* || *hunting horn* cuerno de caza || FIG *on the horns of a dilemma* entre la espada y la pared | *to blow one's own horn* echarse flores | *to draw in one's horns* bajársele a uno los humos, moderarse.

horn [hɔːn] *vt* dar una cornada a, cornear.
◆ *vi to horn in* entrometerse (*on* en).

hornbeam ['hɔːnbiːm] *n* BOT carpe *m*.

hornblende ['hɔːnblend] *n* MIN hornablenda *f*.

hornbook ['hɔːnbuk] *n* abecedario *m*.

horned ['hɔːnid] *adj* con cuernos (animals) || — US ZOOL *horned owl* búho *m* || ZOOL *horned toad* lagarto cornudo | *horned viper* víbora cornuda.

hornet ['hɔːnit] *n* ZOOL avispón *m* (wasp) || — FAM *to bring a hornet's nest about one's ears, to stir up a hornet's nest* meterse en un avispero *or* en un lío.

hornless ['hɔːnlis] *adj* mocho, cha; sin cuernos.

horn owl ['hɔːnaul] *n* ZOOL búho *m*.

hornpipe ['hɔːnpaip] *n* MUS chirimía *f* (instrument) | baile *m* de marineros (dance).

horn-rimmed ['hɔːnrimd] *adj* de concha (glasses).

hornswoggle ['hɔːns,wɔgl] *vt* US FAM embaucar, engañar (to hoax).

horny ['hɔːni] *adj* córneo, a (of or like horn) || calloso, sa (hands) || con cuernos (horned).

horologe ['hɔrələdʒ] *n* reloj *m*.

horologer [-ə*]; **horologist** [-ist] *n* relojero, ra.

horoscope ['hɔrəskəup] *n* horóscopo *m*; *to cast a horoscope* hacer un horóscopo.

horrendous [hɔ,rendəs] *adj* horrendo, da.

horrent ['hɔrənt] *adj* erizado, da || horrorizado, da.

horrible ['hɔrəbl] *adj* horrible, horroroso, sa; horrendo, da; *horrible weather* un tiempo horroroso; *a horrible sight* una visión horrible || *don't be horrible!* ¡no seas antipático!

horribly [-i] *adv* horriblemente (in a horrible manner) || terriblemente (to a horrible degree) || *it's horribly cold* hace un frío espantoso.

horrid ['hɔrid] *adj* antipático, ca; odioso, sa (unkind) || horrible, horroroso, sa (horrible) || inaguantable, insoportable (a child) || *to be horrid to s.o.* tratar muy mal a alguien.

horrific [hɔ'rifik] *adj* horrendo, da; horroroso, sa.

horrify ['hɔrifai] *vt* horrorizar || *I was horrified at the idea* me horrorizaba la idea.

horripilation [hɔripi'leiʃən] *n* horripilación *f*.

horror ['hɔrə*] *n* horror *m*, pavor *m* (fear); *pale with horror* pálido de horror || horror *m*; *the horrors of war* los horrores de la guerra || ansia *f*, angustia *f* (of death) || diablo *m*; *this child is a horror* este niño es un diablo || — *horror film* película *f* de miedo || *it gives me the horrors* me da horror || *to have a horror of* tener horror a || *you horror!* ¡antipático!

horror-stricken [-,strikən]; **horror-struck** [-strʌk] *adj* horrorizado, da.

hors d'oeuvre [ɔː'dəːvr] *n* CULIN entremés *m*.
— OBSERV El plural de esta palabra es *hors d'oeuvres*.

horse [hɔːs] *n* caballo *m* (animal) || caballete *m* (of a carpenter) || potro *m* (in gymnastics) || MIL caballería *f* (cavalry) || caballo *m* (in chess) || MAR marchapié *m* || FIG & FAM caballo *m* (heavy-featured person) || — *cart horse* caballo de tiro || *change of horse* relevo *m* || FIG *don't look a gift horse in the mouth* a caballo regalado no le mires el diente || FIG & FAM *hold your horses!* ¡no te sulfures! (control your temper), ¡echa el freno!, ¡para el carro! (not so fast) || MIL *horse soldier* soldado *m* de a caballo || *saddle horse* caballo de montar *or* de silla || SP *side* o *pommelled horse* potro *m* con arzón || FIG *that's a horse of a different colour* eso es otro cantar, eso es harina de otro costal | *to be flogging a dead horse* azotar el aire | *to be on* o *to get on one's high horse, to mount* o *to ride the high horse* tener muchos humos, darse importancia *or* pisto *or* aires | *to change horses in midstream* efectuar un cambio a mitad de camino | *to come down off one's high horse* bajársele a uno los humos | *to eat like a horse* comer como un sabañón, comer como un regimiento || *to get on* o *to mount a horse* subir a *or* montar a caballo || FIG *to get sth. straight from the horse's mouth* saber algo de buena tinta || *to horse!* ¡a caballo! || *to play the horses* apostar en las carreras de caballos || FIG *white horses* cabrillas *f pl* (of waves) | *wild horses could not drag it out of him* no se puede sacárselo ni con tenazas || *wooden horse (of Troy)* o *Trojan horse* caballo de Troya.
◆ *adj* de caballos (race) || montado, da (artillery) || FIG basto, ta (coarse).

horse [hɔːs] *vt* proveer de caballos || FAM tomar el pelo a (to kid).
◆ *vi* estar salida (a mare) || US *to horse around* hacer el tonto, bromear.

horseback [-bæk] *n* *on horseback* a caballo.
horsebean [-biːn] *n* BOT haba *f* panosa.
horse block [-blɔk] *n* montadero *m*.
horse box [-bɔks] *n* vagón *m* para transportar caballos (railway) ‖ furgón *m* para el transporte de caballos (car).
horsebreaker [-ˌbreikə*] *n* domador *m* de caballos.
horse butcher's [-ˈbutʃə*] *n* expendeduría *f* de carne de caballo, carnicería *f* hipofágica.
horse chestnut [-ˈtʃesnʌt] *n* BOT castaña *f* de Indias (fruit) | castaño *m* de Indias (tree).
horsecloth [-klɔθ] *n* manta *f* para caballos.
horsedealer [-ˌdiːlə*] *n* chalán *m*, tratante *m* de caballos.
horse doctor [-ˌdɔktə*] *n* veterinario *m* ‖ FIG & FAM matasanos *m inv* (doctor).
horse-drawn [-drɔːn] *adj* tirado por caballos, de tracción de sangre.
horseflesh [-fleʃ] *n* carne *f* de caballo ‖ caballos *m pl*; *a good judge of horseflesh* un entendido en caballos.
horsefly [-flai] *n* tábano *m* (insect).
Horse Guards [-gɑːdz] *pl n* guardia *f sing* montada.
horsehair [-hɛə*] *n* crin *f*.
horselaugh [-lɑːf] *n* carcajada *f*, risotada *f*.
horseless [-lis] *adj* sin caballo ‖ *horseless carriage* automóvil *m*.
horse mackerel [-ˈmækrəl] *n* jurel *m* (fish).
horseman [-mən] *n* jinete *m*, caballista *m* (rider).
— OBSERV El plural de esta palabra es *horsemen*.
horsemanship [-mənʃip] *n* equitación *f*.
horse opera [-ˈɔpərə] *n* US película *f* del Oeste.
horseplay [-plei] *n* payasadas *f pl* ‖ pelea *f* (boisterous fun).
horse pond [-pɔnd] *n* abrevadero *m* de caballos.
horsepower [-ˌpauə*] *inv n* caballo *m* de vapor, caballo *m*; *a four horsepower car* un coche de cuatro caballos ‖ potencia *f*; *brake horsepower* potencia al freno ‖ COMM *treasury horsepower* caballo fiscal.
horse racing [-ˈreisiŋ] *n* carreras *f pl* de caballos, hipismo *m*.
horseradish [-ˌrædiʃ] *n* rábano *m* picante.
horse riding [-ˌraidiŋ] *n* equitación *f* ‖ *to go horse riding* montar a caballo.
horse's ass [-zæs] *n* FAM burro *m*, necio *m*.
horse sense [-sens] *n* FIG & FAM sentido *m* común.
horseshoe [-ʃuː] *n* herradura *f* ‖ *horseshoe arch* arco *m* de herradura.
horse show [-ʃəu] *n* concurso *m* hípico.
horsetail [-teil] *n* BOT cola *f* de caballo.
horse thief [-θiːf] *n* cuatrero *m*.
horse trade [-treid] *n* chalaneo *m*.
horsewhip [-wip] *n* látigo *m*.
horsewhip [-wip] *vt* dar latigazos a, azotar.
horsewoman [-ˌwumən] *n* caballista *f*, amazona *f*.
— OBSERV El plural de esta palabra es *horsewomen*.
horsiness [-inis] *n* afición *f* a los caballos ‖ aspecto *m* caballuno.
horsy [-i] *adj* caballuno, na; *horsy features* rasgos caballunos ‖ hípico, ca ‖ aficionado a los caballos y a las carreras ‖ *a horsy smell* un olor a caballo.
hortative [ˈhɔːtətiv]; **horatory** [ˈhɔːtətəri] *adj* exhortador, ra; exhortatorio, ria.
horticultural [ˌhɔːtiˈkʌltʃərəl] *adj* hortícola.
horticulture [ˈhɔːtikʌltʃə*] *n* horticultura *f*.
horticulturist [ˌhɔːtiˈkʌltʃərist] *n* horticultor *m*.
hosanna [həuˈzænə] *n* REL hosanna *m*.
hose [həuz] *n* manguera *f*, manga *f* (flexible tube) ‖ medias *f pl* (women's stockings) ‖ calcetines *m pl* (socks) ‖ (ant) calzas *f pl* (mediaeval tights).
— OBSERV Esta palabra es invariable excepto cuando significa *manguera*.
hose [həuz] *vt* regar con una manga (to water) ‖ limpiar con una manga (to clean).
hosier [ˈhəuziə*] *n* calcetero, ra.
hosiery [-ri] *n* calcetería *f*, géneros *m pl* de punto (goods) ‖ medias *f pl* y calcetines (in a store).
hospice [ˈhɔspis] *n* hospicio *m*.
hospitable [ˈhɔspitəbl] *adj* hospitalario, ria; acogedor, ra ‖ FIG abierto, ta; receptivo, va; *a person hospitable to new ideas* una persona abierta a las nuevas ideas.
hospitably [-i] *adv* con hospitalidad, de una manera hospitalaria.
hospital [ˈhɔspitl] *n* MED hospital *m*; *hospital train* tren hospital; *hospital ship* buque hospital ‖ HIST hospicio *m* ‖ — MIL *field hospital* hospital de sangre ‖ *maternity hospital* casa *f* de maternidad ‖ *mental hospital* manicomio *m*.
hospitaler [-ə*] *n* US capellán *m*.
Hospitaler [-ə*] *n* US REL caballero *m* hospitalario, hospitalario *m*.
hospitality [ˌhɔspiˈtæliti] *n* hospitalidad *f*.
hospitalization [ˌhɔspitəlaiˈzeiʃən] *n* hospitalización *f*.
hospitalize [ˈhɔspitəlaiz] *vt* hospitalizar.
hospitaller [ˈhɔspitlə*] *n* capellán *m* (in a hospital).
Hospitaller [ˈhɔspitlə*] *n* REL caballero *m* hospitalario, hospitalario *m*.
host [həust] *n* anfitrión, ona; huésped, da (at a meal, etc.) ‖ BIOL & BOT huésped *m* (plant, animal) ‖ hostelero *m*, mesonero *m* (of an inn) ‖ multitud *f* (multitude) ‖ montón *m* (of ideas, etc.) ‖ hueste *f* (of angels, enemies) ‖ presentador *m* (in cabaret, etc.) ‖ — INFORM *host computer* ordenador *m* central ‖ *host nation* país organizador (of a competition, etc.) ‖ FIG *to reckon without one's host* no contar con la huéspeda.
Host [həust] *n* REL Hostia *f* ‖ *Lord God of Hosts* Señor *m* de los ejércitos.
hostage [ˈɔstidʒ] *n* rehén *m*; *to hold hostage* tener como rehén.
hostel [ˈhɔstəl] *n* residencia *f* (for students) ‖ albergue *m*; *youth hostel* albergue juvenil ‖ hotel *m*, parador *m*.
hostelry [-ri] *n* hostal *m*.
hostess [ˈhəustis] *n* anfitriona *f*, huéspeda *f* (at a meal, etc.) ‖ hostelera *f*, mesonera *f* (of an inn) ‖ azafata *f* (air hostess) ‖ presentadora *f* (in cabaret, etc.).
hostile [ˈhɔstail] *adj* hostil, enemigo, ga; *a hostile nation* una nación hostil ‖ de hostilidad; *hostile act* acto de hostilidad ‖ *to be hostile to* estar en contra de (reform, etc.).
hostility [hɔsˈtiliti] *n* hostilidad *f*.
◆ *pl* hostilidades *f*; *to begin, to renew hostilities* romper, reanudar las hostilidades.
hot [hɔt] *adj* caliente; *hot water* agua caliente; *the radiator is hot* el radiador está caliente ‖ cálido, da; caluroso, sa (climate) ‖ caluroso, sa; de calor (day) ‖ abrasador, ra (sun) ‖ CULIN picante (spicy) ‖ fuerte, subido, da (colours) ‖ fresco, ca; reciente (scent, trail) ‖ ELECTR de alta tensión (wire) ‖ TECH en caliente (working metals) | radioactivo, va (radioactive) ‖ FIG acalorado, da (argument) | vivo, va (temper) | muy discutido, da; controvertido, da (controversial) | muy delicado, da (situation) | peligroso, sa (dangerous) | porfiado, da (pursuit) | ardiente (follower, supporter) | apasionado, da (passionate) | feroz (battle) | caliente (in children's games); *now you're hot* caliente, caliente ‖ FIG & FAM robado, da (stolen) | estupendo, da; extraordinario, ria (very good) ‖ POP caliente ‖ — FIG *a hot contest* una lucha muy reñida ‖ *boiling hot* ardiendo, abrasando ‖ FIG *hot air* música *f* celestial, palabras *f pl* al aire | *hot and strong* muy fuerte | *hot favourite* gran favorito *m* (horse racing, etc.) | *hot for* ansioso de | *hot from London* recién llegado de Londres | *hot line* teléfono rojo (between Washington and Moscow) | *hot music* «swing» *m* | *hot news* noticia *f* bomba (big news), noticias *f pl* de última hora (latest news) | *hot potato* patata *f* caliente, asunto *m* delicado | *hot seat* silla eléctrica (electric chair), apuro *m*, aprieto *m* (tight spot) | *hot tip* informe seguro | *hot words* palabras *f* mayores | *hot work* trabajo duro | *news hot from the press* noticias *f pl* de última hora | *not so hot* no tan bueno ‖ *to be hot* tener calor (person); *I am very hot* tengo mucho calor; hacer calor (weather); *it's very hot today* hoy hace mucho calor; estar caliente (things); *the soup is very hot* la sopa está muy caliente ‖ FIG *to be hot on* ser muy aficionado a (to be fond of), ser perito en (to be an expert on) | *to be hot on s.o.'s track* o *on s.o.'s trail* seguir de cerca a alguien, estar sobre la pista de alguien ‖ FAM *to be hot stuff* ser cachondo, da (lecherous) ‖ FIG *to be hot stuff at geography* ser un hacha en geografía | *to be hot stuff at tennis* ser un as en tenis | *to blow hot and cold* jugar con dos barajas (to play a double game), cambiar de opinión cada dos por tres (to hesitate) | *to get all hot and bothered* ponerse nervioso y colorado, sofocarse (to get flustered) ‖ *to get hot* acalorarse (angry person), calentarse (thing), empezar a hacer calor (weather) ‖ FIG *to get o.s. into hot water* meterse en un aprieto *or* en un lío | *to give it s.o. hot* echar un rapapolvo a alguien | *to have a hot temper* tener un genio violento *or* fuerte *or* vivo | *to make a place too hot for s.o.* hacer que la situación sea inaguantable para alguien | *to put s.o. in the hot sea* ponerle a uno en un aprieto ‖ *white hot* calentado al rojo blanco.
◆ *adv* con calor ‖ calurosamente ‖ acaloradamente ‖ ardientemente ‖ vehementemente ‖ apasionadamente ‖ violentamente.
hot [hɔt] *vt* FAM calentar.
hot-air balloon [-ɛə*bəˌluːn] *n* globo *m* aerostático.
hot baths [-bɑːðz] *pl n* termas *f*.
hotbed [-bed] *n* estercolero *m* (dunghill) ‖ FIG semillero *m* (of vice, disease, etc.).
hot-blooded [-ˈblʌdid] *adj* *to be hot-blooded* tener la sangre caliente, ser muy apasionado.
hot cross bun [-krɔsˌbʌn] *n* bollo *m* marcado con una cruz típico de Cuaresma.
hotchpotch [-ʃpɔtʃ]; **hodgepodge** [ˈhɔdʒpɔdʒ] *n* CULIN ropa *f* vieja (stew) ‖ FIG mezcolanza *f*, batiburrillo *m* (mixture).
hot dog [ˈhɔtˈdɔg] *n* perro *m* caliente (sandwich).
hotel [həuˈtel] *n* hotel *m*; *at* o *in a hotel* en un hotel.
hotelier [həuteliə*] *n* hotelero, ra.
hotelkeeper [-ˈkiːpə*] *n* hotelero, ra.
hotfoot [ˈhɔtfut] *adv* FAM a toda prisa (very fast).
hotfood [ˈhɔtfut] *vt/vi* *to hotfoot it* volar, ir corriendo (to go quickly).
hothead [ˈhɔthed] *n* FAM impulsivo, va.

hotheated ['hɔt'hedid] *adj* impulsivo, va; impetuoso, sa (impetuous) || enfadadizo, za (quick-tempered) || exaltado, da (excitable).

hothouse ['hɔthaus] *n* invernadero *m* (for plants).

hotly ['hɔtli] *adv* de cerca; *hotly pursued* seguido de cerca || con pasión (fiercely) || acaloradamente || violentamente.

hotness ['hɔtnis] *n* lo picante (of a spice) || FIG ardor *m* (of passions).

hot pants ['hɔtpænts] *pl n* shorts *m*, pantalones *m* cortos (garment).

hot plate ['hɔtpleit] *n* calientaplatos *m inv* || hornillo *m* (portable stove).

hot pot ['hɔtpɔt] *n* CULIN estofado *m* (stewed meat and vegetables).

hot-press ['hɔtpres] *n* TECH calandria *f*.

hot rod ['hɔtrɔd] *n* US FAM bólido *m* (fast car).

hotshot [hɔtʃɔt] *adj* US FAM brillante, de primera.

hot spot ['hɔtspɔt] *n* FIG situación *f* crítica | sitio *m* donde la situación es crítica | sala *f* de fiestas (nightclub).

hot springs ['hɔt'spriŋz] *pl n* aguas *f* termales.

Hottentot ['hɔtntɔt] *adj/n* hotentote, ta.

hot-water bottle [hɔt'wɔːtəˌbɔtl] *n* bolsa *f* de agua caliente.

hound [haund] *n* perro *m* (de caza), podenco *m* (hunting dog) || FIG canalla *m* || — *pack of hounds* jauría *f* || *to follow the hounds, to ride to hounds* cazar con jauría.

hound [haund] *vt* acosar, perseguir (to harass, to pursue) || cazar con perros || azuzar (a dog) || — *to hound s.o. down* acosar a alguien || *to hound s.o. on* incitar a uno (*to* a).

hound's tongue ['haundzˌtʌŋ] *n* BOT cinoglosa *f*.

hound's-tooth check ['haundzˌtuːθ'tʃek] *n* US pata *f* de gallo (fabric).

hour [auə*] *n* hora *f*; *there are sixty minutes in an hour* hay sesenta minutos en una hora; *dinner hour* la hora de comer; *at an early hour* a una hora temprana; *at this hour he's usually having a nap* a esta hora suele dormir la siesta; *the fateful hour* la hora fatal || FIG hora *f*, momento *m* || — *a good hour* una hora larga (easily an hour) || *a hundred miles an hour* cien millas por hora || *an eight-hour day* una jornada de ocho horas || *an hour and a half* una hora y media || *a quarter of an hour* un cuarto de hora || *at an hour's notice* con aviso previo de una hora || *at the eleventh hour* a última hora || *by the hour* por horas || *children's hour* programa *m* infantil (on the radio, etc.) || *half an hour, half hour* media hora || FIG *his hour has come* ha llegado su hora || *hour by hour* de hora en hora || *hour of truth* hora de la verdad || *off-peak hour* horas de menos afluencia *or* tráfico (transport), horas de menor consumo (gas, etc.) || *on the hour* a la hora en punto || *per hour* por hora (speed, production, etc.), a la hora, por hora (wages) || *rush hour* hora de mayor afluencia, hora punta || *the news is broadcast on the hour and on the half hour* dan las noticias a las horas y a las medias || *the questions of the hour* los problemas actuales || *to strike the hour* dar la hora || *zero hour* hora H.
◆ *pl* horario *m sing*; *to keep reasonable hours* respetar un horario razonable || REL horas *f* || — *after hours* fuera de horas || *at all hours* a todas horas || *hours on end* horas enteras || *office* o *business hours* horas de oficina || *peak hours* horas de mayor consumo (gas, etc.), horas punta *or* de mayor afluencia (transport, etc.) || *small hours* altas horas || *to keep good hours* acostarse temprano || *to keep late hours* acostarse tarde, trasnochar || *to keep regular hours* llevar una vida ordenada || *to take hours over sth.* tardar horas en hacer algo || *to work long hours* trabajar muchas horas || *visiting hours* horas de visita || *working hours* horas de trabajo.

hour circle [-'səːkl] *n* ASTR círculo *m* horario.

hourglass [-glɑːs] *n* reloj *m* de arena.

hour hand [-hænd] *n* horario *m*, manecilla *f* de las horas.

houri ['huəri] *n* hurí *f*.

hourly ['auəːli] *adj* de cada hora || cada hora (trains, etc.); *there is an hourly train to London* hay un tren para Londres cada hora || por hora (wage, output) || incesante (continual) || *on an hourly basis* por hora.
◆ *adv* cada hora (every hour); *the medicine should be taken hourly* se debe tomar el medicamento cada hora || por hora, por horas (to pay) || de un momento a otro (at any moment); *we're expecting news hourly* esperamos noticias de un momento a otro.

house [haus] *n* casa *f*; *a three-story house* una casa de tres pisos; *publishing house* casa editorial || cámara *f* (of legislative body); *the House of Lords* la Cámara de los Lores || colegio *m* mayor (of students' residence) || casa *f* (of a noble family); *the House of Bourbon* la Casa de Borbón || COMM casa *f* (commercial establishment) || THEATR sala *f* (theatre) | público *m* (audience) || ASTR casa *f* || — THEATR *a good house* mucho público (a big audience), buen público (a good audience) || *at my house* en casa, en mi casa || *country house* casa de campo || FIG *disorderly house* casa *f* de lenocinio (brothel), casa *f* de juego (gambling house) || *doll's house* casa de muñecas || *eating house* restaurante *m* || *fashion house* casa de modas || *from house to house* de casa en casa || *full house* (teatro) lleno (theatre), no hay localidades (notice outside theatre), full *m* (poker) || *gambling house* casa de juego || *have a drink on the house* tómate una copa, invita *or* paga la casa || *house of cards* castillo *m* de naipes || *House of Commons* Cámara de los Comunes || *house of correction* correccional *m*, reformatorio *m* || US *House of Representatives* Cámara de Representantes || *Houses of Parliament* Parlamento *m sing* || *Lower House* Cámara Baja || *mother house* casa matriz || *on the house* regalo *m* de cortesía *f* de la casa || *out of house and home* sin casa ni hogar, en la calle || *parents' house* casa paterna || *the House of God* la casa de Dios || THEATR *to bring the house down* ser un exitazo || US *to clean house* hacer las labores domésticas || FIG *to get on like a house on fire* llevarse de maravilla (to get on very well), progresar rápidamente (to progress) || *to keep house* llevar la casa || *to keep open house* tener mesa franca *or* casa abierta || *to keep to the house* quedarse en casa || *to make a House* obtener el quórum || *to move house* mudarse || *to run the house* llevar la casa || FIG *to set one's own house in order* cuidarse de los asuntos propios || *to set up house* poner casa || *Upper House* Senado *m*, Cámara Alta.

house [hauz] *vt* alojar; *the new wing will house fifty students* la nueva ala podrá alojar a cincuenta alumnos || albergar, alojar (to put up) || dar alojamiento para (on a large scale); *to house immigrants* dar alojamiento para los inmigrantes || almacenar (to store) || entrojar (grain) || poner a cubierto *or* al abrigo (to shelter) || contener (to contain) || TECH encajar || MAR calar (the mast) | amainar (a sail) || aparcar (a car).
◆ *vi* alojarse, vivir.

house agent [-ˌeidʒənt] *n* agente *m* inmobiliario.

house arrest [-ə'rest] *n* arresto *m* domiciliario.

houseboat [-bəut] *n* casa *f* flotante.

housebound [-baund] *adj* confinado, da en su casa [por motivos de salud].

housebreak [-breik] *vi* robar con fractura.
◆ *vt* enseñar (animals).

housebreaker [-breikə*] *n* ladrón *m*, atracador *m* (robber) || demoledor de casas (who dismantles houses).

housebreaking [-'breikiŋ] *n* JUR allanamiento *m* de morada | robo *m* con fractura (robbery) || demolición *f* de un edificio.

houseclean [-kliːn] *vt/vi* limpiar (la casa), hacer la limpieza de (la casa) || FIG limpiar.

housecleaning [-'kliːniŋ] *n* limpieza *f* de la casa.

housecoat [-kəut] *n* bata *f*.

housedress [-dres] *n* bata *f*.

housefly [-flai] *n* mosca *f* doméstica.

household [-həuld] *n* casa *f*, familia *f*; *theirs is a happy household* su casa es una casa feliz || casa *f*; *to look after the household* ocuparse de la casa || *the Royal Household* la Corte.
◆ *adj* casero, ra; doméstico, ca; *the household chores* los quehaceres domésticos || de la casa; *household expenses* gastos de la casa || casero, ra; *household remedy* remedio casero; *household bread* pan casero || familiar, común (common) || real (royal); *household troops* guardia real || — *household gods* dioses *m* lares || *household word* nombre muy conocido, palabra muy conocida.

householder [-'həuldə*] *n* cabeza *m* de familia (head of a family) || dueño *m or* dueña *f* de una casa (owner) || inquilino, na (tenant).

househunting [-'hʌntiŋ] *n* búsqueda *f* de una casa.

housekeeper [-'kiːpə*] *n* ama *f* de casa (housewife); *his wife is a good housekeeper* su mujer es una buena ama de casa || ama *f* de llaves (woman paid to run a home).

housekeeping [-'kiːpiŋ] *n* gobierno *m* de la casa (running of a house) || quehaceres *m pl* domésticos (housework) || dinero *m* para gastos domésticos.

houseleek [-liːk] *n* BOT siempreviva *f* mayor.

houseline [-lain] *n* MAR piola *f*.

housemaid [-meid] *n* criada *f* [AMER mucama *f*] || MED *housemaid's knee* higroma *m*, hidrartrosis *f*.

house martin [-ˌmaːtin] *n* avión *m* común (bird).

housemaster [-ˌmaːstə*] *n* profesor *m* encargado de un pabellón de alumnos en un internado.

house organ ['ɔːgən] *n* publicación *f* interna.

house painter [-'peintə*] *n* pintor *m* de brocha gorda.

house party [-'pɑːti] *n* estancia *f* en la casa de campo de un amigo (gathering) || invitados *m pl*, convidados *m pl* (guests).

house physician [-fiˌziʃən] *n* MED interno *m* (in a hospital).

houseplant [-ˌplaːnt] *n* planta *f* de interior.

house-proud [-praud] *adj* *to be very house-proud* tener la casa como una plata.

houseroom [-rum] *n* *I wouldn't give it houseroom* no lo tendría en casa || *there's houseroom for everybody* hay sitio en casa para todos || *to find houseroom for s.o.* encontrar sitio en su casa para alguien.

house surgeon [-'səːdʒən] *n* MED cirujano *m* interno (in a hospital).

house-to-house [-tə'haus] *adj* de casa en casa (from house to house); *house-to-house inquiries* investigaciones de casa en casa.
◆ *adv* de casa en casa.

housetop [-tɔp] *n* tejado *m* (roof) ‖ FIG *to claim sth. from the housetops* gritar algo a los cuatro vientos, pregonar algo a voz en grito.

house-train [-trein] *vt* enseñar (an animal).

housewares [-wεə:z] *pl n* utensilios *m* domésticos.

housewarming [-ˈwɔ:miŋ] *n* inauguración *f* de una casa ‖ *to have a housewarming party* inaugurar la casa.

housewife [-waif] *n* ama *f* de casa ‖ madre *f* de familia (mother) ‖ sus labores *f pl* (on official forms); *profession: housewife* profesión: sus labores.
— OBSERV El plural de esta palabra es *housewives*.

housewife [ˈhʌzif] *n* costurero *m* (sewing kit).
— OBSERV El plural de esta palabra es *housewives*.

housewifery [ˈhausˌwaifəri] *n* gobierno *m* de la casa (housekeeping).

housework [ˈhauswə:k] *n* quehaceres *m pl* domésticos.

housing [ˈhausiŋ] *n* alojamiento *m* (accommodation) ‖ vivienda *f*; *Ministry of Housing* Ministerio de la Vivienda; *housing shortage* crisis de la vivienda; *housing plan* proyecto relativo a la vivienda ‖ casas *f pl* (houses) ‖ almacenaje *m* (storage) ‖ entrojamiento *m* (of cereals) ‖ gualdrapa *f* (of a horse) ‖ AUT cárter *m* ‖ TECH bastidor *m* (of a machine) ‖ ARCH empotramiento *m* (of beams) ‖ — *housing association* cooperativa *f* inmobiliaria ‖ *housing estate* o *development* urbanización *f*.

hove [həuv] *pret/pp* MAR ⟶ **heave.**

hovel [ˈhɔvəl] *n* casucha *f*, cuchitril *m* (miserable dwelling) ‖ cobertizo *m* (shed).

hover [ˈhɔvə*] *vi* cernerse (eagle, helicopter) ‖ revolotear (bird, butterfly) ‖ quedarse suspendido *or* flotando en el aire (paper, leaves, embers) ‖ FIG rondar; *he is always hovering around me* está siempre rondando alrededor de mí ‖ — FIG *a smile hovered over her lips* esbozó una sonrisa | *to hover over* cernerse sobre (danger).

hovercraft [-krα:ft] *n* aerodeslizador *m*.

hoverport [-pɔ:t] *n* puerto *m* para aerodeslizadores.

how [hau] *adv* como; *do it how you like* hazlo como quieras ‖ cómo (in what way); *how did he do it?* ¿cómo lo hizo?; *I don't know how to thank you* no sé cómo agradecerle; *you should see how the children run* hay que ver cómo corren los niños; *how he snores!* ¡cómo ronca!; *how big is it?* ¿cómo es de grande?; *how do you like your tea?* ¿cómo quiere su té? ‖ cómo, qué tal; *how was the meal, the film?* ¿qué tal estuvo la comida, la película?; *how do you find it?* ¿qué tal lo encuentras? ‖ qué (in exclamations before an adjective or an adverb); *how pretty she is!* ¡qué guapa es! ‖ lo... que, cómo, cuán (to what extent); *you don't realize how difficult it is* no te das cuenta de lo difícil que es *or* de cómo es de difícil *or* cuán difícil es ‖ que (that); *I told him how I had spoken to you* le dije que te había hablado ‖ a cuánto; *how did you buy it?* ¿a cuánto lo compraste?; *how are fruits today?* ¿a cuánto está la fruta hoy? ‖ — *and how!* ¡y cómo! ‖ *how about?* ¿qué te (le, os, etc.) parece si...?; *how about going to the cinema?* ¿qué te parece si vamos al cine?; y... qué; *how about me?, you haven't given me anything* ¿y yo qué?, a mí no me has dado nada ‖ *how are you?* ¿cómo está usted?, ¿qué tal está Vd.? ‖ *how can it be?* ¿cómo puede ser? ‖ *how can you!* ¿no te da vergüenza? ‖ *how come?* ¿cómo es eso? ‖ *how come...?* ¿cómo es que...? ‖ *how do you do?* ¿cómo está usted? (how are you), encantado, da; mucho gusto (pleased to meet you) ‖ *how early* ¿cuándo?, ¿a qué hora? ‖ *how else?* claro (of course), ¿de qué otra manera? (in what other way) ‖ *how far?* ¿a qué distancia? ‖ *how glad I am!* ¡cuánto me alegro! ‖ *how is it that?* ¿cómo es que? ‖ *how is that?* ¿cómo es eso? ‖ *how is that for...?* ¿qué te parece? ‖ *how kind of you!* ¡es Ud. muy amable!, ¡qué amabilidad la suya! ‖ *how late?* ¿cuándo?, ¿a qué hora? ‖ *how long?* ¿cuánto tiempo?, ¿cuánto?; *how long will you be?* ¿cuánto tiempo tardarás?; *how long is the film?* ¿cuánto dura la película?; cómo... de largo; *how long is the rope?* ¿cómo es la cuerda de larga?; *how long do you want it?* ¿cómo lo quieres de largo? ‖ *how many?* ¿cuántos, tas?; *how many times?* ¿cuántas veces? ‖ *how much?* ¿cuánto, ta? ‖ *how much is it?* ¿cuánto vale? ‖ *how now?* ¿y entonces? ‖ *how often?* ¿cuántas veces? ‖ *how old are you?* ¿qué edad tienes?, ¿cuántos *or* qué años tienes? ‖ *how on earth, how the devil, how the dickens?* ¿cómo diablos?, ¿cómo demonios? ‖ *how pleased I am to see you* ¡cuánto me alegro de verle! ‖ *how so?* ¿cómo es eso? ‖ *how soon can you come?* ¿cuándo puedes venir? ‖ *how sorry I am!* ¡cuánto lo siento! ‖ *that was how...* así fue como... ‖ *to know how to do sth.* saber hacer algo, saber cómo se hace algo ‖ *to learn how to do sth.* aprender a hacer algo.

◆ *n* modo *m*, forma *f*, manera *f* ‖ — *the hows and whys* el cómo y el porqué ‖ *the how, the when and the wherefore* todos los detalles.

howdah [-də] *n* silla *f* de elefante.

howdy [-di] *interj* ¡hola!, ¿qué hay?

how-d'ye-do [-diˈdu:] *n* FAM lío *m* (annoying situation).

however [-hauˈevə*] *adv* por... que (with subjunctive); *however much I should like to* por mucho que me guste; *however much you insist* por más que te empeñes; *however cold it is* por mucho frío que haga ‖ como (with subjunctive); *do it however you can* hazlo como puedas ‖ de cualquier manera que (with subjunctive); *however he may do it* de cualquier manera que lo haga ‖ cómo (how); *however did he manage it?* ¿cómo lo consiguió? ‖ sin embargo, no obstante; *I do not, however, agree with the second method* sin embargo no estoy de acuerdo con el segundo método ‖ — *however it may be* o *that may be* sea lo que sea ‖ *however much he may admire you* aunque le admire mucho ‖ *however you may decide* decida lo que decida.

howitzer [ˈhauitsə*] *n* MIL obús *m* (short cannon).

howl [haul] *n* aullido *m* (of dogs, wolves) ‖ rugido *m*, bramido *m* (of wind) ‖ alarido *m* (of pain) ‖ berrido *m* (of a crying child) ‖ gritos *m pl*, abucheo *m* (hoot) ‖ *howl of laughter* carcajada *f*.

howl [haul] *vi* aullar (dogs, wolves) ‖ gritar, vociferar (crowds) ‖ dar alaridos; *to howl with pain* dar alaridos de dolor ‖ rugir, bramar (the wind) ‖ berrear (to cry like a child) ‖ — *to howl with laughter* reír a carcajadas ‖ *to howl with rage* bufar de cólera.

◆ *vi* gritar ‖ *to howl a speaker down* callar a un orador a gritos *or* abucheándole.

howler [-ə*] *n* plancha *f*, pifia *f*, error *m* garrafal (bad mistake); *to make a howler* tirarse una plancha, cometer una pifia, hacer una falta garrafal ‖ ZOOL aullador *m*, mono *m* aullador (monkey).

howling [-iŋ] *adj* aullador, ra (that howls) ‖ rugiente (wind) ‖ furioso, sa (storm, etc.) ‖ FAM garrafal (mistake) | escandaloso, sa (injustice) | clamoroso, sa (success) | lúgubre (wilderness).

◆ *n* aullido *m* (of dog, etc.) ‖ alaridos *m pl* (of pain) ‖ rugido *m*, bramido *m* (of wind).

howsoever [hausəuˈevə*] *adv* comoquiera que, de cualquier manera que (in whatever way) ‖ por muy... que (to whatever extent).

hoy [hɔi] *interj* ¡eh!

hoyden [ˈhɔidn] *n* marimacho *m*, machona *f* (tomboy).

hoydenish [-iʃ] *adj* poco femenino, na; hombruno, na.

hub [hʌb] *n* cubo *m* (of a wheel) ‖ FIG centro *m*, eje *m*; *London is the hub of the financial world* Londres es el eje del mundo financiero.

hubble-bubble [ˈhʌblˌbʌbl] *n* narguile *m* (pipe) ‖ algarabía *f* (hubbub) ‖ borboteo *m* (gurgling).

hubbub [ˈhʌbʌb] *n* alboroto *m*, barullo *m*, jaleo *m* (tumult) ‖ vocerío *m*, algarabía *f* (of voices).

hubby [ˈhʌbi] *n* FAM marido *m*.

hubcap [ˈhʌbkæp] *n* tapacubos *m inv* (of a car).

huckle [ˈhʌkl] *n* ANAT cadera *f* (hip).

huckleberry [ˈhʌklberi] *n* BOT arándano *m*.

hucklebone [ˈhʌklbəun] *n* ANAT cía *f*, hueso *m* de la cadera (hipbone) ‖ US ANAT astrágalo *m*, taba *f* (knucklebone).

huckster [ˈhʌkstə*] *n* buhonero *m*, vendedor *m* ambulante (pedlar) ‖ FAM mercachifle *m* ‖ US FAM agente *m* de publicidad (advertising man).

huddle [ˈhʌdl] *n* grupo *m* (apretado), turba *f*, tropel *m* (group); *a huddle of people sheltering from the rain* un grupo de personas resguardándose de la lluvia ‖ montón *m* (of things) ‖ confusión *f*, batiborrillo *m* (confusion, muddle) ‖ US *to go into a huddle* conferenciar *or* discutir en secreto.

huddle [hʌdl] *vt* amontonar, apiñar (to bunch together) ‖ — *to huddle on* ponerse sin cuidado (one's clothes) ‖ *to huddle o.s. up* acurrucarse ‖ *to huddle over* o *through* o *up* hacer de prisa y corriendo (a piece of work).

◆ *vi* amontonarse, apiñarse, apretarse unos contra otros ‖ *to huddle up* acurrucarse.

hue [hju:] *n* tinte *m* (colour) ‖ matiz *m* (shade) ‖ vocerío *m* (in hunting) ‖ FIG matiz *m* ‖ — *hue and cry* protesta clamorosa, grito *m* de indignación (protest), griterío *m* (shouting), persecución *f* (pursuit) ‖ *to raise a hue and cry against* protestar *or* gritar contra.

hued [-d] *adj* colorado, da ‖ — *many-hued* de muchos colores, multicolor ‖ *yellow-hued* de color amarillo.

huff [hʌf] *n* enfado *m*, enojo *m* (anger) ‖ mal humor *m* (bad temper) ‖ soplo *m* (in draughts) ‖ — *to be in a huff* estar enojado, haberse picado ‖ *to go off in a huff* o *to get into a huff* picarse, amoscarse.

huff [hʌf] *vt* ofender, enojar, picar (to offend, to annoy) ‖ maltratar (to bully) ‖ comerse, soplar (a piece in draughts).

◆ *vi* picarse (to take offence) ‖ enojarse (to become angry) ‖ bufar, resoplar (to snort) ‖ *to huff and puff* echar pestes.

huffily [-ili] *adv* de mal talante, de malhumor.

huffiness [-inis] *n* susceptibilidad *f* (touchiness) ‖ malhumor *m* (bad temper).

huffy [-i] *adj* enojadizo, za; enfadadizo, za; susceptible (touchy) ‖ enojado, da (angry) ‖ *to be huffy about* picarse por, enfadarse por.

hug [hʌg] *n* abrazo *m*; *he gave her a hug* le dio un abrazo.

hug [hʌg] *vt* abrazar (to embrace) ‖ ahogar, apretar (a bear) ‖ FIG aferrarse a (an opinion) | acariciar (an idea) ‖ arrimarse a, no apartarse de (the coast, a wall) ‖ ceñirse a, pegarse a; *to hug the kerb* pegarse a la acera ‖ *to hug o.s.* congratularse.

huge [hju:dʒ] *adj* enorme; *a huge animal* un animal enorme ‖ inmenso, sa; enorme; *a huge* *building* un edificio inmenso || amplio, plia; *a huge collection of samples* un amplio muestrario || altísimo, ma (prices) || descomunal (colossal); *a man of huge physical strength* un hombre de una fuerza descomunal.

hugely [-li] *adv* enormemente (to a huge extent) || muchísimo (very much).

hugeness [-nis] *n* inmensidad *f*.

hugger-mugger ['hʌgə,mʌgə*] *adj* (ant) secreto, ta (secret) || desordenado, da.
◆ *adv* (ant) en secreto (secretly) || desordenadamente (in a disorderly fashion).
◆ *n* desorden *m*, confusión *f* (jumble) || (ant) secreto *m* (secrecy); *in hugger-mugger* en secreto.

Hugh [hju:]; **Hugo** ['hju:gəu] *pr n* Hugo *m*.

Huguenot ['hju:gənɔt] *adj/n* hugonote, ta.

hulk [hʌlk] *n* casco *m* (hull of a ship) || armatoste *m* (sth. or s.o. big and clumsy) || carraca *f* (old boat).

hulking [-iŋ] *adj* grande y pesado, voluminoso, sa.

hull [hʌl] *n* MAR casco *m* (of boat) || AVIAT casco *m* || BOT cáscara *f* (shell) | vaina *f* (pod) || casquillo *m* (of a cartridge).

hull [hʌl] *vt* perforar el casco de [un barco] (with a torpedo, etc.) || desvainar (peas) || cascar (nuts) || mondar (barley) || descascarillar (oats).

hullabaloo [,hʌləbə'lu:] *n* FAM jaleo *m*, follón *m*, bullicio *m*, lío *m*.

hullo ['hʌ'ləu]; **hallo** ['hə'ləu] *interj* ¡hola! (greeting) || ¡diga! (answering the phone) || ¡oiga! (calling by phone) || ¡oiga!, ¡oye! (call) || ¡vaya! (surprise).

hum [hʌm] *n* tarareo *m*, canturreo *m* (of a song) || zumbido *m* (of bees, bombs, bullets, engine) || murmullo *m* (murmur).
◆ *interj* ¡ejem!

hum [hʌm] *vt* tararear, canturrear (a tune) || arrullar (a child to sleep).
◆ *vi* tararear, canturrear; *he always hums when he is happy* siempre tararea cuando está contento || zumbar (bees, bombs, bullets, engine) || FIG hervir (with activity) || FAM apestar (to smell bad) || — *business is humming* los negocios marchan bien || *to hum and haw* vacilar || *to make things hum, to start things humming* desplegar gran actividad, activar las cosas || *town humming with activity* ciudad muy activa.

human ['hju:mən] *adj* humano, na || — *human being* ser humano || *human error* error *m* humano || *human nature* naturaleza humana || *human rights* derechos *m pl* humanos.
◆ *n* humano *m*.

humane [hju:'mein] *adj* humano, na; *he has a very humane relationship with his employees* tiene un trato muy humano con sus empleados || humanístico, ca (of the humanities) || *humane studies* humanidades *f*.

humaneness [-nis] *n* humanidad *f*, sentimientos *m pl* humanos.

humanism ['hju:mənizəm] *n* humanismo *m*.

humanist ['hju:mənist] *adj/n* humanista.

humanistic [,hju:mə'nistik] *adj* humanístico, ca.

humanitarian [hju:,mæni'tɛəriən] *adj* humanitario, ria.
◆ *n* filántropo, pa; persona *f* humanitaria.

humanitarianism [-izəm] *n* humanitarismo *m*.

humanity [hju:'mæniti] *n* humanidad *f*, género *m* humano (mankind) || naturaleza *f* humana (human nature) || humanidad *f* (kindness of heart).
◆ *pl* humanidades *f*; *to study humanities* estudiar humanidades.

humanization [,hju:mənai'zeiʃən] *n* humanización *f*.

humanize ['hju:mənaiz] *vt* humanizar.

humankind ['hju:mən'kaind] *n* humanidad *f*, género *m* humano, especie *f* humana.

humanly ['hju:mənli] *adv* humanamente || *humanly impossible* humanamente imposible.

humble ['hʌmbl] *adj* humilde; *my humble abode* mi humilde morada; *in my humble opinion* en mi humilde parecer || — *of humble birth* de humilde cuna || *your humble servant* su humilde servidor.

humble ['hʌmbl] *vt* humillar || *to humble o.s.* humillarse.

humble-bee [-bi:] *n* ZOOL abejorro *m*.

humbleness [-nis] *n* humildad *f*.

humbling [-iŋ] *adj* humillante.

humbly [-i] *adv* humildemente, con humildad.

humbug ['hʌmbʌg] *n* bola *f*, embuste *m* (lie) || engaño *m* (deceit) || tonterías *f pl*, disparates *m pl* (nonsense) || farsa *f* (farce) || farsante *m* (person) || caramelo *m* de menta (sweet).

humbug ['hʌmbʌg] *vt* embaucar, engañar (to mislead).

humdinger [hʌm'diŋgə*] *n* FAM maravilla *f*; *she's a humdinger of a girl* es una maravilla de chica.

humdrum ['hʌmdrʌm] *adj* monótono, na (monotonous) || rutinario, ria (routine) || aburrido, da (boring) || vulgar (commonplace).
◆ *n* monotonía *f* (monotony) || rutina *f* (routine) || pelma *m* & *f* (person) || lata *f*, pesadez *f* (nuisance).

humeral ['hju:mərəl] *adj* ANAT humeral.
◆ *n* REL humeral *m* (veil).

humerus ['hju:mərəs] *n* ANAT húmero *m* (bone).
— OBSERV El plural de esta palabra es *humeri*.

humid ['hju:mid] *adj* húmedo, da.

humidifier [-faiə*] *adj* humedecedor, ra.
◆ *n* humedecedor *m*.

humidify [hju:'midifai] *vt* humedecer.

humidity [hju:'miditi] *n* humedad *f*.

humidor ['hju:midɔ:*] *n* bote *m* que mantiene húmedo el tabaco || humedecedor *m* (humidifier).

humiliate [hju:'milieit] *vt* humillar.

humiliating [-iŋ] *adj* humillante.

humiliation [hju:,mili'eiʃən] *n* humillación *f*.

humility [hju:'militi] *n* humildad *f*.

humming ['hʌmiŋ] *adj* que zumba (bees, bombs, bullets, engine) || FAM en pleno desarrollo, que funciona bien, que pita (affair) | muy fuerte (blow).
◆ *n* tarareo *m*, canturreo *m* (of a tune) || zumbido *m* (of bees, bombs, bullets, engine) || murmullo *m* (murmur).

hummingbird [-bə:d] *n* colibrí *m*, pájaro *m* mosca.

humming top [-tɔp] *n* peonza *f*, trompo *m*.

hummock ['hʌmək] *n* morón *m*, montecillo *m* (of heart) || montículo *m* de hielo (of ice).

humor ['hju:mə*] *n* US → **humour.**

humoral [-əl] *adj* ANAT humoral.

humoresque [,hju:mə'resk] *n* MUS capricho *m*.

humorist; humourist ['hju:mərist] *n* humorista *m* & *f* (writer or teller of jokes) || gracioso, sa (funny person) || bromista *m* & *f* (joker).

humoristic [,hju:mə'ristik] *adj* humorístico, ca.

humorless ['hju:məlis] *adj* US → **humourless.**

humorous ['hju:mərəs] *adj* humorístico, ca; humorista (writer) || gracioso, sa; divertido, da; chistoso, sa (person, remark, etc.).

humorously [-li] *adv* con gracia, humorísticamente || con tono jocoso, jocosamente.

humorousness [-nis] *n* humorismo *m*, gracia *f*.

humour ['hju:mə*] *n* humor *m*; *sense of humour* sentido del humor; *in a good humour* de buen humor || gracia *f* (of a joke); *I don't see the humour of it* no le veo la gracia || capricho *m* (whim) || ANAT humor *m* (fluid); *aqueous, vitrous humor* humor ácueo, vítreo || — *bad* o *ill humour* malhumor *m*, mal humor || *out of humour* de mal humor || *to be in no humour for laughing* no tener humor para reírse || *to be lacking in humour* no tener sentido del humor.

humour; US **humor** ['hju:mə*] *vt* seguir el humor a (to play s.o.'s game) || complacer (to oblige, to please).

humourist [-rist] *n* → **humorist.**

humourless; US **humorless** [-lis] *adj* sin sentido del humor || que no tiene gracia (joke).

hump [hʌmp] *n* joroba *f*, corcova *f*, giba *f* (of person's back) || joroba *f*, giba *f* (of camel) || montecillo *m* (in the ground) || FIG malhumor *m*; *to have the hump* estar de malhumor | nostalgia *f* || — FIG *to be over the hump* haber vencido una dificultad | *to give s.o. the hump* jorobar *or* fastidiar a uno.

hump [hʌmp] *vt* FIG & FAM cargar con, llevar (to carry) || *to hump one's back* encorvarse (person), arquear el lomo (cat).
◆ *vi* US FAM matarse (to exert o.s.) | darse prisa (to hurry).

humpback [-bæk] *n* joroba *f*, corcova *f*, giba *f* (back) || jorobado, da; corcovado, da (person) || *humpback bridge* puente *m* peraltado.

humpbacked [-bækt]; **hunchbacked** [hʌntʃbækt] *adj* jorobado, da; corcovado, da.

humph [hʌmf] *interj* ¡bah!

humpy ['hʌmpi] *adj* desigual (ground) || jorobado, da (humpbacked).

humus ['hju:məs] *n* AGR mantillo *m*, humus *m*.

Hun [hʌn] *n* HIST huno *m* || FAM alemán, ana.

hunch [hʌntʃ] *n* joroba *f*, giba *f*, corcova *f* (hump) || trozo *m* (small piece) || FIG presentimiento *m*, idea *f*, corazonada *f*; *I've got a hunch he won't come* tengo la idea de que no va a venir.

hunch [hʌntʃ] *vt* *to hunch one's back* encorvarse || *to sit hunched up* estar sentado con el cuerpo encorvado || *with hunched shoulders* con la cabeza muy metida entre los hombros.
◆ *vi* US empujar (to shove, to jostle).

hunchback [-bæk] *n* jorobado, da; corcovado, da (person) || joroba *f*, corcova *f*, giba *f* (hump).

hunchbacked [-bækt] *adj* → **humpbacked.**

hundred ['hʌndrəd] *adj* cien, ciento (see OBSERV) || *the Hundred Years' War* la Guerra de los Cien Años.
◆ *n* ciento *m*; *a hundred oysters* un ciento de ostras || centenar *m*; *a hundred men* un centenar de hombres; *by the hundred, by the hundreds, in hundreds* por *or* a centenares || centena *f*; *hundreds of times* centenas de veces || HIST división *f* administrativa del condado || — *a hundred miles away* a cien leguas || *a hundred miles per hour* cien por hora || FIG *a hundred per cent* cien por cien | *a hundred times* cientos de veces, un montón de veces | *a hundred to one it will be a success* apuesto a que va a ser un éxito || *five hundred* quinientos, tas || *hundreds*

and thousands of people miles y miles de personas || *in 1900 (nineteen hundred)* en 1900 [mil novecientos] || *nine hundred* novecientos, tas || FIG *ninety times out of a hundred* la mayoría de las veces, casi siempre || *not one in a hundred* ni uno || *one hundred* cien, ciento || *to get six hundred a year* ganar seiscientas libras al año || *to live to be a hundred* llegar a los cien años || *two hundred* doscientos, tas; *two hundred women* doscientas mujeres || *two hundred and one* doscientos uno.

— OBSERV The form *ciento* is only used when the number stands alone or is followed by another number, by tens or by units: *ciento* a hundred; *ciento cinco* a hundred and five; *ciento treinta* a hundred and thirty. It is automatically apocopated to the form *cien* when followed by a noun or by the numbers *mil, millón, billón, etc.*: *cien libros* a hundred books; *cien casas* a hundred houses; *cien mil hombres* a hundred thousand men. Multiples of *ciento* are written as one word with plural form: *doscientos diez* two hundred and ten; *página seiscientas dos* page six hundred and two.

hundredfold [-fəuld] *adj* céntuplo, pla.
◆ *n* céntuplo *m* || — *to increase a hundredfold* centuplicar, aumentar cien veces || *to repay a hundredfold* devolver ciento por uno.

hundredth ['hʌndrədθ] *adj* centésimo, ma (in a series) || centésimo, ma; centavo, va (being one of 100 equal parts).
◆ *n* centésima parte *f*, centésimo *m*, centavo *m* (one of 100 parts) || centésimo, ma (in hundredth position).

hundredweight ['hʌndrədweit] *n* quintal *m*.

hung [hʌŋ] *pret/pp* → **hang.**

Hungarian [hʌŋ'gɛəriən] *adj/n* húngaro, ra.

Hungary ['hʌŋgəri] *pr n* GEOGR Hungría *f*.

hunger ['hʌŋgə*] *n* hambre *f* (craving for food); *to satisfy one's hunger* aplacar el hambre || FIG sed *f*; *hunger for adventure* sed de aventuras || — FIG *hunger is a poor adviser* el hambre es mala consejera | *hunger is the best sauce* a buen hambre no hay pan duro | *hunger sharpens the wit* el hambre aguza el ingenio || *hunger strike* huelga *f* del hambre || *to be weak from hunger* estar muerto de hambre || *to die from hunger* morir *or* morirse de hambre || *to stave off hunger* engañar *or* matar el hambre.

hunger ['hʌŋgə*] *vi* tener hambre (to be hungry) || FIG *to hunger after* o *for* tener sed *or* hambre de.
◆ *vt* hacer pasar hambre.

hung over ['hʌŋəuvə*] *adj* con resaca; *to be hung over* estar conresaca, tener resaca.

hungrily ['hʌŋgrili] *adv* ávidamente || con ansia; *he looked hungrily at the cake* miraba el pastel con ansia.

hungry ['hʌŋgri] *adj* hambriento, ta (feeling hunger) || de hambre; *hungry look* cara de hambre || FIG ávido, da; sediento, ta; *hungry for news* ávido de noticias || AGR pobre (land) || — *I am ravenously hungry* o *as hungry as a wolf* o *hungry enough to eat a horse* tengo un hambre que no veo *or* un hambre canina || *to be* o *to feel hungry* tener hambre || *to be very hungry* tener mucha hambre || *to go hungry* pasar hambre || *to look hungry* tener cara de hambre || *to make s.o. hungry* darle hambre a uno.

hung up [hʌŋʌp] *adj* FAM obsesionado, da.

hunk [hʌnk] *n* trozo *m*, pedazo *m*; *a hunk of bread* un trozo de pan.

hunkers ['hʌŋkəz] *pl n* *to be on one's hunkers* estar en cuclillas.

hunks [hʌŋki] *n* FAM avaro *m*, tacaño *m* (miser) || persona *f* de malhumor.

hunky ['hʌŋki] *n* US FAM inmigrante *m* de Europa Central.

hunky-dory [-'dɔ:ri] *adj* US FAM muy bien.

Hunnish ['hʌniʃ] *adj* de los hunos || FAM bárbaro, ra.

hunt [hʌnt] *n* caza *f*, cacería *f*, partida *f* de caza (of small game) || cacería *f*, montería *f* (of big game) || cazadores *m pl* (huntsmen) || búsqueda *f*, busca *f*; *the hunt for the criminal* la búsqueda del criminal || persecución *f* (pursuit) || *to go on a hunt for* ir en busca de, buscar.

hunt [hʌnt] *vt* perseguir (to pursue) || cazar; *to hunt foxes, whales* cazar zorros, ballenas || recorrer, cazar en; *to hunt an area for foxes* recorrer una región en busca de zorros || cazar con (hounds) || buscar (to search for) || — *to hunt down* acorralar (to corner), dar con (to find) || *to hunt out* echar (s.o.), conseguir encontrar (sth.), descubrir (truth) || *to hunt up* encontrar (to find), buscar (to look for).
◆ *vi* cazar, ir de cacería (small game) || ir de cacería *or* de montería (big game) || FIG buscar (to search) || — *to go hunting* ir de caza *or* de cacería || *to hunt about for* buscar por todas partes || *to hunt after* o *for* buscar.

— OBSERV En Inglaterra *to hunt* se suele emplear para la caza de pelo mientras *to shoot* se aplica más generalmente a la caza de pluma. En cambio, en Estados Unidos, *to hunt* se usa para cualquier tipo de caza.

hunter [-ə*] *n* cazador *m* (someone who hunts) || caballo *m* de caza (horse) || perro *m* de caza (dog) || saboneta *f* (watch) || FIG cazador *m*.

hunting ['hʌntiŋ] *n* caza *f*, cacería *f* (small game) || cacería *f*, montería *f* (big game) || FIG caza *f*.
◆ *adj* de caza; *hunting knife* cuchillo de caza.

hunting box [-bɔks] *n* pabellón *m* de caza.

hunting dog [-dɔg] *n* perro *m* de caza.

hunting field [-fi:ld]; **hunting ground** [-graund] *n* terreno *m* de caza.

hunting horn [-hɔ:n] *n* cuerno *m*, trompa *f*.

hunting lodge [-lɔdʒ] *n* US pabellón *m* de caza.

hunting watch [-'wɔtʃ] *n* saboneta *f* (watch).

huntress ['hʌntris] *n* cazadora *f*.

huntsman ['hʌntsmən] *n* cazador *m* || montero *m* (of big game).

— OBSERV El plural de esta palabra es *huntsmen*.

hunt the slipper [hʌntðə'slipə*]; **hunt the thimble** [hʌntðə'θimbl] *n* zurriago *m* escondido (game).

hurdle ['hə:dl] *n* valla *f* (fence) || SP valla *f* || FIG barrera *f*, obstáculo *m* || SP *the one hundred metres hurdles* los cien metros vallas.

hurdle ['hə:dl] *vt* vallar, cercar con vallas (to surround) || SP saltar (to jump) || FIG salvar, vencer (an obstacle).
◆ *vi* saltar vallas || SP participar en una carrera de vallas.

hurdler [-ə*] *n* SP corredor *m* de vallas.

hurdle race [-reis] *n* SP carrera *f* de vallas, carrera *f* de obstáculos.

hurdy-gurdy ['hə:di,gə:di] *n* MUS organillo *m* (barrel organ) || (ant) zanfonía *f*.

hurl [hə:l] *n* lanzamiento *m*, tiro *m*.

hurl [hə:l] *vt* lanzar, arrojar (to throw) || soltar (insults, etc.) || — *to hurl back* rechazar || *to hurl down* derribar || *to hurl o.s.* lanzarse (into sth.) || *to hurl o.s. at sth.* abalanzarse sobre algo || *to hurl o.s. from* tirarse de.

hurler [-ə*] *n* lanzador *m* (baseball).

hurly-burly ['hə:li,bə:li] *n* barullo *m*, tumulto *m*, alboroto *m*.
◆ *adj* tumultuoso, sa; alborotado, da.

Huron ['hjuərən] *adj/n* hurón, ona.

Huron (Lake) ['hjuərən] *pr n* GEOGR Lago *m* Hurón.

hurrah [hu'rɑ:]; **hurray** [hu'rei] *interj* ¡hurra! || *hurrah for...!* ¡viva...!
◆ *n* vítor *m*.

hurrah [hu'rɑ:] *vt* vitorear, aclamar.
◆ *vi* dar vítores.

hurricane ['hʌrikən] *n* huracán *m*.

hurricane deck [-dek] *n* MAR cubierta *f* superior.

hurricane lamp [-læmp] *n* farol *m*.

hurried ['hʌrid] *adj* apresurado, da (done quickly) || hecho de prisa (done quickly and badly) || rápido, da (reading) || — *to have a hurried meal* comer de prisa || *we were hurried when we wrote this letter* teníamos mucha prisa cuando escribimos esta carta.

hurriedly [-li] *adv* apresuradamente, precipitadamente || *he left the room hurriedly* salió corriendo de la habitación.

hurry ['huri] *n* prisa *f* || precipitación *f* (rush) || — *are you in a hurry for this translation?* ¿le corre prisa esta traducción? || *in a hurry* de prisa; *he ate in a hurry* comió de prisa; tan pronto; *I will not return in a hurry* no voy a volver tan pronto || *is there any hurry?* ¿corre prisa? || *there is no hurry* no hay prisa || *to be in a hurry* tener prisa; *to be in a hurry to do sth.* tener prisa por hacer algo || *to be in no hurry* no tener prisa || *to leave in a hurry* salir corriendo || *what's your hurry?* ¿por qué te das tanta prisa?, ¿qué prisa tienes?

hurry ['hʌri] *vt* dar prisa a (to make move quickly); *don't hurry me!* ¡no me des prisa! || hacer de prisa; *to hurry work* hacer el trabajo de prisa || acelerar; *to hurry negotiations through* acelerar la conclusión de las negociaciones || llevar a toda prisa; *I hurried her to the hospital* le llevé al hospital a toda prisa || — *to hurry s.o. into a car* meter a alguien de prisa en un coche || *to hurry s.o. into doing sth.* dar prisa a alguien para que haga algo.
◆ *vi* darse prisa, apresurarse; *don't hurry!* ¡no te des prisa! || ir *or* irse de prisa; *to hurry to a place* ir de prisa a un sitio.
◆ *phr v* ***to hurry after*** correr detrás de || ***to hurry along*** ir de prisa (to walk) | pasar de prisa | acelerar (sth.) || llevar *or* llevarse rápidamente (s.o.) || ***to hurry away*** llevar *or* llevarse rápidamente (s.o.) | irse corriendo, irse de prisa (to depart rapidly) || ***to hurry back*** hacer volver rápidamente [a un sitio] (to bring back) | volver rápidamente *or* corriendo (to come back) || ***to hurry down*** hacer bajar rápidamente (to take down) | bajar rápidamente *or* corriendo (to descend) || ***to hurry in*** entrar corriendo || ***to hurry off*** llevar *or* llevarse rápidamente (s.o.) | irse de prisa *or* corriendo || ***to hurry on*** dar prisa a (people) | acelerar (things) | apresurar *or* acelerar el paso (walking) || ***to hurry out*** sacar rápidamente, hacer salir rápidamente (to make leave) | salir corriendo *or* de prisa (to leave) || ***to hurry over*** hacer de prisa y corriendo (a task) || ***to hurry up*** apresurar | subir rápidamente *or* corriendo (to climb) | darse prisa, apresurarse (to speed up) || — *hurry up!* ¡dese prisa!, ¡rápido!

hurry-scurry [-'skʌri] *n* precipitación *f*.
◆ *adv* en desorden (in a disorderly manner) || precipitadamente, atropelladamente (hurriedly).

hurry-scurry [-'skʌri] *vi* precipitarse.

hurst [hə:st] *n* colina *f* (hill) || bosquecillo *m* (small wood) || banco *m* de arena (sandbank).

hurt [hə:t] *n* daño *m*, mal *m* (harm) || herida *f* (wound) || FIG daño *m*, perjuicio *m* (damage) | golpe *m* (to s.o.'s pride).

hurt* [hə:t] *vt* hacer daño, lastimar (to cause bodily injury) || doler (to cause physical pain); *it hurts me* me duele; *where does it hurt?* ¿dónde le duele? || herir (to wound) || SP lesionar

(to injure) || estropear, dañar; *the storm hurt his crop* la tormenta ha dañado su cosecha || perjudicar; *to hurt s.o.'s interests* perjudicar los intereses de uno || doler, herir (mental pain); *his words hurt me* me han dolido sus palabras || ofender (to offend) || — FIG *he wouldn't hurt a fly* es incapaz de matar una mosca || *to get hurt* hacerse daño, lastimarse (to hurt o.s.), ser herido (to be wounded) || *to hurt one's leg* lastimarse la pierna, hacerse daño en la pierna || *to hurt o.s.* hacerse daño, lastimarse || *to hurt s.o.'s feelings* ofenderle a uno.
◆ *vi* doler; *my head hurts* me duele la cabeza || hacer daño || estropearse (to get spoiled) || *nothing hurts like the truth, the truth always hurts* sólo la verdad ofende.
— OBSERV Pret y pp *hurt*.

hurtful [-ful] *adj* dañoso, sa (harmful) || nocivo, va (to the health) || perjudicial (detrimental) || hiriente (words remark).

hurtfulness [-fulnis] *n* nocividad *f*.

hurtle ['hə:tl] *vt* lanzar, arrojar (to hurl).
◆ *vi* lanzarse, precipitarse || caer violentamente (to fall) || — *to hurtle along* ir como un rayo || *to hurtle down* caer estrepitosamente (rocks), llover (missiles) || *to hurtle past* pasar como un rayo.

hurtless ['hə:tlis] *adj* inofensivo, va (harmless) || ileso, sa; sano y salvo, sana y salva (unharmed) || intacto, ta (intact).

husband ['hʌzbənd] *n* marido *m*, esposo *m*.

husband ['hʌzbənd] *vt* ahorrar, economizar; *to husband one's resources* ahorrar fondos || escatimar (one's strenght) || FAM casar.

husbandman [-mən] *n* agricultor *m*, labrador *m*.
— OBSERV El plural de *husbandman* es *husbandmen*.

husbandry ['hʌzbəndri] *n* AGR agricultura *f* || ahorro *m* (saving) || buen gobierno *m* (management) || *animal husbandry* cría *f* de ganado, ganadería *f*.

hush [hʌʃ] *n* silencio *m* (silence) || quietud *f* (stillness); *the hush of the night* la quietud de la noche.
◆ *interj* ¡chitón!, ¡cállate!, ¡cállese!

hush [hʌʃ] *vt* callar, hacer callar (to make silent) || calmar (to calm) || *to hush up* echar tierra a (an affair), hacer callar (a person).
◆ *vi* callarse.

hushaby ['hʌʃəbai] *interj* *hushaby baby!* ¡ea, mi niño!, ¡arrorró mi nene!

hush-hush ['hʌʃ'hʌʃ] *adj* muy secreto, muy secreta.

hush-hush ['hʌʃ'hʌʃ] *vt* hacer callar, callar.

hush money ['hʌʃ,mʌni] *n* FAM mamela *f*, guante *m* (bribe).

husk [hʌsk] *n* cáscara *f* (of nuts, cereals, etc.) || farfolla *f*, envoltura *f* de la mazorca (of maize) || vaina *f* (of peas and beans) || pellejo *m* (of grapes) || erizo *m* (of chestnut) || binza *f*, tela *f* (of onion).
◆ *pl* ahechaduras *f*.

husk [hʌsk] *vt* descascarar (nuts, etc.) || descascarar, descascarillar (cereals) || pelar, desvainar, desgranar (peas and beans) || pelar, mondar (chestnuts, onions) || despellejar (grapes).

huskily ['hʌskili] *adv* con voz ronca.

huskiness ['hʌskinis] *n* ronquera *f*, enronquecimiento *m*.

husky ['hʌski] *adj* con cáscara (nuts, cereals, etc.) || con vaina (peas and beans) || ronco, ca (voice) || US FAM fuerte, fornido, da (strong).
◆ *n* ZOOL perro *m* esquimal || esquimal *m* & *f* (eskimo).

hussar [hu'zɑ:*] *n* MIL húsar *m*.

Hussite ['hʌsait] *adj/n* HIST husita.

hussy ['hʌsi] *n* FAM fresca *f* (saucy girl) | lagarta *f* (immoral woman).

hustings ['hʌstiŋz] *pl n* elecciones *f* (election) || tribuna *f sing* electoral (platform) || FIG tribuna *f*, plataforma *f*.

hustle ['hʌsl] *n* prisa *f* (hurry) || empujón *m* (shove) || empuje *m* (energy) || bullicio *m* (activity) || FAM estafa *f*, timo *m* (swindle) || — *the hustle and bustle of modern life* el ajetreo de la vida moderna || US FAM *to get a hustle on* darse prisa.

hustle ['hʌsl] *vt* empujar; *they hustled him out of the station* le empujaron fuera de la estación || sacudir (to shake) || dar prisa a (to hurry s.o.) || acelerar (sth.) || FAM robar (to steal) | estafar, timar (to swindle) || — *he was hustled into agreement* le obligaron a llegar rápidamente a un acuerdo || *to hustle things on* llevar las cosas a buen paso.
◆ *vi* abrirse paso a codazos (to push one's way); *he hustled through the crowd* se abrió paso a codazos entre la muchedumbre || darse prisa, apresurarse (to hurry) || US ajetrearse, moverse (to bustle).

hustler [-ə*] *n* FAM despabilado, da (energetic person) | puta *f*, ramera *f* (whore).

hut [hʌt] *n* cabaña *f*, choza *f* (log cabin) || cobertizo *m* (garden shed) || casucha *f*, chabola *f* (small house, hovel) || MIL barraca *f* || *mountain hut* albergue *m* de montaña.

hutch [hʌtʃ] *n* conejera *f* (cage) || MIN vagoneta *f* (truck) || artesa *f* (trough) || hucha *f*, arca *f* (large box) || FAM chabola *f*, casucha *f* (hovel) || US aparador *m* (cupboard).

huzza [hu'zɑ:] *interj* ¡hurra!
◆ *n* vítor *m*, viva *m*.

hyacinth ['haiəsinθ] *n* jacinto *m* (flower, gem).

hyaena [hai'i:nə] *n* ZOOL hiena *f*.

hyaline ['haiəlin] *adj* hialino, na.
◆ *n* CHEM hialina *f* || mar *m* transparente (sea) || cielo *m* diáfano (sky).

hyalite ['haiəlait] *n* MIN hialita *f*.

hybrid ['haibrid] *adj* híbrido, da.
◆ *n* híbrido *m* || mestizo, za (person).

hybridism ['haibridizəm]; **hybridity** [haibri'diti] *n* carácter *m* híbrido, hibridismo *m*.

hibridization [haibridai'zeiʃən] *n* hibridación *f*.

hybridize ['haibridaiz] *vt* hibridizar.

hydatid ['haidətid] *n* MED hidátide *f*.

hydra ['haidrə] *n* MYTH & ZOOL hidra *f*.

hydracid [hai'dræsid] *n* CHEM hidrácido *m*.

hydrangea [hai'dreindʒə] *n* BOT hortensia *f*.

hydrant ['haidrənt] *n* boca *f* de riego || *fire hydrant* boca *f* de incendio.

hydrargyriasis [haidrɑ:'dʒiriəzis]; **hydrargyrism** [haidrɑ:'dʒirizəm] *n* MED hidrargirismo *m*.

hydrargyrum [hai'drɑ:dʒirəm] *n* CHEM hidrargiro *m*.

hydrarthrosis [haidrɑ:'θrəuzis] *n* MED hidrartrosis *f*.

hydratable ['haidrətəbl] *adj* CHEM hidratable.

hydrate ['haidreit] *n* CHEM hidrato *m*.

hydrate ['haidreit] *vt* CHEM hidratar.
◆ *vi* hidratarse.

hydration [hai'dreiʃən] *n* CHEM hidratación *f*.

hydraulic [hai'drɔ:lik]; **hydraulical** [-əl] *adj* hidráulico, ca; *hydraulic brake, cement* freno, cemento hidráulico; *hydraulic press* prensa hidráulica; *hydraulic power* fuerza hidráulica; *hydraulic jack* gato hidráulico.

hydraulics [-s] *n* hidráulica *f* (science).

hydric ['haidrik] *adj* hídrico, ca.

hydride ['haidraid] *n* CHEM hidruro *m*.

hydro ['həidrəu] *n* estación *f* termal, balneario *m*.

hydrobromic [,haidrəu'brəumik] *adj* CHEM bromhídrico, ca (acid).

hydrocarbon [,haidrəu'kɑ:bən] *n* CHEM hidrocarburo *m*.

hydrocarbonate [-eit] *n* CHEM hidrocarbonato *m*.

hydrocele ['haidrəusi:l] *n* MED hidrocele *f*.

hydrocephalic [,haidrəuse'fælik] *adj/n* MED hidrocéfalo, la.

hydrocephalous [haidrəu'sefələs] *adj* MED hidrocéfalo, la.

hydrocephalus ['haidrəu'sefələs] *n* MED hidrocefalia *f*.

hydrochloric ['haidrəu'klɔrik] *adj* CHEM clorhídrico, ca.

hydrochloride ['haidrəu'klɔ:raid] *n* CHEM clorhidrato *m*.

hydrocyanic [,haidrəusai'ænik] *adj* CHEM cianhídrico, ca.

hydrodynamic ['haidrəudai'næmik]; **hydrodynamical** [-ikəl] *adj* hidrodinámico, ca.

hydrodynamics [-s] *n* hidrodinámica *f* (science).

hydroelectric [,haidrəui'lektrik] *adj* hidroeléctrico, ca.

hydroelectricity ['haidrəuilek'trisiti] *n* hidroelectricidad *f*.

hydrofluoric ['haidrəuflu'ɔrik] *adj* fluorhídrico, ca.

hydrofoil ['haidrəfɔil] *n* MAR patín *m* (fin) | aerodeslizador *m* (craft).

hydrogel ['haidrədʒel] *n* CHEM hidrogel *m*.

hydrogen ['haidridʒən] *n* CHEM hidrógeno *m*; *heavy hydrogen* hidrógeno pesado || — *hydrogen bomb* bomba *f* de hidrógeno || *hydrogen chloride* hidrocloruro *m*.

hydrogenate [hai'drɔdʒineit] *vt* hidrogenar.

hidrogenize [hai'drɔdʒinaiz] *vt* hidrogenar.

hydrogenous [hai'drɔdʒinəs] *adj* hidrogenado, da.

hydrogen peroxide ['haidridʒənpə'rɔksaid] *n* CHEM agua *f* oxigenada.

hydrographer [hai'drɔgrəfə*] *n* hidrógrafo, fa.

hydrographic [,haidrəu'græfik]; **hydrographical** [-əl] *adj* hidrográfico, ca.

hydrography [hai'drɔgrəfi] *n* hidrografía *f*.

hydrologist [hai'drɔlədʒist] *n* hidrólogo *m*.

hydrology [hai'drɔlədʒi] *n* hidrología *f*.

hydrolyse; hydrolyze ['haidrəlaiz] *vt* hidrolizar.

hydrolysis [hai'drɔlisis] *n* CHEM hidrólisis *f*.
— OBSERV El plural de *hydrolysis* es *hydrolyses*.

hydromechanics [,haidrəumi'kæniks] *n* hidromecánica *f*.

hydromel ['haidrəmel] *n* hidromel *m*, aguamiel *m*.

hydrometer [hai'drɔmitə*] *n* hidrómetro *m*.

hydrometric [,haidrəu'metrik]; **hydrometrical** [-əl] *adj* hidrométrico, ca.

hydrometry [hai'drɔmitri] *n* hidrometría *f*.

hydrophilic [,haidrəu'filik]; **hydrophile** ['haidrəufail] *adj* hidrófilo, la.

hydrophobe [,haidrəu'fəub] *n* hidrófobo, ba.

hydrophobia [,haidrəu'fəubjə] *n* MED hidrofobia *f*.

hidrophobic [ˌhaidrəuˈfəubik] *adj* hidrófobo, ba.

hidropic [haiˈdrɔpik] *adj* MED hidrópico, ca.

hydroplane [ˈhaidrəuplein] *n* AVIAT hidroavión *m*, hidroplano *m* (seaplane) || MAR hidroplano *m*.

hydropneumatic [haidrənjuˈmætik] *adj* hidroneumático, ca.

hydropower [haidrəˈpauə*] *n* fuerza *f* hidroeléctrica.

hydrops [ˈhaidrɔps]; **hydropsy** [-i] *n* MED hidropesía *f*.

hydroscope [ˈhaidrəskəup] *n* hidroscopio *m*.

hydrosilicate [ˌhaidrəˈsilikeit] *n* hidrosilicato *m*.

hydrosphere [ˈhaidrəsfiə] *n* hidrosfera *f*.

hydrostatic [ˌhaidrəuˈstætik] *adj* hidrostático, ca.

hydrostatics [-s] *n* hidrostática *f*.

hydrotherapeutic [ˈhaidrəˌθerəˈpjuːtik]; **hydrotherapeutical** [-əl] *adj* hidroterápico, ca.

hydrotherapeutics [-s] *n* hidroterapia *f*.

hydrotherapy [ˈhaidrəuˈθerəpi] *n* hidroterapia *f*.

hydrous [ˈhaidrəs] *adj* CHEM hidratado, da || acuoso, sa.

hydroxide [haiˈdrɔksaid] *n* hidróxido *m*.

hydroxyl [haiˈdrɔksil] *n* hidroxilo *m*, oxhidrilo *m*.

hydrozoan [ˌhaidrəˈzəuən] *n* ZOOL hidrozoario, *m*.

hyena [haiˈiːnə] *n* ZOOL hiena *f*.

hyetograph [haiˈtəgrɑːf] *n* mapa *m* pluviométrico.

hygiene [ˈhaidʒiːn] *n* higiene *f* (system).

hygienic [haiˈdʒiːnik]; **hygienical** [-əl] *adj* higiénico, ca.

hygienics [-s] *n* higiene *f* (science).

hygienist [-ist] *n* higienista *m*.

hygroma [ˈhaiˈgrəumə] *n* MED higroma *m*.

hygrometer [haiˈgrɔmitə*] *n* higrómetro *m*.

hygrometric [ˌhaigrəuˈmetrik]; **hygrometrical** [-əl] *adj* higrométrico, ca.

hygrometry [haiˈgrɔmitri] *n* higrometría *f*.

hygroscope [ˈhaigrəskəup] *n* higroscopio *m*.

hygroscopic [-ik] *adj* higroscópico, ca.

hymen [ˈhaimen] *n* ANAT himen *m* || himeneo *m* (marriage).

hymenoptera [haimənˈɔptərə] *pl n* ZOOL himenópteros *m*.

hymenopteran; *US* **hymenopteron** [haimenˈɔptərən] *n* ZOOL himenóptero *m*.

hymn [him] *n* himno *m*.

hymn [him] *vt* cantar alabanzas; *let us hymn God* cantemos alabanzas al Señor.
◆ *vi* cantar himnos.

hymnal [ˈhimnəl]; **hymnbook** [ˈhimbuk] *n* REL libro *m* de himnos, himnario *m*.

hymnody [ˈhimnəudi] *n* himnos *m pl* (hymns).

hyoid [ˈhaiɔid] *adj* ANAT hioides, hioideo, a.
◆ *n* ANAT hioides *m*.

hype [haip] *n* FAM bombo *m* publicitario (exagerated promotion) | engaño *m*, superchería *f* (deception) | drogadicto, ta (drug addict).

hype [haip] *vt* FAM dar bombo (to promote) | engañar (to cheat) | excitar (with drugs).
◆ *vi* FAM chutarse (to shoot up), colocarse (to get high).

hyped-up [ˈhaiptʌp] *adj* FAM excitado, da.

hyperacidity [ˌhaipərəˈsiditi] *n* MED hiperacidez *f*.

hyperactive [ˌhaipəˈæktiv] *adj* hiperactivo, va.

hyperbaton [haiˈpəːbətɔn] *n* GRAMM hipérbaton *m*.
— OBSERV El plural de la palabra inglesa es *hyperbatons* o *hyperbata*.

hyperbola [haiˈpəːbələ] *n* MATH hipérbola *f*.
— OBSERV El plural de la palabra inglesa es *hyperbolas* o *hyperbolae*.

hyperbole [haiˈpəːbəli] *n* GRAMM hipérbole *f*.

hyperbolic [ˌhaipəːˈbɔlik]; **hyperbolical** [-əl] *adj* hiperbólico, ca.

hyperboloid [haiˈpəːbəlɔid] *n* MATH hiperboloide *m*.

hyperborean [ˌhaipəbɔːˈriən] *adj* hiperbóreo, a; hiperboreal || FAM del norte.

hyperchlorhydria [haipəːklɔːˈriːdriə] *n* MED hiperclorhidria *f*.

hipercritical [ˈhaipəˈkritikəl] *adj* hipercrítico, ca.

hyperdulia [ˌhaipədjuːˈlaiə] *n* REL hiperdulía *f*.

hyperfocal [ˌhaipəˈfəukəl] *adj* hiperfocal; *hyperfocal distance* distancia hiperfocal.

hyperinflation [ˌhaipəinˈfleiʃən] *n* ECON hiperinflación *f*.

hypermarket [ˌhaipəˈmaːkit] *n* hipermercado *m*.

hypermetropia [ˌhaipəmiˈtrˈupjə] *n* MED hipermetropía *f* (longsightedness).

hypermnesia [haipəːmˈniziə] *n* MED hipermnesia *f*.

hypernervous [haipəːˈnəːvəs] *adj* hipernervioso, sa.

hyperopia [ˌhaipəˈrəupjə] *n* MED hipermetropía *f*.

hyperopic [ˌhaipəˈrəupik] *adj* MED hipermétrope.

hyperphysical [ˈhaipəˈfizikəl] *adj* sobrenatural.

hypersecretion [haipəːsiˈkriːʃən] *n* MED hipersecreción *f*.

hypersensitive [ˈhaipəˈsensitiv] *adj* hipersensible.

hypersensitivity [ˌhaipəsensiˈtiviti] *n* hipersensibilidad *f*.

hypertension [ˌhaipəˈtenʃən] *n* MED hipertensión *f*.

hypertensive [ˈhaipəˈtensiv] *adj* MED hipertenso, sa.

hyperthermia [haipəːˈθəːmjə] *n* hipertermia *f*.

hyperthyroidism [ˌhaipəˈθairɔidizəm] *n* MED hipertiroidismo *m*.

hypertonic [ˌhaipəˈtɔnik] *adj* hipertónico, ca.

hypertrophic [ˌhaipəˈtrəufik] *adj* MED hipertrófico, ca.

hypertrophy [haiˈpəːtrəfi] *n* MED hipertrofia *f*.

hypertrophy [haiˈpəːtrəfi] *vi* MED hipertrofiarse.
◆ *vt* MED hipertrofiar.

hypervitaminosis [haipəːvitəmiˈnəusis] *n* MED hipervitaminosis *f*.
— OBSERV El plural de *hypervitaminosis* es *hypervitaminoses*.

hyphen [ˈhaifən] *n* guión *m*.

hyphen [ˈhaifən]; **hyphenate** [ˈhaifəneit] *vt* unir con guión, escribir con guión || *US* FAM *hyphenated American* norteamericano de origen extranjero.

hypnosis [hipˈnəusis] *n* hipnosis *f* || *under hypnosis* bajo los efectos de la hipnosis.
— OBSERV El plural de la palabra inglesa es *hypnoses*.

hypnotic [hipˈnɔtik] *adj* hipnótico, ca.
◆ *n* hipnótico *m* (drug) || persona *f* hipnotizada *or* fácil de hipnotizar (person).

hypnotism [ˈhipnətizəm] *n* MED hipnotismo *m*.

hypnotist [ˈhipnətist] *n* MED hipnotizador, ra.

hypnotize [ˈhipnətaiz] *vt* hipnotizar.

hypnotizing [-iŋ] *adj* hipnotizador, ra.

hypo [ˈhaipəu] *n* CHEM hiposulfito *m* sódico || PHOT fijador *m* || *US* FAM inyección *f* (injección) | jeringa *f* (syringe).

hypocaust [ˈhaipəukɔːst] *n* hipocausto *m*.

hypocenter [haipəˈsentə*] *n* hipocentro *m*.

hypochlorhydria [haipəklɔːˈriːdriə] *n* MED hipoclorhidria *f*.

hypochlorite [haipəˈklɔːrait] *n* CHEM hipoclorito *m*.

hypochlorous [ˌhaipəuˈklɔːrəs] *adj* hipocloroso, sa.

hypochondria [ˌhaipəuˈkɔndriə] *n* hipocondría *f*.

hypochondriac [ˌhaipəuˈkɔndriæk] *adj/n* hipocondriaco, ca; hipocondríaco, ca.

hypochondriasis [ˌhaipəukɔnˈdraiəsis] *n* hipocondría *f*.

hipochondrium [ˌhaipəˈkɔndriəm] *n* ANAT hipocondrio *m*.
— OBSERV El plural de la palabra *hypochondrium* es *hypochondria*.

hypocrisy [hiˈpɔkrəsi] *n* hipocresía *f*.

hypocrite [ˈhipəkrit] *n* hipócrita *m* & *f*.

hypocritical [ˌhipəuˈkritikəl] *adj* hipócrita.

hypoderma [ˌhaipəuˈdəːmə] *n* BOT & ZOOL hipodermis *f*.

hypodermal [-əl] *adj* hipodérmico, ca.

hypodermic [-ik] *adj* hipodérmico, ca.
◆ *n* MED jeringa *f* hipodérmica (syringe) | aguja *f* hipodérmica (needle) | inyección *f* hipodérmica (injection).

hypodermis [ˌhaipəˈdəːmis] *n* ANAT hipodermis *f*.

hypogaeum [ˌhaipəˈdʒiːəm] *n* hipogeo *m*.
— OBSERV El plural de esta palabra es *hypogaea*.

hypogastric [ˌhaipəuˈgæstrik] *adj* ANAT hipogástrico, ca.

hypogastrium [ˌhaipəuˈgæstriəm] *n* ANAT hipogastrio *m*.
— OBSERV El plural de *hypogastrium* es *hypogastria*.

hypogeum [haipəˈdʒiːəm] *n* hipogeo *m*.
— OBSERV El plural de esta palabra es *hypogea*.

hypophysis [haiˈpɔfisis] *n* ANAT hipófisis *f*.
— OBSERV El plural de *hypophysis* es *hypophyses*.

hypostyle [ˈhaipəustail] *adj* ARCH hipóstilo, la.

hyposulphite; *US* **hyposulfite** [ˌhaipəuˈsʌlfait] *n* CHEM hiposulfito *m*.

hypotension [ˌhaipəuˈtenʃən] *n* hipotensión *f*.

hypotensive [ˌhaipəuˈtensiv] *adj* hipotenso, sa.

hypotenuse; **hypothenuse** [haiˈpɔtinjuːz] *n* MATH hipotenusa *f*.

hypothalamus [ˌhaipəuˈθæləməs] *n* ANAT hipotálamo *m*.
— OBSERV El plural de *hypothalamus* es *hypothalami*.

hypothec [haiˈpɔθek] *n* JUR hipoteca *f*.

hypothecary [haiˈpɔθikəri] *adj* JUR hipotecario, ria.

hypothecate [haiˈpɔθikeit] *vt* JUR hipotecar.

hypothermia [ˌhaipəu'θəːmjə] *n* MED hipotermia *f.*

hypothesis [hai'pɔθisis] *n* hipótesis *f.*
— OBSERV El plural de *hypothesis* es *hypotheses.*

hypothesize [hai'pɔθəsaiz] *vi* hacer hipótesis.

hypothetic [ˌhaipəu'θetik]; **hypothetical** [-əl] *adj* hipotético, ca.

hypothyroidism [ˌhaipəu'θairɔidizəm] *n* MED hipotiroidismo *m.*

hypotonic [ˌhaipəu'tɔnik] *adj* hipotónico, ca.

hypsometer [hip'sɔmitə*] *n* PHYS hipsómetro *m.*

hypsometry [hip'sɔmitri] *n* PHYS hipsometría *f.*

hyssop ['hisəp] *n* hisopo *m.*

hysterectomy [histə'rektəmi] *n* MED histerectomía *f.*

hysteresis [ˌhistə'riːsis] *n* PHYS histéresis *f.*
— OBSERV El plural de esta palabra es *hystereses.*

hysteria [his'tiəriə] *n* MED histeria *f,* histerismo *m* ‖ FAM ataque *m* de nervios.

hysteric [his'terik]; **hysterical** [-əl] *adj* histérico, ca.

hysterics [-s] *n* MED histerismo *m,* crisis *f* de histeria ‖ FAM ataque *m* histérico, ataque *m* de nervios | nerviosismo *m* ‖ *to go into hysterics* ponerse histérico.

I

i [ai] *n* i *f* (letter of the alphabet).

I [ai] *n* PHIL yo *m*, ego *m*.
◆ *adj* de doble T; *I beam* viga de doble T.
◆ *pers pron* yo; *it is I* soy yo; *shall I do it or will you?* ¿lo hago yo o lo haces tú? ‖ *I am going to Madrid* voy a Madrid.
— OBSERV The English personal pronoun is not usually translated into Spanish unless emphasis is sought: *I find it difficult* lo encuentro difícil, yo lo encuentro difícil; *I for one find it difficult* yo lo encuentro difícil.

IAEA *abbr of [International Atomic Energy Agency]* OIEA, Organismo Internacional para la Energía Atómica.

iamb ['aiæmb] *n* POET yambo *m*.

iambic [ai'æmbik] *adj* POET yámbico, ca.
◆ *n* POET yambo *m* (iambus) | verso *m* yámbico (verse).

iambus [ai'æmbəs] *n* POET yambo *m*.
— OBSERV El plural de *iambus* es *iambi* o *iambuses*.

Iberia [ai'biəriə] *pr n* GEOGR Iberia *f*.

Iberian [-n] *adj* ibérico, ca (of the Iberian peninsula) ‖ ibero, ra (of ancient Iberia) ‖ GEOGR *Iberian Peninsula* Península Ibérica.
◆ *n* ibero, ra; ibérico, ca (a Spaniard or Portuguese) ‖ HIST ibero, ra ‖ lengua *f* ibera (language).

ibex ['aibeks] *n* ZOOL íbice *m*.
— OBSERV El plural de *ibex* es *ibexes* o *ibices*.

ibidem [i'baidem] *lat adv* ibídem.
— OBSERV Abbreviation: *ibid* o *ib* in both languages.

ibis ['aibis] *n* ZOOL ibis *m*.
— OBSERV El plural en inglés es *ibises* o *ibis*.

Ibiza [i'vi:θæ] *pr n* GEOGR Ibiza.

Ibizan [-n] *adj/n* ibicenco, ca.

icaco [i'kɑ:kə] *n* BOT icaco *m*.

Icarus ['aikərus] *pr n* MYTH Ícaro *m*.

ICC *abbr of [International Chamber of Commerce]* CCI, Cámara de Comercio Internacional.

ice [ais] *n* hielo *m* (solidified water); *blocks of ice* hielo en barras; *ice cubes* cubitos de hielo ‖ helado *m* (ice cream) ‖ polo *m* (iced lolly) ‖ CULIN escarcha *f* (icing) ‖ FAM diamantes *m pl* ‖ — *carbonic ice* hielo carbónico ‖ CHEM *dry ice* nieve carbónica ‖ *ice bag* bolsa *f* de hielo ‖ FIG *to break the ice* romper el hielo | *to cut no ice* no tener importancia; no convencer | *to have on ice* tener en el bote *or* en el bolsillo ‖ *to keep on ice* conservar en hielo (food), tener en reserva (to keep handy), haber metido en chirona (to keep in jail) ‖ FIG *to put on ice* dejar para más tarde | *to skate* o *to tread on thin ice* pisar un terreno peligroso.

ice [ais] *vt* helar (to convert into ice) ‖ enfriar, refrescar (to cool) | alcorzar, escarchar, garapiñar (to cover with icing).
◆ *vi* helarse ‖ *to ice over* helarse.

Ice Age [-eidʒ] *n* GEOL período *m* glaciar.

ice axe; *US* **ice ax** [-æks] *n* SP pico *m* de alpinista, piqueta *f*.

iceberg [-bə:g] *n* iceberg *m* ‖ FIG & FAM témpano *m* (unemotional person).

iceblink [-bliŋk] *n* claridad *f* en el horizonte producida por el reflejo de la luz sobre el hielo.

iceboat [-bəut] *n* trineo *m* de vela [para deslizarse sobre el hielo] ‖ rompehielos *m inv* (icebreaker).

icebound [-baund] *adj* MAR detenido por el hielo, preso entre hielos; *an icebound ship* un barco detenido por el hielo ‖ obstruido *or* bloqueado por el hielo; *an icebound harbour* un puerto obstruido por el hielo.

icebox [-bɔks] *n* nevera *f*.

icebreaker [-ˌbreikə*] *n* MAR rompehielos *m inv* (ship) ‖ espolón *m* (of a pier).

ice bucket [-'bʌkit] *n* cubo *m* con hielo para mantener frío el champán u otra bebida.

ice cap [-kæp] *n* casquete *m* glaciar (in the poles) ‖ helero *m*, glaciar *m* (glacier).

ice-cold [-kəuld] *adj* helado, da.

ice cream [-kri:m] *n* helado *m*.

ice-cream cone [-'kri:mkəun] *n* helado *m* de cucurucho (ice cream) ‖ cucurucho *m* de helado (cone-shaped wafer).

ice-cream parlor [-'kri:m'pɑ:lə*] *n US* heladería *f*.

ice-cream soda [-'kri:m'səudə] *n* soda *f* mezclada con helado.

iced [-t] *adj* helado, da ‖ enfriado, da; refrescado, da ‖ CULIN escarchado, da; *iced fruits* fruta escarchada.

icefall [-fɔ:l] *n* cumbre *f* del glaciar (steep part of glacier) ‖ cascada *f* helada (frozen waterfall).

ice fender [-'fendə*] *n* MAR rompehielos *m inv*.

ice field [-fi:ld] *n* banquisa *f*, banco *m* de hielo (sheet of floating ice) ‖ helero *m* (ice cap).

ice floe [-fləu] *n* témpano *m* de hielo.

ice foot [-fut] *n* faja *f* costera de hielo.

ice hockey [-ˌkɔki] *n* SP hockey *m* sobre hielo.

ice house [-haus] *n* nevera *f* (where ice is stored) ‖ fábrica *f* de hielo.

Iceland [-lənd] *pr n* GEOGR Islandia *f*.

Icelander [-'ləndə*] *n* islandés, esa.

Icelandic [-'ləndik] *adj* islandés, esa.
◆ *n* islandés *m* (language).

iceman [-mæn] *n US* fabricante *m* de hielo (who makes ice) | vendedor *m* de hielo (who sells ice) | repartidor *m* de hielo (who delivers ice).
— OBSERV El plural de esta palabra es *icemen*.

ice pack [-pæk] *n* banco *m* de hielo ‖ bolsa *f* de hielo (ice bag).

ice pail [-peil] *n* cubo *m* para el hielo.

ice pick [-pik] *n* piqueta *f* para romper hielo (mountaineer's tool) ‖ punzón *m* para romper hielo (kitchen implement).

ice point [-pɔint] *n* punto *m* de congelación.

ice rink [-riŋk] *n* pista *f* de patinaje.

ice sailing [-'seiliŋ] *n* SP navegación *f* a vela sobre hielo.

ice sheet [-ʃi:t] *n* casquete *m* glaciar (in the poles) ‖ helero *m*, glaciar *m* (glacier).

ice skate [-skeit] *n* SP patín *m* de cuchilla.

ice-skate [-skeit] *vi* SP patinar sobre hielo.

ice skating [-'skeitiŋ] *n* SP patinaje *m* sobre hielo.

ice tray [-trei] *n* bandeja *f* para los cubiletes *or* cubitos de hielo.

ichneumon [ik'nju:mən] *n* ZOOL mangosta *f*, icneumón *m* (mangoose) | icneumón *m* (fly).

ichor ['aikɔ:*] *n* MED icor *m*.

ichorous ['aikərəs] *adj* MED icoroso, sa.

ichthyocolla ['ikθiəkəljə] *n* ictiocola *f*.

ichthyol ['ikθiɔl] *n* CHEM ictiol *m*.

ichthyology [ˌkθi'ɔlədʒi] *n* ictiología *f*.

ichthyophagy [ˌikθi'ɔfədʒi] *n* ictiofagia *f*.

ichthyosaur [ˌikθiə'sɔ:r] *n* ZOOL ictiosauro *m*.

icicle ['aisik'l] *n* carámbano *m*.

icily ['aisili] *adv* fríamente, glacialmente.

iciness ['aisnis] *n* frialdad *f*.

icing ['aisiŋ] *n* CULIN glaseado *m*, escarchado *m* ‖ AVIAT capa *f* de escarcha ‖ — MED *icing liver* cirrosis hepática ‖ FIG *the icing on the cake* el remate.

icing sugar [-ʃugə*] *n* azúcar *m* & *f* en polvo.

ICJ *abbr of [International Court of Justice]* TIJ, Tribunal Internacional de Justicia.

icon ['aikɔn] *n* REL icono *m*.

iconoclasm [ai'kɔnəuklæzəm] *n* REL iconoclasia *f*.

iconoclast [ai'kɔnəuklæst] *n* iconoclasta *m* & *f*.

iconoclastic [ai'kɔnəu'klæstik] *adj* iconoclasta.

iconographer [ˌaikɔ'nɔgrəfə*] *n* iconógrafo *m*.

iconography [ˌaikɔ'nɔgrəfi] *n* iconografía *f*.

iconolatry [ikɔ'nɔlətri] *n* iconolatría *f*.

iconology [ˌikɔ'nɔlədʒi] *n* iconología *f*.

iconoscope [ai'kɔnəskəup] *n* iconoscopio *m*.

icosahedron ['aikəsə'hedrən] *n* MATH icosaedro *m* (solid figure).

icteric [ik'terik] *adj* ictérico, ca.

icterus ['iktərəs] *n* MED ictericia *f*.

ictus ['iktəs] *n* MED ictus *m* (stroke) ‖ GRAMM ictus *m* (stress).

icy ['aisi] *adj* helado, da (hand, foot) ‖ glacial (wind, room) ‖ cubierto de nieve *or* de hielo (mountain) ‖ FIG glacial (look).

id [id] *n* id *m*.

Idaho ['aidəˌhəu] *pr n* GEOGR Idaho.

I'd [aid] contracción of I had, I should, I would.

ID card [ai'di:,ka:d] *n* carné *m or* carnet *m* de identidad.

idea ['aidiə] *n* idea *f*; *that's my idea of America* ésa es mi idea de América; *have you any idea of the time?* ¿tienes idea de la hora que es? ‖ intención *f* (intention) ‖ idea *f* (belief, outline, skill) ‖ plan *m*, proyecto *m* (plan) ‖ — *bright idea* idea luminosa, idea genial ‖ *central, fixed idea* idea central, fija ‖ *no idea!* ¡ni idea! ‖ *not to have the foggiest* o *the slightest idea* no tener la menor *or* la más mínima *or* la más remota idea ‖ *that's the idea!* ¡exacto!, ¡eso es! ‖ *the idea is to go tomorrow* pensamos ir mañana ‖ *to be a good, a bad idea* ser una buena, una mala idea ‖ *to form* o *to get an idea* formarse una idea ‖ *to get an idea into one's head* metérsele a uno una idea en la cabeza ‖ *to get an idea of sth.* hacerse una idea de algo ‖ *to get the idea* captar la idea ‖ *to get used to the idea of* hacerse a la idea de ‖ *to have no idea* no tener ni idea ‖ *to put ideas into s.o.'s head* meterle ideas en la cabeza a alguien ‖ FAM *what's the big idea?* ¿a qué viene eso? ‖ *whose idea was it?* ¿a quién se le ocurrió?

ideal [ai'diəl] *adj* ideal; *the ideal woman* la mujer ideal.
◆ *n* ideal *m* ‖ *man of ideal* hombre de ideales.

idealism [-izəm] *n* idealismo *m*.

idealist [-ist] *n* idealista *m* & *f*.

idealistic [-istik] *adj* idealista.

idealization [ai,diəlai'zeiʃən] *n* idealización *f*.

idealize [ai'diəlaiz] *vt* idealizar.

idealizing [-iŋ] *adj* idealizador, ra.

ideally [ai'diəli] *adv* idealmente ‖ a las mil maravillas, perfectamente (perfectly).

ideate [ai'dieit] *vt* idear, concebir (to construct a mental image of) ‖ imaginar (to imagine).

idée fixe [i:'dei'fi:ks] *n* idea *f* fija.

idem ['aidəm] *adv* ídem.

identical [ai'dentikəl] *adj* idéntico, ca ‖ FAM *this is the identical spot where we stood yesterday* éste es el mismo sitio donde estuvimos ayer.

identifiable [ai'dentifaiəbl] *adj* identificable.

identification [ai,dentifi'keiʃən] *n* identificación *f* ‖ — *identification card* tarjeta *f* de identidad ‖ *identification papers* documentos *f* de identidad ‖ *identification tag* placa *f* de identificación.

identify [ai'dentifai] *vt* identificar ‖ *to identify o.s. with* identificarse con.

identikit [ai'dentikit] *n* fotorrobot *f*.

identity [ai'dentiti] *n* identidad *f*; *identity card* carnet *or* documento de identidad ‖ identidad *f* (exact similarity) ‖ — *identity parade* careo *m* de sospechosos ‖ *mistaken identity* identificación errónea.

ideogram ['idiəugræm] *n* ideograma *m*.

ideograph ['idiəugrɑ:f] *n* ideograma *m*.

ideologic [,aidi'ɔlədʒik]; **ideological** [-əl] *adj* ideológico, ca.

ideologist [,aidi'ɔlədʒist] *n* ideólogo *m*.

ideology [,aidi'ɔlədʒi] *n* ideología *f*.

ides [aidz] *pl n* idus *m*, idos *m*.

idiocy ['idiəsi] *n* idiotez *f*.

idiom ['idiəm] *n* idioma *m*, lenguaje *m* (language of a community) ‖ modismo *m*, idiotismo *m*, locución *f* (expression) ‖ estilo *m* (writer's style).

idiomatic [,idiə'mætik] *adj* idiomático, ca.

idiopathy ['idiə,pæθi] *n* idiopatía *f*.

idiosyncrasy [,idiə'siŋkrəsi] *n* idiosincrasia *f* ‖ *occupational idiosyncrasy* deformación profesional.

idiosyncratic [,idiəsiŋ'krætik] *adj* idiosincrásico, ca.

idiot ['idiət] *n* tonto, ta; imbécil *m* & *f*, idiota *m* & *f* ‖ — *to play the idiot* hacerse el tonto ‖ *village idiot* tonto del pueblo ‖ FAM *you idiot!* ¡idiota!, ¡imbécil!

idiotic [,idi'ɔtik] *adj* idiota, imbécil, tonto, ta.

idiotism ['idiətizəm] *n* US idiotez *f* (idiocy) ‖ idiotismo *m* (idiom).

idle ['aidl] *adj* perezoso, sa; holgazán, ana; vago, ga; gandul (unwilling to work) ‖ ocioso, sa (at leisure) ‖ parado, da; desocupado, da (out of work) ‖ infundado, da; *idle fears* temores infundados ‖ frívolo, la; fútil; *idle talk* conversación frívola ‖ vano, na; inútil (useless) ‖ COMM improductivo, va (capital) ‖ parado, da (machine) ‖ — *idle moment* momento *m* de ocio ‖ TECH *idle wheel* rueda intermedia ‖ *to run idle* funcionar en vacío (machine, engine), girar loco (mechanism).

idle ['aidl] *vi* perder el tiempo (to waste time) ‖ estar ocioso (to be at leisure) ‖ holgazanear, gandulear (to be lazy) ‖ estar parado, estar desocupado (to be out of work) ‖ TECH funcionar en vacío (engine, machine) ‖ girar loco (mechanism).
◆ *vt* *to idle away* perder, desperdiciar; *to idle away the morning* perder la mañana.

idleness [-nis] *n* ociosidad *f* (leisure) ‖ holgazanería *f*, gandulería *f* (laziness) ‖ paro *m*, desocupación *f* (unemployment) ‖ inutilidad *f* (uselessness) ‖ futilidad *f* (futility).

idler [-ə*] *n* ocioso, sa; holgazán, ana; vago, ga; gandul (lazy person) ‖ TECH polea *f* loca (pulley) ‖ rueda *f* intermedia (wheel).

idler pulley [-ə'puli] *n* TECH polea *f* loca.

idler wheel [-əwi:l] *n* US TECH rueda *f* intermedia.

idly ['aidli] *adv* ociosamente (lazily) ‖ inútilmente (uselessly) ‖ distraídamente (absent-mindedly).

idol ['aidl] *n* ídolo *m*.

idolater [ai'dɔlətə*] *n* idólatra *f*.

idolatress [ai'dɔlətris] *n*, idólatra *f*.

idolatrous [ai'dɔlətrəs] *adj* idólatra (person) ‖ idolátrico, ca; *idolatrous cult* culto idolátrico.

idolatry [ai'dɔlətri] *n* idolatría *f*.

idolization [,aidəulai'zeiʃən] *n* idolatría *f*.

idolize ['aidəlaiz] *vt* idolatrar.

idolizer [-ə*] *n* idólatra *m* & *f*.

idyll; idyl ['idil] *n* idilio *m*.

idyllic [ai'dilik] *adj* idílico, ca.

idyllist ['aidilist] *n* autor *m* de idilios.

i.e. [ai'i:] *abbr of* [*id est*] es decir, o sea.

if [if] *conj* si; *if it rains we will stay at home* si llueve nos quedaremos en casa; *do you know if he's in?* ¿sabes si está en casa? ‖ si bien, aunque; *he is kind, if a bit too impulsive* es amable, aunque un poco impulsivo ‖ — *as if by chance* como por casualidad ‖ *he's tall if anything* es más bien alto ‖ *he is tired if anything* quizás esté cansado ‖ *if and when I like* si quiero y cuando quiera ‖ *if I were you* yo en tu lugar, yo que tú ‖ *if not* si no ‖ *if only to speak to him* aunque sea sólo para hablarle ‖ *if only we had known!* ¡si lo hubiésemos sabido!, ¡ojalá lo hubiésemos sabido! ‖ *I'll go tomorrow, if at all* iré mañana, si es que voy ‖ *I shouldn't wonder if it rains* no me extrañaría que lloviera ‖ *if so* si es así, de ser así.
◆ *n* condición *f* (condition) ‖ suposición *f*, hipótesis *f*, supuesto *m* (supposition) ‖ *ifs and buts* pegas *f*.

iffy ['ifi] *adj* FAM dudoso, sa.

igloo; US **iglu** ['iglu:] *n* iglú *m*.

Ignatius [ig'neiʃjəs] *pr n* Ignacio *m*.

igneous ['igniəs] *adj* ígneo, a; *igneous rock* roca ígnea.

ignis fatuus ['ignis'fætjuəs] *n* fuego *m* fatuo.
— OBSERV El plural de *ignis fatuus* es *ignes fatui*.

ignitable [ig'naitəbl] *adj* inflamable.

ignite [ig'nait] *vt* encender, prender fuego a.
◆ *vi* encenderse (to begin to burn).

igniter [ig'naitə*]; **ignitor** [ig'naitə*] *n* deflagrador *m*.

ignition [ig'niʃən] *n* ignición *f* (action) ‖ encendido *m* (in a car, a rocket) ‖ *ignition coil* bobina *f* de encendido.

ignition key [-ki:] *n* llave *f* de contacto.

ignition point [-pɔint] *n* punto *m* de combustión.

ignoble [ig'nəubl] *adj* innoble, vil.

ignominious [,ignəu'miniəs] *adj* ignominioso, sa.

ignominy ['ignəmini] *n* ignominia *f*.

ignoramus [,ignə'reiməs] *n* ignorante *m* & *f*, inculto, ta.

ignorance ['ignərəns] *n* ignorancia *f*; *ignorance of the law is no excuse* la ignorancia de la ley no exime su cumplimiento ‖ — *through ignorance* por ignorancia ‖ *to be in ignorance of* ignorar, desconocer, no saber.

ignorant ['ignərənt] *adj* ignorante ‖ *to be ignorant of* ignorar, no saber, desconocer.

ignore [ig'nɔ:'] *vt* no hacer caso de, hacer caso omiso de; *he ignored their warnings* no hizo caso de sus advertencias ‖ pasar por alto (to leave out) ‖ no hacer caso a (s.o.) ‖ JUR sobreseer.

Iguaçu Falls [,i:gwə'su: fɔ:ls] *pr n* GEOGR cataratas del Iguazú.

iguana [i'gwɑ:nə] *n* ZOOL iguana *f*.

iguanodon [i'gwɑ:nədɔn] *n* ZOOL iguanodonte *m*.

ikon ['aikən] *n* icono *m*.

ileac ['ili:ək]; **ileal** ['ili:əl] *adj* ANAT iliaco, ca; ilíaco, ca.

ileocecal ['iliəsi:kəl] *adj* ANAT ileocecal.

ileum ['ili:əm] *n* ANAT íleon *m*.

ileus ['ili:əs] *n* MED íleo *m*.

ilex ['aileks] *n* BOT encina *f* (holm oak) ‖ acebo *m* (holly).

iliac ['iliæk] *adj* ANAT iliaco, ca; ilíaco, ca.

Iliad ['iliəd] *n* Ilíada *f*.

ilium ['iliəm] *n* ANAT ilion *m*.
— OBSERV El plural de *ilium* es *ilia*.

ilk [ilk] *n* índole *f*, clase *f* (sort); *of that ilk* de esta índole.

I'll [ail] contracción of I will and I shall.

ill [il] *adj* enfermo, ma (sick); *seriously ill* enfermo de gravedad, gravemente enfermo ‖ malo, la (unfortunate); *ill news* malas noticias ‖ malo, la (causing harm); *ill turn* mala jugada; *ill repute* mala fama ‖ FIG enfermo, ma; *to make s.o. ill* poner enfermo a uno ‖ — *to be taken ill, to fall ill* caer enfermo, ponerse enfermo, enfermar ‖ *to feel ill* encontrarse mal, sentirse mal.
◆ *adv* mal (adversely) ‖ difícilmente ‖ — *ill at ease* molesto, ta (uncomfortable); inquieto, ta; intranquilo, la (anxious) ‖ *to be ill spoken of* tener mala fama ‖ *to take sth. ill* tomar algo a mal ‖ *we can ill afford the time* casi no tenemos tiempo ‖ *we can ill afford to refuse* no podemos permitirnos el lujo de negarnos.
◆ *n* mal *m*, desgracia *f*, infortunio *m* (misfortune) ‖ MED mal *m*.

ill-advised [-əd'waizd] *adj* malaconsejado, da; imprudente (person) ‖ poco atinado, da (action).

illation [i'leiʃən] *n* ilación *f*.
illative [i'leitiv] *adj* GRAMM ilativo, va.
ill-behaved ['ilbi'heivd] *adj* mal educado, da; de malos modales.
ill-boding ['il'bəudinŋ] *adj* de mal agüero.
ill-bred ['il'bred] *adj* mal educado, da.
ill-conditioned ['ilkən'diʃənd] *adj* en mal estado (thing) || desabrido, da (person).
ill-considered ['ilkən'sidəd] *adj* poco estudiado, da; poco meditado, da (not properly considered) || apresurado, da (hasty); *ill-considered measures* medidas apresuradas || imprudente (unwise).
ill-defined ['ildi'faind] *adj* mal definido, da.
ill-disposed ['ildis'pəuzd] *adj* mal dispuesto, ta.
illegal [i'li:gəl] *adj* ilegal.
illegality [ili'gæliti] *n* ilegalidad *f*.
illegibility [i,ledʒibiliti] *n* ilegibilidad *f*.
illegible [i'ledʒəbl] *adj* ilegible; *illegible signature* firma ilegible.
illegibly [i'ledʒəbli] *adv* de una manera ilegible.
illegitimacy [,ilidʒitiməasi] *n* ilegitimidad *f*.
illegitimate [,ili'dʒitimit] *adj* ilegítimo, ma (bastard); *illegitimate son* hijo ilegítimo || ilógico, ca (not logical) || ilegítimo, ma (contrary to law).
ill-equipped ['ili'kwipt] *adj* mal equipado, da || FIG mal preparado, da.
ill-fated ['il'feitid] *adj* desafortunado, da; desdichado, da (destined to have bad luck) || fatal; *an ill-fated encounter* un encuentro fatal.
ill-favoured; *US* **ill-favored** ['il'feivəd] *adj* feo, a; poco agraciado, da (ugly) || desagradable (unpleasant).
ill-founded ['il'faundid] *adj* infundado, da; sin fundamento.
ill-gotten ['il'gɔtn] *adj* mal adquirido, da; adquirido por medios ilícitos.
ill health ['il'helθ] *n* mala salud *f*.
ill humour; *US* **ill humor** ['il'hju:mə*] *n* mal genio *m*, malhumor *m*, mal humor *m*.
ill-humoured; *US* **ill-humored** [-d] *adj* malhumorado, da.
illiberal [i'libərəl] *adj* falto de liberalidad || intolerante.
illicit [i'lisit] *adj* ilícito, ta.
illicitness [-nis] *adj* ilicitud *f*.
illimitable [i'limitəbl] *adj* ilimitable || ilimitado, da; infinito, ta (having no limits).
ill-informed ['ilin'fɔ:md] *adj* mal informado, da.
Illinois [,ili'nɔi] *pr n* GEOGR Illinois.
illiteracy [i'litərəsi] *n* analfabetismo *m* || ignorancia *f*.
illiterate [i'litərit] *adj* analfabeto, ta (unable to read or write) || iletrado, da; inculto, ta (lacking culture) || ignorante.
◆ *n* analfabeto, ta.
ill luck ['il'lʌk] *n* mala suerte *f*, desgracia *f*.
ill-mannered ['il'mænəd] *n* maleducado, da; mal educado, da.
ill nature ['il'neitʃə*] *n* mal carácter *m* (unpleasant disposition) || malevolencia *f* (wickedness).
ill-natured [-d] *adj* de mal genio, malhumorado, da || malévolo, la (wicked).
illness ['ilnis] *n* enfermedad *f*; *to recover from a long illness* salir de una larga enfermedad.
illogical [i'lɔdʒikəl] *adj* ilógico, ca.
illogicality ['ilɔdʒi'kæliti] *n* ilogismo *m*, falta *f* de lógica.
ill-omened ['il'əumend] *adj* de mal agüero.
ill-pleased ['il'pli:zd] *adj* descontento, ta.
ill-starred ['il'stɑ:d] *adj* desafortunado, da; desgraciado, da; malhadado, da (person) || aciago, ga (day) || fatal (ill-fated).
ill-suited ['il'sju:təd] *adj* impropio, pia (not appropriate).
ill-tempered ['il'tempəd] *adj* de mal carácter, de mal genio (person) || malhumorado, da (remark, etc.).
ill-timed ['il'taimd] *adj* inoportuno, na; intempestivo, va.
ill-treat ['il'tri:t] *vt* maltratar.
ill-treatment [-mənt] *n* maltratamiento *m*, malos tratos *m pl*.
illuminance [i'ljuminəns] *n* PHYS iluminancia *f*.
illuminate [i'ljumineit]; **illumine** [i'ljumin] *vt* iluminar (to light up) || aclarar; *to illuminate a problem* aclarar un problema || iluminar (with colours, lights).
illuminated [i'lju:mineitid] *adj* iluminado, da || luminoso, sa.
illuminati [i,lu:mi'nɑ:ti] *pl n* iluminados *m*.
illuminating [i'ljumineitiŋ] *n* ⟶ **illumination.**
◆ *adj* de alumbrado; *illuminating gas* gas de alumbrado || luminoso, sa; *illuminating power* potencia luminosa || revelador, ra (remark, etc.) || instructivo, va; *illuminating book* libro instructivo.
illumination; illuminating [i'ljumineitiŋ] [i'ljumineiʃən] *n* iluminación *f*, alumbrado *m* (of buildings) || ARTS iluminación *f* || aclaración *f* (of a problem) || inspiración *f* || PHYS iluminación *f*, iluminancia *f*.
◆ *pl* luces *f*, iluminación *f sing*, iluminaciones *f*.
illuminator [i'ljumineitə*] *n* iluminador, ra.
illumine [i'ljumin] *vt* ⟶ **illuminate.**
illuminism [-izəm] *n* iluminismo *m*.
illuminist [-ist] *n* iluminado, da.
ill-use ['il'ju:z] *vt* maltratar.
illusion [i'lu:ʒən] *n* ilusión *f*; *optical illusion* ilusión óptica.
illusionary [-əri] *adj* ilusorio, ria.
illusionism [i'lu:ʒənizəm] *n* ilusionismo *m*.
illusionist [i'lu:ʒənist] *n* ilusionista *m* & *f*.
illusive [i'lu:siv] *adj* ilusorio, ria.
illusory [i'lu:səri] *adj* ilusorio, ria.
illustrate [i'ləstreit] *vt* ilustrar (a book) || FIG ilustrar, aclarar (to clarify).
illustration [,iləs'treiʃən] *n* ilustración *f* (of a book) || FIG aclaración *f* (clearing up) | ilustración *f*, ejemplo *m* (instance).
illustrative [i'ləstreitiv] *adj* ilustrativo, va; aclaratorio, ria.
illustrator [i'ləstreitə*] *n* ilustrador, ra.
illustrious [i'lʌstriəs] *adj* ilustre.
ill will ['il'wil] *n* mala voluntad *f* (unwillingness) || rencor *m* (grudge).
ILO *abbr of [International Labour Organization]* OIT, Organización Internacional del Trabajo.
I'm [aim] contracción of I am.
image ['imidʒ] *n* imagen *f* || FIG reputación *f*, fama *f* (reputation) || — *he is the living* o *spitting image of his father* es el vivo retrato de su padre || *image maker* imaginero *m* || *in one's own image* a su imagen || *mirror image* reflejo exacto || *poetic images* imágenes poéticas || FIG *to have a bad image of s.o.* tener mal concepto de alguien.
image ['imidʒ] *vt* reflejar (to reflect) || imaginar (to imagine) || representar (to represent) || simbolizar (to symbolize).
imagery ['imidʒəri] *n* imágenes *f pl* (figurative language) || imaginaciones *f pl* (things one imagines) || REL imágenes *f pl* (images) | imaginería *f* (art).
imaginable [i'mædʒinəbl] *adj* imaginable || *the fastest imaginable car* el coche más veloz que uno se puede imaginar.
imaginary [i'mædʒinəri] *adj* imaginario, ria.
imagination [i'mædʒi'neiʃən] *n* imaginación *f*; *don't let your imagination run away with you!* ¡no se deje llevar por la imaginación! || imaginación *f*, imaginativa *f*, inventiva *f* (power).
imaginative [i'mædʒinətiv] *adj* imaginativo, va; *imaginative power* facultad imaginativa.
imagine [i'mædʒin] *vt* imaginar (to conceive, to invent) || figurarse, imaginarse, suponer (to suppose) || — *don't imagine that...* no te vayas a imaginar que... || *imagine that!, just imagine!* ¡imagínate!, ¡fíjate! || *imagine that you are president* imagínate que eres presidente.
imago [i'meigəu] *n* PHIL imagen *f*.
— OBSERV El plural de la palabra inglesa *imago* es *imagines* o *imagos*.
imam; imaum [i'mɑ:m] *n* REL imán *m*.
imamate [i'mɑ:meit] *n* REL imanato *m*.
imbalance [im'bæləns] *n* falta *f* de equilibrio, desequilibrio *m*.
imbecile ['imbisi:l] *adj/n* imbécil.
imbecility [,imbi'siliti] *n* imbecilidad *f*.
imbed [im'bed] *vt* empotrar, encajar.
imbibe [im'baib] *vt* embeber, absorber (to take in liquid) || aspirar (air) || FIG impregnarse de, embeberse de, empaparse de *or* en (ideas, etc.) | beber (to drink).
◆ *vi* beber.
imbibing [-iŋ] *n* imbibición *f*, absorción *f*.
imbricate ['imbrikeit] *vt* imbricar, traslapar.
◆ *vi* superponerse, traslaparse.
imbrication [imbri'keiʃən] *n* imbricación *f*, superposición *f*.
imbroglio [im'brəuliəu] *n* embrollo *m*, lío *m*.
imbrue [im'bru:] *vt* bañar; *to imbrue sth. in blood* bañar algo en sangre.
imbrute [im'bru:t] *vt* embrutecer.
◆ *vi* embrutecerse.
imbue [im'bju:] *vt* empapar (*with* en) (with a liquid) || imbuir (*with* de) (with emotions, etc.).
IMF *abbr of [International Monetary Fund]* FMI, Fondo Monetario Internacional.
imitable ['imitəbl] *adj* imitable.
imitate ['imiteit] *vt* imitar.
imitating [-iŋ] *adj* imitador, ra.
imitation [,imi'teiʃən] *n* imitación *f* || — *beware of imitations* desconfíe de las imitaciones || *in imitation of* a imitación de.
◆ *adj* de imitación, artificial, imitación; *imitation leather* cuero artificial || *imitation jewelry* joyas *f pl* de imitación, bisutería *f*.
imitative ['imitətiv] *adj* imitativo, va.
imitator ['imiteitə*] *n* imitador, ra.
immaculate [i'mækjulit] *adj* inmaculado, da; limpio, pia (very clear) || perfecto, ta (perfect) || REL inmaculado, da; purísimo, ma || REL *the Immaculate Conception* la Inmaculada Concepción.
immanence; immanency ['imənəns] *n* inmanencia *f*.
immanent ['imənənt] *adj* inmanente.
immaterial [,imə'tiəriəl] *adj* inmaterial (having no substance) || indiferente; *it's immaterial to me whether you go or stay* me es indiferente que te vayas o te quedes || *that's immaterial* no importa.

immaterialism [ˌiməˈtiəriəlizəm] *n* PHIL inmaterialismo *m*.

immateriality [ˈiməˌtiəriˈæliti] *n* inmaterialidad *f* ‖ insignificancia *f* (unimportance).

immature [ˌiməˈtjuə*] *adj* BOT inmaduro, ra; no maduro, ra; verde ‖ inmaduro, ra (person) ‖ juvenil (childish).

immaturity [ˌiməˈtjuəriti] *n* inmadurez *f*, falta *f* de madurez.

immeasurability [iˈmeʒərəˈbiliti] *n* inconmensurabilidad *f*.

immediacy [iˈmi:djəsi] *n* inmediación *f*, proximidad *f* (proximity) ‖ urgencia *f* (urgency); *the immediacy of our needs* la urgencia de nuestras necesidades ‖ carácter *m* inminente (of a danger).

immediate [iˈmi:djət] *adj* inmediato, ta; *immediate response* respuesta inmediata ‖ PHIL intuitivo, va ‖ cercano, na; próximo, ma (near); *immediate future* futuro próximo ‖ directo, ta (directly related) ‖ urgente ‖ — *immediate danger* peligro inminente ‖ *immediate need* primera necesidad ‖ *immediate neighbourhood* inmediaciones *f pl* ‖ *to take immediate action* actuar inmediatamente.

immediately [-li] *adv* inmediatamente, en seguida (at once) ‖ directamente (directly) ‖ sin demora, sin retraso (without delay).
◆ *prep* tan pronto como, en cuanto.

immedicable [iˈmedikəbl] *adj* irremediable, incurable.

immemorial [ˌimiˈmɔ:riəl] *adj* inmemorial ‖ *from time immemorial* desde tiempo inmemorial.

immense [iˈmens] *adj* inmenso, sa; enorme ‖ FAM estupendo, da (very good).

immensely [-li] *adv* enormemente ‖ muy (very) ‖ FAM estupendamente.

immensity [-iti] *n* inmensidad *f* ‖ FIG cosa *f* enorme.

immensurable [-jə:rəbl] *adj* inmensurable.

immerge [iˈmə:dʒ]; **immerse** [iˈmə:s] *vt* sumergir, hundir (to dip); *to immerse one's feet in water* sumergir los pies en el agua ‖ REL bautizar por inmersión ‖ FIG enfrascar, sumir; *to immerse o.s. in work* enfrascarse en el trabajo | sumir, absorber; *he was immersed in thought* estaba absorto en sus pensamientos.

immersion [iˈmə:ʃən] *n* inmersión *f* ‖ *immersion heater* calentador *m* de inmersión.

immesh [iˈmeʃ] *vt* enredar.

immethodical [imiˈθɔdikəl] *adj* sin método.

immigrant [ˈimigrənt] *adj/n* inmigrante, inmigrado, da.

immigrate [ˈimigreit] *vi* inmigrar.

immigration [ˌimiˈgreiʃən] *n* inmigración *f*.

immigratory [ˈimigreitəri] *adj* inmigratorio, ria.

imminence [ˈiminəns]; **imminency** [-i] *n* inminencia *f*.

imminent [ˈiminənt] *adj* inminente.

immitigable [iˈmitigəbəl] *adj* que no se puede mitigar.

immix [iˈmiks] *vt* mezclar.

immixture [iˈmikstʃə] *n* mezcla *f* (mixture) ‖ FIG intromisión *f* (meddling).

immobile [iˈməubail] *adj* inmóvil (motionless) ‖ fijo, ja; inmutable (not changing).

immobility [ˌiməuˈbiliti] *n* inmovilidad *f* ‖ inmutabilidad *f*.

immobilization [iˌməubilaiˈzeiʃən] *n* inmovilización *f*.

immobilize [iˈməubilaiz] *vt* inmovilizar.

immoderate [iˈmɔdərit] *adj* inmoderado, da (beyond the proper limits) ‖ desmedido, da; desmesurado, da; excesivo, va (unreasonably large) ‖ descomunal; *immoderate appetite* apetito descomunal.

immoderation [ˈiˌmɔdəˈreiʃən] *n* falta *f* de moderación, exceso *m*.

immodest [iˈmɔdist] *adj* inmodesto, ta (not humble) ‖ indecente, impúdico, ca (indecent) ‖ impudente, desvergonzado, da (bold).

immodesty [iˈmɔdisti] *n* inmodestia *f* (lack of modesty) ‖ impudicia *f*, impudor *m* (indecency) ‖ impudencia *f*, desvergüenza *f* (boldness).

immolate [ˈməuleit] *vt* inmolar.

immolation [ˌiməuˈleiʃən] *n* inmolación *f*.

immolator [ˈiməuleitə*] *n* inmolador, ra.

immoral [iˈmɔrəl] *adj* inmoral ‖ disoluto, ta (life) ‖ vicioso, sa (vicious).

immorality [iməˈræliti] *n* inmoralidad *f*.

immortal [iˈmɔ:t] *adj* inmortal ‖ FIG imperecedero, ra (memories, etc.).
◆ *n* inmortal *m* & *f*.

immortality [ˌimɔ:ˈtæliti] *n* inmortalidad *f*.

immortalize [iˈmɔ:təlaiz] *vt* inmortalizar.

immortelle [ˌimɔ:ˈtel] *n* BOT siempreviva *f*.

immovability [iˌmu:vəˈbiliti] *n* inmovilidad *f* (immobility) ‖ inmutabilidad *f*, impasibilidad *f* (impassibility) ‖ inflexibilidad *f* (firmness) ‖ inamovilidad *f* (of a post).

immovable [iˈmu:vəbl] *adj* inmóvil ‖ impasible, inmutable (unemotional) ‖ inflexible (steadfast) ‖ inamovible (post) ‖ JUR inmueble ‖ REL *immovable feast* fiesta fija.
◆ *n* JUR bienes *m pl* raíces *or* inmuebles.

immune [iˈmju:n] *adj* inmune (*to* a) ‖ FIG exento, ta (*from* de) (taxes).

immunity [iˈmju:niti] *n* inmunidad *f* (*to* contra) ‖ JUR exención *f* (*from* de) ‖ *diplomatic, parliamentary immunity* inmunidad diplomática, parlamentaria.

immunization [ˌimju:naiˈzeiʃən] *n* inmunización *f*.

immunize [ˈimju:naiz] *vt* inmunizar.

immunogenic [ˌimju:nəuˈdʒenik] *adj* inmunizador, ra.

immunology [ˌimju:ˈnɔlədʒi] *n* inmunología *f*.

immure [iˈmjuə*] *vt* emparedar (to shut up within walls) ‖ encerrar (to imprison).

immurement [-mənt] *n* emparedamiento *m*.

immutability [iˌmju:təˈbiliti] *n* inmutabilidad *f*.

immutable [iˈmju:təbl] *adj* inmutable.

imp [imp] *n* diablillo *m*, duendecillo *m*, trasgo *m* (young devil) ‖ FAM pícaro, ra (mischievous person).

impact [ˈimpækt] *n* impacto *m*, choque *m* (shock) ‖ colisión *f*, choque *m* (collision) ‖ FIG impacto *m*, efecto *m* (effect) | repercusiones *f pl*, consecuencias *f pl* (consequences).

impact [imˈpækt] *vt* incrustar.

impair [imˈpɛə*] *vt* dañar, perjudicar, deteriorar.

impairment [-mənt] *n* deterioro *m*, daño *m*.

impale; US **empale** [imˈpeil] *vt* empalar (as punishment) ‖ atravesar (with a sword, etc.).

impalement [-mənt] *n* empalamiento *m*.

impalpability [imˌpælpəˈbiliti] *n* impalpabilidad *f*.

impalpable [imˈpælpəbl] *adj* impalpable ‖ FIG intangible, impalpable.

imparadise [imˈpærədaiz] *vt* llevar al colmo de la felicidad, colmar de felicidad (a person) ‖ convertir en paraíso (a place).

imparity [imˈpæriti] *n* disparidad *f*.

impark [imˈpɑ:k] *vt* acorralar, encerrar (animals) ‖ cercar, vallar (land).

impart [imˈpɑ:t] *vt* impartir, dar (to give) ‖ conceder (to grant) ‖ comunicar (to make known).

impartial [imˈpɑ:ʃəl] *adj* imparcial.

impartiality [ˈimˌpɑ:ʃiˈæliti] *n* imparcialidad *f*.

impartible [imˈpɑ:təbl] *adj* indivisible (estate).

impartment [imˈpɑ:tmənt] *n* comunicación *f*, transmisión *f* (of news).

impassable [imˈpɑ:səbl] *adj* intransitable (street, corridor, roads) ‖ infranqueable (barrier).

impasse [æmˈpɑ:s] *n* callejón *m* sin salida (street) ‖ FIG callejón *m* sin salida, atolladero *m*; *talks have reached an impasse* las negociaciones están en un atolladero.

impassibility [ˈimˌpɑ:siˈbiliti] *n* impasibilidad *f*.

impassible [imˈpæsibl] *adj* impasible.

impassion [imˈpæʃən] *vt* apasionar.

impassioned [-d] *adj* apasionado, da.

impassive [imˈpæsiv] *adj* impasible (not showing emotion) ‖ insensible.

impassiveness [-nis]; **impassivity** [-iti] *n* impasibilidad *f* ‖ insensibilidad *f*.

impaste [imˈpeist] *vt* ARTS empastar ‖ convertir en pasta.

impasto [imˈpɑ:stəu] *n* empaste *m*.

impatience [imˈpeiʃəns] *n* impaciencia *f*.

impatient [imˈpeiʃənt] *adj* impaciente ‖ — *to be impatient of* no soportar (to be unable to endure) ‖ *to be impatient to do sth.* tener muchos deseos de hacer algo, estar impaciente por hacer algo ‖ *to get impatient* perder la paciencia ‖ *to make s.o. impatient* impacientar a uno.

impavid [imˈpævid] *adj* impávido, da (fearless).

impawn [imˈpɔ:n] *vt* empeñar (to put in pawn) ‖ FIG comprometer, arriesgar (to risk).

impeach [imˈpi:tʃ] *vt* JUR acusar (to charge with a crime) | encausar, enjuiciar (to prosecute) | recusar (evidence, a witness) ‖ poner en tela de juicio (to question); *to impeach the veracity of a statement* poner en tela de juicio la veracidad de una declaración ‖ censurar (s.o.'s conduct).

impeachable [-əbl] *adj* JUR acusable (chargeable) | recusable (evidence, a witness) ‖ controvertible, discutible (probity, veracity) ‖ censurable (conduct).

impeacher [-ə*] *n* denunciador, ra.

impeachment [-mənt] *n* JUR acusación *f* (accusation) | enjuiciamiento *m* (prosecution) | recusación *f* (of evidence, a witness) ‖ puesta *f* en tela de juicio (of s.o.'s veracity) ‖ censura *f* (of s.o.'s conduct).

impeccability [imˌpekəˈbiliti] *n* impecabilidad *f*.

impeccable [imˈpekəbl] *adj* impecable.

impecunious [ˌimpiˈkju:njəs] *adj* falto de dinero, sin dinero, pobre, indigente.

impedance [imˈpi:dəns] *n* ELECTR impedancia *f*.

impede [imˈpi:d] *vt* estorbar (to hinder); *to impede the traffic* estorbar el tráfico ‖ *if you want to go on the stage I shall not impede you* si quieres ser actor no te lo voy a impedir.

impediment [imˈpedimənt] *n* estorbo *m* (hindrance) ‖ obstáculo *m*, impedimento *m* (obstacle) ‖ defecto *m* del habla (speech defect) ‖ JUR impedimento *m*; *diriment impediment* impedimento dirimente.

impedimenta [imˌpediˈmentə] *pl n* MIL impedimenta *f sing* ‖ FAM equipaje *m sing*.

impel [im'pel] *vt* impeler, impulsar (to drive forward) ‖ empujar (to push) ‖ mover (to move) ‖ mover, incitar, inducir (to urge); *what impelled him to do such a thing?* ¿qué le incitó a hacer tal cosa? ‖ obligar (to compel); *I feel impelled to do it* me veo obligado a hacerlo.

impellent [-ənt] *adj* impelente.
◆ *n* motor *m* ‖ fuerza *f* impelente.

impeller [-ə*] *n* TECH rueda *f* motriz (wheel) | rotor *m* ‖ FIG instigador, ra.

impelling [-iŋ] *adj* impelente; *impelling force* fuerza impelente.

impend [im'pend] *vi* ser inminente, cernerse.

impendence [im'pendəns] *n* inminencia *f*.

impendent [im'pendənt]; **impending** [im'pendiŋ] *adj* inminente (imminent); *an impending disaster* un desastre inminente ‖ próximo, ma (in the near future).

impenetrability [im'penitrə'biliti] *n* impenetrabilidad *f*.

impenetrable [im'penitrəbl] *adj* impenetrable.

impenitence [im'penitəns]; **impenitency** [-i] *n* impenitencia *f*.

impenitent [im'penitənt] *adj* impenitente.

imperative [im'perətiv] *adj* imperioso, sa (urgent); *imperative need* necesidad imperiosa ‖ imprescindible, indispensable (necessary) ‖ perentorio, ria; imperioso, sa (peremptory) ‖ GRAMM imperativo, va; *the imperative mood* el modo imperativo.
◆ *n* GRAMM imperativo *m*.

imperatorial [im'perə'tɔːriəl] *adj* imperatorio, ria.

imperceptibility ['impə,septə'biliti] *n* imperceptibilidad *f*.

imperceptible [,impə'septəbl] *adj* imperceptible.

imperfect [im'pəːfikt] *adj* imperfecto, ta; defectuoso, sa (defective) ‖ incompleto, ta (incomplete) ‖ GRAMM imperfecto.
◆ *n* GRAMM imperfecto *m*, pretérito *m* imperfecto.

imperfection [,impə'fekʃən] *n* imperfección *f* ‖ imperfección *f*, defecto *m* (defect).

imperforate [im'pəːfərit] *adj* sin perforaciones, sin dentado (stamp).

imperial [im'piəriəl] *adj* imperial; *imperial crown* corona imperial ‖ FIG señorial.
◆ *n* perilla *f* (beard) ‖ imperial *f* (top deck of a coach) ‖ *imperial gallon* galón inglés [4,543 litros].

imperialism [-izəm] *n* imperialismo *m*.

imperialist [-ist] *adj/n* imperialista.

imperialistic [impiəriə'listik] *adj* imperialista.

imperil [im'peril] *vt* arriesgar, poner en peligro.

imperious [im'piəriəs] *adj* imperioso, sa (need) ‖ autoritario, ria (person).

imperiousness [-nis] *n* autoridad *f* ‖ arrogancia *f* ‖ urgencia *f*.

imperishable [im'periʃəbl] *adj* imperecedero, ra.

imperium [im'piəriəm] *n* imperio *m*, poder *m* absoluto (authority).

impermanence [im'pəːmənəns] *n* inestabilidad *f* ‖ temporalidad *f*.

impermanent [im'pəːmənənt] *adj* inestable (unstable) ‖ temporal (temporary).

impermeability [im,pəːmjə'biliti] *n* impermeabilidad *f*.

impermeable [im'pəːmjəbl] *adj* impermeable (*to* a).

impermissible [impəː'misibl] *adj* inadmisible, intolerable.

impersonal [im'pəːsnl] *adj* impersonal.

impersonality [im,pəːsə'næliti] *n* impersonalidad *f*.

impersonate [im'pəːsəneit] *vt* hacerse pasar por (to pretend to be s.o. else) ‖ imitar (to imitate in order to entertain) ‖ representar *or* interpretar el papel de (to act the part of) ‖ FIG encarnar (to embody) | personificar (to personify).

impersonation [im'pəːsə'neiʃən] *n* imitación *f* (as entertainment) ‖ interpretación *f* (of a part) ‖ FIG encarnación *f* (embodiment) | personificación *f* (personification).

impersonator [im'pəːsəneitə*] *n* imitador, ra (entertainer) ‖ intérprete *m* & *f* (actor).

impertinence [im'pəːtinəns] *n* impertinencia *f* (rudeness, rude act or remark) ‖ impertinencia *f*, improcedencia *f* (irrelevance) ‖ inoportunidad *f* (untimeliness) ‖ *a piece of impertinence* una impertinencia.

impertinent [im'pəːtinənt] *adj* impertinente (impudent); *he was impertinent to me* fue impertinente conmigo ‖ impertinente, improcedente (irrelevant) ‖ fuera de lugar, inoportuno, na (inappropriate).

impertinently [-li] *adv* con impertinencia.

imperturbability ['impə,təːbə'biliti] *adj* imperturbabilidad *f*.

imperturbable [,impə'təːbəbl] *adj* imperturbable, impertérrito, ta.

impervious [im'pəːvjəs] *adj* insensible (insensitive); *impervious to pain* insensible al dolor; *impervious to criticism* insensible a las críticas ‖ impenetrable (impenetrable) ‖ *impervious to water* impermeable ‖ *to be impervious to reason* no atender a razones.

imperviousness [-nis] *n* impenetrabilidad *f* ‖ insensibilidad *f* (insensitivity); *his imperviousness to criticism* su insensibilidad a las críticas ‖ TECH impermeabilidad *f*.

impetigo [,impi'taigəu] *n* MED impétigo *m*.

impetrate ['impətreit] *vt* impetrar; *to impetrate divine protection* impetrar la protección divina.

impetration [impə'treiʃən] *n* impetración *f*.

impetrating ['impətreitiŋ] *adj* impetrador, ra; impetrante.

impetuosity [im,petju'ɔsiti] *n* impetuosidad *f*.

impetuous [im'petjuəs] *adj* impetuoso, sa.

impetuousness [-nis] *n* impetuosidad *f*.

impetus ['impitəs] *n* ímpetu *m* (force) ‖ FIG impulso *m*; *the new treaty will give impetus to trade between the two countries* el nuevo tratado dará un impulso al comercio entre los dos países | estímulo *m*, incentivo *m* (incentive).

impiety [im'paiəti] *n* impiedad *f*.

impinge [im'pindʒ] *vi* *to impinge on* o *against* tropezar con, chocar con *or* contra ‖ *to impinge on* o *upon* usurpar (to encroach upon), impresionar (to make an impression).

impingement [-mənt] *n* choque *m* (collision) ‖ impresión *f* (impression) ‖ intrusión *f*, usurpación *f* (encroachment).

impious ['impiəs] *adj* impío, a.

impish ['impiʃ] *adj* travieso, sa; pícaro, ra.

implacability [im'plækə'biliti] *n* implacabilidad *f*.

implacable [im'plækəbl] *adj* implacable.

implant [im'plɑːnt] *n* MED injerto *m*.

implant [im'plɑːnt] *vt* implantar (to plant deeply) ‖ inculcar (to instil firmly in the mind) ‖ MED injertar, implantar.

implantation [,implɑː'nteiʃən] *n* implantación *f*.

implausible [im'plɔːzəbl] *adj* inverosímil.

impledge [im'pledʒ] *vt* empeñar.

implement ['implimənt] *n* herramienta *f* (tool) ‖ utensilio *m* (utensil) ‖ instrumento *m* (instrument) ‖ — *farm implements* aperos *m* de labranza ‖ *writing implements* artículos *m* *or* objetos *m* de escritorio.

implement ['implimənt] *vt* llevar a cabo (to carry out) ‖ realizar, ejecutar (to execute) ‖ cumplir (a promise) ‖ aplicar (a law) ‖ poner en práctica *or* en ejecución (decisions, measures).

implementation [,implimen'teiʃən] *n* realización *f*, ejecución *f* (execution) ‖ aplicación *f* (of a law) ‖ puesta *f* en práctica *or* en ejecución (of decisions, measures).

implicate ['implikeit] *vt* implicar (to imply) ‖ comprometer, implicar, complicar (to involve); *he was implicated in the scandal* fue comprometido en el escándalo.

implication [,impli'keiʃən] *n* implicación *f* (thing implied) ‖ complicidad *f*, implicación *f* (in a crime, etc.) ‖ repercusión *f*, consecuencia *f*, incidencia *f*; *one cannot tell what the implications of his action will be* no se puede decir cuáles serán las consecuencias de su acción ‖ *by implication* por lo tanto.

implicative [im'plikətiv]; **implicatory** [im-pli'keitəri] *adj* implicatorio, ria.

implicit [im'plisit] *adj* implícito, ta (understood though not stated) ‖ absoluto, ta (absolute).

implied [im'plaid] *adj* implícito, ta.

implore [im'plɔː*] *vt* suplicar; *to implore s.o. to do sth.* suplicar a uno que haga algo ‖ implorar; *to implore forgiveness* implorar perdón ‖ *I implore you!* ¡se lo suplico!

imploring [-riŋ] *adj* suplicante.

imploringly [-riŋli] *adv* de modo suplicante.

implosive [im'pləusiv] *adj* GRAMM implosivo, va.

imply [im'plai] *vt* implicar, suponer (to involve); *this implies a great effort from us* esto supone un gran esfuerzo por nuestra parte ‖ presuponer, suponer (to presuppose) ‖ insinuar (to hint) ‖ dar a entender; *without actually saying so he implied that...* sin llegar a decirlo dio a entender que... ‖ significar, querer decir (to mean).

impolicy [im'pɔlisi] *n* política *f* poco hábil, mala política *f*, imprudencia *f*.

impolite [,impə'lait] *adj* mal educado, da; descortés.

impolitely ['-i] *adj* con descortesía, descortesmente.

impoliteness [-nis] *n* mala educación *f*, descortesía *f*.

impolitic [im'pɔlitik] *adj* impolítico, ca; imprudente.

imponderability [im,pɔndərə'biliti] *n* imponderabilidad *f*.

imponderable [im'pɔndərəbl] *adj* imponderable.
◆ *n* imponderable *m*.

import ['impɔːt] *n* COMM artículo *m* importado, mercancía *f* importada (sth. imported) | importación *f*; *a rise in imports* un aumento de las importaciones ‖ significado *m*, sentido *m* (meaning) ‖ importancia *f* (importance) ‖ — COMM *import duty* derechos *m pl* de importación ‖ *import licence* permiso *m or* licencia *f* de importación ‖ *import trade* comercio *m* de importación.

import [im'pɔːt] *vt* importar (goods); *we import Spanish oranges into our country* importa-

mos naranjas españolas en nuestro país ‖ FIG introducir (ideas) | implicar (to imply) | significar, querer decir (to mean).
◆ *vi* importar, tener importancia (to matter).

importable [-əbl] *adj* COMM importable.

importance [-əns] *n* importancia *f* ‖ — *of importance* importante ‖ *of the highest importance, of the first importance* de mucha importancia, primordial ‖ FIG *she is full of her own importance* se da mucho tono ‖ *to be of importance* tener importancia, ser importante.

important [-ənt] *adj* importante ‖ engreído, da (conceited) ‖ — *it's not important* no importa, no tiene importancia ‖ *the important thing is...* lo importante es... ‖ *to try and look important* darse mucho tono.

importantly [-əntli] *adv* dándose mucho tono (to speak).

importation [ˌimpɔːˈteiʃən] *n* importación *f*.

importer [imˈpɔːtə*] *n* importador, ra.

importing [imˈpɔːtiŋ] *adj* importador, ra; *importing country* país importador.

importunate [imˈpɔːtjunit]; **importune** [imˈpɔːtjuːn] *adj* importuno, na (annoyingly persistent) ‖ molesto, ta; pesado, da (bothersome).

importune [imˈpɔːtjuːn] *vt* importunar (to annoy) ‖ molestar (to bother) ‖ hacer proposiciones deshonestas (said of a prostitute).

importunity [ˌimpɔːˈtjuːniti] *n* importunidad *f*.

impose [imˈpəuz] *vt/vi* imponer (conditions, a doctrine, etc.); *to impose one's ideas on s.o.* imponer las ideas propias a otro ‖ COMM gravar con (a tax) ‖ REL & PRINT imponer ‖ — *to impose on* o *upon* engañar a (to cheat), abusar de, aprovecharse de (to take advantage of) ‖ *to impose o.s.* imponerse.

imposing [-iŋ] *adj* imponente, impresionante ‖ PRINT *imposing table* platina *f*.

imposition [ˌimpəˈziʃən] *n* imposición *f*; *the imposition of certain conditions* la imposición de ciertas condiciones ‖ impuesto *m*, gravamen *m* (tax) ‖ abuso *m*; *it is an imposition to ask him for help* es un abuso pedirle ayuda ‖ castigo *m* (at school) ‖ PRINT imposición *f* ‖ FAM engaño *m* (deception) ‖ — REL *imposition of hands* imposición de manos ‖ *would it be too much of an imposition to...?* le resultaría muy molesto...?

impossibility [imˈpɔsəˈbiliti] *n* imposibilidad *f* ‖ cosa *f* imposible, imposible *m*; *to ask for impossibilities* pedir imposibles.

impossible [imˈpɔsəbl] *adj* imposible; *an impossible task* una tarea imposible; *it is impossible for me to do it* me es imposible hacerlo ‖ inaceptable (unacceptable) ‖ insoportable, inaguantable (unbearable); *he's an impossible person!* ¡es una persona inaguantable! ‖ intratable (difficult to get on with) ‖ FIG ridículo, la; *an impossible hat* un sombrero ridículo ‖ — *it's not impossible that...* es posible que... ‖ *lack of ammunition made attack impossible* la falta de municiones imposibilitó el ataque ‖ *to do the impossible* hacer lo imposible ‖ *your decision makes it impossible for me to go* su decisión me quita la posibilidad de ir, su decisión impide que vaya.

impossibly [-i] *adv* imposiblemente ‖ — *it is impossibly expensive* es carísimo, es de lo más caro ‖ *not impossibly* quizás.

impost [ˈimpəust] *n* COMM impuesto *m* (tax) | derecho *m* de aduana (customs duty) ‖ ARCH imposta *f* ‖ SP handicap *m*.

impostor [imˈpɔstə*] *n* impostor, ra.

imposture [imˈpɔstʃə*] *n* impostura *f*, engaño *m*.

impotence [ˈimpətəns]; **impotency** [-i] *n* impotencia *f*.

impotent [ˈimpətənt] *adj* impotente.

impound [imˈpaund] *vt* JUR confiscar, embargar (goods) ‖ meter en la perrera (dogs) ‖ poner en el depósito (cars) ‖ encerrar (to shut up) ‖ US embalsar (water).

impoverish [imˈpɔvəriʃ] *vt* empobrecer (people) ‖ agotar (land).

impoverishment [-mənt] *n* empobrecimiento *m* ‖ AGR agotamiento *m*.

impracticability [imˌpræktikəˈbiliti] *n* impracticabilidad *f*, imposibilidad *f* ‖ cosa *f* impracticable *or* imposible.

impracticable [imˈpræktikəbl] *adj* impracticable, irrealizable, imposible de realizar (plan) ‖ intransitable (road) ‖ intratable (person).

impractical [imˈpræktikəl] *adj* US poco práctico, ca (person, idea, etc.).

imprecate [ˈimprikeit] *vt* imprecar (evil) ‖ echar (curses) ‖ maldecir (to curse).

imprecation [ˌimpriˈkeiʃən] *n* imprecación *f*.

imprecatory [ˈimprikeitəri] *adj* imprecatorio, ria.

imprecise [impriˈsais] *adj* impreciso, sa.

imprecision [impriˈsiʒən] *n* imprecisión *f*.

impregnable [imˈpregnəbl] *adj* inexpugnable (castle, fortification, etc.) ‖ invulnerable (position) ‖ impregnable (that can be impregnated) ‖ FIG inquebrantable (belief).

impregnate [imˈpregnit] *adj* embarazada, preñada (woman) ‖ FIG impregnado, da.

impregnate [ˈimpregneit] *vt* BIOL fecundar ‖ impregnar, empapar (to saturate) ‖ FIG impregnar (to imbue).

impregnation [ˌimpregˈneiʃən] *n* impregnación *f* ‖ BIOL fecundación *f*.

impresario [ˌimpreˈsɑːriəu] *n* THEATR empresario *m*.

imprescriptibility [ˌimpriskriptiˈbiliti] *n* imprescriptibilidad *f*.

imprescriptible [ˌimprisˈkriptəbl] *adj* imprescriptible.

impress [ˈimpres] *n* impresión *f* ‖ sello *m*; *the printer's impress* el sello del impresor ‖ FIG marca *f*, sello *m* (distinguish mark) | huella *f*, impresión *f* (an effect of the mind).

impress [imˈpres] *vt* imprimir (to press a mark on sth.) ‖ estampar (a design, signature, etc.) ‖ sellar (to seal) ‖ imprimir (to print) ‖ grabar (upon s.o.'s mind) ‖ FIG convencer de; *we tried to impress on him the importance of his work* intentamos convencerle de la importancia de su trabajo | inculcar; *to impress an idea on s.o.* inculcar una idea a alguien ‖ impresionar; *he tried to impress me* trató de impresionarme; *he is not easily impressed* no se deja impresionar fácilmente ‖ MIL requisar ‖ — *he impressed me favourably* me hizo *or* me causó buena impresión, me impresionó favorablemente ‖ *how did it impress you?* ¿qué impresión le produjo? ‖ *the incident impressed itself upon my mind* el incidente se me quedó grabado en la memoria ‖ *the story deeply impressed us* el relato nos causó una gran impresión, el relato nos impresionó mucho.
◆ *vi* hacer *or* causar (buena) impresión.

impressible [imˈpresəbl] *adj* imprimible, estampable (capable of being impressed) ‖ impresionable (impressionable).

impression [imˈpreʃən] *n* impresión *f* (an impressing or being impressed) ‖ señal *f*, huella *f*, marca *f* (mark) ‖ PRINT ejemplar *m* (copy made from type) | tirada *f* (group of copies) | impresión *f* (printing) ‖ molde *m* (in dentistry) ‖ FIG impresión *f*; *the film left me with an impression of sadness* la película me dejó una impresión de tristeza; *to have the impression that...* tener la impresión de que...; *to make a bad impression* causar mala impresión ‖ — *to be under the impression that...* tener la impresión de que... ‖ *to make an impression* impresionar ‖ *to make an impression on* o *upon* impresionar a ‖ *your words make no impression on me* tus palabras no me hacen el menor efecto *or* ningún efecto.

impressionability [imˌpreʃnəˈbiliti] *n* impresionabilidad *f*.

impressionable [imˈpreʃnəbl] *adj* impresionable.

impressionism [imˈpreʃnizəm] *n* ARTS impresionismo *m*.

impressionist [imˈpreʃnist] *adj/n* impresionista.

impressionistic [imˌpreʃəˈnistik] *adj* impresionista.

impressive [imˈpresiv] *adj* impresionante.

impressively [-li] *adv* de forma *or* de modo impresionante.

impressiveness [-nis] *n* carácter *m* impresionante, lo impresionante.

impressment [imˈpresmənt] *n* requisa *f*, requisición *f*.

imprest [ˈimprest] *n* préstamo *m*, anticipo *m*.

imprimatur [ˌimpriˈmeitə*] *n* imprimátur *m*.

imprint [ˈimprint] *n* impresión *f*, marca *f* (mark produced by pressure) ‖ FIG sello *m*; *the work bore the imprint of his personality* el trabajo llevaba el sello de su personalidad ‖ PRINT pie *m* de imprenta (printer's mark).

imprint [imˈprint] *vt* imprimir ‖ estampar (on cloth) ‖ FIG grabar (on the mind).

imprison [imˈprizn] *vt* encarcelar, aprisionar, poner en la cárcel.

imprisonment [-mənt] *n* encarcelamiento *m* (action) ‖ cárcel *f*, prisión *f*; *sentenced to five years' imprisonment* condenado a cinco años de cárcel ‖ *false imprisonment* detención *f* ilegal.

improbability [imˌprɔbəˈbiliti] *n* improbabilidad *f* ‖ inverosimilitud *f*.

improbable [imˈprɔbəbl] *adj* improbable (not probable) ‖ inverosímil (hard to believe) ‖ *it seems improbable* parece poco probable.

improbity [imˈprəubiti] *n* improbidad *f*.

impromptu [imˈprɔmptjuː] *adj* improvisado, da.
◆ *adv* improvisadamente, sin preparación (without preparation) ‖ de repente, de improviso (unexpectedly).
◆ *n* MUS impromptu *m* ‖ improvisación *f*.

improper [imˈprɔpə*] *adj* indecente, impropio, pia (indecent) ‖ indecoroso, sa (indecorous) ‖ impropio, pia; inadecuado, da (unfit) ‖ inexacto, ta (wrong) ‖ incorrecto, ta; *it would be improper to decline the invitation* sería incorrecto rehusar la invitación ‖ MATH *improper fraction* fracción impropia.

impropriate [imˈprəuprieit] *vt* REL secularizar.

impropriation [imˌprəupriˈeiʃən] *n* REL secularización *f*.

impropriety [ˌimprəˈpraiəti] *n* impropiedad *f* (of language) ‖ indecencia *f* (unseemliness) ‖ falta *f* de decoro (indecorousness) ‖ incorrección *f*.

improvable [imˈpruːvəbl] *adj* perfectible, mejorable.

improve [imˈpruːv] *vt* mejorar (to make better) ‖ perfeccionar; *to improve one's knowledge of Spanish* perfeccionar sus conocimientos del español ‖ favorecer; *that dress improves her greatly* ese vestido le favorece mucho ‖ hacer mejoras en; *to improve a property* hacer mejoras

en una propiedad || AGR abonar || aumentar (production) || aumentar el valor de (to increase the value of) || cultivar (the mind) || aprovechar (an opportunity) || TECH perfeccionar.
◆ *vi* mejorar, mejorarse; *do you think that his health has improved?* ¿cree Ud. que su salud ha mejorado? || perfeccionarse (knowledge) || hacer progresos (to make progress) || aumentar (production) || subir, aumentar (prices) || — *to improve on* o *upon* mejorar; *to improve on a translation* mejorar una traducción || *to improve on s.o.'s offer* sobrepujar una oferta.

improvement [-mənt] *n* mejora *f*, mejoramiento *m* (a making better) || progreso *m* (progress) || aumento *m* (increase) || ampliación *f* (enlargement) || cultivo *m*, desarrollo *m* (of the mind) || reforma *f*; *to make improvements in a house* hacer reformas en una casa || MED mejoría *f* || aprovechamiento *m* (of the occasion) || TECH perfeccionamiento *m* || AGR abono *m* || — *to be open to improvement* poderse mejorar || *your new house is a great improvement on the last one* su nueva casa es mucho mejor que la anterior.

improver [im'pru:və*] *n* aprendiz *m*.

improvidence [im'prɔvidəns] *n* imprevisión *f*.

improvident [im'prɔvidənt] *adj* imprevisor, ra (without foresight) || gastador, ra (thriftless).

improving [im'pru:viŋ] *adj* FIG instructivo, va; edificante || *the patient is improving* el enfermo está mejor.

improvisation ['imprəvai'zeiʃən] *n* improvisación *f*.

improvisator ['imprəvai'zeitə*] *n* improvisador, ra.

improvise ['imprəvaiz] *vt/vi* improvisar.

improviser [,imprəvaizə*] *n* improvisador, ra.

imprudence [im'pru:dəns] *n* imprudencia *f*.

imprudent [im'pru:dənt] *adj* imprudente.

impubic [im'pjubik] *adj* impúber.

impudence ['impjudəns] *n* impudencia *f*, descaro *m*, desfachatez *f*, desvergüenza *f* (shamelessness) || insolencia *f* (insolence).

impudent ['impjudənt] *adj* impudente, desvergonzado, da; descarado, da (shameless) || insolente.

impudicity [,impju'disiti] *n* impudicia *f*.

impugn [im'pju:n] *vt* impugnar.

impugnable [-əbl] *adj* impugnable.

impugning [im'pju:niŋ] *adj* impugnativo, va (challenging).

impugnment [im'pju:nmənt] *n* impugnación *f*.

impulse ['impʌls] *n* impulso *m*; *his first impulse was to* su primer impulso fue; *to yield to an impulse* dejarse llevar por un impulso || TECH & ELECTR impulso *m*, impulsión *f* || impulso *m*, influjo *m* (in physiology) || — *I bought it on impulse* lo compré sin reflexionar || *man of impulse* hombre impulsivo || *nerve impulse* influjo nervioso.

impulsion [im'pʌlʃən] *n* impulsión *f*, impulso *m*.

impulsive [im'pʌlsiv] *adj* impulsivo, va.

impulsiveness [-nis]; **impulsivity** [-iti] *n* impulsividad *f*.

impunity [im'pju:niti] *n* impunidad *f* || JUR *with impunity* con impunidad.

impure [im'pjuə*] *adj* impuro, ra.

impurity [-riti] *n* impureza *f*.

imputability [im,pju:təbiliti] *n* imputabilidad *f*.

imputable [im'pju:təbl] *adj* imputable, achacable.

imputation [,impju'teiʃən] *n* imputación *f*.

impute [im'pju:t] *vt* imputar, atribuir, achacar.

imputrescible [,impju'tresibl] *adj* imputrescible.

in [in] *prep*

1. PLACE 2. TIME 3. MANNER 4. WEATHER 5. ACTIVITY 6. MEANING RELATING TO 7. WITH VERB 8. AFTER SUPERLATIVE 9. EXPRESSIONS

1. PLACE en; *in France* en Francia; *in Madrid* en Madrid; *in the cage* en la jaula; *in bed, in prison, in school* en la cama, en la cárcel, en el colegio; *wounded in the shoulder* herido en el hombro; *he had a stick in his hand* tenía un palo en la mano || de; *the furniture in the room* los muebles del cuarto || a; *to arrive in England* llegar a Inglaterra; *in the distance* a lo lejos; *in everybody's eyes* a los ojos de todos; *throw it in the fire* échalo al fuego || al, en; *to look at o.s. in the mirror* mirarse en el espejo || con; *I can't go out in this heat* no puedo salir con este calor; *she came in her new dress* vino con el traje nuevo; *you look pretty in that dress* está Ud. muy guapa con ese traje || por; *to walk in the street* pasearse por la calle.
2. TIME en; *in 1970, in the year 1970* en 1970, en el año 1970; *in the 19th century* en el siglo XIX [diez y nueve]; *in winter, in September* en invierno, en septiembre; *he did it in an hour* lo hizo en una hora; *in my youth* en mi juventud; *in my time* en mis tiempos || de; *at two o'clock in the afternoon* a las dos de la tarde || por; *in the morning, in the afternoon, in the evening* por la mañana, por la tarde, por la noche || dentro de; *he will be along in a while, in an hour* estará aquí dentro de un rato, dentro de una hora || durante, de; *in the daytime* durante el día, de día || durante, bajo; *in the reign of* durante el reinado de || — *early in the morning* de madrugada, por la mañana temprano || *I haven't seen my cousin in years* no veo a mi primo desde hace años, hace años que no veo a mi primo || *in the thirties, in the twenties* en los años treinta, en los años veinte || *in time* a tiempo || *I was back in a month* volví al cabo de un mes, volví al mes.
3. MANNER en; *in a loud, a low voice* en voz alta, baja; *to write in verse* escribir en verso; *he said it in English* lo dijo en inglés; *in cash* en metálico; *in these circumstances* en estas circunstancias || de; *in uniform* de uniforme; *in wood* de madera; *covered in mud* cubierto de barro; *dressed in black* vestido de negro; *in fashion* de moda; *in civilian clothes* de paisano; *in an amusing way* de una manera graciosa; *in mourning* de luto; *in good humour* de buen humor || a, con; *in ink* a tinta || a; *in hundreds, in dozens, in millions* a cientos, a docenas, a millones || por; *in writing* por escrito; *in alphabetical order* por orden alfabético; *cut in half* cortado por la mitad; *packed in dozens* empaquetados por docenas || con; *in anger* con ira; *people in good health* gente con buena salud; *in all frankness* con toda franqueza; *to speak in a raucous voice* hablar con voz ronca || — *any man in his senses* cualquiera que esté en su sano juicio, cualquier hombre sensato || *in a big way* a lo grande || *in chains* encadenado, da || *in despair* desesperado, da || *in tears* llorando || *in the European fashion* a la europea, al estilo europeo || *she was in trousers* llevaba pantalones || *the girl in black* la chica vestida de negro || *to be in difficulties* estar en un aprieto || *to be in poor health* estar mal de salud || *to line up in fours* formar en filas de a cuatro, alinearse de cuatro en fondo.
4. WEATHER a; *to sit in the sun* sentarse al sol || bajo; *in the rain* bajo la lluvia.
5. ACTIVITY en; *he is somebody in chemicals* es una persona importante en la industria química; *the latest thing in shoes* lo último en zapatos; *to be in the army* estar en el ejército || de; *to buy shares in a company* comprar acciones de una compañía || — *he is in the diamond business* trabaja en el sector de los diamantes || *he spends all his time in reading* se pasa el tiempo leyendo || *he travels in shoes* es viajante de zapatos || *those in teaching* los profesores, los que se dedican a la enseñanza || *to engage in trade* abrir *or* poner un negocio (to open a business), tener relaciones comerciales (to have commercial relations) || *to have shares in steel* tener acciones de las acerías.
6. MEANING *RELATING TO* de; *better in health* mejor de salud; *blind in one eye* ciego de un ojo; *a rise in prices* una subida de precios; *five kilometres in length* cinco kilómetros de largo; *lame in one foot* cojo de un pie || en; *he is very bad in Latin* es muy malo en latín; *slow in acting* lento en obrar; *to believe in God* creer en Dios; *my trust in him will never die* mi confianza en él nunca morirá || por; *to be interested in s.o., in sth.* interesarse por alguien, por algo || — *a change in tactics* un cambio de táctica || *long in the leg* de piernas largas || *to differ in opinion* tener opiniones distintas || *to differ in opinion with* no compartir la opinión de || *short in height* de baja estatura.
7. WITH VERB al; *in crossing the street* al cruzar la calle; *in saying this* al decir esto; *in touring the world he matured a lot* al dar la vuelta al mundo adquirió mucha madurez; *in working so hard he lost his health* al trabajar tanto perdió la salud || mientras (while)
8. AFTER SUPERLATIVE de; *the best in the world* el mejor del mundo; *the biggest city in the world* la ciudad más grande del mundo.
9. EXPRESSIONS *a chance in a million* una oportunidad entre mil || *a one in ten gradient* una pendiente del diez por ciento || *four in ten* cuatro de cada diez || *in all* en total || *in fact* de hecho, en realidad || *in particular* en particular || *in that* porque, ya que || *the person in question* la persona en cuestión || *to have it in one to do sth.* ser capaz de hacer algo.
◆ *adv* dentro, adentro; *in here, in there* aquí dentro, allí dentro; *in you go!* ¡para dentro!, ¡vete para adentro! || — *all in* todo incluido || *day in day out* día tras día || FAM *he's in for it* la va a pagar, se va a armar la gorda | *he's in for trouble* se la va a cargar || *in and out* entrando y saliendo || *my luck is in* estoy de suerte || *on the way in* al entrar || *oysters, asparragus are in* es la temporada de las ostras, de los espárragos || *the sun is in* el sol se ha ido || *to be all in* estar rendido *or* agotado || *to be in* estar, estar en casa (at home); *is Fred in?* ¿está Federico en casa?, ¿está Federico?; estar (at the office), estar en la cárcel (to be in prison), estar en el poder; *the Liberals are in* los liberales están en el poder; estar de moda; *trousers are in this year* este año están de moda los pantalones; estar recogido; *the potatoes are in* las patatas están recogidas; haber llegado; *the train is in* ha llegado el tren; batear (in cricket and baseball) || *to be in for* ir a; *it looks like we are in for rain* parece que va a llover; tomar parte en, participar en (a competition), ser candidato a (a post), presentarse a (an exam) || *to be in on* estar enterado de, estar al tanto de || *to be in on the secret* estar en el secreto || *to be in with s.o.* estar en buenas relaciones con alguien (to be on good terms with s.o.), ser amigo de *or* tener amistad con alguien (to be friendly with s.o.), estar a favor de alguien (to be in s.o.'s favour) || *to feel all in* estar rendido *or* agotado || FAM *to have it in for s.o.* tenerla tomada con alguien | *we're in for an unpleasant time* vamos a pasar un momento desagradable || FAM *you*

don't know what you're in for no sabes la que te espera.
◆ *adj* de entrada; *the in door* la puerta de entrada ‖ interior, de adentro (inner) ‖ de moda (fashionable) ‖ moderno, na (modern) ‖ en el poder (party).
◆ *n* *the ins* los que están en el poder, los que mandan ‖ US FAM influencia *f* ‖ *the ins and outs* los pormenores, los detalles.
— OBSERV «*In*» se emplea frecuentemente después de varios verbos (*to come, to get, to give, to go, etc.*) cuyo sentido modifica. Por lo tanto, remitimos a cada uno de ellos para sus distintas traducciones.

inability [inə'biliti] *n* incapacidad *f*.

inaccessibility ['inæk,sesə'biliti] *n* inaccesibilidad *f*.

inaccessible [,inæk'sesəbl] *adj* inaccesible (place, height) ‖ inasequible (prices, etc.).

inaccuracy [in'ækjurəsi] *n* inexactitud *f* (lack of accuracy) ‖ equivocación *f*, error *m* (mistake).

inaccurate [in'ækjurit] *adj* inexacto, ta (not accurate) ‖ incorrecto, ta; erróneo, a (in error).

inaction [in'ækʃən] *n* inacción *f*.

inactive [in'æktiv] *adj* inactivo, va ‖ — MIL *inactive list* escalafón *m* de reserva | *inactive status* situación *f* de reserva.

inactivity [,inæk'tiviti] *adj* inactividad *f* ‖ ociosidad *f* (idleness).

inadaptable [,inə'dæptəbl] *adj* inadaptable.

inadequacy [in'ædikwəsi] *n* inadecuación *f* (unsuitability) ‖ insuficiencia *f*.

inadequate [in'◆ikwit] *adj* inadecuado, da (unsuitable) ‖ insuficiente (insufficient).

inadmissibility ['inəd,misə'biliti] *n* inadmisibilidad *f* ‖ JUR improcedencia *f*.

inadmissible [,inəd'misəbl] *adj* inadmisible ‖ JUR improcedente.

inadvertence [,inəd'və:təns] *n* inadvertencia *f*.

inadvertency [-i] *n* inadvertencia *f*.

inadvertent [,inəd'və:tənt] *adj* inadvertido, da; descuidado, da (negligent) ‖ involuntario, ria (unintentional).

inadvertently [-li] *adv* por inadvertencia.

inadvisability [,inəd'vaizə'biliti] *n* inconveniencia *f*.

inadvisable [,inəd'vaizəbl] *adj* poco aconsejable, desaconsejable, inconveniente.

inaesthetic [inis'θetik] *adj* inestético, ca.

inalienability [in,eiljənə'biliti] *n* inalienabilidad *f*.

inalienable [in'eiljənəbl] *adj* inalienable.

inalterability [i,nɔ:ltərə'biliti] *n* inalterabilidad *f*.

inalterable [i'nɔ:ltərəbl] *adj* inalterable.

inamorata [in,æmə'rɑ:tə] *n* enamorada *f*, amada *f*.

inamorato [in,æmə'rɑ:təu] *n* enamorado *m*, amado *m* (male lover).

in-and-in ['inə'nin] *adj/adv* por consanguinidad.

inane [i'nein] *adj* inane, fútil (futile) ‖ necio, cia (silly) ‖ vacío, a (empty).
◆ *n* vacío *m*.

inanimate [in'ænimit] *adj* inanimado, da.

inanition [,inə'niʃən] *n* MED inanición *f*.

inanity [i'næniti] *n* inanidad *f*, futilidad *f* (futility) ‖ necedad *f* (stupidity).

inappetence [i'næpitəns]; **inappetency** [-i] *n* inapetencia *f*.

inappetent [i'næpitənt] *adj* inapetente.

inapplicability ['in,æplikə'biliti] *n* falta *f* de aplicabilidad.

inapplicable [in'æplikəbl] *adj* inaplicable.

inapposite [in'æpəzit] *adj* inadecuado, da.

inappreciable [,inə'pri:ʃəbl] *adj* inapreciable, insignificante.

inappreciative [inə'pri:ʃiətiv] *adj* que no sabe apreciar.

inapprehensible [inæpri'hensibl] *adj* incomprensible.

inapprehension [inæpri'henʃən] *n* incomprensión *f*.

inapproachability ['inə,prəutʃəbiliti] *n* inaccesibilidad *f*.

inapproachable [,inə'prəutʃəbl] *adj* inaccesible.

inappropriate [,inə'prəupriit] *adj* impropio, pia; inadecuado, da (unsuitable) ‖ inconveniente (inconvenient) ‖ impropio, pia (word).

inappropriateness [-nis] *n* impropiedad *f*.

inapt [in'æpt] *adj* inepto, ta; inhábil (lacking skill) ‖ torpe (awkward) ‖ inadecuado, da (inappropriate).

inaptitude [in'æptitju:d] *n* inaptitud *f*, ineptitud *f*, incapacidad *f*.

inarch [in'ɑ:tʃ] *vt* AGR injertar por aproximación.

inarm [in'ɑ:m] *vt* estrechar, abrazar (to embrace).

inarticulate [,inɑ:'tikjulit] *adj* inarticulado, da (sounds, speech) ‖ incapaz de expresarse (person) ‖ *he was inarticulate with grief* tenía la voz embargada por el dolor.

in articulo mortis [inɑ:'tikjulə'mɔ:tis] *adv* in articulo mortis.

inartificial [inɑ:ti'fiʃəl] *adj* natural, sin artificio (unaffected) ‖ sin arte, poco artístico, ca (lacking art).

inartistic [,inɑ:'tistik] *adj* poco artístico, ca; sin arte.

inasmuch [inəz'mʌtʃ] *adv* *inasmuch as* puesto que, visto que, en vista de que, ya que (since, because), en la medida en que (insofar as).

inattention [,inə'tenʃən] *n* falta *f* de atención, inatención *f*, desatención *f*, distracción *f*.

inattentive ['inə'tentiv] *adj* poco atento, ta; desatento, ta; distraído, da.

inattentively [-li] *adv* distraídamente.

inaudible [in'ɔ:dəbl] *adj* inaudible.

inaudibly [-i] *adv* de modo inaudible ‖ *she said it almost inaudibly* lo dijo de modo que apenas se oía.

inaugural [i'nɔ:gjurəl] *adj* inaugural.
◆ *n* discurso *m* inaugural *or* de apertura (speech) ‖ inauguración *f* (ceremony).

inaugurate [i'nɔ:gjureit] *vt* dar posesión de un cargo a (an official) ‖ inaugurar (a new building, an exhibition, etc.) ‖ descubrir (a statue) ‖ FIG inaugurar, introducir.

inauguration [i,nɔ:gju'reiʃən] *n* inauguración *f* (of a building, exhibition, etc.) ‖ investidura *f*, toma *f* de posesión (of an official).

inaugurator [i'nɔ:gjureitə*] *n* inaugurador, ra.

inauspicious [,inɔ:s'piʃəs] *adj* desfavorable, poco propicio, cia.

inauspiciously [-li] *adv* en condiciones desfavorables, bajo malos auspicios.

inbeing [in'bi:iŋ] *n* esencia *f*.

in-between [inbi'twi:n] *adj* intermedio, dia.

inboard ['in'bɔ:d] *adv/adj* MAR dentro del casco.

inborn ['in:bɔ:n] *adj* innato, ta ‖ MED congénito, ta.

inbreathe ['in'bri:ð] *vt* inspirar.

inbred ['inbred] *adj* procreado en consanguinidad, consanguíneo, a (animals) ‖ engendrado por endogamia (people) ‖ innato, ta (innate).

inbreed ['in'bri:d] *vt* procrear en consanguinidad (animals) ‖ engendrar por endogamia (people).

inbreeding [-iŋ] *n* endogamia *f* (of people) ‖ procreación *f* en consanguinidad (of animals).

inbuilt [in'bilt] *adj* innato, ta (people) ‖ incorporado, da (machine).

Inca ['iŋkə] *n* inca *m* & *f*.
◆ *adj* incaico, ca; incásico, ca.

incalculable [in'kælkjuləbl] *adj* incalculable (countless) ‖ imprevisible (unpredictable).

Incan ['iŋkən] *adj* incaico, ca; incásico, ca.

incandesce [inkæn'des] *vi* ponerse incandescente.

incandescence ['inkæn'desns] *n* incandescencia *f*.

incandescent ['inkæn'desnt] *adj* incandescente ‖ *incandescent lamp* lámpara *f* incandescente *or* de incandescencia.

incantation [,inkæn'teiʃən] *n* conjuro *m* (spell).

incantatory [in'kæntə,tɔri] *adj* mágico, ca.

incapability [in,keipə'biliti] *n* incapacidad *f*.

incapable [in'keipəbl] *adj* incapaz (not capable) ‖ incompetente ‖ JUR incapaz (person).

incapacious [inkə'peiʃəs] *adj* estrecho, cha (having little capacity) ‖ (ant) atrasado mental.

incapacitate [,inkə'pæsiteit] *vt* incapacitar (to make incapable); *incapacitated by illness* incapacitado por la enfermedad ‖ SP descalificar ‖ JUR incapacitar.

incapacitation ['inkə,pæsi'teiʃən] *n* JUR privación *f* de capacidad.

incapacity [,inkə'pæsiti] *n* incapacidad *f*; *incapacity to govern* incapacidad para gobernar; *legal incapacity* incapacidad legal.

incarcerate [in'kɑ:səreit] *vt* encarcelar.

incarceration [in,kɑ:sə'reiʃən] *n* encarcelamiento *m*, encarcelación *f*.

incarnadine [in'kɑ:nədain] *adj* encarnado, da.
◆ *n* encarnado *m* (colour).

incarnadine [in'kɑ:nədain] *vt* encarnar (to make flesh-coloured) ‖ volver encarnado *or* rojo (to turn red).

incarnate [in'kɑ:nit] *adj* encarnado, da; *the incarnate God* Dios encarnado ‖ encarnado, da (flesh-coloured) ‖ — *beauty incarnate* la encarnación de la belleza ‖ *to become incarnate* encarnar.

incarnate ['inkɑ:neit] *vt* encarnar.

incarnation [,inkɑ:'neiʃən] *n* encarnación *f*.

incase [in'keis] *vt* ⟶ **encase.**

incaution [in'kɔ:ʃən] *n* descuido *m*, negligencia *f* (negligence) ‖ imprudencia *f*.

incautious [in'kɔ:ʃəs] *adj* descuidado, da; negligente ‖ imprudente, incauto, ta (lacking in prudence).

incendiary [in'sendjəri] *adj* incendiario, ria ‖ *incendiary device* artefacto *m* incendiario.
◆ *n* incendiario, ria; pirómano, na (person) ‖ bomba *f* incendiaria (bomb) ‖ FIG agitador, ra.

incense ['insens] *n* incienso *m* ‖ FIG incienso *m* (flattery).

incense ['insens] *vt* incensar.
◆ *vi* quemar incienso.

incense [in'sens] *vt* encolerizar, sulfurar, sacar de sus casillas (to anger).

incense bearer [-'bɛərə*] *n* turiferario *m*.

incense boat [-bəut] *n* naveta *f*.

incense burner [-'bəːnə*] *n* pebetero *m*.

incensory ['insensəri] *n* incensario *m*.

incentive [in'sentiv] *adj* estimulante.
◆ *n* incentivo *m*, estímulo *m*, aliciente *m*, acicate *m*; *an incentive to work* un incentivo para trabajar ‖ *incentive scheme* plan *m* de incentivos (salariales).

incept [in'sept] *vt* BIOL ingerir ‖ FIG empezar.

inception [in'sepʃən] *n* principio *m*, comienzo *m* (origin) ‖ MED ingestión *f*.

inceptive [in'septiv] *adj* inicial (initial) ‖ GRAMM incoativo, va.
◆ *n* GRAMM verbo *m* incoativo.

incertitude [in'səːtitjuːd] *n* incertidumbre *f*.

incessant [in'sesnt] *adj* incesante, continuo, nua; constante.

incessantly [-li] *adv* sin cesar, incesantemente, constantemente.

incest ['insest] *n* incesto *m*.

incestuous [in'sestjuəs] *adj* incestuoso, sa.

inch [intʃ] *n* pulgada *f* [unidad de medida equivalente a 2,54 cm.] (measure) ‖ FIG pizca *f*; *he hasn't an inch of common sense* no tiene ni pizca de sentido común ‖ — FIG *by inches* poco a poco | *every inch a lady* una señora de pies a cabeza | *give him an inch and he'll take a yard* dale la mano y te cogerá el brazo | *inch by inch* poco a poco (little by little), palmo a palmo (to gain ground, etc.) | *not an inch of room was there* no cabía un alfiler | *they scoured every inch of the beach* registraron la playa palmo a palmo *or* minuciosamente | *to know every inch of* conocer palmo a palmo | *within an inch of* a dos pasos de.

inch [intʃ] *vt* hacer avanzar *or* retroceder poco a poco.
◆ *vi* *to inch forward* avanzar poco a poco.

inchoate ['inkəueit] *adj* JUR incoado, da ‖ rudimentario, ria ‖ incipiente (initial).

inchoation [ˌinkəu'eiʃən] *n* incoación *f*.

inchoative ['inkəueitiv] *adj* incoativo, va.
◆ *n* GRAMM verbo *m* incoativo.

incidence ['insidəns] *n* PHYS incidencia *f*; *angle of incidence* ángulo de incidencia ‖ frecuencia *f* (frecuency) ‖ FIG alcance *m* (reach) | extensión *f* (of a disease) | peso *m* (of a tax) | efecto *m* (effect).

incident ['insidənt] *adj* incidente ‖ *incident to* que acompaña a, inherente a, propio de; *risks incident to a profession* los riesgos que acompañan a una profesión.
◆ *n* incidente *m*; *a diplomatic incident* un incidente diplomático ‖ incidentes *m pl*; *the meeting took place without incident* la reunión tuvo lugar sin incidentes; *a life full of incident* una vida llena de incidentes ‖ episodio *m* (in a novel, a play).

incidental [ˌinsi'dentl] *adj* incidente; *incidental question* cuestión incidente ‖ incidental; *incidental observation* observación incidental ‖ imprevisto, ta; accesorio, ria (expense) ‖ de fondo (music) ‖ fortuito, ta (casual) ‖ secundario, ria (secondary) ‖ — *incidental clause* inciso *m* ‖ *incidental to* que acompaña a, inherente a, propio de; *the worries incidental to motherhood* las preocupaciones propias de la maternidad.
◆ *n* elemento *m* accesorio *or* secundario.
◆ *pl* COMM imprevistos *m*.

incidentally [-i] *adv* a propósito, dicho sea de paso (by the way) ‖ incidentemente.

incinerate [in'sinəreit] *vt* incinerar (body) ‖ quemar (rubbish).

incineration [inˌsinə'reiʃən] *n* incineración *f*.

incinerator [in'sinəreitə*] *n* quemador *m* *or* incinerador *m* de basuras (for rubbish) ‖ crematorio *m*, horno *m* crematorio (crematorium).

incipience [in'sipiəns]; **incipiency** [-i] *n* comienzo *m*, principio *m* (beginning).

incipient [in'sipiənt] *adj* incipiente.

incise [in'saiz] *vt* cortar, hacer una incisión en (to make a cut in) ‖ grabar (to engrave, to carve) ‖ MED sajar.

incision [in'siʒən] *n* incisión *f*.

incisive [in'saisiv] *adj* incisivo, va; cortante, mordaz (tone, style) ‖ incisivo, va; cortante (instrument) ‖ penetrante (mind) ‖ incisivo, va (tooth).

incisiveness [in'saisivnis] *n* mordacidad *f* (of words) ‖ penetración *f* (of mind).

incisor [in'saizə*] *n* diente *m* incisivo, incisivo *m*.

incite [in'sait] *vt* incitar; *the soldier incited his comrades to rise against their officers* el soldado incitó a sus compañeros a que se sublevaran contra sus oficiales ‖ provocar; *insults incite resentment* los insultos provocan el resentimiento.

incitement [-mənt] *n* incitamiento *m*, incitación *f*; *incitement to crime* incitación al crimen ‖ estímulo *m*, incentivo *m* (stimulus).

inciter [-ə*] *n* incitador, ra.

inciting [-iŋ] *adj* incitador, ra; incitante.

incivility [ˌinsi'viliti] *n* descortesía *f*, incivilidad *f*.

in-clearing ['inkliəriŋ] *n* COMM cheques *m pl* recibidos por un banco a través de la cámara de compensación.

inclemency [in'klemənsi] *n* inclemencia *f*.

inclement [in'klemənt] *adj* inclemente ‖ inclemente, riguroso, sa (weather).

inclinable [in'klainəbl] *adj* propenso, sa; inclinado, da (*to* a) (prone) ‖ que se puede inclinar (a table, stand, etc.).

inclination [inkli'neiʃən] *n* inclinación *f*; *the inclination of a roof* la inclinación de un tejado; *an inclination of the head* una inclinación de la cabeza ‖ pendiente *f* (slope) ‖ FIG inclinación *f*, tendencia *f*, propensión *f* (leaning, tendency) ‖ — *he has an inclination to lie* tiene tendencia a mentir ‖ *he has an inclination towards women* le gustan las mujeres ‖ *my inclination is towards the second alternative* prefiero la segunda solución.

incline [in'klain] *n* pendiente *f*, cuesta *f* (slope).

incline [in'klain] *vt* inclinar (to slope) ‖ FIG inclinar (to give a tendency to) | inducir (to induce) ‖ — FIG *I am inclined to believe him* me inclino a creerle, estoy dispuesto a creerle | *it is inclined to warp* tiene tendencia a alabearse | *they are that way inclined* son así | *to be well inclined towards s.o.* estar bien dispuesto con alguien | *to incline one's steps towards...* dirigir sus pasos hacia... | *when he feels that way inclined* cuando le da la gana, cuando le apetece.
◆ *vi* inclinarse ‖ MED tener propensión (*to* a) (towards an illness) ‖ *green that inclines to blue* verde que tira a azul.

inclined [-d] *adj* inclinado, da; *inclined plane* plano inclinado.

inclining [-iŋ] *adj* inclinador, ra; inclinante.
◆ *n* inclinación *f* (slanting).

inclinometer [ˌinkli'nɔmitə*] *n* AVIAT clinómetro *m*.

inclose [in'kləuz] *vt* ⟶ **enclose.**

inclosure [in'kləuʒə*] *n* ⟶ **enclosure.**

include [in'kluːd] *vt* incluir; *to include an item in the bill* incluir un artículo en la cuenta; *the price includes meals* el precio incluye la comida ‖ adjuntar (in a letter) ‖ *I hope you don't include me in that remark* espero que esta observación no va dirigida también a mí.

included [-id] *adj* incluido, da; *all* o *everything included* todo incluido ‖ incluso, incluido, da; *all his property was sold, his house included* se vendieron todos sus bienes, incluso su casa.

including [-iŋ] *adj* incluso, inclusive, con inclusión de ‖ — *everyone, including the President* todos, incluso *or* inclusive el Presidente ‖ *I have five including this one* con éste tengo cinco ‖ *including service* servicio comprendido *or* incluido.

inclusion [in'kluːʒən] *n* inclusión *f*.

inclusive [in'kluːsiv] *adj* inclusivo, va ‖ inclusive; *pages ten to fifteen inclusive* de la página diez a la quince inclusive ‖ — *inclusive of transport* transporte incluido ‖ *inclusive terms* precio *m* todo incluido ‖ *to be inclusive of* incluir.

inclusively [-li] *adv* inclusive.

incoagulable [inkəˈægjuləbl] *adj* incoagulable.

incoercible [inkəu'əːsibl] *adj* incoercible.

incognito [in'kɔgnitəu] *adj* incógnito, ta.
◆ *adv* de incógnito; *to travel incognito* viajar de incógnito.
◆ *n* incógnito *m*; *to preserve one's incognito* guardar el incógnito.

incognizance [in'kɔgnizəns] *n* ignorancia *f*, desconocimiento *m*.

incognizant [in'kɔgnizənt] *adj* ignorante.

incoherence [ˌinkəu'hiərəns]; **incoherency** [-i] *n* incoherencia *f*.

incoherent [ˌinkəu'hiərənt] *adj* incoherente.

incoherently [-li] *adv* de modo incoherente.

incombustibility ['inkəmˌbʌstə'biliti] *n* incombustibilidad *f*.

incombustible [ˌinkəm'bʌstəbl] *adj* incombustible.
◆ *n* sustancia *f* incombustible.

income ['inkʌm] *n* ingresos *m pl*; *his income as a lawyer* sus ingresos de abogado ‖ renta *f* (private income) ‖ rédito *m* (interest) ‖ — *earned income* ingresos profesionales ‖ *gross income* renta bruta ‖ *he cannot live on his income* no puede vivir con su sueldo *or* con lo que gana ‖ *income group* o *bracket* categoría *f* de contribuyentes ‖ *income return* declaración *f* de impuestos ‖ *incomes policy* política *f* de rentas ‖ *income tax* impuesto *m* sobre la renta ‖ *national income* renta nacional ‖ *real income* poder adquisitivo (purchasing power) ‖ *to live on one's private income* vivir de sus rentas.

incomer ['inˌkʌmə*] *n* inmigrante *m* & *f* (immigrant) ‖ recién llegado, recién llegada (newcomer) ‖ intruso, sa (intruder).

incoming ['inˌkʌmiŋ] *adj* que entra, entrante ‖ entrante; *the incoming year* el año entrante ‖ nuevo, va; *the incoming President* el nuevo Presidente ‖ MAR ascendente (tide).
◆ *n* entrada *f* (entrance) ‖ llegada *f* (arrival).
◆ *pl* ingresos *m*.

incommensurable [ˌinkə'menʃərəbl] *adj* inconmensurable.

incommensurate [ˌinkə'menʃərit] *adj* inconmensurable ‖ desproporcionado, da (out of proportion).

incommode [ˌinkə'məud] *vt* incomodar, molestar (to cause annoyance to) ‖ estorbar (to hinder).

incommodious [ˌinkə'məudjəs] *adj* incómodo, da (uncomfortable).

incommodity [inkə'mɔditi] *n* incomodidad *f*.

incommunicability [inkəmjunikə'biliti] *n* incomunicabilidad *f*.

incommunicable ['inkə'mju:nikəbl] *adj* incomunicable.

incommunicado ['inkəm,ju:ni'kɑ:dəu] *adj* incomunicado, da.

incommunicative [inkə'mju:nikeitiv] *adj* poco expansivo, va; reservado, da.

incommutability [,inkəmju:tə'biliti] *n* inconmutabilidad *f*.

incommutable [,inkə'mju:təbl] *adj* inconmutable.

incompact [inkəm'pækt] *adj* no compacto, ta || blando, da (soft).

incomparability [in,kɔmpərə'biliti] *n* excelencia *f*.

incomparable [in'kɔmpərəbl] *adj* incomparable.

incompassionate [inkəm'pæʃənit] *adj* incompasivo, va.

incompatibility ['inkəm,pætə'biliti] *n* incompatibilidad *f*.

incompatible [,inkəm'pætəbl] *adj* incompatible || INFORM incompatible.

incompetence [in'kɔmpitəns]; **incompetency** [-i] *n* incompetencia *f*.

incompetent [in'kɔmpitənt] *adj/n* incompetente.

incomplete [,inkəm'pli:t] *adj* incompleto, ta || inacabado, da; sin terminar (unfinished) || imperfecto, ta (not perfect).

incompleteness [,inkəm'pli:tnis]; **incompletion** [,inkəm'pli:ʃən] *n* estado *m* incompleto || *due to the incompletion of the book* puesto que el libro no está terminado.

incompliance [inkəm'plaiəns]; **incompliancy** [-i] *n* inflexibilidad *f* || desobediencia *f*.

incompliant [inkəm'plaiənt] *adj* inflexible || desobediente.

incomprehensibility [in,kɔmprihensə'biliti] *n* incomprensibilidad *f*.

incomprehensible [in,kɔmpri'hensəbl] *adj* incomprensible.

incomprehension [inkɔmpri'henʃən] *n* incomprensión *f*.

imcomprehensive [inkɔmpri'hensiv] *adj* incomprensivo, va; poco comprensivo, va (understanding little) || limitado, da (including little).

imcompressibility ['inkəm,presə'biliti] *n* incompresibilidad *f*.

incompressible [,inkəm'presəbl] *adj* incomprensible, incomprimible.

incomputable [,inkəm'pju:təbl] *adj* incalculable.

inconceivability ['inkən,si:və'biliti] *n* lo inconcebible.

inconceivable [,inkən'si:vəbl] *adj* inconcebible.

inconciliable [,inkən'siljəbl] *adj* inconciliable (irreconcilable).

inconclusive [,inkən'klu:siv] *adj* poco concluyente, poco convincente (not convincing) || no decisivo, va (indecisive).

incondensable [inkən'densəbl] *adj* no condensable.

incondite [in'kɔndit] *adj* mal construido, da (literary work) || tosco, ca; basto, ta (coarse).

incongruent [in'kɔŋgruənt] *adj* incongruente || inadecuado, da (inappropriate).

incongruity [,inkɔŋ'gru:iti] *n* incongruidad *f*, incongruencia *f* || inadecuación *f*.

incongruous [in'kɔŋgruəs] *adj* incongruo grua; incongruente || incompatible || inadecuado, da || *incongrous colours* colores que no van uno con otro.

incongruousness [-nis] *n* incongruencia *f*.

inconsequence [in'kɔnsikwəns] *n* inconsecuencia *f*.

inconsequent [in'kɔnsikwənt] *adj* inconsecuente (mind) || ilógico, ca (reasoning) || inconexo, xa (ideas).

inconsequential [inkɔnse'kwenʃəl] *adj* de poca importancia, sin trascendencia, insignificante (unimportant) || inconsecuente, ilógico, ca (inconsequent).

inconsiderable [,inkən'sidərəbl] *adj* insignificante.

inconsiderate [,inkən'sidərit] *adj* desconsiderado, da (without consideration for others) || inconsiderado, da (thoughtless) || *that was inconsiderate of him!* ¡qué falta de consideración por su parte!

inconsiderateness [,inkən'sidəritnis]; **inconsideration** ['inkən,sidə'reiʃən] *n* inconsideración *f*, irreflexión *f* (thoughtlessness) || falta *f* de consideración (towards others).

inconsistency [,inkən'sistənsi] *n* inconsistencia *f* (of a substance) || inconsecuencia *f*, falta *f* de lógica (inconsequence) || contradicción *f*.

inconsistent [,inkən'sistənt] *adj* inconsistente (substance) || inconsecuente, ilógico, ca (ideas, actions) || contradictorio, ria || *inconsistent with* que se contradice con, que no concuerda con, que contradice.

inconsolable [inkən'səuləbl] *adj* inconsolable, desconsolado, da (person) || inconsolable (grief).

inconsonance [in'kɔnsənəns] *n* desacuerdo *m*, discordancia *f*.

inconsonant [in'kɔnsənənt] *adj* discordante || *to be inconsonant with* no concordar con.

inconspicuous [,inkən'spikjuəs] *adj* discreto, ta; que no llama la atención || *I try to be as inconspicuous as possible* procuro no llamar la atención.

inconstancy [in'kɔnstənsi] *n* inconstancia *f* (fickleness) || inestabilidad *f* (unsteadiness).

inconstant [in'kɔnstənt] *adj* inconstante (fickle) || inestable (unsteady).

inconstructible [inkən'strʌktibl] *adj* inconstruible.

inconsumable [inkən'sju:məbl] *adj* incombustible (by fire) || COMM no consumible.

incontestability ['inkən,testə'biliti] *n* incontestabilidad *f*.

incontestable [,inkən'testəbl] *adj* incontestable, indiscutible, incontrovertible.

incontinence [in'kɔntinəns] *n* incontinencia *f*.

incontinent [in'kɔntinənt] *adj* incontinente.

incontrovertible ['inkɔntrə'və:təbl] *adj* incontrovertible, indiscutible.

inconvenience [,inkən'vi:njəns] *n* inconvenientes *m pl*, molestia *f*; *the inconvenience of living in a small house* los inconvenientes de vivir en una casa pequeña || *I was put to great inconvenience by his late arrival* me causó mucha molestia su llegada tardía.

inconvenience [,inkən'vi:njəns] *vt* incomodar, molestar, causar molestia.

inconvenient [,inkən'vi:njənt] *adj* incómodo, da (house) || molesto, ta (person) || inoportuno, na (time) || *if it is not inconvenient for you* si no le sirve de molestia.

inconveniently [-li] *adv* inoportunamente, en un momento inoportuno (untimely) || de un modo incómodo (uncomfortably).

inconvertibility [inkən,və:tə'biliti] *n* no convertibilidad *f*.

inconvertible [,inkən'və:təbl] *adj* inconvertible.

inconvincible [inkən'vinsibl] *adj* imposible de convencer, inconvencible.

incoordination [inkə,ɔ:di'neiʃən] *n* incoordinación *f*, falta *f* de coordinación.

incorporable [in'kɔ:pərəbl] *adj* incorporable.

incorporate [in'kɔ:pərit] *adj* incorporado, da (incorporated) || incorpóreo, a (incorporeal).

incorporate [in'kɔ:pəreit] *vt* incorporar, incluir; *to incorporate in* o *into* incluir *or* incorporar en || contener (to contain) || incorporar, admitir como miembro || JUR constituir en sociedad (a firm).

◆ *vi* incorporarse || unirse (to join) || JUR constituirse en sociedad, formar una sociedad.

incorporated [-id] *adj* incorporado, da || JUR constituido en sociedad.

incorporation [in,kɔ:pə'reiʃən] *n* incorporación *f* || unión *f* || JUR constitución *f* en sociedad (of a company).

incorporeal [,inkɔ:'pɔ:riəl] *adj* incorpóreo, a.

incorporeity [in,kɔ:pɔ:'ri:iti] *n* incorporeidad *f*.

incorrect [,inkə'rekt] *adj* incorrecto, ta (behaviour, style) || inexacto, ta (statement) || erróneo, a (views) || inadecuado, da (clothes).

incorrectness [-nis] *n* incorrección *f* (of behaviour, style) || inexactitud *f* (of statement) || lo erróneo (of views).

incorrigibility [in,kɔridʒə'biliti] *n* incorregibilidad *f*.

incorrigible [in'kɔridʒəbl] *adj* incorregible.

incorrodible [inkə'rəudibl] *adj* inatacable (metal).

incorrupt [,inkə'rʌpt] *adj* incorrupto, ta.

incorruptibility ['inkə,rʌptə'biliti] *n* incorruptibilidad *f*.

incorruptible [,inkə'rʌptəbl] *adj* incorruptible.

increase ['inkri:s] *n* aumento *m*; *a fifty per cent increase* un aumento del cincuenta por ciento; *an increase in production* un aumento de la producción || aumento *m*, subida *f* (of prices) || *to be on the increase* aumentar, ir creciendo.

increase [in'kri:s] *vt* aumentar, incrementar; *to increase exports* incrementar las exportaciones || aumentar (prices).

◆ *vi* aumentarse, aumentar || subir, aumentar (prices).

increasing [-iŋ] *adj* creciente.

increasingly [-iŋli] *adv* cada vez más; *this work gets increasingly difficult* este trabajo se pone cada vez más difícil.

increate [inkri'eit] *adj* REL increado, da.

incredibility [in,kredi'biliti] *n* incredibilidad *f*.

incredible [inkredəbl] *adj* increíble.

incredulity [,inkri'dju:liti] *n* incredulidad *f*.

incredulous [in'kredjuləs] *adj* incrédulo, la; descreído, da (person) || incrédulo, la; *an incredulous look* una mirada incrédula.

incredulously [-li] *adv* con incredulidad.

increment ['inkrimənt] *n* aumento *m*, incremento *m* (increase) || MATH & INFORM incremento *m* || *unearned increment* plusvalía *f*.

increment ['inkrimənt] *vt* INFORM incrementar.

incriminate [in'krimineit] *vt* incriminar.

incriminating [in'krimineitiŋ]; US **incriminatory** [in'kriminətəri] *adj* incriminatorio, ria; incriminador, ra.

incrimination [in,krimi'neiʃən] *n* incriminación *f*.

incrust [in'krʌst] *vt* encostrar, incrustar (to cover with) ‖ incrustar (with gems, etc.).

incrustation [ˌinkrʌs'teiʃən] *n* incrustación *f.*

incubate ['inkjubeit] *vt* incubar ‖ empollar, incubar (to sit on an egg).
◆ *vi* incubar.

incubation [ˌinkju'beiʃən] *n* incubación *f; incubation period* período de incubación.

incubator ['inkjubeitə*] *n* incubadora *f.*

incudes ['iŋkju:di:z] *pl n* → **incus.**

inculcate ['inkʌlkeit] *vt* inculcar.

inculcation [ˌinkʌl'keiʃən] *n* inculcación *f.*

inculcator ['inkʌlkeitə*] *n* inculcador, ra.

inculpability [inˌkʌlpə'biliti] *n* inculpabilidad *f.*

inculpable [in'kʌlpəbl] *adj* inculpable.

inculpate ['inkʌlpeit] *vt* inculpar.

inculpation [ˌinkʌl'peʃən] *n* inculpación *f.*

inculpatory [in'kʌlpətəri] *adj* acusador, ra.

incumbency [in'kʌmbənsi] *n* incumbencia *f.*

incumbent [in'kʌmbənt] *adj* apoyado, da ‖ *it is incumbent on you* te incumbe a ti.
◆ *n* REL beneficiado *m* ‖ titular *m* (of an office).

incunable [in'kju:nəbl] *n* incunable *m.*

incunabula [ˌinkju'næbjulə] *pl n* incunables *m.*

incunabular [ˌinkju'næbjulə*] *adj* incunable.

incunabulum [ˌinkju'næbjuləm] *n* incunable *m.*
— OBSERV El plural de la palabra inglesa es *incunabula.*

incur [in'kə:*] *vt* incurrir en; *to incur the king's disfavour, punishment, hatred* incurrir en la desgracia del rey, en castigo, en odio ‖ contraer (debt, obligation) ‖ sufrir (a loss) ‖ incurrir en (expenses).

incurability [inˌkjuərə'biliti] *n* incurabilidad *f.*

incurable [in'kjuərəbl] *adj* incurable ‖ FIG irremediable.
◆ *n* enfermo *m* incurable, incurable *m.*

incuriosity [inkjuəri'ɔsiti] *n* falta *f* de curiosidad, indiferencia *f.*

incurious [in'kjuəriəs] *adj* poco curioso, sa; indiferente.

incursion [in'kə:ʃən] *n* incursión *f.*

incursive [in'kə:siv] *adj* agresor, ra; invasor, ra.

incurvate ['inkə:vit] *adj* encorvado, da.

incurvate ['inkə:veit] *vt* encorvar.

incurvation [ˌinkə:'veiʃən] *n* encorvamiento *m,* encorvadura *f.*

incurve ['in'kə:v] *vt* encorvar.
◆ *vi* encorvarse.

incus ['iŋkəs] *n* ANAT yunque *m* (in the ear).
— OBSERV El plural de *incus* es *incudes.*

indebted [in'detid] *adj* endeudado, da (*to* con) (owing money) ‖ FIG agradecido, da (grateful); *she is very indebted to you* le está muy agradecida.

indebtedness [-nis] *n* deuda *f* (debt) ‖ FIG agradecimiento *m.*

indecency [in'di:snsi] *n* indecencia *f.*

indecent [in'di:snt] *adj* indecente, indecoroso, sa ‖ — JUR *indecent assault* atentado *m* contra el pudor | *indecent exposure* exhibicionismo *m.*

indeciduous [indi'sidjuəs] *adj* perenne.

indecipherable [ˌindi'saifərəbl] *adj* indescifrable.

indecision [ˌindi'siʒən] *n* indecisión *f,* irresolución *f.*

indecisive [ˌindi'saisiv] *adj* indeciso, sa; irresoluto, ta (person) ‖ que no resuelve nada (not conclusive).

indecisiveness [-nis] *n* indecisión *f,* irresolución *f.*

indeclinable [ˌindi'klainəbl] *adj* indeclinable.

indecorous [in'dekərəs] *adj* indecoroso, sa; impropio, pia; incorrecto, ta.

indecorum ['indi'kɔ:rəm] *n* indecoro *m,* falta *f* de decoro.

indeed [in'di:d] *adv* efectivamente, en efecto; *indeed, he was the only one* efectivamente, fue el único ‖ realmente (really) ‖ — *did he indeed?* ¿de verdad?, ¿de veras? ‖ *indeed?* ¿de verdad?, ¿de veras? ‖ *thank you very much indeed* muchísimas gracias ‖ *that's a gift indeed* eso sí que es un regalo ‖ *very glad indeed* realmente muy contento ‖ *yes indeed!* ¡naturalmente!, ¡claro que sí!, ¡ya lo creo!

indefatigability ['indiˌfætigə'biliti] *n* fuerzas *f pl* inagotables.

indefatigable [ˌindi'fætigəbl] *adj* infatigable, incansable.

indefeasibility ['indiˌfi:zə'biliti] *n* irrevocabilidad *f.*

indefeasible [ˌindi'fi:zəbl] *adj* irrevocable.

indefectibility ['indiˌfektə'biliti] *n* indefectibilidad *f.*

indefectible [ˌindi'fektəbl] *adj* indefectible.

indefensible [ˌindi'fensəbl] *adj* indefensible, indefendible ‖ insostenible (theory) ‖ injustificable (unjustifiable).

indefinable [ˌindi'fainəbl] *adj* indefinible.

indefinite [in'definit] *adj* indefinido, da; impreciso, sa; *indefinite plans* proyectos indefinidos ‖ indefinido, da; indeterminado, da; *indefinite period* período indeterminado ‖ GRAMM indefinido, da; indeterminado, da; *indefinite article, adjective, pronoun* artículo, adjetivo, pronombre indefinido | *past indefinite* pretérito indefinido ‖ *you're being very indefinite* es muy impreciso *or* es muy vago lo que dices.

indehiscent [ˌindi'hisənt] *adj* BOT indehiscente.

indeliberation ['indiˌlibə'reiʃən] *n* indeliberación *f.*

indelibility [inˌdeli'biliti] *n* indelebilidad *f.*

indelible [in'delibl] *adj* indeleble, imborrable.

indelicacy [in'delikəsi] *n* indelicadeza *f,* falta *f* de delicadeza.

indelicate [in'delikit] *adj* indelicado, da; poco delicado, da.

indemnification [inˌdemnifi'keiʃən] *n* indemnización *f.*

indemnify [in'demnifai] *vt* asegurar (*against* contra) (to secure) ‖ indemnizar (to compensate).

indemnity [in'demniti] *n* indemnidad *f* (security) ‖ indemnización *f,* reparación *f,* compensación *f.*

indemonstrable [in'demənstrəbl] *adj* indemostrable.

indent ['indent] *n* muesca *f* (notch) ‖ hendidura *f or* quebradura *f* de la costa (on the coastline) ‖ COMM pedido *m* ‖ requisición *f.*

indent [in'dent] *vt* dentar, hacer muescas en (to notch) ‖ abollar (to dent) ‖ PRINT sangrar ‖ JUR hacer por duplicado (to duplicate) | cortar en dos partes [un documento] ‖ pedir, hacer un pedido de (goods).
◆ *vi to indent on s.o. for sth.* pedir algo a alguien.

indentation [ˌinden'teiʃən] *n* muesca *f* (notch) ‖ hendidura *f or* quebradura *f* en la costa ‖ PRINT sangría *f.*

indention [in'denʃən] *n* PRINT sangría *f.*

indenture [in'dentʃə*] *n* documento *m* cortado en dos partes (divided document) ‖ contrato *m* (contract).

indenture [in'dentʃə*] *vt* ligar por un contrato.

independence [ˌindi'pendəns] *n* independencia *f; to gain independence* conseguir la independencia.

independency [ˌindi'pendənsi] *n* estado *m* independiente (state) ‖ independencia *f* (independence).

independent [ˌindi'pendənt] *adj* independiente ‖ — *independent school* escuela *m* privada ‖ *to become independent of* independizarse de ‖ *to be independent of* no depender de.
◆ *n* independiente *m* & *f.*

in-depth *adj* a fondo, exhaustivo, va; *an in-depth study* un estudio exhaustivo.

indescribable [ˌindis'kraibəbl] *adj* indescriptible.

indestructibility ['indisˌtrʌktə'biliti] *n* indestructibilidad *f.*

indestructible [ˌindis'trʌktəbl] *adj* indestructible.

indeterminable [ˌindi'tə:minəbl] *adj* indeterminable.

indeterminate [ˌindi'tə:minit] *adj* indeterminado, da (not fixed) ‖ indefinido, da (undefined) ‖ MATH indeterminado, da ‖ BOT racimoso, sa.

indetermination ['indiˌtə:mi'neiʃən] *n* indeterminación *f,* indecisión *f,* irresolución *f.*

indeterminism [ˌindi'tə:minizəm] *n* indeterminismo *m* (theory).

indeterminist [ˌindi'tə:minist] *adj/n* indeterminista.

index ['indeks] *n* índice *m,* señal *f,* indicio *m,* prueba *f; the number of new cars is an index of prosperity* el número de coches nuevos es un índice de prosperidad ‖ índice *m* (forefinger) ‖ índice *m* (of a book) ‖ indicador *m* (of an instrument) ‖ PRINT manecilla *f* ‖ MATH exponente *m,* índice *m* ‖ REL índice *m* ‖ — *index card* ficha *f* ‖ REL *Index Expurgatorius* Índice Expurgatorio | *Index Librorum Prohibitorum* Índice de libros prohibidos ‖ PHYS *index of refraction, refractive index* índice de refracción ‖ *the cost-of-living index* el índice del coste de la vida.
— OBSERV El plural de la palabra *index* es *indexes* o *indices.*

index [ˌindeks] *vt* poner un índice a (a book) ‖ poner en el índice (an entry) ‖ clasificar (to file).

index finger [-'fiŋgə*] *n* dedo *m* índice.

indexing ['indeksiŋ] *n* INFORM indexación *f.*

index-linked [-liŋkt] *adj* ECON indexado, da; indiciado, da; vinculado, da a un índice.

index number [-'nʌmbə*] *n* índice *m,* indicador *m* [de precios, etc.].

India ['indjə] *pr n* GEOGR India *f.*
— OBSERV The article must be used in Spanish with the name of this country.

India ink [-iŋk] *n* tinta *f* china.

Indiaman [-mən] *n* barco *m* que hace el servicio de las Indias Orientales.

Indian [-n] *adj* indio, dia.
◆ *n* indio, dia (person) ‖ indio *m* (language).

Indiana [ˌindi'ænə] *pr n* GEOGR Indiana.

Indian club [-klʌb] *n* SP maza *f* de gimnasia.

Indian corn [-kɔ:n] *n* BOT maíz *m.*

Indian file [-fail] *n* fila *f* india.

Indian giver [-'givə*] *n* US FAM persona *f* que hace un regalo a otra y luego pide que le sea devuelto.

Indian hemp [-hemp] *n* BOT cáñamo *m* de la India.

Indian ink [-iŋk] *n* tinta *f* china.

Indianism [-nizəm] *n* indianismo *m* | indigenismo *m* (latin-american politico-literary movement in favour of the Indians).

Indian meal [-mi:l] *n* harina *f* de maíz.

Indian millet ['milit] *n* BOT alcandía *f*.

Indian Ocean [-'əuʃən] *pr n* GEOGR Océano *m* Índico.

Indian reed [-ri:d] *n* BOT cañacoro *m*.

Indian summer [-ʌmə*] *n* veranillo *m* de San Martín *or* del membrillo.

India paper ['indjə'peipə*] *n* papel *m* de China.

India rubber ['indjə'rʌbə*] *n* goma *f* de borrar (rubber eraser) || caucho *m* (natural rubber).

indicate ['indikeit] *vt* indicar, señalar (to point out, to show).

indication [,indi'keiʃən] *n* indicación *f*, señal *f* (sign) || indicación *f*.

indicative [in'dikətiv] *adj* indicativo, va; indicador, ra (giving an indication) || GRAMM indicativo || *to be indicative of* indicar.

◆ *n* GRAMM indicativo *m*.

indicator ['indikeitə*] *n* indicador *m* || AUT indicador *m*, intermitente *m* || TECH indicador *m*.

indices ['indisi:z] *pl n* → **index.**

indict [in'dait] *vt* JUR acusar (*for* de), procesar || JUR *to indict sth. as false* tachar algo de falsedad.

indictable [-əbl] *adj* procesable.

indiction [in'dikʃən] *n* indicción *f*.

indictment [in'daitmənt] *n* acusación *f*; *bill of indictment* acta de acusación.

indie ['indi] *n* FAM compañía *m* discográfica independiente.

Indies ['indiz] *pl n* GEOGR Indias *f*; *the West Indies* las Indias Occidentales; *the East Indies* las Indias Orientales.

indifference [in'difrəns] *n* indiferencia *f* (*to* ante) (lack of interest).

indifferent [in'difrəns] *n* indiferente; *it is indifferent to him* le es indiferente || insignificante, poco importante (insignificant) || FIG regular (neither good nor bad) || CHEM neutro, tra.

indifferently [in'difrəntli] *adv* indiferentemente || *he paints indifferently* su pintura es muy regular.

indigence ['indidʒəns] *n* indigencia *f*.

indigenous [in'didʒinəs] *adj* indígena, nativo, va.

indigent ['indidʒənt] *adj* indigente.

indigested [indi'dʒestid] *adj* mal digerido, da (food) || mal asimilado, da (knowledge) || confuso, sa (text).

indigestibility ['indi,dʒestə'biliti] *n* indigestibilidad *f*.

indigestible [,indi'dʒestəbl] *adj* indigesto, ta.

indigestion [,indi'dʒestʃən] *n* indigestión *f*, empacho *m*; *to suffer from indigestion* tener una indigestión.

indign [in'dain] *adj* indigno, na.

indignant [in'dignənt] *adj* indignado, da || — *to get indignant* indignarse || *to make s.o. indignant* indignar a uno.

indignantly [-li] *adv* con indignación.

indignation [,indig'neiʃən] *n* indignación *f* || *indignation meeting* reunión *f* de protesta.

indignity [in'digniti] *n* indignidad *f* (lack of dignity) || ultraje *m*, afrenta *f* (outrage).

indigo ['indigəu] *n* índigo *m* (dye, plant) || añil *m*, índigo *m* (colour).

◆ *adj* de color añil, añil.

indigo bird [-bə:d]; **indigo bunting** [-'bʌntiŋ] *n* ZOOL azulejo *m*.

indirect [,indi'rekt] *adj* indirecto, ta (not direct) || FIG sucio, cia (dishonest) || — US GRAMM *indirect discourse* estilo indirecto || *indirect lighting* luz indirecta || GRAMM *indirect object* complemento indirecto | *indirect speech* estilo indirecto || *indirect tax* impuesto indirecto.

indiscernible [,indi'sə:nəbl] *adj* indiscernible, imperceptible.

indiscipline [in'disiplin] *n* indisciplina *f*.

indiscreet [,indis'kri:t] *adj* indiscreto, ta; imprudente.

indiscrete [,indis'kri:t] *adj* homogéneo, a.

indiscretion [,indis'kreʃən] *n* indiscreción *f*, imprudencia *f*.

indiscriminate [,indis'kriminit] *adj* indistinto, ta || sin criterio (person).

indiscriminately [-li] *adv* indistintamente || sin criterio.

indispensable [,indis'pensəbl] *adj* indispensable, imprescindible (essential) || ineludible, obligatorio, ria (inevitable).

indispose [,indis'pəuz] *vt* indisponer.

indisposed [-d] *adj* indispuesto, ta.

indisposition [,indispə'ziʃən] *n* indisposición *f* (slight illness) || aversión *f* (disinclination).

indisputability ['indispju:tə'biliti] *n* indisputabilidad *f*, incontestabilidad *f*.

indisputable ['indis'pju:təbl] *adj* indisputable, indiscutible, incontestable, incontrovertible.

indisputably [-i] *adv* incontestablemente, sin duda alguna.

indissolubility [,indi'sɔlju'biliti] *n* indisolubilidad *f*.

indissoluble [,indi'sɔljubl] *adj* indisoluble.

indistinct [,indis'tiŋkt] *adj* indistinto, ta; confuso, sa (not clear) || indistinto, ta (not plainly defined).

indistinctive [,indis'tiŋktiv] *adj* común y corriente.

indistinctness [,indis'tiŋktnis] *n* falta *f* de claridad.

indistinguishable [,indis'tiŋgwiʃəbl] *adj* indistinguible (not easy to differentiate).

indite [in'dait] *vt* redactar (text, letter) || componer (verse).

inditement [-mənt] *n* redacción *f*, composición *f*.

inditer [-ə*] *n* redactor, ra; escritor, ra.

indium [indiəm] *n* CHEM indio *m*.

individual [,indi'vidjuəl] *adj* individual (existing as a complete and separate entity) || personal, particular, propio, pia; *a very individual style of dress* un estilo de vestido muy personal; *their individual qualities* sus cualidades particulares || — *add up the individual marks* suma cada una de las notas || *the guests all have individual telephones* cada invitado tiene su propio teléfono *or* su teléfono.

◆ *n* individuo *m* || *private individual* particular *m*.

individualism [-izəm] *n* individualismo *m*.

individualist [-ist] *n* individualista *m* & *f*.

individualistic [,indi,vidjuə'listik] *adj* individualista.

individuality [,indi,vidju'æliti] *n* individualidad *f* || personalidad *f* (special characteristics).

individualization [,indi,vidjuəlai'zeiʃən] *n* individualización *f*.

individualize [,indi'vidjuəlaiz] *vt* individualizar (to make individual) || particularizar.

individually [,indi'vidjuəli] *vt* individualmente || personalmente (personally).

individuate [indi'vidjueit] *vt* individuar.

individuation ['indi,vidju'eiʃən] *n* individuación *f*.

indivisibility [,indi,vizi'biliti] *n* indivisibilidad *f*.

indivisible [,indi'vizəbl] *adj* indivisible.

indivision [indi'viʒən] *n* indivisión *f*.

Indochina ['indəu'tʃainə] *pr n* GEOGR Indochina *f*.

Indochinese; Indo-Chinese ['indəutʃai'ni:z] *adj* indochino, na.

◆ *n* indochino, na (person) || indochino *m* (language).

indocile [in'dəusail] *adj* indócil.

indocility [,indəu'siliti] *n* indocilidad *f*.

indoctrinate [in'dɔktrineit] *vt* adoctrinar.

indoctrination [in,dɔktri'neiʃən] *n* adoctrinamiento *m*.

Indo-European ['indəu,juərə'pi:ən] *adj/n* indo-europeo, a.

Indo-Germanic ['indəudʒə:'mænik] *adj/n* indo-germánico, ca.

indolence ['indələns] *n* indolencia *f*.

indolent ['indələnt] *adj* indolente (lazy) || indoloro, ra (painless).

indomitable [in'dɔmitəbl] *adj* indomable, indómito, ta.

Indonesia [,indəu'ni:zjə] *pr n* GEOGR Indonesia *f*.

Indonesian [-n] *adj/n* indonesio, sia.

indoor ['indɔ:*] *adj* interior; *indoor aerial* antena interior || — *indoor activities* actividades caseras || *indoor clothes* traje *m* de casa || *indoor games* juegos *m* de sociedad || *indoor lavatory* retrete *m* en la casa || *indoor life* vida casera *or* de familia || *indoor sports* deportes *m* en sala || *indoor swimming pool* piscina cubierta.

indoors ['in'dɔ:z] *adv* dentro; *we'll be more comfortable indoors* estaremos mejor dentro || en casa; *to be, to stay indoors* estar, quedarse en casa || — *indoors and outdoors* dentro y fuera de la casa || *indoors it is decorated with red velvet* el interior está decorado con terciopelo rojo || *let's go indoors, it's warmer* entremos, que hace más calor dentro.

indophenol [ində'fi:nɔl] *n* CHEM indofenol *m*.

indorse [in'dɔ:s] *vt* → **endorse.**

indraught; US **indraft** ['indra:ft] *n* corriente *f* || aspiración *f* de aire.

indubitable [in'dju:bitəbl] *adj* indudable, indubitable.

indubitably [in'dju:bitəbli] *adv* indudablemente, sin duda.

induce [in'dju:s] *vt* inducir, persuadir (to convince); *I have induced him to accompany us* le persuadí de que nos acompañara, le induje a que nos acompañara || causar, ocasionar, producir, provocar (to cause) || PHYS inducir || (ant) inducir (to infer).

inducement [-mənt] *n* incentivo *m*, estímulo *m*, aliciente *m* (incentive) || atractivo *m* (attractiveness) || móvil *m* (motive).

inducer [-ə*] *n* inducidor, ra; provocador, ra.

inducing [-iŋ] *adj* inducidor, ra; inductor, ra.

induct [in'dʌkt] *vt* instalar (into a position, office) || admitir (in a society) || iniciar (to initiate) || PHYS inducir || US MIL incorporar a filas.

inductance [in'dʌktəns] *n* PHYS inductancia *f*.

inductee [indʌk'ti:] *n* MIL recluta *m*.

inductile [in'dʌktail] *adj* PHYS indúctil, no dúctil || FIG inflexible.

induction [in'dʌkʃən] *n* PHIL & ELECTR inducción *f* || TECH admisión *f* || instalación *f* (installation) || admisión *f* (in a society) || iniciación *f* (iniciation) || US MIL incorporación *f*.

induction coil [-kɔil] *n* ELECTR bobina *f or* carrete *m* de inducción.

induction course [-kɔːs] *n* curso *m* de introducción (education).

inductive [in'dʌktiv] *adj* inductivo, va (logic) || inductor, ra (inducing) || ELECTR inductor, ra (of electric or magnetic induction) | inductivo, va (of inductance).

inductively [-li] *adv* por inducción.

inductor [in'dʌktə*] *n* ELECTR & CHEM inductor *m*.

indue [in'djuː] *vt* ⟶ **endue.**

indulge [in'dʌldʒ] *vt* mimar, consentir (to pamper) || consentir, ceder a (to comply with); *to indulge s.o.'s wishes* consentir los caprichos de uno || dar rienda suelta a (to let loose); *to indulge one's anger* dar rienda suelta a su cólera || complacer (a person) || COMM conceder un plazo a || *to indulge o.s.* darse gusto.
◆ *vi I don't indulge* no fumo (in smoking), no bebo (in drinking) || *to indulge in* entregarse a (vice, pleasures, etc.), permitirse el lujo de, darse el gusto de.

indulgence [in'dʌldʒəns] *n* indulgencia *f*, complacencia *f* (pampering) || tolerancia *f*, indulgencia *f* (tolerance, leniency) || satisfacción *f* (of desire, etc.) || exceso *m*, desenfreno *m* (self-indulgence) || vicio *m* (a habit indulged in) || COMM moratoria *f* || REL indulgencia *f*.

indulgent [in'dʌldʒənt] *adj* indulgente (*towards* con).

indult [in'dʌlt] *n* REL indulto *m*.

indurate ['indjuəreit] *vt* endurecer || FIG endurecer (feelings) || MED indurar.
◆ *vi* endurecerse || MED indurarse || FIG endurecerse.

induration [indjuə'reiʃən] *n* endurecimiento *m* || MED induración *f* || FIG endurecimiento *m*.

Indus ['indəs] *n* GEOGR Indo *m*.

industrial [in'dʌstriəl] *adj* industrial || — *industrial accident* o *injury* accidente *m* de trabajo *or* laboral || *industrial action* huelga *f*; *to take industrial action* declararse en huelga || *industrial disease* enfermedad *f* profesional || *industrial estate*, US *industrial park* polígono *m* industrial || *industrial tribunal* magistratura *f* de trabajo || *industrial relations* relaciones *f* profesionales.
◆ *n* industrial *m*.
◆ *pl* valores *m* industriales.

industrialism [in'dʌstriəlizəm] *n* industrialismo *m*.

industrialist [in'dʌstriəlist] *n* industrial *m*.

industrialization [in,dʌstriəlai'zeiʃən] *n* industrialización *f*.

industrialize [in'dʌstriəlaiz] *vt* industrializar.

industrious [in'dʌstriəs] *adj* trabajador, ra; industrioso, sa; laborioso, sa || estudioso, sa; aplicado, da (studious).

industriousness [-nis] *n* laboriosidad *f* || aplicación *f*.

industry ['indəstri] *n* industria *f*; *heavy industry* industria pesada; *light industry* industria ligera; *iron and steel industry* industria siderúrgica || laboriosidad *f*, diligencia *f* (industriousness) || aplicación *f* || *the tourist industry* el turismo.

indwell ['in'dwel] *vt* residir en, morar en.
◆ *vi* residir, morar.

indweller [-ə*] *n* habitante *m* & *f*, residente *m* & *f*.

inebriant [in'iːbriənt] *adj* embriagador, ra; embriagante.

inebriate [i'niːbrieit] *vt* embriagar, emborrachar (to intoxicate) || FIG embriagar.

inebriate [i'niːbriit] *adj* ebrio, a; embriagado, da; borracho, cha.
◆ *n* borracho, cha.

inebriated [-id] *adj* ebrio, a; embriagado, da.

inebriation [i,niːbri'eiʃən] *n* embriaguez *f*, ebriedad *f*.

inedible [in'edibl] *adj* incomible, incomestible.

inedited [in'editid] *adj* inédito, ta (unpublished).

ineducable [in'edjukəbl] *adj* ineducable.

ineffability [inefə'biliti] *n* inefabilidad *f*.

ineffable [in'efəbl] *adj* inefable.

ineffaceable [,ini'feisəbl] *adj* indeleble, imborrable.

ineffective [,ini'fektiv] *adj* ineficaz (without effect) || inútil (useless) || ineficaz (person) || *to prove ineffective* no surtir efecto.

ineffectiveness [-nis] *n* ineficacia *f*.

ineffectual [,ini'fektjuəl] *adj* ineficaz, inútil.

inefficacious [,inefi'keiʃəs] *adj* ineficaz.

inefficacy [in'efikəsi] *n* ineficacia *f*.

inefficiency [ini'fiʃənsi] *n* ineficacia *f*, inutilidad *f* (of an act) || incompetencia *f*, ineficacia *f* (of a person).

inefficient [,ini'fiʃənt] *adj* ineficaz, inútil (useless) || ineficaz, incompetente.

inelastic [,ini'læstik] *adj* no elástico, ca (not elastic) || FIG inflexible (not adaptable) | fijo, ja (supply and demand).

inelasticity [,inilæs'tisiti] *n* falta *f* de elasticidad || FIG inflexibilidad *f*.

inelegance [in'eligəns] *n* inelegancia *f*.

inelegant [in'eligənt] *adj* poco elegante.

ineligibility [in,elidʒə'biliti] *n* inelegibilidad *f*.

ineligible [in,elidʒəbl] *adj* inelegible (not eligible) || inadecuado, da (unsuited) || no apto (for military service).

ineluctability ['ine,lʌktə'biliti] *n* calidad *f* de ineluctable, inevitabilidad *f*.

ineluctable [ine'lʌktəbl] *adj* ineluctable, inevitable.

ineludible [inə'ludəbl] *adj* ineludible.

inept [i'nept] *adj* inepto, ta; incapaz (incompetent) || inadecuado, da (unfit) || inepto, ta; estúpido, da.

ineptitude [i'neptitjuːd] *n* ineptitud *f*, incapacidad *f* (incompetence) || inepcia *f*, necedad *f*, ineptitud *f* (inept action).

ineptness [i'neptnis] *n* ineptitud *f*, incapacidad *f*.

inequality [,ini'kwɔliti] *n* desigualdad *f* (lack of equality) || injusticia *f* (injustice) || desigualdad *f* (unevenness) || ASTR & MATH desigualdad *f*.

inequation [in'ikwei'ʃən] *n* MATH inecuación *f*.

inequitable [in'ekwitəbl] *adj* injusto, ta.

inequity [in'ekwiti] *n* injusticia *f*, falta *f* de equidad.

ineradicable [ini'rædikəbl] *adj* inextirpable || indeleble (ineffaceable).

inerrability [inerə'biliti] *n* infalibilidad *f*.

inerrable [i'nerəbl] *adj* infalible.

inert [i'nəːt] *adj* inerte || FIG inerte || *inert gas* gas *m* inerte.

inertia [i'nəːʃjə] *n* inercia *f*.

inertial [i'nəːʃjəl] *adj* de inercia; *inertial force* fuerza de inercia || — *inertial guidance* dirección *f* por inercia || *inertial mass* masa inerte.

inertness [i'nəːtnis] *n* inercia *f*.

inescapable [,inis'keipəbl] *adj* ineludible, inevitable.

inessential ['ini'senʃəl] *adj* no esencial, accesorio, ria.
◆ *n* lo accesorio.

inestimable [in'estiməbl] *adj* inestimable.

inevitability [in,evitə'biliti] *n* inevitabilidad *f*.

inevitable [in'evitəbl] *adj* inevitable, ineludible.
◆ *n* lo inevitable.

inexact [,inig'zækt] *adj* inexacto, ta.

inexactitude [,inig'zæktitjuːd] *n* inexactitud *f*.

inexactly [,inig'zæktli] *adv* de modo inexacto.

inexcusable [,iniks'kjuːzəbl] *adj* imperdonable, inexcusable.

inexecutable [in'eksikjutəbl] *adj* inejecutable.

inexecution [in,eksi'kjuːʃən] *n* inejecución *f*, incumplimiento *m*.

inexhaustible [,inig'zɔːstəbl] *adj* inagotable.

inexigible [in'igzidʒibl] *adj* inexigible.

inexistent [inik'sistənt] *adj* inexistente.

inexorability [in,eksərə'biliti] *n* inexorabilidad *f*.

inexorable [in'eksərəbl] *adj* inexorable.

inexpediency [,iniks'piːdjənsi] *n* inoportunidad *f*, inconveniencia *f*.

inexpedient [,iniks'piːdjənt] *adj* inoportuno, na; inconveniente.

inexpensive [,iniks'pensiv] *adj* barato, ta; económico, ca; poco costoso, sa.

inexperience [,iniks'piəriəns] *n* inexperiencia *f*, falta *f* de experiencia.

inexperienced [-t] *adj* inexperto, ta; sin experiencia.

inexpert [,ineks'pəːt] *adj* inexperto, ta.

inexpiable [in'ekspiəbl] *adj* inexpiable.

inexplicability [in,eksplikə'biliti] *adj* carácter *m* inexplicable.

inexplicable [in'eksplikəbl] *adj* inexplicable.

inexplicit [,iniks'plisit] *adj* poco explícito, ta.

inexpressibility [inikspresi'biliti] *adj* inefabilidad *f*.

inexpressible [iniks'presəbl] *adj* inexpresable, indecible, inefable.

inexpressive [,iniks'presiv] *adj* inexpresivo, va (devoid of expression); *an inexpressive style* un estilo inexpresivo || reservado, da; callado, da (reserved).

inexpugnable [,iniks'pʌgnəbl] *adj* inexpugnable.

inextensible [,inik'stensəbl] *adj* inextensible.

in extenso [,inik'stensəu] *adv phr* in extenso.

inextinguishable [,iniks'tiŋgwiʃəbl] *adj* inextinguible (passion, etc.) || inapagable (fire, light, etc.).

inextirpable [iniks'təːpəbl] *adj* inextirpable.

in extremis [iniks'treimis] *adv phr* in extremis.

inextricable [in'ekstrikəbl] *adj* inextricable.

infallibility [in,fælə'biliti] *n* infalibilidad *f*.

infallible [in'fæləbl] *adj* infalible.

infamous ['infəməs] *adj* de mala fama, infame (of ill repute) || infame, odioso, sa (arousing horror) || JUR infame (crime, person) | infamante (punishment).

infamy ['infəmi] *n* infamia *f*.

infancy ['infənsi] *n* infancia *f*, niñez *f* || FIG principio *m*, infancia *f*, comienzo *m*; *it is in its* *infancy* está en sus comienzos || JUR minoría *f* de edad, menor edad *f*.

infant ['infənt] *n* niño, ña (very young child) || párvulo, la (young pupil) || JUR menor *m* & *f* de edad (minor) || *the infant Jesus* el niño Jesús.
◆ *adj* FIG naciente (industry, etc.) || de párvulos (school) || *infant mortality rate* mortalidad *f* infantil.

infanta [in'fæntə] *n* infanta *f* (princess).

infante [in'fænti] *n* infante *m* (prince).

infanticide [in'fæntisaid] *n* infanticidio *m* (the killing of a child) || infanticida *m* & *f* (murderer).

infantile ['infəntail] *adj* infantil || MED *infantile paralysis* parálisis *f* infantil.

infantine ['infəntain] *adj* infantil, pueril.

infantry ['infəntri] *n* MIL infantería *f*.

infantryman [-mən] *n* MIL soldado *m* de infantería, infante *m*.
— OBSERV El plural de esta palabra es *infantrymen*.

infarct [in'fɑːkt] *n* MED infarto *m*; *infarct of the myocardium* infarto del miocardio.

infatuate [in'fætjueit] *vt* atontar (to make foolish) || enamorar locamente, chiflar (to inspire with foolish passion).

infatuated [-id] *adj to be infatuated with* estar encaprichado por (an idea), estar chiflado por *or* locamente enamorado de (a person).

infatuation [in'fætju'eiʃən] *n* enamoramiento *m*, encaprichamiento *m*.

infeasible [in'fiːzibl] *adj* no factible, imposible de hacer.

infect [in'fekt] *vt* infectar, inficionar; *to infect a wound* infectar una herida || contaminar, contagiar (to contaminate) || FIG corromper || FIG *he infected everybody with his indignation* contagió a todos su indignación.

infection [in'fekʃən] *n* infección *f* || contaminación *f*, contagio *m*.

infectious [in'fekʃəs] *adj* infeccioso, sa; contagioso, sa; *an infectious disease* una enfermedad contagiosa || FIG *infectious laughter* risa contagiosa.

infectiousness [-nis] *n* contagiosidad *f*.

infective [in'fektiv] *adj* infeccioso, sa.

infecund [in'fikʌnd] *adj* infecundo, da.

infecundity [,infi'kʌnditi] *n* infecundidad *f*.

infelicitous [,infi'lisitəs] *adj* inapropiado, da; poco afortunado, da; desacertado, da (not appropriate) || desgraciado, da (not happy).

infelicity [,infi'lisiti] *n* inoportunidad *f* (unsuitability) || desacierto *m*, metedura *f* de pata (blunder) || (ant) desgracia *f*, infelicidad *f* (misfortune).

infer [in'fəː*] *vt* inferir, deducir (to deduce).

inferable [-rəbl] *adj* deducible.

inference ['infərəns] *n* inferencia *f*, deducción *f* || *by inference* por deducción.

inferential [,infə'renʃəl] *adj* que se deduce, que se infiere.

inferior [in'fiəriə*] *adj* inferior, de poca calidad (of poor quality) || inferior (of poorer quality, of lower rank or status) || inferior (placed lower down).
◆ *n* inferior *m*.

inferiority [in,fiəri'ɔriti] *n* inferioridad *f*; *inferiority complex* complejo de inferioridad.

infernal [in'fəːnl] *adj* infernal (of hell) || FAM infernal, endemoniado, da; *infernal noise* ruido endemoniado || — *infernal machine* máquina *f* infernal || FAM *why won't this infernal contraption work?* ¿por qué no funciona este maldito cacharro?

infernally [in'fəːnli] *adv* terriblemente || *it is infernally hot* hace un calor de mil demonios.

inferno [in'fəːnəu] *n* infierno *m* (hell, or place resembling it) || FIG hoguera *f* (blazing building) | llamas *f pl*; *the girders melted in the inferno* las vigas se derritieron entre las llamas || *Dante's Inferno* el Infierno de Dante.

infertile [in'fəːtail] *adj* estéril (land) || infecundo, da; estéril (people).

infertility [infəː'tiliti] *n* esterilidad *f* (of land) || infecundidad *f*, esterilidad *f* (of a person).

infest [in'fest] *vt* infestar, plagar.

infeudation [,infju'deiʃən] *n* enfeudación *f*.

infidel ['infidəl] *adj/n* infiel, pagano, na.

infidelity [,infi'deliti] *n* infidelidad *f* || FIG deslealtad *f* (disloyalty).

infield [infiːld] *n* SP terreno *m* central (ground near the wicket in cricket) | jugadores *m pl* centrales (players in this area) | cuadro *m* interior (playing square in baseball) | jugadores *m pl* del cuadro interior (players in this area) || tierras *f pl* alrededor de una granja (lands near a farmhouse).

infielder [-ə*] *n* SP jugador *m* central (in cricket) | jugador *m* del cuadro interior (in baseball).

infighting ['infaitiŋ] *n* SP lucha *f* cuerpo a cuerpo (in boxing).

infiltrate ['infiltreit] *n* MED infiltrado *m*.

infiltrate ['infiltreit] *vi* infiltrarse (*into* en).
◆ *vt* infiltrar || infiltrarse en; *to infiltrate an organization* infiltrarse en una organización.

infiltration [,infil'treiʃən] *n* infiltración *f*.

infinite ['infinit] *adj* infinito, ta || — GRAMM *infinite verb* forma sustantiva del verbo || *to do infinite harm* hacer muchísimo daño.
◆ *n* infinito *m*.

infinitesimal [,infini'tesiməl] *adj* infinitesimal, infinitésimo, ma || MATH *infinitesimal calculus* cálculo *m* infinitesimal.
◆ *n* MATH cantidad *f* infinitesimal.

infinitive [in'finitiv] *adj* GRAMM infinitivo.
◆ *n* GRAMM infinitivo *m*.

infinitude [in'finitjuːd] *n* infinitud *f*, infinidad *f*.

infinity [in'finiti] *n* infinidad *f* (quality of being infinite, a large amount or quantity) || MATH infinito *m*.

infirm [in'fəːm] *adj* enfermizo, za; débil (physically weak) || JUR nulo, la (document) || FIG *infirm of purpose* indeciso, sa; irresoluto, ta.

infirmary [-əri] *n* enfermería *f* (of school, etc.) || hospital *m*.

infirmity [-iti] *n* enfermedad *f*, achaque *m* (illness) || debilidad *f* (weakness) || FIG debilidad *f*, flaqueza *f*.

infix ['infiks] *n* GRAMM infijo *m*.

infix ['infiks] *vt* inculcar (to instill) || intercalar (to insert) || fijar (to set in).

inflame [in'fleim] *vt* inflamar (to set on fire) || MED inflamar || FIG avivar (passion) | encender; *anger inflamed her cheeks* la cólera encendía sus mejillas.
◆ *vi* inflamarse, encenderse (to catch fire) || MED inflamarse || FIG inflamarse, acalorarse.

inflammability [in,flæmə'biliti] *n* inflamabilidad *f*.

inflammable [in'flæməbl] *adj* inflamable (easily set on fire) || FIG irritable (easily angered or excited).
◆ *n* sustancia *f* inflamable.

inflammation [,inflə'meiʃən] *n* inflamación *f* || MED inflamación *f* || FIG acaloramiento *m*.

inflammatory [in'flæmətəri] *adj* MED inflamatorio, ria || FIG incendiario, ria (that stirs up feelings).

inflatable [in'fleitəbl] *adj* inflable.

inflate [in'fleit] *vt* hinchar, inflar (to cause to swell with gas or air) || COMM provocar la inflación de || *to inflate s.o. with pride* llenar a uno de orgullo, engreír a alguien.

inflated [-id] *adj* hinchado, da; inflado, da (full of air or gas) || FIG pomposo, sa; rimbombante (language, style) | henchido, da; engreído, da (elated with pride) || COMM en situación inflacionista, inflacionario, ria | excesivo, va (prices).

inflation [in'fleiʃən] *n* inflado *m* (with air or gas) || pomposidad *f*, rimbombancia *f* (of language) || ECON inflación *f*; *runaway inflation* inflación galopante.

inflationary [in'fleiʃnəri] *adj* inflacionario, ria; inflacionista || ECON *inflationary spiral* espiral *f* inflacionaria.

inflationism [in'fleiʃnizəm] *n* inflacionismo *m*.

inflation-proof [in'fleiʃənpruːf] *adj* resistente a cambios inflacionistas.

inflator [in'fleitə*] *n* bomba *f* [para hinchar neumáticos] || inflador *m*.

inflect [in'flekt] *vt* GRAMM declinar | conjugar || torcer, doblar (to bend) || MUS modular.

inflection [in'flekʃən] *n* inflexión *f*.

inflexibility [in'fleksə'biliti] *n* inflexibilidad *f*.

inflexible [in'fleksəbl] *adj* inflexible.

inflexion [in'flekʃən] *n* inflexión.

inflict [in'flikt] *vt* infligir, imponer (a punishment, penalty) || dar, asestar (blow) || hacer, causar (wounds, grief, harm) || *to inflict o.s. on s.o.* imponer su presencia a alguien.

infliction [in'flikʃən] *n* imposición *f* (act of inflicting punishment) || castigo *m* (punishment).

in-flight ['inflait] *adj* durante el vuelo (meal, entertainment).

inflorescence [inflɔ'resəns] *n* BOT florescencia *f*.

inflow ['infləu] *n* afluencia *f*.

influence ['influəns] *n* influencia *f* (*on, over* sobre; *with* con) (indirect power) || ELECTR inducción *f* || — *a man of influence* un hombre influyente || *to be an influence* tener influencia || *to bring every influence to bear* utilizar toda su influencia || *to get sth. by influence* conseguir algo por influencias || *to have an influence over s.o.* ejercer una influencia sobre uno || FIG *to have influence at court* tener buenas aldabas || *under the influence of drink, of drugs* bajo los efectos del alcohol, de las drogas.

influence ['influəns] *vt* influenciar (a person) || influir en (a decision, etc.) || *he is easily influenced* es influenciable.

influent ['influənt] *adj* afluente.
◆ *n* afluente *m*.

influential [,influ'enʃəl] *adj* influyente.

influenza [,influ'enzə] *n* MED gripe *f*.

influenzal [-l] *adj* MED gripal.

influx ['inflʌks] *n* entrada *f* (of liquid, gas, etc.) || desembocadura *f* (of a river in the sea) || afluencia *f*; *the influx of tourists* la afluencia de turistas.

info ['infəu] *n* FAM información *f*.

inform [in'fɔːm] *vt* informar (*about* sobre), poner al corriente (*about* de) (to communicate information to) || informar, avisar (*of* de) (to tell) || inspirar (to inspire) || (ant) formar, moldear (the mind) || — *I am pleased to inform you that...* tengo el placer de comunicarle que... || *to keep o.s. informed* mantenerse al corriente || *to keep s.o. informed* tener a alguien al corriente.
◆ *vi to inform against* o *on* denunciar a, delatar a.

informal [in'fɔ:ml] *adj* sencillo, lla (person) ‖ sin cumplidos, entre amigos, sin etiqueta, sin ceremonia; *an informal dinner* una cena entre amigos ‖ familiar (tone) ‖ no oficial, extraoficial, oficioso, sa (unofficial) ‖ *informal dress* traje *m* de calle.

informality [ˌinfɔ:'mæliti] *n* sencillez *f* (of a person) ‖ carácter *m* íntimo (intimacy) ‖ ausencia *f* de ceremonia (of a dinner, etc.).

informally [in'fɔ:məli] *adv* sin ceremonia (without ceremony) ‖ en tono de confianza (speaking) ‖ sencillamente (dressed) ‖ oficiosamente (unofficially).

informant [in'fɔ:mənt] *n* informante *m* & *f*.

information [ˌinfə'meiʃən] *n* información *f* (the communication of news, knowledge, etc.) ‖ datos *m pl*, información *f*; *to have no information regarding...* no tener información sobre...; *to feed a machine with information* introducir información *or* datos en una máquina ‖ JUR denuncia *f*, acusación *f* (complaint of accusation) ‖ conocimientos *m pl* (knowledge); *the information we have today about hormone behaviour* los conocimientos que hoy tenemos sobre el comportamiento de las hormonas ‖ — *a piece of information* una información, un dato ‖ *by way of information* a título de información, a título informativo ‖ *classified information* información de difusión secreta *or* reservada ‖ *for your information* para que lo sepa Ud., para su información ‖ INFORM *information flow* flujo *m* de información | *information retrieval* recuperación *f* de la información ‖ *information service* servicio *m* de información ‖ INFORM *information technology* tecnología *f* de la información ‖ *to ask for information* pedir informes *or* información ‖ *to give information to the police* proporcionar información a la policía ‖ JUR *to lay an information against s.o.* denunciar *or* delatar a alguien.

information bureau [-bjuə'rəu] *n* centro *m* de informaciones.

information desk [-desk] *n* informaciones *f pl*; *where is the information desk?* ¿dónde están las informaciones?

informative [in'fɔ:mətiv] *adj* informativo, va.

informed [in'fɔ:md] *adj* informado, da; al corriente, al tanto (having much information) ‖ culto, ta (having much education).

informer [in'fɔ:mə*] *n* denunciante *m* & *f*, delator, ra ‖ confidente *m* (of the police).

infraction [in'frækʃən] *n* infracción *f*.

infractor [in'fræktə*] *n* infractor, ra.

infra dig ['infrə'dig] *adj* indigno (*for* de).

infrangible [in'frændʒibl] *adj* irrompible ‖ FIG inquebrantable.

infrared ['infrə'red] *adj* infrarrojo, ja.
◆ *n* infrarrojo.

infrasonic ['infrə'sɔnik] *adj* *infrasonic wave* infrasonido *m*.

infrastructure ['infrəˌstrʌktʃə*] *n* infraestructura *f*.

infrequency [in'fri:kwənsi] *n* poca frecuencia *f*, rareza *f*.

infrequent [in'fri:kwənt] *adj* poco frecuente, infrecuente, raro, ra.

infrequently [-li] *adv* raramente, raras veces.

infringe [in'frinʒ] *vt* infringir, violar (law, etc.).
◆ *vi* *to infringe on* o *upon* usurpar (s.o.'s rights).

infringement [-mənt] *n* infracción *f*, violación *f* (of a law) ‖ usurpación *f* (encroachment).

infulae ['infjuli] *pl n* ínfulas *f*.

infuriate [in'fjuərieit] *vt* enfurecer, poner furioso (to make furious); *sometimes you infuriate me* a veces me pones furioso ‖ exasperar; *all this gossip infuriates me* todo este chismorreo me exaspera.

infuriating [-iŋ] *adj* exasperante.

infuriation [in'fjuəri'eiʃən] *n* exasperación *f*, enfurecimiento *m*.

infuse [in'fju:z] *vt* FIG infundir (to instil) ‖ hacer una infusión de (to soak tea, etc.).

infusion [in'fju:ʒən] *n* infusión *f*.

infusoria [infju:'zɔ:riə] *pl n* ZOOL infusorios *m*.

ingathering ['inˌgæðəriŋ] *n* recolección *f*, recogida *f* (of harvest).

ingeminate [in'dʒemineit] *vt* repetir, reiterar (to repeat).

ingemination [inˌdʒemi'neiʃən] *n* repetición *f*, reiteración *f*.

ingenious [in'dʒi:njəs] *adj* ingenioso, sa.

ingeniousness [-nis] *n* ingeniosidad *f*, ingenio *m*.

ingénue [ɛ̃:nʒei'nju:] *n* THEATR ingenua *f*.

ingenuity [ˌindʒi'nju:iti] *n* ingeniosidad *f*, ingenio *m* (ingeniousness) ‖ cosa *f* ingeniosa (ingenious device).

ingenuous [in'dʒenjuəs] *adj* ingenuo, nua; cándido, da (naïve) ‖ franco, ca; sincero, ra (frank, candid).

ingest [in'dʒest] *vt* ingerir.

ingestion [-ʃən] *n* ingestión *f*.

ingle ['ingl] *n* fuego *m* de chimenea, lumbre *f* (fire) ‖ hogar *m*, chimenea *f* (fireplace).

inglenook [-nuk] *n* rincón *m* de la chimenea (chimney corner) ‖ *in the inglenook* junto a la chimenea, al amor de la lumbre.

inglorious [in'glɔ:riəs] *adj* vergonzoso, sa; ignominioso, sa (shameful) ‖ sin fama, desconocido, da (not famous).

in-goal ['ingəul] *n* SP zona *f* de meta (in rugby).

ingoing ['inˌgəuiŋ] *adj* entrante, que entra.

ingot ['ingət] *n* lingote *m*, barra *f*; *gold ingots* lingotes de oro, oro en barras; *ingot steel* acero en lingotes ‖ lingotera *f* (mould).

ingrain ['in'grein] *vt* FIG inculcar (habits, tastes, etc.) ‖ teñir (to dye).

ingrain carpet [-'kɑ:pit] *n* alfombra *f* reversible.

ingrained [-d] *adj* inculcado, da ‖ arraigado, da (firmly established).

ingrate [in'greit] *adj/n* ingrato, ta.

ingratiate [in'greiʃieit] *vt* *to ingratiate o.s. with* congraciarse con.

ingratiating [-iŋ] *adj* zalamero, ra.

ingratitude [in'grætitju:d] *n* ingratitud *f*.

ingravescent [in'grævesənt] *adj* MED que se agrava.

ingredient [in'gri:djənt] *n* ingrediente *m*.

ingress ['ingres] *n* acceso *m* (access, entrance) ‖ entrada *f*, ingreso *m* (going in).

ingrowing ['ingrəuiŋ] *adj* que crece hacia dentro ‖ *ingrowing nail* uñero *m*, uña encarnada.

ingrown ['ingrəun] *adj* crecido hacia dentro ‖ FIG innato, ta ‖ *ingrown nail* uñero *m*, uña encarnada.

inguinal ['ingwinl] *adj* ANAT inguinal.

ingurgitate [in'gə:dʒiteit] *n* ingurgitar, engullir.

ingurgitation [ingə:dʒi'teiʃən] *n* ingurgitación *f*.

inhabit [in'hæbit] *vt* habitar (to occupy) ‖ vivir en (to live in).

inhabitable [-əbl] *adj* habitable.

inhabitant [-ənt] *n* habitante *m*.

inhabitation [inˌhæbi'teiʃən] *n* habitación *f*.

inhabited [in'hæbitid] *adj* habitado, da; poblado, da.

inhalant [in'heilənt] *n* medicamento *m* para inhalación *or* para inhalar.
◆ *adj* inhalador, ra; para inhalar.

inhalation [ˌinhə'leiʃən] *n* inhalación *f*.

inhale [in'heil] *vt* MED inhalar ‖ aspirar, inhalar (air) ‖ tragar (tobacco smoke).

inhaler [-ə*] *n* inhalador *m*.

inharmonic [inhɑ:'mɔunik] *adj* inarmónico, ca.

inharmonious [ˌinhɑ:'məunjəs] *adj* inarmónico, ca (sounds) ‖ FIG falto de *or* sin armonía, poco armonioso, sa (colours, relations, etc.).

inharmony [inhɑ:'məuni] *n* inarmonía *f*.

inhere [in'hiə*] *vi* ser inherente (*in* a), ser propio (*in* de).

inherence [in'hiərəns]; **inherency** [-i] *n* inherencia *f*.

inherent [in'hiərənt] *adj* inherente (*in* a), propio, pia (*in* de), intrínseco, ca.

inherit [in'herit] *vt* heredar (a fortune, a title).
◆ *vi* heredar.

inheritability [-əbiliti] *n* transmisibilidad *f* (of property, title) ‖ capacidad *f* para heredar (of person).

inheritable [in'heritəbl] *adj* transmisible (property, title) ‖ capaz de heredar, que puede heredar (person).

inheritance [in'heritəns] *n* herencia *f*; *to receive an inheritance* recibir una herencia ‖ sucesión *f*; *intestate, testate inheritance* sucesión intestada, testada ‖ FIG & MED herencia *f* ‖ — *inheritance tax* impuesto *m* sobre sucesiones ‖ *to come into an inheritance* heredar.

inheritor [in'heritə*] *n* heredero *m* (heir).

inheritress [in'heritris]; **inheritrix** [in'heritriks] *n* heredera *f* (heiress).

inhibit [in'hibit] *vt* inhibir, reprimir (to restrain, to hold in check) ‖ impedir (to prevent).

inhibition [ˌinhi'biʃən] *n* inhibición *f*.

inhibitor [in'hibitə*] *n* CHEM inhibidor *m*.

inhibitory [in'hibitəri] *adj* inhibitorio, ria.

inhospitable [in'hɔspitəbl] *adj* inhóspito, ta (place) ‖ inhospitalario, ria (person).

inhospitality ['inˌhɔspi'tæliti] *n* inhospitalidad *f*, falta *f* de hospitalidad.

in-house ['inˌhaus] *adj* interno, na, en *or* de la propia empresa, de la casa ‖ *in-house magazine* revista *f* de circulación interna.

inhuman [in'hju:mən] *adj* inhumano, na (lacking human mercy) ‖ insensible, frío, a (insensitive) ‖ sobrehumano, na (superhuman).

inhumane [ˌinhju'mein] *adj* inhumano, na.

inhumanity [ˌinhju:'mæniti] *n* inhumanidad *f*.

inhumation [ˌinhju:'meiʃən] *n* inhumación *f*.

inhume [in'hju:m] *vt* inhumar.

inimical [i'nimikəl] *adj* hostil (hostile) ‖ contrario, ria; que va en contra de; *inimical to the national interest* contrario al interés nacional.

inimitable [i'nimitəbl] *adj* inimitable.

iniquitous [i'nikwitəs] *adj* inicuo, cua.

iniquity [i'nikwiti] *n* iniquidad *f*.

initial [i'niʃəl] *adj* inicial, primero, ra (of or occurring at the beginning) ‖ COMM inicial (capital).
◆ *n* inicial *f* (first letter) ‖ letra *f* florida (large decorative letter).

◆ *pl* iniciales *f* (of a name) ‖ siglas *f* (used as abbreviation); *ILO are the initials of the International Labour Organization* OIT son las siglas de la Organización Internacional del Trabajo.

initial [i'niʃəl] *vt* poner iniciales a, poner las iniciales a ‖ firmar con las iniciales (to sign) ‖ JUR rubricar (a document).

initialization [i,niʃəlai'zeiʃən] *n* INFORM inicialización *f*.

initialize [i'niʃəlaiz] *vt* INFORM inicializar.

initially [-i] *adv* inicialmente, al principio.

initiate [i'niʃieit] *vt* iniciar; *to initiate an investigation* iniciar una investigación; *to initiate s.o. into a practice* iniciar a uno en una práctica ‖ entablar, iniciar (negotiations) ‖ entablar (proceedings) ‖ admitir (into a secret society).

initiate [i'niʃiit] *adj/n* iniciado, da.

initiation [i,niʃi'eiʃən] *n* iniciación *f*, principio *m*, comienzo *m* (beginning) ‖ iniciación *f* (into a practice, a society).

initiative [i'niʃiətiv] *n* iniciativa *f*; *to take the initiative* tomar la iniciativa; *on one's own initiative* por iniciativa propia; *to use one's initiative* actuar por iniciativa propia.
◆ *adj* preliminar.

initiator [i'niʃieitə*] *n* iniciador, ra.

initiatory [i'niʃiətəri] *adj* iniciador, ra ‖ preliminar (preliminary) ‖ de iniciación (ceremonies).

inject [in'dʒekt] *vt* inyectar, poner una inyección de; *to inject penicillin* inyectar penicilina ‖ inyectar en, poner una inyección en; *to inject an infected tissue with a liquid* inyectar un líquido en un tejido infectado ‖ poner una inyección a (to administer an injection to) ‖ TECH inyectar ‖ FIG introducir (to introduce into) ‖ infundir (enthusiasm, etc.).

injectable [-əbl] *adj* inyectable.

injection [in'dʒekʃən] *n* TECH inyección *f*; *injection feeding* alimentación por inyección ‖ MED inyección *f*; *to put o.s. an injection* ponerse una inyección.

injector [in'dʒektə*] *n* inyector *m*.

injudicious [,indʒu:'diʃəs] *adj* poco juicioso, sa; imprudente.

injunction [in'dʒʌŋkʃən] *n* mandato *m*, orden *f* (command) ‖ JUR requerimiento *m*, intimación *f* (summons) ‖ entredicho *m* (prohibition).

injure ['indʒə*] *vt* herir (to wound) ‖ lastimar, dañar, hacer daño (to hurt) ‖ FIG herir (feelings) ‖ perjudicar (reputation, etc.) ‖ ofender (to offend) ‖ estropear (to spoil) ‖ SP lesionar ‖ JUR causar perjuicio a ‖ — *he injured his leg* se lesionó una pierna ‖ *the injured* los heridos ‖ JUR *the injured party* la parte perjudicada.

injurious [in'dʒuəriəs] *adj* injurioso, sa; ofensivo, va (offensive) ‖ nocivo, va; perjudicial (harmful).

injury ['indʒəri] *n* herida *f*, lesión *f* (physical damage) ‖ daño *m* (physical hurt) ‖ ofensa *f* (offensive treatment) ‖ JUR perjuicio *m*, daño *m* ‖ — *to do o.s. an injury* hacerse daño, lastimarse ‖ *to the injury of* en detrimento de, en perjuicio de.

injury time [-taim] *n* SP descuento *m*.

injustice [in'dʒʌstis] *n* injusticia *f* ‖ *to do s.o. an injustice* hacerle una injusticia a alguien (to treat s.o. badly), juzgar mal a alguien, ser injusto con alguien (to misjudge s.o.).

ink [iŋk] *n* tinta *f* (for pen, of fish) ‖ — *Indian* o *India ink* tinta china ‖ *in ink* con tinta ‖ *invisible ink* tinta simpática ‖ *printer's ink* tinta de imprenta.

ink [iŋk] *vt* entintar (a plate for engraving) ‖ *to ink in* o *over* marcar *or* repasar con tinta.

inker [-ə*] *n* PRINT rodillo *m* entintador.

inkhorn [-hɔ:n] *n* (ant) tintero *m* [en forma de asta].
◆ *adj* culto, ta; *inkhorn terms* palabras cultas.

inking [-iŋ] *n* PRINT entintado *m*.
◆ *adj* PRINT entintador, ra.

ink-jet printer ['ŋkdʒet printə*] *n* INFORM impresora *f* por chorros de tinta.

inkling [-liŋ] *n* idea *f*; *I had no inkling that you were there* no tenía ni idea de que estabas allí ‖ impresión *f* (feeling, impression) ‖ algo *m*, tinte *m*; *there is an inkling of truth in what he says* hay algo de verdad en lo que dice ‖ indicio *m* (hint) ‖ sospecha *f* (suspicion) ‖ *to have some inkling of* tener cierta idea de *or* una ligera idea de.

ink pad [-pæd] *n* almohadilla *f*, tampón *m*.

inkpot [-pɔt] *n* tintero *m*.

inkslinger [-sliŋgə*] *n* FAM chupatintas *m inv*.

inkstand [-stænd] *n* tintero *m* de despacho.

inkwell [-wel] *n* tintero *m* [de pupitre].

inky [-i] *adj* manchado de tinta (stained with ink) ‖ parecido a la tinta (resembling ink) ‖ negro, gra (black).

inlaid ['inleid] *pret/pp* ⟶ **inlay.**

inland [-lənd] *n* interior *m* (interior of a country).
◆ *adj* interior (away from the coast) ‖ interior, nacional (trade, post, etc.) ‖ nacional (produce) ‖ del interior (roads, town, etc.) ‖ *inland navigation* navegación *f* fluvial.

inland [in'lænd] *adv* hacia el interior, tierra adentro.

Inland Revenue ['inlənd'revinju] *n* contribuciones *f pl* (government income) ‖ hacienda *f*, fisco *m* (government department) ‖ *inland revenue stamp* timbre fiscal.

Inland Sea ['inlənd,si:] *pr n* GEOGR mar *m* del Japón.

in-law [in'lɔ:] *n* pariente *m* político.
◆ *pl* familia *f sing* política.

inlay ['inlei] *n* incrustación *f* ‖ taracea *f* (with different coloured woods) ‖ damasquinado *m* (with gold or silver) ‖ empaste *m* (for a tooth).

inlay ['in'lei] *vt* incrustar; *to inlay mother-of-pearl into wood* incrustar nácar en madera ‖ adornar con incrustaciones de; *to inlay a box with mother-of-pearl* adornar una caja con incrustaciones de nácar ‖ taracear, adornar con marquetería (with different coloured woods) ‖ damasquinar (with a decoration of gold or silver) ‖ montar (a picture) ‖ *to inlay a floor with mosaic* poner mosaicos en el suelo.

inlet ['inlet] *n* cala *f*, ensenada *f* (small bay) ‖ brazo *m* de mar (narrow arm of sea) ‖ brazo *m* (of river) ‖ TECH entrada *f*, admisión *f*; *inlet valve* válvula de admisión.

inlier ['inlaiə*] *n* GEOL afloramiento *m* de rocas viejas rodeadas de otras más jóvenes.

inlying ['inlaiiŋ] *adj* del interior (inland).

inmate ['inmeit] *n* habitante *m* & *f*, inquilino, na (occupant of a dwelling) ‖ internado, da (of a mental home, camp, etc.) ‖ enfermo, ma (in a hospital) ‖ preso *m*, presidiario *m* (prisoner).

inmost ['inməust] *adj* más íntimo, ma; más profundo, da; más secreto, ta (most private or secrete) ‖ situado más adentro (room, etc.).

inn [in] *n* posada *f*, hostería *f*, mesón *m*, venta *f* (a type of hotel) ‖ taberna *f* (tavern) ‖ *Inns of Court* Colegio *m* de abogados de Londres.

innards ['inə:dz] *pl n* FAM tripas *f*, entrañas *f* (entrails) ‖ FIG entrañas *f*.

innate ['i'neit] *adj* innato, ta.

innavigable [i'nævigəbl] *adj* innavegable.

inner ['inə*] *adj* interior; *inner court* patio interior; *inner rooms* habitaciones interiores; *inner dock* dársena interior ‖ interior, interno, na; *the inner part* la parte interna ‖ FIG oculto, ta; secreto, ta (hidden); *the inner meaning* el sentido oculto ‖ interior; *inner life* vida interior ‖ íntimo, ma ‖ *inner city* barrios *m pl* céntricos ‖ ANAT *inner ear* oído interno.
◆ *n* primer espacio *m* después de la diana (ring of a target) ‖ tiro *m* que da en este espacio (shot).

innermost [-məust] *adj* más íntimo, ma; más profundo, da; más secreto, ta (most private or secret) ‖ situado más adentro; *the innermost room* la habitación situada más adentro.

inner tube [-tju:b] *n* cámara *f* (of tyre).

innervate ['inə:veit] *vt* inervar.

innervation [,inə:'veiʃən] *n* ANAT inervación *f*.

innerve [i'nə:v] *vt* inervar.

inning ['iniŋ] *n* SP entrada *f*, turno *m*.

innings [-z] *n* SP entrada *f*, turno *m* (in cricket, baseball) ‖ FIG *to have had a good innings* haber tenido una vida larga y buena.
— OBSERV Esta palabra se construye tanto con el singular como con el plural.

innkeeper ['in,ki:pə*] *n* posadero, ra; mesonero, ra (of an hotel) ‖ tabernero, ra (of a tavern).

innocence ['inəsəns] *n* inocencia *f*; *in all innocence* con toda inocencia.

innocent ['inəsnt] *adj* inocente (free from guilt or evil, naïve, harmless); *an innocent young girl* una chica inocente; *an innocent joke* una broma inocente ‖ desprovisto, ta; sin; *a room innocent of furniture* una habitación desprovista de muebles ‖ autorizado, da (authorized).
◆ *n* inocente *m* & *f*.

Innocent ['inəsnt] *pr n* Inocencio *m*.

innocuity [inɔ'kju:iti] *n* inocuidad *f*.

innocuous [i'nɔkjuəs] *adj* inocuo, cua; inofensivo, va.

innominate [i'nɔminit] *adj* innominado, da; *innominate bone* hueso innominado.

innovate ['inəuveit] *vt/vi* innovar.

innovation [,inəu'veiʃən] *n* innovación *f*.

innovative ['inəuveitiv] *adj* innovador, ra.

innovator ['inəuveitə*] *n* innovador, ra.

innovatory ['inəuveitəri] *adj* innovador, ra.

innoxious [i'nɔkʃəs] *adj* inocuo, cua.

innoxiousness [-nis] *n* inocuidad *f*.

innuendo [,inju'endəu] *n* indirecta *f*, insinuación *f* (malicious insinuation) ‖ JUR insinuación *f*.
— OBSERV El plural de *innuendo* es *innuendoes*.

innumerability [i,nju:mərə'biliti] *n* innumerabilidad *f*.

innumerable [i'nju:mərəbl] *adj* innumerable ‖ *there are innumerable difficulties* hay muchísimas dificultades *or* una infinidad de dificultades *or* un sinnúmero de dificultades.

innutrition [,inju:'triʃən] *n* MED desnutrición *f*.

innutritious [,inju'triʃəs] *adj* poco nutritivo, va (food).

inobservance [,inəb'zə:vəns]; **inobservancy** [-i] *n* falta *f* de atención, desatención *f*, descuido *m* (lack of attention) ‖ inobservancia *f* (of a law, custom, etc.) ‖ incumplimiento *m* (of a promise).

inobservant [,inəb'zə:vənt] *adj* desatento, ta (inattentive) ‖ inobservante (of a law, custom).

inoculate [i'nɔkjuleit] *vt* MED inocular; *to inoculate s.o. with a virus* inocular un virus a uno || *to get inoculated* vacunarse.

inoculation [i,nɔkju'leiʃən] *n* MED inoculación *f*.

inodorous [in'əudərəs] *adj* inodoro, ra.

inoffensive [,inə'fensiv] *adj* inofensivo, va.

inofficious [,inə'fiʃəs] *adj* JUR inoficioso, sa.

inoperable [in'ɔpərəbl] *adj* MED inoperable; *inoperable tumour* tumor inoperable || impracticable (not practicable).

inoperative [in'ɔpərətiv] *adj* inoperante.

inopportune [in'ɔpətj'u:n] *adj* inoportuno, na.

inordinacy [in'ɔ:dinəsi] *n* desmesura *f*, exceso *m* (excess) || desorden *m* (disorder).

inordinate [i'nɔ:dinit] *adj* desmesurado, da; excesivo, va (not within reasonable limits) || desordenado, da (disorderly).

inorganic [,inɔ:'gænik] *adj* inorgánico, ca; *inorganic chemistry* química inorgánica.

inorganization [inɔ:gənai'zeiʃən] *n* falta *f* de organización.

inosculate [i'nɔskjuleit] *vt* ANAT unir por anastomosis.
◆ *vi* anastomosarse.

inosculation [i,nəskjuleiʃən] *n* ANAT anastomosis *f*.

inoxidizable [inɔksi'daizəbl] *adj* inoxidable.

inpatient ['in,peiʃənt] *n* enfermo *m* internado en un hospital.

in petto [in'petəu] *adv phr* in péctore.

input ['input] *n* entrada *f* (terminal for the introduction of power or energy to a machine) || TECH energía *f* de entrada (power or energy put into a machine) || INFORM entrada *f*; *input/output system* sistema de entrada/salida || COMM factor *m* de producción [*AMER* insumo *m*].

inquest ['inkwest] *n* investigación *f*, encuesta *f*.

inquietude [in'kwaiitju:d] *n* desasosiego *m*, inquietud *f*.

inquiline ['inkwilain] *n* ZOOL inquilino, na.

inquire; enquire [in'kwaiə*] *vt* informarse de, preguntar; *to inquire the price* informarse del precio || pregunta; *to inquire sth. of s.o.* preguntar algo a alguien; *to inquire a person's name* preguntar el nombre de una persona.
◆ *vi* preguntar; «*how are you?*», *he inquired* «¿cómo estás?», preguntó || — *inquire at number twenty* razón; número veinte || *inquire within* razón aquí.
◆ *phr v* ***to inquire about*** informarse de; *he inquired about the price* se informó del precio | preguntar por; *your uncle inquired about you yesterday* tu tío preguntó por ti ayer | pedir informes sobre (to make inquiries about) | hacerse preguntas sobre; *people are beginning to inquire about his absence* la gente empieza a hacerse preguntas sobre su ausencia || ***to inquire after*** preguntar por || ***to inquire for*** preguntar por || ***to inquire into*** investigar *or* hacer investigaciones sobre; *the police are inquiring into his sudden death* la policía está haciendo investigaciones sobre su muerte repentina; *to inquire into s.o.'s private life* hacer investigaciones sobre la vida privada de alguien | hacer una investigación sobre, estudiar, examinar (to make a study of).

inquirer [in'kwaiərə*] *n* el que pregunta, la que pregunta (s.o. who asks) || investigador, ra (researcher).

inquiring [in'kwaiəriŋ] *adj* curioso, sa || interrogativo, va; inquisitivo, va; inquisidor, ra (look).

inquiry; enquiry [in'kwaiəri] *n* pregunta *f* (question) || investigación *f* (investigation, study of a particular subject); *to hold an inquiry into alcoholism* hacer una investigación sobre el alcoholismo || encuesta *f*, investigación *f*, pesquisa *f* (police investigation); *to set up an inquiry* hacer una encuesta || petición *f* de información (request for information) || — *all inquiries to* dirigirse a || *Board of Inquiry* Comisión *f* de investigación || *expression of inquiry* mirada interrogativa *or* inquisitiva *or* inquisidora || *inquiries* información (sign) || *inquiries at number twenty* razón: número veinte || *to make inquiries* hacer investigaciones (*about* sobre) (police), pedir informes *or* información (*about* sobre) (to seek information) || *upon* o *on inquiry, he was told that...* a su pregunta contestaron que.

inquiry agent [-'eidʒənt] *n* detective *m* privado.

inquiry desk [-desk] *n* mostrador *m* de información.

inquiry office [-'ɔfis] *n* oficina *f* de informaciones.

inquisition [,inkwi'ziʃən] *n* inquisición *f*, investigación *f* (close investigation) || *the Inquisition* la Inquisición.

inquisitive [in'kwizitiv] *adj* preguntón, ona (prying) || curioso, sa (interested, curious) || *inquisitive look* mirada inquisidora *or* inquisitiva.

inquisitively [-li] *adv* con curiosidad (curiously) || indiscretamente (indiscreetly).

inquisitiveness [-nis] *n* curiosidad *f*.

inquisitor [in'kwizitə*] *n* JUR investigador *m* || REL inquisidor *m*.

inquisitorial [in,kwizi'tɔ:riəl] *adj* inquisitorial.

inroad ['inrəud] *n* MIL incursión *f* (raid) || FIG intrusión *f* | usurpación *f* (*into* de) (encroachment) || — FIG & FAM *to make inroads on one's capital* mermar su capital | *to make inroads on s.o.'s time* hacerle perder el tiempo a alguien.

inrush ['inrʌʃ] *n* irrupción *f* || afluencia *f*; *inrush of tourists* afluencia de turistas || entrada *f* repentina (of air, fluid, etc.).

insalivate [in'sæliveit] *vt* BIOL insalivar.

insalivation [insæli'veiʃən] *n* BIOL insalivación *f*.

insalubrious [,insə'lu:briəs] *adj* insalubre.

insalubrity [,insə'lu:briti] *n* insalubridad *f*.

insane [in'sein] *adj* loco, ca; demente (person) || FIG insensato, ta; loco, ca (action) || — *insane asylum* manicomio *m* || *the insane* los locos || *to drive s.o. insane* volver loco a alguien.

insanitary [in'sænitəri] *adj* insalubre, antihigiénico, ca; malsano, na.

insanity [in'sæniti] *n* locura *f*, demencia *f* || JUR enajenación *f* mental || FIG locura *f*, insensatez *f* (foolish act); *pure insanity* pura locura.

insatiability [in,seiʃjə'biliti] *n* insaciabilidad *f*.

insatiable [in'seiʃjəbl] *adj* insaciable.

insatiate [in'seiʃiit] *adj* FIG insaciable (never satisfied).

inscribable [in'skraibəbl] *adj* MATH inscribible.

inscribe [in'skraib] *vt* inscribir (to write, to enrol) || grabar (to engrave) || dedicar (to dedicate) || MATH inscribir || COMM registrar (stock).

inscribed [-d] *adj* inscrito, ta || COMM registrado, da (stock).

inscription [in'skripʃən] *n* inscripción *f* || dedicatoria *f* (in a book) || COMM registro *m* | valores *m pl* registrados.

inscrutability [in,skru:tə'biliti] *n* inescrutabilidad *f*.

inscrutable [in'skru:təbl] *adj* inescrutable.

insect ['insekt] *n* insecto *m* || FIG bicho *m* || *insect repellent* loción *f* repelente de insectos.

insecticide [in'sektisaid] *n* insecticida *m*.

insectivora [in'sektivərə] *pl n* insectívoros *m*.

insectivorous [,insek'tivərəs] *adj* insectívoro, ra.

insecure [,insi'kjuə*] *adj* inseguro, ra (uncertain, unsure) || poco seguro, ra; *the ice is insecure* el hielo está poco seguro || inestable (unstable); *an insecure table* una mesa inestable.

insecurity [-riti] *n* inseguridad *f*.

inseminate [in'seminit] *vt* inseminar.

insemination [in,semi'neiʃən] *n* inseminación *f*; *artificial insemination* inseminación artificial.

insensate [in'senseit] *adj* insensato, ta (foolish) || insensible (unfeeling).

insensibility [in,sensi'biliti] *n* insensibilidad *f* || MED inconsciencia *f*.

insensible [in'sensəbl] *adj* insensible; *insensible to cold, to sorrow* insensible al frío, al dolor || inconsciente (unaware); *insensible of the risk* inconsciente del peligro || insensible, imperceptible (imperceptible) || MED inconsciente (unconscious) || *to drink o.s. insensible* beber hasta perder el conocimiento.

insensitive [in'sensitiv] *adj* insensible.

insensitiveness [-nis]; **insensitivity** [in,sensə'tiviti] *n* insensibilidad *f*.

insentient [in'senʃənt] *adj* inconsciente.

inseparability [in,seperə'biliti] *n* inseparabilidad *f*.

inseparable [in'sepərəbl] *adj* inseparable; *inseparable friends* amigos inseparables.
◆ *pl n* amigos *m* inseparables (friends) || cosas *f* inseparables (things).

insert [insə:t] *n* encarte *m* (in a book, magazine, etc.) || entredós *m* (in sewing).

insert [in'sə:t] *vt* introducir; *to insert a key in the lock* introducir una llave en la cerradura || introducir, insertar, incluir; *to insert a clause in a contract* introducir una cláusula en un contrato || insertar (advertisement in a newspaper) || intercalar (between pages).

insertable [-əbl] *adj* insertable, incluible.

inserted [in'sə:tid] *adj* BOT & ZOOL inserto, ta.

insertion [in'sə:ʃən] *n* inserción *f* (an inserting, a thing inserted) || encarte *m* (in a book, magazine) || anuncio *m* (advertisement) || BOT & ANAT inserción *f* || entredós *m* (band of lace or embroidery).

in-service ['in,sə:vis] *adj* *in-service training* formación *f* profesional en el trabajo.

inset ['inset] *n* recuadro *m* (in a picture, map, etc.) || encarte *m* (extra page of a book) || entredós *m* (of material).

inset ['in'set] *vt* insertar (to insert) || encartar (in a book).

— OBSERV El verbo *inset* no varía en el pretérito y en el participio pasivo *(inset)*, excepto cuando significa *encartar* en cuyo caso se usa la forma *insetted*.

inshore ['in'ʃɔ:*] *adj* cercano a la orilla (near the shore) || costero, ra (coastal).
◆ *adv* hacia la orilla; *to drift inshore* ser empujado hacia la orilla || cerca de la orilla (near the shore) || *to be inshore of sth.* estar entre algo y la orilla.

inside ['in'said] *adj* interior; *inside wall* pared interior; *inside diameter* diámetro interior; *inside pages of a paper* páginas interiores de un periódico || confidencial, secreto, ta; *inside information* información confidencial.
◆ *adv* dentro, adentro; *wait inside* espera dentro; *stay inside* quédate adentro || para

adentro, adentro (movement towards); *go inside* vete para adentro || por dentro; *red outside, green inside* rojo por fuera, verde por dentro || abajo (in a bus) || en la cárcel (in jail) || — FAM *inside of* en menos de; *inside of a week* en menos de una semana; dentro de (within) || *please, step inside* pase, por favor || *to come inside* entrar || *to go inside* entrar (to enter), ir a la cárcel (to go to jail).

◆ *prep* dentro de.

◆ *n* interior *m* (interior) || parte *f* de adentro, parte *f* interior (inner part of pavement, etc.) || forro *m* (lining) || — *on the inside* por dentro || *to know the inside of an affair* conocer las interioridades de un asunto || *to overtake on the inside* adelantar por la derecha (for those driving on the right), adelantar por la izquierda (for those driving on the left) || *to see sth. from the inside* estudiar algo por dentro.

◆ *pl* FAM tripas *f* (stomach and intestines).

inside forward [ˈinsaidˈfɔːwəd] *n* SP interior *m*.

inside job [inˈsaidʒɔb] *n* FAM crimen *m* cometido con la complicidad de una persona allegada a la víctima || *this must be an inside job* esto debe hacerlo alguien de la casa.

inside lane [ˈinsaidlain] *n* carril *m* interior.

inside left [ˈinsaidˈleft] *n* SP interior *m* izquierda.

inside out [inˈsaidaut] *adv* al revés (the wrong way round) || — *to know sth. inside out* conocer algo a fondo (to know thoroughly) || *to turn sth. inside out* registrar de arriba abajo (to search), volver algo del revés (to put sth. the wrong way round).

insider [inˈsaidə*] *n* persona *f* enterada || ECON *insider dealing* tráfico *m* de influencias.

inside right [ˈinsaidˈrait] *n* SP interior *m* derecha.

inside story [ˈinsaidˌstɔːri] *n* interioridades *f pl* de un asunto.

inside track [ˈinsaidˈtræk] *n* SP pista *f* interior || FIG ventaja *f*.

insidious [inˈsidiəs] *adj* insidioso, sa.

insidiousness [-nis] *n* insidia *f*.

insight [ˈinsait] *n* perspicacia *f*, penetración *f* (perspicacity) || idea *f*; *to get an insight into* hacerse una idea de.

insignia [inˈsigniə] *pl n* insignias *f*.

— OBSERV En Inglaterra *insignia* se considera como un sustantivo plural. En Estados Unidos se puede emplear como singular. En este último caso el plural es *insignias*.

insignificance [ˌinsigˈnifikəns] *n* insignificancia *f*.

insignificant [ˌinsigˈnifikənt] *adj* insignificante.

insincere [ˌinsinˈsiə*] *adj* insincero, ra; poco sincero, ra (not sincere) || hipócrita (hypocritical).

insincerity [ˌinsinˈseriti] *n* insinceridad *f*, falta *f* de sinceridad || hipocresía *f*.

insinuate [inˈsinjueit] *vt* insinuar || — *to insinuate o.s. into* insinuarse en || *to insinuate that* insinuar que, dar a entender que.

insinuating [-iŋ] *adj* insinuante.

insinuation [inˌsinjuˈeiʃən] *n* insinuación *f*.

insipid [inˈsipid] *adj* soso, sa; insípido, da (tasteless) || FIG soso, sa; insulso, sa (dull).

insipidity [ˌinsiˈpiditi]; **insipidness** [inˈsipidnis] *n* insipidez *f*, sosería *f* || FIG sosería *f*, insulsez *f*.

insist [inˈsist] *vi* insistir, empeñarse; *if you insist, you will only make him angry* si insistes sólo conseguirás que se enfade || — *to insist on* o *upon doing sth.* empeñarse en hacer algo, insistir en hacer algo || *to insist on* o *upon sth.* exigir algo, insistir en algo.

◆ *vt* insistir en; *he insists that it was so* insiste en que fue así; *he insists that you apologize* insiste en que pidas disculpas.

insistence [inˈsistəns] *n* insistencia *f*, empeño *m* || *he came at my insistence* vino ante mi insistencia.

insistency [-i] *n* insistencia *f*, empeño *m*.

insistent [inˈsistənt] *adj* insistente || *they were most insistent that I bring you* insistieron mucho en que te trajera.

insistently [-li] *adv* con insistencia, insistentemente.

in situ [inˈsitu] *adv phr* en el lugar de origen, en el sitio.

insobriety [insəuˈbraiəti] *n* intemperancia *f*.

insofar [ˈinsəuˈfɑː] *adv* *insofar as* en la medida en que.

insolate [ˈinsəleit] *vt* insolar.

insolation [ˌinsəuˈleiʃən] *n* insolación *f*.

insole [ˈinsəul] *n* plantilla *f* (for shoes).

insolence [ˈinsələns] *n* insolencia *f*, descaro *m*.

insolent [ˈinsələnt] *adj* insolente, descarado, da.

insolubility [inˌsɔljuˈbiliti] *n* insolubilidad *f*.

insoluble [inˈsɔljubl] *adj* insoluble.

insolvency [inˈsɔlvənsi] *n* COMM insolvencia *f*.

insolvent [inˈsɔlvənt] *adj/n* COMM insolvente || *to declare o.s. insolvent* declararse en quiebra.

insomnia [inˈsɔmniə] *n* MED insomnio *m*.

insomniac [-k] *n* insomne *m* & *f*.

insomnious [-s] *adj* insomne (sleepless).

insomuch [ˌinsəuˈmʌtʃ] *adv* *insomuch as* puesto que, ya que (since, because) || *insomuch that* hasta tal punto que.

insouciance [inˈsuːsjəns] *n* despreocupación *f*.

insouciant [inˈsuːsjənt] *adj* despreocupado, da.

inspect [inˈspekt] *vt* inspeccionar, examinar, registrar || MIL pasar revista a (troops).

inspection [inˈspekʃən] *n* inspección *f*, registro *m*, examen *m* || MIL revista *f*.

inspector [inˈspektə*] *n* inspector *m*.

inspectorate [inˈspektərit] *n* cargo *m* de inspector (office) || cuerpo *m* de inspectores (staff of inspectors) || distrito *m* asignado a un inspector (district under an inspector).

inspectorship [inˈspektəʃip] *n* cargo *m* de inspector.

inspiration [ˌinspəˈreiʃən] *n* inspiración *f* || aspiración *f*, inspiración *f* (inhaling) || *his courageous behaviour was an inspiration for all of us* su valor nos infundió ánimo a todos.

inspirational [ˌinspəˈreiʃənl] *adj* inspirador, ra (persons, etc.) || inspirado, da (inspired).

inspiratory [inˈspaiərətəri] *adj* ANAT inspirador, ra; *inspiratory muscles* músculos inspiradores.

inspire [inˈspaiə*] *vt* inspirar (to give inspiration) || sugerir, inspirar (to suggest) || dar, infundir; *to inspire s.o. with fear* infundir miedo a alguien || aspirar, inspirar (to inhale) || *to inspire s.o. to do sth.* incitar a alguien a que haga algo.

◆ *vi* inspirar, aspirar.

inspired [-d] *adj* inspirado, da; de inspiración; *in an inspired moment* en un momento de inspiración || genial; *his performance was absolutely inspired* su actuación fue absolutamente genial.

inspirer [-rə*] *n* inspirador, ra.

inspiring [-iŋ] *adj* inspirador, ra.

inspirit [inˈspirit] *vt* alentar, animar.

inspiriting [-iŋ] *adj* alentador, ra; estimulante.

inspissate [inˈspiseit] *vt* espesar (to thicken) || condensar (to condense).

◆ *vi* espesarse (to thicken) || condensarse (to condense).

inspissation [inspiˈseiʃən] *n* espesamiento *m* (thickening) || condensación *f* (condensación).

inst. [ˈinstənt] *abbr of* *[instant]* del actual, del corriente; *the 9th inst.* el nueve del corriente.

instability [ˌinstəˈbiliti] *n* inestabilidad *f*, instabilidad *f* (lack of stability).

instable [insˈteibl] *adj* inestable, instable.

install [inˈstɔːl] *vt* instalar; *to install electricity* instalar la electricidad; *they have installed a hundred poor families in the neighbourhood* han instalado cien familias pobres en el barrio || *to install o.s.* instalarse.

installation [ˌinstəˈleiʃən] *n* instalación *f*.

instalment; US **installment** [inˈstɔːlmənt] *n* plazo *m* (of payment); *to pay by* o *in instalments* pagar a plazos || fascículo *m* (of a book) || instalación *f* (an installing) || — *annual instalment* anualidad *f* || *instalment plan* venta *f* or compra *f* a plazos || *monthly instalment* mensualidad *f*.

instance [ˈinstəns] *n* ejemplo *m* (example) || caso *m* (case) || — *at the instance of* a petición de || JUR *court of first instance* tribunal *m* de primera instancia || *for instance* por ejemplo || *in many instances* en muchos casos || *in that instance* en ese caso || *in the first instance* en primer lugar.

instance [ˈinstəns] *vt* ilustrar; *he instanced his speech with several examples* ilustró su discurso con varios ejemplos || citar como ejemplo (to quote).

instancy [-i] *n* inminencia *f* (of a danger) || urgencia *f* (of a need) || insistencia *f* (of a request).

instant [ˈinstənt] *adj* urgente (urgent) || inminente (imminent) || inmediato, ta (immediate) || insistente (request) || instantáneo, a (coffee, soup, etc.) || *your letter of the 10th instant* su carta del 10 del corriente *or* del actual.

◆ *n* instante *m*, momento *m*; *in an instant* en un instante || — *come this instant* ven ahora mismo || *on the instant* al instante, inmediatamente || *the instant he arrived* en cuanto llegó || *the instant he arrives* en cuanto llegue.

instantaneity [instæntəˈniːiti] *n* instantaneidad *f*.

instantaneous [ˌinstənˈteinjəs] *adj* instantáneo, a.

instantly [ˈinstəntli] *adv* instantáneamente, al instante, inmediatamente.

instauration [instɔːˈreiʃən] *n* restauración *f*.

instaurator [ˈinstɔːreitə*] *n* restaurador *m*.

instead [inˈsted] *adv* en su lugar || — *instead of* en vez de, en lugar de || *we did not go to Rome but to Venice instead* en vez de ir a Roma fuimos a Venecia.

instep [ˈinstep] *n* empeine *m* (of human foot) || caña *f* (of horse).

instigate [ˈinstigeit] *vt* instigar, incitar (s.o.) || fomentar (rebellion, etc.).

instigating [-iŋ] *adj* instigador, ra.

instigation [ˌinstiˈgeiʃən] *n* instigación *f*; *at* o *on the instigation of* a instigación de.

instigator [ˈinstigeitə*] *n* instigador, ra.

instil; US **instill** [inˈstil] *vt* instilar || FIG infundir, inculcar (*into* a) (ideas, etc.).

instinct [ˈinstiŋkt] *n* instinto *m*; *by instinct* por instinto; *self-preservation instinct* instinto de conservación; *maternal instinct* instinto materno.

◆ *adj instinct with* lleno de.

instinctive [in'stiŋktiv] *adj* instintivo, va.

institute ['institju:t] *n* instituto *m* (research organization); *geographical institute* instituto geográfico ‖ asociación *f*, institución *f* (welfare organization) ‖ centro *m* social (social centre) ‖ US seminario *m* (seminar).
◆ *pl* JUR instituciones *f* ‖ *the institutes of Justinian* la Instituta.
— OBSERV La palabra inglesa *institute* no tiene nunca el significado de *instituto de segunda enseñanza*.

institute ['institju:t] *vt* instituir, fundar, establecer (to found) ‖ iniciar, empezar (to begin) ‖ investir (to invest) ‖ JUR entablar; *to institute proceedings* entablar un proceso.

institution [,insti'tju:ʃən] *n* institución *f*; *welfare institution* institución benéfica; *cricket is an English institution* el criquet es una institución en Inglaterra ‖ establecimiento *m*, creación *f*, institución *f*; *the institution of the National Health Service helped the poor* la creación del Seguro de Enfermedad fue una ayuda a los pobres ‖ asociación *f* (society) ‖ manicomio *m* (madhouse) ‖ hospicio *f* (for abandoned children) ‖ investidura *f* (investiture) ‖ JUR iniciación *f* (of proceedings) ‖ FAM institución *f* (familiar person); *he is a local institution* es una institución local.
◆ *pl* JUR instituciones *f*.

institutional [-l] *adj* institucional ‖ con instituciones benéficas (religion) ‖ US de prestigio (publicity).

institutionalization [insti'tju:ʃənəlai'zeiʃən] *n* institucionalización *f*.

institutionalize [insti'tju:ʃənəlaiz] *vt* institucionalizar ‖ FAM meter en una institución.

instruct [in'strʌkt] *vt* dar instrucciones a (to command formally, to advise, i. e. a jury) ‖ instruir (to teach) ‖ ordenar, mandar (to order) ‖ avisar (to notify) ‖ — *the Committee has not been instructed to deal with this question* la Comisión no ha sido encargada de ocuparse de esta cuestión ‖ *to instruct s.o. in Latin* enseñar latín a uno.

instruction [in'strʌkʃən] *n* instrucción *f* enseñanza *f* (teaching) ‖ INFORM instrucción *f* ‖ — *instruction manual* manual *f* de instrucciones ‖ *to give driving instruction* dar clases de conducir.
◆ *pl* instrucciones *f*; *instructions for use* instrucciones para el uso; *to follow s.o.'s instructions perfectly* seguir las instrucciones de alguien al pie de la letra ‖ *on the instructions of* por orden de, siguiendo las instrucciones de.

instructional [-l] *adj* de instrucción.

instructive [in'strʌktiv] *adj* instructivo, va.

instructor [in'strʌktə*] *n* instructor *m* ‖ profesor *m* (teacher) ‖ maestro *m*; *fencing instructor* maestro de esgrima ‖ MIL instructor *m* ‖ SP instructor *m*, monitor *m* ‖ US profesor *m* auxiliar.

instructress [in'strʌktris] *n* profesora *f*.

instrument ['instrumənt] *n* instrumento *m* (tool, etc.) ‖ FIG & AVIAT & MUS & JUR instrumento *m* ‖ — *musical instrument* instrumento músico ‖ *string, brass, percussion, wind instrument* instrumento de cuerda, de metal, de percusión, de viento ‖ *to play an instrument* tocar un instrumento.
◆ *pl* MED instrumental *m sing*; *a surgeon's instruments* el instrumental de un cirujano.

instrument ['instrumənt] *vt* MUS instrumentar, orquestar.

instrumental [,instru'mentl] *adj* instrumental; *instrumental music* música instrumental ‖ *to be instrumental in* o *to* contribuir a.

instrumentalism [-lizəm] *n* instrumentalismo *m*.

instrumentalist [,instru'mentəlist] *n* MUS instrumentalista *m* & *f*.

instrumentality [,instrumen'tæliti] *n through the instrumentality of* por intermedio de, por mediación de (a person), por medio de (a thing).

instrumentation [,instrumen'teiʃən] *n* MUS instrumentación *f* ‖ empleo *m* de instrumentos.

instrument board ['instruməntbɔ:d] *n* tablero *m* de mandos, salpicadero *m* (of a car) ‖ tablero *m or* cuadro *m* de instrumentos (of an aircraft).

instrument flying ['instruməntflaiiŋ] *n* AVIAT vuelo *m* con instrumentos.

instrument landing system ['instrumənt'lændiŋ'sistim] *n* AVIAT sistema *m* de aterrizaje por instrumentos.

instrument panel ['instrumənt'pænl] *n* AVIAT tablero *m or* cuadro *m* de instrumentos ‖ AUT tablero *m* de mandos, salpicadero *m*.

insubmergible [,insəb'mə:dʒəbl]; **insubmersible** [insəb'mə:səbl] *adj* insumergible.

insubordinate [,insə'bɔ:dinit] *adj* insubordinado, da.

insubordination ['insə,bɔ:di'neiʃən] *n* insubordinación *f*.

insubstantial [,insəb'stænʃəl] *adj* insubstancial (soul) ‖ inconsistente, flojo, ja (weak); *insubstantial arguments* argumentos flojos ‖ infundado, da (unreal); *insubstantial fears* temores infundados ‖ insignificante.

insubstantiality [insəbstænʃi'æliti] *n* insubstancialidad *f* (of soul) ‖ poco peso *m*, inconsistencia *f* (weakness) ‖ falta *f* de fundamento, irrealidad *f* (unreality).

insufferable [in'sʌfərəbl] *adj* insufrible, inaguantable, insoportable (not to be tolerated).

insufferably [in'sʌfərəbli] *adv* de modo intolerable ‖ *insufferably selfish* de lo más egoísta.

insufficiency [,insə'fiʃənsi] *n* insuficiencia *f* (inadequacy) ‖ limitación *f*; *to know one's own insufficiencies* conocer sus propias limitaciones ‖ MED insuficiencia *f*.

insufficient [,insə'fiʃənt] *adj* insuficiente.

insufflate ['insʌfleit] *vt* insuflar.

insufflation [insʌ'fleiʃən] *n* insuflación *f*.

insufflator ['insʌfleitə*] *n* insuflador *m*.

insular ['insjulə*] *adj* insular (inhabiting or forming an island) ‖ FIG estrecho de miras (narrow-minded) | aislado, da (insulated) ‖ MED insular.

insularity [,insju'læriti] *n* insularidad *f* ‖ FIG estrechez *f* de miras.

insulate ['insjuleit] *vt* PHYS aislar ‖ FIG aislar, apartar (to isolate).

insulating [-iŋ] *adj* aislante, aislador, ra; *insulating tape* cinta aislante.

insulation [,insju'leiʃən] *n* PHYS aislamiento *m* ‖ FIG aislamiento *m*.

insulator ['insjuleitə*] *n* aislador *m*, aislante *m*.

insulin ['insjulin] *n* insulina *f*.

insult ['insʌlt] *n* insulto *m*, injuria *f* ‖ US MED trauma *m* ‖ *to add insult to injury* para colmo de males.

insult [in'sʌlt] *vt* insultar, injuriar ‖ *to feel insulted* ofenderse, sentirse ofendido.

insulter [-ə*] *n* insultador, ra.

insulting [-iŋ] *adj* insultante, ofensivo, va.

insuperable [in'sju:pərəbl] *adj* insuperable.

insupportable [,insə'pɔ:təbl] *adj* insoportable, inaguantable (unbearable).

insuppressible [,insə'presəbl] *adj* irreprimible.

insurable [in'ʃuərəbl] *adj* asegurable.

insurance [in'ʃuərəns] *n* seguro *m*; *insurance against theft* seguro contra robo; *insurance on new cars is high* el seguro de los coches nuevos es alto; *the insurance on this is five hundred pounds* esto tiene un seguro de quinientas libras; *accident insurance* seguro contra accidentes; *insurance policy* póliza de seguro; *insurance premium* prima de seguro ‖ — *fire insurance* seguro contra incendios ‖ *fully comprehensive insurance* seguro a todo riesgo ‖ *insurance agent, broker, company* agente, corredor, compañía de seguros ‖ *life, mutual, third party insurance* seguro de vida *or* sobre la vida, mutuo, contra terceros ‖ *national* o *social insurance* seguros sociales ‖ *to take out an insurance* hacerse un seguro.

insure [in'ʃuə*] *vt* asegurar.
◆ *vi* asegurarse.

insured [-d] *adj/n* asegurado, da.

insurer [-rə*] *n* asegurador, ra.

insurgence [in'sə:dʒəns] *n* insurrección *f*, levantamiento *m*.

insurgency [in'sə:dʒənsi] *n* rebelión *f* ‖ insurrección *f*, levantamiento *m* (insurgence).

insurgent [in'sə:dʒənt] *adj/n* insurrecto, ta; insurgente.

insurmountable [,insə'mauntəbl] *adj* insalvable (obstacle) ‖ insuperable (difficulty).

insurrection [,insərekʃən] *n* insurrección *f*.

insurrectionary [-əri] *adj* insurreccional, insurrecto, ta; insurgente.
◆ *n* insurrecto, ta; insurgente *m* & *f*.

insurrectionist [-ist] *n* insurrecto, ta; insurgente *m* & *f*.

insusceptibility ['insə,septə'biliti] *n* insensibilidad *f* ‖ falta *f* de susceptibilidad.

insusceptible [,insə'septəbl] *adj* insensible (not affected emotionally) ‖ no susceptible (not sensitive).

inswinger [in'swiŋə*] *n* SP lanzamiento *m* con efecto (in cricket).

intact [in'tækt] *adj* intacto, ta.

intaglio [in'tɑ:liəu] *n* talla *f* (engraved design) ‖ piedra *f* preciosa grabada en hueco (gem) ‖ *intaglio engraving* grabado *m* en hueco, huecograbado *m*.

intake ['inteik] *n* toma *f*, entrada *f* (of air) ‖ toma *f* (of water) ‖ AUT entrada *f* de aire (of a carburettor) | admisión *f* | válvula *f* de admisión (entry for fuel, water, steam, etc.) ‖ MIN pozo *m* de ventilación ‖ consumo *m* (thing taken in) ‖ aspiración *f* ‖ número *m* de personas admitidas (in a college, club, etc.) ‖ MIL reclutas *m pl* ‖ menguado *m* (in knitting) ‖ *food intake* ración *f*.

intangibility [in,tændʒə'biliti] *n* intangibilidad *f*.

intangible [in'tændʒəbl] *adj* intangible (not tangible).
◆ *n* cosa *f* intangible.

intarsia [in'tɑ:siə] *n* ARTS marqueteria *f*, taracea *f*.

integer ['intidʒə*] *n* MATH entero *m*, número *m* entero ‖ FIG totalidad *f*.

integrable ['intigrəbl] *adj* MATH integrable.

integral ['intigrəl] *adj* integrante; *an integral part of his studies* una parte integrante de sus estudios; *a part integral with the whole* una parte integrante del todo ‖ integral, íntegro, gra (complete) ‖ MATH *integral calculus* cálculo *m* integral.
◆ *n* MATH integral *f*.

integrality [inte'græliti] *n* integridad *f* (wholeness).

integrant ['intigrənt] *adj* integrante.
◆ *n* parte *f* integrante, elemento *m*, componente *m* (component, part).

integrate ['intigreit] *vt* integrar.
◆ *vi* integrarse (*into* en).

integrated *adj* integrado, da; *integrated circuit* circuito integrado || abierto, ta; *integrated school* escuela abierta a diferentes razas *or* grupos || INFORM *integrated program* programa integrado.

integration [,inti'greiʃən] *n* integración *f*.

integrationist [,inti'græʃnist] *n* integracionista *m* & *f* (s.o. in favour of integration).

integrative ['intigreitiv] *adj* integrador, ra.

integrator ['intigreitə*] *n* integrador *m*.

integrity [in'tegriti] *n* integridad *f* (probity, soundness) || totalidad *f*, integridad *f* (wholeness).

intellect ['intilekt] *n* intelecto *m*, inteligencia *f* (intelligence) || FIG intelectual *m* & *f* (person of superior reasoning power) | intelectuales *m pl*, intelectualidad *f* (intelligentsia).

intellection [inti'lekʃən] *n* idea *f* (thought).

intellectual [,inti'lektjuəl] *adj/n* intelectual.

intellectualism [,inti'lektjuəlizəm] *n* PHIL intelectualismo *m*.

intellectualist [,intilek'tjuəlist] *adj/n* intelectualista.

intellectuality ['inti'lektju'æliti] *n* intelectualidad *f*.

intellectualize [,inti'lektjuəlaiz] *vt* intelectualizar.

intelligence [in'telidʒəns] *n* inteligencia *f*; *intelligence test* test *or* prueba de inteligencia || noticia *f*, información *f* (news) || MIL información *f* (secret information) | servicio *m* de información (service) || — MIL *intelligence bureau* o *department* servicio *m* de información || *intelligence quotient* cociente *m* intelectual *or* de inteligencia.

intelligencer [-ə*] *n* informador, ra (s.o. who brings news) || espía *m* & *f*, agente *m* secreto (spy).

intelligent [in'telidʒənt] *adj* inteligente.

intelligentsia [in'teli'dʒentsiə] *n* intelectualidad *f*, intelligentsia *f*.

intelligibility [in,telidʒə'biliti] *n* inteligibilidad *f*.

intelligible [in'telidʒəbl] *adj* inteligible.

intemperance [in'tempərns] *n* intemperancia *f*, falta *f* de moderación.

intemperate [in'tempərit] *adj* intemperante, inmoderado, da (person) || excesivo, va (zeal) || inclemente (climate) || violento, ta (wind).

intend [in'tend] *vt* querer hacer; *I intended no harm* no quería hacer daño || tener la intención *or* el propósito de; *I intend going* tengo la intención de ir || querer decir (to mean) || — *I hope that remark was not intended for me* espero que esta observación no iba dirigida a mí || *to intend for* destinar a; *this book is not intended for young girls* este libro no está destinado a chicas jóvenes || *to intend to* tener la intención *or* el propósito de; *to intend to do sth.* tener la intención de hacer algo; pretender, querer; *I intend to be obeyed* pretendo que se me obedezca || *we fully intend to continue* tenemos la firme intención *or* el firme propósito de continuar.

intendance [-əns] *n* intendencia *f*.

intendant [-ənt] *n* intendente *m*.

intended [-id] *adj* proyectado, da (planned) || deliberado, da; intencional (intentional) || futuro, ra (husband, wife).
◆ *n* FAM prometido, da; novio, via.

intendment [-mənt] *n* JUR espíritu *m* (of a law, etc.).

intense [in'tens] *adj* intenso, sa; fuerte (heat, pain, colour) || profundo, da (look) || ardiente, apasionado, da (highly emotional) | enorme, sumo, ma (interest, etc.) || PHOT reforzado, da.

intensification [in,tensifi'keiʃən] *n* intensificación *f*.

intensifier [in'tensifaiə*] *n* PHOT reforzador *m*.

intensify [in'tensifai*] *vt* intensificar (trade, pain, measures, etc.) || aumentar (joy) || PHOT reforzar.
◆ *vi* intensificarse || aumentar.

intension [in'tenʃən] *n* PHIL comprensión *f* || intensidad *f* (intensity) || intensificación *f* (intensification) || determinación *f*.

intensity [in'tensiti] *n* intensidad *f*.

intensive [in'tensiv] *adj* intensivo, va; *intensive course* curso intensivo; *intensive cultivation* o *farming* cultivo intensivo || profundo, da; *to make an intensive study of* hacer un estudio profundo de || GRAMM intensivo, va (giving emphasis) || MED *intensive care unit* unidad *f* de vigilancia intensiva.
◆ *n* palabra *f* intensiva.

intent [in'tent] *adj* atento, ta; profundo, da; *an intent gaze* una mirada atenta || constante (application) || *intent on* o *upon* resuelto a, determinado a (with firm intention to), absorto en (engrossed in), atento a (with one's attention concentrated on).
◆ *n* intención *f*, propósito *m* || — *to all intents and purposes* prácticamente || *with malicious intent* con fines delictivos *or* criminales.

intention [in'tenʃən] *n* intención *f*; *it is my intention to* tengo la intención de; *first intention* primera intención; *healing by first, second intention* cura de *or* por primera, de *or* por segunda intención; *the intentions of a Mass* las intenciones de una misa || *I have no intention of going* no tengo ninguna intención de ir, no me propongo ir.

intentional [-əl] *adj* intencional, deliberado, da.

intentionality [-əliti] *n* intencionalidad *f*.

intentionally [-əli] *adv* intencionalmente, intencionadamente, a propósito, adrede.

intentioned [in'tenʃənd] *adj* intencionado, da.

intently [in'tentli] *adv* atentamente.

intentness [in'tentnis] *n* gran atención *f*, aplicación *f* (*on* a).

inter [in'tə:*] *vt* enterrar (to bury).

interact ['intərækt] *n* THEATR entreacto *m*.

interact [,intər'ækt] *vi* actuar recíprocamente.

interaction [,intər'ækʃən] *n* interacción *f*, acción *f* recíproca || INFORM interacción *f*.

interactive [,intər'æktiv] *adj* recíproco, ca || INFORM interactivo, va.

interallied ['intər:ə'laid] *adj* interaliado, da.

interamerican [int,:ə'merikən] *adj* interamericano, na.

interandean [intə:'ændi:n] *adj* interandino, na.

interbreed ['intə'bri:d] *vt* cruzar.
◆ *vi* cruzarse.

intercadence ['intə:'keidəns] *n* MED intercadencia *f* (of pulse).

intercadent ['intə:'keidənt] *adj* MED intercadente.

intercalary [in'tə:kələri] *adj* intercalar; *intercalary day* día intercalar || bisiesto (year) || intercalado, da (inserted).

intercalate [in'tə:kəleit] *vt* intercalar.

intercalation [in,tə:kə'leiʃən] *n* intercalación *f*.

intercede [,intə:'si:d] *vi* interceder; *to intercede with s.o. for another* interceder con *or* cerca de alguien por otro.

interceder [-ə*] *n* intercesor, ra.

interceding [-iŋ] *adj* intercesor, ra.

intercellular ['intə:'seljulə*] *adj* intercelular.

intercept [,intə:'sept] *vt* interceptar (a message) || parar *or* detener en el camino (to stop s.o.) || parar (s.o.'s escape) || cortar (s.o.'s retreat) || cortar (line, circuit) || MATH cortar.

interception [,intə:'sepʃən] *n* intercepción *f*, interceptación *f* || MATH intersección *f*.

interceptive ['intə:'septiv] *adj* que intercepta.

interceptor [,intə'septə*] *n* AVIAT interceptador *m* || persona *f* que intercepta.

intercession [,intə'seʃən] *n* intercesión *f*.

intercessor [,intə'sesə*] *n* intercesor, ra.

intercessory [,intə'sesəri] *adj* intercesor, ra.

interchange ['intə:'tʃeindʒ] *n* intercambio *m*; *interchange of letters* intercambio de cartas || cambio *m*; *interchange of ideas* cambio de impresiones || pasos *m pl* elevados a distintos niveles (of roads) || alternación *f* (of day and night).

interchange [,intə:'tʃeindʒ] *vt* intercambiar, cambiar || alternar (to alternate).

interchangeable [,intə:'tʃeindʒəbl] *adj* intercambiable.

intercity ['intə:'siti] *adj* interurbano, na.
◆ *n* tren *m* interurbano.

intercollegiate ['intə:kə'li:dʒiit] *adj* entre varios colegios *or* varias universidades.

intercolumnar [intə:kə'lʌmnə*] *adj* ARCH entre columnas.

intercolumniation [intə:kəlʌmni'eiʃən] *n* ARCH intercolumnio *m*.

intercom ['intə:kɔm] *n* sistema *m* de intercomunicación, intercomunicador *m* (of boats, etc.) || interfono *m* (in factories, etc.).

intercommunicate [,intə:kə'mju:nikeit] *vi* comunicarse, intercomunicarse.

intercommunication ['intə:kə,mju:ni'keiʃən] *n* intercomunicación *f*.

interconnect ['intə:kə'nekt] *vt* ELECTR interconectar || conectar.
◆ *vi* conectar.

interconnected [-id] *adj* que se comunican (rooms) || AVIAT conectado, da (rudders) || ligado, da; íntimamente relacionado (facts).

interconnection; interconnexion ['intə:kə'nekʃən] *n* ELECTR interconexión *f* || conexión *f*.

intercontinental ['intə:,kɔnti'nentl] *adj* intercontinental.

intercostal [,intə:'kɔ:stl] *adj* ANAT intercostal.

intercourse ['intə:kɔ:s] *n* trato *m* (social dealings) || relaciones *f pl* (commercial, political dealings) || intercambio *m* (interchange) || contacto *m* sexual (sexual union).

intercrop ['intə:'krɔp] *vi* AGR alternar cultivos.

intercurrent ['intə:kʌrənt] *adj* intercalado, da.

interdenominational ['intə:di,nɔmi'neiʃənl] *adj* entre varias confesiones *or* religiones.

interdental ['intə:'dentl] *adj* interdental.

interdepartmental ['intə:,di:pɑ:t'mentl] *adj* interdepartamental.

interdepend [,intə:di'pend] *vi* depender el uno del otro.

interdependence [,intə:di'pendəns]; **interdependency** [-i] *n* interdependencia *f*.

interdependent [ˌintəːdiˈpendənt] *adj* interdependiente.

interdict [ˈintəːdikt] *n* REL interdicto *m*, entredicho *m* ‖ JUR interdicto *m* ‖ interdicción *f*, prohibición *f*.

interdict [ˌintəːˈdikt] *vt* poner en entredicho ‖ prohibir (to forbid).

interdiction [ˌintəːˈdikʃən] *n* JUR & REL interdicto *m* ‖ interdicción *f*, prohibición *f*.

interdictory [ˈintəːˈdiktəri] *adj* JUR prohibitivo, va; prohibitorio, ria.

interdigital [ˈintəːˈdidʒitl] *adj* ZOOL interdigital.

interest [ˈintrist] *n* interés *m*; *he looked at me with interest* me miró con interés; *public interest* interés público ‖ beneficio *m*, provecho *m*; *in one's own interest* en beneficio propio ‖ COMM interés *m*, participación *f* (participation) | interés *m*, rédito *m* (on money lent); *to lend at interest* prestar con interés; *a ten per cent interest* un interés del *or* de un diez por ciento ‖ — *compound interest* interés compuesto ‖ *his main interest is music* la música es lo que más le interesa ‖ *in the interest of peace* en pro de la paz ‖ *it is not in your interest* no va en beneficio suyo ‖ *simple interest* interés simple ‖ *to be of interest* tener interés, ser interesante, interesar; *it is of no interest to me* no me interesa ‖ *to have a controlling interest in a firm* tener la mayor parte de las acciones de una compañía ‖ *to pay back with interest* pagar con creces (figurative sense), pagar con interés (literal sense) ‖ *to show an interest in* mostrar interés en *or* por ‖ *to take an interest in* tomarse interés por, interesarse por *or* en ‖ COMM *to yield a high interest* dar un interés elevado ‖ *vested interest* derecho adquirido (legal term), interés *m* personal; *many vested interests are involved in this affair* muchos intereses personales entran en juego en este asunto; intereses *m pl*; *to have a vested interest in a concern* tener intereses en una empresa.
◆ *pl* industria *f sing*; *the steel interests* la industria del acero, la industria siderúrgica ‖ negocios *m*; *he has mining interests in South Africa* tiene negocios en Sudáfrica relacionados con las minas ‖ — *business interests* los negocios, el mundo de los negocios ‖ *the landed interests* los terratenientes.

interest [ˈintrist] *vt* interesar.

interested [-id] *adj* interesado, da; *the interested party* la parte interesada ‖ *to be interest in sport* interesarle a uno el deporte, interesarse en *or* por el deporte.

interest-free [-friː] *adj* sin intereses.

interesting [-iɛ] *adj* interesante ‖ FIG *in an interesting condition* en estado interesante (pregnant).

interface [ˈintəːfeis] *n* superficie *f* de contacto ‖ INFORM interface *f*, interfaz *m*; *interface adaptor* adaptador de interfaz.

interfacial [ˌintəːˈfeiʃəl] *adj* MATH diedro (angle).

interfere [ˌintəˈfiə*] *vi* entrometerse; *stop interfering!* ¡deja de entrometerte! ‖ PHYS interferir ‖ JUR reclamar la prioridad de un invento ‖ *to interfere with* estorbar, dificultar (to hinder), tocar (to touch), estropear (to ruin), entrometerse *or* meterse en (other people's business), producir interferencias en (a radio), oponerse a, chocar con (interests).

interference [-rəns] *n* intromisión *f*, ingerencia *f* (the act of interfering) ‖ SP obstrucción *f* ‖ PHYS interferencia *f* ‖ RAD parásitos *m pl*, interferencias *f pl*.

interfering [ˌintəːˈfiəriŋ] *adj* interferente ‖ entrometido, da (person).

interfuse [ˌintəːˈfjuːz] *vt* mezclar.
◆ *vi* mezclarse, fundirse.

interfusion [ˌintəːˈfjuːʒən] *n* mezcla *f* (mixing).

intergalactic [ˌintəːgəlæktik] *adj* intergaláctico, ca.

interglacial [ˈintəːˈgleisjəl] *adj* interglacial.

intergovernmental [ˈintəːˈgʌvənˈmentl] *adj* intergubernamental.

interim [ˈintərim] *n* ínterin *m* (interval) ‖ *in the interim* en el ínterin, entretanto.
◆ *adj* provisional, interino, na; *an interim decision* una decisión provisional.

interior [inˈtiəriə*] *adj* interior; *the interior market* el mercado interior ‖ interno, na (internal) ‖ profundo, da; *the interior meaning of the play* el significado profundo de la obra ‖ — MATH *interior angle* ángulo interno ‖ *interior decorator* decorador, ra de interiores ‖ *interior monologue* monólogo *m* interior.
◆ *n* interior *m*.

interiority [intiəˈriɔriti] *n* interioridad *f*.

interjacent [intəːˈdʒeisənt] *adj* interyacente.

interject [ˌintəːˈdʒekt] *vt* interponer.

interjection [ˌintəːˈdʒekʃən] *n* GRAMM interjección *f* ‖ interposición *f*.

interjectory [ˌintəːˈdʒektəri] *adj* interpuesto, ta.

interlace [ˌintəːˈleis] *vt* entrelazar (to cross things over and under) ‖ entremezclar (to mix).
◆ *vi* entrelazarse ‖ entremezclarse.

interlacement [-mənt] *n* entrelazamiento *m*.

interlard [ˌintəːˈlɑːd] *vt* entreverar.

interleaf [ˈintəliːf] *n* página *f* blanca intercalada.

interleave [ˌintəːˈliːv] *vt* interfoliar, interpaginar.

interline [ˌintəːˈlain] *vt* interlinear (to write between lines) ‖ entretelar (in sewing).

interlinear [ˌintəːˈliniə*] *adj* interlineal.

interlineation [ˈintəːˌliniˈeiʃən] *n* interlineación *f*, interlineado *m*.

interlining [ˌintəːˈlainiŋ] *n* entretela *f* (in sewing) ‖ interlineado *m*, interlineación *f* (interlineation).

interlock [ˌintəːˈlɔk] *vt* engranar (teeth of a mechanism) ‖ enganchar (to hook together) ‖ encajar (to insert) ‖ trabar, entrelazar (to connect).
◆ *vi* engranar ‖ engancharse ‖ encajar (to fit) ‖ trabarse, entrelazarse (to be connected).

interlocution [ˌintələuˈkjuːʃən] *n* conversación *f*, interlocución *f*.

interlocutor [ˌintəˈlɔkjutə*] *n* interlocutor, ra.

interlocutory [-ri] *adj* JUR interlocutorio, ria; *to award an interlocutory decree* formar auto interlocutorio.

interlope [ˌintəːˈləup] *vi* entrometerse (to meddle) ‖ hacer negocios fraudulentos.

interloper [ˈintəːləupə*] *n* intruso, sa (in s.o. else's property) ‖ entrometido, da (in s.o. else's affairs) ‖ traficante *m*.

interloping [ˌintəːləupiŋ] *adj* intérlope, fraudulento, ta.

interlude [ˈintəluːd] *n* MUS interludio *m* ‖ THEATR entremés *m* (short play) | entreacto *m* (entr'acte) ‖ intervalo *m* (interval).

intermarriage [ˌintəˈmæridʒ] *n* matrimonio *m* mixto (between different races, etc.) ‖ matrimonio *m* entre consanguíneos (between close relations).

intermarry [ˈintəˈmæri] *vi* casarse entre consanguíneos *or* entre parientes (between close relations) ‖ casarse [personas de distintas razas, etc.] ‖ *these tribes have intermarried for centuries* estas tribus se han casado entre sí durante siglos.

intermaxillary [intəˈmækˈsiləri] *adj* ANAT intermaxilar.

intermeddle [ˌintəˈmedl] *vt* intervenir, inmiscuirse, entremeterse, entrometerse (*with* en).

intermeddling [-iŋ] *n* intervención *f*, intromisión *f*, entremetimiento *m*.

intermediary [ˌintəˈmiːdjəri] *adj* intermediario, ria (acting between persons) ‖ intermedio, dia (intermediate).
◆ *n* intermediario, ria (mediator) ‖ etapa *f* intermedia (phase).

intermediate [ˌintəˈmiːdjət] *adj* intermedio, dia ‖ INFORM *intermediate memory* memoria *f* intermedia.
◆ *n* intermediario, ria (mediator).

intermediate [ˌintəˈmiːdieit] *vi* intermediar, mediar.

intermediation [ˌintəːmiˈdieiʃən] *n* mediación *f*.

interment [inˈtəːmənt] *n* entierro *m*.

intermezzo [ˌintəˈmetsəu] *n* MUS intermezzo *m*.
— OBSERV El plural de la palabra inglesa es *intermezzi* o *intermezzos*.

interminable [inˈtəːminəbl] *adj* interminable.

intermingle [ˌintəːˈmiŋgl] *vt* entremezclar.
◆ *vi* entremezclarse.

interministerial [ˌintəːminisˈtiəriəl] *adj* interministerial.

intermission [ˌintəˈmiʃən] *n* intermisión *f*, interrupción *f* (interruption) ‖ CINEM descanso *m* ‖ THEATR entreacto *m*, descanso *m* ‖ MED intermitencia *f*.

intermissive [ˌintəˈmisiv] *adj* intermitente.

intermit [ˈintəːˈmit] *vt* interrumpir.
◆ *vi* interrumpirse ‖ MED ser intermitente.

intermittence [ˌintəˈmitəns]; **intermittency** [-i] *n* intermitencia *f*.

intermittent [ˌintəˈmitənt] *adj* intermitente ‖ — ELECTR *intermittent current* corriente *f* intermitente ‖ MED *intermittent fever* fiebre *f* intermitente.

intermix [ˌintəˈmiks] *vt* entremezclar.
◆ *vi* entremezclarse.

intermixture [ˌintˈmikstʃə*] *n* mezcla *f*.

intermolecular [ˌintəˈːməuˈlekjulə*] *adj* intermolecular.

intermuscular [ˌintəˈmʌskjulə*] *adj* ANAT intermuscular.

intern [ˌintəːn] *n* MED interno *m*.

intern; interne [inˈtəːn] *vt* internar.
◆ *vi* trabajar como interno.

internal [-l] *adj* interno, na; *internal injuries* lesiones internas; *internal organs* órganos internos ‖ interior; *internal trade* comercio interior ‖ interno, na; intestino, na; *internal conflicts* luchas intestinas ‖ intrínseco, ca (intrinsic) ‖ — MATH *internal angle* ángulo interno ‖ *internal medicine* medicina interna ‖ US *Internal Revenue* rentas públicas.
◆ *pl n* ANAT órganos *m* internos ‖ FIG cualidades *f* esenciales.

internal-combustion engine [inˈtəːnlkəmˈbʌstʃənˈendʒin] *n* motor *m* de combustión interna.

internally [inˈtəːnəli] *adv* interiormente ‖ MED *not to be used internally* uso externo.

international [ˌintəˈnæʃənl] *adj* internacional ‖ — GEOGR *international date line* línea *f* de cambio de fecha ‖ *international law* derecho *m* internacional ‖ *international relations* relaciones *f pl* internacionales.

◆ *n* SP internacional *m* & *f* (sportsman) | partido *m* internacional (match) ‖ Internacional *f* (organization); *the First International* la Primera Internacional.

Internationale [ˌintənæʃəˈnɑːl] *n* Internacional *f* (hymn).

internationalism [ˌintəˈnæʃnəlizəm] *n* internacionalismo *m*.

internationalist [ˌintəˈnæʃnəlist] *n* internacionalista *m* & *f*.

internationalization [ˈintəˌnæʃnəlaiˈzeiʃən] *n* internacionalización *f*.

internationalize [ˌintəˈnæʃnəlaiz] *vt* internacionalizar.

interne [ˈintəːn] *n* MED ⟶ **intern.**

internecine [ˌintəˈniːsain] *adj* de aniquilación mutua (mutually destructive); *internecine war* guerra de aniquilación mutua ‖ mortífero, ra (deadly).

internee [ˌintəːˈniː] *n* internado, da.

internist [inˈtəːnist] *n* MED internista *m* & *f*, médico *m* internista.

internment [inˈtəːnmənt] *n* MIL internamiento *m* ‖ JUR internación *f*.

internode [ˈintəːnəud] *n* BOT entrenudo *m*.

inter nos [intəːˈnɔs] *adv phr* entre nosotros.

internship [ˈintəːnʃip] *n* US puesto *m* de interno.

internuncio [ˌintəːˈnʌnʃiəu] *n* REL internuncio *m*.

interoceanic [ˈintəːrˌəuʃiˈænik] *adj* interoceánico, ca.

interosculate [ˈintəːˈɔskjuleit] *vi* entremezclarse, confundirse (to intermix) ‖ BOL tener características comunes.

interpage [intəːˈpeidʒ] *vt* interpaginar.

interpaliamentary [ˈintəːˌpɑːləˈmentəri] *adj* interparlamentario, ria.

interparietal [ˌintəːpəˈraiitl] *adj* ANAT interparietal.

interpellate [inˈtəːpeleit] *vt* interpelar.

interpellation [inˌtəːpeˈleiʃən] *n* interpelación *f*.

interpellator [inˈtəːpeleitə*] *n* interpelador, ra; interpelante *m* & *f*.

interpenetrate [ˌintəːˈpenitreit] *vt* penetrar.
◆ *vi* compenetrarse.

interpenetration [ˈintəːˌpeniˈtreiʃən] *n* compenetración *f* ‖ interpenetración *f*.

interpersonal [ˌintəːˈpəːsnl] *adj* interpersonal.

interphone [ˈintəːfəun] *n* teléfono *m* interior, interfono *m*.

interplanetary [ˌintəˈplænitəri] *adj* interplanetario, ria.

interplay [ˈintəˈplei] *n* interacción *f*.

interplay [ˈintəˈplei] *vi* actuar recíprocamente.

Interpol [ˈintəpɔl] *n* Interpol *f*.

interpolate [inˈtəːpəuleit] *vt* interpolar.

interpolating [-iŋ] *adj* interpolador, ra.

interpolation [inˌtəːpəuˈleiʃən] *n* interpolación *f*.

interpolator [inˈtəːpəuleitə*] *n* interpolador, ra.

interposal [ˌintəːˈpəuzl] *n* interposición *f* ‖ intervención *f*.

interpose [ˌintəˈpəuz] *vt* interponer.
◆ *vi* interponerse (to come between) ‖ intervenir (to intervene) ‖ interrumpir (to interrupt).

interposition [inˌtəːpəˈziʃən] *n* interposición *f*.

interpret [inˈtəːprit] *vt* interpretar.
◆ *vi* hacer de intérprete (to act as an interpreter).

interpretable [-əbl] *adj* interpretable.

interpretation [inˌtəːpriˈteiʃən] *n* interpretación *f*.

interpretative [inˌtəːpritətiv] *adj* interpretativo, va.

interpreter [inʒtəːˈitə*] *n* intérprete *m* & *f*.

interpretive [inˈtəːpritiv] *adj* US interpretativo, va.

interprofessional [ˌintəːprəˈfeʃənl] *adj* interprofesional.

interracial [ˌintəːˈreiʃəl] *adj* interracial.

interregnum [ˌintəˈregnəm] *n* interregno *m*.
— OBSERV El plural de la palabra *interregnum* es *interregnums* o *interregna*.

interrelate [ˌintəːriˈleit] *vt* interrelacionar.

interrelated [intəːriˈleitid] *adj* relacionado, da; estrechamente ligado, estrechamente vinculado.

interrelation [intəːriˈleiʃən] *n* correlación *f* ‖ relación *f*.

interrogate [inˈterəugeit] *vt* interrogar.

interrogation [inˌterəuˈgeiʃən] *n* interrogatorio *m*; *a police interrogation* un interrogatorio de la policía ‖ interrogación *f* (question, questioning) ‖ US *interrogation mark* signo *m* de interrogación.

interrogative [ˌintəˈrɔgətiv] *adj* interrogativo, va; *interrogative sentence* oración interrogativa ‖ interrogador, ra; *an interrogative look* una mirada interrogadora.
◆ *n* palabra *f or* oración *f* interrogativa.

interrogator [inˈterəugeitə*] *n* interrogador, ra.

interrogatory [ˌintəˈrɔgətəri] *adj* interrogador, ra.
◆ *n* JUR interrogatorio *m*.

interrupt [ˌintəˈrʌpt] *vt* interrumpir.
◆ *vi* interrumpir.

interrupter [-ə*] *n* ELECTR interruptor *m*.

interruption [ˌintəˈrʌpʃən] *n* interrupción *f*.

intersect [ˌintəˈsekt] *vt* cruzar (to cross) ‖ MATH cortar.
◆ *vi* MATH intersecarse ‖ cruzarse (roads).

intersection [-ʃən] *n* intersección *f* ‖ cruce *m* (crossroads).

intersession [ˈintəˌseʃən] *n* US vacaciones *f pl* semestrales universitarias.

intersex [ˈintəseks] *n* individuo *m* con características intersexuales.

intersexual [ˌintəˈseksjuəl] *adj* intersexual.

interspace [ˈintəˈspeis] *n* intervalo *m*, espacio *m* intermedio.

interspace [ˈintəˈspeis] *vt* espaciar.

intersperse [ˌintəˈspəːs] *vt* esparcir, entremezclar; *daisies interspersed amongst the poppies* margaritas esparcidas entre las amapolas ‖ salpicar; *a field interspersed with poppies* un campo salpicado de amapolas; *to intersperse a lecture with anecdotes* salpicar de anécdotas una conferencia.

interspersion [ˌintəˈspəːʃən] *n* mezcla *f*.

interstate [intəˈsteit] *adj* entre estados.

interstellar [ˈintəˈstelə*] *adj* interestelar, intersideral.

interstice [inˈtəːstis] *n* intersticio *m*.

interstitial [intəˈstiʃəl] *adj* intersticial.

intertrigo [ˌintəˈtraigəu] *n* MED intertrigo *m*.

intertropical [ˌintəˈtrɔpikəl] *adj* intertropical.

intertwine [ˌintəˈtwain] *vt* entrelazar.
◆ *vi* entrelazarse.

interurban [ˌintəːˈəːbən] *adj* interurbano, na.

interval [ˈintəvəl] *n* intervalo *m* (period of time, space between two points) ‖ entreacto *m*, descanso *m* (in theatre) ‖ descanso *m* (in cinema, in sports events) ‖ descanso *m*, pausa *f* (short break) ‖ MUS intervalo *m* ‖ — *at intervals* de vez en cuando, a intervalos (from time to time), de trecho en trecho, a intervalos (here and there) ‖ *bright intervals* claros *m* (in meteorology).

intervene [ˌintəˈviːn] *vi* intervenir, mediar; *to intervene in s.o.'s defence* intervenir en defensa de alguien ‖ ocurrir (to happen) ‖ transcurrir, mediar (time) ‖ mediar (distance) ‖ *in the intervening days* durante los días intermedios.

intervention [ˌintəˈvenʃən] *n* intervención *f*.

interventionism [ˌintəˈvenʃənizəm] *n* intervencionismo *m*.

interventionist [ˌintəˈvenʃənist] *n* intervencionista.

interview [ˈintəvjuː] *n* entrevista *f*, interviú *f*.

interview [ˈintəvjuː] *vt* entrevistar.

interviewee [-i] *n* entrevistado, da.

interviewer [-ə*] *n* entrevistador, ra.

interweave* [ˌintəˈwiːv] *vt* entretejer ‖ FIG entremezclar.
◆ *vi* entremezclarse.
— OBSERV Pret *interwove*; pp *interwoven*.

interweaving [-iŋ] *n* entretejido *m*.

interwove [ˌintəˈwəuv] *pret* ⟶ **interweave.**

interwoven [-ən] *pp* ⟶ **interweave.**

intestacy [inˈtestəsi] *n* JUR hecho *m* de morir intestado | falta *f* de testamento.

intestate [inˈtestit] *adj/n* JUR intestado, da.

intestinal [inˈtestinl] *adj* intestinal ‖ US *intestinal fortitude* valor *m*, estómago *m* (*fam*).

intestine [inˈtestin] *n* ANAT intestino *m*; *small, large intestine* intestino delgado, grueso.
◆ *adj* intestino, na; *intestine conflicts* luchas intestinas.

intimacy [ˈintiməsi] *n* intimidad *f* (state of being intimate) ‖ relaciones *f pl* íntimas (sexual relations).

intimate [ˈintimit] *adj* íntimo, ma; *intimate friends* amigos íntimos; *intimate feelings* sentimientos íntimos ‖ amoroso, sa (loving) ‖ personal; *an intimate style of writing* un estilo personal ‖ profundo, da; *intimate knowledge* conocimiento profundo ‖ — *to become intimate with s.o.* intimar con alguien ‖ *to be intimate with s.o.* tener relaciones íntimas con alguien.
◆ *n* íntimo, *m*.

intimate [ˈintimeit] *vt* insinuar, dar a entender (to hint) ‖ anunciar, notificar (to announce).

intimating [ˈintimeitiŋ] *adj* intimatorio, ria.

intimation [ˌintiˈmeiʃən] *n* insinuación *f* (hint) ‖ indicio *m* (insight) ‖ indicación *f* (indication).

intimidate [inˈtimideit] *vt* intimidar.

intimidation [inˌtimiˈdeiʃən] *n* intimidación *f*.

intimidator [inˈtimideitə*] *n* persona *f* que intimida.

intimist [ˈintimist] *adj/n* intimista.

intimity [inˈtimiti] *n* intimidad *f*.

intitule [inˈtitjul] *vt* titular (a legislative act).

into [ˈintu] *prep* en; *to enter into* entrar en; *to fall into enemy hands* caer en manos del enemigo; *to come into contact with* entrar en contacto con; *to change from one thing into another* convertirse de una cosa en otra; *to fold into four* doblar en cuatro ‖ a; *to open into the street* dar a la calle; *to translate into French* traducir al francés ‖ hacia; *they went off into the setting sun* se fueron hacia el sol poniente; *a journey into the future* un viaje hacia el futuro ‖ contra; *to crash into* estrellarse contra ‖ contra, con; *to* *bump into a tree* tropezar contra un árbol; *to bump into an old friend* tropezar con un viejo amigo || dentro; *get into the sack* métete dentro del saco || — *three into twelve goes four* doce entre tres son cuatro || *to grow into a man* hacerse un hombre || *to work into the night* trabajar hasta muy entrada la noche.

— OBSERV La preposición *into* se emplea muy frecuentemente después de varios verbos (*to come, to fall, to get, to go, etc.*) cambiando su sentido. Por lo tanto remitimos a cada uno de ellos para sus distintas traducciones.

intolerability [in,tɔlərəbiliti] *n* inadmisibilidad *f*.

intolerable [in'tɔlərəbl] *adj* intolerable, inadmisible.

intolerance [in'tɔlərəns] *n* intolerancia *f*.

intolerant [in'tɔlərənt] *adj/n* intolerante (*of* con, para).

intonate ['intəuneit] *vt* ⟶ **intone.**

intonation [,intəu'neiʃən] *n* entonación *f*.

intone [in'təun]; **intonate** [,intəuneit] *vt* salmodiar (to chant) || entonar (to sing the opening phrase of).

in toto [inðəu'təu] *adv* en su totalidad.

intoxicant [in'tɔksikɔnt] *adj* embriagador, ra.
◆ *n* bebida *f* alcohólica (alcoholic drink) || sustancia *f* que embriaga (drug).

intoxicate [in'tɔksikeit] *vt* embriagar, emborrachar (to make drunk) || MED intoxicar || FIG embriagar (joy, etc.).

intoxicating [-iŋ] *adj* embriagador, ra.

intoxication [in,tɔksi'keiʃən] *n* embriaguez *f*, borrachera *f* || MED intoxicación *f* || FIG embriaguez *f*.

intracellular [,intrə'seljulə*] *adj* intracelular.

intractability [in,træktə'biliti] *n* indocilidad *f* (of a person) || insolubilidad *f* (of a problem) || dificultad *f* (difficulty).

intractable [in'træktəbl] *adj* intratable (difficult to manage) || indisciplinado, da (unruly) || insoluble (problem) || TECH difícil de labrar || MED incurable || incultivable (land).

intradermic [intrə'dəːmik] *adj* intradérmico, ca.

intrados [in'treidɔs] *n* ARCH intradós *m*.

intramural ['intrə'mjuərəl] *adj* situado intramuros.

intramuscular ['intrə'mʌskjulə*] *adj* intramuscular; *intramuscular injection* inyección intramuscular.

intransigence [in'trænsidʒəns] *n* intransigencia *f*.

intransigent [in'trænsidʒənt] *adj* intransigente.

intransitive [in'trænsitiv] *adj* intransitivo, va.
◆ *n* intransitivo *m*.

intransmissible [intræns'misibl] *adj* intrasmisible.

intranuclear [intra'njuːkliə*] *adj* PHYS intranuclear.

intrastate [,intrə'steit] *adj* US interior.

intrauterine [intrə'jutərain] *adj* MED intrauterino, na.

intravenous [intrə'viːnəs] *adj* intravenoso, sa.

intravenously [-li] *adv* por vía intravenosa.

in-tray ['intrei] *n* bandeja *f* de entradas *or* de asuntos pendientes.

intreat [in'triːt] *vt* suplicar, implorar, rogar.

intrench [in'trenʃ] *vt/vi* ⟶ **entrench.**

intrepid [in'trepid] *adj* intrépido, da.

intrepidity [intri'piditi] *n* intrepidez *f*.

intricacy ['intrikəsi] *n* intrincamiento *m* || dédalo *m*, laberinto *m* (of a town) || complejidad *f* (of a problem).

intricate ['intrikit] *adj* intrincado, da || complejo, ja; complicado, da (problem).

intrigant ['intrigənt] *n* intrigante *m*.

intrigante [intri'gɑːnt] *n* intrigante *f*.

intrigue [in'triːg] *n* intriga *f* (plot, etc.) || (ant) relaciones *f pl* amorosas ilícitas.

intrigue [in'triːg] *vt/vi* intrigar; *she intrigues me* me intriga; *they remained intriguing late into the night* se quedaron intrigando hasta muy avanzada la noche.

intriguer [-ə*] *n* intrigante *m* & *f*.

intriguing [-iŋ] *adj* intrigante, enredador, ra (scheming) || fascinante, misterioso, sa; curioso, sa; intrigante (fascinating).

intrinsic [in'trinsik] *adj* intrínseco, ca.

intro ['intrəu] *n* FAM introducción *f*.

introduce [,intrə'djuːs] *vt* presentar; *may I introduce you to my wife?* le presento a mi mujer; *to introduce s.o. into society* presentar a alguien en sociedad || introducir; *to introduce a new fashion* introducir una nueva moda; *to introduce one's products into foreign markets* introducir sus productos en el mercado exterior; *to introduce s.o. into high society* introducir a alguien en la alta sociedad || lanzar; *to introduce a new toothpaste* lanzar una nueva pasta de dientes || iniciar; *to introduce a bill before Parliament* presentar un proyecto de ley ante el Parlamento || prologar (to preface a book) || — *he was introduced into a room* lo hicieron entrar en una habitación || *I was introduced into his presence* me llevaron ante él || *to introduce a question* hacer una pregunta (to ask), abordar un tema (to bring a subject up).

introduction [,intrə'dʌkʃən] *n* introducción *f* || presentación *f* (of one person to another); *letter of introduction* carta de presentación || introducción *f*, prólogo *m* (of a book) || MUS preludio *m*.

introductive [,intrə'dʌktiv]; **introductory** [,intrə'dʌktəri] *adj* preliminar, introductorio, ria.

introit ['intrɔit] *n* REL introito *m*.

intromission [,intrəu'miʃən] *n* introducción *f* (inserting) || intromisión *f* (interference) || admisión *f* (admission).

intromit [,intrəu'mit] *vt* introducir, insertar (to put in) || admitir.

introspect [,intrəu'spekt] *vi* practicar la introspección.

introspection [,intrəu'spekʃən] *n* introspección *f*.

introspective [,intrəu'spektiv] *adj* introspectivo, va.

introversion [,intrəu'vəːʃən] *n* introversión *f*.

introversive [,intrəu'vəːsiv] *adj* introverso, sa.

introvert ['intrəuvəːt] *adj/n* introvertido, da.

introvert [,intrəu'vəːt] *vt* volver hacia sí mismo (to direct upon o.s.) || MED invaginar.

introverted [-id] *adj* introvertido, da.

intrude [in'truːd] *vt* imponer (to force upon) || meter por fuerza || GEOL introducir (to force between rock strata).
◆ *vi* entrometerse, inmiscuirse; *we were talking but he kept on intruding* estábamos charlando, pero él seguía entrometiéndose || imponerse (to impose) || — *am I intruding?* ¿estorbo?, ¿molesto? || *to intrude upon a conversation* interrumpir una conversación; meterse en; *to intrude upon s.o.'s privacy* meterse en la vida privada de alguien.

intruder [-ə*] *n* intruso, sa.

intrusion [in'truːʒən] *n* entremetimiento *m* (meddling) || JUR intrusión *f*, usurpación *f* || GEOL intrusión *f*.

intrusive [in'truːsiv] *adj* intruso, sa.

intubate ['intjubeit] *vt* MED intubar.

intubation [intju'beiʃən] *n* MED intubación *f*.

intuit [in'tjuːit] *vt/vi* intuir.

intuition [,intjuː'iʃən] *n* intuición *f*.

intuitional [,intjuː'iʃənl] *adj* intuitivo, va.

intuitive [in'tjuːitiv] *adj* intuitivo, va.

intumesce [,intjuː'mes] *vi* hincharse.

intumescence [-ns] *n* intumescencia *f*, tumefacción *f*, hinchazón *f*.

intumescent [-nt] *adj* intumescente, tumefacto, ta; hinchado, da.

intussuscept [,intəssə'sept] *vt* MED invaginar.

inunction [in'ʌŋkʃən] *n* untura *f*, unción *f* (ointing) || ungüento *m* (ointment).

inundate ['inʌndeit] *vt* inundar.

inundation [,inʌn'deiʃən] *n* inundación *f*.

inurbane [,inəː'bein] *adj* inurbano, na; descortés.

inurbanity [,inəː'bæniti] *n* descortesía *f*.

inure [i'njuə*] *vt* habituar, acostumbrar (to accustom) || endurecer (to harden).
◆ *vi* JUR entrar en vigor, aplicarse (to take effect).

inurement [-mənt] *n* hábito *m*, costumbre *f* (custom) || endurecimiento *m* (hardening) || JUR entrada *f* en vigor, aplicación *f*.

inurn [in'əːn] *vt* poner en una urna.

inutile [in'juːtail] *adj* inútil.

inutility [,injuː'tiliti] *n* inutilidad *f*.

in vacuo [in'vækjuəu] *adv* en vacío.

invade [in'veid] *vt* invadir (a country, region, etc.); *a city invaded by tourists* una ciudad invadida por los turistas || meterse en; *to invade s.o.'s privacy* meterse en la vida privada de alguien || usurpar (s.o.'s rights).

invader [-ə*] *n* invasor, ra.

invaginate [invædʒineit] *vt* MED invaginar.
◆ *vi* MED invaginarse.

invagination [invædʒi'neiʃən] *n* MED invaginación *f*.

invalid ['inváliːd] *adj* inválido, da (disabled) || enfermo, ma (sick) || enfermizo, za (sickly) || para enfermos (for sick people).
◆ *n* inválido *m*, persona *f* inválida (incapacitated person) || enfermo, ma (sick person).

invalid [in'vælid] *adj* nulo, la; *an invalid contract* un contrato nulo || *to become invalid* caducar.

invalid [,invə'liːd] *vt* dejar inválido (to disable) || poner enfermo (to make sick) || *to invalid out* dar de baja por invalidez (from military service).
◆ *vi* quedarse inválido || ponerse enfermo || darse de baja por invalidez.

invalidate [in'vælideit] *vt* invalidar, anular.

invalidation [in,væli'deiʃən] *n* invalidación *f*, anulación *f*.

invalidity [,invə'liditi] *n* MED invalidez *f* (infirmity) | enfermedad *f*, mala salud *f* (sickness) || JUR invalidez *f*, nulidad *f*.

invaluable [in'væljuəbl] *adj* inestimable, inapreciable.

invar [in'vɑː*] *n* invar *m* (metal).

invariability [in,vɛəriə'biliti] *n* invariabilidad *f*.

invariable [in'vɛəriəbl] *adj* invariable.

invariably [in'vɛəriəbli] *adv* invariablemente || siempre, constantemente (always).

invariant [in'vɛəriənt] *adj* invariable, constante.

invasion [in'veiʒən] *n* invasión *f* (an invading or being invaded) || JUR usurpación *f* (of s.o.'s rights) || entretenimiento *m* (intrusion).

invasive [in'veisiv] *adj* invasor, ra.

invective [in'vektiv] *n* invectiva *f*; *to thunder invectives against s.o.* fulminar invectivas contra alguien.

inveigh [in'vei] *vi* *to inveigh against* lanzar invectivas contra, vituperar.

inveigle [in'vi:gl] *vt* embaucar, engatusar (to cajole); *he inveigled me into doing such a thing* me embaucó para que hiciese tal cosa.

inveiglement [-mənt] *n* embaucamiento *m*, engatusamiento *m*.

invent [in'vent] *vt* inventar.

invention [in'venʃən] *n* invención *f*, invento *m*; *of his own invention* de su propia invención || inventiva *f* (inventiveness) || mentira *f* (untrue story).

inventive [in'ventiv] *adj* inventivo, va.

inventiveness [-nis] *n* inventiva *f*.

inventor [in'ventə*] *n* inventor, ra.

inventory ['invəntri] *n* inventario *m* (itemized list) || existencias *f pl* (stock).

inventory ['invəntri] *vt* inventariar, hacer un inventario de.

inverness [,invə'nis] *n* macfarlán *m*, macferlán *m*.

inverse ['in'və:s] *adj* inverso, sa.
◆ *n* lo inverso (opposite) || lo contrario *m* (contrary).

inversion [in'və:ʃən] *n* inversión *f* (an inverting or sth. inverted) || GRAMM inversión *f* || MATH inversión *f* || inversión *f* (sexual) (homosexuality).

invert [ixinvə:t] *n* invertido, da.
◆ *adj* invertido, da (sugar).

invert [in'və:t] *vt* invertir.

invertebrata [in,və:ti'brɑ:tə] *pl n* invertebrados *m*.

invertebrate [in'və:tibrit] *adj* ZOOL invertebrado, da.
◆ *n* ZOOL invertebrado *m*.

inverted commas [in'və:tid'kɔməz] *pl n* comillas *f*.

inverted snob [in'və:tid'snɔb] *n* intelectualoide *m* & *f*.

invest [invest] *vt* invertir; *to invest money in a business* invertir dinero en un negocio || investir (to install in office) || conferir (with a dignity, etc.) || envolver; *invested with an air of mystery* envuelto en un aire de misterio || MIL sitiar, cercar (to besiege).
◆ *vi* hacer una inversión, invertir dinero || FIG & FAM *to invest in* comprarse; *I invested in a new dress yesterday* ayer me compré un nuevo traje.

investigate [in'vestigeit] *vt* investigar || examinar (to examine) || estudiar (to study).
◆ *vi* hacer una investigación.

investigating [-iŋ] *adj* investigador, ra.

investigation [in,vesti'geiʃən] *n* investigación *f* || estudio *m* (study).

investigative [in'vestigeitiv] *adj* investigador, ra.

investigator [in'vestigeitə*] *n* investigador, ra.

investigatory [in'vestigeitəri] *adj* investigador, ra.

investiture [in'vestitʃə*] *n* investidura *f*.

investment [in'vestmənt] *n* inversión *f*; *a two hundred pound investment* una inversión de doscientas libras || MIL sitio *m*, cerco *m* || JUR & REL investidura *f* (investiture) || *investment trust* sociedad *f* de inversión *or* inversionista.
◆ *pl* inversiones *f* (money invested) || valores *m* en cartera (shares).

investor [in'vestə*] *n* inversionista *m* & *f*.

inveteracy [in'vetərəsi] *n* lo arraigado (of a habit) || costumbre *f* arraigada (long standing habit).

inveterate [in'vetərit] *adj* inveterado, da; empedernido, da (smoker, etc.) || arraigado, da (habit).

invidious [in'vidiəs] *adj* odioso, sa (odious); *invidious comparisons* comparaciones odiosas || que produce envidia (causing envy).

invigilate [in'vidʒileit] *vt* vigilar [a los candidatos].

invigilator [-ə*] *n* vigilante *m*.

invigorate [in'vigəreit] *vt* vigorizar, dar vigor a, fortificar (to give vigour to) || animar, estimular (to enliven).

invigorating [-iŋ] *adj* tónico, ca; que da vigor || estimulante.

invigoration [in,vigə'reiʃən] *n* fortalecimiento *m*.

invigorator [in'vigə,reitə*] *n* tónico *m*.

invincibility [in,vinsi'biliti] *n* invencibilidad *f*.

invincible [in'vinsəbl] *adj* invencible.

inviolability [in,vaiələ'biliti] *n* inviolabilidad *f*.

inviolable [in'vaiələbl] *adj* inviolable.

inviolate [in'vaiəlit] *adj* inviolado, da.

invisibility [in,vizə'biliti] *n* invisibilidad *f*.

invisible [in'vizəbl] *adj* invisible || *invisible ink* tinta simpática.
◆ *n* lo invisible || *the Invisible* Dios (God), el mundo invisible (unseen world).

invitation [,invi'teiʃən] *n* invitación *f*; *invitation card* tarjeta de invitación.

invitatory [in'vaitətətəri] *n* REL invitatorio *m* (in church services).

invite [in'vait] *n* FAM invitación *f*.

invite [in'vait] *vt* invitar, convidar; *to invite s.o. to dinner* invitar a alguien a cenar || pedir, solicitar (to ask for) || solicitar (questions, opinions) || incitar (to incite) || provocar (to cause); *his suggestion invited a lot of criticism* su sugerencia provocó muchas críticas || buscarse; *to invite trouble* buscarse problemas.

inviting [-iŋ] *adj* atractivo, va (attractive) || tentador, ra (tempting) || seductor, ra (seductive) || provocativo, va (provocative) || apetitoso, sa (food).

invitingly [-iŋli] *adv* de forma atractiva *or* tentadora || *the door was invitingly open* la puerta abierta invitaba a entrar.

in vitro [in'vi:trəu] *adj* in vitro; *in vitro fertilization* fecundación in vitro.

invocation [,invəu'keiʃən] *n* . invocación *f* || *under the invocation of* bajo la advocación de.

invocatory [in'vɔkətəri] *adj* invocatorio, ria.

invoice ['invɔis] *n* COMM factura *f*; *pro forma invoice* factura pro forma || — *as per invoice* según factura || *invoice clerk* facturador, ra || *to make out an invoice* extender una factura.

invoice ['invɔis] *vt* COMM facturar.

invoke [in'vəuk] *vt* invocar (to appeal to in prayer) || invocar (evil spirits) || recurrir a, acogerse a, invocar (to fall back on); *he invoked his special powers to justify the action* recurrió a sus poderes especiales para justificar su acción || suplicar, implorar (to implore) || pedir (to ask for); *to invoke s.o.'s aid* pedir la ayuda de alguien.

invoker [-ə*] *n* invocador, ra.

involucrate [,invə'lu:krət] *adj* involucrado, da.

involuntarily [in'vɔləntərili] *adv* sin querer, involuntariamente.

involuntary [in'vɔləntəri] *adj* involuntario, ria.

involute ['invəlu:t] *n* MATH involuta *f*.
◆ *adj* enrevesado, da; complicado, da (involved) || espiral, en espiral.

involution [,invə'lu:ʃən] *n* complicación *f* (entanglement) || MATH & BIOL & MED involución *f*.

involve [in'vɔlv] *vt* concernir, atañer; *this problem involves us all* este problema nos concierne a todos || afectar (to affect) || suponer, implicar (to imply); *this job involves little work* este empleo supone poco trabajo || acarrear, ocasionar (to entail) || comprometer, complicar; *to involve s.o. in a theft* comprometer a uno en un robo || mezclar, envolver, meter; *don't involve me in the argument* no me mezcles a mí en la discusión || requerir, exigir (to require); *it involves a large labour force* requiere un gran número de trabajadores || comprender (to include) || enredar, complicar (to complicate) || (ant) envolver (to wrap) || MATH elevar a cierta potencia || — *a question of honour is involved* el honor está en juego, se trata de una cuestión de honor || *the forces involved* las fuerzas en juego || *those involved* los interesados || *to be involved in* estar metido *or* complicado en || *to get involved in* meterse en, enredarse en.

involved [-d] *adj* complicado, da; enrevesado, da || —→ **involve.**

involvement [-mənt] *n* envolvimiento *m* (an involving) || complication *f*, enredo *m* (complicated state of affairs) || compromiso *m* (in politics, etc.) || participación *f*, implicación *f* (in a plot).

invulnerability [in,vʌlnərə'biliti] *n* invulnerabilidad *f*.

invulnerable [in'vʌlnərəbl] *adj* invulnerable.

inwall ['inwɔ:l] *vt* US cercar con un muro.

inward ['inwəd] *adj* interior, interno, na; *inward peace* paz interior || íntimo, ma; *inward thoughts* pensamientos íntimos.
◆ *adv* hacia adentro.

inward-flow [-fləu] *adj* centrípeto, ta.

inwardly [-li] *adv* interiormente || *to laugh inwardly* reír para sus adentros.

inwardness [-nis] *n* espiritualidad *f* (spirituality) || esencia *f* (inner nature) || sentido *m* profundo (meaning).

inwards ['inwədz] *adv* hacia dentro.
◆ *pl n* FAM tripas *f*, entrañas *f*.

inweave* ['in'wi:v] *vt* entretejer.
— OBSERV Pret *inwove*; pp *inwoven*.

inwrap ['inræp] *vt* envolver.

inwrought ['in'rɔ:t] *adj* bordado, da || incrustado, da (inlaid) || entretejido, da (interwoven).

IOC *abbr of [International Olympic Committee]* COI, Comité Olímpico Internacional.

iodate ['aiəudeit] *n* CHEM yodato *m*.

iodate ['aiəudeit] *vt* tratar con iodo, yodar.

iodic [ai'ɔdik] *adj* CHEM yódico, ca; *iodic acid* ácido yódico.

iodide ['aiəudaid] *n* CHEM yoduro *m*.

iodine ['aiəudi:n] *n* CHEM yodo *m*.

iodism ['aiəudizəm] *n* MED yodismo *m*.

iodization [aiəudai'zeiʃən] *n* yoduración *f*.

iodize ['aiəudaiz] *vt* yodar.

iodoform [ai'ɔdəfɔ:m] *n* CHEM yodoformo *m*.

ion ['aiən] *n* CHEM & PHYS ion *m* || *ion exchange* intercambio *m* de iones.

Ionia [ai'əunjə] *pr n* GEOGR Jonia *f*.

Ionian [-n] *adj/n* jonio, nia; jónico, ca || GEOGR *Ionian Sea* mar Jónico.

ionic [ai'ɔnik] *adj* CHEM iónico, ca.

Ionic [ai'ɔnik] *adj* jónico, ca.

ionization [ˌaiənai'zeiʃən] *n* CHEM & PHYS ionización *f*.

ionize ['aiənaiz] *vt* CHEM & PHYS ionizar.
◆ *vi* CHEM & PHYS ionizarse.

ionosphere [ai'ɔnəsfiə*] *n* ionosfera *f*.

iota [ai'əutə] *n* iota *f* (letter of the Greek alphabet) ‖ pizca *f*, ápice *m* (a very small amount); *not an iota of truth* ni una pizca de verdad.

IOU ['aiəu'ju:] *n* pagaré *m*.

Iowa ['aiəuə] *pr n* GEOGR Iowa.

ipecac ['ipikæk] *n* BOT ipecacuana *f*.

ipecacuanha [ˌipikækju'ænə] *n* BOT ipecacuana *f*.

ipso facto ['ipsəu'fæktəu] *adv phr* ipso facto.

IQ *abbr of [intelligence quotient]* cociente de inteligencia.

IRA *abbr of [Irish Republican Army]* IRA *m*.

Irak [i'rɑ:k] *pr n* GEOGR Irak *m*, Iraq *m*.

Iran [i:'rɑ:n] *pr n* GEOGR Irán *m*.

Iranian [i'reinjən] *adj* iranio, nia; iraní.
◆ *n* iranio, nia *m* & *f* (inhabitant of Iran) ‖ iranio *m* (language).

Iraq [i'rɑ:k] *pr n* GEOGR Irak *m*, Iraq *m*.

Iraqi [-i]; **Iraqian** [-iən] *adj* iraquí, iraqués, esa.
◆ *n* iraquí *m* & *f*, iraqués, esa (inhabitant of iraq) ‖ iraquí *m*, iraqués *m* (language).

irascibility [iˌræsi'biliti] *n* irascibilidad *f*.

irascible [i'ræsibl] *adj* irascible, colérico, ca.

irate [ai'reit] *adj* airado, da; furioso, sa.

ire ['aiə*] *n* ira *f*, cólera *f*.

ireful [-ful] *adj* iracundo, da.

Ireland ['aiələnd] *pr n* GEOGR Irlanda *f*; *Northern Ireland* Irlanda del Norte.

Irene [ai'ri:ni] *pr n* Irene *f*.

irenic [-k]; **irenical** [-kəl] *adj* REL pacífico, ca.

iridaceae [irideisi:i] *pl n* BOT iridáceas *f*.

iridescence [iri'desns] *n* iridiscencia *f*, irisación *f*.

iridescent [iri'desnt] *adj* iridiscente, irisado, da.

iridium [ai'ridiəm] *n* CHEM iridio *m*.

iris ['aiəris] *n* ANAT iris *m* ‖ BOT lirio *m* ‖ iris *m*, arco *m* iris (rainbow).
— OBSERV El plural de la palabra inglesa es *irises* o *irides*.

iris diaphragm [-'daiəfræm] *n* PHOT diafragma *m* iris.

Irish ['aiəriʃ] *adj* Irlandés, esa ‖ *Irish Free State* Estado *m* libre de Irlanda.
◆ *n* irlandés *m* (language) ‖ *the Irish* los irlandeses.

Irish coffee [-'kɔfi] *n* café *m* irlandés, café *m* con whisky y nata.

Irishman [-mən] *n* irlandés *m*.
— OBSERV El plural de *Irishman* es *Irishmen*.

Irish potato [-pə'teitəu] *n* BOT patata *f* blanca.

Irish Sea [-si:] *pr n* GEOGR mar *m* de Irlanda.

Irish whiskey [-'wiski] *n* whisky *m* irlandés.

Irishwoman [-ˌwumən] *n* irlandesa *f*.
— OBSERV El plural de *Irishwoman* es *Irishwomen*.

irk [ə:k] *vt* molestar, fastidiar.

irksome [-səm] *adj* molesto, ta; fastidioso, sa.

iron ['aiən] *n* MIN hierro *m* (metal); *red-hot iron* hierro candente ‖ plancha *f* (for pressing clothes) ‖ hierro *m* candente (for branding) ‖ SP palo *m* de golf (golf club) ‖ FIG hierro *m*, acero *m*; *a man of iron* un hombre de hierro ‖ FAM revólver *m*, pistola *f* (firearm) ‖ — *cast iron* hierro colado, arrabio *m*, fundición *f* ‖ *corrugated iron* chapa ondulada ‖ *curling iron* tenacillas *f pl* de rizar, rizador *m* para el pelo ‖ *iron plate* pletina *f* ‖ *merchant iron* hierro comercial ‖ *old iron* chatarra *f*, hierro viejo ‖ *pig iron* arrabio *m*, hierro colado, hierro en lingotes ‖ *round, soft iron* hierro redondo, dulce ‖ *square iron bar* hierro cuadradillo *or* cuadrado ‖ FIG *strike while the iron is hot* al hierro candente batir de repente ‖ *will of iron* voluntad de hierro, voluntad férrea ‖ *wrought iron* hierro forjado.
◆ *pl* hierros *m*, grilletes *m*, grillos *m* (chains) ‖ — *in irons* encadenado ‖ FIG *to have many irons in the fire* tener muchas actividades (to be busy), tener muchos recursos (to be resourceful).

iron ['aiən] *vt* planchar (to press) ‖ herrar (to guarnish with iron) ‖ *to iron out* planchar (a crease), hacer desaparecer, suprimir (to remove), allanar (difficulties).
◆ *vi* planchar.

Iron Age [-eidʒ] *n* GEOL Edad *f* de hierro.

ironbound [-baund] *adj* zunchado, da (bound with iron) ‖ inflexible, férreo, a (inflexible) ‖ escabroso, sa (rocky).

ironclad [-klæd] *adj* acorazado, da (protected by iron plates) ‖ US riguroso, sa (rigorous, strict).
◆ *n* MAR acorazado *m*.

Iron Curtain [-'kə:tn] *n* FIG Telón *m* de acero.

ironer ['aiənə*] *n* planchador, ra.

iron foundry [ˌfaundri] *n* fundición *f* de hierro.

iron grey [-'grei] *adj* gris oscuro ‖ entrecano, na (hair).
◆ *n* gris *m* oscuro.

iron horse [-hɔ:s] *n* FAM locomotora *f* (locomotive) ‖ ferrocarril *m* (train).

ironic [airɔnik]; **ironical** [-əl] *adj* irónico, ca.

ironing ['aiəniŋ] *n* planchado *m* ‖ *when I finish the ironing* cuando termine de planchar.

ironing board [-bɔ:d] *n* tabla *f or* mesa *f* de planchar.

ironist ['aiənist] *n* ironista *m* & *f*.

iron lung ['aiənlʌŋ] *n* MED pulmón *m* de acero.

ironmaster [-'mɑ:stə*] *n* fabricante *m* de hierro.

iron mold [-məuld] *n* US mancha *f* de tinta *or* de moho.

ironmonger [-ˌmʌŋgə*] *n* quincallero *m*, ferretero *m* (hardware dealer).

ironmongery [-ˌmʌŋgəri] *n* quincallería *f*, ferretería *f* (place) ‖ quincalla *f*, ferretería *f* (wares).

iron mould [-məuld] *n* mancha *f* de tinta *or* de moho.

iron ore [-ɔ*] *n* mineral *m* de hierro.

ironside [-said] *n* hombre *m* valiente.

Ironsides [-saidz] *pl n* HIST caballería *f sing* de Cromwell en la guerra civil inglesa.

ironstone [-stəun] *n* MIN mineral *m* de hierro.

ironware [-wɛə*] *n* quincalla *f*, ferretería *f*.

ironwood [-wud] *n* BOT quiebrahacha *m*, jabí *m*.

ironwork [-wə:k] *n* herrajes *m pl*; *the ironwork on a trunk* los herrajes de un baúl ‖ carpintería *f* metálica, armazón *f* de hierro (iron framework).

ironworks [-wə:ks] *n* fundición *f* de hierro (iron foundry) ‖ fábrica *f* siderúrgica (iron and steel works).

irony ['aiəni] *adj* de hierro.

irony ['aiərəni] *n* ironía *f* ‖ *the irony is that...* lo gracioso es que...

irradiance [i'reidjəns] *n* irradiación *f*, radiación *f* ‖ resplandor *m* (brightness).

irradiant [i'reidjənt] *adj* radiante ‖ resplandeciente (brilliant).

irradiate [i'reidieit] *vt* irradiar ‖ FIG iluminar.
◆ *vi* lucir, brillar.

irradiation [ˌireidi'eiʃən] *n* irradiación *f*.

irradiative [i'reidiˌeitiv] *adj* radiante (irradiant) ‖ FIG que ilumina (for the soul, etc.).

irrational [i'ræʃənl] *adj* irracional.
◆ *n* MATH número *m* irracional.

irrationalism [i'ræʃənəlizm] *n* PHIL irracionalismo *m*.

irrationality [i'ræʃə'næliti] *n* irracionalidad *f*, sinrazón *f* (quality) ‖ absurdo *m* (act).

irreceivability [iriˌsi:və'biliti] *n* inadmisibilidad *f*.

irreceivable [iri'si:vəbl] *adj* JUR inadmisible.

irreclaimable [ˌiri'kleiməbl] *adj* incorregible (person) ‖ incultivable (land).

irrecognizable [i'rekəgnaizəbl] *adj* irreconocible.

irreconcilability [i'rekənsailəbiliti] *n* imposibilidad *f* de reconciliar (of enemies) ‖ incompatibilidad *f* (of opinions).

irreconcilable [i'rekənsailəbl] *adj* irreconciliable (enemies) ‖ inconciliable, incompatible (ideas).
◆ *n* persona *f* intransigente.
◆ *pl* ideas *f* inconciliables.

irrecoverable [ˌiri'kʌvərəbl] *adj* irrecuperable (object) ‖ irrecuperable, incobrable (money) ‖ FIG irremediable (loss).

irrecusable [iri'kju:zəbl] *adj* irrecusable.

irredeemable [ˌiri'di:məbl] *adj* irredimible (that cannot be bought back) ‖ COMM no amortizable (government loan or annuity) ‖ inconvertible (paper money) ‖ FIG irremediable (without remedy) ‖ incorregible (incorrigible) ‖ irreparable (fault).

irredentism [ˌiri'dentizəm] *n* irredentismo *m*.

irreducibility [ˌiridju:si'biliti] *n* irreductibilidad *f*.

irreducible [ˌiri'dju:səbl] *adj* irreducible, irreductible.

irrefragability [iˌrefrəgə'biliti] *n* incontestabilidad *f*, indiscutibilidad *f*.

irrefragable [i'refrəgəbl] *adj* incontestable, indiscutible, irrefragable.

irrefrangible [ire'frændʒibl] *adj* inviolable (law).

irrefutable [i'refjutəbl] *adj* irrefutable, irrebatible.

irregular [i'regjulə*] *adj* irregular; *irregular attendance, conduct* asistencia, conducta irregular; *irregular verb* verbo irregular ‖ desigual (surface).
◆ *n* MIL soldado *m* irregular.

irregularity [iˌregju'læriti] *n* irregularidad *f* ‖ desigualdad *f* (of a surface).

irrelevance [i'relivəns]; **irrelevancy** [-i] *n* falta *f* de pertinencia, impertinencia *f* ‖ observación *f* fuera de lugar (irrelevant remark) ‖ JUR improcedencia *f*.

irrelevant [i'relivənt] *adj* fuera de propósito, fuera de lugar (remark) ‖ impertinente, no pertinente (not to the point) ‖ JUR improcedente ‖ *questions that are irrelevant to the subject being discussed* cuestiones que no tienen nada que ver con el tema discutido *or* ajenas al tema discutido.

irrelievable [iri'li:vəbl] *adj* imposible de aplacar *or* de aliviar ‖ irremediable.

irreligion [ˌiriˈlidʒən] *n* irreligión *f*.

irreligious [ˌiriˈlidʒəs] *adj* irreligioso, sa.

irreligiousness [-nis] *n* irreligiosidad *f*.

irremediable [ˌiriˈmiːdjəbl] *adj* irremediable.

irremissible [iriˈmisibl] *adj* irremisible (unpardonable) || inevitable (unavoidable).

irremovability [ˈiriˌmuːvəˈbiliti] *n* inamovilidad *f* (of civil servant).

irremovable [iriˈmuːvəbl] *adj* inamovible || inmutable (immutable) || FIG invencible, insuperable (obstacle).

irreparable [iˈrepərəbl] *adj* irreparable (that cannot be repaired) || irremediable (that cannot be remedied).

irreplaceable [ˌiriˈpleisəbl] *adj* irreemplazable, irremplazable, insustituible.

irreprehensible [ˌiripriˈhensəbl] *adj* irreprensible.

irrepressible [ˌiriˈpresəbl] *adj* incontenible; *irrepressible laughter* risa incontenible || incontrolable.

irreproachable [ˌiriˈprəutʃəbl] *adj* irreprochable, intachable, irreprensible.

irresistibility [ˈiriˌzistəˈbiliti] *n* lo irresistible.

irresistible [ˌiriˈzistəbl] *adj* irresistible.

irresolute [iˈrezəluːt] *adj* irresoluto, ta; indeciso, sa.

irresolution [ˈiˌrezəˈluːʃən]; **irresoluteness** [iˈrezəluːtnis] *n* irresolución *f*, indecisión *f*.

irresolvable [ˌiriˈzɔlvəbl] *adj* irresoluble, insoluble (unsolvable) || CHEM irreducible.

irrespective [ˌirisˈpektiv] *adj* desconsiderado, da || *irrespective of* sin tomar en consideración, sin tener en cuenta.

irrespirable [iˈrespirəbl] *adj* irrespirable.

irresponsibility [ˌirisˈpɔnsəˈbiliti] *n* irreflexión *f*, irresponsabilidad *f*, falta *f* de seriedad || JUR irresponsabilidad *f*.

irresponsible [ˌirisˈpɔnsəbl] *adj* irreflexivo, va; irresponsable; poco serio, ria || JUR irresponsable.

irresponsive [ˌirisˈpɔnsiv] *adj* poco entusiasta, frío, a (not enthusiastic) || insensible (insensitive); *irresponsive to entreaties* insensible a las súplicas.

irresponsiveness [-nis] *n* frialdad *f*, insensibilidad *f* (insensitiveness).

irretentive [ˌiriˈtentiv] *adj* *irretentive memory* mala memoria.

irretrievable [ˌiriˈtriːvəbl] *adj* irrecuperable || irreparable, irremediable (error).

irreverence [iˈrevərəns] *n* irreverencia *f*, falta *f* de respeto.

irreverent [iˈrevərət] *adj* irreverente, irrespetuoso, sa.

irreversibility [iriˌvəːsəˈbiliti] *n* irreversibilidad *f* || irrevocabilidad *f* (of a decision).

irreversible [ˌiriˈvəːsəbl] *adj* irreversible || irrevocable (decision).

irrevocability [iˌrevəkəˈbiliti] *n* irrevocabilidad *f*.

irrevocable [iˈrevəkəbl] *adj* irrevocable.

irrigable [ˈirigəbl] *adj* irrigable || *irrigable lands* tierras de regadío.

irrigate [ˈirigeit] *vt* AGR irrigar, regar || MED irrigar.

irrigation [ˌiriˈgeiʃən] *n* AGR irrigación *f*, riego *m* || MED irrigación *f* || *irrigation channel* acequia *f*, canal *m* de riego.

irrigator [ˈiriˈgeitə*] *n* AGR regador, ra (person) | regadera *f* (implement) || MED irrigador *m*.

irritability [ˌiritəˈbiliti] *n* irritabilidad *f*.

irritable [ˈiritəbl] *adj* irritable.

irritably [-i] *adv* con tono malhumorado, de mal talante.

irritant [ˈiritənt] *adj* irritante.
◆ *n* agente *m* irritante.

irritate [ˈiriteit] *vt* MED irritar (organ, skin) | enconar (wound) || FIG irritar, poner nervioso || *to get irritated* irritarse, ponerse nervioso.

irritating [-iŋ] *adj* irritante; *an irritating effect on the skin* un efecto irritante en la piel || molesto, ta; enojoso, sa (annoying).

irritation [ˌiriˈteiʃən] *n* irritación *f*.

irritative [ˈiriteitiv] *adj* MED que irrita, irritante.

irrupt [iˈrʌpt] *vi* irrumpir (*into* en).

irruption [iˈrʌpʃən] *n* irrupción *f*.

is [iz] *3rd pers sing pres indic* ⟶ **be.**

Isaac [ˈaizək] *pr n* Isaac *m*.

Isabel [ˈizəbel]; **Isabella** [izəˈbelə] *pr n* Isabel *f*.

Isabelline [izəˈbelin] *adj/n* isabelino, na.

Isaiah [aiˈzaiə] *pr n* Isaías *m*.

isba [ˈizbə] *n* isba *f*.

ISBN *abbr of [International Standard Book Number]* ISBN, número internacional uniforme para los libros.

ischemia [isˈkiːmiə] *n* MED isquemia *f*.

ischium [ˈiskiəm] *n* ANAT isquion *m*.
— OBSERV El plural de la palabra inglesa es *ischia*.

Ishmael [ˈiʃmeiəl] *pr n* Ismael *m*.

Isidore [ˈizidɔː*] *pr n* Isidoro *m*, Isidro *m*.

Isidorian [ˌiziˈdɔːriən] *adj* isidoriano, na.

isinglass [ˈaiziŋglɑːs] *n* ictiocola *f*, cola *f* de pescado (glue) || MIN mica *f* (mica).

Isis [ˈaisis] *pr n* Isis *f*.

Islam [ˈizlɑːm] *n* Islam *m*.

Islamabad [izˈlɑːməbæd] *pr n* GEOGR Islamabad.

Islamic [izˈlæmik] *adj* islámico, ca.

Islamism [ˈizləmizəm] *n* islamismo *m*.

Islamite [ˈizləmait] *adj/n* islamita.

islamization [izləmiˈzeiʃən] *n* islamización *f*.

islamize [ˈizləmaiz] *vt* islamizar.

island [ˌilənd] *n* isla *f* (in the sea) || isleta *f*, refugio *m* (traffic island) || MAR superestructura *f* (of an aircraft carrier) || *small island* isla pequeña, islote *m*.

island [ˈailənd] *vt* aislar (to isolate) || salpicar (to intersperse with).

islander [-ə*] *n* isleño, ña; insular *m* & *f*.

isle [ail] *n* islote *m*, isleta *f* (small island) || isla *f*; *the Isle of Wight* la isla de Wight; *the British Isles* las islas Británicas.

islet [ˈailit] *n* islote *m*.

ism [ˈizəm] *n* FAM ismo *m* (theory).

isn't [ˈiznt] contraction of is not.

isobar [ˈaisəubɑː*] *n* isobara *f*.

isobaric [aisəˈbærik] *adj* isobárico, ca.

isochromatic [aisəukrəuˈmætik] *adj* isocromático, ca.

isochronous [aiˈsɔkrənəs] *adj* isócrono, na.

isoclinal [aisəˈklainəl] *adj* GEOL isoclinal || isoclino, na; *isoclinal line* línea isoclina.

isocline [ˌisəklain] *n* GEOL pliegue *m* isoclinal.

isogamous [aiˈsɔgəməs] *adj* BIOL isógamo, ma.

isogamy [aiˈsɔgəmi] *n* BIOL isogamia *f*.

isogloss [ˌisəuglɔs] *n* isoglosa *f*.

isogonal [aiˈsɔgənəl] *adj* isógono, na.

isogonic [aisəˈgɔnik] *adj* isógono, na.

isolate [ˈaisəleit] *vt* aislar.

isolated [-id] *adj* aislado, da; *an isolated example* un caso aislado.

isolating [-iŋ] *adj* aislador, ra.

isolation [ˌaisəuˈleiʃən] *n* aislamiento *m* || *in isolation* por separado.

isolationism [ˌaisəuˈleiʃnizəm] *n* aislacionismo *m*.

isolationist [ˌaisəuˈleiʃnist] *adj/n* aislacionista.

isolator [ˈaisəleitə*] *n* aislante *m*, aislador *m*.

isomer [ˈaisəmə*] *n* isómero *m*.

isomeric [ˌaisəuˈmerik] *adj* isómero, ra.

isomerism [aiˈsɔmərizm] *n* CHEM isomería *f*.

isomerous [aiˈsɔmerəs] *adj* isómero, ra.

isometric [ˌaisəuˈmetrik]; **isometrical** [-əl] *adj* isométrico, ca.

isomorph [ˌaisəuˈmɔːf] *n* cuerpo *m* isomorfo.

isomorphic [-ik] *adj* isomorfo, fa.

isomorphism [-izəm] *n* isomorfismo *m*.

isomorphous [-əs] *adj* isomorfo, fa.

isopod [ˈaisəpɔd] *n* ZOOL isópodo *m* (crustacean).
◆ *adj* ZOOL isópodo, da.

isosceles [aiˈsɔsiliːz] *adj* MATH isósceles; *isosceles triangle* triángulo isósceles.

isotherm [ˈaisəuθəːm] *n* isoterma *f*.

isothermal [ˌaisəuˈθəːməl] *adj* isotermo, ma; isotérmico, ca.

isothermic [ˌaisəuˈθəːmik] *adj* isotérmico, ca.

isotonic [aisəuˈtɔnik] *adj* PHYS isotónico, ca; isótono, na.

isotonicity [aisəutəˈnisiti] *n* PHYS isotonía *f*.

isotope [ˈaisəutəup] *n* CHEM isótopo *m*.

isotopic [ˌaisəuˈtɔpik] *adj* CHEM isotópico, ca.

isotopy [aiˈsɔtəpi] *n* CHEM isotopía *f*.

isotropic [aisəuˈtrɔpik] *adj* BIOL & PHYS isótropo, pa.

isotropous [aiˈsɔtrəpəs] *adj* BIOL & PHYS isótropo, pa.

isotropy [aiˈsɔtrəpi] *n* BIOL & PHYS isotropía *f*.

Israel [ˈizreiəl] *pr n* GEOGR Israel *m*.

Israeli [izˈreili] *adj/n* israelí.

Israelite [ˈizriəlait] *adj/n* israelita.

Israelitish [ˈizriəlaitiʃ] *adj* israelítico, ca.

issei [ˈiˈsei] *n* US inmigrante *m* japonés.
— OBSERV El plural de *issei* es *issei* o *isseis*.

issuable [ˈiʃuːəbl] *adj* JUR en litigio.

issuant [ˈiʃuənt] *adj* HERALD naciente, saliente.

issue [ˈiʃuː] *n* salida *f* (exit) || derrame *m* (of a liquid) || flujo *m*, desagüe *m*, salida *f* (of water) || desembocadura *f* (of a river) || emisión *f* (of shares, paper money, stamps, etc.) || publicación *f* (publication) || edición *f*, tirada *f* (edition) || número *m* (copy); *back issue* número atrasado || expedición *f* (of a passport) || distribución *f*, reparto *m* (distribution) || venta *f* (of tickets) || MED exutorio *m* (of ulcer, etc.) | derrame *m* (of blood, etc.) || resultado *m*, consecuencia *f* (outcome) || cuestión *f*, punto *m*, problema *m* (question under discussion) || asunto *m* (matter, affair) || JUR progenie *f*, prole *f*, descendencia *f* (offspring) || beneficio *m* (profit) || — *at issue* en discusión (point), en juego (interests), en litigio (legal matter), en desacuerdo (persons) || *in the issue* finalmente, al final || *side issue* cuestión secundaria || *to avoid the issue* andar con rodeos || *to bring an affair to an issue* llevar un asunto a un punto decisivo || *to force the issue* forzar una decisión || *to join issue with* discutir con (to discuss), estar en desacuerdo con (to disagree) || *to make an issue of sth.* hacer un lío por algo || *to raise* *the issue of* plantear el problema de || *to take issue with* estar en desacuerdo con.

issue [ˈiʃuː] *vi* salir (to come out) || ser descendiente (from de) || resultar (to result) || — *to issue forth* o *out* brotar (blood, liquid), salir (to come out) || *to issue from* descender de, proceder de (a family), derivarse de, resultar de (a cause) || *to issue in* llegar a, resultar en.
◆ *vt* publicar (to publish) || distribuir, repartir (*to* entre) (to distribute); *to issue children with milk* repartir leche entre los niños || dar (to give) || emitir, poner en circulación (shares, stamps, banknotes) || promulgar (a decree) || dar (an order) || expedir (a certificate, passport, etc.) || expender (tickets) || extender (a cheque, a warrant) || facilitar, dar (a licence) || asignar, conceder (credits) || conceder, otorgar (a loan) || pronunciar (a verdict) || *when is the newspaper issued?* ¿cuándo se publica el periódico?

issueless [-lis] *adj* sin descendencia (person) || sin salida (street, etc.).

issuing [-iŋ] *adj* descendiente (*from* de) (born) || COMM emisor, ra; *issuing bank* banco emisor.

Istanbul [ˌistænˈbuːl] *pr n* GEOGR Estambul.

Isthmian [ˈisθmiən] *adj* ístmico, ca; *Isthmian games* juegos ístmicos.
◆ *n* istmeño, ña.

isthmus [ˈisməs] *n* istmo *m*.
— OBSERV El plural de la palabra inglesa es *isthmuses* o *isthmi*.

it [it] *pron* él, ella, ello (subject of verb, but generally omitted in Spanish); *where is the book? it is here* ¿dónde está el libro? está aquí || lo, la (accusative, usually placed before the verb, except after the infinite, the imperative and the gerund); *I saw it* lo *or* la vi; *I believe it* lo creo; *I want to see it* quiero verlo, lo quiero ver; *look at it closely* míralo de cerca || le (dative case); *give it a turn* dale la vuelta || él, ella, ello (after prepositions); *we spoke about it* hablamos de ello; *I'll see to it* me ocuparé de ello || — *I don't think it necessary to arrive early* no considero que sea necesario llegar temprano || *that's it!* ¡eso es! (agreement), ¡ya está!, ¡está bien! (it's all right), ¡se acabó!, ¡hemos terminado! (on finishing sth.) || *that's just it* ahí está || *the worst of it is that...* lo peor del caso es que... || *this is it!* ¡ha llegado el momento!, ¡ha llegado la hora! || *what is it?* ¿qué es eso? || FIG & FAM *with it* al corriente, al tanto, al día (person), a la moda, de moda (clothes).
◆ *n* aquél *m*, atractivo *m*, no sé qué *m*; *she's got it* tiene un no sé qué || FAM vermut *m*; *gin and it* vermut con ginebra || — *he thinks he's it* se lo tiene creído || *you're it, I'm it* tú te quedas, yo me quedo (playing tag).
— OBSERV En muchas expresiones impersonales *it* no se traduce en español: *he considers it bad to kill* considera que es malo matar; *how is it that you have such a big house?* ¿cómo es que tiene Ud. una casa tan grande?; *I have heard it said that...* he oído decir que...; *it is a long way to Madrid* Madrid está muy lejos; *it's Peter* soy Pedro; *it is not in me to do it* no soy capaz de hacerlo, no es propio de mí hacer eso; *it is snowing* está nevando; *it is said that...* se dice que...; *it is six o'clock* son las seis; *oh! it's you!* ¡ah! eres tú; *it is I, it is me* soy yo.

Italian [iˈtæljən] *adj* italiano, na.
◆ *n* italiano, na (inhabitant of Italy) || italiano *m* (language).

italianate [iˈtæljəneit] *adj* de estilo italiano.

italianism [iˈtæljənizəm] *n* italianismo *m*.

italianize [iˈtæljənaiːz] *vt* italianizar.
◆ *vi* italianizarse.

italic [iˈtælik] *adj* PRINT bastardilla, cursiva.
◆ *n* bastardilla *f*, cursiva *f*.
◆ *pl* bastardilla *f sing*, cursiva *f sing*.

Italic [iˈtælik] *adj* itálico, ca.

italicize [iˈtælisaiz] *vt* escribir *or* imprimir en bastardilla *or* en cursiva || subrayar (to underline).

Italy [ˈitəli] *pr n* GEOGR Italia *f*.

itch [itʃ] *n* MED picazón *f*, picor *m*, comezón *f* (sensation) || FIG prurito *m*, ganas *f pl* (desire) || — MED *the itch* la sarna (scabies) || FIG *to have an itch* o *the itch to* estar impaciente por, tener el prurito de, tener muchas ganas de.

itch [itʃ] *vi* picar (to irritate); *my hand itches* me pica la mano || FIG anhelar (to long) || *to be itching to* estar impaciente por, tener el prurito de, tener muchas ganas de.

itchiness [ˈitʃinis] *n* picazón *f*, comezón *f*, picor *m* (itch).

itching [ˈitʃiŋ] *adj* MED que pica, que produce comezón || irresistible (desire) || — *itching powder* polvos *m pl* de picapica || FIG *to have an itching palm* ser codicioso, sa.
◆ *n* —> **itch**.

itchy [ˈitʃi] *adj* picante || *I have an itchy hand* me pica la mano, siento comezón en la mano || FIG & FAM *to have itchy feet* tener muchas ganas de viajar.

it'd [ˈitd] contraction of it would and it had.

item [ˈaitəm] *adv* ítem, además.
◆ *n* artículo *m* (article) || THEATR número *m* (number) || noticia *f*, suelto *m* (piece of news) || detalle *m* (detail) || punto *m* (on an agenda); *the first item on the agenda* el primer punto del orden del día || punto *m* (point) || COMM partida *f*, asiento *m*.

itemize [ˈaitəmaiz] *vt* detallar || especificar.

iterate [ˈitəreit] *vt* iterar, repetir, reiterar.

iteration [ˌitəˈreiʃən] *n* iteración *f*, repetición *f*, reiteración *f* || INFORM iteración *f*; *iteration loop* lazo de iteración.

iterative [ˈitərətiv] *adj* iterativo, va; reiterativo, va || GRAMM frecuentativo, va || INFORM iterativo, va; *iterative process* proceso iterativo.

itineracy [iˈtinərəasi]; **itinerancy** [iˈtinərənsi] *n* carácter *m* itinerante (itinerant nature) || vida *f* itinerante (itinerant life) || cambio *m* frecuente de residencia (change of residence).

itinerant [iˈtinərənt] *adj* itinerante, ambulante.

itinerary [aiˈtinərəri] *n* itinerario *m* (route) || relación *f* de un viaje (account) || guía *f* (guidebook).
◆ *adj* itinerario, ria.

itinerate [iˈtinəreit] *vi* viajar *or* desplazarse constantemente.

it'll [ˈitl] contraction of it will and it shall.

its [its] *poss adj* su, sus.
— OBSERV The English possessive adjective is often translated by the definite article in Spanish: *its handle came off* se le desprendió el asa; *when the lion leaves its den* cuando el león sale de la leonera.

it's [ˈits] contraction of it has and it is.

itself [itˈself] *pron* se; *the dog has hurt itself* el perro se ha hecho daño || (él) mismo, (ella) misma, (ello) mismo; *the horse itself knows the way* el caballo mismo sabe el camino; *it drank the water itself* él mismo se bebió el agua || sí (mismo), sí (misma) (after preposition); *the speech was all right in itself* el discurso en sí *or* en sí mismo estuvo bien || mismo, ma (emphasis); *Lewis spent the night in the palace itself* Luis pasó la noche en el mismo palacio || — *by itself* solo, la; *the doll sits up by itself* la muñeca se incorpora sola; aislado, da; *the house stands by itself* la casa está aislada || *he is kindness itself* es la bondad misma, es la bondad personificada.

ITU *abbr of [International Telecommunication Union]* UIT, Unión Internacional para las Telecomunicaciones.

ITV *abbr of [Independent Television]* canal de televisión británico.

IUCD; IUD *abbr of [intrauterine* (contraceptive) *device]* DIU, dispositivo intrauterino.

I've [aiv] contraction of «I have».

ivory [ˈaivəri] *n* marfil *m* (substance) || color *m* marfil (colour).
◆ *pl* FAM teclas *f* (piano keys) | dientes *m* (teeth) | bolas *f* (in billiards) | dados *m* (dice) || FAM *to tickle the ivories* tocar el piano.
◆ *adj* de marfil, marfileño, ña (of ivory) || de color marfil, marfileño, ña (ivory coloured) || ebúrneo, a; de marfil, marfileño, ña (resembling ivory) || — *ivory black* negro *m* de marfil || BOT *ivory nut* tagua *f*, marfil *m* vegetal | *ivory palm* tagua *f* || FIG *ivory tower* torre *f* de marfil.

Ivory Coast [-kəust] *pr n* GEOGR Costa *f* de Marfil.

ivy [ˈaivi] *n* BOT hiedra *f*, yedra *f* || US *Ivy league* grupo de universidades de prestigio de los EE.UU.

izard [ˈizəd] *n* ZOOL gamuza *f*, rebeco *m*.

J

j [dʒei] *n* j *f* (letter); *a capital j* una j mayúscula.

jab [dʒæb] *n* golpe *m* seco (a blow, poke) || pinchazo *m* (a stab) || estocada *f* (with a sword) || codazo *m* (with elbow) || FAM inyección *f*, pinchazo *m*.

jab [dʒæb] *vt* pinchar; *he jabbed my finger with a needle* me pinchó el dedo con una aguja || herir (with a sword, bayonet, etc.) || dar un codazo a (with the elbow) || dar un puñetazo a (with the fist) || señalar; *he jabbed his finger at the headlines* señaló los titulares con el dedo || *to jab into* clavar en, hundir en.
◆ *vi* *to jab at s.o. with a knife* intentar clavarle un cuchillo a alguien.

jabber [-ə*] *n* algarabía *f* (noise of many loud voices) || farfulla *f*, chapurreo *m* (fast, unintelligible speech) || charloteo *m*, cotorreo *m*.

jabber [-ə*] *vt* farfullar, chapurrear || decir atropelladamente.
◆ *vi* farfullar, chapurrear (unintelligibly) || charlotear, cotorrear (to chatter) || hablar atropelladamente (to speak fast).

jabiru [ˈdʒæbiruː] *n* ZOOL jabirú *m*.

jaborandi [ˌdʒæbəˈrændi] *n* BOT jaborandi *m* (bird).

jabot [ˈʒæbəu] *n* chorrera *f*.

jacamar [ˈdzækəˌmɑː] *n* ZOOL jacamar *m*, jacamara *f*.

jacaranda [ˌdʒækəˈrændə] *n* BOT jacarandá *f*.

jacinth [ˈdʒæsinθ] *n* MIN jacinto *m* || naranja *m* (colour).

jack [dʒæk] *n* gato *m* [AMER cric *m*] (a tool) || sacabotas *m inv* (bootjack) || MAR pabellón *m*, bandera *f* de proa (national flag) | marinero *m* (sailor) || valet *m*, jota *f* (card) || sota *f* (Spanish cards) || ELECTR enchufe *m* hembra || lucio *m* pequeño (fish) || macho *m* (male of some animals) || SP boliche *m* (in bowls) || POP pasta *f* (money).
◆ *pl* tabas *f*, cantillos *m*; *to play jacks* jugar a las tabas.

jack [dʒæk] *vt* levantar con el gato; *we jacked up the car* levantamos el coche con el gato || aumentar, subir (to raise); *to jack up prices* aumentar los precios || FAM *to jack in* dejar, abandonar.

Jack [dʒæk] *pr n* Juan *m*, Juanito *m* || — FIG *before you could say Jack Robinson* en un decir Jesús | *every Jack has his Jill* cada oveja con su pareja | *every man Jack* cada quisque | *I'm all right, Jack* ande yo caliente y ríase la gente.

jack-a-dandy [ˈdʒækəˈdændi] *n* dandy *m*.

jackal [ˈdʒækɔːl] *n* ZOOL chacal *m*.

jackanapes [ˈdʒækəneips] *n* mequetrefe *m* (conceited boy) || mono *m* (monkey) || diablillo *m* (naughty child).

jackass [ˈdʒækæs] *n* burro *m*, asno *m* || FIG burro *m* (foolish person).

jackboot [ˈdʒækbuːt] *n* bota *f* alta.

jackdaw [ˈdʒækdɔː] *n* ZOOL chova *f* (bird).

jacket [ˈdʒækit] *n* chaqueta *f*, americana *f* [AMER saco *m*] (of man's suit) || chaqueta *m* (of a woman's suit, of pyjamas, etc.) || sobrecubierta *f* (of a book) || forro *m* (of a record) || carpeta *f* (file) || camisa *f* (casing for tubes, cylinders, pipes) || casquillo *m* (of a bullet) || cáscara *f* (of a fruit) || piel *f* (of potatoes) || — FIG & FAM *to dust s.o.'s jacket* sacudirle el polvo a uno || *strait jacket* camisa *f* de fuerza.

jacket [ˈdʒækit] *vt* cubrir.

Jack Frost [ˈdʒækˈfrɔst] *n* helada *f* (freeze) || escarcha *f* (frost) || invierno *m* (winter) || tiempo *m* frío (cold weather).

jack-in-office [ˈdʒækinˈɔfis] *n* funcionario *m* meticuloso.

jack-in-the box [ˈdʒækinðəbɔks] *n* caja *f* sorpresa.

— OBSERV El plural de la palabra *jack-in-the-box* es *jacks-in-the-box* o *jack-in-the-boxes*.

Jack Ketch [ˈdʒækˈketʃ] *n* verdugo *m*.

jackknife [ˈdʒæknaif] *n* navaja *f* (a knife) || SP salto *m* de la carpa (a dive).

jackknife [ˈdʒæknaif] *vi* hacer el salto de la carpa (to dive) || colear [un camión articulado] (a lorry).

jack mackerel [ˈdʒækˈmækrəl] *n* jurel *m* (fish).

jack-of-all-trades [ˈdʒækəvˈɔːltreidz] *n* persona *f* apañada *or* mañosa (skilful person) || factótum *m* (factotum) || *jack-of-all-trades, master of none* hombre de muchos oficios, maestro de ninguno.

jack-o'-lantern [ˈdʒækəuˌlæntən] *n* fuego *m* fatuo (will-o'-the wisp) || linterna *f* hecha con una calabaza (pumpkin lamp).

jack plane [ˈdʒækplein] *n* TECH garlopa *f*.

jack plug [ˈdʒækˈplʌg] *n* ELECTR jack.

jackpot [ˈdʒækpɔt] *n* premio *m* gordo (main prize) || bote *m* (cards) || *to hit the jackpot* dar en el blanco (to be successful), sacar el premio gordo, tocarle a uno el premio gordo.

jack-pudding [ˈdʒækˈpudiŋ] *n* payaso *m*, bufón *m*.

jackrabbit [ˈdʒækˌræbit] *n* liebre *f* americana.

jackstone [ˈdʒækstəun] *n* US taba *f*, cantillo *m*.
◆ *pl* US tabas *f*, cantillos *m*.

jackstraw [ˈdʒækstrɔː] *n* palillo *m* || FIG muñeco *m* de paja.
◆ *pl* palillos *m*.

Jack-tar [ˈdʒækˈtɑː*] *n* FAM marinero *m*.

Jacob [ˈdʒeikəb] *pr n* Jacob *m*.

Jacobean [ˌdʒækəˈbiːən] *adj* de la época de Jacobo I, jacobino, na.

Jacobin [ˈdʒækəubin] *adj/n* jacobino, na.

Jacobite [ˈdʒækəbait] *n* jacobita *m* & *f*.

jactation [ˌdʒækˈteiʃən] *n* jactancia *f* (a boast) || MED agitación *f*.

jactitation [ˈdʒæktiˈteiʃən] *n* MED agitación *f* || JUR impostura *f*.

jade [dʒeid] *n* MIN jade *m* || color *m* jade (colour) || FAM jamelgo *m*, penco *m* (horse) | mujerzuela *f* (woman).

jaded [-id] *adj* harto, ta; ahíto, ta (satiated) || agotado, da; reventado, da (tired out).

jag [dʒæg] *n* mella *f* (of a break) || siete *m* (of a tear) || diente *m* (tooth of saw) || punta *f* (sharp projection) || FAM juerga *f* (spree) || FAM *to have a jag on* estar trompa *or* borracho [AMER estar mamado].

jag [dʒæg] *vt* dentar (edge of cloth) || mellar (a knife edge).

jagged [-id]; **jaggy** [-i] *adj* dentado, da || mellado, da || serrado, da (serrated).

jaggery [ˈdʒægəri] *n* azúcar *m* de palmera.

jaggy [ˈdʒgægi] *adj* ⟶ **jagged.**

jaguar [ˈdʒægjuə*] *n* ZOOL jaguar *m*.

jai alai [ˈhailai] *n* SP jai alai *m*, pelota *f* vasca.

jail [dʒeil] *n* cárcel *f*; *to go to jail* ir a la cárcel; *to be in jail* estar en la cárcel || prisión *f*, cárcel *f*; *sentenced to 10 years' jail* condenado a diez años de prisión.

jail [dʒeil] *vt* encarcelar.

jailbird [-bəːd] *n* presidiario *m* reincidente, preso *m* reincidente.

jailbreak [-breik] *n* evasión *f*, fuga *f*.

jailer; jailor [-ə*] *n* carcelero *m*.

Jakarta [dʒəˈkɑːtə] *pr n* GEOGR Yakarta.

Jakuzzi [dʒəˈkuːzi] *n* jacuzzi (registered trademark).

jalap [ˈdʒæləp] *n* BOT jalapa *f*.

Jalapan [ˈdʒæləpən] *adj/n* jalapeño, ña.

jalopy; jaloppy [dʒəˈlɔpiː] *n* FAM cafetera *f*, cacharro *m* (car) | cacharro *m* (plane).

jalousie [ˈʒæluziː] *n* celosía *f* (blind).

jam [dʒæm] *n* mermelada *f* (food); *bread and jam* pan con mermelada || atasco *m* (a blockage) || agolpamiento *m* (of people) || machucamiento *m* (crushing) || embotellamiento *m*, atasco *m*; *the traffic jam was a mile long* el embotellamiento del tráfico se extendía sobre una milla || barrera *f* (of ice in a river) || FAM apuro *m*, lío *m* (difficult situation); *to be in a jam* estar en un apuro; *to get into a jam* meterse en un lío; *to get out of a jam* salir de un apuro || FAM *what do you want?, jam on it?* ¿qué quieres encima?, ¿que te lo traiga en bandeja de plata?

jam [dʒæm] *vt* meter a la fuerza (to force to enter); *he jammed the coin into the slot* metió a la fuerza la moneda en la ranura || pillar (to catch); *to jam one's fingers in a door* pillarse los dedos en una puerta || apretar, apiñar (to squash); *to jam people against a wall* apretar a la gente contra un muro || atestar, atiborrar; *the room was jammed with people* el cuarto estaba atestado de gente || llenar hasta los topes (to fill to the brim) || atorar, atascar (to clog); *rubbish jammed the pipes* la basura atoró la tubería || bloquear (to block) || atascar (a nut, a moving part) || causar un embotellamiento de; *the demonstration jammed the traffic* la manifestación causó el embotellamiento del tráfico || RAD interferir (radio signals) | causar interferencia en (to cause interference) || — *to jam on one's hat* encasquetarse el sombrero || *to jam on the brakes* frenar en seco, dar un frenazo ||

to jam the door shut atrancar la puerta || *we can't jam any more in* ya no caben más cosas.
◆ *vi* atrancarse (to become fixed or wedged); *the door has jammed* se ha atrancado la puerta || atascarse, atorarse (to get clogged) || encasquillarse (a firearm) || agarrotarse (brakes).

Jamaica [dʒə'meikə] *pr n* GEOGR Jamaica *f.*

Jamaican [-n] *adj/n* jamaicano, na.

jamb [dʒæm] *n* ARCH jamba *f.*

jamboree [dʒæmbə'riː] *n* jamboree *m*, reunión *f* internacional de exploradores || FAM juerga *f* (spree).

James [dʒeimz] *pr n* Jaime *m*, Jacobo *m*, Diego *m*, Santiago *m*.
— OBSERV *Jacobo* is used specifically for the king of Scotland. *Jaime* is used above all in Aragon, Valencia, Catalonia and the Balearic Islands.

jamming ['dʒæmiŋ] *n* atascamiento *m*, atrancamiento *m* || RAD interferencia *f.*

jam-packed ['dʒæmpækt] *adj* FAM a tope, a reventar.

jam session [-'seʃən] *n* MUS concierto *m* de jazz improvisado.

Jane [dʒein] *pr n* Juana *f* || *to be a plain Jane* tener poco atractivo, ser del montón.

jangle ['dʒæŋgl] *n* ruido *m* de chatarra (metallic noise) || cascabeleo *m* (of small bells), cencerreo *m* (of cow bells) || riña *f* (quarrel) || parloteo *m* (chattering).

jangle ['dʒæŋgl] *vt* hacer sonar.
◆ *vi* hacer un ruido de chatarra (tins, etc.) || cencerrear (bells) || reñir, discutir (to bicker).

janissary ['dʒænisəri] *n* MIL jenízaro *m*.

janitor ['dʒænitə*] *n* portero *m*.

janitress ['dʒænitris] *n* portera *f.*

janizary ['dʒænisəri] *n* MIL jenízaro *m*.

Jansenism ['dʒænsnizəm] *n* REL jansenismo *m*.

Jansenist ['dʒænsnist] *adj/n* jansenista.

January ['dʒænjuəri] *n* enero *m*.

Jap [dʒæp] *adj/n* FAM japonés, esa.

japan [dʒə'pæn] *n* laca *f* de China, laca *f* de Japón.

japan [dʒə'pæn] *vt* barnizar con laca de China *or* de Japón.

Japan [dʒə'pæn] *pr n* GEOGR Japón *m*.

Japanese [ˌdʒæpə'niːz] *adj* japonés, esa.
◆ *n* japonés, esa (inhabitant) || japonés *m* (language) || *the Japanese* los japoneses.

jape [dʒeip] *n* broma *f.*

jape [dʒeip] *vi* bromear.

japonica [dʒə'pɔnikə] *n* BOT membrillo *m* japonés.

jar [dʒɑː*] *n* tarro *m* (jam pot) || tinaja *f* (a large earthenware pot) || cántaro *m* (water picher) || jarra *f* (jug) || vasija *f* (recipient, vessel) || choque *m*, sacudida *f* (an impact) || sonido *m* discordante (discordant sound) || FIG conflicto *m* (conflict) | choque *m*, golpe *m* (blow, shock) || — *Leyden jar* botella *f* de Leyden || *on the jar* entreabierto, ta; entornado, da.

jar [dʒɑː*] *vt* sacudir (to shake) || mover (to move) || lastimar (sounds); *to jar one's ears* lastimar los oídos de uno || herir (feelings) || irritar (the nerves).
◆ *vi* chirriar (harsh sounds) || desentonar, sonar mal (music) || chocar (colours) || sacudirse, vibrar (to shake) || FIG reñir (to argue) || — *to jar on* chocar contra || FIG *to jar on* o *upon* irritar, molestar | *to jar on s.o.'s nerves* ponerle a uno los nervios de punta | *to jar with* no concordar con.

jardinière [ʒɑːdi'njɛə*] *n* jardinera *f* (box for plant pots) || macetón *m* (ornamental plant pot) || CULIN menestra *f.*

jargon ['dʒɑːgən] *n* jerga *f*; *medical jargon* jerga médica || jerigonza *f*, galimatías *f* (gibberish).

jarring ['dʒɑːriŋ] *adj* que chocan (colours) || discordante (sound) || FIG discorde (opinion, etc.).

jarvey ['dʒɑːvi] *n* FAM cochero *m*.

jasmin; jasmine ['dʒæsmin] *n* BOT jazmín *m*.

jasper ['dʒæspə*] *n* MIN jaspe *m*.

jaundice ['dʒɔːndis] *n* MED ictericia *f* || FIG celos *m pl*, envidia *f* (envy).

jaundice ['dʒɔːndis] *vt* MED dar ictericia a || FIG dar envidia *or* celos a.

jaundiced [-t] *adj* MED ictérico, ca || cetrino, na; amarillo, lla (yellow) || FIG amargado, da (embittered) | envidioso, sa (envious).

jaunt [dʒɔːnt] *n* paseo *m*, excursión *f* corta.

jaunt [dʒɔːnt] *vi* ir de paseo.

jauntiness [-inis] *n* viveza *f* (liveliness) || desenvoltura *f* (self-confidence) || garbo *m* (grace).

jaunty [-i] *adj* vivaz (lively) || desenvuelto, ta (free and easy); *jaunty manner* aire desenvuelto || garboso, sa (graceful).

Java ['dʒɑːvə] *pr n* GEOGR Java.

Javan [-n]; **Javanese** [ˌdʒɑːvə'niːz] *adj/n* javanés, esa.

javelin ['dʒævlin] *n* (ant) venablo *m* (weapon) || SP jabalina *f*; *throwing the javelin* lanzamiento de la jabalina.

jaw [dʒɔː] *n* ANAT mandíbula *f* (of person) || ZOOL quijada *f* (of animal) || TECH mordaza *f*, mandíbula *f* (of vice, pliers, pincers) || embocadura *f* (of a channel) || FAM charla *f* (chat) || ola *f* (wave) || mar *m* (sea) || — FAM *hold your jaw!* ¡cierra el pico!, ¡cállate! | *it's a lot of a jaw* todo son palabras || *jaw clutch* embrague *m* de mordaza || *jaw coupling* acoplamiento dentado.
◆ *pl* boca *f sing*, fauces *f* || FIG *the jaws of death* la boca del lobo (great danger).

jaw [dʒɔː] *vt* regañar, echar una bronca a (to scold).
◆ *vi* hablar por los codos (to talk and talk) || charlar (to chat).

jawbone [-bəun] *n* ANAT mandíbula *f*, maxilar *m* (of people) || quijada *f* (of animals).

jawbreaker [-ˌbreikə*] *n* FAM trabalenguas *m inv* (tongue twister) | caramelo *m* de goma (sweet) || triturador *m* (of stones, etc.).

jay [dʒei] *n* arrendajo *m* (bird) || FIG cotorra *f* (chatterbox) | tonto, ta (fool).

jaywalk [-wɔːk] *vi* cruzar la calle imprudentemente.

jaywalker [-'wɔːkə*] *n* peatón *m* imprudente.

jazz [dʒæz] *n* MUS jazz *m* || FAM palabrería *f* (hot air).
◆ *adj* del jazz.

jazz [dʒæz] *vt* arreglar para jazz || FIG *to jazz up* alegrar, animar.
◆ *vi* tocar jazz (to play jazz) || bailar jazz (to dance jazz).

jazz band [-bænd] *n* MUS orquesta *f* de jazz.

jazzman [-mæn] *n* MUS músico *m* de jazz.
— OBSERV El plural de *jazzman* es *jazzmen*.

jazzy [-i] *adj* MUS de jazz | animado, da (lively) | sincopado, da (syncopated) || de colores chillones, llamativo, va (brightly coloured).

jealous ['dʒeləs] *adj* celoso, sa; *jealous of one's rights* celoso de sus derechos; *a jealous husband* un marido celoso || envidioso, sa (envious, resentful) || *to be jealous of* tener celos de, estar celoso de.

jealousy ['dʒeləsi] *n* celos *m pl* || envidia *f* (envy).

Jean [dʒiːn] *pr n* Juana *f.*

jeans [dʒiːnz] *pl n* pantalones *m* vaqueros (trousers) || mono *m sing* (overalls).

jeep [dʒiːp] *n* MIL jeep *m*, todo terreno *m* [AMER coche campero *m*].

jeer [dʒiə*] *n* mofa *f*, burla *f*, escarnio *m* (mockery) || abucheo *m* (boo).
◆ *pl* MAR drizas *f* (rigging).

jeer [dʒiə*] *vt* mofarse de, burlarse de (to mock) || abuchear (to boo) || insultar (to insult).
◆ *vi* mofarse, burlarse || *to jeer at* mofarse de, burlarse de, hacer escarnio de (to mock), abuchear a (to boo), insultar a (to insult).

jeering [-riŋ] *adj* burlón, ona; *a jeering smile* una sonrisa burlona.
◆ *n* abucheo *m* (booing) || burla *f*, mofa *f*, escarnio *m* (mockery) || insultos *m pl* (insults).

jehad [dʒi'hɑːd] *n* REL guerra *f* santa.

Jehoshaphat [dʒi'hɔʃəfæt] *pr n* GEOGR Josafat.

Jehovah [dʒi'həuvə] *pr n* REL Jehová *m*.

Jehovah's Witness [-z'witnis] *pr n* REL testigo *m* de Jehová.

jejune [dʒi'dʒuːn] *adj* árido, da; seco, ca (dry) || aburrido, da; sin interés (lacking interest) || US inmaduro, ra.

jejuneness [-nis] *n* aridez *f* (dryness) || FIG falta *f* de interés (lack of interest) | aridez *f* (of style) || US inmadurez *f.*

jejunum [-əm] *n* ANAT yeyuno *m*.
— OBSERV El plural de *jejunum* es *jejuna*.

jell [dʒel] *vt* FIG moldear, dar forma (to cause to take shape).
◆ *vi* cuajar || FIG tomar forma, cristalizarse (to take shape).

jellied ['dʒelid] *adj* CULIN en gelatina.

jellify ['dʒeilifai] *vt* convertir en gelatina.

jelly ['dʒeli] *n* CULIN gelatina *f* (gelatinous food) || jalea *f*; *citron jelly* jalea de cidra || — *jelly baby* muñeco *m* de caramelo || *petroleum jelly* vaselina *f* || *to pound into a jelly* hacer trizas *or* papilla.

jellyfish [-fiʃ] *n* ZOOL medusa *f* || FAM calzonazos *m inv* (man).

Jello ['dʒeləu] *n* US jalea *f* (registered trademark).

jemmy ['dʒemi] *n* palanqueta *f*, ganzúa *f* (tool) || CULIN cabeza *f* de cordero (sheep's head).

Jennerian [dʒe'niːəriən] *adj* jenneriano, na.

jenny ['dʒeni] *n* hembra *f* (female animal) || burra *f* (female ass) || TECH máquina *f* de hilar.

jeopardize ['dʒepədaiz] *vt* arriesgar, poner en peligro (to endanger) || comprometer.

jeopardy ['dʒepədi] *n* riesgo *m*, peligro *m* || *to be in jeopardy* estar en peligro.

jerboa [dʒəː'bəuə] *n* ZOOL jerbo *m*, gerbo *m*.

jeremiad [ˌdʒeri'maiəd] *n* jeremiada *f* (lamentation).

Jeremiah [ˌdʒeri'maiə] *pr n* Jeremías *m*.

Jericho ['dʒerikəu] *pr n* GEOGR Jericó.

jerk [dʒəːk] *n* sacudida *f* (sudden movement); *by jerks* a sacudidas || tirón *m* (sudden pull) || empujón *m* (shove) || espasmo *m* (reflex action) || CULIN cecina *f* [AMER charqui *m*] (dry meat) || US FAM idiota *m* & *f* (idiot) | pelmazo, za; latoso, sa (nuisance) || — FAM *physical jerks* ejercicios físicos || *put a jerk in it!* ¡ánimo!, ¡date prisa! || *to have the jerks* tener el baile de San Vito (illness), tener hormiguillo.

jerk [dʒəːk] *vt* mover a tirones (to move by tugging) ‖ sacudir, dar una sacudida a (to shake) ‖ lanzar bruscamente (to throw) ‖ dar un tirón a (to give a sharp pull) ‖ acecinar [AMER charquear], curar al sol (to cure meat) ‖ — *jerked meat* cecina *f* [AMER charqui *m*] ‖ *to jerk o.s. free* librarse de un tirón ‖ *to jerk sth. off* quitar algo de un tirón ‖ *to jerk sth. out* decir algo a trompicones (to say), sacar algo de un tirón (to take out).
◆ *vi* moverse a trompicones (to move in stops and starts) ‖ *the door jerked open* la puerta se abrió de golpe.

jerkin ['dʒəːkin] *n* (ant) jubón *m*, justillo *m*.

jerkwater ['dʒəːkˌwɔːtə*] *adj* US FAM de poca monta (poor, trivial) ‖ *a jerkwater town* un pueblecito perdido.

jerky ['dʒəːki] *adj* espasmódico, ca ‖ desigual (road) ‖ que traquetea (car).
◆ *n* cecina *f*, tasajo *m* [AMER charqui *m*] (dry meat).

jeroboam [ˌdʒerə'bəuəum] *n* botella *f* grande.

Jerome [dʒə'rəum] *pr n* Jerónimo *m*.

jerrican ['dʒerikæn] *n* bidón *m*.

jerry ['dʒeri] *n* FAM orinal *m* (chamber pot) ‖ MIL soldado *m* alemán.
◆ *adj* de mala calidad.

jerry-building [-ˌbildiŋ] *n* construcción *f* de baja calidad, mala construcción *f*.

jerry-built [-bilt] *adj* construido con materiales de mala calidad, mal construido, da.

jerry can [-kæn] *n* bidón *m*.

jerrymander [-ˌmændə*] *vt* ⟶ **gerrymander.**

jersey ['dʒəːzi] *n* jersey *m* (garment) ‖ tejido *m* de punto (material).

Jerusalem [dʒə'ruːsələm] *pr n* Jerusalén.

Jerusalem artichoke [-'ɑːtitʃəuk] *n* aguaturna *f*, pataca *f*.

jess; jesse [dʒes] *n* US pihuela *f*.

jessamine ['dʒesəmin] *n* BOT jazmín *m* (jasmine).

jest [dʒest] *n* broma *f*, burla *f*, mofa *f* (mocking) ‖ chiste *m* (joke) ‖ hazmerreír *m* (laughingstock) ‖ *in jest* en broma.

jest [dʒest] *vi* bromear (to speak jokingly) ‖ mofarse, burlarse (*about* de) (to speak tauntingly).

jester [-ə*] *n* bromista *m* & *f* (person who jests) ‖ (ant) bufón *m* (buffoon).

jesting [-iŋ] *adj* guasón, ona.
◆ *n* chistes *m pl* (jokes) ‖ bromas *f pl* (practical jokes).

Jesuit ['dʒezjuit] *adj/n* REL jesuita *m*.

Jesuitical [-əl] *adj* REL jesuítico, ca.

Jesuitism ['dʒezjuitizəm] *n* jesuitismo *m*.

Jesus ['dʒiːzəs] *pr n* REL Jesús *m* ‖ — REL *Jesus Christ* Jesucristo *m* ‖ *Society of Jesus* Compañía *f* de Jesús.

jet [dʒet] *n* chorro *m* (of water, steam, blood, etc.) ‖ surtidor *m* (pipe) ‖ surtidor *m*, pulverizador *m*, chicler *m* (of the carburetter) ‖ llama *f* (flame) ‖ mechero *m* (gas burner) ‖ AVIAT avión *m* de reacción, reactor *m* (plane) | reactor *m* (engine) ‖ MIN azabache *m* (black mineral).

jet [dʒet] *vt* lanzar en chorro.
◆ *vi* salir a chorros ‖ volar en avión de reacción.

jet-black [-blæk] *adj* negro como el azabache.

jet engine [-'endʒin] *n* AVIAT reactor *m*.

jet fighter [-'faitə*] *n* AVIAT avión *m* de caza de reacción.

jet lag [-læg] *n* jet lag *f*.

jetliner [-'lainə*] *n* avión *m* de reacción, reactor *m* [de pasajeros].

jet plane [-plein] *n* AVIAT avión *m* de reacción, reactor *m*.

jet-propelled [-prə'peld] *adj* de propulsión a chorro, de reacción.

jet propulsion [-prə'pʌlʃən] *n* propulsión *f* a chorro.

jetsam [-səm] *n* MAR echazón *f*, carga *f* arrojada al mar ‖ FIG desecho *m*.

jet set [-set] *n* jet set *f*.

jet sprayer [-ˌspreiə*] *n* pulverizador *m*.

jet stream [-striːm] *n* corriente *f* en chorro (in meteorology) ‖ chorro *m* (of a jet).

jettison ['dʒetisn] *vt* MAR echar (la carga) al mar ‖ FIG deshacerse de (to get rid of).

jetty ['dʒeti] *n* malecón *m*, muelle *m*, escollera *f*.
◆ *adj* negro como el azabache.

Jew [dʒuː] *n* judío, a.

jewel ['dʒuːəl] *n* joya *f*, alhaja *f* (bracelet, ring, etc.) ‖ piedra *f* preciosa (precious stone) ‖ rubí *m* (in a watch); *a watch with 21 jewels* un reloj de 21 rubíes ‖ FIG joya *f*, perla *f* (person) ‖ *jewel case, jewel box* joyero *m*.

jewel ['dʒuːəl] *vt* alhajar, enjoyar.

jeweled; US jewelled [-d] *adj* alhajado, da; enjoyado, da (person, dress) ‖ adornado con piedras preciosas (object) ‖ con rubíes (watch).

jeweller; US jeweler [-ə*] *n* joyero *m* ‖ *jeweller's* o *jeweler's* joyería *f*.

jewellery; (US jewelery) ['dʒuːəlri] *n* joyería *f* (shop) ‖ joyas *f pl*, alhajas *f pl* (jewels).

Jewess ['dʒuːis] *n* judía *f*.

Jewish ['dʒuːiʃ] *adj* judío, a.

Jewishness ['dʒuːiʃnis] *n* judaísmo *m*.

Jewry ['dʒuəri] *n* pueblo *m* judío (the Jewish people) ‖ (ant) judería *f* (district).

jew's harp; jews' harp ['dʒuːz'hɑːp] *n* MUS birimbao *m*, guimbarda *f*.

jib [dʒib] *n* MAR foque *m* (sail) ‖ TECH aguilón *m* (of crane).

jib; jibb; gibb [dʒib] *vt* MAR poner a la capa (to gybe).
◆ *vi* plantarse (a horse) ‖ resistirse (a person) ‖ *to jib at sth.* resistirse *or* oponerse a algo.

jibboom ['dʒib'buːm] *n* MAR botalón *m*.

jibe [dʒaib] *vi* US concordar, estar de acuerdo.

jibe [dʒaib] *n* ⟶ **gibe.**

jibe [dʒaib] *vt/vi* MAR ⟶ **gybe.**

jiffy ['dʒifi] *n* FAM momento *m* ‖ FAM *it was done in a jiffy* lo hizo en un decir Jesús *or* en un santiamén *or* en un periquete.

Jiffy bag [-bæg] *n* sobre *m* acolchado (registered trademark).

jig [dʒig] *n* giga *f* (dance and its music) ‖ TECH gálibo *m*, calibre *m*, plantilla *f* (gauge) ‖ MIN criba *f* ‖ anzuelo *m* de cuchara (hook) ‖ FIG & FAM *the jig is up* todo se acabó.

jig [dʒig] *vt* MIN separar por vibración y lavado, cribar (ore) ‖ TECH pasar por la plantilla (a part).
◆ *vi* bailar la giga (to dance) ‖ andar a saltitos (to move with little jumps) ‖ dar saltitos (to jump up and down) ‖ *he keeps jigging up and down* no puede estarse quieto.

jigger ['dʒigə*] *n* bailarín *m* de giga (dancer) ‖ ELECTR transformador *m* ‖ MIN criba *f* ‖ MAR balandra *f* (boat) | palo *m* de mesana, contramesana *f* (mast) | anzuelo *m* de cuchara (hook) ‖ SP apoyo *m* (in billiard) ‖ ZOOL nigua *f* (chigoe) ‖ FAM chisme *m*, artefacto *m* ‖ US medida *f* para líquidos (for drinks).

jiggered ['dʒigəd] *adj* FAM *I'm jiggered if...* que me lleven los demonios si... | *well I'm jiggered!* ¡vaya por Dios!

jiggermast ['dʒigəˌmɑːst] *n* MAR contramesana *f*, palo *m* de mesana.

jiggery-pokery ['dʒigəri'pəukəri] *n* FAM trampa *f*.

jiggle ['dʒigl] *vi* menearse, zangolotearse.
◆ *vt* menear, zangolotear.

jigsaw ['dʒigsɔː] *n* TECH sierra *f* de vaivén (saw) ‖ rompecabezas *m inv* (puzzle) ‖ *jigsaw puzzle* rompecabezas.

jihad [dʒi'hɑːd] *n* REL guerra *f* santa.

jilt [dʒilt] *vt* dejar plantado a (a fiancé) ‖ dar calabazas a (to reject a suitor).

Jim [dʒim] *pr n* Santiago *m*, Santi *m* ‖ *Jim Crow* negro *m* (Negro), discriminación *f* racial (discrimination).

jimjams ['dʒimdʒæmz] *pl n* US FAM delírium tremens *m*.

jimmy ['dʒimi] *n* ganzúa *f*, palanqueta *f*.

jimmy ['dʒimi] *vt* forzar (con una ganzúa).

jimsonweed ['dʒimsənˌwiːd] *n* BOT estramonio *m*.

jingle ['dʒiŋgl] *n* cascabeleo *m*, tintineo *m* (sound of bells) ‖ tintineo *m*, sonido *m* (of glassware, of coins, etc.) ‖ cascabel *m* (of tambourine) ‖ rima *f* infantil (childish rhyme) ‖ canción *f*, copla *f* (song) ‖ anuncio *m* comercial cantado (advertisement).

jingle ['dʒiŋgl] *vi* cascabelear (bells) ‖ tintinear, sonar (glasses, coins, etc.).
◆ *vt* hacer cascabelear, sonar (bells) ‖ agitar (keys, coins).

jingly ['dʒiŋgli] *adj* que tintinea ‖ metálico, ca (sound).

jingo ['dʒiŋgəu] *adj/n* jingoísta, patriotero, ra ‖ *by jingo!* ¡caramba!

jingoism [-izəm] *n* jingoísmo *m*, patriotería *f*.

jingoist [-ist] *n* jingoísta *m* & *f*, patriotero, ra.

jingoistic [dʒiŋgəu'istik] *adj* jingoísta, patriotero, ra.

jinks [dʒiŋks] *pl n* jolgorio *m sing*, juerga *f sing*; *the girls were up to (high) jinks in the dormitory* las niñas estaban en pleno jolgorio en el dormitorio.

jinn [dʒin] *n* genio *m*.

jinx [dʒiŋks] *n* FAM gafe *m*, cenizo *m* (person) | maleficio *m* (spell); *to break the jinx* romper el maleficio | cenizo *m*, mala suerte *f* (bad luck) ‖ — FAM *this car is a jinx* este coche trae mala suerte | *to put a jinx on* echar mal de ojo a.

jinx [dʒiŋks] *vt* FAM traer mala suerte a.

jinxed [-t] *adj* FAM gafe, gafado, da.

jipijapa [ˌhiːpi'hɑːpə] *n* jipijapa *m* (hat).

jitney ['dʒitni] *n* US FAM moneda *f* de cinco centavos (coin) | colectivo *m* (bus, car).

jitter ['dʒitə*] *vi* FAM temblar de miedo, tener mieditis.

jitters ['dʒitəz] *pl n* FAM nervios *m*, miedo *m*, canguelo *m*, mieditis *f* ‖ — FAM *to give s.o. the jitters* darle miedo a alguien | *to have the jitters* tener miedo *or* mieditis, tener canguelo.

jittery ['dʒitəri] *adj* FAM *to be jittery* tener canguelo | *to get jittery* entrarle miedo a uno.

Jivaro ['hiːvərəu] *n* jíbaro, ra.

Jivaroan [-ən] *adj* jíbaro, ra.

jive [dʒaiv] *n* MUS «swing» *m* ‖ US FAM «argot» *m*, jerga *f* (slang).

jive [dʒaiv] *vi* bailar el «swing» ‖ US FAM burlarse.

Joachim ['dʒəuəkim] *pr n* Joaquín *m*.

Joan [dʒəun] *pr n* Juana *f* ‖ *Joan of Arc* Juana de Arco.

job [dʒɔb] *n* trabajo *m* (work); *I've got a job for you* tengo un trabajo para ti ‖ trabajo *m*, empleo *m*; *to look for a job* buscar un empleo, buscar trabajo ‖ cometido *m*, función *f*; *his job is to file them* su cometido es archivarlos ‖ asunto *m* (affair) ‖ FAM chanchullo *m* (dishonest practice) | golpe *m* (robbery) ‖ destajo *m* (piecework); *to work by the job* trabajar a destajo ‖ pinchazo *m* (jab) ‖ — FIG *a bad job* un mal asunto (bad state of affairs) ‖ *and a good job too!* ¡menos mal! ‖ *I had a job to do it* me costó trabajo hacerlo ‖ *it's not my job!* ¡eso no es cosa mía! ‖ *just the job!* ¡justo lo que nos hacía falta!, ¡estupendo! ‖ *that car is just the job* ese coche es exactamente lo que buscaba ‖ *to be on the job* estar trabajando ‖ *to be out of a job* estar sin trabajo, estar parado ‖ *to create jobs* crear puestos de trabajo ‖ FAM *to do a job on s.o.* perjudicar mucho a alguien ‖ *to fall down on the job* no estar a la altura del trabajo, fallar en el trabajo ‖ *to know one's job* saber *or* conocer su oficio ‖ *to lose one's job* perder su trabajo ‖ *to make a good job of sth.* hacer algo bien ‖ *to make the best of a bad job* poner a mal tiempo buena cara ‖ *to throw it in as a bad job* darse por vencido ‖ *what a good job he was there!* ¡menos mal que estaba allí!
◆ *adj* a destajo, a tanto alzado (by the piece) ‖ laboral, del trabajo (labour) ‖ alquilado, da (rent).

job [dʒɔb] *vt* dar (trabajo) a tanto alzado *or* a destajo (to give work to s.o. else) ‖ comprar y vender como intermediario (as a middleman) ‖ comprar y vender [acciones] (on Stock Exchange) ‖ meter; *he jobbed his son into the post* metió a su hijo en el puesto ‖ alquilar (horses, carriages) ‖ pinchar (to jab).
◆ *vi* trabajar a destajo (to work by the job) ‖ trabajar como corredor (as an agent) ‖ US trabajar de vez en cuando (to do casual jobs).

Job [dʒəub] *pr n* Job *m*.

jobber [dʒɔbə*] *n* intermediario *m* (middleman) ‖ COMM corredor *m* de Bolsa (middleman on the Stock Exchange) | agiotista *m* (speculator) ‖ trabajador *m* a destajo (pieceworker) ‖ FAM chanchullero *m* (corrupt person).

jobbery [-əri] *n* chanchullos *m pl*, intrigas *f pl* (underhand business) ‖ *a piece of jobbery* un chanchullo, una intriga.

jobbing ['dʒɔbiŋ] *adj* que trabaja a destajo (worker).

jobbing printer ['dʒɔbiŋ'printə*]; US **job printer** [dʒɔb'printə*] *n* PRINT impresor *m* de circulares, prospectos, etc. [y no de libros y revistas].

job centre ['dʒɔb,sentə*] *n* oficina *f* estatal de empleo.

jobless ['dʒɔblis] *adj* sin trabajo.

job lot ['dʒɔblɔt] *n* partida *f* de artículos vendidos a bajo precio (lot of cheap goods) ‖ surtido *m* (set of goods).

job printer [dʒɔb'printə*] *n* US ⟶ **jobbing printer.**

jobsharing ['dʒɔb,ʃεəriŋ] *n* empleo *m* compartido.

jockey ['dʒɔki] *n* jinete *m*, «jockey» *m*.

jockey ['dʒɔki] *vt* embaucar (to deceive) ‖ manejar (to handle) ‖ montar (to horse) ‖ — *to jockey s.o. into doing sth.* persuadirle a alguien a que haga algo ‖ *to jockey s.o. out of sth.* quitar algo a alguien con artimañas.
◆ *vi* maniobrar.

jockstrap ['dʒɔkstræp] *n* suspensorio *m*.

jocose [dʒə'kəus]; **jocular** [dʒɔkjulə*] *adj* jocoso, sa; gracioso, sa; divertido, da (amusing); *jocose remarks* observaciones jocosas ‖ burlón, ona; bromista (full of jokes) ‖ alegre (happy).

jocosity [dʒəu'kɔsiti] *n* jocosidad *f*.

jocular ['dʒɔkjulə*] *adj* ⟶ **jocose.**

jocularity [,dʒɔkju'læriti] *n* jocosidad *f*.

jocund ['dʒɔkənd] *adj* jocoso, sa (inspiring laughter) ‖ jocundo, da; jovial (cheerful).

jocundity [dʒəu'kʌnditi] *n* jocundidad *f*, jovialidad *f* (cheerfulness).

jodhpurs ['dʒɔdpuəz] *pl n* pantalones *m* de montar.

jog [dʒɔg] *n* empujón *m*, sacudida *f* (little push) ‖ codazo *m* (blow with the elbow) ‖ trote *m* corto (slow run) ‖ FIG estímulo *m* ‖ US saliente *m* (on a wall) ‖ FIG *to give s.o.'s memory a jog* refrescarle la memoria a uno.

jog [dʒɔg] *vt* dar un empujón a (to give a slight push) ‖ refrescar (la memoria) (memory) ‖ sacudir (to shake) ‖ *to jog s.o.'s elbow* darle ligeramente en el codo a uno.
◆ *vi* *to jog along* ir tranquilamente (to go peacefully along), andar con un traqueteo (a horse-drawn coach), andar a trote corto *or* a paso lento (horse), avanzar poco a poco (to progress slowly), ir tirando (to manage).

jogger [dʒɔgə] *n* persona *f* que practica el footing.

jogging ['dʒɔgiŋ] *n* footing *m*.
— OBSERV In Spanish *footing* is used for *jogging* but it is not correct. *To go jogging* can be translated by *correr*.

joggle ['dʒɔgl] *n* TECH lengüeta *f*, espiga *f*, barbilla *f* ‖ sacudida *f* ligera (a shake).

joggle [dʒɔgl] *vt* menear (to jiggle) ‖ mover (to move) ‖ TECH ensamblar (to join wood).
◆ *vi* menearse (to jiggle) ‖ *to joggle along* andar con un traqueteo (an old car, carriage, etc.).

jogtrot ['dʒɔg'trɔt] *n* trote *m* corto (of horses); *at a jogtrot* a trote corto ‖ FIG rutina *f* (routine).

john [dʒɔn] *n* US FAM retrete *m* [*AMER* inodoro *m*, baño *m*] (lavatory).

John [dʒɔn] *pr n* Juan *m* ‖ — FAM *John Barleycorn* licor *m* ‖ *John Bull* héroe *m* de una novela que personifica a Inglaterra ‖ US *John Doe* Fulano *m* de Tal ‖ *John the Baptist* San Juan Bautista.

John dory [-'dɔri] *n* pez *m* de san Pedro.

Johnny ['dʒɔni] *pr n* Juanito *m* ‖ FAM sujeto *m*, individuo *m*, tipo *m* (person).

johnnycake; jonnycake [-keik] *n* US pan *m* or torta *f* de maíz.

join [d'ɔin] *n* juntura *f*, unión *f* ‖ costura *f* (seam).

join [dʒɔin] *vt* juntar, unir; *to join two things together* juntar dos cosas; *to join the tables* juntar las mesas ‖ unir; *to join two people in matrimony* unir a dos personas en matrimonio; *a line joins two points* una línea une dos puntos ‖ ir a dar a, empalmar con; *the path which joins the road* el camino que va a dar a la carretera ‖ hacer frontera con, lindar con; *the United States of America joins Canada in the north* los Estados Unidos de América hacen frontera con Canadá por el norte ‖ reunirse con, juntarse con; *to join one's friends* reunirse con sus amigos ‖ entrar en, ingresar en; *he joined the company last year* entró en la empresa el año pasado ‖ afiliarse a (a party) ‖ MIL incorporarse a (one's unit) | alistarse en (the army) ‖ hacerse socio de (to become a member of a club) ‖ TECH ensamblar, unir (two pieces) ‖ — *he will be joining us next week* llegará la semana que viene ‖ *to join end to end* unir por la punta ‖ *to join battle* trabar batalla ‖ *to join forces with s.o.* unirse con alguien ‖ FIG *to join hands* darse la mano (to shake hands), asociarse ‖ MAR *to join one's ship* regresar a bordo ‖ *to join s.o. in a glass of cognac* tomar una copa de coñac con alguien ‖ *to join together in wishing s.o...* unirse todos para desearle a alguien... ‖ *to join with s.o. in an opinion* compartir con alguien una opinión, hacerse eco de la opinión de alguien ‖ *will you join us for dinner?* ¿quieren cenar con nosotros?
◆ *vi* unirse (to become united) ‖ empalmar (lines) ‖ confluir (rivers) ‖ hacerse socio (of a club or society) ‖ MIL alistarse (in the army).
◆ *phr v* *to join in* tomar parte en, participar en (to take part); *everybody joined in the argument* todos participaron en la discusión | intervenir en (a debate, discussion) | ponerse (todos) a; *everybody joined in the applause, in the singing* todos se pusieron a aplaudir, a cantar ‖ *to join up* alistarse (in the army) | juntar (two things) | unirse (two roads, etc.) | reunirse (people).

joinder ['dʒɔində*] *n* reunión *f*, unión *f*.

joiner ['dʒɔinə*] *n* carpintero *m*, ebanista *m*.

joinery ['dʒɔinəri] *n* carpintería *f*, ebanistería *f*.

joining ['dʒɔiniŋ] *n* unión *f* ‖ bisagra *f* (of a door).

joint [dʒɔint] *adj* unido, da ‖ colectivo, va; combinado, da; en común (collective, combined); *joint effort* esfuerzo colectivo ‖ conjunto, ta; *joint naval exercises* maniobras navales conjuntas; *joint declaration* declaración conjunta ‖ mutuo, tua (agreement) ‖ solidario, ria (responsibility) ‖ COMM conjunto, ta (account) ‖ — *joint author* coautor *m* ‖ *joint commission, joint committee* comisión mixta, comisión conjunta, comisión paritaria ‖ *joint estate* copropiedad *f* ‖ *joint guardian* cotutor *m* ‖ *joint heir* coheredero *m* ‖ *joint manager* codirector, ra ‖ *joint owner* copropietario, ria ‖ *joint ownership* copropiedad *f* ‖ *joint partner* copartícipe *m* & *f* ‖ *joint stock* capital *m* social.
◆ *n* juntura *f*, unión *f*, junta *f* (join) ‖ ensambladura *f* (in wood) ‖ TECH articulación *f* ‖ ANAT articulación *f* ‖ BOT nudo *m* ‖ GEOL grieta *f* ‖ CULIN corte *m* para asar (meat for roasting) | asado *m* (roast meat) ‖ bisagra *f* (of a door) ‖ FAM antro *m* (place) | porro *m* (marijuana) ‖ — *gambling joint* garito *m* ‖ *hinged joint* articulación *f* ‖ FIG *joint in the harness* punto débil *or* flaco *or* vulnerable ‖ *out of joint* dislocado, da (dislocated); descentrado, da (disordered) ‖ *rheumatism of the joints* reúma *m* articular ‖ *to come out of joint* dislocarse ‖ *to put out of joint* dislocar, desencajar ‖ TECH *universal joint* junta cardán *or* universal ‖ *to throw out of joint* dislocarse (a bone).

joint [dʒɔint] *vt* juntar, unir (to join) ‖ ensamblar (to join wood) ‖ descuartizar (animals into joints) ‖ articular.

jointed ['dʒɔintid] *adj* articulado, da ‖ desmontable (fishing rod) ‖ BOT nudoso, sa.

jointer ['dʒɔintə*] *n* garlopa *f* (plane).

jointly [dʒɔintli] *adv* conjuntamente, en común.

jointress [-ris] *n* viuda *f* usufructuaria.

joint-stock company [-'stɔk,kʌmpəni] *n* COMM sociedad *f* anónima.

jointure ['dʒɔintʃə*] *n* JUR viudedad *f*.

joist ['dʒɔist] *n* ARCH vigueta *f*.

jojoba [həu'həubə] *n* BOT jojoba *f*.

joke [dʒəuk] *n* chiste *m* (funny story); *he told me a joke* me contó un chiste ‖ broma *f* (funny situation, prank); *he must have his little joke* le encanta gastar bromas; *I can take a joke* yo sé tomar las bromas; *it is no joke* no es broma; *practical joke* broma pesada ‖ hazmerreír *m*; *he's the joke of the office* es el hazmerreír del despacho ‖ payaso, sa; bufón, ona (buffoon) ‖ — *as a joke* en broma, bromeando ‖ *I did it for a joke* lo hice en broma ‖ *I don't see the joke* no le veo la gracia ‖ *it's no joke working with him* no tiene ninguna gracia trabajar con él ‖ *to crack a joke* hacer un chiste (to say sth. witty), contar un chiste (to tell a funny story) ‖ *the joke is that...* lo gracioso es que... ‖ *the joke was* *on him* fue él quien pagó la broma, él fue la víctima de la broma ‖ FIG & FAM *to go beyond a joke* pasar de castaño oscuro ‖ *to know how to take a joke* saber tomar las bromas ‖ *to make of joke of everything* no tomar nada en serio, tomar todo en broma ‖ *to play a (practical) joke on s.o.* gastarle una broma a alguien ‖ *to take as a joke* tomar en broma.

joke [dʒəuk] *vi* bromear; *he is joking* está bromeando ‖ contar chistes (to tell jokes) ‖ — *and he wasn't joking* y hablaba en serio, y no era broma ‖ *joking apart* hablando en serio, bromas aparte ‖ *to be in a joking mood* estar de broma ‖ *to joke about sth.* bromear sobre algo ‖ *you must be joking!* ¡no hablarás en serio!
◆ *vt* dar una broma a, gastar bromas a.

joker [-ə*] *n* bromista *m* & *f* (s.o. who jokes a lot) ‖ chistoso, sa (wit) ‖ payaso, sa; bufón, ona (buffoon) ‖ comodín *m* (in a pack of cards) ‖ FAM tipo *m*, individuo *m*, sujeto *m* (bloke); *what's that joker doing here?* ¿qué hace este tipo aquí? ‖ US disposición *f* engañosa (in a legal document).

joking [-iŋ] *adj* humorístico, ca; gracioso, sa.
◆ *n* bromas *f pl* ‖ chistes *m pl*.

jokingly [-iŋli] *adv* en broma.

jollification [ˌdʒɔlifiˈkeiʃən] *n* FAM jolgorio *m*.

jollify [ˈdʒɔlifai] *vi* FAM pasarlo en grande.

jolliness [ˈdʒɔlinis] *n* jovialidad *f*.

jollity [ˈdʒɔliti] *n* jovialidad *f* (joviality) ‖ alegría *f*, regocijo *m* (gaiety) ‖ jolgorio *m* (merrymaking).

jolly [ˈdʒɔli] *adj* jovial, alegre (jovial); *a jolly fellow* un tipo jovial ‖ FAM divertido, da (amusing) | piripi (a little drunk); *to get jolly* ponerse piripi | bueno, na (used intensively); *a jolly mess* un buen lío ‖ bonito, ta (pretty) ‖ — FAM *he gave her a jolly hiding* le dio una buena tunda | *it's a jolly shame* es una verdadera vergüenza | *jolly fool* tonto *m* de remate ‖ *the jolly God* Baco ‖ FAM *to have a jolly time* pasarlo en grande | *to make a jolly din* armar mucho jaleo.
◆ *adv* FAM muy, la mar de (very); *jolly tired* muy cansado ‖ — *a jolly good hiding* una buena tunda ‖ *he's jolly well right* tiene toda la razón ‖ *I'll do what I jolly well like* haré lo que me dé la gana ‖ *jolly good!* ¡estupendo! ‖ *take jolly good care of her* cuídala muy bien.

jolly [ˈdʒɔli] *vt* convencer; *to jolly s.o. into doing sth.* convencer a uno para que haga algo ‖ seguirle el humor a (to humour) ‖ animar (to encourage).
◆ *vi* burlarse.

jolly boat [-bəut] *n* MAR bote *m*, esquife *m*.

Jolly Roger [-ˈrɔdʒə*] *n* (ant) pabellón *m* pirata, bandera *f* negra (flag).

jolt [dʒəult] *n* sacudida *f* (jerk); *the car gave a jolt* el coche dio una sacudida ‖ choque *m* (bump); *the jolt of the car against the kerb* el choque del coche contra el borde de la acera ‖ FIG susto *m* (fright); *it gave me quite a jolt* ¡menudo susto me dio! ‖ — *the car stopped with a jolt* el coche se paró en seco ‖ FIG *the news of his death was a jolt for her* la noticia de su muerte le impresionó mucho.

jolt [dʒəult] *vt* sacudir (to shake) ‖ dar un empujón *or* una sacudida a (to give a shove) ‖ — *he jolted the glass out of my hand* me dio un empujón que me hizo soltar el vaso ‖ *to jolt s.o. back to reality* hacer que uno vuelva bruscamente a la realidad.
◆ *vi* moverse a sacudidas (to move jerkily) ‖ traquetear (vehicle) ‖ *to jolt along* avanzar dando tumbos.

Jonah [ˈdʒəunə] *pr n* Jonás *m* ‖ FIG gafe *m* (jinx).

Jonathan [ˈdʒɔnəθən] *pr n* Jonatán *m*.

jongleur [ʒ˜ɔːŋˈgləː*] *n* (ant) juglar *m*.

jonnycake [ˈdʒɔnikeik] *n* US —> **johnnycake.**

jonquil [ˈdʒɔŋkwil] *n* BOT junquillo *m*.

Jordan [ˈdʒɔːdn] *pr n* GEOGR Jordán *m* (river) | Jordania *f* (country).

Jordan [ˈdʒɔːdn]; **Jordanian** [dʒɔːˈdeinjən] *adj/n* jordano, na.

jorum [ˈdʒɔːrəm] *n* tazón *m*.

Joseph [ˈdʒəuzif] *pr n* José *m*.

Josephine [ˈdʒəuzifiːn] *pr n* Josefina *f*.

josh [dʒɔʃ] *n* broma *f*.

josh [dʒɔʃ] *vt* US FAM tomar el pelo a (to tease); *stop joshing him* deja de tomarle el pelo.
◆ *vi* US FAM bromear, estar de broma.

Joshua [ˈdʒɔʃwə] *pr n* Josué *m*.

joss [dʒɔs] *n* REL ídolo *m* chino.

Joss house [-haus] *n* REL templo *m* chino.

joss stick [-stik] *n* pebete *m*.

jostle [ˈdʒɔsl] *n* empujones *m pl* (shoving).

jostle [ˈdʒɔsl] *vt* empujar, dar empujones a (to push) ‖ *to jostle one's way through the crowd* abrirse paso a codazos entre la multitud.
◆ *vi* codear (to elbow) ‖ empujar, dar empujones (to push) ‖ abrirse paso a empujones; *to jostle for tickets* abrirse paso a empujones para ir a comprar billetes ‖ — *to jostle against* chocar contra ‖ *to jostle with* mezclarse con.

jot [dʒɔt] *n* jota *f*; *I don't understand a jot* no entiendo ni jota; *not a jot* ni jota ‖ pizca *f*, poco *m* (tiny amount) ‖ *I don't care a jot* me importa poco.

jot [dʒɔt] *vt* *to jot down* tomar nota de, anotar, apuntar; *jot it down* apúntalo.

jotter [-ə*] *n* bloc *m* (notepad).

jotting [-iŋ] *n* apunte *m*, nota *f*.

joule [dʒuːl] *n* PHYS julio *m*, joule *m*.

journal [ˈdʒəːnl] *n* diario *m* (daily record, diary) ‖ periódico *m* (newspaper) ‖ revista *f* (magazine) ‖ COMM diario *m* (in bookkeeping) ‖ boletín *m* (of a club, learned society, etc.) ‖ MAR diario *m* de a bordo ‖ TECH gorrón *m*, muñón *m*.

journal box [-bɔks] *n* TECH cojinete *m* (bearing).

journalese [dʒəːnəˈliːz] *n* lenguaje *m* periodístico.

journalism [ˈdʒəːnəlizəm] *n* periodismo *m*.

journalist [ˈdʒəːnəlist] *n* periodista *m* & *f*.

journalistic [ˌdʒəːnəˈlistik] *adj* periodístico, ca.

journalize [ˈdʒəːnəlaiz] *vt* contabilizar (in book-keeping) ‖ apuntar en un diario.
◆ *vi* escribir un diario (to keep a diary).

journey [ˈdʒəːni] *n* viaje *m*; *a long journey* un viaje largo; *outward, return journey* viaje de ida, de vuelta; *four journeys to the kitchen* cuatro viajes a la cocina; *I was on a journey* estaba de viaje ‖ — *have a nice journey!* ¡buen viaje! ‖ *to break one's journey* hacer un alto en el viaje ‖ *to go a journey* ir de viaje ‖ FIG & FAM *to go on one's last journey* irse al otro mundo, irse al otro barrio (to die).

journey [ˈdʒəːni] *vi* viajar.

journeyman [ˈdʒəːnimən] *n* oficial *m* (qualified worker).
— OBSERV El plural de *journeyman* es *journeymen*.

journeywork [ˈdʒəːniwəːk] *n* trabajo *m* realizado por un oficial ‖ FIG trabajo *m* rutinario.

joust [dʒaust] *n* (ant) justa *f*, torneo *m*.

joust [dʒaust] *vi* (ant) participar en una justa.

Jove [dʒəuv] *pr n* MYTH Júpiter *m* ‖ *by Jove!* ¡por Júpiter!, ¡por Dios!

jovial [ˈdʒəuvjəl] *adj* jovial.

joviality [ˌdʒəuviˈæliti] *n* jovialidad *f*.

Jovian [ˈdʒəuvjən] *adj* joviano, na.

jowl [dʒaul] *n* papada *f* (fleshy part under the jaw) ‖ mandíbula *f* (jawbone of people) ‖ quijada *f* (jawbone of animals) ‖ mejilla *f*, carrillo *m* (cheek) ‖ ZOOL papada *f* (of oxen) | barba *f* (of birds) ‖ FIG *cheek by jowl* cara a cara.

joy [dʒɔi] *n* alegría *f*, júbilo *m* (great gladness) ‖ deleite *m*, placer *m* (pleasure) ‖ — *her voice was a joy to the ear* su voz era un regalo para el oído ‖ *it is a joy to hear her* da gusto oírla *or* escucharla, es un placer escucharla ‖ *it's a joy to see* da gusto verlo ‖ *I wish you joy* le doy la enhorabuena (congratulations), le deseo suerte (good luck) ‖ *she is her mother's joy* es la alegría de su madre ‖ *the joys of country life* los placeres de la vida en el campo ‖ *to beam with joy* estar radiante de alegría ‖ *to be beside o.s. with joy* estar loco de alegría ‖ *to jump for joy* saltar de alegría.

joyful [-ful] *adj* alegre, contento, ta.

joyfulness [-fulnis] *n* alegría *f*, gozo *m*.

joyless [ˈdʒɔilis] *adj* triste, sin alegría.

joyous [ˈdʒɔiəs] *adj* alegre, gozoso, sa (happy) ‖ *a joyous event* un feliz acontecimiento.

joyride [ˈdʒɔiraid] *n* FAM paseo *m* en coche [sin autorización].

joy stick [ˈdʒɔistik] *n* AVIAT FAM palanca *f* de mando.

jubbah; US **jubba** [ˈdʒəbə] *n* aljuba *f*.

jubilance [ˈdʒuːbiləns] *n* júbilo *m*, alborozo *m*.

jubilant [ˈdʒuːbilənt] *adj* jubiloso, sa; alborozado, da.

jubilate [ˈdʒuːbileit] *vi* exultar de alegría.

jubilation [ˌdʒuːbiˈleiʃən] *n* júbilo *m*, regocijo *m*, alborozo *m*.

jubilee [ˈdʒuːbiliː] *n* quincuagésimo aniversario *m* (fiftieth anniversary) ‖ aniversario *m* (anniversary) ‖ HIST & REL jubileo *m* ‖ júbilo *m* (jubilation).
◆ *adj* jubilar.

Judaea [dʒuːˈdiə] *pr n* GEOGR Judea *f*.

Judaeo-Christian [dʒuːˈdiəuˈkristjən] *adj/n* judeocristiano, na.

Judaeo-German [-ˈdʒəːmən] *n* judeoalemán *m*.

Judaeo-Spanish [-ˈspæniʃ] *adj/n* judeoespañol.

Judah [ˈdʒuːdə] *pr n* Judá *m*.

Judaic [dʒuˈdeiik] *adj* judaico, ca.

Judaism [ˈdʒuːdeiizəm] *n* REL judaísmo *m*.

Judaist [ˈdʒuːdeiist] *n* judaizante *m* & *f*.

Judaize [ˈdʒuːdeiaiz] *vt* convertir al judaísmo.
◆ *vi* judaizar.

Judas [ˈdʒuːdəs] *pr n* Judas ‖ FIG Judas *m* (traitor) ‖ *Judas Iscariot* Judas Iscariote.

judas hole [-həul] *n* mirilla *f*.

Judas tree [-triː] *n* BOT ciclamor *m*.

judder [dʒʌdə*] *vi* trepidar, vibrar.

Judea [dʒuːˈdiə] *pr n* GEOGR Judea *f*.

judge [dʌdʒ] *n* JUR juez *m*; *judge of the court of first instance* juez de primera instancia ‖ juez *m* (in a competition) ‖ árbitro *m* (in a dispute) ‖ SP juez *m*; *the line judges* los jueces de línea ‖ entendido, da; conocedor, ra; *a good judge of music* un entendido en música ‖ — *I am a poor judge of music* no entiendo de música ‖ *judge advocate* auditor *m* militar ‖ *the Divine Judge* el Juez Supremo ‖ *to be a poor judge of character* no saber juzgar a la gente ‖ *to be no judge of* no poder juzgar.

Judge [dʒʌdʒ] *n* juez *m* (in Jewish history) ‖ *the Book of Judges* el libro de los Jueces.

judge [dʒʌdʒ] *vt* JUR juzgar; *to judge a case* juzgar un caso | declarar; *they judged him guilty* le declararon culpable ‖ SP arbitrar | juzgar (in a competition) ‖ considerar, estimar, juzgar (to consider); *it has been judged necessary* se ha juzgado necesario ‖ calcular, evaluar; *he judged the distance well* calculó bien la distancia ‖ — *it is difficult* o *hard to judge* es difícil de juzgar ‖ FIG *one can't judge a book by its cover* no se puede juzgar por las apariencias.
◆ *vi* opinar, formarse una opinión (to arrive at an opinion) ‖ juzgar; *don't judge too hastily* no juzgues apresuradamente ‖ ser juez, juzgar, actuar como juez (to act as a deciding body) ‖ — *how did the jury judge?* ¿cuál ha sido el veredicto del jurado? ‖ *judging by* o *from the weight of it* a juzgar por el peso ‖ *one cannot judge by appearances* no se puede juzgar por las apariencias ‖ *to judge well, ill of s.o.* tener una buena, una mala opinión de alguien.

judgement ['dʒʌdʒmənt] *n* → **judgment.**

judgemental [dʒʌdʒ'mentəl] *adj* → **judgmental.**

Judges ['dʒʌdʒiz] *n* REL libro *m* de los Jueces.

judgeship [-ʃip] *n* judicatura *f*, magistratura *f*.

judgment; judgement ['dʒʌdʒmənt] *n* JUR juicio *m* (trial) | sentencia *m*, fallo *m* (legal sentence); *judgment by default* sentencia en rebeldía ‖ juicio *m*; *a man of sound judgment* un hombre de mucho juicio ‖ opinión *f* (opinion); *in your judgment* en su opinión ‖ REL juicio *m*; *Last Judgment* Juicio Final; *Judgment Day* Día del Juicio ‖ apreciación *f*; *an error of judgment* un error de apreciación ‖ — *against my better judgement* en contra de lo que me parece mejor ‖ *in the judgment of many* para muchos, a los ojos de muchos ‖ FAM *it's a judgment on you* es un castigo de Dios ‖ *judgment seat* tribunal *m* ‖ *sense of judgment* juicio ‖ *to form a judgment on sth.* formarse una opinión sobre algo ‖ *to give one's judgment on sth.* dar su opinión sobre algo ‖ *to make a judgment about sth.* emitir un juicio sobre algo ‖ *to pass judgment* pronunciar una sentencia (in court), juzgar (to judge) ‖ *to reserve judgement* reservarse la opinión, no opinar ‖ *to the best of my judgment* por lo que puedo juzgar, según mi entender.

judgmental; judgemental [dʒʌd'ʒmentəl] *adj* crítico, ca.

judicature ['dʒuːdikətʃə*] *n* JUR judicatura *f* (administration, body of judges) | juzgado *m*, tribunal *m* (a law court).

judicial [dʒuː'diʃəl] *adj* JUR judicial; *judicial powers* poderes judiciales | legal; *judicial separation* separación legal ‖ sensato, ta; juicioso, sa (judicious) ‖ imparcial (unbiased) ‖ *judicial faculty* sentido crítico, discernimiento *m*.

judiciary [dʒu'diʃiəri] *n* JUR magistratura *f* (the apparatus of law and its administrators) ‖ poder *m* judicial; *the legislative, the executive and the judiciary* el poder legislativo, ejecutivo y judicial.
◆ *adj* judicial.

judicious [dʒu'diʃəs] *adj* juicioso, sa; sensato, ta.

judiciousness [-nis] *n* sensatez *f*, juicio *m*, buen sentido *m*.

Judith ['dʒuːdiθ] *pr n* Judit *f*.

judo ['dʒuːdəu] *n* SP judo *m*.

judoka ['dʒuːdəukə] *n* judoka *m*.

jug [dʒʌg] *n* jarra *f* (for water, beer, etc.) ‖ FAM chirona *f*, trena *f* (prison); *to be in the jug* estar en la trena, estar en chirona.

jug [dʒʌg] *vt* CULIN estofar ‖ FAM encarcelar, meter en chirona ‖ *jugged hare* encebollado *m* de liebre.

juggernaut ['dʒʌgənɔːt] *n* monstruo *m* que destruye a los hombres ‖ fuerza *f* irresistible.

juggle ['dʒʌgl] *n* juegos *m pl* malabares (tricks of dexterity) ‖ juego *m* de manos (magic trick) ‖ FIG timo *m* (swindle) | truco *m*, treta *f*, trampa *f* (trick).

juggle ['dʒʌgl] *vi* hacer juegos malabares (to perform tricks of dexterity) ‖ hacer juegos de manos (a magician) ‖ — *to juggle s.o. out of* quitar engañosamente a alguien ‖ *to juggle with* hacer juegos malabares con (in a circus, etc.), dar vueltas a (ideas), hacer malabarismos con; *to juggle skilfully with numbers* hacer malabarismos con los números; falsificar, hacer trampas con (to falsify, to manipulate).
◆ *vt* hacer juegos malabares con (to perform tricks of dexterity with) ‖ FIG falsear, falsificar (to falsify) | embaucar (to cheat) ‖ *to juggle away* escamotar, escamotear (to make vanish).

juggler [-ə*] *n* malabarista *m* & *f* ‖ prestidigitador *m*, ilusionista *m* & *f* (magician).

jugglery ['dʒʌgləri]; **juggling** ['dʒʌgliŋ] *n* juegos *m pl* malabares (tricks of dexterity) ‖ juegos *m pl* de manos, prestidigitación *f* (magic trick) ‖ FIG timo *m*, fraude *m* (swindle) | trampas *f pl* (tricks) | manipulación *f* (manipulation) | falsificación *f* (falsification).

jughead ['dʌghed] *n* FAM testarudo, da; cabezota *m* & *f* (stubborn) | mentecato, ta (idiot).

Jugoslav ['juːgəu'slaːv] *adj/n* yugoslavo, va.

Jugoslavia ['juːgəu'slaːvjə] *pr n* Yugoslavia *f*.

jugular ['dʒʌgjulə*] *adj* ANAT yugular; *jugular vein* vena yugular.
◆ *n* yugular *f* (vein).

jugulate ['dʒʌgjuleit] *vt* degollar ‖ FIG detener (a disease, an epidemic).

juice [dʒuːs] *n* jugo *m* (fluid) ‖ jugo *m* (of meat) ‖ zumo *m*, jugo *m* (of fruits, etc.) ‖ FAM lo picante (of a story) | gasolina *f* (petrol) | corriente *f* (electricity) ‖ *gastric juice* jugo gástrico.

juiciness ['dʒuːsinis] *n* jugosidad *f* ‖ FAM lo picante.

juicy ['dʒuːsi] *adj* jugoso, sa (rich in juice); *a juicy orange* una naranja jugosa ‖ FAM sustancioso, sa (profitable); *juicy profits* beneficios sustanciosos | picante, sabroso, sa (racy); *a juicy story* una historia picante.

jujitsu [dʒuː'dʒitsuː] *n* jiu-jitsu *m*.

juju ['dʒuːdʒuː] *n* grisgrís *m*, talismán *m*.

jujube ['dʒuːdʒuːb] *n* BOT azufaifa *f* (fruit) | azufaifo *m* (plant) ‖ pastilla *f* de azufaifa (sweet).

jujutsu [dʒuː'dʒutsuː] *n* jiu-jitsu *m*.

jukebox ['dʒuːkbɔks] *n* máquina *f* de discos.

julep ['dʒuːlep] *n* julepe *m* (drink).

Jules ['dʒuːlz] *pr n* Julio *m*.

Julian [dʒuːljən] *pr n* Julián *m* ‖ Juliano *m* (Roman emperor).
◆ *adj* juliano, na; *Julian calendar* calendario juliano.

Juliana [ˌdʒuːli'ɑːnə] *pr n* Juliana *f*.

julienne [ˌdʒuːli'en] *n* juliana *f*, sopa *f* juliana.

Juliet ['dʒuːljət] *pr n* Julieta *f*.

July [dʒu'lai] *n* julio *m*; *on the nineteenth of July 1982* el 19 [diez y nueve] de julio de 1982.

jumble ['dʒʌmbl] *n* revoltijo *m*, embrollo *m*, confusión *f*, mezcolanza *f* (confused collection) ‖ FIG confusión *f* (mental) ‖ — *a jumble of books* un montón de libros revueltos ‖ *to get into a jumble* hacerse un lío, embrollarse.

jumble ['dʒʌmbl] *vt* embrollar, confundir (to confuse) ‖ mezclar (to mix) ‖ *jumbled papers* papeles revueltos.

jumble sale [-seil] *n* venta *f* por liquidación (clearance sale) ‖ venta *f* de caridad.

jumbo ['dʒʌmbəu] *adj* muy grande, enorme, colosal, gigantesco, ca (very big) ‖ *jumbo jet* jumbo *m*, avión *m* de reacción de gran capacidad.
◆ *n* coloso *m* (big animal) ‖ FAM elefante *m*.

jump [dʒʌmp] *n* salto *m*; *with a jump he avoided the puddle* salvó el charco de un salto *or* dando un salto; *it was a difficult jump, but he made it* era un salto difícil, pero logró darlo ‖ aumento *m* grande, salto *m* (of prices) ‖ salto *m* (short trip) ‖ sobresalto *m* (of surprise) ‖ acción *f* de comer [en damas] (in draughts) ‖ SP obstáculo *m* (in a race) | salto *m*; *high jump* salto de altura; *long jump* salto de longitud; *to take a jump* dar un salto (a horse) ‖ — FIG *now he is in for the high jump!* ¡ahora se va a enterar! ‖ *there has been a big jump in sales* las ventas han experimentado un aumento muy grande ‖ *to be one jump ahead of s.o.* llevar ventaja a alguien ‖ *to give a jump* dar un salto ‖ *to give s.o. a jump* dar un susto a alguien ‖ *to have the jump on s.o.* llevar ventaja a alguien ‖ *to take a running jump at* coger impulso para saltar.

jump [dʒʌmp] *vi* saltar; *he hurt his leg when he jumped* se hizo daño en la pierna al saltar ‖ tirarse, saltar (from a height) ‖ botar, rebotar (to bounce) ‖ sobresaltarse (to start); *she jumped when I called her* se sobresaltó cuando le llamé ‖ dar un salto; *the cost of living, the temperature jumped* el coste de la vida, la temperatura dio un salto ‖ comerse una ficha [en damas] (in draughts) ‖ — FIG *and jump to it!* ¡y hazlo volando!, ¡rápido! ‖ *he jumped on the bus* subió de un salto al autobús ‖ FIG *I nearly jumped out of my skin!* ¡qué susto me pegué! | *I was criticizing her and John jumped down my throat* estaba criticándola y Juan se puso furioso ‖ *to jump about* dar saltos, brincar, saltar ‖ *to jump across* o *over sth.* salvar *or* cruzar algo de un salto ‖ *to jump ahead* ponerse el primero de un salto ‖ *to jump at a chance* aprovechar una oportunidad ‖ *to jump at s.o.* echarse encima a alguien ‖ *to jump back* dar un salto atrás ‖ *to jump down* bajar de un salto ‖ *to jump for joy* saltar de alegría ‖ FIG *to jump from one thing to another* saltar de un tema a otro ‖ *to jump in* saltar a, subir de un salto (car), saltar a (water) ‖ FIG *to jump in at the deep end* coger el toro por los cuernos ‖ *to jump in the water* tirarse al agua ‖ FIG *to jump on s.o.* echarse encima de alguien ‖ *to jump out from behind* salir de repente de detrás de ‖ *to jump out of, to jump from* saltar de ‖ *to jump to conclusions* sacar conclusiones precipitadas ‖ *to jump up* levantarse de golpe *or* de un salto ‖ *to jump with* concordar con, coincidir con ‖ *to make s.o. jump* sobresaltar a uno.
◆ *vt* saltar, salvar (to cross by leaping); *he jumped the wall* saltó el muro ‖ SP hacer saltar; *he jumped the horse over the fence* hizo saltar la valla al caballo | presentar en un concurso (to present in a competition) | levantar (game) ‖ saltarse (to miss out); *you jumped a few details* se saltó algunos detalles ‖ usurpar (to usurp) ‖ comer (in draughts); *he jumped my king* me comió la dama ‖ FAM agredir, atacar (to attack) | escapar de, fugarse de (a prison) | largarse de (a town) ‖ — *to jump a bid* marcar más alto (in bridge) ‖ *to jump a claim* usurpar una concesión minera ‖ *to jump a queue* colarse ‖ US FAM *to jump a train* subirse a un tren en marcha para no pagar billete ‖ FAM *to jump the lights* saltarse el semáforo ‖ *to jump the rails* o *the tracks* descarrilar, salirse de las vías.

jumped-up ['dʒʌmptʌp] *adj* FAM creído, da.

jumper ['dʒʌmpə*] *n* saltador, ra (s.o. who jumps) ‖ ELECTR cable *m* de conexión ‖ MIN barrena *f* || jersey *m* [cerrado] (pullover) || *US* vestido *m* sin mangas (dress) | pelele *m* (rompers) | mono *m* (for workmen).

jumpiness ['dʒʌmpinis] *n* nerviosismo *m*.

jumping ['dʒʌmpiŋ] *n* SP pruebas *f pl* de saltos (in athletics) || *show jumping* concurso hípico.

jumping bean [-bi:n] *n* BOT judía *f* saltadora [*AMER* frijol *or* poroto saltador].

jumping jack [-djæk] *n* buscapiés *m inv* (firework) || pelele *m* (child's toy).

jumping-off place [-ɔ:fpleis] *n* lugar *m* remoto || FIG situación *f* extrema.

jump jet ['dʒʌmpdʒet] *n* AVIAT avión *m* de despegue vertical.

jump leads ['dʒʌmp,li:dz] *n* cables *m pl* de empalme.

jump-off ['dʒʌmpɔf] *n* salida *f* (in a race).

jump rope ['dʒʌmprəup] *n* *US* saltador *m*, comba *f* (skipping rope).

jump seat ['dʒʌmpsi:t] *n* traspuntín *m*, traspontín *m* (in a car).

jump suit ['dʒʌmpsju:t] *n* mono *m* (garment).

jumpy ['dʒʌmpi] *adj* nervioso, sa (nervous) || asustadizo, za (easily frightened) || que traquetea (train, etc.) || cortado, da (style).

juncaceae [dʒʌŋ'keisi:i] *pl n* BOT juncáceas *f*.

junction ['dʒʌŋkʃən] *n* empalme *m* (of railway) || estación *f* de empalme (railway station) || unión *f*, juntura *f* (join) || cruce *m* (of roads) || ELECTR empalme *m* || confluencia *f* (of rivers).

junction box [-bɔks] *n* ELECTR caja *f* de empalme.

juncture ['dʒʌŋktʃə*] *n* unión *f*, juntura *f* (join) || ANAT coyuntura *f* || confluencia *f* (of rivers) || momento *m* (moment) || coyuntura *f* (time with relation to circumstances); *at this juncture* en esta coyuntura.

June [dʒu:n] *n* junio *m*; *on the fourth of June 1901* el cuatro de junio de 1901.

June beetle [-'bi:tl] *n* *US* ZOOL escarabajo *m*.

June bug [-bʌg] *n* *US* ZOOL escarabajo *m*.

jungle ['dʒʌŋgl] *n* selva *f*, jungla *f*; *tropical jungle* selva tropical || FIG maraña *f* (tangle, jumble) | laberinto *m* (maze) || FIG *the concrete jungle* el mundo del hormigón, el universo del hormigón.

junior ['dʒu:njə*] *adj* hijo; *John Brown junior* John Brown hijo || subalterno, na; inferior (lower in grade); *junior officer* oficial subalterno || más nuevo, va; más reciente (more recent); *their club is two years junior to ours* su club es dos años más reciente que el nuestro || de menor antigüedad; *the junior members of the committee* los miembros de menor antigüedad de la comisión || más joven, menor (younger) || SP juvenil; *the junior team* el equipo juvenil || *US* de penúltimo año.

◆ *n* subalterno, na (lower in grade) || menor *m* & *f* (younger person) || jovencito *m*; *come here, junior* ven aquí, jovencito || *US* estudiante *m* & *f* de penúltimo año (student) || pequeño, ña (in school); *the seniors and the juniors* los mayores y los pequeños || SP juvenil *m* & *f* || — *she is two years my junior* le llevo dos años, es dos años más joven que yo || SP *to play for the juniors* jugar en el equipo juvenil.

junior college [-'kɔlidʒ] *n* *US* colegio *m* universitario para los dos primeros años.

juniper ['dʒu:nipə*] *n* BOT enebro *m*.

junk [dʒiŋk] *n* MAR junco *m* (eastern vessel) | cuerda *f* gastada (old rope) | cecina *f* (meat) || FAM sandeces *f pl* (nonsense) | trastos *m pl* viejos (useless objects) | chatarra *f* (old iron, metal) || — FAM *he talks a lot of junk* no dice más que tonterías | *the book is a load of junk* el libro es una porquería | *where did you buy this junk?* ¿dónde compraste esta porquería *or* estas porquerías?

junk [dʒʌŋk] *vt* *US* desechar, tirar a la basura | hacer chatarra.

junket ['dʒʌŋkit] *n* dulce *m* de leche cuajada (sweet) || *US* excursión *f* (excursion) | viaje *m* (journey) | fiesta *f* (party).

junket ['dʒʌŋkit] *vi* *US* ir de excursión (to go on an excursion).

junk food ['dʒʌŋkfu:d] *n* comida *f* de plástico.

junk heap [dʒʌŋkhi:p] *n* vertedero *m*.

junkie ['dʒʌŋki] *n* FAM toxicómano, na; drogadicto, ta.

junk mail ['dʒʌŋk meil] *n* propaganda *f* enviada por correo.

junkman ['dʒʌŋkmən]; **junk merchant** ['dʒʌŋk'mə:tʃənt] *n* trapero *m*.

— OBSERV El plural de *junkman* es *junkmen*.

junk market ['dʒʌŋkma:kit] *n* rastro *m*, mercado *m* de objetos de lance.

junkshop ['dʒʌŋkʃɔp] *n* baratillo *m*.

junkyard ['dʒʌŋkja:d] *n* depósito *m* de chatarra.

junta ['dʒʌntə] *n* HIST junta *f*.

junto ['dʒʌntə] *n* facción *f*.

Jupiter ['dʒu:pitə*] *pr n* MYTH Júpiter *m*.

jural ['dʒuərəl] *adj* jurídico, ca; legal.

Jurassic [dʒu'ræsik] *adj* GEOL jurásico, ca.

◆ *n* GEOL período *m* jurásico, jurásico *m*.

jurat [dʒuəræt] *n* escritura *f* notarial.

juratory ['dʒuərətəri] *adj* JUR bajo juramento (declaration) | jurado, da (obligation).

jurel [hu'rel] *n* ZOOL jurel *m* (fish).

juridical [dʒuə'ridikəl] *adj* jurídico, ca.

jurisconsult ['dʒuəriskən,sʌlt] *n* jurisconsulto *m*.

jurisdiction [,dʒuəris'dikʃən] *n* jurisdicción *f* || *to fall* o *to come under s.o.'s jurisdiction* caer bajo la jurisdicción de uno, ser de la competencia de uno.

jurisprudence ['dʒuəris,pru:dəns] *n* jurisprudencia *f* || *medical jurisprudence* medicina *f* legal.

jurisprudent [θdʒuəris,pru:dənt] *n* jurisperito *m*.

jurist ['dʒuərist] *n* jurista *m* & *f*.

juristical [dʒuə'ristikəl] *adj* jurídico, ca.

juror ['dʒuərə*] *n* jurado, da (person).

jury ['dʒuəri] *n* jurado *m*; *to sit on the jury* ser miembro del jurado || tribunal *m* (for exams).

jury box [-bɔks] *n* tribuna *f* *or* banco *m* del jurado.

juryman [-mən] *n* miembro *m* de un jurado, jurado *m*.

— OBSERV El plural de *juryman* es *jurymen*.

jurymast [-ma:st] *n* MAR bandola *f*.

jury rig [-rig] *n* MAR aparejo *m* provisional.

jurywoman [-'wumən] *n* jurado *m*.

— OBSERV El plural de *jurywoman* es *jurywomen*.

jussive ['dʒʌsiv] *adj* GRAMM imperativo, va.

◆ *n* GRAMM imperativo *m*.

just [dʒʌst] *adj* justo, ta (fair, deserved, honest); *a just decision* una decisión justa; *a just price, man* un precio, un hombre justo || justificado, da; fundado, da; justo, ta (well-founded, justified); *just grounds for complaint* motivo justificado de queja || exacto, ta; justo, ta (accurate) || — *as is just* como es justo || *to get one's just reward* o *deserts* recibir su merecido || *to plead for a just cause* abogar por una causa justa.

◆ *pl n* *the just* los justos; *to sleep the sleep of the just* dormir el sueño de los justos.

◆ *adv* justo; *just in front, behind, opposite* justo delante, detrás, en frente; *just enough* justo lo suficiente || justamente, justo; *I was just calling you when you arrived* te estaba llamando justamente cuando llegaste || exactamente, precisamente; *it's just what I expected* es exactamente lo que esperaba; *it's just a year ago that...* hace un año exactamente que...; *just what did he say?* ¿qué dijo exactamente?; *that's just what I mean* es precisamente lo que quiero decir; *just how much I couldn't say* no te podría decir exactamente cuánto; *he does just as he pleases* hace exactamente lo que le da la gana || en punto, justo (with time); *it was just two o'clock* eran justo las dos, eran las dos en punto || sólo, solamente, no... más que; *there is just one left* sólo queda uno, no queda más que uno; *it's just the postman* no es más que el cartero; *but he's just a caporal* pero es solamente un cabo; *it'll just take me a moment* sólo tardaré un momento || sólo, solamente, nada más; *just once* una vez nada más; *just a little* un poquito nada más; *just you and I* tú y yo nada más || ahora mismo (now); *I'm just leaving* salgo ahora mismo; *it's just starting to rain* ahora mismo empieza a llover; *the train is just arriving* el tren está llegando ahora mismo || sencillamente (simply); *I just refused* me negué sencillamente; *just tell him to leave you alone* dile sencillamente que te deje en paz || francamente, sencillamente; *it's just incredible* es francamente increíble; *it was just wonderful, perfect* fue sencillamente maravilloso, perfecto || recién (newly); *those just arrived* los recién llegados; *a record just out* un disco recién salido || de pronto (suddenly); *he just arrived without warning* llegó de pronto sin avisar || mismo; *just here* aquí mismo; *just by the door* al lado mismo de la puerta || — *a book which just came out* un libro recién publicado *or* que acaba de publicarse || *he had just arrived* acababa de llegar || *he has just left school* acaba de terminar el colegio *or* los estudios secundarios || *he only just escaped drowning* por poco se ahoga || *he only just managed to reach the top* llegó con mucha dificultad a la cima || *I just can't understand her* no la llego a comprender || *I just missed the train* perdí el tren por muy poco || *I'm just starving* me muero de hambre || *I only just caught the bus* cogí el autobús por los pelos || *I only just finished in time* terminé justo a tiempo || *it's just as good* es lo mismo || *it's just as well you were there* menos mal que estabas allí || *it would be just as well for you to reconsider* más vale que lo vuelvas a pensar || *I've got just enough to live on* tengo justo lo suficiente para vivir || *just about* poco más o menos; *there were just about a hundred people there* había cien personas poco más o menos; por; *I lost it just about here* lo perdí por aquí; a punto de; *they were just about to leave* estaban a punto de marcharse; justo; *I had just about enough* tenía justo lo suficiente; ya; *I'm just about fed up with it* ya estoy harto || *just a moment* un momento || *just as* nada más, justo al; *just as we left it started raining* nada más salir nosotros *or* justo al salir nosotros se puso a llover; tal como, tal y como; *we found everything just as we had left it* encontramos todo tal y como lo habíamos dejado; *come just as you are* ven tal y como estás; justo cuando, justo en el momento en que; *they arrived just as the fight started* llegaron justo en el momento en que empezó la pelea; *it happened just as you called* ocurrió justo en el momento en que llamaste || *just as I thought* ya me lo figuraba, lo que me figuraba || *just as you please* como usted quiera || *just before, after* justo antes, después || *just here* aquí mismo, aquí || *just imagine!, just think!* ¡fíjate!, ¡imagínate! || *just let me see him!* ¡como lo vea! || *just listen* escucha un momento || *just now* actualmente; *business is bad just now* los negocios van mal actualmente; en este momento, ahora mismo; *I'm busy just now* estoy ocupado en este momento; hace un momento; *he came just now* vino hace un momento || FAM *just shut up about it, will you?* cállate ya, ¿quieres? || *just taste this* prueba un poco de esto || *just then* en ese momento, en ese mismo momento || *just the same* sin embargo (nevertheless), exactamente igual (exactly the same, in the same way) || *just this once* por una vez || *not just yet* todavía no || *she dances just as well as you* ella baila tan bien como tú || *she's just a child* no es más que una niña || *that's just it!* ¡ahí está! || *that's just too bad* ¡qué lástima!, ¡qué pena! || *the car just missed him* casi le atropelló el coche || *to do sth. just as a joke* hacer algo en plan de broma || *to do sth. just for a laugh* hacer algo en plan de broma *or* para divertirse || *we were just discussing that* precisamente estábamos hablando de eso || FAM *won't* o *wouldn't* o *don't I just!* ¡ya lo creo! || *you just missed him* ácaba de marcharse || *you just missed the bull's-eye* poco te faltó para dar en el blanco || *you're just in time to see the show* llegas justo a tiempo *or* llegas a punto para ver el espectáculo.

justice ['dʒʌstis] *n* justicia *f* (equity); *I doubt the justice of the decision* dudo de la justicia de la decisión || JUR justicia *f* (administration of law); *the forces of justice* las fuerzas de la justicia; *justice has been done* se ha hecho justicia | juez *m* (judge); *justice of the peace* juez de paz || — *in justice to* para ser justo con || *let justice be done* que la justicia se cumpla || *Mr. Justice Brown* el magistrado señor Brown || *the dress does not do her justice* el traje no le favorece || *their marks didn't do them justice* merecían una nota más alta || *the photo doesn't do you justice* no estás favorecido *or* no has salido bien en la foto || *to administer justice* administrar (la) justicia || *to bring s.o. to justice* llevar a uno ante la justicia *or* ante los tribunales || *to demand justice* pedir justicia || *to do a meal justice* hacer honor a la comida || *to do s.o. justice* hacer justicia a (a criminal, etc.) || *to do o.s. justice* quedar bien.

justiceship [-ʃip] *n* judicatura *f*.

justiciar [dʒʌs'tiʃiɑ:*] *n* HIST justicia *m* mayor.

justiciary [dʒʌs'tiʃiəri] *n* HIST justicia *m* mayor.

justifiable ['dʒʌstifaiəbl] *adj* justificable || JUR *justifiable homicide* homicidio *m* inculpable.

justification [ˌdʒʌstifi'keiʃən] *n* justificación *f* || PRINT justificación *f*.

justificative ['dʒʌstifikeitiv] *adj* justificativo, va.

justificatory ['dʒʌstifikeitəri] *adj* justificador, ra.

justify ['dʒʌstifai] *vt* justificar; *the end justifies the means* el fin justifica los medios || PRINT justificar || — *am I justified in refusing?* ¿tengo razón en negarme? || *to justify o.s.* justificarse.

Justinian [dʒʌs'tiniən] *pr n* Justiniano *m*.

justly ['dʒʌstly] *adv* con justicia, justamente (fairly) || con razón; *she justly remarked that...* con razón observó que...

justness ['dʒʌstnis] *n* justicia *f* || rectitud *f* || exactitud *f* (of a remark, etc.).

jut [dʒʌt] *n* ARCH salidizo *m*, saliente *m* || saliente *m* (of rock).

jut [dʒʌt] *vi* sobresalir || *to jut out* sobresalir.

jute [dʒu:t] *n* BOT yute *m*.

juvenile ['dʒu:vinail] *adj* juvenil; *juvenile delinquency* delincuencia juvenil; *juvenile behaviour* comportamiento juvenil || infantil (childish) || de menores (for the young); *juvenile court* tribunal de menores.

◆ *n* joven *m* & *f*, menor *m* & *f*, adolescente *m* & *f* (young person) || publicación *f* juvenil, libro *m* para niños (book for young people) || US galán *m* joven (in a play).

juvenile lead [-'li:d] *n* THEATR papel *m* de galán joven (part) | galán *m* joven (actor).

juvenilia [ˌdzu:vi'niljə] *pl n* obras *f* de juventud.

juxtalinear [ˌdʒʌkstə'liniə*] *adj* yuxtalineal.

juxtapose ['dʒʌkstəpəuz] *vt* yuxtaponer.

juxtaposition [ˌdʒʌkstəpə'ziʃən] *n* yuxtaposición *f*.

K

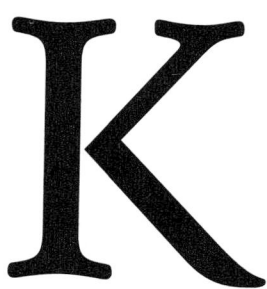

k [kei] *n* k *f* (letter); *a small, capital k* una k minúscula, mayúscula.

Kabul ['kɑːbl] *pr n* GEOGR Kabul.

Kabyle [kə'bail] *n* Cabila *m & f.*

kadi ['kɑːdi] *n* REL cadí *m.*

kaftan ['kæftən] *n* caftán *m.*

kainite ['kainait] *n* CHEM kainita *f.*

kaiser ['kaizə*] *n* káiser *m.*

kaki ['kɑːki] *n* BOT caqui *m*, kaki *m* (Japanese persimmon).

Kalahari Desert (the) [,kælə'hɑːri] *pr n* GEOGR Kalahari *m.*

kale [keil] *n* BOT col *f* rizada ‖ *US* FAM pasta *f* [*AMER* plata *f*] (money).

kaleidoscope [kə'laidəskəup] *n* calidoscopio *m*, caleidoscopio *m.*

kaleidoscopic [kə'laidə'skɔpik] *adj* calidoscópico, ca; caleidoscópico, ca.

kalends ['kælendz] *pl n* HIST calendas *f.*

Kalmuck ['kælmək] *adj/n* calmuco, ca.

kamikaze [,kɑːmi'kɑːziː] *n* kamikase *m.*

Kampala [kæm'pɑːlə] *pr n* GEOGR Kampala.

Kanaka ['kænəkə] *n* canaco, ca.

kangaroo [,kæŋgə'ruː] *n* ZOOL canguro *m.*

kangaroo court [-kɔːt] *n* *US* tribunal *m* desautorizado.

Kansas ['kænzəs] *pr n* GEOGR Kansas.

Kantian ['kæntiən] *adj/n* PHIL kantiano, na.

kaolin; *US* **kaoline** ['keiəlin] *n* MIN caolín *m.*

kapok ['keipɔk] *n* BOT kapok *m*, capoc *m*, miraguano *m* (fibre).

kappa ['kæpə] *n* kappa *f* (Greek letter).

kaput [kə'put] *adj* FAM estropeado, da.

karakul [,kɑːrɑː'kʌl] *n* ZOOL caracul *m* (sheep) ‖ astracán *m* (fur).

karat ['kærət] *n* quilate *m*; *18 karat gold* oro de 18 quilates.

karate [kə'rɑːti] *n* SP karate *m.*

karting ['kɑːtiŋ] *n* SP carrera *f* de karts, karting *m.*

karyoplasm ['kæriə,plæzəm] *n* BIOL carioplasma *m* (nuclear protoplasm).

Kashmir ['kæʃmiə*] *pr n* GEOGR Cachemira *f.*

katabolic [,kætə'bɔlik] *adj* catabólico, ca.

katabolism [kə'tæbəlizəm] *n* catabolismo *m.*

Katanganese [kæ,tæŋgə'niːz] *adj/s* katangueño, ña.

Katar, Qatar [kæta:] *pr n* GEOGR Qatar.

katharsis [kə'θɑːsis] *n* catarsis *f.*

Katherine ['kæθərin]; **Kathleen** ['kæθliːn] *pr n* Catalina *f.*

Katmandou, Katmandu [,kætmæn'duː] *pr n* GEOGR Katmandú.

katydid ['keitidid] *n* ZOOL saltamontes *m inv.*

kauri ['kauri] *n* BOT pino *m* de Nueva Zelanda.

kayak ['kaiæk] *n* kayac *m.*

kebab [kə'bæb] *n* pincho *m*, broqueta *f*, brocheta *f.*

kedge [kedʒ] *n* MAR anclote *m.*

kedge [kedʒ] *vt* MAR espiar por un anclote.

kedgeree [kedʒə'riː] *n* CULIN plato *m* a base de arroz, pescado y huevos.

keel [kiːl] *n* MAR, AVIAT & ZOOL quilla *f* ‖ MAR barco *m* (boat) | chalana *f* (long, flat boat) ‖ — MAR *bilge keel* quilla de balance ‖ *to be on an even keel* no tener diferencia de calado (a ship), estar en equilibrio (to be well balanced).

keel [kiːl] *vt* MAR dar de quilla; *to keel a boat* dar de quilla a un barco.

◆ *vi* MAR zozobrar, volcar ‖ *to keel over* zozobrar (a boat), volcarse (a thing), desplomarse (a person).

keelhaul [-hɔːl] *vt* HIST pasar por debajo de la quilla (as punishment).

keelson ['kelsn] *n* MAR sobrequilla *f.*

keen [kiːn] *adj* afilado, da (sharp); *a keen blade* una hoja afilada ‖ agudo, da; *a keen mind* una mente aguda; *keen eyesight* vista aguda; *a keen sense of humour* un sentido agudo del humor ‖ agudo, da (pain) ‖ fino, na; *a very keen ear* un oído muy fino ‖ penetrante; *a keen stare* una mirada penetrante; *a keen wind* un viento penetrante ‖ fuerte, vivo, va; intenso, sa (feelings); *a keen desire* un vivo deseo ‖ vivo, va; profundo, da; *a keen interest* un vivo interés ‖ concienzudo, da (conscientious) ‖ entusiasta (enthusiastic) ‖ cortante (cold) ‖ deseoso, sa; ansioso, sa (greedy); *keen to arrive at the truth* deseoso de llegar a la verdad ‖ competitivo, va (prices) ‖ fuerte (competition) ‖ — *to be a keen cyclist* ser muy aficionado al ciclismo ‖ *to be keen on* gustarle a uno; *I'm keen on that girl* me gusta esta chica; *I'm keen on Beethoven* me gusta Beethoven; *I'm not keen on custard* no me gustan las natillas; ser aficionado a; *he's keen on football* es aficionado al fútbol ‖ *to be keen to do sth.* tener muchas ganas de hacer algo, tener un vivo deseo de hacer algo ‖ *to have a keen appetite* tener buen apetito ‖ *try to seem keen* intenta demostrar un poco de entusiasmo ‖ *we're not all that keen to go* no nos entusiasma la idea de ir.

◆ *n* lamento *m* fúnebre [con que se acompaña en Irlanda la muerte de una persona].

keen [kiːn] *vi* cantar un lamento fúnebre.

keenly [-li] *adv* con entusiasmo; *the match was keenly fought* el partido se jugó con entusiasmo ‖ profundamente, vivamente; *keenly interested in* profundamente interesado por; *keenly affected* profundamente afectado ‖ fijamente; *he looked at her keenly* la miró fijamente ‖ — *a keenly disputed point* un punto muy controvertido ‖ *to listen keenly* escuchar con mucha atención.

keenness [-nis] *n* lo afilado, lo cortante (of a knife blade) ‖ rigor *m* (of the cold) ‖ agudeza *f* (of mind, sight) ‖ profundidad *f*, intensidad *f* (of emotion) ‖ finura *f* (of sense of smell, hearing) ‖ entusiasmo *m* (enthusiasm); *keenness to do sth.* entusiasmo en hacer algo ‖ deseo *m* (desire) ‖ *the keenness of the wind* el viento penetrante.

keep [kiːp] *n* HIST torre *f* de homenaje (of a castle) ‖ sustento *m*; *to earn one's keep* ganarse el sustento ‖ subsistencia *f* (maintenance) ‖ — *for keeps* para siempre (for ever) ‖ *he's not worth his keep* no sirve para nada ‖ *it's yours for keeps* te lo puedes quedar ‖ *to play for keeps* jugar de veras.

keep* [kiːp] *vt* guardar; *I am keeping old newspapers* estoy guardando periódicos viejos; *to keep silence* guardar silencio; *to keep a secret* guardar un secreto; *keep it till I come back* guárdalo hasta que yo vuelva; *keep me a place in the queue* guárdame un sitio en la cola; *to keep the commandments* guardar los mandamientos ‖ quedarse; *I lent him my book and he kept it* le presté mi libro y se quedó con él ‖ mantener; *to keep a family* mantener una familia; *to keep order* mantener el orden; *to keep a car in good condition* mantener un coche en buenas condiciones; *to keep one's composure* mantener la compostura; *to keep a door open* mantener una puerta abierta ‖ reservar, guardar; *I keep this whisky for special friends* este whisky lo reservo para amigos especiales ‖ tener; *it keeps me very busy* me tiene muy ocupado; *to keep an open mind* tener amplitud de ideas; *to keep s.o. in prison* tener a alguien en la cárcel; *to keep the workers happy* tener a los trabajadores contentos ‖ hacer (to make); *to keep s.o. working* hacer trabajar a uno; *he kept me waiting* me hizo esperar; *she keeps him very happy* le hace muy feliz ‖ observar; *to keep the law* observar la ley ‖ cumplir; *to keep a promise* cumplir una promesa ‖ acudir a; *to keep an appointment* acudir a una cita ‖ tener; *to keep a maid, a shop* tener criada, una tienda ‖ criar (to raise livestock) ‖ llevar; *to keep accounts* llevar la contabilidad *or* las cuentas ‖ entretener, detener, retener; *can I keep you for a few minutes?* ¿le puedo entretener unos minutos?; *what kept you?* ¿qué te entretuvo?; *to keep s.o. to dinner* retener a alguien a cenar ‖ conservar, mantener; *keep it warm* consérvalo caliente ‖ contener, dominar; *to keep one's temper* contener el malhumor ‖ cuidar; *to keep s.o.'s dog whilst he o she is away* cuidar el perro de alguien mientras está de viaje ‖ seguir (a track, a way, a direction) ‖ quedarse en; *he kept his house* se quedó en casa; *she keeps her room* se queda en su cuarto ‖ celebrar (to celebrate); *to keep a feast* celebrar una fiesta ‖ defender; *to keep goal* defender la portería ‖ salvar (to save); *to keep s.o. from despair* salvar a alguien de la desesperación ‖ — *God keep you!* ¡Dios le guarde! ‖ *he can't keep a job* no puede quedarse en ningún trabajo ‖ *keep it out of harm's way* guárdalo en un sitio seguro ‖ FAM *keep it under your hat* no se lo digas a nadie ‖ *keep the change* quédese con la vuelta ‖ *keep your hands to yourself!* ¡las manos quietas! ‖ *keep your town tidy* mantenga limpia la ciudad ‖ *this shop doesn't keep snails* en esta tienda no se venden caracoles ‖ *to keep a diary* escribir *or* llevar un diario ‖ *to keep a little money by* tener un poco de dinero apartado ‖ *to keep a note of* apuntar ‖ *to keep* *boarders* tener huéspedes || *to keep company* acompañar || *to keep going* mantener; *he managed to keep the firm going* consiguió mantener la empresa; mantener con vida; *the doctors kept him going* los médicos le mantuvieron con vida; hacer funcionar (a machine, a motor, etc.), mantener (to maintain), hacer durar (to make last) || *to keep one's distance* guardar las distancias || *to keep one's seat* permanecer sentado (audience, etc.), conservar el escaño (in an election) || *to keep one's word* cumplir su palabra || *to keep s.o. quiet* hacer callar a alguien || *to keep s.o. somewhere* no dejar a alguien salir de un sitio, tener a alguien encerrado en un sitio || *to keep sth. dry* impedir que se moje algo || *to keep to o.s.* guardarse; *he kept the secret to himself* se guardó el secreto || *to keep under lock and key* guardar bajo siete llaves, guardar bajo llave.

◆ *vi* seguir, continuar (to continue); *to keep singing* seguir cantando; *keep on this path* siga por este camino || conservarse; *wine doesn't keep once the bottle is opened* el vino no se conserva una vez abierta la botella || mantenerse; *he keeps in good health* se mantiene en buena salud || permanecer, seguir siendo (to remain); *to keep faithful to one's wife* seguir siendo fiel a su mujer || quedarse; *to keep in bed* quedarse en cama || no dejar de (to do sth. persistently); *he keeps asking me the time* no deja de preguntarme la hora || estarse, quedarse; *keep still!* ¡quédate quieto! || esperar (to wait); *that can keep till later* eso puede esperar hasta más tarde || vivir (to lodge) || — *how are you keeping?* ¿qué tal estás?, ¿cómo estás? || FIG *keep cool* no te pongas nervioso, tómatelo con calma || *to keep clear of* evitar, evitar todo contacto con || *to keep going* seguir (to persevere with an action); *you keep going until you come to a church* siga usted hasta llegar a una iglesia; *he kept going until she was exhausted* siguió hasta agotarla; seguir viviendo *or* con vida (to stay alive), ir tirando (to manage), seguir funcionando (a machine), continuar (to continue), durar (to last) || *to keep quiet* o *silent about* guardar silencio sobre || *to keep right* circular por la derecha, ceñirse a la derecha || *to keep well* estar bien de salud.

◆ *phr v* **to keep at** seguir con; *to keep at work* seguir con su trabajo | US importunar (to nag) || — *keep at it!* ¡ánimo! || *to keep at it* perseverar (to make an effort), insistir (to insist) || **to keep away** mantener a distancia (to stop from coming nearer); *to keep the photographers away* mantener a distancia a los fotógrafos | mantenerse a distancia (to stay at a distance) | alejar (to ward off); *to keep the devil away* alejar al demonio | no ir (not to go) | impedir (to prevent) || — *keep away!*; ¡no te acerques! || *to keep away from* no acercarse a (not to go near), evitar (to avoid), mantener alejado de (to prevent from going near) || *to keep medicines away from children* poner las medicinas fuera del alcance de los niños || **to keep back** contener; *the police kept back the crowd* la policía contuvo a la multitud; *to keep back one's tears* contener el llanto | no acercarse, mantenerse a distancia; *the crowd kept back* la gente no se acercó | ocultar; *he kept some of the facts back* ocultó algunos hechos | quedarse con; *I've kept back half of your money* me he quedado con la mitad de su dinero | retrasar (to delay) || **to keep down** contener (a rebellion) | oprimir (people) | mantenerse agachado (to avoid being spotted) | mantener bajo (temperature, price) || — *keep your head down* no levantes la cabeza || **to keep from** impedir; *they kept me from going out* me impidieron salir | evitar (to avoid) | mantener alejado de (to prevent from approaching) | ocultar; *he kept the facts from me* me ocultó los hechos | abstenerse de (to refrain from) || — *he kept me from being too bored* consiguió que no me aburriese demasiado || *I do it to keep from putting on weight* lo hago para no engordar || **to keep in** disimular; *he kept in his sadness* disimuló su tristeza | quedarse en casa, no salir (to stay indoors) | impedir salir, no dejar salir (to prevent from going out) | castigar a salir más tarde [del colegio] (school punishment) | mantener encendido, no dejar que se apague (a fire) || — *to keep in mind* acordarse de, recordar (to remember), tener en cuenta, tener presente (to take into account) || *to keep in with s.o.* mantenerse en buenos términos con alguien || **to keep off** mantenerse lejos *or* a distancia (de) (to stay away from) | mantener a distancia (to hold at a distance) | alejar (to ward off) | cerrar el paso a (to put a stop to) || — *if the rain keeps off* si no llueve || *keep off the grass* prohibido pisar el césped || *keep the dog off* no suelte al perro || *keep your hands off!* ¡no toques! || *private property, keep off* propiedad privada, prohibido el paso || *to keep off a subject* evitar un tema, no mencionar un tema || *to keep the sun, the rain off sth.* resguardar algo del sol, de la lluvia || **to keep on** no quitarse; *keep your coat on* no te quites el abrigo | seguir; *to keep on dancing* seguir bailando; *to keep on with sth.* seguir con algo | no dejar de; *he keeps on asking me* no deja de preguntarme | insistir; *don't keep on!* ¡no insistas! | no despedir, quedarse con (a servant), no apagar (lights) || — *to keep on at s.o.* estar siempre encima de alguien || **to keep out** no entrar, quedarse fuera | no dejar entrar, no admitir (not to admit) | no meterse (not to get involved in); *I'm keeping out of this* yo no me meto en eso; *to keep out of trouble* no meterse en líos || — *keep out* prohibida la entrada (sign) || *this coat will keep the cold out* este abrigo te resguardará del frío || **to keep to** quedarse en; *to keep to the house* quedarse en la casa | limitarse a (to restrict o.s. to) | cumplir con (a promise) | seguir (a direction) || — *he should keep to swimming* debería dedicarse a la natación || *to keep o.s. to o.s.* vivir apartado || *to keep s.o. to his* o *her word* cogerle a uno la palabra || *to keep sth. to o.s.* negarse a compartir algo || *to keep to one's bed* guardar cama || *to keep to the left* circular por la izquierda, ceñirse a la izquierda || *to keep to the original plan* seguir el proyecto original || **to keep together** poner juntos; *keep all the relevant papers together* ponga juntos todos los documentos pertinentes | mantenerse unidos || — *only the children keep their marriage together* sólo siguen juntos por los niños || *please keep together* no se separen || *put some string round it to keep it together* sujételo con una cuerda || **to keep under** dominar (one's passions) | someter, oprimir (people) || **to keep up** levantar; *keep your spirits up* levanta el ánimo | continuar, seguir; *the rain kept up all day* la lluvia continuó todo el día | tener en vela; *the baby kept me up all night* el niño me tuvo en vela toda la noche | no retrasarse en, no quedarse atrás en; *to keep up the payments* no retrasarse en el pago | seguir con; *I want to keep up my French* quiero seguir con el francés | mantener; *to keep up a property, a motor, traditions* mantener una propiedad, un motor, las tradiciones | sostener; *this keeps the ceiling up* esto sostiene el techo | sujetar; *my belt keeps my trousers up* el cinturón me sujeta los pantalones | mantener alto (a price) | FAM alojar (to lodge) || — *he'll never keep it up* no podrá resistir *or* aguantar || *I hope I'm not keeping you up* espero que no le estoy entreteniendo demasiado || *keep it up!* ¡sigue! || *to keep up appearances* guardar las apariencias || *to keep up with* seguir; *it is difficult to keep up with the class* es difícil seguir la clase || *he couldn't keep up with me* no podía mantenerse a mi ritmo || *to keep up with one's work* tener el trabajo al día || *to keep up with the Joneses* achantar a los vecinos || *to keep up with the times* ser muy de su época.

— OBSERV Pret y pp *kept*.

keeper [-ə*] *n* guarda *m* (guard) || dueño, ña (of a shop, boardinghouse) || guardabosque *m* (gamekeeper) || guarda *m*, guardián *m* (of zoo) || carcelero *m* (of a jail) || loquero *m* (of asylum) || conservador, ra (in museums, etc.) || archivero *m* (in records office) || ELECTR armadura *f* || pestillo *m* (small latch) || seguro *m* (safety latch) || *these apples are good keepers* estas manzanas se conservan muy bien.

keep fit [-fit] *n* ejercicios *m pl* físicos de mantenimiento.

keeping [-iŋ] *n* cargo *m*, cuidado *m* (care); *in s.o.'s keeping* al cuidado de alguien || observación *f*, cumplimiento *m* (of the law) || mantenimiento *m*, conservación *f* (upkeep) || — *in keeping with* de acuerdo con || *in safe keeping* en buenas manos, en lugar seguro || *out of keeping with* no de acuerdo con; *his behaviour is out of keeping with his profession* su comportamiento no está de acuerdo con su profesión || *wine improves with keeping* el vino mejora con el tiempo.

keepsake [-seik] *n* recuerdo *m*.

kefir [ke'fi:ə*] *n* kéfir *m*.

keg [keg] *n* barril *m*, cuñete *m*.

kelp [kelp] *n* BOT varec *m*, alga *f* marina.

kelson ['kelsn] *n* MAR sobrequilla *f*.

kelt [kelt] *n* ZOOL salmón *m* zancado.

Kelt [kelt] *n* celta *m* & *f* (Celt).

Keltic [-ik] *adj* celta (Celtic).

◆ *n* celta *m* (language).

ken [ken] *n* vista *f* (sight) || *beyond my ken* fuera de mis conocimientos *or* de mi alcance.

ken [ken] *vt* saber (to have knowledge of) || comprender (to understand) || conocer (to be acquainted with) || reconocer (to recognize).

kendo ['kendəu] *n* SP kendo *m*.

kennel [kenl] *n* caseta *f* para el perro (for a dog).

◆ *pl* perrera *f sing* (place where dogs are kept) || jauría *f sing* (pack of dogs).

kenotron ['kenə,trɔn] *n* kenotrón *m*.

Kentucky [ken'tʌki] *pr n* GEOGR Kentucky.

Kenya ['kenjə] *pr n* GEOGR Kenia.

Kenyan ['kenjən] *adj/n* keniano, na.

kepi ['keipi] *n* quepis *m* (cap).

kept [kept] *pret/pp* → **keep** || *kept woman* mujer mantenida.

keratin ['kerətin] *n* queratina *f*.

kerb [kə:b] *n* bordillo *m* (of the pavement) || brocal *m* (of a well) || *kerb crawler* conductor *m* que busca prostitutas desde su coche.

kerbstone ['kə:bstəun] *n* piedra *f* del bordillo.

kerchief ['kə:tʃif] *n* pañuelo *m* de cabeza.

kerf [kə:f] *n* corte *m*.

kerfuffle [kə'fʌfl] *n* FAM follón *m*.

kermes ['kə·miz] *n* quermes *m* (of an insect) || BOT coscoja *f*.

kermes oak [-'əuk] *n* BOT coscoja *f*.

kermess; kermis ['kə:mis] *n* kermesse *f*, quermese *f*, verbena *f*.

kernel ['kə:nl] *n* FIG meollo *m*, núcleo *m*, médula *f* (centre of argument, etc.) || pepita *f* (of a fruit) || grano *f* (of wheat).

kerosene; kerosine ['kerəsi:n] *n* queroseno *m*.

kerseymere ['kə:zimiə*] *n* cachemira *f* (cloth).

kestrel ['kestrəl] *n* cernícalo *m* (bird).

ketch [ketʃ] *n* MAR queche *m*.

ketchup ['ketʃəp] *n* salsa *f* de tomate.

ketone ['ki:təun] *n* CHEM acetona *f*.

kettle ['ketl] *n* hervidor *m* [en forma de tetera] (for boiling water) ‖ US olla *f* (large pot) ‖ — FIG *that's a different kettle of fish* eso es harina de otro costal | *to get into a fine kettle of fish* meterse en un berenjenal.

kettledrum [-drʌm] *n* MUS timbal *m*.

kevel ['kevl] *n* MAR cornamusa *f*.

key [ki:] *n* llave *f* (for a lock, for clockwork) ‖ clave *f* (of a code, map, diagram, etc.) ‖ TECH chaveta *f*, clavija *f* (pin, wedge in metalwork) | espiga *f*, clavija *f* (in woodwork) | cuña *f* (wedge for a stretch frame) ‖ ARCH clave *f* (keystone) ‖ MUS tono *m*; *major key* tono mayor | tecla *f* (of a piano) | llave *f*, pistón *m* (of wind instruments) ‖ tecla *f* (of typewriter); *back space key* tecla de retroceso ‖ FIG llave *f*; *that port is the key to the country* ese puerto es la llave del país | clave *f*; *the key to the problem, to the puzzle* la clave del problema, del enigma ‖ clave *f* (book of answers) ‖ ELECTR llave *f*, conmutador *m* (switch which opens or cuts a circuit) | manipulador *m* (of a telegraph) ‖ GEOGR cayo *m*, isleta *f* (reef or low island) ‖ FIG tono *m*; *speaking in a plaintive key* hablando en tono lastimero ‖ — *master key* llave maestra ‖ MUS *off key, out of key* desafinado, da (out of tune) ‖ *skeleton key* ganzúa *f* ‖ MUS *to be in key* llevar el tono, estar afinado | *to play, to sing out of key* desafinar ‖ FIG *to touch the right key* tocar la cuerda sensible (to find s.o.'s soft spot).
◆ *adj* clave (essential); *key industry* industria clave; *key position* posición clave.

key [ki:] *vt* TECH calzar con chavetas (metalwork) | acuñar (to tighten a stretch frame) ‖ MUS afinar (to tune up) ‖ FIG poner a tono con (to harmonize with) ‖ — INFORM *to key in* entrar, introducir (data) ‖ FIG *to key up* emocionar, excitar.

keyboard [-bɔ:d] *n* teclado *m* (of piano, typewriter, etc.).

keyhole [-həul] *n* ojo *m* de la cerradura.

keyman [-mæn] *n* hombre *m* clave.
— OBSERV El plural es *keymen* (hombres clave).

keymask [-ma:sk] *n* INFORM máscara *f*.

keynote [-nəut] *n* MUS nota *f* tónica, tónica *f* ‖ FIG piedra *f* angular, idea *f* fundamental ‖ FIG *keynote address* discurso *m* inaugural, discurso *m* de apertura.

keypad [-pæd] *n* teclado *m* numérico.

key punch [-pʌntʃ] *n* perforadora *f* (for computers).

key ring [-riŋ] *n* llavero *m*.

key signature [-'signitʃə*] *n* MUS armadura *f*.

keystone [-stəun] *n* ARCH clave *f* ‖ FIG piedra *f* angular.

keystroke [-strəuk] *n* pulsación *f* de una tecla.

Key West [-'west] *pr n* GEOGR Cayo *m* Hueso.

keyword [-wɔ:d] *n* INFORM palabra *f* clave.

khaki ['ka:ki] *n* caqui *m* (colour) ‖ tela *f* caqui (cloth).
◆ *adj* caqui *inv*.

khan [ka:n] *n* kan *m* (title) ‖ mesón *m* (inn).

khanate [ka:neit] *n* kanato *m*.

Khartoum [ka:'tu:m] *pr n* GEOGR Jartum.

khedive [ke'di:v] *n* jedive *m*.

kibbutz [ki'buts] *n* kibutz *m*.
— OBSERV El plural de *kibbutz* es *kibbutzim*.

kibitzer ['kibətsə*] *n* FAM mirón, ona.

kibosh ['kaibɔʃ] *n* FAM tonterías *f pl* ‖ *to put the kibosh on sth.* poner término a algo.

kick [kik] *n* patada *f*, puntapié *m* (act or instance of kicking); *to give s.o. a kick in the pants* darle a uno una patada en el trasero ‖ coz *f* (of an animal) ‖ retroceso *m*, culatazo *m* (recoil of a firearm) ‖ FIG fuerza *f* (energy) ‖ SP tiro *m* (in football); *a kick at goal* un tiro a gol | golpe *m*; *free kick* golpe franco | patada *f* (in rugby) | piernas *f pl*, movimiento *m* de las piernas (in swimming); *you must improve your kick* tienes que mejorar el movimiento de las piernas ‖ — FAM *not to get a kick out of sth.* no encontrar la gracia a algo ‖ SP *to be* o *to have a good kick* tener buen tiro (in football), tener buena patada (in rugby) ‖ FAM *to do sth. for kicks* hacer algo porque le hace gracia a uno, hacer algo para divertirse | *to get a kick out of sth.* encontrar placer en algo | *to have a kick* ser muy fuerte, ser tónico, ca; *this drink has a kick in it* esta bebida es tónica.

kick [kik] *vt* dar un puntapié a, dar una patada a (a person or an object) ‖ dar una coz a (animals) ‖ dar culatazo en (a firearm) ‖ SP marcar, meter (to score); *to kick a goal, a penalty* marcar un gol, un penalty | pasar (de una patada); *he kicked the ball to me* me pasó la pelota ‖ mandar de una patada; *he kicked the bottle across the room* de una patada mandó la botella al otro lado de la habitación ‖ dar patadas a; *he walked down the road kicking a ball* bajó la calle dando patadas a una pelota ‖ mover; *to kick one's legs* mover las piernas | FAM librarse de (to get rid of) ‖ — FIG *he could have kicked himself* se comió los puños de rabia, se dio de cabeza contra la pared ‖ *to kick a man when he's down* dar patadas a un hombre cuando ya está en el suelo (real sense), dar la puntilla (figurative sense) ‖ FIG *to kick one's heels* estar de plantón | *to kick s.o. upstairs* deshacerse de alguien dándole un puesto honorífico | *to kick the bucket* estirar la pata, hincar el pico (to die).
◆ *vi* dar patadas, dar puntapiés (to strike out with the foot) ‖ dar coces (animals) ‖ dar culatazo, retroceder (to recoil, of a firearm) ‖ SP mover las piernas (in swimming) | chutar (in football) ‖ FIG protestar mucho ‖ — FIG & FAM *to be alive and kicking* estar vivito y coleando | *to be still kicking* no haber abandonado la lucha.
◆ *phr v* ***to kick against*** oponerse a ‖ ***to kick around*** o ***about*** dar patadas a (a ball) | tratar a patadas, dar malos tratos a (a person) | andar rodando (to hang about) | dar vueltas a (an idea, a project, etc.) ‖ — *it's kicking around here somewhere* está rodando por aquí ‖ ***to kick aside*** apartar con una patada ‖ ***to kick back*** devolver (a football) | retroceder (a crank) | dar culatazo (a gun) | FIG devolver golpe por golpe (to strike back) ‖ ***to kick down*** derribar ‖ ***to kick in*** derribar a patadas (a door) | tirar de una patada; *he kicked her in the river* le tiró de una patada al agua | FAM estirar la pata (to die) ‖ ***to kick off*** empezar; *to kick off a party with a song* empezar una fiesta cantando | hacer el saque de centro (in sports) | US FAM estirar la pata (to die) ‖ ***to kick out*** echar a patadas, poner de patitas en la calle; *they kicked him out of the bar* le echaron a patadas del bar | dar patadas, dar puntapiés (to strike out with the foot) | dar coces (an animal) ‖ ***to kick over*** tirar de una patada ‖ ***to kick up*** levantar (dust) | ponerse furioso (to get angry) | subir, aumentar (prices, etc.) | FAM *to kick up a dust* o *a row* armar un escándalo; *to kick up a fuss* armar un escándalo, armar un follón; *to kick up one's heels* echar una cana al aire.

kickback [-bæk] *n* retroceso *m*, culatazo *m* (of firearm) ‖ US comisión *f* (money) | reacción *f* (of a person).

kicker [-ə*] *n* SP chutador *m* ‖ coceador, ra [AMER pateador, ra] ‖ FIG & FAM *to be a kicker* tener agallas (to be a fighter).

kickoff [-'ɔf] *n* SP saque *m* del centro ‖ FIG & FAM principio *m*, comienzo *m* ‖ FIG & FAM *for a kickoff* para empezar.

kickshaw [-ʃɔ:] *n* FAM golosina *f* (tidbit) | fruslería *f* (trinket).

kickstand [-stænd] *n* soporte *m* (on bikes, motorcycles).

kick starter [-'sta:tə*]; **kick-start** [-sta:t] *n* arranque *m*, pedal *m* de arranque.

kid [kid] *n* ZOOL cabrito *m* ‖ cabritilla *f* (skin); *kid gloves* guantes de cabritilla ‖ cría *f* (young of various animals) ‖ niño, ña; crío, cría (child, young person) ‖ — FIG *to handle with kid gloves* tratar con guante blanco | *kid stuff, kid's stuff* cosas *f pl* de niños (childish), facilísimo, tirado (very easy); *it's kid's stuff* está tirado, es facilísimo.

kid [kid] *vt* FAM meter la trola de; *David kidded me that he'd broken his arm* David me metió la trola de que se había roto el brazo | tomar el pelo a; *stop kidding me* deja de tomarme el pelo ‖ *to kid o.s. that* hacerse la ilusión de que.
◆ *vi* bromear ‖ parir (a goat) ‖ — *¿are you kidding?* ¿en serio? ‖ *he was only kidding* estaba bromeando, lo decía en broma ‖ *no kidding!* ¡no me digas! ‖ *you're kidding!* ¡no me digas!, ¡no estarás hablando en serio!

kidder [-ə*] *n* bromista *m* & *f*.

kiddy ['kidi] *n* crío, cría (child).

kidnap ['kidnæp] *vt* raptar, secuestrar.

kidnapper [-ə*] *n* raptor, ra; secuestrador, ra.

kidnapping [-iŋ] *n* rapto *m*, secuestro *m*.

kidney ['kidni] *n* ANAT riñón *m* ‖ FIG índole *f* ‖ CULIN riñón *m*.

kidney bean [-bi:n] *n* judía *f*, alubia *f* [AMER frijol *m*, poroto *m*] (bean) ‖ US alubia *f* pinta.

kidney machine [-mə'ʃi:n] *n* MED riñón *m* artificial.

kidney stone [-stəun] *n* MED cálculo *m* renal.

kidskin ['kidskin] *n* cabritilla *f*.

kier [kiə*] *n* TECH autoclave *m* para blanquear.

kieselguhr; kieselgur ['ki:zəlgu:ə] *n* MIN kieselgur *m*.

kieserite ['ki:zə,rait] *n* MIN kieserita *f*.

kif [kif] *n* kif *m*.

kilderkin ['kildəkin] *n* pequeño barril *m*.

Kilimanjaro (Mount) [,kilimən'dʒa:rəu] *pr n* GEOGR monte Kilimanjaro.

kill [kil] *n* muerte *f* (in hunting, bullfighting) ‖ caza *f*, cacería *f* (the animals killed in a hunt).

kill [kil] *vt* matar; *the dog was killed by a car* el perro fue matado por un coche; *he killed his wife's lover* mató al amante de su mujer ‖ FIG echar abajo; *to kill a bill* echar abajo un proyecto de ley | acabar con, arruinar; *this has killed my hopes* esto ha acabado con mis esperanzas | amortiguar (sound) | matar, acabar con; *this work is killing me* este trabajo me está matando, este trabajo acabará conmigo | hacer morir de risa; *that joke killed me* ese chiste me hizo morir de risa | hundir (a boat) ‖ FIG & FAM apagar, parar (a motor) ‖ SP parar (in football) ‖ sacrificar, matar (to slaughter animals) ‖ FIG suprimir (to prevent publication of) ‖ — FIG *the suspense was killing me* el suspenso me tenía en vilo | *this will kill you!* ¡te vas a morir de risa! | *to kill off* exterminar ‖ *to kill o.s.* matarse ‖ FIG *to kill the flavour of sth.* quitar el sabor de algo | *to kill time* matar el tiempo | *to kill two birds with one stone* matar dos pájaros de un tiro.
◆ *vi* matar (to destroy life) ‖ FIG *to be dressed to kill* estar de punta en blanco *or* de tiros largos.

killer [-ə*] *n* asesino, na (one who kills) ‖ — *this disease is a killer* esta enfermedad es mortal || FAM *this joke is a killer* este chiste es para morirse de risa.

killer whale ['kilə'weil] *n* ZOOL orca *f.*

killick ['kilik] *n* piedra *f* que sirve de ancla.

killing ['kiliŋ] *adj* mortal (mortal) || asesino, na (murderous) || FAM agotador, ra; matador, ra (exhausting) | para morirse de risa (irresistibly funny) | asesino, na (fierce); *a killing glance* una mirada asesina.

◆ *n* asesinato *m* (murder) || matanza *f* (slaughter, massacre) || US FAM buena operación *f,* éxito *m* (financial coup) || FAM *to make a killing* hacer su agosto, forrarse.

killjoy ['kildʒɔi] *n* aguafiestas *m* & *f inv.*

kill-or-cure ['kilɔ:'kjuə*] *adj* FAM de caballo (remedy).

kiln [kiln] *n* horno *m.*

kiln-dry [-drai] *vt* secar al horno.

kilo ['ki:ləu] *n* kilo *m.*

kilobyte ['ki:ləubait] *n* INFORM kilobyte *m.*

kilocalorie ['ki:ləu,kæləri] *n* kilocaloría *f.*

kilocycle ['ki:ləu,saikl] *n* kilociclo *m.*

kilogram; kilogramme ['kiləugræm] *n* kilogramo *m.*

kilogram calorie [-'kæləri] *n* kilocaloría *f.*

kilogram-metre; US **kilogram-meter** ['kiləugræ,mi:tə*] *n* kilográmetro *m.*

kilohertz ['kiləu,hə:ts] *n* kilohercio *m.*

kilojoule ['ki:ləudʒu:l] *n* kilojulio *m.*

kilolitre; US **kiloliter** ['ki:ləu,li:tə*] *n* kilolitro *m.*

kilometre; US **kilometer** ['kiləu,mi:tə*] *n* kilómetro *m.*

kilometric ['kiləu,metrik] *adj* kilométrico, ca.

kiloton ['ki:ləutʌn] *n* kilotón *m* (en física nuclear).

kilovolt ['ki:ləuvəult] *n* kilovoltio *m.*

kilowatt ['kiləuwɔt] *n* kilovatio *m.*

kilowatt-hour [-'auə*] *n* kilovatio-hora *m.*

kilt [kilt] *n* falda *f* escocesa, «kilt» *m.*

kilt [kilt] *vt* plegar (to pleat).

kimono [ki'məunəu] *n* kimono *m,* quimono *m.*

kin [kin] *n* parientes *m pl,* familia *f* (relatives) || *next of kin* pariente más cercano, parientes más cercanos.

◆ *adj* emparentado, da (kindred).

kinaesthesia [,kainis'θi:zjə] *n* cinestesia *f.*

kinaesthesis; kinesthesis [,kainis'θi:sis] *n* cinestesia *f.*

kind [kaind] *adj* amable, amistoso, sa (friendly, helpful); *kind words* palabras amables || bueno, na; cariñoso, sa; *kind to animals* cariñoso con los animales || amable, bondadoso, sa (well-disposed); *kind to his servants* amable con sus sirvientes || comprensivo, va (understanding) || favorable (favourable) || benigno, na; *a kind climate* un clima benigno || bueno, na (beneficial); *kind to the skin* bueno para el cutis || — *be so kind as to...* sea tan amable de..., tenga la bondad de... || *it is very kind of you* es muy amable de su parte || *kind regards* muchos recuerdos || *that wasn't very kind of them* no fue muy simpático de su parte || *the critics were not kind to his book* los críticos han sido bastante duros con su libro || *they were kind enough to...* tuvieron la amabilidad de... || *would you be so kind as to...?* ¿me haría Ud. el favor de...? ¿tendría Ud. la bondad de...?

◆ *n* clase *f,* tipo *m; a different kind of wine* una clase diferente de vino || tipo *m; what kind of car do you drive?* ¿qué tipo de coche conduces? || clase *f,* tipo *m; I am not that kind of person* no soy de esa clase de personas || índole *f,* carácter *m; they are different in kind* son de distinta índole || cantidad *f; I haven't got that kind of money* no tengo esa cantidad de dinero || especie *f; a kind of grey* una especie de gris || género *m,* especie *f; other animals of their kind* otros animales de su misma especie; *human kind* especie humana || REL especie *f* (for communion) || — *a kind of* cierto, ta; *there is a kind of harmony* hay una cierta armonía || *in a kind way* en cierta manera || *in kind* en especie; *payment in kind* pago en especie || *nothing of the kind* nada por el estilo || *of a kind* de la misma especie *or* clase (belonging to the same group), una especie de; *coffee of a kind* una especie de café || *of all kinds* de todas clases, toda clase de; *food of all kinds* toda clase de comida || *of the kind* parecido, casi igual, por el estilo; *he has sth. of the kind* tiene algo parecido || *they are the kind who don't care* son de los que no se preocupan || *they are two of a kind* son tal para cual || FIG *to repay in kind* pagar con la misma moneda.

◆ *adv* FAM *I kind of liked her* en cierta manera la quería | *I'm kind of tired* estoy como *or* algo cansado | *it's kind of round* es como redondo | *I've kind of got a headache* tengo una especie de dolor de cabeza, tengo como un dolor de cabeza.

kindergarten ['kindəgɑ:tn] *n* jardín *m* de la infancia, colegio *m* de párvulos, «kindergarten» *m* (school for young children).

kindhearted ['kaind'hɑ:tid] *adj* bondadoso, sa; de buen corazón.

kindheartedness [-nis] *n* bondad *f,* buen corazón *f* (kindness).

kindle ['kindl] *vt* encender || FIG encender, atizar, provocar; *to kindle anger, passion* encender la ira, la pasión | despertar (interest, suspicions).

◆ *vi* encenderse || FIG inflamarse.

kindliness ['kaindlinis] *n* bondad *f,* amabilidad *f* (goodness) || benignidad *f* (of climate).

kindling ['kindliŋ] *n* encendimiento *m* (act of lighting) || leña *f,* astillas *f pl* (firewood) || FIG encendimiento *m* (of passion, etc.).

kindly ['kaindli] *adj* amable, bondadoso, sa (person) || amable, cariñoso, sa (remark) || agradable (place) || benigno, na (climate) || favorable (wind).

◆ *adv* amablemente (nicely) || bondadosamente (gently) || por favor; *kindly come this way* venga por aquí, por favor || — *to look kindly on sth.* mirar algo con buenos ojos || *to take kindly to* aceptar gustoso || *to take sth. kindly* tomar algo bien, apreciar algo.

kindness ['kaindnis] *n* amabilidad *f,* bondad *f* (*to* con) (quality of being kind); *he had the kindness to bring me flowers* tuvo la amabilidad de traerme flores || buen trato *m* (*to* de) (animals) || atención *f,* consideración *f* (consideration) || — *to do s.o. a kindness* hacerle un favor a alguien, tener una amabilidad con alguien || *to show kindness to s.o.* mostrarse amable con alguien.

kindred ['kindrid] *adj* emparentado, da (related by blood) || de tronco común (of common origin); *kindred languages* idiomas de tronco común || similar, semejante, afín (similar) || *kindred spirits* almas gemelas.

◆ *n* parientes *m pl* (kin) || parentesco *m* (kinship).

kine [kain] *pl n* (ant) vacas *f* (cows) || ganado *m sing* (cattle).

— OBSERV La palabra *kine* es el plural antiguo de *cow.*

kinematic [,kaini'mætik] *adj* cinemático, ca.

kinematics [-s] *n* cinemática *f.*

kinematograph [,kaini'mætəugrɑ:f] *n* cinematógrafo *m.*

kinescope ['kinəskəup] *n* cinescopio *m.*

kinesitherapy [kinisi'θerəpi] *n* kinesiterapia *f.*

kinesthesia [,kainis'θi:zjə] *n* cinestesia *f.*

kinetic [kai'netik] *adj* cinético, ca || *kinetic energy* energía cinética.

kinetics [-s] *n* cinética *f.*

kinfolk ['kinfəuk] *pl n* US (ant) parientes *m.*

king [kiŋ] *n* rey *m; King Charles* el rey Carlos; *the lion is the king of the jungle* el león es el rey de la selva; *the king of Spanish football* el rey del fútbol español || rey *m* (in chess, card games) || dama *f* (in draughts) || — *book of Kings* libro *m* de los Reyes || *King of kings* Rey de reyes || *King of Rome* Rey de Roma || *the Sun king* el rey Sol || *the three Kings* los Reyes Magos || *to live, to treat like a king* vivir, tratar a cuerpo de rey.

kingbolt [-bəult] *n* TECH clavija *f* maestra, pivote *m* central.

king cobra [-'kəubrə] *n* ZOOL cobra *f* real.

kingcup ['kiŋkʌp] *n* BOT botón *m* de oro.

kingdom [-dəm] *n* reino *m* || — FAM *kingdom come* el otro mundo; *to blast s.o. to kingdom come* enviar a alguien al otro mundo || *the animal kingdom* el reino animal || *the plant kingdom* el reino vegetal || FAM *till kingdom come* hasta el Día del Juicio.

kingfisher [-,fiʃə*] *n* martín *m* pescador (bird).

kinglet [-lit] *n* reyezuelo *m.*

kingly [-li] *adj* real.

king of arms [-əv'ɑ:mz] *n* rey *m* de armas.

kingpin [-pin] *n* bolo *m* central (in bowling) || TECH clavija *f* maestra, pivote *m* central || FIG persona *f* clave (key person) | alma *f* (of a team) | piedra *f* angular (essential thing).

king post [-pəust] *n* ARCH pendolón *m.*

Kings [-z] *n* REL libro *m* de los Reyes (in the Bible).

King's Bench [-z'bentʃ] *n* HIST & JUR Tribunal *m* Supremo.

king's bishop [-z'biʃəp] *n* alfil rey *m.*

king's evil [-z'i:vl] *n* escrófula *f.*

kingship [-ʃip] *n* realeza *f,* majestad *f* (royalty) || monarquía *f* (monarchy) || trono *m* (throne).

king-size [-saiz] *adj* enorme, gigante (huge) || *king-size cigarettes* cigarrillos largos.

Kingston ['kiŋstən] *pr n* GEOGR Kingston.

kink [kiŋk] *n* retorcimiento *m* (twist or loop in a cable, pipe, etc.) || rizo *m* (in hair) || arruga *f,* pliegue *m* (crease, fold) || MED tortícolis *f inv* || FAM chifladura *f,* manía *f* (mental twist) || fallo *m,* defecto *m* (defect).

kink [kiŋk] *vt* retorcer (to twist).

◆ *vi* retorcerse || ensortijarse, rizarse (hair).

kinky [kiŋki] *adj* retorcido, da (twisted) || ensortijado, da; rizado, da (curly) || FAM chiflado, da (crazy) | extraño, ña; raro, ra (strange).

kino ['ki:nəu] *n* quino *m.*

kinsfolk ['kiŋzfəuk] *pl n* parientes *m.*

Kinshasa [kin'ʃæsə] *pr n* GEOGR Kinshasa.

kinship ['kiŋʃip] *n* parentesco *m* (family relationship) || afinidad *f* (similarity).

kinsman ['kinzmən] *n* pariente *m.*

— OBSERV El plural de *kinsman* es *kinsmen.*

kinswoman ['kinz,wumən] *n* parienta *f.*

— OBSERV El plural de *kinswoman* es *kinswomen.*

kiosk [ki'ɔsk] *n* quiosco *m,* kiosco *m.*

kip [kip] *n* piel *f* de cordero *or* de becerro (animal hide) || FAM catre *m,* piltra *f* (bed) | pensión *f* (boardinghouse) | alojamiento *m* (lodging) || — FAM *to have a kip* echar una cabezada | *you* *ought to get some kip* deberías dormir un poco *or* echar una cabezada.

kip [kip] *vi* dormir; *he's kipping* está durmiendo.

kipper [-ə*] *n* arenque *m or* salmón *m* ahumado y salado.

kipper [-ə*] *vt* curar, ahumar.

kirk [kəːk] *n* iglesia *f* ‖ *the Kirk* la Iglesia (Presbiteriana) de Escocia.

kirsch [kiəʃ] *n* kirsch *m*.

kismet ['kismet] *n* destino *m*.

kiss [kis] *n* beso *m*; *give me a kiss* dame un beso ‖ roce *m* (light touch) ‖ merengue *m* (sweet) ‖ — *the kiss of life* respiración *f* boca a boca ‖ *to blow s.o. a kiss* enviar un beso a alguien.

kiss [kis] *vt* besar; *to kiss the hand* besar la mano ‖ rozar (to touch lightly) ‖ — *to kiss away* hacer olvidar con besos | *to kiss s.o. goodbye* dar un beso de despedida a alguien ‖ FIG *to kiss sth. goodbye* despedirse de algo, decir adiós a algo | *to kiss the ground* besar el suelo.
◆ *vi* besarse ‖ rozarse (balls in billiards) ‖ *they kissed* se besaron, se dieron un beso.

kissagram ['kisəugræm] *n* telegrama *m* entregado con un beso.

kiss-curl [-kəːl] *n* caracol *m* (of hair).

kisser [-ə*] *n* FAM besucón, ona (person) | morro *m*, boca *f* (mouth) | jeta *f* (face).

kissproof [-pruːf] *adj* indeleble (lipstick).

kit [kit] *n* herramientas *f pl* (tools); *a plumber's kit* las herramientas del fontanero ‖ caja *f* de las herramientas (box) ‖ botiquín *m* (first-aid) ‖ MIL & SP equipo *m* ‖ equipaje *m*, equipo *m* (equipment, gear) ‖ grupo *m*, conjunto *m* (group) | maqueta *f* (toy model to be assembled) | avíos *m pl*; *washing kit* avíos de aseo; *shoe cleaning kit* avíos de limpiar zapatos ‖ conjunto *m* de piezas [para montar un coche, una radio, etc.] ‖ FAM *the whole kit and caboodle* toda la pesca.

kit [kit] *vt* equipar ‖ *to kit out* equipar.

kit bag [-bæg] *n* macuto *m* (knapsack) ‖ bolsa *f* (canvas bag).

kitchen [kitʃin] *n* cocina *f*.

kitchen boy [-bɔi] *n* pinche *m*.

kitchener [-ə*] *n* cocinero *m*.

kitchenette [ˌkitʃi'net] *n* cocina *f* pequeña.

kitchen garden ['kitʃin'gɑːdn] *n* huerto *m*.

kitchen maid ['kitʃinmeid] *n* ayudanta *f* de cocinera.

kitchen police ['kitʃinpə'liːs] *n* US MIL servicio *m* de cocina.

kitchen range ['kitʃinreindʒ] *n* cocina *f* económica.

kitchen sink ['kitʃin'siŋk] *n* fregadero *m*, pila *f* de cocina.

kitchen-sink drama [-'drɑːmə] *n* THEATR comedia *f* de costumbres.

kitchenware ['kitʃiɛwɛə*] *n* utensilios *m pl* de cocina, batería *f* de cocina.

kite [kait] *n* ZOOL milano *m* (bird) ‖ cometa *f* (toy) ‖ COMM cheque *m* sin fondos ‖ FIG *to fly a kite* lanzar una idea para tantear el terreno.
◆ *pl* MAR sobrejuanete *m sing*.

Kite-mark [-maːk] *n* marchamo *m* oficial de calidad.

kith [kiθ] *n* amigos *m pl* (friends) ‖ *kith and kin* parientes y amigos.

kit inspection [kitin'spekʃən] *n* revista *f*.

kitsch [kitʃ] *adj* kitsch, cursi, de mal gusto.
◆ *n* kitsch *m*.

kitten ['kitn] *n* gatito *m* ‖ — FAM *she'll have kittens!* ¡le dará un ataque! | *we almost had kittens!* ¡casi nos morimos del susto!

kitten ['kitn] *vi* parir (a cat).

kittenish [-iʃ] *adj* coquetón, ona.

kittiwake ['kitiweik] *n* ZOOL gaviota *f* (sea gull).

kitty ['kiti] *n* plato *m*, platillo *m*, bote *m* (into which each player puts a stake) ‖ FAM fondo *m* común, reserva *f* (of money, goods, etc.) | gatito *m* (kitten).

kiwi ['kiːwi] *n* ZOOL kiwi *m* (bird).

kiwi fruit *n* BOT kiwi *m*.

KKK *abbr of [Ku Klux Klan]* Kukluxklán (United States).

klaxon ['klæksn] *n* claxon *m*, klaxon *m*.

kleptomania [ˌkleptəu'meinjə] *n* cleptomanía *f*.

kleptomaniac [ˌkleptəu'meiniæk] *n* cleptómano, na.

knack [næk] *n* facilidad *f*; *a knack for remembering names* facilidad para recordar nombres ‖ tranquillo *m*, truco *m*; *it's easy once you get the knack* es fácil una vez que le coges el tranquillo ‖ habilidad *f*, maña *f*; *to have the knack of doing sth.* tener maña para hacer algo ‖ don *m*; *to have the knack of doing the right thing* tener el don de hacer lo que se debe.

knacker [-ə*] *n* matarife *m*, descuartizador *m* (for horses) ‖ desguazador *m* (for cars, etc.).

knackered [-əd] *adj* FAM hecho, cha polvo; molido, da.

knag [næg] *n* nudo *m* (in wood).

knap [næp] *vt* golpear (to knock) ‖ picar (stones) ‖ mordisquear (to bite).

knapsack [-sæk] *n* mochila *f*.

knar [nɑː*] *n* nudo *m* (in wood).

knave [neiv] *n* bribón *m*, granuja *m*, bellaco *m* (rogue) ‖ sota *f* (in Spanish cards) ‖ jota *f* (in international cards).

knavery ['neivəri] *n* bribonada *f*, bribonería *f*, bellaquería *f*, picardía *f*.

knavish ['neiviʃ] *adj* bribón, ona; bellaco, ca; picaresco, ca (roguish).

knead [niːd] *vt* amasar (dough, clay) ‖ dar masaje a (to massage) ‖ FIG formar, moldear (to shape).

kneading trough [-iŋtrɔf] *n* artesa *f*, amasadera *f*.

knee [niː] *n* ANAT rodilla *f*; *he was on his knees* estaba de rodillas; *down on one's knees* de rodillas; *to bend* o *to bow the knee* doblar la rodilla ‖ TECH codo *m* ‖ rodillera *f* (part of a garment that covers the knee) ‖ — *to bring s.o. to his* o *her knees* poner a alguien de rodillas ‖ *to go down on one's knees* arrodillarse ‖ *to go down on one's knees to s.o.* suplicar a alguien de rodillas.

knee [niː] *vt* dar con la rodilla a.

knee breeches [-britʃiz] *pl n* calzón *m sing* corto.

kneecap [-kæp] *n* ANAT rótula *f*.

knee-deep [-diːp] *adj* *the water was knee-deep* el agua llegaba hasta las rodillas ‖ *to be knee-deep in water* estar metido en el agua hasta las rodillas.

knee-high [-hai] *adj* *the grass was knee-high* la hierba llegaba hasta las rodillas.

kneehole desk ['niːhəul'desk] *n* mesa *f* con un hueco para meter las rodillas, mesa *f* de despacho.

knee jerk ['niːdʒəːk] *n* reflejo *m* rotuliano *or* de la rótula.

knee joint ['niːdʒɔint] *n* ANAT articulación *f* de la rodilla ‖ TECH junta *f* articulada.

kneel* [niːl] *vi* arrodillarse ‖ — *to be kneeling* estar de rodillas ‖ *to kneel down* ponerse de rodillas, arrodillarse.
— OBSERV Pret y pp *knelt, kneeled*.

knee-length ['niːleŋə] *adj* hasta las rodillas.

kneeling chair ['niːliŋtʃɛə*] *n* REL reclinatorio *m*.

kneepad ['niːpæd] *n* rodillera *f*.

kneepan ['niːpæn] *n* ANAT rótula *f*.

knees-up ['niːsʌp] *n* FAM juerga *f*.

knell [nel] *n* toque *m* de difuntos, tañido *m* fúnebre ‖ FIG fin *m* (end); *to sound the knell of* anunciar el fin de.

knelt [nelt] *pret/pp* ⟶ **kneel.**

knew [njuː] *pret* ⟶ **know.**

knickerbockers ['nikəbɔkəz] *pl n* bombachos *m* (trousers).

knickers ['nikəz] *pl n* bragas *f* (women's panties) ‖ bombachos *m* (knickerbockers).

knickknack ['niknæk] *n* chuchería *f*.

knife [naif] *n* cuchillo *m* (cutting instrument); *bread, butter knife* cuchillo para el pan, para la mantequilla ‖ navaja *f* (with folding blade) ‖ cuchilla *f* (cutting blade in a machine) ‖ MED bisturí *m* (scalpel) ‖ — *knife and fork* cubierto *m* (cutlery) ‖ *to get one's knife into s.o.* tener rabia *or* manía a alguien.
— OBSERV El plural de *knife* es *knives*.

knife [naif] *vt* cortar con cuchillo (to cut with a knife) ‖ apuñalar (to stab) ‖ US FIG dar una puñalada trapera (to stab s.o. in the back).

knife-edge [-edʒ] *n* filo *m* ‖ FIG *to be balancing on a knife-edge* estar pendiente de un hilo.

knife grinder [-ˌgraində*] *n* afilador *m*.

knife switch [-switʃ] *n* ELECTR interruptor *m* de cuchilla.

knifing ['naifiŋ] *n* pelea *f* con navajas.

knight [nait] *n* caballero *m*; *the knights of the Round Table* los caballeros de la Tabla Redonda ‖ caballo *m* (in chess).

knight [nait] *vt* armar caballero ‖ FIG conceder el título de «Sir» a.

knight-errant [-'erənt] *n* caballero *m* andante ‖ FIG Don Quijote *m* (defender of just causes).
— OBSERV El plural de *knight-errant* es *knights-errant*.

knight-errantry ['erəntri] *n* caballería *f* errante ‖ FIG quijotismo *m* (defence of just causes).

knighthood [-hud] *n* caballería *f* (knights) ‖ título *m* de caballero (rank) ‖ FIG título *m* de «Sir».

knightly [-li] *adj* caballeresco, ca; *knightly deeds* hazañas caballerescas.

Knight Templer [-'templə*] *n* templario *m*.

knit [nit] *n* punto *m* (a stitch in knitting) ‖ *knit goods* géneros *m* de punto.

knit* [nit] *vt* tejer; *to knit a dress* tejer un traje ‖ juntar, unir (to join together) ‖ — *to knit one's brows* fruncir el ceño *or* el entrecejo ‖ FIG *to knit up* poner punto final a.
◆ *vi* hacer punto [AMER hacer malla, tejer, tricotar] ‖ *Elena likes knitting* a Elena le gusta hacer punto ‖ unirse, soldarse (to unite) ‖ soldarse (bones).
— OBSERV Pret y pp *knit, knitted*.

knitter [-ə*] *n* persona *f* que hace punto.

knitting [-iŋ] *n* tejido *m* de punto (cloth) ‖ punto *m* de aguja, labor *f* de punto (process) ‖ *I must do some knitting* tengo que hacer punto.

knitting machine ['nitiŋməʃiːn] *n* máquina *f* de hacer punto, tricotosa *f*.

knitting needle ['nitiŋˌniːdl] *n* aguja *f* de hacer punto [AMER aguja de tejer].

knitwear ['nitwɛə*] *n* artículos *m pl or* géneros *m pl* de punto.

knives [naivz] *pl n* ⟶ **knife.**

knob [nɔb] *n* bulto *m*, protuberancia *f* (protuberance) || tirador *m* (of a drawer) || botón *m* (of a radio) || nudo *m* (on a tree) || pomo *m* (of a door, stick, sword) || terrón *m*; *sugar knob* terrón de azúcar || pedazo *m* (of butter, coal) || US loma *f*, montículo *m* (hillock).

knobble [nɔbl] *n* bulto *m* pequeño.

knobbly ['nɔbly]; **knobby** ['nɔbi] *adj* nudoso, sa; *knobbly tree* árbol nudoso || lleno de bultos (covered with knobs).

knobkerrie ['nɔbkeri] *n* clava *f* (club).

knock [nɔk] *n* golpe *m*, llamada *f*, toque *m* (at the door) || golpe *m*, choque *m* || FIG revés *m*, golpe *m* (of bad luck or misfortune) || TECH picado *m*, golpeteo *m* (in motor) || FIG & FAM crítica *f* (criticism); *a knock at the monarchy* una crítica de la monarquía || — *there was a knock at the door* llamaron a la puerta || *to get a knock on the head* recibir un golpe en la cabeza || FIG *to take a hard knock* sufrir un gran revés, recibir un golpe duro.

knock [nɔk] *vt* golpear, pegar (to hit) || chocar contra (to collide with) || FAM meterse con (to find fault with) | poner por los suelos, dar un palo a (to criticize) || — FIG *our plans have been knocked on the head* han dado al traste con nuestros planes || *to knock a hole in sth.* hacer *or* abrir un agujero en algo || *to knock sth. flying* enviar algo por los aires || FIG *to knock one's head against a brick wall* darse de cabeza contra la pared (in anger) || *to knock one's head on the luggage rack* dar con la cabeza en la redecilla || *to knock the bottom out of* quitar el fondo de (a box), acabar con (to destroy), ser el fin de; *the accident knocked the bottom out of his world* el accidente fue el fin del mundo para él || *to knock to pieces* hacer pedazos.

◆ *vi* golpear || llamar; *to knock at the door* llamar a la puerta || picar (a motor) || FAM criticar || FAM *he's knocking on seventy* va para los setenta (age).

◆ *phr v* ***to knock about*** maltratar (to subject to rough treatment) | golpear (to hit) | zarandear, zamarrear (in a crowd) | rodar; *they knock about the streets all day* pasan el día rodando por las calles || ***to knock against*** dar contra || ***to knock back*** beber (de un trago) (to drink) || ***to knock down*** atropellar (a person) | derribar (an object) | tirar (to make fall) | rebajar (the price) | adjudicar (in an auction); *it was knocked down to him for 500 pounds* le ha sido adjudicado en 500 libras || ***to knock in*** hacer entrar a golpes | clavar (a nail) | abollar (to dent) | aplastar; *to knock s.o.'s head in* aplastar la cabeza a alguien | derribar (a door) || ***to knock into*** hacer entrar a golpes | chocar con || ***to knock off*** tirar; *to knock sth. off the table* tirar algo de la mesa | romper (to break off) | hacer saltar a golpes | rebajar en; *to knock one pound off an article* rebajar un artículo en una libra | bajar en, mejorar en; *to knock two seconds off the world record* bajar el récord mundial en dos segundos | despachar (to do sth. hurriedly) | poner fin a (to finish) | terminar; *the men knock off at six* los trabajadores terminan a las seis | FAM birlar, mangar (to steal), detener (to arrest), cargarse, liquidar (to kill) || — *knock it off!* ¡basta ya! || FIG *to knock s.o.'s head off* pegar una buena paliza a uno || ***to knock out*** vaciar; *to knock out a pipe* vaciar una pipa | dejar KO, noquear, dejar fuera de combate (in boxing) | dejar sin conocimiento (to make unconscious) | SP eliminar (to eliminate) | quitar (to remove) | partirse; *to knock two teeth out* partirse dos dientes | FAM dejar pasmado (to amaze) || ***to knock over*** tirar (a glass, etc.) | atropellar (a pedestrian) || ***to knock together*** golpear (to strike) | golpearse (to hit each other) | hacer de prisa y corriendo (to make hurriedly) || ***to knock up*** despertar (to awaken) | construir precipitadamente (a house) | hacer de prisa y corriendo (to make quickly) | marcar (in cricket) | pelotear (in tennis) | reventar, derrengar (to exhaust) | POP dejar embarazada || — *to knock up against* tropezar con (difficulties, people).

knockabout [-əbaut] *adj* de diario (clothes) || de risa (a play) || bullicioso, sa (boisterous).

◆ *n* yate *m* pequeño (yacht) || *to have a knockabout with a ball* jugar con un balón, dar patadas a un balón.

knockdown [-'daun] *adj* que derriba (a blow) || US desmontable; *knockdown table* mesa desmontable || *knockdown price* precio *m* de saldo.

◆ *n* SP caída *f* (in boxing) || golpe *m* muy fuerte.

knocker [-ə*] *n* aldaba *f*, aldabón *m* (of door) || FAM criticón, ona (faultfinder).

knocking [-iŋ] *n* golpeo *m*, golpeteo *m* || golpes *m pl*; *we heard a knocking at the door* oímos golpes en la puerta.

knock-kneed [-niːd] *adj* patizambo, ba; zambo, ba.

knock-on ['nɔkɔn] *adj* *knock-on effect* reacción *f* en cadena.

knockout [-aut] *n* SP «knock out» *m*, KO *m*, fuera de combate *m* (boxing) || FIG maravilla *f*; *she is a knockout* es una maravilla.

◆ *adj* FAM maravilloso, sa (marvellous) || que deja sin conocimiento (a blow) || que pone fuera de combate, que noquea (in boxing) || SP & FAM *knockout drops* narcótico *m sing*.

knockup [-ʌp] *n* SP peloteo *m* (in tennis) || *to have a knockup* pelotear.

knoll [nəul] *n* loma *f*, montículo *m*.

knot [nɔt] *n* nudo *m*; *he tied a knot* hizo un nudo || lazo *m* (ornamental ribbon) || MIL galón *m* || grupo *m* (a group); *a knot of people* un grupo de personas || MED haz *m* (of nerves) || BOT nudo *m*, nudosidad *f* || MAR nudo *m* || FIG nudo *m* (of problem, question) | vínculo *m*, lazo *m* (of marriage) || — *knot of hair* enmarañamiento *m* del pelo (tangle), moño *m* (bun) || FIG *to get tied up in knots* enmarañarse, enredarse, liarse || MAR *to make ten knots* hacer diez nudos || *to tie a knot in one's handkerchief* hacer un nudo en el pañuelo || FIG *to tie the knot* echar las bendiciones || *to untie a knot* deshacer *or* desatar un nudo.

knot [nɔt] *vt* atar con un nudo (to tie with a knot) || anudar; *he knotted the rope* anudó la cuerda || enmarañar, enredar, liar (to tangle) || fruncir (the eyebrows).

◆ *vi* anudarse || enredarse (to get tangled) || agruparse (to crowd).

knotgrass [-grɑːs] *n* BOT centinodia *f*.

knothole [-həul] *n* hueco *m* que queda en la madera al desprenderse un nudo.

knotty [-i] *adj* nudoso, sa (having knots) || FIG espinoso, sa; intrincado, da (hard to solve).

knout [naut] *n* knut *m* (whip).

knout [naut] *vt* azotar con un knut.

know [nəu] *n* *to be in the know* estar enterado, estar al tanto.

know* [kəu] *vt* saber; *he knows how to swim* sabe nadar; *he knows French* sabe francés; *I don't know how you do it* no sé cómo lo haces; *I know it by heart* lo sé de memoria; *I always knew that it would happen* ya sabía yo que sucedería; *to know one for what one is* saber muy bien lo que es uno; *not to want to know anything* no querer saber nada || conocer (acquaintance); *do you know my father?* ¿conoces a mi padre?; *do you know Athens?* ¿conoces Atenas?; *to know poverty* conocer la miseria; *he knows me by sight* me conoce de vista || reconocer (recognize); *I knew him from* o *by his voice* le reconocí por la voz || distinguir; *to know truth from falsehood* distinguir la verdad de la mentira; *I know one from another* distingo uno de otro || ver; *she had never been known to weep* nunca se le había visto llorar; *I've never known anyone to lie like he does* nunca he visto a uno que mienta tanto como él || — *as is well known* como es sabido || *be it known that...* se da a conocer que... || *don't I know it!* ¡y usted que lo diga! || FIG *everyone knows on which side his* o *her bread is buttered* cada uno sabe dónde le aprieta el zapato || *he is known to be weak* se sabe que es débil || *he knows everything* se lo sabe todo, sabe todo || *I knew him for a Spaniard* le tomaba por español || *it is a known fact that..., it is known that...* se sabe que... || *not to know anything about anything* no saber nada de nada || FIG *not to know s.o. from Adam* no conocer a uno ni por asomo || *not to know the first thing about sth.* no saber ni jota de algo || *not to know what to do with o.s.* no saber dónde meterse || *she knows all about cars* entiende mucho de coches || *there's no knowing* no se puede saber || *to be known as, to be known to be* ser conocido como (reputation), ser conocido por el nombre de (name) || *to be worth knowing* ser digno de saberse (a fact), valer la pena de ser conocido (place, person) || *to get to know s.o.* conocer; *when you get to know each other a bit better* cuando os conozcáis un poco mejor || *to get to know sth.* enterarse de algo (to be informed), conocer; *to get to know a country* conocer un país || FIG *to know all the tricks of the trade* conocer muy bien el percal *or* el paño *or* el asunto || *to know a thing or two* saber algo, conocer cuatro cosas || FIG *to know a woman* conocer a una mujer (in the biblical sense) || *to know each other* conocerse || *to know for sure* estar seguro de, saber a punto fijo || FIG *to know how many beans make five* saber cuántas son cinco || *to know how to do sth.* saber hacer algo || *to know how to get by* saber arreglárselas || *to know more than one says* saber más de lo que uno dice || *to know one's own mind* saber lo que se quiere || *to know one's own weaknesses* saber dónde le aprieta el zapato a uno, conocer sus propios defectos || *to know one to be a good teacher* saber que uno es un buen profesor || *to know only too well that...* saber de sobra que... || *to know o.s.* conocerse a sí mismo || FIG *to know s.o. inside out* conocer el pie que calza uno | *to know sth. backwards* saber algo al dedillo *or* como el padre nuestro || *to know sth. like the back of one's hand* conocer algo como la palma de la mano || *to know too much* saber más de la cuenta || *to know what's what* saber cuántas son cinco || *to let s.o. know sth.* avisar algo a alguien, dar a conocer algo a alguien || *to make it known to s.o. that* dar a conocer a alguien que, informar a alguien de que || *to make o.s. known* darse a conocer || *what do you know?* ¿tú qué sabes? || *without his (my, etc.) knowing it* sin saberlo él (yo, etc.) || *you don't know what you're letting yourself in for* no sabes dónde te metes || *you wouldn't know him from a Frenchman* se lo tomaría por un francés.

◆ *vi* saber; *as far as I know!* ¡que yo sepa! || — *do you know about Peter?* ¿sabes lo de Pedro? || *Goodness knows!, God only knows!* ¡sabe Dios!, ¡vete a saber! || *he's not young, you know* no te creas que es joven || *how should I know!* ¡yo qué sé!, ¡qué sé yo! || *I don't know about you, but I'm leaving* no sé lo que vas a hacer tú, pero yo me voy || *if only I'd known!* ¡de haberlo sabido antes || *I know!* ¡ya lo sé! || *I know better than anyone!* ¡lo sé mejor que nadie! || *I ought to know!* ¡lo sabré yo! || *so now you know!* ¡conque ya lo sabes! || *they didn't want to know* no quisieron saber nada || *three hours is a long time, you know* tres horas son muchas, ¿sabes? || *to know about* entender de (to have a knowledge of), saber; *I didn't know about that* eso no lo sabía || *to know better than to...* saber que no se debe...; *I know better than to play with fire*

sé que no se debe jugar con fuego; guardarse de; *he knew better than to believe them* se guardó de creerlos || *to know of* saber de; *I know of s.o. who can help you* sé de alguien que te puede ayudar || FIG *to know where the shoe pinches* saber uno dónde le aprieta el zapato || *to let s.o. know of sth.* informar a alguien de algo || *who knows?* ¿quién sabe?, ¡vete a saber! || *you know best* usted lo sabe mejor que nadie || *you ought to know better!* ¡ya tenías que saber esas cosas!
— OBSERV Pret *knew*; pp *known*.

knowable [-əbl] *adj* conocible.

know-all [-ɔːl] *n* sabelotodo *m* & *f*, sabihondo, da (pedant).

know-how [-hau] *n* habilidad *f*, destreza *f* (skill) || conocimientos *m pl* (knowledge); *scientific know-how* conocimientos científicos.

knowing [-iŋ] *adj* astuto, ta; sagaz (shrewd) || deliberado, da (deliberate) || instruido, da; culto, ta (educated) || de complicidad, de entendimiento (glance, wink).
◆ *n* conocimiento *m*.

knowingly [-iŋli] *adv* astutamente, sagazmente || a sabiendas, deliberadamente; *he started the fire knowingly* provocó el incendio deliberadamente.

know-it-all [-itɔːl] *n* US FAM sabelotodo *m* & *f*, sabihondo, da.

knowledge ['nɔlidʒ] *n* conocimiento *m*; *intuitive knowledge* conocimiento intuitivo || conocimientos *m pl*, saber *m*; *to apply one's knowledge* aplicar sus conocimientos || — *a little knowledge is a dangerous thing* es mejor no saber nada que saber poco || *a working knowledge of French* conocimientos sólidos de francés || *I had no knowledge of it* no tenía conocimiento de ello, no sabía nada de ello || *it has come to my knowledge* me enteré, ha llegado a mi conocimiento || *it is common knowledge that...* es del dominio público que... (a piece of news), todo el mundo sabe que... (everybody knows that...) || *knowledge is power* saber es poder || *not to my knowledge* que yo sepa no || *to have a thorough knowledge of* conocer a fondo, dominar || *to my knowledge* que yo sepa || *with full knowledge of the facts* con conocimiento de causa || *without my knowledge* sin saberlo yo.

knowledgeable [-əbl] *adj* informado, da (informed) || erudito, ta (erudite) || *he is knowledgeable about Spanish art* sabe mucho de arte español.

known [nəun] *pp* —> **know.**

know-nothing [-'nʌθiŋ] *n* ignorante *m* & *f*.

knuckle [nʌkl] *n* ANAT nudillo *m* (of finger) || jarrete *m* (of an animal) || CULIN jarrete *m*; *knuckle of pork* jarrete de cerdo || TECH junta *f* articulada || FIG *near the knuckle* rayando en la indecencia.
◆ *pl* llave *f sing* inglesa, manopla || *to rap s.o.'s knuckles* pegar en los nudillos a alguien.

knuckle [nʌkl] *vt* golpear con los nudillos.
◆ *vi* *to knuckle down to* ponerse seriamente a (hacer) || *to knuckle under* pasar por el aro, someterse.

knucklebone [-bəun] *n* ANAT nudillo *m* (of people) || taba *f* (of animals).
◆ *pl* tabas *f* (game).

knuckle-duster [-ˌdʌstə*] *n* manopla *f*, llave *f* inglesa.

knur [nəː*] *n* BOT nudo *m* (in tree trunks).

knurl [nəːrl] *n* BOT nudo *m* || grafilado *m* (in metalwork).

knurled [nəːrld] *adj* nudoso, sa (tree trunk) || grafilado, da (coin, etc.).

koala [kəu'ɑːlə] *n* ZOOL koala *m*.

Kodiak bear ['kəudiækbɛə*] *n* ZOOL oso *m* americano.

kohlrabi [kəul'rɑːbi] *n* BOT colinabo *m*.

kola nut ['kəulənʌt] *n* BOT nuez *f* de cola.

kola tree ['kəulətriː] *n* BOT cola *f*.

kolinsky [kə'linski] *n* ZOOL visón *m* de Siberia.

kolkhoz [kɔl'kɔz] *n* koljoz *m*, granja *f* colectiva (in USSR).
— OBSERV El plural de *kolkhoz* es *kolkhozy* o *kolkhozes*.

kook [kuːk]; **kooky** [kuːki] *adj* US FAM chalado, da.

Kremlin ['kremlin] *n* Kremlin *m*.

kopeck ['kəupek] *n* copec *m*, kopek *m* (currency).

Koran [kɔ'rɑːn] *pr n* REL Corán *m*, Alcorán *m*.

Koranic [-ik] *adj* coránico, ca.

Korea [kə'riə] *pr n* GEOGR Corea *f*.

Korean [kə'riən] *adj/n* coreano, na.

koruna ['kɔːrənɑː] *n* corona *f* checa (currency).
— OBSERV El plural es *koruny* o *korunas*.

kosher ['kəuʃə*] *adj* permitido por la religión judía (food) || *kosher butcher* carnicero *m* que vende carne preparada para los judíos.

koumiss ['kuːmis] *n* kumis *m* (drink).

kowtow ['kau'tau] *vi* hacer una reverencia china [arrodillarse y tocar el suelo con la frente] || FIG demostrar sumo respeto || *to kowtow to s.o.* humillarse ante alguien.

kraft [krɑːft] *n* kraft *m*, papel *m* de envolver.

krater ['kreitə*] *n* crátera *f* (vase).

kris [kriːs] *n* puñal *m* malayo, cris *m*.

krona ['kruːnæ] *n* corona *f* sueca (currency).
— OBSERV El plural de *krona* es *kronor*.

krypton ['kriptɔn] *n* CHEM criptón *m*.

kudos ['kjuːdɔs] *n* prestigio *m*, gloria *f*, fama *f*.

Ku Klux Klan ['kuːklʌks'klæn] *n* kukluxklán *m*.

kulak ['kjuːlæk] *n* kulak *m*.

kumiss ['kuːmis] *n* kumis *m* (drink).

kümmel ['kuməl] *n* cúmel *m*, kummel *m* (liquor).

kumquat ['kʌmkwɔt] *n* BOT quinoto *m*, naranja *f* china.

kung fu [kʌŋ'fuː] *n* SP kung fu *m*.

Kurd [kəːd]; **Kurdish** [-iʃ] *adj/n* curdo, da; kurdo, da.

Kurdistan [ˌkəːdi'stɑːn] *pr n* GEOGR Kurdistán.

Kuwait [ku'weit] *pr n* GEOGR Kuwait || GEOGR *Kuwait City* Kuwait.

Kuwaiti [ku'weiti] *adj/n* kuwaití.

kyphosis [kai'fəusis] *n* MED cifosis.

kyrie eleison [kirieie'leis'n] *n* REL kirieeleisón *m*.

L

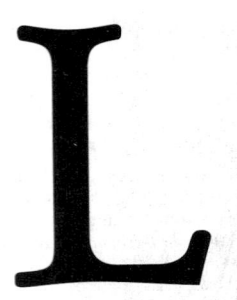

l [el] *n* l *f* (letter of alphabet) || libra *f* (pound) || *L plate* placa obligatoria que lleva en el coche el aprendiz de conductor o la autoescuela.
◆ *adj* en forma de L.

la [lɑ:] *n* MUS la *m* (fixed notation) | superdominante *f* (movable notation).

lab [læb] *n* FAM laboratorio *m*.

labefaction [ˌlæbiˈfækʃən] *n* decrepitud *f*.

label [ˈleibl] *n* etiqueta *f* (tag) || etiqueta *f*, rótulo *m*, membrete *m*, marbete *m* (on merchandise) || letrero *m* (notice) || tejuelo *m* (on the spine of a book) || cinta *f* (ribbon to hold the seal) || FIG etiqueta *f*; *political labels* etiquetas políticas | designación *f*, calificación *f* || FAM apodo *m* (nickname) || INFORM etiqueta *f* || ARCH goterón *m* || HERALD lambel *m*.

label [ˈleibl] *vt* poner etiqueta a, etiquetar (to attach a label) || rotular, poner un letrero a || facturar (luggage) || FAM apodar (to nickname) || FIG clasificar | calificar || CHEM marcar.

labelling; *US* **labeling** [-iŋ] *n* etiquetado *m* || FIG clasificación *f* | calificación *f*, designación *f*.

labia [ˈleibjə] *pl n* ⟶ **labium**.

labial [ˈleibjəl] *adj* labial.
◆ *n* GRAMM labial *f* || MUS caño *m* de boca (of an organ).

labialize [ˈleibiəlaiz] *vt* labializar.

labiate [ˈleibiət] *adj* BOT labiado, da.
◆ *n* BOT labiada *f*.

labiodental [ˈleibiəuˈdentl] *adj* GRAMM labiodental.
◆ *n* GRAMM labiodental *f*.

labiovelar [ˈleibiəuˈvi:lə] *adj* GRAMM labiovelar.
◆ *n* GRAMM labiovelar *f*.

labium [ˈleibiəm] *n* BOT labio *m*.
◆ *pl* ANAT labios *m* (of vulva).
— OBSERV El plural de esta palabra es *labia*.

labor [ˈleibə*] *n* *US* ⟶ **labour** || — *labor union* sindicato *m* (trade union) || *labor unionist* sindicalista *m* & *f* (trade unionist).
◆ *adj* *US* ⟶ **labour**.

laboratory [ləˈbɔrətəri] *n* laboratorio *m*.

labored [ˈleibəd] *adj* *US* ⟶ **laboured**.

laborer [ˈleibərə*] *n* *US* ⟶ **labourer**.

laboring [ˈleibəriŋ] *adj/n* *US* ⟶ **labouring**.

laborious [ləˈbɔ:riəs] *adj* laborioso, sa; penoso, sa; difícil (involving hard work); *a laborious task* una tarea penosa || trabajador, ra; laborioso, sa (hard-working).

laboriousness [-nis] *n* laboriosidad *f* (of a person) || dificultad *f*; *the laboriousness of a task* la dificultad de una tarea.

laborite [ˈleibərait] *n* *US* ⟶ **labourite**.

laborsaving [ˈleibə*ˌseiviŋ] *adj/n* *US* ⟶ **laboursaving**.

labour; *US* **labor** [ˈleibə*] *n* trabajo *m* (work); *manual labour* trabajo manual || labor *f*, tarea *f* (task) || faena *f* (hard task) || esfuerzo *m*, esfuerzos *m pl*, trabajo *m* (effort); *lost labour* trabajo en vano; *after much labour* tras grandes esfuerzos || MED parto *m* (childbirth); *to be in labour* estar de parto | dolores *m pl* del parto (pains) || mano *f* de obra, trabajadores *m pl* (manpower); *labour shortage* falta de mano de obra || obreros *m pl*, clase *f* obrera (the workers) || laborismo *m*, partido *m* laborista (party) || — *hard labour* trabajos forzados *or* forzosos || *International Labour Office* Oficina *f* Internacional del Trabajo || *International Labour Organization* Organización *f* Internacional del Trabajo || FIG *labour of love* trabajo desinteresado, trabajo hecho por amor al arte (without payment), trabajo agradable (pleasant) || *Ministry of Labour* Ministerio *m* de Trabajo || *skilled labour* mano de obra especializada || *the Herculean labours* los trabajos de Hércules.
◆ *adj* laborista; *Labour Party* Partido laborista || laboral; *labour dispute* conflicto laboral; *labour relations* relaciones laborales || obrero, ra; *labour movement* movimiento obrero || de la mano de obra; *labour cost* coste de la mano de obra || de trabajo; *labour camp* campo de trabajo || — *Labour Day* Día *m* del Trabajo || *labour exchange* Bolsa *f* de Trabajo || *labour force* mano *f* de obra || *labour market* mercado *m* del trabajo.

labour [ˈleibə*] *vi* trabajar (to work); *I was labouring under difficulties* estuve trabajando en condiciones difíciles || esforzarse, hacer esfuerzos, afanarse (to dedicate o.s. diligently); *to labour for* afanarse por || desplazarse penosamente, moverse con dificultad, avanzar difícilmente (to move very slowly) || estar de parto (woman) || MAR balancear y cabecear (a ship) || — *the engine is beginning to labour* el motor empieza a funcionar con dificultad || *to labour under* ser víctima de || *to labour under a delusion* estar engañado *or* equivocado (to be wrong) || *to labour up the hill* subir con dificultad la pendiente.
◆ *vt* insistir en, machacar en; *to labour a point* insistir en un punto; *you needn't labour the point* no hace falta que insistas en esto || pulir, trabajar (one's style) || AGR labrar.

laboured; *US* **labored** [-d] *adj* forzado, da; pesado, da (style) || penoso, sa; dificultoso, sa (movement) || dificultoso, sa; penoso, sa; fatigoso, sa (respiration).

labourer; *US* **laborer** [-rə*] *n* trabajador *m*, obrero *m* (worker) || jornalero *m* (day worker) || peón *m* (unskilled worker); *bricklayer's labourer* peón de albañil || AGR bracero *m*, peón *m*, labriego *m* (farm worker).

labouring; *US* **laboring** [-riŋ] *n* trabajo *m* manual, labor *f*.
◆ *adj* obrero, ra (class) || laborable (day) || jadeante (breast) || anhelante (soul).

labour-intensive [-inˈtensiv] *adj* con mucha necesidad de mano de obra.

labourite; *US* **laborite** [ˈleibərait] *n* laborista *m* & *f*.

laboursaving; *US* **laborsaving** [ˈleibəˌseiviŋ] *adj* que ahorra trabajo || que economiza mano de obra.
◆ *n* economía *f* de trabajo *or* de mano de obra.

Labrador [ˈlæbrədɔ:*] *n* ZOOL labrador.

labradorite [ˈlæbrədɔrait] *n* MIN labradorita *f*.

labret [ˈleibrit] *n* adorno *m* de piedra, de hueso o de concha que se colocan en el labio ciertas tribus primitivas.

labrum [ˈleibrəm] *n* labio *m* (lip) || ZOOL labro *m*.
— OBSERV El plural de *labrum* es *labra*.

laburnum [ləˈbə:nəm] *n* BOT codeso *m*.

labyrinth [ˈlæbərinθ] *n* laberinto *m*.

labyrinthian [ˌlæbəˈrinθiən]; **labyrinthine** [ˌlæbəˈrinθain] *adj* laberíntico, ca.

lac [læk] *n* laca *f*.

laccolite [ˈlækəlait]; **laccolith** [ˈlækəliθ] *n* GEOL lacolito *m*.

lace [leis] *n* encaje *m* (fabric) || cinta *f* (ribbon) || galón *m*, trencilla *f* (braid) || galón *m* (of gold, silver) || cordón *m* (of shoes, etc.) || — *bobbin lace* encaje de bolillos || *lace curtains* visillos *m*.

lace [leis] *vt* atar (shoes, corset) || adornar con encajes (to adorn with lace) || poner una cinta *or* un cordón a (to put a ribbon or a lace on) || ajustar el corsé a (body) || entrelazar (to interlace) || rayar (to streak) || FAM dar una paliza a (to beat) | rociar, echar (a drink); *he likes to lace his coffee with brandy* le gusta rociar el café con coñac, le gusta echar coñac al café || *to lace up* atar los cordones.
◆ *vi* atarse con cordones *or* cintas || FAM *to lace into s.o.* ponerle verde a uno.

lace-up [ˈleisʌp] *n* zapato *m* de cordones (shoe).

Lacedaemon [ˌlæsiˈdi:mən] *pr n* GEOGR Lacedemonia *f*.

lace glass [ˈleisglɑ:s] *n* vidrio *m* afiligranado.

lace maker [ˈleisˌmeikə*] *n* encajero, ra.

lace pillow [ˈleisˈpiləu] *n* cojín *m*, almohadilla *f*.

lacerate [ˈlæsəreit] *vt* lacerar (to tear) || FIG herir (feelings).

lacerate [ˈlæsərit]; **lacerated** [ˈlæsəreitid] *adj* lacerado, da.

laceration [ˌlæsəˈreiʃən] *n* laceración *f* || MED desgarrón *m*.

lacework [ˈleiswə:k] *n* encajes *m pl* (lace) || pasamanería *f* (trimmings).

laches [ˈleitʃiz] *n* JUR negligencia *f*.

lachryma christi [ˈlækriməˈkristi] *n* lácrima christi *m* (wine).

lachrymal; *US* **lacrimal** [ˈlækriməl] *adj* ANAT lagrimal, lacrimal || lacrimatorio (vase).
◆ *n* lacrimatorio *m* (vase).

lachrymator [ˈlækrimeitə*] *n* gas *m* lacrimógeno (tear gas).

lachrymatory; *US* **lacrimatory** [ˈlækrimətəri] *adj* lacrimatorio (vase) || lacrimógeno, na (producing tears).
◆ *n* vaso *m* lacrimatorio.

lachrymose [ˈlækriməus] *adj* lloroso, sa; llorón, ona; lagrimoso, sa; lacrimoso, sa.

lacing ['leisiŋ] *n* atadura *f* (act) ‖ cordón *m* (shoelace) ‖ galón *m* (of gold, silver) ‖ FAM paliza *f* (thrashing).

lack [læk] *n* falta *f*, carencia *f*, escasez *f* (shortage); *lack of cereals* carencia de cereales ‖ falta *f* (absence); *lack of judgment* falta de juicio ‖ necesidad *f* (necessity) ‖ — *for lack of* por falta de, a falta de ‖ *there is no lack of examples* no faltan ejemplos, hay bastantes ejemplos ‖ *through lack of* por falta de, a falta de ‖ *to supply the lack* proporcionar lo que falta.

lack [læk] *vt* carecer de, faltarle a uno, no tener; *to lack money* carecer de dinero; *he lacks authority* carece de autoridad; *he lacks experience* le falta experiencia, no tiene experiencia ‖ necesitar (to need); *what is it that I lack?* ¿qué es lo que necesito?
◆ *vi* faltar; *money is lacking for the plan* falta dinero para el proyecto ‖ *to be lacking in* faltarle a uno, carecer de; *he is lacking in courage* carece de valor, le falta valor.

lackadaisical [,lækə'deizikəl] *adj* tardo, da; lento, ta (slow) ‖ apático, ca; indolente (listless) ‖ descuidado, da (careless) ‖ poco enérgico, ca; lánguido, da (weak) ‖ vago, ga; perezoso, sa (lazy) ‖ distraído, da (dreamy) ‖ afectado, da (affected).

lackaday ['lækədei] *interj* ¡ay!

lackey ['læki] *n* lacayo *m* (servant) ‖ FIG lacayo *m*.

lacking ['lækiŋ] *adj* *lacking in* sin; *lacking in meaning* sin sentido ‖ *she is lacking in courage* le falta valor, carece de valor ‖ *subject on which books are lacking* tema sobre el cual no hay libros.

lackustre; *US* **lackluster** ['læk,lʌstə*] *adj* sin brillo, sin vida, apagado, da (dull) ‖ soso, sa (colourless).

Laconia [lə'kəunjə] *pr n* GEOGR Laconia *f*.

laconic [lə'kɔnik] *adj* lacónico, ca.

lacquer ['lækə*] *n* laca *f* (hair spray, varnish, ware coated with this varnish) ‖ pintura *f* al duco, pintura *f* esmalte (hard gloss paint).

lacquer ['lækə*] *vt* pintar con laca, dar laca, laquear (to coat with varnish) ‖ echar laca a, poner laca en (to spray hair) ‖ pintar al duco.

lacquey ['læki] *n* lacayo *m*.

lacrima christy ['lækrimə'kristi] *n* lácrima christi *m* (wine).

lacrimal ['lækriməl] *adj/n* → **lachrymal.**

lacrimation ['lækri'meiʃən] *n* lágrimas *f pl*.

lacrimator ['lækrimeitə*] *n* gas *m* lacrimógeno (tear gas).

lacrimatory ['lækrimətəri] *adj/n* → **lachrymatory.**

lacrimose ['lækriməus] *adj* lloroso, sa; llorón, na; lagrimoso, sa; lacrimoso, sa.

lacrosse [lə'krɔs] *n* juego *m* parecido a la vilorta.

lactary ['læktəri] *adj* lácteo, a.
◆ *n* *US* lechería *f* (dairy).

lactase ['lækteis] *n* CHEM lactasa *f*.

lactate ['lækteit] *n* CHEM lactato *m*.

lactate ['lækteit] *vi* secretar leche (to secrete milk) ‖ lactar (to suckle young).

lactation [læk'teiʃən] *n* lactancia *f* (suckling) ‖ secreción *f* de leche.

lacteal ['læktiəl] *adj* lácteo, a; *lacteal fever* fiebre láctea ‖ ANAT lácteo, a; quilífero, ra.
◆ *n* ANAT vaso *m* lácteo *or* quilífero.

lactescent [læk'tesənt] *adj* lactescente.

lactic ['læktik] *adj* láctico, ca; *lactic acid* ácido láctico.

lactiferous [læk'tifərəs] *adj* lactífero, ra.

lactone ['læktəun] *n* CHEM lactona *f*.

lactose ['læktəus] *n* CHEM lactosa *f*.

lacuna [lə'kju:nə] *n* laguna *f* (break in continuity) ‖ BIOL laguna *f*.
— OBSERV El plural de *lacuna* es *lacunae* o *lacunas*.

lacunar [lə'kju:nə*] *n* ARCH artesón *m*, lagunar *m*.

lacustrine [lə'kʌstrain] *adj* lacustre.

lacy ['leisi] *adj* de encaje ‖ parecido al encaje ‖ FIG fino, na.

lad [læd]; **laddie** ['lædi] *n* chaval *m*, chico *m*, muchacho *m* (boy) ‖ mozo *m* de cuadra (stableboy) ‖ — *he's a bit of a lad!* ¡qué tío! ‖ *the lads* los amigos.

ladder ['lædə*] *n* escalera *f* de mano, escala *f* (for climbing) ‖ escala *f* (of rope) ‖ FIG escalón *m*, peldaño *m*; *on the ladder to success* en los peldaños del éxito | escala *f*, jerarquía *f*; *the social ladder* la escala social | escala *f* (of salaries) | carrera *f*, carrerilla *f* (in a stocking); *to make a ladder in* hacerse una carrerilla en ‖ — MAR *accommodation ladder* escala real ‖ FIG *at the top of the ladder* en la cumbre ‖ *rope ladder* escala de cuerda.

ladder ['lædə*] *vt* hacerse una carrera *or* una carrerilla en (una media).
◆ *vi* correrse.

ladder-back [-bæk] *adj* con respaldo de barrotes horizontales (chair back).

ladderless [-lis] *adj* indesmallable.

ladder mender [-,mendə*] *n* zurcidora *f* (person) ‖ máquina *f* para coger puntos en las medias (tool).

ladderproof [-pru:f] *adj* indesmallable.

ladder stitch [-stitʃ] *n* calado *m* (in embroidery).

ladder truck [-trʌk] *n* *US* coche *m* de bomberos con escalera.

laddie ['lædi] *n* → **lad.**

lade* [leid] *vt* MAR cargar (to load) | embarcar (to take on board).
— OBSERV Pret *laded*; pp *laden*.

laden [leidn] *pp* → **lade.**
◆ *adj* cargado, da (*with* de) (loaded) ‖ FIG agobiado, da.

la-di-da ['lɑ:di'dɑ:] *adj* FAM afectado, da; presuntuoso, sa; presumido, da.

ladies ['leidiz] *pl n* → **lady.**

Ladin [lə'di:n] *n* ladino *m* (language).

lading ['leidiŋ] *n* MAR cargamento *m*, flete *m* ‖ MAR *bill of lading* conocimiento *m* de embarque.

Ladino [lə'di:nəu] *n* ladino *m* [lenguaje judeoespañol].

ladle ['leidl] *n* cucharón *m* (for serving) ‖ cazo *m* (for kitchen) ‖ TECH caldero *m* de colada.

ladle ['leidl] *vt* servir (con cucharón) (to serve) ‖ FIG repartir; *he ladled out compliments to everybody* repartió cumplidos a todos ‖ TECH colar.

ladleful ['leidlful] *n* cucharón *m*.

lady ['leidi] *n* señora *f*; *act like a lady* pórtese como una señora ‖ — *a perfect lady* toda una señora ‖ *first lady* primera dama ‖ *his good lady* su mujer, su señora ‖ *his young lady* su novia ‖ *how is your good lady?* ¿cómo está su señora? ‖ *lady of loose living* mujer *f* de la vida, mujer *f* de vida airada ‖ *lady of the house* señora de la casa ‖ REL *Our Lady* Nuestra Señora ‖ FIG *painted lady* fulana *f* ‖ *young lady* señorita *f*.
◆ *pl* servicios *m* de señoras, aseos *m* de señoras (toilet); *where is the ladies?* ¿dónde están los servicios de señoras? ‖ señoras *f* (sign on door) ‖ *ladies and gentlemen* señoras y señores, señoras y caballeros.
◆ *adj* *ladies' hairdresser's* peluquería *f* de señoras ‖ *ladies' man, lady's man* hombre mujeriego ‖ *Lady chapel* capilla *f* de la Virgen ‖ *Lady Day* Anunciación *f* ‖ *lady doctor* médica *f*, doctora *f* ‖ *lady dog* perra *f* ‖ *lady help* asistenta *f* ‖ *lady lawyer* abogada *f* ‖ *lady mayoress* alcaldesa *f*.
— OBSERV *Lady* se emplea también como título nobiliario (duquesas, condesas, etc.).

ladybird ['leidibə:d]; *US* **ladybug** ['leidibʌg] *n* ZOOL mariquita *f*.

ladyfinger ['leidi,fiŋgə*] *n* CULIN lengua *f* de gato (biscuit).

lady-in-waiting ['leidiin'weitiŋ] *n* dama *f* de honor, azafata *f*.
— OBSERV El plural es *ladies-in-waiting*.

lady-killer ['leidi,kilə*] *n* FAM castigador *m*, ladrón *m* de corazones, tenorio *m*.

ladylike ['leidilaik] *adj* elegante, fino, na; distinguido, da ‖ FAM afeminado, da (effeminate).

ladylove ['leidilʌv] *n* amada *f* (sweetheart).

lady's companion ['leidizkəm'pænjən] *n* señora *f* de compañía.

Ladyship ['leidiʃip] *n* *Your Ladyship* su señoría.

lady's maid ['leidizmeid] *n* doncella *f*.

lag [læg] *n* revestimiento *m* calorífugo *or* termoaislante (lagging) ‖ intervalo *m* (length of time between two events) ‖ retraso *m* (delay) ‖ ELECTR retardo *m* ‖ listón *m* (strip, lath) ‖ FAM presidiario *m* (convict) | condena *f* (sentence).

lag [læg] *vt* poner un revestimiento termoaislante *or* calorífugo a (to cover with lagging) ‖ revestir, cubrir (to cover) ‖ FAM encarcelar (to jail).
◆ *vi* retrasarse (to be behind time) ‖ rezagarse, quedarse atrás (walking) ‖ *to lag behind* estar retrasado, estar rezagado, tener retraso.

lagan ['lægən] *n* MAR mercancías *f pl* arrojadas al mar y marcadas con una boya para poder ser recogidas.

lager ['lɑ:gə*] *n* cerveza *f* dorada.

laggard ['lægəd] *adj* rezagado, da (who lags behind) ‖ tardo, da; lento, ta (sluggish) ‖ remolón, ona; vago, ga (lazy).
◆ *n* vago, ga; remolón, ona (lazy) ‖ rezagado, da; retrasado, da (loiterer).

lagger ['lægə*] *n* vago, ga; remolón, ona (lazy) ‖ rezagado, da; retrasado, da (loiterer).

lagging ['lægiŋ] *n* revestimiento *m* calorífugo *or* termoaislante (covering to reduce heat loss) ‖ revestimiento *m*, forro *m* (covering) ‖ retraso *m* (time lag).
◆ *adj* retrasado, da; rezagado, da.

lagoon [lə'gu:n] *n* laguna *f*.

Lagos ['leigɔs] *pr n* GEOGR Lagos.

lah-di-dah; **la-di-da** [,la:di'da] *adj* afectado, da (voice).
◆ *adv* afectadamente, con afectación.

laic ['leiik] *adj/n* laico, ca; seglar.

laical [-əl] *adj* laico, ca.

laicism ['leiisizəm] *n* laicismo *m*.

laicization [,leiisai'zeiʃən] *n* laicización *f* [*AMER* laicalización *f*].

laicize ['leiisaiz] *vt* laicizar, dar carácter laico a [*AMER* laicalizar].

laid [leid] *pret/pp* → **lay.**

laid-back [-bæk] *adj* FAM pancho, cha.

laid paper [-'peipə*] *n* papel *m* vergé.

lain [lein] *pp* → **lie** (meaning «echarse»).

lair [lɛə*] *n* guarida *f* (of wild animals) ‖ FIG guarida *f*.

lair [lɛə*] *vi* recogerse en su guarida.

laird [lɛəd] *n* terrateniente *m* (Scottish landlord).

laisser-faire; **laissez-faire** ['leisei'fɛə*] *n* liberalismo *m*.

laity ['leiiti] *n* laicado *m*, seglares *m pl* ‖ FIG profanos *m pl*, legos *m pl*.

lake [leik] *n* GEOGR lago *m* ‖ laca *f* (dye) ‖ *ornamental lake* estanque *m*.
◆ *adj* lacustre, de lago; *lake plant* planta lacustre ‖ *the Lake District* la Región de los Lagos (in England).

lake dweller [-ˌdwelə*] *n* habitante *m* & *f* de una vivienda lacustre.

lake dwelling [-ˌdweliŋ] *n* vivienda *f* lacustre.

Lake poet [-ˌpəuit] *n* lakista *m* & *f*.

Lake school [-sku:l] *n* lakismo *m*.

lakeside [-said] *n* orilla *f* (de un lago).

lallation [læ'leiʃən] *n* lambdacismo *m*.

lam [læm] *n* US FAM huida *f* ‖ US FAM *to take it on the lam* tomar las de Villadiego, largarse.

lam [læm] *vt* FAM dar una paliza.
◆ *vi* US FAM huir.

lama ['lɑ:mə] *n* lama *m* (priest).

Lamaism ['lɑ:məizəm] *n* REL lamaísmo *m*.

lamasery ['lɑ:məsəri] *n* REL lamasería *f*.

lamb [læm] *n* cordero *m* (animal and meat) ‖ piel *f* de cordero, cordero *m* (lambskin) ‖ FIG cordero *m* (mild person) | cielo *m* (good lovable person) ‖ — *lamb chop* chuleta *f* de cordero ‖ *the Lamb of God* el Cordero de Dios.

lamb [læm] *vt/vi* parir [la oveja].

lambast; lambaste [læm'beist] *vt* dar una paliza (to thrash) ‖ poner como un trapo (to scold).

lambda ['læmdə] *n* lambda *f* (Greek letter).

lambdacism ['læmdəsizəm] *n* lambdacismo *m*.

lambency ['læmbənsi] *n* palidez *f* (paleness) ‖ vacilación *f* (movement).

lambent ['læmbənt] *adj* macilento, ta; pálido, da (softly glowing) ‖ vacilante (dancing, flickering) ‖ FIG brillante (humour, eyes, etc.).

lambing ['læmiŋ] *n* época *f* en que paren las ovejas.

lambkin ['læmkin] *n* corderito *m*, corderillo *m* ‖ FAM cielo *m*.

lamblike ['læmlaik] *adj* manso como un cordero.

lambskin ['læmskin] *n* piel *f* de cordero, cordero *m* (skin, fur).

lamb's wool ['læmzwul] *n* lana *f* de cordero.

lame [leim] *adj* cojo, ja (unable to walk, run, etc.); *a lame woman* una mujer coja; *he was lame* era cojo; *I am lame today* estoy cojo hoy ‖ lisiado, da (injured in the foot or leg) ‖ FIG poco convincente, débil, malo, la; *a lame excuse* una excusa mala | flojo, ja (an argument) | cojo, ja; *a lame verse* un verso cojo ‖ — US *a lame back* dolor *m* de espalda ‖ *lame person* cojo, ja ‖ *to go lame* empezar a cojear ‖ *to walk lame* cojear ‖ *you are lame in one foot* cojeas de un pie.
◆ *n* hoja *f* (of metal).

lame [leim] *vt* dejar cojo (to cause to limp) ‖ lisiar (to injure) ‖ incapacitar (to render unfit).

lamé ['lɑ:mei] *n* lamé *m*.

lame duck ['leim'dʌk] *n* incapaz *m* & *f* (ineffectual person) ‖ cosa *f* inútil (useless thing) ‖ persona *f* incapacitada (physically handicapped person) ‖ especulador *m* insolvente (insolvent speculator) ‖ US FAM cesante *m*, funcionario *m* cesante (official) | diputado *m* no reelegido (congressman).

lamella [lə'melə] *n* ANAT laminilla *f*, lámina *f* ‖ BOT laminilla *f*.
— OBSERV El plural es *lamellae* o *lamellas*.

lamellar [lə'melə*] *adj* laminar, laminoso, sa.

lamellate; lamellated ['læməleit] *adj* laminoso, sa.

lamellibranch [lə'meliˌbræŋk] *n* ZOOL lamelibranquio *m*.
— OBSERV El plural de esta palabra es *lamellibranchia*.

lamellicorn [lə'meliˌkɔ:n] *adj* ZOOL lamelicornio.
◆ *n* ZOOL lamelicornio *m*.
— OBSERV El plural de esta palabra es *lamellicornia*.

lamellirostres [lə'meli'rɔstriz] *pl n* lamelirrostros *m* (birds).

lamely ['leimli] *adj* cojeando, renqueando (to walk) ‖ FIG con poca convicción (when arguing).

lameness ['leimnis] *n* cojera *f* ‖ FIG debilidad *f*, flojedad *f* (weakness) | falta *f* de convicción (in arguing).

lament [lə'ment] *n* lamento *m* (of grief) ‖ queja *f* (complaint) ‖ MUS endecha *f*.

lament [lə'ment] *vi* *to lament for* o *over* lamentarse por *or* de (to feel great sorrow), llorar (to show great sorrow); *to lament for a friend* llorar a un amigo.
◆ *vt* lamentar, llorar (to mourn); *he laments the death of his friend* llora la muerte de su amigo ‖ sentir, lamentar, lamentarse de (to regret deeply); *to lament having done sth.* sentir haber hecho algo ‖ *it is much to be lamented that...* es de lamentar que...

lamentable ['læməntəbl] *adj* lamentable (pitiable); *he is in a lamentable state* está en un estado lamentable ‖ lastimero, ra (mournful).

lamentation [ˌlæmen'teiʃən] *n* lamentación *f* (lamenting) ‖ lamento *m* (lament).

lamented [lə'mentid] *adj* llorado, da (dead person).

lamenting [lə'mentiŋ] *n* lamentación *f*.

lamina ['læminə] *n* hoja *f* (of metal) ‖ BOT lámina *f* ‖ ANAT laminilla *f*, lámina *f*.
— OBSERV El plural de la palabra inglesa *lamina* es *laminae* o *laminas*.

laminable ['læminəbl] *adj* laminable.

laminal ['læminəl]; **laminar** ['læminə*] *adj* laminar; *laminar structure* estructura laminar.

laminate ['læminət] *adj* laminado, da.
◆ *n* laminado *m*.

laminate ['læmineit] *vt* laminar (to roll) ‖ dividir en láminas (to split into thin plates) ‖ contrachapar, contrachapear (to unite superimposed layers).
◆ *vi* dividirse en láminas, estratificarse.

laminated [-id] *adj* laminado, da ‖ hojoso, sa (sheet) ‖ contrachapado, da (wood).

lamination [ˌlæmi'neiʃən] *n* laminación *f*, laminado *m*.

laminose ['læminəus]; **laminous** ['læminəs] *adj* laminoso, sa.

Lammas ['læməs] *n* *Lammas Day* primero *m* de agosto.

lammergeyer; US **lammergeier** ['læməgaiə*] *n* ZOOL quebrantahuesos *m inv*.

lamp [læmp] *n* lámpara *f*; *electric, gas, oil lamp* lámpara eléctrica, de gas, de aceite; *lamp bracket* brazo de lámpara ‖ farol *m*, farola *f* (in the street) ‖ faro *m* (of cars, etc.); *rear lamp* faro trasero ‖ MAR luz *f* de navegación ‖ linterna *f* (pocket torch) ‖ ELECTR bombilla *f* (bulb) ‖ — *arc lamp* lámpara de arco ‖ *bracket* o *wall lamp* aplique *m* ‖ *hanging lamp* lámpara suspendida ‖ *incandescent lamp* lámpara de incandescencia *or* incandescente ‖ *infrared lamp* lámpara de rayos infrarrojos ‖ *mercury vapour lamp* lámpara de vapor de mercurio ‖ *miner's* o *safety lamp* lámpara de minero *or* de seguridad ‖ *pocket lamp* linterna *f* ‖ *reading lamp* lámpara para la mesilla de noche ‖ *spirit lamp* lámpara de alcohol ‖ *sun-ray lamp* lámpara solar ‖ *ultraviolet lamp* lámpara de rayos ultravioletas.
◆ *pl* FAM luceros *m*, sacáis *m*, pajarillas *f* (eyes).

lamp [læmp] *vt* poner lámparas ‖ iluminar ‖ US FAM echar el ojo a.

lampblack [-blæk] *n* negro *m* de humo.

lamp chimney [-ˌtʃimni] *n* tubo *m* de cristal de lámpara.

lamp dealer [-ˌdi:lə*] *n* lamparero *m*.

lamp holder [-ˌhəuldə*] *n* casquillo *m*, portalámparas *m inv*.

lampion ['læmpiən] *n* farolillo *m*.

lamplight ['læmplait] *n* luz *f* de lámpara; *by lamplight* a la luz de la lámpara ‖ luz *f* de un farol (in the street).

lamplighter [-ə*] *n* farolero *m*.

lamp maker ['læmpˌmeikə*] *n* lamparero *m*.

lamp oil ['læmpɔil] *n* aceite *m* lampante ‖ petróleo *m* lampante.

lampoon [læm'pu:n] *n* pasquín *m*, libelo *m* (piece of satirical writing).

lampoon [læm'pu:n] *vt* escribir pasquines contra, satirizar.

lamppost ['læmppəust] *n* poste *m* de alumbrado (post) ‖ farol *m*, farola *f* (streetlight).

lamprey ['læmpri] *n* ZOOL lamprea *f* (fish).

lampshade ['læmpʃeid] *n* pantalla *f*.

LAN [læn] *abbr of* *[local area network]* red (de área) local.

lanate ['leineit] *adj* BOT velloso, sa; lanado, da.

Lancashire ['læŋkəʃiə*] *pr n* GEOGR Lancaster (county).

Lancaster ['læŋkəstə*] *pr n* Lancaster.

lance [lɑ:ns] *n* lanza *f* (weapon) ‖ lancero *m* (soldier) ‖ arpón *m* (for fishing) ‖ MED lanceta *f* ‖ lanza *f* (of a hosepipe) ‖ US & ZOOL amodita *f* (launce) ‖ *lance head* moharra *f*, punta *f* de la lanza.

lance [lɑ:ns] *vt* lancear (to pierce with a lance) ‖ MED abrir (con una lanceta).

lance corporal [-'kɔ:pərəl] *n* MIL cabo *m* interino.

lancelet ['lɑ:nslət] *n* anfioxo *m* (marine animal).

Lancelot ['lɑ:nslət] *pr n* Lancelote *m*, Lanzarote *m*.

lanceolar ['lɑ:nsiələ*]; **lanceolate** ['lɑ:nsiələt] *adj* ARCH & BOT lanceolado, da.

lancer ['lɑ:nsə*] *n* MIL lancero *m*.
◆ *pl* lanceros *m* (dance).

lance sergeant ['lɑ:ns'sɑ:dʒənt] *n* MIL sargento *m* interino.

lancet ['lɑ:nsit] *n* MED lanceta *f* ‖ ARCH ojiva *f* ‖ — *lancet arch* arco apuntado ‖ *lancet window* ventana *f* ojival.

lanciform ['lɑ:nsifɔ:m] *adj* lanciforme.

lancinate ['lɑ:nsineit] *vi* lancinar, dar punzadas.

lancinating [-iŋ] *adj* punzante, lancinante.

lancination [ˌlɑ:nsi'neiʃən] *n* punzada *f*.

land [lænd] *n* tierra *f*; *to travel over land and sea* viajar por tierra y mar; *to sight land* divisar tierra ‖ país *m*, tierra *f* (country, state) ‖ país *m*, pueblo *m* (people) ‖ tierra *f*; *the land here is good for farming* la tierra aquí es buena para el cultivo ‖ suelo *m*, tierra *f* (soil); *poor land* suelo pobre ‖ campo *m*; *I want to get back to the land* deseo volver al campo ‖ tierras *f pl*, finca *f* [AMER estancia *f*, hacienda *f*] (of an owner); *he has 1 000 hectares of land* tiene 1 000 hectáreas de tierras, tiene una finca de 1 000 hectáreas ‖ JUR bienes *m pl* raíces ‖ zona *f* (area); *fo-*

rest land zona forestal || TECH parte *f* plana entre las estrías (of a riffle, etc.) || — AGR *arable land* tierra de cultivo || *by land* por tierra || *drift from the land* éxodo *m* rural, abandono *m* del campo || *dry land* tierra firme (opposed to sea), tierra de secano (in agriculture) || *flight from land* éxodo *m* rural, despoblación *f* del campo || *irrigated land* tierra de regadío || *land ho!* ¡tierra! || FIG *land of milk and honey* tierra de Jauja, paraíso *m* terrenal | *land of nod* sueño *m* | *land of plenty* tierra de abundancia || *native land* tierra *or* país natal, patria *f* || MIL *no man's land* tierra de nadie || *on land* en tierra || *piece of land* terreno *m* || *promised land, land of promise* tierra de promisión || *to make land* llegar a tierra (ship), aterrizar, tomar tierra (aircraft) || *to see how the land lies* tantear el terreno (before taking action) || *tract of land* terreno *m*.

◆ *adj* terrestre; *land defenses* defensas terrestres || de tierra; *land breeze* viento de tierra || agrario, ria; *land reform* reforma agraria.

land [lænd] *vt* hacer aterrizar (a plane) || desembarcar (to disembark) || descargar (goods) || dejar (to drop) || sacar (to bring a fish to shore) || hacer llegar; *to land a golf ball next to the hole* hacer llegar una pelota de golf junto al hoyo || FIG asestar, dar (a blow) | conseguir, lograr (a good job, contract, prize, etc.) | meter; *to land somebody in trouble* meter a alguien en un lío | llevar; *his crime landed him in prison* su crimen le llevó a la cárcel || FAM *to get landed with* tener que cargar con.

◆ *vi* aterrizar (a plane on land) || amerizar, amarar (on the sea) || alunizar (on the Moon) || posarse (birds, etc.) || desembarcar (to disembark) || llegar (to arrive) || MAR atracar, arribar (to reach port) || caer; *I jumped off the wall and landed badly* salté del muro y caí mal || dar (to hit); *the dart landed on the target* la flecha dio en el blanco || — FIG *to land on* caer encima; *he landed on me unexpectedly* me cayó encima sin avisar || *to land on one's feet* caer de pie (from a fall), salir adelante (to emerge safely from a situation) || *to land on one's head* caer de cabeza || *to land up somewhere* ir a parar a cierto sitio.

land agent [-ˌeidʒənt] *n* administrador *m* (manager of an estate) || corredor *m* de fincas (seller).

landau [-ɔː] *n* landó *m* (carriage) || coche *m* descapotable (car).

landaulet [-ɔːˈlet] *n* landó *m* pequeño (carriage) || coche *m* descapotable (car).

land bank [-bæŋk] *n* banco *m* hipotecario.

land crab [-kræb] *n* ZOOL cangrejo *m* de tierra.

landed [-id] *adj* hacendado, da; terrateniente, que tiene tierras (owning land) || que consiste en tierras (consisting of land) || — *landed gentry* terratenientes *m pl* || *landed property* bienes *m pl* raíces || *loan on landed property* crédito hipotecario.

landfall [-fɔːl] *n* MAR recalada *f* (sighting of land) | arribada *f* (arrival at land) || AVIAT vista *f* de tierra | aterrizaje *m* (landing).

land forces [-fɔːsiz] *pl n* MIL fuerzas *f* terrestres, ejército *m sing* de tierra.

land grant [-grɑːnt] *n* concesión *f* de terrenos *or* de tierras.

landgrave [-greiv] *n* landgrave *m*.

landholder [-ˌhəuldə*] *n* terrateniente *m* & *f*.

landholding [-ˌhəuldiŋ] *n* tenencia *f* de tierras, posesión *f* de tierras.

landing [ˈlændiŋ] *n* desembarco *m* (of passengers, troops) || desembarque *m* (of cargo) || AVIAT aterrizaje *m* (of a plane on land); *emergency o forced landing* aterrizaje forzoso | amerizaje *m*, amaraje *m* (of a plane on the sea) || alunizaje *m* (on the Moon) || desembarcadero *m* (jetty) || descansillo *m*, rellano *m* (of a staircase).

landing barge [-bɑːdʒ] *n* MIL lancha *f* de desembarco.

landing carriage [-ˈkæridʒ] *n* tren *m* de aterrizaje.

landing craft [-krɑːft] *n* MIL lancha *f* de desembarco.

landing deck [-dek] *n* cubierta *f* de aterrizaje (of an aircraft carrier).

landing field [-fiːld] *n* AVIAT campo *m* de aterrizaje.

landing force [-fɔːs] *n* cuerpo *m* expedicionario.

landing gear [-giə*] *n* AVIAT tren *m* de aterrizaje.

landing ground [-graund] *n* AVIAT campo *m* de aterrizaje.

landing net [-net] *n* salabardo *m*, manguilla *f*, sacadera *f*.

landing party [-ˌpɑːti] *n* MIL destacamento *m* de desembarco.

landing stage [-steidʒ] *n* MAR desembarcadero *m*.

landing strip [-strip] *n* AVIAT pista *f* de aterrizaje.

landlady [ˈlændˌleidi] *n* patrona *f*, dueña *f* (of a boardinghouse) || propietaria *f* (of land) || propietaria *f*, casera *f* (of a rented house).

landless [ˈlændlis] *adj* sin tierras.

landlocked [ˈlændlɔkt] *adj* cercado *or* rodeado de tierra; *a landlocked bay* una bahía rodeada de tierra || que no tiene acceso al mar; *a landlocked country* un país que no tiene acceso al mar.

landlord [ˈlændlɔːd] *n* patrón *m*, dueño *m* (of a pub, a boardinghouse) || propietario *m* (of land) || propietario *m*, casero *m* (of a rented house).

landlordism [-izəm] *n* sistema *m* de arrendamiento de tierras.

landlubber [ˈlændˌlʌbə*] *n* FAM marinero *m* de agua dulce.

landmark [ˈlændmɑːk] *n* señal *f* (mark) || mojón *m* (for marking a route or boundary) || MAR marca *f*, señal *f* || FIG hito *m*, acontecimiento *m* decisivo.

land mine [ˈlændmain] *n* MIL mina *f* terrestre.

land office [ˈlændˌɔfis] *n* oficina *f* del catastro.

land-office business [-ˈbiznis] *n* US FIG negocio *m* magnífico.

landowner [ˈlændˌəunə*] *n* terrateniente *m* & *f*, propietario, ria.

landownership [-ʃip] *n* posesión *f* de tierras, tenencia *f* de tierras.

land-poor [ˈlændpuə*] *adj* que no puede explotar sus tierras por falta de recursos.

land power [ˈlændˌpauə*] *n* potencia *f* militar terrestre.

land reclamation [ˈlændˌrekləˈmeiʃən] *n* tierra *f* ganada al mar (creation of land) || puesta *f* en cultivo de las tierras, aprovechamiento *m* de las tierras (improvement of land).

land register [ˈlændˌredʒistə*] *n* registro *m* de la propiedad.

Land-Rover [ˈlændˌrəuvə*] *n* Land-Rover (registered trademark).

landscape [ˈlændskeip] *n* paisaje *m* || — *landscape architect* arquitecto *m* paisajista || *landscape architecture* profesión *f* de arquitecto paisajista || *landscape gardener* jardinero *m* paisajista || *landscape gardening* profesión *f* de jardinero paisajista || *landscape painter* paisajista *m* & *f*.

landscape [ˈlændskeip] *vt* ajardinar.

landscapist [-ist] *n* paisajista *m* & *f* (painter).

land settlement [ˈlændˈsetlmənt] *n* colonización *f*.

landslide [ˈlændslaid] *n* corrimiento *m or* desprendimiento *m* de tierras || FIG triunfo *m* electoral aplastante.

landslip [ˈlændslip] *n* corrimiento *m or* desprendimiento *m* de tierras.

landsman [ˈlændzmən] *n* hombre *m* que vive en la tierra || FIG marinero *m* inexperto, marinero *m* de agua dulce.

— OBSERV El plural de esta palabra es *landsmen*.

land survey [ˈlænˈsəːvei]; **land surveying** [-iŋ] *n* agrimensura *f*, topografía *f*.

land surveyor [ˈlændsəˈveiə*] *n* agrimensor *m*.

land tax [ˈlændtæks] *n* impuesto *m* territorial.

land tenure [ˈlændˈtejuə*] *n* régimen *m* de la propiedad agrícola.

land use [ˈlændjuːs]; **land utilization** [ˈlændˌjuːtilaiˈzeiʃən] *n* explotación *f* del suelo.

landward [ˈlændwədz] *adj* más cerca de la tierra.

◆ *adv* hacia la tierra.

landwards [ˈlændwədz] *adv* hacia la tierra.

lane [lein] *n* camino *m* (in the country) || callejuela *f*, callejón *m* (in the town) || carril *m*, vía *f*, banda *f* (of a motorway) || calle *f* (rows of people); *to forme a lane* hacer calle || MAR & AVIAT ruta *f* || SP calle *f* (in athletics, swimming) | pista *f* (in bowling).

lang syne; **langsyne** [ˈlæŋˈsain] *adv* antaño || *auld lang syne* tiempos *m pl* de antaño, tiempos remotos.

language [ˈlæŋgwidʒ] *n* lenguaje *m* (faculty, mode, style of speech); *language is man's method of communication* el lenguaje es el medio de comunicación del hombre; *don't use that language with me* no uses ese lenguaje conmigo; *scientific language* lenguaje científico || lengua *f*, idioma *f* (of a country); *he speaks three languages* habla tres idiomas || — *agglutinative language* lengua aglutinante || *bad language* palabrotas *f pl* || *dead language* lengua muerta || *he uses bad language, his language is very bad* es muy mal hablado || *language laboratory* laboratorio *m* de lenguas *or* de idiomas || *living language* lengua viva || *modern languages* lenguas modernas || *native language* lengua materna *or* nativa || *strong language* palabras mayores *or* fuertes.

◆ *adj* de idiomas; *language school, teacher* escuela, profesor de idiomas.

langue d'oc [lɑgdɔk] *n* lengua *f* de oc.

langue d'oil [lɑgdɔil] *n* lengua *f* de oil.

languid [ˈlæŋgwid] *adj* lánguido, da.

languidness [-nis] *n* languidez *f*.

languish [ˈlæŋgwiʃ] *vi* languidecer (to become languid) || FIG consumirse (in prison) | decaer (interest) | languidecer (conversation) | echar una mirada lánguida [para ganarse la simpatía] || *to languish for* consumirse por (to pine for).

languishing [-iŋ] *adj* que va decayendo (interest) || lánguido, da (look, eyes) || que se consume (lover).

languishment [-mənt] *n* languidez *f* || MED postración *f* || FIG mirada *f* lánguida.

languor [ˈlæŋgə*] *n* languidez *f*.

languorous [-rəs] *adj* lánguido, da.

laniary [ˈlænjəri] *adj* canino (tooth).

◆ *n* canino *m*, diente *m* canino.

laniferous [ləˈnifərəs]; **lanigerous** [ləˈnidʒərəs] *adj* ZOOL lanífero, ra.

lank [læŋk] *adj* larguirucho, cha; desgarbado, da; desmadejado, da (tall and thin) ‖ flaco, ca; seco, ca (thin) ‖ lacio, cia (hair) ‖ hundido, da (cheeks).

lankiness [-inis] *n* flacura *f* (thinness) ‖ desmadejamiento *m* (gawkiness).

lanky [-i] *adj* larguirucho, cha (tall and thin) ‖ desgarbado, da; desmadejado, da (gawky).

lanolin ['lænəuli:n]; **lanoline** ['lænəuli:n] *n* lanolina *f*.

lansquenet ['lɑ:nskənet] *n* HIST lansquenete *m*.

lantern ['læntən] *n* farol *m*, linterna *f* (portable light) ‖ ARCH linterna *f* ‖ MAR linterna *f* (of lighthouse) | fanal *m*, farol *m* (in a ship) ‖ linterna *f* mágica (magic lantern) ‖ — *Chinese lantern* farolillo *m* ‖ *lantern lecture* conferencia *f* con proyecciones.

lantern fly [-flai] *n* cocuyo *m* (insect).

lantern-jawed [-'dʒɔ:d] *adj* FAM chupado de cara.

lantern pinion [-'pinjən] *n* linterna *f*.

lantern slide [-slaid] *n* diapositiva *f*.

lantern wheel [-wi:l] *n* linterna *f*.

lanthanum ['lænθənəm] *n* CHEM lantano *m*.

lanuginous [lə'nju:dʒinəs] *adj* lanuginoso, sa.

lanyard ['lænjəd] *n* MAR acollador *m*.

Laodicea [,leiəudi'siə] *pr n* GEOGR Laodicea *f*.

Laos [lauz] *pr n* GEOGR Laos *m*.

Laotian ['lauʃiən] *adj/n* laosiano, na.

lap [læp] *n* rodillas *f pl*, regazo *m*; *she was sitting with the child on her lap* estaba sentada con el niño en sus rodillas ‖ faldón *m* (of a coat) ‖ regazo *m* (of an apron, etc.) ‖ GEOGR depresión *f* (of a valley) ‖ ARCH revestimiento *m* ‖ ELECTR aislante *m* ‖ chapoteo *m*; *the lap of the water on the shore* el chapoteo del agua contra la orilla ‖ lametón *m*, lengüetada *f* (of a dog drinking) ‖ TECH rueda *f* de pulir, bruñidor *m* (polishing disk) ‖ SP vuelta *f*; *lap of honour* vuelta de honor; *four laps of the track* cuatro vueltas a la pista ‖ ANAT lóbulo *m* (of ear) ‖ vuelta *f* (part which overlaps) ‖ imbricación *f* (of tiles) ‖ FIG etapa *f* (stage); *the last lap of a journey* la etapa final de un viaje | seno *m* (bosom) ‖ — FIG *it dropped into my lap* me llegó a las manos | *it is in the lap of the gods* está en manos de Dios | *to live in the lap of luxury* vivir *or* nadar en la abundancia.

lap [læp] *vi* chapotear (water) ‖ dar lengüetadas (a dog) ‖ imbricarse, traslaparse (to overlap) ‖ SP dar una vuelta ‖ *to lap over* sobresalir (to project), imbricarse, traslaparse (to overlap).
◆ *vt* beber a lengüetadas (animals); *the cat was lapping its milk* el gato bebía su leche a lengüetadas ‖ chocar suavemente contra, lamer; *the waves lapped the side of the boat* las olas chocaban suavemente contra el borde del barco ‖ doblar (to fold) ‖ traslapar, solapar, imbricar (tiles, etc.) ‖ empalmar a media madera (to join by overlapping) ‖ TECH pulir (to polish) | esmerilar (metal) ‖ ELECTR enfundar, revestir, forrar ‖ envolver (to wrap) ‖ SP sacar una vuelta de ventaja, adelantar; *to lap s.o. twice* adelantar a alguien dos veces | dar una vuelta a (a track of course) ‖ FIG *to lap up* beber a lengüetadas (animals), sorber (to drink quickly and noisily), disfrutar con (to enjoy), tragarse (to believe).

lapdog ['læpdɔg] *n* ZOOL perro *m* faldero.

lapel [lə'pel] *n* solapa *f* (of coat, etc.).

lapful ['læpful] *n* *he had a lapful of books* tenia un montón de libros en las rodillas.

lapidary ['læpidəri] *adj* lapidario, ria.
◆ *n* lapidario *m*.

lapidate ['læpideit] *vt* lapidar.

lapidation [,læpi'deiʃən] *n* lapidación *f* (stoning).

lapidify [læ'pidifai] *vt* lapidificar, petrificar.
◆ *vi* lapidificarse, petrificarse.

lapilli [lə'pilai] *pl n* GEOGR lapilli *m*.

lapis lazuli [,læpis'læzjulai] *n* MIN lapislázuli *m* ‖ azul *m* de ultramar (colour).

lap joint ['læpdʒɔint] *n* empalme *m* a media madera.

Lapland ['læplænd] *pr n* GEOGR Laponia *f*.

Laplander [-ə*] *n* lapón, ona.

Lapp [læp] *adj/n* lapón, ona.
◆ *n* lapón *m* (language).

lappet ['læpit] *n* orejera *f* (of cap) ‖ caída *f* (of lady's headdress) ‖ faldón *m* (of garment) ‖ solapa *f* (of pocket) ‖ pliegue *m*, doblez *f* (of clothing) ‖ lóbulo *m* (of the ear) ‖ pliegue *m* (of a membrane) ‖ moco *m*, carúncula *f* (of a turkey cock) ‖ escudo *m* (of a keyhole).

lapping ['læpiŋ] *n* chapoteo *m* (of water).

lap robe ['læp'rəub] *n* manta *f* de viaje (heavy blanket).

lapse [læps] *n* lapso *m*, período *m* (period); *a short lapse of time* un breve lapso de tiempo ‖ transcurso *m*; *the lapse of time* el transcurso del tiempo ‖ fallo *m*; *a memory lapse* un fallo de memoria ‖ lapso *m*, lapsus *m* (mistake when speaking) ‖ equivocación *f*, error *m* (mistake) ‖ desliz *m*, falta *f*, error *m* (moral mistake) ‖ caída *f*; *lapse into heresy* caída en la herejía ‖ caída *f* en desuso (falling into desuse) ‖ derogación *f* (of one's principles) ‖ JUR caducidad *f* (of laws) | prescripción *f* (of rights) ‖ — *lapse from one's duty* falta a su deber ‖ *lapse of the pen* lapsus cálami ‖ *lapse of the tongue* lapsus linguae.

lapse [læps] *vi* transcurrir, pasar (time) ‖ JUR caducar ‖ caer, incurrir; *to lapse into bad habits* incurrir en malas costumbres ‖ caer en el error, equivocarse (to err) ‖ cometer un desliz (morally) ‖ faltar; *to lapse from duty* faltar a su deber ‖ recaer, reincidir (to relapse) ‖ recurrir; *to lapse into one's own language* recurrir a su propia lengua ‖ desaparecer (to cease to be) ‖ caer en desuso (habits, customs) ‖ — *to lapse into silence* quedarse callado, no decir palabra ‖ *to lapse into unconsciousness* perder el conocimiento.

lapsed [-t] *adj* REL lapso, sa ‖ JUR caducado, da.

lapstrake ['læpstreik]; **lapstreak** ['læpstri:k] *adj* de tingladillo.
◆ *n* barco *m* de tingladillo.

laptop ['læptɔp]; **laptop computer** ['læptɔp kəm'pju:tə*] *n* INFORM ordenador *m* portátil.

lapwing ['læpwiŋ] *n* ZOOL avefría *f*.

lar [lɑ:*] *n* lar *m*.
◆ *pl* dioses lares.
— OBSERV El plural de esta palabra es *lares* tanto en inglés como en español.

larboard ['lɑ:bəd] *adj* MAR de babor.
◆ *adv* a babor.
◆ *n* babor *m*.

larcener ['lɑ:sinə*]; **larcenist** ['lɑ:sinist] *n* ratero *m* (thief).

larcenous ['lɑ:sinəs] *adj* culpable de robo *or* de hurto (person) ‖ *larcenous action* robo *m*.

larceny ['lɑ:səni] *n* ratería *f*, hurto *m*, robo *m*, latrocinio *m* ‖ *petty larceny* robo de menor cuantía, hurto, ratería.

larch [lɑ:tʃ] *n* BOT alerce *m*.

lard [lɑ:d] *n* CULIN manteca *f* de cerdo.

lard [lɑ:d] *vt* CULIN mechar, lardar ‖ FIG entreverar, sembrar (*with* de) (a speech, a text).

larder ['lɑ:də*] *n* despensa *f* (pantry).

lardon ['lɑ:dən]; **lardoon** [lɑ:du:n] *n* CULIN mecha *f*, lonja *f* de tocino.

lardy ['lɑ:di] *adj* mantecoso, sa.

lardy-dardy [-'dɑ:di] *adj* FAM presuntuoso, sa.

large [lɑ:dʒ] *adj* grande; *a large farm* una finca grande ‖ grande, abundante, copioso, sa (meal) ‖ grande, importante; *a large sum of money* una gran cantidad de dinero; *a large company* una sociedad importante ‖ grande, voluminoso, sa (parcel) ‖ grande, numeroso, sa (family) ‖ amplio, plia; *to have large views* tener miras amplias ‖ liberal, espléndido, da (generous) ‖ amplio, plia; extenso, sa (powers) ‖ grande (size of clothes) ‖ MAR favorable (wind) ‖ — *as large as life* de tamaño natural (life-size), en persona (in person) ‖ *on a large scale* en gran escala ‖ *to a large extent* en gran parte.
◆ *adv* MAR con viento a la cuadra ‖ — *at large* en libertad, libre, suelto, ta; *the fugitive is still at large* el fugitivo está aún en libertad; en general; *the public at large* el público en general; extensamente, largamente; *to speak at large* hablar extensamente ‖ US *congressman-at-large* diputado *m* que representa una región entera.

large-handed [-'hændid] *adj* de manos grandes ‖ FIG dadivoso, sa; generoso, sa; espléndido, da (generous).

large-hearted [-'hɑ:tid] *adj* dadivoso, sa; desprendido, da; magnánimo, ma (generous).

large intestine [-in'testin] *n* ANAT intestino *m* grueso.

largely ['lɑ:dʒli] *adv* en gran parte (mainly) ‖ considerablemente, ampliamente (much) ‖ generosamente (generously) ‖ *largely sufficient* más que suficiente.

large-minded ['lɑ:dʒ'maindid] *adj* tolerante, de ideas *or* miras amplias.

largeness ['lɑ:dʒnis] *n* tamaño *m* (in space) ‖ grosor *m* (in mass) ‖ FIG amplitud *f* (of mind) | magnitud *f*.

larger ['lɑ:dʒə*] *comp adj* más grande, mayor.

larger-than-life [-ðən,laif] *adj* exagerado, da; desmedido, da.

large-scale ['lɑ:dʒskeil] *adj* en gran escala.

large-sized ['lɑ:dʒsaizd] *adj* de gran tamaño.

largess; largesse [lɑ:'dʒes] *n* dádiva *f* (gift) ‖ largueza *f*, generosidad *f* (generosity).

larghetto [lɑ:'getəu] *adv* MUS larghetto.
◆ *n* MUS larghetto *m*.

largish ['lɑ:dʒiʃ] *adj* bastante largo, ga; más bien largo, ga.

largo ['lɑ:gəu] *adv* MUS largo.
◆ *n* MUS largo *m*.

lariat ['læriət] *n* lazo *m* (lasso) ‖ cabestro *m* (for picketing horses).

lark [lɑ:k] *n* ZOOL alondra *f* (bird) ‖ FAM broma *f* (joke); *to have a lark with s.o.* gastar una broma a uno; *this wedding lark cost me a fortune* la broma de la boda me costó un dineral | travesura *f* (mischievous action) | juerga *f*, parranda *f* (binge, spree); *what a lark we had!* ¡qué juerga nos corrimos!; *to go on a lark* irse de juerga ‖ — FAM *to do sth. for a lark* hacer algo para divertirse | *to get up with the lark* levantarse con el alba *or* con las gallinas | *what a lark!* ¡qué divertido!

lark [lɑ:k] *vi* FAM andar de juerga | divertirse (to amuse o.s.) ‖ — FAM *stop larking about!* ¡déjate de tonterías *or* de sandeces *or* de bromas! | *to lark about* hacer el tonto | *to lark about with sth.* juguetear con algo.

larkspur [-spə:*] *n* BOT espuela *f* de caballero.

larky ['lɑ:ki] *adj* FAM bromista.

larrikin ['lærikin] *n* FAM golfo *m*, gamberro *m*.

larrup ['lærəp] *vt* dar una paliza a.

larva ['lɑːvə] *n* ZOOL larva *f*.
— OBSERV El plural de la palabra inglesa es *larvae*.

larval [-l] *adj* ZOOL larval ‖ MED larvado, da.

larvicolous [lɑː'vikələs] *adj* larvícola.

laryngeal [,lærin'dʒiːəl] *adj* laríngeo, a.

laryngectomy [,lærin'dʒektəmi] *n* MED laringectomía *f*.

laryngitis [,lærin'dʒaitis] *inv n* MED laringitis *f*.

laryngology [læriŋ'gɔlədzi] *n* laringología *f*.

laryngoscope [lə'riŋgəskəup] *n* MED laringoscopio *m* (instrument for examining the larynx).

laryngotomy [,læriŋ'gɔtəmi] *n* MED laringotomía *f*.

larynx ['læriŋks] *n* ANAT laringe *f*.
— OBSERV El plural de la palabra inglesa es *larynges* o *larynxes*.

lasagne [lə'zænjə] *n* CULIN lasaña *f*.

lascivious [lə'siviəs] *adj* lascivo, va; lujurioso, sa.

lasciviousness [-nis] *n* lascivia *f*, lujuria *f*.

laser [leizə*] *n* láser *m*; *laser beam* rayo láser ‖ INFORM *laser printer* impresora *f* láser.

lash [læʃ] *n* tralla *f* (striking part of whip) ‖ latigazo *m*, azote *m* (blow with the whip) ‖ azote *m* (punishment) ‖ FIG coletazo *m* (of a tail) | azote *m* (of wind) | embate *m* (of waves) ‖ ANAT pestaña *f* (eyelash) ‖ MAR amarra *f* (rope) ‖ FIG aguijonamiento *m*, incitación *f* (of desire) | sarcasmo *m*, pulla *f* (remark).

lash [læʃ] *vt* azotar a, dar latigazos a (to whip) ‖ azotar; *the waves lashed the rocks* las olas azotaban las rocas; *the rain lashed the windows* la lluvia azotaba los cristales ‖ sacudir; *the wind lashed the trees* el viento sacudía los árboles ‖ FIG incitar (to excite) | atacar violentamente, fustigar (when speaking) ‖ atar (to bind) ‖ MAR amarrar, trincar ‖ — *to lash its tail* dar coletazos ‖ *to lash o.s. into a fury* ponerse furioso.
◆ *vi* dar coletazos, agitarse (tail) ‖ azotar el aire (swords, etc.).
◆ *phr v* ***to lash against*** azotar (wind, rain) ‖ ***to lash down*** caer con fuerza (rain, hail) | sujetar, atar firmemente (to bind) ‖ ***to lash on*** hacer andar a latigazos ‖ ***to lash out*** dar una coz, dar coces (a horse, etc.) | repartir golpes a diestro y siniestro (a person with his fists) | estallar (with anger) | gastar (money) ‖ — *to lash out at* dar un latigazo a (a horse), lanzar una indirecta a, tirar una pulla a (to criticize).

lashing [-iŋ] *n* azotaina *f*, azotes *m pl*, flagelación *f* (whipping) ‖ azotes *m pl* (of rain) ‖ FIG bronca *f* (scolding) ‖ ligadura *f*, atadura *f* (tying) ‖ MAR amarra *f*, trinca *f* (rope).
◆ *pl* FAM montones *m*; *lashing of cream* montones de nata.

lass [læs] *n* muchacha *f*, chica *f* (young girl) ‖ novia *f* (sweetheart).

lassie ['læsi] *n* muchacha *f*, chica *f*.

lassitude ['læsitjuːd] *n* lasitud *f*, cansancio *m*.

lasso [læ'suː] *n* lazo *m*.

lasso [læ'suː] *vt* coger con el lazo.

last [lɑːst] *adj* último, ma; *the last time* la última vez; *the last row* la última fila; *his last three books* sus tres últimos libros; *you are my last hope* eres mi última esperanza; *the last Saturday of the year* el último sábado del año; *he is the last person I would have suspected it from* es la última persona a quien hubiera sospechado; *my last offer* mi última oferta ‖ último, ma; final; *the last stage* la etapa final; *the last match of the season* el partido final de la temporada ‖ pasado, da; *last month* el mes pasado; *last Saturday* el sábado pasado; *on Saturday last* el sábado pasado ‖ sumo, ma; extremo, ma (greatest) ‖ — *before last* penúltimo, ma; *the house before last* la penúltima casa; antepasado, da; *the week before last* la semana antepasada ‖ *every last one* todos y cada uno ‖ *I haven't seen him these last two years* hace dos años que no le veo ‖ *last but not least* o *by no means least* el último en orden aunque no en importancia ‖ *last but one* penúltimo, ma; *the last house but one* la penúltima casa ‖ *last honours* honras *f* fúnebres ‖ *last night* anoche, ayer por la noche (yesterday), último día, última función *or* representación (of a play), último día (of a film) ‖ *last November* el mes de noviembre pasado ‖ *last thing at night* al final del día ‖ *that's the last thing that's worrying me* es lo que menos me preocupa ‖ *the Last Judgment* el Juicio Final ‖ FIG *the last thing* o *the last word in hats* el último grito en sombreros ‖ *the night before last* antes de anoche, anteanoche ‖ *this day last week* hace exactamente una semana ‖ *to be the last* o *the last one* o *the last person to do sth.* ser el último en hacer algo ‖ *to have the last word* tener la última palabra ‖ *to pay one's last respects* rendir el último homenaje.
◆ *adv* el último, la última, lo último; *we'll do this last* haremos esto lo último; *they arrived last* ellos llegaron los últimos ‖ el último, la última, en último lugar, en la última posición (in a competition or race) ‖ por última vez, la última vez; *we last saw him in Paris* la última vez le vimos en París; *when did it last happen?* ¿cuándo ocurrió por última vez? ‖ en último lugar (at the end) ‖ por último, finalmente; *and last we'll go to the cinema* y por último iremos al cine ‖ *to leave sth. till last* dejar algo para el final.
◆ *n* último, ma; *who is the last in the queue?* quién es el último de la cola? ‖ lo que queda, el resto; *would anyone like the last of the cheese?* ¿quiere alguien el resto del queso? ‖ final *m*, fin *m*; *to be true to the last* ser fiel hasta el final ‖ último día *m*; *the last of the month* el último día del mes ‖ anterior *m* & *f*; *that apple was better than the last* esa manzana era mejor que la anterior ‖ unidad *f* de peso y de capacidad (measure) ‖ horma *f* (for shoes) ‖ COMM última *f* (letter); *in my last* en mi última ‖ — *at last* por fin ‖ *at long last* por fin, al fin y al cabo ‖ FIG *stick to your last!* ¡zapatero, a tus zapatos! ‖ *the last of the apples* la última manzana ‖ FIG *to be near one's last* estar en las últimas | *to breath one's last* exhalar el último suspiro ‖ *to have seen the last of s.o.* haber visto a alguien por última vez ‖ *to speak one's last* pronunciar su última palabra ‖ *you haven't heard the last of this* volverás a oír hablar del asunto ‖ *you haven't seen the last of me* volverás a verme.

last [lɑːst] *vi* durar; *his illness lasted a week* su enfermedad duró una semana; *this coat has lasted a long time* este abrigo ha durado mucho tiempo ‖ permanecer; *his memory will last* permanecerá su recuerdo ‖ aguantar, resistir; *I can't last much longer* no puedo aguantar mucho más ‖ llegarle a uno, alcanzar; *I don't think my money will last* no creo que me llegue el dinero ‖ conservarse (a custom, etc.) ‖ — *made to last* duradero, ra ‖ *this is too good to last* esto es demasiado bueno para que dure ‖ *to last out* resistir (to survive), llegarle a uno, alcanzar; *will the food last out till the end of the week?* ¿nos llegará la comida hasta el final de la semana?
◆ *vt* durar; *those shoes didn't last you long* estos zapatos no te han durado mucho tiempo ‖ *to last out* aguantar, resistir; *my coat will not last the winter out* mi abrigo no aguantará todo el invierno; sobrevivir a (to outlive); *he lasted the war out* sobrevivió a la guerra.

last-ditch [-ditʃ] *adj* FIG último, ma; desesperado, da; *a last-ditch effort* un último esfuerzo | hasta el extremo (resistance, etc.).

Lastex ['læsteks] *n* Lástex *m* (trademark).

lasting ['lɑːstiŋ] *adj* duradero, ra; *a lasting peace* una paz duradera ‖ resistente (strong) ‖ constante (fear, etc.) ‖ profundo, da; *it created a lasting impression on me* me produjo una profunda impresión.
◆ *n* tela *f* fuerte ‖ FIG resistencia *f*.

lastly ['lɑːstli] *adv* por último, finalmente.

last-minute ['lɑːst'minit] *adj* de última hora (news, decision, etc.).

last name ['lɑːst'neim] *n* apellido *m*.

last offices ['lɑːst'ɔfisiz] *pl n* REL oficio *m sing* de difuntos.

last quarter ['lɑːst'kwɔːtə*] *n* cuarto *m* menguante (of the moon).

last rites ['lɑːst'raits] *pl n* REL extremaunción *f sing*.

last sleep ['lɑːst'sliːp] *n* último sueño *m* (death).

last straw ['lɑːst'strɔː] *n* colmo *m*, acabóse *m* ‖ FIG *it's the last straw* es el colmo, es la última gota que hace rebasar la copa, es el acabóse.

Last Supper ['lɑːst'sʌpə*] *n* REL Última Cena *f*.

latch [lætʃ] *n* picaporte *m*, pestillo *m* (of a door) ‖ pestillo *m* [de golpe] (of window) ‖ — *on the latch* cerrado con picaporte ‖ *to drop the latch* correr *or* echar el pestillo.

latch [lætʃ] *vt* cerrar [con el picaporte].
◆ *vi* *to latch on to* pegarse a (a person), darse cuenta de (a fact), agarrarse a (to grasp).

latchet ['lætʃit] *n* cordón *m* del zapato.

latchkey ['lætʃkiː] *n* llave *f* (de picaporte).

late [leit] *adj* tardío, a; *his late arrival* su llegada tardía; *late middle English* inglés medio tardío; *it is a late summer* es un verano tardío ‖ último, ma (last); *in the late war* en la última guerra; *in the late years* en los últimos años ‖ reciente (recent) ‖ retrasado, da (delayed) ‖ atrasado, da (delivery) ‖ GRAMM tardío (latin) ‖ de fines de; *a late 16th century church* una iglesia de fines del siglo XVI ‖ ex, antiguo, gua (former); *the late Foreign Minister* el ex ministro de Asuntos Exteriores ‖ fallecido, da; difunto, ta; *my late husband* mi difunto marido ‖ avanzado, da (age, hour, season); *at a late hour* a una hora avanzada ‖ — *a late party* una reunión que acaba tarde ‖ *he is late* ya tenía que estar aquí (before arriving), ha llegado tarde (upon arriving) ‖ *in the late afternoon* hacia el final de la tarde ‖ *in the late nineteenth century* a fines *or* a finales del siglo diez y nueve ‖ *it is late* es tarde ‖ *it is too late* es demasiado tarde ‖ *I was late in coming* llegué tarde ‖ *of late years* en estos últimos años ‖ US *the late late show* la película nocturna [en la televisión] ‖ *the late show* la última función ‖ *to be late* llegar tarde (a person), llevar retraso (a train, etc.), tardar; *he was late in going to bed* tardó en acostarse; caer tarde (feast, event) ‖ *to get* o *to grow late* hacerse tarde; *it's getting late* se está haciendo tarde ‖ *to make s.o. late* retrasar a uno, hacer llegar tarde a uno, entretener a uno.
◆ *adv* tarde; *to arrive late* llegar tarde; *very late in the night* muy tarde por la noche ‖ con retraso (after the appointed time) ‖ tardíamente, tarde (too late) ‖ recientemente (recently) ‖ anteriormente; *late of York* anteriormente domiciliado en York ‖ — *as late as* todavía en; *this custom existed as late as last century* esta costumbre existía todavía en el siglo pasado; hasta (until) ‖ *as late as yesterday* no más tarde que ayer, ayer mismo ‖ *better late than never* más vale tarde que nunca ‖ *late in* hacia fines de; *late in the year* hacia fines de año ‖ *late in life* a una edad avanzada ‖ *late in*

the afternoon a última hora de la tarde || FIG *late in the day* tarde || *late in years* de edad avanzada || *late last century* hacia finales del siglo pasado || *late of Oxford* antiguo de Oxford || *of late* últimamente, recientemente || *to arrive ten minutes late* llegar con diez minutos de retraso || *to keep s.o. late* entretener a alguien hasta muy tarde || *to stay up late* quedarse levantado hasta muy tarde.

latecomer [-'kʌmə*] *n* rezagado, da (who lags behind) || retrasado, da; persona *f* que llega tarde (who arrives late) || recién llegado, recién llegada, nuevo, va (newcomer).

lateen [lə'ti:n] *adj* MAR latina (sail).
◆ *n* MAR vela *f* latina || *lateen yard* entena *f*.

lately ['leitli] *adv* últimamente, recientemente || hace poco; *until lately* hasta hace poco.

latency [-si] *n* estado *m* latente.

lateness ['leitnis] *n* retraso *m* (of train, of person's arrival, etc.) || llegada *f* tardía (of a person) || lo avanzado (of the hour) || fecha *f* reciente (of an event) || *lateness will be punished* será castigado el que llegue tarde.

late-night ['leitnɑit] *adj* de madrugada (show), abierto, ta hasta tarde (shop).

latent ['leitənt] *adj* latente; *latent heat* calor latente; *in a latent state* en estado latente || oculto, ta (defect, qualities).

later ['leitə*] *comp adj* → **late** || posterior; *his later works* sus obras posteriores; *a later date* una fecha posterior || último, ma (last) || más reciente; *this picture is later than the other* este cuadro es más reciente que el otro.
◆ *comp adv* → **late** || después, más tarde; *three years later* tres años después || — *later on* más tarde, después || *no later than yesterday* ayer mismo, no más tarde que ayer || *see you later* hasta luego, hasta pronto.

lateral ['lætərəl] *adj* lateral.

laterally [-i] *adv* lateralmente.

Lateran ['lætərən] *adj* REL lateranense.
◆ *n* REL Letrán *m*.

latest ['leitist] *superl adj* → **late** || último, ma; *the latest news* las últimas noticias || más reciente (recent) || *the latest thing in hats* el último grito en sombreros.
◆ *superl adv* → **late.**
◆ *n* última noticia *f* (latest news); *have you heard the latest?* ¿has oído la última noticia? || lo último || — *at the latest* a más tardar || *the latest that suits me is* lo más tarde que me conviene es || *the very latest* el último grito (in fashion).

latex ['leiteks] *n* BOT látex *m*.
— OBSERV El plural de *latex* es *latices* o *latexes*.

lath [lɑ:θ] *n* listón *m* || FAM *as thin as a lath* como un fideo.

lathe [leið] *n* torno *m* (for pottery) || torno *m* (machine tool).

lathe [leið] *vt* tornear.

lathe operator [-'ɔpəreitə*] *n* tornero *m*.

lather ['lɑ:ðə*] *n* espuma *f* (of soap, etc.) || sudor *m* (on a horse).

lather ['lɑ:ðə*] *vi* hacer espuma (soap) || estar cubierto de sudor (of sweat).
◆ *vt* enjabonar (with soap) || FAM dar una paliza, zurrar (to thrash).

lather ['leiðə*] *n* tornero *m* (of machine tool) || alfarero *m* (in pottery).

lathery ['lɑ:ðəri] *adj* espumoso, sa (liquid) || lleno de espuma (chin) || sudoroso, sa (covered in sweat).

lathing ['lɑ:θiŋ] *n* enlistonado *m*, listonado *m* (lathwork) || listones *m pl*.

latices ['lætisi:z] *pl n* → **latex.**

latifundium [læti'fʌndiəm] *n* latifundio *m*.
— OBSERV El plural de la palabra inglesa es *latifundia*.

Latin ['lætin] *adj* latino, na.
◆ *n* latino, na (person) || latín *m* (language); *low Latin* bajo latín; *vulgar Latin* latín vulgar *or* rústico || FAM *dog Latin* latín de cocina *or* macarrónico.

Latin America [-ə'merikə] *pr n* GEOGR América Latina *f*, Latinoamérica *f*.

Latin American [-ə'merikən] *n* latinoamericano, na.

Latin-American [-ə'merikən] *adj* latinoamericano, na.
— OBSERV *Latinoamericano* is the term used by Latin Americans. In Spain *hispanoamericano* and *iberoamericano* are more commonly used.

Latinism ['lætinizəm] *n* latinismo *m*.

Latinist ['lætinist] *n* latinista *m* & *f*.

Latinity [lə'tiniti] *n* latinidad *f*.

Latinization [,lætini'zeiʃən] *n* latinización *f*.

Latinize ['lætinaiz] *vt/vi* latinizar.

latish ['leitiʃ] *adj* un poco tardío.
◆ *adv* un poco tarde.

latitude ['lætitju:d] *n* latitud *f* || FIG latitud *f*, amplitud *f*, libertad *f* (freedom to act).

latitudinal [,læti'tju:dinl] *adj* latitudinal, transversal.

Latium ['leiʃjəm] *pr n* GEOGR Lacio *m*.

Latona [lə'təunə] *pr n* MYTH Latona *f*.

latria [lə'traiə] *n* REL latría *f*.

latrine [lə'tri:n] *n* letrina *f*, retrete *m*.

latten ['lætn] *n* latón *m* (brass alloy) || hojalata *f* (tin).

latter ['lætə*] *adj* segundo, da; último, ma; *the latter half of the week* la segunda mitad de la semana || último, ma; más reciente; *his latter works* sus últimas obras.
◆ *pron* éste, ésta; *the former... the latter* aquél... éste.

latter-day [-dei] *adj* moderno, na; reciente, de nuestros días.

Latter-day Saint [-deiseint] *n* REL santo *m* del último día, mormón, ona.

latterly ['lætəːli] *adv* últimamente, recientemente (recently) || después, más tarde (after).

lattice ['lætis] *n* celosía *f*, enrejado *m* || HERALD celosía *f* || PHYS retículo *m* (of a reactor).
◆ *adj* enrejado, da (door) || de celosía (girder, etc.) || de celosía, enrejado, da (window).

latticed [-t] *adj* enrejado, da; con celosía.

latticework [-wə:k] *n* celosía *f*, enrejado *m*.

Latvia ['lætviə] *pr n* GEOGR Letonia *f*.

Latvian [-n] *adj/n* letón, ona.
◆ *n* letón *m* (language).

laud [lɔ:d] *n* alabanza *f* (praise).
◆ *pl* REL laudes *f*.

laud [lɔ:d] *vt* alabar, elogiar, encomiar.

laudability [,lɔ:də'biliti] *n* lo encomiable, lo elogiable.

laudable ['lɔ:dəbl] *adj* laudable, loable.

laudanum ['lɔdnəm] *n* láudano *m*.

laudative ['lɔ:dətiv]; **laudatory** ['lɔ:dətəri] *adj* laudatorio, ria; elogioso, sa; encomiástico, ca.

laugh [lɑ:f] *n* risa *f* (expression of amusement); *mocking laugh* risa burlona || broma *f* (joke) || — *a loud laugh* una carcajada, una risotada || *good for a laugh* divertido, da || *he is a good laugh* es un tipo gracioso || *just for a laugh* o *for laughs* sólo para divertirse || *to give a forced laugh, to force a laugh* reír de dientes afuera, reír con risa de conejo || *to have the last laugh* ser el que ríe el último || *to raise a laugh* causar risa || *we had a good laugh the other day* nos reímos mucho el otro día || *what a laugh!* ¡qué risa!

laugh [lɑ:f] *vi* reír, reírse; *to start laughing* echarse a reír || — *he who laughs last laughs longest, he laughs best who laughs last* quien ríe el último ríe mejor, al freír será el reír || *to burst out laughing* soltar la carcajada, echarse a reír a carcajadas || *to die laughing* morirse de risa || *to laugh about* o *over* reírse de || *to laugh at* reírse de; *to laugh at s.o.* reírse de uno || *to laugh heartily* reír con ganas || *to laugh in s.o.'s face* reírse de uno en su cara *or* en sus barbas || *to laugh one's head off* partirse de risa || FIG *to laugh on the other* o *the wrong side of one's face* llorar || *to laugh out loud* reírse a carcajadas || FIG *to laugh s.o. out of court* poner a alguien en ridículo || *to laugh until one's sides ache* reír a mandíbula batiente || *to laugh up one's sleeve* o *to o.s.* reírse para su capote *or* para su sayo *or* para su coleto *or* para sus adentros *or* a solas *or* por lo bajo || *to make one laugh* dar risa || *to make s.o. laugh on the other* o *on the wrong side of his face* quitarle a uno las ganas de reír || *to split one's sides laughing* partirse de risa.
◆ *vt* decir riendo || — *they laughed their approval* aprobaron riendo || *to laugh away* tomar a risa || *to laugh away the time with jokes* matar el tiempo contando chistes || *to laugh down* ridiculizar || *to laugh off* tomar a risa || *we laughed him out of his bad humour* le hicimos reír tanto que se puso de buen humor.

laughable [-əbl] *adj* ridículo, la; absurdo, da || irrisorio, ria; *a laughable offer* una oferta irrisoria || *to be laughable* dar que reír, ser de risa.

laughing [-iŋ] *adj* risueño, ña; *laughing eyes* ojos risueños; *a laughing fountain* una fuente risueña || — *it's no laughing matter* no es cosa de risa || *laughing gas* gas *m* hilarante || *to have a laughing fit* tener un ataque de risa.
◆ *n* risas *f pl*.

laughingly [-li] *adv* riendo.

laughingstock ['lɑ:fiŋstɔk] *n* hazmerreír *m inv*; *to be a laughingstock of everyone* ser el hazmerreír de todo el mundo.

laughter ['lɑ:ftə*] *n* risa *f*, risas *f pl*, carcajadas *f pl*; *the laughter of the audience* las risas del público || — *roar* o *peals of laughter* carcajadas || *to burst into laughter* soltar la carcajada || *uncontrollable laughter* risa nerviosa.

launce [lɑ:ns] *n* amodita *f* (sea fish).

Launcelot ['lɑ:nslət] *pr n* Lancelote *m*, Lanzarote *m* (Lancelot).

launch [lɔ:ntʃ] *n* lancha *f* (craft); *motor launch* lancha motora || botadura *f* (launching).

launch [lɔ:ntʃ] *vt* botar (a ship) || lanzar (a missile, an actor, a new product) || echar al mar, sacar al mar (a lifeboat) || crear, fundar (a new company) || estrenar (play, film) || emprender (a project, an attack) || emitir (to emit, to issue) || lanzar (to throw) || FAM *to launch into eternity* mandar al otro mundo.
◆ *vi* lanzarse || — *to launch forth* o *into* lanzarse en (explanations) || *to launch out on* lanzarse en, emprender (an enterprise).

launcher [-ə*] *n* lanzador *m* || — MIL *grenade launcher* lanzagranadas *m inv* | *rocket launcher* lanzacohetes *m inv*.

launching [-iŋ] *n* lanzamiento *m* (of a missile, of a probe) || botadura *f* (of a ship) || estreno *m* (of play, of film) || lanzamiento *m* (of a campaign, etc.) || iniciación *f* (beginning) || fundación *f*, creación *f* (foundation) || puesta *f* en servicio (making operational) || — *launching pad* plataforma *f* de lanzamiento || *launching ramp* rampa *f* de lanzamiento || *launching site* rampa *f* de lanzamiento.

launder ['lɔ:ndə*] *n* MIN reguera *f* de la colada.

launder ['lɔːndə*] *vt* lavar (to wash) || lavar y planchar (to wash and iron).
◆ *vi* lavar la ropa (to wash) || resistir el lavado (to bear washing).

launderer [-rə*] *n* lavadero *m*.

launderette [ˌlɔːndə'ret] *n* lavandería *f* automática.

laundress ['lɔːndris] *n* lavandera *f*.

laundromat ['lɔːndrə'mæt] *n* US lavandería *f* automática.

laundry ['lɔːndri] *n* lavandería *f* (place) || ropa *f* sucia (dirty clothes) || ropa *f* limpia (clean clothes) || *laundry basket* cesto *m* de la ropa sucia.

laundryman [-mæn] *n* lavandero *m*.
— OBSERV El plural de esta palabra es *laundrymen*.

laundrywoman [-'wumən] *n* lavandera *f*.
— OBSERV El plural de esta palabra es *laundrywomen*.

laureate ['lɔːriit] *adj/n* laureado, da.

laurel ['lɔrəl] *n* BOT laurel *m* || US BOT rododendro *m* | azalea *f* || BOT *cherry laurel* laurel cerezo *or* real.
◆ *pl* FIG laureles *m* (award); *laden with laurels* cargado de laureles || — FIG *to cast a stain on one's laurels* mancillar sus laureles | *to look to one's laurels* no dormirse en los laureles | *to rest on one's laurels* dormirse en los laureles | *to win laurels* cosechar *or* conquistar laureles.

laurel ['lɔrəl] *vt* laurear.

Laurence ['lɔrəns] *pr n* Lorenzo *m*.

lav [læv] *n* FAM ⟶ **lavatory**.

lava ['lɑːvə] *n* lava *f* (of a volcano); *lava flows* torrentes de lava.

lavabo [lə'veibəu] *n* REL lavatorio *m*, lavabo *m*.

lavage [læ'vɑːʒ] *n* MED lavado *m* (of stomach, etc.).

lavaret ['lævəret] *n* farra *f* (fish).

lavatory ['lævətəri] *n* retrete *m* (a water closet) || US lavabo *m*, servicios *m pl*, cuarto *m* de aseo (washroom) || — *lavatory paper* papel *m* higiénico || *public lavatory* servicios (públicos).

lave [leiv] *vt* lavar (to wash) || bañar (river, sea).

lavender ['lævində*] *n* BOT espliego *m*, lavanda *f*, alhucema *f* || azul *m*, color *m* de lavanda (colour) || *lavender water* lavanda *f*.
◆ *adj* azul (de) color de lavanda.

lavish ['læviʃ] *adj* pródigo, ga; generoso, sa (generous); *to be lavish of* ser pródigo de || abundante, profuso, sa (abundant) || lujoso, sa (luxurious) || desconsiderado, da; desmesurado, da (disproportionate) || *to be lavish with one's money* no escatimar gastos, despilfarrar el dinero.

lavish ['læviʃ] *vt* prodigar.

lavishly [-li] *adv* generosamente (generously) || profusamente, con profusión (abundantly) || lujosamente (luxuriously).

lavishness [-nis] *n* prodigalidad *f*, generosidad *f* (generosity) || abundancia *f*, profusión *f* (abundance) || lujo *m* (luxury).

law [lɔː] *n* JUR ley *f* (governing customs); *to break the law* quebrantar la ley; *law in force* ley vigente | derecho *m*; *administrative, canon, civil, commercial, constitutional, common* o *consuetudinary* o *customary, criminal, international, maritime law* derecho administrativo, canónico, civil, mercantil [AMER comercial], político, consuetudinario, penal, internacional, marítimo | derecho *m*, leyes *f pl* (study); *to read law* estudiar derecho *or* leyes | ley *f* (bill in Parliament) | lo contencioso; *law department* servicio de lo contencioso | jurisprudencia *f* (jurisprudence) || ley *f*; *the law of gravitation* la ley de la gravedad; *the law of supply and demand* la ley de la oferta y la demanda || SP regla *f*, ley *f*; *the offside law* la regla del fuera de juego || FAM policía *f* || — *according to law* según la ley || *as the law at present stands* según la legislación vigente || *by law* según la ley || *custom has the force of law* la costumbre hace ley *or* tiene fuerza de ley || *his word is law* su palabra es ley, lo que dice va a misa (*fam*) || JUR *ignorance of the law is no excuse* la ignorancia de la ley no excusa su cumplimiento || *in law* según la ley || *law and order* orden público || *law of contradiction* principio *m* de la contradicción || *law of mass action* ley de la acción de las masas || *law of nature* ley natural || PHYS *law of reflection, of refraction* ley de la reflexión, de la refracción || *law of the jungle* ley de la selva || *law of thermodynamics* principios termodinámicos || *laws are made to be broken* hecha la ley, hecha la trampa || *law school* facultad *f* de derecho || JUR *martial law* ley marcial | *officer of the law* representante *m* de la ley || *one law for o.s. and one for everyone else, one law for the rich another for the poor* la ley del embudo || JUR *prohibition law* ley seca | *salic law* ley sálica || *the forces of law and order* las fuerzas del orden || REL *the Law* la Ley (de Moisés) || FIG *the strong man is a law unto himself* allá van las leyes do *or* donde quieren reyes || *to be above the law* estar por encima de la ley || FIG *to be a law unto o.s.* dictar sus propias leyes || JUR *to be at law* estar en pleito | *to be outside the law* estar fuera de la ley | *to come under the law* estar condenado por la ley | *to go to law* recurrir a la justicia, poner pleito | *to have force of law* tener fuerza de ley | *to have the law on s.o.* llevar ante los tribunales a alguien, poner pleito a alguien || *to keep within the law* obrar legalmente || *to lay down the law* dictar la ley || JUR *to practise law* ejercer la profesión de abogado || *to take the law into one's own hands* tomarse la justicia por su mano || JUR *to take to law* citar ante la justicia, llevar ante los tribunales.
◆ *adj* jurídico, ca; *law term* término jurídico || legal.

law-abiding [-əˌbaidiŋ] *adj* observante de la ley, respetuoso de las leyes.

law adviser [-ədˌvaizə*] *n* asesor *m* jurídico.

lawbreaker [-ˌbreikə*] *n* infractor *m* de la ley, violador *m* de la ley.

lawbreaking [-ˌbreikiŋ] *n* violación *f* de la ley.

lawcourt [-kɔːt] *n* tribunal *m* de justicia.

lawful [-ful] *adj* legal (in accordance with the law) || lícito, ta (permitted by law) || legítimo, ma (recognized by law) || válido, da (contract) || justo, ta (just) || *lawful day* día *m* hábil.

lawfulness [-fulnis] *n* legalidad *f* || legitimidad *f* (legitimacy).

lawgiver [-ˌgivə*] *n* legislador, ra.

law Latin [-'lætin] *n* latín *m* macarrónico.

lawless [-lis] *adj* ilegal, ilícito, ta (illegal) || sin leyes (without law) || ingobernable, desordenado, da (unorderly) || anárquico, ca.

lawlessness [-lisnis] *n* anarquía *f* || desorden *m*, licencia *f*.

lawmaker [-ˌmeikə*] *n* legislador, ra.

lawmaking [-ˌmeikiŋ] *n* elaboración *f* de las leyes.
◆ *adj* legislativo, va.

law merchant [-'məːtʃənt] *n* derecho *m* mercantil [AMER derecho *m* comercial].

lawn [lɔːn] *n* césped *m* (grass) || linón *m* (fabric).

lawn mower [-ˌməuə*] *n* cortacéspedes *m inv*.

lawn tennis [-'tenis] *n* SP tenis *m* sobre hierba.

law officer ['lɔːˌɔfisə*] *n* JUR consejero *m* jurídico [de la corona].

Lawrence ['lɔrəns] *pr n* Lorenzo *m*.

lawrencium [lɔ'rensjəm] *n* CHEM laurencio *m*.

lawsuit ['lɔːsjuːt] *n* JUR pleito *m*, juicio *m*, proceso *m* (case presented before a civil court).

lawyer ['lɔːjə*] *n* jurista *m* & *f* (legal expert) || US abogado *m*.
— OBSERV En inglés la palabra *lawyer* se aplica a asesorar a cualquier jurista que esté autorizado a asesorar a sus clientes en cuestiones jurídicas. Por lo tanto puede designar tanto a un procurador de los tribunales como a un abogado.

lax [læks] *adj* flojo, ja (untensed) || elástico, ca (conscience) || laxo, xa; relajado, da (discipline, morals) || negligente, descuidado, da (negligent) || vago, ga; confuso, sa (ideas) || MED flojo, ja; suelto, ta (bowels) || flojo, ja; fláccido, da; flácido, da (flesh).

laxation [læk'seiʃən] *n* laxación *f*, laxamiento *m*, relajamiento *m*.

laxative ['læksətiv] *adj* laxante.
◆ *n* MED laxante *m*.

laxity ['læksiti]; **laxness** ['læksnəs] *n* laxitud *f* (looseness) || flojedad *f* (of a rope) || flaccidez *f*, flacidez *f* (of flesh) || elasticidad *f* (of conscience) || relajamiento *m* (of discipline, of morals) || negligencia *f*, descuido *m* (negligence).

lay [lei] *adj* laico, ca; seglar; *a lay preacher* un predicador seglar || profano, na; lego, ga (not expert) || REL lego, ga; *lay brother* hermano lego; *lay sister* hermana lega.
◆ *n* lay *m*, endecha *f* (song, poem) || configuración *f* (nature of land) || orientación *f* || situación *f*, disposición *f* (situation) || ocupación *f* || guarida *f* (animal lie) || — *hen in lay* gallina ponedora || POP *she is an easy lay* es una mujer fácil || *to come into lay* empezar a poner huevos || *to go out of lay* dejar de poner huevos || FIG *to study the lay of the land* estudiar el terreno.

lay* [lei] *vt* poner, colocar (to place); *to lay a carpet, bricks* poner una alfombra, ladrillos || disponer (to arrange) || poner; *to lay the table, the tablecloth* poner la mesa, el mantel || tender (pipe line, cable, railway line) || preparar (fire) || cubrir (to cover) || echar (foundations) || derribar, tirar al suelo (to knock s.o. down) || derribar (to flatten) || echar abajo (to destroy) || alisar (to smooth) || asentar (dust) || calmar (wind) || acostar (to put to bed); *to lay a child on a sofa* acostar a un niño en un sofá || presentar, exponer (facts) || presentar, formular (a claim) || valorar (damages) || echar (the blame) || hacer (an accusation) || dar (an information) || dar (*on, upon* a) (importance) || atribuir (a responsibility) || formar, hacer (a plan) || urdir, tramar (a plot) || poner, imponer (a fine, a tax, etc.) || situar (a play, etc.) || aquietar, calmar, acallar (fears) || conjurar (ghost) || SP hacer (a bet) | apostar (a horse, etc.) | apostar (a sum) || AGR encamar (corn) | poner (eggs) || MIL apuntar (to aim a gun) | tender (a trap, an ambush) || MAR trazar, marcar (the course) | corchar (a rope) | sembrar (a mine) || FAM acostarse con || — *the story is laid in Spain* la historia se sitúa en España || *to lay an axe to a tree* dar un hachazo a un árbol || *to lay bare* poner al descubierto || *to lay eyes on* ver; *I haven't laid eyes on him for ten years* hace diez años que no le he visto; mirar (to look at) || *to lay flat* arrasar; *to lay a town flat* arrasar una ciudad; extender; *to lay sth. flat on the table* extender algo sobre la mesa || *to lay hands on* echar mano a (to take), tocar (to touch), ponerle la mano encima a, alzarle la mano a (to injure), imponer las manos a (in blessing, in confirming, etc.), encontrar (to find) || *to lay hold of* agarrar || *to lay low* derribar (to overthrow), postrar (en cama) (to make bedridden) || *to lay open* abrir (to open), exponer (to expose); *to lay o.s. open to criticism* exponerse a las críticas ‖ *to lay siege to* asediar, poner sitio a, sitiar ‖ FIG *to lay to rest* enterrar ‖ *to lay waste* devastar, asolar.

◆ *vi* poner huevos (a hen) ‖ estar, estar situado (to be situated) ‖ poner la mesa; *lay for five* pon la mesa para cinco ‖ apostar (to bet).

◆ *phr v* ***to lay about*** repartir golpes a diestro y siniestro ‖ ***to lay aside*** dejar a un lado (sth. that is unwanted) | guardar (to save) | dejar de lado (scruples, prejudices) ‖ ***to lay away*** guardar (to store) ‖ ***to lay before*** presentar, exponer; *he laid the problem before me* me presentó el problema; someter; *to lay a bill before Parliament* someter un proyecto de ley al Parlamento ‖ ***to lay by*** guardar (to save) ‖ ***to lay down*** deponer, rendir (arms) | dejar, soltar (a burden) | dejar a un lado (pen, tools) | dar, ofrendar, sacrificar; *he laid down his life* dio su vida | imponer, fijar, poner (conditions) | establecer, dictar (a rule) | sentar, formular (a principle) | sentar, establecer (a precedent) | sostener (an opinion) | afirmar; *he laid down the fact that he disagreed* afirmó que no estaba de acuerdo | guardar (to save) | poner en el suelo (to put on the ground) | acostar (to put to bed) | echarse *or* tumbarse en el suelo (o.s.) | apostar (to bet) | conservar (wine) | trazar, proyectar, fijar (a plan) | cubrir (a surface) | MAR poner en un dique seco *or* en los astilleros (a ship) | hacer el tendido de, tender (a railway) | levantar, trazar (a map) | dimitir (one's office) | poner en el tapete (cards) ‖ ***to lay in*** proveerse de, abastecerse de (to provide o.s. with) | ahorrar (to save) | acumular (to amass) | comprar (to buy) ‖ ***to lay into*** dar una paliza a (to thrash) ‖ ***to lay off*** despedir (to dismiss) | dejar de; *to lay off smoking* dejar de fumar | dejar de utilizar (a machine) | dejar de trabajar (to stop working) | trazar (a line) | extender (a paint) | MAR alejarse | FAM dejar en paz (to leave alone) ‖ — *lay off it!* ¡ya está bien! ‖ ***to lay on*** proveer de (to provide) | instalar, poner (to install) | conectar (to connect) | dar, asestar, propinar (blows) | pegar (to beat) | imponer (taxes) | REL imponer (hands) | atacar (to attack) | aplicar (paint) | FAM *to lay it on thick* recargar *or* cargar las tintas, exagerar (to exaggerate), adular (to flatter) | *to lay one's hopes on* cifrar sus esperanzas en ‖ ***to lay out*** presentar (to present); *he laid out the facts to us* nos presentó los hechos | invertir, emplear (to invest money) | desembolsar (to spend money) | tender, extender (to stretch out) | estirar, alargar (cable) | exponer (to exhibit for people to see) | trazar, levantar (a map, a plan) | disponer (to arrange in a certain order) | servir (a meal) | acondicionar (a mine) | MIL levantar (a camp) | trazar, construir (a road) | amortajar, preparar (un cadáver) para un entierro (a corpse) | FAM liquidar, cargarse, matar (to kill) | FAM poner fuera de combate (to knock out), hacer besar la lona (to floor a boxer) ‖ — *to lay o.s. out* hacer todo lo posible ‖ ***to lay over*** diferir (to postpone) | parar (to stop over) ‖ MAR *to lay to* pairar ‖ ***to lay up*** encerrar en el garaje (a car) | desarmar (a warship) | atracar (a boat) | dejar de lado (to leave aside) | obligar a guardar cama (to confine to bed) | enfermar (to make ill) | guardar, almacenar (to store) | ahorrar (to save) | acumular, amasar (to amass) | FIG prepararse (troubles) ‖ — *to be laid up* guardar cama.

— OBSERV Pret y pp ***laid***.

lay [lei] *pret* ⟶ **lie** (meaning «echarse», etc.).

layabout [-əbaut] *n* holgazán, ana; vago, ga.

lay-by [-bai] *n* área *f* de aparcamiento (on motorway) ‖ apartadero *m* (railways) ‖ FAM ahorros *m pl* (savings).

lay days [-'deiz] *pl n* MAR días *m* de estadía.

layer [-ə*] *n* capa *f*; *layer of cream, of paint* capa de nata, de pintura ‖ capa *f*, lámina *f* (of wood, of metal) ‖ GEOL estrato *m* ‖ gallina *f* ponedora (hen) ‖ AGR acodo *m*, mugrón *m* (shoot) ‖ ostral *m* (oyster bed) ‖ MIL apuntador *m* (who lays guns) ‖ instalador *m* (who lays pipes, railway lines).

layer ['leiə*] *vt* AGR acodar (a rose tree).

◆ *vi* AGR encamarse (corn).

layerage [-ridʒ]; **layering** [-riŋ] *n* AGR acodadura *f*.

layette [lei'et] *n* canastilla *f*, ajuar *m* de niño.

lay figure ['lei'figə*] *n* maniquí *m* & *f* (model) ‖ FIG pelele *m*, fantoche *m*.

laying ['leiŋ] *n* colocación *f*, instalación *f* (placing) ‖ tendido *m* (of pipe, of cable) ‖ puntería *f* (of a gun) ‖ puesta *f* (of an egg).

laying down [-'daun] *n* colocación *f* (placing) ‖ establecimiento *m*, asentamiento *m* (of a principle) ‖ fijación *f*, imposición *f* (of conditions) ‖ formulación *f* (of a doctrine) ‖ tendido *m* (of pipe, cable, railway) ‖ levantamiento *m*, trazado *m* (of a map) ‖ dimisión *f* (of one's office) ‖ sacrificio *m* (of one's life) ‖ MAR colocación *f* en el dique.

laying in [-'in] *n* almacenamiento *m*.

laying on [-'ɔn] *n* imposición *f* (of taxes, of hands) ‖ colocación *f*, instalación *f* (of gas, of water) ‖ aplicación *f* (of paint).

laying out [-'aut]; **layout** ['leiəut] *n* disposición *f* (arrangement) ‖ presentación *f*, exposición *f* (exhibition) ‖ presentación *f* (of proof) ‖ trazado *m* (of a map, of a plan) ‖ MIL levantamiento *m* (of a camp) ‖ amortajamiento *m* (of a corpse) ‖ inversión *f* (investment) ‖ gasto *m*, desembolso *m* (of money) ‖ FAM liquidación *f* (elimination) | puesta *f* fuera de combate (of a boxer) ‖ PRINT composición *f*.

laying up [-'ʌp] *n* desarme *m* (of a warship) ‖ atraque *m* (of a boat) ‖ encierro *m* en un garaje (of a car) ‖ acumulación *f* (of money) ‖ preparación *f* (of troubles).

layman ['leimən] *n* seglar *m*, lego *m*, laico *m* ‖ FIG lego *m*, profano *m*.

— OBSERV El plural de esta palabra es *laymen*.

layoff ['leiɔf] *n* paro *m* involuntario *or* forzoso (unemployment) ‖ despido *m* (dismissal) ‖ cierre *m* (closing).

layout ['leiaut] *n* ⟶ **laying out**.

layover ['leiəuvə*] *n* escala *f* (travelling by plane, by boat) ‖ parada *f* (travelling by train, by car).

lay reader ['lei'ri:də*] *n* REL lego *m* autorizado a dirigir oficios religiosos.

lazar ['læzə*] *n* leproso *m* ‖ *lazar house* leprosería *f*.

lazaret [,læzə'ret]; **lazaretto** [-əu] *n* lazareto *m*.

Lazarist ['læzərist] *n* REL lazarista *m*.

Lazarus ['læzərəs] *pr n* Lázaro *m*.

laze [leiz] *n* descanso *m* ‖ *to have a laze* holgazanear (to be idle), descansar (to rest).

laze [leiz] *vi* holgazanear (to be idle) ‖ descansar, no hacer nada (to rest).

◆ *vt* *to laze away* desperdiciar, perder (el tiempo).

lazily [-ili] *adv* perezosamente (idly) ‖ lentamente (slowly).

laziness [-inis] *n* pereza *f*, holgazanería *f*.

lazulite ['læzjulait] *n* MIN lazulita *f*.

lazy ['leizi] *adj* perezoso, sa; holgazán, ana; vago, ga (idle) ‖ lento, ta (slow); *lazy pace* paso lento ‖ de pereza; *lazy days* días de pereza.

lazybones [-,bəunz] *n* FAM gandul, la; vago, ga; holgazán, ana.

lazy Susan [-'su:zn] *n* US bandeja *f* giratoria para servir la comida en la mesa.

LCD *abbr of [liquid crystal display]* visualización en cristales líquidos.

lea [li:] *n* prado *m* ‖ ovillo *m*, madeja *f* (of yarn).

leach [li:tʃ] *n* sustancia *f* para lixiviar (substance) ‖ lixiviación *f* (leaching).

leach [li:tʃ] *vt* lixiviar ‖ *to leach away* o *out* extraer por lixiviación.

lead [li:d] *n* correa *f* (for dog) ‖ traílla *f* (for hunting dog) ‖ THEATR primer papel *m* (role); *she has the lead in this play* tiene el primer papel en esta obra de teatro | primer actor *m* (male actor) | primera actriz *f* (female actor) ‖ MUS tema *m* principal ‖ GEOL pasadizo *m* (in ice field) ‖ MIN filón *m*, veta *f* ‖ TECH avance *m* (mechanics) | acequia *f* (irrigation canal) | caz *m* (of a mill) ‖ ELECTR cable *m* ‖ mano *f* (in cards); *it's my lead* soy mano, es mi mano ‖ SP golpe *m* inicial (in boxing) ‖ pista *f*, indicación *f* (clue); *he gave me a good lead to find a job* me dio una buena indicación para encontrar una colocación ‖ introducción *f* (of a newspaper article) ‖ noticia *f* más importante (important piece of news) ‖ dirección *f*, mando *m* (direction) ‖ supremacía *f* (supremacy) ‖ ejemplo *m*; *to follow s.o.'s lead* seguir el ejemplo de alguien ‖ iniciativa *f* (initiative) ‖ ventaja *f*; *to have a lead of two kilometres* llevar una ventaja de dos kilómetros ‖ primer lugar *m*, cabeza *f*; *to be in* o *to have the lead* ir en primer lugar *or* en cabeza ‖ — *to give s.o. a lead* guiar a uno, orientar a uno ‖ *to give the lead* dar el tono ‖ *to return the lead* volver a jugar una carta del mismo palo (in cards) ‖ *to take the lead* ponerse a la cabeza (of a procession), desempeñar el primer papel (in a play), llevar la batuta (the command), tomar la delantera (in a race); *he took the lead over me* me tomó la delantera.

lead* [li:d] *vt* llevar, conducir; *this road leads you to London* esta carretera le lleva a Londres; *he led the police to the hideout* condujo a la policía al escondrijo; *lead me to him* lléveme a verlo; *what led me to Paris?* ¿qué me llevó a París?; *his discovery led him to the solution of the mystery* su descubrimiento le condujo a la solución del misterio ‖ inducir a, llevar a, hacer; *what lead you to study Chinese?* ¿qué le indujo a estudiar chino?; *what lead you to believe that?* ¿qué te hizo creer eso? ‖ inducir; *he led me into error* me indujo a error ‖ guiar (to guide) ‖ remitir; *each reference led him to another* cada referencia le remitía a otra ‖ canalizar, encauzar (to channel) ‖ MUS dirigir (an orchestra) | ser primer violín (to play first violin) ‖ ir a la cabeza de (a race) ‖ encabezar, ir a la cabeza de (a procession) ‖ encabezar (a movement, an organization) ‖ dirigir (a country, a team, an expedition) ‖ estar a la cabeza de; *this country leads the world in agriculture* este país está a la cabeza del mundo en agricultura ‖ llevar la delantera a; *Peter led the field during the first half of the race* Pedro llevó la delantera a los demás corredores durante la primera mitad de la carrera ‖ llevar una ventaja *or* un adelanto de; *he led me by one hour* me llevaba una ventaja de una hora ‖ llevar; *to lead s.o. into evil ways* llevar a alguien por mal camino ‖ ganar a; *England is leading Spain, two one* Inglaterra gana a España dos a uno ‖ salir con (in cards) ‖ llevar (a life); *he led a dog's life* llevaba una vida de perros ‖ apuntar delante de [la pieza] (in shooting) ‖ — *she led him a hard life* le hizo llevar una vida imposible ‖ *to be easily led* ser muy influenciable ‖ *to be led to the conclusion that* llegar a la conclusión de que ‖ FIG *to lead s.o. on a wild goose chase, to lead s.o. a merry dance* mandar a alguien de la ceca a la meca, traerle a uno al retortero ‖ *to lead s.o. out to dance* sacar a alguien a bailar ‖ *to lead s.o. to Christ* convertir a

alguien a la fe de Cristo || FIG *to lead s.o. up the garden path* hacer tragar el anzuelo a alguien || *to lead the field* ir el primero, estar en cabeza (to be first), ganar (to win) || *to lead the way* ir el primero, ir en cabeza (to go first), enseñar el camino (to show the way), dar el ejemplo (to set an example).
◆ *vi* ir delante (to go first) || ir a la cabeza, ir en primer lugar (in a procession, in a race) || ponerse delante (to go in front) || ir, conducir, llevar (to be a way to); *this road leads to London* esta carretera va a Londres || producir, causar || conducir; *the information led to his arrest* la información condujo a su detención || ser el jefe, tener el mando, mandar (to be in command) || dirigir (to direct) || salir (in cards) || SP iniciar (in boxing) | ir en cabeza (in a race) | ganar, ir ganando; *Scotland is leading two nil* Escocia gana dos a cero; *to be leading two sets to one* ganar dos juegos a uno || — *to lead for the defence* ser el abogado principal de la defensa || *to lead to nothing* no llevar a nada *or* a ninguna parte.
◆ *phr v* ***to lead astray*** llevar por mal camino || ***to lead away*** llevar (to take away) | FIG apartar (to keep away from) || ***to lead back*** volver a llevar; *lead the horse back to the stable* vuelve a llevar el caballo a la cuadra || — *this road leads back to London* por esta carretera se vuelve a Londres || ***to lead in*** hacer entrar en (to bring in) | ELECTR traer (current) || ***to lead off*** empezar (to start) | abrir (the conversation) | entablar (negotiations) | SP abrir el juego | salir (cards) | salir de; *the street leads off the main road* la calle sale de la carretera principal | comunicar con; *the room leads off the kitchen* la habitación comunica con la cocina | llevarse (to take away) || ***to lead on*** llevar, conducir (to take forward) | seducir a (to seduce) | animar a, incitar a (to encourage) | FIG engañar (to deceive) | *to lead s.o. on to believe that* hacer creer a alguien que || ***to lead up to*** llevar a, conducir a (to cause) | preparar el terreno para (to prepare the way for) || — *what are you leading up to?* ¿a dónde quiere Ud. llegar?
— OBSERV Pret y pp ***led***.

lead [led] *n* plomo *m* (metal and objects made of it) || mina *f* (of a pencil) || MAR sonda *f*, escandallo *m* || PRINT regleta *f* || plomo *m*, tiras *f pl* de plomo (in window) || — FIG *it is as heavy as lead* pesa más que el plomo || *red lead* minio *m* (paint) || FAM *to fill s.o. full of lead* acribillar a uno a balazos | *to swing the lead* hacerse el remolón || *white lead* albayalde *m*.

lead [led] *vt* forrar con plomo (to line) || cubrir con plomo (to cover) || emplomar (a window) || PRINT regletear, interlinear, espaciar.

leaden ['ledn] *adj* de plomo, plúmbeo, a (of lead) || plomizo, za (colour) || FIG de plomo, pesado, da (dull) | desanimado, da (depressed) || — *a leaden sky* un cielo grisáceo *or* plomizo || *a leaden weight* un peso enorme || *his pace was leaden* andaba con paso pesado.

leader ['li:də*] *n* guía *m* & *f* (guide) || jefe *m* & *f* dirigente *m* & *f* (who organizes or directs) || cabecilla *f* (of thieves, of a gang, of rebels) || jefe *m*, líder *m* (in politics) || caudillo *m* (of military forces) || conductor *m* (of masses) || primero, ra (first person of a moving group) || JUR abogado *m* principal || MUS primer violín *m* (first violin) | director *m* (of a band) || editorial *m*, artículo *m* de fondo (in newspapers) || TECH conducto *m* || MIN filón *m* || guía *f*, caballo *m* delantero (in a team of horses) || COMM artículo *m* de reclamo || BOT brote *m* terminal || sotileza *f* (of a fishing line) || SP líder *m* || *he's a born leader* nació para mandar.
◆ *pl* PRINT puntos *m* conductores para guiar la vista.

leadership [-ʃip] *n* dirección *f*, mando *m*; *to have powers of leadership* tener dotes de mando; *under the leadership of* bajo la dirección de; *to take over the leadership* tomar el mando || jefatura *f*, liderato *m*, liderazgo *m* (in politics) || caudillaje *m* (of military forces).

lead-free ['ledfri:] *adj* sin plomo; *lead-free petrol* gasolina sin plomo.

lead-in ['li:d'in] *n* RAD bajada *f* de antena || introducción *f*, entrada *f* (introduction).
◆ *adj* ELECTR de entrada.

leading [li:diŋ] *adj* que va a la cabeza, que va en cabeza, que encabeza; *the leading car of a race* el coche que va a la cabeza de la carrera *or* que encabeza la carrera || primero, ra; *the leading runners are now in sight* los primeros corredores están a la vista ahora || TECH conductor, ra (wire) || MAR que impulsa (wind) || AUT delantero, ra; *leading axle* eje delantero || AVIAT de ataque; *leading edge* borde de ataque || COMM de propaganda, de reclamo (goods) || MIL de vanguardia; *leading column* columna de vanguardia || FIG dominante (idea) | notable, destacado, da; eminente, importante (people) || JUR que sienta jurisprudencia (case) | principal (counsel) || primero, ra; principal (character, part in theatre) || — *leading article* artículo *m* de fondo, editorial *m* || THEATR *leading lady* primera dama, primera actriz || *leading man* primer galán, primer actor (theatre), jefe *m*, dirigente *m* (chief) || *leading note* o *tone* nota *f* sensible || *leading power* fuerza *f* motriz || *leading question* pregunta *f* hecha de tal manera que sugiere la respuesta deseada || *leading strings* andadores *m*.
◆ *n* conducción *f* || dirección *f* (of a company, etc.) || mando *m* (command).

lead line ['led,lain] *n* MAR sonda *f*.

leadoff ['li:d'ɔf] *n* US comienzo *m*, principio *m*.

lead pencil ['led'pensl] *n* lápiz *m* de mina, lapicero *m*.

lead poisoning ['ledpɔizniŋ] *n* MED saturnismo *m*.

leadsman ['ledzmən] *n* MAR sondeador *m*.
— OBSERV El plural de *leadsman* es *leadsmen*.

leaf [li:f] *n* BOT hoja *f* (of tree, of stem); *deciduous leaf* hoja caduca; *dead leaf* hoja seca; *to come into leaf* echar hojas | pétalo *m* (of flower) || hoja *f* (of paper) || página *f* (of a book) || hoja *f* abatible (of table) || hoja *f*, batiente *m* (of door, of shutter, etc.) || lonja *f* (of bacon) || TECH hoja *f* (of spring, of metals) || — *a tree in leaf* un árbol con hojas *or* cubierto de hojas || *gold leaf* pan *m* de oro, oro batido || *lead bud* yema *f* [de un árbol] || *leaf tobacco* tabaco *m* en rama || *loose* o *mobile leaf* hoja suelta *or* volante || *tea leaves* posos *m* (dregs), hojas de té (of the plant) || FIG *to shake like a leaf* temblar como un azogado | *to take a leaf out of s.o.'s book* seguir el ejemplo *or* tomar ejemplo de alguien | *to turn over a new leaf* hacer borrón y cuenta nueva, volver la hoja, empezar nueva vida.
— OBSERV El plural de *leaf* es *leaves*.

leaf [li:f] *vt* *to leaf through a book* hojear un libro.
◆ *vi* echar hojas.

leafless [-lis] *adj* deshojado, da; sin hojas.

leaflet [-lit] *n* folleto *m* (pamphlet) || prospecto *m* (publicity sheet) || BOT folíolo *m*, hojuela *f* || *propaganda leaflet* octavilla *f* (single sheet), folleto *m* de propaganda (booklet).

leaf mould; US **leaf mold** [-məuld] *n* AGR mantillo *m*.

leaf spring [-spriŋ] *n* TECH ballesta *f*.

leafstalk [-stɔ:k] *n* BOT pecíolo *m*.

leafy [-i] *adj* frondoso, sa.

league [li:g] *n* liga *f* (sporting) || asociación *f* (political association) || liga *f* (alliance) || legua *f* (measure of distance) || — *Hanseatic League* Liga Hanseática || *Holy League* Santa Liga || *League of Nations* Sociedad *f* de Naciones || SP *league table* tabla *f* de clasificación de la liga || *to be in league with s.o.* estar asociado con alguien (in business), estar conchabado con alguien (secret agreement) || *to form a league against* aliarse contra.

league [li:g] *vi* *to league together* unirse, aliarse, coligarse.
◆ *vt* unir, aliar.

leak [li:k] *n* vía *f* de agua (in a boat); *the boat has a leak* el buque tiene una vía de agua || gotera *f*; *there is a leak in the roof* hay una gotera en el tejado || agujero *m* (hole) || escape *m*, salida *f*, pérdida *f*, fuga *f* (of gas or liquid) || pérdida *f* (loss) || FIG fuga *f* (of money) | filtración *f* (of secret information) || *to spring a leak* empezar a hacer agua, hacerse una vía de agua (a boat), tener un escape (a pipe).

leak [li:k] *vi* hacer agua (a boat) || salirse (a container); *the pot is leaking* la olla se sale || tener un escape, perder (a pipe) || gotear (a roof) || hacer agua, dejar entrar el agua (shoes) || salirse (liquid) || salirse, escaparse (gas) || FIG filtrarse (information) || *to leak out* trascender (news), filtrarse (secret information), descubrirse (to be discovered).
◆ *vt* dejar salir, dejar escapar (liquid, gas) || rezumar (to exude); *to leak water* rezumar agua || FIG pasar; *to leak information to the enemy* pasar información al enemigo.

leakage [-idʒ] *n* → **leak** || ELECTR *earth leakage* pérdida *f* a tierra.

leakproof [-pru:f] *adj* estanco, ca; hermético, ca.

leaky [-i] *adj* que hace agua, que tiene vías de agua (boat) || que deja entrar el agua (shoe) || que tiene goteras (roof) || agujereado, da (with holes) || que tiene escapes, que se sale (container, pipe) || FIG que tiene fallos, que falla (memory) | indiscreto, ta (person).

lean [li:n] *adj* magro, gra; sin grasa (meat) || flaco, ca; delgado, da (person) || enjuto, ta (face) || frugal (diet) || pobre (soil) || malo, la; escaso, sa (crop) || malo, la; *a lean year for farmers* un mal año para los labradores || — *lean years* años *m pl* de escasez, vacas flacas || *to grow lean* enflaquecer.
◆ *n* carne *f* magra, carne *f* sin grasa, magro *m* (meat) || inclinación *f* (of a wall, etc.) || *on the lean* inclinado, da.

lean* [li:n] *vi* inclinarse, ladearse; *the lamppost leans dangerously* el farol se inclina peligrosamente || FIG inclinarse; *he leans towards communism* se inclina hacia el comunismo || — *do not lean out of the window* prohibido asomarse al exterior (in trains) || *to lean against, to lean back against* apoyarse en *or* contra || *to lean back in a chair* reclinarse *or* respaldarse en una silla || *to lean forward* inclinarse || *to lean on* apoyarse en; *to lean on the table* apoyarse en la mesa || FIG *to lean on s.o.* presionar a uno | *to lean on s.o. for support* contar con el apoyo de uno || *to lean out of* asomarse a; *to lean out of the window* asomarse a la ventana || FIG *to lean over backwards to* no escatimar esfuerzos para || *to lean over s.o.* inclinarse sobre uno || *to lean to* inclinarse hacia *or* a.
◆ *vt* inclinar (to incline) || apoyar, poner; *lean it against the wall for a moment* apóyalo contra la pared un minuto; *lean your head on my shoulder* apoya la cabeza sobre mi hombro || — *to lean one's elbows on the table* acodarse en la mesa, apoyar los codos en la mesa || *to lean one's head back* echar la cabeza hacia atrás.
— OBSERV Pret y pp ***leaned, leant***.

leaning [-iŋ] *n* inclinación *f* || FIG inclinación *f*, propensión *f* (sympathy) | predilección *f* (*to, towards* por) (liking) | tendencia *f* (tendency).
◆ *adj* inclinado, da; *the leaning tower of Pisa* la torre inclinada de Pisa.

leanness [-nis] *n* flaqueza *f*, delgadez *f* (of a person) || magrez *f* (of meat) || FIG escasez *f*, carestía *f* (shortage).

leant [lent] *pret/pp* ⟶ **lean.**

lean-to ['li:ntu:] *n* cobertizo *m*.
◆ *adj* de una sola vertiente (roof).
— OBSERV El plural de esta palabra es *lean-tos*.

leap [li:p] *n* salto *m*, brinco *m* (jump); *he cleared the stream with one leap* cruzó el arroyo de un salto || obstáculo *m* que hay que salvar (obstacle) || FIG salto *m*, paso *m*; *a great leap forwards* un gran paso hacia adelante | cambio *m* (change) | vuelco *m*; *his heart gave a leap* el corazón le dio un vuelco || — FIG *a leap in the dark* un salto en el vacío | *by leaps and bounds* a pasos agigantados || *leap day* día *m* intercalar (29th of February) || *leap year* año bisiesto.

leap* [li:p] *vi* saltar (to jump) || dar un salto (to give a jump) || echarse, lanzarse; *she leapt into his arms* se echó en sus brazos || dar un vuelco (the heart) || — *to leap about* dar saltos || *to leap at* saltarle (a uno) encima (s.o.), no dejar escapar, aprovechar (an offer, an opportunity) || *to leap down* bajar de un salto || *to leap for joy* dar botes *or* saltos de alegría || *to leap off* bajar de un salto de || *to leap on to* subir de un salto a || *to leap out of* saltar de || *to leap over* saltar por encima de, salvar de un salto || *to leap to one's feet* ponerse de pie de un salto || *to leap up* pegar un salto, saltar (a person), elevarse, brotar (a flame).
◆ *vt* saltar por encima de, salvar de un salto (to jump over) || hacer saltar (a horse).
— OBSERV Pret y pp ***leaped, leapt***.

leaper [-ə*] *n* saltador, ra.

leapfrog [-frɔg] *n* pídola *f*, piola *f*; *to play leapfrog* jugar a la pídola.

leapfrog [-frɔg] *vi* jugar a la pídola.
◆ *vt* saltar por encima de (to jump over).

leaping [-iŋ] *adj* saltador, ra.
◆ *n* salto *m*.

leapt [lept] *pret/pp* ⟶ **leap.**

learn* [lə:n] *vt* aprender; *to learn to swim* aprender a nadar; *how long have you been learning Spanish?* ¿cuánto tiempo llevas aprendiendo español? || instruirse (*about* en) (to instruct o.s.) || enterarse de, saber (to find out about); *I have not yet learned if everything went right* no sé todavía si todo ha ido bien || — *to learn by heart* aprender de memoria || *to learn how to do sth.* aprender a hacer algo || *to learn one's lesson* aprenderse la lección; escarmentar || *to learn sth. up* esforzarse por aprender algo.
◆ *vi* aprender || — *I have learnt better since then* ahora me sé la lección || *it's never too late to learn* cada día se aprende algo nuevo || *to learn from experience* aprender por experiencia || *to learn from one's mistakes* aprender por experiencia || *to learn from other people's mistakes* escarmentar en cabeza ajena || *to learn of* enterarse de, saber (to find out about), saber de, conocer; *have you learnt of any good restaurant around here?* ¿conoce algún buen restaurante por aquí?.
— OBSERV Pret y pp ***learned, learnt***.

learned [-id] *adj* instruido, da; culto, ta (educated) || sabio, bia (wise) || erudito, ta (erudite) || docto, ta (form of address); *my learned friend* mi docto colega || liberal (profession) || cultural (society) || *learned word* palabra culta.

learner ['lə:nə*] *n* principiante *m* & *f* (beginner) || aprendiz, za (apprentice, driver) || estudiante *m* & *f* (student) || *to be a quick learner* aprender rápidamente.

learner driver ['lə:nə*'draivə*] *n* conductor *m* principiante, aprendiz *m* de conductor, aprendiza *f* de conductora.

learning [-'lə:niŋ] *n* saber *m*, erudición *f*, conocimientos *m pl*, conocimiento *m* (knowledge); *a man of great learning* un hombre de gran saber || estudio *m* (study) || *seat of learning* centro *m* de estudios.

learnt [lə:nt] *pret/pp* ⟶ **learn.**

lease [li:s] *n* JUR arrendamiento *m*, arriendo *m* (contract) | contrato *m* de arrendamiento (document when leasing land) | contrato *m* de inquilinato *or* de alquiler (document when leasing a house, etc.) | período *m* de arrendamiento (period) || — FIG *to give s.o. a new lease of life* dar nuevas fuerzas a uno || *to let out on lease* dar en arriendo, arrendar || FIG *to take on a new lease of life* empezar una nueva vida || *to take on lease* tomar en arrendamiento *or* en arriendo, arrendar.

lease [li:s] *vt* JUR arrendar, dar *or* ceder en arriendo (to let out) | arrendar, tomar en arriendo (to take on lease) | alquilar (to rent, to hire).

leasehold [-həuld] *adj* arrendado, da; en arriendo.
◆ *n* JUR propiedad *f or* casa *f* arrendada (property) | arrendamiento *m* (right of holding property).

leaseholder [-həuldə*] *n* arrendatario, ria.

lease-lend [-lend] *n* préstamo *m* y arriendo.

leash [li:ʃ] *n* correa *f* (for dogs, etc.) || traílla *f* (for hunting dogs) || pihuela *f* (for a hawk) || — *the dog is on the leash* el perro está atado || FIG *to hold in leash* mantener a raya, dominar | *to strain at the leash* mantener a raya, dominar | *to strain at the leash* procurar sacudir el yugo.

leash [li:ʃ] *vt* atar (to tie up) || poner la correa a (a dog) || atraillar, poner la traílla a (hunting dogs).

leasing [-'li:siŋ] *n* arrendamiento *m*, alquiler *m* || «leasing» *m* [arrendamiento con opción de compra].

least [li:st] *adj* menor, (más) mínimo, ma; más pequeño, ña; *he hasn't got the least chance* no tiene la más mínima posibilidad; *the least offence is heavily punished* el menor delito es severamente castigado; *the least noise startles her* el ruido más pequeño le asusta || menor (smallest in size, amount, importance, age) || — *not least* especialmente; *all employees, not least Mr. Smith* todos los empleados, especialmente el Sr. Smith || *not the least bit* en absoluto; *I am not the least bit annoyed* no estoy enfadado en absoluto || MATH *the least common multiple* el mínimo común múltiplo.
◆ *n* lo menos; *that is the least you could do* eso es lo menos que podrías hacer || el menor, la menor, el más pequeño; la más pequeña; *that is the least of my problems* ése es el menor de mis problemas || — *at least* por lo menos; *he is at least 40* tiene por lo menos 40 años; por lo menos, al menos; *you could at least say thank you* al menos podrías dar las gracias || *at the very least* como mínimo || *in the least* en lo más mínimo || *not in the least* nada, en absoluto; *it does not matter in the least* no importa en absoluto || *that's the least of my worries* esto es lo que menos me preocupa || *to say the least* para no decir otra cosa peor.
◆ *adv* menos; *the least possible* lo menos posible; *I am the least able to do it* yo soy el que menos puede hacerlo; *the least happy* el menos contento || — *he least of all* él menos que nadie || *least of all* sobre todo, y menos que a nadie; *don't tell anyone, least of all your mother* no se lo digas a nadie, sobre todo a tu madre; menos; *he deserves it least of all* él es el que menos se lo merece || *least of all would I want to criticize you* no tengo la más mínima intención de criticarle.

leastways [-weiz]; **leastwise** [-waiz] *adv* por lo menos (at least).

leat [li:t] *n* saetín *m* (of a mill).

leather ['leðə*] *n* piel *f*, cuero *m*; *a leather coat, belt* un abrigo, un cinturón de cuero; *leather gloves, bags* guantes, bolsos de piel || gamuza *f* (for washing cars, windows, etc.) || SP & FAM cuero *m*, pelota *f* (ball) || — *fancy leather goods* tafiletería *f*, marroquinería *f* || *leather bottle* bota *f*, odre *m* || *patent leather* charol *m*.
◆ *adj* de cuero, de piel; *leather case* estuche de cuero.

leather ['leðə*] *vt* cubrir con cuero (to cover with leather) || FAM zurrar (to tan s.o.'s hide).

leatherback [-bæk] *n* ZOOL laúd *m* (marine turtle).

leather-bound [-baund] *adj* encuadernado en cuero.

leather dresser [-'dresə*] *n* curtidor *m* de pieles.

leatherette [,leðə'ret] *n* similicuero *m* (imitation leather).

leathern ['leðə:n] *adj* de cuero (of leather) || parecido al cuero (like leather).

leatherneck ['leðənek] *n* US FAM soldado *m* de infantería de marina.

leatheroid ['leðərɔid] *n* similicuero *m*, cuero *m* artificial.

leathery ['leðəri] *adj* parecido al cuero (like leather) || FIG correoso, sa (meat) | curtido, da (skin).

leave [li:v] *n* permiso *m* (permission); *to beg leave to* pedir permiso para; *by your leave* con su permiso || MIL permiso *m*, licencia *f*; *to be on leave* estar de permiso || — *leave of absence* permiso para ausentarse || *on ticket of leave* en libertad condicional || FIG *to have taken leave of one's senses* haber perdido la cabeza | *to take French leave* despedirse a la francesa || *to take leave of s.o., to take one's leave of s.o.* despedirse de alguien || FIG *without so much as a by your leave* sin pedir permiso.

leave* [li:v] *vi* irse, marcharse; *he is leaving tomorrow* se va mañana || salir; *he is leaving for Madrid* sale para Madrid; *the train is leaving* el tren sale.
◆ *vt* dejarse (to forget); *he left his lighter in the bar* se dejó el encendedor en el bar || dejar; *to leave a tip* dejar una propina; *to leave things lying about* dejar las cosas desparramadas; *leave what you don't like* deja lo que no te guste; *I leave it to your sense of fairness* lo dejo a su sentido de la justicia; *leave it until tomorrow* déjalo para mañana; *leave the door open* deja la puerta abierta; *let's leave it at that* dejemos las cosas así, dejémoslo así; *she left a note for him* le dejó una nota || salir de (to go out of); *he left the cinema* salió del cine || dejar; *I must leave you* debo dejaros || marcharse de, irse de (home, job) || dejar, abandonar; *to leave one's wife* abandonar a su mujer || JUR legar, dejar (in a will) || — *I leave it to you* lo dejo en sus manos || *leave me alone!* ¡déjame en paz! || *leave that radio alone* deja de tocar la radio || *leave your nails alone* deja de morderte las uñas || *take it or leave it* lo toma o lo deja || *to be left* quedar (to remain); *how many are there left?* ¿cuántos quedan?; quedarse (s.o.) || *to have left* quedarle a uno; *I have four left* me quedan cuatro || *to leave be* dejar en paz (to stop annoying) || *to leave go, to leave hold of* soltar || *to leave much to be desired* dejar mucho que desear || *to leave room for* dejar sitio para (physically), dejar lugar para *or* a (hope, doubt) || *to leave school* salir del colegio; *what time do you leave school in the afternoon?* ¿a qué hora sales del colegio por la tarde?; dejar de ir al colegio; *some people leave school at 16* algunos dejan de ir al colegio a los 16 años; dejar el colegio, salirse del colegio; *his father's death forced him to leave school* la muerte de su padre le obligó a salirse del colegio || *to leave the road* salirse de la carretera ||

to leave the table levantarse de la mesa || *to leave the track* o *the rails* salirse de la vía, descarrilar || *to leave to chance* dejar a la suerte, dejar en manos del destino || *to leave undone* no hacer; no terminar || MATH *two from six leaves four* seis menos dos son cuatro.
◆ *phr v* **to leave about** dejar tirado, dejar rodando, no dejar en su sitio; *why do you always leave your clothes about?* ¿por qué deja siempre la ropa tirada? | dejar por medio; *you shouldn't leave so much money about* no debería dejar tanto dinero por medio || **to leave aside** omitir, dejar de lado, prescindir de (to omit) | olvidar (to forget) || **to leave behind** dejar atrás; *slow down, you are leaving me behind* ve más despacio, me estás dejando atrás | olvidarse, dejarse; *wait, I've left my umbrella behind* espera, que me he olvidado el paraguas | dejar; *this leaves a nasty smell behind* esto deja mal olor || **to leave off** dejar de; *to leave off smoking* dejar de fumar | no ponerse; *leave your coat off* no te pongas el abrigo | pararse (rain) | acabar; *where did we leave off?* ¿dónde acabamos? || **to leave out** omitir, saltarse (to omit) | dejar fuera (washing, etc.) | dejar a mano; *I'll leave the records out for you* te dejaré los discos a mano | excluir (to exclude); *to feel left out* sentirse excluido || **to leave over** dejar, aplazar (to postpone) || — *to be left over* sobrar (to be over); *there are ten left over* sobran diez.
— OBSERV Pret y pp ***left***.

leave [liːv] *vi* echar hojas.

leaved [liːvd] *adj* cubierto de hojas (in leaf) || de hojas (door) || con largueros (table).

leaven ['levn] *n* levadura *f* || FIG estímulo *m* (stimulus) | fermento *m*, germen *m*.

leaven ['levn] *vt* leudar (dough) || FIG impregnar (*with* de) (to spread through) | transformar, modificar (to change).

leavening [-iŋ] *n* fermentación *f* || levadura *f* (leaven).

leaver [liːvə*] *n* estudiante *m* & *f* a punto de dejar la escuela *or* la universidad.

leaves [liːvz] *pl n* ⟶ **leaf.**

leave-taking [liːv'teikiŋ] *n* despedida *f*.

leaving ['liːviŋ] *n* salida *f* (departure).
◆ *pl* restos *m*, sobras *f*.

Lebanese [ˌlebə'niːz] *adj/n* libanés, esa.

Lebanon ['lebənən] *pr n* GEOGR Líbano *m*.

lecher ['letʃə*] *n* lascivo, va; libertino, na.

lecherous ['letʃərəs] *adj* lascivo, va; libertino, na; lujurioso, sa.

lechery ['letʃəri] *n* lascivia *f*, lujuria *f*, libertinaje *m* (lewdness).

lectern ['lektəːn] *n* atril *m*, facistol *m*.

lection ['lekʃən] *n* REL lección *f*.

lector ['lektɔː*] *n* REL lector *m*.

lecture ['lektʃə*] *n* conferencia *f*; *lecture room* sala de conferencias; *a lecture on birth control* una conferencia sobre la regulación de nacimientos || clase *f*, curso *m* (in university); *to attend lectures on* dar clases de, seguir un curso de || FIG sermón *m*, reprimenda *f* (reprimand); *to read s.o. a lecture* echar un sermón a uno.

lecture ['lektʃə*] *vi* dar una conferencia; *to lecture on space travel* dar una conferencia sobre viajes espaciales || dar conferencias (to give lectures) || dar clase *or* clases (in university) || hablar (to speak); *I haven't heard anyone lecture so well* nunca oí hablar a nadie tan bien.
◆ *vt* dar una conferencia *or* conferencias a || dar clase *or* clases a (in university) || FIG sermonear a, echar un sermón *or* una reprimenda a (to reprimand).

lecture hall [-hɔːl] *n* aula *f* (classroom) || sala *f* de conferencias.

lecturer [-rə*] *n* profesor, ra (in university); *assistant lecturer* profesor adjunto || conferenciante *m* & *f* [AMER conferencista *m* & *f*] (who gives lectures).

lectureship [-ʃip] *n* cargo *m* de profesor, cátedra *f* (in a college or in university).

lecture theatre ['lektʃə*θiətə*] *n* aula (classroom) || sala *f* de conferencias.

led [led] *pret/pp* ⟶ **lead.**

LED *abbr of [light-emitting diode]* LED, diodo electroluminiscente.

ledge [ledʒ] *n* saliente *m* (part which juts out) || repisa *f*, anaquel *m* (shelf) || antepecho *m* (of a window) || ARCH cornisa *f* (cornice) || MIN vena *f*, veta *f* (stratum rich in ore) || banco *m* de arrecifes (reef).

ledger [-ə*] *n* COMM libro *m* mayor (in bookkeeping) || lápida *f* sepulcral (tombstone) || travesaño *m* de andamio (of a scaffold).

ledger line [-lain] *n* MUS línea *f* suplementaria.

ledger paper [-'peipə*] *n* papel *m* de cuentas.

lee [liː] *adj* MAR de sotavento, a sotavento.
◆ *n* MAR sotavento *m* || FIG abrigo *m* (shelter); *in the lee of* al abrigo de.

lee board [-bɔːd] *n* MAR orza *f* de deriva.

leech [liːtʃ] *n* sanguijuela *f* (animal) || FIG parásito *m*, sanguijuela *f* (parasite) | lapa *f* (clinging person) || MAR grátil *m*, gratil *m* (of a sail) || (ant) médico *m*.

leek [liːk] *n* BOT puerro *m*.

leer [liə*] *n* mirada *f* de reojo lasciva (of lust) || mirada *f* de soslayo maliciosa (malicious).

leer [liə*] *vi* echar una mirada de soslayo *or* de reojo, mirar de soslayo *or* de reojo [de manera lasciva o maliciosa].

leering [-riŋ] *adj* de reojo, de soslayo (glance) || lascivo, va; impúdico, ca (lustful).

leery [-ri] *adj* US suspicaz; receloso, sa (suspicious) | malicioso, sa; astuto, ta (knowing).

lees [liːz] *pl n* heces *f*, poso *m sing* (dregs) || FIG hez *f sing* (of society) || FIG *to drain* o *to drink the cup to the lees* apurar el cáliz hasta las heces.

lee side ['liːsaid] *n* MAR banda *f* de sotavento, sotavento *m*.

leeward ['liːwəd] *adj* MAR de sotavento, a sotavento.
◆ *adv* MAR a sotavento.
◆ *n* MAR sotavento *m*.

Leeward Islands [-'ailəndz] *pl n* GEOGR islas *f* de Sotavento.

leeway ['liːwei] *n* MAR & AVIAT deriva *f* (drift) || FIG atraso *m*, atrasos *m pl*; *to have a lot of leeway to make up* tener muchos atrasos que recuperar | campo *m*, libertad *f* (for action) | margen *m* (spare time, spare money) || MAR *to make leeway* abatir, derivar.

left [left] *pret/pp* ⟶ **leave.**

left [left] *adj* izquierdo, da; *the left bank of the river* la orilla izquierda del río; *the left hand* la mano izquierda; *the left side* el lado izquierdo || izquierdista, de izquierda (in politics) || *left hook* gancho *m* de izquierda (in boxing).
◆ *adv* a *or* hacia la izquierda; *to turn left* torcer a la izquierda.
◆ *n* izquierda *f*; *to turn to the left* torcer a la izquierda; *on your left* a su izquierda || mano *f* izquierda, izquierda *f*, zurda *f* (left hand) || pie *m* izquierdo (left foot) || directo *m* de izquierda, izquierdazo *m* (in boxing) || izquierda *f* (in politics) || *on the left* a la izquierda; *a little further down on the left* un poco más abajo a la izquierda; por la izquierda; *to drive on the left* conducir por la izquierda.

left-hand [-hænd] *adj* izquierdo, da; de la izquierda || — *left-hand drive* conducción *f* a la izquierda || *left-hand side* izquierda *f*, lado izquierdo.

left-handed [-'hændid] *adj* zurdo, da; zocato, ta (person) || para zurdos; *left-handed golf club* palo de golf para zurdos || FIG torpe, desmañado, da (clumsy) | ambiguo, gua; equívoco, ca (compliments) || FIG *left-handed marriage* matrimonio por detrás de la iglesia.
◆ *adv* con la mano izquierda.

left-hander [-'hændə*] *n* zurdo, da; zocato, ta (left-handed person) || directo *m* de izquierda, izquierdazo *m* (blow with the left hand).

Leftism ['leftizəm] *n* izquierdismo *m*.

Leftist ['leftist] *adj* izquierdista, de izquierdas.
◆ *n* izquierdista *m* & *f*.

left luggage ['left'lʌgidʒ] *n* equipaje *m* en consigna.

left-luggage office ['left'lʌgidʒˌɔfis] *n* consigna *f*.

left-of-centre ['leftɔf'sentə*] *adj* de centro izquierda (in politics).

leftover ['leftˌəuvə*] *adj* restante, sobrante.

leftovers [-z] *pl n* sobras *f*, restos *m*.

leftward ['leftwəd] *adj/adv* hacia la izquierda.

left wing ['left'wiŋ] *n* izquierda *f* (in politics) || SP extremo *m* izquierda (in football, in hockey) | ala *f* izquierda (in rugby).

left-wing ['left'wiŋ] *adj* izquierdista, de izquierdas; *left-wing policy* política izquierdista.

left winger [-ə*] *n* izquierdista *m* & *f* (in politics) || SP extremo *m* izquierda (in football, in hockey) | ala *f* izquierda (in rugby).

lefty ['lefti] *n* FAM izquierdista *m* & *f* (in politics) | zurdo, da; zocato, ta (left-handed person).

leg [leg] *n* pierna *f* (of a person) || pata *f* (of animals, etc.) || pata *f*, pie *m* (of furniture) || soporte *m* (support) || pernera *f* (of trousers) || caña *f* (of boots) || CULIN pierna *f* (joint); *a leg of lamb* una pierna de cordero | muslo *m* (of chicken) | anca *f* (of frogs) | pernil *m* (of venison, of pork) || pierna *f* (of compass, of triangle, etc.) || cateto *m* (of right-angled triangle) || etapa *f* (stage of a journey, of a race) || MAR trayecto *m* (distance covered) | bordada *f* (in sailing) || — SP *leg before wicket* eliminación *f* del bateador por obstrucción de la pelota con la pierna || *leg of pork* jamón *m* || FIG *not to have a leg to stand on* carecer de fundamento, no tener en qué apoyarse | *to be on one's (o its) last legs* estar dando las diez de últimas, estar en las últimas | *to find one's legs* recobrarse, levantarse (after a setback), establecerse (to establish o.s.) || *to give s.o. a leg up* ayudar a alguien a subir (to get on a horse, etc.), echar una mano a alguien (to help) || FIG *to have been on one's legs all day* no haberse sentado en todo el día, no haber tenido un momento de respiro en todo el día | *to have the legs of s.o.* correr más rápido que alguien | *to keep one's legs* mantenerse de pie | *to pull s.o.'s leg* tomarle el pelo a uno | *to run as fast as one's legs will carry one* correr a toda marcha *or* a todo gas | *to set s.o. on his legs* ayudar a alguien a levantar cabeza || FIG & FAM *to shake a leg* darse prisa, volar (to hurry up), mover el esqueleto, bailar (to dance) | *to show a leg* levantarse de la cama || FIG *to stand on one's own legs* valerse por sí mismo | *to stretch one's legs* estirar las piernas (to take a walk) | *to take to one's legs* poner pies en polvorosa | *to walk s.o. off his legs* dejar agotado a alguien || *wooden leg* pata de palo.

leg [leg] *vt* *to leg it* ir a pie, ir a pata, ir andando (to walk), largarse (to run).

legacy ['legəsi] *n* legado *m*, herencia *f* || FIG patrimonio *m*, herencia *f*.

legal ['li:gəl] *adj* jurídico, ca; *legal procedure* procedimientos jurídicos || legal (in accordance with the law) || lícito, ta (permitted by law) || legítimo, ma (recognized by law) || civil (year) || — JUR *legal adviser* asesor jurídico | *legal age* mayoría *f* de edad | *legal aid* abogacía *f* de pobres | *legal costs* costas *f* | *legal document* acta legalizada | *legal entity* persona jurídica | *legal expert* asesor jurídico | *legal holiday* fiesta *f* legal | *legal profession* abogacía *f* | *legal responsibility* responsabilidad *f* civil | *legal status* o *capacity* personalidad jurídica | *legal tender* moneda *f* de curso legal (currency) | *of legal age* mayor de edad | *to take legal action against s.o.* entablar un pleito contra alguien.

legalism [-izəm] *n* legalismo *m*.

legalist [-ist] *n* legalista *m* & *f*.

legalistic ['li:gə'listik] *adj* legalista.

legality [li'gæliti] *n* legalidad *f*.
◆ *pl* trámites *m* jurídicos (legal formalities).

legalization [,li:gəlai'zeiʃən] *n* legalización *f*.

legalize ['li:gəlaiz] *vt* legalizar.

legally ['li:gəli] *adv* legalmente.

legate ['legit] *n* legado *m*.

legate [li'geit] *vt* legar.

legatee [,legə'ti:] *n* JUR legatario, ria.

legation [li'geiʃən] *n* legación *f*.

legator [li'geitə*] *n* JUR testador, ra.

legend ['ledʒənd] *n* leyenda *f* (story) || pie *m* (of a cartoon) || clave *f*, signos *m pl* (of a map) || inscripción *f* || *black legend* leyenda negra.

legendary ['ledʒəndəri] *adj* legendario, ria.

legerdemain ['ledʒədə'mein] *n* juego *m* de manos, prestidigitación *f* (conjuring) || truco *m* (trick).

legged [legd] *adj* de piernas (people); *long-legged* de piernas largas || de patas (animals, furniture, etc.); *round-legged* de pata redonda.

leggings ['leginz] *pl n* polainas *f*.

leg guards [leggɑ:dz] *pl n* defensas *f* (on motorbike) || SP espinilleras *f*.

leggy ['legi] *adj* zanquilargo, ga; patilargo, ga.

leghorn ['leghɔ:n] *n* paja *f* italiana (straw) || sombrero *m* de paja italiana (hat) || gallina *f* leghorn, leghorn *f* (hen).

Leghorn ['leg'hɔ:n] *pr n* GEOGR Liorna.

legibility [,ledʒi'biliti] *n* legibilidad *f*.

legible ['ledʒəbl] *adj* legible.

legion ['li:dʒən] *n* legión *f*; *the Foreign Legion* la Legión Extranjera || FIG legión *f* (great number) || *Legion of Honour* Legión de Honor.

legionary [-əri] *adj* legionario, ria; de la legión.
◆ *n* legionario *m*.

legionnaire [,li:dʒə'nɛə*] *n* US MIL legionario *m* || MED *legionnaire's disease* enfermedad *f* del legionario.

legislate ['ledʒisleit] *vi* JUR legislar.
◆ *vt* establecer por ley.

legislation [,ledʒis'leiʃən] *n* JUR legislación *f*.

legislative ['ledʒislətiv] *adj* JUR legislativo, va; *legislative assembly* asamblea legislativa.
◆ *n* cuerpo *m* legislativo.

legislator ['ledʒis,leitə*] *n* JUR legislador *m*.

legislature ['ledʒis,leitʃə*] *n* JUR legislatura *f* || cuerpo *m* legislativo (lawmaking body).

legist ['li:dʒist] *n* JUR legista *m*.

legitimacy [li'dʒitiməsi] *n* legitimidad *f*.

legitimate [li'dʒitimit] *adj* legítimo, ma (claim, child, king, etc.) || válido, da; justo, ta; *a legitimate argument* un argumento válido || auténtico, ca (theatre, music).

legitimate [li'dʒitimeit] *vt* legitimar.

legitimist [li'dʒitimist] *adj/n* legitimista.

legitimization [,lidʒitimi'zeiʃən] *n* legitimación *f*.

legitimize [li'dʒitimaiz] *vt* legitimar.

legless ['leglis] *adj* sin piernas (person) || sin patas (furniture, animal).

leg-of-mutton ['legəv'mʌtn] *adj* de jamón (sleeve) || MAR triangular (sail).

leg-pull ['legpul] *n* FAM tomadura *f* de pelo, broma *f*.

leg-puller [-ə*] *n* FAM bromista *m* & *f*.

legroom ['legru:m] *n* sitio *m* para las piernas.

legume ['legju:m] *n* BOT legumbre *f*.

leguminous [le'gju:minəs] *adj* leguminoso, sa.

leg-warmers ['legwɔ:mə*] *n pl* calientapiernas *f*.

leister ['li:stə*] *n* arpón *m* de tres púas.

leisure ['leʒə*] *n* ocio *m*; *a life of leisure* una vida de ocio || tiempo *m* libre (free time); *I have the leisure to do it* tengo tiempo libre para hacerlo || — *at leisure* desocupado, da; libre; *he is at leisure* está desocupado; con tiempo, con tranquilidad, sin prisa (peacefully) || *at one's leisure* en sus momentos de ocio, en sus ratos libres (in one's spare time), cuando uno tenga tiempo *or* un rato; *do it at your leisure* hazlo cuando tengas tiempo || *leisure occupation* pasatiempo *m* || *leisure time* tiempo libre, ratos *m pl* libres, momentos *m pl* de ocio.

leisured [-d] *adj* desocupado, da; ocioso, sa (not occupied) || pausado, da; sin prisa (unhurried).

leisurely [-li] *adj* pausado, da; sin prisa.
◆ *adv* sin prisa, despacio.

leitmotiv; leitmotif ['laitməu,ti:f] *n* leitmotiv *m*, tema *m* central.

lemma ['lemə] *n* lema *m* (in logic and mathematics).
— OBSERV El plural de la palabra inglesa *lemma* es *lemmata* o *lemmas*.

lemming ['lemiŋ] *n* ZOOL lemming *m*, ratón *m* campestre.

lemnaceae [lem'neisii] *pl n* lemnáceas *f*.

lemniscus [lem'niskəs] *n* ANAT lemnisco *m*.
— OBSERV El plural de la palabra inglesa es *lemnisci*.

lemon ['lemən] *n* BOT limonero *m* (tree) | limón *m* (fruit); *lemon juice* zumo de limón || amarillo *m* limón (colour) || US FAM primo, ma; lila *m* & *f* (twit) || — *lemon balm* toronjil *m* || *lemon curd* crema *f* de limón || *lemon drop* caramelo *m or* pastilla *f* de limón || *lemon grove* limonar *m* || *lemon squash* zumo *m* de limón || *lemon squeezer* exprimelimones *m inv*, exprimidor *m*.
◆ *adj* amarillo limón, cetrino, na.

lemonade [,lemə'neid] *n* limonada *f*, limón *m* natural (lemon drink) || gaseosa *f* (fizzy drink).

lempira [lem'piræ] *n* lempira *m* (monetary unit of Honduras).

lemur ['li:mə*] *n* ZOOL lémur *m*.

lemures ['lemjuəri:z] *pl n* MYTH lémures *m*.

lend* [lend] *vt* prestar; *can you lend me ten pounds?* ¿me puede prestar diez libras? || FIG dar, conferir; *to lend a touch of gaiety* dar una nota de alegría || — FIG *to lend a hand* echar una mano || *to lend o.s. to* prestarse a; *the sentence lends itself to several interpretations* la frase se presta a varias interpretaciones.
◆ *vi* prestar dinero.
— OBSERV Pret y pp ***lent***.

lender [-ə*] *n* prestamista *m* & *f* (professional) || prestador, ra (accidental).

lending [-iŋ] *n* préstamo *m*, otorgamiento *m* de un préstamo || *lending library* biblioteca *f* de préstamo || ECON *lending rate* tipo *m* de interés de *or* sobre los préstamos, tipo *m* activo.

lend-lease [-'li:s] *n* préstamo *m* y arriendo || *Lend-Lease Act* ley *f* de préstamo y arriendo.

length [leŋθ] *n* longitud *f*, largo *m*; *length over all* longitud total; *seven metres in length* siete metros de largo *or* de longitud; *the length of a football field* la longitud de un campo de fútbol; *the length of a skirt* la longitud de una falda || largo *m*; *three lengths of material* tres largos de tela; *ten lengths of the swimming pool* diez largos de la piscina || longitud *f* (of a story, of a joke) || lo largo, longitud *f* (of parts of the body) || largo *m* (of hair) || duración *f* (of time); *the length of a film* la duración de una película || extensión *f* (extension); *the length of a letter* la extensión de una carta || espacio *m* (space) || distancia *f* (distance) || tramo *m* (part of a road, of a track, etc.) || recorrido *m* (of route) || pedazo *m*, trozo *m* (piece) || GRAMM cantidad *f* (amount of stress) || MAR eslora *f*, largo *m* (of a boat) || SP largo *m* (length of a bicycle) | cuerpo *m* (in swimming and horse racing); *to win by a length* ganar por un cuerpo || — *along the whole length of* a lo largo de todo || *at full length* a todo lo largo (to lie), con todo detalle (to explain) || *at great length* con muchos detalles || *at length* finalmente, por fin (at last), con todo detalle; *to explain at length* explicar con todo detalle || *focal length* distancia focal || *for what length of time?* ¿durante cuánto tiempo? || *some length of time* algún tiempo, bastante tiempo || *the length and breadth of* todo, da; entero, ra; *over the length and breadth of the country* por el país entero || *the length of time required to do sth.* el tiempo requerido para hacer algo || *to fall full length* caer cuan largo es uno || FIG *to go to any lengths* ser capaz de hacer cualquier cosa | *to go to great lengths* hacer un gran esfuerzo | *to go to the length of* llegar hasta el extremo de | *to keep at arm's length* mantener a distancia | *to measure one's length on the floor* medir el suelo (to fall down) || *to walk the length of* recorrer; *we walked the whole length of the train* recorrimos todo el tren || *what length is it?* ¿cuánto mide?, ¿cuánto tiene de largo?

lengthen ['leŋθən] *vi* alargarse, prolongarse || crecer (days).
◆ *vt* alargar; *to lengthen a dress* alargar un vestido || alargar, prolongar (time).

lengthening [-iŋ] *n* alargamiento *m* || prolongación *f* (of time).

lengthily ['leŋθili] *adv* largamente, extensamente.

lengthiness ['leŋθinis] *n* duración *f* excesiva, prolijidad *f* (of a speech).

lengthways ['leŋθweiz] *adv* longitudinalmente, a lo largo || *to measure sth. lengthways* medir el largo de algo.

lengthwise ['leŋθwaiz] *adv* longitudinalmente, a lo largo.
◆ *adj* longitudinal.

lengthy ['leŋθi] *adj* largo, ga (in distance) || largo, ga; prolongado, da (in time) || FAM larguísimo, ma; demasiado largo, ga; *a lengthy journey* un viaje larguísimo.

lenience ['li:njəns]; **leniency** [-i] *n* clemencia *f*, indulgencia *f*, poca severidad *f*.

lenient ['li:njənt] *adj* clemente, indulgente, poco severo, ra.

Leninism ['leninizəm] *n* leninismo *m*.

Leninist ['leninist]; **Leninite** ['leninait] *adj/n* leninista.

lenitive ['lenitiv] *adj* lenitivo, va.
◆ *n* MED lenitivo *m* || FIG lenitivo *m*.

lenity ['leniti] *n* lenidad *f*, poca severidad *f*, indulgencia *f*.

lens [lenz] *n* PHYS lente *f*; *magnifying lens* lente de aumento || lupa *f* (magnifying glass) || PHOT objetivo *m* || ANAT cristalino *m* || *contact lens* lente de contacto, lentilla *f*.
— OBSERV El plural de *lens* es *lenses*.

Lent [lent] *n* REL Cuaresma *f*.

lent [lent] *pret/pp* —→ **lend.**

Lenten ['lentən] *adj* cuaresmal, de Cuaresma || FIG escaso, sa; pobre (meager) | sin carne (meatless).

lenticular [len'tikjulə*] *adj* lenticular.

lentil ['lentil] *n* BOT lenteja *f*.

lentiscus [len'tiskəs]; **lentisk** ['lentisk] *n* BOT lentisco *m*.

Leo ['li:əu] *pr n* León *m* (Christian name) || ASTR Leo *m*, León *m*.

leonine ['li:əunain] *adj* leonino, na.

leopard ['lepəd] *n* ZOOL leopardo *m* || HERALD león *m* rampante || FIG *the leopard cannot change his spots* genio y figura hasta la sepultura.

leopardess [-is] *n* ZOOL leopardo *m* hembra.

leotard ['liəta:d] *n* leotardo *m*.

leper ['lepə*] *n* leproso, sa || *leper colony* leprosería *f*.

lepidopteran; lepidopteron [ˌlepi'dɔptərən] *n* ZOOL lepidóptero *m*.
— OBSERV El plural de la palabra inglesa *lepidopteron* es *lepidoptera*.

leporine ['lepərain] *adj* leporino, na.

leprechaun ['leprəkɔ:n] *n* MYTH duende *m*, gnomo *m* [irlandés].

leprosarium [ˌleprə'sεəriəm] *n* leprosería *f*.

leprosy ['leprəsi] *n* MED lepra *f*.

leprous ['leprəs] *adj* leproso, sa || FIG desconchado, da (walls).

Lerna ['lə:nə] *pr n* Lerna.

Lernaean ['lə:ni:ən] *adj* MYTH *Lernaean hydra* hidra *f* de Lerna.

lesbian ['lezbiən] *adj/n* lesbiano, na; lesbio, bia.
◆ *n* lesbiana *f* (homosexual woman).

lesbianism ['lezbiənizəm] *n* lesbianismo *m*.

Lesbos ['lezbɔs] *pr n* GEOGR Lesbos.

lese majesty ['li:z'mædʒisti] *n* JUR crimen *m* de lesa majestad.

lesion ['li:ʒən] *n* lesión *f*.

less [les] *adj* menos; *he has less money than I* tiene menos dinero que yo; *no less than three members* no menos de tres miembros; *to spend less money* gastar menos dinero; *less customers than the year before* menos clientes que el año anterior; *ten shillings is less than a pound* diez chelines son menos que una libra || inferior, menor; *the price is less than last year's* el precio es inferior al *or* menor que el del año pasado; *5 is less than 7* cinco es inferior a siete; *speeds less than 90 k.p.h.* velocidades inferiores a noventa km/h || menor; *the danger is less now* el peligro es menor ahora || — *in less than no time* en un abrir y cerrar de ojos, en menos de nada || *it's nothing less than terrifying* es francamente espantoso || *it was nobody less than the King!* o *no less a person than the King!* ¡era nada menos que el rey!, ¡era el mismísimo rey! || *less of it!* ¡ya está bien! || *no less than* por lo menos (at least); *there were no less than 10 000 people* había por lo menos 10 000 personas; nada menos que (as much as); *he earns no less than a million a year* gana nada menos que un millón al año || *nothing less than* nada menos que || *Saint James the Less* Santiago el Menor || *that was given me by the King, no less* eso me lo dio el mismo rey || *the answer was sth. less* o *somewhat less than polite* la conversación no fue nada cortés || *to be nothing less than* ser un verdadero; *it is nothing less than a crime* es un verdadero crimen.
◆ *adv* menos; *my head aches less now* ahora me duele menos la cabeza; *he is less happy* está menos alegre; *this is worth less than the other* éste vale menos que el otro; *it is worth less than 100 pesetas* vale menos de 100 pesetas; *it is worth 100 pesetas less* vale 100 pesetas menos; *some of his less known works* algunas de sus obras menos conocidas; *if we were one man less* si fuéramos uno menos; *not a penny less* ni un penique menos; *he spoke less than I expected* habló menos de lo que yo me esperaba || — *even less* aun menos || *I was less offended than angry* me enfadé más que me ofendí || *less and less* cada vez menos || *less than* ni mucho menos; *to be less than easy* no ser fácil ni mucho menos || *more or less* más o menos; *more or less easy* más o menos fácil || *none the less* sin embargo, a pesar de todo; *none the less he is a good runner* sin embargo es un buen corredor || *so much the less* tanto menos || *still less* todavía menos || *the less... the less* mientras menos... menos, cuanto menos... menos; *the less you read, the less you learn* cuanto menos lees menos aprendes || *the less you think of it the better* cuanto menos lo pienses mejor || *to grow less* disminuir.
◆ *prep* menos; *1 000 francs less certain deductions* 1 000 francos menos ciertos descuentos; *a year less a week* un año menos una semana; *seven less five is two* siete menos cinco son dos.
◆ *n* menor *m* & *f*; *of the two evils it is the less* de los dos males es el menor || menos; *less was given than should have been* dieron menos de lo que se debía; *people have died for less* hay quien ha muerto por menos.

lessee [le'si:] *n* JUR inquilino, na (of a house) | arrendatario, ria (of lands).

lessen ['lesn] *vt* disminuir, reducir.
◆ *vi* disminuir, reducirse.

lessening [-iŋ] *n* disminución *f*, reducción *f*.

lesser ['lesə*] *comp adj* menor; *the lesser evil* el mal menor || menor, más pequeño, ña; *the lesser half* la mitad más pequeña || de menos categoría; *one of the lesser officials* uno de los funcionarios de menos categoría || *Lesser Antilles* Antillas *f* Menores.

lesson ['lesn] *n* lección *f*; *to recite a lesson* dar la lección || clase *f*; *to give Spanish lessons* o *lessons in Spanish* dar clases de español || lectura *f*, lección *f* (Bible reading) || — FIG *let that be a lesson to you* que eso te sirva de lección | *now I'm going to teach them a lesson* ahora les voy a dar una lección | *to learn one's lesson* escarmentar | *to make a child say his lesson* tomarle la lección a un niño || *to take Spanish lessons* dar clases de español.

lesson ['lesn] *vt* dar una lección a.

lessor [le'sɔ:*] *n* JUR arrendador, ra.

lest [lest] *conj* por miedo a que, por temor a que (for fear that); *I didn't do it lest he should beat me* no lo hice por miedo a que me pegase || para que no; *they kept quiet lest he should wake up* se callaron para que no se despertase || para no (followed by the infinitive); *they did not come lest they should disturb you* no vinieron para no molestarle || que (after verbs of fearing); *he was anxious lest I should miss the train* temía que yo perdiese el tren.
— OBSERV *Para no* can only be used to translate *lest* when the subject of the two clauses is the same.

let [let] *n* alquiler *m* (renting of a house) || arrendamiento *m*, arriendo *m* (renting of land) || obstáculo *m*, traba *f* (hindrance) || SP let *m*, servicio *m* nulo (tennis, etc.) || *without let or hindrance* sin estorbo ni obstáculo.
— OBSERV The term *net* is sometimes used incorrectly in Spanish for *let*.

let* [let] *vt* dejar, permitir; *he let me do it* me dejó hacerlo; *let me see your injury* déjame ver tu herida; *will you let me give you a piece of advice?* ¿me permite que le dé un consejo? || alquilar (to rent a house) || arrendar (to rent land) || — *he doesn't speak French, let alone Chinese* no habla francés y aun menos chino || *house to let* se alquila (inscription) || *I didn't even see him, let alone speak to him* ni siquiera le vi, ¿cómo iba a hablarle? || *to let alone, to let be* dejar en paz, dejar tranquilo || MED *to let blood* sangrar, hacer una sangría || *to let fall* soltar, dejar caer (to drop), echar, decir, soltar; *to let fall a hint* soltar una indirecta; soltar; *he let fall a few oaths* soltó unos tacos; trazar; *to let fall a perpendicular* trazar una perpendicular || FIG *to let fly* disparar (weapon), soltar (insults), salir de sus casillas (with anger), empezar a repartir golpes (to start hitting out) | *to let fly at s.o.* arremeter contra uno (shouting), asestarle un golpe a uno (to hit out at), disparar contra alguien (with a firearm) || *to let go* soltar (to release), dejar en libertad (to set free), fondear, anclar (to drop anchor) || *to let go of* soltar || *to let know* avisar; *let me know if anyone calls* avísame si llama alguien; dar a conocer, informar (to inform) || *to let loose* dar rienda suelta a; *he let loose his anger* dio rienda suelta a su cólera; enfadarse, echar una bronca; *he let loose at her* se enfadó con ella; írsele a uno la lengua (to speak harshly), soltar (abuse) || *to let* o *to set loose* poner en libertad, soltar (person, animal) || *to let o.s.* dejarse; *to let o.s. be caught* dejarse coger; *to let o.s. be seen* dejarse ver || *to let o.s. go* dejarse llevar, abandonarse (to lose one's inhibitions), abandonarse (dejarse, descuidarse (to cease to have pride in o.s.) || *to let o.s. go on a subject* dejarse llevar por un tema || *to let slip* dejar pasar (an opportunity), revelar (a secret) || *to let well alone* o *well enough alone* dejar (una cosa) como está || *well, let it go at that* dejémoslo así || *without letting any blood* sin derramamiento de sangre.
◆ *vi* alquilarse (house) || arrendarse (land) || *to let* se alquila (inscription).
◆ *phr v* *to let by* dejar pasar || **to let down** bajar; *to let a basket down on a rope* bajar una cesta con una cuerda | descender, bajar (s.o.) | fallar; *the car, the weather let us down* el coche, el tiempo nos falló | alargar (to lengthen) | soltarse (hair) | desinflar, deshinchar (to deflate) | aflojar (a spring) | FIG defraudar (to deceive), fallar; *he let me down* me falló; abandonar (a friend) || — FIG *to be let down* llevarse un chasco | FIG *to let one's hair down* soltarse el pelo | FIG *to let o.s. down* no estar a la altura de sus compromisos | *to let o.s. down by a rope* descolgarse *or* bajar por una cuerda | *to let s.o. down gently* ser indulgente con alguien || **to let in** dejar entrar; *they let me in* me dejaron entrar; *a hole that lets the cold in* un agujero que deja entrar el frío | hacer entrar, dejar entrar; *when he came I let him in* cuando vino le dejé entrar | abrir; *it was his mother who let me in* fue su madre quien me abrió | permitir, dar paso a; *these measures will let in too many excuses* estas medidas permitirán demasiadas excusas | estafar, timar (to swindle) | engañar (to mislead) | encajar (to insert) || — *I got let in for 500 pesetas* tuve que pagar 500 pesetas | *let him in!* ¡dile que entre! | *to let o.s. in* abrir la puerta | *to let o.s. in for* meterse en; *to let o.s. in for trouble* meterse en un lío; comprometerse a; *to let o.s. in for a speech* comprometerse a hacer un discurso | *to let s.o. in for difficulties* crearle problemas a alguien, ocasionarle dificultades a alguien | *to let s.o. in on a secret* revelar un secreto a alguien || **to let into** empotrar; *to let a cupboard into a wall* empotrar un armario en una pared | abrir; *to let a door into a wall* abrir una puerta en una pared | revelar (a secret) | dejar entrar a (to al-

low to enter); *he let me into his house* me dejó entrar en su casa || — FAM *to let into s.o.* atacar a alguien, arremeter contra alguien || ***to let off*** dispensar de (to exempt) | perdonar (to forgive) | disparar (a gun) | tirar (a rocket) | hacer explotar (a bomb) | hacer estallar (firework) | aflojar (a spring) | dejar salir (the steam) | emitir (to emit, to give off) | alquilar (to hire) || — *to be let off with a light sentence* sacar una condena muy leve | *to be let off with a warning* escapar con una amonestación | FIG *to let off steam* desfogarse || ***to let on*** decir; *don't let on!* ¡no lo digas!; *don't let on that it was me* no digas que he sido yo | fingirse, hacerse; *he let on that he was dead* se hizo el muerto | fingir; *he let on that his father was rich* fingió que su padre era rico | hacerse pasar por; *he let on that he was a policeman* se hizo pasar por un policía || — *he never let on that he was angry* disimuló su enfado | *to let on about* revelar || ***to let out*** poner en libertad, dejar salir (to set free) | ensanchar (a garment) | revelar, divulgar (a secret) | dejar apagarse (a fire) | soltar (a scream, a yell) | dejar salir (air from a tyre) | aflojar (to loosen) | acompañar a la puerta (person who is leaving) | alquilar (to rent a house) | arrendar (to rent land) | MAR largar (sails) | US repartir (trabajo) (to portion out work), conceder (un contrato) (to assign a contract) || — *to let out a contract to s.o.* contratar a alguien | FIG *to let out at s.o.* decirle a uno cuatro verdades | *to let out at s.o. with one's fist* soltar un puñetazo a alguien || ***to let through*** dejar pasar (to allow to pass) || ***to let up*** disminuir (to lessen) | moderarse (to become moderate) | dejar de trabajar (to stop working) | aflojar, disminuir los esfuerzos (to slacken) || — *to let up on* ser menos exigente con | *when the rain lets up* cuando llueva menos.

◆ *v aux* (1st and 3rd pers of imperative let everyone know) que todos sepan || *let him live* que viva || *let's get out of here!* ¡vayámonos de aquí! || *let's go!* ¡vamos!, ¡vámonos!, ¡vayámonos! || *let's not be silly* no seas idiota, no hagamos el tonto || *let's not lose our heads* no perdamos la cabeza || *let's see* a ver, veamos; *let's see what you've done wrong* a ver lo que has hecho mal || *let there be light* hágase la luz || *let us sing* cantemos || *let X be equal to Y* supongamos que X es igual a Y.

— OBSERV Pret y pp ***let***.

letdown [-'daun] *n* decepción *f*, desilusión *f*, chasco *m* (disappointment) || disminución *f*.

lethal ['li:θəl] *adj* mortífero, ra; *a lethal weapon* un arma mortífera || mortal; *a lethal dose* una dosis mortal; *a lethal wound* una herida mortal || MED letal.

lethargic [le'θɑ:dʒik] *adj* letárgico, ca.

lethargically [-əli] *adv* letárgicamente.

lethargy ['leθədʒi] *n* letargo *m*.

let's [lets] contraction of «let us».

Lett [let] *n* letón, ona.

letter ['letə*] *n* letra *f*; *the letter «f»* la letra «f» || carta *f*; *to write s.o. a letter* escribirle una carta a alguien; *covering letter* carta adjunta; *registered letter* carta certificada || PRINT tipo *m*, carácter *m*, letra *f* (type) || FIG letra *f* (literal meaning) || *by letter post* como carta || *capital letter* mayúscula *f* || PRINT *compound letter* signo *m* doble || *cursive letter* letra cursiva || *dead letter* letra muerta || *dominical letter* letra dominical || *letter of advice* aviso *m*, notificación *f* || *letter of attorney* poder *m* || *letter of condolence* carta de pésame || COMM *letter of credit* carta de crédito || *letter of dismissal* carta de despido || *letter of introduction* carta de presentación *or* de recomendación || MAR *letter* o *letters of marque* patente *f* de corso || *letter of sponsorship* carta de llamada || *love letter* carta de amor || *open letter* carta abierta || *small capital letter* letra versalita || *small letter* minúscula *f* || *to the letter* al pie de la letra; *to carry out instructions to the letter* cumplir las instrucciones al pie de la letra.

◆ *pl* letras *f* (literature); *a man of letters* un hombre de letras || — *block letters* letras de molde || *italic letters* letra bastardilla || *letter* o *letters of credence, letters credential, credential letters* cartas credenciales || *letters patent of nobility* ejecutoria *f sing*.

letter ['letə*] *vt* rotular (to inscribe) || PRINT imprimir *or* estampar con letras (to impress letters) || poner un título a (a book).

letter ['letə*] *n* alquilador, ra.

letter book [-buk] *n* libro *m* copiador.

letter box [-bɔks] *n* buzón *m*.

lettercard [-kɑ:d] *n* billete *m* postal.

letter carrier [-ˌkæriə*] *n* US cartero *m* (postman).

lettered [-d] *adj* rotulado, da || estampado *or* marcado con letras (marked with letters) || culto, ta (cultured) || letrado, da; erudito, ta (learned).

letterer [-rə*] *n* rotulador *m*.

letter file [-fail] *n* carpeta *f*.

letterhead [-hed] *n* membrete *m* (heading) || papel *m* con membrete (headed paper).

lettering [-riŋ] *n* rotulado *m*, rotulación *f* (act of making letters) || letras *f pl*, rótulo *m*, inscripción *f*.

letter-lock [-lɔk] *n* candado *m* de combinación.

letter opener [-ˌəupənə*] *n* abrecartas *m inv*.

letter paper [-ˌpeipə*] *n* papel *m* de escribir.

letter-perfect [-'pə:fikt] *adj* al pie de la letra; *he knows his part letter-perfect* sabe su papel al pie de la letra || exacto, ta (correct).

letter press [-pres] *n* prensa *f* de copiar.

letterpress [-pres] *n* PRINT texto *m* impreso (printed text) | impresión *f* tipográfica (printing).

letter scales [-skeilz] *pl n* pesacartas *m inv*.

letters rogatory ['letə*z'rɔgətəri] *pl n* JUR exhorto *m sing*.

letter writer ['letəˌraitə*] *n* manual *m* de correspondencia (book) || el que escribe cartas, escritor *m* de cartas (person).

Lettic ['letik]; **Lettish** ['letiʃ] *adj* letón, ona.

◆ *n* letón *m* (language).

letting ['letiŋ] *n* arrendamiento *m*.

lettre de cachet [letrədəkæʃei] *n* HIST carta *f* cerrada con el sello real que exigía el encarcelamiento o destierro de una persona.

lettuce ['letis] *n* BOT lechuga *f* || US FAM pasta *f* (money).

letup ['letʌp] *n* descanso *m*, tregua *f* (rest) || interrupción *f* || moderación *f* (moderation) || reducción *f*, disminución *f* (reduction).

leucaemia; US **leucemia** [lju'ki:miə] *n* MED leucemia *f*.

leucaemic; US **leucemic** [lju'ki:mik] *adj* MED leucémico, ca.

leucoblast ['lju:kəblæst] *n* BIOL leucoblasto *m*.

leucocyte ['lju:kəusait] *n* BIOL leucocito *m*.

leucocytosis [ˌlju:kəusai'təusis] *n* MED leucocitosis *f inv*.

leucoma [lju:'kəumə] *n* MED leucoma *m*.

leucoplast ['lju:kəplæst] *n* BOT leucoplasto *m*.

leucorrhoea [ˌlju:kə'ri:ə] *n* MED leucorrea *f*.

leucosis [lju:'kəusis] *n* MED leucosis *f*.

leud [lju:d] *n* HIST leude *m*.

leukaemia; US **leukemia** [lju:'ki:miə] *n* MED leucemia *f*.

leukaemic; US **leukemic** [lju:'ki:mik] *adj* MED leucémico, ca.

leukoblast ['lju:kəblæst] *n* US BIOL leucoblasto *m*.

leukocyte ['lju:kəusait] *n* US BIOL leucocito *m*.

leukocytosis [ˌlju:kəusai'təusis] *n* US MED leucocitosis *f inv*.

leukoma [lju:'kəumə] *n* US MED leucoma *m*.

leukorrhea [ˌlju:kə'ri:ə] *n* US MED leucorrea *f*.

leukosis [lju:'kəusis] *n* US MED leucosis *f*.

Levant [li'vænt] *pr n* Levante *m*.

levanter [-ə*] *n* viento *m* de Levante (wind).

Levantine ['levəntain] *adj/n* levantino, na.

levator [li'veitə*] *n* ANAT elevador *m*.

— OBSERV El plural de *levator* es *levatores*.

levee ['levi] *n* HIST recepción *f* dada por un rey al principio de la tarde o cuando se levanta por la mañana (reception) || US dique *m* (dike) | malecón *m* (jetty) | recepción *f* (held by a high official).

level ['levl] *adj* horizontal (horizontal) || a nivel (even) || llano, na; plano, na (flat) || raso, sa; *level spoonful* cucharada rasa || igual (equal) || igualado, da (of two moving objects); *they were level until the last straight* estaban igualados hasta la recta final || estable (stable); *a level temperature* una temperatura estable || uniforme; *a level tone* un tono uniforme || sin emoción, tranquilo, la; *a level voice* una voz sin emoción || ecuánime (equable) || ordenado, da; *a level life* una vida ordenada || flemático, ca; *the Englishman is very level* el inglés es muy flemático || penetrante; *a level look* una mirada penetrante || PHYS equipotencial (equipotential) || — *dead level* al mismo nivel (objects), completamente igualados (moving objects, people) || *level with* al nivel de || *level with the ground* a ras de tierra, a flor de tierra || *one's level best* todo lo posible, el máximo || *to be level with* estar a la misma altura *or* al mismo nivel que || *to draw level with* igualar.

◆ *adv* a nivel || horizontalmente (horizontally).

◆ *n* nivel *m* (instrument); *spirit level* nivel de burbuja || nivel *m*; *sea level* nivel del mar; *water level* nivel del agua; *at ministerial level* al nivel ministerial; *the general level is very high* el nivel general es muy alto; *level of language* nivel de lenguaje || altura *f*, nivel *m*; *to come down to s.o.'s level* ponerse a la altura de alguien; *at shoulder level* a la altura del hombro; *to be on the same level* estar a la misma altura; *difference of level* diferencia de nivel || índice *m*; *the alcohol level in the blood* el índice de alcohol en la sangre; *intelligence level* índice de inteligencia || línea *f* visual (of a gun) || llano *m*, superficie *f* llana, llanura *f* (flat place) || — *at eye level* a la altura del ojo || *at ground level* a ras de tierra || *noise level* intensidad *f* del ruido || *on a level with* al nivel de, a la misma altura que (at the same height as), equiparable con, parangonable con, comparable con (comparable with) || *on the level* honrado, da; serio, ria (person, offer, etc.), en serio; *to tell s.o. sth. on the level* decirle algo a alguien en serio || *out of level* desnivelado, da || *to find one's own level* encontrar su sitio en la sociedad || *to take a level* nivelar (in topography).

level ['levl] *vt* nivelar, allanar, aplanar (to make flat) || nivelar (in surveying) || arrasar (to raze); *the school was levelled by the hurricane* el huracán arrasó el colegio || apuntar (to aim a weapon) || FIG dirigir (an accusation) | igualar, nivelar (to make equal) || — *to level away* nivelar, allanar || *to level down* rebajar al mismo nivel, igualar || *to level up* elevar al mismo nivel, igualar.

◆ *vi* nivelarse (to become balanced) || estabilizarse (prices) || *to level off* o *out* nivelarse (to become balanced), estabilizarse (prices), ponerse en una trayectoria horizontal [antes de aterrizar] (an aircraft).

level crossing [-'krɔsiŋ] *n* paso *m* a nivel.

leveler [-ə*] *n* US nivelador, ra.

level-headed [-'hedid] *adj* sensato, ta; juicioso, sa.

leveling [-iŋ] *n* US ⟶ **levelling.**

leveller [-ə*] *n* nivelador, ra.

levelling [-iŋ] *n* nivelación *f* (topography) || aplanamiento *m*, allanamiento *m* (flattening).

levelling rod; US **leveling rod** ['levliŋrɔd]; **levelling staff**; US **leveling staff** ['levliŋstɑ:f] *n* jalón *m*, mira *f*.

level pegging ['levlpegiŋ] *adj* igualada, da; empatado, da (contestants, teams).

lever ['li:və*] *n* palanca *f* || FIG apoyo *m*, palanca *f* (influence).

lever ['li:və*] *vt* apalancar || *to lever up* levantar con una palanca.

leverage [-ridʒ] *n* apalancamiento *m* || fuerza *f* de la palanca || FIG influencia *f* | ventaja *f*.

leveret [levərit] *n* ZOOL lebrato *m*.

leviable ['leviəbl] *adj* percibible, recaudable (tax) || imponible (person).

Leviathan [li'vaiəθən] *pr n* REL Leviatán *m*.

levigation [,levi'geiʃən] *n* levigación *f*.

levitate ['leviteit] *vt* elevar *or* mantener en el aire por levitación.

◆ *vi* elevarse *or* mantenerse en el aire por levitación.

levitation [,levi'teiʃən] *n* levitación *f*.

Levite ['li:vait] *n* REL levita *m*.

Leviticus [li'vitikəs] *pr n* REL Levítico *m*.

levity ['leviti] *n* ligereza *f*.

levy ['levi] *n* exacción *f* (imposing of a tax) || recaudación *f*, percepción *f* (collecting of a tax) || impuesto *m* (amount paid) || sobretasa *f* (surcharge) || MIL leva *f* (recruitment) || JUR embargo *m* (of property, etc.).

levy ['levi] *vt* exigir (to exact taxes) || recaudar, percibir (to collect taxes) || imponer (a fine) || MIL reclutar, hacer una leva de (soldiers) || JUR embargar (to seize property) || — *to levy a duty on sth.* gravar algo con un impuesto || *to levy war on* hacer la guerra a.

◆ *vi* JUR imponer un embargo.

levy in mass [-in'mæs] *n* movilización *f* general.

lewd [lu:d] *adj* lascivo, va; lúbrico, ca (lascivious) || indecente, obsceno, na (indecent).

lewdness [-nis] *n* lascivia *f*, lubricidad *f* (lasciviousness) || obscenidad *f*.

Lewis ['lu:is] *pr n* Luis *m* || MIL *Lewis gun* ametralladora *f*.

lexical ['leksikəl] *adj* léxico, ca; lexicológico, ca.

lexicographer [,leksi'kɔgrəfə*] *n* lexicógrafo, fa.

lexicographic [,leksikəu'græfik]; **lexicographical** [-əl] *adj* lexicográfico, ca.

lexicography [,leksi'kɔgrəfi] *n* lexicografía *f*.

lexicologic [,leksikəu'lɔdʒik]; **lexicological** [-əl] *adj* lexicológico, ca.

lexicologist [,leksi'kɔlədʒist] *n* lexicólogo, ga.

lexicology [,leksi'kɔlədʒi] *n* lexicología *f*.

lexicon ['leksikən] *n* léxico *m*.

Leyden ['laidn] *pr n* GEOGR Leyden || *Leyden jar* botella *f* de Leyden.

liability [,laiə'biliti] *n* responsabilidad *f* (legal responsibility) || sujeción *f*; *liability to duties* sujeción a impuestos || tendencia *f* (propensity); *liability to catch cold* tendencia a constiparse; *liability to explode* tendencia a explotar || probabilidad *f* (probability) || inconveniente *m* (drawback); *owning a car can be a liability* tener un coche puede ser un inconveniente || estorbo *m* (nuisance) || — *liability insurance* seguro *m* de responsabilidad civil || *limited-liability company* sociedad (de responsabilidad) limitada.

◆ *pl* COMM pasivo *m sing*, debe *m sing*; *assets and liabilities* el activo y el pasivo, el debe y el haber | deudas *f* (debts); *he met his liabilities* satisfizo sus deudas | compromisos *m* (obligations).

liable ['laiəbl] *adj* JUR responsable; *to be liable for s.o.'s debts* ser responsable de las deudas de alguien || sujeto, ta; sometido, da; *liable to duties* sujeto a impuestos || expuesto, ta; *liable to a fine* expuesto a una multa; *liable to a good hiding* expuesto a una buena paliza || susceptible de; *liable to change* susceptible de cambio || propenso, sa; *liable to catch cold* propenso a constiparse || capaz; *she is liable to change her mind* es capaz de cambiar de opinión || — *to be liable for military service* estar obligado a hacer el servicio militar || *to be liable to snow* ser probable que nieve || US *we are liable to be in Seattle next month* puede ser que *or* es probable que estemos en Seattle el mes que viene.

liaise [li'eiz] *vi* MIL establecer el enlace.

liaison [li'eiz⁻ɔ] *n* MIL enlace *m* || coordinación *f*, enlace *m* (coordination) || GRAMM enlace *m* (between words) || aventura *f* (love affair) || MIL *liaison officer* oficial *m* de enlace.

liana [li'ɑ:nə]; **liane** [li'a:n] *n* BIT bejuco *m*, liana *f*.

liar ['laiə*] *n* mentiroso, sa; embustero, ra.

Lias ['laiəs] *n* GEOL lías *m*, liásico *m*.

libation [lai'beiʃən] *n* libación *f*.

libel ['laibəl] *n* escrito *m* difamatorio, libelo *m* (published statement) || difamación *f* (act of publishing such a statement); *libel suit* pleito por difamación || FIG calumnia *f* (slander).

libel ['laibəl] *vt* difamar [por escrito] (to publish a libel about) || FIG calumniar (to slander).

libeller; US **libeler** [-ə*]; **libellist**; US **libelist** [-ist] *n* JUR libelista *m* & *f* || difamador, ra (defamer) || calumniador, ra (slanderer).

libellous; US **libelous** ['laibləs] *adj* difamatorio, ria || calumnioso, sa.

libellula [li'beljulə] *n* libélula *f* (insect).

liber ['laibə*] *n* registro *m* (book) || BOT líber *m*.

liberal ['libərəl] *adj* liberal || libre; *a liberal interpretation of the rules* una libre interpretación de las reglas || generoso, sa; liberal (generous); *a liberal reward* una recompensa generosa || — *liberal arts* artes *f* liberales || *liberal education* educación *f* humanista || *liberal ideas* ideas *f* liberales || *the Liberal Party* el Partido liberal.

◆ *n* liberal *m* & *f* || *the Liberals* los liberales (political party).

liberalism ['libərəlizəm] *n* liberalismo *m*.

liberality [,libə'ræliti] *n* liberalidad *f* || amplitud *f* de miras (broad-mindedness).

liberalization [,libərəlai'zeiʃən] *n* liberalización *f*.

liberalize ['libərəlaiz] *vt* liberalizar.

◆ *vi* liberalizarse.

liberally ['libərəli] *adv* liberalmente || liberalmente, generosamente (generously) || libremente (to translate, etc.).

liberal-minded ['libərəl'maindid] *adj* amplio, plia (ideas) || tolerante (conscience) || liberal (person).

liberal-mindedness ['libərəl'maindidnis] *n* amplitud *f* de miras (broad-mindedness) || tolerancia *f* (tolerance).

liberate ['libəreit] *vt* liberar, libertar (to free) || poner en libertad (a prisoner) || liberar (a country) || librar (from obligations) || CHEM desprender, liberar (to give off a gas).

liberating [-iŋ] *adj* liberador, ra.

liberation [,libə'reiʃən] *n* liberación *f* || CHEM desprendimiento *m*, liberación *f* (of gas).

liberator ['libəreitə*] *n* libertador, ra; liberador, ra.

liberatory ['libərətəri] *adj* liberatorio, ria.

Liberia [lai'biəriə] *pr n* GEOGR Liberia *f*.

Liberian [-n] *adj/n* liberiano, na.

libertarian [,libər'tɛəriən] *adj/n* libertario, ria.

libertinage ['libətinidʒ] *n* libertinaje *m*.

libertine ['libətain] *adj/n* libertino, na.

liberty ['libəti] *n* libertad *f*; *liberty of action, of thought* libertad de acción, de pensamiento || MAR licencia *f*, permiso *m* (leave) || FAM libertad *f*, confianza *f* (familiarity) || privilegio *m* || — *liberty boat* barco *m* de los marineros que están de permiso || *liberty cap* gorro frigio || US *liberty ship* barco *m* mercante || *to be at liberty* estar en libertad (to be free), estar libre, estar desocupado (to be at leisure), estar autorizado, tener derecho; *not to be at liberty to disclose sth.* no estar autorizado a revelar una cosa; *to be at liberty to do sth.* tener derecho a hacer algo || *to pledge one's liberty* hipotecar la libertad || *to set at liberty* poner en libertad || *to take liberties* tomarse libertades || *to take the liberty of* o *to* tomarse la libertad de.

libidinal [li'bidinəl]; **libidinous** [li'bidinəs] *adj* libidinoso, sa.

libido [li'bi:dəu] *n* libido *f*.

Libra ['laibrə] *pr n* ASTR Libra *f*.

librarian [lai'brɛəriən] *n* bibliotecario, ria.

librarianship [-ʃip] *n* cargo *m* de bibliotecario.

library ['laibrəri] *n* biblioteca *f*; *reference, lending, public library* biblioteca de consulta, de préstamo, pública; *circulating* o *mobile library* biblioteca circulante || INFORM biblioteca *f* || — *library book* libro *m* de biblioteca || *newspaper library* hemeroteca *f*.

librate ['laibreit] *vi* balancearse, oscilar.

libratory ['laibrə,tɔri] *adj* que se balancea, oscilatorio, ria.

librettist [li'bretist] MUS libretista *m* & *f*.

libretto [li'bretəu] *n* MUS libreto *m*.

— OBSERV El plural de la palabra inglesa es *librettos* o *libretti*.

Libya ['libiə] *pr n* GEOGR Libia *f*.

Libyan [-n] *adj/n* libio, bia.

lice [lais] *pl n* ⟶ **louse.**

licence; US **license** ['laisəns] *n* licencia *f*, permiso *m*; *hunting, fishing licence* licencia de caza, de pesca; *export licence* licencia de exportación || autorización *f* (authorization) || carnet *m*, permiso *m*; *driving licence* carnet de conducir, permiso de conducción || licencia *f*; *poetic licence* licencia poética || libertad *f* (freedom); *he was allowed some licence in interpreting the play* le fue concedida cierta libertad en la interpretación de la obra || licencia *f*, libertinaje *m* (socially undesirable behaviour) || — *licence number* matrícula *f*, número *m* de matrícula || *licence plate* placa *f* de matrícula, matrícula *f* || *licence tax* impuesto *m* sobre patente || *road tax licence* impuesto *m* de circulación || ECON *under licence* con licencia; *manufacturing under licence* fabricación con licencia.

licence; **license** ['laisəns] *vt* conceder una licencia *or* un permiso a || autorizar; *licenced to sell* autorizado para vender || permitir (to permit) || *licensed premises* establecimiento autorizado para vender bebidas alcohólicas.

licencee [,laisən'si:] *n* ⟶ **licensee.**

license ['laisəns] *n/vt* ⟶ **licence.**

licensee; licencee [ˌlaisən'siː] *n* persona *f* que tiene un permiso *or* una licencia, concesionario *m* ‖ persona *f* autorizada para vender bebidas alcohólicas.

licenser ['laisənsə*] *n* persona *f* que concede un permiso *or* una licencia.

licensing hours ['laisənsiŋˌauəz] *pl n* horas *f* autorizadas de venta de alcohol al público (in English pubs).

licensing laws [-ˌlɔːz] *pl n* normas *f* reguladoras de la venta y consumo de alcohol.

licentiate [lai'senʃiit] *n* licenciado, da.

licentious [lai'senʃəs] *adj* licencioso, sa.

licentiousness [-nis] *n* libertinaje *m*, licencia *f*.

lichen ['laikən] *n* BOT liquen *m*.

lich-gate [litʃgeit] *n* entrada *f* de cementerio.

licit ['lisit] *adj* lícito, ta.

licitness [-nis] *n* licitud *f*.

lick [lik] *n* lamedura *f*, lamido *m*, lengüetazo *m*, lengüetada *f* (the act of licking) ‖ mano *f* (light coating); *a lick of paint* una mano de pintura ‖ salina *f* (salt lick) ‖ FAM poco *m* (little) | golpe *m* (blow) ‖ — FAM *he won't do a lick of work* no dará ni golpe | *to give o.s. a lick and a promise* lavarse rápidamente | *to go at a great* o *at full lick* ir a todo gas.

lick [lik] *vt* lamer; *he licked the ice cream* lamió el helado ‖ acariciar; *the waves licked the beach* las olas acariciaban la playa ‖ FAM dar una paliza a (to beat) ‖ — *to lick clean* lamer ‖ FIG *to lick into shape* pulir, poner a punto (an article), formar; *travel licks a young man into shape* los viajes forman a los jóvenes; pulir, desbastar (an uncouth person) ‖ *to lick off* quitar de un lametazo ‖ FIG & FAM *to lick one's chops* o *one's lips* relamerse | *to lick s.o.'s shoes* o *boots, to lick up to s.o.* hacer la pelotilla a alguien, dar coba a alguien | *to lick the dust* morder el polvo ‖ *to lick up* beber a lengüetadas.

lickerish [-əriʃ] *adj* ávido, da (eager) ‖ goloso, sa (greedy) ‖ lascivo, va (lecherous) ‖ apetitoso, sa (appetizing).

lickety-split [ˌlikəti'split] *adv* FAM pelotillero, ra; cobista *m* & *f*.

licking [likiŋ] *n* lamido *m* (act of one who licks) ‖ FIG & FAM paliza *f*; *to give s.o. a licking* dar una paliza a alguien ‖ FIG & FAM *licking up* pelotilla *f*, coba *f*.

lickspittle ['likspitl] *n* FAM pelotillero, ra; cobista *m* & *f*.

licorice ['likəris] *n* regaliz *m*.

lictor ['liktə*] *n* HIST lictor *m*.

lid [lid] *n* tapa *f*, tapadera *f* (cover) ‖ FAM güito *m* (hat) ‖ ANAT párpado *m* (of the eye) ‖ BOT opérculo *m* ‖ — FAM *to flip one's lid* volverse loco | *to flip one's lid for* o *over* chiflarse por, volverse loco por | *to put the lid on* rematar.

lido ['laidəu] *n* piscina *f* pública descubierta.

lie [lai] *n* mentira *f*, embuste *m* ‖ — *it's a pack of lies* es una sarta de mentiras ‖ *lie detector* detector *m* de mentiras ‖ *one lie makes many* de una mentira nacen ciento ‖ *to act a lie* actuar con falsedad ‖ *to give the lie to* demostrar que (algo) es falso (to prove false), dar el mentís a (person), desmentir (a report) ‖ *to tell a lie* decir una mentira, mentir ‖ *white lie* mentira piadosa.

lie [lai] *vi* mentir ‖ *to lie o.s. out of a scrape* conseguir salir de un apuro por medio de mentiras.

lie [lai] *n* posición *f*, situación *f* (place) ‖ dirección *f*, orientación *f* (direction) ‖ configuración *f* (nature) ‖ guarida *f* (of a wild animal) ‖ — FIG *the lie of the land* el estado de las cosas | *to study the lie of the land* estudiar el terreno.

lie* [lai] *vi* echarse, acostarse, tumbarse, tenderse (to assume a horizontal posture); *to lie on the floor* echarse en el suelo ‖ estar tendido, estar echado, estar acostado, estar tumbado (to be in a horizontal posture); *he was lying on the floor* estaba tumbado en el suelo ‖ estar acostado, dormir (to sleep) ‖ estar; *he lay dead on the ground* estaba muerto en el suelo; *to lie hidden* estar escondido; *to lie resting* estar descansando; *the difference lies in the fact that* la diferencia está en el hecho de que ‖ estar, estar situado; *the town lies to the south* la ciudad está al sur; *his grave lies over the hill* su tumba está situada al otro lado de la colina ‖ yacer, reposar, estar enterrado (the dead); *here lies Snow White* aquí yace Blancanieves ‖ quedarse (to remain); *to lie still* quedarse inmóvil; *to lie in bed* quedarse en cama ‖ estribar, radicar, residir; *you know where your interest lies* ya sabes donde radica tu interés ‖ extenderse; *a pall of smoke lies over the town* una capa de humo se extiende sobre la ciudad; *the town lay before us* la ciudad se extendía ante nosotros ‖ depender; *the decision lies with you* la decisión depende de ti ‖ pertenecer, incumbir (to concern) ‖ cuajar (snow) ‖ estar depositado (money) ‖ MIL acampar ‖ MAR estar anclado (to be at anchor) ‖ JUR ser admisible *or* procedente ‖ — *the fault lies with him* la culpa es suya ‖ *the route lay across a desert* el camino atravesaba un desierto ‖ *the water lay two metres deep* había dos metros de agua ‖ *to lie asleep* estar durmiendo ‖ *to lie heavy on the conscience* pesar en la conciencia ‖ *to lie idle* estar parado (factory) ‖ *to lie in ruins* estar en ruinas ‖ *to lie in state* estar de cuerpo presente ‖ *to lie under a charge of* estar bajo la acusación de ‖ *to lie under obligation to* tener la obligación de ‖ *to lie with a woman* conocer mujer.

◆ *phr v* ***to lie about*** estar tirado, estar rodando; *her clothes were lying about all over the room* su ropa estaba tirada por toda la habitación ‖ — *books were lying about everywhere* había libros por todas partes | *it's lying about here somewhere* anda rodando por aquí | *we lay about in the sun all day* pasamos el día tumbados al sol ‖ ***to lie back*** recostarse (in an armchair, etc.) | estar retranqueado, da (house) ‖ ***to lie by*** estar sin utilizar (to be unused) | descansar, pararse (to rest) | estar a mano, estar cerca (to be near) ‖ ***to lie down*** acostarse, tenderse, tumbarse, echarse; *to lie down on the floor* tenderse en el suelo; *why don't you lie down for a while?* ¿por qué no te echas un rato? | estar acostado *or* tendido *or* echado *or* tumbado (state) ‖ — *lie down!* ¡échate! (to a dog) | *to lie down under an insult* aguantar un insulto | *to take sth. lying down* aguantar algo sin chistar ‖ ***to lie in*** estar de parto (to be confined due to childbirth) | quedarse en cama (to stay in bed) ‖ ***to lie off*** mantenerse a distancia (boats) | reservarse (for later on) | descansar (to rest from work) ‖ ***to lie over*** aplazarse, quedar aplazado (to be postponed) | *it can lie over* nada se pierde con esperar ‖ ***to lie to*** pairar, estar al pairo (a ship) ‖ ***to lie up*** estar sin utilizar (a vehicle) | desarmar (a ship) | guardar cama (during an illness) | esconderse (to hide) | descansar (to rest).

— OBSERV Pret ***lay***; pp ***lain***.

lie-abed [-əbed] *n* FAM remolón, ona; perezoso, sa.

Liechtenstein ['liktənstain] *pr n* GEOGR Liechtenstein *m*.

lied [liːt] *n* MUS lied *m*.

— OBSERV El plural es *lieder* en ambos idiomas.

lie-down ['laidaun] *n* siestecita *f* ‖ *to have a lie-down* echarse.

lief [liːf] *adv* *I had as lief* o *I would as lief go as stay* me da igual irme que quedarme ‖ *I would as lief have died* hubiera preferido morir.

liege [liːdʒ] *adj* HIST ligio (subject) | feudal (lord).

◆ *n* HIST señor *m* feudal (lord) | vasallo *m* (vassal).

liegeman ['liːdʒmæn] *n* HIST vasallo *m*.

— OBSERV El plural de *liegeman* es *liegemen*.

lie-in ['laiin] *n* *to have a lie-in* levantarse tarde.

lien [liən] *n* JUR carga *f*, gravamen *m* (encumbrance) | derecho *m* de retención (on a property).

lierne [li'əːn] *n* ARCH nervio *m* secundario [de una bóveda].

lieu [ljuː] *n* lugar *m* ‖ *in lieu of* en vez de, en lugar de.

lieutenancy [lef'tenənsi] *n* lugartenencia *f* ‖ MIL tenientazgo *m*.

lieutenant [lef'tenənt] *n* lugarteniente *m* (deputy) ‖ MIL teniente *m* ‖ MAR alférez *m* de navío ‖ — MIL *lieutenant colonel* teniente coronel ‖ MAR *lieutenant commander* capitán *m* de corbeta ‖ MIL *lieutenant general* teniente general ‖ *lieutenant governor* vicegobernador *m* ‖ US MAR *lieutenant junior grade* alférez de navío ‖ MIL *second lieutenant* subteniente *m*.

life [laif] *n* vida *f*; *life and death* vida y muerte; *expectation of life* esperanza de vida; *she has lived all her life in Dublin* ha vivido toda su vida en Dublín; *city, home, family, private life* vida de ciudad, casera, de familia, privada *or* íntima; *bird life* la vida de los pájaros; *is there life on Mars?* ¿hay vida en Marte? ‖ duración *f*, vida *f* (of a carpet, of a light bulb, etc.) ‖ biografía *f*, vida *f*; *he is writing the life of Disraeli* está escribiendo la biografía de Disraeli ‖ vida *f*, alma *f*, animación *f* (at a party) ‖ vida *f*, vitalidad *f*; *full of life* lleno de vida ‖ vigencia *f* (validity) ‖ JUR cadena *f* perpetua (life imprisonment) ‖ víctima *f* (being); *how many lives were lost?* ¿cuántas víctimas hubo?; *no lives were lost* no hubo víctimas ‖ — *a matter of life and death* una cuestión de vida o muerte ‖ *animal life* los animales; *there is not much animal life here* aquí no hay muchos animales; la vida animal; *animal or plant life* la vida animal o vegetal ‖ *as large as life* de tamaño natural (life-size); *a statue as large as life* una estatua de tamaño natural; en persona (in person) ‖ *at my time of life* a mi edad ‖ *early life* juventud *f*, años *m pl* juveniles ‖ *eternal life* vida eterna ‖ *for dear life* desesperadamente; *he ran for dear life* corrió desesperadamente ‖ *for life* de por vida ‖ *for one's life* desesperadamente ‖ *from life* del natural (painting) ‖ *how's life?* ¿cómo va la vida?, ¿qué cuentas? ‖ *I can't for the life of me remember his name* por mucho que lo intente no puedo acordarme de su nombre ‖ *I wouldn't go there for the life of me* no iría allí por nada en el mundo ‖ *later life* los últimos años ‖ *low life* hampa *f* ‖ *my life!* ¡Dios mío! ‖ *never in my life have I seen such a thing* en mi vida he visto tal cosa ‖ *not on your life!* ¡ni hablar! ‖ *one's whole life through* durante toda su vida ‖ *run for your life!* ¡sálvese quien pueda! ‖ ARTS *still life* bodegón *m*, naturaleza muerta ‖ *such is life!* ¡así es la vida! ‖ *that's life!* ¡son cosas de la vida!, ¡la vida es así! ‖ *the cat has nine lives* el gato tiene siete vidas ‖ *the good life* la buena vida ‖ *the high life* la alta sociedad ‖ *the life and soul of the party* el alma de la fiesta ‖ *this is the life!* ¡eso es vida! ‖ *to bear a charmed life* escaparse por milagro de todos los peligros ‖ *to begin life as a carpenter* empezar de carpintero ‖ *to bring (back) to life* reanimar, resucitar ‖ *to come to life* resucitar (to resuscitate, to wake up), recobrar el conocimiento, volver en sí (to regain consciousness) ‖ *to depart this life* partir de esta vida ‖ *to escape with one's life from an accident* escaparse con vida de un accidente ‖ *to have seen life* haber vivido mucho ‖ FAM *to have the time of one's life* pasárselo en grande ‖ *to lay*

down one's life dar *or* ofrendar *or* sacrificar la vida || *to lead a dog's life* llevar una vida de perros || *to live the life of Riley* darse buena vida || *to pay with one's life* pagar con la vida || *to put new life into sth.* dar vida a algo, infundir nueva vida a algo || *to see life* ver mundo || *to sell one's life dearly* vender cara la vida || *to send s.o. to prison for life* mandarle a uno a la cárcel para toda su vida || *to take one's life in one's hands* jugarse la vida || *to take one's own life* quitarse la vida, atentar contra su vida || *to take s.o.'s life* quitar la vida a uno || *true to life* conforme a la realidad || *what a life!* ¡qué vida ésta!, ¡qué vida! || *with all the pleasure in life* con muchísimo gusto.
◆ *adj* de la vida || vitalicio, cia (annuity, etc.) || vital; *life force* fuerza vital.
— OBSERV El plural de *life* es *lives*.

life-and-death [-ən,deθ] *adj* FIG encarnizado, da; a vida y muerte; *a life-and-death struggle* una lucha encarnizada *or* a vida y muerte.

life annuity [-ə'njuiti] *n* JUR renta *f* vitalicia, vitalicio *m*.

life assurance [-ə'ʃuərəns] *n* → **life insurance.**

life belt [-belt] *n* cinturón *m* salvavidas.

lifeblood [-blʌd] *n* sangre *f* (blood) || alma *f*, nervio *m*, parte *f* vital (sth. of vital importance).

lifeboat [-bəut] *n* bote *m* salvavidas, lancha *f* de salvamento.

lifeboatman [-mæn] *n* tripulante *m* de una lancha de salvamento.

life buoy [-bɔi] *n* boya *f* salvavidas.

life cycle [-'saikl] *n* ciclo *m* vital.

life expectancy [-iks'pektənsi] *n* esperanza *f* de vida.

life-giving [-giviŋ] *adj* vivificante, que da vida.

lifeguard [-gɑːd] *n* bañero *m* (on beach, in swimming pool).

Life Guards [-gɑːdz] *pl n* regimiento *m sing* de caballería al servicio del soberano británico.

life history [-'histəri] *n* ciclo *m* biológico.

life imprisonment [-im'priznmənt] *n* cadena *f* perpetua.

life insurance [-in'ʃuərəns]; **life assurance** [-ə'ʃuərəns] *n* seguro *m* de vida.

life interest [-'intrist] *n* vitalicio *m*.

life jacket [-,dʒækit] *n* chaleco *m* salvavidas.

lifeless [-lis] *adj* sin vida, muerto, ta || FIG flojo, ja; soso, sa (dull) | sin vida, sin animación.

lifelessness [-lisnis] *n* falta *f* de vida.

lifelike [-laik] *adj* que parece vivo (that seems alive) || natural (that is well reproduced) || parecido, da; que está hablando (portrait).

lifeline [-lain] *n* cuerda *f* de salvamento (for sea rescue) || cordel *m* de señales (of a diver) || FIG cordón *m* umbilical (vital supply line) | línea *f* de la vida (in palmistry).

lifelong [-lɔŋ] *adj* de toda la vida, de siempre.

life member [-'membə*] *n* miembro *m* vitalicio.

life peer [-piə*] *n* par *m* vitalicio.

life preserver [-pri,zəːvə*] *n* salvavidas *m inv* (buoy, jacket) || vergajo *m* (for self-defence).

lifer [-ə*] *n* FAM condenado *m* a cadena perpetua (prisoner) | condena *f* a cadena perpetua (sentence).

life raft [-rɑːft] *n* balsa *f* salvavidas.

lifesaver [-,seivə*] *n* bañero *m* (lifeguard) || FIG salvación *f*.

lifesaving [-,seiviŋ] *n* salvamento *m* y socorrismo || *livesaving jacket* chaleco *m* salvavidas.

life-size [-'saiz]; **life-sized** [-'saizd] *adj* de tamaño natural.

life span [-spæn] *n* vida *f*.

life-style [-stail] *n* estilo *m* de vida.

life-support system ['laifsə,pɔːt'sistim] *n* MED respirador *m* artificial || equipo *m* de vida (for spaceman).

life table [-,teibl] *n* tabla *f* de mortalidad.

lifetime [-taim] *n* vida *f*; *the lifetime of sth.* la vida de algo; *in my lifetime* en mi vida || — *the chance of a lifetime (for you)* la ocasión de tu vida || *the work of a lifetime* el trabajo de toda una vida.
◆ *adj* de toda una vida.

life vest [-vest] *n* chaleco *m* salvavidas.

lifework [-'wəːk] *n* trabajo *m* de la vida [de alguien]; *his lifework* el trabajo de su vida.

lift [lift] *n* elevación *f*, levantamiento *m*, alzamiento *m* (act of lifting) || empuje *m* (upward support) || levantamiento *m* (of a weight) || elevación *f* (in the ground) || ascensión *f* (upward movement) || agitación *f*, levantamiento *m* (of the waves) || diferencia *f* de nivel (of level) || altura *f* de elevación (of a crane, etc.) || porte *m* (of s.o.'s head) || AVIAT fuerza *f* de ascensión | empuje *m* (that raises an aircraft) | sustentación *f*, fuerza *f* de sustentación | puente *m* aéreo (airlift) || ascensor *m* [AMER elevador *m*] (elevator) || montacargas *m inv* (hoist) || carga *f* (load that is lifted) || TECH gato *m*, levantacoches *m inv* (jack) | carrera *f* (of a valve) || MAR amantillo *m* || escalón *m* (section in a mine) || tapa *f* (in the heel of a shoe) || FIG exaltación *f* (of mind) || — *I got a lift from Madrid to Seville* me cogió un coche de Madrid a Sevilla || *to give s.o. a lift* llevar en coche; *give me a lift to the next town* lléveme en coche hasta la próxima ciudad; reanimar, levantar la moral *or* el ánimo; *your letter gave me a lift* su carta me reanimó mucho || *to give s.o. a lift with sth.* echar una mano a alguien, ayudar; *can you give me a lift with that suitcase?* ¿puede echarme una mano para llevar esta maleta?

lift [lift] *vt* levantar; *he can lift 200 kilos* levanta 200 kilos || levantar, elevar, alzar; *the crane lifted the load* la grúa levantó la carga || coger (to pick up) || levantar en brazos (a child) || quitarse (a hat) || levantar, elevar, subir (one's eye, arm) || alzar, levantar, erguir (a spire) || izar (the flag) || subir (to raise to a specified place); *it lifted the load to the third floor* subió la carga hasta el tercer piso || levantar, suprimir (an embargo, restrictions, etc.) || levantar (blockade) || levantar, alzar (siege) || AGR arrancar (potatoes) | desplantar (seedlings) || transportar (by plane) || transportar por puente aéreo (to transport by airlift) || MIL alargar (the fire) || MED hacer el estirado de la piel (s.o.'s face) || FIG exaltar, elevar (heart, mind) | elevar (in rank, in dignity) || FAM robar, mangar, birlar (to steal) | copiar (to plagiarize) | llevarse, ganarse; *they lifted all the prizes* se llevaron todos los premios || US cancelar, redimir (a mortgage) || — *he doesn't lift a finger to help* no mueve un dedo para ayudar || *she has had her face lifted* le han estirado la piel (de la cara) || *to lift down* bajar || *to lift one's hand against* levantar la mano contra || *to lift one's voice against* levantar *or* alzar la voz contra || *to lift up* levantar (to raise off a surface), dar; *can you lift me up that box?* ¿me das esa caja?; levantar, alzar (one's head, one's voice).
◆ *vi* elevarse (to go up) || levantarse; *the nose of the plane lifted* el morro del avión se levantó || disiparse (fog, gloom) || alabearse (the floor) || aparecer (land) || AVIAT despegar.

lift attendant [-ə,tendənt] *n* ascensorista *m* & *f*.

lift boy [-bɔi] *n* ascensorista *m*.

lifting [-iŋ] *n* levantamiento *m* (of a weight) || AVIAT sustentación *f*; *lifting force* fuerza de sustentación.

lifting gear [-giə*] *n* torno *m* elevador.

lifting jack [-dʒæk] *n* TECH gato *m*.

liftman [-mæn] *n* ascensorista *m*.
— OBSERV El plural de *liftman* es *liftmen*.

lift-off [ɔf] *n* despegue *m* (of a plane or rocket).

lift pump [-pʌmp] *n* bomba *f* aspirante.

lift shaft [-ʃɑːft] *n* caja *f* del ascensor, hueco *m* del ascensor.

lift-up [-ʌp] *adj* abatible (seat).

lift valve [-vælv] *n* válvula *f* de movimiento vertical.

ligament ['ligəmənt] *n* ANAT ligamento *m*.

ligamental [,ligə'mentl]; **ligamentary** [,ligə'mentəri]; **ligamentous** [,ligə'mentəs] *adj* ANAT ligamentoso, sa.

ligate ['laigeit] *vt* MED ligar, hacer una ligadura a.

ligation [lai'geiʃən] *n* ligación *f* || MED ligadura *f*.

ligature ['ligətʃuə*] *n* ligadura *f* || PRINT ligado *m* || MUS ligado *m*, ligadura *f*.

ligature ['ligətʃuə*] *vt* ligar, atar || MED ligar, hacer una ligadura a.

light [lait] *adj* ligero, ra; liviano, na (see OBSERV) (burden, material, meal, food, wine, coffee, sleep) || fino, na (rain) || ligero, ra; *to walk with a light step* andar con paso ligero || suave (wind, breeze) || de poco peso, ligero, ra (not heavy) || no muy fuerte (tax) || de poca monta, poco, ca (expenses) || suave; *light grade* pendiente suave || ligero, ra; despreocupado, da (spirits) || ligero, ra (conduct); *a light woman* una mujer ligera || leve (wound, punishment, error) || ligero, ra (music, comedy, reading) || alegre, contento, ta; *a light heart* un corazón alegre || débil (sound) || ligero, ra; *a light blow* un golpe ligero || fácil, ligero, ra; *light work* trabajo fácil || ligero, ra (soil) || delicado, da (hand, touch) || vacío, a (purse) || MIL ligero, ra (artillery, infantry, tanks) | de pequeño calibre (gun) || MAR en lastre || vacío, a; sin carga (train) || de vía estrecha (railway) || TECH ligero, ra; *a light metal* un metal ligero | feble, falto de peso (coin) || falto de peso (underweight) || GRAMM débil || luminoso, sa; *light image* imagen luminosa; *light ray* rayo luminoso || claro, ra; *light blue* azul claro; *a light room* una habitación clara; *light eyes* ojos claros || rubio, bia (hair) || blanco, ca (skin); *light complexion* tez blanca || — *a light sleeper* una persona que tiene un sueño ligero || *as light as a feather* tan ligero como una pluma || *light in the head* ligero de cascos || *to be light on one's feet* ser ligero de pies, andar con mucha agilidad || *to get light* amanecer || *to grow light* clarear, hacerse de día || *to make light of* no tomar en serio, hacer poco caso de || *to make light work of* hacer con facilidad (to accomplish with ease), vencer con facilidad a (to defeat with ease) || *with a light heart* contento, ta.
◆ *adv* *to travel light* viajar con poco equipaje.
— OBSERV The word *liviano* is used mainly in Latin America.

light* [lait] *vi* bajar || — *to light into* atacar || *to light on o upon* posarse; *a fly lighted on his nose* una mosca se le posó en la nariz; tropezar con (to meet, to find) || FAM *to light out* largarse, irse.
— OBSERV Pret y pp ***lighted, lit.***

light [lait] *n* luz *f*; *light and dark* luz y oscuridad; *light and shade* luz y sombra; *the light of day* la luz del día; *the light of reason* la luz de la razón ‖ luz *f*; *electric light* luz eléctrica; *turn on the light* enciende la luz; *black light* luz negra ‖ lámpara *f*, luz *f* (lamp); *overhead light* lámpara de techo ‖ vela *f* (candle) ‖ linterna *f* (lantern) ‖ farol *m* (streetlight) ‖ faro *m* (lighthouse) ‖ AUT faro *m* (headlight) | luz *f*; *the lights on this car don't work* las luces de este coche no funcionan ‖ fuego *m*, lumbre *f* (flame); *have you got a light?* ¿tiene fuego? ‖ brillo *m*; *the light in her eyes* el brillo de sus ojos ‖ día *m* (daylight); *it is light* es de día ‖ disco *m*, luz *f*, semáforo *m* (in the street); *red light* disco rojo ‖ ARCH luz *f*, lumbrera *f* (window) | cristal *m*, vidrio *m* (of a leaded window) ‖ ARTS luz *f* (in painting) ‖ FIG aspecto *m*, apariencia *f* (aspect); *I see things in a new light* veo las cosas bajo otro aspecto | lumbrera *f* (outstanding person) ‖ — *against the light* a trasluz (to look at sth.), a contraluz (photography) ‖ FIG *a shining light* una lumbrera ‖ *at first light* al rayar la luz del día, a primera luz ‖ *bengala light* bengala *f* ‖ *by the light of* a la luz de ‖ *in the light of* a la luz de; *in the light of recent information* a la luz de las noticias recientes ‖ *in this light* desde este punto de vista ‖ *leading light* figura *f* principal ‖ *let there be light!* ¡hágase la luz! ‖ *parking light* luz de estacionamiento ‖ *pavement light* cristal *m* ‖ *pilot* o *warning light* piloto *m* ‖ *point of light* punto luminoso ‖ *this room has a poor light* esta habitación tiene poca luz ‖ SP *to appeal against the light* pedir la suspensión de un partido por falta de luz ‖ FIG *to appear in one's true light* mostrarse como se es ‖ *to be in one's own light* estar en la sombra ‖ *to be light* hacerse de día ‖ FIG *to bring sth. to light* sacar algo a luz, revelar algo | *to cast* o *to throw* o *to shed light on sth.* aclarar algo, arrojar luz sobre algo | *to come to light* salir a la luz | *to give s.o. the green light* dar la luz verde a alguien | *to portray s.o. in a favourable light* mostrar el lado bueno de alguien ‖ *to put a light to* encender ‖ FIG *to see the light* nacer, ver la luz (to be born), salir a la luz (work), ver claramente las cosas (to understand), convertirse (to be converted) ‖ *to set light to sth.* prender fuego a algo, encender algo ‖ *to shine a light on sth.* enfocar algo ‖ *to show s.o. a light* iluminar a alguien ‖ *to stand in s.o.'s light* quitarle la luz a alguien ‖ *to strike a light* encender una cerilla *or* un fósforo.

◆ *pl* luces *f*; *city lights* las luces de la ciudad ‖ semáforos *m*, luces *f* de tráfico (traffic lights) ‖ iluminaciones *f*, iluminación *f sing*; *Christmas lights* la iluminación de Navidad ‖ candilejas *f* (of the stage) ‖ FIG luces *f* (intelligence, culture) ‖ — *according to one's lights* según lo que uno sabe ‖ *advertising lights* letreros luminosos ‖ *driving lights* luces de carretera ‖ *lights out!* ¡apaguen! ‖ *northern lights* aurora *f* boreal ‖ AUT *rear* o *tail lights* pilotos *m*, luces posteriores ‖ *to see one's name in lights* ver su nombre en los carteles.

light* [lait] *vt* encender; *to light a lamp, a cigarette, a fire* encender una lámpara, un cigarrillo, un fuego ‖ iluminar, alumbrar; *to light the way for s.o.* iluminar el camino a alguien; *to light a building* iluminar un edificio; *to light the streets* iluminar las calles ‖ FIG iluminar (s.o.'s eyes, face) ‖ *to light up* iluminar.

◆ *vi* encenderse; *the fire wouldn't light* el fuego no se encendía ‖ encender, encenderse (a lamp, etc.) ‖ FIG iluminarse (eyes, face) ‖ *to light up* iluminarse (to become illuminated); *the house lit up* la casa se iluminó; *her face lit up* se le iluminó la cara; encender un cigarrillo (to begin to smoke).

— OBSERV Pret y pp ***lighted, lit.***

light aircraft [-'ɛəkrɑ:ft] *n* avión *m* ligero, avioneta *f*.

light ale [-eil] *n* cerveza *f* ligera.

light-armed [-'ɑ:md] *adj* MIL con armas ligeras.

light bulb [-bʌlb] *n* bombilla *f*.

light buoy [-bɔi] *n* boya *f* luminosa.

lighten [-n] *vt* aligerar; *to lighten the load* aligerar la carga ‖ alijar (to unload); *to lighten a ship* alijar un barco ‖ aliviar (to relieve); *to lighten a sorrow* aliviar una pena ‖ amenizar (to make more amusing) ‖ iluminar; *the sun lightened the room* el sol iluminó la habitación ‖ aclarar; *to lighten a colour* aclarar un color ‖ FIG iluminar (s.o.'s face).

◆ *vi* aligerarse, hacerse más ligero (to become lighter) ‖ aliviarse (sorrow) ‖ iluminarse, alegrarse (to become brighter) ‖ clarear (to grow light) ‖ aclararse, despejarse (sky) ‖ relampaguear (to flash); *it's lightening again* vuelve a relampaguear.

lightening [-niŋ] *n* aligeramiento *m* (of a load) ‖ alivio *m* (relief) ‖ iluminación *f* (brightening) ‖ aclaramiento *m* (of the weather).

lighter [-ə*] *n* encendedor *m*, mechero *m* (for cigarettes) ‖ encendedor, ra (person) ‖ TECH encendedor *m* ‖ MAR barcaza *f*, gabarra *f*.

lighter [-ə*] *vt* transportar en barcaza *or* en gabarra.

lighterage [-əridʒ] *n* transporte *m* por medio de barcazas (transportation by lighter) ‖ coste *m* del transporte en barcazas (cost).

lighterman [-əmən] *n* gabarrero *m*.

— OBSERV El plural de esta palabra es *lightermen.*

light-fingered [-,fiŋgəd] *adj* FIG largo *or* listo de manos.

light-footed [-'futid] *adj* de paso ligero, ligero de pies.

light-haired [-'hɛəd] *adj* rubio, bia.

light-headed [-'hedid] *adj* mareado, da (from drink) ‖ delirante (delirious) ‖ casquivano, na; ligero de cascos (scatterbrained).

lighthearted [-'hɑ:tid] *adj* alegre, contento, ta (gay) ‖ sin preocupaciones, despreocupado, da (free from care).

light heavyweight [-'heviweit] *n* SP peso *m* semipesado.

light horse [-'hɔ:s] *n* MIL caballería *f* ligera.

light-horseman [-'hɔ:smən] *n* MIL soldado *m* de caballería ligera.

— OBSERV El plural de esta palabra es *light-horsemen.*

lighthouse [-haus] *n* faro *m* ‖ *lighthouse lamp* fanal *m*.

lighthouse keeper [-haus,ki:pə*] *n* torero *m*.

lighting [-iŋ] *n* alumbrado *m* (system) ‖ iluminación *f* (act of illuminating) ‖ encendido *m* (of a fire) ‖ luz *f* (of a picture) ‖ — *direct lighting* alumbrado directo ‖ *lighting effects* efectos luminosos ‖ *lighting engineer* luminotécnico *m*, técnico *m* en iluminación, ingeniero *m* de luces ‖ *lighting engineering* luminotecnia *f* ‖ *street lighting* alumbrado público.

lighting-up [-ʌp] *adj* *lighting-up time* hora *f* de encendido de luces (for cars, etc.).

lightly [-li] *adv* ligeramente (gently, to a small degree) ‖ con paso ligero (with a light step); *she walked lightly* andaba con paso ligero ‖ a la ligera; *to take sth. lightly* tomar algo a la ligera ‖ alegremente (cheerfully) ‖ levemente (wounded) ‖ *lightly clad* vestido con muy poca ropa.

light meter [-,mi:tə*] *n* PHOT exposímetro *m*, fotómetro *m*.

light-minded [-'maindid] *adj* frívolo, la; ligero de cascos.

lightness [-nis] *n* ligereza *f*, poco peso *m* (quality of being by no means heavy) ‖ carácter *m* leve, levedad *f* (of a wound) ‖ facilidad *f* (easiness) ‖ agilidad *f*, ligereza *f* (agility) ‖ ligereza *f* (fickleness) ‖ luminosidad *f*, claridad *f* (degree of illumination) ‖ claridad *f* (of a colour).

lightning ['laitniŋ] *n* relámpago *m* (flash) ‖ rayo *m* (stroke); *lightning hit the church tower* cayó un rayo en el campanario de la iglesia ‖ FIG *as quick as lightning* como un rayo.

◆ *adj* relámpago; *a lightning visit* una visita relámpago ‖ *lightning strike* huelga *f* sin previo aviso.

lightning arrester [-ə,restə*] *n* pararrayos *m inv*.

lightning bug [-bʌg] *n* ZOOL luciérnaga *f*.

lightning conductor [-kən,dʌktə*] *n* pararrayos *m inv*.

lightning rod [-rɔd] *n* US pararrayos *m inv*.

light-o'-love ['laitəlʌv] *n* mujer *f* ligera.

light opera ['lait'ɔpərə] *n* opereta *f*.

light quantum ['lait'kwɔntəm] *n* PHYS fotón *m*.

lights [laits] *pl n* bofes *m* (of slaughtered cattle).

light shell ['laitʃel] *n* proyectil *m* luminoso.

lightship ['laitʃip] *n* MAR buque *m* faro.

light show ['laitʃəu] *n* juego *m* de luces.

lightsome ['laitsəm] *adj* luminoso, sa; claro, ra (full of light) ‖ gracioso, sa (graceful) ‖ ágil (nimble) ‖ alegre (cheerful) ‖ frívolo, la (frivolous).

light source [laitsɔ:s] *n* fuente *f* luminosa.

lights-out ['laitsaut] *n* MIL retreta *f* ‖ *lights-out is at ten o'clock* las luces se apagan a las diez (in boarding schools, etc.).

light spot ['laitspɔt] *n* punto *m* luminoso.

light wave ['laitweiv] *n* onda *f* luminosa.

lightweight ['laitweit] *adj* ligero, ra; de poco peso.

◆ *n* SP peso *m* ligero (boxer) ‖ US FAM persona *f* de poco peso *or* de poca entidad.

lightwood ['laitwud] *n* madera *f* resinosa que se enciende fácilmente.

light-year ['laitjə:*] *n* ASTR año *m* luz, año *m* de luz.

lignaloe [lai'næləu] *n* áloe *m* (drug).

ligneous ['ligniəs] *adj* leñoso, sa.

lignification [,lignifi'keiʃən] *n* BOT lignificación *f*.

lignify ['lignifai] *vi* BOT lignificarse.

◆ *vt* BOT convertir en madera.

lignite ['lignait] *n* MIN lignito *m*.

lignum vitae ['lignəm'vaiti:] *n* BOT guayaco *m* (tree) | palo *m* santo (wood).

Ligures [li'gjuəri:z] *pl n* HIST ligures *m*.

Liguria [li'gjuəriə] *pr n* GEOGR Liguria *f*.

Ligurian [-n] *adj/n* ligur.

likable ['laikəbl] *adj* amable, agradable, simpático, ca (person) ‖ agradable, grato, ta (thing).

likableness [-nis] *n* simpatía *f*, amabilidad *f*.

like [laik] *adj* parecido, da; semejante, similar; *two like cases* dos casos parecidos; *two people of like tastes* dos personas de gustos similares ‖ igual, equivalente; *like poles* polos iguales ‖ mismo, ma; *the like period last year* la misma época del año pasado ‖ análogo, ga; *cholera and other like illnesses* el cólera y otras enfermedades análogas ‖ — *like father like son* de tal palo tal astilla ‖ *something like twenty pounds* unas veinte libras, algo así como veinte libras ‖ *they are as like as two peas* se parecen como dos gotas de agua ‖ *to be like to* ser probable que; *it is like to give us trouble* es probable que nos cause problemas; ser capaz de; *he is like to come at any moment* es capaz de venir a cualquier momento.

◆ *prep* como; *there is nothing like swimming* no hay nada como nadar; *to fight like a man* luchar como un hombre; *to run like a hare* co-

rrer como una liebre || igual que, del mismo modo que, como; *you think like my father* piensas igual que mi padre; *he treated me like a brother* me trataba como a un hermano || como, igual que; *a car like mine* un coche igual que el mío; *eyes like diamonds* ojos como diamantes || — *I never saw anything like it* nunca he visto cosa igual || *it's not like him to do that* no es de él hacer eso, no es propio de él hacer eso || *it looks like a fine day tomorrow* parece que mañana hará buen tiempo || *like that* así; *I can't do it like that* no lo puedo hacer así; *Spaniards are like that* los españoles son así; como ése, como ésa; *I want a skirt like that* quiero una falda como ésa || *that's just like him!* ¡eso es muy de él!, ¡es muy propio de él! || *that's more like it!* ¡eso está mejor! || *to be like* parecerse a (to resemble); *they are very much like their mother* se parecen mucho a su madre || *to be nothing like so rich* estar lejos de ser tan rico || *to be nothing like as happy as s.o. else* no estar, ni mucho menos, tan contento como otro || *to feel like* apetecer; *do you feel like a beer?* ¿te apetece una cerveza?; tener ganas de; *I feel like going to the pictures* tengo ganas de ir al cine; parecer; *it feels like wool* parece lana || *to look like* parecerse a; *he looks like his mother* se parece a su madre; parece que; *it looks like snow* parece que va a nevar; parecer; *it looks like glass* parece cristal || *what does she sing like?* ¿qué tal canta?, ¿cómo canta? || *what is she like?* ¿qué tal es?, ¿cómo es? || *who is she like?* ¿a quién se parece? || *you are like a brother to me* eres como un hermano para mí.
◆ *adv* *as like as not, like as not, like enough, very like* probablemente, a lo mejor || FAM *it's like big* es más bien grande, es como grande || *it's nothing like* no se parece en nada.
◆ *conj* FAM como; *do it like he does* hazlo como él; *it was like when you were at home* era como cuando estabas en casa.
◆ *n* igual *m* & *f*, semejante *m* & *f*; *we shall never see her like again* nunca volveremos a ver una igual || — *and the like* y cosas por el estilo || *to do the like* hacer lo mismo.
◆ *pl* gustos *m* || — *I have my likes and dislikes* tengo mis preferencias || *the likes of* personas como; *it is not for the likes of you* no es para personas como tú.

— OBSERV *Like* se emplea como sufijo y significa entonces *parecido a, propio de*, etc.: *woodlike* parecido a la madera; *childlike* propio de un niño; *to behave in adultlike fashion* comportarse como un adulto.

like [laik] *vt/vi* gustarle (a uno); *do you like tea?* ¿le gusta el té?; *how do you like your tea?* ¿cómo le gusta el té?; *I like flamenco* a mí me gusta el flamenco; *I like reading* me gusta leer || gustarle (a uno), tenerle simpatía (friends and acquaintances); *I like Charles* le tengo simpatía a Carlos, me gusta Carlos || querer a (close friends); *I like my parents* quiero a mis padres || querer (to wish); *I don't like to interrupt* no quiero interrumpir; *you can say what you like* puede decir lo que quiera; *as you like* como quiera; *when you like* cuando quiera; *would you like another cup of tea?* ¿quiere otra taza de té? || gustarle (a uno); *I should like to talk to you* me gustaría hablar con Ud.; *would you like to go tomorrow?* ¿le gustaría ir mañana?; *I like you to be near me* me gusta que esté cerca de mí || — *as much as (ever) you like* todo lo que quiera || *how do you like my article?* ¿qué le parece mi artículo? || *if you like* si quiere || *I like milk but milk doesn't like me* me gusta la leche pero me sienta mal || FIG *I like that!* ¡qué bien!, ¡estupendo! || *I would like a dozen eggs, please* quisiera una docena de huevos, por favor || *this plant likes sunshine* le sienta bien el sol a esta planta || *to do what one likes with sth.* hacer lo que uno quiere con algo || *to like best* gustarle más (a uno) || *to like better* preferir || *what would you like to drink?* ¿qué quiere beber? || *whether you like it or not* le guste o no le guste, quiera o no quiera || *would you like to do me a favour?* ¿quiere hacerme un favor? || *would you like to go for a walk?* ¿le apetece dar un paseo?, ¿le gustaría dar un paseo?

likeable [-əbl] *adj* amable, agradable, simpático, ca (person) || agradable, grato, ta (thing).

likeableness [-əblnis] *n* simpatía *f*, amabilidad *f*.

likelihood [-lihud]; **likeliness** [-linis] *n* posibilidad *f*; *there is little likelihood of* hay poca posibilidad de || probabilidad *f* (probability); *in all likelihood* con toda probabilidad || verosimilitud *f* (credibility).

likely [-li] *adj* probable (probable) || posible (possible) || plausible, verosímil (plausible) || apropiado, da (suitable); *what is the likeliest moment to find you at home?* ¿cuál es el momento más apropiado para encontrarle en casa? || prometedor, ra (promising); *a likely lad* un joven prometedor || — *it is likely to be wet* es probable que esté húmedo || FIG *that's a likely story!* ¡puro cuento! || *they are likely to cause trouble afterwards* puede ser que *or* es probable que ocasionen problemas después || *to be not likely that* ser poco probable que; *it is not likely that it will rain* es poco probable que llueva || *where are you likely to be this evening?* ¿dónde piensas estar esta noche?
◆ *adv* probablemente || — *as likely as not, likely as not* probablemente, a lo mejor || *likely enough* probablemente.

like-minded [-maindid] *adj* de la misma opinión.

liken [-ən] *vt* comparar (*with, to* con).

likeness [-nis] *n* semejanza *f*, parecido *m* (similarity) || retrato *m* (portrait) || verosimilitud *f* (credibility) || forma *f*, apariencia *f*; *in the likeness of* bajo la forma de || — *family likeness* parecido de familia || *the picture is a good likeness* el retrato se parece mucho *or* está muy conseguido || *to catch the likeness* coger el parecido.

likewise [-waiz] *adv* del mismo modo, lo mismo, igualmente (the same way) || también, asimismo (also) || además (moreover) || *to do likewise* hacer lo mismo.

liking [-iŋ] *n* cariño *m*, simpatía *f* (for a person); *I took a liking to him* le cogí simpatía, le tomé cariño || afición *f*, gusto *m* (for a thing) || preferencia *f*, predilección *f* (preference) || — *for one's liking* para el gusto de uno || *he took a liking to it* le cogió gusto || *to have a liking for* ser aficionado a (sth.), tener simpatía a (s.o.) || *to one's liking* del gusto *or* del agrado de uno.

lilac ['lailək] *n* BOT lila *f* || lila *m* (colour).
◆ *adj* de color lila, lila.

liliaceae [,lili'eiʃii] *pl n* BOT liliáceas *f*.

Lilliput ['lilipʌt] *pr n* Liliput.

Lilliputian [,lili'pju:ʃjən] *adj/n* liliputiense.

Lilo ['lailəu] *n* (registered trademark) colchoneta *f*.

lilt [lilt] *n* canción *f* alegre (song) || deje *m* (singsong accent) || balanceo *m* (light swaying) || ritmo *m*, cadencia *f* (rhythm).

lilt [lilt] *vt/vi* cantar melodiosamente.

lilting [-iŋ] *adj* melodioso, sa (song, voice) || rítmico, ca (movement).

lily ['lili] *n* azucena *f* (flower) || HERALD flor *f* de lis || — BOT *calla lily* cala *f*, lirio *m* de agua | *lily of the valley* lirio *m* de los valles, muguete *m* | *water lily* nenúfar *m* | *white lily* lirio blanco, azucena.
◆ *adj* blanco como la azucena *or* como la nieve (white) || inocente, puro, ra (pure).

lily-livered [-'livəd] *adj* cobarde, miedoso, sa.

lily pad [-pæd] *n* BOT hoja *f* de nenúfar.

lily-white [-wait] *adj* blanco como la azucena *or* como la nieve || FIG inocente, puro, ra (innocent).

Lima ['li:mə, US 'laimə] *pr n* GEOGR Lima.

Lima bean [-bi:n] *n* BOT fríjol *m*, frijol *m*.

limb [lim] *n* ANAT miembro *m* || BOT rama *f* (branch of a tree) | limbo *m* (of a petal) || brazo *m* (of a cross) || estribación *f* (of a mountain) || GRAMM período *m* (of a sentence) || ASTR & MATH limbo *m* || FAM representante *m* (of the law, etc.) | chiquillo *m* travieso, golfillo *m* (child) || — FIG *out on a limb* en una situación precaria | *to risk life and limb* jugarse la vida || *to tear limb from limb* despedazar.

limb [lim] *vt* desmembrar (a person) || despedazar (an animal) || podar (a tree).

limbed [-d] *adj* de miembros; *strong-limbed* de miembros fuertes.

limber [-bə*] *adj* flexible (thing) || ágil (person).
◆ *n* MIL armón *m* (of a gun carriage).
◆ *pl* MAR imbornales *m* de cuaderna.

limber [-bə*] *vt* enganchar el armón a || *to limber up* volver ágil *or* flexible.
◆ *vi* *to limber up* hacer ejercicios de precalentamiento (an athlete), prepararse.

limbless [-lis] *adj* falto de un brazo *or* una pierna, tullido, da.

limbo ['limbəu] *n* REL limbo *m* || FIG olvido *m* (oblivion) | mazmorra *f*, cárcel *f* (prison).

lime [laim] *n* CHEM cal *f*; *lime cast* enlucido con cal; *slaked lime* cal muerta || liga *f* (birdlime) || BOT limero *m*, lima *f* (tree) | lima *f* (fruit) | tilo *m* (linden tree).

lime [laim] *vt* encalar (to spread lime over) || AGR abonar con cal || apelambrar (hides) || untar con liga (to smear with birdlime) || coger con liga (birds).

limeburner [-'bə:nə*] *n* calero *m*.

lime-green [-gri:n] *adj* de color verde lima.

limekiln [-kiln] *n* calera *f*, horno *m* de cal.

limelight [-lait] *n* THEATR foco *m*, proyector *m* || luz *f* de calcio || FIG *to be in limelight* estar en el candelero, estar en la primera plana de la actualidad.
◆ *pl* candilejas *f* (footlights).

limen ['laimən] *n* umbral *m*.

limerick ['limərik] *n* quintilla *f* humorística.

limestone ['laimstəun] *n* piedra *f* caliza, caliza *f*.

lime tree ['laimtri:] *n* BOT tilo *m*.

lime-twig ['laimtwig] *n* vareta *f*.

limewash ['laimwɔʃ] *n* lechada *f* de cal.

limewater ['laim,wɔ:tə*] *n* agua *f* de cal.

limey ['laimi] *n* FAM inglés, esa.

liminal ['liminl] *adj* liminal.

liminary ['liminəri] *adj* liminar (introductory).

limit ['limit] *n* límite *m*; *the limits of his knowledge* los límites de sus conocimientos; *speed limit* límite de velocidad || máximo *m* (maximum) || mínimo *m* (minimum) || MATH límite *m* || — *age limit* edad máxima || *he o that is the limit!* ¡es el colmo! || *off limits* de acceso prohibido (area) || *to know no limits* ser infinito, no tener límites || *within limits* dentro de ciertos límites || *within the limits of the city* dentro de la ciudad || *without limit* sin límite, ilimitado, da.

limit ['limit] *vt* limitar; *I have to limit my expenses* tengo que limitar mis gastos || *to limit o.s. to* limitarse a.

limitary [-əri] *adj* limitador, ra (restrictive) || limitado, da (limited) || limítrofe (bordering).

limitation [,limi'teiʃən] *n* limitación *f* || limitación *f*, restricción *f* || JUR prescripción *f*.

limitative [ˌlimiˈteitiv] *adj* limitativo, va || *clause limitative* cláusula restrictiva.

limited [ˈlimitid] *adj* limitado, da; *limited knowledge* conocimientos limitados || escaso, sa; reducido, da (small) || — COMM *limited company, limited-liability company* sociedad (de responsabilidad) limitada || *limited edition* tirada *f* de un número reducido de ejemplares || *limited mobilization* movilización *f* parcial || *limited monarchy* monarquía *f* constitucional || *limited partnership* sociedad *f* en comandita.

limiting [ˈlimitiŋ] *adj* restrictivo, va || GRAMM determinativo, va.

limitless [ˈlimitlis] *adj* ilimitado, da; sin límites.

limn [lim] *vt* pintar (to paint, to draw) || retratar, pintar (to portray in words).

limner [-nə*] *n* pintor, ra.

limonite [ˈlaimənait] *n* MIN limonita *f*.

limousine [ˈlimu:zi:n] *n* limusina *f* (car).

limp [limp] *adj* fláccido, da; flácido, da; blando, da; fofo, fa (floppy) || débil (weak) || debilitado, da; *limp with the heat* debilitado por el calor || poco enérgico, ca (lacking energy) || blandengue (lacking firmness) || desmayado, da (voice) || TECH flexible (bookbinding) || FIG *as limp as a rag* como un trapo.
◆ *n* cojera *f*; *a slight limp* una ligera cojera || *to walk with a limp* cojear.

limp [limp] *vi* cojear || POET cojear (verse) || — *he limped off* se marchó cojeando || FIG *the ships limped into harbour* los barcos llegaron con dificultad al puerto.

limpet [ˈlimpit] *n* ZOOL lapa *f* (shellfish) || FIG lapa *f* || MIL *limpet mine* mina *f* que se coloca en el casco de un barco.

limpid [ˈlimpid] *adj* límpido, da; claro, ra.

limpidity [limˈpiditi] *n* limpidez *f*, claridad *f*.

limpness [ˈlimpnis] *n* flojedad *f*.

limy [ˈlaimi] *adj* calizo, za (of caustic lime) || untado de liga (with birdlime) || pegajoso, sa (sticky).

linaceae [laiˈneisii:] *pl n* BOT lináceas *f*.

linaceous [laiˈneiʃəs] *adj* lináceo, a.

linage; lineage [ˈlainidʒ] *n* número *m* de líneas (number of lines) || pago *m* por líneas (payment).

linchpin [ˈlintʃpin] *n* TECH pezonera *f* (of an axle) || FIG lo esencial, parte esencial (vital part) | eje *m*; *he is the linchpin of the organization* es el eje de la organización.

linctus [ˈliŋktəs] *n* MED jarabe *m* para la tos.

linden [ˈlindən] *n* BOT tilo *m* (tree) | tila *f* (infusion) || madera *f* de tilo (wood).

line [lain] *n* línea *f*, trazo *m*, raya *f* (by a pencil, by a pen) || línea *f*, renglón *m* (of writing) || MUS línea *f* [del pentagrama] || MATH línea *f*; *straight line* línea recta || línea *f*, contorno *m* (outline) || línea *f* (of the hand) || línea *f*, rasgo *m* (feature) || arruga *f* (wrinkle) || fila *f* (row); *in a line* en fila; *in line* en filas || línea *f*, hilera *f* (of trees) || fila *f* (of parked cars) || cola *f* (of traffic, of people) || serie *f*, sucesión *f* (series) || verso *m* (verse) || líneas *f pl*, letras *f pl* (brief letter); *drop me a line* escríbeme cuatro letras, ponme unas líneas || línea *f*, corte *m* (of a dress) || línea *f* (of a vehicle) || línea *f* (telephone) || línea *f*, conferencia *f* (speaking on the telephone) || ELECTR línea *f*; *high-tension line* línea de alta tensión | cable *m* (wire) | cordón *m*, flexible *m* (flex) || INFORM línea *f* || cuerda *f* (rope) || línea *f* (rail) || vía *f* (track); *down, up line* vía descendente, ascendente || AVIAT línea *f* || línea *f*; *bus line* línea de autobuses || vía *f*; *lines of communication* vías de comunicación || línea *f* (in factory); *assembly line* línea de montaje || ARCH cordel *m*; *in the straight line* tirado a cordel | alineación *f* (of a street); *building line* alineación de los edificios | tubería *f*, cañería *f* (pipe) | gola *f*, cimacio *m* (cyma) || PHYS raya *f* (of the spectrum) | línea *f* (of television) || MAR cabo *m* (cord) | línea *f*; *ship of the line* barco de línea | compañía *f*; *shipping line* compañía naviera | sedal *m*, cuerda *f* (for fishing) || MIL línea *f*; *front line* primera línea; *line of battle* línea de batalla || límite *m*; *to draw the line* marcar *or* trazar el límite; *State line* límite de un Estado || SP raya *f* (on a court) | línea *f*; *goal line* línea de meta; *forward line* línea delantera || GEOGR Ecuador *m* || COMM artículo *m* (article) | surtido *m* (range of goods) || FIG línea *f* (of conduct) | directiva *f*; *to work on the lines of* trabajar siguiendo las directivas de | postura *f*, actitud *f* (position) | especialidad *f*, rama *f* (department of activity); *that's not in my line* eso no es de mi especialidad | ramo *m*; *in the building line* en el ramo de la construcción | línea *f*; *the party line* la línea del partido | límite *m*, límites *m pl*; *one must draw the line somewhere* hay que fijar ciertos límites | familia *f*; *he comes of a good line* procede de buena familia | línea *f*, linaje *m* (of descent) | línea *f*; *we are descended in direct line from* descendemos en línea directa de | pista *f*, indicación *f* (clue); *to give a line on* poner sobre la pista de, dar una indicación sobre | cuento *m* (patter) || — *all along the line* en toda la línea || *demarcation line* línea de demarcación || *dotted line* línea de puntos || *he is in line for promotion* va a ser ascendido || *he is in line for trouble!* ¡va a tener problemas!, ¡se puede preparar! || *hold the line!* ¡no cuelgue!, ¡no se retire! || FIG *hot line* teléfono rojo || *it is more in my line* me va mejor || MAR *line abreast* línea de frente | *line astern* uno detrás de otro, en fila india || *line of fire* línea de fuego *or* de tiro || *line of force* línea de fuerza || FIG *line of least resistance* ley *f* del mínimo esfuerzo || *line of route* itinerario *m* || *line of thought* hilo *m* del pensamiento || *line of vision* visual *f* || *next* o *new line* punto y aparte (in dictation) || *of the male line* de la línea masculina || *on the line of* en la línea de || MAR *plimsoll line* línea de máxima carga || *royal line* familia real || *to be in line with* estar de acuerdo con || *to be out of line with* no estar de acuerdo con || *to bring into line* alinear (to line up), poner al día (to bring up to date), poner de acuerdo (to make agree), llamar al orden (to bring under control) || FIG *to come into line with* conformarse con la opinión de | *to draw the line at* no ir más allá de || *to fall into line* alinearse || FIG *to fall into line with* conformarse con (s.o.'s ideas), conformarse con las ideas de (s.o.) | *to get a line on* obtener información sobre, informarse sobre | *to give s.o. line enough* soltar la rienda a alguien | *to have a good line* tener mucha labia | *to have a line on* tener una idea de (idea), tener información sobre (information) | *to hold the line* aguantar | *to keep one's men in line* mantener la disciplina entre sus hombres | *to know where to draw the line* saber dónde pararse || FIG *to lay on the line* dar (sum of money) || FAM *to shoot a line* darse postín *or* bombo || FIG *to sign on the dotted line* aprobar a ciegas || *to stand in line* hacer cola || FIG *to step out of line* salir de las reglas || *to toe the line* pisar la línea (in a race), conformarse (to conform) || FIG *to toe the party line* seguir la línea del partido | *what line are you in?, what's your line?* ¿a qué se dedica Ud.?
◆ *pl* FAM partida *f sing* de matrimonio | destino *m sing* (destiny) || papel *m sing* (actor's part) || *along the lines of* de acuerdo con || — *along these lines* de esta manera || FIG *hard lines!* ¡mala suerte! || *on the following lines* de la manera siguiente || *sth. along these lines* algo por el estilo || *to be on the right lines* ir por buen camino || *to lay down the broad lines of* trazar las grandes líneas de || *to leave the lines* descarrilar (train) || *to read between the lines* leer entre líneas.

line [lain] *vt* rayar (to cover with lines); *lined paper* papel rayado || alinearse por (to stand in a line along) || bordear; *road lined with poplars* carretera bordeada de álamos || surcar, arrugar (to wrinkle) || surcar (a field) || forrar (to provide with an inner layer); *she lined her coat with silk* forró su abrigo con seda || forrar (in bookbinding) || TECH revestir | entibar (a well) | guarnecer (brakes) | encamisar (a gun) || MAR reforzar (sails) || llenar, cubrir (to cover) || — FAM *to line one's pockets* forrarse, llenarse los bolsillos (to make money) | *to line one's stomach* hartarse, ponerse como un quico || *to line up* alinear, poner en fila (to arrange in a line).
◆ *vi* *to line up* alinearse, ponerse en fila (people), hacer cola (to queue), formarse (troops, teams).

lineage [ˈlaiˈnidʒ] *n* → **linage.**

lineage [ˈliniidʒ] *n* linaje *m*.

lineal [ˈliniəl] *adj* lineal (linear) || en línea directa (descent).

lineally [-i] *adv* en línea directa.

lineament [ˈliniəmənt] *n* lineamiento *m*, lineamento *m*.
◆ *pl* rasgos *m*, facciones *f* (facial features).

linear [ˈliniə] *adj* lineal || — TECH *linear accelerator* acelerador *m* lineal || MATH *linear equation* ecuación *f* lineal *or* de primer grado || *linear measure* medida *f* de longitud || *linear perspective* perspectiva *f* lineal.

lineation [ˌliniˈeiʃən] *n* líneas *f pl* || trazado *m*.

line drawing [ˈlainˈdrɔ:iŋ] *n* dibujo *m* lineal.

line engraving [ˈlaininˈgreiviŋ] *n* ARTS grabado *m* en dulce, grabado *m* con buril.

line fishing [ˈlainˌfiʃiŋ] *n* pesca *f* con caña.

lineman [ˈlainmən] *n* ELECTR instalador *m* de líneas || guardavía *m* (railway).
— OBSERV El plural de esta palabra es *linemen*.

linen [ˈlinin] *n* hilo *m*, lino *m* (textile) || mantelería *f* (of table) || ropa *f*; *clean, dirty linen* ropa limpia, sucia || ropa *f* blanca (of the house) || ropa *f* interior (underclothes) || ropa *f* de cama (bed linen) || — FIG *don't wash your dirty linen in public* los trapos sucios se lavan en casa || *linen basket* canasta *f* or cesto *m* de la ropa || *linen closet, linen cupboard* armario *m* de la ropa || *linen clothes* o *drapery* lencería *f* || *linen room* lencería *f*.
◆ *adj* de hilo, de lino; *linen cloth* tela de hilo.

linendraper [-ˌdreipə*] *n* lencero, ra || *linendraper's* lencería *f*.

line-out [ˈlainaut] *n* SP saque *m* de banda.

line printer [ˈlainˌprintə*] *n* INFORM impresora *f* de líneas.

liner [ˈlainə*] *n* transatlántico *m* (ship) || AVIAT avión *m* de línea || TECH forro *m*, revestimiento *m* (lining) | camisa *f* (of a cylinder).

linesman [ˈlainzmən] *n* SP juez *m* de línea, juez *m* de banda || guardavía *m* (on railway) || MIL soldado *m* de línea || US ELECTR instalador *m* de líneas.
— OBSERV El plural de *linesman* es *linesmen*.

line spacer [ˈlainˌspeisə*] *n* interlineador *m* (of a typewriter).

lineup [ˈlainʌp] *n* SP alineación *f*, formación *f* (football, rugby) || hilera *f* de personas (file).

ling [liŋ] *n* bacalao *m*, abadejo *m* (fish) || BOT brezo *m*.

linger [ˈliŋgə*] *vi* rezagarse (to dawdle, to lag behind) || callejear, vagabundear (to loiter) || persistir, subsistir (use, hope, doubts, etc.) || tardar; *to linger to go* tardar en ir || quedarse (to stay) || tardar en morirse || hacerse largo (to be too long); *the film lingers* la película se hace larga || — *to linger on* o *upon* dilatarse en (to expatiate) || *to linger over* no darse prisa en hacer, tardar en hacer; *to linger over a job* tardar en

hacer un trabajo; dilatarse en (to expatiate) || *to linger over a meal* tardar en comer.
◆ *vt* *to linger away* perder (one's time) || *to linger out one's life* arrastrar su vida.

lingerer [-rə*] *n* rezagado, da.

lingerie ['lẽnʒəri] *n* ropa *f* interior, ropa *f* blanca (women's).

lingering ['liŋgəriŋ] *adj* lento, ta (death) || persistente (doubt, smell) || fijo, ja (look) || MED crónico, ca (disease).

lingo ['liŋgəu] *n* FAM lengua *f*, idioma *m* (language) | jerga *f* (jargon).
— OBSERV El plural de esta palabra es *lingoes*.

lingua ['liŋgwə] *n* lengua *f*.
— OBSERV El plural de *lingua* es *linguae*.

lingual ['liŋgwəl] *adj* lingual (like or near the tongue) || GRAMM lingual.
◆ *n* GRAMM lingual *f*.

linguiform ['liŋgwi,fɔːm] *adj* en forma de lengua, lingüiforme.

linguist ['liŋgwist] *n* lingüista *m* & *f* (specialist in linguistics) || políglota, ta (polyglot).

linguistic [liŋ'gwistik] *adj* lingüístico, ca.

linguistics [-s] *n* lingüística *f*.

lingulate ['liŋgjəleit] *adj* en forma de lengua, lingüiforme.

liniment ['linimənt] *n* linimento *m*.

lining ['lainiŋ] *n* forro *m* (of clothes) || TECH revestimiento *m*, forro *m* | guarnición *f*, forro *m* (of brakes) || forro *m* (in bookbinding) || MIN entibación *f*, entibado *m*.

link [liŋk] *n* eslabón *m* (of a chain) || FIG vínculo *m*, lazo *m*; *the child was the only link between them* el niño era el único vínculo existente entre ellos; *the links of friendship* los lazos de la amistad | relación *f* (relationship, connection) || malla *f* (of knitting) || enlace *m*; *a rail link* un enlace ferroviario || TECH vástago *m* || AUT biela *f* de acoplamiento || antorcha *f* (torch) || — *missing link* eslabón perdido | *weak link* punto flaco.
◆ *pl* gemelos *m* (cuff links).

link [liŋk] *vt* unir, enlazar (to join) || acoplar (trains, spaceships) || FIG vincular, unir || conectar (*to* con) (by telephone) || INFORM enlazar || — *this is linked to what I said earlier* eso está relacionado con lo que dije anteriormente || *to link arms* cogerse del brazo, darse el brazo || *to link together* unir.
◆ *vi* unirse, enlazarse || empalmar (two trains) || acoplarse (to couple) || FIG unirse || — *to link on to* unirse a || *to link together* unirse.
— OBSERV *To link* va seguido frecuentemente por *up* sin que cambie su sentido.

linkage ['liŋkidʒ] *n* enlace *m* || unión *f* || conexión *f* (telephone) || eslabonamiento *m*, encadenamiento *m* (of facts) || articulación *f* (joint) || acoplamiento *m* (coupling) || BIOL & CHEM enlace *m* || TECH varillaje *m* || FIG vinculación *f*.

linker [liŋkə*] *n* INFORM montador *m*, editor *m* de enlaces.

linking ['liŋkiŋ] *n* unión *f* || enlace *m* || encadenamiento *m*, eslabonamiento *m* (of facts) || acoplamiento *m* (coupling) || articulación *f* (joint) || FIG vinculación *f*.

links [liŋks] *pl n* SP campo *m sing* de golf || terreno *m sing* arenoso (sandy ground).

Link trainer ['liŋk'treinə*] *n* simulador *m* de vuelo.

linkup ['liŋkʌp] *n* conexión *f* (by telephone) || encuentro *m* (meeting of people, of chiefs, etc.) || unión *f* (of approaching forces) || acoplamiento *m* (of spacecraft).

linnet ['linit] *n* pardillo *m* (bird).

lino ['lainəu] *n* linóleo *m* (linoleum) || PRINT linotipia *f*.

linocut ['lainəkʌt] *n* estampa *f* impresa en linóleo.

linoleum [li'nəuljəm] *n* linóleo *m*.

linotype ['lainətaip] *n* PRINT linotipia *f* || *linotype operator* linotipista *m* & *f*.

linotyper [-ə*]; **linotypist** [-ist] *n* PRINT linotipista *m* & *f*.

linseed ['linsiːd] *n* linaza *f*; *linseed meal* harina de linaza; *linseed oil* aceite de linaza.

linstock ['linstɔk] *n* (ant) botafuego *m*.

lint [lint] *n* hilas *f pl* (for bandaging) || pelusa *f* (fluff).

lintel ['lintl] *n* ARCH dintel *m* (of doors).

linter ['lintə*] *n* US desfibradora *f* de algodón.
◆ *pl* borra *f sing*.

lion ['laiən] *n* ZOOL león *m* || celebridad *f*, persona *f* famosa (celebrity) || FIG león *m* (brave man) || HERALD león *m* || — ZOOL *sea lion* león marino || FIG *the lion's share* la parte del león, la mejor tajada | *to put one's head in the lion's mouth* meterse en la boca del lobo.

Lion ['laiən] *n* ASTR Leo *m*, León *m*.

lioness [-is] *n* ZOOL leona *f*.

lionet [-et] *n* ZOOL cachorro *m* de león.

lionhearted [-,hɑːtid] *adj* valiente.

lionize [-aiz] *vt* agasajar mucho a, poner en primer plano a.

lip [lip] *n* labio *m* (of mouth, of wound); *lower, upper lip* labio inferior, superior || belfo *m*, morro *m*, labio *m* (of an animal) || pico *m* (of a jug) || borde *m* (of a cup) || boquilla *f* (of a wind instrument) || saliente *m*, reborde *m* (protuberance) || FAM impertinencia *f*, insolencia *f* (impertinence) || — FAM *none of your lip!* ¡no te insolentes!, ¡no seas descarado! || FIG *to bite one's lip* morderse los labios | *to hang on s.o.'s lips* estar pendiente de los labios *or* de las palabras de alguien | *to keep a stiff upper lip* poner a mal tiempo buena cara | *to lick* o *to smack one's lips* relamerse | *to open one's lips* despegar los labios | *to screw up one's lips* apretar los labios | *to seal s.o.'s lips* sellarle a uno los labios.
◆ *adj* GRAMM labial; *lip consonant* consonante labial || FIG falso, sa; hipócrita.

lip [lip] *vt* mojar los labios en (a cup) || bañar (the coast) || llevar a la boca, embocar (p us) llevar a la boca, embocar (a trumpet, etc.) || besar (to kiss) || FIG decir con la boca chiquita.

lipase ['laipeis] *n* BIOL lipasa *f*.

lipid ['lipaidʀ US 'lipid]; **lipide** ['lipaid] *n* lípido *m*.

lipoid ['lipɔid] *adj* lipoideo, a.
◆ *n* lipoide *m*.

lipoma [li'pəumə] *n* MED lipoma *m*.
— OBSERV El plural de la palabra inglesa es *lipomata* o *lipomas*.

lipped [lipt] *adj* de labios (person); *thin-lipped* de labios finos || con pico (pitcher).

lip-read* ['lipriːd] *vt/vi* leer en los labios, interpretar por el movimiento de los labios.
— OBSERV Pret y pp ***lip-read***.

lip-reader ['lip,riːdə*] *n* persona *f* que comprende por el movimiento de los labios.

lipreading ['lip,riːdiŋ] *n* comprensión *f* del lenguaje hablado mediante la observación del movimiento de los labios.

lipsalve ['lipsɑːv] *n* MED pomada *f* rosada || FIG coba *f* (flattering).

lip service ['lip,səːvis] *n* jarabe *m* de pico, palabras *f pl* || FIG *to pay lip service to* hablar de boquilla de; fingir estar de acuerdo con.

lipstick ['lipstik] *n* barra *f* de labios, lápiz *m* de labios.

liquate ['laikweit] *vt* licuar.

liquation [lik'weiʃən] *n* licuación *f*.

liquefaction [,likwi'fækʃən] *n* licuefacción *f*.

liquefacient [,likwi'fæʃən]; **liquefactive** [,likwi'fæktiv] *adj* licuefactivo, va.

liquefiable ['likwifaiəbl] *adj* licuable, licuefactible.

liquefier ['likwifaiə*] *n* aparato *m* de licuefacción, licuador *m*.

liquefy ['likwifai] *vt* licuar, licuefacer.
◆ *vi* licuarse.

liquefying [-iŋ] *adj* licuante.

liquescent [lik'wesənt] *adj* licuescente.

liqueur [li'kjuə*] *n* licor *m* || — *liqueur brandy* coñac fino || *liqueur wine* vino licoroso.

liquid ['likwid] *adj* líquido, da (fluid) || para líquidos (measure) || claro, ra; transparente, puro, ra (clear, transparent) || MUS claro, ra (sound) || GRAMM líquido, da || COMM líquido, da; *liquid cash* dinero líquido; *liquid debt* deuda líquida || — *liquid air* aire líquido || COMM *liquid assets* activo [líquido].
◆ *n* líquido *m* || GRAMM consonante *f* líquida.

liquidambar [,likwi'dæmbə*] *n* BOT liquidámbar *m*.

liquidate ['likwideit] *vt* COMM liquidar, saldar (a debt) | liquidar (a business) || FIG liquidar (to get rid of, to kill).

liquidating [-iŋ] *adj* liquidador, ra.

liquidation [,likwi'deiʃən] *n* liquidación *f* (of a debt, of a business, of enemies); *to go into liquidation* entrar en liquidación.

liquidator ['likwideitə*] *n* COMM liquidador, ra.

liquid crystal ['likwid'kristl] *n* cristal *m* líquido.

liquid fire ['likwid'faiə*] *n* MIL líquido *m* incendiario.

liquidity [likwiditi] *n* liquidez *f*, fluidez *f*.

liquidize ['likwidaiz] *vt* liquidar, licuar.
◆ *vi* liquidarse, licuarse.

liquidizer [-ə*] *n* licuadora *f*.

liquidness ['likwidnis] *n* liquidez *f*, fluidez *f*.

liquor ['likə*] *n* bebida *f* alcohólica; *liquor trade* comercio de bebidas alcohólicas || licor *m* (in chemistry, in pharmacy) || jugo *m*, salsa *f* (of meat) || FIG & FAM *to be in liquor, to be the worse for liquor* haber bebido más de la cuenta, estar borracho.

liquor ['likə*] *vt* FAM *to liquor s.o. up* emborrachar a uno.
◆ *vi* FAM *to liquor up* beber, empinar el codo.

liquor cabinet [-,kæbinit] *n* licorera *f*.

liquorice ['likəris] *n* BOT regaliz *m*.

lira ['liərə] *n* lira *f*.
— OBSERV El plural de la palabra inglesa es *lire* o *liras*.

Lisbon ['lizbən] *pr n* GEOGR Lisboa.

lisle [lail] *n* hilo *m* de Escocia.

lisp [lisp] *n* ceceo *m* (speech defect) || balbuceo *m* (of a child) || FIG murmullo *m*, susurro *m* (of stream, of leaves) || *to speak with a lisp, to have a lisp* cecear.

lisp [lisp] *vt* decir ceceando.
◆ *vi* cecear || balbucear, balbucir (a child).

lisping [-iŋ] *adj* que cecea || balbuciente (a child) || FIG murmurador, ra.

lissom; US **lissome** ['lisəm] *adj* ágil (nimble) || flexible.

list [list] *n* orillo *m*, orilla *f* (of cloth) || lista *f*, raya *f* (stripe) || listón *m* (of wood) || lista *f* (enumeration); *price list* lista de precios || escalafón *m* (of officials) || catálogo *m* (catalogue) || INFORM lista *f* || MAR escora *f* || inclinación *f* || — *casualty list* lista de bajas || *honours* o *prize list* lista de premios || MIL *on the active list* en

activo || *waiting list* lista de espera || *wine list* carta *f* de vinos.
◆ *pl* liza *f sing*, palestra *f*; *he entered the lists* salió a la palestra.

list [list] *vt* hacer una lista (to make a list of); *I listed all my records* hice una lista de todos mis discos || poner en una lista, inscribir (to put on a list) || enumerar (to enumerate) || COMM cotizar || poner un orillo a (a cloth) || *it is not listed* no está en la lista, no figura en la lista.
◆ *vi* MAR escorar || MIL alistarse || (ant) querer (to wish).

listed building [-id'bildiŋ] *n* edificio *m* de interés histórico.

listel ['listl] *n* ARCH listón *m*, listel *m*.

listen ['lisn] *vi* escuchar, oír; *listen to me instead of gazing out of the window* escúchame en vez de mirar por la ventana || prestar atención (to pay attention) || — *not to listen to reason* no atender a razones || *to listen for* estar atento a || *to listen in* escuchar la radio || *to listen in to* escuchar (radio programme), escuchar (a hurtadillas) (telephone conversation).

listen ['lisn] *n* *to be on the listen* estar a la escucha, escuchar || *to have a listen* escuchar.

listener ['lisnə*] *n* oyente *m* & *f* || radioyente *m* & *f*, radioescucha *m* & *f* (to the radio) || *to be a good listener* saber escuchar.

listening ['lisniŋ] *n* escucha *f* || MIL *listening post* puesto *m* de escucha.

listing ['listiŋ] *n* inscripción *f* en una lista || INFORM listado *m*.

listless ['listlis] *adj* decaído, da (lacking energy) || indiferente, apático, ca (uninterested).

listlessness [-nis] *n* apatía *f*, inercia *f*, indiferencia *f*.

list price ['listprais] *n* precio *m* de catálogo.

lit [lit] *pret/pp* ⟶ **light.**

litany ['litəni] *n* REL letanía *f*.

liter ['li:tə*] *n* US litro *m*.

literacy ['litərəsi] *n* capacidad *f* de leer y escribir || *literacy campaign* campaña *f* de alfabetización.

literal ['litərəl] *adj* literal; *in the literal sense of the word* en el sentido literal de la palabra; *literal translation* traducción literal || prosaico, ca (prosaic) || crudo, da; sin disimulo (truth) || *literal error* errata *f*.
◆ *n* PRINT errata *f*.

literalism ['litərəlizəm] *n* carácter *m* literal (literal interpretation) || realismo *m* (realism).

literalize ['litərəlaiz] *vt* tomar literalmente (to interpret) || traducir literalmente (to translate).

literally ['litərəli] *adv* literalmente, al pie de la letra; *he translates literally* traduce literalmente || literalmente, verdaderamente (really).

literary ['litərəri] *adj* literario, ria; *literary criticism* crítica literaria || — *literary man* hombre *m* de letras, literato *m* || *literary property* propiedad literaria.

literate ['litərit] *adj* letrado, da (erudite) || que sabe leer y escribir (able to read and write).
◆ *n* persona *f* letrada || persona *f* que sabe leer y escribir.

literati [ˌlitə'rɑ:ti] *pl n* literatos *m*, hombres *m* de letras.

literatim [ˌlitə'rɑ:tim] *adv* literalmente, al pie de la letra.

literature ['litəritʃə*] *n* literatura *f*; *English literature* literatura inglesa || profesión *f* de escritor || obras *f pl* literarias (literary works) || información *f*, folletos *m pl* publicitarios (printed matter) || documentación *f* (on a subject).

lithe [laið] *adj* ágil (nimble) || flexible.

litheness [-nis] *n* agilidad *f* (nimbleness) || flexibilidad *f*.

lithesome [-səm] *adj* ágil (nimble) || flexible.

lithic ['liθik] *adj* lítico, ca.

lithium ['liθiəm] *n* litio *m* (metal).

lithochromy [ˌliθə'krəumi] *n* litocromía *f*.

lithograph ['liθəugrɑ:f] *n* litografía *f*.

lithographer [li'θɔgrəfə*] *n* litógrafo *m*.

lithographic [ˌliθəu'græfik] *adj* litográfico, ca.

lithography [li'θɔgrəfi] *n* litografía *f*.

lithophagous [li'θɔfəgəs] *adj* ZOOL litófago, ga.

lithophyte ['liθəfait] *n* BOT litófito *m*.

lithoprint ['liθəuprint] *vt* litografiar.

lithosphere ['liθəusfiə*] *n* GEOL litosfera *f*.

lithotypography [ˌliθəutai'pɔgrəfi] *n* litotipografía *f*.

Lithuania [ˌliθju:'einjə] *pr n* GEOGR Lituania *f*.

Lithuanian [-n] *adj* lituano, na.
◆ *n* lituano, na (person) || lituano *m* (language).

litigant ['litigənt] *adj/n* litigante, pleiteante.

litigate ['litigeit] *vt* litigar sobre, pleitear sobre.
◆ *vi* litigar.

litigation [ˌliti'geiʃən] *n* litigio *m*, pleito *m*.

litigious [li'tidʒəs] *adj* litigioso, sa (point) || pleitista (person).

litmus ['litməs] *n* tornasol *m* || — *litmus paper* papel *m* de tornasol || FIG *litmus test* prueba *f* definitiva *or* contundente.

litotes ['laitəuti:z] *inv n* litote *f*.

litre ['li:tə*] *n* litro *m*.

litter ['litə*] *n* basura *f* (rubbish) || papeles *m pl* (scraps of paper) || desorden *m* (disorder); *in a litter* en desorden || camada *f* (offspring of animals) || cama *f* de paja, pajaza *f* (for animals) || estiércol *m* (manure) || mantillo *m* (humus) || camilla *f* (a stretcher) || litera *f* (ancient carriage).

litter ['litə*] *vt* ensuciar; *papers littered the street* unos papeles ensuciaban la calle || esparcir (to scatter) || cubrir; *the wreckage of the plane littered the mountainside* los restos del avión cubrían la ladera de la montaña || llenar; *he littered the room with chairs* llenó la habitación de sillas || desordenar (to jumble) || andar rodando por, estar esparcido por; *several books littered the table* varios libros andaban rodando por la mesa || preparar una cama de paja a (to bed down) || parir (to give birth to).
◆ *vi* parir (animals).

litterateur ['litərə'tə:*] *n* hombre *m* de letras (literary man).

litter basket ['litə*ˌbɑ:skit]; **litter bin** ['litə*bin] *n* papelera *f*.

litterburg [-bʌg] *n* persona *f* que tira papeles usados en la vía pública.

little ['litl] *adj* pequeño, ña (small in size, stature, number); *little hands* manos pequeñas; *a little person* una persona pequeña; *a little child* un niño pequeño; *a little herd* un rebaño pequeño || poco, ca (small in degree, in quantity); *we had little difficulty* tuvimos poca dificultad; *of little importance* de poca importancia; *we have little time left* nos queda poco tiempo; *there is little space* hay poco sitio; *a little money* un poco de dinero; *a little water* un poco de agua || pequeño, ña; poco, ca; corto, ta (in distance, in duration) || poco, ca (in force) || estrecho, cha; *little minds* mentes estrechas || REL menor (hours, office) || ASTR Menor (Bear) || — *a little kindness* un poco de amabilidad || *a little while* un rato || *a nice little house* una casita muy mona || *has Johnny hurt his little arm?* ¿te duele el bracito Juan? || *little finger* dedo *m* meñique || *little if any, little or no* muy poco || *little toe* dedo pequeño del pie || *my little man* hijo mío || *poor little boy* pobrecito || *the little ones* los pequeños || *the little people* los duendes || *with no little fear* con bastante miedo.
◆ *n* poco *m*; *give me a little* dame un poco; *he did little to help* hizo poco para ayudar || lo poco; *they took the little that I had* me robaron lo poco que tenía; *the little that I could do* lo poco que podía hacer || — *after a little* al poco tiempo || *a little* un rato, un poco (time); *stay a little* quédate un rato; un poco (distance); *go down the road a little* baja la calle un poco; algo, un poco; *a little better* algo mejor || *every little helps* muchos pocos hacen un mucho || *for a little* un poco, un rato || *in little* en pequeño || *little by little* poco a poco || *little or nothing* poco o nada, casi nada || *not a little* mucho, no poco (amount), muy (degree) || *to make little of* hacer caso omiso de, hacer poco caso de (to pay no attention to), sacar poco provecho de (to get little benefit from) || *to think little of* tener en poco, tener mala opinión de (to think badly of), dar poca importancia a, hacer poco caso de (to pay little attention to), no dudar en (not to hesitate) || *wait a little!* ¡espera un momento! || *we had little to do with it* poco tuvimos que ver en aquello.
◆ *adv* poco; *she dances little* baila poco; *I see him very little* lo veo muy poco; *a little more than five years ago* hace poco más de cinco años; *little known* poco conocido || — *as little as possible* lo menos posible || *little did he know that* no tenía la menor idea de que.

littleness [-nis] *n* pequeñez *f* || FIG pequeñez *f*, mezquindad *f*.

little theater [-'θiətə*] *n* teatro *m* experimental.

littoral ['litərəl] *adj* GEOGR litoral.
◆ *n* GEOGR litoral *m*.

lit up ['lit'ʌp] *adj* FAM achispado, da; alegre.

liturgical [li'tə:dʒikəl] *adj* REL litúrgico, ca.

liturgics [li'tə:dʒiks] *n* REL liturgia *f*.

liturgy ['litə:dʒi] *n* REL liturgia *f*.

livable; liveable ['livəbl] *adj* habitable; *a very livable house* una casa muy habitable || llevadero, ra; *a livable life* una vida llevadera || *he's very livable with* es muy fácil vivir con él.

live [laiv] *adj* vivo, va (living); *is that a live snake?* ¿está viva esta serpiente? || vivo, va; activo, va (lively) || encendido, da; en ascuas (coal) || encendido, da (match, fire) || vivo, va (colour) || de actualidad, de interés actual, candente (question) || ELECTR con corriente, cargado, da (conductor, wire) || en directo (broadcast) || motor, ra (axle) || sin explotar, cargado, da; *a live bomb* una bomba sin explotar || cargado, da (cartridge) || útil; *live weight* carga útil || en vivo (animal weight) || — *a real live cowboy* un vaquero de verdad, un vaquero en carne y hueso || *live coals* ascuas *f*.

live [liv] *vt* vivir, llevar, tener; *to live a wonderful life* llevar una vida maravillosa || vivir, tener (an experience) || — *to live a lie* vivir en la mentira || *to live a part* identificarse con un personaje || *to live it up* echar una cana al aire, pegarse la vida padre.
◆ *vi* vivir; *to live well* vivir bien; *to live together* vivir juntos || permanecer; *his name will live* su nombre permanecerá || — *as long as I live* mientras viva || *as ye live so shall ye die* quien mal anda mal acaba || *long live the queen!* ¡viva la reina! || *the times we live in* en los tiempos en que vivimos || *they all lived happily ever after* vivieron felices, comieron perdices y a mí no me dieron (in tales) || *to live and learn*

vivir para ver || *to live and let live* vivir y dejar vivir || *to live from one day to the next* vivir al día || *to live like a king* vivir como un rey, vivir a cuerpo de rey, vivir como un pachá.
◆ *phr v* **to live by** vivir de; *he lives by his pen* vive de su pluma || **to live down** conseguir que se olvide || **to live in** ser interno (at school, etc.) | vivir en (a house, a town) | vivir en la casa (a maid, etc.) || **to live off** vivir de || **to live on** seguir viviendo | perdurar; *his memory lives on* su memoria perdura || **to live on** o **upon** vivir (de); *what does she live on?* ¿de qué vive?; *he lives on charity* vive de limosna; *I don't earn enough to live on* no gano bastante para vivir; *to live on hope* vivir de esperanzas; vivir a expensas de; *he still lives on his parents* vive todavía a expensas de sus padres; vivir con; *he lives on twenty pounds a month* vive con veinte libras al mes || **to live out** acabar; *he lived out his days in exile* acabó sus días en el exilio | no vivir en la casa (maid, etc.) | ser externo; *as a student I lived out* cuando era estudiante era externo || — *she won't live out the week* no acabará la semana con vida || **to live through** sobrevivir a (a war) | vivir (an experience); *I lived through all these events* viví todos estos acontecimientos || **to live up to** cumplir con; *he lived up to his promise* cumplió con su promesa | vivir según; *he lives up to his income* vive según sus ingresos | vivir de acuerdo con; *he lived up to his principles* vivió de acuerdo con sus principios.

liveable ['livəbl] *adj* ⟶ **livable.**

lived [lived] *adj* *short-lived* de corta vida, de breve vida.

live-in ['livin] *adj* que vive en la casa (maid, servant).

livelihood ['laivlihud] *n* sustento *m* (subsistence) || — *to earn a livelihood* ganarse la vida *or* el sustento || *to earn an honest livelihood* ganarse honradamente la vida.

liveliness ['laivlinis] *n* viveza *f*, vivacidad *f*, vida *f* (briskness) || animación *f*, vida *f* (activity).

live load ['laivləud] *n* carga *f* móvil.

livelong ['livlɔŋ] *adj* entero, ra; todo, da || *all the livelong day* todo el santo día.

lively ['laivli] *adj* vivo, va (vivacious) || activo, va (active) || enérgico, ca (forceful) || gráfico, ca (graphic) || realista (realistic) || animado, da (party, debate) || alegre (tune) || rápido, da (pace, pitch) || agudo, da (intense); *a lively sense of humour* un sentido agudo del humor || vivo, va (bright, lucid, fresh); *lively colours* colores vivos || AUT que responde bien; *I've got a lively car* tengo un coche que responde bien || — *to make things lively for s.o.* complicar la vida a alguien || *to take a lively interest in sth.* interesarse vivamente en algo.

liven [laivn] *vt* *to liven up* animar.
◆ *vi* *to liven up* animarse.

live oak ['laiv'əuk] *n* BOT roble *m*.

liver ['livə*] *n* ANAT hígado *m*; *liver complaint* enfermedad del hígado || CULIN hígado *m* || — FAM *fast* o *loose liver* vividor, ra; juerguista *m & f* | *good liver* persona *f* que se da buena vida.

liveried ['livərid] *adj* que lleva librea.

liverish ['livəriʃ] *adj* que padece del hígado, hepático, ca (having liver disorder) || *to feel liverish* estar pachucho, no encontrarse bien.

Liverpool ['livəpu:l] *pr n* GEOGR Liverpool.

liverwort ['livəwə:t] *n* BOT hepática *f*.

livery ['livəri] *n* librea *f* (dress, costume of a servant) || cuadra *f* de caballos de alquiler (stable) || JUR entrega *f* (of property) || JUR *livery of seisin* toma *f* de posesión.

livery company [-,kʌmpəni] *n* gremio *m* de la ciudad de Londres.

liveryman [-mən] *n* miembro *m* de un gremio de la ciudad de Londres || propietario *m* de caballos de alquiler *or* de carruajes de alquiler.
— OBSERV El plural de *liveryman* es *liverymen*.

livery stable [-,steibl] *n* cuadra *f* de caballos de alquiler.

lives [laivz] *pl n* ⟶ **life.**

livestock ['laivstɔk] *n* ganado *m* (cattle) || ganadería *f* (stock farming).

live wire ['laiv,waiə*] *n* ELECTR alambre *m* con corriente *or* cargado || FIG persona *f* enérgica.

livid ['livid] *adj* plomizo, za (lead-coloured) || lívido, da (discoloured) || FAM furioso, sa (angry).

lividity [li'viditi]; **lividness** ['lividnis] *n* lividez *f*.

living ['liviŋ] *adj* vivo, va; viviente (having life); *living beings* seres vivientes || viviente, contemporáneo, a; *the greatest living sculptor* el mejor escultor viviente || lleno de vida (image, style, picture) || vivo, va; *she is the living image of her mother* es el vivo retrato de su madre || de vida; *living conditions* condiciones de vida || vivo, va (water, force) || de mantenimiento (expenses) || suficiente para vivir; *living wage* sueldo suficiente para vivir || — *living death* muerte *f* en vida || *living language* lengua viva || *living or dead* muerto o vivo || *no living man could do better* nadie lo haría mejor || *not a living soul* ni un alma.
◆ *n* vivos *m pl*; *the living and the dead* los vivos y los muertos || vida *f*; *to earn one's living* ganarse la vida; *his living alone made him sad* su vida solitaria le entristecía; *clean living* vida ordenada; *loose living* vida disoluta || REL beneficio *m* || — *they make a bare living* ganan lo justo para vivir || *to make a living* ganarse la vida || *to make a living for s.o.* mantener a alguien || *to work for one's living* ganarse la vida trabajando.

living allowance [-ə'lauəns] *n* dietas *f pl*.

living death [-deθ] *n* muerte *f* en vida.

living quarters [-'kwɔ:təz] *pl n* alojamiento *m sing*, residencia *f sing*.

living room [-rum] *n* cuarto *m* de estar, sala *f* de estar.

living space [-speis] *n* espacio *m* vital.

living standard [-'stændəd] *n* nivel *m* de vida.

lixiviate [lik'sivieit] *vt* lixiviar.

lizard ['lizəd] *n* ZOOL lagarto *m* (big), lagartija *f* (small).

llama ['lɑ:mə] *n* ZOOL llama *f*.

llanos ['lɑ:nəus] *pl n* GEOGR llanos *m*.

lo [ləu] *interj* ¡he aquí! || *lo and behold there he was!* ¡y allí estaba!

loach [ləutʃ] *n* ZOOL locha *f* (fish).

load [ləud] *n* carga *f* (burden) || cabida *f*; *this washing machine takes a load of six pounds* esta lavadora tiene una cabida de seis libras || peso *m* (weight) || cargamento *m*, carga *f* (of vehicles, of animals) || carretada *f* (cartful) || MIL carga *f* (of a gun) || TECH carga *f* | rendimiento *m* (of an engine); *at full load* con pleno rendimiento | resistencia *f* || ELECTR carga *f* || FIG peso *m*; *you have taken a load off my mind* me has quitado un peso de encima || — *dead load* peso muerto || FAM *get a load of this!* ¡mira esto! | *it's a load of rubbish* es una porquería, no vale absolutamente nada || *peak load* carga máxima || *useful load* carga útil.
◆ *pl* FAM cantidades *f*, montones *m*; *loads of money* cantidades de dinero.

load [ləud] *vt* cargar; *to load coal on a lorry* cargar carbón en un camión || hacer más pesado (to make heavier) || cargar; *to load the dice* cargar los dados || MIL cargar; *to load a rifle* cargar un fusil || cargar (wine) || ELECTR cargar || INFORM cargar || poner, cargar con; *to load a film in a camera* poner un rollo en una cámara, cargar una cámara con un rollo || recargar (an insurance premium) || FIG agobiar; *to be loaded with debts* estar agobiado de deudas | colmar, llenar (*with* de) (honours) | acompañar; *he loaded his arguments with examples* acompañó sus argumentos con ejemplos || — *everything was loaded against him* todo iba en contra suya || *to load o.s. with* cargarse de *or* con.
◆ *vi* cargar || tomar carga (to take a load on) || cargarse; *how did this gun load?* ¿cómo se carga este fusil? || cargarse (a camera).

load displacement [-dis'pleismənt] *n* MAR desplazamiento *m* (del buque) con carga.

loaded [-id] *adj* cargado, da (animal, vehicle, dice, camera, gun, etc.) || *to be loaded* estar cargado, estar tajado (drunk), estar forrado de dinero (rich).

loader [-ə*] *n* cargador *m* (person) || cargadora *f* (machine).

load factor [-,fæktə*] *n* coeficiente *m* de carga.

loading [-iŋ] *n* carga *f* (of goods); *loading and unloading* carga y descarga || sobreprima *f* (insurance).
◆ *adj* de carga.

loading bay [-bei] *n* cargadero *m*.

load line [-lain] *n* MAR línea *f* de flotación [del buque con carga].

loadstar [-stɑ:*] *n* ⟶ **lodestar.**

loadstone [-stəun] *n* ⟶ **lodestone.**

loaf [ləuf] *n* pan *m* (bread) || barra *f* (french bread) || pan *m* de azúcar (of sugar) || callejeo *m* (wandering) || — FIG *half a loaf is better than none* mejor que nada, menos da una piedra || FAM *use your loaf* piensa con la cabeza.
— OBSERV El plural de *loaf* es *loaves*.

loaf [ləuf] *vt* pasar (el tiempo) ociosamente.
◆ *vi* holgazanear; *I spent the whole day loafing* me pasé el día holgazaneando || *to loaf about* o *around* callejear (along the streets), holgazanear (to laze).

loafer [-ə*] *n* holgazán, ana (lazy person) || azotacalles *m inv* (on the street) || US mocasín *m* (shoes).

loam [ləum] *n* marga *f* (rich soil of clay and sand) || mezcla *f* de barro y arcilla (for making bricks, moulds, etc.) || ARCH adobe *m* || AGR mantillo *m*.

loan [ləun] *n* préstamo *m* (sth. lent); *loan on trust* préstamo de honor || COMM empréstito *m* (of the State); *government loan* empréstito del Estado; *a loan at 3% interest* un empréstito al 3% || palabra *f* tomada de otra lengua (loanword) || — *on loan* prestado, da || *to ask for the loan of* pedir prestado || *to issue a loan* conceder un préstamo (s.o.), hacer un empréstito (the state) || *to raise* o *to float a loan* emitir *or* lanzar un empréstito.

loan [ləun] *vt* prestar.

loan office [-'ɔfis] *n* casa *f* de préstamos.

loan shark [ʃɑ:k] *n* FAM usurero *m*.

loanword [-wə:d] *n* palabra *f* tomada de otra lengua.

loath; loth [ləuθ] *adj* reacio, cia || — *nothing loath* de buena gana || *to be loath to* ser reacio a, estar poco dispuesto a.

loathe [ləuð] *vt* aborrecer, odiar; *I loathe vice* aborrezco el vicio; *to loathe doing sth.* aborrecer hacer algo.

loathing [-iŋ] *n* aborrecimiento *m* (*of* de), odio *m* (*of* a), aversión (*of* por, a) (of s.o.) || repugnancia *f*, asco *m*, aversión *f* (*of* a) (of sth.)

|| *it fills me with loathing* me asquea, me repugna.

loathsome [-səm] *adj* repugnante, asqueroso, sa (disgusting) || odioso, sa (hateful).

loathsomeness [-səmnis] *n* lo odioso || lo repugnante, lo asqueroso.

loaves [ləuvz] *pl n* → **loaf.**

lob [lɔb] *n* volea *f* alta, «lob» *m* (in tennis).

lob [lɔb] *vt* SP lanzar (la pelota) por debajo del brazo (in cricket) | volear, lanzar (la pelota) voleada (in tennis) | bombear (in football) || FAM tirar, dar; *lob it to me, will you?* tíramelo.
◆ *vi* andar con dificultad (to walk) || SP lanzar la pelota voleada.

lobar ['ləubə*] *adj* lobular.

lobate ['ləubeit] *adj* BOT lobulado, da.

lobby ['lɔbi] *n* pasillo *m* (corridor) || antecámara *f* (anteroom) || sala *f* de espera (waiting room) || vestíbulo *m* (vestibule) || pasillo *m* de una cámara legislativa (in a legislative building) || grupo *m*, grupo *m* de presión; *the industrial reform lobby* el grupo a favor de la reforma industrial.

lobby ['lɔbi] *vt* hacer aprobar (a bill) por medio de presiones || ejercer presiones sobre.
◆ *vi* ejercer presiones, cabildear.

lobbying [-iŋ] *n* presiones *f pl*, cabildeo *m*.

lobbyist [-ist] *n* el que ejerce presiones, cabildero *m*.

lobe [ləub] *n* lóbulo *m*.

lobectomy [ləu'bektəmi] *n* MED lobectomía *f*.

lobed [ləubd] *adj* lobulado, da.

lobotomy [ləu'bɔtəmi] *n* MED lobotomía *f*.

lobscouse ['lɔbskaus] *n* guisado *m*, guiso *m*.

lobster ['lɔbstə*] *n* ZOOL langosta *f* | bogavante *m* (with claws) || *spiny lobster* langosta *f*.

lobster boat [-bəut] *n* MAR langostero *m*.

lobster pot [-pɔt] *n* MAR nasa *f*.

lobular ['lɔbjulə*]; **lobulate** ['lɔbjulit] *adj* lobular, lobulado, da.

lobule ['lɔbju:l] *n* lóbulo *m*.

local ['ləukəl] *adj* local (restricted to a particular place); *local customs* costumbres locales; *local colour* color local || limitado, da; restringido, da (outlook) || ciudad, interior (on a letter) || urbano, na; *local telephone service* servicio telefónico urbano || del barrio (doctor) || pueblerino, na; *local quarrels* luchas pueblerinas || vecinal; *local road* camino vecinal || de cercanías (trains) || de línea (bus) || local (authority, team, agent, dealer, radio station) || MED local (anaesthetic) | externo, na (remedy) || GRAMM de lugar (adverb) || — *a local man* un hombre de aquí || *local authority* autoridad *f* municipal (in town), autoridad comarcal *or* provincial (in county) || *local call* llamada *f* urbana || SP *local derby* derby *m* entre equipos locales || *local government* gobierno *m* municipal || *local option* derecho *m* concedido a una región de determinar si una ley es aplicable o no en su territorio || *local time* hora *f* local.
◆ *n* tren *m* de cercanías (train) || autobús *m* de línea (bus) || informaciones *f pl* locales (news) || equipo *m* local (team) || COMM agente *m* local || FAM bar *m* del barrio (pub) || escenario *m* (of events) || sello *m* de correos válido únicamente en cierta área (stamp) || examen *m* regional (examination) || indígena *m* & *f*, nativo, va (person) || US sección *f* local (of an organization) || *the locals are very friendly* los vecinos de esta población son muy simpáticos, la gente del lugar es muy simpática.

locale [ləu'kɑ:l] *n* lugar *m* (place) || escenario *m* (of events).

localism ['ləukəlizəm] *n* localismo *m* || provincianismo *m*, regionalismo *m* (word, etc.) || mentalidad *f* pueblerina, espíritu *m* localista (interest in local affairs).

locality [ləu'kæliti] *n* localidad *f* (neighbourhood) || sitio *m*, lugar *m* (place) || región *f* || situación *f*, lugar *m* (situation) || orientación *f*; *poor sense of locality* mal sentido de la orientación || residencia *f*, domicilio *m*; *I don't know his present locality* no conozco su residencia actual.

localization [,ləukəlai'zeiʃən] *n* localización *f*.

localize ['ləukəlaiz] *vt* localizar.

locally ['ləukəli] *adv* localmente || en la localidad, en el lugar, en la región || en el sitio; *staff engaged locally* personal contratado en el sitio.

locate [ləu'keit] *vt* localizar (to look for and discover); *they have located the thief* han localizado al ladrón || encontrar, hallar (to find); *can you locate the town on this map?* ¿puede encontrar la ciudad en este mapa? || situar [AMER ubicar] (to situate); *where is your house located?* ¿dónde está situada su casa? || *to be located somewhere* estar domiciliado en algún sitio (people).
◆ *vi* US establecerse.

locating [-iŋ] *n* → **location.**

location [ləu'keiʃən] *n* localización *f* (finding) || situación *f*, sitio *m*, posición *f* (place) [AMER ubicación *f*] || colocación *f* [AMER ubicación *f*] (placing) || CINEM exteriores *m pl* || US MIN concesión *f* || CINEM *to film on location in Spain* rodar en España.

locative ['lɔkətiv] *adj* GRAMM locativo, va.
◆ *n* GRAMM locativo *m*.

loch [lɔk] *n* lago *m* (lake) || ría *f* (estuary). •

loci ['ləusai] *pl n* → **locus.**

lock [lɔk] *n* mecha *f*, mechón *m* (curl of hair) || vedija *f*, vellón *m* (of wool) || copo *m* (of cotton) || cerradura *f* (on door, box, drawer, etc.); *he cut a hole in the door for the lock* hizo un agujero en la puerta para la cerradura || candado *m* (for a bicycle, a trunk, etc.) || cerrojo *m* (bolt) || SP llave *f* (in wrestling) || llave *f* (of a firearm) || TECH tope *m*, retén *m* (blocking device) || esclusa *f* (on a canal) || esclusa *f* de aire (on submarines, on spacecrafts, etc.) || AUT ángulo *m* de giro || FIG embotellamiento *m*, atasco *m* (traffic jam) | callejón *m* sin salida (deadlock) || — FIG *lock, stock and barrel* completamente, por completo || *under lock and key* bajo siete llaves, bajo llave.
◆ *pl* cabellera *f sing* (hair).

lock [lɔk] *vt* cerrar con llave (to fasten) || encerrar (to shut in); *lock these prisoners in their cells* encierre a esos prisioneros en sus celdas || juntar, unir (to fit parts tightly together) || TECH bloquear, trabar || enclavar (railway points, signals) || enredar; *they locked their horns* se enredaron los cuernos || PRINT ajustar || hacer pasar por una esclusa (a boat) || — *to be locked in each other's arms* estar estrechamente abrazados, estar unidos en un abrazo || *to be locked in mortal combat* estar enzarzados en una batalla mortal || *to lock one's arms around s.o.'s neck* echar los brazos al cuello de uno.
◆ *vi* cerrarse con llave (to shut with a key) || unirse, juntarse (to fit tightly together) || pasar por esclusas (a boat) || bloquearse (mechanism).
◆ *phr v* *to lock away* guardar bajo llave || *to lock in* encerrar || *to lock into* engranarse en || *to lock out* dejar fuera a, cerrar la puerta a (to prevent from entering) | declarar el cierre patronal *or* el «lock-out» (in a factory) || *to lock up* cerrar; *to lock up the house* cerrar la casa | dejar bajo llave; *to lock up money* dejar dinero bajo llave | encarcelar (to imprison) | encerrar (to shut in) | COMM inmovilizar, bloquear (capital) | concluir, terminar (a stock).

lockable ['lɔkəbl] *adj* que se puede cerrar con llave.

lockage [-idʒ] *n* cierre *m* con esclusas, sistema *m* de esclusas (lock system) || paso *m* de un barco por una esclusa || peaje *m* para pasar por una esclusa (toll).

lock bolt [-bəult] *n* pestillo *m*.

lock chamber [-,tʃeimbə*] *n* MAR esclusa *f*.

locker [-ə*] *n* casillero *m* (shelf with pigeonholes) || armario *m* (cupboard) || cajón *m* [AMER gaveta *f*] (drawer) || MAR pañol *m* (storeroom) | cajón *m* || US cámara *f* frigorífica.

locker room [ərum] *n* vestuario *m* con casilleros *or* armarios.

locket [-it] *n* relicario *m* (for any souvenir) || guardapelo *m* (for a lock of hair).

locking [-iŋ] *n* cierre *m* con llave || TECH bloqueo *m* (jam) || → **lockage.**
◆ *adj* de fijación.

lockjaw [-dʒɔ:] *n* MED trismo *m*.

lockkeeper [-,ki:pə*] *n* esclusero *m*.

locknut [-nʌt] *n* TECH contratuerca *f*.

lockout [-aut] *n* cierre *m* patronal, «lockout» *m*.

locksman [-smən] *n* esclusero *m*.
— OBSERV El plural de *locksman* es *locksmen*.

locksmith [-smiθ] *n* cerrajero *m*.

lockstitch [-stitʃ] *n* punto *m* de cadeneta.

lockup [-ʌp] *n* encierro *m* (of a person) || cierre *m* de una puerta (of a house) || FAM calabozo *m* (prison cell) | cárcel *f*, jaula *f*, chirona *f* (prison building) || garaje *m*, jaula *f* (garage) || almacén *m* (shop) || COMM inmovilización *f* (of capital).

lock-up [-ʌp] *adj* con cerradura (desk, etc.).

loco ['ləukəu] *n* BOT especie *f* de astrágalo || FAM locomotora *f*, máquina *f* (locomotive).
◆ *adj* US FAM loco, ca; chiflado, da (crazy).

locomobile ['ləukə,məubil] *adj* locomovible, locomóvil.

locomotion [,ləukə'məuʃən] *n* locomoción *f*.

locomotive ['ləukə,məutiv] *n* locomotora *f*.
◆ *adj* locomotor, ra.

locomotor [,ləukə'məutə*] *adj* locomotor, ra || MED *locomotor ataxy* ataxia locomotriz.

locoweed ['ləukəu,wi:d] *n* BOT especie *f* de astrágalo.

locum (tenens) ['ləukəm'ti:nenz] *n* interino, na; suplente *m* & *f*.

locus ['ləukəs] *n* MATH lugar *m* geométrico || BIOL posición *f* [de un gene] || situación *f*, sitio *m*, lugar *m* (exact place of sth.) || teatro *m*, escenario *m* (of a crime).
— OBSERV El plural de *locus* es *loci*.

locust ['ləukəst] *n* ZOOL langosta *f* (cricket) | cigarra *f* (cicada) || BOT algarroba *f* (fruit) || — BOT *locust bean* algarroba *f* | *locust tree* algarrobo *m*.

locution [ləu'kju:ʃən] *n* locución *f*.

locutory ['lɔkjutəri] *n* locutorio *m* (visiting room).

lode [ləud] *n* MIN veta *f*, filón *m*.

loden ['ləudn] *n* loden *m* (material).

lodestar; loadstar ['ləudstɑ:*] *n* estrella *f* polar (star) || FIG norte *m*, guía *m*.

lodestone; loadstone ['ləudstəun] *n* magnetita *f*, piedra *f* imán.

lodge [lɔdʒ] *n* casa *f* del guarda (of a caretaker) || portería *f* (porter's house) || pabellón *m*; *a hunting* o *a shooting lodge* un pabellón de caza || posada *f* (inn) || logia *f* (masonic) || madriguera *f* (of beavers, of otters) || tienda *f* [de indio] (tepee).

lodge [lɔdʒ] *vt* alojar, hospedar; *she lodges students in her house* aloja estudiantes en su casa || albergar; *the house lodges three of us* la casa alberga a tres de nosotros || encajar (to wedge) || colocar (to place) || contener (to contain) || clavar (an arrow, a sword) || alojar, meter (a bullet); *he lodged a bullet in my arm* me metió una bala en el brazo || plantar (a blow) || depositar (to deposit); *I lodged my money in the bank* he depositado mi dinero en el banco || conferir (to vest) || meter (an idea) || presentar (a proof, a complaint) || interponer (an appeal) || AGR encamar || *to lodge in a gaol* meter en la cárcel.

◆ *vi* alojarse, hospedarse (to live) || alojarse, meterse; *the bullet lodged in his head* la bala se alojó en su cabeza || clavarse (knife, arrow) || AGR encamarse.

lodgement [-mənt] *n* ⟶ **lodgment.**

lodger [-ə*] *n* huésped, da (in a boarding-house) || inquilino, na (in a rented house).

lodging [-iŋ] *n* pensión *f*; *board and lodging* pensión completa || alojamiento *m* (act) || MIL alojamiento *m* (of troops) || JUR presentación *f* (of complaint) || depósito *m* (of money) || *lodging house* casa *f* de huéspedes.

◆ *pl* habitación *f sing*, habitaciones *f* || *to take lodgings* alojarse.

lodgment; lodgement [-mənt] *n* MIL posición *f* firme (foothold) || JUR depósito *m* de dinero || depósito *m* (an accumulation of sth.) || alojamiento *m* (of guests) || pensión *f*, alojamiento *m* (house).

loess ['ləuis] *n* loess *m*.

— OBSERV Esta palabra es invariable en ambos idiomas.

loft [lɔft] *n* desván *m* (attic) || pajar *m* (for hay) || palomar *m* (dovecote) || galería *f*, triforio *m* (of a church) || SP inclinación *f* (of a golf club) | golpe *m* alto || US piso *m* alto (in a warehouse).

loft [lɔft] *vt* SP lanzar (la pelota) en alto.

lofter [-ə*] *n* SP palo *m* de golf [para lanzar la pelota en alto].

loftily [-ili] *adv* en alto || FIG con arrogancia, con altanería (haughtily).

loftiness [-inis] *n* altura *f* (height) || FIG arrogancia *f*, altanería *f* (haughtiness) | elevación *f*, nobleza *f* (of principles, of sentiments) | elevación *f* (of style).

lofty [-i] *adj* alto, ta (high) || FIG arrogante, altanero, ra; altivo, va (haughty) | elevado, da; noble (principles, sentiments) | elevado, da (style).

log [lɔg] *n* tronco *m* (large section of tree) || leño *m*, tronco *m* (used for fuel) || AVIAT diario *m* de vuelo || MAR corredera *f* (speed gauge) | cuaderno *m* de bitácora, libro *m* de navegación, diario *m* de a bordo (book) || diario *m* (on a journey, etc.) || MATH logaritmo *m* || — FIG *as easy as falling off a log* más fácil que beber un vaso de agua; tirado, da | *to sleep like a log* dormir como un tronco.

log [lɔg] *vt* cortar (trees) || anotar, apuntar (to record) || MAR navegar a (to sail at) | anotar en el cuaderno de bitácora || — *he has logged two thousand flying hours* tiene dos mil horas de vuelo || *he logged one hundred kilometres yesterday* ayer recorrió cien kilómetros || *to log a piece of forest* cortar los árboles de una parte del bosque.

◆ *vi* cortar y transportar árboles || — INFORM *to log in* iniciar una sesión, entrar en el sistema | *to log out* clausurar una sesión, salir del sistema.

loganberry ['ləugənbəri] *n* BOT frambueso *m* (bush) | frambuesa *f* (fruit).

logarithm ['lɔgəriðəm] *n* logaritmo *m* || *logarithm table* tabla *f* de logaritmos.

logarithmic [,lɔgə'riðmik] *adj* logarítmico, ca.

logbook ['lɔgbuk] *n* MAR cuaderno *m* de bitácora, libro *m* de navegación, diario *m* de a bordo || AVIAT diario *m* de vuelo || diario *m* (on a journey, etc.) || cuaderno *m* de trabajo (of workmen) || RAD libro *m* de escucha || INFORM diario *m* de bitácora.

log cabin ['lɔg,kæbin] *n* cabaña *f* de troncos.

log chip ['lɔg,tʃip] *n* MAR barquilla *f* de la corredera, guindola *f*.

loge [ləuʒ] *n* US THEATR palco *m*.

log fire ['lɔg,faiə*] *n* fuego *m* de madera.

logger ['lɔgə*] *n* leñador *m* (woodcutter) || maderero *m*, negociante *m* en maderas.

loggerhead ['lɔgəhed] *n* TECH instrumento *m* de hierro para calentar brea || ZOOL tortuga *f* marina (turtle) || FIG *to be at loggerheads* estar a mal *or* disgustado *or* a matar.

loggia ['lɔdʒə] *n* ARCH logia *f*.

logging ['lɔgiŋ] *n* explotación *f* forestal || transporte *m* de troncos.

log hut ['lɔghʌt] *n* cabaña *f* de troncos.

logic ['lɔdʒik] *n* lógica *f* || *in logic* lógicamente.

logical [-əl] *adj* lógico, ca || INFORM *logical operator* operador *m* lógico.

logically [-i] *adv* lógicamente.

logician [ləu'dʒiʃən] *n* lógico, ca.

logistic [ləu'dʒistik] *adj* logístico, ca.

logistician [,lɔdʒis'tiʃən] *n* logístico *m*.

logistics [ləu'dʒistik] *n* logística *f*.

log line ['lɔglain] *n* MAR cordel *m* de la corredera.

logo ['ləugəu] *n* logotipo *m*.

logogram ['lɔgəugræm] *n* signo *m* taquigráfico.

logographer [ləu'gɔgrəfə*] *n* logógrafo *m*.

logogriph ['lɔgəugrif] *n* logogrifo *m*.

logomachy [lɔ'gɔməki] *n* logomaquia *f*.

logos ['lɔgɔs] *n* PHIL logos *m* || REL verbo *m* (Jesus).

logroll ['lɔgrəul] *vt* US conseguir la aprobación de [una ley] | conducir en armadías (logs).

◆ *vi* US prestarse una ayuda recíproca [en las votaciones].

logrolling [-iŋ] *n* publicidad *f* mutua entre dos escritores || US transporte *m* de troncos en armadía (transport of timber) | intercambio *m* de favores políticos (arrangement between legislators to get their own projects carried out).

log ship ['lɔgʃip] *n* MAR barquilla *f* de la corredera, guindola *f*.

logwood ['lɔgwud] *n* BOT palo *m* campeche.

logy ['ləugi] *adj* US torpe.

loin [lɔin] *n* ANAT lomo *m* || ijada *f*, ijar *m* (of animals) || CULIN solomillo *m* (of beef) | lomo *m* (of pork, of veal) || FIG *to gird up one's loins* prepararse para la lucha.

loincloth ['lɔinklɔθ] *n* taparrabo *m*.

loiter ['lɔitə*] *vi* callejear (to hang about) || retrasarse, rezagarse (to lag behind) || holgazanear (to idle) || perder el tiempo (to waste time) || entretenerse; *don't loiter on the way* no te entretengas por el camino || JUR merodear; *to loiter with intent* merodear con fines criminales.

◆ *vt* *to loiter away* perder (time).

loiterer [-rə*] *n* paseante *m* & *f*, ocioso, azotacalles *m* & *f inv* || JUR merodeador, ra.

loll [lɔl] *vi* colgar (to hang) || echarse (to lie) || repantigarse (to slouch) || — *to loll about* no dar golpe (to do nothing), repantigarse (to slouch) || *to loll against* o *back on* recostarse en, apoyarse en || *to loll out* colgar (to hang).

◆ *vt* dejar colgar.

lollipop ['lɔlipɔp] *n* chupón *m*, pirulí *m* [AMER chupete *m*] (sweet) || polo *m* (iced).

lollop ['lɔləp] *vi* FAM moverse torpemente.

lolly ['lɔli] *n* FAM chupón *m*, pirulí *m* [AMER chupete *m*] | polo *m* (iced) || POP pasta *f*, parné *m* (money).

lollypop ['lɔlipɔp] *n* US chupón *m*, pirulí *m* [AMER chupete *m*] | polo *m* (iced).

lombard ['lɔbəd] *n* MIL lombarda *f* (cannon).

Lombardy ['lɔmbədi] *pr n* GEOGR Lombardía *f*.

Lomé ['ləumei] *pr n* GEOGR Lomé.

London ['lʌndən] *pr n* GEOGR Londres.

◆ *adj* londinense, de Londres.

Londoner [-ə*] *n* londinense *m* & *f*.

lone [ləun] *adj* solitario, ria (single, alone) || solo, la (on one's own) || aislado, da (isolated); *a lone place* un sitio aislado || desierto, ta (deserted) || — FIG *a lone wolf* una persona solitaria || *to play a lone hand* actuar solo.

loneliness [-linis]; **lonesomeness** [ləunsəmnis] *n* soledad *f* || aislamiento *m* (isolation).

lonely [-li] *adj* solo, la (solitary); *I feel very lonely* me siento muy solo || aislado, da (isolated) || solitario, ria (without companions); *he lives a lonely life* lleva una vida solitaria || solitario, ria; poco frecuentado, da (unfrequented); *this must be a lonely place in winter* esto tiene que ser un lugar solitario en invierno.

loner [-ə*] *n* solitario, ria.

lonesome [-səm] *adj* solo, la (lonely) || solitario, ria (solitary) || aislado, da (isolated) || *on one's lonesome* solo, la.

lonesomeness [-səmnis] *n* ⟶ **loneliness.**

long [lɔŋ] *adj* largo, ga; *a long road* una carretera larga; *the long side of the room* la parte larga de la habitación; *a long life* una vida larga; *two long miles* dos millas largas || mucho, cha; *a long time* mucho tiempo || de largo, de longitud; *two feet long* dos pies de largo || de longitud (measure) || bueno, na; *a long memory* una buena memoria || fuerte, largo, ga (suit in cards) || grande (figure) || elevado, da; alto, ta; grande (price) || de largo alcance (far-reaching) || viejo, ja; *a long friendship* una vieja amistad || de cuerpo entero (mirror) || alto, ta (tall) || GRAMM largo, ga (vowel) || RAD largo, ga (wave) || — *a long face* una cara larga || *a long time ago* hace mucho tiempo || *as long as your arm* larguísimo, ma || *at long last* por fin, al fin y al cabo || *how long is it?* ¿qué longitud tiene? (distance), ¿cuánto tiempo dura? (time) || *in the long run* a la larga || *it is a long time since I saw you* hace mucho tiempo que no te he visto || *it's a long way to* hay una gran distancia a || *it will take a long time* tardará mucho, necesitará mucho tiempo || FIG *long home* última morada || *long in the leg* de piernas largas || *long odds* apuesta arriesgada || MIL *long service* alistamiento *m* a largo plazo || *long shot* plano largo (of film), posibilidad remota (possibility), apuesta arriesgada (bet) || FIG *not by a long shot* ni mucho menos || *of long standing* de larga duración || FIG *the long arm of the law* el brazo de la justicia || *they are a long time in coming* tardan mucho en llegar || *this play is two hours long* esta obra de teatro dura dos horas || *to be long in getting ready* tardar mucho en prepararse || FAM *to be long in the tooth* tener ya muchos años || *to be long of* tener muchas reservas de || *to be long on practical experience* tener mucha experiencia práctica || *to get* o *to grow longer* alargarse || FIG *to have a face as long as a mile* llegarle a uno la cara a los pies | *to have a long head* tener vista, tener buen olfato | *to have a long tongue* tener la lengua suelta | *to make a*

long nose hacer un palmo de narices | *to pull a long face* poner cara larga.
◆ *n* mucho tiempo *m*; *not for long* no por mucho tiempo || GRAMM larga *f* (syllable) || — *before long* en breve, dentro de poco, muy pronto || *the long and the short of the matter* los pormenores del asunto, el asunto con todos los detalles || *the long and the short of the matter is* en resumidas cuentas || *to take long* tomar mucho tiempo, tardar || *will you be there for long?* ¿vas a quedarte allí mucho tiempo?
◆ *pl* pantalones *m* largos (trousers).
◆ *adv* (durante) mucho tiempo (for a long time) || — *all day long* (durante) todo el día, el día entero || *as long as* mientras; *I am not going out as long as it is raining* mientras llueva no saldré; hasta donde; *as long as the eye can see* hasta donde alcanza la vista; tanto como, todo el tiempo que; *keep it as long as you like* quédatelo todo el tiempo que quieras; con tal que (provided that) || *don't be long!* ¡no tardes mucho!, ¡vuelve pronto! || FIG *he is not long for this world* le queda poco || *how long?* ¿cuánto tiempo? || *long ago* o *since* hace mucho tiempo || *long before he arrived* mucho antes de que llegase || *long before now* hace mucho tiempo || *long live the King!* ¡viva el rey! || *not long ago* o *since* hace poco || *not long before* poco tiempo antes || *not to live long* morir pronto || FAM *so long!* ¡hasta luego!, ¡hasta pronto! || *so long as* con tal que (provided that) || COMM *to lend long* prestar a largo plazo || *to live long* vivir mucho || *to speak long about* hablar largamente *or* mucho tiempo de || *we shan't be long* en seguida acabamos, no tardaremos mucho.

long [lɔŋ] *vi* *to long for* desear con ansia, anhelar || *to long to* anhelar, desear ardientemente, tener muchas ganas de.

longanimity [-gəˈnimiti] *n* longanimidad *f*.

long-armed [-ɑːmd] *adj* de brazos largos.

long-awaited [-əˈweitid] *adj* esperado, da desde hace mucho tiempo.

longbill [-bil] *n* agachadiza *f* (bird).

longboat [-bəut] *n* MAR chalupa *f*, lancha *f*.

longbow [-bəu] *n* arco *m* || FAM *to draw the longbow* decir cuchufletas.

longcloth [-klɔθ] *n* percal *m* (material).
◆ *pl* pañales *m*.

long-dated [-ˈdeitid] *adj* a largo plazo.

long distance [-ˈdistəns] *n* conferencia *f*.

long-distance [-ˈdistns] *adj* de larga distancia || interurbano, na; *a long-distance telephone call* una conferencia interurbana || *long-distance runner* corredor *m* de fondo, fondista *m*.

long division [-diˈviʒən] *n* MATH división *f* de más de una cifra.

long-drawn-out [-drɔːnˈaut] *adj* muy prolongado, da; interminable (sigh) || FIG interminable.

long drink [-driŋk] *n* cubalibre *m*, bebida *f* larga.

longe [lʌndʒ] *n* ⟶ **lunge.**

longe [lʌndʒ] *vt* domar, amaestrar.

long-eared [ˈlɔŋiəd] *adj* de orejas largas || ZOOL *long-eared bat* orejudo *m*.

longed-for [ˈlɔŋdfɔː*] *adj* ansiado, da; deseado ardientemente.

longer [ˈlɔŋgə*] *comp adv* más tiempo || más; *ten hours longer* diez horas más; *to live longer than* vivir más que || — *how much longer?* ¿hasta cuándo? || *no longer* ya no; *he is no longer a minister* ya no es ministro.
◆ *comp adj* ⟶ **long.**

longeron [ˈlɔndgərən] *n* AVIAT larguero *m*.

longevity [lɔnˈdʒeviti] *n* longevidad *f*.

long-faced [ˈlɔŋˈfeist] *adj* descontento, ta.

long green [ˈlɔnˈgriːn] *n* US FAM billete *m*.

longhair [ˈlɔŋhεə*] *adj/n* FAM intelectual.

long-haired [lɔŋˈhεəd] *adj* de pelo largo.

longhand [ˈlɔŋhænd] *n* escritura *f* normal.

long-headed [ˈlɔŋˈhedid] *adj* dolicocéfalo, la || FAM *to be long-headed* tener buen olfato.

long hop [ˈlɔŋhɔp] *n* SP tiro *m* corto (in cricket).

longhouse [ˈlɔŋhaus] *n* casa *f* comunal.

long hundredweight [ˈlɔŋˈhʌndrədweit] *n* unidad *f* de medida que equivale a 112 libras.

longing [ˈlɔŋiŋ] *adj* anhelante, ansioso, sa; impaciente.
◆ *n* anhelo *m*, deseo *m*, ansia *f* (desire) || nostalgia *f*, añoranza *f* (nostalgia) || antojo *m* (of pregnant woman) || *sexual longing* apetito *m* sexual.

longingly [-li] *adv* con ansia.

longish [ˈlɔŋiʃ] *adj* bastante largo, más bien largo.

longitude [ˈlɔndʒitjuːd] *n* longitud *f*.

longitudinal [ˌlɔndʒiˈtjuːdinl] *adj* longitudinal.

long johns [ˈlɔnˈdʒɔnz] *pl n* FAM calzones *m* largos.

long jump [ˈlɔŋdʒʌmp] *n* SP salto *m* de longitud.

long-lasting [ˈlɔŋˈlɑːstiŋ] *adj* duradero, ra; que dura mucho tiempo.

long-legged [ˈlɔŋlegd] *adj* de piernas largas, zanquilargo, ga.

long-life [ˈlɔŋlaif] *adj* de larga duración (battery) || de larga conservación (milk).

long-lived [ˈlɔŋˈlivd] *adj* de larga vida, longevo, va (people) || duradero, ra (things) || FIG persistente (error).

long-lost [ˈlɔŋlɔst] *adj* perdido, da de vista desde hace mucho tiempo.

long-necked [ˈlɔŋnekt] *adj* de cuello largo, largo de cuello.

long off [ˈlɔŋˈɔf] *n* SP jugador *m* a la derecha del bateador (in cricket).

long on [ˈɔŋˈɔn] *n sp* jugador *m* a la izquierda del bateador (in cricket).

long play [ˈlɔŋˈplei] *n* disco *m* de larga duración, microsurco *m*.

long-playing [ˈlɔŋˈpleiiŋ] *adj* de larga duración; *a long-playing record* un disco de larga duración.

long primer [ˈlɔŋˈpraimə*] *n* PRINT entredós *m*.

long-range [ˈlɔŋˈreindʒ] *adj* MIL de largo alcance || de larga distancia, transcontinental (plane, etc.) || de mucho alcance (plan, etc.).

long-running [ˈlɔŋˈrʌniŋ] *adj* que permanece mucho tiempo en cartelera (play, film).

longshanks [ˈlɔŋʃæŋks] *n* ZOOL zancuda *f* (bird).

long-shaped [ˈlɔŋʃeipt] *adj* largo, ga (face).

longshore [ˈlɔŋʃɔː*] *adj* MAR costero, ra.

longshoreman [-mən] *n* MAR estibador *m*, cargador *or* descargador de muelle.
— OBSERV El plural de *longshoreman* es *longshoremen*.

long sight [ˈlɔŋˈsait] *n* buena vista *f* || FIG perspicacia *f*, previsión *f*.

longsighted [ˈlɔŋˈsaitid] *adj* MED présbita || FIG previsor, ra; perspicaz.

longsightedness [-nis] *n* MED presbicia *f* || FIG previsión *f*, perspicacia *f*.

long-sleeved [ˈlɔŋˈsliːvd] *adj* de mangas largas.

longsome [ˈlɔŋsəm] *adj* larguísimo, ma.

long-spun [ˈlɔŋspʌm] *adj* interminable.

long-standing [ˈlɔŋˈstændiŋ] *adj* antiguo, gua; viejo, ja; de muchos años.

long stop [ˈlɔŋstɔp] *n* SP jugador *m* detrás del guardameta (in cricket).

long-suffering [ˈlɔŋˈsʌfəriŋ] *adj* sufrido, da; resignado, da; paciente.
◆ *n* paciencia *f*, resignación *f*.

long suit [ˈlɔŋsjuːt] *n* palo *m* fuerte (in cards) || FIG especialidad *f*, punto *m* fuerte.

long-term [ˈlɔŋˈtəːm] *adj* a largo plazo; *a long-term credit* un crédito a largo plazo.

long ton [ˈlɔŋˈtən] *n* tonelada *f* inglesa, tonelada *f* larga [1,016 toneladas métricas].

long-tongued [ˈlɔŋˈtʌŋd] *adj* que tiene la lengua suelta, parlanchín, ina (talkative) || chismoso, sa (gossipy).

long vacation [ˈlɔŋvəˈkeiʃən] *n* vacaciones *f pl* de verano (at schools, University).

long-wave [ˈlɔŋˈweiv] *adj* RAD de onda larga.

longways [ˈlɔŋweiz]; **longwise** [ˈlɔŋwaiz] *adv* a lo largo, longitudinalmente.

long weekend [ˈlɔŋˈwiːkend] *n* puente *m*.

long-winded [ˈlɔŋˈwindid] *adj* prolijo, ja (person) || interminable (story).

loo [luː] *n* FAM retrete *m* || FAM *loo roll* rollo *m* de papel higiénico.

looby [ˈluːbi] *n* patán *m*.

loofah [ˈluːfɑː] *n* esponja *f* vegetal (sponge).

look [luk] *n* mirada *f* (glance); *to have a look at* echar una mirada a || ojeada *f*; *take a look at this report* échele una ojeada a este informe || aspecto *m*, apariencia *f*, apariencias *f pl* (appearance); *by the look of it* según las apariencias; *by the look of her* a juzgar por su aspecto || criterio *m*, manera *f* de ver, punto *m* de vista (viewpoint) || — *by the look of things* según parece || *do you want a look?* ¿quieren verlo? || *have a look!* ¡mire! || *he gave me a severe look* me echó una mirada severa || *I don't like the look of things* no me gusta el aspecto de las cosas, estas cosas me dan mala espina (*fam*) || *I don't like her looks* o *the look of her* no me gusta || *let me* o *let's have a look!* ¡déjeme ver! || *new look* nueva moda, nuevo estilo (fashion), nuevo aspecto (aspect) || *odd look* mirada de extrañeza, mirada extraña || *the portrait has a look of your mother* el retrato se parece bastante a su madre || *to give a look* mirar || *to have* o *to take a look at* mirar, echar un vistazo *or* una mirada a || *to have a look for* buscar || *to have a look round* recorrer con la mirada (to scan), visitar (to visit), inspeccionar (to inspect) || *to have a quick look at* dar *or* echar un vistazo a || *to take a good* o *a long look at* mirar bien, mirar cuidadosamente || *to take a long hard look before doing it* pensarlo bien antes de hacerlo.
◆ *pl* belleza *f sing* || — *good looks* belleza *f* || *she has her mother's looks* se parece a su madre, tiene cierto parecido con su madre || *to have good looks* ser guapo, pa || *to have looks and youth* ser guapo y joven || *to judje by looks* juzgar por las apariencias.

look [luk] *vi* mirar; *we looked but couldn't find it* miramos pero no lo pudimos encontrar || estar; *how pretty you look!* ¡qué guapa estás! || parecer; *he looks ill* parece enfermo; *everything looks all right to me* todo me parece muy bien; *he looked about to die* parecía que estaba a punto de morirse; *it looks as if there is going to be a strike* parece que va a haber una huelga || fijarse; *look and see how clever she is* fíjate y verás qué lista es || mirar, tener cuidado; *look where you put your feet* ten cuidado donde pones los pies || estar orientado hacia, mirar a, dar a (to face) || — *he did look a fool* hizo el ridículo, quedó en ridículo || *how does her hat look?* ¿qué tal le sienta *or* le va el sombrero? || *how does it look?* ¿qué le parece? || *just look!* ¡mira! || *look alive!* ¡muévete!, ¡menéate! || FIG *look before you leap* antes de que te cases mira lo que haces ‖ *look here!* ¡oye!, ¡mira! ‖ *look sharp!* ¡date prisa!, ¡pronto!, ¡rápido! ‖ *look who is talking!* ¡mira quién habla! ‖ *look you!* ¡oye tú! ‖ *to look alike* parecerse ‖ *to look like* parecerse a; *he looks like his mother* se parece a su madre; parecer que; *it looks like snow* parece que va a nevar; parecer; *it looks like glass* parece cristal ‖ *to look well* tener buena cara (person), tener buen aspecto (thing) ‖ *to look well on s.o.* quedarle bien a uno (a garment).

◆ *vt* mirar (to regard intensely, to examine) ‖ expresar con la mirada *or* con los ojos (a feeling); *he looks his despair* expresa con los ojos su desesperación ‖ parecer; *he looks a thief* parece un ladrón ‖ representar; *he looks his age* representa su edad ‖ — *he looks sadness itself* es la viva imagen de la tristeza ‖ *not to look o.s.* no tener buena cara; *he doesn't look himself today* hoy no tiene buena cara ‖ *to look the other way* mirar para el otro lado ‖ *to look the part* encajar muy bien en el papel ‖ *you don't look your usual self today* hoy te encuentro cambiado.

◆ *phr v* **to look about** mirar alrededor de, echar una mirada alrededor de; *to look about one* mirar a su alrededor ‖ — *to look about for* buscar (con los ojos) ‖ **to look after** cuidar de, cuidar a, ocuparse de (to take care of) | encargarse de, ocuparse de (to attend to) | vigilar (to watch over) ‖ **to look ahead** mirar hacia adelante (while driving, etc.) | mirar el porvenir, mirar el futuro ‖ **to look around** echar una mirada alrededor ‖ **to look at** mirar; *don't look at me like that* no me mires así | considerar (to consider) | examinar (to examine) | mirar, enfocar (a situation) ‖ — *fair to look at* agradable a la vista | *he wouldn't look at it* no quiso ni verlo | *to look at her, you wouldn't know she was ill* por su aspecto no dirías que está enferma, al verla no creerías que está enferma ‖ **to look away** apartar la mirada ‖ **to look back** mirar hacia atrás; *he looked back as he left* miró hacia atrás al irse | FIG volverse atrás; *you can't look back at this stage of the work* no se puede volver atrás en esta etapa del trabajo | FIG volver; *I'll look back later* volveré más tarde ‖ — *he never looked back after his first sale* no dejó de prosperar después de su primera venta | *to look back on* recordar ‖ **to look down** recorrer con la mirada (to scan) | bajar la mirada, bajar los ojos (to lower one's eyes) | bajar (price) ‖ — *to look down on* o *upon* mirar por encima del hombro, mirar despectivamente (to disdain), dominar (to dominate); *the tower looks down on the valley* la torre domina el valle ‖ **to look for** buscar (to search); *we are looking for a flat* estamos buscando un piso; *go and look for your book* ve a buscar tu libro | esperar (to expect) ‖ **to look forward** considerar el futuro ‖ — *to look forward to* esperar [con ansia]; *I look forward to seeing you again* espero volverle a ver ‖ **to look in** mirar la televisión (to watch television) | hacer una visita rápida (to visit) ‖ — *to look in at the window* mirar por la ventana | *to look in on s.o.* pasar por casa de alguien (to call) ‖ **to look into** recorrer, hojear (a book) | examinar, estudiar (a question); *I'll look into the matter* estudiaré el asunto ‖ **to look on** mirar | considerar; *he looks on her as a daughter* la considera como a una hija | dar a (to command a view) ‖ **to look out** mirar fuera | escoger (to choose) | buscar (to search); *look out some clothes* busca algunos vestidos | tener cuidado (to be careful) ‖ — *look out!* ¡cuidado! | *to look out for* tener cuidado con (to be careful), estar atento a (to pay attention to), esperar (to wait), vigilar (to keep an eye on), acechar (to watch) | *to look out of* asomarse a, mirar por (the window) | *to look out onto* o *over* dar a; *my window looks out over the street* mi ventana da a la calle; tener vistas a, dar a ‖ **to look over** mirar por encima, echar un vistazo, echar una ojeada a (to look at superficially); *I looked over the document* miré el documento por encima, eché un vistazo al documento | revisar (to check) | inspeccionar, registrar (a place) ‖ — *to look sth. all over* mirar algo por los cuatro costados ‖ **to look round** mirar alrededor (around one) | volver la cabeza (to turn round) | inspeccionar (to visit, to inspect) | *to look round for* buscar ‖ **to look through** echar un vistazo; *to look through a list* echar un vistazo a una lista | mirar por; *he looked through the window* miró por la ventana | mirar sin ver; *he looked right through me* me miró sin verme | registrar (to search) | hojear (a book) | examinar cuidadosamente (to examine carefully) ‖ **to look to** mirar a, dar a; *building that looks to the south* edificio que da al sur | buscar, recurrir a; *I always looked to my father for help* siempre buscaba la ayuda de mi padre | contar con (to count on); *to look to s.o. to* contar con alguien para | cuidar de, velar por (to take care of) | ocuparse de (to attend to) | tender a (to tend to) ‖ **to look up** ponerse mejor, mejorar; *things are looking up* las cosas se están poniendo mejor | mirar para arriba, levantar los ojos (to gaze upwards) | consultar (a list) | buscar, mirar; *I have to look this word up in a dictionary* tengo que buscar esta palabra en un diccionario | venir a ver, venir a visitar (to come and see); *look me up when you come back* ven a verme cuando vuelvas | ir a ver, ir a visitar (to go and see) ‖ — *to look s.o. up and down* mirar a alguien de arriba abajo | *to look up to* respetar, apreciar ‖ **to look upon** mirar, considerar.

look-alike [ˈlukəˈlaik] *n* doble *m* & *f*.

looked-for [ˈluktfɔː*] *adj* esperado, da.

looker [ˈlukə*] *n* espectador, ra ‖ US FAM guapa *f*.

looker-on [ˈlukərˈɔn] *n* espectador, ra.

— OBSERV El plural de *looker-on* es *lookers-on*.

look-in [ˈlukin] *n* visita *f* rápida (quick visit); *I gave her a look-in* le hice una visita rápida.

looking [ˈlukiŋ] *adj* *a queer-looking person* una persona extraña.

— OBSERV Este adjetivo va siempre precedido por otro del cual se separa por un guión.

looking glass [-glɑːs] *n* espejo *m* (mirror).

lookout [ˈlukˈaut] *n* guardia *f* (action of keeping watch) ‖ MIL centinela *m* (man) | mirador *m*, atalaya *f* (post for a guard) | vigilancia *f* (vigilance) ‖ MAR vigía *m* (man) | puesto *m* del vigía (post) ‖ FAM panorama *m*, perspectiva *m* (prospect) | asunto *m*; *if he wants to go, that's his lookout* si quiere ir, es asunto suyo ‖ — *to be on the lookout for* estar al acecho de ‖ *to keep a lookout* estar ojo avizor.

look-see [ˈluksiː] *n* vistazo *m*, ojeada *f*.

loom [luːm] *n* TECH telar *m* (for textiles) ‖ MAR guión *m* (of an oar) ‖ somorgujo *m* (bird) ‖ silueta *f* borrosa (indistinct outline) ‖ aparición *f* (appearance).

loom [luːm] *vi* dibujarse, perfilarse (to appear in silhouette) ‖ surgir, aparecer (to arise) ‖ surgir amenazadoramente (to threaten) ‖ — *to loom large* cobrar mucha importancia ‖ *to loom up out of, to loom up from* surgir de.

loon [luːn] *n* somorgujo *m* (bird) ‖ bobo, ba (simpleton).

loony [-i] *adj* FAM chiflado, da; chalado, da (crazy) ‖ FAM *loony bin* casa *f* de locos.

loop [luːp] *n* lazo *m*, lazada *f*; *a loop in a rope* un lazo en una cuerda ‖ sinuosidad *f*, curva *f* (of a river, of a road) ‖ espira *f* (of a spiral) ‖ presilla *f* (for a button, of a belt) ‖ apartadero *m* (in a railway line) ‖ PHYS antinodo *m* ‖ ELECTR circuito *m* cerrado ‖ AVIAT rizo *m* (in aerobatics); *to loop the loop* rizar el rizo ‖ SP bucle *m* (ice skating) ‖ US *to knock* o *to throw for a loop* asombrar, desconcertar (to throw into bewilderment), trastornar, descomponer (to upset).

loop [luːp] *vt* hacer un lazo en (a rope) ‖ arrollar, enroscar (to roll) ‖ asegurar con presilla (a button) ‖ atar con un lazo (to fasten) ‖ AVIAT rizar; *to loop the loop* rizar el rizo ‖ — *to loop back* recoger con un alzapaño (drapery) ‖ *to loop up* recoger.

◆ *vi* serpentear (to move in loops) ‖ hacer un lazo (a rope) ‖ AVIAT hacer un rizo.

looper [-ə*] *n* ZOOL oruga *f* geómetra [AMER oruga *f* medidora].

loophole [-həul] *n* MIL aspillera *f*, tronera *f* (of a castle) ‖ FIG escapatoria *f*, evasiva *f*, pretexto *m*.

loophole [-həul] *vt* MIL hacer aspilleras *or* troneras en.

loop stitch [-ˈstitʃ] *n* punto *m* de cadeneta.

loopy [-i] *adj* FAM turulato, ta (slightly crazy).

loose [luːs] *adj* holgado, da (not fitting tightly); *a loose coat* un abrigo holgado ‖ suelto, ta; *loose papers* papeles sueltos; *the sheep roamed loose on the hill* las ovejas andaban sueltas por la colina; *loose rein* rienda suelta ‖ flojo, ja (knot, texture, screw) ‖ suelto, ta (hair) ‖ desatado, da (untied) ‖ flojo, ja; *there's a loose button on my shirt* tengo un botón flojo en la camisa; *loose bandage* venda floja ‖ poco firme (earth) ‖ FIG vago, ga; poco preciso, sa; poco exacto, ta; *a loose definition* una definición poco exacta | libre; *a loose translation* una traducción libre | relajado, da; *loose morals* moralidad relajada | licencioso, sa; disoluto, ta (life) | fácil (woman) | desatado, da; suelto, ta; *loose tongue* lengua desatada | sin ilación, inconexo, xa (ideas) | deshilvanado, da (style) | soez, grosero, ra (talk) ‖ MED que se mueve (tooth) | fofo, fa; fláccido, da; flácido, da (skin) | suelto, ta (bowels) ‖ MIL disperso, sa (order) ‖ SP abierto, ta (in rugby) | flojo, ja (fielding in cricket) ‖ COMM a granel, suelto, ta (goods); *do you sell coffee in packages or loose?* ¿vende el café en paquetes o suelto? ‖ TECH desmontable (plant) | flojo, ja (rope) | loco, ca (wheel) ‖ CHEM libre ‖ ELECTR desconectado, da ‖ — SP *a loose ball* una pelota suelta ‖ *loose change, loose cash* suelto *m*, dinero suelto ‖ TECH *loose pulley* polea loca ‖ *of loose build* desgarbado, da; desgalichado, da ‖ *that man is a loose character* aquel hombre es un perdido ‖ *to break* o *to get loose* escaparse ‖ *to cast loose* soltar ‖ *to come* o *to get* o *to work loose* desatarse, aflojarse (knot, rope), desprenderse (part) ‖ *to cut loose* soltar; *to cut a rope loose* soltar una cuerda; soltar las amarras (boat), liberarse (to free o.s. from domination), pasárselo en grande (to enjoy o.s.),soltarse el pelo (to drop all restraint) ‖ *to cut loose from* independizarse de ‖ *to give s.o. a loose rein* dar a alguien rienda suelta ‖ *to hang loose* estar colgado, colgar ‖ FAM *to have a loose tongue* írsele a uno la lengua, no poder callarse, tener la lengua suelta | *to have a screw loose* faltarle a uno un tornillo ‖ FIG *to let loose* dar rienda suelta a; *he let loose his anger* dio rienda suelta a su cólera; enfadarse, echar una bronca; *he let loose at her* se enfadó con ella; írsele a uno la lengua (to speak harshly), soltar (abuse) ‖ *to let* o *to set loose* poner en libertad, soltar (person), soltar (animal).

◆ *n* SP juego *m* abierto (in rugby) ‖ — *on the loose* en libertad (free), suelto, ta (uncontrolled) ‖ *to be* o *to go on the loose* irse de juerga *or* de parranda.

loose [luːs] *vt* poner en libertad, soltar (to set free) ‖ desatar (to untie) ‖ soltar (to unfasten) ‖ aflojar (screw, knot) ‖ soltar (hair) ‖ FIG soltar, desatar (tongue) | desencadenar, desatar (passions) ‖ MAR largar, soltar ‖ REL absolver ‖ — *to loose hold of* soltar ‖ *to loose off* disparar.

◆ *vi* *to loose off* disparar.

loose cover [-ˌkʌvə*] *n* funda *f* (on furniture).

loose end [-end] *n* extremo *m* suelto (sth. hanging free) || FIG cabo *m* suelto (sth. still to be done) || — FIG *at a loose end* desocupado, da | *at loose ends* en desorden | *to tie up the loose ends* no dejar cabo suelto, atar cabos.

loose-fitting [-'fitiŋ] *adj* suelto, ta.

loose-jointed [-'dʒɔintid] *adj* desvencijado, da (thing) || desgarbado, da; desgalichado, da (person).

loose-leaf [-li:f] *adj* de hojas sueltas.

loose-living [-'liviŋ] *adj* de vida alegre.

loosely [-li] *adv* aproximadamente (approximately) || holgadamente (amply) || sin apretar (not tight) || licenciosamente, disolutamente (immorally) || imprecisamente, vagamente (imprecisely).

loosen [-n] *vt* aflojar, soltar (to slacken); *to loosen a screw, a knot* aflojar un tornillo, un nudo || desatar, soltar, deshacer (to untie) || FIG soltar, desatar; *drink loosened his tongue* la bebida le desató la lengua || aliviar, descargar (the bowels) || relajar; *to loosen discipline* relajar la disciplina || AGR mullir (soil) || SP *to loosen up* desentumecer (muscles).

◆ *vi* desatarse || soltarse, aflojarse || MED aliviarse, descargarse (the bowels) || — *my cough has loosened up* se me ha aliviado la tos || SP *to loosen up* calentarse.

looseness [-nis] *n* relajamiento *m* (of morals, of discipline) || aflojamiento *m* (of a rope, of screw) || holgura *f* (of a coat, of a part) || friabilidad *f*, falta *f* de firmeza (of soil) || MED soltura *f* de vientre (of bowels) | flacidez *f*, flaccidez *f* (of skin) | movilidad *f* (of a tooth) || FIG imprecisión *f*, vaguedad *f*, falta *f* de precisión (vagueness).

loose-tongued [-'tʌŋd] *adj* que tiene la lengua suelta.

loot [lu:t] *n* botín *m*, presa *f* (booty) || FAM ganancias *f pl* (earnings) | pasta *f* (money).

loot [lu:t] *vt* saquear (to pillage) || llevar como botín (to carry off).

◆ *vi* entregarse al saqueo.

looter [-ə*] *n* saqueador, ra.

looting [-iŋ] *n* saqueo *m*.

lop [lɔp] *n* recortes *m pl* (cuttings of trees) || chapoteo *m* (of waves).

lop [lɔp] *vt* cortar (branches from a tree) || podar (a tree) || *to lop off* cortar (to cut), llevarse; *taxes lop off half his salary* los impuestos se llevan la mitad de su salario; cercenar (to reduce).

◆ *vi* caer (ears) || colgar (to hang) || saltar (to bound) || chapotear (waves) || *to lop down in* dejarse caer en (an armchair).

lope [ləup] *n* paso *m* largo.

lope [ləup] *vi* andar con paso largo || andar muy de prisa (to walk quickly).

◆ *phr v* *to lope along* andar *or* correr con paso largo || *to lope away* o *off* alejarse con paso largo.

lop-eared ['lɔpiəd] *adj* de orejas gachas, de orejas caídas.

lopsided ['lɔp'saidid] *adj* ladeado, da; torcido, da (drooping at one side) || cojo, ja (table, chair) || desproporcionado, da (unsymmetrical) || desequilibrado, da (unbalanced) || MAR escorado, da (ship).

loquacious [ləu'kweiʃəs] *adj* locuaz.

loquacity [ləu'kwæsiti] *n* locuacidad *f*.

loquat ['ləukwæt] *n* BOT níspero *m* del Japón.

loran ['lɔ:ræn] *n* RAD & AVIAT loran *m* (long range navigation).

lord [lɔ:d] *n* lord *m* (title); *House of Lords* Cámara de los Lores || señor *m* (ruler, feudal estate owner) || REL señor *m* || magnate *m*; *the cotton lords* los magnates del algodón || — FAM *drunk as a lord* borracho como una cuba || *good Lord!* ¡Dios mío! || *lord and master* dueño *m* y señor || REL *Lord of Hosts* Señor de los Ejércitos || *lord of the manor* señor feudal || *my Lord* su Ilustrísima (bishop), su señoría (judge), mi señor (noble) || *Our Lord* Nuestro Señor || REL *the Lord* el Señor || *the Lords* la Cámara de los Lores || *to live like a lord* vivir como un señor.

— OBSERV El título de *Lord* se concede a los duques, marqueses, condes, vizcondes y barones ingleses (en este caso antecede directamente al apellido: *the Earl of Leicester* tiene el título de *Lord Leicester*), a los hijos menores de los duques y marqueses (en cuyo caso antecede al nombre y apellido) y a ciertos dignatarios como el *Lord Mayor* (alcalde).

lord [lɔ:d] *vi* *to lord it* dárselas de gran señor || *to lord it over s.o.* dominar a alguien, tratar despóticamente a alguien.

lord lieutenant [-lef'tenənt] *n* gobernador *m* (of a county) || HIST virrey *m* (in Ireland).

— OBSERV El plural de esta palabra es *lords lieutenant* o *lord lieutenants*.

lordiness [-linis] *n* carácter *m* señorial, señorío *m* || altivez *f*, arrogancia *f* (arrogance).

lordling [-liŋ] *n* hidalgüelo *m*, hidalgo *m* de gotera || FAM señorito *m*.

lordly [-li] *adj* señorial (magnificent) || noble || arrogante, altivo, va (haughty) || *to put on a lordly air* dárselas de gran señor.

Lord Mayor [-'mɛə*] *n* alcalde *m*.

Lord Privy Seal [-'privisi:l] *n* guardasellos *m inv*.

Lord's day ['lɔ:dz'dei] *n* REL día *m* del Señor.

lordship ['lɔ:dʃip] *n* señorío *m*, señoría *f* (dignity) || señorío *m* (lands or estate) || señorío *m* (authority) || *His Lordship* Su Señoría.

Lord's Prayer ['lɔ:dz'prɛə*] *n* Padrenuestro *m*.

lore [lɔ:*] *n* ciencia *f*, saber *m* (knowledge) || *the local lore* la tradición local.

lorgnette [lɔ:'njet] *n* impertinentes *m pl* (eyeglasses) || gemelos *m pl* (opera glasses).

lorica [lə'raikə] *n* loriga *m* (coat of mail).

lorn [lɔ:n] *adj* (ant) solitario, ria.

lorry ['lɔri] *n* camión *m* (truck) || batea *f* (railway carriage) || *lorry driver* camionero *m*.

lose* [lu:z] *vt* perder; *to lose a leg* perder una pierna; *he lost his son* perdió a su hijo; *to lose an opportunity* perder una oportunidad; *he lost the train* perdió el tren; *to lose a match, a battle* perder un partido, una batalla; *all is lost* todo está perdido; *the horse lost the race* el caballo perdió la carrera; *he lost no time in telling us* no perdió tiempo en decírnoslo; *we lost the thread of the conversation* perdimos el hilo de la conversación; *she lost most of the sermon* perdió la mayor parte del sermón || no poder salvar la vida de (a patient) || hacer perder, costar; *her rudeness lost her the job* su grosería le costó el trabajo || atrasar; *my watch loses ten minutes a day* mi reloj atrasa diez minutos por día || — *get lost!* ¡vete al diablo! || *I'm lost without her* estoy perdido sin ella || *not to lose a word of* no perderse una palabra de || *sarcasm is lost on her* el sarcasmo no le hace ningún efecto || *she has not lost by it* no ha perdido nada con eso || *the joke, the music is lost on me* no entiendo el chiste, la música || *the motion is lost* la moción queda rechazada || MAR *to be lost at sea* morir ahogado (people), perderse en el mar, hundirse (boat) || *to be lost in amazement* quedarse asombrado || *to be lost in thought* estar ensimismado *or* absorto en sus pensamientos || *to get lost* perderse || *to give up for lost* dar por perdido || *to look lost* parecer perdido || *to lose ground* perder terreno || *to lose heart* descorazonarse, desanimarse || *to lose one's heart to* enamorarse de, dar su corazón a || *to lose interest* perder interés || *to lose one's head* perder la cabeza || *to lose one's mind* perder la razón *or* el juicio || *to lose one's temper* perder los estribos || *to lose one's voice* perder la voz, quedarse afónico || *to lose one's way* perderse, extraviarse [en el camino] || *to lose o.s.* perderse (on one's way), perderse, perder el hilo (in speaking, in reading) || *to lose o.s. in thought* ensimismarse, abstraerse || *to lose sight of* perder de vista || *to lose weight* perder peso, adelgazar || *to stand to lose nothing* no tener nada que perder.

◆ *vi* perder (to fail to win, to suffer loss); *to lose heavily* perder estrepitosamente || atrasar; *my watch is losing* mi reloj atrasa || *to lose out* salir perdiendo, perder.

— OBSERV Pret y pp ***lost***.

loser [-ə*] *n* perdedor, ra || — *to be a bad loser* no saber perder || *to be a good loser* saber perder || *to be a loser* sufrir *or* tener una pérdida (to suffer a loss), salir siempre perdiendo (to lose always) || *to come off the loser* salir perdiendo.

losing [-iŋ] *adj* vencido, da; derrotado, da (team) || no agraciado, no premiado (number in a lottery) || que deja pérdidas (business) || con pérdida (bargain) || perdedor, ra (card, etc.) || perdido de antemano (game) || malo, la; desventajoso, sa (proposition).

◆ *n* pérdida *f*.

loss [lɔs] *n* pérdida *f* (a losing); *he met with a loss* sufrió una pérdida || daño *m* (damage) || MED pérdida *f* (of blood, of sight, etc.) || derrota *f* (defeat) || COMM pérdida *f*; *to sell at a loss* vender con pérdida || PHYS pérdida *f* (of heat) || TECH pérdida *f* (energy wasted in a machine) || — FIG *at a loss for an answer* sin saber qué contestar || *dead loss* pérdida *f* total (of money), nulidad *f*, birria *f* (things); *the film is a dead loss* la película es una birria; inútil *m* & *f*, nulidad *f* (person) || *it's his loss* es él quien pierde || *loss in transit* objeto perdido durante el transporte || *loss of life* víctimas *f pl*; *there was no loss of life in the accident* en el accidente no hubo víctimas || *loss of memory* pérdida de memoria, amnesia *f* || *to be at a loss* estar perdido, estar desorientado || *to be at a loss for words* no encontrar palabras con que expresarse || *to be at a loss to do sth.* no saber cómo hacer algo.

◆ *pl* pérdidas *f* (of money) || MIL bajas *f* || *to cut one's losses* reducir pérdidas (strict meaning), cortar por lo sano (figurative meaning).

loss leader [-ˌli:də*] *n* artículo *m* de lanzamiento.

lost [lɔst] *pret/pp* ⟶ **lose.**

◆ *adj* perdido, da; *lost property* objetos perdidos; *many lost hours* muchas horas perdidas; *a lost opportunity* una oportunidad perdida; *twenty matches lost* veinte partidos perdidos; *he's lost without his glasses* está perdido sin las gafas || perdido, da; condenado, da; *a lost soul* un alma perdida || insensible (*to* a) (insensible) || absorto, ta; ensimismado, da (engrossed) || — *lost and found* o *lost property office* depósito *m* de objetos perdidos || *lost cause* causa perdida || FIG *lost to* perdido para | *lost to the world* absorto, ta; en otro mundo.

lot [lɔt] *n* porción *f*, parte *f*, lote *m* (portion) || lote *m* (at auction) || lote *m*, partida *f* (set of articles for sale) || parcela *f* (of ground) || solar *m*, terreno *m* (plot in town) || destino *m*, suerte *f* (destiny, fate); *it's the common lot* es el destino de todos || sorteo *m* (draw in lottery) || FAM panda *f*; *they are a lot of criminals* son una panda de criminales | gente *f*; *the wife's parents are a queer lot* los padres de mi mujer son gente muy rara | tipo *m*, individuo *m*, tío *m* (individual); *a dangerous lot* un tipo peligroso | grupo *m*; *a fine lot of people* un grupo de gente simpática | colección *f*; *a fine lot of books* una buena colección de libros | serie *f* (series) || — FAM *a bad lot* una mala persona | *a fat lot* *of good he is!* ¡no sirve para nada! ‖ *a lot* cantidad; *what a lot of money!* ¡qué cantidad de dinero!; mucho, mucha; *a lot of luck* mucha suerte; *thanks a lot* muchas gracias; mucho; *I write a lot* escribo mucho; *he is a lot better today* está mucho mejor hoy ‖ *an awful lot* una barbaridad ‖ *by lots* por sorteo ‖ *in one lot* en bloque ‖ *lots* cantidades, mucho, mucha ‖ *lots of* cantidades de, mucho, mucha; *lots of money* cantidades de dinero; mucho, mucha; *lots of love* mucho cariño ‖ *quite a lot of* bastante; *quite a lot of books* bastantes libros ‖ *such a lot* tanto, ta; *such a lot of lamps* tantas lámparas ‖ *the lot* todo, la totalidad; *that's the lot* eso es todo; *he got the lot* se lo llevó todo ‖ *the whole lot of them* todos ellos ‖ *to cast in one's lot with* probar fortuna con ‖ *to cast* o *to draw lots* echarlo a suertes, echar suertes ‖ *to cast* o *to draw lots for sth.* sortear algo, echar algo a suertes ‖ *to fall to s.o.'s lot* caerle a uno en suerte; incumbirle a uno ‖ *to throw in one's lot with s.o.* compartir la suerte de alguien ‖ *what a lot of!* ¡cuánto!, ¡cuánta!, ¡cuántos!, ¡cuántas!; *what a lot of people!* ¡cuánta gente!

lot [lɔt] *vt* repartir en lotes (to divide).
◆ *vi* US echar suertes.

loth [ləuθ] *adj* ⟶ **loath.**

lotion ['ləuʃən] *n* loción *f.*

lottery ['lɔtəri] *n* lotería *f.*

lotto ['lɔtəu] *n* lotería *f* (game).

lotus ['ləutəs] *n* BOT loto *m* ‖ *lotus position* posición *f* de loto (yoga).

lotus-eater [-,i:tə*] *n* FIG soñador, ra.

loud [laud] *adj* alto, ta; fuerte; *a loud voice* una voz fuerte; *the music is too loud* la música está demasiado alta ‖ fuerte, grande; *a loud noise* un ruido fuerte ‖ ruidoso, sa (noisy); *a loud district* un barrio ruidoso ‖ estrepitoso, sa (laugh) ‖ clamoroso, sa (applause) ‖ sonoro, ra (bell) ‖ categórico, ca; rotundo, da (denial) ‖ flagrante, patente (lie) ‖ chillón, ona; llamativo, va; *loud colours* colores chillones; *a loud shirt* una camisa llamativa ‖ cursi, de mal gusto (in bad taste) ‖ vulgar (unrefined behaviour, person) ‖ — *in a loud voice* en voz alta ‖ *to be loud in one's admiration* manifestar calurosamente su admiración ‖ *to be loud in one's complaints* quejarse a voz en grito ‖ *to be loud in one's praises of* cantar las alabanzas de.
◆ *adv* alto; *to speak loud* hablar alto | fuerte; *a loud thicking clock* un reloj que suena fuerte ‖ ruidosamente (noisily) ‖ estrepitosamente (to laugh) ‖ *to hear loud and clear* oír claramente *or* perfectamente ‖ *to say sth. out loud* decir algo en voz alta.

louden ['laudn] *vt* intensificar.
◆ *vi* intensificarse.

loud-hailer ['laud'heilə*] *n* megáfono *m.*

loudly ['laudli] *adv* en voz alta; *to talk loudly* hablar en voz alta ‖ ruidosamente (noisily) ‖ estrepitosamente (to laugh) ‖ a voz en grito (to shout).

loudmouth ['laud'mauð] *n* FAM gritón, ona (who shouts) | fanfarrón, ona (braggart).

loudmouthed ['laud'mauðd] *adj* FAM gritón, ona (shouting) | fanfarrón, ona (boastful).

loudness ['laudnis] *n* fuerza *f,* intensidad *f* (of a noise) ‖ sonoridad *f* (sonority) ‖ lo chillón (of a dress) ‖ vulgaridad *f* (of behaviour).

loudspeaker ['laud'spi:kə*] *n* altavoz *m* [AMER altoparlante *m*].

lough [lɔk] *n* lago *m* (lake) ‖ ría *f* (an arm of the sea).

louis ['lu:i]; **louis d'or** [-'dɔ:*] *n* luis *m* (coin).

Louis ['lu:i] *pr n* Luis *m.*

Louisa [lu:'izə]; **Louise** [lu'i:z] *pr n* Luisa *f.*

Louisiana [lu:'i:zi'ænə] *pr n* GEOGR Luisiana *f.*

lounge [laundʒ] *n* salón *m* (sitting room) ‖ salón *m* (in hotel, club, bar, etc.) ‖ sofá *m* (long sofa).

lounge [laundʒ] *vi* repantigarse (to sit or stand in a lazy manner) ‖ vagar, gandulear (to saunter idly) ‖ *to lounge about* o *around* repantigarse (to sit in a lazy manner), holgazanear, gandulear (to do nothing).
◆ *vt* *to lounge away* malgastar, desperdiciar, perder ganduleando (time).

lounge car [-kɑ:*] *n* US coche *m* salón.

lounge chair [-tʃɛə*] *n* tumbona *f.*

lounger [-ə*] *n* gandul, la; haragán, ana (idler) ‖ azotacalles *m* & *f inv* (who roams the streets).

lounge suit ['laundz'su:t] *n* traje *m* de calle.

lour; lower ['lauə*] *n* ceño *m,* entrecejo *m* (of a person) ‖ encapotamiento *m* (of the sky).

lour; lower [,lauə*] *vi* fruncir el ceño *or* el entrecejo (to scowl) ‖ FIG amenazar; *the clouds loured on the horizon* las nubes amenazaban en el horizonte | encapotarse (the sky).

louse [laus] *n* piojo *m* (insect) ‖ FIG canalla *m* & *f,* sinvergüenza *m* & *f.*
— OBSERV El plural de *louse* es *lice* cuando se trata del insecto y *louses* en el sentido figurado.

louse [lauz] *vt* FAM *to louse sth. up* echar algo a perder.

lousy [-i] *adj* piojoso, sa (infested with lice) ‖ FAM fatal, malísimo, ma; *the weather is lousy* hace un tiempo fatal ‖ — FAM *a lousy trick* una cochinada | *to be lousy with* estar plagado de; *the place was lousy with detectives* el sitio estaba plagado de detectives; estar forrado de; *he is lousy with money* está forrado de dinero.

lout [laut] *n* bruto *m,* patán *m* (rough fellow).

loutish [-iʃ] *adj* bruto, ta; palurdo, da (boorish).

Louvain ['lu:vɛ̃:ŋ] *pr n* GEOGR Lovaina.

louver; louvre ['lu:və*] *n* persiana *f* (blind, moveable arrangement of slats for ventilation) ‖ respiradero *m* (fixed arrangement of slats for ventilation) ‖ lumbrera *f* (in medieval architecture) ‖ listón *m* (long slat) ‖ tablilla *f* (small slat) ‖ AUT rejilla *f* de ventilación.

louver board [-bɔ:d] *n* tablilla *f.*

louvered [-d] *adj* de tablillas.

louvre ['lu:və*] *n* ⟶ **louver.**

lovable ['lʌvəbl] *adj* adorable, encantador, ra.

love [lʌv] *n* amor *m*; *his love for his wife* su amor por su mujer; *she was the love of his life* ella era el amor de su vida; *mother love* amor materno; *love for thy neighbour* amor al prójimo; *love of money* amor al dinero ‖ amor *m* (loved person); *an old love of his* un viejo amor suyo ‖ cariño *m,* afecto *m* (affection) ‖ pasión *f,* afición *f*; *his love for cricket* su pasión por el cricket, su afición al cricket ‖ amorcillo *m* (cupid) ‖ encanto *m* (lovable person); *your child is a love* su niño es un encanto ‖ SP nada, cero (in tennis); *love, fifteen* nada a quince; *fourty love* cuarenta a cero ‖ — *a labour of love* trabajo desinteresado, trabajo hecho por amor al arte (without payment), trabajo agradable (pleasant) ‖ FAM *cupboard love* amor interesado ‖ *for love* por amor (lovingly); *he did it for love* lo hizo por amor; gratis (free) ‖ *for the love of* por el amor de ‖ *for the love of God!* ¡por Dios!, ¡por el amor de Dios! ‖ *for the love of it* por amor al arte; *to do sth. for the love of it* hacer algo por amor al arte ‖ FAM *for the love of Mike!* ¡por Dios!, ¡por el amor de Dios! ‖ *give my love to your parents* dale recuerdos a tus padres ‖ *he is a little love* es un cielo ‖ *in love with* enamorado de ‖ *love* un abrazo (in letters) ‖ *love at first sight* flechazo *m* ‖ FAM *love in a cottage* contigo pan y cebolla ‖ *love is blind* el amor es ciego ‖ *love letter* carta *f* de amor ‖ *love life* vida *f* amorosa ‖ *my love* mi amor, amor mío ‖ *neither for love nor money, not for love nor money* por nada del mundo, por nada en el mundo, por todo el oro del mundo; *I wouldn't do it for love nor money* no lo haría por todo el oro del mundo ‖ *there is no love lost between them* no se aprecian ‖ *to be in love* estar enamorado ‖ *to fall in love with* enamorarse de ‖ *to make love to* hacer la corte a, hacer el amor a (to court), hacer ei amor con (to have sexual intercourse) ‖ *to marry for love* casarse por amor ‖ *to send one's love to s.o.* enviar cariñosos saludos a ‖ *to work for love* trabajar para el obispo *or* para el rey de Roma ‖ *with much love* con todo el cariño de (in letters) ‖ *with my love* abrazos *m pl* (in letters).

love [lʌv] *vt* querer, amar (to feel love for s.o.); *he loves his parents* quiere a sus padres ‖ tener cariño a (to feel affectionate) ‖ ser muy aficionado a; *he loves tennis* es muy aficionado al tenis ‖ gustarle (a uno) muchísimo, encantarle (a uno); *I should love to go with you* me gustaría muchísimo ir contigo; *I love cakes* me gustan muchísimo los pasteles; *I love cooking* me encanta guisar; *I love this book* me encanta este libro ‖ — *he loves me, he loves me not* me quiere, no me quiere (pulling petals off a daisy) ‖ *I'd love to!* ¡con mucho gusto! ‖ *love me, love my dog* quien quiere a Beltrán, quiere a su can.
◆ *vi* estar enamorado, querer.

loveable ['lʌvəbl] *adj* adorable, encantador, ra.

love affair ['lʌvə,fɛə*] *n* amores *m pl,* amorío *m* (romance) ‖ aventura *f,* intriga *f* amorosa (intrigue).

love apple ['lʌv,æpl] *n* tomate *m.*

lovebird ['lʌvbə:d] *n* ZOOL periquito *m.*
◆ *pl* FIG tórtolos *m* (people in love).

love child ['lʌvtʃaild] *n* hijo *m* natural, hijo *m* del amor.
— OBSERV El plural de *love child* es *love children.*

love feast ['lʌvfi:st] *n* REL ágape *m.*

love-in-a-mist ['lʌvnə'mist] *n* BOT arañuela *f.*

love knot ['lʌvnɔt] *n* lacito *m.*

loveless ['lʌvlis] *adj* sin amor; *loveless marriage* matrimonio sin amor.

loveliness ['lʌvlinis] *n* encanto *m,* belleza *f.*

lovelock ['lʌvlɔk] *n* caracol *m,* rizo *m* en la sien.

lovelorn ['lʌvlɔ:n] *adj* abandonado por su amor (forsaken) ‖ herido de amor, suspirando de amor (languishing).

lovely ['lʌvli] *adj* encantador, ra (lovable); *her grandmother is a lovely person* su abuela es una persona encantadora ‖ precioso, sa; bonito, ta [AMER lindo, da] (beautiful); *isn't it lovely?* ¡qué bonito! ‖ hermoso, sa; precioso, sa; bello, lla [AMER lindo, da] (attractive) ‖ delicioso, sa (delightful) ‖ *to have a lovely time* pasarlo maravillosamente, pasarlo muy bien.
◆ *n* belleza *f.*

lovemaking ['lʌv,meikiŋ] *n* galanteo *m* (courting) ‖ relaciones *f pl* sexuales (sexual intercourse).

love match ['lʌv,mʃ] *n* matrimonio *m* de amor.

love-potion ['lʌv'pəuʃən] *n* filtro *m* de amor.

lover ['lʌvə*] *n* amante *m* & *f* ‖ novio *m* (boyfriend) ‖ novia *f* (girlfriend) ‖ amante *m* & *f*; aficionado, da; amigo, ga; *he is a lover of good music* es un amante de la buena música, es un aficionado a la buena música, es amigo de la buena música.

love seat ['lʌvsi:t] *n* confidente *m* (couch).

lovesick [ˈlʌvsik] *adj* enfermo de amor.

love song [ˈlʌvsɔŋ] *n* MUS romanza *f*, canción *f* de amor.

love story [ˈlʌv,stɔːri] *n* historia *f* de amor.

love token [ˈlʌv,təukən] *n* prueba *f* de amor, prende *f* de amor.

loving [ˈlʌviŋ] *adj* cariñoso, sa (affectionate); *a loving son* un hijo cariñoso ‖ amoroso, sa (feeling or expressing love); *a loving look* una mirada amorosa ‖ aficionado, da (fond of) ‖ *a loving friend* un fiel amigo.

loving cup [-kʌp] *n* copa *f* de la amistad.

loving-kindness [-ˈkaindnis] *n* bondad *f*.

lovingly [-li] *adv* cariñosamente, con cariño (affectionately) ‖ amorosamente (amorously); *he looked at her lovingly* la miró amorosamente.

lovingness [-nis] *n* cariño *m*.

low [ləu] *adj* bajo, ja (in degree, height, intensity, sonority, cost, price, value, wages, speed); *low intelligence* inteligencia baja; *low land* tierra baja; *low number* número bajo; *low price* precio bajo; *in a low voice* en voz baja; *low temperatures* temperaturas bajas ‖ estrecho, cha; poco, ca; *he has a low forehead* tiene poca frente, tiene una frente estrecha ‖ escotado, da (dress, neckline) ‖ pequeño, ña; bajo, ja; reducido, da (small); *profits have been low* los beneficios han sido pequeños ‖ escaso, sa; *supplies are low* los abastecimientos son escasos; *we are low on petrol* estamos escasos de gasolina ‖ poco, ca; poco numeroso, sa; *losses were low in the battle* las bajas fueron pocas en la batalla ‖ bajo, ja; poco profundo, da (shallow) ‖ profundo, da; *a low bow* una reverencia profunda ‖ grosero, ra; vulgar; *a low remark* una observación grosera ‖ vil (mean) ‖ malo, la; *low company* malas compañías; *a low opinion* mala opinión; *a low trick* una mala jugada ‖ humilde (birth, rank); *I am not ashamed of my low birth* no me avergüenzo de mi humilde cuna ‖ deprimido, da; abatido, da (depressed); *to feel low* estar deprimido ‖ desanimado, da; desalentado, da (downhearted) ‖ débil (weak); *a low moan was heard* se oyó un débil quejido ‖ REL rezada (mass) ‖ GEOGR & MAR bajo, ja ‖ MED bajo, ja (blood pressure) ‖ BIOL primitivo, va ‖ tenue, bajo, ja (light) ‖ CULIN lento, ta (fire) ‖ MUS grave, bajo, ja ‖ bajo (Latin, German) ‖ — *low season* temporada *f* baja ‖ *to be in low spirits* estar desanimado ‖ *to get low* empezar a escasear ‖ FIG *to keep a low profile* no llamar la atención, ser discreto ‖ *to lay low* derribar (to overthrow), postrar (en cama) (to make bedridden) ‖ *to lie low* permanecer escondido (to keep hidden), mantenerse quieto (to keep quiet).
◆ *adv* bajo; *to fly low* volar bajo; *to speak, to sing low* hablar, cantar bajo ‖ profundamente; *to bow low* inclinarse profundamente ‖ poco; *to play low* jugar poco; *to bet low* apostar poco ‖ barato, ta (cheap); *to be sold low* venderse barato ‖ recientemente (recently) ‖ — *cut low* (muy) escotado, da (dress) ‖ *lowest paid workers* los obreros peor pagados ‖ FIG *to fall as low as to* caer en una bajeza tal que | *to fall low* caer muy bajo ‖ MED *to feed low* ponerse a dieta ‖ *to hit low* dar un golpe bajo.
◆ *n* AUT primera *f* (first gear); *put the car in low* ponga el coche en primera ‖ area *f* de baja presión, depresión *f* (in meteorology) ‖ FIG lo más bajo, punto *m* más bajo (low level) ‖ FAM *to be at an all-time low* estar más bajo que nunca.

low [ləu] *n* mugido *m* (moo of a cow).

low [ləu] *vi* mugir (a cow).

low-altitude [-ˈæltitjud] *adj* a poca altura.

lowborn [-ˈbɔːn] *adj* de familia humilde, de humilde cuna, de origen modesto.

lowboy [-bɔi] *n* US cómoda *f*.

lowbred [-bred] *adj* mal educado, da; malcriado, da.

lowbrow [-brau] *n* persona *f* de poca cultura, ignorante *m* & *f*.
◆ *adj* de poca cultura, ignorante.

Low Church [-ˈtʃəːtʃ] *n* iglesia *f* anglicana que no da mucha importancia a los ritos y al dogma.

low-class [-klɑːs] *adj* de clase baja, de clase humilde.

low comedy [-ˈkɔmidi] *n* farsa *f*.

low-cost [-ˈkɔst] *adj* económico, ca; barato, ta.

Low Countries [-ˈkʌntriz] *pl prn* GEOGR Países *m* Bajos.

low-cut [-kʌt] *adj* (muy) escotado, da (dress).

low-down [-daun] *adj* FAM vil, bajo, ja.

lowdown [-daun] *n* FAM *to give s.o. the lowdown* dar informes confidenciales a alguien (to inform), decir la verdad a alguien (to tell the truth).

lower [-ə*] *comp adj* más bajo ‖ inferior; *the lower jaw* la mandíbula inferior ‖ bajo, ja ‖ reciente (recent) ‖ ⟶ **low.**
◆ *comp adv* más bajo ‖ ⟶ **low.**

lower [-ə*] *vt* bajar ‖ bajar (the voice) ‖ lanzar (lifeboats) ‖ arriar (flag, sails) ‖ reducir, disminuir, bajar, aminorar (to reduce) ‖ rebajar, bajar (price) ‖ debilitar (to weaken) ‖ FIG rebajar, humillar ‖ FIG *to lower o.s.* rebajarse.
◆ *vi* bajar.

lower [ˈlauə*] *n/vi* ⟶ **lour.**

lowercase [ˈləuəkeis] *n* PRINT caja *f* baja.

lower class [ˈləuə,klɑːs] *n* clase *f* baja.

lower-class [ˈləuə,klɑːs] *adj* de clase baja.

Lower House [ˈləuə,haus] *n* Cámara *f* Baja.

lowering [ˈlauəriŋ] *adj* amenazador, ra (weather) ‖ ceñudo, da; con el entrecejo fruncido (person) ‖ encapotado, da; cubierto, ta (sky).

lowermost [ˈləuəməust] *adj* más bajo, ja.

lowest [ˈləuist] *superl adj* más bajo, ja; *the lowest score* la puntuación más baja ‖ mínimo, ma; *lowest price* precio mínimo ‖ MATH *lowest common denominator, multiple* mínimo común denominador, múltiplo.
◆ *n* mínimo *m*; *at the lowest* como mínimo; *prices are at their lowest* los precios han bajado al mínimo ‖ *the lowest of the low* de lo peor que hay.

low-fat [-fæt] *adj* descremado, da; bajo en calorías (dairy products).

low frequency [-ˈfriːkwənsi] *n* baja frecuencia *f*.

low-frequency [ˈləuˈfriːkwənsi] *adj* de baja frecuencia.

low gear [ˈləuˈgiə*] *n* AUT primera velocidad *f*, primera *f*; *the car was in low gear* el coche estaba en primera.

low-grade [ˈləuˈgreid] *adj* de baja calidad.

low-heeled [ˈləuˈhiːld] *adj* con tacones bajos.

lowing [ˈləuiŋ] *n* mugidos *m pl* (of a cow).

low-key [ˈləukiː] *adj* discreto, ta.

lowland [ˈləulənd] *n* tierra *f* baja.
◆ *pl* *the Lowlands* la Baja Escocia.
◆ *adj* de tierra baja ‖ de la Baja Escocia.

lowlander [-ə*] *n* habitante *m* & *f*, de tierra baja ‖ habitante *m* & *f*, de la Baja Escocia.

low-level [ˈləuˈlevl] *adj* de bajo nivel ‖ de grado inferior, subalterno, na (staff).

lowliness [ˈləulinis] *n* humildad *f*, modestia *f* (humbleness).

lowly [ˈləuli] *adj* humilde, modesto, ta (humble) ‖ inferior.
◆ *adv* humildemente.

low-lying [ˈləuˈlaiiŋ] *adj* bajo, ja.

low-minded [ˈləuˈmaindid] *adj* vulgar, chabacano, na.

low-necked [ˈləuˈnekt] *adj* escotado, da (dress).

lowness [ˈləunis] *n* falta *f* de altura, poca altura *f* (lack of height) ‖ poca estatura *f* (in stature) ‖ FIG bajeza *f* (meanness) | humildad *f*, condición *f* modesta (humbleness) | desánimo *m*, desaliento *m* (discouragement) ‖ baratura *f*, lo barato (of price) ‖ gravedad *f* (of voice).

low-paid *adj* mal pagado, da (worker, job).
◆ *pl n* trabajadores *m* con sueldos bajos.

low-pitched [ˈləuˈpitʃt] *adj* MUS bajo, ja; grave (voice) ‖ ARCH poco inclinado, da (roof) | de techo bajo (room) ‖ FIG poco elevado, da (ideals).

low pressure [ˈləuˈpreʃə*] *n* baja presión *f*.

low-pressure [ˈləuˈpreʃə*] *adj* de baja presión.

low-priced [ˈləuˈpraist] *adj* barato, ta (cheap).

low relief [ˈləuriˈliːf] *n* ARTS bajorrelieve *m*, bajo relieve *m*.

low-spirited [ˈləuˈspiritid] *adj* deprimido, da; desanimado, da.

Low Sunday [ˈləuˈsʌndi] *n* Domingo *m* de Cuasimodo.

low-tension [ˈləuˈtenʃən] *adj* de baja tensión, de bajo voltaje.

low tide [ˈləuˈtaid] *n* marea *f* baja, bajamar *f*.

low water [ˈləuˈwɔːtə*] *n* marea *f* baja, bajamar *f* ‖ FIG decadencia *f* (decline) ‖ FIG *to be in low water* estar apurado.

low-water mark [-mɑːk] *n* estiaje *m*.

lox [lɔks] *n* CULIN salmón *m* ahumado ‖ oxígeno *m* líquido.

loyal [ˈlɔiəl] *adj* leal (true to one's ruler); *loyal subjects* súbditos leales ‖ fiel (faithful); *loyal supporters* fieles partidarios.

loyalist [-ist] *n* leal *m* & *f* ‖ legitimista *m* & *f* (in England).

loyalty [ˈlɔiəlti] *n* lealtad *f*, fidelidad *f* (to a king) ‖ fidelidad *f* (to a person, to a cause, etc.).

lozenge [ˈlɔzindʒ] *n* rombo *m* (four-sided figure) ‖ pastilla *f*, tableta *f* (medicinal sweet) ‖ HERALD losange *m*.

LP [ˈelˈpiː] *adj* de larga duración.
◆ *n* disco *m* de larga duración, microsurco *m* (record).
— OBSERV *LP* son las iniciales de *long-playing*.

L-plate *n* placa *f* de la ele (for driving learner).

Luanda [luːˈændə] *pr n* GEOGR Luanda.

Ltd; ltd *abbr of [limited (liability)]* SA, sociedad anónima.

lubber [ˈlʌbə*] *n* marinero *m* de agua dulce (landlubber) ‖ palurdo *m* (clumsy person).

lubberly [-li] *adj* palurdo, da; torpe.
◆ *adv* torpemente.

lubricant [ˈluːbrikənt] *n* lubricante *m*, lubrificante *m* (grease, oil, etc.).
◆ *adj* lubricante, lubrificante.

lubricate [ˈluːbrikeit] *vt* lubricar, lubrificar ‖ FAM *lubricated* tajado, da (drunk).

lubricating [-iŋ] *adj* lubricante, lubrificante.

lubrication [,luːbriˈkeiʃən] *n* lubricación *f*, lubrificación *f*, engrase *m*.

lubricator ['lu:brikeitə*] *n* lubricante *m*, lubrificante *m* (lubricant).

lubricity [lu:'brisiti] *n* lubricidad *f* (slipperiness) || FIG lubricidad *f* (lewdness) | duplicidad *f*, carácter *m* esquivo (trickiness).

lubricous ['lu:brikəs] *adj* lúbrico, ca; resbaladizo, za (slippery) || FIG lúbrico, ca (lewd) || huidizo, za; esquivo, va (tricky).

luce [lu:s] *n* lucio *m* (fish).

lucency ['lu:snsi] *n* claridad *f*, luminosidad *f*.

lucent ['lu:snt] *adj* luminoso, sa (luminous) || translúcido, da; transparente (transparent).

lucern; lucerne [lu:'sə:n] *n* BOT alfalfa *f*.

lucid ['lu:sid] *adj* claro, ra; lúcido, da; resplandeciente (clear) || MED lúcido, da; *a lucid interval* un intervalo lúcido || FIG lúcido, da (mind) | claro, ra (style, speech).

lucidity [lu:'siditi] *n* lucidez *f*, brillantez *f*, claridad *f* (clarity) || FIG lucidez *f* (of thinking) | claridad *f* (of style, of speech) || MED lucidez *f*.

lucifer ['lu:sifə*] *n* fósforo *m* (match).

Lucifer ['lu:sifə*] *pr n* REL Lucifer *m* || ASTR Venus *m*, Lucífero *m*, Lucifer *m*.

luciferous [lu:'sifərəs] *adj* lucífero, ra.

luck [lʌk] *n* suerte *f* (good fortune); *to wish s.o. luck* desearle a uno suerte || destino *m*, suerte *f* (fate) || — *as luck would have it* el azar *or* la suerte quiso que || *a stroke of luck* una suerte, un golpe de suerte, un momento de suerte || *beginner's luck* suerte del principiante || *better luck next time* otra vez será || *good luck!* ¡buena suerte!, ¡suerte! || *good luck to you!* ¡que tengas suerte! || *hard* o *bad luck* mala suerte || *here's luck!* ¡mucha suerte! || *just my luck!* ¡mi mala suerte de siempre!, ¡qué mala suerte la mía! || *luck is blind* la suerte es ciega || *no such luck!* ¡ojalá! || *that's your hard luck!* ¡peor para ti!, ¡allá tú! || *the best of luck!* ¡qué tengas mucha suerte! || *the luck has turned* la suerte ha cambiado || *to be in luck* estar de *or* con suerte || *to be out of luck, to be down on one's luck* no tener suerte, estar de mala suerte, estar de malas || *to bring bad luck* traer *or* dar mala suerte || *to do sth. trusting to luck* hacer algo confiando en la suerte || *to have the luck of the devil* tener una suerte de mil demonios || *to keep sth. for luck* conservar algo pensando que puede traer suerte || *to push one's luck* tentar la suerte || *to trust to luck that* confiar que || *to try one's luck* probar fortuna || FAM *what rotten luck!* ¡qué suerte más negra *or* más perra! || *with a bit of luck, with any luck* con un poco de suerte || *worse luck* mala suerte; *I can't go out, worse luck!* no puedo salir, ¡mala suerte!

luckily [-ili] *adv* por suerte, afortunadamente, por fortuna.

luckiness [-inis] *n* suerte *f*, fortuna *f*.

luckless [-lis] *adj* desafortunado, da.

lucky [-i] *adj* afortunado, da; *a lucky event* un acontecimiento afortunado || afortunado, da; con suerte; *a lucky person* una persona con suerte; *lucky in love* afortunado en amores || que trae suerte (charm, etc.) || oportuno, na; *he came at a lucky moment* llegó en un momento oportuno || propicio, cia (hour) || favorable, de buen agüero (day) || — *how lucky!* ¡qué suerte! || *it was lucky for you that* menos mal que || *lucky dip* caja *f* de las sorpresas || *lucky strike* suerte || *thank your lucky stars!* ¡bendice tu buena estrella! || *third time lucky* a la tercera va la vencida || *to be a lucky sort* tener mucha suerte || *to be born lucky* o *under a lucky star* haber nacido con buena estrella || *to be lucky enough to* tener la suerte de || *to be lucky in that* tener la suerte de que || *to be lucky to* tener la suerte de.

lucrative ['lu:krətiv] *adj* lucrativo, va.

lucre ['lu:kə*] *n* lucro *m* || *filthy lucre* el vil metal.

Lucretia [lu:'kri:ʃjə] *pr n* Lucrecia *f*.

Lucretius [lu:'kri:ʃjəs] *pr n* HIST Lucrecio *m*.

lucubrate ['lu:kjubreit] *vi* lucubrar, elucubrar.

lucubration [,lu:kju'breiʃən] *n* lucubración *f*, elucubración *f*.

ludicrous ['lu:dikrəs] *adj* absurdo, da; ridículo, la; grotesco, ca.

ludicrousness [-nis] *n* ridiculez *f*, lo ridículo, lo absurdo, lo grotesco.

ludo ['lu:dəu] *n* parchís *m*, parchesi *m*.

luff [lʌf] *n* MAR orza *f*.

luff [lʌf] *vi* MAR orzar.

luffa ['lʌfə] *n* US estropajo *m*.

lug [lʌg] *n* MAR vela *f* al tercio (lugsail) || agarradero *m* [AMER agarradera *f*] (handle) || asa *f* (of a casserole) || TECH espiga *f*, saliente *m* (spike) || ELECTR lengüeta *f* de conexión (for soldering wires) || tirón *m* (a tug, pull) || orejera *f* (of a cap) || ZOOL arenícola *f*, gusano *m* (lugworm) || FAM oreja *f* (ear).

lug [lʌg] *vt* arrastrar (to drag) || — *to lug sth. about* cargar con algo || *to lug in a subject* sacar un tema a colación || *to lug s.o. off* llevarse a alguien.

◆ *vi* arrastrar.

luge [lu:dʒ] *n* SP trineo *m* (sledge).

luggage ['lʌgidʒ] *inv m* equipaje *m* (baggage) || maletas *f pl* (suitcases and trunks) || *luggage in advance* equipaje facturado.

luggage boot [-bu:t] *n* AUT maleta *f*, maletero *m*.

luggage carrier [-,kæriə*] *n* portaequipajes *m inv*.

luggage porter [-,pɔ:tə*] *n* mozo *m* de equipajes.

luggage rack [-ræk] *n* AUT portaequipajes *m inv*, baca *f* || redecilla *f* (in a train, a coach, a plane).

luggage trolley [-,trɔli] *n* carretilla *f*.

luggage van [-væn] *n* furgón *m* de equipajes.

lugger ['lʌgə*] *n* MAR lugre *m* (ship).

lugsail ['lʌgseil] *n* MAR vela *f* al tercio.

lugubrious [lu:'gu:briəs] *adj* lúgubre, lóbrego, ga; tétrico, ca.

lugworm ['lʌgwə:m] *n* ZOOL arenícola *f*, gusano *m*.

Luke [lu:k] *pr n* Lucas *m* || *the Gospel according to St Luke* el Evangelio según San Lucas.

lukewarm [-wɔ:m] *adj* tibio, bia; templado, da (tepid) || FIG tibio, bia; poco entusiasta (half-hearted).

lull [lʌl] *n* calma *f*, recalmón *m* (in storm, in wind) || FIG tregua *f*, momento *m* de calma, pausa *f*, respiro *m* (truce) || FIG *the lull before the storm* una tensa calma que anuncia la tempestad.

lull [lʌl] *vt* calmar, sosegar (to calm, to soothe) || MAR calmar (sea, wind) || acallar (to quiet) || *to lull to sleep* arrullar, adormecer (to send to sleep), mecer, acunar (to rock).

◆ *vi* calmarse (to become less intense) || amainar, encalmarse (wind, storm) || calmarse (sea).

lullaby ['lʌləbai] *n* canción *f* de cuna, nana *f*.

lumbago [lʌm'beigəu] *n* MED lumbago *m*.

lumbar ['lʌmbə*] *adj* ANAT lumbar.

lumber ['lʌmbə*] *n* trastos *m pl* viejos (junk) || maderos *m pl*, madera *f* (wood).

lumber ['lʌmbə*] *vt* abarrotar, atestar, cargar; *the room was lumbered with old furniture* la habitación estaba abarrotada de muebles viejos || amontonar (to pile up) || talar (to fell timber) || — FIG *to lumber s.o. with sth.* hacer que alguien cargue con algo || *to lumber together* amontonar.

◆ *vi* talar, cortar madera (to fell timber) || moverse *or* andar pesadamente (to move clumsily).

lumberer [-rə*] *n* leñador *m* (woodcutter) || FIG torpe.

lumbering [-riŋ] *adj* torpe, pesado, da (moving heavily) || pesado, da (heavy).

◆ *n* explotación *f* forestal (timber industry).

lumberjack ['lʌmbədʒæk] *n* leñador *m* (woodcutter).

lumberman ['lʌmbəmən] *n* leñador *m* (woodcutter) || maderero *m*, negociante *m* en maderas (who deals in timber).

— OBSERV El plural de *lumberman* es *lumbermen*.

lumber mill ['lʌmbəmil] *n* aserradero *m*.

lumber room ['lʌmbərum] *n* cuarto *m* trastero, cuarto *m* de los trastos.

lumber trade ['lʌmbətreid] *n* industria *f* maderera.

lumberyard ['lʌmbəja:d] *n* almacén *m or* depósito *m* de madera.

lumen ['lumən] *n* lumen *m* [unidad de flujo luminoso] (measure of light) || ANAT abertura *f*.

— OBSERV El plural de la palabra inglesa es *lumina* o *lumens*.

luminary ['lu:minəri] *n* ASTR luminar *m*, cuerpo *m* luminoso || FIG lumbrera *f* (outstanding person).

luminescence [,lu:mi'nesns] *n* PHYS luminiscencia *f*, luminescencia *f*.

luminescent [,lu:mi'nesnt] *adj* PHYS luminiscente, luminescente.

luminiferous [,lu:mi'nifərəs] *adj* luminoso, sa.

luminosity [,lu:mi'nɔsiti] *n* luminosidad *f*.

luminous ['lu:minəs] *adj* luminoso, sa; *luminous flux* flujo luminoso || *luminous energy* energía *f* radiante.

lummox ['lʌməks] *n* US FAM ganso *m*, tonto *m*.

lummy ['lʌmi] *interj* FAM ¡caray!

lump [lʌmp] *n* trozo *m*, pedazo *m*; *a lump of coal* un trozo de carbón || terrón *m* (of sugar, of earth) || bloque *m* (of stone) || grumo *m* (in cooking) || masa *f*, montón *m* (mass) || pella *f*; *a lump of clay* una pella de arcilla || protuberancia *f*, bulto *m* (swelling) || MED chichón *m* (bruise) || FIG nudo *m*; *to have a lump in one's throat* tener un nudo en la garganta | conjunto *m*, masa *f*, totalidad *f* (whole) || FIG & FAM pelmazo, za; pelma *m* & *f* (bore); *he is a lump* es un pelmazo | imbécil *m* & *f*, bobo, ba (fool).

lump [lʌmp] *vt* amontonar (to put together) || agrupar (to treat alike) || FAM aguantar (to bear); *you'll just have to lump it* tendrás que aguantarte.

◆ *vi* hacerse grumos (in cooking) || apelmazarse (clay) || aterronarse (earth, etc.) || *to lump about* o *along* andar *or* moverse pesadamente.

lumper [-ə*] *n* MAR cargador *m*, descargador *m*, estibador *m* (docker).

lumpish [-iʃ] *adj* FAM bobalicón, ona (stupid) | torpe (clumsy) | pesado, da (heavy, boring).

lumpishness [-iʃnis] *n* FAM necedad *f* (stupidity) | torpeza *f* (clumsiness) | pesadez *f* (bore).

lump sugar [-'ʃugə*] *n* azúcar *m* en terrones *or* de cortadillo.

lump sum [-ˈsʌm] *n* cantidad *f* total, suma *f* global (total amount) || precio *m* a tanto alzado (overall estimate).

lumpy [-i] *adj* apelmazado, da (clay) || aterronado, da (earth) || en terrones (sugar) || grumoso, sa (sauce, food) || granuloso, sa (skin) || con chichones (with bruises) || cubierto de protuberancias *or* bultos (surface) || picado, da (sea) || lleno de bultos (bed) || torpe (clumsy).

lunacy [ˈluːnəsi] *n* locura *f* || *it's sheer lunacy!* ¡es una locura!, ¡es un disparate!

lunar [ˈluːnə*] *adj* lunar.

lunar landing [ˈluːnə*ˈlændiŋ] *n* alunizaje *m*, aterrizaje *m* en la Luna.

lunar month [ˈluːnə*ˈmʌnθ] *n* mes *m* lunar.

lunar year [ˈluːnə*jəː*] *n* año *m* lunar.

lunate [ˈluːneit] *adj* lunado, da; en forma de media Luna.

lunatic [ˈluːnətik] *adj* loco, ca (insane) || lunático, ca (whimsical) || descabellado, da; *a lunatic plan* un proyecto descabellado.
◆ *n* loco, ca.

lunatic asylum [-əˈsailəm] *n* manicomio *m*.

lunatic fringe [-frindʒ] *n* extremistas *m pl*, fanáticos *m pl*.

lunation [luːˈneiʃən] *n* ASTR lunación *f*.

lunch [lʌntʃ]; **luncheon** [ˈlʌntʃən] *n* almuerzo *m* (midday meal) || US refrigerio *m*, bocado *m* (snack) || — *buffet lunch* lunch *m* || *lunch hour* hora *f* de comer || *to have* o *to take lunch* almorzar, comer.

lunch [lʌntʃ] *vi* almorzar.
◆ *vt* convidar a almorzar a.

lunch basket [-ˌbɑːskit] *n* cesta *f* de la comida.

lunch counter [ˌkauntə*] *n* cafetería *f*, snack-bar *m*.

luncheon [ˈlʌntʃən] *n* ⟶ **lunch.**

luncheon basket [-ˌbɑːskit] *n* cesta *f* de la comida.

luncheonette [ˌlʌnʃənˈet] *n* US cafetería *f*, snack-bar *m*.

luncheon meat [ˈlʌntʃənˌmiːt] *n* CULIN embutido *m* de cerdo en lata.

luncher [ˈlʌntʃə*] *n* persona *f* que almuerza.

lunchroom [ˈlʌntʃrum] *n* US restaurante *m* pequeño.

lunchtime [ˈlʌntʃtaim] *n* hora *f* de comer, hora *f* del almuerzo.

lune [luːn] *n* MATH lúnula *f*.

lunes [-z] *pl n* ataques *m* de locura.

lunette [luːˈnet] *n* ARCH luneto *m* || MIL luneta *f*.

lung [lʌŋ] *n* ANAT pulmón *m*; *iron lung* pulmón de acero; *lung cancer* cáncer del pulmón || FIG *to shout at the top of one's lungs* gritar a voz en cuello *or* a voz en grito *or* con todas las fuerzas de los pulmones.

lunge; **longe** [lʌndʒ] *n* embestida *f*, arremetida *f* (sudden forward movement) || SP estocada *f* (in fencing) || ronzal *m*, cabestro *m* (rope for training horses).

lunge [lʌndʒ] *vt* domar, amaestrar (to train horses).
◆ *vi* lanzarse, arremeter, embestir (to move forwards suddenly) || SP atacar, tirarse a fondo (in fencing) || *to lunge (out) at* arremeter contra.

lunger [ˈlʌŋə*] *n* US FAM tísico, ca.

lunula [ˈluːnjulə] *n* MATH lúnula *f* || lúnula *f*, blanco *m* de las uñas (of nails).
— OBSERV El plural de la palabra inglesa es *lunulae*.

lunule [ˈluːnjuːl] *n* lúnula *f*, blanco *m* de las uñas.

Lupercalia [ˌluːpəːˈkeiljə] *pl n* Lupercales *f*.

lupin; US **lupine** [ˈluːpin] *n* BOT altramuz *m*, lupino *m*.

lurch [ləːtʃ] *n* guiñada *f*, bandazo *m* (of a boat) || bandazo *m* (of a vehicle, person, moving object) || sacudida *f* (jolt) || FAM *to leave s.o. in the lurch* dejar a alguien en la estacada.

lurch [ləːtʃ] *vi* dar bandazos, guiñar (boat) || dar bandazos (vehicle, person) || dar sacudidas (to jolt) || *to lurch along* ir dando bandazos (vehicle), ir tambaleándose, ir dando bandazos (drunkard).

lurcher [-ə*] *n* ratero, ra; mangante *m* & *f*, ladronzuelo, la (thief) || cazador *m* furtivo (poacher) || perro *m* de cazador furtivo (dog).

lure [ljuə*] *n* señuelo *m* (in falconry) || cebo *m* (device to attract animals) || FIG señuelo *m*, añagaza *f* (bait) | aliciente *m*, atractivo *m* (incentive); *the lure of adventure* el aliciente de la aventura | atractivo *m*, encanto *m*; *the lures of a woman* los encantos de una mujer.

lure [ljuə*] *vt* engañar con el señuelo (in falconry) || FIG atraer || — *to lure s.o. away from* apartar a uno de || *to lure s.o. into a trap* hacer que alguien caiga en una trampa || *to lure s.o. into doing sth.* convencer a alguien de que haga algo.

lurid [ˈljuərid] *adj* espeluznante (violent and shocking) || sensacionalista, sensacional || lívido, da; pálido, da (pale, ashen) || chillón, ona; llamativo, va (gaudy).

lurk [ləːk] *vi* estar escondido, esconderse (to be hidden) || estar al acecho (to lie in wait) || FIG rondar (to be constantly present); *the suspicion lurked in her mind* la sospecha rondaba por su mente.

lurker [-ə*] *n* persona *f* que está al acecho || espía *m* (spy).

lurking [-iŋ] *adj* oculto, ta; vago, ga || *lurking place* escondite *m* (hiding place), puesto *m* (of hunter).

Lusaka [luːˈsɑːkə] *pr n* GEOGR Lusaka.

luscious [ˈlʌʃəs] *adj* exquisito, ta; delicioso, sa (smells, tastes, etc.) || exquisito, ta (colours) || apetitoso, sa (woman) || voluptuoso, sa (impressions, feelings) || dulzón, ona (sickeningly sweet) || empalagoso, sa (style).

lusciousness [-nis] *n* exquisitez *f* || voluptuosidad *f* (voluptuousness).

lush [lʌʃ] *adj* exuberante, lujuriante (vegetation) || verde (grass) || FIG exuberante, florido, da (writing).
◆ *n* FAM borracho, cha (drunkard).

lushy [-i] *adj* FAM tajado, da (drunk).

Lusiads (the) [ˈluːsiædz] *pl prn* los Lusiadas.

Lusitania [ˌluːsiˈteinjə] *pr n* GEOGR Lusitania *f*.

Lusitanian [-n] *adj/n* lusitano, na.

lust [lʌst] *n* lujuria *f*, lascivia *f* (sexual desire) || ansia *f*, anhelo *m*, apetito *m*, gran deseo *m* (great desire) || REL concupiscencia *f*.

lust [lʌst] *vi* *to lust for* o *after* codiciar (sth.), desear (s.o.).

luster [-ə*] *n/vt* US ⟶ **lustre.**

lusterless [-əlis] *adj* US ⟶ **lustreless.**

lusterware [-əwɛə*] *n* US ⟶ **lustreware.**

lustful [-ful] *adj* lujurioso, sa; lascivo, va; lúbrico, ca; libidinoso, sa (person) || lleno de deseo (look).

lustfulness [-fulnis] *n* lujuria *f*, lascivia *f*.

lustily [-ili] *adv* fuertemente.

lustiness [-inis] *n* fuerza *f*, vigor *m*.

lustrate [ˈlʌstreit] *vt* purificar, lustrar.

lustration [lʌsˈtreiʃən] *n* purificación *f*, lustración *f*.

lustre; US **luster** [ˈlʌstə*] *n* lustre *m* (gloss) || brillo *m* (radiance, brightness) || lustre *m*, brillo *m* (on a cloth) || aguas *f pl* (of a diamond) || colgante *m* (glass pendant) || araña *f* (chandelier hung with pendants) || barniz *m* vítreo, vidriado *m* (on pottery) || cerámica *f or* loza *f* vidriada, cerámica *f* decorada con reflejos metálicos (lustreware) || FIG lustre *m* (renown, distinction) || lustrina *f* (fabric) || lustro *m* (period of five years).

lustre [ˈlʌstə*] *vt* lustrar, dar brillo || lustrar (cloth) || vidriar (pottery).

lustreless; US **lusterless** [-lis] *adj* sin brillo, deslustrado, da.

lustreware; US **lusterware** [-wɛə*] *n* cerámica *f or* loza *f* vidriada, cerámica *f* decorada con reflejos metálicos.

lustring [ˈlʌstriŋ] *n* lustrina *f*.

lustrous [ˈlʌstrəs] *adj* brillante.

lustrum [ˈlʌstrəm] *n* lustro *m* (five years).
— OBSERV El plural de la palabra inglesa es *lustra* o *lustrums*.

lusty [ˈlʌsti] *adj* fuerte, robusto, ta (person) || fuerte (shout).

lutanist [ˈluːtənist] *n* tañedor *m* de laúd.

lute [luːt] *n* zulaque *m* (cement for pipes) || MUS laúd *m*.

lute [luːt] *vt* zulacar, tapar con zulaque.

lutein [ˈljuːtiin] *n* luteína *f*.

luteous [ˈljuːtiəs] *adj* lúteo, a; amarillento, ta.

lute player [ˈluːtˌpleiə*] *n* tañedor *m* de laúd.

lutestring [ˈljuːtstriŋ] *n* lustrina *f*.

Lutetia [luˈtiːʃjə] *pr n* HIST Lutecia *f*.

lutetium [luˈtiʃiəm] *n* lutecio *m* (metal).

Luther [ˈluːθə*] *pr n* Lutero *m*.

Lutheran [-rən] *adj/n* luterano, na.

Lutheranism [-rənizəm] *n* luteranismo *m*.

lutist [ˈluːtist] *n* tañedor *m* de laúd (player) || fabricante *m* de laúdes (maker).

luv [lʌv] *n* FAM cielo *m*, chato, ta.

lux [lʌks] *n* PHYS lux *m*.
— OBSERV El plural de la palabra inglesa *lux* es *lux* o *luxes*.

luxate [ˈlʌkseit] *vt* dislocar, producir una luxación en.

luxation [lʌkˈseiʃən] *n* MED luxación *f*.

luxe [luks] *n* lujo *m* || *de luxe* de lujo.

Luxembourg; **Luxemburg** [ˈlʌksəmbəːg] *pr n* GEOGR Luxemburgo *m*.

Luxembourger; **Luxemburger** [-ə*] *n* luxemburgués, esa.

Luxembourgian; **Luxemburgian** [-iən] *adj* luxemburgués, esa.

Luxor [ˈlʌksɔː*] *pr n* GEOGR Luxor.

luxuriance [lʌgˈzjuəriəns] *n* exuberancia *f*.

luxuriant [lʌgˈzjuəriənt] *adj* exuberante.

luxuriate [lʌgˈzjuərieit] *vi* disfrutar (*in* de, con), deleitarse (*in* con) (to revel in, to enjoy) || crecer exuberantemente *or* con profusión (vegetation).

luxurious [lʌgˈzjuəriəs] *adj* lujoso, sa (sumptuous); *a luxurious flat* un piso lujoso || fastuoso, sa; *a luxurious life* una vida fastuosa || voluptuoso, sa; *a luxurious sense of well-being* un sentido voluptuoso del bienestar || sensual.

luxury [ˈlʌkʃəri] *n* lujo *m*; *a life of luxury* una vida de lujo; *the luxury of having two cars* el lujo de tener dos coches || placer *m*, gusto *m*; *what a luxury to be able to rest at last!* ¡qué gusto poder descansar por fin! || — *luxury car, flat* coche, piso de lujo || *luxury goods* productos *m pl* de lujo || *luxury tax, article* impuesto, artículo de lujo || *luxury trade* comercio *m* de artículos de lujo || *to live in luxury* vivir espléndidamente.

lycanthrope [ˈlaikənθrəup] *n* MED licántropo *m*.

lyceum [lai'siəm] *pr n* liceo *m* (at Athens) || auditorio *m*, sala *f* de conferencias (lecture hall) || ateneo *m* (organization providing lectures, etc.).

lychee ['laitʃiː] *n* lichi *m*.

lych-gate ['litʃgeit] *n* ARCH entrada *f* de cementerio.

lye [lai] *n* CHEM lejía *f*.

lying [-iŋ] *adj* mentiroso, sa (telling untruths) || falso, sa (not true) || tendido, da; echado, da (laid down) || situado, da (situated).
◆ *n* mentira *f* (the telling of lies) || mentiras *f pl* (lies) || lecho *m*, cama *f* (bed) || descanso *m*, reposo *m* (rest).

lying-in [-iŋ'in] *n* MED parto *m* || *lying-in hospital* maternidad *f*.

lymph [limf] *n* ANAT linfa *f* || *lymph gland* o *node* ganglio linfático.

lymphangitis [limfæn'dʒaitis] *n* MED linfangitis *f*.

lymphatic [lim'fætik] *adj* linfático, ca.
◆ *n* vaso *m* linfático.

lymphocyte ['limfəˌsait] *n* ANAT linfocito *m*.

lymphocytosis [ˌlimfəsai'təsis] *n* linfocitosis *f*.

lymphoid ['limfɔid] *adj* linfoide.

lyncean [lin'siən] *adj* de lince (eye) || con ojos de lince (person).

lynch [lintʃ] *vt* linchar.

lynching [-iŋ] *n* linchamiento *m*.

lynx [liŋks] *n* ZOOL lince *m*.
— OBSERV El plural de esta palabra es *lynxes* o *lynx*.

lynx-eyed [-aid] *adj* con ojos de lince.

lyophilize [lai'ɔfəlaiz] *vt* liofilizar.

Lyra ['laiərə] *pr n* ASTR Lira *f*.

lyre ['laiə*] *n* MUS lira *f*.

lyrebird [-bəːd] *n* ave *f* lira, menura *m* (bird).

lyric ['lirik] *adj* lírico, ca.
◆ *n* poema *m* lírico (lyric poem).
◆ *pl* poesía *f sing* lírica, lírica *f sing* (genre) || letra *f sing* (words of a song).

lyrical [-əl] *adj* lírico, ca || FIG *to get lyrical about sth.* entusiasmarse por algo.

lyrically [-əli] *adv* líricamente || FIG entusiásticamente, con entusiasmo.

lyricism ['lirisizəm] *n* lirismo *m*.

lyricist ['lirisist] *n* lírico *m* (poet) || autor *m* de la letra de una canción (song writer).

lyrist ['laiərist] *n* lírico *m* (lyric poet) || MUS tañedor *m* de lira.

Lysistrata [lai'sistrətə] *pr n* Lisistrata *f*.

M

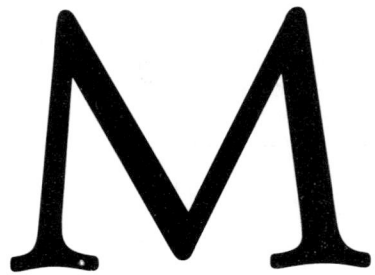

m [em] *n* m *f* (letter).

ma [mɑː] *n* FAM mamá *f*.

ma'am [mæm, mɑːm] *n* señora *f*.
— OBSERV Esta palabra es una forma abreviada de *madam* que se utiliza para dirigirse ya a la reina o a una princesa, ya a una mujer en señal de cortesía.

mac [mæk] *n* FAM impermeable *m* (mackintosh).

macabre; US **macaber** [məˈkɑːbr] *adj* macabro, bra; *danse macabre* danza macabra.

macaco [məˈkɑːkəu] *n* ZOOL ayeaye *m* (lemur) | macaco *m* (macaque).

macadam [məˈkædəm] *n* macadán *m*, macadam *m*.

macaque [məˈkɑːk] *n* macaco *m* (monkey).

macaroni [ˌmækəˈrəuni] *n* macarrones *m pl* (pasta) || FIG petimetre *m* (dandy) || FAM italiano, na.

macaronic [ˌmækəˈrɔnik] *adj* macarrónico, ca.
◆ *pl n* versos *m* macarrónicos.

macaroon [ˌmækəˈruːn] *n* macarrón *m*, mostachón *m* (cake).

macaw [məˈkɔː] *n* ara *m* (parrot).

Maccabee [ˈmækəbiː] *pr n* Macabeo *m*.

mace [meis] *n* maza *f* (club, ornamental staff of office) || macero *m* (mace-bearer).

mace-bearer [-ˌbɛərə*] *n* macero *m*.

macedoine [mæseiˈdwɑːn] *n* macedonia *f* (dish).

Macedonia [ˌmæsiˈdəunjə] *pr n* GEOGR Macedonia *f*.

Macedonian [-n] *adj/n* macedónico, ca; macedonio, nia.

macer [ˈmeisə*] *n* macero *m* (mace-bearer).

macerate [ˈmæsəreit] *vt* macerar.
◆ *vi* macerar, macerarse.

maceration [ˌmæsəˈreiʃən] *n* maceración *f*, maceramiento *m*.

Macfarlane [məkˈfɑːlən] *n* macfarlán *m*, macferlán *m* (overcoat).

Mach [mæk] *n* PHYS mach *m* (number).

machete [məˈtʃeiti] *n* machete *m*.

Machiavelli [ˌmækiəˈveli] *pr n* Maquiavelo *m*.

Machiavellian [ˌmækiəˈveliən] *adj* maquiavélico, ca.

machicolation [mæˌtʃikəuˈleiʃən] *n* ARCH matacán *m* (of a castle).

machinate [ˈmækineit] *vt* maquinar, complotar.

machination [ˌmækiˈneiʃən] *n* maquinación *f*, intriga *f*.

machinator [ˈmækineitə*] *n* maquinador, ra; intrigante *m* & *f*.

machine [məˈʃiːn] *n* máquina *f*; *sewing, washing, adding machine* máquina de coser, de lavar, de sumar || FIG máquina *f* (person) | máquina *f*, maquinaria *f* (machinery); *the political machine* la maquinaria política | bicicleta *f*, máquina *f* (bicycle) | moto *f* (motorcycle) | coche *m*, máquina *f* (car) | avión *m*, aparato *m* (aeroplane) || INFORM máquina *f* (computer) || THEATR tramoya *f* || US bomba *f* de incendios (fire pump) || — *accounting machine* máquina contabilizadora, máquina contable || *calculating machine* máquina de calcular || *copying machine* copiadora *f* || *fruit* o *slot machine* máquina tragaperras || *infernal machine* máquina infernal || *reaping machine* segadora *f*.
◆ *adj* a máquina; *machine wound* enrollado a máquina || mecánico, ca; *machine winding* enrollamiento mecánico || — INFORM *machine language* lenguaje *m* de máquina | *machine translation* traducción *f* asistida por ordenador.

machine [məˈʃiːn] *vt* TECH mecanizar, trabajar con máquina herramienta || coser a máquina (to sew).

machine gun [-gʌn] *n* MIL ametralladora *f*.

machine-gun [-gʌn] *vt* ametrallar.

machine gunner [-gʌnə*] *n* MIL ametrallador *m*.

machine-made [-meid] *adj* hecho a máquina.

machinery [məˈʃiːnəri] *n* maquinaria *f* (machines); *agricultural machinery* maquinaria agrícola || mecanismo *m* (mechanism) || FIG mecanismo *m*, maquinaria *f*; *administrative machinery* el mecanismo administrativo || THEATR tramoya *f*.

machine-readable [məˈʃiːnˈriːdəbl] *adj* INFORM legible *or* procesable por máquina.

machine shop [məˈʃiːnʃɔp] *n* taller *m* de construcción y de reparación de máquinas.

machine tool [məˈʃiːntuːl] *n* máquina *f* herramienta.

machining [məˈʃiːniŋ] *n* TECH mecanizado *m* || costura *f* a máquina (swing).

machinist [məˈʃiːnist] *n* mecánico *m* (who repairs) || maquinista *m* (who operates) || maquinista *f* (sewing machine operator) || THEATR tramoyista *m*, maquinista *m*.

machismo [mæˈtʃizməu] *n* machismo *m*.

macho [ˈmætʃəu] *adj* FAM machista, de macho.

mack [mæk] *n* FAM impermeable *m* (raincoat).

mackerel [ˈmækrəl] *n* caballa *f* (fish).
◆ *adj* aborregado, da (sky).

mackintosh [ˈmækintɔʃ] *n* impermeable *m* (raincoat) || gabardina *f* (cloth).

mackle; **macle** [ˈmækl] *n* PRINT mácula *f*, maculatura *f*.

mackle; **macle** [ˈmækl] *vt* PRINT macular.

macle [ˈmækl] *n* MIN macla *f* (twinned crystal).

macramé; US **macrame** [məˈkrɑːmi] *n* agremán *m* (lace, trimming).

macrobiotic [ˌmækrəbaiˈɔtik] *adj* macrobiótico, ca.

macrobiotics [-s] *n* macrobiótica *f*.

macrocephalic [ˌmækrəuseˈfælik]; **macrocephalous** [ˌmækrəuˈsefələs] *adj* MED macrocéfalo, la.

macrocosm [ˈmækrəukɔzəm] *n* macrocosmo *m*.

macrocyte [ˈmækrəuˌsait] *n* BIOL macrocito *m*.

macrodactyl [mækrəuˈdæktil] *adj* macrodáctilo, la.

macrogamete [ˌmækrəuˈgæmiːt] *n* BIOL macrogameto *m*.

macromolecular [ˌmækrəuməuˈlekjulə*] *adj* macromolecular.

macromolecule [ˌmækrəuˈmɔlikjuːl] *n* macromolécula *f*.

macrophage [ˌmækrəˈfeidʒ] *n* macrófago *m*.

macrophotography [ˌmækrəufəˈtɔgrəfi] *n* macrofotografía *f*.

macropodid [məˈkrɔpədid] *adj* macrópodo, da.
◆ *n* macrópodo *m*.

macroscopic [ˌmækrəuˈskɔpik] *adj* macroscópico, ca.

macrosporange [ˌmækrəuˈspɔrændʒ] *n* BOT macrosporangio *m*.

macrospore [ˈmækrəuˌspɔː] *n* BOT macrospora *f*.

macruran [məˈkruərən] *adj* macruro, ra.
◆ *n* macruro *m*.

macula [ˈmækjulə]; **macule** [ˈmækjuːl] *n* MED mácula *f* || mancha *f*, mácula *f* (on the sun, moon) || ANAT *macula lutea* mácula *f* (of the eye).
— OBSERV El plural de la palabra inglesa es *maculae*.

maculate [ˈmækjuleit] *vt* macular || manchar (to stain) || FIG manchar, mancillar (honour, etc.).

maculation [ˌmækjuˈleiʃən] *n* mácula *f* (spot, stain) || FIG mancha *f*, mancilla *f*.

mad [mæd] *adj* loco, ca (insane); *he is mad* está loco || loco, ca; insensato, ta (foolish); *a mad idea* una idea insensata || FIG furioso, sa; *he was mad at* o *with her* estaba furioso con *or* contra ella || loco, ca (compass) || rabioso, sa (dog) || — FAM *as mad as a hatter* o *as a March hare* o *as they come* loco de atar *or* de remate *or* rematado, más loco que una cabra || FIG *like mad* como un loco; *to run like mad* correr como un loco; muchísimo (a lot) | *mad with fear* muerto de miedo || *raving mad, stark mad* loco furioso, loco perdido || *that was a mad thing to do* fue una locura || FIG *to be mad keen on doing sth.* estar loco por hacer algo | *to be mad on* o *about* esar loco por | *to be mad with joy* estar loco de alegría | *to drive s.o. mad* volverle loco a uno | *to get mad* ponerse furioso, enfadarse || *to go mad* enloquecer, volverse loco || FIG *to make mad* enfurecer, poner furioso.

MAD *abbr of [mutual assured destruction]* equilibrio del terror.

Madagascan [ˌmædəˈgæskən] *adj/n* malgache.

Madagascar [,mædə'gæskə*] *pr n* Madagascar.

madam ['mædəm] *n* señora *f* (polite title) || patrona *f* (of a brothel) || FIG *to be a bit of a madam* tener muchos humos.
— OBSERV El plural de *madam* es *mesdames* cuando se emplea como tratamiento de cortesía y *madams* si significa *patrona*. Esta palabra no va nunca seguida por el apellido.

Madame ['mædəm] *n* señora *f*.
— OBSERV El plural de eta palabra es *Mesdames*.

madcap ['mædkæp] *adj* atolondrado, da; sin seso.
◆ *n* cabeza *f* de chorlito, locuelo, la.

madden ['mædn] *vt* enloquecer, volver loco (to make insane) || FIG volver loco || *it is maddening* es para volverse loco.
◆ *vi* enloquecer, volverse loco || FIG volverse loco.

maddening [-iŋ] *adj* enloquecedor, ra || exasperante (infuriating) || *it is maddening* es para volverse loco.

madder ['mædə*] *n* rubia *f* (plant).

madding ['mædiŋ] *adj* enloquecido, da (frenzied) || *to live far from the madding crowd* vivir lejos del mundanal ruido.

made [meid] *pp/pret* → **make.**

madeira [mə'diərə] *n* madera *m* (wine).

Madeira [mə'diərə] *pr n* GEOGR Madera *f* (island).

made-to-measure ['meidtuː'meʒə*] *adj* hecho, cha a (la) medida (clothes).

made-to-order ['meidtuː'ɔːdə*] *adj* hecho, cha de encargo.

made-up ['meidʌp] *adj* inventado, da; ficticio, cia (fictitious); *a made-up story* una historia inventada || compuesto, ta (put together); *a made-up page* una página compuesta || maquillado, da (face) || pintado, da (lips).

madhouse ['mædhaus] *n* manicomio *m* (mental hospital) || FIG casa *f* de locos.

madly ['mædli] *adv* locamente || como un loco; *to shout madly* gritar como un loco || FIG terriblemente (extremely); *madly jealous* terriblemente envidioso || *to be madly in love with* estar locamente enamorado de.

madman ['mædmən] *n* loco *m*.
— OBSERV El plural de *madman* es *madmen*.

madness ['mædnis] *n* locura *f* (insanity) || furia *f*, rabia *f* (rage) || rabia *f* (of dogs).

Madonna [mə'dɔnə] *n* REL madona *f*.

madras [mə'drɑːs] *n* madrás *m* (fabric).

madreporaria [,mædripɔː'rɛəriə] *pl n* ZOOL madreporarios *m*.

madrepore [,mædripɔː*] *n* ZOOL madrépora *f*.

Madrid [mə'drid] *pr n* GEOGR Madrid.

madrigal ['mædrigəl] *n* madrigal *m*.

Madrilenian [mædri'liːniən] *adj/n* madrileño, ña.

madrona [mə'drəunə] *n* BOT madroño *m*.

madwoman ['mædwumən] *n* loca *f*.
— OBSERV El plural es *madwomen*.

Maecenas [mi'siːnæs] *n* mecenas *m*.

maelstrom ['meilstrəum] *n* maelstrom *m* (whirlpool) || FIG torbellino *m*, remolino *m*.

maenad ['miːnæd] *n* MYTH ménade *f* (bacchante).
— OBSERV El plural de *maenad* es *maenads* o *maenades*.

maestoso [,mɑːes'təuzəu] *adv* MUS maestoso.

maestro [mɑː'estrəu] *n* MUS maestro *m*.
— OBSERV El plural de la palabra inglesa *maestro* es *maestros* o *maestri*.

Mae West ['mei'west] *n* chaleco *m* salvavidas.

maffia; mafia ['mɑːfjə] *n* mafia *f*, maffia *f*.

mafioso [,mɑfi'əuzəu] *n* mafioso *m*.
— OBSERV El plural de *mafioso* es *mafiosi*.

mag [mæg] *n* FAM revista *f* (magazine).

magazine [,mægə'ziːn] *n* revista *f* (publication) || almacén *m* (warehouse) || polvorín *m* (for explosives) || pañol *m* de municiones (of a warship) || recámara *f* (of a rifle) || carga *f* (of a camera) || *magazine gun* fusil *m* de repetición.

magazinist [-ist] *n* colaborador *m* de una revista.

Magdalen; Magdalene ['mægdəlin] *pr n* Magdalena *f*.

Magdalenian [,mægdə'liːnjən] *adj* magdaleniense.
◆ *n* magdaleniense *m*.

Magellan [mə'gelən] *pr n* Magallanes || *Strait of Magellan* estrecho *m* de Magallanes.

magenta [mə'dʒentə] *adj* magenta.

maggot ['mægət] *n* gusano *m*, cresa *f* (larva) || FIG capricho *m*, antojo *m* (whim).

maggoty [-i] *adj* agusanado, da || FIG caprichoso, sa; antojadizo, za.

Magi ['meidʒai] *pl n* *the three Magi* los tres Reyes Magos.

magic ['mædʒik] *adj* mágico, ca; *magic power* poder mágico; *magic lantern* linterna mágica || *magic wand* varita *f* de las virtudes, varita mágica.
◆ *n* magia *f*; *white, black magic* magia blanca, negra || FIG magia *f* (charm) || *by magic, as if by magic* por arte de magia, como por encanto.

magical [-əl] *adj* mágico, ca.

magically [-əli] *adv* por arte de magia.

magician [mə'dʒiʃən] *n* mago *m* (wizard) || hechicero *m* (of a tribe) || ilusionista *m* & *f* (in a theatre).

magisterial [,mædʒis'tiəriəl] *adj* magistral (of a master) || autoritario, ria (authoritative) || magistral (with masterly skill) || de magistrado (of a magistrate) || *with a magisterial tone* en tono magistral.

magistracy ['mædʒistrəsi] *n* magistratura *f*.

magistral [mə'dʒistrəl] *adj* magistral.

magistrate ['mædʒistreit] *n* magistrado *m* (judicial officer) || juez *m* municipal (judge) || — *examining magistrate* juez de instrucción || *magistrate's court* juzgado *m* de paz.

magistrature ['mædʒistrə,tjuə*] *n* magistratura *f*.

magma ['mægmə] *n* magma *m*.
— OBSERV El plural de la palabra inglesa *magma* es *magmata* o *magmas*.

Magna Carta; Magna Charta ['mægnə'kɑːtə] *pr n* Carta *f* Magna.
— OBSERV La Carta Magna, que garantizaba las libertades civiles y políticas del pueblo inglés, fue concedida por el rey Juan Sin Tierra el 15 de junio de 1215.

Magna Graecia ['mægnə'griːʃiːə] *pr n* Magna Grecia *f*.

magnanimity [,mægnə'nimiti] *n* magnanimidad *f*.

magnanimous [mæg'næniməs] *adj* magnánimo, ma.

magnate ['mægneit] *n* magnate *m*.

magnesia [mæg'niːʃə] *n* CHEM magnesia *f*.

magnesian [-n] *adj* CHEM magnesiano, na.

magnesic [mæg'niːsik] *adj* CHEM magnésico, ca.

magnesiferous [mægniː'sifərəs] *adj* magnesífero, ra.

magnesite ['mægnisait] *n* MIN magnesita *f*.

magnesium [mæg'niːzjəm] *n* CHEM magnesio *m*.

magnet ['mægnit] *n* imán *m*.

magnetic [mæg'netik] *adj* magnético, ca; *magnetic equator, field, pole* ecuador, campo, polo magnético; *magnetic induction, mine, needle, storm* inducción, mina, aguja, tempestad magnética || magnetofónico, ca; magnético, ca; *magnetic tape* cinta magnetofónica; *magnetic recording* grabación magnética || FIG atractivo, va (person, look) || — INFORM *magnetic card* tarjeta *f* magnética | *magnetic core* núcleo *m* magnético | *magnetic disk* disco *m* magnético | *magnetic drum* tambor *m* magnético | *magnetic memory* memoria *f* magnética | *magnetic strip* banda *f* magnética | *magnetic tape* cinta *f* magnética.

magnetic compass [-'kʌmpəs] *n* brújula *f*.

magnetic recorder [-ri'kɔːdə*] *n* magnetófono *m* [AMER grabadora *f*].

magnetics [-s] *n* magnetismo *m* (science).

magnetism ['mægnitizəm] *n* magnetismo *m* || FIG magnetismo *m*, atractivo *m* (charm).

magnetite ['mægnətait] *n* MIN magnetita *f*.

magnetization [,mægnitai'zeiʃən] *n* magnetización *f*, imantación *f*, imanación *f*.

magnetize [,mægnitaiz] *vt* magnetizar || imantar, imanar, magnetizar; *to magnetize a needle* imantar una aguja || FIG magnetizar, atraer.

magneto [mæg'niːtəu] *n* magneto *f*.

magnetoelectric [,mægniːtəui'lektrik] *adj* magnetoeléctrico, ca.

magnetometer [,mægnə'tɔmitə*] *n* PHYS magnetómetro *m*.

magnetophone [mæg'nitə,fəun] *n* magnetófono *m* [AMER grabadora *f*].

magnetoscope [mæg'nitə,skəup] *n* PHYS magnetoscopio *m*.

magnetron ['mægnitrɔn] *n* TECH magnetrón *m*.

magnific [mæg'nifik]; **magnifical** [-əl] *adj* magnífico, ca.

Magnificat [mæg'nifikæt] *n* REL magnificat *m*.

magnification [,mægnifi'keiʃən] *n* PHYS aumento *m*, ampliación *f* || FIG enaltecimiento *m*, glorificación *f* (glorification) | exageración *f* (exaggeration).

magnificence [mæg'nifisns] *n* magnificencia *f*.

magnificent [mæg'nifisnt] *adj* magnífico, ca.

magnifier ['mægnifaiə*] *n* PHYS lupa *f*, lente *f* de aumento (magnifying glass) || FIG exagerado, da.

magnify ['mægnifai] *vt* aumentar (to increase) || FIG exagerar; *he is inclined to magnify the difficulties* tiene tendencia a exagerar las dificultades | enaltecer, exaltar, glorificar (to glorify) | magnificar (God) || PHYS aumentar, ampliar (an image) | amplificar (a sound).

magnifying [-iŋ] *adj* PHYS de aumento || — *magnifying glass* lente *f* de aumento, lupa *f* || *magnifying power* aumento *m* (magnification).

magniloquence [mæg'niləukwəns] *n* grandilocuencia *f*.

magniloquent [mæg'niləukwənt] *adj* grandilocuente (ostentatious).

magnitude ['mægnitjuːd] *n* magnitud *f* || FIG magnitud *f*, envergadura *f*; *a project of great magnitude* un proyecto de gran magnitud *or* de mucha envergadura || volumen *m* (of sound) || ASTR & MATH magnitud *f*.

magnolia [mæg'nəuljə] *n* BOT magnolio *m*, magnolia *f* (tree) | magnolia *f* (flower).

magnoliaceae [mægnəul'jəsii] *pl n* BOT magnoliáceas *f*.

magnum ['mægnəm] *n* botella *f* de dos litros.

magnum opus [-'əupəs] *n* obra *f* maestra (masterpiece).

magpie ['mægpai] *n* urraca *f* (bird) || FIG cotorra *f* (chatterbox).

maguey ['mægwei] *n* BOT magney *m* pita *f*.

magus ['meigəs] *n* mago *m* (Zoroastrian priest) || REL Rey *m* Mago || *Simon Magus* Simón Mago.

— OBSERV El plural de la palabra inglesa es *magi*.

Magyar ['mægjɑː*] *adj/n* magiar (Hungarian).

maharaja; maharajah [ˌmɑːhə'rɑːdʒə] *n* maharajá *m* (Hindu prince).

maharanee; maharani [ˌmɑːhə'rɑːniː] *n* maharani *f* (wife of a maharaja).

mahatma [mə'hɑːtmə] *n* mahatma *m*.

Mahdi ['mɑːdi] *n* profeta *m* (Moslem prophet).

mahlstick ['mɔːlstik] *n* ARTS tiento *m* (maulstick).

mahogany [mə'hɔgəni] *n* caoba *f* (tree, wood).

◆ *adj* de caoba; *mahogany table* mesa de caoba || caoba (colour).

Mahomet [mə'hɔmit] *pr n* Mahoma *m*.

Mahometan [mə'hɔmitən] *adj/n* mahometano, na.

mahout [mə'haut] *n* cornaca *m* (elephant driver).

maid [meid] *n* criada *f* [AMER mucama *f*] (servant) || camarera *f* (in a hotel) || doncella *f* (virgin, young girl) || — *lady's maid* doncella *f* || *maid of all work* criada para todo || *maid of honour* dama *f* de honor || *old maid* solterona *f* || HIST *the maid of Orléans* la Doncella de Orleáns (Joan of Arc).

maiden ['meidn] *n* doncella *f* (girl, virgin) || guillotina *f*.

◆ *adj* virgen, virginal (virgin) || soltera (unmarried) || de soltera; *maiden name* apellido de soltera || primero, ra; *maiden trip* primer viaje || inaugural; *maiden speech* discurso inaugural || SP que no ha ganado ninguna carrera (horse).

maidenhair [-hεə*] *n* BOT culantrillo *m*.

maidenhead [-hed] *n* virginidad *f* (quality) || ANAT himen *m*.

maidenhood [-hud] *n* soltería *f* || virginidad *f*.

maidenly [-li] *adj* virginal || recatado, da; modesto, ta (modest).

◆ *adv* recatadamente, modestamente.

maid-in-waiting ['meidin'weitiŋ] *n* dama *f* de compañía.

— OBSERV El plural es *maids-in-waiting*.

maidservant ['meidˌsəːvənt] *n* criada *f*, sirvienta *f* [AMER mucama *f*].

maieutics [mei'juːtiks] *n* mayéutica *f*.

mail [meil] *n* correo *m*; *air mail* correo aéreo; *the morning mail* el correo de la mañana; *by return mail* a vuelta de correo || correspondencia *f*; *to do one's mail* escribir la correspondencia || cartas *f pl*; *I got a lot of mail this morning* he recibido un montón de cartas esta mañana || correo *m* (train, boat) || cota *f* de mallas (armour) || caparazón *m* (of turtles, of lobsters, etc.) || *Royal Mail* Correos, Servicio *m* de Correos.

◆ *adj* postal; *mail plane* avión postal || de correo.

mail [meil] *vt* mandar por correo (to send) || echar al correo (in a letter box).

mailbag [-bæg] *n* saca *f* de correspondencia.

mailboat [-bəut] *n* buque *m* correo.

mailbox; mail box [-bɔks] *n* buzón *m*.

mail car [-kɑː*] *n* coche *m* de correos, furgón *m* or vagón *m* postal.

mail coach [-'kəutʃ] *n* diligencia *f* || coche *m* de correos, furgón *m* or vagón *m* postal (mail car).

mailing list [-iŋlist] *n* lista *f* de personas a quienes se mandan propaganda o documentos.

mailman [-mən] *n* US cartero *m* (postman).

— OBSERV El plural de *mailman* es *mailmen*.

mail order [-ˌɔːdə*] *n* pedido *m* hecho por correo.

mailshot ['meilʃɔt] *n* envío *m* de publicidad a domicilio.

mail train [-trein] *n* tren *m* correo.

mail van [-væn] *n* furgoneta *f* postal (lorry) || furgón *m* or vagón *m* postal (in railways).

maim [meim] *vt* mutilar, tullir, lisiar (a limb) || FIG mutilar (a text).

main [mein] *adj* principal; *the main problems* los problemas principales || mayor; *main street* calle mayor || general, de primer orden; *main road* o *highway* carretera general || principal (floor) || MAR mayor (mast, sail) | principal; *main deck* cubierta principal | maestro, tra; *main frame* cuaderna maestra || AVIAT de sustentación (wing) || principal (railway line) || GRAMM principal (clause) || fuerte; *main course, main dish* plato fuerte || — *by main force* a viva fuerza || *main body* grueso *m* (of an army) || INFORM *main file* fichero *m* principal || *main office* oficina *f* central || *main sewer* colector *m* || *main shaft* árbol *m* de transmisión (of a car) || *the main thing* lo principal, lo esencial || *to look to the main chance* velar por su propio interés.

◆ *n* parte *f* principal *or* fundamental || cañería *f* principal (principal pipe system) || colector *m* (sewer) || ELECTR cable *m* principal (main cable) || línea *f* principal (railways) || pelea *f* de gallos (cockfight) || POET alta mar *f* (high sea) | palo *m* mayor (mainmast) | vela *f* mayor (sail) || — *in the main* por lo general, en general || ELECTR *the mains* la red eléctrica | *to plug sth. into the mains* enchufar algo | *to run off the mains* funcionar con electricidad || *with might and main* con todas sus fuerzas.

Main [main] *pr n* GEOGR Meno *m*.

Maine [mein] *pr n* GEOGR Maine.

mainframe (computer) ['meinfreim] *n* INFORM unidad *f* central, ordenador *m* principal.

mainland ['meinlənd] *n* continente *m*, tierra *f* firme.

mainline ['meinlɑin] *adj* principal (station).

mainly ['meinli] *adv* principalmente, sobre todo, especialmente.

mainmast ['meinmɑːst] *n* MAR palo *m* mayor.

mainsail ['meinseil] *n* MAR vela *f* mayor.

mainsheet ['mainʃiːt] *n* MAR escota *f* mayor.

mainspring ['mainspriŋ] *n* muelle *m* real (of a clock) || FIG causa *f* principal, móvil *m* esencial.

mainstay ['meinstei] *n* MAR estay *m* mayor || FIG fundamento *m*, sostén *m*, punto *m* de apoyo, pilar; *the mainstays of religion* los fundamentos de la religión.

mainstream ['mainstriːm] *n* corriente *f* principal.

maintain [mein'tein] *vt* mantener, conservar, cuidar (sth. unimpaired) || mantener (speed) || alimentar, mantener (fire) || mantener, sustentar (a family, etc.) || mantener, sostener (relations, correspondance, conversation) || mantener (friendship) || guardar (advantage, silence) || conservar, mantenerse en (one's post) || mantener, sostener (an opinion, one's reputation); *he maintains that he is innocent* sostiene que es inocente || JUR defender (a cause, one's rights) | mantener (order) || MIL sostener (a siege) || FIG *to maintain one's ground* mantenerse en sus trece.

maintenance ['meintənəns] *n* conservación *f*, mantenimiento *m*, entretenimiento *m*, cuidado *m* (of sth. unimpaired); *maintenance costs* gastos de mantenimiento || defensa *f*, mantenimiento *m* (of order, peace, family, etc.) || defensa *f*, mantenimiento *m* (of one's rights) || — *in maintenance of* en apoyo de || *maintenance allowance* pensión alimenticia || JUR *maintenance obligations* obligación alimentaria.

maintop ['meintɔp] *n* MAR cofa *f* mayor.

main-topgallant mast [-'gæləntmɑːst] *n* MAR mastelerillo *m* de juanete mayor.

main-topgallant sail [-'gæləntseil] *n* MAR juanete *m* mayor.

main-topmast [-mɑːst] *n* MAR mastelero *m* de gavia *or* mayor.

main-topsail [-seil] *n* MAR gavia *f*.

main yard ['meinjɑːd] *n* MAR verga *f* mayor.

Mainz [maintz] *pr n* GEOGR Maguncia.

maisonette [ˌmeizə'net] *n* dúplex *m* (two-storey flat) || casita *f* (small house).

maitre d'hôtel ['metrədəu'tel] *n* jefe *m* de comedor (headwaiter) || mayordomo *m* (of a large household).

maize [meiz] *n* BOT maíz *m*; *toasted maize* maíz tostado || *maize field* maizal *m*.

majestic [mə'dʒestik]; **majestical** [-əl] *adj* majestuoso, sa.

majesty ['mædʒisti] *n* majestad *f* || — *God, the Divine Majesty* Su Divina Majestad || *Her Majesty the Queen* Su Graciosa Majestad || *His Catholic Majesty* Su Majestad Católica (king of France) || *His Christian Majesty* Su Majestad Cristianísima (King of Spain) || *His* o *Her* o *Your Majesty* Su Majestad.

majolica [mə'jɔlikə] *n* mayólica *f*.

major ['meidʒə*] *adj* mayor; *the major part* la mayor parte || importante (of great magnitude) || principal (main) || grave (illness, wound) || JUR mayor de edad || MUS & PHIL mayor || prioritario, ria (road) || REL mayor (orders) || US de la especialidad, de especialización (academic subject, field) || — MIL *major general* general *m* de división || *major party* partido mayoritario || *major suit* palo *m* mayor (cards).

◆ *n* JUR persona *f* mayor de edad, mayor *m* & *f*, de edad || PHIL mayor *f* (premise) || MIL comandante *m* || US especialidad *f* (of studies).

major ['meidʒə*] *vi* US especializarse (in education); *to major in Spanish* especializarse en español.

Majorca [mə'dʒɔːkə] *pr n* GEOGR Mallorca.

Majorcan [-n] *adj/n* mallorquín, ina.

majordomo ['meidʒə'dəuməu] *n* mayordomo *m*.

majorette [ˌmeidʒə'ret] *n* bastonera *f*.

majority [mə'dʒɔriti] *n* mayoría *f*; *the majority were happy* la mayoría estaba contenta; *a majority of three* tres votos de mayoría; *overwhelming majority* mayoría abrumadora || mayoría *f*, mayor parte *f*; *the majority of the participants* la mayor parte de los participantes || JUR mayoría *f*, mayoría *f* de edad (full legal age) || MIL grado *m* de comandante || *the silent majority* la mayoría silenciosa.

make [meik] *n* marca *f* (provenance of manufacture); *he knows all the makes of French cars* conoce todas las marcas de coches franceses || hechura *f*; *she does not like the make of the coat* no le gusta la hechura del abrigo || forma *f* (of an object) || fabricación *f* (manufacture); *of Spanish make* de fabricación española || estatura *f* (of a person) ‖ CULIN confección *f* ‖ ELECTR cierre *m* ‖ FIG calidad *f* (quality of personality) ‖ FIG & FAM *to be on the make* intentar prosperar por todos los medios (businessman), buscar aventuras galantes, intentar conquistar a una mujer (man).

make* [meik] *vt* hacer; *to make impossible* hacer imposible; *to make a noise* hacer ruido; *to make a journey* hacer un viaje; *to make a machine work* hacer funcionar una máquina; *to make the bed* hacer la cama; *bread is made of wheat* el pan está hecho con trigo; *to make an effort* hacer un esfuerzo ‖ hacer, fabricar; *to make barrels* hacer barriles; *to make a machine* fabricar una máquina ‖ hacer (remark, statement, proposal, offer) ‖ hacer (to total); *that makes 50* esto hace 50 ‖ hacer, preparar; *to make a meal, tea* hacer una comida, té ‖ hacer, elaborar; *to make plans* hacer planes | hacer, confeccionar (clothes) ‖ hacer, crear (to create); *God made man* Dios hizo al hombre ‖ hacer, nombrar; *they made him their president* le hicieron presidente; *to make s.o. one's heir* hacerle a alguien heredero ‖ hacer; *to make s.o. a knight, an earl* hacer a alguien caballero, conde ‖ hacer, componer; *to make an opera* hacer una ópera ‖ hacer, obligar (to compel); *she was made to stop* le hicieron detenerse | tomar (decision) ‖ cometer, hacer (error); *he made a mistake* cometió una falta ‖ efectuar (payment) ‖ dar; *to make an appointment with* dar cita a ‖ pronunciar, hacer (speech) ‖ celebrar, concertar (agreement) ‖ presentar (excuse) ‖ hacer de; *to make one's son a doctor* hacer de su hijo un médico ‖ convertir, transformar (*into* en) ‖ ser; *he will make a good doctor* será un buen médico; *this makes the third time* es la tercera vez ‖ ser, hacer, equivaler, ser equivalente *or* igual a; *two halves make a whole* dos mitades hacen un entero; *five and five make ten* cinco y cinco son diez ‖ poner, volver; *to make s.o. sad* ponerle a uno triste ‖ hacer, poner; *that will make her happy* eso la hará feliz ‖ sacar (conclusion) ‖ pensar, deducir (to infer); *what does he make of that?* ¿qué piensa de eso? ‖ servir de; *this stone will make a good hammer for me* esta piedra me servirá perfectamente de martillo ‖ servir para hacer; *silk makes elegant clothes* la seda sirve para hacer trajes elegantes ‖ hacer; *to make many friends* hacer muchos amigos ‖ recorrer, hacer (distance); *to make 60 miles in a day* recorrer sesenta millas en un día ‖ visitar (a place during a journey) ‖ llegar a; *will they make the finals?* ¿llegarán a la final? ‖ sacar; *to make a profit* sacar un beneficio ‖ sacar, ganar (to earn); *he makes two thousand pounds a year* gana dos mil libras por año ‖ alcanzar, conseguir; *to make a high score* alcanzar un tanteo elevado ‖ intentar (to try); *he made to run but he couldn't* intentó correr pero no pudo ‖ calcular (to evaluate); *he made the distance about forty miles* calculó la distancia en cuarenta millas aproximadamente ‖ creer, imaginarse (to believe); *he is not so bad as you make him* no es tan malo como te lo imaginas ‖ poner (to say); *let's make it ten pounds, 3 o'clock* pongamos diez libras, las tres ‖ establecer como; *to make a rule that* establecer como principio que ‖ hacer famoso a, dar fama a; *the cotton trade is what made Manchester* el comercio de algodón es lo que hizo a Manchester famoso ‖ causar (to provoke); *to make trouble* causar problemas ‖ hacer de (to represent) ‖ ganar (a trick in cards) ‖ barajar (to shuffle cards) ‖ GRAMM ser; *«to see» in the past tense makes «saw»* el pretérito de «to see» es «saw»; *«mouse» makes «mice» in the plural* el plural de «mouse» es «mice» ‖ MIL hacer (peace, war) ‖ navegar a (knots) ‖ llegar a, alcanzar (land) ‖ divisar (to perceive) ‖ navegar con; *the ship made bad weather* el barco navegó con mal tiempo ‖ hacerse a; *to make sail* hacerse a la vela ‖ ELECTR cerrar (a circuit) | establecer (a contact) ‖ SP entrar en; *to make the team* entrar en el equipo ‖ US FAM seducir (a girl) | birlar (to steal) ‖ — *he is a made man* tiene un porvenir asegurado ‖ FAM *he's as cute as they make'em* es de lo más astuto que hay ‖ *I don't know what to make of it* no lo acabo de entender ‖ *made in Spain* hecho en España, de fabricación española ‖ *make believe* supongamos que, pongamos que (in games) ‖ *to be made for* estar hecho para; *you are made for this kind of thing* estás hecho para esta clase de cosas ‖ *to be made of* estar hecho con, ser de; *it is made of silver* es de plata ‖ *to make a bid* pujar (in an auction), declarar (to make a contract in bridge), cumplir el contrato (to score in bridge) ‖ *to make a bid for* intentar conseguir ‖ FAM *to make a bit on the side* ganar algún dinero más ‖ FIG *to make a break with s.o.* reñir con alguien ‖ *to make a change* cambiar ‖ JUR *to make a complaint* presentar una demanda ‖ *to make faces* hacer muecas ‖ *to make a fool of o.s.* hacer el ridículo, ridiculizarse ‖ *to make a fortune* hacerse rico ‖ *to make a habit of* acostumbrar, tener la costumbre de ‖ *to make a living* ganarse la vida ‖ *to make a name* hacerse un nombre ‖ PHOT *to make a print* hacer una copia ‖ *to make a record* establecer un récord ‖ *to make a start* empezar ‖ *to make available to* poner a la disposición de ‖ *to make believe* fingir ‖ *to make clear* poner en claro ‖ *to make default* faltar ‖ *to make do with sth.* arreglárselas con algo ‖ *to make fast* asegurar (to fasten) ‖ *to make fire* encender un fuego (to light a fire) ‖ *to make friends with* trabar amistad con, hacerse amigo de (to become friends), hacer las paces con, reconciliarse con (to become reconciled) ‖ *to make fun of* reírse de ‖ *to make good time* ganar tiempo; *I can make a good time on this road* puedo ganar tiempo por esta carretera ‖ *to make haste* darse prisa, apresurarse ‖ *to make it* aguantar (to endure), llegar (to arrive), tener éxito (to succeed), conseguir lo deseado (to obtain) ‖ FAM *to make it with s.o.* conseguir acostarse con alguien ‖ *to make known* dar a conocer ‖ *to make life impossible for s.o.* hacerle la vida imposible a uno ‖ *to make little of* hacer caso omiso de, hacer poco caso de (to pay no attention to), sacar poco provecho de (to get little benefit from) ‖ *to make love* hacer el amor ‖ *to make much of* dar mucha importancia a (to attach importance to), sacar mucho provecho de (to benefit by), tratar muy bien a (a person) ‖ *to make one's contract* cumplir un contrato (in card games) ‖ *to make one's way* abrirse paso (to open a path), salir bien (to come out all right), progresar, adelantar (to make progress) ‖ *to make or break, to make or mar* hacer la fortuna o ser la ruina de ‖ *to make peace* hacer las paces ‖ *to make o.s. an authority* llegar a ser una autoridad ‖ *to make o.s. a reputation* cobrar buena fama, adquirir fama, hacerse famoso ‖ *to make o.s. indispensable* hacerse indispensable ‖ *to make o.s. sick* ponerse enfermo ‖ *to make o.s. uneasy* preocuparse ‖ *to make people respect one* hacerse respetar ‖ *to make pleasant reading* ser agradable de leer ‖ *to make port* llegar a buen puerto ‖ *to make room* dejar sitio ‖ *to make sail* zarpar ‖ *to make sense* tener sentido ‖ *to make s.o. ashamed* darle vergüenza a uno ‖ *to make s.o. hungry* darle hambre a uno ‖ *to make s.o. laugh* darle risa a uno, hacerle gracia a uno ‖ *to make s.o. sleepy* darle sueño a uno ‖ *to make s.o. wonder* o *think* darle que pensar a uno ‖ *to make sth. ready* preparar algo ‖ *to make strong* fortalecer ‖ *to make the best of* sacar el mejor partido de ‖ *to make the most of it* sacar el mayor partido *or* el mayor provecho de ello, aprovecharlo al máximo ‖ *to make the train* coger el tren, alcanzar el tren ‖ *to make time* ganar tiempo ‖ *to make use of* hacer uso de, utilizar, servirse de, emplear ‖ *to make war* hacer la guerra ‖ FAM *to show what one is made of* mostrar de lo que uno es capaz, revelar lo que uno lleva dentro ‖ *what do you make of it?* ¿qué le parece? ‖ *what do you make of this book, of this girl?* ¿qué le parece este libro, esta chica? ‖ *what do you make the time?* ¿qué hora es?, ¿qué hora tienes?

◆ *vi* ir, dirigirse (*for, towards* a, hacia) (to go) ‖ abalanzarse (*at* sobre) (to attack) ‖ disponerse a; *she made to go* se dispuso a salir ‖ mostrarse (to prove to be) ‖ formarse (ice, flood, etc.) ‖ MAR subir (tide) ‖ — *to make against* perjudicar, ser dañino *or* nocivo para (to be harmful) ‖ ELECTR *to make and break* encenderse y apagarse ‖ *to make as if* o *as though* simular que, fingir que, hacer el paripé de ‖ *to make certain of* asegurarse de ‖ US *to make like* imitar, hacer como ‖ *to make merry* divertirse ‖ *to make ready* prepararse ‖ *to make so bold as to* ser tan atrevido como para ‖ *to make sure of* asegurarse de (to find out about).

◆ *phr v* ***to make after*** perseguir (to chase, to follow) ‖ ***to make at*** atacar a ‖ — ***to make away*** irse (to go) | *to make away with* llevarse, alzarse con (to steal), despilfarrar (fortune), suprimir, eliminar (to kill), destruir, hacer desaparecer (to get rid of) | *to make away with o.s.* suicidarse (to kill o.s.) ‖ ***to make down*** achicar (a dress) ‖ ***to make for*** ir hacia *or* a, dirigirse hacia (to go) | contribuir a *or* servir para crear; *it makes for difficulties* contribuye a crear dificultades ‖ ***to make into*** convertir en, transformar en ‖ ***to make off*** irse, largarse (to go away) ‖ — *to make off with* arramblar con, alzarse con, llevarse (to steal) ‖ ***to make out*** hacer (list) | extender (check, document) | redactar (report) | rellenar, llenar (a form) | distinguir, divisar, vislumbrar (to perceive) | descifrar (writing) | comprender, (acabar de) entender (to understand); *I can't make it out* no lo entiendo | creer, imaginarse (to believe); *he is not such a fool as people make out* no es tan tonto como se imagina la gente | considerar (to regard) | pretender, dar a entender (to claim); *to make out that* pretender que | llegar a (una conclusión); *how did you make that out?* ¿cómo llegó a esa conclusión? | US FAM arreglárselas; *don't worry, I'll make out* no se preocupe, me las arreglaré | ir tirando (to get by) | salir (to come out) ‖ — *how did you make out in that matter?* ¿cómo le fue en ese asunto? | *to make s.o. out to be a liar* decir que alguien es un embustero ‖ ***to make over*** ceder, traspasar (to hand over) | US arreglar (dress, house) ‖ ***to make up*** inventar (story) | completar, suplir (sth. lacking) | maquillar (to apply cosmetics to s.o.) | maquillarse, pintarse (one's face) | preparar (a prescription) | confeccionar, hacer (dress) | montar (to assemble) | hacer (parcel, list, balance) | envolver, empaquetar (goods into a parcel) | constituir, componer (to constitute) | reunir (to gather) | echar carbón a (a fire) | arreglar, concertar (a marriage, a pact) | compaginar, confeccionar (page) | recuperar, compensar; *to make up lost time by extra work* recuperar el tiempo perdido haciendo horas extraordinarias | compensar (a loss) | recuperar (lost ground) | colmar (a deficit) | pagar (to pay) | hacer las paces, reconciliarse; *I don't think they'll make up* no creo que vayan a reconciliarse | US repetir (an academic course, an examination) ‖ — *the standing committee is made up of five persons* la comisión permanente está integrada *or* constituida por cinco personas | *to make it up again* hacer las paces, reconciliarse | *to make it up to s.o. for sth.* indemnizar a alguien por algo | *to make up a quarrel* hacer las paces, reconciliarse | *to make up for* recuperar (to recover), compensar (to compensate), enmendar (one's faults), suplir (sth. lacking) | *to make up one's mind* decidirse | *to make up to s.o.* acercarse a alguien (to come near), halagar a alguien (to flatter).

— OBSERV Pret y pp **made**.

make and break [-əndbreik] *n* ELECTR interruptor *m* automático.

make-believe [-bi,liːv] *n* simulación *f*, fingimiento *m* (pretence) || — *all this cordiality is but make-believe* toda esta cordialidad es pura comedia || *a world of make-believe* un mundo de ensueño.
◆ *adj* fingido, da; simulado, da || de mentirijillas; *make-believe soldiers* soldados de mentirijillas.

make-do [-duː] *adj* improvisado, da.
◆ *n* improvisación *f*.

make-peace [-piːs] *n* mediador *m*, pacificador *m*.

maker [-ə*] *n* fabricante *m* (manufacturer) || constructor *m* (of machine) || JUR firmante *m* || autor, ra (of a book) || REL *the Maker* el Hacedor, el Creador (God).

makeshift [-ʃift] *n* expediente *m*, arreglo *m* provisional.
◆ *adj* provisional (temporary) || improvisado, da; *a makeshift dinner* una cena improvisada.

makeup [-ʌp] *n* construcción *f*, composición *f* (of several parts) || estructura *f* (structure) || carácter *m*, temperamento *m* (nature); *stolid makeup* carácter impasible || maquillaje *m* (beauty products and art of applying them) || confección *f* (of clothes) || PRINT compaginación *f*, confección *f*, ajuste *m* || FAM cuento *m*, historia *f* inventada (story) || *makeup assistant* maquillador, ra || *makeup base* maquillaje de fondo || *makeup girl* maquilladora *f*.

makeweight [-weit] *n* complemento *m* (de peso) || FIG tapaagujeros *m inv*, comodín *m* (person) | relleno *m* (padding).

making ['meikiŋ] *n* fabricación *f* (manufacture) || construcción *f* (of a bridge) || confección *f* (of clothes) || preparación *f* (of meals) || preparación *f*, formación *f* (training) || composición *f* (of a poem) || creación *f* (of the world, of a post) || hechura *f* (shape) || — *revolution in the making* revolución *f* en potencia || *that's history in the making* son acontecimientos históricos *or* que pasarán a la historia || *the marriage was none of her making* no era responsable del matrimonio || *the skirt was of her own making* la falda era obra suya || *to be still in the making* estar haciéndose || *to be the making of s.o.* ser la causa del éxito *or* del triunfo *or* de la fortuna de alguien (to cause the success of), formar a alguien; *this failure was the making of him* este fracaso le ha formado.
◆ *pl* cualidades *f*, madera *f sing*; *he has the makings of a leader* tiene las cualidades de un jefe, tiene madera de jefe || ganancias *f* (earnings).

making-up [-'ʌp] *n* maquillaje *m*.

Malabo [mə'lɑːbəu] *pr n* GEOGR Malabo [antiguamente Santa Isabel].

Malacca [mə'lækə] *pr n* GEOGR Malaca.

malachite ['mæləkait] *n* MIN malaquita *f*.

malacopterygian [mæləkɔptə'ridʒiən] *adj* malacopterigio, gia.
◆ *n* malacopterigio *m*.

maladjusted ['mælə'dʒʌstid] *adj* TECH mal ajustado, da || FIG inadaptado, da.

maladjustment ['mælə'dʒʌstmənt] *n* TECH mal ajuste *m* || FIG inadaptación *f*.

maladminister ['mæləd'ministə*] *vt* US administrar mal.

maladministration ['mæləd,minis'treiʃən] *n* mala administración *f*.

maladroit ['mælə'drɔit] *adj* torpe.

malady ['mælədi] *n* MED enfermedad *f* (disease).

Malaga ['mæləgə] *n* málaga *m* (wine).

Málaga ['mæləgə] *pr n* GEOGR Málaga.

Malagasy [,mælə'gæsi] *adj/n* malgache.

malaguena [,mælə'geinjə] *n* malagueña *f*.

malaise [mæ'leiz] *n* malestar *m*.

malapropism ['mæləprɔpizəm] *n* barbarismo *m*.

malapropos ['mæl'æprəpəu] *adj* inoportuno, na.
◆ *adv* inoportunamente.

malar ['meilə*] *adj* ANAT malar || *malar bone* malar *m*, pómulo *m*.
◆ *n* ANAT malar *m*, pómulo *m*.

malaria [mə'lɛəriə] *n* MED malaria *f*, paludismo *m*.

malarial [-l]; **malarian** [-n]; **malarious** [-s] *adj* palúdico, ca (fever) || de la malaria, del paludismo (mosquito).

malaxate ['mæləkseit] *vt* malaxar, amasar.

malaxation [,mælək'seiʃən] *n* malaxación *f*, amasamiento *m*.

Malay [mə'lei]; **Malayan** [-ən] *adj/n* malayo, ya.

Malaysia [mə'leiziə] *pr n* GEOGR Malasia *f*, Malaysia *f*.

Malaysian [-n] *adj/n* malasio, sia.

malcontent ['mælkən,tent] *adj/n* descontento, ta.

Maldive Islands ['mɔːldiv'ailəndz] *pl prn* GEOGR islas *f* Maldivas.

male [meil] *adj* BOT & ZOOL macho; *male panther* pantera macho; *male fern* helecho macho || varón; *male issue* hijos varones; *male child* hijo varón || masculino, na; *male sex* sexo masculino || de hombres; *male ward in a hospital* sala de hombres en un hospital || viril, varonil (manly) || TECH macho || — TECH *male screw* tornillo *m* || *male chauvinist pig* machista *m*, falócrata *m*.
◆ *n* BOT & ZOOL macho *m* || varón *m* (person).

malediction [,mæli'dikʃən] *n* maldición *f*.

malefaction [,mæli'fækʃən] *n* mala acción *f*, fechoría *f*.

malefactor ['mælifæktə*] *n* malhechor, ra.

maleficence [mə'lefisns] *n* maleficencia *f*.

maleficent [mə'lefisnt] *adj* maléfico, ca (malefic) || perjudicial (harmful) || criminal.

malevolence [mə'levələns] *n* malevolencia *f*.

malevolent [mə'levələnt] *adj* malévolo, la.

malevolently [-li] *adv* malévolamente, con malevolencia.

malfeasance [mæl'fiːzəns] *n* JUR hecho *m* delictivo.

malformation ['mælfɔː'meiʃən] *n* malformación *f*.

malformed [mælfɔːmd] *adj* malformado, da; deforme.

malfunction ['mæl'fʌnkʃən] *n* funcionamiento *m* defectuoso.

malic ['mælik] *adj* málico, ca (acid).

malice ['mælis] *n* maldad *f* (ill will) || rencor *m* (*to, towards* a) (grudge); *I bear her no malice* no le guardo rencor || JUR intención *f* delictuosa || *malice aforethought* premeditación *f*.

malicious [mə'liʃəs] *adj* malo, la; malévolo, la (wicked) || rencoroso, sa (rancorous) || JUR delictuoso, sa; delictivo, va (intent) | delictivo, va (act) || JUR *malicious damage* daño doloso.

maliciously [-li] *n* con maldad || por rencor, rencorosamente || JUR con premeditación.

maliciousness [-nis] *n* malicia *f*, mala intención *f*.

malign [mə'lain] *adj* maligno, na; malévolo, la (malevolent) || perjudicial, pernicioso, sa; *a malign influence* una influencia perjudicial || MED maligno, na.

malign [mə'lain] *vt* calumniar, difamar (to slander) || hablar mal de (to speak evil of).

malignancy [mə'lignənsi]; **malignity** [mə'ligniti] *n* malignidad *f*, maldad *f*, malevolencia *f* || MED malignidad *f*.

malignant [mə'lignənt] *adj* malvado, da; malo, la (person) || perjudicial (harmful) || MED maligno, na.

malignity [mə'ligniti] *n* → **malignancy.**

Malines [mæ'liːn] *pr n* GEOGR Malinas.

malinger [mə'liŋgə*] *vi* fingirse enfermo [para no trabajar o eludir una responsabilidad].

malingerer [-rə*] *n* enfermo *m* fingido, enferma *f* fingida, remolón, ona; simulador, ra.

malingering [-riŋ] *n* remolonería *f*, simulación *f*.

mall [mɔːl] *n* paseo *m* (avenue) || mazo *m*, mallo *m* (hammer) || mallo *m* (game).

mallard ['mæləd] *n* lavanco *m*, pato *m* silvestre (duck).

malleability [,mæliə'biliti] *n* maleabilidad *f*.

malleable ['mæliəbl] *adj* maleable.

malleolus [mə'liːələs] *n* ANAT maléolo *m*.
— OBSERV El plural es *malleoli*.

mallet ['mælit] *n* mazo *m*.

malleus ['mæliəs] *n* ANAT martillo *m* (of the ear).
— OBSERV El plural es *mallei*.

mallow ['mæləu] *n* BOT malva *f* || BOT *rose mallow* malvarrosa *f*.

malmsey ['mɑːmzi] *n* malvasía *f* (wine).

malnutrition ['mælnjuː'triʃən] *n* desnutrición *f*.

malodorous [mæ'ləudərəs] *adj* maloliente.

malpractice ['mæl'præktis] *n* JUR negligencia *f*, incuria *f* (negligence) | procedimientos *m pl* ilegales *or* desleales, hecho *m* delictivo.

malt [mɔːlt] *n* malta *f* (grain) || — *malt liquor* cerveza *f* || *malt sugar* maltosa *f* || *malt whisky* whisky *m* de malta.

malt [mɔːlt] *vt* maltear; *malted milk* leche malteada.

Malta ['mɔːltə] *pr n* GEOGR Malta; *Knight of Malta* caballero de Malta.

maltase ['mɔːlteis] *n* maltasa *f*.

Maltese ['mɔːl'tiːz] *adj/n* maltés, esa || *Maltese cross* cruz de Malta.

malthouse ['mɔːlthaus] *n* maltería *f*, fábrica *f* de malta.

Malthusian [mæl'θjuːzjən] *adj/n* maltusiano, na.

malting ['mɔːltiŋ] *n* malteado *m*, maltaje *m*.

maltose ['mɔːltəus] *n* CHEM maltosa *f*.

maltreat [mæl'triːt] *vt* maltratar.

maltreatment [-mənt] *n* malos tratos *m pl*, maltratamiento *m*, maltrato *m*.

malvaceae [mæl'veisiiː] *pl n* BOT malváceas *f*.

malvasia [,mælvə'siə] *n* malvasía *f* (grape).

malversation [,mælvəː'seiʃən] *n* JUR malversación *f*.

mama [mə'mɑː] *n* FAM mamá *f*.

Mameluke ['mæmiluːk] *n* mameluco *m*.

mamilla [mæ'milə] *n* ANAT pezón *m*.
— OBSERV El plural de *mamilla* es *mamillae*.

mamillary ['mæmiləri] *adj* ANAT mamilar.

mamma [mə'mɑː] *n* FAM mamá *f*.

mamma ['mæmə] *n* ANAT mama *f*, teta *f*.
— OBSERV El plural es *mammae*.

mammal ['mæməl] *n* ZOOL mamífero *m*.

mammalia [mæ'meiljə] *n* ZOOL mamíferos *m pl* (class).

mammalian [-n] *adj* ZOOL mamífero, ra.
◆ *n* mamífero *m*.

mammary ['mæməri] *adj* ANAT mamario, ria.

mammiferous [mæ'mifərəs] *adj* ZOOL mamífero, ra.

mammilla [mæ'milə] *n* ANAT pezón *m*.
— OBSERV El plural de *mammilla* es *mammillae*.

mammillary ['mæmiləri] *adj* ANAT mamilar.

mammoth ['mæməθ] *n* mamut *m*.
◆ *adj* descomunal; *mammoth sale* venta descomunal || gigante, ta; *a mammoth coach* un autocar gigante.

mammy ['mæmi] *n* mamá *f*, mamaíta *f* || US niñera *f* negra.

man [mæn] *n* hombre *m*, ser *m* humano, persona *f* (human being) || humanidad *f*, hombre *m*, género *m* humano (human race) || hombre *m* (adult male); *how many men are there here?* ¿cuántos hombres hay aquí?; *men and women* hombres y mujeres || varón *m* (male) || uno; *a man must live* uno tiene que vivir || criado *m*, sirviente *m* (valet) || MAR ordenanza *m* (orderly) | marinero *m* (sailor) || MIL ordenanza *m* (orderly) | soldado *m* (soldier) || TECH obrero *m* (workman) || COMM empleado *m* (employee) | mozo *m* (boy) || SP ficha *f* (in draughts) | pieza *f* (in chess) | jugador *m* (player) || JUR ciudadano *m* (citizen) | habitante *m* (inhabitant) || FAM hombre *m*, marido *m* (husband) | hombre *m*, amante *m* (lover) || estudiante *m*; *he's an Oxford man* es un estudiante de Oxford || vendedor *m*; *here comes the newspaper man* ahí viene el vendedor de periódicos || — *all good men and true* todos los que tienen derecho a llamarse hombres || *all to a man* todos sin exceptuar a nadie || *a man is as old as he feels* uno no tiene más edad que la que representa || *a man of the world* un hombre de mundo || *an old man* un anciano, un viejo || *any man* cualquier hombre, cualquiera || *as one man* como un solo hombre, unánimemente || *best man* padrino *m* del novio || *between man and man* de hombre a hombre || *every man* todo el mundo || *every man for himself!* ¡sálvese quien pueda! || *family man* padre de familia (father), hombre casero (devoted to his home) || *good man!* ¡muy bien! || *great man* gran hombre || *he is a Manchester man* es de Manchester || *he is quite a little man already* está ya hecho un hombre || *he is the man for me* es mi tipo de hombre (for a woman), es el hombre que necesito (for a job) || *he seems to be the very man for the job* parece ser la persona más adecuada para este trabajo || *I am your man* soy el hombre que usted necesita, soy su hombre || *I have lived here man and boy for forty years* vivo aquí desde mi más tierna infancia, es decir desde hace cuarenta años || *in the face of all men* abiertamente, a la vista de todos || *it is not fit for man or beast* no hay quien se lo trague (food) || *like a man* como un hombre || FAM *man!* ¡hombre!; *come here, man!* ¡ven aquí, hombre! || *man for man the teams were matched* hombre por hombre, los equipos estaban igualados || FIG *man Friday* factótum *m* || *man of his word* hombre de palabra || *man of letters* hombre de letras, literato *m* || *man of means* o *of property* hombre muy rico || *man of straw* testaferro *m*, hombre de paja || *man proposes, God disposes* el hombre propone y Dios dispone || *man servant* criado, sirviente || *man shall not live on bread alone* no sólo de pan vive el hombre || *man trap* cepo *m* || *men say that* dicen que, se dice que || *men's room* servicios *m pl* para caballeros || *my good man* buen hombre; *here, my good man!* ¡tenga, buen hombre! || *my little man* hijo mío || FAM *my old man* mi padre (father), mi marido (my husband) || *my young man* mi novio || *no man* nadie || *no man can serve two masters* no se puede servir a Dios y al diablo || *no man's land* tierra *f* de nadie || FAM *old man* hombre; *good-bye, old man* adiós, hombre || *old man of the sea* viejo lobo de mar || *red man* piel *m* roja || *sandwich man* hombre anuncio || *that man Smith* ese Smith || *the average man* el hombre medio || *the man in the street* el hombre de la calle || *the man of the moment* o *of the day* el hombre del día || *the old man* el jefe (the boss), el director [de una escuela, de un colegio] (the headmaster) || *the rights of man* los derechos del hombre || *they were slain to a man* mataron hasta el último, murieron todos || *to be one's own man* ser dueño de sí mismo, hacer lo que uno quiere || *to fight man to man* luchar cuerpo a cuerpo || *to live as man and wife* vivir como marido y mujer || *to make a man of* hacer un hombre; *the army will make a man of him* el ejército le hará un hombre || *to talk man to man* hablar de hombre a hombre || *what are you, man or mouse?* ¿eres hombre o no? || *young man* joven *m*.
— OBSERV El plural de *man* es *men*.

man [mæn] *vt* MIL guarnecer [de hombres] (to place men on) | servir (a gun, a post) | armar (a battery) || MAR & AVIAT tripular (to crew) || contratar personal para (a factory) || *manned flight* vuelo tripulado || *man the pumps!* ¡todos a las bombas!

man-about-town [-əˌbaut'taun] *n* hombre *m* de mundo.
— OBSERV El plural es *men-about-town*.

manacle ['mænəkl] *n* manilla *f*.
◆ *pl* esposas *f* (handcuffs).

manacle ['mænəkl] *vt* esposar, poner esposas || FIG estorbar (to hamper).

manage ['mænidʒ] *vt* manejar (tool, instrument) || conducir, llevar [AMER manejar] (a car) || gobernar (a ship) || conducir, dirigir (an undertaking) || dirigir, llevar; *to manage the affairs of the nation* dirigir los asuntos del país || administrar, dirigir, llevar (an affair, a company, a bank, etc.); *to manage a hotel* llevar un hotel || administrar (property) || llevar (affairs, a person); *he manages his own affairs* lleva él mismo sus negocios || domar (an animal) || dominar (to dominate); *to manage one's husband* dominar a su marido || conseguir, arreglárselas; *he managed to do it* consiguió hacerlo, se las arregló para hacerlo; *he managed to see the president* se las arregló para ver al presidente || hacer (a piece of work); *he managed it very cleverly* lo ha hecho de una manera muy inteligente || poder comer *or* beber; *I could manage a bit more of lamb* podría comer un poco más de cordero || querer; *can you manage another drink?* ¿quieres otra copa? || FIG manejar (s.o.) || — *can you manage ten o'clock?* ¿puedes venir a las diez? || *fifty pounds is the most that I can manage* no puedo darle más que cincuenta libras || *I can't quite manage to do it* no puedo hacerlo.
◆ *vi* arreglárselas; *how do you manage alone?* ¿cómo te las arreglas solo? || llevar *or* dirigir los negocios (to direct business) || FAM conseguir su objetivo, lograr su propósito || — *how does he sing? he manages* ¿qué tal canta? se defiende || *how will you do it? I'll manage* ¿cómo lo harás? me las arreglaré || *manage the best you can* arreglátelas como puedas || *to manage without sth., without s.o.* prescindir de algo, de alguien.

manageability [ˌmænidʒə'biliti] *n* manejabilidad *f* (of tool) || docilidad *f* (of person, animal) || flexibilidad *f*.

manageable ['mænidʒəbl] *adj* manejable (tool) || dócil (person, animal) || factible (undertaking).

management ['mænidʒmənt] *n* dirección *f*, administración *f*, gestión *f* (administration) || dirección *f*, consejo *m* de administración, junta *f* directiva (board of directors) || habilidad *f* (skill) || manejo *m* (of tools, of persons).

manager ['mænidʒə*] *n* director *m*, gerente *m* (in business); *sales manager* director de ventas || administrador *m* (of an estate) || empresario *m*, apoderado *m* (of artists, of sportsmen) || manager *m* (of boxers) || jefe *m*; *departmental manager* jefe de servicio || US jefe *m* (of a political party) || — *business manager* director comercial || *his wife is a good manager* su mujer es una buena administradora (in the home).

manageress ['mænidʒə'res] *n* directora *f*, administradora *f*.

managerial [ˌmænə'dʒiəriəl] *adj* directivo, va; directorial, administrativo, va || *managerial staff* personal *m* dirigente, ejecutivos *m pl*.

managership ['mænidʒəʃip] *n* dirección *f*, administración *f*, gestión *f*.

managing ['mænidʒiŋ] *adj* gerente; *managing director* director gerente || FIG mandón, ona.
◆ *n* ⟶ **management.**

man-at-arms ['mænət'ɑːmz] *n* hombre *m* de armas.
— OBSERV El plural es *men-at-arms*.

manatee [ˌmænə'tiː] *n* ZOOL manatí *m* (mammal).

manchineel [ˌmæntʃi'niːl] *n* manzanillo *m* (tree).

Manchu [mæn'tʃuː] *adj/n* manchú, úa.

Manchurian [-n] *adj/n* manchú, úa.

manciple ['mænsipl] *n* ecónomo *m* (of a college).

Mancunian [mæŋ'kjuːnjən] *adj* de Manchester.
◆ *n* persona *f* de Manchester.

mandamus [mæn'deiməs] *n* JUR mandamiento *m* judicial.

mandarin ['mændərin] *n* mandarín *m* (in China) || BOT mandarina *f* (fruit) || mandarino *m*, mandarinero *m* (tree).
◆ *adj* mandarino, na.

mandatary ['mændətəri] *n* mandatario *m*.

mandate ['mændeit] *n* JUR mandato *m* (given to a representative) | mandamiento *m* judicial, orden *f* (order) | mandato *m* (over a territory) | territorio *m* bajo fideicomiso *or* mandato (mandated territory).

mandate ['mændeit] *vt* poner bajo el mandato (*to* de); *New Guinea was mandated to Australia* Nueva Guinea fue puesta bajo el mandato de Australia.

mandated [-id] *adj* bajo mandato, bajo fideicomiso; *mandated territory* territorio bajo mandato.

mandator [mæn'deitə*] *n* JUR mandante *m*.

mandatory ['mændətəri] *adj* obligatorio, ria (compulsory) || *mandatory writ* mandamiento *m* judicial.
◆ *n* mandatario *m*.

mandible ['mændibl] *n* mandíbula *f*.

Mandingo [mæn'dingəu] *n* mandingo *m* (people of África).

mandola [mæn'dəulə] *n* MUS mandora *f*.

mandolin; mandoline ['mændəlin] *n* MUS mandolina *f*.

mandragora [mæn'drægərə]; **mandrake** ['mændreik] *n* BOT mandrágora *f* (plant).

mandrel ['mændrəl]; **mandril** ['mændril] *n* TECH mandril *m*.

mandril ['mændril] *n* mandril *m* (monkey).

manducate ['mændjukeit] *vt* masticar (to chew).

mane [mein] *n* crin *f*, crines *f pl* (of horse) || melena *f* (of lion, of person).

man-eater ['mæn,i:tə*] *n* antropófago *m*, caníbal *m* (person) || animal *m* que come carne humana.

man-eating ['mæn,i:tiŋ] *adj* antropófago, ga; caníbal (person) || que come carne humana (animal).

manège [mæ'neiʒ] *n* equitación *f* (hosermanship) || picadero *m* (riding school).

manes ['mɑ:neiz] *pl n* manes *m* (the souls of the dead).

maneuver [mə'nu:və*] *n/vt/vi* US ⟶ **manoeuvre.**

maneuverability [mə,nu:vrə'biliti] *n* US ⟶ **manoeuvrability.**

maneuverable [mə'nuvərəbl] *adj* US manejable, maniobrable.

manful ['mænful] *adj* valiente (brave) || resuelto, decidido (resolute) || varonil (manly).

manfulness [-nis] *n* valentía *f* (bavery) || resolución *f* (determination) || virilidad *f*, hombría *f* (manliness).

manganate ['mæŋgənət] *n* CHEM manganato *m*.

manganese [,mæŋgə'ni:z] *n* CHEM manganeso *m* || CHEM *manganese dioxide* manganesa *f*, manganesia *f*.

manganesian [-iən] *adj* manganésico, ca.

manganic [mæŋ'gænik] *adj* mangánico (acid).

manganite ['mæŋgənait] *n* manganita *f*.

manganous ['mæŋgənəs] *adj* manganésico, ca; manganoso, sa.

mange [meindʒ] *n* MED sarna *f* (skin disease).

mangel-wurzel ['mæŋgl'wə:zl] *n* BOT remolacha *f* forrajera (beet).

manger ['meindʒə*] *n* pesebre *m*.

mangetout pea [mɔnʒ'tu:pi:] *n* BOT chícharo *m*.

mangle ['mæŋgl] *n* máquina *f* de planchar (to press) || escurridor *m* (to squeeze out water).

mangle ['mæŋgl] *vt* planchar con máquina (to press) || destrozar, despedazar (to hack, to cut) || FIG deformar (a word) | mutilar (a text) || FAM destrozar (in performing).

mango ['mæŋgəu] *n* BOT mango *m* (tree, fruit).
— OBSERV El plural de la palabra inglesa *mango* es *mangoes* o *mangos*.

mangold ['mæŋgəld]; **mangold-wurzel** [-'wə:zl] *n* BOT remolacha *f* forrajera (beet).

mangosteen ['mæŋgəusti:n] *n* BOT mangostán *m* (tree, fruit).

mangrove ['mæŋgrəuv] *n* BOT mangle *m* (tree) || *mangrove swamp* manglar *m*.

mangy ['meindʒi] *adj* MED sarnoso, sa (with mange) || FAM asqueroso, sa (shabby) || FAM *mangy trick* mala jugada, cochinada *f*.

manhandle ['mæn,hændl] *vt* TECH manipular (to move by manual force) || FAM maltratar, tratar duramente; *the police began manhandling the demonstrators* la policía empezó a maltratar a los manifestantes.

manhole ['mænhəul] *n* registro *m*, boca *f* [de acceso].

manhood ['mænhud] *n* hombres *m pl* (men) || virilidad *f*, edad *f* viril, madurez *f* (state) || hombría *f*, virilidad *f* (manly qualities).

man-hour ['mæn,auə*] *n* trabajo *m* realizado por un hombre en una hora.

manhunt ['mænhʌnt] *n* caza *f* del hombre.

mania ['meinjə] *n* manía *f*; *persecution mania* manía persecutoria; *to have a mania for* tener la manía de.

maniac ['meiniæk] *adj/n* maníaco, ca || FIG fanático, ca.

maniacal [mə'naiəkəl] *adj* maníaco, ca.

manic ['mænik] *adj* maníaco, ca || *manic-depressive psychosis* manía depresiva.

Manichaean; Manichean [,mæni'ki:ən] *adj/n* maniqueo, a.

Manichaeism; Manicheism [,mæni'ki:izəm] *n* maniqueísmo *m*.

manicure ['mænikjuə*] *n* manicura *f* (care); *to give s.o. a manicure* hacerle a uno la manicura || manicuro, ra (manicurist).

manicure ['mænikjuə*] *vt* hacer la manicura a (s.o.) || arreglar (nails).

manicurist [-ist] *n* manicuro, ra.

manifest ['maenifest] *adj* manifiesto, ta; evidente.
◆ *n* MAR manifiesto *m* (list of a ship's cargo).

manifest ['mænifest] *vt* manifestar || MAR registrar en un manifiesto.

manifestant [mæni'festənt] *n* US manifestante *m* & *f* (demonstrator).

manifestation [,mænifes'teiʃən] *n* manifestación *f*.

manifesto [,mænifes'festəu] *n* manifiesto *m*.
— OBSERV El plural es *manifestoes* o *manifestos*.

manifold ['mænifəuld] *ajd* multicopista; *manifold writer* máquina multicopista || FIG múltiple, numeroso, sa (numerous) | variado, da; diverso, sa (varied) | consumado, da; notorio, ria (thief, liar, etc.).
◆ *n* copia *f* hecha con multicopista || colector *m* (pipe) || MATH multiplicidad *f* || PHIL diversidad *f*.

manifold ['mænifəuld] *vt* tirar *or* hacer con multicopista, multicopiar (documents) || multiplicar.

manifolder [-ə*] *n* multicopista *f*, máquina *f* multicopista.

manikin; mannequin; mannikin ['mænikin] *n* maniquí *m* (of taylors, etc.) || maniquí *f*, modelo *f* (of fashion) || FIG enano *m*, retaco *m* (tiny man).

Manila [mə'nilə] *pr n* GEOGR Manila.

Manila; Manilla [mə'nilə] *n* manila *m* (cigar) || — *Manila hemp* cáñamo *m* de Manila, abacá *m* || *Manila paper* papel *m* de pruebas.

manille [mə'nil] *n* malilla *f* (in cards).

manioc ['mæniɔk] *n* BOT mandioca *f*, yuca *f*.

maniple ['mænipl] *n* REL manípulo *m*.

manipulate [mə'nipjuleit] *vt* manipular, manejar (to handle) || accionar (a lever, a knob, etc.) || falsear, amañar (election results, etc.) || influir en (the market).

manipulation [mə,nipju'leiʃən] *n* manipulación *f*, manejo *m* || falseamiento *m*, amaño *m* (falsification).

manipulative [mə'nipjulətiv] *adj* manipulador, ra.

manipulator [mə'nipjuleitə*] *n* manipulador *m*.

manitou ['mænitu:] *n* manitú *m*.

mankind [mæn'kaind] *n* humanidad *f*, género *m* humano (the human race) || hombres *m pl* (men).

manlike ['mænlaik] *adj* varonil, masculino, na (of a man) || de hombre, hombruno, na (resembling a man) || hombruna (woman).

manliness ['mænlinis] *n* virilidad *f*, masculinidad *f*, hombría *f*.

manly ['mænli] *adj* varonil, viril (virile) || de hombres, masculino, na; *manly sports* deportes de hombres.

man-made ['mænmeid] *adj* hecho por la mano del hombre, artificial.

manna ['mænə] *n* maná *m* (godsend) || BOT maná *m* (of trees) || FIG *like manna from heaven* como maná llovido del cielo.

manned [mænd] *adj* tripulado, da.

mannequin ['mænikin] *n* ⟶ **manikin.**

manner ['mænə*] *n* manera *f*, modo *m*; *I don't like his manner of talking* no me gusta su manera de hablar || modo *m*, forma *f*, manera *f* (of payment) || clase *f* (kind); *all manner of things* toda clase de cosas || comportamiento *m*, modo *m* de ser *or* de portarse (behaviour) || aire *m*; *his easy manner* su aire desenvuelto || ARTS estilo *m*, manera *f* || — *adverb of manner* adverbio de modo || *after the manner of* a la manera de || *after this manner* de esta manera || *as if to the manner born* como si estuviese acostumbrado desde la cuna || *by no manner of means* de ninguna manera *or* forma, de ningún modo || *in a manner* en cierto modo, en cierto sentido || *in a manner of speaking* como si dijéramos, por decirlo así || *in like manner* de la misma manera || *in such a manner that* de tal manera que || *in the same manner as* del mismo modo que || *in this manner* de esta manera || *it's a manner of speaking* es un decir.
◆ *pl* modales *m*; *distinguished manners* modales distinguidos || educación *f sing*; *it is bad manners to interrupt* es de mala educación interrumpir; *lack of manners* falta de educación || costumbres *f*; *comedy of manners* comedia de costumbres || — *don't forget your manners!* ¡conserve los buenos modales! || *road manners* comportamiento en la carretera || *where are your manners?* ¡vaya modales!

mannered ['mænəd] *adj* de modales; *a well-mannered person* una persona de buenos modales || amanerado, da; *a mannered style of writing* un estilo amanerado.

mannerism ['mænərizəm] *n* amaneramiento *m* (affectation) || ARTS manierismo *m* || peculiaridad *f*.

mannerist ['mænərist] *n* manierista *m* & *f*.

mannerless ['mænəlis] *adj* sin educación, de malos modales, maleducado, da.

mannerliness ['mænəlinis] *n* cortesía *f*, buenos modales *m pl*, buena educación *f*.

mannerly ['mænəli] *adj* cortés, bien educado, da; de buenos modales.

mannikin ['mænikin] *n* ⟶ **manikin.**

mannish ['mæniʃ] *adj* hombruna, viril (woman) || masculino, na (dress).

mannishness [-nis] *n* aspecto *m* hombruno, masculinidad *f*.

manoeuvrability [mə,nu:vrə'biliti]; US **maneuverability** *n* manejo *m*, maniobrabilidad *f*, manejabilidad *f*.

manoeuvrable [mə'nu:vrəbl] *adj* manejable, maniobrable.

manoeuvre [mə'nu:və*]; US **maneuver** *n* maniobra *f*.

manoeuvre [mə'nu:və*]; US **maneuver** *vt* MIL & MAR hacer maniobrar || FIG maniobrar, manejar (s.o.) | maquinar, tramar (sth.) || — FIG *to manoeuvre a friend into a good job* arreglárselas hábilmente para conseguir un buen puesto a un amigo || *to manoeuvre sth. into position* poner algo en posición.
◆ *vi* MIL & MAR maniobrar || FIG maniobrar.

man-of-war ['mænəv'wɔ:*] *n* MAR buque *m* de guerra.
— OBSERV El plural de esta palabra es *men-of-war*.

manometer [mə'nɔmitə*] *n* manómetro *m*.

manor ['mænə*] *n* señorío *m*, feudo *m* (under the feudal system) || *manor house* casa solariega.

manorial [mə'nɔ:riəl] *adj* señorial, feudal (constituting a manor) || solariego, ga (house).

manpower ['mænpauə*] *n* TECH mano *f* de obra || MIL soldados *m pl* || hombres *m pl* (men).

manrope ['mænrəup] *n* MAR barandilla *f*.

mansard ['mænsɑːd] *n* tejado *m* abuhardillado (roof) || buhardilla *f* (garret).

manse [mæns] *n* casa *f* de un pastor protestante.

manservant ['mæn,səːvənt] *n* criado *m*, sirviente *m* [AMER mucamo *m*].

— OBSERV El plural de esta palabra es *menservants*.

mansion ['mænʃən] *n* casa *f* solariega (manor house) || gran casa *f* de campo (in the country) || palacete *m*, hotelito *m* (in town) || *Mansion House* casa consistorial del alcalde de Londres.

◆ *pl* casa *f sing* de vecindad, casa *f* de vecinos (apartment house).

man-size ['mænsaiz]; **man-sized** [-d] *adj* de hombres, para hombres; *a man-size job* un trabajo de hombres || muy grande (very big).

manslaughter ['mæn,slɔːtə*] *n* JUR homicidio *m* involuntario.

manslayer ['mæn,sleiə*] *n* JUR homicida *m* & *f*.

mantel ['mæntl] *n* manto *m* (of a fireplace).

mantelet; mantlet ['mæntlit] *n* mantelete *m* (shelter) || esclavina *f* (short cape) || pantalla *f* contra balas (screen).

mantelpiece ['mæntlpiːs] *n* manto *m* (mantel) || repisa *f* de chimenea (mantelshelf) || chimenea *f* (fireplace).

mantelshelf ['mæntlʃelf] *n* repisa *f* de chimenea.

— OBSERV El plural de *mantelshelf* es *mantelshelves*.

mantilla [mæn'tilə] *n* mantilla *f*.

mantis ['mæntis] *n* ZOOL *mantis prawn* o *shrimp* esquila *f*, camarón *m* | *praying mantis* santateresa *f*, predicador *m* (insect).

— OBSERV El plural es *mantises* o *mantes*.

mantissa [mæn'tisə] *n* mantisa *f* (of a logarithm).

mantle ['mæntl] *n* capa *f*, manto *m* (sleeveless cloak) || FIG manto *m*; *under the mantle of night* bajo el manto de la noche || TECH camisa *f* exterior (of a furnace) | manguito *m* (incandescent device) || manto *m* (of molluscs) || ARCH paramento *m*.

mantle ['mæntl] *vt* cubrir con un manto || FIG cubrir (to cover) | ocultar, tapar (to conceal).

◆ *vi* hacer espuma, cubrirse de espuma (liquid) || FIG enrojecerse, ruborizarse (to blush) | subirse (blood).

mantlet ['mæntlit] *n* → **mantelet.**

man-to-man [mæntəmæn] *adj* de hombre a hombre.

mantrap ['mæntræp] *n* trampa *f*.

manual ['mænjuəl] *adj* manual; *manual work* o *labour* trabajo manual || — *manual alphabet* alfabeto *m* de sordomudos || MIL *manual exercise* instrucción *f* con armas.

◆ *n* manual *m* (book) || MUS teclado *m* de un órgano.

manually [-li] *adv* a mano, manualmente.

manufacturable [,mænju'fæktʃərəbl] *adj* manufacturable.

manufacture [,mænju'fæktʃə*] *n* fabricación *f* (act) || producto *m* manufacturado (product).

manufacture [,mænju'fæktʃə*] *vt* fabricar, manufacturar || confeccionar (clothes) || FIG fabricar en serie (art, literature) | fabricar, inventar, forjar (a story).

manufacturer [-rə*] *n* fabricante *m*; *boiler manufacturer* fabricante de calderas || industrial *m* || FIG autor, ra.

manufacturing [-riŋ] *adj* industrial, fabril, manufacturero, ra.

◆ *n* fabricación *f* || confección *f* (of clothes).

manumission [,mænju'miʃən] *n* JUR manumisión *f*.

manumit [,mænju'mit] *vt* emancipar, libertar, manumitir (slaves).

manure [mə'njuə*] *n* AGR abono *m*, estiércol *m* || *manure heap* estercolero *m*.

manure [mə'njuə*] *vt* abonar, estercolar.

manuscript ['mænjuskript] *adj* manuscrito, ta (written by hand).

◆ *n* manuscrito *m* (documento written by hand) || original *m* (typewritten document).

Manx [mæŋks] *adj* de la isla de Man || sin cola (cat).

◆ *n* lengua *f* hablada en la isla de Man || *the Manx* los habitantes de la isla de Man.

Manxman [-mən] *n* natural *m* de la isla de Man.

— OBSERV El plural de *Manxman* es *Manxmen*.

many ['meni] *adj* muchos, muchas (with plural terms); *he has been here many times* ha estado aquí muchas veces; *many of us* muchos de nosotros || mucho, mucha (with collective nouns); *many people* mucha gente || — *a great many people* un gran número de personas, muchísima gente || *as many as* hasta, no menos de; *as many as ten saw it* hasta diez lo vieron; tantos *or* tantas como; *as many as you want* tantos como quieras; cuantos, cuantas; *to as many as are present I would say* a cuantos están presentes afirmo que || *as many... as* tantos *or* tantas.... como; *as many times as you* tantas veces como tú; *I have as many books as you* tengo tantos libros como tú || *ever so many times* no sé cuántas veces || *for many years* durante muchos años || *how many are there?* ¿cuántos hay? || *in as many* en el mismo número de; *they have had ten children in as many years* han tenido diez hijos en el mismo número de años || *many a man* más de uno || *many a time* más de una vez, muchas veces; *he has been here many a time* ha estado aquí más de una vez || *many is the time* más de una vez || *not very many* no muchos, no muchas || *of many kinds* de muchas clases || *one too many* uno de más, uno de sobra; *one card too many* una carta de más || *so many* tantos, tantas; *so many men, so many minds* tantos hombres, tantos pareceres || *they were so many* eran tantos, eran tantas || *too many* demasiado, da; *too many flowers* demasiadas flores || *twice as many* dos veces más, el doble || *you are none too many to* ninguno de ustedes sobra para.

◆ *pron* muchos, muchas.

◆ *n* mayoría *f*; *the will of the many* la voluntad de la mayoría || *a good* o *a great many* muchísimos, mas; un gran número.

— OBSERV El comparativo de *many* es *more* y el superlativo *most*.

many-coloured [-'kʌləd] *adj* multicolor.

manyfold [-fəuld] *adv* muchas veces.

◆ *adj* → **manifold.**

manyplies [-plaiz] *n* ZOOL libro *m* (omasum).

many-sided [-'saidid] *adj* de muchos lados || FIG complejo, ja (question) | polifacético, ca; diverso, sa; variado, da (talent).

many-sidedness [-'saididnis] *n* FIG complejidad *f* (of a question) | diversidad *f*, variedad *f* (of a talent).

manzanilla [,mænzə'nilə] *n* manzanilla *f* (wine) || manzanillo *m* (tree).

Maoism ['mæuizəm] *n* maoísmo *m*.

Maoist ['mæuist] *adj/n* maoísta.

Maori ['mauri] *adj/n* maorí.

map [mæp] *n* mapa *m*; *blank* o *outline* o *skeleton map* mapa mudo; *to draw up a map* levantar un mapa; *relief map* mapa en relieve || plano *m*; *map of a town* plano de una ciudad || carta *f* (chart) || US POP jeta *f*, hocico *m* (mug) || — *map of the world* mapamundi *m* || FAM *off the map* en el otro mundo, donde Cristo dio las tres voces (place), que no es de actualidad (question) | *to disappear from the map* desaparecer del mapa | *to put on the map* poner en el primer plano de la actualidad | *to wipe off the map* hacer desaparecer del mapa (to destroy).

map [mæp] *vt* levantar un mapa de (to make a map) || indicar en el mapa (to represent on a map) || trazar, dibujar (a plan) || FIG *to map out* proyectar, planear, organizar; *he mapped out his holidays* planeó sus vacaciones.

maple ['meipl] *n* BOT arce *m* (tree, wood); *maple sugar, syrup* azúcar, jarabe de arce.

map maker ['mæp,meikə*] *n* cartógrafo, fa.

map making [-iŋ] *n* cartografía *f*.

mapping ['mæpiŋ] *n* cartografía *f* || levantamiento *m* de planos.

Maputo [mə'puːtəu] *pr n* GEOGR Maputo.

maquette [mæ'ket] *n* maqueta *f*.

maquis ['mæki] *n* monte *m* bajo, soto *m* (copse) || resistencia *f* de los franceses contra los alemanes en la segunda guerra mundial.

mar [mɑː*] *vt* estropear, echar a perder (to damage) || desfigurar (s.o.) || — *to mar one's enjoyment* aguarle la fiesta a uno || *to mar one's joy* entristecer a uno.

marabou; marabout ['mærəbuː] *n* marabú *m*.

marabout ['mærəbuː] *n* morabito *m* (moslem hermit).

maraca [mə'rɑːkə] *n* MUS maraca *f* (percussion instrument).

maraschino [,mærəs'kiːnəu] *n* marrasquino *m* (liqueur).

marasmus [mə'ræzməs] *n* MED marasmo *m*.

— OBSERV *Marasmus* no tiene el sentido figurado y familiar que tiene *marasmo* en español (falta de energía, estancamiento).

marathon ['mærəθən] *n* maratón *m* (race).

maraud [mə'rɔːd] *vi* merodear.

marauder [-ə*] *n* merodeador, ra.

marauding [-iŋ] *adj* merodeador, ra.

◆ *n* merodeo *m*.

maravedi [,mærə'veidi] *n* maravedí *m* (coin).

marble ['mɑːbl] *n* mármol *m* (statue, stone); *sculpted in marble* esculpido en mármol || canica *f*, bola *f* (ball); *to play marbles* jugar a las canicas.

◆ *adj* de mármol; *marble pavement* enlosado de mármol || del mármol; *marble industry* industria del mármol || marmóreo, a; de mármol (whiteness).

marble ['mɑːbl] *vt* jaspear, vetear.

marble cutter [-,kʌtə*] *n* marmolista *m* (worker) || *marble-cutter's workshop* marmolería *f*.

marbleize ['mɑːblaiz] *vt* US jaspear, vetear (to marble).

marblework ['mɑːbl'wəːk] *n* marmolería *f*.

marbling ['mɑːbliŋ] *n* jaspeado *m*, veteado *m*.

marbly ['mɑːbli] *adj* jaspeado, da; veteado, da.

marc [mɑːk] *n* orujo *m*.

marcasite ['mɑːkəsait] *n* marcasita *f* (pyrite).

march [mɑːtʃ] *n* marcha *f*; *on the march* en marcha; *to organize a protest march* organizar una marcha de protesta || paso *m*; *double march* paso gimnástico || MUS marcha *f*; *wedding march* marcha nupcial || FIG marcha *f*, adelanto *m*, progreso *m* (progress) ‖ HIST marca *f* (border territory) ‖ — *day's march* etapa *f* ‖ *forced march* marcha forzada ‖ FAM *to steal a march on* aventajar a, tomar la delantera a, ganar por la mano a.

march [mɑːtʃ] *vi* marchar, caminar (to walk) ‖ desfilar (in a procession) ‖ MIL hacer una marcha ‖ FIG avanzar, progressar (to advance) | MIL *forward march!, quick march!* ¡de frente!, ¡ar! ‖ *to march away* o *off* irse ‖ *to march in* entrar ‖ *to march on* seguir su camino; pasar; *times marches on* el tiempo pasa ‖ *to march out* salir ‖ MIL *to march past* o *by* desfilar ‖ *to march upon* o *with* lindar con (territory).

◆ *vt* MIL hacer marchar, hacer efectuar una marcha ‖ llevar andado, marchar (a distance) ‖ *to march s.o. off* llevarse a uno.

March [mɑːtʃ] *n* marzo *m*; *5th March 1983* el 5 de marzo de 1983.

marcher [mɑːtʃə*] *n* manifestante *m* & *f*.

marching orders ['mɑːtʃiŋ,ɔːdəz] *pl n* MIL orden *f sing* de ponerse en marcha ‖ FIG despido *m sing* (dismissal) ‖ FIG *to give s.o. his marching orders* despedir a uno.

marchioness ['mɑːʃənis] *n* marquesa *f*.

marchland ['mɑːtʃlənd] *n* región *f* fronteriza, marca *f*.

marchpane ['mɑːtʃpein] *n* CULIN mazapán *m*.

march-past ['mɑːtʃpɑːst] *n* desfile *m*.

marconigram [mɑː'kəunigræm] *n* radiograma *m*.

Marcus ['mɑːkəs] *pr n* Marco *m* ‖ *Marcus Aurelius* Marco Aurelio.

Mardi Gras ['mɑːdi'grɑː] *n* Martes *m* de Carnaval.

mare [mɛə*] *n* yegua *f* (female horse).

mare's nest ['mɛəznest] *n* FAM parto *m* de los montes, descubrimiento *m* ilusorio (worthless discovery) | engaño *m* (hoax).

mare's tail ['mɛəzteil] *n* BOT cola *f* de caballo (aquatic plant) ‖ cirro *m* (cloud).

Margaret ['mɑːgərit] *pr n* Margarita *f*.

margarine [,mɑːdʒə'riːn] *n* margarina *f*.

margarite ['mɑːgə,rait] *n* margarita *f* (pearl).

marge [mɑːdʒ] *n* FAM margarina *f* (margarine).

margin ['mɑːdʒin] *n* margen *f* (of a river) ‖ lindero *m*, linde *f* (of a wood) ‖ margen *m*; *in the margin* al margen; *bottom, head margin* margen inferior, superior; *the margin of a page* el margen de una página; *profit margin* margen de beneficio; *safety margin* margen de seguridad ‖ provisión *f*, reserva *f* (reserve) ‖ cobertura *f* (in finance) ‖ FIG límite *m*, margen *m* (limit) ‖ — *by a narrow margin* por un escaso margen ‖ *to allow s.o. some margin* dejarle margen a uno.

margin ['mɑːdʒin] *vt* dejar un margen a (page) ‖ poner al margen (notes) ‖ hacer una reserva de, tener una cobertura de (in finance).

marginal [-əl] *adj* marginal (note, profits) ‖ PHYS periférico, ca (rays) ‖ — *marginal case* caso *m* marginal, caso *m* límite ‖ *marginal stop* tecla *f* marginal.

marginalia [,mɑːdʒi'neiljə] *pl n* notas *f* marginales.

marginate ['mɑːdʒineit] *vt* marginar.

margrave ['mɑːgreiv] *n* margrave *m*.

margravine ['mɑːgrəviːn] *n* mujer *f* del margrave.

marguerite [,mɑːgə'riːt] *n* margarita *f* (daisy).

Marguerite [,mɑːgə'riːt] *pr n* Margarita *f*.

Maria [mə'riːə] *pr n* Maria *f* ‖ FAM *Black Maria* coche *m* celular.

Marian ['mɛəriən] *adj* mariano, na; marial (of the Virgin Mary).

Mariana [,mɛəri'ænə] *pr n* GEOGR *Mariana Islands* islas Marianas.

marianism ['mɛəriənizəm] *n* marianismo *m*.

marianist ['mɛəriənist] *adj/n* marianista.

marigold ['mærigəuld] *n* BOT maravilla *f*, caléndula *f*.

marigraph ['mærigræf] *n* mareografo *m*.

marijuana [,mæri'hwɑːnə] *n* marihuana *f*, marijuana *f*.

marimba [mə'rimbə] *n* MUS marimba *f*.

marina [mə'riːnə] *n* US puerto *m* deportivo.

marinade [,mæri'neid] *n* CULIN adobo *m*, escabeche *m* (for meat) | escabeche *m* (for fish).

marinade [,mæri'neid] ; **marinate** ['mærineit] *vt* CULIN adobar, escabechar (meat) | escabechar, marinar (fish).

marine [mə'riːn] *adj* MAR marino, na; *marine life* vida marina | naval (forces, engineer) | de marina (infantry) | marítimo, ma (insurance) | náutico, ca (chart).

◆ *n* soldado *m* de infantería de marina ‖ marina *f*; *the merchant marine* la marina mercante ‖ marina *f* (painting).

◆ *pl* infantería *f sing* de marina ‖ FAM *tell that to the marines!* ¡cuéntaselo a tu abuela!

mariner ['mærinə*] *n* marinero *m*, marino *m*.

marionette [,mæriə'net] *n* marioneta *f*, títere *m*.

Marist ['mɛərist] *adj/n* REL marista.

marital ['mæritl] *adj* marital ‖ matrimonial ‖ *marital status* estado *m* civil.

maritime ['mæritaim] *adj* marítimo, ma.

marjoram ['mɑːdʒərəm] *n* BOT mejorana *f*.

mark [mɑːk] *n* huella *f* (trace); *the tyres left marks on the road* los neumáticos dejaron huellas en la carretera; *marks of old age* huellas de la vejez ‖ signo *m* (sign); *his business shows all the marks of success* su negocio presenta todos los signos de prosperidad ‖ signo *m*, señal *f*; *as a mark of my esteem* en señal de mi aprecio ‖ señal *f*; *it is a mark of good weather* es señal de buen tiempo ‖ marca *f* (brand, trademark) ‖ marca *f*, etiqueta *f* (label) ‖ huella *f*, señal *f*; *marks of a blow* las huellas de un golpe ‖ signo *m*, cruz *f*; *he cannot write, he makes his mark* no sabe escribir, firma con un signo ‖ mancha *f* (stain) ‖ prueba *f* testimonio *m*; *marks of friendship* pruebas de amistad ‖ sello *m*; *his works bear his mark* sus obras llevan su sello ‖ signo *m*; *punctuation marks* signos de puntuación; *exclamation mark* signo de admiración; *question mark* signo de interrogación ‖ llamada *f* (asterisk, etc.) ‖ nota *f* (in an examination); *he had a bad mark* tuvo una mala nota ‖ puntuación *f*; *what marks did you get?* ¿qué puntuación sacó? ‖ cotización *f* (stock exchange) ‖ punto *m*; *reference mark* punto de referencia ‖ SP línea *f* de partida (in a race) | tanto *m* (point of a score) ‖ objetivo *m*, meta *f*, blanco *m* (targe, aim); *to hit the mark* alcanzar el objetivo ‖ MAR señal, *f* [de boya o de baliza] (on buoy) ‖ ANAT boca *f* del estómago (pit of the stomach) ‖ boliche *m* (bowls) ‖ nivel *m* (level); *water mark* nivel de agua ‖ marco *m* (German money) ‖ picadura *f* (of smallpox) ‖ FIG nivel *m* (standard) ‖ — FIG *a man of mark* una persona notable *or* relevante | *beside the mark* fuera de lugar | *beyond the mark* fuera de todo límite ‖ FAM *easy mark* primo, ma; tonto, ta ‖ SP *on your marks!, get set!, go!* ¡preparados!, ¡listos!, ¡ya! ‖ *printer's mark* pie *m* de imprenta ‖ FIG *to be near, over, under, wide of the mark* estar cerca de, por encima de, por debajo de, lejos de la verdad *or* de la realidad ‖ *to be quick, slow off the mark* arrancar rápidamente, lentamente (motor), ser rápido, lento (person) ‖ FIG *to be up to the mark* estar a la altura (in ability), estar en perfecto estado de salud (in health), estar en forma (on form) | *to come up to the mark* estar a la altura ‖ *to fall* o *to go wide of the mark* no dar en el blanco (a shot) ‖ FIG *to hit he mark* dar en el clavo, acertar | *to leave one's mark* dejar su huella | *to make one's mark* distinguirse, señalarse ‖ *to miss the mark* no dar en el blanco.

mark [mɑːk] *vt* marcar (clothes) ‖ señalar, indicar (a passage) ‖ señalar, marcar; *to mark the place with a cross* señalar el sitio con una cruz ‖ poner, señalar [el precio de]; *to mark (the price of) an article* poner el precio a un artículo ‖ poner la marca *or* la etiqueta a (to label) ‖ señalar; *this event marked the beginning of the revolution* este suceso señaló el comienzo de la revolución ‖ poner una nota, calificar, puntuar; *to mark an exercise* poner una nota a un ejercicio ‖ picar; *his face was marked by smallpox* tenía la cara picada de viruelas ‖ señalar (with a blow) ‖ indicar, revelar, mostrar; *his silence marked his anger* su silencio indicaba su enfado ‖ COMM cotizar (stock exchange) ‖ SP marcar (to watch a player, to indicate the score); *to mark an opposing player* marcar a un jugador contrario ‖ MUS llevar, marcar; *to mark the rhythm* llevar el compás ‖ caracterizar; *the friendship which has marked our relations* la amistad que ha caracterizado nuestras relaciones ‖ distinguir, señalar; *the qualities which mark a leader* las cualidades que distinguen a un dirigente ‖ observar; *I marked her closely* la observé atentamente ‖ darse cuenta, observar; *mark that there is a difference* dese cuenta de que hay una diferencia ‖ prestar atención a, fijarse en, escuchar; *mark my words* fíjese en mis palabras ‖ marcar (cards) ‖ — *mark you, he did say he might be late* cuidado, que dijo que a lo mejor llegaría tarde ‖ *to mark down* rebajar (the price), apuntar, señalar; *he has marked down the items he wants* ha señalado los artículos que quiere ‖ *to mark off* delimitar (to indicate the limit), amojonar, jalonar (a road) ‖ *to mark out* trazar (boundaries), amojonar, jalonar (field) ‖ *to mark s.o. off* o *out from* distinguir a uno de ‖ *to mark s.o. out for* escoger *or* señalar a uno para, destinar a uno a ‖ *to mark time* marcar el paso (in a military march), no avanzar nada, estancarse (to stagnate), hacer tiempo (waiting) ‖ *to mark up* aumentar (prices).

◆ *vi* SP marcar.

Mark [mɑːk] *pr n* Marcos *m* ‖ *Mark Antony* Marco Antonio.

markdown [-daun] *n* rebaja *f*, disminución *f* (of price).

marked [-t] *adj* marcado, da ‖ acusado, da; acentuado, da; pronunciado, da; *a marked difference* una diferencia pronunciada ‖ apreciable, notable, sensible; *marked improvement* mejora apreciable ‖ destacado, da (enjoying notoriety) ‖ fichado, da (regarded with suspicion).

marker [-ə*] *n* marcador *m*.

marker pen [-pen] *n* rotulador *m*.

market [-it] *n* mercado *m* (place); *fish market* mercado de pescado; *Sunday is market day* el domingo hay mercado; *to go to market* ir al mercado ‖ salida *f*, mercado *m* (demand); *how is the market for this product?* ¿qué salida tiene este producto? ‖ mercado *m* (sale); *open, unofficial market* mercado libre, paralelo; *foreign exchange market* mercado de cambios ‖ bolsa *f* (stock exchange) ‖ mercado *m* (region); *the American market* el mercado americano ‖ FIG tráfico *m* ‖ — *at market price* al precio del mercado ‖ *black market* mercado negro, estraperlo *m* ‖ *buyer's market* mercado favorable al comprador ‖ *Common Market* Mercado Común ‖ *home market* mercado interior *or* nacional ‖ *into* o *on the market* en venta, en el mercado ‖ *market forces* tendencias *f pl or* fuerzas *f pl* de mercado || *market price* precio *m* de mercado *or* corriente || *market value* valor *m* comercial || *overseas market* mercado exterior || *ready market* fácil venta *f*, fácil salida || *seller's market* mercado favorable al vendedor || *steady, quiet market* mercado sostenido, encalmado || *Stock market* Bolsa *f*, mercado de valores || *there is a good market for* hay mucho mercado para, hay una gran demanda de || *to be in the market for* ser comprador de, estar dispuesto a comprar || *to come into the market* ponerse en venta, salir al mercado || *to corner the market in* acaparar el mercado de || *to flood the market with* inundar el mercado de || *to make a market for* crear un mercado para || FIG *to make a market of* malvender || *to play the market* jugar a la Bolsa || *to put on the market* poner en venta, sacar al mercado || *world market* mercado mundial.

market [-it] *vt* poner en venta *or* a la venta, vender (to sell) || comercializar.
◆ *vi* hacer la compra, ir al mercado (for provisions).

marketable [-itəbl] *adj* de fácil venta, vendible || comercial.

marketeer [ˌmɑːkiˈtiːə*]; **marketer** [ˌmɑːkitə*] *n* vendedor, ra (market dealer, seller) || partidario *m* del Mercado Común || *black marketeer* estraperlista *m* & *f*.

market garden [ˈmɑːkitˌgɑːdn] *n* huerto *m* (small), huerta *f* (large).

market gardener [-ə*] *n* hortelano *m*.

market gardening [-iŋ] *n* cultivo *m* de hortalizas.

marketing [ˈmɑːkitiŋ] *n* estudio *m or* investigación *f* de mercados (market research) || comercialización *f* (of goods).

market order [ˈmɑːkitˌɔːdə*] *n* orden *f* de compra (to buy) || orden *f* de venta (to sell).

marketplace [ˈmɑːkitpleis] *n* mercado *m*, plaza *f* (del mercado).

market research [ˈmɑːkitriˈsəːtʃ] *n* estudio *m* de mercados, investigación *f* de mercados.

market town [ˈmɑːkittaun] *n* mercado *m*, población *f* con mercado.

marking [ˈmɑːkiŋ] *n* marca *f*, señal *f* (mark) || marcado *m* || SP marcaje *m* || cotización *f* (stock exchange) || pinta *f* (on animals, etc.) || nota *f*, calificación *f* (at school).

marking gauge [-geidʒ] *n* gramil *m*.

marksman [ˈmɑːksmən] *n* tirador *m*.
— OBSERV El plural de *marksman* es *marksmen*.

marksmanship [-ʃip] *n* puntería *f* excelente.

markup [ˈmɑːkʌp] *n* subida *f*, alza *f*, aumento *m* (of prices) || margen *m* de beneficio (profit margin).

marl [mɑːl] *n* marga *f*.

marl [mɑːl] *vt* margar, abonar con marga.

marlinespike; marlinspike [ˈmɑːlinˌspaik] *n* MAR pasador *m*.

marlpit [ˈmɑːlpit] *n* margal *m*, marguera *f*.

marmalade [ˈmɑːməlәid] *n* mermelada *f* de naranja amarga.

marmoreal [ˌmɑːˈmɔːrjəl] *adj* marmóreo, a.

marmoset [ˈmɑːməuzet] *n* tití *m* (monkey).

marmot [ˈmɑːmət] *n* ZOOL marmota *f*.

Maronite [ˈmærənait] *adj/n* maronita.

maroon [məˈruːn] *adj* castaño, ña.
◆ *n* castaño *m* (colour) || petardo *m* (firework) || cimarrón *m* (slave) || MAR persona *f* abandonada en una isla desierta.

maroon [məˈruːn] *vt* MAR abandonar en una isla desierta || FIG aislar.

marque [mɑːk] *n* patente *f* de corso.

marquee [mɑˈkiː] *n* gran tienda *f* de campaña (tent) || US marquesina *f* (rooflike projection).

marquess [ˈmɑːkwis] *n* marqués *m*.

marquetry; marqueterie [ˈmɑːkitri] *n* marquetería *f*, taracea *f*.

marquis [ˈmɑːkwis] *n* marqués *m*.

marquisate [ˈmɑːkwizit] *n* marquesado *m*.

marquise [mɑːˈkiːz] *n* marquesa *f* (title) || lanzadera *f* (ring) || FIG *to put on airs like a marquise* dárselas de marquesa.
— OBSERV Este título nobiliario sólo se aplica a las personas que no son inglesas. A estas últimas se les llama *marchioness*.

marriage [ˈmæridʒ] *n* matrimonio *m*; *to take in marriage* o *to contract marriage with* contraer matrimonio con; *marriage of convenience* matrimonio de conveniencia *or* de interés; *civil marriage* matrimonio civil || boda *f*, casamiento *m* (ceremony) || tute *m* (at cards) || FIG unión *f*, asociación *f* (intimate union) || — *by marriage* político (family); *uncle by marriage* tío político || *marriage by proxy* matrimonio por poderes || *marriage lines, certificate of marriage* partida *f* de matrimonio || FAM *marriage over the broomstick* matrimonio por detrás de la iglesia || *marriage portion* dote *f* || *non-consummated marriage* matrimonio rato.

marriageable [-əbl] *adj* casadero, ra; en edad de casarse || núbil (age).

married [ˈmærid] *adj* casado, da; *to be married* estar casado || de casados, conyugal; *married life* vida de casados || matrimonial; *married state* estado matrimonial || — *married couple* matrimonio *m* || *married name* apellido *m* de casada || *to get married to* casarse con.

marron glacé [ˈmærənˈglæsei] *n* castaña *f* confitada, «marron *m* glacé».

marrow [ˈmærəu] *n* MED médula *f*; *spinal marrow* médula espinal || CULIN tuétano *m* || FIG meollo *m* (essential part) || — FIG *to the marrow* hasta los tuétanos || *vegetable marrow* calabacín *m*.

marrowbone [-bəun] *n* CULIN hueso *m* con tuétano || FAM *on your marrowbones!* ¡de rodillas!

marrowfat [-fæt] *n* guisante *m* de semilla grande.

marrowless [-lis] *adj* CULIN sin tuétano || FIG poco enérgico, ca; sin nervio.

marry [ˈmæri] *vt* casar (to join in marriage); *they were married by the bishop* los casó el obispo || casarse con, casar con (to get married); *he married her last month* se casó con ella el mes pasado || casar; *he married his daughter last month* casó a su hija el mes pasado; *he married his daughter to a foreigner* casó a su hija con un extranjero || FIG unir (to join closely) || — *they married each other* se casaron (los dos) || FAM *to marry money* casarse por interés || *to marry off* casar.
◆ *vi* casarse || — *to marry a second time* volver a casarse, casarse en segundas nupcias || *to marry beneath one* malcasarse || *to marry into* emparentar con.

Mars [mɑːz] *pr n* Marte *m* (god, planet).

Marseilles [mɑːˈseilz] *pr n* GEOGR Marsella.

marsh [mɑːʃ] *n* zona *f* pantanosa, pantano *m* (bog) || marisma *f* (near the sea or a river).
◆ *adj* pantanoso, sa.

marshal [-əl] *n* MIL mariscal *m* | comandante *m* supremo, jefe *m* supremo || maestro *m* de ceremonias (master of ceremonies) || US jefe *m* de policía (sheriff) | oficial *m* de justicia | jefe *m* de bomberos.

marshal [-əl] *vt* formar (troops) || poner en orden, ordenar (to arrange in order).

marshalling yard; US **marshaling yard** [-əliŋjɑːd] *n* estación *f* de apartado *or* de clasificación (railway).

marsh fever [-ˈfiːvə*] *n* MED paludismo *m*, fiebre *f* palúdica, malaria *f*.

marsh gas [-gæs] *n* gas *m* de los pantanos, metano *m*.

marsh hen [-hen] *n* ZOOL polla *f* de agua.

marshmallow [-ˈmæləu] *n* BOT malvavisco *m* || CULIN melcocha *f*.

marsh marygold [-ˈmærigəuld] *n* BOT calta *f*.

marshy [-i] *adj* pantanoso, sa.

marsupial [mɑːˈsjuːpjəl] *adj* marsupial.
◆ *n* marsupial *m*.

mart [mɑːt] *n* centro *m* comercial (trading centre) || martillo *m* (for auction sale).

marten [ˈmɑːtin] *n* ZOOL marta *f*.

martial [ˈmɑːʃəl] *adj* marcial; *martial law* ley marcial || bélico, ca (war-minded) || militar; *martial songs* canciones militares || SP *martial arts* artes *f pl* marciales.

Martian [ˈmɑːʃjən] *adj/n* marciano, na.

martin [ˈmɑːtin] *n* vencejo *m*, avión *m* (bird).

Martin [ˈmɑːtin] *pr n* Martín *m*.

martinet [ˌmɑːtiˈnet] *n* jefe *m* muy autoritario, ordenancista *m*, sargento *m*.

martingale [ˈmˌgɑːtiŋgeil] *n* gamarra *f*, amarra *f* (of a horse) || MAR moco *m* del bauprés || martingala *f*, combinación *f* (in gambling).

Martinique [ˌmɑːtiˈniːk] *pr n* GEOGR La Martinica.

Martinmas [ˈmɑːtinməs] *n* día *m* de San Martín (11th november).

martlet [ˈmɑːtlit] *n* ZOOL vencejo *m*, avión *m* (martin).

martyr [ˈmɑːtə*] *n* mártir *m* & *f* || — FIG *to be a martyr to* ser víctima de, padecer, estar aquejado de (an illness) | *to make a martyr of o.s.* dárselas de mártir.

martyr [ˈmɑːtə*] *vt* martirizar.

martyrdom [-dəm] *n* martirio *m*.

martyrize [ˈmɑːtəraiz] *vt* martirizar.

martyrology [ˌmɑːtəˈrɔlədʒi] *n* martirologio *m*.

martyry [ˈmɑːtiri] *n* santuario *m* en honor a un mártir.

marvel [ˈmɑːvəl] *n* maravilla *f*; *to work marvels* hacer maravillas; *what a marvel!* ¡qué maravilla! || *it's marvel to me that* me maravilla que.

marvel [ˈmɑːvəl] *vi* maravillarse, asombrarse; *I marvel at his patience* me maravillo con su paciencia; *I marvel that you should remain so calm* me maravilla que se quede tan tranquilo.

marvellous; US **marvelous** [-əs] *adj* maravilloso, sa || FIG *isn't it marvellous?* ¡qué bien!

marvel-of-Peru [-əvpəˈruː] *n* BOT dondiego *m*, maravilla *f*.

Marxian [ˈmɑːksjən] *adj/n* marxista.

Marxism [ˈmɑːksizəm] *n* marxismo *m*; *Marxism-Leninism* marxismo-leninismo.

Marxist [ˈmɑːksist] *adj/n* marxista.

Mary [ˈmɛəri] *pr n* María *f* || FAM *Bloody Mary* vodka *m* con jugo de tomate.

Maryland [ˈmɛərilænd] *pr n* GEOGR Maryland.

marzipan [ˌmɑːziˈpæn] *n* mazapán *m* (sweet).

mascara [mæsˈkɑːrə] *n* rimel *m*.

mascle [ˈmɑːskl] *n* HERALD macla *f*.

mascot [ˈmæskət] *n* mascota *f*.

masculine [ˈmæskjulin] *adj* masculino, na || *masculine rhyme* rima asonantada.
◆ *n* masculino *m* (gender).

masculinity [ˌmæskjuˈliniti] *n* masculinidad *f*.

maser [meizə*] *n* PHYS maser *m*.

mash [mæʃ] *n* CULIN puré *m* de patatas ‖ AGR afrecho *m* remojado (animal food) ‖ malta *f* remojada (in brewing) ‖ mezcla *f* (mixture) ‖ FIG papilla *f*; *to reduce sth. to mash* hacer algo papilla ‖ FAM *to have a mash on s.o.* estar encaprichado por alguien.

mash [mæʃ] *vt* triturar (to grind) ‖ machacar (to crush) ‖ mezclar (to mix) ‖ — *mashed potatoes* puré *m* de patatas ‖ FAM *to be mashed on s.o.* estar encaprichado por alguien ‖ *to mash potatoes* hacer un puré de patatas.

masher [-ə*] *n* FAM seductor *m*.

mask [mɑːsk] *n* máscara *f*, careta *f* (covering, disguise); *carnival mask* máscara de carnaval ‖ enmascarado, da (person) ‖ máscara *f*; *gas mask* máscara antigás ‖ mascarilla *f*; *oxygen mask* mascarilla de oxígeno; *death mask* mascarilla mortuoria ‖ ARCH mascarón *m* ‖ PHOT ocultador *m* ‖ INFORM máscara *f* ‖ — FIG *to throw off the mask* quitarse la máscara | *under the mask of* bajo el disfraz de.

mask [mɑːsk] *vt* enmascarar ‖ FIG ocultar, disfrazar, disimular ‖ PHOT ocultar, poner un ocultador a ‖ MIL camuflar (a battery) ‖ MED poner una mascarilla a ‖ *to mask one's face* enmascararse, ponerse una careta.

masked ball [ˈmɑːsktˈbɔːl] *n* baile *m* de disfraces *or* de máscaras.

masker [ˈmɑːskə*] *n* máscara *f*, enmascarado, da.

masking tape [ˈmɑːskiŋˌteip] *n* cinta *f* adhesiva.

masochism [ˈmæsəukizəm] *n* masoquismo *m*.

masochist [ˈmæsəukist] *n* masoquista *m* & *f*.

masochistic [ˌmæsəuˈkistik] *adj* masoquista.

mason [ˈmeisn] *n* albañil *m* (in building industry) ‖ cantero *m* (stonemason).

Mason [ˈmeisn] *n* masón *m* (freemason).

mason [ˈmeisn] *vt* mampostear, construir con mampostería.

mason bee [ˈmeisnˌbiː] *n* abeja *f* albañila.

Masonic [məˈsɔnik] *adj* masónico, ca; *Masonic lodge* logia masónica.

masonry [ˈmeisnri] *n* albañilería *f* (trade of a mason) ‖ fábrica *f*, mampostería *f*, obra *f* de albañilería (brickwork, stonework).

Masonry [ˈmeisnri] *n* masonería *f* (freemasonry).

masque [mɑːsk] *n* THEATR mascarada *f*.

masquerade [ˌmæskəˈreid] *n* mascarada *f*, baile *m* de máscaras (ball) ‖ disfraz *m* (costume) ‖ FIG farsa *f*, mascarada *f*.

masquerade [ˌmæskəˈreid] *vi* disfrazarse (to put on a disguise); *a prince who masquerades as a peasant* un príncipe que se disfraza de campesino ‖ hacerse pasar (*as* por) (to pretend to be).

mass [mæs] *n* PHYS masa *f*; *the mass of a solid* la masa de un cuerpo sólido; *critical mass* masa crítica ‖ masa *f*; *the lake became a mass of ice* el lago se convirtió en una masa de hielo ‖ FIG montón *m*, cantidad *f*; *masses of money* cantidades de dinero ‖ mayoría *f*, mayor parte *f*; *the mass of Englishmen* la mayoría de los ingleses ‖ — FIG *he was a mass of bruises* era un puro cardenal ‖ *in the mass* en conjunto ‖ *mass executions* ejecuciones en masa ‖ *the masses* la masa, las masas ‖ FIG *to be a mass of nerves* ser un manojo de nervios.

Mass [mæs] *n* REL misa *f* ‖ — *Black Mass* misa negra ‖ *High Mass* misa mayor ‖ *Low Mass* misa rezada ‖ *Mass for the dead* misa de difuntos ‖ *Midnight Mass* misa del gallo ‖ *Morning Mass* misa del alba ‖ *Outdoor Mass* misa de campaña ‖ *Pontifical Mass* misa pontifical ‖ *Requiem, funeral Mass* misa de cuerpo presente ‖ *Sung Mass* misa cantada ‖ *to attend Mass* ir a misa (to go), oír misa (to hear) ‖ *to go to Mass* ir a misa ‖ *to hear Mass* oír misa ‖ *to ring for Mass* tocar a misa ‖ *to say Mass* decir misa ‖ *to serve at Mass* ayudar a misa ‖ *to sing* o *to say one's first Mass* cantar misa (a newly-ordained priest).

mass [mæs] *vt* reunir en masa, agrupar ‖ MIL concentrar (troops).

◆ *vi* reunirse en masa, agruparse, congregarse ‖ MIL concentrarse (troops).

Massachusetts [ˌmæsəˈtʃuːsits] *pr n* GEOGR Massachusetts.

massacre [ˈmæsəkə*] *n* matanza *f* [AMER masacre *f*] (killing).

massacre [ˈmæsəkə*] *vt* matar en masa, hacer una matanza de.

massage [ˈmæsɑːʒ] *n* masaje *m*.

massage [ˈmæsɑːʒ] *vt* dar masajes a.

massé [mæˈsei] *n* SP massé *m* (billiard).

masseter [mæˈsiːtə] *n* ANAT masetero *m*.

masseur [mæˈsəː*] *n* masajista *m*.

masseuse [mæˈsəːz] *n* masajista *f*.

massif [ˈmæsiːf] *n* GEOGR macizo *m*.

massing [ˈmæsiŋ] *n* congregación *f* (of persons) ‖ amontonamiento *m* (of things) ‖ MIL concentración *f* (of troops).

massive [ˈmæsiv] *adj* macizo, za (weighty) ‖ masivo, va; *a massive price increase* un aumento masivo de precio ‖ macizo, za (gold, silver) ‖ imponente (large and imposing).

massiveness [-nis] *n* lo macizo, macicez *f*.

mass market [ˈmæsˈmɑːkit] *adj* de gran consumo (product).

mass media [ˈmæsˈmiːdiə] *n* medios *m pl* informativos, medios *m pl* de comunicación de masa (press, radio, etc.).

mass meeting [ˈmæsˈmiːtiŋ] *n* mitin *m* popular.

mass memory [ˈmæsˈmeməri] *n* INFORM memoria *f* masiva.

mass-produce [ˈmæsprəˌdjuːs] *vt* fabricar en serie.

mass production [ˈmæsprəˌdʌkʃən] *n* fabricación *f* en serie.

massy [ˈmæsi] *adj* macizo, za.

mast [mɑːst] *n* MAR palo *m*, mástil *m* ‖ RAD poste *m* (post) ‖ TECH torre *f* ‖ AGR bellota *f* ‖ — MAR *fore-topgallant mast* mastelerillo *m* de juanete de proa | *main-topgallant mast* mastelerillo *m* de juanete mayor | *mizzen-topgallant mast* mastelero *m* de perico | *topgallant mast* mastelerillo *m* | *to sail before the mast* servir como marinero.

mast [mɑːst] *vt* MAR arbolar.

mastaba [ˈmæstəbə] *n* mastaba *f* (tomb).

mastectomy [mæsˈtektəmi] *n* MED mastectomía *f*.

master [ˈmɑːstə*] *n* amo *m* (of animals, of slaves) ‖ señor *m* (of household); *the master of the house* el señor de la casa ‖ jefe *m*, patrón *m* (of workmen) ‖ dueño *m* (owner) ‖ maestre *m* (of a military order) ‖ maestro *m* (in primary school) ‖ profesor *m* (in secondary school) ‖ director *m* (head of a college) ‖ licenciado, da (university graduate); *Master of Arts* licenciado en Letras; *Master of Sciences* licenciado en Ciencias (see OBSERV) ‖ MAR capitán *m* (of ship) | patrón *m* (of boat) ‖ ARTS maestro *m* ‖ maestro *m* (in chess) ‖ — *fencing master* maestro de armas ‖ FIG *he's met his master* ha dado con la horma de su zapato | *I am the master now* ahora mando yo | *like master like man* de tal palo tal astilla ‖ *Master John Smith* Señor Don John Smith ‖ *master of ceremonies* maestro de ceremonias (at a formal event), presentador *m* (of a show) ‖ *the young master* el señorito ‖ *to be a master of* dominar ‖ *to be a past master at sth.* ser experto *or* maestro en algo ‖ *to be master in one's own house* mandar en su propia casa ‖ *to be master of the situation* ser dueño de la situación ‖ *to be one's own master* no depender de nadie ‖ *to make o.s. master of a situation* llegar a dominar una situación.

◆ *adj* maestro, tra; *master key* llave maestra ‖ principal; *master joint* junta principal ‖ directivo, va; rector, ra (idea) ‖ original (print, record) ‖ dominante (passion) ‖ — *master bedroom* dormitorio *m* principal ‖ *master plan* plan *m* maestro ‖ *master switch* interruptor *m* general.

— OBSERV No hay equivalencia exacta entre los títulos otorgados por las universidades de lengua española y las de Gran Bretaña o Estados Unidos. El grado de *Master* se encuentra entre el de *licenciado* y el de *doctor*.

master [ˈmɑːstə*] *vt* dominar; *to master one's passions* dominar las pasiones; *to master one's opponent* dominar a su adversario ‖ domar (a horse) ‖ superar, vencer (difficulties) ‖ dominar, llegar a ser experto en; *to master a language* dominar un idioma.

master-at-arms [-rəˈtɑːms] *n* MAR sargento *m* de marina.

— OBSERV El plural es *masters-at-arms*.

master builder [-bildə] *n* maestro *m* de obras.

masterful [-ful] *adj* dominante, autoritario, ria (domineering) ‖ magistral (showing mastery); *a masterful speech* un discurso magistral.

master hand [-hænd] *n* maestro, tra; experto, ta (expert) ‖ maestría *f* (great skill).

masterliness [-linis] *n* maestría *f*.

masterly [-li] *adj* magistral, genial; *masterly work* obra genial ‖ maestro, tra; *masterly stroke* golpe maestro ‖ *in a masterly manner* de mano maestra.

master mason [-meisn] *n* maestro *m* de albañilería.

mastermind [-ˌmaind] *n* cerebro *m* (person with superior brains).

mastermind [-ˌmaind] *vt* ser el cerebro de.

masterpiece [-piːs] *n* obra *f* maestra.

master's [-z]; **master's degree** [-zdiˈgriː] *n* título *m* universitario entre la licenciatura y el doctorado.

master sergeant [-sɑːdʒənt] *n* MIL sargento *m* mayor.

mastership [-ʃip] *n* magisterio *m* (position of a shoolmaster) ‖ maestría *f* (ability) ‖ autoridad *f* (dominion) ‖ dominio *m* (of a subject).

masterstroke [-strəuk] *n* golpe *m* maestro.

mastery [-ri] *n* dominio *m* (control) ‖ supremacía *f*, superioridad *f*, dominio *m* (supremacy) ‖ maestría *f* (skill) ‖ *to gain the mastery over* llegar a dominar.

masthead [ˈmɑːsthed] *n* MAR tope *m* (highest part of a ship's mast) | vigía *m* (lookout).

masthead [ˈmɑːsthed] *vt* MAR mandar (a alguien) al tope del palo (a sailor) | izar (a flag, etc.).

mastic [ˈmæstik] *n* almáciga *f* (resin) ‖ BOT lentisco *m* (tree) ‖ masilla *f* (cement).

masticate [ˈmæstikeit] *vt* masticar.

mastication [ˌmæstiˈkeiʃən] *n* masticación *f*.

masticatory [ˈmæstikətəri] *adj* masticador, ra; masticatorio, ria.

◆ *n* masticatorio *m*.

mastiff [ˈmæstif] *n* mastín *m* (dog).

mastitis [mæsˈtaitis] *n* MED mastitis *f*.

mastodon ['mæstədɔn] *n* mastodonte *m.*

mastoid ['mæstɔid] *adj* mastoideo, a; mastoides.
◆ *n* ANAT mastoides *f.*

mastoiditis [,mæstɔi'daitis] *n* MED mastoiditis *f.*

masturbate ['mæstə:beit] *vt* masturbar.
◆ *vi* masturbarse.

masturbation [,mæstə:'beiʃən] *n* masturbación *f.*

mat [mæt] *n* estera *f* (floor covering) ‖ felpudo *m*, esterilla *f* (behind a door) ‖ salvamanteles *m inv* (table cover) ‖ tapete *m* (under vases, etc.) ‖ greña *f*; *a mat of hair* una greña de pelo ‖ MAR pallete *m* ‖ SP colchoneta *f* (in gymnastics) ‖ FIG maraña *f.*

mat [mæt] *vt* esterar (to cover with mats) ‖ enredar, enmarañar (to entangle).
◆ *vi* enredarse, enmarañarse (to get entangled).

mat; matt; matte [mæt] *n* US orla *f* (of a picture) ‖ superficie (f), mate (of metals) ‖ PRINT matriz *f.*
◆ *adj* mate.

mat; matt [mæt] *vt* deslustrar, poner mate (metal) ‖ esmerilar (glass).

matador ['mætədɔ:*] *n* matador *m*, diestro *m.*

match [mætʃ] *n* igual *m* (person or thing equal to another) ‖ pareja *f*; *they are a good match* hacen una buena pareja ‖ matrimonio *m* (a marriage) ‖ partido *m* (mate); *he is a good match* es un buen partido ‖ SP partido *m* (of football, of tennis) | combate *m* (in boxing) | encuentro *m*, competición *f*; *an athletics match* un encuentro de atletismo ‖ fósforo *m*, cerilla *f*; *a box of matches* una caja de fósforos ‖ MIL mecha *f* ‖ — SP *deciding, return match* partido de desempate, de vuelta ‖ *to be a bad match* no hacer juego ‖ *to be a good match* hacer juego; *her hat and shoes are a good match* su sombrero y sus zapatos hacen juego, su sombrero hace juego con sus zapatos ‖ *to be a match for s.o.* poder competir con uno ‖ FIG *to be more than a match for s.o.* darle ciento y raya a uno | *to make a match of it* casarse | *to meet one's match* encontrar la horma de su zapato ‖ *wax match* cerilla *f.*

match [mætʃ] *vt* enfrentar (to bring into competition); *to match s.o. against s.o.* enfrentar a una persona con otra ‖ igualar, equiparar (to equal) ‖ casar, combinar (colours) ‖ parear, emparejar (gloves) ‖ hacer juego con; *the carpet should match the curtains* la alfombra tendría que hacer juego con las cortinas ‖ corresponder a; *his actions don't match his ideas* sus acciones no corresponden a sus ideas ‖ rivalizar con, competir con (to compete); *no one can match him in archery* nadie puede rivalizar con él en el tiro al arco ‖ encajar (to fit) ‖ casar, unir (to marry) ‖ US echar al aire (to toss) ‖ — US *I'll match you to see who goes first* echaremos a suertes quién va el primero ‖ *to be well matched* hacer una buena pareja (married people), ser muy iguales (opponents).
◆ *vi* hacer juego; *ribbons that do not match with the dress* cintas que no hacen juego con el vestido.

matchbox [-bɔks] *n* caja *f* de fósforos *or* de cerillas.

matchet [-it] *n* machete *m.*

matching [-iŋ] *adj* que hace juego.
◆ *n* combinación *f* (of colours).

matchless [-lis] *adj* incomparable, sin igual, sin par (having no equal).

matchmaker [-,meikə*] *n* casamentero, ra (who arranges marriages) ‖ fabricante *m* de fósforos (who makes matches) ‖ SP organizador, ra.

matchmaking [-,meikiŋ] *n* afición *f* a casar a los demás ‖ fabricación *f* de fósforos ‖ organización *f* de encuentros deportivos.

matchmark [-mɑ:k] *n* señal *f* (on machine parts).

match point [-'pɔint] *n* SP última jugada *f*, punto *m* decisivo.

matchstick ['mætʃstik] *n* palo *m* de la cerilla, cerilla *f*, fósforo *m.*

matchwood [-wud] *n* madera *f* para fósforos ‖ astillas *f pl* (splinters) ‖ FIG *to make matchwood of* hacer trizas.

mate [meit] *n* compañero, ra; camarada *m* & *f* (companion, fellow worker) ‖ amigo, ga (friend) ‖ cónyuge *m* & *f*, compañero, ra (spouse) ‖ ZOOL macho *m*, hembra *f* (of animals) ‖ piloto *m* (on a merchant ship) ‖ ayudante *m*; *carpenter's mate* ayudante de carpintero ‖ mate *m* (in chess).

mate [meit] *vt* dar jaque mate a (in chess) ‖ aparear, acoplar (animals, birds) ‖ casar (to marry) ‖ FIG hermanar, emparejar.
◆ *vi* acoplarse (animals) ‖ casarse (to get married) ‖ *mate!* ¡jaque mate! (in chess).

maté ['mætei] *n* mate *m* (plant, tea).

mateless ['meitlis] *adj* solo, la.

matelote [mæt'ləut] *n* CULIN guiso *m* de pescado.

mater ['meitə*] *n* FAM madre *f* ‖ — ANAT *dura mater* duramáter *f*, duramadre *f* | *pia mater* piamáter *f*, piamadre *f.*

material [mə'tiəriəl] *adj* material (physical); *material necessities* necesidades materiales ‖ materialista; *material point of view* punto de vista materialista ‖ esencial, fundamental (essential); *material facts* hechos fundamentales ‖ profundo, da (change) ‖ grande, enorme (service) ‖ JUR pertinente.
◆ *n* material *m*; *heatproof material* material refractario ‖ tela *f*, tejido *m* (cloth) ‖ PHYS materia *f*; *fissionable material* materia escindible *or* fisible ‖ MIL material; *war material* material de guerra ‖ — *advertising material* material de publicidad ‖ *raw material* materia prima.
◆ *pl* materiales *m*; *building materials* materiales de construcción ‖ material *m sing*; *teaching materials* material escolar ‖ artículos *m*, objetos *m*; *office materials* artículos de escritorio ‖ FIG hechos *m*, datos *m*, elementos *m* (facts).

materialism [mə'tiəriəlizəm] *n* materialismo *m.*

materialist [mə'tiəriəlist] *adj/n* materialista.

materialistic [mə,tiəriə'listik] *adj* materialista.

materiality [mə,tiəri'æliti] *n* materialidad *f* (being material) ‖ JUR importancia *f* (importance).

materialization [mə,tiəriəlai'zeiʃən] *n* materialización *f* (apparition) ‖ realización *f* (realization).

materialize [mə'tiəriəlaiz] *vt* realizar, hacer realidad, materializar (plans) ‖ materializar (a spirit).
◆ *vi* realizarse, concretarse; *his plans never materialized* sus planes no se realizaron ‖ concretarse (ideas) ‖ materializarse (to appear).

materiel [mə,tiəri'el] *n* MIL material *m.*

maternal [mə'tə:nl] *adj* maternal; *maternal instincts* instintos maternales ‖ materno, na; *maternal uncle* tío materno.

maternity [mə'tə:niti] *n* maternidad *f* ‖ — *maternity belt* faja *f* de embarazo ‖ *maternity dress* vestido *m* de maternidad ‖ *maternity hospital* casa *f* de maternidad.

matey ['meiti] *adj* simpático, ca (friendly) ‖ *to get matey with s.o.* hacerse amigo de alguien.

math [mæθ] *n* US FAM matemáticas *f pl.*

mathematical [,mæθi'mætikəl] *adj* matemático, ca.

mathematically [-i] *adv* matemáticamente ‖ FIG por A más B (to prove).

mathematician [,mæθimə'tiʃən] *n* matemático, ca.

mathematics [,mæθi'mætiks] *n* matemáticas *f pl*; *pure, applied mathematics* matemáticas puras, aplicadas.

maths [mæθs] *pl n* FAM matemáticas *f.*

matinal ['mætənəl] *adj* matinal.

matinée; US matinee ['mætinei] *n* primera sesión *f* (cinema) ‖ función *f* de la tarde (theatre) ‖ FAM *matinée idol* ídolo *m* del público.

mating ['meitiŋ] *n* unión *f* (of persons) ‖ acoplamiento *m*, apareamiento *m* (of animals) ‖ *mating season* época *f* de celo.

matins ['mætins] *pl n* REL maitines *m.*

matrass ['mætrəs] *n* CHEM matraz *m.*

matriarch ['meitriɑ:k] *n* mujer *f* que manda [en su familia o tribu].

matriarchal [-əl] *adj* matriarcal.

matriarchate [-eit] *n* matriarcado *m.*

matriarchy [-i] *n* matriarcado *m.*

matrices ['meitrisi:z] *pl n* matrices *f.*

matricide ['meitrisaid] *n* matricidio *m* (murder) ‖ matricida *m* & *f* (murderer).

matriculate [mə'trikjuleit] *vt* matricular.
◆ *vi* matricularse.

matriculation [mə,trikju'leiʃən] *n* matrícula *f*, matriculación *f* (inscription) ‖ examen *m* de ingreso (exam).

matrilineal [,meitri'linjəl] *adj* por línea materna.

matrimonial [,mætri'məunjəl] *adj* matrimonial.

matrimony ['mætriməni] *n* matrimonio *m* (wedding) ‖ vida *f* conyugal (married life).

matrix ['meitriks] *n* TECH matriz *f* (mould) ‖ GEOL & MATH matriz *f* ‖ ANAT matriz *f.*
— OBSERV El plural de *matrix* es *matrices.*

matron ['meitrən] *n* matrona *f* (elderly lady) ‖ enfermera *f* jefe (in hospital) ‖ matrona *f* (prison guard) ‖ ama *f* de llaves (in schools) ‖ *matron of honour* dama *f* de honor.

matronly [-li] *adj* de matrona ‖ FIG maduro, ra; de edad.

matt; matte [mæt] *n/adj/vt* → **mat.**

matte [mæt] *n* TECH mata *f.*

matted ['mætəd] *adj* enmarañado, da.

matter ['mætə*] *n* materia *f*; *mind and matter* el espíritu y la materia ‖ materia *f*, sustancia *f*; *colouring matter* materia colorante ‖ importancia *f* (importance); *it makes no matter* no tiene importancia ‖ asunto *m*, cuestión *f*; *a matter requiring attention* un asunto que requiere atención; *it's a matter of great concern to me* es una cuestión que me preocupa mucho ‖ tema *m* (of a speech) ‖ cuestión *f*; *it's a matter of taste* es cuestión de gustos ‖ MED pus *m*, materia *f* ‖ PHYS & JUR materia *f* ‖ PRINT plomo *m* (type) | material *m* ‖ — *as a matter of fact* en realidad ‖ *as if nothing was the matter* como si nada, como si tal cosa ‖ *as matters stand* tal y como están las cosas ‖ *business matters* negocios *m pl* ‖ *form and matter* forma *f* y fondo ‖ *for that matter* respecto a eso ‖ *grey matter* materia gris ‖ *in all matters of* en todo lo que se refiere a ‖ *in the matter of* en cuanto a, en materia de ‖ *in this matter* al respecto ‖ *it's an easy matter* es fácil ‖ *it's no great matter* no importa, es poca cosa ‖ *it will be a matter of ten days* será cosa de diez días ‖ *matter of conscience* caso *m* de conciencia ‖ *matter of course* cosa *f* normal, cosa que cae de su peso ‖ *matter of fact* cuestión de hecho ‖ *matter of state* asunto de Estado ‖ *no* *matter* no importa || *no matter how fast you run* por mucho que corras || *no matter how well you do it* por muy bien que lo hagas || *nothing's the matter* no pasa nada || *on the matter* al respecto, sobre eso || *printed matter* impresos *m pl* || *something must be the matter* debe de pasar algo || *that's quite another matter* eso es harina de otro costal || *there's sth. the matter* pasa algo || *there's sth. the matter with him* algo le pasa || *to carry matters too far* llevar las cosas demasiado lejos || *to go into the matter* entrar en materia || *what matter!* ¡qué más da!, ¡qué importa! || *what's the matter?* ¿qué pasa?, ¿qué ocurre? || *what's the matter with going home?* ¿qué inconveniente hay en ir a casa? || *what's the matter with you?* ¿qué te pasa?, ¿qué te ocurre?

matter ['mætə*] *vi* importar; *it doesn't matter* no importa; *what does it matter to him?* ¿qué le importa? || MED supurar (to suppurate).

matter-of-course [-əv'kɔ:s] *adj* natural (manner) || que cae de su peso (words) || normal.

matter-of-fact [-əv'fækt] *adj* prosaico, ca (prosaic) || práctico, ca (practical) || realista (sticking to facts).

Matthew ['mæθju:] *pr n* Mateo *m* || REL *the Gospel according to St. Matthew* el Evangelio según San Mateo.

matting ['mætiŋ] *n* deslustrado *m* (dulling) || superficie *f* mate (dull surface) || orla *f*, marco *m* (of a painting) || estera *f* (floor covering) || enmarañamiento *m* (tangle).

mattock ['mætək] *n* pico *m*, azadón *m*.

mattras ['mætrəs] *n* CHEM matraz *m* (rounded glass container).

mattres ['mætris] *n* colchón *m* (of a bed); *wool mattress* colchón de lana || somier *m*; *wire mattress* somier metálico.

maturate ['mætjureit] *vi* madurar.

maturation [mætju'reiʃən] *n* maduración *f*.

mature [mə'tjuə*] *adj* maduro, ra; *a mature person* una persona madura; *a mature fruit* una fruta madura || madurado, da; pensado, da; *a mature decision* una decisión madurada || largo, ga; *after mature deliberations* después de largas deliberaciones || COMM vencido, da (in finance) || *mature student* estudiante *m* & *f* mayor de 25 años.

mature [mə'tjuə*] *vt* madurar.
◆ *vi* madurar || COMM vencer.

maturing [-riŋ] *n* maduramiento *m*.

maturity [-riti] *n* AGR & FIG madurez *f* || COMM vencimiento *m*.

matutinal [,mætju:'tainl] *adj* matutino, na.

maud [mɔ:d] *n* manta *f* escocesa.

maudlin [-lin] *adj* llorón, ona; *maudlin voice* voz llorona || sensiblero, ra (weakly sentimental).

maul [mɔ:l] *n* mazo *m*.

maul [mɔ:l] *vt* herir gravemente (to injure) || maltratar (to treat roughly) || vapulear, apalear (to beat) || FIG vapulear, dar un palo (to criticize) || FAM manosear (to paw) || US partir con un mazo (wood).

maulstick [-stik] *n* ARTS tiento *m*.

maunder ['mɔ:ndə*] *vi* divagar (to drivel) || vagar, errar (to wander).

Maundy ['mɔ:ndi] *pr n* REL lavatorio *m* || — *Maundy money* limosna *f* que se da el Jueves Santo || *Maundy Thursday* Jueves Santo.

Maurice ['mɔris] *pr n* Mauricio *m*.

Mauritania [,mɔri'teinjə] *pr n* GEOGR Mauritania *f*.

Mauritanian [-n] *adj/n* mauritano, na.

Mauritius [mə'riʃəs] *pr n* GEOGR Mauricio (island).

mauser ['mauzə*] *n* MIL máuser *m* (gun).

mausoleum [,mɔ:sə'liəm] *n* mausoleo *m*.
— OBSERV El plural es *mausoleums* o *mausolea*.

mauve [məuv] *n* malva *m*.
◆ *adj* malva.

maverick ['mævrik] *n* US FAM inconformista *m* & *f* (nonconformist) | disidente *m* & *f* (of a political party) | res *f* sin marcar (animal).

mavis ['meivis] *n* tordo *m*, zorzal *m* (bird).

maw [mɔ:] *n* ZOOL cuajar *m* (of a ruminant) | buche *m* (of a granivorous bird) | fauces *f pl* (of lions) || FAM *to fill one's maw* llenarse el buche.

mawkish [-kiʃ] *adj* sensiblero, ra (weakly sentimental) || empalagoso, sa (cloingly sentimental).

mawkishness [-kiʃnis] *n* sensiblería *f* || lo empalagoso.

maxilla [mæk'silə] *n* ANAT maxilar *m* superior.
— OBSERV El plural de la palabra inglesa *maxilla* es *maxillae* o *maxillas*.

maxillary [-əri] *adj* ANAT maxilar.
◆ *n* maxilar *m* (bone).

maxim ['mæksim] *n* máxima *f*.

maximal [-əl] *adj* máximo, ma.

maximize ['mæksimaiz] *vt* llevar al máximo.

maximum ['mæksiməm] *n* máximo *m*; *law of maxima* ley de los máximos; *production reached a maximum* la producción llegó al máximo || *to the maximum* al máximo.
◆ *adj* máximo, ma; *maximum temperature* temperatura máxima.
— OBSERV El plural de *maximum* es *maxima* o *maximums*.

maxiskirt ['mæksi,skə:t] *n* maxifalda *f*.

maxwell ['mækswəl] *n* PHYS maxvelio *m*, maxwell *m* (eletromagnetic unit).

May [mei] *n* mayo *m*; *first of May* primero de mayo.

may [mei] *n* BOT *f* del espino (flower of the hawthorn) | espino *m* (hawthorn).

may* [mei] *v aux* poder (permission); *you may go now* se puede ir ahora || poder, ser posible (probability); *you may be right* puede que tengas razón; *it may snow* es posible que nieve || poder (possibility); *he works so that he may eat* trabajar para poder comer || — *as you might expect* como era de esperar || *be that as it may* sea como sea, sea como fuere || *come what may* pase lo que pase || *how many may you be?* ¿cuántos van a ser? || *how old may* o *might she be?* ¿qué edad puede tener? || *if I may* si me lo permite || *if I may say so* si se me permite || *I hope it may be true* espero que sea verdad || *it may* o *might be that* puede ser que *or* podría ser que || *it may not be true* puede ser que no sea verdad || *may he rest in peace!* ¡que en paz descanse! || *may I?* ¿se permite? || *may I come in? you may* ¿puedo pasar? sí, por supuesto || *may I have the pleasure of this dance?* ¿quiere Ud. concederme este baile? || *may they both be happy!* ¡ojalá sean felices! || *might it not be well to warn him?* ¿no estaría bien que le avisáramos? || *run as he might he could not overtake me* por mucho que corrió no me pudo adelantar || *that's as may be* puede ser, puede que sea así || *we may as well stay here* más vale que nos quedemos aquí || *whatever you may say* por más que diga || *will you go? I may* ¿vas a ir? quizás, puede ser || *you might open the window!* ¡podrías abrir la ventana!
— OBSERV La contracción de la forma negativa *may not* es *mayn't*. El pretérito de *may* es ***might***.

Maya ['mæijə] *n* maya *m* & *f* (person) || maya *m* (language).

Mayan [-n] *adj/n* maya.

maybe ['meibi:] *adv* quizá, quizás, tal vez.

May Day ['meidei] *n* Primero *m* de Mayo.

Mayday ['meidei] *n* señal *f* de socorro, SOS.

mayflower ['mei,flauə*] *n* BOT espino *m*.

mayfly ['meiflai] *n* ZOOL cachipolla *f*, efímera *f*.

mayhem ['meihem] *n* JUR mutilación *f* criminal.

maying ['meiiŋ] *n* celebración *f* del primero de mayo.

mayn't ['meint] contraction of «may not» ⟶ **may.**

mayonnaise [,meiə'neiz] *n* CULIN mayonesa *f*, salsa *f* mahonesa.

mayor [mɛə*] *n* alcalde *m* || *mayor of the palace* mayordomo *m* de palacio.

mayoralty ['mɛərəlti] *n* alcaldía *f* (office and term).

mayoress ['mɛəris] *n* alcaldesa *f*.

maypole ['meipəul] *n* mayo *m* (pole) || FAM zangolotino *m*, espingarda *f* (tall person).

maze [meiz] *n* laberinto *m* || FIG *to be in a maze* estar perplejo.

maze [meiz] *vt* dejar perplejo.

mazer ['meizə*] *n* escudilla *f* (drinking bowl).

mazurka [mə'zə:kə] *n* MUS mazurca *f*.

mazy ['meizi] *adj* laberíntico, ca || FIG perplejo, ja (person) | intrincado, da; enmarañado, da (things).

MB *abbr of [megabyte]* MB, megabyte.

MBA *abbr of [Master of Business Administration]* MBA, máster en administración de empresas.

me [mi:] *pron* me; *he looked at me* me miró || mi (after preposition); *he came to me* vino hacia mí; *it's for me* es para mí || — *ah me!* ¡pobre de mí! || FAM *it's me* soy yo || *with me* conmigo.

mead [mi:d] *n* aguamiel *f*, hidromiel *m* || (ant) prado *m*, pradera *f* (meadow).

meadow ['medəu] *n* prado *m*, pradera *f*.

meadowsweet [-swi:t] *n* BOT reina *f* de los prados.

meagre; US **meager** ['mi:gə*] *adj* FIG exiguo, gua; escaso, sa; *meagre rewards* exigua recompensa | pobre; *a meagre supper* una cena pobre | seco, ca; mediocre (style), poco, ca (clothing) || flaco, ca (thin).

meagreness; US **meagerness** [-nis] *n* flaqueza *f* (thinness) || FIG escasez *f*.

meal [mi:l] *n* harina *f* (of grain) || comida *f* (food) || *to make a meal of* comer.

mealie [-i] *n* BOT maiz *m*.

meals on wheels [mi:lzɔnwi:lz] *pl n* comidas *f* a domicilio para personas imposibilitadas.

mealtime [-taim] *n* hora *f* de comer.

mealworm [-wə:m] *n* ZOOL gusano *m* de la harina.

mealy [-i] *adj* harinoso, sa (farinaceous) || descolorido, da; pálido, da (complexion) || enharinado, da (covered with meal) || empolvado, da (covered with powder) || salpicado, da (spotted with a colour) || FAM meloso, sa; camandulero, ra (mealymouthed).

mealymouthed [-imauðd] *adj* FAM camandulero, ra; meloso, sa.

mean [mi:n] *adj* medio, dia (average); *mean temperature* temperatura media || mediano, na (quality) || inferior, mediocre (inferior) || humilde, pobre (humble) || tacaño, ña; agarrado, da (stingy) || mezquino, na (petty); *it's mean of him* es mezquino de su parte || ruin, vil, despreciable; *mean character* carácter ruin || malo, la (bad); *mean opinion* mala opinión || malo, la (unkind) || avergonzado, da (ashamed) || *US* desagradable, pajolero, ra; *mean job* trabajo pajolero | muy malo; *mean weather* tiempo muy malo || — *mean trick* mala jugada || *she is no mean cook* es una cocinera excelente || *US to feel mean* encontrarse mal.

◆ *n* promedio *m* (average) || MATH media *f*; *mean proportional* media proporcional || término *m* medio (middle term) || *golden mean* justo medio.

◆ *pl* medios *m*, medio *m sing*; *by what means did you get it?* ¿con qué medios lo conseguiste? || medio *m sing*, manera *f sing*; *I must find means to do it* tengo que encontrar la manera de hacerlo || medios *m*, recursos *m*; *economic means* medios económicos || medios *m* (of production, of transport) || — *a man of means* un hombre adinerado || *by all manner of means* por todos los medios, de todos modos || *by all means!* ¡no faltaba más!, ¡naturalmente!, ¡por supuesto! || *by all means come when you like* venga por supuesto cuando quiera, por favor venga cuando quiera || *by any means* de cualquier modo || *by fair means or foul* por las buenas o por las malas || *by means of* por medio de, mediante || *by no means* de ningún modo, de ninguna manera (certainly not), nada (far from); *he is by no means a scholar* no es nada erudito || *means test* comprobación *f* de medios de vida || *the end justifies the means* el fin justifica los medios || *to live beyond one's means* gastar más de lo que se tiene, vivir por encima de sus posibilidades.

mean* [mi:n] *vt* tener la intención de, querer; *she didn't mean to force you* no tenía la intención de forzarte || pensar, tener la intención de (to intend); *what do you mean to do?* ¿qué piensas hacer? || destinar; *this remark was meant to offend him* esta observación estaba destinada a molestarle || dirigir; *that remark was meant for you* esta observación estaba dirigida contra usted || querer; *I mean you to speak* quiero que hable || significar (to signify, to denote); *the Spanish word «mesa» means «table»* la palabra española «mesa» significa «table»; *it doesn't mean much* no significa gran cosa; *I can't tell you what it has meant to me* no puedo decirle lo que ha significado para mí || querer decir; *what do you mean by that?* ¿qué quieres decir con eso? || aludir a, referirse a (to refer to); *do you mean him?* ¿se refiere usted a él? || suponer, implicar (to involve) || — *he meant it for a joke* lo dijo en broma || *this term doesn't mean anything to me* este término no me suena || *to be meant for* servir para (to be for), nacer para (vocation), estar dirigido a (remarks) || *to mean business* hablar *or* actuar en serio || *to mean it* decirlo en serio; *I'm sure you don't mean it* estoy seguro de que no lo dices en serio || *to mean well* o *no harm* tener buenas intenciones || *without meaning it* sin querer.

— OBSERV Pret y pp ***meant***.

meander [mi'ændə*] *n* meandro *m* (of a river) || ARCH meandro *m* (in Greek ornament).

◆ *pl* FIG meandros *m*.

meander [mi'ændə*] *vi* serpentear (a river) || vagar, errar (to wander).

meaning ['mi:niŋ] *n* significado *m*, sentido *m*; *I don't know the meaning of this word* no conozco el sentido de esta palabra || acepción *f*, sentido *m*; *the first meaning of a word* la primera acepción de una palabra || intención *f*, propósito *m* (purpose) || FIG significación *f* (importance) || — *double meaning* doble sentido || *what's the meaning of?* ¿qué significa?, ¿qué quiere decir?

◆ *adj* significativo, va (expressive); *a meaning smile* una sonrisa significativa || intencionado, da; *well-meaning words* unas palabras bien intencionadas.

meaningful [-ful] *adj* significativo, va.

meaningless [-lis] *adj* sin sentido, que carece de sentido.

meanness ['mi:nnis] *n* mezquindad *f* || tacañería *f* (stinginess) || humildad *f* (humbleness) || mediocridad *f* (mediocrity) || maldad *f* (evil) || bajeza *f*, vileza *f* (low character).

means [mi:nz] *n* medio *m*; *a means of transport* un medio de transporte.

meant [ment] *pret/pp* → **mean.**

meantime ['mi:n'taim]; **meanwhile** ['mi:n'wail] *adv* mientras tanto, entretanto.

◆ *n* *in the meantime* mientras tanto, entretanto.

measles ['mi:zlz] *n* MED sarampión *m* || VET cisticercosis *f* muscular (in pigs) || MED *German measles* rubéola *f*.

measly ['mi:zli] *adj* FAM ínfimo, ma (very small) || MED que tiene sarampión (infected with measles).

measurability [,meʒərə'biliti] *n* mensurabilidad *f*.

measurable ['meʒərəbl] *adj* mensurable, medible.

measurably [-i] *adv* sensiblemente.

measure ['meʒə*] *n* medida *f*; *measure of length* medida de longitud; *square, cubic measure* medida de superficie, de volumen; *full measure* medida exacta || medida *f* (in dressmaking) || metro *m* (tape measure, yardstick) || JUR medida *f*; *to take drastic measures* tomar medidas drásticas | proyecto *m* de ley (bill) | ley *f* (act) || FIG moderación *f*, mesura *f* || TECH justificación *f*, anchura *f*, ancho *m* (in printing) || MUS compás *m* || CHEM probeta *f* graduada (utensil) || MATH divisor *m* || POET metro *m*, medida *f* || — *beyond* o *out of measure* excesivamente (exceedingly) || *for good measure* por añadidura || *in a large measure* en gran parte || *in a measure* hasta cierto punto, en cierto modo || *in due measure* con mesura || *in great measure* en gran parte || *in some measure* hasta cierto punto || *made to measure* hecho a la medida || *sense of measure* mesura, ponderación *f* || FIG *to give one's measure* mostrar de lo que uno es capaz || *to take s.o.'s measure* tomarle a uno las medidas || FIG *to take the measure of* calibrar.

◆ *pl* GEOL yacimiento *m sing* || FIG *to set measures to* poner coto a.

measure ['meʒə*] *vt* medir; *he measured the table* midió la mesa; *to measure in litres* medir por litros; *thermometers measure temperature* los termómetros miden la temperatura || tomar las medidas (in dressmaking); *they measured him for a suit* le tomaron las medidas para un traje || medir la estatura de (s.o.) || FIG pesar, medir (words) | sopesar, ponderar (acts) || — FIG *he measured his length* midió el suelo, se cayó cuan largo era || *to measure off* medir (fabric) || *to measure one's strength* o *o.s. against* competir con, medirse con || *to measure out* medir (a specified length), repartir (to distribute) || *to measure up* medir (wood).

◆ *vi* medir; *it measures two feet and a half* mide dos pies y medio || *to measure up to* estar a la altura de.

measured [-d] *adj* medido, da (space, time) || acompasado, da (tread) || moderado, da; comedido, da; mesurado, da (language) || prudente (statement) || *with measured steps* con pasos contados.

measureless [-lis] *adj* sin medida, inmensurable, inconmensurable, inmenso, sa.

measurement [-mənt] *n* medida *f*, medición *f* (action) || medida *f* (dimensión, length) || COMM dimensiones *f pl* (of goods).

◆ *pl* medidas *f* (in dressmaking).

measurer [-rə*] *n* medidor *m*.

measuring [-riŋ] *n* medición *f*, medida *f*.

measuring chain [-riŋtʃein] *n* cadena *f* de agrimensor.

measuring cup [-riŋ,kʌp] *n* vaso *m* graduado.

measuring tape [-riŋ,teip] *n* cinta *f* métrica.

measuring worm [-riŋ,wə:m] *n* ZOOL oruga *f* geómetra *or* medidora.

meat [mi:t] *n* CULIN carne *f* (flesh) || comida *f* (food, meal) || FIG meollo *m*, sustancia *f* (the essence, the main part) | materia *f* (for reflexion) || — *cold meat* fiambre *m* || FIG *it was meat and drink to them* disfrutaron con ello | *one man's meat is another man's poison* lo que es bueno para uno no lo es para todos.

meatball [-bɔ:l] *n* albóndiga *f*.

meat fly [-flai] *n* ZOOL moscarda *f*, moscón *m*.

meat grinder [-,graində*] *n* máquina *f* de picar carne.

meat hook [-huk] *n* gancho *m*, garabato *m*.

meatless [-lis] *adj* sin carne || REL de vigilia (day).

meatman [-mən] *n* *US* carnicero *m*.

— OBSERV El plural es *meatmen*.

meat pie [-'pai] *n* empanada *f*, pastel *m* de carne.

meat safe [-seif] *n* fresquera *f*.

meatus [mi'eitəs] *n* ANAT meato *m*.

— OBSERV El plural de *meatus* es *meatus* o *meatuses*.

meaty ['mi:ti] *adj* carnoso, sa (fleshy) || lleno de carne (full of meat) || FIG jugoso, sa; sustancioso, sa (full of substance).

Mecca ['mekə] *pr n* REL La Meca *f* || FIG lugar *m* predilecto, la meca *f*.

— OBSERV Esta palabra no va nunca precedida por el artículo en inglés.

Meccan [-n] *adj/n* mecano, na (from Mecca).

Meccano [mi'kɑ:nəu] *n* mecano *m* (toy).

mechanic [mi'kænik] *n* mecánico *m*.

mechanical [-əl] *adj* mecánico, ca (art, power, civilization, engineer) || FIG mecánico, ca; maquinal || — *mechanical drawing* dibujo *m* industrial || *mechanical engineering* ingeniería *f* mecánica.

mechanics [-s] *n* PHYS mecánica *f*; *wave mechanics* mecánica ondulatoria || FIG mecanismo *m*.

mechanism ['mekənizəm] *n* TECH & FIG mecanismo *m*; *firing, ejector mechanism* mecanismo de disparo, de expulsión || MUS técnica *f*.

mechanistic [mekə'nistik] *adj* mecánico, ca.

mechanization [,mekənai'zeiʃən] *n* mecanización *f*.

mechanize ['mekənaiz] *vt* mecanizar; *mechanized accountancy* contabilidad mecanizada || AGR *mechanized farming* motocultivo *m*.

mechanotherapy [,mekənə'θerəpi] *n* MED mecanoterapia *f*.

Mechlin ['meklin] *pr n* GEOGR Malinas || *Mechlin lace* encaje *m* de Malinas, malinas *f*.

meconium [mi'kəuniəm] *n* BIOL meconio *m*.

medal ['medl] *n* medalla *f*; *to award s.o. a medal* conceder una medalla a uno.

medalist; *US* **medalist** ['medlist] *n* *US* → **medallist.**

medallion [mi'dæljən] *n* medallón *m*.

medallist ['medlist] *n* medallista *m* & *f* (engraver) || galardonado *or* premiado con una medalla (recipient of a medal); *gold medallist* galardonado con una medalla de oro || campeón, ona (champion) || condecorado con una medalla (decorated with a medal).

meddle ['medl] *vi* *to meddle in* meterse en, entrometerse en, entremeterse en ‖ *to meddle with* meterse en (to interfere), toquetear (to tamper).

meddler [-ə*] *n* entrometido, da; entremetido, da.

meddlesome [-səm] *adj* entrometido, da; entremetido, da.

meddlesomeness [-səmnis] *n* intromisión *f*, entrometimiento *m*, entremetimiento *m*.

meddling [-iŋ] *adj* entrometido, da; entremetido, da.
◆ *n* intromisión *f*, entrometimiento *m*, entremetimiento *m*.

Mede [mi:d] *n* HIST medo, da.

Media ['mediə] *pr n* HIST Media *f*.

media *pl n* ⟶ **medium.**

mediaeval [,medi'i:vəl] *adj* medieval.

mediaevalist [-ist] *n* medievalista *m* & *f*.

medial ['mi:djəl] *adj* intermedio, dia; central (in the middle) ‖ medio, dia (average).

median ['mi:djən] *adj* mediano, na.
◆ *n* MATH mediana *f* (line) | valor *m* mediano (quantity).

Median ['mi:djən] *adj/n* medo, da.

mediate ['mi:diit] *adj* mediato, ta.

mediate ['mi:dieit] *vt* ser mediador en, servir de intermediario para llegar a; *to mediate an agreement* servir de intermediario para llegar a un acuerdo ‖ transmitir, comunicar (to convey).
◆ *vi* mediar; *to mediate between two enemies* mediar entre dos enemigos; *to mediate in an affair* mediar en un asunto.

mediating [-iŋ] *adj* mediador, ra.

mediation [,mi:di'eiʃən] *n* mediación *f*.

mediative [,mi:diətiv] *adj* mediador, ra.

mediatize ['mi:diətaiz] *vt* mediatizar.

mediator ['mi:dieitə*] *n* mediador, ra.

mediatory ['mi:diətəri] *adj* mediador, ra.

mediatress ['mi:diətrəs]; **mediatrix** ['mi:diətrix] *n* mediadora *f*.

medic ['medik] *n* FAM médico, ca (doctor) | estudiante *m* de medicina (student).

medicable [-əbl] *adj* curable.

medical [-əl] *adj* médico, ca; *medical attention* asistencia médica; *medical treatment* tratamiento médico ‖ de medicina (book, school, student) ‖ — *medical adviser* consejero médico ‖ *medical certificate* certificado *m* médico ‖ *medical consultant* médico consultor *or* de apelación *or* de consulta ‖ *medical corps* servicio *m* de sanidad ‖ *medical examination* reconocimiento médico ‖ US *medical examiner* médico *m* forense ‖ *medical jurisprudence* medicina *f* legal *or* forense ‖ *medical kit* botiquín *m* ‖ *medical man* médico *m* ‖ MIL *medical officer* médico *m* militar *or* castrense ‖ *Medical school* Facultad *f* de Medicina ‖ *medical staff* cuadro médico *or* facultativo.
◆ *n* FAM reconocimiento *m* médico.

medicament [me'dikəmənt] *n* medicamento *m*, medicina *f*.

medicaster ['medikæstə*] *n* medicastro *m*, medicucho *m*.

medicate ['medikeit] *vt* medicinar (s.o.).

medicated [-id] *adj* hidrófilo (cotton) ‖ medicinal (soap, water).

medication [,medi'keiʃən] *n* medicación *f*.

medicinal [me'disinl] *adj* medicinal.

medicine ['medsin] *n* MED medicina *f* (art, science); *forensic medicine* medicina forense *or* legal ‖ medicina *f*, medicamento *m* (drug) ‖ rito *m or* objeto *m* mágico (among savages) ‖ FAM purga *f* ‖ — *patent medicine* específico *m* ‖ FIG *to give s.o. a taste of his own medicine* pagarle a uno con la misma moneda | *to take one's medicine* cargar con las consecuencias.

medicine ['medsin] *vt* medicinar, tratar.

medicine ball [-bɔ:l] *n* balón *m* medicinal (heavy stuffed leather ball).

medicine cabinet [-'kæbinit]; **medicine chest** [-tʃest]; **medicine cupboard** [-,kʌbəd] *n* botiquín *m*.

medicine man [-mæn] *n* hechicero *m* (priestly healer or sorcerer).
— OBSERV El plural de *medicine man* es *medicine men*.

medico ['medikəu] *n* FAM médico *m* (doctor) | estudiante *m* de medicina (student).

medico-legal [-'li:gəl] *adj* medicolegal.

medieval [,medi'i:vəl] *adj* medieval.

medievalist [-ist] *n* medievalista *m* & *f*.

mediocre [,mi:di'əukə*] *adj* mediocre, mediano, na.

mediocrity [,mi:di'ɔkriti] *n* mediocridad *f*, medianía *f* (quality) ‖ mediocridad *f* (person).

meditate ['mediteit] *vt* meditar; *to meditate a speech* meditar un discurso ‖ planear; *to meditate an incursion* planear una incursión.
◆ *vi* meditar ‖ *to meditate on* o *upon* reflexionar sobre.

meditation [,medi'teiʃən] *n* meditación *f*.

meditative ['meditətiv] *adj* meditabundo, da.

meditatively ['meditətivli] *adv* con aire meditabundo.

meditator ['mediteitə*] *n* pensador *m*.

Mediterranean [,meditə'reinjən] *adj* mediterráneo, a; *Mediterranean climate* clima mediterráneo; *Mediterranean Sea* Mar Mediterráneo.
◆ *n* GEOGR Mediterráneo *m*.

medium ['mi:djəm] *adj* mediano, na (height, quality) ‖ RAD medio, dia (wave) ‖ CULIN medio hecho ‖ SP *medium distance race* carrera *f* de medio fondo.
◆ *n* instrumento *m*, medio *m* (means) ‖ término *m* medio (middle quality) ‖ medio *m* ambiente (environment) ‖ médium *m* & *f* (spiritualism) ‖ PHYS & BIOL medio *m* ‖ ARTS medio *m* de expresión ‖ CHEM caldo *m* de cultivo (for culture growth) | agente *m* (liquid for suspending pigment) ‖ — *happy medium* justo medio ‖ COMM *medium of exchange* instrumento *or* medio de cambio ‖ *through the medium of* por medio de.
◆ *pl* medios *m* [de información]; *advertising media* medios de publicidad.
— OBSERV El plural de *medium* es *mediums* o *media*.

medium-fine [-fain] *adj* entrefino, na; semifino, na.

medium-haul [-hɔ:l] *adj* de distancias medias, continental (aircraft).

medium-sized [-saizd] *adj* mediano, na; de tamaño mediano.

medlar ['medlə*] *n* níspero *m* (tree, fruit).

medley ['medli] *n* mezcla *f*, mezcolanza *f* (mixture) ‖ miscelánea *f* (miscellany) ‖ confusión *f*; *a medley of voices* una confusión de voces ‖ MUS popurrí *m*.
◆ *adj* mezclado, da (mixed) ‖ heteróclito, ta (motley) ‖ SP *medley relay* o *race* relevo *m* estilos.

medulla [mə'dʌlə] *n* ANAT & BOT médula *f*; *medulla spinalis* médula espinal; *medulla oblongata* médula oblonga.
— OBSERV El plural de *medulla* es *medullas* o *medullae*.

medullary [-ri] *adj* ANAT & BOT medular.

medusa [mi'dju:zə] *n* (ant) medusa *f* (jellyfish).
— OBSERV El plural de la palabra inglesa *medusa* es *medusae*.

Medusa [mi'dju:zə] *n* MYTH Medusa *f*.

meed [mi:d] *n* recompensa *f* (reward).

meek [mi:k] *adj* dócil, manso, sa (mild) ‖ *as meek as a lamb* manso como un cordero.

meekness [-nis] *n* docilidad *f*, mansedumbre *f*.

meerschaum ['miəʃəm] *n* espuma *f* de mar (mineral) ‖ pipa *f* de espuma de mar (pipe).

meet [mi:t] *n* reunión *f* (meeting) ‖ partida *f* de caza (hunt) ‖ SP encuentro *m*.
◆ *adj* conveniente (fitting); *it is meet that you go* es conveniente que vaya.

meet* [mi:t] *vt* encontrar, encontrarse a *or* con (to come upon); *to meet s.o. in the street* encontrarse a uno en la calle ‖ entrevistarse con; *the minister will meet his colleague tomorrow* el ministro se entrevistará con su colega mañana ‖ encontrar, tropezar con, encontrarse con; *to meet a problem* tropezar con un problema ‖ ver (to see); *I hope to meet her tomorrow* espero verla mañana | conocer; *I met my wife in Paris* conocí a mi mujer en París; *I am very pleased to meet you* estoy encantado de conocerle ‖ enfrentarse con; *to meet the enemy* enfrentarse con el enemigo; *he will meet him in the semifinals* se enfrentará con él en las semifinales; *to meet a danger, a difficulty* enfrentarse con un peligro, con una dificultad ‖ recibir, ir a recibir, ir a buscar; *to meet s.o. at the station* recibir a alguien en la estación ‖ cruzarse con (to come across); *here the road meets the railway* la carretera se cruza aquí con la vía férrea; *to meet another car* cruzarse con otro coche ‖ confluir con (two rivers) ‖ desembocar en (streets) ‖ unirse con; *this road meets the main road a mile from here* esta carretera se une con la carretera general a una milla de aquí ‖ empalmar con, enlazar con; *this flight meets all trains* este vuelo empalma con todos los trenes ‖ satisfacer (demand, need); *it does not meet my desires* esto no satisface mis deseos; *production can't meet demand* la producción no puede satisfacer la demanda ‖ hacer honor a, cumplir con; *to meet an engagement* hacer honor a un compromiso ‖ cumplir con, satisfacer, llenar; *to meet all the requirements* satisfacer todos los requisitos ‖ cumplir con (obligations) ‖ conformarse con, acceder a (claims) ‖ costear, hacer frente a, sufragar, correr con; *I can meet all the expenses* puedo costear todos los gastos ‖ pagar (a bill) ‖ pagar, satisfacer (debt) ‖ cubrir (deficit) ‖ llegar a; *a noise met my ear* un ruido llegó a mis oídos ‖ mirar; *she dared not meet my eye* no se atrevía a mirarme a los ojos ‖ coger, tomar (the bus) ‖ recibir (a reward) ‖ responder a (an objection) ‖ — *meet Mr Warham* le presento al Señor Warham ‖ *pleased to meet you!* ¡mucho gusto!, ¡encantado de conocerle! ‖ *there is more to it than meets the eye* hay más de lo que parece a primera vista, aquí hay gato encerrado ‖ *to arrange to meet s.o.* dar cita a uno, citar a uno ‖ *to meet one's death* encontrar la muerte, morir ‖ FIG *to meet s.o. halfway* llegar a un arreglo con alguien ‖ *to meet s.o.'s eye* tropezar con la mirada de alguien ‖ *to meet the case* convenir, ser apropiado ‖ *to meet the eye* saltar a la vista.
◆ *vi* encontrarse, verse; *they met in Salford* se vieron en Salford; *when shall we meet again?* ¿cuándo nos veremos otra vez? ‖ conocerse (to become acquainted); *we met yesterday* nos conocimos ayer ‖ reunirse; *the assembly meets in London* la asamblea se reúne en Londres ‖ unirse (to join); *four lines that meet* cuatro líneas que se unen ‖ confluir; *the rivers meet outside the city* los ríos confluyen en las afueras de la ciudad ‖ enfrentarse; *the finalists meet to-*

morrow los finalistas se enfrentan mañana || cruzarse; *our eyes met* nuestras miradas se cruzaron || — *extremes meet* los extremos se tocan || *to arrange to meet* citarse, darse cita || *to meet up with* encontrar || *to meet with* encontrar, encontrarse con (to encounter), tener (to have), recibir (a refusal), sufrir, experimentar (a loss), sufrir (accident), encontrar (violent death) || *until we meet again!* ¡hasta la vista!
— OBSERV Pret y pp ***met***.

meeting [-iŋ] *n* encuentro *m* (coming together) || reunión *f*; *a committee meeting* la reunión de una comisión || reunión *f*, mitin *m* (political) || sesión *f* (of an assembly); *open meeting* sesión pública; *to open the meeting* abrir la sesión; *to adjourn* o *to close the meeting* levantar la sesión; *opening, plenary meeting* sesión de apertura, plenaria || entrevista *f*; *the two ministers will have an official meeting tomorrow* los dos ministros celebrarán una entrevista mañana || cita *f*; *I had a meeting with the director* tuve una cita con el director || duelo *m*, desafío *m* (duel) || confluencia *f* (of two rivers) || empalme *m* (of roads) || SP reunión *f* hípica | encuentro *m* deportivo || — *the meeting is open* o *is declared open* se abre la sesión || *to address the meeting* tomar la palabra || *to hold a meeting* celebrar una sesión *or* una reunión.

meetinghouse ['miːtiŋhaus] *n* REL templo *m*.

meeting place ['miːtiŋpleis] *n* lugar *m* de reunión, punto *m* de reunión.

megabyte ['megəbait] *n* INFORM megabyte *m*, megaocteto *m*.

megacephalic [,megəse'fælik]; **megacephalous** [,megə'sefələs] *adj* megacéfalo, la.

megacycle ['megə,saikl] *n* megaciclo *m*.

megahertz ['megə,həːts] *n* RAD megahercio *m*.

megalith ['megəliθ] *n* megalito *m*.

megalithic [,megə'liθik] *adj* megalítico, ca.

megalocephalic [,megələuse'fælik]; **megalocephalous** [,məgələu'sefələs] *adj* megalocéfalo, la.

megalomania ['megələu'meinjə] *n* megalomanía *f*.

megalomaniac ['megələu'meiniæk] *adj/n* megalómano, na.

megaphone ['megəfəun] *n* megáfono *m*.

megathere ['megəθiə] *n* megaterio *m* (fossil).

megaton ['megətʌn] *n* PHYS megatón *m*.

megavolt ['megəvəult] *n* PHYS megavoltio *m*.

megawatt ['megəwɔt] *n* PHYS megavatio *m*.

megohm ['megəum] *n* PHYS megohmio *m*.

megrim ['miːgrim] *n* MED jaqueca *f* (migraine) || vértigo *m* (in horses) || FIG capricho *m* (whim).
◆ *pl* FAM moral *f sing* baja (low spirits).

meharist; mehariste [mə'heirist] *n* meharista *m*.

meiosis [mai'əusis] *n* BIOL meiosis *f*.

Meknès [mek'nes] *pr n* GEOGR Mequínez *m*.

melancholia [,melən'kəuljə] *n* MED melancolía *f*.

melancholiac [,melən'kəuljək] *adj/n* MED melancólico, ca.

melancholic [,melən'kɔlik] *adj* melancólico, ca.

melancholy ['melənkəli] *adj* melancólico, ca; *to make s.o. melancholy* volver melancólico a uno || deprimente, triste (saddening).
◆ *n* melancolía *f*.

Melanesia [,melə'niːzjə] *pr n* GEOGR Melanesia *f*.

Melanesian [-n] *adj/n* melanesio, sia.

mélange [mei'lɑːnʒ] *n* mezcla *f*, mezcolanza *f*.

melba toast ['melbə'teust] *n* US pan *m* tostado.

Melbourne ['melbən] *pr n* GEOGR Melbourne.

Melchior ['melkiɔː*] *pr n* Melchor *m*.

meld [meld] *vt* cantar, declarar, anunciar (in card games).

mêlée; US melee ['melei] *n* pelea *f* confusa, refriega *f* || lucha *f*, conflicto *m* (conflict) || confusión *f*.

meliorate ['miːliəreit] *vt/vi* mejorar.

melioration [,miːliə'reiʃən] *n* mejora *f*, mejoramiento *m*.

melissa [me'lisə] *n* BOT toronjil *m*.

melliferous [me'lifərəs] *adj* melífero, ra.

mellifluous [me'lifluəs] *adj* melifluo, flua; *mellifluous words* palabras melifluas.

mellow ['meləu] *adj* suave (voice) || melodioso, sa (instrument) || suave (colour, light) || tierno, na (soft) || maduro, ra (fruit) || añejo, ja (wine) || maduro, ra (character) || FAM achispado, da (tipsy) || AGR mollar (soil).

mellow ['meləu] *vt* madurar (people, fruit) || suavizar (voice, colour, wine) || AGR mullir (soil).
◆ *vi* madurar (people, fruit) || suavizarse (voice, colour, wine).

mellowing [-iŋ] *n* maduración *f* (of people, of fruit) || suavización *f* (of voice, colour, wine) || AGR mullidura *f*.

mellowness [-nis] *n* madurez *f* (of people, of fruit) || AGR riqueza *f* || suavidad *f* (of voice, colour, wine) || lo melodioso (of an instrument).

melodic [mi'lɔdik] *adj* MUS melódico, ca.

melodious [mi'ləudjəs] *adj* MUS melodioso, sa.

melodiousness [-nis] *n* lo melodioso (of an instrument) || melodía *f*, armonía *f* (of music).

melodist ['melədist] *n* MUS melodista *m*, compositor *m* de melodías.

melodize [-'daiz] *vt* poner música a.

melodrama ['meləu,drɑːmə] *n* melodrama *m*.

melodramatic [,meləudrə'mætik] *adj* melodramático, ca.

melodramatically [-əli] *adv* melodramáticamente.

melody ['melədi] *n* MUS melodía *f* || *melody writer* melodista *m*, compositor *m* de melodías.

melomane ['meləmein] *adj* melómano, na.

melomania [melə'meiniə] *n* melomanía *f*.

melon ['melən] *n* BOT melón *m* (muskmelon) | sandía *f* (watermelon) || US FAM ganancias *f pl* (profit) || — *melon patch* melonar *m* || US FAM *to cut a melon* repartir el bacalao.

melopoeia [,melə'pijə] *n* MUS melopea *f*.

melt [melt] *n* colada *f* (molten metal) || fundición *f* (melting) || fusión *f*, derretimiento *m* (liquefaction).

melt [melt] *vt* derretir (to make liquid); *the sun melts the snow* el sol derrite la nieve || fundir (metals) || disolver (to dissolve) || mezclar, combinar (to mix) || FIG ablandar || *to melt down* fundir.
◆ *vi* derretirse (to become liquid) || disolverse (to dissolve) || fundirse (metals) || FIG derretirse, ablandarse (to be moved) || — FIG *butter wouldn't melt in his mouth* parece que no ha roto un plato en su vida | *money melts in his hands* parece que tiene un boquete en la mano || *to melt away* derretirse (snow), fundirse (metal), desvanecerse (confidence), desaparecer (money, person), disiparse (crowd) || *to melt in one's mouth* derretirse en la boca || *to melt into* fundirse en (colours), desaparecer en (to disappear), deshacerse en; *he melted into tears* se deshizo en lágrimas; confundirse en (distance), mezclarse con (to mix).

meltdown [-daun] *n* PHYS fusión *f* del núcleo del reactor nuclear (nuclear accident).

melting [-iŋ] *n* fundición *f*, fusión *f* (of metal) || derretimiento *m*, fusión *f* (thawing) || disolución *f* (dissolution).
◆ *adj* que se derrite (butter, snow) || que se funde (metal) || FIG enternecedor, ra || *melting point* punto *m* de fusión.

melting pot [-iŋpɔt] *n* crisol *m* (crucible) || FIG crisol *m* (country) | amalgama *f* de gente (mixed society) || FIG *to put everything back into the melting pot* volver a ponerlo todo en tela de juicio.

melton [-ən] *n* muletón *m*.

meltwater [-,wɔːtə*] *n* aguanieve *f*.

member ['membə*] *n* miembro *m* (person); *a member of the family* un miembro de la familia || ANAT miembro *m* || miembro *m*, socio *m* (of a society) || diputado *m* (of Parliament) || MATH & GRAMM miembro *m* || — *full-fledged* miembro de pleno derecho || *life member* miembro vitalicio || ANAT *mala member* miembro viril || *member of Parliament* diputado *m*, miembro del Parlamento (in general), procurador *m* en Cortes (in Spain) || *«members only»* «sólo para socios» || *ordinary member of the public* persona *f* cualquiera, cuidadano *m*.
◆ *adj* miembro; *member state* Estado miembro.

membership [-ʃip] *n* calidad *f* de miembro || calidad *f* de socio || número *m* de socios *or* miembros (members) || ingreso *m*; *to apply for membership of the United Nations* pedir su ingreso en las Naciones Unidas || — *membership dues* cuota *f* de socio || *membership is obligatory* es obligatorio ser miembro || *to acquire membership* hacerse miembro *or* socio.

membrane ['membrein] *n* membrana *f* (thin tissue).

membranous [mem'breinəs] *adj* membranoso, sa.

memento [mi'mentəu] *n* recuerdo *m* (reminder) || REL memento *m*.
— OBSERV El plural de la palabra inglesa *memento* es *mementoes* o *mementos*.

memo ['meməu] *n* FAM memorándum *m*.

memo book [-buk] *n* agenda *f*.

memo pad [-pæd] *n* bloc *m* de notas.

memoir ['memwɑː*] *n* memoria *f* || biografía *f*, reseña *f* biográfica (biography) || nota *f* necrológica (obituary).
◆ *pl* memorias *f*.

memorabilia [,memərə'biliə] *pl n* acontecimientos *m* memorables (events) || recuerdos *m* (things).

memorable ['memərəbl] *adj* memorable.

memorandum [,memə'rændəm] *n* memorándum *m*.
— OBSERV El plural de la palabra inglesa *memorandum* es *memorandums* o *memoranda*.

memorial [mi'mɔːriəl] *adj* conmemorativo, va (festival, monument) || *memorial faculty* facultad *f* de recordar.
◆ *n* monumento *m* conmemorativo (monument) || memorial *m* (petition) || recuerdo *m* (reminder) || — US *Memorial Day* día *m* de conmemoración de los Caídos || *war memorial* monumento *m* a los Caídos.

Satisfacer todos los requisitos

:ri-
rar
un

memorization [ˌmemərai'zeiʃən]; **memorizing** [ˌmeməraiziŋ] *n* memorización *f.*

memorize ['meməraiz] *vt* memorizar, aprender de memoria.

memory ['meməri] *n* memoria *f*; *I have a good memory* tengo buena memoria; *to lose one's memory* perder la memoria; *it slipped my memory* se me fue de la memoria || recuerdo *m*; *memories of childhood* recuerdos de la infancia; *of happy memory* de feliz recuerdo || INFORM memoria *f*; *memory capacity* capacidad de memoria || — *from memory* de memoria || *if my memory serves me right* si mal no recuerdo, si la memoria no me falta || *in memory* o *to the memory of* en memoria de || *memory book* álbum *m* de recuerdos (scrapbook), álbum *m* de firmas (autograph book) || INFORM *memory cell* celda *f* de memoria | *memory expansion* expansión *f* de memoria | *memory location* emplazamiento *m* de memoria || *to bring away a pleasant memory of* guardar *or* conservar un recuerdo agradable de || *to call to memory* recordar || *to commit to memory* aprender de memoria || *to erase from one's memory* borrar de la memoria || *to have a memory like a sieve* tener una memoria como un colador || *to keep s.o.'s memory alive* conservar el recuerdo de alguien || *to the best of my memory* que yo recuerde || *within living memory* que se recuerda; *it's the coldest winter within living memory* es el invierno más frío que se recuerda || *within my memory* que yo recuerde.

Memphite ['memfait] *adj/n* menfita.

men [men] *pl n* ⟶ **man.**

menace ['menəs] *n* amenaza *f* (threat) || FAM pesado, da (nuisance).

menace ['menəs] *vt/vi* amenazar.

menacing [-iŋ] *adj* amenazador, ra.

ménage [me'nɑːʒ] *n* casa *f* (household) || economía *f* doméstica.

menagerie [mi'nædʒəri] *n* casa *f* de fieras.

mend [mend] *n* reparación *f* (in roads, in China, etc.) || remiendo *m* (patch) || zurcido *m* (darn) || mejoría *f* (improvement) || FIG *to be on the mend* estar mejorando.

mend [mend] *vt* remendar; *to mend a jacket shoes* remendar una chaqueta, unos zapatos || zurcir (to darn) || arreglar, reparar (roads) || lañar, remendar (china) || echar carbón a (fire) || enmendar, corregir (to correct) || mejorar (to improve); *to mend matters* mejorar las cosas || arreglar; *now we must try and mend the situation* ahora tenemos que intentar arreglar la situación || — FIG *to mend one's pace* apresurar el paso | *to mend one's ways* enmendarse.
◆ *vi* mejorar, mejorarse (from an illness) || FIG enmendarse.

mendacious [men'deiʃəs] *adj* mendaz, mentiroso, sa.

mendacity [men'dæsiti] *n* mendacidad *f* (quality or state of being mendacious) || mentira *f*, embuste *m* (lie).

mendelevium [ˌmendə'liːvjəm] *n* CHEM mendelevio *m* (radioactive element).

Mendelian [men'diːliən] *adj* mendeliano, na.

Mendelianism [-izəm]; **Mendelism** ['mendəlizəm] *n* mendelismo *m.*

mendicant ['mendikənt] *adj/n* mendicante, mendigo, ga || REL mendicante; *the mendicant orders* las órdenes mendicantes.

mendicity [men'disiti] *n* mendicidad *f.*

mending ['mendiŋ] *n* reparación *f*, arreglo *m* (repair) || zurcido *m* (darning) || ropa *f* por zurcir (clothes).

menfolk ['menfəulk] *pl n* hombres *m.*

menhir ['menhiə*] *n* menhir *m.*

menial ['miːnjəl] *adj* doméstico, ca (suited for a servant) || bajo, ja (low, mean).
◆ *n* criado, da (domestic servant) || FIG lacayo *m* (servile person).

meningeal [mə'nindʒjəl] *adj* meníngeo, a.

meninges [mə'nindʒiːz] *pl n* meninges *f.*

meningitis [ˌmenin'dʒaitis] *n* MED meningitis *f.*
— OBSERV El plural de la palabra inglesa *meningitis* es *meningitides.*

meningococcus [məˌniŋgəu'kɔkəs] *n* MED meningococo *m.*
— OBSERV El plural es *meningococci.*

meninx ['miːniŋks] *n* meninge *f.*
— OBSERV El plural de *meninx* es *meninges.*

menippean [me'nipiən] *adj* menipeo, a.

meniscus [mə'niskəs] *n* menisco *m.*
— OBSERV El plural es *menisci* o *meniscuses.*

Mennonite ['menənait] *n* menonita *m.*

menopausal [menəu'pɔːzəl] *adj* menopáusico, ca.

menopause ['menəupɔːz] *n* MED menopausia *f.*

Menorca [me'nɔrkəː] *pr n* GEOGR Menorca.

menorrhagia [menə'reidʒiə] *n* MED menorragia *f.*

menorrhoea [menə'riːə] *n* menorrea *f.*

menses ['mensiːz] *pl n* MED menstruo *m sing*, reglas *f*, menstruación *f sing.*

Menshevik ['menʃəvik] *n* menchevique *m.*
— OBSERV El plural es *Mensheviki* o *Menshevikѕ.*

men's room ['menzˌruːm] *n* US servicios *m pl* para caballeros.

menstrual ['menstruəl] *adj* MED menstrual; *menstrual cycle* ciclo menstrual || mensual (monthly).

menstruate ['menstrueit] *vi* MED menstruar.

menstruation [ˌmenstru'eiʃən] *n* menstruación *f.*

mensurability [ˌmenʃurə'biliti] *n* mensurabilidad *f.*

mensurable ['menʃurəbl] *adj* mensurable, medible.

mensuration [ˌmensjuə'reiʃən] *n* medida *f*, medición *f.*

menswear ['menzwɛə*] *n* ropa *f* para hombres.

mental ['mentl] *adj* mental (of the mind); *mental faculties* facultades mentales; *mental patient* enfermo mental || psiquiátrico, ca; *mental hospital* hospital psiquiátrico || de las enfermedades mentales (specialist) || del mentón (of the chin) || FAM chiflado, da, chalado, da (crazy); *she must be a bit mental* debe de estar un poco chalada || — *mental age* edad *f* mental || *mental arithmetic* cálculo *m* mental || *mental block* bloqueo *m* mental || *mental deficiency* deficiencia *f* mental || *mental derangement* alienación *f* mental || *mental reservation* reserva *f* mental || *mental retardation* retraso *m* mental || *mental telepathy* transmisión *f* del pensamiento || *mental test* prueba *f* de inteligencia.

mentality [men'tæliti] *n* mentalidad *f*; *sometimes it is difficult to understand the Spanish mentality* a veces resulta difícil comprender la mentalidad española; *what a mentality!* ¡vaya mentalidad!

menthol ['menθɔl] *n* CHEM mentol *m* || *menthol cigarettes* cigarrillos mentolados.

mentholated [-eitid] *adj* mentolado, da.

mention ['menʃən] *n* mención *f*; *honourable mention* mención honorífica || *to make mention of* hacer mención de, mencionar.

mention ['menʃən] *vt* mencionar, hablar de, aludir a; *I avoided mentioning his divorce* evité hablar de su divorcio || mencionar; *I don't want to mention his name* no quiero mencionar su nombre || citar; *he was mentioned in the dispatches* fue citado en la orden del día || JUR mencionar (in a will) || — *don't mention it* no lo menciones, no hables de eso (don't speak about it), de nada, no hay de qué (thanks are unnecessary), no hay de qué (apology is unnecessary) || *I'll mention it when I see him* se lo diré cuando lo vea || *I need hardly mention that* huelga decir que || *not to mention* sin mencionar, por no decir nada de, además de || *not worth mentioning* sin importancia || *to make mention of* hacer mención de || *too numerous to mention* demasiado numerosos para citarlos aquí.

mentor ['mentɔː*] *n* mentor *m.*

menu ['menjuː] *n* carta *f*, lista *f* de platos (a la carta) || menú *m*, minuta *f* (fixed meal) || FIG *what's on the menu?* ¿qué hay de comer? || INFORM menú; *drop-down menu* menú drop-down *or* desenvolvente.

meow [miː'au] *n* maullido *m* (sound made by a cat) || miau *m* (onomatopoeia).

meow [miː'au] *vi* maullar.

MEP *abbr of [Member of the European Parliament]* eurodiputado.

Mephistopheles [ˌmefis'tɔfiliːz] *pr n* Mefistófeles *m.*

mephitic [me'fitik] *adj* mefítico, ca.

mephitis [me'faitis] *n* vapor *m or* olor *m* fétido, emanación *f* mefítica.

mercantile ['məːkəntail] *adj* mercantil, comercial; *mercantile operation* operación mercantil || comercial (affairs, nation, establishment) || JUR mercantil || MAR *mercantile marine* marina *f* mercante.

mercantilism ['məːkəntilizəm] *n* mercantilismo *m.*

mercantilist ['məːkəntilist] *n* mercantilista *m & f.*

mercedarian [ˌməːsə'dærjən] *n* mercedario, ria (monk, nun).

mercenary ['məːsinəri] *adj* mercenario, ria || *I have a purely mercenary interest in the matter* mi interés en el asunto es puramente material.
◆ *n* mercenario *m.*

mercer ['məːsə*] *n* (ant) mercero, ra.

mercerize ['məːsəraiz] *vi* mercerizar.

mercery ['mθːsəri] *n* comercio *m* de tejidos de seda (trade) || tejidos *m pl* de seda (goods) || mercería *f* (haberdashery).

merchandise ['məːtʃəndaiz] *n* mercancías *f pl* [AMER mercaderías *f pl*].

merchandise ['məːtʃəndaiz] *vt* comercializar || comerciar con *or* en.
◆ *vi* comerciar, negociar.

merchant ['məːtʃənt] *n* comerciante *m & f*, negociante *m & f* (person who directs large-scale trade); *grain merchant* negociante en granos || US comerciante *m* al por menor, detallista *m & f*, minorista *m & f* (retailer) | tendero, ra; vendedor, ra (shopkeeper) || mercader *m*; *the Merchant of Venice* el Mercader de Venecia.
◆ *adj* mercante; *merchant marine* o *navy* marina mercante || comercial; *merchant bank* banco comercial || mercantil; *Law merchant* derecho mercantil.

merchantable [-əbəl] *adj* comerciable.

merchantman [-mən] *n* MAR buque *m* mercante.
— OBSERV El plural es *merchantmen.*

merciful ['məːsiful] *adj* clemente, compasivo, va; misericordioso, sa.

mercifulness [-nis] *n* clemencia *f*, compasión *f*, misericordia *f.*

merciless ['mə:silis] *adj* despiadado, da; sin piedad.

mercurial [mə:'kjuəriəl] *adj* CHEM mercurial, mercúrico, ca || mercurial (pertaining to the god or planet) || FIG vivo, va (lively) | despierto, ta; despabilado, da (quick-witted) | cambiadizo, za; voluble, versátil (changeable).

mercurialism [-izəm] *n* MED hidrargirismo *m*.

mercuriality [-iti] *n* viveza *f* (liveliness) || inconstancia *f*, carácter *m* cambiadizo.

mercuric [mə:'kjuərik] *adj* mercúrico, ca || — CHEM *mercuric chloride* cloruro *m* de mercurio | *mercuric sulphide* sulfuro *m* de mercurio.

mercurochrome [mə:'kjuərəukrəum] *n* mercurocromo *m*.

mercurous ['mə:kjurəs] *adj* CHEM mercurioso.

mercury ['mə:kjuri] *n* CHEM mercurio *m*, azogue *m* || — *mercury arc* arco *m* de mercurio || *mercury barometer* barómetro *m* de mercurio || *mercury chloride* cloruro *m* de mercurio || *mercury-vapour lamp* lámpara *f* de vapor de mercurio.

Mercury ['mə:kjuri] *pr n* Mercurio *m* (planet, god).

mercy ['mə:si] *n* misericordia *f*, clemencia *f*, compasión *f*; *to beg for mercy* pedir clemencia || suerte *f*; *it's a mercy that the doctor arrived in time* es una suerte que el médico llegara a tiempo || merced *f*; *at the mercy of* a merced de || — *for mercy's sake!* ¡por piedad! || *I must be thankful for small mercies* algo tengo que agradecer || *to have mercy on s.o.* tener compasión de uno || FIG *to leave to the tender mercies of s.o.* dejar en las manos poco compasivas de alguien || *to show no mercy to s.o.* no tener la menor compasión de || *to throw o.s. on s.o.'s mercy* abandonarse a la merced de uno || *without mercy* sin piedad, despiadadamente || *works of mercy* obras *f* de caridad.

mercy killing [-'kiliŋ] *n* eutanasia *f*.

mere [miə*] *adj* mero, ra; simple, puro, ra; *mere foolishness* una simple tontería || — *a mere glance* una simple ojeada || *it's mere trifle* es una nadería *or* una fruslería || *it's mere talk* es pura palabrería || *she's a mere child* no es más que una niña, es solamente una niña.

◆ *n* estanque *m* (pond) || lago *m* (lake) || pantano *m* (marsh).

merely [-li] *adv* meramente, simplemente, solamente; *they are not opposite, but merely different* no son opuestos sino simplemente diferentes || sólo, solamente; *I merely asked his name* sólo pregunté su nombre || *she merely smiled* se limitó simplemente a sonreír.

meretricious [,meri'triʃəs] *adj* de oropel (superficially attractive) || engañoso, sa (fallacious) || ampuloso, sa; enfático, ca (style).

meretrix ['meritrix] *n* (ant) meretriz *f*.

merganser [mə:'gænsə*] *n* mergo *m* (bird).

merge [mə:dʒ] *vt* unir (to join) || fusionar (companies, political parties, etc.) || fundir (colours).

◆ *vi* unirse (to join together) || fusionarse; *the three parties have merged* los tres partidos se han fusionado || fundirse; *the green merges into the yellow* el verde se funde con el amarillo || *motorways merge* empalme *m* de autopistas.

mergence [-əns] *n* fusión *f* || unión *f*.

merger [-ə*] *n* unión *f* (joining) || fusión *f* (of companies, of parties).

meridian [mə'ridiən] *adj* meridiano, na || FIG máximo, ma.

◆ *n* ASTR & GEOGR meridiano *m* || FIG cenit *m*, apogeo *m*.

meridional [mə'ridiənl] *adj* meridional, del sur.

◆ *n* meridional *m* & *f*.

meringue [mə'ræŋ] *n* CULIN merengue *m*.

merino [mə'ri:nəu] *adj* merino, na.

◆ *n* merino *m* (sheep).

merit ['merit] *n* mérito *m*; *to treat everyone according to their merits* tratar a cada uno según sus méritos; *a work of little merit* una obra de poco mérito || cualidad *f*; *patience is one of his greatest merits* la paciencia es una de sus mayores cualidades.

◆ *pl* JUR fondo *m sing*; *to judge the merits of a case* juzgar el fondo de un caso.

merit ['merit] *vt* merecer, ser digno de (to deserve); *he doesn't merit your friendship* no merece tu amistad.

◆ *vi* hacer méritos.

meritocracy [meri'tɔkrəsi] *n* meritocracia *f*.

meritorious [,meri'tɔ:riəs] *adj* meritorio, ria; que tiene mérito.

merlin ['mə:lin] *n* esmerejón *m* (bird).

Merlin ['mə:lin] *pr n* Merlín *m*.

mermaid ['mə:meid] *n* sirena *f*.

merman ['mə:mæn] *n* tritón *m*.

— OBSERV El plural de esta palabra es *mermen*.

Merovaeous; Meroveous [merə'vi:əs] *pr n* Meroveo *m*.

Merovingian [,merəu'vindʒiən] *adj/n* HIST merovingio, gia.

merriment ['merimənt] *n* alegría *f*, júbilo *m* (gaiety) || risas *f pl* (laughter) || fiesta *f* (festivity) || diversión *f* (entertainment) || *there is no cause for merriment* no tiene ninguna gracia, no hay por qué alegrarse.

merriness ['merinis] *n* alegría *f*, regocijo *m*.

merry ['meri] *adj* alegre; *he has a merry disposition* tiene un carácter alegre || divertido, da; gracioso, sa; *a merry joke* un chiste gracioso || achispado, da (slightly drunk) || — *Merry Christmas* Felices Pascuas, Felices Navidades || *the more the merrier* cuantos más mejor || *to make merry* pasarlo bien, divertirse || *to make merry over* burlarse de, reírse de.

Merry-Andrew [-'ændru:] *n* payaso *m*.

merry-go-round [-gəu,raund] *n* tiovivo *m*.

merrymaker [-,meikə*] *n* juerguista *m* & *f*, parrandero, ra.

merrymaking [-,meikiŋ] *n* diversión *f*, fiestas *f pl*.

◆ *adj* alegre, festivo, va.

merrythought [-θɔ:t] *n* espoleta *f* (wishbone).

mésalliance [me'zæliəns] *n* casamiento *m* desigual, mal casamiento *m*.

mescal ['meskæl] *n* BOT mezcal *m*.

mescaline ['meskəli:n] *n* CHEM mezcalina *f*.

mesdames ['meidæm] *pl n* señoras *f*.

meseems [mi'si:mz] *v impers* (ant) me parece.

mesencephalon [,mesən'kefə,lɔn] *n* ANAT mesencéfalo *m*.

mesentery ['mezəntəri] *n* ANAT mesenterio *m*.

mesh [meʃ] *n* malla *f*; *fine mesh stocking* medias de malla fina || FIG red *f*; *caught up in a mesh of intrigue* enmarañado en una red de intrigas || engranaje *m* (of gears) || — TECH *in mesh* engranado, da || *wire mesh* tela metálica.

◆ *pl* FIG red *f sing*.

mesh [meʃ] *vt* coger con red || TECH engranar (to engage) || encajar bien (to fit).

◆ *vi* cogerse en la red, enredarse || TECH engranar (to engage) || encajar (to fit).

meshwork [-wə:k] *n* red *f* (network).

mesial ['mi:zjəl] *adj* BIOL mediano, na.

mesmerist ['mezmərist] *n* hipnotizador, ra.

mesmerize ['mezməraiz] *vt* hipnotizar.

mesne [mi:n] *adj* JUR intermediario, ria.

mesoblast ['mesəu,blɑ:st] *n* BIOL mesoblasto *m*.

mesocarp ['mesəu,kɑ:p] *n* BOT mesocarpo *m*, mesocarpio *m*.

mesocephalic [,mesəusə'fælik] *adj* ANAT mesocéfalo, la.

mesoderm ['mesəu,də:m] *n* BIOL mesodermo *m*.

Mesolithic [,mesəu'liθik] *adj* GEOL mesolítico, ca.

◆ *n* GEOL mesolítico *m*.

meson ['mi:zɔn] *n* PHYS mesón *m*.

Mesopotamia [,mesəpə'teimjə] *pr n* GEOGR Mesopotamia *f*.

Mesopotamian [-n] *adj/n* mesopotámico, ca.

mesosphere ['mesəusfiə*] *n* mesosfera *f*.

mesothelium [,mesəu'θi:liəm] *n* BIOL mesotelio *m*.

— OBSERV El plural de *mesothelium* es *mesothelia*.

mesothorax [,mesəu'θɔ:ræks] *n* ANAT mesotórax *m*.

— OBSERV El plural es *mesothoraxes* o *mesothoraces*.

mesotron ['mesəutrɔn] *n* PHYS mesotrón *m*.

Mesozoic [,mesəu'zəuik] *adj* GEOL mesozoico, ca.

mess [mes] *n* porquería *f*, asquerosidad *f*, suciedad *f* (dirt) || porquería *f*; *the cat has made a mess on the floor* el gato ha hecho una porquería en el suelo || confusión *f*, desorden *m* (disorderly state of things); *the room is in a mess* la habitación está en desorden || revoltijo *m*, follón *m* (disorderly things); *the filing cabinet is a mess* el fichero está hecho un revoltijo || lío *m*, follón *m* (awkward or confused situation); *his personal life is a mess* su vida privada es un lío; *to get into a mess* meterse en un lío; *to get out of a mess* salir de un lío || lío *m* (mental); *when I try to speak French I get into an awful mess* cuando intento hablar francés me armo un lío tremendo || (ant) ración *f*, plato *m* (portion of food); *mess of pottage* plato de lentejas || MIL rancho *m* (for soldiers) | comida *f* (officers' food) | comedor *m* de la tropa (place where meals are taken) || comida *f* (for dogs) || — MIL *mess hall* comedor *m* | *mess tin* escudilla *f* | *officers' mess* imperio *m* de oficiales || *to be in a mess* estar revuelto *or* desordenado (disorderly), estar metido en un lío (in an awkward situation), estar hecho un lío (confused) || *to make a mess of* desordenar (to disarrange), ensuciar (to dirty), hacer con los pies (a job), echar a perder (one's life) || *what a mess!* ¡qué asco!, ¡qué porquería! (something dirty), ¡qué lío!, ¡qué follón! (situation).

mess [mes] *vt* MIL dar el rancho a (to supply with meals) || — *to mess, to mess up* ensuciar (to dirty), desordenar (to disarrange), despeinar (hair), estropear, echar a perder (to spoil) || *to mess s.o. about* fastidiarle a uno.

◆ *vi* MIL comer el rancho || — FAM *stop messing about!* ¡déjate de tonterías! || *to mess about* o *around* no hacer nada de particular, hacer esto y lo otro; *I spend the weekends messing about in the garden* paso los fines de semana haciendo esto y lo otro en el jardín || *to mess about with* o *around with* entretenerse con; *he likes messing about with cars* le gusta entretenerse con coches; enredar con; *stop messing around with that gun* deja de enredar con ese fusil || *to mess around with s.o. else's wife* tener un lío con la mujer de otro || *to mess in* o *with* entrometerse *or* meterse en.

message ['mesidʒ] *n* recado *m* (non-official communication from person to person); *may*

I have a message? ¿puedo dejar un recado? || encargo *m*, recado *m* (errand); *to run messages* hacer los encargos || mensaje *m* (official or important communication, teaching); *the Gospels are the message of Christ* los Evangelios son el mensaje de Cristo; *a film with a message for modern youth* una película con un mensaje para la juventud actual || FAM *to get the message* comprender, caer en la cuenta.

message ['mesidʒ] *vt* mandar por intermedio de un recadero || transmitir por medio de señales.

Messalina [mesə'lainə] *pr n* Mesalina *f.*

messenger ['mesindʒə*] *n* mensajero, ra; *a messenger of the gods* un mensajero de los dioses || recadero, ra (in an office, bank) || MAR virador *m* (of a capstan).

Messiah [mi'saiə] *n* Mesías *m.*

messianic [,mesi'ænik] *adj* mesiánico, ca.

messieurs ['mesəz] *pl n* señores *m.*

messiness ['mesinis] *n* desorden *m* (disorder) || suciedad *f* (dirtiness).

messmate ['mesmeit] *n* compañero *m* de rancho.

Messrs. ['mesəz] *pl n* Sres. (abbreviation).

messuage ['meswidʒ] *n* JUR casa *f* con sus dependencias y tierras.

mess-up ['mesʌp] *n* FAM lío *m*, follón *m* (confusion); *the ceremony was an awful mess-up* el acto fue un lío espantoso.

messy ['mesi] *adj* desordenado, da; en desorden (disorganized) || sucio, cia (dirty); *the inside of the car is messy* el interior del coche está sucio || confuso, sa (confused) || lioso, sa; *a very messy affair* un asunto muy lioso || *prawns are very messy to peel* las gambas ensucian mucho al pelarlas.

mestiza [mes'ti:zə] *n* mestiza *f.*

mestizo [mes'ti:zəu] *n* mestizo, za.

met [met] *pret/pp* ⟶ **meet.**

metabolic [,metə'bɔlik] *adj* metabólico, ca.

metabolism [me'tæbəlizəm] *n* BIOL metabolismo *m.*

metacarpal [,metə'kɑ:pl] *adj* metacarpiano, na.
◆ *n* hueso *m* metacarpiano.

metacarpus [,metə'kɑ:pəs] *n* ANAT metacarpo *m.*

metal ['metl] *n* metal *m*; *metal engraver* grabador en metal || grava *f* (for surfacing roads) || balasto *m* (of railways) || vidrio *m* fundido (molten glass) || plomo *m* (printing types) || (ant) FIG ⟶ **mettle** || HERALD metal *m* || *sheet metal* lámina *f* de metal.
◆ *pl* rieles *m*, raíles *m* (rails of railway line) || *precious metals* metales preciosos.

metal ['metl] *vt* cubrir con metal (to cover with metal) || cubrir con grava (to surface a road with metal).

metaldehyde [me'tældihaid] *n* CHEM metaldehído *m.*

metaling ['metliŋ] *n* firme *m* (of a road).

metallic [mi'tælik] *adj* metálico, ca.

metalliferous [,metə'lifərəs] *adj* metalífero, ra.

metalling ['metliŋ] *n* firme *m* (of a road).

metallization; *US* **metalization** [metəlai'zeiʃən] *n* metalización *f.*

metallize; *US* **metalize** ['metəlaiz] *vt* metalizar (a surface) || vulcanizar (rubber).

metalloid ['metəlɔid] *n* metaloide *m.*

metallurgic [metə'lə:dʒik] *adj* metalúrgico, ca.

metallurgical [-əl] *adj* metalúrgico, ca.

metallurgist [me'tælədʒist] *n* metalúrgico *m.*

metallurgy [me'tælədʒi] *n* metalurgia *f.*

metalwork ['metəlwə:k] *n* metalistería *f*, trabajo *m* del metal (craft) || objetos *m pl* de metal.

metalworking [-iŋ] *n* metalistería *f*, trabajo *m* del metal.

metamorphic [,metə'mɔ:fik] *adj* metamórfico, ca.

metamorphism [,metə'mɔ:fizəm] *n* GEOL metamorfismo *m* || metamorfosis *f* (metamorphosis).

metamorphose [,metə'mɔ:fəuz] *vt* metamorfosear, transformar.
◆ *vi* metamorfosearse, transformarse (*into, to* en).

metamorphosis [,metə'mɔ:fəsis] *n* BIOL metamorfosis *f* || transformación *f* metamorfosis *f* (change of character, of form, etc.).
— OBSERV El plural de *metamorphosis* es *metamorphoses.*

metaphase ['metəfeiz] *n* BIOL metafase *f.*

metaphor ['metəfə*] *n* metáfora *f.*

metaphoric [,metə'fɔrik]; **metaphorical** [-əl] *adj* metafórico, ca.

metaphorize ['metəfəraiz] *vt* metaforizar.

metaphrase ['metəfreiz] *n* traducción *f* literal.

metaphrastic [metə'fræstik] *adj* literal.

metaphysical [,metə'fizikəl] *adj* metafísico, ca.

metaphysician [,metəfi'ziʃən] *n* metafísico *m.*

metaphysics [,metə'fiziks] *n* metafísica *f.*

metaplasm ['metəplæzəm] *n* GRAMM metaplasmo *m.*

metapsychic [metə'saikik]; **metapsychical** [-əl] *adj* metapsíquico, ca.

metapsychology [,metəsai'kɔlədʒi] *n* metapsíquica *f.*

metastasis [me'tæstisis] *n* metástasis *f.*
— OBSERV El plural de la palabra inglesa es *metastases.*

metatarsal [,metə'tɑ:səl] *adj* ANAT metatarsiano, na.

metatarsus [,metə'tɑ:sis] *n* ANAT metatarso *m.*
— OBSERV El plural de *metatarsus* es *metatarsi.*

metathesis [me'tæθəsis] *n* GRAMM metátesis *f.*
— OBSERV El plural de *metathesis* es *metatheses.*

metathorax [,metə'θɔ:ræks] *n* ZOOL metatórax *m.*

métayer ['metəiei] *n* AGR aparcero *m.*

metazoan [,metə'zəuən] *adj* ZOOL metazoario, ria.
◆ *n* metazoario *m*, metazoo *m.*

mete [mi:t] *vt* medir || — *to mete out* repartir, distribuir || *to mete out punishment* dar un castigo.

metempsychosis [,metempsi'kəusis] *n* metempsicosis *f.*
— OBSERV El plural de *metempsychosis* es *metempsychoses.*

meteor ['mi:tjə*] *n* meteoro *m.*

meteoric [,mi:ti'ɔrik] *adj* meteórico, ca || *US* atmosférico, ca (phenomenon) || FIG meteórico, ca; fugaz, rápido, da.

meteorism ['mi:tjərizəm] *n* meteorismo *m.*

meteorite ['mi:tjərait] *n* meteorito *m.*

meteoroid ['mi:tjərɔid] *n* meteorito *m.*

meteorologic [,mi:tjərə'lɔdʒik]; **meteorological** [-əl] *adj* meteorológico, ca.

meteorologist [,mi:tjə'rɔlədʒist] *n* meteorólogo, ga; meteorologista *m & f.*

meteorology [,mi:tjə'rɔlədʒi] *n* meteorología *f.*

meter ['mi:tə*] *n* contador *m* (instrument) || *US* metro *m* (measure, rhythmic pattern); *square, cubic meter* metro cuadrado, cúbico; *to measure in meters* medir por metros.

meter ['mi:tə*] *vt* medir [con contador] || *US* franquear [sellos] (to frank mail).

meterage [-ridʒ] *n* medición *f* con contador.

methane ['mi:θein] *n* CHEM metano *m.*

methanol ['mi:θənɔl] *n* CHEM metanol *m*, alcohol *m* metílico.

methinks [mi'θiŋks] *v impers* me parece, creo.
— OBSERV El pretérito es ***methought.***

method ['meθəd] *n* método *m* (*of* para) || manera *f*, modo *m* (of payment) || procedimiento *m* (means) || JUR modalidad *f* (of application) || FIG *there's method in his madness* es menos loco de lo que parece.

methodic [mi'θɔdik]; **methodical** [-əl] *adj* metódico, ca.

Methodism ['meθədizəm] *n* REL metodismo *m.*

Methodist ['meθədist] *adj/n* REL metodista.

methodize ['meθədaiz] *vt* metodizar, sistematizar.

methodological [,meθədə'lɔdʒikəl] *adj* metodológico, ca.

methodology [,meθə'dɔlədʒi] *n* metodología *f.*

methought [mi'θɔ:t] *pret* ⟶ **methinks.**

meths [meθs] *n* FAM alcohol *m* desnaturalizado.

Methuselah [mi'θju:zələ] *pr n* Matusalén *m* || FIG *as old as Methuselah* más viejo que Matusalén.

methyl ['meθil] *n* CHEM metilo *m* || *methyl alcohol* alcohol metílico, metanol *m.*

methylate ['meθileit] *vt* desnaturalizar, mezclar con metanol || *methylated spirit* alcohol desnaturalizado.

methylene ['meθili:n] *n* CHEM metileno *m* || *methylene blue* azul *m* de metileno.

methylic [me'θilik] *adj* metílico, ca.

meticulosity [me,tikju'lɔsiti] *n* meticulosidad *f.*

meticulous [mi'tikjuləs] *adj* meticuloso, sa.

métier ['meitjei] *n* oficio *m*, profesión *f* || especialidad *f.*

métis; **metis** ['meitis] *n* mestizo, za.

metol ['metɔl] *n* CHEM metol *m.*

metonymical [metə'nimikəl] *adj* metonímico, ca.

metonymy [mi'tɔnimi] *n* metonimia *f.*

metope ['metəup] *n* ARCH metopa *f.*

metre ['mi:tə*] *n* metro *m* (measure, rhythmic pattern); *square, cubic metre* metro cuadrado, cúbico; *to measure in metres* medir por metros.

metric ['metrik] *adj* métrico, ca; *metric ton* tonelada métrica || *metric system* sistema métrico.

metrical [-əl] *adj* métrico, ca.

metrication [,metri'keiʃən] *n* adopción *f* del sistema métrico || conversión *f* al sistema métrico.

metrics [-s] *n* POET métrica *f.*

metrification [,metrifi'keiʃən] *n* metrificación *f.*

metrify ['metrifai] *vt* metrificar.

metrist ['metrist] *n* versificador, ra; metrificador, ra.

metritis [me'traitis] *n* MED metritis *f.*

metro ['metrəu] *n* metro *m* (underground).

metrology [me'trɔlədʒi] *n* metrología *f.*

metronome ['metrənəum] *n* metrónomo *m.*

metronymic [ˌmetrə'nimik] *adj* del apellido materno.
◆ *n* apellido *m* materno.

metropolis [mi'trɔpəlis] *n* metrópoli *f.*

metropolitan [ˌmetrə'pɔlitən] *adj* metropolitano, na || *Metropolitan Police* cuerpo *m* de policía de Londres.
◆ *n* REL metropolitano *m.*

mettle ['metl] *n* ánimo *m*, valor *m*, temple *m* || — FIG *to be on one's mettle* estar dispuesto a mostrar su valor | *to put s.o. on his mettle* picar a uno en su amor propio | *to show one's mettle* mostrar lo que uno vale, mostrar su valor.

mettlesome [-səm] *adj* ardiente, fogoso, sa; animoso, sa; valiente.

Meuse [məːz] *pr n* GEOGR Mosa *m.*

mew [mjuː] *n* maullido *m* (noise made by a cat) || miau (onomatopoeia) || grito *m* (noise of a gull) || ZOOL gaviota *f* (gull) || jaula *f* (cage).

mew [mjuː] *vi* maullar (a cat) || gritar (a gull) || mudar (to moult).
◆ *vt* enjaular (to put in a cage).

mewing [-iŋ] *n* maullido *m* (of a cat) || muda *f* (moulting).

mewl [mjuːl] *vi* lloriquear (to whimper) || maullar (a cat).

mews [mjuːz] *n* caballerizas *f pl* (stables) || callejuela *f* (back street).

Mexican ['meksikən] *adj/n* mejicano, na; mexicano, na.

Mexico ['meksikəu] *pr n* GEOGR Méjico, México || — *Mexico City* Méjico, México [capital] || *gulf of Mexico* golfo *m* de Méjico *or* de México.
— OBSERV See at *México* in the Spanish-English part.

mezzanine ['metsəniːn] *n* entresuelo *m* (storey between two main ones) || US entresuelo *m.*

mi [miː] *n* MUS mi *m.*

miaow [miː'au] *n* maullido *m* (sound made by a cat) || miau *m* (onomatopoeia).

miaow [miː'au] *vi* maullar.

miasma [mi'æzmə] *n* miasma *m.*
— OBSERV El plural de la palabra inglesa *miasma* es *miasmas* o *miasmata*. El género de la palabra española *miasma* es masculino aunque se usa a menudo el femenino erróneamente.

miaul [mi'aul] *vi* maullar.

mica ['maikə] *n* MIN mica *f.*

micaceous [mai'keiʃəs] *adj* micáceo, a.

mice [mais] *pl n* ⟶ **mouse.**

micelle [mi'sel] *n* BIOL & CHEM micela *f.*

Michael ['maikl] *pr n* Miguel *m.*

Michaelmas ['miklməs] *n* día *m* de San Miguel (29th September).

Michelangelo [ˌmaikəl'ændʒiləu] *pr n* Miguel Ángel *m.*

Michigan ['miʃigən] *pr n* GEOGR Michigan || *Michigan Lake* lago *m* Michigan.

mickey ['miki] *n* FAM *to take the mickey out of* tomar el pelo a.

mickle ['mikl] *n* *many a little makes a mickle* muchos pocos hacen un mucho.

micro ['maikrəu]; **microcomputer** ['maikrəu'kɔmpjuːtə*] *n* INFORM micro *m*, microordenador *m*, microcomputador, ra.

microampere [ˌmaikrə'æmpɛə*] *n* ELECTR microamperio *m.*

microanalysis [ˌmaikrəuə'nælisis] *n* CHEM microanálisis *m.*

microbe ['maikrəub] *n* microbio *m.*

microbial [mai'krəubiəl]; **microbic** [mai'krəubik] *adj* microbiano, na.

microbicide [mai'krəubəsaid] *n* microbicida *m.*

microbiology [ˌmaikrəubai'ɔlədʒi] *n* microbiología *f.*

microcephalic ['maikrəusə'fælik]; **microcephalous** ['maikrəu'sefələs] *adj* microcéfalo, la.

microcephaly [ˌmaikrəu'sefəli] *n* microcefalia *f.*

microchip ['maikrəutʃip] *n* INFORM microchip *f.*

microclimate ['maikrəuˌklaimit] *n* microclima *m.*

microcomputer ['maikrəu'kɔmpjuːtə*] *n* ⟶ **micro.**

microcomputing ['maikrəu'kɔmpjuːtiŋ] *n* INFORM microinformática *f.*

microcosm ['maikrəukɔzəm] *n* microcosmo *m.*

microcosmic ['maikrəuˌkɔzmik] *adj* microcósmico, ca.

microfarad [ˌmaikrəu'færəd] *n* PHYS microfaradio *m.*

microfiche ['maikrəufiːʃ] *n* microficha *f.*

microfilm ['maikrəufilm] *n* microfilm *m*, microfilme *m* (very small photographic film).

microfilm ['maikrəufilm] *vt* microfilmar.

micrography [mai'krɔgrəfi] *n* micrografía *f.*

microgroove ['maikrəugruːv] *n* microsurco *m.*

microhm ['maikrəum] *n* ELECTR microhmio *m*, microhm *m.*

micrometer [mai'krɔmitə*] *n* micrómetro *m.*

micrometric [maikrə'metrik]; **micrometrical** [-əl] *adj* micrométrico, ca.

micron ['maikrən] *n* micra *f*, micrón *m.*
— OBSERV El plural de la palabra inglesa es *microns* o *micra.*

Micronesia [ˌmaikrəu'niːʃiə] *pr n* GEOGR Micronesia *f.*

Micronesian [-n] *adj* micronesio, sia.
◆ *n* micronesio, sia (person) || micronesio *m* (language).

microorganism ['maikrəu'ɔːgənizəm] *n* microorganismo *m.*

microphone ['maikrəfəun] *n* micrófono *m*; *to speak through* o *over the microphone* hablar por el micrófono.

microphotograph ['maikrəu'fəutəgrɑːf] *n* microfotografía *f.*

microphotography [ˌmaikrəufə'tɔgrəfi] *n* microfotografía *f.*

microphysics [ˌmaikrəu'fiziks] *n* microfísica *f.*

microprocessor ['maikrəuprəu'sesə*] *n* INFORM microprocesador *m.*

microprogram ['maikrəu'prəugræn] *n* INFORM microprograma *f.*

microprogramming ['maikrə'səːdʒəri] *n* INFORM microprogramación *f.*

microscope ['maikrəskəup] *n* microscopio *m*; *electron microscope* microscopio electrónico.

microscopic [ˌmaikrəs'kɔpik]; **microscopical** [-əl] *adj* microscópico, ca.

microscopy [mai'krɔskəpi] *n* microscopia *f.*

microsecond [ˌmaikrəu'sekənd] *n* microsegundo *m.*

microsurgery ['maikrə'səːdʒəri] *n* MED microcirugía *f.*

microtherm ['maikrəθəːm] *n* microtermia *f.*

microwave ['maikrəweiv] *n* onda *f* ultracorta, microonda *f.*

micturate ['miktjureit] *vi* orinar.

micturition [ˌmiktju'riʃən] *n* micción *f.*

mid [mid] *adj* medio, dia; *the mid afternoon break* el descanso de media tarde; *in mid journey* a medio camino; *in mid course* a media carrera || GRAMM intermedio, dia (vowel) || — *from mid March to mid August* de mediados de marzo a mediados de agosto || *in mid air* entre cielo y tierra, en pleno aire || *in mid ocean* en medio del océano.
◆ *prep* en medio de, entre.
— OBSERV La palabra *mid* se emplea generalmente en la composición de palabras compuestas como *midday, midnight* etc.

midbrain [-brein] *n* ANAT mesencéfalo *m*, cerebro *m* medio.

midday [-dei] *n* mediodía *m.*
◆ *adj* del mediodía.

midden [-n] *n* yacimiento *m* arqueológico || AGR muladar *m*, estercolero *m* (dunghill).

middle [-l] *adj* central, de en medio; *you have to go through the middle door* tienes que pasar por la puerta de en medio; *middle axle* eje central || intermedio, dia (intermediate); *middle management* mandos intermedios || mediano, na (middling) || medio, dia; *of middle height* de estatura media || mediano, na; *middle age* edad mediana || ARCH medianero, ra (wall) || SP medio (weight) || medio, dia (voice).
◆ *n* medio *m*, media *f*; *in the middle of the night, of the road* en medio de la noche, de la calle || centro *m*; *right in the middle of the target* en el mismo centro del blanco || mitad *f*; *cut it down the middle* córtalo por la mitad || FAM cintura *f* (waist); *round the middle* alrededor de la cintura || — *in the middle of* en el centro de, en medio de (in the centre), en pleno; *in the middle of one's work* en pleno trabajo || *in the middle of August* a mediados de agosto || FAM *in the middle of nowhere* en el quinto pino (very far) || *in the very middle of* en pleno centro de (just in the centre), en medio de; *in the very middle of the night* en medio de la noche || *they are in the middle of dinner* están cenando.

middle ['midl] *vt* centrar || MAR doblar en dos || SP centrar.

middle-aged [-'eidʒd] *adj* de mediana edad.

Middle Ages [-'eidʒiz] *pl prn* Edad *f sing* Media.

middlebrow [-brau] *adj* de cultura mediana.

middle class [-klɑːs] *n* clase media || burguesía *f* (bourgeoisie).

middle class [-klɑːs] *adj* de la clase media || burgués, esa (bourgeois).

middle distance [-'distəns] *n* ARTS segundo término *m*, segundo plano *m* || SP medio fondo *m.*

middle ear [-iə*] *n* ANAT oído *m* medio.

Middle East [-'iːst] *pr n* GEOGR Oriente *m* Medio.

Middle English [-'iŋgliʃ] *n* inglés *m* hablado entre los siglos XII y XV.

middle finger [-'fiŋgə*] *n* dedo *m* medio *or* del corazón.

middleman [-mæn] *n* COMM intermediario *m* || FAM alcahuete *m* (pimp).
— OBSERV El plural de esta palabra es *middlemen.*

middlemost [-məust] *adj* central.

middle of the road [-əvðə'rəud] *n* política *f* moderada *or* centrista.

middle-of-the-road [-əvðə'rəud] *adj* centrista, moderado, da (policy).

middle-sized [-'saizd] *adj* de tamaño mediano (thing) || de mediana estatura (person).

middle term [-'təːm] *n* término *m* medio.

middleweight [-weit] *n* SP peso *m* medio.

middling ['midliŋ] *adj* mediano, na; regular.
◆ *pl n* AGR acemite *m sing* || COMM productos *m* de calidad media.
◆ *adv* regular || *middling good* medianamente bueno, regular.

middy ['midi] *n* FAM guardiamarina *m*, guardia *m* marina (midshipman) || US marinera *f* (blouse) || US *middy blouse* marinera *f*.

midfield [midfi:ld] *n* SP centrocampo *m*, centro *m* del campo.
◆ *adj* SP centrocampista (player).

midge [midʒ] *n* mosca *f* enana.

midget ['midʒit] *n* enano, na (dwarf).
◆ *adj* pequeñísimo, ma; en miniatura || *midget submarine* submarino *m* de bolsillo.

Midianite ['midiənait] *n* REL madianita *m*.

midland ['midlənd] *adj* de tierra adentro, del interior.
◆ *n* región *f* central || *the Midlands* región *f* central de Inglaterra.

midmost ['midməust] *adj* central, en pleno centro.
◆ *adv* en pleno centro.
◆ *n* centro *m*.

midnight ['midait] *adj* de medianoche; *midnight sun* sol de medianoche || — *midnight Mass* misa *f* del gallo || FAM *to burn the midnight oil* quemarse las pestañas.
◆ *n* medianoche *f*.

midrib ['midrib] *n* BOT nervio *m* central (of a leaf).

midriff ['midrif] *n* ANAT diafragma *m* || traje *m* de dos piezas (woman's garment).

midsection ['mid'sekʃən] *n* sección *f* media.

midship ['midʃip] *adj* MAR en medio del barco || — *midship frame* cuaderna maestra || *midship gangway* crujía *f*.

midshipman ['midʃipmən] *n* MAR guardamarina *m*, guardia *m* marina.
— OBSERV El plural de *midshipman* es *midshipmen*.

midships ['midʃips] *adv* MAR en medio del barco.

midst [midst] *n* *in our midst* entre nosotros || *in the midst of* en medio de (in the middle of), en pleno; *in the midst of winter* en pleno invierno.
◆ *prep* entre.

midstream ['midstri:m] *n* medio *m* del río || FAM *to change horses in midstream* cambiar de camisa.

midsummer ['mid,sʌmə*] *n* pleno verano *m* (middle of the summer) || solsticio *m* de verano (period of the summer solstice) || — *a Midsummer Night's Dream* el sueño de una noche de verano || *Midsummer Day* el día de San Juan (24th of June).

midterm ['midtə:m] *n* mitad *f* del trimestre (of a school term) || mitad *f* del mandato (of a term of office) || US FAM examen *m* parcial a mitad del trimestre.

midway ['mid'wei] *adj/adv* a medio camino, a mitad del camino.
◆ *n* US avenida *f* central (of a fair).

midweek ['midwi:k] *adj/adv* entre semana.
◆ *n* medio *m or* mitad *f* de la semana.

Midwest ['mid'west] *n* US GEOGR mediooeste *m* norteamericano.

midwife ['midwaif] *n* comadrona *f*, partera *f*.
— OBSERV El plural de *midwife* es *midwives*.

midwifery ['midwifəri] *n* obstetricia *f*.

midwinter ['mid'wintə*] *n* pleno invierno *m* || solsticio *m* de invierno (solstice).

midyear ['midjə:*] *n* mediados *or* mitad *f* del año || US FAM examen *m* parcial a mitad de curso, examen *m* semestral.
◆ *adj* semestral.

mien [mi:n] *n* semblante *m*, aire *m* (face) || aspecto *m* (aspect) || porte *m* (bearing).

miff [mif] *n* US FAM disgusto *m*.

miff [mif] *vt* US FAM ofender, disgustar.

might [mait] *n* fuerza *f*, poder *m* (strength) || *with all one's might, with might and main* con todas sus fuerzas.

might [mait] *pret* ⟶ **may**.

might-have-been [-hæv,bi:n] *n* lo que hubiera podido suceder (event) || fracasado, da (person).

mightily [-ili] *adv* con fuerza, poderosamente || FAM sumamente, extremadamente (extremely).

mightiness [-inis] *n* fuerza *f*, poder *m*, poderío *m*.

mightn't ['maitnt] contraction of «might not».

might've ['maitəv] contraction of «might have».

mighty ['maiti] *adj* fuerte (strong) || poderoso, sa (powerful); *a mighty country* un país poderoso || extraordinario, ria; *he made a mighty effort* hizo un esfuerzo extraordinario || enorme (great).
◆ *adv* FAM muy; *a mighty big man* un hombre muy grande || *to be mighty sorry* sentirlo enormemente.

mignonette [,minjə'net] *n* BOT reseda *f*.

migraine ['mi:grein] *n* MED jaqueca *f*.

migrant ['maigrənt] *adj* migratorio, ria.
◆ *n* trabajador *m* que se traslada de un sitio a otro || ave *f* migratoria (bird).

migrate [mai'greit] *vi* emigrar (people, animals, plants) || CHEM desplazarse (atoms, ions, etc.).

migrating [-iŋ] *adj* migratorio, ria.

migration [mai'greiʃən] *n* migración *f* (of people, of animals, etc.) || CHEM migración *f*.

migratory ['maigrətəri] *adj* migratorio, ria.

mihrab ['mirab] *n* mihrab *m* (of a mosque).

mikado [mi'kɑ:dəu] *n* micado *m*.

mike [maik] *n* FAM micro *m*.

Mike [maik] *pr n* FAM Miguelín *m*, Miguelito *m* || *for the love of Mike!* ¡por Dios!, ¡por el amor de Dios!

mil [mil] *n* milésima *f* de pulgada.

milady [mi'leidi] *n* miladi *f*.

Milan [mi'læn] *pr n* GEOGR Milán.

Milanese [,milə'ni:z] *adj/n* milanés, esa || HIST Milanesado *m*.

milch [miltʃ] *adj* lechero, ra; *milch cow* vaca lechera.

mild [maild] *adj* poco riguroso, sa; poco severo, ra (punishment, rule) || templado, da; benigno, na (climate, weather) || suave (wind) || bondadoso, sa; dulce, apacible (person, character) || dulce (look) || suave (slope) || flojo, ja (food, drink) || suave (tobacco, cheese, medicine) || benigno, na (disease, illness) || dulce (steel) || *mild success* éxito *m* de prestigio.

milden ['maildən] *vt* suavizar.
◆ *vi* suavizarse.

mildew ['mildju:] *n* moho *m* || mancha *f* de humedad (stain) || AGR añublo *m*, tizón *m* (on plants) | mildiu *m*, mildeu *m* (on vine).

mildew ['mildju:] *vt* enmohecer || manchar de humedad (to stain) || AGR atizonar, añublar (plants) | atacar de mildiu (vine).
◆ *vi* enmohecerse || mancharse de humedad || AGR atizonarse, añublarse (plants) | estar atacado de mildiu (vine).

mildewy [-i] *adj* mohoso, sa || manchado de humedad || AGR atizonado, da; añublado, da (plant) | atacado de mildiu (vine).

mildly ['maildli] *adv* suavemente (softly) || ligeramente (lightly, slightly) || *to put it mildly* para no decir más.

mild-mannered ['maild,mænəd] *adj* dulce, apacible.

mildness ['maildnis] *n* poca severidad *f* (of punishment) || benignidad *f* (of climate, of illness) || dulzura *f*, suavidad *f* (of a person) || bondad *f*, afabilidad *f* (of character) || dulzura *f* (of a look) || suavidad *f* (of tobacco, of slope, etc.).

mile [mail] *n* milla *f* [unidad de medida que equivale a 1 609 m] || MAR milla *f* [unidad de medida que equivale a 1 852 m] || — *it is miles away* está muy lejos || FIG *it stands out a mile* se ve a la legua || *I walked miles* anduve kilómetros y kilómetros || FIG *he is miles away* está en la luna | *you are miles out* o *off* estás lejos de la cuenta (you are very much mistaken).

mileage ['mailidʒ] *n* distancia *f* en millas (distance from one place to another) || recorrido *m* en millas (distance travelled) || gastos *m pl* de viaje por millas recorridas (travel allowance per mile) || coste *m* de transporte por milla (transport cost per mile) || kilometraje *m*, kilómetros *m pl*; *what is the mileage of this car?* ¿qué kilometraje tiene este coche?, ¿cuántos kilómetros ha recorrido este coche? || — *mileage indicator* cuentakilómetros *m inv* || *mileage ticket* billete kilométrico de ferrocarril.
— OBSERV The word *kilometraje* refers to the number of kilometres travelled.

mileometer [mai'lɔmitə*] *n* ⟶**milometer.**

milepost ['mailpəust] *n* mojón *m* [kilométrico].

miler ['mailə*] *n* SP corredor *m* de la milla (runner) || caballo *m* cuya especialidad es correr la milla.

milestone ['mailstəun] *n* mojón *m* [kilométrico] || FIG jalón *m*, hito *m* (in s.o.'s life).

milfoil ['milfɔil] *n* BOT milenrama *f*.

miliary ['miliəri] *adj* MED miliar; *miliary fever* fiebre miliar.

milieu ['mi:ljə:] *n* medio ambiente *m*, entorno *m* (environment).

militancy ['militənsi] *n* belicosidad *f*, combatividad *f* (fighting spirit) || actividad *f* de un militante (in politics).

militant ['militənt] *adj* combatiente (engaged in fighting) || belicoso, sa (aggressive) || militante; *a militant socialist* un socialista militante || REL militante.
◆ *n* militante *m* & *f*.

militarism ['militərizəm] *n* militarismo *m*.

militarist ['militərist] *adj/n* militarista.

militaristic [,militə'ristik] *adj* militarista.

militarization ['militərai'zeiʃən] *n* militarización *f*.

militarize ['militəraiz] *vt* militarizar.

military ['militəri] *adj* militar; *military academy* academia militar; *military attaché* agregado militar; *military service* servicio militar; *military training* instrucción militar || — *military government* gobierno *m* militar || *military law* código *m* militar || *military man* militar *m* || *military police* policía *f* militar || *military record* cartilla *f* militar || *the military* los militares.

militate ['militeit] *vi* militar; *much evidence militates in his favour* militan muchas pruebas en su favor.

militia [mi'liʃə] *n* milicia *f*.

militiaman [-mən] *n* miliciano *m*.
— OBSERV El plural de *militiaman* es *militiamen*.

milk [milk] *n* leche *f* || — *coconut milk* leche de coco || FIG *it is no use crying over spilt milk* a lo hecho, pecho || *milk chocolate* chocolate *m* con leche || *milk diet* dieta láctea || *powdered milk* leche en polvo || *skim milk* leche desnatada || FIG *the milk of human kindness* la amabilidad personificada.

milk [milk] *vt* ordeñar (an animal) || sacar (juice, sap) || FIG exprimir (to exploit in order to get money from) | sacar a (to get from) | chupar; *they are milking me of my money* me están chupando el dinero.
◆ *vi* dar leche.

milk-and-water [-ən'wɔːtə*] *adj* insulso, sa; insípido, da; soso, sa.

milk bar [-bɑː*] *n* cafetería *f*.

milk can [-kæn] *n* cántara *f or* cántaro *m* de leche, lechera *f*.

milk churn ['milktʃəːn] *n* lechera *f*, cántaro *m or* cántara *f* de leche.

milker [-ə*] *n* ordeñador, ra (person who milks) || ordeñadora *f*, máquina *f* de ordeñar (machine) || vaca *f* lechera (milch cow).

milk fever [-ˌfiːvə*] *n* MED & VET fiebre *f* láctea.

milk-float [-fləut] *n* carro *m* de la leche.

milkiness [-inis] *n* aspecto *m* lechoso (appearance) || color *m* lechoso (colour).

milking [-iŋ] *adj* lechero, ra || *milking machine* ordeñadora mecánica.
◆ *n* ordeño *m*.

milk-livered [-ˌlivəd] *adj* FAM que tiene sangre de horchata, cobarde.

milkmaid [-meid] *n* mujer *f* que trabaja en una lechería, lechera *f* (dairymaid) || ordeñadora *f* (who milks cows).

milkman [-mən] *n* lechero *m* (who sells milk) || repartidor *m* de la leche, lechero *m* (who delivers milk).
— OBSERV El plural de *milkman* es *milkmen*.

milk of lime [-əv'laim] *n* lechada *f* de cal.

milk of magnesia [-əvmæg'niːʃə] *n* leche *f* de magnesia.

milk pail [-peil] *n* ordeñadero *m*.

milk round [-raund] *n* reparto *m* diario de la leche.

milk shake [-'ʃeik] *n* batido *m* de leche [AMER leche *f* malteada].

milksop [-sɔp] *n* FAM persona *f* que tiene sangre de horchata (person without spirit) | gallina *m* (coward) | marica *m* (effeminate man).

milk sugar [-'ʃugə*] *n* lactosa *f*.

milk toast [-təust] *n* CULIN torrija *f*.

milk tooth [-tuːθ] *n* diente *m* de leche.
— OBSERV El plural de *milk tooth* es *milk teeth*.

milkweed [-wiːd] *n* BOT algodoncillo *m*.

milk-white [-ˌwait] *adj* lechoso, sa; blanco como la leche.

milky [-i] *adj* lechoso, sa || FIG timorato, ta (timid).

Milky Way ['milki'wei] *pr n* ASTR Vía *f* Láctea.

mill [mil] *n* molino *m* (for grain, for flour) || molinillo *m* (grinder for coffee, for pepper) || pasapuré *m* (for vegetables) || fábrica *f* (factory); *textile mill* fábrica de tejidos || papelera *f*, fábrica *f* de papel (for paper) || serrería *f*, aserradero *m* (for sawing wood) || prensa *f* (for stamping) || prensa *f* de acuñar monedas (for coins) || taller *m* (in general, a small manufacturing works) || fresa *f* (cutter) || laminador *m*, laminadora *f* (rolling mill) || US milésima *f* parte de un dólar || — *spinning mill* fábrica de hilados, hilandería *f* || FAM *to go through the mill* pasarlas negras *or* moradas | *to put s.o. through the mill* someter a alguien a duras pruebas.

mill [mil] *vt* moler (grain, beans, coffee, pepper, etc.) || batir (cream) || hacer puré (vegetables) || abatanar (textiles) || acordonar (to cut grooves on a coin) || TECH pulir (to polish) | laminar (with a rolling mill) | fresar, avellanar (gears) || MIN machacar, triturar (ore) || FAM pegar, moler a golpes (to beat).
◆ *vi* arremolinarse, apiñarse (to crowd around) || FAM pegar, pegarse.

millboard [-bɔːd] *n* cartón *m* piedra.

millcourse [-kɔːs] *n* saetín *m*, caz *m*.

milldam [-dæm] *n* presa *f* de molino.

millenary [mi'lenəri] *adj* milenario, ria.
◆ *n* milenario *m* (a thousandth anniversary) || milenio *m*, milenario *m* (millennium).

millenial [mi'leniəl] *adj* milenario, ria.

millennium [mi'leniəm] *n* milenio *m*, milenario *m* (a thousand years) || FIG edad *f* de oro.
— OBSERV El plural de *millennium* es *millenniums* o *millenia*.

millepede ['milipiːd] *n* ZOOL milpiés *m inv*.

miller ['milə*] *n* molinero, ra || harinero *m* (of power-driven mill) || TECH fresadora *f*, máquina *f* fresadora (machine) | fresador *m* (person) || ZOOL mariposa *f*.

miller's thumb [-z'θʌm] *n* ZOOL coto *m* (fish).

millesimal [mi'lesiməl] *adj* milésimo, ma.

millet ['milit] *n* BOT mijo *m*.

mill hand ['milhænd] *n* obrero, ra.

mill hopper ['mil'hɔpə*] *n* tolva *f*.

milliammeter ['mili'æmitə*] *n* ELECTR miliamperímetro *m*.

milliampere [mili'æmpɛə*] *n* ELECTR miliamperio *m* (one thousand of an ampere).

milliard ['miljɑːd] *n* mil millones *m pl*.

milliary ['miliəri] *adj* miliar.

millibar ['miliba:*] *n* PHYS milibar *m*.

millicurie ['mili,kjuəri] *n* PHYS milicurie *m*.

millier [mil'jei] *n* tonelada *f* métrica.

milligram; milligramme ['miligræm] *n* miligramo *m*.

millilitre; US **milliliter** ['mili,liːtə*] *n* mililitro *m* (one thousandth of a litre).

millimetre; US **millimeter** ['mili,miːtə*] *n* milímetro *m*.

millimetric [,mili'metrik] *adj* milimétrico, ca.

millimicron ['mili,maikrɔn] *n* milimicrón *m*, milimicra *f*.

milliner ['milinə*] *n* sombrerero, ra || *milliner's* tienda *f* de sombreros, sombrerería *f*.

millinery ['milinəri] *n* sombrerería *f* (milliner's work or business) || sombreros *m pl* de señora (woman's hats).

milling ['miliŋ] *n* molienda *f* (act) || fábrica *f* de harina (flour factory) || almacén *m* de harina (warehouse) || enfurtido *m*, batanadura *f* (of cloth) || fresado *m* (of gears) || trituración *f* (of ore) || cordoncillo *m* (of coin) || — *milling cutter* fresa *f* || *milling machine* fresadora *f*.

million ['miljən] *n* millón *m* || — *a million dollar cheque* un cheque de un millón de dólares || *by the million* o *in millions* a millones, por millones || *millions of* millones de || *one million pounds* un millón de libras || US *to feel like a million* estar en plena forma || *two million pesetas* dos millones de pesetas || FIG *you are one in a million* eres un mirlo blanco | *you look like a million* estás guapísima.

millionaire [,miljə'nɛə*] *n* millonario.

millionairess [,miljə'nɛəris] *n* millonaria *f*.

millionfold ['miljən,fəuld] *adj* multiplicado por un millón.
◆ *adv* un millón de veces.

millionth ['miljənθ] *adj/n* millonésimo, ma.

millipede ['milipiːd] *n* ZOOL milpiés *m inv*.

millitherm ['miliθəːm] *n* PHYS militermia *f*.

millivolt ['milivəult] *n* PHYS milivoltio *m*.

milliwatt ['miliwɔt] *n* PHYS milivatio *m*.

millowner ['mil,əunə*] *n* industrial *m*, propietario *m* de una fábrica.

millpond ['milpɔnd] *n* represa *f* de molino.

millrace ['milreis] *n* saetín *m*, caz *m*.

millstone ['milstəun] *n* muela *f*, piedra *f* de molino || FIG *it's a millstone round his neck* lleva una cruz a cuestas.

millstream ['milstriːm] *n* agua *f* que pasa por el saetín.

mill wheel ['milwiːl] *n* rueda *f* de molino.

millwright ['milrait] *n* constructor *m* de molinos.

milometer; mileometer [mai'lɔmitə*] *n* cuentamillas *m inv*.

milord [mi'lɔːd] *n* milord *m*.

milt [milt] *n* lecha *f*, lechaza *f* (of fish).

milt [milt] *vt* ZOOL fecundar [las huevas].

milter ['miltə*] *n* pez *m* macho [en el tiempo de la freza].

mime [maim] *n* mimo *m*, pantomima *f* (entertainment) || mimo *m* (actor) || payaso *m* (clown).

mime [maim] *vt* imitar, remedar.
◆ *vi* actuar de mimo.

mimeograph ['mimiəgrɑːf] *n* multicopista *f* [AMER mimeógrafo *m*] (machine) || copia *f* a multicopista (copy).

mimeograph ['mimiəgrɑːf] *vt* tirar a multicopista, sacar copias de [en la multicopista], reproducir en la multicopista [AMER mimeografiar].

mimeographing [-iŋ] *n* reproducción *f* de documentos [AMER mimeografía *f*].

mimesis [mi'miːsis] *n* mimetismo *m*.

mimetic [mi'metik] *adj* mimético, ca || FIG imitativo, va.

mimic ['mimik] *adj* mímico, ca; imitativo, va || fingido, da; ficticio, cia; simulado, da (pretended) || *mimic art* mímica *f*.
◆ *n* mimo *m* (mime) || imitador, ra (imitator).

mimic ['mimik] *vt* imitar, remedar (to imitate).
— OBSERV Pret y pp ***mimicked***.

mimicry ['mimikri] *n* mímica *f* (art) || imitación *f*, remedo *m* (imitation) || ZOOL & BOT mimetismo *m*.

mimographer [mai'mɔgrəfə*] *n* mimógrafo *m*.

mimosa [mi'məuzə] *n* BOT mimosa *f*.

minacious [mi'neiʃəs] *adj* amenazador, ra; amenazante.

minaret ['minəret] *n* alminar *m*, minarete *m*.

minatory ['minətəri] *adj* amenazador, ra; amenazante || JUR conminatorio, ria.

mince [mins] *n* carne *f* picada (minced meat) || *mince pie* bizcocho *m* con frutas picadas.

mince [mins] *vt* picar (meat) || desmenuzar || FIG *not to mince matters, not to mince one's words* no tener pelos en la lengua, no andar con rodeos.
◆ *vi* andar con pasos medidos (to walk) || hablar remilgadamente (to speak).

mincemeat ['minsmiːt] *n* carne *f* picada (meat) || conserva *f* de fruta picada y especias || FIG *to make mincemeat of* hacer trizas *or* picadillo a (a person), echar abajo (an argument).

mincer ['minsə*] *n* máquina *f* de picar carne.

mincing ['minsiŋ] *adj* melindroso, sa; remilgado, da ‖ *mincing machine* máquina *f* de picar carne.

mind [maind] *n* mente *f* (seat of consciousness); *conscious mind* mente consciente ‖ inteligencia *f* (intelligence); *he has a very quick mind* tiene una inteligencia muy viva ‖ opinión *f*, parecer *m* (opinion); *they were of the same mind* eran de la misma opinión ‖ cabeza *f*; *he got that idea fixed in his mind* se metió esa idea en la cabeza; *he can't get it out of his mind* no se lo puede quitar de la cabeza ‖ cerebro *m*; *he is one of the great minds of the century* es uno de los grandes cerebros del siglo ‖ mentalidad *f* (mentality); *a liberal mind* una mentalidad liberal ‖ juicio *m* (sanity); *in one's right mind* en su sano juicio ‖ intención *f*, mente *f* (intention); *nothing is further from my mind* no hay nada más lejos de mi intención; *it's not in my mind to* no está en mi mente ‖ pensamiento *m*, idea *f* (idea) ‖ espíritu *m*, alma *f* (soul); *peace of mind* tranquilidad de espíritu ‖ memoria *f* (memory) ‖ — *he had no mind to do it* no tenía intención de hacerlo ‖ *mind's eye* imaginación *f* ‖ *my mind is made up* he tomado mi decisión ‖ *not to be clear in one's mind about* no acordarse bien de (not to remember), no ver claramente (to be confused) ‖ *of unsound mind* que no está en su sano juicio ‖ *sound in mind* cuerdo, da ‖ *state of mind* estado *m* de ánimo ‖ *the mind boggles* uno puede imaginarse cualquier cosa ‖ *to bear in mind* recordar (to remember), tener en cuenta, tener presente (to take into account); *bearing that in mind* teniéndolo en cuenta ‖ *to be of a mind* estar de acuerdo ‖ *to be of a mind to do sth.* estar dispuesto a hacer algo ‖ *to be of sound mind* estar en su sano juicio ‖ *to be in two minds* estar indeciso, dudar ‖ *to be out of one's mind* estar fuera de juicio, haber perdido el juicio ‖ *to be to one's mind* gustar a uno (to be to one's liking) ‖ *to be uneasy in one's mind* no estar tranquilo ‖ *to bring one's mind to bear on sth.* examinar algo ‖ *to bring to mind* recordar ‖ *to call to mind* acordarse de, recordar (to remember); *I cannot call it to mind* no me puedo acordar de ello; recordar, traer a la memoria *or* a la mente (to remind); *that calls to mind a story I know* esto me trae a la memoria una historia que conozco ‖ *to change one's mind* cambiar *or* mudar de opinión (way of thinking), cambiar de idea *or* de intención (idea) ‖ *to come to s.o.'s mind, to enter s.o.'s mind* ocurrírsele a uno, venir a la mente de uno ‖ *to cross one's mind* pasarle por la cabeza a uno ‖ *to give one's mind to sth.* prestar atención a algo (to pay attention), dedicarse a algo (to dedicate o.s.) ‖ *to give s.o. a piece* o *a bit of one's mind* decir a alguien cuatro verdades *or* las verdades del barquero ‖ *to go* o *to pass out of mind* olvidarse, caer en el olvido ‖ *to go out of one's mind* perder el juicio ‖ *to have a good mind* o *a mind* o *a great mind to do sth.* tener (muchas) ganas de hacer algo ‖ *to have half a mind to do sth.* tener ciertas ganas de hacer algo ‖ *to have it in mind to do sth.* tener la intención de hacer algo, pensar hacer algo ‖ *to have set one's mind on doing sth.* estar resuelto a hacer algo ‖ *to have sth., s.o. in mind* pensar en algo, en alguien; *have you anyone in mind for the job?* ¿ha pensado en alguien para este trabajo? ‖ *to have sth. on one's mind* tener algo en la conciencia (to have sth. on one's conscience), estar pensando constantemente en algo, estar preocupado por algo (to worry about sth.) ‖ *to keep an open mind* tener amplitud de ideas ‖ *to keep in mind* acordarse de, recordar (to remember), tener en cuenta, tener presente (to take into account) ‖ *to keep one's mind on* prestar atención a ‖ *to know one's mind* saber lo que uno quiere; *he doesn't even know his own mind* ni siquiera sabe lo que quiere ‖ *to lose one's mind* perder la cabeza *or* el juicio ‖ *to make up one's mind* decidirse; *come, make up your mind!* ¡venga, decídase! ‖ *to my mind* a mi parecer, en mi opinión, a mi modo de ver; *that, to my mind, is excellent advice* eso, a mi parecer, es un consejo excelente ‖ *to put s.o. in mind of* recordar a alguien; *she puts me in mind of her mother* me recuerda a su madre ‖ *to put s.o. in the mind for doing sth.* dar a alguien ganas de hacer algo ‖ *to put sth. from* o *out of one's mind* olvidarse de algo ‖ *to read s.o.'s mind* adivinar el pensamiento de alguien ‖ *to set one's mind on* estar resuelto a; *I have my mind set on going shopping today* estoy dispuesto a ir de compras hoy ‖ *to set one's mind on sth.* estar resuelto a conseguir algo ‖ *to slip s.o.'s mind* írsele completamente de la cabeza *or* de la memoria a uno, olvidársele (a uno); *his name has slipped my mind* se me ha olvidado su nombre ‖ *to speak one's mind* decir lo que uno piensa, hablar sin rodeos ‖ *to take a great weight off s.o.'s mind* quitarle a alguien un peso de encima ‖ *to take s.o.'s mind off sth.* distraer a alguien de algo (to distract), quitar a alguien algo de la cabeza (to make s.o. forget sth.) ‖ *to tell s.o. one's mind* decirle a alguien lo que uno piensa ‖ *turn of mind* espíritu, mentalidad ‖ *with an open mind* con amplitud de ideas ‖ *with one mind* por unanimidad, unánimemente.

mind [maind] *vt* cuidar (to take care of); *to mind the baby* cuidar al niño ‖ tener cuidado (to be careful); *mind how you cross the street* ten cuidado al cruzar la calle ‖ vigilar, cuidar (to guard) ‖ procurar; *mind you're not late* procure no llegar tarde ‖ prestar atención a, hacer caso de (to pay attention); *never mind what he says* no hagas caso de lo que dice ‖ hacer caso a (to listen to); *if you had minded me* si me hubieras hecho caso ‖ cumplir (rules) ‖ preocuparse por *or* de (to worry about); *don't mind the weather* no te preocupes por el tiempo; *don't mind what people say* no te preocupes de lo que diga la gente ‖ pensar en, acordarse de (not to forget); *mind you phone him* acuérdese de telefonearle ‖ — *do you mind if I open the window?* ¿le importa que abra la ventana? ‖ *do you mind my smoking?* ¿le importa que fume? ‖ *I don't mind the cold* a mí no me importa *or* no me molesta el frío ‖ *I don't mind trying* lo puedo intentar ‖ *I shouldn't mind a cup of tea* me gustaría tomarme una taza de té ‖ *mind my words!* ¡presta atención a lo que te digo! ‖ *mind out* ¡cuidado! ‖ *mind the paint!* ¡cuidado con la pintura! ‖ *mind what you are doing!* ¡cuidado con lo que haces! ‖ *mind you* en realidad, la verdad es que; *mind you, it was not his fault* en realidad no era culpa suya ‖ *mind you don't fall!* ¡ten cuidado de no caerte! ‖ *mind your language!* ¡cuidado con lo que dices! ‖ FAM *mind your own business* no te metas en lo que no te importa ‖ *mind yourself* ten cuidado con lo que haces ‖ *never mind him* no le hagas caso (take no notice of him), no te preocupes por él (don't worry about him) ‖ *never mind that* no te preocupes por eso ‖ FAM *never you mind!* ¿y a ti qué te importa? ‖ *would you mind shutting the door?* ¿le importaría cerrar la puerta? ‖ *you don't mind my smoking, do you?* no le importa que fume, ¿verdad?
◆ *vi* preocuparse; *don't mind about the gossip* no se preocupe de las habladurías ‖ — FAM *do you mind!* ¡vaya!, ¡por Dios! ‖ *I don't mind* no me importa, me da igual ‖ *if no one minds I will close the window* si no le importa a nadie voy a cerrar la ventana ‖ *if you don't mind* si no le importa, si le parece ‖ *mind and do not be late* procure no llegar tarde ‖ *never mind* no se preocupe (don't worry), no importa, da igual (it doesn't matter) ‖ *would you like a glass of wine? I don't mind* ¿quieres un vaso de vino? Sí, con mucho gusto.

mind-bending [-,bendiŋ] *adj* FAM alucinante.

mind cure [-,kjuə*] *n* psicoterapia *f*.

minded [-id] *adj* dispuesto, ta; *she is not minded to do it* no está dispuesta a hacerlo ‖ — *he is commercially minded* tiene una mentalidad mercantil ‖ *if you are so minded* si le apetece, si quiere ‖ *weak-minded* pobre de espíritu.

minder [maində*] *n* cuidador, ra ‖ FAM gorila *m*, guardaespaldas *m* & *f inv* ‖ — *child minder* niñera *f* ‖ *machine minder* operador, ra.

mindful [-ful] *adj* cuidadoso, sa; atento, ta ‖ — *to be mindful of others* pensar en los demás ‖ *to be mindful of sth.* tener algo presente *or* en cuenta ‖ *to be mindful to do sth.* no olvidar hacer algo.

mindless [-lis] *adj* sin inteligencia, estúpido, da (senseless) ‖ despreocupado, da (careless) ‖ — *to be mindless of danger* ser inconsciente del peligro ‖ *to be mindless of one's health* no preocuparse por su salud ‖ *to be mindless of s.o.'s generosity* no acordarse de la generosidad de alguien.

mind picture [-,piktʃə*] *n* representación *f* mental.

mind reader [-,ri:də*] *n* adivinador *m* de los pensamientos.

mind reading [-,ri:diŋ] *n* lectura *f or* adivinación *f* de los pensamientos.

mine [main] *poss pron* (él) mío, (la) mía, (los) míos, (las) mías, (lo) mío; *this book is mine* este libro es mío, este libro es el mío; *these are mine* éstos son míos, éstos son los míos; *that's mine* eso es mío ‖ mío, mía; *the fault is mine* la culpa es mía ‖ el mío, la mía; *give me mine* dame el mío ‖ *of mine* mío, mía; *a friend of mine* un amigo mío.

— OBSERV Téngase en cuenta que el pronombre posesivo *mine* se puede aplicar tanto a un objeto como a varios: *give me mine* dame el mío, dame los míos.

mine [main] *n* MIN, MIL & MAR mina *f* ‖ FIG mina *f*; *a mine of information* una mina de información ‖ — MIL *antitank, delayed-action, antipersonnel, floating, submarine mine* mina anticarro, de acción retardada, contra personal, flotante, submarina ‖ MIN *coal mine* mina de carbón ‖ MIL *land mine* mina terrestre ‖ MIL *to lay a mine* poner una mina | *to lay mines* fondear minas (in the sea), sembrar minas (in the ground).

mine [main] *vt* minar, socavar (the earth) ‖ cavar (a hole) ‖ extraer (minerals) ‖ explotar (a mine) ‖ MIL & MAR poner *or* sembrar *or* fondear minas en, minar (to lay mines) | volar *or* destruir con minas (to blow up) ‖ FIG minar (to undermine).
◆ *vi* cavar una mina (to dig a mine) ‖ extraer minerales ‖ poner *or* sembrar *or* fondear minas (to lay mines) ‖ trabajar en las minas *or* en la minería.

mine detector [-di'tektə*] *n* MIL & MAR detector *m* de minas.

minefield [-fi:ld] *n* MIL campo *m* de minas, campo *m* minado.

minelayer [-,leiə*] *n* minador *m* (ship).

mine laying [-,leiiŋ] *n* minado *m*.

miner [-ə*] *n* MIN minero *m* ‖ MIL minador *m*, zapador *m*.

mineral ['minərəl] *adj* mineral; *mineral water* agua mineral; *mineral oil* aceite mineral ‖ minero, ra; *mineral deposit* yacimiento minero; *mineral belt* zona minera.
◆ *n* mineral *m*.

mineralize ['minərəlaiz] *vt* mineralizar.

mineralogical [,minərə'lɔdʒikəl] *adj* mineralógico, ca.

mineralogist [,minə'rælədʒist] *n* mineralogista *m* & *f*.

mineralogy [ˌminəˈrælədʒi] *n* mineralogía *f.*

Minerva [miˈnəːvə] *n* MYTH Minerva *f.*

mine shaft [mainʃɑːft] *n* pozo *m* de extracción.

minestrone [ˌminesˈtrəuni] *n* sopa *f* de verduras, sopa *f* milanesa.

minesweeper [ˈmainˌswiːpə*] *n* MAR dragaminas *m inv.*

minesweeping [-ˌswiːpiŋ] *n* MAR dragado *m* de minas, rastreo *m* de minas.

mine thrower [-ˌθrəuə*] *n* MIL lanzaminas *m inv.*

minever [ˈminivə*] *n* armiño *m.*

mingle [ˈmingl] *vt* mezclar.
◆ *vi* mezclarse; *the water mingled with the ink* el agua se mezcló con la tinta ‖ confundirse; *his voice mingled with mine in song* su voz se confundía con la mía en el canto ‖ mezclarse; *he mingles with a bad crowd* se mezcla con mala gente.

mingy [ˈmindʒi] *adj* FAM tacaño, ña; cicatero, ra; mezquino, na (stingy).

miniature [ˈminjətʃə*] *adj* miniatura, en miniatura; *miniature train* tren miniatura ‖ FAM diminuto, ta; pequeñísimo, ma (very small) ‖ — *miniature golf* minigolf *m* ‖ *miniature model* maqueta *f* ‖ *miniature painter* miniaturista *m* & *f.*
◆ *n* miniatura *f* ‖ *in miniature* en miniatura.

miniaturist [ˈminjətjuərist] *n* miniaturista *m* & *f.*

miniaturization [ˌminjətjəraiˈzeiʃən] *n* miniaturización *f.*

miniaturize [ˈminjətjuəraiz] *vt* miniaturizar.

minibus [ˈminibʌs] *n* microbús *m.*

minicab [ˈminikæb] *n* microtaxi *m.*

minicomputer [ˌminikəmˈpjuːtə*] *n* miniordenador *m.*

minim [ˈminim] *n* CHEM gota *f* (drop) ‖ MUS mínima *f*, blanca *f* ‖ REL mínimo *m* ‖ palo *m*, trazo *m* (in writing) ‖ pizca *f* (small portion).

minimal [ˈminiml] *adj* mínimo, ma.

minimize [ˈminimaiz] *vt* minimizar, reducir al mínimo, empequeñecer (to reduce to a minimum) ‖ FIG menospreciar, minimizar (to underestimate).

minimum [ˈminiməm] *adj* mínimo, ma; *the minimum temperature* la temperatura mínima.
◆ *n* mínimo *m*, mínimum *m*; *to reduce to a minimum* reducir al mínimo ‖ *keep expenses to a minimum* gaste lo menos posible *or* el mínimo.
— OBSERV El plural de *minimum* es *minimums* o *minima.*

minimum wage [-ˈweidʒ] *n* salario *m* mínimo (legally fixed wage) ‖ mínimo *m* vital (living wage).

mining [ˈmainiŋ] *n* minería *f* (work) ‖ MIL minado *m* (mine laying).
◆ *adj* minero, ra; *mining zone* zona minera ‖ MIL minador, ra ‖ de minas; *mining ingeneer* ingeniero de minas.

minion [ˈminjən] *n* favorito, ta; valido *m* (of the king) ‖ favorito, ta; predilecto, ta (favourite) ‖ secuaz *m* (servile follower) ‖ FAM enchufado, da; paniaguado, da (of the government) ‖ miñona *f* (letter in printing) ‖ FAM *minion of the law* poli *m.*

miniskirt [ˈminiskəːt] *n* minifalda *f.*

minister [ˈministə*] *n* ministro *m*; *Minister of Finance* ministro de Hacienda; *Minister of Labour* ministro de Trabajo; *minister plenipotentiary* ministro plenipotenciario; *minister of religion* ministro de la Iglesia; *minister without portfolio* ministro sin cartera; *Prime Minister* primer ministro; *Minister of Education* ministro de Educación; *Minister of Health* ministro de Sanidad ‖ REL pastor *m* (protestant clergyman).

minister [ˈministə*] *vi* *to minister to* atender a; *to minister to the needs of the poor* atender a las necesidades de los pobres; ayudar a, contribuir a (to help), servir en (a parish).
◆ *vt* administrar (a sacrament) ‖ suministrar (to provide).

ministerial [ˌminisˈtiəriəl] *adj* ministerial (of ministry) ‖ gubernamental (of government) ‖ REL pastoral ‖ *to be ministerial to* servir para, contribuir a.

ministration [ˌminisˈtreiʃən] *n* ayuda *f*, servicio *m* (help) ‖ REL ministerio *m.*

ministry [ˈministri] *n* ministerio *m* ‖ REL sacerdocio *m* | clero *m* (clergy) ‖ — *Ministry of Education* Ministerio de Educación ‖ *Ministry of Finance* Ministerio de Hacienda ‖ *Ministry of Foreign Affairs* Ministerio de Asuntos Exteriores [AMER Ministerio de Relaciones Exteriores] ‖ *Ministry of Housing* Ministerio de la Vivienda ‖ *Ministry of Labour* Ministerio de Trabajo ‖ *Ministry of Public Works* Ministerio de Obras Públicas ‖ *Ministry of the Interior* Ministerio del Interior.

minium [ˈminiəm] *n* CHEM minio *m.*

miniver [ˈminivə*] *n* armiño *m* (ermine).

mink [miŋk] *n* visón *m* (animal, fur).

minnesinger [ˈminiˌsiŋə*] *n* HIST trovador *m* alemán, minnesinger *m.*

Minnesota [ˌminiˈsəutə] *pr n* GEOGR Minnesota.

minnow [ˈminəu] *n* pececillo *m.*

minor [ˈmainə*] *adj* menor, más pequeño, ña (smaller, junior) ‖ menor de edad (younger than legal age) ‖ GEOGR, PHIL & REL menor; *minor orders* órdenes menores ‖ secundario, ria (secondary) ‖ menudo, da (small); *minor expenses* gastos menudos ‖ sin importancia, de poca importancia, nimio, mia; *a minor detail* un detalle sin importancia ‖ poco, ca; *of minor interest* de poco interés ‖ MUS menor; *E minor* mi menor; *minor key* tono menor ‖ minoritario, ria (party).
◆ *n* menor *m* & *f* de edad ‖ MUS tono *m* menor (key) ‖ PHIL menor *f* ‖ REL hermano *m* menor ‖ US asignatura *f* secundaria (academic subject).

minor [ˈmainə*] *vi* US estudiar como asignatura secundaria; *to minor in Basque* estudiar el vasco como asignatura secundaria.

Minorca [miˈnɔːkə] *pr n* GEOGR Menorca.

Minorcan [-n] *adj/n* menorquín, ina.

Minorite [ˈmainərait] *n* REL fraile *m* franciscano, menor *m.*

minority [maiˈnɔriti] *n* minoría *f* (less than half) ‖ minoría *f*, menor edad *f* (of age) ‖ minoría *f* (small group); *England is Protestant but with a Catholic minority* Inglaterra es protestante con una minoría católica ‖ — *a minority government* un gobierno minoritario ‖ *to be in a* o *the minority* estar en minoría, ser minoría.

Minotaur [ˈmainətɔː*] *n* MYTH Minotauro *m.*

minster [ˈminstə*] *n* REL catedral *f* (cathedral) | iglesia *f* de un monasterio (monastery church).

minstrel [ˈminstrəl] *n* trovador *m*, juglar *m* ‖ FIG poeta *m* | músico *m* ‖ US artista *m* que parodia a los negros cantando o contando chistes.

minstrelsy [-si] *n* canto *m* de trovador *or* de juglar (song) ‖ arte *m* del trovador *or* del juglar, juglaría *f* (art) ‖ grupo *m* de trovadores *or* juglares (group) ‖ mester *m* de juglaría (poetry).

mint [mint] *adj* nuevo, va (not marred) ‖ de menta; *mint sauce* salsa de menta ‖ *in mint condition* como nuevo.
◆ *n* BOT menta *f*, hierbabuena *f* ‖ menta *f* (peppermint) ‖ pastilla *f or* caramelo *m* de menta (sweet) ‖ casa *f* de la moneda, ceca *f* (ant) (where coins are made) ‖ FIG mina *f*; *a mint of ideas* una mina de ideas ‖ FAM *to spend a mint* gastar un dineral *or* una fortuna.

mint [mint] *vt* acuñar; *to mint money* acuñar dinero ‖ FIG forjar, idear, inventar (to make up, to fabricate) | acuñar (a word).

mintage [ˈmintidʒ] *n* acuñación *f* (act of minting) ‖ moneda *f* acuñada (minted money) ‖ cuño *m*, sello *m* (stamp on a coin) ‖ FIG invención *f*, creación *f* | acuñación *f* (of a word).

minter [ˈmintə*] *n* monedero *m*, acuñador *m.*

minuend [ˈminjuend] *n* MATH minuendo *m.*

minuet [minjuˈet] *n* MUS minué *m.*

minus [ˈmainəs] *adj* negativo, va; *a minus quantity* una cantidad negativa; *a minus number* un número negativo ‖ de sustracción, menos; *minus sign* signo menos *or* de sustracción ‖ — FIG & FAM *a minus quantity* una cantidad despreciable | *he is a minus quantity* es un cero a la izquierda ‖ *minus difference* diferencia *f* en menos.
◆ *n* cantidad *f* negativa (negative quantity) ‖ menos *m*, signo *m* menos, signo *m* de sustracción *or* de resta (mathematical sign).
◆ *prep* menos; *seven minus five* siete menos cinco ‖ FAM sin; *he came back minus his hat* volvió sin sombrero ‖ *minus zero temperature* temperatura *f* bajo cero.

minuscule [ˈminəskjuːl] *adj* minúsculo, la.
◆ *n* minúscula *f* (letter).

minute [maiˈnjuːt] *adj* menudo, da; diminuto, ta; muy pequeño, ña (small) ‖ minucioso, sa; detallado, da (precise); *he gave us a minute account of what had happened* nos hizo una relación detallada de lo que había ocurrido ‖ insignificante, ínfimo, ma; nimio, mia (of little importance).

minute [ˈminit] *n* minuto *m* (time, section of a degree) ‖ FIG minuto *m*, momento *m*, instante *m* (a moment); *he will come in a minute* vendrá dentro de un momento; *wait a minute* espera un momento ‖ nota *f*, minuta *f* (note) ‖ — *at the last minute* a última hora ‖ *come at 9 o'clock to the minute* ven a las 9 en punto | *I'll do it in a minute* lo haré en un minuto ‖ *I was expecting him any minute* le esperaba de un momento a otro ‖ *just a minute!* ¡un momento! ‖ *the minute (that)* en el momento en que ‖ *this very minute* al momento, ahora mismo ‖ *up to the minute news* noticias *f pl* de última hora ‖ *up to the minute style* último grito, última moda.
◆ *pl* actas *f*, acta *f sing* (of a meeting); *to keep* o *to draw up the minutes* preparar *or* redactar las actas; *to place on record in the minutes* hacer constar en las actas.

minute [ˈminit] *vt* anotar, apuntar, tomar nota de (to take note) ‖ minutar (contracts) ‖ levantar acta de (of a meeting) ‖ cronometrar (a race).

minute book [-buk] *n* libro *m* de actas ‖ JUR minutario *m.*

minute gun [-gʌn] *n* cañón *m* de salvas.

minute hand [-hænd] *n* minutero *m.*

minutely [-li] *adj/adv* a cada minuto.

minutely [maiˈnjutli] *adv* detalladamente, minuciosamente.

minuteman [ˈminitmən] *n* US miliciano *m* [durante la Guerra de la Independencia].
— OBSERV El plural de esta palabra es *minutemen.*

minuteness [maiˈnjutnis] *n* minuciosidad *f* ‖ pequeñez *f* (smallness).

minutiae [maiˈnjuːʃiiː] *pl n* pequeños detalles *m*, minucias *f.*

minx [minks] *n* FAM fresca *f* || FAM *a sly minx* una lagarta.

Miocene ['maiəusi:n] *adj* GEOL mioceno.
◆ *n* GEOL mioceno *m*.

miracle ['mirəkl] *n* milagro *m*; *Jesus's first miracle was the changing of water into wine* el primer milagro de Jesús fue la conversión del agua en vino || FIG milagro *m*, prodigio *m* || — *by a miracle* de milagro, por milagro || *miracle play* milagro *m*, auto *m* sacramental.

miraculous [mi'rækjuləs] *adj* milagroso, sa (supernatural) || FIG milagroso, sa; prodigioso, sa; maravilloso, sa.

mirador [,mirə'dɔ] *n* mirador *m*.

mirage ['mirɑ:ʒ] *n* espejismo *m* (natural phenomenon) || FIG espejismo *m* (illusion).

mire ['maiə*] *n* fango *m*, lodo *m*, cieno *m* (mud) || lodazal *m*, ciénaga *f* (muddy place).

mire [maiə*] *vt* enlodazar, encenagar (to cover with mud) || atascar, empantanar (to bog down) || manchar de barro, salpicar de barro (to soil).
◆ *vi* atascarse, empantanarse (to stick in mud).

mirk [mə:k] *n* ⟶ **murk.**

mirkiness [-inis] *n* ⟶ **murk.**

mirky [-i] *adj* oscuro, ra; lóbrego, ga; tenebroso, sa.

mirror ['mirə*] *n* espejo *m* || FIG espejo *m*, reflejo *m* (representation); *his novel is a mirror of today's society* su novela es un espejo de la sociedad de hoy | modelo *m*, ejemplo *m* (model) || retrovisor *m* (on a car).

mirror ['mirə*] *vt* reflejar || *life is mirrored in his book* la vida se refleja en su libro.

mirth [mə:θ] *n* alegría *f*, júbilo *m* (glee) || hilaridad *f* (hilarity) || risas *f pl*, carcajadas *f pl* (laughter).

mirthful [-ful] *adj* alegre, risueño, ña (merry).

mirthless [-lis] *adj* triste, sin alegría.

miry ['maiəri] *adj* fangoso, sa; lodoso, sa; cenagoso, sa (muddy) || sucio, cia (dirty).

misadventure ['misəd'ventʃə*] *n* desgracia *f* (misfortune) || accidente *m* (accident) || contratiempo *m* (mishap) || *death by misadventure* muerte accidental.

misadvise ['misəd'vaiz] *vt* aconsejar mal, dar malos consejos a.

misalliance ['misə'laiəns] *n* casamiento *m* desigual, mal casamiento *m* || FIG unión *f* or asociación *f* desacertada.

misanthrope ['mizənθrəup] *n* misántropo *m*.

misanthropic [,mizən'θrɔpik] *adj* misantrópico, ca.

misanthropist [mi'zænθrəpist] *n* misántropo *m*.

misanthropy [mi'zænθrəpi] *n* misantropía *f*.

misapplication ['mis,æpli'keiʃən] *n* uso *m* indebido (ill use) || mala aplicación *f* || malversación *f* (of funds).

misapply ['misə'plai] *vt* usar indebidamente || aplicar mal || malgastar; *to misapply one's efforts* malgastar los esfuerzos || malversar (funds).

misapprehend ['mis,æpri'hend] *vt* comprender mal || interpretar mal.

misapprehension ['mis,æpri'henʃən] *n* malentendido *m*, equivocación *f* || mala interpretación *f*; *misapprehension of the facts* mala interpretación de los hechos || — *to be under a misapprehension* estar equivocado || *to be under the misapprehension that* creer erróneamente que, creer equivocadamente que.

misappropriate ['misə'prəuprieit] *n* malversar, desfalcar (to embezzle) || hacer mal uso de (to appropriate to a bad use).

misappropriation ['misə,prəupri'eiʃən] *n* malversación *f*, desfalco *m* (embezzlement) || mal uso *m* (bad use).

misbecame ['misbi'keim] *pret* ⟶ **misbecome.**

misbecome* ['misbi'kʌm] *vt* no ir, ir mal, no convenir; *it misbecomes him to criticize* no le va el criticar.
— OBSERV Pret ***misbecame***; pp ***misbecome***.

misbecoming [-iŋ] *adj* impropio, pia (*to* de).

misbegotten ['misbi,gɔtn] *adj* ilegítimo, ma; bastardo, da (child) || extravagante, descabellado, da; estrafalario, ria; *another of his misbegotten plans* otro de sus proyectos descabellados.

misbehave ['misbi'heiv] *vi* portarse mal, comportarse mal (to behave badly) || ser malo (a child).

misbehaviour; US **misbehavior** ['misbi'heivjə*] *n* mala conducta *f*, mal comportamiento *m*.

misbelief ['misbi'li:f] *n* REL herejía *f*, falsa creencia *f*, creencia *f* errónea (wrong belief) || opinión *f* errónea, error *m* (mistaken opinion).

misbeliever ['misbi'li:və*] *n* REL hereje *m* & *f*, incrédulo, la.

miscalculate ['mis'kælkjuleit] *vt/vi* calcular mal.

miscalculation ['mis,kælkju'leiʃən] *n* cálculo *m* erróneo, error *m* de cálculo || FIG desacierto *m*, equivocación *f*, error *m*.

miscall ['mis'kɔ:l] *vt* llamar equivocadamente, llamar erróneamente; *he was miscalled «the champion»* era llamado erróneamente «el campeón» || FAM insultar.

miscarriage [mis'kæridʒ] *n* MED aborto *m* || error *m*; *a miscarriage of justice* un error judicial || extravío *m*, pérdida *f* (of a letter) || FIG fracaso *m* (failure).

miscarry [mis'kæri] *vi* MED abortar || extraviarse, perderse (a letter) || FIG fracasar (to fail).

miscast* [mis'kɑ:st] *vt* dar un papel poco apropiado a (an actor) || distribuir mal los papeles en [una obra de teatro] (a play) || sumar mal (to add up badly).
— OBSERV Pret y pp ***miscast***.

miscegenation [,misidʒi'neiʃən] *n* cruce *m* de razas, mestizaje *m*.

miscellanea [,misi'leinjə*] *pl n* miscelánea *f sing* (literary miscellany).

miscellaneous [,misi'leinjəs] *adj* variado, da; vario, ria; diverso, sa (news) || ecléctico, ca (writer).

miscellany [mi'seləni] *n* miscelánea *f*, mezcla *f*.

mischance [mis'tʃɑ:ns] *n* mala suerte *f*, infortunio *m*, desgracia *f* || *by some mischance* por desgracia.

mischief ['mistʃif] *n* travesura *f*, diablura *f* (of a child) || daño *m*, perjuicio *m* (harm); *to do s.o. a mischief* causar un daño a alguien || maldad *f*, mala intención *f* (evil); *there is no mischief in him* no tiene ninguna maldad || discordia *f* (discord); *to make mischief between* sembrar la discordia entre || pícaro, ra; diablillo, lla (mischievous child) || — *the mischief of it is that* lo malo de esto es que || *to be up to (some) mischief* estar pensando en hacer de las suyas || *to get into mischief* hacer tonterías | *to keep s.o. out of mischief* impedir a alguien que haga tonterías or disparates.

mischief-maker [-,meikə*] *n* lioso, sa; persona *f* enredadora.

mischievous ['mistʃivəs] *adj* travieso, sa (child) || malo, la (wicked) || lioso, sa; enredador, ra (troublemaking) || nocivo, va; dañino, na (harmful) || perjudicial (damaging) || malicioso, sa (look).

mischievousness [-nis] *n* picardía *f* (of a child) || travesura *f* (prank) || maldad *f* (wickedness).

miscible ['misibl] *adj* miscible, mezclable.

miscolour; US **miscolor** [mis'kʌlə*] *vt* deformar, desnaturalizar, representar bajo un aspecto engañoso; *to miscolour the facts* deformar los hechos.

misconceive ['miskən'si:v] *vi* tener un concepto erróneo (*of* de).
◆ *vt* comprender *or* interpretar mal.

misconception ['miskən'sepʃən] *n* concepto *m* erróneo, concepto *m* falso, idea *f* falsa || equivocación *f*, malentendido *m* (misunderstanding).

misconduct [mis'kɔndʌkt] *n* mala conducta *f* (misbehaviour) || mala administración *f* (mismanagement) || JUR adulterio *m* (adultery).

misconduct ['miskən'dʌkt] *vt* administrar *or* dirigir mal (to mismanage) || *to misconduct o.s.* portarse mal.

misconstruction ['miskəns'trʌktʃən] *n* mala interpretación *f*.

misconstrue ['miskən'stru:] *vt* interpretar mal.

miscount [mis'kaunt] *n* error *m* de cálculo, cálculo *m* erróneo.

miscount ['mis'kaunt] *vi* calcular mal, equivocarse en la cuenta.
◆ *vt* calcular mal.

miscreant ['miskriənt] *adj* bellaco, ca (villainous) || infiel, herético, ca.
◆ *n* bellaco, ca (villain) || infiel *m* & *f*, hereje *m* & *f*.

miscue ['mis'kju:] *n* pifia *f* (in billiards).

miscue ['mis'kju:] *vi* pifiar (in billiards) || THEATR equivocarse.

misdeal ['mis'di:l] *n* error *m* en el reparto de las cartas.

misdeal* ['mis'di:l] *vt/vi* repartir mal.
— OBSERV Pret y pp ***misdealt***.

misdealt ['mis'delt] *pret/pp* ⟶ **misdeal.**

misdeed ['mis'di:d] *n* delito *m* (crime) || fechoría *f* (villainy).

misdemeanant [-ənt] *n* JUR delincuente *m* & *f*.

misdemeanour; US **misdemeanor** [,misdi'mi:nə*] *n* JUR infracción *f*, delito *m* menor || FIG fechoría *f* (misdeed) | mala conducta *f* (bad behaviour).

misdirect ['misdi'rekt] *vt* dirigir mal (to give wrong directions) || poner mal las señas en (a letter) || JUR instruir mal [al jurado] (a jury) || dirigir mal (to aim badly).

misdirection ['misdi'rekʃən] *n* dirección *f* errónea, mala dirección *f* (in a letter) || información *f* errónea (wrong information) || JUR malas instrucciones *f pl* [al jurado] (of the jury).

misdoing ['mis'du:iŋ] *n* delito *m* (crime) || fechoría *f*, mala acción *f* (villainy) || falta *f* (falta).

misdoubt ['mis'daut] *vt* dudar (to have doubt about) || sospechar (to suspect).

miser ['maizə*] *n* avaro, ra.

miserable ['mizərəbl] *adj* desgraciado, da; desdichado, da (unfortunate); *I have never seen a man so miserable* nunca vi a un hombre tan desgraciado || triste (sad) || fatal, mal (sick); *I feel miserable* me encuentro fatal || desagradable (disagreeable) || miserable (wretched) || de pena (distressing) || deplorable, lamentable (deplorable) || vil, despreciable (contemptible) || sin valor (valueless) || indecente, miserable; *a miserable salary* un sueldo miserable || malo, la; *miserable weather* mal tiempo || miserable; *after four years he had saved a miserable twenty pounds* al cabo de cuatro años sólo había ahorrado veinte miserables libras.

miserere [mizəˈriəri] *n* REL & MUS miserere *m* (psalm).

misericord; *US* **misericorde** [miˈzerikɔ:d] *n* relajación *f* de las reglas monásticas || refectorio *m* [donde las reglas del ayuno son menos severas] (refectory) || puñal *m*, misericordia *f* (dagger) || misericordia *f*, coma *f* (seat).

— OBSERV Esta palabra no tiene nunca el sentido de *compasión* o *perdón* que se traducen por *mercy*.

miserliness [ˈmaizəlinis] *n* avaricia *f*, mezquindad *f*, tacañería *f*.

miserly [ˈmaizəli] *adj* mezquino, na; avaro, ra; tacaño, ña; avariento, ta.

misery [ˈmizəri] *n* miseria *f*, pobreza *f* (poverty) || desgracia *f*, infelicidad *f* (unhappiness) || sufrimiento *m*, dolor *m* (pain) | sufrimiento *m*, aflicción *f* (affliction) || — FAM *she makes my life a misery* me amarga la vida || *to put a horse out of its misery* rematar un caballo.

misestimate [misˈestimeit] *n* cálculo *m* erróneo, estimación *f* errónea.

misestimate [misˈestimeit] *vt* calcular mal, estimar erróneamente.

misfeasance [misˈfi:zəns] *n* JUR abuso *m* de autoridad.

misfire [ˈmisˈfaiə*] *n* fallo *m* de tiro (of a gun) || fallo *m* de encendido (of a motor).

misfire [ˈmisˈfaiə*] *vi* fallar (a gun) || tener fallos, fallar (a car) || FAM no tener éxito, fallar; *the joke misfired* el chiste no tuvo éxito.

misfit [ˈmisfit] *n* inadaptado, da (person) || traje *m* que no cae bien (suit).

misfortune [misˈfɔ:tʃən] *n* desgracia *f*, infortunio *m*, desdicha *f* (ill fortune); *he had the misfortune to be blind* tuvo la desgracia de ser ciego; *companion in misfortune* compañero de infortunio || desgracia *f* (mishap).

misgave [ˈmisˈgeiv] *pret* ⟶ **misgive.**

misgive* [ˈmisˈgiv] *vt* hacer dudar (to cause doubt) || hacer sospechar (to cause suspicion) || hacer temer (to cause fear) || *my heart misgives me that* tengo el presentimiento de que.

— OBSERV Pret ***misgave***; pp ***misgiven***.

misgiven [ˈmisˈgivn] *pp* ⟶ **misgive.**

misgiving [-iŋ] *n* duda *f*, recelo *m* (mistrust); *with some misgiving* con cierto recelo | inquietud *f*, aprensión *f*, presentimiento *m*.

misgovern [ˈmisˈgʌvən] *vt* gobernar mal (a country) || administrar mal (a business).

misgovernment [-mənt] *n* mal gobierno *m*, desgobierno *m* (of a country) || mala administración *f* (of a business).

misguidance [ˈmisˈgaidəns] *n* mala dirección *f* || mala orientación *f* || malos consejos *m pl* (bad advice).

misguide [ˈmisˈgaid] *vt* dirigir mal (to direct badly) || orientar mal (to guide badly) || aconsejar mal (to advise badly) || descaminar (to mislead).

misguided [-d] *adj* mal aconsejado, da (badly advised) || descaminado, da (mislead) || poco afortunado, da (attempt, conduct).

mishandle [ˈmisˈhændl] *vt* tratar mal, maltratar | manejar mal (to handle badly) || llevar mal, tratar mal (a matter).

mishap [ˈmishæp] *n* contratiempo *m*, accidente *m*, desgracia *f*.

mishear* [ˈmishiə*] *vt* oír mal.

— OBSERV Pret y pp ***misheard***.

misheard [ˈmisˈhə:d] *pret/pp* ⟶ **mishear.**

mishmash [ˈmiʃmæʃ] *n* mezcla *f*, revoltijo *m*.

misinform [ˈmisinˈfɔ:m] *vt* informar mal.

misinformation [misinfɔ:ˈmeiʃən] *n* información *f* errónea.

misinterpret [ˈmisinˈtə:prit] *vt* interpretar mal.

misinterpretation [ˈmisinˌtə:priˈteiʃən] *n* interpretación *f* errónea, mala interpretación *f*.

misjudge [ˈmisˈdʒʌdʒ] *vt/vi* juzgar mal.

misjudgment; misjudgement [-mənt] *n* juicio *m* equivocado, estimación *f* errónea.

mislaid [misˈleid] *pret/pp* ⟶ **mislay.**

mislay* [misˈlei] *vt* extraviar, perder.

— OBSERV Pret y pp ***mislaid***.

mislead* [misˈli:d] *vt* engañar (to deceive) || equivocar, descaminar (to lead into error) || descarriar, corromper (to corrupt).

— OBSERV Pret y pp ***misled***.

misleading [-iŋ] *adj* engañoso, sa.

misled [misˈled] *pret/pp* ⟶ **mislead.**

mismanage [ˈmisˈmænidʒ] *vt* dirigir mal, administrar mal.

mismanagement [-mənt] *n* mala dirección *f*, mala administración *f*.

mismatch [ˈmisˈmætʃ] *vt* emparejar mal.

misname [ˈmisˈneim] *vt* dar un nombre equivocado a, llamar equivocadamente.

misnomer [ˈmisˈnəumə*] *n* nombre *m* equivocado || nombre *m* inapropiado || JUR error *m* en el nombre.

misogamy [miˈsɔgəmi] *n* misogamia *f*.

misogynist [maiˈsɔdʒinist] *n* misógino, na.

misogynous [maiˈsɔdʒinəs] *adj* misógino, na.

misogyny [maiˈsɔdʒini] *n* misoginia *f*.

misplace [ˈmisˈpleis] *vt* colocar mal *or* fuera de su lugar || extraviar, perder (to lose) || colocar mal (an accent) || FIG dar indebidamente *or* inmerecidamente (one's affection, one's confidence).

misplaced [-t] *adj* mal colocado, da || extraviado, da; perdido, da (lost) || fuera de lugar, impropio, pia (word) || inmerecido, da (affection).

misplacement [-mənt] *n* mala colocación *f*, colocación *f* fuera de lugar || extravío *m* (loss).

misprint [ˈmisˈprint] *n* errata *f*, error *m* de imprenta, falta *f* tipográfica.

misprint [ˈmisˈprint] *vt* imprimir mal.

misprision [misˈpriʒən] *n* JUR ocultación *f*, encubrimiento *m* (of a crime).

mispronounce [ˈmisprəˈnauns] *vt* pronunciar mal.

mispronunciation [ˈmisprəˌnʌnsiˈeiʃən] *n* mala pronunciación *f*.

misquotation [ˈmiskwəuˈteiʃən] *n* cita *f* errónea.

misquote [ˈmisˈkwəut] *vt* citar incorrectamente.

misread* [ˈmisˈri:d] *vt* leer mal (to read badly) || interpretar mal (to interpret badly).

— OBSERV Pret y pp ***misread*** [ˈmisˈred].

misremember [ˈmisriˈmembə*] *vt* acordarse mal de, recordar mal.

misrepresent [ˈmisˌrepriˈzent] *vt* representar mal || desnaturalizar, desfigurar, desvirtuar (to distort).

misrepresentation [ˈmisˌreprizenˈteiʃən] *n* representación *f* falsa || desnaturalización *f*, desfiguración *f* (of a fact).

misrule [ˈmisˈru:l] *n* mala administración *f*, mal gobierno *m* (misgovernment) || desorden *m* (disorder).

misrule [ˈmisˈru:l] *vt* gobernar mal.

miss [mis] *n* señorita *f*; *Miss Jones* la señorita Jones; *good morning, Miss* buenos días, señorita || *Miss World* Miss Mundo.

miss [mis] *n* tiro *m* errado, fallo *m* (shot) || fracaso *m*, fallo *m* (failure) || — FIG *a miss is as good as a mile* por un clavo se pierde una herradura || *to give a miss* prescindir de; *I can give tobacco a miss* puedo prescindir del tabaco; no asistir a (a conference, etc.), no visitar (a monument) || *to score a near miss* acercarse al blanco.

miss [mis] *vt* no dar en; *to miss the target* no dar en el blanco || errar, fallar; *he missed his shot* erró el tiro || perder; *to miss the train* perder el tren || perder, dejar pasar, desperdiciar; *to miss an opportunity* dejar pasar una oportunidad || notar la ausencia de (to note the absence of); *we missed him yesterday* notamos su ausencia ayer || echar de menos; *I miss you very much* te echo mucho de menos || no conseguir, no alcanzar, fallar (one's aim) || faltar a; *to miss class, an appointment* faltar a clase, a una cita || no asistir a, no acudir a (a meeting) || dejar de encontrar; *you can't miss my house* no puede dejar de encontrar mi casa || perderse en, equivocarse de (one's way) || perderse; *I mustn't miss this play* no debo perderme esta comedia || no encontrar; *I missed her at the hotel* no la encontré en el hotel || saltarse; *to miss a page* saltarse una página || omitir (to omit) || perder; *I missed my lighter in the underground* perdí mi encendedor en el metro || no entender, no comprender; *to miss a joke* no entender un chiste || no acertar; *to miss the solution* no acertar la solución || — *I missed what you said* se me escapó lo que dijiste || *it just missed me* por poco me dio || *the bullet just missed me* la bala me pasó rozando || *to miss one's footing* perder pie || *to miss out* perder (to let go by), saltar, omitir (to omit) || FAM *to miss the boat* perder el tren, perder la oportunidad || *to miss the mark* no dar en el blanco || *to miss the point* no comprender || *you are much missed* se te echa mucho de menos || *you did not miss much* no te perdiste gran cosa || *you just missed going to prison* por poco te metían en la cárcel.

◆ *vi* errar *or* fallar el tiro || no dar en el blanco || fallar, tener fallos (a motor) || faltar; *you have never missed* nunca has faltado; *is anything missing?* ¿falta algo? || fallar; *it can't miss!* ¡es imposible que falle!

missal [ˈmisəl] *n* REL misal *m*.

missel thrush [-θrʌʃ] *n* ZOOL cagaaceite *m*, tordo *m* mayor (bird).

misshapen [ˈmisˈʃeipən] *adj* deformado, da (hat) || deforme, contrahecho, cha (person).

missile [ˈmisail] *n* proyectil *m*, cohete *m*, misil *m*; *guided missile* proyectil teledirigido || arma *f* arrojadiza.

◆ *adj* arrojadizo, za (weapon).

missing [ˈmisiŋ] *adj* perdido, da (lost) || ausente (absent); *four pupils are missing* cuatro alumnos están ausentes || desaparecido, da (disappeared) || que falta (lacking) || — *number of dead and missing* número de muertos y desaparecidos || *to be missing* faltar; *how many are missing?* ¿cuántos faltan?; no haber vuelto, haber desaparecido; *four planes are missing* cuatro aviones no han vuelto.

mission [ˈmiʃən] *n* misión *f*; *to carry out a mission* cumplir una misión || REL misión *f* || *US* embajada *f* (embassy) || — *goodwill mission* misión de buena voluntad || *trade mission* misión comercial.

missionary [ˈmiʃnəri] *adj* misional, misionero, ra.

◆ *n* REL misionero, ra.

missis ['misiz]; **missus** ['misəs] *n* FAM señora *f* (used by servants) | parienta *f* (the wife).

Mississippi [ˌmisi'sipi] *pr n* GEOGR Misisipí *m*, Mississippi *m*.

missive ['misiv] *n* misiva *f* (letter).

Missouri [mi'zuəri] *pr n* GEOGR Misuri *m*, Missouri *m*.

misspell* ['mis'spel] *vt* escribir mal, ortografiar mal.
— OBSERV Pret y pp ***misspelt***.

misspelling [-iŋ] *n* falta *f* de ortografía.

misspelt ['mis'spelt] *pret/pp* ⟶ **misspell.**

misspend* ['mis'spend] *vt* gastar mal, malgastar (money) || desperdiciar, perder (one's time).
— OBSERV Pret y pp ***misspent***.

misstate ['mis'steit] *vt* exponer mal (to state incorrectly) || desnaturalizar (to distort).

misstatement [-mənt] *n* afirmación *f* or declaración *f* errónea (incorrect statement) || error *m*.

misstep ['mis'step] *n* paso *m* en falso, tropezón *m*, traspié *m* || FIG desliz *m*.

missus ['misəs] *n* FAM ⟶ **missis.**

missy ['misi] *n* US señorita *f*.

mist [mist] *n* niebla *f*, neblina *f* (fog) || bruma *f* (at sea) || calina *f* (haze) || vaho *m* (of glasses) || FIG velo *m*; *a mist of tears* un velo de lágrimas || — *Scotch mist* llovizna *f* || FIG *the mist of time* la noche de los tiempos.

mist [mist] *vt* cubrir de niebla || empañar (a mirror, the eyes).
◆ *vi* cubrirse de niebla || empañarse || *to mist up* o *over* cubrirse de niebla (landscape), empañarse (mirror), llenarse de lágrimas (eyes).

mistakable [mis'teikəbl] *adj* que puede confundirse; *the two boys are easily mistakable* los dos chicos se pueden confundir fácilmente || ambiguo, gua; equívoco, ca (ambiguous).

mistake [mis'teik] *n* equivocación *f*, error *m*; *he made the mistake of* cometió el error de; *I acknowledged my mistake* confesé mi equivocación || GRAMM falta *f*; *spelling mistake* falta de ortografía || — *and no mistake!* ¡sin duda alguna!, ¡ciertamente!, ¡ya lo creo! || *by mistake* sin querer (unintentionally), por equivocación || *let there be no mistake* o *make no mistake about it* que quede bien claro || *sorry, my mistake* lo siento, ha sido culpa mía || *to make a mistake* equivocarse, cometer un error.

mistake* [mis'teik] *vt* entender or interpretar mal (to misunderstand); *you mistook my words* interpretaste mal mis palabras || equivocarse en, confundirse respecto a (to be wrong) || equivocarse de (one's way) || — *there is no mistaking his voice* su voz es inconfundible || *to mistake s.o. for* tomar a alguien por, confundir a alguien con.
◆ *vi* equivocarse.
— OBSERV Pret ***mistook***; pp ***mistaken***.

mistaken [-ən] *pp* ⟶ **mistake.**
◆ *adj* equivocado, da (wrong); *you are mistaken* estás equivocado || erróneo, a; inexacto, ta (inexact); *a mistaken declaration* una declaración inexacta || mal comprendido, da; mal interpretado, da (word) || — *if I am not mistaken* si no me equivoco || *mistaken ideas* ideas falsas || *mistaken identity* identificación errónea || *to be mistaken about* o *as to* estar equivocado or equivocarse acerca de or en cuanto a || *you are mistaken in thinking that* te engañas si piensas que, estás equivocado al pensar que.

mister ['mistə*] *n* señor *m*; *good morning, Mister Jones* buenos días, señor Jones || FAM señor *m*; *give us a shilling, Mister* me da un chelín, señor.

mistime ['mis'taim] *vt* hacer or decir a destiempo || calcular mal el momento de; *they mistimed the strike* calcularon mal el momento de la huelga || — *to mistime an answer* contestar a destiempo || *to mistime an entry* entrar a destiempo.

mistiness ['mistinis] *n* estado *m* brumoso, nebulosidad *f*.

mistle thrush ['misəlθrʌʃ] *n* US ZOOL cagaaceite *m*, tordo *m* mayor (bird).

mistletoe ['misltəu] *n* BOT muérdago *m* (plant).

mistook [mis'tuk] *pret* ⟶ **mistake.**

mistral ['mistrəl] *n* mistral *m* (wind).

mistranslate ['minstræns'leit] *vt* traducir mal.

mistranslation ['mistræns'leiʃən] *n* mala traducción *f*, traducción *f* errónea.

mistreat ['mis'tri:t] *vt* maltratar, tratar mal.

mistreatment [-mənt] *n* trato *m* malo, malos tratos *m pl*, maltrato *m*.

mistress ['mistris] *n* amante *f*, querida *f* (lover); *she was the king's mistress* era la amante del rey || señora *f*; *the mistress of the house* la señora de la casa || dueña *f*; *the dog's mistress* la dueña del perro || profesora *f*; *the French mistress* la profesora de francés || — *Mistress Jones* la señora Jones || *Mistress Mary* Doña María || *school mistress* maestra *f* de escuela || *she is a mistress in the art of cookery* es una experta en el arte de cocinar || *she was mistress of the situation* era dueña de or dominaba la situación.

mistrial ['mis'traiəl] *n* JUR juicio que se declara nulo [por falta de unanimidad del jurado o por error de procedimiento].

mistrust ['mis'trʌst] *n* recelo *m* (suspicion) || desconfianza *f* (lack of confidence).

mistrust ['mis'trʌst] *vt* recelar de, desconfiar de (to regard with suspicion); *I mistrust him* desconfío de él || dudar de, no tener confianza en (to feel no confidence in); *he mistrusts his own capacities* no tiene confianza en sus propias posibilidades.

mistrustful [-ful] *adj* receloso, sa; desconfiado, da.

misty ['misti] *adj* de niebla; *a misty day* un día de niebla || brumoso, sa (in the sea) || FIG vago, ga; confuso, sa; nebuloso, sa (vague) || empañado, da; *misty glass* cristal empañado; *misty eyes* la mirada empañada.

misunderstand* ['misʌndə'stænd] *vt* comprender or entender mal || interpretar mal || *he misunderstood you* no comprendió lo que le dijo.
— OBSERV Pret y pp ***misunderstood***.

misunderstanding [-iŋ] *n* error *m*, equivocación *f*, equívoco *m*, malentendido *m* (mistake); *there must be some misunderstanding* debe de haber alguna equivocación || desavenencia *f*, desacuerdo *m* (dissension) || concepto *m* erróneo.

misunderstood ['misʌndə'stud] *pret/pp* ⟶ **misunderstand.**
◆ *adj* mal comprendido, da; mal interpretado, da (thing) || incomprendido, da (person).

misusage ['mis'ju:sidʒ] *n* ⟶ **misuse.**

misuse ['mis'ju:s] *n* mal uso *m*, uso *m* incorrecto (of words) || maltrato *m* (ill treatment) || mal empleo *m*, mal manejo *m* (of a machine, etc.) || JUR abuso *m*; *misuse of authority* abuso de autoridad || JUR *fraudulent misuse of funds* malversación de fondos (embezzlement).

misuse ['mis'ju:z] *vt* emplear mal (words, etc.) || maltratar, tratar mal (to mistreat) || manejar or emplear mal (a machine, etc.) || JUR abusar de, hacer mal uso de | malversar (funds).

MIT *abbr of [Massachussets Institute of Technology]* Instituto de Tecnología de Massachussets [United States].

mite [mait] *n* arador *m*, acárido *m* (insect) || REL ardite *m* (coin of very little value) || FIG pizca *f* (small quantity) | chiquillo, lla (child) | óbolo *m* (small contribution) || FIG *it's a mite heavy* es algo pesado.

miter ['maitə*] *n/vt* US ⟶ **mitre.**

miter box [-bɔks] *n* US caja *f* de ingletes.

mitered [-d] *adj* US mitrado, da.

miter joint [-dʒɔint] *n* US inglete *m*.

Mithridates [ˌmiθri'deiti:z] *pr n* HIST Mitrídates *m*.

mitigate ['mitigeit] *vt* mitigar, aliviar (a penalty) || aligerar, aliviar (burden) || temperar, templar, suavizar (climate) || aliviar, hacer llevadero (pain, sorrow) || atenuar (a fault) || calmar, aplacar, moderar (wrath).

mitigating ['mitigeitiŋ] *adj* JUR atenuante (circumstances).

mitigation [ˌmiti'geiʃən] *n* mitigación *f*, alivio *m* (of a penalty) || aligeramiento *m*, alivio *m* (of a burden) || atenuación *f* (of a fault) || alivio *m* (of a pain, of a sorrow) || aplacamiento *m*, moderación *f* (of wrath).

mitigator ['mitigeitə*] *n* mitigador, ra.

mitigatory ['mitigətəri] *adj* mitigador, ra; mitigante.

mitosis [mi'təusis] *n* BIOL mitosis *f*.

mitral ['maitrəl] *adj* mitral || ANAT *mitral valve* válvula *f* mitral.

mitre; US **miter** ['maitə*] *n* REL mitra *f* (headdress) || inglete *m* (in carpentry).

mitre; US **miter** ['maitə*] *vt* unir con ingletes || REL conferir la mitra a.

mitre box [-bɔks] *n* caja *f* de ingletes.

mitred [-d] *adj* mitrado, da; *mitred abbot* abad mitrado.

mitre joint [-dʒɔint] *n* inglete *m*.

mitt [mit] *n* mitón *m* (fingerless glove) || guante *m* (glove) || FAM puño *m* (fist) | mano *f* (hand).

mitten ['mitn] *n* manopla *f* (glove with single division for fingers) || mitón *m* (mitt) || FAM guante *m* (glove) || FIG *to give s.o. the mitten* dar calabazas a uno.

mittimus ['mitimʌs] *n* JUR orden *f* de detención, auto *m* de prisión.

mix [miks] *n* mezcla *f*.

mix [miks] *vt* mezclar (to bring together several ingredients) || amasar (flour, plaster, cement, etc.) || preparar (drinks) || aliñar, aderezar (to prepare a salad) || mover (to turn over a salad) || hacer (a mayonnaise) || FIG combinar, compaginar; *to mix business with pleasure* combinar los negocios con el placer | reunir; *the party mixed old and young people* la fiesta reunió a ancianos y jóvenes || — *I don't want to get mixed up in it* no quiero meterme en eso, no quiero estar comprometido en eso || *to get all mixed up* hacerse un lío || FAM *to mix it* llegar a las manos || *to mix up* mezclar (to give a mix), confundir; *he mixed me up with Peter* me confundió con Pedro; meter, complicar, implicar, comprometer (in an affair).
◆ *vi* mezclarse (to become mixed) || asociarse (to associate) || mezclarse, frecuentar, alternar; *he mixes with a bad crowd* se mezcla con mala gente || *he doesn't mix well* no se lleva bien con la gente.

mixed [mikst] *adj* mezclado, da (blended) || mixto, ta; *mixed school* escuela mixta || variado, da (varied) || BOT mezclado, da || surtido, da; variado, da (sweets) || AGR mixto, ta; *mixed fertilizers* abonos mixtos || — FIG *mixed blessing* bendición *f* a medias || SP *mixed doubles* mixtos *m*, doble mixto *m sing* || *mixed economy* economía *f* mixta || *mixed farming* sistema *m* de cultivo alternado || *mixed feelings* sentimientos contradictorios || *mixed ice* helado *m* de varios gustos || *mixed marriage* matrimonio *m* mixto || *mixed salad* ensalada mixta.

mixed-ability [-ə'biliti] *adj* para alumnos de distinto nivel (class, teaching system).

mixed-up [-ʌp] *adj* mezclado, da || confuso, sa (confused) || revuelto, ta (in disorder) || FIG confuso, sa.

mixer ['miksə*] *n* mezcladora *f* || hormigonera *f*, mezcladora *f* (of mortar) || CULIN batidora *f* || ELECTR mezclador *m* [de sonidos] (of sound) || CINEM operador *m* de sonido || FAM persona *f* sociable (sociable person) || — *mixer tap* grifo *m* mezclador || FAM *to be a good mixer* tener don de gentes, ser sociable.

mixing ['miksiŋ] *n* mezcla *f* || *mixing bowl* gol *m* grande.

mixture ['mikstʃə*] *n* mezcla *f* || MED mixtura *f* || CHEM mezcla *f* || tela *f* de mezclilla (fabric).

mix-up ['miks'ʌp] *n* FAM lío *m*, enredo *m*, confusión *f* (confusion) | pelea *f* (fight).

mizen; mizzen ['mizn] *n* MAR artimón *m* mesana *f* (sail) | palo *f* de mesana (mast).

mizen; mizzenmast [-mɑːst] *n* MAR palo *m* de mesana.

mizzen-topgallant mast [-tɔp'gæləntmɑːst] *n* MAR mastelero *m* de perico.

mizzen-topmast; mizzen-topmast [-'tɔpmɑːst] *n* MAR mastelero *m* de sobremesana.

mizzen-topsail [-'tɔpseil] *n* MAR sobremesana *f*.

mizzle ['mizl] *n* llovizna *f*.

mizzle ['mizl] *v impers* lloviznar (to drizzle).
◆ *vi* FAM largarse (to go).

mnemonic [ni'mɔnik] *adj* mnemotécnico, ca; nemotécnico, ca.

mnemonics [-s] *n* mnemotecnia *f*, mnemotécnica *f*, nemotecnia *f*.

Moabite ['məuəbait] *adj/n* moabita.

moan [məun] *n* gemido *m*, quejido *m*, lamento *m* (sound) || queja *f* (complaint) || *to have a moan about sth.* quejarse de algo.

moan [məun] *vi* gemir (to groan) || quejarse, lamentarse (*about* de) (to complain).
◆ *vt* decir gimiendo (to groan) || llorar (a dead person) || deplorar, lamentar (one's fate).

moaning [-iŋ] *adj* que gime (groaning) || quejoso, sa (complaining).
◆ *n* gemido *m* (sound) || queja *f* (complaint).

moat [məut] *n* foso *m* (of a castle).

mob [mɔb] *n* multitud *f*, muchedumbre *f* (crowd) || tropel *m*, turba *f* (unruly crowd) || pandilla *f* (gang) || clase *f* baja (low class) || populacho *m*, masa *f* (masses) || gentuza *f*, chusma *f* (rabble) || bandada *f* (of birds) || — *mob law* ley *f* de Lynch || *to join the mob* echarse a la calle.

mob [mɔb] *vt* asaltar, atropellar, acosar (to attack in masses) || acosar, rodear; *the bullfighter was mobbed by his fans* el torero fue rodeado por los aficionados || atestar; *the streets were mobbed with people* las calles estaban atestadas de gente.
◆ *vi* agruparse, aglomerarse, apiñarse.

mobcap [-kæp] *n* cofia *f* (hat).

mobile ['məubail] *adj* móvil, movible || transportable, portátil (portable) || ambulante (itinerant) || orientable (antenna) || móvil (facial expressions) || FIG voluble, cambiadizo, za (character) || FAM *when we are mobile again* cuando estemos de nuevo motorizados.
◆ *n* ARTS móvil *m*.

mobile home [-həum] *n* casa *f* rodante.

mobility [məu'biliti] *n* movilidad *f* || FIG volubilidad *f* || *mobility allowance* subsidio *m* de desplazamiento para impedidos.

mobilizable [məubi'laizəbl] *adj* movilizable.

mobilization [ˌməubilai'zeiʃən] *n* movilización *f*.

mobilize ['məubilaiz] *vt* movilizar.

mobster ['mɔbstə*] *n* US FAM gángster *m*.

moccasin ['mɔkəsin] *n* mocasín *m* (shoe) || ZOOL mocasín *m* (snake).

mocha ['mɔkə] *n* moca *m* (coffee).

mock [mɔk] *adj* simulado, da; fingido, da (sham); *mock laugh* risa fingida || falso, sa; *mock modesty* falsa modestia || imitado, da (imitated) || burlesco, ca; cómico, ca (burlesque) || COMM de imitación, artificial; *mock bronze* bronce de imitación || — *mock battle* simulacro *m* de combate || *mock jewelry* joyas *f pl* de imitación, bisutería *f*.
◆ *n* mofa *f*, burla *f* (sneer) || hazmerreír *m* (laughingstock) || simulacro *m* (simulacrum) || *to make a mock of sth.* ridiculizar algo, hacer mofa de algo.

mock [mɔk] *vt* burlarse de, mofarse de, reírse de (to scoff at); *the other children mocked him* los demás chicos se rieron de él || ridiculizar (to ridicule) || frustrar (to thwart, to frustrate) || remedar, imitar a (to mimic) || defraudar (to deceive) || burlar (the law).
◆ *vi* burlarse, reírse; *to mock at* burlarse de.

mocker [-ə*] *n* mofador, ra; burlón, ona.

mockery ['mɔkəri] *n* burla *f*, mofa *f* (sneer) || hazmerreír *m* (laughingstock) || parodia *f*, simulacro *m*; *a mockery of the truth* una parodia de la verdad || imitación *f*, remedo *m* (imitation) || *to make a mockery of* ridiculizar.

mock-heroic ['mɔkhi'rəuik] *adj* heroicoburlesco, ca; heroicocómico, ca.

mocking ['mɔkiŋ] *adj* burlón, ona; mofador, ra.
◆ *n* burla *f*, mofa *f* (mockery).

mockingbird [-bəːd] *n* ZOOL sinsonte *m*.

mock orange ['mɔk'ɔrindʒ] *n* BOT jeringuilla *f*.

mock-up ['mɔkʌp] *n* maqueta *f*, modelo *m* a escala.

mod [mɔd] *adj* FAM moderno, na || *complete with all mod cons* equipado, da todo confort (house, flat).

modal ['məudl] *adj* GRAMM & MUS & PHIL & JUR modal.

modality [məu'dæliti] *n* modalidad *f*.

mode [məud] *n* modo *m*, manera *f*, forma *f* (manner); *a mode of life* una manera de vivir || moda *f* (fashion) || MUS & PHIL & GRAMM modo *m*.

model ['mɔdl] *n* maqueta *f* (of a monument, of a statue, etc.) || modelo *m* (of a car, etc.) || FIG modelo *m*, dechado *m*, ejemplo *m* (example); *he is a model of virtue* es un dechado de virtudes || modelo *m* & *f* (for pictures) || maniquí *m*, modelo *m* & *f* (who demonstrates clothes) || patrón *m*, modelo *m* (pattern) [in dressmaking] || MAR gálibo *m*, vitola *f* || *scale model* maqueta.
◆ *adj* ejemplar, modelo; *a model student* un estudiante ejemplar; *Carmen is a model wife* Carmen es una esposa modelo || modelo; *a model house* una casa modelo; *model company* empresa modelo || en miniatura, de tamaño reducido (railway, car, plane) || *model maker* modelista *m* & *f* (designer), maquetista *m* & *f* (of a scale model).

model ['mɔdl] *vt* modelar; *to model clay, a bust* modelar arcilla, un busto || construir (a imitación de); *to model a house after* o *on* o *upon a castle* construir una casa a imitación de un castillo || presentar (a dress) || — *his work is modelled on Shakespeare* su obra está inspirada en Shakespeare || *to model o.s. on s.o.* seguir el modelo *or* el ejemplo de alguien.
◆ *vi* modelar (to make a model) || modelarse; *clay models well* la arcilla se modela bien || posar (for an artist) || pasar modelos, ser modelo, ser maniquí (for clothes).

modeller; US **modeler** ['mɔdlə*] *n* modelador, ra; modelista *m* & *f*.

modelling; US **modeling** ['mɔdliŋ] *n* modelado *m* || profesión *f* de modelo *or* maniquí || creación *f* de modelos.

modem [məudem] *n* INFORM modem *m*.

moderate ['mɔdərit] *adj* moderado, da; comedido, da; mesurado, da (not extreme) || razonable, módico, ca; moderado, da (reasonable); *moderate prices* precios módicos || regular, mediano, na; mediocre (average); *moderate skill* habilidad mediocre.
◆ *n* moderado, da.

moderate ['mɔdəreit] *vt* moderar; *you have to moderate your enthusiasm* tiene que moderar su entusiasmo || aplacar (s.o.'s anger) || presidir [una asamblea] (to preside over).
◆ *vi* moderarse (to become less extreme) || amainar (the wind) || presidir una asamblea (to preside) || arbitrar, servir de moderador (to act as a moderator).

moderating ['mɔdəreitiŋ] *adj* moderador, ra.

moderation [ˌmɔdə'reiʃən] *n* moderación *f*; *in* o *with moderation* con moderación.

moderator ['mɔdəreitə*] *n* mediador, ra; árbitro *m*, moderador, ra (mediator) || presidente *m* del tribunal de exámenes (in a university) || PHYS moderador *m*.

modern ['mɔdən] *adj* moderno, na.
◆ *n* persona *f* moderna, moderno, na.

modernism [-izəm] *n* modernismo *m*.

modernist [-ist] *adj/n* modernista.

modernistic [mɔdə'nistik] *adj* modernista.

modernity [mɔ'dəːniti] *n* modernidad *f*, modernismo *m*.

modernization [ˌmɔdənai'zeiʃən] *n* modernización *f*.

modernize ['mɔdənaiz] *vt* modernizar.

modest ['mɔdist] *adj* modesto, ta; humilde (not conceited) || púdico, ca; modesto, ta; recatado, da (decent, reserved); *a modest woman* una mujer recatada || moderado, da; discreto, ta; *a modest success* un éxito discreto || módico, ca; *a modest wage* un sueldo módico.

modesty [-i] *n* modestia *f*, humildad *f* (humility) || modestia *f*, recato *m*, pudor *m* (sense of decency) || moderación *f* (moderation) || modicidad *f* (of expenses, etc.).

modicum ['mɔdikəm] *n* pequeña cantidad *f*, pizca *f*.

modifiable ['mɔdifaiəbl] *adj* modificable.

modification [ˌmɔdifi'keiʃən] *n* modificación *f*.

modificatory ['mɔdifikeitəri] *adj* modificador, ra.

modifier ['mɔdifaiə*] *n* modificador, ra (person) || GRAMM calificativo *m*.

modify ['mɔdifai] *vt* modificar || JUR atenuar.
◆ *vi* modificarse.

modillion [məu'diljən] *n* ARCH modillón *m*.

modish ['məudiʃ] *adj* de moda.

modishly [-li] *adj* elegantemente, a la moda.

modiste [məu'diːst] *n* modisto, ta (dressmaker) || sombrerero, ra (milliner).

modulate ['mɔdjuleit] *vt* modular (voice, sound) || adaptar (*to* a).
◆ *vi* MUS & RAD modular.

modulation [ˌmɔdjuˈleiʃən] *n* modulación *f* || *frequency modulation* modulación de frecuencia, frecuencia modulada.

modulator [ˈmɔdjuleitə*] *n* modulador *m*.

module [ˈmɔdjul] *n* módulo *m*.

modulus [ˈmɔdjuləs] *n* módulo *m*, coeficiente *m* || *modulus of elasticity* módulo de elasticidad.
— OBSERV El plural de *modulus* es *moduli*.

modus operandi [ˈmɔdəsˌɔpəˈrændiː] *n* procedimiento *m*.

modus vivendi [ˈmɔdəsviˈvendi] *n* modus vivendi *m*.

mofette; moffette [məuˈfet] *n* GEOL mofeta *f*.

Mogadiscio; Mogadishu [mɔgəˈdiʃuː] *pr n* GEOGR Mogadischo.

moggy [ˈmɔgi] *n* FAM minino *m*.

Mogul [məuˈgʌl] *adj/n* mogol, la; mongol, la || US FAM magnate *m* (important person).

mohair [ˈməuhɛə*] *n* mohair *m*.

Mohammed [məuˈhæmed] *pr n* REL Mahoma *m*.

Mohammedan [məuˈhæmidən] *adj/n* REL mahometano, na.

Mohammedanism [-izəm] *n* REL mahometismo *m*.

Mohican [ˈməuikən] *adj/n* mohicano, na.

moiety [ˈmɔiəti] *n* mitad *f* (half) || parte *f*, porción *f* (share).

moil [mɔil] *n* trabajo *m* penoso.

moil [mɔil] *vi* trabajar duramente, afanarse.

moiré [ˈmwɑːrei] *n* muaré *m*, moaré *m* (fabric).

moist [mɔist] *adj* húmedo, da; *a moist climate* un clima húmedo; *eyes moist with tears* ojos húmedos de lágrimas || mojado, da (wet).

moisten [ˈmɔisn] *vt* humedecer, mojar || humedecer (the skin).
◆ *vi* humedecerse, mojarse.

moistness [ˈmɔistnis] *n* humedad *f*.

moisture [ˈmɔistʃə*] *n* humedad *f* (dampness) || vaho *m*, empañamiento *m* (of mirror).

moisturize [-raiz] *vt* humedecer || *moisturizing cream* crema *f* hidratante.

moke [məuk] *n* ZOOL burro *m*, asno *m* (donkey).

mol [məul] *n* CHEM mol *m*.

molar [ˈməulə*] *n* muela *f*, molar *m* (tooth).
◆ *adj* molar.

molasses [məuˈlæsiz] *n* melaza *f* (treacle).

mold [məuld] *n/vt/vi* US ⟶ **mould.**

moldable [-əbl] *adj* US moldeable.

moldboard [ˈməuldˌbɔːd] *n* US ⟶ **mouldboard.**

molder [ˈməuldə*] *n* US moldeador, ra.

molder [ˈməuldə*] *vi* US desmoronarse.

moldiness [ˈməuldinis] *n* US enmohecimiento *m*, estado *m* mohoso.

molding [ˈməuldiŋ] *n* US ⟶ **moulding.**

moldy [ˈməuldi] *adj* US ⟶ **mouldy.**

mole [məul] *n* topo *m* (animal) || lunar *m* (on skin); *she has a mole on her face* tiene un lunar en la cara || malecón *m* (jetty, breakwater) || muelle *m* (harbour) || CHEM mol *m* || ZOOL *mole cricket* grillo *m* cebollero *or* real.

molecular [məuˈlekjulə*] *adj* molecular; *molecular mass* masa molecular; *molecular weight* peso molecular.

molecule [ˈmɔlikjuːl] *n* molécula *f*; *gram molecule* molécula gramo.

molehill [ˈməulhil] *n* topera *f*.

moleskin [ˈməulskin] *n* molesquín (fabric).
◆ *pl* pantalones *m* de molesquín (trousers).

molest [məuˈlest] *vt* importunar, molestar.

molestation [ˌməulesˈteiʃən] *n* molestia *f*, importunidad *f*.

molester [məuˈlestə*] *n* persona *f* que comete abusos deshonestos.

moll [mɔll] *n* POP amiga *f* (girlfriend) | prostituta *f*.

mollification [ˌmɔlifiˈkeiʃən] *n* aplacamiento *m*, apaciguamiento *m*.

mollify [ˈmɔlifai] *vt* aplacar, apaciguar.

mollusc [ˈmɔləsk] *n* ZOOL molusco *m*.

mollusk [ˈmɔləsk] *n* US ZOOL molusco *m*.

mollycoddle [ˈmɔlikɔdl] *n* FAM niño *m* mimado (spoilt boy) | gallina *m* (coward) | marica *m* (effeminate man).

mollycoddle [ˈmɔlikɔdl] *vt* FAM mimar.

Molotov cocktail [ˈmɔlətɔvˈkɔkteil] *n* cóctel *m* Molotov.

molt [məult] *n/vt/vi* US ⟶ **moult.**

molten [ˈməultən] *adj* fundido, da; derretido, da || *molten lava* lava líquida.

molybdenum [mɔˈlibdinəm] *n* CHEM molibdeno *m*.

mom [mɔm] *n* FAM mamá *f*, mamaíta *f*.

moment [ˈməumənt] *n* momento *m*; *wait a moment* espérate un momento; *when the moment came to do it* cuando llegó el momento de hacerlo || importancia *f* (importance); *of great moment* de gran importancia || PHYS momento *m*; *moment of inertia* momento de inercia || — *a few moments later* momentos después || *at any moment* de un momento a otro || *at that moment* en aquel momento || *at the moment* de momento, ahora || *at the very moment when* en el momento en que || *at this moment* en este momento || *crucial, fatal, psychological moment* momento crucial, fatídico, psicológico || *every moment* a cada momento || *for the moment* por el momento || *from that moment* desde ese momento, a partir de ese momento || *from the moment when* desde el momento en que || *in a moment* dentro de un momento || *just a moment!* ¡un momento! || *last moments* últimos momentos || *moment of truth* hora *f* de la verdad || *not a moment ago* hace un momento || *not for a moment* en absoluto || *this moment* ahora mismo || *to be the man of the moment* ser el hombre del momento || *to have one's (good) moments* tener buenos momentos.

momenta [məuˈmentə] *pl n* ⟶ **momentum.**

momentarily [ˈməuməntərili] *adv* momentáneamente (for a short moment) || de un momento a otro (at any moment).

momentariness [ˈməuməntərinis] *n* carácter *m* momentáneo, poca duración *f*.

momentary [ˈməuməntəri] *adj* momentáneo, a; pasajero, ra.

momentous [məuˈmentəs] *adj* de gran importancia, trascendental.

momentousness [-nis] *n* gran importancia *f*, trascendencia *f*.

momentum [məuˈmentəm] *n* PHYS momento *m* || ímpetu *m*, velocidad *f* (speed); *to gather momentum* adquirir velocidad || impulso *m*.
— OBSERV El plural de *momentum* es *momentums* o *momenta*.

momma [ˈmɔmə]; **mommy** [ˈmɔmi] *n* US FAM mamá, mami *f*.

monachism [ˈmɔnəkizəm] *n* monacato *m*.

Monaco (the Pricipality of) [ˈmɔnəkəu] *pr n* GEOGR el Principado de Mónaco.

monad [ˈmɔnæd] *n* mónada *f*.

monarch [ˈmɔnək] *n* monarca *m* (king).

monarchal [mɔˈnɑːkəl]; **monarchial** [mɔˈnɑːkjəl] *adj* monárquico, ca.

monarchic [mɔˈnɑːkik]; **monarchical** [-əl] *adj* monárquico, ca.

monarchism [ˈmɔnəkizəm] *n* monarquismo *m*.

monarchist [ˈmɔnəkist] *adj/n* monárquico, ca.

monarchistic [ˈmɔnəˈkistik] *adj* monárquico, ca.

monarchy [ˈmɔnəki] *n* monarquía *f*.

monastery [ˈmɔnəstəri] *n* monasterio *m*.

monastic [məˈnæstik] *adj* monacal, monástico, ca.
◆ *n* monje *m* (monk).

monasticism [məˈnæstisizəm] *n* monacato *m*.

Monday [ˈmʌndi] *n* lunes *m*; *I shall come on Monday morning* vendré el lunes por la mañana; *last Monday* el lunes pasado; *next Monday* el lunes que viene.

Monegasque [ˈmɔnigæsk] *adj/n* monegasco, ca.

monetarism [ˈmʌnitərizm] *n* monetarismo.

monetarist [mʌnitərist] *adj* monetarista.
◆ *n* monetarista *m* & *f*.

monetary [ˈmʌnitəri] *adj* monetario, ria.

monetization [ˌmʌnitaiˈzeiʃən] *n* monetización *f*.

money [ˈmʌni] *n* dinero *m*; *minted money* dinero acuñado || — *counterfeit money* moneda falsa || FAM *for my money he's drunk!* ¿a que está borracho? | *it's money for jam* o *for old rope* es una ganga | *money burns a hole in his pocket* el dinero le quema en el bolsillo | *money does not grow on trees* el dinero no nace en macetas, no se atan los perros con longanizas || *money in hand* dinero disponible || FIG *money is welcome though it comes in a dirty clout* el dinero no tiene olor | *money makes money* el dinero llama al dinero || *money matters* asuntos económicos || *money of account* moneda de cuenta, moneda imaginaria || *money payment* pago *m* en metálico, pago *m* en numerario || *money's worth* valor *m* en metálico || FIG *money talks* poderoso caballero es don Dinero || *paper money* papel *m* moneda || *pocket money* dinero para gastos menudos *or* de bolsillo || *ready money* dinero líquido || *there is good money in business* se puede sacar mucho dinero de los negocios || *there is money in it* se le puede sacar mucho dinero, es un buen negocio || FIG *time is money* el tiempo es oro | *to be in the money* ser rico | *to be made of money, to be rolling in money* estar nadando en dinero, ser millonario || *to be short of money* andar escaso de dinero || FAM *to bring in big money* ganar el dinero a espuertas, ganar más dinero que un torero || *to coin money* acuñar moneda (to make coins), forrarse de dinero (to earn much money) || *to come into money* heredar dinero || FIG & FAM *to cost a mint of money* costar un dineral *or* una fortuna || *to do sth. for money* hacer algo por dinero || FIG *to give s.o. a run for his money* hacer pasar un mal rato a alguien (to give a bad time), permitir a alguien que le saque jugo al dinero (to give good value) | *to have money to burn* estar forrado, nadar en dinero *or* en la abundancia || *to make money* hacer dinero (a person), dar dinero (a business) || *to make tons of money* ganar dinero a espuertas || *to marry money* casarse por interés || *to mint money* acuñar *or* labrar *or* batir moneda || *to part with one's money* desembolsar dinero || *to put money into* colocar *or* invertir dinero en || *to put money on* apostar a (to bet) || FIG *to spend money like water, to throw money down the drain* tirar el dinero por la ventana | *we got our money's worth* le sacamos jugo al di-

nero || *with my own money* con mi dinero || *your money or your life!* ¡la bolsa o la vida!
◆ *pl* fondos *m*, dinero *m sing; public moneys* fondos públicos || cantidades *f* de dinero.
— OBSERV El plural de la palabra *money* es *monies* o *moneys*.

moneybag [-bæg] *n* cartera *f*, monedero *m*.

moneybags [-bægz] *n* FAM ricachón, ona (rich person) | dineral *m*, fortuna *f* (wealth).

money box [-bɔks] *n* hucha *f*, alcancía *f*.

money changer [-ˌtʃeindʒə*] *n* cambista *m* & *f*.

moneyed [-d] *adj* rico, ca; adinerado, da.

moneygrubber [-grʌbə*] *n* avaro, ra.

moneylender [-ˌlendə*] *n* prestamista *m* & *f*.

moneyless [-lis] *adj* sin dinero, pobre.

moneymaker [-ˌmeikə*] *n* amasador *m* de dinero (person) || fuente *f or* mina *f* de dinero (thing).

moneymaking [-ˌmeikiŋ] *adj* rentable, productivo, va (business) || que saca dinero de todo (person).
◆ *n* ganancia.

money market [-ˌmɑːkit] *n* mercado *m* de valores, bolsa *f*.

money-minded [-ˌmaindid] *adj* interesado, da.

money order [-ˌɔːdə*] *n* giro *m* postal.

money-spinner *n* mina *f* (source of wealth) || *this business is a money-spinner* este negocio es una mina.

monger [ˈmʌŋgə*] *n* COMM traficante *m*, negociante *m*, vendedor, ra.
— OBSERV *Monger* se emplea sobre todo en palabras compuestas: *ironmonger* ferretero; *fishmonger* vendedor de pescado, pescadero.

Mongol [ˈmɔŋgɔl] *adj/n* mongol, la; mogol, la (mogul).

Mongolia [mɔŋˈgəuljə] *pr n* GEOGR Mongolia *f*.

Mongolian [-n] *adj* mongol, la (of Mongolia) || MED mongólico, ca.
◆ *n* mongol, la (inhabitant of Mongolia) || mongol *m* (language).

Mongolic [mɔŋˈgəulik] *adj* mongólico, ca.
◆ *n* mongol *m* (language).

Mongolism [ˈmɔŋgəlizəm] *n* MED mongolismo *m*.

Mongoloid [ˈmɔŋgəlɔid] *adj/n* MED mongoloide.

mongoose [ɔɔŋguːs] *n* ZOOL mangosta *f*.

mongrel [ˈmʌŋgrəl] *n* perro *m* mestizo *or* cruzado || mestizo, za (person).
◆ *adj* mestizo, za.

monies [ˈmʌniz] *pl n* → **money.**

monism [ˈmɔnizəm] *n* PHIL monismo *m*.

monition [məuˈniʃən] *n* admonición *f*, advertencia *f* || JUR citación *f*.

monitor [ˈmɔnitə*] *n* monitor *m*, instructor *m* || alumno *m* encargado de mantener la disciplina (in school) || RAD radioescucha *m* (a person) | monitor *m*, receptor *m* de control (apparatus) || MAR monitor *m* || ZOOL varano *m*.

monitor [ˈmɔnitə*] *vt* controlar, comprobar (to check) || escuchar, oír (to listen) || PHYS determinar [la contaminación radioactiva de] || INFORM monitor *m*.

monitoring [mɔniˈtɔriŋ] *n* RAD control *m* | servicio *m* de escucha.

monitor room [ˈmɔnitərum] *n* cabina *f* de escucha || cabina *f* de control.

monk [mʌnk] *n* REL monje *m*.

monkery [-əri] *n* FAM monasterio *m* (monastery) | vida *f* monástica.

monkey [ˈmʌŋki] *n* ZOOL mono *m* (ape), mona *f* (female ape) || FIG & FAM diablillo *m*, mico *m* (child) || TECH maza *f* (hammer) | bigotera *f* (of a blast furnace) || FAM quinientas libras *f pl* | US quinientos dólares *m pl* | FAM *to make a monkey out of s.o.* tomar el pelo a alguien (to pull s.o.'s leg), ridiculizar a alguien (to make a fool of).

monkey [ˈmʌŋki] *vi* FAM hacer tonterías *or* payasadas (to play the fool) || — FAM *to monkey about* entretenerse, perder el tiempo | *to monkey about with* enredar *or* jugar con (to play with), manosear (to finger), meterse con (a person).
◆ *vt* remedar, imitar.

monkey bread [-bred] *n* BOT pan *m* de mono, fruto *m* del baobab (fruit) | baobab *m* (tree).

monkey business [-ˌbiznis] *n* FAM diablura *f*, travesura *f* (mischief) | tejemanejes *m pl*, trampas *f pl* (trickery).

monkey jacket [-ˌdʒækit] *n* chaqueta *f* corta (short dress jacket).

monkey-like [-laik] *adj* de mono, simiesco, ca.

monkey-nut [-nʌt] *n* cacahuete *m* [AMER maní *m*] (groundnut).

monkeyshines [-ʃainz] *pl n* US FAM diabluras *f*, travesuras *f* (mischief).

monkey suit [-sjuːt] *n* uniforme *m* || traje *m* de etiqueta (man's dress suit).

monkey tricks [-triks] *pl n* diabluras *f*, travesuras *f* (mischief).

monkey wrench [-rentʃ] *n* TECH llave *f* inglesa, llave *f* de cremallera.

monkhood [ˈmʌnkhud] *n* monacato *m*.

monkish [ˈmʌŋkiʃ] *adj* frailuno, na; monacal, monástico, ca.

mono [ˈmɔnəu] *adj* mono (system of sound recording).

monoacid [ˈmɔnəuˈæsid] *adj* CHEM monoácido, da.
◆ *n* CHEM monoácido *m*.

monobasic [ˈmɔnəˈbeisik] *adj* monobásico, ca.

monobloc [ˈmɔnəblɔk] *adj* monobloque.

monochord [ˈmɔnəkɔːd] *n* MUS monocordio *m*.

monochromatic [ˈmɔnəkrəuˈmætik] *adj* monocromático, ca.

monochrome [ˈmɔnəkrəum] *adj* monocromo, ma; de un solo color.
◆ *n* monocromo *m*.

monochromy [-i] *n* monocromía *f*.

monocle [ˈmɔnɔkl] *n* monóculo *m*.

monocoque [ˈmɔnəkɔk] *adj* monocasco.

monocotyledon [ˈmɔnəˌkɔtiˈliːdən] *n* BOT monocotiledóneo *m*.

monocracy [mɔˈnəkrəsi] *n* autocracia *f*.

monoculture [ˈmɔnəˌkʌltʃə*] *n* monocultivo *m*.

monody [ˈmɔnədi] *n* MUS monodia *f* (single voice ode) | treno *m* (threnody).

monogamist [mɔˈnɔgəmist] *n* monógamo, ma.

monogamous [mɔˈnɔgəməs] *adj* monógamo, ma.

monogamy [mɔˈnɔgəmi] *n* monogamia *f*.

monogram [ˈmɔnəgræm] *n* monograma *m*.

monograph [ˈmɔnəgrɑːf] *n* monografía *f*.

monographic [ˌmɔnəˈgræfik] *adj* monográfico, ca.

monolingual [ˌmɔnəˈliŋgwəl] *adj* monolingüe.

monolith [ˈmɔnəuliθ] *n* monolito *m*.

monolithic [ˌmɔnəuˈliθik] *adj* monolítico, ca.

monolog [ˈmɔnəlɔg] *n* US monólogo *m*.

monologize [mɔˈnɔlədʒaiz] *vi* monologar.

monologue [ˈmɔnəlɔg] *n* monólogo *m*.

monomania [ˈmɔnəuˈmeinjə] *n* monomanía *f*.

monomaniac [ˈmɔnəuˈmeiniæk] *n* monomaníaco, ca.

monometallic [ˌmɔnəumeˈtælik] *adj* monometalista.

monometallism [ˌmɔnəuˈmetælizəm] *n* monometalismo *m*.

monomial [məˈnəumiəl] *n* MATH monomio *m*.

mononuclear [ˈmɔnəuˈnjuːkliə*] *adj* mononuclear.

mononucleosis [ˈmɔnəuˌnuːkliˈəusis] *n* MED mononucleosis *f*.

monophase [ˈmɔnəfeiz] *adj* ELECTR monofásico, ca.

Monophysite [məˈnɔfəˌsait] *n* monofisita *m*.

monoplane [ˈmɔnəplein] *n* monoplano *m*.

monopolist [məˈnɔpəlist] *n* monopolizador, ra.

monopolization [məˌnɔpəlaiˈzeiʃən] *n* monopolización *f*.

monopolize [məˈnɔpəlaiz] *vt* monopolizar.

monopolizer [-ə*] *n* monopolizador, ra.

monopolizing [-iŋ] *adj* monopolizador, ra.

monopoly [mɔˈnɔpəli] *n* monopolio *m*.

monorail [ˈmɔnəureil] *adj* monocarril, monorriel.
◆ *n* monocarril *m*, monorriel *m*.

monosaccharide [ˈmɔnəuˌsækəraid] *n* CHEM monosacárido *m*.

monosodium glutamate [ˈmɔnəuˈsəudiəm ˈgluːtəmeit] *n* glutamato *m* de monosodio.

monosyllabic [ˈmɔnəusiˈlæbik] *adj* monosílabo, ba (word) || monosilábico, ca (language).

monosyllable [ˈmɔnəˌsiləbl] *n* monosílabo *m*.

monotheism [ˈmɔnəuθiːˌizəm] *n* REL monoteísmo *m*.

monotheist [ˈmɔnəuθiːist] *n* REL monoteísta *m* & *f*.

monotheistic [ˈmɔnəuθiːistik] *adj* REL monoteísta.

monotone [ˈmɔnətəun] *adj* monótono, na.
◆ *n* monotonía *f* || *in a monotone* con una voz monótona, con monotonía.

monotonous [məˈnɔtnəs] *adj* monótono, na.

monotony [məˈnɔtni] *n* monotonía *f*.

monotremata [ˌmɔnəuˈtriːmətə] *pl n* ZOOL monotremas *m*.

monotype [ˈmɔnəutaip] *n* PRINT monotipo *m* (machine) | monotipia *f* (process).

monovalent [ˈmɔnəuˌveilənt] *adj* monovalente.
◆ *n* monovalente *m*.

Monrovia [mənˈrəuviə] *pr n* GEOGR Monrovia.

Monseigneur; Monsignor [mɔnˈsiːnjə*] *n* monseñor *m*.

monsoon [mɔnˈsuːn] *n* monzón *m* (wind).

monster [ˈmɔstə*] *n* monstruo *m*.
◆ *adj* monstruoso, sa.

monstrance [ˈmɔnstrəns] *n* custodia *f*.

monstrosity [mɔnsˈtrɔsiti] *n* monstruosidad *f*.

monstrous [ˈmɔnstrəs] *adj* monstruoso, sa.

monstrousness [-nis] *n* monstruosidad *f*.

montage [mɔnˈtɑːʒ] *n* montaje *m*.

Montagues ['mɔntəgju:z] *pl prn* Montescos *m*.

Montana [mɔn'tænə] *pr n* GEOGR Montana.

Mont Blanc [,mɔ̃'blɑ] *pr n* GEOGR Mont Blanc.

monteith [mɔn'ti:θ] *n* ponchera *f* de plata.

Montevidean [,mɔntivi'deiən] *adj/n* montevideano, na.

Montevideo [,mɔntivi'deiəu] *pr n* GEOGR Montevideo.

month [mʌnθ] *n* mes *m*; *a hundred pounds a month* cien libras al *or* por mes || — *calendar month* mes civil || *current month* mes corriente || FIG *it will take you a month of Sunday* tardará siglos en hacerlo, tardará una eternidad en hacerlo || *last month* el mes pasado || *lunar month* mes lunar || *month's pay* sueldo *m* mensual, mensualidad *f* || FIG *never in a month of Sunday* nunca || *to go on for months* durar meses y meses, durar meses.

monthly [-li] *adj* mensual; *monthly wage* salario mensual || *monthly instalment, monthly payment* mensualidad *f*.
◆ *adv* mensualmente, una vez al mes, todos los meses || mensualmente, por meses; *they pay him monthly* le pagan por meses.
◆ *n* mensual *m*, revista *f* mensual (publication).
◆ *pl* MED & FAM mes *m sing* (menses).

monticule ['mɔntikjul] *n* montículo *m*.

monument ['mɔnjumənt] *n* monumento *m* (building, memorial, work) || US mojón *m* (boundary mark).

monumental [,mɔnju'mentl] *adj* monumental || FIG monumental, enorme (stupidity) | monumental (literary work) | garrafal (mistake).

monumentalize [,mɔnju'mentəlaiz] *vt* conmemorar con un monumento.

moo [mu:] *n* mugido *m* (of a cow).

moo [mu:] *vi* mugir.

mooch [mu:tq] *vi* vagar, haraganear (to idle) || US FAM gorronear (to cadge).
◆ *vt* US FAM dar un sablazo; *he mooched ten dollars off me* me dio un sablazo de diez dólares | birlar (to steal).

moocher [-ə*] *n* US FAM gorrón *m*, parásito *m* (parasite) | sablista *m* (sponger).

mood [mu:d] *n* humor *m*; *to be, to put in a bad mood* estar, poner de mal humor || GRAMM & PHIL modo *m* || — *I am not in the mood* no me apetece || *I am not in the mood for* no estoy para, no tengo ganas de || *to be in the mood for* estar de humor para, tener ganas de.
◆ *pl* mal humor *m sing*, malhumor *m sing*, momentos *m* de mal humor (bad mood) || caprichos *m* (whims).

moodily [-ili] *adv* malhumoradamente || caprichosamente.

moodiness [-inis] *n* malhumor *m*, mal humor *m* (bad mood) || tristeza *f*, melancolía *f* (sadness) || humor *m* cambiadizo (instability) || caprichos *m pl* (whims).

moody [-i] *adj* malhumorado, da (bad-tempered) || triste, melancólico, ca; taciturno, na (sad) || de humor cambiadizo (fickle) || caprichoso, sa (whimsical).

moon [mu:n] *adj* lunar; *moon capsule* cápsula lunar.
◆ *n* luna *f*; *full moon* luna llena; *new moon* luna nueva; *crescent moon* media luna || ASTR lunación *f* || FIG mes *m* (month) || — *april moon* luna de abril || FIG *many moons ago* hace muchas lunas *or* mucho tiempo | *once in a blue moon* de Pascuas a Ramos, de higos a brevas | *to ask for the moon* pedir la Luna | *to bark* o *to bay at the moon* ladrar a la Luna | *to be over the moon* volverse loco de alegría | *to promise the moon* prometer la luna *or* el oro y el moro || *waning moon* luna menguante || *waxing moon* luna creciente.

moon [mu:n] *vi* mirar a las musarañas, estar en la Luna.
◆ *vt* *to moon one's time away* pasarse el tiempo mirando a las musarañas.

moonbeam [-bi:m] *n* rayo *m* de luna.

moon blindness [-'blaindnis] *n* ceguera *f* nocturna.

mooncalf [-kɑ:f] *n* idiota *m* & *f*.

moonfaced [-feist] *adj* de cara redonda.

moonfish [-fiʃ] *n* ZOOL pez *m* luna.

moonish [-iʃ] *adj* variable (changeable) || caprichoso, sa (capricious).

moonless [-lis] *adj* sin luna.

moonlight [-lait] *n* claro *m* de luna, luz *f* de la luna; *by moonlight, in the moonlight* a la luz de la luna, con el claro de luna || — *it was moonlight* había luna || *to do a moonlight flit* mudarse a escondidas, irse a la chita callando (to move out secretly), desaparecer de la noche a la mañana (to disappear overnight).

moonlighting [-laitiŋ] *n* pluriempleo *m*.

moonlit [-lit] *adj* iluminado por la luna || de luna (night).

moonrise [-raiz] *n* salida *f* de la luna.

moonscape [-skeip] *n* paisaje *m* lunar.

moonset [-set] *n* puesta *f* de la luna.

moonshine [-ʃain] *n* claro *m* de luna, luz *f* de la luna (moonlight) || FAM pamplinas *f pl* (nonsense) || US FAM alcohol *m* ilegalmente destilado || FAM *that's just moonshine* eso es música celestial, no son más que pamplinas.

moonshiner [-ʃainə*] *n* US FAM destilador *m* ilegal de alcohol | contrabandista *m* de alcohol.

moonstone [-stəun] *n* piedra *f* de la luna.

moonstruck [-strʌk] *adj* lunático, ca; chiflado, da (mentally deranged) || turulato, ta (flabbergasted).

moony [-i] *adj* de la luna || parecido a la luna (moonlike) || semilunar (crescent-shaped) || distraído, da; en la luna (absentminded) || soñador, ra (dreamy).

moor [muə*] *n* páramo *m*, brezal *m* (heath) || terreno *m* pantanoso (marsh) || coto *m* de caza (game preserve).

moor [muə*] *vt* MAR amarrar (with cables or chains) | anclar (with an anchor).
◆ *vi* MAR echar las amarras | echar el ancla.

Moor [muə*] *n* moro, ra.

moorage [-ridʒ] *n* MAR amarradura *f*, amarre *m* (action) | amarradero *m* (place) | amarraje *m* (charge).

moorcock [-kɔk] *n* ZOOL lagópedo *m* de Escocia.

moorhen [-hen] *n* ZOOL polla *f* de agua (gallinule) | hembra *f* del lagópedo de Escocia (female of the red grouse).

mooring [-riŋ] *n* MAR amarradura *f*, amarre *m*.
◆ *pl* MAR amarras *f* (cables) || amarradero *m sing* (place).

Moorish [-riʃ] *adj* moro, ra; morisco, ca || árabe (architecture) || *Moorish district* morería *f*.

moorland [-lənd] *n* páramo *m*.

moose [mu:s] *n* ZOOL alce *m*, anta *f*.

moot [mu:t] *adj* discutible (point).
◆ *n* asamblea *f* de ciudadanos (assembly) || JUR debate *m*.

moot [mu:t] *vt* discutir, debatir (a point) || someter a discusión (an idea).

mop [mɔp] *n* fregona *f* (for washing floors) || mueca *f* (grimace) || MAR lampazo *m* || FAM greñas *f pl*, pelambrera *f* (hair) || FAM *Mrs. Mop* la asistenta.

mop [mɔp] *vt* fregar (a floor) || enjugarse, secarse (one's brow) || MAR fregar con lampazo || *to mop up* secar, limpiar (spilt liquids, etc.), dar una paliza a (to defeat), acabar con (the enemy, etc.), limpiar (territory), beberse (to drink up), llevarse (profits).
◆ *vi* hacer muecas (to grimace).

mope [məup] *n* melancólico, ca (person).
◆ *pl* melancolía *f sing*, moral *f sing* baja, abatimiento *m sing* (low spirits).

mope [məup] *vi* estar abatido, tener ideas negras || *to mope about* o *around* andar abatido, da.

moped ['məuped] *n* ciclomotor *m*.

mopish ['məupiʃ] *adj* abatido, da; alicaído, da; melancólico, ca.

mopishness ['məupiʃnis] *n* abatimiento *m*, decaimiento *m*, depresión *f*, melancolía *f* || desaliento *m*, descorazonamiento *m* (discouragement).

mop-up ['mɔpʌp] *n* MIL & FAM limpieza *f*.

moquette [mɔ'ket] *n* moqueta *f*.

moraine [mɔ'rein] *n* GEOL morrena *f*, morena *f*.

moral ['mɔrəl] *adj* moral; *a moral problem* un problema moral || con moralidad, honrado, da; recto, ta (man) || virtuoso, sa; decente (woman) || moral; *moral law, obligation* ley, obligación moral; *moral victory* victoria moral; *moral support* apoyo moral || de moral (book).
◆ *n* moraleja *f*; *the moral of a tale* la moraleja de un cuento; *he drew a moral from* sacó una moraleja de.
◆ *pl* moral *f sing* (principles of conduct) || moralidad *f sing*; *a man with no morals* un hombre sin moralidad || *loose morals* costumbres relajadas.

morale [mɔ'rɑ:l] *n* moral *f*, estado *m* de ánimo; *our morale is high* nuestra moral es alta || *to undermine the morale of* desmoralizar a.

moralism ['mɔrəlizəm] *n* moralismo *m*.

moralist ['mɔrəlist] *n* moralista *m* & *f* (student, writer) || moralizador, ra (person who moralizes) || persona *f* con moralidad, persona *f* honrada.

moralistic [mɔrə'listik] *adj* moralizador, ra.

morality [mə'ræliti] *n* moralidad *f* (rightness) || moral *f* (ethics) || precepto *m* moral.

morality play [-plei] *n* moralidad *f*.

moralization [,mɔrəlai'zeiʃən] *n* moralización *f*.

moralize ['mɔrəlaiz] *vi* moralizar.
◆ *vt* sacar la moraleja de (a fable) || interpretar según la moral (an event) || moralizar (s.o.).

moralizer [-ə*] *n* moralizador, ra.

moral philosophy ['mɔrəlfi'lɔsəfi] *n* moral *f*, ética *f*.

morass [mə'ræs] *n* pantano *m*, marisma *f* (marsh) || FIG lío *m*, embrollo *m*.

moratorium [,mɔrə'tɔ:riəm] *n* JUR moratoria *f*.
— OBSERV El plural de *moratorium* es *moratoria* o *moratoriums*.

moratory ['mɔrətəri] *adj* moratorio, ria.

moray [mə'rei] *n* morena *f* (fish).

morbid ['mɔ:bid] *adj* MED patológico, ca (anatomy) | mórbido, da; *morbid state* estado mórbido || malsano, na; enfermizo, za; morboso, sa (mind) || morboso, sa (gruesome); *the morbid details* los detalles morbosos || malsano, na (curiosity) || pesimista (depressed).

morbidity [mɔ:'biditi]; **morbidness** ['mɔ:bidnis] *n* morbosidad *f* (incidence of disease, gruesomeness) || morbosidad *f*, lo malsano, lo enfermizo (of mind) || pesimismo *m* (depression).

mordacious [mɔː'deiʃəs] *adj* mordaz, cáustico, ca; *mordacious speech* discurso mordaz.

mordacity [mɔː'dæsiti] *n* mordacidad *f*, causticidad *f* (causticity).

mordant ['mɔːdənt] *adj* mordiente (acids) || mordaz, cáustico, ca (speech).
◆ *n* TECH mordiente *m*.

more [mɔː*] *adj* más; *would you like some more wine?* ¿quieres más vino?; *a few more days* unos días más; *he has more books than I* tiene más libros que yo; *to spend more money* gastar más dinero; *more than one pound* más de una libra || superior; *the price is more than last year's* el precio es superior al del año pasado; *speeds of more than 100 k. p. h* velocidades superiores a 100 km/h || mayor; *the danger is more than it was* el peligro es mayor de lo que era || — *no more nonsense!* ¡basta de tonterías! || *without more ado* sin más ni más.
◆ *adv* más; *you must eat more* tienes que comer más; *this is far more serious* esto es mucho más grave; *some of Picasso's more famous pictures* algunos de los cuadros más famosos de Picasso; *this is worth more than the other* éste vale más que el otro; *it is worth more than 100 dollars* vale más de 100 dólares; *it is worth 100 dollars more* vale cien dólares más; *if we were one man more* si fuéramos uno más; *not a penny more* ni un penique más || más, más bien; *is it a story? no, it's more a play* ¿es una novela? no, es más bien una obra de teatro || — *all the more* aun más || *all the more... since* o *because* tanto más... cuanto que || *if it happens any more* si vuelve a ocurrir || *I won't do it any more* no lo haré más || *more and more* cada vez más, más y más; *he was getting more and more angry* se estaba enfadando cada vez más || *more or less* más o menos || *more than ever* más que nunca || *neither more nor less* ni más ni menos || *never more* nunca más || *no more no less* ni más ni menos || *once more* una vez más, otra vez, de nuevo || *still more* más aún, todavía más || *that is not done any more* eso ya no se hace || *that's more like it!* ¡eso está mejor! || *the more* más aún; *I was the more happy because* me alegré más aún porque || *the more..., the less* cuanto más..., menos || *the more..., the more* cuanto más..., más; *the more you read, the more you learn* cuanto más lees, más aprendes || *there's not much more to go* ya nos queda poco por hacer || *to be more offended than angry* ofenderse más que enfadarse || *to be more than* ser *or* estar más que; *I'm more than happy, I'm delighted* estoy más que contento, estoy encantado || *to be no more* haber dejado de existir (to exist no longer), haber fallecido (to be dead) || *to have more than achieved sth.* haber cumplido algo con creces.
◆ *n* más; *Peter asked for more* Pedro pidió más; *more than expected* más de lo esperado; *would you like some more?* ¿quieres más? || — *and what is more* y lo que es más, y además || *I hope to see more of you* espero volverle a ver (to meet again), espero verle más a menudo (to meet more often) || *many failed but more succeeded* muchos fracasaron pero más aún triunfaron || *much of his work is good, but more is terrible* gran parte de su obra es buena, pero la mayor parte es infame || *that's more than enough* es más que suficiente || *the more the merrier* cuanto más mejor || *to be no more than* no ser más que; *he is no more than a child* no es más que un niño.

moreish ['mɔːriʃ] *adj* FAM apetitoso, sa (food).

morel [mɔ'rel] *n* BOT cagarria *f*, morilla *f* (mushroom) | hierba *f* mora (nightshade).

morello [mə'reləu] *n* BOT guinda *f* (cherry).

moreover [mɔː'rəuvə*] *adj* además, por otra parte.

mores ['mɔːriz] *pl n* costumbres *f*, usos *m*, tradiciones *f*.

Moresque [mɔ'ːresk] *adj* árabe (art, architecture).

morganatic [ˌmɔːgə'nætik] *adj* morganático, ca.

morgue [mɔːg] *n* depósito *m* de cadáveres (mortuary) || US archivos *m pl* (of a newspaper).

moribund ['mɔribʌnd] *adj* moribundo, da.

morion ['mɔːriən] *n* morrión *m*.

Morisco [məu'riskəu] *adj/n* morisco, ca.
— OBSERV El plural de la palabra inglesa es *Moriscos* o *Moriscoes*.

Mormon ['mɔːmən] *adj* REL mormónico, ca.
◆ *n* REL mormón, ona.

Mormonism [-izəm] *n* REL mormonismo *m*.

morn [mɔːn] *n* POET mañana *f* (morning) | alborada *f* (dawn).

morning ['mɔːniŋ] *adj* matutino, na; de la mañana (breeze) || del alba (star) || *morning paper* diario *m* de la mañana.
◆ *n* mañana *f*; *in the morning* por la mañana; *the following morning* a la mañana siguiente; *at six o'clock in the morning* a las seis de la mañana; *all the morning* la mañana entera, toda la mañana; *tomorrow morning* mañana por la mañana; *this morning* esta mañana || FIG comienzo *m* (beginning) || — *first thing in the morning* por la mañana a primera hora || *good morning* buenos días || *in the grey of the morning* al rayar el día, al despuntar el alba, de madrugada || *morning, noon and night* mañana, tarde y noche || FIG *the morning after* la mañana después de la borrachera || *to get up early in the morning* madrugar, levantarse temprano.

morning-after pill [-ɑːftə* pil] *n* píldora *f* abortiva.

morning coat [-'kəut] *n* chaqué *m*.

morning glory [-'glɔri] *n* BOT maravilla *f*, dondiego *m* de día.

mornings [-z] *adv* por la mañana.

morning sickness [-'siknis] *n* náuseas *f pl* [que se sienten por la mañana].

morning star [-'stɑː*] *n* lucero *m* del alba.

Moroccan [mə'rɔkən] *adj/n* marroquí.

morocco [mə'rɔkəu] *n* marroquí *m*, tafilete *m* (leather).

Morocco [mə'rɔkəu] *pr n* GEOGR Marruecos.

moron ['mɔːrɔn] *n* MED retrasado *m* mental (subnormal) || FAM imbécil *m* & *f*, idiota *m* & *f* (stupid).

moronic [mə'rɔnik] *adj* MED retrasado mental || FAM idiota.

morose [mə'rəus] *adj* malhumorado, da; taciturno, na (gloomy).

morpheme ['mɔːfiːm] *n* GRAMM morfema *m*.

Morpheus ['mɔːfjuːs] *pr n* MYTH Morfeo *m*.

morphia ['mɔːfjə] *n* CHEM morfina *f*.

morphine ['mɔːfiːn] *n* CHEM morfina *f* || *morphine addict* morfinómano, na.

morphinomaniac [mɔːfinə'meiniæk] *n* MED morfinómano, na.

morphologic [ˌmɔːfə'lɔdʒik]; **morphological** [-əl] *adj* morfológico, ca.

morphologist [mɔː'fɔlədʒist] *n* experto *m* en morfología.

morphology [mɔː'fɔlədʒist] *n* morfología *f*.

morphosis [mɔː'fəusis] *n* BIOL morfosis *f*.
— OBSERV El plural de morphosis es *morphoses*.

morrow ['mɔrəu] *n* día *m* siguiente || FIG porvenir *m*, futuro *m* || *on the morrow* al día siguiente, el día después.

Morse code [mɔːskəud] *n* Morse *m*, alfabeto *m* Morse.

morsel ['mɔːsəl] *n* bocado *m* (mouthful) || pedazo *m* (a piece) || poco *m*; *they gave us a morsel to eat* nos dieron un poco de comer || *choice morsel* bocado de cardenal.

mort [mɔːt] *n* toque *f* de muerte (in hunting).

mortadella [ˌmɔːtə'delə] *n* mortadela *f*.

mortal ['mɔːtl] *adj* mortal; *man is mortal* el hombre es mortal; *mortal combat* combate mortal; *mortal hatred* odio mortal; *mortal agony* agonía mortal; *mortal wound* herida mortal; *mortal sin* pecado mortal; *mortal remains* restos mortales || humano, na (of a man) || FIG mortal (tedious); *the film was mortal* la película era mortal | terrible (extreme); *mortal fear* miedo terrible || FIG *it's no mortal good to anyone* no es nada bueno para nadie.
◆ *n* mortal *m*, ser *m* mortal; *a happy mortal* un feliz mortal || FAM individuo *m*, tipo *m*.

mortality [mɔː'tæliti] *n* mortalidad *f* (mortal nature, death rate); *infantile mortality* mortalidad infantil || mortandad *f* (death); *heavy mortality* gran mortandad || mortales *m pl*, humanidad *f* (mankind) || — *mortality rate* tasa *f* de mortalidad || *mortality tables* tablas *f* de mortalidad.

mortally ['mɔːtəli] *adv* mortalmente; *mortally wounded* mortalmente herido || FIG mortalmente (grievously) | terriblemente (very).

mortar ['mɔːtə*] *n* mortero *m*, almirez *m* (recipient) || mortero *m*, argamasa *f* (building material) || MIL mortero *m*.

mortar ['mɔːtə*] *vt* argamasar (in building) || MIL bombardear con morteros.

mortarboard ['mɔːtəbɔːd] *n* birrete *m* (hat) || esparavel *m* (in building).

mortgage ['mɔːgidʒ] *n* hipoteca *f*; *to raise a mortgage* hacer una hipoteca; *to pay off a mortgage* levantar una hipoteca || — *mortgage bank* banco hipotecario || *mortgage credit, deed, loan* crédito, contrato, préstamo hipotecario.

mortgage ['mɔːgidʒ] *vt* hipotecar (property) || FIG hipotecar, empeñar; *to mortgage one's independence* hipotecar su independencia.

mortgageable [-əbl] *adj* hipotecable.

mortgagee ['mɔːgə'dʒiː] *n* acreedor *m* hipotecario.

mortgager; mortgagor [ˌmɔːgə'dʒɔː*] *n* deudor *m* hipotecario.

mortice ['mɔːtis] *n/vt* → **mortise.**

mortician [mɔː'tiʃən] *n* empresario *m* de pompas fúnebres (undertaker).

mortification [ˌmɔːtifi'keiʃən] *n* mortificación *f* || MED gangrena *f*.

mortify ['mɔːtifai] *vt* mortificar || MED gangrenar.
◆ *vi* mortificarse || MED gangrenarse.

mortifying [-iŋ] *adj* mortificador, ra; mortificante.

mortise; mortice ['mɔːtis] *n* muesca *f*, mortaja *f*, escopleadura *f* || — *mortise gauge* gramil *m* || *mortise lock* cerradura *f* de mortaja.

mortise; mortice ['mɔːtis] *vt* escoplear, hacer muesca en (to cut a mortise in) || ensamblar a espiga (to fasten).

mortmain ['mɔːtmein] *n* JUR manos *f pl* muertas.

mortuary ['mɔːtjuəri] *adj* mortuorio, ria.
◆ *n* depósito *m* de cadáveres (morgue).

mosaic [məu'zeiik] *adj* de mosaico; *mosaic floor* suelo de mosaico.
◆ *n* mosaico *m* (floor, wall, etc.) || AVIAT aerofotografía *f* || FIG mosaico *m*.

Mosaic [məu'zeiik] *adj* mosaico, ca (of Moses).

Moscow ['mɔskəu] *pr n* GEOGR Moscú.

Moses ['məuziz] *pr n* Moisés *m* || *Moses basket* moisés *m* (of a baby).

mosey ['məuzi] *vi* US deambular (to stroll) | irse (to go away).

Moslem ['mɔzlem] *adj/n* musulmán, ana.

Moslemism [-izəm] *n* religión *f* musulmana.

mosque [mɔsk] *n* mezquita *f*.

mosquito [məs'ki:təu] *n* mosquito *m* (insect); *mosquito bite* picadura de mosquito.

— OBSERV El plural de la palabra inglesa *mosquito* es *mosquitoes* o *mosquitos*.

mosquito boat [-bəut] *n* lancha *f* torpedera.

mosquito curtain [-,kə:tn]; **mosquito net** [-net] *n* mosquitero *m*.

moss [mɔs] *n* BOT musgo *m* || pantano *m* (bog).

moss [mɔs] *vt* cubrir con musgo.

mossback [-bæk] *n* US FAM retrógrado, da.

moss-grown [-grən] *adj* musgoso, sa (covered with moss) || FAM anticuado, da.

moss-trooper [-'tru:pə*] *n* bandido *m*, bandolero *m* (royalist freebooter).

mossy ['mɔsi] *adj* cubierto de musgo, musgoso, sa.

most [məust] *adj* más; *who has most books?* ¿quién tiene más libros?; *they are the most beautiful girls I've ever seen* son las chicas más guapas que he visto en mi vida || la mayoría de, la mayor parte de; *in most cases* en la mayoría de los casos; *most people like the sun* a la mayoría de la gente le gusta el sol || *for the most part* en su mayor parte; por lo general (generally).

◆ *adv* más; *he is the most intelligent* es el más inteligente; *which do you like most?* ¿cuál es el que más te gusta? || de lo más, sumamente, muy (very); *the play was most amusing* la obra fue de lo más entretenida || US FAM casi (almost) || — *most likely* muy probablemente || *most of all* sobre todo.

◆ *n* la mayoría; *most were in agreement* la mayoría estaba de acuerdo || la mayor parte; *most of the country is forest* la mayor parte del país es bosque || lo máximo, lo más; *that's the most I can pay* esto es lo máximo que puedo pagar || — *at most, at the most* a lo más, a lo sumo, como máximo || *the very most* lo más que || *to make the most of* sacar el mayor provecho de *or* el mayor partido de, aprovechar al máximo.

— OBSERV *Most* se emplea en la formación del superlativo de los adjetivos polisílabos y del superlativo relativo. Se utiliza igualmente como superlativo de *much* y de *many*. Sin embargo *most* no debe emplearse cuando existe una comparación entre dos elementos, así no hay que decir *of those two men, John is the most intelligent* sino *the more intelligent*.

Most High [-hai] *n* Altísimo *m* (God).

mostly [-li] *adv* principalmente, sobre todo (chiefly); *they are found mostly in the South* se encuentran principalmente en el Sur || la mayoría de las veces, casi siempre, generalmente (in the main) || en su mayor parte (for the most part).

mot [məu] *n* ocurrencia *f*, agudeza *f* (witticism) || *mot juste* palabra adecuada.

MOT *abbr of [Ministry of Transport]* ministerio británico de transportes || *abbr of [Ministry of Transport test]* inspección técnica oficial de vehículos.

mote [məut] *n* mota *f* (spot, speck) || FIG *to see the mote in another's eye and not the beam in one's own* ver la paja en el ojo ajeno y no la viga en el propio.

motel [məu'tel] *n* motel *m*.

motet [məu'tet] *n* MUS motete *m*.

moth [mɔθ] *n* ZOOL mariposa *f* [nocturna] | polilla *f* (in clothes).

mothball [-bɔ:l] *n* bola *f* de naftalina.

moth-eaten [-,i:tn] *adj* apolillado, da || FIG anticuado, da (outdated).

mother ['mʌðə*] *n* madre *f* (parent) || REL madre *f* || CULIN madre *f*; *mother of vinegar* madre del vinagre || FIG madre; *Greece, mother of democracy* Grecia, madre de la democracia || — *every mother's son* todo quisque, todo hijo de vecino || *foster mother* madre adoptiva || *Queen Mother* reina madre.

◆ *adj* materno, na (love) || madre (country) | matriz (church) || materno, na (tongue).

mother ['mʌðə*] *vt* dar a luz (to give birth) || servir de madre a (to act as mother) || FIG concebir | reconocerse autor de || cuidar como una madre, cuidar como a un hijo (to care for) || mimar (to spoil).

motherboard [-bɔ:d] *n* INFORM placa *f* madre, tarjeta *f* madre.

Mother Church [-'tʃə:tʃ] *n* REL Santa Madre Iglesia *f*.

mother country [-,kʌntri] *n* madre patria *f*.

motherhood [-hud] *n* maternidad *f*.

mother-in-law [-inlɔ:] *n* suegra *f*, madre *f* política.

— OBSERV El plural de *mother-in-law* es *mothers-in-law*.

motherland [-lənd] *n* madre patria *f*.

motherless [-lis] *adj* huérfano de madre, sin madre.

motherliness [-linis] *n* cariño maternal, sentimientos *m pl* maternales.

motherly [-li] *adj* maternal.

◆ *adv* maternalmente.

mother-of-pearl [-əv'pə:l] *adj* nacarado, da.

◆ *n* madreperla *f*, nácar *m*.

mother's boy ['mʌðəzbɔi] *n* hijo *m* de su mamá.

Mother's Day ['mʌðəzdei] *n* día *f* de la Madre.

mother ship ['mʌðəʃip] *n* buque *m* nodriza.

mother superior [-sju'piəriə*] *n* superiora *f*, madre *f* superiora.

mother-to-be ['mʌðətə'bi:] *n* futura madre *f*.

mother tongue [-tʌŋ] *n* lengua *f* materna (native language) || lengua *f* madre (from which others are derived).

mother wit [-'wit] *n* sentido *m* común.

moth hole ['mɔθhəul] *n* picadura *f* de polilla.

moth killer ['mɔθ,kilə*] *n* matapolillas *m inv*.

mothy ['mɔθi] *adj* lleno de polillas (infested with moths) || apolillado, da (moth-eaten).

motif [məu'ti:f] *n* MUS & ARTS motivo *m* || tema *m* (main subject).

motile ['məutail] *adj* BIOL movible, móvil.

motility [məu'tiliti] *n* BIOL motilidad *f*, movilidad *f*.

motion ['məuʃən] *n* movimiento *m*; *all her motions are clumsy* todos sus movimientos son torpes || señas *f pl*, gesto *m*, señal *f* (signal); *to make motion to* hacer señas a || ademán *m*; *he made motion to get up* hizo ademán de levantarse || marcha *f*; *to be in motion* estar en marcha; *to set in motion* poner en marcha || movimiento *m* (of a clock) || mecanismo *m* (of a machine) || moción *f* (in an assembly); *censure motion* moción de censura; *to second a motion* apoyar una moción; *the motion is carried by 20 votes to 7 with 3 abstentions* queda aprobada la moción por 20 votos a favor, 7 en contra y 3 abstenciones; *the motion is rejected* o *lost* se rechaza la moción || MUS cambio *m* de tono || MED deposición *f*, evacuación *f* del vientre, deyección *f* || JUR pedimento *m* || — PHYS *in motion* en movimiento || *motion camera* cámara *f* tomavistas || *motion picture* película *f* || *motion pictures* cine *m* || *perpetual motion* movimiento perpetuo || *substantive motion* moción sobre el fondo de la cuestión || *to bring forward a motion* presentar una moción || *to carry a motion* aprobar una moción || *to declare a motion receivable* declarar una moción admisible || *to go through the motions* hacer algo como es debido || *to table a motion* presentar una moción (to propose), aplazar una moción sine die (to postpone) || *to vote on a motion* votar una moción || *would this motion be in order?* ¿se puede aceptar esta moción?

motion ['məuʃən] *vt* indicar con la mano; *he motioned me to come forward* me indicó con la mano que avanzara.

◆ *vi* hacer señas *or* una señal.

motionless [-lis] *adj* inmóvil || *to remain motionless* no moverse, permanecer inmóvil.

motivate ['məutiveit] *vt* motivar.

motivation [,məuti'veiʃən] *n* motivo *m*, motivación *f*.

motive ['məutiv] *adj* motor, motriz; *motive power* fuerza motriz || PHYS cinético, ca (energy).

◆ *n* motivo *m* (reason); *hidden motives* motivos ocultos || móvil *m*; *the motive of a crime* el móvil de un crimen || ARTS motivo *m* || *profit motive* afán *m* de lucro.

motivity [məu'tiviti] *n* movilidad *f* || TECH energía *f* cinética | fuerza *f* motriz (motive power).

motley ['mɔtli] *adj* abigarrado, da; multicolor; *a motley crowd* una multitud abigarrada || vario, ria; variado, da; diversificado, da (heterogeneous).

◆ *n* botarga *f* (costume) || mezcla *f* abigarrada de colores || FIG revoltijo *m*, mezcolanza *f* (incongruous mixture).

moto-cross ['məutəkrɔs] *n* motocross *m*.

motor ['məutə*] *n* motor *m*; *electric motor* motor eléctrico || coche *m*, automóvil *m* (car).

◆ *pl* acciones *f* [de fábricas de automóviles] (securities).

◆ *adj* motor, motriz || de motor, impulsado por un motor (motor-driven) || ANAT motor, ra.

motor ['məutə*] *vi* ir *or* viajar en coche.

motor bicycle [-,baisikl] *n* motocicleta *f* || US velomotor *m*.

motorbike [-baik] *n* motocicleta *f*, moto *f* || US velomotor *m*.

motorboat [-bəut] *n* motora *f*, lancha *f* motora.

motor bus [-bʌs] *n* autobús *m*.

motorcade [-keid] *n* caravana *f or* desfile *m* de automóviles.

motorcar [-kɑ:*] *n* automóvil *m*, coche *m* (car).

motor coach [-kəutʃ] *n* autocar *m*.

motorcycle [-,saikl] *n* motocicleta *f*, moto *f*.

motorcycling [-,saikliŋ] *n* motorismo *m*, motociclismo *m*.

motorcyclist [-,saiklist] *n* motorista *m* & *f*, motociclista *m* & *f*.

motor-driven [-drivn] *adj* impulsado por un motor.

motordrome [-drəum] *n* autódromo *m*.

motor fuel [-fjuəl] *n* carburante *m*.

motor generator [-'dʒenəreitə*] *n* ELECTR grupo *m* convertidor.

motoring [-riŋ] *n* automovilismo *m* || *school of motoring, motoring school* autoescuela *f*.

◆ *adj* de automóvil, automovilístico, ca.

motorist [-rist] *n* automovilista *m* & *f* || conductor, ra (driver) || *racing motorist* corredor *m* de coches.

motorization [ˌməutərai'zeiʃən] *n* motorización *f*.

motorize ['məutəraiz] *vt* motorizar.

motorized [-d] *adj* motorizado, da || *motorized farming* motocultivo *m*.

motor launch ['məutəlɔːntʃ] *n* lancha *f* motora.

motorless ['məutəlis] *adj* sin motor (plane).

motor lorry ['məutəˌlɔri] *n* camión *m*.

motorman ['məutəmən] *n* US conductor *m*, maquinista *m* (of trains) | conductor *m* (of tram).

— OBSERV El plural de *motorman* es *motormen*.

motor propellor ['məutəprə'pelə*] *n* TECH motopropulsor *m*.

motor pump ['məutəpʌmp] *n* motobomba *f*.

motor sailer ['məutəˌseilə*] *n* motovelero *m*.

motor scooter ['məutəˌskuːtə*] *n* scooter *m*.

motor scythe ['məutəsaið] *n* AGR motosegadora *f*.

motor ship ['məutəʃip] *n* motonave *f*.

motor show ['məutəʃəu] *n* salón *m* del automóvil.

motor tractor ['məutə'træktə*] *n* mototractor *m*.

motor truck ['məutətrʌk] *n* US camión *m*.

motorway ['məutəwei] *n* autopista *f*.

mottle ['mɔtl] *n* mancha *f* or veta *f* de color (spot) || superficie *f* abigarrada.

mottle ['mɔtl] *vt* abigarrar || motear, jaspear.

mottled [-d] *adj* abigarrado, da || veteado, da; jaspeado, da (grained) || de mezclilla, de varios colores (cloth) || con manchas (skin) || moteado, da (animal).

motto ['mɔtəu] *n* lema *m* || HERALD divisa *f*, lema *m* || epígrafe *m* (in a literary work) || MUS tema *m*, motivo *m* || consigna *f*, santo y seña *m* (watchword) || máxima *f* (maxim).

— OBSERV El plural de *motto* es *mottoes* o *mottos*.

moue [muː] *n* mueca *f*.

mouflon; moufflon ['muːflɔn] *n* musmón *m* (animal).

mouillé [muː'jei] *adj* GRAMM palatalizado, da; palatal.

moujik ['muːʒik] *n* mujic *m*.

moulage ['muːlɑːʒ] *n* molde *m* (plaster mould).

mould [məuld] *n* molde *m* (hollow container) || pieza *f* moldeada || CULIN molde *m* || ARCH moldura *f* || matriz *f* (in printing) || MAR gálibo *m*, vitola *f* || modelo *m*, patrón *m*, plantilla *f* (pattern) || forma *f* (shape) || FIG temple *m*, carácter *m*; *a man cast in a heroic mould* un hombre de temple heroico || AGR mantillo *m* (vegetable matter) || moho *m* (fungus) || ANAT fontanela *f* || FIG *cast in the same mould* cortado con el mismo patrón.

mould [məuld] *vt* moldear (to shape) || moldear, vaciar (statues) || ceñir; *dress which moulds the body* traje que ciñe el cuerpo || FIG formar, moldear (one's character) | amoldar (*on* a, según) (to adapt) || ARCH moldurar || FIG *to mould o.s. on s.o.* tomar como modelo a alguien.

◆ *vi* enmohecerse (to go mouldy).

mouldable [-əbl] *adj* moldeable.

mouldboard; US moldboard [-bɔːd] *n* vertedera *f* del arado.

moulder [-ə*] *n* moldeador, ra.

moulder [-ə*] *vi* desmoronarse.

mouldiness [-inis] *n* enmohecimiento *m*, estado *m* mohoso.

moulding; US molding [-iŋ] *n* moldeado *m*, moldeamiento *m* (action) || vaciado *m* (of statues) || ARCH moldura *f* || ELECTR junquillo *m*, moldura *f* || FIG formación *f* (formation).

mouldy; US moldy [-i] *adj* mohoso, sa; enmohecido, da (covered with mould) || FAM anticuado, da (old-fashioned) | aburrido, da (boring) | fatal (very bad) | cochino, na (disreputable).

moult [məult] *n* muda *f*.

moult [məult] *vt* mudar.

◆ *vi* mudar la piel (a snake) or las plumas (a bird).

mound [maund] *n* montón *m* (heap) || montículo *m* (small hill) || terraplén *m* (artificial bank of earth) || túmulo *m* (over a grave) || HERALD globo *m*, mundo *m* || US SP elevación *f*, altura *f*, montículo *m* [donde se pone el lanzador en béisbol].

mound [maund] *vt* amontonar (to heap up) || terraplenar (to build up a bank).

mount [maunt] *n* GEOGR monte *m* (mountain) || montículo *m* (hillock) || montura *f*, cabalgadura *f* (horse) || engaste *m*, montura *f* (of jewels) || soporte *m*, base *f* (support, base) || fondo *m* (of a drawing, etc.) || borde *m* (of photo) || portaobjeto *m* (of a microscope) || fijasellos *m inv* (for stamps) || MIL cureña *f* (of cannon).

mount [maunt] *vi* subir (to climb) || montar a caballo (on a horse) || aumentar (to increase) || *to mount up to* elevarse hasta.

◆ *vt* subir (to climb) || subir a (a table, a throne) || montar a, subirse a (a horse) || subir a, montar en (bicycle) || proveer de caballo or caballos (to equip with horses) || ayudar a subir a caballo || montar, armar (an engine) || montar (a picture, a statue, a play, an exhibition, etc.) || engastar, montar (a jewel) || fijar, pegar (stamps) || MAR & MIL montar (guns) | estar armado con (to be armed with) || — MIL *to mount an offensive* lanzar or efectuar una ofensiva || *to mount the guard* montar la guardia.

mountain ['mauntin] *n* montaña *f* || FIG montón *m*; *a mountain of debts* un montón de deudas || FIG *to make a mountain out of a molehill* hacerse de todo una montaña.

◆ *adj* montañoso, sa (mountainous) || montañés, esa (people, costumes) || de montaña; *mountain artillery* artillería de montaña.

mountain ash [-'æʃ] *n* BOT serbal *m*.

mountain cat [-kæt] *n* ZOOL puma *m* (cougar) | lince *m* | gato *m* montañés (wildcat).

mountain chain [-tʃein] *n* cordillera *f*, sierra *f*.

mountain climber [-ˌklaimə*] *n* montañero, ra; alpinista *m* & *f* [AMER andinista *m* & *f*].

mountain climbing [-ˌklaimiŋ] *n* montañismo *m*, alpinismo *m* [AMER andinismo *m*].

mountain dew [-'djuː] *n* FAM whisky *m* [de contrabando].

mountain dweller [-ˌdwelə*] *n* montañés, esa.

mountaineer [ˌmaunti'niə*] *n* montañero, ra; alpinista *m* & *f* [AMER andinista *m* & *f*] (mountain climber) || montañés, esa; serrano, na (dweller).

mountaineer [ˌmaunti'niə*] *vi* hacer alpinismo, escalar montañas.

mountaineering [-riŋ] *n* montañismo *m*, alpinismo *m* [AMER andinismo *m*] || *mountaineering school* escuela *f* de montañismo.

mountain goat [-gəut] *n* ZOOL cabra *f* de las Montañas Rocosas.

mountain lion [-'laiən] *n* ZOOL puma *m*.

mountainous ['mauntinəs] *adj* montañoso, sa || FIG enorme, monumental.

mountain range ['mauntinreindʒ] *n* cordillera *f*, sierra *f*.

mountain sheep [-ʃiːp] *n* ZOOL musmón *f* de las Montañas Rocosas.

mountain sickness [-'siknis] *n* mal *m* de montaña [AMER soroche *m*, puna *f*].

mountainside ['mauntinˌsaid] *n* falda *f* or ladera *f* de montaña.

mountaintop ['mauntinˌtɔp] *n* cumbre *f* or cima *f* de una montaña.

mountebank ['mauntibæŋk] *n* saltimbanqui *m* || FIG charlatán *m* (quack).

mounted police ['məuntidpə'lis] *n* policía *m* montada.

mounter ['mauntə*] *n* montador, ra.

Mountie ['maunti] *n* FAM miembro *m* de la policía montada canadiense.

mounting ['mauntiŋ] *n* subida *f* (climbing) || engaste *m*, montura *f* (of jewels) || fondo *m* (of drawing, etc.) || soporte *m*, base *m* (support) || THEATR & CINEM montaje *m* || TECH montaje *m*.

mounting block [-blɔk] *n* montador *m*.

Mounty ['maunti] *n* FAM miembro *m* de la policía montada canadiense.

mourn ['mɔːn] *vt* llorar (la muerte de) || lamentar (to lament) || llevar luto por (to wear mourning for).

◆ *vi* estar de luto (to be in mourning) || lamentarse || *to mourn for* llorar la muerte de (the death of), deplorar, lamentar (a loss).

mourner [-ə*] *n* persona *f* que está de luto (person in mourning) || acompañante *m* & *f*, doliente *m* & *f* (at a funeral) || plañidera *f* (hired mourner) || *chief mourner* el que preside un entierro.

mournful [-ful] *adj* triste, lúgubre (sad) || afligido, da (grieved).

mournfulness [-fulnis] *n* tristeza *f*.

mourning [-iŋ] *n* luto *m*, duelo *m* (period) || luto *m* (clothes) || aflicción *f*, tristeza *f* (sadness) || — *deep mourning* luto riguroso || *half mourning* medio luto || *house of mourning* casa mortuoria || *mourning band* brazalete *m* || *mourning dress* traje *m* de luto || *to be in mourning* estar de luto || *to be in mourning for* llevar luto por || *to come out of deep mourning* aliviar el luto || *to come out of mourning* dejar or quitarse el luto || *to go into mourning* ponerse or vestirse de luto.

◆ *adj* de luto.

moussaka [mu'sɑːkə] *n* CULIN mousaka *f*.

mouse [maus] *n* ZOOL ratón *m* || FIG tímido, da (shy person) | cobarde *m* & *f* (coward) || MAR trinca *f* (of a hook) | barrilete *m* (knot) || US FAM ojo *m* a la funerala.

— OBSERV El plural de *mouse* es *mice*.

mouse [maus] *vi* cazar ratones || INFORM ratón *m* || FAM *to mouse about* fisgar.

mouse-ear [-iə*] *n* BOT oreja *f* de ratón.

mousehole [-həul] *n* ratonera *f*.

mouser ['mauzə*] *n* gato *m* cazador de ratones.

mousetrap ['maustræp] *n* ratonera *f*.

mousey ['mausi] *adj* → **mousy**.

mousse [muːs] *n* CULIN crema *f* batida; *chocolate mousse* crema batida de chocolate.

moustache [məs'tɑːʃ] *n* bigote *m*, bigotes *m pl*.

Mousterian [ˌmuːs'tiəriən] *adj* GEOL musteriense.

mousy; mously ['mausi] *adj* ratonesco, ca; ratonil || lleno de ratones (infested with mice)

|| FAM pardusco, ca (colour) || FIG tímido, da (shy) | silencioso, sa (quiet).

mouth [mauθ] *n* ANAT boca *f*; *I've got a bad taste in my mouth* tengo mal sabor de boca || abertura *f* (of a tube, etc.) || desembocadura *f*, bocas *f pl* (of a river) || entrada *f*; *he stopped at the mouth of the cave* se detuvo a la entrada de la cueva || MUS boquilla *f*, boca *f* (of an instrument) || boca *f*, abertura *f* (of an oven, sewer, well, etc.) || boca *f* (of a pitcher, of a volcano) || tragante *m* (of a blast furnace) || gollete *m* (of a bottle) || mueca *f*, gesto *m* (grimace) || — FIG *by word of mouth* de viva voz | *from mouth to mouth* de boca en boca | *I've got seven mouths to feed* tengo siete bocas que alimentar | *never look a gift horse in the mouth* a caballo regalado no le mires el diente | *not to open one's mouth* no abrir *or* no descoser la boca || FAM *shut your mouth!* ¡a callarse la boca! || FIG *to be down in the mouth* estar deprimido, estar cariacontecido *or* cabizbajo | *to foam at the mouth* echar espumarajos por la boca (with anger) | *to get sth. straight from the horse's mouth* saber algo de buena tinta | *to give mouth to* expresar || FAM *to have a big mouth* ser un bocazas || FIG *to keep one's mouth shut* no decir esta boca es mía | *to live from hand to mouth* vivir al día | *to look down in the mouth* estar con la cara larga | *to make one's mouth water* hacérsele (a uno) la boca agua | *to put words into s.o.'s mouth* poner palabras en boca de uno | *to shoot one's mouth off* hablar más de la cuenta | *to stop s.o.'s mouth* cerrar el pico a uno | *to take the words right out of s.o.'s mouth* quitarle a uno las palabras de la boca.

mouth [mauð] *vt* articular (to form with the lips) || pronunciar con afectación (to say in an affected manner) || proferir (insults) || acostumbrar al bocado (a horse) || tomar *or* coger en la boca (to take into the mouth).
◆ *vi* hablar con rimbombancia || hacer una mueca (to grimace).

mouth-filling ['mauθ,filiŋ] *adj* rimbombante (bombastic).

mouthful ['mauθful] *n* bocado *m* (eating) || bocanada *f* (of air, of smoke, etc.) || US FAM *you've said a mouthful!* ¡así se habla!, ¡muy bien dicho!

mouth organ ['mauθ,ɔːgən] *n* MUS armónica *f*.

mouthpiece ['mauθpiːs] *n* MUS boquilla *f* || micrófono *m* (of a telephone) || boquilla *f* (of a pipe) || FIG portavoz *m* [*AMER* vocero *m*] (spokesman).

mouth-to-mouth respiration ['mauθtə'mauθ,respə'reiʃən] *n* boca a boca *m*.

mouthwash ['mauθwɔʃ] *n* enjuague *m*.

mouth-watering ['mauθ,wɔːtəriŋ] *adj* muy apetitoso, sa; que hace la boca agua.

mouthy ['mauði] *adj* rimbombante (bombastic).

movability [,muːvə'biliti]; **movableness** ['muːvəblnis] *n* movilidad *f*.

movable; moveable ['muːvəbl] *adj* movible, móvil || móvil; *movable feast* fiesta móvil || desmontable (detachable) || JUR mobiliario, ria (effects) | mueble (property).
◆ *pl n* muebles *m* (furniture) || JUR bienes *m* muebles.

move [muːv] *n* FIG paso *m*; *he made the first move towards peace* dio el primer paso hacia la paz; *false move* paso en falso | marcha *f*; *Mexico is a nation on the move* México es una nación en marcha | medida *f*, gestión *f*, acción *f*; *that was a wasted move* fue una gestión inútil | maniobra *f* (manoeuvre) || movimiento *m* (movement); *she made a move towards the door* hizo un movimiento hacia la puerta || mudanza *f* (of house) || traslado *m* (of person) || jugada *f* (in chess, etc.); *mate in four moves* mate en cuatro jugadas || turno *m*, vez *f* (turn) || — *a wise move* una buena jugada, una buena maniobra || *don't make a move!* ¡no se mueva! || FAM *get a move on!* ¡date prisa!, ¡apresúrate! (be quick), ¡menéate!, ¡muévete! (do sth.) || *it is your move* tú juegas, te toca a ti || FAM *to be always on the move* no parar ni un momento, estar siempre moviéndose || *to be on the move* estar de acá para allá (to be moving), estar en camino (on the way), estar en movimiento (in motion), estar de viaje (travelling) || *to be up to every move* sabérselas todas || *to get a move on* darse prisa, apresurarse || *to have been on the move all day* no haber parado en todo el día || *to have first move* salir (in games) || FIG *to know every move in the game* sabérselas todas || *to make a move* dar un paso (to take a step), tomar medidas (to take action), ponerse en marcha (to get started), irse (to go), levantarse (to stand up), jugar, hacer una jugada (in games) || FAM *to make s.o. get a move on* dar *or* meter prisa a uno | *we must be on the move* hay que irse || *what's the next move?* ¿qué hacemos ahora? || *whose move is it?* ¿quién juega?, ¿a quién le toca?

move [muːv] *vt* cambiar de; *to move one's position* cambiar de lugar; *he moved his job* cambió de empleo || cambiar de sitio, trasladar; *let's move the table* vamos a cambiar la mesa de sitio || mudarse de; *to move house* mudarse de casa || mover, menear (head, arm, etc.) || mover; *the wind moved the leaves* el viento movía las hojas || trasladar (from one place to another) || transportar (to transport) || trasladar; *to move an official* trasladar a un funcionario || mover, poner en movimiento *or* en marcha (to set in motion) || poner en marcha *or* en funcionamiento (to switch on) || mover, accionar; *moved by electricity* accionado eléctricamente || remover (to stir up) || sacudir, menear (to shake) || mover, jugar (in chess, etc.); *he moved a piece* movió una pieza || propulsar, impeler (to propel) || mover a, incitar a, inducir a; *he moved me to speak* me indujo a que hablara || emocionar, conmover, afectar; *these demonstrations move me very little* esas demostraciones me conmueven muy poco; *much moved by the news* muy afectado por las noticias || hacer cambiar de parecer; *nothing will move me* nada me hará cambiar de parecer || proponer; *I move that the meeting be postponed* propongo que se aplace la reunión || COMM vender || exonerar (the bowels) || — *easily moved* muy emocionable || *moved with anger* movido por la cólera || FIG *not to move hand or foot* no moverse, no mover un dedo || *to move a proposal* hacer *or* formular una propuesta || FIG *to move s.o.'s heart* conmover el corazón de alguien || *to move s.o. to anger* provocar la cólera de uno || *to move s.o. to laughter* hacer reír a alguien || *to move s.o. to pity* mover a uno a compasión || *to move s.o. to tears* hacer llorar a uno || *when the spirit moves one* cuando le venga a uno en gana.
◆ *vi* moverse; *don't move!* ¡no te muevas!; *I can't move* no puedo moverme; *stop moving* deja de moverte; *the Earth moves round the Sun* la Tierra se mueve alrededor del Sol || trasladarse (from one place to another) || cambiarse; *I am going to move to another seat* me voy a cambiar de sitio || andar (to walk) || estar en movimiento (to be moving) || circular; *the crowd moving in the street* la muchedumbre que circula por la calle || ir; *to move at high speed* ir a gran velocidad; *things are moving slowly* las cosas van lentamente || irse, marcharse (to go); *it is time we were moving* ya es hora de marcharnos || cubrir, hacer; *I moved 600 kilometres that day* hice seiscientos kilómetros aquel día || mudarse; *last year we moved into town* el año pasado nos mudamos a la ciudad || mudar de casa (to move house) || hacer una jugada, jugar (in games) || tocar jugar, jugar; *who moves next?* ¿a quién le toca jugar ahora?, ¿quién juega ahora? || moverse (chess pieces) || moverse, menearse (to shake) || hacer progresos, adelantar (to progress) || dar un paso (to take steps) || hacer gestiones, tomar medidas (to take action) || ponerse en marcha (to start up) || funcionar; *this machine moves by hand* esta máquina funciona a mano || venderse bien (to sell well) || — *keep moving!* ¡circulen! || *this article is not moving* este artículo tiene mala salida *or* es de difícil venta || *to keep the traffic moving* mantener una circulación fluida || *to move for* proponer; *I move for a postponement of the meeting* propongo un aplazamiento de la reunión || *to move freely* tener juego *or* holgura (a part) || *to move one step* dar un paso.
◆ *phr v* ***to move about*** cambiar de sitio; *when I arrived they were moving the furniture about* cuando llegué estaban cambiando los muebles de sitio | moverse (to be in motion) | ir y venir (to come and go) || — *to move about freely* circular libremente || ***to move along*** hacer circular | circular; *move along!* ¡circulen! | avanzar (to go forward) || ***to move aside*** poner a un lado (sth.), ponerse a un lado || ***to move away*** alejar, apartar (sth.) | alejarse, apartarse || ***to move back*** hacer retroceder | retroceder (to go backwards) | echarse para atrás (to stand back) || ***to move down*** bajar || ***to move forward*** avanzar | hacer avanzar, hacer progresar (to help progress) | adelantar (a meeting) || ***to move in*** instalarse (into a house) | entrar (to enter) || — *to move in high society* alternar con la alta sociedad || ***to move off*** alejarse (to go away) | ponerse en camino (to set off) | irse (to go) | salir (a train) || ***to move on*** hacer circular (a crowd) | circular; *to make the crowd move on* hacer circular la muchedumbre; *move on!* ¡circulen! | seguir su camino (to continue on one's way) | avanzar (to go forward) | pasar, transcurrir (the time) | irse, marcharse (to go) || ***to move over*** cambiar de sistema (to transfer) | ceder el puesto (to step aside) | dejar sitio, hacerse a un lado (to budge up) || ***to move out*** sacar (to take out) | echar (to throw out) | mudar (furniture) | irse (to leave) | mudarse, mudar de casa (to change one's residence) || ***to move up*** subir (to make go up) | correr (to take out of the way) | adelantar (a date) | subir (to go up) | correrse (to make room) | ser ascendido (to be promoted) || — *to be moved up* cambiarse a la clase superior (in school).

moveability [,muːvə'biliti]; **moveableness** ['muːvəblnis] *n* movilidad *f*.

moveable ['muːvəbl] *adj* → **movable.**

movement ['muːvmənt] *n* movimiento *m*; *the movement of the waves* el movimiento de las olas; *the separatist movement* el movimiento separatista || gesto *m*, ademán *m* (gesture); *he made a movement of impatience* hizo un gesto de impaciencia || acto *m*, acción *f* (act) || impulso *m* (impulse) || arrebato *m* (of anger) || tendencia *f* (trend) || transporte *m* (transport) || traslado *m* (of goods, of an official) || movimiento *m* (of a person) || tráfico *m*, movimiento *m* (of ships, etc.) || tráfico *m*, circulación *f* (of cars) || MAR & MIL maniobra *f* | movimiento *m* || MUS movimiento *m* (division of a work) | tiempo *m* (tempo) || TECH mecanismo *m* | marcha *f*, funcionamiento *m* (working) | juego *m*, holgura *f* (of a part) || COMM actividad *f* (activity) | variación *f* (of price) || MED evacuación *f* [del vientre] (of the bowels) || *upward movement* movimiento ascendente.
◆ *pl* actividades *f*, idas *f* y venidas.

mover ['muːvə*] *n* motor *m* (moving force) || autor, ra (of a motion) || inspirador, ra; instigador, ra (of a plot, etc.) || US mozo *m* de mudanzas (of furniture).

movie ['muːvi] *n* US película *f* (film) | cine *m* (cinema).
◆ *pl* US cine *m sing*; *to go to the movies* ir al cine.

movie camera [-,kæmərə] *n* cámara *f*, tomavistas *m inv*.

moviegoer [-gəuə*] *n* US aficionado, da al cine.

movie house [-haus] *n* US cine *m*.

movie star [-stɑ:*] *n* US estrella *f* de cine.

moving ['mu:viŋ] *adj* móvil; *a moving target* un blanco móvil || en movimiento (in motion) || en marcha; *moving tram* tranvía en marcha || motriz (force) || motor, ra (driving) || mecánico, ca (staircase) || FIG conmovedor, ra; *a moving story* una historia conmovedora.
◆ *n* movimiento *m* (movement) || traslado *m* || mudanza *f* (of house).

moving picture [-'piktʃə*] *n* película *f* [cinematográfica].

moving sidewalk [-'saidwɔ:k] *n* US pasillo *m* rodante.

moving staircase [-'stɛəkeis]; **moving stairway** [-'stɛəwei] *n* escalera *f* mecánica.

moving van [-væn] *n* camión *m* de mudanzas.

mow [məu] *n* US granero *m*, henil *m* (barn) | montón *m* de heno *or* de gavillas (heap of hay).

mow* [məu] *vt* segar, cortar (grass) || segar (corn) || FIG segar || FIG *they mowed down the enemy with a machine gun* barrieron al enemigo con una ametralladora.
— OBSERV Pret ***mowed***; pp ***mown, mowed***.

mower [-ə*] *n* cortacéspedes *m inv* (for a garden) || AGR segadora *f* (machine) | segador, ra (person).

mowing [-iŋ] *n* siega *f* (reaping) || corte *m* (in the garden) || *mowing machine* segadora *f* (for corn), cortacéspedes *m inv* (for a garden).

mown [məun] *pp* → **mow.**

Mozambique [,məuzæm'bi:k] *pr n* GEOGR Mozambique.

Mozarab [məu'zærəb] *n* mozárabe *m & f*.

Mozarabic [məu'zærəbik] *adj* mozárabe.

mozzetta; mozetta [məu'zetə] *n* muceta *f* (short cape).

MP *abbr of [Member of Parliament]* miembro *m* del Parlamento, diputado *m* || *abbr of [Military Police]* Policía *f* Militar || *abbr of [Mounted Police]* Policía *f* Montada.

Mr ['mistə*] *mister* Sr., señor.

Mrs ['misiz] *mistress* Sra., señora.

ms *abbr of [manuscript]* ms, manuscrito.

MSC *abbr of [Manpower Services Commission]* el instituto de empleo británico.

mu [mju:] *n* my *f* (Greek letter).

much [mʌtʃ] *adj* mucho, cha; *much attention* mucha atención || — *as much courage as* tanto valor como || *how much* cuánto, ta; *how much wine shall I buy?* ¿cuánto vino compro?; *when I think how much time I waste* al pensar cuánto tiempo pierdo || *I don't eat very much fruit* no como mucha fruta || *so much* tanto, ta; *so much money* tanto dinero || *too much* demasiado, da; *too much wine* demasiado vino || *twice as much water* el doble de agua.
◆ *adv* mucho; *do you drink much?* ¿bebes mucho?; *much better* mucho mejor; *it doesn't matter much* no importa mucho; *much more* mucho más || muy (before a past participle); *much annoyed* muy enfadado || con mucho; *it much exceeds my expectations* sobrepasa con mucho mis esperanzas || — *as much as* tanto como; *it is as much your fault as mine* es tanto su culpa como la mía; todo lo que, cuanto; *do as much as you can* haz todo lo que puedas || *as much as to say* como si dijera || *ever so much* muchísimo; *ever so much more intelligent* muchísimo más inteligente || *however much* por mucho que || *how much?* ¿cuánto?; *how much is it?* ¿cuánto vale? || *I don't want two, much less five* no quiero dos y menos aún cinco || *it's as much as I can do to remain awaken* apenas puedo quedarme despierto || *it was as much as I could do not to laugh* poco faltó para que me riese || *much as I should like* por mucho *or* por más que yo quisiera || *much the largest* el más grande con mucho || *much the same* poco más o menos lo mismo || *much the same age* más o menos de la misma edad || *much to my surprise* con gran sorpresa mía || *not much* no mucho, poco || FAM *not much!* ¡ya lo creo!, ¡y cómo! (and how), ¡esto te lo crees tú! (I don't believe you) || *not so much as* ni siquiera (not even) || *not so much... as* no... sino más bien || *so much* tanto, ta; *so much money* tanto dinero; tanto; *so much has been said that...* tanto se ha dicho que... || *so much for that* ?qué le vamos a hacer¿ || *so much so that* tanto que || *so much the better* tanto mejor || *thank you very much* muchas gracias || FAM *that's too much of a good thing!* ¡eso es demasiado! || *too much* demasiado; *it costs too much* cuesta demasiado; de más; *she gave me ten pounds too much* me dio diez libras de más || *very much* muchísimo; *I like it very much* me gusta muchísimo; *very much better* muchísimo mejor; muy; *I am very much pleased* estoy muy contento || *you can't have too much of a good thing* lo que abunda no daña.
◆ *n* mucho; *much remains to be done* queda mucho por hacer; *there is not much to see* no hay mucho que ver || gran parte *f*; *much of the land was flooded* se inundó gran parte del terreno || — *as much* tanto; *as much again* otro tanto; otro tanto; *can you do as much?* ¿puede hacer otro tanto? || *do you see much of one another?* ¿os veis a menudo? || *half as much again* la mitad más || *he's not much of a sportsman* dista mucho de ser un deportista, le falta mucho para ser un deportista, es un deportista de poca entidad *or* de poca categoría || *I don't think much of it* no me parece gran cosa, en mi opinión no vale gran cosa || *I thought as much* ya me lo figuraba, ya me lo imaginaba || FAM *it is not up to much* no vale mucho || *I will say this much for him* diré esto en su favor || *there is not much in him* no vale mucho || *there is not much of it* no hay mucho || *this, that much* tanto como esto, tanto como eso || *to make much of* dar mucha importancia a (to attach importance to), sacar mucho provecho de (to benefit by), tratar muy bien a (a person).

muchness [-nis] *n* magnitud *f* || FAM *it's much of a muchness* viene a ser lo mismo, es poco más o menos lo mismo.

mucillage ['mju:silidʒ] *n* BOT mucílago *m* || US goma *f* de pegar (adhesive).

mucilaginous [,mju:si'lædʒinəs] *adj* mucilaginoso, sa.

muck [mʌk] *n* estiércol *m* (manure) || US mantillo *m* (fertile soil) || suciedad *f* (dirt) || lodo *m* (mud) || FAM porquería *f*, basura *f* || — *it was in a muck* estaba asqueroso *or* sucio || FAM *to make a muck up of* echar a perder.

muck [mʌk] *vt* estercolar (to manure) || FAM ensuciar (to dirty) | echar a perder (to spoil) || — FAM *to muck about* fastidiar (s.o.) | *to muck out* limpiar | *to muck up* ensuciar (to dirty), echar a perder (to spoil).
◆ *vi* FAM *to muck about* perder el tiempo | *to muck about with* manosear, juguetear con (to handle), entretenerse con (to amuse o.s.), estropear, echar a perder (to ruin) | *to muck in with* compartir un alojamiento con.

mucker [-ə*] *n* patán *m* (coarse person) || persona *f* soez (vulgar person) || porrazo *m*, caída *f* (cropper) || *to come a mucker* darse un porrazo, caerse.

muckiness [-inis] *n* suciedad *f*, asquerosidad *f*.

muckrake ['mʌkreik] *vi* descubrir *or* revelar escándalos.

muckraker [-ə*] *n* revelador *m* de escándalos.

muckraking [-iŋ] *n* revelación *f* de escándalos.

muckworm ['mʌkwə:m] *n* gusano *m* del estiércol || FIG avaro, ra (miser).

mucky ['mʌki] *adj* asqueroso, sa; sucio, cia; puerco, ca || *to get mucky* ensuciar.

mucosa [mju:'kəusə] *n* ANAT mucosa *f*.
— OBSERV El plural de la palabra inglesa *mucosa* es *mucosae*, *mucosa* o *mucosas*.

mucosity [mju:'kɔsiti] *n* mucosidad *f*.

mucous ['mju:kəs] *adj* mucoso, sa || *mucous membrane* mucosa *f*.

mucus ['mju:kəs] *n* mucosidad *f*, moco *m*.

mud [mʌd] *n* barro *m*, lodo *m* || fango *m* (thick mud) || cieno *m*, limo *m* (in a river) || lodo *m* (in drilling) || ARCH adobe *m* || FIG cieno *m*, lodo *m*, fango *m* (dirt) || — FIG *his name is mud* tiene muy mala fama || *mud hat* cabaña *f* de barro || *to get stuck in the mud* empantanarse, atascarse en el fango (cart), embarrancarse (ship) || FIG *to sling* o *to throw* o *to fling mud at s.o.* calumniar a alguien, arrastrar a alguien por los suelos.

mud bath [-bɑ:θ] *n* baño *m* de lodo.

muddiness [-inis] *n* fangosidad *f* (of the ground) || turbiedad *f* (of a liquid) || FIG confusión *f*.

muddle ['mʌdl] *n* confusión *f* embrollo *m* (mental confusion) || desorden *m* (disorder) || revoltijo *m*, follón *m*; *a muddle of papers* un revoltijo de papeles || embrollo *m*, lío *m* (mixup); *what a muddle!* ¡qué lío! || — *he was all in a muddle* estaba hecho un lío || *it was a dreadful muddle* era un lío espantoso || *to get into a muddle* embrollarse, enredarse, armarse un lío.

muddle ['mʌdl] *vt* confundir, embrollar || dejar confuso *or* perplejo, aturdir (to daze) || embotar (with drink) || formar un lío con, enredar (to make a mess of) || — *to get muddled* armarse un lío || *to muddle up* confundir, embrollar.
◆ *vi* obrar confusamente *or* sin ton ni son || — *to muddle along* ir tirando || *to muddle through* salir del paso, arreglárselas.

muddlehead [-hed] *n* lioso, sa; persona *f* que lo enreda todo.

muddleheaded [-,hedid] *adj* atontado, da; lioso, sa; despistado, da (person) || confuso, sa (ideas).

muddler ['mʌdlə*] *n* lioso, sa; persona *f* que lo enreda todo || varilla *f* para mezclar cócteles.

muddy ['mʌdi] *adj* fangoso, sa; lleno de barro *or* de lodo; *a muddy path* un sendero fangoso || con cieno, cenagoso, sa (river) || lleno de barro; *your clothes are all muddy* tu ropa está llena de barro || turbio, bia (liquid) || macilento, ta (light) || terroso, sa (complexion) || oscuro, ra (dark) || turbio, bia; confuso, sa (ideas).

muddy ['mʌdi] *vt* manchar de barro || enturbiar (a liquid) || poner de color terroso (the complexion) || turbar (one's mind).
◆ *vi* enturbiarse (a liquid).

Mudejar [mu:'dehɑ*] *adj/n* mudéjar.

mud flat ['mʌdflæt] *n* marisma *f*, terreno *m* bajo que se inunda con la marea alta.

mudguard ['mʌdgɑ:d] *n* guardabarros *m inv* (of a motorcycle, etc.) || guardabarros *m inv*, aleta *f* (of a car).

mudlark ['mʌdlɑ:k] *n* FAM galopín *m* (child).

mudpack ['mʌdpæk] *n* mascarilla *f*.

mudslinging ['mʌd,sliŋiŋ] *n* calumnia *f*, ataque *m* calumnioso.

mud wall ['mʌd'wɔ:l] *n* tapia *f*.

muesli ['mju:zli] *n* CULIN muesli *m*.

muezzin [mu'ezin] *n* almuecín *m*, almuédano *m*, muecín *m*.

muff [mʌf] *n* manguito *m* (for the hands) ‖ SP mala jugada *f*, fallo *m* ‖ FAM chapucería *f* (sth. badly done) | zopenco, ca (person).

muff [mʌf] *vt* SP dejar escapar (the ball) | fallar, errar (a shot) ‖ desperdiciar, perder (a chance) ‖ *to muff an interview* hacer mal una entrevista.

muffin ['mʌfin] *n* CULIN mollete *m*, panecillo *m*.

muffle ['mʌfl] *n* hocico *m*, morro *m* (of a cow) ‖ guante *m* (glove) ‖ sordina *f* (of a piano) ‖ TECH mufla *f* (in a furnace).

muffle ['mʌfl] *vt* tapar; *to muffle one's throat* taparse la garganta ‖ amortiguar (a sound) ‖ enfundar (to put a cover on) ‖ tapar la cara *or* la boca a (to prevent from seeing or speaking) ‖ *to muffle up* embozar (with a cloak).

muffler [-ə*] *n* bufanda *f* (scarf) ‖ MUS sordina *f* ‖ AUT silenciador *m* (of exhaust pipe).

mufti ['mʌfti] *n* REL mufti *m* ‖ traje *m* de paisano (civil dress) ‖ *in mufti* vestido de paisano.

mug [mʌg] *n* tazón *m* (cup) ‖ jarra *f* (of beer) ‖ vaso *m* (for toothbrush) ‖ FAM jeta *f*, hocico *m* (face) | primo, ma (dupe) ‖ *US* FAM rufián *m*.

mug [mʌg] *vt* atacar, asaltar (to attack) | fotografiar (to photograph).
◆ *vi* FAM exagerar los gestos (an actor) ‖ FAM *to mug up* empollar (to study).

mugger [-ə*] *n* asaltante *m* & *f*.

mugginess [-inis] *n* bochorno *m* (of weather).

mugging [-iŋ] *n* FAM asalto *m*, ataque *m*.

muggins ['mʌginz] *inv n* FAM primo, ma; tonto, ta.

muggy ['mʌgi] *adj* bochornoso, sa (weather).

mugwump ['mʌgwʌmp] *n* *US* independiente *m* (in politics).

Muhammad [mʌ'hæmed] *pr n* Mahoma *m*.

Muhammadan [mʌ'hæmidən] *adj/n* mahometano, na.

Muhammadanism [-izəm] *n* REL mahometismo *m* (Islam).

mujaheddin [mu:dʒəhə'di:n] *pl n* muyahidin *m pl* (Islamic fighter).

mujik ['mu:ʒik] *n* mujic *m*.

mulatto [mju'lætəu] *adj/n* mulato, ta.
— OBSERV El plural de *mulatto* es *mulattoes*.

mulattress [mju'lætris] *n* mulata *f*.

mulberry ['mʌlbəri] *n* BOT mora *f* (berry) | morera *f*, moral *m* (tree) ‖ color *m* morado (colour) ‖ — *mulberry field* moreral *m* ‖ *mulberry tree* morera *f*, moral *m*.

mulch [mʌltʃ] *n* AGR pajote *m*.

mulch [mʌltʃ] *vt* AGR cubrir con pajote.

mulct [mʌlkt] *n* multa *f*.

mulct [mʌlkt] *vt* multar ‖ FIG sacar (money, etc.).

mule [mju:l] *n* babucha *f* (slipper) ‖ ZOOL mulo *m* (male) | mula *f* (female) ‖ FIG testarudo, da; mula *f*; *as stubborn as a mule* testarudo como una mula ‖ BIOL híbrido *m* estéril ‖ TECH máquina *f* de hilar (spinning machine).
◆ *adj* mular, mulero, ra.

mule jenny [-'dʒeni] *n* TECH máquina *f* de hilar.

mule skinner [-,skinə*] *n* *US* FAM mulero *m*, muletero *m*, arriero *m*.

muleteer [,mju:li'tiə*] *n* mulero *m*, muletero *m*, arriero *m*.

mule track ['mju:ltræk] *n* camino *m* de herradura.

mulish ['mju:liʃ] *adj* testarudo, da; terco, ca (stubborn).

mulishness [-nis] *n* testarudez *f*, terquedad *f*.

mull [mʌl] *n* muselina *f* fina.

mull [mʌl] *vt/vi* calentar con especias (to heat and spice) ‖ FAM *to mull over* reflexionar sobre, rumiar sobre.

mullah ['mulə] *n* mulá *m* (Muslim teacher).

mullein ['mʌlin] *n* BOT gordolobo *m*.

muller ['mʌlə*] *n* moleta *f*.

mullet ['mʌlit] *n* mújol *m* (fish) ‖ *red mullet* salmonete *m* (fish).

mulligan ['mʌligən] *n* *US* FAM guisado *m*, guiso *m*.

mullion ['mʌliən] *n* ARCH parteluz *m*, mainel *m*.

mullion ['mʌliən] *vt* dividir con parteluces *or* maineles.

multi-access system ['mʌlti'ækses'sistim] *n* INFORM sistema *m* de acceso múltiple.

multicellular [,mʌlti'seljulə*] *adj* BIOL multicelular, pluricelular.

multichannel ['mʌlti'tʃænl] *adj* de varios canales (television).

multicoloured; *US* **multicolored** [,mʌlti'kʌləd] *adj* multicolor, policromo, ma.

multifarious [,mʌlti'fɛəriəs] *adj* múltiple, vario, ria; diverso, sa; variado, da.

multifold ['mʌlti,fəuld] *adj* múltiple.

multiform ['mʌltifɔ:m] *adj* multiforme.

multilateral ['mʌlti'lætərəl] *adj* multilateral.

multilingual [,mʌlti'liŋgwəl] *adj* poligloto, ta; polígloto, ta (person) ‖ plurilingüe (text, etc.).

multi media; multi-media ['mʌlti'mi:diə] *adj* INFORM multimedia.

multimillionaire ['mʌltimiljə'nɛə*] *adj/n* multimillonario, ria.

multinational [,mʌlti'næʃənl] *adj* multinacional.

multinomial [,mʌlti'nəumiəl] *adj* polinómico, ca.
◆ *n* polinomio *m*.

multipara [mʌl'tipərə] *n* multípara *f*.
— OBSERV El plural de la palabra inglesa es *multiparae*.

multiparous [mʌl'tipərəs] *adj* multíparo, ra.

multiphase ['mʌltifeiz] *adj* ELECTR polifásico, ca.

multiplane ['mʌltiplein] *n* AVIAT multiplano *m*.

multiple ['mʌltipl] *adj* múltiple ‖ MATH múltiplo, pla ‖ ELECTR en paralelo (connection) ‖ AGR de varias rejas (plough) ‖ — COMM *multiple shop* o *store* sucursal *f* [de una cadena de establecimientos] ‖ INFORM *multiple system* multiprocesador *m*.
◆ *n* MATH múltiplo *m*.

multiple-choice [-tʃɔis] *adj* *multiple-choice exam* examen *m* en el que las preguntas van seguidas de varias contestaciones entre las cuales se encuentra la solución exacta ‖ *multiple-choice question* pregunta *f* que va seguida de varias contestaciones entre las cuales está incluida la solución exacta.

multiple sclerosis [-skliə'rəusis] *n* MED esclerosis *f* en placas.

multiplex ['mʌltipleks] *adj* múltiple (manifold) ‖ ELECTR múltiplex.

multiplex ['mʌlti'pleks] *vt* transmitir por sistema múltiplex.

multipliable ['mʌltiplaiəbl]; **multiplicable** ['mʌltiplikəbl] *adj* multiplicable.

multiplicand [,mʌltiplikænd] *n* multiplicando *m*.

multiplication [,mʌltipli'keiʃən] *n* multiplicación *f* ‖ — *multiplication sign* signo *m* de multiplicar ‖ *multiplication table* tabla *f* de multiplicar.

multiplicative [,mʌlti'plikətiv] *adj* multiplicativo, va.

multiplicity [,mʌltiplisiti] *n* multiplicidad *f*.

multiplier ['mʌltiplaiə*] *n* multiplicador *m*.

multiply ['mʌltiplai] *vt* multiplicar.
◆ *vi* multiplicarse.

multiplying ['mʌltiplaiiŋ] *adj* multiplicador, ra.

multiprocessor ['mʌltiprəsesə*] *n* INFORM multiprocesador *m*.

multiprogramming ['mʌlti'prəugræmiŋ] *n* INFORM multiprogramación *f*.

multipurpose ['mʌlti'pə:pəs] *adj* multiuso.

multiracial ['mʌlti'reiʃəl] *adj* multirracial.

multi-storey ['mʌlti'stɔ:ri] *adj* de varios pisos (building, car park).

multitasking; multi-tasking ['mʌlti'tɑ:skiŋ] *n* INFORM multitarea.

multi-terminal system ['mʌlti'tə:minl'sistim] *n* INFORM multipuesto *m*.

multitude ['mʌltitju:d] *n* multitud *f*, muchedumbre *f* (of persons) ‖ multitud *f*, infinidad *f* (of things) ‖ — *for a multitude of motives* por múltiples motivos ‖ *the multitude* la masa.

multitudinous [,mʌlti'tju:dinəs] *adj* multitudinario, ria ‖ muy numeroso, sa.

multi-user [,mʌlti'ju:zə*] *adj* INFORM multiusuario ‖ *multi-user system* multiusuario *m*.

multivalence [,mʌlti'veiləns] *n* polivalencia *f*.

multivalent [,mʌlti'veilənt] *adj* polivalente.

multure ['mʌltjə*] *n* maquila *f*.

mum [mʌm] *interj* ¡chitón! ‖ *mum's the word!* ¡punto en boca!
◆ *adj* silencioso, sa ‖ *to keep mum* mantenerse callado, no decir esta boca es mía, guardar silencio.

mum [mʌm] *n* FAM mamá *f* (mother) ‖ *US* BOT crisantemo *m* ‖ cerveza *f* fuerte (beer).

mum [mʌm] *vi* disfrazarse.

mumble ['mʌmbl] *n* refunfuño *m* ‖ *to say in a mumble* decir entre dientes.

mumble ['mʌmbl] *vt/vi* mascullar, decir *or* hablar entre dientes (to speak indistinctly).

mumbling [-iŋ] *adj* *to say sth. in a mumbling voice* decir algo entre dientes.
◆ *n* *stop that mumbling!* ¡habla claro! (speak clearly), ¡silencio!

mumbo jumbo ['mʌmbəu'dʒʌmbəu] *n* fetiche *m* (fetish) ‖ conjuro *m* (spell) ‖ farsa *f*, comedia *f* (sham) ‖ galimatías *m* (gibberish).

mummer ['mʌmə*] *n* mimo *m* (in a pantomime) ‖ máscara *m* & *f*, enmascarado, da (masked person).

mummery [-ri] *n* mascarada *f*, farsa *f* (mascarade) ‖ THEATR pantomima *f*.

mummification [,mʌmifi'keiʃən] *n* momificación *f*.

mummify ['mʌmifai] *vt* momificar.
◆ *vi* momificarse.

mummy ['mʌmi] *n* mamá *f* (mother) ‖ momia *f* (preserved body).

mummy ['mʌmi] *vt* momificar.

mummy cloth [-klɔθ] *n* venda *f*.

mumpish ['mʌmpiʃ] *adj* malhumorado, da; desabrido, da.

mumps [mʌmps] *pl n* MED paperas *f*.
munch [mʌntʃ] *vt/vi* mascar, ronzar.
mundane ['mʌndein] *adj* mundano, na (worldly) ‖ terrestre, terrenal (earthly).
mungo ['mʌngəu] *n* lana *f* de baja calidad.
Munich ['mju:nik] *pr n* GEOGR Munich.
municipal [mju:'nisipəl] *adj* municipal ‖ *municipal council* concejo *m* municipal.
municipality [mju:,nisi'pæliti] *n* municipio *m*.
municipalize [mju:'nisipəlaiz] *vt* municipalizar.
munificence [mju:'nifisns] *n* munificencia *f*, generosidad *f*, liberalidad *f*.
munificent [mju:'nifisnt] *adj* munificente, munífico, ca; generoso, sa; liberal.
muniments ['mju:nimənts] *pl n* JUR documentos *m*.
munition [mju:'niʃən] *vt* amunicionar.
munitions [mju:'niʃənz] *pl n* MIL municiones *f*.
muraena [mju:'ri:nə] *n* morena *f* (fish).
mural ['mjuərəl] *adj* mural; *mural painting* pintura mural.
◆ *n* ARTS mural *m*, pintura *f* mural, fresco *m*.
muralist [-ist] *n* pintor *m* de murales.
murder ['mə:də*] *n* JUR asesinato *m*, homicidio *m* (killing as a crime); *premeditated murder, murder in the first degree* homicidio premeditado ‖ FIG asesinato *m*; *war is mass murder* la guerra es un asesinato en masa ‖ FAM cosa *f* espantosa *or* horrible ‖ — FAM *it was murder crossing the mountain* fue matador cruzar la montaña ‖ *to commit murder* cometer un asesinato ‖ FIG *to cry blue murder* protestar enérgicamente, poner el grito en el cielo | *to get away with murder* salirse con la suya | *to go through murder* pasar las de Caín.
murder ['mə:də*] *vt* asesinar (to kill unlawfully) ‖ matar, asesinar; *the bombing murdered most of the civilian population* el bombardeo mató a la mayoría de la población civil ‖ FIG destrozar, interpretar *or* ejecutar desastrosamente; *to murder a sonata* interpretar desastrosamente una sonata | desfigurar, deformar (a quotation) | chapurrear, hablar mal (a foreign language) | degollar (a play).
◆ *vi* cometer un asesinato.
murderer [-rə*] *n* asesino *m*.
murderess ['mə:dəris] *n* asesina *f*.
murderous ['mə:dərəs] *adj* asesino, na; homicida ‖ *murderous weapon* arma mortífera.
murex ['mjuəreks] *n* ZOOL múrice *m*, múrex *m*.
— OBSERV El plural de *murex* es *murices* o *murexes*.
murk; mirk [mə:k]**; murkiness; mirkiness** [-inis] *n* oscuridad *f*, tinieblas *f pl*, lobreguez *f*.
murky [-i] *adj* oscuro, ra; lóbrego, ga.
murmur ['mə:mə*] *n* murmullo *m* (of voice, of river, etc.) ‖ susurro *m*, murmullo *m* (of wind) ‖ murmullo *m*, queja *f* (of disapproval) ‖ MED soplo *m* cardiaco (of the heart).
murmur ['mə:mə*] *vi* murmurar ‖ *to murmur against s.o.* murmurar de alguien.
◆ *vt* murmurar.
murmuring [-iŋ] *adj* murmurador, ra; murmurante.
murphy ['mə:fi] *n* FAM papa *f* (potato).
Murphy bed [-bed] *n* cama *f* empotrada.
murrain ['mʌrin] *n* VET epizootia *f*.
muscadel [mʌskə'del] *n* moscatel *m* (wine).
muscadine ['mʌskədain] *n* BOT uva *f* moscatel, moscatel *m*.
muscat ['mʌskət] *n* BOT uva *f* moscatel, moscatel *m* (grape).
Muscat ['mʌskæt] *pr n* GEOGR Mascate.
muscatel [,mʌskə'tel] *n* moscatel *m* (wine).
muscle ['mʌsl] *n* ANAT músculo *m* ‖ — *he has a lot of muscle* tiene muchos músculos ‖ FAM *not to move a muscle* no inmutarse, permanecer impasible.
muscle ['mʌsl] *vi* FAM *to muscle in* meterse (por fuerza) en.
muscle-bound [-baund] *adj* con los músculos agarrotados.
muscovado [,mʌskə'vɑ:də] *n* azúcar *f* mascabada (unrefined sugar).
muscovite ['mʌskəuvait] *n* MIN mica *f*.
Muscovite ['mʌskəuvait] *adj/n* moscovita.
Muscovy ['mʌskəuvi] *pr n* GEOGR Moscovia *f*.
muscular ['mʌskjulə*] *adj* muscular; *muscular tissue* tejido muscular ‖ musculoso, sa (having strong muscles) ‖ MED *muscular dystrophy* distrofia *f* muscular.
muscularity [,mʌskju'læriti] *n* musculatura *f*.
musculature ['mʌskjulətʃuə] *n* musculatura *f*.
muse [mju:z] *n* meditación *f* (meditation) ‖ musa *f* (source of inspiration).
muse [mju:z] *vt/vi* meditar, reflexionar (to ponder) ‖ contemplar (to watch) ‖ decir pensativamente (to say).
Muse [mju:z] *pr n* MYTH Musa *f*.
musette [mju'zet] *n* MUS gaita *f*, cornamusa *f* (bagpipe).
musette bag [-bæg] *n* MIL mochila *f*.
museum [mju'ziəm] *n* museo *m*; *the Prado Museum* el Museo del Prado.
museum piece [-pi:s] *n* pieza *f* de museo ‖ FAM pieza *f* de museo (person).
mush [mʌʃ] *n* gachas *f pl* (porridge) ‖ RAD interferencia *f* ‖ FAM lío *m*, confusión *f* (mess) | majaderías *f pl*, pamplinas *f pl* (silly things) | sensiblería *f*, sentimentalismo *m* (maudlin sentimentality) ‖ viaje *m* en trineo por la nieve (journey across snow).
◆ *interj* ¡arre!
mush [mʌʃ] *vi* viajar en trineo.
mushroom [-rum] *n* BOT seta *f*, hongo *m* ‖ CULIN champiñón *m*, seta *f*.
◆ *adj* de champiñones; *mushroom salad* ensalada de champiñones ‖ en forma de hongo (like a mushroom in shape) ‖ FIG de crecimiento rápido (town) ‖ TECH de campana (insulator) ‖ — *mushroom cloud* hongo atómico ‖ *to grow* o *to spring up like mushrooms* crecer como hongos.
mushroom [-rum] *vi* crecer como hongos (to grow quickly) ‖ esparcirse (smoke, a cloud, etc.) ‖ tomar la forma de un hongo (to resemble a mushroom) ‖ recoger setas (to pick mushrooms) ‖ FIG *to mushroom into* convertirse en poco tiempo en.
mushy [-i] *adj* blando, da; mollar (soft) ‖ empapado, da (ground) ‖ blando, da; en papilla (food) ‖ FAM sentimentaloide ‖ RAD con interferencias.
music ['mju:zik] *n* música *f*; *chamber, instrumental, sacred, vocal, background music* música de cámara, instrumental, sacra, vocal, de fondo ‖ partitura *f* (score) ‖ — FIG *to face the music* afrontar las consecuencias ‖ *to set a poem to music* poner música a un poema.
musical [-əl] *adj* de música; *musical box* caja de música ‖ musical (ear, evening) ‖ de música, músico, ca (instrument) ‖ de músicos; *Bach was a member of a musical family* Bach pertenecía a una familia de músicos ‖ aficionado a la música; *my family is very musical* mi familia es muy aficionada a la música ‖ armonioso, sa; melodioso, sa (sound, voice, verse) ‖ — *musical chairs* juego *m* de las sillas vacías (game), cambio *m* de puestos (in politics) ‖ *musical comedy* comedia *f* musical.
◆ *n* comedia *f* musical.
musicale [,mju:zi'kæl] *n* US MUS velada *f* musical.
musicality [-iti]**; musicalness** [-nis] *n* musicalidad *f*.
music book ['mju:zikbuk] *n* libro *m* de música.
music box [-bɔks] *n* caja *f* de música.
music hall ['mju:zikhɔ:l] *n* teatro *m* de variedades, music-hall *m* ‖ US sala *f* de conciertos (for musical productions).
musician [mju:'ziʃən] *n* músico, ca.
music lover ['mju:zik,lʌvə*] *n* melómano, na.
musicographer [,mju:zi'kɔgrəfə*] *n* musicógrafo, fa.
musicologist [,mju:zi'kɔlədʒist] *n* musicólogo, ga.
musicology [,mju:zi'kɔlədʒi] *n* musicología *f*.
music paper ['mju:zik,peipə*] *n* papel *m* pautado.
music stand ['mju:zikstænd] *n* atril *m*.
music stool ['mju:zikstu:l] *n* taburete *m* de piano.
musing ['mju:ziŋ] *adj* meditativo, va; pensativo, va.
◆ *n* meditación *f*.
musk [mʌsk] *n* almizcle *m* ‖ ZOOL *musk deer* almizclero *m*.
muskeg ['mʌskeg] *n* terreno *m* pantanoso.
muskellunge ['mʌskə'lʌndʒ] *n* sollo *m* (fish).
musket ['mʌskit] *n* mosquete *m*.
musketeer ['mʌski'tiə*] *n* mosquetero *m*.
musketoon [,mʌski'tu:n] *n* mosquetón *m*.
musketry ['mʌskitri] *n* mosquetería *f* (musketeers) ‖ mosquetes *m pl* (muskets) ‖ fusilería *f* (firing).
muskmelon ['mʌsk,melən] *n* BOT melón *m*.
muskrat ['mʌskræt] *n* ZOOL ratón *m* almizclero.
musk rose ['mʌskrəuz] *n* BOT rosa *f* almizcleña.
musky ['mʌski] *adj* almizclero, ra; almizcleño, ña.
Muslim ['muslim] *adj/n* musulmán, ana.
muslin ['mʌzlin] *n* muselina *f* ‖ *cambric muslin* percal *m*.
musquash ['mʌskwɔʃ] *n* ZOOL ratón *m* amizclero.
muss [mʌs] *n* US FAM desorden *m* (disorder) | riña *f* (squabble).
muss [mʌs] *vt* US FAM desordenar | arrugar, chafar (dress) ‖ *to muss s.o.'s hair up* despeinar a uno.
mussel ['mʌsl] *n* mejillón *m* (mollusc).
mussy ['mʌsi] *adj* US FAM desordenado, da (disorganized) | sucio, cia (dirty) | arrugado, da (rumpled).
must [mʌst] *n* moho *m* (mould) ‖ mosto *m* (of grapes) ‖ → **celo** *m* (of an elephant, etc.); *on* o *in must* en celo.
must [mʌst] *v aux* deber, tener que (expressing obligation); *this is what he must do* esto es lo que debe hacer; *you must respect your father's wishes* debes respetar la voluntad de tu padre; *man must eat to live* el hombre tiene que comer para vivir ‖ deber de (expressing supposition); *it must be your sister* debe de ser tu hermana;

her name is Pilar, so she must be Spanish se llama Pilar, por lo tanto debe de ser española; *he said that he must have made a mistake* dijo que debía de haber cometido un error || tener que (expressing fatality); *why must it always rain on Sundays?* ¿por qué tiene que llover todos los domingos?; *why must he always be talking?* ¿por qué tiene que estar siempre hablando? || tener que (expressing invitation, recommendation); *you must come to visit us* tienes que venir a vernos; *you must get to know him* tienes que conocerle || — *it must be* es más que probable, seguramente || *one must be careful* hay que tener cuidado.
— OBSERV *Must* se emplea siempre en el presente, incluso cuando se refiere al pasado: *I told him what he must do* le dije lo que debía hacer.

must [mʌst] *n* cosa *f* indispensable, imperativo *m*, necesidad *f*; *it is an absolute must* es de absoluta necesidad || *this film, this book is a must* no deje de ver esta película, de leer este libro; es imprescindible ver esta película, leer este libro.

mustache [məs'tɑːʃ] *n* bigote *m*, bigotes *m pl*.

mustachios [mʌs'tæʃiəuz] *pl n* bigote *m sing*, bigotes *m*.

mustang ['mʌstæŋ] *n* ZOOL mustang *m*, mustango *m* (horse).

mustard [mʌstəd] *n* mostaza *f*.

mustard gas [-gæs] *n* gas *m* mostaza, yperita *f*.

mustard oil [-ɔil] *n* aceite *m* de mostaza.

mustard plaster [-ˌplɑːstə*] *n* cataplasma *f* de mostaza, sinapismo *m*.

mustard-seed shot [-siːd'ʃɔt] *n* mostacilla *f*.

muster ['mʌstə*] *n* MIL revista *f* (inspection) || reunión *f* (meeting) || asamblea *f* (assembly) || — *muster roll* lista *f* de revista (of troops), rol *m* de la tripulación (of crew) || FIG *to pass muster* ser aceptable.

muster ['mʌstə*] *vt* MIL formar || reunir (to gather) || — US MIL *to muster in* enrolar, alistar | *to muster out* licenciar, dar de baja || *to muster up* cobrar (strength) || *to muster up one's courage* revestirse *or* armarse de valor.
◆ *vi* reunirse (to gather together).

musth [mʌst] *n* celo *m* (of an elephant, etc.); *on* o *in musth* en celo.

mustiness ['mʌstinis] *n* olor *m* a cerrado *or* a humedad (smell).

mustn't ['mʌsənt] contraction of «must not».

must've ['mʌstəv] contraction of «must have».

musty ['mʌsti] *adj* mohoso, sa (mouldy) || que huele a cerrado *or* a humedad || FIG anticuado, da; viejo, ja; pasado de moda (old-fashioned) || *it smells musty here* aquí huele a cerrado *or* a humedad.

mutability [ˌmjuːtə'biliti] *n* mutabilidad *f* || inconstancia *f* (fickleness).

mutable ['mjuːtəbl] *adj* mudable, variable || cambiadizo, za; inconstante (fickle).

mutant ['mjuːtənt] *adj/n* BIOL mutante.

mutate [mjuː'teit] *vt* mudar, cambiar, transformar.
◆ *vi* experimentar un cambio, cambiar, transformarse.

mutation [mju'teiʃən] *n* mutación *f*.

mute [mjuːt] *adj* mudo, da (unable to speak, speechless) || GRAMM mudo, da (letter) || JUR *to stand mute* negarse a responder al interrogatorio del tribunal.
◆ *n* mudo, da (person who cannot speak) || GRAMM letra *f* muda || MUS sordina *f*.

mute [mjuːt] *vt* apagar, amortiguar, ensordecer (to deaden a sound) || MUS poner sordina a.

muted [-id] *adj* sordo, da (noise).

muteness [-nis] *n* mutismo *m* (silence) || MED mudez *f*.

mutilate ['mjuːtileit] *vt* mutilar.

mutilation [ˌmjuːti'leiʃən] *n* mutilación *f*.

mutilator ['mjuːtileitə*] *n* mutilador, ra.

mutineer [ˌmjuːti'niə*] *n* amotinador *m*, amotinado *m*, rebelde *m*.

mutinous ['mjuːtinəs] *adj* amotinado, da; sedicioso, sa (crew, sailor) || FIG rebelde.

mutiny ['mjuːtini] *n* motín *m*, rebelión *f*, sedición *f*.

mutiny ['mjuːtini] *vi* amotinarse, sublevarse, rebelarse.

mutt [mʌt] *n* FAM perro *m* mestizo (mongrel) | bobo, ba; tonto, ta (stupid person).

mutter ['mʌtə*] *n* murmullo *m* (murmur) || refunfuño *m* (grumbling).

mutter ['mʌtə*] *vt* murmurar, decir entre dientes || refunfuñar (angrily).
◆ *vi* murmurar, hablar entre dientes || refunfuñar (angrily) || quejarse (to complain); *he's always muttering about sth.* siempre se está quejando de algo.

muttering [-riŋ] *n* refunfuño *m*.

mutton ['mʌtn] *n* cordero *m*; *leg, shoulder of mutton* pierna, espaldilla de cordero || FIG *mutton dressed as lamb* vejestorio emperifollado.

mutton chop [-'tʃɔp] *n* chuleta *f* de cordero.

muttonchops [-'tʃɔps] *pl n* patillas *f* (side whiskers).

muttonhead [-hed] *n* FAM bobo, ba.

mutual ['mjuːtʃuəl] *adj* mutuo, tua; *mutual insurance* seguros mutuos || mutuo, tua; recíproco, ca; *mutual admiration* admiración mutua || FAM común (common); *by mutual consent* de común acuerdo || — *mutual aid* ayuda mutua || *mutual benefit society* mutualidad *f*, mutua *f*, mutual *f*.

mutualist ['mjuːtjuəlist] *n* mutualista *m* & *f*.

mutualistic [ˌmjuːtjuə'listik] *adj* mutualista.

mutuality [ˌmjuːtju'æliti] *n* mutualidad *f* || reciprocidad *f*.

mutule ['mjuːtjuːl] *n* ARCH mútulo *m*.

Muzak ['mjuzæk] *n* hilo *m* musical (registered trademark).

muzhik; muzjik ['muːʒik] *n* mujic *m*.

muzziness [mʌzinis] *n* atontamiento *m* (from drinking) || borrosidad *f* (of sight, of ideas).

muzzle ['mʌzl] *n* hocico *m*, morro *m* (part of animal's head) || bozal *m* (to prevent an animal from biting) || boca *f* (of a weapon).

muzzle ['mʌzl] *vt* abozalar, poner bozal a (a dog, etc.) || FIG amordazar.

muzzle-loader [-ˌləudə*] *n* MIL arma *f* que se carga por la boca.

muzzle velocity [-vi'lɔsiti] *n* MIL velocidad *f* inicial (of a shell).

muzzy ['mʌzi] *adj* atontado, da (with drink) || borroso, sa (ideas, vision) || deprimente (day).

MW *abbr of [medium wave]* OM, onda media.

my [mai] *poss adj* mi; *my book* mi libro; *my friends* mis amigos || mío, mía; *listen, my sons* escuchadme, hijos míos || FAM *my!* ¡madre mía!
— OBSERV The English possessive adjective is often translated by the definite article in Spanish: *I took my gloves from my bag* saqué los guantes del bolso.

myalgia [mai'ældʒə] *n* MED mialgia *f*.

mycelium [mai'siːliəm] *n* BOT micelio *m*.
— OBSERV El plural de *mycelium* es *mycelia*.

Mycenae [mai'siːni] *pr n* Micenas (in Greece).

mycosis [mai'kəusis] *n* MED micosis *f*.
— OBSERV El plural de la palabra inglesa es *mycoses*.

mydriasis [mi'draiəsis] *n* MED midriasis *f*.

myelin; myeline ['maiəlin] *n* mielina *f*.

myelitis [ˌmaiə'laitis] *n* MED mielitis.

mygale ['migəli] *n* migala *f* (spider).

myocarditis [ˌmaiəkɑː'daitis] *n* MED miocarditis *f*.

myocardium [ˌmaiə'kɑːdiəm] *n* ANAT miocardio *m*.
— OBSERV El plural de *myocardium* es *myocardia*.

myograph ['maiəgræf] *n* MED miógrafo *m*.

myoma [mai'əumə] *n* MED mioma.
— OBSERV El plural de la palabra inglesa es *myomata* o *myomas*.

myope ['maiəup] *n* MED miope *m* & *f*.

myopia [mai'əupjə] *n* MED miopía *f*.

myopic [mai'ɔpik] *adj* MED miope.

myosotis [ˌmaiə'səutis] *n* BOT miosota *f*, raspilla *f*.

myriad ['miriəd] *adj* innumerable (countless).
◆ *n* miríada *f*.

myriagramme; myriagram ['miriəgræm] *n* miriagramo *m*.

myriametre; US **myriameter** ['miriəmitə*] *n* miriámetro *m*.

myriapod; myriopod ['miriəpɔd] *adj* ZOOL miriápodo, da.
◆ *n* ZOOL miriápodo *m*.

myrmidon ['məːmidən] *n* secuaz *m* (loyal follower) || esbirro *m* (subordinate) || asesino *m* a sueldo (hired killer).

myrrh [məː*] *n* mirra *f*.

myrtaceae [məː'teisiiː] *pl n* BOT mirtáceas *f*.

myrtle ['məːtl] *n* BOT arrayán *m*, mirto *m*.

myself [mai'self] *pron* yo mismo, yo misma (emphatic); *I gave him the money myself* le di el dinero yo mismo || me (reflexive); *I hurt myself* me he hecho daño || mí (mismo), mí (misma) (after preposition); *I didn't buy it for myself* no lo compré para mí || — *I am sorry I blew up, I am not myself lately* discúlpeme por haberme puesto furioso, no soy el mismo últimamente || *I did it by myself* lo hice (completamente) solo || *I stayed by myself all morning* me quedé (completamente) solo toda la mañana.

mysterious [mis'tiəriəs] *adj* misterioso, sa || *to act in a mysterious manner* andar con misterios, hacer misterios, ser muy misterioso.

mysteriousness [-nis] *n* misterio *m*, carácter *m* misterioso.

mystery ['mistəri] *n* misterio *m* || enigma *m* || REL misterio *m* || auto *m* sacramental, misterio *m* (medieval religious drama) || — *mystery man* hombre misterioso || *mystery novel* novela policíaca || *wrapped in mystery* misterioso, sa.

mystic ['mistik] *adj* esotérico, ca (rites) || mágico, ca (formula) || oculto, ta (power) || sobrenatural (truth) || misterioso, sa; enigmático, ca (mysterious) || REL místico, ca.
◆ *n* iniciado, da || REL místico, ca.

mystical [-əl] *adj* místico, ca || *mystical theology* mística *f*.

mysticism ['mistisizəm] *n* misticismo *m* || mística *f* (literary genre).

mystification [ˌmistifi'keiʃən] *n* mistificación *f*, engaño *m* (deceit) || complejidad *f*, misterio *m*, oscuridad *f* (of a question) || perplejidad *f*, confusión *f* (perplexity).

mystify ['mistifai] *vt* engañar (to deceive) || desconcertar, dejar perplejo (to disconcert) || desorientar, despistar (to confuse) || llenar de misterio, oscurecer, complicar, enmarañar (a question).

mystique [mis'ti:k] *n* mística *f* || misterio *m* (mystery).

myth [miθ] *n* mito *m*.

mythic [-ik]; **mythical** [-ikəl] *adj* mítico, ca.

mythicize ['miθəsaiz] *vt* dar un sentido mítico a.

mythologer [mi'θɔlədʒə*] *n* mitólogo *m*.

mythological [,miθə'lɔdʒikəl] *adj* mitológico, ca.

mythology [mi'θɔlədʒi] *n* mitología *f*.

mythomania [,miθəu'meiniə] *n* mitomanía *f*.

mythomaniac [,miθəu'meiniæk] *adj/n* mitómano, na.

myxomatosis [,miksəumə'təusis] *n* mixomatosis *f*.

myxomycetes [,miksə'maisi:ti:z] *pl n* BOT mixomicetos *m*.

N

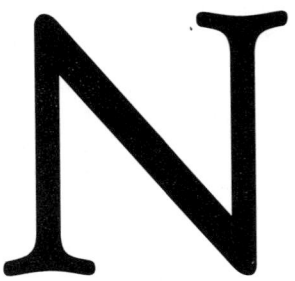

n [en] *n* n *f* (letter) ‖ FIG *it's the nth. time I've told you* es la enésima vez que te lo digo.

nab [næb] *vt* FAM coger, pescar (s.o.) | coger, mangar, birlar (sth.).

nabob ['neibɔb] *n* nabab *m*.

nacelle [næ'sel] *n* AVIAT barquilla *f*.

nacre ['neikə*] *n* nácar *m*.

nacreous ['neikriəs]; **nacred** ['neikəd] *adj* nacarado, da; anacarado, da.

nadir ['neidiə*] *n* ASTR nadir *m* ‖ FIG punto *m* más bajo.

naevus ['ni:vəs] *n* nevo *m*.
— OBSERV El plural de *naevus* es *naevi*.

naff [næf] *adj* POP chungo, ga ‖ *a naff book* una porquería *f* de libro.

nag [næg] *n* rocín *m* (old horse) ‖ regañón, ona; quejica *m* & *f* (complainer) ‖ quejas *f pl* (complaints).

nag [næg] *vt* regañar, reñir (to tell off) ‖ FIG remorder (the conscience) | fastidiar, molestar (to annoy) | machacar (to bother insistently) | asaltar; *I was nagged by doubts* me asaltaron las dudas.
◆ *vi* regañar, reñir (to tell off) ‖ quejarse (to complain) ‖ criticar (to criticize) ‖ gritar (to shout) ‖ *to nag at* molestar, fastidiar.

nagger [-ə*] *n* regañón, ona; criticón, ona (faultfinding person) ‖ quejica *m* & *f* (complaining person).

nagging [-iŋ] *adj* regañón, ona; criticón, ona (faultfinding) ‖ quejica (complaining) ‖ FIG continuo, nua; persistente (constant) | punzante, lancinante (pain).
◆ *n* quejas *f pl*.

naiad ['naiæd] *n* náyade *f*.
— OBSERV El plural es *naiads* o *naiades*.

nail [neil] *n* uña *f* (of the finger, of the toe) ‖ garra *f* (claw) ‖ clavo *m* (metal spike) ‖ — *to bang a nail in* clavar un clavo ‖ FIG *to be as hard as nails* ser muy resistente (to be resistant), tener un corazón de piedra (to be hardhearted) ‖ *to bite one's nails* comerse *or* morderse las uñas ‖ *to drive a nail home* remachar un clavo (to bang in), remachar el clavo (to insist) ‖ FIG *to fight tooth and nail* luchar a brazo partido, defenderse como gato panza arriba | *to hit the nail on the head* dar en el clavo, acertar | *to pay on the nail* pagar a tocateja.

nail [neil] *vt* clavar, sujetar con clavos (*on, to* en); *to nail a lid on a box* clavar una tapa en una caja ‖ clavetear (to decorate with nails) ‖ FIG fijar (eyes, attention) | averiguar, descubrir (to find out) ‖ FIG & FAM coger, agarrar (to catch) ‖ — FIG *to nail a lie to the counter* descubrir una mentira ‖ *to nail down* clavar, sujetar con clavos (sth.), poner entre la espada y la pared (to corner a person), comprometer (to make s.o. give a promise) ‖ *to nail up* cerrar con clavos.

nailbrush [-brʌʃ] *n* cepillo *m* para las uñas, cepillo *m* de uñas.

nail claw [-klɔ:] *n* arrancaclavos *m inv*, sacaclavos *m inv*.

nail clippers [-'klipəz] *n* cortaúñas *m inv*.

nailer [-ə*] *n* fabricante *m* de clavos (nail maker) ‖ FAM as *m*, hacha *m* (person) | cosa *f* estupenda (thing).

nailery [-əri] *n* fábrica *f* de clavos.

nail file [-fail] *n* lima *f* de uñas.

nailing [-iŋ] *n* clavado *m* (of case) ‖ claveteado *m* (of boots) ‖ clavos *m pl* (nails).

nail polish [-'pɔliʃ] *n* US esmalte *m* de uñas *or* para las uñas.

nail puller [-pulə*] *n* arrancaclavos *m inv*, sacaclavos *m inv*.

nail-scissors [-'sizəz] *pl n* tijeras *f* para las uñas.

nail varnish [-'va:niʃ] *n* esmalte *m* de uñas, esmalte *m* para las uñas.

Nairobi [nai'rəubi] *pr n* GEOGR Nairobi.

naïve; naive [na:'i:v] *adj* ingenuo, nua; cándido, da.

naïveté; naiveté [na:'i:vtei] *n* ingenuidad *f*, candidez *f*.

naja ['neidʒə] *n* naja *f* (snake).

naked ['neikid] *adj* desnudo, da (body, part of body) ‖ descubierto, ta (head) ‖ descalzo, za (feet) ‖ FIG pelado, da; desnudo, da (landscape) | sin hojas, desnudo, da (tree) | desnudo, da; sin adornos (wall) | sin pantalla (light) | sin protección (flame) | desenvainado, da (a sword) ‖ indefenso, sa (helpless) ‖ JUR unilateral | sin garantía (contract) ‖ — *invisible to the naked eye* invisible a simple vista ‖ *the naked truth* la verdad escueta, la verdad desnuda ‖ *to strip (o.s.) naked* desnudarse.

nakedness [-nis] *n* desnudez *f* ‖ FIG claridad *f*, evidencia *f*.

namby-pamby ['næmbi'pæmbi] *adj/n* soso, sa; ñoño, ña.

name [neim] *n* nombre *m* (Christian name) ‖ apellido *m* (family name) ‖ nombre *m* (of places, of things, etc.) ‖ apodo *m* (nickname); *the last name they gave him was «lefty»* el último apodo que le dieron era «zurdo» ‖ fama *f*, reputación *f* (reputation) ‖ título *m* (title) ‖ linaje *m* (lineage) ‖ personalidad *f*, celebridad *f* (celebrity) ‖ — FIG *big name* gran figura *f* ‖ *by* o *under another name* bajo otro nombre ‖ *by name* por el nombre (to call people), de nombre (to know s.o.) ‖ *by the name of* llamado, da ‖ *Christian name* nombre de pila, nombre ‖ *family name* apellido ‖ *first name* nombre de pila, nombre ‖ *full name* nombre y apellidos ‖ *I'll do it or my name is not Brown* lo haré, como me llamo Brown ‖ *in one's name* en nombre de uno ‖ *in name, in name only* sólo de nombre ‖ *in the name of* en nombre de; *in the name of the law* en nombre de la ley ‖ REL *in the name of the Father* en el nombre del Padre ‖ *maiden name* apellido de soltera ‖ *married name* apellido de casada ‖ *my name is Michael* me llamo Miguel ‖ FIG *not to have a penny to one's name* no tener un céntimo *or* un real ‖ *pet name* nombre cariñoso ‖ *proper name* nombre propio ‖ *registered name* nombre registrado ‖ *to answer to the name of* responder al nombre de, tener por nombre, llamarse ‖ FIG *to call s.o. names* poner verde a alguien ‖ *to get o.s. a bad name* hacerse una mala reputación ‖ *to go by the name of* llamarse (real name), ser conocido por el nombre de (ficticious name) ‖ *to know by name* conocer de nombre ‖ *to make a name for o.s.* darse a conocer, hacerse un nombre ‖ *to put one's name down* inscribirse, apuntarse ‖ *what name shall I say?* ¿de parte de quién? (on the phone), ¿a quién debo anunciar? (announcing arrival) ‖ *what's your name?* ¿cómo te llamas?

name [neim] *vt* llamar, poner; *what are you going to name your baby?* ¿cómo vas a llamar al niño?, ¿cómo le vas a poner al niño? ‖ llamar, denominar, dar nombre a (a new product) ‖ nombrar (to appoint); *to name s.o. to an office* nombrar a uno para un cargo ‖ dar el nombre de; *the victim named his attacker* la víctima dio el nombre del agresor ‖ mencionar (to mention) ‖ elegir (to choose); *name your weapon* elige el arma ‖ dar, fijar (date, price) ‖ bautizar con el nombre de (a ship) ‖ — *he is named Frederick Pelayo* se llama Federico Pelayo ‖ *name it* pide lo que quieras ‖ *to be named in a list* figurar en una lista ‖ *to name a child after his father* poner a un niño el nombre de su padre.

name day [-dei] *n* santo *m*, día *m* onomástico, onomástica *f*.

name-dropping [-'drɔpiŋ] *n* FAM farol *m* (practice of mentioning important people to impress others).

nameless [-lis] *adj* anónimo, ma; sin nombre (without a name) ‖ FIG sin nombre; *nameless atrocities were committed* se cometieron atrocidades sin nombre | indecible (dread, grief) ‖ *the accused, who shall remain nameless* el acusado, cuyo nombre debe permanecer en el anonimato.

namely [-li] *adv* a saber (that is to say).

nameplate [-pleit] *n* placa *f or* letrero *m* con el nombre.

namesake [-seik] *n* tocayo, ya; homónimo, ma.

naming [-iŋ] *n* elección *f* de un nombre (of a child) ‖ denominación *f* (of things) ‖ nombramiento *m* (appointment).

nan [næn]; **nana** ['nænæ] *n* FAM abuelita.

nandu ['næn,du] *n* ZOOL ñandú *m*.

nandubay [nja:ndəbai] *n* ñandubay *m*.

nanduti ['nandʌti] *n* ñandutí *m*.

nanism ['nei,nizəm] *n* MED enanismo *m*.

nankeen [næŋ'ki:n] *n* nanquín *m*, mahón *m* (cloth).

nanny; nannie ['næni] *n* niñera *f* (child's nurse).

nanny goat [-gəut] *n* ZOOL & FAM cabra *f* (female goat).

nanosecond ['neinə'sekənd] *n* nanosegundo *m*.

nap [næp] *n* siesta *f* (short sleep) ‖ lanilla *f*, pelusa *f* (of cloth) ‖ BOT pelusa *f* ‖ informe *m* seguro (in racing) ‖ — *to go against the nap* ir a contrapelo ‖ FIG *to go nap* jugárselo todo ‖ *to* *take* o *to have a nap* dormir la siesta, descabezar un sueño.

nap [næp] *vt* levantar hacia atrás (the pile of a cloth) || recomendar (a horse).
◆ *vi* dormitar (to sleep lightly) || descabezar un sueño, dormir la siesta (to have a nap) || FIG *to catch s.o. napping* coger a uno desprevenido.

napalm ['neipɑ:m] *n* napalm *m*; *napalm bomb* bomba de napalm.

nape [neip] *n* ANAT cogote *m*, nuca *f*.

napery ['neipəri] *n* mantelería *f* (table linen).

naphtha ['næfθə] *n* nafta *f*.

naphthalene [-li:n] *n* CHEM naftalina *f*.

naphthene ['næfθi:n] *n* nafteno *m*.

naphtol ['næfθɔl] *n* CHEM naftol *m*.

Napierian [nə'piəriən] *adj* MATH neperiano, na.

napiform ['neipifɔ:m] *adj* nabiforme.

napkin ['næpkin] *n* servilleta *f* (used at table) || pañal *m* (for a baby) || US compresa *f* higiénica, paño *m* higiénico (sanitary towel).

napkin ring [-riŋ] *n* servilletero *m*.

Naples ['neiplz] *pr n* GEOGR Nápoles.

napoleon [nə'pəuljən] *n* napoleón *m* (coin) || milhojas *m inv* (pastry).

Napoleon [nə'pəuljən] *pr n* Napoleón *m*.

Napoleonic [nə,pəuli'ɔnik] *adj* napoleónico, ca.

nappy ['næpi] *n* pañal *m* (napkin).
◆ *adj* que tiene pelusa (cloth) || fuerte (ale).

narcissism [nɑ:'sisizm] *n* narcisismo *m*.

narcissist [nɑ:'sisist] *n* narcisista *m* & *f*.

narcissistic [,nɑ:si'sistik] *adj* narcisista.

narcissus [nɑ:'sisəs] *n* BOT narciso *m*.
— OBSERV El plural de *narcissus* es *narcissuses* o *narcissi*.

Narcissus [nɑ:'sisəs] *pr n* Narciso *m*.

narcoanalysis [nɑ:kəuə'næləsis] *n* MED narcoanálisis *m*.

narcosis [nɑ:'kəusis] *n* MED narcosis *f*.
— OBSERV El plural de la palagra inglesa es *narcoses*.

narcotic [nɑ:'kɔtik] *adj* MED narcótico, ca; estupefaciente.
◆ *n* MED narcótico *m*, estupefaciente *m*.

narcotine ['nɑ:kə,tin] *n* CHEM narcotina *f*.

narcotism ['nɑ:kətizəm] *n* MED narcotismo *m*, narcosis *f*.

narcotize ['nɑ:kətaiz] *vt* MED narcotizar.

nard [nɑ:d] *n* BOT nardo *m*.

narghile ['nɑ:gili] *n* narguile *m* (pipe).

nark [nɑ:k] *n* FAM soplón *m*.

nark [nɑ:k] *vt* FAM fastidiar (to annoy) || FAM *to get narked* ponerse furioso.

narratable [nə'reitəbl] *adj* narrable.

narrate [nə'reit] *vt* narrar, relatar, referir, contar.

narration [nə'reiʃən] *n* narración *f*, relato *m*.

narrative ['nærətiv] *adj* narrativo, va.
◆ *n* narrativa *f*, narración *f* (art of relating stories) || historia *f*, relato *m* (story).

narrator [nə'reitə*] *n* narrador, ra || MUS solista *m* & *f*.

narrow ['nærəu] *adj* estrecho, cha; angosto, ta (street, path, etc.); *a narrow bridge* un puente estrecho || estrecho, cha (tight); *my trousers are narrow* mi pantalón es estrecho || FIG de miras estrechas (person) | estrecho, cha (views) | escaso, sa; pequeño, ña; reducido, da (small); *a narrow majority* una mayoría escasa | restringido, da; limitado, da; *a narrow interpretation* una interpretación restringida | minucioso, sa (precise) || COMM poco activo, va (market) || — *in the narrowest sense of the word* en el sentido más estricto de la palabra || FAM *the narrow bed* la tumba || *to grow narrow* estrecharse, angostarse || *to have a narrow escape* o *shave* o *squeak* librarse por los pelos, escaparse por un pelo *or* por los pelos || *to live in narrow circumstances* vivir estrechamente, vivir con estrechez.
◆ *n* paso *m* estrecho *or* angosto (narrow passage) || estrecho *m* (strait).

narrow ['nærəu] *vt* estrechar, hacer más estrecho (to make less wide) || — *to narrow down* limitar, reducir || *to narrow sth. down to* reducir algo a || *to narrow the eyes* entrecerrar los ojos.
◆ *vi* estrecharse, angostarse, hacerse más estrecho (a road, etc.) || reducirse || entrecerrarse (eyes) || *to narrow down to* reducirse a.

narrow-gauge [-geidʒ] *adj* de vía estrecha (railway) || FIG de miras estrechas.

narrowing [-iŋ] *n* estrechamiento *m* (of a road) || menguado *m* (in knitting) || FIG limitación *f*.

narrowly [-li] *adv* estrechamente || de cerca, minuciosamente (closely) || *he narrowly missed being run over* no le atropellaron por muy poco, faltó muy poco para que le atropellaran.

narrow-minded [-'maindid] *adj* de miras estrechas.

narrow-mindedness [-'maindidnis] *n* estrechez *f* de miras.

narrowness [-nis] *n* estrechez *f* || FIG lo reducido, lo limitado (of possibilities, etc.) | minuciosidad *f* (of an inspection) | estrechez *f* (of ideas).

narrows [-z] *pl n* paso *m* estrecho *or* angosto (narrow passage) || estrecho *m sing* (strait).

narthex ['nɑ:θeks] *n* ARCH nártex *m*.

narwal; narwhal; narwhale ['nɑ:wəl] *n* ZOOL narval *m*.

NASA *abbr of [National Aeronautics and Space Administration]* NASA, agencia espacial norteamericana.

nasal ['neizəl] *adj* nasal; *nasal sounds* sonidos nasales; *nasal fossae* fosas nasales || gangoso, sa; *nasal voice* voz gangosa.
◆ *n* GRAMM nasal *f*.

nasality [nei'zæliti] *n* nasalidad *f*.

nasalization [,neizəlai'zeiʃən] *n* nasalización *f*.

nasalize ['neizəlaiz] *vt* nasalizar.
◆ *vi* ganguear, hablar con voz gangosa.

nasally ['neizəli] *adv* con voz gangosa.

nascent ['næsnt] *adj* naciente.

naseberry ['neizbəri] *n* BOT zapote *m* (fruit) | zapotillo *m*, chicozapote *m* (tree).

Nassau ['næsɔ:] *pr n* GEOGR Nassau.

nastily ['nɑ:stili] *adv* de mala manera (in an unpleasant way) || muy mal; *to behave nastily* portarse muy mal || suciamente (dirtily) || groseramente (rudely) || peligrosamente (dangerously) || gravemente (seriously).

nastiness ['nɑ:stinis] *n* sabor *m* horrible (taste) || peste *f* (odour) || obscenidad *f* (obscenity) || maldad *f* (wickedness) || antipatía *f* (unfriendliness) || suciedad *f* (dirtiness).

nasturtium [nəs'tə:ʃəm] *n* BOT capuchina *f*.

nasty ['nɑ:sti] *adj* sucio, cia; asqueroso, sa (dirty); *the bottom of the dustbin was really nasty* el fondo del cubo de la basura estaba realmente asqueroso || repugnante; repulsivo, va (repugnant) || horrible, espantoso, sa; asqueroso, sa (taste, smell, weather) || desagradable (unpleasant); *nasty remark* observación desagradable || antipático, ca (unfriendly); *she is a nasty girl* es una chica antipática || malo, la; malévolo, la (wicked) || vivo, va (temper) || grosero, ra (rude) || obsceno, na; asqueroso, sa (obscene) || molesto, ta; *she has a very nasty cough* tiene una tos muy molesta || feo, a (wound, cut) | grave (accident) || peligroso, sa (dangerous); *a nasty corner* una esquina peligrosa || difícil (difficult) || — *nasty business* asunto malo *or* feo (affair), trabajo molesto (job) || *nasty habit* mala costumbre || *nasty trick* mala jugada || *to be nasty to s.o.* portarse mal con uno, tratar mal a alguien || *to have a nasty mind* ser un mal pensado *or* una mal pensada || FIG *to leave a nasty taste in the mouth* dejar mal sabor de boca || *to smell nasty* oler mal || *to taste nasty* saber mal, tener mal sabor || *to turn nasty* ponerse feo (an affair, the weather) || *to turn nasty on s.o.* volverse antipático con alguien.

natal ['neitl] *adj* natal || de nacimiento; *natal day* día de nacimiento.

natality [nə'tæliti] *n* natalidad *f*; *natality rate* índice de natalidad.

natation [nə'teiʃən] *n* SP natación *f*.

natatorial [,neitə'tɔ:riəl]; **natatory** [nə'teitəri] *adj* natatorio, ria.

natatorium [,neitə'tɔ:riəm] *n* US piscina *f* cubierta (swimming pool).
— OBSERV El plural es *natatoriums* o *natatoria*.

nation ['neiʃən] *n* nación *f*; *the United Nations* las Naciones Unidas.

national ['næʃənl] *adj* nacional; *national anthem* himno nacional; *national income* renta nacional || — *gross national product* producto nacional bruto || *national debt* deuda pública || *national grid* red *f* nacional de electricidad (electrical network), sistema *m* de coordenadas de los mapas británicos (coordinates system) || *national park* parque *m* nacional || *National Trust* organización *f* del gobierno británico para la conservación del patrimonio.
◆ *n* nacional *m*, natural *m*.

nationalism ['næʃnəlizəm] *n* nacionalismo *m*.

nationalist ['næʃnəlist] *adj/n* nacionalista.

nationalistic [,næʃnə'listik] *adj* nacionalista.

nationality [,næʃə'næliti] *n* nacionalidad *f*; *dual nationality* doble nacionalidad.

nationalization [,næʃnəlai'zeiʃən] *n* nacionalización *f* (of industry) || naturalización *f* (of person).

nationalize ['næʃnəlaiz] *vt* nacionalizar (industry) || naturalizar (person).

nationally ['næʃnəli] *adv* nacionalmente || desde el punto de vista nacional (from a national point of view) || a escala nacional; *to plan future constructions nationally rather than regionally* planear construcciones futuras a escala nacional y no regional || por toda la nación, por todo el país (throughout a nation); *the company is divided nationally into fifteen branches* la compañía está dividida por todo el país en quince sucursales.

National Socialism ['næʃənl'səuʃəlizəm] *n* nacionalsocialismo *m*.

National Syndicalism ['næʃənl'sindikəlizəm] *n* nacionalsindicalismo *m*.

nationhood ['neiʃənhud] *n* categoría *f* de nación || *to achieve nationhood* alcanzar la independencia nacional.

nationwide ['neiʃənwaid] *adj* a todo el país, a toda la nación (appeal, broadcast) || por todo el país, por toda la nación (tour) || nacional, a escala nacional; *nationwide scandal* escándalo nacional.

native ['neitiv] *adj* nativo, va (inhabitant); *a native Spaniard* un español nativo || natal (country, town) || materno, na; nativo, va (language) || del país (product) || nacional (painter, writer) || indígena, del país (labour) || indígena

(indigenous) || innato, ta (innate) || natural (simple) || MIN nativo, va; *native gold* oro nativo || originario, ria; *customs native to England* costumbres originarias de Inglaterra || FAM *to go native* vivir como los indígenas.
◆ *n* natural *m* & *f*, nativo, va; *I am a native of Scotland* soy natural de Escocia || nativo, va; indígena *m* & *f*, autóctono, na (original inhabitant of a country) || BOT & ZOOL originario, ria; *the elephant is a native of Asia* el elefante es originario de Asia || *you speak English like a native* habla inglés como un inglés.

native-born [-bɔːn] *adj* de nacimiento; *a native-born Englishman* un inglés de nacimiento.

nativism ['neitivizəm] *n* PHIL nativismo *m* || nacionalismo *m* (in politics).

nativist ['neitivist] *adj/n* nativista.

nativity [nə'tiviti] *n* nacimiento *m* (birth) || ASTR horóscopo *m*.

Nativity [nə'tiviti] *n* REL Natividad *f* || Navidad *f*, Natividad *f* (Christmas) || ARTS natividad *f* (painting) | nacimiento *m*, belén *m* (crib).

NATO ['neitəu] *abbr of* [*North Atlantic Treaty Organization*] OTAN, Organización del Tratado Atlántico Norte.

natron ['neitrən] *n* MIN natrón *m*.

natter ['nætə*] *n* FAM charla *f*.

natter ['nætə*] *vi* FAM charlar, charlotear (to chatter).

nattily ['nætili] *adv* elegantemente, con gusto.

nattiness ['nætinis] *n* elegancia *f*, buen gusto *m* (smartness) || habilidad *f*, maña *f* (skill).

natty ['næti] *adj* elegante (smart) || hábil, mañoso, sa (skilful) || ingenioso, sa (clever).

natural ['nætʃrəl] *adj* natural; *natural resources* recursos naturales; *natural gas* gas natural || natural, sencillo, lla (simple) || innato, ta; de nacimiento (innate) || nato, ta; *he is a natural orator* es un orador nato || MATH & MUS natural || — *natural child* hijo *m* natural || *natural death* muerte *f* natural || *natural features* geografía física || *natural historian* naturalista *m* & *f* || *natural history* historia *f* natural || *natural law* derecho *m* natural, ley *f* natural || MATH *natural logarithm* logaritmo *m* natural || *natural person* persona física || *natural sciences* ciencias *f pl* naturales || *natural to* propio de || *to be natural that* ser natural *or* lógico que.
◆ *n* FAM persona *f* particularmente dotada (gifted person) | cosa *f* sensacional (good thing) || MUS nota *f* natural (note) | becuadro *m* (sign) || tonto *m* de nacimiento, tonta *f* de nacimiento (half-wit) || — FAM *he is a natural for the job* es la persona más adecuada para este trabajo || *the natural* lo natural.

natural-born [-bɔːn] *adj* de nacimiento (native-born) || nato, ta; *a natural-born pianist* un pianista nato.

naturalism ['nætʃrəlizəm] *n* naturalismo *m*.

naturalist ['nætʃrəlist] *adj/n* naturalista.

naturalistic [,nætʃrə'listik] *adj* naturalista.

naturalization [,nætʃrəlai'zeiʃən] *n* naturalización *f* (of an alien) || BOT & ZOOL aclimatación *f* || *naturalization papers* carta *f sing* de ciudadanía *or* de naturaleza.

naturalize ['nætʃrəlaiz] *vt* naturalizar (an alien) || BOT & ZOOL aclimatar || *to become naturalized* naturalizarse.
◆ *vi* naturalizarse (person) || aclimatarse (plants, animals, etc.) || BOT herborizar.

naturally ['nætʃrəli] *adv* naturalmente, por supuesto, desde luego, claro (of course) || por naturaleza; *he is naturally generous* es generoso por naturaleza || con naturalidad, naturalmente; *people don't know how to behave naturally* la gente no sabe comportarse con naturalidad.

naturalness ['nætʃrəlnis] *n* naturalidad *f*.

nature ['neitʃə*] *n* naturaleza *f* (physical universe, essential characteristic or property); *nature is at its best in spring* la naturaleza está en todo su esplendor en primavera; *human nature* naturaleza humana; *the nature of the problem* la naturaleza del problema || natural *m*, temperamento *m*, carácter *m*; *to be a happy nature* ser de natural alegre || índole *f*, género *m*, clase *f*, tipo *m*; *other things of that nature* otras cosas de esta índole || esencia *f* (essence) || — *against nature* contra la naturaleza, contra natura || *by nature* por naturaleza || *from nature* del natural || *good nature* amabilidad *f*, buen carácter || *in a state of nature* en estado natural || *in the nature of things it's unlikely* normalmente es improbable || *it is not in his nature to shout* no es propio de él gritar || *it's the nature of things that* es natural que || *learning languages is a second nature to him* tiene mucha facilidad para los idiomas || *Mother Nature* la Madre Naturaleza || *nature lover* amante *m* & *f* de la naturaleza || *nature reserve* reserva *f* natural || *nature study* historia *f* natural || *return to nature* vuelta *f* a la naturaleza || *something in the nature of* una especie de || *the laws of nature* las leyes de la naturaleza || *the nature of fish is to swim* lo propio de los peces es nadar || *to draw from nature* dibujar del natural || FIG *to relieve nature* hacer de *or* del cuerpo.

naturism ['neitʃərizəm] *n* naturismo *m* (nudism).

naturist ['neitʃərist] *n* naturista *m* & *f* (nudist).

naturistic [neitʃə'ristik] *adj* naturista.

naught; nought [nɔːt] *n* POET nada *f* || MATH cero *m* || — *all for naught* en balde, para nada || *to bring to naught* frustrar (to ruin) || *to come to naught* fracasar, reducirse a nada || *to set at naught* hacer caso omiso de, despreciar.
◆ *adj* sin valor, inútil.

naughtily [-ili] *adv* mal; *to behave naughtily* portarse mal.

naughtiness [-inis] *n* picardía *f*, travesuras *f pl* (mischief) || desobediencia *f* (disobedience) || mala conducta *f* (bad behaviour) || picardía *f*, lo verde (of a story).

naughty [-i] *adj* travieso, sa; pícaro, ra (mischievous) || desobediente (disobedient) || malo, la (bad); *he's been a very naughty boy* ha sido muy malo || atrevido, da; verde, picante (slightly indecent); *a naughty joke* un chiste atrevido.

nausea ['nɔːsiə] *n* náusea *f* (sickness) || FIG náuseas *f pl*, asco *m* (strong disgust).

nauseate ['nɔːsieit] *vt* dar náuseas a || FIG dar asco a, repugnar a, dar náuseas a.
◆ *vi* tener náuseas (to be sick) || FIG asquear, dar náuseas (to disgust).

nauseating [-iŋ] *adj* nauseabundo, da; repugnante, asqueroso, sa.

nauseous ['nɔːsjəs] *adj* nauseabundo, da (causing nausea) || FIG nauseabundo, da; repugnante, asqueroso, sa (disgusting).

nauseousness [-nis] *n* náuseas *f pl* (nausea) || FIG asco *m*, asquerosidad *f*.

nautical ['nɔːtikəl] *adj* MAR náutico, ca; *nautical chart* carta náutica | marítimo, ma; *nautical term* término marítimo | marino, na; *nautical mile* milla marina.

nautilus ['nɔːtiləs] *n* ZOOL nautilo *m* (small sea animal).
— OBSERV El plural de *nautilus* es *nautiluses* o *nautili*.

naval ['neivəl] *adj* MAR naval; *naval forces* fuerzas navales; *naval engagement* combate naval || — *naval attaché* agregado *m* naval || *naval base* base *f* naval || *naval college* escuela *f* naval [militar] || *naval hospital* hospital *m* de marina || *naval officer* oficial *m* de marina || *naval power* potencia marítima || *naval station* base *f* naval.

Navarre [nə'vɑː*] *pr n* GEOGR Navarra *f*.

Navarrese [nævə'riːz] *adj/n* navarro, rra.

nave [neiv] *n* ARCH nave *f* || cubo *m* (of a wheel).

navel ['neivəl] *n* ANAT ombligo *m* || FIG ombligo *m*, centro *m* || — *navel orange* naranja *f* navel || *navel string* cordón *m* umbilical.

navelwort [-wəːt] *n* BOT ombligo *m* de Venus.

navicert ['nævisəːt] *n* MAR navicert *m*, licencia *f* de navegación (certificate).

navicula [nə'vikjələ] *n* REL naveta *f*.

navigability [,nævigə'biliti] *n* MAR navegabilidad *f*.

navigable ['nævigəbl] *adj* MAR navegable (river, etc.) || gobernable, dirigible (steerable).

navigate ['nævigeit] *vt* MAR navegar por (river, seas) | gobernar (ship) || pilotar (plane) || FIG *to navigate a bill through Parliament* llevar un proyecto de ley a buen término.
◆ *vi* navegar.

navigation [,nævi'geiʃən] *n* navegación *f* (art); *submarine, aerial navigation* navegación submarina, aérea || náutica *f* (science) || — *coastal navigation* navegación costera *or* de cabotaje || *navigation chart* carta náutica, carta aeronáutica || *navigation laws* código marítimo || *river navigation* navegación fluvial.

navigator ['nævigeitə*] *n* MAR & AVIAT navegante *m*.

navvy ['nævi] *n* peón *m* caminero.

navy ['neivi] *n* marina *f* [de guerra] (organization and manpower) || armada *f*, flota *f* (ships) || *merchant navy* marina mercante.
◆ *adj* de marina; *Navy Department* Ministerio de Marina || marino; *navy blue* azul marino.

nay [nei] *n* voto *m* en contra (in voting); *four ayes against three nays* cuatro votos a favor y tres en contra || negativa *f* (refusal) || *to say s.o. nay* decir que no a alguien.
◆ *adv* no (no) || más aún, mejor dicho, más bien (or even); *I suspect, nay, I am certain, that he is wrong* creo, mejor dicho, estoy seguro de que está equivocado.

Nazarene [,næzəriːn] *adj/n* nazareno, na.

Nazareth ['næzəriθ] *pr n* GEOGR Nazaret.

naze [neiz] *n* GEOGR cabo *m*.

Nazi ['nɑːtsi] *adj/n* nazi.

Nazism ['nɑːtsizəm] *n* nazismo *m*.

NBC *abbr of* [*National Broadcasting Company*] NBC, cadena de radiotelevisión norteamericana.

neap [niːp] *n* MAR marea *f* muerta.
◆ *adj* MAR *neap tide* marea muerta.

Neapolitan [niə'pɔlitən] *adj/n* napolitano, na.

near [niə*] *adj* cercano, na; *a near relative* un pariente cercano || íntimo, ma (friend) || estrecho, cha (friendship) || cercano, na; próximo, ma (nearby); *the nearest inn* la venta más cercana || próximo, ma; cercano, na (in time); *the near future* el futuro próximo || grande (resemblance) || bastante acertado, da (guess, estimate) || directo, ta; corto, ta (road) || AUT izquierdo, da; de la izquierda (when driving on the left) | derecho, cha; de la derecha (when driving on the right) || literal; *near translation* traducción literal || artificial; *near silk* seda artificial || delicado, da; minucioso, sa (work) || tacaño, ña (stingy) || SP reñido, da (race) || — *it was a near thing* me he librado por los pelos || *near distance* plano intermedio || *near one's end* cercano a su fin || *one's nearest and dearest* los parientes y amigos íntimos || *or near offer* pre-

cio a discutir (in advertisements) || *the near side* el lado izquierdo (when driving on the left), el lado derecho (when driving on the right) || *to have a near escape* librarse por los pelos || *to take it to the nearest pound* redondear la cifra hasta la libra más próxima.
◆ *adv* cerca; *he lives near* vive cerca; *you live near to my house* vives cerca de mi casa || FAM con parquedad, parcamente || — *as near as I can remember* que yo recuerde || *far and near* en todas partes || *he was very near asleep* estaba casi dormido || *I am nothing near so rich* estoy muy lejos de ser tan rico || *near at hand* a mano, muy cerca (object), a un paso, muy cerca (death, place, etc.), próximo, ma (time) || *near by* cerca || *near on* casi || *near to Easter* un poco antes de Pascua || *near upon* cerca de || *quite near* muy cerca || FIG *that's near enough* está bien || *to be as near as could be to doing sth.* estar a punto de hacer algo || *to bring near* acercar || *to come near* acercarse a (s.o.), estar a punto de *or* a dos dedos de, faltar poco para; *I came near fainting* estuve a punto de desmayarme || *to draw near* acercarse || *to keep as near as posible to the text* ajustarse lo más posible al texto, acercarse lo más posible al texto.
◆ *prep* cerca de; *near the door* cerca de la puerta; *near death* cerca de la muerte || casi; *we must have been near fifty* debíamos de ser casi cincuenta || — *near here* aquí cerca, cerca de aquí || *near the end of the month* hacia fines de mes || *near the end of the text* hacia el final del texto.

near [niə*] *vt* acercarse a, aproximarse a (a place) || acercarse a (s.o.) || acercarse a; *she is nearing sixty* se acerca a los sesenta || — *it was nearing midnight* la medianoche se acercaba || *summer is nearing its end* el fin del verano se acerca, el verano está a punto de terminarse || *to be nearing ruin* estar al borde de la ruina, estar muy cerca de la ruina.

nearby [-bai] *adj* cercano, na; próximo, ma.
◆ *adv* cerca.

Near East [-i:st] *pr n* GEOGR Cercano Oriente *m*.

nearly [-li] *adv* casi; *it is nearly midnight* son casi las doce de la noche; *he is nearly as old as her* es casi tan viejo como ella; *we are nearly there* casi hemos llegado || de cerca (to affect s.o.); *the matter concerns me nearly* el asunto me afecta de cerca || por poco, casi (in verbal constructions); *he nearly killed me* por poco me mata, casi me mata || — *not nearly* ni con mucho, ni mucho menos; *that will not be nearly enough for my journey* no será ni mucho menos suficiente para el viaje || *or nearly so* o casi || *to be nearly acquainted with* estar íntimamente relacionado con || *very nearly* casi, casi.

near-miss [-'mis] *n* tiro *m* cercano || *to be a near-miss* casi acertar, fallar por poco.

nearness [-nis] *n* proximidad *f*, cercanía *f* (of place) || proximidad *f* (in time) || intimidad *f* (of friends) || fidelidad *f* (of translation) || FAM parquedad *f* || *nearness of relationship* parentesco cercano.

nearsighted [-'saitid] *adj* MED miope, corto de vista.

nearsightedness [-'saitidnis] *n* MED miopía *f*.

neat [ni:t] *adj* limpio, pia; pulcro, cra (person, clothes) || limpio, pia (house, written work, worker) || bien cuidado, da (garden) || ordenado, da (orderly) || esmerado, da; bien hecho, cha (job) || elegante, pulcro, cra; pulido, da (style) || claro, ra (handwriting) || bien hecho, cha (speech) || bien hecho, cha; bien proporcionado, da (shapely) || fino, na (ankle) || elegante (smart) || ingenioso, sa (ingenious) || hábil (skilful) || solo, la (drinks); *a neat whisky* un whisky solo || — *as neat as a pin* limpio como una patena || US FAM *that's neat!* ¡qué bien!

neat [ni:t] *n* animal *m* vacuno.

neaten ['ni:tən] *vt* ordenar, arreglar, adecentar || *to neaten up one's hair* arreglarse el pelo.

neatherd [-hə:d] *n* vaquero *m*.

neatly [-li] *adv* con cuidado, con esmero || pulcramente || con gusto, elegantemente; *neatly dressed* vestido con gusto || hábilmente (skilfully).

neatness [-nis] *n* pulcritud *f*, limpieza *f* (of persons, of clothes) || limpieza *f* (of house, written work, worker) || orden *m* (order) || lo cuidado (of garden) || esmero *m* (care) || gusto *m*, elegancia *f* (of dress) || elegancia *f*, pulcritud *f* (of style) || claridad *f* (of handwriting) || lo bien hecho (of speech, of figure) || ingenio *m* (ingenuity) || destreza *f*, habilidad *f* (skill).

neb [neb] *n* pico *m* (beak) || punta *f* (projecting tip).

Nebraska [ni'bræskə] *pr n* GEOGR Nebraska.

Nebuchadnezzar [ˌnebjukəd'nezə*] *pr n* Nabucodonosor *m*.

nebula ['nebjulə] *n* ASTR nebulosa *f* || MED nube *f* (on eye).
— OBSERV El plural de esta palabra es *nebulae*.

nebulosity [ˌnebju'lɔsiti] *n* nebulosidad *f*.

nebulous ['nebjuləs] *adj* ASTR nebuloso, sa || FIG vago, ga; nebuloso, sa; confuso, sa.

NEC *abbr of [National Exhibition Centre]* parque de exposiciones cerca de Birmingham en Inglaterra.

necessarily ['nesisərili] *adv* necesariamente.

necessary ['nesisəri] *adj* necesario, ria; indispensable, imprescindible || — *if (it is) necessary* si es necesario, si es preciso || *it is necessary for you to do it, it is necessary that you do it* es necesario *or* es preciso que lo hagas, tienes que hacerlo || *to make it necessary for s.o. to do sth.* obligar a alguien a que haga algo.
◆ *n* lo necesario, lo esencial, lo imprescindible | necesidad *f* (necessity) || *to do the necessary* hacer lo necesario.
◆ *pl* lo necesario *sing* || — *the bare necessaries* lo estrictamente necesario || *the necessaries of life* lo indispensable.

necessitarianism [niˌsesitɛə'rijənizəm] *n* PHIL determinismo *m*.

necessitate [ni'sesiteit] *vt* necesitar, hacer necesario, exigir, requerir; *process that necessitates high pressures* procedimiento que exige presiones elevadas.

necessitous [ni'sesitəs] *adj* necesitado, da; pobre, indigente (poor) || urgente, apremiante (urgent).

necessity [ni'sesiti] *n* necesidad *f*; *necessity is the mother of invention* la necesidad aguza el ingenio || requisito *m* indispensable (requisite) || necesidad *f*, indigencia *f* (poverty) || — *a car is a necessity nowadays* el coche es una necesidad actualmente || *a case of absolute* o *of sheer necessity* un caso de fuerza mayor || PHIL *doctrine of necessity* determinismo *m* || *in case of necessity* si fuese necesario, en caso de necesidad || *necessity knows no law* la necesidad carece de ley || *of necessity, out of necessity* por necesidad, por fuerza, forzosamente || *there is no necessity for him to do it* no es necesario que lo haga || *to be in necessity* estar necesitado || *to be under the necessity of* verse obligado a || *to make a virtue of necessity* hacer de la necesidad virtud.
◆ *pl* artículos *m* de primera necesidad || *the necessities of life* lo indispensable || *to take the bare necessities* tomar lo estrictamente necesario.

neck [nek] *n* ANAT cuello *m* (of a man) || pescuezo *m* (of an animal) || cuello *m* (of garment) || cuello *m*, gollete *m* (of bottle, etc.) || mástil *m*, mango *m* (of violin, of guitar, etc.) || istmo *m* (isthmus) || estrecho *m* (strait) || ARCH collarino *m* || ANAT cuello *m* (of tooth, of womb) || TECH estrangulamiento *m* (of pipe) | garganta *f* (of axle) | cuello *m* (of retort) || SP cabeza *f*; *to win by a neck* ganar por una cabeza || — *low neck* escote *m* || *neck and neck* parejos; *to be neck and neck* ir parejos || *roll neck* cuello vuelto || MED *stiff neck* tortícolis *f* || FIG *to be in it up to the neck* estar metido en ello hasta el cuello | *to break one's neck* romperse la crisma (after a fall), deslomarse (working), matarse (to obtain sth.) | *to break s.o.'s neck* partir la cara a uno (to beat s.o. up) | *to fall on s.o.'s neck* echar los brazos al cuello de alguien || FIG & FAM *to get it in the neck* cargársela | *to have a neck* tener mucha cara | *to risk one's neck* jugarse el tipo | *to save one's neck* salvar el pellejo | *to stick one's neck out* arriesgarse (to take a risk), dar la cara (to face up to sth.) || *to throw* o *to fling one's arms around s.o.'s neck* echarle a uno los brazos al cuello || FIG & FAM *to throw s.o. out neck and crop* ponerle a uno de patitas en la calle || *to wring s.o.'s neck* retorcerle a uno el pescuezo || *V neck* cuello de pico.

neck [nek] *vi* besuquearse (to kiss) || abrazarse (to hug) || acariciarse (to caress).
◆ *vt* besuquear || abrazar || acariciar.

neckband [-bænd] *n* tirilla *f* (of a shirt).

neckerchief [-ətʃif] *n* pañuelo *m*.

necking [-iŋ] *n* ARCH collarino *m* || FAM besuqueo *m* (kissing) | abrazos *m pl* (hugging) | caricias *f pl* (caresses).

necklace [-lis] *n* collar *m*.

necklet [-lit] *n* collar *m* (necklace) || cuello *m* (of fur).

neckline [-lain] *n* escote *m* (of a dress).

necktie [-tai] *n* corbata *f*.

necrological [nekrə'lɔdʒikəl] *adj* necrológico, ca.

necrologist [ne'krɔlədʒist] *n* necrólogo *m*.

necrology [ne'krɔlədʒi] *n* necrología *f*.

necromancer ['nekrəumænsə*] *n* nigromante *m* & *f*, nigromántico, ca.

necromancy ['nekrəumænsi] *n* nigromancia *f*.

necrophagous [ne'krɔfəgəs] *adj* necrófago, ga.

necrophilia [ˌnekrəu'filiə] *n* necrofilia *f*.

necrophobia [ˌnekrəu'fəubiə] *n* necrofobia *f*.

necropolis [ne'krɔpəlis] *n* necrópolis *f*.
— OBSERV El plural de la palabra inglesa es *necropolises* o *necropoles* o *necropoleis* o *necropoli*.

necropsy ['nekrɔpsi] *n* necropsia *f*.

necrosis [ne'krəusis] *n* MED necrosis *f*.
— OBSERV El plural de la palabra inglesa es *necroses*.

nectar ['nektə*] *n* néctar *m*.

nectareous [nek'tɛəriəs] *adj* nectáreo, a.

nectarine ['nektərin] *n* nectarina *f* (variety of peach).

née; nee [nei] *adj* de soltera; *Mrs Mary Brown née Watson* la Sra. María Brown, de soltera Watson.

need [ni:d] *n* necesidad *f*; *the need for reinforcements* la necesidad de refuerzos; *a little money is enough to satisfy my needs* poco dinero me hace falta para satisfacer mis necesidades || requisito *m* indispensable (requisite) || necesidad *f*, indigencia *f* (poverty) || carencia *f*, falta *f* (lack) || necesidad *f*, apuro *m* (trouble); *in times of need* en momentos de apuro || — *if need be, in case of need* en caso de necesidad, si fuera necesario, si hiciera falta || *no need to hurry* no es necesario *or* no hace falta darse prisa || *no* *need to say that* huelga decir que, no es necesario decir que || *there is no need to* no es necesario, no hace falta || *to be badly in need of* o *in urgent need of* necesitar urgentemente, tener gran necesidad de || *to be in need* estar necesitado (poor) || *to have need of, to stand in need of* necesitar, tener necesidad de, hacerle falta a uno; *he has need of money* necesita dinero, tiene necesidad de dinero, le hace falta dinero || *to have need to do* tener que hacer.

◆ *pl* necesidades *f* (wants); *to supply the needs of* satisfacer las necesidades de || FAM necesidades *f*; *bodily needs* necesidades corporales || *my needs are easily satisfied* soy fácil de contentar.

need [ni:d] *vt* necesitar, hacerle falta a uno; *I need to rest* necesito descansar, me hace falta descansar; *I need twenty pounds* necesito *or* me hacen falta veinte libras || requerir, exigir (to require); *a job which needs a lot of care* un trabajo que requiere mucho cuidado || necesitar; *the soil needs rain* la tierra necesita lluvia || carecer de, faltar (to lack) || tener que, deber (to have to); *to need to do sth.* tener que hacer algo || hacer falta; *these clothes need to be ironed* hace falta planchar esta ropa || — *that needs no saying* ni que decir tiene || *they need to be told everything* hay que decírselo todo || *things needn't be that way* las cosas no tienen por qué ser así.

◆ *vi* estar necesitado (to be needy).

◆ *v aux* tener que, deber; *you needn't go if you don't want to* no tienes que ir si no quieres; *need I do it?* ¿tengo que hacerlo?, ¿debo hacerlo?

◆ *v impers* hacer falta, ser necesario; *it needs much skill to do this work* hace falta *or* es necesaria mucha habilidad para este trabajo.

— OBSERV El verbo auxiliar es invariable en 3ª persona del singular del presente del indicativo y en el pretérito. No tiene ni participio pasivo ni gerundio. Va siempre seguido por el infinitivo sin *to*.

needed [-id] *adj* necesario, ria || *to be needed* necesitarse, hacer falta, ser necesario.

needful [-ful] *adj* necesario, ria (necessary).

◆ *n* lo necesario; *do the needful* haz lo necesario || dinero *m* necesario (money).

neediness [-inis] *n* necesidad *f*, indigencia *f*.

needle ['ni:dl] *n* aguja *f* (for knitting and sewing); *crochet needle* aguja de ganchillo || MED & BOT aguja *f* || punta *f* (for engraving) || ARCH obelisco *m* || TECH aguja *f* || — *darning needle* aguja de zurcir || *knitting needle* aguja mechera || *magnetic needle* aguja imantada *or* magnética || BOT *shepherd's needle* aguja de pastor *or* de Venus || FIG *to be as sharp as a needle* ser un lince | *to look for a needle in a haystack* buscar una aguja en un pajar.

needle ['ni:dl] *vt* coser (to sew) || FAM hacer rabiar, pinchar, meterse con (to annoy); *stop needling him* deja de pincharle || US cargar (a drink).

needle case [-keis] *n* alfiletero *m*.

needlecord [-kɔ:d] *n* pana *f* de bordones estrechos.

needlecraft [-krɑ:ft] *n* costura *f*, labor *f* de aguja.

needlefish [-fiʃ] *n* ZOOL aguja *f*.

needleful [-ful] *n* hebra *f* (of thread).

needlepoint [-pɔint] *n* encaje *m* de aguja, puntas *f pl* (lace) || punta *f* seca (of a compass) || FIG minuciosidad *f*.

needless ['ni:dlis] *adj* innecesario, ria; inútil (unnecessary) || inútil (useless) || *needless to say* ni que decir tiene que, huelga decir que, está de más decir que; *I was, needless to say, working* huelga decir que yo estaba trabajando.

needlessness [-nis] *n* inutilidad *f* (of sth.) || inoportunidad *f* (of a remark).

needle valve ['ni:dlvælv] *n* válvula *f* de aguja.

needlewoman ['ni:dl'wumən] *n* costurera *f* || *to be a good needlewoman* coser bien.

— OBSERV El plural es *needlewomen*.

needlework ['ni:dlwə:k] *n* costura *f*, labor *f* de aguja (sewing) || bordado *m* (embroidery).

needn't ['ni:dnt] contracción de «need not».

needs [ni:dz] *adv* necesariamente, forzosamente || — *if needs must* si hace falta || *they must needs return* no tienen más remedio que volver.

— OBSERV *Needs* sólo se emplea antes o después de *must*.

needy ['ni:di] *adj* necesitado, da; indigente.

◆ *n* *the needy* los necesitados.

ne'er [nɛə*] *adv* nunca, jamás (never).

ne'er-do-well [-du,wel] *adj/n* inútil.

nefarious [ni'fɛəriəs] *adj* infame, inicuo, cua.

negate [ni'geit] *vt* negar (to deny) || anular, invalidar (to invalidate).

negation [ni'geiʃən] *n* negación *f*.

negative ['negətiv] *adj* negativo, va; *a negative reply* una contestación negativa; *negative personality, criticism* personalidad, crítica negativa || MATH & ELECTR negativo, va.

◆ *n* negativa *f*; *to reply in the negative* contestar con una negativa || MATH cantidad *f* negativa, término *m* negativo || PHOT negativo *m* || ELECTR polo *m* negativo || GRAMM negación *f* || *two negatives make an affirmative* o *a positive* dos negaciones equivalen a una afirmación.

negative ['negətiv] *vt* rechazar, no aprobar (to reject) || refutar (to refute) || negar (to deny) || contradecir (to contradict) || neutralizar (to counteract).

negaton ['negətɔn]; **negatron** ['negətrɔn] *n* PHYS negatón *m*.

neglect [ni'glekt] *n* negligencia *f*, descuido *m*, dejadez *f*, desidia *f*; *from* o *through* o *out of neglect* por negligencia; *neglect for one's own cleanliness* negligencia en el aseo personal || inobservancia *f* (of a rule) || incumplimiento *m* (of duties) || abandono *m* (abandon); *in total neglect* en el más completo abandono || dejadez *f* (self-neglect) || desaliño *m*, dejadez *f* (in style) || desatención *f* (*of* con) (inattention) || — *neglect of one's duty* negligencia en el cumplimiento del deber || *to die in neglect* morir abandonado.

neglect [ni'glekt] *vt* faltar a, no cumplir con, no cumplir (one's duty) || no observar (a rule) || dejar de; *don't neglect to post the letter* no dejes de echar la carta; *why did you neglect to go?* ¿por qué dejaste de ir? || descuidar, desatender; *she neglects her house, her child* descuida la casa, al niño || descuidar (a garden) || no hacer caso de, despreciar, desdeñar (to disregard advice) || abandonar (to abandon) || no aprovechar, desperdiciar (an opportunity) || hacer poco caso de (one's friends) || omitir, olvidar (to omit) || ignorar (to ignore).

neglected [-id] *adj* descuidado, da; desaliñado, da (appearance, style) || abandonado, da; dejado, da (person, garden).

neglectful [-ful]; **negligent** ['neglidʒənt] *adj* descuidado, da; negligente (careless) || olvidadizo, za (forgetful) || *to be neglectful of* descuidar, desatender.

négligé; negligee ['negli:ʒei] *n* salto *m* de cama, bata *f*, «negligé» *m*.

negligence ['neglidʒəns] *n* negligencia *f*, descuido *m*; *through negligence* por descuido || *a piece of negligence* un descuido.

negligent ['neglidʒənt] *adj* ⟶ **neglectful.**

negligible ['neglidʒəbl] *adj* insignificante (insignificant) || despreciable, desdeñable; *the reward is by no means negligible* la recompensa no es nada despreciable.

negotiable [ni'gəuʃjəbl] *adj* negociable || FAM transitable (road) | salvable, franqueable (obstacle) || — COMM *negotiable paper* efecto *m* || *not negotiable* que no se puede negociar.

negotiant [ni'gəuʃiənt] *n* negociador, ra.

negotiate [ni'gəuʃieit] *vi* negociar || *to negotiate for* negociar para obtener, entablar negociaciones para.

◆ *vt* negociar, gestionar; *to negotiate the sale of an estate* gestionar la venta de una finca || negociar; *to negotiate a bill of exchange* negociar una letra de cambio; *to negotiate a treaty* negociar un tratado || FIG salvar, franquear (obstacle) | tomar (bends) | subir (a hill).

negotiating [-iŋ] *adj* negociador, ra.

negotiation [ni,gəuʃi'eiʃən] *n* negociación *f*, gestión *f*; *the negotiation of a contract* la negociación de un contrato || negociación *f*; *to enter into* o *to open negotiations with* entablar negociaciones con || — *to be in negotiation with* estar negociando con || *under negotiation* en negociación.

negotiator [ni'gəuʃieitə*] *n* negociador, ra.

negotiatress [ni'gəuʃieitris]; **negotiatrix** [ni'gəuʃieitriks] *n* negociadora *f*.

Negress ['ni:gris] *n* negra *f*.

Negrillo [ne'griləu] *n* negrito, ta (from Africa).

— OBSERV El plural de la palabra inglesa *Negrillo* es *Negrillos* o *Negrilloes*.

Negrito [ne'gri:təu] *n* negrito, ta (from Asia and Oceania).

— OBSERV El plural de la palabra inglesa *Negrito* es *Negritos* o *Negritoes*.

negritude ['nigrə,tjud] *n* negritud *f*.

Negro ['ni:grəu] *adj* negro, gra.

◆ *n* negro *m*.

— OBSERV El plural de la palabra inglesa *Negro* es *Negroes*.

Negroid ['ni:grɔid] *adj* negroide.

negus ['ni:gəs] *n* bebida *f* caliente de vino, agua y especias.

Negus ['ni:gəs] *n* Negus *m* (Ethiopian ruler).

neigh [nei] *n* relincho *m*.

neigh [nei] *vi* relinchar.

neighbour; US **neighbor** ['neibə*] *n* vecino, na || REL prójimo *m*; *love thy neighbour* ama a tu prójimo || — *Good Neighbour Policy* política *f* de buena vecindad || *the new building dwarfs its neighbours* el nuevo edificio empequeñece las casas colindantes.

neighbour; US **neighbor** ['neibə*] *vt* lindar con, estar contiguo a; *his land neighbours the river* sus tierras lindan con el río *or* están contiguas al río.

◆ *vi* *to neighbour on* o *upon* lindar con, estar contiguo a (to be next to), rayar en; *his language neighboured on vulgarity* sus palabras rayaban en la vulgaridad.

neighbourhood; US **neighborhood** [-hud] *n* barrio *m* (district) || vecindad *f*; *my friend lives in the neighbourhood* mi amigo vive en la vecindad || vecindad *f*, vecindario *m*, vecinos *m pl*; *the whole neighbourhood came to the meeting* todo el vecindario vino a la reunión || alrededores *m pl*, cercanías *f pl*; *Manchester and its neighbourhood* Manchester y sus alrededores || — *in the neighbourhood of* alrededor de, cerca de, aproximadamente (approximately), cerca de (near) || *neighbourhood watch* vigilancia *f* vecinal.

neighbouring; US **neigboring** [-riŋ] *adj* vecino, na; *neighbouring country* país vecino || cercano, na (near).

neighbourliness; US **neighborliness** [-linis] *n* buenas relaciones *f pl* entre vecinos, relaciones *f pl* de buena vecindad.

neighbourly; *US* **neighborly** [-li] *adj* de buena vecindad (relations) ‖ amable, amistoso, sa (action, person).

neither ['naiðə*, *US* 'ni:ðə*] *adj* ninguno de los dos, ninguna de las dos (not either of two); *neither concert pleased me* no me gustó ninguno de los dos conciertos.
◆ *pron* ninguno, na; ninguno de los dos, ninguna de las dos; *neither of the books is of any use to me* ninguno de los dos libros me sirve para nada ‖ — *neither of them* ninguno de ellos, ninguno de los dos, ni el uno ni el otro ‖ *neither of the parents* ninguno de los padres.
◆ *adv* ni tampoco, tampoco; *he didn't know the answer and neither did she* él no conocía la respuesta ni ella tampoco ‖ tampoco; *if you don't work neither shall I* si tú no trabajas yo tampoco trabajaré ‖ — *neither... nor* ni... ni, no... ni... ni; *I want neither milk nor sugar* no quiero ni leche ni azúcar; *neither wind nor rain will make me change my mind* ni el viento ni la lluvia me harán cambiar de idea, no me harán cambiar de idea ni el viento ni la lluvia; *neither you nor I* ni tú ni yo; *neither one nor the other* ni uno ni otro ‖ FIG *to be neither here nor there* no tener nada que ver, no hacer al caso.

nemathelminths [,nemə'θelminθz] *pl n* ZOOL nematelmintos *m.*

nematodes ['nemətəudz] *pl n* ZOOL nematodos *m.*

nemesis ['nemisis] *n* justo castigo *m* (punishment) ‖ vengador *m* (avenger).
— OBSERV El plural de la palabra inglesa es *nemeses.*

nenuphar ['nenjufa:*] *n* BOT nenúfar *m.*

neo ['ni:əu] *pref* neo [con el sentido de «nuevo»].

neo-Catholicism [,ni:əukə'θɔlisizəm] *n* neocatolicismo *m.*

Neocene ['ni:ə,si:n] *n* GEOL neógeno *m.*

neo-Christianity [,ni:əu,kristi'æniti] *n* neocristianismo *m.*

neoclassic [,ni:əu'klæsik]**; neoclassical** [-əl] *adj* neoclásico, ca.

neoclassicism [,ni:əu'klæsisizəm] *n* neoclasicismo *m.*

neoclassicist [,ni:əu'klæsisist] *n* neoclásico, ca.

neocolonialism [,ni:əukə'ləunjəlizəm] *n* neocolonialismo *m.*

neocolonialist [,ni:əukə'ləunjəlist] *adj/n* neocolonialista.

neofascism [,ni:əu'fæʃizəm] *n* neofascismo *m.*

neo-Gothic [,ni:əu'gɔθik] *adj* neogótico, ca.

neo-Greek [,ni:əu'gri:k] *adj* neogriego, ga.

neo-Impressionism [,ni:əuim'preʃnizəm] *n* neoimpresionismo *m.*

neo-Latin ['ni:əu'lætin] *adj* neolatino, na; románico, ca.

Neolithic [,ni:əu'liθik] *adj* neolítico, ca.

neologism [ni:'ɔlədʒizəm] *n* neologismo *m.*

neologist [ni:'ɔlədʒist] *n* neólogo, ga.

neo-Malthusianism [,ni:əumæl'θju:ziənizəm] *n* neomaltusianismo *m.*

neon ['ni:ən] *n* neón *m; neon lighting* alumbrado de neón.

neophyte ['ni:əufait] *n* neófito, ta.

Neoplatonism ['ni:əu'pleitənizəm] *n* PHIL neoplatonismo *m.*

Neoplatonist ['ni:əu'pleitənist] *n* neoplatónico, ca.

neopositivism [,ni:əu'pɔzitivizəm] *n* PHIL neopositivismo *m.*

neorealism [,ni:əu'riəlizəm] *n* neorrealismo *m.*

neorealist [,ni:əu'riəlist] *adj/n* neorrealista.

neoromantic [,ni:əurəu'mæntik] *adj/n* neorromántico, ca.

neoromanticism [,ni:əurəu'mæntisizəm] *n* neorromanticismo *m.*

neo-Scholastic [,ni:əuskə'læstik] *adj* neoescolástico, ca.

neo-Scholasticism [,ni:əuskə'læstisizəm] *n* neoescolástica *f.*

neo-Thomism ['ni:əu'təmizəm] *n* neotomismo *m.*

Neozoic [,ni:əu'zəuik] *adj* GEOL neozoico, ca.

Nepal [ni'pɔ:l] *pr n* Nepal *m.*

Nepalese [,nepɔ:'li:z] *adj/n* nepalés, esa ‖ *the Nepalese* los nepaleses.

nephew ['nevju:] *n* sobrino *m.*

nephralgia [ne'frældʒiə] *n* MED nefralgia *f.*

nephritic [nə'fritik] *adj* MED nefrítico, ca.

nephritis [nə'fraitis] *n* MED nefritis *f.*

nepotism ['nepətizəm] *n* nepotismo *m.*

Neptune ['neptju:n] *pr n* MYTH Neptuno *m.*

Neptunian [nep'tju:njən] *adj* GEOL neptúnico, ca ‖ POET neptúneo, a.

neptunium [nep'tju:njəm] *n* CHEM neptunio *m.*

Nereid ['niəriid] *n* MYTH Nereida *f.*

Nero ['niərəu] *pr n* Nerón *m.*

nervate ['nə:vit] *adj* BOT nerviado, da.

nerve [nə:v] *n* ANAT nervio *m; optic nerve* nervio óptico ‖ BOT nervio *m* (of a leaf) ‖ nervadura *f* (of insects) ‖ ARCH nervadura *f,* nervio *m* (rib) ‖ FIG nervio *m; his nerves are on edge* tiene los nervios de punta; *he has nerves of steel* tiene nervios de acero ‖ valor *m* (courage); *I have not the nerve to do it* no tengo valor para llevarlo a cabo ‖ FAM cara *f,* caradura *f,* descaro *m* (cheek, insolence); *what a nerve!* ¡qué descaro!; *he has got a nerve!* ¡tiene una caradura! ‖ — *nerve specialist* neurólogo, ga ‖ FIG *to lose one's nerve* rajarse (to back down), ponerse nervioso (to get nervous) ‖ *to strain every nerve to* hacer todo lo posible para.
◆ *pl* FAM nerviosismo *m sing,* nerviosidad *f sing; he couldn't control his nerves* no podía dominar su nerviosismo; *to soothe s.o.'s nerves* quitar a uno el nerviosismo ‖ — *a fit of nerves* un ataque de nervios ‖ FIG *to be a bundle of nerves* estar hecho un manojo de nervios ‖ *to be in a state of nerves* estar muy nervioso ‖ *to get on s.o.'s nerves* crisparle los nervios a uno, ponerle nervioso a uno, ponerle a uno los nervios de punta ‖ *to have steady nerves* tener los nervios bien templados ‖ *to set one's nerves on edge* ponerle a uno los nervios de punta ‖ *war of nerves* guerra *f* de nervios.

nerve [nə:v] *vt* animar, dar ánimos a ‖ *to nerve o.s. to* animarse a.

nerve cell [-sel] *n* ANAT neurona *f,* célula *f* nerviosa.

nerve centre; *US* **nerve center** [-'sentə*] *n* ANAT centro *m* nervioso ‖ FIG punto *m* neurálgico.

nerve gas [-gæs] *n* gas *m* nervioso.

nerve impulse [-'impʌls] *n* impulso *m* nervioso.

nerveless [-lis] *adj* sin nervios (spiritless) ‖ BOT sin nervadura ‖ MED sin nervios.

nerve-racking; nerve-wracking [-'rækiŋ] *adj* crispante (sound, etc.) ‖ desgarrador, ra (blood-curdling) ‖ horripilante (terrifying) ‖ exasperante (exasperating) ‖ muy agudo, da (pain).

nerviness ['nə:vinis]**; nervosity** [nə:'vɔsiti] *n* nerviosidad *f,* nerviosismo *m.*

nervous ['nə:vəs] *adj* MED nervioso, sa (disease, system) ‖ ARTS vigoroso, sa; enérgico, ca ‖ tímido, da (timid) ‖ miedoso, sa (apprehensive) ‖ nervioso, sa; *nervous laugh* risa nerviosa ‖ nervioso, sa; irritable (irritable) ‖ inquieto, ta; preocupado, da (worried) ‖ — *don't be nervous* no tengas miedo, no te asustes ‖ *nervous breakdown* depresión nerviosa ‖ FAM *to be a nervous wreck* estar hecho un manojo de nervios ‖ *to be nervous of* tener miedo a.

nervously [-li] *adv* tímidamente, con miedo ‖ nerviosamente.

nervousness [-nis] *n* nerviosismo *m,* nerviosidad *f* (agitated mood) ‖ timidez *f* (shyness) ‖ miedo *m* (fear) ‖ vigor *m,* fuerza *f* (strength).

nervure ['nə:vjuə*] *n* nervadura *f* (of insects) ‖ BOT nervio *m,* nervadura *f.*

nervy ['nə:vi] *adj* nervioso, sa (nervous) ‖ *US* FAM descarado, da; fresco, ca (brazen).

nescience ['nesiəns] *n* ignorancia *f* ‖ PHIL agnosticismo *m.*

nescient ['nesiənt] *adj* ignorante.
◆ *adj/n* REL agnóstico, ca.

ness [nes] *n* promontorio *m,* cabo *m.*

nest [nest] *n* nido *m* (of birds) ‖ nidal *m* (of hens) ‖ madriguera *f* (of mice, of rabbits, etc.) ‖ nidada *f* (brood) ‖ hormiguero *m* (of ants) ‖ avispero *m* (of wasps) ‖ FIG nido *m* (house) ‖ guarida *f,* cueva *f* (of criminals) ‖ — *nest box* ponedero *m,* nidal *m* ‖ *nest of drawers* archivador *m* (for office), costurero *m,* «chiffonnier» *m* (for room) ‖ *nest of machine guns* nido de ametralladoras ‖ *nest of shelves* casillero *m* ‖ *nest of tables* mesas *f pl* de nido ‖ FIG *to feather one's nest* hacer su agosto.

nest [nest] *vt* encajar (to fit into) ‖ empalmar (to join).
◆ *vi* anidar (birds) ‖ TECH empalmar (to join); *pipes that nest in each other* tubos que empalman unos con otros ‖ encajar (to fit into) ‖ buscar nidos (an egg collector).

nest egg ['nesteg] *n* nidal *m* (in a hen's nest) ‖ FIG ahorrillos *m pl,* ahorros *m inv* (savings).

nestful [-ful] *n* nidada *f.*

nestle ['nesl] *vi* arrellanarse; *he nestled in an armchair* se arrellanó en un sillón ‖ acurrucarse (in s.o.'s arms) ‖ recostar la cabeza; *she nestled against his shoulder* recostó la cabeza sobre su hombro ‖ anidar (to nest) ‖ — *to nestle down* acurrucarse, hacerse un ovillo ‖ *to nestle up* arrimarse a ‖ *village nestling in a valley* pueblo situado en el fondo de un valle.
◆ *vt* recostar (the head) ‖ poner con mimo; *she nestled the bird in her hand* puso con mimo el pájaro en su mano.

nestling [-iŋ] *n* pajarito *m,* cría *f* de pájaro.

Nestorian [nes'tɔ:riən] *adj/n* nestoriano, na.

net [net] *n* red *f; net fishing* pesca con red; *to cast the net* echar la red ‖ redecilla *f; hair net* redecilla para el pelo ‖ redecilla *f* (for shopping, luggage rack) ‖ malla *f* (mesh) ‖ tul *m* (fabric) ‖ SP red *f,* malla *f* ‖ ganancia *f* neta (benefit) ‖ peso *m* neto (weight) ‖ cantidad neta (amount) ‖ FIG red *f,* trampa *f; to fall into the net* caer en la red ‖ *to sleep under a mosquito net* dormir con mosquitero.
◆ *adj* neto, ta; *a net profit* un beneficio neto; *net weight* peso neto.

net [net] *vt* coger [con red] (to catch with a net) ‖ pescar [con red] (fish) ‖ SP dar en la red con (the ball) ‖ tejer en forma de malla ‖ COMM ganar neto (to earn) ‖ producir neto (to yield).

netball [-bɔ:l] *n* SP baloncesto *m* femenino.

netful [-ful] *n* *a netful of fish* una red llena de peces.

nether ['neðə*] *adj* inferior; *the nether lip* el labio inferior ‖ *the nether regions, the nether* *world* el infierno (hell), el otro mundo (the next world).

Netherlander ['neðələndə*] *n* holandés, esa; neerlandés, esa.

Netherlands ['neðələndz] *pl n* GEOGR Holanda *f sing*, Países Bajos *m*.
— OBSERV *Netherlands* lleva siempre el artículo en inglés como *Países Bajos* en español, mientras que *Holanda* no lo lleva.

nethermost ['neðəməust] *adj* más profundo, más bajo.

nett [net] *adj* neto, ta; *a net profit* un beneficio neto; *net weight* peso neto.

nett [net] *vt* COMM ganar neto (to earn) | producir neto (to yield).

netting [-iŋ] *n* fabricación *f or* confección *f* de redes ‖ colocación *f* de redes (for fishing or hunting) ‖ red *f* (net) ‖ redes *f pl* (nets) ‖ tul *m* (fabric) ‖ malla *f* (mesh).

nettle ['netl] *n* BOT ortiga *f* ‖ MED *nettle rash* urticaria *f*.

nettle ['netl] *vt* picar con una ortiga (to sting) ‖ FAM picar, hacer rabiar, irritar (to irritate).

network ['netwə:k] *n* malla *f*, red *f* (net) ‖ red *f* (of railways, rivers, roads, telephones, etc.); *rail network* red de ferrocarriles ‖ RAD canal *m*, cadena *f* (channel) ‖ INFORM red *f*; *network architecture* arquitectura de red; *network processor* procesador de red ‖ FIG tejido *m*, sarta *f*; *it is a network of lies* es un tejido de mentiras | red *f*; *a network of drug pushers* una red de vendedores de drogas.

neume [nju:m] *n* MUS neuma *m*.

neural ['njuərəl] *adj* de los nervios, nervioso, sa; neural.

neuralgia [njuə'rældʒə] *n* MED neuralgia *f*.

neuralgic [njuə'rældʒik] *adj* MED neurálgico, ca.

neurasthenia [,njuərəs'θi:njə] *n* MED neurastenia *f*.

neurasthenic [,njuərəs'θenik] *adj/n* MED neurasténico, ca.

neuritic [njuə'ritik] *adj* MED neurítico, ca.

neuritis ['njuə'raitis] *n* MED neuritis *f*.

neuroblast ['njuərə,blæst] *n* BIOL neuroblasto *m*.

neurological [,njuərə'lɔdʒəkəl] *adj* MED neurológico, ca.

neurologist [njuə'rɔlədʒist] *n* MED neurólogo *m*.

neurology [njuə'rɔlədʒi] *n* MED neurología *f*.

neuroma [njuə'rəumə] *n* MED neuroma *m*.
— OBSERV El plural de la palabra inglesa *neuroma* es *neuromata* o *neuromas*.

neuron ['njuərɔn] *n* MED neurona *f* (cell).

neuropath ['njuərəpæθ] *n* MED neurópata *m*.

neuropathology [,njuərəpæ'θɔlədʒi] *n* MED neuropatología *f*.

neuropathy [njuə'rɔpəθi] *n* MED neuropatía *f*.

neuroptera [njuə'rɔptərə] *pl n* neurópteros *m*.

neuropteran [njuə'rɔptərən] *adj* neuróptero (insect).
◆ *n* neuróptero *m* (insect).

neurosis [njuə'rəusis] *n* neurosis *f*.
— OBSERV El plural de la palabra inglesa es *neuroses*.

neuroskeleton [,njuərə'skelitn] *n* neuroesqueleto *m*.

neurosurgery [,njuərə'sə:dʒəri] *n* neurocirugía *f*.

neurotic [njuə'rɔtik] *adj/n* neurótico, ca.

neurotomy [njuə'rɔtəmi] *n* MED neurotomía *f*.

neurovegetative [,njuərə'vedʒitətiv] *adj* neurovegetativo, va.

neuter ['nju:tə*] *adj* neutro, tra ‖ GRAMM neutro, tra (gender) | neutro, tra; intransitivo, va (verb).
◆ *n* GRAMM neutro *m*; *in the neuter* en neutro ‖ obrera *f* (worker bee) ‖ animal *m* castrado (castrated animal).

neuter ['nju:tə*] *vt* castrar (to castrate).

neutral ['nju:trəl] *adj* neutro, tra ‖ JUR & MIL neutral; *to remain neutral* permanecer neutral ‖ CHEM & ELECTR neutro, tra.
◆ *n* neutral *m* & *f* ‖ AUT punto *m* muerto (of gearshift).

neutralism [-izəm] *n* neutralismo *m*.

neutralist [-ist] *adj/n* neutralista, neutral.

neutrality [nju:'træliti] *n* neutralidad *f*.

neutralization [,nju:trəlai'zeiʃən] *n* neutralización *f*.

neutralize ['nju:trəlaiz] *vt* neutralizar.

neutralizer [-ə*] *n* neutralizador *m*, neutralizante *m*.

neutralizing [-iŋ] *adj* neutralizador, ra.

neutrino [nju:'tri:nəu] *n* PHYS neutrino *m*.

neutron ['nju:trɔn] *n* PHYS neutrón *m*.

never ['nevə*] *adv* nunca, jamás; *he never came* nunca vino, no vino nunca; *never again, never more* nunca más; *never yet* jamás hasta ahora; *she said never a word about it* nunca dijo una palabra sobre aquello ‖ — *I never expected it* no me lo esperaba ‖ *I never heard anything like it* no he oído nunca una cosa parecida ‖ *never!, you never did!* ¡no me digas! ‖ *never a* ni; *never a care in the world* ni una preocupación en el mundo ‖ *never a one* ni siquiera uno ‖ *never fear* no tema ‖ *never in all my life* jamás en la vida, en mi vida ‖ *never mind* no importa, da igual (it doesn't matter), no se preocupe (don't worry) ‖ *never never, never ever* nunca jamás; *I shall never ever forget her* no la olvidaré nunca jamás ‖ *surely you never did it?* ¿no me digas que lo has hecho? ‖ *well I never!* ¡no me digas!

never-ceasing [-'si:siŋ] *adj* incesante.

never-dying [-'daiiŋ] *adj* imperecedero, ra.

never-ending [-'endiŋ] *adj* sin fin, interminable.

never-fading [-'feidiŋ] *adj* imperecedero, ra.

never-failing [-'feiliŋ] *adj* infalible.

nevermore [-'mɔ:*] *adv* nunca más; *nevermore shall I hear her voice* nunca más oiré su voz; *nevermore to return* para no volver más.

never-never [-'nevə*] *n* FAM compra *f* a plazos ‖ — *never-never land* país *m* de ensueños ‖ FAM *to buy sth. on the never-never* comprar algo a plazos.

nevertheless [-ðə'les] *adv* sin embargo, no obstante.

nevus ['ni:vəs] *n* US nevo *m*.
— OBSERV El plural de *nevus* es *nevi*.

new [nju:] *adj* nuevo, va; *a new house* una nueva casa, una casa nueva (see OBSERV; *there is nothing new* no hay nada nuevo; *new moon* luna nueva; *new pupil* alumno nuevo; *new suit* traje nuevo ‖ tierno (bread) ‖ fresco, ca (fish) ‖ nuevo, va; *new to one's job* nuevo en el oficio ‖ — *are you new to this technique?* ¿es nueva esta técnica para ti? ‖ *it's as good as new* está como nuevo, está nuevo ‖ *New Year* Año Nuevo ‖ *New Year's Day* primer día *m* del año, día *m* de Año Nuevo ‖ *New Year's Eve* Nochevieja *f* ‖ *New World* Nuevo Mundo ‖ *there is nothing new under the sun* no hay nada nuevo bajo el sol ‖ *to be new in* o *to a town* acabar de llegar a una ciudad ‖ *to be new to the college* ser nuevo en el colegio ‖ *what's new?* ¿qué hay de nuevo?
◆ *n* lo nuevo; *to throw out the old and keep the new* tirar lo viejo y quedarse con lo nuevo.
◆ *adv* recién, recientemente; *new-made* recién hecho.
— OBSERV The translation *una nueva casa* would tend to suggest a recently acquired house, whereas *una casa nueva* would indicate a newly built house.

new arrival [-ə'raivəl] *n* recién llegado, da.

newborn [-bɔ:n] *adj* recién nacido, da.

New Caledonia [-,kæli'dəunjə] *pr n* GEOGR Nueva Caledonia *f*.

newcomer [-'kʌmə*] *n* recién llegado, da; nuevo, va.

New Delhi [-'deli] *pr n* GEOGR Nueva Delhi.

newel [-əl] *n* ARCH nabo *m*, eje *m* (of stairs) | pilastra *f* (at bottom of handrail).

New England [-'iŋglənd] *pr n* GEOGR Nueva Inglaterra *f*.

newfangled [-,fæŋgld] *adj* moderno, na; recién inventado, da.

newfound [-'faund] *adj* nuevo, va.

Newfoundland [-fənd'lænd] *pr n* GEOGR Terranova *f* ‖ *Newfoundland dog* terranova *m*.

New Guinea [-'gini] *pr n* GEOGR Nueva Guinea *f*.

New Hampshire [-'hæp,ʃə] *pr n* GEOGR Nueva Hampshire.

New Jersey [-'dʒə:zi] *pr n* GEOGR Nueva Jersey.

new-laid [-leid] *adj* recién puesto, fresco (egg).

newly [-li] *adv* nuevamente (in a new way) ‖ recién, recientemente; *newly painted wall* pared recién pintada ‖ *he is newly arrived* acaba de llegar.

newlywed [-li'wed] *n* recién casado, da.

New Mexico [-'meksi,kəu] *pr n* GEOGR Nuevo México.

newness [-nis] *n* novedad *f* (novelty) ‖ FIG inexperiencia *f* (of s.o.).

New Orleans [-'ɔ:liənz] *pr n* GEOGR Nueva Orleáns *f*.

news [nju:z] *n* noticia *f* (piece of news), noticias *f pl*; *this is good news* es una buena noticia; *to send news of s.o.* dar noticias de uno ‖ noticias *f pl*, informaciones *f pl*; *financial news* informaciones financieras ‖ crónica *f*; *musical news* crónica musical ‖ actualidad *f*; *to be in the news* ser de actualidad ‖ diario *m* hablado, noticias *f pl* (on the radio) ‖ noticias *f pl*, telediario *m* (on television) ‖ CINEM noticiario *m* (film) ‖ — *a piece of news* una noticia ‖ *have I got news for you!* ¡menuda noticia tengo que darte! ‖ *have you heard the news?* ¿te has enterado de la última noticia? ‖ *if the news breaks* si la noticia llega a oídos del público ‖ *it was news to me* me cogió de nuevas ‖ *latest news* últimas noticias ‖ *no news is good news* las malas noticias llegan las primeras ‖ *that's no news* eso no es ninguna novedad ‖ *to break the news to s.o.* dar una noticia a alguien ‖ *what news?, what's the news?* ¿qué hay de nuevo?
— OBSERV *News* se construye siempre con el verbo en singular. Sin embargo es incorrecto decir *a news*. En su lugar debe emplearse *a piece of news* o *a news item*.

news agency [-'eidʒənsi] *n* agencia *f* de información *or* de prensa.

newsagent [-,eidʒənt] *n* vendedor *m* de periódicos.

newsboard [-bɔ:d] *n* tablero *m or* tablón *m* de anuncios.

newsboy [-bɔi] *n* muchacho *m* vendedor de periódicos (seller) ‖ muchacho *m* que reparte periódicos (deliverer).

news bulletin [-'bulitin] *n* boletín *m* informativo, noticias *f pl*, noticiario *m*.

newscast [-kɑːst] *n* noticiario *m*, noticias *f pl*.

newscaster [-'kɑːstə*] *n* presentador, ra; locutor, ra [del telediario] (on television) || locutor, ra [del boletín informativo] (on radio).

news conference [-'kɔnfərəns] *n* rueda *f* de prensa, conferencia *f* de prensa.

news correspondent [-ˌkɔris'pɔndənt] *n* corresponsal *m* & *f* [de prensa, de radio o televisión].

news dealer [-'diːlə*] *n* US vendedor *m* de periódicos.

news flash [-flæʃ] *n* noticia *f* de última hora, flash *m*.

news item [-'aitəm] *n* noticia *f*.

newsletter [-'letə*] *n* hoja *f* informativa, boletín *m* (printed sheet).

newsman [-mən] *n* vendedor *m* de periódicos (newsagent) || periodista *m*, reportero *m* (reporter) || locutor *m* [del boletín informativo] (newscaster on radio) || presentador *m*, locutor *m* [del telediario] (newscaster on television).
— OBSERV El plural de *newsman* es *newsmen*.

newsmonger [-'mʌŋgə*] *n* chismoso, sa.

newspaper [-'peipə*] *n* periódico *m*, diario *m* (daily) || — *newspaper correspondent* corresponsal *m* de periódico || *weekly newspaper* semanario *m*.

newpaperman [-'peipəmən] *n* periodista *m*.
— OBSERV El plural de *newspaperman* es *newspapermen*.

newspaperwoman [-ˌpeipəˌwumən] *n* periodista *f*.
— OBSERV El plural es *newspaperwomen*.

newsprint [-print] *n* papel *m* de periódico.

newsreel [-riːl] *n* noticiario *m* (film).

newsroom [-rum] *n* sala *f* de lectura de los periódicos (in a library) || sala *f* de redacción (in a newspaper office, in a radio station, etc.).

newsstand [-stænd] *n* quiosco *m* or puesto *m* de periódicos.

newsworthy [-ˌwəːði] *adj* de interés periodístico.

newsy [-i] *adj* US lleno de noticias.

newt [njuːt] *n* ZOOL tritón *m*.

newton ['njuːtn] *n* newton *m*, neutonio *m* (unit of force).

Newtonian [njuː'təunjən] *adj* neutoniano, na; newtoniano, na.

new town ['njuːtaun] *n* ciudad *f* de nueva planta.

New York ['njuː'jɔːk] *pr n* GEOGR Nueva York *f*.

New Yorker [-ə*] *n* neoyorquino, na.

New Zealand ['njuː'ziːlənd] *pr n* GEOGR Nueva Zelanda *f*, Nueva Zelandia *f*.

New Zealander [-ə*] *n* neocelandés, esa; neozelandés, esa.

next [nekst] *adj* vecino, na; de al lado; *the next room* la habitación de al lado || próximo, ma; *the next train to London* el próximo tren para Londres; *(the) next time I sing* la próxima vez que cante; *the next stop* la próxima parada || siguiente; *the next chapter* el capítulo siguiente; *the next day, morning* el día, la mañana siguiente || que viene, próximo, ma; *next year* el año que viene || — *next best* el segundo (en calidad) || *next door* (en) la casa de al lado || *next door but one to me* dos casas más allá de la mía || *next please!* ¡el siguiente por favor! || *on Sunday next* el próximo domingo, el domingo que viene || *on 23rd November next* el 23 de noviembre próximo || *the next but one* el segundo después de éste || *the next day but one* dos días después || *the next larger size* una talla más grande, un número más grande || *the next life* la otra vida || *next of kin* pariente más cercano, parientes más cercanos || *this time next month, next year* el mes, el año que viene por estas fechas || *to be next after s.o.* ser el primero después de alguien || *to live next door to* ser vecino de || *what next?* y ahora ¿qué? || *what next, please?* ¿algo más? (in shop) || *who is next?* ¿a quién le toca?, ¿quién es el siguiente?, ¿de quién es el turno?
◆ *adv* después, luego; *next came the bishop* luego vino el obispo || ahora (now) || la próxima vez; *when we next see each other* cuando nos veamos la próxima vez || *who comes next?* ¿a quién le toca?, ¿quién es el siguiente?, ¿de quién es el turno?
◆ *prep* cerca de, junto a, al lado de (s.o., sth.); *she was sitting next me* estaba sentada junto a mí or a mi lado || — *for next to nothing* por casi nada || *next to* cerca de, junto a, al lado de || *next to impossible* casi imposible || *next to nobody* casi nadie || FAM *the thing next my heart* lo que más aprecio, lo más entrañable para mí || *to come next to s.o.* acercarse a uno || *to wear wool next to one's skin* llevar lana en contacto con la piel.

next-door ['neks'dɔː*] *adj* de al lado.

nexus ['neksəs] *n* nexo *m*, vínculo *m*.
— OBSERV El plural de *nexus* es *nexus* o *nexuses*.

NHS *abbr of [National Health Service]* Seguridad Social británica.

niacin ['naiəsin] *n* ácido *m* nicotínico.

Niagara [nai'ægərə] *pr n* GEOGR Niágara *m*; *Niagara Falls* Cataratas del Niágara.

Niamey [ni'aːmei] *pr n* GEOGR Niamey.

nib [nib] *n* plumilla *f*, plumín *m* (of a pen) || punta *f*, pico *m* (of tool) || pico *m* (of bird).

nibble ['nibl] *n* mordisqueo *m*, mordedura *f* (act of nibbling) || mordisco *m* (bite) || roedura *f* (of mice) || pizca *f*, pedacito *m* (bit) || bocado *m* (bite to eat) || mordida *f*, picada *f* (in fishing) || — *I never had a nibble all day* no han picado en todo el día || *to have a nibble* picar un poco (at food).

nibble ['nibl] *vt* roer, mordisquear; *mice have been nibbling the cheese* los ratones han mordisqueado el queso || picar (fish).
◆ *vi* mordisquear, mordiscar; *to nibble at a biscuit* mordisquear una galleta || picar (fish at the bait) || FIG sentirse tentado; *to nibble at an offer* sentirse tentado por una oferta || *to nibble at one's food* comisquear.

Nibelungen ['niːbəluŋən] *pl prn* Nibelungos *m*.

nibs [nibz] *n* FAM *his nibs* su señoría.

Nicaragua [ˌnikə'rægjuə] *pr n* GEOGR Nicaragua *f*.

Nicaraguan [-n] *adj/n* nicaragüense.

nice [nais] *adj* simpático, ca (likeable); *she is very nice* es muy simpática || amable [AMER gentil] (kind); *that is very nice of you* es usted muy amable || bueno, na; agradable (agreeable); *nice dinner* buena cena; *nice evening* velada agradable || bonito, ta [AMER lindo, da]; *nice car* bonito coche || mono, na; guapo, pa; bonito, ta [AMER lindo, da] (pretty); *you're looking very nice* estás muy mona || ameno, na (pleasant); *a nice book* un libro ameno || agradable; *to say nice things* decir cosas agradables || bueno, na (weather) || difícil, delicado, da (finicky) || difícil, exigente, escrupuloso, sa; meticuloso, sa (punctilious) || minucioso, sa; meticuloso, sa (enquiry) || sutil (distinction) || delicado, da; difícil (experiment, point) || bueno, na; *to have a nice ear for music* tener buen oído para la música || atinado, da; acertado, da; *a nice judgment* un juicio atinado || preciso, sa (accurate) || agudo, da (eye) || delicado, da; fino, na (refined taste, manners) || bien; *it smells, it tastes nice* huele, sabe bien || decente; *it is not a nice joke* no es un chiste decente || FAM menudo, da (unsatisfactory); *a nice mess we are in now!* ¡en menudo lío nos hemos metido!; *a nice friend you turned out to be!* ¡menudo amigo me has salido! || — *a nice little sum* una buena cantidad || *as nice as nice can be* de lo más agradable || *how nice!* ¡qué amable! (kind), ¡qué precioso!, ¡qué bonito! (pretty) || *how nice of you to come!* ¡qué amable haber venido! || *it's nice and warm in here* hace un calor agradable aquí dentro || *it's nice here* se está bien aquí || *nice and* bien, bastante (quite); *it is nice and easy* es bien fácil; bien, muy (very); *nice and friendly* bien simpático || *nice people* buena gente || *there's a nice thing to say!* ¡qué agradable! (with irony) || *to be a nice fellow* ser un buen chico || *to have a nice time* pasarlo bien, divertirse || *what a nice gesture!* ¡qué detalle más delicado!

nice-looking [-'lukiŋ] *adj* guapo, pa; mono, na; bien parecido, da [AMER lindo, da] (person) || precioso, sa; bonito, ta [AMER lindo, da] (object).

nicely [-li] *adv* amablemente [AMER gentilmente] (kindly) || agradablemente (pleasantly) || cuidadosamente (carefully) || bien; *very nicely, thank you* muy bien, muchas gracias; *she speaks very nicely about you* habla muy bien de ti; *we're very nicely situated* estamos muy bien situados || *that will do nicely* así está muy bien.

niceness [-nis] *n* amabilidad *f*, simpatía *f* [AMER gentileza *f*] (kindness) || lo agradable (pleasantness) || meticulosidad *f* (punctiliousness) || delicadeza *f* (refinement) || sutileza *f*, sutilidad *f*, fineza *f*.

nicety [-ti] *n* precisión *f*, exactitud *f* (exactness) || sutileza *f* (subtlety) || delicadeza *f* || — *niceties* sutilezas || *to a nicety* perfectamente.

niche [niːʃ] *n* hornacina *f*, nicho *m* (in a wall) || FIG hueco *m* (place); *he found his niche in administration* encontró un hueco en la administración | buena colocación *f* (good job).

nick [nik] *n* muesca *f* (notch) || cran *m* (in printing) || uña *f*, muesca *f* (for opening penknife) || mella *f* (in edge of blade) || hendidura *f* (in screw head) || desportillado *m*, desportilladura *f* (of a dish) || rasguño *m* (slight wound) || FAM chirona *f* (jail) || — FAM *in good nick* en buen estado, en buenas condiciones || FIG *in the nick of time* en el momento preciso or oportuno, a punto (at the right moment), justo a tiempo (just in time).

nick [nik] *vt* hacer muescas en (to make nicks) || cortar (to cut) || hacer una hendidura en (a screw head) || señalar, marcar (cards) || desportillar (a dish) || mellar (a blade) || ganar (in dice games) || FAM acertar (to guess) | coger, pillar, pescar, agarrar (to arrest) | birlar (to steal).
◆ *vi* *to nick at* criticar || *to nick in* meterse en.

Nick [nik] *pr n* Nico *m*, Nicolás *m* (diminutive of «Nicholas») || FAM *Old Nick* Patillas (the Devil).

nickel ['nikl] *n* níquel *m* (metal) || US moneda *f* de cinco centavos || — *nickel bronze* cuproníquel *m* || *nickel silver* plata alemana.

nickel ['nikl] *vt* niquelar.

nickel-plate [-'pleit] *vt* niquelar.

nickel-plating [-'pleitiŋ] *n* niquelado *m*.

nickname ['nikneim] *n* apodo *m*, mote *m* (name) || diminutivo *m* (diminutive).

nickname ['nikneim] *vt* apodar, poner de apodo or de mote; *they nicknamed him «toothy»* le pusieron de mote «el dientes» || llamar con un diminutivo.

Nicosia [ˌnikə'siːə] *pr n* GEOGR Nicosia.

nicotine ['nikətiːn] *n* nicotina *f*.

nictation [nik'teiʃən] *n* nictación *f.*

nictitating ['niktiteitiŋ] *adj* ZOOL nictitante.

nidation [ni'deiʃən] *n* nidación *f.*

nidification [,nidifi'keiʃən] *n* nidificación *f.*

nidify ['nidifai] *vi* hacer el nido, anidar, nidificar.

nidus ['naidəs] *n* ZOOL nido *m* (of insects) || MED foco *m*, centro *m.*
— OBSERV El plural de *nidus* es *nidi* o *niduses.*

niece [ni:s] *n* sobrina *f.*

niello [ni'eləu] *n* TECH niel *m* (of metal) | nielado *m* (process).
— OBSERV El plural de niello es *nielli* o *niellos.*

niff [nif] *n* FAM peste *f*, hedor *m.*

niff [nif] *vi* FAM apestar.

niffy [-i] *adj* FAM apestoso, sa.

nifty ['nifti] *adj* FAM formidable, estupendo, da (splendid).

nigella [nai'dʒelə] *n* neguilla *f.*

Niger ['naidʒə*] *pr n* Níger *m.*

Nigeria [nai'dʒiəriə] *pr n* GEOGR Nigeria *f.*

Nigerian [-n] *adj/n* nigeriano, na.

niggard ['nigəd] *adj/n* tacaño, ña; avaro, ra (stingy).

niggardliness [-linis] *n* avaricia *f*, tacañería *f.*

niggardly [-li] *adj* avaro, ra; tacaño, ña || miserable (portion, amount).
◆ *adv* tacañamente, mezquinamente.

nigger ['nigə*] *n* FAM negro, gra || — FAM *there is a nigger in the woodpile* aquí hay gato encerrado | *to work like a nigger* trabajar como un negro.
— OBSERV La palabra *nigger* es muy despectiva.

niggle ['nigl] *vi* reparar en minucias, pararse en pequeñeces.

niggling [-iŋ] *adj* insignificante, de poca monta (trifling) || demasiado meticuloso, sa; demasiado cuidadoso, sa (punctilious) || molesto, ta (annoying).

nigh [nai] *adv* (ant) cerca || *nigh on* casi.
◆ *prep* (ant) cerca de.

night [nait] *n* noche *f*; *in the silence of the night* en el silencio de la noche || FIG noche *f*, oscuridad *f*, tinieblas *f pl*; *the night of ignorance* las tinieblas de la ignorancia; *the dark nights of the soul* las noches oscuras del alma || THEATR representación *f*, función *f* || velada *f* (musical evening) || — *all night, the whole night* o *all night long* toda la noche || *at night, by night* por la noche, de noche || *dark night* noche cerrada || *far into the night* hasta altas horas de la noche, hasta muy entrada la noche || *first night* noche de estreno, primera representación (first performance) || *good night!* ¡buenas noches! || *I am used to late nights* estoy acostumbrado a acostarme tarde || *in the night* por la noche, durante la noche || *it is my night off* o *out* es mi noche libre || *it is night* es de noche || *it was 10 o'clock at night* eran las 10 de la noche || *last night* anoche, ayer por la noche (yesterday), último día, última función *or* representación (of a play), último día (of a film) || *night is falling* o *is coming on* está anocheciendo, se hace de noche, se está haciendo de noche || *night out* noche de fiesta || *sleepless night* noche en blanco, noche en claro, noche toledana || *The Arabian Nights* Las mil y una noches || *the night before* la noche anterior || *the night before last* antes de anoche, anteanoche || *the night before the journey* la víspera del viaje || *Thursday is my chess night* los jueves por la noche juego al ajedrez || *to have a bad night* pasar una mala noche, no poder dormir, dormir mal || *to make a night of it* pasarse la noche de juerga || *tomorrow night* mañana por la noche || *to pass the night* pasar la noche || *to say good night to s.o.* dar las buenas noches a uno || *to spend the night* pasar la noche || *to stay up all night* pasar la noche en claro *or* en blanco || *to turn day into night* hacer de la noche día || *to work day and night* trabajar noche y día || *to work nights* trabajar de noche || *wedding night* noche de bodas || *when night fell* al caer la noche.
◆ *adj* nocturno, na; de noche; *night boat, train, flight* barco, tren, vuelo nocturno.

night bird [-bə:d] *n* pájaro nocturno (in zoology) || noctámbulo *m*, trasnochador *m*, pájaro nocturno (person).

night blindness [-'blaindnis] *n* ceguera *f* nocturna.

nightcap [-kæp] *n* gorro *m* de dormir (worn in bed) || bebida *f* tomada antes de acostarse (drink).

nightclothes [-kləuðz] *pl n* ropa *f sing* de dormir.

nightclub [-klʌb] *n* club *m* nocturno, sala *f* de fiestas, «night club» *m.*

nightdress [-dres] *n* camisón *m*, camisa *f* de dormir.

nightfall [-fɔ:l] *n* caída *f* de la noche, anochecer *m*; *at nightfall* al anochecer.

nightgown [-gaun] *n* camisón *m*, camisa *f* de dormir.

nighthawk [-hɔ:k]; **night owl** [naitaul] *n* ZOOL chotacabras *m inv* (bird) || FAM pájaro *m* nocturno, trasnochador *m*, noctámbulo *m* (person).

nightie [-i] *n* FAM camisón *m.*

nightingale [-iŋgeil] *n* ruiseñor *m* (bird).

nightjar [-dʒɑ:*] *n* chotacabras *m inv* (bird).

night lamp [-læmp] *n* lamparita *f* de noche.

night letter [-'letə*] *n* telegrama *m* de noche.

night life [-laif] *n* vida *f* nocturna.

night-light [-lait] *n* lamparilla *f.*

nightlong [-lɔŋ] *adj* que dura toda la noche.
◆ *adv* durante toda la noche.

nightly [-li] *adj* nocturno, na; de noche || de cada noche.
◆ *adv* por las noches (at night) || todas las noches, cada noche (every night).

nightmare [-mɛə*] *n* pesadilla *f.*
◆ *adj* de pesadilla; *a nightmare journey* un viaje de pesadilla.

nightmarish [-mɛəriʃ] *adj* de pesadilla.

night owl [-aul] *n* → **nighthawk.**

night porter [-'pɔ:tə*] *n* portero, ra de noche.

night-robe [-rəub] *n* camisón *m*, camisa *f* de dormir.

nights [-s] *adv* FAM por la noche, de noche; *to work nights* trabajar de noche.

night safe [-seif] *n* caja *f* nocturna (in a bank).

night school [-sku:l] *n* escuela *f* nocturna.

nightshade [-ʃeid] *n* BOT hierba *f* mora || *deadly nightshade* belladona *f.*

night shift [-ʃift] *n* turno *m* de noche.

nightshirt [-ʃə:t] *n* camisón *m*, camisa *f* de dormir (for men).

night soil [-sɔil] *n* estiércol *m* (fertilizer).

night spot [-spɔt] *n* sala *f* de fiestas.

nightstick [-stik] *n* US porra *f* (of a policeman).

night table [-'teibl] *n* mesilla *f* de noche.

nighttime [-taim] *n* noche *f* || *at nighttime, in the nighttime* por la noche, de noche.

night watch [-wɔtʃ] *n* guarda *m* nocturno, vigilante *m* nocturno [*AMER* nochero *m*] (person) || sereno *m* (for houses in Spain) || guardia *f* de noche *or* nocturna (period of duty) || ronda *f* nocturna (of guard, of watchman).

night watchman [-'wɔtʃmən] *n* guarda *m* nocturno [*AMER* nochero *m*] || sereno *m* (for houses in Spain).
— OBSERV El plural de *night watchman* es *night watchmen.*

nightwear [-wɛə*] *n* ropa *f* de dormir.

nighty [-i] *n* FAM camisón *m.*

nigrescent [nai'gresnt] *adj* negruzco, ca.

nigritude ['nigritju:d] *n* negrura *f.*

nihilism ['naiilizəm] *n* nihilismo *m.*

nihilist ['naiilist] *adj/n* nihilista.

nihilistic [naii'listik] *adj* nihilista.

nil [nil] *n* nada *f* || ninguno, na (on an official form) || SP cero *m*; *we beat them three nil* les ganamos por tres a cero.

Nile [nail] *pr n* GEOGR Nilo *m* (river); *Upper, Blue Nilo* Alto Nilo, Nilo Azul.

nimble ['nimbl] *adj* ágil (person, etc.); *nimble at doing sth.* ágil para hacer algo || ágil, vivo, va; rápido, da (mind).

nimbleness [-lnis] *n* agilidad *f* || vivacidad *f*, agilidad *f*, rapidez *f* (of mind).

nimbly [-li] *adv* ágilmente.

nimbostratus ['nimbəu,streitəs] *n* nimboestrato *m* (cloud).

nimbus ['nimbəs] *n* nimbo *m* (cloud) || aureola *f*, nimbo *m* (halo).
— OBSERV El plural de *nimbus* es *nimbuses* o *nimbi.*

nincompoop ['ninkəmpu:p] *n* FAM lelo, la; memo, ma; mentecato, ta (idiot).

nine [nain] *adj* nueve || *nine times out of ten* en el noventa por ciento de los casos.
◆ *n* nueve *m* (number, card) || — FAM *dressed up to the nines* de punta en blanco || *nine o'clock* las nueve || *ten past nine* las nueve y diez || MATH *to cast out the nines* hacer la prueba del nueve.

ninefold [-fəuld] *adj* multiplicado por nueve.
◆ *adv* nueve veces.

nine hundred [-'hʌndrəd] *adj/n* novecientos, tas.

ninehundredth [-'hʌndrədθ] *adj/n* noningentésimo, ma.

ninepin ['nainpin] *n* bolo *m* (skittle).
◆ *pl* juego *m sing* de bolos.

nineteen ['nain'ti:n] *adj* diecinueve, diez y nueve || FIG *to talk nineteen to the dozen* hablar como una cotorra *or* por los codos.
◆ *n* diecinueve *m*, diez y nueve *m.*

nineteenth [-θ] *adj* decimonoveno, na; decimonono, na (ordinal) || diecinueveavo, va (partitive); *nineteenth part* diecinueveava parte || *the nineteenth century* el siglo diecinueve.
◆ *n* decimonoveno, na; diez y nueve *m* & *f*, diecinueve *m* & *f* (in a series) || diecinueveavo *m*, diecinueveava parte *f* (fraction) || diecinueve, diez y nueve; *John XIX (the nineteenth)* Juan XIX [diez y nueve] || diecinueve *m*, día *m* diecinueve (date); *the nineteenth of May* el diecinueve de mayo.

ninetieth ['naintiiθ] *adj* nonagésimo, ma; noventavo, va.
◆ *n* nonagésimo, ma; noventa *m* & *f* (in a series) || nonagésimo *m*, nonagésima parte *f* (fraction).

ninety ['nainti] *adj* noventa.
◆ *n* noventa *m*; *ninety-four* noventa y cuatro || — *the nineties* los años noventa (period) || *to be in one's nineties* tener unos noventa años.

ninetyfold [-fəuld] *adj* multiplicado por noventa.
◆ *adv* noventa veces.

ninny ['nini] *n* FAM memo, ma; mentecato, ta (idiot).

ninth [nainθ] *adj* noveno, na; *the ninth house* la novena casa.
◆ *n* noveno, na; *I was the ninth in the queue* era el noveno en la cola || novena parte *f* (fraction) || nueve *m*, día *m* nueve (day of the month); *the ninth of May* el día nueve de mayo || nono; *Pious IX (the ninth)* Pío IX [nono] || noveno, na; *Alphonse IX (the ninth)* Alfonso IX [noveno] || MUS novena *f*.

ninthly [-li] *adv* en noveno lugar.

niobium [nai'əubiəm] *n* CHEM niobio *m*.

nip [nip] *n* pizca *f*, gota *f* (of liquid) || trago *m* (drink) || pellizco *m* (pinch) || mordisco *m*, mordedura *f* (bite) || estrechamiento *m* (narrowing) || frío *m* seco (in the air) || AGR helada *f* (freeze) || FIG palabras *f pl* mordaces, pulla *f* (cutting words) || MAR doblez *f*, vuelta *f* (in a cable) || GEOGR recorte *m* (of coastline) || — US *the race was nip and tuck* la carrera estuvo muy reñida || *there was a nip in the air* hacía algo de frío || *to feel the nip of the wind* sentir el viento penetrante.

nip [nip] *vt* pellizcar (to pinch) || morder (to bite) || coger, pillar; *to nip one's fingers in the door* cogerse los dedos con la puerta || atenazar (with pincers) || beber a traguitos (to drink) || AGR helar, quemar (a plant by the frost) || cortar, recortar (to cut) || cortar (cold) || FAM birlar (to steal) || FIG *to nip in the bud* cortar de raíz.
◆ *vi* FAM correr (to run, to go fast); *we were nipping along at 100 m p h* corríamos a 100 millas por hora || beber a traguitos (to drink) || — *nip across to the baker's for me* pega un salto a la panadería, por favor || *nip along!* ¡date prisa! || *to nip in* entrar un momento || *to nip off* largarse || *to nip on a bus* coger al vuelo un autobús || *to nip out for a moment* salir un rato.

Nip [nip] *n* US FAM nipón, ona (Japanese).
— OBSERV La palabra *Nip* es sumamente despectiva.

nipper ['nipə*] *n* FAM chiquillo *m*, chaval *m* (young boy) || boca *f*, pata *f* (of a crustacean) || pala *f* (of a horse).
◆ *pl* alicates *m* (pliers) || tenazas *f* (pincers) || pinzas *f* (forceps).

nipping ['nipiŋ] *adj* cortante (cold) || mordiente, mordaz (remark).

nipple ['nipl] *n* pezón *m* (of female mammals) || tetilla *f* (of male mammals) | tetina *f*, tetilla *f*, boquilla *f* (of an infant's feeding bottle) || protuberancia *f* (protuberance) || cerro *m*, montecillo *m* (hill) || TECH pezón *m* de engrase (for greasing) | boquilla *f* de unión (connexion) || AUT tuerca *f* (of a wheel) || chimenea *f* (of a gun).

Nippon ['nipɔn] *pr n* Japón *m* (Japan)

Nipponese [,nipɔ'ni:z] *adj/n* nipón, ona; *they are Nipponese* son japoneses.

nippy ['nipi] *adj* FAM rápido, da (person) | rápido, da; veloz (vehicle) | que tiene buena aceleración (car) || cortante, vivo, va (air) || fresquito, ta (day) || *and be nippy about it* y date prisa.

Nirvana [niə'vɑ:nə] *pr n* REL nirvana *m*.

nisei ['ni,sei] *n* US nisei, ciudadano de los Estados Unidos de padres japoneses.
— OBSERV El plural de *nisei* es *nisei* o *niseis*.

nisi ['naisai] *adj* bajo condición (decision) || provisional (decree).

Nissen hut ['nisən hʌt] *n* barraca *f* prefabricada.

nit [nit] *n* liendre *f* (of a louse) || FAM papanatas *m inv*, imbécil *m* & *f* (idiot).

niter ['naitə*] *n* US —> **nitre.**

nit-picking ['nitpikiŋ] *adj* FAM quisquilloso, sa.
◆ *n* FAM nimiedades *f pl* || *I'm fed up with your nit-picking* estoy harto de que le pongas pegas a todo.

nitrate ['naitreit] *n* CHEM nitrato *m*; *sodium nitrate* nitrato sódico.

nitrate ['naitreit] *vt* CHEM nitratar.

nitrated [-id] *adj* CHEM nitrado, da; nitratado, da.

nitration [nai'treiʃən] *n* CHEM nitratación *f*, nitración *f*.

nitre ['naitə*]; US **niter** *n* nitro *m*, nitrato *m* potásico, salitre *m*.

nitre bed [-bed] *n* nitral *m*, nitrería *f*.

nitric ['naitrik] *adj* CHEM nítrico, ca.

nitride ['naitraid] *n* CHEM nitruro *m*.

nitriding [-iŋ] *n* CHEM nitruración *f*.

nitrification [,naitrifi'keiʃən] *n* CHEM nitrificación *f*.

nitrify ['naitrəfai] *vt* CHEM nitrificar.

nitrifying [-iŋ] *adj* CHEM nitrificador, ra.

nitrile ['naitril] *n* CHEM nitrilo *m*.

nitrite ['naitrait] *n* CHEM nitrito *m*.

nitrobenzene ['naitrəu,benzi:n] *n* CHEM nitrobenceno *m*.

nitrocellulose ['naitrəu,seljuləus] *n* CHEM nitrocelulosa *f*.

nitrogen ['naitrədʒən] *n* CHEM nitrógeno *m*.

nitrogenation [,naitrədʒə'neiʃən] *n* nitruración *f*.

nitrogenization [nai,trɔdʒənai'zeiʃən] *n* nitrogenización *f*.

nitrogenize [nai'trɔdʒənaiz] *vt* nitrogenar.

nitrogenous [nai'trɔdʒinəs] *adj* nitrogenado, da.

nitroglycerine; nitroglycerin [,naitrəuglisə'ri:n] *n* CHEM nitroglicerina *f*.

nitrotoluene [,naitrəu'tɔljuin] *n* CHEM nitrotolueno *m*.

nitrous ['naitrəs] *adj* CHEM nitroso, sa.

nitty ['niti] *adj* lleno de liendres.

nitty-gritty ['niti'griti] *n* FAM meollo *m*, quid *m* || FAM *to get down to o to come to the nitty-gritty* ir al grano.

nitwit ['nitwit] *n* FAM burro, rra; mentecato, ta; cretino, na (idiot).

niveous ['niviəs] *adj* nevoso, sa; níveo, a.

nix [niks] *n* FAM nada.
◆ *interj* ¡ni hablar!

no [nəu] *adj* ninguno, na; *he's no genious* no es ningún genio; *it's no trouble* no es ninguna molestia || — *he's no artist* de artista no tiene nada, no es ningún artista || *he's no friend of mine* no es amigo mío || *he's no great walker* no es aficionado a andar || *make no mistake about it* no lo dudes || *no admittance* prohibida la entrada || *no fooling, no kidding* en serio, sin broma || *no man* nadie, ninguno (nobody) || *no matter* no importa || *no... no* sin... no hay; *no contestants, no championship* sin competidores no hay campeonato || *no nonsense!* ¡sin tonterías! || *no one* nadie, ninguno, na (nobody); *no one else* nadie más || *no one man can do it* es demasiado para un hombre solo || *no parking* prohibido estacionar, prohibido aparcar || *no smoking* se prohibe fumar, prohibido fumar || *no thoroughfare* calle *f* sin salida (no through road), calle interceptada (road blocked), prohibido el paso (no entry) || *no two men think alike* no hay dos hombres que piensen igual || *no use* inútil || *of little or no interest* de casi ningún interés || *orders or no orders, I'm staying* no me importan las órdenes, me quedo || *say no more* no digas mas || *she's no beauty* no es nada guapa || *there is no agreeing with him* es imposible ponerse de acuerdo con él || *to no purpose* en vano (in vain), sin objetivo (aimlessly) || *we have no tea* no tenemos té || *with no* sin; *with no money* sin dinero.
◆ *n* no *m*; *he wouldn't take no for an answer* no estaba dispuesto a aceptar un no como respuesta || voto *m* en contra (vote); *ayes and noes* votos a favor y votos en contra || *the noes have it* hay mayoría de votos en contra.
◆ *adv* no; *no sir!* ¡no señor!; *no better than before* no mejor que antes; *whether he likes it or no* le guste o no || — FAM *no can do* imposible || *no less than* no menos de || *no longer* ya no, no... más || *no more* ya no || *no more than* no más de || *no sooner* apenas, no bien; *I had no sooner arrived than they called me* apenas había llegado cuando me llamaron, no bien llegué me llamaron || *no sooner said than done* dicho y hecho || *she is no nicer than you* no es más mona que tú || *to say no* decir que no.

no-account [-ə'kaunt] *adj* US FAM insignificante, sin importancia.

Noah ['nəuə] *pr n* REL Noé *m* || *Noah's ark* el arca de Noé.

nob [nɔb] *n* FAM pez *m* gordo (important person) | melón *m*, chola *f* (head).

no ball ['nəu'bɔ:l] *n* SP lanzamiento *m* nulo (cricket) | pelota *f* mala *or* nula (tennis).

nobble ['nɔbl] *vt* drogar (a racehorse, a greyhound) || sobornar (a person) || FAM birlar (to steal) | coger, pescar (to arrest).

nobelium [nəu'beliəm] *n* CHEM nobelio *m*.

Nobel prize ['nəubl'praiz] *n* premio *m* Nobel.

nobiliary [nəu'biliəri] *adj* nobiliario, ria.

nobility [nəu'biliti] *n* nobleza *f*.

noble [nəubl] *n* noble; *of noble birth* de noble cuna; *of noble descent* de noble alcurnia *or* linaje; *noble sentiments* sentimientos nobles; *noble metal* metal noble || magnánimo, ma; generoso, sa; *noble gesture* acción magnánima || grandioso, sa; magnífico, ca; *a noble mansion* una mansión grandiosa || *noble gas* gas *m* inerte.
◆ *n* noble *m* & *f* (peer or peeress)

nobleman [-mən] *n* noble *m*.
— OBSERV El plural de *nobleman* es *noblemen*.

nobleness [-nis] *n* nobleza *f* || grandiosidad *f* (majesty).

noblewoman [-'wumən] *n* noble *f*.
— OBSERV El plural de *noblewoman* es *noblewomen*.

nobody ['nəubədi] *pron* nadie; *nobody came* no vino nadie; *I spoke to nobody* no hablé con nadie || — *nobody but* nadie más que || *nobody else* nadie más.
◆ *n* FAM nadie, don nadie *m*.

nock [nɔk] *n* muesca *f*.

nock [nɔk] *vt* ajustar, empulgar (to place an arrow) || hacer una muesca en (to notch).

noctambulant [nɔk'tæmbjulənt] *adj* noctámbulo, la || sonámbulo, la; somnámbulo, la (sleepwalking).

noctambulism [nɔk'tæmbjulizəm] *n* noctambulismo *m* || sonambulismo *m*, somnambulismo *m* (sleepwalking).

noctivagation [,nɔktivi'geiʃən] *n* noctambulismo *m*.

nocturnal [nɔk'tə:nl] *adj* nocturno, na.

nocturne ['nɔktə:n] *n* MUS nocturno *m* || ARTS escena *f* nocturna.

nod [nɔd] *n* inclinación *f* de cabeza || saludo *m* con la cabeza || cabezada *f* (when falling asleep) || — FIG *a nod is as good as a wink* a buen entendedor con pocas palabras basta | *a nod is as good as a wink to a blind horse* es como si hablara a la pared | *the land of Nod* el mundo de los sueños || *to give the nod* asentir, aprobar.

nod [nɔd] *vi* asentir con la cabeza (as a sign of agreement) ‖ saludar con la cabeza (as a greeting) ‖ dar cabezadas (because of sleepiness) ‖ balancearse, mecerse; *the poppies nodded in the wind* las amapolas se balanceaban con el viento ‖ — *she nodded to him to begin* inclinó la cabeza para que empezara, le hizo una señal con la cabeza para que empezase ‖ *to nod off* quedarse dormido, da; echar una cabezada.
◆ *vt* inclinar, mover (the head) ‖ — *to nod a greeting* saludar con una inclinación de cabeza ‖ *to nod assent, to nod one's head* asentir con la cabeza.

nodal ['nəudl] *adj* ASTR & PHYS nodal ‖ *nodal point* punto nodal.

nodding ['nɔdiŋ] *adj* que se balancea.
◆ *n* inclinación *f* de cabeza ‖ cabezada *f* (when sleepy) ‖ balanceo *m* (swaying motion) ‖ — *they are nodding acquaintances of mine* sólo los conozco de vista ‖ *to have a nodding acquaintance with s.o.* conocer a alguien de vista.

noddle ['nɔdl] *n* FAM chola *f*, melón *m* (head) | mollera *f* (brain).

node [nəud] *n* BOT nudo *m* ‖ ASTR, PHYS, ANAT & MED nodo *m* ‖ nudo *m* (of a story, of a play).

nodose ['nəudəus] *adj* nudoso, sa.

nodosity [nəu'dɔsiti] *n* nudosidad *f*.

nodular ['nɔdjulə*] *n* nodular.

nodule ['nɔdju:l] *n* nódulo *m*.

nodulose ['nɔdju:ləus]; **nodulous** ['nɔdju:ləs] *adj* nodular.

noël; noel [nəu'el] *n* villancico *m* (Christmas carol).

Noël; Noel [nəu'el] *n* Navidad *f*.

nog [nɔg] *n* tarugo *m* de madera en la pared ‖ CULIN ponche *m* de huevo (eggnog) | cerveza *f* muy fuerte (ale).

noggin ['nɔgin] *n* jarra *f* pequeña (small mug) ‖ copita *f* (glass) ‖ cuarto *m* de pinta (spirit measure).

no-go ['nəu,gəu] *adj* de acceso prohibido; *a no-go area* una zona de acceso prohibido.

no-good ['nəugud] *adj* FAM malísimo, ma (very bad) | inútil (useless).
◆ *n* US FAM inútil *m* & *f* (person).

nohow ['nəuhau] *adv* de ninguna manera.

noise [nɔiz] *n* ruido *m*; *the noise of traffic* el ruido del tráfico; *to make a noise* hacer ruido; *clanging noise* ruido metálico ‖ ruido *m* parásito, interferencia *f* (in radio, in acoustics, etc.) ‖ zumbido *m* (in the ears) ‖ FIG sensación *f* ‖ — FAM *big noise* pez gordo ‖ FIG *to make a lot of noise about* hablar mucho de.

noise [nɔiz] *vt* divulgar, propalar ‖ — *to be noised* rumorearse (to be rumoured), propagarse, divulgarse (to become known) ‖ *to noise abroad* divulgar.
◆ *vi* hacer ruido ‖ hablar mucho.

noise abatement [-ə'beitmənt] *n* defensa *f* contra el ruido ambiental.

noiseless [-lis] *adj* silencioso, sa; sin ruido ‖ TECH insonorizado, da (soundproof).

noisemaker [-'meikə*] *n* persona *f* or cosa *f* que hace ruido ‖ US matraca *f* (rattle).

noisemaking [-'meikiŋ] *adj* que hace ruido.
◆ *n* ruido *m*.

noiseproof [-pru:f] *adj* insonorizado, da.

noisiness ['nɔizinis] *n* ruido *m* (noise) ‖ lo ruidoso (being noisy).

noisome ['nɔisəm] *adj* fétido, da (stinking) ‖ dañino, na; nocivo, va (harmful, injurious) ‖ asqueroso, sa (repulsive).

noisomeness [-nis] *n* fetidez *f* (stench) ‖ nocividad *f* (harmfulness) ‖ asquerosidad *f* (repulsiveness).

noisy ['nɔizi] *adj* ruidoso, sa ‖ bullicioso, sa; *a noisy crowd* una muchedumbre bulliciosa ‖ FIG chillón, ona; llamativo, va (colours, clothes, etc.) | clamoroso, sa; vivo, va (protest).

nomad ['nəuməd] *adj/n* nómada.

nomadic [nəu'mædik] *adj* nómada.

nomadism ['nəumædizəm] *n* nomadismo *m*.

no-man's-land ['nəumænzlænd] *n* tierra *f* de nadie.

nom de plume ['nɔmdə'plu:m] *n* seudónimo *m*.
— OBSERV El plural es *nom de plumes*.

nomenclature [nəu'menklətʃə*] *n* nomenclatura *f*.

nominal ['nɔminl] *adj* nominal, sólo de nombre; *the nominal leader* el jefe nominal ‖ COMM nominal; *nominal value* valor nominal | nominativo, va (shares) ‖ GRAMM nominal.

nominalism [-izəm] *n* nominalismo *m*.

nominalist [-ist] *adj/n* nominalista.

nominalistic [nɔminə'listik] *adj* nominalista.

nominate ['nɔmineit] *vt* designar (to propose for appointment, to designate) ‖ nombrar (to appoint); *to nominate s.o. as secretary* nombrar secretario a uno ‖ proponer la candidatura de (to name as a candidate) ‖ nombrar (to name).

nomination [,nɔmi'neiʃən] *n* designación *f* (designation) ‖ nombramiento *m* (appointment) ‖ propuesta *f* (as a candidate) ‖ — *to accept nomination* aceptar ser candidato ‖ *to put s.o.'s name in nomination for* poner a alguien entre los candidatos para ‖ *to support a nomination* apoyar una candidatura.

nominative ['nɔminətiv] *n* GRAMM nominativo *m* ‖ *nominative absolute* nominativo absoluto.
◆ *adj* GRAMM nominativo, va ‖ nombrado, da (appointed) ‖ designado, da (designated) ‖ nominativo, va (shares).

nominator ['nɔmineitə*] *n* nominador, ra ‖ persona *f* que designa *or* que nombra *or* que propone.

nominee [nɔmi'ni:] *n* candidato *m*.

nonabsorbent [,nɔnəb'sɔ:bənt] *adj* impermeable, que no absorbe.

nonacceptance [,nɔnək'septəns] *n* no aceptación *f*, falta *f* de aceptación, rechazo *m*.

nonage ['nəunidʒ] *n* minoría *f* (minority) ‖ juventud *f* (youth).

nonagenarian [,nəunədʒi'nɛəriən] *adj/n* nonagenario, ria; noventón, ona.

nonaggression [,nɔnə'greʃən] *n* no agresión *f*; *nonaggression pact* pacto de no agresión.

nonalcoholic ['nɔn,ælkə'hɔlik] *adj* no alcohólico, ca.

nonaligned [,nɔnə'laind] *adj* no alineado, da; *nonaligned country* país no alineado.

nonalignment [,nɔnə'lainmənt] *n* no alineación *f*.

nonappearance [,nɔnə'piərəns] *n* JUR incomparecencia *f*.

nonattendance [,nɔnə'tendəns] *n* ausencia *f*, falta *f* de asistencia.

nonbelligerancy ['nɔnbi'lidʒərənsi] *n* no beligerancia *f*.

nonbelligerent [,nɔnbi'lidʒəripnt] *adj/n* no beligerante.

nonbreakable [nɔn'breikəbl] *adj* irrompible.

nonce [nɔns] *n* *for the nonce* por el momento ‖ *nonce word* palabra inventada para una circunstancia especial.

nonchalance ['nɔnʃələns] *n* tranquilidad *f*, sangre *f* fría (casualness) ‖ indiferencia *f* (indifference) ‖ negligencia *f* ‖ inmutabilidad *f*, imperturbabilidad *f* (calmness) ‖ aplomo *m* (self-confidence).

nonchalant ['nɔnʃələnt] *adj* indiferente (unenthusiastic) ‖ imperturbable, inmutable (unperturbed) ‖ negligente (negligent) ‖ tranquilo, la (calm).

nonchalantly [-li] *adv* con indiferencia, indiferentemente (indifferently) ‖ con aplomo, con calma (calmly) ‖ negligentemente (negligently).

noncollapsible [,nɔnkə'læpsəbl] *adj* indesmontable.

noncollectible ['nɔnkə'lektəbl] *adj* incobrable.

noncom ['nɔnkɔm] *n* MIL & FAM suboficial *m*.

noncombatant [,nɔn'kɔmbətənt] *adj/n* no combatiente.

noncombustible [nɔnkəm'bʌstəbl] *adj* incombustible.

noncommissioned officer [,nɔnkə'miʃənd'ɔfisə*] *n* MIL suboficial *m* ‖ MIL *noncommissioned officers* clases *f* de tropa, suboficiales.

noncommittal ['nɔnkə'mitl] *adj* evasivo, va (evasive) ‖ reservado, da (reserved) ‖ que no compromete a nada (answer, etc.) ‖ *to answer in a noncommittal way* contestar de forma poco comprometedora, contestar con evasivas.

noncompliance ['nɔnkəm'plaiəns] *n* incumplimiento *m* (*with* de) (failure to comply) ‖ desobediencia *f* (disobedience).

nonconductor ['nɔnkən,dʌktə*] *n* aislante *m*.

nonconformist ['nɔnkən'fɔ:mist] *adj/n* REL disidente, no conformista.

nonconformity ['nɔnkən'fɔ:miti] *n* no conformismo *m*, no conformidad *f* ‖ disconformidad *f* (between two things) ‖ REL disidencia *f*, no conformismo *m*.

noncontagious [nɔnkən'teidʒəs] *adj* no contagioso, sa.

noncooperation ['nɔnkəu,ɔpə'reiʃən] *n* no cooperación *f*, falta *f* de cooperación.

nondelivery ['nɔndi'livəri] *n* falta *f* de entrega (of goods).

nondescript ['nɔndiskript] *adj* indescriptible ‖ inclasificable (unclassifiable) ‖ anodino, na (mediocre).

none [nʌn] *pron* nadie, ninguno, na (nobody); *none but he can do it* nadie sino él lo puede hacer; *none of them could do it* ninguno de ellos lo pudo hacer ‖ ninguno, na (not any, not one); *none of the books is mine* ninguno de los libros es mío ‖ nada (no part); *he understood none of the book* no entendió nada del libro ‖ — *it is none of your business* no es asunto suyo ‖ *none at all* nada en absoluto; *is there any left? no, none at all* ¿queda algo? no, nada en absoluto; ninguno; *are there any left? no, none at all* ¿queda alguno? no, ninguno; nada; *a half is better than none at all* la mitad es mejor que nada ‖ *none but* solamente ‖ *none other than* nada menos que; *he was none other than the King* era nada menos que el rey ‖ *we'll have none of that here* ¡nada de esto aquí!
◆ *adv* de ningún modo, de ninguna manera, no; *I am none the happier for the experience* no estoy de ningún modo más contento con la experiencia; *I'm none the worse for it* no estoy peor por ello ‖ — *none the less* sin embargo, a pesar de todo ‖ *none too* nada; *the pay is none too good* el sueldo no es nada bueno ‖ *none too soon* en buena hora ‖ *reply gave he none* respuesta no la dio ‖ *to be none the better off* no haber avanzado nada.

noneffective [,nɔni'fektiv] *adj* ineficaz (ineffective) ‖ MIL inhabilitado (man) ‖ JUR no vigente.

nonego ['nɔ'ni:gəu] *n* PHIL no yo *m*.

nonentity [nɔ'nentiti] *n* cero *m* a la izquierda, nulidad *f* (insignificant person) || inexistencia *f*, no existencia *f*, nada *f* (nonexistence).

nones [nəunz] *pl n* HIST nonas *f* (day) || REL nona *f sing* (hour).

nonessential ['nɔni'senʃəl] *adj* no esencial.

nonesuch; nonsuch ['nʌnsʌtʃ] *n* persona *f or* cosa *f* sin igual *or* sin par.

nonetheless [nʌnðə'les] *adv* US sin embargo, no obstante.

nonevent [nɔni'vent] *n* fracaso *m*, decepción *f* || *the film was a nonevent* la película no fue nada del otro mundo.

nonexecution ['nɔn,eksi'kju:ʃən] *n* incumplimiento *m* (of an order).

nonexigibility ['nɔn,eksidʒi'biliti] *n* inexigibilidad *f*.

nonexistence ['nɔnnig'zistəns] *n* inexistencia *f*, no existencia *f*.

nonexistent ['nɔnig'zistənt] *adj* inexistente, no existente.

nonfattening ['nɔn'fætniŋ] *adj* que no engorda.

nonfeasance ['nɔn'fi:zəns] *n* JUR omisión *f*, incumplimiento *m*.

nonferrous [nɔn'ferəs] *adj* no ferroso, sa.

nonfiction [nɔn'fikʃən] *n* literatura *f* no novelesca.

nonfulfilment; US **nonfulfillment** ['nɔnful'filmənt] *n* JUR incumplimiento *m*.

noninflammable ['nɔnin'flæməbl] *adj* ininflamable.

nonintervention ['nɔn,intə:'venʃən] *n* no intervención *f*.

noniron [nɔn'aiən] *adj* que no necesita plancha.

nonjuror ['nɔn'dʒuərə*] *n* HIST clérigo *m* no juramentado.

nonmember ['nɔn,membə*] *n* no miembro *m*.

nonmetal [nɔn'metl] *n* CHEM metaloide *m*.

nonnegotiable ['nɔnni'gəuʃjəbl] *adj* COMM no negociable.

nonobservance ['nɔnəb'zə:vəns] *n* incumplimiento *m* (of a rule).

nonofficial ['nɔnə'fiʃəl] *adj* oficioso, sa.

no-nonsense ['nəu'nɔnsəns] *adj* sensato, ta; práctico, ca (person) || directo, ta (approach).

nonpareil ['nɔnpərəl] *adj* sin par, sin igual.
◆ *n* persona *f* sin par *or* sin igual || cosa *f* sin par *or* sin igual.

nonpartisan ['nɔn,pɑ:ti'zæn] *adj* independiente.

nonparty [nɔn'pɑ:ti] *adj* independiente.

nonpayment ['nɔn'peimənt] *n* falta *f* de pago.

nonperformance ['nɔnpə'fɔ:məns] *n* incumplimiento *m* (of contract, etc.).

nonplus ['nɔn'plʌs] *vt* asombrar, anonadar, dejar anonadado *or* perplejo.

nonproductive ['nɔnprə'dʌktiv] *adj* improductivo, va.

nonprofessional ['nɔnprə'feʃənl] *adj* no profesional.

nonprofitmaking [,nɔn'prɔfit,meikiŋ] *adj* no lucrativo, va.

nonrecurring ['nɔnri'kə:riŋ] *adj* COMM extraordinario, ria (expenditure).

nonrenewable ['nɔnri'nju:əbl] *adj* no renovable || COMM no prorrogable.

nonresident ['nɔn'rezidənt] *adj/n* no residente.

nonresistance [,nɔnri'zistəns] *n* falta *f* de resistencia, pasividad *f*.

nonrestrictive ['nɔnri'striktiv] *adj* sin restricción.

nonreturnable [,nɔnri'tə:nəbl] *adj* sin devolución.

nonreversible [,nɔnri'və:səbl] *adj* irreversible.

nonscheduled ['nɔn'ʃedju:ld] *adj* no regular (airline, etc.).

nonsectarian [,nɔnsek'tɛəriən] *adj* no sectario, ria.

nonsense ['nɔnsəns] *n* tonterías *f pl*, disparates *m pl*; *to talk nonsense* decir tonterías || — *a nonsense, a piece of nonsense* una tontería, un disparate || *I want no more of your nonsense!* ¡déjate de tonterías! || *that's nonsense* esto es absurdo || *to make nonsense* no tener sentido.
◆ *interj* ¡tonterías!, ¡bobadas!

nonsensical [nɔn'sensikəl] *adj* disparatado, da; absurdo, da.

non sequitur ['nɔn'sekwitə*] *n* PHIL conclusión *f* errónea.
— OBSERV El plural de *non sequitur* es *non sequiturs*.

nonshrink ['nɔnʃriŋk] *adj* inencogible.

nonskid ['nɔn'skid] *adj* AUT antideslizante.

nonsmoker ['nɔn'sməukə*] *n* persona *f* que no fuma.

nonstarter ['nɔn'stɑ:tə*] *n* *to be a nonstarter* no tener futuro, ser imposible (plan, scheme).

nonstop ['nɔn'stɔp] *adj* directo *m* (train) || sin escalas; *nonstop flight* vuelo sin escalas || continuo, nua; *nonstop show* sesión continua.
◆ *adv* sin parar; *to drive nonstop to Rome* conducir a Roma sin parar || directamente (by train) || sin escalas (by plane).

nonsuch ['nʌnsʌtʃ] *n* ⟶ **nonesuch.**

nonsuit ['nɔn'sju:t] *n* JUR desestimación *f*, denegación *f*.

nonsuit ['nɔn'sju:t] *vt* JUR desestimar, denegar.

nonsupport [,nɔnsə'pɔ:t] *n* JUR falta *f* de pago de la pensión alimenticia.

nontaxable [,nɔn'tæksəbl] *adj* exento de impuestos, no imponible.

nontransferable [,nɔntræns'fə:rəbl] *adj* intransferible.

non-U [,nɔn'ju:] *adj* impropio, pia; vulgar (behaviour, language).

nonunion [,nɔn'ju:njən] *adj* no sindicado, da (not belonging to a union).

nonviolence [nɔn'vaiələns] *n* no violencia *f*.

nonviolent [nɔn'vaiələnt] *adj* pacífico, ca; no violento, ta.

noodle ['nu:dl] *n* FAM melón *m*, chola *f* (head) | lelo, la; memo, ma (idiot).
◆ *pl* CULIN fideos *m* (cylindrical) | tallarines *m* (flat).

nook [nuk] *n* rincón *m* (recess, corner) || refugio *m* (refuge) || escondrijo *m* (hiding place) || *in every nook and cranny* en todos los recovecos.

noon [nu:n] *n* mediodía *m*; *at moon* al mediodía || FIG apogeo *m*.
◆ *adj* de mediodía.

moonday [-dei] *n* mediodía *m* || — *the noonday meal* el almuerzo || *the noonday sun* el sol de mediodía.

no one ['nəuwʌn] *pron* nadie; *no one heard me* nadie me oyó; *I saw no one* no vi a nadie; *I spoke to no one* no hablé con nadie.

noose [nu:s] *n* nudo *m* corredizo (knot) || lazo *m* (for snaring animals, etc.) || dogal *m*, soga *f* (of hangman's rope) || FIG vínculo *m*, lazo *m* (link) | trampa *f* (trap) || FIG *to have one's head in the noose* estar con la soga al cuello.

noose [nu:s] *vt* coger con un lazo (to catch in a noose) || hacer un nudo corredizo en (to make a noose in) || ahorcar (to hang).

nopal ['nəupəl] *n* BOT nopal *m*, chumbera *f* [AMER tuna *f*].

nope [nəup] *interj* US FAM ¡no!

nor [nɔ:*] *conj* ni; *he is neither big nor small* no es ni grande ni pequeño; *neither you nor I* ni tú ni yo || ni, ni tampoco; *they don't know him, nor do they want to* no lo conocen, ni tampoco quieren conocerlo || tampoco; *nor had I forgotten the bread* tampoco se me había olvidado el pan; *he had not gone there, nor had I* él no había ido allí, yo tampoco.

Nordic ['nɔ:dik] *adj/n* nórdico, ca.

Norfolk jacket ['nɔ:fək'dʒækit] *n* cazadora *f*.

noria ['nɔ:riə] *n* noria *f*.

norm [nɔ:m] *n* norma *f* (standard) || *to deviate from the norm* salir de lo normal.

normal [-əl] *adj* normal; *normal temperature* temperatura normal; *a normal person* una persona normal; *a normal reaction for a child of his age* una reacción normal para un niño de su edad; *normal production figures* cifras normales de producción || MATH perpendicular, normal || CHEM normal, neutro, tra (salt) | normal (solution chain of atoms) || *normal school* escuela *f* normal.
◆ *n* lo normal; *above (the) normal* por encima de lo normal, superior a lo normal || estado *m* normal || MATH normal *f*, perpendicular *f* || normalidad *f*; *to return to normal* volver a la normalidad.

normalcy ['nɔ:məlsi] *n* normalidad *f*.

normality [nɔ:'mæliti] *n* normalidad *f*.

normalization [,nɔ:məlai'zeiʃən] *n* normalización *f*.

normalize ['nɔ:məlaiz] *vt* normalizar.

normally ['nɔ:məli] *adv* normalmente.

Norman ['nɔ:mən] *adj/n* normando, da.

Normandy ['nɔ:məndi] *n* GEOGR Normandía *f*.

Norman-French ['nɔ:mən'frentʃ] *n* normando *m*.

normative ['nɔ:mətiv] *adj* normativo, va.

Norse [nɔ:s] *n* nórdico *m* (language) || noruego, ga (Norwegian) || escandinavo, va; nórdico, ca (Scandinavian).
◆ *adj* noruego, ga (of Norway) || escandinavo, va; nórdico, ca (Scandinavian).

Norseman [-mən] *n* nórdico *m*, escandinavo *m*.
— OBSERV El plural de *Norseman* es *Norsemen*.

north [nɔ:θ] *adj* del norte, norteño, ña (belonging to or situated towards the north) || que da al norte (facing north) || (que sopla) del norte (wind).
◆ *adv* hacia el norte, al norte.
◆ *n* norte *m* || *the North* el Norte *m*.

North Africa [-'æfrikə] *pr n* GEOGR África *f* del Norte.

North African [-'æfrikən] *adj/n* norteafricano, na.

North America [-ə'merikə] *pr n* GEOGR América *f* del Norte, Norteamérica *f*.

North American [-ə'merikən] *adj/n* norteamericano, na.

northbound [-baund] *adj* que se dirige hacia el norte.

Northbound [-baund] *adj* de dirección norte, que va hacia el norte.

north by east [-bai'i:st] *n* MAR norte *m* cuarta al nordeste.

north by west [-bai'west] *n* MAR norte *m* cuarta al noroeste.

North Carolina [-,kærə'lainə] *pr n* GEOGR Carolina del Norte.

North Dakota [-də'kəutə] *pr n* GEOGR Dakota del Norte.

northeast [-'i:st] *adj* del nordeste, nordeste.
◆ *adv* hacia el nordeste.
◆ *n* nordeste *m*, noreste *m*.

northeast by east [-'i:stbai'i:st] *n* MAR nordeste *m* cuarta al este.

northeast by north ['i:stbai'nɔ:θ] *n* MAR nordeste *m* cuarta al norte.

northeaster [-'i:stə*] *n* nordeste *m* (wind).

northeasterly [-'i:stəli] *adj* nordeste, del nordeste.
◆ *adv* hacia el nordeste.
◆ *n* nordeste *m* (wind).

northeastern [-'i:stən] *adj* del nordeste.

norheastward [-'i:stwəd] *adj/adv* hacia el nordeste.

northeastwards [-'i:stwədz] *adv* hacia el nordeste.

northerly ['nɔ:ðəli] *adj* norte, del norte || (que sopla) del norte (wind) || *the most northerly point* el punto más septentrional.
◆ *adv* hacia el norte.
◆ *n* norte *m*, viento *m* del norte.

northern ['nɔ:ðən] *adj* del norte, septentrional (situated in the north) || del Norte, norteño (of the North) || — *northern hemisphere* hemisferio norte *or* boreal || *northern lights* aurora *f sing* boreal.

Northerner [-ə*] *n* norteño, ña (of a northern region) || nórdico, ca (of a northern country).

Northern Ireland [-'aiələnd] *pr n* GEOGR Irlanda *f* del Norte.

northernmost [-məust] *adj* más septentrional; *the northernmost point* el punto más septentrional.

northing ['nɔ:θiŋ] *n* MAR rumbo *m* norte.

Northland ['nɔ:θlənd] *n* norte *m* (of a country).

Northman ['nɔ:θmən] *n* escandinavo *m*.
— OBSERV El plural de *Northman* es *Northmen*.

north-northeast ['nɔ:θnɔ:θ'i:st] *adj* nornordeste.
◆ *n* nornordeste *m*.

north-northwest ['nɔ:θnɔ:θ'west] *adj/adv* nornoroeste, nornorueste.
◆ *n* nornoroeste *m*, nornorueste *m*.

North Pole ['nɔ:θpəul] *n* GEOGR Polo *m* Norte.

North Sea ['nɔ:θsi:] *n* GEOGR mar *m* del Norte.

North Star ['nɔ:θsta:*] *n* ASTR Estrella *f* polar.

North Vietnam ['nɔ:θ'vjet'næm] *pr n* GEOGR Vietnam *m* del Norte.

North Vietnamese [-i:z] *adj/n* vietnamita del Norte, norvietnamita.

northward ['nɔ:θwəd] *adj/adv* hacia el norte.
◆ *n* dirección *f* norte.

northwards [-z] *adv* hacia el norte.

northwest ['nɔ:θ'west] *adj* del noroeste, noroeste || (que sopla) del noroeste (wind).
◆ *adv* hacia el noroeste || (que sopla) del noroeste (wind).
◆ *n* noroeste *m*.

northwest by north [-bai'nɔ:θ] *n* MAR noroeste *m* cuarta al norte.

northwest by west [-bai'west] *n* MAR noroeste *m* cuarta al oeste.

northwester [-ə*] *n* noroeste *m* (wind).

northwesterly [-əli] *adj* noroeste, del noroeste.
◆ *adv* hacia el noroeste.
◆ *n* noroeste *m* (wind).

northwestern [-ən] *adj* del noroeste.

northwestward [-wəd] *adj/adv* hacia el noroeste.

northwestwards [-wədz] *adv* hacia el noroeste.

Norway ['nɔ:wei] *n* GEOGR Noruega.

Norwegian [nɔ:'wi:dʒən] *n* noruego, ga (person) || noruego *m* (language).
◆ *adj* noruego, ga.

nose [nəuz] *n* ANAT nariz *f* || ZOOL hocico *m* (of many animals) | nariz *f* (of dog, etc.) || FIG olfato *m* (perspicacity); *to have a nose for business* tener olfato para los negocios | olfato *m* (sense of smell) | morro *m*, nariz *f* (front of an aircraft) | nariz *f*, proa *f* (of a ship) | morro *m* (of a car) | boca *f*, aroma *m* (of a wine, of a drink) | aroma *m* (of tobacco, of herbs, etc.) || TECH boca *f* (of a tool) || — *aquiline* o *Roman, turned-up, snub, flat, hooked nose* nariz aguileña, respingona, chata, aplastada, de gancho || FIG & FAM *he gets up my nose* me pone negro, me joroba || FIG *it is (right) under your nose* está delante de tus narices || FIG & FAM *keep your nose out of it!* ¡no te metas donde no te importa! || FIG *not to be able to see further than the end of one's nose* no ver más allá de sus narices | *to be as plain as the nose on one's face* estar más claro que el agua || *to blow one's nose* sonarse, sonarse la nariz || FIG *to cut off one's nose to spite one's face* fastidiarse a sí mismo por querer fastidiar a los demás | *to follow one's nose* seguir recto (to go straight ahead), dejarse llevar por el instinto (to follow one's instinct) || *to hold one's nose* taparse la nariz || FAM *to keep one's nose out of sth.* no meter las narices en algo || FIG *to keep one's nose to the grindstone* trabajar con ahínco (to work hard) | *to lead s.o. by the nose* manejar a uno a su antojo, tener a uno agarrado por las narices | *to look down one's nose at* mirar por encima del hombro a | *to make a long nose* hacer un palmo de narices | *to pay through the nose* pagar un dineral || *to pick one's nose* hurgarse la nariz || FIG & FAM *to poke* o *to stick one's nose into other people's business* meter la nariz *or* las narices en los asuntos de los demás | *to put s.o.'s nose out of joint* enfadar a alguien || *to speak through the nose* hablar con *or* por la nariz, hablar con voz gangosa || FIG *to thumb one's nose at s.o.* hacer un palmo de narices a alguien | *to turn up one's nose at* despreciar, hacer una mueca de desprecio ante (sth.) || *your nose is bleeding* estás echando sangre *or* sangrando por la nariz *or* por las narices.

nose [nəuz] *vt* olfatear (to smell out) || — *to nose one's way through* abrirse paso con cuidado entre || *to nose out* olfatear, husmear (an animal), conseguir descubrir (a secret).
◆ *vi* *to nose about* o *around* curiosear || *to nose forward* avanzar con cuidado || *to nose in* o *into* meterse en, meter la nariz *or* las narices en.

nose bag [-bæg] *n* morral *m*.

noseband [-bænd] *n* muserola *f*.

nosebleed [-bli:d] *n* hemorragia *f* nasal.

nose cone [-kəun] *n* morro *m* (of a rocket).

nose dive [-daiv] *n* AVIAT picado *m*.

nose-dive [-daiv] *vi* AVIAT descender en picado.

nose flute [-flu:t] *n* MUS flauta *f* nasal.

nosegay [-gei] *n* ramillete *m* de flores.

nosepiece [-pi:s] *n* puente *m* (of glasses) || muserola *f* (noseband) || lanza *f* (of a pipe).

nose ring [-riŋ] *n* nariguera *f* (ornament) || aro *m* [que ponen en la nariz a los cerdos y a los toros].

nosey [-i] *adj* FAM entrometido, da || *nosey parker* entrometido, da; metomentodo *m* & *f*.

no-show ['nəu'ʃəu] *n* pasajero *m* que no utiliza su reservación sin cancelarla.

nosh-up ['nɔʃʌp] *n* comilona *f*.

nosing [-iŋ] *n* ARCH borde *m* saliente (edge of a step) | saliente *m* (projection).

nostalgia [nɔst'ældʒiə] *n* nostalgia *f*.

nostalgic [nɔst'ældʒik] *adj* nostálgico, ca.

nostril ['nɔstril] *n* ANAT ventanilla *f or* ventana *f* de la nariz || ollar *m* (of a horse).
◆ *pl* narices *f*.

nostrum ['nɔstrəm] *n* panacea *f*.

nosy ['nəuzi] *adj* FAM entrometido, da (nosey).

not [nɔt] *adv* no; *they did not come* no vinieron; *not everybody* no todos; *not a little* no poco; *not a few* no pocos; *I think not* creo que no; *you like him, don't you?* le gusta, ¿no?; *don't* o *do not do it* no lo hagas; *I don't care whether he comes or not* me da igual que venga o no; *we told you not to go* te dijimos que no fueras || ¿no?, ¿verdad?; *he is here, isn't he?* está aquí, ¿verdad?; *it is this one, is it not?* es éste, ¿verdad? || ni; *not one of them knew it* ni uno de ellos lo sabía || como no; *not wanting to disturb them, he kept quiet* como no quería molestarles, se calló || sin; *not thinking that* sin pensar que || — *absolutely not!* ¡en absoluto! || *certainly not!* ¡de ninguna manera!, ¡por supuesto que no!, ¡ni hablar! || *not a hope!, not a chance!* ¡ni pensarlo! || *not any* ninguno, na || *not any more* ya no || *not... at all* no... nada, no... en absoluto; *I do not like him at all* no me gusta nada; *he is not handsome at all* no es nada guapo || *not at all* no hay de qué; *thank you not at all* gracias no hay de qué; nada, en absoluto; *are you cross? not at all* ¿estás enfadado? ¡en absoluto! || *not even* ni siquiera || JUR *not guilty* inocente || *not likely!* ¡ni hablar! || *not much!* ¡ya lo creo!, ¡y cómo! (and how), ¡eso te lo crees tú! (I don't believe you) || *not only... but also* no sólo... sino también; *not only small but also bald* no sólo bajo sino también calvo || *not she!* ¡ella no! || *not that* no es que; *not that I don't want to go* no es que no quiera ir || *not to say* por no decir || *not yet, still not* todavía no, aún no || *of course not* claro que no || *why not?* ¿por qué no?, ¿cómo no?
— OBSERV El adverbio *not* se suele contraer y combinar con los verbos que acompaña, particularmente en la lengua hablada: *don't* (do not), *won't* (will not), *isn't* (is not).

nota bene ['nəutə'bi:ni] *loc lat* nota bene.

notability ['neutə'biliti] *n* notabilidad *f* (quality, person).

notable ['nəutəbl] *adj* notable (admirable, noteworthy); *a notable success* un éxito notable.
◆ *n* notabilidad *f*, notable *m* (person).

notarial [nəu'tɛəriəl] *adj* notarial; *notarial deeds* actas notariales.

notarize ['nəutəraiz] *vt* US hacer certificar por notario.

notary ['nəutəri] *n* notario *m* [*AMER* escribano *m*].

notary public [-'pʌblik] *n* notario *m*.
— OBSERV El plural de *notary public* es *notaries public*.

notation [nəu'teiʃən] *n* anotación *f* (note) || MATH & MUS notación *f*.

notch [nɔtʃ] *n* muesca *f*, corte *m* (a cut, an indentation) || grado *m*, punto *m* (a degree) || US desfiladero *m* (between mountains).

notch [nɔtʃ] *vt* hacer una muesca en, cortar (to make a cut in) || *to notch up* apuntarse (to mark up); *the team notched up its third consecutive victory* el equipo se apuntó la tercera victoria consecutiva.

note [nəut] *n* nota *f*; *he wrote me a note to say he wasn't coming* me escribió una nota para decirme que no venía; *diplomatic note* nota diplomática; *translator's note* nota del traductor || MUS nota *f* (sound, symbol) | tecla *f* (key of piano, of organ, etc.); *the black notes* las teclas negras || sonido *m* (sound) || canto *m* (of a bird) || billete *m*; *a hundred peseta note* un billete de cien pesetas || tono *m*, nota *f*; *a note of irony in his voice* una nota de ironía en su voz || importancia *f*; *a person of note* una persona de importancia || renombre *m*; *a restaurant of note* un restaurante de renombre || marca *f*, señal *f* (mark, sign) || PRINT signo *m*; *note of exclamation* signo de admiración || — *nothing of note* nada especial || *promissory note* pagaré *m* || FIG *to change one's note* cambiar de tono || *to make a note of* tomar nota de, apuntar || FIG *to strike a false note* desentonar | *to strike the right note* hacer *or* decir lo apropiado, acertar || *to take note* prestar atención || *to take note of* tomar nota de || *worthy of note* digno de mención.
◆ *pl* apuntes *m*; *to take notes in a history lesson* tomar apuntes en una clase de historia || notas *f*; *to make notes during a journey* tomar notas durante un viaje || — FIG *to compare notes* cambiar impresiones || *to speak from notes* pronunciar un discurso utilizando notas *or* apuntes.

note [nəut] *vt* fijarse en, tomar nota de; *note carefully what I am about to say* fíjense bien en lo que voy a decir || darse cuenta de, tener en cuenta; *but note that he is only ten years old* pero date cuenta de que tiene sólo diez años || anotar, apuntar; *I noted the details in my exercise book* anoté los detalles en mi cuaderno || tomar nota de; *we have noted your request* hemos tomado nota de su solicitud || señalar; *the report noted a drop in sales* el informe señaló un descenso en las ventas || notar, observar, advertir; *to note a difference between* notar una diferencia entre; *I noted that he had holes in his shoes* advertí que tenía agujeros en los zapatos || *to note down* apuntar, anotar.

notebook [-buk] *n* cuaderno *m*, libreta *f*.

notecase [-keis] *n* billetero *m*, billetera *f* (wallet).

noted [-id] *adj* notable, eminente (eminent) || famoso, sa; célebre (famous).

note of hand [-əvhænd] *n* COMM pagaré *m*.

notepad [-pæd] *n* bloc *m* de notas.

notepaper [-ˌpeipə*] *n* papel *m* de escribir, papel *m* de cartas.

noteworthy [-ˌwəːði] *adj* digno de mención, notable || *it is noteworthy that* es de notar que.

nothing [ˈnʌθiŋ] *n* no... nada; *to eat nothing* no comer nada; *nothing happened* no pasó nada || nada; *nothing new* nada nuevo; *nothing else* nada más; *nothing at all* nada de nada || cero *m* (zero) || — *a mere nothing* una fruslería, una bagatela || *as though it were nothing at all* como si nada || *for nothing* para nada (in vain), por nada, gratis (free), sin razón (for no reason) || *it's nothing to laugh about* no tiene ninguna gracia || *it's nothing to me* me da igual (I don't care) || *man risen from nothing* hombre *m* salido de la nada || *next to nothing* casi nada || *nothing but* sólo || *nothing but the truth* nada más que la verdad || *nothing doing!* ¡ni hablar! || *nothing if not* más que todo, antes que nada; *you are nothing if not selfish* eres egoísta antes que nada || *nothing much* poca cosa || *nothing on earth* nada en el mundo || FIG *nothing to write home about* nada del otro mundo || *nothing ventured, nothing gained* quien no se arriesga no pasa la mar || *sweet nothings* ternezas *f* || *there's nothing for it but to* no hay más remedio que || *there's nothing in it* no dice nada (not profound), es falso (untrue), no se puede sacar nada de ello (unprofitable), van muy iguales (in race) || *there is nothing like* no hay nada mejor que, no hay nada como || *there is nothing much to be said* no hay mucho que decir || *there is nothing stupid about her* no es nada tonta || *there is nothing to it* es facilísimo, está tirado || *think nothing of it* no hay de qué || *to be nothing of a teacher* ser muy mal profesor || *to come to nothing* reducirse a nada, quedar en nada, fracasar || *to have nothing to do with* no tener nada que ver con || *to make nothing of* no sacar nada en limpio de (to be unable to understand), no dar importancia a (to treat as unimportant), desaprovechar (to waste) || *to make nothing of doing sth.* hacer algo como si nada || *to mean nothing to* no significar nada para, no querer decir nada para || *to say nothing of* por no hablar de || *to think nothing of* no suponer nada para uno; *he thinks nothing of working sixteen hours a day* para él no supone nada trabajar dieciséis horas diarias; no encontrarle nada (not to like); *I'm afraid I think nothing of her* lo siento, pero yo no le encuentro nada.
◆ *adv* de ninguna manera, de ningún modo || — *it's nothing like as good as the first one* no es ni mucho menos tan bueno como el primero || *it looks nothing like you* no se te parece nada || *nothing less than* nada menos que.

nothingness [-nis] *n* nada *f*; *God created the world out of nothingness* Dios creó el mundo de la nada || insignificancia *f*; *to realize one's own nothingness* darse cuenta de su propia insignificancia.

notice [ˈnəutis] *n* atención *f* (attention); *to come into notice, to attract notice* llamar la atención || anuncio *m* (announcement, advert) || letrero *m* (sign); *the notice said «keep off the grass»* el letrero decía «no pisar el césped» || cartel *m* (poster) || reseña *f* (review of a book) || aviso *m*, notificación *f*; *subject to change without previous notice* sujeto a cambio sin previo aviso *or* sin notificación previa || despido *m*, aviso *m* de despido; *the firm gave him his notice* la firma le comunicó su despido || dimisión *f*; *he handed in his notice* presentó su dimisión || desahucio *m* (of a tenant) || aviso *m*; *the landlady gave him notice to leave* la dueña de la casa le dio el aviso de que se marchara || plazo *m*; *a week's notice* una semana de plazo || — *an event which attracted a lot of notice* un acontecimiento que llamó mucho la atención || *at a moment's notice* en seguida, inmediatamente (at once) || *at short notice* a corto plazo, con poco tiempo de antelación || *at such short notice* con tan poco plazo || *on short notice* en poco tiempo || *take notice that* le advierto que || *to bring to s.o.'s notice that* hacer observar a uno que || *to come to one's notice* llegar al conocimiento de uno || *to escape one's notice* pasarle desapercibido a uno, escapársele a uno || *to give notice of* avisar de || *to give notice to* despedir (an employee), despedirse (one's master), presentar la dimisión (one's employer) || *to give s.o. notice* despedir a uno (to dismiss) || *to give two weeks notice* avisar con dos semanas de anticipación || *to serve notice on* hacer saber, notificar, avisar || FIG *to sit up and take notice* prestar atención || *to take notice of s.o.* hacer caso a alguien || *to take notice of sth.* observar (to observe), prestar atención a algo, hacer caso de algo (to pay attention) || *under notice* avisado, da; dimitido, da || *until further notice* hasta nuevo aviso || *without notice* sin previo aviso (without warning), desapercibido, da (unnoticed) || *worthy of notice* digno de atención.

notice [ˈnəutis] *vt* darse cuenta de, advertir (to realize, to see); *I noticed that it was getting dark* me di cuenta de que estaba oscureciendo || fijarse, reparar en; *I had never noticed that picture before* no me había fijado nunca en ese cuadro || observar, notar; *notice the harmony of colour* observe la armonía de colores || ver, reconocer; *I noticed him in the crowd* lo vi entre la multitud || prestar atención a (to pay attention) || hacer la reseña de (to review) || avisar (to notify).

noticeable [-əbl] *adj* notable, sensible; *a noticeable difference* una diferencia notable; *a noticeable increase* un aumento sensible || evidente, obvio, via (obvious) || — *is the hole in my trousers very noticeable?* ¿se ve mucho el agujero en mi pantalón? || *it is hardly noticeable* casi no se nota.

notice board [-bɔːd] *n* tablón *m* de anuncios (for pinning notices) || letrero *m* (for inscription) || AUT señal *f* de tráfico.

notifiable [ˈnəutifaiəbl] *adj* de declaración obligatoria, que hay que declarar a las autoridades (diseases).

notification [ˌnəutifiˈkeiʃən] *n* notificación *f*, aviso *m*.

notify [ˈnəutifai] *vt* avisar, comunicar, notificar; *they notified me of your arrival* me avisaron de su llegada, me comunicaron *or* me notificaron su llegada.

notion [ˈnəuʃən] *n* idea *f*, concepto *m*; *his notion of a good novel is different to mine* su idea de una buena novela es diferente de la mía || concepto *m*, noción *f*; *the notion of law* el concepto de la ley || impresión *f*; *I have a notion he is right* tengo la impresión de que tiene razón || teoría *f* (theory) || idea *f*; *Anthony had no notion what was going on* Antonio no tenía ni idea de lo que estaba pasando; *I haven't the slightest notion* no tengo la más mínima idea || intención *f*; *to have a notion to do sth.* tener intención de hacer algo || FAM capricho *m*; *Victoria always acts as the notion takes her* Victoria actúa siempre según su capricho.
◆ *pl* US artículos *m* de mercería.

notional [ˈnəuʃənl] *adj* especulativo, va; teórico, ca (theoretical) || imaginario, ria (imaginary) || US caprichoso, sa (capricious).

notoriety [ˌnəutəˈraiəti] *n* notoriedad *f* (fame) || celebridad *f* (a celebrity) || mala fama *f*, notoriedad *f* (ill repute).

notorious [nəuˈtɔːriəs] *adj* célebre, famoso, sa; notorio, ria; muy conocido, da; *a notorious criminal* un criminal notorio; *a place notorious for crime* un sitio muy conocido por los crímenes que se cometen.
— OBSERV *Notorious* casi siempre tiene un sentido despectivo en inglés.

no-trump [ˈnəuˈtrʌmp] *adj* sin triunfo.

no-twithstanding [ˌnɔtwiθˈstændiŋ] *prep* a pesar de.
◆ *adv* sin embargo, no obstante.
◆ *conj* a pesar de que, por más que.

nougat [ˈnuːgɑː] *n* turrón *m* de almendras.

nought [nɔːt] *n* → **naught.**

noughts-and-crosses [ˈnɔːtsəndˈkrɔsiz] *n* tres en raya *m* (game).

noumenon [ˈnuːməˌnɔn] *n* PHIL nóumeno *m*.
— OBSERV El plural de la palabra inglesa es *noumena*.

noun [naun] *n* GRAMM nombre *m*, sustantivo *m* || GRAMM *proper noun* nombre propio.
◆ *adj* GRAMM sustantivo, va.

nourish [ˈnʌriʃ] *vt* alimentar, nutrir (with food) || FIG abrigar (hopes, etc.) | fomentar (to encourage).

nourishing [-iŋ] *adj* nutritivo, va; alimenticio, cia.

nourishment [-mənt] *n* alimento *m* (food) || alimentación *f*, nutrición *f* (feeding).

nous [naus] *n* PHIL mente *f*, intelecto *m* || FAM sentido *m* común.

nouveau riche ['nuːvəu'riːʃ] *n* nuevo rico *m*, nueva rica *f*.

nova ['nəuvə] *n* ASTR nova *f*.
— OBSERV El plural de la palabra inglesa *nova* es *novae* o *novas*.

Nova Scotia ['nəuvə'skəuʃə] *pr n* GEOGR Nueva Escocia *f*.

novation [nə'veiʃən] *n* JUR novación *f*.

novel ['nɔvəl] *n* novela *f*; *clock-and-dagger novel* novela de capa y espada; *serialized novel* novela por entregas.
◆ *adj* nuevo, va (new) || original, ingenioso, sa (new and ingenious).

novelette [ˌnɔvə'let] *n* novela *f* corta (short novel) || novela *f* rosa (sentimental novel).

novelist ['nɔvəlist] *n* novelista *m* & *f*.

novelistic [nɔvə'listik] *adj* novelístico, ca.

novelize ['nɔvəlaiz] *vt* novelar, novelizar.

novelty ['nɔvəlti] *n* novedad *f* || COMM novedad *f*, fantasía *f*.

November [nəu'vembə*] *n* noviembre *m*; *on the fifth of November* el cinco de noviembre.

novena [nəu'viːnə] *n* REL novena *f*.
— OBSERV El plural de la palabra inglesa es *novenae*.

novice ['nɔvis] *n* principiante *m* & *f*, novato, ta; novicio, cia (beginner) || REL novicio, cia | recién convertido, da (convert).

noviciate [nəu'viʃiit]; **novitiate** [nəu'viʃiit] *n* REL noviciado *m* || período *m* de aprendizaje || novicio, cia; principiante (novice).

novocaine ['nəuvəˌkein] *n* CHEM novocaína *f*.

now [nau] *adv* ahora; *how do you feel now?* ¿cómo te sientes ahora?; *I want to go now* quiero irme ahora; *now or never* ahora o nunca || ahora bien; *now, while this was happening* ahora bien, mientras esto ocurría || entonces; *the general now changed his plan* entonces el general cambió su plan || ya; *I have worked here a long time now* hace ya mucho tiempo que trabajo aquí; *all was now ready* todo estaba ya listo || ya, ahora; *it's six o'clock now* ya son las seis, son las seis ahora; *you can go now* ya te puedes marchar || inmediatamente (immediately) || actualmente (at present) || — *he won't be long now* ya no puede tardar || *I can't help you just now* no le puedo ayudar en este momento *or* ahora mismo || *I saw him just now* lo he visto ahora mismo, acabo de verlo || *not now* ahora no || *now and again, now and then* de vez en cuando, de cuando en cuando || *now... now* ya..., ya; ora..., ora || *now, now!* ¡vamos, vamos! || *now then, where have you been?* ahora bien, ¿dónde has estado? || *right now* ahora mismo.
◆ *conj* ya que, ahora que; *now (that) you have come you may stay* ahora que has venido te puedes quedar.
◆ *n* *by now* ya || *for now* por ahora || *from now* dentro de; *three days from now* dentro de tres días || *from now on* de ahora en adelante, a partir de ahora || *long before now* hace mucho tiempo ya || *till now* hasta ahora || *up to now* hasta ahora.

nowadays [-ədeiz] *adv* hoy, actualmente, ahora, hoy día, hoy en día.

noways ['nəuweiz] *adv* US de ninguna manera.

nowhere ['nəuwɛə*] *adv* por ninguna parte; *he was nowhere to be found* no se le encontraba por ninguna parte || a ninguna parte; *where are you going? nowhere* ¿a dónde vas? a ninguna parte || en ninguna parte; *nowhere in the world* en ninguna parte del mundo || — *nowhere else* en ninguna otra parte || *nowhere near* nada cerca; *it's nowhere near London* no está nada cerca de Londres; ni mucho menos; *it was nowhere near as difficult as he expected* no fue ni mucho menos tan difícil como pensaba || *there's nowhere I can think of* no se me ocurre ningún sitio || *to appear out of* o *from nowhere* salir de la nada || *to be nowhere as good as* distar mucho de ser tan bueno como || FIG *to come nowhere in a race* quedarse muy atrás en una carrera | *to get nowhere* no conseguir nada.
◆ *n* nada *f*; *a man came out of nowhere and shot me* un hombre salió de la nada y me disparó || *at the back of nowhere* en el quinto pino, en el quinto infierno.

nowise ['nəuwaiz] *adv* de ninguna manera.

noxious ['nɔkʃəs] *adj* nocivo, va; perjudicial (harmful) || nocivo, va; pernicioso, sa; dañino, na (corrupting).

nozzle ['nɔzl] *n* boca *f*, boquilla *f* (serving as an outlet for a fluid, etc.) || TECH tobera *f*, inyector *m* || cánula *f* (of a syringe) || FAM napias *f pl* (nose).

nth [enθ] *adj* enésimo, ma || *for the nth time* por enésima vez || *for the nth degree* al máximo.

nu [njuː] *n* ny *f* (greek letter).

nuance [nju'ɑːns] *n* matiz *m*.

nub [nʌb] *n* trocito *m* (small lump or piece) || nudo *m* (crucial part of problem, etc.) || — *that's the nub of it* ahí está el quid || *to be worn to the nub* estar molido (to be exhausted).

nubbin ['nʌbin] *n* US AGR mazorca *f* defectuosa (stunted corn) | verdura *f* or fruta *f* defectuosa (defective fruit).

nubecula [nju'biːkjulə] *n* MED nefelión *m*.

nubile ['njuːbail] *adj* núbil, casadera.

nubility [njuː'biliti] *n* nubilidad *f*.

nucha ['njuːkə] *n* ANAT nuca *f*.

nuchal [-l] *adj* de la nuca.

nuclear ['njuːkliə*] *adj* nuclear; *nuclear energy, physics, warfare* energía, física, guerra nuclear; *nuclear physicist, reactor, fission, fusion* físico, reactor, fisión, fusión nuclear; *nuclear weapons* armas nucleares || *nuclear power* energía *f* nuclear (energy), potencia *f* nuclear (country).

nuclear-free ['njuːkliə*friː] *adj* desnuclearizado, da; *nuclear-free zone* zona desnuclearizada.

nucleate ['njuːkliit] *adj* nucleado, da.

nucleate ['njuːklieit] *vi* formar núcleo.

nuclei ['njuːkliai] *pl n* → **nucleus**.

nucleic [njuː'kliik] *adj* nucleico, ca; *nucleic acid* ácido nucleico.

nuclein ['njuːkliːin] *n* nucleína *f*.

nucleolar ['njuːkliəulə*] *adj* del nucléolo.

nucleolus [njuː'kliːələs] *n* nucléolo *m*.
— OBSERV El plural de *nucleolus* es *nucleoli*.

nucleon ['njuːkliɔn] *n* PHYS nucleón *m*.

nucleonic [njuːkli'ɔnik] *adj* nucleónico, ca.

nucleonics [-s] *n* PHYS nucleónica *f*.

nucleoplasm ['njuːkliːəplæzəm] *n* nucleoplasma *m*.

nucleoprotein ['njuːkliəu'prəutiːn] *n* nucleoproteína *f*.

nucleus ['njuːkliəs] *n* núcleo *m*; *atomic nucleus* núcleo atómico || FIG núcleo *m*; *the nucleus of guerrillas grew into an army* el núcleo de guerrilleros se transformó en un ejército.
— OBSERV El plural de *nucleus* es *nuclei* o *nucleuses*.

nude [njuːd] *adj* desnudo, da (naked) || de color carne (stockings).
◆ *n* desnudo *m* || *in the nude* desnudo, da.

nudge [nʌdʒ] *n* codazo *m*.

nudge [nʌdʒ] *vt* dar un codazo a.

nudism ['njuːdizəm] *n* nudismo *m*, desnudismo *m*.

nudist ['njuːdist] *adj/n* nudista.

nudity ['njuːditi] *n* desnudez *f* || desnudo *m* (arts).

nugatory ['njuːgətəri] *adj* insignificante (of no importance) || ineficaz (ineffective).

nugget ['nʌgit] *n* MIN pepita *f*; *gold nugget* pepita de oro.

nuisance ['njuːsns] *n* fastidio *m*, molestia *f*, pesadez *f*, lata *f* (thing); *these flies are a nuisance* estas moscas son una pesadez || pesado, da; latoso, sa; persona *f* molesta (person); *what a nuisance he is!* ¡qué pesado es! || JUR perjuicio *m*, daño *m* || — *to make a nuisance of o.s.* dar la lata, ponerse pesado || *what a nuisance!* ¡qué pesadez!

nuke [njuːk] *n* US FAM arma *f* nuclear.

nuke [njuːk] *vt* US FAM bombardear con armas nucleares.

null [nʌl] *adj* nulo, la || inútil (useless) || JUR *null and void* nulo y sin valor.
◆ *n* cero *m*.

nullification [ˌnʌlifi'keiʃən] *n* anulación *f*.

nullify ['nʌlifai] *vt* anular.

nullipara [nʌlipərə] *n* MED nulípara *f*.
— OBSERV El plural de la palabra inglesa es *nulliparae*.

nullity ['nʌliti] *n* JUR nulidad *f*.

Numantian [nju'mænʃiən] *adj/n* numantino, na.

numb [nʌm] *adj* entumecido, da; *my feet were numb with cold* tenía los pies entumecidos de frío || FIG petrificado, da; paralizado, da; *numb with fear* petrificado de miedo || *my foot has gone numb* se me ha dormido el pie.

numb [nʌm] *vt* entumecer; *the cold numbed my feet* el frío me entumeció los pies || FIG dejar helado, paralizar; *the sad news numbed me completely* la triste noticia me dejó completamente helado.

number ['nʌmbə*] *n* número *m*; *one is a number* uno es un número; *the May number of a magazine* el número de mayo de una revista; *reference number* número de referencia; *the next number on the programme* el próximo número del programa || grupo *m*; *she was not among their number* no estaba en el grupo || total *m*, número *m* (total) || GRAMM número *m* || MIL número *m* || SP dorsal *m*, número *m* (worn by footballers, by athletes) || — FIG & FAM *a nice little number* una niña muy mona || *a number of things to do* varias cosas que hacer || *any number of times* muchísimas veces || *atomic number* número atómico || *beyond number* innumerable || *cardinal number* número cardinal || GRAMM *dual number* número dual || *golden number* número áureo || *number one* número uno (best), primero, ra (first), mi menda, este cura (o.s.) || *odd number* número impar || *on a number of occasions* en varias *or* diversas ocasiones || FIG *opposite number* colega *m* & *f* || *ordinal number* número ordinal || *prime number* número primo || *registration number* número de matrícula (of a car) || *they were four in number* eran cuatro || *they were not of our number* no eran de los nuestros || *to be few in number* ser pocos || US FIG *to have s.o.'s number* tener a uno calado, conocer a alguien a fondo || *to make up the number* hacer número, rellenar || *to take care of* o *to look after number one* cuidarse de sí mismo || *to the number of ten* hasta el número diez || *whole number* número entero || *winning number* número premiado || *without number* sin número, innumerable || FIG *your number is up* te llegó la hora, te llegó tu turno (you are going to die).
◆ *pl* números *m*; *he is no good at numbers* no se le dan bien los números || cantidades *f*; *they attacked in great numbers* atacaron en grandes cantidades || versos *m* (in poetry) || REL Números *m* (Bible) || — REL *Book of Numbers* Libro *m* de los Números || *by the numbers* mecáni-

camente; de uno en uno (file) || *in round numbers* en números redondos || *law of large numbers* ley *f* de los grandes números || US *the numbers* la lotería clandestina || *there is strength in numbers* la unión hace la fuerza || *to swell the numbers* hacer bulto.

number ['nʌmbə*] *vt* numerar, poner número a; *he numbered the pages, the seats* numeró las páginas, las sillas || contar (to count); *my days are numbered* mis días están contados; *he numbered them among his friends* los contaba entre sus amigos || ascender a, sumar (to amount to); *the population numbered ten thousand* la población ascendía a diez mil.
◆ *vi to number off* numerarse.

number-crunching [-'krʌntʃiŋ] *n* INFORM cálculo *m* complejo.

numbering ['nʌmbəriŋ] *n* enumeración *f*, recuento *m* (counting) || numeración *f* (of pages, etc.) || TECH *numbering machine* numerador *m*.

numberless ['nʌmbəlis] *adj* innumerable.

number plate ['nʌmbə*pleit] *n* matrícula *f* (of car).

numbers pool ['nʌmbəzpu:l] *n* US lotería *f* clandestina.

Number Ten ['nʌmbə*ten] *pr n* residencia *f* oficial del Primer Ministro británico.

numbles ['nʌmblz] *pl n* asaduras *f* (of deer).

numbness ['nʌmnis] *n* entumecimiento *m* (from cold, etc.) || FIG parálisis *f*.

numbskull ['nʌmskʌl] *n* lelo, la; tonto, ta.

numen ['nju:mən] *n* MYTH numen *m*.
— OBSERV El plural de la palabra inglesa es *numina*.

numerable ['nju:mərəbl] *adj* numerable.

numeral ['nju:mərəl] *adj* numeral.
◆ *n* número *m*, cifra *f*; *Roman, Arabic numerals* números romanos, arábigos.

numerary ['njumərəri] *adj* numerario, ria.

numerate ['nju:mərət] *adj* con conocimientos matemáticos básicos (person).

numeration [,nju:mə'reiʃən] *n* numeración *f* || INFORM *numeration system* sistema *m* de numeración.

numerator ['nju:məreitə*] *n* numerador *m*.

numerical [nju:'merikəl]; **numeric** [nju:'merik] *adj* numérico, ca.

numerical-control [nju:'merikəl] *adj* INFORM de control numérico || *numerical-control machine tool* máquina *f* herramienta de control numérico.

numerosity [nju:mə'rɔsiti] *n* numerosidad *f*.

numerous ['nju:mərəs] *adj* numeroso, sa; *a numerous family* una familia numerosa; *on numerous occasions* en numerosas ocasiones.

numismatic ['nju:miz'mætik] *adj* numismático, ca.

numismatics [-s] *n* numismática *f*.

numismatist [nju:'mizmətist] *n* numismático, ca.

nummulite ['nʌmjulait] *n* numulita *f* (fossil).

numskull ['nʌmskʌl] *n* lelo, la; tonto, ta.

nun [nʌn] *n* monja *f*, religiosa *f*; *to become a nun* meterse a monja.

nunciature ['nʌnsiətʃə*] *n* REL nunciatura *f*.

nuncio ['nʌnʃiəu] *n* REL nuncio *m*; *papal nuncio* nuncio apostólico.

nunnery ['nʌnəri] *n* convento *m* de monjas.

nuptial ['nʌpʃəl] *adj* nupcial.
◆ *pl n* nupcias *f*.

nurse [nə:s] *n* MED enfermera *f* || niñera *f* (nanny) || ama *f* seca (dry nurse) || nodriza *f*, ama *f* de cría (wet nurse) || ZOOL obrera *f* (bee) || MED *male nurse* enfermero.

nurse [nə:s] *vt* cuidar, atender, asistir (sick people, etc.) || criar, amamantar (to suckle an infant) || mecer (to cradle a child) || cuidar (plants) || curar (to try to cure) || FIG guardar, reservar (one's strength) | abrigar (hopes) | acariciar (plans) | cultivar (one's popularity) | fomentar (a business) || juntar (billiard balls) || *to nurse a grudge against s.o.* guardar rencor a uno.
◆ *vi* ser enfermera (to be a nurse) || ser niñera (to be a nursemaid) || dar de mamar (to suckle) || mamar (to feed at the breast).

nurse-child ['nə:s,tʃaild] *n* niño *m* de pecho.

nurseling ['nə:sliŋ] *n* lactante *m*, niño *m* de pecho.

nursemaid [-meid] *n* niñera *f*.

nursery ['nə:səri] *n* habitación *f* de los niños (in a house) || guardería *f* infantil (day nursery) || escuela *f* de párvulos (school) || AGR vivero *m* (for young plants) || vivero *m* (for young animals) || FIG vivero *m*, cantera *f*, semillero *m* (of politicians, etc.).

nurseryman [-mən] *n* encargado *m* de un vivero, arbolista *m*.
— OBSERV El plural de *nurseryman* es *nurserymen*.

nursery nurse ['nə:sri nə:s] *n* puericultor, ra.

nursery rhyme ['nə:sri,raim] *n* poesía *f* infantil.

nursery school ['nə:srisku:l] *n* escuela *f* de párvulos.

nursery slope ['nə:srisləups] *n* SP pista *f* para principiantes.

nursing ['nə:siŋ] *adj* lactante (mother) || *nursing staff* enfermeras *f pl*.
◆ *n* profesión *f* or trabajo *m* de enfermera (profession) || cuidado *m*, asistencia *f* (of patient) || lactancia *f* (suckling).

nursing bottle [-'bɔtl] *n* biberón *m*.

nursing home [-həum] *n* MED clínica *f*.

nursling ['nə:sliŋ] *n* nutrición *f*, alimentación *f* (nourishment) || alimento *m* (food) || educación *f*, crianza *f* (upbringing).

nurture ['nə:tʃə*] *n* nutrición *f*, alimentación *f* (nourishment) || alimento *m* (food) || educación *f*, crianza *f* (upbringing).

nurture ['nə:tʃə*] *vt* nutrir, alimentar (to nourish) || educar, criar (to educate) || FIG alimentar.

nut [nʌt] *n* nuez *f* (dry fruit) || TECH tuerca *f* || MUS ceja *f* (of stringed instruments) | nuez *f* (of violin bow) || MAR cepo *m* (of an anchor) || carbón *m* de bola (coal) || FAM melón *m*, chola *f* (head) || FAM chiflado, da; chalado, da (crazy person) || — FIG & FAM *a hard nut to crack* un hueso duro de roer | *to be off one's nut* estar como una cabra | *to do one's nut* echar el resto.
◆ *pl* FAM huevos *m* (testicles) || FIG & FAM *nuts!* ¡naranjas de la China!

nut-brown ['nʌtbraun] *adj* de color avellana (colour) || castaño claro (hair).

nutcase ['nʌtkeis] *n* FAM chiflado, da; chalado, da.

nutcracker ['nʌt,krækə*] *n* cascanueces *m inv* || ZOOL cascanueces *m inv* (bird).

nutgall ['nʌtgɔ:l] *n* BOT agalla *f*.

nuthatch ['nʌthætʃ] *n* trepatroncos *m inv* (bird).

nutmeg ['nʌtmeg] *n* BOT nuez *f* moscada.

nutria ['nju:triə] *n* ZOOL nutria *f*.

nutrient ['nju:triənt] *adj* nutritivo, va.
◆ *n* alimento *m* nutritivo.

nutriment ['nju:trimənt] *n* alimento *m* nutritivo.

nutrition [nju:'triʃən] *n* nutrición *f*, alimentación *f*.

nutritional [-əl] *adj* nutritivo, va; alimenticio, cia.

nutritious [nju:'triʃəs] *adj* nutritivo, va; alimenticio, cia; nutricio, cia.

nutritiousness [-nis] *n* valor *m* nutritivo.

nutritive ['nju:tritiv] *adj* nutritivo, va; alimenticio, cia.

nuts [nʌts] *adj* FAM chiflado, da; chalado, da (crazy); *he is nuts about music* está chiflado por la música || — FAM *to drive s.o. nuts* volver loco a alguien | *to go nuts* volverse loco.

nutshell ['nʌtʃel] *n* cáscara *f* de nuez || FIG *to put it in a nutshell* decirlo en pocas palabras.

nutter ['nʌtə*] *n* FAM chiflado, da; chalado, da.

nutty ['nʌti] *adj* que sabe a nuez (taste) || que da nueces (tree) || con nueces (cake) || FAM tonto, ta; chiflado, da; chalado, da; loco, ca; *to be nutty about* estar loco por; *to be as nutty as a fruitcake* estar más loco que una cabra.

nux vomica ['nʌks'vɔmikə] *n* BOT nuez *f* vómica.

nuzzle ['nʌzl] *vt* hocicar, hozar (a dog).
◆ *vi* hocicar || arrimarse cómodamente || acurrucarse (to nestle).

nyctalopia ['niktə,ləupiə] *n* MED nictalopía *f*.

nylon ['nailən] *n* nylon *m*, nilón *m*, nailon *m* (material).
◆ *pl* medias *f* de nilón.
◆ *adj* de nilón.

nymph [nimf] *n* MYTH & ZOOL ninfa *f*.

nympha ['nimfə] *n* ZOOL ninfa *f*.

nymphaea ['nimfi] *n* BOT nínfea *f*, nenúfar *m*.

nymphomania [,nimfə'meiniə] *n* MED ninfomanía *f*.

nymphomaniac [,nimfəu'meinjæk] *n* MED ninfómana *f*, ninfomaníaca *f*.

NYSE *abbr of [New York Stock Exchange]* Bolsa de Nueva York.

O

o [əu] *n* o *f* (letter) ‖ cero *m* (zero).
◆ *interj* ¡oh!

oaf [əuf] *n* FAM zoquete *m*, ceporro *m*, bruto *m*.
— OBSERV El plural de *oaf* es *oafs* u *oaves*.

oafish [-iʃ] *adj* FAM lerdo, da; tonto, ta; bruto, ta.

oafishness [-iʃnis] *n* FAM necedad *f*, tontería *f* (foolishness) | torpeza *f* (clumsiness).

oak [əuk] *n* BOT roble *m* (tree) ‖ — BOT *holm oak* encina *f* | *oak grove* robledal *m*, robleda *f*, robledo *m* ‖ FIG *to sport one's oak* cerrar la puerta.
◆ *adj* de roble.

oak apple [-æpl] *n* BOT agalla *f*.

oaken [-ən] *adj* de roble.

oak gall [-gɔːl] *n* BOT agalla *f*.

oakum [-əm] *n* estopa *f*.

oakwood [-wud] *n* roble *m* (wood) ‖ robledo *m*, robledal *m*, robleda *f* (grove of oaks).

oar [ɔː*] *n* MAR remo *m* (wooden shaft) | remero *m* (oarsman) ‖ — FIG & FAM *to put* o *to shove* o *to stick one's oar in* meter baza, entrometerse ‖ *to rest on one's oars* dormirse en los laureles (to rest on one's laurels), dejar de remar (to stop rowing).

oar [ɔː*] *vi* MAR remar.
◆ *vt* MAR hacer avanzar con el remo.

oarlock [ɔː*lɔk] *n* MAR escálamo *m*, tolete *m*.

oarsman [ˈɔːzmən] *n* MAR remero *m*.
— OBSERV El plural de *oarsman* es *oarsmen*.

oarsmanship [-ʃip] *n* arte *m* de remar.

oarswoman [ˈɔːzˌwumən] *n* MAR remera *f*.
— OBSERV El plural de *oarswoman* es *oarswomen*.

OAS *abbr of [Organization of American States]* OEA, Organización de Estados Americanos.

oasis [əuˈeisis] *n* oasis *m inv* ‖ FIG remanso *m*, oasis *m*; *an oasis of peace* un remanso de paz.
— OBSERV El plural de la palabra inglesa *oasis* es *oases*.

oast [əust] *n* secadero *m* para el lúpulo, el tabaco o la malta (kiln).

oasthouse [-haus] *n* secadero *m* para el lúpulo, el tabaco o la malta (building).

oat [əut] *n* BOT avena *f*.
◆ *pl* BOT avena *f sing* ‖ — CULIN *rolled oats* copos *m* de avena ‖ FIG *to be off one's oats* estar indispuesto, no estar en forma | *to feel one's oats* sentirse en plena forma (to feel frisky), estar muy ancho (to feel important) | *to sow one's wild oats* andar de picos pardos, correrla ‖ BOT *wild oats* avena loca.

oatcake [-keik] *n* torta *f* hecha con harina de avena.

oaten [ˈəutn] *adj* de avena.

oatfield [ˈəutfiːld] *n* avena *m*, campo *m* de avena.

oat grass [ˈəutgrɑːs] *n* BOT avena *f* loca.

oath [əuθ] *n* juramento *m*; *to administer the oath to* tomar juramento a ‖ reniego *m*, voto *m*, blasfemia *f*, juramento *m* (blasphemy) ‖ — *on* o *upon* o *under oath* bajo juramento ‖ *taking of an oath* jura *f* ‖ *to break one's oath* romper un juramento ‖ *to make* o *to swear* o *to take an oath* prestar juramento, jurar ‖ *to put s.o. on oath* tomar juramento a alguien, hacer prestar juramento a alguien ‖ *to take one's oath of allegiance* jurar bandera (in the army) ‖ *upon my oath* palabra de honor (honestly), ¡por Dios!, ¡voto a tal! (expression of surprise) ‖ *witness on oath* testigo juramentado.

oatmeal [ˈəutmiːl] *n* harina *f* de avena.

oats [əuts] *pl n* ⟶ **oat.**

OAU *abbr of [Organization of African Unity]* OUA, Organización para la Unidad Africana.

obduracy [ˈɔbdjurəsi] *n* obstinación *f*, terquedad *f* (stubbornness) ‖ inflexibilidad *f*, inexorabilidad *f* (hardness) ‖ REL impenitencia *f*.

obdurate [ˈɔbdjurit] *adj* obstinado, da; terco, ca (stubborn) ‖ inflexible, inexorable (unyielding) ‖ duro, ra (hardhearted) ‖ endurecido, da (hardened) ‖ REL impenitente.

obeah [ˈəubiə] *n* fetichismo *m*, hechicería *f* (witchcraft) ‖ fetiche *m* (fetish).

obedience [əˈbiːdjəns] *n* obediencia *f*; *blind obedience* obediencia ciega ‖ REL obediencia *f* ‖ — *in obedience to* conforme a, en *or* de conformidad con ‖ *to compel obedience from* exigir obediencia de.

obedient [əˈbiːdjənt] *adj* obediente ‖ dócil (docile) ‖ *to be obedient to* obedecer a.

obediently [-li] *adv* con obediencia, obedientemente ‖ dócilmente ‖ COMM *Yours obediently* queda siempre a su disposición *or* a sus órdenes.

obeisance [əuˈbeisəns] *n* reverencia *f* (curtsy) ‖ homenaje *m* (homage) ‖ *to do* o *to make* o *to pay obeisance to* rendir homenaje a.

obelisk [ˈɔbilisk] *n* obelisco *m* (stone shaft) ‖ PRINT obelisco *m* (dagger).

obese [əuˈbiːs] *adj* obeso, sa.

obesity [-iti] *n* obesidad *f*.

obey [əˈbei] *vt* obedecer; *to obey s.o.* obedecer a alguien ‖ cumplir (an order) ‖ acatar, respetar (the law) ‖ observar (the rules) ‖ obedecer a; *to obey the helm* obedecer al timón.
◆ *vi* obedecer.

obeyer [-ə*] *n* *obeyer of the laws* persona que acata la ley.

obfuscate [ˈɔbfʌskeit] *vt* ofuscar.

obfuscation [ˌɔbfʌsˈkeiʃən] *n* ofuscación *f*.

obi [ˈəubi] *n* faja *f* de seda japonesa (sash) ‖ fetichismo *m*, hechicería *f* (witchcraft) ‖ fetiche *m* (fetish).

obit. [ˈɔbit] *n* US necrología *f*, obituario *m*.

obituarist [əˈbitjuərist] *n* necrólogo *m*.

obituary [əˈbitjuəri] *adj* necrológico, ca ‖ — *obituary column* necrología *f* ‖ *obituary notice* nota necrológica; esquela *f* de defunción.
◆ *n* necrología *f*, obituario *m*.

object [ˈɔbdʒikt] *n* objeto *m*; *a bag containing a round object* una bolsa que contiene un objeto redondo ‖ objeto *m*, cosa *f* (thing) ‖ FIG objetivo *m*, meta *f*, objeto *m* (aim); *to accomplish one's object* alcanzar su objetivo | propósito *m*, fin *m*, objeto *m*; *this law has several objects* esta ley tiene varios propósitos | objeto *m*; *why is he the object of such strong dislike?* ¿por qué es objeto de una antipatía tan grande? ‖ PHIL objeto *m* ‖ GRAMM complemento *m*; *direct object* complemento directo ‖ INFORM objeto *m* ‖ — *to become an object of ridicule* ponerse en ridículo ‖ FIG *there is no object in doing that* no sirve para nada hacer eso | *to be no object* no importar; *money is no object* el dinero no importa ‖ *to make s.o. the object of* hacerle a alguien objeto de ‖ *with this object* con este fin, con este objeto.

object [əbˈdʒekt] *vi* oponerse; *no one objected to the decision* nadie se opuso a la decisión; *he objected to my going out* se opuso a que saliese ‖ poner reparos, hacer objeciones (to raise objections) ‖ molestar; *do you object to my smoking?* ¿le molesta que fume? ‖ *I object (to that remark)!* ¡protesto!
◆ *vt* objetar; *I objected that it was impossible* objeté que era imposible.

object ball [ˈɔbdʒiktbɔːl] *n* mingo *m* (in billiards).

object glass [ˈɔbdʒiktglɑːs] *n* PHYS objetivo *m*.

objectification [əbˌdʒektifiˈkeiʃən] *n* objetivación *f*.

objectify [əbˈdʒektifai] *vt* objetivar.

objecting [əbˈdʒektiŋ] *adj* objetante.

objection [əbˈdʒekʃən] *n* objeción *f*; *to raise an objection* hacer una objeción ‖ reparo *m*, objeción *f*; *he raises objections to everything* pone reparos a todo, hace objeciones a todo ‖ inconveniente *m*, dificultad *f* (difficulty); *can you see any objection?* ¿ves algún inconveniente? ‖ — *have you any objection to my smoking?* ¿le molesta que fume? ‖ *if you have no objection* si no tiene nada que objetar ‖ *we have no objection to your staying* no tenemos inconveniente en que se quede.

objectionable [əbˈdʒekʃnəbl] *adj* censurable (criticizable); *objectionable conduct* comportamiento censurable ‖ desagradable, molesto, ta (unpleasant) ‖ grosero, ra; *objectionable language* palabras groseras ‖ *I found the idea most objectionable* la idea me pareció inaceptable.

objective [əbˈdʒektiv] *adj* objetivo, va ‖ GRAMM objetivo, va (case).
◆ *n* objetivo *m*.

objectivism [əbˈdʒektivizəm] *n* objetivismo *m*.

objectivity [ˈɔbdʒekˈtiviti] *n* objetividad *f*.

object lesson [ˈɔbdʒiktˌlesn] *n* lección *f* práctica ‖ FIG ejemplo *m*.

objector [əbˈdʒektə*] *n* objetante *m* ‖ *conscientious objector* objetor *m* de conciencia.

objurgate [ˈɔbdʒəːgeit] *vt* reprender, amonestar.

objurgation [ˌɔbdʒəːˈgeiʃən] *n* reprensión *f*, amonestación *f*, censura *f*.

oblate ['ɔbleit] *adj* achatado por los polos (spheroid).
◆ *adj/n* REL oblato, ta.

oblation [əu'bleiʃən] *n* REL oblación *f* (offering) | oblata *f* (eucharist).

obligate ['ɔbligeit] *vt* obligar.

obligation [,ɔbli'geiʃən] *n* obligación *f*; *to fulfil one's obligations* cumplir con sus obligaciones; *marital obligations* obligaciones matrimoniales || COMM compromiso *m*; *without obligation* sin compromiso; *to meet one's obligations* cumplir sus compromisos || — *I don't want him to put me under an obligation* no quiero tener que agradecerle algo || REL *of obligation* de precepto, de guardar || *to be under an obligation to do sth.* tener la obligación de hacer algo, estar obligado a hacer algo || *to be under an obligation to s.o.* estarle muy agradecido a uno || *to put s.o. under an obligation to do sth.* obligarle a uno a hacer algo.

obligatory [ɔ'bligətəri] *adj* obligatorio, ria || *to make it obligatory upon s.o. to do sth.* obligarle a uno a que haga algo.

oblige [ə'blaidʒ] *vt* obligar (to compel); *he obliged me to resign* me obligó a dimitir || hacer un favor (to assist); *oblige me by thinking no more about it* hágame el favor de no pensar más en eso; *can you oblige me with a light?* ¿me haría el favor de darme lumbre? || complacer (to please); *I'll do it in order to oblige you* lo haré para complacerte || — *I'm not obliged to do it* nada me obliga a hacerlo || *much obliged!* ¡muy agradecido!, ¡muchas gracias! || *to be obliged to do sth.* verse *or* estar obligado a hacer algo || *to be much obliged to s.o.* estarle muy agradecido a uno || *to be much obliged to s.o. for his help* agradecerle mucho a uno su ayuda.

obligee [,ɔbli'dʒi:] *n* JUR acreedor, ra.

obliger [ə'blaidʒə*] *n* persona *f* a quien uno tiene que estar agradecido.

obliging [ə'blaidʒiŋ] *adj* complaciente, servicial (helpful) || atento, ta; amable (kind).

obligor [,ɔbli'gɔ:*] *n* JUR deudor, ra.

oblique [ə'bli:k] *adj* oblicuo, cua; *oblique angle* ángulo oblicuo || FIG indirecto, ta (ways, means); *oblique criticism* crítica indirecta.
◆ *n* ANAT oblicuo *m* (muscle) || MATH oblicua *f* (line).

oblique [ə'bli:k] *vi* oblicuar (*to* hacia).

oblique-angled [-æŋgld] *adj* oblicuángulo, la.

obliqueness [ə'bli:knis]; **obliquity** [ə'blikwiti] *n* oblicuidad *f*, inclinación *f* || FIG falta *f* de rectitud (lack of rectitude) | rodeos *m pl* (obscure statement).

obliterate [ə'blitəreit] *vt* borrar (to blot out, to erase) || quitar (to remove) || tachar (to cross out) || eliminar (to wipe out) || arrasar, destruir (a town) || MED obliterar || matar, poner el matasellos sobre (a stamp).

obliterating [-iŋ] *adj* MED obliterador, ra.

obliteration [ə'blitə'reiʃən] *n* borradura *f* (erasure) || tachadura *f* (crossing out) || eliminación *f* (elimination) || destrucción *f*, arrasamiento *m* (destruction) || MED obliteración *f* || matado *m* (of a stamp).

obliterator [ə'blitəreitə*] *n* matasellos *m inv*.

oblivion [ə'bliviən] *n* olvido *m*; *to fall into oblivion* caer en el olvido || inconsciencia *f* (unconsciousness) || JUR amnistía *f* || — *to cast into oblivion* echar al olvido || *to rescue from oblivion* sacar del olvido.

oblivious [ə'bliviəs] *adj* olvidadizo, za (forgetful) || inconsciente; *oblivious of o to danger* inconsciente del peligro || *oblivious of my presence he started singing* olvidando mi presencia empezó a cantar.

oblong ['ɔblɔŋ] *adj* oblongo, ga.
◆ *n* rectángulo *m*.

obloquy ['ɔbləkwi] *n* calumnia *f* (abusive condemnation) || deshonra *f*, oprobio *m* (shame).

obnoxious [əb'nɔkʃəs] *adj* odioso, sa (odious) || odiado, da (*to* por) (hated) || desagradable, molesto, ta (unpleasant) || repugnante; *obnoxious smell* olor repugnante || *I find him o it exceedingly obnoxious* me repugna.

obnubilation [əbnjubi'leiʃən] *n* obnubilación *f*, obcecación *f*.

oboe ['əubəu] *n* MUS oboe *m* (instrument) | juego *m* de lengüetas (of an organ).

oboe player [-'pleiə*]; **oboist** ['əubəuist] *n* oboe *m*, oboísta *m* & *f*.

obol ['ɔbɔl]; **obolus** [-əs] *n* óbolo *m*.

obscene [əb'si:n] *adj* obsceno, na; indecente (indecent) || grosero, ra (coarse).

obscenity [əb'si:niti] *n* obscenidad *f* | grosería *f*, obscenidad *f* (coarse language); *to utter obscenities* decir obscenidades.

obscurant [ɔb'skjuərənt] *n* oscurantista, obscurantista.

obscurantism [,ɔbskjuə'ræntizəm] *n* oscurantismo *m*, obscurantismo *m*.

obscurantist [,ɔbskjuə'ræntist] *adj/n* oscurantista, obscurantista.

obscuration [,ɔbskjuə'reiʃən] *n* oscurecimiento *m* || ASTR ocultación *f*.

obscure [əb'skjuə] *adj* oscuro, ra (dim); *obscure corner* rincón oscuro || FIG oscuro, ra (undistinguishable, abstruse) | recóndito, ta; aislado, da; retirado, da (hidden); *to live in an obscure place in the country* vivir en un lugar recóndito del campo | oscuro, ra; desconocido, da (not famous).

obscure [əb'skjuə*] *vt* oscurecer (to darken) || FIG ocultar, disimular (the truth) | esconder, ocultar (to hide); *a lake obscured by trees* un lago escondido entre árboles | ocultar; *to obscure sth. from s.o.'s view* ocultar algo a la vista de alguien | ofuscar (the understanding) | eclipsar (to overshadow) || FIG *to obscure the issue* complicar las cosas.

obscureness [-nis] *n* falta *f* de claridad (of style, etc.).

obscurity [əb'skjuəriti] *n* oscuridad *f*; *the obscurity of the sky* la oscuridad del cielo; *to live in obscurity* vivir en la oscuridad.

obsequies ['ɔbsikwiz] *pl n* exequias *f*.

obsequious [əb'si:kwiəs] *adj* obsequioso, sa.

obsequiousness [-nis] *n* obsequiosidad *f*.

observable [əb'zə:vəbl] *adj* observable || — *as is observable* como se puede comprobar *or* observar || *no observable reaction* ninguna reacción perceptible.

observance [əb'zə:vəns] *n* observancia *f*, cumplimiento *m* (of a command) || acatamiento *m*, observancia *f* (of the law) || observancia *f* (of a religious order) || *strict observance* observancia regular, estricta observancia.
◆ *pl* prácticas *f*; *religious observances* prácticas religiosas.

observant [əb'zə:vənt] *adj* observador, ra (quick to observe) || atento, ta (attentive) || cumplidor, ra (of one's duty) || acatador, ra (of the law) || observante (strict in observance) || *he is very observant* se fija en todo, no se le escapa nada.
◆ *n* REL observante *m*.

observantly [-li] *n* con cuidado.

observation [,ɔbzə:'veiʃən] *n* observación *f* (remark, note, care, watching) || observancia *f* (of rules, etc.) || — MIL *observation post* puesto *m* de observación || *patient under observation* enfermo *m* en observación || *to escape observation* pasar inadvertido || *to keep under observation* vigilar.

observation car [-kɑ:*] *n* US coche *m* panorámico, coche *m* con techo transparente (railway coach).

observatory [əb'zə:vətri] *n* ASTR observatorio *m* || mirador *m* (lookout).

observe [əb'zə:v] *vt* observar (to look at with attention) || cumplir, observar (rules) || acatar, respetar (the law) || guardar (silence) || observar; *to observe an eclipse* observar un eclipse || guardar (religious feasts) || observar, notar (to notice) || ver (to see); *I observed him stopping* le vi pararse || decir (to say) || — *he observed to me that* me advirtió que, me hizo observar que || *to observe care in* tener cuidado en.
◆ *vi* observar || hacer una observación *or* observaciones (*on, upon* sobre) (to comment) || decir (to say).

observer [-ə*] *n* observador, ra.

observing [-iŋ] *adj* observador, ra (quick to observe) || observante (strict in observance).

obsess [əb'ses] *vt* obsesionar (*with, by* por); *it obsesses him* le obsesiona.

obsession [əb'seʃən] *n* obsesión *f* || *to have an obsession about* estar obsesionado por.

obsessional [-əl]; **obsessive** [əb'sesiv] *adj* obsesivo, va.

obsidian [ɔb'sidiən] *n* MIN obsidiana *f* (dark volcanic rock).

obsolescence [,ɔbsəu'lesns] *n* caída *f* en desuso || BIOL atrofia *f*.

obsolescent [,ɔbsəu'lesnt] *adj* que cae en desuso || BIOL atrofiado, da.

obsolete ['ɔbsəli:t] *adj* caído en desuso, anticuado, da [AMER obsoleto] (out of usage); *obsolete word* palabra caída en desuso || pasado de moda (out of fashion) || que ha caducado (expired) || MED atrofiado, da || TECH & AVIAT & MIL anticuado, da; fuera de uso.

obstacle ['ɔbstəkl] *n* obstáculo *m*; *to overcome an obstacle* superar *or* vencer un obstáculo; *to put obstacles in the way of* poner obstáculos a || *obstacle race* carrera *f* de obstáculos.

obstetric [ɔb'stetrik]; **obstetrical** [-əl] *adj* MED obstétrico, ca.

obstetrician [,ɔbste'triʃən] *n* MED tocólogo *m*.

obstetrics [ɔb'stetriks] *n* MED obstetricia *f*, tocología *f*.

obstinacy ['ɔbstinəsi] *n* obstinación *f*, terquedad *f* (stubbornness) || MED persistencia *f* (of a disease).

obstinate ['ɔbstinit] *adj* obstinado, da (not yielding to reason) || terco, ca; obstinado, da (stubborn) || FIG rebelde (stubbornly resisting) || MED rebelde; *an obstinate disease* una enfermedad rebelde || — *as obstinate as a mule* terco *or* testarudo como una mula || *to be obstinate in one's refusal to help* negarse rotundamente a ayudar.

obstreperous [əb'strepərəs] *adj* ruidoso, sa (noisy) || revoltoso, sa (unruly) || protestón, ona (defying commands).

obstruct [əb'strʌkt] *vt* obstruir (a road, etc.) || atorar, atascar, obstruir (pipes) || estorbar (to hinder); *to obstruct the traffic* estorbar el tráfico; *to obstruct s.o. in the execution of his duty* estorbarle a uno en el desempeño de sus funciones || dificultar (to make it difficult) || tapar (the view) || MED obstruir.

obstruction [əb'strʌkʃən] *n* obstrucción *f* (obstructing) || atoramiento *m*, atasco *m*, obstrucción *f* (of pipes) || obstáculo *m* (obstacle) || estorbo *m* (hindrance) || obstrucción *f* (in Parliament) || MED obstrucción *f*, oclusión *f*.

obstructionism [-izəm] *n* obstruccionismo *m*.

obstructionist [-ist] *adj/n* obstruccionista.

obstructive [əb'strʌktiv] *adj* que obstruye ‖ MED obstructor, ra ‖ de obstrucción; *obstructive tactics* tácticas de obstrucción ‖ obstruccionista (Member of Parliament).

obstructor [əb'strʌktə*] *n* obstructor, ra.

obstruent ['ɔbstruənt] *adj* MED obstructor, ra.

obtain [əb'tein] *vt* obtener, conseguir, lograr (to get); *to obtain good results* conseguir buenos resultados ‖ adquirir (to acquire) ‖ sacar; *to obtain sugar from beet* sacar azúcar de la remolacha ‖ valer; *his merits obtained him the post* sus méritos le valieron el puesto.
◆ *vi* prevalecer (to prevail) ‖ existir (to exist).

obtainable [-əbl] *adj* que se puede conseguir ‖ *obtainable in your local supermarket* de venta en el supermercado de su barrio.

obtaining [-iŋ] *n* obtención *f*, consecución *f*.

obtainment [-mənt] *n* obtención *f*, consecución *f*.

obtrude [əb'tru:d] *vt* imponer; *he is always obtruding his opinions upon others* siempre impone sus opiniones a los demás ‖ sacar (to thrust out) ‖ — *to obtrude o.s. into* entrometerse en ‖ *to obtrude o.s. on s.o.* imponerse a alguien.
◆ *vi* manifestarse.

obtrusion [əb'tru:ʒən] *n* intrusión *f* ‖ entrometimiento *m*.

obtrusive [əb'tru:siv] *adj* importuno, na; molesto, ta (annoying) ‖ entrometido, da (meddlesome) ‖ presumido, da (conceited) ‖ llamativo, va (too eye-catching) ‖ penetrante (smell).

obtrusiveness [-nis] *n* importunidad *f*.

obturate ['ɔbtjuəreit] *vt* obturar.

obturating [-iŋ] *adj* obturador, ra.

obturation [,ɔbtjuə'reiʃən] *n* obturación *f*.

obturator ['ɔbtjuəreitə*] *n* obturador *m*.

obtuse [əb'tju:s] *adj* MATH obtuso, sa ‖ obtuso, sa; romo, ma (blunt) ‖ FIG tardo en comprender, torpe, obtuso, sa (dim-witted); *how can you be so obtuse?* ¿cómo puedes ser tan obtuso? | sordo (pain).

obtuse-angled [-æŋgld] *adj* MATH obtusángulo; *obtuse-angled triangle* triángulo obtusángulo.

obtuseness [-nis] *n* embotadura *f* embotamiento *m* (bluntness) ‖ FIG torpeza *f*, estupidez *f* (stupidity).

obverse ['ɔbvə:s] *adj* del anverso.
◆ *n* anverso *m* (of a medal).

obvert [ɔb'və:t] *vt* invertir.

obviate ['ɔbvieit] *vt* obviar; *to obviate a difficulty* obviar una dificultad ‖ evitar (a danger) ‖ adelantarse a (an objection).

obvious ['ɔbviəs] *adj* obvio, via; evidente, patente (evident) ‖ vistoso, sa; llamativo, va (showy) ‖ — *an obvious remark* una perogrullada ‖ *it was the obvious thing to do* era lo que había que hacer ‖ *to be glaringly obvious* saltar a la vista.
◆ *n* lo evidente ‖ *to state the obvious* constatar algo evidente.

obviously [-li] *adv* evidentemente, naturalmente, con toda evidencia ‖ claro, por supuesto, naturalmente (in answers); *do you think she is right? obviously* ¿crees que tiene razón? por supuesto ‖ — *he was obviously impressed* se veía que estaba impresionado ‖ *they were not obviously convinced* no parecían estar muy convencidos.

obviousness [-nis] *n* evidencia *f*.

ocarina [ɔkə'ri:nə] *n* MUS ocarina *f*.

OCAS *abbr of [Organization of Central American States]* Odeca, Organización de Estados Centroamericanos.

occasion [ə'keiʒən] *n* ocasión *f*, oportunidad *f* (opportunity); *he took occasion to speak* aprovechó la oportunidad para hablar; *the banquet was a good occasion for talking* el banquete fue una buena ocasión para hablar ‖ motivo *m* (cause); *you have no occasion to be alarmed* no tiene ningún motivo para preocuparse ‖ lugar *m*; *to give occasion to a rebellion* dar lugar a una rebelión ‖ caso *m*; *should the occasion arise, please mention it* si viene al caso menciónelo ‖ ocasión *f*, acontecimiento *m* (ceremony); *or great occasions* en grandes ocasiones ‖ momento *m*, ocasión *f*; *should the occasion arise, you know what to do* si llega el momento *or* si se presenta la ocasión ya sabes lo que tienes que hacer ‖ circunstancia *f*, ocasión *f*; *a speech prepared for the occasion* un discurso preparado para la circunstancia ‖ — *as occasion requires* eventualmente ‖ *on a certain occasion* en cierta oportunidad, otro día ‖ *on occasion* de vez en cuando ‖ *on several occasions* en varias ocasiones, varias veces ‖ *on the occasion of* con motivo de, con ocasión de ‖ *on the present occasion* actualmente (at present), en esta oportunidad, esta vez (this time) ‖ *to be equal to the occasion* estar a la altura de las circunstancias ‖ *to make it an occasion* celebrarlo ‖ *to rise to the occasion* ponerse a la altura de las circunstancias ‖ *upon occasion* de vez en cuando.

occasion [ə'keiʒən] *vt* ocasionar, causar, provocar (to cause) ‖ incitar; *to occasion s.o. to do sth.* incitar a alguien a que haga algo.

occasional [-əl] *adj* ocasional (fortuitous) ‖ que ocurre de vez en cuando (ocurring from time to time) ‖ para el caso; *an occasional poem* un poema para el caso ‖ alguno que otro; *despite our being so isolated we do get the occasional visitor* a pesar de estar tan aislados tenemos alguna que otra visita ‖ para casos de necesidad; *an occasional chair* una silla para casos de necesidad ‖ *we give the occasional party* damos una fiesta de vez en cuando.

occasionalism [ə'keiʒnəlizəm] *n* ocasionalismo *m*.

occasionally [ə'keiʒənəli] *adv* de vez en cuando, alguna que otra vez, ocasionalmente.

Occident ['ɔksidənt] *n* Occidente *m*.

Occidental [,ɔksi'dentl] *adj* occidental.

Occidentalism [,ɔksi'dentəlizəm] *n* occidentalismo *m*.

Occidentalization [,ɔksidentəlai'zeiʃən] *n* occidentalización *f*.

occipital [ɔk'sipitl] *adj* ANAT occipital (bone).
◆ *n* ANAT occipital *m*.

occiput ['ɔksipʌt] *n* ANAT occipucio *m* (back part of the skull).
— OBSERV El plural de la palabra *occiput* es *occipita*.

occlude [ɔ'klu:d] *vt* obstruir (a passage) ‖ MED & CHEM ocluir ‖ *occluded front* oclusión *f* (in meteorology).
◆ *vi* encajarse, ocluirse (in dentistry).

occlusion [ɔ'klu:ʒən] *n* obstrucción *f* ‖ MED CHEM oclusión *f* ‖ oclusión *f* [de las muelas] (in dentistry).

occlusive [ɔ'klu:siv] *adj* oclusivo, va.
◆ *n* oclusiva *f* (consonant).

occult [ɔ'kʌlt] *adj* oculto, ta ‖ *occult sciences* o *arts* ciencias ocultas.
◆ *n* ciencias *f pl* ocultas.

occult [ɔ'kʌlt] *vt* ASTR ocultar.
◆ *vi* ASTR ocultarse.

occultation [,ɔkəl'teiʃən] *n* ASTR ocultación *f*.

occultism ['ɔkəltizəm] *n* ocultismo *m*.

occultist ['ɔkəltist] *adj/n* ocultista.

occupancy ['ɔkjupənsi] *n* ocupación *f* ‖ posesión *f* (of a post).

occupant ['ɔkjupənt] *n* ocupante *m* & *f* (of house, etc.) ‖ posesor, ra; titular (of a post).

occupation [,ɔkju'peiʃən] *n* ocupación *f* (of a house, a country); *the Roman occupation* la ocupación romana ‖ profesión *f*, ocupación *f* (employment); *what is your occupation?* ¿cuál es su profesión? ‖ trabajo *m* (work) ‖ pasatiempo *m* (pastime).

occupational [-l] *adj* profesional; *occupational disease* enfermedad profesional ‖ — *occupational hazards* o *risks* gajes *m pl* del oficio ‖ *occupational therapy* reeducación basada en un trabajo manual o intelectual.

occupier ['ɔkjupaiə*] *n* ocupante *m* & *f* ‖ inquilino, na (tenant).

occupy ['ɔkjupai] *vt* ocupar, vivir en (to reside in); *my friends don't occupy the whole house* mis amigos no ocupan toda la casa ‖ ocupar (by military force) ‖ ocupar (a space, post, period of time); *his work occupies all his time* el trabajo le ocupa todo el tiempo; *is that seat occupied?* ¿está ocupado este sitio? ‖ emplear, ocupar; *to occupy one's time in doing sth.* emplear su tiempo en hacer algo ‖ ocupar (one's mind) ‖ emplear, dar trabajo, ocupar (to keep employed) ‖ — *she is occupied in translating* está traduciendo ‖ *to occupy o.s. in doing sth.* ocuparse de algo *or* en hacer algo.

occur [ə'kə:*] *vi* ocurrir, suceder, acontecer (to happen); *the accident occurred in the afternoon* el accidente ocurrió por la tarde ‖ tener lugar (to take place); *festival that occurs every five years* festival que tiene lugar cada cinco años ‖ producirse; *a complete change has occurred* se ha producido un cambio completo ‖ presentarse (opportunity) ‖ encontrarse; *these plants rarely occur in this country* estas plantas se encuentran muy poco en este país ‖ ocurrirse; *it occurred to me that* se me ocurrió que ‖ *I hope it won't occur again* espero que no vuelva a suceder.

occurrence [ə'kʌrəns] *n* acontecimiento *m*, suceso *m* (event); *an unusual occurrence* un suceso extraño ‖ caso *m* (case) ‖ existencia *f*, presencia *f* (of minerals, of plants, etc.) ‖ REL coincidencia *f* ‖ — *to be a common occurrence* suceder *or* ocurrir frecuentemente ‖ *to be of frequent occurrence* ocurrir frecuentemente *or* a menudo.

ocean ['əuʃən] *n* océano *m*; *the Atlantic Ocean* el Océano Atlántico ‖ FIG mar *m*, océano *m*; *an ocean of sand* un mar de arena.
◆ *pl* FAM *oceans of* la mar de, un montón de.
◆ *adj* oceánico, ca; *ocean currents* corrientes oceánicas.

oceangoing [-'gəuiŋ] *adj* MAR transatlántico, ca (liner) | de alta mar (capable of sailing across oceans) ‖ *an oceangoing liner* un transatlántico.

Oceania [əuʃi'einjə] *pr n* GEOGR Oceanía *f*.

Oceanian [-n] *adj/n* oceánico, ca (of Oceania).

oceanic [,əuʃi'ænik] *adj* oceánico, ca (of the ocean).

Oceanic [,əuʃi'ænik] *adj* Oceánico, ca (Oceanian).

Oceanid [əu'si:ənid] *n* oceánida *f* (nymph).

oceanographer [,əuʃjə'nɔgrəfə*] *n* oceanógrafo, fa.

oceanographic [,əuʃjənəu'græfik]; **oceanographical** [-əl] *adj* oceanográfico, ca.

oceanography [,əuʃjə'nɔgrəfi] *n* oceanografía *f*.

ocellus [əu'seləs] *n* ocelo *m* (eye, mark).
— OBSERV El plural de *ocellus* es *ocelli*.

ocelot ['əusilɔt] *n* ocelote *m* (wildcat).

ocher ['əukə*] *n* US ocre *m*.

ocherous ['əukərəs] *adj* US ocre.

ochre ['əukə*] *n* ocre *m*; *red ochre* ocre rojo.

ochreous ['əukriəs]; **ochrous** ['əukrəs] *adj* ocre.

o'clock [ə'klɔk] *adv* *at three o'clock* a las tres ‖ *it is one o'clock* es la una ‖ *it is six o'clock* son las seis.

octagon ['ɔktəgən] *n* MATH octógono *m*, octágono *m*.

octagonal [ɔk'tægənl] *adj* octagonal, octogonal, octágono, na; octógono, na.

octahedral ['ɔktə'hedrəl] *adj* octaédrico, ca.

octahedron ['ɔktə'hedrən] *n* MATH octaedro *m*.
— OBSERV El plural de *octahedron* es *octahedrons* u *octahedra*.

octane ['ɔktein] *n* octano *m*; *octane number* índice de octano ‖ *high-octane fuel* supercarburante *m*.

octave ['ɔktiv] *n* MUS & POET octava *f*.

octave ['ɔkteiv] *n* REL octava *f*.

Octavian [ɔk'teivjən] *pr n* Octavio *m*.
◆ *adj* octaviano, na; *Octavian peace* paz octaviana.

octavo [ɔk'teivəu] *adj* en octavo (book).
◆ *n* libro *m* en octavo.

octennial [ɔk'tenjəl] *adj* que ocurre cada ocho años (occurring) ‖ que dura ocho años (lasting).

octet; octette [ɔk'tet] *n* MUS octeto *m*.

October [ɔk'təubə*] *n* octubre *m*; *on the 12th of October 1492* el 12 de octubre de 1492.

octogenarian [,ɔktəudʒi'nεəriən] *adj/n* octogenario, ria.

octopod ['ɔktəpɔd] *n* ZOOL octópodo *m* pulpo *m* (octopous).
◆ *adj* ZOOL octópodo, da.

octopoda [ɔk'tɔpədə] *pl n* ZOOL octópodos *m*.

octopus ['ɔktəpəs] *n* pulpo *m* (mollusc).
— OBSERV El plural de *octopus* es *octopuses* u *octopodes*.

octosyllabic ['ɔktəusi'læbik] *adj* octosilábico, ca; octosílabo, ba.
◆ *n* octosílabo *m* (verse).

octosyllable ['ɔktəu,siləbl] *adj* ⟶ **octosyllabic.**
◆ *n* octosílabo *m* (verse).

octuple ['ɔktju:pl] *vt* multiplicar por ocho.

ocular ['ɔkjulə*] *adj* ocular.
◆ *n* ocular *m* (of an optical instrument).

oculist ['ɔkjulist] *n* oculista *m* & *f*.

odalisque; odalisk ['əudəlisk] *n* odalisca *f*.

odd [ɔd] *adj* impar; *odd day* día impar ‖ impar, non (number) ‖ unos, unas; y pico; *a hundred-odd pounds* cien libras y pico, unas cien libras ‖ pequeño, ña (amount) ‖ sobrante, de más (left over) ‖ suelto, ta (isolated) ‖ descabalado, da; deshermanado, da; desparejado, da; *an odd shoe* un zapato desparejado ‖ alguno, na; alguno que otro, alguna que otra; *on odd occasions* en algunas ocasiones; *to receive the odd client* recibir a algún que otro cliente ‖ suelto, ta (money); *a few odd coins* algunas monedas sueltas ‖ cualquier, cualquiera; *in an odd corner* en cualquier rincón ‖ apartado, da (out-of-the-way) ‖ poco corriente; *an odd size* una talla poco corriente ‖ extraño, ña; raro, ra (strange); *an odd person* una persona rara; *how very odd!* ¡qué raro!; *the odd thing is that* lo raro es que ‖ — *odd job man* factótum *m* (who does all kinds of work), hombre mañoso (skilful man) ‖ *odd jobs* pequeños arreglos *or* reparaciones; *to do odd jobs around the house* hacer pequeños arreglos en toda la casa; trabajitos *m pl* [que uno hace de vez en cuando]; *he lives by odd jobs he picks up* vive de los trabajitos que hace de vez en cuando ‖ *odd man out* excepción *f* (unlike the others), persona *f* sobrante (person left over) ‖ *odd moments* momentos *m* de ocio, ratos perdidos ‖ *to eat the odd meal* comer de vez en cuando ‖ *to play at odds or evens* jugar a pares o nones.

oddball ['ɔdbɔ:l] *adj* raro, ra; excéntrico, ca.
◆ *n* persona *f* rara *or* excéntrica.

oddity ['ɔditi] *n* rareza *f*, singularidad *f* (quality) ‖ curiosidad *f*, cosa *f* rara (thing) ‖ excéntrico, ca; original *m* & *f* (person) ‖ *she has her oddities* tiene sus cosas raras.

oddly ['ɔdli] *adv* extrañamente ‖ — *oddly enough* por extraño que parezca ‖ *to behave oddly* comportarse extrañamente *or* de una manera rara.

oddments ['ɔdmənts] *pl n* COMM saldos *m* | retales *m* (of fabric) ‖ cosillas *f* (odds and ends).

oddness ['ɔdnis] *n* carácter *m* impar (of day, of number) ‖ FIG excentricidad *f*, extravagancia *f*, rareza *f* (of a person) | singularidad *f* (of a thing).

odds [ɔdz] *pl n* desigualdad *f sing*, disparidad *f sing* (inequality); *overwhelming odds in his favour* desigualdad enorme a su favor ‖ fuerzas *f* superiores; *to fight against odds* luchar contra fuerzas superiores ‖ posibilidades *f*, probabilidades *f* (chances) ‖ diferencia *f sing* (difference) ‖ SP ventaja *f sing* | apuesta *f sing*; *the odds are four to one* las apuestas están cuatro contra uno ‖ — *against the odds* a pesar de las circunstancias adversas ‖ *by all odds* indiscutiblemente, sin duda alguna ‖ *it makes no odds* da lo mismo, no importa ‖ *odds and ends* pedazos *m*, trozos *m* (bits), cosillas *f*; *I've just a few odds and ends left to pack* sólo me quedan algunas cosillas por poner en la maleta; fruslerías *f* (curios), restos *m* (food) ‖ *the odds are in his favour* tiene muchas posibilidades de ganar ‖ *the odds are that* es probable que ‖ *to be at odds with s.o.* estar peleado con uno, estar de punta con uno ‖ *to give odds* dar ventaja ‖ *to put* o *to set two people at odds* enemistar a dos personas, sembrar la discordia entre dos personas ‖ FAM *what's the odds?* ¿qué más da?, ¿qué importa?

odds-on ['ɔdzɔn] *adj* seguro, ra ‖ — *he has an odds-on chance of winning* tiene mucha probabilidad de ganar ‖ *odds-on favourite* caballo favorito (horse), favorito, ta (person).

ode [əud] *n* oda *f* (poetry).

Odense ['ɔdənsə] *pr n* GEOGR Odense.

odeon [əudjən]; **odeum** ['əudjəm] *n* odeón *m*.
— OBSERV El plural de *odeum* es *odeums* u *odea*.

odious ['əudjəs] *adj* odioso, sa.

odium ['əudjəm] *n* odio *m* (hatred) ‖ oprobio *m* (ignominy) ‖ reprobación *f* (condemnation) ‖ *to lose one's odium* dejar de ser odiado.

odometer [ɔ'dɔmitə*] *n* odómetro *m*.

odontologist [,ɔdɔn'tɔlədʒist] *n* odontólogo *m*.

odontology [,ɔdɔn'tɔlədʒi] *n* odontología *f*.

odor ['əudə*] *n* US ⟶ **odour.**

odoriferous [,əudə'rifərəs] *adj* odorífero, ra.

odorless ['əudəlis] *adj* inodoro, ra.

odorous ['əudərəs] *adj* odorante, oloroso, sa ‖ perfumado, da; fragante.

odour; US **odor** ['əudə*] *n* olor *m* (smell) ‖ perfume *m* (fragrance) ‖ — *in the odour of sanctity* en olor de santidad ‖ FAM *to be in bad odour with* estar mal visto por, no ser santo de la devoción de | *to be in good odour with* ser muy bien visto por.

odourless [-lis] *adj* inodoro, ra.

Odyssey ['ɔdisi] *pr n* Odisea *f*.

OECD *abbr of [Organization for Economic Cooperation and Development]* OCDE, Organización para la Cooperación y el Desarrollo Económico.

oecological [i:kə'lɔdʒikəl] *adj* ecológico, ca.

oecology [i:'kɔlədʒi] *n* ecología *f*.

oecumene ['i:kju:min:n] *n* REL ecumene *m*.

oecumenical [,i:kju'menikəl] *adj* REL ecuménico, ca.

oecumenicalism [-izəm]; **oecumenism** ['i:kjumənizəm] *n* REL ecumenismo *m*.

oedema [i'di:mə] *n* MED edema *m*.

oedematous [i'demətəs] *n* MED edematoso, sa.

Oedipus ['i:dipəs] *pr n* Edipo *m* ‖ *Oedipus complex* complejo *m* de Edipo.

oenological [inə'lɔdʒikəl] *adj* enológico, ca.

oenologist [i:'nɔlədʒist] *n* enólogo, ga.

oenology [i:'nɔlədʒi] *n* enología *f*.

o'er ['əuə*] *prep/adv* POET ⟶ **over.**

oersted ['ə:sted] *n* oersted *m*, oerstedio *m*.

oesophagus [i:'sɔfəgəs] *n* ANAT esófago *m*.
— OBSERV El plural de oesophagus es *oesophagi*.

oestrogen ['i:strədʒin] *n* MED estrógeno *m*.

oestrus ['i:strəs] *n* estro *m* (rut, insect).

of [ɔv]ʁ[əv] *prep* de (in most senses); *the events of last year* los acontecimientos del año pasado; *she is proud of her daughter* está orgullosa de su hija; *of good family* de buena familia; *citizens of London* ciudadanos de Londres; *the novels of Faulkner* las novelas de Faulkner; *cured of his illness* curado de su enfermedad; *a group of women* un grupo de mujeres; *a basket of apples* un cesto de manzanas; *one of his brothers* uno de sus hermanos; *three of us went to university* tres de nosotros fueron a la universidad; *made of gold* (hecho) de oro ‖ que tiene, de; *a man of resources* un hombre de recursos; *a person of distinction* una persona que tiene distinción ‖ en; *doctor of medicine* doctor en medicina ‖ de parte de; *it is very kind of you* es muy amable de su parte ‖ por; *it can move of itself* puede moverse por sí solo ‖ de; *of a child he was very naughty* de niño era muy malo ‖ por; *of an evening* por la noche | US menos, para (of time); *it is five of one* es la una menos cinco, faltan cinco minutos para la una ‖ — *a beauty of beauties* la belleza por excelencia ‖ *a child of seven* un niño de siete años ‖ *a fine figure of a man* un hombre bien hecho *or* bien proporcionado ‖ *a friend of mine, yours, etc.* un amigo mío, tuyo, etc. ‖ *a friend of my father's* un amigo de mi padre ‖ *all of them* todos ellos ‖ *a love of animals, of nature* un amor a los animales, a la naturaleza ‖ *a smell of paint* un olor a pintura ‖ *a terror of a child* un monstruo de niño, un niño terrible ‖ *dresses of her own making* vestidos hechos por ella misma ‖ *fleet of foot* veloz, rápido, da ‖ *hard of hearing* duro de oído ‖ *hard of heart* duro de corazón, de corazón duro ‖ *heart of gold* corazón de oro ‖ *it was cruel of her* fue una crueldad de su parte ‖ *king of kings* rey de reyes ‖ *of age* mayor de edad ‖ *of a Sunday* los domingos (on Sundays), un domingo (one Sunday) ‖ *of late* últimamente, recientemente ‖ *of o.s.* de motu propio ‖ *she is a marvel of marvels* es de lo más maravilloso que hay ‖ *she is the queen of queens* es la reina de las reinas ‖ *south of, north of* al sur de, al norte de ‖ *the best of friends* los mejores amigos del mundo, muy buenos amigos; *we are the best of friends* somos muy buenos amigos ‖ *the fool of my brother* el tonto de mi hermano ‖ *the love of God* el amor de Dios ‖ *there were lots of us* éramos muchos ‖ *today of all days* hoy precisamente ‖ *what of it?* ¿y qué? (so what?), ¿qué te parece? (how about it?) ‖ *you are no friend of mine* no eres amigo mío ‖

you, of all men o *of all people, should have more sense* tú, más que nadie, tendrías que ser más sensato.

— OBSERV Esta preposición se traduce de varias maneras cuando acompaña ciertos verbos como *to think, to smell, to taste*, etc. Consúltense los artículos dedicados a estos verbos para encontrar la traducción adecuada.

off [ɔf] *adv* a (away); *the dam is twenty miles off* la presa está a veinte millas; *some way off* a cierta distancia ‖ a distancia; *to keep s.o. off* mantener a alguien a distancia ‖ MAR viento en popa (with the wind) | mar adentro, hacia alta mar, en alta mar (out to sea) ‖ THEATR fuera de escena, entre bastidores (off stage) ‖ en off; *voice off* voz en off ‖ — *a long way off* muy lejos (time, distance), muy equivocado (a guess, etc.); *to be a long way off in one's calculations* estar muy equivocado en sus cálculos ‖ *be off with you!* ¡fuera de aquí! ‖ *further off* más lejos, más allá ‖ *off and on, on and off* de vez en cuando ‖ *off in the distance* allá lejos ‖ *off we go!* ¡vámonos! ‖ *off with him, with you!* ¡fuera!, ¡fuera de aquí! ‖ *off with his head!* ¡que le corten la cabeza! ‖ *off with your boots!* ¡quítate las botas! ‖ *right off, straight off* inmediatamente, en seguida (at once), de un tirón (in one go), seguidos, das (one after the other) ‖ FAM *that's a bit off!* ¡no hay derecho! ‖ *the party is four days off* la fiesta tendrá lugar dentro de cuatro días, faltan cuatro días para la fiesta ‖ *there are two shillings off* hay un descuento de dos chelines ‖ POP *to be having it off with* hacer el amor con ‖ *to be off* irse; *I'm off* me voy; *I think it's time we were off* creo que ya es hora de que nos vayamos *or* de irnos; *I'm off to Madrid this weekend* me voy a Madrid este fin de semana; despegar (an aircraft), acabar de tomar la salida (in sports); *they're off!* ¡acaban de tomar la salida!; estar fuera (absent) ‖ *to give s.o. ten per cent off* hacerle a uno un descuento del diez por ciento ‖ *to take a day off* tomar un día de descanso ‖ *why is the lid of the pan off?* ¿por qué está destapada la cacerola?
◆ *prep* fuera de; *our house is off the main road* nuestra casa está fuera de la carretera principal ‖ de; *it fell off the table* cayó de la mesa; *take that off the table* quita eso de la mesa; *not far off each other* no lejos uno de otro ‖ a... de; *three yards off me* a tres metros de mí ‖ desde, de; *he jumped off the cliff* saltó desde el acantilado ‖ que arranca de, que sale de; *street off the main road* calle que arranca de la carretera principal ‖ en; *to eat off gold plate* comer en vajilla de oro ‖ de, con; *to feed off vegetables* alimentarse de verduras ‖ a; *to borrow money off s.o.* pedirle dinero prestado a uno ‖ MAR a la altura de; *sailing off Gibraltar* navegando a la altura de Gibraltar ‖ — *height off the ground* altura del suelo ‖ *he is off tobacco for life* ha dejado definitivamente de fumar ‖ *I've gone right off the cinema* ya no me gusta el cine ‖ MAR *off the wind* viento en popa ‖ *ten per cent off all our prices* descuento del diez por ciento sobre todos los precios ‖ *that's a load off my mind!* ¡qué peso me he quitado de encima! ‖ *to be off a job* haber dejado un trabajo ‖ *to be off centre* estar descentrado (crooked), no dar en el blanco (a shot) ‖ *to be off form* no estar en forma ‖ *to be off one's food* no tener apetito ‖ *to be off work* no trabajar ‖ FAM *to be right off it* estar completamente equivocado (wrong) ‖ *to catch s.o. off guard* cogerle a uno desprevenido ‖ *to dine off* cenar ‖ *to live off s.o.* vivir a costa de alguien ‖ *to take a fortnight off work* tomarse quince días de vacaciones ‖ *you have a button off your coat* te falta un botón del abrigo.
◆ *adj* malo, la; pasado, da (meat, fish, fruit, vegetables) ‖ cortada (milk) ‖ agriado, da (wine) ‖ rancio, cia (butter) ‖ malo, la (not up to standard); *an off day* un día malo ‖ suspendido, da; cancelado, da; *the match, the trip is off* el partido, el viaje ha sido suspendido ‖ apagado, da (electrical appliances); *the lights were off* las luces estaban apagadas ‖ cerrado, da (tap) ‖ cortado, da (water) ‖ suelto, ta; quitado, da (brake) ‖ libre (free); *are you off on Thursday?* ¿estás libre el jueves? ‖ lateral; *an off street* una calle lateral ‖ equivocado, da; erróneo, a (wrong); *his answer was slightly off* su contestación fue ligeramente errónea ‖ remoto, ta; lejano, na (remote); *an off chance* una lejana posibilidad ‖ secundario, ria; *an off issue* una cuestión secundaria ‖ derecho, cha (part of an animal) ‖ SP derecho, cha (in cricket) ‖ MAR mar adentro ‖ — *chicken is off* no hay pollo, no queda pollo (on a menu) ‖ *for off consumption* para llevar (goods) ‖ *his shirt was off* se había quitado la camisa ‖ *in the off position* (en posición de) cerrado (a switch), en posición de paro (lever) ‖ *in the off season* fuera de temporada ‖ *off season prices* precios de fuera de temporada (in hotels), precios de temporada baja (of airlines) ‖ AUT *off side* lado izquierdo (when driving on the right), lado derecho (when driving on the left) ‖ *to be badly off* andar mal de dinero ‖ *to be badly off for* andar mal de; *I am badly off for money* ando mal de dinero ‖ *to be better off* andar mejor de dinero (moneywise), estar mejor (of conditions) ‖ *to be well off* estar muy bien; *she is well off in her new job* está muy bien en su nuevo trabajo; estar acomodado *or* desahogado (to enjoy financial comfort) ‖ *to be with* o *to have one's coat off* estar sin abrigo, haberse quitado el abrigo ‖ *to be worse off for* estar *or* andar peor de ‖ *to have sth. off* quitarse (to take off), estar sin (to be without) ‖ *to walk with one's shoes off* ir descalzo ‖ *we are only thirty pounds off* sólo nos faltan treinta libras ‖ *we came on the off chance of finding you* vinimos pensando que a lo mejor le encontraríamos, vinimos a ver si le encontrábamos ‖ *we'll go on the off chance* iremos por si acaso, iremos a ver ‖ *your aim was off* apuntaste mal.
◆ *n* SP salida *f* (start) | campo *m* derecho (in cricket).

— OBSERV Como la palabra *off* modifica frecuentemente el sentido de los verbos que acompaña, es preciso consultar los artículos dedicados a estos verbos para encontrar la traducción adecuada.

off [ɔf] *vi* MAR hacerse mar adentro ‖ irse (to go away).

offal [-əl] *n* menudos *m pl*, despojos *m pl*, asaduras *f pl* (of cattle) ‖ menudillos *m pl* (of poultry) ‖ desechos *m pl* (waste product) ‖ basuras *f pl* (refuse).

off-balance [-ˌbæləns] *adj* sin equilibrio ‖ FIG desprevenido, da.

offbeat [-biːt] *adj* US original, excéntrico, ca.

off-centre [-ˌsentə*] *adj* descentrado, da.

off-colour; US **off-color** [-ˈkʌlə*] *adj* pálido, da (pale) ‖ indispuesto, ta; malo, la (not in normal health); *he was feeling off-colour* se encontraba indispuesto ‖ desteñido, da (material) ‖ defectuoso, sa; que no es del color debido; *an off-colour diamond* un diamante defectuoso ‖ subido de color; *an off-colour joke* un chiste subido de color.

offcut [-kʌt] *n* recorte *m*.

offence; US **offense** [əˈfens] *n* ofensa *f* (act of offending s.o.) ‖ escándalo *m* (scandal) ‖ JUR delito *m* ‖ REL ofensa *f*, pecado *m*, falta *f* (sin) ‖ MIL ataque *m*, ofensiva *f* ‖ SP falta *f* (foul) ‖ — JUR *capital offence* crimen *m* que merece la pena capital | *minor offence* contravención *f*, infracción *f* ‖ *no offence, no offence meant* sin intención de ofenderle ‖ *no offence was intended* no tenía la intención de ofender ‖ JUR *second offence* reincidencia *f* ‖ FIG *to be an offence to the ear* herir *or* lastimar el oído ‖ *to cause offence to s.o.* ofender a alguien (to create resentment), escandalizar a alguien (to shock) ‖ *to give offence* ofender ‖ *to take offence at* ofenderse por, sentirse ofendido por (to get resentful), escandalizarse por (to be shocked at) ‖ *without offence to you* sin intención de ofenderle.

offenceless [-lis] *adj* inofensivo, va ‖ inocente.

offend [əˈfend] *vt* ofender; *the remark offended him* la observación le ofendió; *to offend s.o.'s dignity* ofender la dignidad de uno ‖ escandalizar (to shock) ‖ FIG lastimar, herir (the eyes, the ears) ‖ — *to be easily offended* picarse *or* enfadarse fácilmente ‖ *to be offended at* ofenderse por, estar enfadado por, tomar a mal ‖ *to be offended with s.o.* estar enfadado con alguien.
◆ *vi* *to offend against* infringir, violar (the law, a regulation, etc.), pecar contra (to sin).

offender [-ə*] *n* ofensor, ra; ofendedor, ra ‖ REL pecador, ra (sinner) ‖ JUR delincuente *m* & *f* | infractor, ra ‖ — JUR *a first offender* un delincuente sin antecedentes penales | *old offender* reincidente *m* & *f*.

offending [-iŋ] *adj* ofendedor, ra; ofensor, ra.

offense [əˈfens] *n* US → **offence.**

offenseless [-lis] *adj* US inofensivo, va ‖ inocente.

offensive [-iv] *adj* ofensivo, va; insultante (insulting) ‖ repugnante (revolting); *an offensive smell* un olor repugnante ‖ chocante (shocking) ‖ MIL ofensivo, va; *offensive weapons* armas ofensivas ‖ — *morally offensive* que ofende la moral (book) ‖ *word offensive to the ear* palabra malsonante *or* grosera.
◆ *n* MIL ofensiva *f*; *to take the offensive* tomar la ofensiva.

offensiveness [-ivnis] *n* lo ofensivo (of insulting words, etc.) ‖ lo chocante ‖ repugnancia *f* ‖ grosería *f* (rudeness).

offer [ˈɔfə*] *n* oferta *f*; *a firm offer* una oferta en firme; *to decline an offer* rechazar una oferta ‖ propuesta *f* (proposal) ‖ — *offer of marriage* petición *f* de mano ‖ *on offer* en venta (on sale), en rebaja (cheap) ‖ *that's my last offer* es mi última oferta *or* mi última palabra, no puedo ofrecer más.

offer [ˈɔfə*] *vt* ofrecer, regalar (a gift) ‖ ofrecer; *can I offer you a cigarette?* ¿le puedo ofrecer un cigarrillo? ‖ ofrecer (a post) ‖ proponer, ofrecer; *he offered his services* propuso sus servicios ‖ ofrecerse; *to offer to do a job* ofrecerse para hacer un trabajo ‖ proponer (to present for consideration); *to offer a plan* proponer un proyecto ‖ ofrecer; *to offer a little resistance* ofrecer poca resistencia ‖ hacer (a remark) ‖ manifestar, expresar (an opinion) ‖ presentar (difficulties) ‖ presentar, ofrecer; *to offer few possibilities of success* ofrecer pocas posibilidades de éxito; *to offer certain advantages* ofrecer ciertas ventajas ‖ ofrecer (to bid); *to offer a good price for sth.* ofrecer un buen precio por algo ‖ hacer como si, hacer el paripé de (to pretend to) ‖ REL ofrecer (a sacrifice) | ofrendar, ofrecer; *to offer one's soul to God* ofrendar su alma a Dios ‖ — *to offer an apology* pedir disculpas ‖ COMM *to offer goods (for sale)* vender mercancías ‖ *to offer one's arm* ofrecer su brazo ‖ *to offer one's help* ofrecer su ayuda ‖ *to offer o.s.* ofrecerse; presentarse; *to offer o.s. to a post* presentarse a un puesto.
◆ *vi* presentarse (occasion) ‖ REL hacer una ofrenda.

offerer [-rə*] *n* oferente *m* & *f*.

offering [-riŋ] *n* oferta *f* (action) ‖ regalo *m* (gift, present) ‖ REL ofrenda *f* (sacrifice) | don *m*, ofrenda *f* (donation) ‖ — REL *burnt offering* holocausto *m* ‖ *to send a girl flowers as a peace offering* mandar *or* regalar flores a una chica para hacer las paces || REL *votive offering* exvoto *m*.

offertory ['ɔfətəri] *n* REL ofertorio *m* (part of the mass) | colecta *f* (collection of money).

offhand ['ɔf'hænd] *adj* improvisado, da (without preparation); *offhand speech* discurso improvisado || desenvuelto, ta (casual) || brusco, ca (brusque).
◆ *adv* sin pensarlo, a primera vista (at once) || improvisadamente, sin preparación (without preparation) || de una manera desenvuelta, con desenvoltura (casually) || bruscamente (abruptly) || — *I can't remember offhand* no me acuerdo en este momento *or* ahora mismo || *I couldn't tell you offhand* no se lo puedo decir así como así.

offhanded [-id] *adj* improvisado, da (without preparation); *offhand speech* discurso improvisado || desenvuelto, ta (casual) || brusco, ca (brusque).

office ['ɔfis] *n* oficina *f* (premises); *business office* oficina comercial; *head office* oficina central || oficina *f*, despacho *m* (room); *manager's office* despacho del director || bufete *m* (of a lawyer) || oficio *m* (service); *through s.o.'s good offices* gracias a los buenos oficios de uno || favor *m* (favour); *to do s.o. a good office* hacer a uno un gran favor || funciones *f pl* (function); *to take office* entrar en funciones || cargo *m*; *public office* cargo público; *to hold office* ocupar un cargo || ministerio *m* (ministry); *Foreign Office* Ministerio de Asuntos Exteriores [AMER Ministerio de Relaciones Exteriores]; *Home Office* Ministerio del Interior; *War Office* Ministerio de Defensa (in Spain), Ministerio de la Guerra (in other countries) || cartera *f* de ministro (portfolio); *to be called to office* recibir una cartera de ministro || poder *m* (power); *the government in office* el gobierno que está en el poder || oficina *f*; *Tourist Office* oficina de turismo; *lost property office* [US *lost and found office*] oficina de objetos perdidos || negociado *m* (administrative division) || REL oficio *m*; *office for the dead* oficio de difuntos || US consulta *f*, consultorio *m* (of a doctor) || — *Holy Office* Santo Oficio || *International Labour Office* Oficina Internacional del Trabajo || *office block* edificio *m* de oficinas || *office hours* horas *f* de oficina || *to leave office* dimitir.
◆ *pl* dependencias *f* (of a house) || *last offices* oficio *m sing* de difuntos.

office boy [-bɔi] *n* recadero *m*.

office clerk [-klɑ:k] *n* oficinista *m* & *f*.

officeholder [-,həuldə*] *n* US funcionario, ria.

officer ['ɔfisə*] *n* funcionario, ria (who holds a public appointment) || policía *m*, agente *m* de policía (policeman) || director *m* (of a company) || MIL oficial *m*; *naval, army officer* oficial de marina, del ejército || dignatario *m* (of an order) || — *customs officer* aduanero *m* || MAR *executive officer* segundo comandante || MIL *field officer* jefe *m* | *officer of the day, of the watch* oficial de servicio, de guardia | *reserve officer* oficial retirado, de reserva || *sanitary officer* oficial de sanidad.

officer ['ɔfisə*] *vt* MIL proveer de mandos || mandar (to command) || *to be well officered* tener buenos mandos.

office seeker [-'si:kə*] *n* político *m* que intenta conseguir una cartera.

office work [-wə:k] *n* trabajo *m* de oficina.

office worker [wə:kə*] *n* oficinista *m* & *f*.

official [ə'fiʃəl] *adj* oficial; *an official report* un informe oficial; *the queen's official birthday* el cumpleaños oficial de la reina; *official news* noticias oficiales || titular (holding an office) || MED oficinal || *in one's official capacity* oficialmente.
◆ *n* funcionario, ria; *high officials* altos funcionarios || REL provisor *m*, oficial *m* (of an ecclesiastical court).

officialdom [-dəm] *n* burocracia *f* (bureaucracy) || funcionarios *m pl* (officials).

officialese [ə,fiʃə'li:z] *n* lenguaje *m* administrativo.

officialism [ə'fiʃəlizəm] *n* burocracia *f*.

officiality [ə,fiʃi'æliti] *n* oficialidad *f*.

officially [ə'fiʃəli] *adv* oficialmente.

official receiver [ɔ'fiʃəl ri'si:və*] *n* administrador *m* judicial.

officiant [ə'fiʃiənt] *n* celebrante *m*, oficiante *m* (priest, minister).

officiary [ə'fiʃiəri] *adj* por el cargo ocupado (title).
◆ *n* autoridades *f pl*.

officiate [ə'fiʃieit] *vt/vi* oficiar, celebrar (a religious service) || FAM ejercer las funciones (*as* de).

officinal [,əfi'sainl] *adj* MED oficinal.

officious [ə'fiʃəs] *adj* oficioso, sa (unofficial); *officious talks* conversaciones oficiosas || entrometido, da; oficioso, sa (meddlesome).

officiousness [-nis] *n* oficiosidad *f*, carácter *m* oficioso.

offing ['ɔfiŋ] *n* MAR alta mar *f*, lontananza *f* || FIG *in the offing* en perspectiva.

offish ['ɔfiʃ] *adj* distante, altivo, va.

off-key ['ɔfki:] *adj* desafinado, da.

off-licence ['ɔf'laisəns] *n* bodega *f* (shop) || taberna *f*, tasca *f* (public house) || permiso *m* que concede el derecho de vender bebidas alcohólicas para consumo externo (licence).

off-line ['ɔflain] *adj* INFORM fuera de línea, autónomo, ma.

off-load *vt* FAM sacarse de encima || FAM *to off-load some of one's work onto s.o.* descargar parte del trabajo en alguien.

off-peak ['ɔfpi:k] *adj* de menor consumo (electricity) || de menos tráfico, de menos afluencia (transport) || *off-peak season* temporada baja.

offprint ['ɔfprint] *n* separata *f*.

off-putting ['ɔfputiŋ] *adj* antipático, ca (person) || desagradable (remark, manner).

offscourings ['ɔfskauəriŋz] *pl n* heces *f*, hez *f sing*; *the offscourings of humanity* la hez de la humanidad.

offset ['ɔfset] *n* BOT renuevo *m*, vástago *m* || AGR acodo *m* (layer) || rama *f* (of a family) || ARCH resalto *m* || GEOL estribación *f*, contrafuerte *m* (mountains) || offset *m* (in printing) || TECH codo *m* (bend in a pipe) | desviación *f* (deviation) || ELECTR ramal *m* || ordenada *f*, perpendicular *f* (in surveying) || FIG compensación *f*; *to be an offset to losses* ser una compensación a las pérdidas | contraste *m* (contrast).

offset ['ɔfset] *vt* compensar (to balance); *his winnings offset my losses* sus ganancias compensan mis pérdidas || desviar (to deviate) || hacer un doble codo en, acodar (a pipe) || PRINT imprimir por el procedimiento offset (to print).
◆ *vi* BOT echar renuevos *or* vástagos || PRINT emplear el procedimiento offset.

offshoot ['ɔfʃu:t] *n* vástago *m*, retoño *m*, renuevo *m* (from a main stem) || FIG ramificación *f* (subsidiary activity) | vástago *m* (of a family).

offshore ['ɔfʃɔ:*] *adj* de la costa, de tierra; *an offshore wind* un viento de la costa || de altura (away from the shore) || — *offshore derrick* torre *f* de perforación en el mar || *offshore islands* islas cercanas a la costa.
◆ *adv* mar adentro.

off side ['ɔf'said] *adj* SP fuera de juego.

offside ['ɔf'said] *n* SP fuera de juego *m* || AUT lado *m* derecho (when driving on the left), lado *m* izquierdo (when driving on the right).

offspring ['ɔfspriŋ] *n* progenitura *f*, progenie *f*, descendencia *f* (children) || hijo, ja (child) || FIG fruto *m*, resultado *m* (result).

offstage ['ɔfsteidʒ] *adj/adv* entre bastidores, fuera del escenario || FIG entre bastidores.

offtake ['ɔfteik] *n* salida *f* (of goods).

off-the-cuff [ɔfðəkʌf] *adj* espontáneo, nea; *an off-the-cuff reply* una respuesta espontánea.
◆ *adv* sin pensar, espontáneamente.

off-the-peg [ɔfθə'peg] *adj* de confección (clothes).

off-the-record ['ɔfðə'rekɔ:d] *adj* oficioso, sa (unofficial) || confidencial.

off-the-wall [ɔfðəwɔ:l] *adj* US FAM raro, ra; extraño, ña.

off-white ['ɔfwait] *adj* blancuzco, ca; de color hueso.

oft [ɔft] *adv* POET ⟶ **often.**

often ['ɔfn] *adv* a menudo, frecuentemente; *I often get angry with Michael* me enfado a menudo con Miguel || muchas veces (many times) || — *as often as* cada vez que, siempre que (each time that), con tanta frecuencia como || *as often as not* la mitad de las veces || FAM *every so often* alguna que otra vez || *how often* cuántas veces (how many times), cada cuánto (at what intervals) || *it's not often that one sees such generosity* no es corriente ver a una persona tan generosa || *more often than not* la mayoría de las veces || *not every often* pocas veces || *too often* con demasiada frecuencia.

ofttimes ['ɔftaimz] *adv* (ant) a menudo.

ogee ['əudʒi:] *n* ARCH cimacio *m*, talón *m*, gola *f*.

ogee arch [-ɑ:tʃ] *n* ARCH arco *m* conopial.

ogival [əu'dʒaivqpl] *adj* ARCH ojival, en ojiva.

ogive ['əudʒaiv] *n* ARCH ojiva *f*.
◆ *adj* ojival, en ojiva.

ogle ['əugl] *n* mirada *f* ávida.

ogle ['əugl] *vt* comerse con los ojos.
◆ *vi* guiñar el ojo (to make eyes at).

ogre ['əugə*] *n* ogro *m* (monster).

ogreish [riʃ]; **ogrish** [-iʃ] *adj* monstruoso, sa.

ogress ['əugris] *n* ogresa *f* (monster).

oh [əu] *interj* ¡oh!

Ohio [əu'haiəu] *pr n* GEOGR Ohio.

ohm [əum] *n* ELECTR ohmio *m*, ohm *m*.

ohmic [-ik] *adj* ELECTR óhmico, ca.

OHMS *abbr of [On His or Her Majesty's Service]* al servicio de su majestad.

oidium [əu'idiəm] *n* BOT oídio *m*.
— OBSERV El plural de *oidium* es *oidia*.

oil [ɔil] *n* aceite *m* (greasy substance) || CULIN aceite *m* (cooking oil); *olive, groundnut oil* aceite de oliva, de cacahuete || ARTS óleo *m* (painting) || MIN petróleo *m* || TECH aceite *m* (lubricant) || fuel *m*, fuel-oil *m*, mazut *m* || REL óleo *m* || US FAM coba *f* (flattery) || — *castor oil* aceite de ricino || *cod-liver oil* aceite de hígado de bacalao || *heavy oil* aceite pesado || *linseed oil* aceite de linaza || *oil bottle* aceitera *f* || *oil of vitriol* aceite de vitriolo || *paraffin oil* petróleo lampante, queroseno *m* || *siccative oil* aceite secante || *the Holy Oil* los Santos Óleos || *thick oil* aceitón *m* || FIG *to burn the midnight oil* quemarse las pestañas || *to check the oil* mirar el nivel del aceite (in a car) || FIG *to know one's oil* ser baquiano || *to paint in oils* pintar al óleo || FIG *to pour oil on the flames* echar aceite *or* leña al fuego | *to pour oil on troubled waters* calmar la tempestad | *to spread like oil* extenderse como mancha de aceite || *to strike oil* encontrar petróleo (to find oil), encontrar una mina de oro

(to make a lot of money) || *vegetable oil* aceite vegetal.
◆ *adj* aceitero, ra; de aceite; *oil production* producción aceitera || petrolero, ra (industry, etc.) || de petróleo; *oil refinery* refinería de petróleo.

oil [ɔil] *vt* aceitar, lubricar (to lubricate) || echar aceite a (in cooking) || — FIG & FAM *to be well oiled* estar como una cuba | *to oil one's tongue* hablar con un tono meloso | *to oil s.o.'s hand* o *s.o.'s palm* untar la mano a alguien.

oil-bearing [-bɛəriŋ] *adj* petrolífero, ra.

oil cake [-keik] *n* torta *f* de aceite (fodder).

oilcan [-kæn] *n* aceitera *f*, alcuza *f* (for lubricating machinery, etc.) || bidón *m* de aceite (large can).

oilcloth [-klɔθ] *n* hule *m*.

oil colour; US **oil color** [-ˌkʌlə*] *n* óleo *m*.

oil cruet [-ˈkruːit] *n* aceitera *f*.

oil engine [-ˈendʒin] *n* motor *m* de petróleo.

oiler [-ə*] *n* engrasador *m* (person) || aceitera *f*, alcuza *f* (oilcan) || MAR petrolero *m*.
◆ *pl* US FAM impermeable *m sing* de hule.

oil field [-fiːld] *n* yacimiento *m* petrolífero.

oil-fired [-ˌfaiəd] *adj* alimentado con mazut *or* fuel-oil || *oil-fired central heating* calefacción *f* central de mazut *or* de fuel-oil.

oil gun [-gʌn] *n* bomba *f* de engrase, engrasador *m*.

oiliness [-inis] *n* lo aceitoso || FIG zalamerías *f pl*.

oiling [-iŋ] *n* aceitado *m*, engrase *m*, lubricación *f* (lubrication).

oil lamp [-læmp] *n* quinqué *m*, lámpara *f* de aceite.

oilman [-mən] *n* petrolero *m* || engrasador *m* (greaser).
— OBSERV El plural de *oilman* es *oilmen*.

oil mill [-mil] *n* molino *m* de aceite, almazara *f*.

oil paint [-peint] *n* pintura *f* al óleo.

oil painting [-peintiŋ] *n* pintura *f* al óleo.

oil palm [ˈɔilpɑːm] *n* BOT palmera *f* de aceite.

oilrig [-rig] *n* plataforma *f* petrolera.

oilseed [-siːd] *n* BOT semilla *f* oleaginosa.

oil seller [-selə*] *n* aceitero *m*.

oil shale [-ʃeil] *n* pizarra *f* bituminosa.

oilskin [-skin] *n* hule *m*.
◆ *pl* traje *m sing* de hule (suit) || impermeable *m sing* de hule (raincoat).

oil slick [-slik] *n* capa *f* de aceite en la superficie del mar.

oilstone [-stəun] *n* afiladera *f*, piedra *f* de afilar.

oilstove [-stəuv] *n* estufa *f* de mazut *or* de fuel-oil.

oil tanker [-ˈtæŋkə*] *n* MAR petrolero *m*.

oil well [-wel] *n* pozo *m* de petróleo.

oily [ˈɔili] *adj* aceitoso, sa (food) || grasiento, ta (machines, etc.) || graso, sa; *oily skin* cutis graso || FIG & FAM zalamero, ra.

ointment [ˈɔintmənt] *n* ungüento *m*, pomada *f*.

OK; okay [ˈəuˈkei] *adj* bien, muy bien; *it is OK* está bien || — *is it OK with you if I stay the night?* ¿te importa *or* te molesta que pase la noche aquí? | *it's OK with me* estoy de acuerdo.
◆ *adv* muy bien.
◆ *n* visto *m* bueno, aprobación *f* (approval).
◆ *interj* ¡de acuerdo!, ¡muy bien!, ¡vale!

OK; okay [ˈəuˈkei] *vt* dar el visto bueno a, aprobar (to approve).

okapi [əuˈkɑːpi] *n* okapí *m* (African animal).

Oklahoma [əukləˈhəumə] *pr n* GEOGR Oklahoma.

okoume; okume [əukəˈmei] *n* okumé *m* (tree and wood).

okra [ˈɔkrə] *n* BOT quingombó *m* [planta de origen africano].

old [əuld] *adj* viejo, ja (aged); *his father is very old* su padre es muy viejo || mayor (adult) || viejo, ja; antiguo, gua (ancient); *old silver* plata vieja || antiguo, gua (former); *our old school* nuestro antiguo colegio; *an old pupil* un antiguo alumno || viejo, ja; usado, da (clothes) || pasado, da (food) || sentado, da; duro, ra (bread) || añejo (wine, cologne) || viejo, ja (colour); *old rose* rosa viejo || conocido, da; familiar; *the same old faces* las mismas caras conocidas || viejo, ja; *he is an old friend of mine* es un viejo amigo mío || antiguo, gua; *Old English* inglés antiguo || — *a little old lady* una viejecita, una ancianita || *an old family* una familia antigua || FIG *an old hand* un perro viejo, un veterano | *an old head on young shoulders* una persona joven con mentalidad de viejo || *an old maid* una solterona || FIG *an old salt* un lobo de mar (sailor) || *an old woman* una anciana, una vieja || *any old how* de cualquier forma, de cualquier manera; *she dresses any old how* se viste de cualquier forma || *any old thing* cualquier cosa || *as old as the hills* más viejo que Matusalén *or* que andar a pie || *at ten years old* a los diez años (de edad) || *a woman is as old as she feels* una mujer no tiene más edad que la que representa || *come any old time* ven cuando quieras || *he is old enough to know better* tiene bastante edad para ser más sensato || *he is older than I am* es mayor que yo || *he is three years older than I* tiene tres años más que yo || *he is twelve years old today* hoy cumple doce años || *how old are you?* ¿qué edad tienes?, ¿cuántos años tienes? || *I am the oldest* soy el mayor || *in days of old* antaño, en tiempos antiguos || *in the good old days* en los buenos tiempos, en la buena época || *in the old days* antaño, en tiempos antiguos || FAM *my dear old fellow* mi querido amigo || *never too old to learn* nunca se es demasiado viejo para aprender || *of old* antiguamente, antaño (formerly), de antaño; *knights of old* los caballeros de antaño; de antiguo, desde hace mucho tiempo; *to know s.o. of old* conocer a alguien de antiguo; por experiencia; *I know it of old* lo sé por experiencia || *old age* vejez *f* || *old bachelor* solterón *m* || *older and wiser* el tiempo no pasa en balde || *old gold* oro viejo || FAM *old John* el tío Juan | *old man* pariente *m*, media naranja *f*, marido *m* (husband), viejo *m*, padre *m* (father), jefe *m* (boss), viejo *m*; *a poor old man* un pobre viejo; hombre *m*; *hello, old man!* ¡hola, hombre! || *Old Testament* Antiguo Testamento || FAM *that's old hat* está más visto que el tebeo || *the old* los ancianos, los viejos || *the old country* la madre patria || FAM *the old lady, the old woman* la parienta, la media naranja (the wife) || *the old world* el viejo mundo || *to be five years old* tener cinco años (person, building), existir desde hace cinco años (firm, organization) || *to be old enough to do sth.* tener edad suficiente para hacer algo || *to be old in sin* ser un pecador impenitente || *to grow old* envejecer || *to live to a ripe old age* vivir hasta una edad muy avanzada || *to live to be ninety years old* vivir hasta los noventa años || *to make old* envejecer || *to throw out all the old things* tirar todo lo viejo || FIG *you can't teach an old dog new tricks* loro viejo no aprende a hablar, es un perro viejo.

Old Bailey [-ˈbeili] *n* JUR tribunal *m* de lo criminal en Londres.

old boy [-bɔi] *n* antiguo alumno *m*, ex alumno *m* (former pupil) || FAM viejo *m* (old man) | hombre *m*; *hello, old boy!* ¡hola, hombre! | pariente *m* (husband).

Old Castile [-kæsˈtiːl] *pr n* GEOGR Castilla la Vieja.

old chap [-tʃæp] *n* hombre *m*.

old-clothes [ˈəuldˈkləuðz] *adj* *old-clothes shop* ropavejería *f*.

old-clothesman [-ˌmæn] *n* ropavejero *m*.
— OBSERV El plural es *old-clothesmen*.

olden [ˈəuldən] *adj* antiguo, gua || *in olden days* o *times* antaño, en tiempos antiguos.

old-established [ˈəuldisˈtæbliʃt] *adj* antiguo, gua (brand, firm, etc.).

old-fashioned [ˈəuldˈfæʃənd] *adj* antiguo, gua (ancient) || chapado a la antigua, anticuado, da (out-of-date); *old-fashioned opinions* opiniones chapadas a la antigua || anticuado, da; pasado de moda (out-of-fashion).

old fogy; old fogey [ˈəuldˈfəugi] *n* FAM → **fogy.**

old-fogyish; old-fogeyish [-iʃ] *adj* chapado a la antigua.

old girl [ˈəuldgəːl] *n* antigua alumna *f*, ex alumna *f* (former pupil) || FAM vieja *f* (old woman) | parienta *f* (wife) | mujer *f*; *come here, old girl!* ¡ven aquí, mujer!

Old Glory [ˈəuldˈglɔːri] *n* US FAM bandera *f* de los Estados Unidos.

Old Harry [ˈəuldˈhæri] *n* US FAM Pedro Botero (the Devil).

oldish [ˈəuldiʃ] *adj* algo viejo, ja.

Old Latin [ˈəuldˈlætin] *n* latín *m* clásico.

old-line [ˈəuldlain] *adj* antiguo, gua (old) || chapado a la antigua, conservador, ra (conservative).

old-maidish [ˈəuldˈmeidiʃ] *adj* remilgado, da.

old master [ˈəuldˈmɑːstə*] *n* ARTS gran maestro *m* (painter of the 16th and 17th cc).

Old Nick [ˈəuldnik] *n* FAM Pedro Botero (the Devil).

old school [ˈəuld-skuːl] *n* vieja escuela, *f*; *the old school attitudes* las ideas de la vieja escuela.

old school tie [ˈəuldskuːltai] *n* corbata *f* de antiguo alumno de un colegio británico (tie) || conservadurismo *m* (attitude).

oldster [ˈəuldstə*] *n* US viejo, ja.

old-style [ˈəuldˌstail] *adj* antiguo, gua.

old-time [ˈəuldtaim] *adj* antiguo, gua; de antaño.

old-timer [-ə*] *n* veterano, na (veteran) || anciano, na; viejo, ja (old person) || persona *f* chapada a la antigua (old-fashioned person).

old wives' tale [ˈəuldwaivzteil] *n* cuento *m* de viejas.

old-world [ˈəuldwəːld] *adj* GEOGR del viejo mundo || clásico, ca; chapado a la antigua (old-fashioned) || antiguo, gua; *an old-world town* un pueblo antiguo || de los tiempos antiguos; *old-world charm* encanto de los tiempos antiguos || *the old-world charm of central Madrid* el encanto del Madrid viejo.

oleaceae [əuliˈeisiiː] *pl n* BOT oleáceas *f*.

oleaginous [ˌəuliˈædʒinəs] *adj* oleaginoso, sa.

oleander [ˌəuliˈændə*] *n* adelfa *f* (shrub).

oleaster [ˌəuliˈæstə*] *n* acebuche *m* (shrub).

olecranon [ˌəuliˈkreinɔn] *n* ANAT olécranon *m*, olecráneo *m*.

oleiferous [əuliˈifərəs] *adj* oleífero, ra.

olein [ˈəuliːin] *n* CHEM oleína *f*.

oleo [ˈəuliːəu] *n* US FAM margarina *f*.

oleograph [ˈəuliəugrɑːf]; **oleography** [ˌəuliˈɔgrəfi] *n* oleografía *f*.

oleometer [əuliˈɔmitə*] *n* PHYS oleómetro *m*.

oleum [ˈəuliəm] *n* CHEM óleum *m*.

O level [ˈəuˌlevl] *n* crédito *m* de enseñanza primaria.

olfaction [ɔl'fækʃən] *n* olfato *m*.

olibanum [ɔ'libənəm] *n* olíbano *m*, incienso *m*.

oligarch ['ɔligɑːk] *n* oligarca *m*.

oligarchic [ˌɔli'gɑːkik]; **oligarchical** [-əl] *adj* oligárquico, ca.

oligarchy ['ɔligɑːki] *n* oligarquía *f*.

oligist ['ɔlidʒist] *n* MIN oligisto *m*.

Oligocene [ɔ'ligəusiːn] *adj* GEOL oligoceno, na.
◆ *n* GEOL oligoceno *m*.

oligophrenia [ˌɔligəu'friniə] *n* MED oligofrenia *f*.

olivaceous [ˌɔli'veiʃəs] *adj* oliváceo, a.

olive ['ɔliv] *n* aceituna *f*, oliva *f* (fruit); *stuffed olive* aceituna rellena || BOT olivo *m* (tree) || olivo *m* (wood) || verde *m* oliva (colour) || — *crescent olive* aceituna picudilla || *Garden of Olives* Huerto *m* de los Olivos || *Mount of Olives* Monte *m* de los Olivos || *queen olive* aceituna gordal.
◆ *adj* olivarero, ra; oleícola (olive-growing) || verde oliva (colour) || aceitunado, da (complexion).

olive branch [-brɑːntʃ] *n* ramo *m* de olivo.

olive drab [-dræb] *n* US verde *m* oliva pardusco.

olive green [-griːn] *n* verde *m* oliva.

olive grove [-grəuv] *n* olivar *m*.

olive-growing [-grəuiŋ] *adj* olivarero, ra; oleícola.

olive-oil [-ɔil] *n* aceite *m* de oliva.

oliviferous [ˌɔli'vifərəs] *adj* olivífero, ra.

olivine [ˌɔli'viːn] *n* MIN olivina *f*, olivino *m*.

olla podrida ['ɔləpɔ'driːdə] *n* CULIN olla *f* podrida.

Olympia [əu'limpiə] *pr n* GEOGR Olimpia.

Olympiad [əu'limpiæd] *n* olimpiada *f*, olimpíada *f*.

Olympian [əu'limpiən] *adj* olímpico, ca.
◆ *n* MYTH dios *m* olímpico || SP participante *m* & *f* en los juegos olímpicos.

Olympic [əu'limpik] *adj* olímpico, ca; *Olympic games* juegos olímpicos; *Olympic village* ciudad olímpica.
◆ *pl n* juegos *m* olímpicos.

Olympus [əu'limpəs] *n* MYTH & GEOGR Olimpo *m*.

Oman [ə'mɑːn] *pr n* GEOGR Omán.

omasum [əu'meisəm] *n* omaso *m*, libro *m* (of ruminants).
— OBSERV El plural de *omasum* es *omasa*.

ombre ['ɔmbə*] *n* tresillo *m* (card game).

ombu [ɔm'buː] *n* ombú *m* (tree).

ombudsman ['ɔmbudzmən] *n* mediador *m*.

omega ['əumigə] *n* omega *f*.

omelet; omelette ['ɔmlit] *n* CULIN tortilla *f*.

omen ['əumən] *n* presagio *m*, augurio *m*, agüero *m* || — *bird of ill omen* pájaro de mal agüero || *it's a good omen* es un buen presagio.

omen ['əumən] *vt* augurar, presagiar.

omentum [əu'mentəm] *n* ANAT omento *m*.
— OBSERV El plural de *omentum* es *omenta*.

omicron [əu'maikrən] *n* ómicron *f* (Greek letter).

ominous ['ɔminəs] *adj* siniestro, tra; inquietante, de mal agüero, ominoso, sa || *that sounds ominous* eso no augura nada bueno.

ominously [-li] *adv* de manera amenazadora (menacingly) || de manera inquietante; *the building shook ominously* el edificio tembló de una manera inquietante || *the room was ominously quiet* había un silencio impresionante en la sala, en la sala reinaba un silencio que no auguraba nada bueno.

omission [ə'miʃən] *n* omisión *f*; *omission of accents* omisión de acentos || olvido *m*, descuido *m* (slip); *it was an omission on your part* fue un descuido tuyo.

omit [ə'mit] *vt* omitir; *I shall omit all mention of the matter* omitiré toda referencia al asunto; *when I made the list I accidentally omitted two names* al hacer la lista omití sin querer dos nombres || suprimir; *this chapter may be omitted* se puede suprimir este capítulo || olvidar; *don't omit any name on the list* no olvides ningún nombre en la lista || *to omit to* dejar de (deliberately), dejar de, olvidarse de (accidentally); *I omitted to mention it* dejé de mencionarlo, se me olvidó mencionarlo.

Ommiads [ɔ'maiædz] *n* HIST Omeyas *m*.

omnibus ['ɔnibəs] *n* antología *f* (book) || ómnibus *m*, autobús *m* (bus); *omnibus route* línea de autobús || *omnibus train* ómnibus.
◆ *adj* que abarca varias cosas || — *omnibus bill* proyecto *m* de ley que abarca varias medidas || *omnibus edition* antología *f*.

omnidirectional [ˌɔmnidi'rekʃənl] *adj* omnidireccional.

omnifarious [ˌɔni'fɛəriəs] *adj* muy variado, da; de todas clases.

omnipotence [ɔm'nipətəns] *n* omnipotencia *f*.

omnipotent [ɔm'nipətənt] *adj* omnipotente.
◆ *n the Omnipotent* el Todopoderoso (God).

omnipresence [ɔni'prezəns] *n* omnipresencia *f*.

omnipresent ['ɔni'prezənt] *adj* omnipresente.

omniscience [ɔm'nisiəns] *n* omnisciencia *f*.

omniscient [ɔm'nisiənt] *adj* omnisciente.

omnium-gatherum ['ɔmniəm'gæðərəm] *n* mezcolanza *f* (hotchpotch) || reunión *f* a la cual se invita a toda clase de personas.

omnivore ['ɔnivɔ*] *n* omnívoro *m*.

omnivorous [ɔm'nivərəs] *adj* omnívoro, ra || FIG *omnivorous reader* persona *f* que lee todo lo que se publica.

on [ɔn][ən] *prep* en; *to sit on a chair* sentarse en una silla; *to strike on the face* golpear en la cara; *a house on Madison Avenue* una casa en Madison Avenue; *on page four* en la página cuatro; *there is a good programme on channel one* hay un buen programa en el primer canal; *there is a mirror on the wall* hay un espejo en la pared; *on the Continent* en el Continente; *I had a meal on the plane* me dieron de comer en el avión; *on the high seas* en alta mar || en, sobre, encima de (on top of); *the book is on the table* el libro está en la mesa; *it fell on my foot* me cayó en el pie || en, sobre; *he carved his name on a tree* grabó su nombre en un árbol || sobre; *stone on stone* piedra sobre piedra || tras; *he sent me letter on letter* me mandó carta tras carta || en, por; *he was walking on the road* iba andando por la carretera || de; *to live on one's income* vivir de sus ingresos; *the stain on the ceiling* la mancha del techo; *the mirror on the wall is broken* el espejo de la pared está roto; *on a journey* de viaje || sobre; *he has a great influence on me* tiene una gran influencia sobre mí || en, sobre (about); *we don't agree on that* no estamos de acuerdo sobre eso; *a tax on luxury goods* un impuesto en los productos de lujo || sobre, acerca de (concerning); *we could speak for a long time on that subject* podríamos hablar mucho tiempo sobre ese tema || según (according to); *both houses are built on the same model* las dos casas están construidas según el mismo modelo || por; *to swear on one's honour* jurar por su honor; *on the orders of* por mandato de; *on the afternoon of the 5th March* el 5 de marzo por la tarde || el (day); *he came on Sunday* vino el domingo; *I usually go to the cinema on Thursdays* generalmente voy al cine los jueves; *on the twenty-second of February* el veintidós de febrero || a; *on his request* a petición suya || bajo; *on the recommendation of* bajo la recomendación de || mediante; *on presentation of your ticket* mediante presentación de su billete || contra (against); *an onslaught on the régime* un ataque violento contra el régimen || con; *on whose authority?* ¿con permiso de quién?; *I live on twenty pounds a week* vivo con veinte libras a la semana || a; *on his arrival* a su llegada || al (with gerund); *on entering the room* al entrar en la habitación || a costa de, a expensas de; *he lives on his brother* vive a costa de su hermano || — *a curse on it!* ¡maldito sea! || *bent on learning English* decidido a aprender inglés || *fate smiles on him* la suerte le sonríe || *have a drink on me* le invito a una copa || *have pity on me* tenga piedad de mí || *he has money on him* lleva dinero encima *or* consigo || *he is on drugs* se droga || *he is on pills* toma píldoras || *he was on TV last night* anoche salió en la televisión || *it is a new one on me* es nuevo para mí || *Madrid is on the Manzanares* Madrid está a orillas del Manzanares, el Manzanares pasa por Madrid || JUR *on a charge of* acusado de || *on a fine day* un buen día || *on all sides* por todas partes (everywhere), por todos los lados (on each side) || *on an equal footing* en un pie de igualdad || *on appearance* por las apariencias || *on average* por término medio || *on certain conditions* bajo ciertas condiciones || *on foot* andando, a pie || *on his arrival* a su llegada || *on holiday* de vacaciones || *on or after the 27th* el día 27 o después || *on our way to* en el camino de, camino de, yendo a || *on pain of death* so pena de muerte || *on principle* por principio || *on sale* en venta || *on strike* en huelga || *on that occasion* en aquella ocasión || *on that side, on this side* del otro lado, de este lado || *on the first day* el primer día || *on the next day* al día siguiente || *on the quiet* o *the sly* a escondidas || *on the right* a la derecha; *it is on the right* está a la derecha; por la derecha; *to drive on the right* conducir por la derecha || *on the spot* en el lugar; *police were on the spot within five minutes* la policía se personó en el lugar en cinco minutos; en el momento; *he dealt with it on the spot* se ocupó de ello en el momento; en el acto; *killed on the spot* matado en el acto || *on time* a tiempo || *the drinks are on me* las bebidas corren de mi cuenta || *the enemy was nearly on them* el enemigo estaba a punto de caer sobre ellos || *to be based on* estar basado en, basarse en || *to be on a diet* estar a régimen || *to be on a grapefruit diet* seguir un régimen a base de pomelos || *to be on an errand* estar haciendo un recado || *to be on the committee* formar parte del comité, ser miembro del comité || *to be on the staff* estar en plantilla || *to bet on a horse* aposar a *or* por un caballo || *to depend on* depender de || *to hang on the wall* estar colgado de la pared || *to have sth. on s.o.* tener algún informe sobre alguien (information), tener algo sobre alguien; *do you have sth. on Freud?* ¿tienes algo sobre Freud? || *to live on bread and water* vivir de pan y agua, comer pan y agua || *to march on London* marchar sobre Londres || *to play sth. on the piano* tocar algo al piano || *to send s.o. on an errand* mandar a alguien a hacer un recado || *to swear on the Bible* jurar sobre la Biblia || *what is on TV tonight?* ¿qué ponen en la televisión esta noche?
◆ *adv* más; *further on* más lejos; *later on* más tarde || más lejos, adelante (further) (see OBSERV) || — *and so on* y así sucesivamente, etcétera || *from now on* a partir de ahora, de ahora en adelante || *from that year on* a partir de ese *or* de aquel año || *have you anything on tonight?* ¿tienes algún plan para esta noche?, ¿tienes algo proyectado *or* previsto para esta noche?

|| *he danced on and on* bailó sin parar || *he is on in five minutes* va a actuar dentro de cinco minutos || *he is on one Sunday in two* trabaja un domingo sí y otro no || FAM *it's not on* eso no se hace (it's not done) || *on and off* de vez en cuando || *on and on* sin cesar, sin parar || *on to* hacia (towards) || *on with the show* que empiece *or* que siga el espectáculo || *on with your coat* ponte el abrigo || *sing on!* ¡siga cantando! || *the police are on to him* la policía le sigue la pista || *they talked on into the early hours of the morning* siguieron hablando hasta la madrugada || *to be on* poner (film); *what film is on?* ¿qué película ponen?; dar; *the show is now on in Madrid* ahora dan el espectáculo en Madrid; estar en escena (actor) || *to be on to s.o.* meterse con uno (to criticize), estar detrás de uno; *she is always on to me to clean the windows* está siempre detrás de mí para que limpie los cristales || *to be on to sth.* enterarse de algo, comprender algo, caer en la cuenta de algo; *he was on to it at once* se enteró en seguida || *to be on to sth. good* haber encontrado algo bueno || *to walk on* seguir andando || *well on in the night* muy entrada la noche || *«what's on in London»* «cartelera de espectáculos londinenses».

◆ *adj* encendido, da; puesto, ta (electrical appliances); *the television is always on* la televisión está siempre encendida || puesto, ta; *the coffee is on* el café está puesto; *the brake is on* el freno está puesto || abierto, ta (tap) || empezado, da; *the programme is already on* ya ha empezado el programa || en marcha (machine) || en el sitio (consumption) || FAM bueno, na (day).

— OBSERV Cuando *on* acompaña ciertos verbos, como *to get, to go, to come*, etc., no se puede traducir literalmente. Por consiguiente es imprescindible consultar el artículo referente al verbo de que se trata.

onager ['ɔnəgə*] *n* ZOOL onagro *m*.

— OBSERV El plural de la palabra inglesa es *onagri* u *onagers*.

onanism ['ɔnənizəm] *n* onanismo *m*.

once [wʌns] *adv* una vez; *she saw him once* le vio una vez; *once a day* una vez al día || antes; *once he was young* antes era joven || hace tiempo; *I knew her once* le conocí hace tiempo || alguna vez; *if once the news got out* si alguna vez saliese la noticia || — *all at once* de repente (suddenly), de una vez (at one go), todos al mismo tiempo (all together) || *at once* en seguida (immediately), al mismo tiempo (at the same time), de una vez (at one go) || *for once* por una vez || *just this once* esta vez nada más || *more than once* más de una vez || *not once* jamás, ni una (sola) vez || *once and for all* de una vez para siempre || *once in a while* de vez en cuando || *once more* una vez más, otra vez || *once or twice* un par de veces, una o dos veces || *once upon a time* hace siglos (a long time ago) || *once upon a time there was* érase una vez, érase que se era (in stories).

◆ *conj* una vez que; *once he starts he goes well* una vez que empieza va bien || si alguna vez; *once he found out he would be furious* si alguna vez se enterase se pondría furioso || en cuanto; *once they arrive we can begin* en cuanto lleguen podemos empezar.

once-over [-ˌuvə*] *n* FAM mirada *f*, ojeada *f*, vistazo *m*; *to give sth. the once-over* echar una mirada a algo.

oncoming ['ɔnˌkʌmiŋ] *adj* que viene, que se aproxima || venidero, ra; *the oncoming century* el siglo venidero.

◆ *n* llegada *f*; *the oncoming of winter* la llegada del invierno.

one [wʌn] *adj* uno, una; *one house* una casa; *one man* un hombre; *one day an old man came to see me* un día un anciano vino a verme || primero, ra; *item one on the agenda* primer punto del orden del día || único, ca; solo, la; *this is the one thing we can feel certain about* es la única cosa de la cual podemos estar seguros; *the one person I know* la única persona que conozco || mismo, ma; *we go all in one direction* vamos todos en la misma dirección || un tal; *one Mr. X* un tal Sr. X || — *for one thing* primero || FIG *his one and only* su Dulcinea || *it's all one* viene a ser lo mismo || *it's all one to me* me da igual || *no one man* ningún hombre, nadie || *one and the same* el mismo, la misma || *one or two mistakes* unas pocas faltas || *that's the one thing I needed* es exactamente lo que necesitaba || *the last but one* el penúltimo, la penúltima || *the one and only* el único, la única; *the one and only house in the street* la única casa de la calle || *to become one* casarse || *to be one with s.o.* estar de acuerdo con alguien || *to be one with sth.* formar un conjunto con algo || *with one voice* a una voz.

◆ *indef pron* uno, una; *one of them* uno de ellos; *have you one?* ¿tienes uno? || una persona, alguien; *he is one whom everybody admires* es una persona a quien todos admiran || uno, una; *one cannot always be right* uno no puede tener siempre razón || uno, una, se; *one cannot be working all day without stopping* uno no puede estar trabajando todo el día sin parar, no se puede trabajar todo el día sin parar || se; *one does not smoke in high society* no se fuma en la alta sociedad || — *all in one* a la vez || *any one of us* cualquiera de nosotros || *for one* por lo menos; *I, for one, do not believe it* yo, por lo menos, no me lo creo || *he is not one to complain* no es el tipo de persona que se queja || FAM *he's a one!* ¡es único!, ¡es un caso! | *he's a real one for football* le gusta muchísimo el fútbol || *many a one* muchos, muchas || *one after the other* uno tras otro || *one and all* todo el mundo, absolutamente todos || *one another* se; *they love one another* se quieren || *one by one* uno tras otro, uno por uno || *one of my friends* uno de mis amigos, un amigo mío || *one's* su; *to give one's opinion* dar su opinión; *to visit one's friends* ir a ver a sus amigos; el, la; *to cut one's hand* cortarse la mano || *the one and the other* el uno y el otro || *the one... the other* uno... el otro || *to be one of the family* ser de la familia || FAM *to have one up on s.o.* tener ventaja sobre alguien.

◆ *dem pron that one* ése *or* aquél, ésa *or* aquélla || FAM *that's a good one!* ¡ésa sí que es buena! || *that's the one* ése es || *the big one* el grande, la grande || *the Evil One* el demonio || *the green one* el verde, la verde || *the little ones* los pequeños || *the one on the table* el que está en la mesa || *the ones who* los que, las que || *the one who* el que, la que || *the one whom* al que, a la que || *this one* éste, ésta || *which one do you prefer?* ¿cuál prefieres?

◆ *n* uno *m* (the number) || COMM unidad *f* || uno, una; *two volumes in one* dos volúmenes en uno || la una (one o'clock); *he'll arrive between one and two* llegará entre la una y las dos || un chelín; *one and three (pence)* un chelín con tres peniques || punto *m* (point) || — *all in one* de una sola pieza || FAM *a quick one* un trago || *one of two things* una de dos || FAM *she gave him one with her handbag* le dio un golpe con el bolso || *they are at one* están de acuerdo || FAM *to have one for the road* tomar la espuela *or* la última copa [antes de marcharse].

— OBSERV La palabra inglesa *one* no se emplea como artículo indefinido sino solamente para distinguir entre una cosa y varias. El artículo indefinido inglés es *a*.

one-act [-'ækt] *adj* de un (solo) acto.

one-armed [-'ɑːmd] *adj* manco, ca || FIG *one-armed bandit* máquina *f* tragaperras.

one-cylinder [-'silində*] *adj* monocilíndrico, ca.

one-eyed [-'aid] *adj* tuerto, ta.

one-handed [-'hændid] *adj* manco, ca.

◆ *adv* con una sola mano.

one-horse [-'hɔːs] *adj* de un caballo; *a one-horse carriage* un carro de un caballo || de segunda categoría, de poca monta; *a one-horse show* un espectáculo de segunda categoría || *a one-horse town* un poblacho.

oneiric [əu'nairik] *adj* onírico, ca.

one-legged ['wʌn'legd] *adj* con una sola pierna (person).

one-liner ['wʌn'lainə] *n* FAM frase *f* ingeniosa *or* cómica (funny remark).

one-man ['wʌn'mæn] *adj* que consiste en una sola persona (committee, staff) || para una sola persona (job, play) || individual; *one-man boat* barco individual.

oneness ['wʌnnis] *n* unidad *f* || identidad *f* (of opinions).

one-off ['wʌnɔf] *adj* único, ca; irrepetible, fuera de serie.

◆ *n* original *m*.

one-parent [wʌn'pɛərənt] *adj* monoparental; *a one-parent family* una familia monoparental.

one-piece ['wʌnpiːs] *adj* de una pieza.

onerous ['ɔnərəs] *adj* oneroso, sa || pesado, da (responsibility).

oneself [wʌn'self] *pron* se (reflexive); *to wash oneself* lavarse || sí, sí mismo, sí misma; *to speak of oneself* hablar de sí mismo || uno mismo, una misma (emphatic) || — *by oneself* solo, la; *it is impossible to do it by oneself* es imposible hacerlo solo; *it is sad to be by oneself* es triste estar solo || *to be oneself* ser natural, comportarse con naturalidad || *to come to oneself* volver en sí || *to say sth. to oneself* decir algo para su capote *or* para sus adentros *or* para sí || *to take sth. upon oneself* encargarse de algo || *with oneself* consigo mismo.

one-sided ['wʌn'saidid] *adj* unilateral; *a one-sided decision* una decisión unilateral || parcial (biased) || desigual (unequal) || que sólo tiene un lado (having only one side) || asimétrico, ca.

one-sidedness [-nis] *n* parcialidad *f*.

onetime ['wʌntaim] *adj* antiguo, gua (former); *a onetime teacher* un antiguo profesor.

one-to-one ['wʌntə'wʌn] *adj* exacto, ta; *one-to-one correspondence* correspondencia exacta.

one-track ['wʌn'træk] *adj* de una sola vía, de un solo carril (road) || FIG *to have a one-track mind* no poder pensar más que en una cosa.

one-upmanship [wʌn'ʌpmənʃip] *n* arte *m* que consiste en aventajar a los demás.

one-way ['wʌn'wei] *adj* de dirección única; *one-way street* calle de dirección única || de ida; *one way ticket* billete de ida || *«one way traffic»* «dirección única» (road sign).

ongoing ['ɔngəuiŋ] *adj* en curso, actual (in process) || progresivo, va (making progress).

onion ['ʌnjən] *n* BOT cebolla *f* || FAM chola *f* (head) || — FAM *to know one's onions* conocer muy bien la materia || BOT *welsh onion* cebollino *m*.

onion bed [-bed] *n* AGR cebollar *m*.

onionskin [-skin] *n* binza *f*, tela *f* de cebolla || PRINT papel *m* cebolla.

on-licence ['ɔnˌlaisəns] *n* licencia *f* para vender bebidas alcohólicas que se tienen que consumir en el mismo establecimiento.

onlooker ['ɔnˌlukə*] *n* espectador, ra || mirón, ona; *there were many onlookers around the building site* había muchos mirones alrededor del solar.

only ['əunli] *adj* solo, la; único, ca; *this is the only example I can give you* es el único ejemplo que puedo darle || único, ca (child, son) || — *the only thing is that* lo único es que || *you were not*

the only one who noticed it no fue el único en darse cuenta de ello.
◆ *adv* sólo, solamente; *I can tell you only what I know* sólo le puedo decir lo que sé || — *I am only the charlady* no soy más que la asistenta || *if only I had an orange!* ¡ojalá tuviera una naranja! || *I only just caught the train* por poco pierdo el tren || *I saw him only last week* no hace más de una semana que le he visto || *not only... but* no sólo... sino (también) || *only too pleased to* encantado de || *only to think of it* con sólo pensarlo || *take him if only for the company* llévale por lo menos para estar acompañado || *they have only just left* acaban de marcharse ahora mismo || *you have only to take it* no tiene más que cogerlo.
◆ *conj* pero, sólo que; *I wanted to do it only I could not* quería hacerlo pero no pude.

only-begotten [-bi'gɔtn] *adj* unigénito, ta.

onomastics [ˌɔnəu'mæstiks] *n* onomástica *f*.

onomatopoeia [ˌɔnəumætəu'pi:ə] *n* onomatopeya *f*.

onomatopoeic [ˌɔnəumætəu'pi:ik]; **onomatopoetic** [ˌɔnəumætəu'pi:tik] *adj* onomatopéyico, ca.

onrush ['ɔnrʌʃ] *n* riada *f*, avalancha *f*, oleada *f*; *onrush of tourists* avalancha de turistas || arremetida *f*, ataque *m* (of an army) || embestida *f* (of a bull) || fuerza *f*, ímpetu *m* (of water).

on-screen ['ɔnskri:n] *adj* INFORM en pantalla; *on-screen display* presentación en pantalla.

onset ['ɔnset] *n* principio *m*, comienzo *m* (beginning) || MED ataque *m*, acceso *m* || MIL ataque *m*, arremetida *f* || — *at the onset* al principio || *from the onset* desde el principio.

onshore ['ɔnʃɔ:*] *adj* que sopla hacia la tierra (wind).
◆ *adv* hacia la tierra.

on side ['ɔnsaid] *adj/adv* SP en posición correcta.

onslaught ['ɔnslɔ:t] *n* MED & MIL ataque *m* violento || FIG crítica *f* violenta, ataque *m* violento.

Ontario (Lake) [ɔn'tɛəriəu] *pr n* GEOGR lago *m* Ontario.

onto ['ɔntu] *prep* ⟶ **on** *adv* (*on to*).

ontological [ˌɔntəu'lɔdʒikəl] *adj* PHIL ontológico, ca.

ontologist [ɔn'tɔlədʒist] *n* PHIL ontólogo *m*.

ontology [ɔn'tɔlədʒi] *n* PHIL ontología *f*.

onus ['əunəs] *n* responsabilidad *f* || *the onus lies upon the government to* le incumbe al gobierno.

onward ['ɔnwəd] *adj* hacia adelante; *the onward march* la marcha hacia adelante.
◆ *adv* hacia adelante || — *from that time onwards* desde entonces || *from the 19th century onwards* del siglo XIX en adelante, a partir del siglo XIX.

onwards [-z] *adv* hacia adelante || — *from that time onwards* desde entonces || *from the 19th century onwards* del siglo XIX en adelante, a partir del siglo XIX.

onyx ['ɔniks] *n* ónice *m* & *f*, ónix *m*.

oocyte ['əuəsait] *n* BIOL ovocito *m*.

oodles ['u:dlz] *pl n* FAM montones *m*, cantidad *f sing* (lots); *oodles of people* cantidad de gente.

oof [u:f] *n* FAM pasta *f*.

oolong ['u:lɔŋ] *n* té *m* negro (black tea).

oomph [umf] *n* FAM atractivo *m*, «sex-appeal» *m* (personal charm) | magnetismo *m* | ánimo *m* (energy).

oops! [ups] *interj* ¡ay!

oosphere ['əuəsfiə*] *n* oosfera *f*.

oospore ['əuəspɔ:*] *n* BOT oospora *f*.

ooze [u:z] *n* cieno *m* (mud) || agua *f* de casca (for tanning leather).

ooze [u:z] *vi* rezumarse, rezumar (to flow) || exudar (to sweat) || — FIG *to ooze away* faltar, acabarse; *he felt his courage oozing away* sentía que le faltaba el valor, sentía que se le acababa el valor | *to ooze with pride* rebosar de orgullo.
◆ *vt* rezumar || sudar (to sweat) || FIG rebosar de.

oozy [-i] *adj* legamoso, sa; cenagoso, sa (muddy) || húmedo, da (exuding liquid).

opacity [əu'pæsiti] *n* opacidad *f* || FIG torpeza *f* (mental obtuseness) | oscuridad *f* (of meaning).

opah ['əupə] *n* ZOOL pez *m* luna.

opal ['əupəl] *n* MIN ópalo *m*.

opalescence [ˌəupə'lesns] *n* opalescencia *f*.

opalescent [ˌəupə'lesnt] *adj* opalescente.

opaline ['əupəli:n] *adj* opalino, na.
◆ *n* opalina *f*.

opaque [əu'peik] *adj* opaco, ca (not transparent) || FIG obtuso, sa (obtuse) | oscuro, ra (obscure).
◆ *n* PHOT pintura *f* opaca.

OPEC *abbr of [Organization of Petroleum Exporting Countries]* OPEP, Organización de Países Exportadores de Petróleo.

open ['əupən] *adj* abierto, ta; *an open window* una ventana abierta; *an open book* un libro abierto; *open shop* tienda abierta; *open to the public* abierto al público; *he is open to suggestions* está abierto a las sugerencias || poco tupido, da (material) || descubierto, ta; *open car* coche descubierto || destapado, da (bottle) || destapado, da; descubierto, ta; *open pot* puchero destapado || despejado, da; *open view* vista despejada || expuesto, ta; *open to attacks* expuesto a los ataques || desplegado, da; extendido, da (unfolded); *the plan was open on the desk* el plano estaba desplegado sobre el escritorio || abierto, ta; *an open rose* una rosa abierta || franco, ca; abierto, ta; *he was very open with me* fue muy franco conmigo || manifiesto, ta (patent) || abierto a todos; *open tournament* competición abierta a todos || público, ca; *open trial* juicio público || sin resolver, pendiente (unsolved) || MIL abierto, ta; *open ranks* filas abiertas || vacante (post); *the job is still open* el puesto queda vacante || libre; *he keeps Saturday open* tiene el sábado libre || MED dilatado, da (pores) | abierto, ta; *an open wound* una herida abierta || MAR alto, ta; *open sea* alta mar | claro, ra (not foggy) || GRAMM abierto, ta; *open vowel* vocal abierta || COMM libre (market) | abierto, ta (account, credit) || MUS no pisado, da; *open string* cuerda no pisada || PRINT espaciado, da || INFORM abierto, ta || — *half open* entreabierto, ta; entornado, da || *in the open country* en descampado || *it is open to you to do so* Ud. puede perfectamente hacerlo || *membership is only open to retired officers* sólo los oficiales retirados pueden hacerse socios || *my invitation is still open* mi invitación vale todavía || *on the open road* por la carretera || *open air* aire libre; *in the open air* al aire libre || *open arrest* arresto *m* simple || CHEM *open chain* cadena abierta || *open cheque* cheque abierto || ELECTR *open circuit* circuito abierto || MIL *open city* ciudad abierta || *open date* fecha *f* que queda por fijar || FIG *open door* libre acceso *m* || *open enemy* enemigo declarado || *open letter* carta abierta || *open mine* mina *f* a cielo abierto || *open market* mercado *m* abierto *or* libre || *open marriage* pareja *f* abierta || *open order* orden abierta (commercial meaning), orden abierto (military meaning) || *open revolt* franca rebeldía || *open season* temporada *f* de caza y pesca || *open secret* secreto *m* a voces || *open shop* fábrica *f* que emplea obreros que son miembros o no de un sindicato || MIL *open sight* alza *f* de ranura (of gun) || *open to doubt* dudoso, sa || *open to improvement* susceptible de mejora || *Open University* Universidad *f* a Distancia || *open verdict* veredicto *m* que no especifica ni el autor ni las circunstancias de un crimen || MIL *open warfare* guerra declarada || *our way lay open* ya no quedaba ningún obstáculo en el camino || *the meeting is open* se abre la sesión || *the road is open* la vía está libre || *the season is open* se ha levantado la veda || *to be open to misinterpretation* poder interpretarse mal || *to be unable to keep one's eyes open* cerrársele a uno los ojos de sueño, tener sueño || *to give with an open hand* dar a manos llenas || *to have an open hand* ser generoso || *to keep open house* tener mesa franca *or* casa abierta || *to lay a wound open* descubrir una herida || *to lay open* abrir (to open), exponer (to expose) || *to lay o.s. open to criticism* exponerse a las críticas, dar pie *or* dar pábulo a la crítica || *to leave sth. open to s.o.* dar a elegir algo a alguien, dejar algo a la elección de alguien; *he left it open to me* me lo dio a elegir || *to leave the matter open* dejar el asunto *or* la cuestión pendiente || *to throw open* abrir de par en par || *two courses are open to you* le quedan dos posibilidades || *wide open* abierto de par en par || *you have only one course open to you* sólo le queda una posibilidad.
◆ *n* *in the open* al aire libre (in the open air), en el campo (in the country), en campo abierto; *to attack the enemy in the open* atacar al enemigo en campo abierto || *to bring into the open* revelar, sacar a luz || *to come into the open* salir a luz (to appear), decir lo que piensa uno (to say what one thinks).

open ['əupən] *vt* abrir; *to open a door* abrir una puerta; *to open a parcel* abrir un paquete; *to open a road, a tunnel* abrir una carretera, un túnel; *to open a hole* abrir un agujero; *to open a bank account* abrir una cuenta en el banco; *to open a testament* abrir un testamento; *to open ranks* abrir filas; *to open a wound* abrir una herida; *to open one's eyes* abrir los ojos; *that opens new prospects for him* esto le abre nuevas perspectivas || desplegar (to unfold) || abrir, poner (a shop) || inaugurar (an exhibition) || AGR roturar || despejar (to clear) || entablar, iniciar, empezar (negotiations, conversation) || abrir (session, debate, ball) || emprender (business) || empezar; *my name opens the list* mi nombre empieza la lista || ELECTR abrir (a circuit) || JUR exponer (a case) || iniciar (an institution) || abrir (in cards) || revelar (one's intentions) || — *to open fire* romper el fuego || FIG *to open one's heart to s.o.* abrir su pecho a alguien (to confide one's feelings) | *to open the door to* abrir la puerta a.
◆ *vi* abrirse (shop, book, window, door, floor, etc.) || empezar, comenzar (to begin); *the book opens with a long dialogue* el libro empieza con un largo diálogo || THEATR estrenarse || abrir (in cards) || *the shops open at eight in the morning* las tiendas (se) abren a las ocho de la mañana.
◆ *phr v* **to open into** dar a, comunicar con; *this door opens into the bedroom* esta puerta comunica con el dormitorio || **to open on to** dar a; *this room opens on to the street* este cuarto da a la calle || **to open out** desplegar (to unfold) | ensanchar (a hole) | extenderse; *the moor opened out before us* el páramo se extendía ante nosotros | abrirse; *the flowers will open out in spring* las flores se abrirán en primavera | desplegarse; *this map opens out* este mapa se despliega || desarrollarse (to develop) | acelerar a fondo (to accelerate) || — *to open out to s.o.* confiarse a alguien, abrirse con alguien || **to open up** abrir (mine, road, shop) | abrir; *open up!* ¡abran! | abrir, conquistar; *to open up new outlets* abrir nuevos mercados | abrir, crear (possibilities) | explorar (to explore) | desarrollar

(to develop) | inaugurar; *to open up a new house* inaugurar una casa | iniciarse; *trade opened up between the two countries* las relaciones comerciales se iniciaron entre los dos países | empezar, comenzar (to begin) | revelar (to disclose) | abrirse (to speak freely) | romper el fuego (to start shooting).

open-air [-'ɛə*] *adj* al aire libre.

open-and-shut ['əupnən'ʃʌt] *adj* US FAM claro, ra; evidente, obvio, via.

opencast ['əupənkɑːst] *adj* MIN a cielo abierto.

opencut ['əupənkʌt] *adj* US MIN a cielo abierto.

open-door ['əupən'dɔː*] *adj* de puertas abiertas.

open-ended ['əupən'endid] *adj* abierto, ta.

opener ['əupənə*] *n* abrelatas *m inv* (for tins) || SP primer partido *m* (first game).
◆ *pl* cartas *f* que por su valor permiten al jugador abrir (in cards).

open-eyed ['əupən'aid] *adj* con los ojos abiertos || FIG boquiabierto, ta (with surprise).

open-faced ['əupn'feist] *adj* sincero, ra (frank).

openhanded ['əupn'hændid] *adj* generoso, sa.

openhandedness [-nis] *n* generosidad *f*.

open-heart ['əupən'hɑːt] *adj* MED a corazón abierto.

openhearted [-id] *adj* sincero, ra; franco, ca (frank) || cordial (kindly) || generoso, sa.

openheartedness [-idnis] *n* sinceridad *f*, franqueza *f* (sincerity) || generosidad *f*.

open-hearth ['əupən'hɑːθ] *adj* TECH *open-hearth furnace* horno *m* de hogar abierto.

opening ['əupniŋ] *n* abertura *f* (aperture) || grieta *f*, abertura *f* (in a wall) || apertura *f* (act of opening); *the opening of the conference* la apertura de la conferencia || oportunidad *f* (opportunity); *it's a fine opening for you* es una buena oportunidad para ti || vacante *f* (vacancy) || principio *m*, comienzo *m* (beginning) || brecha *f* (breach) || claro *m* (in forest, clouds) || estreno *m* (première of a play, etc.) || inauguración *f* (of an exhibition) || apertura *f* (in chess).
◆ *adj* inaugural, de apertura (inaugural) || —*opening hours* horas *f pl* de apertura || *opening night* noche *f* de estreno || *opening price* cotización *f* inicial (in the stock exchange) || *opening time* hora *f* de apertura.

openly ['əupənli] *adv* francamente (frankly) || abiertamente (undisguisedly) || públicamente (publicly).

open-minded ['əupn'maindid] *adj* liberal || imparcial (impartial).

open-mindedness [-nis] *n* liberalidad *f* || imparcialidad *f*.

openmouthed ['əupn'mauðd] *n* boquiabierto, ta.

open-necked ['əupnnekt] *adj* con el cuello desabrochado (shirt, blouse).

openness ['əupənnis] *n* franqueza *f*.

open-plan ['əupn'plæn] *adj* ARCH *open-plan house* casa *f* cuya disposición se deja al arbitrio del dueño.

openwork ['əupnwəːk] *n* calado *m* || MIN explotación *f* a cielo abierto.

opera ['ɔpərə] *n* MUS ópera *f* (musical play) | ópera *f* (theatre) | compañía *f* de ópera (company) || — *comic opera* ópera bufa || *grand opera* ópera || *light opera* opereta *f*.

opera ['ɔpərə] *pl n* ⟶ **opus.**

operability [ɔpərə'biliti] *n* INFORM operabilidad *f*.

operable ['ɔpərəbl] *adj* MED operable || factible (practicable).

opéra bouffe ['ɔpərə'buːf] *n* MUS ópera *f* bufa.

opéra comique ['ɔpeiræ'kɔmiːk] *n* MUS ópera *f* cómica, zarzuela *f*.

opera glasses ['ɔpərə'glɑːsiz] *pl n* prismáticos *m*, gemelos *m*.

opera hat ['ɔpərəhæt] *n* clac *m*, sombrero *m* de muelles.

opera house ['ɔpərə'haus] *n* MUS ópera *f* [teatro].

operand [‚ɔpə'rænd] *n* INFORM operando *m*.

operate ['ɔpəreit] *vt* manejar, hacer funcionar; *to operate a machine* manejar una máquina || dirigir (to direct) || efectuar, realizar, llevar a cabo; *to operate a plan* realizar un proyecto || llevar; *to operate an affair* llevar un asunto || producir (to bring about) || accionar (a lever) || hacer funcionar; *the switch operates the light* el interruptor hace funcionar la luz || impulsar (to propel) || — *the machine is operated by electricity* la máquina funciona con electricidad || FAM *to operate a switch* efectuar un cambio (to make a change).
◆ *vi* funcionar; *the lift is not operating* el ascensor no funciona || surtir efecto, operar; *is the aspirin operating yet?* ¿ha surtido efecto ya la aspirina? || obrar, actuar; *to operate freely* obrar con libertad || trabajar; *the company operates on an international scale* la compañía trabaja a escala internacional || cometer un delito (criminal, etc.); *the thief operated by night* el ladrón cometió su delito por la noche || MED operar, efectuar una operación || COMM especular || — MED *to operate on s.o. for sth.* operar a alguien de algo | *to operate on s.o.'s heart* operar a alguien del corazón.

operatic [‚ɔpə'rætik] *adj* MUS operístico, ca; de ópera.

operating ['ɔpəreitiŋ] *adj* MED que opera (surgeon) || COMM de explotación; *operating expenses* gastos de explotación || INFORM *operating software* software *m* operativo | *operating system* sistema *m* operativo.
◆ *n* funcionamiento *m* || acción *f* (of a medicine) || MED operación *f* || COMM explotación *f*.

operating room ['ɔpəreitiŋruːm] *n* MED quirófano *m*, sala *f* de operaciones.

operating table ['ɔpəreitiŋteibl] *n* MED mesa *f* de operaciones.

operating theatre; US **operating theater** ['ɔpəreitiŋ'θiətə*] *n* MED quirófano *m*, sala *f* de operaciones.

operation [‚ɔpə'reiʃən] *n* MATH, MED & COMM operación *f* || manejo *m*; *the operation of a crane* el manejo de una grúa || funcionamiento *m*; *the operation of the valves is bad* el funcionamiento de las válvulas es malo || MIL operación *f* || maniobra *f* (manoeuvre) || aplicación *f* (of a law, of a rule) || actividad *f* (activity) || — *shady operations* maniobras turbias || *to be in operation* estar en vigor, ser vigente (law, rule), estar funcionando (to be working), estar en funcionamiento; *not all our machines are in operation yet* todavía no están en funcionamiento todas nuestras máquinas || *to bring* o *to put into operation* poner en funcionamiento (a machine), poner en vigor, empezar a aplicar (a law) || *to come into operation* entrar en vigor (a law) || MED *to perform an operation on s.o. for cataract* operar a alguien de catarata | *to undergo an operation* ser operado, sufrir una operación (*for* de).
◆ *pl* obras *f* (work); *operations begin tomorrow* las obras empiezan mañana.

operational [‚ɔpə'reiʃənl] *adj* MIL operacional | de operaciones || en buen estado, capaz de funcionar (in working order) || — MIL *operational flight* vuelo *m* de servicio || *we're not fully operational yet* todavía no estamos en pleno funcionamiento.

operative ['ɔpə'ətiv] *adj* operativo, va; operante || en vigor; *this law will be operative as from today* esta ley entra en vigor hoy || eficaz (efficient) || MED operatorio, ria || *operative part* parte resolutiva, parte dispositiva (of a resolution).
◆ *n* operario, ria; obrero, ra (workman) || US detective *m* privado (private detective).

operator ['ɔpəreitə*] *n* operario, ria; maquinista *m* & *f* (of machine) || telefonista *m* & *f* (of telephone) || operador *m* (in the cinema) || MATH & MED operador *m* || US especulador, ra (speculator) | explotador *m* (of mine, of airline, etc.) | empresario *m* (an industrial) | negociante *m* (dealer) | conductor, ra (driver) | FAM estafador, ra (swindler) | ladrón *m* (thief) || INFORM operador, ra || — *tour operator* agente *m* de viajes || MIL & MAR *wireless operator* radio *m*, radiotelegrafista *m*.

operculum [ə'pəːkjuləm] *n* opérculo *m*.
— OBSERV El plural de *operculum* es *opercula* o *operculums*.

operetta [‚ɔpə'retə] *n* MUS opereta *f* | zarzuela *f* (in Spain).

Ophelia [ɔ'fiːljə] *pr n* Ofelia *f*.

ophidian [ɔ'fidiən] *n* ZOOL ofidio *m*.
◆ *adj* ZOOL ofidio, dia.

ophthalmia [ɔf'θælmiə] *n* MED oftalmía *f*.

ophthalmic [ɔf'θælmik] *adj* MED oftálmico, ca.

ophthalmologic [‚ɔfθæl'mɔlədʒik]; **ophthalmological** [‚ɔfθælmə'lɔdʒikəl] *adj* MED oftalmológico, ca.

ophthalmologist [‚ɔfθæl'mɔlədʒist] *n* MED oftalmólogo *m*.

ophthalmology [‚ɔfθæl'mɔlədʒi] *n* MED oftalmología *f*.

ophthalmoscope [ɔf'θælməskəup] *n* MED oftalmoscopio *m*.

ophthalmoscopy [ɔfθæl'mɔskəpi] *n* MED oftalmoscopia *f*.

opiate ['əupieit] *n* narcótico *m*.

opiate ['əupieit] *vt* dormir con opio (to put to sleep) || mezclar con opio (to mix with opium).

opine [əu'pain] *vt/vi* opinar.

opiner [-ə*] *n* opinante *m* & *f*.

opinion [ə'pinjən] *n* opinión *f* || — *advisory opinion* dictamen *m* || *I am of your opinion* estoy de acuerdo con Ud, comparto su opinión, soy de la misma opinión que Ud || *I didn't ask your opinion* no te he pedido tu opinión *or* tu parecer || *in my opinion it is possible* a mi parecer *or* a mi juicio *or* en mi opinión es posible || *in the opinion of* según opinión *or* la opinión de || *opinion of the experts* dictamen *m* pericial || *public opinion poll* sondeo *m* de la opinión pública || *that is a matter of opinion* es cuestión de opinión || *to be of the opinion that* ser de opinión que, ser del parecer que || *to form an opinion* formarse una opinión || *to have a high opinion of o.s.* ser muy creído || *to have a high, a low opinion of s.o.* tener buen, mal concepto de alguien || *to share the opinion of* compartir la opinión de || FIG *to stick to one's opinion* casarse con su opinión, aferrarse a una opinión || *what was your opinion of it?* ¿qué le pareció?

opinionated [-eitid]; **opinionative** [-eitiv] *adj* testarudo, da; obstinado, da.

opium ['əupjəm] *n* opio *m*.

opium addict [-'ædikt] *n* opiómano, na.

opium addiction [-ə'dikʃən] *n* opiomanía *f*.

opium den [-den] *n* fumadero *m* de opio.

opiumism [-izəm] *n* opiomanía *f*.

opium poppy [-'pɔpi] *n* BOT adormidera *f*.

opium smoker [-'sməukə*] *n* fumador *m* de opio.

Oporto [əu'pɔːtəu] *pr n* GEOGR Oporto.

opossum [ə'pɔsəm] *n* ZOOL oposum *m*, zarigüeya *f*.

opponent [ə'pəunənt] *n* adversario, ria; contrario, ria; oponente *m* & *f*, contrincante *m* & *f* (adversary) || competidor, ra (competitor).
◆ *adj* opuesto, ta; contrario, ria || ANAT oponente (muscle).

opportune ['ɔpətjuːn] *adj* oportuno, na; *he has come at an opportune moment* llega en un momento oportuno.

opportunism ['ɔpətjuːnizəm] *n* oportunismo *m*.

opportunist ['ɔpətjuːnist] *adj/n* oportunista.

opportunistic [ɔpətjuː'nistik] *adj* oportunista.

opportunity [ˌɔpə'tjuːniti] *n* oportunidad *f*, ocasión *f*; *if I get the opportunity* si la ocasión se presenta || oportunidad *f*; *equality of opportunity* igualdad de oportunidades; *to have the opportunity of* tener la oportunidad de || — *opportunity makes the thief* la ocasión hace al ladrón || *to seize, to miss an opportunity* aprovechar, perder una oportunidad || *we should like to take this opportunity to* quisiéramos aprovechar esta ocasión *or* esta oportunidad para.

opposable [ə'pəuzəbl] *adj* oponible.

oppose [ə'pəuz] *vt* oponerse a; *to oppose a motion, a plan* oponerse a una moción, a un proyecto || oponer; *to oppose two teams* oponer dos equipos.
◆ *vi* oponerse.

opposed [-d] *adj* opuesto, ta || — *as opposed to* en comparación con || *to be opposed to* oponerse a, estar en contra de (not to agree), ir en contra de; *what you say is opposed to all reason* lo que Ud dice va en contra del sentido común.

opposer [-ə*] *n* oponente *m* & *f*, adversario, ria.

opposing [-iŋ] *adj* adversario, ria; contrario, ria; opuesto, ta; *opposing team* equipo adversario.

opposite ['ɔpəzit] *adj* opuesto, ta; contrario, ria; *in the opposite direction* en dirección contraria || de enfrente; *he ran to the opposite house* corrió a la casa de enfrente || contrario, ria; *a member of the opposite faction* un miembro de la facción contraria || opuesto, ta; *his tastes were completely opposite to mine* sus gustos eran completamente opuestos a los míos; *the opposite page* la página opuesta; *the opposite bank* la ribera opuesta || PHYS & MATH opuesto, ta; *opposite angles* ángulos opuestos || BOT opuesto, ta || — *opposite number* colega *m* & *f* || *the opposite sex* el otro sexo || *to hold an opposite view to* no estar de acuerdo con || *to hold opposite views* no estar de acuerdo || *to take the opposite view* defender la opinión contraria || *your house is opposite to mine* su casa está frente a la mía *or* enfrente de la mía.
◆ *n* lo opuesto, lo contrario; *she says one thing but means the opposite* dice una cosa pero piensa lo contrario; *«big» is the opposite of «small»* «grande» es lo contrario de «pequeño» || *the opposite is true of women* es todo lo contrario para las mujeres.
◆ *adv* enfrente; *the post office is opposite* Correos está enfrente.
◆ *prep* enfrente de, frente a; *the hotel is opposite the church* el hotel está frente a la iglesia.

opposition [ˌɔpə'ziʃən] *n* oposición *f*, desacuerdo *m*; *I am in opposition to the policies of the country* estoy en oposición *or* en desacuerdo con la política del país || oposición *f*, partido *m* de la oposición (party not in power) || oposición *f* (group opposed to plan, to policy, etc.) || resistencia *f*; *they met with little opposition* encontraron poca resistencia || ASTR oposición *f* || COMM competencia *f* (competition) || — *the opposition party, the party in opposition* el partido de la oposición || *to be in opposition* estar en la oposición (a party).

oppositionist [ɔpə'ziʃənist] *n* oposicionista *m* & *f*.

oppress [ə'prəs] *vt* oprimir; *the tyrant oppressed the poor* el tirano oprimía a los pobres || oprimir, agobiar (mentally).

oppressed [-t] *adj* oprimido, da.
◆ *pl n* oprimidos *m*.

oppression [ə'preʃən] *n* opresión *f*.

oppressive [ə'presiv] *adj* opresor, ra; opresivo, va; tiránico, ca; *an oppressive government* un gobierno opresivo || sofocante, bochornoso, sa; *the oppressive heat* el calor sofocante || agobiante (mental burden).

oppressiveness [-nis] *n* opresión *f* (of government, etc.) || bochorno *m* (of the atmosphere).

oppressor [ə'presə*] *n* opresor, ra.

opprobrious [ə'prəubriəs] *adj* oprobioso, sa.

opprobrium [ə'prəubriəm] *n* oprobio *m*.

oppugn [ɔ'pjuːn] *vt* opugnar, atacar.

oppugnation [ɔpju'neiʃən] *n* opugnación *f*, ataque *m* (attack).

oppugner [ɔ'pjuːnə*] *n* opugnador *m*.

opt [ɔpt] *vi* *to opt for* optar por, escoger (to choose) || *to opt in* optar por participar *or* colaborar || *to opt out* optar por no participar *or* no colaborar || *to opt to* optar por.

optative ['ɔptətiv] *adj* GRAMM optativo, va.
◆ *n* GRAMM optativo *m*.

optic ['ɔptik] *adj* óptico, ca; *optic nerve, angle* nervio, ángulo óptico.
◆ *n* FAM ojo *m* (eye).

optical [-əl] *adj* óptico, ca; *optical instruments* instrumentos ópticos || — INFORM *optical character recognition* reconocimiento *m* óptico de caracteres || *optical disk* disco *m* óptico || *optical fibre* fibra *f* óptica || *optical illusion* ilusión óptica || *optical telegraph* telégrafo óptico.

optician [ɔp'tiʃən] *n* MED óptico *m*.

optics ['ɔptiks] *n* PHYS óptica *f*.

optimism ['ɔptimizəm] *n* optimismo *m*.

optimist ['ɔptimist] *n* optimista *m* & *f*.

optimistic [ˌɔpti'mistik] *adj* optimista.

optimistically [-əli] *adv* con optimismo.

optimize ['ɔptimaiz] *vt* mejorar *or* perfeccionar lo más posible.

optimum ['ɔptiməm] *adj* óptimo, ma; *optimum conditions* condiciones óptimas.
◆ *n* lo óptimo.
— OBSERV El plural de *optimum* es *optimums* u *optima*.

option ['ɔpʃən] *n* opción *f*; *to rent a house with the option of purchase* alquilar una casa con opción a compra; *to take out an option on* tomar una opción sobre || posibilidad *f* || elección *f* (choice) || — *I had no option but to go* no tuve más remedio que ir || *to make one's option between* escoger entre.

optional ['ɔpʃənl] *adj* facultativo, va (not compulsory) || — *dress optional* traje de etiqueta o de calle || *it is optional with you whether you go or stay* puede irse o quedarse.

opulence ['ɔpjuləns] *n* opulencia *f*.

opulent ['ɔpjulənt] *adj* opulento, ta (rich, full) || abundante.

opus ['əupəs] *n* MUS obra *f*, opus *m*.
— OBSERV El plural de la palabra inglesa *opus* es *opuses* u *opera*.

opuscule [ɔ'pʌsk'juːl] *n* opúsculo *m*.

opusculum [ɔ'pʌskjələm] *n* opúsculo *m*.
— OBSERV El plural de la palabra inglesa es *opuscula*.

or [ɔː*] *n* HERALD oro *m*.

or [ɔː*] *conj* o; *clean or dirty* limpio o sucio; *the sea can be blue or green* el mar puede ser azul o verde; *his accent is good, or at least not bad* su acento es bueno o por lo menos no es malo || ni (with negation); *with no house or money* sin casa ni dinero; *he cannot walk or run* no puede andar ni correr || — *a dozen or so* una docena poco más o menos || *or else* si no || *or not* o no.
— OBSERV In Spanish *o* changes to *u* before a word beginning with *o* or *ho*: *shame or pride* vergüenza u orgullo; *woman or man* mujer u hombre.

oracle ['ɔrəkl] *n* oráculo *m*.

oracular [ɔ'rækjulə*] *adj* del oráculo || oscuro, ra (mysterious) || sentencioso, sa || profético, ca.

oral ['ɔːrəl] *adj* oral; *oral medicine* medicina oral; *to pass the oral exams* aprobar los exámenes orales.
◆ *n* examen *m* oral, oral *m* (examination).

orally [-i] *adv* oralmente, de palabra.

orange ['ɔrindʒ] *n* BOT naranjo *m* (tree) | naranja *f* (fruit) || naranja *m* (colour) || *orange tree* naranjo.
◆ *adj* naranja *inv*, de color naranja.

Orange ['ɔrindʒ] *pr n* HIST Orange.

orangeade ['ɔrindʒ'eid] *n* naranjada *f*.

orange blossom ['ɔrindʒblɔsəm] *n* BOT azahar *m*.

orangle-flower water ['ɔrindʒ'flauə*'wɔːtə*] *n* agua *f* de azahar.

orange grove ['ɔrindʒ'grəuv] *n* BOT naranjal *m*.

orange grower ['ɔrindʒgrəuə*] *n* naranjero, ra.

orange juice ['ɔrindʒdʒuːs] *n* zumo *m* de naranja, jugo *m* de naranja.

orangery ['ɔrindʒəri] *n* invernadero *m* de naranjos.

orange seller ['ɔrindʒ'selə*] *n* naranjero, ra.

orange stick ['ɔrindʒstik] *n* palito *m* de naranjo (in manicuring).

orangewood ['ɔrindʒwud] *n* naranjo *m*, madera *f* de naranjo.

orangoutang ['ɔːrəŋ'uːtæŋ]; **orangutan** ['ɔːrəŋ'uːtæn] *n* ZOOL orangután *m*.

orant ['ɔrənt] *n* estatua *f* orante.

orate [ɔː'reit] *vi* perorar.

oration [ɔː'reiʃən] *n* oración *f*, discurso *m* || *funeral oration* oración fúnebre.

orator ['ɔrətə*] *n* orador, ra.

Oratorian [ɔrə'tɔːriən] *n* REL oratoriano *m*.

oratorical [ˌɔrə'tɔrikəl] *adj* oratorio, ria; *oratorical style* estilo oratorio.

oratorio [ˌɔrə'tɔːriəu] *n* MUS oratorio *m*.

oratory ['ɔrətəri] *n* REL oratorio *m* (chapel) || oratoria *f* (art of speech).

orb [ɔːb] *n* orbe *m*.

orbit ['ɔːbit] *n* ASTR órbita *f* || ANAT órbita *f* || FIG esfera *f*, órbita *f* || — *in orbit* en órbita || *putting into orbit* puesta *f* en órbita || *to put into orbit* poner en órbita.

orbit ['ɔːbit] *vi* estar en órbita (satellite) || dar vueltas, girar (to revolve); *the Moon orbits around the Earth* la Luna da vueltas alrededor de la Tierra.
◆ *vt* estar en órbita alrededor de (to be in orbit) || poner en órbita (to put into orbit) || dar vueltas a, girar alrededor de (a planet).

orbital [-əl] *adj* orbital; ***orbital flight*** vuelo orbital || orbitario, ria; ***orbital index*** índice orbitario.

orc [ɔːk] *n* ZOOL orca *f* (grampus).

orchard [ˈɔːtʃəd] *n* huerto *m* (in general) ‖ — *apple orchard* manzanal *m* ‖ *pear orchard* peral *m*.

orchestra [ˈɔːkistrə] *n* MUS orquesta *f* ‖ foso *m* de orquesta (pit) ‖ patio *m* de butacas (in theatre, in cinema) ‖ — *orchestra pit* foso de orquesta ‖ *orchestra seat* butaca *f* de patio.

orchestral [ɔːˈkestrəl] *adj* orquestal.

orchestrate [ˈɔːkistreit] *vt* MUS orquestar.

orchestration [ˌɔːkesˈtreiʃən] *n* MUS orquestación *f*.

orchid [ˈɔːkid] *n* BOT orquídea *f*.

orchidaceae [ˌɔːkiˈdeisiiː] *pl n* BOT orquidáceas *f*.

ordain [ɔːˈdein] *vt* REL ordenar; *to ordain s.o. deacon* ordenar a uno diácono ‖ decretar, ordenar (to decree) ‖ FIG destinar (to destine) ‖ *to be ordained* ser ordenado, ordenarse.

ordainer [-ə*] *n* REL ordenador *m*.

ordaining [-iŋ] *adj* REL ordenador, ra.

ordeal [ɔːˈdiːl] *n* prueba *f* muy dura, sufrimiento *m*; *twenty four hours of walking is an ordeal* veinticuatro horas de marcha es una prueba muy dura ‖ *after such an ordeal* después de tanto sufrir.
◆ *pl* HIST ordalías *f*.

order [ˈɔːdə*] *n* orden *m*; *in alphabetical, in chronological order* en *or* por orden alfabético, en *or* por orden cronológico; *to put one's affairs in order* poner sus asuntos en orden; *in order of seniority* por orden de antigüedad; *order of priority* orden de prioridad ‖ orden *m*; *law and order* el orden público; *the police kept order* la policía mantuvo el orden; *to call to order* llamar al orden; *to keep order in a class* mantener el orden en una clase ‖ regla *f*; *your licence is in order* su permiso está en regla; *it's all in order* todo está en regla ‖ orden *f* (title); *the Order of the British Empire, of the Garter* la Orden del Imperio Británico, de la Jarretera; *order of knighthood, Order of the Golden Fleece* orden de caballería, Orden del Toisón de Oro ‖ condecoración *f* (medal) ‖ MIL orden *f*; *to give orders* cumplir las órdenes | orden *m*; *in battle order* en orden de combate; *close, open order* orden cerrado, abierto ‖ REL orden *m* (of the angels) | orden *f*; *monastic order* orden monástica; *the Dominican Order* la orden dominicana; *Holy Orders* órdenes sagradas ‖ JUR fallo *m*, sentencia *f* (of the court) | mandato *m*, mandamiento *m*, orden *f* (of the judge) ‖ COMM pedido *m*; *to place an order with* hacer un pedido a; *order form* orden de pedido; *order number* número de pedido; *rush order* pedido urgente | giro *m*; *postal, banker's order* giro postal, bancario ‖ ARCH & BOT orden *m*; *Gothic, Ionic order* orden gótico, jónico ‖ MATH grado *m*; *equation of the first order* ecuación de primer grado ‖ FIG calidad *f*, orden *m*, categoría *f*; *of the first order* de primera calidad | tipo *m*, índole *f* (kind); *problems of a different order* problemas de distinto tipo ‖ ZOOL orden *m*; *of the orthopteran order* del orden de los ortópteros ‖ — *am I in order?* ¿me autoriza el reglamento? ‖ *at the order of* por orden de ‖ MIL *at your orders!* ¡a la orden! ‖ COMM *bill to order* pagaré *m*, billete *m* a la orden ‖ *by order of* por orden de ‖ COMM *cheque to order* cheque nominativo | *delivery order* orden *f* de expedición ‖ JUR *departmental order* orden *f* ministerial ‖ *he gave me orders to do it* me mandó hacerlo, me mandó que lo hiciera ‖ MIL *in gala order* en uniforme de gala ‖ *in order* en orden (in the correct disposition), bien; *a piece of toast would be in order* una tostada me vendría bien; que funciona (working); *is the machine in order again?* ¿funciona ahora la máquina?; pertinente; *your question is in order, sir* su pregunta es pertinente, señor; aceptable, admisible (motions, amendment), en regla; *your papers are in order* sus papeles están en regla ‖ *in order of appearance* por orden de aparición ‖ *in order that* para que; *I did it in order that he should come out* lo hice para que saliese ‖ *in order to* para; *in order to be able to go* para poder ir; para, a; *I went to London in order to see the Queen* me fui a Londres para ver a la reina ‖ US *in short order* en seguida (at once) ‖ *in working order* que funciona; *everything is in working order* todo funciona ‖ *it is in order for me to suggest sth.?* ¿puedo proponer algo?, ¿me permiten que proponga algo? ‖ *made to order* hecho a la medida ‖ *of the order of* del mismo estilo que, parecido a (similar); *my village is of the order of yours* mi pueblo es del mismo estilo que el tuyo; del orden de; *sth. of the order of five pounds* una cantidad del orden de cinco libras ‖ *on order* pedido, da; *we have twenty thousand books on order* tenemos pedidos *or* hemos pedido veinte mil libros ‖ *order of arrest* orden *f* de detención *or* de arresto ‖ *Order of Council* Real Orden *f* ‖ MIL *order of the day* orden *f* del día ‖ COMM *pay to the order of* páguese a la orden de ‖ *point of order* cuestión *f* de orden ‖ *sailing orders* últimas instrucciones [dadas al capitán de un barco] ‖ COMM *standing order* pedido regular ‖ *that's an order!* ¡es una orden! ‖ FIG *that's a tall* o *a large order* eso es mucho pedir ‖ *the meeting is called to order* se abre la sesión ‖ *the new, the old order* el nuevo, el antiguo régimen ‖ *to be out of order* no funcionar (a machine); *the lift is out of order* el ascensor no funciona; estar en desorden (not in the correct sequence); *these pages are out of order* estas páginas están en desorden; hablar cuando no se debe (in meetings, etc.), no ser pertinente (a question), estar descompuesto; *my tummy is out of order* tengo el vientre descompuesto; estar fuera de lugar (out of place) ‖ FIG *to be the order of the day* estar de moda ‖ MIL *to come to order* descansar armas ‖ *to declare a candidature out of order* rechazar una candidatura ‖ *to get out of order* estropearse ‖ *to keep order* mantener el orden ‖ *to put in order* poner en orden, ordenar (to arrange), poner en orden, arreglar (a matter) ‖ *to put sth. on order* pedir algo ‖ *to restore order* restablecer el orden ‖ *to rule a question out of order* rechazar una pregunta.
◆ *pl* clase *f sing* (class); *the lower orders* la clase baja ‖ — REL *major, minor, mendicant orders* órdenes *f* mayores, menores, mendicantes ‖ *no-one gives me orders!* ¡a mí nadie me da órdenes!, ¡a mí nadie me manda! ‖ REL *to be in holy orders* ser sacerdote ‖ *standing orders* reglamento *m* general (of committee, etc.) ‖ *till further orders* hasta nueva orden ‖ SP *to be under starter's orders* estar esperando la orden de salida ‖ *to be under the orders of* estar bajo las órdenes *or* el mando de ‖ FIG *to get one's marching orders* ser despedido ‖ FIG *to give s.o. his marching orders* despedir a uno ‖ COMM *unfilled orders* pedidos pendientes ‖ REL *to take holy orders* tomar las órdenes sagradas, ordenarse.

order [ˈɔːdə*] *vt* ordenar, poner en orden; *to order one's affairs* poner en orden sus asuntos ‖ clasificar (to classify) ‖ organizar (one's life) ‖ ordenar, mandar; *I order you to do it* le ordeno que lo haga ‖ mandar; *to order s.o. in, out, back* mandar a uno entrar, salir, volver ‖ COMM pedir, encargar, hacer un pedido de (goods) ‖ encargar; *yesterday I ordered a coat* ayer encargué un abrigo ‖ pedir, encargar (in restaurant, etc.) ‖ MED mandar; *the doctor ordered him to stay in bed* el médico le mandó que se quedara en cama | recetar (to prescribe) ‖ MIL mandar (to send, to command) ‖ — *order, arms!* ¡descansen!, ¡ar! ‖ *to order s.o. about* mandar a uno de acá para allá, estar siempre dándole órdenes a uno ‖ *to order s.o. off* mandar a uno que se vaya (to send away), expulsar (a player in sports).

order blank [-blæŋk] *n* orden *f* de pedido.

order book [-buk] *n* libro *m* de pedidos.

ordered [ˈɔːdəd] *adj* ordenado, da.

ordering [ˈɔːdəriŋ] *n* ordenamiento *m* ‖ INFORM clasificación *f*.

orderliness [ˈɔːdəlinis] *n* orden *m* ‖ método *m* ‖ disciplina *f*.

orderly [ˈɔːdəli] *adj* ordenado, da; en orden (tidy) ‖ ordenado, da; metódico, ca (careful) ‖ pacífico, ca; disciplinado, da; tranquilo, la; *an orderly crowd* una multitud disciplinada.
◆ *n* MIL ordenanza *m* ‖ US MED enfermero *m* (nurse) ‖ — *orderly officer* oficial *m* de servicio ‖ *orderly room* oficina *f* de la compañía.

ordinal [ˈɔːdinl] *adj* ordinal.
◆ *n* número *m* ordinal, ordinal *m* ‖ REL ordinal *m*.

ordinance [ˈɔːdinəns] *n* JUR ordenanza *f* ‖ REL rito *m* (rite) | eucaristía *f*.

ordinarily [ˈɔːdnrili] *adv* generalmente, en general, ordinariamente.

ordinariness [ˈɔːdnrinis] *n* mediocridad *f*.

ordinary [ˈɔːdnri] *adj* corriente, habitual, usual; *in the ordinary way* de la manera corriente ‖ corriente, ordinario, ria; *the ordinary model* el modelo corriente ‖ corriente, cualquiera; *it cannot be done with an ordinary pencil* no se puede hacer con un lápiz cualquiera ‖ simple; *he was just an ordinary tourist* no era más que un simple turista ‖ medio, dia; *the ordinary reader* el lector medio; *the ordinary Spaniard* el español medio ‖ regular, ordinario, ria; mediocre (mediocre); *a very ordinary piece of work* un trabajo muy ordinario ‖ — *in ordinary use* empleado normalmente *or* habitualmente ‖ MAR *ordinary seaman* marinero *m* ‖ *ordinary shares* acciones ordinarias.
◆ *n* lo corriente, lo ordinario (the usual) ‖ REL ordinario *m* (bishop) | ordinario *m* de la Misa (order of service) ‖ JUR ordinario *m* (judge) ‖ — *above the ordinary* fuera de lo común ‖ *in ordinary* habitual; *purveyor in ordinary to* proveedor habitual de ‖ *out of the ordinary* extraordinario, ria; fuera de lo común, excepcional; *the film was nothing out of the ordinary* la película no era nada excepcional.

ordinate [ˈɔːdnit] *n* MATH ordenada *f*.

ordination [ˌɔːdiˈneiʃən] *n* REL ordenación *f* (of a priest) ‖ disposición *f*, ordenación *f* (arrangement).

ordnance [ˈɔːdnəns] *n* MIL artillería *f* (artillery); *ordnance officer* oficial de artillería | material *m* de guerra (material) | servicio *m* de material de guerra (department) ‖ — *Ordnance Survey* servicio *m* oficial de topografía y cartografía ‖ *ordnance survey map* mapa *m* de estado mayor.

ordure [ˈɔːdjuə*] *n* basura *f* (rubbish) ‖ porquería *f* (filth) ‖ excremento *m* (excrement) ‖ estiércol *m* (manure).

ore [ɔː*] *n* MIN mineral *m*, mena *f*; *iron ore* mineral de hierro.

oread [ˈɔːriæd] *n* MYTH oréada *f*, oréade *f*.

oregano [ɔˈregəunəu] *n* orégano *m*.

Oregon [ˈɔrigən] *pr n* GEOGR Oregón.

organ [ˈɔːgən] *n* MUS órgano *m* ‖ ZOOL, ANAT & BOT órgano *m*; *the organs of digestion* los órganos de la digestión ‖ FIG órgano *m*; *the organ of the democratic party* el órgano del partido democrático ‖ MUS *barrel organ* organillo *m*, órgano de manubrio.

organdie; US **organdy** [ˈɔːgəndi] *n* organdí *m*.

organ-grinder [ˈɔːgəngraində*] *n* organillero, ra.

organic [ɔːˈgænik] *adj* orgánico, ca; *organic chemistry* química orgánica.

organism [ˈɔːgənizəm] *n* organismo *m*.

organist ['ɔːgənist] *n* MUS organista *m* & *f*.

organization [,ɔːgənai'zeiʃən] *n* organización *f*.

organize ['ɔːgənaiz] *vt* organizar; *to organize a party* organizar una fiesta; *he organizes the trade union* organiza el sindicato || *to get organized* organizarse.
◆ *vi* organizarse.

organized [-d] *adj* organizado, da || *organized labour* obreros sindicados.

organizer [-ə*] *n* organizador, ra || BIOL organizador *m*.

organizing [-iŋ] *adj* organizador, ra.
◆ *n* organización *f* (action).

organ stop ['ɔːgən,stɔp] *n* MUS registro *m* de órgano.

organum ['ɔːgənəm] *n* MUS organum *m*.

organzine ['ɔːgənziːn] *n* torzal *m*.

orgasm ['ɔːgæzəm] *n* orgasmo *m*.

orgeat ['ɔːʒə] *n* horchata *f*.

orgiastic [,ɔːdʒi'æstik] *adj* orgiástico, ca.

orgy ['ɔːdʒi] *n* orgía *f* (debauchery) || FIG orgía *f*; *an orgy of colour* una orgía de colores.

oriel ['ɔːriəl] *n* mirador *m*.

orient ['ɔːriənt] *n* oriente *m* (lustre) || perla *f* fina (pearl) || oriente *m* (east) || *the Orient* el Oriente.
◆ *adj* brillante || oriental.

orient ['ɔːriənt] *vt* orientar || *to orient o.s.* orientarse.

Oriental [,ɔːri'entl] *adj/n* oriental.

Orientalism [,ɔːri'entəlizəm] *n* orientalismo *m*.

orientalize [,ɔːri'entəlaiz] *vt* orientalizar.
◆ *vi* orientalizarse.

orientate ['ɔːrienteit] *vt* orientar || *to orientate o.s.* orientarse.

orientation [,ɔːrien'teiʃən] *n* orientación *f*.

orienteering [,ɔːrien'tiːriŋ] *n* SP marcha *f* de orientación.

orifice ['ɔrifis] *n* orificio *m*.

oriflamme ['ɔriflæm] *n* oriflama *f*.

origan ['ɔrigən] *n* BOT orégano *m*.

origin ['ɔridʒin] *n* origen *m* || origen *m*, procedencia *f*; *country of origin* país de origen.
◆ *pl* origen *m sing*; *of humble origins* de origen humilde.

original [ə'ridʒənl] *adj* original; *original work, sin* obra, pecado original || primero, ra; *one of the original members* uno de los primeros miembros || original, primero, ra; *original sense of a word* primer sentido de una palabra || original (not common); *original taste* gusto original.
◆ *n* original *m* (work); *the original of this copy is in Paris* el original de esta copia está en París || persona *f* original (an eccentric).

originality [ə,ridʒi'næliti] *n* originalidad *f*.

originally [ə'ridʒnəli] *adv* en un principio, al principio, originariamente (initially) || con originalidad (in an original manner).

originate [ə'ridʒineit] *vt* originar, causar, provocar; *the spring thaw originates floods* el deshielo primaveral origina inundaciones || crear, inventar (to create).
◆ *vi* comenzar, empezar (to begin); *how did your friendship originate?* ¿cómo empezó vuestra amistad? || ser originario de; *the custom originated in Wales* la costumbre es originaria de Gales || — *the plan originated with him* es el autor del proyecto || *to originate from* ser descendiente de || *to originate from* o *in* tener su origen en.

origination [ə,ridʒi'neiʃən] *n* origen *m* (source) || creación *f*, invención *f* (creation) || principio *m* (beginning).

originative [ə'ridzineitiv] *adj* inventivo, va; creador, ra.

originator [ə'ridzineitə*] *n* autor, ra; creador, ra.

Orinoco [,ɔri'nəukəu] *pr n* GEOGR Orinoco *m*.

oriole ['ɔːriəul] *n* oropéndola *f* (bird).

Orion [ə'raiən] *pr n* ASTR Orión *m*.

orison ['ɔrizən] *n* plegaria *f*, oración *f*.

Orkney Islands ['ɔːkni'ailəndz] *pl prn* GEOGR Orcadas *f*.

Orkneys ['ɔːkniz] *pl prn* GEOGR Orcadas *f*.

orle [ɔːl] *n* HERALD orla *f*.

Orlon ['ɔːlɔn] *n* orlón *m* (fabric).

orlop ['ɔːlɔp] *n* MAR sollado *m*.

ormer ['ɔːmə*] *n* ZOOL oreja *f* de mar (shell).

ormolu ['ɔːməuluː] *n* oro *m* molido.

ornament ['ɔːnəmənt] *n* ornamento *m*, adorno *m* (embellishment) || honra *f* (person) || REL ornamento *m* || AUT embellecedor *m*.
◆ *pl* MUS floreos *m*, adornos *m*.

ornament ['ɔːnəmənt] *vt* adornar, ornamentar, ornar.

ornamental [,ɔːnə'mentl] *adj* ornamental, decorativo, va; de adorno.

ornamentation [,ɔːnəment'teiʃən] *n* ornamentación *f*, decoración *f* || adornos *m pl*, decoración *f* (ornaments).

ornamenter ['ɔːnəməntə*] *n* decorador, ra.

ornate [ɔː'neit] *adj* adornado, da; ornado, da (adorned) || recargado, da (overadorned) || FIG florido, da (style).

ornateness [-nis] *n* adornos *m pl* excesivos || FIG estilo *m* florido.

ornery ['ɔnəri] *adj* US FAM terco, ca; tozudo, da.

ornithological [,ɔːniθə'lɔdʒikl] *adj* ornitológico, ca.

ornithologist [,ɔːni'θɔlədʒist] *n* ornitólogo *m*.

ornithology [,ɔːni'θɔlədʒi] *n* ornitología *f*.

ornithorhynchus [,ɔːniθə'riŋkəs] *n* ZOOL ornitorrinco *m*.

orogenesis [,ɔrəu'dʒenisis] *n* GEOL orogénesis *f*.

orogenic [ɔrə'dʒenik] *n* GEOL orogénico, ca.

orogeny [ɔ'rɔdʒəni] *n* GEOL orogenia *f*.

orographic [,ɔrəu'græfik]; **orographical** [-əl] *adj* orográfico, ca.

orography [ɔ'rɔgrəfi] *n* orografía *f*.

orometry [ɔ'rɔmetri] *n* orometría *f*.

orotund ['ɔrətʌnd] *adj* sonoro, ra (voice) || pomposo, sa; rimbombante (bombastic).

orphan ['ɔːfən] *adj/n* huérfano, na.

orphan ['ɔːfən] *vt* dejar huérfano.

orphanage ['ɔːfənidʒ] *n* orfanato *m*, asilo *m* de huérfanos (institution) || orfandad *f* (condition).

orphaned ['ɔːfənd] *adj* huérfano, na.

orphanhood ['ɔːfənhud] *n* orfandad *f*.

orphanize ['ɔːfənaiz] *vt* dejar huérfano.

Orphean [ɔː'fiən] *adj* órfico, ca.

Orpheus ['ɔːfjuːs] *pr n* Orfeo *m*.

Orphic ['ɔːfik] *adj* órfico, ca || FIG esotérico, ca | embelesador, ra (entrancing).

orrery ['ɔrəri] *n* planetario *m*.

orthocentre; *US* **orthocenter** [ɔːθə'sentə*] *n* MATH ortocentro *m*.

orthochromatic ['ɔːθəukrəu'mætik] *adj* ortocromático, ca.

orthodox ['ɔːθədɔks] *adj* ortodoxo, xa.

orthodoxy ['ɔːθədɔksi] *n* ortodoxia *f*.

orthoepy ['ɔːθəuepi] *n* ortología *f*.

orthogenesis [ɔːθə'dʒenesis] *n* ortogénesis *f*.

orthogenetic [ɔːθədʒi'netik] *adj* ortogenético, ca.

orthognathism [ɔː'θɔgnəθizəm] *n* ortognatismo *m*.

orthogonal [ɔː'θɔgənl] *adj* MATH ortogonal.

orthograpic [,ɔːθəu'græfik]; **orthographical** [-əl] *adj* ortográfico, ca || MATH ortogonal.

orthography [ɔː'θɔgrəfi] *n* GRAM ortografía *f* MATH proyección *f* ortogonal.

orthopaedic; *US* **orthopedic** [,ɔːθəu'piːdik] *adj* ortopédico, ca.

orthopaedics; *US* **orthopedics** [-s] *n* MED ortopedia *f*.

orthopaedist; *US* **orthopedist** [,ɔːθəu'piːdist] *n* ortopedista *m* & *f*, ortopédico, ca.

orthopteran [ɔː'θɔptərən] *adj* ortóptero, ra.
◆ *n* ZOOL ortóptero *m*.

orthopteron [ɔː'θɔptərən] *n* ZOOL ortóptero *m*.
— OBSERV El plural de la palabra inglesa es *orthoptera*.

orthopterous [ɔː'θɔptərəs] *adj* ZOOL ortóptero, ra.

orthotropic [,ɔːθəu'trɔpik] *adj* BOT ortótropo, pa.

ortolan ['ɔːtələn] *n* ZOOL hortelano *m* (European bunting).

Oscar ['ɔskə*] *n* Oscar *m* (reward).

oscillate ['ɔsileit] *vt* hacer oscilar.
◆ *vi* oscilar (to swing) || FIG oscilar, fluctuar, variar (to fluctuate); *the prices oscillate* los precios oscilan | vacilar (to be indecisive).

oscillating [-iŋ] *adj* oscilante.

oscillation [,ɔsi'leiʃən] *n* oscilación *f* || FIG fluctuación *f*, variación *f* (fluctuation) | vacilación *f*, oscilación *f* (hesitation).

oscillator ['ɔsileitə*] *n* oscilador *m*.

oscillatory ['ɔsilətəri] *adj* oscilatorio, ria; oscilante || vibratorio, ria.

oscillogram [ɔ'siləugræm] *n* PHYS oscilograma *m*.

oscillograph [ɔ'siləugræf] *n* PHYS oscilógrafo *m*.

oscilloscope [ɔ'siləskəup] *n* PHYS osciloscopio *m*.

osculate ['ɔskjuleit] *vt* besar (to kiss).
◆ *vi* besarse.

osculation [,ɔskju'leiʃən] *n* ósculo *m*, beso *m* (kiss).

osculum ['ɔskjuləm] *n* ósculo *m* (in sponges).
— OBSERV El plural de *osculum* es *oscula*.

osier ['əuʒə*] *n* BOT mimbrera *f*, mimbre *m* (tree) || mimbre *m* (rod).
◆ *adj* de mimbre || *osier bed* mimbrera *f*, mimbreral *m*, mimbral *m*.

osiery [-ri] *n* mimbreral *m*, mimbral *m*, mimbrera *f* (osier bed) || cestería *f* (basketwork).

Osiris [əu'saiəris] *pr n* MYTH Osiris *m*.

Oslo ['ɔzləu] *pr n* GEOGR Oslo.

osmanli [ɔz'mænli] *adj/n* osmanlí, otomano, na.

osmic ['ɔzmik] *adj* CHEM ósmico, ca.

osmium ['ɔzmiəm] *n* CHEM osmio *m*.

osmometer [ɔz'mɔmitə*] *n* PHYS osmómetro *m*.

osmosis [ɔz'məusis] *n* ósmosis *f*.

osmotic [ɔz'mɔtik] *adj* osmótico, ca.

osmous ['ɔzməus] *adj* ósmico, ca.

osprey ['ɔspri] *n* quebrantahuesos *m inv*, pigargo *m* (bird) || airón *m* (trimming).

ossein ['ɔsiin] *n* oseína *f*.

osseous ['ɔsiəs] *adj* óseo, a.

ossification [ˌɔsifiˈkeiʃən] *n* osificación *f.*

ossifrage [ˈɔsifridʒ] *n* ZOOL quebrantahuesos *m inv*, pigargo *m* (bird) ‖ airón *m* (trimming).

ossify [ˈɔsifai] *vt* osificar.

◆ *vi* osificarse.

ossuary [ˈɔsjuəri] *n* osario *m.*

osteal [ˈɔstiəl] *adj* óseo, a.

ostein [ˈɔstiin] *n* CHEM osteína *f.*

osteitis [ɔstiˈaitis] *n* MED osteítis *f.*

ostensible [ɔsˈtensəbl] *adj* aparente.

ostensibly [ɔsˈtensəbli] *adv* aparentemente.

ostensive [ɔsˈtensiv] *adj* aparente ‖ ostensible, manifiesto, ta (obvious).

ostensory [ɔsˈtensəri] *n* REL custodia *f.*

ostentation [ˌɔstenˈteiʃən] *n* ostentación *f.*

ostentatious [ˌɔstenˈteiʃəs] *adj* ostentoso, sa.

ostentatiousness [-nis] *n* ostentación *f.*

osteoarthritis [ɔstiəuɑːrˈθraitis] *n* MED osteoartritis *f.*

osteoblast [ˈɔstiəblæst] *n* osteoblasto *m.*

osteologic [ˌɔstiəˈlɔdʒik]; **osteological** [-əl] *adj* osteológico, ca.

osteologist [ˌɔstiˈɔlədʒist] *n* osteólogo, ga.

osteology [ɔstiˈɔlədʒi] *n* osteología *f.*

osteoma [ɔstiˈəumə] *n* MED osteoma *m.*

— OBSERV El plural de la palabra inglesa es *osteomas* u *osteomata.*

osteomyelitis [ɔstiəmaiəˈlaitis] *n* MED osteomielitis *f.*

osteopath [ˈɔstiəpæθ] *n* MED osteópata *m* & *f.*

osteopathic [ˌɔstiəˈpæθik] *adj* MED osteopático, ca.

osteopathy [ˌɔstiˈɔpəθi] *n* MED osteopatía *f.*

osteoplasty [ɔstiəˈplæsti] *n* MED osteoplastia *f.*

osteoporosis [ˌɔstiəupəˈrəusis] *n* MED osteoporosis *f inv.*

osteotomy [ɔstiˈɔtəmi] *n* MED osteotomía *f.*

ostiary [ˈɔstiəri] *adj* ostiario *m.*

ostler [ˈɔstlə*] *n* mozo *m* de cuadra, palafrenero *m.*

ostmark [ˈɔstmɑːk] *n* marco *m* [de Alemania Oriental].

ostracism [ˈɔstrəsizəm] *n* ostracismo *m.*

ostracize [ˈɔstrəsaiz] *vt* condenar al ostracismo.

ostreiculture [ˈɔstriikʌltʃə*] *n* ostricultura *f.*

ostrich [ˈɔstritʃ] *n* avestruz *m* (bird).

Ostrogoth [ˈɔstrəugɔθ] *n* HIST ostrogodo, da.

Ostrogothic [-ik] *adj* ostrogodo, da.

otalgia [əˈtældʒiə] *n* MED otalgia *f.*

otalgic [əˈtældʒik] *adj* otálgico, ca.

otary [ˈəutəri] *n* ZOOL otaria *f.*

Othello [əuˈθeləu] *pr n* Otelo *m.*

other [ˈʌðə*] *adj* otro, tra; *your other hand* tu otra mano; *no other place to go* ningún otro sitio a donde ir; *some other examples* algunos otros ejemplos; *the youth of other days* la juventud de otros tiempos; *the other day* el otro día; *the other world* el otro mundo ‖ diferente, distinto, ta; *his tastes are quite other than mine* sus gustos son bastante diferentes a *or* de los míos ‖ — *among* o *amongst other things* entre otras cosas ‖ *every other day* cada dos días, un día sí y otro no ‖ *on the other hand* por otra parte, por otro lado ‖ *other people* otros ‖ *other people's property* los bienes ajenos ‖ *some day or other* un día u otro ‖ *the other one* el otro, la otra.

◆ *n/pron* otro, tra; *show me the others* enséñeme los otros; *open the other* abra el otro ‖ — *a few others* otros pocos ‖ *among others* entre otros ‖ *each other* uno a otro, el uno al otro ‖ *many others* otros muchos ‖ *no other* ningún otro ‖ *no other than* nadie más que (person) ‖ *one after the other* uno después del otro, uno tras otro ‖ *one or other of you* uno de vosotros ‖ *someone or other* uno u otro ‖ *some other* otra persona, otro ‖ *the others* los otros, los demás.

◆ *adv other than* de otra manera que.

otherwise [-waiz] *adj* distinto, ta; diferente, otro, tra; *if circumstances were otherwise* si las circunstancias fuesen distintas.

◆ *adv* de otra manera, de otro modo (in a different way) ‖ si no, de lo contrario; *do it now, otherwise you will forget* hazlo ahora, si no lo olvidarás ‖ aparte de eso, por lo demás (in other respects); *he broke a leg but was otherwise unhurt* se rompió una pierna, pero aparte de eso no le pasó nada.

otherworldliness [-ˈwəːldlinis] *n* alejamiento *m or* desapego *m* del mundo.

otherworldly [-ˈwəːldli] *adj* alejado del mundo, desapegado del mundo.

otiose [ˈəuʃiəus] *adj* ocioso, sa (idle) ‖ ocioso, sa; inútil (useless).

otiosity [əuʃiɔsiti] *n* ociosidad *f* (idleness) ‖ inutilidad *f* (uselessness).

otitis [əuˈtaitis] *n* MED otitis *f.*

otolaryngology [ˌɔtəulæriŋˈgɔlədʒi] *n* MED otolaringología *f.*

otologist [əuˈtɔlədʒist] *n* MED otólogo *m.*

otology [əuˈtɔlədʒi] *n* MED otología *f.*

otorhinolaryngology [ˌɔtəurainəulæriŋˈgɔlədʒi] *n* MED otorrinolaringología *f.*

otoscope [ˈəutəskəup] *n* otoscopio *m.*

Ottawa [ˈɔtəwə] *pr n* GEOGR Ottawa.

otter [ˈɔtə*] *n* nutria *f* (animal, fur).

Ottoman [-mən] *n* otomano, na; *Ottoman Empire* Imperio Otomano.

ottoman [-mən] *n* otomana *f* (divan).

oubliette [ˌuːbliˈet] *n* mazmorra *f* (dungeon).

ouch [autʃ] *interj* ¡ay!

ought [ɔːt] *v aux* deber; *we ought to tell them* deberíamos decírselo; *to sleep more than one ought* dormir más de lo que se debe ‖ tener que; *you ought to have been with us yesterday* tenías que haber estado con nosotros ayer.

— OBSERV El verbo *ought* va seguido por el infinitivo con *to.*

ought [ɔːt] *n* —→ **aught.**

oughtn't [ɔːtnt] contracción de «ought not».

ouija [ˈwiːdʒɑː] *n* tabla *f* con signos.

ounce [auns] *n* onza *f* (weight of 28.35 g) ‖ FAM pizca *f*; *not an ounce of sympathy* ni una pizca de simpatía ‖ ZOOL onza *f.*

our [ˈauə*] *poss adj* nuestro, nuestra; nuestros, nuestras; *our sisters* nuestras hermanas.

ours [-z] *poss pron* nuestro, nuestra, el nuestro, la nuestra, nuestros, nuestras, los nuestros, las nuestras; *this book is ours* este libro es nuestro, este libro es el nuestro; *these are ours* éstos son nuestros, éstos son los nuestros ‖ el nuestro, la nuestra, los nuestros, las nuestras; *your house is larger than ours* su casa es más grande que la nuestra ‖ nuestro, nuestra, nuestros, nuestras; *the fault is ours* la culpa es nuestra ‖ — *it is not ours to blame him* no somos quienes para criticarle ‖ *of ours* nuestro, nuestra; *a friend of ours* un amigo nuestro; *it is no business of ours* no es asunto nuestro ‖ FAM *that gardener of ours!* ¡ese maldito jardinero!

ourself [-ˈself] *pron* (ant) nos (myself).

◆ *pl* nos (reflexive); *we can wash ourselves* podemos lavarnos ‖ nosotros, nosotras, nosotros mismos, nosotras mismas; *we always speak of ourselves* siempre hablamos de nosotros ‖ nosotros mismos, nosotras mismas (emphatic).

— OBSERV El plural de *ourself* es *ourselves.*

oust [aust] *vt* expulsar, echar (to eject) ‖ desahuciar, desalojar (a tenant) ‖ desalojar, expulsar (the enemy) ‖ derribar (government) ‖ desbancar (s.o. from a post) ‖ destituir (to remove from office) ‖ JUR desposeer (to dispossess) ‖ FIG desbancar, sustituir, suplantar.

ouster [-ə*] *n* JUR desposeimiento *m.*

out [aut] *adv* fuera; *to lock s.o. out* dejar a alguien fuera ‖ en huelga (on strike); *the workers are all out* todos los trabajadores están en huelga ‖ MED dislocado, da (joint) ‖ MIL preparado, da (troops) ‖ largado, da; soltado, da (rope) ‖ desplegado, da (sail) ‖ — *all out* a toda velocidad ‖ *day out* día *m* libre ‖ *inside out* al revés ‖ *it's my day out* es el día en que salgo ‖ *out and away* con mucho ‖ *out and out* completamente ‖ *out at sea* en alta mar, mar adentro ‖ *out here* por aquí (in these parts), aquí fuera (here outside) ‖ *out loud* en voz alta ‖ *out there* por allí (in those parts), allí fuera (outside) ‖ FAM *out with it!* ¡desembucha! ‖ *out with you!* ¡fuera de aquí! ‖ *right* o *straight out* sin rodeos ‖ *the tide is out* es marea baja ‖ *the voyage out* el viaje de ida ‖ *to be far* o *a long way out* estar muy equivocado (to make a mistake), estar muy lejos; *the house is far out* la casa está lejos ‖ *to be out* estar fuera, haber salido, no estar en casa; *Mrs Smith is out* la señora Smith ha salido; estar de viaje (traveling), pasar fuera; *to be out a lot* pasar mucho tiempo fuera; salir; *I was out with some friends yesterday* salí ayer con unos amigos; estar fuera, estar libre (prisoner), haber salido, haberse publicado; *the book is out* ha salido el libro; haber salido (sun), estar abierto (flower), haber salido del cascarón (bird), estar sin conocimiento; *he was out for seven seconds* estuvo sin conocimiento durante siete segundos; haberse apagado; *my cigarette is out* se ha apagado mi cigarrillo; estar apagado; *the fire is out* el fuego está apagado; acabarse, terminarse; *before the month is out* antes de que se acabe el mes; haberse agotado; *my patience is out* se me ha agotado la paciencia; haber pasado de moda, no estar ya de moda; *the miniskirt is out* ya no está de moda la minifalda; haberse descubierto; *the secret is out* el secreto se ha descubierto; estar fuera del poder; *now that my party is out* ahora que mi partido está fuera del poder; quedar descartado (possibility), estar eliminado (player), estar fuera de juego (ball), estar fuera de combate (boxer), estar desenvainado (sword), estar equivocado (to be mistaken); *you are out in your accounts* está equivocado en sus cuentas; faltar (to have too little); *I am five pounds out* me faltan cinco libras; adelantar (to be fast); *his watch is ten minutes out* su reloj adelanta diez minutos; atrasar (to be slow); *his watch is two minutes out* su reloj atrasa dos minutos; haber vencido (lease), haber sido presentada en sociedad (young girl) ‖ *to be out and about again* estar de nuevo en pie (after an illness) ‖ *to be out cold* haber perdido completamente el sentido *or* el conocimiento ‖ *to be out for* buscar; *to be out for revenge* buscar venganza ‖ *to be out to do sth.* estar decidido a *or* tener la intención de hacer algo ‖ *to be the best out* ser el mejor que ha habido; *she is the best singer out* es la mejor cantante que ha habido ‖ *to go all out to win* hacer todo lo posible para ganar ‖ *to go out to sea* hacerse a la mar ‖ *to have a day out on the beach* pasar un día en la playa ‖ *to have fallen out with* haber reñido con ‖ *to have one's cry out* llorar hasta más no poder ‖ *to hear out* escuchar hasta el final ‖ *to run out* salir corriendo.

◆ *prep* US por ‖ — *out of* fuera de aquí; *out of the house* fuera de la casa; *out of danger* fuera de peligro; *out of place* fuera de lugar; *out of season* fuera de temporada; *out of wedlock* fuera del matrimonio; por; *to jump out of the window* saltar por la ventana; *out of necessity*

por necesidad; *out of curiosity* por curiosidad; entre; *one criticism out of many* una crítica entre otras muchas; de cada; *ten out of fifteen* diez de cada quince; de; *a paragraph out of a chapter* un párrafo de un artículo; *built out of stone* hecho de piedra; en; *he took a cigarette out of my case* tomó un cigarrillo en mi petaca; sin; *out of breath* sin aliento || «*out of order*» «no funciona» || COMM *out of print* agotado, da || *out of reach* fuera del alcance || *out of sight, out of mind* ojos que no ven, corazón que no siente || *out of the corner of one's eye* con el rabillo del ojo || *out of work* sin trabajo, parado, da || *to be out of* habérsele agotado (a uno), no tener; *I am out of patience* se me ha agotado la paciencia; habérsele acabado (a uno), no tener; *I am out of money* se me ha acabado el dinero || *to be out of it* no estar metido en un asunto, quedar excluido (to be left out), no estar en el ajo (to be unaware) || *to be out of sight* no poder verse || *to drink out of* beber en (a glass), beber de (a bottle) || *to feel out of it* sentirse aislado || FAM *we're well out of it!* ¡de buena nos hemos librado!
◆ *adj* exterior, externo, na (part) || muy grande (size).
◆ *interj* ¡fuera!
◆ *n* PRINT bordón *m* || US FAM salida *f* (way out).
◆ *pl* US partido *m sing* que está fuera del poder || *the ins and outs* los pormenores, los detalles.
— OBSERV Cuando *out* acompaña un verbo, en general no puede traducirse literalmente. Es imprescindible, por consiguiente, consultar el artículo referente al verbo de que se trata.

out [aut] *vi* descubrirse; *the truth will out* la verdad se descubrirá.
◆ *vt* expulsar, echar.

out-and-out [autnd'aut] *adj* empedernido, da; redomado, da; cien por cien (thorough); *an out-and-out drunkard* un borracho empedernido; *an out-and-out liar* un mentiroso empedernido || cien por cien; *an out-and-out nationalist* un nacionalista cien por cien || acérrimo, ma (supporter).

outback ['autbæk] *n* interior *m*.

outbalance [aut'bæləns] *vt* exceder de peso, pesar más que (to weigh more) || superar (to be more important).

outbid* [aut'bid] *vt* pujar más alto que, sobrepujar.
— OBSERV Pret y pp ***outbid***.

outboard ['autbɔ:d] *adj* fuera borda, fuera bordo; *two outboard motors* dos motores fuera borda || exterior.
◆ *adv* fuera de la embarcación.
◆ *n* motor *m* fuera borda *or* fuera bordo (engine) || fuera borda *m inv*, fuera bordo *m inv* (boat).

outbound ['autbaund] *adj* que sale (ship, etc.).

outbrave [aut'breiv] *vt* arrostrar; *to outbrave the danger* arrostrar el peligro || ser más valiente que (to exceed in courage).

outbreak ['autbreik] *n* comienzo *m*; *the outbreak of war* el comienzo de la guerra || erupción *f* (of pimples) || brote *m* (of an epidemic) || epidemia *f* (of a disease); *an outbreak of influenza* una epidemia de gripe || motín *m*, insurrección *f*, sublevación *f* (insurrection) || ola *f*; *an outbreak of violence* una ola de violencia; *a crime outbreak* una ola de crímenes || arrebato *m*; *outbreak of temper* arrebato de cólera || — *at the outbreak of war* cuando estalló la guerra || *new outbreak* recrudescencia *f*.

outbred ['autbred] *pret/pp* ⟶ **outbreed.**

outbreed* ['autbri:d] *vt* criar por cruce de razas.
— OBSERV Pret y pp ***outbred***.

outbreeding ['aut'bri:diŋ] *n* cría *f* por cruce de razas || US matrimonio *m* entre razas o grupos sociales distintos.

outbuilding ['aut'bildiŋ] *n* dependencia *f*.

outburst ['autbə:st] *n* explosión *f* || arrebato *m*; *outburst of rage, of enthusiasm* arrebato de ira, de entusiasmo || arranque *m*; *outburst of generosity* arranque de generosidad || ataque *m* (of laughter) || — *outburst of applause* salva *f* de aplausos || *outburst of temper* arrebato de cólera, momento *m* de mal humor.

outcast ['autkɑ:st] *adj* proscrito, ta.
◆ *n* paria *m* & *f*, proscrito, ta || *to be a social outcast* vivir rechazado por la sociedad.

outcaste ['autkɑ:st] *n* paria *m* & *f*.

outclass [aut'klɑ:s] *vt* aventajar con mucho, ser muy superior a, superar.

outcome ['autkʌm] *n* resultado *m*; *what was the outcome of the match?* ¿cuál fue el resultado del partido? || consecuencias *f pl*.

outcrop ['autkrɔp] *n* GEOL afloramiento *m*.

outcry ['autkrai] *n* protesta *f* || alboroto *m* (din) || *to raise an outcry* protestar ruidosamente, poner el grito en el cielo (to protest), provocar fuertes protestas (to provoke protest).

outdated [aut'deitid] *adj* anticuado, da; pasado de moda.

outdid [autdid] *pret* ⟶ **outdo.**

outdistance [aut'distəns] *vt* dejar atrás.

outdo* [-'du:] *vt* superar, aventajar; *to outdo s.o. in sth.* aventajar a uno en algo || vencer, derrotar (to defeat) || — *not to be outdone* para no ser menos, para no quedarse atrás || *to outdo o.s.* superarse; *this time you have outdone yourself in generosity* esta vez se ha superado en generosidad.
— OBSERV Pret ***outdid***; pp ***outdone***.

outdone [aut'dʌn] *pp* ⟶ **outdo.**

outdoor ['autdɔ:*]; **out-of-door** [autəv'dɔ:] *adj* al aire libre; *an outdoor restaurant, sport* un restaurante, un deporte al aire libre || de calle (clothes) || externo, na (hospital activities, etc.) || JUR a domicilio (relief) || — CINEM *outdoor scenes* exteriores *m* || *to lead an outdoor life* vivir al aire libre.

outdoors [aut'dɔ:z]; **out-of-doors** ['autəv'dɔ:z] *adv* fuera; *clean your boots outdoors* límpiate las botas fuera || al aire libre (in the open air); *to eat outdoors* comer al aire libre.
◆ *n* aire *m* libre.

outer ['autə*] *adj* exterior, externo, na (side) || — *outer ear* oído externo || *outer space* espacio *m* exterior, espacio interplanetario.
◆ *n* círculo *m* exterior del blanco (ring of target).

outermost ['autə:məust] *adj* más exterior || más alejado, da; extremo, ma (part of a city) || *to travel to the outermost parts of the globe* recorrer las regiones más remotas de la Tierra.

outface [aut'feis] *vt* hacer bajar los ojos (to stare down) || desafiar (to defy).

outfall ['autfɔ:l] *n* desembocadura *f* (of a river) || desagüe *m*, desaguadero *m* (of a drain).

outfield ['autfi:ld] *n* SP parte *f* del campo más lejana del bateador (field).

outfit ['autfit] *n* equipo *m* (gear); *camping outfit* equipo de camping || juego *m* de herramientas (tools) || piezas *f pl* (components) || ropa *f* (clothes); *summer outfit* ropa de verano || traje *m* (suit) || conjunto *m* (lady's costume); *to wear a new outfit for the first time* estrenar un nuevo conjunto || uniforme *m* (uniform) || MIL unidad *f* || FAM grupo *m* (group); *the whole outfit was against him* todo el mundo estaba en contra suya | equipo *m*, cuadrilla *f* (of workers).

outfitter ['aut'fitə*] *n* vendedor *m* de ropa confeccionada para caballero, camisero *m* || *outfitter's* camisería *f*.

outflank [aut'flæŋk] *vt* MIL desbordar, rebasar || FIG burlar (to outwit).

outflow ['autfləu] *n* salida *f* (flowing out) || corriente *f* (of lava) || desagüe *m*, salida *f* (of a sewer).

outgeneral [aut'dʒenərəl] *vt* superar en estrategia *or* en táctica.

outgo ['autgəu] *n* US salida *f* (outflow) | gastos *m pl* (expense).

outgo* [aut'gəu] *vt* superar (to outdo).
— OBSERV Pret ***outwent***; pp ***outgone***.

outgoer [-,gəuə*] *n* el *or* la que se va || *the outgoer must vacate the flat before 1st January* el que ocupa actualmente el piso tiene que desalojarlo antes del primero de enero.

outgoing ['aut,gəuiŋ] *adj* saliente; *the outgoing president* el presidente saliente || que sale; *the outgoing ship* el barco que sale || saliente; *the outgoing tide* la marea saliente || US sociable.
◆ *n* salida *f*.
◆ *pl* gastos *m* (expenditure).

outgone [aut'gɔn] *pp* ⟶ **outgo.**

outgrew [aut'gru:] *pret* ⟶ **outgrow.**

outgrow* [aut'grəu] *vt* crecer más que; *he has outgrown his elder brother* ha crecido más que su hermano mayor || perder con la edad; *you will outgrow your shyness* perderás tu timidez con la edad || — *to outgrow one's clothes* quedarle la ropa pequeña a uno || *to outgrow one's youthful habits* perder las costumbres que se tenían de joven.
— OBSERV Pret ***outgrew***; pp ***outgrown***.

outgrown [aut'grəun] *pp* ⟶ **outgrow.**

outgrowth ['autgrəuθ] *n* excrecencia *f* (sth. which grows) || consecuencia *f*, resultado *m* (result).

outhaul ['authɔ:l] *n* MAR driza *f*.

out-Herod [aut'herəd] *vt* FAM *to out-Herod Herod* ser peor que Herodes.

outhouse ['authaus] *n* dependencia *f* [de un edificio] || US retrete *m* (outside lavatory).

outing ['autiŋ] *n* excursión *f*; *to go on a car outing* ir de excursión en coche || paseo *m*, vuelta *f* (walk).

outlander ['aut,lændə*] *n* extranjero, ra.

outlandish [aut'lændiʃ] *adj* extraño, ña; raro, ra (bizarre) || extravagante (behaviour) || apartado, da; alejado, da; *an outlandish place* un lugar alejado || tosco, ca (uncouth) || (ant) extranjero, ra (foreign).

outlandishness [aut'lændiʃnis] *n* aspecto *m* extraño, lo extraño || extravagancia *f* (of behaviour).

outlast [aut'lɑ:st] *vt* durar más (tiempo) que; *the tyres have outlasted the car* los neumáticos han durado más tiempo que el coche || sobrevivir a (person).

outlaw ['autlɔ:] *n* proscrito, ta; persona *f* fuera de la ley.

outlaw ['autlɔ:] *vt* proscribir, declarar fuera de la ley; *the rebels have been outlawed* los rebeldes han sido proscritos || prohibir, declarar ilegal; *the use of several medicines has been outlawed* el uso de varias medicinas ha sido prohibido.

outlawry ['aut,lɔ:ri] *n* proscripción *f* || bandolerismo *m*, bandidaje *m* (banditry).

outlay ['autlei] *n* gastos *m pl*, desembolso *m*.

outlet ['autlet] *n* salida *f* (way out) || desagüe *m*, desaguadero *m* (of a drain) || desagüe *m* (of a lake) || COMM mercado *m*, salida *f*; *the product has no outlet* el producto no tiene mercado | distribuidor *m*, sucursal *f* (agency) || ELECTR toma *f* || — FIG *an outlet for one's energies* la posibilidad de emplear su energía || COMM *retail outlet* tienda *f*.

outlier ['aut,laiə*] *n* GEOL afloramiento *m* [separado del macizo principal] || persona *f* que vive lejos de donde trabaja.

outline ['autlain] *n* contorno *m* (line showing the boundary of an object) || perfil *m*; *the outline of a mountain, of a building* el perfil de una montaña, de un edificio || silueta *f* (indistinct); *a shadowy outline* una silueta vaga || bosquejo *m*, esbozo *m* (draft); *a short outline of a plan* un pequeño bosquejo de un proyecto || ARTS bosquejo *m*, boceto *m*, esbozo *m* (sketch); *to draw a quick outline* hacer un bosquejo rápido || trazado *m* (of a map) || resumen *m* (summary); *here is an outline of his speech* aquí tiene un resumen de su discurso || esquema *m*; *I will give you an outline of the organization* le haré un esquema de la organización || signo *m* taquigráfico (symbol) || introducción *f*, reseña *f*; *outline of Spanish history* introducción a *or* reseña de la historia de España || *in broad outline* en líneas generales.

◆ *pl* líneas *f* generales.

outline ['autlain] *vt* perfilar (to draw the outline of) || bosquejar, esbozar (to sketch) || trazar las líneas generales de (to give the main points of) || resumir (to summarize) || *the tower was outlined against the sky* la torre se perfilaba en el cielo.

outlive [aut'liv] *vt* durar más que (to last longer than) || sobrevivir a (s.o., a disgrace).

outlook ['autluk] *n* vista *f* (view) || panorama *m*, perspectiva *f*, perspectivas *f pl*; *there is a bad outlook for trade* las perspectivas relativas al comercio no son buenas || punto *m* de vista; *he has an optimistic outlook* tiene un punto de vista optimista || concepto *m*; *outlook upon life* concepto de la vida.

outlying [aut,laiiŋ] *adj* exterior, alejado del centro (lying away from the centre) || remoto, ta; alejado, da; aislado, da; *outlying villages* pueblos remotos.

outmanoeuvre; *US* **outmaneuver** [autmə'nu:və*] *vt* superar en estrategia || superar a (to put o.s. in a stronger position than).

outmarch [aut'mɑ:tʃ] *vt* dejar atrás.

outmatch [aut'mætʃ] *vt* aventajar, superar.

outmoded [aut'məudid] *adj* anticuado, da; pasado de moda.

outmost ['autməust] *adj* más exterior || más alejado, da; extremo, ma || *at the outmost* como máximo.

outnumber [aut,nʌmbə*] *vt* exceder en número, ser más numeroso que || *they were outnumbered twenty to one* éramos veinte veces más que ellos.

out-of-date [autəv'deit] *adj* pasado de moda, anticuado, da (old-fashioned) || anticuado, da (not current, obsolete).

out-of-door [autəv'dɔ:] *adj* ⟶ **outdoor.**

out-of-doors ['autəv'dɔ:z] *adv/n* ⟶ **outdoors.**

out-of-pocket ['autəv'pɔkit] *adj* efectivo, en efectivo || *out-of-pocket expenses* gastos *m*, desembolsos *m*.

out-of-school [autəv'sku:l] *adj* extraescolar.

out-of-the-way [autəvðə'wei] *adj* apartado, da; aislado, da; remoto, ta (distant); *a little out-of-the-way village* un pueblecito aislado || poco corriente (unusual); *an out-of-the-way expression* una expresión poco corriente || inaccesible, inasequible (price).

outpace [aut'peis] *vt* dejar atrás.

outpatient ['aut,peiʃənt] *n* MED paciente *m* no internado, enfermo *m* no hospitalizado.

outplay [aut'plei] *vt* jugar mejor que || *we were completely outplayed right from the beginning* nos dominaron completamente desde el primer momento.

outpoint [aut'point] *vt* puntuar más alto que, sacar más puntos que (an opponent).

outport ['autpɔ:t] *n* MAR antepuerto *m* (outer part of a port) | puerto marítimo (of a city).

outpost ['autpəust] *n* MIL avanzada *f* (detachment) | puesto *m* avanzado (post) | puesto *m* fronterizo (on a frontier).

outpouring ['aut'pɔ:riŋ] *n* efusión *f* (of heart) || profusión *f* (of abuses).

output ['autput] *n* producción *f* || TECH rendimiento *m* (of a machine) | potencia *f*, energía *f* (power) || ELECTR salida *f* (of a computer) || INFORM salida *f*; *output device* unidad de salida; *output unit* unidad de salida.

outrage ['autreidʒ] *n* ultraje *m*, atropello *m*, agravio *m* (on people's rights, feelings or property) || desafuero *m* (against order to principles) || ataque *m*, atentado *m*; *a wave of outrages and assassinations* una ola de ataques y asesinatos || atrocidad *f* (atrocity) || — *bomb outrage* atentado con bomba || *it's an outrage!* ¡no hay derecho!, ¡es escandaloso! || *to commit an outrage against s.o.* ultrajar a alguien, agraviar a alguien.

outrage ['autreidʒ] *vt* ultrajar, agraviar (to subject to an outrage) || violentar (to do violence to) || violar (to rape) || atentar contra, ofender (public opinion) || atropellar (the law) || ir en contra de (common sense).

outrageous [aut'reidʒəs] *adj* ultrajante (constituting an outrage) || extravagante (extravagant) || escandaloso, sa (provoking disapproval); *his outrageous behaviour lost him many friends* perdió muchos amigos con su conducta escandalosa || infame (accusation) || flagrante (injustice) || exorbitante, escandaloso, sa (price) || FAM horrible || — *how outrageous!* ¡qué vergüenza!, ¡qué barbaridad!, ¡es escandaloso! || *it is outrageous that he be allowed to do it* es indignante que se le permita hacerlo.

outrageously [aut'reidʒəsli] *adv* de una manera escandalosa.

outrageousness [aut'reidʒəsnis] *n* carácter *m* ultrajante *or* escandaloso.

outran [aut'ræn] *pret* ⟶ **outrun.**

outrange [aut'reindʒ] *vt* tener un alcance mayor que || FIG superar.

outrank [autræŋk] *vt* ser superior a.

outré ['u:trei] *adj* exagerado, da; extravagante (exaggerated) || chocante (shocking).

outreach [aut'ri:tʃ] *vt* tener un alcance mayor que || superar (to exceed).

outridden [zut'ridn] *pp* ⟶ **outride.**

outride* [aut'raid] *vt* cabalgar mejor *or* más rápido que, adelantar (to surpass in riding) || MAR capear (a storm).

— OBSERV Pret ***outrode***; pp ***outridden***.

outrider ['aut,raidə*] *n* persona *f* que escolta a caballo (on horseback) || motorista *m* de escolta (on motorcycle).

outrigger ['aut,rigə*] *n* MAR batanga *f*, balancín *m* (float) | bote *m* con batanga (boat equipped with a float) | escálamo *m* (rowlock) | «outrigger» *m* (racing boat with projecting rowlocks) | tangón *m*, botalón *m* (extending spar) || AVIAT larguero *m* de soporte del plano fijo.

outright ['autrait] *adj* completo, ta; absoluto, ta; total; *outright dishonesty* una falta completa de honradez || rotundo, da; categórico, ca; *outright denial* negación rotunda || absoluto, ta; incondicional (unconditional) || franco, ca (forthright).

outright [aut'rait] *adv* francamente (openly); *I told him outright he was mistaken* le dije francamente que estaba equivocado || en el acto (at once); *to be killed outright* ser matado en el acto || al contado; *to pay outright* pagar al contado || en su totalidad (entirely) || rotundamente, categóricamente (to refuse) || abiertamente (to laugh).

outrival [aut'raivəl] *vt* superar, aventajar.

outrode [aut'rəud] *pret* ⟶ **outride.**

outrun* [aut'rʌn] *vt* correr más deprisa que, dejar atrás (to run faster than) || FIG rebasar, sobrepasar; *his ambition outruns his talents* su ambición sobrepasa su talento.

— OBSERV Pret ***outran***; pp ***outrun***.

outsail [aut'seil] *vt* MAR adelantar, dejar atrás.

outscore [aut'skɔ:*] *vt* puntuar más alto que.

outsell* [aut'sel] *vt* vender más que (to sell more than) || venderse mejor que (a product).

— OBSERV Pret y pp ***outsold***.

outset ['autset] *n* principio *m*, comienzo *m*; *at the outset* al principio; *from the outset* desde el principio.

outshine* [aut'ʃain] *vt* brillar más que (to shine brighter than) || FIG eclipsar; *she outshone all rivals* eclipsó a todas sus rivales.

— OBSERV El pretérito y el participio pasivo de ***outshine*** son ***outshone***, aunque en Estados Unidos se emplea también ***outshined***.

outshoot [aut'ʃu:t] *vt* disparar mejor que.

◆ *vi* sobresalir (to protrude).

outside ['aut'said] *n* exterior *m*; *the outside of the house* el exterior de la casa || superficie *f* (surface) || piso *m* superior (of a bus) || apariencia *f* (appearance) || SP extremo *m*; *outside left* extremo izquierda || — *at the outside* como mucho, como máximo || *from the outside* desde fuera || *on the outside* por fuera.

◆ *adj* exterior, externo, na; *the outside wheel* la rueda exterior; *outside interests* intereses exteriores || al aire libre (done outdoors) || ajeno, na; *outside opinion* opinión ajena || remoto, ta; *outside chance of living* remota posibilidad de vivir || más elevado, da (highest); *they have exceeded the outside estimate* han rebasado las previsiones más elevadas || máximo, ma; más elevado, da (price) || del piso superior (of a bus) || exterior, que trabaja fuera de la empresa (worker) || independiente (independent) || RAD exterior || — RAD *outside broadcast* emisión *f* remota || *outside lane* carril *m* de adelantamiento || *outside line* línea *f* exterior (telephone) || *outside market* bolsín *m* || *the outside world* el mundo exterior.

◆ *adv* fuera, afuera; *he is outside* está fuera; *he went outside* salió fuera || en la calle (in the street), a la calle (into the street) || fuera de la empresa; *work done outside* trabajo realizado fuera de la empresa || en el piso superior (on bus).

◆ *prep* fuera de; *waiting outside the office* esperando fuera de la oficina; *outside the family* fuera de la familia || más allá de, fuera de (beyond); *outside the city boundary* más allá de los límites de la ciudad || — *interests outside work* intereses ajenos al trabajo || *outside of* fuera de.

outsider [-ə*] *n* intruso, sa (stranger to a group of people) || FIG forastero, ra (stranger to a place) || SP caballo *m* no favorito (horse) || candidato *m* poco conocido (in an election) || persona *f* independiente (not included in a party).

outsize ['ausaiz] *adj* de talla muy grande.

◆ *n* talla *f* muy grande.

outskirts ['autskə:ts] *pl n* afueras *f*, cercanías *f*.

outsmart [aut'smɑ:t] *vt* *US* burlar, ser más listo que.

outsold [aut'səuld] *pret/pp* ⟶ **outsell.**

outspoken [aut'spəukən] *adj* franco, ca; abierto, ta || *to be outspoken* no tener pelos en la lengua.

outspokenness [-nis] *n* franqueza *f*.

outspread ['aut'spred] *adj* extendido, da || desplegado, da (sails).
◆ *n* extensión *f* || despliegue *m*.

outstanding [aut'stændiŋ] *adj* destacado, da; notable; *an outstanding event* un acontecimiento notable || sobresaliente; *outstanding features* características sobresalientes || eminente, notable, destacado, da (person) || excepcional, fuera de lo común; *an outstanding success* un éxito excepcional || sin pagar, pendiente (unpaid); *outstanding debts* deudas sin pagar || sin resolver, pendiente (unsolved) || por hacer, pendiente (still to be done).

outstare [aut'stɛə*] *vt* hacer bajar los ojos.

outstay [aut'stei] *vt* quedarse más tiempo que (to remain longer than) || aguantar más que (to resist more than) || *to outstay one's welcome* quedarse más tiempo de lo conveniente.

outstretched [aut'stretʃt] *adj* extendido, da.

outstrip [aut'strip] *vt* dejar atrás (to leave behind, to surpass).

outtake ['autteik] *n* RAD & CINEM descarte *m*.

out tray ['auttrei] *n* bandeja *f* de salida (documents).

outturn ['aut,tə:n] *n* producción *f* || rendimiento *m* (yield).

outvalue [aut'vælju:] *vt* sobrepasar en valor a, valer más que.

outvote [aut'vəut] *vt* vencer en una elección *or* en una votación || *to be outvoted* perder en una elección *or* en una votación.

outwalk [aut'wɔ:k] *vt* andar más rápidamente que, dejar atrás (to walk faster) || andar más que (to walk longer).

outward ['autwəd] *adj* de ida; *outward journey* viaje de ida || exterior, externo, na (exterior) || MED externo, na (application).
◆ *adv* hacia afuera || exteriormente.
◆ *n* exterior *m*.

outward bound; outward-bound [-baund] *adj* que sale || — *to be outward bound for Bilbao* salir *or* ir rumbo a Bilbao || *to be outward bound from Southampton* haber salido de Southampton.

outwardly [-li] *adj* exteriormente, por fuera (externally) || aparentemente (apparently).

outwards [-z] *adv* hacia fuera || exteriormente.

outwear* [aut'wɛə*] *vt* durar más que (to last longer than); *this skirt will outwear the other one* esa falda durará más que la otra || gastar, desgastar (to wear out) || deshacerse de (to get rid of); *to outwear a habit* deshacerse de una costumbre.
— OBSERV Pret ***outwore***; pp ***outworn***.

outweigh [aut'wei] *vt* pesar más que; *the advantages outweigh the disadvantages* las ventajas pesan más que los inconvenientes || valer más que (to be more valuable).

outwent [aut'went] *pret* → **outgo.**

outwit [aut'wit] *vt* burlar, ser más listo que; *the thief outwitted the police and escaped* el ladrón burló a la policía y se escapó.

outwore [aut'wɔ:*] *pret* → **outwear.**

outwork ['autwə:k] *n* MIL defensa *f* exterior, obra *f* accesoria || trabajo *m* hecho fuera de la empresa (outside work).

outwork [aut'wə:k] *vt* trabajar mejor *or* más rápido que.

outworn [aut'wɔ:n] *pp* → **outwear.**
◆ *adj* gastado, da; desgastado, da (worn-out) || trillado, da (excessively used); *outworn phrase* expresión trillada || anticuado, da; caduco, ca; *outworn ideas* ideas caducas.

ouzel ['u:zl] *n* mirlo *m* (bird).

ova ['əuvə] *pl n* → **ovum.**

oval ['əuvəl] *adj* oval, ovalado, da.
◆ *n* óvalo *m*.

ovalize ['əuvəlaiz] *vt* ovalizar.

ovarian [əu'vɛəriən] *adj* ovárico, ca.

ovariectomy [əu,vɛəri'ektəmi] *n* MED ovariotomía *f*, ovariectomía *f* (removal of one or both ovaries).

ovariotomy [əu,vɛəri'ətəmi] *n* MED ovariotomía *f*, ovariectomía *f* (ovariectomy) | incisión *f* de un ovario (incision).

ovary ['əuvəri] *n* ANAT & BOT ovario *m*.

ovate ['əuveit] *adj* ovado, da; aovado, da.

ovation [əu'veiʃən] *n* ovación *f* || — *to give s.o. an ovation* o *a standing ovation* ovacionar a alguien || *to receive an ovation* ser ovacionado.

oven ['ʌvn] *n* horno *m*; *baker's oven* horno de panadero || FIG estufa *f*, horno *m* (hot place) || *oven gloves* manoplas *f pl* para el horno.

ovenbird [-bə:d] *n* ZOOL hornero *m* (passerine bird).

ovenproof [-pru:f] *adj* de horno (dish).

oven-ready [-,redi] *adj* listo, ta para hornear.

over ['əuvə*] *prep* sobre; *the umbrella over his head* el paraguas sobre su cabeza; *he increased his lead over the others* aumentó su ventaja sobre los demás; *he has a great influence over me* tiene una gran influencia sobre mí || sobre, por encima de; *the plane flew over the house* el avión voló por encima de la casa || sobre, encima de; *books spread over the table* libros esparcidos sobre la mesa || por encima de; *to throw a ball over a wall* lanzar una pelota por encima de un muro; *he jumped over the fence* saltó por encima de la valla; *he was over his ankles in water* tenía agua por encima de los tobillos || encima de; *the clouds are over our heads* las nubes están encima de nuestras cabezas || más de; *over a million* más de un millón; *he is over fourty* tiene más de cuarenta años; *to sleep for over three hours* dormir más de tres horas || superior; *numbers over fifteen win a prize* los números superiores a quince ganan un premio || junto a; *sitting over the fire* sentado junto al fuego || al otro *or* del otro lado de; *Charles lives over the hill* Carlos vive al otro lado de la colina || del otro lado de; *I live over the street* vivo del otro lado de la calle || por; *we got this information over the phone* recibimos esta información por teléfono; *to drive over a new road* conducir por una nueva carretera; *to throw o.s. over a precipice* despeñarse por un precipicio; *to fight over a woman* pelearse por una mujer || durante; *over several days* durante varios días; *can you stay over the weekend?* ¿puede quedarse durante el fin de semana? || hasta; *stay over Peter's birthday* quédate hasta el cumpleaños de Pedro || en, con; *how long will you be over it?* ¿cuánto tiempo vas a estar con eso *or* vas a tardar en ello? || con; *to stumble over a mat* tropezar con un felpudo || — *all over the house* por toda la casa || *all over the world* en el mundo entero, en todo el mundo || *let's talk over a glass of beer* hablemos mientras tomamos un vaso de cerveza || *over and above* además de (in addition to), superior a (besides) || *over the river* que cruza el río (bridge), en la otra orilla del río (house, etc.) || *over the road* de enfrente; *the house over the road* la casa de enfrente || *over the seas* allende los mares || *to be all over s.o.* tener muchas atenciones con alguien || *to have an advantage over s.o.* llevar ventaja a uno || *to help s.o. over the road* ayudar a alguien a cruzar la calle || *what's come over you?* ¿qué le pasa? || *with his hat over his eyes* con el sombrero calado hasta los ojos.
◆ *adv* encima, por encima; *this one goes over* éste pasa por encima || más; *it weighs three tons and a bit over* pesa tres toneladas y algo más || todo, da; *to search Paris over* registrar todo París || hasta el final; *to read over* leer hasta el final || — *all over* por todas partes (everywhere), completamente (completely) || *all the world over* en el mundo entero, en todo el mundo || *children of fifteen and over* mayores de quince años, chicos de quince años para arriba || *he is over from Spain* viene de España || *he is his father all over* es su padre cien por cien || *he is Scottish all over* es escocés cien por cien *or* hasta la médula || *I ache all over* me duele todo el cuerpo || *I am over for the weekend* he venido a pasar el fin de semana || *it's all over!* ¡se acabó! || *it's all over with me* estoy perdido || *over again* otra vez || *over against* en frente de, frente a || *over and over (again)* repetidas veces, una y otra vez || *over here* aquí, acá || *over in China they eat rice* allá en China se come arroz || *over there* allí, allá || *sixteen divided by five equals three and one over* dieciséis dividido por cinco da tres de cociente y queda uno de resto || *that's over and done with!* ¡se acabó! || *that's you all over* eso es muy suyo || *to ask s.o. over* pedir a alguien que venga || *to be all over dust* estar cubierto de polvo || *to bend over* doblar (sth.), inclinarse || *to be over* haberse terminado *or* acabado; *the film is over* la película se ha acabado; quedar; *is there any soup over?* ¿queda algo de sopa? || *to boil over* salirse (milk) || *to cross over* atravesar, cruzar || *twice over* dos veces [seguidas] || *we have a pound over* tenemos una libra de más, nos sobra una libra || *what is left over* lo que sobra.
◆ *n* MIL tiro *m* largo || SP serie *f* de seis saques (cricket) || COMM excedente *m*, superávit *m* (surplus).
— OBSERV Cuando el adverbio *over* acompaña ciertos verbos no se puede traducir literalmente. Es preciso, por lo tanto, consultar el artículo referente al verbo de que se trata. En algunos casos este adverbio implica una idea de repetición que se puede expresar en español por *volver a* u *otra vez*: *to sing over* volver a cantar; *to do over* hacer otra vez.

overabundance [-ə'bʌndəns] *n* superabundancia *f*, sobreabundancia *f*.

overabundant [-ə'bʌndənt] *adj* superabundante, sobreabundante.

overact [-'ækt] *vt* THEATR exagerar (a part).
◆ *vi* THEATR exagerar el papel.

overacting [-'æktiŋ] *n* THEATR exageración *f*.

overactive [-'æktiv] *adj* demasiado activo, va.

overage [-idʒ] *n* US COMM excedente *m* de mercancías.

overage [,uvər'eidʒ] *adj* US con más edad de la requerida, demasiado viejo, ja.

overall ['əuvər,ɔ:l] *adj* global, de conjunto (including everything) || total; *the overall cost* el coste total || — *overall dimensions* dimensiones exteriores || MAR *overall length* eslora *f* total, longitud máxima.

overall [,əuvər'ɔ:l] *adv* en conjunto (generally) || por todas partes (everywhere).

overalls ['əuvərɔ:lz] *n* guardapolvo *m sing* (child's) || bata *f sing* (woman's) || mono *m* (worker's).

overambitious ['əuvəræm'biʃəs] *adj* demasiado ambicioso, sa.

overanxious ['əuvər'æŋkʃəs] *adj* demasiado preocupado, da (worried) || excesivamente deseoso, sa (eagerly wishing) || *I am not overanxious to do it* no tengo muchas ganas de hacerlo.

overarm ['əuvərɑ:m] *adv* SP por encima de la cabeza (to throw).

overate [,əuvər'et] *pret* → **overeat.**

overawe [,əuvər'ɔ:] *vt* intimidar, imponer respeto a, impresionar.

overbalance [ˌəuvəˈbæləns] *vt* hacer perder el equilibrio (to throw off balance) ‖ pesar más que (to weigh more than).
◆ *vi* perder el equilibrio (to lose one's balance) ‖ volcar (to overturn).

overbear* [ˌəuvəˈbɛə*] *vt* oprimir (to press) ‖ FIG intimidar (s.o.) | hacer caso omiso de, no hacer caso de, no tener en cuenta (s.o.'s wishes) ‖ dominar (to domineer over).
◆ *vi* dar demasiados frutos.
— OBSERV Pret ***overbore***; pp ***overborne***.

overbearing [-riŋ] *adj* imperioso, sa; autoritario, ria (domineering).

overbid [ˈəuvəˌbid] *n* sobrepuja *f* (at auction) ‖ declaración *f* más alta (in bridge).

overbid* [ˌəuvəˈbid] *vt* pujar más que, sobrepujar, hacer una mejor oferta que (to bid more than) ‖ ofrecer más del valor de (to bid more than the value of) ‖ declarar más que (in bridge).
◆ *vi* ofrecer más que otro ‖ hacer una declaración más alta [que lo que permite su mano] (in bridge).
— OBSERV Pret y pp ***overbid***.

overbidding [-iŋ] *n* sobrepuja *f*.

overblown [ˈəuvipbləun] *adj* demasiado abierto, ta (flowers) ‖ pomposo, sa; rimbombante, ampuloso, sa (style).

overboard [ˈəuvəbɔːd] *adv* por la borda ‖ — *man overboard!* ¡hombre al agua! ‖ US FIG *to go overboard* pasarse de la raya ‖ *to throw overboard* tirar por la borda.

overbold [ˌuvəˈbəuld] *adj* temerario, ria; muy osado, da; muy atrevido, da.

overbook [ˌəuvəˈbuk] *vt* reservar más plazas de las disponibles (hotel, plane).
◆ *vi* practicar la sobreventa.

overbooking [ˌəuvəˈbukiŋ] *n* overbooking *m*, sobreventa *f*, sobrecontratación *f*, saturación.

overbore [ˌəuvəˈbɔː] *pret* ⟶ **overbear.**

overborne [-n] *pp* ⟶ **overbear.**

overbought [ˈəuvəˈbɔːt] *pret/pp* ⟶ **overbuy.**

overbuild* [ˈəuvəˈbild] *vt* construir demasiado en (an area).
— OBSERV Pret y pp ***overbuilt***.

overburden [ˌəuvəˈbəːdn] *n* sobrecarga *f* (excess of burden) ‖ FIG agobio *m*.

overburden [ˌəuvəˈbəːdn] *vt* sobrecargar ‖ FIG agobiar, abrumar; *not overburdened with scruples* poco agobiado por los escrúpulos.

overbuy* [ˈəuvəbai] *vt/vi* comprar demasiado.
— OBSERV Pret y pp ***overbought***.

overcall [ˌəuvəˈkɔːl] *n/vt/vi* ⟶ **overbid.**

overcame [ˌəuvəˈkeim] *pret* ⟶ **overcome.**

overcapitalization [ˈəuvəˌkæpitəlaiˈzeiʃən] *n* supercapitalización *f*.

overcast [ˈəuvəkɑːst] *adj* nublado, da; encapotado, da; cubierto, ta (the sky).
◆ *n* sobrehilado *m* (in sewing) ‖ revestimiento *m* (coating).

overcast* [ˈəuvəkɑːst] *vt* sobrehilar (in sewing) ‖ encapotar, cubrir (sky) ‖ oscurecer (to darken).
— OBSERV Pret y pp ***overcast***.

overcautious [ˈəuvəˈkɔːʃəs] *adj* demasiado *or* excesivamente cauteloso, sa.

overcharge [ˈəuvəˈtʃɑːdʒ] *n* carga *f* excesiva, sobrecarga *f* (weight) ‖ precio *m* excesivo (very high price) ‖ recargo *m*, sobreprecio *m* (extra charge).

overcharge [ˈəuvəˈtʃɑːdʒ] *vt* cobrar más de lo debido a (to charge too high a price) ‖ recargar (price) ‖ cobrar de más (a certain amount) ‖ sobrecargar (to overload).
◆ *vi* sobrecargar ‖ cobrar demasiado.

overcloud [ˌəuvəˈklaud] *vt* nublar, cubrir, encapotar (to cover over with clouds) ‖ FIG oscurecer, entristecer; *fear of madness overclouded her last years* el miedo a la locura oscureció sus últimos años.
◆ *vi* encapotarse, nublarse, cubrirse (sky).

overcoat [ˈəuvekəut] *n* abrigo *m*.

overcome* [ˌəuvəˈkʌm] *vt* vencer; *to overcome one's enemies* vencer al enemigo ‖ salvar, vencer, superar (difficulty, obstacle) ‖ *she was overcome by fear* estaba muerta de miedo.
◆ *vi* vencer, triunfar, salir victorioso.
— OBSERV Pret ***overcame***; pp ***overcome***.

overconfidence [ˈəuvəˈkɔnfidəns] *n* exceso *m* de confianza, confianza *f* excesiva ‖ presunción *f*, suficiencia *f* (self-conceit).

overconfident [ˈəuvəˈkɔnfidənt] *adj* demasiado confiado, da ‖ presumido, da; suficiente (conceited).

overconsumption [ˈəuvəkənˈsʌmpʃən] *n* consumo *m* excesivo.

overcook [ˈəuvəˈkuk] *vt* cocer demasiado, recocer ‖ requemar (to burn).

overcrop [ˈəuvəˈkrɔp] *vt* esquilmar, agotar (land).

overcrossing [ˈəuvəˈkrɔsiŋ] *n* paso *m* superior (railway).

overcrowd [ˈəuvəˈkraud] *vt* atestar (*with* de) ‖ superpoblar (a town).

overcrowded [-id] *adj* atestado, da (de gente); *the bus is overcrowded* el autobús está atestado de gente ‖ superpoblado, da (a town, a country).

overcrowding [-iŋ] *n* atestamiento *m* (de gente) ‖ superpoblación *f* (in a town, in a country).

overdevelop [-diˈveləp] *vt* desarrollar demasiado.

overdeveloped [-t] *adj* demasiado desarrollado, da; superdesarrollado, da.

overdevelopment [-mənt] *n* desarrollo *m* excesivo, superdesarrollo *m*.

overdid [ˌəuvədid] *pret* ⟶ **overdo.**

overdo* [ˈəuvəˈduː] *vt* exagerar (to exaggerate) ‖ agotar (to exhaust) ‖ CULIN cocer demasiado ‖ *to overdo it* exagerar (to go too far), excederse; *I think I'm overdoing it at work* creo que me estoy excediendo en el trabajo; recargar las tintas.
— OBSERV Pret ***overdid***; pp ***overdone***.

overdone [ˌəuvəˈdʌn] *pp* ⟶ **overdo.**
◆ *adj* exagerado, da ‖ CULIN muy hecho, cha (meat) | pasado, da (rice, etc.).

overdose [ˈəuvədəus] *n* dosis *f* excesiva.

overdraft [ˈəuvədrɑːft] *n* COMM giro *m* en descubierto (sum overdrawn) | saldo *m* deudor, descubierto *m* (on account) ‖ corriente *f* de aire [en un horno].

overdrank [ˈəuvəˈdræŋk] *pret* ⟶ **overdrink.**

overdraw* [ˈəuvəˈdrɔː] *vt* COMM girar en descubierto ‖ exagerar (to exaggerate) ‖ *to be overdrawn* tener un saldo deudor *or* un descubierto en su cuenta.
◆ *vi* COMM girar en descubierto.
— OBSERV Pret ***overdrew***; pp ***overdrawn***.

overdrawn [ˈəuvəˈdrɔːn] *pp* ⟶ **overdraw.**

overdress [ˈəuvəˈdres] *vt* vestir con exageración.
◆ *vi* ponerse de tiros largos (too elegantly) ‖ vestirse con exageración (too showily).

overdrew [ˈəuvəˈdruː] *pret* ⟶ **overdraw.**

overdrink* [ˈəuvəˈdriŋk] *vi* beber demasiado.
— OBSERV Pret ***overdrank***; pp ***overdrunk***.

overdrive [ˈəuvəˈdraiv] *n* AUT superdirecta *f* (gear).

overdrive* [ˈəuvəˈdraiv] *vt* hacer trabajar con exceso (to give too much work) ‖ agotar (to exhaust).
— OBSERV Pret ***overdrove***; pp ***overdriven***.

overdriven [ˈəuvəˈdrivn] *pp* ⟶ **overdrive.**

overdrove [ˈəuvəˈdrəuv] *pret* ⟶ **overdrive.**

overdrunk [ˈəuvəˈdrʌŋk] *pp* ⟶ **overdrink.**

overdue [ˈəuvəˈdjuː] *adj* atrasado, da (train, rent, etc.) ‖ COMM vencido y sin pagar ‖ FIG requerido *or* esperado desde hace tiempo (reform, etc.) ‖ *the train is twenty minutes overdue* el tren tiene veinte minutos de retraso.

overeat* [ˈəuvərˈiːt] *vi* comer excesivamente *or* demasiado.
— OBSERV Pret ***overate***; pp ***overeaten***.

overeaten [-n] *pp* ⟶ **overeat.**

overeating [-iŋ] *n* comida *f* excesiva.

overelaborate [ˈəuvəriˈlæbərit] *adj* demasiado complicado, da ‖ con muchos detalles (with many details) ‖ muy rebuscado, da (affected).

overemphasize [ˈəuvərˈemfəsaiz] *vt* recalcar *or* enfatizar con exceso.

overestimate [-ˈestimit] *n* sobrestimación *f*, estimación *f* excesiva.

overestimate [ˈəuvərˈestimeit] *vt* sobrestimar.

overexcite [ˈəuvərikˈsait] *vt* sobreexcitar, sobrexcitar.

overexcitement [-mənt] *n* sobreexcitación *f*, sobrexcitación *f*.

overexert [ˈəuvərigˈzəːt] *vt* agotar ‖ *to overexert o.s.* hacer un esfuerzo excesivo.
◆ *vi* hacer un esfuerzo excesivo.

overexertion [ˈəuvərigˈzəːʃən] *n* esfuerzo *m* excesivo ‖ agotamiento *m* (exhaustion).

overexpose [ˈəuvəriksˈpəuz] *vt* PHOT sobreexponer, exponer demasiado.

overexposure [ˈəuvəriksˈpəuʒə*] *n* PHOT exposición *f* excesiva, sobreexposición *f*.

overfall [ˈəuvəfɔːl] *n* vertedero *m*.

overfamiliar [ˈəuvəfəˈmiljə*] *adj* demasiado familiar, que se toma demasiada confianza [con los demás].

overfatigue [ˈəuvəfəˈtiːg] *n* cansancio *m* excesivo, agotamiento *m*.

overfatigue [ˈəuvəfəˈtiːg] *vt* agotar, cansar demasiado.

overfed [ˈəuvəˈfed] *pret/pp* ⟶ **overfeed.**

overfeed* [ˈəuvəˈfiːd] *vt* sobrealimentar.
◆ *vi* comer demasiado.
— OBSERV Pret y pp ***overfed***.

overfeeding [-iŋ] *n* sobrealimentación *f*.

overfill [ˈəuvəˈfil] *vt* sobrellenar.

overflew [ˈəuvəfluː] *pret* ⟶ **overfly.**

overflow [ˈəuvəfləu] *n* desbordamiento *m* (of river, etc.) ‖ derrame *m* (from small containers) ‖ cañería *f* de desagüe (pipe) ‖ inundación *f* (flooding) ‖ FIG exceso *m*.

overflow [ˈəuvəˈfləu] *vt* inundar (to flood) ‖ derramarse de (to flow over) ‖ *the river overflowed its banks* el río se desbordó *or* se salió de madre.
◆ *vi* desbordarse (river, dam, etc.) ‖ derramarse, rebosar; *your cup is overflowing* tu taza se está derramando ‖ FIG rebosar; *to overflow with joy* rebosar de alegría.

overflown [ˈəuvəˈfləun] *pp* ⟶ **overfly.**

overfly* [ˈəuvəˈflai] *vt* sobrevolar, volar por encima de.
— OBSERV Pret ***overflew***; pp ***overflown***.

overfull [ˈəuvəˈful] *adj* rebosante (*of, with* de).

overgarment [ˈəuvəgɑːmənt] *n* abrigo *m* (overcoat) ‖ guardapolvo *m* (protective clothing).

overgild [ˌəuvəˈgild] *vt* sobredorar.

overglaze ['əuvə'gleiz] *vt* vidriar.

overgrew ['əuvə'gru:] *pret* → **overgrow.**

overgrow* ['əuvə'grəu] *vt* cubrir (plants).
— OBSERV Pret *overgrew*; pp *overgrown*.

overgrown [-n] *pp* → **overgrow.**
◆ *adj* cubierto de hierba; *an overgrown garden* un jardín cubierto de hierba ‖ cubierto, ta; *a field overgrown with mushrooms* un campo cubierto de hongos ‖ demasiado crecido para su edad (too big for one's age).

overgrowth ['əuvə'grəuθ] *n* crecimiento *m* excesivo (excessive growth) ‖ vegetación *f* frondosa, frondosidad *f*.

overhand ['əuvə'hænd] *adj* de arriba abajo ‖ SP por alto (stroke).
◆ *adv* por alto.

overhang ['əuvə'hæŋ] *n* saliente *m* (projection) ‖ ARCH alero *m*.

overhang* ['əuvəhæŋ] *vt* sobresalir por encima de ‖ adornar [con colgaduras] (a balcony) ‖ FIG amenazar (to threaten).
◆ *vi* sobresalir.
— OBSERV Pret y pp *overhung*.

overhanging [-iŋ] *adj* saliente, sobresaliente.

overhaul ['əuvəhɔ:l]; **overhauling** ['əuvəhɔ:liŋ] *n* revisión *f*, examen *m* detenido ‖ TECH revisión *f* | reparación *f*, arreglo *m*.

overhaul ['əuvə'hɔ:l] *vt* revisar (to examine) ‖ examinar detenidamente (to look into) ‖ TECH arreglar (to repair) ‖ alcanzar (to catch up) ‖ adelantar (to pass).

overhauling [-iŋ] *n* → **overhaul.**

overhead ['əuvəhed] *adj* de arriba ‖ COMM general (expenses) ‖ a tanto alzado (price) ‖ — *overhead cable* o *wire* cable aéreo ‖ *overhead projector* retroproyector *m*, proyector *m* de transparencias ‖ *overhead railway* ferrocarril aéreo.
◆ *pl n* COMM gastos *m* generales.

overhead ['əuvə'hed] *adv* por encima de la cabeza, arriba.

overhear* [,əuvə'hiə*] *vt* oír [por casualidad] (to hear) ‖ sorprender (a conversation).
— OBSERV Pret y pp *overheard*.

overheard [,əuvə'hə:d] *pret/pp* → **overhear.**

overheat ['əuvə'hi:t] *vt* recalentar, calentar demasiado ‖ FIG acalorar.
◆ *vi* recalentarse, calentar demasiado.

overheating [-iŋ] *n* recalentamiento *m* ‖ FIG acaloramiento *m*.

overhung ['əuvə'hʌŋ] *pret/pp* → **overhang.**

overindulge ['əuvərin'dʌldʒ] *vt* mimar demasiado a, ser demasiado indulgente con (s.o.) ‖ dar rienda suelta a (a passion).
◆ *vi* *to overindulge in* abusar de; *he overindulges in drinking* abusa de la bebida.

overindulgence [-əns] *n* indulgencia *f* excesiva ‖ abuso *m*, exceso *m* (*in* de).

overindulgent [-ənt] *adj* demasiado indulgente.

overissue ['əuvər'iʃu:] *vt* COMM emitir en exceso.

overjoy [,əuvə'dʒɔi] *vt* llenar de alegría ‖ *to be overjoyed at sth.* no caber en sí de contento por algo.

overkill ['əuvəkil] *n* capacidad *f* de destrucción superior al de las fuerzas enemigas.

overlaid [,əuvə'leid] *pret/pp* → **overlay.**

overlain [,əuvə'lein] *pp* → **overlie.**

overland ['əuvəlænd] *adv* por tierra, por vía terrestre.
◆ *adj* terrestre (road) ‖ que viaja por tierra.

overlap ['əuvəlæp]; **overlapping** [,əuvə'læpiŋ] *n* imbricación *f*, superposición *f*, traslapo *m* ‖ *overlapping with other meetings* coincidencia *f* con otras reuniones.

overlap [,əuvə'læp] *vt* traslapar, superponerse a (to cover partially) ‖ FIG coincidir parcialmente con.
◆ *vi* traslaparse, solaparse ‖ sobresalir (to jut out) ‖ FIG coincidir parcialmente.

overlay ['əuvəlei] *n* cubierta *f* (cover) ‖ chapa *f* (of wood, of metal, etc.) ‖ capa *f* (coat) ‖ revestimiento *m* (new surface) ‖ colcha *f* (of a bed) ‖ colchón *m* (mattress) ‖ PRINT alza *f*.

overlay* [,əuvə'lei] *vt* revestir, cubrir (to cover) ‖ asfixiar, ahogar (to overlie) ‖ oprimir (to oppress).
— OBSERV Pret y pp *overlie*.

overlay [,əuvə'lei] *pret* → **overlie.**

overleaf [-'li:f] *adv* a la vuelta ‖ *see overleaf* véase al dorso.

overleap* ['əuvə'li:p] *vt* saltar, salvar (to leap over) ‖ saltar más lejos que ‖ FIG pasar por alto, omitir.
— OBSERV Pret y pp *overleaped, overleapt*.

overlie* [,əuvə'lai] *vt* cubrir (to cover) ‖ asfixiar, ahogar [a un niño echándose sobre él].
— OBSERV Pret *overlay*; pp *overlain*.

overload ['əuvələud] *n* sobrecarga *f*.

overload ['əuvə'ləud] *vt* sobrecargar.

overlook [,əuvə'luk] *vt* dar a, tener vista a (to command a view); *my window overlooks the sea* mi ventana da al mar ‖ dominar; *the Eiffel Tower overlooks all Paris* la Torre Eiffel domina todo París ‖ mirar desde lo alto (to look at from above) ‖ pasar por alto (to pretend not to notice) ‖ no hacer caso de (to ignore) ‖ dejar pasar (to excuse); *to overlook an error* dejar pasar un error ‖ vigilar (to look after) ‖ inspeccionar, supervisar (to supervise).

overlooker [-ə*] *n* vigilante *m* (watchman) ‖ supervisor, ra; inspector, ra.

overlord ['əuvəlɔ:d] *n* señor *m* feudal ‖ jefe *m* supremo (supreme ruler).

overlordship [-ʃip] *n* soberanía *f* or señorío *m* feudal ‖ jefatura *f* suprema, mando *m* supremo.

overly ['əuvəli] *adv* excesivamente, demasiado.

overman ['əuvəmæn] *n* capataz *m*.
— OBSERV El plural de *overman* es *overmen*.

overman ['əuvə'mæn] *vt* emplear a más personal de lo necesario en.

overmanning [,əuvə'mæniŋ] *n* ECON exceso *m* de personal.

overmaster [,əuvə'mɑ:stə*] *vt* dominar.

overmastering [,əuvə'mɑ:stəriŋ] *adj* dominante, dominador, ra ‖ FIG irresistible.

overmatch [,əuvə'mætʃ] *vt* dominar, superar, patentizar una superioridad manifiesta sobre ‖ *to be overmatched* ser dominado en todos los terrenos.

overmuch ['əuvə'mʌtʃ] *adj* demasiado, da.
◆ *adv* demasiado, excesivamente.

overnice ['əuvə'nais] *adj* empalagoso, sa (too kind).

overnight ['əuvə'nait] *adj* de noche (journey) ‖ por una noche; *to have overnight guest* tener invitados por una noche ‖ de la noche anterior ‖ — *overnight bag* neceser *m* ‖ *to be an overnight success* tener éxito de la noche a la mañana.
◆ *adv* por la noche (during the night) ‖ de la noche a la mañana; *he changed his mind overnight* cambió de parecer de la noche a la mañana ‖ — *the milk won't keep overnight* la leche no se conservará fresca hasta mañana ‖ *to stay overnight* pernoctar, pasar la noche.

overornate ['əuvərɔ:'neit] *adj* recargado, da.

overpaid ['əuvə'peid] *pret/pp* → **overpay.**
◆ *adj* pagado con exceso, demasiado pagado, da.

overparticular ['əuvəpə'tikjulə*] *adj* melindroso, sa ‖ — *he is not overparticular about money* no le importa mucho el dinero ‖ *he is not overparticular in how he gets his money* tiene pocos escrúpulos para conseguir dinero.

overpass [ixəuvə,pɑ:s] *n* paso *m* superior.

overpass [,əuvə'pɑ:s] *vt* atravesar (a country) ‖ salvar, superar (an obstacle) ‖ sobrepasar (the limits) ‖ superar (s.o.).

overpay* ['əuvə'pei] *vt* pagar con exceso a, pagar demasiado a (s.o.) ‖ pagar demasiado por (sth.).
— OBSERV Pret y pp *overpaid*.

overpayment [-mənt] *n* pago *m* excesivo.

overpersuade ['əuvepə'sweid] *vt* persuadir.

overplacement ['əuvə'pleismənt] *n* superposición *f*.

overplay ['əuvə,plei] *vt* exagerar (a part) ‖ SP lanzar la pelota más allá de (the green).

overplus ['əuvəplʌs] *n* excedente *m*.

overpopulated ['əuvə'pɔpjuleitid] *adj* superpoblado, da.

overpopulation ['əuvə,pɔpju'leiʃən] *n* exceso *m* de población, superpoblación *f*.

overpower [,əuvə'pauə*] *vt* vencer, dominar (to beat) ‖ abrumar, agobiar; *the heat overpowered him* el calor le abrumaba ‖ dar demasiada potencia a.

overpowering [-riŋ] *adj* abrumador, ra ‖ irresistible (desire).

overpraise ['əuvə'preiz] *vt* alabar con exceso.

overpressure ['əuvə'preʃə*] *n* TECH superpresión *f* ‖ FIG agotamiento *m*.

overprint ['əuvəprint] *n* sobrecarga *f* (postmark) ‖ sello *m* con sobrecarga (stamp) ‖ PRINT & PHOT sobreimpresión *f*.

overprint ['əuvə'print] *vt* PRINT & PHOT sobreimprimir ‖ imprimir demasiados ejemplares de (to print too many copies of) ‖ poner sobrecarga a (stamp).

overprize [,əuvə'praiz] *vt* supervalorar, sobrestimar.

overproduce ['əuvəprə'dju:s] *vt* producir con exceso.

overproduction ['əuvəprə'dʌkʃən] *n* superproducción *f*.

overproof ['əuvəpru:f] *adj* con una proporción de alcohol superior al cincuenta por ciento.

overprotective ['əuvəprə'tektiv] *adj* excesivamente protector, ra.

overran [,əuvə'ræn] *pret* → **overrun.**

overrate ['əuvə'reit] *vt* supervalorar, sobrestimar.

overrated [-id] *adj* sobreestimado, da.

overreach [,əuvə'ri:tʃ] *vt* llegar más allá de, rebasar (to extend beyond) ‖ engañar (to cheat) ‖ *to overreach o.s.* extralimitarse.
◆ *vi* alcanzarse (horses).

overreact ['əuvəri:'ækt] *vi* reaccionar exageradamente.

overrefine ['əuvəri'fain] *vt* refinar con exceso (a metal) ‖ alambicar (style).

overrefinement [-mənt] *n* afectación *f* ‖ preciosidad *f* (of style).

override* [,əuvə'raid] *vt* pasar por encima de (to ride over) ‖ pisotear (to trample down) ‖ no hacer caso de, hacer caso omiso de, no tener en cuenta (to disregard); *to override orders* hacer caso omiso de las órdenes ‖ anular (to invalidate) ‖ dejar a un lado (to set aside) ‖ dominar (to dominate) ‖ extralimitarse en, so-

brepasar (to exceed) || agotar, reventar (a horse).
— OBSERV Pret *overrode*; pp *overridden*.

overridden [ˌəuvəˈridn] *pp* ⟶ **override.**

overriding [ˌəuvəˈraidiŋ] *adj* principal, primordial, esencial (principal) || — *overriding clause* cláusula derogatoria || *overriding principle* principio absoluto.

overripe [ˈəuvəˈraip] *adj* demasiado maduro, ra; pasado, da (fruit) || pasado, da; demasiado hecho (cheese).

overrode [ˌəuvəˈrəud] *pret* ⟶ **override.**

overrule [ˌəuvəˈruːl] *vt* denegar (to refuse) || no aceptar (an objection) || rechazar [una protesta] || anular (to rescind) || dominar (to prevail over).

overrun [ˈəuvəˌrʌn] *n* PRINT recorrido *m* || zona *f* libre de obstáculos en un aeropuerto dispuesta para un aterrizaje forzoso.

overrun* [ˌəuvəˈrʌn] *vt* invadir (to invade) || inundar (to flood) || rebasar (to exceed) || ELECTR aumentar el voltaje de || PRINT recorrer || pasar (a traffic signal) || *to overrun o.s.* correr hasta el agotamiento.
◆ *vi* rebosar (liquid) || desbordarse (river) || AUT correr más rápido que el motor.
— OBSERV Pret *overran*; pp *overrun*.

overrunning [-iŋ] *n* invasión *f* (by people) || inundación *f* (flood) || ELECTR aumento *m* de voltaje, sobrevoltaje *m*, sobretensión *f*.

oversaw [ˈəuvəˈsɔː] *pret* ⟶ **oversee.**

overscrupulous [ˈəuvəˈskruːpjuləs] *adj* ⟶ **overparticular.**

oversea [ˈəuvəˈsiː]; **overseas** [-z] *adv* en *or* a ultramar (beyond the sea) || por el extranjero, en el extranjero, al extranjero (abroad).
◆ *adj* ultramarino, na; de ultramar || exterior (debt, trade) || extranjero, ra (foreign).

oversee* [ˈəuvəˈsiː] *vt* supervisar (to supervise) || vigilar (to watch).
— OBSERV Pret *oversaw*; pp *overseen*.

overseen [-n] *pp* ⟶ **oversee.**

overseer [ˈəuvəsiə*] *n* supervisor, ra || vigilante *m* (watchman) || capataz *m* (foreman) || regente *m* (in printing).

oversell* [ˈəuvəˈsel] *vt* COMM vender con exceso | hacer una propaganda excesiva de.
— OBSERV Pret y pp *oversold*.

oversensitive [ˈəuvəˈsensitiv] *adj* hipersensible, demasiado sensible.

overset* [ˈəuvəˈset] *vt* ⟶ **upset.**
— OBSERV Pret y pp *overset*.

oversew* [ˈəuvəˈsəu] *vt* sobrehilar (to overcast).
— OBSERV Pret *oversewed*; pp *oversewn, oversewed*.

oversewn [-n] *pp* ⟶ **oversew.**

overshade [ˌəuvəˈʃeid] *vt* sombrear.

overshadow [ˌəuvəˈʃædəu] *vt* oscurecer, sombrear (to cast a shadow over) || FIG eclipsar; *he is overshadowed by his brother* es eclipsado por su hermano.

overshoe [ˈəuvəʃuː] *n* bota *f* de goma, chanclo *m*.

overshoot* [ˈəuvəˈʃuːt] *vt* ir *or* llegar más allá de (to go beyond) || llegar más allá de [la pista] (an aeroplane) || FIG & FAM *to overshoot the mark* pasarse de la raya, rebasar los límites.
— OBSERV Pret y pp *overshot*.

overshot [ˈəuvəˈʃɔt] *pret/pp* ⟶ **overshoot.**
◆ *adj* ZOOL con la mandíbula superior saliente || *overshot wheel* rueda *f* de cangilones.

oversight [ˈəuvəsait] *n* descuido *m* (neglect); *by* o *through oversight* por descuido || supervisión *f* (supervision) || vigilancia *f*.

oversimplification [ˈəuvəˌsimplifiˈkeiʃən] *n* simplificación *f* excesiva.

oversimplify [ˈəuvəˈsimplifai] *vt* simplificar excesivamente *or* demasiado.

oversize [ˈəuvəsaiz] *adj* demasiado grande (too large) || de tamaño descomunal (unusually large).
◆ *n* tamaño *m* descomunal.

overskirt [ˈəuvəskəːt] *n* sobrefalda *f*.

oversleep* [ˈəuvəˈsliːp] *vi* dormir más de lo previsto, dormir demasiado, quedarse dormido más de la cuenta, no despertarse a la hora deseada || *I overslept this morning* se me pegaron las sábanas esta mañana (*fam*).
— OBSERV Pret y pp *overslept*.

overslept [ˈəuvəˈslept] *pret/pp* ⟶ **oversleep.**

oversold [ˈəuvəˈsəuld] *pret/pp* ⟶ **oversell.**

overspend* [ˈəuvəˈspend] *vt/vi* gastar excesivamente *or* demasiado || gastar más que.
— OBSERV Pret y pp *overspent*.

overspent [ˈəuvəˈspent] *pret/pp* ⟶ **overspend.**

overspill [ˈəuvəˈspil] *n* traslado *m* de población || exceso *m* de población.

overspread* [ˌəuvəˈspred] *vt* extender sobre.
— OBSERV Pret y pp *overspread*.

overstaffed [ˈəuvəˈstɑːft] *adj* con exceso de personal (company).

overstate [ˈəuvəˈsteit] *vt* exagerar.

overstatement [-mənt] *n* exageración *f*.

overstay [ˈəuvəˈstei] *vt* *to overstay one's leave* o *one's welcome* quedarse más tiempo de lo conveniente.

overstep [ˈəuvəˈstep] *vt* sobrepasar, pasar de || FIG *to overstep the mark* pasarse de la raya.

overstitch [ˈəuvəˈstitʃ] *n* punto *m* por encima.

overstock [ˈəuvəˈstɔk] *vt* *to be overstocked with* poseer existencias excesivas de.

overstrain [ˈəuvəˈstrein] *n* cansancio *m* excesivo, agotamiento *m* (exhaustion) || hipertensión *f* (nervous).

overstrain [ˈəuvəˈstrein] *vt* cansar excesivamente, agotar (to exhaust) || producir hipertensión en (nervously) || — *overstrained relations* relaciones muy tensas || *to overstrain o.s.* agotarse.
◆ *vi* agotarse.

overstress [ˈəuvəˈstres] *vt* sobrecargar || FIG insistir demasiado en.

overstrung [ˈəuvəˈstrʌŋ] *adj* hipertenso, sa; sobreexcitado, da (very nervous) || muy sensible (sensitive).

oversubscribe [ˈəuvəsəbˈskraib] *vt* COMM suscribir en exceso de la emisión (shares, etc.).

oversupply [ˈəuvəsəˈplai] *vt* proveer en exceso.

overt [ˈəuvəːt] *adj* abierto, ta; público, ca || evidente, manifiesto, ta (patent).

overtake* [ˌəuvəˈteik] *vt* adelantar, pasar [AMER rebasar] (to pass); *I overtook his car* adelanté su coche || alcanzar (to catch up) || sorprender; *a storm overtook them two hours later* una tormenta les sorprendió dos horas después || abatirse; *misfortune overtook his family* la desgracia se abatió sobre su familia || apoderarse; *panic overtook the crowd* el pánico se apoderó de la muchedumbre.
◆ *vi* adelantar, pasar.
— OBSERV Pret *overtook*; pp *overtaken*.

overtaken [-ən] *pp* ⟶ **overtake.**

overtaking [-iŋ] *n* adelantamiento *m* || *no overtaking* prohibido adelantar.

overtask [ˈəuvəˈtɑːsk] *vt* agobiar de trabajo.

overtax [ˈəuvəˈtæks] *vt* exigir demasiado a (to strain).

over-the-counter [ˈəuvəðəˈkauntə*] *adj* negociado fuera de la Bolsa (stocks).

overthrew [ˌəuvəˈθruː] *pret* ⟶ **overthrow.**

overthrow [ˈəuvəθrəu] *n* derrocamiento *m* (of a government) || derrumbamiento *m* (of an empire) || derrota *f* (of an army) || desbaratamiento *m* (of plans).

overthrow* [ˌəuvəˈθrəu] *vt* derrocar, derribar; *to overthrow a government* derrocar un gobierno || derrumbar (an empire) || derrotar (an army) || volcar (to overturn) || echar abajo, desbaratar (plans).
— OBSERV Pret *overthrew*; pp *overthrown*.

overthrown [-n] *pp* ⟶ **overthrow.**

overtime [ˈəuvətaim] *adv* fuera de hora (beyond the usual hours) || US SP fuera del tiempo reglamentario || *to work overtime* hacer horas extraordinarias.
◆ *n* horas *f pl* extraordinarias (work) || US SP prórroga *f* || *an hour's overtime* una hora extraordinaria.

overtime [ˈəuvəˈtaim] *vt* PHOT sobreexponer.

overtire [ˈəuvəˈtaiə*] *vt* cansar demasiado, agotar.

overtone [ˈəuvətəun] *n* MUS armónico *m* || FIG insinuación *f*, alusión *f*; *a reply full of overtones* una contestación llena de insinuaciones.

overtook [ˈəuvəˈtuk] *pret* ⟶ **overtake.**

overtop [ˈəuvətɔp] *vt* descollar entre, sobresalir entre.

overtrain [ˈəuvətrein] *vt* entrenar con exceso, sobreentrenar.
◆ *vi* entrenarse con exceso, sobreentrenarse.

overtrick [ˈəuvətrik] *n* baza *f* de más (in card games).

overtrump [ˈəuvəˈtrʌmp] *vt/vi* contrafallar (in card games).

overture [ˈəuvətjuə*] *n* propuesta *f*, proposición *f*, oferta *f* (proposal); *we have made overtures of peace* hemos hecho propuestas de paz || MUS obertura *f*.

overturn [ˌəuvəˈtəːn] *vt* volcar (to turn upside down) || MAR hacer zozobrar (a ship) || derrocar, derribar (a government, etc.) || trastornar (to disarrange).
◆ *vi* volcar (car, airplane, etc.) || MAR zozobrar (a ship).

overturning [ˌəuvəˈtəːniŋ] *n* vuelco *m* (of a car) || vuelco *m*, zozobra *f* (of a ship) || derrocamiento *m* (of a government, etc.).

overuse [ˈəuvəˈjuːs] *n* empleo *m* excesivo, uso *m* excesivo.

overuse [ˈəuvəˈjuːz] *vt* emplear *or* usar excesivamente.

overvaluation [ˈəuvəˌvæljuˈeiʃən] *n* sobrestimación *f*, supervaloración *f*.

overvalue [ˈəuvəˈvæljuː] *vt* supervalorar, sobrestimar.

overview [ˈəuvəvjuː] *n* visión *f* general.

overweening [ˌəuvəˈwiːniŋ] *adj* presuntuoso, sa; vanidoso, sa; arrogante.

overweight [ˈəuvəˈweit] *adj* de peso excesivo, demasiado pesado, da || — *to be overweight* pesar demasiado, ser demasiado pesado || *to be two pounds overweight* pesar dos libras de más.
◆ *n* sobrepeso *m*, exceso *m* de peso || exceso *m* (of luggage).

overweight [ˈəuvəˈweit] *vt* dar demasiada importancia a (to emphasize to excess) || sobrecargar (to overload).

overwhelm [ˌəuvəˈwelm] *vt* inundar, sumergir (to inundate) || aplastar, arrollar (in a discussion, an opponent) || abrumar; *they were overwhelmed at the news* la noticia les abrumó || agobiar, confundir; *overwhelmed by s.o.'s kind-*

ness confundido por la amabilidad de alguien || agobiar, abrumar; *overwhelmed with work* agobiado de trabajo || colmar; *to overwhelm with honours* colmar de honores || *to be overwhelmed with joy* rebosar de alegría.

overwhelming [-iŋ] *adj* abrumador, ra; aplastante, arrollador, ra (defeat) || agobiante, abrumador, ra (work) || irresistible (desire).

overwind* [ˈəuvəˈwaind] *vt* tensar demasiado la cuerda de (a watch).
— OBSERV Pret y pp ***overwound***.

overwork [ˈəuvəˈwəːk] *n* exceso *m* de trabajo, trabajo *m* excesivo.

overwork [ˈəuvəˈwəːk] *vt* hacer trabajar demasiado (to make work excessively) || usar demasiado, abusar de; *to overwork an expression* usar demasiado una expresión || *an overworked expression* una expresión trillada.
◆ *vi* trabajar demasiado (to work excessively) || trabajar horas extraordinarias (to work overtime).

overwound [ˈəuvəˌwaund] *pret/pp* ⟶ **overwind.**

overwrought [ˈəuvəˈrɔːt] *adj* sobreexcitado, da; *an overwrought child* un niño sobreexcitado || agotado por el trabajo excesivo, con los nervios destrozados (exhausted) || recargado, da; *an overwrought style* un estilo recargado.

Ovid [ˈɔvid] *pr n* Ovidio *m*.

ovidae [ˈəuvidiː] *pl n* ZOOL óvidos *m*.

oviduct [ˈəuvidʌkt] *n* oviducto *m*.

oviform [ˈəuvifɔːm] *adj* oviforme.

ovine [ˈəuvain] *adj* ZOOL ovino, na; lanar.

oviparity [əuviˈpæriti] *n* ZOOL oviparidad *f*.

oviparous [əuˈvipərəs] *adj* ZOOL ovíparo, ra.

oviposit [əuviˈpɔzit] *vi* ZOOL poner huevos.

ovipositor [-ə*] *n* ZOOL oviscapto *m*.

ovoid [ˈəuvɔid] *adj* ovoide.
◆ *n* ovoide *m*.

ovolo [ˈəuvələu] *n* ARCH óvolo *m*.
— OBSERV El plural de la palabra inglesa es *ovoli*.

ovoviviparous [əuvəviˈvipərəs] *adj* ZOOL ovovivíparo, ra.

ovular [ˈəuvjulə*] *adj* ovular.

ovulate [ˈəuvjuleit] *vi* ovular.

ovulation [əuvjuˈleiʃən] *n* ovulación *f*.

ovule [ˈəuvjuːl] *n* óvulo *m*.

ovum [ˈəuvum] *n* ARCH ovo *m* || BIOL óvulo *m*.
— OBSERV El plural de *ovum* es *ova*.

owe [əu] *vt* deber; *to owe s.o. money* deber dinero a alguien || deber; *to owe respect to s.o.* deber respeto a alguien; *to owe allegiance to one's country* deber lealtad al propio país *or* a la patria; *she owes her life to the doctors* debe su vida a los médicos || *I owe him my thanks* le tengo que estar agradecido.
◆ *vi* tener deudas.

owing [ˈəuiŋ] *adj* que se debe; *a small quantity of money is owing* se debe una pequeña cantidad de dinero || *owing to* debido a, a causa de, por razones de.

owl [aul] *n* ZOOL lechuza *f* común (barn) | mochuelo *m* (little) | búho *m* (long-eared) | cárabo *m*, autillo *m* (tawny) || — *eagle owl* búho real || *horned owl* búho *m* || FIG & FAM *night owl* ave nocturna || US FAM *owl train* tren *m* de noche.

owlet [ˈaulit] *n* ZOOL mochuelo *m*.

owlish [ˈauliʃ] *adj* de búho || FIG & FAM serio, ria.

own [əun] *adj* propio, pia; *her own money* su propio dinero; *I saw it with my own eyes* lo he visto con mis propios ojos || — *of one's own accord* de motu propio || SP *own goal* gol *m* en propia portería || *she makes her own dresses* hace ella misma sus vestidos.
◆ *n* lo mío, lo tuyo, lo suyo, etc.; *to look after one's own* ocuparse de lo suyo || los míos, los tuyos, los suyos (relatives) || — *for my own* para mí solo || *my, your, his own* mío, mía, tuyo, tuya, suyo, suya; *the house is my own* la casa es mía || *of my, your, his etc. own* mío, mía, tuyo, tuya, suyo, suya, etc.; *she has money of her own* tiene dinero suyo; *he has nothing of his own* no tiene nada suyo; propio, pia; *for reasons of his own* por motivos propios; muy mío, muy mía, muy tuyo, muy tuya, muy suyo, muy suya, etc.; *she has a style of her own* tiene un estilo muy suyo || *on one's own* solo, sola; *he did it on his own* lo hizo solo; de motu propio (on one's own initiative), por su cuenta; *to work on one's own* trabajar por su cuenta || *to come into one's own* tomar posesión de lo suyo; conseguir lo que uno se merece || *to get one's own back* desquitarse || *to hold one's own* mantenerse firme (not to give away), poder competir *or* rivalizar; *I can hold my own with you* puedo competir con usted; defenderse; *I hold my own in English* me defiendo en inglés || *to make sth. one's own* apoderarse de algo.

own [əun] *vt* poseer, tener (to possess); *I own a boat* tengo un barco || reconocer (a child, a king, an authority) || reconocer, admitir, confesar; *I own I was wrong* reconozco que estaba equivocado || *who owns this land?* ¿a quién pertenece este terreno?
◆ *vi* *to own to* reconocer, confesar || *to own up* confesar || *to own up to* confesar.

owner [-ə*] *n* dueño, ña; propietario, ria (of house, of land, etc.) || poseedor, ra (possessor) || — *joint owner* copropietario, ria || JUR *rightful owner* propietario legítimo, derecho habiente *m*.

ownerless [-əlis] *adj* sin dueño.

owner-occupier [-ˈɔkjəpaiə*] *n* propietario, ria que reside en su propia vivienda.

ownership [əʃip] *n* propiedad *f*; *bare ownership* nuda propiedad || posesión *f* || — *common ownership* copropiedad *f* || *«under new ownership»* «cambio de propietario».

ox [ɔks] *n* buey *m* (animal).
— OBSERV El plural de *ox* es *oxen*.

oxalic [ɔkˈsælik] *adj* CHEM oxálico, ca (acid).

oxalidaceae [ɔksæliˈdeisiːi] *pl n* BOT oxalidáceas *f*.

oxbow [ˈɔksbəu] *n* collera *f* de yugo || US recodo *m* de un río (of a river).

oxcart [ˈɔkskɑːt] *n* carreta *f* de bueyes.

oxeye daisy [ˈɔksaiˈdeizi] *n* BOT margarita *f*.

Oxfam [ˈɔksfæm] *n* organización *f* benéfica de ayuda al Tercer Mundo [Gran Bretaña].

Oxford [ˈɔksfəd] *pr n* GEOGR Oxford.

Oxfordian [ˈɔksˈfɔdjən] *adj/n* oxoniense.

oxhide [ˈɔkshaid] *n* cuero *m* de buey.

oxidation [ˌɔksiˈdeiʃən] *n* oxidación *f*.

oxide [ˈɔksaid] *n* CHEM óxido *m*; *copper oxide* óxido de cobre.

oxidizable [ˈɔksidaizəbl] *adj* oxidable.

oxidize [ˈɔksidaiz] *vt* oxidar.
◆ *vi* oxidarse.

oxidizer [-ə*] *n* oxidante *m*.

oxidizing [-iŋ] *adj* oxidante.
◆ *n* oxidación *f*.

oxlip [ˈɔkslip] *n* BOT prímula *f*.

Oxonian [ɔkˈsəunjən] *adj/n* oxoniense.

oxtail [ˈɔksteil] *n* rabo *m* de buey.

oxtongue [ˈɔkstʌŋ] *n* BOT lengua *f* de buey.

oxyacetylene [ˈɔksiəˈsetiliːn] *adj* CHEM oxiacetilénico, ca || — *oxyacetylene torch* soplete oxiacetilénico, soplete de soldadura autógena || *oxyacetylene welding* soldadura autógena *or* oxiacetilénica.

oxyacid [ˈɔksiˈæsid] *n* CHEM oxácido *m*.

oxygen [ˈɔksidʒən] *n* CHEM oxígeno *m* || — *oxygen acid* oxácido *m* || *oxygen cylinder* balón *m* de oxígeno || *oxygen mask* máscara *f* de oxígeno || *oxygen tent* cámara *f* de oxígeno || *oxygen treatment* oxigenoterapia *f*.

oxygenate [ɔkˈsidʒineit] *vt* CHEM oxigenar.

oxygenation [ˌɔksidʒiˈneiʃən] *n* CHEM oxigenación *f*.

oxygen-hydrogen welding [ˈɔksidʒənˈhaidridʒənˈweldiŋ] *n* soldadura *f* oxhídrica.

oxygenize [ˈɔksidʒənaiz] *vt* oxigenar.

oxyhaemoglobin; oxyhemoglobin [ˈɔksihiːməˈgləubin] *n* BIOL oxihemoglobina *f*.

oxyhydrogen [ˈɔksiˈhaidridʒən] *adj* oxhídrico, ca; *oxyhydrogen torch* soplete oxhídrico.

oxytone [ˈɔksitəun] *adj* GRAMM oxítono, na.
◆ *n* GRAMM oxítono *m*.

oxyuris [ɔksiˈjuəris] *n* oxiuro *m*.

oyer and terminer [ˈɔiə*ændˈtəːminə*] *n* JUR audiencia *f* de lo criminal.

oyes; oyez [əuˈjes] *interj* ¡atención!, ¡oíd!

oyster [ˈɔistə*] *n* ZOOL ostra *f* || — *oyster bed* o *farm* criadero *m* de ostras, ostral *m*, ostrero *m* || *oyster catcher* ostrero *m* (bird) || *oyster culture* o *farming* ostricultura *f* || *oyster culturist* o *farmer* ostricultor *m* || *oyster seller* ostrero, ra || *the oyster industry* la industria ostrícola.

oysterroot [-ruːt] *n* BOT salsifí *m*.

ozonation [əuzəuˈneiʃən] *n* CHEM ozonización *f*.

ozonator [əuzəuˈneitə*] *n* CHEM ozonador *m*, ozonizador *m*.

ozone [ˈəuzəun] *n* CHEM ozono *m* || *ozone layer* capa *f* de ozono.

ozone-friendly [-ˌfrendli] *adj* que no daña la capa de ozono.

ozonic [əuˈzɔnik] *adj* CHEM ozonizado, da.

ozonization [əuzəunaiˈzeiʃən] *n* CHEM ozonización *f*.

ozonize [ˈəuzəunaiz] *vt* CHEM ozonizar, ozonar, ozonificar.

ozonometer [əuzəuˈnɔmitə*] *n* ozonómetro *m*.

ozonosphere [əuˈzəunəˌsfiə*] *n* ozonosfera *f*.

P

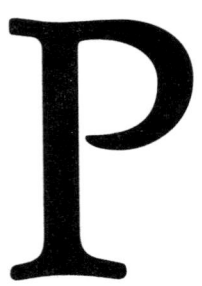

p [piː] *n* p *f; capital p, small p* p mayúscula, p minúscula || FIG *to mind one's P's and Q's* darle siete vueltas a la lengua antes de hablar, tener cuidado de no meter la pata.

pa [pɑː] *n* FAM papá *m*.

pabulum ['pæbjuləm] *n* alimento *m*, pábulo *m* (nourishment) || FIG *mental pabulum* alimento del espíritu.

paca ['pækə] *n* ZOOL paca *f* (rodent).

pacay [pə'kai] *n* AMER pacay *m* (tree).

pace [peis] *n* paso *m* (step); *ten paces off* o *away* a diez pasos || paso *m* (speed); *to walk at a brisk pace* andar con paso rápido; *to slacken one's pace* aminorar el paso || ritmo *m*; *the present building pace* el ritmo actual de la construcción || — *at a good pace* a buen paso || *at a slow pace* a paso lento || *at a walking pace* al paso || *at one's own pace* al paso de uno (walk), al ritmo de uno (work) || FIG *to go at a snail's pace* andar a paso de tortuga *or* de buey *or* de carreta || *to keep pace with s.o.* andar al mismo paso que alguien || FIG *to keep pace with sth.* correr parejas con algo, seguir el mismo ritmo que algo (to develop at the same speed), mantenerse al tanto de (to keep up to date with) || *to put through his* o *its paces* poner a prueba (to test), entrenar (to train) || *to quicken one's pace* apretar *or* alargar *or* acelerar *or* aligerar el paso || FIG *to set the pace* dar la pauta.

pace [peis] *vi* ir al paso, andar al paso || amblar (a horse) || *to pace up and down the room* ir y venir por la habitación.
◆ *vt* medir a pasos (to measure); *to pace a room* medir una habitación a pasos || DEP marcar el paso para (runner, etc.) || ir y venir por (a room) || *to pace off* o *out fifteen metres* medir quince metros a pasos.

pacemaker [-ˌmeikə*] *n* persona *f* que da la pauta, líder *m* (s.o. who takes the lead) || SP el que marca el paso (in a race) || MED marcapasos *m inv*, regulador *m* cardiaco, marcador *m* de paso.

pacer ['peisə*] *n* SP el que marca el paso.

pacesetter ['peisˌsetə*] *n* persona *f* que da la pauta, líder *m*.

pachyderm ['pækidəːm] *n* ZOOL paquidermo *m*.

pachydermatous [ˌpæki'dəːmətəs] *adj* ZOOL paquidermo, ma || FIG insensible.

pacific [pə'sifik] *adj* pacífico, ca.

Pacific [pə'sifik] *adj* pacífico; *Pacific Ocean* Océano Pacífico.

pacifically [pə'sifikəli] *adv* pacíficamente.

pacification [ˌpæsifi'keiʃən] *n* pacificación *f*.

pacifier ['pæsifaiə*] *n* pacificador, ra || US chupete *m* (for babies).

pacifism ['pæsifizəm] *n* pacifismo *m*.

pacifist ['pæsifist] *adj/n* pacifista.

pacify ['pæsifai] *vt* apaciguar, calmar, tranquilizar (s.o.) || pacificar (a country).

pack [pæk] *n* bulto *m*, fardo *m* (bundle) || paquete *m* (packet) || manada *f* (of wolves) || jauría *f* (of hounds) || baraja *f* (of cards) || MIL mochila *f* || MED paño *m* [caliente] | compresa *f* || emplasto *m* (cosmetic treatment) || partida *f*, pandilla *f*, panda *f* (gang of people) || serie *f*, montón *m* (of troubles) || montón *m*, tejido *m*, sarta *f*; *a pack of lies* una sarta de mentiras || SP «pack» *m*, delanteros *m pl* (in rugby) || banquisa *f*, banco *m* de hielo (of ice) || albarda *f* (carried by an animal) || envase *m* (wrapping) || US cajetilla *f* (of cigarettes).

pack [pæk] *vt* llenar (to fill a container with sth.) || embalar (to put sth. in a container); *a vacuum cleaner packed in a box* una aspiradora embalada en una caja || envasar; *to pack flour in sacks* envasar harina en sacos; *to pack milk in cartons* envasar leche en cartones || envolver (to wrap) || enlatar (to put in a tin) || embotellar (to put in a bottle) || empaquetar (to put in a packet or in a parcel) || poner en cajas (to put in boxes) || empacar (wool) || embarrilar (to put into barrels) || poner en la maleta; *I have to pack my things* tengo que poner mis cosas en la maleta || hacer; *to pack a suitcase* hacer la maleta || albardar (a horse) || llenar hasta los topes, atestar (to fill tightly); *a train packed with people* un tren atestado de gente || TECH guarnecer (a piston) || llenar de partidarios (a committee, a jury) || US llevar, cargar (a parcel, etc.) | llevar [un arma] (to carry a gun) || — *the film is packing them in* la película atrae a mucha gente || *the town is packed with tourists* la ciudad está llena de turistas || *to pack down* apretar (to press), pisotear (with the feet) || *to pack in* apiñar (people), llenar de bote en bote, atestar (a place) || FAM *to pack it in* dejarlo | *to pack one's bags* liar el petate (to leave) | *to pack s.o. off* mandar a alguien a paseo, echar *or* despedir a alguien con cajas destempladas (to tell s.o. to leave), mandar, despachar (to send) || *to pack up a tent* recoger una tienda || *to pack up one's bits and pieces* preparar sus bártulos || FAM *to send s.o. packing* echar *or* despedir a alguien con cajas destempladas.
◆ *vi* hacer la maleta *or* las maletas (to put one's things into a suitcase) || volverse compacto, endurecerse (to become compact) || apiñarse (to crowd together); *the crowd packed round the minister* la muchedumbre se apiñó en torno al ministro || caber en la maleta; *small things pack easily* las cosas pequeñas caben fácilmente en la maleta || — *to pack badly* arrugarse en la maleta || FAM *to pack off* o *away* largarse (to leave) || *to pack together* apretarse || *to pack up* hacer la maleta *or* las maletas (for a trip, etc.), amontonarse (to pile up), averiarse, estropearse (to break down), liar el petate (to die, to depart) || *to pack well* no arrugarse en la maleta.

package ['pækidʒ] *n* paquete *m* (parcel) || bulto *m* (bundle) || embalaje *m* (packing) || envase *m* (of liquids, etc.) || FIG conjunto *m* de medidas (series of measures taken at one time) | acuerdo *m* global que supone concesiones mutuas (deal) || INFORM paquete *m* de programas || — FIG *package deal* acuerdo global que supone concesiones mutuas (agreement), venta *f* global de varios artículos (sale) | *package holiday* o *tour* viaje *m* todo comprendido || US *package store* bodega *f*.

package ['pækidʒ] *vt* embalar (to pack) || envasar (liquids, grain, etc.).

packaging [-iŋ] *n* embalaje *m* (packing) || envase *m* (of liquids, etc.).

pack animal ['pækˌænimәl] *n* animal *m* de carga, acémila *f*.

packed [pækt] *adj* lleno, na.

packed lunch [-lʌntʃ] *n* almuerzo *m* frío para llevar.

packed-out [-ɑut] *adj* abarrotado, da; atestado, da.

packer ['pækə*] *n* embalador, ra; empaquetador, ra || envasador, ra (of liquids, etc.).

packet ['pækit] *n* paquete *m* (small package) || cajetilla *f* (of cigarettes) || sobre *m* (of tea, etc.) || paquebote *m* (packet boat) || FAM dineral *m* (money).

packet ['pækit] *vt* empaquetar, embalar || envasar.

packet boat [-bəut] *n* paquebote *m*.

packhorse ['pækhɔːs] *n* caballo *m* de carga.

pack ice ['pækais] *n* banquisa *f*, banco *m* de hielo.

packing ['pækiŋ] *n* embalaje *m* (in boxes); *the packing of goods* el embalaje de mercancías || empaquetado *m* || envase *m*, envasado *m* (of liquids, of powders) || embalaje *m* (material used); *to throw away the packing* tirar el embalaje || envase *m* (recipient for liquids, for flour, etc.) || relleno *m* (filling) || MED paño *m* caliente || TECH guarnición *f* (of a piston) || *to do one's packing* hacer las maletas.

packing case [-ˌkeis] *n* cajón *m*, caja *f* de embalaje.

packing ring [-riŋ] *n* TECH arandela *f*.

packman ['pækmən] *n* (ant) vendedor *m* ambulante, buhonero *m*.
— OBSERV El plural de *packman* es *packmen*.

packsaddle ['pækˌsædl] *n* albarda *f*.

packthread ['pækθred] *n* bramante *m*, guita *f*.

packtrain ['pæktrein] *n* reata *f* de animales de carga.

pact [pækt] *n* pacto *m*; *nonaggresion pact* pacto de no agresión.

pad [pæd] *n* almohadilla *f*, cojín *m* (cushion) || rodete *m* (to carry loads) || almohadilla *f*, tampón *m* (for inking) || carpeta *f* (for blotting) || bloc *m*, taco *m* (of paper) || taco *m* (of a calendar) || relleno *m*, almohadilla *f* (soft material to fill) || hombrera *f*, almohadilla *f* (for shoulders) || SP espinillera *f* (for cricket, for hockey, etc.) | peto *m* (for fencing) || ZOOL almohadilla *f* (sole of the paw) | pata *f* (paw) || MED cataplasma *f* || TECH portaherramientas *m inv* (for several tools) || pisada *f* silenciosa (muffled step) || FAM camino *m* (road) | casa *f* (house, flat) || pista *f* de despegue *or* de aterrizaje (for helicopters) || plataforma *f* de lanzamiento (for launching a rocket) || hoja *f* grande (of water plants) || — FAM *gentleman of the pad* salteador *m* de caminos, bandolero *m* | *to be on the pad* vagabundear.

pad [pæd] *vt* acolchar, acolchonar, enguatar (door, material, etc.) || rellenar (a cushion) || poner hombreras (shoulders) || FIG rellenar, meter paja en; *to pad a book, a speech* meter paja en un libro, en un discurso || — *padded cell* loquera *f* || FAM *to pad it, to pad the hoof* ir en el coche de San Fernando || FIG *to pad out* meter paja en, rellenar.

◆ *vi* andar, caminar (to walk) || andar a pasos quedos *or* silenciosos (with muffled steps) || FAM vagabundear (unhurriedly).

padding [-iŋ] *n* acolchado *m*, acolchonado *m*, enguatado *m* (operation) || relleno *m* (material) || FIG relleno *m*, paja *f*; *two chapters of pure padding* dos capítulos de pura paja.

paddle ['pædl] *n* pagaya *f*, zagual *m*, canalete *m* (oar) || paseo *m* en canoa (voyage) || álabe *m*, paleta *f* (of waterwheel) || ZOOL aleta *f* (flipper) || paleta *f* (for mixing, for beating clothes) || FAM *to go for a paddle* ir a mojarse los pies.

paddle ['pædl] *vt* MAR hacer avanzar con pagaya || mover con una paleta (a liquid) || *US* FAM azotar (to spank).

◆ *vi* remar con pagaya (to row) || mojarse los pies, chapotear (in the sea, etc.).

paddle boat [-bəut] *n* MAR vapor *m* de ruedas | hidropedal *m* (pedal boat).

paddle box [-bɔks] *n* MAR tambor *m* de ruedas (of a boat).

paddler [-ə*] *n* remero, ra; persona *f* que rema con pagaya.

paddle steamer [-sti:mə*] *n* MAR vapor *m* de ruedas.

paddle wheel [-wi:l] *n* rueda *f* de paletas *or* de álabes.

paddling pool [-iŋpu:l] *n* estanque *m* para niños.

paddock ['pædək] *n* potrero *m*, «paddock» *m* (grassy enclosed area) || «paddock» *m* (racecourse enclosure).

paddy ['pædi] *n* arroz *m* con cáscara (rice) || arrozal *m* (rice field) || FAM rabieta *f*, berrinche *m*; *to get into a paddy* coger una rabieta.

paddy wagon [-'wægən] *n* FAM coche *m* celular.

padlock ['pædlɔk] *n* candado *m*.

padlock ['pædlɔk] *vt* cerrar con candado.

padre ['pɑ:dri] *n* MIL & MAR capellán *m*.

paean ['pi:ən] *n* peán *m*, himno *m* de alegría, himno *m* triunfal.

paederast ['pedəræst] *n* pederasta *m*.

paederasty [-i] *n* pederastia *f*.

paediatrician [,pi:diə'triʃən]; **paediatrist** [,pidi'ætrist] *n* MED pediatra *m*, pedíatra *m*.

paediatrics [,pi:di'ætriks] *n* MED pediatría *f*.

paedophile; *US* **pedophile** ['pi:dəfɑi] *n* pedófilo, la.

pagan ['peigən] *adj/n* pagano, na.

paganism ['peigənizəm] *n* paganismo *m*.

paganize ['peigənaiz] *vt* paganizar.

page [peidʒ] *n* página *f* (of a book, etc.); *on page 2* en la página 2 || PRINT plana *f* || FIG página *f* || paje *m* (at court, at a wedding) || botones *m inv* (in a hotel) || acomodador *m* (in a theatre) || — *full page* a toda plana || *on the front page* en primera plana.

page [peidʒ] *vt* paginar, foliar (to number the pages) || PRINT compaginar || mandar llamar por el botones (in a hotel) || servir como paje (at court).

pageant ['pædʒənt] *n* cabalgata *f or* desfile *m* histórico (historical procession) || espectáculo *m* histórico (historical spectacle) || pompa *f*, aparato *m*, boato *m* (pageantry) || *air pageant* fiesta *f* aeronáutica.

pageantry [-ri] *n* pompa *f*, aparato *m*, boato *m* (display) || espectáculo *m* (spectacle).

page boy [peidʒbɔi] *n* paje *m* (at court, at a wedding) || botones *m inv* (in a hotel).

page proof [peidʒpru:f] *n* PRINT prueba *f* de imprenta.

pager ['peidʒə*] *n* buscapersonas *m inv*.

paginate [pædʒineit] *vt* paginar.

pagination [,pædʒi'neiʃən] *n* paginación *f*.

pagoda [pə'gəudə] *n* pagoda *f*.

paid [peid] *adj* pagado, da; a sueldo (receiving wages) || pagado, da; *paid holidays* vacaciones pagadas || ⟶ **pay** || — *paid assassin* asesino pagado *or* a sueldo || *to put paid to* acabar con, poner término a.

paid-up [-'ʌp] *adj* COMM liberado, da (share, capital) || *to be a paid-up member* haber pagado su cotización (of a union, etc.).

pail [peil] *n* cubo *m* (bucket) || MAR balde *m*, cubo *m*.

pailful [-ful] *n* cubo *m*.

paillasse ['pæliæs] *n* jergón *m*, colchón *m* de paja (palliasse).

paillette [pæl'jet] *n* lentejuela *f*.

pain [pein] *n* dolor *m* (physical); *to cry out with pain* gritar de dolor || pena *f*, dolor *m* (mental) || sufrimiento *m* (suffering) || — *on* o *upon* o *under pain of* so pena de, bajo pena de || FIG & FAM *to be a pain in the neck* ser un pesado (s.o.), ser una lata (sth.) || *to be in pain* estar sufriendo, tener dolores || *to be out of pain* haber dejado de sufrir || FIG & FAM *to give s.o. a pain in the neck* fastidiarle *or* darle la lata *or* chincharle a alguien || *to have a pain in one's arm* dolerle a uno el brazo.

◆ *pl* MED dolores *m* del parto || esfuerzos *m*, trabajo *m sing*; *to take pains to do sth.* hacer grandes esfuerzos *or* darse mucho trabajo para hacer algo || — *that's all I got for my pains* esto es todo lo que me dieron para recompensarme || *to be at pains to do sth.* esmerarse *or* esforzarse en hacer algo || *to spare no pains to get sth.* no escatimar esfuerzos para lograr algo || *to take pains over* esmerarse en.

pain [pein] *vt* doler (physically); *my foot pains me* me duele el pie || afligir, apenar, dar lástima, dar pena, doler (mentally); *it pains me to see him like that* me duele verle así || *it pains me to say so* me cuesta decirlo, me duele decirlo.

pained [-d] *adj* dolorido, da; apenado, da (voice) || afligido, da (expression).

painful [-ful] *adj* doloroso, sa; *a painful wound* una llaga dolorosa; *a painful blow* un golpe doloroso || dolorido, da (as a result of a blow) || penoso, sa; difícil (task) || afligente, lastimoso, sa; penoso, sa (spectacle) || difícil, angustioso, sa (decision) || doloroso, sa; desagradable; *it is painful to me to have to say so* me es desagradable tener que decir estas cosas || — *a painful performance* una actuación deplorable *or* lamentable || *it was painful to see her* daba pena verla || *my back is painful* me duele la espalda.

painfully [-fuli] *adv* penosamente, con dificultad || FIG muy, terriblemente || FIG *it is painfully obvious* está clarísimo.

pain killer [-kilə*] *n* MED calmante *m*, analgésico *m*.

painless [-lis] *adj* sin dolor, indoloro, ra (physically) || sin dificultad, fácil (task, etc.) || *painless childbirth* parto *m* sin dolor.

painstaking ['peinz,teikiŋ] *adj* cuidadoso, sa; esmerado, da; *a painstaking schoolboy* un alumno cuidadoso || cuidadoso, sa (requiring great care) || hecho con cuidado, esmerado, da (piece of work).

◆ *n* cuidado *m*, esmero *m*.

paint [peint] *n* pintura *f*; *a box of paints* una caja de pinturas; *a coat of paint* una mano de pintura || FAM pintura *f* (cosmetics) || *«wet paint»* «cuidado con la pintura».

paint [peint] *vt* pintar; *to paint a landscape* pintar un paisaje; *to paint the ceiling white* pintar el techo de blanco || pintarse (with cosmetics); *to paint one's face* pintarse la cara || MED dar unos toques a, untar (a throat, etc.) || FIG describir, pintar || — *to paint al fresco, in oils* pintar al fresco, al óleo || *to paint out* tapar con una mano de pintura || FIG & FAM *to paint the town red* irse de juerga, irse de parranda.

◆ *vi* pintar || ser pintor.

paintbox [-bɔks] *n* caja *f* de pinturas.

paintbrush [-brʌʃ] *n* pincel *m* (for an artist) || brocha *f* (for house painters).

painter [-ə*] *n* pintor, ra (artist) || pintor *m* de brocha gorda (who paints walls, etc.) || MAR amarra *f*, boza *f* || FIG *to cut the painters* soltar las amarras.

painting [-iŋ] *n* pintura *f*; *to study painting* estudiar pintura; *painting in oils* pintura al óleo || cuadro *m* (picture) || FIG descripción *f*, pintura *f* || MED pincelada *f*, toque *m* || — *cave painting* pintura rupestre || *spray painting* pintura con pistola.

paint roller [-rəulə*] *n* rodillo *m*.

paint spray [-sprei] *n* pistola *f* [para pintar].

paint-stripper [-,stripə*] *n* quitapinturas *f inv*.

paintwork [-wə:k] *n* pintura *f*.

pair [pεə*] *n* par *m*; *a pair of shoes, of stockings* un par de zapatos, de medias; *a pair of scissors* un par de tijeras || pareja *f* (of people, of animals) || tronco *m* (of horses) || yunta *f* (of oxen) || pareja *f* (in cards) || TECH par *m*; *a pair of gears* un par de engranajes || — *carriage and pair* carruaje tirado por dos caballos || *pair of pants* calzoncillos *m pl* || *pair of pyjamas* pijama *m* || *pair of scales* balanza *f* || *pair of spectacles* gafas *f pl* || *pair of suspenders* tirantes *m pl* || *pair of trousers* pantalón *m*, pantalones *m pl* || *the happy pair* la feliz pareja, los novios || *these two candlesticks are a pair* estos dos candeleros hacen juego.

pair [pεə*] *vt* emparejar; *to pair gloves* emparejar guantes || emparejar, juntar (people) || BIOL aparear.

◆ *vi* emparejarse (to form a pair) || emparejar, hacer pareja; *this glove pairs with the other* este guante empareja con el otro || BIOL aparearse (animals) || formar parejas (people).

— OBSERV La preposición *off* acompaña a veces este verbo sin cambiar por ello su significado.

pairing [-iŋ] *n* apareamiento *m* (of animals) || emparejamiento *m*.

paisley ['peizli] *n* cachemira *f* (material, design).

pajamas [pə'dʒɑ:məz] *pl n* *US* pijama *m sing* [*AMER* piyama *m sing*].

Paki ['pæki] *n* FAM paquistaní *m* & *f*, pakistaní *m* & *f*.

Pakistan [,pɑ:kis'tɑ:n] *pr n* GEOGR Paquistán *m*, Pakistán *m*.

Pakistani [,pɑ:kis'tɑ:ni] *adj/n* paquistaní, pakistaní.

pal [pæl] *n* *US* FAM amigote *m*, camarada *m* & *f*, amigo, ga (close friend) || *US* FAM *pen pal* amigo por carta.

pal [pæl] *vi* *US* FAM *to pal up* hacerse amigos | *to pal up with* hacerse amigo de.

PAL *abbr of [phase alternating line]* PAL, línea de fase alternativa [norma de televisión en color].

palace ['pæləs] *n* palacio *m*; *Royal Palace* Palacio Real; *bishop's palace* palacio episcopal.

paladin ['pælədin] *n* paladín *m*.

palaeogeography [,pæliəudʒi'ɔgrəfi] *n* paleogeografía *f* (paleogeography).

palaeographer [,pæli'ɔgrəfə*] *n* paleógrafo *m*.

palaeographic [,pæliəu'græfik] *adj* paleográfico, ca.

palaeography [,pæli'ɔgrəfi] *n* paleografía *f*.

Palaeolithic [,pæliəu'liθik] *adj* paleolítico, ca.

palaeologist [pæli'ɔlədʒist] *n* paleólogo *m*.

Palaeologus [pæli'ɔləgəs] *pr n* Paleólogo.

palaeontologic [,pæliɔntə'lɔdʒik] *adj* paleontológico, ca (paleontologic).

palaeontologist [,pæliɔn'tɔlədʒist] *n* paleontólogo *m*.

palaeontology [,pæliɔn'tɔlədʒi] *n* paleontología *f*.

Palaeozoic [pæliə'zəuik] *adj* paleozoico, ca.
◆ *n* paleozoico *m*.

palafitte ['pæləfit] *n* palafito *m* (lake dwelling).

palatability [pælətə'biliti] *n* lo sabroso, sabor *m* agradable.

palatable ['pælətəbl] *adj* sabroso, sa (pleasant to taste) || comestible, que se puede comer (eatable) || FIG agradable, aceptable.

palatal ['pælətl] *adj* GRAMM palatal.
◆ *n* GRAMM palatal *f*.

palatalization ['pælətəlai'zeiʃən] *n* GRAMM palatalización *f*.

palatalize ['pælətəlaiz] *vt* GRAMM palatalizar.

palate ['pælit] *n* ANAT & FIG paladar *m*; *to have a refined palate* tener el paladar delicado || — ANAT *soft palate* velo *m* del paladar || *the pleasures of the palate* los placeres de la mesa.

palatial [,pə'leiʃəl] *adj* magnífico, ca; espléndido, da; suntuoso, sa (splendid) || palaciego, ga (of palace).

Palatinate [pə'lætinit] *pr n* GEOGR Palatinado *m*.

palatine ['pælətain] *adj/n* palatino, na.

palaver [pə'lɑːvə*] *n* conferencia *f*, discusión *f* (discussion); *a lengthy palaver between the union and the management* una larga discusión entre el sindicato y la dirección || lío *m*, follón *m* (fuss); *what a palaver just to get a passport!* ¡qué lío sólo para conseguir un pasaporte! || palabrería *f* (worthless talk) || charlatanería *f* (misleading talk) || engatusamiento *m* (cajolery) || asunto *m* (affair); *that's his palaver* es asunto suyo || *there's no need for all that palaver!* ¡no es para tanto!

palaver [pə'lɑːvə*] *vi* palabrear (to talk profusely) || discutir (to converse).
◆ *vt* FAM engatusar (to cajole); *he palavered me into signing* me engatusó de tal manera que firmé.

pale [peil] *adj* pálido, da; *her face was pale* su cara estaba pálida; *two pale blue ties* dos corbatas de color azul pálido || — *pale as death, deadly pale* blanco como el papel, más pálido que un muerto || *to go* o *to turn pale* ponerse pálido.
◆ *n* estaca *f* (of a fence) || HERALD palo *m* || FIG límites *m pl* || — FIG *beyond the pale* al margen de la sociedad | *within the pale of* en el seno de.

pale [peil] *vi* palidecer.
◆ *vt* poner pálido, hacer palidecer.

paleface [-feis] *n* rostro *m* pálido.

paleness [-nis] *n* palidez *f*.

paleogeography [,pæliəudʒi'ɔgrəfi] *n* paleogeografía *f*.

paleographer [,pæli'ɔgrəfə*] *n* paleógrafo *m*.

paleographic [,pæliəu'græfik] *adj* paleográfico, ca.

paleography [,pæli'ɔgrəfi] *n* paleografía *f*.

paleolithic [,pæliəu'liθik] *adj* GEOL paleolítico, ca.

paleologist [,pæli'ɔlədʒist] *n* Paleólogo *m*.

Paleologus [pæli'ɔləgəs] *pr n* paleólogo.

paleontologic [,pæliɔn'tɔlədʒik] *adj* paleontológico, ca.

paleontologist [,pæliən'tɔlədʒist] *n* paleontólogo *m*.

paleontology [,pæliɔn'tɔlədʒi] *n* paleontología *f*.

Paleozoic [pæliə'zəuik] *adj* GEOL paleozoico, ca.
◆ *n* GEOL Paleozoico *m*.

Palermo [pə'ləːməu] *pr n* GEOGR Palermo.

Palestine ['pælistain] *pr n* GEOGR Palestina *f*.

Palestinian [,pæles'tiniən] *adj/n* palestino, na.

palette ['pælit] *n* ARTS paleta *f*.

palette knife [-naif] *n* ARTS espátula *f*.

palfrey ['pɔːlfri] *n* palafrén *m*.

palimpsest ['pælimpsest] *n* palimpsesto *m*.

palindrome ['pælindrəum] *n* palíndromo *m*.

palindromic [-ik] *adj* palíndromo, ma.

paling ['peiliŋ] *n* estacada *f* (fence) || estaca *f* (stake).

palingenesis [,pælin'dʒenisis] *n* palingenesia *f*.

palinode ['pælinəud] *n* palinodia *f*.

palisade [,pæli'seid] *n* empalizada *f*, estacada *f*, vallado *m*.

palish ['peiliʃ] *adj* paliducho, cha.

pall [pɔːl] *n* paño *m* mortuorio (over a coffin) || féretro *m* (coffin) || REL palio *m* (pallium) || HERALD palio *m* || FIG cortina *f*, velo *m* (of smoke) | manto *m*, capa *f* (of snow, etc.).

pall [pɔːl] *vi* perder su sabor (*on* para) (to become insipid) || cansar, dejar de gustar (*on* a) (to become unattractive) || cansarse; *to pall of too much music* cansarse de un exceso de música.
◆ *vt* saciar, hartar (appetite).

palladium [pə'leidjəm] *n* CHEM paladio *m* (metal) || paladión *m* (statue) || FIG paladión *m* (safeguard).

Pallas ['pælæs] *pr n* MYTH Palas *f*.

pallbearer ['pɔːl,bεərə*] *n* portador *m* del féretro.

pallet ['pælit] *n* jergón *m* (hard bed, mattress) || paleta *f*, espátula *f* (wooden tool, of painters) || TECH trinquete *m* (of a ratchet) | paleta *f* (of a clock) | paleta *f* (portable platform) || MUS válvula *f* (of an organ pipe).

pallet truck [-trʌk] *n* carretilla *f* elevadora.

palliasse ['pæliæs] *n* jergón *m*, colchón *m* de paja.

palliate ['pælieit] *vt* paliar, mitigar, atenuar; *to palliate a pain* mitigar un dolor || reducir, disminuir (boredom).

palliative ['pæliətiv] *adj* paliativo, va.
◆ *n* paliativo *m*.

pallid ['pælid] *adj* pálido, da.

pallidity [-iti]; **pallidness** [-nis] *n* palidez *f*.

pallium ['pæliəm] *n* REL palio *m* || manto *m* (of mollusks, of birds).
— OBSERV El plural de *pallium* es *pallia* o *palliums*.

pallor ['pælə*] *n* palidez *f*.

pally ['pæli] *adj* FAM amistoso, sa || *to be pally with s.o.* ser amigote de alguien.

palm [pɑːlm] *n* palma *f* (of the hand, of a glove) || pala *f* (of an implement); *the palm of a paddle* la pala de una pagaya || palmo *m* (measure) || BOT palma *f*, palmera *f* (tree) | palma *f* (leaf) || FIG palma *f* (success); *to carry off the palm* llevarse la palma || MAR uña *f* (of the anchor) || pala *f* (of an antler) || — *coconut palm* cocotero *m* || *date palm* palma datilera || *palm cake* palmera *f* || *royal palm* palmiche *m*, palma *f* real || FIG & FAM *to grease s.o.'s palm* untarle la mano a alguien | *to have an itching palm* ser codicioso | *to hold* o *to have s.o. in the palm of one's hand* tener a alguien en el bolsillo *or* en la palma de la mano *or* en el bote | *to know like the palm of one's hand* conocer como la palma de la mano | *to yield the palm to* conceder la victoria a.

palm [pɑːm] *vt* escamotear, escamotar || FIG *to palm sth. off on s.o.* colar *or* encajar algo a alguien.

Palma ['pælmə]; **Palma de Mallorca** [-dəmə'ljɔːkə] *pr n* GEOGR Palma (de Mallorca).

palmar ['pælmə*] *adj* ANAT de la palma, palmar; *palmar muscle* músculo palmar.

palmary [-ri] *adj* sobresaliente.

palmate ['pælmit] *adj* palmeado, da.

palmer ['pɑːmə*] *n* palmero *m* (pilgrim).

palmetto [pæl'metəu] *n* BOT palmito *m*.
— OBSERV El plural de la palabra inglesa es *palmettos* o *palmettoes*.

palm grove ['pɑːm'grəuv] *n* palmar *m*, palmeral *m*.

palm heart [pɑːmhɑːt] *n* CULIN palmito *m*.

palmiped ['pælmiped] *adj* ZOOL palmípedo, da.
◆ *n* ZOOL palmípeda *f*.

palmist ['pɑːmist] *n* quiromántico, ca [*AMER* palmista *f*].

palmistry [-ri] *n* quiromancia *f*.

palm leaf ['pɑːmliːf] *n* palma *f*.

palm oil ['pɑːmɔil] *n* aceite *m* de palma.

Palm Sunday ['pɑːm'sʌndi] *pr n* REL Domingo *m* de Ramos.

palm tree ['pɑːmtriː] *n* BOT palma *f*, palmera *f*.

palm wine ['pɑːm'wain] *n* vino *m* de palma.

palmy ['pɑːmi] *adj* FIG próspero, ra; *palmy days* días prósperos.

palp [pælp] *n* ZOOL palpo *m*.

palpability [,pælpə'biliti] *n* palpabilidad *f* || FIG evidencia *f*.

palpable ['pælpəbl] *adj* palpable || FIG palpable, patente, evidente; *palpable falsehood* falsedad patente.

palpably ['pælpəbli] *adv* palpablemente, evidentemente.

palpate ['pælpeit] *vt* palpar.

palpation [pæl'peiʃən] *n* palpación *f*, palpadura *f*, palpamiento *m*.

palpitate ['pælpiteit] *vi* palpitar.

palpitating [-iŋ] *adj* palpitante (throbbing).

palpitation [,pælpi'teiʃən] *n* palpitación *f*; *to suffer from palpitations* tener palpitaciones.

palsied ['pɔːlzid] *adj* MED paralizado, da.

palsy ['pɔːlzi] *n* parálisis *f*.

palter ['pɔːltə*] *vi* tergiversar (to talk insincerely) || regatear (to bargain) || no tomar en serio; *to palter with a question* no tomar una cuestión en serio.

paltriness ['pɔːltrinis] *n* mezquindad *f*.

paltry ['pɔːltri] *adj* ínfimo, ma; miserable; insignificante; *a paltry sum* una cantidad ínfima || mezquino, na (mean).

paludal [pæ'ljuːdl] *adj* palúdico, ca.

paludism ['pæljə,dizəm] *n* MED paludismo *m*.

pampas ['pæmpəs] *pl n* pampa *f sing*.

pampean ['pæmpiən] *adj/n* pampero, ra.

pamper ['pæmpə*] *vt* mimar, consentir ‖ *he lead a pampered childhood* se crió entre algodones.

pamphlet ['pæmflit] *n* folleto *m*, opúsculo *m* (booklet) ‖ octavilla *f* (one sheet handout) ‖ panfleto *m*, libelo *m* (lampoon).

pamphleteer [,pæmfli'tiə*] *n* folletista *m* ‖ panfletista *m* (lampoonist).

pan [pæn] *n* cacerola *f*, cazo *m* (metal container) ‖ cazuela *f* (of earthenware) ‖ sartén *f* (for frying) ‖ batea *f* (for washing gold) ‖ mortero *m* (for crushing) ‖ platillo *m* (of a balance) ‖ taza *f* (of lavatory) ‖ MIL cazoleta *f* (of a musket) ‖ BOT betel *m* ‖ US FAM jeta *f*, cara *f* (face) ‖ *pots and pans* batería *f* de cocina.

pan [pæn] *vt* lavar con batea (gold) ‖ CINEM tomar una vista panorámica de *or* con ‖ FAM poner por los suelos, poner de vuelta y media (to criticize).
◆ *vi* extraer oro ‖ FIG *to pan out* salir; *things did not pan out as I wanted* las cosas no salieron como quería; salir bien, ser un éxito (to turn out well).

Pan [pæn] *pr n* MYTH Pan *m*.

panacea [,pænə'siə] *n* panacea *f*.

panache [pa'næʃ] *n* estilo *m*, brillantez *f*, lustre *m*.

Pan-African ['pæn'æfrikən] *adj* panafricano, na.

Pan-Africanism ['pæn'æfri'kənizəm] *n* panafricanismo *m*.

panama [,pænə'mɑ:] *n* jipijapa *m*, panamá *m* (hat).

Panama [,pænə'mɑ:] *pr n* GEOGR Panamá *m* (country) ‖ *Panama Canal* canal *m* de Panamá.

Panama city [-'siti] *pr n* GEOGR Panamá (capital).

Panamanian [,pænə'meinjən] *adj/n* panameño, ña.

Pan-American ['pænə'merikən] *adj* panamericano, na ‖ *Pan-American Highway* carretera panamericana.

Pan-Americanism ['pænə'merikənizəm] *n* panamericanismo *m*.

Pan-Arabism ['pænə'ræbizəm] *n* panarabismo.

pancake ['pænkeik] *n* tortita *f*, «pancake» *m* [AMER panqueque *m*] ‖ AVIAT desplome *m* ‖ FAM *flat as a pancake* completamente llano, na; liso como la palma de la mano (ground), totalmente liso (uniform), aplastado, da (crushed).

pancake ['pænkeik] *vi* AVIAT desplomarse.

Pancake Day [-dei] *n* Martes *m* de carnaval.

pancake landing [-'lændiŋ] *n* AVIAT aterrizaje *m* en desplome.

panchromatic ['pænkrəu'mætik] *adj* pancromático, ca.

pancreas ['pæŋkriəs] *n* ANAT páncreas *m*.

pancreatic [,pæŋkri'ætik] *adj* ANAT pancreático, ca; *pancreatic juice* jugo pancreático.

panda ['pændə] *n* ZOOL panda *m*.

panda car [-kɑ:] *n* coche *m* patrulla.

Pandects ['pændekts] *pl n* JUR Pandectas *f*.

pandemia [pæn'dimiə] *n* pandemia *f*.

pandemic [pæn'demik] *adj* MED pandémico, ca.
◆ *n* MED pandemia *f*.

pandemonium [,pændi'məunjəm] *n* pandemonio *m*, pandemónium *m* ‖ FIG jaleo *m*; *it was absolute pandemonium* había un jaleo tremendo.

pander ['pændə*] *n* alcahuete *m*, proxeneta *m*.

pander ['pændə*] *vi* alcahuetear (to act as a pander) ‖ *to pander to* complacer; *he is always pandering to the director* siempre está complaciendo al director; consentir (a child), agradar, contentar; *television programmes which pander to the lowest taste* programas de televisión que agradan el gusto más vulgar.

pandit ['pændit] *n* pandit *m*.

Pandora [pæn'dɔ:rə] *pr n* MYTH Pandora *f*; *Pandora's box* la caja de Pandora.

pane [pein] *n* cristal *m*, vidrio *m* (sheet of glass) ‖ cara *f*, lado *m* (flat side of an object).

panegyric [,pæni'dʒirik] *n* panegírico *m*.

panegyrist [,pæni'dʒirist] *n* panegirista *m* & *f*.

panegyrize ['pænidʒiraiz] *vt* panegirizar.

panel ['pænl] *n* ARCH lienzo *m* (of a wall) | panel *m*, cuarterón *m*, entrepaño *m* (of a door) | artesón *m* (of a ceiling) ‖ panel *m*, tablero *m* (of plywood) ‖ paño *m* (of a dress) ‖ tablero *m* (of controls or instruments) ‖ ARTS tabla *f* ‖ grupo *m*; *a panel of experts* un grupo de expertos | jurado *m* (jury in a competition) ‖ MED lista *f* de médicos del seguro social.

panel ['pænl] *vt* revestir con paneles de madera (walls) ‖ artesonar (ceilings) ‖ dividir en paños (a dress) ‖ JUR elegir jurado.

panel board [-bɔ:d] *n* tablero *m* de mandos.

panel doctor [-'dɔktə*] *n* médico *m* que presta sus servicios en el seguro social.

panel game [-geim] *n* RAD concurso *m* por equipos.

panel heating [-'hi:tiŋ] *n* calefacción *f* por radiación.

panelist ['pænələst] *n* miembro *m* del jurado.

panelling; US **paneling** ['pænliŋ] *n* revestimiento *m* de madera (of walls) ‖ artesonado *m* (of a ceiling).

panel pin [-pin] *n* alfiler *m* de espiga.

Pan-European ['pæn,juərə,pi:ən] *adj/n* paneuropeo, a.

pang [pæŋ] *n* punzada *f* (of pain) ‖ FIG remordimiento *m*; *pangs of conscience* remordimientos de conciencia | punzada *f* (of hunger) | herida *f* (of love) | angustia *f*, tormento *m* (of jealousy) ‖ — *the pangs of childbirth* los dolores del parto ‖ *the pangs of death* las ansias de la muerte.

Pan-Germanism ['pæn'dʒə:mənizəm] *n* pangermanismo *m*.

Pan-Germanist ['pæn'dʒə:mənist] *adj/n* pangermanista.

pangolin [pæn'gəulin] *n* pangolín *m* (mammal).

panhandle ['pæn'hændl] *n* US faja *f* estrecha de un territorio que entra en otro.

panhandle ['pæn'hændl] *vi* US pordiosear, mendigar, pedir limosna.

panhandler [-ə*] *n* US pordiosero *m*, mendigo *m*.

Panhellenism ['pæn'helənizəm] *n* panhelenismo *m*.

panic ['pænik] *adj* pánico, ca ‖ — *panic fear o terror* miedo cerval *or* pánico, pavor *m* ‖ *it was panic stations* cundió el pánico.
◆ *n* pánico *m*; *he got into a panic* le entró un pánico ‖ *to throw into a panic* meter el miedo en el cuerpo a (a person), sembrar el pánico entre (a group of people).

panic ['pænik] *vi* asustarse, entrarle a uno pánico.
◆ *vt* sembrar el pánico entre.
— OBSERV Pret y pp ***panicked***.

panic grass [-grɑ:s] *n* BOT panizo *m*.

panicky [-i] *adj* lleno de pánico (person) ‖ alarmista (report) ‖ *to get panicky* entrarle a uno pánico, asustarse.

panic-stricken [-,strikən]; **panic-struck** [-,strʌk] *adj* preso de pánico.

Pan-Islamism ['pæn'izləmizəm] *n* panislamismo *m*.

panjandrum [pən'dʒændrəm] *n* FAM archipámpano *m* (person of great self-importance).

panne [pæn] *n* pana *f* (soft fabric).

pannier ['pæniə*] *n* cesto *m* (basket) ‖ serón *m* (on a mule) ‖ cartera *f* (on a bicycle) ‖ miriñaque *m* (of a dress).

pannier bag [-bæg] *n* cartera *f* (on a bicycle) ‖ serón *m* (on a mule).

pannikin ['pænikin] *n* cubilete *m* (metal cup).

panoplied ['pænəplid] *adj* de punta en blanco (elaborately dressed).

panoply ['pænəpli] *n* panoplia *f* ‖ FIG boato *m*, pompa *f* (pomp).

panorama [,pænə'rɑ:mə] *n* panorama *m* ‖ CINEM panorámica *f*.

panoramic [,pænə'ræmik] *adj* panorámico, ca; *panoramic windows* ventanas panorámicas; *panoramic view* vista panorámica.

panpipe ['pænpaip] *n* MUS zampoña *f*.

Pan-Slavism ['pæn'slɑ:vizəm] *n* paneslavismo *m*.

Pan-Slavist ['pæn'slɑ:vist] *adj/n* paneslavista.

pansy ['pænzi] *n* BOT pensamiento *m*, trinitaria *f* ‖ FIG & FAM marica *m*.

pant [pænt] *n* jadeo *m* (laboured breathing) ‖ latido *m*, palpitación *f* (of the heart) ‖ resoplido *m* (of an engine).

pant [pænt] *vi* jadear (to breathe quickly) ‖ palpitar, latir (to throb rapidly) ‖ — *to pant for* o *after* suspirar por ‖ *to pant for breath* estar sin aliento, jadear.
◆ *vt* *to pant out* decir con palabras entrecortadas.

pantagruelism [pæntə'gruelizəm] *n* pantagruelismo *m*.

pantaloons [,pæntə'lu:nz] *pl n* pantalones *m*.

pantechnicon [pæn'teknikən] *n* camión *m* de mudanzas (furniture van).

pantheism ['pæntθi:izəm] *n* panteísmo *m*.

pantheist ['pænθi:ist] *n* panteísta *m* & *f*.

pantheistic [,pænθi:'istik] *adj* panteísta, panteístico, ca.

pantheon ['pænθiən] *n* panteón *m*.

panther ['pænθə*] *n* ZOOL pantera *f* ‖ US ZOOL puma *m* | jaguar *m* ‖ US FIG *Black Panthers* Panteras Negras.

panties ['pæntiz] *pl n* bragas *f*, braga *f sing*.

pantile ['pæntail] *n* teja *f* flamenca.

panting ['pæntiŋ] *n* jadeo *m*.
◆ *adj* jadeante.

panto ['pæntəu] *n* FAM pantomima *f* (dumb show) ‖ representación *f* teatral navideña (Christmas play).

pantograph ['pæntəugrɑ:f] *n* pantógrafo *m*.

pantomime ['pæntəmaim] *n* THEATR pantomima *f* (dumb show) | mimo *m* (actor) | representación *f* musical basada en cuentos de hadas que se da sobre todo por Navidades ‖ FAM *it's a pantomime, what a pantomime!* ¡es una farsa!, ¡qué farsa!

pantry ['pæntri] *n* despensa *f* (food store) ‖ oficio *m* (for preparing food).

pants [pænts] *pl n* calzoncillos *m* (underpants) ‖ pantalones *m*, pantalón *m sing* (trousers).

panty ['pænti] *n* bragas *f pl* (panties) ‖ *panty girdle* faja *f* pantalón.

pantywaist ['pæntiweist] *n* US FAM afeminado *m*.

Panzer ['pæntsə*] *adj* MIL blindado, da; *Panzer division* división blindada.

pap [pæp] *n* papilla *f* (for babies, etc.) || (ant) teta *f*, pezón *m* (of breast) | pico *m* (of a mountain) || US FIG enchufe *m* (political patronage) | tonterías *f pl* (insubstantial reading matter, talk, etc.).

papa [pə'pɑː] *n* papá *m*.

papacy ['peipəsi] *n* papado *m*, pontificado *m*.

papain [pə'peiin] *n* CHEM papaína *f*.

papal ['peipəl] *adj* papal; *papal decrees* decretos papales || — *Papal Chancery* Cancillería Apostólica || *papal nuncio* nuncio apostólico || *Papal States* Estados Pontificios.

paparazzi [pæpə'rætzi] *pl n* paparazzi *m*.

papaveraceae [pəpeivə'reisii] *pl n* BOT papaveráceas *f*.

papaverine [pə'peivərin] *n* CHEM papaverina *f*.

papaw; pawpaw [pə'pɔː]; **papaya** [pə'paiə] *n* BOT papaya *f* (fruit) | papayo *m* (tree).

paper ['peipə*] *n* papel *m* (for writing, wrapping, covering the walls, etc.); *ordinary paper* papel corriente; *corrugated paper* papel ondulado || documento *m*; *working papers* documentos de trabajo || periódico *m*, diario *m* (newspaper); *morning paper* periódico de la mañana; *evening paper* diario de la tarde *or* vespertino || prueba *f* (examination); *to set a history paper* poner una prueba de historia || comunicación *f*, ponencia *f*, informe *m* (learned composition to be read aloud); *to read a paper* leer una comunicación || artículo *m* (written article) || pases *m* de favor (in theatre) || COMM efecto *m* || paquete *m* (of pins, etc.) || — *autographic paper* papel autográfico || *ballot paper* papeleta *f* || *bible paper* papel biblia || *blotting paper* papel secante || *brown paper* papel de estraza || *carbon paper* papel carbón || *cigarette paper* papel de fumar || *coated paper* papel cuché || *drawing paper* papel de dibujo || *emery paper* papel esmerilado *or* de lija, lija *f* || *examination paper* preguntas *f pl* del examen (questions), respuestas *f pl* del examen (answers) || *fashion paper* revista *f* de modas || *filter paper* papel filtro || *glossy paper* papel glaseado || *greaseproof paper* papel vegetal || *India paper* papel de China || *laid paper* papel vergé *or* verjurado || *litmus paper* papel de tornasol || *music paper* papel de música *or* pautado || *on paper* por escrito; *to put down on paper* poner por escrito; sobre el papel, en teoría; *the project is a good one on paper* el proyecto es bueno en teoría || INFORM *paper bin* alimentador *m* de papel || *pelure paper* papel cebolla || *rice paper* papel de arroz || *silver paper* papel de plata || *sports paper* periódico deportivo || *squared paper* papel cuadriculado || *stamp* o *stamped paper* papel sellado || *sticky* o *gummed paper* papel de pegar *or* engomado || *tissue paper* papel de seda || *to commit to paper* apuntar || *toilet paper* papel higiénico *or* sánico || *to put pen to paper* comenzar a escribir || *tracing paper* papel de calcar || *trade paper* revista *f* comercial || *untrimmed paper* papel de barba || *vellum paper* papel vitela || *waste paper* papeles *pl* || *waste paper basket* cesto *m* de los papeles, papelera *f* || *weekly paper* semanario *m* || *wrapping paper* papel de envolver *or* de embalar || *writing paper* papel de escribir *or* de cartas.
◆ *pl* documentación *f sing*, documentos *m*, papeles *m* (to prove s.o.'s identity) || papeles *m* (private documents) || — MIL *call-up papers* llamamiento *m sing* a filas || MAR *ship's papers, boarding papers* papeles de a bordo || FIG *to send in one's papers* presentar la dimisión.
◆ *adj* de papel; *a paper bag, handkerchief* una bolsa, un pañuelo de papel || papelero, ra; *paper industry* industria papelera || FIG poco seguro, ra (hypothetical) || *a project still in the paper stage* un proyecto todavía poco seguro.

paper ['peipə*] *vt* envolver (to wrap) || empapelar (walls) || FIG *to paper over* disimular, ocultar (problem).

paperback [-bæk] *n* libro *m* en rústica || *paperback edition* edición *f* en rústica.

paperbacked [-bækt] *adj* en rústica.

paper basket [-'bɑːskit] *n* cesto *m* de los papeles, papelera *f*.

paperboard [-bɔːd] *n* cartón *m*.

paperbound [-baund] *adj* en rústica.

paperboy [-bɔi]; **papergirl** [-gəːl] *n* repartidor, ra de periódicos.

paper chase [-tʃeis] *n* juego *m* que consiste en alcanzar a dos personas que han salido antes que los demás y que van sembrando papeles para señalar el camino que siguen.

paper clip [-klip] *n* sujetapapeles *m inv*, clip *m*.

paper cutter ['peipəkʌtə] *n* guillotina *f*.

paper fastener [-'fɑːsnə*] *n* grapa *f*.

paper folder [-fəuldə*] *n* plegadera *f*.

paperhanger [-,hæŋə*] *n* empapelador *m*.

papering [-riŋ] *n* empapelado *m*.

paper knife [-naif] *n* cortapapeles *m inv*, plegadera *f*.

paper mill [-mil] *n* fábrica *f* de papel, papelera *f*.

paper money [-mʌni] *n* papel *m* moneda || billete *m* de banco.

paperweight [-weit] *n* pisapapeles *m inv*.

paper work [-wəːk] *n* papeleo *m*.

papery ['peipəri] *adj* parecido al papel.

papier mâché ['pæpjei'mɑːʃei] *adj* de cartón piedra.
◆ *n* cartón *m* piedra.

papilionaceae [pəpiliə'neisiiː] *pl n* BOT papilionáceas *f*.

papilla [pə'pilə] *n* ANAT papila *f*.
— OBSERV El plural de *papilla* es *papillae*.

papillary [pə'piləri] *adj* ANAT papilar.

papilloma [pæpi'ləumə] *n* MED papiloma *m* (tumour).
— OBSERV El plural de *papilloma* es *papillomata* o *papillomas*.

papillote ['pæpi,ləut] *n* papillote *m*.

papism ['peipizəm] *n* REL papismo *m*.

papist ['peipist] *adj/n* papista.

papistry ['peipistri] *n* papismo *m*.

pappy ['pæpi] *adj* pastoso, sa; pulposo, sa || FIG blando, da (character).
◆ *n* FAM papá *m*, papi *m*.

paprika ['pæprikə] *n* paprika *f*, pimiento *m* picante molido.

Papua ['pæpjuə] *pr n* GEOGR Papuasia *f*.

Papuan [-n] *adj/n* papú.

Papua New Guinea ['pæpjuənjuː'gini] *pr n* GEOGR Papúa-Nueva Guinea.

papyrus [pə'pairəs] *n* papiro *m*.
— OBSERV El plural de la palabra inglesa *papyrus* es *papyri* o *papyruses*.

par [pɑː] *n* igualdad *f* (equality) || COMM par *f*, paridad *f*; *at par* a la par; *to be under, over par* estar por debajo de, por encima de la par || valor *m* nominal || promedio *m* (average) || SP par *m*, recorrido *m* normal (in golf) || FAM párrafo *m* (paragraph) || salmoncillo *m* (parr) || — *to be on a par with* estar en un pie de igualdad con, correr parejas con || FIG *to feel below par* no sentirse bien, no estar en forma || SP *to get round the course in four under par* hacer el recorrido con cuatro por debajo del par || *to put sth. on a par with* equiparar algo con, poner algo en un pie de igualdad con.
◆ *adj* normal || COMM a la par.

para ['pærə] *n* MIL & FAM paraca *m* & *f* (paratrooper).

parable ['pærəbl] *n* REL parábola *f*; *the parable of the prodigal son* la parábola del hijo pródigo.

parabola [pə'ræbələ] *n* MATH parábola *f*.

parabolic [,pærə'bɔlik] *adj* parabólico, ca.

parabolize [pə'ræbəlaiz] *vt* parabolizar.

paracetamol [pærə'siːtəmɔl] *n* MED paracetamol *m*.

parachute ['pærəʃuːt] *n* paracaídas *m inv* || — *parachute drop* lanzamiento *m* en paracaídas || *parachute flare* bengala *f* con paracaídas || *parachute jump* salto *m* en paracaídas || *parachute troops* tropas *f* paracaidistas.

parachute ['pærəʃuːt] *vi* saltar con paracaídas.
◆ *vt* lanzar con paracaídas.

parachuting [-iŋ] *n* lanzamiento *m* en paracaídas (of arms, etc.) || paracaidismo *m*; *to go in for parachuting* practicar el paracaidismo.

parachutist [-ist] *n* paracaidista *m* & *f*.

parade [pə'reid] *n* alarde *m*, ostentación *f*, gala *f*; *to make a parade of learning* hacer alarde de erudición || paseo *m* público (a promenade) || MIL desfile *m*; *parade of troops* desfile de tropas | revista *f* (for inspection) || desfile *m* (non-military procession); *parade of floats* desfile de carrozas || desfile *m*, presentación *f*; *fashion parade* presentación de modelos || SP quite *m*, parada *f* (fencing) || *shopping parade* zona *f* comercial || *to be on parade* estar en formación.

parade [pə'reid] *vt* hacer alarde de, hacer ostentación de, hacer gala de, alardear de; *to parade one's talent* hacer alarde de su talento || pasear (a banner, a placard) || MIL pasar revista a (for inspection) | formar (a regiment) | hacer desfilar a (troops).
◆ *vi* pavonearse (to attract attention) || desfilar (strikers, a model) || MIL desfilar (troops) || *to parade up and down* pasearse (por); *in the evening many Madrilenians parade up and down the Gran Via* por la tarde muchos madrileños se pasean por la Gran Vía.

parade ground [-graund] *n* MIL plaza *f* de armas.

paradigm ['pærədaim] *n* GRAMM paradigma *m* (example).

paradigmatic [,pærədig'mætik] *adj* paradigmático, ca.

paradisaic [pærədi'seiik]; **paradisaical** [-əl] *adj* paradisiaco, ca; paradisíaco, ca.

paradisal [,pærə'daisəl] *adj* paradisiaco, ca; paradisíaco, ca.

paradise ['pærədais] *n* paraíso *m*, Gloria *f*, Cielo *m* (heaven); *to go to paradise* ir al Cielo || FIG paraíso *m* (wonderful place); *a tourists's paradise* el paraíso de los turistas || — *bird of paradise* ave *f* del paraíso || *earthly paradise* edén *m*.

paradisiac [,pærə'disiæk]; **paradisiacal** [,pærədi'saiəkəl] *adj* paradisiaco, ca; paradisíaco, ca.

paradox ['pærədɔks] *n* paradoja *f*.

paradoxical [,pærə'dɔksikəl] *adj* paradójico, ca.

paraffin ['pærəfin] *n* parafina *f* (solid) || petróleo *m*, queroseno *m* (fuel); *paraffin lamp, stove* lámpara, estufa de petróleo || — *liquid paraffin* aceite *m* de parafina, vaselina *f* || *paraffin oil* petróleo lampante, queroseno || *paraffin wax* parafina *f*.

paraffin ['pærəfin] *vt* parafinar.

paragoge [ˌpærəˈgəudʒi] *n* paragoge *f*.

paragogic [ˌpærəˈgɔdʒik] *adj* paragógico, ca.

paragon [ˈpærəgən] *n* dechado *m*, modelo *m*; *a paragon of virtue* un modelo de virtud || diamante *m* sin defecto.

paragraph [ˈpærəgrɑːf] *n* párrafo *m* [AMER acápite *m*]; *a short paragraph* un párrafo corto || suelto *m* (short article in a newspaper); *the accident got a paragraph in the Times* hubo un suelto en el Times sobre el accidente || apartado *m* (subdivision); *the last paragraph of article three* el último apartado del artículo tres || *new paragraph* punto y aparte.

paragraph [ˈpærəgrɑːf] *vt* dividir en párrafos.
◆ *vi* escribir sueltos *or* artículos cortos (in a newspaper).

paragrapher [-ə*]; **paragraphist** [-ist] *n* gacetillero, ra.

Paraguay [ˈpærəgwai] *pr n* GEOGR Paraguay *m*.

Paraguayan [ˌpærəˈgwaiən] *adj/n* paraguayo, ya.

parakeet [ˈpærəkiːt] *n* perico *m*, periquito *m* (bird).

parallax [ˈpærəlæks] *n* PHYS paralaje *f*.

parallel [ˈpærələl] *adj* MATH paralelo, la; *to draw line AB parallel to CD* trazar la línea AB paralela a CD || FIG paralelo, la; similar, semejante, análogo, ga (similar); *parallel situations* situaciones similares | correspondiente; *the progress of medicine and the parallel drop in the death rate* el progreso de la medicina y la disminución correspondiente de la mortalidad || — ELECTR *in parallel* en paralelo || SP *parallel bars* barras paralelas || *to run parallel to* correr paralelo a.
◆ *n* MATH paralela *f* || GEOGR paralelo *m*; *the 38th parallel* el paralelo 38 || ELECTR circuito *m* paralelo || FIG paralelo *m*; *one can draw a parallel between industrialization and pollution* se puede hacer un paralelo entre la industrialización y la contaminación || — FIG *his behaviour is without* o *have no parallel* su conducta es única *or* no tiene paralelo || INFORM *parallel port* puerto *m* paralelo.
◆ *pl* PRINT barras *f*.

parallel [ˈpærələl] *vt* comparar con, paragonar con (to compare); *to parallel the English parliamentary system with the French* comparar el sistema parlamentario inglés con el francés || igualar a, ser comparable con, correr parejas con (to be comparable to); *his generosity parallels his amiability* su generosidad es comparable con su amabilidad.

parallelepiped [ˌpærəleˈlepiped] *n* MATH paralelepípedo *m*.

parallelism [ˈpærəlelizəm] *n* paralelismo *m*.

parallelogram [ˌpærəˈleləugræm] *n* MATH paralelogramo *m*.

paralogism [pəˈrælədʒizəm] *n* paralogismo *m*.

paralyse; paralyze [ˈpærəlaiz] *vt* paralizar; *paralysed in one leg* paralizado de una pierna || FIG paralizar; *the strike paralysed the country* la huelga paralizó el país.

paralyser [-ə*] *n* paralizador, ra; paralizante *m* & *f*.

paralysing [-iŋ] *adj* paralizador, ra; paralizante.

paralysis [pəˈrælisis] *n* MED parálisis *f*; *creeping paralysis* parálisis progresiva || FIG parálisis *f*, paralización *f*.
— OBSERV El plural de la palabra inglesa es *paralyses*.

paralytic [ˌpærəˈlitik] *adj* paralítico, ca || FAM como una cuba (drunk).
◆ *n* paralítico, ca.

paralyzation [ˈpærəliˈzeiʃən] *n* paralización *f*.

paralyze [ˈpærəlaiz] *vt* → **paralyse.**

paramagnetic [pærəmægˈnetik] *adj* paramagnético, ca.

paramagnetism [pærəˈmægnətizəm] *n* paramagnetismo *m*.

Paramaribo [ˌpærəˈmæriˌbəu] *pr n* GEOGR Paramaribo.

paramedical [ˈpærəˈmedikəl] *adj* paramédico, ca.

parament [ˈpærəmənt] *n* paramento *m*.

parameter [pəˈræmitə*] *n* MATH parámetro *m*.

parametric [pærəˈmetrik] *adj* paramétrico, ca.

paramilitary [pærəˈmilitəri] *adj* paramilitar.

paramnesia [ˈpærəmˈniːzjə] *n* paramnesia *f*.

paramo [ˈpæræməu] *n* páramo *m*.

paramount [ˈpærəmaunt] *adj* supremo, ma; extremo, ma; sumo, ma; *of paramount importance* de extrema importancia || soberano, na (lord) || *work is paramount with him* el trabajo para él es lo más importante de todo.

paramour [ˈpærəmuə*] *n* amante *m* & *f* (lover).

parang [ˈpɑːræŋ] *n* machete *m* malayo.

paranoia [pærəˈnɔiə] *n* MED paranoia *f*.

paranoiac [-k] *adj/n* MED paranoico, ca.

paranoid [ˈpærənɔid] *adj/n* MED paranoico, ca.

paranormal [ˌpærəˈnɔːməl] *adj* paranormal.

parapet [ˈpærəpit] *n* ARCH pretil *m*, antepecho *m* (of a bridge, of a balcony, etc.) || MIL parapeto *m* (of a trench) || *parapet walk* camino *m* de ronda.

paraph [ˈpæræf] *n* rúbrica *f* (of a signature).

paraph [ˈpæræf] *vt* rubricar.

paraphernal [pærəˈfəːnl] *adj* JUR parafernal.

paraphernalia [pærəfəːˈneiljə] *n* trastos *m pl*, chismes *m pl*, avíos *m pl* (belongings) || jaleo *m* (fuss) || JUR bienes *m pl* parafernales.

paraphrase [ˈpærəfreiz] *n* paráfrasis *f inv*.

paraphrase [ˈpærəfreiz] *vt* parafrasear, hacer una paráfrasis de.

paraphrastic [pærəˈfræstik] *adj* parafrástico, ca.

paraplegia [ˌpærəˈpliːdʒə] *n* MED paraplejía *f*.

paraplegic [-ik] *adj/n* MED parapléjico, ca.

parapsychology [ˈpærəsaiˈkɔlədʒi] *n* parasicología *f*.

paraselene [pærəsəˈliːni] *n* paraselene *f* (on the lunar halo).
— OBSERV El plural de la palabra inglesa es *paraselenae*.

parasite [ˈpærəsait] *n* parásito *m* || FIG parásito *m*.

parasitic [ˌpærəˈsitik]; **parasitical** [-əl] *adj* parásito, ta; parasitario, ria.

parasiticide [pærəˈsitisaid] *n* parasiticida *m*.
◆ *adj* parasiticida.

parasitism [ˈpærəsaitizəm] *n* parasitismo *m*.

parasol [ˈpærəsɔl] *n* parasol *m*, sombrilla *f*, quitasol *m* (umbrella).

parasympathetic [ˈpærəsimpəˈθetik] *adj* ANAT parasimpático, ca.
◆ *n* nervio *m* parasimpático.

parathyroid [pærəˈθairɔid] *adj* paratiroides.
◆ *n* paratiroides *f*.

paratroop [ˈpærətruːp] *adj* paracaidista.

paratrooper [-ə*] *n* soldado *m* paracaidista.

paratroops [-s] *n* tropas *f pl* paracaidistas.

paratuberculosis [ˈpærətjuːˌbəːkjuːləusis] *n* MED paratuberculosis *f*.

paratuberculous [ˈpærətjuːˈbəːkjuləs] *adj* MED paratuberculoso, sa.

paratyphoid [ˈpærəˈtaifɔid] *adj* MED paratifoideo, a.
◆ *n* MED paratifoidea *f*.

paravane [ˈpærəvein] *n* MAR dispositivo *m* contra las minas.

parboil [ˈpɑːbɔil] *vt* CULIN cocer a medias, sancochar.

parbuckle [ˈpɑːbʌkl] *n* MAR tiravira *f* (rope).

Parcae [ˈpɑːsiː] *pl n* MYTH Parcas *f* (fates).

parcel [ˈpɑːsl] *n* paquete *m*; *to make, to wrap a parcel* hacer, envolver un paquete || parcela *f* (of land) || grupo *m* (collection of things) || partida *f* (of goods); *he bought the house and its contents in a single parcel* compró la casa y su contenido en una sola partida || paquete *m* (of shares) || FAM sarta *f*, montón *m*, retahíla *f* (of lies) || — *parcel delivery* reparto *m* de paquetes || *parcel post* servicio *m* de paquetes postales en Correos || *parcels office* despacho *m* de paquetes (in a railway station) || *postal parcel* paquete postal [AMER encomienda *f*] || *to do up into parcels* empaquetar.

parcel [ˈpɑːsl] *vt* empaquetar (to make into a parcel) || envolver (to wrap) || — *to parcel out* repartir (to share), parcelar (land) || *to parcel up* empaquetar, embalar.

parcelling; US **parceling** [-iŋ] *n* empaquetado *m* (making into a parcel) || MAR preçinta *f* (a strip of canvas) || parcelación *f* (of land) || reparto *m*, distribución *f* (sharing out).

parcenary [ˈpɑːsənəri] *n* JUR herencia *f* pro indiviso, copropiedad *f*.

parcener [ˈpɑːsənə*] *n* JUR heredero *m* pro indiviso, coheredero *m*.

parch [pɑːtʃ] *vt* tostar (to roast) || secar (to dry beans, grain, etc.) || abrasar (fever) || resecar, agostar (sun) || *to be parched with thirst* abrasarse de sed.
◆ *vi* resecarse.

parcheesi [pəˈtʃisi] *n* parchís *m*, parchesi *m* (game).

parchment [ˈpɑːtʃmənt] *n* pergamino *m* || *parchment paper* papel *m* pergamino, pergamino vegetal.

parchment-like [-laik] *adj* apergaminado, da.

pardon [ˈpɑːdn] *n* perdón *m*; *to beg s.o.'s pardon* pedir perdón a alguien || JUR indulto *m* (release from a penalty) || REL indulgencia *f* || — JUR *general pardon* amnistía *f* || *I beg your pardon* dispénseme, usted perdone, discúlpeme (excuse me) || *I beg your pardon?, pardon?* ¿cómo? [AMER ¿mande?] (what did you say?).

pardon [ˈpɑːdn] *vt* perdonar; *to pardon s.o. sth.* perdonar algo a alguien || disculpar, dispensar, excusar (to excuse) || JUR indultar (to grant a pardon to) || — *pardon me* dispénseme, discúlpeme, perdóneme || *pardon my saying so* perdone que se lo diga.

pardonable [-əbl] *adj* perdonable, excusable, disculpable.

pardonably [-əbli] *adv* con toda la razón; *he was pardonably furious* estaba furioso y con toda la razón.

pardoner [-ə*] *n* REL vendedor *m* de indulgencias.

pare [pɛə*] *vt* pelar, mondar (fruit) || cortar (nails) || refilar (in bookbinding) || *to pare down* disminuir, reducir (to reduce).

parenchyma [pəˈreŋkimə] *n* parénquima *m*.

parent [ˈpɛərənt] *n* padre *m*, madre *f* (father, mother) || FIG madre *f*, causa *f*, origen *m* (source); *wealth is the parent of idleness* la riqueza es madre de la ociosidad || — *parent branch* rama *f* principal (of a tree) || *parent company, establishment* casa central, casa matriz || *parent ship* barco *m* nodriza || *parent state* madre *f* patria.

◆ *pl* padres *m*; *our first parents* nuestros primeros padres.

parentage [-idʒ] *n* extracción *f*, linaje *m*, familia *f* || *born of humble parentage* de humilde cuna.

parental [pəˈrentl] *adj* de los padres, paternal, maternal.

parenthesis [pəˈrenθisis] *n* paréntesis *m inv*; *in parentheses* entre paréntesis.
— OBSERV El plural de esta palabra es *parentheses*.

parenthesize [pəˈrenθesaiz] *vt* poner entre paréntesis.

parenthetic [pærənˈθetik]; **parenthetical** [-əl] *adj* entre paréntesis.

parenthood [ˈpɛərənthud] *n* paternidad *f*, maternidad *f* || *the joys of parenthood* la alegría de tener hijos.

par excellence [pɑːrˈeksəlɑːns] *adv* por excelencia.

parget [ˈpɑːdʒit] *n* enlucido *m*.

parget [ˈpɑːdʒit] *vt* enlucir.

parhelion [pɑːˈhiːljən] *n* ASTR parhelio *m*, parhelia *f*.
— OBSERV El plural de la palabra inglesa es *parhelia*.

pariah [ˈpæriə] *n* paria *m* & *f*.

parietal [pəˈraiitl] *adj* ANAT parietal || *parietal bone* parietal *m*.

pari-mutuel [ˈpæriˈmjuːtjuəl] *n* apuestas *f pl* mutuas (betting system) || totalizador *m* (machine).

paring [ˈpɛəriŋ] *n* mondadura *f*, peladura *f* (of a fruit) || corte *m* (of nails) || refilado *m* (of books).

pari passu [ˈpæriˈpæsuː] *adv* al mismo ritmo.

Paris [ˈpæris] *pr n* Paris *m* (son of Priam).

Paris [ˈpæris] *pr n* GEOGR París (capital of France).

parish [ˈpæriʃ] *n* REL parroquia *f* (of a church) || municipio *m* (division of local government) || — *parish church* parroquia, iglesia *f* parroquial || *parish clerk* sacristán *m* || *parish council* concejo *m* municipal || *parish priest* párroco *m* || *parish register* registro *m* parroquial || *to go on the parish* correr a cargo del municipio.

parishioner [pəˈriʃənə*] *n* REL feligrés, esa.

parish-pump [ˈpæriʃpʌmp] *adj* FAM pueblerino, na; localista; *parish-pump politics* política pueblerina.

Parisian [pəˈrizjən] *adj/n* parisiense, parisino, na.

parisyllabic [ˈpærisiˈlæbik] *adj* parisílabo, ba; parisilábico, ca.

parity [ˈpæriti] *n* igualdad *f*, paridad *f* (equality) || COMM paridad *f*; *the parity of the dollar* la paridad del dólar; *exchange parities* paridades de cambio.

park [pɑːk] *n* parque *m*; *public park* parque público || US terreno *m* (baseball) || — *car park* aparcamiento *m* de coches, parking *m* || MIL *gun park* parque de artillería || *oyster park* criadero *m* de ostras, ostral *m*, ostrero *m*.

park [pɑːk] *vt* estacionar, aparcar [AMER parquear] (a vehicle) || AGR meter en el aprisco (sheep) || MIL poner en un parque de artillería || FAM dejar (to deposit) || FAM *to park o.s.* instalarse.
◆ *vi* estacionarse, aparcar [AMER parquear].

parka [ˈpɑːkə] *n* trenca *f*.

parkerization [pɑːkəraiˈzeiʃən] *n* TECH parkerización *f*.

parkin [ˈpɑːkin] *n* bizcocho *m* de avena y melaza.

parking [ˈpɑːkiŋ] *n* aparcamiento *m*, estacionamiento *m* (of cars) || — *no parking* prohibido aparcar || *parking attendant* guardacoches *m inv* || *parking lights* luces *f pl* de estacionamiento || *parking lot* aparcamiento [AMER playa *f* de estacionamiento] || *parking meter* parcómetro *m*, parquímetro *m*, contador *m* de aparcamiento || *parking space* aparcamiento, sitio *m* para aparcar.

Parkinson's disease [ˈpɑːkinsənzdiˈziːz] *n* MED enfermedad *f* de Parkinson.

parkland [ˈpɑːklænd] *n* paisaje *m* modelado.

parkway [ˈpɑːkwei] *n* avenida *f*.

parky [ˈpɑːki] *adj* FAM frío, a; fresquito, ta.

parlance [ˈpɑːləns] *n* habla *f*, lenguaje *m* || *in common parlance* en la lengua hablada, en el habla corriente.

parley [ˈpɑːli] *n* conversación *f*, negociaciones *f pl*, parlamento *m* || *to hold a parley with* parlamentar con.

parley [ˈpɑːli] *vi* parlamentar.

parliament [ˈpɑːləmənt] *n* parlamento *m* || Cortes *f pl* (in Spain) || — *Houses of Parliament* Parlamento *m* || *Member of Parliament* miembro *m* del Parlamento, diputado *m*.

parliamentarian [ˌpɑːləmenˈtɛəriən] *adj/n* parlamentario, ria.

parliamentarianism [ˌpɑːləmenˈtɛərianizm] *n* parlamentarismo *m*.

parliamentary [ˌpɑːləmenˈtəri] *adj* parlamentario, ria || *parliamentary elections* elecciones legislativas.

parlour; US **parlor** [ˈpɑːlə*] *n* salón *m*, sala *f* de recibir (in a house) || locutorio *m* (of convent) || — *bar parlour* reservado *m* (in an inn) || *beauty parlour* salón *m* de belleza, instituto *m* de belleza || *funeral parlour* funeraria *f* || *hairdressing parlour* peluquería *f* || *ice-cream parlour* heladería *f* || US *parlor car* coche *m* salón || *parlour game* juego *m* de sociedad.

parlourmaid; US **parlormaid** [-meid] *n* doncella *f*, criada *f* de cuerpo de casa [AMER mucama *f*].

parlous [ˈpɑːləs] *adj* alarmante, peligroso, sa.

Parmesan [ˌpɑːmiˈzæn] *adj/n* parmesano, na || *Parmesan cheese* queso parmesano.

Parnassian [pɑːˈnæsiən] *adj/n* parnasiano, na.

Parnassus [pɑːˈnæsəs] *pr n* GEOGR Parnaso *m*.

parochial [pəˈrəukjəl] *adj* REL parroquial, de la parroquia (of a parish) || municipal (of a civil parish) || FIG localista, pueblerino, na; *to have a parochial outlook* tener una mentalidad pueblerina.

parochialism [-izəm] *n* mentalidad *f* pueblerina, mentalidad *f* localista (narrowness of opinions).

parodic [ˈpərɔdik]; **parodical** [-əl] *adj* paródico, ca.

parodist [ˈpærədist] *n* parodista *m*.

parody [ˈpærədi] *n* parodia *f*.

parody [ˈpærədi] *vt* parodiar, hacer una parodia de.

parole [pəˈrəul] *n* palabra *f* de honor (promise) || libertad *f* bajo palabra (of a prisoner) || US libertad *f* condicional || MIL santo *m* y seña || — *to break parole* o *one's parole* faltar a su palabra || *to put* o *to release on parole* liberar bajo palabra.

parole [pəˈrəul] *vt* liberar bajo palabra || US poner en libertad condicional.

parolee [ˌpærəuˈliː] *n* US persona *f* en libertad condicional.

paronomasia [pærɔnəˈmeiziə] *n* paronomasia *f*.

paronym [ˈpærənim] *n* GRAMM parónimo *m*.

paronymous [pəˈrɔniməs] *adj* GRAMM paronímico, ca; parónimo, ma.

parotid [pəˈrɔtid] *n* ANAT parótida *f*.

parotitis [pærəˈtaitəs] *n* MED parotiditis *f*.

paroxysm [ˈpærəksizəm] *n* paroxismo *m* || FIG paroxismo *m* (extreme stage) | crisis *f*, ataque *m* (of laughter, of rage, etc.).

paroxytone [pəˈrɔksitəun] *adj* GRAMM paroxítono, na.
◆ *n* GRAMM paroxítono *m*.

parpen [ˈpɑːpen] *n* ARCH perpiaño *m*.

parquet [ˈpɑːkei] *n* entarimado *m*, parqué *m* (floor) || US patio *m* de butacas (theatre).

parquet [ˈpɑːkei] *vt* entarimar, poner parqué a.

parquet flooring [-ˈflɔːriŋ] *n* entarimado *m*.

parquetry [ˈpɑːkətri] *n* entarimado *m*.

parr [pɑː*] *n* salmoncillo *m*, cría *f* de salmón (fish).

parrakeet [pærəˈkiːt] *n* perico *m*, periquito *m* (bird).

parricide [ˈpærisaid] *n* parricida *m* & *f* (person) || parricidio *m* (crime).

parrot [ˈpærət] *n* loro *m*, papagayo *m* (bird) || FIG loro *m*, cotorra *f*, papagayo *m* (who repeats mechanically) || — MED *parrot disease* o *fever* psitacosis *f inv* || FIG *parrot fashion* como un loro, mecánicamente.

parrot [ˈpærət] *vt* repetir como un loro.

parry [ˈpæri] *n* quite *m*, parada *f*.

parry [ˈpæri] *vt* parar (a blow) || parar, quitar (in fencing) || rechazar (an attack) || FIG evitar, sortear (a difficulty) | eludir (a question).

parse [pɑːz] *vt* GRAMM analizar gramaticalmente.

parsec [pɑːsek] *n* ASTR parsec *m*.

parsimonious [pɑːsiˈməunjəs] *adj* parsimonioso, sa; parco, ca (sparing) || frugal, escaso, sa; *parsimonious meal* comida frugal || parsimonioso, sa; avaro, ra (mean).

parsimony [ˈpɑːsiməni] *n* parsimonia *f*, parquedad *f*, escasez *f* (frugality) || parsimonia *f*, avaricia *f* (meanness).

parsley [ˈpɑːsli] *n* BOT perejil *m*.

parsnip [ˈpɑːsnip] *n* BOT pastinaca *f*, chirivía *f*.

parson [ˈpɑːsn] *n* REL sacerdote *m*, cura *m* (priest) || pastor *m* (protestant) || FAM *parson's nose* curcusilla *f*, rabadilla *f* (of a chicken).

parsonage [-idʒ] *n* casa *f* del cura *or* parroquial, rectoral *f*.

part [pɑːt] *n* parte *f*; *part of the book is damaged* una parte del libro está estropeada; *fifteen minutes is a fourth part of an hour* quince minutos son la cuarta parte de una hora; *the greater part* la mayor parte; *to be part of* formar parte de || parte *f*; *on my part* de mi parte; *on the part of* de parte de; *on the one part..., on the other part* por una parte..., por otra || partido *m* (side); *to take s.o.'s part* tomar el partido de alguien || deber *m* (duty); *to do one's part* cumplir con su deber || TECH pieza *f* (of a machine); *spare parts* piezas de recambio *or* de repuesto || fascículo *m*, entrega *f* (of a serial publication) || THEATR papel *m*; *to play a part* desempeñar un papel; *how did he play his part?* ¿cómo representó su papel? || MUS parte *f*; *to sing the baritone part* cantar la parte del barítono || GRAMM parte *f*; *parts of speech* partes de la oración | tiempo *m* (of a verb) || JUR parte *f* (in a transaction, in a dispute); *the other part* la parte adversaria || US raya *f* del pelo (in hair) || — *aliquot part* parte alícuota || THEATR *bit part* papel secundario || *for my part* en cuanto a mí, por lo que a mí se refiere, por mi parte || *for the most part* en la mayor parte || *in part* en parte || *in the early part of the week* al principio de la semana || FIG *part and parcel* parte integrante *or* esencial || *the best part was when he...* lo mejor fue cuando... || *the difficult part* la parte difícil, lo difícil || *the funny part about it is that...* lo gracioso del caso es que... || FIG *to be just playing a part* hacer teatro || *to have a part in* tener algo que ver en || *to have no part in* no tener nada que ver en || *to look the part* encajar muy bien en el papel || FIG *to play a part in* desempeñar un papel en || *to sing in parts* cantar a varias voces || *to take in good, in bad part* tomar en buena, en mala parte || *to take part in* participar en, tomar parte en || *to want no part in...* no querer tener nada que ver con... || *X parts of whisky to Y of water* X partes de whisky e Y de agua.

◆ *pl* regiones *f*, parajes *m*; *in tropical parts* en regiones tropicales || FIG talento *m sing* (abilities); *a man of parts* un hombre de talento || ANAT partes *f* (genitales) || — *in foreign parts* en el extranjero || *in parts* en parte; *the film is good in parts* la película es buena en parte || *in these parts* en estos parajes, por aquí || ANAT *private parts* partes pudendas *or* vergonzosas || *to be three parts gone* haberse gastado *or* consumido las tres cuartas partes.

◆ *adj* parcial.

◆ *adv* en parte; *it is part finished* está en parte terminado; *it is part wool, part nylon* es en parte lana y en parte nylon.

part [pɑ:t] *vt* dividir [en dos] (to divide) || separar; *he parted the fighting dogs* separó a los perros que se peleaban || abrirse paso entre (the crowd) || repartir (to share) || MAR romper (a cable) || — *to part company with* separarse de || *to part one's hair* hacerse la raya.

◆ *vi* separarse (to separate); *he parted from her on bad terms* se separó de ella en malos términos || despedirse, separarse (to say goodbye); *we parted at 10 o'clock* nos separamos a las diez || abrirse (to draw apart); *the curtains parted* las cortinas se abrieron || apartarse; *the crowd parted* se apartó la multitud || romperse; *the rope parted in the middle* la cuerda se rompió por en medio || bifurcarse (a road) || *to part with* tener que separarse de; *I hate parting with my piano* no me gusta tener que separarme del piano; deshacerse de (to get rid of), gastar (money), pagar, gastar (a certain sum); *I had to part with ten pounds* tuve que gastar diez libras.

partake* [pɑ:'teik] *vi* participar, tomar parte (*in* en) (to take part) || — *to partake of* compartir (to share); *to partake of s.o.'s meal* compartir la comida con alguien; comer (to eat); *he partook of his dinner alone* comió la cena solo; beber, tomar (to drink); *to partake of a glass of wine* beber una copa de vino; tener algo de, participar de (to have some of the qualities of) || REL *to partake of the Sacrament* acercarse a la Sagrada Comunión, confesarse y comulgar.

— OBSERV Pret ***partook***; pp ***partaken***.

partaken [-ən] *pp* ⟶ **partake.**

partaker [-ə*] *n* participante *m* & *f*.

parterre [pɑ:'tɛə*] *n* cuadro *m*, arriate *m* (of a garden) || patio *m* de butacas (theatre).

part exchange [pɑ:tiks'tʃeindʒ] *n* COMM cambio *m* de un objeto por otro mejor pagando la diferencia || COMM *to offer, to take a car in part exchange* ofrecer, tomar un coche como pago parcial de otro.

parthenogenesis [pɑ:θinəu'dʒenisis] *n* partenogénesis *f*.

Parthenon [pɑ:θinən] *pr n* Partenón *m*.

Parthian ['pɑ:θjən] *adj/n* HIST parto, ta; *Parthian shot* flecha del parto.

partial ['pɑ:ʃəl] *adj* parcial; *a partial explanation* una explicación parcial; *partial eclipse* eclipse parcial || parcial (biased); *a partial judgment* un juicio parcial || FAM aficionado, da (fond of); *David is very partial to claret* David es muy aficionado al clarete.

partiality [ˌpɑ:ʃi'æliti] *n* parcialidad *f* (bias) || FAM predilección *f*, afición *f*, inclinación *f* (fondness); *a partiality for sweets* una afición a los dulces.

partially ['pɑ:ʃəli] *adv* parcialmente, con parcialidad.

partible ['pɑ:təbl] *adj* divisible, que se puede dividir.

participant [pɑ:'tisipənt] *adj/n* participante, partícipe.

participate [pɑ:'tisipeit] *vi* participar, tomar parte (to take part); *to participate in a game* participar en un juego || FAM tener algo (*of* de) (to have some of the qualities of).

participating [-iŋ] *adj* participante || *participating stock* acciones *f pl* preferenciales.

participation [pɑ:ˌtisi'peiʃən] *n* participación *f*.

participle ['pɑ:tisipl] *n* GRAMM participio *m*; *present participle* participio de presente *or* activo; *past participle* participio pasivo *or* de pretérito.

particle ['pɑ:tikl] *n* partícula *f* || grano *m* (of dust) || FIG pizca *f*, átomo *m* (of common sense, of truth) || GRAMM partícula *f* || PHYS partícula *f*; *particle accelerator* acelerador *m* de partículas.

parti-coloured; *US* **parti-colored** ['pɑ:tiˌkʌləd] *adj* abigarrado, da; con colores entremezclados, multicolor.

particular [pə'tikjulə*] *adj* particular; *I have nothing particular to do* no tengo nada particular que hacer || concreto, ta; *each particular case* cada caso concreto || cierto, ta; determinado, da; *a particular object* cierto objeto, un objeto determinado || especial; *take particular care not to offend him* ten especial cuidado en no ofenderle; *she left me for no particular reason* me dejó sin ninguna razón especial || detallado, da; minucioso, sa (with details); *a particular account of what occurred* un relato detallado de lo que ocurrió || exigente (demanding); *he is very particular about punctuality* es muy exigente con la puntualidad || exigente, delicado, da (about food); *she is very particular about what she eats* es muy delicada con lo que come || personal; *my own particular sentiments* mis propios sentimientos personales || íntimo, ma; *he is a particular friend of mine* es un íntimo amigo mío || — *I'm not particular about it* me da igual, me da lo mismo, le doy poca importancia || *in particular* particularmente, especialmente, principalmente || *that particular person* aquella persona en particular.

◆ *n* detalle *m*, pormenor *m* (detail); *he gave me full particulars* me dio todos los detalles || — *for further particulars apply to* si desea más información diríjase a || *in every particular* en todos los detalles || *please give full particulars* se ruega dar una información completa || *to go into particulars* entrar en pormenores.

particularism [-rizəm] *n* particularismo *m*.

particularist [-rist] *adj/n* particularista.

particularity [pəˌtikju'læriti] *n* particularidad *f* || minuciosidad *f*, lo detallado (of a description).

particularization [pətikjulərai'zeiʃən] *n* particularización *f*.

particularize [pə'tikjuləraiz] *vt* particularizar.

◆ *vi* especificar, concretar, entrar en detalles.

particularly [pə'tikjuləli] *adv* particularmente, especialmente (especially); *it is particularly well done* está especialmente bien hecho || en particular, sobre todo, particularmente (in particular) || *I am not particularly rich* no soy muy rico.

parting ['pɑ:tiŋ] *n* separación *f* || despedida *f* (departure) || ruptura *f* (of a cable) || raya *f* (in the hair) || FIG *to be at the parting of the ways* estar en la encrucijada *or* en el momento crucial (critical point), haber llegado al momento de separarse (point of separation).

◆ *adj* de despedida (farewell); *parting visit* visita de despedida || último, ma (words) || FIG *parting shot* último comentario *m or* reproche *m*.

partisan; partizan [ˌpɑti'zæn] *adj* partidista (of a party); *partisan spirit* espíritu partidista || partidario, ria (of a supporter) || MIL de guerrilleros (of guerrillas).

◆ *n* partidario, ria (adept) || seguidor, ra; partidario, ria (of a doctrine) || MIL guerrillero *m* (in guerrilla warfare) || *partisan warfare* guerrilla *f*.

partisanship [-ʃip] *n* partidismo *m*.

partition [pɑ:'tiʃən] *n* división *f* || parte *f* (section) || tabique *m* (thin wall); *wooden partition* tabique de madera.

partition [pɑ:'tiʃən] *vt* dividir || repartir (to share) || poner un tabique a, tabicar (a room) || *to partition off* separar con un tabique.

partitive ['pɑ:titiv] *adj* partitivo, va.

◆ *n* GRAMM partitivo *m*.

partizan [ˌpɑ:ti'zæn] *n* ⟶ **partisan.**

partly ['pɑ:tli] *adv* en parte.

partner ['pɑ:tnə*] *n* asociado, da; socio, cia (in business); *senior partner* socio más antiguo || asociado, da; miembro asociado (of an organization); *our Common Market partners* los demás asociados del Mercado Común || firmante *m* & *f*, partícipe *m* & *f* (of a treaty) || interlocutor, ra (in a conversation) || pareja *f* (in dancing); *take your partners, please* elijan su pareja por favor || compañero, ra; pareja *f* (in cards, etc.) || SP pareja *f* || cónyuge *m* & *f*, consorte *m* & *f* (husband, wife) || — *partner in crime* codelincuente *m* & *f* || COMM *sleeping partner* socio comanditario.

◆ *pl* TECH fogonadura *f sing*.

partner ['pɑ:tnə*] *vt* estar asociado con, asociarse con || acompañar, ser pareja de (in a dance).

partnership [-ʃip] *n* asociación *f* || sociedad *f* (firm); *limited partnership* sociedad en comandita || vida *f* conyugal (married life) || — *to go into partnership with* asociarse con || *to take into partnership* tomar como socio.

partook [pɑ:'tuk] *pret* ⟶ **partake.**

part owner ['pɑ:t'əunə*] *n* copropietario, ria.

partridge ['pɑ:tridʒ] *n* perdiz *f* (bird) || *young partridge* perdigón *m*.

part-song ['pɑ:tsɔŋ] *n* MUS canción *f* a varias voces.

part time ['pɑ:t'taim] *adv* (a) media jornada; *to work part time* trabajar media jornada.

◆ *n* *to be on part time* trabajar media jornada.

part-time ['pɑ:t'taim] *adj* de media jornada; *a part-time job* un trabajo de media jornada || que trabaja a media jornada; *a part-time typist* un mecanógrafc que trabaja a media jornada.

parturition [ˌpɑ:tjuə'riʃən] *n* parto *m* (childbirth).

partway ['pɑ:t'wei] *adv* en parte, parcialmente.

party ['pɑ:ti] *n* partido *m*; *political parties* partidos políticos; *Labour, Liberal, Conservative party* partido laborista, liberal, conservador || partida *f*; *a shooting party* una partida de caza || grupo *m*; *will you join our party?* ¿quiere unirse a nuestro grupo?; *a party of tourists* un grupo de turistas || JUR parte *f* (in a dispute, in an agreement, etc.); *contracting parties* partes contratantes || reunión *f* (gathering) || fiesta *f* (reception); *to give a birthday party* dar una fiesta de cumpleaños || guateque *m*, fiesta *f* (young people's gathering) || equipo *m*; *rescue party* equipo de salvamento || cuadrilla *f* (of workers, of bandits) || MIL destacamento *m* || cómplice *m* & *f*; *to be party to a crime* ser cómplice en un crimen || FAM individuo *m* (person); *a party of the name of Brown* un individuo llamado Brown || — *dancing party* baile *m* || *dinner party* cena *f* || MIL *firing party* pelotón *m* de ejecución, piquete *m* de ejecución || *party dress* traje *m* de vestir || *party games* juegos *m* de sociedad || *party line* línea política del partido (of a political group), línea telefónica compartida entre varios abonados (telephone), linde *f*, lindero *m* (between two properties) || FAM *party piece* numerito *m* de fiesta || RAD *party political broadcast* espacio *m* para propaganda electoral || *party politics* política *f* de partidos (system), politiqueo *m* (political jobbery) || *party spirit* partidismo *m* || *party ticket* billete *m* de grupo || *party wall* pared medianera || *tea party* té *m* || JUR *third party* tercero *m* || *third party insurance* seguro *m* contra tercera persona || *to be a party to* participar en, tener algo que ver con (to participate), estar interesado en (financially) || *to be a party to an agreement* firmar un acuerdo || *to be one of the party* ser miembro del grupo.

parvenu ['pɑːvənjuː] *n* nuevo rico, nueva rica; advenedizo, za; arribista *m* & *f*.

parvis ['pɑːvis] *n* ARCH atrio *m*.

pas [pɑː] *inv n* paso *m*.

pascal ['pæskæl] *n* pascal *m* (pressure unit).

paschal ['pɑːskəl] *adj* pascual; *paschal lamb* cordero pascual; *paschal candle* cirio pascual.

pasha ['pɑːʃə] *n* bajá *m*, pachá *m*.

pasquinade [pæskwi'neid] *n* pasquín *m* (lampoon).

pass [pɑːs] *n* GEOGR puerto *m*, desfiladero *m* || MAR paso *m*, pasaje *m* || aprobado *m* (in an examination) || pase *m* (document); *you need a pass to get into the research laboratories* hace falta un pase para entrar en los laboratorios de investigación || MIL permiso *m*; *to be on pass* estar con permiso || SP pase *m* (in football, etc.); *forward pass* pase adelantado || pase *m* (in bullfighting, in fencing) || pasa *f* (in cards) || pase *m* (of a conjurer) || pase *m* de favor (in a theatre) || billete *m* de favor (on the railway) || FIG paso *m*, situación *f* (situation); *things have come to a pretty pass* las cosas están en un mal paso || TECH pasada *f* || — *it came to a pass that* ocurrió que || *to bring to pass* llevar a cabo || *to get a pass in* aprobar en (an exam) || FIG *to make a pass at* intentar conquistar | *to sell the pass* traicionar al país *or* al partido.

pass [pɑːs] *vi* pasar (to move along); *to pass before one's eyes* pasar ante los ojos de uno; *will you pass into the dining room please?* ¿quieren ustedes pasar al comedor, por favor? || pasar, transcurrir (time); *a fortnight passed* pasaron quince días || pasar, ocurrir (to happen); *I know what has passed* sé lo que ha pasado || desaparecer (to disappear); *to pass into darkness* desaparecer en la oscuridad || aprobar (in an examination); *to pass in maths* aprobar en matemáticas || ser aprobado *or* adoptado (bill) || ser aceptado (theory) || tener curso legal (coin) || aceptarse, admitirse; *what passes in Sweden* lo que se admite en Suecia || SP pasar, hacer un pase || pasar (in cards) || — *be it said in passing* dicho sea de paso || *he passes for a liberal* pasa por liberal || *to let sth. pass* dejar pasar algo, tolerar algo (a fault), dejar pasar (an opportunity) || *to pass into oblivion* ser olvidado, caer en el olvido || *to pass out of sight* perderse de vista.

◆ *vt* pasar, cruzar, atravesar (to cross over); *to pass a river* pasar un río; *to pass the frontier* cruzar la frontera || pasar por delante de; *I passed your house yesterday* pasé por delante de su casa ayer || cruzarse con; *I passed her on the street* me crucé con ella en la calle || pasar; *to pass the thread through the eye of the needle* pasar el hilo por el ojo de la aguja; *pass the sponge over the table* pasa la esponja por la mesa || pasar (time); *they passed ten days in San Sebastian* pasaron diez días en San Sebastián || aprobar (an examination, a candidate) || aprobar, adoptar (a bill, a motion) || COMM aprobar (an invoice) || aprobar, dar el visto bueno a; *the censor has passed the play* la censura ha dado el visto bueno a la obra || ser aprobado *or* ser adoptado por; *bill that has passed the House of Commons* ley que ha sido aprobada por la Cámara de los Comunes || tener el visto bueno de, ser aprobado por; *to pass the censor* tener el visto bueno de la censura || superar, sobrepasar (to surpass) || pasar; *please, pass me that book, the salt* por favor pásame ese libro, la sal || pasar (counterfeit money) || escamotear (conjurer) || AUT pasar, adelantar (to overtake); *he passed me at a hundred miles an hour* me adelantó a cien millas por hora || expresar (an opinion) || hacer (a comment) || JUR pronunciar, dictar (a judgment) || SP pasar (ball) | adelantar, dejar atrás (to overtake) || CULIN pasar, colar (through a sieve) || MED evacuar (faeces) || — *to pass each other* cruzarse || *to pass in review* pasar revista a || *to pass s.o. fit* dar a alguien de alta (after illness), declarar a alguien apto (for military service).

◆ *phr v* ***to pass across*** cruzar (street) | pasar (a ball) || ***to pass along*** pasar por (street) | pasar; *the procession passed along in perfect order* el desfile pasó en un orden perfecto | pasar; *pass along the tray* pasa la bandeja || — *pass along!* ¡pasen para adelante! || ***to pass away*** pasar, desaparecer (to disappear) | pasar a mejor vida (to die) | pasar (time) || ***to pass by*** pasar (to go past) | pasar por (to call in at); *I'll pass by your house tomorrow* pasaré por su casa mañana | pasar de largo (to go straight past) | pasar por alto, dejar de lado (to ignore) | hacer caso omiso de (not to take into account) | dejar pasar (a fault) || ***to pass down*** pasar para adelante || ***to pass in*** entrar || ***to pass off*** pasar | pasar (counterfeit money) | hacer pasar (*as* por) (to make sth. out to be) || — *to pass off with* disimular con | *to pass o.s. off as* hacerse pasar por || ***to pass on*** pasar; *to pass on to a new subject* pasar a un nuevo tema | pasar a mejor vida (to die) | seguir para adelante | pasar, transmitir (news) | dar; *to pass a message on to s.o.* dar un mensaje a alguien | pasar; *read this and pass it on to the others* lee esto y pásalo a los demás || ***to pass out*** salir (to go out) | desmayarse (to faint) | pasar a mejor vida (to die) | repartir, distribuir (to give out) | graduarse (from school, from academy) || ***to pass over*** cruzar (to cross over) | hacer caso omiso de, pasar por alto, dejar de lado (to ignore) | pasarse; *the soldier passed over to the enemy* el soldado se pasó al enemigo | dar, transmitir (to give) | decir (to say) | alejarse (a storm) | disiparse (clouds) || — FIG *to pass s.o. over* postergar a uno || ***to pass round*** dar la vuelta a (an obstacle, a village) | pasar de mano en mano; *the book passed round* el libro pasó de mano en mano | pasar; *pass round the pastries* pasa los pasteles || ***to pass through*** pasar por; *to pass through Madrid* pasar por Madrid || cruzar, atravesar (to cross); *we passed through Germany in two days* cruzamos Alemania en dos días | FIG pasar por; *the economy is passing through a crisis* la economía está pasando por una crisis || ***to pass up*** rechazar (to decline); *to pass up an offer* rechazar una oferta | dejar pasar (an opportunity) | renunciar a (hopes).

passable [-əbl] *adj* pasable, tolerable, admisible, aceptable, pasadero, ra (good enough) || atravesable (river) || transitable (road) || promulgable (law).

passably [-i] *adv* bastante; *passably good* bastante bueno.

passacaglia [,pæsə'kɑːljə] *n* MUS pasacalle *m*.

passade [pə'seid] *n* pasada *f* (of a horse).

passage ['pæsidʒ] *n* pasaje *m*, paso *m* (way); *underground passage* pasaje subterráneo || callejón *m* (alley) || corredor *m*, pasillo *m*, pasadizo *m* (in a house) || paso *m*; *the passage of time* el paso del tiempo || trozo *m*, pasaje *m* (of a book); *selected passages* trozos escogidos || aprobación *f*; *the passage of a bill through Parliament* la aprobación de un proyecto de ley por el Parlamento || paso *m* (passing) || MAR travesía *f* (crossing) | pasaje *m* (ticket) || ANAT tubo *m* || paso *m*; *birds of passage* aves de paso || MUS pasaje *m* || paso *m* de costado (of a horse) || — *free passage* o *access* paso franco *or* libre || *passage of arms* combate *m*.

passage money [-'mʌni] *n* MAR pasaje *m*.

passageway [-wei] *n* callejón *m* (alley) || corredor *m*, pasillo *m* (in a house).

passant ['pæsənt] *adj* HERALD pasante.

passbook ['pɑːsbuk] *n* libreta *f* de depósitos.

pass degree ['pɑːsdi'griː] *n* aprobado *m*.

passé ['pɑːsei] *adj* pasado de moda.

passementerie [pæs'mɑːntri] *n* pasamanería *f*.

passenger ['pæsindʒə*] *n* pasajero, ra; viajero, ra (traveller) || FIG persona *f* inútil || — *passenger loading bridge* pasarela *f* de acceso || *passenger train, ship* tren, buque de pasajeros.

passe-partout ['pæspɑːtuː] *n* orla *f*, «passe-partout» *m* (frame of binding) || llave *f* maestra (key).

passer-by; passerby ['pɑːsə'bai] *n* transeúnte *m* & *f*.

— OBSERV El plural es *passers-by* y *passersby*.

passibility [,pæsi'biliti] *n* sensibilidad *f*.

passible ['pæsibl] *adj* sensible.

passing ['pɑːsiŋ] *adj* de paso, que pasa; *passing traveller* viajero de paso || pasajero, ra; efímero, ra; *passing desire* deseo pasajero || hecho de paso, de pasada; *passing remark* observación hecha de paso || — *a passing glance* un vistazo rápido || *passing bell* toque *m* de difuntos || US *passing mark* aprobado *m*.

◆ *n* paso *m* (of a train, of birds, etc.) || adelantamiento *m* (overtaking) || desaparición *f* (disappearance) || paso *m*, transcurso *m* (of time) || fallecimiento *m*, muerte *f* (death) || adopción *f*, aprobación *f* (of a bill) || — *in passing* de paso || *with the passing of time* andando el tiempo.

◆ *adv* (ant) sumamente, extremadamente; *passing fair* sumamente bello.

passion ['pæʃən] *n* pasión *f*; *to master one's passions* dominar sus pasiones; *the debate aroused strong passions* el debate despertó fuertes pasiones || cólera *f*, ira *f* (anger); *fit of passion* ataque de cólera || pasión *f*, amor *m* (love); *to conceive a passion for* tener una pasión por || REL pasión *f* || — *I have a passion for strawberries* me encantan las fresas, adoro las fresas || *Passion Week* Semana Santa, Semana de la Pasión || *to be in a passion* estar furioso || *to fly into a passion* encolerizarse, ponerse furioso || *to put s.o. into a passion* encolerizar *or* poner furioso a alguien.

passional [-əl] *n* REL martirologio *m* (book).

◆ *adj* pasional.

passionate [-it] *adj* apasionado, da (emotional); *a passionate speech* un discurso apasionado || fervoroso, sa; ardiente, vehemente; *a passionate supporter* un ardiente partidario || enfadado, da; furioso, sa (angry) || irascible, colérico, ca (quick-tempered) || ardiente (desire).

passionflower [-ˌflauə*] *n* BOT pasionaria *f*, pasiflora *f*.

passion fruit [-fruːt] *n* BOT fruta *f* de la pasión.

passionless [-lis] *adj* desapasionado, da.

Passion play [-plei] *n* auto *m* sacramental, misterio *m*.

passive [ˈpæsiv] *adj* pasivo, va; *passive resistance* resistencia pasiva || GRAMM pasivo, va || AVIAT sin motor.
◆ *n* GRAMM voz *f* pasiva.

passively [-li] *adv* pasivamente || GRAMM en voz pasiva.

passiveness [-nis]; **passivity** [pæˈsiviti] *n* pasividad *f*.

passkey [ˈpɑːskiː] *n* llave *f* maestra.

Passover [ˈpɑːsˌəuvə*] *n* REL Pascua *f* [de los judíos].

passport [ˈpɑːspɔːt] *n* pasaporte *m*; *to issue a passport* expedir un pasaporte || FIG *passport to fame* pasaporte a la fama.

password [ˈpɑːswəːd] *n* contraseña *f*, santo y seña *m*.

past [pɑːst] *adj* pasado, da; *his past life* su vida pasada; *in times past* en tiempos pasados; *the past week* la semana pasada || anterior, último, ma (former); *the past president* el presidente anterior || GRAMM pasado, da || — *for some time past* desde hace cierto tiempo || *past participle* participio pasivo *or* de pretérito || *past perfect* pluscuamperfecto *m* || *past tense* pretérito *m* || *the past few years* estos últimos años || *to be past* haber pasado.
◆ *n* pasado *m*, lo pasado; *let us forget the past* olvidemos el pasado; *to relive the past* resucitar el pasado || antecedentes *m pl* (record); *a man with a doubtful past* un hombre con unos antecedentes dudosos || FAM historia *f*; *a woman with a past* una mujer con historia || GRAMM pretérito *m*; *past absolute* o *historic, anterior* pretérito indefinido, anterior || — *in the past* antes, anteriormente || *it's a thing of the past* pertenece al pasado || *that's all in the past* son cosas pasadas || *Toledo is a town with a past* Toledo es una ciudad llena de historia.
◆ *prep* por delante de; *to walk past the house* pasar por delante de la casa || más allá de; *it's just past the church* está un poco más allá de la iglesia || más de; *he is past fifty* tiene más de cincuenta años || — *bullets whistled past our ears* las balas silbaban en nuestros oídos || *he is past dancing* ya no tiene edad para bailar || *he pushed past me* me empujó para pasar || *I am past caring* ya me trae sin cuidado || *I am past worrying* ya no me preocupa || *it's half past* es la media || *it's past belief* es increíble || *it's past endurance* es insoportable || *it's past ten o'clock* son las diez dadas, son más de las diez, son las diez y pico || *it's past tolerance* es intolerable || *I wouldn't put it past you* no me extrañaría de tu parte || *my trousers are past mending* mis pantalones están tan viejos que ya no se pueden arreglar || *ten past eight* las ocho y diez || FAM *to be past it* ya no estar para esos trotes.
◆ *adv* *to drive past* pasar en coche || *to fly past* pasar volando || *to go* o *to walk past* pasar || *to march past* desfilar || *to run past* pasar corriendo.

pasta [ˈpæstə] *n* pastas *f pl*.

paste [peist] *n* masa *f* (for pastry crust) || pasta *f*; *anchovy paste* pasta de anchoas || pasta *f*; *paste for teeth* pasta dentífrica || estrás *m* (for jewelry) || barro *m* (clay) || engrudo *m* (adhesive) || FAM puñetazo *m* (blow).

paste [peist] *vt* pegar (to stick) || engrudar (to cover with paste) || FAM pegar (to hit) || SP FAM dar una paliza a (to beat) || FAM *to paste up* pegar (to stick).

pasteboard [-bɔːd] *n* cartón *m* (for boxes) || cartulina *f* (for visiting cards) || tarjeta *f* de visita (visiting card) || carta *f*, naipe *m* (playing card) || billete *m* [AMER boleto *m*] (ticket).
◆ *adj* de cartón (box) || de cartulina (visiting card).

pastel [pæsˈtel] *n* pastel *m* (painting, colour) || — *pastel blue* azul *m* pastel || *pastel drawing* dibujo *m* al pastel.

pastellist [pæsˈtəlist]; **pastelist** [ˈpæstəlist] *n* pastelista *m* & *f*.

pastern [ˈpæstəːn] *n* cuartilla *f* (of a horse).

paste-up [ˈpeistˈʌp] *n* PRINT maqueta *f*.

pasteurization [ˌpæstərəraiˈzeiʃən] *n* pasterización *f*, pasteurización *f*.

pasteurize [ˈpæstəraiz] *vt* pasterizar, pasteurizar.

pasticcio [pæsˈtitʃəu]; **pastiche** [pæsˈtiːʃ] *n* pastiche *m* (imitation).

pastil [ˈpæstəl]; **pastille** [pæsˈtiːl] *n* pastilla *f*.

pastime [ˈpɑːstaim] *n* pasatiempo *m*.

pastiness [ˈpeistinis] *n* pastosidad *f*.

pasting [ˈpeistiŋ] *n* FAM paliza *f* (beating, criticism); *what a pasting I got!* ¡menuda paliza me dieron!; *they gave him a pasting* le dieron una paliza.

past master [ˈpɑːstˈmɑːstə*] *n* FAM *to be a past master in* o *at* ser maestro en, ser perito en.

pastor [ˈpɑːstə*] *n* REL pastor *m*.

pastoral [ˈpɑːstərəl] *adj* pastoral, pastoril (relating to country life) || pastoral, pastoril (literature) || REL pastoral; *pastoral ring* anillo pastoral.
◆ *n* pastoral *f* (poem) || REL pastoral *f* (letter).

pastorale [ˌpæstəˈrɑːli] *n* MUS pastoral *f*.

pastose [pæsˈtəus] *adj* pastoso, sa (paint).

pastosity [pæsˈtɔsiti] *n* pastosidad *f*.

pastourelle [ˌpæstəˈrel] *n* pastorela *f*.

pastrami [pəsˈtrɑːmi] *n* CULIN pastrami *m*, carne *f* de buey adobada.

pastry [ˈpeistri] *n* pasta *f* (dough) || pasteles *m pl* (cakes).

pastrycook [-kuk] *n* pastelero, ra; repostero, ra.

pastry shop [-ʃɔp] *n* pastelería *f*, repostería *f*.

pasturable [ˈpɑːstjurəbl] *adj* pacedero, ra.

pasturage [ˈpɑːstjuridʒ] *n* pasto *m*, dehesa *f* (field) || pasto *m* (grass) || pasto *m*, pastoreo *m* (feeding) || *common pasturage* pasto comunal.

pasture [ˈpɑːstʃə*] *n* pasto *m*.

pasture [ˈpɑːstʃə*] *vt* apacentar, pastorear (cattle) || pacer (grass).
◆ *vi* pastar, pacer.

pastureland [-lænd] *n* pastizal *m*.

pasty [ˈpæsti] *n* pastel *m*, empanada *f*.

pasty [ˈpeisti] *adj* pastoso, sa (like paste) || pálido, da (complexion).

pat [pæt] *adj* adecuado, da; oportuno, na; *pat answer* contestación adecuada || *he always has an excuse pat* siempre tiene una excusa preparada.
◆ *adv* oportunamente, en el momento oportuno; *the reply came pat* la contestación llegó en el momento oportuno || — *to answer pat* responder inmediatamente || *to know sth. off pat* saber algo al dedillo || *to stand pat* mantenerse en sus trece (to stand firm).
◆ *n* palmadita *f*, golpecito *m* (gentle stroke) || caricia *f* (caress) || porción *f* (small lump) || ruido *m* ligero (noise) || *to give s.o. a pat on the back* dar a alguien palmaditas en la espalda (to tap lightly), felicitar a alguien (to congratulate).

pat [pæt] *vt* dar palmaditas; *to pat s.o. on the back* dar palmaditas a alguien en la espalda || acariciar (a dog) || dividir en porciones (butter, etc.) || — FIG *to pat o.s. on the back* congratularse | *to pat s.o. on the back* felicitar a alguien.

Patagonia [ˌpætəˈgəunjə] *pr n* GEOGR Patagonia *f*.

Patagonian [-n] *adj* patagón, ona; patagónico, ca.
◆ *n* patagón, ona.

patch [pætʃ] *n* pieza *f*, remiendo *m* (mend); *to put a patch on a coat* echar *or* poner un remiendo a un abrigo || parche *m* (to cover a scratch, wound, puncture, etc.) || bancal *m*; *potato patch* bancal de patatas || parcela *f* (of land) || parte *f*, trozo *m* (of a book, etc.) || mancha *f* (of oil, of colour) || charco *m* (of water) || lunar *m* (beauty spot) || — *a bad patch of road* un tramo malo de carretera || *bald patch* calva *f* || *eye patch* parche *m* || FIG *not to be a patch on* no tener ni punto de comparación con || *patch of blue sky* claro *m*, trozo *m* de cielo azul || *patch pocket* bolsillo *m* de parche || FIG *to strike a bad patch* tener mala suerte, pasar por un mal momento, tener una mala racha.

patch [pætʃ] *vt* remendar, poner un remiendo a; *to patch a hole* remendar un roto || poner un parche a (a tyre) || *to patch up* arreglar; *to patch up an old bicycle* arreglar una vieja bicicleta; remendar (clothing), arreglar (diferences) || FIG *to patch together* armar *or* formar de cualquier manera.

patchouli [ˈpætʃuli] *n* pachulí *m*.

patch test [ˈpætʃtest] *n* MED prueba *f* para descubrir una alergia.

patchwork [ˈpætʃwəːk] *n* labor *f* hecha a trozos de varios colores || — *a patchwork of fields* un mosaico de campos || *patchwork quilt* centón *m*, manta *f* hecha con trozos de varios colores.

patchy [ˈpætʃi] *adj* desigual (unequal).

pate [peit] *n* FAM coronilla *f* (top of the head) | sesos *m pl* (brains) || *bald pate* calva *f*.

pâté [ˈpɑːtei] *n* CULIN pastel *m* de carne || *pâté de foie gras* pasta *f* de hígado de ganso, «foie gras» *m*.

patella [pəˈtelə] *n* ANAT rótula *f*.
— OBSERV El plural de *patella* es *patellae* o *patellas*.

patellar [pəˈtelə*] *adj* ANAT rotular.

paten [ˈpætən] *n* REL patena *f*.

patent [ˈpeitənt] *adj* patente, evidente, manifiesto, ta (obvious); *you can't deny patent facts* no puede negar hechos evidentes || COMM patentado, da (an invention); *patent goods* artículos patentados | de patente (right) | de patentes (office) || particular; *a patent way of pickling onions* una manera particular de conservar cebollas || MED abierto, ta (unobstructed) || — *patent leather* charol *m* || *patent medicine* específico *m*.
◆ *n* patente *f*; *to take out a patent* obtener una patente || *infringement of patent* imitación fraudulenta.

patent [ˈpeitənt] *vt* patentar.

patently [ˈpeitəntli] *adv* evidentemente || *to be patently obvious* o *clear* estar clarísimo.

patentee [ˌpeitənˈtiː] *n* poseedor *m* de una patente.

pater [ˈpeitə*] *n* FAM padre *m* (father).

paterfamilias [ˈpeitəfəˈmiliæs] *n* paterfamilias *m inv* (in ancient Rome) || jefe *m* de la familia.
— OBSERV El plural es *patresfamilias*.

paternal [pəˈtəːnl] *adj* paternal (of or like a father) || paterno, na; *paternal grandmother* abuela paterna.

paternalism [pəˈtəːnəlizəm] *n* paternalismo *m*.

paternalistic [pəˌtəːnəˈlistik] *adj* paternalista.

paternity [pəˈtəːniti] *n* paternidad *f* (fatherhood) ‖ FIG paternidad *f* ‖ JUR *paternity suit* litigio *m* de paternidad.

paternoster [ˈpætəˈnɔstə*] *n* REL paternóster *m*, padrenuestro *m*.

path [pɑːθ] *n* camino *m*, sendero *m*, senda *f* (way); *he took the path that runs along the river* cogió el camino que va a lo largo del río ‖ calle *f* (of a garden) ‖ camino *m*; *the police cleared a path through the crowd for him* la policía le abrió camino entre la multitud ‖ pista *f* (track) ‖ órbita *f* (of a planet) ‖ curso *m* (of a star) ‖ curso *m*, recorrido *m* (of sun) ‖ trayectoria *f* (of bullet) ‖ FIG paso *m*; *his path through life was hard* su paso por la vida fue difícil | camino *m*; *path to glory* camino hacia la gloria ‖ — FIG *our paths had crossed before* ya nos hemos visto antes | *the straight and narrow path* el buen camino.

pathetic [pəˈθetik]; **pathetical** [-əl] *adj* patético, ca; lastimoso, sa (arousing pity) ‖ FAM malísimo, ma; *the bullfighter was pathetic* el torero fue malísimo | pobre; *she is a pathetic creature* es una pobre mujer.

pathfinder [ˈpɑːθˌfaində*] *n* explorador, ra (explorer) ‖ pionero *m*, adelantado *m* (pioneer).

pathless [ˈpɑːθlis] *adj* sin senderos *or* caminos (without paths) ‖ inexplorado, da (unexplored).

pathogen [ˈpæθədʒən]; **pathogene** [pæθəˈdʒiːn] *n* agente *m* patógeno.

pathogenesis [pæθəˈdʒenesis] *n* MED patogenesia *f*, patogenia *f*.

pathogenetic [pæθədʒəˈnetik] *adj* patógeno, na.

pathogenic [pæθəˈdʒenik] *adj* patógeno, na.

pathogeny [pəˈθɔdʒəni] *n* MED patogenia *f*.

pathologic [ˌpæθəˈlɔdʒik]; **pathological** [-əl] *adj* patológico, ca.

pathologist [pəˈθɔlədʒist] *n* MED patólogo, ga.

pathology [pəˈθɔlədʒi] *n* patología *f*.

pathos [ˈpeiθɔs] *n* patetismo *m*.

pathway [ˈpɑːθwei] *n* camino *m*, senda *f*, sendero *m* (path) ‖ acera *f* [AMER vereda *f*] (pavement).

patience [ˈpeiʃəns] *n* paciencia *f*; *to have patience* tener paciencia; *to lose one's patience* perder la paciencia; *my patience is exhausted* se me ha agotado la paciencia ‖ solitario *m* (card game); *to play patience* hacer solitarios ‖ — *to be out of patience* habérsele agotado a uno la paciencia ‖ *to have no patience with* o *for* no aguantar; *I have no patience with that singer* no aguanto a ese cantante ‖ *to possess one's soul in patience* armarse de paciencia ‖ *to tax* o *to try s.o.'s patience* probarle a alguien la paciencia.

patient [ˈpeiʃənt] *adj* paciente.
◆ *n* paciente *m* & *f*, enfermo, ma.

patiently [-li] *adv* con paciencia, pacientemente.

patina [ˈpætinə] *n* pátina *f*; *to coat with a patina* dar pátina a.

patinate [ˈpætineit] *vt* patinar.

patio [əætiəu] *n* patio *m* ‖ *patio doors* puerta *f* acristalada de entrada al patio.

patois [ˈpætwɑː] *n* dialecto *m*.

patriarch [ˈpeitriɑːk] *n* patriarca *m*.

patriarchal [ˌpeitriˈɑːkəl] *adj* patriarcal.

patriarchate [ˈpeitriɑːkit]; **patriarchy** [ˈpeitriɑːki] *n* patriarcado *m*.

patrician [pəˈtriʃən] *adj/n* patricio, cia.

patricidal [ˈpætrisaidəl] *adj* parricida.

patricide [ˈpætrisaid] *n* parricidio *m* (crime) ‖ parricida *m* & *f* (criminal).

Patrick [ˈpætrik] *pr n* Patricio *m*.

patrilineal [pætrəˈliniəl] *adj* por línea paterna.

patrimonial [ˈpætriˈməunjəl] *adj* patrimonial.

patrimony [ˈpætriməni] *n* patrimonio *m*.

patriot [ˈpeitriət] *n* patriota *m* & *f*.

patriotic [ˌpætriˈɔtik] *adj* patriótico, ca; patriota.

patriotism [ˈpætriətizəm] *n* patriotismo *m*.

patristic [pəˈtristik]; **patristical** [-əl] *adj* REL patrístico, ca.

patristics [pəˈtristiks] *n* REL patrística *f*.

patrol [pəˈtrəul] *n* patrulla *f* ‖ US ronda *f* (of a policeman) ‖ *to be on patrol* estar de patrulla.

patrol [pəˈtrəul] *vt* hacer una ronda por; *he patrolled the area* hizo una ronda por la región ‖ hacer la ronda en, vigilar; *that watchman patrols this street* aquel sereno hace la ronda en esta calle *or* vigila esta calle ‖ patrullar por, estar de patrulla por; *police patrol the streets* la policía patrulla por la calle ‖ estar de patrulla; *soldiers patrol the border* unos soldados están de patrulla en la frontera ‖ FIG rondar.
◆ *vi* patrullar.

patrol boat [-bəut] *n* patrullero *m*.

patrol car [-kɑː*] *n* coche *m* patrulla.

patrol leader [-ˈliːdə*] *n* jefe *m* de patrulla.

patrolman [-mən] *n* US policía *m*, guardia *m*.
— OBSERV El plural de *patrolman* es *patrolmen*.

patrol wagon [-ˈwægən] *n* US coche *m* celular.

patron [ˈpeitrən] *n* patrocinador, ra (person who gives practical support to a cause) ‖ patrón *m*, patrono *m*, patrona *f*; *St Christopher is the patron of travellers* San Cristóbal es el patrón de los viajeros ‖ mecenas *m inv* (of arts) ‖ patrono *m* (of a charity) ‖ cliente *m* & *f* (customer) ‖ REL *patron saint* santo patrón, santa patrona.

patronage [ˈpætrənidʒ] *n* patrocinio *m* (sponsorship); *under the patronage of* bajo el patrocinio de ‖ patronato *m*; *royal patronage* patronato real ‖ mecenazgo *m* (of arts) ‖ clientela *f* (customers).

patronal [pəˈtrəunl] *adj* REL patronal.

patroness [ˈpeitrənis] *n* REL patrona *f* ‖ patrocinadora *f* (of a cause).

patronize [ˈpætrənaiz] *vt* patrocinar; *to patronize a firm* patrocinar una empresa; *campaign patronized by* campaña patrocinada por ‖ favorecer, proteger (an artist) ‖ fomentar (arts) ‖ tratar con condescendencia *or* con aire protector (to be condescending towards) ‖ ser cliente de (to be customer at) ‖ *this cinema is well patronized* este cine tiene mucha clientela *or* atrae a mucha gente.

patronizing [-iŋ] *adj* protector, ra.

patronymic [ˌpætrəˈnimik] *adj* patronímico, ca.
◆ *n* patronímico *m*.

patten [ˈpætn] *n* zueco *m*, chanclo *m*.

patter [ˈpætə*] *n* jerga *f* (jargon) ‖ charloteo *m* (chat) ‖ charlatanería *f* (of a salesman) ‖ golpecitos *m pl*, golpeteo *m* (noise) ‖ tamborileo *m*, repiqueteo *m* (of rain) ‖ — *a patter of feet* unos pasos ligeros y apresurados ‖ *to have a good patter* tener mucha labia.

patter [ˈpætə*] *vt* chapurrear (a language) ‖ farfullar (to mumble) ‖ repetir mecánicamente (prayers, etc.).
◆ *vi* charlar (to chatter) ‖ tamborilear, repiquetear (rain) ‖ andar con paso ligero (walking) ‖ *to patter about* corretear.

pattern [ˈpætən] *n* dibujo *m* (design) ‖ estampado *m*, dibujo *m* (on cloth) ‖ dibujo *m*, diseño *m* (on china) ‖ muestra *f* (sample) ‖ forma *f* (form) ‖ TECH patrón *m* (in dressmaking) | escantillón *m*, plantilla *f* (for making moulds) ‖ dispersión *f* (of shots on a target) ‖ FIG modelo *m*, ejemplo *m*; *to take s.o. as a pattern* coger a alguien como modelo | pauta *f*; *to follow a fixed pattern* seguir una pauta fija ‖ INFORM *pattern recognition* reconocimiento *m* de formas.

pattern [ˈpætən] *vt* adornar con dibujos (to decorate with a pattern) ‖ estampar (cloth) ‖ — *to pattern o.s. on s.o.* seguir el ejemplo de alguien, imitar a alguien ‖ *to pattern sth. after* o *on* o *upon* hacer algo según el modelo de.

pattern book [-buk] *n* libro *m* de muestras.

patternmaker [-meikə*] *n* modelista *m* & *f*.

patty [ˈpæti] *n* empanada *f* (fried meat pie) ‖ fritura *f*.

paucity [ˈpɔːsiti] *n* escasez *f* (shortness, lack) ‖ falta *f* (of money).

Paul [pɔːl] *pr n* Pablo *m* ‖ *Paul VI (the sixth)* Paulo VI [sexto], Pablo VI [sexto].

Pauline [ˈpɔːlain] *adj* de San Pablo; *the Pauline Epistles* las Epístolas de San Pablo.

Paulist [ˈpɔːlist] *n* REL paulista *m*.

paunch [pɔːntʃ] *n* barriga *f*, panza *f* (belly).

paunch [pɔːntʃ] *vt* destripar.

paunchy [-i] *adj* panzudo, da; barrigón, ona.

pauper [ˈpɔːpə*] *n* pobre *m* & *f* ‖ *pauper's grave* fosa *f* común.

pauperism [-rizəm] *n* pauperismo *m*.

pauperization [ˌpɔːpəraiˈzeiʃən] *n* empobrecimiento *m*, pauperización *f*.

pauperize [ˈpɔːpəraiz] *vt* empobrecer, depauperar.

pause [pɔːz] *n* pausa *f* ‖ descanso *m*; *after a brief pause I continued my work* después de un breve descanso seguí trabajando ‖ silencio *m*; *there was a pause in the conversation* hubo un silencio en la conversación ‖ MUS & POET pausa *f* ‖ *to give pause to s.o.*, *to give s.o. pause* hacer vacilar a alguien.

pause [pɔːz] *vi* hacer una pausa (to make a pause) ‖ detenerse, pararse; *I paused at every shop-window* me paré delante de todos los escaparates ‖ descansar (in working) ‖ vacilar (to hesitate); *to make s.o. pause* hacer vacilar a alguien ‖ *to pause on a word* recalcar una palabra.

pavan [ˈpævən]; **pavane** [ˈpævæn] *n* pavana *f*.

pave [peiv] *vt* pavimentar (with asphalt) ‖ adoquinar (with cobbles) ‖ enlosar (with flagstones) ‖ enladrillar (with bricks) ‖ empedrar (with stones) ‖ — FIG *the road to hell is paved with good intentions* el camino del infierno está empedrado de buenas intenciones | *to pave the way for* preparar el terreno para.

pavement [ˈpeivmənt] *n* acera *f* [AMER vereda *f*] (for pedestrians) ‖ pavimento *m* (paved surface) ‖ US calzada *f* (roadway) ‖ — *brick pavement* enladrillado *m* ‖ *cobblestone pavement* adoquinado *m* ‖ *flagstone pavement* enlosado *m* ‖ *stone pavement* empedrado *m*.

pavement artist [-ˈɑːtist] *n* pintor *m* callejero.

Pavia [pəˈviːə] *pr n* GEOGR Pavía.

pavilion [pəˈviljən] *n* pabellón *m*; *the Spanish pavilion* el pabellón español ‖ vestuario *m* (changing room) ‖ quiosco *m* (bandstand) ‖ ANAT pabellón *m* (outer ear) ‖ pabellón *m* (of a precious stone, in heraldry).

paving [ˈpeiviŋ] *n* pavimento *m* ‖ — *brick paving* enladrillado *m* ‖ *cobblestone paving* adoquinado *m* ‖ *flagstone paving* enlosado *m* ‖ *paving roller* apisonadora *f* ‖ *paving stone* adoquín *m* (brick), losa *f* (flagstone) ‖ *stone paving* empedrado *m*.

paw [pɔː] *n* pata *f* (of animals) ‖ garra *f* (of cats) ‖ zarpa *f* (of lions) ‖ FAM manaza *f* (hand) ‖ FAM *keep your paws off!* ¡las manos quietas!

paw [pɔː] *vt* dar zarpazos a (a clawed animal) || tocar con la pata (any animal) || FAM toquetear, manosear, sobar (to touch) || — FAM *stop pawing me!* ¡las manos quietas! || *to paw the ground* piafar (a horse).
◆ *vi* piafar (horse) || FAM manosear, toquetear, sobar (to touch).

pawkiness [-kinis] *n* astucia *f*.

pawky [-ki] *adj* astuto, ta; ladino, na.

pawl [pɔːl] *n* TECH trinquete *m*.

pawn [pɔːn] *n* peón *m* (in chess) || FIG instrumento *m*, juguete *m* (person used by others) || prenda *f* (object left as a deposit); *in pawn* en prenda || — *pawn ticket* papeleta *f* del monte de piedad || *to be in pawn* estar empeñado, da || FIG *to be in pawn to* estar en manos de || *to put in pawn* empeñar, dejar en prenda.

pawn [pɔːn] *vt* empeñar.

pawnage ['pɔːnidʒ] *n* empeño *m*.

pawnbroker [-ˌbrəukə*] *n* prestamista *m* & *f* || *pawnbroker's shop* casa *f* de empeños, monte *m* de piedad.

pawnshop [-ʃɔp] *n* casa *f* de empeños, monte *m* de piedad.

pawpaw [pə'pɔː] *n* ⟶ **papaw.**

pax [pæks] *n* REL paz *f*.
◆ *interj* ¡me rindo!

pay [pei] *n* paga *f*; *extra pay* paga extraordinaria || sueldo *m* (of employee) || salario *m* (of workman) || jornal *m* (of day worker) || emolumentos *m pl* (of Member of Parliament) || MIL paga *f* || — *equal pay* igualdad *f* de salarios || *holidays with pay* vacaciones retribuidas *or* pagadas || *in the pay of* pagado por, a sueldo de || *retirement pay* pensión *f*, jubilación *f*, retiro *m* || FIG *to be in the pay of* estar al servicio de || *to draw one's pay* cobrar || *to stop sth. out of s.o.'s pay* descontar *or* deducir algo del sueldo de alguien.

pay* [pei] *vt* pagar (to hand over in payment); *to pay five pounds* pagar cinco libras; *to pay one's debts* pagar las deudas; *to pay s.o. to do sth.* pagar a alguien para que haga algo || producir, dar; *our investment paid five per cent* nuestra inversión produjo el cinco por ciento || hacer (visit, compliment) || rendir (homage) || presentar (respects) || prestar; *to pay attention* prestar atención || FIG compensar; *it will pay you to take that trip* te compensará hacer ese viaje | ser rentable *or* ser provechoso para (to be profitable) | pagar; *she paid his kindness with insults* le pagó su amabilidad con insultos; *to pay the consequences* pagar las consecuencias; *to pay sth. with one's life* pagar algo con la vida || MAR calafatear (to make waterproof) || — *to be paid every week* cobrar todas las semanas || FIG & FAM *to pay a visit* ir al excusado || *to pay cash* o *on the nail* pagar al contado *or* a tocateja || FIG *to pay court to* cortejar a || *to pay expenses* cubrir gastos || *to pay in cash* pagar en metálico *or* en efectivo || *to pay in instalments* pagar a plazos || *to pay in kind* pagar en especie || *to pay money into an account* ingresar dinero en una cuenta || *to pay on account* pagar a cuenta || *to pay one's way* pagar su parte (to pay one's share), ser solvente (to be solvent).
◆ *vi* pagar; *have you paid yet?* ¿has pagado ya? | FIG compensar; *crime does not pay* el crimen no compensa | ser rentable *or* provechoso (to be profitable) || — FIG *it pays* vale *or* merece la pena; *it pays not to eat too much* merece la pena no comer demasiado; es rentable (to be profitable) || *to pay in advance* pagar por adelantado || *to pay in full* pagarlo todo.
◆ *phr v* **to pay away** soltar (a rope) | pagar || **to pay back** reembolsar, devolver (money) | pagar (s.o.) | devolver (an insult, etc.) || — FIG *to pay s.o. back in his own coin* pagar a alguien con la misma moneda || **to pay down** pagar al contado (cash) | dejar una señal de, hacer un desembolso inicial de (as a first payment) || **to pay for** pagar; *he paid for the cigarettes* pagó los cigarrillos | pagar por, pagar; *I paid five pounds for my watch* pagué cinco libras por mi reloj, pagué mi reloj cinco libras | FIG pagar por, pagar; *he paid for his crimes* pagó por sus crímenes || — *to pay for the sins of others* pagar las culpas ajenas || *you shall pay for it!* ¡ya me las pagarás! || **to pay in** ingresar || **to pay off** saldar, liquidar; *to pay off one's debts* saldar las deudas | reembolsar (creditor) | redimir (mortgage) | despedir (employee, servant) | licenciar (troops) | MAR despedir (crew), arriar (rope) | merecer la pena; *it was a risk but it paid off* fue un riesgo pero mereció la pena | dar resultado || **to pay out** pagar (s.o.) | desembolsar (money) | distribuir (to distribute) | arriar, soltar (rope) || — FIG *I'll pay you out for that!* ¡ya me las pagarás! | *to pay s.o. out* pagar a alguien con la misma moneda || **to pay over** pagar || **to pay up** pagar.
— OBSERV Pret y pp ***paid***.
— OBSERV Cuando este verbo significa *calafatear* se emplea también el pretérito y el participio pasivo *payed*.

payable [-əbl] *adj* pagadero, ra; *payable at sight, in instalments, to bearer* pagadero a la vista, a plazos, al portador || *to make a cheque payable to s.o.* extender un cheque a favor de alguien.

pay-as-you-earn [peiæzjuəːn] *n* deducción *f* del sueldo para los impuestos.

pay bill [-bil] *n* vale *m*.

payday [-dei] *n* día *m* de paga.

paydesk [-desk] *n* caja *f*.

pay dirt [-dəːt] *n* US suelo *m* rico en minerales (soil) | información *f* interesante (useful information) | filón *m* (remunerative discovery).

payee [pei'iː] *n* beneficiario, ria (of a cheque, of a postal order) || tenedor, ra (of a bill).

payer ['peiə*] *n* pagador, ra || *slow payer* moroso, sa.

paying ['peiiŋ] *adj* que paga (who pays) || rentable, provechoso, sa (profitable) || *paying guest* huésped, da de pago.
◆ *n* reembolso *m* (of a creditor) || liquidación *f*, pago *m* (of debt) || pago *m* (of money).

payload ['peiləud] *n* carga *f* útil || MIL carga *f* explosiva.

paymaster ['peiˌmaːstə*] *n* pagador *m* || MIL pagador *m*, habilitado *m*.

payment ['peimənt] *n* pago *m*; *to make a payment* efectuar *or* hacer un pago; *payment in (hard) cash* pago en metálico || FIG recompensa *f*, pago *m* (reward) || — *advance payment, payment in advance* pago adelantado *or* anticipado, anticipo *m* || *as* o *in payment for* en pago de || *cash payment* pago al contado || *deferred payment* pago a plazos || *down payment* desembolso *m* inicial || *monthly payment* mensualidad *f* || *net payment* líquido *m* || *on payment of two pounds* mediante el pago de dos libras, pagando dos libras || *payment by instalments* pago a plazos || *payment in full* pago íntegro, liquidación *f* || *payment in kind* pago en especie || *payment on account* pago a cuenta || *to present a cheque for payment* presentar un cheque al cobro, cobrar un cheque || *to stop payments* suspender los pagos || *without payment* sin pagar, gratuitamente; *to get sth. without payment* conseguir algo sin pagar; sin cobrar, gratuitamente; *I'll do it without payment* lo haré gratuitamente.

payoff ['peiɔf] *n* US FAM pago *m* (payment) | día *m* de paga (payday) | rentabilidad *f* (income) | pago *m*, recompensa *f* (reward) | resultado *m* final (result) | momento *m* or factor *m* decisivo | desenlace *m* (of a story).

pay office ['pei'ɔfis] *n* caja *f*, pagaduría *f*.

pay-out ['peiaut] *n* FAM pago.

pay-packet ['peiˌpækit] *n* sobre *m* de paga || FIG paga.

payphone ['peifəun] *n* teléfono *m* público de monedas.

pay rise ['pei'raiz] *n* aumento *m* de sueldo.

payroll ['peirəul]; **paysheet** ['peiʃiːt] *n* nómina *f*; *he has 20 people on his payroll* tiene una nómina de veinte personas.

pay slip ['peiˌslip] *n* hoja *f* de paga.

pay station ['pei'steiʃən]; **pay telephone** ['pei'telifiəun] *n* US teléfono *m* público.

PC *abbr of [personal computer]* PC, ordenador personal.

PCB *abbr of [printed circuit board]* tarjeta de circuito impreso.

pea [piː] *n* BOT guisante *m* [AMER arveja *f*, chícharo *m*] || — BOT *green peas* guisantes | *sugar pea* guisante mollar | *sweet pea* guisante de olor || FIG *to be as like as two peas* o *like two peas in a pod* parecerse como dos gotas de agua.

peace [piːs] *n* paz *f* (between countries) || orden *m* público (in a country); *to break the peace* alterar el orden público || armonía *f* (between people) || paz *f*, tranquilidad *f* (tranquillity) || — *at peace* en paz (countries), en armonía (people) || *go in peace!* ¡vaya en paz! || *my conscience is at peace* tengo la conciencia tranquila || *Octavian peace* paz octaviana || *peace be with you* la paz sea con vosotros || *peace of mind* tranquilidad de espíritu || *peace pipe* pipa *f* de la paz || *peace to his ashes!* ¡paz a sus cenizas! || *peace treaty* tratado *m* de paz || *the King's peace, the Queen's peace* el orden público || *to give s.o. no peace* no dejar a uno en paz || *to hold* o *to keep one's peace* guardar silencio, callarse || *to keep the peace* poner paz (between two people), mantener la paz (internationally), mantener el orden (in a country) || *to leave s.o. in peace* dejar a alguien en paz || *to live in peace* vivir en paz || *to make one's peace with* hacer las paces con || *to make peace* hacer las paces (individuals), firmar la paz (after war), poner paz (to stop a fight) || *to rest in peace* descansar en paz; *may he rest in peace* que en paz descanse.

peaceable [-əbl] *adj* pacífico, ca.

peaceably [-əbli] *adv* pacíficamente, de modo pacífico; *to behave peaceably* comportarse de modo pacífico || en paz; *to live peaceably* vivir en paz.

peaceful [-ful] *adj* pacífico, ca; *peaceful coexistence* coexistencia *or* convivencia pacífica; *peaceful tribes* tribus pacíficas || tranquilo, la (quiet).

peacefulness [-fulnis] *n* tranquilidad *f*, sosiego *m*, calma *f* (tranquility) || carácter *m* pacífico.

peace-keeping [-ˌkiːpiŋ] *adj* de pacificación; *peace-keeping forces* fuerzas *or* tropas de pacificación.
◆ *n* mantenimiento *m* de la paz.

peace-loving [-ˌlʌviŋ] *adj* amante de la paz.

peacemaker [-ˌmeikə*] *n* pacificador, ra || conciliador, ra.

peace offering [-ˌɔfəriŋ] *n* REL ofrenda *f* propiciatoria || FIG regalo *m* hecho para hacer las paces con una persona || oferta *f* de paz (to make peace).

peacetime [-taim] *n* tiempo *m* de paz.

peach [piːtʃ] *n* BOT melocotonero *m* [AMER durazno *m*] (tree) | melocotón *m* [AMER durazno *m*] (fruit) || color *m* melocotón (colour) || — BOT *peach tree* melocotonero *m* [AMER duraznero *m*] || FAM *she is a peach* es un bombón, es una monada.
◆ *adj* de color melocotón.

peach [piːtʃ] *vi* FAM chivarse (*on* de), delatar (*on* a).
◆ *vt* FAM soplar, delatar.

Peach Melba [-'melbə] *n* CULIN postre *m* Melba.

peachy [-i] *adj* FIG aterciopelado, da.

peacock ['piːkɔk] *n* ZOOL pavo *m* real, pavón *m* ‖ FIG *to be as proud as a peacock* ser más orgulloso que un pavo real.

peacock ['piːkɔk] *vi* pavonearse.

peacock blue [-bluː] *n* azul *m* eléctrico (colour).

peacock butterfly [-'bʌtəflai] *n* ZOOL pavón *m*.

peafowl ['piːfaul] *n* ZOOL pavo *m* real, pava *f* real.

pea green ['piː'griːn] *n* verde *m* claro.

pea-green ['piː'griːn] *adj* verde claro.

peahead ['piːhed] *n* FAM mentecato *m*.

peahen ['piː'hen] *n* ZOOL pava *f* real.

peajacket ['piːˌdʒækit] *n* chaquetón *m* de marinero.

peak [piːk] *n* pico *m* (mountain) ‖ cumbre *f*, cima *f* (summit) ‖ visera *f* (of a cap) ‖ punta *f* (point) ‖ MAR puño *m* de boca (of a sail) | penol *m* (of lateen yard) | uña *f* (of anchor) ‖ ELECTR carga *m* máxima ‖ FIG apogeo *m*, auge *m* (in a course of development) | cumbre *f* (of glory) | punto *m* máximo *or* más alto; *the peak of production* horas *f* punta *or* de mayor afluencia (transport), horas de mayor consumo (gas, etc.) ‖ *peak load* carga máxima ‖ *peak rate* tarifa *f* de horas punta ‖ *peak season* temporada alta.

peak [piːk] *vt* MAR embicar ‖ FIG encumbrar.
◆ *vi* alcanzar el máximo.

peaked [-t] *adj* con visera (cap) ‖ puntiagudo, da (sharp-pointed) ‖ *peaked features* cara cansada.

peaky [-i] *adj* FAM paliducho, cha.

peal [piːl] *n* repique *m*, repiqueteo *m* (of bells) ‖ sonido *m* (of organ) ‖ estruendo *m* (loud noise) ‖ — *peals of laughter* carcajadas *f* ‖ *peals of thunder* truenos *m*.

peal [piːl] *vt* repicar (bells).
◆ *vi* repicar, repiquetear (bells) ‖ retumbar (thunder) ‖ resonar (laugh).

peanut ['piːnʌt] *n* BOT cacahuete *m* [*AMER* cacahuate *m*, maní *m*] ‖ FIG & FAM insignificancia *f*.
◆ *pl* FIG & FAM miseria *f*; *to work for peanuts* trabajar por una miseria | nada (something small) ‖ — *peanut butter* manteca *f* de cacahuete ‖ US THEATR *peanut gallery* gallinero *m* ‖ *peanut oil* aceite *m* de cacahuete.

pear [pɛə] *n* BOT pera *f* (fruit) | peral *m* (tree) ‖ BOT *pear tree* peral *m*.

pearl [pəːl] *n* perla *f*; *cultured pearl* perla cultivada; *real pearl* perla fina ‖ madreperla *f*, nácar *m* (mother-of-pearl) ‖ FIG joya *f*, perla *f*, alhaja *f* (person) ‖ PRINT perla *f* (four-point type) ‖ gris *m* perla (colour) ‖ FIG *to cast pearls before swine* echar margaritas a los cerdos *or* a los puercos.
◆ *adj* de perlas (necklace) ‖ de perlas; *pearl diver* o *fisher* pescador de perlas; *pearl fishing* pesca de perlas ‖ de color perla (colour) ‖ perlero, ra (industry).

pearl [pəːl] *vi* pescar perlas (to fish for pearls) ‖ gotear (moisture, etc.).

pearl barley [-'bɑːli] *n* BOT cebada *f* perlada.

pearl grey [-grei] *n* gris *m* perla.

pearl oyster [-'ɔistə*] *n* ZOOL madreperla *f*, ostra *f* perlífera.

pearl-shaped [-ʃeipt] *adj* perlado, da; en forma de perla.

pearl shell [-ʃel] *n* concha *f* de perla.

pearly ['pəːli] *adj* nacarado, da; color de perla (colour) ‖ de perla (made of pearl).

pearly nautilus [-'nɔːtiləs] *n* ZOOL nautilo *m*.

pear-shaped ['pɛəʃeipt] *adj* en forma de pera ‖ FIG suave (mellow).

peasant ['pezənt] *adj/n* campesino, na ‖ FIG paleto, ta; cateto, ta; palurdo, da.

peasantry [-ri] *n* campesinos *m pl*.

pease [piːz] *n* guisantes *m pl* (peas).

peashooter ['piːˌʃuːtə*] *n* cerbatana *f*.

pea soup ['piːsuːp] *n* puré *m* de guisantes (soup) ‖ US FAM niebla *f* espesa de color amarillento (fog).

pea-souper [-ə*] *n* niebla *f* espesa de color amarillento (fog).

peat [piːt] *n* turba *f* ‖ *peat bog* turbera *f*.

peaty [-i] *adj* turboso, sa.

pebble ['pebl] *n* guijarro *m* (stone) ‖ FAM *you aren't the only pebble on the beach* no eres el único en el mundo.

pebbledash ['pebldæʃ] *n* enlucido *m* granuloso.

pebbly [-i] *adj* guijarroso, sa.

pecan [pi'kæn] *n* BOT pacana *f* (tree, nut).

peccadillo [ˌpekə'diləu] *n* pecadillo *m*, falta *f* leve, peccata minuta *f*.
— OBSERV El plural de la palabra inglesa es *peccadilloes* o *peccadillos*.

peccant ['pekənt] *adj* culpable, pecador, ra.

peccary ['pekəri] *n* ZOOL pecarí *m*, pécari *m* [*AMER* saíno *m*].

peck [pek] *n* medida *f* de áridos parecida al celemín (measure) ‖ picotín *m* (of oats) ‖ picotazo *m* (of a bird, mark) ‖ picadura *f* (of an insect) ‖ FAM beso *m* (kiss) ‖ FIG montón *m*; *a peck of trouble* un montón de problemas.

peck [pek] *vt* picotear (bird) ‖ FAM besar (to kiss).
◆ *vi* *to peck at* picotear (bird), picar (to nibble at food) ‖ *to peck out* sacar a picotazos (the eyes).

pecker [-ə*] *n* FAM *to keep one's pecker up* no dejarse desanimar.

peckerwood ['pekəwud] *n* pájaro *m* carpintero (woodpecker).

pecking ['pekiŋ] *n* picoteo *m*.

pecking order [-'ɔːdə*] *n* FIG la ley del más fuerte.

peckish ['pekiʃ] *adj* FAM hambriento, ta (hungry) ‖ US FAM irritable (irritable) ‖ FAM *to feel peckish* tener gazuza.

pectineal [pek'tiniəl] *adj* ANAT pectíneo, a (muscle).

pectoral ['pektərəl] *adj* ANAT pectoral ‖ REL *pectoral cross* pectoral *m*.
◆ *n* ANAT músculo *m* pectoral ‖ MED & REL pectoral *m* ‖ pectoral *m* (ornament).

peculate ['pekjuleit] *vt/vi* JUR desfalcar, malversar.

peculation [ˌpekju'leiʃən] *n* JUR malversación *f*, desfalco *m*, peculado *m* (embezzlement).

peculator ['pekjuleitə*] *n* malversador, ra; desfalcador, ra; concusionario, ria.

peculiar [pi'kjuːljə*] *adj* raro, ra; extraño, ña (odd); *a peculiar girl* una chica extraña ‖ característico, ca; típico, ca; propio, pia; peculiar; *custom peculiar to a country* costumbre típica de un país ‖ propio, pia; *this gait is peculiar to him* esta manera de andar es propia de él ‖ especial, particular (special) ‖ — *the condor is peculiar to the Andes* el cóndor es un animal de los Andes ‖ *he is a bit peculiar* está algo chalado (slightly mad).

peculiarity [piˌkjuːli'æriti] *n* particularidad *f*, peculiaridad *f* (particularity) ‖ rareza *f* (oddity) ‖ característica *f*, rasgo *m* característico (special characteristic) ‖ — *everyone has his peculiarities* todo el mundo tiene sus manías ‖ *special peculiarities* señas *f* particulares (on passport).

peculiarly [pi'kjuːljəli] *adv* particularmente; *peculiarly difficult* particularmente difícil ‖ de una manera extraña (strangely); *she dresses peculiarly* se viste de una manera extraña.

peculium [pi'kjuːljəm] *n* peculio *m*.
— OBSERV El plural de peculium es *peculia*.

pecuniary [pi'kjuːnjəri] *adj* pecuniario, ria ‖ *pecuniary troubles* apuros de dinero *or* monetarios.

pedagog ['pedəgɔg] *n* US pedagogo *m*.

pedagogic [ˌpedə'gɔdʒik]; **pedagogical** [-əl] *adj* pedagógico, ca.

pedagogics [-s] *n* pedagogía *f*.

pedagogue ['pedəgɔg] *n* pedagogo *m*.

pedagogy ['pedəgɔdzi] *n* pedagogía *f*.

pedal ['pedl] *n* pedal *m*; *the pedals of a bicycle* los pedales de una bicicleta; *clutch, brake pedal* pedal de embrague, de freno ‖ — MUS *loud pedal* pedal fuerte | *soft pedal* sordina *f*.

pedal ['pedl] *vt* dar a los pedales de (to move the pedals of); *to pedal a bicycle hard* darle fuerte a los pedales de una bicicleta.
◆ *vi* pedalear.

pedal bin [-bin] *n* papelera *f or* cubo *m* de basura con pedal.

pedal boat [-bəut] *n* hidropedal *m*.

pedal brake [-breik] *n* freno *m* de pie.

pedalling; pedaling [-iŋ] *n* pedaleo *m*.

pedant ['pedənt] *n* pedante *m* & *f*.

pedantic [pi'dæntik]; **pedantical** [-əl] *adj* pedante (person) ‖ pedantesco, ca; pedante (manner).

pedantically [-əli] *adv* con pedantería, de una manera pedante, pedantescamente.

pedanticism [pe'dəntisizəm]; **pedantism** ['pedəntizəm] *n* pedantismo *m*, pedantería *f*.

pedantry ['pedəntri] *n* pedantería *f*.

peddle ['pedl] *vt* vender de puerta en puerta ‖ FIG divulgar, difundir.
◆ *vi* vender de puerta en puerta.

peddler [-ə*] *n* vendedor *m* ambulante, buhonero *m*.

peddling [-iŋ] *n* venta *f* ambulante, buhonería *f*.

pederast ['pedəræst] *n* US pederasta *m*.

pederasty [-i] *n* US pederastia *f*.

pedestal ['pedistl] *n* pedestal *m* ‖ *to put* o *to set s.o. on a pedestal* poner a alguien en un pedestal *or* por las nubes.

pedestal lamp [-læmp] *n* lámpara *f* de pie.

pedestal table [-'teibl] *n* velador *m*.

pedestrian [pi'destriən] *adj* pedestre (relating to people on foot) ‖ FIG vulgar, pedestre (commonplace) | prosaico, ca (style).
◆ *n* peatón *m*.

pedestrian crossing [-'krɔsiŋ] *n* paso *m* de peatones.

pedestrianize [pi'destriənaiz] *vt* peatonalizar.

pedestrian precinct [-'priːsiŋkt] *n* zona *f* peatonal.

pedestrian traffic [-'træfik] *n* peatones *m pl*; *the town center is reserved for pedestrian traffic* el centro de la ciudad está reservado a los peatones.

pediatric [ˌpiːdi'ætrik] *adj* MED pediátrico, ca.

pediatrician [ˌpiːdiə'triʃən]; **pediatrist** [ˌpiːdi'ætrist] *n* US MED pediatra *m*, pedíatra *m*.

pediatrics [ˌpiːdi'ætriks] *n* US MED pediatría *f*.

pedicular [pe'dikjulə*] *adj* pedicular.

pedicure ['pedikjuə*] *n* pedicuro, ra; callista *m* & *f* (chiropodist) || pedicura *f*, quiropodia *f* (chiropody).

pedicurist [-rist] *n* pedicuro, ra; callista *m* & *f*.

pedigree ['pedigri:] *n* árbol *m* genealógico (family tree) || genealogía *f*, «pedigree» *m*, pedigrí *m*, carta *f* de origen (of animals) || linaje *m* (ancestry) || — *man of pedigree* hombre *m* de alta alcurnia || *pedigree animal* animal *m* de raza.

pediment ['pedimənt] *n* ARCH frontón *m*.

pedlar ['pedlə*] *n* vendedor *m* ambulante, buhonero *m*.

pedology [pe'dɔlədʒi] *n* pedología *f*, edafología *f* (soil science) || pedología *f* (study of the development of children).

pedometer [pi'dɔmitə*] *n* MED podómetro *m*.

peduncle [pi'dʌŋkl] *n* BOT & ANAT pedúnculo *m*.

peduncular [pe'dʌŋkjulə*] *adj* peduncular.

pedunculate [pe'dʌŋkjulət]; **pedunculated** [pe'dʌŋkju,leitid] *adj* pedunculado, da.

pee [pi:] *n* FAM pis *m*; *to have a pee* hacer pis.

pee [pi:] *vi* FAM hacer pis.

peek [pi:k] *n* ojeada *f*, mirada *f*; *to take a peek at* echar una ojeada a.

peek [pi:k] *vi* mirar a hurtadillas (to look furtively) || echar una ojeada (to glance).

peekaboo ['pi:kə'bu:] *n* cucú *m* (game).

peel [pi:l] *n* piel *f* (skin) || pala *f* (shovel) || monda *f*, mondadura *f*, cáscara *f*, peladura *f* (removed skin of oranges, of potatoes) || pellejo *m* (of grapes) || — *candied peel* piel *f* almibarada *or* confitada || *slice of peel* cáscara *f* (in cocktails).

peel [pi:l] *vt* pelar, mondar (to take the skin off); *to peel an orange, potatoes* pelar una naranja, patatas || descortezar (bark) || descascarillar (nuts) || — *to peel off* quitar, despegar (wallpaper, etc.), quitarse (clothes) || FIG *to keep one's eyes peeled* estar ojo avizor.
◆ *vi* pelarse; *apples that peel easily* manzanas que se pelan fácilmente || *to peel off* desconcharse (paint), caerse a tiras, despegarse (wallpaper, etc.), despellejarse (skin), desnudarse (to undress), descortezarse (bark), descascarillarse (nails).

peeler [-ə*] *n* (ant) policía *m* (policeman) || FAM mujer *f* que hace strip-tease || *potato peeler* pelapatatas *m inv*.

peeling [-iŋ] *n* peladura *f* (of fruit, etc.).
◆ *pl* peladuras *f*, mondaduras *f*.

peen [pin] *n* boca *f* (of a hammer).

peep [pi:p] *n* mirada *f* furtiva, ojeada *f* (look); *to have o to take a peep at* echar una ojeada a || pío pío *m*, pío *m* (of birds) || grito *m* agudo (of a mouse) || — *at peep of day* o *of dawn* al amanecer || || — *to get a peep at sth.* conseguir ver algo un poco || FAM *we have not had a peep out of him all day* no ha dicho ni pío en todo el día.

peep [pi:p] *vi* mirar furtivamente, echar una ojeada *or* una mirada furtiva (*at* a) (to look) || piar (a bird) || — *to peep out* asomar; *his head peeped out from behind the wall* su cabeza asomó detrás del muro; aparecer, salir; *the moon peeped out from behind the clouds* la luna salió detrás de las nubes || *to peep through the curtains* atisbar detrás de los visillos || *to peep through the keyhole* mirar por el ojo de la cerradura.
◆ *vt* asomar; *he peeped his head out of the window* asomó la cabeza por la ventana.

peeper [-ə*] *n* FAM ojo *m* (eye) | mirón, ona (person) || pollito *m* (bird).

peephole [-həul] *n* mirilla *f* (in the door).

peeping Tom [-iŋtɔm] *n* mirón *m*, curioso *m*.

peep show ['pi:pʃəu] *n* mundonuevo *m* (box) || FAM espectáculo *m* sicalíptico.

peep sight [-sait] *n* alza *f* (of a gun).

peer [piə*] *n* par *m* (nobleman) || igual *m*, semejante *m* (equal) || — *peer group* grupo *m* paritario || *peer of the realm* par del reino || *peer pressure* presión *f* de los pares || *you will not find his peer* no encontrará otro igual.

peer [piə*] *vi* mirar (to look) || mirar con atención *or* con ojos de miope, entornar los ojos (to look closely) || aparecer, asomar (to peep out) || — *to peer at s.o.* mirar a alguien de hito en hito || *to peer into* mirar dentro de.
◆ *vt* elevar a la dignidad de par.

peerage [-ridʒ] *n* pares *m pl* (the peers of a country) || dignidad *f* de par (rank of a peer) || libro *m* nobiliario (book) || nobleza *f* (nobility) || *to get a peerage* recibir un título de nobleza.

peeres [-ris] *n* paresa *f*.

peerless [-lis] *adj* sin par, sin igual.

peeve [pi:v] *n* FAM malhumor *m*; *he got up in a peeve* se levantó de malhumor || *a pet peeve* un motivo de enfado.

peeve [pi:v] *vt* FAM irritar, poner de malhumor *or* furioso || — FAM *to be peeved* estar furioso *or* de malhumor | *to get peeved* ponerse furioso *or* de malhumor.
◆ *vi* irritarse, ponerse de malhumor *or* furioso.

peevish [-iʃ] *adj* picajoso, sa (irritable) || quejica (complaining) || malhumorado, da; de malhumor (bad-tempered) || terco, ca; testarudo, da (stubborn).

peevishly [-iʃli] *adv* con malhumor, malhumoradamente || quejándose.

peevishness [-iʃnis] *n* malhumor *m* (bad temper) || terquedad *f* (stubbornness).

peewit ['pi:wit] *n* avefría *f* (bird).

peg [peg] *n* pinza *f* (for clothes) || percha *f* (for hats, for coats, etc.) || gancho *m* (hook) | estaca *f* (for tent) || TECH clavija *f* || MUS clavija *f* || trago *m* (of spirits) || FIG escalón *m*, grado *m*; *to move up a peg in an organization* ascender un escalón en una organización || nivel *m* (of prices) || pretexto *m* (pretext); *he looked for a peg* buscó un pretexto || estaca *f* (croquet) || punto *m* de apoyo (of an argument) || FAM pata *f* (leg) || — *off the peg* de confección (clothes) || FIG *to be a square peg in a round hole* estar como pez fuera del agua | *to come down a peg (or two)* bajársele a uno los humos | *to take s.o. down a peg (or two)* bajar los humos a alguien.

peg [peg] *vt* fijar con clavijas, enclavijar || estabilizar (stock exchange, prices) || SP marcar (the score) || — *to peg down* sujetar con estacas, estacar || *to peg out* jalonar, señalar con estacas (to mark with pegs), tender (clothes).
◆ *vi* *to peg away* trabajar con ahínco || — *to peg away at* afanarse por || *to peg out* acabar la partida (in croquet), estirar la pata (to die).

pegasus ['pegəsəs] *n* pegaso *m* (fish).

Pegasus ['pegəsəs] *pr n* MYTH Pegaso *m*.

pegbox ['peg,bɔks] *n* MUS clavijero *m*.

pegleg ['pegleg] *n* pata *f* de palo.

peg top ['pegtɔp] *n* peonza *f*.

peignoir ['peinwɑ:*] *n* bata *f*, salto *m* de cama.

pejorative ['pi:dʒərətiv] *adj* peyorativo, va; despectivo, va.
◆ *n* palabra *f* peyorativa *or* despectiva.

peke [pi:k] *n* pequinés *m*, pekinés *m* (dog).

Pekinese [pi:ki'ni:z] *adj/n* → **Pekingese.**

Peking [pi:'kiŋ] *pr n* GEOGR Pekín, Pequín.

Pekingese [,pi:kiŋ'i:z]; **Pekinese** [pi:ki'ni:z] *adj* pekinés, esa; pequinés, esa.
◆ *n* pekinés, esa; pequinés, esa (person) || pequinés *m* (dog).

pelage ['pelidʒ] *n* pelaje *m*, pelo *m* (fur).

pelagian [pə'leidʒiən] *adj/n* REL pelagiano, na.

pelagic [pə'lædʒik] *adj* pelágico, ca; *pelagic fauna* fauna pelágica.

Pelagius [pə'leidʒiəs] *pr n* Pelagio *m*.

Pelasgian [pə'læzgiən] *adj/n* HIST pelasgo, ga.

pelerine ['peləri:n] *n* esclavina *f* (woman's cape).

pelf [pelf] *n* FAM vil metal *m* (money).

pelican ['pelikən] *n* pelicano *m*, pelícano *m* (bird).

pelican crossing [-'krɔsiŋ] *n* paso *m* de peatones.

pelisse [pe'li:s] *n* pelliza *f*.

pellagra [pe'lægrə] *n* MED pelagra *f*.

pellet ['pelit] *n* bola *f*, bolita *f* (little ball) || perdigón *m* (of a gun) || MED píldora *f* (pill).

pellicle ['pelikl] *n* película *f*.

pellicular [pe'likjulə*] *adj* pelicular.

pellitory ['pelitəri] *n* BOT parietaria *f* || BOT *pellitory of Spain* pelitre *m*.

pellmell; pell-mell ['pel'mel] *adv* atropelladamente || confusamente, desordenadamente.
◆ *adj* en desorden, confuso, sa.

pellucid [pe'lju:sid] *adj* translúcido, da; transparente || FIG lúcido, da; claro, ra (mind) | claro, ra (explanation).

pellucidity [pelju'siditi] *n* transparencia *f*, translucidez *f* || FIG lucidez *f*, claridad *f* (of mind) | claridad *f* (of explanation).

Peloponnese ['peləpəni:s] *pr n* GEOGR Peloponeso *m*.

Peloponnesian [,peləpə'ni:ʃən] *adj/n* peloponense.

pelota [pe'ləutə] *n* SP pelota *f* vasca || *pelota player* pelotari *m* & *f*.

pelt [pelt] *n* lluvia *f* (of stones) || pellejo *m*, piel *f* (skin of an animal) || golpe *m* (blow) || FAM piel *f*, pellejo *m* (skin) || — *at full pelt* a toda mecha, a toda velocidad, a todo meter || *pelt of rain* lluvia persistente *or* recia.

pelt [pelt] *vt* tirar, lanzar, arrojar; *they pelted us with snowballs* nos tiraron bolas de nieve || apedrear (to stone) || acribillar (with questions) || colmar (with abuse).
◆ *vi* llover a cántaros (to rain) || FAM correr a todo meter (to run) || — *he pelted away* se fue corriendo || *it's pelting down* está lloviendo a cántaros || *pelting rain* lluvia recia || *to pelt at* golpear fuertemente, aporrear.

peltry ['peltri] *n* peletería *f*.

pelure paper [pə'ljuə*peipə*] *n* papel *m* cebolla.

pelvic ['pelvik] *adj* ANAT pélvico, ca; pelviano, na.

pelvis ['pelvis] *n* ANAT pelvis *f*.
— OBSERV El plural de la palabra inglesa *pelvis* es *pelves*.

pen [pen] *n* gallinero *m* (enclosure for hens) || aprisco *m*, redil *m* (for sheep) || pocilga *f* (for pigs) || corral *m* (for farm animals) || toril *m* (at a bullring) || hembra *f* del cisne (female swan) || pluma *f* (writing instrument, bird's feather) || pluma *f*, plumilla *f* (nib) || parque *m*, jaula *f* (child's play area) || FIG pluma *f*; *a journalist lives by his pen* el periodista vive de su pluma || FAM chirona *f* (jail) || — *ball-point pen* bolígrafo *m* || *felt-tipped pen* rotulador *m* || *fountain pen* pluma estilográfica || *to have a ready pen* tener facilidad para escribir || *to let one's pen run on* escribir al correr de la pluma *or* a vuela pluma || *to put pen to paper* tomar la pluma.

pen [pen] *vt* escribir || *to pen in* o *up* encerrar, acorralar.

penal ['pi:nl] *adj* penal; *penal code* código penal || castigable (legally punishable) || — *penal colony* penal *m* || *penal servitude* trabajos *m pl* forzados || *penal servitude for life* cadena perpetua.

penalization [pi:nəlai'zeiʃən] *n* castigo *m*, penalización *f*.

penalize ['pi:nəlaiz] *vt* penar, castigar, penalizar (to inflict punishment on) || perjudicar; *the tobacco tax penalizes the smoker* los impuestos sobre el tabaco perjudican al fumador || SP castigar, penalizar.

penalty ['penlti] *n* pena *f* (punishment for breaking a law, etc.); *death penalty* pena de muerte || multa *f* (fine) || FIG castigo *m*; *his hangover was a penalty for drinking too much* la resaca fue su castigo por haber bebido demasiado | precio *m*, contrapartida *f*; *penalty of fame* precio de la gloria | consecuencias *f pl*; *to pay the penalty of* pagar las consecuencias de || SP penalty *m*, castigo *m* máximo (in football), hockey | penalización *f* (in golf) | tiro *m* de castigo *or* de penalidad (rugby) || multa *f* (in bridge) || — *on* o *upon* o *under penalty of* bajo pena de || SP *penalty area* o *box* área *f* de castigo || *penalty clause* cláusula *f* penal || SP *penalty kick* penalty | *penalty spot* punto *m* de penalty.

penance ['penəns] *n* REL penitencia *f* || — *as penance* como penitencia || *to do one's penance* cumplir la penitencia || *to do penance* hacer penitencia || *to give s.o. a penance* imponer una penitencia a uno.

pen-and-ink ['penənd'iŋd] *adj* a pluma (drawing).

penates [pe'nɑ:teis] *pl n* penates *m*.

pence [pens] *pl n* → **penny.**

penchant ['pɑ:ŋʃɑ:ŋ] *n* inclinación *f*; *to have a penchant for music* tener inclinación por la música.

pencil ['pensl] *n* lápiz *m*, lapicero *m*; *coloured pencil* lápiz de color; *eyebrow pencil* lápiz de ojos || PHYS haz *m* (narrow beam of light) || — *in pencil* a *or* con lápiz || *pencil drawing* dibujo *m* a lápiz || *propelling pencil* lapicero, portaminas *m inv*.

pencil ['pensl] *vt* escribir con lápiz (to write) || dibujar a lápiz (to draw) || pintarse con lápiz (one's eyebrows).

pencil box [-bɔks]; **pencil case** [-keis] *n* estuche *m* para lápices, plumero *m*.

pencil holder [-ˌhəuldə*] *n* portalápiz *m*.

pencil sharpener [-'ʃɑ:pnə*] *n* sacapuntas *m inv*, afilalápices *m inv*.

pendant ['pendənt] *n* colgante *m*, dije *m* (of necklace, chain, etc.) || pendiente *m* (earring) || colgante *m* (of a chandelier) || colgante *m*, lámpara *f* colgante (electrical fixture) || MAR grímpola *f*, gallardete *m*, banderín *m* (pennant) || pareja *f* (companion piece of a picture, etc.).
◆ *adj* pendiente, colgante (hanging) || que sobresale, sobresaliente (overhanging) || pendiente (pending).

pendent ['pendənt] *adj* pendiente, colgante (hanging) || que sobresale, sobresaliente (overhanging) || pendiente (pending).

pendentive [pendentiv] *n* ARCH pechina *f*.

pending ['pendiŋ] *adj* pendiente; *the case is still pending* el caso está todavía pendiente; *pending orders* pedidos pendientes || *pending tray* bandeja *f* de asuntos pendientes.
◆ *prep* hasta; *a temporary arrangement pending a final settlement* un arreglo temporal hasta una solución definitiva || durante; *pending the discussions there are to be no troop movements* durante las conversaciones, no debe haber movimiento de tropas.

pendular ['pendjulə*] *adj* pendular.

pendulous ['pendjuləs] *adj* colgante (hanging or bending down) || oscilante (swinging to and fro).

pendulum [pendjuləm] *n* péndulo *m*.

peneplain; peneplane ['pi:niplein] *n* GEOL penillanura *f*.

penetrability [ˌpenitrə'biliti] *n* penetrabilidad *f*.

penetrable ['penitrəbl] *adj* penetrable.

penetrate ['penitreit] *vt* penetrar en (to go into by piercing); *the shell penetrated the hull* el proyectil penetró en el casco || extenderse por; *the smell penetrated the whole house* el olor se extendió por toda la casa || FIG penetrar, descubrir (to discern, to see through); *to penetrate a secret* penetrar un secreto.
◆ *vi* penetrar; *the bullet penetrated to the lung* la bala penetró hasta el pulmón; *to penetrate into the jungle* penetrar en la selva || entrar, penetrar; *water is penetrating everywhere* el agua está entrando por todas partes || *to penetrate through sth.* atravesar algo.

penetrating [-iŋ] *adj* penetrante; *a penetrating gaze, wind* una mirada, un viento penetrante || agudo, da (cry) || perspicaz; *a penetrating mind* una mente perspicaz || *to have a penetrating eye* tener la vista aguda *or* penetrante.

penetration [ˌpeni'treiʃən] *n* penetración *f*.

penetrative ['penitrətiv] *adj* penetrante.

penfriend ['penfrend] *n* persona *f* con quien uno se cartea.

penguin ['peŋgwin] *n* ZOOL pingüino *m*.

penholder ['penˌhəuldə*] *n* portaplumas *m inv*, mango *m* de la pluma.

penicillin [ˌpeni'silin] *n* MED penicilina *f*.

penicillium [peni'siliəm] *n* BOT penicillium *m*.
— OBSERV El plural de la palabra inglesa es *penicillia*.

peninsula [pi'ninsjulə] *n* península *f*; *the Iberian Peninsula* la Península Ibérica.

peninsular [-*] *adj* peninsular || HIST *the Peninsular War* la Guerra de Independencia (in Spain).

penis ['pi:nis] *n* ANAT pene *m*.
— OBSERV El plural de *penis* es *penes* o *penises*.

penitence ['penitəns] *n* penitencia *f* || arrepentimiento *m*.

penitent ['penitənt] *adj/n* penitente || arrepentido, da; *a penitent thief* un ladrón arrepentido.

penitential [ˌpeni'tenʃəl] *adj* penitencial.

penitentiary [ˌpeni'tenʃəri] *n* penitenciaría *f*, penal *m* (prison) || reformatorio *m*, correccional *m* (institution to reform offenders) || REL penitenciaría *f* (office) | penitenciario *m* (officer).
◆ *adj* penitenciario, ria; *penitentiary system* régimen penitenciario || US *penitentiary offence* delito castigado con el encarcelamiento en un penal.

penknife ['pennaif] *n* navaja *f*, cortaplumas *m inv*.
— OBSERV El plural de esta palabra es *penknives*.

penman ['penmən] *n* calígrafo *m* || escritor *m* (writer).
— OBSERV El plural de *penman* es *penmen*.

penmanship [-ʃip] *n* caligrafía *f* || pluma *f* (style).

penna ['penə] *n* pena *f* (feather).
— OBSERV El plural de *penna* es *pennae*.

pen name ['penneim] *n* seudónimo *m*.

pennant ['penənt] *n* MAR gallardete *m*, grímpola *f* || banderín *m* (small flag).

pennate ['penet] *adj* BOT pinado, da || ZOOL alado, da.

pen nib ['penib] *n* plumilla *f* (of fountain pen) || punta *f*.

penniless ['penilis] *adj* sin dinero || *to be penniless* estar sin un céntimo *or* sin un real.

Pennine Chain ['penaintʃein] *pr n* GEOGR Montes *m pl* Peninos.

Pennines ['penainz] *pl prn* GEOGR Peninos *m*, Montes *m* Peninos.

pennon ['penən] *n* HIST pendón *m* (of a knight) || MAR gallardete *m*, grímpola *f* || banderín *m* (small flag).

Pennsylvania [ˌpensil'veinjə] *pr n* GEOGR Pensilvania *f*.

penny ['peni] *n* penique *m*; *a new penny* un nuevo penique; *sevenpence* siete peniques || US centavo *m* || FIG céntimo *m* || — *a penny for your thoughts* ¿en qué estás pensando? || FIG *bad pennies always turn up* bicho malo nunca muere | *he is a bad penny* es un gamberro | *I am not a penny the wiser* no me he enterado todavía || *not to have a penny to one's name* o *to bless o.s. with* no tener un céntimo *or* un real || FIG *take care of the pennies and the pounds will take care of themselves* poco a poco la vieja hila el copo | *the penny just dropped* ahora caigo (en la cuenta), acabo de caer en la cuenta | *to be two* o *ten a penny* haber a patadas | *to cost a pretty penny* costar un dineral | *to look twice at every penny* reparar en gastos, ser tacaño | *to make a pretty penny out of it* sacar buen provecho de ello || FIG & FAM *to spend a penny* llamar por teléfono (to go to the toilet) || *to turn an honest penny* ganarse honradamente la vida.
— OBSERV La palabra *penny* tiene dos plurales: *pence* (forma más empleada hoy) y *pennies*.
— OBSERV La libra, hasta el año 1971, se dividía en 240 peniques, y desde entonces se divide en 100, o sea que en la actualidad el penique es la centésima parte de la libra.

penny-a-liner ['peniə'lainə*] *n* escritorzuelo *m* (bad writer).

penny dreadful ['peni'dredful] *n* novela *f* de muy poca categoría *or* barata, revista *f* de muy poca categoría *or* barata.

penny-in-the-slot machine ['peniinðə'slɔtməʃi:n] *n* máquina *f* tragaperras.

penny-pinching ['penipintʃiŋ] *adj* US FAM tacaño, ña.

pennyweight ['peniweit] *n* peso *m* que equivale aproximadamente a un gramo y medio.

penny-wise ['peniwaiz] *adj* que escatima en cosas pequeñas || *to be penny-wise and pound-foolish* hacer economías de chicha y nabo.

pennyworth ['penəθ,ʲəd'peniwerθ] *n* valor *m* de un penique; *to buy a pennyworth of* comprar por el valor de un penique || FIG pizca *f* || FIG *there is not a pennyworth of food in the house* no hay absolutamente nada de comer en la casa.

penologist [pi:'nɔlədʒist] *n* JUR penalista *m* & *f*, criminalista *m* & *f*.

penology [pi:'nɔlədʒist] *n* JUR criminología *f*.

penpusher ['penˌpuʃə*] *n* chupatintas *m inv*.

pension ['penʃən] *n* jubilación *f* (given to workers) | MIL retiro *m* || pensión *f* (allowance) || subvención *f* (given to artists) || — *old-age pension, retirement pension* jubilación *f* (of workers), retiro *m* (of soldiers), subsidio *m* de vejez, pensión *f* (state aid) || *pension fund* fondo *m* de pensiones || *to retire on a pension* jubilarse (a worker), retirarse (a soldier).

pension ['pɑ:ŋsi'ɔ:ə] *n* pensión *f* (board, lodging) || internado *m* (school).

pension ['penʃən] *vt* pensionar, dar una pensión a || *to pension off* jubilar (a worker), retirar (a soldier).

pensionable [-əbl] *adj* con derecho a la jubilación (a worker) || con derecho al retiro (soldier) || *pensionable age* edad *f* de la jubilación (of a worker), edad *f* del retiro (of a soldier).

pensionary [-əri] *n* pensionado, da (who receives a pension) || jubilado, da (worker) || retirado, da (soldier) || mercenario *m* (hireling).

pensioner [-ə*] *n* pensionista *m* & *f*, pensionado, da || inválido *m* (in institution) || pensionista *m* & *f* (student).

pensive ['pensiv] *adj* pensativo, va; meditabundo, da.

penstock ['penstɔk] *n* compuerta *f* (sluice gate) || caz *m* (millrace).

pent [pent] *adj* ⟶ **pent-up.**

pentagon ['pentəgən] *n* pentágono *m* || *the Pentagon* el Pentágono.

pentagonal [pen'tægənl] *adj* MATH pentagonal, pentágono, na.

pentahedron [pentə'hi:drən] *n* MATH pentaedro.

pentarchy ['pentɑ:rki] *n* pentarquía *f*.

pentasyllabic [pentəsi'læbik] *adj* pentasílabo *m*.

pentasyllable [pentə'siləbl] *n* pentasílabo *m*.

Pentateuch ['pentətju:k] *n* REL Pentateuco *m*.

pentathlon [pen'tæθlɔn] *n* SP pentatlón *m*.

Pentecost ['pentikɔst] *n* REL Pentecostés *m*.

Pentecostal [,penti'kɔstl] *adj* de Pentecostés.

penthouse ['penthaus] *n* cobertizo *m* (shed) || ático *m* (flat) || alero *m* (over door or window).

pentode ['pentəud] *n* PHYS pentodo *m*.

pentothal ['pentəθɔl] *n* MED pentotal *m*.

pent-up ['pentʌp]; **pent** [pent] *adj* encerrado, da (confined) || reprimido, da; contenido, da (emotion).

penult [pi'nʌlt] *n* penúltima sílaba *f*.

penultimate [pi'nʌltimit] *adj* penúltimo, ma.
◆ *n* penúltimo, ma || penúltima sílaba *f*.

penumbra [pi'nʌmbrə] *n* penumbra *f*.
— OBSERV El plural de la palabra inglesa *penumbra* es *penumbrae* o *penumbras*.

penurious [pi'njuəriəs] *adj* parsimonioso, sa; avaro, ra (stingy) || mezquino, na (mean) || pobre; *penurious family* familia pobre || poco fértil (barren).

penury ['penjuri] *n* penuria *f*, escasez *f* (lack) || pobreza *f*, miseria *f* (extreme poverty); *to live in penury* vivir en la miseria || pobreza *f* (of ideas, of language, etc.).

peon [pju:n,ʃeḍ'pi:ən] *n* peón *m*, bracero *m* (labourer) || criado *m* (servant).

peonage ['piənidʒ] *n* condición *f* de peón || FIG esclavitud *f* (servitude).

peony ['piəni] *n* BOT peonía *f*, saltaojos *m inv*.

people ['pi:pl] *n* personas *f pl*; *five hundred people* quinientas personas || gente *f*; *what will people say?* ¿qué dirá la gente?; *many people* mucha gente; *the country people* la gente del campo; *business people* gente de negocios; *all sorts of people* toda clase de gente; *people say* la gente dice || pueblo *m*, nación *f*; *the Spanish people* el pueblo español; *to call on the people* hacer un llamamiento al pueblo || súbditos *m pl* (of a king) || nacionales *m pl* (of a country) || pueblo *m*; *government by the people* gobierno por el pueblo || habitantes *m pl* (of a town) || familia *f*; *to write to one's people* escribir a la familia || amigos *m pl* (friends) || antepasados *m pl* (ancestors) || — *coloured people* gente de color || *I am going to write to my people* voy a escribir a los míos *or* a mi familia || *lower class people* pueblo bajo || *man of the people* hombre *m* del pueblo || *most people* la mayoría de la gente || *ordinary people* gente de la calle || *people's court* tribunal *m* del pueblo || *people's front* frente *m* popular || *people's republic* república *f* popular || *the common people* el pueblo, la plebe || *the people at large* la gente en general || *what do you people think?* ¿qué piensan ustedes? || *young people* gente joven, jóvenes *m pl*.
— OBSERV Cuando tiene un sentido colectivo *people* permanece invariable, pero se construye con el plural; en los demás casos la forma plural es *peoples*.

people ['pi:pl] *vt* poblar; *densely peopled country* país muy poblado; *thinly peopled* poco poblado.

pep [pep] *n* FAM energía *f*; *full of pep* lleno de energía.

pep [pep] *vt* *to pep up* animar (conversation, dance, person).

peplum [pepləm] *n* peplo *m*.
— OBSERV El plural de *peplum* es *peplums* o *pepla*.

pepper ['pepə*] *n* pimienta *f*; *black pepper* pimienta negra || BOT pimentero *m* (plant) | pimiento *m*; *red pepper* pimiento rojo; *sweet pepper* pimiento morrón || FAM tocino *m* (in skipping).

pepper ['pepə*] *vt* sazonar con pimienta (to season with pepper) || acribillar; *they peppered him with shot* le acribillaron a balazos || FIG salpicar; *to pepper a speech with anecdotes* salpicar un discurso con anécdotas.

pepper-and-salt [-ən'sɔ:lt] *adj* de mezclilla (cloth) || entrecano, na (hair).

pepperbox [-bɔks] *n* pimentero *m*.

peppercorn [-kɔ:n] *n* grano *m* de pimienta || FIG *peppercorn rent* alquiler *m* nominal.

pepper mill [-mil] *n* molinillo *m* de pimienta.

peppermint [-mint] *n* BOT hierbabuena *f*, yerbabuena *f*, menta *f* || menta *f* (flavour) || pipermín *m* (liqueur) || pastilla *f* de menta (sweet).

pepper patch [-pætʃ] *n* pimental *m*.

pepper pot [-pɔt] *n* pimentero *m* (pepperbox) || CULIN guiso *m* indio compuesto de carne *or* pescado y pimientos rojos | estofado *m* muy picante (highly seasoned stew).

pepper shaker [-ʃeikə*] *n* US pimentero *m*.

peppery [-ri] *adj* picante (tasting of pepper) || irascible, enojadizo, za (quick-tempered) || mordaz, picante (language).

pep pill ['pep'pil] *n* MED estimulante *m*.

peppy ['pepi] *adj* lleno de vida.

pepsin ['pepsin] *n* CHEM pepsina *f*.

peptalk ['peptɔ:k] *n* FAM discurso *m or* palabras *f pl* destinados a levantar los ánimos.

per [pə:*] *prep* por; *three shillings per person* tres chelines por persona; *three per cent* tres por ciento; *an increase of ten per cent* un aumento del diez por ciento; *to decrease by five per cent* bajar en un cinco por ciento || por, por medio de (by means of) || a, por; *per annum* al año || — *as per invoice* según factura || *as per usual* como de costumbre || *per capita* per cápita, por cabeza || *per hour* por hora; *one hundred miles per hour* cien millas por hora; por horas; *to work per hour* trabajar por horas || *thirty pence per pound* treinta peniques la libra.

peradventure [pərəd'ventʃə*] *adv* (ant) quizás, tal vez (perhaps) || por casualidad (by chance).
◆ *n* (ant) *beyond* o *without peradventure* sin duda alguna.

perambulate [pə'ræmbjuleit] *vt* recorrer; *to perambulate the countryside* recorrer el campo.
◆ *vi* andar, pasear.

perambulation [pə,ræmbju'leiʃən] *n* paseo *m* (stroll) || viaje *m* (trip) || inspección *f*.

perambulator ['præmbjuleitə*] *n* cochecito *m* de niño (pram) || paseante *m* & *f* (person walking).

perborate [pə:'bɔ:reit] *n* CHEM perborato *m*.

percale [pə:'keil] *n* percal *m*.

perceivable [pə'si:vəbl] *adj* perceptible.

perceive [pə'si:v] *vt* percibir (to hear); *he perceived a faint sound* percibió un leve ruido || divisar (to see); *I perceived a boat in the distance* divisé un barco a lo lejos || notar, darse cuenta (to notice); *he perceived that he was being watched* se dio cuenta de que le estaban observando || comprender (to understand).

percent [pə'sent] *adj* del... por ciento; *nine percent interest* interés del nueve por ciento.
◆ *n* tanto *m* por ciento, porcentaje *m* || por ciento; *a commission of ten percent* una comisión del diez por ciento || *to agree a hundred per cent* estar completamente de acuerdo, estar cien por cien de acuerdo.

percentage [-idʒ] *n* porcentaje *m*, tanto por ciento *m*; *to allow a percentage on all transactions* conceder un tanto por ciento en todas las transacciones || porcentaje *m*, parte *f*; *only a small percentage of pupils were successful* sólo una pequeña parte de los alumnos aprobó || proporción *f* (of acid, of alcohol, etc.) || FIG provecho *m* (profit).
◆ *adj* porcentual.

per centum [pə'sentəm] *n* ⟶ **percent.**

percept [pə:sept] *n* percepción *f*.

perceptibility [pə,septə'biliti] *n* perceptibilidad *f*.

perceptible [pə'septəbl] *adj* perceptible || sensible; *perceptible difference* diferencia sensible || — *perceptible to the ear* audible, oíble || *perceptible to the eye* visible.

perception [pə'sepʃən] *n* percepción *f* (the act of perceiving) || sensibilidad *f* || comprensión *f*.

perceptive [pə'septiv] *adj* perceptivo, va; *perceptive faculties* facultades perceptivas || perspicaz (perspicacious).

perceptivity [-iti] *n* facultad *f* perceptiva.

perch [pə:tʃ] *n* perca *f* (fish) || percha *f*, vara *f* (for birds) || FIG posición *f*; *he had a good view from his perch on the rooftop* tenía muy buena vista desde su posición en el tejado || medida *f* de longitud de unos 5 metros || FAM *to knock s.o. off his perch* derribar *or* desbancar a alguien.

perch [pə:tʃ] *vt* encaramar; *a castle perched on a rock* un castillo encaramado en una roca || colocar [en un sitio elevado].
◆ *vi* posarse (bird) || encaramarse; *the child perched on a stool* el niño se encaramó en un taburete || subirse (to climb up).

perchance [pə'tʃɑ:ns] *adv* (ant) tal vez, quizás (perhaps) || por casualidad (by chance).

percheron ['pə:ʃərɔn] *n* percherón *m* (horse).

perchlorate [pə:'klɔ:ret] *n* CHEM perclorato *m*.

perchloride [pə:'klɔraid] *n* CHEM percloruro *m*.

percipient [pə:'sipiənt] *adj/n* perceptor, ra.

percolate ['pə:kəleit] *vt* colar, filtrar (to filter) || filtrar (coffee).
◆ *vi* filtrarse, colarse (liquid) || filtrarse (coffee) || FIG infiltrarse.

percolation [,pə:kə'leiʃən] *n* filtración *f*, filtrado *m* || FIG infiltración *f*.

percolator ['pə:kəleitə*] *n* cafetera *f* de filtro, percolador *m*.

percuss [pə:'kʌs] *vt* MED percutir.

percussion [pə'kʌʃən] *n* percusión *f*; *percussion instruments* instrumentos de percusión; *percussion gun* arma de percusión ‖ — *percussion cap* cápsula *f*, pistón *m* (of firearm) ‖ *percussion hammer* percusor *m*.

percussionist [pə'kʌʃənist] *n* MUS percusionista *m* & *f*.

per diem [pəː'daiem] *adv* diariamente.
◆ *adj* diario, ria.
◆ *n* US dietas *f pl* (allowance).

perdition [pəː'diʃən] *n* perdición *f*.

perdurability [pəː,djuərə'biliti] *n* perdurabilidad *f*.

perdurable [pəː'djuərəbl] *adj* perdurable.

peregrinate ['perigrineit] *vi* peregrinar.

peregrination [,perigri'neiʃən] *n* peregrinación *f*.

peregrine ['perigrin] *n* ZOOL halcón *m* peregrino.

peremptorily [pə'remptərili] *adv* perentoriamente.

peremptoriness [pə'remptərinis] *n* perentoriedad *f*.

peremptory [pə'remptəri] *adj* perentorio, ria; *in a peremptory tone* con tono perentorio ‖ autoritario, ria (person) ‖ JUR *peremptory plea* excepción perentoria.

perennial [pə'renjəl] *adj* perenne ‖ *perennial youth* juventud eterna.
◆ *n* planta *f* perenne.

perestroika [peres'trɔikə] *n* perestroika *f*.

perfect ['pəːfikt] *adj* perfecto, ta; *a perfect example* un ejemplo perfecto; *perfect knowledge* conocimiento perfecto ‖ perfecto, ta; verdadero, ra; *a perfect gentleman* un verdadero caballero ‖ perfecto, ta; consumado, da; completo, ta; *a perfect idiot* un idiota completo ‖ absoluto, ta; *perfect silence* silencio absoluto ‖ BOT completo, ta; *perfect flower* flor completa ‖ MATH, MUS & GRAMM perfecto, ta; *a perfect square* un cuadrado perfecto; *perfect cadence* cadencia perfecta; *perfect tense* tiempo perfecto ‖ — GRAMM *future perfect* futuro perfecto | *present perfect* pretérito perfecto ‖ *she is a perfect stranger to me* no la conozco absolutamente nada.
◆ *n* GRAMM pretérito *m* perfecto.

perfect [pə'fekt] *vt* perfeccionar.

perfectibility [pə,fekti'biliti] *n* perfectibilidad *f*.

perfectible [pə'fektəbl] *adj* perfectible.

perfection [pə'fekʃən] *n* perfección *f* ‖ perfeccionamiento *m* ‖ — *to be the perfection of kindness* ser la bondad misma ‖ *to bring sth. to perfection* rematar algo ‖ *to do sth. to perfection* hacer algo a la perfección *or* a las mil maravillas.

perfectioning [-iŋ] *n* perfeccionamiento *m*.

perfectionist [-ist] *n* perfeccionista *m* & *f*.

perfectly ['pəːfiktli] *adv* perfectamente ‖ — *it's perfectly silly* es completamente tonto ‖ *to be perfectly happy* ser muy feliz.

perfervid [pəː'fəːvid] *adj* ardiente, férvido, da.

perfidious [pəː'fidiəs] *adj* pérfido, da.

perfidy ['pəːfidi] *n* perfidia *f*.

perfoliate [pəː'fəuliət] *adj* BOT perfoliado, da.

perforate ['pəːfəreit] *vt* perforar ‖ *perforated stamp* sello dentado.
◆ *vi* perforarse ‖ penetrar (*into* en).

perforating [-iŋ] *adj* perforador, ra; perforante ‖ MED *perforating ulcer* úlcera *f* perforante.
◆ *n* perforado *m* (punching).

perforation [,pəːfə'reiʃən] *n* perforación *f*, perforado *m* ‖ agujero *m* (hole) ‖ MED perforación *f* ‖ trepado *m*, dentado *m* (of stamps).

perforator ['pəːfəreitə*] *n* perforador, ra (person) ‖ perforadora *f* (machine).

perforce [pə'fɔːs] *adv* (ant) forzosamente, por fuerza.

perform [pə'fɔːm] *vt* hacer, llevar a cabo, ejecutar, realizar (to carry out); *the work being performed* el trabajo que se está realizando ‖ cumplir (duty, promise) ‖ desempeñar (functions) ‖ THEATR representar (a play) ‖ desempeñar, interpretar (a part) ‖ ejecutar, interpretar, tocar (piece of music) ‖ celebrar (a ceremony, rite) ‖ *to perform wonders* hacer maravillas.
◆ *vi* actuar, trabajar (actors); *who performs in that play?* ¿quién trabaja en esa obra? ‖ tocar (musicians); *to perform on the flute* tocar la flauta ‖ cantar (singers) ‖ hacer un número, hacer trucos (animals) ‖ TECH funcionar; *the engine performs well* el motor funciona bien | portarse; *how does this car perform on slippery roads?* ¿cómo se porta este coche en las carreteras resbaladizas?

performable [-əbl] *adj* hacedero, ra; realizable (task) ‖ representable (play) ‖ ejecutable (piece of music).

performance [-əns] *n* ejecución *f*, cumplimiento *m*, realización *f* (of a task) ‖ desempeño *m* (of functions) ‖ representación *f* (of a play) ‖ actuación *f* interpretación *f* (of an actor, of a musician) ‖ interpretación (of a piece of music, of a part) ‖ sesión *f* (in cinema); *the evening performance* la sesión de la tarde ‖ función *f* (in theatre) ‖ hazaña *f* (deed) ‖ celebración *f* (of ceremony, rite) ‖ SP actuación *f* (of a team, athlete, horse, etc.) | marca *f*, resultado *m*; *best performance* mejor marca ‖ TECH funcionamiento *m* (of a machine) | rendimiento *m* (of a motor, of an aircraft, etc.); *best performance* rendimiento máximo | cualidades *f pl* técnicas (of a car) ‖ — *continuous performance* sesión continua ‖ *first performance* primera representación, estreno *m* ‖ *no performance tonight* no hay función esta noche ‖ FAM *what a performance!* ¡qué jaleo!

performer [-ə*] *n* THEATR actor *m*, actriz *f*, artista *m* & *f* ‖ MUS músico *m*, intérprete *m* & *f*, ejecutante *m* & *f*.

performing [-iŋ] *adj* amaestrado, da; *performing seals* focas amaestradas.

perfume ['pəːfjuːm] *n* perfume *m* ‖ — *perfume atomizer* atomizador *m*, vaporizador *m*, pulverizador *m* ‖ *perfume burner* o *pan* pebetero *m*.

perfume [pə'fjuːm] *vt/vi* perfumar.

perfumed [-d] *adj* perfumado, da.

perfumery [-əri] *n* perfumería *f*.

perfunctorily [pə'fʌŋktərili] *adv* a la ligera; *to perform a piece of work perfunctorily* hacer un trabajo a la ligera ‖ superficialmente ‖ mecánicamente.

perfunctoriness [pə'fʌŋktərinis] *n* negligencia *f*, descuido *m* (carelessness) ‖ superficialidad *f* ‖ indiferencia *f* (lack of interest).

perfunctory [pə'fʌŋktəri] *adj* negligente, descuidado, da (careless) ‖ superficial, somero, ra (superficial); *a perfunctory inspection* una inspección somera ‖ hecho a la ligera; *perfunctory work* trabajo hecho a la ligera ‖ mecánico, ca (done as a duty or routine).

perfuse [pəː'fjuːz] *vt* inundar (to cover with liquid) ‖ introducir, hacer penetrar (to force a liquid through).

perfusion [pəː'fjuːʒən] *n* aspersión *f* ‖ MED perfusión *f*.

pergola ['pəːgələ] *n* pérgola *f*.

perhaps [pə'hæps] *adv* quizá, quizás, tal vez ‖ *perhaps so* puede ser, quizás.

perianth ['periænθ] *n* BOT periantio *m*.

periapt ['periæpt] *n* amuleto *m*, talismán *m*.

pericardium [,peri'kɑːdjɔm] *n* ANAT pericardio *m*.
— OBSERV El plural de *pericardium* es *pericardia*.

pericarp ['perikɑːp] *n* BOT pericarpio *m*.

pericranium [peri'kreiniəm] *n* ANAT pericráneo *m*.
— OBSERV El plural de *pericranium* es *pericrania*.

peridot ['peridɔt] *n* MIN peridoto *m*.

perigee ['peridʒiː] *n* ASTR perigeo *m*.

peril ['peril] *n* peligro *m* (danger) ‖ riesgo *m* (risk) ‖ — *at o to one's own peril* por su cuenta y riesgo ‖ *in peril of* en peligro de ‖ *in peril of one's life* en peligro de muerte ‖ *to face the peril* arrostrar el peligro.

perilous [-əs] *adj* peligroso, sa; arriesgado, da.

perimeter [pə'rimitə*] *n* perímetro *m*.

perimetric [peri'metrik] *adj* perimétrico, ca.

perineum [peri'niːəm] *n* ANAT perineo *m*.
— OBSERV El plural de la palabra inglesa es *perinea*.

period ['piəriəd] *n* período *m*, periodo *m*, época *f*; *the Elizabethan period* el período isabelino ‖ período *m*; *a period of two months* un período de dos meses ‖ época *f*; *period costume* traje de época ‖ clase *f*; *the school day is divided into seven periods* el día escolar está dividido en siete clases ‖ plazo *m*; *within a period of two months* en un plazo de dos meses ‖ PHYS, MATH & MUS período *m* ‖ GRAMM período *m* ‖ punto *m* (orthography) ‖ pausa *f* (natural pause in speaking) ‖ SP tiempo *m* (division of play) ‖ MED período *m* (a single menstruation, stage of a disease) ‖ GEOL & ASTR período *m*; *lunar period* período lunar ‖ — *bright period* clara *f* (weather) ‖ MED *period pains* dolores *m pl* menstruales ‖ *probationary period, period of instruction* período de prácticas ‖ *to put a period to* poner punto final a.
◆ *adj* del período ‖ de época (costume, furniture).

periodic [,piəri'ɔdik] *adj* periódico, ca; *the periodic motion of the planets* el movimiento periódico de los planetas ‖ CHEM *periodic table* tabla *f* periódica.

periodical [-əl] *adj* periódico, ca.
◆ *n* periódico *m*, revista *f*, publicación *f* periódica.

periodicity [,piəriə'disiti] *n* periodicidad *f* ‖ frecuencia *f*.

periosteum [peri'ɔstiəm] *n* ANAT periostio *m*.
— OBSERV El plural de la palabra inglesa es *periostea*.

peripatetic [,peripə'tetik] *adj* ambulante ‖ PHIL peripatético, ca.
◆ *n* PHIL peripatético, ca.

peripeteia [peripə'tiə]; **peripetia** [peripə'taiə] *n* peripecia *f*.

peripheral [pə'rifərəl]; **peripheric** [peri'ferik] *adj* periférico, ca ‖ INFORM *peripheral device* dispositivo *m* periférico.
◆ *n* INFORM periférico *m*.

periphery [pə'rifəri] *n* periferia *f*.

periphrase ['perifreiz] *vi* perifrasear.

periphrasis [pə'rifrəsis] *n* perífrasis *f*.
— OBSERV El plural de la palabra inglesa es *periphrases*.

periphrastic [,peri'fræstik] *adj* perifrástico, ca.

periplus ['periplʌs] *n* periplo *m*.
— OBSERV El plural de *periplus* es *peripli*.

periscope ['periskəup] *n* periscopio *m*.

periscopic [peri'skɔpik] *adj* periscópico, ca.

perish ['periʃ] *vi* perecer, fallecer, morir (person) ‖ echarse a perder, estropearse (subst-

ance) || — *perish the thought!* ¡Dios nos libre! || FAM *to perish with cold* morirse de frío.
◆ *vt* estropear, echar a perder.

perishable [-əbl] *adj* perecedero, ra; *perishable goods* productos perecederos || efímero, ra; de corta duración; *perishable glory* gloria efímera.
◆ *pl n* productos *m* perecederos.

perisher [-ə*] *n* FAM individuo *m* || FAM *you little perisher!* ¡sinvergüenza!

perishing [-iŋ] *adj* FAM *it's perishing* hace un frío de perros, hace un frío que pela.

peristaltic [ˌperi'stæltik] *adj* ANAT peristáltico, ca.

peristyle ['peristail] *n* ARCH peristilo *m*.

perisystole ['perisistəl] *n* BIOL perisístole *f*.

peritoneum; peritonaeum [ˌperitəu'niːəm] *n* ANAT peritoneo *m*.
— OBSERV El plural de las palabras inglesas es *peritonea* y *peritonaea*.

peritonitis [ˌperitəu'naitis] *n* MED peritonitis *f*.

periwig ['periwig] *n* peluca *f* (wig).

periwinkle ['periˌwiŋkl] *n* vincapervinca *f* (plant) || bígaro *m*, bigarro *m*, caracol *m* de mar (mollusc).

perjure ['pəːdʒə*] *vt* perjurar || *to perjure o.s.* perjurar, perjurarse.

perjured [pəːdʒəd] *adj* perjuro, ra.

perjurer [pəːdʒərə*] *n* perjuro, ra.

perjury ['p'ːdʒəri] *n* perjurio *m* || JUR *to commit perjury* jurar en falso (to swear), prestar falso testimonio (to testify).

perk [pəːk] *vt* *to perk up* entonar, animar (to make cheerful), levantar (one's head), levantar (the tail) || *to perk up its ears* aguzar las orejas (dog).
◆ *vi* *to perk up* entonarse, animarse (after depression), reponerse (after an illness).

perkily [-ili] *adv* con desenvoltura || con descaro (saucily).

perkiness [-inis] *n* desenvoltura *f* (assurance) || descaro *m*, frescura *f* (sauciness) || alegría *f* (gaiety).

perks [-s] *pl n* ⟶ **perquisite.**

perky [-i] *adj* despabilado, da; despierto, ta (alert) || desenvuelto, ta (assured) || descarado, da; fresco, ca (saucy) || alegre, de buen humor (gay).

perm [pəːm] *n* FAM permanente *f* (hairdressing); *to have a perm* hacerse la permanente.

perm [pəːm] *vt* FAM *to have one's hair permed* hacerse una permanente.

permanence ['pəːmənəns] *n* permanencia *f* || estabilidad *f* (of law) || duración *f* (of conquest).

permanency [-i] *n* permanencia *f* (permanence) || algo definitivo (permanent thing) || puesto *m* fijo (job, post).

permanent ['pəːmənənt] *adj* permanente || definitivo, va || estable (stable) || duradero, ra (lasting) || — *permanent address* domicilio *m* || *permanent post* puesto fijo || *permanent president* presidente vitalicio || *permanent wave* permanente *f* (hairdressing) || *permanent way* vía férrea.
◆ *n* permanente *f* (hairdressing).

permanganate [pəː'mæŋgənit] *n* CHEM permanganato *m*.

permeability [ˌpəːmjə'biliti] *n* permeabilidad *f*.

permeable ['pəːmjəbl] *adj* permeable.

permeate ['pəːmieit] *vt* penetrar (to penetrate) || empapar, impregnar (to soak); *the soil was permeated with water* el suelo estaba empapado de agua.
◆ *vi* penetrar.

permeation [ˌpəːmi'eiʃən] *n* penetración *f* || empapamiento *m*, impregnación *f* (soaking).

Permian ['pəːmiən] *adj* GEOL pérmico, ca; permiano, na.
◆ *n* GEOL Pérmico *m*.

permissible [pə'misəbl] *adj* permisible, lícito, ta || *would it be permissible to say that...?* ¿podemos decir que...?

permission [pə'miʃən] *n* permiso *m*; *to ask, to give, to have permission* pedir, dar, tener permiso; *with your permission* con su permiso.

permissive [pə'misiv] *adj* permisivo, va || tolerante; *permissive society* sociedad tolerante || facultativo, va (optional).

permit ['pəːmit] *n* permiso *m* (permission) || permiso *m*, licencia *f*; *export, import permit* licencia de exportación, de importación || pase *m* (allowing free movement).

permit [pə'mit] *vt* permitir; *he permitted them to come* les permitió que viniesen; *smoking is not permitted in this theatre* no está permitido fumar en este teatro.
◆ *vi* permitir || dejar lugar; *your conduct permits of no other explanation* su conducta no deja lugar a otra explicación || *weather permitting* si el tiempo no lo impide.

permutability [pəːmjutə'biliti] *n* permutabilidad *f*.

permutable [pə'mjuːtəbl] *adj* permutable.

permutation [ˌpəːmju'teiʃən] *n* permutación *f* (change).

permute [pə'mjuːt] *vt* permutar.

pernicious [pəː'niʃəs] *adj* pernicioso, sa (harmful) || funesto, ta (evil); *pernicious habits* costumbres funestas || peligroso, sa (dangerous); *pernicious doctrine* doctrina peligrosa || MED *pernicious anaemia* anemia perniciosa.

pernickety [pə'nikiti]; US **persnickety** [pə'snikəti] *adj* quisquilloso, sa; puntilloso, sa (person) || delicado, da; minucioso, sa (work) || *to be pernickety about one's food* ser muy exigente para la comida.

peroneal [perəu'niːəl] *adj* peroneo, a; del peroné (of the fibula).

perorate ['perəreit] *vi* perorar.

peroration [ˌperə'reiʃən] *n* peroración *f*, perorata *f*.

peroxid; peroxide [pə'rɔksaid] *n* CHEM peróxido *m* || — *hydrogen peroxide* agua oxigenada || FAM *peroxide blonde* rubia oxigenada.

perpend [pə'pend] *n* US ARCH perpiaño *m*.

perpend [pə'pend] *vt* considerar, meditar (to ponder sth.) || pesar, medir, sopesar (words).
◆ *vi* reflexionar, meditar.

perpendicular [ˌpəːpən'dikjulə*] *adj* perpendicular; *line perpendicular to another* línea perpendicular a *or* con otra || vertical (cliff) || ARCH flamígero, ra (English Gothic style).
◆ *n* MATH perpendicular *f* || plomada *f* (plumb line) || *to be out of (the) perpendicular* no estar a plomo.

perpendicularity ['pəːpənˌdikju'læriti] *n* perpendicularidad *f*.

perpetrate ['pəːpitreit] *vt* JUR perpetrar, cometer; *to perpetrate a crime* perpetrar un crimen || hacer; *to perpetrate a pun* hacer un juego de palabras.

perpetration [ˌpəːpi'treiʃən] *n* perpetración *f*.

perpetrator ['pəːpitreitə*] *n* autor, ra; *the perpetrator of the joke* el autor de la broma || JUR perpetrador, ra.

perpetual [pə'petʃuəl] *adj* perpetuo, tua; *perpetual calendar* calendario perpetuo || continuo, nua; incesante; *perpetual chatter* charla continua || eterno, na; *perpetual damnation* condena eterna || *perpetual motion* movimiento continuo *or* perpetuo.

perpetuate [pə'petʃueit] *vt* perpetuar; *the pyramids perpetuate the memory of the pharaohs* las pirámides perpetúan el recuerdo de los faraones.

perpetuation [pə'petʃu'eiʃən] *n* perpetuación *f*.

perpetuity [ˌpeːpi'tjuːiti] *n* perpetuidad *f* || JUR renta *f* perpetua (perpetual annuity) || *in o to perpetuity* a perpetuidad, para siempre (for ever).

perplex [pə'pleks] *vt* dejar perplejo (to astonish) || complicar, enredar, embrollar (a situation, etc.).

perplexed [-t] *adj* perplejo, ja (astonished) || embrollado, da; enredado, da (entangled).

perplexing [-iŋ] *adj* que causa perplejidad || confuso, sa; poco claro, ra; *a perplexing author* un autor poco claro || complicado, da (complex).

perplexity [pə'pleksiti] *n* perplejidad *f* || confusión *f* || *to be in perplexity* estar perplejo.

perquisite ['pəːkwizit] *n* gratificación *f*, propina *f* (tip) || ganancia *f* extra (extra profit).

perron ['perən] *n* ARCH escalinata *f* (stairs).

perry ['peri] *n* sidra *f* de pera.

per se ['pəːsei] *adv* en sí (as such) || de por sí (in itself).

persecute ['pəːsikjuːt] *vt* perseguir (for religious or political reasons) || acosar, agobiar, atormentar (to harass); *to persecute a man with questions* acosar a un hombre con preguntas || molestar (to worry).

persecution [ˌpəːsi'kjuːʃən] *n* persecución *f* || *persecution mania* manía persecutoria.

persecutor ['pəːsikjuːtə*] *n* perseguidor, ra.

persecutory [-ri] *adj* persecutorio, ria.

perseverance [ˌpəːsi'viərəns] *n* perseverancia *f*.

persevere [ˌpəːsi'viə*] *vi* perseverar (*with, in* en); *to persevere in one's work* perseverar en su trabajo || persistir (*in* en); *he perseveres in doing it* persiste en hacerlo.

persevering [-riŋ] *adj* perseverante.

Persia ['pəːʃə] *pr n* Persia *f*.

Persian [-n] *adj/n* persa (of Persia) || — *Persian blinds* persianas *f* || *Persian cat* gato *m* persa || *Persian lamb* caracul *m*.

Persian Gulf [-gʌlf] *pr n* GEOGR golfo *m* Pérsico.

persiflage [ˌpɛəsi'flɑːʒ] *n* zumba *f*, guasa *f*, burla *f*.

persimmon [pəː'simən] *n* caqui *m* (tree, fruit).

persist [pə'sist] *vi* persistir || empeñarse (to continue insistently); *he persists in asking me the same question* se empeña en hacerme la misma pregunta || *to persist in one's opinion* aferrarse a su opinión.

persistence [pə'sistəns]; **persistency** [-i] *n* persistencia *f*; *persistence in error* persistencia en el error || empeño *m* (insistence) || perseverancia *f* (tenacity).

persistent [pə'sistənt] *adj* persistente || continuo, nua; constante; *persistent attacks* ataques continuos || perseverante (persevering) || firme; *persistent in his intention to* firme en su intención de.

persistently [-li] *adv* continuamente (continually, repeatedly) || con empeño (perseveringly).

persnickety [pə'snikəti] *adj* US ⟶ **pernickety.**

person ['pəːsn] *n* persona *f* (human being); *he is a very important person* es una persona muy importante || GRAMM persona *f*; *in the first person* en primera persona || — JUR *artificial person* persona jurídica *or* social *or* civil || *in the person of* en la persona de || JUR *natural person* persona natural || *no person* nadie || *private person* particular *m* || *some person said* alguien dijo || *to be delivered to the addressee in person* a entregar en propia mano || *to come in person* venir en persona || *to have about one's person* llevar encima (things) || *without respect of persons* sin acepción de personas.

persona [pəː'səunə] *n* persona *f*; *persona non grata* persona no grata, persona non grata.
— OBSERV El plural de la palabra inglesa es *personae*.

personable ['pəːsnəbl] *adj* de buen ver, bien parecido, da (good-looking).

personage ['pəːsnidʒ] *n* personaje *m*.

personal ['pəːsnl] *adj* personal; *a personal opinion* una opinión personal; *personal needs* necesidades personales; *personal effects* efectos personales; *personal business* asunto personal || íntimo, ma; *personal friend* amigo íntimo || privado, da; particular, personal (private) || individual; *personal liberty* libertad individual || GRAMM personal (pronoun) || — *personal assistant* secretaria *f* personal || *personal column* mensajes *m pl* personales (in newspapers) || INFORM *personal computer* ordenador *m* personal || *personal equation* factor *m* personal (personal reason), opinión *f* personal (opinion) || *personal estate* o *property* bienes *m pl* muebles || *personal file* expediente *m* personal || *personal injury* daños *m pl* corporales || *personal stereo* minicasete *m*, casete *m* de bolsillo (Walkman) || *to be personal* hacer alusiones personales, personalizar; *don't be personal* no hagas alusiones personales || *to make a personal appearance* presentarse personalmente, personarse.
◆ *pl* mensajes *m* personales || ecos *m* de sociedad (society column).

personalism [-izəm] *n* personalismo *m*.

personality [,pəːsə'næliti] *n* personalidad *f*; *to lack personality* carecer de personalidad || personalidad *f*, personaje *m*, figura *f* (famous person) || *personality cult* culto a la personalidad.
◆ *pl* alusiones *f* personales.

personalization [pəːsənəlai'zeiʃən] *n* personalización *f*, personificación *f*.

personalize ['pəːsnəlaiz] *vt* personalizar, personificar.

personalized [-d] *adj* con las iniciales *or* el nombre de uno (be longings) || personalizado, da (service).

personally ['pəːsnəli] *adv* personalmente; *personally, I see no objection* personalmente no veo ninguna objeción || *don't take that remark personally* no se dé por aludido, no se lo tome como si fuera una alusión personal.

personalty ['pəːsnlti] *n* JUR bienes *m pl* muebles.

personate ['pəːsəneit] *vt* hacerse pasar por, usurpar la personalidad de (s.o.) || THEATR hacer el papel de.

personation [,pəːsə'neiʃən] *n* usurpación *f* de personalidad || THEATR representación *f* || personificación *f* (of a quality).

personator ['pəːsəneitə*] *n* THEATR intérprete *m* & *f* || impostor, ra (fake).

personification [pə,sɔnifi'keiʃən] *n* personificación *f* || *he is the personification of selfishness* es el egoísmo personificado, es la encarnación del egoísmo.

personify [pəː'sɔnifai] *vt* personificar; *the poets personify the Sun and Moon* los poetas personifican el Sol y la Luna; *he is avarice personified* es la avaricia personificada.

personnel [,pəːsə'nel] *n* personal *m* || — *personnel department* departamento *m* de personal || *personnel officer* jefe, fa de personal.

perspective [pə'spektiv] *n* perspectiva *f* || vista *f*, perspectiva *f* (view) || — *in perspective* en perspectiva || *to get sth. into perspective* juzgar en consideración || FIG *to see a matter in its true perspective* ver un asunto como es, apreciar un asunto en su justo valor.
◆ *adj* perspectivo, va; en perspectiva.

Perspex ['pəːspeks] *n* plexiglás *m*.

perspicacious [,pəːspi'keiʃəs] *adj* perspicaz.

perspicacity [,pəːspi'kæsiti] *n* perspicacia *f*.

perspicuity [,pəːspi'kjuːiti] *n* claridad *f*.

perspicuous [pə'spikjuəs] *adj* claro, ra; perspicuo, cua; *a perspicuous explanation* una explicación clara.

perspiration [,pəːspə'reiʃən] *n* transpiración *f*, sudor *m*; *to be dripping with perspiration* estar bañado en sudor.

perspiratory [pəː'spaiərətəri] *adj* sudorífero, ra; sudoríparo, ra (glands, etc.) || MED sudorífico, ca.

perspire [pəs'paiə*] *vi* transpirar, sudar.

persuadable [pə'sweidəbl] *adj* fácil de convencer.

persuade [pə'sweid] *vt* persuadir; *they persuaded me to do it* me persuadieron a que lo hiciese || convencer; *I am almost persuaded of his honesty* estoy casi convencido de su honradez || *to persuade s.o. not to do sth.* disuadir a alguien de hacer algo.

persuasible [pə'sweizəbl] *adj* fácil de convencer.

persuasion [pə'sweiʒən] *n* persuasión *f*; *he spoke with great persuasion* habló con gran persuasión || convicción *f*, creencia *f* (conviction) || opinión *f*; *they are both of the same persuasion* los dos son de la misma opinión || REL creencia *f* religiosa (belief) | secta *f* (religious sect) || *it is my persuasion that* estoy convencido de que.

persuasive [pə'sweisiv] *adj* persuasivo, va; convincente.

persuasively [-li] *adv* de modo convincente.

persuasiveness [-nis] *n* persuasión *f*, persuasiva *f*.

persulphate; US **persulfate** [pəː'sʌlfeit] *n* CHEM persulfato *m*.

pert [pəːt] *adj* impertinente, insolente; *a pert answer* una respuesta impertinente || alegre (jaunty); *a pert little spring outfit* un alegre trajecito de primavera || animado, da (in good spirits) || muy vivaracho, cha; *she is a pert little thing* es una chiquilla muy vivaracha.

pertain [pəː'tein] *vi* pertenecer (to belong) || ser propio de (to be characteristic); *the enthusiasm pertaining to youth* el entusiasmo que es propio de la juventud || relacionarse (*to* con) (to relate to) || — *pertaining to* relacionado con, referente a, relativo a; *subjects pertaining to religion* temas relacionados con la religión || *this does not pertain to my office* esto no es de mi incumbencia.

pertinacious [,pəːti'neiʃəs] *adj* pertinaz.

pertinaciousness [-nis]; **pertinacity** [,pəːti'næsiti] *n* pertinacia *f*.

pertinence ['pəːtinəns]; **pertinency** [-i] *n* pertinencia *f* (of a reason) || oportunidad *f*, pertinencia *f* (of a remark, etc.).

pertinent ['pəːtinənt] *adj* pertinente, oportuno, na; *a pertinent remark* una observación pertinente || pertinente (reason) || *pertinent to* relacionado con, referente a, relativo a.

pertly ['pəːtli] *adv* impertinentemente, insolentemente || alegremente || animadamente.

pertness ['pəːtnis] *n* impertinencia *f*, insolencia *f* || alegría *f* (jauntiness) || animación *f* (liveliness).

perturb [pə'təːb] *vt* perturbar, turbar (to disturb) || preocupar, inquietar (to worry).

perturbation [,pəːtə'beiʃən] *n* perturbación *f* || preocupación *f*, inquietud *f* (worry).

perturbing [pə'təːbiŋ] *adj* perturbador, ra || inquietante (worrying).

Peru [pə'ruː] *pr n* GEOGR Perú *m*.

peruke [pə'ruːk] *n* peluca *f* (wig).

perusal [pə'ruːzəl] *n* examen *m* (examination) || lectura *f* atenta (reading).

peruse [pə'ruːz] *vt* examinar (to examine) || leer atentamente (to read).

Peruvian [pə'ruːvjən] *adj/n* peruano, na || *Peruvian bark* chinchona *f*, quina *f*.

pervade [pəː'veid] *vt* extenderse por, difundirse por (to spread) || impregnar, empapar (to soak).

pervasion [pəː'veiʒən] *n* difusión *f* || impregnación *f*, empapamiento *m* (soaking).

pervasive [pəː'veisiv] *adj* penetrante || que lo impregna todo.

perverse [pə'vəːs] *adj* perverso, sa (wicked) || obstinado, da; terco, ca; contumaz (obstinate) || adverso, sa; contrario, ria; *perverse circumstances* circunstancias adversas.

perverseness [-nis] *n* perversidad *f* (wickedness) || obstinación *f*, terquedad *f* (stubbornness).

perversion [pə'vəːʃən] *n* perversión *f* || desnaturalización *f* (of facts).

perversity [pə'vəːsiti] *n* perversidad *f* (wickedness) || obstinación *f*, terquedad *f* (stubbornness).

perversive [pə'vəːsiv] *adj* pervertidor, ra.

pervert ['pəːvəːt] *n* pervertido, da; *sexual pervert* pervertido sexual.

pervert [pə'vəːt] *vt* pervertir (a person) || desvirtuar, desnaturalizar (words, facts) || estragar, pervertir (taste) || prostituir (talent).

perverted [-id] *adj* pervertido, da (person) || perverso, sa; retorcido, da (imagination, mind).

perverter [-ə*] *n* pervertidor, ra.

pervious ['pəːvjəs] *adj* permeable.

perviousness ['pəːvjəsnis] *n* permeabilidad *f*.

peseta [pə'setə] *n* peseta *f* (Spanish monetary unit).

pesky ['peski] *adj* US FAM maldito, ta; *what pesky weather!* ¡maldito tiempo!

peso ['peisəu] *n* peso *m* (monetary unit).

pessary ['pesəri] *n* MED pesario *m*.

pessimism ['pesimizəm] *n* pesimismo *m*.

pessimist ['pesimist] *n* pesimista *m* & *f*.

pessimistic [,pesi'mistik] *adj* pesimista.

pessimistically [-əli] *adv* con pesimismo.

pest [pest] *n* insecto *m or* animal *m* nocivo *or* dañino, parásito *m* || FIG lata *f*, tostón *m* (tiresome person) | lata *f* (boring thing) | peste *f*; *what pests these children are!* ¡estos niños son la peste!

pester [-ə*] *vt* molestar, importunar, fastidiar (to annoy) || acosar; *to pester s.o. with questions* acosar a alguien con preguntas || *to pester s.o. for sth.* pedir algo a alguien con insistencia.

pesticide ['pestisaid] *n* pesticida *m*.

pestiferous [pes'tifərəs] *adv* nocivo, va; dañino, na (insects) || pestífero, ra; pestilente (air) || FIG pernicioso, sa (harmful) | pesado, da; molesto, ta; fastidioso, sa; latoso, sa (annoying).

pestilence ['pestiləns] *n* MED pestilencia *f*, peste *f*.

pestilent ['pestilənt] *adj* pestífero, ra; pestilente || FIG pernicioso, sa; nocivo, va (harmful) | pesado, da; latoso, sa (annoying).

pestilential [ˌpesti'lenʃəl] *adj* pestífero, ra; pestilencial, pestilente || pestilente (smell) || FIG pesado, da; latoso, sa (annoying) | pernicioso, sa; nocivo, va (harmful).

pestle ['pesl] *n* mano *m*, maja *f* (of a mortar).

pestle ['pesl] *vt* majar (in a mortar).

pet [pet] *n* animal *m* favorito || ojo *m* derecho, favorito, ta; preferido, da (favourite person) || — *he is a real pet* es un cielo, es un encanto || *my pet!* ¡mi cielo! || *teacher's pet* ojo derecho *or* favorito del maestro || *to be in a pet* estar de mal humor || *to make a pet of* mimar a || *to take pet* ofenderse.
◆ *adj* mimado, da || — *her pet cat* su gato || *pet aversion* pesadilla *f* || *pet name* nombre cariñoso || *pet panther* pantera domesticada || *pet subject* tema preferido, manía *f*.

pet [pet] *vt* mimar (to pamper) || acariciar (to caress).
◆ *vi* acariciarse (to caress) || estar enfadado (to be angry).

petal ['petl] *n* pétalo *m* (of a flower).

petard [pe'tɑːd] *n* petardo *m* || FIG *hoist with one's own petard* cogido en sus propias redes.

petcock ['petkɔk] *n* TECH llave *f* de purga.

Pete [piːt] *pr n* FAM Perico *m*.
— OBSERV Esta palabra es el diminutivo de *Peter*.

peter [-ə*] *vi* *to peter out* agotarse (a mine, a stream), desaparecer (to disappear), quedarse en agua de borrajas (a plan), pararse (an engine).

Peter [-ə*] *pr n* Pedro *m* || — MAR *blue Peter* bandera *f* de salida || *Peter's pence* dinero *m* de San Pedro || FIG *to rob Peter to pay Paul* desnudar a un santo para vestir a otro.

petersham ['piːtəʃəm] *n* abrigo *m* de ratina (coat) || ratina *f* (material).

petiole ['petiəul] *n* BOT peciolo *m*, pecíolo *m*.

petit bourgeois ['petiˌbuəʒwɑː] *adj/n* pequeño burgués.

petite [pə'tit] *adj* chiquita (woman).

petition [pi'tiʃən] *n* petición *f*, solicitud *f*, instancia *f* (request) || ruego *m*, súplica *f* (to God) || JUR demanda *f*, petición *f*, recurso *m* || *petition for divorce* demanda de divorcio.

petition [pi'tiʃən] *vt* solicitar a, presentar una solicitud a, dirigir una petición a || JUR presentar demanda a || rogar; *to petition s.o. to do sth.* rogar a alguien que haga algo || *to petition for sth.* pedir *or* solicitar algo.
◆ *vi* presentar una petición, hacer una solicitud (to make a petition).

petitionary [pi'tiʃənəri] *adj* petitorio, ria.

petitioner [-ə*] *n* solicitador, ra; solicitante *m* & *f* || JUR demandante *m* & *f*.

Petrarch ['petrɑːk] *pr n* Petrarca.

Petrarchan [-ən] *adj* petrarquista.

Petrarchism [-izəm] *n* petrarquismo *m*.

petrel ['petrəl] *n* petrel *m* (bird).

petrifaction [ˌpetri'fækʃən]; **petrification** [ˌpetrifi'keiʃən] *n* petrificación *f*.

petrify ['petrifai] *vt* petrificar || FIG petrificar, paralizar || FIG *we were petrified* nos quedamos de piedra.
◆ *vi* petrificarse.

petrifying [-iŋ] *adj* petrificante.

petrochemical [petrəu'kemikəl] *adj* petroquímico, ca.
◆ *n* producto *m* petroquímico.

petrochemistry [petrəu'kemistri] *n* petroquímica *f*.

petrography [pe'trɔgrəfi] *n* petrografía *f*.

petrol ['petrəl] *n* gasolina *f* [AMER nafta *f*]; *petrol pump* surtidor de gasolina || *high-grade petrol* supercarburante *m*, súper *f*, gasolina *f* plomo.

petrol bomb [-bɔm] *n* cóctel *m* Molotov.

petrol can [-kæn] *n* bidón *m* de gasolina.

petroleum [pi'trəuljəm] *n* petróleo *m* (mineral oil) || — *petroleum-bearing* petrolífero, ra [AMER petrolero, ra] || *petroleum-producing* petrolífero, ra [AMER petrolero, ra].

petrol gauge ['petrlgeidʒ] *n* indicador *m* del nivel de gasolina.

petroliferous ['petrə'lifərəs] *adj* petrolífero, ra [AMER petrolero, ra].

petrology [pe'trɔlədʒi] *n* petrología *f*.

petrol pump ['petrəlpʌmp] *n* bomba *f* de gasolina (in engine) || surtidor *m* de gasolina (in a garage).

petrol station ['petrəl'steiʃən] *n* gasolinera *f*, surtidor *m* de gasolina.

petrol tank ['petrəltæŋk] *n* depósito *m* de gasolina.

petrous ['petrəs] *adj* pétreo, a.

petticoat ['petikəut] *n* enaguas *f pl*, enagua *f* (underskirt) || FAM mujer *f* || — FAM *petticoat chaser* mujeriego *m* | *petticoat government* dominación *f* de la mujer.

pettifogger ['petifɔgə*] *n* picapleitos *m inv*, leguleyo *m*, abogadillo *m*.

pettifoggery [ˌpeti'fɔgəri] *n* argucia *f* *or* trapacería *f* de abogados.

pettifogging ['petifɔgiŋ] *adj* pleitista (lawyer) || quisquilloso, sa (person) || insignificante (detail).

pettiness ['petinis] *n* pequeñez *f* || mezquindad *f*.

petting ['petiŋ] *n* FAM caricias *f pl*.

pettish ['petiʃ] *adj* de mal humor, malhumorado, da (sulky).

pettitoes ['petitəuz] *pl n* CULIN manos *f* de cerdo.

petty ['peti] *adj* pequeño, ña; insignificante, sin importancia (minor, trivial); *petty reforms* reformas insignificantes || quisquilloso, sa (hairsplitting) || mezquino, na (narrow-minded) || — *petty cash* dinero *m* *or* fondo *m* para gastos menores || *petty larceny* hurto *m*, ratería *f* || *petty monarch* reyezuelo *m* || MAR *petty officer* contramaestre *m* || *petty thief* ladronzuelo *m*, ratero *m*.

petty-minded [-ˌmaindid] *adj* mezquino, na.

petulance ['petjuləns] *n* irritabilidad *f*, susceptibilidad *f* (irritability) || malhumor *m* (ill humour).
— OBSERV *Petulancia* in Spanish means *arrogance*.

petulant ['petjulənt] *adj* irritable, susceptible, enojadizo, za (irritable) || malhumorado, da; de mal humor (bad-tempered).
— OBSERV *Petulante* in Spanish means *arrogant*.

petunia [pi'tjuːnjə] *n* petunia *f* (flower).

pew [pjuː] *n* banco *m* de iglesia || FAM *take a pew* tome asiento.

pewee ['piwi] *n* papamoscas *m inv* norteamericano (bird).

pewit ['piːwit] *n* avefría *f* (lapwing) || papamoscas *m inv* norteamericano (pewee).

pewter ['pjuːtə*] *n* estaño *m*, peltre *m* (metal).

peyotl [pei'ɔtl]; **peyote** [pei'əuti] *n* peyote *m*.

phaeton ['feitn] *n* faetón *m* (carriage).

phagocyte ['fægəusait] *n* fagocito *m*.

phagocitosis [fægəsai'təusis] *n* fagocitosis *f*.

phalaena [fə'liːnə] *n* falena *f* (moth).

phalange ['fælændʒ] *n* falange *f*.

phalanger [-ə*] *n* falangero *m* (animal).

phalanges [-iz] *pl n* ⟶ **phalanx.**

phalanstery ['fælənstəri] *n* falansterio *m*.

phalanx ['fælæŋks] *n* ANAT & HIST falange *f*.
— OBSERV El plural es *phalanxes* o *phalanges* cuando se refiere al sentido histórico y *phalanges* en el otro caso.

phallic ['fælik] *adj* fálico, ca.

phallus ['fæləs] *n* falo *m*.
— OBSERV El plural es *phalli* o *phalluses*.

phanerogam ['fænərəugæm] *n* BOT fanerógama *f*.

phanerogamic [ˌfænərəu'gæmik]; **phanerogamous** [ˌfænə'rɔgəməs] *adj* BOT fanerógamo, ma.

phantasm ['fæntæzəm] *n* fantasma *m* (spectre) || ilusión *f*.

phantasmagoria [ˌfæntæzmə'gɔriə] *n* fantasmagoría *f*.

phantasmagoric [ˌfæntæzmə'gɔrik] *adj* fantasmagórico, ca.

phantasmal [fæn'tæzməl] *adj* fantasmal.

phantasy ['fæntəsiː] *n* ⟶ **fantasy.**

phantom ['fæntəm] *adj* fantasma; *the phantom ship* el buque fantasma || FIG ilusorio, ria; inexistente.
◆ *n* fantasma *m*.

Pharaoh ['fɛərəu] *n* faraón *m* (Egyptian king).

Pharaonic [fɛə'rɔnik] *adj* faraónico, ca.

Pharisaic [ˌfæri'seiik]; **Pharisaical** [-əl] *adj* farisaico, ca.

Pharisaism ['færiseiizəm]; **Phariseeism** ['færiseiizəm] *n* farisaísmo *m*, fariseísmo *m*.

Pharisee ['færisiː] *n* fariseo *m*.

pharmaceutic [ˌfɑːmə'sjuːtik]; **pharmaceutical** [-əl] *adj* farmacéutico, ca.

pharmaceutics [-s] *n* farmacia *f*.

pharmaceutist [ˌfɑːmə'sjuːtist] *n* farmacéutico, ca.

pharmacist ['fɑːməsist] *n* farmacéutico, ca.

pharmacological [fɑːməkə'lɔdʒikəl] *adj* farmacológico, ca.

pharmacologist [ˌfɑːmə'kɔlʃʒut] *n* farmacólogo, ga.

pharmacology [ˌfɑːmə'kɔlədʒi] *n* farmacología *f*.

pharmacopoeia [ˌfɑːməkə'piːə] *n* farmacopea *f*.

pharmacy ['fɑːməsi] *n* farmacia *f*.

pharyngal [fə'riŋgəl]; **pharyngeal** [ˌfærin'dʒiːəl] *adj* faríngeo, a.

pharynges [fərindʒiz] *pl n* ⟶ **pharynx.**

pharyngitis [ˌfærin'dʒaitis] *n* MED faringitis *f*.

pharynx ['færiŋks] *n* ANAT faringe *f*.
— OBSERV El plural es *pharynges* o *pharynxes*.

phase [feiz] *n* fase *f*; *the phases of an illness* las fases de una enfermedad; *the Moon's phases* las fases de la Luna || ELECTR fase *f* || *out of phase* desfasado, da.

phase [feiz] *vt* ELECTR poner en fase || escalonar (to plan in stages) || — *to phase in* introducir *or* hacer aparecer progresivamente || *to phase out* eliminar *or* hacer desaparecer progresivamente.

phasing [-iŋ] *n* ELECTR ajuste *m* de fase.

PhD *abbr of* *[Doctor of Philosophy]* doctor en Filosofía.

pheasant ['feznt] *n* faisán *m* (bird) ‖ — *hen pheasant* faisán hembra, faisana *f* ‖ *young pheasant* pollo *m* de faisán.

Phenicia [fi'niʃiə] *pr n* GEOGR Fenicia *f* (phoenicia).

Phenician [fi'niʃiən] *adj/n* fenicio, cia.

phenix ['fiːniks] *n* fénix *m* (phoenix).

phenol ['fiːnɔl] *n* CHEM fenol *m*.

phenomena [fi'nɔminə] *pl n* ⟶ **phenomenon.**

phenomenal [-l] *adj* fenomenal.

phenomenalism [-lizəm] *n* fenomenismo *m*, fenomenalismo *m*.

phenomenologist [fi,nɔmi'nɔlədʒist] *n* fenomenólogo *m*.

phenomenology [fi,nɔmi'nɔlədʒi] *n* fenomenología *f*.

phenomenon [fi'nɔminən] *n* fenómeno *m*; *the phenomena of nature* los fenómenos de la naturaleza.

— OBSERV El plural es *phenomena* o *phenomenons*.

phenyl ['fiːnil] *n* fenilo *m*.

phew [fjuː] *interj* ¡uy!

phi [fai] *n* fi *f* (Greek letter).

phial ['faiəl] *n* frasco *m* (small bottle) ‖ ampolla *f* (ampoule).

Philadelphia [,filə'delfjə] *pr n* GEOGR Filadelfia.

philander [fi'lændə*] *vi* flirtear (to flirt) ‖ mariposear (to have many love affairs).

philanderer [-rə*] *n* galanteador *m* (who flirts) ‖ mariposón *m* (who has many love affairs).

philandering [-riŋ] *adj* mariposón.
◆ *n* flirteo *m*.

philanthropic [,filən'θrɔpik]; **philanthropical** [-əl] *adj* filantrópico, ca.

philanthropist [fi'lænθrəpist] *n* filántropo, pa.

philanthropy [fi'lænθrəpi] *n* filantropía *f*.

philatelic [,filə'telik] *adj* filatélico, ca.

philatelist [fi'lætəlist] *n* filatelista *m* & *f*.

philately [fi'lætəli] *n* filatelia *f*.

philharmonic [,filɑː'mɔnik] *adj* MUS filarmónico, ca.

philhellene ['fil,heliːn] *n* filheleno, na.

philhellenism [fil'helinizəm] *n* filhelenismo *m*, helenismo *m*.

Philip ['filip] *pr n* Felipe *m* (actual name) ‖ Filipo *m* (king of Macedon).

Philippe [fi'liːp] *pr n* Felipe *m* (king of France).

Philippians [fi'lipiənz] *pl prn* Filipenses *m*; *Epistle to the Philippians* Epístola a los Filipenses.

philippic [fi'lipik] *n* filípica *f* (angry tirade).

Philippine ['filipiːn] *adj/n* filipino, na ‖ GEOGR *Philippine Islands* islas Filipinas.

Philippines [-z] *pl prn* GEOGR Filipinas *f*.

Philistine ['filistain] *adj/n* HIST filisteo, a.
◆ *n* FIG filisteo *m*.

philodendron [,filə'dendrən] *n* BOT filodendro *m*.

philologic [,filə'lɔdʒik]; **philological** [-əl] *adj* filológico, ca.

philologist [fi'lɔlədʒist] *n* filólogo, ga.

philology [fi'lɔlədʒi] *n* filología *f*.

philosophaster [fi'lɔsəfæstə*] *n* filosofastro *m*.

philosopher [fi'lɔsəfə*] *n* filósofo, fa ‖ — *moral philosopher* moralista *m* ‖ *philosopher's* o *philosophers' stone* piedra *f* filosofal.

philosophic [,filə'sɔfik]; **philosophical** [-əl] *adj* filosófico, ca.

philosophize [fi'lɔsəfaiz] *vi* filosofar.

philosophizer [fi'lɔsəfaizə*] *n* filosofador, ra.

philosophy [fi'lɔsəfi] *n* filosofía *f* ‖ *moral philosophy* moral *f*.

philtre; US **philter** ['filtə*] *n* filtro *m*, bebedizo *m*, poción *f* (magic potion).

phimosis [fai'məusis] *n* MED fimosis *f*.

phiz [fiz] *n* FAM jeta *f*, cara *f* (face).

phlebitis [fli'baitis] *n* MED flebitis *f*.

phlebotomize [fli'bɔtəmaiz] *vi* MED hacer una sangría.
◆ *vt* MED sangrar.

phlebotomy [fli'bɔtəmi] *n* MED flebotomía *f*, sangría *f*.

phlegm [flem] *n* MED flema *f* ‖ FIG flema *f*.

phlegmatic [fleg'mætik]; **phlegmatical** [-əl] *adj* flemático, ca.

phlegmon ['flegmɔn] *n* MED flemón *m*.

phloem ['fləuem] *n* BOT líber *m*.

phlogiston [flɔ'dʒistən] *n* flogisto *m*.

phobia ['fəubiə] *n* fobia *f*.

Phocian ['fəuʃjən] *adj/n* focense.

Phoebus ['fiːbəs] *pr n* Febo *m* (the Sun).

Phoenicia [fi'niʃiə] *pr n* Fenicia *f*.

Phoenician [-n] *adj/n* fenicio, cia.

phoenix ['fiːniks] *n* fénix *m* (bird).

phon [fɔn] *n* fono *m*, fon *m*, fonio *m* (unit of loudness).

phonate [fəu'neit] *vi* pronunciar un sonido.

phonation [fəu'neiʃən] *n* fonación *f*.

phone [fəun] *n* GRAMM fonema *m* ‖ FAM teléfono *m* ‖ — *phone book* guía *f* telefónica ‖ *phone box* o *booth* cabina telefónica ‖ *phone call* llamada *f* telefónica ‖ *phone card* tarjeta *f* de teléfonos ‖ *phone number* número *m* de teléfono ‖ *phone tapping* escucha *f* telefónica ‖ *to be on the phone* estar hablando (por teléfono).

phone [fəun] *vt/vi* telefonear, llamar por teléfono.

phoneme ['fəuniːm] *n* GRAMM fonema *m*.

phonetic [fəu'netik] *adj* fonético, ca.

phonetician ['fəuni'tiʃən] *n* fonetista *m* & *f*.

phonetics [fəu'netiks] *n* GRAMM fonética *f*.

phoney ['fəuni] *adj/n* ⟶ **phony.**

phoniatrician [fəuni'ætriʃən] *n* MED foniatra *m*.

phoniatrics [fəuni'ætriks] *n* MED foniatría *f*.

phonic ['fəunik] *adj* fónico, ca.

phonics [-s] *n* acústica *f* ‖ fonética *f*.

phoniness ['fəuninis] *n* FAM falsedad *f*.

phonogram ['fəunəgræm] *n* fonograma *m*.

phonograph ['fəunəgrɑːf] *n* fonógrafo *m*.

phonographic [,fəunə'græfik] *adj* fonográfico, ca.

phonologist [fəu'nɔlədʒist] *n* fonólogo, ga.

phonology [fəu'nɔlədʒi] *n* fonología *f*.

phonometer [fəu'nɔmitə*] *n* fonómetro *m*.

phonometry [fəu'nɔmətri] *n* fonometría *f*.

Phnom Penh [,nɔm'pen] *pr n* GEOGR Phnom Penh.

phony; **phoney** ['fəuni] *adj* FAM falso, sa (not genuine); *a phony diamond* un diamante falso.
◆ *n* FAM farsante *m* & *f*, camelista *m* & *f* (person) | camelo *m* (thing).

phosgene ['fɔzdʒiːn] *n* CHEM fosgeno *m*.

phosphate ['fɔsfeit] *n* CHEM fosfato *m*; *phosphate of lime, calcium phosphate* fosfato de cal.

phosphatic [fɔs'fætik] *adj* CHEM fosfático, ca.

phosphatize ['fɔsfətaiz] *vt* CHEM fosfatar.

phosphene ['fɔsfiːn] *n* fosfeno *m*.

phosphite ['fɔsfait] *n* CHEM fosfito *m*.

phosphor ['fɔsfə*] *n* fósforo *m*.

phosphorate [-reit] *vt* fosforar.

phosphoresce [,fɔsfə'res] *vi* fosforecer, fosforescer.

phosphorescence [-ns] *n* fosforescencia *f*.

phosphorescent [-nt] *adj* fosforescente.

phosphoric [fɔs'fɔrik] *adj* CHEM fosfórico, ca.

phosphorism ['fɔsfərizəm] *n* MED fosforismo *m*.

phosphorous ['fɔsfərəs] *adj* fosforoso, sa.

phosphorus ['fɔsfərəs] *n* CHEM fósforo *m*.

phot [fɔt] *n* foto *m*, fot *m* (unit of illumination).

photo ['fəutəu] *n* foto *f*.

photo ['fəutəu] *vt/vi* ⟶ **photograph.**

photocell [-sel] *n* célula *f* fotoeléctrica.

photochemistry [-'kemistri] *n* fotoquímica *f*.

photochrome [-krəum] *n* fotocromía *f* (colour photograph).

photochromy [-,krəumi] *n* fotocromía *f* (colour photography).

photocomposition [-,kɔmpə'ziʃən] *n* fotocomposición *f*.

photoconductive [-kən'dʌktiv] *adj* fotoconductor, ra.

photocopier [-,kɔpiə*] *n* fotocopiadora *f*.

photocopy [-,kɔpi] *n* fotocopia *f*.

photocopy [-,kɔpi] *vt* fotocopiar.

photocurrent [-,kʌrənt] *n* corriente *f* fotoeléctrica.

photoelasticity [-,elæs'tisiti] *n* PHYS fotoelasticidad *f*.

photoelectric [-i'lektrik]; **photoelectrical** [-i'lektrikəl] *adj* PHYS fotoeléctrico, ca; *photoelectric cell* célula fotoeléctrica.

photoelectricity [-ilek'trisiti] *n* PHYS fotoelectricidad *f*.

photoelectron [-i'lektrɔn] *n* PHYS fotoelectrón *m*.

photoemission [-i'miʃən] *adj* PHYS fotoemisión *f*.

photoengrave [-in'greiv] *vt* fotograbar.

photoengraver [-in'greivə*] *n* fotograbador *m*.

photoengraving [-in'greiviŋ] *n* fotograbado *m*.

photo finish [-'finiʃ] *n* SP final *m* de carrera muy reñido (close race finish) ‖ FIG competición *f* muy reñida (close contest).

Photofit [-fit] *n* (registered trademark) fotorrobot *f*.

photoflash [-flæʃ] *n* PHOT flash *m*, luz *f* relámpago.

photoflood [-flʌd] *n* lámpara *f* incandescente de gran voltaje.

photogenic [,fəutəu'dʒenik] *adj* fotogénico, ca.

photogram ['fəutəugræm] *n* fotograma *m*.

photogrammetry ['fəutə'græmətri] *n* fotogrametría *f*.

photograph ['fəutəgrɑːf] *n* fotografía *f*; *to take a photograph* sacar una fotografía; *to have one's photograph taken* hacerse *or* sacarse una fotografía ‖ — *aerial photograph* fotografía aérea, aerofotografía *f* ‖ *photograph library* fototeca *f*.

photograph; **photo** ['fəutəu] ['fəutəgrɑːf] *vt* fotografiar, hacer una fotografía, sacar una foto de.

◆ *vi* salir en una fotografía; *she photographs well* sale bien en las fotografías.

photographer [fəˈtɔgrəfə*] *n* fotógrafo, fa; *street photographer* fotógrafo callejero.

photographic [ˌfəutəˈgræfik] *adj* fotográfico, ca.

photographically [fəutəˈgræfikəli] *adv* fotográficamente.

photography [fəˈtɔgrəfi] *n* fotografía *f* || *aerial photography* fotografía aérea, aereofotografía *f.*

photogravure [ˌfəutəgrəˈvjuə*] *n* fotograbado *m.*

photolith [ˈfəutəuliθ]; **photolitho** [ˈfəutəuˈlaiθəu] *n* fotolito *m.*

photolithograph [ˈfəutəˈliθəgrɑ:f] *n* fotolitografía *f.*

photolithography [ˈfəutəliˈθɔgrəfi] *n* fotolitografía *f.*

photoluminescence [ˈfəutəulu:miˈnesəns] *n* PHYS & CHEM fotoluminescencia *f.*

photolysis [fəuˈtɔlisis] *n* fotólisis *f.*

photomap [ˈfəutəumæp] *n* mapa *m* hecho con una fotografía aérea.

photomechanical [ˈfəutəuməˈkænikəl] *adj* PRINT fotomecánico, ca.

photometer [fəuˈtɔmi:tə*] *n* fotómetro *m.*

photometric [fəutəˈmetrik]; **photometrical** [-əl] *adj* fotométrico, ca.

photometry [fəˈtɔmetri] *n* fotometría *f.*

photomicrography [fəutəmaiˈkrɔgrəfi] *n* fotomicrografía *f.*

photomontage [ˈfəutəumɔnˈtɑ:ʒ] *n* fotomontaje *m,* montaje *m* fotográfico.

photon [ˈfəutɔn] *n* PHYS fotón *m.*

photophore [ˈfəutəfɔ:*] *n* fotóforo *m.*

photophoresis [ˈfəutəufəˈrisis] *n* fotoforesis *f.*

— OBSERV El plural de *photophoresis* es *photophoreses.*

photoprint [ˈfəutəuprint] *n* fotocalco *m.*

photosensitive [fəutəuˈsensitiv] *adj* fotosensible.

photosphere [ˈfəutəusfiə*] *n* fotosfera *f.*

photostat [ˈfəutəustæt] *n* fotostato *m,* copia *f* fotostática.

photostat [ˈfəutəustæt] *vt* hacer una copia fotostática, fotocopiar.

photostatic [ˌfəutəuˈstætik] *adj* fotostático, ca.

photosynthesis [fəutəˈsinθəsis] *n* BOT fotosíntesis *f.*

phototherapy [fəutəˈθerəpi] *n* MED fototerapia *f.*

phototropism [fəˈtɔtrəpizəm] *n* fototropismo *m.*

phototype [ˈfəutətaip] *n* PRINT fototipo *m.*

phototypesetting [-ˈsetiŋ] *n* PRINT fotocomposición *f.*

phototypography [fəutətaiˈpɔgrəfi] *n* PRINT fototipografía *f.*

phototypy [ˈfəutətipi] *n* PRINT fototipia *f.*

phrasal verb [ˈfreizəlˌvə:b] *n* verbo *m* adverbial *or* preposicional.

phrase [freiz] *n* locución *f,* expresión *f,* frase *f* || GRAMM locución *f; adverbial phrase* locución adverbial || MUS frase *f* || — *proverbial phrase* frase proverbial || *set* o *stock phrase* frase hecha *or* acuñada *or* estereotipada.

phrase [freiz] *vt* expresar (a thought) || redactar (to write); *well-phrased letter* carta bien redactada || frasear (to express in phrases) || MUS frasear.

◆ *vi* frasear.

phrase book [ˈfreizbuk] *n* repertorio *m* de expresiones.

phraseology [ˌfreiziˈɔlədʒi] *n* fraseología *f.*

phrasing [ˈfreiziŋ] *n* expresión *f* (of thought) || redacción *f* (of a letter) || estilo *m* (style) || fraseología *f* (phraseology) || MUS fraseo *m.*

phratry [ˈfreitri] *n* fratría *f* (in Athens).

phreatic [friˈætik] *adj* freático, ca.

phrenetic [friˈnetik] *adj* frenético, ca.

phrenic [ˈfrenik] *adj* ANAT frénico, ca.

phrenologist [friˈnɔlədʒist] *n* frenólogo *m.*

phrenology [friˈnɔlədʒi] *n* frenología *f.*

Phrygia [ˈfridʒiə] *pr n* GEOGR Frigia *f* (ancient country in Asia Minor).

Phrygian [-n] *adj/n* frigio, gia; *Phrygian cap* gorro frigio.

phthalein [ˈfθæliin] *n* CHEM ftaleína *f.*

phthisic [ˈθaisik]; **phthisical** [-əl] *adj* MED tísico, ca.

phthisis [ˈθaisis] *n* MED tisis *f.*

— OBSERV El plural de *phtisis* es *phtises.*

phut [fʌt] *adv to go phut* estropearse (an engine), hundirse (a business), fracasar, fallar (a project).

phycomycete [faikəuˈmaisi:t] *n* BOT ficomiceto *m.*

phylactery [fiˈlæktəri] *n* filacteria *f.*

phylloxera [ˌfilɔkˈsiərə] *n* filoxera *f.*

phylum [ˈfailəm] *n* BIOL filo *m.*

— OBSERV El plural de esta palabra es *phyla.*

physic [ˈfizik] *n* MED medicamento *m,* medicina *f,* remedio *m.*

physical [-əl] *adj* físico, ca (culture, force) || físico, ca; *a physical change in a substance* un cambio físico en una sustancia || FIG físico, ca; material; *physical impossibility* imposibilidad física || — *physical chemistry* fisicoquímica *f* || *physical education* educación física || *physical examination* reconocimiento médico || *physical fitness* buena salud || *physical geography* geografía física || *physical sciences* ciencias *f pl* físicas || *physical therapy* fisioterapia *f* || *physical training* educación *f* física.

◆ *n* reconocimiento *m* médico.

physically [-əli] *adv* físicamente || *physically handicapped* impedido físico.

physician [fiˈziŋən] *n* médico *m* (doctor).

physicist [ˈfizisist] *n* físico, ca (specialist in physics).

physicochemical [ˈfisikəˈkemikəl] *adj* fisicoquímico, ca.

physics [ˈfiziks] *n* física *f; nuclear physics* física nuclear.

physio [ˈfisiəu] *n* FAM fisioterapia *f* (therapy) | fisioterapeuta *m* & *f* (doctor).

physiocracy [fiziˈɔkrəsi] *n* fisiocracia *f.*

physiocrat [ˈfiziəkræt] *n* fisiócrata *m* & *f.*

physiognomic [ˌfiziəˈnɔmik]; **physiognomical** [-əl] *adj* fisonómico, ca.

physiognomist [ˌfiziˈɔnəmist] *n* fisonomista *m* & *f,* fisónomo, ma.

physiognomy [ˌfiziˈɔnəmi] *n* fisonomía *f.*

physiographer [fiziˈɔgrəfə*] *n* fisiógrafo *m.*

physiography [ˌfiziʒɔgrəfi] *n* fisiografía *f* || geografía *f* física.

physiologic [ˌfiziəˈlɔdʒik]; **physiological** [-əl] *adj* fisiológico, ca.

physiologist [ˌfiziˈɔlədʒist] *n* fisiólogo, ga.

physiology [ˌfiziˈɔlədʒi] *n* fisiología *f.*

physiotherapist [fiziəuˈθerəpist] *n* fisioterapeuta *m* & *f.*

physiotherapy [fiziəˈθerəpi] *n* fisioterapia *f.*

physique [fiˈzi:k] *n* constitución *f* (of a person's body) || físico *m* (of a person).

physostome [ˈfaisəstəum]; **physostomous** [faisəsˈtəuməs] *adj* fisóstomo, ma (fish).

phytography [faiˈtɔgrəfi] *n* fitografía *f.*

phytology [faiˈtɔlədʒi] *n* fitología *f* (botany).

phytophagous [faiˈtɔfəgəs] *adj* fitófago, ga (planteating).

phytozoon [faitəˈzəuɔn] *n* BIOL fitozoario *m,* zoófito *m.*

— OBSERV El plural de esta palabra es *phytozoa.*

pi [pai] *n* pi *f* (Greek letter) || MATH pi *f* || PRINT pastel *m.*

piacular [paiˈækjulə*] *adj* expiatorio, ria || pecaminoso, sa (requiring atonement).

pia mater [ˈpaiəˈmeitə*] *n* ANAT piamadre *f,* piamáter *f.*

pianissimo [pjæˈnisiməu] *adj/adv* MUS pianísimo.

pianist [ˈpiənist] *n* MUS pianista *m* & *f.*

piano [piˈænəu] *n* MUS piano *m; grand, upright piano* piano de cola, vertical *or* recto; *baby grand piano* piano de media cola.

piano [ˈpjɑ:nəu] *adv* MUS piano (softly).

pianoforte [ˌpjænəuˈfɔ:ti] *n* MUS piano *m,* pianoforte *m.*

pianola [piəˈnəulə] *n* MUS pianola *f.*

piano tuner [piˈænəuˌtju:nə*] *n* afinador *m* de pianos.

piastre; piaster [piˈastə*] *n* piastra *f.*

piazza [piˈætsə] *n* plaza *f* (square) || soportales *m pl,* pórtico *m* (portico) || US galería *f,* porche *m* (veranda).

pibroch [ˈpi:brɔk] *n* MUS pieza *f* de música tocada con la gaita.

pica [ˈpaikə] *n* cícero *m* (printing) || MED pica *f.*

picador [ˈpikədɔ:*] *n* picador *m* (bullfighting).

picaresque [ˌpikəˈresk] *adj* picaresco, ca.

picaroon [ˌpikəˈru:n] *n* pícaro, ra; bribón, ona (rogue) || pirata *m,* corsario *m* (pirate).

picayune [piki:ˈju:n] *adj* US de poco valor, de poca monta, insignificante (of little value) | baladí (trivial).

◆ *n* US fruslería *f,* nadería *f,* nonada *f* || FAM *it's not worth a picayune* no vale un pepino.

piccalilli [ˈpikəlili] *n* CULIN macedonia *f* de verduras con salsa picante.

piccaninny [ˈpikənini] *n* negrito, ta.

piccolo [ˈpikələu] *n* MUS flautín *m.*

pick [pik] *n* elección *f,* selección *f* (choice) || piqueta *f,* pico *m* (tool) || ganzúa *f* (picklock) || MUS plectro *m* || cosecha *f,* recolección *f* (of fruit) || — *take your pick* escoja el que quiera || FIG *the pick of the bunch* lo más escogido, la flor y nata, lo más selecto, lo mejor de lo mejor || *to have the pick of* poder escoger entre || *to take one's pick* elegir a su gusto.

pick [pik] *vt* escoger (to choose); *to pick the best cake* escoger el mejor pastel || seleccionar (to select carefully); *to pick a team* seleccionar un equipo || coger (flowers) || recoger (fruit) || cavar (in the earth) || escarbar (with the nails) || abrir; *to pick a hole* abrir un agujero *or* un boquete || mondarse, escarbarse (the teeth) || hurgarse (one's nose) || rascarse (a pimple, a wound) || desplumar (to pluck poultry) || picotear, picar (to peck, of a bird) || roer (a bone) || clasificar, seleccionar (minerals) || forzar, abrir con ganzúa (a lock) || picar (rocks) || puntear, pulsar (a guitar, etc.) || buscar (to seek); *to pick a quarrel with* buscar camorra con || sacar (threads) || deshilachar (a material) || — FIG *to have a bone to pick with* tener que ajustarle las cuentas a || *to pick acquaintance with* conocer a, trabar amistad con ‖ FIG *to pick holes in* encontrar defectos en (sth. done), criticar, desbaratar (an argument), criticar, poner verde (a person) ‖ *to pick one's steps* o *way* andar con tiento *or* con mucho cuidado (to go carefully), abrirse camino (*through* entre) (through a crowd, etc.) ‖ *to pick one's words* elegir las palabras ‖ *to pick pockets* robar carteras ‖ FIG *to pick s.o.'s brains* explotar los conocimientos de alguien ‖ *to pick s.o.'s pocket* robar algo del bolsillo de alguien ‖ *to pick to pieces* poner de vuelta y media, poner verde (to criticize), hacer polvo, no dejar un hueso sano (to beat up), desbaratar (an argument), hacer trizas (to break to pieces).

◆ *vi* picar (with a pick) ‖ picar, picotear (to eat); *to pick at one's food* picar la comida ‖ picotear (a bird) ‖ cogerse, recogerse (fruit, flowers, etc.) ‖ criticar (to criticize) ‖ *to pick and choose* ser muy exigente, escoger con sumo cuidado.

◆ *phr v* *to pick off* quitar (to remove) | eliminar *or* matar uno a uno (to kill) ‖ *to pick on* escoger, elegir (to choose) | criticar (to criticize) | meterse con; *stop picking on your little brother* deja de meterte con tu hermanito ‖ *to pick out* escoger, elegir (to select) | ver, descubrir (to discover); *he hoped no one would pick him out in the crowd* esperaba que nadie le descubriese en la muchedumbre | distinguir (to distinguish) | discernir (to discern) | hacer resaltar (to make sth. stand out) | subrayar (to underline); *important words are picked out in red* las palabras importantes están subrayadas en rojo | sacar, tocar de oído (a tune) ‖ *to pick over* buscar en (to look for) ‖ *to pick up* coger (to take); *pick the baby up* coge al niño | levantar (to lift); *I can't pick it up, it's too heavy* no lo puedo levantar, es demasiado pesado | recoger (to lift, to collect) | descolgar, coger (telephone) | recoger, reunir (information) | sacar, lograr (a profit) | recoger (to fetch); *I shall pick you up at your house* le recogeré en su casa | adquirir (to acquire) | comprar (to buy) | tomar, coger (a train) | encontrar (to meet, to find) | coger; *to pick up speed* coger velocidad | recobrar (strength, etc.) | entonar (to tone up) | recuperarse (to recover) | mejorar (to get better) | aprender (to learn) | enterarse de, saber (a piece of news) | captar (a message on the radio, signals, etc.) | coger, detener (to arrest) | FAM ligar con (a girl) | ganarse; *to pick up a living* ganarse la vida ‖ — *to pick o.s. up* levantarse ‖ FIG *to pick up the pieces* volver a empezar después de un fracaso ‖ *to pick up with* conocer a, trabar amistad con.

pickaback [-əbæk] *adv* a cuestas, en los hombros.

◆ *n* paseo *m* a cuestas.

pickanniny ['pikənini] *n* negrito, ta.

pickaxe; pickax [-æks] *n* piocha *f*, piqueta *f*, zapapico *m*.

picked [-t] *adj* escogido, da; selecto, ta.

picker [-ə*] *n* recogedor, ra ‖ desmotadora *f* (of cotton).

pickerel [-ərəl] *n* lucio *m* (fish).

picket [-it] *n* piquete *m*, pelotón *m* (of soldiers) ‖ piquete *m* (during a strike) ‖ huelguista *m* & *f*, miembro *m* de un piquete (person) ‖ manifestación *f* (riot, demonstration) ‖ manifestante *m* & *f* (demonstrator) ‖ retén *m* (of firemen) ‖ estaca *f*, poste *m* (pointed stake) ‖ jalón *m*, mojón *m* (in surveying) ‖ poste *m* (for horses) ‖ *picket line* piquete.

picket [-it] *vt* vallar *or* cercar con estacas (with a picket fence) ‖ atar al poste (an animal) ‖ vigilar las inmediaciones de (strikers, soldiers) ‖ poner de guardia a un piquete de huelguistas alrededor de (a factory) ‖ poner de guardia a unos soldados alrededor de (a mil itary camp).

◆ *vi* vigilar, estar de guardia.

picketer [-itə*] *n* miembro *m* de un piquete de huelguistas.

picking ['pikiŋ] *n* recolección *f*, cosecha *f* (of fruit) ‖ selección *f* (choice) ‖ forzamiento *m* (of a lock).

◆ *pl* sobras *f*, restos *m* (leftovers) ‖ ganancias *f* (profits) ‖ botín *m sing* (booty).

pickle ['pikl] *n* adobo *m*, salmuera *f* (for preserving meat) ‖ escabeche *m* (for fish) ‖ conserva *f* en vinagre, encurtido *m* (preserve in vinegar) ‖ TECH baño *m* de ácido para desoxidar ‖ FAM lío *m*, aprieto *m*, apuro *m* (awkward situation) | diablillo *m* (mischievous child) ‖ — FIG & FAM *to be in a nice* o *in a fine pickle* estar metido en un lío | *to get into a pickle* meterse en un lío.

pickle ['pikl] *vt* conservar en vinagre, encurtir (to preserve in vinegar) ‖ adobar (meat) ‖ escabechar (fish) ‖ TECH desoxidar.

pickled [-d] *adj* adobado, da; en adobo (meat) ‖ escabechado, da; en escabeche (fish) ‖ en vinagre; *pickled onions* cebollas en vinagre ‖ FIG *to be pickled* estar piripi (to be drunk).

picklock ['piklɔk] *n* ganzúa *f* (device for picking locks) ‖ ladrón *m* de ganzúa (burglar).

pick-me-up ['pikmiʌp] *n* tónico *m*, reconstituyente *m*, estimulante *m* (drink).

pickpocket ['pikˌpɔkit] *n* ratero, ra; carterista *m*.

pickup ['pikʌp] *n* recogida *f* de la pelota (cricket) ‖ recolección *f*, recogida *f* (harvest) ‖ TECH fonocaptor *m* (of a gramophone) ‖ recepción *f*, toma *f*, captación *f* (of sound or light) ‖ receptor *m* (of a transmitter) ‖ recuperación *f*, restablecimiento *m* (of health) ‖ recuperación *f* (business recovery) ‖ FAM ligue *m* (of a person) ‖ ganga *f* (bargain) ‖ camioneta *f* de reparto, furgoneta *f* de reparto (delivery truck) ‖ aceleración *f*, poder *m* de aceleración (of a car) ‖ arresto *m*, detención *f* (arrest) ‖ *pickup truck* camión *m* de reparto.

picky ['piki] *adj* US FAM difícil (finical).

picnic ['piknik] *n* excursión *f* al campo, merienda *f or* comida *f* campestre ‖ merienda *f*, comida *f* (food) ‖ FAM placer *m*; *life is not a picnic* la vida no es ningún placer | cosa *f* tirada (easy thing) ‖ — *picnic lunch* bolsa *f* de comida (given in a hotel, etc.), bocadillos *m pl* (sandwiches) ‖ *to go for a picnic* ir a merendar al campo.

picnic ['piknik] *vi* merendar *or* comer en el campo ‖ *we picnicked by the lake* merendamos a orillas del lago.

— OBSERV El pretérito y el participio pasivo de *picnic* son *picnicked* y el participio de presente es *picniking*.

picnicker [-ə*] *n* excursionista *m* & *f*.

picot ['piːkəu] *n* puntilla *f* (of a ribbon).

picric ['pikrik] *adj* pícrico, ca.

Pict [pikt] *adj/n* picto, ta (people of Scotland).

Pictish [-iʃ] *adj* picto, ta.

pictograph ['piktəugrɑːf] *n* pictografía *f*.

pictographic [pikt'əgræfik] *adj* pictográfico, ca.

pictography [pik'tɔgrəfi] *n* pictografía *f*.

pictorial [pik'tɔːriəl] *adj* pictórico, ca (of pictures); *pictorial art* arte pictórica ‖ gráfico, ca; *a very pictorial style of writing* una manera de escribir muy gráfica ‖ ilustrado, da (magazine).

◆ *n* revista *f* ilustrada (magazine).

pictorially [-i] *adv* pictóricamente ‖ gráficamente (graphically) ‖ con ilustraciones (through pictures).

picture ['piktʃə*] *n* cuadro *m* (painting) ‖ dibujo *m* (drawing) ‖ grabado *m*, lámina *f* (engraving) ‖ ilustración *f* (in a magazine) ‖ película *f* (film) ‖ retrato *m* (portrait) ‖ fotografía *f*, foto *f* (photograph); *to have one's picture taken* sacarse una fotografía ‖ FIG retrato *m*; *Alexander is the picture of his father* Alejandro es el retrato de su padre ‖ representación *f*, imagen *f*; *Mary is the picture of happiness* María es la imagen de la felicidad ‖ imagen *f* (mental image) ‖ pintura *f*, descripción *f*, cuadro *m*; *picture of the morals of the period* descripción de las costumbres de la época ‖ visión *f*; *these facts give you the general picture* estos hechos le dan una visión general ‖ situación *f* (panorama); *have you understood the picture?* ¿has comprendido la situación? ‖ facha *f* (ridiculous sight); *what a picture you looked!* ¡qué facha tenías!, ¡estabas hecho una facha! ‖ — FIG *I get the picture* ya veo | *in the picture* al corriente (well informed), de actualidad (of the moment) | *out of the picture* fuera de lugar ‖ FIG *the roses were a picture this year* las rosas eran preciosas este año | *to come into the picture* entrar en escena ‖ *to give a good picture* dar buena imagen (TV set) ‖ FIG *to paint a very black picture of sth.* pintar algo muy negro | *to put s.o. in the picture* poner a uno al corriente | *to see the other side of the picture* ver el reverso de la medalla ‖ *to take a picture* sacar una fotografía ‖ FIG *what a picture!* ¡qué cuadro!, ¡había que verlo!

◆ *pl* cine *m sing* (movies) ‖ — *silent pictures* cine mudo ‖ *talking pictures* cine sonoro ‖ *to go to the pictures* ir al cine.

picture ['piktʃə*] *vt* describir, pintar (to depict) ‖ pintar (to paint) ‖ *to picture (to o.s.)* imaginarse, figurarse, representarse (to imagine); *can you picture the situation?* ¿os imagináis la situación?

picture book [-buk] *n* libro *m* ilustrado.

picture card [-kɑːd] *n* figura *f*.

picture frame [-freim] *n* marco *m*.

picture gallery [-gæləri] *n* museo *m* de pintura, pinacoteca *f* (art museum) ‖ galería *f* (small exhibition room).

picturegoer [-gəuə*] *n* aficionado *m* al cine.

picture hat [-hæt] *n* pamela *f*.

picture house [-haus]; **picture palace** [-'pælis] *n* cine *m*.

picture postcard [-'pəustkɑːd] *n* tarjeta *f* postal.

picturesque [ˌpiktʃə'resk] *adj* pintoresco, ca; *a picturesque village* un pueblo pintoresco ‖ gráfico, ca (style) ‖ típico, ca (typical).

picture theatre ['piktʃə*'θiətə*] *n* cine *m*.

picture window ['piktʃəˌwindəu] *n* ventanal *m*.

picture writing ['piktʃəˌraitiŋ] *n* pictografía *f*.

piddle [pidl] *vi* FAM hacer pipí ‖ US malgastar el tiempo.

piddling ['pidliŋ] *adj* FAM menudo, da.

piddock ['pidək] *n* dátil *m* de mar (mollusc).

pidgin ['pidʒin] *n* lengua *f* macarrónica ‖ — *pidgin English* «pidgin English» *m*, inglés macarrónico ‖ FAM *that's his pidgin, not yours* eso es asunto suyo y no tuyo ‖ *to talk pidgin* hablar como los indios.

pie [pai] *n* ZOOL urraca *f* (bird) ‖ CULIN pastel *m* de carne, empanada *f* (with meat) | pastel *m* (of fruit) ‖ pastel *m* (printing) ‖ US tarta *f* (cake) ‖ — FIG *it's pie in the sky* son ilusiones, son castillos en el aire, es como prometer la luna ‖ CULIN *shepherd's pie* pastel *m* de carne picada con puré de patatas ‖ FIG *to be as easy as pie* estar tirado, ser muy fácil | *to eat humble pie* reconocer su error | *to have a finger in every pie* estar metido en todo, meter las manos en todo | *to have had a finger in the pie* haber metido las manos *or* estar pringado en el asunto.

piebald ['paibɔ:ld] *adj* pío, a; picazo, za (horse) || con lunares de colores, moteado, da (with patches of different colours).
◆ *n* caballo *m* pío, caballo *m* picazo.

piece [pi:s] *n* pedazo *m*, trozo *m*; *a piece of bread* un pedazo de pan || parte *f* (part) || pieza *f*; *a dinner service of 48 pieces* una vajilla de 48 piezas || pieza *f* (of material) || muestra *f* (sample) || momento *m* (moment) || moneda *f*, pieza *f* (of money); *a five pence piece* una moneda de cinco peniques || pieza *f* (chess, draughts, etc.) || MUS & THEATR obra *f*, pieza *f* (musical composition, play) || pasaje *m* (part of a work) || MIL pieza *f* (of artillery) || parcela *f* (of land) || poesía *f* (poem) || — *all of one piece, all in one piece* de un solo bloque, de una sola pieza || *a piece of advice* un consejo || *a piece of carelessness* un descuido || *a piece of folly* una locura || *a piece of insolence* una insolencia || *a piece of luck* una suerte || *a piece of luggage* un bulto || *a piece of news* una noticia || *a piece of rubbish* una sandez || FIG *a pretty piece* una preciosidad, una monería (girl, object) || *by the piece* a destajo, por piezas || *in pieces* destrozado, da (destroyed), desmontado, da (machine), por piezas (piece by piece), hecho pedazos (in bits) || *it comes to pieces* es desmontable, se puede desmontar *or* desarmar || *of a piece with* parecido a || *piece by piece* pieza por pieza, pieza a pieza || *piece of furniture* mueble *m* || *piece of ground* o *of land* solar *m*, terreno *m*, parcela *f* || *piece of water* estanque *m* || *to arrive in one piece* llegar sano y salvo, llegar indemne *or* ileso (a person), llegar en buen estado (a thing) || *to be of a piece with* formar una sola pieza con (to be a whole), estar de acuerdo con, concordar con (to agree with) || *to be in pieces* estar hecho pedazos (broken), estar desmontado *or* desarmado (taken apart) || *to be smashed to pieces* romperse en mil pedazos || *to break sth. in pieces* o *to pieces* hacer algo trizas *or* pedazos || *to come* o *to fall to pieces* caerse a pedazos (house, person), hacerse pedazos (to break up, to fall apart), hundirse (business) || *to cut to pieces* cortar en pedazos || *to fly to pieces* hacerse pedazos || FIG *to give s.o. a piece of one's mind* decir a uno cuatro verdades | *to go to pieces* venirse abajo (to break up physically or morally), perder el dominio de sí mismo (to lose self-control) || *to pay by the piece* pagar a destajo (a workman) || *to pick to pieces* poner de vuelta y media, poner verde (to criticize), hacer polvo, no dejar un hueso sano (to beat up), desbaratar (an argument), hacer trizas (to break to pieces) || *to pull* o *to tear to pieces* hacer pedazos (to break), echar abajo, echar por tierra (an argument), poner como un trapo, poner por los suelos (to criticize) || *to say one's piece* decir su parecer || *to take to pieces* desmontar, desarmar (a machine), deshacer (a dress).

piece [pi:s] *vt* poner una pieza a (to add a piece) || — *to piece out* completar || FIG *to piece things together* atar cabos || *to piece together* juntar, juntar las partes de (to join), montar, armar (a machine), hacer (a jigsaw puzzle).

pièce de résistance [pjɛsdəreizistɑ:s] *n* atracción *f* principal (main attraction) || CULIN plato *m* fuerte *or* principal.

piecemeal ['pi:smi:l] *adj* hecho por partes *or* poco a poco || poco sistemático, ca (not methodical).
◆ *adv* por partes, poco a poco.

piecework ['pi:swə:k] *n* trabajo *m* a destajo || — *piecework price* precio *m* a destajo || *to be on piecework, to do piecework* trabajar a destajo.

pieceworker [-ə*] *n* destajista *m* & *f*, trabajador *m* a destajo.

piecrust ['paikrʌst] *n* CULIN pasta *f*.

pied [paid] *adj* de varios colores, moteado, da || *Pied Piper* el Flautista de Hamelín.

pied-à-terre [,pieitæ'tɛə*] *n* apeadero *m*.

Piedmont ['pi:dmənt] *pr n* GEOGR Piamonte *m*.

Piedmontese [,pi:dmən'ti:z] *adj/n* GEOGR piamontés, esa.

pie-eyed ['paiaid] *adj* FAM mona; *to be pie-eyed* estar mona.

pier [piə*] *n* malecón *m*, rompeolas *m inv*, espigón *m* (breakwater masonry) || muelle *m*, embarcadero *m* (access to vessels) || ARCH pilar *m*, machón *m* (on an arch) | entrepaño *m* (between two doors), entreventana *f* (between two windows) | pila *f* (of a bridge).

pierce [piəs] *vt* perforar, taladrar (to bore, to punch a hole in) || agujerear (to make a hole in) || atravesar, traspasar (to go through); *the bullet pierced his heart* la bala le atravesó el corazón || penetrar en (to penetrate) || entrar en (to go into); *the arrow pierced his eye* la flecha le entró en el ojo || abrirse paso por (to break through) || FIG traspasar (to heart) | herir (with cries); *her cries pierced my ears* sus gritos me hirieron los oídos | conmover, afectar (with emotions); *the news pierced him deeply* la noticia le conmovió profundamente | penetrar, adivinar (a mystery, a secret) | comprender (to understand) || — *a ray of light pierced the darkness* un rayo de luz atravesó la oscuridad || *a scream pierced the silent night* un chillido rompió el silencio de la noche || *the glass pierced the tyre* el cristal pinchó la rueda || *to pierce a hole in sth.* hacer un agujero en algo || *to pierce s.o. through* atravesar a uno (with a spear, etc.), traspasarle el corazón a uno (with grief) || *to pierce the lid of a tin* perforar una lata || *when did you have your ears pierced?* ¿cuándo le hicieron los agujeros en las orejas?
◆ *vi* salir (the teeth).

piercing [-iŋ] *adj* penetrante, agudo, da (cold, look, sound) || punzante, agudo, da (pain) || desgarrador, ra (cry) || cortante (wind) || TECH perforador, ra; *piercing dies* matrices perforadoras.
◆ *n* perforación *f*.

pier glass ['piəglɑ:s] *n* espejo *m* de cuerpo entero.

pierrot ['piərəu] *n* pierrot *m* (comic character).

pier table ['piə*teibl] *n* consola *f*.

Pietà [,piə'tɑ:] *pr n* ARTS Piedad *f*.

pietism ['paiətizəm] *n* REL pietismo *m* (doctrine) || piedad *f* (piety) || beatería *f* (excessive piety).

pietistic [,paiə'tistik] *adj* devoto, ta (pious) || beato, ta (excessively pious).

piety ['paiəti] *n* piedad *f* || *affected piety* beatería *f*.

piezoelectric [paiəzəi'lektrik] *adj* piezoeléctrico, ca.

piezoelectricity [,paiəzəilek'trisiti] *n* piezoelectricidad *f*.

piezometer [paiə'zɔmi:tə*] *n* PHYS piezómetro *m*.

piezometry [paiə'zɔmetri] *n* piezometría *f*.

piffle ['pifl] *n* FAM pamplina *f*, disparate *m*, tontería *f* (nonsense); *his argument was piffle* su argumento era una pamplina || FAM *a load of piffle* pamplinas, disparates, tonterías.

piffle ['pifl] *vi* FAM decir pamplinas, decir tonterías, soltar disparates, disparatar.

piffling [-iŋ] *adj* fútil, trivial (trivial) || disparatado, da (nonsensical) || insignificante, de poca importancia (insignificant).

pig [pig] *n* cerdo *m*, puerco *m* [AMER chancho *m*, guarro *m*] (animal) || US cochinillo *m* (piglet) || TECH lingote *m* de arrabio (of iron) | galápago *m* (of lead) | lingotera *f* (mould in which metal is cast) || FAM cerdo, da; cochino, na (dirty person); *what a pig!* ¡qué cerdo! || — FIG *greedy pig* tragón, ona; comilón, ona || *pig breeding* cría *f* de cerdos || *roast pig* cochinillo asado || *sucking pig* lechón *m*, cochinillo *m* de leche || FIG *to buy a pig in a poke* comprar a ciegas | *to make a pig of o.s.* hincharse como un cerdo | *to sell s.o. a pig in a poke* dar a alguien gato por liebre | *when pigs fly* o *have wings* cuando las ranas críen pelos || *wild pig* jabalí *m* (wild boar) || FAM *you dirty pig!* ¡qué cerdo eres!, ¡eres un guarro!, ¡qué guarro eres!

pig [pig] *vi* parir (the sow) || FAM vivir como cerdos (to live like pigs).

pig bed [-bed] *n* TECH era *f* de colada.

pigeon ['pidʒin] *n* ZOOL paloma *f*; *domestic, crested, carrier* o *homing, wild, wood, rock pigeon* paloma casera, de moño, mensajera, silvestre, torcaz, zurita || SP pichón *m* (bird) | plato *m* (clay pigeon) || CULIN pichón *m* || — SP *clay pigeon shooting* tiro *m* al plato || FAM *that's his pigeon* es asunto suyo.

pigeonhole [-həul] *n* casilla *f* || *(set of) pigeonholes* casillas *f pl*, casillero *m sing*.

pigeonhole [-həul] *vt* archivar (to store away) || encasillar, clasificar (to classify) || dar carpetazo a (to shelve).

pigeon house [-haus]; **pigeon loft** [-lɔft] *n* palomar *m*.

pigeon shooting [-'ʃu:tiŋ] *n* tiro *m* de pichón.

pigeon-toed [-təud] *adj* con los pies torcidos hacia dentro.

piggery ['pigəri] *n* pocilga *f*, porqueriza *f* (pigsty) || FIG pocilga *f* (a filthy place) | porquería *f* (filthiness).

piggish ['pigiʃ] *adj* glotón, ona (greedy) || puerco, ca; cochino, na (dirty) | testarudo, da (stubborn).

piggy ['pigi] *adj* guarro, rra (dirty) || glotón, ona (greedy).
◆ *n* cochinillo *m*, lechón *m*, cerdito *m*.

piggyback [-bæk] *adv* a cuestas, en los hombros; *to carry s.o. piggyback* llevar a alguien a cuestas || US sobre vagones plataformas.
◆ *n* US sistema *m* de transporte sobre vagones plataformas || paseo *m* a cuestas (pickaback ride).

piggy bank [-bæŋk] *n* hucha *f*, alcancía *f* (money box).

pigheaded [-'hedid] *adj* testarudo, da; terco, ca; cabezón, ona.

pigheadedness [-'hedidnis] *n* terquedad *f*, testarudez *f*, cabezonería *f*.

pig iron [-,aiən] *n* arrabio *m*, hierro *m* colado, hierro *m* en lingotes.

pig Latin [-'lætin] *n* jerga *f*.

piglet [-lit] *n* cochinillo *m*, lechón *m*.

pigman [-mən] *n* porquero *m*, porquerizo *m*.
— OBSERV El plural de *pigman* es *pigmen*.

pigment ['pigmənt] *n* pigmento *m*.

pigment [pigmənt] *vt* pigmentar.

pigmentary [-məntəri] *adj* pigmentario, ria.

pigmentation [,pigmən'teiʃən] *n* pigmentación *f*.

pigmy ['pigmi] *n* → **pygmy.**

pignus ['pignəs] *n* prenda *f*.
— OBSERV El plural de *pignus* es *pignora*.

pignut ['pignʌt] *n* BOT pacana *f*.

pigpen ['pigpen] *n* US pocilga *f*, porqueriza *f*.

pigskin ['pigskin] *n* piel *f* de cerdo (skin) || FAM silla *f* de montar (saddle) | balón *m*, pelota *f* (ball).

pigsty ['pigstai] *n* pocilga *f*, porqueriza *f* || FIG pocilga *f* (dirty place).

pigswill ['pigswil] *n* bazofia *f*.

pigtail [ˈpigteil] *n* coleta *f* (of Chinese, of bullfighter) || coleta *f*, trenza *f* (of girl).

pike [paik] *n* punta *f* (sharp tip) || pica *f* (weapon) || lucio *m* (fish) || *US* peaje *m* (toll) | barrera *f* (toll bar) | carretera *f* de peaje (toll road).

pikeman [-mən] *n* MIL piquero *m*.
— OBSERV El plural de *pikeman* es *pikemen*.

piker [-ə*] *n* *US* FAM tacaño, ña; roñoso, sa (skinflint).

pikestaff [-stɑːf] *n* asta *f* de la pica (weapon staff) || báculo *m* de peregrino (walking stick) || *as plain as a pikestaff* clarísimo, ma.
— OBSERV El plural es *pikestaffs* o *pikestaves*.

pilaf; pilaff [ˈpilæf] *n* CULIN plato *m* oriental a base de arroz.

pilaster [piˈlæstə*] *n* ARCH pilastra *f*.

Pilate [ˈpailət] *pr n* HIST Pilato *m*.

pilau [piˈlau] *n* CULIN plato *m* oriental a base de arroz.

pilchard [ˈpiltʃəd] *n* sardina *f* (fish).

pile [pail] *n* ARCH pilote *m* (support); *built on piles* construido sobre pilotes || estaca *f* (stake); *to drive piles in the ground* clavar estacas en la tierra || montón *m*, pila *f*; *a pile of books* un montón de libros || FAM pila *f*, montón *m*; *a pile of things to do* una pila de cosas que hacer | fortuna *f* (fortune) || pira *f* funeraria (funeral pyre) || ELECTR pila *f*, batería *f* || PHYS pila *f*; *atomic pile* pila atómica || mole *f* (building) || pelo *m* (of carpets); *to have a thick pile* tener el pelo largo || MIL pabellón *m* (of arms) || MED almorrana *f*.

pile [pail] *vt* ARCH sostener con pilotes (to support) || hincar pilotes en (to drive piles into) || amontonar, apilar (to place in a heap); *he piled the books one on top of the other* amontonó los libros uno encima de otro || abarrotar (to cram) || — MIL *to pile arms* formar pabellones || *to pile a table with books* llenar una mesa de libros, amontonar libros sobre una mesa.
◆ *vi* amontonarse, apiñarse (in a heap) || acumularse (to accumulate).
◆ *phr v* ***to pile in*** o ***into*** meterse, amontonarse; *they all piled into the car* se amontonaron todos en el coche | entrar en tropel (to crowd in) || — *pile in everyone!* ¡todos adentro! || ***to pile on*** echar un montón de; *to pile wood on the fire* echar un montón de leña al fuego | aumentar, intensificar (to intensify) || — FIG *to pile it on* exagerar | *to pile on the agony* cargar las tintas || ***to pile out*** salir en tropel || ***to pile up*** amontonar, apilar (to put in a heap) | cargar (to load) | acumular; *he piled up evidence* acumuló pruebas | amontonarse, acumularse; *the books piled up* se amontonaban los libros; *the debts piled up* se acumulaban las deudas | chocar uno contra otro (several cars) || — *to pile up against* o *on* estrellarse contra.

pile driver [-ˌdraivə*] *n* TECH martinete *m*.

pile dwelling [-ˌdweliŋ] *n* vivienda *f* sostenida por pilotes, vivienda *f* lacustre.

piles [-z] *pl n* MED almorranas *f*.

pileup [-ʌp] *n* accidente *m* múltiple.

pileus [ˈpailiəs] *n* sombrerillo *m* (of a mushroom).

pilewort [ˈpailwəːt] *n* BOT celidonia *f* menor.

pilfer [ˈpilfə*] *vt/vi* sisar, hurtar, robar.

pilferer [-rə*] *n* ladronzuelo, la.

pilfering [-riŋ] *n* sisa *f*, hurto *m*, robo *m*.

pilgrim [ˈpilgrim] *n* peregrino, na.

Pilgrim [ˈpilgrim] *n* HIST padre *m* Peregrino (one of the Pilgrim Fathers).

pilgrimage [-idʒ] *n* peregrinación *f*; *to go on a pilgrimage* ir en peregrinación.

Pilgrim Father [-ˈfɑːðə*] *n* HIST padre *m* Peregrino.

piliferous [paiˈlifərəs] *adj* BOT pilífero, ra.

piliform [ˈpailifɔːm] *adj* piliforme.

piling [-iŋ] *n* pilotaje *m*.

pill [pil] *n* píldora *f* (medicine) || FIG & FAM lata *f* (person) | bala *f* (bullet) || pelota *f* (ball) || — FIG *it was a bitter pill to swallow* era una píldora difícil de tragar | *to sugar* o *to gild the pill* dorar la píldora | *to swallow the bitter pill* tragarse la píldora.

pillage [ˈpilidʒ] *n* pillaje *m*, saqueo *m*.

pillage [ˈpilidʒ] *vt/vi* saquear, pillar.

pillar [ˈpilə*] *n* ARCH pilar *m* | columna *f* || FIG pilar *m*, soporte *m*, puntal *m*; *the pillars of the Church* los pilares de la Iglesia | columna *f*; *a pillar of smoke* una columna de humo || — FIG *he is a pillar of strength* es firme como una roca || *Pillars of Hercules* Columnas de Hércules || FIG *to be driven from pillar to post* tener que ir de la Ceca a la Meca.

pillar box [-bɔks] *n* buzón *m* (for letters).

pillbox [ˈpilbɔks] *n* cajita *f* para pastillas *or* píldoras (for tablets) || sombrero *m* sin ala (hat) || MIL fortín *m*.

pillion [ˈpiljən] *n* asiento *m* trasero (of a motorcycle) || silla *f* ligera de montar (saddle) || grupera *f* (pad) || *to ride pillion* ir en el asiento trasero (on a motorcycle), montar a la grupa (on a horse).

pillory [ˈpiləri] *n* picota *f*.

pillory [ˈpiləri] *vt* poner en la picota (to punish) || FIG poner en la picota, exponer a la vergüenza pública (to ridicule).

pillow [ˈpiləu] *n* almohada *f* (cushion for the head) || TECH cojinete *m* || mundillo *m*, almohadilla *f* (in lace making).

pillow [ˈpiləu] *vt* apoyar en una almohada (to lean on a pillow) || servir de almohada para (to serve as a pillow) || *to pillow one's head on one's arms* reposar la cabeza en los brazos.

pillow block [-blɔk] *n* TECH cojinete *m*.

pillowcase [-keis] *n* funda *f* de almohada.

pillow lace [-leis] *n* encaje *m* de bolillos.

pillowslip [-slip] *n* funda *f* de almohada.

pilose [ˈpailəus] *adj* piloso, sa.

pilosity [paiˈlɔsiti] *n* pilosidad *f*.

pilot [ˈpailət] *n* MAR piloto *m*, práctico *m* (of the harbour) | timonel *m*, piloto *m* (of a boat) || AVIAT piloto *m* || piloto *m* (light) || FIG guía *m* & *f* (guide) || *US* quitapiedras *m inv* (of a locomotive) || TECH guía *f* || — *airline pilot* piloto de línea || *automatic pilot* piloto automático || *coast pilot* práctico *m* || *test pilot* piloto de pruebas.
◆ *adj* modelo, piloto; *a pilot factory* una fábrica modelo; *pilot scheme* o *study* proyecto *m* *or* experiencia *f* piloto.

pilot [ˈpailət] *vt* pilotar (a plane, a ship, etc.) || guiar, dirigir (to guide) || — *to pilot a bill through Parliament* defender un proyecto de ley en el Parlamento || *to pilot through* llevar a buen término (talks, etc.), guiar (people, etc.).

pilotage [-idʒ] *n* pilotaje *m*.

pilot balloon [-bəˈluːn] *n* globo *m* sonda.

pilot boat [-bəut] *n* MAR barco *m* del práctico.

pilot engine [-ˈendʒin] *n* locomotora *f* exploradora.

pilot fish [-fiʃ] *n* pez *m* piloto (fish).

pilothouse [-haus] *n* *US* MAR timonera *f*, cabina *f* del piloto.

pilot lamp [-læmp] *n* piloto *m*, lámpara *f* indicadora.

pilot light [-lait] *n* piloto *m*, lámpara *f* indicadora.

pilous [ˈpailəs] *adj* piloso, sa.

pilular [ˈpiljulə*] *adj* en forma de píldora.

pimento [piˈmentəu] *n* BOT pimienta *f* de Jamaica || pimiento *m* morrón (pimiento).
— OBSERV El plural de *pimento* es *pimento* o *pimentos*.

pimiento [piˈmentəu] *n* pimiento *m* morrón.

pimp [pimp] *n* chulo *m*, rufián *m*, proxeneta *m*, alcahuete *m*.

pimp [pimp] *vi* alcahuetear || *to pimp for* ser alcahuete de.

pimpernel [ˈpimpənel] *n* BOT murajes *m pl*, pimpinela *f* (creeping plant).

pimple [-l] *n* grano *m*; *I came out in pimples* me salieron granos || espinilla *f*, grano *m* (on the face).

pimpled [-ld]; **pimply** [-li] *adj* espinilloso, sa; con espinillas (face) || con granos (body).

pin [pin] *n* alfiler *m* (used in sewing, etc.) || horquilla *f* (hairpin) || imperdible *m* (safety pin) || broche *m* (brooch) || insignia *f* (emblem) || pinza *f*, alfiler *m* (for washing) || clavija *f* (peg) || MUS clavija *f* (string instruments) || macho *m* (of a dovetail joint) || rodillo *m* (rolling pin) || TECH pezonera *f* (linchpin) | chaveta *f* (cotter) | paletón *m* (of key) | perno *m* (bolt) || FIG & FAM pimiento *m*; *it's not worth a pin* no vale un pimiento || SP banderín *m* (in golf) | bolo *m* (skittle) || barrilete *m* (cask) || — FIG *alike as two pins* como dos gotas de agua | *as clean as a new pin* limpio como los chorros del oro, limpio como un espejo *or* como una patena || MAR *belaying pin* cabilla *f* || *drawing pin* chincheta *f* || *firing pin* percutor *m* || *rolling pin* rodillo *m* | FIG *you could have heard a pin drop* se podía oír el vuelo de una mosca.
◆ *pl* FAM zancas *f*, patas *f* (legs) || — *for two pins I'd hit him* un poco más y le pego || FIG & FAM *he is shaky on his pins* le flaquean las piernas || FIG *pins and needles* hormigueo *m*.

pin [pin] *vt* prender con alfileres; *to pin the hem of a dress* prender el dobladillo de un vestido con alfileres || sujetar (to hold, to fix) || prender *or* coger con un alfiler; *to pin banknotes together* prender billetes de banco con un alfiler || ARCH apuntalar (a wall) || TECH enclavijar (with pegs) | enchavetar (with cotters) | sujetar con perno (with a bolt).
◆ *phr v* ***to pin down*** sujetar a la fuerza (to hold down) | sujetar (to fix, to attach); *pin it down with a few nails* sujétalo con unos clavos | hacer que alguien concrete (to make s.o. specify) | encontrar, localizar (to find) | precisar; *there's sth. wrong but I can't quite pin it down* hay algo que no va, pero no puedo precisar lo que es | inmovilizar (the enemy, etc.) || — *to pin sth. down to* atribuir algo especialmente a || ***to pin on*** prender (a brooch, a medal); *to pin a brooch on one's lapel* prender un broche en la solapa | prender con alfiler (with pins) | poner, cifrar; *to pin one's hopes on sth.* poner sus esperanzas en algo | acusar; *they tried to pin the robbery on him* intentaron acusarle del robo || ***to pin out*** extender con el rodillo (dought) || ***to pin up*** fijar, sujetar; *how can I pin this po.ter up?* ¿cómo puedo sujetar este cartel? | sujetar [con horquillas] (hair) | sujetar con chinchetas (with drawing pins) | ARCH apuntalar.

PIN *abbr of [personal identification number]* NIP, número de identificación personal.

pinafore [-əfɔː*] *n* delantal *m* (apron) || *US* babero *m* (for baby) || *pinafore dress* falda *f* con peto.

pinaster [paiˈnæstə*] *n* BOT pino *m* rodeno.

pinball table [ˈpinbɔːlˌteibl] *n* billar *m* automático.

pince-nez [ˈpɛ̃ːnsnei] *inv n* quevedos *m pl*.

pincers [ˈpinsəz] *pl n* TECH tenazas *f*, tenaza *f sing* || ZOOL pinzas *f* || MIL *pincers movement* movimiento *m* de tenazas.

pinch [pintʃ] *n* pellizco *m*; *she gave him a pinch* le dio un pellizco || pizca *f*; *a pinch of salt* una pizca de sal || pulgarada *f* (of tobacco) || FIG necesidad *f* (need) || FAM robo *m* (robbery) | pesca *f*, captura *f* (arrest) || — FIG *at a pinch* en caso de necesidad | *to feel the pinch* empezar a pasar apuros | *to feel the pinch of hunger* empezar a sentir hambre | *to take sth. with a pinch of salt* admitir algo con reservas | *when it comes to the pinch* cuando llega el momento decisivo.

pinch [pintʃ] *vt* pellizcar; *to pinch s.o.'s arm* pellizcar a alguien en el brazo || pillarse, cogerse; *he pinched his finger in the door* se pilló el dedo con la puerta || apretar; *do the new shoes pinch you?* ¿te aprietan los zapatos nuevos? || FIG herir (pride) | poner en un apuro *or* en un aprieto (to put in a tight spot) | atenazar (hunger) || FAM mangar, birlar (to steal); *he had his car pinched* le mangaron el coche | robar (an idea) | coger (to grab) | quitar (to take away) | agarrar, pescar (to arrest) || — *pinched features* cara cansada || *pinched with cold* aterido, transido de frío || *to be pinched for* andar mal de, andar escaso de (to be short of) || *to pinch off* quitar con los dedos || *to pinch pennies* escatimar gastos.
◆ *vi* apretar; *these shoes pinch* estos zapatos aprietan || economizar (to economize) || tacañear, escatimar (to overeconomize) || FIG *he knows where the shoe pinches* sabe donde le aprieta el zapato.

pinch bar [-bɑː*] *n* pie *m* de cabra, alzaprima *f*.

pinchbeck [-bek] *n* imitación *f*.
◆ *adj* de pacotilla, de imitación.

pinchcock [-kɔk] *n* TECH abrazadera *f*.

pinched [-t] *adj* → **pinch.**

pinchers [-əz] *pl n* TECH tenazas *f*, tenaza *f sing*.

pinch-hit [-hit] *vi* US SP batear en sustitución del titular (in baseball) || US FAM sustituir a otro en un momento de apuro (to substitute in an emergency).

pinch hitter [-ˌhitə*] *n* US SP bateador *m* suplente || US FAM sustituto *m* en un momento de apuro.

pinchpenny [-ˈpeni] *adj* tacaño, ña.

pincushion [ˈpinˌkuʃən] *n* acerico *m*.

Pindar [ˈpində*] *pr n* Píndaro *m* (Greek author).

pine [pain] *n* BOT pino *m* (tree, wood) || FAM piña *f* (pineapple) || — *Aleppo pine* pino carrasco || *cluster pine* pino marítimo *or* rodeno || *Scotch pine* pino albar *or* royo || *stone* o *umbrella pine* pino piñonero *or* real.

pine [pain] *vi* desfallecer, languidecer || — *to pine away* consumirse, languidecer || *to pine for* anhelar, suspirar por.

pineal body [ˈpiniəlˈbɔdi]; **pineal gland** [ˈpiniəlglænd] *n* ANAT glándula *f* pineal.

pineapple [ˈpainˌæpl] *n* piña *f*, ananás *m*.

pinecone [ˈpainkəun] *n* BOT piña *f*.

pine grove [ˈpaingrəuv] *n* pinar *m*.

pine kernel [ˈpainˌkəːnl] *n* piñón *m*.

pine marten [ˈpainˌmɑːtin] *n* ZOOL marta *f*.

pine needle [ˈpainˌniːdl] *n* BOT aguja *f* de pino.

pinery [ʒpainəri] *n* BOT plantación *f* de piñas *or* ananás (pineapple plantation) | pinar *m* (pine grove).

pine seed [ˈpainsiːd] *n* piñón *m*.

pine tree [ˈpaintriː] *n* pino *m*.

pinetum [paiˈniːtəm] *n* BOT pinar *m*.
— OBSERV El plural de *pinetum* es *pineta*.

pinewood [ˈpainwud] *n* pinar *m* (forest) || pino *m*, madera *f* de pino (wood).

pinfeather [ˈpinfeðə*] *n* ZOOL cañón *m*.

pinfold [ˈpinfəuld] *n* perrera *f* (for stray dogs) || depósito *m* (for stray animals).

ping [piŋ] *n* sonido *m* corto y metálico || silbido *m* (of a bullet).

ping [piŋ] *vi* producir un sonido corto y metálico || silbar, zumbar (a bullet) || AUT picar.

ping-pong [ˈpiŋpɔŋ] *n* SP ping-pong *m*, tenis *m* de mesa.

pinguid [ˈpiŋgwid] *adj* pingüe || feraz (soil).

pinhead [ˈpinhed] *n* cabeza *f* de alfiler || FIG nimiedad *f*, insignificancia *f* || US FAM tonto, ta; mentecato, ta (idiot).

pinhole [ˈpinhəul] *n* agujero *m* de alfiler.

pinion [ˈpinjən] *n* ala *f* (wing) || TECH piñón *m* || *pinion drive* transmisión *f* por engranaje.

pinion [ˈpinjən] *vt* cortar las alas a (birds) || maniatar (people).

pink [piŋk] *n* clavel *m* (flower, plant) || rosa *m* (colour) || levita *f* roja (hunting coat) || FIG modelo *m*, dechado *m* (example) || FAM rojillo, lla (leftist) || *in the pink of health* rebosante de salud.
◆ *adj* rosa (colour) || FAM rojillo, lla (leftwing) || — FIG & FAM *strike me pink!* ¡caray! || FIG *to tickle (s.o.) pink* encantar, gustar mucho; *he was tickled pink by the present* le encantó el regalo; divertir mucho, hacer mucha gracia a (to amuse intensely).

pink [piŋk] *vt* picar (to ornament with holes) || festonear (to edge) | herir levemente (to wound) || *to pink out* embellecer.
◆ *vi* AUT picar.

pinkeye [ˈpiŋkai] *n* MED conjuntivitis *f* aguda.

pinkie [ˈpiŋki] *n* FAM dedo *m* meñique.

pinking shears [ˈpiŋkiŋʃiəz] *pl n* tijeras *f* dentadas.

pinkish [piŋkiʃ] *adj* rosáceo, a.

pin money [ˈpinˌmʌni] *n* dinero *m* para gastos menudos.

pinna [ˈpinə] *n* BOT pina *f*, folíolo *m* || ZOOL ala *f* (of birds) | aleta *f* (of fishes) || ANAT pabellón *m* de la oreja.

pinnace [ˈpinis] *n* MAR pinaza *f*.

pinnacle [ˈpinəkl] *n* pináculo *m* (turret) || pico *m*, cima *f* (peak) || FIG cumbre *f*, apogeo *m*, pináculo *m*; *on the pinnacle of one's glory* en la cumbre de la gloria.

pinnacle [ˈpinəkl] *vt* coronar, rematar (to top, to crown) || FIG poner en un pedestal.

pinnate [ˈpinit] *adj* BOT pinada (leaf).

pinniped [ˈpiniped] *adj* ZOOL pinnípedo, da.

pinny [ˈpini] *n* delantal *m*.

pinole [pəˈnəuliː] *n* pinole *m*.

pinpoint [ˈpinpɔint] *n* punta *f* de alfiler.
◆ *adj* preciso, sa; exacto, ta (exact) || de precisión (shooting).

pinpoint [ˈpinpɔint] *vt* localizar con toda precisión (to locate) || apuntar con precisión (to aim) || señalar (to point out) || determinar con precisión (to determine).

pinprick [ˈpinprik] *n* alfilerazo *m* (with a pin) || pinchazo *m* (small puncture) || FIG puya *f*, pinchazo *m* (malicious remark).

pinstripe [ˈpinstraip] *adj* rayado, da; a rayas.

pint [paint] *n* pinta *f* [medida de líquido equivalente a 0, 568 litros en Gran Bretaña y a 0, 473 en Estados Unidos] || FAM cerveza *f* (beer) | caña *f* (pot of beer).

pinta [ˈpintə] *n* MED pinta *f*.

pintail [ˈpinteil] *n* ZOOL ánade *m* de cola larga.

pintle [ˈpintəl] *n* TECH perno *m* (bolt) || MAR macho *m* (of rudder).

pinto [ˈpintəu] *n* caballo *m* pinto (horse) || judía *f* pinta (bean).

pinto bean [-biːn] *n* judía *f* pinta.

pint-size [-saiz]; **pint-sized** [-d] *adj* muy pequeño, ña; diminuto, ta.

pinup [ˈpinʌp] *n* FAM fotografía *f* de una modelo | mujer *f* atractiva || *she is his pinup* para él es la mujer ideal.

pinup girl [-gəːl] *n* FAM modelo *f* fotográfica | mujer *f* atractiva.

pinwheel [ˈpinwiːl] *n* US rueda *f* de fuegos artificiales, girándula *f* (fireworks) | molinillo (toy).

pinworm [ˈpinwəːm] *n* lombriz *f* intestinal.

piolet [ˈpiːəlei] *n* «piolet» *m*, bastón *m* de montañero [AMER piqueta *f*].

pioneer [ˌpaiəˈniə*] *n* colonizador *m*, pionero *m* (early settler) || MIL zapador *m* || FIG pionero *m*, iniciador *m*, adelantado *m*; *a pioneer of flying* un pionero de la aviación.

pioneer [ˌpaiəˈniə*] *vt* promover (to foster) || sentar las bases de (to lay the foundations for) || iniciar, ser el iniciador de (to initiate) || colonizar (to colonize).
◆ *vi* abrir *or* enseñar el camino.

pioneering [ˌpaiəˈniəriŋ] *adj* pionero, ra; innovador, ra.

pious [ˈpaiəs] *adj* piadoso, sa (devout) || FAM beato, ta (excessively religious) || FIG digno de alabanza; *pious intention* intención digna de alabanza.

piousness [ˈpaiəsnis] *n* piedad *f* || FAM beatería *f* (religious bigotry).

pip [pip] *n* VET moquillo *m* (of birds) || punto *m* (on dice, playing cards) || MIL estrella *f* (on uniform) || BOT flor *f* (flower) | pipa *f*, pepita *f* (seed) || RAD señal *f* [para dar las horas] (time signal) || FAM alhaja *f*, perla *f* (highly prized person) || — FAM *to give s.o. the pip* ponerle a uno enfermo | *to have the pip* estar disgustado.

pip [pip] *vt* romper (el cascarón) (a bird hatching) || vencer (to beat) || fastidiar (to spoil) || dar en (to hit) || suspender (to fail s.o. in an examination) || ser suspendido en (to fail an examination) || hacer el vacío a (to ignore) || FIG *to pip s.o. at the post* ganarle a uno por la mano.
◆ *vi* romper el cascarón (a bird) || perder (to lose) || fracasar (to fail) || FAM *to pip out* estirar la pata (to die).

pipage [ˈpaipidʒ] *n* transporte *m* por tuberías (transportation) || precio *m* del transporte por tuberías (cost) || tuberías *f pl* (pipes).

pipe [paip] *n* pipa *f* (cask) || tubo *m*, tubería *f*, cañería *f*, conducto *m*; *gas pipe* tubo de gas || MUS caramillo *m*, flautín *m*, flauta *f* (small flute) | tubo *m* (of bagpipes) | tubo *m*, cañón *m* (of an organ) || MAR pito *m* (whistle) || pipa *f* (smoking device) || — *pipe of peace* pipa de la paz || FAM *put that in your pipe and smoke it!* ¡chúpate ésa!
◆ *pl* MUS gaita *f sing* (bagpipes) || tubería *f sing*, cañería *f sing*, tubos *m*; *the water pipes* la tubería del agua (see OBSERV).
— OBSERV Technically speaking, the words *tubería* and *cañería* mean a *set of pipes*. They are however commonly used to denote a single *pipe* and the plural form *tuberías* and *cañerías* to denote *pipes*.

pipe [paip] *vt* conducir por tubería (water, etc.) || transportar por oleoducto (oil) || instalar tuberías en (to furnish with pipes) || MUS interpretar *or* tocar con el caramillo || adornar con ribete (to adorn cloth with piping) || — *to pipe one's eye* llorar || *to pipe the captain aboard* pitar cuando sube el capitán a bordo.
◆ *vi* MUS tocar la gaita (to play the pipes) | tocar el caramillo (flute) || chillar (to make a shrill sound) || MAR convocar a la tripulación

(to summon the crew) || — FAM *to pipe down* callarse | *to pipe up* empezar a hablar.

pipe clay ['paipklei] *n* espuma *f* de mar (for making pipes) || blanco *m* de España (for cleaning).

pipe-clay ['paipklei] *vt* limpiar con blanco de España.

pipe cleaner [-,kli:nə*] *n* limpiapipas *m inv.*

piped music [-d,mju:zik] *n* hilo *m* musical.

pipe dream [-dri:m] *n* FIG castillos *m pl* en el aire, ilusiones *f pl.*

pipefish [-fiʃ] *n* ZOOL aguja *f.*

pipeful [-ful] *n* pipa *f* (of tobacco).

pipeline [-lain] *n* oleoducto *m* (for oil) || gasoducto *m* (for gas) || tubería *f* (for water) || FIG conducto *m* (of information) || *to be in the pipeline* estar en trámite.

pipe organ [-,ɔ:gən] *n* MUS órgano *m.*

piper [-ə*] *n* MUS gaitero *m* | flautista *m* || — FIG *he who pays the piper calls the tune* manda el que paga | *to pay the piper* pagar el pato *or* los vidrios rotos.

piperaceae [pipə'reisii] *pl n* piperáceas *f.*

pipe tobacco ['paiptə,bækəu] *n* tabaco *m* de pipa.

pipette; *US* **pipet** [pi'pet] *n* CHEM pipeta *f.*

piping ['paipiŋ] *n* sonido *m* de la gaita (music of pipes) || sonido *m* de la flauta (of a flute) || gorjeo *m* (of birds) || pitido *m* (whistle) || tubería *f*, tuberías *f pl* (system of pipes) || ribete *m* (decoration on cloth) || adorno *m* hecho sobre un pastel (on cakes).

◆ *adj* agudo, da; aflautado, da; *a piping voice* una voz aguda.

◆ *adv* *to be piping hot* estar hirviendo.

pipistrelle [,pipi'strel] *n* pipistrelo *m* (bat).

pipit ['pipit] *n* pitpit *m* (bird).

pipkin ['pipkin] *n* puchero *m* de barro.

pippin ['pipin] *n* reineta *f* (apple).

pipsqueak ['pipskwi:k] *n* FAM cero *m* a la izquierda.

piquancy ['pi:kənsi] *n* picante *m*, lo picante.

piquant ['pi:kənt] *adj* picante.

piquantly [-li] *adv* de modo picante.

pique [pi:k] *n* resentimiento *m*, pique *m* (resentment) || — *he did it out of pique* lo hizo por resentimiento || *to be in a pique* estar resentido.

pique [pi:k] *vt* FIG herir (to hurt); *to pique s.o. with a remark* herir a alguien con una observación || picar (to annoy) || FIG picar; *to pique s.o.'s curiosity* picarle a alguien la curiosidad.

piqué ['pi:kei] *n* piqué *m* (material).

piquet [pi'ket] *n* juego *m* de los cientos.

piracy ['paiərəsi] *n* piratería *f* || edición *f* pirata (of books).

Piraeus [pai'ri:əs] *pr n* GEOGR El Pireo *m.*

piragua [pi'rægwə] *n* piragua *f* (boat).

piranha [pi'rænə] *n* piraña *f*, piraya *f* (fish).

pirate ['paiərit] *n* pirata *m* || — FIG *pirate edition* edición *f* pirata | *pirate of the air* pirata del aire | *pirate radio* radio *f* pirata.

pirate ['paiərit] *vt* hacer una edición pirata de.

◆ *vi* piratear.

piratical [pai'rætikəl] *adj* pirata, pirático, ca.

pirogue [pi'rəug] *n* piragua *f* (boat).

pirouette [,piru'et] *n* pirueta *f*, cabriola *f.*

pirouette [,piru'et] *vi* hacer piruetas, hacer cabriolas.

Pisces ['pisi:z] *pl n* ASTR Piscis *m.*

pisciculture ['pisikʌltʃə*] *n* piscicultura *f.*

pisciculturist [,pis'ikʌltʃərəst] *n* piscicultor *m.*

pisciform ['pisifɔ:m] *adj* pisciforme.

piscina [pi'si:nə] *n* REL piscina *f* || vivero *m* de peces (for fishes).

— OBSERV El plural de la palabra inglesa *piscina* es *piscinas* o *piscinae.*

piscine ['pisain] *adj* pisciforme (like a fish) || de peces (relating to fish).

piscivorous [pi'sivərəs] *adj* ZOOL piscívoro, ra.

pisiform ['pisifɔ:m] *adj* pisiforme.

pismire ['pismaiə*] *n* hormiga *f* (ant).

piss [pis] *n* POP meada *f.*

piss [pis] *vi* POP mear || POP *piss off!* ¡vete al cuerno!

pissed [-t] *adj* POP trompa (drunk) || — POP *he got pissed* cogió una trompa, se puso trompa || POP *to be pissed off at* estar furioso con.

pistache [pis'tɑ:ʃ]; **pistachio** [pis'tɑ:ʃiəu] *n* pistachero *m*, alfóncigo *m* (tree) || pistacho *m*, alfóncigo *m* (fruit).

pistil ['pistil] *n* BOT pistilo *m.*

pistol ['pistl] *n* pistola *f* || *pistol shot* pistoletazo *m*, tiro *m* de pistola.

piston ['pistən] *n* TECH émbolo *m*, pistón *m* || MUS llave *f*, pistón *m.*

piston ring [-riŋ] *n* AUT aro *m* del émbolo, segmento *m* del émbolo.

piston rod [-rɔd] *n* AUT vástago *m* del émbolo.

piston stroke [-strəuk] *n* AUT carrera *f* del émbolo.

piston travel [-,trævl] *n* AUT recorrido *m* del émbolo.

piston valve [-vælv] *n* MUS llave *f*, pistón *m.*

pit [pit] *n* pozo *m*, hoyo *m* (natural or man-made hole) || trampa *f* (trap) || MIN mina *f* (of coal, etc.) || cantera *f* (quarry) || picadura *f*, señal *f* (of smallpox) || pozo *m* (in a garage) || reñidero *m* (for fighting cocks) || SP taller *m*, box *m* (in motor racing) | foso *m* (of jumpers) || THEATR patio *m* de butacas (seats) | foso *m* de la orquesta (orchestra space) || ANAT boca *f* (of the stomach) || FIG abismo *m* (abyss) | infierno *m* (hell) || *US* mercado *m*, bolsa *f* (exchange) | hueso *m* (of fruits) || — SP *pit stop* parada *f* en boxes (in motor racing) || FIG *to dig a pit for* tender una trampa a.

◆ *pl* FIG & FAM infierno *m sing.*

pit [pit] *vt* oponer; *to pit one thing against another* oponer una cosa a otra || picar; *face pitted by smallpox* cara picada de viruelas || llenar de hoyitos, hacer hoyos en (a surface); *the sand was pitted by the rain* la arena estaba llena de hoyitos después de la lluvia || echar a pelear; *to pit two animals* echar a pelear a dos animales || almacenar (to store) || *US* deshuesar (a fruit) || *to pit o.s. against s.o.* medirse con alguien, luchar con alguien || *to pit one's wits against* medirse con (in a test of knowledge, etc.).

◆ *vi* estar picado de viruelas (with smallpox) || llenarse de agujeros.

pita ['pi:tə] *n* BOT pita *f*, agave *m* [AMER maguey *m*].

pit-a-pat ['pitə'pæt] *n* latido *m*, palpitación *f* (beating) || paso *m* ligero (footstep).

◆ *adv* *her heart went pit-a-pat* su corazón latía rápidamente.

pit-a-pat ['pitə'pæt] *vi* ir con paso ligero (to move) || latir rápidamente (heart).

pitch [pitʃ] *n* pez *f*, brea *f* (black sticky substance) || resina *f* (resin) || puesto *m* (space in market, etc.); *a beggar in his usual pitch* un mendigo en su puesto habitual || charlatanería *f* (sales patter) || SP campo *m*; *football pitch* campo de fútbol || tiro *m*, lanzamiento *m* (a throw) || MUS tono *m* (tone of sound) || grado *m* de inclinación, inclinación *f* (of slope) || grado *m*, nivel *m* (of joy, etc.) || MIN & GEOL buzamiento *m* (dip) || TECH paso *m* (of screw, gearwheel, propellor) || ARCH pendiente *f* (of a roof) || MAR cabezada *f* (rolling of ship) || — *feelings were raised to a high pitch* el ambiente estaba tenso || *he ran full pitch into the door* se dio de narices con la puerta || *to reach fever pitch* llegar a su punto culminante (emotion, tensión, etc.) || *to reach such a pitch that* llegar a tal extremo que.

pitch [pitʃ] *vt* armar, montar; *to pitch a tent* armar una tienda || colocar (to place) || echar, lanzar, tirar, arrojar (to throw); *to pitch hay* echar heno || SP tirar, lanzar (to deliver the ball) || MUS entonar || embrear (to tar) || calafatear (to caulk) || contar; *to pitch s.o. a story* contar una historia a alguien || — *US* FIG *to be in there pitching* estar luchando, estar bregando (to strive) || *to be pitched off one's horse* ser desarzonado, caerse del caballo || MIL *to pitch battle* trabar combate || *to pitch camp* acampar || FIG *to pitch it strong* exagerar | *to pitch one's aims very high* picar muy alto || *to pitch s.o. out* echar a alguien || *to pitch sth. away* tirar algo.

◆ *vi* acampar (to encamp) || instalarse (to install o.s.) || MAR cabecear (a ship) || caerse, caer (to fall); *he pitched sideways* se cayó de costado; *he pitched off his horse* se cayó del caballo || inclinarse (to dip) || lanzar (in baseball, etc.) || — *to pitch in* ponerse a trabajar (to start working), echar una mano (to lend a hand), contribuir (to contribute) || *to pitch into* atacar (to attack), arremeter contra (to attack verbally), echar un rapapolvo a (to scold severely), echarse encima de (a meal), emprender con energía (a job) || *to pitch upon* tropezar con (to bump into, to come across), decidirse por (to choose).

pitch and toss ['pitʃən'tɔs] *n* rayuela *f.*

pitch-black ['pitʃ'blæk] *adj* negro como el carbón (intensely black) || oscuro como boca de lobo (extremely dark).

pitchblende ['pitʃblend] *n* MIN pechblenda *f*, pecblenda *f.*

pitch-dark ['pitʃdɑ:k] *adj* oscuro como boca de lobo.

pitched battle ['pitʃt'bætl] *n* batalla *f* campal.

pitcher ['pitʃə*] *n* cántaro *m*, cántara *f*, jarra *f*, jarro *m* (jug) || *US* SP lanzador *m* (in baseball).

pitchfork ['pitʃfɔ:k] *n* horca *f*, bieldo *m.*

pitchfork ['pitʃfɔ:k] *vt* echar con la horca (hay, etc.) || FIG catapultar (into a post).

pitching ['pitʃiŋ] *n* cabeceo *m* (of a boat) || lanzamiento *m* (throwing).

pitch pine ['pitʃpain] *n* BOT pino *m* tea.

pitch pipe ['pitʃpaip] *n* MUS diapasón *m.*

pitchy ['pitʃi] *adj* negro, gra (black) || oscuro, ra (dark) || parecido a la pez (like pitch).

piteous ['pitiəs] *adj* patético, ca; lastimoso, sa.

pitfall ['pitfɔ:l] *n* FIG escollo *m*, peligro *m* (danger) | trampa *f* (trap) | dificultad *f*, pega *f* (difficulty).

pith [piθ] *n* médula *f* (medulla) || FIG médula *f*, meollo *m*, esencia *f*; *the pith of a matter* el meollo de una cuestión | vigor *m* (vigour).

pith [piθ] *vt* matar cortando la médula (to kill by breaking spinal cord) || quitar la médula a (to remove pith from a plant).

pithead ['pithed] *n* MIN bocamina *f.*

pithecanthrope [,piθikæn'θrəup]; **pithecanthropus** [,piθikæn'θrəupəs] *n* pitecántropo *m.*

— OBSERV El plural de la palabra inglesa *pithecanthropus* es *pithecanthropi.*

pit helmet ['piθ,helmit] *n* salacot *m.*

pithiness ['piθinis] *n* fuerza *f* (vigour) || concisión *f* (conciseness).

pithy [piθi] *adj* FIG conciso, sa (concise) | sustancial | expresivo, va ‖ meduloso, sa (like or containing pith).

pitiable [ˈpitiəbl] *adj* lastimoso, sa; lastimero, ra (arousing pity) ‖ lamentable (bad) ‖ *it was a pitiable sight* daba lástima *or* pena verlo.

pitiful [ˈpitiful] *adj* lastimoso, sa; lastimero, ra; digno de compasión (arousing pity) ‖ despreciable, lamentable (contemptible) ‖ *it was pitiful* daba lástima.

pitifully [-i] *adv* lastimosamente, lastimeramente (arousing pity) ‖ lamentablemente (lamentably) ‖ *to cry pitifully* llorar que da lástima.

pitiless [ˈpitilis] *adj* despiadado, da; cruel, implacable.

pitman [ˈpitmən] *n* minero *m* (miner) ‖ pocero *m* (well digger) ‖ US TECH barra *f* de conexión.

— OBSERV El plural de *pitman* es *pitmen*, cuando significa *minero* o *pocero*, y *pitmans* cuando significa *barra de conexión*.

piton [ˈpiːtɔn] *n* pitón *m*, clavija *f* de escala (in mountaineering).

pitprop [ˈpitprɔp] *n* puntal *m*.

pit saw [ˈpitsɔː] *n* TECH sierra *f* abrazadera.

pitta bread [ˈpiːtəˌbred] *n* pan *m* griego *or* árabe.

pittance [ˈpitəns] *n* miseria *f*; *his wage is a pittance* tiene un sueldo de miseria.

pitted [pitid] *adj* picado de viruelas (pockmarked) ‖ US deshuesado, da (fruit).

pitter-patter [ˈpitəˌpætə*] *n* golpeteo *m* (tapping) ‖ tamborileo *m* (of rain) ‖ pasos *m pl* ligeros (light steps).

◆ *adv* *to go pitter-patter* golpetear (to tap), tamborilear, repiquetear (rain).

pitter-patter [ˈpitəˌpætə*] *vi* golpetear (to tap) ‖ tamborilear, repiquetear (rain).

pituita [piˈtjuːitə] *n* ANAT pituita *f*.

— OBSERV El plural de la palabra inglesa es *pituitae*.

pituitary [piˈtjuːtəri] *adj* pituitario, ria; *pituitary gland* o *body* glándula pituitaria.

◆ *n* ANAT pituitaria *f*, glándula *f* pituitaria.

pit viper [ˈpitˌvaipə*] *n* crótalo *m* (snake).

pity [ˈpiti] *n* compasión *f* (sympathy); *to move s.o. to pity* mover a uno a compasión, inspirar compasión a uno ‖ lástima *f*, pena *f*; *it's a pity that it's raining* es una lástima que esté lloviendo ‖ — *for pity's sake* ¡por amor de Dios!, ¡por piedad! ‖ *man without pity* hombre sin piedad *or* despiadado ‖ *more's the pity* tanto peor ‖ *out of pity* por piedad ‖ *to have* o *to take pity on, to feel pity for* tener lástima de, compadecerse *or* apiadarse de ‖ *what a pity!* ¡qué lástima!, ¡qué pena!

pity [ˈpiti] *vt* compadecerse de, apiadarse de ‖ — *I pity him* me da lástima ‖ *you are to be pitied* eres digno de compasión, mereces compasión.

pitying [-iŋ] *adj* de lástima, compasivo, va.

Pius [ˈpaiəs] *pr n* Pío *m*; *Pius IX* Pío Nono.

pivot [ˈpivət] *n* TECH gorrón *m*, pivote *m* ‖ SP pivote *m* (in basketball) ‖ FIG eje *m*, base *f* (central element).

◆ *adj* giratorio, ria; que gira (which pivots) ‖ FIG esencial, fundamental.

pivot [ˈpivət] *vt* montar sobre un gorrón *or* un pivote (to mount on a pivot) ‖ hacer girar (to spin).

◆ *vi* girar sobre su eje, dar vueltas sobre su eje (to turn) ‖ FIG *to pivot on* depender de, basarse en.

pivotal [-l] *adj* giratorio, ria; que gira (which pivots) ‖ FIG esencial, fundamental (fundamental).

pixie [ˈpiksi] *n* duendecillo *m*.

pixilated; pixillated [ˈpiksileitid] *adj* US FAM chiflado, da.

pixy [ˈpiksi] *n* duendecillo *m*.

pizza [ˈpiːtsə] *n* CULIN «pizza» *f*.

pizzeria [pitsəˈriːə] *n* «pizzería» *f*.

pizzicato [ˌpitsiˈkaːtəu] *n* MUS pizzicato *m*.

◆ *adj/adv* pizzicato, punteado.

— OBSERV El plural del sustantivo inglés *pizzicato* es *pizzicatos* o *pizzicati*.

pizzle [ˈpizəl] *n* vergajo *m*.

PP *abbr of [Place]* Pl., plaza.

placable [ˈplækəbl] *adj* aplacable, apacible.

placard [ˈplækaːd] *n* cartel *m* (poster, bill) ‖ letrero *m* (notice).

placard [ˈplækaːd] *vt* colocar *or* pegar carteles en (to place placards) ‖ anunciar en carteles (to advertise).

placate [pləˈkeit] *vt* apaciguar, aplacar.

placatory [ˈplækətəri] *adj* apaciguador, ra.

place [pleis] *n* lugar *m*, sitio *m* (spot, position); *a place for everything and everything in its place* un sitio para cada cosa y cada cosa en su sitio; *this is a pleasant place* es un lugar agradable; *a very elegant place* un sitio muy elegante; *he lost his place in the queue* perdió el sitio en la cola ‖ puesto *m*, empleo *m*, colocación *f* (post) ‖ página *f*; *I lost my place in the book* perdí la página en el libro ‖ parte *f*, momento *m*; *she always cries at the sad places in the book* siempre llora en las partes tristes del libro ‖ local *m* (premises) ‖ edificio *m* (building) ‖ plaza *f* (square) ‖ casa *f* (house); *let's all go to my place* vayamos todos a mi casa; *his place in the country* su casa de campo ‖ sitio *m* (seat, etc.); *are there any places left?* ¿queda sitio? ‖ cubierto *m* (at table); *to lay a place for* poner un cubierto para ‖ asiento *m*, localidad *f* (seat in theatre, etc.) ‖ SP lugar *m*, posición *f*; *in first place* en primer lugar ‖ — *all over the place* por todas partes ‖ FIG *another place* la otra Cámara (in Parliament) ‖ *any place* en cualquier sitio (without motion), a cualquier sitio (motion towards) ‖ *from place to place* de un sitio para otro ‖ *if I were in your place I would not do that* yo en tu lugar *or* yo que tú no haría eso ‖ *in another place* en otra parte ‖ *in no place* en ninguna parte ‖ *in place* en su sitio ‖ *in place of* en lugar de, en vez de ‖ *in the first place* en primer lugar ‖ *in the next place* luego ‖ *it is not your place to criticize* no eres quien para criticar ‖ *market place* mercado *m* ‖ *out of place* fuera de lugar ‖ *people in high places* gente bien situada ‖ *place of business* despacho *m* (office), comercio *m* (shop), domicilio *m* social (premises) ‖ *place of decimal* decimal *m* ‖ *place of refuge* refugio *m* ‖ *place of residence* domicilio *m* ‖ *place of worship* lugar de culto ‖ REL *the Holy Places* los Santos Lugares ‖ *there's no place for you here* estás de más aquí, estás sobrando aquí ‖ *this is no place for children* éste no es lugar para niños, este sitio no es para niños ‖ *to back a horse for a place* apostar a un caballo colocado ‖ *to change places* cambiar de sitio ‖ FIG *to fall into place* encajar (set of events, facts) ‖ *to give place to* ceder el paso a ‖ FAM *to go places* llegar lejos (to get ahead), viajar (to travel), hacer progresos (to make progress), tener éxito (to be successful) ‖ *to hold sth. in place* sujetar algo ‖ *to keep one in his place* mantener a alguien en su lugar ‖ *to know one's place* saber cuál es su sitio ‖ *to put o.s. in s.o.'s place* ponerse en el lugar de alguien ‖ *to put s.o. in his place* poner a alguien en su sitio ‖ *to put sth. back in its place* devolver algo a su sitio ‖ *to take place* suceder, ocurrir, tener lugar (to happen), tener lugar, celebrarse (a meeting, etc.) ‖ *to take the place of* sustituir a.

place [pleis] *vt* colocar, poner (to put) ‖ situar; *I knew his face but I couldn't place him* su cara me era familiar, pero no la pude situar; *your house is very well placed* su casa está muy bien situada ‖ reconocer (to recognize) ‖ hacer; *place your bets!* ¡hagan juego! ‖ poner; *to place one's confidence in* o *on* o *upon s.o.* poner su confianza en alguien; *to place a matter in s.o.'s hands* poner un asunto en manos de alguien ‖ entonar [la voz] (in speech) ‖ emplear, colocar (to employ) ‖ lograr que se publique, hacer publicar (one's book) ‖ COMM invertir, colocar (money) | colocar, hacer (an order) | encontrar salida para, vender, colocar (to find a market for) ‖ — *to be placed* colocarse, llegar; *to be placed third* colocarse en tercer lugar; clasificarse, quedar clasificado (to be in the first three) ‖ *to be well placed* estar en buena posición ‖ *to place before* someter a (a project, etc.) ‖ *to place one's trust in* fiarse de, confiar en ‖ *we are better placed now* hemos mejorado de posición.

◆ *vi* SP clasificarse.

place-kick [ˈpleiskik] *n* SP tiro *m* libre (in rugby).

placeman [ˈpleismən] *n* arribista *m*.

— OBSERV El plural de *placeman* es *placemen*.

place mat [ˈpleismæt] *n* mantel *m* individual.

placement [ˈpleismənt] *n* colocación *f*.

place-name [ˈpleisneim] *n* topónimo *m*.

◆ *pl* toponimia *f sing*.

placenta [pləˈsentə] *n* ANAT & BOT placenta *f*.

— OBSERV El plural de la palabra inglesa *placenta* es *placentas* o *placentae*.

placer [ˈpleisə*] *n* GEOL placer *m* (of gold).

placer mining [-ˌmainiŋ] *n* MIN explotación *f* de placeres.

placet [ˈpleiset] *n* plácet *m*.

placid [ˈplæsid] *adj* apacible, plácido, da.

placidity [plæˈsiditi] *n* placidez *f*.

placing [ˈpleisiŋ] *n* colocación *f*.

placket [ˈplækit] *n* abertura *f*.

plagal [ˈpleigəl] *adj* MUS plagal.

plagiarism [ˈpleidʒjərizəm] *n* plagio *m*.

plagiarist [ˈpleidʒjərist] *n* plagiario, ria.

plagiarize [ˈpleidʒjəraiz] *vt/vi* plagiar.

plagiary [ˈpleidʒjəri] *n* plagiario, ria (person) ‖ plagio *m* (plagiarism).

plagiostomi [ˌpleidʒiˈɔstəmai] *pl n* plagióstomos *m*.

plague [pleig] *n* peste *f* (disease) ‖ plaga *f* (social scourge); *a plague of vandalism* una plaga de vandalismo ‖ FIG molestia *f*, fastidio *m* (annoyance) ‖ — *plague on it!* ¡maldito sea! ‖ *the ten plagues of Egypt* las diez plagas de Egipto ‖ *to avoid s.o. like the plaga* huir de alguien como de la peste *or* del demonio ‖ *to hate s.o. like the plague* aborrecer *or* odiar a uno ‖ *what a plague she is!* ¡qué pesada es!

plague [pleig] *vt* plagar, infestar; *plagued by insects* plagado de insectos ‖ FIG atormentar; *the memory plagued him* le atormentaba el recuerdo | plagar; *plagued with debts* plagado de deudas | *to plague s.o. with questions* asar a alguien con preguntas.

plaguy; US plaguey [-i] *adj* FAM latoso, sa; molesto, ta; fastidioso, sa; pesado, da.

plaice [pleis] *n* platija *f* (fish).

plaid [plæd] *n* gabán *m* escocés (cloak) ‖ tartán *m* (cloth).

◆ *adj* escocés, esa; de cuadros; *a plaid skirt* una falda escocesa.

plain [plein] *adj* claro, ra; evidente (clear, obvious); *it is plain* está claro, es evidente ‖ simple, sencillo, lla (simple) ‖ completo, ta; *that is plain madness* es una locura completa ‖ sencillo, lla (food) ‖ puro, ra; natural (unmixed) ‖ franco, ca; abierto, ta (frank) ‖ honrado, da (dealings) ‖ natural (unsophisticated) ‖ sin atractivo (unattractive) ‖ simple, sin lujo (living) ‖ — *a plain answer* una respuesta clara

(clear), una respuesta categórica (categorical) || *he made it plain that* dijo claramente que (verbally), dio a entender que (by attitude) || *in plain language* en lenguaje corriente || *is that plain?* ¿está claro? || *it was plain to see that* estaba muy claro que || *let me make this plain* quiero que quede claro || *plain clothes* traje *m sing* de paisano || *plain English* palabras *f pl* claras || *plain flour* harina *f* común || *plain speaking* palabras claras, franqueza *f* || *she's very plain* no vale nada, no es ninguna belleza || *the plain truth* la verdad llana y lisa, la pura verdad || *to do some plain talking* hablar claro || *to make sth. plain (to s.o.)* poner algo de manifiesto (ante alguien); *his question made it plain that he had not been listening* su pregunta puso de manifiesto que no había escuchado || *under plain cover, in a plain envelope* con la mayor discreción (in advertisements), en un sobre blanco.
◆ *n* llanura *f*, planicie *f*, llano *m*.
◆ *adv* claramente (clearly) || lisa y llanamente, claramente (candidly) || francamente (frankly).

plainchant ['pleintʃɑ:nt] *n* MUS & REL canto *m* llano.

plainclothesman [plein'kləuðzmən] *n* policía *m* en traje de paisano (when on duty).
— OBSERV El plural es *plainclothesmen*.

plainly ['pleinli] *adj* claramente, evidentemente (obviously) || claramente, con claridad (with clarity) || sencillamente, simplemente (with simplicity) || francamente (frankly) || *to put it plainly* para ser claro.

plainness ['pleinnis] *n* claridad *f*, evidencia *f* || simpleza *f*, sencillez *f* || franqueza *f* (frankness) || fealdad *f*, falta *f* de atractivo (unattractiveness).

plainsman ['pleinzmən] *n* llanero *m*, hombre *m* de la llanura.
— OBSERV El plural de *plainsman* es *plainsmen*.

plainsong ['pleinsɔŋ] *n* MUS & REL canto *m* llano.

plainspoken ['plein'spəukən] *adj* franco, ca.

plaint [pleint] *n* JUR querella *f*, demanda *f*.

plaintiff [-if] *n* JUR demandante *m* & *f*, querellante *m* & *f*.

plaintive [-iv] *adj* quejumbroso, sa; lastimero, ra; *a plaintive voice* una voz quejumbrosa.

plait [plæt] *n* trenza *f* (hair) || pliegue *m*, frunce *m* (fold) || *in plaits* trenzado (hair), fruncido, da; plisado, da (folded).

plait [plæt] *vt* trenzar (hair) || fruncir, plisar (to fold).

plan [plæn] *n* plano *m* (design, map) || plan *m*, proyecto *m* (scheme, schedule); *work plan* plan de trabajo; *what are your plans now?* ¿ahora qué proyectos tiene?; *to make plans* hacer proyectos || ARCH plano *m*; *to draw up a plan of* trazar el plano de || — *development plan* plan de desarrollo || *five-year plan* plan quinquenal || *have you any plans for tomorrow?* ¿tienes algún plan para mañana?, ¿tienes algún compromiso para mañana? || *if everything goes according to plan* si todo sale como está previsto || *it all went according to plan* todo salió como estaba previsto || *plan of action* plan de acción || MIL *plan of campaign* plan de campaña || *the best plan would be to wait* lo mejor sería esperar || *the Marshall Plan* el Plan Marshall.

plan [plæn] *vt* hacer el plano de (to design) || planificar (production, economy) || planear; *to plan a coup, a journey, a reform* planear un golpe de estado, un viaje, una reforma || hacer el plan de (a book, holidays, etc.) || hacer planes para (the future) || — *I plan to go out tonight* pienso salir esta noche, tengo la intención de salir esta noche || FAM *to plan on* tener pensado.
◆ *vi* hacer planes, hacer proyectos || *to plan out* planificar detalladamente.

planch [plɑ:ʃ] *n* plancha *f*.

planchet ['plɑ:nʃət] *n* cospel *m*.

planchette [plɑ:n'ʃet] *n* tabla *f* usada en sesiones de espiritismo.

plane [plein] *n* TECH cepillo *m* (of a carpenter) || MATH plano *m* (surface) || FIG plano *m*, nivel *m* (level of thought, etc.); *to be on another plan* estar en otro plano || AVIAT avión *m* (aircraft); *to go by plane* ir en avión (people), ir por avión (goods, post) | plano *m* (stabilizer) || BOT plátano *m*.
◆ *adj* plano, na; *plane geometry* geometría plana.

plane [plein] *vt* cepillar (a carpenter).
◆ *vi* cepillar (to work with a plane) || planear (to glide) || viajar en avión (to go by aircraft).

plane sailing [-,seiliŋ] *n* MAR → **sailing.**

planet ['plænit] *n* ASTR planeta *m* || TECH *planet gear* piñón planetario.

planetarium [,plæni'tɛəriəm] *n* planetario *m*.
— OBSERV El plural de la palabra inglesa es *planetariums* o *planetaria*.

planetary ['plænitəri] *adj* planetario, ria.

planetoid ['plænətɔid] *n* ASTR planetoide *m*, asteroide *m*.

planet wheel ['plænitwi:l] *n* TECH rueda *f* planetaria.

plangent ['plændʒənt] *adj* resonante || plañidero, ra (plaintive).

planimetry [plæ'nimətri] *n* planimetría *f*.

planing [pleiniŋ] *n* cepillado *m*.

planish ['plæniʃ] *vt* aplanar, alisar (metals).

planisphere ['plænisfiə] *n* planisferio *m*.

plank [plæŋk] *n* tablón *m*, tabla *f* (wooden board) || FIG punto *m* (in a policy) || — *deck planks* tablazón *f* de cubierta (of a ship) || *to walk the plank* ser castigado a arrojarse al mar desde un tablón que sobresale de la nave.

plank [plæŋk] *vt* entablar, entarimar (to cover with boards) || CULIN hacer a la plancha || *to plank down* tirar con violencia (to throw down with force), desembolsar (to pay out).

planking [-iŋ] *n* entarimado *m*, entablado *m* || MAR tablazón *f* de cubierta.

plankton ['plæŋktən] *n* BIOL plancton *m*.

planned [plænd] *adj* planificado, da; *planned economy* economía planificada.

planner [plænə*] *n* planificador, ra.

planning ['plæniŋ] *n* planificación *f* || — *family planning* planificación familiar || *planning permission* licencia *f* de obras.
◆ *adj* planificador, ra.

plano-concave ['plænəukɔn'keiv] *adj* planocóncavo, va.

plano-convex ['plænəukɔn'veks] *adj* planoconvexo, xa.

plant [plɑ:nt] *n* BOT planta *f* || planta *f*, fábrica *f* (factory) || instalación *f* (installation) || maquinaria *f* (machinery) || FAM trampa *f* (trap) | estratagema *f* (stratagem) || — *in plant* en crecimiento || *plant kingdom* reino *m* vegetal || *plant life* las plantas, la vida vegetal.

plant [plɑ:nt] *vt* plantar (plants); *he planted roses in the garden* plantó rosas en el jardín || sembrar (a field); *to plant a field with corn* sembrar un campo de trigo || cultivar (the land) || colocar (to place) || instalar, establecer (to establish) || FIG inculcar (ideas) | plantar; *he planted himself in front of the door* se plantó delante de la puerta || FAM colocar a escondidas; *they planted marked notes in the drawer* colocaron a escondidas billetes marcados en el cajón | asestar, plantar; *he planted him a blow on the nose* le asestó un puñetazo en la nariz || — *to plant out* trasplantar (to transplant) || *to plant sth. on s.o.* comprometer a uno escondiendo un objeto robado en su ropa *or* habitación.

plantain ['plæntin] *n* BOT llantén *m*, plantaina *f* | plátano *m* (banana tree) || BOT *water plantain* llantén de agua.

plantar ['plæntɑ:*] *adj* ANAT plantar, de la planta del pie.

plantation [plæn'teiʃən] *n* plantación *f*, plantío *m* (of plants) || hacienda *f* (large estate) || plantel *m* (of young trees) || HIST colonia *f* (colony) || — *banana plantation* platanal *m*, plantanar *m* || *coffee plantation* cafetal *m*.

planter ['plɑ:ntə*] *n* plantador, ra (person) || plantadora *f* (machine) || HIST colono *m* (colonist).

plantigrade ['plæntigreid] *adj/n* ZOOL plantígrado, da.

plant louse ['plɑ:nt,laus] *n* ZOOL pulgón *m*.

plantpot ['plɑ:nt,pɔt] *n* maceta *f*, tiesto *m*.

plaque [plɑ:k] *n* placa *f*; *commemorative plaque* placa conmemorativa.

plaquette [plæ'ket] *n* plaqueta *f*.

plash [plæʃ] *n* salpicadura *f* (splashing) || chapoteo *m* (sound) || charca *f* cenagosa (pool).

plash [plæʃ] *vt* salpicar (to splash) || chapotear en || entrelazar, entretejer (to interweave).
◆ *vi* chapotear.

plashy [-i] *adj* cenagoso, sa.

plasm ['plæzəm]; **plasma** ['plæzmə] *n* plasma *m*.

plaster ['plɑ:stə*] *n* yeso *m* (for walls, for ceilings, etc.) || MED emplasto *m*, parche *m* | escayola *f* (for injured leg, etc.) | esparadrapo *m* (sticking plaster) || — MED *mustard plaster* sinapismo *m* | *to have one's arm in plaster* tener el brazo escayolado.

plaster ['plɑ:stə*] *vt* enyesar, enlucir (walls, etc.) || cubrir; *his hands were plastered with paint* tenía las manos cubiertas de pintura || pegar, fijar (to stick) || MED aplicar un emplasto a | enyesar, escayolar (a broken leg, etc.) || FIG colmar, llenar (with praise, etc.) | bombardear (to bomb) || — FAM *to be plastered* estar trompa (to be drunk) || *to plaster down one's hair* ponerse fijador en el pelo || *to plaster over a crack* tapar una grieta con yeso, enyesar una grieta.

plasterboard [-bɔ:d] *n* cartón *m* yeso.

plaster cast [-kɑ:st] *n* ARTS vaciado *m* en yeso || MED enyesado *m* || *to have one's leg in a plaster cast* tener la pierna escayolada.

plasterer ['plɑ:stərə*] *n* yesero *m*, enlucidor *m*.

plastering ['plɑ:stəriŋ] *n* enlucido *m* (of a wall) || FAM paliza *f* (thrashing); *to give s.o. a plastering* dar *or* pegar una paliza a alguien.

plaster of Paris ['plɑ:stərəv'pæris] *n* yeso *m* blanco.

plastic ['plæstik] *adj* plástico, ca; *plastic substance* materia plástica; *plastic arts* artes plásticas || de plástico (made of plastic) || — *plastic bomb* bomba *f* de plástico || *plastic bullet* bala *f* de goma || *plastic explosive* plástico *m* || FAM *plastic money* tarjeta *f* de crédito.
◆ *n* plástico *m*, materia *f* plástica.

plasticene; plasticine ['plæstisi:n] *n* ARTS arcilla *f* de moldear.

plasticity [plæs'tisiti] *n* plasticidad *f*.

plasticization [plæstisi'zeiʃən] *n* plastificado *m*, plastificación *f*.

plasticize ['plæstisaiz] *vt* plastificar.

plastics ['plæstiks] *n* plástica *f*.

plastic surgery ['plæstik'sə:dʒəri] *n* MED cirugía *f* plástica.

plastify ['plæstifai] *vt* plastificar.

plastifying [-iŋ] *adj* plastificante.

plastron ['plæstrɔn] *adj* ZOOL peto *m*, plastrón *m* || peto *m*, plastrón *m* (breastplate) || pechera *f* postiza (dicky) || plastrón *m* (of fencer).

plat [plæt] *n* US parcela *f* (piece of land) | plano *m* (plan) | mapa *m* (map).

plat [plæt] *vt* US hacer un plano de (to make a map of).

plate [pleit] *n* plato *m* (dish) || placa *f* (plaque) || chapa *f*, lámina *f*, plancha *f* (of metal) || vajilla *f* (tableware) || PHOT placa *f* || MED placa *f* de la dentadura postiza || FAM dentadura *f* postiza (false teeth) || REL bandeja *f*, platillo *m* (for collection) || PRINT estereotipo *m*, plancha *f*, clisé *m* (stereotype) | lámina *f*, grabado *m* (illustration) || ARCH viga *f* horizontal (of a roof) || MIL plancha *f* de blindaje, blindaje *m* || SP premio *m*, copa *f* de oro *or* de plata (in horse racing) || US SP base *f* del bateador (in baseball) || ANAT & ZOOL lámina *f* || TECH revestimiento *m* (coating) || plancha *f* (grill) || ELECTR placa *f*, ánodo *m* || AUT matrícula *f* (number plate) || — FIG *it was given to him on a plate* se lo dieron en una bandeja de plata || *number plate, license plate* matrícula *f*, placa *f* de matrícula || FIG *to have a lot on one's plate* tener tela de que cortar.

plate [pleit] *vt* blindar (to armour) || chapar (with metal) || niquelar (with nickel) || dorar (with gold) || platear (with silver) || PRINT hacer un clisé *or* un estereotipo de.

plate armour; US plate armor [-'ɑ:mə*] *n* MIL blindaje *m* (of tank, of ship).

plateau ['plætəu] *n* GEOGR meseta *f* [AMER altiplano *m*].

— OBSERV El plural de *plateau* es *plateaus* o *plateaux*.

plated ['pleitid] *adj* chapado, da (metals) || blindado, da (armoured).

plateful ['pleitful] *n* plato *m*; *a plateful of chips* un plato de patatas fritas.

plate glass ['pleit'glɑ:s] *n* TECH vidrio *m* cilindrado, luna *f*.

platelayer ['pleit,leiə*] *n* asentador *m* de vías.

platelet ['pleitlət] *n* BIOL plaqueta *f*.

plate mark ['pleit,mɑ:k] *n* contraste *m* (hallmark).

platen; platten ['plætən] *n* PRINT platina *f* (of a press) | rodillo *m* (of typewriter).

plater ['pleitə*] *n* chapista *m* (with metal) || plateador *m* (with silver) || dorador *m* (with gold) || niquelador *m* (with nickel) || SP caballo *m* de segunda categoría (horse).

plate rack ['pleitræk] *n* escurreplatos *m inv*.

plateresque [,plætə'resk] *adj* ARCH plateresco, ca.

Plate River ['pleit'rivə*] *pr n* GEOGR Río *m* de la Plata.

platform ['plætfɔ:m] *n* plataforma *f* (raised planking) || andén *m* (of railway station); *people waiting on the platform* gente esperando en el andén || vía *f*; *the train standing at platform three* el tren que está en la vía tres || plataforma *f* (on a bus or tram, for artillery, raised piece of ground) || estrado *m* (stage) || tribuna *f*, plataforma *f* (at a meeting, etc.) || tablado *m* (for dancing, etc.) || andamio *m* (of builders) || programa *m* [político] (of a party).

platform car [-kɑ:*] *n* US batea *f*, vagón *m* plataforma (flatcar).

platform ticket [-'tikit] *n* billete *m* de andén.

plating ['pleitiŋ] *n* enchapado *m*, chapado *m* || capa *f* metálica (layer of metal) || blindaje *m* (armour) || — *gold plating* dorado *m* || *nickel plating* niquelado *m* || *silver plating* plateado *m*.

platinize ['plætinaiz] *vt* platinar.

platinous ['plætinəs] *adj* platinoso, sa.

platinum ['plætinəm] *n* platino *m*.

platinum black [-'blæk] *n* CHEM negro *m* de platino.

platinum blonde [-'blɔ:nd] *n* mujer *f* rubia platino.

◆ *adj* rubio platino (hair) || rubia platino (woman).

platitude ['plætitju:d] *n* tópico *m*, lugar *m* común.

platitudinize [,plæti'tju:dinaiz] *vi* decir tópicos.

platitudinous [,plæti'tju:dinəs] *adj* tópico, ca; trivial.

Plato ['pleitəu] *pr n* Platón *m*.

Platonic [plə'tɔnik] *adj* platónico, ca; *platonic love* amor platónico.

Platonism ['pleitəunizəm] *n* PHIL platonismo *m*.

platoon [plə'tu:n] *n* MIL pelotón *m*.

platten ['plætən] *n* ⟶ **platen.**

platter ['plætə*] *n* (ant) plato *m* (dish) || US fuente *f* (serving dish) | disco *m* (record).

platyhelminth [,plæti'helminθ] *n* ZOOL platelminto *m* (flatworm).

platypus ['plætipəs] *n* ZOOL ornitorrinco *m*.

platyrrhine ['plaetirain] *n* ZOOL platirrino *m*.

plaudits ['plɔ:dits] *pl n* aplausos *m*.

plausibility [,plɔ:zə'biliti] *n* plausibilidad *f*.

plausible ['plɔ:zəbl] *adj* plausible; *a plausible excuse* una excusa plausible || convincente pero poco de fiar (person).

play [plei] *n* juego *m*, entretenimiento *m*, diversión *f* (amusement) || SP juego *m* (manner of playing); *fair, foul play* juego limpio, sucio | jugada *f* (manoeuvre); *a good play* una buena jugada || THEATR obra *f* de teatro; *Lorca's plays* las obras de teatro de Lorca | teatro *m*; *to go to the play* ir al teatro || juego *m* (gambling) || TECH juego *m*, holgura *f* (looseness) || FIG rienda *f* suelta (free rein) || — *a smart bit of play, a smart piece of play* una buena jugada || *at play* en juego || FIG *child's play* juego de niños || *influences in play* influencias *f* en juego || *in play* en broma, de broma (joking); *to do sth. in play* hacer algo en broma; en juego (sports) || *it's your play* te toca a ti || *out of play* fuera de juego || SP *play has started* ha empezado el partido || *play of light* juego de luces || *play on words* juego de palabras || *to bring, to come into play* poner, entrar en juego || FIG *to give full play to* dar rienda suelta a || *to make play of* burlarse de || *to watch the children at play* mirar cómo juegan los niños, ver jugar a los niños.

play [plei] *vt* jugar a; *to play rugby, tennis, cards* jugar al rugby, al tenis, a las cartas || MUS tocar (an instrument, a song) | interpretar (a song, a composer); *to play sth. on the piano* tocar algo al piano || THEATR hacer de, desempeñar *or* hacer el papel de (a role) | representar, poner, dar; *they played Macbeth* representaron Macbeth | actuar en; *they played Madrid for two months* actuaron en Madrid durante dos meses || acompañar (to accompany) || gastar, dar; *to play a joke on* gastar una broma a || enfocar, dirigir; *to play a hose on* dirigir la manguera hacia || jugar (in cards); *to play an ace* jugar un as || jugarse (to gamble away) || apostar por (to bet on) || SP colocar, mandar; *he played the ball into the net* colocó la pelota en la red | jugar contra; *Wales played France* Gales jugó contra Francia | alinear, hacer jugar; *England is playing a good kicker for this match* Inglaterra hace jugar a un buen chutador para este partido | jugar de; *Joseph plays right half* José juega de medio derecho || mover, jugar (a chessman) || jugar a; *to play pirates* jugar a los piratas || FIG dárselas de, echárselas de; *to play the big shot* dárselas de hombre importante || COMM jugar a; *to play the stock exchange* jugar a la Bolsa || dejar que se canse; *to play a fish* dejar que se canse un pez || — *to play a dirty trick on s.o.* hacerle una mala jugada *or* hacerle una jugarreta a alguien, jugarle una mala pasada a alguien || *to play a game of bridge* jugar *or* echar una partida de bridge || MUS *to play by ear* tocar de oído || *to play false* traicionar (to betray) || FIG *to play one's part well* desempeñar bien su papel | *to play s.o.'s game* hacer el juego de alguien | *to play the arbitrator* desempeñar el papel de árbitro | *to play the fool* hacer el tonto.

◆ *vi* jugar; *the children are playing* los niños están jugando; *stop playing with your food!* ¡deja de jugar con la comida!; *he played badly in the last match* jugó mal en el último partido || bailar; *the shadows played on the walls* las sombras bailaban en las paredes || fingirse (to pretend to be); *to play ill* fingirse enfermo || conducirse, portarse (to behave) || MUS tocar; *he plays rather well* toca bastante bien | sonar; *this piano plays better now* este piano suena mejor ahora || THEATR & CINEM actuar, trabajar; *he played at the best theatre in town* actuó en el mejor teatro de la ciudad | desempeñar (a role) || estar funcionando (a fountain) || ser; *this court plays very slow* esta pista es muy lenta || retozar (to gambol) || jugar (to gamble) || bromear (to joke); *they are only playing* están sólo bromeando || TECH tener juego, tener holgura (a steering wheel, etc.) | funcionar (to work) || — FIG *are you sure he's not just playing with you?* ¿estás segura de que no está jugando contigo? || SP *how much time is left to play?* ¿cuánto tiempo queda de juego? || FIG *I'm playing with the idea* estoy dándole vueltas en la cabeza a la idea || *love is not a thing to be played with* con el amor no se juega || *run away and play!* ¡vete a jugar! || *they are not people to be played with* con esa gente no se juega || *to play dead* hacerse *or* hacer el muerto || *to play fair, dirty* jugar limpio, sucio || *to play for money* jugar por dinero || *to play for time* hacer tiempo || *to play foul* jugar sucio || FIG *to play into s.o.'s hands* hacerle el juego a alguien | *to play to the gallery* actuar para la galería | *to play upon words* hacer juegos de palabras, jugar del vocablo | *to play with fire* jugar con fuego | *to play with one's health* jugar con la salud | *to play with the cards on the table* jugar con las cartas boca arriba || *what's playing at the theatre?* ¿qué ponen en el teatro?

◆ *phr v* ***to play along*** seguir la corriente (*with s.o.* a alguien) | ***to play around*** o ***about*** hacer el tonto (to play the fool) | juguetear (to fiddle) | jugar; *he's playing about with you* está jugando contigo || ***to play at*** jugar a; *to play at chess* jugar al ajedrez; *children playing at being adults* niños jugando a adultos || — FAM *what are you playing at?* ¿qué haces? (what are you doing?), ¿a qué jugáis? (game) || ***to play back*** poner, volver a poner [algo grabado] | oír, escuchar [una cinta]; *let's play it back* vamos a escucharlo || — *play it back for me* déjeme oírlo || ***to play down*** quitar importancia a, intentar minimizar || ***to play off*** oponer; *to play one person off against another* oponer a dos personas | SP jugar un partido de desempate || ***to play on*** aprovecharse de, explotar (to make use of) | seguir jugando *or* tocando | disparar (a gun) || — *to play on s.o.'s nerves* hacerle la guerra de nervios a alguien (to wage a war of nerves on), atacarle los nervios a alguien (to irritate) || ***to play out*** acabar (to finish) | agotar (to exhaust) | representar hasta el final || ***to play up*** jugar con toda el alma, darse por entero (to play heartily) | jugar con más ánimo, jugar mejor (to play better) | fastidiar, dar guerra (to annoy) | hinchar (news, incident) | exagerar (to exaggerate) || — *to play up to* adular.

playable [-əbl] *adj* MUS interpretable, que se puede interpretar ‖ THEATR representable (a play).

playact [-ækt] *vi* hacer teatro (to pretend) ‖ THEATR desempeñar un papel.

playacting [-,æktiŋ] *n* comedia *f*, teatro *m*.

playback [-bæk] *n* reproducción *f* (of a tape) ‖ — *playback head* cabeza auditiva ‖ *to listen to the playback* escuchar una cinta.

playbill [-bil] *n* cartel *m* [anunciador de una obra de teatro] (poster) ‖ US programa *m*.

playboy [-bɔi] *n* «playboy» *m*.

play-by-play [-bai'plei] *adj* US punto por punto, detallado, da.

playday [-dai] *n* día *m* de fiesta.

playdown [-daun] *n* desempate *m*, partido *m* de desempate.

played out ['pleidaut] *adj* agotado, da (exhausted) ‖ acabado, da (worn-out).

player [pleiə*] *n* jugador, ra (in games, in sport, etc.) ‖ MUS intérprete *m* & *f*, músico, ca; ejecutante *m* & *f* ‖ THEATR actor *m*, actriz *f* | (ant) cómico, ca ‖ — *guitar player* guitarrista *m* & *f* ‖ *piano player* pianista *m* & *f* ‖ *violin player* violinista *m* & *f*.

player piano [-pi'ænəu] *n* MUS pianola *f*.

playfellow ['plei,feləu] *n* compañero *m* de juego, compañera *f* de juego, amigo, ga.

playful ['pleiful] *adj* juguetón, ona; retozón, ona (who likes to play) ‖ travieso, sa (mischievous) ‖ alegre (happy) ‖ guasón, ona (joking) ‖ festivo, va (humorous).

playfully ['pleifuli] *adv* jugando ‖ alegremente ‖ en broma (jokingly).

playfulness [-nis] *n* alegría *f* (happiness) ‖ tono *m* guasón (in voice).

playgoer ['plei,gəuə*] *n* aficionado al teatro.

playground ['pleigraund] *n* patio *m* (of a school) ‖ campo *m* de juegos (place for children to play) ‖ FIG lugar *m* de predilección; *a millionaires' playground* un lugar de predilección para los millonarios.

playgroup ['plei,gru:p] *n* guardería *f*.

playhouse ['pleihaus] *n* teatro *m* (theatre) ‖ US casa *f* de muñecas (doll's house).

playing card ['pleiiŋka:d] *n* carta *f*, naipe *m*.

playing field ['pleiiŋfi:ld] *n* campo *m* de deportes.

playmate ['pleimeit] *n* compañero *m* de juego, compañera *f* de juego, amigo, ga.

play-off ['plei,ɔf] *n* SP partido *m* de desempate (to decide a tie).

playpen ['plei,pen] *n* parque *m*, corral *m* (for children).

playroom ['plei,ru:m] *n* cuarto *m* de jugar.

playschool ['plei,sku:l] *n* jardín *m* de infancia.

plaything ['pleiθiŋ] *n* juguete *m*.

playtime ['plei,taim] *n* recreo *m* (at school).

playwright ['plei,rait] *n* autor *m* de teatro.

plc *abbr of [public limited company]* SA, sociedad anónima.

plea [pli:] *n* súplica *f* (appeal); *to ignore s.o.'s pleas* no escuchar las súplicas de alguien ‖ petición *f* (request) ‖ excusa *f*, disculpa *f* (excuse) ‖ pretexto *m* (pretext); *with the plea of* con el pretexto de ‖ JUR alegato *m* ‖ — JUR *his plea was not guilty* se declaró inocente ‖ *to make a plea for mercy* pedir clemencia, pedir gracia.

pleach [pli:tʃ] *vt* entretejer.

plead [pli:d] *vi* implorar; *now you plead for mercy* ahora imploras clemencia ‖ suplicar; *to plead and plead with s.o.* suplicar mil veces a alguien ‖ JUR hacer un alegato, abogar (*for* por) ‖ defender, abogar (*for* por); *to plead for s.o.'s cause* defender la causa de alguien ‖ intervenir (to intervene); *he pleaded for me* intervino en mi favor.

◆ *vt* JUR alegar (to cite in defence); *to plead extenuating circumstances* alegar circunstancias atenuantes | defender; *to plead a case* defender un caso ‖ — JUR *to plead guilty* declararse culpable ‖ *to plead ignorance* pretextar su ignorancia ‖ JUR *to plead not guilty* declararse inocente | *to plead self-defence* alegar legítima defensa.

pleader [-ə*] *n* JUR abogado *m* defensor ‖ intercesor *m*.

pleading [-iŋ] *n* súplicas *f pl*; *to give way to s.o.'s pleading* ceder ante las súplicas de alguien ‖ JUR alegato *m*, defensa *f*.

pleasant ['pleznt] *adj* agradable; *a pleasant surprise, evening* una sorpresa, una velada agradable ‖ simpático, ca; agradable (person) ‖ *to have a pleasant time* pasarlo muy agradablemente.

pleasantly [-li] *adv* agradablemente ‖ *we were pleasantly surprised* fue una sorpresa agradable.

pleasantness [-nis] *n* agrado *m*, lo agradable ‖ simpatía *f* (of a person).

pleasantry [-ri] *n* chanza *f*, broma *f*, chiste *m* (joke) ‖ jocosidad *f* (jocularity).

please [pli:z] *vt* gustar, agradar; *do you think this tie will please him?* ¿cree que le gustará esta corbata?; *it pleases him to take a walk* le gusta dar un paseo; *your essay pleased me considerably* su ensayo me ha gustado mucho ‖ contentar, complacer, agradar; *he is easy to please* es fácil de contentar ‖ caer bien, gustar, agradar; *you really pleased my mother when you met* caíste muy bien a mi madre cuando os conocisteis; *do you think I please him?* ¿crees que le gusto? ‖ dar gusto, agradar, gustar; *it pleases me to think that* me gusta pensar que ‖ satisfacer, contentar (to satisfy); *there's no pleasing him* no hay manera de satisfacerle ‖ complacer; *it pleases me to announce that* me complace comunicar que ‖ ser un placer para, agradar; *to please the ear, the eye* ser un placer para el oído, para la vista ‖ — *if it so please you* si usted quiere, si le parece bien ‖ FIG *it might please you to know* le interesará saber (with irony) ‖ *please yourself!* ¡haga lo que quiera! ‖ *to be hard to please* ser difícil de contentar, ser muy exigente ‖ *to be pleased to* tener el agrado de ‖ *to be pleased with* estar satisfecho con ‖ *where shall I sit? please yourself* ¿dónde me siento? donde quiera *or* donde le parezca.

◆ *vi* agradar, gustar; *it is sure to please* agradará sin duda alguna ‖ querer, parecer; *to do as one pleases* hacer lo que quiera uno, hacer lo que le parezca a uno; *he will do just as he pleases* hará exactamente lo que quiera; *as you please* como quiera; *when you please* cuando quiera ‖ — *if you please* por favor, tenga la amabilidad de (please), haga el favor de; *stop that noise if you please* haga el favor de callarse; con su permiso (with your permission), ¡fíjate!, ¡fíjese!, ¡imagínate!, ¡imagínese!; *he called me a pig if you please!* ¡fíjate que me trató de cerdo!; por raro que parezca (strange as it may seem) ‖ *may I come in? please do!* ¿puedo entrar? ¡por supuesto! *or* ¡por favor! ‖ *please* por favor; *please come in* pase por favor ‖ *please be seated, please take a seat* siéntese por favor, tenga a bien sentarse ‖ *«please do not speak to the driver»* «se ruega no hablar con el conductor» ‖ *please stop that noise!* ¡haga el favor de no hacer ese ruido!

pleased [-d] *adj* contento, ta (content); *he is pleased with his new job* está contento con su nuevo trabajo ‖ contento, ta; alegre (happy); *everyone looked very pleased* todos parecían muy contentos ‖ de satisfacción (of satisfaction); *a pleased smile* una sonrisa de satisfacción ‖ satisfecho, cha (satisfied); *she was pleased with the result* estaba satisfecha del resultado; *he is very pleased with himself* está muy satisfecho de sí mismo; *to be pleased with s.o.* estar satisfecho con alguien ‖ — *I am pleased to announce that* tengo el placer de comunicarles que, me complace comunicarles que, me complazco en comunicarles que ‖ *I am pleased to hear it* me alegra saberlo, me alegro ‖ *I was pleased at the news* me alegré de la noticia ‖ *pleased to meet you* encantado de conocerle ‖ *to be all but pleased, to be far from pleased* no estar nada contento ‖ *to be as pleased as Punch* estar como unas Pascuas.

pleasing [-iŋ] *adj* agradable.

pleasurable; US **pleasureable** ['pleʒərəbl] *adj* grato, ta; agradable.

pleasurably [-i] *adv* agradablemente ‖ *we were pleasurably surprised* fue una agradable sorpresa.

pleasure ['pleʒə*] *n* placer *m*, gusto *m*; *with pleasure* con gusto; *I have the pleasure of welcoming you here* tengo el placer de darles la bienvenida; *with great pleasure* con mucho gusto; *it is a pleasure to know that* es un placer saber que, da gusto saber que; *what pleasure do you find in fishing?* ¿qué placer encuentras en la pesca? ‖ voluntad *f*; *at pleasure* a voluntad ‖ — *all the pleasures of Paris* todos los placeres de París ‖ *I do it because it gives me pleasure* lo hago porque me gusta ‖ *it gives me a certain amount of pleasure* me da cierto placer ‖ *it gives me pleasure to introduce to the audience* tengo el placer de *or* me complace presentar al público ‖ *it's a pleasure to see you* da gusto verte ‖ *may I have the pleasure?* ¿quiere usted bailar? ‖ *the pleasure is mine* de nada, no hay de qué (returning thanks), el gusto es mío (returning a greeting) ‖ *to allow o.s. the pleasure of* darse el gusto de ‖ *to be a pleasure lover* ser amante de los placeres ‖ *to be at s.o.'s pleasure* estar a la merced de alguien (at s.o.'s service) ‖ *to be to one's pleasure* ser del gusto de alguien ‖ *to find pleasure in cards* disfrutar jugando a las cartas ‖ *to take pleasure in* disfrutar (to delight); *to take great pleasure in reading* disfrutar mucho leyendo; *to take pleasure in music* disfrutar con la música; divertirse (to amuse o.s.) ‖ *what is your pleasure?* ¿en qué puedo servirle? ‖ *with the greatest of pleasure* con sumo gusto ‖ *you may go or stay at your pleasure* puede irse o quedarse, según prefiera.

pleasure boat [-bəut] *n* barco *m* de recreo.

pleasure ground [-graund] *n* parque *m* de atracciones.

pleasure trip [-trip] *n* viaje *m* de recreo.

pleat [pli:t] *n* pliegue *m*.

pleat [pli:t] *vt* plisar, hacer pliegues en.

pleated [-id] *adj* plisado, da ‖ *pleated skirt* falda *f* plisada *or* tableada.

pleb [pleb] *n* FAM plebeyo *m*, persona *f* ordinaria ‖ — FAM *don't be such a pleb* no seas tan ordinario | *the plebs* la plebe *f sing*.

plebeian; US **plebian** [pli'biən] *adj/n* plebeyo, ya.

plebiscite ['plebisit] *n* plebiscito *m*.

plectognath ['plectɔgnæθ] *adj* plectognato, ta.

◆ *n* plectognato *m*.

plectron ['plektrɔn] *n* US MUS púa *f*, plectro *m*.

plectrum ['plektrəm] *n* MUS púa *f*, plectro *m*.
— OBSERV El plural de *plectrum* es *plectra* o *plectrums*.

pledge [pledʒ] *n* prenda *f*, garantía *f* (guarantee); *in pledge of my good faith* en prenda de mi buena fe, como garantía de mi buena fe ‖ promesa *f* solemne (promise) ‖ JUR pignoración *f*, empeño *m* (pawning) ‖ compromiso *m* (commitment); *the country will honour its* *pledges* el país hará honor a sus compromisos || (ant) brindis *m* (a toast) || — *as a pledge of* en señal de || *to keep the pledge* cumplir la promesa || *to put in pledge* empeñar (to pawn), dar en prenda (to offer as a token) || *to take out of pledge* desempeñar || *to take the pledge* hacer la promesa solemne de dejar de beber.

pledge [pledʒ] *vt* empeñar, pignorar (to pawn) || dar en prenda; *to pledge sth. as a sign of one's good intentions* dar algo en prenda como señal de sus buenas intenciones || comprometer (to commit) || prometer (to promise); *to pledge assistance to s.o.* prometer su ayuda a alguien || jurar (to swear); *to pledge allegiance* jurar lealtad; *to be pledged to secrecy* haber jurado guardar el secreto || (ant) brindar por (to toast) || *to pledge one's word* dar *or* empeñar su palabra || *to pledge o.s. to do sth.* comprometerse a hacer algo.

pleiad ['plaiəd] *n* pléyade *f.*

Pleiades ['plaiədiz] *pl n* ASTR & MYTH Pléyades *f.*

Pleiocene ['plaiəusi:n] *n* GEOL Plioceno *m.*

Pleistocene ['plaistəusi:n] *n* GEOL Pleistoceno *m.*

◆ *adj* pleistoceno, na.

plenary ['pli:nəri] *adj* plenario, ria; *plenary session* sesión plenaria; *plenary indulgence* indulgencia plenaria || completo, ta.

plenipotentiary [ˌplenipəu'tenʃəri] *adj* plenipotenciario, ria.

◆ *n* plenipotenciario *m.*

plenitude ['plenitju:d] *n* plenitud *f* (fullness) || abundancia *f* (abundance).

plenteous ['plentjəs] *adj* abundante (abundant); *a plenteous harvest* una cosecha abundante || bueno, na; abundante (supply) || copioso, sa (food) || *oranges are plenteous this year* hay abundancia de naranjas *or* abundan las naranjas este año.

plentiful ['plentiful] *adj* ⟶ **plenteous.**

plenty ['plenti] *n* abundancia *f*; *years of plenty* años de abundancia || cantidad *f* suficiente (sufficiency) || — *in plenty* en abundancia || *plenty of* suficiente, bastante (enough); *I have plenty of money to pay for both of us* tengo bastante dinero para pagar por los dos; mucho, cha (many, much); *he has plenty of friends* tiene muchos amigos; de sobra (more than enough); *there is plenty of time* hay tiempo de sobra.

◆ *adj* abundante (abundant) || suficiente (sufficient).

◆ *adv* más que; *this is plenty large enough* es más que suficiente || US *I like it plenty* me gusta mucho.

plenum ['pli:nəm] *n* PHYS espacio *m* lleno || asamblea *f* plenaria, pleno *m* (assembly).

— OBSERV El plural de *plenum* es *plenums* o *plena.*

pleonasm ['pli:ənæzəm] *n* GRAMM pleonasmo *m.*

pleonastic [pliə'næstik] *adj* GRAMM pleonástico, ca.

plesiosaur ['pli:siə'sɔ*] *n* plesiosauro *m* (fossil).

plethora ['pleθərə] *n* MED & FIG plétora *f.*

plethoric [ple'θɔrik] *adj* MED pletórico, ca || FIG pletórico, ca | ampuloso, sa (sentences).

pleura ['pluərə] *n* ANAT & ZOOL pleura *f.*

— OBSERV El plural de la palabra inglesa *pleura* es *pleurae* o *pleuras.*

pleurisy ['pluərisi] *n* MED pleuresía *f*, pleuritis *f.*

pleuritis [pluə'ritəs] *n* MED pleuritis *f*, pleuresía *f.*

plexiglass; plexiglas ['pleksəglɑ:s] *n* TECH plexiglás *m.*

plexor ['pleksɔ:*] *n* MED martillo *m* para comprobar los reflejos.

plexus ['pleksəs] *n* ANAT plexo *m*; *solar plexus* plexo solar || FIG entrelazamiento *m* (interwoven structure).

pliability [ˌplaiə'biliti]; **pliancy** ['plaiənsi] *n* flexibilidad *f* || FIG docilidad *f*, flexibilidad *f.*

pliable ['plaiəbl]; **pliant** ['plaiənt] *adj* flexible || FIG dócil, flexible.

pliancy ['plaiənsi] *n* ⟶ **pliability.**

pliant ['plaiənt] *adj* ⟶ **pliable.**

plica ['plaikə] *n* plica *f.*

— OBSERV El plural de la palabra inglesa es *plicae.*

plicate ['plaikeit]; **plicated** [-id] *adj* BOT & ZOOL plegado, da.

plication [plai'keiʃən] *n* plegamiento *m*, plegadura *f* (folding) || pliegue *m* (fold) || GEOL plegamiento *m* (fold in a stratum).

pliers ['plaiəz] *pl n* alicates *m* (tool).

plight [plait] *n* apuro *m*, aprieto *m* (tight spot) || situación *f* || situación *f* difícil, crisis *f.*

plight [plait] *vt* dar, empeñar (one's word) || — *to plight one's troth* dar palabra de matrimonio *or* de casamiento || *to plight o.s. to* celebrar esponsales con.

Plimsoll line ['plimsəllain] *n* MAR línea *f* de máxima carga.

Plimsoll mark ['plimsəlmɑ:k] *n* MAR línea *f* de máxima carga.

plimsolls ['plimsəlz] *pl n* zapatos *m* de lona *or* de tenis, playeras *f.*

plinth [plinθ] *n* ARCH plinto *m* (of a column) | zócalo *m* (of a wall) | peana *f* (of a statue).

Pliny ['plini] *pr n* Plinio *m*; *Pliny the Elder, the Younger* Plinio el Viejo, el Joven.

Pliocene ['plaiəusi:n] *n* GEOL Plioceno *m.*

PLO *abbr of [Palestine Liberation Organization]* OLP, Organización para la Liberación de Palestina.

plod [plɔd] *n* paso *m* pesado || — *it's a long plod to the town* queda mucho camino *or* una gran caminata para llegar a la ciudad || *to go at a steady plod* andar despacio pero sin parar.

plod [plɔd] *vt/vi* andar con paso pesado *or* con dificultad (to walk) || trabajar laboriosamente (to work slowly) || — *to plod away at a dull task* seguir haciendo un trabajo pesado a pesar de las dificultades que presenta || *to plod one's way* andar con paso pesado *or* con dificultad.

plodder [-ə*] *n* FAM empollón, ona (student) | persona que trabaja mucho sin tener grandes aptitudes (worker).

plodding [-iŋ] *adj* laborioso, sa.

plonk [plɔŋk] *n* FAM pirriaque *m*, morapio *m* (cheap wine) || ruido *m* sordo (dull, short sound) || rasgueo *m*, punteo *m* (noise of a banjo, of a guitar, etc.) || golpe *m* seco (forceful blow) || FAM dólar *m.*

plonk [plɔŋk] *vt/vi* ⟶ **plunk.**

plop [plɔp] *n* plaf *m* || *to go plop* hacer plaf.

plop [plɔp] *vi* hacer plaf (to make a sound) || caerse haciendo plaf (to fall with a plop) || *to plop down into a chair* desplomarse pesadamente en un sillón.

plosive ['pləusiv] *adj* GRAMM explosivo, va.

◆ *n* explosiva *f.*

plot [plɔt] *n* parcela *f*, terreno *m* (of ground) || cuadro *m* (in a garden); *a little vegetable plot* un pequeño cuadro de hortalizas || solar *m* (for building) || conspiración *f*, complot *m* (conspiracy) || intriga *f* (intrigue) || argumento *m*, trama *f* (story of a book, etc.) || MATH gráfico *m* (graph) || US plano *m.*

plot [plɔt] *vt* tramar, urdir, maquinar, fraguar (a scheme); *to plot s.o.'s downfall* tramar la caída de alguien || hacer el plano de (to map) || idear el argumento de [un libro] (of a book, etc.) || hacer un gráfico de (to make a graph of) || trazar (to trace); *to plot one's course* trazar su itinerario || marcar, señalar (points) || FIG tramar, maquinar, urdir; *what are you two plotting now?* ¿qué estáis tramando ahora vosotros dos?

◆ *vi* conspirar, intrigar || *they are plotting to overthrow the government* están urdiendo un complot para derribar el gobierno.

plotter ['plɔtə*] *n* conspirador, ra (conspirator) || maquinador, ra (schemer) || INFORM plotter *m*, trazador *m*, tabla *f* trazadora.

plotting paper ['plɔtiŋ'peipə*] *n* papel *m* cuadriculado (graph paper).

plough [plau] *n* AGR arado *m* (implement) | tierra *f* arada (ploughed land) || guillotina *f* (in bookbinding) || guimbarda *f* (grooving plane) || ASTR *the Plough* el Carro, la Osa Mayor.

plough [plau] *vt* arar || abrir; *to plough one's way through a crowd* abrirse paso entre la multitud || surcar (ships through the water) || acanalar (in carpentry) || guillotinar (in bookbinding) || FAM cargar, suspender (to fail an exam); *I was ploughed in English* me cargaron en inglés.

◆ *vi* arar (to work with a plough) || ararse; *this field ploughs easily* este campo se ara fácilmente || trabajar con una guillotina (in bookbinding) || trabajar con una guimbarda (in carpentry).

◆ *phr v* COMM ***to plough back*** reinvertir (to reinvest) || ***to plough in*** enterrar arando (seeds) || ***to plough into*** atacar (to attack) | precipitarse contra; *the lorry ploughed into the crowd* el camión se precipitó contra la multitud || ***to plough through*** abrirse camino por (to make a path through) || — *I managed to plough through it* conseguí acabarlo (book, work, etc.) | *to plough through a book* leer un libro con dificultad || ***to plough under*** enterrar (to bury) || ***to plough up*** arar, roturar; *to plough up a piece of ground* arar un terreno | destrozar, levantar; *the rugby match has ploughed up the pitch* el partido de rugby ha destrozado el campo | arrancar con el arado (to dig up with a plough) | FIG descubrir (to find out).

ploughboy; plowboy [-bɔi] *n* mozo *m* de labranza.

ploughing; plowing [-iŋ] *n* arada *f.*

ploughland; ploudand [-lænd] *n* AGR tierra *f* de labranza.

ploughman; plowman [-mən] *n* arador *m*, labrador *m* || *ploughman's lunch* almuerzo *m* a base de pan, queso y encurtidos.

— OBSERV El plural de *ploughman* es *ploughmen.*

ploughshare; plowshare [-ʃɛə*] *n* reja *f* del arado.

ploughtail; plowtail [-teil] *n* esteva *f.*

plover ['plʌvə*] *n* chorlito *m* (bird).

plow [plau] *n/vt/vi* US ⟶ **plough.**

plowboy[plaubɔi] *n* US ⟶ **ploughboy.**

plowing [plauiŋ] *n* ⟶ **ploughing.**

plowland [plaulænd] *n* ⟶ **ploughland.**

plowman [plaumən] *n* ⟶ **ploughman.**

plowshare [plauʃɛə*] *n* ⟶ **ploughshare.**

plowtail [plauteil] *n* ⟶ **ploughtail.**

ploy [plɔi] *n* trabajo *m*, actividad *f* (activity) || táctica *f* (tactic) || truco *m*, estratagema *f* (trick) || diversión *f* (amusement).

pluck [plʌk] *n* tirón *m* (a sharp pull) || asadura *f* (heart, liver, etc. of an animal) || valor *m*, arrojo *m* (courage) || agallas *f pl* (guts) || MUS plectro *m* || — *I didn't have the pluck to ask him* no tuve el valor de preguntárselo || *it takes a lot of pluck* hace falta tener agallas, hace falta mucho valor.

pluck [plʌk] *vt* arrancar (to pull out sharply); *he plucked it out of my hand* me lo arrancó de la mano || desplumar; *to pluck a fowl* desplumar un ave || MUS pulsar, puntear (a stringed instrument) || coger (flowers, etc.) || FAM robar, estafar (to rob) | suspender (in an exam) || *to pluck one's eyebrows* depilarse las cejas.
◆ *phr v* ***to pluck at*** tirar de, dar un tirón a; *he plucked at my sleeve* me tiró ligeramente de la manga || ***to pluck off*** arrancar || ***to pluck up*** animarse; *I wish he'd pluck up a bit* ojalá se anime un poco | reunir (strength); *to pluck up enough strength* reunir bastantes fuerzas | arrancar, coger bruscamente (to pick up suddenly) || — *he'll never pluck up the courage* nunca tendrá el valor | *to pluck up the* o *enough courage to* armarse de valor para.

pluckiness [-inis] *n* valor *m*, ánimo *m*.

plucking [-iŋ] *n* MUS punteado *m*, punteo *m*.

plucky [-i] *adj* valiente, valeroso, sa.

plug [plʌg] *n* tapón *m* (in sink, in bath, etc.) || taco *m* de madera (wood for filling holes, etc.) || ELECTR enchufe *m*; *a two, three pin plug* un enchufe bipolar, de tres polos; *there is only one plug in this room* sólo hay un enchufe en este cuarto || clavija *f* (of telephone exchange) || AUT bujía *f* (sparking plug) || andullo *m* (of tobacco) || boca *f* de incendio (fireplug) || US FAM penco *m* (old horse) || tiro *m* (shot) || FAM *to give sth. a plug on the radio* dar publicidad a algo en la radio (to publicize), mencionar algo en la radio (to mention).

plug [plʌg] *vt/vi* taponar (a sink, etc.) || tapar (a hole) || empastar (a tooth) || enchufar (radio, etc.) || atascar (to block up) || FAM dar publicidad a (to publicize) | repetir (to repeat) | poner constantemente (a record) | hacer hincapié en, insistir en (to emphasize); *they plug the advantages and ignore the disadvantages* insisten en las ventajas y dejan de lado los inconvenientes | pegar (to hit) | pegar un tiro a (to shoot) || — FAM *to plug away at* perseverar en (to persevere), aporrear (to hit) || ELECTR *to plug in* enchufar || *to plug up* atascarse, atorarse; *the sink has plugged up* el labavo se ha atascado.

plugged [-d] *adj* atascado, da; atorado, da (blocked) || falsificado, da (money).

plughole [-həul] *n* desagüe *m*, desaguadero *m*.

plug-in [-in] *adj* con enchufe.

plum [plʌm] *n* ciruela *f* (fruit) || ciruelo *m* (tree) || FAM chollo *m*, breva *f* (sth. advantageous) || *plum duff, plum pudding* pudín *m*, budín *m* de pasas.

plumage ['plu:midʒ] *n* plumaje *m*.

plumb [plʌm] *n* plomada *f*, plomo *m* (for indicating verticality) || MAR plomo *m*, plomada *f*, sonda *f* || — *plumb bob* plomo *m* || *plumb line* plomada *f*, cuerda *f* de plomada (in construction), sonda *f* (for measuring the depth of water) || *to be in plumb* estar a plomo || *to be out of plumb* no estar a plomo.
◆ *adj* vertical, a plomo (vertical) || FAM completo, ta; *plumb nonsense* disparate completo.
◆ *adv* a plomo, verticalmente || US FAM completamente; *plumb crazy* completamente loco | de lleno (full); *it landed plumb in his eye* le dio de lleno en el ojo.

plumb [plʌm] *vt* aplomar (to test for verticality) || MAR sondar || FIG sondear; *to plumb s.o.'s mind* sondear el pensamiento de alguien || — FIG *he plumbed the depths of despair* su desesperación no conocía límites || *to plumb in* instalar (bath, toilet).

plumbaginaceae [plʌm,bædʒə'neisii] *pl n* BOT plumbagináceas *f*.

plumbago [-'beigəu] *n* MIN plombagina *f* || BOT plumbaginácea *f*.

plumbeous ['plʌmbiəs] *adj* plúmbeo, a (of or like lead) || plomizo, za (lead coloured).

plumber ['plʌmə*] *n* fontanero *m*.

plumbiferous [plʌm'bifərəs] *adj* plomífero, ra.

plumbing ['plʌmiŋ] *n* fontanería *f* (the craft of a plumber) || instalación *f* de cañerías, instalación *f* sanitaria (water-supply and drainage system).

plumbism ['plʌm,bizəm] *n* MED saturnismo *m* (lead poisoning).

plumbum ['plʌmbəm] *n* plomo *m*.

plume [plu:m] *n* pluma *f* (feather) || penacho *m* (on hat) || *plume of smoke* penacho de humo.

plume [plu:m] *vt* emplumar (to adorn with feathers) || — *to plume o.s.* arreglarse las plumas (the birds) || FIG *to plume o.s. on* vanagloriarse de.

plumed [-d] *adj* plumado, da (feathered) || con penacho, empenachado, da (helmet).

plummet ['plʌmit] *n* plomo *m* (of plumb line, of fishing line, etc.) || pesa *f* (of a clock) || plomada *f* (plumb line) || MAR sonda *f* || FIG lastre *m*, peso *m*.

plummet ['plʌmit] *vi* caer en picado (a bird, a plane) || caer a plomo (object, person) || caer verticalemente (prices).

plummy ['plʌmi] *adj* pastoso, sa (voice).

plump [plʌmp] *adj* rellenito, ta; regordete, ta (persons) || gordo, da (animals) || categórico, ca; terminante (denial).
◆ *n* ruido *m* sordo (sound) || *to fail with a plump* caer pesadamente.
◆ *adv* con un ruido sordo (with a dull sound) || pesadamente (heavily) || justo (straight down) || categóricamente, terminantemente (categorically).

plump [plʌmp] *vt* soltar bruscamente, dejar caer pesadamente (to drop) || engordar (to fatten).
◆ *vi* caer de golpe, dejarse caer pesadamente (to fall heavily) || ponerse regordete (to put on weight) || — *to plump for* votar por; decidirse por || *to plump out* o *up* hincharse (sails, etc.), engordar (people).

plumpness [-nis] *n* gordura *f*.

plumule ['plu:mju:l] *n* BOT plúmula *f* || plumón *m* (small or downy feather).

plumy ['plu:mi] *adj* plumoso, sa.

plunder ['plʌndə*] *n* saqueo *m*, pillaje *m* (the act of plundering) || botín *m* (the goods obtained).

plunder ['plʌndə*] *vt* saquear, cometer pillaje en, pillar (a town, etc.) || robar (a safe, tomb, pantry).
◆ *vi* robar.

plunderer [-rə*] *n* saqueador *m*.

plundering ['plʌndəriŋ] *n* saqueo *m*.

plunge [plʌndʒ] *n* zambullida *f*, chapuzón *m* (short dive into water) || salto *m* (leap, high dive) || inmersión *f* (swim under water) || piscina *f* (pool) || SP estirada *f* (dive in rugby, etc.) | caída *f* (fall) || baño *m*, remojón *m* (dip); *I'm going for a plunge* voy a darme un baño || *to take the plunge* aventurarse, dar un paso decisivo.

plunge [plʌndʒ] *vt* hundir, meter; *to plunge a knife into sth.* hundir el cuchillo en algo; *to plunge one's hand into one's pocket* meter la mano en el bolsillo || hundir, clavar (a dagger) || sumergir (to submerge) || hundir, sumir; *plunged into despair* hundido en la desesperación || templar (steel) || *the room, the town was plunged into darkness* el cuarto, la ciudad quedó a oscuras.
◆ *vi* arrojarse (to throw o.s.) || tirarse [de cabeza], zambullirse (into water) || saltar (to dive) || caer (to fall) || sumergirse; *the submarine plunged* el submarino se sumergió || cabecear (a ship) || corcovear (a horse) || ser muy escotado (a dress) || precipitarse (to move suddenly) || hundirse, sumirse (into despair) || lanzarse; *he plunged into his speech* se lanzó a hablar; *I hesitated before plunging* vacilé antes de lanzarme || actuar precipitadamente, precipitarse; *he always plunges into things* siempre actúa precipitadamente || jugar fuerte (to bet) || arriesgar mucho dinero (in the stock exchange).

plunger [-ə*] *n* TECH émbolo *m* (piston) || desatascador *m* (for clearing drains, for pipes, etc.).

plunging [-iŋ] *adj* muy bajo (neckline).

plunk [plʌŋk] *n* ruido *m* sordo (dull, short sound) || rasgueo *m*, punteo *m* (noise of a banjo, of a guitar, etc.) || golpe *m* seco (forceful blow) || FAM dólar *m*.
◆ *adv* con un ruido sordo *or* seco.

plunk; plonk [plɔŋk] [plʌŋk] *vt* dejar caer pesadamente (to put down suddenly and heavily) || rasguear, puntear (a banjo, a guitar, etc.).
◆ *vi* dejarse caer pesadamente (into a chair).

pluperfect ['plu:'pə:fikt] *n* GRAMM pluscuamperfecto *m*.

plural ['pluərəl] *adj* plural; *plural noun* sustantivo plural || plural, del plural (form, ending).
◆ *n* plural *m*.

pluralism [-izəm] *n* pluralismo *m* || REL multiplicidad *f* de cargos.

pluralist [-ist] *n* pluralista *m* & *f*.

plurality [pluə'ræliti] *n* pluralidad *f* || mayoría *f*, pluralidad *f*; *by a plurality of votes* por mayoría de votos.

pluralize ['pluərəlaiz] *vt* pluralizar.

pluricellular [,pluəri'seljulə*] *adj* pluricelular.

plus [plʌs] *prep* más; *four plus two is six* cuatro más dos son seis || FAM más, además de; *he arrived with a trunk plus a large suitcase* llegó con un baúl más una maleta grande.
◆ *adj* positivo, va; *plus number* número positivo || de ingresos, de entradas; *the plus column of an account* la columna de ingresos de una cuenta || ELECTR positivo, va || más; *the plus sign* el signo más || — *plus sign* signo *m* más || *to be plus five pounds on a sale* ganar cinco libras en una venta || *twenty pounds plus* algo más de veinte libras.
◆ *n* cantidad *f* positiva (a positive quantity) || signo *m* más (plus sign).
— OBSERV El plural del sustantivo *plus* es *plusses* en Gran Bretaña y *pluses* en Estados Unidos.

plus fours ['plʌs'fɔ:z] *pl n* pantalones *m* de golf, pantalones *m* bombachos.

plush [plʌʃ] *n* felpa *f*.
◆ *adj* afelpado, da; de felpa || FIG lujoso, sa (luxurious).

plushy [-i] *adj* afelpado, da; de felpa || FIG lujoso, sa (luxurious).

Plutarch ['plu:tɑ:k] *pr n* Plutarco *m*.

Pluto ['plu:təu] *pr n* MYTH & ASTR Plutón *m*.

plutocracy [plu:'tɔkrəsi] *n* plutocracia *f*.

plutocrat ['plu:təukræt] *n* plutócrata *m* & *f*.

plutocratic [,plu:təu'krætik] *adj* plutocrático, ca.

plutonium [plu:'təunjəm] *n* plutonio *m*.

pluvial [plu:vjəl] *adj* pluvial.
◆ *n* REL capa *f* pluvial.

pluviograph ['plu:viəgrɑ:f] *n* pluviógrafo *m*.

pluviometer [plu:vi'ɔmitə*] *n* pluviómetro *m*.

pluviometry [pluvi'ɔmitri] *n* pluviometría *f*.

pluviosity [plu:vi'ɔsiti] *n* pluviosidad *f*.

pluvious ['plu:vjəs] *adj* pluvioso, sa; lluvioso, sa.

ply [plai] *n* cabo *m*; *two-ply wool* lana de dos cabos || chapa *f* (layer of plywood) || capa *f* (of fabric).

ply [plai] *vt* manejar, emplear; *to ply an axe* manejar el hacha || ejercer (a trade, etc.) || aplicarse a (to dedicate o.s.) || MAR hacer el trayecto de, ir y venir por; *this boat plies the Channel* este barco hace el trayecto del Canal de la Mancha || *to ply with* acosar con; *to ply s.o. with questions* acosar a alguien con preguntas; ofrecer *or* dar constantemente (to supply persistently).

◆ *vi* *to ply between* hacer el servicio entre, ir y venir entre || *to ply for hire* estar a la espera de clientes.

plywood [-wud] *n* contrachapado *m*, madera *f* contrachapada.

PM *abbr of [prime minister]* primer ministro.

pneumatic [nju:'mætik] *adj* neumático, ca || *pneumatic tyre* neumático *m*.

pneumatic drill [-dril] *n* taladradora *f* neumática.

pneumatics [-s] *n* PHYS neumática *f*.

pneumococcus [ˌnju:məu'kɔkəs] *n* neumococo *m*.

— OBSERV El plural de *pneumococcus* es *pneumococci*.

pneumogastric [ˌnju:məu'gæstrik] *adj* ANAT neumogástrico, ca.

◆ *n* ANAT nervio *m* neumogástrico, neumogástrico *m*.

pneumonia [nju'məunjə] *n* MED pulmonía *f*, neumonía *f*.

pneumonic [nju'mɔnik] *adj* MED neumónico, ca.

pneumothorax [ˌnju:məu'θɔ:ræks] *n* MED neumotórax *m*.

Po [pəu] *pr n* GEOGR Po *m*.

poach [pəutʃ] *vt* CULIN escalfar (eggs) | hervir (fish) || cazar furtivamente, cazar en vedado (to hunt illegally) || pescar furtivamente, pescar en vedado (to fish illegally) || pisotear (to trample ground) || FIG robar (to steal).

◆ *vi* cazar furtivamente, cazar en vedado (to hunt illegally) || pescar furtivamente, pescar en vedado (to fish illegally) || enfangarse (to become soggy) || FIG *to poach on s.o.'s preserves* meter la hoz en mies ajena.

poached [-t] *adj* escalfado, da (egg).

poacher [-ə*] *n* cazador *m* furtivo (hunter) || pescador *m* furtivo (fisherman).

poaching [-iŋ] *n* caza *f* furtiva (hunting) || pesca *f* furtiva (fishing).

pock [pɔk] *n* MED picadura *f*, señal *f*.

pocket [-it] *n* bolsillo *m* (on a garment); *flap pocket* bolsillo con cartera || hueco *m*, cavidad *f* (small hollow) || MIN bolsa *f* (deposit of oil, of gas, etc.) | filón *m* (of metal, of mineral, etc.) || AVIAT bache *m* (air pocket) || tronera *f* (of a billiard table) || bolsa *f* (under the eyes) || MIL foco *m*; *pocket of resistance* foco de resistencia || ZOOL bolsa *f* (external pouch) || — *breast pocket* bolsillo de pecho || FIG *empty pockets* persona *f* sin dinero || *patch pocket* bolsillo de parche || *pocket battleship* acorazado *m* de bolsillo || US *pocket billiards* billar *m* americano | US *pocket book* libro *m* de bolsillo || HIST *pocket borough* municipio *m* en el que han sido comprados los votos || *pocket calculator* calculadora *f* de bolsillo || *pocket dictionary, edition* diccionario *m*, edición *f* de bolsillo || *pocket handkerchief* pañuelo *m* de bolsillo || *pocket money* dinero *m* para gastos menudos, dinero de bolsillo || *to be ten pounds out of pocket, in pocket* salir perdiendo, ganando diez libras || *to dip in one's own pocket* poner de su bolsillo || FIG *to have s.o. in one's pocket* tener a alguien en el bolsillo | *to have sth. in one's pocket* tener algo en el bolsillo (to be sure of victory, of success, etc.) | *to line one's pockets* llenarse los bolsillos, forrarse | *to live beyond one's pocket* vivir por encima de sus posibilidades económicas || *to pay s.o. out of one's own pocket* pagar a alguien de su bolsillo || FIG *to put one's hand in one's pocket* echar mano al bolsillo | *to put one's pride in one's pocket* tragarse el orgullo.

pocket [-it] *vt* meterse en el bolsillo; *he pocketed the keys* se metió las llaves en el bolsillo || FIG embolsarse; *he had pocketed fifty pounds of the company's money* se había embolsado cincuenta libras del dinero de la compañía || FIG & FAM birlar, mangar (to pinch); *someone must have pocketed my lighter* alguien me debe haber mangado el mechero || meter en la tronera (a billiard ball) || SP cerrar el paso a (in a race) || FIG tragarse; *to pocket one's pride* tragarse el orgullo.

pocketbook [-itbuk] *n* cartera *f*, monedero *m*, billetero *m*, billetera *f* (purse, wallet) || bolso *m* [AMER cartera *f*] (handbag).

pocketful [-itful] *n* bolsillo *m* (content).

pocketknife [-itnaif] *n* navaja *f*.

pocket-size [-itsaiz] *adj* de bolsillo.

pocket veto ['pɔkit'vi:təu] *n* US veto *m* indirecto.

pockmark ['pɔkma:k] *n* picadura *f* de viruela, señal *f* de viruela.

pockmarked [-t] *adj* picado de viruelas.

pod [pɔd] *n* BOT vaina *f* (of peas, of beans, etc.) | capullo *m* (cocoon, etc.) || ZOOL manada *f* (of seals or whales) || TECH ranura *f* (groove, channel) || mandril *m* (of a drill).

pod [pɔd] *vt* desvainar, pelar (peas).

◆ *vi* hincharse (to swell) || producir vainas (to produce pods).

podagra [pəu'dægrə] *n* MED podagra *f*.

podgy ['pɔdʒi] *adj* gordinflón, ona; regordete, ta.

podium ['pəudjuəm] *n* podio *m* || MUS estrado *m* (of the conductor).

— OBSERV El plural de *podium* es *podia* o *podiums*.

podology [pɔ'dɔlədʒi] *n* MED podología *f*.

podzol ['pɔdzɔl] *n* podzol *m*.

poem ['pəuim] *n* poesía *f*, poema *m* (short poem); *the poems of Lorca* las poesías de Lorca || poema *m* (long); *Homer's poems* los poemas de Homero.

poesy ['pəuizi] *n* poesía *f*.

poet ['pəuit] *n* poeta *m*.

poetaster [ˌpəui'tæstə*] *n* poetastro *m*.

poetess ['pəuitis] *n* poetisa *f*.

poetic [pəu'etik]; **poetical** [-əl] *adj* poético, ca; *poetic licence* licencia poética || FIG *poetic justice* justicia divina.

poeticize [pəu'etisaiz] *vt* poetizar.

poetics [pəu'etiks] *n* poética *f*, arte *m* poética.

poetize ['pəuitaiz] *vt* poetizar.

poet laureate ['pəuit'lɔ:riit] *n* poeta *m* laureado.

— OBSERV El plural es *poet laureates* o *poets laureate*.

poetry ['pəuitri] *n* poesía *f*.

pogo stick ['pəugəustik] *n* saltador *m* (toy).

pogrom ['pɔgrəm] *n* pogrom *m*, pogromo *m*.

poignancy ['pɔinənsi] *n* patetismo *m* (sadness) || intensidad *f* (intensity) || mordacidad *f* (of a satire).

poignant ['pɔinənt] *adj* conmovedor, ra (moving) || intenso, sa; agudo, da (grief, pain) || profundo, da; enorme; *of poignant interest* de un interés enorme || mordaz (satire).

point [pɔint] *n* punto *m*; *four main points* cuatro puntos principales; *to agree on a point* estar de acuerdo en un punto; *point of departure* punto de partida; *point of interest* punto de interés; *melting, boiling point* punto de fusión, de ebullición || cuestión *f*, punto *m* (problem) || punto *m*, lugar *m* (place) || aspecto *m* (aspect) || momento *m* (moment) || significado *m*, sentido *m*; *the point of a story* el significado de una historia || gracia *f*, chiste *m* (of a joke) || cualidad *f*; *generosity is not one of her better points* la generosidad no es una de sus mejores cualidades; *to have one's good points* tener sus cualidades || motivo *m*, interés *m*, razón *f*; *I see no point in it* no le veo el interés; *is there any point in going on?* ¿hay algún motivo para continuar? || punta *f* (sharp end); *to sharpen the point of a pencil* sacar punta a un lápiz; *the point of the arrow* la punta de la flecha || objeto *m* puntiagudo (sharp object) || punto *m* (full stop) || MATH punto *m* (in geometry) | coma *f* (in decimals); *five point seven (5.7)* cinco coma siete [5,7] || grado *m* (of thermometer); *to rise two points* subir dos grados || COMM entero *m*; *the shares dropped three points* las acciones bajaron de tres enteros || PRINT punto *m* || GEOGR cabo *m*, punta *f*, promontorio *m* || SP ataque *m* (in fencing) | posición *f* de uno de los jugadores (cricket) | tanto *m*, punto *m*; *to score a point* marcar un tanto || muestra *f* (of gundogs) || cuerna *f* (of a deer) || característica *f* principal, cualidad *f* (of an animal) || MAR punto *m* (compass) || MIL punta *f* || punto *m* (in braille) || ELECTR contacto *m* (contact) || — *at the point of death* a punto de morirse, in articulo mortis || *at the point where* allí donde, donde (there where), cuando (when) || *at this point* al llegar a este punto || *at this point in time* en este momento || *beside the point* fuera de propósito, que no viene al caso || *critical point* punto crítico || *focal point* punto focal || *he was severe to the point of cruelty* fue severo hasta la crueldad || *high point* punto álgido || *in point* que viene al caso (relevant), de que se trata, en cuestión (in question) || *in point of* en cuanto a, por lo que se refiere a; *in point of numbers* por lo que se refiere al número || *in point of fact* en realidad || *not to put too fine a point on it* hablando sin rodeos || *off the point* fuera de propósito, que no viene al caso || *on a point of clarification* para una aclaración || *on that point* en ese momento (at that moment), en cuanto a eso (regarding that) || *on the point of* a punto de; *he was on the point of falling* estaba a punto de caerse || *penalty point* punto de penalty || *point by point* punto por punto || *point duty* dirección *f* del tráfico, control *m* de la circulación || *point of conscience* caso *m* de conciencia || *point of fact* hecho *m* || *point of honour* punto de honor || *point of impact* punto de impacto || *point of order* cuestión de orden || *point of reference* punto de referencia || *point of view* punto de vista || *starting point* punto de partida || *strong point* punto fuerte || *supporting point* punto de apoyo || *that's just the point!* ¡eso es!, ¡ahí está! || *that's not the point* eso no tiene nada que ver, no es eso || *the point at issue* el punto en cuestión || *the point is that* el caso es que || *this is the point* esto es lo importante, esto es lo que cuenta || *to a certain point* hasta cierto punto || *to be beside* o *off the point* no venir al caso, no tener nada que ver || *to be to the point* venir al caso || *to carry one's point* conseguir lo que uno quiere || *to catch the point* comprender || *to get back to the point* volver al tema || *to get* o *to wander off the point* salirse del tema || *to get the point* comprender || *to get* o *to come to the point* ir al grano || *to give a twenty point advantage* dar veinte puntos de

ventaja || *to give point to an objection* dar valor *or* importancia a una objeción || *to keep* o *to stick to the point* no salirse del tema, ceñirse al tema || *to make a point* hacer una observación, llamar la atención sobre un punto || *to make a point of* creerse en la obligación de || *to make one's point* lograr lo que uno quiere, salirse con la suya || *to miss the point* no comprender; *he has completely missed the point* no ha comprendido absolutamente nada || *to press the point that* insistir en que, hacer hincapié en que || *to speak to the point* ceñirse al tema || *to stretch a point* hacer una excepción || *to such a point* hasta tal punto || *to taper to a point* terminarse en punta || *to the point* pertinente || *up to a point* hasta cierto punto || *weak point* punto débil *or* flaco || *we have reached the point of no return* no podemos volver atrás || *what's the point of having a horse?* ¿para qué sirve tener un caballo?
◆ *pl* extremidades *f* (of a horse) || agujas *f* (of railway) || — *cardinal points* puntos cardinales || *suspension points* puntos suspensivos || *to reach all points in England* llegar a todos los puntos de Inglaterra || SP *to win on points* ganar por puntos (boxing).

point [pɔint] *vt* afilar, sacar punta a; *to point a pencil* sacar punta a un lápiz || apuntar; *to point a gun at s.o.* apuntar a uno con un arma || TECH mampostear || poner los puntos a (jewish writing) || señalar, indicar; *Carol pointed the way* Carol indicó el camino.
◆ *vi* señalar; *the compass needle always points north* la aguja de la brújula siempre señala el norte || mostrar la caza, pararse (hunting dog).
◆ *phr v* **to point at** señalar; *to point a finger at* señalar con el dedo | apuntar (to aim) || **to point out** señalar, hacer notar, hacer observar; *Carol pointed out my mistake* Carol señaló mi error; *she pointed out that it was not David's fault* hizo notar que no era culpa de David | advertir; *she pointed out to me that it was dangerous* me advirtió que era peligroso | señalar, indicar; *I'd like to point out that* me gustaría señalar que || **to point to** señalar; *an arrow pointing to Raymond's house* una flecha señalando la casa de Ramón | indicar; *everything points to his guilt* todo indica que es culpable | marcar; *the hands pointed to nine o'clock* las manecillas marcaban las nueve || **to point up** poner de relieve.

point-blank [-'blæŋk] *adv* a boca de jarro, a quema ropa; *she shot him point-blank* le disparó a quema ropa || sin rodeos, directamente, a boca de jarro, a quema ropa; *he asked her point-blank* se lo preguntó sin rodeos || categóricamente; *she refused point-blank* se negó categóricamente.
◆ *adj* disparado a quema ropa *or* a boca de jarro (shot) || directo, ta; hecho a quema ropa *or* a boca de jarro; *a point-blank question* una pregunta directa || categórico, ca; *a point-blank refusal* una negativa categórica.

pointed [-id] *adj* puntiagudo, da (having a sharp point) || FIG mordaz (critical); *a pointed attack* un ataque mordaz | intencionado, da (intended); *pointed rudeness* descortesía intencionada | picante (lively, piquant) || ARCH *pointed arch* arco ojival *or* apuntado.

pointedly [-idli] *adv* con mordacidad (cuttingly) || intencionadamente (deliberately).

pointer [-ə*] *n* indicador *m* (needle) || manecilla *f* (of a clock) || fiel *m* (of scales) || FIG indicación *f* (indication, clue) | consejo *m* (suggestion) || perro *m* de muestra (dog) || puntero *m* (for blackboard) || INFORM puntero *m*.

pointillism ['pwæntilizəm] *n* ARTS puntillismo *m*.

pointillist ['pwæntilist] *n* ARTS puntillista *m* & *f*.

pointless ['pɔintlis] *adj* sin punta (without a point) || FIG insustancial, sin sentido (meaningless); *a pointless conversation* una conversación insustancial | inútil; *it's pointless continuing* es inútil continuar | sin sentido, que carece de sentido (existence).

pointlessly [-lisli] *adv* inútilmente (uselessly).

pointlessness [-lisnis] *n* inutilidad *f* (uselessness) || insensatez *f*, falta *f* de sentido (senselessness).

poise [pɔiz] *n* PHYS poise *m* (viscosity unit) || equilibrio *m* (balance) || porte *m* (bearing) || elegancia *f* (elegance) || aplomo *m*, serenidad *f* (mental stability).

poise [pɔiz] *vt* poner en equilibrio (to balance) || preparar; *to poise o.s. for an ordeal* prepararse para una prueba.
◆ *vi* estar en equilibrio || estar suspendido (to hang as if suspended) || cernerse (to hover).

poised [-d] *adj* suspendido, da (suspended) || listo, ta; preparado, da (ready for action) || sereno, na (calm).

poison [-n] *n* veneno *m*, ponzoña *f*; *deadly poison* veneno mortífero; *selfishness is the poison of mankind* el egoísmo es el veneno de la humanidad || — FIG *to hate like poison* odiar a muerte || FAM *what's your poison?* ¿con qué te quieres envenenar?, ¿qué quieres tomar? (drink).
◆ *adj* venenoso, sa; ponzoñoso, sa (snake, etc.) || tóxico, ca (gas, drug, etc.) || — *a poison arrow* una flecha envenenada || *poison hemlock* cicuta *f*.

poison [-n] *vt* envenenar || FIG envenenar, emponzoñar.

poisoner [-nə*] *n* envenenador, ra.

poisoning [-niŋ] *n* envenenamiento *m* || *to die of poisoning* morir envenenado.

poisonous [-nəs] *adj* venenoso, sa; ponzoñoso, sa (snake, etc.) || tóxico, ca (drug, gas, etc.) || FIG odioso, sa (hateful) | nefasto, ta; pernicioso, sa (harmful) | malísimo, ma (very bad).

poison-pen ['pɔizn'pen] *adj* *poison-pen letter* carta *f* ofensiva anónima.

poke [pəuk] *n* hurgonada *f* (with a poker) || empujón *m* con el dedo (with a finger) || pinchazo *m* (with sth. sharp) || codazo *m* (with the elbow); *he gave me a poke in the ribs* me dio un codazo en las costillas || golpe *m* (blow) || trangallo *m* (for animals) || bolsa *f*, saco *m* (bag) || — FIG *to buy a pig in a poke* comprar a ciegas || *to give the fire a poke* atizar el fuego.

poke [pəuk] *vt* atizar, hurgar; *to poke the fire* atizar el fuego || hurgarse (one's nose) || dar con la punta del dedo (with the finger); *he poked me in the arm* me dio con la punta del dedo en el brazo || dar un codazo (with the elbow) || meter; *to poke one's finger into a hole* meter el dedo en un agujero; *he poked his finger in my eye* me metió el dedo en el ojo; *to poke one's hand through a letterbox* meter la mano en un buzón || hacer; *he poked a hole in the wall* hizo un agujero en la pared || empujar (to push) || asomar; *Raymond poked his head round the door* Ramón asomó la cabeza por la puerta || FAM dar un golpe *or* un puñetazo a (to hit) || — *to poke fun at* reírse de || FIG *to poke one's nose into* meter la nariz en, meter las narices en.
◆ *vi* hurgar (to make digs); *to poke at sth. with a stick* hurgar algo con un bastón || asomar; *his head poked through the window* su cabeza asomó por la ventana.
◆ *phr v* **to poke about** o **around** fisgonear, hurgar (to search); *to poke around in a drawer* fisgonear en un cajón | entrometerse (to meddle) | husmear (to sniff around) | curiosear; *to poke around in the shops* curiosear en las tiendas || **to poke out** sacar; *he poked her eye out* le sacó un ojo | asomar, sacar (one's head) | salirse; *a car poked out from the row* un coche se salió de la fila.

poker [-ə*] *n* hurgón *m*, atizador *m* (for a fire) || póker *m*, póquer *m* (card game); *poker of aces* póker de ases || FIG *as stiff as a poker* más tieso que un palo.

poker face [-əfeis] *n* FAM cara *f* inmutable.

poky; US **pokey** ['pəuki] *adj* diminuto, ta (very small) || US lento, ta || — *a poky little room* un cuartucho || *a poky old town* un pueblucho.

Poland ['pəulənd] *pr n* Polonia *f*.

polar ['pəulə*] *adj* polar; *polar circle* círculo polar; *polar coordinates* coordenadas polares || FIG opuesto, ta; *polar views* ideas opuestas || — *polar bear* oso *m* polar || *polar cap* casquete *m* polar || *polar climate* clima *m* polar || *polar lights* aurora *f* boreal.

polarimeter [,pəulə'rimitə*] *n* PHYS polarímetro *m*.

Polaris [pəu'læris] *pr n* estrella *f* polar.

polariscope [pəu'læriskəup] *n* PHYS polariscopio *m*.

polarity [pəu'læriti] *n* polaridad *f*.

polarization [,pəulərai'zeiʃən] *n* polarización *f*.

polarize ['pəuləraiz] *vt* polarizar.

polarizing ['pəuləraiziŋ] *adj* polarizador, ra.

Polaroid ['pəulərɔid] *n* polaroid *m*.

polder ['pɔldə*] *n* pólder *m*.

pole [pəul] *n* ELECTR, MATH & BIOL polo *m*; *negative pole* polo negativo; *magnetic pole* polo magnético || palo *m*, vara *f* (long piece of wood) || barra *f* (of metal) || poste *m*; *telegraph pole* poste telegráfico || estaca *f*, poste *m* (of a tent) || lanza *f* (of carriage) || MAR mástil *m* (mast) || asta *f*; *flag pole* asta de bandera || pértiga *f* (for propelling a punt) || palo *m*, estaca *f* (for climbing plants) || SP pértiga *f* [AMER garrocha *f*]; *pole vault* salto de pértiga || medida *f* de longitud de 5,03 m || — *greasy pole* palo ensebado || *pole horse* caballo *m* de tronco || FIG *to be poles apart* ser polos opuestos | *to be up the pole* estar como una cabra (crazy), estar metido en líos (in trouble).

pole [pəul] *vt* empujar con una pértiga (to propel with a pole).

Pole [pəul] *n* polaco, ca (native of Poland) || polo *m*; *North Pole* Polo Norte.

poleaxe; US **poleax** [-æks] *n* HIST alabarda *f* (lonz-handled axe) | hacha *f* de abordaje (for grappling an enemy vessel) | hacha *f* de armas (battle axe).

poleaxe; US **poleax** [-æks] *vt* desnucar.

pole bean [-biːn] *n* BOT judía *f* trepadora [AMER fríjol *m* trepador].

polecat [-kæt] *n* ZOOL turón *m* || US mofeta *f* (skunk).

polemic [pɔ'lemik] *adj* polémico, ca.
◆ *n* polémica *f* (controversy) || polemista *m* & *f* (person involved in a controversy).

polemical [pɔ'lemikəl] *adj* polémico, ca.

polemicist [pɔ'lemisist] *n* polemista *m* & *f*.

polemicize [pɔ'leməsaiz] *vt* polemizar.

polemics [pɔ'lemiks] *n* polémica *f*.

polenta [pəu'lentə] *n* CULIN polenta *f*.

polestar ['pəulstɑː*] *n* estrella *f* polar.

police [pə'liːs] *n* policía *f*; *to join the police* entrar en la policía || US mantenimiento *m* del orden (keeping in order) | control *m* (control) || US MIL limpieza *f* (cleaning).
◆ *pl* policía *f sing*; *a squad of mounted police* una escuadra de la policía montada; *the police were called in* llamaron a la policía.

police [pə'liːs] *vt* vigilar, mantener el orden en; *the match will be policed by a detachment of forty* el partido será vigilado por un destacamento de cuarenta hombres; *twenty men policed the town* veinte hombres mantuvieron el orden en la ciudad || vigilar; *to police the border* vigilar la frontera || tener un servicio de policía en (to provide with police) || supervisar, vigilar (to supervise) || *US* MIL limpiar (to clean up).

police car [-kɑ:*] *n* coche *m* de policía.

police constable [-'kʌnstəbl] *n* policía *m*, guardia *m*.

police dog [-dɔg] *n* perro *m* policía.

police force [-fɔ:s] *n* cuerpo *m* de policía; *to join the police force* entrar en el cuerpo de policía || fuerza *f* pública; *the police force intervened* intervino la fuerza pública || policía *f*; *this town has an efficient police force* esta ciudad tiene una policía eficiente.

police headquarters [-'hed'kwɔ:təz] *n* jefatura *f* de policía.

policeman [-mən] *n* policía *m*, guardia *m*.
— OBSERV El plural de *policeman* es *policemen*.

police power [-'pauə*] *n* fuerza *f* pública.

police record [-'rekɔ:d] *n* antecedentes *m pl* penales.

police state [-'steit] *n* estado *m* policíaco.

police station [-'steiʃən] *n* comisaría *f* de policía.

policewoman [-,wumən] *n* mujer *f* policía.
— OBSERV El plural de *policewoman* es *policewomen*.

policlinic [pɔli'klinik] *n* policlínica *f* [*AMER* policlínico *m*].

policy ['pɔlisi] *n* política *f* (of a government); *foreign policy* política exterior; *a revolutionary policy* una política revolucionaria || norma *f*, principio *m*, sistema *m* (principle); *our policy is to satisfy our customers* tenemos por norma satisfacer a nuestros clientes; *it is always my policy to ask people's opinion* tengo por principio pedir a la gente su opinión || táctica *f*; *would it be good policy to accept the invitation* ¿sería buena táctica aceptar la invitación? || póliza *f*; *insurance policy* póliza de seguros || *US* lotería *f* clandestina (lottery) || — *good-neighbour policy* política de buena vecindad || *to change one's policy* cambiar de política *or* de táctica.

policyholder [-,həuldə*] *n* asegurado, da.

polio ['pəuliəu] *n* MED polio *f*.

poliomyelitis ['pəuliəumaiə'laitis] *n* MED poliomielitis *f*.

Polish ['pəuliʃ] *adj* polaco, ca.
◆ *n* polaco *m* (language).

polish ['pɔliʃ] *n* pulimento *m* (act of polishing) || lustre *m*, brillo *m* (shine, lustre); *it loses its polish very easily* pierde su brillo muy fácilmente || esmalte *m* para las uñas, laca *f* para las uñas (for nails) || cera *f* (for furniture, for floors, etc.) || betún *m* [*AMER* cera *f*, bola *f*] (for shoes) || FIG refinamiento *m*, finura *f*, elegancia *f*; *a show which lacks polish* un espectáculo que carece de refinamiento || — *a high polish* mucho brillo || *to give sth. a polish* pulir algo, dar brillo a algo || FIG *to have polish* ser fino (person, show), ser pulido (style) | *your style lacks polish* su estilo no es muy pulido, le hace falta perfeccionar el estilo.

polish ['pɔliʃ] *vt* encerar (the floor, furniture) || limpiar [*AMER* embolar] (shoes) || limpiar, dar brillo a (silverware) || pulir, bruñir (metals) || FIG pulir, refinar; *this child needs a little polishing* a este niño hace falta pulirle un poco | pulir, perfeccionar (to perfect) | pulir (the style) || TECH pulir || — FAM *to polish off* zampar, zamparse (to costume quickly); *he polished off three chickens* se zampó tres pollos; despachar (work), despachar, liquidar, cepillarse (to kill) || *to polish up* dar brillo a (to shine up), perfeccionar, pulir (to revise and improve).

polished [-t] *adj* pulido, da (cleaned with polish) || FIG refinado, da; fino, na (refined) | pulido, da (style, etc.).

polisher [-ə*] *n* pulidor, ra (person) || pulidora *f* (machine) || enceradora *f* (floor-polishing machine).

polishing [-iŋ] *adj* pulidor, ra || — TECH *polishing machine* pulidora *f* || *polishing wax* cera *f*.
◆ *n* pulido.

Politburo [pɔ'litbjuərəu] *n* Politburó *m*.

polite [pə'lait] *adj* cortés (tactful, correct); *a polite answer* una respuesta cortés || educado, da; fino, na (refined); *in polite society* entre gente educada || atento, ta (considerate) || — *it is not polite to yawn* es de mala educación bostezar || *she was very polite to me* me trató con mucha cortesía *or* educación, estuvo muy atenta conmigo || *this word is not in polite usage* esta palabra es incorrecta.

politeness [-nis] *n* cortesía *f*, educación *f*, urbanidad *f* (good manners, etc.) || atenciones *f pl* (consideration).

politic ['pɔlitik] *adj* diplomático, ca; prudente (prudent) || astuto, ta; sagaz (astute) || ingenioso, sa (clever).

political [pə'litikəl] *adj* político, ca || — *political economy* economía política || *political jobbery* politiqueo *m* || *political prisonner* prisionero político, prisionera política || *political sciences* ciencias políticas.

politicaster [pə'liti,kɑ:stə*] *n* politicastro *m*.

politician [,pɔli'tiʃən] *n* político *m* || *petty politician* politicastro *m*.

politicize [pə'litisaiz] *vt* politizar.

politics ['pɔlitiks] *n* política *f*; *to talk politics* hablar de política.
◆ *pl* política *f sing*; *the politics of the last government were heavily criticized* la política del último gobierno fue muy criticada.

politization [,pəlitiˈzeiʃən] *n* politización *f*.

polity ['pɔliti] *n* gobierno *m* (organized government) || constitución *f* (constitution) || estado *m* (state).

polje ['pəuljə] *n* GEOL poljé *m* (depression).

polka ['pɔlkə] *n* polca *f* (dance).

polka dot [-dɔt] *n* lunar *m* || tela *f* de lunares (material).

poll [pəul] *n* votación *f* (the casting of votes, the number of votes cast); *a heavy poll* una votación masiva || escrutinio *m* (scrutiny) || elecciones *f pl* (elections) || sondeo *m*, encuesta *f*; *public opinion poll* sondeo de la opinión pública || capitación *f* (tax) || TECH cotillo *m* (blunt end of a hammer) || — *there was a poll of 65 %* ha votado el 65 % del electorado || *to hold a Gallup poll on rising prices* hacer una encuesta *or* un sondeo de la opinión pública sobre el alza de los precios.
◆ *pl* centro *m sing* electoral; *the polls shut at nine* el centro electoral cierra a las nueve || *to go to the polls* ir a las urnas, votar.

poll [pəul] *vt* obtener; *he polled two thousand votes* obtuvo dos mil votos || registrar los votos de (to record the votes of) || sondear; *to poll public opinion* sondear la opinión pública || descornar (to cut off the horns of) || esquilar (to cut off wool, etc.) || trasquilar (to cut off hair) || desmochar (a tree).
◆ *vi* votar (to vote).

pollard ['pɔləd] *n* árbol *m* desmochado (tree) || animal *m* mocho (animal).

pollee [,pəu'li] *n* entrevistado, da.

pollen ['pɔlin] *n* BOT polen *m* || *pollen count* índice *m* de polen contenido en el aire.

pollinate [-eit] *vt* BOT polinizar.

pollination [,pɔli'neiʃən] *n* BOT polinización *f*.

polling ['pəuliŋ] *n* votación *f*.

polling booth [-bu:θ] *n* cabina *f* electoral.

polling day [-dei] *n* día *m* de elecciones.

polling place [-pleis]; **polling station** [-'steiʃən] *n* centro *m or* colegio *m* electoral.

polliniferous [pɔli'nifərəs] *n* BOT polinífero, ra.

polliwog ['pɔliwɔg] *n* renacuajo *m* (tadpole).

pollster ['pəulstə*] *n* entrevistador, ra; encuestador, ra.

poll tax ['pəultæks] *n* capitación *f*.

pollutant [pə'lu:tənt] *n* contaminante *m*, agente *m* contaminador.

pollute [pə'lu:t] *vt* contaminar || REL profanar || FIG corromper (to corrupt).

polluting [-iŋ] *adj* contaminante.

polluting agent [-iŋ'eidʒənt] *n* contaminante *m*, agente *m* contaminador.

pollution [pə'lu:ʃən] *n* contaminación *f*, polución *f* || contaminación *f* del medio ambiente (of the environment) || REL profanación *f* || *air, river pollution* contaminación del aire, de los ríos.

Pollux ['pɔləks] *pr n* Pólux *m*.

pollywog ['pɔliwɔg] *n* renacuajo *m* (tadpole).

polo ['pəuləu] *n* SP polo *m* | polo *m* acuático (water polo).

poloist [-ist] *n* polista *m*, jugador *m* de polo.

polonaise [,pɔlə'neiz] *n* MUS polonesa *f*.

poloneck ['pəuləunek] *n* cuello *m* vuelto (collar) || jersey *m* de cuello vuelto (sweater).

polonium [pə'ləunjəm] *n* CHEM polonio *m*.

polo shirt ['pəuləuʃə:t] *n* polo *m*.

poltergeist ['pɔltəgaist] *n* duende *m*.

poltroon [pɔl'tru:n] *adj/n* cobarde.

poltroonery [-əri] *n* cobardía *f*.

poly ['pɔli] *n* FAM escuela *f* politécnica.

polyandry ['pɔliændri] *n* poliandria *f*.

polyanthus [,pɔli'ænθəs] *n* BOT prímula *f*.
— OBSERV El plural es *polyanthuses* o *polyanthi*.

polycephalous [pɔlike'fæləs] *adj* policéfalo, la.

polychroism ['pɔli,krəuizəm] *n* PHYS policroísmo *m*.

polychromatic [,pɔlikrə'mætik] *adj* policromo, ma.

polychrome ['pɔlikrəum] *adj* policromado, da; policromo, ma.

polychromy [-i] *n* policromía *f*.

polyclinic [,pɔli'klinik] *n* *US* policlínica *f* [*AMER* policlínico *m*].

polydactyl [,pɔli'dæktil] *adj/s* polidáctilo, la.

polyester ['pɔliestə*] *n* CHEM poliéster *m*.

polyethylene [,pɔli'eθəli:n] *n* CHEM polietileno *m*.

polygamist [pɔ'ligəmist] *n* polígamo, ma.

polygamous [pɔ'ligəməs] *adj* polígamo, ma.

polygamy [pɔ'ligəmi] *n* poligamia *f*.

polyglot ['pɔliglɔt] *adj* políglota, ta.
◆ *n* políglota, ta (person) || libro *m* políglota (book) || *the Polyglot Bible* la Biblia Políglota.

polygon ['pɔligən] *n* polígono *m*.

polygonaceae [pəligə'neisi:i] *pl n* poligonáceas *f*.

polygonal [pɔ'ligənl] *adj* poligonal.

polygraph ['pɔligrɑ:f] *n* polígrafo *m*.

polygraphy [pə'ligrafi] *n* poligrafía *f*.

polygyny [pɔ'lidʒini] *n* poliginia *f*.

polyhedral ['pɔli'hedrəl] *adj* MATH poliédrico, ca.

polyhedron ['pɔli'hedrən] *n* MATH poliedro *m*.
— OBSERV El plural de *polyhedron* es *polyhedra* o *polyhedrons*.

polymer ['pɔlimə*] *n* CHEM polímero *m*.

polymerism ['pɔlimerizəm] *n* CHEM polimería *f*.

polymerization [pəˌlimərai'zeiʃən] *n* polimerización *f*.

polymerize [pə'liməraiz] *vt* polimerizar.

polymorph ['pɔliˌmɔːf] *n* BIOL organismo *m* polimorfo || MIN sustancia *f* polimorfa.

polymorphic [ˌpɔli'mɔːfik] *adj* polimórfico, ca.

polymorphism [ˌpɔli'mɔːfizəm] *n* polimorfismo *m*.

polymorphous [ˌpɔli'mɔːfəs] *adj* polimorfo, fa.

Polynesia [ˌpɔli'niːzjə] *pr n* GEOGR Polinesia *f*.

Polynesian [-n] *adj/n* GEOGR polinesio, sia.

polynomial [ˌpɔli'nəumjəl] *adj* MATH polinómico, ca.
◆ *n* MATH polinomio *m*.

polyp ['pɔlip] *n* ZOOL pólipo *m*.

polypary ['pɔlipəri] *n* ZOOL polípero *m*.

polypeptide [ˌpɔli'peptaid] *n* CHEM polipéptido *m*.

polypetalous [pɔli'petələs] *adj* BOT polipétalo, la.

polyphase ['pɔlifeiz] *adj* ELECTR polifásico, ca.

polyphonic [ˌpɔli'fɔnik] *adj* polifónico, ca.

polyphony [pə'lifəni] *n* polifonía *f*.

polypus ['pɔlipəs] *n* MED pólipo *m*.
— OBSERV El plural de *polypus* es *polypi* o *polypuses*.

polysaccharide [pɔli'sækəraid] *n* CHEM polisacárido *m*.

polysemy ['pɔlisəmi] *n* polisemia *f*.

polystyrene [ˌpɔli'stairiːn] *n* CHEM poliestireno *m*.

polysyllabic ['pɔlisi'læbik]; **polysyllabical** [-əl] *adj* polisílabo, ba; polisilábico, ca.

polysyllable ['pɔliˌsiləbl] *n* polisílabo *m*.

polytechnic [ˌpɔli'teknik] *adj* politécnico, ca.
◆ *n* escuela *f* politécnica.

polytheism ['pɔliθiːizəm] *n* politeísmo *m*.

polytheistic [ˌpɔliθiː'istik]; **polytheistical** [-əl] *adj* politeísta.

polythene ['pɔliθiːn] *n* CHEM polietileno *m*.

polyunsaturated [pɔliʌn'sætjureitid] *adj* poliinsaturado, da; bajo, ja en colesterol.

polyurethane [pɔli'juərəθein] *n* poliuretano *m*.

polyvalence ['pɔli'veiləns] *n* polivalencia *f*.

polyvalent [ˌpɔli'veilənt] *adj* polivalente.

polyvinyl [ˌpɔli'vainil] *n* CHEM polivinilo *m*.

pomace ['pʌmis] *n* pulpa *f* de manzana (apple pulp) || pulpa *f* (of seeds).

pomaceous [pəu'meiʃəs] *adj* BOT pomáceo, a.

pomade [pə'mɑːd] *n* pomada *f*.

pomander [pəu'mændə*] *n* almohadilla *f* perfumada.

pomatum [pəu'meitəm] *n* pomada *f*.

pomegranate ['pɔmˌgrænit] *n* BOT granada *f* (fruit) | granado *m* (tree).

pomelo ['pɔmiləu] *n* BOT pomelo *m* (grapefruit).

pomfret ['pɔmfrət] *n* japuta *f* (fish).

pommel ['pʌml] *n* pomo *m* (knob on sword handle) || perilla *f* (of a saddle).

pommel ['pʌml] *vt* aporrear.

pommy ['pɔmi] *n* FAM inglés, esa [palabra despectiva empleada en Australia].

pomp [pɔmp] *n* pompa *f*.

pompadour ['pɔmpəduə*] *n* copete *m* (hairstyle).

pompano ['pɔmpənəu] *n* ZOOL pámpano *m* (fish).
— OBSERV El plural de la palabra inglesa *pompano* es *pompano* o *pompanos*.

Pompeii [pɔm'piːai] *pr n* GEOGR Pompeya *f*.

Pompeius [pɔm'peiəs] *pr n* Pompeyo *m* (Sextus).

Pompey ['pɔmpi] *pr n* Pompeyo *m* (Magnus).

pom-pom ['pɔmpɔm] *n* MIL cañón *m* antiaéreo.

pompon ['p˜ɔːmp˜ɔːŋ] *n* borla *f* (on a hat) || BOT rosa *f* de pitiminí | variedad *f* de crisantemo.

pomposity [pɔm'pɔsiti] *n* pomposidad *f* (splendour, grandiloquence) || presunción *f*, ostentación *f* (pretentiousness).

pompous ['pɔmpəs] *adj* pomposo, sa (style, occasion, etc.) || presumido, da; ostentoso, sa (pretentious).

ponce [pɔns] *n* FAM chulo *m*.

poncho ['pɔntʃəu] *n* poncho *m*.

pond [pɔnd] *n* charca *f* (natural) || estanque *m* (artificial) || vivero *m* (for breeding fish).

ponder [-ə*] *vt* considerar, examinar, sopesar.
◆ *vi* meditar, reflexionar || *to ponder on* o *over* meditar *or* reflexionar sobre.

ponderable [-ərəbl] *adj* ponderable.

ponderous [-ərəs] *adj* laborioso, sa; pesado, da; *ponderous style, movement* estilo, movimiento laborioso || pesado, da (heavy).

pone [pəun] *n* US pan *m* de maíz, borona *f* [AMER arepa *f*].

pong [pɔŋ] *vi* FAM apestar, heder.

poniard ['pɔnjəd] *vt* apuñalar.

pons [pɔns] *n* ANAT puente *m* de Varolio || FIG *pons asinorum* puente *m* de los asnos.

pontifex ['pɔntifeks] *n* HIST pontífice *m*.
— OBSERV El plural de *pontifex* es *pontifices*.

pontiff ['pɔntif] *n* REL pontífice *m* || *Sovereign Pontiff* Sumo Pontífice.

pontifical [pɔn'tifikəl] *adj* REL pontifical, pontificio, cia; *pontificial mass* misa pontifical || FIG presuntuoso, sa (pretentious) | dogmático, ca; sentencioso, sa (dogmatic).
◆ *n* REL pontifical *m* (book).
◆ *pl* pontifical *m sing* (garments and insignia).

pontificate [pɔn'tifikit] *n* REL pontificado *m*.

pontificate [pɔn'tifikeit] *vi* pontificar.

pontifices [pɔn'tifisiːz] *pl n* ⟶ **pontifex.**

Pontius Pilate ['pɔntjəs'pailət] *pr n* Poncio Pilato *m*.

ponton ['pɔntən] *n* US MIL pontón *m*.

pontoneer; US **pontonier** [ˌpɔntə'niə*] *n* MIL pontonero *m*.

pontoon [pɔn'tuːn] *n* pontón *m* (bridge of boats) || AVIAT flotador *m* || veintiuna *f* (card game) || *pontoon bridge* puente de pontones.

pony ['pəuni] *n* poney *m*, jaca *f* (horse) || FAM veinticinco libras *f pl* || US FAM chuleta *f* [para exámenes] (crib) | copa *f* de licor (liqueur glass) ||— US *pony express* sistema *m* postal que consistía en enviar el correo por el intermediario de hombres a caballo || *pony trekking* excursión *f* en poney.

ponytail [-teil] *n* cola *f* de caballo (hairstyle).

pooch [putʃ] *n* US FAM perro *m*.

poodle ['puːdl] *n* perro *m* de lanas, caniche *m*.

poof [puf] *n* POP marica *m*.

pooh [puː] *interj* ¡bah!

pooh-pooh [puː'puː] *vt* despreciar, desdeñar (to treat with contempt).

pool [puːl] *n* estanque *m* (artificial pond) || charca *f* (natural pond) || pozo *m* (in stream or river) || charco *m*; *a pool of blood, rainwater* un charco de sangre, de agua de lluvia || piscina *f* [AMER pileta *f*] (swimming pool) || pozo *m*, bote *m*, banca *f*, plato *m* (in card games) || guerra *f* (game of billiards played for money) || billar *m* americano (pocket billiards) || COMM fondos *m pl* comunes, capital *m* común (common fund) | recursos *m pl* comunes (combination of resources) | consorcio *m* (consortium) || FIG reserva *f* (reserve) | fuente *f* (source) ||— *pool table* billar *m*, mesa *f* de billar || *typing pool* servicio *m* de mecanografía.
◆ *pl* quinielas *f* (football pools).

pool [puːl] *vt* aunar, unir (knowledge, strength) || poner en un fondo común (money) || reunir (resources).

poolroom [-ruːm] *n* billar *m*, sala *f* de billar.

poop [puːp] *n* MAR popa *f* (stern) | toldilla *f* (poop deck).

poop [puːp] *vt* MAR recibir (un golpe de mar) por la popa || romper sobre la popa de [un barco] (waves).

poop deck [-dek] *n* MAR toldilla *f*.

poor [puə*] *adj* pobre; *the poor countries of the world* los países pobres del mundo; *the tragedy of being old and poor* la tragedia de ser viejo y pobre || pobre, necesitado, da; *a poor family* una familia pobre || malo, la; *poor quality* mala calidad; *poor memory* mala memoria; *to have a poor night* pasar una mala noche; *to be a poor actor* ser mal actor; *poor excuse* mala excusa || escaso, sa; poco numeroso, sa; *poor attendance* asistencia poco numerosa || pobre; *poor in vitamins* pobre en vitaminas || escaso, sa; malo, la (scanty); *a poor harvest* una cosecha escasa; *poor soil* terreno pobre || mediocre (lacking excellence); *a poor speaker* un orador mediocre; *a poor worker* un trabajador mediocre || tontaina, necio, cia (stupid); *poor character* persona tontaina || malo, la; delicado, da; *poor health* salud delicada || humilde (humble) || pobre; *I am but a poor tramp* no soy sino un pobre vagabundo || desgraciado, da (unfortunate, wretched) || poco favorable; *to have a poor opinion of* tener una opinión poco favorable de || FIG pobre, pobrecito, ta; *poor child!* ¡pobrecito niño!; *poor me!* ¡pobre de mí!; *poor John broke his neck* el pobre (de) Juan se rompió la nuca || — *I have but a poor chance of success* tengo poca probabilidad de éxito || *poor thing!* ¡pobrecito!, ¡pobrecita! || *to be a poor liar* mentir mal, no saber mentir || *to be as poor as a church mouse* ser más pobre que las ratas || *to be poor at* ser flojo en, ser poco fuerte en; *I am poor at mathematics* soy flojo en matemáticas || *to be two hundred pounds the poorer* salir perdiendo doscientas libras || FIG *to give a poor performance* hacer un pobre papel.
◆ *n the poor* los pobres.

poor box [-bɔks] *n* cepillo *m* de los pobres.

poorhouse [-haus] *n* US asilo *m* para los pobres.

poorly [-li] *adv* mal; *poorly fed* mal alimentado || pobremente ||— *to be doing poorly* ir mal || *to think poorly of* tener mala opinión de.
◆ *adj to be poorly* estar malo || *you are looking very poorly* tienes muy mala cara.

poorness [-nis] *n* pobreza *f* (poverty) || mala calidad *f* (bad quality).

poor-spirited [puə'spiritid] *adj* pusilánime, apocado, da.

pop [pɔp] *n* explosión *f*, detonación *f* (sound) | taponazo *m* (of a bottle opening) || FAM bebida *f* gaseosa (fizzy drink) | gaseosa *f* (le-

monade) || FAM papá *m* (father) || — FAM *in pop* empeñado (in pawn) || *to go pop* explotar, hacer pum.
◆ *adj* popular || — *pop art* pop art, arte *m* pop || *pop concert, festival* concierto *m*, festival *m* de música popular || *pop group* grupo *m* pop || *pop music* música «pop».
◆ *interj* ¡pum!

pop [pɔp] *vt* pinchar, hacer reventar (to burst with sth. sharp) || meter; *to pop sth. into one's mouth* meterse algo en la boca || hacer saltar (a cork) || FAM empeñar (to pawn) || — *to pop one's head out* asomar (de repente) la cabeza || FIG *to pop the question* declararse.
◆ *vi* explotar, estallar; reventar; *the balloon popped* el globo explotó || saltar (a cork) || disparar (to shoot).
◆ *phr v* **to pop across** o **by** o **over** o **round** acercarse, pasar; *pop by the baker's on your way back* acércate a la panadería de la vuelta; *pop by and see me* acércate a verme || **to pop in** entrar un momento; *are you sure won't pop in?* ¿está seguro de que no quiere entrar un momento? | asomarse; *he only popped in at the meeting* no hizo más que asomarse a la reunión | acercarse, pasar; *John popped in this morning* Juan pasó esta mañana; *pop in at the baker's for me* pasa por la panadería por favor | venir (to come) || **to pop off** irse, marcharse (to go) | FAM palmar (to die) || **to pop out** saltar (a cork, etc.) | salir; *he's just popped out for a moment* ha salido un momento; *pop out and buy some milk* sal un momento a comprar leche | salir de pronto; *to pop out from behind a tree* salir de pronto de detrás de un árbol || **to pop up** aparecer de pronto (to appear suddenly) | surgir (to arise); *this question has popped up before* esta cuestión ha surgido ya.

popcorn [-kɔːn] *n* palomitas *f pl* de maíz, rosetas *f pl* de maíz.

pope [pəup] *n* REL papa *m*; *Pope Pious IX* el Papa Pío IX || pope *m* (orthodox priest).

popedom [-dəm] *n* papado *m*.

popery ['pəupəri] *n* REL papismo *m*.

popeyed ['pɔpaid] *adj* de ojos saltones || *he looked at her popeyed* le miró con los ojos desorbitados.

popgun ['pɔpgʌn] *n* pistola *f* de aire comprimido (toy).

popinjay ['pɔpindʒei] *n* petimetre *m*, pedante *m*.

popish ['pəupiʃ] *adj* papista.

poplar ['pɔplə*] *n* BOT álamo *m* || US tulipero *m*, tulipanero *m* || — *black poplar* álamo negro, chopo *m* || *white poplar* álamo blanco.

poplin ['pɔplin] *n* popelín *m*, popelina *f*.

popliteal [pɔ'plitiəl] *adj* ANAT poplíteo, a.

poppadom; poppadum ['pɔpədəm] *n* CULIN oblea *f* frita india.

popper ['pɔpə*] *n* corchete *m* (on clothes).

poppet ['pɔpet] *n* TECH cabezal *m* (lathe head) || MAR escálamo *m* || FAM *my poppet* hijo mío, hija mía.

poppethead [-hed] *n* TECH cabezal *m* (of a lathe).

popping crease ['pɔpiŋkriːs] *n* SP línea *f* del bateador (in cricket).

popple ['pɔpl] *n* chapoteo *m* (of water).

popple ['pɔpl] *vi* chapotear.

poppy ['pɔpi] *n* BOT amapola *f* (red flower) | adormidera *f* (used in pharmacy).

poppycock [-kɔk] *n* tonterías *f pl*, necedades *f pl* (nonsense).

popsy ['pɔpsi] *n* FAM chica *f*, niña *f*.

populace ['pɔpjuləs] *n* pueblo *m*, vulgo *m* (common people) || populacho *m* (rabble).

popular ['pɔpjulə*] *adj* popular; *a popular play* una obra popular; *popular prices* precios populares || democrático, ca; *a popular election* una elección democrática || corriente, generalizado, da; *popular opinions* opiniones corrientes || estimado, da; *officer popular amongst his friends* oficial estimado por sus amigos || popular, de moda (fashionable) || — *popular front* frente popular || *to be popular with the girls* tener éxito con las chicas.

popularity [,pɔpju'læriti] *n* popularidad *f*.

popularization ['pɔpjulərai'zeiʃən] *n* popularización *f*, vulgarización *f*.

popularize ['pɔpjuləraiz] *vt* popularizar, vulgarizar.

popularly ['pɔpjuləli] *adv* generalmente, por la gran mayoría || *he's popularly known as Big Joe* la mayoría de la gente lo llama Big Joe.

populate ['pɔpjuleit] *vt* poblar.

population [,pɔpju'leiʃən] *n* población *f*; *working population* población activa; *the population of Spain* la población española; *an increase in population* un aumento de la población || BIOL población *f* || *the population explosion* la explosión demográfica.

Populist ['pɔpjulist] *n* populista *m* & *f*.

populous ['pɔpjuləs] *adj* muy poblado, da; populoso, sa.

pop-up ['pɔpʌp] *adj* con ilustraciones en relieve (book) || automático, ca (toaster) || INFORM *pop-up menu* menú *m* desenvolvente.

porcelain ['pɔːsəlin] *n* porcelana *f*.
◆ *adj* de porcelana.

porcellaneous; porcelaneous [,pɔːsə'leinjəs] *adj* de porcelana (made of porcelain) || de la porcelana (relative to porcelain) || frágil.

porch [pɔːtʃ] *n* pórtico *m* (of a building) || US porche *m*, portal *m*.

porcine ['pɔːsain] *adj* porcino, na.

porcupine ['pɔːkjupain] *n* ZOOL puerco *m* espín.

pore [pɔː*] *n* ANAT & BOT poro *m*.

pore [pɔː*] *vi* *to pore over* estudiar detenidamente (to study), reflexionar sobre (to think about).

porgy ['pɔːdʒi] *n* pargo *m*, pagro *m* (fish).
— OBSERV El plural de *porgy* es *porgies* o *porgy*.

pork [pɔːk] *n* CULIN cerdo *m*, carne *f* de cerdo; *pork chop* chuleta de cerdo || CULIN *pork sausage* salchicha *f*.

pork barrel [-'bærəl] *n* FAM fondos *m pl* públicos asignados a un proyecto local para fines electorales.

pork butcher [-'butʃə*] *n* chacinero, ra; salchichero, ra [AMER chanchero, ra] || *pork butcher's* chacinería *f*, salchichería *f* [AMER chanchería *f*].

porker [-ə*] *n* cebón *m*.

porkpie [-,pai] *n* empanada *f* de carne de cerdo || sombrero *m* de copa baja (hat).

porky [-i] *adj* FAM gordo, da; gordinflón, ona.

porn [pɔːn] *n* FAM pornografía *f*.

pornographer [pɔː'nɔgrəfə*] *n* pornógrafo *m*.

pornographic [,pɔːnə'græfik] *adj* pornográfico, ca.

pornography [pɔː'nɔgrəfi] *n* pornografía *f*.

porosity [pɔː'rɔsiti] *n* porosidad *f*.

porous ['pɔːrəs] *adj* poroso, sa.

porousness [-nis] *n* porosidad *f*.

porphyritic [pɔːfi'ritik] *adj* MIN porfídico, ca; porfírico, ca.

porphyry ['pɔːfiri] *n* MIN pórfido *m*, pórfiro *m*.

porpoise ['pɔːpəs] *n* ZOOL marsopa *f*, marsopla *f* (cetacean).

porridge ['pɔridʒ] *n* CULIN gachas *f pl* de avena.

porringer ['pɔrindʒə*] *n* plato *m* hondo (small bowl).

port [pɔːt] *n* MAR puerto *m* (harbour); *sea port* puerto marítimo; *fishing port* puerto pesquero; *port of entry* puerto de entrada | babor *m* (left side) | portilla *f* (porthole) | porta *f* (gunhole) || TECH lumbrera *f* || oporto *m* (wine) || — FIG *any port in a storm* la necesidad carece de ley || *commercial o trading port* puerto comercial || *free port* puerto franco *or* libre || *outer port* antepuerto *m* || MAR *port of call* puerto de escala *or* de arribada | *port of registry, home port* puerto de amarre *or* de matrícula || *to come into port, to put into port* tomar puerto, arribar || *to get safely into port* llegar a buen puerto.
◆ *adj* portuario, ria; *port duties* derechos portuarios; *port authority* autoridad portuaria; *port facilities* instalaciones portuarias.

port [pɔːt] *vt* MAR poner a babor || MIL presentar; *port arms!* ¡presenten armas! || MAR *to port the helm* poner el timón a babor, virar a babor.
◆ *vi* MAR virar a babor.

portability [,pɔːtə'biliti] *n* INFORM portabilidad *f*.

portable [-əbl] *adj* portátil; *portable typewriter* máquina de escribir portátil.
◆ *n* objeto *m* portátil || máquina *f* de escribir portátil (typewriter) || INFORM portátil *m* (computer).

portage [-idʒ] *n* porteo *m*, transporte *m*, porte *m* (transportation) || porte *m* (cost).

portal ['pɔːtl] *adj* ANAT porta; *portal vein* vena porta.
◆ *n* ARCH pórtico *m*, portal *m* || ANAT vena *f* porta.

portal-to-portal pay ['pɔːtəltə'pɔrtəl'pei] *n* US remuneración *f* que tiene en cuenta el tiempo pasado entre la empresa y el sitio donde se efectúa realmente el trabajo.

portative ['pɔːtətiv] *adj* portátil (portable).

Port-au-Prince [pɔːtəuprɛs] *pr n* GEOGR Puerto Príncipe (Haití).

portcullis [pɔːt'kʌlis] *n* rastrillo *m*.

portend [pɔː'tend] *vt* presagiar, augurar || anunciar; *dark clouds that portend a storm* nubarrones que anuncian una tempestad.

portent ['pɔːtent] *n* presagio *m*, augurio *m* (omen) || portento *m*, prodigio *m* (prodigy).

portentous [pɔː'tentəs] *adj* de mal agüero, siniestro, tra (ominous); *portentous news* noticias de mal agüero || portentoso, sa; prodigioso, sa (prodigious).

porter ['pɔːtə*] *n* portero, ra (doorkeeper) || conserje *m* (in government buildings) || maletero *m*, mozo *m* (baggage carrier) || mozo *m* de cuerda (person who carries things) || mozo *m* (attendant) || cerveza *f* negra (dark-brown beer).

porterage [-ridʒ] *n* COMM porte *m*, transporte *m* (transport, cost).

porterhouse [-haus] *n* mesón *m* || CULIN *porterhouse steak* bistec *m* de solomillo.

porter's lodge [-z,lɔdʒ] *n* portería *f*.

portfolio [pɔːt'fəuljəu] *n* cartera *f* (briefcase) || carpeta *f* (folder) || cartera *f*; *minister without portfolio* ministro sin cartera || COMM cartera *f*; *securities in portfolio* valores en cartera.

porthole ['pɔːthəul] *n* MAR portilla *f* (window) || MIL tronera *f*, cañonera *f* (for cannon, etc.).

portico ['pɔːtikəu] *n* ARCH pórtico *m*.
— OBSERV El plural de la palabra inglesa es *porticos* o *porticoes*.

portion ['pɔːʃən] *n* porción *f*, parte *f* ‖ parte *f*; *he got the biggest portion of the profits* obtuvo la mayor parte de los beneficios ‖ ración *f* (of food); *a portion of cheese* una ración de queso ‖ trozo *m*, porción *f* (of cake) ‖ JUR parte *f* (of inheritance) ‖ dote *f* (dowry) ‖ sino *m*, destino *m* (destiny).

portion ['pɔːʃən] *vt* dividir (to divide) ‖ repartir, distribuir (to distribute) ‖ dotar (to endow).
— OBSERV Este verbo va seguido muchas veces por *out* sin que cambie su sentido.

portionless [-lis] *adj* sin dote.

Portland cement ['pɔːtləndsi'ment] *n* Portland *m*.

portliness ['pɔːtlinis] *n* corpulencia *f*, gordura *f*.

Port Louis [,pɔːt'luːi] *pr n* GEOGR Port-Louis.

portly ['pɔːtli] *adj* corpulento, ta; gordo, da (stout).

portmanteau [pɔːt'mæntəu] *n* maleta *f* (suitcase).
— OBSERV El plural de la palabra inglesa es *portmanteaus* o *portmanteaux*.

portmanteau word [-wəːd] *n* GRAMM palabra *f* formada por la combinación de otras dos.

Port Moresby [,pɔːt'mɔːzbi] *pr n* GEOGR Port Moresby.

Port of Spain [,pɔːtɔf'spein] *pr n* GEOGR Puerto España.

Porto Rican [,pɔːtəu'riːkən] *adj/n* puertorriqueño, ña; portorriqueño, ña.

Porto Rico [,pɔːtəu'riːkəu] *pr n* GEOGR Puerto Rico.

portrait ['pɔːtrit] *n* retrato *m*; *half-length portrait* retrato de medio cuerpo; *full-length portrait* retrato de cuerpo entero ‖ — *to have one's portrait painted, to sit for one's portrait* hacerse retratar ‖ *to take s.o.'s portrait* retratar a alguien.

portraitist [-ist] *n* retratista *m* & *f*.

portraiture ['pɔːtritʃə] *n* retrato *m* ‖ FIG descripción *f*.

portray [pɔː'trei] *vt* retratar, pintar (in painting) ‖ retratar (with a camera) ‖ FIG pintar, describir (to describe) | representar (to represent).

portrayal [pɔː'treiəl] *n* retrato *m* (portrait) ‖ FIG descripción *f* | representación *f*.

portress ['pɔːtris] *n* portera *f* (doorkeeper).

Portugal ['pɔːtjugəl] *pr n* GEOGR Portugal *m*.

Portuguese [,pɔːtju'giːz] *adj* portugués, esa.
◆ *n* portugués, esa (people) ‖ portugués *m* (language) ‖ *the Portuguese* los portugueses.

pose [pəuz] *n* postura *f*, actitud *f* (of the body) ‖ FIG afectación *f*, pose *f* (pretence).

pose [pəuz] *vt* colocar, hacer tomar una postura (model) ‖ plantear (a problem) ‖ formular, hacer (question); *I don't like the way you pose the question* no me gusta su manera de formular la pregunta ‖ dejar perplejo (to puzzle).
◆ *vi* posar (model) ‖ FIG darse tono, presumir (to be conceited) ‖ FIG *to pose as* dárselas de; *he poses as an intellectual* se las da de intelectual.

Poseidon [pɔ'saidən] *pr n* MYTH Poseidón *m*.

poser ['pəuzə*] *n* pregunta *f* difícil (question) ‖ cuestión *f* or problema *m* difícil (problem).

poseur [pəu'zəː*] *n* presumido, da.

posh [pɔʃ] *adj* FAM elegante, distinguido, da (elegant); *posh clothes* ropa elegante; *I live in a posh district* vivo en un barrio elegante | de lujo (luxurious); *a posh hotel* un hotel de lujo | afectado, da; *he speaks with a posh accent* habla con un acento afectado | cursi (in bad taste).
◆ *adv* *to talk posh* hablar con un tono afectado.

posh [pɔʃ] *vt* *to posh o.s. up* arreglarse ‖ *to posh up* arreglar.

posit ['pɔzit] *vt* postular (to postulate) ‖ proponer (to propose) ‖ colocar, situar (to situate).

position [pə'ziʃən] *n* posición *f*, situación *f* (place) ‖ sitio *m*; *from this position you can see the whole field* desde este sitio se puede ver todo el campo ‖ posición *f*, postura *f* (of the body, etc.); *vertical position* posición vertical ‖ situación *f*; *what is the position in Europe?* ¿cuál es la situación en Europa? ‖ punto *m* de vista (point of view) ‖ opinión *f*; *to state one's position* manifestar su opinión ‖ posición *f*, postura *f*; *to take up a position on a problem* adoptar una postura sobre un problema ‖ posición *f* (social), categoría *f*, rango *m* (rank) ‖ condiciones *f pl*; *in a position to marry* en condiciones de casarse ‖ puesto *m*; *he has a good position in a ministry* tiene un buen puesto en un ministerio ‖ cargo *m*, puesto *m*, empleo *m* (employment) ‖ puesto *m* (in a class) ‖ taquilla *f* (at the post office) ‖ MIL & MAR posición *f* ‖ — *in a position to* en condición *or* en condiciones de ‖ *out of position* fuera de lugar ‖ *put yourself in my position* ponte en mi lugar ‖ *to be in a position of trust* tener *or* ocupar un puesto de confianza ‖ FIG *to know one's position* saber cuál es su sitio ‖ *to place in position* colocar.

position [pə'ziʃən] *vt* situar, colocar, disponer.

position light [-lait] *n* MAR & AVIAT luz *f* de situación.

positive ['pɔzətiv] *adj* seguro, ra (convinced); *I am positive about* o *of it* estoy seguro de ello ‖ formal (order) ‖ tajante, categórico, ca; *positive tone of voice* tono categórico ‖ verdadero, ra; auténtico, ca; *it's a positive robbery* es un verdadero robo; *a positive miracle* un milagro auténtico ‖ evidente; *positive proof* prueba evidente ‖ afirmativo, va; categórico, ca (affirmative); *don't be so positive* no sea tan categórico ‖ enérgico, ca; *he is a very positive person* es una persona muy enérgica ‖ positivo, va (not negative); *we reached a positive conclusion* llegamos a una conclusión positiva ‖ PHYS, BIOL & CHEM positivo, va; *positive ray* rayo positivo; *positive electricity* electricidad positiva ‖ PHIL, GRAMM & MATH positivo, va ‖ COMM firme, en firme; *positive offer* oferta firme ‖ — PHOT *positive print* positiva *f* ‖ *positive discrimination* apoyo *m* a grupos discriminados.
◆ *n* PHOT positiva *f* ‖ GRAMM positivo *m* ‖ ELECTR polo *m* positivo ‖ lo positivo.

positively [-li] *adv* afirmativamente, positivamente (affirmatively); *I answered him positively* le contesté afirmativamente ‖ categóricamente, rotundamente; *I positively refused to go* me negué rotundamente a ir ‖ verdaderamente, realmente; *he is positively stupid* es realmente estúpido ‖ totalmente (completely) ‖ *I can't speak positively* no puedo asegurar nada.

positivism ['pɔzitivizəm] *n* PHIL positivismo *m*.

positivist ['pɔzitivist] *n* PHIL positivista *m* & *f*.

positron ['pɔzitrɔn] *n* PHYS positrón *m*, positón *m*.

posology [pə'sɔlədʒi] *n* MED posología *f*.

posse ['pɔsi] *n* pelotón *m* (of police) ‖ grupo *m* (of people).

possess [pə'zes] *vt* poseer, tener; *he possesses an aeroplane* posee un avión; *to possess endless patience* tener una paciencia inagotable ‖ poseer; *he is possessed by the devil* está poseído por el demonio ‖ dominar (to command); *he possesses French* domina el francés ‖ poseer (a woman) ‖ — *to be possessed of* tener (a quality, a property) ‖ *to possess o.s. in patience* armarse de paciencia ‖ *to possess o.s. of* apoderarse de ‖ *what possessed him to kill her?* ¿cómo se le ocurrió matarla?

possessed [pə'zest] *adj* poseído, da; poseso, sa (controlled by a spirit) ‖ obsesionado, da; *possessed with an idea* obsesionado por una idea ‖ poseído, da (by fear, etc.) ‖ *to scream like one possessed* gritar como un endemoniado *or* como un poseído.

possession [pə'zeʃən] *n* posesión *f* (act, object); *to take possession of* tomar posesión de ‖ REL posesión *f* (by a devil) ‖ posesión *f* (colony) ‖ JUR tenencia *f*; *illicit possession of arms* tenencia ilícita de armas ‖ — *house for sale with vacant possession* casa que se vende desocupada ‖ *in full possession of one's faculties* con pleno dominio de sus facultades ‖ *to be in possession of* tener ‖ *to be in the possession of* estar en manos de ‖ *to come into possession of* adquirir ‖ *to come into the possession of* llegar a las manos de ‖ *to have sth. in one's possession* tener algo (en su poder).
◆ *pl* bienes *m* (estate).

possessive [pə'zesiv] *adj* posesivo, va ‖ GRAMM posesivo, va.
◆ *n* GRAMM posesivo *m*.

possessor [pə'zesə*] *n* poseedor, ra.

possibility [,pɔsə'biliti] *n* posibilidad *f*; *I admit the possibility of your being right* admito la posibilidad de que tenga razón ‖ posibilidad *f*, eventualidad *f* (event); *to foresee all the possibilities* prever todas las posibilidades ‖ — *if by any possibility* si por casualidad ‖ *there is no possibility of my going there* es imposible que vaya allí ‖ *to have possibilities* ser prometedor (artist, project, etc.) ‖ *within the bounds of possibility* dentro de lo posible.

possible ['pɔsəbl] *adj* posible; *a possible success* un posible éxito ‖ aceptable (reasonably satisfactory) ‖ — *as best as possible* lo mejor posible ‖ *as far as possible* en la medida de lo posible, en lo posible ‖ *as much as possible* todo lo posible ‖ *as often as possible* lo más frecuentemente posible ‖ *as soon as possible* tan pronto como sea posible, lo antes posible, cuanto antes ‖ *if possible* de ser posible, si es posible ‖ *it is possible that* puede ser que, es posible que ‖ *the best, the worst possible* lo mejor, lo peor posible ‖ *to make* o *to render possible* hacer posible, posibilitar.
◆ *n* máximo *m* (maximum score) ‖ candidato *m* posible; *there are two possibles for the post* hay dos candidatos posibles para el puesto.

possibly [-i] *adv* probablemente, posiblemente ‖ quizás, tal vez (perhaps) ‖ *I cannot possibly do it* no puedo hacerlo.

possum ['pɔsəm] *n* ZOOL zarigüeya *f* ‖ FAM *to play possum* hacerse el muerto.

post [pəust] *n* poste *m* (pole) ‖ estaca *f*, palo *m* (stake) ‖ SP línea *f* de llegada, llegada *f*, meta *f* (finishing) | línea *f* de salida (starting) ‖ Correos *m pl*, oficina *f* de correos (post office); *to take a letter to the post* llevar una carta a correos ‖ recogida *f* (collection of letters); *at what time does the post go?* ¿a qué hora es la recogida? ‖ correo *m*; *has the post come?* ¿ha venido el correo?; *registered post* correo certificado; *by post* por correo ‖ cartas *f pl*; *did you have any post this morning?* ¿tuviste cartas esta mañana? ‖ reparto *m* (delivery of mail); *first post* primer reparto ‖ HIST posta *f* ‖ MIL puesto *m* (position); *advanced post* puesto avanzado; *to stay at one's post* quedarse en su puesto ‖ puesto *m*, empleo *m*; *he has been given a post in industry* se le ha asignado un puesto en la industria ‖ cargo *m*; *to take up one's post* tomar posesión de su cargo ‖ factoría *f* (a trading post) ‖ — *by return of post* a vuelta de correo ‖ MIL *last post* toque *m* de retreta ‖ FIG *there has been a general post* *in the Cabinet* ha habido una reorganización ministerial || FAM *to be as deaf as a post* estar más sordo que una tapia | *to be as straight as a post* estar más tieso que un poste || FIG *to be left at the post* quedarse en la estacada.

post [pəust] *vt* fijar, pegar; *post no bills* prohibido fijar carteles || poner; *results will be posted on the notice board* los resultados se pondrán en el tablón de anuncios || fijar en; *to post a wall with notices* fijar carteles en una pared || declarar; *to post s.o. missing* declarar a alguien desaparecido || anunciar (to advertise by poster) || echar (al correo); *to post a letter* echar una carta || mandar, enviar; *post me the photos* mándame las fotos || COMM pasar (in bookkeeping) || informar, poner al tanto *or* al corriente (to inform) || MIL destinar, enviar; *posted to Germany* destinado a Alemania | apostar (a sentry) || nombrar, designar; *to post s.o. as captain* nombrar a alguien capitán; *to post s.o. to a command* designar a alguien para un mando || — *to keep s.o. posted about the situation* tener a alguien al tanto *or* al corriente de la situación || *to post up* fijar, pegar (bills, advertisements), poner al día (in bookkeeping), poner al corriente (s.o.).
◆ *vi* viajar en posta.

postage ['pəustidʒ] *n* franqueo *m* || *postage paid* franco de porte, porte pagado.
◆ *pl* gastos *m* de correo.

postage stamp [-stæmp] *n* sello *m* [AMER estampilla *f*].

postal ['pəustəl] *adj* postal; *postal order* giro postal || — *postal card* postal *f*, tarjeta *f* postal || *postal reply coupon* respuesta pagada.
◆ *n* US FAM tarjea *f* postal, postal *f*.

postbag ['pəustbæg] *n* saca *f* || FIG & FAM correspondencia *f* (of a company).

postbellum ['pəust'beləm] *adj* de la posguerra.

postbox ['pəustbɔks] *n* buzón *m*.

postboy ['pəustbɔi] *n* (ant) postillón *m*.

postcard ['pəustkɑːd] *n* tarjeta *f* postal, postal *f*.

post chaise ['pəustʃeiz] *n* HIST silla *f* de posta.

postcode ['pəustkəud] *n* código *m* postal.

postdate ['pəust'deit] *vt* poner fecha posterior a la verdadera, posfechar (to assign a later date to).

postdiluvian ['pəustdai'luːvjən] *adj* postdiluviano, na.

posted ['pəustid] *adj* al corriente, al tanto (informed) || con postes (with poles).

poster ['pəustə*] *n* cartel *m* (notice) || cartelero *m* (person).

poster designer [-di'zainə*] *n* cartelista *m* & *f*.

poste restante ['pəust'restɑːnt] *n* lista *f* de correos [AMER poste restante *f*].

posterior [pɔs'tiəriə*] *adj* posterior, trasero, ra (situated behind) || posterior (following) || ANAT posterior.
◆ *n* FAM trasero *m*.

posteriority [pɔs,tiəri'ɔriti] *n* posterioridad *f*.

posterity [pɔs'teriti] *n* posteridad *f*.

postern ['pəustəːn] *n* postigo *m* || MIL poterna *f*.

post exchange ['pəustiks'tʃeindʒ] *n* MIL cantina *f*.

postfix ['pəust'fiks] *n* GRAMM sufijo *m*, postfijo *m*.

postfix ['pəust'fiks] *vt* GRAMM añadir (un sufijo) a.

post-free ['pəust'friː] *adj* franco de porte, con porte pagado.

postglacial ['pəust'gleisjəl] *adj* GEOL postglacial.

postgraduate ['pəust'grædjuit] *adj* graduado, da; diplomado, da (person) || para graduados *or* diplomados (course).
◆ *n* graduado, da; diplomado, da.

posthaste ['pəust'heist] *adv* a toda prisa.

post horse ['pəusthɔːs] *n* caballo *m* de posta.

posthumous ['pɔstjuməs] *adj* póstumo, ma.

posthumously [-li] *adv* después de la muerte.

postilion; postillion [pəs'tiljən] *n* postillón *m*.

postimpressionism ['pəustim'preʃnizəm] *n* postimpresionismo *m*.

postimpressionist ['pəustim'preʃnist] *adj/n* postimpresionista.

post-industrial ['pəustinədʌstriəl] *adj* postindustrial.

posting ['pəustiŋ] *n* destino *m* (appointment to a post).

postman ['pəustmən] *n* cartero *m*.
— OBSERV El plural de *postman* es *postmen*.

postmark ['pəustmɑːk] *n* matasellos *m inv*; *letter with a London postmark* carta con el matasellos de Londres.

postmark ['pəustmɑːk] *vt* matasellar, matar || *the letter was postmarked London* la carta llevaba el matasellos de Londres.

postmaster ['pəust,mɑːstə*] *n* administrador *m* de Correos || *postmaster general* director *m* general de Correos.
— OBSERV El plural de esta palabra es *postmasters general* o *postmaster generals*.

postmeridian ['pəustmə'ridiən] *adj* postmeridiano, na; de la tarde.

post meridiem ['pəustmə'ridiəm] *adv* de la tarde (of the afternoon) || de la noche (of the night).
— OBSERV La expresión *post meridiem* se usa normalmente en forma abreviada, *p. m.*: *seven p. m.* las siete de la tarde; *nine p. m.* las nueve de la noche.

postmistress ['pəust,mistris] *n* administradora *f* de Correos.

postmortem ['pəust'mɔːtəm] *adj* MED que sucede después de la muerte || MED *postmortem examination* autopsia *f*.
◆ *n* MED autopsia *f*.

postnatal ['pəust'neitl] *adj* postnatal.

post office ['pəust,ɔfis] *n* Correos *m pl*, oficina *f* de correos, casa *f* de correos (office); *I have to go to the post office* tengo que ir a correos || — *district post office* estafeta *f* de correos || *General Post Office* Administración *f* de Correos || *post-office box* apartado *m* de correos [AMER casilla *f* postal].

postoperative ['pəust'ɔpərətiv] *adj* postoperatorio, ria.

postpaid ['pəust'peid] *adj* con porte pagado, franco de porte (parcel) || franqueo concertado (letter, newspaper).

postpalatal [pəust'pælətəl] *adj* postpalatal.

postpone [pəust'pəun] *vt* aplazar; *to postpone a matter for a week* aplazar un asunto hasta la semana siguiente.
◆ *vi* MED tardar.

postponement [-mənt] *n* aplazamiento *m*.

postposition ['pəustpə'ziʃən] *n* GRAMM posposición *f*.

postprandial ['pəust'prændjəl] *adj* de sobremesa (speech, talk, etc.) || que se da después de comer (walk).

postscript ['pəusskript] *n* posdata *f*, post scriptum *m* (in a letter) || nota *f* final de un libro, advertencia *f* final (in a book) || comentario *m* (commentary).

postsynchronization ['pəust,siŋkrənai'zeiʃən] *n* CINEM postsincronización *f*.

postsynchronize [pəust'siŋkrənaiz] *vt* CINEM postsincronizar.

postulant ['pɔstjulənt] *n* postulante, ta.

postulate ['pɔstjulit] *n* postulado *m*.

postulate ['pɔstjuleit] *vt* postular, pedir (to demand) || considerar como un postulado || dar por sentado (to assume).
◆ *vi* *to postulate for* pedir, postular.

postulation [,pɔstju'leiʃən] *n* postulación *f* (petition) || supuesto *m* (assumption) || postulado *m* (postulate).

postulator ['pɔstjuleitə*] *n* REL postulador *m*.

posture ['pɔstʃə*] *n* postura *f*, actitud *f* (of the body) || situación *f* (of affairs).

posture ['pɔstʃə*] *vi* adoptar una postura (to pose) || fingir ser, dárselas de; *posturing as an intellectual* fingiendo ser un intelectual || darse tono, presumir (to be conceited).
◆ *vt* poner en una postura.

postwar ['pəust'wɔː*] *adj* de la posguerra || *the postwar period* la posguerra.

posy ['pəuzi] *n* ramillete *m* de flores (bouquet) || US flor *f* (flower) | lema *m*, inscripción *f* (motto).

pot [pɔt] *n* olla *f*, marmita *f*, puchero *m* (for cooking) || tarro *m* (for preserving) || tiesto *m*, maceta *f* (for flowers) || nasa *f* (for fishing) || orinal *m* (chamberpot) || platillo *m*, pozo *m*, puesta *f* (in card games) || SP & FAM copa *f* (cup) || premio *m* (prize) || FAM sombrerete *m* (of chimney) | marihuana *f*, marijuana *f*, mariguana *f* || — FAM *big pot* pez gordo || *pot plant* planta *f* de maceta || FAM *to go to pot* echarse a perder | *to keep the pot boiling* calentar el puchero, ganarse la vida *or* el cocido.
◆ *pl* FAM montones *m*; *pots of money* montones de dinero || *pots and pans* batería *f* de cocina.

pot [pɔt] *vt* poner en tiesto *or* en maceta (plants) || meter en la tronera (billiards) || conservar en tarros (to preserve food) || guisar en una olla (to cook) || matar (to shoot animals).
◆ *vi* tirar, disparar || *to pot at s.o.* disparar a alguien.

potable ['pəutəbl] *adj* potable.

potash ['pɔtæʃ] *n* CHEM potasa *f*.

potassic [pə'tæsik] *adj* CHEM potásico, ca.

potassium [pə'tæsjəm] *n* CHEM potasio *m*.

potations [pəu'teiʃənz] *pl n* libaciones *f*.

potato [pə'teitəu] *n* BOT patata *f* [AMER papa *f*]; *early* o *new potato* patata temprana; *boiled potatoes* patatas al vapor || — *mashed potatoes* puré *m* de patatas || *potato straws* patatas paja || *sweet potato* batata *f*.
— OBSERV El plural de *potato* es *potatoes*.

potato beetle [-biːtl] *n* ZOOL dorifora *f*, escarabajo *m* de la patata.

potato chipper [-'tʃipə*] *n* freidora *f* de patatas.

potato chips [-tʃips] *pl n* patatas *f* fritas [AMER papas *f* fritas] || US patatas *f* fritas a la inglesa [AMER papas *f* fritas a la inglesa].

potato crisps [-krisps] *pl n* patatas *f* fritas a la inglesa [AMER papas *f* fritas a la inglesa].

potato field [-fiːld] *n* campo *m* de patatas, patatar *m*, patatal *m*.

potato masher [-'mæʃə*] *n* pasapurés *m inv*.

potato peeler [-piːlə*] *n* pelapatatas *m inv*.

potbellied ['pɔt,belid] *adj* barrigudo, da; barrigón, ona.

potbelly ['pɔt͵beli] *n* barriga *f*, tripa *f* (stomach) ‖ barrigudo, da (person) ‖ US salamandra *f* (stove).

potboiler ['pɔt͵bɔilə*] *n* obra *f* sin ningún valor hecha para ganar dinero.

poteen [pɔ'ti:n] *n* whisky *m* irlandés [destilado ilegalmente].

potency ['pəutənsi] *n* potencia *f*, fuerza *f* (power, strength) ‖ potencia *f*, potencialidad *f* (potentiality).

potent ['pəutənt] *adj* potente (person) ‖ poderoso, sa (argument, poison) ‖ fuerte (drink) ‖ eficaz (remedy) ‖ HERALD *potent cross* potenza *f*, cruz potenzada.

potentate ['pəutənteit] *n* potentado *m*.

potential [pəu'tenʃəl] *adj* posible, potencial, en potencia ‖ GRAMM potencial ‖ PHYS potencial; *potential energy* energía potencial.
◆ *n* potencial *m* ‖ posibilidad *f* ‖ GRAMM, PHYS & MATH potencial *m* ‖ ELECTR voltaje *m*.

potentiality [pəu͵tenʃi'æliti] *n* potencialidad *f*.

potentially [pəu'tenʃəli] *adv* potencialmente, en potencia.

potentiometer [pə͵tenʃi'ɔmitə*] *n* ELECTR potenciómetro *m*.

pother ['pɔðə*] *n* confusión *f*, lío *m* ‖ *to make a pother about sth.* armar un lío por algo.

potherb ['pɔthə:b] *n* hierba *f* (to flavour food).

pothole ['pɔthəul] *n* GEOL marmita *f* de gigante | cueva *f* (cave) ‖ bache *m* (in a road).

pothole ['pɔthəul] *vi* dedicarse a la espeleología.

potholer [-ə*] *n* espeleólogo *m*.

potholing [-iŋ] *n* espeleología *f*.

pothook ['pɔthuk] *n* gancho *m*, llares *m pl* (for hanging a pot) ‖ garabato *m* (writing).

pothunter ['pɔt͵hʌntə*] *n* cazador *m* que mata cualquier animal (hunter) ‖ cazador *m* de premios (contestant).

potion ['pəuʃən] *n* MED dosis *f*, pócima *f*, poción *f* ‖ *love potion* filtro *m* de amor.

pot lead ['pɔtled] *n* grafito *m*.

pot-lead ['pɔtled] *vt* cubrir con grafito.

potluck ['pɔt'lʌk] *n* lo que haya; *to take potluck* tomar lo que haya.

potpie ['pɔtpai] *n* US CULIN pastel *m* de carne.

potpourri [pəu'puri] *n* MUS popurrí *m* ‖ CULIN olla *f* podrida ‖ FIG popurrí *m* ‖ pebete *m* (to scent a room).

pot roast ['pɔtrəust] *n* CULIN carne *f* asada.

potsherd ['pɔtʃə:d] *n* tiesto *m*, casco *m*.

potshot ['pɔt'ʃɔt] *n* tiro *m* al azar (at random) ‖ *to take a potshot at* disparar al azar contra.

pottage ['pɔtidʒ] *n* sopa *f*, potaje *m* ‖ FIG *to sell one's birthright for a mess of pottage* vender su primogenitura por un plato de lentejas.

potted ['pɔtid] *adj* en conserva (food) ‖ en tiesto, en maceta (plant).

potter ['pɔtə*] *n* alfarero *m* ‖ ceramista *m* & *f* (artistic) ‖ *potter's wheel* torno *f* de alfarero.

potter; US **putter** ['pɔtə*] *vi* *to potter about* o *around* ocuparse de trabajos de poca importancia, no hacer nada en particular.

potter's clay [-z͵klei] *n* arcilla *f* figulina.

pottery ['pɔtəri] *n* alfarería *f* (craft) ‖ alfarería *f* (workshop) ‖ cacharros *m pl* de barro (pots) ‖ cerámica *f* (artistic).

potting compost ['pɔtiŋ'kɔmpɔst] *n* tierra *f* abonada para plantas, mantillo *m*.

potty ['pɔti] *adj* FAM insignificante (trivial) | chiflado, da (crazy) ‖ — FIG *to be potty about* estar chiflado por | *to drive s.o. potty* volver loco a uno.
◆ *n* FAM orinal *m* (chamberpot).

potty ['pɔti] *n* orinal *m*.

potty-trained [-treind] *adj* que no usa más pañales.

pouch [pautʃ] *n* bolsa *f* pequeña (small bag) ‖ petaca *f* (for tobacco) ‖ cartuchera *f* (for ammunition) ‖ morral *m* (of hunters) ‖ ZOOL bolsa *f* (abdominal sack) | abazón *m* (cheek sack) ‖ bolsa *f* (under the eyes) ‖ valija *f* (locked bag for mail, etc.).

pouch [pautʃ] *vt* embolsar (to put in a bag) ‖ poner en una valija (to put in a locked bag) ‖ tragar (to swallow) ‖ formar bolsas en (to cause to form bags).

pouffe; pouf [pu:f] *n* puf *m*, taburete *m* bajo de asiento relleno (seat).

poult [pəult] *n* pollo *m* (chicken) ‖ pavipollo *m* (turkey).

poulterer [-ərə*] *n* vendedor *m* de aves, pollero, ra ‖ *poulterer's shop* pollería *f*.

poultice ['pəultis] *n* MED cataplasma *f*.

poultry ['pəultri] *n* aves *f pl* de corral.

poultry dealer [-'di:lə*] *n* pollero, ra; vendedor *m* de aves.

poultry farm [-fa:m] *n* granja *f* avícola.

poultry farming [-fa:miŋ] *n* avicultura *f*, cría *f* de aves de corral.

poultry house [-haus] *n* gallinero *m*.

poultry keeping [-ki:piŋ] *n* avicultura *f*.

poultryman [-mən] *n* avicultor *m*.
— OBSERV El plural de esta palabra es *poultrymen*.

poultry yard [-ja:d] *n* corral *m*.

pounce [pauns] *n* ZOOL garra *f* ‖ arenilla *f* (powder) ‖ cisquero *m* (charcoal) ‖ salto *m*, ataque *m*; *the lion's pounce* el ataque del león ‖ salto *m* repentino (spring).

pounce [pauns] *vt* estampar en relieve, repujar (to emboss) ‖ polvorear con arenilla (to sprinkle with fine powder) ‖ estarcir (to transfer a design).
◆ *vi* saltar ‖ *to pounce on* o *upon* o *at* saltar sobre; *the lion pounces on the sheep* el león salta sobre la oveja; abalanzarse sobre (birds), precipitarse sobre; *they pounced on the evening newspaper* se precipitaron sobre el periódico de la tarde; no perder (an opportunity).

pound [paund] *n* libra *f* (weight, money); *pound sterling* libra esterlina; *to sell by the pound* vender por libras; *half a pound* media libra ‖ aprisco *m*, redil *m* (for sheep) ‖ perrera *f* (for dogs) ‖ depósito *m* (for animals, for cars) ‖ garlito *m*, nasa *f* (fish trap) ‖ ruido *m* (noise) ‖ FIG *a question of pounds, shillings and pence* un asunto de dinero.

pound [paund] *vt* aporrear (to thump) ‖ martilliear (with a hammer) ‖ moler (to grind) ‖ machacar (to crush) ‖ azotar, batir; *the waves pounded the ship* las olas azotaban el barco ‖ FAM dar una paliza, aporrear (to beat) ‖ MIL machacar, martillear a cañonazos *or* con bombas ‖ aporrear (a piano, a table) ‖ — *to pound sth. to pieces* destrozar algo a martillazos ‖ US FAM *to pound the asphalt* callejear.
◆ *vi* dar golpes, aporrear (to strike) ‖ palpitar, latir violentamente (heart) ‖ picar (machine) ‖ resonar; *we heard feet pounding up the stairs* oímos pasos que resonaban en las escaleras.
◆ *phr v* *to pound along* andar *or* ir con paso pesado ‖ *to pound at* dar golpes en, aporrear; *he was pounding at the door* estaba aporreando la puerta ‖ *to pound away* machacar ‖ *to pound on* aporrear, dar golpes en.

poundage [-idʒ] *n* impuesto *m or* comisión *f* por cada libra.

pounder [-ə*] *n* mazo *m* (big hammer) ‖ maja *f* (kitchen utensil) ‖ pisón *m* (beetle) ‖ — *a twenty-five pounder* un cañon de veinticinco ‖ *ten-pounder* algo que pesa diez libras.

pound-foolish [-'fu:liʃ] *adj* gastador, ra; manirroto, ta; derrochador, ra.

pounding [-iŋ] *n* golpeteo *m* (noise) ‖ embate *m*, azote *m* (of the sea) ‖ trituración *f* (crushing) ‖ molienda *f* (grinding) ‖ MIL bombardeo *m*, martilleo *m*, machaqueo *m*.

pound net [-net] *n* nasa *f*, garlito *m* (fish trap).

pound sterling [-'stə:liŋ] *n* libra *f* esterlina.

pound-weight [-weit] *n* PHYS libra *f*.

pour [pɔ:*] *vt* derramar, verter; *he poured the wine all over the table* derramó el vino por toda la mesa ‖ echar; *pour me a glass of wine* échame un vaso de vino ‖ servir; *may I pour the coffee?* ¿sirvo el café? ‖ colar (metal) ‖ — *to pour away* o *off* vaciar, verter ‖ FIG *to pour cats and dogs* llover a cántaros ‖ *to pour out* servir, echar (tea, etc.), echar (smoke) ‖ *to pour out abuse on s.o.* llenar a uno de improperios ‖ *to pour out one's feelings* expansionarse ‖ *to pour out one's heart* abrir el corazón, desahogar su corazón ‖ *to pour out one's thanks* dar las gracias efusivamente ‖ *to pour out one's troubles* confiar sus penas ‖ *to pour out threats* desatarse en amenazas.
◆ *vi* diluviar, llover a cántaros (to rain) ‖ correr, fluir (water) ‖ salir a borbotones (to come out with a rush) ‖ servir; *the tea is ready, you pour* el té está preparado, sírvelo tú ‖ — *it is pouring down* está lloviendo a cántaros ‖ FIG *it never rains but it pours* llueve sobre mojado ‖ *the crowds poured out of the theatre* la gente salía del teatro en tropel ‖ *the letters were pouring in* las cartas llegaban en abundancia ‖ *to pour in* entrar a raudales *or* en tropel.

pouring [-riŋ] *adj* torrencial; *pouring rain* lluvia torrencial.

pout [paut] *n* FAM mala cara *f* ‖ ZOOL abadejo *m* (fish) ‖ *to have the pouts* poner mala cara, hacer pucheros.

pout [paut] *vt* *to pout one's lips* poner mala cara, hacer pucheros.
◆ *vi* poner mala cara, hacer pucheros.

pouter [-ə*] *n* paloma *f* buchona (pigeon).

poverty ['pɔvəti] *n* pobreza *f*; *the poverty of the land* la pobreza de la tierra; *to live in poverty* vivir en la pobreza ‖ carencia *f*, escasez *f*; *poverty of ideas* carencia de ideas ‖ — *extreme poverty* miseria *f* ‖ FIG *poverty is no crime* pobreza no es vileza.

poverty-stricken [-͵strikn] *adj* menesteroso, sa; necesitado, da; indigente.

pow! [pau] *interj* FAM ¡pum!

powder [͵paudə*] *n* polvo *m*; *he reduced it to powder* lo redujo a polvo ‖ pólvora *f* (gun powder) ‖ polvos *m pl* (cosmetic) ‖ arenilla *f* (pounce) ‖ — FIG *to keep one's powder dry* no gastar pólvora en salvas ‖ US FIG *to take a powder* poner pies en polvorosa.

powder ['paudə*] *vt* reducir a polvo, pulverizar (to pulverize) ‖ espolvorear (to sprinkle) ‖ *to powder one's face* ponerse polvos en la cara.
◆ *vi* reducirse a polvo ‖ ponerse polvos en la cara (to use cosmetic powder).

powder blue [-blu:] *n* azul *m* pálido.

powder box [-bɔks] *n* polvera *f*.

powder compact [-'kɔmpækt] *n* polvera *f*.

powdered [-d] *adj* en polvo.

powder flask [-fla:sk] *n* frasco *m* para la pólvora.

powder keg [-keg] *n* FIG polvorín *m*.

powder magazine [-mægə͵zi:n] *n* polvorín *m* ‖ MAR santabárbara *f*.

powder monkey [-'mʌŋki] *n* MAR grumete *m* encargado de la pólvora.

powder puff [-pʌf] *n* borla *f*.

powder room [-ru:m] *n* US aseos *m pl*, servicios *m pl*.

powdery [-ri] *adj* en polvo; *powdery snow* nieve en polvo || pulverizado, da (pulverized) || polvoriento, ta; empolvado, da (dusty) || quebradizo, za (friable).

power ['pauə*] *n* poder *m* (authority, control); *to be in the power of* estar en poder *or* bajo el poder de; *to hand over power* entregar los poderes; *with full power* o *powers* con plenos poderes || potencia *f* (country); *the Great Powers* las grandes potencias; *atomic power* potencia atómica; *world power* potencia mundial || poderío *m* (supremacy) || facultad *f*, capacidad *f*, posibilidad *f*, poder *m* (gift); *the power to fly* la facultad de volar || facultad *f*; *mental powers* facultades mentales *or* intelectuales; *my powers are failing* mis facultades decaen || fuerza *f*, potencia *f* (strength) || fuerza *f*, poder *m*; *attractive power* poder de atracción || ascendiente *m*, influencia *f* (influence) || autoridad *f*, poder *m*, capacidad *f*, facultad *f* (legal authority); *to have the power to dismiss an employee* tener capacidad para despedir a un empleado || PHYS, ELECTR & TECH potencia *f* (rate of work done) | fuerza *f*; *motive power* fuerza motriz | energía *f* (energy); *electric, water power* energía eléctrica, hidráulica | potencia *f* (of a lense) || MATH potencia *f*; *to raise a number to the power of four* o *to the fourth power* elevar un número a la cuarta potencia; *to the nth. power* a la enésima potencia || — *absolute, executive, judicial, legislative power* poder absoluto, ejecutivo, judicial, legislativo || FAM *a power of people* una multitud || *as far as lies within my power* en la medida de lo posible || *five to the power of three, of two* cinco elevado al cubo, al cuadrado || *it is not within my power to help you* no puedo ayudarle, no entra dentro de mis posibilidades ayudarle || FIG *more power to your elbow!* ¡que le acompañe el éxito! || *nuclear power* energía nuclear || *power base* base *f* de poder || JUR *power of attorney* poderes, poder, procuración *f* || *purchasing power* poder adquisitivo || *to be in power* estar en el poder || *to come to power* subir al poder; tomar el mando || *to do all in one's power to* hacer todo lo posible para || FAM *to do a power of good* sentar bien, hacer mucho bien a (a remedy) || *to fall into s.o.'s power* caer en poder de alguien || *to have s.o. in one's power* tener a uno en su poder || FAM *to make a power of money* ganar un dineral.
◆ *pl* potestades *f* (of angels) || — *the powers that be* las autoridades || *to exceed one's powers* excederse.

power ['pauə*] *vt* *to be powered by* estar impulsado *or* accionado por.

power axle [-'æksl] *n* eje *m* de transmisión.

powerboat [-bəut] *n* lancha *f* fuera borda.

power brakes [-breiks] *pl n* AUT frenos *m* asistidos, servofrenos *m*.

power cable [-'keibl] *n* cable *m* de energía eléctrica, cable *m* de transmisión.

power cut [-kʌt] *n* corte *m* de corriente, apagón *m*.

power dive [-daiv] *n* AVIAT picado *m* con motor.

power drill [-drill] *n* TECH taladradora *f* mecánica *or* eléctrica.

power-driven [-'drivn] *adj* con motor || mecánico, ca (tool).

powerful [-ful] *adj* poderoso, sa; *a powerful nation* una nación poderosa || potente (machine, engine) || fuerte (strong) || enérgico, ca; eficaz (medicines, etc.) || FIG intenso, sa (feelings) | convincente (argument).

powerfully [-fuli] *adv* poderosamente || *to be powerfully built* ser fuerte *or* fornido.

power hammer [-'hæmə*] *n* martillo *m* pilón.

powerhouse [-haus] *n* central *f* eléctrica || US FIG persona *f* enérgica.

powerless [-lis] *adj* impotente (helpless) || ineficaz (remedy, etc.) || sin autoridad, sin poder (not empowered) || — *to be powerless in a matter* no poder hacer nada en un asunto || *to be powerless to help s.o.* no poder *or* ser incapaz de ayudar a alguien.

power line [-lain] *n* línea *f* de fuerza eléctrica, línea *f* de conducción *or* de transmisión eléctrica.

power plant [-plɑ:nt] *n* central *f* eléctrica || grupo *m* electrógeno (of a factory) || *nuclear power plant* central nuclear.

power point [-pɔint] *n* ELECTR toma *f* de corriente.

power politics [-,pɔlitiks] *n* política *f* de fuerza.

power saw [-sɔ:] *n* TECH sierra *f* mecánica.

power-sharing [-ʃɛəriŋ] *n* reparto *m* del poder.

power shovel [-ʃʌvl] *n* excavadora *f*, pala *f* mecánica.

power station [-,steiʃən] *n* central *f* eléctrica || grupo *m* electrógeno (of a factory) || *nuclear power station* central nuclear.

power steering [-,stiəriŋ] *n* AUT dirección *f* asistida.

power tool [-tu:l] *n* herramienta *f* mecánica *or* eléctrica.

power unit [-'ju:nit] *n* unidad *f* de potencia (for measurement) || motor *m* (motor) || ELECTR generador *m* | grupo *m* electrógeno.

power worker [-wə:kə*] *n* trabajador, ra de una central eléctrica.

powwow ['pauwau] *n* conferencia *f*.

pox [pɔks] *n* FAM sífilis *f* (syphilis) || viruela *f*, viruelas *f pl* (smallpox) || varicela *f* (chicken pox) || *a pox on her!* ¡maldita sea!

pozzolana [pɔtsə'lɑ:nə]; **pozzuolana** [pɔttswə'lɑ:nə] MIN puzolana *f*.

practicability ['præktikə'biliti] *n* practicabilidad *f*, factibilidad *f*.

practicable ['præktikəbl] *adj* factible, practicable, hacedero, ra; posible, realizable (which can be done); *a practicable plan* un proyecto factible || utilizable (capable of being used) || transitable (route) || THEATR practicable.

practical ['præktikəl] *adj* práctico, ca; *practical experience* experiencia práctica; *practical idea* idea práctica || — *practical exam* examen práctico || *practical lesson* clases prácticas || *practical training period* período *m* de prácticas || *the first night was a practical disaster* el estreno fue casi un fracaso.

practicality [,prækti'kæliti] *n* espíritu *m* práctico, sentido *m* práctico (of a person) || factibilidad *f* (of a project).

practical joke ['præktikəldʒəuk] *n* broma *f* pesada.

practically ['præktikəli] *adv* de manera práctica, eficazmente || prácticamente, casi (virtually); *practically a year ago* hace prácticamente un año.

practical nurse ['præktikəlnə:s] *n* US enfermera *f* sin título [que ha adquirido sus conocimientos gracias a la práctica].

practice ['præktis] *n* práctica *f* (not theory); *in theory it is easy in practice impossible* en teoría es fácil, pero en la práctica es imposible; *to put into practice* poner en práctica || costumbre *f*; *to make a practice of dining early* tener la costumbre de cenar temprano || práctica *f* (exercise); *to learn by practice* aprender con la práctica || ejercicios *m pl* (on the piano) || SP entrenamiento *m* (training); *practice match* partido de entrenamiento || ejercicio *m* (of a profession); *to devote o.s. to the practice of medicine* dedicarse al ejercicio de la medicina || clientela *f*; *a dentist with a large practice* un odontólogo con una clientela numerosa; *to sell one's practice* vender su clientela || JUR procedimiento *m*, práctica *f* (procedure) | bufete *m* (lawyer's business); *to set up in practice* poner un bufete || estratagema *f* (stratagem) || — *he is no longer in practice* ya no ejerce (a profession) || *it is not my practice to do that* no acostumbro hacer eso || *practice makes perfect* machacando se aprende el oficio || *restrictive practices* normas restrictivas || *sharp practices* mañas *f* || SP *to be in practice* estar bien entrenado, estar en forma | *to be out of practice* no estar bien entrenado, no estar en forma || *to make it a practice to do sth.* acostumbrar hacer algo.

practice ['præktis] *vt/vi* US → **practise.**

practiced [-t] *adj* US → **practised.**

practician [præk'tiʃən] *n* practitioner.

practicing ['præktisiŋ] *adj/n* US → **practising.**

practise; US practice ['præktis] *vt* practicar; *to practise a policy of neutrality* practicar una política de neutralidad; *to practise one's English* practicar el inglés; *to practise a religion* practicar una religión || tener; *to practise patience, good manners* tener paciencia, buenos modales || ejercer (a profession); *to practise medicine* ejercer la medicina || ejercitarse en (to exercise o.s. in) || MUS hacer ejercicios en (an instrument) || mandar hacer ejercicios sobre; *to practise a class in irregular verbs* mandar hacer ejercicios sobre los verbos irregulares a una clase || SP practicar (a stroke, a shot, a punch, etc.) | entrenarse en (a sport); *to practise rugby* entrenarse en el rugby || — *to practise punctuality* ser puntual || *to practise what one preaches* predicar con el ejemplo.
◆ *vi* ejercer (*as* de) (professionally) || ejercitarse (to exercise o.s.) || hacer ejercicios; *to practise on the piano* hacer ejercicios en el piano || SP entrenarse.

practised [-t] *adj* experto, ta; experimentado, da (expert) || muy entrenado, da (well-trained).

practising [-iŋ] *adj* que ejerce, en ejercicio; *practising doctor, lawyer* médico, abogado en ejercicio || REL practicante.
◆ *n* ejercicio *m* (of a profession) || REL práctica *f* (of a faith) || ejercicios *m pl* (exercises) || SP entrenamiento *m* (training).

practitioner [præk'tiʃnə*] *n* persona *f* que ejerce una profesión || MED facultativo *m*, médico *m* || MED *general practitioner* internista *m*.

praedial ['pri:diəl] *adj* predial.

praenomen [pri:'nəumen] *n* prenombre *m*.
— OBSERV El plural es *praenomens* o *praenomina*.

praesidium [pri'sidiəm] *n* presidium *m*.
— OBSERV El plural de la palabra *praesidium* es *praesidia* o *praesidiums*.

praetexta [pri':tekstə] *n* pretexta *f*.

praetor; pretor ['pri:tə*] *n* pretor *m*.

praetorian; pretorian [pri'tɔ:riən] *adj* pretorial, pretoriano, na || HIST *Praetorian Guard* guardia pretoriana.
◆ *n* pretoriano *m*.

praetorianism; pretorianism [pritɔ'riə,nizəm] *n* pretorianismo *m*.

praetorium; pretorium [pri'tɔriəm] *n* pretorio *m*.

praetorship; pretorship ['pri:təʃip] *n* pretoría *f*.

pragmatic [præg'mætik]; **pragmatical** [-əl] *adj* pragmático, ca || dogmático, ca (dogmatic) || práctico, ca (practical) || entrometido, da (meddling).

pragmatics [præg'mætiks] *n* pragmática *f.*

pragmatism ['prægmətizəm] *n* pragmatismo *m.*

pragmatist ['prægmətist] *n* pragmatista *m* & *f.*

Prague [prɑ:g] *pr n* GEOGR Praga.

prairie ['prεəri] *n* pradera *f,* llanura *f* [AMER pampa *f*].

prairie schooner [-'sku:nə*] *n* US HIST carromato *m* en el que viajaban los pioneros.

prairie wolf [-wulf] *n* ZOOL coyote *m.*

praise [preiz] *n* alabanza *f,* alabanzas *f pl,* elogio *m* || — *praise be to God!* ¡alabado sea Dios! || *to heap praises on s.o.* cubrir a alguien de alabanzas || *to sing* o *to shout the praises of* cantar las alabanzas de.

praise [preiz] *vt* alabar, elogiar, ensalzar || alabar (god) || FIG *to praise to the skies* poner por las nubes.

praiser [-ə*] *n* ensalzador, ra; elogiador, ra; alabador, ra.

praiseworthy [-,wə:ði] *adj* laudable, loable, digno de elogio.

Prakrit ['prɑ:krit] *n* pracrito *m,* prácrito *m* (Indic language).

praline ['prɑ:li:n] *n* almendra *f* garapiñada.

pram [præm] *n* cochecito *m* de niño (perambulator).

prance [prɑ:ns] *n* cabriola *f.*

prance [prɑ:ns] *vi* encabritarse (to rear up) || hacer cabriolas (to move by leaps) || pavonearse (to swagger) || — *to prance with glee* dar saltos *or* brincos de alegría || *to prance with rage* patalear de rabia.

prandial ['prændiəl] *adj* de la comida (of a meal) || de la cena (of dinner).

prang [præŋ] *vt* FAM derribar (an aircraft) | bombardear (a building) | chocar contra (to bump into).

◆ *vi* FAM estrellarse (an aircraft).

prank [præŋk] *n* travesura *f* (a piece of mischief) || broma *f* (joke); *to play a prank on s.o.* gastar una broma a alguien.

prank [præŋk] *vt* ataviar, engalanar (to adorn).

prankish [-iʃ] *adj* travieso, sa; pícaro, ra.

prankster [-stə*] *n* bromista *m* & *f.*

praseodymium [,preiziə'dimiəm] *n* CHEM praseodimio *m.*

prat [præt] *n* FAM imbécil *m* & *f.*

prate [preit] *n* charla *f,* parloteo *m,* cháchara *f.*

prate [preit] *vi* parlotear, charlar.

prater [-ə*] *n* charlatán, ana.

prating [-iŋ] *adj* parlanchín, ina; charlatán, ana.

pratique ['præti:k] *n* MAR libre plática *f.*

prattle ['prætl] *n* balbuceo *m* (of a child) || cháchara *f,* parloteo *m* (chatter).

prattle ['prætl] *vi* charlar, parlotear (to chatter).

◆ *vt* balbucear.

prattler [-ə*] *n* charlatán, ana.

prawn [prɔ:n] *n* ZOOL camarón *m* (small) | gamba *f,* langostino *m* (large) || CULIN *prawn cocktail* cóctel *m* de gambas.

praxis ['præksis] *n* práctica *f.*

— OBSERV El plural de *praxis* es *praxes.*

pray [prei] *vi* rezar, orar; *to pray for s.o.* rezar por alguien || rogar (to beg); *to pray for rain* rogar que llueva || *he's past praying for* ya no se puede salvar.

◆ *vt* rogar, suplicar (to beg); *to pray s.o. to do sth.* rogar a alguien que haga algo || — *pray be seated* siéntese por favor, haga el favor de sentarse || *pray tell me* le ruego me diga || *what, pray, is the meaning of this?* ¿qué significa esto, por favor?

prayer [prεə*] *n* REL oración *f,* rezo *m* || súplica *f,* ruego *m* (entreaty) || — REL *book of Common Prayer* libro *m* de oraciones de la Iglesia Anglicana | *evening prayers* vísperas *f* | *Lord's Prayer* padrenuestro *m* | *morning prayers* maitines *m* | *to say a prayer* o *prayers for* rezar por | *to say one's prayers* rezar sus oraciones, rezar | *to spend one's life in prayer* pasarse la vida rezando.

prayer beads [-bi:dz] *pl n* REL rosario *m sing.*

prayer book [-buk] *n* REL devocionario *m.*

prayerful [-ful] *adj* devoto, ta; piadoso, sa (devout).

prayer meeting [-,mi:tiŋ] *n* REL reunión *f* de fieles para rezar.

prayer rug [-rʌg] *n* REL alfombra *f* de rezo.

prayer shawl [-ʃɔ:l] *n* REL taled *m.*

prayer stool [-stu:l] *n* REL reclinatorio *m.*

prayer wheel [-wi:l] *n* molinillo *m* de oraciones.

praying mantis ['preiŋ'mæntis] *n* predicador *m,* santateresa *f* (insect).

pre [pri:] *pref* pre [con el sentido de «antelación»].

preach [pri:tʃ] *vi* predicar; *he preaches very well* predica muy bien || dar un sermón; *to preach about tolerance* dar un sermón sobre la tolerancia || sermonear; *he is always preaching at his children* está siempre sermoneando a sus hijos.

◆ *vt* predicar (the gospel) || dar, pronunciar (a sermon) || FIG aconsejar; *to preach moderation* aconsejar la moderación.

preacher [-ə*] *n* predicador, ra (s.o. who preaches) || pastor *m* (minister).

preachify [-ifai] *vi* FAM sermonear.

preaching [-iŋ] *adj* sermoneador, ra (tone).

◆ *n* predicación *f* || sermón *m* || FAM sermoneo *m* (tiresome moral advice).

preachy [-i] *adj* FAM sermoneador, ra.

preamble [pri:'æmbl] *n* preámbulo *m.*

preamplifier ['pri:'æmplifaiə*] *n* RAD preamplificador *m.*

prearrange ['pri:ə'reindʒ] *vt* organizar de antemano (to organize in advance); *a prearranged visit* una visita organizada de antemano || preparar de antemano; *to ask a prearranged question* hacer una pregunta preparada de antemano.

prebend ['prebənd] *n* prebenda *f* (stipend) || prebendado *m* (prebendary).

prebendary [-əri] *n* prebendado *m.*

prebook ['pri:buk] *vt* reservar de antemano.

Precambrian [pri'kæmbriən] *adj* GEOL precámbrico, ca; precambriano, na.

◆ *n* Precámbrico *m.*

precarious [pri'kεəriəs] *adj* precario, ria.

precariousness [-nis] *n* precariedad *f,* carácter *m* precario.

precast [pri:'kɑ:st] *adj* vaciado de antemano (concrete) || prefabricado, da (concrete block, house).

precatory ['prekətəri] *adj* suplicante.

precaution [pri'kɔ:ʃən] *n* precaución *f; as a precaution* por precaución; *to take the precaution of doing sth.* tomar la precaución de hacer algo.

precautionary [-əri] *adj* preventivo, va; de precaución; *precautionary measures* medidas preventivas.

precautious [pri'kɔ:ʃəs] *adj* precavido, da; cauteloso, sa; cauto, ta.

precede [pri'si:d] *vt* preceder, anteceder (in time, position, importance); *the stillness that precedes a storm* la quietud que precede la tormenta || empezar, comenzar; *to precede a ceremony with a speech of welcome* comenzar una ceremonia con un discurso de bienvenida.

◆ *vi* preceder, anteceder.

precedence [pri'si:dəns] *n* precedencia *f; an archbishop has precedence over a bishop* un arzobispo tiene precedencia sobre un obispo || prioridad *f,* preferencia *f,* prelación *f; exports take precedence over home production* las exportaciones tienen prioridad sobre la producción para el mercado nacional.

precedent [pri'si:dənt] *adj* precedente.

precedent ['presidənt] *n* precedente *m; to establish a precedent* sentar un precedente; *without precedent* sin precedente; *there is no precedent for it* no tiene precedente.

preceding [pri'si:diŋ] *adj* precedente, anterior.

precentor [pri'sentə*] *n* REL chantre *m.*

precept ['pri:sept] *n* precepto *m* (rule) || JUR mandato *m* judicial.

preceptist [-ist] *n* preceptista *m* & *f.*

preceptive [pri'septiv] *adj* preceptivo, va.

preceptor [pri'septə*] *n* preceptor *m.*

precession [pri'seʃən] *n* ASTR precesión *f.*

precinct ['pri:siŋkt] *n* recinto *m* (grounds); *the cathedral precinct* el recinto de la catedral || zona *f; pedestrian precinct* zona reservada para peatones; *shopping precinct* zona comercial [reservada para peatones] || frontera *f,* límite *m* (boundary) || US distrito *m* electoral | barrio *m* (neighbourhood).

◆ *pl* contornos *m,* alrededores *m.*

preciosity [,preʃi'ɔsiti] *n* preciosismo *m,* amaneramiento *m* (of style).

precious ['preʃəs] *adj* precioso, sa; *precious metals* metales preciosos; *precious stone* piedra preciosa || inapreciable (priceless); *a precious friendship* una amistad inapreciable || preciosista (exhibiting preciosity); *a precious writer* un escritor preciosista || rebuscado, da (style); *a precious turn of phrase* una locución rebuscada || afectado, da (manners) || precioso, sa (term of endearment); *hello, precious!* ¡hola, preciosa! || querido, da (beloved); *he will be furious if you damage his precious car* se pondrá furioso si estropeas su querido coche || *a precious fool* un perfecto imbécil.

◆ *adv* muy (very); *precious little* muy poco; *precious few* muy pocos.

preciousness [-nis] *n* preciosidad *f* || valor *m* inapreciable.

precipice ['presipis] *n* precipicio *m.*

precipitance [pri'sipitəns]; **precipitancy** [-i] *n* precipitación *f.*

precipitant [pri'sipitənt] *adj* precipitado, da (hasty).

precipitate [pri'sipitit] *adj* precipitado, da (hasty).

◆ *n* CHEM precipitado *m.*

precipitate [pri'sipiteit] *vt* arrojar, precipitar (to hurl downward) || apresurar, precipitar; *the assassination precipitated the war* el asesinato precipitó la guerra || causar, producir, provocar (to cause) || CHEM precipitar || condensar (vapour) || *to precipitate o.s.* precipitarse, arrojarse.

◆ *vi* CHEM precipitarse || condensarse (vapour).

precipitation [pri,sipi'teiʃən] *n* precipitación *f* (haste); *his precipitation cost him his life* su precipitación le costó la vida || CHEM precipitación *f* | precipitado *m* (precipitate) || precipitación *f* (rain, snow, etc.).

precipitous [pri'sipitəs] *adj* empinado, da; escarpado, da (steep) || precipitado, da; precipitoso, sa (hasty).

précis ['preisi:] *n* resumen *m*.

precise [pri'sais] *adj* preciso, sa; exacto, ta (detailed, exact); *a precise account* un relato preciso || preciso, sa; claro, ra (clear) || preciso, sa; mismo, ma; *at that precise moment* en aquel momento preciso || meticuloso, sa (finicky) || — *it is the precise word I was looking for* es precisamente *or* exactamente la palabra que estaba buscando || *to be precise* para ser preciso.

precisely [-li] *adv* precisamente, justamente, exactamente; *it is precisely what I want* es precisamente lo que quiero || con precisión; *to speak, to write precisely* hablar, escribir con precisión || meticulosamente (meticulously) || en punto; *it is precisely one o'clock* es la una en punto || — *at precisely six o'clock* a las seis en punto || *precisely!* ¡eso es!, ¡exactamente!

preciseness [-nis] *n* precisión *f*, exactitud *f* (accuracy) || precisión *f* (in speaking, in writing).

precisian [pri'siʒən] *n* rigorista *m* & *f*.

precision [pri'siʒən] *n* precisión *f*, exactitud *f* || *precision instrument* instrumento de precisión.

précis writer ['preisi:'raitə*] *n* redactor *m or* secretario *m* de actas.

preclude [pri'klu:d] *vt* impedir (to prevent); *to preclude s.o. from doing sth.* impedir a alguien que haga algo || imposibilitar, impedir; *the use of one system precludes the use of another* el uso de un sistema imposibilita el uso de otro || evitar; *to preclude any misunderstanding* para evitar todo malentendido || excluir; *it does not preclude the possibility of* no excluye la posibilidad de.

preclusion [pri'klu:ʒən] *n* prevención *f* (prevention) || exclusión *f* (exclusion).

preclusive [pri'klu:siv] *adj* que impide, que evita; *preclusive of a misunderstanding* que evita un malentendido.

precocious [pri'kəuʃəs] *adj* precoz; *a precocious child* un niño precoz.

precociousness [-nis]; **precocity** [pri'kɔsiti] *n* precocidad *f*.

precognition [pri:kɔg'niʃən] *n* precognición *f* (foreknowledge).

pre-Columbian [,pri:kə'lʌmbjən] *adj* precolombino, na.

precombustion [pri:kəm'bʌstʃən] *n* precombustión *f*.

precompression [,pri:kəm'preʃən] *n* precompresión *f*.

preconceive ['pri:kən'si:v] *vt* preconcebir.

preconception ['pri:kən'sepʃən] *n* preconcepción *f*, idea *f* preconcebida (preconceived idea) || prejuicio *m* (prejudice).

preconcert ['pri:kən'sə:t] *vt* concertar de antemano.

precondition [prikən'diʃən] *n* condición *f* previa.

preconization [prikənai'zeiʃən] *n* REL preconización *f*.

preconize ['pri:kɔnaiz] *vt* preconizar (a bishop) || preconizar, encomiar (to extol).

precook [pri:kuk] *vt* precocinar.

precooked [pri:kukt] *adj* precocinado, da.

precursive [pri:'kə:siv] *adj* precursor, ra.

precursor [pri'kə:sə*] *n* precursor, ra.

precursory [-ri] *adj* precursor, ra (which precedes) || preliminar (preliminary).

predaceous; predacious [pri'deiʃəs] *adj* de rapiña, rapaz (animal).

predacity [pri'dæsiti] *n* rapacidad *f*.

predate [pri:'deit] *vt* preceder (to come before).

predator ['predətə*] *n* animal *m* de rapiña || depredador, ra (person).

predatory ['predətəri] *adj* de rapiña, rapaz (animal) || depredador, ra (person).

predecease ['pri:di'si:s] *vt* morir antes que.

predecessor ['pri:disesə*] *n* predecesor, ra; antecesor, ra || antepasado, da (forefather).

predestinate [pri'destinit] *adj* predestinado, da.

predestinate [pri'destineit] *vt* predestinar.

predestination [pri,desti'neiʃən] *n* predestinación *f*.

predestine [pri'destin] *vt* predestinar.

predeterminate [,pri:di'tə:mineit] *adj* predeterminado, da.

predetermination ['pri:di,tə:mi'neiʃən] *n* predeterminación *f*.

predetermine ['pri:di'tə:min] *vt* predeterminar; *my fate is already predetermined* mi destino está ya predeterminado || determinar de antemano; *we must predetermine the consequences* debemos determinar de antemano las consecuencias.

predetermining [-iŋ] *adj* predeterminante.

predial ['pri:diəl] *adj* predial.

predicable ['predikəbl] *adj* predicable.
◆ *n* predicable *m*.

predicament [pri'dikəmɛt] *n* apuro *m*, situación *f* difícil || PHIL predicamento *m* (category) || *what a predicament to be in!* ¡menudo lío!

predicant ['predikənt] *adj* predicante.
◆ *n* predicador *m*.

predicate ['predikit] *n* GRAMM & PHIL predicado *m*.

predicate ['predikeit] *vt* afirmar (to affirm) || implicar (to imply) || US basar (to base).

predication [,predi'keiʃən] *n* afirmación *f* (affirmation) || PHIL predicación *f*.

predicative [pri'dikətiv] *adj* GRAMM predicativo, va.

predict [pri'dikt] *vt* predecir, pronosticar; *to predict rain* pronosticar lluvia.

predictable [-əbl] *adj* previsible; *a predictable move* una maniobra previsible || de reacciones previsibles (person).

predicted [-id] *adj* previsto, ta.

prediction [pri'dikʃən] *n* predicción *f*, pronóstico *m*.

predictive [pri'diktiv] *adj* profético, ca.

predigest [,pri:dai'dʒest] *vt* predigerir.

predigested [pri:did'ʒestid' pri:daid'ʒestid] *adj* predigerido, da.

predigestion [pridə'dʒestʃən] *n* predigestión *f*.

predilection [,pri:di'lekʃən] *n* predilección *f*.

predispose ['pri:dis'pəuz] *vt* predisponer.

predisposition ['pri:,dispə'ziʃən] *n* predisposición *f*, propensión *f*.

predominance [pri'dɔminəns]; **predominancy** [pri'dɔminənsi] *n* predominio *m*.

predominant [pri'dɔminənt] *adj* predominante.

predominantly [pri'dɔminəntli] *adv* predominantemente, mayormente.

predominate [pri'dɔmineit] *vi* predominar, prevalecer.

predominating [-iŋ] *adj* predominante.

predomination [pri,dɔmi'neiʃən] *n* predominio *m*.

preeminence [pri'eminəns] *n* preeminencia *f*.

preeminent [pri'eminənt] *adj* preeminente.

preempt [pri'empt] *vt* comprar con derecho preferente || US adueñarse de (un terreno) para conseguir el derecho preferente de compra || apropiarse de (to acquire).

preemption [pri'empʃən] *n* JUR derecho *m* preferente de compra (right) | adquisición *f or* apropiación *f* por derecho preferente de compra.

preemptive [pri'emptiv] *adj* con derecho preferente || MIL *preemptive strike* ataque *m* preventivo.

preen [pri:n] *vt* arreglarse (feathers) || FIG *to preen o.s.* pavonearse (to show vanity), atildarse (to dress up).

preestablish [,pri:es'tæbliʃ] *vt* preestablecer, establecer de antemano.

preexist ['pri:ig'zist] *vi* preexistir.
◆ *vt* existir antes que.

preexistence [-əns] *n* preexistencia *f*.

preexisting [-iŋ] *adj* preexistente.

prefab ['pri:fæb] *n* FAM casa *f* prefabricada.

prefabricate ['pri:'fæbrikeit] *vt* prefabricar.

prefabricated [-id] *adj* prefabricado, da.

prefabrication ['pri,fæbri'keiʃən] *n* prefabricación *f*.

preface ['prefis] *n* prólogo *m*, prefacio *m* (of a book) || FIG prólogo *m* || REL prefacio *m*.

preface ['prefis] *vt* prologar (a book, etc.) || introducir (to begin).

prefactorial [,prefə'tɔ:riəl]; **prefatory** ['prefətəri] *adj* preliminar, a modo de prólogo.

prefect ['pri:fekt] *n* prefecto *m*.

prefecture ['pri:fektjuə*] *n* prefectura *f*.

prefer [pri'fə:*] *vt* preferir; *I prefer this house to that one* prefiero esta casa a aquélla; *I prefer not to think about it* prefiero no pensar en ello || JUR presentar (a complaint, etc.) | entablar (an action) | formular (a request) | dar prioridad a (a creditor) || ascender (to promote) | JUR *to prefer a charge against s.o.* acusar a alguien.

preferable ['prefərəbl] *adj* preferible.

preferably [-i] *adv* preferentemente, preferiblemente.

preference ['prefərəns] *n* preferencia *f* || JUR preferencia *f*, prioridad *f* || *in preference to* preferentemente a.
◆ *adj* preferencial (tariff) || preferente; *preference shares* acciones preferentes.

preferential [,prefə'renʃəl] *adj* preferente, preferencial; *preferential treatment* trato preferente || privilegiado, da (creditor, debt) || COMM *preferential tariff* aranceles *m pl* preferenciales, tarifa *f* preferencial.

preferment [pri'fə:mənt] *n* ascenso *m* || *to get preferment* ser ascendido.

preferred stock [pri'fə:dstɔk] *n* US acciones *f pl* preferentes.

prefiguration [pri,figjə'reiʃən] *n* prefiguración *f*.

prefigure [pri'figə*] *vt* prefigurar (to represent beforehand) || figurarse de antemano (to imagine).

prefix ['pri:fiks] *n* GRAMM prefijo *m* || JUR título *m*.

prefix [pri:'fiks] *vt* GRAMM poner un prefijo || FIG anteponer (to place before) || prefijar (to fix beforehand).

preform ['pri:'fɔ:m] *vt* preformar.

preformation [ˌpriːfɔːˈmeiʃən] *n* preformación *f.*

preglacial [priːˈgleisjəl] *adj* preglaciar.

pregnable [ˈpregnəbl] *adj* MIL conquistable, vulnerable, expugnable ‖ FIG controvertible, discutible.

pregnancy [ˈpregnənsi] *n* embarazo *m* (of a woman) ‖ *pregnancy test* prueba *f or* test *m* del embarazo.

pregnant [ˈpergnənt] *adj* embarazada *m* (of woman).

pregnant [ˈpregnənt] *adj* embarazada, encinta, en estado (a woman), preñada (a female animal); *to be three months pregnant* estar embarazada de tres meses ‖ FIG muy significativo, va | preñado, da; lleno, na; cargado, da (*with* de) (full) | fecundo, da (fruitful).

preheat [ˈpriːˈhiːt] *vt* precalentar.

preheater [-ə*] *n* TECH precalentador *m.*

preheating [-iŋ] *n* TECH precalentamiento *m.*

prehensile [priˈhensail] *adj* prensil; *prehensile tail* cola prensil.

prehension [priˈhenʃən] *n* ZOOL prensión *f* ‖ comprensión *f*, aprehensión *f* (mental).

prehistorian [priːhisˈtɔriən] *n* prehistoriador, ra.

prehistoric [ˈpriːhisˈtɔrik]; **prehistorical** [-əl] *adj* prehistórico, ca.

prehistory [ˈpriːˈhistəri] *n* prehistoria *f.*

Pre-Inca [priːˈiŋkə] *adj* HIST preincaico, ca.

preindustrial [ˈpriːinˈdʌstriəl] *adj* preindustrial.

prejudge [ˈpriːˈdʒʌdʒ] *vt* prejuzgar ‖ juzgar de antemano (s.o.).

prejudgment; prejudgement [-mənt] *n* prejuicio *m* (prejudice).

prejudice [ˈpredʒudis] *n* prejuicio *m*; *racial prejudice* prejuicio racial ‖ parcialidad *f* (bias) ‖ — *in prejudice of* en detrimento de, con menoscabo de, en perjuicio de ‖ *without prejudice to* sin perjuicio de.

prejudice [ˈpredʒudis] *vt* predisponer, prevenir (to cause to have a prejudice) ‖ perjudicar (to harm).

prejudiced [-t] *adj* parcial (partial) ‖ predispuesto, ta; *to be prejudiced against, in favour of* estar predispuesto contra, a favor de.

prejudicial [ˌpredʒuˈdiʃəl]; **prejudicious** [predʒudiʃəs] *adj* perjudicial.

prelacy [ˈpreləsi] *n* REL prelacía *f*, prelatura *f* (office, dignity) | episcopado *m* (prelates).

prelate [ˈprelit] *n* REL prelado *m.*

prelature [ˈprelətjə*] *n* REL prelatura *f*, prelacía *f.*

prelect [priˈlekt] *vi* dar una conferencia.

prelection [priˈlekʃən] *n* conferencia *f.*

prelector [priˈlektə*] *n* conferenciante *m.*

prelibation [prilaibeiʃən] *n* anticipación *f* (foretaste).

prelim [ˈpriːlim] *n* preliminar *m* ‖ examen *m* preliminar.

◆ *pl* preliminares *m*, preparativos *m* ‖ páginas *f* preliminares (of a book).

preliminary [priˈliminəri] *adj* preliminar.

◆ *n* preliminar *m* ‖ examen *m* preliminar (examination).

◆ *pl* preliminares *m*, preparativos *m.*

prelude [ˈpreljuːd] *n* preludio *m*; *the discussions were a prelude to the treaty* las discusiones fueron el preludio del tratado ‖ MUS preludio *m.*

prelude [ˈpreljuːd] *vt/vi* preludiar.

prelusive [priˈljuːsiv] *adj* preliminar.

premarital [priːˈmæritl] *adj* premarital, prenupcial.

premature [ˌpreməˈtjuə] *adj* prematuro, ra; *a premature baby* un niño prematuro; *a premature crop* una cosecha prematura ‖ precoz.

prematurity [priməˈtjuriti] *n* precocidad *f*, carácter *m* prematuro.

premaxilla [ˌpriːmækˈsilə] *n* ANAT & ZOOL premaxilar *m.*

— OBSERV El plural de la palabra *premaxilla* es *premaxillae.*

premeditate [priˈmediteit] *vt* premeditar.

premeditation [priˌmediˈteiʃən] *n* premeditación *f.*

premeditative [priˈmeditətiv] *adj* premeditado, da.

premier [ˈpremjə*] *adj* primero, ra.

◆ *n* primer ministro *m*, presidente *m* del consejo (Prime Minister).

première; premiere [ˈpremiɛə*] *n* THEATR estreno *m* (first public performance) ‖ US THEATR primera estrella *f*, protagonista *f* (female star).

premiership [ˈpremjə*ʃip] *n* cargo *m* de primer ministro, presidencia *f* del consejo.

premilitary [priˈmilitəri] *adj* premilitar.

premise [ˈpremis] *n* premisa *f* (in logic).

◆ *pl* parte *f sing* inicial (of a deed) ‖ local *m sing* (site) ‖ edificio *m sing* (building) ‖ *on the premises* en el local, en el sitio.

premise [priˈmaiz] *vt* sentar como premisa (in logic) ‖ FIG hacer preceder (*with* de), empezar (*whit* por).

premiss [ˈpremis] *n* premisa *f.*

premium [ˈpriːmjəm] *n* premio *m* (award) ‖ prima *f* (extra salary) ‖ prima *f* (in commerce, in insurance) ‖ — *to be at a premium* estar sobre la par (above normal value), ser muy solicitado, da (to be in demand) ‖ *to put a premium on* dar un gran valor a (to value highly).

premium bond [-bɔnd] *n* bono *m* del Estado que participa en un sorteo nacional.

premolar [priːˈməulə*] *adj* premolar.

◆ *n* premolar *m.*

premonish [priˈmɔniʃ] *vt* avisar, advertir, prevenir.

premonition [ˌpriːməˈniʃən] *n* premonición *f*, presentimiento *m* (presentiment) ‖ advertencia *f* (forewarning).

premonitory [priˈmɔnitəri] *adj* premonitorio, ria.

prenatal [ˈpriːˈneitl] *adj* prenatal.

prenuptial [priˈnʌpʃəl] *adj* prenupcial.

preoccupancy [priˈɔkjupənsi] *n* ocupación *f* anterior.

preoccupation [priˌɔkjuˈpeiʃən] *n* preocupación *f.*

preoccupied [priˈɔkjupaid] *adj* preocupado, da (worried); *to be preoccupied about* estar preocupado por ‖ absorto, ta; ensimismado, da (lost in thought); *to be preoccupied with* estar absorto en ‖ ocupado anteriormente (occupied before).

preoccupy [priˈɔkjupai] *vt* preocupar (to worry) ‖ absorber, ensimismar (to absorb) ‖ ocupar anteriormente (a house).

preordain [ˈpriːɔːˈdein] *vt* predeterminar.

prep [prep] *n* deberes *m pl* (homework) ‖ escuela *f* preparatoria.

prepacked [ˈpriːˈpækt] *adj* empaquetado, da previamente.

prepaid [ˈpriːˈpeid] *adj* pagado con antelación *or* con anticipación *or* por adelantado ‖ franqueado, da (letter) ‖ pagado, da (carriage, etc.) ‖ franco de porte, con el porte pagado (carriage paid, postpaid).

preparation [ˌprepəˈreiʃən] *n* preparación *f*; *the preparation of the meal takes two hours* la preparación de la comida requiere dos horas ‖ deberes *m pl* (homework) ‖ preparación *f*, preparado *m* (chemical substance, medicine).

◆ *pl* preparativos *m*; *have you made all the preparations for the trip?* ¿ha hecho todos los preparativos para el viaje?

preparative [priˈpærətiv] *adj* preparativo, va; preparatorio, ria.

◆ *n* preparativo *m.*

preparatory [-i] *adj* preparatorio, ria; preliminar (preliminary) ‖ — *preparatory school* escuela preparatoria ‖ *preparatory to* antes de (before), con miras a (with a view to).

prepare [priˈpɛə*] *vt* preparar, disponer (to get ready) ‖ CULIN preparar; *I am preparing dinner* estoy preparando la cena ‖ preparar (s.o., document) ‖ FIG *to prepare the way for* preparar el terreno para.

◆ *vi* prepararse; *he is preparing for an examination* se está preparando para un examen ‖ MIL *to prepare for action* entrar en batería.

prepared [-d] *adj* listo, ta; preparado, da; dispuesto, ta ‖ — *be prepared* estad siempre listos ‖ *to be prepared for anything* estar preparado para cualquier cosa ‖ *to be prepared to* estar dispuesto a ‖ *we were not prepared for this* no contábamos con esto ‖ *we were prepared for it* lo teníamos previsto.

preparedness [-dnis] *n* preparación *f*, estado *m* de preparación.

preparer [-rə*] *n* preparador, ra.

prepay* [ˈpriːˈpei] *vt* pagar por adelantado *or* por anticipado ‖ franquear (a letter).

— OBSERV pret y pp ***prepaid.***

prepayment [-mənt] *n* pago *m* por adelantado *or* por anticipado ‖ franqueo *m* (of a letter).

prepense [priˈpens] *adj* premeditado, da ‖ *with malice prepense* con premeditación.

preponderance [priˈpɔndərəns] *n* preponderancia *f*, predominio *m.*

preponderant [priˈpɔndərənt] *adj* preponderante, predominante.

preponderate [priˈpɔndəreit] *vi* preponderar, prevalecer, predominar.

preposition [ˌprepəˈziʃən] *n* GRAMM preposición *f.*

prepositional [ˌprepəˈziʃənl] *adj* GRAMM prepositivo, va; *prepositional phrase* locución prepositiva.

prepositive [priˈpɔzitiv] *adj* GRAMM prepositivo, va.

prepossess [ˌpriːpəˈzes] *vt* predisponer (*in favour of* a favor de) ‖ obseder, obsesionar, preocupar (to preoccupy).

prepossessing [-iŋ] *adj* atractivo, va; agradable.

prepossession [ˌpriːpəˈzeʃən] *n* prejuicio *m*, predisposición *f.*

preposterous [priˈpɔstərəs] *adj* absurdo, da; ridículo, la; extravagante.

preposterousness [-nis] *n* lo absurdo, lo ridículo, ridiculez *f.*

prepotency [priˈpəutənsi] *n* predominio *m* ‖ BIOL prepotencia *f.*

prepotent [priˈpəutənt] *adj* predominante ‖ BIOL prepotente.

preppy [ˈprepi] *n* US FAM alumno, na de colegio privado ‖ pijo, ja.

prepuce [ˈpriːpjuːs] *n* ANAT prepucio *m.*

Pre-Raphaelite [ˈpriːˈræfəlait] *adj/n* prerrafaelista.

Pre-Raphaelitism [priˈræfəlaitizəm] *n* prerrafaelismo *m.*

prerecord [priri'kɔːd] *vt* grabar antes, grabar de antemano.

prerequisite ['priː'rekwizit] *adj* previamente necesario.
◆ *n* requisito *m* previo, condición *f* previa (precondition).

prerogative [pri'rɔgətiv] *adj* privilegiado, da.
◆ *n* prerrogativa *f*.

Preromanticism [prirə'mæntisizəm] *n* prerromanticismo *m*.

presage ['presidʒ] *n* presagio *m* (that which foretells) ‖ presentimiento *m* (presentiment).

presage ['presidʒ] *vt* presagiar (to portend, to predict) ‖ presentir, tener el presentimiento de (to have a presentiment of).

presbyopia [ˌprezbi'əupjə] *n* MED presbicia *f*.

presbyopic [prezbi'ɔpik] *adj* présbita.

presbyter ['prezbitə*] *n* REL presbítero *m*.

presbyterate [pres'bitərət] *n* REL presbiterado *m*.

presbyterial [ˌprezbi'tiːəriəl] *adj* REL presbiteral.

Presbyterian [ˌprezbi'tiəriən] *adj/n* presbiteriano, na.

Presbyterianism [-izəm] *n* REL presbiterianismo *m*.

presbytery ['prezbitəri] *n* ARCH presbiterio *m* (part of a church) ‖ casa *f* del cura, casa *f* parroquial (priest's house).

preschool [priː'skuːl] *adj* preescolar.

prescience ['presiəns] *n* presciencia *f*.

prescient ['presiənt] *adj* que tiene presciencia, presciente.

prescind [pri'sind] *vt* separar (to isolate).
◆ *vi* *to prescind from* prescindir de.

prescribe [pris'kraib] *vt* prescribir (to order) ‖ MED recetar (a medicine) | mandar, ordenar; *the doctor prescribed complete rest* el médico le mandó reposo absoluto ‖ JUR prescribir ‖ — *in the prescribed time* dentro del plazo fijado por la ley ‖ *in the prescribed way* de conformidad con lo prescrito.
◆ *vi* establecer una norma, fijar una norma (to lay down a rule) ‖ MED hacer una receta ‖ JUR prescribir.

prescript ['priːskript] *n* norma *f*, regla *f*, precepto *m* (rule).

prescriptible [pri'skriptibl] *adj* prescriptible.

prescription [pris'kripʃən] *n* prescripción *f* (act of prescribing) ‖ norma *f*, regla *f*, precepto *m* (prescript) ‖ MED receta *f*, prescripción *f*; *on prescription* con receta ‖ JUR prescripción *f*.

prescriptive [pris'kriptiv] *adj* preceptivo, va ‖ establecido, da (established by usage).

presealed [priː'siːld] *adj* precintado, da.

preselection [priːsi'lekʃən] *n* RAD preselección *f*.

preselector [priːse'lektə*] *n* RAD preselector *m*.

presence ['prezns] *n* presencia *f*; *nobody noticed his presence in the room* nadie advirtió su presencia en la sala; *of good presence* de buena presencia; *supernatural presence* presencia sobrenatural ‖ asistencia *f*, presencia *f* (attendance) ‖ personalidad *f* (personality) ‖ — *in the presence of* en presencia de ‖ *presence of mind* presencia de ánimo ‖ *to be admitted to the Presence* ser recibido en audiencia por el rey ‖ *to make one's presence felt* imponerse, hacerse notar ‖ *your presence is requested* se ruega su asistencia.

presence chamber [-'tʃeimbə*] *n* sala *f* de audiencia.

present ['preznt] *adj* presente (in a place); *everybody was present* todos estaban presentes ‖ presente; *in the present case* en el caso presente ‖ presente, actual (time) ‖ GRAMM presente; *present tense* tiempo presente ‖ — *all present* todos los presentes ‖ *at the present time* en el momento actual, en este momento ‖ *present company excepted* mejorando lo presente ‖ *the present letter* la presente carta, la presente ‖ *the present writer* el que esto suscribe ‖ *the present year* el año en curso ‖ *those present* los presentes ‖ *to be present* asistir (to attend), haber; *nobody else was present* no había nadie más ‖ *to be present at* asistir; *we were present at the banquet* asistimos al banquete; ser testigo de, presenciar; *he was present at the ceremony* presenció la ceremonia.
◆ *n* regalo *m*, presente *m* (gift); *did you give him a present for his birthday?* ¿le hizo un regalo para su cumpleaños? ‖ presente *m*, actualidad *f* (time) ‖ GRAMM presente *m* (tense) ‖ — *at present* en la actualidad, actualmente, ahora (at the present day), por ahora (for the moment) ‖ JUR *by these presents* por la presente ‖ *for the present* por ahora, por el momento ‖ *to make s.o. a present of sth.* regalar algo a alguien ‖ *up to the present* hasta ahora.
◆ *interj* ¡presente!

present [pri'zent] *vt* presentar; *to present a candidate* presentar a un candidato; *may I present Mrs. Robinson?* le presento a la señora Robinson; *to present a bill* presentar un proyecto de ley; *to present a report* presentar un informe ‖ exponer, presentar (an argument, a case, etc.) ‖ presentar; *matter that presents many difficulties* asunto que presenta muchas dificultades ‖ plantear; *the dog presents a problem* el perro plantea un problema ‖ JUR presentar (a charge, etc.) ‖ ofrecer, presentar; *to present a dismal aspect* ofrecer un aspecto lúgubre ‖ regalar, obsequiar (to give as a gift); *to present s.o. with a gold watch* regalar a alguien un reloj de oro a alguien, obsequiar a alguien con un reloj de oro ‖ presentar (in theatre, in cinema, etc.) ‖ REL designar, proponer, presentar (to an ecclesiastical benefice) ‖ — *presenting X as Romeo* con X en el papel de Romeo ‖ MIL *to present arms* presentar armas ‖ *to present one's compliments to s.o.* presentar sus respetos a alguien ‖ *to present o.s.* presentarse.

presentability [priˌzentə'biliti] *n* buena presencia *f*.

presentable [pri'zentəbl] *adj* presentable ‖ *she is quite presentable* tiene buena presencia.

presentation [ˌprezen'teiʃən] *n* presentación *f* ‖ entrega *f*, ceremonia *f* de entrega (ceremony) ‖ obsequio *m*, regalo *m* (gift) ‖ THEATR presentación *f* (manner of presenting) | representación *f* (performance) ‖ REL presentación *f* ‖ MED presentación *f* (of a foetus) ‖ — *a presentation copy* un ejemplar de cortesía, un ejemplar con la dedicatoria del autor (of a book) ‖ *on presentation of* al presentar.

presentative [pri'zentətiv] *adj* REL colativo, va ‖ PHIL perceptible | intuitivo, va.

present-day ['prezntdei] *adj* actual, de hoy en día.

presentee [ˌprezən'tiː] *n* persona *f* presentada ‖ REL presentado *m*.

presenter [pri'zentə*] *n* presentador, ra.

presentient [pri'senʃiənt] *adj* *to be presentient of* presentir, tener el presentimiento de.

presentiment [pri'zentimənt] *n* presentimiento *m*, corazonada *f* ‖ *to have the presentiment that* tener el presentimiento de que.

presently ['prezntli] *adv* dentro de poco, luego (in a little while); *I'll come along presently* iré dentro de poco ‖ pronto (soon) ‖ US ahora, en el momento presente (at present).

presentment [pri'zentmənt] *n* presentación *f* ‖ REL reclamación *f*, queja *f* (complaint) ‖ THEATR & ARTS representación *f* ‖ JUR declaración *f* del jurado ‖ FIG descripción *f* (of a place, etc.).

present participle ['preznt'pɑːtisipl] *n* GRAMM gerundio *m*, participio *m* de presente.

present perfect ['preznt'pəːfikt] *n* GRAMM pretérito *m* perfecto.

preservable [pri'zəːvəbl] *adj* conservable.

preservation [ˌprezə'veiʃən] *n* conservación *f*; *preservation of fruit* conservación de frutas ‖ preservación *f* (protection) ‖ *in good preservation* bien conservado, da.

preservative [pri'zəːvətiv] *adj* preservativo, va.
◆ *n* preservativo *m* ‖ producto *m* para la conservación, producto *m* de conservación (for food).

preserve [pri'zəːv] *n* coto *m*, vedado *m* (for game or fish) ‖ conserva *f* (of food) ‖ confitura *f*, compota *f* (jam) ‖ FIG terreno *m*; *to trespass on s.o.'s preserve* meterse en terreno ajeno.

preserve [pri'zəːv] *vt* conservar, poner en conserva (foodstuffs) ‖ preservar, proteger (to protect) ‖ proteger (game) ‖ conservar (memory, custom) ‖ conservar, guardar, mantener (one's dignity, peace, etc.) ‖ observar, guardar (silence).

preserved [-d] *adj* en conserva ‖ *preserved food* conservas *f pl*.

preserving [-iŋ] *n* conservación *f*.

preset ['priː'set] *vt* programar, predefinir.

preshrunk ['pri'ʃrʌŋk] *adj* encogido de antemano, inencogible.

preside [pri'zaid] *vi* presidir; *to preside at o over a meeting* presidir una reunión.

presidency ['prezidənsi] *n* presidencia *f* ‖ dirección *f* (of a bank, etc.) ‖ US rectoría *f* (of a university).

president ['prezidənt] *n* presidente *m*, presidenta *f* ‖ director *m* (of a bank, etc.) ‖ US rector *m* (of a university).

presidential [ˌprezi'denʃəl] *adj* presidencial.

presidentship ['prezidəntʃip] *n* presidencia *f* ‖ dirección *f* (of a bank, etc.) ‖ US rectorado *m* (of a university).

presidio [pri'sidiəu] *n* presidio *m*.

presidium [pri'sidiəm] *n* presidium *m*.

press [pres] *n* presión *f* (pressure) ‖ apretón *m* (of hand) ‖ muchedumbre *f*, multitud *f* (crowd) ‖ apiñamiento *m* (crush of people) ‖ prisa *f*, urgencia *f* (urgency) ‖ apresuramiento *m* (haste) ‖ prensa *f*; *hydraulic press* prensa hidráulica ‖ PRINT imprenta *f* (printing office); *to send to press* mandar a la imprenta | impresión *f* (printing); *the edition is ready to go to press* la edición está lista para la impresión | personal *m* de imprenta (staff) ‖ prensa *f* (journalist, newspapers collectively); *will the press be admitted to the conference?* ¿se admitirá a la prensa en la conferencia? ‖ prensa *f*, crítica *f*; *the play received a good press* la obra tuvo muy buena prensa ‖ ropero *m* (cupboard) ‖ SP presa *f* (in wrestling) | levantada *f* (in weight lifting) | prensa *f* (for a tennis racket) ‖ leva *f* forzosa de marineros y soldados ‖ — *freedom of the press* libertad *f* de prensa ‖ *in the press* en prensa ‖ *off the press* recién salido de la imprenta ‖ *press campaign* campaña *f* de prensa ‖ *printing press* prensa (machine) ‖ *rotary press* rotativa *f* ‖ *to get a good, bad press* tener buena, mala prensa ‖ *to go to press* entrar en prensa ‖ *to pass for press* dar el tírese ‖ *to write for the press* escribir en los periódicos ‖ FIG *yellow press* prensa sensacionalista.

press [pres] *vt* prensar (in a mechanical press) ‖ apretar, presionar (to push) ‖ apretar; *they press me here* me aprietan aquí ‖ planchar (to iron clothes); *to press a skirt* planchar una falda ‖ pulsar, presionar, dar a (a button, a lever, etc.); *press the button* dale al botón || tocar (a bell) || apretar (trigger, hand, etc.) || exprimir (fruits to obtain juice) || estrujar (to squeeze) || secar (flowers) || prensar (a record) || FIG instar, apremiar, urgir (to urge); *to press s.o. to do sth.* instar a alguien a que haga algo | insistir en (to insist upon); *to press one's opinion* insistir en su opinión | hacer hincapié en (to emphasize) | acosar, acuciar, apremiar (to harass); *to press a debtor for payment* acosar a un deudor para que pague | imponer; *to press one's opinions on others* imponer sus opiniones a otros | hostigar, acosar (the enemy) | seguir muy de cerca, ir pisándole los talones a (in pursuit) || TECH calandrar (a fabric) | sobar, adobar (hides) | pisar, prensar (grapes) | prensar (apples, olives) | estampar, embutir (metals) | satinar (paper) || levar por fuerza (soldiers, sailors) || — *he didn't need much pressing* no hubo que repetírselo dos veces, no se hizo de rogar || *to be pressed for time, for money* andar escaso de tiempo, de dinero || *to press a claim* insistir en una petición || *to press a gift on s.o.* obligar a alguien a aceptar un regalo || *to press a point home* conseguir convencer a alguien de algo || *to press for payment* apremiar para el pago || *to press one's face to the window* pegar la cara contra el cristal || FIG *to press s.o. for an answer* insistir en que alguien conteste || *to press s.o. into service* recurrir a alguien || *to press s.o. to one's heart* abrazar a alguien estrechamente || *to press sth. into service* utilizar algo.

◆ *vi* apretar; *to press hard* apretar fuerte *or* mucho || apretujarse, apiñarse (crowds) || abrirse paso (through a crowd) || apremiar, urgir, ser urgente (to be urgent); *the matter does not press* el asunto no urge || apremiar (time); *time is pressing* el tiempo apremia || pesar; *great responsibilities press on him* grandes responsabilidades pesan sobre él || ejercer presión (to put pressure on).

◆ *phr v* ***to press back*** rechazar (the enemy) | contener (tears, desire) || ***to press down*** apretar | *to press down on sth.* apretar algo (to force down), apoyarse en algo (to rest on, to lean on) || ***to press for*** pedir con insistencia || ***to press forward*** activar, apresurar (to hasten) | apresurarse (to make haste) || — seguir adelante (to advance with resolution) || ***to press in*** clavar (a drawing pin) | meter a presión || ***to press on*** activar, apresurar (to hasten) | seguir adelante (to advance with resolution) | apresurarse (to make haste) | *to press on with* activar, apresurar || ***to press out*** exprimir (a fruit) | planchar (creases) | expulsar a presión || ***to press up*** apretujarse, apretarse; *to press up to* apretujarse contra.

press agency [-ˌeidʒənsi] *n* agencia *f* de prensa.

press agent [-ˌeidʒənt] *n* agente *m* de publicidad, agente *m* de prensa.

press baron [-'bærən] *n* magnate *m* de la prensa.

press box [-bɔks] *n* tribuna *f* de la prensa.

press button [-'bʌtn] *n* botón *m*.

press clipping [-'klipiŋ] *n* recorte *m* de periódico *or* de prensa.

press conference [-ˌkɔnfərəns] *n* rueda *f or* conferencia *f* de prensa.

press corps [-kɔː] *n* US grupo *m* de periodistas acreditados en un mismo lugar.

press cutting [-ˌkʌtiŋ] *n* recorte *m* de periódico *or* de prensa.

presser [-ə*] *n* prensador, ra (press operator).

press fastener [-ˌfɑːsenə*] *n* → **press stud.**

presser foot [-ə*fut] *n* pie *m* prensatelas, prensilla *f* (of sewing machine).

press gallery [-'gæləri] *n* tribuna *f* de la prensa.

press-gang [-gæŋ] *n* MIL & MAR patrulla *f* de enganche.

press house [-haus] *n* lagar *m* (for olives, for grapes and apples) || prensa *f* (for fruits and grains).

pressing [-iŋ] *adj* urgente; *he had a pressing engagement elsewhere* tenía un compromiso urgente en otra parte || apremiante, acuciante; *a pressing need* una necesidad apremiante || insistente.

◆ *n* prensado *m* (of fruits, of records) || planchado *m* (ironing) || calandrado *m* (of fabric) || estampado *m*, embutido *m* (of metals) || satinado *m* (of paper).

pressman [-mən] *n* prensador *m* (press operator) || impresor *m* (of a printing press) || periodista *m* (journalist).

— OBSERV El plural de *pressman* es *pressmen*.

pressmark [-mɑːk] *n* signatura *f* (on books).

press money [-'mʌni] *n* prima *f* de enganche.

press of canvas [-əv'kænvəs]; **press of sail** [-əv'seil] *n* MAR velamen *m* máximo.

press officer [-'ɔfisə*] *n* encargado, da de prensa (of an organization).

press photographer [-fə'tɔgrəfə*] *n* fotógrafo *m* de prensa, reportero *m* gráfico.

press proof [-pruːf] *n* PRINT última prueba *f* de imprenta.

press release [-ri'liːs] *n* comunicado *m* de prensa.

press roll [-rəul] *n* rodillo *m* de presión.

pressroom [-ruːm] *n* taller *m* de imprenta.

press stud [-stʌd]; **press fastener** [-ˌfɑːsenə*] *n* automático *m*.

press-up [-ʌp] *n* tracción *f* (in gymnastics).

pressure ['preʃə*] *n* PHYS & TECH presión *f*; *atmospheric pressure* presión atmosférica || peso *m* (weight) || fuerza *f* (strength) || ELECTR tensión *f*, voltaje *m* || MED tensión *f*; *blood pressure* tensión arterial; *low blood pressure* tensión baja || FIG presión *f*, apremio *m*; *under the pressure of circumstances* bajo la presión de las circunstancias | influencia *f*, presión *f* (influence) || — *at full pressure* a toda presión || *to act under pressure* obrar bajo presión || *to bring pressure to bear on s.o.* ejercer presión sobre alguien || *to do sth. under pressure from s.o.* hacer algo presionado por alguien || *to exert pressure on* ejercer presión sobre || *tyre pressure* presión de los neumáticos || *under the pressure of* apremiado por, bajo la presión de.

pressure ['preʃə*] *vt* ejercer presión sobre.

pressure cabin [-ˌkæbin] *n* cabina *f* presurizada.

pressure cooker [-ˌkukə*] *n* olla *f* de presión.

pressure feed [-fiːd] *n* alimentación *f* a presión.

pressure gauge [-geidʒ] *n* manómetro *m*.

pressure group [-gruːp] *n* grupo *m* de presión (in politics).

pressurization [preʃərai'zeiʃən] *n* presurización *f*.

pressurize ['preʃəraiz] *vt* presurizar, sobrecomprimir.

presswork ['preswəːk] *n* PRINT impresión *f*, tirada *f*.

Prestel ['prestel] *n* videotex *m* británico (registered trademark).

Prester John ['prestə:'dʒɔn] *pr n* Preste Juan.

prestidigitation ['prestiˌdidʒi'teiʃən] *n* prestidigitación *f*.

prestidigitator [ˌpresti'didʒiteitə*] *n* prestidigitador *m*.

prestige [pres'tiːʒ] *n* prestigio *m*.

prestigious [pres'tidʒəs] *adj* prestigioso, sa.

presto ['prestəu] *adj/adv* MUS presto.

prestress ['prestris] *vt* pretensar; *prestressed concrete* hormigón pretensado.

presumable [pri'zjuːməbl] *adj* probable, presumible.

presumably [pri'zjuːməbli] *adv* probablemente; *presumably she will come* probablemente vendrá.

presume [pri'zjuːm] *vt* suponer, imaginarse, figurarse, presumir (to suppose); *I presume that he will come tomorrow* supongo que vendrá mañana || tomarse la libertad de, permitirse, atreverse a (to dare).

◆ *vi* presumir (to be presumptuous) || abusar; *to presume on s.o.'s hospitality* abusar de la hospitalidad de alguien.

presumed [-d] *adj* presunto, ta; supuesto, ta.

presuming [-iŋ] *adj* osado, da; atrevido, da (daring) || presuntuoso, sa; presumido, da (conceited).

presumption [pri'zʌmpʃən] *n* presunción *f*, suposición *f* (supposition) || presunción *f*, presuntuosidad *f* (vanity, conceit) || atrevimiento *m*, osadía *f* (daring) || JUR presunción *f*.

presumptive [pri'zɔptiv] *adj* presunto, ta; supuesto, ta || JUR presuntivo, va; *presumptive evidence* pruebas presuntivas || *heir presumptive* heredero presunto.

presumptuous [pri'zʌmptjuəs] *adj* presuntuoso, sa; presumido, da (conceited) || atrevido, da; osado, da (daring).

presumptuousness [-nis] *n* presuntuosidad *f*, presunción *f* (vanity) || atrevimiento *m*, osadía *f* (daring).

presuppose [ˌpriːsə'pəuz] *vt* presuponer, suponer.

presupposition [ˌpriːsʌpə'ziʃən] *n* presuposición *f*, presupuesto *m*.

pretence; US **pretense** [pri'tens] *n* pretensión *f* (claim, pretentiousness); *no pretence to originality* ninguna pretensión de originalidad || pretexto *m* (pretext) || apariencia *f* (appearance) || simulación *f*, fingimiento *m* (false show) || ostentación *f* (display); *devoid of all pretence* sin ninguna ostentación || JUR procedimiento *m* fraudulento || — *false pretences* fraude *m sing* || *his anger was only pretence* su cólera era fingida || *to make a pretence of* simular que, hacer como si || *to make no pretence to know* no pretender saber || *to obtain sth. under false pretences* obtener algo por fraude *or* fraudulentamente || *under the pretence of* so pretexto de, con el pretexto de.

pretend [pri'tend] *n* FAM simulacro *m* || FAM *his anger was all pretend* su cólera era fingida.

pretend [pri'tend] *vt* fingir, aparentar, simular; *to pretend ignorance* fingir ignorancia || pretender (to claim); *he didn't pretend to know it* no pretendía saberlo || suponer, imaginarse (to imagine); *let's pretend that we are on an island* vamos a suponer que estamos en una isla || — *to pretend to be* fingirse, fingir; *he pretends to be dead* se finge muerto, finge estar muerto; dárselas de; *he pretended he was a doctor* se las daba de médico.

◆ *vi* disimular, fingir (to hide feelings, etc.); *don't pretend with me* no disimules conmigo || — *let's not pretend to each other* no nos engañemos uno a otro || *to pretend to cleverness* dárselas de listo, pretender ser listo || *to pretend to the throne* pretender el trono.

pretended [-id] *adj* fingido, da; simulado, da (emotion) || supuesto, ta (person).

pretender [-ə*] *n* pretendiente *m* & *f*; *pretender to the throne* pretendiente al trono ‖ simulador, ra (s.o. who pretends).

pretense [pri'tens] *n* US ⟶ **pretence.**

pretension [pri'tenʃən] *n* pretensión *f* (claim) ‖ presunción *f*, pretensión *f* (pretentiousness).

pretentious [pri'tenʃəs] *adj* pretencioso, sa; presuntuoso, sa; presumido, da (conceited, showy) ‖ cursi (showy and in bad taste).

pretentiousness [-nis] *n* presunción *f*, presuntuosidad *f*, pretensión *f* (conceit) ‖ cursilería *f* (snobbishness).

preterite; preterit ['pretərit] *adj* GRAMM pretérito ‖ FIG pretérito, ta; pasado, da.
◆ *n* GRAMM pretérito *m*.

preterition [pri:tə'riʃən] *n* preterición *f* (omission) ‖ JUR preterición *f*.

pretermission [ˌpri:tə'miʃən] *n* preterición *f*.

pretermit [ˌpri:tə'mit] *vt* omitir, preterir (to omit).

pretext ['pri:tekst] *n* pretexto *m* ‖ — *under the pretext of* so pretexto de, con el pretexto de ‖ *under the pretext that* con el pretexto de que.

pretext ['pri:tekst] *vt* pretextar, dar como pretexto.

pretexta [-ə] *n* pretexta *f*.

pretor ['pri:tə*] *n* ⟶ **praetor.**

pretorian ['pri'tɔ:riən] *adj* ⟶ **praetorian.**

pretorianism [pritɔ'riəˌnizəm] *n* ⟶ **praetorianism.**

pretorium [pri'tɔriəm] *n* ⟶ **praetorium.**

pretorship ['pri:təʃip] *n* ⟶ **praetorship.**

prettification [ˌpritifi'keiʃən] *n* embellecimiento *m*.

prettify ['pritifai] *vt* embellecer.

prettily ['pritili] *adv* bonitamente, lindamente ‖ bien; *to behave prettily* portarse bien.

prettiness ['pritinis] *n* lo bonito, lo mono, lo lindo, lindeza *f*, belleza *f* (beauty) ‖ preciosidad *f* (in style).

pretty ['priti] *adj* bonito, ta; mono, na; lindo, da (thing) ‖ mono, na; guapo, pa; lindo, da (person) ‖ FAM menudo, da; *a pretty mess* menudo lío | importante, considerable, bueno, na (sum etc.) ‖ FIG *to cost pretty penny* costar caro, costar mucho dinero, costar un dineral.
◆ *adv* bastante; *pretty good* bastante bueno; *I am pretty busy* estoy bastante ocupado ‖ *pretty much the same* más o menos lo mismo.
◆ *n* cosa *f* bonita *or* linda ‖ *my pretty* mi vida, mi cielo, guapa.

pretzel ['pretsəl] *n* galleta *f* tostada cubierta con sal.

prevail [pri'veil] *vi* prevalecer; *truth will prevail* la verdad prevalecerá; *the tradition still prevails in the South* la tradición prevalece todavía en el Sur ‖ triunfar, vencer; *we prevailed over* o *against the enemy* vencimos al enemigo, triunfamos sobre el enemigo ‖ predominar; *a region where strong winds prevail* una región donde predominan vientos fuertes ‖ imperar, predominar, regir, reinar; *the conditions that then prevailed* las condiciones que imperaban entonces ‖ — *to be prevailed upon to* dejarse convencer *or* persuadir de ‖ *to prevail on* o *upon* persuadir, convencer.

prevailing [-iŋ] *adj* reinante, imperante, predominante; *the prevailing wind* el viento predominante; *the prevailing cold* el frío imperante ‖ común (opinion) ‖ actual (present); *under prevailing conditions* en las condiciones actuales.

prevalence ['prevələns] *n* uso *m* corriente, costumbre *f* (common practice) ‖ predominio *m*; *the prevalence of good over evil* el predominio del bien sobre el mal ‖ frecuencia *f* (frequency).

prevalent ['prevələnt] *adj* predominante, que prevalece, que reina, que impera; *disease that is prevalent in a country* enfermedad que impera en un país ‖ extendido, da (widespread) ‖ corriente (common) ‖ actual (present-day); *the prevalent fashion* la moda actual ‖ frecuente (frequent).

prevaricate [pri'værikeit] *vi* andar con rodeos, tergiversar (to avoid the issue) ‖ mentir (to lie) ‖ JUR prevaricar.

prevarication [priˌværi'keiʃən] *n* tergiversación *f*, equívocos *m pl*, evasivas *f pl* ‖ mentira *f* (lie) ‖ JUR prevaricación *f*.

prevaricator [pri'værikeitə*] *n* tergiversador, ra ‖ mentiroso, sa (liar) ‖ JUR prevaricador *m*.

prevenient [pri'vi:njənt] *adj* previo, via; anterior (previous) ‖ MED preventivo, va.

prevent [pri'vent] *vt* impedir; *illness prevented him from coming* o *prevented his coming* la enfermedad le impidió venir ‖ evitar (to avoid); *to prevent a serious accident* evitar un accidente grave.

preventable; preventible [pri'ventəbl] *adj* evitable.

preventative [pri'ventətiv] *adj/n* ⟶ **preventive.**

preventer [pri'ventə*] *n* impedimento *m*, obstáculo *m* ‖ — MAR *preventer stay* contraestay *m* | *preventer tack* contraamura *f*.

prevention [pri'venʃən] *n* prevención *f* ‖ impedimento *m* (hindrance); *in case of prevention* en caso de impedimento ‖ protección *f* ‖ — *for the prevention of accidents* para evitar accidentes ‖ *prevention is better than cure* más vale prevenir que curar ‖ *prevention of unemployment* medidas preventivas contra el paro *or* desempleo ‖ *society for the prevention of cruelty to* sociedad protectora de.

preventive [pri'ventiv]**; preventative** [pri'ventətiv] *adj* preventivo, va.
◆ *n* medida *f* preventiva ‖ MED medicamento *m* profiláctico.

preventorium [priven'tɔ:riəm] *n* MED preventorio *m* (for preventive care or treatment).

preview ['pri:vju:] *n* CINEM & THEATR presentación *f* a los críticos | trailer *m*, avance *m* (film extract).

preview; US **prevue** ['pri:'vju:] *vt* asistir a la presentación (de una película u obra de teatro) a los críticos ‖ presentar a los críticos (to present) ‖ ver antes que los demás.

previous ['pri:vjəs] *adj* anterior, previo, via; *the previous meeting* la reunión anterior; *without previous notice* sin previo aviso ‖ FAM prematuro, ra (premature) | apresurado, da (hasty) ‖ JUR *previous question* cuestión previa.
◆ *adv* *previous to* antes de; *to check one's work previous to handing it in* revisar el trabajo antes de entregarlo.

previously [-li] *adv* antes, anteriormente, previamente; *he didn't know what had happened previously* no sabía lo que había ocurrido antes ‖ *previously to* antes de.

previse [pri'va:iz] *vt* prever (to foresee) ‖ prevenir, advertir (to warn).

prevision [pri'viʒən] *n* previsión *f*.

previsional [-əl] *adj* previsor, ra.

prevue ['pri:'vju:] *n/vt* US ⟶ **preview.**

prewar ['pri:'wɔ:*] *adj* de antes de la guerra ‖ *the prewar period* la preguerra.

prey [prei] *n* presa *f* (of an animal) ‖ FIG víctima *f*; *he fell prey to robbers* fue víctima de los ladrones ‖ ZOOL *bird of prey* ave *f* de rapiña *or* de presa.

prey [prei] *vi* atacar (to attack) ‖ pillar (to plunder) ‖ aprovecharse de (to exploit) ‖ FIG reconcomer, carcomer; *doubts preyed on him* las dudas lo reconcomían | remorder (one's conscience) ‖ alimentarse (*on* de) (animals) ‖ *to prey on one's mind* preocupar mucho.

price [prais] *n* precio *m*; *asking, cash, cost, list net price* precio ofrecido, al contado, de coste, de lista, neto; *price fixing* fijación de precios; *price rise* subida de precio *or* de precios ‖ COMM cotización *f*; *closing, opening price* cotización de cierre, inicial ‖ FIG precio *m*, valor *m* (value) ‖ — FIG *at any price* a toda costa, cueste lo que cueste ‖ *at a price* a un precio muy alto ‖ *at cost price* a precio de coste ‖ *beyond price* inapreciable, sin precio ‖ *factory price* precio de fábrica ‖ *fixed price* precio fijo ‖ *full price* precio fuerte ‖ *low price* precio barato *or* bajo ‖ *manufacturer's price* precio de fábrica ‖ *market price* precio de mercado, precio corriente ‖ FIG *not at any price* por nada del mundo ‖ *price ceiling, maximum price* precio tope ‖ *price control* control *m* de precios, intervención *f* ‖ *price free on board* precio franco a bordo ‖ *price list* lista *f* de precios, tarifa *f* ‖ *price of money* tipo *m* de descuento, interés *m* ‖ *price range* gama *f* de precios ‖ *price support* mantenimiento *m* de los precios ‖ *price tag* etiqueta *f* del precio ‖ *purchase price* precio de compra ‖ *reserve price* precio mínimo ‖ *rock-bottom* o *cheapest possible price* precio mínimo ‖ *sale price* precio de venta ‖ *top* o *ceiling price* precio tope ‖ *to put a price on* poner precio a ‖ FIG *to put a price on s.o.'s head* poner a precio la cabeza de uno | *to set a high price on sth.* dar mucha importancia a algo ‖ *unit price* precio por unidad ‖ *whatever the price* a cualquier precio ‖ *what price autonomy?* y la autonomía, ¿qué? ‖ *wholesale price* precio al por mayor.

price [prais] *vt* COMM poner precio a, tasar, valorar (*at* en) (to fix the price of) ‖ preguntar el precio de (to ask the price of) ‖ FIG estimar, evaluar, valorar, tasar (to estimate the value of) ‖ — COMM *all the commodities are priced* todos los artículos llevan precio | *to be priced at* costar, tener un precio de | *to be priced out of the market* no poder competir en los mercados internacionales [a causa de su elevado precio], no ser competitivo.

priceless [-lis] *adj* inapreciable, inestimable, que no tiene precio (invaluable) ‖ FAM divertidísimo, ma; graciosísimo, ma (highly amusing) ‖ *to be priceless* no tener precio; ser divertidísimo.

price [-i] *adj* FAM carillo, lla.

prick [prik] *n* pinchazo *m* (act, pain, perforation) ‖ picadura *f* (of an insect) ‖ alfilerazo *m* (with a pin) ‖ pinchazo *m* (of a needle) ‖ aguijonazo *m* (with a goad) ‖ espolazo *m*, espolada *f* (with a spur) ‖ POP polla *f* (penis) ‖ FIG *prick of conscience* remordimiento *m* de conciencia.

prick [prik] *vt* pinchar, picar, punzar; *to prick sth. with a pin* pinchar algo con un alfiler ‖ pinchar; *to prick a balloon* pinchar un globo ‖ pinchar (a part of the body); *he pricked his finger* se pinchó el dedo ‖ abrir, reventar (an abscess) ‖ agujerear (to mark with holes) ‖ aguijar, aguijonear (to goad) ‖ espolear (to spur a horse) ‖ levantar, erguir (an animal its ears) ‖ trasplantar (to transplant) ‖ FIG remorder; *his conscience pricked him* le remordía la conciencia ‖ — *to prick out* trasplantar (flowers) ‖ *to prick up one's ears* aguzar el oído, prestar atención (a person), levantar *or* erguir las orejas (an animal).
◆ *vi* causar comezón (to hurt) ‖ pinchar (to be prickly) ‖ agriarse, echarse a perder (a beverage) ‖ espolear (on horseback) ‖ MED hormiguear (limbs) ‖ erguirse (ears, etc.).

prick-eared [-iəd] *adj* con las orejas levantadas *or* erguidas (animal) ‖ que aguza el oído (person).

pricker [-ə*] *n* punzón *m* (sharp instrument) ‖ montero *m* de caza (in hunting).

pricket ['prikət] *n* ZOOL corzo *m* [de un año] || pincho *m* en un candelabro que sirve para sujetar la vela.

pricking [-iŋ] *adj* que pincha || punzante (pain).
◆ *n* pinchazo *m* || punzada *f* || MED punción *f* (of an abscess) | hormigueo *m* (of a limb).
◆ *pl* remordimientos *m* (of conscience).

prickle ['prikl] *n* BOT espina *f*, pincho *m*, púa *f* (thorn) || ZOOL púa *f* || picor *m*, picazón *f* (prickly sensation).

prickle ['prikl] *vt* picar (to cause a prickly sensation) || pinchar (to prick).
◆ *vi* sentir picor *or* picazón || hormiguear (a limb).

prickling [-iŋ] *n* picazón *f*, picor *m* (on the skin) || hormigueo *m* (of a limb).

prickly [-li] *adj* espinoso, sa; lleno de pinchos *or* púas || FIG espinoso, sa; delicado, da | quisquilloso, sa; susceptible (touchy) || — MED *prickly heat* sarpullido causado por exceso de calor || BOT *prickly pear* nopal *m*, chumbera *f* (plant), higo chumbo (fruit).

pride [praid] *n* orgullo *m*; *to wound s.o.'s pride* herir el orgullo de uno; *he is the pride of his family* es el orgullo de la familia || amor *m* propio (self-esteem) || dignidad *f* (dignity) || soberbia *f*, arrogancia *f* (arrogance) || grupo *m* (of lions) || brío *m* (of horse) || FIG apogeo *m*, esplendor *m* || — *false pride* vanidad *f* || *in the full pride of youth* en la flor de la edad || *it is a source of pride to us that* es para nosotros un motivo de orgullo que || *peacock in his pride* pavo *m* real haciendo la rueda || FIG *puffed* o *blown up with pride* hinchado de orgullo || *to be s.o.'s pride and joy* ser el orgullo de alguien || *to have* o *to take pride of place* ocupar un puesto de honor || *to pocket one's pride* tragarse el orgullo *or* el amor propio || *to take pride in* enorgullecerse *or* vanagloriarse de, estar orgulloso de (to be proud of), esmerarse en (one's work, appearance, etc.).

pride [praid] *vt* *to pride o.s. on* o *upon* enorgullecerse de, vanagloriarse de, estar orgulloso de.

prideful [-ful] *adj* orgulloso, sa || arrogante (conceited).

prie-dieu ['pri:djə:] *n* reclinatorio *m*.
— OBSERV El plural es *prie-dieux* o *prie-dieus*.

prier ['praiə*] *n* FAM fisgón, ona.

priest [pri:st] *n* REL sacerdote *m* || — *high priest* Sumo Sacerdote || *parish priest* párroco *m*, cura *m* párroco.

priestcraft [-kra:ft] *n* clericalismo *m*.

priestess [-is] *n* REL sacerdotisa *f*.

priesthood [-hud] *n* sacerdocio *m* (office) || clero *m* (clergy) || *to enter the priesthood* hacerse sacerdote, ordenarse de sacerdote.

priestly [-li] *adj* sacerdotal.

priest-ridden [-ˌridn] *adj* dominado por el clero.

prig [prig] *n* mojigato, ta; gazmoño, ña (prude) || presumido, da; pedante *m* & *f* (pedant).

priggish [-iʃ] *adj* presumido, da; pedante (pedantic) || mojigato, ta; gazmoño, ña (prudish).

priggishness [-iʃnis] *n* presunción *f*, pedantería *f* (pedantry) || mojigatería *f*, gazmoñería *f* (prudery).

prim [prim] *adj* remilgado, da (fussy) || forzado, da (smile) || etiquetero, ra; estirado, da (formal) || recatado, da (demure).

prim [prim] *vt* *to prim o.s. up* acicalarse, arreglarse || *to prim up one's mouth* poner boca de corazoncito.

prima ballerina [ˈpri:məˌbæləˈri:nə] *n* primera bailarina *f*.

primacy ['praiməsi] *n* primacía *f*.

primadonna [ˈpri:məˈdɔnə] *n* diva *f*, prima donna *f*.

prima facie ['praimə'feiʃii] *adv* a primera vista.

prima-facie evidence [-evidəns] *n* JUR prueba *f* suficiente a primera vista.

primage ['praimidʒ] *n* MAR prima *f* de flete.

primal ['praiməl] *adj* primitivo, va; original || principal, fundamental, primordial (most important).

primarily ['praimərili] *adv* ante todo, en primer lugar, principalmente, esencialmente (mainly) || primitivamente (originally).

primary ['praiməri] *adj* primario, ria; *primary school* escuela primaria; *primary instincts* instintos primarios || básico, ca; esencial, fundamental, principal (fundamental) || primero, ra (not derived); *primary meaning of a word* primer sentido de una palabra || ELECTR & GEOL & CHEM & ASTR & MED primario, ria || — *primary accent* acento primario || *primary education* primera enseñanza, enseñanza primaria.
◆ *n* lo principal (most important thing) || pluma *f* primaria (feather) || color *m* primario (colour) || ASTR planeta *m* primario || ELECTR primario *m* || US elección *f* primaria *or* preliminar para nombrar candidatos.

primary cell [-sel] *n* pila *f*.

primate ['praimit] *n* REL primado *m*.

primate ['praimeit] *n* ZOOL primate *m* (ape).

prime [praim] *adj* primero, ra (first) || principal, fundamental, primordial (fundamental) || original, primitivo, va (primary) || de primera calidad *or* categoría, selecto, ta (top-quality) || MATH primo, ma (number) || — *in prime condition* en perfecto estado, en estado excelente || *of prime importance* primordial, sumamente importante || COMM *prime cost* coste *m* de producción || *prime meridian* primer meridiano || *Prime Minister* primer ministro || *prime mover* fuerza motriz (of a machine), causa primera (in philosophy), promotor, ra; instigador, ra (person behind an action) || *prime time* horas *f pl* de audiencia.
◆ *n* flor *f* de la vida *or* de la edad; *to be cut off in one's prime* morir en la flor de la vida; *to be in one's prime* estar en la flor de la vida || POET albor *m*, principio *m* (beginning); *the prime of the world* el albor del mundo | flor y nata *f*, lo mejor, lo más escogido (the best) || MATH número *m* primo || REL prima *f* || PRINT virgulilla *f* (apostrophe) || átomo *m* simple (atom) || SP primera posición *f* (in fencing) || MUS sonido *m* fundamental || *to be past one's prime* haber pasado lo mejor de la vida.

prime [praim] *vt* cebar (a gun, a pump, a motor) || preparar (a surface, etc.) || ARTS imprimar, aprestar || FIG preparar (a person for an interview) | informar; *they had primed him as to what to do* le habían informado de lo que tenía que hacer | emborrachar (to make drunk) || FIG *to be well primed* estar alegre (to be drunk), estar bien preparado (for an examination).

primeness [-nis] *n* calidad *f* superior, excelencia *f*.

primer [-ə*] *n* cartilla *f* (for learning to read) || libro *m* elemental (elementary text book) || cebador *m* (of a pump) || cartucho *m* cebo (of a gun) || fulminante *m* (for firing a bomb) || REL libro *m* de horas || *primer coat* primera mano.

primeval [prai'mi:vəl] *adj* primitivo, va; prístino, na || virgen (forest).

priming ['praimiŋ] *adj* de cebar.
◆ *n* ARTS imprimación *f*, apresto *m* | primera mano *f* (first coat) || cebado *m* (of pump etc.) || cebo *m* (of a gun).

primipara [prai'mipərə] *n* primeriza *f*, primípara *f*.
— OBSERV El plural es *primiparae* o *primiparas*.

primiparous [prai'mipərəs] *adj* primeriza, primípara.

primitive ['primitiv] *adj* primitivo, va; *a primitive tribe* una tribu primitiva || sencillo, lla; primitivo, va; primario, ria; rudimentario, ria; *primitive weapons* armas rudimentarias || BIOL & GRAMM & ARTS primitivo, va || GEOL primario, ria.
◆ *n* primitivo *m*, hombre *m* primitivo || ARTS primitivo *m*.

primitiveness [-nis] *n* carácter *m* primitivo.

primness ['primnis] *n* lo estirado, lo etiquetero (formality) || remilgo *m* (fussiness).

primogenitor [ˌpraiməu'dʒenitə*] *n* primer antepasado *m* (earliest ancestor) || FAM antepasado *m*.

primogeniture [ˌpraiməu'dʒenitʃə*] *n* primogenitura *f*.

primordial [prai'mɔ:djəl] *adj* primordial.

primp [primp] *vt* acicalar, emperejilar.
◆ *vi* acicalarse, emperejilarse.

primrose ['primrəuz] *n* primavera *f*, prímula *f* (flower) || amarillo *m* claro (colour) || FIG *primrose path* camino *m* de flores, camino *m* de rosas.
◆ *adj* amarillo claro.

primula ['primjulə] *n* BOT prímula *f* (flower).

primulaceae [ˌprimju'leisii:] *pl n* primuláceas *f*.

Primus ['praiməs] *n* hornillo *m* de camping (registered trademark).

prince [prins] *n* príncipe *m*; *Prince of Wales* Príncipe de Gales || — *crown prince* príncipe heredero || *Prince Charming* el Príncipe Azul || *prince consort* príncipe consorte || *Prince of Darkness* príncipe de las tinieblas || *prince royal* príncipe real.

princedom [-dəm] *n* principado *m*.

princekin [-kin]; **princeling** [-liŋ] *n* principito *m* (insignificant prince).

princely [-li] *adj* principesco, ca || FIG regio, gia; magnífico, ca; *a princely reward* una magnífica recompensa.

princess [prin'ses] *n* princesa *f* || *princess royal* princesa real.

principal ['prinsəpəl] *adj* principal || GRAMM *principal parts* formas *f* principales (of a verb).
◆ *m* director, ra (of a school, of a factory, etc.) || rector, *m* (of a university) || jefe *m* (of a firm) || mandante *m*; *principal and agent* mandante y mandatario || JUR autor *m* (of a crime) || COMM capital *m*, principal *m* (sum of money) || THEATR primera figura *f* || MUS solista *m* & *f* | principal *m* (organ stop) | tema *m* principal (of a fugue).

principality [ˌprinsi'pæliti] *n* principado *m*.
◆ *pl* REL principados *m* (order of angels).

principally ['prinsəpli] *adv* principalmente.

principalship ['prinsəpəlʃip] *n* dirección *f* (of a school, of a factory) || rectorado *m* (of a university).

principle ['prinsəpl] *n* principio *m*; *Archimedes' principle* el principio de Arquímedes; *my principles won't allow me to do it* mis principios no me permiten hacerlo || — *a man of principle* un hombre de principios || *I make it a principle never to do that* tengo por principio no hacer nunca eso, tengo por norma jamás hacer eso || *in principle* en principio || *it is a matter* *of principle* es una cuestión de principios || *on principle* por principio || *to go back to first principles* volver a los principios fundamentales || *to have high principles* tener elevados *or* nobles principios || *to lay it down as a principle that* sentar el principio de que.

principled [-d] *adj* de principios.

prink [priŋk] *vt* emperejilar, emperifollar || *to prink o.s. up* emperejilarse, emperifollarse.

print [print] *n* huella *f* (of finger) || huella *f*, señal *f* (of foot) || marca *f*, impresión *f* (impression) || prueba *f*, positiva *f* (photography) || copia *f* (of a photograph) || impreso *m*, texto *m* impreso (printed paper) || tirada *f* (edition) || impresión *f* (printing) || imprenta *f* (printing office) || letras *f pl* de imprenta *or* de molde (handwriting) || caracteres *m pl*, letra *f* (letters in a book) || tipo *m* (type) || molde *m* (mould) || estampado *m* (cloth, dress); *cotton prints* estampados de algodón || estampa *f*, grabado *m* (picture) || — *in print* impreso, sa (in printed form), en venta, disponible (available) || *out of print* agotado, da || *to find o.s. in print* ver sus obras publicadas || *to get into print* publicarse; *I don't want that to get into print* no quiero que eso se publique || *to rush into print* publicar algo precipitadamente.
◆ *pl* huellas *f* dactilares *or* digitales (fingerprints).
◆ *adj* estampado, da (dress, material).

print [print] *vt* imprimir; *where was this book printed?* ¿dónde imprimieron este libro? || tirar, hacer una tirada de (an edition) || publicar (to publish); *the letter was printed in yesterday's paper* la carta se publicó en el periódico de ayer || imprimir, grabar (drawings, etc.) || dejar (huellas), imprimir, estampar (marks, traces, e. g. in the snow) || estampar (seal) || estampar (cloth, textiles) || sacar, tirar, positivar (copies of a negative) || escribir con letras de imprenta *or* de molde (when writing); *print your name, please* por favor escriba su nombre con letras de imprenta || FIG grabar, imprimir (sth. on the mind) || INFORM *to print out* imprimir, sacar por impresora.
◆ *vi* imprimirse (book) || escribir con letras de imprenta *or* de molde || PHOT *to print well* salir bien (a negative).

printable [-əbl] *adj* imprimible.

printed [-id] *adj* impreso, sa (newspapers, books) || estampado, da (cloth, seal) || de imprenta, de molde (letter) || — *printed circuit* circuito impreso || *printed matter* impresos *m pl*.

printer [-ə*] *n* impresor *m* (of books) || INFORM impresora *f* || — *printer's devil* aprendiz *m* de imprenta || *printer's error* errata *f*, error *m* de imprenta || *printer's ink* tinta *f* de imprenta || *printer's mark* pie *m* de imprenta || *printer's reader* corrector *m* de pruebas.

printery [-əri] *n* US imprenta *f* (printing house) || fábrica *f* de estampados.

printing [-iŋ] *n* impresión *f* (action); *colour printing* impresión en color || imprenta *f* (art, profession); *to know everything about printing* conocer perfectamente la imprenta || impresión *f* (quality of print) || tipografía *f* (layout, etc.) || tirada *f* (quantity printed) || letras *f pl* de imprenta *or* de molde (handwriting) || PHOT tiraje *m*, positivado *m* (of a negative).

printing frame [-iŋfreim] *n* prensa *f* de copiar.

printing house [-iŋhaus] *n* imprenta *f*.

printing machine [-iŋməʃi:n] *n* prensa *f*.

printing office [-iŋˌɔfis] *n* imprenta *f*, talleres *m pl* gráficos.

printing press [-iŋˌpres] *n* prensa *f*.

printless [-lis] *adj* sin señal, sin marca, sin huellas.

printout [-aut] *n* INFORM impresión *f*, salida *f* de impresora.

print room [-ru:m] *n* sección *f* de estampas.

prior ['praiə*] *adj* anterior (previous) || más importante, preferente (more important).
◆ *adv* *prior to* antes de (before).
◆ *n* REL prior *m*.

priorate ['praiəret] *n* REL priorato *m*.

prioress ['praiəris] *n* REL priora *f*.

priority [prai'ɔriti] *n* prioridad *f* (in order, in importance) || anterioridad *f* (in time) || — *according to priority* por orden de prelación, por orden de prioridad || *priority share* acción privilegiada.

priorship ['praiəʃip] *n* REL priorato *m* (rank, office).

priory ['praiəri] *n* REL priorato *m*.

prise [praiz] *n* apalancamiento *m* (leverage) || palanca *f* (lever).

prise [praiz] *vt* *to prise open, up* abrir, levantar por fuerza *or* con una palanca.

prism ['prizəm] *n* MATH & PHYS prisma *m*.

prismatic [priz'mætik] *adj* prismático, ca || *prismatic colours* colores *m* del prisma.

prison ['prizn] *n* cárcel *f*, prisión *f* (building, punishment) || MIL prisión *f* || — *model prison* cárcel modelo || *sent to prison* encarcelado, da (civil person), prisionero, ra (military man) || *to go to prison for three years* ser condenado a tres años de prisión *or* de cárcel *or* de encarcelamiento || *to put s.o. in prison, to send s.o. to prison* encarcelar a alguien, meter a alguien en la cárcel || *to put s.o. in prison for three years, to send s.o. to prison for three years* condenar a alguien a tres años de prisión *or* de cárcel *or* de encarcelamiento.
◆ *adj* carcelario, ria || — *prison breaking* evasión *f* || *prison camp* campamento *m* para prisioneros || *prison house* cárcel *f*, prisión *f* || *prison life* la vida en la cárcel || *prison population* población reclusa || *prison sentence of 20 years* condena *f* a veinte años de cárcel *or* de prisión *or* de encarcelamiento || *prison system* régimen penitenciario || *prison van* coche *m* celular || *prison yard* patio *m* de la cárcel.

prison ['prizn] *vt* encarcelar.

prisoner [-ə*] *n* preso, sa (in a prison) || detenido, da (under arrest) || JUR acusado, da (in the court-room) || MIL prisionero, ra; *to take s.o. prisoner* hacerle prisionero a uno || — *prisoner of war* prisionero de guerra || FIG *to be a prisoner of* estar aprisionado por || *to hold s.o. prisoner* tener detenido a uno || *to take s.o. prisoner* hacer prisionero a uno.

prisoner's base ['priznəzbeis] *n* marro *m* (children's game).

prissy ['prisi] *adj* remilgado, da (very prim).

pristine ['pristain] *adj* prístino, na; original, primitivo, va.

prithee ['priði] *interj* ¡te lo ruego!, ¡por favor!

privacy ['privəsi] *n* intimidad *f*; *in the privacy of one's own home* en la intimidad del hogar; *to respect s.o.'s privacy* respetar la intimidad de uno || vida *f* privada; *he doesn't get any privacy* no tiene ninguna vida privada || aislamiento *m*, soledad *f* (isolation); *desire for privacy* deseo de soledad || secreto *m* (secrecy).

private [praivit] *adj* privado, da; *private property* propiedad privada; *private life* vida privada; *private law* derecho privado; *private interview* entrevista privada || personal (personal); *private motives* motivos personales; *my private opinion* mi opinión personal; *private use* uso personal || privado, da; íntimo, ma (thoughts) || secreto, ta (secret) || reservado, da; *she is very private about her affairs* es muy reservada en sus cosas || confidencial (confidential) || particular (lessons, arrangement, car, house, etc.) || en la intimidad (wedding) || privado, da; no público, ca (party) || aislado, da; íntimo, ma (place) || MIL raso; *private soldier* soldado raso || — *private bill* proyecto *m* de ley de interés local || *private citizen* particular *m* || *private detective* detective privado || *private enterprise* empresa privada || US MIL *private first class* soldado *m* de primera || *private fishing* coto vedado || *private income* renta *f* || ANAT *private parts* partes pudendas || THEATR *private performance* representación privada || *private practice* medicina *f* privada || *private school* colegio privado || *private secretary* secretario *m* particular, secretaria *f* particular || CINEM *private showing* sesión privada || *private view* inauguración privada (of an exhibition) || *the ceremony was private* la ceremonia se celebró en la intimidad || *to have private means* tener una fortuna personal || *to keep a matter private* no divulgar un asunto, mantener secreto un asunto.
◆ *n* MIL soldado *m* raso || *in private* en privado; *they discussed the matter in private* discutieron el asunto en privado; en secreto, confidencialmente (confidentially), a puerta cerrada (a meeting), en la intimidad (a ceremony).
◆ *pl* ANAT partes *f* pudendas (private parts).

privateer [ˌpraivə'tiə*] *n* MAR corsario *m* (ship, sailor).

privateering [-iŋ] *n* MAR corso *m*, expedición *f*.

privateersman [-zmən] *n* MAR corsario *m*.
— OBSERV El plural de esta palabra es *privateersmen*.

privately ['praivitli] *adv* en privado, privadamente (in private) || en secreto, confidencialmente (confidentially) || personalmente; *I spoke privately to him* le hablé personalmente || a puerta cerrada; *the meeting was held privately* la reunión se celebró a puerta cerrada || en la intimidad; *privately married* casado en la intimidad || en el fondo; *privately I was quite worried* en el fondo estaba muy preocupado || *privately printed book* libro editado por cuenta del autor.

privation [prai'veiʃən] *n* privación *f* || estrechez *f*, miseria *f*; *to live in privation* vivir en la estrechez || apuro *m*; *he suffered many privations* pasó muchos apuros.

privative ['privətiv] *adj* privativo, va || FIG negativo, va (quality).
◆ *n* GRAMM prefijo *m* privativo, sufijo *m* privativo.

privatize ['praivitaiz] *vt* privatizar.

privet ['privit] *n* BOT alheña *f*.

privilege ['privilidʒ] *n* privilegio *m*, prerrogativa *f* || honor *m*; *it has been a privilege to meet you* ha sido un honor conocerle || *parliamentary privilege* inmunidad parlamentaria.

privilege ['privilidʒ] *vt* privilegiar || *to privilege s.o. to do sth.* conceder a alguien el privilegio de hacer algo.

privileged [-d] *adj* privilegiado, da (favoured) || que goza del privilegio (*to* de) || que goza de la inmunidad parlamentaria || — *to be privileged from sth.* estar dispensado por privilegio de algo || *to be privileged to do sth.* gozar del privilegio de hacer algo, tener el privilegio de hacer algo.

privily ['privili] *adv* en privado, en secreto.

privity ['priviti] *n* JUR vínculo *m* legal, relación *f* | obligación *f*; *privity in law* obligación legal || conocimiento *m* (knowledge).

privy ['privi] *adj* privado, da (private) || secreto, ta (secret) || — *Privy Council* consejo privado || ANAT *privy parts* partes pudendas || *privy purse* gastos *m* personales del monarca ||

privy seal sello *m* real || *to be privy to* estar al tanto de.
◆ *n* JUR derechohabiente *m*, interesado *m* || cómplice *m* & *f* (abettor) || FAM retrete *m*, excusado *m* (toilet).

prize [praiz] *n* premio *m*; *to win first prize, to carry off the prize* ganar *or* llevarse el primer premio || FIG recompensa *f*, premio *m*, galardón *m*; *cash prize* premio en metálico; *a prize worthy of all the effort* una recompensa digna del esfuerzo; *to award a prize* conceder un premio || MAR presa *f* (captured vessel) || TECH palanca *f* (lever) | apalancamiento *m* (leverage) || — *consolation prize* premio de consolación || *first prize* premio gordo, primer premio (in a lottery) || *to take the prize* llevarse el premio.
◆ *adj* premiado, da; galardonado, da (prizewinning) || digno de premio (worthy of a prize) || de primera categoría (first-class) || FAM *you are a prize idiot* eres un tonto de remate.

prize [praiz] *vt* apreciar, estimar (to value) || MAR capturar (a ship) || *to prise open, up* abrir, levantar por fuerza *or* con una palanca.

prize court [-kɔːt] *n* JUR tribunal *m* de presas marítimas.

prizefight [-,fait] *n* combate *m* de boxeo profesional.

prizefighter [-,faitə*] *n* SP boxeador *m* profesional.

prizefighting [-,faitiŋ] *n* boxeo *m* profesional.

prizegiving [-,giviŋ] *n* reparto *m* de premios.

prize money [-,mʌni] *n* premio *m* en metálico || SP bolsa *f* (in boxing) || MAR parte *f* de presa.

prize ring [-riŋ] *n* SP cuadrilátero *m*, ring *m* (boxing ring) | boxeo *m* profesional (prizefighting).

prizewinner [-,winə*] *n* premiado, da; galardonado, da.

prizewinning [-'winiŋ] *adj* premiado, da; galardonado, da.

pro [prəu] *pref* pro [con el sentido de «a favor de»].

pro [prəu] *prep* en pro de, pro.
◆ *adv* a favor.
◆ *adj* favorable || SP profesional.
◆ *n* SP profesional *m* & *f* || *the pros and cons* el pro y el contra (arguments for and against), los votos a favor y los votos en contra (votes).

probabilism ['prɔbəbilizəm] *n* probabilismo *m*.

probabilist ['prɔbəbilist] *adj/n* probabilista.

probability [,prɔbə'biliti] *n* probabilidad *f*; *in all probability* según toda probabilidad.

probable ['prɔbəbl] *adj* probable; *rain isn't very probable* no es muy probable que llueva || verosímil (credible).

probably [-i] *adv* probablemente || *most probably* seguramente.

probang ['prəubæŋ] *n* MED sonda *f*.

probate ['prəubit] *n* JUR legalización *f* de un testamento.

probate ['prəubeit] *vt* US JUR legalizar (a will).

probation [prə'beiʃən] *n* período *m* de prueba (trial period) || JUR libertad *f* vigilada *or* condicional || — *on probation* a prueba (on trial); *to put on probation* poner a prueba; en *or* bajo libertad vigilada *or* condicional (a convicted offender) || JUR *probation officer* encargado *m* de la vigilancia de los que están en libertad condicional.

probationary [prə'beiʃnəri] *adj* de prueba, probatorio, ria || JUR *probationary period* período *m* de libertad vigilada *or* condicional.

probationer [prə'beiʃnə*] *n* JUR persona *f* que está en libertad vigilada || persona *f* a prueba.

probative ['prəubətiv] *adj* probatorio, ria.

probatory ['prəubətəri] *adj* probatorio, ria.

probe [prəub] *n* MED sonda *f* (instrument) || sondeo *m* (act) || investigación *f*, encuesta *f* (*into* sobre) (an investigation) || exploración *f* (*into* de) || *space probe* sonda espacial.

probe [prəub] *vt* MED sondear, sondar (with a medical probe) || sondear (ground, etc.) || examinar (to examine) || investigar (to investigate) || explorar (to explore) || tantear (to judge the possibilities, etc.) || sondear (opinion).
◆ *vi* *to probe into* tantear (possibilities), examinar (to examine), investigar (to investigate), explorar (to explore).

probing [-iŋ] *adj* minucioso, sa; meticuloso, sa (thorough) || penetrante (penetrating).
◆ *n* sondeo *m* || investigación *f* (investigation) || exploración *f* || toma *f* de muestras (in the ground).

probity ['prəubiti] *n* probidad *f*.

problem ['prɔbləm] *n* problema *m*; *that presents no problem* no plantea ningún problema; *the housing problem* el problema de la vivienda; *he poses me a lot of problems* me plantea innumerables problemas.
◆ *adj* problemático, ca || difícil (difficult); *a problem child* un niño difícil || — *problem page* consultorio *m* || *problem play* obra *f* de tesis (theatre).

problematic [,prɔbli'mætik]; **problematical** [-əl] *adj* problemático, ca || dudoso, sa (doubtful).

proboscideans; proboscidians [prɔbɔ'sidiənz] *pl n* ZOOL proboscidios *m*.

proboscis [prəu'bɔsis] *n* ANAT probóscide *f*, trompa *f* || FAM napia *f* (nose).
— OBSERV El plural de *proboscis* es *proboscises* o *proboscides*.

procain ['prəukein] *n* CHEM procaína *f*.

procedural [prə'siːdʒərəl] *adj* JUR procesal; *procedural law* derecho procesal || de procedimiento; *a procedural question* una cuestión de procedimiento || INFORM *procedural language* lenguaje *m* de procedimiento.

procedure [prə'siːdʒə*] *n* procedimiento *m*; *legal procedure* procedimiento legal; *to open a debate on procedure* abrir un debate sobre el procedimiento || trámites *m pl* (things one has to do) || procedimiento *m*, proceder *m* (course of action) || — *rules of procedure* reglamento interno || *the correct procedure would be* lo mejor sería || *the usual procedure is* lo que se suele hacer es.

procedure-oriented [-ə'riəntid] *adj* INFORM orientado, da al procedimiento; *procedure-oriented language* lenguaje *m* orientado al procedimiento.

proceed [prə'siːd] *vi* seguir, continuar (to continue); *they proceeded to Leeds* siguieron hacia Leeds; *to proceed on one's way* seguir su camino; *the letter proceeds thus* la carta continúa así || ir (to go); *before we proceed any further* antes de ir más lejos; *the car proceeded at thirty kilometres per hour* el coche iba a treinta kilómetros por hora || pasar, irse; *let us proceed to the dining room* pasemos al comedor || obrar, actuar, proceder; *how should we proceed?* ¿cómo hemos de proceder?, ¿cómo debemos actuar?; *this is a delicate matter, so please proceed with caution* esto es un asunto delicado, así que por favor obren con cuidado || avanzar; *crossing a mine field, you must proceed with caution* al cruzar un campo de minas se debe avanzar con cuidado || ponerse a, proceder a; *to proceed to do sth.* ponerse a hacer algo; *to proceed to a vote* proceder a votar || pasar a; *let us proceed to the next item on the agenda* pasemos al punto siguiente del orden del día || venir, provenir, proceder (*from* de); *the confusion proceeded from a misunderstanding* la confusión vino de un malentendido || desarrollarse, suceder; *things are proceeding as usual* las cosas se están desarrollando normalmente || JUR proceder *against* contra) || — *the negotiations now proceeding in our country* las negociaciones en curso en nuestro país || *to proceed to blows* llegar a las manos || *to proceed with* seguir con, proseguir.

proceeding [-iŋ] *n* proceder *m* (way) || acción *f* (action).
◆ *pl* debates *m*; *to conduct the proceedings* dirigir los debates || reunión *f sing* (meeting) || actas *f* (minutes); *according to the proceedings of the last meeting* según las actas de la última reunión || JUR proceso *m sing*; *to take proceedings against s.o.* entablar un proceso contra alguien.

proceeds ['prəusiːdz] *pl n* ganancias *f*, beneficios *m*; *he is entitled to one half of the proceeds* tiene derecho a la mitad de los beneficios || ingresos *m*, producto *m sing* (of a sale).

process ['prəuses] *n* proceso *m*; *the historic process* el proceso histórico; *process of the mind* proceso mental || procedimiento *m*; *the manufacturing process* el procedimiento de fabricación || procedimiento *m*, método *m*, sistema *m* (method) || JUR & ANAT proceso *m* || — *in process* en curso || *in process of* en vías de, en curso de || *in the process of time* con el tiempo, andando el tiempo || TECH *process engraving* fotomecánica *f*.

process ['prəuses] *vt* tratar; *to process milk* tratar la leche || transformar (raw materials) || elaborar (to elaborate) || tratar (data) || JUR procesar || PHOT revelar (a negative) || PRINT reproducir por procedimientos fotomecánicos (to reproduce).

process [prə'ses] *vi* ir en procesión, desfilar.

processing ['prəusesiŋ] *n* tratamiento *m* (of food, of information, etc.) || procedimiento *m* || transformación *f*; *processing industry* industria de transformación || *data processing* informática *f* (science), tratamiento *m* de la información, proceso *m or* procesamiento *m* de datos.

procession [prə'seʃən] *n* procesión *f*, desfile *m* (of people, of animals) || cortejo *m*, comitiva *f* (royal, wedding, etc.) || REL procesión *f* || FIG serie *f* (sting).

procession [prə'seʃən] *vi* desfilar || REL ir en procesión.

processional [-l] *adj* procesional.
◆ *n* himno *m* procesional (hymn) || procesionario *m* (book).

processionary [-əri] *adj* procesionaria.

processor [prəusesə*] *n* INFORM procesador.

proclaim [prə'kleim] *vt* proclamar (to announce publicly) || declarar (war) || proclamar (a king) || revelar (to reveal) || prohibir (to prohibit) || *to proclaim the banns* correr las amonestaciones.

proclamation [,prɔklə'meiʃən] *n* proclamación *f* (act) || proclama *f* (document) || bando *m* (edict) || declaración *f* || publicación *f* (of banns).

proclitic [prəu'klitik] *adj* GRAMM proclítico, ca.
◆ *n* GRAMM proclítico *m*.

proclivity [prə'kliviti] *n* propensión *f*, tendencia *f*, inclinación *f*.

proconsul [prəu'kɔnsəl] *adj* procónsul *m*.

proconsular [prəu'kɔnsjulə*] *adj* proconsular.

proconsulate [prəu'kɔnsjulit] *n* proconsulado *m*.

procrastinate [prəu'kræstineit] *vi* andar con dilaciones, no decidirse, aplazar *or* diferir una decisión.
◆ *vt* aplazar, diferir.

procrastination [prəuˌkræsti'neiʃən] *n* dilación *f*.

procrastinator [prəu'kræstineitə*] *n* indeciso, sa; persona *f* que anda con dilaciones.

procreant ['prəukriənt] *adj* procreador, ra.

procreate ['prəukrieit] *vt/vi* procrear.

procreation [ˌprəukri'eiʃən] *adj* procreación *f*.

procreative ['prəukrieitiv] *adj* procreador, ra.

procreator ['prəukrieitə*] *n* procreador, ra.

proctor ['prɔktə*] *n* oficial *m* encargado de la disciplina (in a university) || US vigilante *m* (in an examination) || JUR procurador *m*.

procumbent [prəu'kʌmbənt] *adj* BOT procumbente, rastrero, ra || boca abajo (face down).

procurable [prə'kjuərəbl] *adj* asequible, alcanzable.

procurance [prəu'kjurəns] *n* adquisición *f*, obtención *f* (obtaining) || consecución *f* (bringing about, achieving).

procuration [ˌprɔkjuə'reiʃən] *n* adquisición *f*, obtención *f* (obtaining) || consecución *f* (achieving, bringing about) || procuración *f*, poder *m* (power of attorney) || proxenetismo *m* (procuring).

procurator ['prɔkjuəreitə*] *n* HIST procurador *m* || JUR apoderado *m*.

procuratory ['prɔkjuərətəri] *n* JUR procuración *f*, poder *m*.

procure [prə'kjuə*] *vt* proporcionar, obtener, conseguir, lograr; *I procured a flat for him* le proporcioné un piso || llevar a la prostitución (a woman).
◆ *vi* dedicarse al proxenetismo.

procurement [-mənt] *n* adquisición *f*, obtención *f* (obtaining) || consecución *f* (achievement).

procurer [-rə*] *n* proxeneta *m* (who procures prostitutes).

procuress [-ris] *n* alcahueta *f*, proxeneta *f*.

procuring [-riŋ] *n* proxenetismo *m*.

prod [prɔd] *n* golpe *m*, golpecito [que se da con la punta de algo] || pincho *m*, instrumento *m* puntiagudo (sharp instrument) || aguijón *m* (goad) || pinchazo *m* (prick) || FIG acicate *m*, aguijón *m*, estímulo *m* (incentive).

prod [prɔd] *vt* darle (a algo o a alguien) con la punta del dedo, de un bastón, etc. (with finger, with stick, etc.) || picar, pinchar (to prick) || FIG aguijonear, estimular (to urge).

prodigal ['prɔdigəl] *adj* pródigo, ga || — *prodigal of* pródigo en || *the Prodigal Son* el Hijo Pródigo.

prodigality [ˌprɔdi'gæliti] *n* prodigalidad *f* (lavishness) || derroche *m* (extreme abundance).

prodigious [prə'didʒəs] *adj* prodigioso, sa; portentoso, sa (wonderful) || enorme, ingente (huge).

prodigy ['prɔdidʒi] *n* prodigio *m* || *a child prodigy* un niño prodigio.

prodrome ['prɔdrəm] *n* MED pródromo *m* (symptom).

produce ['prɔdjuːs] *n* productos *m pl*; *farm produce* productos agrícolas || producción *f* (gield) || FIG fruto *m* (of efforts).

produce [prə'djuːs] *vt* presentar, mostrar, enseñar (to show); *I had to produce my passport* tuve que enseñar el pasaporte || sacar (to take out); *he produced a handkerchief from his pocket* se sacó un pañuelo del bolsillo || producir; *this author hasn't produced much lately* este autor no ha producido mucho últimamente; *the factory produces a thousand cars a week* la fábrica produce mil coches por semana || fabricar, hacer (to manufacture) || producir, dar; *to produce profit* producir beneficios || dar, producir (fruit) || producir, ocasionar, causar (to cause, to give rise to) || MATH prolongar (a line) || THEATR dirigir (the making of a play) | presentar (to present) || CINEM producir || realizar (in television) || JUR presentar (a witness, a proof).
◆ *vi* producir.

producer [-ə*] *n* productor, ra || fabricante *m* (manufacturer) || THEATR escenógrafo *m*, director *m* de escena || CINEM productor, ra || realizador, ra (in television) || gasógeno *m* (for cars).

producer gas [-ə*gæs] *n* gas *m* pobre.

producer goods [-ə*gudz] *pl n* elementos *m* de producción || materias *f* primas (raw materials).

producible [prə'djuːsəbl] *adj* producible.

producing [prə'djuːsiŋ] *adj* productor, ra.

producive [prə'djuːsiv] *adj* productivo, va || *to be producive of* producir.

product ['prɔdʌkt] *n* producto *m*; *manufactured products* productos manufacturados || producto *m*, resultado *m* (result) || producción *f* (of literature) || MATH producto *m* || *gross national product* producto nacional bruto.

production [prə'dʌkʃən] *n* producción *f* || presentación *f* (showing) || fabricación *f* (manufacture) || rendimiento *m* (output) || producto *m* (product) || obra *f* (artistic work) || THEATR dirección *f* escénica, escenografía *f* (of a play) | representación *f* (performance) | dirección *f* (of actors) || producción *f* (of a film) || realización *f* (in television).
◆ *adj* de serie; *production car* coche de serie || *production line* línea *f* de montaje, cadena *f* de montaje.

productive [prə'dʌktiv] *adj* productivo, va || AGR fértil || FIG fecundo, da; fértil (*of* en) (fruitful) || *to be productive of* producir.

productivity [ˌprɔdʌk'tiviti]; **productiveness** [prə'dʌktivnis] *n* productividad *f*.

proem ['prəuem] *n* proemio *m*.

prof [prɔf] *n* FAM profe *m* (professor).

profanation [ˌprɔfə'neiʃən] *n* profanación *f*.

profanatory [prə'fænətəri] *adj* profanador, ra.

profane [prə'fein] *adj* profano, na (worldly, irreverent, uninitiated) || impío, a; sacrílego, ga (sacrilegious) || blasfemo, ma (blasphemous) || soez (language) || malhablado, da (person) || *profane word* blasfemia *f*, palabrota *f*.

profane [prə'fein] *vt* profanar.

profaner [-ə*] *n* profanador, ra.

profanity [prə'fæniti] *n* lo profano, carácter *m* profano || impiedad *f*, sacrilegio *m* (irreverence) || blasfemia *f* (blasphemy) || palabrota *f*, taco *m* (swearword).

profess [prə'fes] *vt* pretender (to claim); *he doesn't profess to be an expert* no pretende ser experto || declarar, manifestar (to state) || asegurar, afirmar (to affirm); *he professed to be sorry* aseguraba sentirlo || profesar (a religion, an opinion, esteem) || ejercer, profesar (a profession) || enseñar (to teach).

professed [-t] *adj* declarado, da (avowed); *a professed atheist* un ateo declarado || fingido, da; supuesto, ta (pretended) || llamado, da (so-called) || REL profeso, sa (monk, nun).

professedly [-idli] *adv* declaradamente, abiertamente (avowedly) || supuestamente (supposedly) || *he is professedly an authority on the subject* pretende ser una autoridad en la materia.

profession [prə'feʃən] *n* profesión *f*; *medical profession* profesión médica; *to make a profession of* hacer profesión de || profesión *f*, oficio *m* (trade) || profesión *f*, miembros *m pl* de la profesión; *an insult to the profession* un insulto a la profesión || manifestación *f*, declaración *f* (declaration) || profesión *f*, declaración *f*; *profession of loyalty* declaración de lealtad || REL profesión *f* (of faith, vows) || — *by profession* de profesión; *by profession he is an architect* es arquitecto de profesión || *teaching profession* profesorado *m*.

professional [-əl] *adj* profesional, de profesión; *professional player* jugador profesional || — SP *professional foul* falta *f* profesional || *professional diplomat* diplomático de carrera.
◆ *n* profesional *m* & *f*.

professionalism [prə'feʃnəlizəm]; **professionality** [prəfəʃə'næliti] *n* profesionalismo *m*.

professionalize [prə'feʃənəlaiz] *vt* profesionalizar, hacer profesional (a sport) || hacer un oficio de (an occupation).

professor [prə'fesə*] *n* profesor, ra; catedrático, ca (at university) || *assistant, full, visiting professor* profesor auxiliar, titular, visitante.

professorate [prə'fesərit] *n* profesorado *m* (function) || profesorado *m*, cuerpo *m* de profesores, cuerpo *m* docente (professors).

professorial [ˌprɔfe'sɔːriəl] *adj* profesoral.

professoriate [ˌprɔfe'sɔːriit] *n* profesorado *m*.

professorship [prə'fesəʃip] *n* cátedra *f*; *to be appointed to a professorship* ser nombrado a una cátedra || profesorado *m* (function).

proffer ['prɔfə*] *n* oferta *f*, propuesta *f* (offer).

proffer ['prɔfə*] *vt* ofrecer, proponer.

proficiency [prə'fiʃənsi] *n* pericia *f*, destreza *f*, habilidad *f* (skilfulness) || capacidad *f*, competencia *f* (competence).

proficient [prə'fiʃənt] *adj* capaz, competente (capable) || experto, ta; perito, ta (expert) || diestro, tra; hábil (skilful).
◆ *n* experto, ta; perito, ta.

profile ['prəufail] *n* perfil *m* (of the face) || silueta *f* (of the body) || contorno *m*, perfil *m* (outline) || línea *f* (of a car) || sección *f*, corte *m* (cross section) || FIG retrato *m*, reseña *f* biográfica (concise biography) | descripción *f* (written study) || GEOL & ARCH perfil *m* || TECH perfil *m* | calibre *m* (gauge) || *in profile* de perfil.

profile ['prəufail] *vt* perfilar.

profit ['prɔfit] *n* provecho *m* (advantage, good); *with profit* con provecho; *to derive profit from* sacar provecho de || ganancia *f*, lucro *m* (financial gain) || COMM beneficios *m pl*, beneficio *m*, ganancia *f*, utilidades *f pl*; *to make a profit on* sacar beneficios de || — *gross profit* beneficio bruto || *margin of profit* margen *m* de beneficio || *net profit, net profits* beneficio neto || *profit and loss account* cuenta *f* de ganancias y pérdidas || *to my profit* en mi provecho, en provecho mío || *to sell sth. at a profit* vender algo con ganancia || *to show a profit* dar beneficios || *to the profit of* en provecho de || *to turn sth. to profit* sacar provecho de algo.

profit ['prɔfit] *vi* ganar; *we profited from that deal* ganamos en aquel negocio || sacar provecho, beneficiarse (*by* de) (to benefit).
◆ *vt* servir a, aprovechar a (to be of advantage to).

profitability [ˌprɔfitə'biliti] *n* rentabilidad *f*.

profitable ['prɔfitəbl] *adj* provechoso, sa; beneficioso, sa (advantageous) || útil (useful) || rentable, productivo, va (economical) || lucrativo, va (lucrative).

profitableness [-nis] *n* utilidad *f*, carácter *m* provechoso (usefulness) || rentabilidad *f* || carácter *m* lucrativo (financially).

profit balance ['prɔfit,bæləns] *n* saldo *m* positivo.

profit-earning ['prɔfit,əːniŋ] *adj* rentable, productivo, va ‖ *profit-earning capacity* rentabilidad *f*.

profiteer [,prɔfi'tiə*] *n* aprovechado, da.

profiteer [,prɔfi'tiə*] *vi* aprovecharse.

profiteering [-riŋ] *n* ganancias *f pl* excesivas (extortionate profits) ‖ mercantilismo *m*.

profitless ['prɔfitlis] *adj* improductivo, va; no rentable, que no rinde (financially) ‖ inútil (useless).

profit-making ['prɔfit'meikiŋ] *n* obtención *f* de beneficios.
◆ *adj* rentable, lucrativo, va.

profit margin ['prɔfit,mɑːdʒin] *n* margen *m* de beneficio.

profit-seeking ['prɔfit,siːkiŋ] *adj* interesado, da (person) ‖ de fines lucrativos, lucrativo, va (society).

profit sharing ['prɔfit,ʃɛəriŋ] *n* participación *f* en los beneficios (by workers) ‖ reparto *m* de los beneficios (by a company).

profit taking ['prɔfit,teikiŋ] *n* COMM realización *f* de beneficios.

profit tax ['prɔfit,tæks] *n* impuesto *m* de utilidades.

profligacy ['prɔfligəsi] *n* libertinaje *m* (dissolution) ‖ prodigalidad *f* (lavishness) ‖ FAM profusión *f*.

profligate ['prɔfligit] *adj/n* libertino, na; disoluto, ta (dissolute) ‖ despilfarrador, ra; pródigo, ga; derrochador, ra (lavish).

pro forma invoice [prəu'fɔːmə'invɔis] *n* factura *f* pro forma.

profound [prə'fɔund] *adj* profundo, da; *profound poverty* miseria profunda.
◆ *n* profundidades *f pl*.

profoundness [-nis]; **profundity** [prə'fʌnditi] *n* profundidad *f*.

profuse [prə'fjuːs] *adj* profuso, sa; abundante; *profuse praise* alabanzas profusas ‖ pródigo, ga (a person); *he is profuse in his praise* es pródigo de *or* en alabanzas ‖ MED profuso, sa (sweat).

profusion [prə'fjuːʒən] *n* profusión *f*, abundancia *f* (abundance) ‖ prodigalidad *f*, liberalidad *f* (lavishness).

progenitor [prəu'dʒenitə*] *n* progenitor *m* ‖ antepasado *m* (forefather).

progeny ['prɔdʒini] *n* progenie *f* (offspring) ‖ descendientes *m pl* (issue) ‖ FIG resultado *m*, consecuencia *f*.

progesterone [prəu'dʒestərəun] *n* progesterona *f*.

progestin [prəu'dʒestin] *n* progestina *f*.

prognathic [prɔg'næθik] *adj* prognato, ta.

prognathism ['prɔgnəθizəm] *n* prognatismo *m*.

prognathous [prɔg'neiθəs] *adj* prognato, ta.

prognosis [prɔg'nəusis] *n* MED pronóstico *m*.
— OBSERV El plural de *prognosis* es *prognoses*.

prognostic [prɔg'nɔstik] *n* pronóstico *m* (forecast) ‖ augurio *m*, presagio *m* (omen).

prognosticate [prəg'nɔstikeit] *vt* pronosticar.

prognostication [prəg,nɔsti'keiʃən] *n* pronóstico *m* (forecast) ‖ augurio *m*, presagio *m* (omen) ‖ presentimiento *m* (foreboding).

prognosticative [prəg'nɔstikətiv] *adj* profético, ca ‖ *prognosticative of* que anuncia.

prognosticator [prəg'nɔstikeitə*] *n* pronosticador, ra.

programmable [prəu'græməbl] *adj* INFORM programable; *programmable storage* memoria *f* programable.

programme; US **program** ['prəugræm] *n* programa *m* ‖ INFORM *program call* llamada *f* a programa | *program loop* bucle *m or* lazo *m* de programa.

programme; US **program** ['prəugræm] *vt* programar (a computer) ‖ planear, programar; *to programme one's day* planear el día; *to programme a reform* programar una reforma.

programmer; US **programer** [-ə*] *n* programador, ra ‖ INFORM programador *m* (device) | programador, ra (person); *programmer analyst* analista *m* programador.

programming; US **programing** [-iŋ] *n* programación *f* ‖ INFORM *programming language* lenguaje *m* de programación.
◆ *adj* programador, ra.

programme music; US **program music** [-'mjuːzik] *n* música *f* descriptiva.

programme seller; US **program seller** [-'selə*] *n* THEATR vendedor *m* de programas.

progress ['prəugres] *n* progreso *m*, marcha *f*, avance *m* (forward movement) ‖ progreso *m*, curso *m* (of a disease) ‖ curso *m* (of events) ‖ progresos *m pl*; *he has made good progress at school* ha hecho grandes progresos en el colegio ‖ progreso *m*, adelanto *m* (of mankind, of science) ‖ viaje *m* oficial (official journey) ‖ etapa *f*, fase *f* (of career, of life) ‖ — *in progress* en curso; *the negotiations in progress* las negociaciones en curso ‖ *progress report* informe *m* sobre la marcha de los trabajos ‖ *we don't seem to be making any progress* parece que no avanzamos mucho, parece que no avanzamos nada.

progress [prəu'gres] *vi* progresar, avanzar (to advance) ‖ ir; *how is the boy progressing?* ¿cómo va el niño? ‖ hacer progresos, hacer adelantos, progresar, avanzar; *he has progressed well* ha hecho muchos progresos, ha avanzado mucho ‖ MED mejorar, progresar (patient) ‖ hacer un viaje (official).

progression [prəu'greʃən] *n* progresión *f* ‖ MUS & MATH progresión *f*; *arithmetic, geometric, harmonic progression* progresión aritmética, geométrica, armónica.

progressionist [prəu'greʃnist] *n* progresista *m* & *f*.

progressist [prəu'gresist] *n* progresista *m* & *f*.

progressive [prəu'gresiv] *adj* progresivo, va; *progressive development* desarrollo progresivo; *progressive taxes* impuestos progresivos ‖ progresista (political and social ideas); *progressive newspaper* periódico progresista ‖ GRAMM progresivo, va (form).
◆ *n* progresista *m* & *f*.

progressiveness [-nis] *n* progresividad *f* ‖ progresismo *m* (in politics).

progressivism [-izəm] *n* progresismo *m*.

prohibit [prə'hibit] *vt* prohibir; *smoking is prohibited* está prohibido *or* se prohibe fumar ‖ impedir, imposibilitar (to prevent); *his broken leg prohibits him from playing rugby* la pierna rota le impide jugar al rugby, la pierna rota le imposibilita para jugar al rugby.

prohibition [,prəui'biʃən] *n* prohibición *f* ‖ US prohibicionismo *m*, prohibición *f*.

prohibitionism [,prəui'biʃnizəm] *n* prohibicionismo *m* (of liquor).

prohibitionist [,prəui'biʃnist] *adj/n* prohibicionista.

prohibitive [prə'hibitiv] *adj* prohibitivo, va; *prohibitive prices* precios prohibitivos.

prohibitory [prə'hibitəri] *adj* prohibitorio, ria.

project ['prɔdʒekt] *n* proyecto *m* (plan); *to carry out a project* llevar a cabo un proyecto; *it is just a project* no es más que un proyecto.

project [prə'dʒekt] *vt* proyectar (a missile, a film, a shadow, plans, etc.) ‖ proyectar, planear (a trip) ‖ MATH proyectar (a line) ‖ hacer resaltar (to cause to stick out) ‖ FIG *to project o.s. into* imaginarse en.
◆ *vi* sobresalir, destacar, resaltar (to protrude).

projectile [prəu'dʒektail] *adj* arrojadizo, za; *projectile weapons* armas arrojadizas.
◆ *n* proyectil *m*.

projecting [prə'dʒektiŋ] *adj* saliente, saledizo, za.

projection [prə'dʒekʃən] *n* proyección *f* ‖ saliente *m*, resalto *m* (part which sticks out) ‖ GEOGR planisferio *m* ‖ MATH proyección *f* ‖ FIG concepción *f* (of a plan) ‖ *projection room* o *booth* cabina *f* de proyección.

projectionist [-ist] *n* operador *m* de cine.

projective [prə'dʒektiv] *adj* MATH descriptivo, va (geometry).

projector [prə'dʒektə*] *n* proyector *m*, aparato *m* de proyección (of films) ‖ proyectista *m* & *f* (planner) ‖ promotor, ra.

prolapse ['prəulæps] *n* MED prolapso *m*.

prolapsus [prəu'læpsəs] *n* MED prolapso *m*.

prole [prəul] *n* FAM proletario, ria.

prolegomenon [,prəule'gɔminən] *n* prolegómeno *m*.
— OBSERV El plural de *prolegomenon* es *prolegomena*.

prolepsis [prəu'lepsis] *n* prolepsis *f*.
— OBSERV El plural de la palabra inglesa es *prolepses*.

proletarian [,prəuli'tɛəriən] *adj/n* proletario, ria.

proletarianization [,prəuli,tɛəriənai'zeiʃən] *n* proletarización *f*.

proletarianize [prəuli'tɛəriənaiz] *vt* proletarizar.

proletariat [,prəuli'tɛəriət] *n* proletariado *m*.

proliferate [prəu'lifəreit] *vi* proliferar.

proliferation [prəu,lifə'reiʃən] *n* proliferación *f*, multiplicación *f*.

proliferous [prə'lifərəs] *adj* prolífero, ra.

prolific [prəu'lifik] *adj* prolítico, ca (*of* en) ‖ fecundo, da.

prolificness [-nis] *n* fecundidad *f*.

prolix ['prəuliks] *adj* prolijo, ja.

prolixity [prəu'liksiti] *n* prolijidad *f*.

prolocutor [prəu'lɔkjutə*] *n* portavoz *m* [AMER vocero *m*] (spokesman) ‖ presidente *m* (chairman).

prologize ['prəulәgaiz] *vi* escribir prólogos.

prologue ['prəulɔg] *n* prólogo *m* (*to* de).

prologue ['prəulɔg] *vt* prologar.

prologuize ['prəuləgaiz] *vi* escribir prólogos.

prolong [prəu'lɔŋ] *vt* prolongar.

prolongate ['prəulɔŋgeit] *vt* prolongar.

prolongation [,prəulɔŋ'geiʃən] *n* prolongación *f*.

prolonge [prə'lɔndʒ] *n* MIL prolonga *f*.

prom [prɔm] *n* FAM concierto *m* en el que una parte del público no tiene localidades sentadas (concert) | paseo *m* marítimo (on the seafront) ‖ US FAM baile *m* de gala (dance).

promenade [,prɔmi'nɑːd] *n* paseo *m* (place, walk, part of dance) ‖ paseo *m* marítimo (on the seafront) ‖ pasillo *m* [sitio donde los espectadores están de pie] (theatre) ‖ — *promenade concert* concierto *m* en el que una parte del público no tiene localidades sentadas ‖ MAR *promenade deck* cubierta *f* de paseo.

promenade [,prɔmi'nɑ:d] *vi* pasearse.
◆ *vt* pasear (to take for a walk or ride) || pasearse por (the streets) || FIG hacer alarde de (to show).

Prometheus [prə'mi:θju:s] *pr n* MYTH Prometeo *m*.

promethium [prə'mi:θiəm] *m* CHEM prometeo *m*.

prominence ['prɔminəns] *n* prominencia *f* (hill, elevation) || protuberancia *f*; *solar prominence* protuberancia solar || FIG importancia *f* || — FIG *to bring into prominence* hacer resaltar | *to come into prominence* empezar a destacar.

prominent ['prɔminənt] *adj* prominente (jutting out) || saliente (tooth, cheekbone) || saltón, ona (eye) || FIG preeminente (eminent) | destacado, da, notable (outstanding) | que llama la atención (striking).

promiscuity [,prɔmis'kjuiti] *n* promiscuidad *f*.

promiscuous [prə'miskjuəs] *adj* promiscuo, cua (mixed) || heterogéneo, a || libertino, na (person) || FAM al azar (casual).

promiscuousness [prə'miskjuəsnis] *n* promiscuidad *f* (promiscuity).

promise ['prɔmis] *n* promesa *f* (pledge); *to keep one's promise* cumplir su *or* con su promesa; *to break a promise* faltar a una promesa; *empty promises* promesas vanas || esperanza *f*, promesa *f* (hope) || — *full of promise* o *of great promise* muy prometedor, ra || *promise of marriage* promesa *or* palabra de matrimonio || *to be of great promise* prometer || *to hold* o *to keep s.o. to his promise* hacer que alguien cumpla lo prometido || *to release s.o. from his promise* liberar a alguien de su promesa || *to show promise* prometer, ser prometedor, ra || *under promise of* bajo palabra de || FIG *wild promise* promesa de borracho.

promise ['prɔmis] *vt* prometer; *you promised to help me* prometió que me ayudaría; *to promise s.o. a rise* prometerle a uno un aumento de sueldo || presagiar, augurar (to augur) || — *the production promises to be good* la producción se anuncia muy buena, la producción promete ser muy buena || FIG *to promise the moon* prometer la luna *or* el oro y el moro || *to promise o.s.* prometerse.
◆ *vi* prometer (to make a promise) || *to promise well* prometer mucho.

promised [-t] *adj* prometido, da || *Promised Land* Tierra de Promisión.

promisee [prɔmi'si:] *n* persona *f* que tiene una promesa.

promiser ['prɔmisə*] *n* prometedor, ra.

promising ['prɔmisiŋ] *adj* prometedor, ra; que promete; *he is a promising tennis player* es un tenista que promete.

promisor ['prɔmisɔ:*] *n* JUR prometedor *m*.

promissory ['prɔmisəri] *adj* promisorio, ria; *promisory oath* juramento promisorio || COMM *promissory note* pagaré *m*.

promo ['prəuməu] *n* FAM publicidad *f* (advertising) || video *m* promocional [de un disco, programa televisivo, etc.]

promontory ['prɔməntri] *n* GEOGR promontorio *m* || ANAT protuberancia *f*, promontorio *m*.

promote [prə'məut] *vt* ascender (to raise in rank); *to promote s.o. captain* ascender a uno a capitán || promover, ascender; *he has been promoted to foreman* lo han ascendido a capataz || promocionar (product) || promover, fomentar (disorder) || suscitar, provocar, fomentar (hatred) || fomentar, estimular (to encourage) || contribuir (a result) || financiar (to finance) || fundar (a company) || presentar (a bill in Parliament) || CHEM provocar (a reaction) || cambiar (un peón) por una pieza anteriormente comida (in chess) || pasar de año (at school).

promoter [-ə*] *n* promotor, ra (originator) || promotor, ra; fundador, ra (of a company) || COMM promotor, ra || promotor *m* (in sports).

promotion [prə'məuʃən] *n* ascenso *m* (rise in rank) || promoción *f* (of an employee, a product) || fundación *f* (of a company) || fomento *m* (encouragement) || presentación *f* (of a bill in Parliament) || US publicidad *f* || — *promotion list* escalafón *m* || *promotion match* partido *m* de promoción.

promotive [prə'məutiv] *adj* promotor, ra.

prompt [prɔmpt] *adj* pronto, ta; rápido, da (quick) || inmediato, ta; rápido, da; *a prompt reply* una respuesta inmediata || puntual; *be prompt* sea puntual || rápido, da (service) || COMM disponible.
◆ *adv* en punto; *at five o'clock prompt* a las cinco en punto.
◆ *n* COMM plazo *m* límite (time limit) | aviso *m* (reminder) || THEATR réplica *f* || sugerencia *f* (suggestion) || *to give an actor a prompt* apuntar a un actor.

prompt [prɔmpt] *vt* incitar, mover, impulsar (to rouse to action); *his anger prompted him to leave* su enfado le movió a marcharse || inspirar, sugerir (to inspire) || sugerir (to suggest) || THEATR apuntar || FIG apuntar, soplar.

prompt box [-bɔks] *n* THEATR concha *f* del apuntador.

prompter [-ə*] *n* THEATR apuntador, ra || instigador, ra; promotor, ra (instigator).

prompter's box [-zbɔks] *n* THEATR concha *f* del apuntador.

prompting [-iŋ] *n* instigación *f* || incitación *f* (incitement).

promptitude ['prɔmptitju:d]; **promptness** ['prɔmptnis] *n* prontitud *f*, presteza *f*.

promptly ['prɔmptli] *adv* enseguida, inmediatamente (immediately) || puntualmente (punctually).

promulgate ['prɔməlgeit] *vt* promulgar (a law) || FIG difundir; *to promulgate culture* difundir la cultura.

promulgating [-iŋ] *adj* promulgador, ra.

promulgation [,prɔməl'geiʃən] *n* promulgación *f* (of a law) || FIG difusión *f*.

promulgator ['prɔməlgeitə*] *n* promulgador, ra.

pronaos [prə'neiɔs] *n* ARCH pronaos *m* (of Greek temple).

pronate ['prəu,neit] *vt* poner en posición prona, poner boca abajo.

pronating [-iŋ] *adj* ANAT pronador, ra.

pronation [prəu'neiʃən] *n* ANAT pronación *f*.

pronator [prəu'neitə*] *n* ANAT pronador *m*.

prone [prəun] *adj* prono, na (hand, etc.) || boca abajo (person) || propenso, sa (inclined); *Mary is prone to fits of laughter* María es propensa a los ataques de risa.

proneness [-nis] *n* propensión *f*, predisposición *f* (propensity).

prong [prɔŋ] *n* diente *m*, púa *f* (of a fork) || pitón *m* (of horns) || uña *f*, diente *m* (in mechanics).

prong [prɔŋ] *vt* AGR remover con la horca *or* el bieldo || pinchar (to prick, to prod).

pronghorn [-hɔ:n] *n* ZOOL berrendo *m* (deer).

pronominal [prəu'nɔminl] *adj* GRAMM pronominal.

pronoun ['prəunaun] *n* GRAMM pronombre *m*.

pronounce [prə'nauns] *vt* pronunciar (words); *to pronounce a word well* pronunciar bien una palabra || declarar (to declare); *the doctor pronounced Peter out of danger* el médico declaró que Pedro estaba fuera de peligro || JUR pronunciar (to pass); *to pronounce sentence* pronunciar un fallo || — *to be pronounced* pronunciarse || *to pronounce o.s.* pronunciarse.
◆ *vi* pronunciar; *to pronounce badly* pronunciar mal || pronunciarse, dar su opinión (to give one's opinion); *to pronounce on a matter* dar su opinión sobre una cuestión; *to pronounce in favour of* pronunciarse a favor de || JUR pronunciarse.

pronounceable [-əbl] *adj* pronunciable.

pronounced [-t] *adj* pronunciado, da; acusado, da; marcado, da; fuerte.

pronouncement [-mənt] *n* declaración *f* (statement); *to make a pronouncement* hacer una declaración.

pronouncing [-iŋ] *n* JUR pronunciamiento *m* (of sentence).

pronouncing dictionary [-iŋ'dikʃənri] *n* diccionario *m* fonético.

pronto ['prɔntə] *adv* US FAM pronto, en seguida, inmediatamente.

pronunciamento [prə,nʌnsiə'mentəu] *n* pronunciamiento *m*, proclama *f*, manifiesto *m*.

pronunciation [prə,nʌnsi'eiʃən] *n* pronunciación *f*.

proof [pru:f] *adj* resistente (*against* a) (resistent to) || al abrigo de, fuera de; *proof against danger* al abrigo de todo peligro || a prueba de; *proof against bullets* a prueba de balas || de graduación normal (alcohol) || FIG insensible (*against* a).
◆ *n* prueba *f*, pruebas *f pl*; *I want proof* quiero una prueba, quiero pruebas; *a proof of one's guilt* una prueba de culpabilidad || prueba *f* (test) || MATH & JUR & PHOT & PRINT prueba *f* || graduación *f* normal (of an alcohol) || — *by way of proof* como prueba || *in proof of* en prueba de || *negative proof* prueba negativa || *proof of death* acta *f* de defunción || *proof of identity* documentos *m pl* de identidad || *the proof of it is* prueba de ello es que || FIG *the proof of the pudding is in the eating* por la muestra se conoce el paño || *to give proof of* dar prueba de || *to put sth. to the proof* poner algo a prueba.
— OBSERV Muy frecuentemente el adjetivo *proof* se combina con un sustantivo para formar una palabra compuesta: *bulletproof* a prueba de balas; *waterproof* estanco, ca; impermeable. El lector tiene, por consiguiente, que consultar los artículos correspondientes a estas palabras.

proof [pru:f] *vt* impermeabilizar (cloth) || hacer hermético, ca (to make watertight) || hacer resistente (against fire, etc.) || PRINT tirar una prueba de (to make a trial proof of) | corregir (to correct).

proofread* [-,ri:d] *vt* PRINT corregir.
◆ *vi* PRINT corregir pruebas.
— OBSERV Pret y pp ***proofread***.

proofreader [-,ri:də*] *n* corrector *m* de pruebas *or* de galeradas.

proofreading [-,ri:diŋ] *n* corrección *f* de pruebas *or* de galeradas.

proof sheet [-ʃi:t] *n* prueba *f*, galerada *f*.

prop [prɔp] *n* puntual *m* (rigid support) || MIN puntual *m*, entibo *m* || AGR rodrigón *m* || MAR escora *f* || FIG sostén *m*, apoyo *m*, pilar *m* || hélice *f* (propeller).
◆ *pl* THEATR accesorios *m*.

prop [prɔp] *vt* apuntalar (a wall) || MIN entibar || apoyar (to lean) || mantener; *prop the door open* mantén la puerta abierta || MAR escorar || AGR poner rodrigones a, rodrigar (plants) || FIG apuntalar, apoyar, sostener || *to prop o.s.*

against apoyarse en *or* contra || *to prop up* apoyar, apuntalar (to support), mantener (prices).

propaganda [ˌprɔpəˈgændə] *n* propaganda *f.*

propagandist [ˌprɔpəˈgændist] *adj/n* propagandista.

propagandize [ˌprɔpəˈgændaiz] *vt* hacer propaganda de.
◆ *vi* hacer propaganda.

propagate [ˈprɔpəgeit] *vt* propagar.
◆ *vi* propagarse.

propagating [-iŋ] *adj* propagador, ra.

propagation [ˌprɔpəˈgeiʃən] *n* propagativo, va; propagador, ra.

propagator [ˈprɔpəgeitə*] *n* propagador, ra; propalador, ra; *propagator of incorrect news* propagador de noticias falsas.

propane [ˈprəupein] *n* CHEM propano *m.*

proparoxytone [ˌprəupəˈrɔksitəun] *adj* proparoxítono, na; esdrújulo, la.
◆ *n* palabra *f* esdrújula.

propel [prəˈpel] *vt* propulsar, impeler, impulsar || *propelled by turbines* propulsado por turbinas.

propellant; propellent [-ənt] *adj* propulsor, ra.
◆ *n* propulsor *m* || propergol *m* (for rockets).

propeller [-ə*] *n* propulsor *m* || hélice *f* (of ship or aircraft).

propeller shaft [-əʃɑːft] *n* AUT árbol *m* de transmisión || MAR eje *m* portahélice.

propelling [-iŋ] *adj* propulsor, ra; impelente.

propelling pencil [-iŋˈpensl] *n* portaminas *m inv,* lapicero *m.*

propense [prəˈpens] *adj* propenso, sa; inclinado, da.

propensity [prəˈpensiti] *n* propensión *f; propensity for lying* propensión a mentir.

proper [ˈprɔpə*] *adj* apropiado, da; adecuado, da (appropriate); *a hat proper to the occasion* un sombrero apropiado para el caso || oportuno, na (opportune); *at the proper time* en el momento oportuno; *to deem it proper to do sth.* juzgar oportuno hacer algo || propio, pia; *in the proper sense of the word* en el sentido propio de la palabra || propio, pia; característico, ca (characteristic); *attitude proper to young people* actitud propia de los jóvenes || propio, pia; mismo, ma; *my office is not in the building proper* mi oficina no está en el propio edificio *or* en el edificio mismo || exacto, ta (accurate); *the proper word* la palabra exacta || correcto, ta; *the proper use of the indicative* el empleo correcto del indicativo || propiamente dicho, cha (properly speaking); *Great Britain proper excludes Ireland* Gran Bretaña propiamente dicha excluye Irlanda || decente, como Dios manda (decent); *she is a very proper girl* es una chica muy decente || de verdad, verdadero, ra (real); *a proper rifle not a toy one* un fusil de verdad no de juguete || FAM verdadero, ra; *a proper idiot* un verdadero idiota || hecho y derecho, cabal; *a proper man* un hombre hecho y derecho || GRAMM propio, pia; *proper noun, proper name* nombre propio || HERALD natural || — *as you think proper* como a usted le parezca || *in proper condition* en buen estado || *in the proper way* de forma adecuada, de la mejor manera || *I think it proper to do this* creo que conviene hacer esto || *it was the proper thing to say* es exactamente lo que había que decir || MATH *proper fraction* fracción propia || FAM *to do the proper thing by s.o.* cumplir con alguien || *to do what is proper* hacer lo que se debe.
◆ *adv* FAM muy || FAM *good and proper* completamente.
◆ *n* REL propio *m.*

properly [-li] *adv* bien; *I like to do things properly* me gusta hacer las cosas bien || debidamente, como es debido; *to thank s.o. properly* dar a alguien las gracias como es debido || apropiadamente, adecuadamente (fitly) || de verdad, verdaderamente (really) || correctamente (correctly) || GRAMM en el sentido propio (word) || FAM completamente (completely); *properly mad* completamente loco || *properly speaking* propiamente dicho; *properly speaking he is not a writer* no es un escritor propiamente dicho.

propertied [ˈprɔpətid] *adj* hacendado, da (landed) || adinerado, da; acaudalado, da; rico, ca (wealthy).

property [ˈprɔpəti] *n* propiedad *f,* posesión *f* (possession) || característica *f,* propiedad *f* (characteristic) || finca *f,* propiedad *f* (land) || bienes *m pl; he left his property to me* me dejó sus bienes || dominio *m,* propiedad *f; public property* dominio público || CHEM, MED & BOT propiedad *f* || THEATR accesorio *m* || — *it became the property of his son* pasó a ser la propiedad de su hijo || *man of property* hombre hacendado, hombre rico || *personal property* bienes muebles || *that's my property* eso es mío, eso es de mi propiedad || *to be common property* ser del dominio público || *whose property is this?* ¿de quién es esto?

property man [-mæn] *n* accesorista *m,* attrezzista *m* (in theatre, in cinema).

property owner [-əunə*] *n* terrateniente *m & f.*

property room [-ruːm] *n* guardarropía *f.*

property tax [-tæks] *n* contribución *f* territorial.

prophase [ˈprəufeiz] *n* BIOL profase *f.*

prophecy [ˈprɔfisi] *n* profecía *f.*

prophesier [ˈprɔfisaiə*] *n* profeta *m,* profetisa *f* || profetizador, ra.

prophesy [ˈprɔfisai] *vt* profetizar (to foretell) || predecir, vaticinar (to predict).
◆ *vi* profetizar.

prophesying [-iŋ] *adj* profetizador, ra.

prophet [ˈprɔfit] *n* REL profeta *m* || adivino *m,* profeta *m* (s.o. who foretells the future) || FIG *an early prophet of socialism* uno de los primeros profetas del socialismo.

prophetess [ˈprɔfitis] *n* profetisa *f.*

prophetic [prəˈfetik]; **prophetical** [-əl] *adj* profético, ca.

prophylactic [ˌprɔfiˈlæktik] *adj* MED profiláctico, ca.
◆ *n* MED medicamento *m* profiláctico.

prophilaxis [ˌprɔfiˈlæksis] *n* MED profilaxis *f,* profilaxia *f.*

propinquity [prəˈpiŋkwiti] *n* cercanía *f,* proximidad *f,* propincuidad *f* (p us) (nearness) || parentesco *m* (kinship) || FIG parentesco *m,* afinidad *f* (of ideas).

propitiate [prəˈpiʃieit] *vt* propiciar, hacer propicio || aplacar (to appease).

propitiation [prəˌpiʃiˈeiʃən] *n* propiciación *f* || aplacamiento *m.*

propitiative [prəˈpiʃiətiv] *adj* propiciatorio, ria; expiatorio, ria.

propitiator [prəˈpiʃieitə*] *n* propiciador, ra.

propitiatory [prəˈpiʃiətəri] *adj* propiciatorio, ria.

propitious [prəˈpiʃəs] *adj* propicio, cia; favorable.

propitiousness [-nis] *n* carácter *m* propicio.

propolis [ˈprɔpəlis] *n* propóleos *m.*

proponent [prəˈpəunənt] *n* autor, ra; proponente *m & f,* proponedor, ra (who makes a proposal) || defensor, ra (who supports a cause).

proportion [prəˈpɔːʃən] *n* proporción *f* || parte *f* (of expenses, of profits) || — MATH *arithmetic proportion* proporción aritmética || *in proportion as* a medida que || *in proportion to* en proporción con || *out of all proportion to* desproporcionado, da en relación con || *sense of proportion* sentido de la medida || *to be out of proportion with* no guardar proporción con.
◆ *pl* dimensiones *f.*

proportion [prəˈpɔːʃən] *vt* proporcionar, adecuar || determinar las dimensiones de || MED dosificar.

proportionable [prəˈpɔːʃnəbl] *adj* proporcionado, da.

proportional [prəˈpɔːʃənl] *adj* proporcional || proporcional, en proporción; *proportional to* proporcional a, en proporción con || MATH proporcional || *proportional representation* representación *f* proporcional (system of election).
◆ *n* MATH número *m* proporcional.

proportionally [prəˈpɔːʃnəli] *adv* proporcionalmente || *proportionally to* proporcionalmente a, en proporción con.

proportionate [prəˈpɔːʃnit] *adj* proporcionado, da (*to* a).

proportionate [prəˈpɔːʃneit] *vt* proporcionar, adecuar.

proportionately [prəˈpɔːʃnitli] *adv* proporcionalmente || *proportionately speaking* guardando las proporciones, teniéndolo todo en cuenta.

proposal [prəˈpəuzəl] *n* proposición *f,* propuesta *f; to make a proposal* hacer una propuesta || oferta *f* (offer) || propuesta *f* de matrimonio, petición *f* de mano (for marriage) || FIG proyecto *m.*

propose [prəˈpəuz] *vt* proponer; *to propose a plan* proponer un proyecto; *to propose s.o. for a post* proponer a alguien para un puesto || proponerse, tener intención de; *he proposes to arrive early* tiene la intención de llegar temprano || brindar por, proponer un brindis por (to toast) || plantear (to pose a problem) || *to propose the health of* brindar por, beber a la salud de.
◆ *vi* proponerse, tener intención (to intend) || pedir la mano, ofrecer matrimonio || FIG *man proposes, God disposes* el hombre propone y Dios dispone.

proposer [-ə*] *n* proponente *m & f,* autor, ra.

proposition [ˌprɔpəˈziʃən] *n* proposición *f,* propuesta *f* (proposal) || oferta *f* (offer) || proyecto *m* (plan) || GRAMM, PHIL & MATH proposición *f* || empresa *f* (undertaking) || tarea *f* (job) || propósito *m* (objective) || perspectiva *f* || US FAM proposición *f* deshonesta (illicit invitation) || FAM tipo *m* (person) | problema *m* (problem) || — FIG *it's a tough proposition* es un asunto difícil de resolver | *that is a different proposition altogether* eso es harina de otro costal.

proposition [ˌprɔpəˈziʃən] *vt* US hacer una proposición a | FAM hacer proposiciones deshonestas a (to propose sexual intercourse to).

propositional [-əl] *adj* PHIL de la proposición || por silogismos (theology).

propound [prəˈpaund] *vt* proponer, exponer, presentar (a plan, a question, etc.) || plantear (a problem).

propraetor; US **propretor** [prəuˈpriːtə*] *n* propretor *m.*

propraetorship; US **propretorship** [-ʃip] *n* propretura *f.*

proprietary [prəˈpraiətəri] *adj* propietario, ria || de propiedad (rights) || patentado, da (article) || REL privado, da (chapel) || MED *proprietary medicines* especialidades farmacéuticas, específicos *m.*

◆ *n* propiedad *f*, derecho *m* de propiedad (ownership) || propietarios *m pl* (proprietors).

proprietor [prə'praiətə*] *n* propietario, ria.

proprietorship [-ʃip] *n* propiedad *f*, posesión *f* || propiedad *f*, derecho *m* de propiedad.

proprietress [prə'praiətris] *n* propietaria *f*.

propriety [prə'praiəti] *n* conveniencia *f* (suitability) || oportunidad *f* (of an action) || decoro *m*, decencia *f* (decent behaviour) || corrección *f* (correctness) || propiedad *f* (of a word) || *breach of propriety* incorrección *f*.
◆ *pl* convenciones *f*, cánones *m* sociales.

propulsion [prə'pʌlʃən] *n* propulsión *f*; *jet propulsion* propulsión a chorro *or* por reacción.

propulsive [prə'pʌlsiv] *adj* propulsivo, va; propulsor, ra; impelente.

propylaeum [ˌprɔpi'liəm] *n* ARCH propileo *m*.
— OBSERV El plural de la palabra inglesa es *propylaea*.

pro rata [prəu'rɑːtə] *adv* a prorrata, a prorrateo, proporcionalmente.

prorate [prəu'reit] *n* US prorrata *f*.

prorate [prəu'reit] *vt* US prorratear.

proration [prəu'reiʃən] *n* US prorrateo *m*.

prorogation [ˌprəurə'geiʃən] *n* prórroga *f*, prorrogación *f*.

prorogue [prə'rəug] *vt* prorrogar.
◆ *vi* ser prorrogado, prorrogarse.

prosaic [prəu'zeiik] *adj* prosaico, ca.

prosaicness [-nis] *n* prosaísmo *m*; *the prosaicness of everyday tasks* el prosaísmo de las tareas cotidianas.

prosaism ['prəuzeiizəm] *n* prosaísmo *m*.

prosaist ['prəuzeiist] *n* prosista *m* & *f* (writer) || FIG persona *f* prosaica.

proscenium [prəu'siːnjəm] *n* THEATR proscenio *m* || — *proscenium arch* embocadura *f* || *proscenium box* palco *m* de proscenio.

proscribe [prəus'kraib] *vt* proscribir.

proscribed [-d] *adj* proscrito, ta.

proscription [prəus'kripʃən] *n* proscripción *f*.

proscriptive [prəus'kriptiv] *adj* proscriptor, ra.

prose [prəuz] *n* prosa *f* (in literature) || FIG prosaísmo *m* (of life) || *prose writer* prosista *m* & *f*.
◆ *adj* en prosa; *prose poem* poema en prosa.

prose [prəuz] *vi* FAM gastar mucha prosa.
◆ *vt* poner en prosa.

prosecutable ['prɔsiˌkjutəbl] *adj* JUR que se puede enjuiciar.

prosecute ['prɔsikjuːt] *vt* JUR procesar, enjuiciar (s.o.) | entablar (an action) || proseguir, continuar (to carry on); *to prosecute a war* proseguir una guerra || llevar a cabo (to carry out) || ejercer (a profession) || hacer (studies) || efectuar, realizar (a voyage).
◆ *vi* JUR entablar una acción judicial.

prosecuting attorney [-iŋə'təːni] *n* US JUR acusador *m* público, fiscal *m*.

prosecution [ˌprɔsi'kjuːʃən] *n* JUR procesamiento *m*, enjuiciamiento *m* (action of prosecuting) | acción *f* judicial; *to start a prosecution against s.o.* entablar una acción judicial contra alguien | proceso *m*, juicio *m* (trial) | parte *f* acusadora (party) | acusación *f*, ministerio *m* público *or* fiscal (public prosecutor) || ejercicio *m* (of a profession) || cumplimiento *m* (of duty) || continuación *f*, prosecución *f* (continuation) || — JUR *counsel for the prosecution* fiscal *m* | *witness for the prosecution* testigo de cargo.

prosecutor ['prɔsikjuːtə*] *n* JUR demandante *m*, querellante *m* (plaintiff) | acusador *m* (lawyer) | fiscal *m*, acusador *m* público (public prosecutor).

prosecutrix ['prɔsiˌkjuːtriks] *n* JUR demandante *f*, querellante *f*.

proselyte ['prɔsilait] *n* prosélito *m*.

proselyte ['prɔsilait] *vi* ganar prosélitos, hacer prosélitos.
◆ *vt* convertir.

proselytize ['prɔsilitaiz] *vt* convertir.
◆ *vi* ganar prosélitos, hacer prosélitos.

prosenchyma [prɔs'enkimə] *n* BOT prosénquima *m*.

proser ['prəuzə*] *n* FAM prosador *m*.

prose writer [prəuz'raitə*] *n* prosista *m* & *f*.

prosimii [prəu'simii] *pl n* ZOOL prosimios *m*.

prosiness ['prəuzinis] *n* prosaísmo *m*.

prosist ['prəusist] *n* prosista *m* & *f* (prose writer).

proslavery [prəu'sleivəri] *adj* esclavista.

prosodic [prə'sɔdik] *adj* prosódico, ca.

prosodist ['prɔsədist] *n* especialista *m* & *f* en prosodia *or* en métrica.

prosody ['prɔsədi] *n* prosodia *f* || métrica *f*.

prosopopoeia [prɔsəpə'piːiə] *n* prosopopeya *f*.

prospect ['prɔspekt] *n* perspectiva *f* (outlook); *the prospect of arriving too late* la perspectiva de llegar demasiado tarde; *a job with good prospects* un puesto con buenas perspectivas || vista *f*, panorama *m* (view); *a place with a splendid prospect* un lugar con una vista espléndida || esperanza *f*, esperanzas *f pl* (hope); *to hold out a prospect of* dar esperanzas de; *there is no prospect of their leaving* hay pocas esperanzas de que se vayan || expectativa *f* (expectation) || posibilidad *f*, probabilidad *f* (possibility); *there is no prospect of agreement* no hay ninguna probabilidad de acuerdo || muestra *f* (of ore) || US cliente *m or* comprador *m* eventual (possible client) | partido *m* (for possible marriage) || — *to have a job in prospect* tener un trabajo en perspectiva || *to have prospects* tener porvenir.

prospect [prəs'pekt] *vt* prospectar, hacer una prospección en [AMER catear].
◆ *vi* hacer una prospección || — *to prospect for* buscar || *to prospect well* ser prometedor, prometer (mine, etc.).

prospect glass ['prɔspektglɑːs] *n* telescopio *m*.

prospecting [prəs'pektiŋ] *n* prospección *f*.

prospection [prəs'pekʃən] *n* prospección *f* (subsoil) || prospección *f* (market).

prospective [prəs'pektiv] *adj* eventual, probable; *a prospective client* un cliente eventual || futuro, ra (future); *prospective mother-in-law* futura suegra.

prospector [prəs'pektə*] *n* explorador, ra (explorer) || buscador *m*, prospector *m* [AMER cateador *m*] (of gold) || prospector *m* (of oil, of clients).

prospectus [prəs'pektəs] *n* prospecto *m*, folleto *m* informativo.

prosper ['prɔspə*] *vi* prosperar, medrar.
◆ *vt* favorecer, hacer prosperar.

prosperity [prɔs'periti] *n* prosperidad *f*.

prosperous ['prɔspərəs] *adj* próspero, ra; *prosperous business* comercio próspero || favorable, propicio, cia (favourable) || favorable (wind) || *happy and prosperous New Year* feliz y próspero Año Nuevo.

prosperousness [-nis] *n* prosperidad *f*.

prostate ['prɔsteit] *adj* MED prostático, ca.
◆ *n* MED próstata *f*.

prostatic [prɔ'stætik] *adj* MED prostático, ca.

prostatitis [prɔstə'taitis] *n* MED prostatitis *f*.

prosthesis ['prɔsθisis] *n* MED prótesis *f* || GRAMM prótesis *f*, próstesis *f*.

prosthetic [prɔs'θetik] *adj* MED protésico, ca || GRAMM protético, ca; prostético, ca.

prostitute ['prɔstitjuːt] *n* prostituta *f*.

prostitute ['prɔstitjuːt] *vt* prostituir || FIG prostituir; *to prostitute one's talent* prostituir su talento || *to prostitute o.s.* prostituirse.

prostitution [ˌprɔsti'tjuːʃən] *n* prostitución *f*.

prostrate ['prɔstreit] *adj* boca abajo (face downwards) || postrado, da; abatido, da (exhausted, defeated, grief-stricken, etc.) || prosternado, da (bowing) || BOT procumbente.

prostrate [prɔs'treit] *vt* postrar || *to prostrate o.s.* postrarse (to lie down), prosternarse (to bow).

prostration [prɔs'treiʃən] *n* postración *f* (lying down, exhaustion) || prosternación *f* (bowing).

prostyle ['prəustail] *n* ARCH próstilo *m*.

prosy ['prəuzi] *adj* prosaico, ca (style) || monótono, na (life) || aburrido, da (boring).

protract [prə'trækt] *vt* prolongar, alargar || *the meeting was protracted* la reunión se ha alargado.

protactinium [ˌprəutˌæk'tiniəm] *n* CHEM protactinio *m* (radioactive element).

protagonist [prəu'tægənist] *n* protagonista *m* & *f*.

protargol [prəu'tɑːgɔl] *n* CHEM protargol *m*.

protean [prəu'tiːən] *adj* proteico, ca.

protect [prə'tekt] *vt* proteger || MAR acorazar (a cruiser) || COMM proteger (industry) | respaldar (a bill of exchange) | salvaguardar (interests) || — *to protect against* proteger contra || *to protect from* proteger de || *protected state* estado bajo protectorado.

protecting [-iŋ] *adj* protector, ra.

protection [prə'tekʃən] *n* protección *f* (defence) || COMM protección *f* || MAR blindaje *m* || salvoconducto *m* (pass) || US dinero *m* pagado a una organización de gángsteres.

protectionism [prə'tekʃənizəm] *n* proteccionismo *m*.

protectionist [prə'tekʃənist] *adj/n* proteccionista.

protective [prə'tektiv] *adj* protector, ra; de protección || proteccionista; *protective tariff* tarifa proteccionista || — ZOOL *protective colouring* color *m* que protege a un animal confundiéndolo con el medio donde se encuentra || JUR *protective custody* detención preventiva.

protector [prə'tektə*] *n* protector *m*.

protectorate [-rit] *n* protectorado *m*.

protectress [prə'tektris] *n* protectora *f*.

protégé ['prəuteʒei] *n* protegido *m*.

protégée ['prəuteʒei] *n* protegida *f*.

proteic [prəu'tiːic] *adj* proteico, ca.

proteid ['prəutiːd] *n* CHEM proteido *m*.

protein ['prəutiːn] *n* proteína *f*.

proteinaceous [prəutiː'neiʃəs]; **proteinic** [prəu'tiːnik]; **proteinous** [prəu'tiːnəs] *adj* proteínico, ca; proteico, ca.

proteles ['prɔtəliːz] *n* ZOOL proteles *m*.

pro tem [prəu'tem]; **pro tempore** ['prəu'tempəri] *adv* por el momento (for the time being) || provisionalmente (temporarily).
◆ *adj* provisional (temporary).

protest ['prəutest] *n* protesta *f*, queja *f* (complaint); *to raise a protest* hacer una protesta || objeción *f*, reparo *m* (objection) || COMM protesto *m* (of a bill of exchange) || MAR declaración *f* de averías || protesta *f* (diplomatic) || *to do sth. under protest* hacer algo de mala gana *or* contra su voluntad.

protest [prə'test] *vt* protestar de; *to protest one's innocence* protestar de su inocencia || JUR

protestar (a bill of exchange, etc.) || poner reparos a (to object to) || US recusar (a witness).
◆ *vi* protestar (to complain).

protestant ['prɔtistənt] *adj* protestador, ra.

Protestant ['prɔtistənt] *adj/n* protestante.

Protestantism [-izəm] *n* protestantismo *m*.

protestation [,prəutes'teiʃən] *n* protesta *f*.

protester [prə'testə*] *n* protestador, ra.

protest march [prə'testmɑːtʃ] *n* manifestación *f*.

Proteus ['prəutjuːs] *pr n* MYTH Proteo *m*.

prothalamium [prəuθə'leimiəm] *n* canto *m* nupcial.
— OBSERV El plural de la palabra inglesa es *prothalamia*.

prothesis ['prɔθisis] *n* REL prótesis *f* || GRAMM prótesis *f*, próstesis *f*.

prothonotary [prəu'θɔnətəri] *n* REL protonotario *m* (protonotary).

prothorax [prəu'θɔːræks] *n* ZOOL protórax *m*.

prothrombin [prəu'θrɔmbin] *n* CHEM protrombina *f*.

protides ['prəutaidz] *pl n* CHEM prótidos *m*.

protocol ['prəutəkəl] *n* protocolo *m*.

protocol ['prəutəkəl] *vt* protocolar, protocolizar.
◆ *vi* hacer un protocolo.

protocolize [-aiz] *vt* protocolar, protocolizar.

protohistoric [,prəutəhis'tɔrik] *adj* protohistórico, ca.

protohistory [,prəutə'histəri] *n* protohistoria *f*.

protomartyr [,prəutə,mɑːtə*] *n* protomártir *m* (first martyr).

proton ['prəutɔn] *n* PHYS protón *m*.

protonic [-ik] *adj* PHYS protónico, ca.

protonotary [,prəutə'nəutəri] *n* REL protonotario *m*; *protonotary apostolic* protonotario apostólico.

protoplasm ['prəutəuplæzəm] *n* BIOL protoplasma *m* (colloidal substance).

protoplasmic [prəutə'plæzmik] *adj* BIOL protoplásmico, ca; protoplasmático, ca.

protoplast ['prəutəplɑːst] *n* BIOL protoplasto *m*.

prototype ['prəutəutaip] *n* prototipo *m*.

protoxide [prəu'tɔksaid] *n* CHEM protóxido *m*.

protozoan [,prəutəu'zəuən] *n* ZOOL protozoario *m*, protozoo *m*.

protozoon [,prəutəu'zəuən] *n* ZOOL protozoo *m*, protozoario *m*.
— OBSERV El plural de la palabra inglesa es *protozoa*.

protract [prə'trækt] *vt* prolongar (to lengthen in duration) || TECH levantar un plano de (to plot) || ZOOL sacar.

protractile [prə'træktail] *adj* protráctil; *protractile tongue* lengua protráctil.

protraction [prə'trækʃən] *n* prolongación *f* (prolongation) || TECH levantamiento *m* or trazado *m* de un plano.

protractor [prə'træktə*] *n* MATH transportador *m* || ANAT músculo *m* protractor.

protrude [prə'truːd] *vt* sacar (to stick out).
◆ *vi* salir (to come out) || sobresalir (to jut out).

protruding [-iŋ] *adj* saliente, sobresaliente || saltón, ona (eyes) || hacia afuera, salido, da (teeth) || saliente (jaw, forehead) || MED herniado, da (bowel).

protrusion [prə'truːʒən] *n* saliente *m*.

protrusive [prɔ'truːsiv] *adj* sobresaliente, saliente (protruding).

protuberance [prə'tjuːbərəns] *n* protuberancia *f*.

protuberant [prə'tjuːbərənt] *adj* protuberante || saltón, ona (eyes).

proud [praud] *adj* orgulloso, sa (self-esteeming, properly satisfied, etc.); *he is proud of his son's success* está orgulloso del éxito de su hijo || soberbio, bia; altivo, va; altanero, ra (arrogant) || soberbio, bia; grandioso, sa; espléndido, da; imponente; *a proud cathedral* una soberbia catedral || glorioso, sa; *a proud moment* un momento glorioso || brioso, sa (a horse) || TECH saliente (rivet) || — *I am proud to* tengo el honor de || FIG *to be as proud as a peacock* ser más orgulloso que un pavo real | *to do o.s. proud* no privarse de nada | *to do s.o. proud* poner a alguien por las nubes (to praise), tratar a alguien a cuerpo de rey (to treat very well).

proud flesh [-fleʃ] *n* MED tejido *m* granulado (exuberant growth).

proudhearted [-'hɑːtid] *adj* orgulloso, sa.

provable ['pruːvəbl] *adj* demostrable.

prove [pruːv] *vt* demostrar, probar (to establish the authenticity with proof, etc.); *I can prove I didn't do it* puedo probar que no lo hice; *to prove s.o.'s innocence* demostrar la inocencia de alguien || probar (one's identity) || probar, poner a prueba (to test); *to prove a method* probar un método || confirmar (to confirm); *to prove an alibi* confirmar una coartada || MATH hacer la prueba a, comprobar (an operation) | demostrar (a theorem) || verificar, comprobar; *to prove a document* verificar un documento || PRINT hacer pruebas de || JUR justificar (damages) | homologar (a will) || — *he was proved innocent* demostró su inocencia || *he was proved right* se demostró que era exacto || *the exception proves the rule* la excepción confirma la regla || *to prove o.s.* dar prueba de sus aptitudes.
◆ *vi* resultar; *it proved to be false* resultó ser falso; *the movie proved to be very bad* la película resultó ser muy mala.

proven [pruːvən] *adj* probado, da; *it is a proven remedy* es un remedio probado.

provenance ['prɔvinəns] *n* procedencia *f*, origen *m*.

Provençal [,prɔvɑːn'sɑːl] *adj* provenzal.
◆ *n* provenzal *m*, lengua *f* de oc (language) || provenzal *m* & *f* (person).

Provence [prɔ'vɑːns] *pr n* GEOGR Provenza *f*.

provender ['prɔvində*] *n* forraje *m* (fodder) || FAM comida *f* (food).

provenience [prəu'viːniəns] *n* US procedencia *f*, origen *m*.

prover ['pruːvə*] *n* TECH cuentahílos *m inv* (for textiles) || PRINT tirador *m* de pruebas.

proverb ['prɔvəːb] *n* refrán *m*, proverbio *m*.

proverbial [prə'vəːbjəl] *adj* proverbial.

Proverbs ['prɔvəːbz] *pl n* REL Proverbios *m*.

provide [prə'vaid] *vt* suministrar; *the underdeveloped countries provide most raw materials* los países subdesarrollados suministran la mayoría de las materias primas || proveer de, dar; *to provide one's son with money* proveer de dinero a su hijo, dar dinero a su hijo || proporcionar, dar; *the tree provides shade* el árbol proporciona sombra || prestar; *to provide support* prestar apoyo || JUR estipular, disponer (to stipulate); *the law provides that* la ley estipula que || — *not to provide a decent living* no dar lo suficiente para vivir || *to provide a topic of conversation* dar que hablar || *to provide o.s. with* proveerse de.
◆ *vi* proveer; *God will provide* Dios proveerá || tomar precauciones, precaverse; *to provide against a storm* tomar precauciones contra una tormenta || satisfacer, atender a (to s.o.'s needs) || — *as provided for in* de acuerdo con lo estipulado en || *to provide for* mantener; *to provide for a family* mantener a una familia; estipular; *the treaty provides for* el tratado estipula; prever; *to provide for an eventuality* prever una posibilidad.

provided [-id] *conj* con tal que, a condición de que, siempre que; *you may come provided it is early* puedes venir con tal que sea temprano || *provided that* con tal que, a condición de que, siempre que.
◆ *adj* previsto, ta; *provided by the statutes* previsto por los estatutos || — *provided with* provisto de, dotado de || *unless otherwise provided* salvo disposición contraria.

providence ['prɔvidəns] *n* Providencia *f*; *Divine Providence* la Providencia Divina, la Divina Providencia || previsión *f* (foresightedness).

provident ['prɔvidənt] *adj* providente || previsor, ra (farsighted).

providential [,prɔvi'denʃəl] *adj* providencial.

provider [prə'vaidə*] *n* proveedor, ra; suministrador, ra; abastecedor, ra.

providing [prə'vaidiŋ] **; providing that** [-ðæt] *conj* con tal que, a condición de que, siempre que.

province ['prɔvins] *n* provincia *f* || FIG esfera *f*, campo *m* (field) | competencia *f*, incumbencia *f*; *it's not within his province* no es de su competencia || JUR jurisdicción *f* || *in the provinces* en la provincia.

provincial [prə'vinʃəl] *adj* provincial, provinciano, na || FIG pueblerino, na; *provincial likes* gustos pueblerinos.
◆ *n* provinciano, na (s.o. who lives in the provinces) || REL provincial *m*.

provincialate [-it] *n* provincialato *m*.

provincialism [prə'vinʃəlizəm] *n* provincialismo *m* || FIG mentalidad *f* pueblerina.

proving ['pruːviŋ] *n* prueba *f* || MIL *proving ground* polígono *m* de pruebas.

provision [prə'viʒən] *n* provisión *f* (providing) || suministro *m*, abastecimiento *m* (supply) || disposición *f* (of treaty, of law, etc.) || — *to make provision for* prever || *to make provision for one's family* atender a las necesidades de su familia; asegurar el porvenir de su familia.
◆ *pl* provisiones *f*, comestibles *m*, suministro *m sing* (food supplies) || *to come within the provisions of the law* estar previsto por la ley *or* por la legislación.

provision [prə'viʒən] *vt* proveer, abastecer, suministrar.

provisional [-l] *adj* provisional; *provisional liberty* libertad provisional || *the provisional IRA* el IRA provisional.

provisioner [-ə*] *n* proveedor, ra; suministrador, ra; abastecedor, ra.

proviso [prə'vaizəu] *n* condición *f*; *with the proviso that* con la condición de que || JUR salvedad *f*.
— OBSERV El plural de *proviso* es *provisoes* o *provisos*.

provisory [prə'vaizəri] *adj* provisional, provisorio, ria (provisional) || condicional (conditional).

Provo ['prəuvəu] *n* FAM miembro *m* del IRA provisional.

provocation [,prɔvə'keiʃən] *n* provocación *f*.

provocative [prə'vɔkətiv] *adj* provocador, ra; provocativo, va.
◆ *n* estimulante *m* || afrodisiaco *m*.

provoke [prə'vəuk] *vt* provocar; *to provoke laughter* provocar la risa; *to provoke a riot* provocar disturbios || incitar, mover (*to* a) (to induce) || provocar, irritar (to annoy).

provoker [-ə*] *n* provocador, ra.

provoking [-iŋ] *adj* provocador, ra || molesto, ta; fastidioso, sa (annoying) || irritante (irritating).

provost ['prɔvəst] *n* director *m* (of a college) || alcalde *m* (Scottish mayor) || REL preboste *m* || US MIL preboste *m* (of military police) || *provost court* tribunal *m* de policía militar || *provost marshal* capitán *m* preboste.

provostship [-ʃip] *n* prebostazgo *m* || alcaldía *f*, cargo *m* de alcalde (in Scotland) || dirección *f* (in a college).

prow [prau] *n* MAR proa *f* || AVIAT morro *m*.

prowess [-is] *n* valor *m* (courage) || habilidad *f* (skill) || *deed of prowess* acto *m* de valor, hazaña *f*, proeza *f*.

prowl [-l] *n* ronda *f* (of police, etc.) || merodeo *m* (of a person) || caza *f* (of animals) || — US *prowl car* coche *m* patrulla || *to be on the prowl* rondar, merodear.

prowl [-l] *vi* rondar (police, etc.) || merodear, vagar, rondar (to roam) || cazar (animals).
◆ *vt* merodear por, rondar; *to prowl the street* merodear por las calles, rondar las calles.

prowler [-lə*] *n* merodeador, ra.

proximate ['prɔksimit] *adj* próximo, ma || aproximado, da (approximate).

proximity [prɔk'simiti] *n* proximidad *f* || *proximity fuse*, US *proximity fuze*, espoleta *f* de proximidad.

proximo ['prɔksimiəu] *adj* COMM del mes próximo, del próximo mes.
— OBSERV La abreviatura *prox.* suele sustituir a la palabra inglesa *proximo*.

proxy ['prɔksi] *n* procuración *f*, poder *m*, poderes *m pl* (authority, document) || poderhabiente *m* & *f*, mandatario, ria; representante *m* & *f*, apoderado *m* (person) || — *by proxy* por poderes; *to vote by proxy* votar por poderes || *to stand proxy for s.o.* tener los poderes de alguien.

prude [pru:d] *n* FAM mojigato, ta; gazmoño, ña.

prudence [-əns] *n* prudencia *f*.

prudent [-ənt] *adj* prudente.

prudential [pru'dənʃəl] *adj* prudencial || industrial (insurance) || US asesor, ra (committee).

prudery ['pru:dəri] *n* mojigatería *f*, gazmoñería *f*.

prudish ['pru:diʃ] *adj* mojigato, ta; pudibundo, da; gazmoño, ña.

prudishness [-nis] *n* mojigatería *f*, gazmoñería *f*, pudibundez *f*.

prune [pru:n] *n* ciruela *f* pasa (fruit) || US FAM mentecato, ta (silly person).

prune [pru:n] *vt* podar, escamondar (trees) || FIG reducir, disminuir, cercenar; *to prune expenses* reducir los gastos | mutilar, cortar; *to prune a text* mutilar un texto.

pruner ['pru:nə*] *n* podador *m*.

pruning ['pru:niŋ] *n* poda *f* || — *pruning hook* o *knife* o *shears* podadera *f* || *pruning season* poda *f*.

prurience ['pruəriəns] *n* lascivia *f* (lewdness) || (ant) comezón *f* (itch).

prurient ['pruəriənt] *adj* lascivo, va (lewd).

prurigo [pru:raigəu] *n* MED prurigo *m*.

pruritus [pru'raitəs] *n* MED prurito *m*.

Prussia ['prʌʃə] *pr n* GEOGR Prusia *f*.

Prussian [-n] *adj/n* prusiano, na || CHEM *Prussian blue* azul *m* de Prusia.

prussiate ['prʌʃiit] *adj/n* CHEM prusiato *m*.

prussic ['prʌsik] *adj* CHEM prúsico, ca; *prussic acid* ácido prúsico.

pry [prai] *n* US palanca *f* (lever).

pry [prai] *vi* fisgar, curiosear, fisgonear (to snoop) || *to pry into* entrometerse en (to meddle).
◆ *vt* US abrir con una palanca (to prise) || *to pry a secret from* o *out of s.o.* sacarle a alguien un secreto.

prying [-iŋ] *adj* fisgón, ona (snooping) || entrometido, da (interfering).
◆ *n* fisgoneo *m*, curioseo *m*.

psalm [sɑ:m] *n* REL salmo *m*.

psalmbook [-buk] *n* salterio *m*.

psalmist [-ist] *n* REL salmista *m*.

psalmodize [-ədaiz] *vi* salmodiar.

psalmody ['sælmədi] *n* REL salmodia *f*.

psalter ['sɔ:ltə*] *n* REL salterio *m*.

psalterium [sɔ:l'ti:riəm] *n* ZOOL omaso *m*.
— OBSERV El plural de la palabra inglesa es *psalteria*.

psaltery ['sɔ:ltəri] *n* MUS salterio *m*.

pseud [sju:d] *n* FAM intelectualoide *m* & *f*.

pseudo ['psju:dəu] *adj* seudo, supuesto, ta.

pseudonym ['psju:dənim] *n* seudónimo *m*.

pseudonymous [psju:'dɔniməs] *adj* seudónimo, ma.

pseudopod ['psju:də'pɔd]; **pseudopodium** [,psju:də'pəudiəm] *n* seudópodo *m*.
— OBSERV El plural de *pseudopodium* es *pseudopodia*.

pshaw! [pʃɔ:] *interj* ¡bah!

psi [psai] *n* psi *f* (Greek letter).

psittacidae [psi'tæsidi:] *pl n* ZOOL psitácidos *m*.

psittacosis [,psitə'kəusis] *n* MED psitacosis *f inv*, sitacosis *f inv*.

psoas ['psəuəs] *n* psoas *m*.

psoriasis [psɔ'raiəsis] *n* MED psoriasis *f*.

psst! [pst] *interj* FAM ¡pst!

psych [saik] *vt* US FAM psicoanalizar, sicoanalizar || — FAM *to psych out* desestabilizar, comer la moral (opponent) | *to psych up* mentalizarse (for contest, difficult task).

psychasthenia ['saikæs'θi:njə] *n* MED psicastenia *f*, sicastenia *f*.

psychasthenic [,saikæs'θi:nik] *adj* MED psicasténico, ca; sicasténico, ca.

psyche ['saiki] *n* psique *f*, psiquis *f* (soul).

Psyche ['saiki] *n* MYTH Psique *f*, Psiquis *f*.

psychedelic ['saiki'delic] *adj* psicodélico, ca; sicodélico, ca.

psychiatric ['saiki'ætrik] *adj* psiquiátrico, ca; siquiátrico, ca.

psychiatrist [sai'kaiətrist] *n* psiquiatra *m* & *f*, siquiatra *m* & *f*.

psychiatry [sai'kaiətri] *n* MED psiquiatría *f*, siquiatría *f*.

psychic ['saikik]; **psychical** [-əl] *adj* psíquico, ca; síquico, ca.
◆ *n* medium *m*.

psychics [-s] *n* metapsíquica *f*.

psychism ['saikizəm] *n* psiquismo *m*, siquismo *m*.

psycho [,saikəv] *n* FAM psicópata *m* & *f*.

psychoanalyse [,saikəu'ænəlaiz] *vt* psicoanalizar, sicoanalizar.

psychoanalysis [,saikəu'æ'eləsis] *n* psicoanálisis *m*, sicoanálisis *m*.

psychoanalyst [,saikəu' əlist] *n* psicoanalista *m* & *f*, sicoanalista *m* & *f*.

psychoanalytic [,saikəuænə'litik]; **psychoanalytical** [-əl] *adj* psicoanalítico, ca; sicoanalítico, ca.

psychoanalyze [,saikəu'ænəlaiz] *vt* psicoanalizar, sicoanalizar.

psychodelic [saikə'delik] *adj* psicodélico, ca; sicodélico, ca.

psychodrama ['saikəu,drɑ:mə] *n* MED psicodrama *m*, sicodrama *m*.

psychologic [,saikə'lɔdʒik]; **psychological** [-əl] *adj* psicológico, ca; sicológico, ca || *psychological warfare* guerra *f* psicológica.

psychologist [sai'kɔlədʒist] *n* psicólogo, ga; sicólogo, ga.

psychology [sai'kɔlədʒi] *n* psicología *f*, sicología *f*.

psychometry [sai'kɔmitri] *n* psicometría *f*, sicometría *f*.

psychomotor ['saikəu'məutə*] *adj* psicomotor, ra; sicomotor, ra.

psychoneurosis ['saikəunjuə'rəusis] *n* MED psiconeurosis *f*, siconeurosis *f*.
— OBSERV El plural de *psychoneurosis* es *psychoneuroses*.

psychopath ['saikəupæθ] *n* MED psicópata *m* & *f*, sicópata *m* & *f*.

psychopathology ['saikəupə'θɔlədʒi] *n* MED psicopatología *f*, sicopatología *f*.

psychopathy [sai'kɔpəθi] *n* MED psicopatía *f*, sicopatía *f*.

psychosis [sai'kəusis] *n* MED psicosis *f*, sicosis *f*.
— OBSERV El plural de *psychosis* es *psychoses*.

psychosomatic [,saikəusəu'mætik] *adj* psicosomático, ca; sicosomático, ca.

psychotechnological ['saikəuteknə'lɔdʒikəl] *adj* psicotécnico, ca; sicotécnico, ca.

psychotherapeutics ['saikəuθerə'pju:tiks] *n* MED psicoterapia *f*, sicoterapia *f*.

psychotherapy [,saikəu'θerəpi] *n* MED psicoterapia *f*, sicoterapia *f*.

psychotic [sai'kɔtik] *adj* psicopático, ca; sicopático, ca.
◆ *n* psicópata *m* & *f*, sicópata *m* & *f*.

PTA *abbr of [Parent-Teacher Association]* asociación de padres y profesores.

ptarmigan ['tɑ,migən] *n* lagópedo *m* (grouse).

PT boat ['pi:ti:'bəut] *n* US MAR lancha *f* torpedera.

pteridophyte ['ptəridəfait] *n* BOT pteridofita *f*.

pterodactyl [,pterəu'dæktil] *n* ZOOL pterodáctilo *m*.

pteropod ['terəpɔd] *n* ZOOL pterópodo *m*.

pterosaur ['pterəusɔ:*] *n* ZOOL pterosaurio *m*.

Ptolemaic [,tɔli'meiik] *adj* ptolemaico, ca; tolemaico, ca.

Ptolemy ['tɔlimi] *pr n* Ptolomeo *m*, Tolomeo *m*.

ptomaine ['təumein] *n* BOT ptomaína *f*, tomaína *f*.

ptosis ['təusis] *n* MED ptosis *f inv*.

PTV *abbr of [pay television]* televisión de pago.

ptyalin ['taiəlin] *n* BIOL ptialina *f*, tialina *f*.

ptyalism ['taiəlizəm] *n* MED ptialismo *m*, tialismo *m* (excessive flow of saliva).

pub [pʌb] *n* FAM taberna *f* (popular drinking place), bar *m* (more refined) || — *pub crawl* chateo *m*, copeo *m*, chiquiteo *m* || *pub crawler* persona *f* a quien le gusta mucho ir de copeo || *to pub crawl* copear, estar de copeo.

puberty ['pju:bəti] *n* pubertad *f*.

pubes ['pju:bi:z] *n* ANAT pubis *m*.

pubescence [pju'besns] *n* BOT pubescencia *f* || MED pubertad *f*, pubescencia *f*.

pubescent [pju'besnt] *adj* BOT pubescente || MED púber, pubescente.

pubic ['pju:bik] *adj* pubiano, na; púbico, ca.

pubis ['pju:bis] *n* ANAT pubis *m*.
— OBSERV El plural de la palabra inglesa *pubis* es *pubes*.

public ['pʌblik] *adj* público, ca; *a public figure* un personaje público; *public convenience* servicios públicos; *public enemy* enemigo público; *public law* derecho público; *public life* vida pública; *public opinion* opinión pública; *public ownership* propiedad pública; *public relations* relaciones públicas; *public thoroughfare* vía pública; *public transport* transporte público; *public works* obras públicas || *public company* sociedad *f* anónima || *to make public* hacer público, publicar.
◆ *n* público *m*; *notice to the public* aviso al público; *the public are requested to remain seated* se ruega al público que permanezca sentado || — *in public* en público || *the general public* el público en general || *the television reaches a large public* la televisión alcanza a un gran auditorio.

public-address system [-ə'dres-'sistim] *n* instalación *f* de altavoces, megafonía *f*.

publican ['pʌblikən] *n* tabernero, ra (in a public house) || publicano, na (tax collector in Rome).

publication [ˌpʌblik'keiʃən] *n* publicación *f* || *Larousse Publications* Ediciones *f* Larousse, Editorial *f sing* Larousse.

public bar ['pʌblik'bɑ:] *n* sala *f* de un pub donde las bebidas son más baratas.

public holiday ['pʌblik'hɔlədi] *n* fiesta *f* legal.

public house ['pʌblik'haus] *n* taberna *f* (popular drinking place) || bar *m* || posada *f* (inn).

publicist ['pʌblisist] *n* publicista *m* & *f*.

publicity [pʌb'lisiti] *n* publicidad *f* || *to give publicity to* dar publicidad a.
◆ *adj* publicitario, ria.

publicize ['pʌblə'saiz] *vt* publicar, hacer público, divulgar.

public prosecutor ['pʌblik'prɔsikju:tə*] *n* JUR fiscal *m*.

public school ['pʌblik'sku:l] *n* colegio *m* privado de enseñanza media (in Great Britain) || instituto *m* (in United States).

public servant ['pʌblik'sə:vənt] *n* funcionario, ria.

public spirit ['pʌblik'spirit] *n* civismo *m*.

public-spirited [-id] *adj* de espíritu cívico, cívico, ca.

public utility ['pʌblikju'tiliti] *n* empresa *f* de servicios públicos, servicio *m* público (business concern) || valores *m pl* de una empresa de servicios públicos (bonds).

publish ['pʌbliʃ] *vt* PRINT publicar, editar || revelar, divulgar, publicar (news) || correr (banns) || — *just published* de publicación reciente || *now publishing* en prensa || *published by* editado por.

publisher [-ə*] *n* editor, ra || US *newspaper publisher* propietario *m* de un periódico.

publishing [-iŋ] *n* publicación *f* || *publishing house* casa *f* editorial, editorial *f*, casa editora.

puce [pju:s] *adj* de color pardo rojizo.
◆ *n* pardo *m* rojizo.

puck [pʌk] *n* SP disco *m* [en hockey sobre hielo] || duende *m* (goblin).

pucker [-ə*] *n* frunce *m*, fruncido *m*, pliegue *m* (pleat) || arruga *f* (wrinkle).

pucker [-ə*] *vt* fruncir (to pleat) || arrugar (to wrinkle) || — *to pucker one's brows* fruncir el ceño || *to pucker up* fruncir.

puckish [-iʃ] *adj* juguetón, ona; travieso, sa (mischievous) || malicioso, sa (cunning).

pudding ['pudiŋ] *n* CULIN pudín *m*, budín *m*, pudding *m* (sweet, pastry, etc.) | FAM postre *m* (dessert) || MAR andullo *m* (fender) || — CULIN *black pudding* morcilla *f* || FAM *pudding face* cara mofletuda | *pudding head* majareta *m* & *f* || *pudding stone* pudinga *f*.

puddle ['pʌdl] *n* charco *m* (small pool) || TECH mezcla *f* de arcilla y grava, argamasa *f*.

puddle ['pʌdl] *vt* TECH pudelar (iron) | mezclar (clay) || enturbiar (water).
◆ *vi* chapotear en el barro || FIG hacer chapucerías (with paints, with clay, etc.).

puddling [-iŋ] *n* TECH pudelado *m*.

puddly [-i] *adj* lleno de charcos, encharcado, da; *a puddly road* una carretera llena de charcos || embarrado, da; fangoso, sa (muddy).

pudency ['pju:dənsi] *n* pudicicia *f*.

pudenda [pju'dendə] *pl n* ANAT partes *f* pudendas.

pudge [pʌdʒ] *n* FAM gordito, ta; rechoncho, cha; gordinflón, ona.

pudgy ['pʌdʒi] *adj* FAM gordito, ta; rechoncho, cha; gordinflón, ona.

pudicity [pju'disiti] *n* pudicicia *f*.

puerile ['pjuərail] *adj* pueril (childish).

puerility [pjuə'riliti] *n* puerilidad *f*.

puerperal [pju'ə:pərəl] *adj* MED puerperal; *puerperal fever* fiebre puerperal.

puerperium [pju:ə'piriəm] *n* puerperio *m*.

Puerto Rican ['pwə:təu'ri:kən] *adj/n* puertorriqueño, ña.

Puerto Rico ['pwə:təu'ri:kəu] *pr n* GEOGR Puerto Rico *m*.

puff [pʌf] *n* soplo *m* (of air) || racha *f*, ráfaga *f* (of wind) || bocanada *f* (of smoke, of cigarette) || chorro *m*, escape *m* (of steam) || resoplido *m* (of breathing, of engine) || borla *f* (for powder) || moña *f* (of ribbon) || edredón *m* (bed covering) || CULIN buñuelo *m* (pastry) || hinchazón *f* (swelling) || FAM bombo *m* (publicity) || bullón *m*, pliegue *m* ahuecado (on a skirt) || CULIN *cream puff* petisú *m*.

puff [pʌf] *vt* soplar (to blow) || echar bocanadas de (to emit whiffs); *the train puffs smoke* el tren echa bocanadas de humo || dar chupadas a (cigarette, pipe, etc.).
◆ *vi* jadear (to pant) || soplar (to emit air through the mouth) || echar humo (to emit smoke) || echar vapor (to emit steam) || *to puff and pant* jadear.
◆ *phr v* *to puff at* dar chupadas a; *to puff at a cigarette* dar chupadas a un cigarro || *to puff out* echar bocanadas de (to emit whiffs) | apagar (a candle, etc.) | cardar (hair) | ahuecar (a skirt) | decir (words) jadeando || — *to be puffed out* estar sin aliento *or* sin resuello (breathless) || *to puff out one's cheeks* hinchar los carrillos || *to puff up* hinchar || — *to puff o.s. up* darse bombo, estar henchido de orgullo.

puffball [-bɔ:l] *n* BOT pedo *m* de lobo.

puffed [-t] *adj* sin aliento (out of breath) || de jamón (sleeve) || hinchado, da (swollen) || FIG henchido, da; *to be puffed up with pride* estar henchido de orgullo | ampuloso, sa (style) || FIG *he was puffed up by his success* se le subió el éxito a la cabeza.

puffer ['pʌfə*] *n* FAM fumador *m* (smoker) | locomotora *f* (locomotive).

puffin ['pʌfin] *n* frailecillo *m* (sea bird).

puffiness ['pʌfinis] *n* hinchazón *f* (swelling) || FIG ampulosidad *f* (of style).

puff pastry ['pʌf'peistri]; **puff paste** ['pʌf-peist] *n* CULIN hojaldre *m*.

puffy ['pʌfi] *adj* hinchado, da (swollen) || ahuecado, da (skirt) || sin aliento (out of breath).

pug [pʌg] *n* arcilla *f* (clay) || doguillo *m* (dog).

pug [pʌg] *vt* amasar (clay) || rellenar con arcilla *or* con argamasa (a wall, floor, etc.).

pugilism ['pju:dʒilizəm] *n* pugilato *m*, pugilismo *m* (boxing).

pugilist ['pju:dʒilist] *n* púgil *m*, pugilista *m* (boxer).

pugnacious [pʌg'neiʃəs] *adj* belicoso, sa; batallador, ra; pugnaz.

pugnaciousness [-nis]; **pugnacity** [pʌg'næsiti] *n* belicosidad *f*, espíritu *m* batallador, pugnacidad *f*.

pug-nosed ['pʌgnəuzd] *adj* chato, ta.

puisne ['pju:ni] *adj* posterior (*to* a) || JUR asesor (judge).
◆ *n* JUR juez *m* asesor.

puke [pju:k] *n* FAM vomitona *f*.

puke [pju:k] *vi* FAM vomitar, cambiar la peseta (to vomit).

puking [-iŋ] *n* FAM vomitona *f*.

pukka ['pʌkə] *adj* FAM auténtico, ca; genuino, na; legítimo, ma.

pulchritude ['pʌlcritu:d] *n* belleza *f*.

pule [pju:l] *vi* gimotear, lloriquear (to whine) || piar (birds).

pull [pul] *n* tracción *f*; *the pull of the engine on the wagons* la tracción de los vagones por la locomotora || tirón *m*; *he gave the elastic a pull* dio un tirón al elástico || arrastre *m* (of the tide) || tensión *f* (of a bow) || tirador *m* (knob, handle) || cuerda *f* (rope of a bell) || cadena *f* (chain) || FIG trecho *m* (distance); *it is a long pull from London to Glasgow* hay un buen trecho de Londres a Glasgow | esfuerzo *m*, trabajo *m*; *it was a hard pull up to the top of the mountain* hubo que hacer un gran esfuerzo para subir hasta la cumbre de la montaña, nos costó mucho trabajo subir hasta la cumbre de la montaña | enchufe *m*, influencia *f* (influence); *you need a lot of pull to get a job* hay que tener mucho enchufe para conseguir un trabajo | ventaja *f*, superioridad *f* (advantage) | atracción *f* (attraction); *the pull of Paris* la atracción de París | rendimiento *m* (efficiency) || FAM chupada *f*; *I took a pull at my cigarette* le di una chupada al cigarrillo | trago *m* (drink) || PHYS atracción *f*, fuerza *f* de atracción (of a magnet) || TECH tracción *f* (movement) | gancho *m* de tracción (between an engine and the wagons) | tiro *m* (of a chimney) || PRINT galerada *f*, primera prueba *f* || SP devolución *f* de la pelota (in cricket) | golpe *m* oblicuo dado a la pelota (in golf) | palada *f*, golpe *m* de remo (oarstroke) | sofrenada *f* (of a horse) | distancia *f* recorrida *or* tiempo *m* pasado remando (distance, period of time) || — *to give a pull at* o *on the bell* tocar la campana || *to give a pull on the trigger* apretar el gatillo || *to give sth. a pull* tirar de algo; *to give the door a pull* tirar de la puerta || *to go for a pull* ir a remar (rowing) || FIG *to have the pull over s.o.* aventajar a alguien || FAM *to take a pull at a bottle* beber de la botella.

pull [pul] *vt* tirar de; *pull the door to open it* tira de la puerta para abrirla; *she pulled his hair* le tiró de los pelos || arrastrar, tirar de (to drag); *the child was pulling a toy car* el niño arrastraba un coche de juguete || sacar, arrancar, extraer (a tooth) || arrancar (to uproot); *they are pulling beetroots* están arrancando remolachas || sacar; *to pull a knife, a gun* sacar un cuchillo, una pistola || tirar; *to pull beer from a barrel* tirar cerveza de un barril || apretar; *to pull the trigger* apretar el gatillo || tensar (a bow) || MAR halar (a rope) | hacer avanzar remando (a boat) | mover (oars) || SP golpear oblicuamente (ball) | sujetar, sofrenar (a horse) || PRINT tirar (a proof) || FAM detener (to arrest) || *US* hacer (to perform); *the police pulled a raid* la policía hizo una incursión || atraer (to attract) || — MED *to have a pulled muscle* tener un tirón en un músculo || FIG *to pull a face* hacer una mueca | *to pull a fast one o a trick on s.o.* hacerle una mala jugada a uno, jugarle una mala pasada a uno || *to pull one's punches* no pegar a fondo (a boxer), andarse con rodeos, hacer críticas moderadas (to criticize halfheartedly) || FIG *to pull s.o.'s leg* tomarle el pelo a uno || *to pull to pieces* hacer pedazos (to break), echar abajo, echar por tierra (an argument), poner como un trapo, poner por los suelos (to criticize).

◆ *vi* tirar; *to pull at a rope* tirar de una cuerda || dar chupadas a (at a pipe) || tirar (a dress) || repropiarse (a horse) || MAR remar || AUT tirar, irse; *this car pulls to the right* este coche tira hacia la derecha || FIG recomendar; *to pull for a candidate* recomendar a un candidato || — *the car pulled to a stop* el coche se paró || FIG *they are pulling different ways* cada uno tira por su lado || *to pull at a bottle* beber de la botella || FIG *to pull with* influenciar a.

◆ *phr v* ***to pull about*** manosear (to finger) | FAM maltratar (to handle roughly) || ***to pull ahead*** destacarse (runner) || ***to pull along*** arrastrar || — *to pull o.s. along* arrastrarse || ***to pull apart*** separar (to separate) | romper, hacer pedazos (to break) | separarse (to become separated) | destrozar, echar abajo, echar por tierra (an argument) || ***to pull away*** separar, apartar (s.o.) | sacar, arrancar (sth.) || — *to pull away from s.o.* apartarse bruscamente de alguien (to move away), dejar a uno atrás (in racing) || ***to pull back*** echar para atrás; *pull the chair back* echa la silla para atrás | retrasar; *his failing the exam pulled him back considerably* el suspenso que sacó en el examen le retrasó enormemente || ***to pull down*** bajar; *pull down the curtain* baja la cortina | encasquetarse (a hat) | tirar; *I pulled him down on the sofa* lo tiré en el sofá | echar abajo, derribar (to demolish); *they are going to pull the building down* van a derribar el edificio | FIG derribar, derrocar; *to pull down a government* derribar a un gobierno; rebajar (price), debilitar mucho; *the disease pulled him down* la enfermedad le ha debilitado mucho; desanimar (to depress), perjudicar (to prejudice) || *US* FAM ***to pull for*** animar || ***to pull in*** entrar (to enter) | entrar en la estación (train) | llegar [en tren]; *we pulled in at four o'clock* llegamos a las cuatro | sujetar, tirar de las riendas (a horse) | tirar de; *let's pull in the line* tiremos de la cuerda | cobrar (a rope) | pararse (to stop) | detener (to arrest) | atraer (to attract) || — *to pull o.s. in* ceñirse la cintura, apretarse la cintura || ***to pull off*** quitar (to take off) | quitarse; *he pulled off his coat* se quitó el abrigo | arrancar; *to pull off a flower's petals* arrancar los pétalos de una flor | FIG conseguir (to obtain), llevar a cabo (to carry out); *to pull off a job* llevar a cabo un trabajo; ganarse, llevarse (a prize, a victory) || ***to pull on*** ponerse (a coat, etc.) | tirar de (a rope) || ***to pull out*** sacar (to take out) | arrancar, sacar (tooth) | irse, marcharse (to go) | salir de la estación (train) | retirarse (troops) | estirar (to stretch) | MAR remar hacia alta mar | salirse [de la fila] (car) || ***to pull over*** ceñirse a; *the car pulled over to the left* el coche se ciñó a la izquierda | volcar (to upset) | acercar (to bring near); *pull the table over* acerca la mesa || ***to pull round*** reanimar; *a glass of sherry will pull him round* una copa de jerez le reanimará || hacer levantar cabeza a (a patient) | volver en sí, recobrar el sentido (to recover consciousness) | recuperarse, reponerse (to recover from an illness) || ***to pull through*** sacar de un apuro (to get out of a difficulty) | salir de un apuro (to survive danger) | salvar, sacar de una enfermedad (to save) | salvarse (to survive illness) | llevar a cabo, llevar a buen término (to carry out) || ***to pull together*** aunar sus esfuerzos, actuar de común acuerdo (to cooperate) || — *to pull o.s. together* serenarse, tranquilizarse (to regain control) || ***to pull up*** levantar, subir (to lift); *pull up the blind* levante la persiana | encabritar (an aircraft) | arremangarse (one's sleeves) | recogerse (one's skirt) | subirse (one's socks) | acercar (to bring near); *pull up a chair* acerca una silla | acercarse (to approach) | AGR arrancar | parar, detener (to make stop) | pararse, detenerse (to come to a halt) | contenerse (to restrain o.s.) | FAM regañar (to scold) | SP acercarse (*with, to* a), recuperar terreno | FIG ayudar (to help) | *to pull s.o. up short* hacer que alguien se pare a pensar.

pullback [-bæk] *adj* de retorno; *pullback spring* muelle de retorno.

◆ *n* obstáculo *m* (hindrance) || retirada *f* (of troops).

puller [-ə*] *n* arrancador, ra || SP remero, ra.

pullet ['pulit] *n* ZOOL polla *f*, pollo *m*.

pulley ['puli] *n* polea *f* || MAR motón *m*.

pulley block [-blɔk] *n* aparejo *m* || MAR cuadernal *m*.

pull-in ['pulin] *n* AUT apartadero *m* (lay-by) | restaurante *m* de carretera (restaurant).

pulling ['puliŋ] *n* tracción *f* || PRINT tirada *f* || *pulling race* carrera *f* de remo.

pulling down [-daun] *n* demolición *f*, derribo *m* (of a building) || FIG derrocamiento *m* (of a government).

pulling in [-in] *n* llegada *f* a la estación (of a train).

pulling out [-aut] *n* extracción *f* (of a tooth) || arranque *m* (of a train) || retirada *f* (of troops).

Pullman [-mən] *n* pullman *m* (railway coach).

pullout [-aut] *adj* corredero, ra; deslizable (slide).

◆ *n* restablecimiento *m* (of an aircraft) || retirada *f* (of troops).

pullover [-əuvə*] *n* jersey *m* (sweater) || nicky *m* (shirt).

pullulate ['pʌljuleit] *vi* pulular.

pullulation [ˌpʌlju'leiʃən] *n* pululación *f*.

pull-up ['pulʌp] *n* SP tracción *f* || parada *f* (stop) || restaurante *m* de carretera (restaurant).

pulmonary ['pʌlmənəri] *adj* ANAT & MED pulmonar; *pulmonary vein, artery* vena, arteria pulmonar.

pulmonate ['pʌlmənit] *adj* ZOOL pulmonado, da.

◆ *n* ZOOL pulmonado *m*.

pulmonic [pʌl'mɔnik] *adj* pulmonar.

pulmotor ['pʌlməutə*] *n* *US* MED pulmón *m* de acero.

pulp [pʌlp] *n* pulpa *f*; *dental pulp* pulpa dentaria, pulpa dental; *pulp of a fruit* pulpa de un fruto || pasta *f*, pulpa *f* (of paper, of wood) || *US* FAM revista *f or* novela *f* de poca categoría || — FIG & FAM *crushed to pulp* hecho papilla || *paper pulp* pulpa de madera, pasta de papel || FIG & FAM *to reduce to pulp* hacer papilla.

pulp [pʌlp] *vt* reducir a pulpa || reducir a pasta (paper) || descascarillar (to husk) || destruir (books).

◆ *vi* volverse pulposo.

pulpit ['pulpit] *n* REL púlpito *m* || FIG predicadores *m pl* (preachers).

pulpitis [pʌl'pitis] *n* MED pulpitis *f*.

— OBSERV El plural de la palabra inglesa es *pulpitides*.

pulpwood ['pʌlpwud] *n* madera *f* para pasta de papel.

pulpy ['pʌlpi] *adj* pulposo, sa.

pulsate [pʌl'seit] *vi* latir, palpitar (to move rhythmically) || vibrar (music) || brillar de forma intermitente (lights) || FIG vibrar, palpitar; *the crowd was pulsating with enthusiasm* la multitud vibraba de entusiasmo.

pulsatile ['pʌlsətail] *adj* pulsátil.

pulsation [pʌl'seiʃən] *n* pulsación *f* (beat) || vibración *f* (vibration).

pulsatory ['pʌlsətəri] *adj* pulsátil, pulsativo, va (throbbing).

pulse [pʌls] *n* pulso *m*; *to take* o *to feel s.o.'s pulse* tomarle el pulso a alguien || pulsación *f*, latido *m* (one single beat of the heart) || compás *m*, cadencia *f*, ritmo *m* (the beat in music) || cadencia *f*, ritmo *m* (the beat of verse) || PHYS pulsación *f* || vibración *f* || RAD impulso *m* || plantas *f pl* leguminosas (leguminous plants) || legumbres *f pl* (seeds of these plants) || — MED *irregular pulse* pulso arrítmico *or* irregular || *pulse of light* luz *f* intermitente || *regular pulse* pulso normal *or* sentado || FIG *to test the pulse of* tomar el pulso a.

pulse [pʌls] *vi* latir, pulsar (to beat) || vibrar (to vibrate) || FIG latir.

pulse-jet engine [-dʒet'endʒin] *n* pulsorreactor *m*.

pulsimeter [pʌl'simitə*] *n* pulsímetro *m*.

pulsometer [pʌl'sɔmitə*] *n* pulsómetro *m*.

pulverizable ['pʌlvəraizəbl] *adj* pulverizable.

pulverization [ˌpʌlvərai'zeiʃən] *n* pulverización *f*.

pulverize ['pʌlvəraiz] *vt* pulverizar || FIG pulverizar; *to pulverize one's opponent, a record* pulverizar a su adversario, un récord | machacar, dar una paliza a; *the team pulverized the opposition* el equipo machacó al equipo contrario || TECH machacar, triturar, pulverizar.

◆ *vi* pulverizarse.

pulverizer [-ə*] *n* pulverizador *m* (for liquid) || TECH machacadora *f*, trituradora *f* (for solids).

pulverulence [pʌl'verjuləns] *n* pulverulencia *f*.

pulverulent [pʌl'verjulənt] *n* polvoriento, ta; pulverulento, ta (covered with powder) || pulverulento, ta (crumbling to powder).

puma ['pju:mə] *n* ZOOL puma *m* (cougar).

— OBSERV El plural de la palabra inglesa es *puma* o *pumas*.

pumice ['pʌmis] *n* piedra *f* pómez.

pumice ['pʌmis] *vt* limpiar *or* pulir con piedra pómez.

pummel ['pʌml] *vt* aporrear.

pummelling [-iŋ] *n* paliza *f*.

pump [pʌmp] *n* bomba *f*; *bicycle pump* bomba de bicicleta; *air pump* bomba de aire; *suction pump* bomba aspirante; *force pump* bomba impelente; *suction and force pump* bomba aspirante impelente || surtidor *m* (in petrol station or car engine); *petrol pump* surtidor de gasolina || zapato *m* bajo de charol, escarpín *m* (evening dress shoe) || zapato *m* de lona, playera *f* (plimsoll) || MAR pompa *f*, bomba *f* || — *injection pump* bomba de inyección || *stomach pump* bomba gástrica || *to give sth. a pump* inflar algo.

pump [pʌmp] *vt* sacar con una bomba, bombear; *to pump water from a boat* sacar agua de un barco con una bomba || sacar [por medio de una bomba]; *Mary is pumping water* María está sacando agua || impulsar; *the heart pumps blood* el corazón impulsa la sangre || inyectar; *to pump air into a machine* inyectar aire en una máquina || echar (con bomba); *to pump water into a bucket* echar agua en un cubo con una bomba || FIG pegar; *the bandit pumped four shots into the detective* el bandido pegó cuatro tiros

al detective | sonsacar; *they pumped the secret out of him* le sonsacaron el secreto | sacar; *they pumped a lot of money out of me* me sacaron mucho dinero | mover de arriba abajo (to shake, to move up and down) | invertir, meter; *to pump money into a new industry* invertir dinero en una nueva industria || — *to pump dry* secar; *to pumb a polder dry* secar un polder; vaciar; *to pump a swimming pool dry* vaciar una piscina || *to pump full of lead* acribillar a tiros || *to pump out* achicar (a boat, a flooded mine, etc.), agotar (to exhaust) || *to pump up* inflar; *to pump up a tyre* inflar un neumático; insuflar aire en (an organ), elevar con una bomba (to raise by pumping).
◆ *vi* accionar una bomba, dar a la bomba (to operate a pump) || impulsar la sangre (the heart) || latir (to beat).

pumpernickel ['pumpənikl] *n* pan integral *m* de centeno.

pump handle [pʌmp'hændl] *n* guimbalete *m*.

pumping ['pʌmpiŋ] *n* de bombeo; *pumping station* estación de bombeo.
◆ *n* bombeo *m* (of water, etc.) || FIG sonsacamiento *m*, sondeo *m*.

pumpkin ['pʌmpkin] *n* BOT calabaza *f*.

pun [pʌn] *n* retruécano *m*, juego *m* de palabras (play on words).

pun [pʌn] *vi* hacer retruécanos, hacer juegos de palabras, jugar del vocablo.

punch [pʌntʃ] *n* puñetazo *m* (blow with the fist) || pegada *f*; *to have a strong punch* tener una gran pegada || FIG fuerza *f*, empuje *m*, vigor *m*; *this story lacks punch* a esta historia le falta fuerza | nervio *m*, energía *f* || TECH sacabocados *m inv*, punzón *m* (instrument for making holes) | punzón *m* de clavo, botador *m* de punta (for driving nails) | perforadora *f* (for cutting holes in paper) | máquina *f* de picar [billetes] (for punching holes in tickets) || ponche *m* (drink) || — INFORM *punched card* ficha *f* perforada || *rabbit punch* golpe *m* en la nuca || *to pack a punch* tener una gran pegada (a boxer), ser muy potente, tener mucha potencia (an engine).

punch [pʌntʃ] *vt* dar un puñetazo a; *he punched him on the nose* le dio un puñetazo en la nariz || golpear, tener pegada, pegar; *Henry punches better than Joseph* Enrique tiene mejor pegada que José || TECH taladrar, agujerear, troquelar (to make a hole in metals) | perforar (in paper); *punched cards* tarjetas perforadas || picar (tickets) || hacer (holes) || US aguijonear (cattle).
◆ *vi* *to punch in* o *out* fichar (employees).

Punch [pʌntʃ] *n* polichinela *m*.

Punch-and-Judy show [,pʌntʃən'dʒudiʃəu] *n* teatro *m* de marionetas.

punchball [-bɔːl]; **punch-bag** [-bæg] *n* SP punching ball *m*, saco *m* de arena.

punch bowl [-bəul] *n* ponchera *f*.

punch card [-kaːd] *n* tarjeta *f* perforada.

punch-drunk [-drʌnk] *adj* SP groggy, aturdido por los golpes.

puncheon ['pʌntʃən] *n* puntal *m*, estribo *m* (strut) || punzón *m*, cuño *m* (patterned die used by silversmiths) || pipa *f*, barril *m* (a cask and its contents).

puncher [əʌntʃə*] *n* empleado *m* que pica los billetes || troquelador *m* (of metal) || sacabocados *m inv* (tool) || perforadora *f*, máquina *f* perforadora (machine) || pegador *m* (boxer) || US vaquero *m* (cowboy).

Punchinello [,pʌntʃi'neləu] *pr n* Polichinela *m*.

punching ['pʌntʃiŋ] *n* TECH taladro *m* || puñetazos *m pl* (blows).

punching bag [-bæg] *n* US SP punching ball *m*, saco *m* de arena.

punching machine [-mə'ʃiːn] *n* TECH taladradora *f*, perforadora *f*.

punch line ['pʌntʃlain] *n* gracia *f* (witty remark).

punch mark ['pʌntʃmaːk] *n* marca *f*, señal *f*.

punch press [,pʌntʃ,pres] *n* TECH prensa *f* troqueladora.

punch-up ['pʌntʃʌp] *n* FAM pelea *f*.

punchy ['pʌntʃi] *adj* FAM con garra (piece of writing).

punctilio [pʌŋk'tiliəu] *n* formalismo *m* || puntillo *m* (point of detail).

punctilious [pʌŋk'tiliəs] *adj* puntilloso, sa; quisquilloso, sa (particular) || formalista, etiquetero, ra (ceremonious).

punctual ['pʌŋtjuəl] *adj* puntual || *the bus was punctual* el autobús llegó a la hora.

punctuality [,pʌŋtju'æliti] *n* puntualidad *f*.

punctuate ['pʌŋktjueit] *vt* GRAMM puntuar (to mark divisions of sentences) || recalcar (to emphasize) || interrumpir (to interrupt); *his speech was punctuated with applause* su discurso fue interrumpido varias veces por los aplausos || *his speech was punctuated with quotations* intercaló citas en su discurso.

punctuation [,pʌŋktju'eiʃən] *n* GRAMM puntuación *f* || *punctuation marks* signos *m* de puntuación.

puncture ['pʌŋktʃə*] *n* pinchazo *m* (in tyre, in sth. inflated) || perforación *f* (perforation) || MED punción *f* || *puncture patch* parche *m*.

puncture ['pʌŋktʃə*] *vt* pinchar (a tyre) || perforar (to perforate) || MED puncionar, hacer una punción a | reventar (an abscess) || *the cyclist punctured a tyre* al ciclista se le pinchó una rueda.
◆ *vi* AUT pinchar (driver, car) || pincharse (tyre).

puncture-proof [-pruːf] *adj* que no se pincha.

pundit ['pʌndit] *n* pandit (in India) || FIG & FAM lumbrera *f*, autoridad *f*.

pungency ['pʌndʒənsi] *n* acritud *f* (of smell) || lo picante (of taste) || FIG mordacidad *f*, causticidad *f* (of words).

pungent ['pʌndʒənt] *adj* acre (smell) || picante, fuerte (taste) || punzante (pain) || FIG mordaz, cáustico, ca (words) | desgarrador, ra (sorrow).

Punic ['pjuːnik] *adj* púnico, ca; *the Punic Wars* las Guerras Púnicas.

puniness ['pjuːninis] *n* debilidad *f* (weakness) || pequeño tamaño *m* (small size).

punish ['pʌniʃ] *vt* castigar (to give a punishment to); *the crime was punished by death* el crimen fue castigado con la pena de muerte || FIG maltratar (to treat harshly) | dar una paliza a (to give s.o. a beating) | castigar (a boxer) | zamparse (food, drink) | aprovecharse hasta el máximo de (to take advantage of).

punishable [-əbl] *adj* castigable, que merece castigo, penable, punible || JUR delictivo, va || *punishable by* merecedor de (a fine, etc.).

punisher [-ə*] *n* castigador, ra || SP pegador *m* (boxer).

punishing [-iŋ] *adj* agotador, ra.

punishment [-mənt] *n* castigo *m*; *corporal punishment* castigo corporal || FIG & FAM paliza *f* (heavy defeat) | castigo *m* (in boxing) || JUR *capital punishment* pena capital *or* de muerte.

punitive ['pjuːnitiv] *adj* punitivo, va; *a punitive expedition* una expedición punitiva.

Punjab [pʌn'dʒaːb] *pr n* GEOGR Pendjab *m*, Penjab *m*, Punjab *m*.

punk [pʌŋk] *adj* US malo, la (of poor quality).
◆ *n* US yesca *f* (tinder) || US FAM mocoso, sa (young inferior person) | novato *m* (beginner) | pobre hombre *m* (inferior person).

punnet ['pʌnit] *n* cestito *m*, canastilla *f*.

punster ['pʌnstə*] *n* aficionado *m* a los juegos de palabras.

punt [pʌnt] *n* batea *f* (boat) || SP patada *f* (in rugby) || apuesta *f* (bet in gambling).

punt [pʌnt] *vt* llevar en batea (to carry s.o. in a punt) || hacer avanzar con el bichero (to propel) || SP dar una patada a, dar un puntapié a, patear (a ball).
◆ *vi* ir en batea (to travel in a punt) || SP dar un puntapié a la pelota, patear la pelota || apostar (to bet) || jugar contra la banca (in gambling).

punter [-ə*] *n* jugador *m* (gambler).

punt pole [-pəul] *n* bichero *m*.

punty [-i] *n* TECH puntel *m* (in glass blowing).

puny ['pjuːni] *adj* endeble, débil, enclenque (weak) || escuchimizado, da (undersized) || insignificante (insignificant).

pup [pʌp] *n* cachorro *m*, cría *f* de perro (of dog) || cría *f* de foca (of seal) || FAM mocoso *m* (conceited young man) || FAM *to sell s.o. a pup* darle a uno gato por liebre.

pup [pəp] *vi* parir [la perra].

pupa ['pjuːpə] *n* ZOOL crisálida *f*.
— OBSERV El plural de *pupa* es *pupas* o *pupae*.

pupil ['pjuːpl] *n* alumno, na (in school) || JUR pupilo, la || ANAT pupila *f* (of the eye).

pupilage; pupillage ['pjuːpilidʒ] *n* JUR pupilaje *m*, tutela *f* (wardship) | minoría *f* (nonage) || escolaridad *f*.

pupillary ['pjuːpiləri] *adj* pupilar.

puppet ['pʌpit] *n* THEATR títere *m*, marioneta *f* || FIG títere *m*, muñeco *m*, pelele *m* || FIG *puppet government* gobierno títere.

puppeteer [,pʌpi'tiə*] *n* THEATR titiritero *m pl*.

puppetry ['pʌpətri] *n* títeres *m pl*.

puppet show [-tʃəu] *n* títeres *m pl*, teatro *m* de marionetas.

puppy ['pʌpi] *n* cachorro *m* (pup) || perrito, ta (young dog) || FIG mocoso *m* (young man).

puppy fat ['pʌpifæt] *n* gordura *f* infantil || *she had a lot of puppy fat when she was a child* de niña era bastante regordeta.

puppy love [-lʌv] *n* amor *m* de jóvenes.

purblind ['pəːblaind] *adj* MED medio ciego, ga (partly blind) || FIG ciego, ga (unable to understand).

purblindness [-nis] *n* ceguera *f* casi total || FIG ceguera *f*, ofuscación *f*.

purchasable ['pəːtʃəsəbl] *adj* adquirible, comprable.

purchase ['pəːtʃəs] *n* compra *f*, adquisición *f* (a buy) || TECH palanca *f* (lever) || agarre *m*, asidero *m* (hold) || apoyo *m*, punto *m* de apoyo (suppport) || MAR aparejo *m*, polipasto *m*.

purchase ['pəːtʃəs] *vt* comprar (to buy) || adquirir (to acquire) || conseguir (to obtain) || MAR levar (the anchor) || apalancar (to lift with a lever).

purchaser [-ə*] *n* comprador, ra (who buys) || adjudicatario, ria (at auction).

purchase tax [-tæks] *n* impuesto *m* sobre la venta.

purchasing [-iŋ] *adj* comprador, ra || *purchasing power* poder adquisitivo.
◆ *n* compra *f*.

purdah ['pəːdə] *n* *in purdah* que se oculta de hombres (of a Hindu or Muslim woman).

pure [pjuə:*] *adj* puro, ra.

pureblood [-blʌd] ; **purebred** [pjuə:bred] *adj* de pura sangre (horse) || de pura raza (other animals).
◆ *n* pura sangre *m*, caballo *m* de pura sangre (horse) || animal *m* de pura raza (any other animal).

purebred [-bred] *adj/n* → **pureblood.**

purée ; US **puree** ['pjuərei] *n* CULIN puré *m*.

purely ['pjuəli] *adj* puramente || *purely by chance* por pura casualidad.

pure-minded ['pjuə,maindid] *adj* sano, na.

purgation [pə:'geiʃən] *n* MED & REL purgación *f*.

purgative ['pə:gətiv] *adj* purgante, purgativo, va.
◆ *n* purgante *m*, purga *f* (a medicine).

purgatorial [,pə:gə'tɔ:riəl] *adj* purificador, ra; expiatorio, ria (expiatory) || REL del purgatorio.

purgatory ['pə:gətəri] *n* REL purgatorio *m* || FIG purgatorio *m*.

purge [pə:dʒ] *n* MED purga *f* (act) | purgante *m*, purga *f* (remedy) || TECH purga *f* || FIG purga *f* (in politics).

purge [pə:dʒ] *vt* MED purgar (the bowels) | purificar (blood) || TECH purgar, limpiar || limpiar (to cleanse) || FIG hacer una purga en; *to purge a political party* hacer una purga en un partido político | deshacerse de (to get rid of) | purgar, expiar; *to purge a sin* purgar un pecado | sanear (the finances) | exonerar (to clear of a charge).

purgecock [-kɔ:k] *n* TECH purgador *m*.

purger [-ə*] *n* TECH purgador *m* || autor *m* de la purga (in politics).

purging buckthorn [pə:dʒiŋ'bʌkθɔ:n] *n* BOT espino *m* cerval.

purification [,pjuərifi'keiʃən] *n* REL purificación *f* || FIG purificación *f* | saneamiento *m* (of finances) || TECH depuración *f*.

purificator ['pjuərifikeitə*] *n* REL purificador *m*.

purificatory ['pjuərifikeitəri] *adj* purificador, ra; purificatorio, ria.

purifier ['pjuərifaiə*] *n* purificador, ra (person who purifies) || TECH depurador, ra.

purify ['pjuərifai] *vt* purificar || TECH purificar, depurar || FIG *to purify s.o. from his sins* librar a alguien de culpa.
◆ *vi* purificarse || TECH purificarse, depurarse.

purifying [-iŋ] *adj* purificador, ra || TECH depurador, ra.
◆ *n* purificación *f* || TECH depuración *f*.

purism ['pjuərizəm] *n* purismo *m*.

purist ['pjuərist] *n* purista *m* & *f*.

puristical [-əl] *adj* purista.

Puritan ['pjuəritən] *adj/n* puritano, na.

puritanical [,pjuəri'tænikəl] *adj* puritano, na.

Puritanism ['pjuəritənizəm] *n* puritanismo *m*.

purity ['pjuəriti] *n* pureza *f*.

purl [pə:l] *n* puntilla *f* (on lace, on ribbon) || ribete *m* de hilo de horo *or* de plata (golden or silver edging) || hilo *m* de oro *or* de plata (thread) || FIG susurro *m*, murmullo *m* (of a stream) || *purl stitch* punto *m* del revés, punto *m* al revés.

purl [pə:l] *vt* ribetear (sewing) || hacer al revés (stitches) || hacer con puntos al revés (garment).
◆ *vi* FIG susurrar, murmurar (a stream).

purler [-ə*] *n* FAM porrazo *m*, batacazo *m*; *to come a purler* pegarse un porrazo, darse un batacazo.

purlieu ['pə:lju:] *n* límites *m pl* (bounds) || lindero *m*, linde *f* (of a forest).
◆ *pl* alrededores *m*, cercanías *f*, inmediaciones *f*.

purlin ['pə:lin] *n* ARCH correa *f*.

purling ['pə:liŋ] *adj* susurrante, murmurador, ra.

purloin [pə:'lɔin] *vt* hurtar, robar (to steal).

purple ['pə:pl] *adj* morado, da; purpúreo, a (colour) || FIG *purple passage* pasaje muy lucido *or* de mucho efecto.
◆ *n* púrpura *f* (crimson cloth, emblem) || morado *m*, violeta *m* (colour) || MED púrpura *f* || AGR añublo *m* || ZOOL púrpura *f* (mollusc).

purple ['pə:pl] *vt* purpurar, enrojecer.

purplish ['pə:pliʃ] ; **purply** ['pə:pli] *adj* violáceo, a; purpurino, na; morado, da.

purport ['pə:pət] *n* significado *m*, sentido *m* (meaning) || intención *f* (purpose) || tenor *m*, contenido *m* (of a document) || objeto *m* (of a letter).

purport ['pə:pət] *vt* pretender (to claim); *this book purports to be an original work* este libro pretende ser original || significar (to mean) || dejar suponer, implicar, dar a entender (to suggest).

purportless [-lis] *adj* sin ningún interés, desprovisto de interés.

purpose ['pə:pəs] *n* propósito *m*, objetivo *m*, intención *f*, deseo *m*; *for the purpose of doing sth. useful* con el propósito de hacer algo útil || destino *m*, fin *m* (destination) || resolución *f*, determinación *f* (determination) || uso *m*; *I have got jeans for everyday purposes* tengo pantalones vaqueros para uso diario || necesidad *f* (need); *for future purposes* para las necesidades futuras || utilidad *f*; *public purpose* utilidad pública || — *fixed purpose* intención precisa || *for all purpose* para todo || *for my purpose* para lo que quiero || *for the above purposes* con los objetivos anteriormente mencionados || *for the purpose* al efecto || *for the purpose of* con el objeto de, con miras a, para || *for this* o *that purpose* con este propósito, con este fin || *infirm of purpose* irresoluto, ta; indeciso, sa || *not to the purpose* que no viene al caso, fuera de lugar || *novel with a purpose* novela *f* de tesis || *of set purpose* deliberadamente, intencionadamente, a propósito || *on purpose* a propósito, adrede, a posta; *I did it on purpose* lo hice adrede || *strength of purpose* firmeza *f*, resolución *f* || *to achieve one's purpose* conseguir el fin deseado, alcanzar su objetivo || *to come to the purpose* ir al grano || *to good purpose* con provecho, fructuosamente, con buenos resultados || *to little purpose* para poco || *to no purpose* para nada, en balde, en vano, sin resultado || *to serve* o *to answer various purposes* servir para varias cosas || *to some purpose* para algo; *all studies serve to some purpose* cualquier estudio sirve para algo || *to speak to the purpose* no salirse del tema, ceñirse al tema || *to the purpose* que viene al caso, a propósito.

purpose ['pə:pəs] *vt* proponerse, tener la intención de (to intend).

purpose-built [-bilt] *adj* construido, da con cierta finalidad.

purposeful [-ful] *adj* decidido, da; determinado, da; resuelto, ta (person) || útil (activity) || lleno de significado (speech).

purposefulness [-fulnis] *n* decisión *f*, determinación *f*, resolución *f* (determination) || utilidad *f* (usefulness) || significado *m* (meaning).

purposeless [-lis] *adj* sin objetivo, sin objeto (aimless) || inútil (useless) || irresoluto, ta (character) || indeciso, sa; irresoluto, ta (person).

purposely [-li] *adj* a propósito, adrede, a posta, deliberadamente, intencionadamente.

purposive ['pə:pəsiv] *adj* deliberado, da; intencionado, da (act) || decidido, da; determinado, da; resuelto, ta (person) || útil (useful) || que desempeña una función (organ).

purpura ['pə:pjurə] *n* MED púrpura *f*.

purpure ['pə:puə*] *n* HERALD púrpura *f*.

purpurin ['pə:pjurin] *n* purpurina *f* (red crystalline compound).

purr [pə:*] *n* ronroneo *m* (of a cat) || zumbido *m* (of an engine).

purr [pə:*] *vi* ronronear (a cat) || zumbar (an engine).

purse [pə:s] *n* monedero *m*, portamonedas *m inv* (for money) || bolsa *f* (a sum of money) || bolsa *f* (of a boxer) || premio *m* (prize) || colecta *f* (collection) || ANAT bolsa *f* || US bolso *m* [AMER cartera *f*] (handbag) || — *belt purse* escarcela *f* || FIG *beyond s.o.'s purse* fuera de las posibilidades de uno, fuera del alcance de alguien || *public purse* erario público || *purse bearer* tesorero, ra || *purse strings* cordones *m* de la bolsa || FIG *to have a common purse* hacer fondo común | *to have a lined purse* tener la bolsa repleta | *to hold the purse strings* manejar los cuartos, administrar el dinero | *to loosen the purse strings* aflojar la bolsa || FIG & FAM *you cannot make a silk purse out of a sow's ear* no se pueden pedir peras al olmo.

purse [pə:s] *vt* fruncir; *to purse one's brows* fruncir el entrecejo, fruncir el ceño || apretar (one's lips).

purse-proud [-praud] *adj* orgulloso de su riqueza.

purser [-ə*] *n* MAR contador *m*.

purslane ['pə:slin] *n* BOT verdolaga *f*.

pursuable [pə:'sjuəbl] *adj* perseguible (punishable, which can be followed) || proseguible (continuable).

pursuance [pə'sjuəns] *n* prosecución *f* (continuation) || ejecución *f*, cumplimiento *m* (carrying out) || *in pursuance of* según, conforme a, de conformidad con.

pursuant [pə'sjuənt] *adv* *pursuant to* según, conforme a, de conformidad con.

pursue [pə'sju:] *vt* perseguir; *to pursue a thief* perseguir a un ladrón || seguir la pista de (an animal) || FIG aspirar a, buscar, perseguir (to strive for) | seguir (a line of conduct, a plan) | ejercer (a profession) | proseguir, continuar (to continue) || JUR demandar, perseguir judicialmente.

pursuer [-ə*] *n* perseguidor, ra || JUR demandante *m* & *f*.

pursuit [pə'sju:t] *n* persecución *f*; *in pursuit of* en persecución de || profesión *f* || ocupación *f*, trabajo *m* (work) || pasatiempo *m* (pastime) || AVIAT caza *f* || FIG búsqueda *f*, busca *f* (of an aim).

pursuit plane [-plein] *n* AVIAT caza *m*, avión *m* de caza.

pursy ['pə:si] *adj* barrigón, ona; barrigudo, da (corpulent) || asmático, ca; que se ahoga (short-winded) || encogido, da; apretado, da (lips) || ricachón, ona (rich).

purulence ['pjuərulәns] *n* MED purulencia *f* (condition) | pus *m* (pus).

purulent ['pjuərulənt] *adj* purulento, ta.

purvey [pə:'vei] *vt/vi* proveer, abastecer, suministrar || *to purvey for a person* ser el proveedor de una persona.

purveyance [-əns] *n* abastecimiento *m*, suministro *m* (supply).

purveying [-iŋ] *adj* proveedor, ra; abastecedor, ra.

purveyor [-ə*] *n* proveedor, ra; abastecedor, ra.

purview ['pəːvjuː] *n* articulado *m*, texto *m* (of a statute) ‖ alcance *m* (extent) ‖ esfera *f* (field) ‖ competencia *f* (concern, province).

pus [pʌs] *n* MED pus *m*.

push [puʃ] *n* empujón *m*; *he gave me a push in the back* me dio un empujón por la espalda ‖ empuje *m*, impulso *m* (force which pushes) ‖ FIG apuro *m*, aprieto *m* (difficult moment) ‖ ARCH empuje *m* ‖ MIL ofensiva *f* ‖ FAM enchufe *m* (influence) | empuje *m* (drive); *he hasn't enough push to succeed as a salesman* no tiene bastante empuje para ser un buen vendedor | empujón *m*; *we have to make a push to finish our work* tenemos que dar un empujón para acabar nuestro trabajo | banda *f* (of thieves) | embestida *f* (of a bull) ‖ — *at a push* en caso de necesidad, en un momento de apuro ‖ FAM *to get the push* ser despedido, ser puesto de patitas en la calle ‖ *to give a push on the bell* tocar el timbre ‖ *to give a push on the button* pulsar el botón ‖ FAM *to give s.o. a push* enchufar a alguien | *to give s.o. the push* despedir a alguien, poner de patitas en la calle a alguien ‖ *to make a push shot* retacar (in billiards) ‖ FIG *when it comes to the push* cuando llega el momento decisivo.

push [puʃ] *vt* empujar; *he pushed the door* empujó la puerta; *the gardener was pushing a wheelbarrow* el jardinero empujaba una carretilla ‖ pisar; *he pushed the accelerator* pisó el acelerador ‖ apretar, pulsar; *he pushed the button* apretó el botón ‖ promocionar (goods, sale); *to push a product* promocionar un producto ‖ fomentar, promover, promocionar (trade, etc.); *the government is pushing agriculture* el gobierno está fomentando la agricultura ‖ extender (to extend) ‖ obligar; *they pushed him into marrying that girl* le obligaron a casarse con esa chica ‖ empujar; *my parents pushed me to go to University* mis padres me empujaron a ir a la Universidad ‖ aprovechar, aprovecharse de (to take advantage of) ‖ recomendar, enchufar (to recommend) ‖ insistir en (a claim) ‖ FIG apremiar; *to push s.o. for payment* apremiar a alguien para que pague ‖ — FAM *don't push him too far!* ¡no le saque de quicio! ‖ *he pushed his finger in his eye* le metió el dedo en el ojo ‖ *I am pushed for time* tengo prisa, ando escaso de tiempo ‖ *to be hard pushed to do sth.* verse en aprietos para hacer algo ‖ *to be pushed for money* andar muy justo de dinero, andar escaso de dinero ‖ *to push one's luck* forzar la suerte ‖ *to push o.s.* darse a fondo (sportsmen) ‖ *to push s.o. out of the way* apartar a alguien empujándole *or* a empujones ‖ *to push sth. open* abrir algo empujándolo ‖ *we are pushed for an answer* nos piden una contestación rápida.

◆ *vi* empujar; *Raymond's car stopped and we all had to push* el coche de Ramón se paró y todos tuvimos que empujar ‖ presionar, ejercer presión; *the trade unions are pushing for better wages* los sindicatos están presionando para que aumenten los salarios ‖ seguir; *we pushed as far as Manchester* seguimos hasta Manchester ‖ adentrarse; *we pushed a good way into Provence* nos adentramos bastante en Provenza ‖ *push* empujen (notice on doors).

◆ *phr v* **to push ahead** seguir adelante | *to push ahead with a plan* llevar adelante un proyecto ‖ **to push around** FAM manejar a su antojo, atropellar ‖ **to push aside** apartar a empujones (people) | apartar con la mano (things) ‖ **to push away** apartar ‖ **to push back** empujar | hacer retroceder; *the police pushed back the crowd* la policía hizo retroceder a la multitud | hacer retroceder, rechazar; *we pushed back the enemy* hicimos retroceder al enemigo | echar hacia atrás (hair, etc.) | empujar hacia atrás | retroceder (to move back) ‖ **to push down** derribar, tirar abajo (a house) | hacer caer (s.o.) | apretar (to press down); *to push down a button* apretar un botón ‖ **to push forward** empujar hacia adelante (s.o.) | avanzar (an army) | *to push forward to the attack* pasar a la ofensiva | *to push o.s. forward* ponerse en evidencia ‖ **to push in** empujar | hincar (a pole, etc.) | entrar a empujones (to get in) | colarse (in a queue) ‖ — FAM *to push s.o.'s face in* romperle a uno la crisma ‖ **to push off** desatracar (a boat) | quitar (to take off) | FAM largarse, irse (to go) | *to push off from* apartarse de | *to push s.o. off a place* echar a alguien de un sitio a empujones ‖ **to push on** activar, apresurar (work) | avanzar; *the enemy pushed on to the village* el enemigo avanzó hasta el pueblo | seguir; *we pushed on to Blackpool* seguimos hasta Blackpool | seguir adelante, continuar; *now that we have rested let's push on* ahora que hemos descansado sigamos adelante | empujar; *to push s.o. on to do sth.* empujar a alguien a hacer algo | hacer adelantar; *to push on a pupil* hacer adelantar a un alumno | irse, ponerse en camino; *it's time to push on* es hora de irnos | **to push out** echar a empujones; *they pushed him out of the room* le echaron a empujones de la habitación | expulsar, deshauciar (a tenant) | eliminar; *to push competitors out of the market* eliminar a los competidores del mercado | echar al agua (a boat) | echar (blossoms, roots) | sacar; *the cat pushed out its claws* el gato sacó las uñas | *to push out into* adentrarse en; *the headland pushes out into the sea* el promontorio se adentra en el mar ‖ **to push over** hacer caer (s.o.) | volcar (sth.); *to push a car over* volcar un coche ‖ **to push through** pasar por, sacar por; *they pushed the table through the window* sacaron la mesa por la ventana | llevar a cabo *or* a buen término (to carry out) | hacer aceptar (a bill in Parliament) | salir (plants) | abrirse paso a empujones entre (the crowd) | *to push one's way through the crowd* abrirse paso a empujones entre la muchedumbre ‖ **to push to** empujar (the door) ‖ **to push up** levantar | hacer subir; *to push up the prices* hacer subir los precios | ayudar a subir [empujándolo] (s.o.) | FIG dar un empujón, ayudar.

push-bike [-baik] *n* FAM bicicleta *f*, bici *f*.

push button [-,bʌtn] *n* pulsador *m*, botón *m*.

push-button control [-,bʌtnkən'trəul] *n* mando *m* por pulsador.

pushcart [-kɑːt] *n* carretilla *f* de mano.

push chair [-tʃɛə*] *n* coche silla *m*.

pusher [-ə*] *n* persona *f* que empuja ‖ FAM persona *f* ambiciosa, arribista *m* & *f* (ambitious person) | vendedor *m* de estupefacientes (narcotic seller) ‖ AVIAT avión *m* de hélice propulsora.

pushful [-ful] *adj* ambicioso, sa (ambitious) ‖ emprendedor, ra; que tiene empuje (energetic).

pushing [-iŋ] *adj* ambicioso, sa (ambitious) ‖ emprendedor, ra; que tiene empuje (energetic) ‖ molesto, ta; insistente.

pushover [-,əuvə*] *n* FAM cosa *f* muy fácil de hacer (easy thing) | persona *f* fácil de convencer (person easily persuaded) ‖ FAM *it's a pushover* está tirado.

pushpin [-pin] *n* chincheta *f* (nail).

push-start [-stɑːt] *n* arranque *m* a empujones (of a motor vehicle).

push-start [-stɑːt] *vt* arrancar a empujones (a motor vehicle).

push-up [-ʌp] *n* tracción *f* (in gymnastics).

pushy [-i] *adj* US FAM molesto, ta; insistente.

pusillanimity [,pjuːsilə'nimiti] *n* pusilanimidad *f*.

pusillanimous [,pjuː'silæniməs] *adj* pusilánime.

puss [pus] *n* minino *m* (cat) ‖ liebre *f* (hare) ‖ FAM chica *f* (girl) ‖ US FAM jeta *f*, cara *f* (face) ‖ — *Puss in Boots* el gato con botas ‖ *to play puss in the corner* jugar a las cuatro esquinas.

pussy [-i] *n* minino *m* (cat) ‖ BOT amento *m* (catkin) ‖ FAM chica *f* (girl).

pussyfoot [-ifut] *vi* andar con mucho sigilo (to move stealthily) ‖ US FAM no comprometerse.

pustular ['pʌstjulə*] *adj* MED pustuloso, sa.

pustulate ['pʌstjuleit] *adj* pustuloso, sa.

pustule ['pʌstjuːl] *n* pústula *f*.

pustulous ['pʌstjuləs] *adj* pustuloso, sa.

put [put] *n sp* lanzamiento *m* (of the shot) ‖ COMM opción *f* de venta.

put [put] *vt* poner; *put all that on the floor* ponga todo eso en el suelo ‖ poner, colocar; *put the books on the table* pon los libros en la mesa ‖ meter (to introduce); *to put the key in the keyhole* meter la llave en la cerradura ‖ echar; *have you put salt in your soup?* ¿le has echado sal a la sopa? ‖ someter (to submit); *to put a proposal before a committee* someter una propuesta a una comisión ‖ exponer, someter; *to put one's case before the jury* o *to the jury* exponerle su caso al jurado ‖ someter, presentar (to propose); *to put a project to the Parliament* presentar un proyecto al Parlamento ‖ someter *or* poner a votación (to a vote); *to put a motion* poner a votación una moción ‖ someter; *to put s.o. to a test* someter a alguien a una prueba ‖ hacer; *he put a question to me* me hizo una pregunta ‖ plantear (a problem) ‖ poner; *put it in writing* ponlo por escrito ‖ gravar con; *to put heavy taxes on alcohol* gravar el alcohol con impuestos elevados ‖ invertir, poner, colocar (to invest); *to put money to a firm* poner *or* invertir dinero en una empresa ‖ poner, meter; *to put money in the savings bank* poner dinero en la caja de ahorros ‖ meter; *I do not want to put you to expense* no quiero meterle en gastos ‖ causar; *to put s.o. to trouble* causar molestias a alguien ‖ echar (to impute to); *they put the blame* o *the responsibility on me* me echaron la culpa ‖ poner (to fix a price); *he put the price at five pounds* puso el precio a cinco libras ‖ echar, calcular (to estimate); *at first glance I would put this at ten pounds* a primera vista le echaría diez libras ‖ calcular; *I put the population of Malaga at 400 000* calculo la población de Málaga en 400 000 habitantes ‖ dar (to attribute); *to put a high value on sth.* dar un gran valor a algo; *to put the proper interpretation on the clause of a contract* dar la interpretación apropiada a la cláusula de un contrato ‖ poner, decir (to state); *if you put in that way* si lo pone así; *let's put it that you were not there* pongamos que no estaba allí ‖ decir (to say); *as Winston Churchill put it in his speech* como dijo Winston Churchill en su discurso; *put it to him nicely* dígaselo con buenos modales ‖ exponer; *to put the case clearly* exponer claramente el caso ‖ expresar; *to put one's thoughts into words* expresar sus pensamientos con palabras ‖ traducir (to translate); *how would you put this into Spanish?* ¿cómo traduciría esto al español? ‖ mandar (to oblige); *they put the troops to digging trenches* mandaron que las tropas abriesen trincheras ‖ poner de, meter a; *he put his boy to* o *into shoemaking* metió a su hijo a zapatero ‖ inscribir; *he put his horse in a race* inscribió su caballo en una carrera ‖ jugarse, poner (to bet); *he put his last penny on that horse* se jugó el último penique en ese caballo ‖ orientar, dirigir (to direct towards) ‖ SP lanzar (the shot) ‖ echar (for reproduction); *to put a cow to a bull* echar una vaca a un toro ‖ — *if I may put it so* por decirlo así ‖ FIG *I put it to you that you are lying* me parece que está usted mintiendo | *I would not put it past him to do sth. silly at the last moment* no me extrañaría que hiciese una tontería en el último momento | *put it there!* ¡chócala! (in a deal) ‖ *to be hard put to do sth.* serle a uno difícil hacer algo; *I'll be hard put to it* me va a ser difícil hacerlo ‖ *to put a bullet in s.o.'s back* pegarle un tiro a alguien por la espalda ‖ *to put a bullet through s.o.* atravesar a alguien de un balazo ‖ *to put a child into a sailor's suit* poner a un niño un traje de marinero, vestir a un niño de marinero ‖ *to put a child to bed* acostar a un niño ‖ *to put a field under potatoes* sembrar un campo de patatas ‖ SP *to put a horse to a fence* hacer que un caballo salte una valla ‖ *to put a knife in s.o.'s back* clavarle un cuchillo a alguien por la espalda (to trick) ‖ *to put a matter into s.o.'s hands* poner un asunto en manos de alguien ‖ *to put an animal out of his misery* acortarle la agonía a un animal, rematar a un animal ‖ *to put an article on the market* poner un artículo en el mercado, lanzar un artículo al mercado ‖ *to put an end* o *a stop to sth.* poner fin *or* término a una cosa ‖ *to put it bluntly* hablando sin rodeos ‖ *to put in danger* poner en peligro ‖ *to put in safekeeping* poner a buen recaudo ‖ FIG *to put one's heart into one's work* poner los cinco sentidos en un trabajo | *to put one's mind to a problem* poner los cinco sentidos en la resolución de un problema | *to put one's pen through a word* tachar una palabra ‖ *to put one's savings into francs, pounds, etc.* cambiar sus ahorros en francos, libras, etc. ‖ *to put one's signature to sth.* firmar algo ‖ *to put on one side* poner a un lado ‖ *to put on the stage* montar, poner en escena (a play) ‖ *to put o.s. in s.o.'s place* ponerse en el lugar de uno ‖ *to put right* o *straight* poner en el buen camino (to put on the right road), desengañar (to show the truth), corregir (to correct), curar (to cure), ordenar, poner en orden, arreglar (to put in order), arreglar (to repair), poner bien (to put in the right position), poner en hora (watch) (adj) ‖ FIG *to put s.o. at ease* tranquilizar a alguien ‖ *to put s.o. in a bad mood* poner de malhumor a alguien ‖ *to put s.o. in a position to* poner a alguien en condiciones de ‖ FIG *to put s.o. in mind of sth.* recordarle algo a alguien ‖ *to put s.o. on the right road to somewhere* indicar a alguien el buen camino para ir a algún sitio ‖ *to put s.o. out of patience* hacerle perder la paciencia a alguien ‖ *to put s.o.'s mind at rest* tranquilizar a alguien ‖ *to put s.o. to death* matar a alguien ‖ FIG *to put s.o. to sleep* darle sueño a alguien (to bore) ‖ *to put s.o. to the sword* pasar a alguien a cuchillo ‖ *to put sth. before sth. else* anteponer una cosa a otra ‖ *to put sth. in doubt* poner algo en duda *or* en tela de juicio ‖ *to put sth. into practice* poner algo en práctica ‖ *to put sth. to good use* hacer buen uso de algo ‖ *to put sth. to a vote* someter *or* poner algo a votación ‖ *to put sth. to one's ear* acercarse algo al oído ‖ FIG *to put the cards on the table* poner las cartas sobre la mesa *or* boca arriba ‖ *to put the enemy to flight* poner en fuga al enemigo ‖ *to put the finishing touch to* dar el último toque a ‖ *to put the matter right* arreglar el asunto ‖ *to put to fire and sword* poner a fuego y a sangre ‖ *to put to the test* poner a prueba ‖ *to stay put* permanecer en el mismo sitio, no moverse (to remain in the same position), seguir igual (in the same condition).

◆ *vi* MAR poner rumbo a (to take a specified course) ‖ — MAR *to put into port* hacer escala en un puerto | *to put to sea* zarpar, hacerse a la mar.

◆ *phr v* **to put about** hacer correr, difundir (a rumour) | preocupar (to worry) | molestar (to trouble) | MAR hacer virar (a boat), virar, cambiar de rumbo (of a boat) ‖ — *he put it about that John was getting married* hizo correr la voz *or* el rumor de que Juan iba a casarse ‖ **to put across** pasar (goods) | hacer aceptar (idea, product) | conseguir, lograr; *the play was put across very well* la obra estaba muy conseguida | cerrar (a deal) | traducir; *the book puts across the seriousness of the problem* el libro traduce la gravedad del problema | transmitir, hacer comprender, comunicar (to communicate) ‖ — FIG *to put it across s.o.* engañar a alguien (to trick), pegar una paliza a alguien (to defeat) ‖ *you can't put that one across me* esto no cuela, esto no me lo creo ‖ **to put aside** poner *or* dejar a un lado | ahorrar (money) | dejar, renunciar a; *to put drinking aside* dejar de beber, renunciar a la bebida | rechazar (to reject) | desechar (fears) ‖ **to put away** poner en su sitio, guardar; *put away your clothes* pon tu ropa en su sitio | poner en el garaje (car) | FIG ahorrar (money), desechar (fears), apartar, alejar (a thought) | repudiar (wife) | FAM zamparse, echarse entre pecho y espalda (drink, food), enjaular, meter en chirona (to jail), meter en un manicomio (a lunatic), suprimir, liquidar (to kill a person), sacrificar (to kill an animal), empeñar (to pawn) ‖ **to put back** volver a poner en su sitio; *put this book back* vuelva a poner este libro en su sitio | volver a poner; *put it back on the table* vuelva a ponerlo en la mesa | atrasar, retrasar (clock, time) | aplazar (to postpone) | MAR volver *or* regresar [al puerto] ‖ **to put by** guardar (to keep) | ahorrar (money) | FIG eludir, evitar (to avoid) ‖ **to put down** bajar; *put your hand down* baja la mano | dejar; *put this pen down on the table* deja esta pluma en la mesa | poner, dejar; *to put sth. down on the ground* poner algo en el suelo | soltar; *put that rifle down* suelta ese fusil | cerrar (an umbrella) | apuntar, poner por escrito (in writting) | poner (on a bill, on an account, etc.) | dejar [bajar] (passengers) | acabar con (to put an end to) | sofocar, reprimir (a rebellion) | reprimir (to repress) | suprimir (an abuse) | disminuir, bajar (prices) | FIG achacar, atribuir (to ascribe); *to put a remark down to bad humour* achacar una observación al mal humor; rebajar (pride), sacrificar (to kill animals), callar, hacer callar (to silence) | degradar (to demote) | MATH poner | MAR fondear (a buoy) | COMM hacer un desembolso inicial de (to deposit), abonar, poner; *put it down to my account* póngalo en mi cuenta ‖ — *to put down as* echar; *I put him down as forty* le echo cuarenta años | *to put down for* tener por, considerar como; *they put him down for a fool* le tienen por tonto | *to put one's name down* apuntar su nombre (on a paper), inscribirse (to enrol) ‖ **to put forth** proponer (to propose) | mostrar (to show) | emplear (one's efforts) | publicar (to issue) | tender, alargar (hand) | extender, alargar (arm) | BOT echar (brotes) | MAR zarpar ‖ **to put forward** proponer, someter (a proposal) | proponer, presentar la candidatura de (to propose as a candidate) | exponer, emitir (an idea) | hacer (a suggestion) | valerse de (to use); *to put forward an argument* valerse de un argumento | adelantar (clock, date) ‖ — FIG *to put o.s. forward* ponerse en evidencia ‖ *to put o.s. forward as* dárselas de ‖ **to put in** meter, introducir (to insert) | dedicar, pasar; *to put in one's time reading* pasarse el tiempo leyendo, dedicar su tiempo a la lectura | JUR presentar; *to put in a claim* presentar una demanda; presentarse, presentar su candidatura (for an election) | AGR sembrar (seeds), plantar (trees, etc.) | FAM decir (a word) | MAR tocar *or* hacer escala (*at en*); *the Queen Mary put in at Malaga* el Queen Mary hizo escala en Málaga | elegir; *the country has put the Conservatives in* el país ha elegido a los conservadores ‖ — FIG *to put a word in* decir una palabra, intervenir en la conversación ‖ *to put in a good word for* hablar por *or* en favor de ‖ *to put in out of one's own pocket* poner de su bolsillo (money) ‖ *to put in some overtime* hacer unas horas extraordinarias ‖ **to put off** quitarse (one's clothes); *he put his coat off* se quitó el abrigo | aplazar, diferir (to postpone); *to put off a date, a payment* aplazar una cita, un pago | aplazar una cita con (s.o.) | cansar, hartar, hastiar (to disgust); *I went to the cinema so often that it put me off* he ido tantas veces al cine que ya estoy harto | dar asco, asquear (to revolt); *the smell of this fish puts me off* el olor de este pescado me da asco | disuadir, quitar de la cabeza; *we put him off his plan* le hemos quitado de la cabeza el proyecto que tenía | desconcertar (to disconcert) | desanimar (to dispirit) | intimidar (to intimidate) | alejar, apartar (to divert) | entretener (with promises) | engañar, dar el pego (to humbug) | SP hacer fallar; *they tried to put me off my shot* intentaron hacerme fallar el tiro | deshacerse de (to get rid of) | MAR hacerse a la mar ‖ — *to put s.o. off his meal* o *off his food* quitarle a uno las ganas de comer ‖ *to put s.o. off the scent* despistar a alguien ‖ *we had to put the guests off* tuvimos que dejar para más tarde la invitación que habíamos hecho ‖ **to put on** ponerse (clothes); *put on your jacket* ponte la chaqueta | encender, dar a (light, radio, etc.) | poner (record player, etc.) | hacer funcionar (a machine) | poner; *in August the airline puts on many extra flights* en agosto la compañía pone muchos vuelos suplementarios | poner a calentar; *I am going to put some water on* voy a poner agua a calentar | servir, poner (a dish) | (brake) | cobrar (speed) | representar, dar (a show) | echar, dar (a film) | montar, poner en escena; *to put a play on* poner una obra en escena | aumentar (to increase) | fingir, simular (to pretend); *his anger was put on* su cólera era fingida | afectar; *that accent isn't real, it's put on* ese acento no es natural, es afectado | engordar; *I put on two pounds in a week* engordé dos libras en una semana | adelantar (a clock) | añadir (to add) | designar (to appoint); *to put s.o. on to a job* designar a alguien para un trabajo | poner, jugarse (to bet) ‖ — FAM *to put it on* darse tono (to be conceited), exagerar (to exaggerate) ‖ *to put on airs* darse tono ‖ *to put on one's Sunday best* ponerse de tiros largos ‖ *to put on weight* engordar ‖ *to put s.o. on* pasar la comunicación a alguien ‖ *to put s.o. on to s.o. else* hablar a una persona de otra, dar a una persona el nombre de otra (to speak to s.o. about s.o. else), poner a una persona con otra (on the telephone) ‖ *who put you on to it?* ¿quién le dio la información? ‖ **to put out** apagar, extinguir (flames, fire) | apagar (light, radio, record player, etc.) | echar, expulsar (to dismiss, to eject) | sacar [por la noche] (a cat) | alargar, tender (one's hand) | alargar, extender (one's arm) | asomar, sacar (one's head) | sacar (one's tongue) | sacar (s.o.'s eye) | sacar; *the snail puts out its horns* el caracol saca los cuernos | BOT echar (leaves) | sacar, enseñar (to show) | sacar, publicar (to issue); *this publisher puts out some very good books* esta editorial publica unos libros muy buenos | extender, hacer correr (a rumour) | hacer (an announcement) | sacar, producir (to produce industrially) | tender, poner a secar (clothes to dry) | dislocar (a joint) | dar fuera (to give work out of the premises) | molestar (to bother, to annoy) | desconcertar (to disconcert) | enfadar (to irritate) | izar (flags) | MAR hacerse a la mar (to head seawards), botar, echar al mar (to launch) | COMM invertir, colocar (money) | SP poner fuera de combate (in boxing), eliminar (in cricket, in baseball) ‖ — *to put o.s. out* molestarse; *don't put yourself out on my account* no se moleste usted por mí ‖ *to put the washing out to dry* poner a secar la ropa ‖ **to put over** hacer aceptar (idea, product) | aplazar, diferir (to postpone) | conseguir (to succeed) | comunicar, hacer comprender (to communicate) ‖ — FIG *to put one over on s.o.* engañar a alguien ‖ *to put o.s. over* impresionar, causar impresión ‖ *to*

put through hacer pasar (suffering) | hacer aceptar (a proposal) | hacer aprobar (a bill) | lleva a cabo (a business deal) | poner; *to put through a telephone call to Madrid* poner una conferencia a Madrid | poner con; *put me through to this number* póngame con este número de teléfono || — *to put s.o. through an examination* hacer sufrir un examen a alguien || FAM *to put s.o. through it* hacerle pasar un mal rato a uno || ***to put to*** enganchar (to harness, to couple) || ***to put together*** unir, reunir, juntar (to join) | comparar (facts) | MATH sumar | confeccionar (a dress) | TECH ensamblar, acoplar (pieces) | montar (a machine) || — FIG *to put two and two together* atar cabos || ***to put up*** levantar (the window of a wagon, one's hand) | colgar, poner (to hang up); *to put up a curtain* colgar una cortina | recogerse (one's hair) | subirse (one's collar) | izar (flag) | oponer (resistance) | librar (a fight) | aumentar, subir (prices) | alojar, hospedar (to provide lodgings); *I can't put you up* no puedo alojarle | alojarse (to lodge); *I put up at a small hotel* me alojo en un hotel pequeño | fijar, pegar (to post up); *to put up a poster* fijar un cartel | colocar, poner (a ladder) | empaquetar, embalar, envolver (to pack) | apostar (to stake money) | COMM proporcionar, dar, poner (funds); *to put up the money for an undertaking* poner el dinero para una empresa | colgar (the telephone receiver) | abrir (umbrella) | envainar (a sword) | construir (to build); *this building was put up in ten months* este edificio fue construido en diez meses | preparar (meal, etc.) | levantar (partridge, etc.) | informar, decir (to inform); *to put s.o. up to a thing* informar a alguien de algo, decir algo a alguien | representar, dar (a play) | dar, ofrecer (prize) | incitar, impulsar (to incite); *they put me up to do it* me incitaron a hacerlo | FAM tramar, urdir, preparar (a dirty trick), inventar (a yarn) || JUR presentar la candidatura de, proponer (s.o. as a candidate), presentar su candidatura, presentarse (o.s.),presentar (a petition) | AUT aparcar (a car) | US poner en conserva, conservar (to preserve fruit, etc.) || — *put them up!* ¡manos arriba! || *to put up a prayer to* rezar a || *to put up banns* correr las amonestaciones || *to put up for auction* subastar, sacar a subasta || *to put up for sale* poner en venta || *to put up with* aguantar, soportar (to stand, to bear), arreglárselas con, conformarse con, contentarse con (to content o.s. with) || ***to put upon*** engañar (to deceive) | molestar (to bother).
— OBSERV Pret y pp ***put***.

putative ['pju:tətiv] *adj* putativo, va (relation) || supuesto, ta (supposed).

put-down ['put,daun] *n* FAM corte *m*.

put-off ['put,ɔf] *n* aplazamiento *m* (postponement).

put-on ['put,ɔn] *n* afectación *f*.

put-out ['putaut] *n* SP eliminación *f* (in baseball).

putrefaction [,pju:tri'fækʃən] *n* putrefacción *f*.

putrefiable ['pju:trifaiəbl] *adj* putrescible.

putrefied ['pju:trifaid] *adj* putrefacto, ta.

putrefy ['pju:trifai] *vt* pudrir, podrir.
◆ *vi* pudrirse, podrirse || MED supurar | gangrenarse || FIG corromperse, pudrirse.

putrescence [pju:'tresns] *n* putrefacción *f*.

putrescent [pju:θtresnt] *adj* putrescente.

putrescible [pju'tresibl] *adj* putrescible.

putrid ['pju:trid] *adj* en putrefacción, pútrido, da; podrido, da; putrefacto, ta (rotten) || FIG depravado, da (depraved) || FAM asqueroso, sa (dirty) | malísimo, ma (very bad) || MED gangrenoso, sa.

putridity [pju:'triditi]; **putridness** ['pju:tridnis] *n* putridez *f*, putrefacción *f*.

putsch [putʃ] *n* golpe *m* de Estado, alzamiento *m*, pronunciamiento *m*, "putsch" *m*.

putt [pʌt] *n* SP golpe *m* corto, tiro *m* al hoyo, "put" *m* (in golf).

putt [pʌt] *vt* SP dar un golpe corto a, tirar al hoyo (the ball).

puttee ['pʌti] *n* polaina *f*.

putter ['pʌtə*] *n* SP palo *m* para los golpes cortos, "putter" *m* (in golf).

putter [pʌtə*] *vi* US ⟶**potter.**

putting ['putiŋ] *n* colocación *f* || COMM concesión *f* (of shares) || FIG presentación *f* || puesta *f*; *putting into cultivation, into orbit, into service* puesta en cultivo, en órbita, en servicio || — *putting about* puesta *f* en circulación (of rumours) || *putting away* colocación *f*, ahorro *m* (of money), colocación *f* en orden (of things), alejamiento *m* (removal) || *putting back* colocación *f* en su sitio (of things), aplazamiento *m* (postponement), regreso *m* al puerto (of a boat), retraso *m* (delay) || *putting by* ahorro *m* (of money) || *putting down* inscripción *f* (in writing), sofocación *f* (of rebellion), rebajamiento *m* (of pride), fondeo *m* (of a buoy) || *putting forth* publicación *f* (of a book), despliegue *m* (display) || *putting forward* adelanto *m* (of a clock), presentación *f*, propuesta *f* (of a theory), exposición *f* || *putting in* introducción *f* (introduction), candidatura *f* (application), presentación *f* (of a legal document), escala *f* (for a boat), ejecución *f* (of an embargo) || *putting off* aplazamiento *m* (postponement) || *putting on* aumento *m*, subida *f* (of prices), adelanto *m* (of a clock), encendido *m* (of light), puesta *f* en marcha (of radio, record player, etc.), colocación *f* (of a dress), montaje *m* (of a play), puesta *f* en servicio (of trains), frenado *m* (of brakes), afectación *f* || *putting out* expulsión *f* (ejection), colocación *f* (of money), extinción *f* (of fire), alargamiento *m* (of arm), luxación *f* (of shoulder) || SP *putting the shot* o *the weight* el lanzamiento del peso || *putting through* conexión *f* (telephone), éxito *m* (success), realización *f* (of a deal) || *putting to* enganche *m* || *putting together* acoplamiento *m*, ensambladura *f* (of pieces), montaje *m* (of machine), comparación *f* (of facts) || MAR *putting to sea* salida *f* || *putting up* colocación *f* (hanging up), alojamiento *m* (lodging), empaquetado *m*, embalaje *m* (packing), aumento *m*, subida *f* (of prices), colocación *f* (of posters), publicación *f* (of bills, of banns), presentación *f* (of a candidate), construcción *f* (building), garaje *m* (of cars).

putting ['pʌtiŋ] *n* SP deporte *m* parecido al golf || *putting green* campo *m* más pequeño que el utilizado para jugar al golf.

putty ['pʌti] *n* masilla *f* (glazier's) || *putty knife* espátula *f* para enmasillar.

putty ['pʌti] *vt* poner masilla a, enmasillar.

put-up ['put'ʌp] *adj* FAM preparado de antemano; *it's a put-up job* es una cosa preparada de antemano | amañado, da (match, etc.).

put-upon ['putə'pɔn] *adj* engañado, da.

puzzle ['pʌzl] *n* enigma *m*, misterio *m*, lío *m* (a problem) || perplejidad *f* (bewilderment) || rompecabezas *m inv* (game); *chinese puzzle* rompecabezas chino || acertijo *m*, adivinanza *f* (riddle) || — *crossword puzzle* crucigrama *m* || *jigsaw puzzle* rompecabezas *m inv* || *to be in a puzzle* estar hecho un lío || *your mother is a real puzzle to me* no acabo de entender a su madre.

puzzle ['pʌzl] *vt* desconcertar, dejar perplejo (to bewilder) || — *he was puzzled how to answer the letter* no sabía cómo contestar la carta || *to puzzle out* descifrar (a letter), esclarecer, aclarar (a mystery), resolver, solucionar (a problem).
◆ *vi* romperse la cabeza, devanarse los sesos [para resolver]; *to puzzle over a problem* romperse la cabeza con un problema.

puzzled [-d] *adj* perplejo, ja; desconcertado, da.

puzzlement [-mənt] *n* perplejidad *f*, desconcierto *m* (bewilderment).

puzzler [-lə*] *n* enigma *m*, misterio *m* || FAM pega *f*; *to ask s.o. puzzlers* plantearle a uno pegas || *that's a puzzler!* ¡qué pregunta más difícil!, ¡qué difícil!

puzzling [-liŋ] *adj* misterioso, sa; enigmático, ca || *it is puzzling that he didn't come* es extraño que no haya venido.

PVC *abbr of [polyvinyl chloride]* PVC, cloruro de polivinilo.

pycnometer [pik'nɔmitə*] *n* picnómetro *m*.

pyelitis [paiə'laitis] *n* MED pielitis *f*.

pygmaean [pig'mi:ən] *adj* pigmeo, a.

Pygmalion [pig'meiljən] *pr n* Pigmalión *m*.

pygmean [pig'mi:ən] *adj* pigmeo, a.

pygmy ['pigmi] *adj/n* enano, na (dwarf).

Pygmy ['pigmi] *adj/n* pigmeo, a.

pyjamas [pə'dʒɑ:məz] *pl n* pijama *m sing*.

pyknic ['piknik] *adj* pícnico, ca.

pylon ['pailən] *n* pilón *m* (of an Egyptian temple) || ELECTR poste *m*, torre *f* metálica (for cables, etc.).

pyloric [pai'lɔrik] *adj* pilórico, ca.

pylorus [pai'lɔ:rəs] *n* ANAT píloro *m*.
— OBSERV El plural de *pylorus* es *pylori*.

pyorrhoea; *US* **pyorrhea** [,paiə'riə] *n* MED piorrea *f*.

pyramid [pirəmid] *n* ARCH & MATH pirámide *f*.

pyramidal [pi'ræmidl] *adj* piramidal.

pyramidion [pirə'midiən] *n* ARCH piramidión *m*.

pyre ['paiə*] *n* pira *f*, hoguera *f* (for burning).

Pyrenean [,pirə'ni:ən] *adj* pirenaico, ca.

Pyrenees [,pirə'ni:z] *pl prn* GEOGR Pirineos *m*.

pyrethrum [pəi'ri:θrəm] *n* BOT pelitre *m*.

pyretic [pai'retik] *adj* pirético, ca.

Pyrex ['paireks] *n* CULIN pirex *m*.

pyrexia [pai'reksiə] *n* MED pirexia *f*.

pyrheliometer [pə:hi:li'ɔmitə*] *n* pirheliómetro *m*.

pyrite ['pairait] *n* MIN pirita *f*.

pyrography [pai'rɔgrəfi]; **pyrogravure** [pairəgrə'vjuə*] *n* pirograbado *m*.

pyrolysis [pai'rɔlisis] *n* CHEM pirolisis *f*.

pyromancy ['pairəumænsi] *n* piromancia *f*.

pyromania [,pairəu'meinjə] *n* piromanía *f*.

pyromaniacal [,pairəumə'naiəkəl] *adj* pirómano, na.

pyrometer [pai'rɔmitə*] *n* pirómetro *m*.

pyrometry [pai'rɔmitri] *n* pirometría *f*.

pyrophosphate [,pairəu'fɔsfeit] *n* CHEM pirofosfato *m* (salt, ester).

pyrophosphoric [,pairəufɔs'fɔrik] *adj* CHEM pirofosfórico (acid).

pyrosis [pai'rəusis] *n* MED pirosis *f*.

pyrosphere ['pairəsfi:ə*] *n* GEOL pirosfera *f*.

pyrotechnic [,pairəu'teknik] *adj* pirotécnico, ca || *pyrotechnic display* fuegos *m pl* artificiales.

pyrotechnics [-s] *n* pirotecnia *f*.

pyrotechnist [ˌpairəu'teknist] *n* pirotécnico *m* artificiero *m*.

pyrotechny [ˌpairəu'tekni] *n* pirotecnia *f*.

pyroxene [pai'rɔksiːn] *n* piroxeno *m*.

pyroxylin; pyroxyline [pai'rɔksilin] *n* piroxilina *f*, algodón *m* pólvora.

pyrrhic ['piric] *adj* pírrico, ca; *pyrrhic victory* victoria pírrica.
◆ *n* pirriquio *m* (poetry).

Pyrrhus ['pirəs] *pr n* Pirro *m*.

Pythagoras [pai'θægəræs] *pr n* Pitágoras *m*.

Pythagorean [paiˌθægə'riən] *adj/n* pitagórico, ca || *Pythagorean table* tabla pitagórica *or* de Pitágoras.

Pythia ['piθiə] *n* pitia *f*.

Pythian [-n] *adj* pitio, tia (of the oracle) || pítico, ca (of the games).

python ['paiθən] *n* pitón *m* (snake).

pythoness ['paiθənes] *n* pitonisa *f*.

pyx [piks] *n* REL copón *m*, píxide *f* || *pyx cloth* paño *m* de cáliz.

Q

q [kjuː] *n* q *f* (letter).

qua [kwei] *adv* como.

quack [kwæk] *adj* falso, sa ‖ de curandero (remedy) ‖ — *quack doctor* curandero *m* ‖ *quack powder* polvos *m pl* de la madre Celestina.
◆ *n* graznido *m* (of a duck) ‖ curandero *m* (fraudulent doctor) ‖ matasanos *m inv* (bad doctor) ‖ charlatán *m* (impostor).

quack [kwæk] *vi* graznar (the duck) ‖ FAM cotorrear (to chatter) | dárselas de listo (to show off).
◆ *vt* encomiar, ensalzar (a remedy, etc.).

quackery [kwækəri] *n* curandería *f*, curanderismo *m* (of a quack doctor) ‖ charlatanismo *m* (of an impostor).

quad [kwɔd] *n* ⟶ **quadrangle** & **quadrat.**
◆ *pl* cuatrillizos, zas (quadruplets).

quadragenarian [ˌkwɔdrədʒəˈnɛəriən] *adj/n* cuadragenario, ria.

Quadragesima [ˌkwɔdrəˈdʒesimə] *n* REL cuadragésima *f*; *Quadragesima Sunday* domingo de la Cuadragésima.

quadrangle [ˈkwɔdræŋgl]; **quad** [kwɔd] *n* MATH cuadrilátero *m* (figure with four sides) | cuadrángulo *m* (figure with four angles) ‖ patio *m* (of a college).

quadrant [ˈkwɔdrənt] *n* cuadrante *m*.

quadraphonic [ˌkwɔdrəˈfɔnik] *adj* cuadrafónico, ca (of sound reproduction).

quadrat [ˈkwɔdrit]; **quad** [kwɔd] *n* PRINT cuadratín *m*.

quadrate [kwɔˈdreit] *vi* cuadrar (*with* con).
◆ *vt* cuadrar ‖ hacer cuadrar (*to, with* con).

quadratic [kwəˈdrætik] *adj* MATH cuadrático, ca; de segundo grado.
◆ *n* MATH ecuación *f* de segundo grado.

quadrature [ˈkwɔdrətʃə*] *n* cuadratura *f*.

quadrennial [ˌkwɔˈdreniəl] *adj* cuadrienal.

quadrennium [kwɔˈdreniːəm] *n* cuadrienio *m*, cuatrienio *m*.
— OBSERV El plural de la palabra *quadrennium* es *quadrenniums* o *quadrennia*.

quadriceps [ˈkwɔdriseps] *n* ANAT cuadríceps *m*.

quadriga [kwəˈdriːgə] *n* cuadriga *f*.
— OBSERV El plural de la palabra inglesa es *quadrigae*.

quadrigeminal [kwɔdriˈdʒeminəl] *adj* ANAT cuadrigémino.

quadrilateral [ˌkwɔdriˈlætərəl] *adj* cuadrilátero, ra.
◆ *n* cuadrilátero *m*.

quadrille [kwəˈdril] *n* cuadrilla *f* (dance) ‖ cuatrillo *m* (card game).

quadrillion [kwɔˈdriljən] *n* cuatrillón *m*.
— OBSERV Esta cifra equivale a 10^{24} en Gran Bretaña y en España y a 10^{15} en Estados Unidos.

quadripartite [ˌkwɔdriˈpɑːtait] *adj* cuadripartido, da; cuadripartito, ta; *quadripartite convention* convenio cuadripartito.

quadrisyllabic [ˈkwɔdrisiˈlæbik] *adj* cuatrisílabo, ba.

quadrisyllable [ˌkwɔdriˈsiləbl] *n* cuatrisílabo *m*.

quadrivalent [ˌkwɔdriˈveilənt] *adj* CHEM tetravalente, cuadrivalente.

quadrivium [kwɔˈdriviəm] *n* cuadrivio *m* (in medieval universities).
— OBSERV El plural de *quadrivium* es *quadrivia*.

quadroon [kwɔˈdruːn] *n* cuarterón, ona.

quadrumane [ˈkwɔdrumein] *n* cuadrumano *m*.

quadrumanous [kwɔˈdruːmənəs] *adj* cuadrumano, na.

quadruped [ˈkwɔdruped] *adj* cuadrúpedo, da.
◆ *n* cuadrúpedo *m*.

quadruple [ˈkwɔdrupl] *adj* cuádruple ‖ MUS *quadruple measure* o *time* compás *m* de dos por cuatro.
◆ *n* cuádruplo *m*.

quadruple [ˈkwɔdrupl] *vt/vi* cuadruplicar, cuadriplicar.

quadruplets [kwɔdruplits] *pl n* cuatrillizos, zas.

quadruplicate [kwɔˈdruːplikit] *adj* cuadruplicado, da; cuadriplicado, da ‖ *in quadruplicate* en cuatro ejemplares, por cuadruplicado.

quadruplicate [kwɔˈdruːplikeit] *vt* sacar cuatro copias de (to make four copies of) ‖ cuadruplicar, cuadriplicar (to quadruple).

quadruplication [kwɔdruːpliˈkeiʃən] *n* cuadruplicación *f*.

quaestor [ˈkwiːstə*] *n* cuestor *m*.

quaestorship [ˈkwiːstəʃip] *n* cuestura *f*.

quaff [kwɑːf] *vt/vi* beber [a grandes tragos].

quag [kwæg] *n* ⟶ **quagmire.**

quaggy [-i] *adj* pantanoso, sa; cenagoso, sa.

quagmire [ˈkwægmaiə*]; **quag** [kwæg] *n* tremedal *m*, ciénaga *f*, cenagal *m* (boggy ground) ‖ FIG atolladero *m*.

quail [kweil] *n* codorniz *f* (bird).

quail [kweil] *vi* acobardarse (*before* ante).

quaint [kweint] *adj* pintoresco, ca (picturesque); *a quaint little village* un pueblecito pintoresco ‖ original, singular; *a quaint person* una persona original ‖ extraño, ña (odd); *a quaint tale* una historia extraña.

quaintness [-nis] *n* lo pintoresco (of a place, of a custom, etc.) ‖ originalidad *f*, singularidad *f* (of a person) ‖ lo extraño, rareza *f* (oddity).

quake [kweik] *n* temblor *m*.

quake [kweik] *vi* temblar (to shake violently); *he was quaking with fear, with cold* temblaba de miedo, de frío; *the earth quaked* tembló la tierra ‖ estremecerse (to shake inwardly) ‖ — *he is quaking at the knees* le flaquean las piernas ‖ FAM *to quake in one's shoes* temblar como un azogado.

Quaker [ˈkweikə*] *n* REL cuáquero, ra.

Quakerism [-rizəm] *n* REL cuaquerismo *m*.

quaking bog [kweikiŋˈbɔg] *n* tremedal *m*.

quaky [ˈkweiki] *adj* tembloroso, sa.

qualification [ˌkwɔlifiˈkeiʃən] *n* reserva *f*, restricción *f*; *we can't accept his statement without qualification* podemos aceptar su declaración sin reserva ‖ aptitud *f*, capacidad *f*, competencia *f*; *to have the necessary qualifications for a post* tener las aptitudes requeridas *or* la competencia requerida para un puesto | requisito *m*; *the qualifications for membership of a club* los requisitos para ser miembro de un club ‖ título *m*; *applicants must bring their qualifications with them* los candidatos tienen que traer sus títulos.

qualified [ˈkwɔlifaid] *adj* competente; *qualified persons* personas competentes ‖ capacitado, da; *he is not qualified to do that job* no está capacitado para hacer ese trabajo ‖ cualificado, da; calificado, da (skilled) ‖ que tiene título, titulado, da; *qualified expert* experto que tiene título ‖ con reservas; *they gave the scheme their qualified approval* aprobaron el proyecto con reservas ‖ limitado, da; restringido, da; *in a qualified sense* en un sentido limitado ‖ JUR capacitado, da; *he is qualified to vote* está capacitado para votar.

qualify [ˈkwɔlifai] *vt* capacitar (to entitle); *he is not qualified to teach English* no está capacitado para enseñar inglés ‖ capacitar, habilitar, dar derecho; *residence qualifies you for membership* la residencia le capacita para hacerse socio ‖ calificar; *would you qualify his behaviour as offensive?* ¿calificaría su comportamiento de ofensivo? ‖ modificar (to modify) ‖ mitigar, atenuar (to mitigate) ‖ limitar, restringir (to limit) ‖ GRAMM calificar; *adverbs qualify verbs* los adverbios califican los verbos ‖ JUR habilitar, capacitar ‖ — *to qualify one's acceptance* aceptar con reservas ‖ *to qualify o.s. for a job* adquirir la competencia *or* sacar los títulos necesarios para un puesto.
◆ *vi* capacitarse ‖ estudiar; *to qualify for medicine* estudiar medicina ‖ sacar el título de; *to qualify as a doctor* sacar el título de médico ‖ satisfacer los requisitos (for a post, for a vote, etc.) ‖ SP clasificarse.

qualifying [-iŋ] *adj* calificativo, va (adjective) ‖ eliminatorio, ria (round, exam).

qualitative [ˈkwɔlitətiv] *adj* cualitativo, va; *qualitative analysis* análisis cualitativo.

quality [ˈkwɔliti] *n* calidad *f*; *of good, of poor quality* de buena, de mala calidad; *we aim at quality rather than quantity* preferimos la calidad a la cantidad ‖ calidad *f*, clase *f*, categoría *f* (degree of excellence); *goods of the first quality* géneros de primera calidad ‖ calidad *f* (status); *person of quality* persona de calidad; *in quality of* en calidad de ‖ cualidad *f* (attribute); *she has many good qualities* tiene muchas buenas cualidades ‖ don *m*; *he has the quality of inspiring confidence* tiene el don de inspirar confianza ‖ MUS timbre *m* ‖ — *quality control* control *m* de calidad ‖ *the quality* la nobleza (nobility), la flor y nata (the best).

◆ *adj* de calidad; *quality goods* productos de calidad.

qualm [kwɑːm] *n* MED náusea *f*, ansias *f pl* (nausea) | mareo *m* (at sea) || FIG escrúpulo *m*; *to have qualms about doing sth.* no tener ningún escrúpulo en hacer algo | remordimiento *m*; *qualms of conscience* remordimientos de conciencia | aprensión *f*, inquietud *f* (worry) | duda *f*, incertidumbre *f* (doubt).

qualmish [-iʃ] *adj* MED que tiene náuseas *or* ansias || FIG escrupuloso, sa | preocupado, da; lleno de aprensión (worried) | dudoso, sa; incierto, ta (uncertain).

quandary ['kɔndəri] *n* dilema *m*; *to be in a quandary* estar en un dilema || apuro *m*, aprieto *m* (difficulty).

quango ['kwæŋgəu] *n* organismo *m* estatal semiautónomo [en Gran Bretaña].

quanta ['kwɔntə] *pl n* ⟶ **quantum.**

quantic ['kwɔntik] *adj* cuántico, ca.

quantification [kwɔntifi'keiʃən] *n* cuantificación *f*.

quantify ['kwɔntifai] *vt* determinar la cantidad de, cuantificar (to determine the quantity of) | PHIL cuantificar.

quantitative ['kwɔntitətiv] *adj* cuantitativo, va; *quantitative analysis* análisis cuantitativo.

quantity ['kwɔntiti] *n* cantidad *f*; *a small quantity of cement* una pequeña cantidad de cemento; *to buy in large quantities* comprar en grandes cantidades || gran cantidad *f*; *a quantity of jewellery* una gran cantidad de joyas || MATH, GRAMM & PHIL cantidad *f* || — FAM *quantity production* producción *f* en serie || *quantity surveyor* aparejador *m* | MATH *unknown quantity* incógnita *f*.

quantum ['kwɔntəm] *n* parte *f* (share) || FIG *quantum leap* gran salto *m*, gran cambio *m* || PHYS quantum *m*, cuanto *m* || — FIG *quantum leap* gran salto *m*, gran cambio *m* || PHYS *quantum number* número cuántico || *quantum theory* teoría *f* de los quanta *or* de los cuanta *or* cuántica.

— OBSERV El plural de la palabra *quantum* es *quanta*.

quarantine ['kwɔrəntiːn] *n* cuarentena *f* (period of isolation); *to put in quarantine* poner en cuarentena || *quarantine service* servicio *m* de sanidad.

quarantine ['kwɔrəntiːn] *vt* poner en cuarentena.

quark [kwɑːk] *n* PHYS cuarc *m*, quark *m*.

quarrel ['kwɔrəl] *n* riña *f*, disputa *f*, pelea *f*, camorra *f* (angry dispute) || — *I have no quarrel with him* no tengo nada en contra suya || *to espouse* o *to take up s.o.'s quarrel* tomar el partido de alguien || *to have a quarrel with* pelearse con, reñir con || *to make up a quarrel* hacer las paces, reconciliarse || *to pick a quarrel with* tener una pelea con || *to try to pick a quarrel with s.o.* buscar camorra con alguien.

quarrel ['kɔrəl] *vi* pelearse, pelear, reñir (to argue); *children sometimes quarrel* a veces los niños se pelean || reñir (to fall out) || regañar; *he quarrelled with me for having done the wrong thing* me regañó por haber hecho lo que no debía || quejarse (*with* de) (to complain).

quarreller; *US* **quarreler** [-ə*] *n* pendenciero, ra; peleón, ona.

quarrelling; *US* **quarreling** [-iŋ] *n* disputas *f pl* (quarrels).

◆ *adj* pendenciero, ra; peleón, ona.

quarrelsome [-səm] *adj* peleón, ona; pendenciero, ra (inclined to quarrel) || enfadadizo, za (quick-tempered).

quarry ['kwɔri] *n* MIN cantera *f* || presa *f* (in hunting) || FIG mina *f*, cantera *f* (source of information, etc.) | presa *f* (prey) | persona *f* acorralada (pursued person) || (ant) encarne *m*, encarna *f* (fleshing of the hounds) || FIG *he became the quarry of the nation's police force* fue acorralado por la policía de todo el país.

quarry ['kwɔri] *vt* MIN extraer, sacar || FIG sacar (information from books).

◆ *vi* MIN explotar una cantera || FIG buscar información.

quarryman [-mən] *n* cantero *m*, picapedrero *m*.

— OBSERV El plural de *quarryman* es *quarrymen*.

quarry tile [-tail] *n* baldosa *f* sin vitrificar.

quart [kwɔːt] *n* cuarto *m* de galón (measure).

quart [kɑːt] *n* ⟶ **quarte.**

quartan ['kwɔːtn] *adj* MED cuartanal.

◆ *n* MED cuartana *f*.

quarte; **quart** [kɑːt] *n* SP cuarta *f* (in fencing) || cuarta *f* (in card games).

quarter ['kwɔːtə*] *n* cuarto *m* (of hour, circle, century, etc.); *quarter of an hour* cuarto de hora; *three quarters* tres cuartos; *to strike the quarters* dar los cuartos; *an hour and a quarter* una hora y cuarto; *a quarter past nine* las nueve y cuarto; *a quarter to seven* las siete menos cuarto || cuarto *m* (of a pound); *a pound and a quarter* una libra y un cuarto || cuarta parte *f*, cuarto *m*; *a quarter of an apple* la cuarta parte de una manzana; *a quarter of the film was boring* una cuarta parte de la película era aburrida; *what's a quarter of 64?* ¿qué es la cuarta parte de 64? || trimestre *m*; *during the first quarter of this year* durante el primer trimestre de este año || alquiler *m* trimestral (rent) || ASTR cuarto *m* (moon); *first, last quarter* cuarto creciente, menguante || SP tiempo *m* (period of playing time) | cuarto *m* de milla, cuatrocientos metros *m pl* (race) || cuarto *m* (of beef, etc.) || barrio *m* (district); *the old quarter of the town* el barrio viejo de la ciudad || MAR cuarta *f* (division of the compass) | cuarto *m* de braza (fourth part of the fathom) | aleta *f* (of a ship) | dirección *f* (of the wind) || FIG lado *m*; *don't look for help from that quarter* no busques ayuda por aquel lado | parte *f*, región *f* (region) | fuente *f*; *information from a reliable quarter* información de fuente fidedigna || cuartel *m*; *to give no quarter to the enemy* no dar cuartel al enemigo || *US* cuarto *m* de dólar, veinticinco centavos *m pl* (value and coin) || HERALD cuartel *m* (division of a shield) || — *it is a quarter as large* es cuatro veces menos ancho || *to ask for quarter, to cry quarter* pedir tregua || *to give quarter to* dar cuartel a || *what quarter is the wind in?* ¿de qué lado sopla el viento?

◆ *pl* cuartos *m* traseros (of an animal) || MAR puesto *m sing* de combate || alojamiento *m sing* (lodgings) || residencia *f sing*, domicilio *m sing*; *to shift one's quarters* cambiar de domicilio || MIL residencia *f sing*; *officers' quarters* residencia de oficiales | cuartel *m sing* (for soldiers); *winter quarters* cuartel de invierno || FAM trasero *m sing* (bottom) || — *at close quarters* muy cerca; *to explode at close quarters* explotar muy cerca; de cerca; *to see s.o. at close quarters* ver a alguien de cerca; cuerpo a cuerpo (to fight) || FIG *from all quarters, from every quarter* de todas partes || *from all quarters of the globe* de todas las partes del mundo || *in high quarters* en las altas esferas || *living quarters* alojamiento, residencia || *to take up one's quarters at* o *in* alojarse en.

quarter ['kwɔːtə*] *vt* dividir en cuartos, cuartear (to divide into four parts) || MIL acuartelar (to lodge troops) || alojar (to lodge) || descuartizar (meat) || HERALD cuartelar || HIST descuartizar (the body of a criminal).

◆ *vi* acuartelarse (troops) || alojarse (to lodge).

quarterback [-bæk] *n* SP quarterback *m* [en fútbol americano].

quarter binding [-'baindiŋ] *n* media pasta *f*, encuadernación *f* a la holandesa.

quarter-bound [-baund] *adj* encuadernado a la holandesa *or* con media pasta.

quarter day [-dei] *n* primer día *m* del trimestre.

quarterdeck; **quarter-deck** [-dek] *n* MAR alcázar *m*.

quarterfinal [-'fainl] *n* SP cuarto *m* de final.

quarter hour [-auə*] *n* *US* cuarto *m* de hora.

quartering [-riŋ] *n* división *f* en cuatro partes (partition) || corte *m* a escuadra (of a log) || descuartizamiento *m* (of a criminal) || alojamiento *m* (lodging) || MIL acuartelamiento *m* || HERALD cuartel *m*.

quarter light [-lait] *n* ventanilla *f* trasera giratoria (in a car).

quarterly [-li] *adj* trimestral.

◆ *adv* trimestralmente, cada tres meses.

◆ *n* publicación *f* trimestral.

quartermaster [-ˌmɑːstə*] *n* MAR cabo *m* de la Marina || MIL oficial *m* de intendencia.

Quartermaster Corps [-ˌmɑːstə*kɔː*] *n* MIL Servicio *m* de Intendencia.

quartermaster general [-ˌmɑːstə*'dʒenərəl] *n* MIL intendente *m* general.

quartermaster sergeant [-ˌmɑːstə*'sɑːdʒənt] *n* MIL sargento *m* mayor.

quartern ['kwɔːtəːn] *n* barra *f* de pan de cuatro libras (loaf) || cuarta parte *f*, cuarto *m* (quarter).

quarter note ['kwɔːtəˌnəut] *n* MUS negra *f*.

quarter-phase ['kwɔːtəˌfeiz] *adj* bifásico, ca.

quarter right ['kwɔːtəˌrait] *n* MIL media vuelta *f* a la derecha.

quarter round ['kwɔːtəraund] *n* ARCH cuarto bocel *m*, óvolo *m*.

quarter sessions ['kwɔːtə'seʃənz] *pl n* audiencia *f sing* trimestral.

quarterstaff ['kwɔːtə*stɑːf] *n* barra *f* (stick).

— OBSERV El plural de esta palabra es *quarterstaves*.

quarter tone ['kwɔːtətəun] *n* cuarto *m* de tono.

quartet; **quartette** [kwɔː'tet] *n* MUS cuarteto *m*.

quartile ['kwɔːtail] *n* MATH cuartila *f*, cuartil *m*.

quarto ['kwɔːtəu] *n* en cuarto *m*, libro *m* en cuarto.

quartz [kwɔːts] *n* MIN cuarzo *m*.

quartzite [θkwɔːtˌsait] *n* MIN cuarcita *f*.

quartzose ['kwɔːtsəus]; **quartzous** ['kwɔːtsəs] *adj* cuarzoso, sa.

quasar ['kweizə*] *n* ASTR quásar *m*.

quash [kwɔʃ] *vt* JUR anular || reprimir, sofocar, ahogar (a feeling, an uprising); *to quash a rebellion* reprimir una rebelión.

quasi ['kwɑːziː] *adv* cuasi, casi || — JUR *quasi contract* cuasicontrato *m* || *quasi delict* cuasidelito *m*.

Quasimodo Sunday [ˌkwɑːzi'məudəu'sʌndi] *n* Domingo *m* de Cuasimodo.

quassia ['kwɔʃə] *n* BOT cuasia *f*.

quatercentenary [ˌkwætəsen'tiːnəri] *n* cuarto centenario *m*.

quaternary [kwə'təːnəri] *adj* cuaternario, ria.

◆ *n* GEOL cuaternario *m*.

quaternion [kwə'təːnjən] *n* MATH cuaternio *m*, cuaternión *m*.

quatrain ['kwɔtrein] *n* cuarteto *m* (poetry).

quatrefoil ['kætrəfɔil] *n* ARCH cuatrifolio *m*.

quaver ['kweivə*] *n* MUS corchea *f* (note) | trino *m* (trill) || temblor *m* (of the voice) || *with a quaver in his voice* con voz trémula.

quaver ['kweivə*] *vi* temblar (voice) || MUS hacer trinos, trinar.
◆ *vt* decir con voz trémula.

quavering [-riŋ]; **quavery** [-i] *adj* tembloroso, sa; trémulo, la; *in a quavering voice* con voz temblorosa.

quay [ki:] *n* muelle *m* (wharf).

quayage [-idʒ] *n* derechos *m pl* de muelle, muellaje *m* (fees) || espacio *m* disponible en un muelle (mooring space).

quayside [-said] *n* muelle *m* (wharf).

quean [kwi:n] *n* mujer *f* perdida (woman) || FIG marica *m* (homosexual).

queasiness ['kwi:zinis] *n* náuseas *f pl*, bascas *f pl* (sick feeling) || FIG escrupulosidad *f*, escrúpulos *m pl*.

queasy ['kwi:zi] *adj* mareado, da; con náuseas (feeling sick) || repugnante, que da náuseas (food) || delicado, da (easily upset) || inquieto, ta; desasosegado, da (uneasy) || FIG escrupuloso, sa (scrupulous) | complicado, da; difícil (difficult).

Quebec [kwi'bek] *pr n* GEOGR Quebec.

quebracho [ke'bra:tʃəu] *n* BOT quebracho *m*.

Quechua ['ketʃuə] *n* quechua *m* & *f*, quichua *m* & *f* (people, language).

Quechuan ['ketʃuən] *adj* quechua, quichua.

queen [kwi:n] *n* reina *f*; *Queen Elizabeth* la reina Isabel; *Queen mother* reina madre; *Queen consort* reina consorte; *Queen regent* reina regente; *Queen dowager* reina viuda || FIG reina *f*; *the queen of jazz* la reina del jazz || ZOOL abeja *f* maestra *or* maesa, reina *f* (of bees) || dama *f*, reina *f* (playing card) || reina *f* (chess) || FAM marica *m* (homosexual) || — FAM *Queen Anne is dead* eso es archisabido || *queen of the meadows* reina de los prados (flower) || ARCH *queen post* péndola *f* || JUR *Queen's Counsel* consejero de la Reina.

queen [kwi:n] *vt* coronar (in chess) || coronar reina (a woman).
◆ *vi* coronarse || FIG *to queen it* darse aires, presumir.

queen bee ['kwi:n'bi:] *n* ZOOL abeja *f* maestra *or* maesa, reina *f*.

queenliness [-linis] *n* majestad *f*, realeza *f*.

queenly [-li]; **queenlike** [-'laik] *adj* regio, gia; de reina, majestuoso, sa.

queer [kwiə*] *adj* raro, ra; extraño, ña (strange); *a queer fish* un tipo raro || curioso, sa (peculiar) || misterioso, sa; turbio, bia; sospechoso, sa (suspicious) || indispuesto, ta; malo, la (unwell) || FAM maricón, marica (homosexual) || — FAM *queer in the head* chiflado, da || *to feel queer* no encontrarse bien, estar indispuesto *or* pachucho.
◆ *n* FAM maricón *m*, marica *m* (homosexual) || US FAM moneda *f* falsa.

queer [kwiə*] *vt* fastidiar, estropear; *to queer s.o.'s pitch* estropear los proyectos de alguien.

queerish [-riʃ] *adj* raro, ra; extraño, ña (strange) || FAM pachucho, cha; malo, la (ill).

queerness [-nis] *n* rareza *f* || FAM indisposición *f*.

quell [kwel] *vt* calmar, mitigar (to mitigate); *to quell one's pains* calmar los dolores || dominar, controlar (fear) || reprimir, sofocar (rebellion) || suprimir (to suppress).

quench [kwentʃ] *vt* apagar (flames) || aplacar, mitigar, apagar (thirst) || TECH templar (hot steel) || ELECTR suprimir (sparks) || FIG sofocar (desire) | apagar, enfriar, aplacar (enthusiasm) | reprimir (emotion) || FAM callar (to shut up).

quenchable [-əbl] *adj* apagable.

quencher [-ə*] *n* bebida *f* refrescante.

quenchless [-lis] *adj* inextinguible, inapagable.

querist ['kwiərist] *n* interrogador, ra.

quern [kwə:n] *n* molinillo *m* de mano.

querulous ['kweruləs] *adj* quejumbroso, sa.

query ['kwiəri] *n* pregunta *f* (question) || duda *f* (doubt) || signo *m* de interrogación (question mark) || FIG interrogante *m*.

query ['kwiəri] *vt* poner en duda, dudar de (to put in doubt) || preguntar (s.o.); *is it true?, he queried* ¿es verdad?, preguntó || US interrogar (to interrogate) || poner el signo de interrogación.
◆ *vi* hacer preguntas, interrogar || *to query whether* preguntarse si.

quest [kwest] *n* búsqueda *f*, busca *f* (search) || *in quest of* en busca de.

quest [kwest] *vt/vi* buscar.

question ['kwestʃən] *n* pregunta *f*; *to ask s.o. a question* hacer una pregunta a alguien; *indiscreet question* pregunta indiscreta; *to ply with questions* acosar con preguntas; *to put a written question* formular una pregunta por escrito; *questions and answers* preguntas y respuestas || problema *m* (in mathematics) || pregunta *f* (in an examination) || cuestión *f*, asunto *m*; *the question of capital punishment* la cuestión de la pena capital; *open question* asunto pendiente; *it is only a question of money* es sólo una cuestión de dinero; *debate on special questions* debate sobre asuntos especiales; *to raise a previous question* plantear una cuestión previa || problema *m* (problem); *that is the question* he aquí el problema; *the gipsy question* el problema gitano || interrogación *f* (interrogation) || cuestión *f* (torture) || — *ask a silly question and you will get a silly answer* a pregunta necia oídos sordos *or* de mercader || *begging the question* petición *f* de principio || *beside the question* que no viene al caso || *beyond all question, beyond question* fuera de toda duda, fuera de duda || *burning question* asunto candente || *committee on legal questions* comisión jurídica || *in question* de que se trata, en cuestión || *it is a question of a quarter of an hour* es cuestión de un cuarto de hora || *it is not out of the question that* es posible que || *out of all question* completamente imposible || *out of the question* imposible (impossible), ni hablar [de eso]; *please may I go out this evening? no, it is out of the question* por favor ¿puedo salir esta noche? no, ni hablar || *that's not the question* no se trata de eso || *there is no question about it* no ofrece la menor duda || *there is no question of going back now* ya no hay posibilidad de volverse atrás || *there was some question of* se habló de || *to call* o *to bring in question* poner en tela de juicio || *to come in question* merecer consideración || *to come into question* plantearse || *to make no question of* no dudar de || *to pop the question* declararse || *to put a question to s.o.* hacer una pregunta a alguien || *to put a question to the vote* poner *or* someter el problema a votación || *what is the question?* ¿de qué se trata? || *without question* sin duda.

question ['kwestʃən] *vt* preguntar; *to question a student* preguntar a un alumno || interrogar (the police, etc.) || poner en duda, dudar de (to query).

questionable ['kwestʃənəbl] *adj* dudoso, sa (doubtful) || discutible, controvertible; *it is a questionable matter* es una cosa discutible.

questionary ['kwestʃənəri] *n* cuestionario *m*.

questioner ['kwestʃənə*] *n* preguntador, ra (p us); interrogador, ra.

questioning ['kwestʃəniŋ] *adj* interrogativo, va.
◆ *n* preguntas *f pl* (questions) || interrogatorio *m* (by the police).

questionless ['kwestʃənlis] *adj* indiscutible, indudable.

question mark ['kwestʃənma:k] *n* signo *m or* punto de interrogación || FIG interrogante *m*.

question-master ['kwestʃən'ma:stə*]; **quiz-master** ['kwizma:stə*] *n* presentador, ra de un concurso.

questionnaire [,kwestiə'nεə*] *n* cuestionario *m*.

question time ['kwestʃəntaim] *n* ruegos y preguntas *m pl* (in Parliament).

questor ['kwi:stə*] *n* cuestor *m*.

quetzal [ket'sɔ:l] *n* quetzal *m*.

queue [kju:] *n* cola *f* (line); *they formed a queue at the ticket window* se pusieron en cola delante de la taquilla; *I was standing in a queue* estaba haciendo cola || coleta *f* (Chinaman's plait) INFORM cola *f*.

queue [kju:] *vi* hacer cola || *to queue up* hacer cola.

quibble ['kwibl] *n* sutileza *f* (subtlety) || subterfugio *m*, evasiva *f* (evasión) || pega *f*, objeción *f*.

quibble ['kwibl] *vi* sutilizar (to split hairs) || utilizar subterfugios (to equivocate) || ser quisquilloso (to find fault with).

quibbler [-ə*] *n* sofista *m* & *f*, casuista *m* & *f* (equivocator).

quibbling [-iŋ] *n* sutilezas *f pl*, sofismas *m pl*.

quiche [ki:ʃ] *n* CULIN quiche *f*.

quick [kwik] *adj* rápido, da (fast); *it is quicker to go through the garden* es más rápido ir por el jardín || vivo, va (alive, lively) || agudo, da (clever) || ágil (agile) || ligero, ra (of feet) || vivo, va (not dead) || pronto, ta (reply) || AGR vivo, va (hedge) || acelerado, da (pulse) || MIL acelerado, da (step) || movedizo, za (ground) || — FIG *as quick as a flash* como un relámpago || *quick temper* genio vivo || FIG *quick with child* embarazada (woman) || *to be quick* darse prisa, apresurarse || *to be quick about sth.* hacer algo rápidamente || FAM *to have a quick one* tomar (rápidamente) una copa || *we had a quick luncheon* almorzamos rápidamente *or* de prisa.
◆ *n* carne *f* viva || — *the quick and the dead* los vivos y los muertos || FIG *to the quick* hasta la médula | *to touch* o *to cut* o *to hurt s.o. to the quick* herir a alguien en lo vivo.
◆ *adv* rápidamente, rápido.

quick-acting [-,æktiŋ] *adj* de acción rápida.

quick assets [-'æsets] *pl n* COMM activo *m* disponible.

quick-change [-,tʃeindʒ] *adj* de cambio rápido || *quick-change artist* transformista *m* & *f*.

quick-eared [-,iəd] *adj* fino de oídos.

quicken ['kwikən] *vt* acelerar, apretar; *to quicken one's pace* apretar el paso || resucitar; *to quicken the dead* resucitar a los muertos || acelerar (the pulse) || estimular; *to quicken s.o.'s interest* estimular el interés de alguien.
◆ *vi* apresurarse, acelerarse (to go faster) || MED moverse (foetus) | sentir los movimientos del feto (a pregnant woman) || FIG vivificarse (hope).

quick-eyed [-,aid] *adj* de vista aguda.

quick-fire [-'faiə*]; **quick-firing** [-riŋ] *adj* de tiro rápido (gun) || FIG rápido, da; hecho a bocajarro (question).

quick-freeze* [-'fri:z] *vt* congelar (rápidamente).
— OBSERV Pret ***quick-froze***; pp ***quick-frozen***.

quick-hedge [-hedʒ] *n* seto *m* vivo.

quickie ['kwiki] *n* cosa *f* hecha rápidamente || *let's pop in a for a quickie* tomemos rápidamente una copa.

quicklime ['kwiklaim] *n* cal *f* viva (lime).

quickly [kwikli] *adv* rápidamente.

quickness ['kwiknis] *n* rapidez *f*, velocidad *f* (speed) || prontitud *f* (promptness) || viveza *f* (liveliness) || agilidad *f* (agility) || agudeza *f* (of ear, eyes, wit) || aceleración *f*, frecuencia *f* (of pulse).

quicksand ['kwiksænd] *n* arena *f* movediza (unstable sand).

quickset ['kwikset] *n* BOT seto *m* vivo (hedge) | plantón *m* (slip) | espino *m* blanco, majuelo *m* (hawthorn).
◆ *adj* vivo, va (hedge).

quick-sighted ['kwik'saitid] *adj* variable.
◆ *n* mercurio *m*, azogue *m* (mercury).

quicksilver ['kwik,silvə*] *vt* azogar.

quicksilvering [-riŋ] *n* azogado *m*.

quickstep ['kwikstep] *n* MIL paso *m* ligero.

quick-tempered ['kwik'tempəd] *adj* de genio vivo, irascible.

quick-witted ['kwik'witid] *adj* agudo, da; perspicaz; listo, ta.

quid [kwid] *n* mascada *f* de tabaco || FAM libra *f* (a pound) || FAM *quids in* forrado de dinero.
— OBSERV La palabra inglesa *quid* tiene como plural *quids* cuando significa *mascada* y *quid* cuando significa *libra* (*it cost me two quid* me costó dos libras).

quiddity [-iti] *n* esencia *f* (essence) || sutileza *f* (subtlety).

quidnunc ['kwidnʌŋk] *n* chismoso, sa (newsmonger).

quid pro quo ['kwidprəu'kwəu] *n* compensación *f*.

quiescence [kwai'esns] *n* quietud *f*, tranquilidad *f*, inactividad *f*, reposo *m*.

quiescent [kwai'esnt] *adj* quieto, ta; inactivo, va; en reposo (at rest).

quiet ['kwaiət] *adj* silencioso, sa; callado, da (silent) || silencioso, sa (a motor) || ligero, ra (footstep) || tranquilo, la (peaceful, calm) || callado, da; reservado, da (reserved) || tranquilo, la (unworried) || descansado, da (soothing) || escondido, da; disimulado, da (secret) || sencillo, lla; discreto, ta (not pretentious) || poco llamativo, va; sobrio, bria (a dress) || privado, da; íntimo, ma (private) || COMM poco activo, va (business) | encalmado, da (stock exchange) || — *all quiet on the front* sin novedad en el frente || *be* o *keep quiet!* ¡cállate! (shut up!), ¡estate quieto! (keep still!) || *it is as quiet as the grave* hay un silencio sepulcral || *to be quiet* callarse (to stop talking), no hacer ruido (to make no noise) || *to keep quiet about sth.* mantener algo en secreto.
◆ *n* tranquilidad *f*, calma *f*, quietud *f*, sosiego *m* (stillness, calm) || silencio *m* (silence) || reposo *m*, descanso *m* (rest) || *on the quiet* a escondidas, a hurtadillas.

quiet [kwaiət] *vt* calmar, tranquilizar, sosegar (to calm) || hacer callar (to silence).
◆ *vi* calmarse, tranquilizarse, sosegarse.

quieten ['kwaiətn] *vt* callar (to silence) || tranquilizar, calmar (to calm).
◆ *vi* callarse (to become silent) || tranquilizarse, calmarse (to calm down) || *to quieten down* tranquilizarse (to calm down), callarse (to shut up).

quietism ['kwaiitizəm] *n* REL quietismo *m*.

quietist ['kwaiitist] *n* REL quietista *m* & *f*.

quietly [kwaiətli] *adv* sin hacer ruido, silenciosamente (silently) || tranquilamente, con calma (calmly) || con sobriedad, discretamente (to be dressed) || en la intimidad (in private).

quietness ['kwaiətnis] *n* → **quiet**.

quietude ['kwaiitju:d] *n* quietud *f*, sosiego *m*.

quietus [kwai'itəs] *n* muerte *f* (death) || golpe *m* de gracia (finishing stroke) || COMM finiquito *m*, descargo *m*.

quiff [kwif] *n* copete *m* (of hair) || US POP suripanta *f*, furcia *f* (woman).

quill [kwil] *n* pluma *f* (feather) || cañón *m* (stem of the feather) || púa *f* (of porcupine) || pluma *f*, cálamo *m* (pen) || canilla *f* (bobbin) || mondadientes *m inv* (toothpick) || púa *f* (plectrum).

quill [kwil] *vt* encanillar (to wind) || encañonar (to goffer).

quillai [ki:'lai] *n* BOT quillay *m*, palo *m* de jabón.

quilling ['kwiliŋ] *n* encañonado *m*.

quilt [kwilt] *n* colcha *f* (coverlet) || US edredón *m* (eiderdown).

quilt [kwilt] *vt* acolchar.

quilted [-id] *adj* acolchado, da.

quilting [-iŋ] *n* acolchado *m* || "piqué" *m* (material).

quinary ['kwainəri] *adj* quinario, ria.

quince [kwins] *n* membrillo *m* (fruit, tree) || *quince jelly* carne *f* de membrillo.

quincentenary [,kwinsen'ti:nəri] *n* quinto centenario *m*.

quincuncial [kwin'kʌŋʃəl] *adj* al tresbolillo.

quincunx ['kwinkʌŋks] *n* AGR tresbolillo *m*.

quinine [kwi'ni:n] *n* CHEM quinina *f*.

quinoa [ki:'nəuə] *n* BOT quinoa *f*, quinua *f*.

quinone [kwi'nəun] *n* CHEM quinona *f*.

quinquagenarian [,kwiŋkwədʒi'nɛəriən] *n* quincuagenario, ria.

Quinquagesima [,kwiŋkwə'dʒesimə] *n* quincuagésima *f*.

quinquennial [kwiŋ'kweniəl] *adj* quinquenal.
◆ *n* quiquenio *m*.

quinquennium [kwiŋ'kweniəm] *n* quiquenio *m*.
— OBSERV El plural de la palabra *quinquennium* es *quinquenniums* o *quinquennia*.

quins [kwinz] *pl n* quintillizos, zas.

quinsy ['kwinzi] *n* MED angina *f*.

quint [kwint] *n* quinta *f* (cards) || MUS quinta *f* || US FAM quintillizo, za (quintuplet).

quintain ['kwintin] *n* estafermo *m*.

quintal ['kwintl] *n* quintal *m*.

quinte [kɛ̃t] *n* SP quinta *f* (in fencing).

quintessence [kwin'tesns] *n* quintaesencia *f*.

quintet; quintette [kwin'tet] *n* MUS quinteto *m*.

quintillion [kwin'tiljən] *n* MATH quintillón *m*, diez elevado a treinta (in England) | trillón *m*, diez elevado a dieciocho (in United States).

quintuple ['kwintjupl] *adj* quíntuplo, pla.
◆ *n* quíntuplo *m*.

quintuple ['kwintjupl] *vt* quintuplicar.
◆ *vi* quintuplicarse.

quintuplets ['kwintjuplits] *pl n* quintillizos, zas.

quip [kwip] *n* pulla *f*, burla *f*, sarcasmo *m*, ocurrencia *f*.

quip [kwip] *vi* tirar pullas.
◆ *vi* decir sarcásticamente.

quipu ['ki:pu:] *n* quipu *m*, quipo *m*.

quire ['kwaiə*] *n* mano *f* de papel || *in quires* en cuadernillos (book).

quirk [kwə:k] *n* peculiaridad *f*, rareza *f* (oddity) || rasgo *m*, floreo *m* (in writing) || ocurrencia *f* (quip) || escapatoria *f* (subterfuge) || capricho *m* (sudden fit) || ARCH mediacaña *f*.

quirky ['kwə:ki] *adj* peculiar, extraño, ña; raro, ra (behaviour, appearance).

quirt [kwə:t] *n* US cuarta *f*, látigo *m* corto.

quirt [kwə:t] *vt* US azotar con cuarta.

quisling ['kwizliŋ] *n* traidor, ra; colaboracionista *m* & *f*.

quit [kwit] *adj* libre; *to be quit of an obligation* estar libre de una obligación.

quit* [kwit] *vt* dejar, abandonar; *to quit one's job* abandonar el empleo; *to quit the army* dejar el ejército || desocupar, dejar, abandonar (a place) || abandonar, dejar; *he quit his wife* dejó a su mujer || irse de (to depart from) || FAM dejar de; *quit shouting!* ¡deja de gritar!
◆ *vi* irse, marcharse (to go away) || dimitir (to resign a job) || dejar de hacer algo; *he was shouting but when s.o. told him to be quiet he quit* estaba gritando pero, cuando alguien le dijo que callase, dejó de hacerlo || abandonar (to give up).
— OBSERV Pret y pp ***quitted, quit***.

quitch [kwitʃ] *n* BOT grama *f*.

quitclaim ['kwitkleim] *n* JUR renuncia *f*.

quitclaim ['kwitkleim] *vt* JUR renunciar.

quite [kwait] *adv* completamente, totalmente; *we are quite alone* estamos completamente solos || bastante; *it is quite near* está bastante cerca; *it is quite good* es bastante bueno || absolutamente, perfectamente (positively); *he quite understood it* lo comprendió perfectamente || verdaderamente, realmente (truly); *he was quite a hero* fue realmente un héroe || exactamente (exactly); *I don't quite know* no sé exactamente || — *it is quite three days ago* hace por lo menos tres días || *quite a few* o *a lot of* o *a bit of* bastante; *three were quite a few cows in the meadow* había bastantes vacas en la pradera || *quite a while* un buen rato, bastante tiempo || *quite so!* ¡así es!, ¡efectivamente!, ¡en efecto! || *quite the thing* muy de moda || *quite the worst* con mucho el peor; *he is quite the worst singer I have ever heard* él es con mucho el peor cantante que he oído || *that's quite enough!* ¡ya está bien! || *you are quite right* tiene toda la razón.

Quito ['ki:təu] *pr n* GEOGR Quito.

quits [kwits] *adj* en paz; *to be quits with s.o.* estar en paz con alguien; *now we are quits* ahora estamos en paz || *to call it quits, to cry quits* hacer las paces.

quittance ['kwitəns] *n* descargo *m* (discharge) || recibo *m* (receipt) || compensación *f*.

quitter ['kwitə*] *n* persona *f* que abandona fácilmente lo que ha iniciado || cobarde *m* & *f* (coward).

quiver ['kwivə*] *n* aljaba *f*, carcaj *m* (for arrow) || temblor *m* (tremble) || estremecimiento *m* (shiver) || temblor *m* (of voice) || parpadeo *m* (of eyelids).

quiver ['kwivə*] *vi* temblar (to tremble) || estremecerse (to shiver) || parpadear (the eyelids) || *to quiver its wings* aletear.

quivering [-riŋ] *adj* tembloroso, sa; *with a quivering voice* con voz temblorosa || parpadeante (eyelids).
◆ *n* → **quiver.**

qui vive [ki:'vi:v] *n* *to be on the qui vive* estar ojo alerta *or* ojo avizor.

Quixote ['kwiksət] *pr n* Quijote *m*.

Quixotic [kwik'sɔtik] *adj* quijotesco, ca.

Quixotism [kwiksɔ,tizəm] *n* quijotismo *m*.

quiz [kwiz] *n* encuesta *f* (enquiry) || acertijo *m* (riddle) || examen *m* (examination) || interrogatorio *m* (questioning) || concurso *m* radiofónico (on radio) || concurso *m* de televisión (on television) || broma *f* (joke) || bromista *m* & *f* (joker).

quiz [kwiz] *vt* interrogar (to interrogate) || mirar con aire burlón (to stare at) || burlarse de (to gibe at).

quizmaster [-mɑːstə*] *n* ⟶**questionmaster.**

quizzical [-ikəl] *adj* curioso, sa; *a quizzical glance* una mirada curiosa ‖ burlón, ona (bantering); *quizzical remarks* observaciones burlonas ‖ extraño, ña (odd).

quizzing [-iŋ] *adj* burlón, ona ‖ *quizzing glass* impertinentes *m pl.*

quod [kwɔd] *n* FAM chirona *f* (prison).

quoin [kɔin] *n* ARCH piedra *f* angular (stone) | esquina *f*, ángulo *m* (corner) | dovela *f* (of an arch) ‖ PRINT cuña *f* (wedge).

quoit [kɔit^{w}ɔit] *n* tejo *m.*
◆ *pl* chito *m sing*, tejo *m sing* (game).

quondam ['kwɔndæm] *adj* antiguo, gua; *my quondam friends* mis antiguos amigos.

quorate ['kwɔːreit] *adj* con quórum (meeting).

quorum ['kwɔːrəm] *n* quórum *m*; *we have a quorum, the quorum is reached* hay quórum.

quota ['kwəutə] *n* cupo *m*; *each has his quota of work for the day* cada uno tiene su cupo de trabajo para el día ‖ COMM cupo *m*, contingente *m*, cuota *f* ‖ cuota *f* (share) ‖ *taxable quota* parte *f* imponible.

quotable ['kwəbəbl] *adj* que merece citarse, citable ‖ COMM cotizable.

quotation [kwəu'teiʃən] *n* cita *f*; *a quotation from the Bible* una cita de la Biblia ‖ COMM cotización *f* ‖ *quotation marks* comillas *f.*

quote [kwəut] *n* cita *f* (quotation) ‖ — *end of quote* fin *m* de la cita ‖ *quote* comienza la cita.
◆ *pl* comillas *f* (quotation marks).

quote [kwəut] *vt* citar (to make a quotation from) ‖ dar (an example) ‖ entrecomillar, poner entre comillas (to enclose with quotation marks) ‖ COMM cotizar.
◆ *vi* hacer citas, citar (from an author, etc.) ‖ *and I quote* y cito sus palabras.

quoth [kwəuθ] *vt* *quoth he* dijo.
— OBSERV Este verbo se emplea únicamente en la primera y tercera personas del singular del pretérito.

quotidian [kwɔ'tidiən] *adj* diario, ria; cotidiano, na (daily).
◆ *n* MED fiebre *f* cotidiana.

quotient ['wəuʃənt] *n* cociente *m.*

qwerty ['kwəːti] *adj* qwerty (keyboard).

R

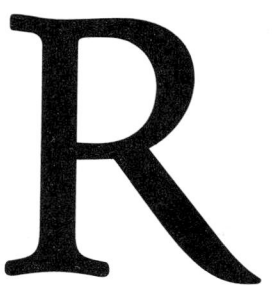

r [ɑː*] *n* r *f* (letter of the alphabet) || *the three R's* lectura, escritura y aritmética.

RA *abbr of* *[Royal Academy]* real academia.

Ra [rɑː] *pr n* MYTH Ra (ancient Egyptian god).

Rabat [rəˈbɑːt] *pr n* GEOGR Rabat.

rabbet [ˈræbit] *n* ranura *f* (groove) || rebajo *m*, renvalso *m* (for doors and windows) || *rabbet plane* guillame *m*.

rabbet [ˈræbit] *vt* hacer una ranura *or* un rebajo en, renvalsar (to make a rabbet) || ensamblar (to join).

rabbi [ˈræbi]; **rabbin** [ˈræbin] *n* REL rabino *m* | rabí *m* (before name) || *chief rabbi* gran rabino.

rabbit [ˈræbit] *n* ZOOL conejo *m*; *Angora rabbit* conejo de Angora || FAM mal jugador *m* || — CULIN *buck rabbit* pan tostado con queso derretido y un huevo frito || ZOOL *doe rabbit* coneja *f* || *rabbit hole* madriguera *f* || *rabbit hutch* conejera *f* || SP *rabbit punch* golpe *m* en la nuca || *rabbit warren* conejal *m*, conejar *m* || *tame rabbit* conejo casero || CULIN *Welsh rabbit* pan tostado con queso derretido || ZOOL *wild rabbit* conejo de campo *or* de monte.

rabbit [ˈræbit] *vi* cazar conejos.

rabble [ˈræbl] *n* multitud *f* ruidosa, gentío *m* (crowd) || TECH hurgón *m* || *the rabble* el populacho, la chusma.

rabble [ˈræbl] *vt* TECH agitar (molten metal).

rabble-rouser [-ˌrauzə*] *n* agitador, ra.

rabble-rousing [-ˌrauziŋ] *n* agitación *f*.

rabid [ˈræbid] *adj* rabioso, sa; *rabid dog* perro rabioso || rábico, ca (virus) || FIG feroz (hate, hunger) | rabioso, sa (thirst) | furioso, sa (opponent) | fanático, ca (supporter).

rabidity [rəˈbiditi]; **rabidness** [-nis] *n* rabia *f* (rabies) || FIG violencia *f* (of passions, of opinions) | fanatismo *m*.

rabies [ˈreibiːz] *n* MED rabia *f*.

RAC *abbr of* *[Royal Automobile Club]* Real Automóvil Club [Gran Bretaña].

raccoon [rəˈkuːn] *n* ZOOL mapache *m*.

race [reis] *n* raza *f*; *the human race* la raza humana || familia *f*; *the race of David* la familia de David || estirpe *f*; *of noble race* de noble estirpe || SP regata *f*; *yatch race* regata de balandros | carrera *f*; *cycling, horse, long-distance race* carrera ciclista, de caballos, de fondo; *walking race* carrera pedestre; *to run a race* participar *or* tomar parte en una carrera || ASTR curso *m*, recorrido *m* (of a star) || curso *m* (of time) || corriente *f* fuerte (current of water) || TECH saetin *m*, caz *m* (of a mill) | anillo *m* de rodadura (of ball bearing) | carrera *f* (of a shuttle) || FIG carrera *f* (rush) | carrera *f*; *arms race* carrera de armamentos || — FIG *his race is run* ha llegado al final de su vida || SP *hurdle race* carrera de vallas || *race against the clock* o *against time* carrera contra el reloj || *race problem* problema *m* racial || *race relations* relaciones *f pl* raciales || *sack race* carrera de sacos || *true to race* de raza (horse, dog, etc.).

◆ *pl* SP carreras *f*; *to go to the races* ir a las carreras.

race [reis] *vt* competir con *or* contra (to compete against) || hacer correr; *to race a horse* hacer correr un caballo || acelerar (un motor) || — *I'll race you home* te echo una carrera a casa || FIG *to race a bill through the House* hacer aprobar un proyecto de ley a toda prisa || *to race away a fortune* perder un dineral en las carreras || *to race s.o. off one's feet* agotar a alguien.

◆ *vi* correr; *I race every Saturday* corro todos los sábados || ir corriendo; *I raced home* fui corriendo a casa || embalarse (an engine) || latir a ritmo acelerado (pulse) || — FIG *to race about* ajetrearse || *to race against time* correr contra el reloj || *to race along* ir corriendo || *to race down the street* bajar la calle corriendo.

race card [-kɑːd] *n* programa *m* de carreras.

racecourse [-kɔːs] *n* hipódromo *m* (for horses) || autódromo *m* (for cars) || pista *f* de carreras de caballos.

racegoer [-ˈgəuə*] *n* aficionado *m* a las carreras de caballos.

race hatred [-ˈheitrid] *n* odio *m* racial.

racehorse [-hɔːs] *n* caballo *m* de carreras.

raceme [rəˈsiːmi] *n* BOT racimo *m*.

race meeting [ˈreisˈmiːtiie] *n* concurso *m* hípico.

racer [ˈreisə*] *n* corredor, ra (person) || caballo *m* de carreras (horse) || coche *m* de carreras (car) || bicicleta *f* de carreras (motorbike) || balandro *m* de carreras (boat).

race riot [ˈreisˈraiət] *n* disturbio *m* racial.

racetrack [ˈreistræk] *n* pista *f* || US hipódromo *m* (racecourse).

Rachel [ˈreitʃəl] *pr n* Raquel *f*.

rachialgia [ˈreikiˈældʒiə] *n* MED raquialgia *f*.

rachidian [rəˈkidiən] *adj* raquídeo, a; *rachidian bulb* bulbo raquídeo.

rachis [ˈreikis] *n* ANAT & BOT raquis *m*.

— OBSERV El plural de *rachis* es *rachises* o *rachides*.

rachitic [ræˈkitik] *adj* raquítico, ca.

rachitis [ræˈkaitis] *n* MED raquitismo *m*.

racial [ˈreiʃəl] *adj* racial; *racial problems* problemas raciales.

racialism [ˈreiʃəlizəm] *n* racismo *m*.

racialist [ˈreiʃəlist] *n* racista *m* & *f*.

raciness [ˈreisinis] *n* picante *m* (of style) || aroma *m*, buqué *m* (of wine).

racing [ˈreisiŋ] *adj* de carreras; *racing car* coche de carreras || embalado, da (engine) || *racing driver* corredor *m*, piloto *m*.

◆ *n* carreras *f pl* (races); *horse racing* carreras de caballos.

racism [ˈreisizəm] *n* racismo *m*.

racist [ˈreisist] *adj/n* racista.

rack [ræk] *n* estante *m*, anaquel *m* (shelf) || perchero *m*, percha *f* (for hats, for coats, etc.) | escurreplatos *m inv* (for plates) || soporte *m* para bicicletas (for bicycles) || redecilla *f*, rejilla *f* (in a train) || adral *m* (on a cart) || pesebre *m* (in a stable) || armero *m* (for arms) || percha *f* (for tools) || taquera *f*, portatacos *m inv* (for billiard cues) || archivador *m* (filing system) || PRINT chibalete *m* || TECH cremallera *f* || potro *m* (torture instrument) || nubes *f pl* (mass of clouds) || pasitrote *m* (horse's gait) || — *bomb rack* dispositivo *m* portabombas || *rack and pinion* engranaje *m* de cremallera y piñón || *roof rack* baca *f* || FIG *to be on the rack* estar atormentado *or* en ascuas | *to go to rack and ruin* venirse abajo | *to put on the rack* atormentar.

rack [ræk] *vt* atormentar; *to be racked by remorse* estar atormentado por los remordimientos || hacer sufrir atrozmente (physical pain) || sacudir; *the cough racked his whole body* la tos le sacudió todo el cuerpo || pedir un alquiler exorbitante; *the landlord racked the tenants* el dueño pedía un alquiler exorbitante a los inquilinos || poner un precio exorbitante (rent) || trasegar (wine) || poner en el pesebre (fodder) || (ant) torturar en el potro || FIG *to rack one's brains* devanarse los sesos.

◆ *vi* andar a pasitrote (a horse) || dispersarse (clouds).

racket [ˈrækit] *n* raqueta *f* (light bat).

◆ *pl* juego *m sing* parecido al frontón.

racket [ˈrækit] *n* alboroto *m*, barullo *m*, jaleo *m* (noise); *to kick up a racket* armar jaleo || FAM timo *m*, estafa *f* (swindle) | chantaje *m* (blackmail) | extorsión *f* (extortion) | tráfico *m*; *drug racket* tráfico de estupefacientes | chanchullo *m*, negocio *m* sucio (dishonest work) || — FIG *to go on the racket* irse de juerga | *to stand the racket* pagar los vidrios rotos.

racket [ˈrækit] *vi* FAM *to racket about* armar jaleo (to make a row), irse de juerga, correrla (to go on a spree).

racketeer [ˌrækiˈtiə*] *n* chantajista *m* (blackmailer) || timador *m*, estafador *m* (swindler).

racketeering [-riŋ] *n* chantaje *m* (blackmail) || crimen *m* organizado.

racket press [ˈrækitpres] *n* prensa *f* de raquetas.

racking [ˈrækiŋ] *adj* muy fuerte, terrible; *a racking pain* un dolor terrible || exorbitante (rent).

◆ *n* trasiego *m* (of wine) || tortura *f* (torment).

rack railway [ˈrækˈreilwei]; **rack railroad** [ˈrækˈreilrəud] *n* ferrocarril *m* de cremallera.

rack rent [ˈrækrent] *n* alquiler *m* exorbitante.

rack wheel [ˈrækwiːl] *n* rueda *f* dentada.

raconteur [ˌrækɔnˈtəː*] *n* anecdotista *m*, persona *f* que cuenta bien anécdotas.

racoon [rəˈkuːn] *n* ZOOL mapache *m*.

racquet [ˈrækit] *n* raqueta *f* (light bat).

racy [ˈreisi] *adj* salado, da (person) || picante (joke) || de raza (animal).

radar [ˈreidə*] *n* radar *m* || — *radar beacon* faro *m* radar || *radar operator* radarista *m*, operador *m* de radar || *radar scanner* antena giratoria de radar || *radar screen* pantalla *f* de radar || *radar trap* radar *m*.

radarman [-mən] *n* operador *m* de radar.

— OBSERV El plural de *radarman* es *radarmen*.

raddle [rædl] *n* almagre *m*, ocre *m* rojo.

raddle [rædl] *vt* almagrar || maquillar exageradamente (a woman).

raddled [rædld] *adj* devastado, da.

radial ['reidjəl] *adj* radial; *radial tyres* neumáticos radiales || *radial engine* motor *m* en estrella.
◆ *n* ANAT nervio *m* radial (nerve) | músculo *m* radial (muscle) | vena *f* radial (vein) | arteria *f* radial (artery).

radian ['reidjən] *n* MATH radián *m*.

radiance ['reidjəns]; **radiancy** [-i] *n* resplandor *m* (brightness) || PHYS radiación *f*.

radiant ['reidjənt] *adj* resplandeciente, radiante (bright); *radiant sun* sol resplandeciente || radiante (smile, face); *he was radiant with joy* estaba radiante de alegría || resplandeciente (beauty) || PHYS radiante || *radiant heating* calefacción *f* por radiación.

radiantly [-li] *adv* con resplandor (to shine) || — *he was radiantly happy* rebosaba de felicidad, estaba radiante de felicidad || *she smiled radiantly at him* le miró con una sonrisa radiante.

radiate ['reidieit] *adj* radiado, da.

radiate ['reidieit] *vt* irradiar (heat) || emitir (rays) || FIG difundir (to spread) || RAD radiar, transmitir.
◆ *vi* irradiar, radiar (to emit rays) || PHYS irradiar, emitir radiaciones || salir; *eight roads radiate from the square* ocho carreteras salen de la plaza || FIG *happiness radiated from her eyes* la felicidad brillaba en sus ojos.

radiating [-iŋ] *adj* radiante; *radiating surface* superficie radiante.

radiation [,reidi'eiʃən] *n* radiación *f* || MED *radiation sickness* enfermedad *f* provocada por la radiación.

radiator ['reidietə*] *n* radiador *m*; *gas radiator* radiador de gas || AUT *radiator cap* tapón *m* del radiador || *radiator grille* calandra *f*, rejilla *f* del radiador (of motor vehicle).

radical ['rædikəl] *adj* radical, fundamental; *radical change* cambio radical; *radical differences* diferencias radicales || radical; *radical point of view* punto de vista radical || MATH, BOT & GRAMM radical || — *Radical Socialism* radicalsocialismo *m* || *Radical Socialist* radicalsocialista *m* & *f*.
◆ *n* GRAMM, MATH & CHEM radical *m*.

radicalism [-izəm] *n* radicalismo *m*.

radicate ['rædikeit] *vt* radicar.

radices ['reidisi:z] *pl n* ⟶ **radix**.

radicle ['rædikl] *n* BOT radícula *f* || CHEM radical *m* (radical).

radii ['reidiəi] *pl n* ⟶ **radius**.

radio ['reidiəu] *n* radio *f* (science, broadcasting); *he is going to talk on the radio* va hablar por la radio; *by radio, on the radio* por radio || radio *m*, aparato *m* de radio, receptor *m* de radio (receiving set).
◆ *adj* de radio (programm, announcer) || radiofónico, ca; *radio advertising* publicidad radiofónica.

radio ['reidiəu] *vt* radiar, transmitir por radio.
◆ *vi* mandar un mensaje por radio (*to* a).

radioactive ['æktiv] *adj* radiactivo, va; radioactivo, va.

radioactivity [-æk'tiviti] *n* radiactividad *f*, radioactividad *f*.

radio altimeter [-'æltimi:tə*] *n* radioaltímetro *m*.

radio amateur [-'æmətə:*] *n* radioaficionado, da.

radio astronomy [-əs'trɔnəmi] *n* radioastronomía *f* (branch of astronomy).

radio beacon [-'bi:kən] *n* radiofaro *m*.

radiobiology [-bai'ɔlədʒi] *n* radiobiología *f*.

radiochemistry [-'kemistri] *n* radioquímica *f*.

radiocobalt [-kəu'bɔ:lt] *n* radiocobalto *m*.

radio compass [-'kʌmpəs] *n* radiocompás *m*.

radioconductor [-kən'dʌktə*] *n* radioconductor *m*.

radio contact [-'kɔntækt] *n* radiocomunicación *f*.

radio control [-kən'trəul] *n* dirección *f* a distancia, teledirección *f*.

radio control [-kən'trəul] *vt* teledirigir.

radio-controlled [-kən'trəuld] *adj* teledirigido, da.

radioelectrical [-i'lektrikəl] *adj* radioeléctrico, ca.

radioelectricity [-ilek'trisiti] *n* radioelectricidad *f*.

radioelement [-'elimənt] *n* radioelemento *m*, ingeniero *m* radiotécnico.

radio engineer [-,endʒi'niə*] *n* radiotécnico *m*, ingeniero *m* radiotécnico.

radio engineering [-,endʒi'niəriŋ] *n* radiotécnica *f*.

radio frequency [-'fri:kwənsi] *n* radiofrecuencia *f*.

radiogoniometer [-gəuni'ɔmitə*] *n* radiogoniómetro *m*.

radiogoniometry [-gəuni'ɔmitri] *n* radiogoniometría *f*.

radiogram [-græm] *n* radiograma *m* (wireless telegram) || MED radiografía *f* (radiograph) || radiogramola *f* (radiogramophone).

radiogramophone [-'græməfəun] *n* radiogramola *f* (wireless receiver and record player).

radiograph [-grɑ:f] *n* radiografía *f*.

radiograph [-grɑ:f] *vt* radiografiar.

radiographer [,reidi'ɔgrəfə*] *n* radiógrafo *m*.

radiographic [,reidiəu'græfik] *adj* radiográfico, ca.

radiography [,reidi'ɔgrəfi] *n* radiografía *f*.

radioisotope ['reidiəu'aisətəup] *n* radioisótopo *m*.

radiolaria [reidiə'lɛəriə] *pl n* ZOOL radiolarios *m*.

radiolocation ['reidiəuləu'keiʃən] *n* radiolocalización *f*.

radiologist [,reidi'ɔlədʒist] *n* MED radiólogo *m*.

radiology [,reidi'ɔlədʒi] *n* MED radiología *f*.

radiometer [,reidi'ɔmitə*] *n* radiómetro *m*.

radiometric [,reidiəu'metrik] *adj* radiométrico, ca.

radiometry [,reidi'ɔmətri] *n* radiometría *f*.

radiomicrometer [,reidiəumai'krɔmitə*] *n* radiomicrómetro *m*.

radio navigation ['reidiəu,nævi'geiʃən] *n* radionavegación *f*.

radio network ['reidiəu'netwə:k] *n* red *f* de emisoras.

radio officer ['reidiəu'ɔfisə*] *n* radionavegante *m*.

radio operator ['reidiəu'ɔpəreitə*] *n* radiotelegrafista *m* & *f*, radiotelefonista *m* & *f*.

radiophone ['reidiəufəun] *n* radiófono *m*.

radiophoto [,reidiəu'fəutəu]; **radiophotograph** [,reidiəu'feutəgrɑ:f] *n* radiofotografía *f*.

radio play ['reidiəu,plei] *n* emisión *f* dramática.

radio receiver ['reidiəuri'si:və*] *n* radiorreceptor *m*.

radioscopic [,reidiəu'skɔpik] *adj* radioscópico, ca.

radioscopy [reidi'ɔskəpi] *n* radioscopia *f*.

radiosensitivity ['reidiəu,sensi'tiviti] *n* radiosensibilidad *f*.

radio set ['reidiəuset] *n* aparato *m* or receptor *m* de radio.

radiosonde ['reidiəu,sɔnd] *n* radiosonda *f*.

radio station ['reidiəu'steiʃən] *n* emisora *f*.

radiotechnologic ['reidiəu,teknə'lɔdʒik]; **radiotechnological** [-əl] *adj* radiotécnico, ca.

radiotechnology ['reidiəutek'nɔlədʒi] *n* radiotécnica *f*.

radiotelegram ['reidiəu'teligræm] *n* radiotelegrama *m* (message transmitted by radiotelegraphy).

radiotelegraph ['reidiəu'teligrɑ:f] *n* aparato *m* de radiotelegrafía.

radiotelegraph ['reidiəu'teligrɑ:f] *vt* radiotelegrafiar.

radiotelephone ['reidiəu'telifəun] *n* radioteléfono *m*.

radiotelephonic ['reidiəu,teli'fɔnik] *adj* radiotelefónico, ca.

radiotelephony ['reidiəuti'lefəni] *n* radiotelefonía *f*.

radio telescope ['reidiəuðeliskəup] *n* radiotelescopio *m*.

radiotherapeutic ['reidiəu'θerə'pju:tik] *adj* radioterápico, ca.

radiotherapist ['reidiəu'θerəpist] *n* radioterapeuta *m* & *f*.

radiotherapy ['reidiəu'θerəpi] *n* radioterapia *f*.

radiothorium ['reidiəu'θɔ:riəm] *n* radiotorio *m*.

radio transmission ['reidiəutrænz'miʃən] *n* radiotransmisión *f*.

radio transmitter ['reidiəutrænz'mitə*] radiotransmisor *m*.

radish ['rædiʃ] *n* BOT rábano *m* || — *radish bed* rabanal *m* || *radish seed* rabaniza *f*.

radium ['reidjəm] *n* CHEM radio *m* || *radium therapy* radioterapia *f*.

radius ['reidjəs] *n* MATH, ANAT & FIG radio *m*; *radius of curvature* radio de curvatura; *within a radius of a hundred kilometres* en un radio de cien kilómetros || AVIAT *operational radius* autonomía *f*.
— OBSERV El plural de *radius* es *radii* o *radiuses*.

radix ['reidiks] *n* MATH base *f* || ANAT & BOT raíz *f*.
— OBSERV El plural de esta palabra es *radices*.

radon ['reidɔn] *n* CHEM radón *m*.

RAF *abbr of* *[Royal Air Force]* Fuerzas Aéreas británicas.

raff [ræf] *n* gentuza *f*, plebe *f*.

raffia ['ræfiə] *n* BOT rafia *f*.

raffish ['ræfiʃ] *adj* chulo, la (flashy) || chabacano, na (vulgar) || disoluto, ta (dissolute).

raffle ['ræfl] *n* rifa *f*.

raffle ['ræfl] *vt* rifar, sortear.
◆ *vi* participar en una rifa.

raft [rɑ:ft] *n* balsa *f* (floating platform) || armadía *f*, almadía *f* (in logging) || masa *f* flotante (of ice) || *US* FIG gran número *m*.

raft [rɑ:ft] *vt* transportar en balsa (to transport) || cruzar en balsa (to cross a river) || construir una balsa con (to make a raft of).
◆ *vi* ir en balsa.

rafter [-ə*] *n* ARCH par *m* (of a roof).

raftsman ['rɑ:ftsmən] *n* ganchero *m*.

— OBSERV El plural de esta palabra es *raftsmen*.

rag [ræg] *n* harapo *m*, andrajo *m* (waste piece of cloth) || trapo *m* (for cleaning) || FAM periodicucho *m* (newspaper) | bandera *f* (flag) || FIG pizca *f* (bit) || FAM payasadas *f pl* (horseplay) | broma *f* (joke) | broma *f* pesada (practical joke) || pizarra *f* (slate) || — FAM *the rag trade* la confección *f* || FIG & FAM *to be like a red rag to a bull* ser como mentar la soga en casa del ahorcado || US FAM *to chew the rag* estar de palique (to chatter) || FAM *to feel like a wet rag* estar hecho polvo.
◆ *pl* trapos *m* viejos (for papermaking) || harapos *m*, andrajos *m* (old clothes) || FAM trapos *m* (clothes) || — FAM *from rags to riches* de la miseria a la riqueza || *in rags* hecho jirones (clothes), andrajoso, sa; con la ropa hecha jirones (person) || *in rags and tafters* desastrado, da || FAM *to put one's glad rags on* ponerse los trapitos de cristianar || *to tear to rags* hacer jirones *or* pedazos.

rag [ræg] *vt* tomar el pelo a (to tease) || dar *or* gastar bromas a (to play practical jokes on) || echar una bronca a (to scold).
◆ *vi* armar jaleo || hacer payasadas.

ragamuffin ['rægə,mʌfin] *n* golfo *m*.

rag-and-bone man ['rægən'bəunmæn] *n* trapero *m*.
— OBSERV El plural es *rag-and-bone men*.

ragbag ['rægbæg] *n* bolsa *f* donde se guardan los trapos || FIG mezcolanza *f* (mixture) | fregona *f* (untidy woman).

rag book ['rægbuk] *n* libro *m* de trapo para niños.

rag doll ['rægdɔl] *n* muñeca *f* de trapo.

rage [reidʒ] *n* furia *f*, rabia *f* || furia *f* (of the sea, etc.) || pasión *f*, fervor *m* (passion) || afán *m* (desire); *the rage of conquest* el afán de conquista || — FIG *to be all the rage* hacer furor, estar en boga || *to fly into a rage* enfurecerse, montar en cólera.

rage [reidʒ] *vi* estar furioso, rabiar (to be furious) || hacer estragos (disease, fire) || estar enfurecido (sea) || bramar (wind).

rag fair ['rægfɛə*] *n* mercado *m* de ropa vieja *or* de cosas viejas, Rastro *m* (in Madrid).

ragged ['rægid] *adj* desigual (surface) || recortado, da (cloud, rock) || mellado, da (edge) || harapiento, ta; andrajoso, sa (people) || roto, ta; hecho jirones (clothes) || FIG desigual (performance, work, style) | descuidado, da (sentence) | discordante (note) | áspero, ra (voice) | desordenado, da (formation) || — US *on the ragged edge* en situación precaria | *on the ragged edge of* al borde de.

raggedly [-li] *adv* con la ropa hecha jirones (in rags) || de una manera discordante (to sing).

raggedness [-nis] *n* estado *m* andrajoso (of clothing) || aspecto *m* harapiento (of people) || desigualdad *f* (of ground) || FIG desigualdad *f* (of style, performance, work) | falta *f* de cohesión (of a team).

raging [reidʒiŋ] *n* furor *m*.
◆ *adj* furioso, sa (person) || encrespado, da (sea) || incontenible, violento, ta (passion, anger) || muy fuerte (fever, headache) || voraz, feroz (hunger) || terrible (thirst) || extraordinario, ria; colosal (success, beauty, etc.).

raglan ['ræglən] *adj* raglán; *rablan sleeve* manga raglán.
◆ *n* raglán *m* (overcoat).

ragman ['ræg,mæn] *n* trapero *m*.
— OBSERV El plural de esta palabra es *ragmen*.

ragout ['rægu:] *n* CULIN ragú *m*, guiso *m*.

ragpicker ['ræg,pikə*] *n* US trapero, ra.

ragtag ['rægtæg] *n* FAM chusma *f* || FAM *ragtag and bobtail* gentuza *f*, chusma *f*.

ragtime ['rægtaim] *n* MUS música *f* de jazz de ritmo sincopado.

ragweed ['rægwi:d] *n* BOT ambrosía *f*.

ragwort ['rægwə:t] *n* BOT hierba *f* cana, zuzón *m*.

raid [reid] *n* correría *f*, incursión *f*, ataque *m* repentino (military attack) || ataque *m*, incursión *f* (aerial attack) || asalto *m* (robbery) || redada *f*, batida *f* (by the police) || maniobra *f* para hacer bajar los precios (stock exchange).

raid [reid] *vt* MIL atacar por sorpresa || asaltar (to rob) || hacer una redada en (the police).
◆ *vi* hacer una incursión.

raider [reidə*] *n* invasor *m* (invader) || MAR buque *m* corsario || AVIAT bombardero *m* || ladrón *m* (thief).

rail [reil] *n* barandilla *f*, baranda *f* (of balcony) || pretil *m*, antepecho *m* (of bridge) || antepecho *m* (of window) || barandilla *f*, baranda *f*, pasamanos *m inv* (of stairs) || barrote *m* (of chair) || pretil *m* (on high building) || barra *f* (bar) || adral *m* (of a cart) || codal *m*, entibo *m* (brace, strut) || MAR barandilla *f*, batayola *f* || cerco *m*, valla *f* (fence) || verja *f* (fence of iron) || cerca *f*, barrera *f* (of a racecourse) || baranda *f* (of billiard table) || riel *m*, rail *m*, carril *m* (for trains, for trams, etc.) || ferrocarril *m*, vía *f* férrea (method of transport); *to send by rail* mandar por ferrocarril || rascón *m* (bird) || — TECH *rail chair* cojinete *m* del carril || *rail network* red ferroviaria || *rail strike* huelga *f* de ferroviarios.
◆ *pl* ferrocarriles *m* (shares) || — FIG *on the rails* en marcha || *to run off the rails* descarrilar.

rail [reil] *vt* poner barandilla a (balcony, staircase) || poner un pretil a (a bridge) || poner un antepecho a (window) || cercar, vallar (to fence) || mandar por ferrocarril (to send by railway) || transportar por ferrocarril (to transport by railway) || poner rieles en (a track) || — *to rail against* o *at* denostar contra || *to rail in* o *off* o *round* cercar.

railcar [-kɑ:*] *n* automotor *m*, autovía *f*.

railcard [-kɑ:d] *n* tarjeta *f* de descuento para el ferrocarril.

railer [-ə*] *n* denigrante *m* & *f* (detractor) || quejica *m* & *f* (grouser).

rail gauge [-geidʒ] *n* ancho *m* de vías.

railhead [-hed] *n* cabeza *f* de línea || MIL cabeza *f* de etapa ferroviaria.

railing ['reiliŋ] *n* valla *f*, cerco *m* (fence of wood) || verja *f* (fence of iron) || barandilla *f*, baranda *f* (of balcony) || pretil *m*, antepecho *m* (of bridge) || pasamanos *m inv* (of stairs) || rieles *m pl*, raíles *m pl* (for trains, for trams, etc.).

raillery ['reiləri] *n* burla *f*.

railroad ['reil,rəud] *n* US vía *f* férrea (track) || ferrocarril *m* || — *railroad car* coche *m* de ferrocarril || *railroad crossing* cruce *m* de vías || *railroad junction* empalme *m* || *railroad siding* o *switch* apartadero *m*.

railroad ['reil,rəud] *vt* US transportar por ferrocarril *or* por vía férrea || US FAM hacer votar apresuradamente (motion, etc.) | encarcelar bajo acusación falsa (to cause to be sent to prison).

railway ['reil,wei] *n* vía *f* férrea (track) || ferrocarril *m* (organization) || línea *f* de ferrocarril (route) || US tranvía *m* (tramcar).
◆ *adj* férreo, a (line) || por ferrocarril, por vía férrea (transport) || ferroviario, ria; *railway traffic, bridge* tráfico, puente ferroviario.

railway car ['reilweikɑ:*] *n* US vagón *m*, coche *m*.

railway carriage [reilwei'kæridʒ] *n* vagón *m*, coche *m*.

railway crossing ['reilwei'krɔsiŋ] *n* cruce *m* *or* intersección *f* de vías || paso *m* a nivel (level crossing).

railway engine ['reilwei'endʒin] *n* locomotora *f*.

railway line ['reilweilain] *n* línea *f or* vía *f* férrea.

railwayman ['reilweimən] *n* ferroviario *m*.
— OBSERV El plural de esta palabra es *railwaymen*.

railway station ['reilwei'steiʃən] *n* estación *f* [de ferrocarril].

railway system ['reilwei'sistim] *n* red *f* ferroviaria.

raiment ['reimənt] *n* vestimenta *f*.

rain [rein] *n* lluvia *f*; *in the rain* bajo la lluvia || FIG lluvia *f* (of bullets, of questions, etc.) | mar *m* (of tears) || — FIG *come rain or shine* llueva o truene, pase lo que pase || *drizzling rain* llovizna *f* || *it looks like rain* parece que va a llover || *the rains* la época de las lluvias.

rain [rein] *v impers* llover || — FIG *it never rains but it pours* las desgracias nunca vienen solas, llueve sobre mojado | *it rained presents that day* llovieron los regalos aquel día | *to rain cats and dogs, to rain buckets* llover a cántaros, caer chuzos de punta.
◆ *vi* llover (blows, etc.) || correr (tears) || *to rain down* llover, caer encima.
◆ *vt* *to rain blows on* llover golpes sobre || *to rain off* suspender por *or* debido a la lluvia.

rain belt ['reinbelt] *n* zona *f* de lluvias.

rainbow ['reinbəu] *n* arco *m* iris.

rainbow-hued ['reinbəu'hjud] *adj* irisado, da.

rainbow-trout ['reinbəutraut] *n* trucha *f* arco iris.

rain chart ['reintʃɑ:t] *n* mapa *m* pluviométrico.

rain check ['reintʃek] *n* US contraseña *f* que se da a los espectadores, cuando se suspende un espectáculo a causa de la lluvia, para que puedan presenciarlo en el momento en que se celebre.

rain cloud ['reinklaud] *n* nubarrón *m*.

raincoat ['reinkəut] *n* impermeable *m*.

raindrop ['reindrɔp] *n* gota *f* de lluvia.

rainfall ['reinfɔ:l] *n* precipitación *f* (falling of rain) || aguacero *m*, chaparrón *m* (shower) || pluviometría *f*, cantidad *f* de lluvia caída durante un tiempo determinado.

rain gauge ['reingeidʒ] *n* pluviómetro *m*.

raininess ['reininis] *n* pluviosidad *f*, lo lluvioso.

rainless ['reinlis] *adj* sin lluvia, seco, ca; *rainless region* región seca.

rainproof ['reinpru:f] *adj* impermeable.

rainproof ['reinpru:f] *vt* impermeabilizar.

rainsquall ['reinskwɔ:l] *n* chubasco *m*.

rainstorm ['reinstɔ:m] *n* tempestad *f* de lluvia, temporal *m*.

raintight ['reintait] *adj* impermeable.

rainwater ['rein,wɔ:tə*] *n* agua *f* de lluvia, agua *f* llovediza.

rainwear ['rein,wɛə*] *n* ropa *f* impermeable, impermeables *m pl*.

rainy ['reini] *adj* lluvioso, sa (climate, region) || lluvioso, sa; de lluvia; *a rainy afternoon* una tarde lluviosa || de las lluvias; *the rainy season* la estación de las lluvias || — *it is rainy* parece que va a llover || FIG *rainy day* tiempos *m or* momentos *m* difíciles; *to save sth. for a rainy day* ahorrar *or* guardar algo para los tiempos difíciles.

raise [reiz] *n* sobremarca *f* (at cards) || US aumento *m*, subida *f* (of prices, of wages, etc.).

raise [reiz] *vt* levantar, alzar (to make stand up); *to raise a fallen statue* levantar una estatua caída || levantar (an object, a weight); *to raise sth. from the floor* levantar algo del suelo || levantar, subir; *would you raise the window, please?* ¿puede subir la ventanilla, por favor? || levantar (one's head, arm, eyes) || levantar, erigir, alzar; *they raised a statue to the mayor* levantaron una estatua al alcalde || levantar, construir (to build); *they have raised a very high building* han construido un edificio muy alto || subir (to heighten); *to raise sth. two metres* subir algo dos metros || dar mayor altura a (a building) || levantar (a piece of ground) || extraer (coal) || aumentar, subir (to increase); *to raise the temperature, the price* subir la temperatura, el precio; *he raised his offer to two hundred pounds* subió la oferta a doscientas libras || aumentar (production) || levantar (a cloud of dust) || izar (a flag) || erizar (feathers, hair) || levantar; *to raise s.o.'s spirits* levantar los ánimos a alguien || ascender, elevar (to a dignity) || provocar, levantar, causar (to provoke); *the joke raised laughter* el chiste provocó la risa; *the book raised considerable controversy* el libro provocó una gran controversia || suscitar (hopes, doubts, etc.) || dar; *he raised a cry* dio un grito || formular, presentar, hacer (a claim, a complaint) || hacer; *I'd like to raise a point* quisiera hacer una observación; *he raised a very good question* hizo una pregunta muy buena || plantear (a problem); *this reform will raise many problems* esta reforma va a plantear muchos problemas || formular, hacer, poner (objection) || alzar, levantar (one's tone, one's voice) || levantar (to remove); *to raise an embargo, an injunction* levantar un embargo, un entredicho || sublevar, alzar, levantar (to incite to rebellion); *to raise the people* sublevar al pueblo || reunir (funds) || conseguir (money) || emitir (loan) || MIL reclutar; *to raise an army of ten thousand men* reclutar un ejército de diez mil hombres | levantar; *to raise a blockade, a siege* levantar un bloqueo, un sitio || ascender (an officer) || MAR levantar, levar (anchor) | guindar, izar (a mast) | poner a flote (a ship) || educar, criar (children) || mantener (a family) || evocar, llamar; *to raise the spirits* evocar los espíritus || envidar (in card games) || REL resucitar; *to raise the dead* resucitar a los muertos || JUR gravar con (a tax) || MED producir, levantar (blisters) || CULIN hacer subir (dough) || AGR criar (livestock) | cultivar (vegetables) || ARTS subir (a colour) || MATH elevar || TECH cardar ||— *to raise game* levantar la caza || *to raise money on* conseguir un préstamo sobre || *to raise one's eyebrows* arquear las cejas || *to raise one's glass to* brindar por || *to raise one's hat* descubrirse || *to raise one's voice in protest* levantar la voz en son de protesta || *to raise o.s. to a sitting position* incorporarse || MUS *to raise the pitch of* subir el tono de || *to raise s.o. from the gutter* sacar a alguien del arroyo || *to raise up* levantar (to lift up).

raisin [ˈreizn] *n* pasa *f.*

raising [ˈreiziŋ] *n* aumento *m*, subida *f* (increase) || levantamiento *m* (of a building, eyes, arm, weight, etc.) || elevación *f* (of one's voice) || evocación *f* (of ghosts) || reclutamiento *m* (of soldiers) || levantamiento *m*, suspensión *f* (of an embargo, of an injunction, etc.) || izado *m* (of a flag) || resurrección *f* (of dead) || elevación *f* (of a wall, etc.) || AGR cría *f*, crianza *f* (of livestock) | cultivo *m* (of vegetables) || extracción *f* (of coal) || aumento *m* (of production) || erizamiento *m* (of hair) || ascenso *m*, elevación *f* (to a dignity) || formulación *f* (of a claim, a complaint, a point) || sublevación *f*, alzamiento *m*, levantamiento *m* (riot) || consecución *f* (of money) || emisión *f* (of a loan) || levantamiento *m* (of a siege) || ascenso *m* (of an officer) || educación *f* (of children) || mantenimiento *m* (of a family) || imposición *f* (with taxes) || envite *m* (in card games) || MATH elevación *f.*

raison d'être [ˈreizˉɔːnˈdeitr] *n* razón *f* de ser.

raj [rɑːdʒ] *n* soberanía *f* || imperio *m*; *the British raj in India* el imperio británico en India.

raja; rajah [ˈrɑːdʒə] *n* rajá *m.*

rake [reik] *n* rastrillo *m* (for gardening) || AGR rastro *m*, rastrillo *m* || hurgón *m* (for the fire) || rastrillo *m*, raqueta *f* (for gambling) || inclinación *f* (slant) || calavera *m* (dissolute man).

rake [reik] *vt* rastrillar; *to rake the garden, the soil* rastrillar el jardín, la tierra || recoger con el rastrillo; *to rake leaves* recoger hojas con el rastrillo || atizar, hurgar; *to rake the fire* hurgar el fuego || FIG rastrear; *the police raked the district for the criminals* la policía rastreó el barrio en busca de los criminales | buscar en; *to rake history for examples* buscar ejemplos en la historia | abarcar [con la mirada] (to scan) | dominar; *window that rakes the valley* ventana que domina el valle || MIL ametrallar, barrer, batir en enfilada (to sweep with gun fire) || inclinar (to incline) || MAR inclinar || — *to rake away* o *off* quitar con el rastrillo || *to rake in* recoger con el rastrillo (gambling chips), amasar (money) || *to rake one's hand through one's hair* pasar la mano por el pelo || *to rake out* quitar las cenizas de (a stove) || FAM *to rake over the coals* echar un rapapolvo *or* una bronca a || *to rake together* o *up* reunir (facts, information) || *to rake up* sacar a luz; *to rake up an old quarrel* sacar a luz una vieja disputa || *to rake up the past* sacar a relucir el pasado.
◆ *vi* inclinarse (to slant).

rake-off [-ˌɔf] *n* FAM comisión *f.*

raker [ˈreikə*] *n* rastrillador, ra.

raking [-iŋ] *n* AGR rastrillado *m*, rastrillaje *m* || FAM *raking over the coals* bronca *f*, rapapolvo *m.*
◆ *adj* MIL de enfilada (fire).

rakish [ˈreikiʃ] *adj* MAR aerodinámico, ca (having a trim appearance) || desenvuelto, ta (jaunty) || libertino, na (dissolute).

rale [rɑːl] *n* MED estertor *m.*

rally [ˈræli] *n* reunión *f*, mitin *m*; *political rally* mitin político || reunión *f*; *youth rally* reunión de jóvenes || SP peloteo *m* (in tennis) || MED & COMM recuperación *f* || AUT rallye *m.*

rally [ˈræli] *vt* reunir (to gather); *to rally troops, supporters* reunir tropas, partidarios || recobrar; *to rally one's spirits* recobrar el ánimo || reanimar (to revive) || reírse de (to mock).
◆ *vi* reunirse (to come together) || reorganizarse (troops) || recuperarse (to regain strength) || reponerse, recuperarse (from an illness) || COMM recuperarse || — *to rally round s.o.* tomar el partido de alguien || *to rally to* adherirse a (a party, s.o.'s opinion).

rallying [-iŋ] *n* reunión *f*; *rallying point* punto de reunión.
◆ *adj* burlón, ona.

ram [ræm] *n* ZOOL carnero *m*, morueco *m* || TECH maza *f*, pilón *m* (of steam hammer) | émbolo *m* (of a pump) | ariete *m* (hydraulic) | pisón *m* (rammer) || MAR espolón *m* (on prow of ship) || MIL ariete *m* (battering ram) || MIN taco *m* || ASTR aries *m* || FAM conquistador *m* (seducer).

ram [ræm] *vt* apisonar (to pound earth, etc.) || hinchar (with a pile driver) || dar con; *he rammed his head against the wall* dio con la cabeza contra la pared || meter a la fuerza, apretar; *he rammed it all into the suitcase* lo metió todo en la maleta a la fuerza || dar con, chocar con; *he rammed the car into the wall* dio con el coche contra la pared || MIL atacar (a charge into a gun) || FIG meter; *to ram ideas into s.o.'s head* meter a alguien ideas en la cabeza || golpear con el ariete (with the battering ram) || embestir con el espolón (ships) || — *to ram down* apisonar (earth), hincar (to drive in) || *to ram in* hincar || FIG *to ram sth. down s.o.'s throat* hacer tragar algo a alguien || *to ram sth. home* dejar algo claro, mostrar algo con claridad (fact, idea) || *to ram up* tapar (a hole).

RAM *abbr of [Random Access Memory]* memoria RAM *or* de acceso aleatorio.

Ramadan [ˌræməˈdɑːn] *n* REL Ramadán *m.*

ramble [ˈræmbl] *n* paseo *m*, vuelta *f* (walk); *to go for a ramble* ir a dar un paseo || FIG divagaciones *f pl* (talk).

ramble [ˈræmbl] *vi* pasear (to go for a walk) || callejear, vagar (to roam) || FIG divagar (to talk or write aimlessly) | serpentear, dar vueltas (stream, road, path, etc.) | trepar, extenderse (plant).

rambler [-ə*] *n* paseante *m* & *f* (walker) || excursionista *m* & *f* (excursionist) || divagador, ra (one who talks without aim) || BOT rosal *m* trepador.

rambling [-iŋ] *adj* de distribución irregular, laberíntico, ca; *a rambling house* una casa de distribución irregular || tortuoso, sa (street) || sin orden ni concierto (conversation) || errante (existence) || sin ilación, incoherente (speech, thoughts) || BOT trepador, ra || *rambling talk* divagaciones *f pl.*
◆ *n* excursiones *f pl*, paseos *m pl* || FIG divagaciones *f pl.*

ramekin; ramequin [ˈræmkin] *n* CULIN pastelillo *m* de queso [AMER quesadilla *f*] || recipiente *m* en el que se sirve el pastelillo de queso (dish).

ramification [ˌræmifiˈkeiʃən] *n* ramificación *f* || FIG ramificación *f*; *the ramifications of a plot* las ramificaciones de una conspiración.

ramify [ˈræmifai] *vt* hacer ramificarse, ramificar.
◆ *vi* ramificarse.

ramjet [ˈræmdʒet] *n* estatorreactor *m.*

rammer [ˈræmə*] *n* pisón *m* (paviour's) || baqueta *f* (ramrod).

ramose [ræˈməus] *adj* ramoso, sa.

ramp [ræmp] *n* rampa *f* (slope) || elevador *m*; *hydraulic ramp* elevador hidráulico || FAM subida *f* injustificada de los precios (price increase) | timo *m*, estafa *f* (swindle).

ramp [ræmp] *vi* inclinarse (to slope) || levantarse sobre las patas traseras (a lion) || HERALD estar en posición rampante (lion) || FIG estar hecho una furia (to rush about in anger) || trepar (plants).

rampage [ræmˈpeidʒ] *n* *to be on a rampage* andar destrozándolo todo a su paso, alborotar.

rampage [ræmˈpeidʒ] *vi* comportarse violentamente (to act wildly) || estar hecho una furia (to rush about in anger) || andar destrozándolo todo a su paso, alborotar (to play havoc).

rampageous [-əs] *adj* alborotador, ra.

rampancy [ˈræmpənsi] *n* abundancia *f*, exuberancia *f* (of vegetation, etc.) || proliferación *f* (of crime, disease, etc.).

rampant [ˈræmpənt] *adj* HERALD rampante (lion) || violento, ta; agresivo, va (aggressive) || exuberante, abundante (vegetation) || desenfrenado, da; *rampant inflation* inflación desenfrenada || ARCH por tranquil (arch) || *to be rampant* estar extendido *or* difundido (plague, vice).

rampart [ˈræmpɑːt] *n* muralla *f*; *the ramparts of a castle* las murallas de un castillo || FIG defensa *f*, amparo *m*, escudo *m.*

rampart [ˈræmpɑːt] *vt* rodear con una muralla.

rampion ['ræmpjən] *n* BOT ruiponce *m*, rapónchigo *m*.

ramrod ['ræmrɔd] *n* MIL baqueta *f* (of rifle) | escobillón *m* (of gun) ‖ FAM *straight as a ramrod* más tieso que un huso.

ramshackle ['ræm,ʃækl] *adj* desvencijado, da.

ran [ræn] *pret* → **run.**

ranch [rɑːntʃ] *n* rancho *m* (in United States) ‖ hacienda *f*, estancia *f* (in Latin America).

ranch [rɑːntʃ] *vi* llevar un rancho (in United States) ‖ llevar una hacienda *or* una estancia (in Latin America).

rancher [-ə*]; **ranchman** [-mən] *n* ranchero *m*, ganadero *m*.

— OBSERV El plural de *ranchman* es *ranchmen*.

rancid ['rænsid] *adj* rancio, cia; *to get rancid* ponerse rancio.

rancidity [ræn'siditi]; **rancidness** ['rænsidnis] *n* rancidez *f*, ranciedad *f*.

rancorous ['ræŋkərəs] *adj* rencoroso, sa.

rancour; *US* **rancor** ['ræŋkə*] *n* rencor *m*.

randiness [-inis] *n* FAM cachondez *f*.

random ['rændəm] *adj* hecho al azar; *random bombing* bombardeo hecho al azar; *a random selection of articles* una selección de artículos hecha al azar ‖ escogido al azar; *a random passage in a boock* un fragmento de un libro escogido al azar ‖ fortuito, ta; *random remark* observación fortuita ‖ aleatorio, ria ‖ — *at a random guess* a ojo de buen cubero ‖ INFORM *random access* acceso *m* aleatorio ‖ *random shot* bala perdida (stray bullet), tiro pegado sin apuntar (chance shot).
◆ *n* *at random* al azar ‖ *to talk at random* hablar sin orden ni concierto *or* sin ton ni son.

randy [ʌxrændi] *adj* FAM cachondo, da.

rang [ræŋ] *pret* → **ring.**

range [˜ɑeindʒ] *n* fila *f*, hilera *f* (row); *a range of houses* una hilera de casas ‖ cadena *f* (of mountains) ‖ extensión *f*, zona *f* (area); *a wide range of meadows* una gran extensión de praderas ‖ alcance *m* (maximum attainable distance); *the range of a rocket, a gun, a telescope* el alcance de un cohete, de un fusil, de un telescopio ‖ distancia *f*; *the gun fired at a range of two hundred metres* el cañón tiró a una distancia de doscientos metros ‖ autonomía *f*, radio *m* de acción (maximum attainable distance without refuelling); *the range of an aircraft* la autonomía de un avión ‖ MIL campo *m* de tiro (for rifles) | polígono *m* (for artillery) ‖ barraca *f* de tiro al blanco (in a fair) ‖ MUS registro *m* (of voice, of instrument) ‖ FIG alcance *m* (scope); *within the range of* al alcance de; *Kant is out of my range* Kant no está a mi alcance | gama *f*, escala *f* (of frequencies, of colours, of prices) | variedad *f*; *a wide range of subjects* una gran variedad de temas | surtido *m*; *this shop has a large range of ties* esta tienda tiene un gran surtido de corbatas | esfera *f*; *the upper ranges of society* las altas esferas de la sociedad | campo *m*; *the range of science* el campo de la ciencia | extensión *f* (of knowledge) ‖ cocina *f* económica (cooking stove) ‖ habitación *f*, área *f* que habita una especie animal *or* vegetal ‖ *US* dehesa *f* (grazing land for cattle) ‖ — *at close range* de cerca ‖ *out of range* fuera de alcance ‖ *range of action* campo de actividad, esfera de acción *or* de actividad ‖ *range of mountains* cordillera *f*, sierra *f* ‖ *range of vision* campo *m* visual ‖ *to be in range* estar al alcance *or* a tiro ‖ *to be in range with* estar alineado con ‖ *to give free range to* dar rienda suelta a (one's imagination) ‖ MIL *to rectify the range* corregir el tiro.

range ['reindʒ] *vt* alinear (to set in a row); *the trees were ranged along the road* los árboles estaban alineados a lo largo de la carretera ‖ colocar (to place) ‖ clasificar (to classify) ‖ recorrer (to wander through); *to range the countryside* recorrer el campo ‖ PRINT alinear (to set type in line) ‖ MAR costear, bordear (the coast) ‖ MIL apuntar; *to range a gun on an enemy ship* apuntar un cañón hacia un barco enemigo ‖ enfocar (a telescope) ‖ *US* apacentar (to graze) ‖ — FIG *to range o.s. against s.o.* ponerse en contra de alguien | *to range o.s. with the opposition* ponerse del lado de la oposición.
◆ *vi* alinearse (to be in line); *the peaks ranged as far as he could see* las cimas se alineaban hasta donde alcanzaba la vista ‖ extenderse; *the frontier ranges from north to south* la frontera se extiende del norte al sur ‖ oscilar, fluctuar, variar; *the temperature ranges between eighty and ninety degrees* la temperatura oscila entre ochenta y noventa grados; *prices range between one and twenty pounds* los precios oscilan entre una y veinte libras ‖ tener un alcance; *this gun ranges over eight miles* este cañón tiene un alcance de más de ocho millas ‖ — *latitudes between which a plant ranges* latitudes entre las cuales se encuentra una planta ‖ *to range along* bordear ‖ *to range over* recorrer; *to range over the country* recorrer el país; *his eyes ranged over the audience* recorrió al público con la mirada; abarcar; *the talk ranged over a number of topics* el discurso abarcó muchos temas; vivir en; *this animal ranges over the southern regions* este animal vive en las regiones del sur ‖ *to range with the great poets* ser uno de los poetas más grandes.

range finder ['reindʒ,faində*] *n* telémetro *m*.

ranger ['reindʒə*] *n* guardabosques *m inv* (park or forest keeper) ‖ MIL soldado *m* de un comando.
◆ *pl* *US* policía *f sing* montada.

Rangoon [ræŋ'guːn] *pr n* GEOGR Rangún.

rangy ['reindʒi] *adj* ágil (agile) ‖ espacioso, sa (wide).

ranidae ['rænədiː] *pl n* ZOOL ránidos *m*.

rank [ræŋk] *n* MIL fila *f* (of soldiers) | graduación *f*, grado *m*; *what rank are you?* ¿qué graduación tiene usted? ‖ fila *f*, hilera *f* (row, line) ‖ categoría *f*, clase *f*; *dancer of the first rank* bailarina de primera categoría; *people of all ranks* gente de todas clases ‖ rango *m*, categoría *f*; *to have the rank of ambassador* tener rango de embajador ‖ calidad *f*; *a man of rank* un hombre de calidad ‖ AUT parada *f* (of taxis) ‖ fila *f* (chess) ‖ — *rank and file* soldados rasos (soldiers), masa *f*, gente *f* del montón (ordinary people), base *f* (of trade unions, etc.) ‖ — MIL *to fall in rank* ponerse en filas.
◆ *pl* MIL tropa *f sing*, soldados *m* rasos ‖ MIL *to be in the ranks* estar en filas | *to break ranks* romper filas | *to close the ranks* estrechar *or* cerrar las filas ‖ *to join the ranks* alistarse (a soldier) ‖ FIG *to join the ranks of* unirse a ‖ MIL *to rise from the ranks* ser ascendido a oficial, ser patatero (fam) | *to serve in the ranks* ser soldado raso.
◆ *adj* exuberante (vegetation) ‖ tupido, da (thick); *rank grass* hierba tupida ‖ fértil, rico, ca (soil) ‖ completo, ta; absoluto, ta (deceit) ‖ manifiesto, ta; flagrante (injustice) ‖ rematado, da; completo, ta; *he is a rank idiot* es un idiota completo ‖ verdadero, ra; auténtico, ca (poison) ‖ grosero, ra; vulgar (coarse) ‖ rancio, cia (rancid) ‖ fétido, da; maloliente (foul-smelling) ‖ — *rank lie* pura mentira ‖ *to smell rank* oler muy mal.

rank [ræŋk] *vt* MIL alinear, poner en fila (soldiers) ‖ situar, colocar, poner (to estimate); *I rank him amongst the greatest* le sitúo entre los mejores ‖ *US* ser superior a (to outrank).
◆ *vi* figurar, estar, encontrarse; *he ranks amongst the best* figura entre los mejores ‖ considerarse; *it ranks as one of his best films* se considera como una de sus mejores películas ‖ — *to rank above* ser superior a ‖ *to rank below* ser inferior a ‖ *to rank high* sobresalir, distinguirse ‖ *to rank with* estar al mismo nivel que.

ranker [-ə*] *n* MIL oficial *m* que antes fue soldado raso, patatero *m* (fam) (officer).

ranking [-iŋ] *adj* de mayor categoría.

rankle ['ræŋkl] *vi* causar rencor ‖ *the insult rankled in her mind* todavía le dolía el insulto.

rankly [-i] *adv* con exuberancia (to grow) ‖ con un olor fétido (to smell).

rankness [-nis] *n* exuberancia *f* (of vegetation) ‖ olor *m* fétido (smell) ‖ rancidez *f*, ranciedad *f* (taste) ‖ enormidad *f* (of a lie).

ransack ['rænsæk] *vt* saquear (to rob) ‖ registrar (to search thoroughly); *to ransack a drawer for a document* registrar un cajón para encontrar un documento.

ransom ['rænsəm] *n* rescate *m* (for a prisoner) ‖ REL redención *f* ‖ — FIG *to be worth a king's ransom* valer su peso en oro ‖ *to hold s.o. to ransom* pedir *or* exigir rescate por uno (for a prisoner), hacer chantaje a alguien (to blackmail).

ransom ['rænsəm] *vt* rescatar (to pay ransom for); *he was ransomed for ten thousand pounds* fue rescatado por diez mil libras ‖ pedir *or* exigir rescate por (to demand ransom for) ‖ REL redimir (of sins).

ransoming [-iŋ] *n* rescate *m*.

rant [rænt] *n* discurso *m* rimbombante.

rant [rænt] *vt* decir con rimbombancia.
◆ *vi* hablar con rimbombancia (to speak bombastically) ‖ divagar, desvariar (to rave) ‖ declamar con exageración (an actor) ‖ vociferar, echar pestes (to be noisily angry).

rantan ['ræn,tæn] *n* FAM *to go on the rantan* ir de francachela, ir de parranda.

ranter [-ə*] *n* orador *m* rimbombante ‖ energúmeno *m*.

ranting [-iŋ] *adj* rimbombante, ampuloso, sa.
◆ *n* discurso *m* rimbombante *or* violento.

ranunculaceae [rænʌŋkju'leisiiː] *pl n* BOT ranunculáceas *f*.

ranunculus [ræ'nʌŋkjuləs] *n* BOT ranúnculo *m*, botón *m* de oro.

— OBSERV El plural de *ranunculus* es *ranunculuses* o *ranunculi*.

rap [ræp] *n* golpecito *m*, golpe *m* seco; *a rap at the door* un golpecito en la puerta ‖ — FIG *not to be worth a rap* no valer un comino | *not to care a rap* importarle a uno un comino | *to give s.o. a rap on the knuckles* llamar a uno al orden, poner a uno en su sitio | *to take the rap* pagar el pato.

rap [ræp] *vt* golpear, dar un golpe en ‖ arrebatar (to stir) ‖ regañar (to scold) ‖ *to rap out* espetar, soltar; *he rapped out a command* espetó una orden; transmitir por golpes (a message).
◆ *vi* *to rap at* o *on* golpear, dar un golpe en.

rapacious [rə'peiʃəs] *adj* de rapiña, rapaz (bird, animal) ‖ FIG rapaz.

rapaciousness [-nis]; **rapacity** [rə'pæsiti] *n* rapacidad *f*.

rape ['reip] *n* JUR violación *f* (forcible sexual intercourse) ‖ FIG asolamiento *m*, saqueo *m* (plundering) | violación *f* (invasión) ‖ BOT colza *f* ‖ orujo *m* (of grapes) ‖ — *rape cake* torta *f* de orujo, borujo *m* ‖ *rape oil* aceite *m* de colza ‖ *the Rape of the Sabine Women* el Rapto de las Sabinas.

rape ['reip] *vt* JUR violar ‖ FIG saquear, asolar (to plunder) | violar (to invade).

rapeseed [-siːd] *n* semilla *f* de colza.

Raphael ['ræfeiəl] *pr n* Rafael *m*.

Raphaelesque [,ræfiə'lesk] *adj* rafaelesco, ca.

rapid ['ræpid] *adj* rápido, da; *rapid movement* movimiento rápido; *to make rapid progress* hacer progresos rápidos || muy empinado, da; muy pendiente (slope).
◆ *n* rápido *m* (in a river); *to shoot the rapids* salvar los rápidos.

rapid-fire [-'faiə*]; **rapid-firing** [-'faiəriŋ] *adj* de tiro rápido (gun).

rapidity [rə'piditi] *n* rapidez *f*.

rapier ['reipjə*] *n* espadín *m*, estoque *m* || *rapier thrust* estocada *f*.

rapine ['ræpain] *n* rapiña *f*, saqueo *m*.

rapist ['reipist] *n* violador *m* || raptor *m*.

rappee [ræ'piː] *n* rapé *m* (snuff).

rapping ['ræpiŋ] *n* golpecitos *m pl*, golpes *m pl* secos.

rapport [ræ'pɔː] *n* relación *f* (connection) || compenetración *f*, armonía *f* (sympathy).

rapporteur [ˌræpɔː'təː*] *n* ponente *m* [AMER relator *m*].

rapprochement [ræ'prɔʃmɑːn] *n* acercamiento *m*, aproximación *f*.

rapscallion [ræp'skæljən] *n* golfo *m*, bribón *m*.

rapt [ræpt] *adj* absorto, ta; ensimismado, da; *rapt in thought* absorto en sus pensamientos || profundo, da; *rapt attention* atención profunda || embelesado, da (enraptured).

raptorial [ræp'tɔːriəl] *adj* ZOOL de rapiña, de presa.

rapture ['ræptʃə*] *n* éxtasis *m*, arrobamiento *m*, embeleso *m* (ecstasy) || — *to be in raptures* estar extasiado || *to go into raptures over* extasiarse por.

rapture ['ræptʃə*] *vt* arrobar, extasiar, embelesar.

rapturous ['ræptʃərəs] *adj* entusiasta (applause, cries) || desbordante (joy) || embelesado, da; extasiado, da; en éxtasis (people).

rare [rɛə*] *adj* raro, ra; poco frecuente; *a rare event* un acontecimiento poco frecuente || poco común (uncommon) || excepcional, raro, ra (extraordinary) || CHEM raro, ra || enrarecido, da (atmosphere) || FAM enorme; *you gave me a rare fright* me has dado un susto enorme | estupendo, da; excelente; *we had a rare meal last night* tuvimos una comida estupenda anoche || CULIN poco hecho (meat).

rarebit ['rɛəbit] *n* *Welsh rarebit* pan *m* tostado con queso derretido.

rarefaction [ˌrɛəri'fækʃən] *n* rarefacción *f*, enrarecimiento *m*.

rarefactive [ˌrɛəri'fæktiv] *adj* rarificativo, va; rarificante.

rarefied ['rɛərifaid] *adj* enrarecido, da (atmosphere).

rarefy ['rɛərifai] *vt* enrarecer, rarificar (gas) || FIG hacer más sutil (to make more subtle) | refinar (to refine).
◆ *vi* enrarecerse, rarificarse (gases).

rarely ['rɛəli] *adv* raramente, raras veces, poco frecuentemente (not frequently) || FAM estupendamente, maravillosamente.

raring ['rɛəriŋ] *adj* deseoso, sa.

rarity ['rɛəriti] *n* rareza *f* (rareness, object); *this object is a rarity* este objeto es una rareza || *rain is a rarity here* es raro que llueva aquí, no llueve casi nunca aquí.

rascal ['rɑːskəl] *n* tunante *m*, bribón *m*, pícaro *m*.

rascality [rɑːs'kæliti] *n* bribonería *f*, picardía *f*.

rascally ['rɑːskəli] *adj* pícaro, ra; bribón, ona || *my rascally son* el pícaro de mi hijo.

rase [reiz] *vt* arrasar.

rash [ræʃ] *adj* precipitado, da; irreflexivo, va (action) || temerario, ria; impetuoso, sa (person) || imprudente (promise, words).
◆ *n* MED sarpullido *m*, salpullido *m*, erupción *f* cutánea.

rasher [-ə*] *n* loncha *f*, lonja *f* (bacon, ham).

rashly [-li] *adj* sin reflexionar (to act) || a la ligera (to speak).

rashness [-nis] *n* precipitación *f* || temeridad *f*, impetuosidad *f* (impetuosity) || irreflexión *f* || imprudencia *f*.

rasp [rɑːsp] *n* TECH escofina *f* (file) || chirrido *m* (noise).

rasp [rɑːsp] *vt* raspar, escofinar (to file) || CULIN rallar (bread) || FIG dañar, lastimar (ears) | herir (s.o.'s feelings) | crispar (to annoy) || — *to rasp away* quitar con la escofina (with a file), rallar (bread) || *to rasp out* decir con voz áspera (an oath, an order).
◆ *vi* chirriar (sound) || hablar con voz áspera.

raspberry ['rɑːzbəri] *n* BOT frambuesa *f* (fruit) | frambueso *m* (plant) || color *m* frambuesa (colour) || — FAM *to blow s.o. a raspberry* hacer un gesto de desprecio a uno, hacer la higa a uno | *to get a raspberry from* recibir una bronca de | *to give s.o. a raspberry* abuchear a alguien (to boo).

raspberry bush [-buʃ]; **raspberry cane** [-kein] *n* BOT frambueso *m*.

rasping [rɑːspiŋ] *n* raspado *m*, raspadura *f* (act) || chirrido *m* (sound).
◆ *pl* CULIN pan *m sing* rallado.
◆ *adj* áspero, ra (voice) || chirriante (sound).

Rasta *adj/n* FAM rasta.

Rastafarian [ˌræstə'fɛəriən] *adj/n* rasta.

rat [ræt] *n* ZOOL rata *f*; *brown rat* rata de alcantarilla; *water rat* rata de agua || FAM esquirol *m* (blackleg) | traidor, ra (betrayer) | delator, ra (accuser) | canalla *m* (comtemptible person) | desertor *m* (quitter) || US FAM postizo *m* (hair) || — *extermination of rats* desratización *f* || FAM *I smell a rat* hay gato encerrado | *like a drowned rat* calado hasta los huesos, hecho una sopa | *rats!* ¡cáscaras! (expression of annoyance), ¡ni hablar! (out of the question!) | *to be caught like a rat in a trap* caer en la ratonera | *to smell a rat* sospechar algo.

rat [ræt] *vi* cazar ratas (to hunt rats) || FAM ser esquirol (worker) | desertar (to let one's side down) | chaquetear, volver casaca (to turn coat) || FAM *to rat on* chivarse de, denunciar; *to rat on a pal* denunciar a un amigote.

ratable ['reitəbl] *adj* ⟶ **rateable.**

ratafia [ˌrætə'fiə] *n* ratafía *f*.

ratal ['reitl] *n* valor *m* imponible.

ratan [rə'tæn] *n* BOT rota *f*, junco *m* de Indias || bastón *m* de caña (walking stick).

ratcatcher ['rætˌkætʃə*] *n* cazador *m* de ratas.

ratch [rætʃ] *n* TECH trinquete *m*.

ratchet [-it] *n* TECH trinquete *m* (hinged catch) | rueda *f* de trinquete (ratched wheel) | uña *f* (of a ratch).

ratchet wheel [-itˌwiːl] *n* TECH rueda *f* de trinquete.

rate [reit] *n* proporción *f* (ratio) || índice *m*, coeficiente *m*; *birth rate* índice de natalidad; *rate of increase* coeficiente de incremento; *rate of growth* índice de crecimiento || velocidad *f* (speed); *he drives at a moderate rate* conduce a una velocidad moderada || ritmo *m*; *the rate of production is very rapid* el ritmo de la producción es muy rápido || precio *m*, tarifa *f* (price); *reduced rate* tarifa reducida; *advertising rates* precios de la publicidad; *buying rate* precio de compra; *free market rate* precio libre; *full rate* precio sin descuento; *selling rate* precio de venta || tanto *m* por ciento, porcentaje *m* (percentage) || tipo *m* (of discount, of interest); *rate of interest* tipo de interés; *bank rate* tipo de descuento bancario || interés *m*; *rates for money on loan* intereses de un préstamo || prima *f* (of insurance); *insurance rate* prima de seguros || nivel *m* (of salaries, etc.) || COMM cotización *f* (in the stock exchange); *market rates* cotizaciones en el mercado; *rate of gold* cotización del oro || MED frecuencia *f* (of the pulse) || — *annual rate* anualidad *f* || *a second-rate hotel* un hotel de segunda categoría || *at any rate* de todos modos, de todas formas, en todo caso || *at that rate* de ese modo || *at the rate of 500 litres per day* a razón de 500 litros por día || *at this rate* si continuamos así || *basic salary rate, base rate* sueldo *m* base || *discount rate* tipo de descuento || *first rate* de primera clase || *freight rate* flete *m* || *inclusive rate* precio a tanto alzado || *inland rate* precio nacional *or* interior || *letter rate* franqueo *m* || *postage rate* tarifa || *rate of exchange* cambio *m*, tipo de cambio || *rate of flow* caudal medio (of water), régimen *m* (of electricity) || *rate of living* tren *m* de vida.
◆ *pl* contribución *f sing* municipal, impuesto *m sing* municipal || — *borough rates* impuestos municipales || *commission rates* comisión *f* || *effective rates* cotización real || *exchange rates* cambio *m*.

rate [reit] *vt* tasar, valorar (*at* en) (to assess the value of) || estimar (to estimate); *to rate s.o. highly* estimar mucho a alguien || considerar; *they rate him as a public menace* le consideran como una amenaza pública || MAR & AUT clasificar || reñir, echar una bronca (to scold) || US merecer (to deserve) | clasificar (a pupil) || — *I rate him among my friends* le cuento entre mis amigos || *what is the house rated at?* ¿cuál es la contribución que hay que pagar por la casa?
◆ *vi* ser considerado (*as* como); *he rates as a fine workman* es considerado como un buen trabajador || FAM *to rate with s.o.* gozar de la estima de alguien.

rateable; ratable [-əbl] *adj* valorable || imponible (value).

ratepayer ['reitˌpeiə*] *n* contribuyente *m* & *f*.

ratepaying ['reitˌpeiiŋ] *adj* contribuyente (taxpayer).
◆ *n* pago *m* de impuestos.

rather ['rɑːðə*] *adv* más bien; *rather long than short* más bien largo que corto || bastante; *this matter is rather important* esta cuestión es bastante importante; *I rather like it* me gusta bastante || algo, un poco (somewhat); *John is rather stupid* Juan es algo estúpido; *rather better* un poco mejor || — *anything rather than* todo menos || *I had rather not, I would rather not* no me apetece || *I rather like it* no me disgusta || *I would rather leave than stay here* preferiría *or* prefiero irme que quedarme aquí || *I would rather not to go* preferiría *or* prefiero no ir || *or rather* mejor dicho.
◆ *interj* ¡ya lo creo!, ¡por supuesto! [AMER ¡cómo no!]; *do you know him? rather!* ¿le conoce? ¡ya lo creo! || *rather not!* ¡claro que no!

raticide ['rætisaid] *n* raticida *m*.

ratification [ˌrætifi'keiʃən] *n* ratificación *f*.

ratify ['rætifai] *vt* ratificar.

ratifying [-iŋ] *adj* ratificatorio, ria.

rating ['reitiŋ] *n* estimación *f*, tasación *f*, valoración *f* (estimate) || rango *m* (rank) || MAR marinero *m* || clasificación *f* (of engines, cars, ships) || SP clase *f*, categoría *f* || crédito *m* (of a business concern) || derrama *f* (of local taxes) || ELECTR condiciones *f pl* normales de funcionamiento || FAM bronca *f* (scolding); *to give s.o. a rating* echarle una bronca a alguien || US clasificación *f* (of a pupil).

ratio ['reiʃiəu] *n* proporción *f*, relación *f*; *the ratio of men to women is two to three* la proporción entre los hombres y las mujeres es de dos a tres; *in the ratio of* en la proporción de || MATH razón *f* || *in direct, indirect ratio to* en razón directa, inversa con.

ratiocinate [ˌrætiˈɔsineit] *vi* raciocinar, razonar.

ratiocination [ˌrætiɔsiˈneiʃən] *n* raciocinio *m*, razonamiento *m*.

ration [ˈræʃən] *n* ración *f* (food) || porción *f* (time) || — *emergency* o *iron ration* reserva *f* de víveres || *to be off the ration* no estar racionado || *to be on the ration* estar racionado || *to put on the ration* racionar.

◆ *pl* víveres *m*, suministro *m sing*, aprovisionamiento *m sing* || FIG *to put on short rations* racionar, poner a media ración.

ration [ˈræʃən] *vt* racionar; *to ration bread* racionar el pan || *to ration out* racionar.

rational [-l] *adj* racional; *man is a rational animal* el hombre es un animal racional; *his criticism is very rational* su crítica es muy racional || razonable, sensato, ta (reasonable) || lógico, ca (logical) || racionalista (tendencies) || MATH racional || FAM práctico, ca.

rationale [ˌræʃəˈnɑːl] *n* razón *f* fundamental, base *f*, fundamento *m* (basis) || análisis *m* razonado, exposición *f* razonada (explanation).

rationalism [ˈræʃnəlizəm] *n* racionalismo *m*.

rationalist [ˈræʃnəlist] *adj/n* racionalista.

rationalistic [ˌræʃnəˈlistik] *adj* racionalista.

rationality [ˌræʃəˈnæliti] *n* racionalidad *f*.

rationalization [ˌræʃnəlaiˈzeiʃən] *n* racionalización *f* (of industry, etc.).

rationalize [ˈræʃnəlaiz] *vt* racionalizar.

ration book [ˈræʃənbuk]; **ration card** [ˈræʃənkɑːd] *n* cartilla *f* de racionamiento.

rationing [ˈræʃniŋ] *n* racionamiento *m*.

ratline [ˈrætlin] *n* MAR flechaste *m*.

rat poison [ˈrætˈpɔizn] *n* matarratas *m inv*, raticida *m*.

rat race [ˈrætreis] *n* FIG competición *f*, competencia *f*, lucha *f* incesante [para triunfar].

rattan [rəˈtæn] *n* BOT rota *f*, junco *m* de Indias || bastón *m* de caña (walking stick).

rat-tat-tat [ˈrætəˈtæt] *interj* ¡pum! ¡pum!

ratteen [rəˈtiːn] *n* ratina *f* (cloth).

ratter [ˈrætə*] *n* perro *m* ratero || FIG & FAM traidor *m* (betrayer) | esquirol *m* (blackleg).

rattle [rætl] *n* sonajero *m* (baby's toy) || carraca *f*, matraca *f* (of football fans) || traqueteo *m* (noise of train, of carriage) || ruido *m* de sonajero (of baby's toy) || ruido *m* metálico (of chains, of bicycle) || tamborileo *m*, repiqueteo *m* (of hail, of train) || golpe *m* (of door, of window, etc.) || chasquido *m*, repiqueteo *m*, tableteo *m* (of machine gun) || castañeteo *m* (of teeth) || ZOOL cascabel *m* (of a snake) || FAM alboroto *m*, jaleo *m* (shindy) || *death rattle* estertor *m* de la muerte.

rattle [rætl] *vt* hacer sonar || agitar, sacudir (to shake) || FIG desconcertar (to disconcert); *the questions rattled the witness* las preguntas desconcertaron al testigo | poner nervioso, crispar (to annoy); *that noise is beginning to rattle me* ese ruido empieza a ponerme nervioso || *to rattle of* o *through* despachar (a piece of work, a speech) || MAR *to rattle up* levantar rápidamente (the anchor).

◆ *vi* hacer un ruido metálico (bicycle, chains) || traquetear (train, carriage); *Raymond's car does not rattle* el coche de Ramón no traquetea || chasquear, repiquetear, tabletear (machine gun) || tamborilear, repiquetear (hail, rain) || golpetear; *the window rattled in the wind* la ventana golpeteaba con el viento || castañetear; *his teeth rattled with fear* le castañeteaban los dientes de miedo || MED tener un estertor || — *to rattle along* traquetar, ir traqueteando || *to rattle at the door* llamar a la puerta (to knock), sacudir la puerta (to shake) || *to rattle away* irse con mucho ruido (coach), charlotear (to talk) || *to rattle down* caer con gran estrépito || *to rattle off* irse con mucho ruido (coach) || *to rattle on* seguir traqueteando (train), seguir hablando (to talk).

rattlebrain [-ˈbrein]; **rattlehead** [-hed]; **rattlepate** [-peit] *n* FAM persona *f* ligera de cascos, cabeza *f* de chorlito.

rattlebrained [-breind] *adj* FAM ligero de cascos, casquivano, na.

rattler [-ə*] *n* FAM tío *m* estupendo (person) | cosa *f* estupenda (thing) || US ZOOL crótalo *m*, serpiente *f* de cascabel || US FAM cacharro *m*, trasto *m* (car).

rattlesnake [-sneik] *n* ZOOL crótalo *m*, serpiente *f* de cascabel.

rattletrap [-træp] *adj* desvencijado, da.

◆ *n* cacharro *m*, trasto *m* (old car).

◆ *pl* cachivaches *m* (baubles).

rattling [-iŋ] *adj* rápido, da (pace) || FAM muy bueno, estupendo, da (extraordinarily good).

◆ *adv* FAM muy.

rattrap [ˈrættræp] *n* ratonera *f*.

ratty [ˈræti] *adj* infestado de ratas (place) || a rata (smell) || FAM furioso, sa.

raucous [ˈrɔːkəs] *adj* ronco, ca (hoarse, harsh) || estridente (shrill).

raucousness [-nis] *n* ronquedad *f*.

raunchy [ˈrɔːntʃi] *adj* FAM verde (joke) || sexy (voice, appearance).

ravage [ˈrævidʒ] *n* destrozo *m*, asolamiento *m* (devastation).

◆ *pl* estragos *m* || FIG *the ravages of time* las injurias del tiempo, los estragos de los años.

ravage [ˈrævidʒ] *vt* destrozar, asolar; *the crops were ravaged by hail* las cosechas fueron destrozadas por el granizo || *face ravaged by disease* cara desfigurada por la enfermedad.

◆ *vi* causar estragos.

rave [reiv] *n* FAM desvarío *m*, delirio *m* (nonsense) | juerga *f* (good time); *the party was quite a rave* la fiesta fue una verdadera juerga || FAM *rave review* relato *m* entusiasta.

rave [reiv] *vi* delirar, desvariar; *he raved in his delirium* desvarió en su delirio || estar desencadenado (wind) || — *to rave about* o *over* deshacerse en alabanzas sobre, entusiasmarse por, estar loco por || *to rave at* o *against s.o.* tronar contra alguien, encolerizarse con alguien || FAM *to rave it up* estar *or* ir de parranda.

ravel [ˈrævəl] *n* enmarañamiento *m* (entanglement) || hilacha *f*, hilacho *m* (ravelled thread) || maraña *f*, embrollo *m* (sth. tangled).

ravel [ˈrævəl] *vt* enredar, enmarañar (to entangle) || *to ravel out* deshilachar (material), desenredar, desenmarañar (threads), desenmarañar, desenredar, aclarar (a matter).

◆ *vi* enredarse, enmarañarse (to become tangled) || *to ravel out* deshilacharse (to fray).

ravelin [ˈrævlin] *n* revellín *m* (of a fort).

ravelling; US **raveling** [ˈrævliŋ] *n* deshilachadura *f* || hilacha *f*, hilacho *m* (ravelled thread).

raven [ˈreivn] *adj* negro como el azabache.

◆ *n* cuervo *m* (bird).

raven [ˈrævn] *vt* devorar.

◆ *vi* buscar una presa (animal) || vivir de rapiña (person) || FIG *to raven for* tener sed de.

ravening [-iŋ] *adj* voraz.

◆ *n* voracidad *f*.

ravenous [ˈrævənəs] *adj* hambriento, ta (very hungry) || voraz (voracious) || *to be ravenous* tener un hambre canina (to be hungry), estar ansioso, tener muchas ganas (*for* de) (to long for).

ravenousness [-nis] *n* voracidad *f* || hambre *f* canina.

ravine [rəˈviːn] *n* barranco *m*.

raving [ˈreiviŋ] *adj* delirante || FIG & FAM extraordinario, ria || *raving mad* loco de atar.

◆ *n* delirio *m*, desvarío *m*.

◆ *pl* divagaciones *f*, desvaríos *m*.

ravioli [ˌrɑviˈəuli] *pl n* CULIN ravioles *m*, raviolis *m* (pasta).

ravish [ˈræviʃ] *vt* raptar (to kidnap) || llevarse, arrebatar (sth.) || violar (a woman) || FIG encantar, embelesar (to enrapture).

ravisher [-ə*] *n* raptor, ra (kidnapper) || violador *m* (rapist).

ravishing [-iŋ] *adj* encantador, ra.

raw [rɔː] *adj* CULIN crudo, da (uncooked); *raw meat* carne cruda || bruto, ta; sin refinar (oil) || en bruto, bruto, ta (metal) || puro, ra; *raw spirit* alcohol puro || sin cocer (brick) || sin curtir, verde, en verde (hide, skins) || en rama (cotton) || ARTS crudo, da (colours) || no aguerrido, da (troops) || vivo, va (flesh) || en carne viva (wound) || a flor de piel (nerves) || FIG frío, a (air) | frío y húmedo (weather) | novato, ta; inexperto, ta (inexperienced) | basto, ta; tosco, ca (uncouth) || FAM verde (story) || — *raw deal* injusticia *f*, tratamiento injusto (injustice), jugarreta *f*, mala pasada (dirty trick) || *raw material* materia *f* prima || *raw silk* seda cruda || *raw umber* ocre *m* natural.

◆ *n* US FAM *in the raw* en cueros (naked), en su estado original (in the original state) || FIG *to touch s.o. on the raw* herir a uno en lo vivo.

rawboned [-bəund] *adj* esquelético, ca; huesudo, da (person) || flaco, ca (horse).

rawhide [-haid] *n* cuero *m* sin curtir *or* verde (untanned skin) || látigo *m* de cuero verde (whip).

rawness [-nis] *n* crudeza *f* || frío *m* húmedo (weather) || FIG falta *f* de experiencia | tosquedad *f* (coarseness).

ray [rei] *n* PHYS rayo *m*; *a ray of light* un rayo de luz; *the sun's rays* los rayos del sol; *cosmic rays* rayos cósmicos; *cathode rays* rayos catódicos || MATH radio *m* (radius) || BOT radio *m*; *medullary ray* radio medular || ZOOL raya *f* (fish) || MUS re *m* (note) || FIG rayo *m*, resquicio *m* (of hope) || ZOOL *electric ray* torpedo *m*.

Raymond [ˈreimənd] *pr n* Raimundo *m*, Ramón *m* (Christian name).

rayon [ˈreiɔn] *n* rayón *m*, rayona *f*, seda *f* artificial (cloth).

raze [reiz] *vt* arrasar (to demolish) || tachar (to erase) || borrar de la memoria (a memory) || arañar (the skin) || *to raze to the ground* arrasar, destruir por completo.

razor [ˈreizə*] *n* navaja *f* de afeitar (with unprotected blade) || maquinilla *f* de afeitar (safety) || máquina *f* de afeitar eléctrica (electric).

razorback [-bæk] *n* rorcual *m* (whale).

razor-backed [-ˈbækt] *adj* en escarpa (hill).

razorbill [-bil] *n* alca *f* (bird).

razor blade [-bleid] *n* hoja *f* de afeitar, cuchilla *f* de afeitar.

razor clam [-klæm] *n* navaja *f* (mollusc).

razor-edge [ˈreizərˈedʒ] *n* filo *m* || FIG *to be on a razor-edge* estar con el agua al cuello, estar en una situación difícil.

razor-sharp [ˈreizəˈʃɑːp] *adj* afilado, da || muy agudo, da (wit).

razor shell [-ʃel] *n* navaja *f* (mollusc).

razor strop [-strɔp] *n* suavizador *m*.

razz [ræz] *vt* US FAM tomar el pelo a (to tease, to rag).

razzia [ˈræziə] *n* razzia *f*.

razzle ['ræzl]; **razzle-dazzle** [-ˌdæzl]] *n* FAM juerga *f*; *to go on the razzle* irse de juerga.

razzmatazz [ˌræzmə'tæz] *n* FAM lado *m* colorista.

R & D *abbr of [research and development]* I + D, investigación y desarrollo.

re [rei] *n* MUS re *m*.

re [riː] *prep* COMM respecto a, relativo a, con referencia a.

reabsorb [riəb'sɔːb] *vt* reabsorber.

reabsorption [riəb'sɔːpʃən] *n* reabsorción *f*.

reach [riːtʃ] *n* alcance *m*; *out of my reach* fuera de mi alcance || tramo *m* (canal) || tramo *m* recto (river) || SP extensión *f* del brazo (boxer) || MAR bordada *f* (tack) || facultad *f* (of mind) || — *beyond s.o.'s reach* fuera del alcance de uno || *Oxford is within easy reach of London* Oxford está muy cerca de Londres || *planets within reach of small telescopes* planetas visibles con telescopios pequeños || *the upper reaches of the Amazon* la cuenca alta del Amazonas || *to make a reach for* intentar alcanzar || *within reach of* al alcance de.

reach [riːtʃ] *vt* llegar a, alcanzar; *we reached Paris at ten o'clock* llegamos a París a las diez; *the plant reaches the ceiling* la planta alcanza el techo || cumplir, llegar a; *to reach fifty* cumplir cincuenta años, llegar a los cincuenta años || llegar a (a conclusion, an agreement, a compromise, perfection) || llegar a las manos de (to come into the possession of); *the letter reached me yesterday* la carta llegó a mis manos ayer || alcanzar, dar en (with a shot) || SP alcanzar; *he could not reach his opponent* no pudo alcanzar a su adversario || pasar, acercar, dar, alargar; *reach me that dictionary* acércame ese diccionario || comunicar con; *we tried to reach John by radio* tratamos de comunicar con Juan por radio || llamar [por teléfono] (to telephone); *you can reach me at this number* me puede llamar a este número || FIG llegar al corazón *or* al alma, impresionar; *his words reached me* sus palabras me llegaron al corazón || — *to reach an amount* ascender *or* alcanzar una cantidad || *to reach down* bajar || *to reach home* llegar a casa || *to reach into one's pocket* meter la mano en el bolsillo || *to reach out one's hand* tender la mano (for money), alargar la mano (to get sth.), dar la mano (to shake hands).

◆ *vi* extenderse (to extend); *the woods reach as far as the river* los bosques se extienden hasta el río || llegar; *I cannot reach* no llego; *she reaches to my shoulder* me llega al hombro || alargar la mano; *he reached over the table* alargó la mano por encima de la mesa || alcanzar; *as far as the eye could reach* hasta donde alcanzaba la vista || intentar alcanzar *or* coger; *he reached for the lighter* intentó alcanzar el mechero || MAR navegar de bolina || — *the books reach up to the ceiling* los libros llegan hasta el techo || *the curtains reach down to the floor* las cortinas llegan hasta el suelo || FIG *to reach for* o *after* aspirar a.

reachable [-əbl] *adj* accesible || — *are you reachable by telephone?* ¿tiene teléfono?, ¿le puedo llamar por teléfono? || *I am always reachable* siempre puede ponerse en contacto conmigo.

reach-me-down [-miˌdaun] *adj* de segunda mano (second-hand) || heredado del hermano *or* de la hermana (handed down).

◆ *n* ropa *f* de segunda mano (second-hand) || ropa *f* heredada (from one's brother or sister).

re-act ['riː'ækt] *vi* volver a representar.

react [ri'ækt] *vi* reaccionar; *how did they react to the news?* ¿cómo reaccionaron ante la noticia? || PHYS & CHEM reaccionar || *to react upon* producir efecto en.

reactance [-əns] *n* ELECTR reactancia *f*.

reaction [ri'ækʃən] *n* reacción *f*; *the decision produced a violent reaction* la decisión provocó una reacción violenta || CHEM & PHYS reacción *f*; *chain reaction* reacción en cadena || — *reaction engine* motor *m* de reacción.

reactionary [-əri] *adj/n* reaccionario, ria.

reactivate [ri'æktiveit] *vt* reactivar.

reactivation [riækti'veiʃən] *n* reactivación *f*.

reactive [ri'æktiv] *adj* reactivo, va.

reactor [ri'æktə*] *n* PHYS reactor *m*; *nuclear reactor* reactor nuclear || CHEM reactivo *m*.

read [red]·*adj* leído, da || leído, da; instruido, da; *he is better read than most* él es más leído que la mayoría de la gente; *to be well-read in history* ser muy leído en historia.

read [riːd] *n* lectura || — *I had a good read in the plane* estuve leyendo un buen rato en el avión || INFORM *read head* cabeza *f* de lectura || *to have a quick read of the paper* echar un vistazo al periódico.

read* [riːd] *vt* leer; *to read a book, music, French* leer un libro, música, en francés; *read me a story* léeme un cuento; *to read fluently* leer de corrido; *to read sth. aloud* leer algo en voz alta || estudiar (at university); *to read history* estudiar historia || PRINT corregir, leer (proofs) || INFORM leer || consultar, mirar, leer (an instrument) || marcar; *the thermometer reads thirty degrees* el termómetro marca treinta grados || interpretar; *it may be read several ways* se puede interpretar de varias maneras || leer; *for "dead" read "lead"* léase «lead» en lugar de "dead" || leer, predecir (to predict) || descifrar (signs, codes) || — MUS *to read at sight* leer a primera vista, repentizar || FIG *to read one a lesson* leerle a uno la cartilla || *to read out* leer en voz alta (aloud), expulsar (from an association) || *to read s.o.'s palm* leerle la mano a uno || *to read s.o.'s thoughts* adivinar *or* leer los pensamientos de alguien || *to read s.o. to sleep* adormecer a alguien leyendo || *to read sth. in s.o.'s eyes* leer algo en los ojos *or* en la mirada de alguien || *to read sth. into a phrase* leer en una frase algo que no hay || *to read sth. over* o *through* leer rápidamente algo, echar un vistazo a algo (to read quickly), volver a leer algo (to reread) || *to read sth. right through* leer algo de cabo a rabo || *to read sth. up* estudiar algo.

◆ *vi* leer; *he is reading aloud* está leyendo en voz alta || leerse; *a magazine which reads easily* una revista que se lee con facilidad || estar escrito; *to read well, badly* estar bien escrito, mal escrito || decir, rezar; *the constitution reads as follows* la constitución dice lo siguiente || poder interpretarse, indicar; *his letter reads as if he isn't coming* su carta parece indicar que no se puede interpretar en el sentido de que no va a venir || — *to read about Churchill* leer un libro sobre Churchill || *to read about sth. in the newspaper* leer un artículo sobre algo *or* ver algo en el periódico || *to read between the lines* leer entre líneas || JUR *to read for the bar* prepararse para el foro || *to read on* seguir leyendo.

— OBSERV Pret y pp ***read*** [red];.

readable [-əbl] *adj* legible (legible) || que merece la pena leerse, entretenido, da (pleasant to read).

readapt ['riːə'dæpt] *vt* readaptar.

readaptation [riˌædæp'teiʃən] *n* readaptación *f*.

readdress ['riːə'dres] *vt* cambiar la dirección en.

reader ['riːdə*] *n* lector, ra (person who reads) || libro *m* de lectura (book) || antología *f* (anthology) || PRINT corrector *m* (proofreader) || INFORM lector *m* || aficionado, da [a la lectura] (person fond of reading) || lector *m* de manuscritos (publisher's critic) || profesor *m* adjunto (of a university staff).

readership [-ʃip] *n* cargo *m* de profesor adjunto (in a university) || lectores *m pl*; *a newspaper with a readership of fifty thousand* un periódico con cincuenta mil lectores.

readily ['redili] *adv* de buena gana (willingly); *I will lend you the money readily* le dejaré el dinero de buena gana || en seguida; *funds are readily available* los fondos están disponibles en seguida || con soltura; *he writes readily* escribe con soltura || pronto; *you must not criticize too readily* no hay que criticar demasiado pronto || libremente; *she talks readily of her divorce* habla libremente de su divorcio || fácilmente (easily); *readily understandable* fácilmente comprensible.

readiness ['redinis] *n* buena disposición *f*; *readiness to help* buena disposición para ayudar || disponibilidad *f* (of funds) || rapidez *f* (of a reply) || soltura *f*; *the readiness with which he writes* la soltura con la cual escribe || agudeza *f* (of s.o.'s wit) || — *to be in readiness* estar listo *or* preparado || *to hold o.s. in readiness* estar listo.

reading ['riːdiŋ] *n* lectura *f*; *the reading of a book* la lectura de un libro; *to be fond of reading* ser aficionado a la lectura || recital *m* (aloud); *a poetry reading* un recital de poesía || versión *f* (textual version) || PRINT corrección *f* (of proofs) || indicación *f* (of instruments) || interpretación *f*; *my reading of the situation differs somewhat* mi interpretación de la situación difiere algo || JUR lectura *f* (of a will, a bill in Parliament) || INFORM lectura *f* || *a man of wide reading* un hombre culto, un hombre que ha leído mucho.

◆ *adj* de lectura (of reading) || de los lectores (of readers) || lector, ra; que lee (who reads) || — *reading desk* mesa *f* de lectura (table), atril *m* (lectern) || INFORM *reading head* cabeza *f* de lectura || *reading lamp* lámpara *f* portátil || *reading matter* lectura *f* || *reading room* sala *f* de lectura.

readjust ['riːə'dʒʌst] *vt* ajustar de nuevo, reajustar, readaptar.

readjustement [-mənt] *n* reajuste *m*.

readmission ['riːəd'miʃən] *n* readmisión *f* || THEATR *readmission ticket* contraseña *f*.

readmit ['riːəd'mit] *vt* readmitir, volver a admitir.

readmittance [-əns] *n* readmisión *f*.

ready ['redi] *adj* listo, ta; preparado, da; *is supper ready?* ¿está la cena preparada?; *ready for use* listo para usar || dispuesto, ta; *she is ready to starve in order to slim* está dispuesta a morirse de hambre para adelgazar || disponible; *a ready supply of money* una cantidad disponible de dinero || rápido, da (reply) || vivo, va; agudo, da (wit) || pronto, ta; dispuesto, ta (prompt); *he is very ready with his criticism* es muy pronto en criticar || a punto de; *she looked ready to drop* parecía a punto de caerse || de buen grado; *he gave me his ready consent* me dio su consentimiento de buen grado || — *now ready, just ready* a punto de publicarse (book) || *ready cash* o *money* dinero *m* contante *or* líquido || *ready reckoner* tabla *f* de cálculo || *ready!, set!, go!, ready!, steady!, go!* ¡preparados!, ¡listos!, ¡ya! || *to be ready to hand* estar a mano || *to get ready* prepararse (to prepare o.s.), arreglarse (before going out) || *to get o to make sth. ready* preparar algo || *to have a ready pen* escribir con soltura || *to have a ready tongue* no tener pelillos en la lengua || *to hold o.s. ready to do sth.* estar listo para hacer algo.

◆ *n* MIL posición *f* de fuego *or* de apresto (firearms) || FAM *the ready* la pasta (money).

ready ['redi] *vt* preparar || *to ready o.s.* prepararse.

ready-made [-'meid] *adj* confeccionado, da; hecho, cha; *ready-made clothing* ropa hecha || *ready-made beliefs* prejuicios *m.*

ready-to-wear [-tə'wɛə*] *adj* confeccionado, da; hecho, cha (clothing).

reaffirm ['ri:ə'fə:m] *vt* reafirmar.

reaffirmation [ri:,æfə'meiʃən] *n* reafirmación *f.*

reafforest ['ri:ə'fɔrist] *vt* repoblar con árboles.

reafforestation ['ri,əfɔris'teiʃən] *n* repoblación *f* forestal.

reagent [ri'eidʒənt] *n* CHEM reactivo *m.*

real [riəl] *adj* real, verdadero, ra; *his pain is real, not imaginary* su dolor es real, no imaginario || auténtico, ca; verdadero, ra; *this is real summer weather* esto es un auténtico tiempo de verano; *a real surprise* una verdadera sorpresa || legítimo, ma; auténtico, ca; genuino, na; *real sherry* vino de Jerez legítimo; *a real pearl* una perla legítima; *real gold* oro legítimo || PHIL, JUR & MATH real || — FAM *for real* de veras || JUR *real estate* o *property* bienes *m pl* raíces | *real estate agency* agencia inmobiliaria || PHYS *real image* imagen real || *real time* tiempo *m* real || FAM *the real McCoy* el auténtico, la auténtica || *the real thing* el original, el auténtico || *they are real men* son hombres de verdad.
◆ *adv* US FAM realmente, verdaderamente; *I am real pleased* estoy verdaderamente contento.
◆ *n* *the real* lo real, la realidad.

real [rei'ɑ:l] *n* real *m* (former spanish coin).

real ale ['riəl,eil] *n* cerveza *f* inglesa fermentada en el barril.

realgar [ri'ælgə*] *n* MIN rejalgar *m.*

realign [ri:ə'lɑin] *vt* realinear, reorganizar.

realise ['riəlaiz] *vt* ⟶ **realize.**

realism ['riəlizəm] *n* realismo *m.*

realist ['riəlist] *n* realista *m* & *f.*

realistic [riə'listik] *adj* realista.

realistically [riə'listikəli] *adv* de una manera realista.

reality [ri'æliti] *n* realidad *f* || realismo *m* (of a description) || — *in reality* en realidad, de hecho || *to get back to realities* volver a la realidad.

realizable ['riəlaizəbl] *adj* realizable, factible || FIG imaginable.

realization ['riəlai'zeiʃən] *n* realización *f* (of a project, assets) || comprensión *f.*

realize; realise ['riəlaiz] *vt* darse cuenta de; *he realized that she was in danger* se dio cuenta de que ella estaba en peligro || realizarse, hacerse realidad; *her wish was realized at last* su deseo al fin se hizo realidad || realizar (to convert into money); *to realize one's assets* realizar sus bienes || sacar, lograr (profit) || — *I realize your position* comprendo su posición || *to realize a high price* venderse caro.

reallocate ['ri:'æləkeit] *vt* asignar de nuevo.

really ['riəli] *adv* realmente, en realidad, de verdad (in reality); *it is not really a storm, just a shower* no es una tormenta de verdad, sino sólo un chubasco || verdaderamente, realmente (truly); *really beautiful weather* tiempo verdaderamente espléndido; *I really like it* me gusta realmente || — *have we really finished?* ¿será verdad que hemos terminado? || *really!* ¡hay que ver! || *really?* ¿de veras?, ¿de verdad?

realm [relm] *n* reino *m* (kingdom) || FIG esfera *f,* terreno *m* (domain) || FIG *within the realm of possibility* dentro de lo posible.

realtor [ri'æltə*] *n* US corredor *m* de fincas.

realty ['riəlti] *n* bienes *m pl* raíces.

ream [ri:m] *n* resma *f* (of paper) || FIG *to write reams about a subject* escribir mucho sobre un tema.
◆ *pl* FIG montones *m,* gran cantidad *f sing.*

ream [ri:m] *vt* TECH abocardar, ensanchar, escariar (to widen or shape with a reamer) || MIL avellanar (to widen the bore with a reamer) || US exprimir (fruit) | extraer con exprimidor (fruit juice).

reamer [-ə*] *n* TECH escariador *m* || MIL avellanador *m* || US exprimelimones *m inv,* exprimidor *m.*

reanimate [ri:'ænimeit] *vt* reanimar.

reanimation [ri:æni'meiʃən] *n* reanimación *f.*

reap [ri:p] *vt* AGR segar (to cut) | recoger, cosechar (to harvest) || FIG cosechar, recoger; *to reap the fruits of one's labours* cosechar los frutos de su trabajo || *to reap the benefits* llevarse los beneficios.
◆ *vi* cosechar, hacer la cosecha.

reaper [-ə*] *n* AGR segador, ra (s.o. who reaps) | segadora *f* (machine) || — *reaper and binder* segadora agavilladora || FIG *the Reaper, the Grim Reaper* la Parca.

reaping [-iŋ] *n* siega *f* || *reaping hook* hoz *f* || *reaping machine* segadora *f* || *reaping time* siega *f.*

reappear ['ri:ə'piə*] *vi* reaparecer.

reappearance ['ri:ə'piərəns] *n* reaparición *f.*

reapply ['ri:ə'plɑi] *vi* presentar una nueva solicitud.

reappoint ['ri:ə'pɔint] *vt* nombrar de nuevo.

reappointment [-mənt] *n* nuevo nombramiento *m.*

reappraisal ['ri:ə'preizəl] *n* replanteamiento *m.*

reappraise ['ri:ə'preiz] *vt* replantear.

reapportion [riə'pɔ:ʃən] *vt* repartir de nuevo.

rear ['ri:ə*] *adj* posterior, de atrás, trasero, ra || MIL de retaguardia || — *rear admiral* contraalmirante *m* || *rear seat, axle* asiento, eje trasero || *rear window, drive* ventanilla, tracción trasera.
◆ *n* parte *f* posterior, parte *f* de atrás (the back of sth.) || MIL retaguardia *f*; *five hundred yards to the rear* quinientas yardas a retaguardia | cola *f* (of a column) || FAM letrina *f* (latrine) | trasero *m* (buttocks) || — *at the rear of* detrás de || *in the rear* atrás; por detrás (to attack) || *to bring up the rear* cerrar la marcha; cubrir la retaguardia (soldiers).

rear [ri:ə*] *vt* levantar, erigir (to erect); *to rear a monument* levantar un monumento || levantar, erguir; *to rear one's head* levantar la cabeza || cultivar (to cultivate) || criar; *to rear dogs* criar perros; *to rear a family* criar niños.
◆ *vi* encabritarse, empinarse (a horse) || levantarse (to rise up).

rear-engined [-r'endʒind] *adj* con motor trasero.

rearguard [-gɑ:d] *n* MIL retaguardia *f*; *rearguard action* acción de retaguardia || FIG *to fight a rearguard action* resistirse inútilmente.

rearing [-iŋ] *n* erección *f* (of a monument, etc.) || erguimiento *m* (of the head) || cultivo *m* (cultivation) || cría *f* (of animals) || crianza *f* (of children) || encabritamiento *m* (of a horse).

rearm ['ri:'ɑ:m] *vt* rearmar.
◆ *vi* rearmarse.

rearmament [-əmənt] *n* MIL rearme *m.*

rearmost ['riəməust] *adj* último, ma.

rearrange ['ri:ə'reindʒ] *vt* volver a arreglar (to arrange again) || disponer de otro modo (to arrange in a different way) || adaptar (to adapt).

rearrangement [-mənt] *n* nuevo arreglo *m,* nueva disposición *f* || adaptación *f.*

rearview ['riəvju:] *adj* AUT *rearview mirror* retrovisor *m.*

rearward ['riəwə:d] *adj* posterior, último, ma.
◆ *adv* hacia atrás.
◆ *n* retaguardia *f.*

reason ['ri:zn] *n* razón *f*; *his reason has shown him the right course* su razón le ha enseñado el buen camino; *to lose one's reason* perder la razón || razón *f,* causa *f,* motivo *m*; *she understands the reason for his behaviour* ella entiende la razón de su comportamiento; *for this reason* por esta razón || PHIL razón *f* || — *all the more reason you should not go* razón de más para que no vaya || *by reason of* en virtud de || *in reason* razonablemente (reasonably), dentro de lo razonable (within reasonable limits) || *it is contrary to reason* no es razonable || *reason of State* razón de Estado || *the reason why* el porqué, la razón por la cual || *to bring to reason* hacer entrar en razón || *to have reason to believe that* tener motivo para creer que || *to listen to reason* avenirse a razones || *to stand to reason* ser evidente || *with good reason* con razón.

reason ['ri:zn] *vt* razonar (to analyse by reasoning) || discutir (to discuss) || — *to reason out* resolver (a problem), llegar a; *to reason out a settlement* llegar a una solución; comprender; *I cannot reason it out* no llego a comprenderlo; disuadir; *to reason s.o. out of doing sth.* disuadir a alguien de hacer algo || *to reason whether...* intentar saber si...
◆ *vi* razonar, raciocinar (to think logically) || discutir (with s.o.).

reasonable ['ri:znəbl] *adj* razonable, sensato, ta (person) || razonable; *a reasonable excuse* una disculpa razonable; *the book had a reasonable success* el libro tuvo un éxito razonable || módico, ca; razonable; *a reasonable rent* un alquiler módico.

reasonableness [-nis] *n* moderación *f,* sensatez *f,* lo razonable.

reasonably *adv* razonablemente (sensibly) || bastante (fairly).

reasoning ['ri:zniŋ] *n* razonamiento *m* || cálculos *m pl*; *according to my reasoning* según mis cálculos.
◆ *adj* dotado de raciocinio, racional.

reasonless ['ri:znlis] *adj* sin razón.

reassemble ['ri:ə'sembl] *vt* reunir, volver a juntar || TECH volver a montar.
◆ *vi* reunirse, volverse a juntar.

reassert ['ri:ə'sə:t] *vt* reafirmar.

reassess ['ri:ə'ses] *vt* revaluar (to revalue) || fijar de nuevo (a tax) || examinar de nuevo (to reconsider).

reassessment [-mənt] *n* revaluación *f,* replanteamiento *m.*

reassume [,ri:ə'sju:m] *vt* reasumir, volver a asumir.

reassumption [,ri:ə'sʌmpʃən] *n* reasunción *f.*

reassurance [,ri:ə'ʃuərəns] *n* tranquilidad *f* || noticia *f* tranquilizadora (reassuring news) || palabras *f pl* tranquilizadoras (words) || promesa *f* tranquilizadora (promise) || COMM reaseguro *m.*

reassure [,ri:ə'ʃuə*] *vt* tranquilizar (to tranquillize) || COMM reasegurar.

reassuring [-riŋ] *adj* tranquilizador, ra.

reattach ['ri:ə'tætʃ] *vt* reatar.

reawaken ['ri:ə'weikən] *vt* volver a despertar.
◆ *vi* volver a despertarse.

reawakening [-iŋ] *n* despertar *m.*

rebaptize [ri:bæp'taiz] *vt* rebautizar.

rebarbative [ri'bɑ:bətiv] *adj* repelente.

rebate [ˈriːbeit] *n* rebaja *f*, descuento *m* (discount) || reembolso *m* (repayment) || TECH rebajo *m* (in carpentry).

rebate [ˈriːbeit] *vt* US rebajar, descontar (to discount) || reembolsar (to repay) || TECH hacer una ranura *or* un rebajo en, renvalsar (to make a rabbet) || ensamblar (to join).

rebec [ˈriːbek] *n* MUS rabel *m*.

Rebecca [riˈbekə] *pr n* Rebeca *f*.

rebel [ˈrebl] *adj/n* rebelde.

rebel [riˈbel] *vi* rebelarse, sublevarse.

rebellion [riˈbeljən] *n* rebelión *f*, sublevación *f*.

rebellious [riˈbeljəs] *adj* rebelde.

rebelliousness [-nis] *n* rebeldía *f*.

rebind* [riːˈbaind] *vt* volver a atar (to fasten again) || reencuadernar (a book).
— OBSERV Pret y pp ***rebound***.

rebirth [ˈriːˈbəːθ] *n* renacimiento *m* (second birth).

rebore [ˈriːˈbɔː*] *n* TECH rectificado *m*.

rebore [ˈriːˈbɔː*] *vt* TECH rectificar.

reborn [ˈriːˈbɔːn] *pp* *to be reborn* renacer, volver a nacer.

rebound [riˈbaund] *n* rebote *m* || FIG *on the rebound* en pleno choque emocional.

rebound [riˈbaund] *vi* rebotar.

rebound [riˈbaund] *pret/pp* ⟶ **rebind.**

rebroadcast [ˈriːˈbrɔːdkɑːst] *n* nueva transmisión *f*.

rebroadcast [ˈriːˈbrɔːdkɑːst] *vt* volver a transmitir.

rebuff [riˈbʌf] *n* negativa *f* (rejection) || desaire *m* (snub).

rebuff [riˈbʌf] *vt* rechazar (to reject) || desairar (to snub).

rebuild* [ˈriːˈbild] *vt* reconstruir.
— OBSERV Pret y pp ***rebuilt***.

rebuilding [-iŋ] *n* reconstrucción *f*.

rebuke [riˈbjuːk] *n* reproche *m*, reprimenda *f*.

rebuke [riˈbjuːk] *vt* reprender, regañar.

rebus [ˈriːbəs] *n* jeroglífico *m* || acertijo *m* (riddle).

rebut [riˈbʌt] *vt* rebatir, refutar, impugnar.

rebuttal [-l] *n* refutación *f*, impugnación *f*.

rebutter [-ə*] *n* JUR contrarréplica *f*.

recalcification [riˌkælsifiˈkeiʃən] *n* recalcificación *f*.

recalcitrance [riˈkælsitrəns] *n* terquedad *f*, obstinación *f*.

recalcitrant [riˈkælsitrənt] *adj* recalcitrante, refractario, ria; reacio, cia || MED que no responde al tratamiento.

recalcitrate [riˈkælsitreit] *vi* oponerse.

recalculate [riˈkæljuleit] *vt* calcular de nuevo.

recall [riˈkɔːl] *n* llamada *f* (the act of recalling) || revocación *f*, anulación *f* || retirada *f* (of a diplomat) || recuerdo *m* (memory) || MIL llamada *f*, toque *m* de llamada || *beyond recall, past recall* irrevocable.

recall [riˈkɔːl] *vt* llamar, hacer volver (to order to return) || retirar; *to recall an ambassador* retirar a un embajador; *to recall an edition from the bookshops* retirar una edición de las librerías || revocar (a decision, a judgment) || retirar (one's word) || MIL llamar a filas (a reservist) || recordar, acordarse de (to remember); *she recalled meeting him last year* se acordó de haberle conocido el año pasado || recordar, hacer pensar en (to remind); *that music recalls my stay in Spain* esa música me recuerda mi estancia en España.

recant [riˈkænt] *vt* retractar.
◆ *vi* retractarse.

recantation [ˌriːkænˈteiʃən] *n* retractación *f* (of a statement).

recap [ˈriˈkæp] *n* FAM recapitulación *f* || recauchutado *m* (of a tyre).

recap [ˈriˈkæp] *vt/vi* FAM recapitular || resumir (to summarize) || recauchutar (a tyre).

recapitalization [ˈriːˌkæˌpitəlaiˈzeiʃən] *n* recapitalización *f*.

recapitulate [ˌriːkəˈpitjuleit] *vt/vi* recapitular || resumir (to summarize).

recapitulation [ˈriːkəˌpitjuˈleiʃən] *n* recapitulación *f*.

recapture [ˈriːˈkæptʃə*] *n* nueva detención *f* (recapturing) || reconquista *f* (of a town).

recapture [ˈriːˈkæptʃə*] *vt* volver a capturar (a prisoner) || reconquistar (a town, an area) || FIG hacer revivir (to recreate); *to recapture the atmosphere of the twenties* hacer revivir el ambiente de los años veinte || JUR recobrar.

recast* [ˈriːˈkɑːst] *vt* refundir (metal) || refundir (a book) || THEATR cambiar el reparto de (a play) || rehacer (to remodel).
— OBSERV Pret y pp ***recast.***.

recasting [-iŋ] *n* refundición *f*.

recede [riˈsiːd] *vi* retroceder, retirarse; *the sea receded* el mar retrocedió || retroceder; *the shore gradually receded* la playa retrocedía gradualmente || descender (tide) || MIL retirarse || disminuir (to lessen) || volverse atrás (to withdraw from a position, from a promise, etc.) || *receding hairline* entradas *f pl*.

receipt [riˈsiːt] *n* recepción *f*, recibo *m* (the act of receiving) || recibo *m* (document); *to ask for a receipt* pedir un recibo || (ant) receta *f* (recipe) || — *I am in receipt of your letter of the third* he recibido *or* obra en mi poder su atenta carta del tres del mes corriente || *on receipt of* al recibo de, al recibir || *to acknowledge receipt of* acusar recibo de || *upon receipt of the goods* al recibir las mercancías.
◆ *pl* ingresos *m*, recaudación *f sing*, entradas *f* (amount collected).

receipt [riˈsiːt] *vt* US acusar recibo de, dar un recibo por.
◆ *vi* US dar un recibo.

receipt book [-buk] *n* talonario *m* de recibos.

receivable [riˈsiːvəbl] *adj* admisible, procedente (that can be accepted or received) || válido, da (candidature) || COMM por cobrar; *receivable bills* cuentas por cobrar.
◆ *pl n* COMM efectos *m or* deudas *f* por cobrar.

receive [riˈsiːv] *vt* recibir; *they received him with applause* le recibieron con aplausos; *to receive good advice* recibir buenos consejos; *to receive a refusal* recibir una negativa; *to receive a letter* recibir una carta; *the canal receives water from several rivers* el canal recibe agua de varios ríos || aceptar (to accept); *if she sends me a gift I shall refuse to receive it* si me manda un regalo me negaré a aceptarlo || acoger (to welcome into one's home); *to receive an orphan for Christmas* acoger a un huérfano para pasar las Navidades || admitir (to admit); *to be received into a society* ser recibido en una sociedad || cobrar; *to receive one's salary* cobrar el sueldo || tener; *to receive serious wounds* tener lesiones graves || JUR ocultar, encubrir (stolen goods) || SP recibir; *to receive a pass* recibir un pase || soportar, aguantar (to take the weight of) || REL recibir (Communion) || contener; *large enough to receive two gallons* suficientemente grande para contener dos galones || RAD captar (a broadcast) || — JUR *he received ten years* le echaron diez años, recibió diez años || GRAMM *received pronunciation* pronunciación generalmente admitida || COMM *received with thanks* recibí || *to be well, badly received* tener una buena, una mala acogida (a play, etc.) || REL *to receive into the Church* recibir en el seno de la Iglesia, bautizar.
◆ *vi* recibir; *to receive on Thursdays* recibir los jueves || REL recibir la comunión, comulgar (to take communion) || JUR ser encubridor.

receiver [-ə*] *n* recibidor, ra; receptor, ra (s.o. who receives) || destinatario, ria (of a letter) || recaudador, ra (tax collector) || JUR síndico *m* (syndic) | ocultador *m*, encubridor *m* (of stolen goods) || auricular *m* (earpiece of a telephone) || RAD receptor *m* (television or radio set) || CHEM recipiente *m* (receptacle) || *to lift the receiver* descolgar el teléfono.

receivership [-ʃip] *n* sindicatura *f* de una quiebra, administración *f* judicial || *to go into receivership* quedar bajo el control de la administración judicial.

receiving [-iŋ] *n* recepción *f* (reception) || JUR encubrimiento *m* (of stolen goods) || — *receiving room* sala *f* de recibo, recibidor *m* || *receiving set* receptor *m* || *receiving station* estación receptora.

recency [ˈriːsnsi] *n* carácter *m* reciente, novedad *f*.

recension [riˈsenʃən] *n* recensión *f*.

recent [ˈriːsnt] *adj* reciente.

recently [-li] *adv* recientemente || *until quite recently* hasta hace poco.

receptacle [riˈseptəkl] *n* receptáculo *m*, recipiente *m* (container) || BOT receptáculo *m*.

reception [riˈsepʃən] *n* recepción *f*, recibo *m*; *reception of goods* recepción de mercancías || admisión *f* (admission) || recibimiento *m*, acogida *f* (welcoming) || recepción *f* (social gathering) || RAD recepción *f* (of radio or television signals) || recepción *f* (part of hotel) || — *reception centre* centro *m* de acogida (for refugees) || *reception clerk* encargado *m* de la recepción, recepcionista *m* & *f* || *reception class* primer curso *m* en una escuela primaria || *reception desk* recepción || *reception room* sala *f* de espera (for receiving the patients of a doctor, of a dentist, etc.), sala *f* de recibir (for receiving guests) || *to get a cold, a warm reception* tener una acogida fría, calurosa.

receptionist [riˈsepʃənist] *n* recepcionista *m* & *f*.

receptive [riˈseptiv] *adj* receptivo, va.

receptiveness [-nis]; **receptivity** [-iti] *n* receptividad *f*.

receptor [riˈseptə*] *n* receptor *m*.

recess [riˈses] *n* ARCH hueco *m* (in a wall) | nicho *m* (for a statue) | alcoba *f* (for a bed) || escondrijo *m* (hiding place) || lugar *m* apartado; *in the farthest recesses of Argentina* en los lugares más apartados de Argentina || parte *f* recóndita; *the recesses of the mind* las partes recónditas de la mente || suspensión *f* (of activity) || descanso *m* (rest) || período *m* de clausura, intermedio *m* (of Parliament) || interrupción *f* (of a meeting) || retroceso *m* (of water) || ANAT fosa *f* || US recreo *m* (period between school classes) || — *to be in recess* estar clausurado (Parliament) || *to have a recess* suspender la sesión.

recess [riˈses] *vt* hacer un hueco en (to construct a recess in) || poner en un hueco (to put into a recess).
◆ *vi* suspender la sesión.

recessed [riˈsest] *adj* en retranqueo (bookshelf, cupboard).

recession [riˈseʃən] *n* retroceso *m*, retirada *f* (retreat) || hueco *m* (receding part) || REL procesión *f* del clero hacia la sacristía || GEOGR retroceso *m* || COMM recesión *f* || JUR retroceso *m*.

recessional [-əl] *adj* REL de la procesión del clero [una vez terminado el servicio] || del período de clausura (Parliament).
◆ *n* himno *m* de fin de oficio.

recessive [ri'sesiv] *adj* que tiende a retroceder || BIOL recesivo, va.

recharge ['riː'tʃɑːdʒ] *vt* recargar.

rechargeable [riː'tʃɑːdʒəbl] *adj* recargable.

recherché [rə'ʃɛəʃei] *adj* rebuscado, da.

rechristen ['ri'krisn] *vt* rebautizar || FIG dar un nuevo nombre a.

recidivism [ri'sidivizəm] *n* reincidencia *f.*

recidivist [ri'sidivist] *adj/n* reincidente.

recipe ['resipi] *n* CULIN & MED receta *f* || FIG receta *f*; *a sure recipe for success* una receta segura para el éxito.

recipient [ri'sipiənt] *adj/n* receptor, ra (receiver) || destinatario, ria (of a letter, of a cheque, etc.).

reciprocal [ri'siprəkəl] *adj* recíproco, ca; mutuo, tua; *reciprocal feelings of affection* sentimientos mutuos de afecto || GRAMM & MATH recíproco, ca.
◆ *n* MATH cantidad *f* recíproca || lo recíproco.

reciprocate [ri'siprəkeit] *vt* corresponder a (to give in return); *to reciprocate s.o.'s love* corresponder al amor de alguien || cambiar, intercambiar (to give and receive mutually); *the two presidents reciprocated expressions of goodwill* los dos presidentes intercambiaron palabras reveladoras de su buena voluntad || TECH producir un movimiento alternativo en.
◆ *vi* corresponder (to respond); *I tried to be nice but she didn't reciprocate* intenté ser amable pero no me correspondió || TECH tener movimiento alternativo.

reciprocating [ri'siprəkeitiŋ] *adj* TECH alternativo, va.

reciprocation [ri,siprə'keiʃən] *n* reciprocidad *f.*

reciprocity [,resi'prɔsiti] *n* reciprocidad *f.*

recital [ri'saitl] *n* relato *m*, relación *f* (a relating of facts, sth. which is related) || recital *m* (of music, of dancing); *organ recital* recital de órgano || recitación *f*, recital *m* (of poetry).

recitation [,resi'teiʃən] *n* relato *m*, relación *f*; *a long recitation of what had happened* una larga relación de lo que había pasado || enumeración *f* (listing) || recitación *f* (of a poem) || poesía *f* (piece of poetry).

recitative [,resitə'tiːv] *adj* recitativo, va.
◆ *n* MUS recitativo *m.*

recite [ri'sait] *vt* recitar (to repeat aloud); *to recite a poem* recitar un poema || relatar, narrar (to give a detailed account of) || enumerar (to list in detail) || JUR exponer (facts).
◆ *vi* recitar.

reciter [-ə*] *n* recitador, ra.

reck [rek] *vt* (ant) preocuparse por.

reckless [-lis] *adj* imprudente (careless); *a reckless driver* un conductor imprudente || arrojado, da; temerario, ria (indifferent to danger) || inconsiderado, da; imprudente (ill-considered); *a reckless thing to say* una declaración inconsiderada || *reckless speed* velocidad peligrosa.

recklessness [-lisnis] *n* imprudencia *f* (carelessness) || temeridad *f* (temerity).

reckon ['rekən] *vt* calcular (to calculate); *reckon how much you have spent* calcule cuánto ha gastado || contar (to count); *she reckons him among her best friends* le cuenta entre sus mejores amigos || estimar, creer; *I reckon she is thirty* creo que tiene treinta años || considerar; *he is reckoned as one of the best runners* está considerado como uno de los mejores corredores || — *reckoning everything* todo incluido, contándolo todo (all included), pensándolo bien, considerándolo todo (everything considered) || *to reckon in* incluir || *to reckon up* calcular.
◆ *vi* calcular (to calculate) || contar; *she reckoned on her fingers* contaba con los dedos; *we are reckoning on a devaluation of the peseta* contamos con una devaluación de la peseta || suponer, imaginar (to suppose) || creer, pensar (to think) || — *reckoning from yesterday* a contar de ayer, a partir de ayer || *to reckon without* prescindir de || *to reckon with s.o.* ajustar cuentas con alguien (to settle accounts with), contar con (to contend with); *if you marry her you will have her mother to reckon with* si se casa con ella tendrá que contar con su madre.

reckoner [-ə*] *n* calculador, ra || MATH tabla *f.*

reckoning [-iŋ] *n* cuenta *f*, cálculo *m*; *to be out in one's reckoning* equivocarse en las cuentas || estimación *f*, apreciación *f*; *to the best of my reckoning* según mi estimación || COMM cuenta *f*, factura *f*, nota *f* (account) | ajuste *m* de cuentas (settling of accounts) || MAR estima *f* || — *it's a lot of money by any reckoning* se mire como se mire representa mucho dinero || FIG *the day of reckoning* el día *m* del juicio final.

reclaim [ri'kleim] *n* *past o beyond reclaim* perdido para siempre.

reclaim [ri'kleim] *vt* reformar (to reform) || sacar (from vice) || AGR roturar, aprovechar || ganar; *land reclaimed from the sea* tierra ganada al mar || sanear (marshland) || TECH recuperar, regenerar; *reclaimed rubber* caucho regenerado || *reclaimed woman* mujer arrepentida.

re-claim [ri'kleim] *vt* reclamar.

reclaimable [-əbl] *adj* enmendable, corregible (reformable) || recuperable; *reclaimable deposit* fianza recuperable || AGR roturable (land) || que puede ser ganado [al mar] (from the sea) || que puede ser saneado (marshland) || TECH recuperable, regenerable.

reclaiming [-iŋ] *n* → **reclamation.**

reclamation [,reklə'meiʃən] *n* enmienda *f*, corrección *f* (moral salvation) || reclamación *f* (claiming back) || AGR roturación *f*, aprovechamiento *m* (of land) || saneamiento *m* (of marshland) || TECH recuperación *f*, regeneración *f.*

recline [ri'klain] *vt* apoyar, reclinar (one's head).
◆ *vi* recostarse, reclinarse (*on* en) || apoyarse, descansar (head).

recluse [ri'kluːs] *n* recluso, sa; solitario, ria.

reclusion [ri'kluːʒən] *n* reclusión *f*, aislamiento *m.*

reclusive [ri'kluːsiv] *adj* recluso, sa; solitario, ria.

recognition [,rekəg'niʃən] *n* reconocimiento *m*; *recognition of a new state* reconocimiento de un nuevo estado; *in recognition of* en reconocimiento de || *it has changed beyond recognition o out of all recognition* ha llegado a ser irreconocible.

recognizable ['rekəgnaizəbl] *adj* reconocible.

recognizance [ri'kɔgnizəns] *n* JUR fianza *f* (guarantee) | compromiso *m* (obligation) || *to enter into recognizances to* comprometerse a.

recognize ['rekəgnaiz] *vt* reconocer; *to recognize s.o. by the way he dresses* reconocer a alguien por su modo de vestirse; *to recognize a new state* reconocer un nuevo estado; *to recognize s.o. as leader* reconocer a alguien como jefe || admitir, reconocer (a mistake) || admitir; *this word is not recognized* esta palabra no está admitida || US dar la palabra a.

recoignage [-idʒ] *n* reacuñación *f*, nueva acuñación *f.*

recoil [ri'kɔil] *n* culatazo *m* (of a gun) || retroceso *m* (of a cannon) || aflojamiento *m* (of a spring) || FIG asco *m*, repugnancia *f*, horror *m* (repugnance) || retirada *f*, retroceso *m* (of soldiers) || *recoil spring* muelle *m* de retroceso.

recoil [ri'kɔil] *vi* dar culatazo (a gun) || retroceder (a cannon) || aflojarse (a spring) || retirarse, retroceder, replegarse (soldiers) || echarse atrás (to draw back) || FIG rechazar, negarse a, rehusar (to refuse); *to recoil from doing sth.* rechazar hacer algo | tener horror a *or* asco a, sentir repugnancia por (to feel disgust) | recaer sobre (to have repercussions); *his dishonesty recoiled on him* su falta de honradez recayó sobre él.

recoilless [-lis] *adj* sin retroceso (gun).

recoin [ri'kɔin] *vt* acuñar de nuevo.

recollect [,rekə'lekt] *vt* recordar, acordarse de (to remember); *as far as I recollect* si mal no recuerdo || *to recolled o.s.* recogerse.

re-collect ['riːkə'lekt] *vt* reunir (to gather) || recuperar (to recover) || *to re-collect o.s.* serenarse.

recollection [,rekə'lekʃən] *n* recuerdo *m* (thing remembered); *I have happy recollections of my stay there* tengo buenos recuerdos de mi estancia allí || memoria *f* (power of recollecting) || recogimiento *m* (spiritual contemplation) || *to the best of my recollection* que yo recuerde.

recommence ['riːkə'mens] *vt/vi* volver a empezar, empezar de nuevo *or* otra vez, recomenzar.

recommend [,rekə'mend] *vt* recomendar; *can you recommend a good restaurant?* ¿puede recomendar un buen restaurante?; *I have been recommended to you* me han recomendado a usted || aconsejar, recomendar (to advise); *I recommend you to accept* le aconsejo que acepte || encomendar; *I recommend my soul to God* encomiendo mi alma a Dios || — *he has little to recommend him* poca cosa tiene que hable en su favor || *not to be recommended* que no es de aconsejar, que no es recomendable, poco aconsejable.

recommendable [-əbl] *adj* recomendable || aconsejable (advisable).

recommendation [,rekəmen'deiʃən] *n* recomendación *f*; *the recommendations of a committee* las recomendaciones de un comité; *when I left he wrote me a good recommendation* cuando me marché me hizo una buena recomendación || consejo *m*, recomendación *f* (advice) || — *in recommendation of* recomendando || *on the recommendation of* por recomendación de || *recommendation to mercy* petición *f* de indulto.

recompense ['rekəmpens] *n* recompensa *f* (reward) || compensación *f*, indemnización *f*, resarcimiento *m* (for damage).

recompense ['rekəmpəns] *vt* recompensar (to reward) || compensar, indemnizar, resarcir (in return for a loss or damage).

recompose ['riːkəm'pəuz] *vt* calmar, tranquilizar, serenar (s.o.) || recomponer (sth.).

recomposition [ri,kɔmə'ziʃən] *n* recomposición *f.*

reconcilable ['rekənsailəbl] *adj* reconciliable (person) || conciliable, compatible (statements).

reconcile ['rekənsail] *vt* reconciliar (persons) || arreglar, poner fin a (a dispute) || conciliar (different statements) || — *to become reconciled to, to reconcile o.s. to* resignarse a, conformarse con (sth.) || *to become reconciled with* reconciliarse con (s.o.).

reconcilement [-mənt]; **reconciliation** [,rekənsili'eiʃən] *n* reconciliación *f* (of two persons) || conciliación *f* (of theories) || arreglo *m* (of a dispute).

reconciliatory [ˌrekənˈsiljətəri] *adj* reconciliador, ra.

recondite [riˈkɔndait] *adj* recóndito, ta; oculto, ta (obscure) || abstruso, sa (difficult to understand).

recondition [ˌriːkənˈdiʃən] *vt* arreglar, poner como nuevo (to restore) || *reconditioned car, engine* coche, motor revisado.

reconfirm [ˈriːkənˈfəːm] *vt* reconfirmar.

reconnaissance; reconnoissance [riˈkɔnisəns] *adj* de reconocimiento; *reconnoissance plane, flight* avión, vuelo de reconocimiento.
◆ *n* reconocimiento *m* || *to go on reconnoissance* reconocer el terreno.

reconnoitre; *US* **reconnoiter** [ˌrekəˈnɔitə*] *vt* reconocer.
◆ *vi* hacer un reconocimiento, reconocer el terreno.

reconnoitrer; *US* **reconnoiterer** [-rə*] *n* MIL explorador *m*.

reconquer [ˈriːˈkɔŋkə*] *vt* reconquistar.

reconquest [ˈriːˈkɔŋkwest] *n* reconquista *f*.

reconsider [ˈriːkənˈsidə*] *vt* volver a considerar, examinar de nuevo, reconsiderar (to consider again) || revisar (a judgment).

reconsideration [ˈriːkənˌsidəˈreiʃən] *n* nuevo examen *m* || revisión *f*.

reconstituent [ˈriːkənsˈtitjuənt] *adj* reconstituyente.
◆ *n* reconstituyente *m*.

reconstitute [ˈriːˈkɔnstitjuːt] *vt* reconstituir || CULIN hidratar (dried food).

reconstitution [ˈriːˌkɔnstiˈtjuːʃən] *n* reconstitución *f*.

reconstruct [ˈriːkənsˈtrʌkt] *vt* reconstruir, reedificar (a building) || reconstruir (a road) || JUR reconstituir (a crime).

reconstruction [ˈriːkənsˈtrʌkʃən] *n* reconstrucción *f*, reedificación *f* (of a building) || reconstrucción *f* (of a road) || JUR reconstitución *f* (of a crime) || *US* reorganización *f*.

reconstructive [ˈriːkənsˈtrʌktiv] *adj* reconstructivo, va.

reconvene [ˈrikənˈviːn] *vt* convocar de nuevo (a meeting).
◆ *vi* reanudar la sesión, volverse a reunir.

reconvention [ˈrikənˈvenʃən] *n* reconvención *f*.

reconversion [ˈriːkənˈvəːʃən] *n* readaptación *f* || TECH reconversión *f*.

reconvert [ˈriːkənˈvəːt] *vt* readaptar || reconvertir.

reconvey [ˈriːkənˈvei] *vt* devolver, restituir (to give back) || JUR hacer la retrocesión de, retroceder.

reconveyance [-əns] *n* JUR retrocesión *f* || devolución *f*, restitución *f*.

recook [ˈriːkuk] *vt* volver a cocer, recocer.

record [ˈrekɔːd] *n* anotación *f*, inscripción *f*, registro *m* (writing down) || registro *m* (register) || documento *m* (document) || relación *f* (account); *a detailed record of what happened* una relación detallada de lo que pasó || actas *f pl*, acta *f* (minutes); *the record of the meeting* las actas de una reunión; *court record* actas de un tribunal || expediente *m* (file); *I'll go and get out your record* voy a sacar su expediente || expediente *m* académico (at university) || historial *m* médico (medical) || historial *m*, hoja *f* de servicios (of s.o.); *I have a good record* tengo una buena hoja de servicios || mención *f*; *there is no record of it in history* no se hace mención de ello en la historia || nota *f*; *to make a record of an observation* tomar nota de una observación || boletín *m*; *official record of a society* boletín oficial de una sociedad || calificación *f*, notas *f pl*; *his son has a good record at school* su hijo tiene buenas notas en el colegio || SP récord *m*, marca *f*, plusmarca *f*; *to break, to hold, to set a record* batir, tener, establecer un récord; *five records fell* se batieron cinco récords || grabación *f* (of sounds) || disco *m* (of gramophone); *long-playing record* disco de larga duración || cinta *f* (of tape recorder) || rollo *m* (of a pianola) || — *matter of record* hecho establecido || *music on record* música grabada || *off the record* confidencialmente, oficiosamente || *off-the-record statement* declaración oficiosa || *police record, criminal record* registro de antecedentes penales || *service record* hoja de servicios, historial || *the Public Record Office* los Archivos Nacionales || *there is no record of it* no hay constancia de ello || *to be on record* estar registrado (to be registered), constar (fact) || *to go on record* declarar públicamente; *the Prime Minister went on record as saying* el Primer Ministro declaró públicamente que; constar; *let it go on record that* que conste que || *to have a clean record* no tener antecedentes penales || *to place on record in the minutes* hacer constar en las actas || *to put a resolution on record* consignar una resolución, hacer constar una resolución || *to put* o *set the record straight* deshacer un error, dejar las cosas bien claras || *verbatim record* actas taquigráficas *or* literales.
◆ *pl* anales *m*, archivos *m* (archives).
◆ *adj* récord, nunca alcanzado, da; *at record speed* a una velocidad nunca alcanzada.

record [riˈkɔːd] *vt* tomar nota de, apuntar (to make a note of); *to record an appointment in one's diary* tomar nota de una cita en su agenda || registrar (to register) || hacer constar, consignar (in the minutes); *to record a resolution* consignar una resolución || informar de, relatar (to relate) || declarar; *to record a birth with the authorities* declarar un nacimiento al registro civil || empadronar, hacer el censo de (population) || grabar (sounds) || marcar (a thermometer, etc.) || — *recorded broadcast* o *transmission* emisión diferida || *to be recorded* constar.

record breaker [ˈrekɔːdˈbreikə*] *n* plusmarquista *m* & *f*, "recordman" *m*, "recordwoman" *f*.

record-breaking [ˈrekɔːdˈbreikiŋ] *adj* récord *m inv* (time, jump, production) || que ha batido muchos récords (team).

record cabinet [rekɔːdˈkæbinit] *n* discoteca *f*, armario *m* para discos.

record card [ˈrekɔːdkɑːd] *n* ficha *f*.

record changer [ˈrekɔːdˈtʃeindʒə*] *n* cambiadiscos *m inv*.

record dealer [ˈrekɔːdˈdiːlə*] *n* vendedor *m* de discos.

recorder delivery [reˈkɔːdid diˈlivəri] *n* correo *m* certificado.

recorder [riˈkɔːdə*] *n* JUR magistrado *m* municipal || secretario *m* del registro civil (registrar) || archivero, ra; archivista *m* & *f* (keeper of records) || MUS flauta *f* (flute) | artista *m* & *f* que graba discos || grabadora *f* (sound recording device) || contador *m*, indicador *m* (recording device); *speed recorder* indicador de velocidad || — AVIAT *flight recorder* registrador *m* de vuelo || *recorder of deeds* registrador *m* de la propiedad || *sound recorder* grabadora *f* || *tape recorder* magnetófono *m*, magnetofón *m* [AMER grabadora *f*].

record holder [ˈrekɔːdˈhəuldə*] *n* SP plusmarquista *m* & *f*, "recordman" *m*, "recordwoman" *f*.

recording [riˈkɔːdiŋ] *adj* JUR encargado del empadronamiento (official) || que graba discos (artist) || de grabación (studio, van, session) || magnetofónico, ca (tape) || *recording head* cabeza sonora.
◆ *n* consignación *f*; *the recording of a motion* la consignación de una moción || narración *f*, relación *f* (narration) || censo *m*, empadronamiento *m* (of the population) || registro *m* (registration) || grabación *f* (of sound) || INFORM grabación *f*.

record library [ˈrekɔːdˈlaibrəri] *n* discoteca *f*.

record player [ˈrekɔːdˌpleiə*] *n* tocadiscos *m inv*.

recount [riˈkaunt] *vt* contar, relatar (a story).

re-count; recount [ˈriːˈkaunt] *n* recuento *m*, segundo escrutinio *m*; *to have a recount* hacer un recuento.

re-count; recount [ˈriːˈkaunt] *vt* hacer el recuento de *or* un segundo escrutinio de, volver a contar (votes).

recountal [riˈkauntəl] *n* relato *m*.

recoup [riˈkuːp] *vt* indemnizar (*for* por) (to compensate) || recuperar, resarcirse (to recover); *to recoup a loss* resarcirse de una pérdida || recobrar (strength) || JUR deducir, descontar (to deduct).

recoupment [-mənt] *n* indemnización *f* (compensation) || recuperación *f*, resarcimiento *m* (of losses) || JUR deducción *f*.

recourse [riˈkɔːs] *n* recurso *m* || *to have recourse to* recurrir a.

recover [riˈkʌvə*] *vt* recuperar, recobrar (the appetite, voice, breath, senses, consciousness, strength, love, etc.) || recuperar (lost time, a town, lost or stolen property) || sacar del agua (sth. floating) || rescatar (to rescue) || sacar, recuperar; *to recover by-products from oil* sacar subproductos del petróleo || obtener (to obtain); *to recover damages from s.o.* obtener daños y perjuicios de alguien || resarcirse de (to make good a loss) || hacer volver en sí (a fainting person) || ganar (land from sea) || cobrar (a debt) || *to recover one's legs* ponerse de pie.
◆ *vi* reponerse, restablecerse, recuperarse (from an illness) || volver en sí, recobrar el sentido (to regain consciousness) || recuperarse; *to recover from civil war* recuperarse de la guerra civil || reponerse, salir; *he recovered from his astonishment* se repuso de su asombro || recuperarse; *the economy has recovered* la economía se ha recuperado || volver a subir (prices) || JUR ganar el pleito.

re-cover [ˈriːˈkʌvə*] *vt* volver a cubrir, cubrir de nuevo (to cover again) || forrar de nuevo (a book, furniture, etc.).

recoverable [-ərəbl] *adj* recuperable || MED curable.

recovery [riˈkʌvəri] *n* recuperación *f* (of sth. lost); *recovery of one's appetite, of lost time, of a stolen car* recuperación del apetito, del tiempo perdido, de un coche robado || MED restablecimiento *m*, recuperación *f* || recuperación *f* (of the economy, of the business) || rescate *m* (rescue) || subida *f* (of prices) || obtención *f* (of damages) || FIG restablecimiento *m* (after a setback) || recuperación *f* (from waste products) || MED *past recovery* en estado desesperado, desahuciado, da.

recreancy [ˈrekriənsi] *n* cobardía *f* (cowardice) || deslealtad *f* (disloyalty).

recreant [ˈrekriənt] *adj/n* cobarde (coward) | traidor, ra; desleal (betrayer).

recreate [ˈrekrieit] *vt* divertir, entretener.
◆ *vi* divertirse, entretenerse.

re-create [ˈriːkriˈeit] *vt* volver a crear, recrear.

recreation [ˌrekriˈeiʃən] *n* esparcimiento *m*, expansión *f*, descanso *m* (leisure-time activity); *a moment of recreation* un momento de esparcimiento || diversión *f*, entretenimiento *m* (pastime); *my favourite recreation* mi diversión preferida || recreo *m* (playtime in school).

re-creation [ˈriːkriˈeiʃən] *n* nueva creación *f*.

recreacional [ˌrekri'eiʃənəl] *adj* recreativo, va; *recreational evening* velada recreativa; *recreational facilities* instalaciones recreativas.

recreative ['rekrieitiv] *adj* recreativo, va.

recrement ['rekrimənt] *n* recremento *m*.

recriminate [ri'krimineit] *vi* recriminar.

recrimination [riˌkrimi'neiʃən] *n* recriminación *f*.

recriminative [ri'krimiˌneitiv]; **recriminatory** [rekrimi'neitəri] *adj* recriminatorio, ria; recriminador, ra.

recross ['riː'krɔs] *vt/vi* volver a cruzar.

recrudesce [ˌriːkruː'des] *vi* recrudecer.

recrudescence [-ns] *n* recrudescencia *f*; *recrudescence of crime* recrudescencia de la criminalidad ‖ recrudecimiento *m*; *recrudescence of the cold weather* recrudecimiento del frío.

recruit [ri'kruːt] *n* MIL recluta *m*, quinto *m* ‖ neófito, ta; nuevo adherente (new member).

recruit [ri'kruːt] *vt* MIL reclutar, alistar (to enlist) ‖ contratar (employees) ‖ recuperar (one's health) ‖ MIL *to recruit supplies* abastecerse.
◆ *vi* MIL reclutar (to take on recruits) | abastecerse (with supplies) ‖ restablecerse, reponerse, recuperarse (one's health).

recruiter [-ə*] *n* reclutador *m*.

recruiting [-iŋ]; **recruitment** [mənt] *n* MIL reclutamiento *m* ‖ contratación *f* (of employees) ‖ MED restablecimiento *m* (recovery) ‖ MIL *recruiting board* junta *f* de clasificación.

rectal ['rektəl] *adj* ANAT rectal, del recto.

rectangle ['rekˌtæŋgl] *n* MATH rectángulo *m*.

rectangular [rek'tæŋgjulə*] *adj* MATH rectangular.

rectifiable ['rektifaiəbl] *adj* rectificable.

rectification [ˌrektifi'keiʃən] *n* rectificación *f*.

rectifier ['rektifaiə*] *n* TECH rectificador *m*.

rectify ['rektifai] *vt* rectificar, corregir; *to rectify an error* rectificar un error ‖ MATH, CHEM & ELECTR rectificar ‖ MIL corregir (a shot).

rectifying [-iŋ] *adj* rectificador, ra.

rectilineal [ˌrekti'liniəl]; **rectilinear** [ˌrekti'liniə*] *adj* rectilíneo, a.

rectitude ['rektitjuːd] *n* rectitud *f*.

recto ['rektəu] *n* recto *m* (of a page).

rector ['rektə*] *n* director *m* (of a school) ‖ rector *m* (of a university) ‖ REL párroco *m* (parish priest) | superior *m* (of a religious order).

rectorate ['rektərit]; **rectorship** ['rektəʃip] *n* rectorado *m*, rectoría *f*.

rectorial [rek'tɔːriəl] *adj* rectoral.

rectory ['rektəri] *n* REL rectoral *f*, rectoría *f*, casa *f* del párroco.

rectum ['rektəm] *n* ANAT recto *m*.
— OBSERV El plural de *rectum* es *rectums* o *recta*.

recumbency [ri'kʌmbənsi] *n* posición *f* yacente *or* recostada.

recumbent [ri'kʌmbənt] *adj* recostado, da ‖ *recumbent statue* estatua *f* yacente.

recuperable [ri'kjuːpərəbl] *adj* recuperable.

recuperate [ri'kjuːpəreit] *vt* recuperar; *to recuperate lost time* recuperar el tiempo perdido ‖ recobrar (one's health) ‖ TECH recuperar (waste products).
◆ *vi* restablecerse, recuperarse, reponerse.

recuperation [riˌkjuːpə'reiʃən] *n* recuperación *f* ‖ restablecimiento *m*, recuperación *f* (of health).

recuperative [ri'kjuːpərətiv] *adj* recuperativo, va.

recur [ri'kəː*] *vi* volver; *this idea recurred to my mind* esta idea volvió a mi mente; *to recur to a subject* volver a un tema ‖ volver a ocurrir, repetirse, reproducirse (to occur again); *the noise recurred several times* el ruido se repitió varias veces ‖ repetirse (a question) ‖ volver a plantearse (a problem) ‖ MATH reproducirse (figures) ‖ MED reproducirse.

recurrence [ri'kʌrəns] *n* vuelta *f* (return) ‖ reaparición *f*, repetición *f* (repetition); *the recurrence of a noise* la reaparición de un ruido ‖ periodicidad *f* (regular repetition) ‖ MED reaparición *f*, reproducción *f* (of a disease).

recurrent [ri'kʌrənt] *adj* que vuelve, que se repite ‖ periódico, ca (at regular intervals) ‖ MED & ANAT recurrente ‖ *it was a recurrent idea in his speech* la idea reapareció constantemente en su discurso.
◆ *n* ANAT nervio *m* recurrente | arteria *f* recurrente.

recurring [ri'kəːriŋ] *adj* periódico, ca.

recusancy ['rekjuzənsi] *n* recusación *f*.

recusant ['rekjuzənt] *adj/n* recusante.

recusation [ˌrekjə'zeiʃən] *n* JUR recusación *f*.

recuse [ri'kjuz] *vt* JUR recusar.

recycle [riː'saikl] *vt* reciclar.

red [red] *adj* rojo, ja; encarnado, da; colorado, da (colour) ‖ rojo, ja (beard, hair) ‖ enrojecido, da; rojo, ja (eyes) ‖ rojo, ja; *red with anger* rojo de ira ‖ colorado, da (with embarrassment); *to go red* ponerse colorado ‖ rojo, ja (in politics) ‖ tinto (wine) ‖ rojo, ja (ink) ‖ ahumado, da (herring) ‖ poco hecha (meat) ‖ FIG sanguinario, ria; *red vengeance* venganza sanguinaria ‖ — FIG *red as a peony* o *as a beetroot* o *as a turkey-cock* o *as a lobster* más rojo que un cangrejo (from the sun), más rojo que un tomate (with embarrassment) ‖ ANAT *red blood cell* glóbulo rojo ‖ SP *red card* tarjeta *f* roja ‖ US FAM *red cent* céntimo *m*, centavo *m* (a trifling sum of money) ‖ *Red Crescent* Creciente *m* Rojo ‖ *Red Cross* Cruz Roja (international organization) ‖ MAR *red duster, red ensign* bandera *f* de la marina mercante británica ‖ *red hands* manos teñidas de sangre ‖ *red hat* capelo cardenalicio ‖ *red heat* calor rojo ‖ CULIN *red herring* arenque ahumado ‖ FAM *red herring* pretexto *m* para desviar la atención | *to draw a red herring across the track* desviar la atención, despistar ‖ *red Indian* piel *m* roja ‖ *red lead* minio *m* ‖ *red light* disco rojo (traffic), luz roja (to draw attention), señal *f* de peligro (danger signal) ‖ *red meat* carne *f* roja ‖ ZOOL *red mullet* salmonete *m* (fish) ‖ *red ochre,* US *red ocher* ocre rojo, almagre *m* ‖ *Red Riding Hood* Caperucita Roja ‖ GEOGR *Red Sea* Mar *m* Rojo ‖ FIG *red tape* papeleo *m*, trámites *m pl* ‖ *to go* o *to turn red* ruborizarse, sonrojarse, ponerse colorado (a person), enrojecer (the sky).
◆ *n* rojo *m*, encarnado *m*, colorado *m*; *dressed in red* vestido de rojo ‖ rojo *m* (in politics) ‖ mingo *m* (ball in billiards) ‖ — *cherry red* rojo cereza ‖ FIG *to be in the red* deber dinero, tener deudas | *to be in the red at the bank* tener la cuenta bancaria en rojo | *to make s.o. see red* sacar a uno de quicio | *to see red* ponerse furioso, ponerse rojo de ira.

redact [ri'dækt] *vt* redactar.

redaction [ri'dækʃən] *n* redacción *f*.

redactor [ri'dæktə*] *n* redactor *m*.

redan [ri'dæn] *n* rediente *m* (fortification).

red-blooded ['red'blʌdəd] *adj* fuerte, vigoroso, sa (vigorous) ‖ enérgico, ca; vigoroso, sa (in writing).

redbreast ['redbrest] *n* petirrojo *m* (bird).

redcap ['redkæp] *n* policía *m* militar ‖ US mozo *m* de equipajes (in a railway station).

red-carpet ['red'kɑːpit] *adj* FAM suntuoso, sa.

redcoat ['redkəut] *n* soldado *m* inglés en la guerra de Independencia de los Estados Unidos.

redcurrant ['redkʌrənt] *n* BOT grosellero *m* (shrub) | grosella *f* (berry).

redden ['redn] *vi* enrojecer (sky) ‖ ruborizarse, ponerse colorado (a person).

reddish ['rediʃ] *adj* rojizo, za.

reddle ['redl] *n* almagre *m*.

redecorate [riː'dekəreit] *vt* volver a decorar, renovar la decoración ‖ volver a pintar, a empapelar.

redeem [ri'diːm] *vt* cancelar, redimir (a mortgage) ‖ recobrar, recuperar (one's rights) ‖ REL redimir (mankind) ‖ liberar, desempeñar (sth. pawned) ‖ amortizar, liberarse de (a debt) ‖ pagar (a bill) ‖ redimir (a slave) ‖ rescatar (by ransom) ‖ cumplir (a promise) ‖ compensar, salvar (a failing) ‖ expiar (a fault) ‖ recuperar (lost time) ‖ *to redeem o.s.* desquitarse.

redeemable [-əbl] *adj* redimible ‖ amortizable (a debt) ‖ liberable (from pawn).

redeemer [-ə*] *n* redentor, ra ‖ *the Redeemer* el Redentor.

redeeming [ri'diːmiŋ] *adj* redentor, ra ‖ compensatorio, ria; que compensa.

redefine ['riːdi'fain] *vt* redefinir.

redemand ['riːdi'maːnd] *vt* pedir de nuevo.

redemption [ri'dempʃən] *n* cancelación *f*, extinción *f* (of a mortgage) ‖ desempeño *m*, liberación *f* (from pawn) ‖ amortización *f* (of a debt) ‖ reembolso *m* (of a loan) ‖ expiación *f* (of a fault) ‖ REL redención *f* ‖ rescate *m* (of a slave) ‖ — *redemption fund* caja *f* de amortización ‖ *past redemption* sin redención, irremediable ‖ *sale with power of redemption* venta *f* con pacto de retro, retroventa *f*.

redemptive [ri'demptiv] *adj* redentor, ra.

Redemptorist [ri'demptərist] *n* REL redentorista *m*.

redeploy ['riːdi'plɔi] *vt* cambiar de frente (military forces).

redeployment [ˌriːdi'plɔimənt] *n* cambio *m* de frente (of troops, of weapons).

redevelop ['riːdi'veləp] *n* reaprovechar ‖ reurbanizar (an area).

redevelopment [ˌriːdi'veləpmənt] *n* reaprovechamiento ‖ reurbanización (of an area).

red-eyed ['redˌaid] *adj* con los ojos inyectados en sangre.

red-faced ['red'feist] *adj* coloradote, ta (with a reddish complexion) ‖ rojo de ira (angry) ‖ colorado, da; avergonzado, da (embarrassed).

red-handed ['red'hændid] *adj* en flagrante delito, con las manos en la masa; *to catch s.o. red-handed* coger a uno con las manos en la masa.

redhead ['red'hed] *n* pelirrojo, ja.

redheaded [-id] *adj* pelirrojo, ja.

redhibition [redhi'biʃən] *n* JUR redhibición *f*.

redhibitory [red'hibitəri] *adj* JUR redhibitorio, ria.

red-hot ['red'hɔt] *adj* al rojo, candente; *to make sth. red-hot* poner algo al rojo ‖ FIG acérrimo, ma (supporter) | ardiente, vehemente (ardent) | de última hora (news, etc.) | muy peligroso, sa (very dangerous) | sensacional, formidable (story) | muy cotizado, da; favorito, ta (favourite) | animado, da (full of pep) ‖ FIG & FAM *red-hot blonde* rubia incendiaria *or* explosiva.

redid [riː'did] *pret* ⟶ **redo.**

redingote ['rediŋgəut] *n* redingote *m*, levita *f*.

redintegrate [re'dintigreit] *vt* reintegrar (s.o.) ‖ volver a dar, devolver (to give back).

redintegration [redinte'greiʃən] *n* reintegro *m* ‖ devolución *f* (restitution).

redirect [ri:di'rekt] *adj* US JUR *redirect examination* segundo interrogatorio de un testigo.

redirect ['ri:dai'rekt] *vt* remitir *or* reexpedir al destinatario, remitir a las nuevas señas del destinatario (a letter).

redirection [-ʃən] *n* reexpedición *f.*

rediscount ['ridis'kaunt] *n* redescuento *m.*

rediscover ['ri:dis'kʌvə*] *vt* descubrir de nuevo, volver a descubrir, redescubrir.

rediscovery ['ridis'kʌvəri] *n* nuevo descubrimiento *m*, redescubrimiento *m.*

redistribute ['ri:dis'tribju:t] *vt* distribuir de nuevo, redistribuir.

redistribution ['ri:,distri'bju:ʃən] *n* nueva distribución *f*, redistribución *f.*

red-letter day ['red'letə*dei] *n* día *m* memorable *or* señalado.

red-light district ['red'lait'distrikt] *n* barrio *m* de mala fama.

redness ['rednis] *n* color *m* rojo.

redo* ['ri:'du:] *vt* volver a hacer, rehacer.
— OBSERV Pret ***redid***; pp ***redone***.

redolence ['redəuləns] *n* perfume *m*, fragancia *f* || FIG evocación *f.*

redolent ['redəulənt] *adj* fragante, oloroso, sa || FIG evocador, ra || *redolent with* impregnado de.

redone [ri'dʌn] *pp* ⟶ **redo.**

redouble [ri'dʌbl] *n* redoble *m* (bridge).

redouble [ri'dʌbl] *vt/vi* redoblar (to intensify); *to redouble one's efforts* redoblar sus esfuerzos || redoblar (bridge).

redoubling [-iŋ] *n* aumento *m*, incremento *m*, redoblamiento *m*, intensificación *f.*

redoubt [ri'daut] *n* MIL reducto *m.*

redoubtable [-əbl] *adj* temible.

redound [ri'daund] *vi* contribuir (to contribute) || recaer (*upon* sobre) (to reflect) || *to redound to* redundar en beneficio de (to benefit).

redpoll ['redpəul] *n* pardillo *m* (bird).

redraft ['ri:'drɑ:ft] *n* nueva redacción *f* || COMM resaca *f.*

redraft ['ri:'drɑ:ft] *vt* redactar de nuevo, escribir de nuevo.

redraw* ['ri:'drɔ:] *vt/vi* volver a dibujar *or* a trazar.
— OBSERV Pret ***redrew***; pp ***redrawn***.

redress [ri'dres] *n* reparación *f*, desagravio *m* (of a wrong) || enmienda *f*, corrección *f* (of an error) || — *beyond redress* irreparable || *to seek redress at s.o.'s hands* exigir un desagravio a alguien.

redress [ri'dres] *vt* restablecer (balance) || corregir, enmendar (an error) || reparar, deshacer, enderezar (a wrong) || aliviar (to relieve).

redresser [-ə*] *n* *redresser of wrongs* desfacedor *m* de entuertos, deshacedor *m* de agravios.

redskin [redskin] *n* piel roja *m* & *f.*

redstart ['redstɑ:t] *n* ZOOL colirrojo *m* (bird).

reduce [ri'dju:s] *vt* reducir; *to reduce expenses* reducir los gastos; *to reduce by a quarter* reducir en una cuarta parte; *to reduce to dust* reducir a polvo; *to reduce s.o. to obedience, to silence* reducir a alguien a la obediencia, al silencio || reducir; *he reduces everything to a simple principle* lo reduce todo a un principio sencillo || consignar; *to reduce sth. to writing* consignar algo por escrito || poner; *to reduce a theory to practice* poner una teoría en práctica || sofocar, reducir (a revolt) || rebajar (to a lower rank) || MIL degradar (an officer) || COMM rebajar, reducir (a price) || acortar (in length) || estrechar (in width) || reducir, aminorar, disminuir (to lessen) || hacer adelgazar (a fat person) || MATH & CHEM & MED reducir || CULIN trabar (a sauce) || PHOT rebajar || — *at reduced prices* a precios reducidos, con rebaja || FIG *in reduced circumstances* apurado, da (poor) | *they were reduced to begging* no tuvieron más remedio que pedir limosna | *to reduce s.o. to poverty* llevar a alguien a la pobreza.
◆ *vi* adelgazar (to slim) || reducirse, disminuir.

reducer [-ə*] *n* reductor *m* || PHOT rebajador *m.*

reducibility [ri,dju:sə'biliti] *n* reductibilidad *f.*

reducible [ri'dju:səbl] *adj* reducible, reductible.

reducing [ri'dju:siŋ] *adj* reductor, ra || — CHEM *reducing agent* reductor *m* || TECH *reducing gear* engranaje desmultiplicador.

reduction [ri'dʌkʃən] *n* reducción *f* (in general) || acortamiento *m* (in length) || estrechamiento *m* (in width) || adelgazamiento *m* (in weight) || MIL degradación *f* (to a lower rank) || MED reducción *f* (of a fracture) || MATH & CHEM reducción *f* || COMM disminución *f* (of prices, of wages) || rebaja *f*, descuento *m* (discount); *to get a good reduction on an article* conseguir un buen descuento en un artículo || baja *f*, disminución *f* (in temperature) || ELECTR disminución *f* (of voltage) || TECH desmultiplicación *f* (gearing down) || PHOT rebajamiento *m* || TECH *reduction gear* engranaje desmultiplicador.

redundance [ri'dʌndəns]; **redundancy** [-i] *n* GRAMM redundancia *f* || superabundancia *f* (exceso) || superfluidad *f* || exceso *m* de mano de obra (of labour) || desempleo *m* (unemployment).

redundant [ri'dʌndənt] *adj* excesivo, va; superfluo, a || GRAMM redundante, pleonástico, ca; tautológico, ca (word) || — *redundant labour* exceso *m* de mano de obra || *to become redundant* perder su empleo (worker).

reduplicate [ri'dju:plikit] *adj* repetido, da || BOT reduplicado, da || GRAMM repetido, da; reduplicado, da.

reduplicate [ri'dju:plikeit] *vt* repetir || BOT reduplicar || GRAMM repetir, reduplicar.

reduplication [ri,dju:pli'keiʃən] *n* repetición *f* || BOT reduplicación *f* || GRAMM repetición *f*, reduplicación *f.*

redwing ['redwiŋ] *n* malvís *m* (bird).

redwood ['redwud] *n* secoya *f* (tree).

redye ['ri:'dai] *vt* teñir de nuevo.

reecho [ri'ekəu] *vi* resonar.
◆ *vt* repetir.

reed [ri:d] *n* BOT caña *f*, junco *m*, carrizo *m* || MUS caramillo *m* (instrument) | lengüeta *f* (in mouthpiece); *reed instrument* instrumento de lengüeta || TECH peine *m* (of a loom) || paja *f*, rastrojo *m* (of a roof) || junquillo *m* (molding).
◆ *pl* MUS instrumentos *m* de lengüeta.

reed [ri:d] *vt* poner lengüeta a (an instrument) || techar con paja (a roof).

reedbed [-bed] *n* cañaveral *m*, carrizal *m*, juncal *m.*

reed mace [-meis] *n* BOT anea *f*, espadaña *f.*

reed organ [-'ɔ:gən] *n* MUS armonio *m.*

reed pipe [-paip] *n* MUS cañón *m* de lengüeta (of an organ) | caramillo *m* (instrument).

reed stop [-stɔp] *n* MUS cañones *m pl* de lengüeta (of an organ).

reeducate ['ri:'edjukeit] *vt* reeducar.

reeducation ['ri:,edju'keiʃən] *n* reeducación *f.*

reedy ['ri:di] *adj* lleno de juncos *or* cañas *or* carrizos || FIG delgado, da (person) | aflautado, da (voice) | agudo, da (sound).

reef [ri:f] *n* MAR arrecife *m*, escollo *m*; *coral reef* arrecife de coral || MIN vena *f*, filón *m* || MAR rizo *m* (in a sail); *to take in a reef* tomar rizos || FIG escollo *m* (hazard) || — FIG *to let out a reef* aflojarse el cinturón | *to take in a reef* apretarse el cinturón || *reef knot* nudo *m* de rizo.

reef [ri:f] *vt* MAR arrizar.

reefer [-ə*] *n* chaquetón *m*, chubasquero *m* (jacket) || guardiamarina *m* (midshipman) || US FAM cigarrillo *m* de marijuana, porro *m* (joint).

reek [ri:k] *n* humo *m* (smoke) || vaho *m*, vapor *m* (vapour) || tufo *m*, mal olor *m*, hedor *m* (unpleasant smell).

reek [ri:k] *vi* humear (sth. burning) || apestar; *this room reeks of tobacco* este cuarto apesta a tabaco || FIG destilar, rebosar de, rezumar; *his speech reeks of hypocrisy* su discurso destila hipocresía || *to reek with blood* estar bañado en sangre.

reel [ri:l] *n* carrete *m*, bobina *f*; *reel of cotton* bobina de algodón || CINEM bobina *f*, cinta *f*; *to change reels* cambiar de bobina || PHOT carrete *m*, rollo *m* || SP carrete *m* (of fishing rod) || baile *m* escocés muy rápido (Scottish dance) || TECH devanadera *f* (spool) | bobina *f* (of paper) || titubeo *m* (staggering) || FIG *off the reel* de un tirón, sin parar.

reel [ri:l] *vi* hacer eses, vacilar, tambalearse (to stagger) || dar vueltas; *my head is reeling* la cabeza me da vueltas || tener vértigo (to feel giddy) || tambalearse (to be shaken) || — FIG *his mind reeled at the thought* este pensamiento le daba vértigo || *to reel down the street* bajar la calle tambaleándose.
◆ *vt* devanar (thread, etc.) || — *to reel in* o *up* cobrar (rope) || *to reel in a fish* sacar un pez del agua enrollando el sedal || *to reel off* devanar (thread, etc.), recitar de un tirón, soltar (to recite without interruption).

reelect ['ri:i'lekt] *vt* reelegir.

reelected [-id] *adj* reelegido, da || reelecto, ta (not yet having taken office).

reelection ['ri:i'lekʃən] *n* reelección *f.*

reeligibility [ri:,elidʒə'biliti] *n* reelegibilidad *f.*

reeligible ['ri:'elidʒəbl] *adj* reelegible.

reembark ['ri:im'bɑ:k] *vt* reembarcar.
◆ *vi* reembarcarse.

reembarkation [,ri:imbɑ:'keiʃən] *n* reembarco *m.*

reemerge ['ri:i'mə:dʒ] *vi* resurgir.

reemphasize ['ri:'emfəsaiz] *vt* volver a recalcar.

reemploy [,ri:im'plɔi] *vt* volver a emplear.

reenact ['ri:i'nækt] *vt* volver a promulgar (law, etc.) || volver a representar (a play) || reconstituir (a crime).

reenforce ['ri:in'fɔ:s] *vt* ⟶ **reinforce.**

reenforcement [-mənt] *n* ⟶ **reinforcement.**

reengage ['ri:in'geidʒ] *vt* contratar de nuevo, volver a contratar (employees).

reengagement [-mənt] *n* nuevo contrato *m.*

reenlist ['ri:in'list] *vt* MIL reenganchar.
◆ *vi* MIL reengancharse.

reenlistment [-mənt] *n* MIL reenganche *m.*

reenter ['ri:'entə*] *vt* volver a entrar; *they never reentered that house* no volvieron nunca a entrar en esa casa || reingresar en, volver a ingresar en; *to reenter an organization* reingresar en una organización || volver a matricular (a child in a school) || volver a apuntar (in a register, etc.).
◆ *vi* volver a entrar; *Raymond went out and reentered* Ramón salió y volvió a entrar || volver a presentarse; *he reentered for his English exam* se volvió a presentar al examen de inglés.

reentrance ['ri:'entrəns] *n* reingreso *m.*

reentrant ['ri:'entrənt] *adj* entrante; *a reentrant angle* un ángulo entrante.
◆ *n* MIL entrante *m* (part of a defence).

reentry [ri:'entri] *n* nueva entrada *f*; *the reentry of a spacecraft into the atmosphere* la nueva entrada de un vehículo espacial en la atmósfera || reingreso *m*; *his reentry into university* su reingreso en la universidad.

reestablish ['ri:is'tæbliʃ] *vt* restablecer; *to reestablish order* restablecer el orden || restaurar; *to reestablish the king on the throne* restaurar al rey en el trono || reintegrar; *to reestablish s.o. in his possessions* reintegrar a alguien sus bienes || *to reestablish one's health* restablecerse, recuperarse, reponerse.

reestablishment [-mənt] *n* restablecimiento *m* (act of reestablishing) || restauración *f* (restoration) || reintegración *f* (of fortune, property) || *reestablishment of one's health* restablecimiento *m*.

reeve [ri:v] *n* baile *m* (king's agent) || presidente *m* del consejo (in Canada).

reeve* [ri:v] *vt* MAR pasar por una polea *or* por un ojal (a rope).
◆ *vi* MAR laborear.
— OBSERV Pret y pp ***rove, reeved***.

reexamination ['ri:ig,zæmi'neiʃən] *n* nuevo examen *m* (second exam) || JUR nuevo interrogatorio *m* (of a witness) || reexaminación *f*.

reexamine ['ri:ig'zæmin] *vt* examinar de nuevo, reexaminar (to examine again) || JUR volver a interrogar.

reexport ['ri:'ekspɔ:t] *n* reexportación *f*; *goods for reexport* mercancías destinadas a la reexportación.

reexport ['ri:'ekspɔ:t] *vt* reexportar.

reexportation ['ri:,ekspɔ:'teiʃən] *n* reexportación *f*.

ref [ref] *n* árbitro *m* (referee).

reface ['ri:'feis] *vt* ARCH rehacer la fachada de || TECH rectificar (a surface) || arreglar (garment).

refashion ['ri:'fæʃən] *vt* rehacer.

refection [ri'fekʃən] *n* colación *f*, refrigerio *m*.

refectory [ri'fektəri] *n* refectorio *m*.

refer [ri'fə:*] *vt* remitir (a matter to s.o.) || remitir; *he referred me to a Spanish dictionary* me remitió a un diccionario español || enviar; *to refer a patient to a specialist* enviar un paciente a un especialista || situar (an event to a date); *historians refer this event to the sixteenth century* los historiadores sitúan este acontecimiento en el siglo dieciséis || atribuir (to attribute); *the discovery of gunpowder is usually referred to China* generalmente el descubrimiento de la pólvora se atribuye a China || atribuir, achacar (an effect to its cause); *he refers his emotional problems to his childhood* atribuye sus problemas emocionales a su infancia || JUR remitir, enviar (an affair to a tribunal) || COMM *to refer a cheque to drawer* negarse a pagar un cheque [por falta de fondos].
◆ *vi* referirse, aludir, mencionar (to allude to); *in his speech he referred to football in Spain* en su discurso se refirió al fútbol en España *or* mencionó el fútbol en España || referirse (to look at for information); *the speaker referred to his notes* el orador se refirió a sus notas || calificar; *he referred to them as idealists* los calificó de idealistas || remitirse; *this man is an idiot, I refer to the facts* ese hombre es un idiota, me remito a los hechos || consultar; *for further information refer to the archives* para mayor información consultar los archivos || — COMM *referring to your letter of the twentieth* con relación a su carta del día veinte || *refer to page 10* véase la página 10.

referable [ri'fə:rəbl] *adj referable to* atribuible a.

referee [,refə'ri:] *n* árbitro *m* (in an argument, in sports) || garante *m* (for character reference).

referee [,refə'ri:] *vt/vi* arbitrar.

reference ['refrəns] *n* referencia *f* (act of referring) || relación *f*; *all parts have reference to one another* todas las partes tienen relación las unas con las otras || alusión *f*, mención *f*, referencia *f*; *to make a reference to a fact* hacer alusión a un hecho || fiador *m*, garante *m* (person giving character reference) || informe *m*, referencia *f* (testimonial) || llamada *f* (mark indicating a footnote) || referencia *f*, nota *f* (footnote) || fuente *f* (source of information) || — *for future reference* para el futuro, para que lo sepas en el futuro || *point of reference* punto *m* de referencia || *reference book* libro *m* de consulta || *reference library* biblioteca *f* de consulta || *reference mark* llamada || *reference number* número *m* de referencia || *terms of reference* mandato *m* || *to make reference to* referirse a, hacer referencia a || *without reference to* sin consultar (without consulting), sin mencionar (without mentioning) || *with reference to* en cuanto a (as regards), con referencia a, con relación a, respecto a (in a business letter).

reference ['refrəns] *vt* poner notas a.

referendum [,refə'rendəm] *n* referéndum *m*; *to have a referendum on a matter* hacer un referéndum sobre un asunto.
— OBSERV El plural de *referendum* es *referendums* o *referenda*.

referential [,refə'renʃəl] *adj* de referencia.

referral [ri'fə:rəl] *n* acción de enviar un paciente a un especialista.

refill ['ri:fil] *n* recambio *m*; *ballpoint refill* recambio de bolígrafo || carga *f*; *gas refill* carga de gas.

refill ['ri:'fil] *vt* rellenar (to fill up) || cargar; *to refill a pen, a lighter* cargar una pluma, un encendedor.

refillable [-əbl] *adj* recargable, recambiable.

refinance [ri'fai,næns] *vt* financiar de nuevo.

refine [ri'fain] *vt* refinar; *to refine oil, sugar* refinar petróleo, azúcar || depurar, purificar (water) || purificar, acrisolar (metal) || FIG refinar, pulir, hacer *or* volver más fino (a person, an accent) | pulir (style) | perfeccionar (a technique).
◆ *vi* refinarse || purificarse || *to refine on* o *upon* sutilizar.

refined [-d] *adj* refinado, da || FIG fino, na.

refinement [-mənt] *n* FIG refinamiento *m* (of a person) | finura *f*, educación *f* (good manners) | elegancia *f* (of style) | perfección *f*, perfeccionamiento *m* (of a technique) || TECH refinado *m*, refinación *f* (of oil, of sugar) | purificación *f* (of metal) | depuración *f* (of water) || — *refinements of cruelty* barbaridades *f* || *refinements of meaning* sutilezas *f*.

refinery [ri'fainəri] *n* TECH refinería *f*.

refining [ri'fainiŋ] *n* TECH refinado *m*, refinación *f*; *oil refining* refinado del petróleo | purificación *f* (of metal) | depuración *f* (of water) || FIG refinamiento *m* (of a person) | perfeccionamiento *m* (of a technique).

refit ['ri:'fit] *n* reparación *f*.

refit ['ri:'fit] *vt* reparar || volver a equipar.

reflate [ri:'fleit] *vt* ECON reactivar, reflotar.

reflation [ri:'fleiʃən] *n* ECON reflación *f*, reactivación *f*.

reflationary [ri:'fleiʃnəri] *adj* ECON de reflación, de reactivación (policy).

reflect [ri'flekt] *vt* reflejar; *mirrors reflect light* los espejos reflejan la luz; *his behaviour reflects his upbringing* su comportamiento refleja su educación || *to reflect credit on* hacer recaer el prestigio en, honrar.
◆ *vi* reflejarse (light, sound) || reflexionar, meditar, pensar (to think); *give him time to reflect* dale tiempo para reflexionar || — *to reflect ill on s.o.* desacreditar a alguien (an action) || *to reflect on* o *upon* perjudicar; *such an act reflects on him* una acción así le perjudica; meditar sobre; *to reflect on the past* meditar sobre el pasado; pensar; *I shall reflect on it* lo pensaré || *to reflect well on o.s.* honrar a alguien (an action).

reflectance [-əns] *n* PHYS reflectancia *f*.

reflected [-id] *adj* reflejado, da || *reflected ray* rayo reflejado *or* reflejo.

reflecting [ri'flektiŋ] *adj* reflectante; *reflecting surface* superficie reflectante.

reflecting telescope [-'teliskəup] *n* PHYS telescopio *m* reflector.

reflection; reflexion [ri'flekʃən] *n* reflexión *f* (act) || reflejo *m* (image produced) || ANAT repliegue *m* (of tissue) || reflexión *f*, meditación *f* (meditation) || reflexión *f*, comentario *m* (opinion) || crítica *f* (criticism); *I don't mean this as any reflection on your work* con eso no quiero hacer ninguna crítica de su trabajo || — *a pale reflection of his former self* una sombra de lo que era || *on reflection* después de pensarlo, pensándolo bien || *to cast reflections on* criticar a || *to see s.o.'s reflection in the mirror* ver la imagen de alguien reflejada en el espejo.

reflective [ri'flektiv] *adj* reflector, ra; *reflective surface* superficie reflectora || reflexivo, va; pensativo, va (pensive) || GRAMM reflexivo, va.

reflector [ri'flektə*] *n* PHYS reflector *m* || AUT catafaro *m*.

reflex ['ri:fleks] *adj* reflejo, ja; *a reflex action* una acción refleja || reflejado, da; *reflex light* luz reflejada.
◆ *n* reflejo *m* || imagen *f* reflejada (image) || — *reflex arc* arco reflejo || PHOT *reflex camera* cámara *f* reflex.

reflexibility [ri,fleksi'biliti] *n* reflexibilidad *f*.

reflexible [ri'fleksibl] *adj* reflexible.

reflexion [ri'flekʃən] *n* → **reflection.**

reflexive [ri'fleksiv] *adj* GRAMM reflexivo, va || reflejo, ja (of a reflex).
◆ *n* GRAMM reflexivo *m*, verbo *m* reflexivo (verb) | pronombre *m* reflexivo (pronoun).

refloat ['ri:'fləut] *vt* MAR desencallar, poner a flote || FIG sacar a flote (a company).

reflourish ['ri'flʌriʃ] *vi* reflorecer.

refluence ['refluəns] *n* reflujo *m*.

refluent ['refluənt] *adj* menguante (tide).

reflux ['ri:flʌks] *n* reflujo *m* || menguante *m*, reflujo *m* (of a tide).

reforest [ri'fɔrist] *vt* US repoblar [con árboles].

reforestation ['ri,fɔris'teiʃən] *n* US repoblación *f* forestal.

reform [ri'fɔ:m*] *n* reforma *f*; *agrarian* o *land reform* reforma agraria || *reform school* reformatorio *m* (reformatory).

reform [ri'fɔ:m] *vt* reformar.
◆ *vi* reformarse.

re-form ['ri:'fɔ:m] *vt* formar de nuevo, volver a formar.
◆ *vi* formarse de nuevo.

reformable [ri'fɔ:məbl] *adj* reformable.

reformation [,refə'meiʃən] *n* reforma *f* || REL *Reformation* la Reforma.

re-formation [,rifɔ'meiʃən] *n* nueva formación *f*.

reformational [,refə'meiʃənəl] *adj* REL de la Reforma.

reformative [ri'fɔ:mətiv] *adj* reformatorio, ria; reformativo, va.

reformatory [ri'fɔ:mətəri] *adj* reformatorio, ria.

◆ *n* reformatorio *m*.

reformed [ri'fɔːmd] *adj* reformado, da; *reformed Church* Iglesia reformada.

reformer [ri'fɔːmə*] *n* reformista *m* & *f*; reformador, ra.

reformist [ri'fɔːmist] *adj/n* reformista.

refract [ri'frækt] *vt* refractar.

refracting telescope [ri'fræktiŋ'teliskəup] *n* telescopio *m* refractor.

refraction [ri'frækʃən] *n* PHYS refracción *f*.

refractive [ri'fræktiv] *adj* refractivo, va; refringente ‖ PHYS *refractive index* índice *m* de refracción.

refractometer [rifræk'tɔmitə*] *n* PHYS refractómetro *m*.

refractory [-ri] *adj* refractario, ria.
◆ *n* material *m* refractario.

refrain [ri'frein] *n* estribillo *m*.

refrain [ri'frein] *vi* abstenerse; *please refrain from smoking* por favor, absténganse de fumar ‖ *I couldn't refrain from making a comment* no pude contenerme e hice una observación.

refrangibility [ri,frændʒi'biliti] *n* PHYS refrangibilidad *f*.

refrangible [ri'frændʒibl] *adj* PHYS refrangible.

refresh [ri'freʃ] *vt* refrescar; *to refresh one's face with a little water* refrescarse la cara con un poco de agua ‖ — *they refreshed themselves in a roadside inn* se restauraron en una posada ‖ *to refresh the memory* refrescar la memoria.
◆ *vi* refrescarse.

refresher [-ə*] *n* refresco *m* (drink) ‖ JUR honorarios *m pl* suplementarios ‖ *refresher course* cursillo *m* de perfeccionamiento *or* de repaso.

refreshing [-iŋ] *adj* refrescante; *a refreshing drink* una bebida refrescante ‖ reparador, ra (sleep) ‖ reconfortante (comforting) ‖ — *it makes a refreshing change to live in the country* irse a vivir al campo representa un cambio muy agradable ‖ *it makes a refreshing change to meet an honest person* da gusto encontrar a una persona honrada.

refresh memory [ri'freʃmeməri] *n* INFORM memoria *f* de regeneración.

refreshment [-mənt] *n* refresco *m* (drink) ‖ — *they offered us some refreshment* nos ofrecieron algo de comer *or* de tomar ‖ *would you like some refreshment?* ¿quiere tomar algo?
◆ *pl* refrigerio *m sing*; *refreshments will be served in the interval* se servirá un refrigerio durante el descanso.

refreshment room [-məntruːm] *n* fonda *f*.

refried [ri'fraid] *adj* refrito, ta.

refrigerant [ri'fridʒərənt] *n* refrigerante *m*.

refrigerate [ri'fridʒəreit] *vt* refrigerar.

refrigeration [ri,fridʒə'reiʃən] *n* refrigeración *f*.

refrigerative [ri'fridʒərətiv] *adj* refrigerante.

refrigerator [ri'fridʒəreitə*] *n* refrigerador *m*, nevera *f*, frigorífico *m* ‖ *refrigerator car, lorry* vagón, camión frigorífico.

refringence [ri'frindʒəns] *n* refringencia *f*.

refry [ri'frai] *vt* volver a freír, refreír.

refuel [ri'fjuəl] *vt* poner combustible *or* carburante a (a boiler, plane, ship) ‖ echar gasolina a (a car).
◆ *vi* repostar, repostarse; *they stopped to refuel in Paris* hicieron escala en París para repostar.

refuge ['refjuːdʒ] *n* refugio *m*; *to seek refuge* buscar refugio ‖ — *to give refuge to* dar refugio a ‖ *to take refuge in* refugiarse en.

refugee [,refju'dʒiː] *n* refugiado, da.

refulgence [ri'fʌldʒəns] *n* refulgencia *f*, resplandor *m* (brightness).

refulgent [ri'fʌldʒənt] *adj* refulgente.

refund ['riːfʌnd] *n* devolución *f*, reembolso *m* (of money) ‖ reembolso *m* (of expenses, of a debt) ‖ *to demand a refund* exigir la devolución *or* el reembolso de su dinero.

refund [riː'fʌnd] *vt* reintegrar, devolver, reembolsar (money) ‖ reembolsar (person); *they refunded him* le reembolsaron; *they refunded his expenses* le reembolsaron los gastos ‖ consolidar (a debt) ‖ *to refund the cost of one's ticket* devolver a uno el importe de la entrada *or* del billete.

refurbish ['riː'fəːbiʃ] *vt* restaurar (an old house, table, etc.).

refurnish ['riː'fəːniʃ] *vt* amueblar de nuevo (with furniture).

refusable [ri'fjuːzəbl] *adj* rechazable.

refusal [ri'fjuːzəl] *n* negativa *f*; *a flat refusal* una negativa rotunda ‖ COMM opción *f* ‖ — *they met the offer with a flat refusal* rechazaron la oferta rotundamente ‖ *your refusal to cooperate caused a lot of difficulty* el hecho de que se negara a cooperar nos causó muchas dificultades.

refuse ['refjuːs] *adj* desechado, da.
◆ *n* basura *f* (rubbish) ‖ desperdicios *m pl* (waste material) ‖ — *refuse bin* cubo *m* de basura ‖ *refuse dump* vertedero *m* ‖ *refuse lorry* camión *m* de la basura.

refuse [ri'fjuːz] *vt* rechazar (to reject); *he refused my offer* rechazó mi oferta ‖ no aceptar, no querer aceptar (invitation, food, present, etc.) ‖ negar, denegar; *to refuse admittance to s.o.* denegar a alguien la entrada ‖ negarse a, rehusar; *he refused to shake hands* se negó a darle la mano ‖ no servir en (in card games) ‖ SP rehusar saltar (a fence) ‖ *to refuse o.s.* privarse de.
◆ *vi* negarse (to make a refusal) ‖ SP pararse, plantarse (a horse).

refutable ['refjutəbl] *adj* refutable, rebatible.

refutal [ri'fjuːtəl]; **refutation** [,refju'teiʃən] *n* refutación *f*, rebatimiento *m*.

refute [ri'fjuːt] *vt* refutar, rebatir (an argument, etc.) ‖ contradecir (s.o.).

regain [ri'gein] *vt* recobrar, recuperar (sth. lost); *to regain one's breath* recobrar el aliento ‖ volver a (to get back to) ‖ — *to regain consciousness* recobrar *or* recuperar el conocimiento, volver en sí ‖ *to regain one's composture* serenarse.

regal ['riːgəl] *adj* real, regio, gia.

regale [ri'geil] *vt* agasajar (to entertain richly) ‖ entretener (to amuse).
◆ *vi* regalarse.

regalia [ri'geiljə] *pl n* insignias *f* (insignia) ‖ atributos *m* (of an office).

regalism ['riːgəlizəm] *n* regalismo *m*.

regalist ['riːgəlist] *n* regalista.

regality [ri'gæliti] *n* soberanía *f*.

regally ['riːgəli] *adv* regiamente.

regard [ri'gɑːd] *n* estima *f* (esteem) ‖ consideración *f*, respeto *m* (consideration) ‖ (ant) mirada *f* (look) ‖ — *having regard to* teniendo en cuenta ‖ *in* o *with regard to* en cuanto a, con respecto a, con relación a ‖ *in this regard* a este respecto, al respecto ‖ *to have no regard to* no tener en cuenta (not to take into account), no tener que ver con (to have nothing to do with) ‖ *to have the highest regard for s.o.* tener a alguien en gran estima ‖ *to pay regard to* hacer caso de ‖ *to show no regard to* no hacer caso de ‖ *to show no regard for other people* no tener ninguna consideración con los demás ‖ *to stand high in s.o.'s regard* gozar de la estima de uno ‖ *without regard to the dangers* indiferente a los peligros.

◆ *pl* recuerdos *m*; *give my regards to your mother* dale recuerdos a tu madre ‖ *with kind regards* con muchos recuerdos.

regard [ri'gɑːd] *vt* considerar, juzgar (to consider); *I regard it as a crime* lo considero un crimen ‖ considerar (to treat); *regard this letter as confidential* considere esta carta como confidencial ‖ concernir, atañer (to concern); *this order does not regard me* esta orden no me concierne ‖ tener en cuenta (to take into account) ‖ tomar en consideración, hacer caso de (to have respect for) ‖ (ant) mirar (to look at) ‖ *as regards your work* con respecto a su trabajo, en cuanto a su trabajo.

regardant [-ənt] *adj* HERALD contornado, da.

regardful [-ful] *adj* atento, ta (heedful); *regardful of my words* atento a mis palabras ‖ respetuoso, sa (of people).

regarding [-iŋ] *prep* con respecto a, en cuanto a, por lo que se refiere a ‖ relativo, va; referente; *everything regarding sales* todo lo relativo *or* todo lo referente a las ventas.

regardless [-lis] *adj* indiferente (*of* a) (indifferent) ‖ insensible (*of* a) (insensitive) ‖ sin tener en cuenta; *regardless of expense* sin tener en cuenta los gastos ‖ *regardless of the cost* a toda costa, cueste lo que cueste; *he wanted to buy it, regardless of the cost* lo quería comprar costase lo que costase.
◆ *adv* a pesar de todo (despite everything) ‖ pase lo que pase (whatever happens) ‖ *I warned him, but he went on regardless* le advertí pero siguió adelante sin hacerme caso.

regatta [ri'gætə] *n* SP regata *f*.

regency ['riːdʒənsi] *n* regencia *f*.

Regency ['riːdʒənsi] *adj* regencia, de estilo regencia.

regeneracy [ri'dʒenərəsi] *n* regeneración *f*.

regenerate [ri'dʒenərit] *adj* regenerado, da.

regenerate [ri'dʒenəreit] *vt* regenerar.
◆ *vi* regenerarse.

regeneration [ri,dʒenə'reiʃən] *n* regeneración *f*.

regenerative [ri'dʒenərətiv] *adj* regenerador, ra.

regenerator [ri'dʒenəreitə*] *n* TECH regenerador *m*.

regent ['riːdʒənt] *adj* regente; *the Prince regent* el príncipe regente.
◆ *n* regente *m* & *f*.

regicidal [,redʒi'saidl] *adj* regicida.

regicide ['redʒisaid] *n* regicidio *m* (crime) ‖ regicida *m* & *f* (person).

regild ['riː'gild] *vt* volver a dorar, redorar.

régime; regime [rei'ʒiːm] *n* régimen *m*; *political régime* régimen político.

regimen ['redʒimən] *n* MED régimen *m*.

regiment ['redʒimənt] *n* MIL regimiento *m* ‖ FIG regimiento *m*, ejército *m*, multitud *f* (large number).

regiment ['redʒimənt] *vt* MIL regimentar ‖ FIG reglamentar estrictamente, regimentar.

regimental [,redʒi'mentl] *adj* MIL de *or* del regimiento.
◆ *pl n* uniforme *m sing* del regimiento ‖ uniforme *m sing* militar.

regimentation [,redʒimen'teiʃən] *n* reglamentación *f* estricta.

regimented [,redʒi'mentid] *adj* reglamentado, da.

region ['riːdʒən] *n* región *f*; *barren region* región árida ‖ zona *f* (area) ‖ ANAT región *f* ‖ *in the region of a hundred pounds* unas cien libras, alrededor de cien libras.

regional [-l] *adj* regional.

regionalist [-əlist] *n* regionalista *m* & *f*.

regionalization [ˌriːdʒənəlaiˈzeiʃən] *n* regionalización *f*.

regionalize [ˈriːdʒənəlaiz] *vt* regionalizar.

regisseur [ˈreiʒiˈsəˈ] *n* THEATR regidor *m* de escena.

register [ˈredʒistəˈ] *n* registro *m*; *hotel register* registro de hotel; *register of births, marriages and deaths* registro civil || lista *f* (in school); *to call the register* pasar lista || MUS & TECH registro *m* (of voice, instrument, stove) || MAR matrícula *f* (list of men, of boats) || registrador *m* (recording instrument) || PRINT registro *m* || indicador *m*, contador *m* (gauge) || INFORM registro *m* || — *cash register* caja registradora || *electoral register* censo *m* or registro electoral || *land register* registro de la propiedad.

register [ˈredʒistəˈ] *vt* registrar (to note in a register) || declarar (birth, deaths) || presentar (a complaint) || facturar (luggage) || registrar (a trademark, an invention) || FIG reflejar, denotar, expresar; *her face registered surprise* su cara reflejaba sorpresa || experimentar; *to register an increase, an improvement* experimentar una subida, una mejora || certificar (a letter); *registered letter* carta certificada || marcar; *the gauge registered 300 revolutions* el indicador marcaba 300 revoluciones || matricular (a car, a boat, students) || TECH hacer corresponder (parts).
◆ *vi* inscribirse (to sign on) || registrarse (in a hotel, in the registrar's office) || matricularse (at university) || coincidir *or* corresponder exactamente (parts) || PRINT estar en registro || *it weighted so little that it didn't register on the scale* pesaba tan poco que no se movía el fiel de la balanza.

registered [-d] *adj* registrado, da; *registered trademark* marca registrada || facturado, da (luggage) || certificado, da (letter) || matriculado, da (student).

registered nurse [-nəːs] *n* enfermera *f* titulada.

register office [-ˈɔfis] *n* US registro *m* civil (for births, marriages, deaths) | registro *m* (for other things).

register ton [-tʌn] *n* MAR tonelada *f* de arqueo.

registrar [ˌredʒisˈtrɑːˈ] *n* registrador *m*, archivero *m* (keeper of a register) || secretario *m* general (of university) || secretario *m* del registro civil (of registry office) || secretario *m* (secretary).

registrate [ˌredʒistreit] *vi* MUS seleccionar el registro.

registration [ˌredʒisˈtreiʃən] *n* inscripción *f* (inscription) || declaración *f* (of a birth, etc.) || registro *m* (of trademark) || matrícula *f* (at university) || certificación *f* (of letters) || facturación *f* (of luggage) || AUT & MAR matrícula *f* (number, nationality) || US MUS registros *m pl* || — *registration number* número *m* de matrícula || *registration plate* placa *f* de matrícula.

registry [ˈredʒistri] *n* registro *m* || — *registry office* registro *m* civil (for births, marriages, deaths), registro *m* (for other things) || *to get married at a registry office* casarse por lo civil.

regius [ˈriːdʒəs] *adj* *regius professor* profesor *m* nombrado por el rey.

reglet [ˈreglet] *n* PRINT regleta *f* || ARCH filete *m*.

regnal [ˈregnəl] *adj* de un reinado || *regnal day* aniversario *m* de la coronación de un monarca.

regnant [ˈregnənt] *adj* reinante; *regnant queen* soberana reinante.

regorge [riːˈgɔːdʒ] *vt* arrojar, vomitar.
◆ *vi* brotar de nuevo.

regress [ˈriːgres] *n* retroceso *m*.

regress [riˈgres] *vi* retroceder.

regression [riˈgreʃən] *n* retroceso *m*, regresión *f*.

regressive [riˈgresiv] *adj* regresivo, va.

regret [riˈgret] *n* arrepentimiento *m* (remorse) || pesar *m*, pena *f*; *the old man's death caused everybody deep regret* la muerte del anciano dio mucha pena a todos || — *much to my regret* con gran sentimiento mío, sintiéndolo mucho, con gran pesar mío || *to express one's regret to s.o.* disculparse con uno (to apologize), dar el pésame a alguien (for s.o.'s death) || *with regret* con pena, con pesar (with sorrow), a disgusto, contra su voluntad (against one's will).
◆ *pl* excusas *f* (on refusing an invitation); *to send one's regrets* enviar sus excusas || *to have no regrets* no arrepentirse de nada.

regret [riˈgret] *vt* sentir, lamentar; *I regret to have to say that* siento tener que decir que; *it is to be regretted that* es de lamentar que || arrepentirse de; *to regret one's sins* arrepentirse de los pecados; *to regret the past* arrepentirse del pasado; *if you go you won't regret it* si vas no te arrepentirás; *he bitterly regretted his action* estaba profundamente arrepentido de lo que había hecho.

regretful [-ful] *adj* arrepentido, da (remorseful) || pesaroso, sa (sorrowful) || — *to be regretful that* lamentar que || *we are not regretful of having done it* no nos arrepentiremos de haberlo hecho, no lamentamos haberlo hecho.

regretfully [-fuli] *adv* con pesar, con sentimiento, sentidamente (with sorrow) || con disgusto (against one's will) || desafortunadamente (unfortunately).

regrettable [-əbl] *adj* lamentable, deplorable.

regrettably [-əbli] *adv* lamentablemente, desgraciadamente.

regroup [ˈriːˈgruːp] *vt* reagrupar.
◆ *vi* reagruparse.

regrouping [-iŋ] *n* reagrupamiento *m*, reagrupación *f*.

regular [ˈregjuləˈ] *adj* regular; *regular pulse* pulso regular || normal; *it's perfectly regular* es completamente normal; *in the regular manner* de manera normal || normal, acostumbrado, da; *his regular job, time* su trabajo acostumbrado, su hora acostumbrada || uniforme; *a regular stroke* una brazada uniforme || regular (features) || corriente (usual) || habitual, asiduo, dua; *a regular customer* un cliente asiduo || permanente (permanent); *regular staff* personal permanente || MIL & REL regular; *regular army, clergy* ejército, clero regular || regular, ordenado, da; *a regular life* una vida regular || BOT, MATH & GRAMM regular; *regular flower, triangle, verb* flor, triángulo, verbo regular || FAM verdadero, ra; auténtico, ca; *a regular idiot* un auténtico idiota | estupendo, da; *a regular guy* un tipo estupendo || — *to be as regular as clockwork* ocurrir con la regularidad de un cronómetro *or* con una regularidad cronométrica || *to make a regular thing of arriving late* tener la costumbre de llegar tarde, llegar siempre tarde || *to make regular use of* emplear con regularidad || *where is your regular assistant?* ¿dónde está la persona que suele ayudarle?
◆ *n* REL & MIL regular *m* || asiduo, dua (of a bar, of a club) || cliente *m* & *f* habitual (of a shop).

regularity [ˌregjuˈlæriti] *n* regularidad *f* || *regularity of attendance* asiduidad *f*.

regularization [ˌregjuləraiˈzeiʃən] *n* regularización *f*.

regularize [ˈregjuləraiz] *vt* regularizar (document, situation, etc.).

regularly [ˈregjuləli] *adv* con regularidad, regularmente || normalmente.

regulate [ˈregjuleit] *vt* regular; *to regulate prices, the flow of water, a machine* regular los precios, la salida del agua, una máquina || reglamentar (to make rules for) || *to regulate one's life by one's work* vivir con arreglo a su trabajo.

regulating [-iŋ] *adj* regulador, ra.

regulation [ˌregjuˈleiʃən] *n* regulación *f* (action); *regulation of a watercourse* regulación de un curso de agua || reglamentación *f* (setting rules for) || regla *f* (a rule).
◆ *pl* reglamento *m sing*, reglas *f* (set of rules).
◆ *adj* reglamentario, ria.

regulative [ˈregjulətiv] *adj* regulativo, va.
◆ *n* regulador *m*.

regulus [ˈregjuləs] *n* CHEM régulo *m* || reyezuelo *m* (bird).

— OBSERV El plural de *regulus* es *reguluses* o *reguli*.

regurgitate [riˈgəːdʒiteit] *vt* vomitar [sin esfuerzo] (to bring up) || FIG reproducir *or* repetir maquinalmente (things learnt).
◆ *vi* regurgitar.

regurgitation [ˌrigəːdʒiˈteiʃən] *n* regurgitación *f* (by animals) || FIG reproducción *f* maquinal.

rehabilitate [ˌriːəˈbiliteit] *vt* rehabilitar (to restore rank, privileges, reputation) || restaurar (to restore to good condition) || MED rehabilitar, reeducar.

rehabilitation [ˈriːəˌbiliˈteiʃən] *n* rehabilitación *f* || restauración *f* (restoration) || reconstrucción *f*, reorganización *f* (of a country) || MED reeducación *f* (of a disabled person).

rehash [ˈriːhæʃ] *n* refrito *m*, refundición *f*; *his last book is just a rehash of his previous works* su último libro es un refrito de sus obras anteriores || comida *f* recalentada (meal) || US repetición *f*.

rehash [ˈriːˈhæʃ] *vt* volver a sacar, volver a repetir, machacar (arguments, ideas) || recalentar (food).

rehearing [ˈriˈhiəriŋ] *n* JUR revisión *f*.

rehearsal [riˈhəːsəl] *n* ensayo *m* (of a play, of a ceremony) || enumeración *f* (enumeration) || — *dress rehearsal* ensayo general || *there was a rehearsal of the fire drill* se hizo un simulacro de incendio.

rehearse [riˈhəːs] *vt* ensayar (a play, a ceremony) || enumerar (to enumerate); *to rehearse a list of complaints* enumerar una lista de quejas.
◆ *vi* ensayar.

reheat [riˈhiːt] *vt* recalentar.

reheating [-iŋ] *n* recalentamiento *m*.

rehouse [ˈriːˈhauz] *vt* proporcionar nueva vivienda a.

rehydrate [riˈhaiˌdreit] *vt* rehidratar, volver a hidratar.

reification [ˌriəfəˈkeiʃən] *n* materialización *f*.

reify [ˈriəˌfai] *vt* materializar, concretar (an abstraction).

reign [rein] *n* reinado *m* (of a monarch); *under the reign of* bajo el reinado de || FIG dominio *m*, predominio *m* (dominion) | régimen *m* (régime); *reign of terror* régimen de terror.

reign [rein] *vi* reinar; *to reign over* reinar sobre || FIG reinar; *silence reigned in the assembly* el silencio reinaba en la asamblea | predominar, imperar (to prevail).

reigning [-iŋ] *adj* reinante (monarch) || FIG dominante, predominante (tendency, etc.).

reimbursable [ˌriːimˈbəːsəbl] *adj* reembolsable.

reimburse [ˌriːimˈbəːs] *vt* reembolsar; *to reimburse s.o.'s expenses* reembolsarle los gastos a uno.

reimbursement [-mənt] *n* reembolso *m.*

reimport ['ri:im'pɔ:t] *n* reimportación *f; reimports amounted to a million pounds* las reimportaciones alcanzaron el valor de un millón de libras || artículo *m* reimportado *or* de reimportación (goods).

reimport ['ri:im'pɔ:t] *vt* reimportar.

reimportation ['ri:impɔ:'teiʃən] *n* reimportación *f.*

reimpression ['ri:im'preʃən] *n* reimpresión *f.*

rein [rein] *n* rienda *f* (for animals) || — *to draw rein* tirar de las riendas || *to give rein to* aflojar las riendas a (to loosen the reins), dar rienda suelta a (the imagination, etc.) || *to keep a tight rein on s.o.* atar corto a uno.
◆ *pl* riendas *f* (for animals) || andadores *m* (for children) || FIG riendas *f; the reins of government* las riendas del gobierno; *to hold the reins* llevar las riendas || *to take the reins* tomar las riendas.

rein [rein] *vtr* poner riendas a || *to rein in* o *up* refrenar.
◆ *vi to rein in* detenerse.

reincarnate [ri:'inka:neit] *vt* reencarnar.

reincarnation ['ri:inka:'neiʃən] *n* reencarnación *f.*

reindeer ['reindiə*] *n* ZOOL reno *m.*
— OBSERV El plural de la palabra *reindeer* es *reindeer* o *reindeers.*

reinforce; reenforce [,ri:in'fɔ:s] *vt* reforzar, fortalecer || armar (concrete).

reinforcement; reenforcement [-mənt] *n* refuerzo *m* (strengthening) || armazón *f* (of concrete).
◆ *pl* MIL refuerzos *m.*

reinsert [,riin'sə:t] *vt* volver a insertar *or* introducir, reinsertar.

reinstall ['ri:in'stɔ:l] *vt* volver a instalar, reinstalar.

reinstate ['ri:in'steit] *vt* reintegrar, reinstalar, restituir; *to reinstate s.o. in a job* reintegrar a uno en su puesto, restituir el puesto a alguien || volver a poner (to put back) || rehabilitar (to rehabilitate) || restablecer (a law, etc.).

reinstatement [-mənt] *n* restablecimiento *m* || reintegración *f*, reinstalación *f* (in a job) || rehabilitación *f.*

reinsurance ['ri:in'ʃuərəns] *n* reaseguro *m.*

reinsure ['ri:in'ʃuə*] *vt* reasegurar.

reintegrate [ri:'intigreit] *vt* reintegrar.

reintegration [ri:,inti'greiʃən] *n* reintegro *m*, reintegración *f.*

reinter ['ri:in'tə*] *vt* volver a enterrar.

reinterpret ['ri:in'tə:prit] *vt* reinterpretar.

reintroduce ['ri:,intrə'dju:s] *vt* volver a presentar (s.o.) || volver a introducir (sth.).

reinvest ['ri:in'vest] *vt* COMM volver a invertir, reinvertir.

reinvestment [-mənt] *n* COMM nueva inversión *f*, reinversión *f.*

reinvigorate ['ri:in'vigəreit] *vt* revigorizar.

reissue ['ri:'iʃu:] *n* reedición *f* (of books) || nueva emisión *f* (of stamps, etc.).

reissue ['ri:'iʃu:] *vt* reeditar (books, etc.) || volver a emitir (stamps, shares, etc.).

reiterate [ri:'itəreit] *vt* reiterar.

reiteration [ri,itə'reiʃən] *n* reiteración *f.*

reiterative [ri:'itərətiv] *adj* reiterativo, va.

reject ['ri:dʒekt] *n* persona *f* rechazada || cosa *f* rechazada, desecho *m* (object).

reject [ri'dʒekt] *vt* rechazar; *to reject an attack, an offer, a request* rechazar un ataque, una oferta, una petición || arrojar (from the stomach).

rejection [ri'dʒekʃən] *n* rechazamiento *m* (action) || cosa *f* rechazada, desecho *m* (reject) || *I've already had two rejections* ya me han rechazado dos veces.

rejig [ri:'dʒig] *vt* reconvertir (a factory, etc.) || reorganizar, reajustar (timetable, etc.).

rejoice [ri'dʒɔis] *vi* alegrarse, regocijarse || disfrutar; *he rejoices in pulling her leg* disfruta tomándole el pelo || *to rejoice in the name of* tener el honor de llamarse.
◆ *vt* alegrar, regocijar.

rejoicing [-iŋ] *n* alegría *f*, regocijo *m*, júbilo *m* (happiness) || fiesta *f; rejoicing went on right through the night* la fiesta continuó toda la noche.
◆ *adj* alegre.

rejoin ['ri:'dʒɔin] *vt* volver a juntarse con, volver a unirse a (two objects) || reincorporarse a (clubs, army, society) || encontrar, reunirse con; *I'll rejoin you at the station* os encontraré en la estación.

rejoin [ri'dʒɔin] *vt* replicar, responder (to reply).
◆ *vi* replicar, responder (to reply) || JUR contestar (to answer to a charge).

rejoinder [-də*] *n* réplica *f*, respuesta *f* (reply) || JUR contestación *f*, contrarréplica *f* (answer).

rejuvenate [ri'dʒu:vineit] *vt* rejuvenecer.
◆ *vi* rejuvenecerse.

rejuvenating [-iŋ] *adj* rejuvenecedor, ra.

rejuvenation [ri'dʒu:vi'neiʃən]; **rejuvenescence** [,ridzu:vi'nesns] *n* rejuvenecimiento *m.*

rejuvenescent [,ridʒu:vi'nesnt] *adj* rejuvenecedor, ra.

rekindle ['ri:'kindl] *vt* volver a encender (a fire) || FIG reavivar, reanimar.

relabel ['ri:'leibl] *vt* volver a etiquetar, etiquetar de nuevo.

relapse [ri'læps] *n* recaída *f*, recidiva *f* (into bad health); *to have a relapse* tener una recaída || reincidencia *f* (into crime, etc.).

relapse [ri'læps] *vi* recaer (into bad health) || reincidir (into crime, etc.) || — REL *relapsed heretic* relapso, sa || JUR *relapsed offender* reincidente *m* & *f* (recidivist).

relatable [ri'leitəbl] *adj* narrable, contable.

relate [ri'leit] *vt* contar, relatar; *to relate a story* relatar una historia || relacionar; *to relate two facts* relacionar dos hechos.
◆ *vi* relacionarse (*to* con), tener que ver (*to* con), estar relacionado (*to* con), ser relativo (*to* a), referirse (*to* a); *everything relating* o *related to aircraft interests him* todo lo que tiene que ver con los aviones le interesa.

related [-id] *adj* relacionado, da; *related subjects, objects* temas, objetos relacionados || emparentado, da (through birth or by marriage) || — *his answer was in no a way related to the question* su respuesta no tenía nada que ver con la pregunta || *she is related to me* es parienta mía || *they are closely related* hay un estrecho parentesco entre ellos, son parientes cercanos (people) || *to be distantly related to* ser pariente lejano de.

relater [-ə*] *n* relator, ra.

relation [ri'leiʃən] *n* relato *m*, narración *f*, relación *f* (account) || pariente, ta (a relative) || parentesco *m; what relation is he to you?* ¿qué parentesco tiene contigo? || relación *f*, conexión *f; the relation between two events* la relación entre dos acontecimientos || JUR relación *f* || — *in* o *with relation to* en relación con, con relación a, en lo que se refiere a || *to bear no relation to reality* no tener ninguna relación *or* nada que ver con la realidad || *to bear relation to* guardar relación con.
◆ *pl* relaciones *f; business relations* relaciones comerciales *or* de negocios; *political relations* relaciones políticas; *good relations* buenas relaciones || — *public relations officer* encargado de relaciones públicas || *sexual relations* relaciones sexuales || *to break off relations with* romper con (a friend), romper las relaciones diplomáticas con (a country).

relationship [-ʃip] *n* relación *f* (connection) || relaciones *f pl; theirs is a strange relationship* tienen unas relaciones muy extrañas || relaciones *f pl* (between countries) || parentesco *m* (kinship); *relationship by marriage* parentesco político; *what is your relationship to her?* ¿qué parentesco tienes con ella? || *theirs is a beautiful relationship* se llevan perfectamente.

relative ['relətiv] *adj* relativo, va; *questions relative to what I have been saying* preguntas relativas a lo que he dicho; *the relative difference between two things* la diferencia relativa entre dos cosas; *relative humidity* humedad relativa || GRAMM relativo, va; *relative pronoun* pronombre relativo || *the mass of the earth relative to that of the sun* la masa de la tierra en relación con la del sol.
◆ *n* pariente, ta (connected by birth or marriage) || GRAMM relativo *m.*

relatively [-li] *adj* relativamente.

relativism ['relətivizəm] *n* relativismo *m.*

relativist ['relativist] *adj/n* relativista.

relativity [,relə'tiviti] *n* relatividad *f.*

relax [ri'læks] *vt* aflojar (to loosen); *to relax one's grip* aflojar la mano || relajar (muscles) || relajar, aflojar (to make less strict); *to relax discipline* relajar la disciplina || disminuir (to diminish); *to relax one's efforts* disminuir los esfuerzos || mitigar (pain) || MED soltar; *to relax the bowels* soltar el vientre.
◆ *vi* relajarse (nerves, muscles, social relations) || descansar, relajarse (after work); *to relax on a golf course* descansar jugando al golf || relajarse (to become less strict) || — *relax!* ¡tranquilo!, ¡cálmate! (take it easy!) || *to relax in one's efforts* disminuir los esfuerzos, aflojar.

relaxant [ri'læksənt] *n* relajante *m.*

relaxation [,ri:læk'seiʃən] *n* relajación *f* (of muscles, of nerves) || relajación *f*, relajamiento *m* (of discipline) || disminución *f* (of efforts) || recreo *m* (recreation) || descanso *m*, desahogo *m*, relajamiento *m*, relajación *f* (after work) || distracción *f; my favourite relaxation* mi distracción preferida.

relaxed [ri'lækst] *adj* tranquilo, la; sosegado, da (peaceful, calm) || relajado, da (muscles, etc.).

relaxing [ri'læksiŋ] *adj* relajante.

relay [ri'lei] *n* relevo *m* (fresh supply of people, of animals, etc.) || posta *f* (of horses) || ELECTR & RAD repetidor *m*, relé *m*, relevador *m; television relay* repetidor de televisión || SP carrera *f* de relevos (race) || — *in relays* por turnos || SP *medley relay* relevo estilos | *relay race* carrera *f* de relevos || *relay station* estación repetidora || SP *the 100 metres relay* los 100 metros relevos.

relay ['ri:'lei] *vt* divulgar, difundir; *to relay the news* divulgar la noticia || retransmitir (to transmit to another station) || transmitir (a message to s.o.) || ELECTR regular con relevador.

re-lay ['ri:'lei] *vt* volver a poner, volver a colocar || volver a tender (rail).

release [ri'li:s] *n* liberación *f*, puesta *f* en libertad (from prison) || orden *f* de puesta en libertad (document) || exención *f*, descargo *m* (from duty or obligation) || salida *f*, estreno *m* (of film, of record, etc.) || anuncio *m*, comunicación *f* (of information, the information itself) || disminución *f* (reduction) || aflojamiento *m* (loosening) || liberación *f* (from difficulties) || alivio *m* (from a pain) || escape *m* (of steam, of gas) || disparo *m* (discharge) || lanzamiento *m* (of a bomb) || suelta *f* (of pigeons) || autorización *f* para publicar (permission to publish news) || JUR cesión *f* (surrender of a right to another) | acta *f* de cesión (document) || TECH disparador *m* || COMM puesta *f* en venta || FIG arrebato *m* (fit); *in a release of rage* en un arrebato de furia || — *press release* comunicado *m* de prensa || *release spring* muelle *m* antagonista || *release valve* válvula *f* de seguridad.

release [ri'li:s] *vt* liberar, poner en libertad (from prison) || liberar, librar, descargar (from a duty, an obligation) || dejar salir (an employee) || JUR ceder (to surrender) || estrenar (a film, a record) || publicar (a book) || poner en venta (to put on sale) || anunciar, comunicar (information) || soltar (to let go); *he released the dog, her arm* soltó el perro, le soltó el brazo || liberar (in a chemical reaction) || echar, desprender, emitir (smoke) || lanzar (a bomb) || arrojar, tirar; *to release waste in the sea* arrojar residuos al mar || PHOT disparar || soltar (a catch) || disparar (a mechanism) || JUR *to release on bail* poner en libertad bajo fianza.

releaser [-ə*] *n* TECH disparador *m*.

relegate ['religeit] *vt* relegar || someter, remitir; *to relegate a matter to s.o.* someter un asunto a alguien || desterrar (to banish) || — *the officer was relegated to the ranks* el oficial fue degradado || *to be relegated* bajar [a una división inferior] (a team).

relegation [,reli'geiʃən] *n* relegación *f* || destierro *m* (banishment) || SP descenso *m*.

relent [ri'lent] *vi* ablandarse, aplacarse (to become less severe) || ceder (to give way).

relentless [-lis] *adj* despiadado, da; implacable, cruel (without pity) || incesante (unceasing).

relet ['ri:'let] *vt* realquilar.

relevance ['relivəns]; **relevancy** [-i] *n* pertinencia *f*.

relevant ['relivənt] *adj* pertinente; *a relevant remark* una observación pertinente || relacionado, da; referente; *information relevant to the matter* información relacionada con el asunto *or* referente al asunto.

reliability [ri,laiə'biliti] *n* seriedad *f*, formalidad *f* (of a person) || TECH fiabilidad *f*, seguridad *f* (of a machine) || exactitud *f* (of figures) || veracidad *f* (of facts).

reliable [ri'laiəbl] *adj* de fiar, de confianza; *a reliable man* un hombre de confianza || seguro, ra; *reliable information* información segura; *a reliable car* un coche seguro || serio, ria (firm, company); *a reliable lawyer* un abogado serio || TECH fiable, seguro, ra (machine) || — *information from a reliable source* información de fuente fidedigna || *reliable friend* amigo de confianza, amigo seguro, amigo del que uno se puede fiar.

reliably [-i] *adv* *to be reliably informed* estar bien informado || *to be reliably informed that* saber de fuente fidedigna que.

reliance [ri'laiəns] *n* dependencia *f* (dependence); *their reliance on foreign aid* su dependencia de la ayuda extranjera || confianza *f* (trust) || *to place reliance on* fiarse de, tener confianza en.

reliant [ri'laiənt] *adj* dependiente || *to be reliant on* depender de (to depend upon), tener confianza en, fiarse de (to trust).

relic ['relik] *n* reliquia *f*, vestigio *m* (of sth. no longer existent) || REL reliquia *f* || FIG vejestorio *m* (old person or thing).

◆ *pl* FIG restos *m* mortales (of a dead person).

relict ['relikt] *n* viuda *f* (widow).

relief [ri'li:f] *n* alivio *m*; *the medicine gave him relief* la medicina le proporcionó alivio; *it is a relief to get outside* es un alivio salir fuera; *to come as a great relief to everybody* ser un gran alivio para todos || socorro *m*, auxilio *m*, ayuda *f*; *relief for refugees* socorro para los refugiados; *to bring relief to a besieged town* llevar auxilio a una ciudad sitiada || beneficencia *f*, auxilio *m* social (for the poor) || alivio *m*, descanso *m*; *a relief for the eyes* un descanso para la vista || relevo *m* (person who carries on work for another) || relieve *m*; *lettering in relief* escritura en relieve || ARTS relieve *m*; *high, low relief* alto, bajo relieve || GEOGR relieve *m*; *the relief of Spain* el relieve de España; *relief map* mapa en relieve || JUR desagravio *m* || — *relief road* carretera *f* de descongestión || *relief train* tren suplementario *or* adicional || *relief valve* válvula *f* de seguridad || *tax relief* desgravación *f* de impuestos || *to go to s.o.'s relief* acudir en ayuda de alguien || *to heave a sigh of relief* dar un suspiro de alivio || *to stand out in relief against* resaltar sobre || *to throw into relief* poner de relieve || *what a relief!* ¡qué alivio!, ¡qué descanso!

relieve [ri'li:v] *vt* aliviar, mitigar (to alleviate pain, distress, anxiety) || liberar, sacar (to free); *to relieve s.o. of his worries* liberar a alguien de sus preocupaciones; *to relieve s.o. from doubt* sacar a alguien de dudas || coger, tomar; *to relieve s.o. of his coat* cogerle el abrigo a alguien || liberar, librar; *to relieve s.o. of an obligation* librar a alguien de una obligación || exonerar (to exonerate) || destituir; *to relieve s.o. of his post* destituirle a uno de su puesto || relevar, sustituir, reemplazar (to replace) || socorrer, auxiliar (a besieged town, the poor, refugees, etc.) || disipar; *to relieve the monotony* disipar la monotonía || alegrar (to brighten up) || MIL relevar (sentries, etc.) || poner de relieve, realzar (to bring out) || JUR desagraviar || FAM limpiar (to steal); *to relieve s.o. of his purse* limpiar a alguien la cartera || — ARCH *relieving arch* arco *m* de descarga || *their intervention relieved the situation momentarily* su intervención remedió la situación momentáneamente || *to relieve one's feelings* desahogarse || *to relieve o.s.* hacer sus necesidades (to go to the toilet) || *to relieve o.s. of a problem* quitarse un problema de encima, liberarse de un problema || FIG *to relieve nature* hacer sus necesidades || *to relieve s.o.'s anxiety* tranquilizarle a uno.

relieved [-d] *adj* aliviado, da; tranquilo, la.

relievo [ri'li:vəu] *n* ARTS relieve *m*.

religion [ri'lidʒən] *n* religión *f* || FIG religión *f*; *football is his religion* el fútbol es su religión || *to take to religion* darle a uno por la religión.

religiosity [ri,lidʒi'ɔsiti] *n* religiosidad *f*.

religious [ri'lidʒəs] *adj* religioso, sa; *to fulfil one's religious duties* cumplir con sus deberes religiosos || FIG religioso, sa; exacto, ta; escrupuloso, sa || *religious wars* guerras de religión.

◆ *n* religioso, sa.

reline ['ri:'lain] *vt* cambiar el forro de (clothes, brakes).

relinquish [ri'liŋkwiʃ] *vt* renunciar a; *to relinquish a right* renunciar a un derecho || soltar (to let go).

relinquishment [-mənt] *n* renuncia *f* (*of* a).

reliquary ['relikwəri] *n* relicario *m*.

relish ['reliʃ] *n* gusto *m*, deleite *m*, fruición *f* (pleasure) || entusiasmo *m* (enthusiasm) || atracción *f*; *the relish of novelty* la atracción de la novedad || CULIN condimento *m*, sazón *f* (seasoning) | gusto *m*, sabor *m* (taste) | pizca *f* (pinch) | gustillo *m* (slight taste) || — *to do sth. with relish* hacer algo con deleite *or* con entusiasmo || *to have a relish for sth.* encantarle algo a alguien, tener mucha afición a algo.

relish ['reliʃ] *vt/vi* CULIN condimentar, sazonar || saborear (to take pleasure in food) || encantar; *I relish oysters* me encantan las ostras || disfrutar con; *Peter relishes a good joke* Pedro disfruta con un buen chiste || — *I don't relish the idea of going* no me gusta mucho *or* no me hace ninguna gracia la idea de ir || *I relish a walk in the country* disfruto dando un paseo por el campo, me encanta dar un paseo por el campo || *to relish of* saber a, tener sabor a.

relive ['ri'liv] *vt* volver a vivir (an experience).

reload ['ri:'ləud] *vt* recargar.

relocate ['ri:ləu'keit] *vt* trasladar.

relocation ['ri:ləu'keiʃən] *n* traslado *m*.

reluct [ri'lʌkt] *vi* sentir repulsión (*at, against* por).

reluctance [ri'lʌktəns] *n* desgana *f*; *to do sth. with reluctance* hacer algo con *or* a desgana || ELECTR reluctancia *f* || *to affect reluctance* hacerse de rogar.

reluctant [ri'lʌktənt] *adj* reacio, cia (reticent) || — *he gave his reluctant consent* consintió de mala gana || *to be reluctant to do sth.* estar poco dispuesto a hacer algo, no querer hacer algo (not to want to), vacilar en hacer algo (to hesitate to) || *to go on a reluctant errand* hacer un recado a disgusto.

reluctantly [-li] *adv* de mala gana, contra su voluntad, a regañadientes, a disgusto.

rely [ri'lai] *vi* depender; *he relied on the money* dependía del dinero || contar, confiar; *to rely on s.o. to do sth.* contar con alguien para hacer algo, confiar en que alguien haga algo || fiarse; *you can't rely on the timetable* uno no se puede fiar del horario.

REM *abbr of [rapid eye movement]* movimiento rápido de los ojos.

remade ['ri:'meid] *pret/pp* → **remake.**

remain [ri'mein] *vi* quedarse, permanecer (to stay); *and they have remained there ever since* y se han quedado allí desde entonces; *to remain silent* permanecer silencioso || quedar, sobrar (to be left over) || quedar; *the few joys that remained to him* las pocas alegrías que le quedaban || quedar, faltar; *nothing remains to be done* nada queda por hacer; *that remains to be seen* eso queda por ver; *it only remains for us but to sign it* ahora sólo nos queda firmarlo || seguir; *I remain certain that* sigo convencido de que; *they remained faithful* siguieron fieles; *the weather remains good* el tiempo sigue bueno || — *I remain yours faithfully* reciba un atento saludo de, le saluda atentamente (in a letter) || *it remains, nevertheless, that* sin embargo || *nothing remained but to go back* no quedaba más remedio que volver || *one thing remains sure* una cosa es segura || *there remains one solution* queda una solución || *to let it remain as it is* dejarlo como es *or* como está || *to remain behind* quedarse (to stay) || *to remain in s.o.'s memory* quedar grabado en la memoria de uno || *to remain with* quedar en manos de.

remainder [ri'meində*] *n* resto *m*; *the remainder of the year, of the money* el resto del año, del dinero || MATH resto *m* (in division, in substraction) || los demás, las demás, los otros, las otras; *some are good, the remainder are bad* algunos son buenos, los demás son malos || *two into nine goes four, remainder one* nueve dividido por dos son cuatro y queda uno.

◆ *pl* saldo *m sing*, restos *m* de edición (books) || COMM saldo *m sing*.

remainder [ri'meində*] *vt* saldar (books).

remaining [ri'meiniŋ] *adj* otro, otra; que queda; *the remaining two were shot* los dos que quedaban *or* los otros dos fueron fusilados || restante, sobrante.

remains [ri'meinz] *pl n* restos *m* (of a building) || vestigios *m* (of a civilization, etc.) || sobras *f*, restos *m* (of a meal) || restos *m* (the dead human body); *mortal remains* restos mortales

|| FIG vestigios *m* (of former beauty, etc.) || obra *f sing* póstuma (of a writer).

remake ['riː'meik] *n* nueva versión *f* (of a film).

remake* ['riː'meik] *vt* rehacer, volver a hacer.
— OBSERV Pret y pp ***remade***.

reman ['riː'mæn] *vt* MAR proveer de nueva tripulación.

remand [ri'mɑːnd] *n* JUR detención *f* (keeping in custody) | libertad *f* condicional (release on bail) | remisión *f* (of a case) || *remand centre* centro *m* de detención preventiva.

remand [ri'mɑːnd] *vt* JUR remitir; *to remand a case to another court* remitir el caso a otro tribunal || — JUR *to remand in custody* mantener bajo custodia | *to remand on bail* liberar bajo fianza.

remanence ['remənəns] *n* PHYS remanencia *f*.

remanent ['remənənt] *adj* remanente.

remark [ri'mɑːk] *n* observación *f*, comentario *m* (comment); *to let sth. by without remark* dejar pasar algo sin hacer comentarios; *to make a remark* hacer una observación || — *his remark went home* su observación tuvo efecto || *introductory remarks* observaciones preliminares || *to escape remark* pasar desapercibido *or* inadvertido || *to make the remark that* observar que || *to pass remarks on* hacer comentarios sobre (to comment), criticar (to criticize) || *worthy of remark* notable.

remark ['ri'mɑːk] *vt* observar, advertir, notar (to say, to notice).
◆ *vi* *to remark on* o *upon* hacer una observación *or* hacer observaciones sobre, comentar.

remarkable [-əbl] *adj* notable; *remarkable for its size* notable por su estatura || extraordinario, ria; excelente (excellent); *a remarkable singer* un cantante extraordinario || admirable; *he did a remarkable piece of work* ha hecho un trabajo admirable || singular (strange).

remarkably [-i] *adv* extraordinariamente.

remarriage ['riː'mæridʒ] *n* segundas nupcias *f pl*, nuevo casamiento *m*.

remarry ['riː'mæri] *vi* volver a casarse.

rematch ['riˌmætʃ] *n* partido *m* de vuelta.

remediable [ri'miːdjəbl] *adj* remediable.

remedial [ri'miːdjəl] *adj* remediador, ra; reparador, ra; *remedial effect* efecto remediador || MED reparador, ra (surgery) | curativo, va (treatment) | correctivo, va (exercises) || *remedial education* enseñanza *f* de niños atrasados.

remediless ['remidilis] *adj* irremediable || MED incurable.

remedy ['remidi] *n* remedio *m*; *there's no remedy for it* no tiene remedio || JUR recurso *m*; *remedy of appeal* recurso de apelación || tolerancia *f* (coinage).

remedy ['remidi] *vt* remediar (to correct by removing a fault); *that should remedy the situation* eso debería remediar la situación || curar (to heal).

remember [ri'membə*] *vt/vi* acordarse de, recordar; *easily remembered* fácil de recordar; *he could not remember your name* no podía acordarse de *or* recordar tu nombre; *to remember a friend on his birthday* acordarse de un amigo en el día de su cumpleaños; *I remember going* recuerdo haber ido, me acuerdo de haber ido || dar recuerdos a; *remember me to your parents* deles recuerdos a sus padres || acordarse de, dar propina a (to give a tip to); *remember the guide* acuérdense del guía || — *as far as I can remember* si mal no recuerdo || *easy to remember* fácil de recordar || *he asked me to remember him to you all* os manda recuerdos a todos || *here's sth. to remember me by* te doy un recuerdo mío || *remember to turn to the left* acuérdate de torcer a la izquierda, que no se te olvide torcer a la izquierda, recuerda que tienes que torcer a la izquierda || *remember where you are!* ¡recuerde de donde está usted! ¿usted dónde se cree?

remembrance [ri'membrəns] *n* recuerdo *m*, rememoración *f* (recollection) || recuerdo *m*, memoria *f* (memory) || recuerdo *m* (souvenir) || — *in remembrance of* en conmemoración de, para conmemorar || *Remembrance Day* día *m* de la conmemoración del armisticio de 1918 || *to have no remembrance of* no recordar, no acordarse de.
◆ *pl* recuerdos *m* (greeting).

remex ['riːmeks] *n* remera *f*, rémige *f* (of a bird's wing).
— OBSERV El plural de *remex* es *remiges*.

remilitarization ['riːˌmilitərai'zeiʃən] *n* remilitarización *f*.

remilitarize ['riː'militəraiz] *vt* remilitarizar.

remind [ri'maind] *vt* recordar; *to remind s.o. of sth.* recordar algo a alguien; *he reminds me of your brother* me recuerda a tu hermano; *remind me to write to her* recuérdame que le escriba || *that reminds me!* ¡por cierto!, ¡a propósito!

reminder [-ə*] *n* recordatorio *m* (of a date) || notificación *f* (of outstanding bill) || advertencia *f* (warning) || recuerdo *m* (souvenir).

reminisce [ˌremi'nis] *vi* recordar el pasado.

reminiscence [ˌremi'nisns] *n* recuerdo *m*, reminiscencia *f* (sth. which is remembered) || recuerdo *m* (souvenir, memory) || *to spend evenings in reminiscence* pasar las tardes recordando el pasado.
◆ *pl* memorias *f* (personal memories).

reminiscent [ˌremi'nisnt] *adj* evocador, ra; que evoca (evocative) || lleno de recuerdos; *reminiscent photographs* fotos llenas de recuerdos || — *a room full of reminiscent old men* una sala llena de ancianos que recuerdan el pasado || *to be reminiscent of* recordar, hacer pensar en; *it is reminiscent of* recordar, hacer pensar en; *it is reminiscent of his first book* recuerda su primer libro.

remintage [riː'mintidʒ] *n* reacuñación *f*.

remise [ri'maiz] *vt* JUR ceder.

remiss [ri'mis] *adj* negligente, descuidado, da (neglectful) || remiso, sa (slack).

remissibility [ˌrimisə'biləti] *n* remisibilidad *f*.

remission [ri'miʃən] *n* remisión *f*, perdón *m*; *the remission of sins* el perdón de los pecados || disminución *f* (decrease in the magnitude of a force, etc.) || exoneración *f* (of a debt, of a fine, etc.) || MED remisión *f* || JUR remisión *f* (of a case) || *to give s.o. six months remission for good conduct* remitirle a uno seis meses de pena por buena conducta.

remissive [ri'misiv] *adj* remisivo, va.

remit [ri'mit] *vt* remitir (to send) || remitir, enviar (money) || remitir (sth. for further consideration) || devolver a un tribunal inferior (to return to a lower court) || aplazar (to postpone) || perdonar, remitir (to forgive) || perdonar, remitir (a debt, of a fine, penalty, etc.).
◆ *vi* moderarse (to moderate) || remitir (fever, storm) | aliviarse (pain).

remittal [-əl] *n* remisión *f*, perdón *m* (forgiveness) || exoneración *f* (of a debt, of a fine, etc.) || JUR remisión *f*.

remittance [-əns] *n* remesa *f*, giro *m* (sending of money) || *remittance man* hombre *m* que vive en el extranjero gracias al dinero que le envían de su casa.

remittee [remi'tiː] *n* destinatario, ria.

remittent [ri'mitənt] *adj* remitente; *remittent fever* fiebre remitente.

remnant ['remnənt] *n* resto *m*, remanente *m* (a remaining part) || retal *m* (piece of fabric); *remnant sale* venta de retales || FIG vestigio *m*.
◆ *pl* saldos *m* (sales).

remodel ['riː'mɔdl] *vt* modelar de nuevo (to give new shape to) || transformar || reorganizar.

remonetization [riˌmʌnitə'zeiʃən] *n* restablecimiento *m* del curso legal (of a metal).

remonetize ['riː'mʌnitaiz] *vt* dar de nuevo curso legal a (a metal).

remonstrance [ri'mɔnstrəns] *n* amonestación *f*, reprimenda *f*, reconvención *f* (reprimand) || protesta *f* (protest) || HIST protesta *f*.

remonstrate ['remənstreit] *vt* decir en señal de protesta.
◆ *vi* protestar (to protest) || amonestar (to reprimand s.o.); *to remonstrate with s.o. upon sth.* amonestar a alguien por algo.

remora ['remərə] *n* rémora *f* (fish).

remorse [ri'mɔːs] *n* remordimiento *m* || — *a twinge of remorse* un remordimiento || *to feel remorse* tener remordimientos || *without remorse* sin piedad.

remorseful [-ful] *adj* lleno de remordimiento, muy arrepentido, da.

remorseless [-lis] *adj* sin remordimiento (without remorse) || despiadado, da; implacable, inexorable (merciless).

remorselessness [-lisnis] *n* implacabilidad *f*, inexorabilidad *f*.

remote [ri'məut] *adj* remoto, ta (in space or time) || lejano, na; distante (distant) || retirado, da; apartado, da (out-of-the-way); *a remote little beach* una playita retirada || lejano, na; *remote theories* teorías lejanas || ligero, ra; remoto, ta (very slight); *a remote possibility* una posibilidad remota, una ligera posibilidad; *I haven't the remotest idea* no tengo la más remota idea || lejano, na; *a remote cousin* un primo lejano || distante (standoffish) || — *remote control* mando *m* a distancia, telemando *m* || INFORM *remote data transmission* transmisión *f* de datos a distancia || FIG *remote from* ajeno a || INFORM *remote maintenance* telemantenimiento *m*.

remote-controlled [-kən'trəuld] *adj* teledirigido, da (operated by remote control).

remotely [ri'məutli] *adv* remotamente.

remoteness [-nis] *n* alejamiento *m*, lejanía *f* (in time or space) || improbabilidad *f* (of a prospect).

remould; *US* **remold** *n* neumático *m* recauchutado.

remould; *US* **remold** *vt* recauchutar.

remount ['riːmaunt] *n* MIL remonta *f*.

remount [riː'maunt] *vt* volverse a montar en (bicycle, horse, etc.) || remontar (to supply with fresh mounts) || volver a subir (a hill) || volver a enmarcar (a photo, etc.).
◆ *vi* volverse a montar.

removability [riˌmuːvə'biliti] *n* amovilidad *f*.

removable [ri'muːvəbl] *adj* movible, móvil, trasladable (moveable) || transportable (machine) || amovible (part, civil servant) || de quita y pon (shirt collar) || que se puede quitar (a stain) || INFORM *removable disk* disco *m* removible.

removal [ri'muːvəl] *n* traslado *m* (transfer) || despido *m*, destitución *f* (discharge from office) || mudanza *f* (moving house) || eliminación *f* (elimination) || supresión *f* (of an article, of a word, etc.) || MED extirpación *f* || alivio *m* (of a suffering) || FAM liquidación *f* (murder) || *removal van* camión *m* de mudanzas.

remove [ri'muːv] *n* grado *m* (degree) || grado *m* de parentesco (of kinship) || distancia *f* (distance) || mudanza *f* (removal) || paso *m* a la clase superior || cambio *m* de platos (eating) || — *cousin at the first remove* tío segundo (one's parent's first cousin), sobrino segundo (one's first cousin's child) || FIG *it is but one remove from* raya en || *not to get one's remove* repetir el curso || *to be many removes from* distar de ser.

remove [ri'mu:v] *vt* quitar (to take off or away); *s.o. has removed my radio* alguien me ha quitado la radio || quitar de en medio (to get sth. out of the way) || quitar (a stain) || eliminar, borrar (traces) || quitarse (to take off); *please remove your coat* quítese el abrigo, por favor || destituir, despedir (to dismiss from office) || trasladar (to transfer) || mudar, trasladar (one's personal effects) || quitar; *he removed the lid* quitó la tapa || suprimir (tax, passage, word) || tachar, borrar (from a list) || disipar (doubt, fear) || eliminar (difficulties, etc.) || deshacerse de (to get rid of) || MED extirpar, quitar (tumour, etc.) || — *the accident removed him from racing* el accidente le hizo abandonar *or* retirarse de las carreras || *to remove o.s.* irse, marcharse (to go away) || *to remove one's hat* descubrirse, quitarse el sombrero || *to remove sth. to another place* cambiar algo de sitio, trasladar algo a otro sitio || *to remove to hospital* o *to the hospital* hospitalizar, llevar al hospital.
◆ *vi* mudarse, trasladarse.

removed [-d] *adj* distante || *first cousin once removed* tío segundo (one's parent's first cousin), sobrino segundo (one's first cousin's child).

remover [-ə*] *n* empresario *m* de mudanzas (agent) || mozo *m* de cuerda *or* de mudanzas (workman) || — *makeup remover* desmaquillador *m* || *nail polish remover* quitaesmalte *m* || *stain remover* quitamanchas *m inv*.

remunerable [ri'mjunərəbl] *adj* remunerable.

remunerate [ri'mju:nəreit] *vt* remunerar, retribuir.

remuneration [ri,mju:nə'reiʃən] *n* remuneración *f*.

remunerative [ri'mju:nərətiv] *adj* remunerativo, va.

remunerator [ri'mju:nə,reitə*] *n* remunerador, ra.

Remus ['ri:məs] *pr n* Remo *m*.

renaissance [rə'neisəns] *n* renacimiento *m* || *the Renaissance* el Renacimiento.

renal ['ri:nəl] *adj* renal.

rename ['ri:'neim] *vt* poner un nuevo nombre a.

renascence [ri'næsns] *n* renacimiento *m* || *the Renascence* el Renacimiento.

renascent [ri'næsnt] *adj* renaciente.

rend* [rend] *vt* rasgar, rajar, hender (to split violently) || rasgar, desgarrar (to tear) || arrancar (to pull away or out) || destrozar (to cause emotional pain to) || dividir (to divide) || — FIG *a cry rent the air* un grito hendió el aire | *to rend one's hair* arrancarse los cabellos | *to rend s.o.'s heart* partirle el corazón a uno || *to rend sth. asunder* partir algo por medio.
— OBSERV Pret y pp ***rent***.

render [-ə*] *n* primera capa *f* de enlucido (building) || contribución *f*.

render [-ə*] *vt* dar; *to render thanks to God* dar gracias a Dios || rendir (homage) || rendir, dar; *to render an account of* dar cuenta de || presentar (to present) || hacer; *to render s.o. a service* hacer un favor a alguien; *to render s.o. happy* hacer feliz a alguien || dar, prestar (assistance) || devolver (to give back) || dejar; *the accident rendered him blind* el accidente le dejó ciego || hacer (to do) || entregar, rendir (to hand over, to surrender) || representar (to represent); *the picture rendered the scene perfectly* el cuadro representaba perfectamente la escena || reproducir (to reproduce) || producir (a benefit) || traducir (to translate) || interpretar (to interprete artistically) || JUR administrar (justice) | pronunciar (a sentence, a verdict) || CULIN derretir (to melt fat) || COMM mandar, presentar (a bill) || ARCH enlucir, dar una capa de enlucido a (building) || TECH extraer derritiendo (to extract fats) || — *for services rendered to the nation* por los servicios prestados a la nación || *the poor soil renders irrigation necessary* la pobreza del suelo hace que sea necesario el regadío || *to render sth. impossible* imposibilitar algo, hacer que algo sea imposible.

rendering [-iŋ] *n* enlucido *m* (of a building) || interpretación *f* (artistic interpretation) || traducción *f* (translation).

rendezvous ['rɔndivu:] *inv n* cita *f*; *to have a rendezvous with* tener cita con || lugar *m* de reunión (place) || MIL punto *m* de reunión.

rendezvous ['rɔndivu:] *vt* MIL reunir (to assemble).
◆ *vi* reunirse.

rendition [ren'diʃən] *n* traducción *f* (translation) || interpretación *f* (artistic interpretation) || rendición *f* (surrender).

renegade ['renigeid] *adj/n* renegado, da.

renegade ['renigeid] *vi* renegar.

renege [ri'ni:g] *n* US renuncio *m* (cards).

renege [ri'ni:g] *vi* US no cumplir una promesa (on a promise) | dar marcha atrás, volverse atrás (on an agreement, etc.) || renunciar (in cards).

renegotiate [,rini'gəuʃi,eit] *vt* negociar de nuevo.

renew [ri'nju:] *vt* renovar; *to renew a passport, vows, a contract* renovar un pasaporte, votos, un contrato || extender, prorrogar (to extend) || reanudar; *to renew one's efforts* reanudar sus esfuerzos; *to renew talks* reanudar las conversaciones; *to renew one's acquaintance with* reanudar una amistad con || reavivar (one's interest) || renovar (to replace) || COMM renovar || — *to renew the attack* volver a atacar || *with renewed strength* con nuevas fuerzas.
◆ *vi* renovarse (strength) || reanudarse (to resume) || COMM hacer una renovación.

renewable [-əbl] *adj* renovable.

renewal [ri'nju:əl] *n* renovación *f* (of passport, subscription, contract, etc.) || prórroga *f*, extensión *f* (extension) || reanudación *f* (continuation after a break) || COMM renovación *f*.

rennet ['renit] *n* cuajo *m* (curdled milk) || cuajar *m* (abomasum) || *rennet stomach* cuajar.

renounce [ri'nauns] *n* renuncio *m* (in cards).

renounce [ri'nauns] *vt* repudiar (to repudiate) || renunciar a (a claim, a right) || denunciar (a treaty).
◆ *vi* renunciar (in cards).

renouncement [-mənt] *n* renuncia *f*.

renovate ['renəuveit] *vt* renovar (to brighten up) || restaurar (to restore).
◆ *vi* renovarse.

renovation [,renəu'veiʃən] *n* renovación *f* || restauración *f* (restoration).

renovator ['renəuveitə*] *n* renovador, ra || restaurador, ra (restorer).

renown [ri'naun] *n* renombre *m*, fama *f*, reputación *f*.

renowned [-d] *adj* renombrado, da; famoso, sa; célebre.

rent [rent] *n* alquiler *m* (for house, car, television, etc.) || arrendamiento *m* (of agricultural land) || raja *f*, hendidura *f* (split) || rasgón *m*, rasgadura *f* (tear) || escisión *f*, división *f* (schism) || — *cars for rent* coches *m* de alquiler || *for rent* se alquila || *I pay five pounds rent* pago cinco libras de alquiler.

rent [rent] *vt* alquilar (house, property); *to rent s.o. a flat* alquilar un piso a alguien; *to rent a house from s.o.* alquilar una casa a alguien || arrendar (land) || *to rent out* alquilar.
◆ *vi* alquilarse; *the house rents at a high price* se alquila la casa a un precio elevado || arrendarse (land).

rent [rent] *pret/pp* → **rend.**

rentable ['rentəbl] *adj* que se alquila, alquilable (house) || arrendable (land).

rental [-əl] *n* alquiler *m* (quantity paid); *monthly rental* alquiler mensual || arriendo *m*, arrendamiento *m* (of agricultural land) || renta *f* (income from rents) || alquiler *m* (renting) || US propiedad *f* alquilada.
◆ *adj* de alquiler.

rent book [-buk] *n* registro *m* de fecha y pago del alquiler.

rent boy [-bɔi] *n* chapero *m*.

renter ['rentə*] *n* inquilino, na (in a house, in a flat) || arrendatario, ria (of land) || CINEM distribuidor, ra (distributor).

rent-free ['rent'fri:] *adv* gratuitamente, sin pagar alquiler.
◆ *adj* exento de alquiler, gratuito, ta (a house).

rentier ['rɔntiei] *n* rentista *m* & *f*.

rent-roll ['rentrəul] *n* registro *m* de propiedades en alquiler (register) || ingresos *m pl* de propiedades en alquiler.

renumber ['ri:'nʌmbə*] *vt* volver a numerar.

renunciation [ri,nʌnsi'eiʃən] *n* renuncia *f*, renunciación *f*.

renunciative [ri'nʌnsiətiv]; **renunciatory** [ri,nʌnsiətəri] *adj* renunciante.

reoccupation ['ri:,ɔkju'peiʃən] *n* nueva ocupación *f*.

reoccupy ['ri:'ɔkjupai] *vt* volver a ocupar.

reopen ['ri:'əupən] *vt* volver a abrir, reabrir (a shop) || JUR volver a estudiar (a case).
◆ *vi* volver a abrirse, reabrirse (a shop) || volverse a estudiar (a case).

reopening [-iŋ] *n* reapertura *f*.

reorder [ri:'ɔ:də*] *n* nuevo pedido *m*.

reorder [ri:'ɔ:də*] *vt* pedir de nuevo *or* hacer un nuevo pedido de (goods) || volver a ordenar *or* a poner en orden (to put in order) || reorganizar (to reorganize).
◆ *vi* hacer un nuevo pedido.

reorganization ['ri:,ɔ:gənai'zeiʃən] *n* reorganización *f*.

reorganize ['ri:'ɔ:gənaiz] *vt* reorganizar.
◆ *vi* reorganizarse.

reorient ['ri:'ɔ:rient] *vt* reorientar, dar nueva orientación a.

reorientation ['ri:,ɔ:rien'teiʃən] *n* nueva orientación *f*.

rep [rep] *n* reps *m* (fabric).

rep [rep] *n* FAM viajante *m*, representante *m* (salesman) | reputación *f*, fama *f*.

repack [ri:'pæk] *vt* volver a embalar (to wrap up again) || volver a hacer (suitcase).

repackage [ri:'pækidʒ] *vt* volver a embalar.

repaid ['ri:'peid] *pret/pp* → **repay.**

repaint [ri:'peint] *vt* volver a pintar, repintar; *to repaint sth. red* repintar algo de rojo.

repair [ri'pεə*]; **repairing** [ri'pεəriŋ] *n* reparación *f* (of a car, of a house, etc.) || remiendo *m* (of clothes) || — *closed for repairs* cerrado por reformas *or* obras || *in bad repair* en mal estado || *it is out of repair* no tiene arreglo, no se puede reparar || *repair kit* caja *f* de herramientas || *repair parts* repuestos *m*, recambios *m* || *repair shop* taller *m* de reparaciones || *repair squad* equipo *m* de reparación || *to be (damaged) beyond repair* no tener arreglo (object, situation) || *to be under repair* estar en reparación (appliance, etc.), estar en obras (house) || *to keep in* *good repair* o *in repair* mantener en buen estado.

repair [ri'pɛə*] *vt* reparar, arreglar, componer (to fix) || remendar (shoes, clothes) || remediar (a wrong) || restablecer (health).
◆ *vi* acudir.

repairing [-riŋ] *n* → **repair.**

repairman [-mæn] *n* reparador *m*.
— OBSERV El plural de *repairman* es *repairmen*.

repaper ['riː'peipə*] *vt* empapelar de nuevo, volver a empapelar.

reparable ['repərəbl] *adj* reparable; *reparable damage* daño reparable.

reparation [ˌrepə'reiʃən] *n* reparación *f* || satisfacción *f* (satisfaction).
◆ *pl* COMM indemnización *f sing* (compensation).

reparative [ri'pærətiv] *adj* reparador, ra.

repartee [ˌrepɑː'tiː] *n* rápida sucesión *f* de réplicas *or* salidas (exchange between speakers) || réplica *f* (art).

repartition ['repɑː'tiʃən] *n* reparto *m*, distribución *f*.

repass ['riː'pɑːs] *vt* volver a pasar (to pass again).
◆ *vi* volver a pasar.

repast [ri'pɑːst] *n* comida *f*.

repatriate [riː'pætrieit] *n* repatriado, da.

repatriate [riː'pætrieit] *vt* repatriar.
◆ *vi* repatriarse.

repatriation ['riːpætri'eiʃən] *n* repatriación *f*.

repay* [riː'pei] *vt* devolver, reembolsar (money) || pagar, liquidar (a debt) || compensar, pagar (s.o.) || corresponder a, devolver (to return); *to repay an invitation* corresponder a una invitación || recompensar (to recompense) || hacer pagar, desquitarse de; *he repaid the trick by setting his dog on them* les hizo pagar la broma echándoles el perro || — *book that repays reading* libro que merece la pena ser leído || *how can I ever repay you?* ¿cómo puedo pagarle? || *I'll repay you for that!* ¡ya me las pagarás! || *to repay s.o. in full* reembolsar a alguien integralmente || FIG *to repay s.o. in kind* pagar a uno con la misma moneda.
◆ *vi* hacer un pago, pagar.
— OBSERV Pret y pp ***repaid***.

repayable [-əbl] *adj* reembolsable, reintegrable.

repayment [-mənt] *n* devolución *f*, pago *m*, reintegro *m*, reembolso *m* (of money) || recompensa *f* (reward).

repeal [ri'piːl] *n* revocación *f* (revocation) || abrogación *f* (abrogation) || anulación *f* (annulment).

repeal [ri'piːl] *vt* revocar || abrogar || anular.

repealing [-iŋ] *adj* derogatorio, ria.

repeat [ri'piːt] *n* repetición *f* (a repeating or sth. repeated) || MUS repetición *f* || CINEM reestreno *m* (of a film) || THEATR reposición *f* (of play) || *this programme is a repeat* es una segunda difusión de este programa.

repeat [ri'piːt] *vt* repetir; *to repeat a sentence* repetir una frase; *to repeat an experience* repetir una experiencia || repetir, volver a hacer; *to repeat a visit* volver a hacer una visita || recitar (to recite) || contar, decir, repetir (sth. one has been told); *don't repeat this to anybody* no se lo cuente a nadie || repetir (a course, a term, etc.) || CINEM volver a poner (a film) || THEATR volver a representar (a play) || *to repeat o.s.* repetirse.
◆ *vi* repetir (a taste, a gun, etc.) || US votar más de una vez [en unas elecciones] || — *garlic repeats on me* el ajo se repite || *not to bear repeating* no merece la pena repetirse.

repeated [-id] *adj* repetido, da.

repeatedly [-idli] *adv* repetidas veces, reiteradamente, reiteradas veces.

repeater [-ə*] *n* reloj *m* de repetición (watch or clock) || arma *f* de repetición (a repeating gun) || repetidor *m* (telegraphy) || US elector *m* que vota más de una vez (elections) | repetidor, ra (student).

repeating [-iŋ] *adj* de repetición (rifle, clock) || MATH *repeating decimal* fracción *f* decimal periódica.

repel [ri'pel] *vt* repeler, rechazar; *to repel an attack* rechazar un ataque || reprimir, contener; *to repel a desire* contener un deseo || rechazar; *to repel an offer of friendship* rechazar un ofrecimiento de amistad || repeler; *this paint repels water* esta pintura repele el agua || PHYS repeler || FIG repeler, repugnar (to repulse).

repellent [-ənt] *adj* repelente || FIG repugnante, repelente.
◆ *n* producto *m* contra los insectos (for repelling insects) || producto *m* para impermeabilizar (to make sth. impermeable).

repent ['riːpənt] *adj* BOT rastrero, ra || ZOOL reptante, que se arrastra.

repent [ri'pent] *vt* arrepentirse de.
◆ *vi* arrepentirse.

repentance [-əns] *n* arrepentimiento *m*.

repentant [-ənt] *adj* arrepentido, da.

repeople ['riː'piːpl] *vt* repoblar.

repercussion [ˌriːpə'kʌʃən] *n* repercusión *f* || reverberación *f*, eco *m* (reverberation) || repercusión *f* (indirect reaction to some event); *to have grave repercussions* tener graves repercusiones.

repertoire ['repətwɑː*]; **repertory** ['repətəri] *n* repertorio *m*; *to have a very varied repertory* tener un repertorio muy variado || *repertory theatre* teatro de repertorio.

repetend [repə'tend] *n* estribillo *m*, cantinela *f*.

repetition [ˌrepi'tiʃən] *n* repetición *f* || recitación *f* || réplica *f* (copy).

repetitious [ˌrepə'tiʃəs] *adj* lleno de repeticiones.

repetitive [ri'petitiv] *adj* reiterativo, va (tending to repeat) || lleno de repeticiones (repetitious).

rephrase ['riː'freiz] *vt* decir con otras palabras, decir de otra manera (when speaking) || volver a redactar (sth. in writing).

repine [ri'pain] *vi* quejarse, afligirse; *to repine at* quejarse de.

repining [-iŋ] *n* quejas *f pl*.

replace [ri'pleis] *vt* reponer, volver a poner en su lugar (to put back) || sustituir, reemplazar; *Smith replaced Brown* Smith sustituyó a Brown; *to replace one thing by another* sustituir una cosa por otra; *he replaced Brown by Smith* reemplazó a Brown por Smith || pagar (to pay for sth. broken) || *please replace the receiver* cuelgue por favor (phone).

replaceable [-əbl] *adj* reemplazable, sustituible.

replacement [-mənt] *n* reposición *f* (action of putting back) || sustitución *f*, reemplazo *m* (action of substituting) || sustituto, ta; suplente *m* & *f* (s.o. who replaces) || repuesto *m*, recambio *m* (spare part) || MIL reemplazo *m* || *I can't find a replacement for the vase I broke* no consigo encontrar un jarrón para sustituir el que rompí.

replant ['riː'plɑːnt] *vt* replantar, volver a plantar.

replanting [-iŋ] *n* replantación *f*.

replay [riː'plei] *n* SP repetición *f* de un partido (match) || repetición *f* (on television).

replay ['riː'plei] *vt* volver a jugar || MUS volver a tocar || THEATR volver a representar.

repleadar [ri'pliːdə*] *n* JUR segundo alegato *m*.

replenish [ri'pleniʃ] *vt* rellenar, llenar de nuevo (to fill again) || abastecer *or* aprovisionar de nuevo (*with* de) || reponer; *to replenish one's stocks* reponer las existencias.

replenishment [-mənt] *n* relleno *m* || reabastecimiento *m*.

replete [ri'pliːt] *adj* repleto, ta; lleno, na.

repletion [ri'pliːʃən] *n* saciedad *f*, repleción *f* || *to eat to repletion* comer hasta hartarse *or* saciarse.

replevin [ri'plevin] *n* JUR desembargo *m*.

replevin [ri'plevin] *vt* US JUR obtener un desembargo de.

replevy [ri'plevi] *n* US JUR desembargo *m*.

replevy [ri'plevi] *vt* JUR obtener un desembargo de.
◆ *vi* JUR obtener un desembargo.

replica ['replikə] *n* copia *f*, reproducción *f*, réplica *f*.

replicate ['replikət] *adj* replegado, da.

replicate ['replikeit] *vt* repetir, duplicar.

replicated [-id] *adj* replegado, da.

replication [repli'keiʃən] *n* copia *f*, reproducción *f*, réplica *f* (copy) || réplica *f* (answer) || JUR réplica *f* || repercusión *f*.

reply [ri'plai] *n* respuesta *f*, contestación *f* || — *in reply they said that...* contestaron que... || COMM *in reply to your letter of the 5th inst.* en respuesta a su atenta del 5 del corriente || *reply coupon* cupón *m* || *reply paid* respuesta pagada.

reply [ri'plai] *vt* responder, contestar; *he replied that he was tired* contestó que estaba cansado.
◆ *vi* contestar, responder; *to reply to s.o.* contestar a uno || *to reply to a letter* contestar una carta.

repolish ['riː'pɔliʃ] *vt* repulir, pulir de nuevo.

repopulate ['riː'pɔpjuleit] *vt* repoblar.

repopulation ['riːpɔpju'leiʃən] *n* repoblación *f*.

report [ri'pɔːt] *n* informe *m* (official); *preliminary, provisional, final report* informe preliminar, provisional, definitivo; *to bring a report up-to-date* poner al día un informe; *to amend a report* enmendar un informe || noticia *f* (piece of news) || reportaje *m* (account in newspaper, on radio) || relato *m*, relación *f* (spoken account) || informe *m*, ponencia *f* (speech at a public meeting) || reputación *f*, fama *f*; *of good report* de buena reputación || boletín *m* (at school, etc.) || rumor *m*, voz *f* (rumour); *there are reports that* corre la voz de que || estampido *m*, detonación *f* (of gun, etc.) || informe *m* (of a policeman) || MIL parte *m*; *to make one's report* dar el parte || — *chairman's report* informe del presidente || *expert report* dictamen *m* pericial, peritaje *m* || *factual report* exposición *f* de hechos || *I have heard reports that he is ill* me han dicho que está enfermo || *information report* nota informativa || *progress report* informe sobre la marcha de los trabajos || COMM *report on activities* o *on the management* informe sobre la gestión || JUR *to draw up a report against s.o.* levantar un atestado contra alguien || *weather report* parte meteorológico.

report [ri'pɔːt] *vt* relatar (to recount) || redactar las actas de (the secretary in a meeting) || hacer la crónica de (a trial, a meeting for a newspaper) || presentar un informe sobre || repetir (a message) || denunciar (to make an official complaint about s.o.); *to report a criminal* denunciar a un criminal; *to report a theft to the police* denunciar un robo a la policía || declarar, anunciar (to declare, to announce) || comuni-

car; *to report the results of an investigation* comunicar los resultados de una investigación ‖ MIL dar parte de ‖ *it is reported that* se dice que.
◆ *vi* presentar un informe (to present a formal report) ‖ hacer un informe (*on* sobre) (to draw up a report) ‖ ser reportero, hacer reportajes (to work as reporter) ‖ presentarse; *to report for work* presentarse para trabajar ‖ — *report back to me when you finish* vuelva a verme cuando acabe ‖ MIL *to report sick* darse de baja por enfermedad | *to report to one's unit* incorporarse a su unidad.

reportage [ˌrepɔːˈtɑːʒ] *n* reportaje *m*.

report card [-kɑːd] *n* US boletín *m* de notas.

reportedly [riˈpɔːtidli] *adv* según dicen *or* se dice.

reporter [riˈpɔːtə*] *n* periodista *m* & *f*, reportero *m* (of a newspaper) ‖ relator *m* (in court, in official meetings, etc.) ‖ presentador, ra (on television).

reporting [riˈpɔːtiŋ] *n* reporterismo *m*.

repose [riˈpəuz] *n* reposo *m*, descanso *m* (rest) ‖ sueño *m* (sleep) ‖ calma *f*, sosiego *m* (calm).

repose [riˈpəuz] *vi* reposar, descansar ‖ — *to repose in state* estar de cuerpo presente ‖ *to repose on* basarse en; *his argument reposes on a new theory* su argumento se basa en una nueva teoría.
◆ *vt* descansar, reposar (to rest) ‖ FIG poner, depositar (confidence).

repository [riˈpɔzitəri] *n* depósito *m* (place for keeping things) ‖ almacén *m* (warehouse) ‖ depositario, ria (person); *repository of one's secrets* depositario de los secretos de uno ‖ fuente *f* (source) ‖ panteón *m* (burial vault) ‖ *furniture repository* guardamuebles *m inv*.

repossess [ˌripəˈzes] *vt* volver a tomar posesión de, recuperar (to take possession of) ‖ devolver (to give back) ‖ *to repossess o.s. of* recuperar, volver a tomar posesión de.

repossession [ˌripəˈzəʃən] *n* recuperación *f* ‖ *repossession order* orden *f* de recuperación de mercancía vendida a plazos.

repoussé [rəˈpuːsei] *adj* TECH repujado, da.
◆ *n* TECH repujado *m*.

repp [rep] *n* reps *m*.

reprehend [ˌrepriˈhend] *vt* reprender; *he reprehended her for bad behaviour* le reprendió por su mala conducta.

reprehensible [ˌrepriˈhensəbl] *adj* reprensible, censurable.

reprehension [ˌrepriˈhenʃən] *n* reprensión *f*, reprobación *f*.

represent [ˌrepriˈzent] *vt* representar; *to represent a minister at the inauguration of a monument* representar a un ministro en la inauguración de un monumento; *the painting represents three Spaniards* el cuadro representa a tres españoles; *this book represents twenty year's work* este libro representa un trabajo de veinte años ‖ equivaler; *that represents a slander* eso equivale a una calumnia ‖ describir (to describe); *you represented it to me quite differently* me lo describió de forma muy diferente ‖ JUR & COMM representar ‖ THEATR representar ‖ *to be well* o *strongly represented* estar bien representado.

re-present [ˈriːˈprizent] *vt* presentar de nuevo, volver a presentar.

representation [ˌreprizenˈteiʃən] *n* representación *f*; *proportional representation* representación proporcional; *a representation of the battle* una representación de la batalla ‖ descripción *f* (description) ‖ representantes *m pl* delegación *f* (representatives) ‖ THEATR representación *f* ‖ *to make a representation* o *representations to* presentar una petición a (to petition), formular *or* elevar una protesta a (to protest).

representational [-əl] *adj* ARTS figurativo, va.

representative [ˌrepriˈzentətiv] *adj* representativo, va; *representative government* gobierno representativo ‖ *a song representative of South American music* una canción representativa de la música sudamericana, una canción que representa la música sudamericana.
◆ *n* representante *m* & *f*; *commercial representative* representante comercial; *to send a representative to a conference* mandar un representante a una conferencia ‖ US diputado *m*, representante *m*.

repress [riˈpres] *vt* reprimir, contener; *to repress an uprising* reprimir una insurrección; *to repress tears* reprimir el llanto.

repression [riˈpreʃən] *n* represión *f*.

repressive [riˈpresiv] *adj* represivo, va; *repressive measures* medidas represivas.

reprieve [riˈpriːv] *n* JUR indulto *m* (pardon) | conmutación *f* (commutation) | suspensión *f* (suspension) ‖ FIG alivio *m*, respiro *m* (relief) ‖ *the right of reprieve* el derecho de gracia.

reprieve [riˈpriːv] *vt* JUR indultar (to pardon) | conmutar la pena de (to commute a sentence) | suspender la pena de (to suspend sentence) ‖ FIG aliviar (to relieve) | aplazar (to postpone).

reprimand [ˈreprimɑːnd] *n* reprimenda *f*, reprensión *f*.

reprimand [ˈreprimɑːnd] *vt* reprender, reconvenir.

reprint [ˈriːˈprint] *n* reimpresión *f*, reedición *f* ‖ separata *f*, tirada *f* aparte (offprint).

reprint [ˈriːprint] *vt* reimprimir (to print again) ‖ tirar aparte (to extract).

reprisal [ripraizəl] *n* represalia *f*; *to take reprisals* ejercer represalias.

reprise [riˈpraiz] *n* MUS repetición *f* ‖ JUR *revenue above reprises* renta neta.

reproach [riˈprəutʃ] *n* reproche *m*, crítica *f*, censura *f* (reproof) ‖ deshonra *f*, oprobio *m* (shame, disgrace) ‖ — *above reproach* sin tacha ‖ *to be a reproach to* ser vergonzoso para ‖ *to be beyond reproach* ser impecable (work, etc.), ser intachable (conduct, reputation, etc.) ‖ *to bring reproach on* ser un oprobio para.

reproach [riˈprəutʃ] *vt* reprochar, criticar, censurar; *to reproach s.o. with* o *for sth.* reprocharle algo a alguien ‖ — *to reproach o.s. with sth.* reprocharse algo ‖ *to reproach s.o. for doing sth.* reprochar a alguien que haya hecho algo.

reproachable [-əbəl] *adj* reprochable, criticable, censurable.

Reproaches [-iz] *pl n* REL improperios *m*.

reproachful [-ful] *adj* reprobador, ra; de reproche (look, etc.) ‖ *to be reproachful of sth.* reprochar algo.

reproachfully [-fuli] *adv* con reproche, de manera reprobatoria.

reprobate [ˈreprəubeit] *adj/n* REL réprobo, ba ‖ malvado, da (wicked).

reprobation [ˌreprəuˈbeiʃən] *n* reprobación *f*.

reprobative [ˈreprəˌbeitiv]; **reprobatory** [ˈreprəbəˌtəri] *adj* reprobatorio, ria.

reproduce [ˌriːprəˈdjuːs] *vt* reproducir.
◆ *vi* reproducirse.

reproducible [ˌriːprəˈdjuːsibl] *adj* reproducible.

reproducing machine [ˌriːprəˈdjuːsiŋməˈʃiːn] *n* máquina *f* reproductora.

reproduction [ˌriːprəˈdʌkʃən] *n* reproducción *f*.

reproductive [ˌriːprəˈdʌktiv] *adj* reproductor, ra ‖ *reproductive organs* órganos reproductores.

reproductivity [ˌriːprədʌkˈtiviti] *n* reproductividad *f* (capacity of being reproductive).

reproof [riˈpruːf] *n* reprobación *f*, censura *f*, reprensión *f*.

reprovable [riˈpruvəbəl] *adj* reprobable, censurable (reproachable).

reproval [riˈpruːvəl] *n* reprobación *f*, censura *f*, reprensión *f*.

reprove [riˈpruːv] *vt* reprobar, condenar, censurar, criticar, reprender.

reproving [-iŋ] *adj* reprobatorio, ria; de reprobación.

reprovingly [riˈpruːviŋli] *adv* con reprobación.

reptant [ˈreptənt] *adj* ZOOL reptante ‖ BOT rastrero, ra; *reptant roots* raíces rastreras.

reptile [ˈreptail] *adj* reptil ‖ FIG rastrero, ra.
◆ *n* reptil *m*.

reptilian [repˈtiliən] *adj* reptil.
◆ *n* reptil *m*.

republic [riˈpʌblik] *n* república *f* ‖ *republic of letters* república de las letras.

republican [-ən] *adj/n* republicano, na ‖ *Republican Party* Partido Republicano.

republicanism [-ənizəm] *n* republicanismo *m*.

republication [ˈriːˌpʌblikeiʃən] *n* reedición *f*.

republish [ˈriːˈpʌbliʃ] *vt* reeditar.

repudiable [riˈpjuːdieibl] *adj* repudiable.

repudiate [riˈpjuːdieit] *vt* repudiar (a person) ‖ rechazar (to reject) ‖ JUR negarse a cumplir (a contract) | negarse a reconocer (debt, claim, etc.).

repudiation [ripjuːˈdieiʃən] *n* repudiación *f*, repudio *m* (of one's wife) ‖ rechazo *m* (rejection) ‖ desconocimiento *m* (of debts, etc.).

repugnance [riˈpʌgnəns]; **repugnancy** [-i] *n* repugnancia *f*, repulsión *f*.

repugnant [riˈpʌgnənt] *adj* repugnante, repulsivo, va; repelente (repellent) ‖ incompatible; *repugnant to* incompatible con ‖ *I find them repugnant* me repugnan.

repulse [riˈpʌls] *n* repulsa *f*, rechazamiento *m* ‖ *he suffered a repulse* fue rechazado.

repulse [riˈpʌls] *vt* rechazar (to drive back) ‖ repeler, rechazar (to reject).

repulsion [riˈpʌlʃən] *n* repulsión *f*, repugnancia *f* (revulsion) ‖ rechazamiento *m*, repulsa *f*, repulsión *f* (rejection) ‖ PHYS repulsión *f*.

repulsive [riˈpʌlsiv] *adj* repulsivo, va; repelente.

repulsiveness [-nis] *n* carácter *m* repulsivo ‖ PHYS fuerza *f* repulsiva.

repurchase [riːˈpəːtʃəs] *n* nueva compra *f*, nueva adquisición *f*.

repurchase [riːˈpəːtʃəs] *vt* volver a comprar, comprar de nuevo.

reputability [ˈrepjutəˈbiliti] *n* buena reputación *f*, honorabilidad *f*.

reputable [ˈrepjutəbl] *adj* reputado, da (well known) ‖ acreditado, da (having a good reputation) ‖ honroso, sa; estimable (honourable) ‖ de confianza, seguro, ra (reliable) ‖ puro, ra; castizo, za (word).

reputation [ˌrepjuˈteiʃən] *n* reputación *f*, fama *f*; *to have a good reputation* tener buena reputación; *to have the reputation of being stupid* tener fama de estúpido ‖ *this region has a reputation for good wine* esta región es famosa por la calidad de sus vinos.

repute [riˈpjuːt] *n* reputación *f*, fama *f*; *a man of good repute* un hombre de buena reputación; *a city of evil repute* una ciudad de mala fama; *to know a person by repute* conocer a una persona por su reputación || *house of ill repute* casa de mala fama || *of repute, of good repute* famoso, sa || *to hold s.o. in high repute* tener a alguien en gran estima.

repute [ri'pjuːt] *vt* considerar || — *he is reputed to have married three times* dicen que se casó tres veces || *it is reputed that Caesar was murdered by Brutus* se supone que César fue asesinado por Bruto || *to be reputed to be rich* tener fama de rico.

reputed [-id] *adj* reputado, da (well known); *highly reputed* muy reputado || supuesto, ta (supposed); *the reputed journalist turned out to be a criminal* el supuesto periodista resultó ser un criminal.

reputedly [-idli] *adj* según dicen, según se dice; *it is reputedly easy to play the piano* según dicen, es fácil tocar el piano.

request [ri'kwest] *n* petición *f*, ruego *m*, solicitud *f*; *to make a request* hacer una petición, dirigir una solicitud || COMM demanda *f* || — *at the request of* a petición de, a instancia de || *by request* a petición del público || *in request* solicitado; *the famous yodeller is very much in request* el célebre cantante tirolés es muy solicitado por el público || *on request* a petición de los interesados, solicite; *a list of prices is available on request* una lista de precios está disponible a petición de los interesados, solicite una lista de precios || *on the request of* a petición de || *request programme* emisión *f* de discos solicitados por los radioyentes || *request stop* parada discrecional || *to send a request for reinforcements* pedir refuerzos.

request [ri'kwest] *vt* pedir, solicitar; *in his speech he requested better conditions for widows* en su discurso pidió mejores condiciones para las viudas; *he requested me to attend the meeting* me pidió que asistiese a la reunión; *I requested that he be shot* pedí que lo fusilaran || rogar; *silence is requested* se ruega silencio || — *Mr. Andrews requests the pleasure of your company for dinner* el señor Andrés tiene el placer de invitarle a cenar || *passengers are requested not to alight between stops* se ruega no bajen entre las paradas || *to request sth. of s.o.* pedir algo a alguien.

requiem ['rekwiəm] *n* REL réquiem *m*.

require [ri'kwaiə*] *vt* disponer, exigir; *the law requires that all criminals be punished* la ley dispone que todos los criminales sean castigados || requerir, necesitar (to need); *this illness requires a lot of care* esta enfermedad requiere muchos cuidados || exigir, requerir (to demand); *the circumstances require that a decision be taken at once* las circunstancias exigen que se tome una decisión en seguida || desear (to desire) || — *if required* si es preciso, en caso de necesidad || *it required all my strength to move it* necesité *or* tuve que aplicar toda mi fuerza para moverlo || *the radiator requires constant filling* hay que rellenar el radiador constantemente || *to be required* necesitarse, requerirse; *a great deal of application is required to study medicine* para estudiar medicina se necesita mucha aplicación || *to require s.o. to do sth.* pedir a alguien que haga algo (to ask), exigir que alguien haga algo (to demand) || *we have all we require* tenemos todo lo que nos hace falta || *what do you require of me?* ¿qué desean que haga yo? (what do you want me to do), ¿qué exigen de mí? (what do you demand of me) || *what if required to make an omelette?* ¿qué hace falta para hacer una tortilla? || *what qualifications are required?* ¿qué títulos se exigen? || *when required* en caso de necesidad || *your presence is required* se requiere su asistencia || *your presence will not be required* su asistencia no es necesaria.

required [-d] *adj* requerido, da; *a table of the required height* una mesa de la altura requerida || necesario, ria; *the required papers* los documentos necesarios || obligatorio, ria (compulsory) || prescrito, ta (fixed); *within the required time* dentro del plazo prescrito.

requirement [-mənt] *n* requisito *m*; *it fulfils all the requirements* satisface todos los requisitos; *the requirements include two foreign languages* entre los requisitos figura el conocimiento de dos idiomas || necesidad *f* (need); *his requirements are very humble* sus necesidades son muy modestas.

requisite ['rekwizit] *adj* → **required.**
◆ *n* requisito *m*.

requisition [ˌrekwi'ziʃən] *n* petición *f* solicitud *f* (formal request) || MIL requisición *f* requisa *f* || JUR requisitoria *f* || *to call into* o *to put in requisition* requisar.

requisition [ˌrekwi'ziʃən] *vt* requisar; *to requisition vehicles* requisar vehículos || requerir; *the householders were requisitioned to open their houses to refugees* se requirió a los dueños de casas que acogiesen a los refugiados.

requital [ri'kwaitl] *n* desquite *m* (retaliation) || compensación *f*, satisfacción *f*.

requite [ri'kwait] *vt* desquitar; *to requite s.o. for breakage caused* desquitar a alguien por los estropicios producidos || devolver; *to requite good for evil* devolver bien por mal || corresponder a; *to requite s.o.'s love* corresponder al amor de alguien || pagar; *she requites me with ingratitude* me paga con ingratitud || desquitarse de, vengarse de (a wrong).

reread ['riː'riːd] *vt* releer, volver a leer.

rereading [-iŋ] *n* relectura *f*.

rerecording [ˌriːri'kɔːdiŋ] *n* MUS regrabación *f*.

reredos ['riədɔs] *n* ARCH retablo *m*.

reroute [ri'rut] *vt* cambiar el itinerario de.

rerun ['riː'rʌn] *n* CINEM reestreno *m*.

rerun* ['riː'rʌn] *vt* CINEM reestrenar (a film).
— OBSERV Pret *reran*; pp *rerun*.

resale [riː'seil] *n* reventa *f*.

reschedule [riː'ʃedjuːl] *vt* reprogramar, volver a programar.

rescind [ri'sind] *vt* rescindir.

rescindable [-əbl]; **rescissible** [ri'sisəbl] *adj* rescindible.

rescission [ri'siʒən] *n* rescisión *f*.

rescript ['riːskript] *n* rescripto *m* || nueva redacción *f* (rewriting) || nueva versión *f*.

rescue ['reskjuː] *n* rescate *m*, salvamento *m*; *rescue party, operations* equipo, operaciones de salvamento; *rescue boat* bote de salvamento || *to go to the rescue of* ir *or* acudir en auxilio de.

rescue ['reskjuː] *vt* rescatar, salvar (a captive, a town, s.o. in danger) || FIG rescatar, salvar; *to rescue from oblivion* rescatar del olvido.

rescuer [-ə*] *n* rescatador, ra; salvador, ra.

resealable [riː'siːəbl] *adj* hermético, ca; *resealable top* o *lid* cierre hermético.

research [ri'səːtʃ] *n* investigación *f*, investigaciones *f pl*; *scientific research* investigación científica || búsqueda *f*, busca *f* (search) || — *market research* estudio *m or* investigación *f* de mercados || *research and development* investigación y desarrollo || *research establishment* o *centre* instituto *m* de investigación, centro *m* de investigación || *research work* trabajo *m* de investigación || *research worker* investigador, ra || *to do the background research for an article* documentarse para escribir un artículo (a reporter) || *to go into research* dedicarse a la investigación.

research [ri'səːtʃ] *vi* investigar || *to research into* investigar, efectuar investigaciones sobre.

researcher [-ə*] *n* investigador, ra.

reseat ['riː'siːt] *vt* TECH rectificar (valves) || poner nuevo asiento en (a chair) || sentar en otro sitio (a person).

resect [riː'sekt] *vt* MED resecar.

resection [riː'sekʃən] *n* MED resección *f*.

reseda ['residə] *n* BOT reseda *f*.

resedaceae [ˌresi'deisii] *pl n* BOT resedáceas *f*.

reseed ['riː'siːd] *vt* replantar.

resell* ['riː'sel] *vt* revender.
— OBSERV Pret y pp *resold*.

resemblance [ri'zembləns] *n* parecido *m* (between people) || semejanza *f* (between things) || — *there is hardly any resemblance between them* no se parecen casi nada || *to bear a strong resemblance to s.o.* parecerse mucho a alguien.

resemble [ri'zembl] *vt* parecerse a; *John resembles his brother* Juan se parece a su hermano; *John and his brother resemble each other a great deal* Juan y su hermano se parecen mucho.

resent [ri'zent] *vt* resentirse de; *I resent what you said* me resiento de lo que dijiste || tomar a mal (to take badly) || ofenderse por (to be offended) || guardar rencor por (to bear a grudge).

resentful [-ful] *adj* resentido, da; ofendido, da.

resentment [-mənt] *n* resentimiento *m*, rencor *m* || *to hold resentment against* o *for s.o.* guardar rencor a alguien.

reservable [ri'zəːvəbl] *adj* reservable.

reservation [ˌrezə'veiʃən] *n* reserva *f* [AMER reservación *f*] (act of booking) || reserva *f* (seat, room, etc. booked) || reserva *f* (for Indians) || reserva *f*; *without reservation* sin reserva; *mental reservation* reserva mental || JUR reserva *f*, salvedad *f* (in a contract) || REL reserva *f* || — *to receive a piece of news with reservation* acoger una noticia con reservas || *we've made the reservation* hemos reservado las plazas.

reserve [ri'zəːv] *n* reserva *f* (of character, of attitude); *without reserve* sin reserva || MIL reservista *m* || COMM reserva *f* || SP reserva *m* & *f*, suplente *m* & *f* || — *cash reserves* reservas en metálico || *game reserve* coto *m* de caza || *in reserve* en reserva, de reserva; *troops in reserve* tropas de reserva; *provisions in reserve* provisiones en reserva || *reserve supplies* provisiones *f* en *or* de reserva || SP *reserve team* equipo *m* de reserva *or* suplente || *to keep in reserve* guardar en reserva.

reserve [ri'zəːv] *vt* reservar; *to reserve seats* reservar asientos; *to reserve one's strength* reservar sus fuerzas || *to reserve one's judgement on* reservarse el juicio acerca de || *to reserve the right to* reservarse el derecho de.

reserved [-d] *adj* reservado, da || *all rights reserved* reservados todos los derechos, es propiedad.

reservedly [-dli] *adv* con reserva, reservadamente.

reservist [-ist] *n* MIL reservista *m*.

reservoir ['rezəvwɑː*] *n* represa *f*, embalse *m* (artificial lake) || depósito *m*, tanque *m*; *petrol reservoir* depósito de gasolina.

reset* ['riː'set] *vt* poner en su sitio (to put in place) || poner en hora (a watch) || MED encajar, volver a encajar (a bone) || volver a engastar (jewel) || PRINT recomponer || TECH reajustar.
— OBSERV Pret y pp *reset*.

resettle ['riː'setl] *vt* volver a establecer (a person) || colonizar de nuevo, volver a colonizar, repoblar (land).
◆ *vi* volver a establecerse.

resettlement [-mənt] *n* nueva colonización *f*, repoblación *f* (colonization) || restablecimiento *m*.

resew* [ˈriːˈsəu] *vt* recoser.
— OBSERV Pret ***resewed***; pp ***resewed, resewn***.

reshape [ˈriːˈʃeip] *vt* reformar, rehacer || reorganizar.

reship [ˈriːˈʃip] *vt* MAR reembarcar || reenviar, reexpedir (to forward).
◆ *vi* MAR reembarcarse.

reshipment [-mənt] *n* reembarque *m* || reenvío *m*, reexpedición *f* (forwarding).

reshuffle [ˈriːˈʃʌfl] *n* reorganización *f* (of a government); *cabinet reshuffle* reorganización del gabinete de ministros || nueva mezcla *f* (of cards).

reshuffle [ˈriːˈʃʌfl] *vt* reorganizar (a government) || volver a barajar (cards).

reside [riˈzaid] *vi* vivir, residir; *to reside in Paris* residir en París || FIG residir, radicar; *there resides the problem* ahí reside el problema; *legislative power resides in Parliament* el poder legislativo reside en el Parlamento.

residence [ˈrezidəns] *n* residencia *f* (building, action, etc.) || permanencia *f*, residencia *f* (stay) || — *hall of residence* residencia || *in residence* en residencia || *official residence* residencia oficial || *place of residence* domicilio *m* (on forms) || *residence permit* permiso *m* de residencia || *to take up one's residence* instalarse (in a house), establecer su residencia (in a country) || *town and country residences for sale* se venden fincas rústicas y urbanas.

residency [-i] *n* residencia *f*.

resident [ˈrezidənt] *adj/n* residente || permanente (servant) || interno, na (doctor) || — *minister resident* ministro *m* residente || *resident population* población fija || *residents' association* asociación *f* de vecinos || *Spaniards resident in France* los españoles residentes en Francia || *to be resident in a town* residir en una ciudad.

residential [ˌreziˈdenʃəl] *adj* residencial; *residential area* barrio residencial.

residentiary [reziˈdenʃəri] *adj* REL residente; *a canon residentiary* un canónigo residente.

residual [riˈzidjuəl] *adj* residual.
◆ *n* residuo *m*.

residuary [riˈzidjuəri] *adj* residual || JUR *residuary legatee* heredero *m* universal.

residue [ˈrezidjuː] *n* residuo *m* || JUR bienes *m pl* residuales.

residuum [riˈzidjuəm] *n* residuo *m* || JUR bienes *m pl* residuales.
— OBSERV El plural de *residuum* es *residua*.

resign [riˈzain] *vt* dimitir, renunciar; *to resign one's charge* dimitir el cargo || renunciar a (task, claim, etc.); *to resign one's rights* renunciar a sus derechos || ceder (to hand over) || *to resing o.s. to* resignarse a, conformarse con; *to resign o.s. to one's fate* resignarse *or* conformarse con su suerte.
◆ *vi* dimitir, presentar la dimisión; *the prime minister has resigned* el primer ministro ha dimitido || abandonar (in chess).

resignation [ˌrezigˈneiʃən] *n* dimisión *f* (from a post) || resignación *f*, conformidad *f* (conformity with a situation); *he accepted with resignation* aceptó con resignación || renuncia *f* (*of* a) (giving up) || *to submit* o *to tender* o *to send in* o *to hand in one's resignation* presentar la dimisión, dimitir.

resigned [riˈzaind] *adj* resignado, da; *to be resigned to* estar resignado a.

resignedly [riˈzainədli] *adv* con resignación.

resignee [riˈzainiː] *n* resignatario *m*.

resilience [riˈziliəns]; **resiliency** [-i] *n* elasticidad *f*, resiliencia *f* (of a body or material) || resistencia *f* (of human body) || FIG fuerza *f* moral (of temperament).

resilient [riˈziliənt] *adj* elástico, ca || resistente (human body) || de carácter fuerte.

resin [ˈrezin] *n* resina *f*.

resinate [ˈrezineit] *vt* untar con resina.

resinous [ˈrezinəs] *adj* resinoso, sa.

resist [riˈzist] *vt* resistir a; *to resist the enemy* resistir al enemigo || resistir (to endure); *I cannot resist the heat as well as I could when I was young* no puedo resistir el calor como cuando era joven; *asbestos resist the heat very well* el amianto resiste muy bien el calor || — *I can't resist chocolate* me encanta el chocolate || *I couldn't resist asking her* no pude resistir la tentación de preguntárselo || *no man could resist her* no había hombre que se le resistiera || *to resist temptation* resistir (a) la tentación.
◆ *vi* resistir; *Madrid resisted for three years* Madrid resistió durante tres años.

resistance [-əns] *n* resistencia *f*; *passive resistance* resistencia pasiva || TECH resistencia *f* || — *French Resistance* Resistencia francesa || MIL *resistance fighter* resistente *m* || *resistance thermometer* termómetro de resistencia || *to offer* o *to put up resistance* oponer resistencia, resistir || *to take the line of least resistance* seguir la ley del mínimo esfuerzo, optar por lo más fácil (to take the easy way).

resistant [-ənt] *adj/n* resistente.

resistible [-əbl] *adj* resistible.

resistivity [riˌzisˈtiviti] *n* ELECTR resistividad *f*.

resistless [riˈzistlis] *adj* incontenible, irresistible (tears, laugh) || ineluctable (unavoidable) || sin defensa, indefenso, sa (defenceless); *a resistless old man* un anciano sin defensa.

resistor [riˈzistə*] *n* ELECTR reóstato *m*.

resit [ˈriːsit] *n* examen *m* de recuperación.

resit [ˈriːsit] *vt* volver a presentarse a un examen.

resold [ˈriːˈsəuld] *pret/pp* ⟶ **resell.**

resole [ˈriːˈsəuld] *vt* poner medias suelas a (to put stick-on soles on) || remontar (to remake the sole of).

resoluble [riˈzɔljubl] *adj* soluble, resoluble.

resolute [ˈrezəluːt] *adj* resuelto, ta; determinado, da.

resoluteness [-nis] *n* resolución *f*, determinación *f*.

resolution [ˌrezəˈluːʃən] *n* resolución *f* (resoluteness) || resolución *f*, propósito *m*; *good resolutions* buenos propósitos || resolución *f* (proposal); *draft joint resolution* proyecto *m* de resolución común || — *to make a resolution* tomar una resolución || *to oppose a resolution* oponerse a una resolución || *to show resolution* mostrarse resuelto.

resolutive [ˈrezəljutiv]; **resolutory** [ˈrezəljutəri] *adj* JUR resolutorio, ria.

resolvable [riˈzɔlvəbl] *adj* soluble, resoluble.

resolve [riˈzɔlv] *n* resolución *f* || *to make a resolve to* resolverse a, decidir.

resolve [riˈzɔlv] *vt* resolver, solucionar (a problem) || resolver, disipar (a doubt) || resolver, decidir; *to resolve to leave* resolver marcharse || MATH, CHEM, PHYS & MED resolver || FIG *to resolve into* convertir en.
◆ *vi* resolverse || MED resolverse || resolver, decidir, acordar (to decide) || *to resolve upon* o *on* decidirse por (with noun), decidirse a (with verb); *they resolved on going* se decidieron a ir.

resolved [riˈzɔlvd] *adj* resuelto, ta.

resolvent [riˈzɔlvənt] *adj* MED resolutivo, va.
◆ *n* MED resolutivo *m*.

resonance [ˈreznəns] *n* resonancia *f*.

resonant [ˈreznənt] *adj* resonante.

resonate [ˈrezɔneit] *vi* resonar.

resonator [-ə*] *n* resonador *m*.

resorb [riˈsɔːb] *vt* resorber.

resorption [riˈsɔːpʃən] *n* resorción *f*.

resort [riˈzɔːt] *n* estación *f*; *seaside resort* estación balnearia; *winter resort* estación de invierno; *summer resort* estación veraniega || centro *m*; *holiday resort, tourist resort* centro de turismo || recurso *m*; *as a last resort* como último recurso || — *a resort for beggars and thieves* un lugar frecuentado por mendigos y ladrones || *in the last resort* en última instancia || *to have resort to* recurrir a || *without resort to violence* sin recurrir a la violencia.

resort [riˈzɔːt] *vi* recurrir; *to resort to torture* recurrir a la tortura || acudir a, frecuentar; *the people resort to church* la gente acude a la iglesia.

resound [riˈzaund] *vt* ensalzar, cantar; *to resound the glory of a nation* cantar la gloria de una nación.
◆ *vi* resonar; *her shout resounded in the empty street* su grito resonó en la calle desierta; *the streets resounded with joyful shouting* gritos de alegría resonaban por las calles || FIG tener resonancias; *a discovery which was to resound the world over* un descubrimiento que tendría resonancia en el mundo entero.

resounding [-iŋ] *adj* resonante, clamoroso, sa; *a resounding victory* un triunfo resonante || retumbante; *resounding thunder* trueno retumbante || sonoro, ra; *a resounding voice* una voz sonora || tremendo, da; *a resounding blow* un golpe tremendo.

resource [riˈsɔːs] *n* recurso *m*, medio *m* (expedient) || habilidad *f*, recursos *m pl*, inventiva *f*, ingenio *m* (skill, resourcefulness).
◆ *pl* distracciones *f* (amusements) || recursos *m*; *to be without resources* estar sin recursos; *natural resources* recursos naturales; *untapped resources* recursos sin explotar || reserva *f sing* (of energy) || *to be at the end of one's resources* haber agotado todos los recursos.

resourceful [-ful] *adj* ingenioso, sa; despabilado, da; listo, ta.

resourcefulness [-fulnis] *n* recursos *m pl*, inventiva *f*, habilidad *f*, ingenio *m*; *to show great resourcefulness in handling a matter* demostrar gran habilidad en el manejo de un negocio.

respect [risˈpekt] *n* respeto *m*; *lack of respect* falta de respeto; *to have great respect for s.o.* tenerle mucho respeto a alguien || consideración *f* (consideration) || respecto *m*; *with respect to what you were saying* con respecto a lo que estaba diciendo; *in this respect* a este respecto || aspecto *m*, punto *m* de vista; *in every respect* en todos los aspectos, desde todos los puntos de vista; *in no respect* en ningún aspecto || — *I have the greatest respect for your opinion, but* tengo el mayor respeto por su opinión, pero || *in other respect* por otro lado || *in respect of* respecto a *or* de || *in that respect* en cuanto a eso || *out of respect for* en consideración a, por respeto a || *to command respect* infundir respeto || *to hold in respect* tener estima a, respetar || *to pay respect to* tomar en consideración || *to show no respect for s.o.* no tener ningún respeto a alguien || *with all due respect* con el respeto debido || *without respect of persons* sin acepción de personas.
◆ *pl* respetos *m*, recuerdos *m*; *give him my respects* preséntale mis respetos || *to pay one's (last) respects to* presentar sus (últimos) respetos a.

respect [risˈpekt] *vt* respetar || — *as respects...* por lo que respecta a... || *my respected colleague* mi estimado colega || *to make o.s. respected* hacerse respetar.

respectability [risˌpektəˈbiliti] *n* respetabilidad *f.*

respectable [risˈpektəbl] *adj* respetable; *a respectable person, place* una persona, un sitio respetable; *a respectable sum of money* una suma respetable de dinero || decente, respetable (decent) || decente; *a respectable performance* una representación decente || *to keep at a respectable distance* mantener a una distancia respetable *or* prudencial.

respectful [risˈpektful] *adj* respetuoso, sa.

respectfully [-i] *adv* respetuosamente || *yours respectfully* le saluda respetuosamente.

respectfulness [-nis] *n* respetuosidad *f.*

respecting [risˈpektiŋ] *prep* respecto a, con respecto a, en cuanto a.

respective [risˈpektiv] *adj* respectivo, va; *they went off with their respective girlfriends* se fueron con sus novias respectivas.

respectively [-li] *adv* respectivamente.

respell* [ˈriːˈspel] *vt* volver a deletrear (to spell again) || transcribir fonéticamente (in phonetics).

— OBSERV El pretérito y el participio pasivo de *to respell* son irregulares: ***respelt***. Además de éstos, en Estados Unidos se usa también la forma ***respelled***.

respelt [-t] *pret/pp* → **respell.**

respiration [ˌrespəˈreiʃən] *n* respiración *f.*

respirator [ˈrespəreitə*] *n* MED respirador *m* || careta *f*, mascarilla *f* (for filtering air) || careta *f* antigás (gas mask).

respiratory [risˈpaiərətəri] *adj* respiratorio, ria.

respire [risˈpaiə*] *vt/vi* respirar.

respite [ˈrespait] *n* respiro *m*, tregua *f*; *to work without respite* trabajar sin respiro; *the pain does not give him a moment's respite* el dolor no le deja ni un momento de respiro || prórroga *f*, plazo *m* (postponement of an obligation) || suspensión *f* (of a sentence).

respite [ˈrespait] *vt* prorrogar, aplazar || suspender (a sentence).

resplendence [risˈplendəns]; **resplendency** [-i] *n* resplandor *m.*

resplendent [risˈplendənt] *adj* resplandeciente || *to be resplendent* resplandecer, ser resplandeciente.

respond [risˈpɔnd] *n* ARCH ménsula *f* || REL responsorio *m.*

respond [risˈpɔnd] *vi* contestar, responder (to reply) || responder; *the patient responded to treatment* el enfermo respondió al tratamiento || reaccionar (to react) || ser sensible a (to be sensitive to) || REL contestar (to make a response).

respondent [-ənt] *n* JUR demandado, da (a defendant).

response [risˈpɔns] *n* contestación *f*, respuesta *f* (reply); *he made no response* no dio contestación || acogida *f*; *the response to a charity campaign* la acogida de una campaña de caridad || reacción *f*; *his response to the treatment is satisfactory* su reacción al tratamiento es satisfactoria; *his question met with no response* su pregunta no suscitó ninguna reacción || REL contestación *f* (words said in answer to the priest) | responsorio *m* (responsory) || — *in response to* en *or* como respuesta a || INFORM *response time* tiempo *m* de respuesta || *the response to the appeal has been poor* la llamada ha suscitado poco interés, la llamada no ha sido acogida con mucho entusiasmo.

responsibility [risˌpɔnsəˈbiliti] *n* responsabilidad *f*; *to take the responsibility of* asumir la responsabilidad de; *on one's own responsibility* bajo su propia responsabilidad || seriedad *f*, formalidad *f* (responsible behaviour) || — *that's not my responsibility* eso no es cosa mía *or* asunto mío || *the decision is your responsibility* le incumbe a Ud. decidir, le corresponde a Ud. decidir.

responsible [risˈpɔnsəbl] *adj* responsable; *to be responsible for* ser responsable de; *a responsible person* una persona responsable; *those responsible* los responsables; *to be responsible to s.o.* ser responsable ante alguien || de responsabilidad; *a responsible position* un cargo de responsabilidad.

responsibly [-i] *adv* con seriedad, con formalidad.

responsive [risˈpɔnsiv] *adj* sensible; *responsive to sympathy* sensible a la simpatía; *a responsive engine* un motor sensible || *they weren't very responsive* no demostraron mucho interés.

responsiveness [-nis] *n* sensibilidad *f* (sensitivity) || interés *m* (interest).

responsory [risˈpɔnsəri] *n* REL responsorio *m.*

respray [ˈriːsprei] *n* repaso *m* de pintura con espray (car).

respray [riːˈsprei] *vt* repasar la pintura con espray (car).

rest [rest] *n* descanso *m*; *a five minute rest* un descanso de cinco minutos; *day of rest* día de descanso; *eternal rest* descanso eterno || reposo *m*, descanso *m*; *to enjoy a well-earned rest* gozar de un bien merecido descanso; *half an hour's rest after dinner* media hora de reposo después de la cena || MUS pausa *f*, silencio *m* (period of silence, symbol thereof) || cesura *f* (in poetry) || pausa *f* (in speech) || taquera *f* (for billiard cue) || apoyo *m*; *the tree made a rest for his back* el árbol le sirvió de apoyo || tranquilidad *f*, sosiego *m*; *I shall have no rest until I find the solution* no tendré un momento de tranquilidad hasta que encuentre la solución || resto *m*; *the rest of the day* el resto del día || resto *m*, lo demás; *take some and leave the rest* toma un poco y deja el resto; *I'll tell you the rest* le contaré lo demás || los demás, las demás, los otros, las otras; *the rest of them didn't mind* a los otros les daba igual; *the rest of the women* las otras *or* las demás mujeres; *we went and the rest stayed* nosotros fuimos y los demás se quedaron || ristre *m* (of lance) || COMM reserva *f* || TECH base *f* (base) | soporte *m* (support) | horquilla *f* (of telephone) || — *after a good night's rest* después de haber pasado una buena noche || *all he needs is a good night's rest* lo que le hace falta es dormir bien una noche || *arm rest* brazo *m* (of chair) || *as for the rest* por lo demás || *at rest* parado, da; *the train was at rest* el tren estaba parado; quieto, ta (motionless), tranquilo, la (quiet), en reposo; *a body at rest* un cuerpo en reposo; en paz; *he is at rest with his family* descansa en paz con su familia || *back rest* respaldo *m* || MED *complete rest* reposo absoluto || *have a good night's rest!* ¡que descanse! || *rest cure* cura *f* de reposo || *to come to rest* pararse (to stop), venir a parar *or* a pararse (car, bird, arrow, etc.) || *to give a rest* dejar descansar || *to have a rest* descansar || *to lay to rest* enterrar || *to lay* o *put an idea to rest* enterrar una idea || *to put* o *to set s.o.'s mind at rest* tranquilizar a alguien || *to take a rest* descansar un rato || *to try and get a little rest* intentar descansar *or* dormir un poco.

rest [rest] *vi* pararse (to stop); *the ball rested at the edge of the hole* la pelota se paró al borde del agujero || descansar; *to rest after a day's work* descansar después de un día de trabajo; *to rest in peace* descansar en paz || descansar, reposar; *you have to rest after meals* tienes que reposar después de las comidas || descansar; *the vase rests on a marble column* el florero descansa sobre una columna de mármol || depender de; *the decision rests on his testimony* la decisión depende de su testimonio; *it rests with France* depende de Francia || quedar; *there the matter rests* allí queda el asunto || radicar, estribar, basarse; *his fame rests in his books* su fama radica en sus libros; *in this rests the problem* en esto radica el problema || pesar sobre; *a great responsibility rests on his shoulders* una gran responsabilidad pesa sobre él || quedarse tranquilo, descansar; *I can't rest till I find the answer* no me quedaré tranquilo *or* no descansaré mientras no encuentre la solución || AGR descansar; *to leave ground to rest* dejar descansar la tierra || JUR terminar su alegato || — FIG *his eyes rested on the object* fijó la mirada en el objeto, sus ojos se posaron en el objeto | *let it rest* déjalo estar | *rest assured that* tenga la seguridad de que | *to rest easy* dormir tranquilo | *to rest on one's oars* o *on one's laurels* dormirse en los laureles.

◆ *vt* apoyar; *to rest a ladder against a wall* apoyar una escalera contra una pared || apoyar, descansar; *to rest one's head on s.o.'s shoulder* descansar la cabeza en el hombro de alguien || descansar; *to rest one's feet* descansar los pies; *these sunglasses rest my eyes* estas gafas de sol me descansan la vista || dejar descansar; *to rest a player* dejar descansar a un jugador || basar; *to rest one's case on the insanity of the accused* basar la defensa en la enajenación mental del acusado || poner (hopes) || — *God rest his soul* que Dios le tenga en su gloria || JUR *to rest one's case* terminar su alegato || *to rest one's eyes on* fijar la mirada en.

restart [ˈriːˈstaːt] *vt* volver a poner en marcha (motor, etc.) || volver a empezar (to begin again).

◆ *vi* volver a arrancar (motor) || volver a empezar.

restate [ˈriːˈsteit] *vt* volver a exponer (case, theory) || volver a plantear (problem) || repetir (to repeat).

restatement [-mənt] *n* nueva exposición *f* || nuevo planteamiento *m* (of problem) || repetición *f.*

restaurant [ˈrestərɔ̃ːŋ] *n* restaurante *m*, restaurant *m*, restorán *m* || *restaurant car* coche *m* restaurante.

restaurateur [ˌrestɔrəˈtəː*] *n* dueño *m* de un restaurante.

restful [ˈrestful] *adj* descansado, da; tranquilo, la; reposado, da; *restful holidays* vacaciones descansadas.

restharrow [restˌhærəu] *n* BOT gatuña *f.*

rest home [ˈresthəum] *n* casa *f* de reposo (for rest cures) || asilo *m* de ancianos (old people's home).

resting-place [ˈrestiŋpleis] *n* lugar *m* de descanso || última morada *f* (of the dead).

restitute [ˈrestiˌtjuːt] *vt* restituir.

restitution [ˌrestiˈtjuːʃən] *n* restitución *f* || indemnización *f.*

restive [ˈrestiv] *adj* intranquilo, la; inquieto, ta (uneasy) || repropio, pia (horse).

restiveness [-nis] *n* inquietud *f*, intranquilidad *f* (uneasiness) || impaciencia *f* (impatience) || agitación *f* (agitation).

restless [ˈrestlis] *adj* agitado, da; inquieto, ta; *a restless sea* un mar agitado || intranquilo, la; agitado, da; inquieto, ta; desasosegado, da; *a restless person* una persona intranquila; *a restless night* una noche agitada || descontento, ta (discontented) || — *the guests are getting restless* los invitados se están impacientando || *the students are restless* los estudiantes se están agitando || *to be restless to do sth.* impacientarse por hacer algo || *to be the restless kind* no poder estarse quieto.

restlessly [-li] *adv* con impaciencia, nerviosamente (impatiently) || con inquietud, nerviosamente (worriedly) || *to toss and turn restlessly in one's bed* agitarse *or* dar vueltas en la cama.

restlessness [-nis] *n* impaciencia *f* (impatience) || inquietud *f*, desasosiego *m* (worry) || agitación *f* (agitation) || descontento *m* (discontent) || insomnio *m* (sleeplessness).

restock ['riː'stɔk] *vt* repoblar (with animals, with trees) || reabastecer (shop with provisions).

◆ *vi* reponer las existencias.

restorable [ris'tɔːrəbl] *adj* rehabilitable.

restoration [ˌrestə'reiʃən] *n* restauración *f* (reparation, reestablishment); *restoration of a painting, of the monarchy* restauración de un cuadro, de la monarquía || restitución *f*, devolución *f* (giving back) || reintegración *f*, restitución *f* (returning to original rank, role) || restablecimiento *m*; *restoration of peace* restablecimiento de la paz || HIST *the Restoration* la Restauración.

restorative [ris'tɔrətiv] *adj* resconstituyente, fortificante.

◆ *n* resconstituyente *m*, fortificante *m*.

restore [ris'tɔː*] *vt* restituir, devolver; *to restore sth. to its owner* restituir algo a su dueño || restaurar (painting, building, monarch) || reconstituir (a text) || reintegrar, restablecer (to bring back to a previous rank or position) || devolver; *to restore s.o. to health* devolver la salud a alguien; *to restore s.o. to liberty* devolverle a alguien la libertad || restablecer; *to restore order* restablecer el orden; *to restore old customs* restablecer viejas costumbres || volver a poner (to put back into place).

restorer [-rə*] *n* restaurador, ra (one who restores) || tónico *m*; *hair restorer* tónico capilar || reconstituyente *m* (reconstituent).

restrain [ris'trein] *vt* impedir (to prevent) || limitar, frenar, restringir (to limit) || contener, reprimir, refrenar (to repress); *he restrained his anger* reprimió su cólera || recluir, encerrar (to confine).

restrained [-d] *adj* comedido, da; sereno, na (tone, voice, manner) || contenido, da (emotion).

restrainedly [-dli] *adv* comedidamente.

restraint [ris'treint] *n* restricción *f*; *restraint of trade* restricción del comercio || limitación *f* (limitation) || traba *f* (hindrance) || represión *f* (of one's feelings) || moderación *f*, reserva *f*, comedimiento *m*; *lack of restraint* falta de moderación || dominio *m* de sí mismo (self-control) || internamiento *m*, reclusión *f* (confinement) || — *to put under restraint* internar, recluir, encerrar || *without restraint* libremente, sin restricción.

restrict [ris'trikt] *vt* restringir, limitar (to limit) || — *to restrict o.s. the main points* limitarse a los puntos principales || *use of the library is restricted to teachers* sólo los profesores pueden utilizar la biblioteca, la biblioteca está reservada a los profesores.

restricted [-id] *adj* restringido, da; limitado, da (limited) || estrecho, cha (mentality, outlook) || *restricted area* zona *f* de velocidad limitada (speed limit), zona prohibida [a ciertas personas] (security zone).

restriction [ris'trikʃən] *n* restricción *f*, limitación *f*.

restrictive [ris'triktiv] *adj* restrictivo, va || ECON *restrictive practices* prácticas restrictivas.

rest room ['restruːm] *n* aseos *m pl*, lavabos *m pl*, tocador *m*.

restructure [riː'strʌktʃə*] *vt* reestructurar.

result [ri'zʌlt] *n* resultado *m*; *the result of the experiment* el resultado del experimento; *the election results* los resultados de las elecciones; *the exam results* los resultados de los exámenes || resultado *m*, consecuencia *f*; *his action had grave results* su acción tuvo consecuencias graves || SP & MATH resultado *m* || — *as a result of* a *or* como consecuencia de, a causa de || *with the result that* con el resultado de que.

result [ri'zʌlt] *vi* resultar; *it resulted badly* resultó mal.

◆ *phr v* ***to result from*** derivarse de; *the consequences resulting from an act* las consecuencias que se derivan de un acto; resultar de; *the misery that results from warfare* la miseria que resulta de la guerra; *it results from this that* de ello resulta que | ser causado *or* producido por (to be produced by); *his death resulted from a fall* su muerte fue provocada por una caída || ***to result in*** tener por *or* como resultado; *the election resulted in an opposition victory* las elecciones tuvieron por resultado la victoria de la oposición | tener como resultado, conducir a; *the modernization resulted in increased productivity* la modernización condujo a un aumento de la productividad | conducir *or* llevar a; *the negotiations resulted in an agreement* las negociaciones condujeron a un acuerdo || dar resultado; *it resulted in nothing* no dio ningún resultado | ser; *the expedition resulted in a failure* la expedición fue un fracaso | *the illness resulted in his death* murió a consecuencia de la enfermedad.

resultant [-ənt] *adj* resultante.

◆ *n* resultante *f*.

resume [ri'zjuːm] *vt* volver a tomar (to take again) || reasumir (one's duties); *to resume command* reasumir el mando || recuperar (a territory, etc.) || reanudar (a journey, a job, etc.); *to resume talks* reanudar las conversaciones || continuar, seguir; *to resume one's speech* seguir su discurso || resumir (to sum up); *to resume the main points of a debate* resumir los puntos principales de un debate || *to resume one's seat* volver a sentarse.

◆ *vi* reanudar sus trabajos || proseguir (to take up an interrupted discourse).

résumé ['rezjuːmei] *n* resumen *m* (summary) || US curriculum vitae *m*.

resumption [ri'zʌmpʃən] *n* reanudación *f* (of talks, of work, etc.) || reasunción *f* (of office) || continuación *f* || *upon the resumption of talks* al reanudarse las conversaciones.

resurface ['riː'səːfis] *vt* rehacer el firme de (road) || revestir (floors, walls, etc.).

◆ *vi* volver a salir a la superficie (submarine).

resurgence [ri'səːdʒəns] *n* resurgimiento *m*, resurrección *f*.

resurgent [ri'ːsəːdʒənt] *adj* que resurge || renaciente.

resurrect [ˌrezə'rekt] *vt* resucitar (to bring back to life) || FIG resucitar (old stories, customs, etc.).

◆ *vi* resucitar.

resurrection [ˌrezə'rekʃən] *n* resurrección *f* || REL *the Resurrection* la Resurrección.

resuscitate [ri'sʌsiteit] *vt/vi* resucitar.

resuscitation [riˌsʌsi'teiʃən] *n* MED resucitación *f*.

ret [ret] *vt* enriar (flax).

retable [ri'teibl] *n* REL retablo *m*.

retail ['riːteil] *n* venta *f* al por menor, venta *f* al detall.

◆ *adj/adv* al por menor, al detall || *retail dealer* detallista *m* & *f*, minorista *m* & *f*, comerciante *m* & *f* al por menor || *retail price* precio *m* de venta al público || *retail price index* índice *m* de precios al consumo.

retail [riː'teil] *vt* vender al por menor, vender al detall (to sell goods) || repetir (gossip).

◆ *vi* venderse al por menor, venderse al detall; *these goods retail at five pounds each* estos artículos se venden al por menor a cinco libras la unidad.

retailer [-ə*] *n* detallista *m* & *f*, minorista *m* & *f*, comerciante *m* & *f* al por menor.

retain [ri'tein] *vt* conservar; *he retained his British sense of humour to the end* conservó el sentido del humor británico hasta el final || retener; *a dyke to retain water* un dique para retener el agua || recordar, acordarse de, retener; *I have great difficulty in retaining names* tengo mucha dificultad en recordar los nombres || contratar; *to retain s.o.'s services* contratar los servicios de alguien || quedarse con (to keep).

retainer [-ə*] *n* dispositivo *m* de retención (device for retaining) || criado, da (servant) || partidario, ria (follower) || JUR anticipo *m* sobre los honorarios (of a barrister) || US contrato *m* con un abogado.

retaining fee [-iŋfiː] *n* anticipo *m*.

retaining wall [-iŋwɔːl] *n* muro *m* de contención.

retake ['riːteik] *n* CINEM repetición *f* de la toma, nueva toma *f* [de una escena].

retake* ['riː'teik] *vt* volver a tomar, recuperar; *the army retook the fortress* el ejército volvió a tomar la fortaleza || capturar (de nuevo), (volver a) capturar; *the fugitive was retaken* capturaron al fugitivo || CINEM volver a rodar *or* a tomar (a scene in a film).

— OBSERV Pret ***retook***; pp ***retaken***.

retaken [-ən] *pp* ⟶ **retake.**

retaliate [ri'tælieit] *vt* devolver (blow, insult, etc.).

◆ *vi* vengarse, tomar represalias; *he is a person who won't retaliate* es el tipo de persona que no toma represalias || desquitarse, vengarse; *he retaliated with a blow* se desquitó con un golpe.

retaliation [riˌtæli'eiʃən] *n* venganza *f*, desquite *m* (revenge) || represalias *f pl* (retaliatory measures) || *in retaliation* para vengarse, para desquitarse, como represalias.

retaliatory [ri'tæliətəri] *adj* vengativo, va || — *a retaliatory bombardment* un bombardeo de represalias || *to take retaliatory measures* tomar *or* ejercer represalias.

retard [ri'tɑːd] *vt* retrasar, retardar; *the storm retarded his arrival by an hour* la tormenta retrasó su llegada en una hora.

◆ *vi* retrasar, atrasar (sth.) || tardar (s.o.).

retardation [ˌriːtɑ'deiʃən] *n* retraso *m*, atraso *m* || MED atraso *m* mental.

retarded [ri'tɑːdid] *adj* atrasado, da || *mentally retarded person* atrasado *m* mental.

retch [retʃ] *n* náusea *f*, basca *f*.

retch [retʃ] *vi* tener náuseas.

retell* ['riː'tel] *vt* volver a contar.

— OBSERV Pret y pp ***retold***.

retention [ri'tenʃən] *n* retención *f* || retentiva *f*, memoria *f* (memory).

retentive [ri'tentiv] *adj* retentivo, va || bueno, na (memory) || *to be retentive of sth.* recordar algo, acordarse de algo.

retentiveness [-nis] *n* retentiva *f*.

retesting ['riː'testiŋ] *n* reensayo *m* (machine).

rethink* ['riː'θiŋk] *vt* volver a pensar.

— OBSERV Pret y pp ***rethought***.

reticence ['retisəns] *n* reserva *f*.

reticent ['retisent] *adj* reservado, da || *to be reticent about sth.* no querer revelar nada sobre algo.

reticle ['retikl] *n* retícula *f*, retículo *m*.

reticular [re'tikjulə*] *adj* reticular.

reticulate [ri'tikjuleit] *vt* dar forma de red a (to give sth. the form of a net).
◆ *vi* esta dividido en forma de red.

reticulated [-id] *adj* reticulado, da.

reticule ['retikju:l] *n* retícula *f*, retículo *m* (reticle) || ridículo *m* (small handbag).

reticulum [re'tikjuləm] *n* ZOOL redecilla *f*, retículo *m* (in ruminants) || BIOL retículo *m* (network structure in cells).
— OBSERV El plural de *reticulum* es *reticula*.

retile ['ri:'tail] *vt* retejar.

retin ['ri:'tin] *vt* restañar.

retina ['retinə] *n* ANAT retina *f*.
— OBSERV El plural de la palabra inglesa es *retinas* o *retinae*.

retinitis [,reti'naitis] *n* MED retinitis *f*.

retinning [ri:tiniŋ] *n* restañadura *f*, restañamiento *m*.

retinue ['retinju:] *n* séquito *m*, comitiva *f*.

retire [ri'taiə*] *vi* jubilarse (from a job, from an occupation) || retirarse (soldier, trader) || retirarse (to draw back, to seek privacy, etc.) || abandonar, retirarse (from a race) || dimitir (to resign) || recogerse (to go to bed) || MIL replegarse, retirarse (troops) || *to retire into o.s.* recogerse en sí mismo.
◆ *vt* COMM retirar (to withdraw) || jubilar (a civilian) || retirar (a soldier) || retirer (bank notes from circulation) || *to apply to be retired on a pension* pedir la jubilación (civilian), pedir el retiro (soldier).

retired [-d] *adj* retirado, da (soldier, trader); *retired officer* oficial retirado || jubilado, da (civilian); *retired civil servant* funcionario jubilado || retirado, da (life) || retirado, da; apartado, da; *a retired corner of the garden* un apartado rincón del jardín || — *a retired person* un jubilado (civilian), un retirado (soldier, trader) || *retired list* escalafón *f* de retirados || *retired pay* retiro *m* (of soldier), jubilación *f* (of civilian).

retirement [-mənt] *n* retiro *m* (of soldiers, of traders); *to reach retirement age* llegar a la edad del retiro || jubilación *f* (from a job) || MIL retirada *f*, repliegue *m* (of troops) || abandono *m* (from a race) || retirada *f* (of an actor) || FIG recogimiento *m* (of a person) || *to live in retirement* vivir apartado del mundo.

retiring [-riŋ] *n* retraído, da; tímido, da; reservado, da (reserved) || saliente; *the retiring president* el presidente saliente || de jubilación, de retiro (pension).

retold ['ri:'təuld] *pret/pp* → **retell.**

retook ['ri:'tuk] *pret* → **retake.**

retort [ri'tɔ:t] *n* CHEM retorta *f* || réplica *f* (reply).

retort [ri'tɔ:t] *vt* devolver (an insult) || replicar; *why should I?, he retorted* ¿por qué yo?, replicó || CHEM destilar en retortas.

retortion [ri'tɔ:ʃən] *n* retorcimiento *m*, retorcedura *f* (bending back) || retorsión *f*, represalia *f* (retaliation).

retouch ['ri:'tʌtʃ] *n* retoque *m* (a retouching) || fotografía *f* retocada (retouched photo).

retouch ['ri:'tʌtʃ] *vt* retocar.

retoucher [-ə*] *n* PHOT retocador, ra.

retrace [ri'treis] *vt* volver a trazar, repasar (to go over again) || reconstruir, reconstituir; *to retrace s.o.'s past* reconstituir el pasado de alguien || remontarse a; *to retrace one's childhood* remontarse a la niñez || *to retrace one's steps* desandar lo andado, volver sobre sus pasos.

retract [ri'trækt] *vt* retractar, retirar (a promise, a statement) || ZOOL meter, encoger (the head, body or limbs) | retraer (the claws) || TECH replegar (the undercarriage, the wheels, etc.).
◆ *vi* retraerse, encogerse (to draw back) || retractarse, desdecirse (to recant) || ZOOL meterse, encogerse (head, body or limbs) | retraerse (claws) || TECH replegarse, meterse (wheels, etc.).

retractable [-əbl] *adj* retractable || replegable, retráctil (the undercarriage, the wheels).

retractation [,ri:træk'teiʃən] *n* retractación *f*.

retractile [ri'træktail] *adj* retráctil.

retracting [ri'træktiŋ] *adj* retráctil.

retraction [ri'trækʃən] *n* retracción *f* (of claws, of wheels, etc.) || retractación *f* (of claim, of promise, etc.).

retractive [ri'træktiv] *adj* retractor, ra.

retractor [ri'træktə*] *n* músculo *m* retractor, retractor *m* || MED retractor *m* (instrument).

retrain ['ri:'trein] *vt* reconvertir (workers).

retraining [-iŋ] *n* reconversión *f* (for another job) || curso *m* de perfeccionamiento (refresher course).

retral ['ri:trəl] *adj* posterior.

retransmission [,ri'trɑ:ns'miʃən] *n* RAD retransmisión *f*.

retread ['ri:'tred] *n* neumático *m* recauchutado.

re-tread* ['ri:'tred] *vt* pisar de nuevo || seguir de nuevo (a path) || volver a (a place).
— OBSERV Pret ***re-trod***; pp ***re-trodden, re-trod***.

retread ['ri:tred] *vt* recauchutar (a tyre).
— OBSERV Este verbo, a diferencia de su homónimo anterior, es regular.

retreat [ri'tri:t] *n* MIL retirada *f* (from battle, from territory, etc.) | retreta *f* (signal); *to sound the retreat* tocar retreta || retirada *f*, retiro *m* (from life) || refugio *m*; *the world of books is his retreat* el mundo de los libros es su refugio; *a country retreat* un refugio en el campo || guarida *f* (of thieves) || retroceso *m*, retirada *f* (of the sea water) || REL retiro; *spiritual retreat* retiro espiritual || — FIG & FAM *to beat a hasty retreat* salir pitando, escaquearse deprisa (from a task, situation, etc.) || MIL *to beat a retreat* batirse en retirada | *to cut off the retreat* cortar la retirada.

retreat [ri'tri:t] *vi* retirarse || MIL retirarse, batirse en retirada || retirarse, aislarse (from life, for spiritual reasons) || retroceder (to draw back) || refugiarse; *to retreat into the mountains* refugiarse en las montañas.
◆ *vt* mover hacia atrás (in chess).

retrench [ri'trentʃ] *vt* reducir, disminuir (to reduce) || restringir (to restrict) || suprimir, quitar (a passage) || cortar (a text) || MIL atrincherar.
◆ *vi* ahorrar.

retrenchment [-mənt] *n* reducción *f*, disminución *f* || supresión *f* || ahorro *m* (saving) || MIL trinchera *f* (trench) | atrincheramiento *m* (entrenchment).

retrial ['ri:'traiəl] *n* nuevo juicio *m* || revisión *f* (of a case).

retribution [,retri'bju:ʃən] *n* pena *f* merecida, castigo *m* justo (merited punishment) || recompensa *f* (reward) || *the Day of Retribution* el día del Juicio Final.

retributive [ri'tribjutiv] *adj* justiciero, ra; *retributive punishment* castigo justiciero || retributivo, va (of reward).

retrievable [ri'tri:vəbl] *adj* recuperable || FIG reparable (error).

retrieval [ri'tri:vəl] *n* recuperación *f* (of sth. lost) || rehabilitación *f* (of reputation, etc.) || reparación *f* (of an error) || restablecimiento *m* (of one's position) || resarcimiento *m* (of damages) || cobranza *f* (in hunting) || *beyond* o *past retrieval* irreparable.

retrieve [ri'tri:v] *n* SP devolución *f* || reparación *f* (of an error) || *beyond* o *past retrieve* irreparable.

retrieve [ri'tri:v] *vt* cobrar (to bring back fallen game) || recuperar, recobrar (sth. lost) || resarcirse de (damages) || rehabilitar (reputation, etc.) || salvar (from ruin, etc.) || enmendar, subsanar, reparar (a mistake) || recoger (to pick up) || SP devolver (to return a difficult shot).
◆ *vi* cobrar (hunting dogs).

retriever [-ə*] *n* perro *m* cobrador.

retroact [,retrəu'ækt] *vi* tener efecto retroactivo (a law, etc.) || reaccionar (to react).

retroaction [,retrəu'ækʃən] *n* retroactividad *f* (of a law, etc.) || reacción *f*.

retroactive [,retrəu'æktiv] *adj* retroactivo, va || *retroactive law* ley con efecto retroactivo.

retroactivity [,retrəuæk'tiviti] *n* retroactividad *f*.

retrocede [,retrəu'si:d] *vi* retroceder (to go backwards).
◆ *vt* devolver (to give back).

retrocession [,retrəu'seʃən] *n* retroceso *m* (backwards movement) || JUR retrocesión *f*.

retrochoir ['retrə,kwaiə*] *n* REL trascoro *m*.

re-trod ['ri:'trɔd] *pret/pp* → **re-tread.**

re-trodden [-ən] *pp* → **re-tread.**

retroflex ['retrəufleks] *adj* vuelto hacia atrás.

retroflexion [,retrəu'flekʃən] *n* MED retroflexión *f*, retroversión *f*.

retrogradation [,retrəugrei'deiʃən] *n* retroceso *m*, regresión *f* || ASTR retrogradación *f*.

retrograde ['retrəugreid] *adj* retrógrado, da; *retrograde movement* movimiento retrógrado || inverso, sa (order) || FIG retrógrado, da.

retrograde ['retrəugreid] *vi* retroceder (to move backwards) || ASTR retrogradar || FIG degenerar.

retrogress [,retrəu'gres] *vi* retroceder || degenerar.

retrogression [,retrəu'greʃən] *n* retroceso *m*, regresión *f* || ASTR retrogradación *f* || FIG degeneración *f*.

retrogressive [,retrəu'gresiv] *adj* retrógrado, da.

retrorocket ['retrəu,rɔkit] *n* retrocohete *m*.

retrorse [ri'trɔ:s] *adj* vuelto hacia atrás.

retrospect ['retrəuspekt] *n* retrospección *f*, examen *m* retrospectivo || *in retrospect* retrospectivamente.

retrospection [,retrəu'spekʃən] *n* retrospección *f*, examen *m* retrospectivo.

retrospective [,retrəu'spektiv] *adj* retrospectivo, va || JUR con efecto retroactivo.

retroussé [rə'tru:sei] *adj* respingona (nose).

retroversion [,retrəu'və:ʃən] *n* MED retroversión *f*.

retry [ri'trai] *vt* volver a juzgar *or* procesar (s.o.) || revisar, volver a examinar (a case).

return [ri'tə:n] *n* vuelta *f*, regreso *m*, retorno *m* (coming back); *on his return* a su vuelta || retorno *m*, vuelta *f*; *the return of the spring* la vuelta de la primavera || reexpedición *f* (of a letter) || cambio *m*; *to give a pen in return for a pencil* dar una pluma a cambio de un lápiz || recompensa *f* (reward) || devolución *f*, restitución *f* (the giving back); *the return of a book to its owner* la devolución de un libro a su dueño || ganancias *f pl* (profit); *to bring a return* proporcionar ganancias || rédito *m*, interés *m* (interest); *return on capital* interés del capital || producto *m*, rendimiento *m* (productivity); *the return for the year* el rendimiento del año || cambio *m*, vuelta *f* (change in a shop) || reembolso *m*, devolución *f* (of a sum); *return of a capital* reembolso de un capital || restablecimiento *m*; *return to public order* restablecimiento del orden público || reelección *f*, elección *f*; *the return of the same members is likely* la reelección de los mismos miembros es probable || estadística *f* (statistic); *the official returns* las estadísticas oficiales || estado *m*; *return of expenses* estado de gastos || informe *m* oficial (report) || censo *m* (of the population) || lista *f*; *return of killed and wounded* lista de muertos y heridos || declaración *f* (of taxes); *to send in one's return of income* enviar la declaración de impuestos || repercusión *f* (of a sound) || retroceso *m* (in typewriter) || réplica *f* (in cards) || respuesta *f* (in fencing) || curva *f* (bend) || ARCH ala *f* || SP devolución *f* (of ball) | resto *m* (in tennis) || TECH rendimiento *m* (of a machine) || — *a return ticket* un billete de ida y vuelta (in Great Britain), un billete de vuelta (in United States) || *as a return for your kindness* para corresponder a su amabilidad || *by return of post, by return mail* a vuelta de correo || *in return* en recompensa (as a reward), a cambio (in exchange) || *on my return home* a mi vuelta a casa || *on sale or return* en depósito (goods) || *quick return* venta rápida || *return address* remite *m*, remitente *m* || *return game* o *match* partido *m* de vuelta || INFORM *return key* tecla *f* de retorno de carro || *return of an illness* recaída *f* || *return spring* muelle *m* antagonista *or* de retorno || *return stroke* carrera *f* de vuelta (of a piston) || *return to school* reapertura *f* del año escolar || *return trip* viaje de ida y vuelta (round trip), viaje de regreso (journey back) || *to bring in a good return* dar mucho beneficio.

◆ *pl* remanente *m sing* de periódicos no vendidos (of unsold newspapers) || resultados *m* (of ballot); *have the election returns come in yet?* ¿han llegado ya los resultados de las elecciones? || COMM ingresos *m*; *gross returns* ingresos brutos || respuestas *f*; *there were enormous returns to our advertisement* ha habido muchas respuestas a nuestro anuncio || *many happy returns (of the day)!* ¡feliz cumpleaños!

return [ri'tə:n] *vt* devolver (to bring back, to give back); *to return a book to its owner* devolver un libro a su dueño; *to return a bill to drawer* devolver una letra de cambio al girador; *to return blow for blow* devolver golpe por golpe; *to return a call* devolver una visita; *to return good for evil* devolver bien por mal || repercutir, devolver; *to return a sound* repercutir un sonido || reflejar (a light) || reembolsar (to refund) || restituir (lost or stolen goods, etc.) || poner de nuevo, volver a colocar (to put back); *to return a book to its place* volver a colocar un libro en su sitio || contestar con, responder con (to reply); *to return a blasphemy* contestar con una blasfemia || corresponder (to s.o.'s love, kindness, etc.); *to return s.o.'s love* corresponder al amor de alguien || COMM declarar (income); *to return one's income to the tax authorities* declarar sus ingresos a Hacienda | evaluar, estimar, valorar (to estimate) | dar, proporcionar, rendir; *investment that returns very good interest* inversión que da muy buenos intereses || elegir, reelegir (to elect) || replicar con, devolver (in cards) || responder (in fencing) || SP devolver (the ball) | restar (tennis) || JUR dar, pronunciar, dictar (a verdict, a sentence, etc.) | declarar (guilty); *the prisoner was returned guilty* declararon culpable al acusado || TECH rendir, producir (productivity) || presentar (to submit statistics, documents, etc.) || dar (las gracias) (thanks) || dar a conocer (results) || hacer retroceder (typewriter carriage) || — *return to sender* devuélvase al remitente (letter) || *to return like for like* pagar en *or* con la misma moneda.

◆ *vi* volver, regresar, retornar (to come back, to go back); *to return home* volver a casa; *to return to poverty* retornar a la pobreza; *my thoughts return to my chilhood* mis pensamientos vuelven a mi niñez; *they are about to return* están a punto de regresar || volver (to a former owner or state) || reanudar; *to return to a task* reanudar un trabajo || volver (*to* a) (a subject) || reaparecer (to reappear) || *to return from the dead* resucitar de entre los muertos.

returnable [-əbl] *adj* que se puede devolver, restituible, reintegrable || JUR devolutivo, va | elegible (candidate) || *non returnable* sin consigna (packing).

returned [-d] *adj* de vuelta (person) || devuelto al remitente (letter, packet) || devuelto, ta; *returned article* artículo devuelto; *returned empties* envases devueltos vacíos.

returning officer [-iŋ,ɔfisə*] *n* escrutador *m*.

retype ['ri:'taip] *vt* volver a escribir a máquina, volver a mecanografiar.

retyre [ri:'taiə*] *vt* poner neumáticos nuevos a.

reunification [ri:'ju:nifi'keiʃən] *n* reunificación *f*.

reunify ['ri:'ju:nifai] *vt* reunificar.

reunion ['ri:'ju:njən] *n* reunión *f*.

reunite ['ri:ju:'nait] *vt* reunir || reconciliar (two friends).

◆ *vi* reunirse || reconciliarse.

reusable [ri:'ju:zəbl] *adj* reutilizable.

reuse ['ri:'ju:z] *vt* volver a emplear.

rev ['rev] *n* FAM revolución *f* (of an engine) | cura *m* (short for reverend) || *rev counter* cuentarrevoluciones *m inv*.

rev [rev] *vt* FAM *to rev up* acelerar (car).

◆ *vi* FAM *to rev up* embalarse (car).

revaccinate ['ri:'væksineit] *vt* MED revacunar.

revaccination ['rivæksi'neiʃən] *n* MED revacunación *f*.

revalorize [ri:'vælәraiz] *vt* revalorizar.

revaluation [ri:vælju'eiʃən] *n* revaluación *f*, revalorización *f*.

revalue ['ri:'vælju:] *vt* revaluar, revalorizar.

revamp ['ri:'væmp] *vt* remendar, arreglar (shoes) || FIG renovar, modernizar.

revanche [rə'vɑ:nʃ] *n* venganza *f*, revancha *f*.

reveal [ri'vi:l] *n* ARCH derrame *m* (of door, of window).

reveal [ri'vi:l] *vt* revelar, manifestar; *to reveal one's real intentions* manifestar sus verdaderas intenciones || revelar, descubrir (to uncover) || revelar, descubrir, divulgar (a secret).

revealer [ri'vi:lə*] *n* revelador, ra.

revealing [ri'vi:liŋ] *adj* revelador, ra; *revealing letter* carta reveladora.

reveille [ri'væli] *n* MIL diana *f*; *to sound reveille* tocar diana.

revel ['revl] *n* diversión *f*, fiesta *f* (amusement) || juerga *f*, jarana *f* (spree).

revel ['revl] *vi* deleitarse, gozar; *she revels in dancing* goza bailando || divertirse (to amuse o.s.) || juerguearse, ir *or* estar de juerga (to have a good time).

◆ *vt* *to revel away* gastar en placeres (money).

revelation [,revi'leiʃən] *n* revelación *f* || *revelations* en Apocalipsis (last book of the New Testament).

reveler; reveller ['revlə*] *n* juerguista *m* & *f*.

revelry ['revlri] *n* jolgorio *m*, jarana *f*, juerga *f*.

revendication [ri,vendi'keiʃən] *n* reivindicación *f*.

revenge [ri'vendʒ] *n* venganza *f* || SP desquite *m*, revancha *f* || — *in revenge for* para vengarse de || *to be full of revenge* arder en deseos de venganza || *to take revenge on s.o. for sth.* vengarse de algo en uno.

revenge [ri'vendʒ] *vt* vengar, vengarse de || *to revenge o.s.* o *to be revenged on s.o.* vengarse en alguien.

revengeful [-ful] *adj* vengativo, va (avenging) || vindicativo, va (vindictive).

revenger [-ə*] *n* vengador, ra.

revenue ['revinju:] *n* entrada *f*, ingreso *m*, renta *f* (income) || fuente *f* de ingresos (source of income) || rentas *f pl* públicas (from taxes, etc.) || Hacienda *f* Pública (administration) || — *Inland Revenue* contribuciones *f pl* (government income), hacienda *f*, fisco *m* (government department) || *Public Revenue* Tesoro Público || *revenue office* oficina *f* de recaudación || *revenue officer* agente *m* de aduanas (of customs), delegado *m* de Hacienda (of finance) || *revenue stamp* timbre *m* fiscal.

◆ *pl* ingresos *m*, entradas *f*, rentas *f*.

revenue cutter [-,kʌtə*] *n* MAR guardacostas *m inv* (boat).

reverberant [ri'və:bərənt] *adj* reverberante.

reverberate [ri'və:bəreit] *vt* reverberar, reflejar (heat and light) || reflejar, reverberar (sound).

◆ *vi* reverberarse, reflejarse (heat and light) || resonar, retumbar, reverberarse (sound).

reverberation [ri,və:bə'reiʃən] *n* reverberación *f* (of heat, of light) || reverberación *f*, repercusión *f*, eco *m* (of sound).

reverberative [ri'və:bəreitiv] *adj* reverberante.

reverberator [ri'və:bəreitə*] *n* reflector *m*.

reverberatory [ri'və:bərətəri] *adj* de reverbero; *reverberatory furnace* horno de reverbero.

◆ *n* horno *m* de reverbero.

revere [ri'viə*] *vt* reverenciar, venerar.

reverence ['revərəns] *n* reverencia *f* (respect, bow) || — *saving your reverence* con perdón sea dicho || *to hold in reverence* reverenciar, venerar || *to pay reverence to* rendir homenaje a || REL *Your Reverence* Su Reverencia.

reverence ['revərəns] *vt* reverenciar, venerar.

reverend ['revərənd] *adj* REL reverendo, da || *most* o *right Reverend* reverendísimo.

◆ *n* REL pastor *m* (Anglican Church) | cura *m*, padre *m* (Roman Catholic Church).

reverent ['revərənt] *adj* reverente.

reverential [,revə'renʃəl] *adj* reverencial.

reverie ['revəri] *n* ensueño *m* || *to be lost in reverie* estar absorto, ta.

revers [ri'viə*] *inv n* solapa *f*.

reversal [ri'və:səl] *n* inversión *f* || JUR revocación *f* (of a judgment) || FIG cambio *m* completo (of opinion).

reverse [ri'və:s] *adj* opuesto, ta; contrario, ria (opposite); *in the reverse direction* en dirección contraria || inverso, sa (inverse); *in reverse order* en orden inverso || AUT de marcha atrás || *the reverse side* el revés, la vuelta (of cloth), el dorso (of a sheet), el reverso (of a medal), el reverso, la cruz (of coin).

◆ *n* lo contrario; *what you say is the reverse of what I say* lo que dice usted es lo contrario de lo que digo yo || revés *m*, vuelta *f* (of cloth) || reverso *m* (of medal) || cruz *f*, reverso *m* (of coin) || dorso *m* (of printed form) || revés *m* (of fortune) || revés *m*, derrota *f* (defeat) || AUT marcha *f* atrás (gear) || — *he is the reverse of polite* no es nada cortés, es todo lo contrario de un hombre cortés || *quite the reverse* todo lo contrario || AUT & FIG *to go into reverse* dar marcha atrás || AUT *to put in* o *into reverse* poner en marcha atrás.

reverse [ri'və:s] *vt* invertir; *a mirror reverses the image* el espejo invierte la imagen || volver al revés (to turn the other way round) || MIL llevar a la funerala (arms) || cambiar completamente (policy, situation) || JUR revocar, anu-

lar, cancelar (a decision) || TECH invertir la marcha de (engine) | invertir (current, steam) || — *to reverse one's car* dar marcha atrás || *to reverse the (telephone) charges* poner una conferencia a cobro revertido.
◆ *vi* AUT dar marcha atrás (to put an engine in reverse) | ir marcha atrás (to drive backwards) || ir en sentido inverso (in dancing).

reverse-charge [-tʃɑːdʒ] *adj* *to make a reverse-charge call* poner una conferencia a cobro revertido.

reverse current [-'kʌrənt] *n* contracorriente *f*.

reverse gear [-giə*] *n* AUT marcha *f* atrás.

reversely [-li] *adv* al revés.

reverser [-ə*] *n* ELECTR inversor *m*.

reversibility [ri,vəːsə'biliti] *n* reversibilidad *f*.

reversible [ri'vəːsəbl] *adj* reversible || JUR revocable (decision) || de dos caras, reversible (material).

reversing light [ri'vəːsiŋ,lait] *n* luz *f* de marcha atrás (in a motor vehicle).

reversion [ri'vəːʃən] *n* reversión *f* (return to a former condition) || BIOL salto *m* atrás, reversión *f* || JUR reversión *f* || PHOT inversión *f*.

reversionary [ri'vəːʃənəri] *adj* de reversión.

reversive [ri'vəːsiv] *adj* reversivo, va.

revert [ri'vəːt] *vi* volver a; *the tribe reverted to paganism* la tribu volvió al paganismo; *reverting to your original statement* volviendo a su declaración inicial || JUR revertir; *property which reverts to the Crown* bienes que revierten a la Corona || BIOL saltar atrás.

revertibility [rivəːti'biliti] *n* JUR reversibilidad *f*.

revertible [ri'vəːtəbl] *adj* JUR reversible.

revet [ri'vet] *vt* revestir.

revetment [-mənt] *n* revestimiento *m*.

revictual ['riː'vitl] *vt* reabastecer.
◆ *vi* reabastecerse.

review [ri'vjuː] *n* examen *m*, análisis *m*; *to take a review of the situation* hacer un análisis de la situación || MIL revista *f* || JUR revisión *f* || crítica *f*, reseña *f* (critic) || revista *f* (magazine) || THEATR revista *f* (revue) || US revisión *f* (revision) || — *review copy* ejemplar *m* para la prensa || *to come under review* ser examinado || *to come up for review* tener que ser revisado, da.

review [ri'vjuː] *vt* examinar, analizar (to consider) || volver a examinar (to reconsider) || MIL pasar revista a; *to review a regiment* pasar revista a un regimiento || hacer una crítica de, hacer una reseña de (a book) || JUR revisar || US revisar (to revise).
◆ *vi* hacer críticas *or* reseñas (to write reviews).

reviewal [-əl] *n* crítica *f*, reseña *f* (of a book) || revisión *f*.

reviewer [-ə*] *n* crítico, ca.

revigorate [ri'vigəreit] *vt* revigorizar.

revile [ri'vail] *vt* insultar, injuriar; *he was reviling his father* estaba insultando a su padre.
◆ *vi* proferir injurias (*against* contra).

revilement [-mənt] *n* insulto *m*, injuria *f*.

reviler [-ə*] *n* injuriador, ra.

reviling [-iŋ] *adj* injurioso, sa.

revindicate ['riː'vindikeit] *vt* reivindicar.

revindication [riːvindi'keiʃən] *n* reivindicación *f*.

revisable [ri'vaizəbl] *adj* que puede ser revisado, revisable.

revisal [ri'vaizəl] *n* revisión *f*.

revise [ri'vaiz] *n* PRINT segunda prueba *f* || *second revise* tercera prueba.

revise [ri'vaiz] *vt* revisar, volver a examinar (to reexamine) || repasar (a lesson) || corregir, revisar (to correct); *to revise a manuscript* revisar un manuscrito || modificar (to modify) || refundir (to make a new version); *to revise a dictionary* refundir un diccionario || PRINT corregir (proofs).

reviser; revisor [-ə*] *n* revisor, ra (who reexamines) || revisor, ra; corrector, ra (who corrects a manuscript) || refundidor, ra (of dictionary, etc.) || PRINT corrector, ra (of proofs).

revision [ri'viʒən] *n* revisión *f* || repaso *m* (of a lesson) || corrección *f*, revisión *f* (of a manuscript) || modificación *f* (modification) || refundición *f* (of a dictionary, etc.) || PRINT correción *f* (of proofs).

revisionism [-izəm] *n* revisionismo *m*.

revisionist [-ist] *adj/n* revisionista.

revisit ['riː'vizit] *vt* volver a visitar.

revisor [ri'vaizə*] *n* → **reviser.**

revisory [ri'vaizəri] *adj* revisor, ra.

revitalization [ri,vaitəlai'zeiʃən] *n* revitalización *f*, revivificación *f*.

revitalize ['riː'vaitəlaiz] *vt* revitalizar, revivificar.

revivable [ri'vaivəbl] *adj* reanimable.

revival [ri'vaivəl] *n* MED reanimación *f* (bringing back to life) | resucitación *f* (of a dead person) | restablecimiento *m* (recovery) || COMM reactivación *f*, nuevo desarrollo *m* (of business, of economy) || REL despertar *m* religioso (awakening of religious fervour) | asamblea *f* evangelística (meeting) || renacimiento *m* (of interest, style of art, etc.) || reaparición *f* (of fashion) || restablecimiento *m* (of an old custom) || resurgimiento *m* (of a country) || THEATR reposición *f*, reestreno *m* (of a play) || JUR restablecimiento *m*, nueva aplicación *f* (of a law, etc.) || ARTS Renacimiento *m* || *the Revival of learning* el Renacimiento.

revivalism [ri'vaivəlizəm] *n* REL evangelismo *m*.

revivalist [ri'vaivəlist] *n* REL evangelista *m*.

revive [ri'vaiv] *vt* MED reanimar (to bring back to consciousness) | resucitar (to bring back to life) || THEATR reponer, reestrenar (a play) || JUR restablecer, volver a aplicar (a law) || volver a poner de moda, resucitar (fashion) || reactivar, dar nueva vida *or* nuevo impulso a (trade) || restablecer (an old custom) || reanimar, animar (the conversation) || resucitar (feelings, memories) || despertar (wish, hopes) || animar (to cheer up) || renovar (interest) || atizar, avivar (fire).
◆ *vi* MED reanimarse, volver en sí, recobrar el sentido (to come back to consciousness) | resucitar (to come back to life) | restablecerse, reponerse, recuperarse (to recover strength) || despertar (nature) || renacer, volver a nacer (to be renewed); *our hopes revived* nuestras esperanzas volvieron a nacer || resucitar (feelings, memories) || renacer (interest) || COMM reactivarse, recuperarse || *his spirits revived* recobró el ánimo.

reviver [ri'vaivə*] *n* reanimador, ra; persona *f* or cosa *f* que reanima || FAM *to have an early morning reviver* matar el gusanillo.

revivify [ri'vivifai] *vt* revivificar.

revocability [,revəkə'biliti] *n* revocabilidad *f*.

revocable ['revəkəbl] *adj* revocable.

revocation [,revə'keiʃən] *n* JUR revocación *f* (of a decree) | suspensión *f* (of a licence).

revocative ['revəkətiv] *adj* revocativo, va.

revocatory ['revəkətəri] *adj* revocatorio, ria.

revokable ['revəkəbl] *adj* revocable.

revoke [ri'vəuk] *n* renuncio *m* (at cards).

revoke [ri'vəuk] *vt* JUR revocar; *to revoke an order, a law, a decree* revocar una orden, una ley, un decreto | suspender (a licence).
◆ *vi* renunciar (at cards).

revolt [ri'vəult] *n* rebelión *f*, sublevación *f*, revuelta *f* (rebellion) || rebeldía *f* (state of mind) || — *in revolt* en rebelión || *to rise in revolt* sublevarse, levantarse || *to stir up to revolt* sublevar, levantar.

revolt [ri'vəult] *vt* repugnar, dar asco, asquear (to fill with repugnance); *snails revolt me* los caracoles me repugnan || escandalizar, indignar (to fill with horror); *the scene revolted him* la escena le escandalizó || sublevar, incitar a la rebelión (to incite to rebellion).
◆ *vi* rebelarse, sublevarse; *to revolt against the government* rebelarse contra el gobierno || sentir repugnancia *or* asco *or* repulsión (to feel disgust) || escandalizarse, indignarse (to be filled with horror); *human nature revolts at such a crime* la naturaleza humana se indigna ante semejante crimen.

revolting [-iŋ] *adj* repugnante, asqueroso, sa (repulsive) || rebelde, sublevado, da (rebellious).

revolution [,revə'luːʃən] *n* revolución *f* (political, social, etc.); *industrial Revolution* la Revolución industrial || TECH rotación *f*, giro *m* (round an axis) | revolución *f* (of a wheel); *40 revolutions per minute* cuarenta revoluciones por minuto || ASTR revolución *f* (round an orbit) | rotación *f* (of heavenly bodies round their axis) || *revolution counter* cuentarrevoluciones *m inv*.

revolutionary [,revə'luːʃnəri] *adj/n* revolucionario, ria.

revolutionize [,revə'luːʃnaiz] *vt* revolucionar (to change completely).

revolvable [ri'vɔlvəbəl] *adj* giratorio, ria.

revolve [ri'vɔlv] *vt* hacer girar (to make turn) || FIG dar vueltas en la cabeza a (problem, thought) | meditar (scheme).
◆ *vi* girar (to move around an axis) || volver, repetirse; *the seasons revolve each year* las estaciones se repiten cada año || — FIG *the problem is revolving in his mind* el problema le está dando vueltas en la cabeza || *to revolve around* girar alrededor de; *to revolve around an axis* girar alrededor de un eje; girar alrededor de, girar en torno a; *all the conversation revolved around politics* toda la conversación giró alrededor de la política.

revolver [-ə*] *n* revólver *m*.

revolving [-iŋ] *adj* giratorio, ria; *revolving door* puerta giratoria || que se repite (year, season) || ASTR rotatorio, ria || *revolving fund* fondo *m* de rotación.

revue [ri'vjuː] *n* THEATR revista *f*.

revulsion [ri'vʌlʃən] *n* MED revulsión *f* || FIG repulsión *f*, repugnancia *f* (repugnance) | cambio *m* brusco (sudden change) | reacción *f* (reaction).

revulsive [ri'vʌlsiv] *adj* MED revulsivo, va.
◆ *n* MED revulsivo *m*.

reward [ri'wɔːd] *n* recompensa *f*; *as a reward for* en recompensa de; *a ten pound reward* diez libras de recompensa.

reward [ri'wɔːd] *vt* recompensar, premiar.

rewarding [-iŋ] *adj* remunerador, ra || que merece la pena, que compensa (experience, film, etc.).

rewind* ['riː'waind] *vt* rebobinar || dar cuerda a (clock, watch).
— OBSERV Pret y pp ***rewound***.

rewinding [-iŋ] *n* rebobinado *m*.

rewire ['riː'waiə*] *vt* poner nueva instalación eléctrica a (a house) || cambiar el alambre de (electric circuit) || telegrafiar de nuevo.

reword ['riː'wəːd] *vt* expresar con otras palabras || volver a redactar.

rework ['riː'wəːk] *vt* revisar (piece of writing) || replantear (idea) || trabajar (material).

rewound ['riː'waund] *pret/pp* ⟶ **rewind.**

rewrite* ['riː'rait] *vt* volver a escribir (to write again) || volver a redactar, redactar con otras palabras (to alter the wording).
— OBSERV Pret *rewrote*; pp *rewritten*.

Reykjavik ['reikjəviːk] *pr n* GEOGR Reikiavik.

Rhaetian ['riːʃjən] *adj/n* rético, ca.

Rhaeto-Romanic ['riːtəurəu'mænik] *n* retorromano *m*, rético *m*.

rhamnaceae [ræm'neisiiː] *pl n* BOT ramnáceas *f*.

rhapsodic [ræp'sɔdik]; **rhapsodical** [-əl] *adj* rapsódico, ca.

rhapsodist ['ræpsədist] *n* rapsoda *m*.

rhapsodize ['ræpsədaiz] *vi* extasiarse (*over* ante), estar entusiasmado (*over* por) || celebrar, poner por las nubes (to praise).

rhapsody ['ræpsədi] *n* rapsodia *f* || FIG *to go into rhapsodies over* poner por las nubes, celebrar.

rhatany ['rætəni] *n* BOT ratania *f*.

rhea [riə] *n* ñandú *m* (bird).

Rhea [riə] *pr n* MYTH Rea *f*.

Rhenish ['riːniʃ] *adj* renano, na || del Rin (wine).
◆ *n* vino *m* del Rin.

rhenium ['riːniəm] *n* CHEM renio *m*.

rheometer [ri'ɔmitə*] *n* reómetro *m*.

rheophore ['riːəfɔː*] *n* PHYS reóforo *m*.

rheostat ['riəustæt] *n* ELECTR reóstato *m*.

rheostatic [riəu'stætik] *adj* reostático, ca.

rhesus ['riːsəs] *n* macaco *m* de la India (monkey) || BIOL *Rhesus factor* factor *m* Rhesus; *Rhesus positive, negative* factor *or* Rh *m* positivo, negativo.

rhetor ['riːtə*] *n* retórico *m*.

rhetoric ['retərik] *n* retórica *f*.

rhetorical [ri'tɔrikəl] *adj* retórico, ca; *rhetorical question* pregunta retórica.

rhetorician [,retə'riʃən] *n* retórico *m*.

rheum [ruːm] *n* MED legaña *f* (in the eyes) | mucosidades *f pl* (in the nose).

rheumatic [ru'mætik] *adj* MED reumático, ca; *rheumatic fever* fiebre reumática.
◆ *n* MED reumático, ca (person).
◆ *pl* FAM reumatismo *m sing*, reúma *m sing* (disease).

rheumatism ['ruːmətizəm] *n* MED reumatismo *m*, reúma *m*.

rheumatoid ['ruːmətɔid] *adj* MED reumatoideo, a || *rheumatoid arthritis* reúma *m* articular.

rheumy ['ruːmi] *adj* MED legañoso, sa (eyes).

rhinal ['rainəl] *adj* ANAT nasal.

Rhine [rain] *pr n* GEOGR Rin *m*.

Rhineland [-lænd] *pr n* GEOGR Renania *f*.

rhinestone ['rainstəun] *n* diamante *m* falso.

rhinitis [rai'naitis] *n* MED rinitis *f inv*.

rhino ['rainəu] *n* FAM rinoceronte *m* (rhinoceros) || FAM parné *m*, pasta *f* (money).

rhinoceros [rai'nɔsərəs] *n* ZOOL rinoceronte *m*.
— OBSERV El plural es *rhinoceroses* o *rhinoceros*.

rhinologist [rai'nɔlədʒist] *n* rinólogo *m*.

rhinology [rai'nɔlədʒi] *n* MED rinología *f*.

rhinopharynx [,rainəu'færiŋks] *n* rinofaringe *f*.

rhinoplasty ['rainəplæsti] *n* MED rinoplastia *f*.

rhizome ['raizəum] *n* BOT rizoma *m*.

rhizophagous [rai'zɔfəgəs] *adj* rizófago, ga (animal).

rhizopod ['raizəɔd] *n* rizópodo *m*.

rhizopoda [rai'zɔpədə] *pl n* rizopodos *m*.

Rhode Island [rəud'ailənd] *pr n* GEOGR Rhode Island.

Rhodes [rəudz] *pr n* GEOGR Rodas.

Rhodesia [rəu'diːzjə] *pr n* GEOGR Rodesia *f*.

Rhodesian [-n] *adj/n* rodesiano, na.

rhodium ['rəudjəm] *n* CHEM rodio *m*.

rhododendron [,rəudə'dendrən] *n* rododendro *m*.

rhomb [rɔm] *n* MATH rombo *m* (rhombus).

rhombic ['rɔmbik] *adj* MATH rómbico, ca; rombal.

rhombohedral [,rɔmbə'hiːdrəl] *adj* MATH romboédrico, ca.

rhombohedron [rɔmbə'hiːdrən] *n* MATH romboedro *m*.
— OBSERV El plural de la palabra inglesa es *rhombohedrons* o *rhombohedra*.

rhomboid ['rɔmbɔid] *adj* MATH romboidal, romboideo, a.
◆ *n* romboide *m*.

rhomboidal [-əl] *adj* MATH romboidal.

rhombus ['rɔmbəs] *n* MATH rombo *m*.
— OBSERV El plural de la palabra rhombus es *rhombuses* o *rhombi*.

Rhône [rəun] *pr n* GEOGR Ródano *m*.

rhotacism ['rəutəsizəm] *n* rotacismo *m* (phonetics).

rhubarb ['ruːbɑːb] *n* BOT ruibarbo *m*.

rhumb [rʌm] *n* MAR rumbo *m*.

rhyme [raim] *n* rima *f* || poesía *f*, versos *m pl* (poetry) || — *in rhyme* en verso || *nursery rhyme* poesía infantil || *to put into rhyme* poner en verso || FIG *without rhyme or reason* a tontas y a locas, sin ton ni son.

rhyme [raim] *vt/vi* rimar.

rhymer [-ə*]; **rhymester** [-stə*] *n* rimador, ra.

rhyming ['raimiŋ] *adj* rimador, ra (person) || rimado, da (words).
◆ *n* versificación *f*.

rhyming dictionary [-'dikʃənri] *n* diccionario *m* de rimas.

rhythm ['riðəm] *n* ritmo *m*; *to put rhythm into* dar ritmo a || MUS *rhythm and blues* rhythm and blues || *rhythm method* método *m* Ogino.

rhythmic ['riðmik]; **rhythmical** [-əl] *adj* rítmico, ca.

rhythmically [-əli] *adv* rítmicamente, de modo rítmico.

rhythmics [-s] *n* rítmica *f*.

ria ['riːə] *n* GEOGR ría *f*.

rib [rib] *n* ANAT costilla *f*; *true, false, floating rib* costilla verdadera, falsa, flotante || ARCH nervio *m*, nervadura *f* (of an arch) | arista *f* (of a vault) || ZOOL & BOT nervio *m* (of leaf, of insect's wing) || cañón *m* (of feather) || MAR cuaderna *f*, costilla *f* || cordoncillo *m* (in knitting) || nervio *m* (in bookbinding) || varilla *f* (of umbrella, of fan, etc.) || CULIN costilla *f* (of meat) || AVIAT costilla *f* || MUS armazón *f* || FAM costilla *f* (wife).

rib [rib] *vt* MAR poner cuadernas a (a ship) || poner nervios a (a book) || US FAM tomar el pelo a (to tease).

ribald ['ribəld] *adj* verde, obsceno, na; chusco, ca.
◆ *n* persona *f* verde *or* chusca.

ribaldry [-ri] *n* chusquería *f*, obscenidad *f*.

riband ['ribənd] *n* ⟶ **ribbon.**

ribband ['ribənd] *n* MAR cinta *f* || ⟶ **ribbon.**

ribbed [ribd] *adj* acanalado, da; *ribbed socks* calcetines acanalados.

ribbon ['ribən]; **riband** ['ribənd] *n* cinta *f* (narrow strip of material) || cordón *m* (of an order) || galón *m* (of a decoration) || — *steel ribbon* fleje *m* || *typewriter ribbon* cinta de máquina de escribir.
◆ *pl* riendas *f* (reins) | FAM jirones *m*, trizas *f*; *the flag was in ribbons* la bandera estaba hecha jirones || FIG *to handle* o *to take the ribbons* tomar las riendas.

ribbon development [-di'veləpmənt] *n* urbanización *f* realizada a lo largo de una carretera.

ribbon saw [-sɔː] *n* TECH sierra *f* de cinta.

rib cage ['ribkeidʒ] *n* ANAT caja *f* torácica.

ribonucleic ['raibəu'njuːkliik] *adj* ribonucleico, ca (acid).

ribwort ['rib,wəːt] *n* BOT llantén *m* menor.

rice [rais] *n* arroz *m*; *husked rice* arroz descascarillado || — *boiled rice* arroz blanco || *broken rice* arroz quebrantado *or* picón || *creamed rice* arroz con leche.

rice [rais] *vt* US CULIN pasar (cooker potatoes).

rice field [-fiːld] *n* arrozal *m*.

rice grower [-grəuə*] *n* arrocero, ra.

rice mill [-mil] *n* molino *m* arrocero.

rice paper [-,peipə*] *n* papel *m* de arroz.

rice pudding [-'pudiŋ] *n* arroz *m* con leche.

ricer [-ə*] *n* US pasapuré *m*.

rich [ritʃ] *adj* rico, ca (wealthy); *a rich property owner* un rico propietario || rico, ca; *person rich in virtues* persona rica en virtudes || magnífico, ca; espléndido, da (splendid); *rich gifts* regalos magníficos || suntuoso, sa (sumptuous) || precioso, sa (elaborate) || rico, ca; *adorned with rich embroidery* adornado con ricos bordados || abundante, rico, ca (abundant); *a rich harvest* una cosecha abundante || AGR fértil, rico, ca (soil) | ubérrimo, ma (pasture) || CULIN rico, ca; sabroso, sa (food) | con mucha materia grasa (pastries) | generoso, sa (wine) || FIG pingüe (earnings, profits) | vivo, va; subido, da (colours) | sonoro, ra; potente (voice) | muy fuerte (perfume) | opíparo, ra (meal) | rico, ca (language) || rico, ca; *ore rich in silver* mineral rico en plata || FAM gracioso, sa; muy divertido, da (funny) | absurdo, da || — *a land rich in minerals* un terreno rico en minerales || *to become* o *to get* o *to grow rich* hacerse rico, enriquecerse || *to be rich in* abundar en || *to make s.o. rich* enriquecer a uno.
◆ *pl n* *the rich* los ricos.

Richard ['ritʃəd] *pr n* Ricardo *m*.

riches ['ritʃiz] *pl n* riquezas *f*, riqueza *f sing*; *to pile up riches* amontonar riquezas.

richly ['ritʃli] *adv* ricamente (in a rich way) || magníficamente, espléndidamente (splendidly) || suntuosamente (sumptuously) || abundantemente (abundantly) || FAM bien; *he richly deserves it* lo tiene bien merecido.

richness ['ritʃnis] *n* riqueza *f* || suntuosidad *f* (sumptuousness) || preciosidad *f* (beauty) || abundancia *f* (abundance) || fertilidad *f* (of soil) || lo sabroso (of food) || sonoridad *f* (of voice).

Richter scale ['riktə*,skeil] *n* GEOL escala *f* de Richter.

rick [rik] *n* almiar *m* (of hay) || esguince *m* (twist).

rick [rik] *vt* amontonar [en almiares] (hay).

rickets ['rikits] *n* MED raquitismo *m*.

rickety ['rikiti] *adj* MED raquítico, ca || FIG cojo, ja (shaky); *a rickety chair* una silla coja | poco seguro, ra (unsteady) | desvencijado, da;

a rickety old car un viejo coche desvencijado | canijo, ja; *a rickety old man* un viejo canijo.

rickshaw ['rikʃɔ:] *n* cochecillo *m* tirado por un hombre.

ricochet ['rikəʃəi] *n* rebote *m*.

ricochet ['rikəʃəi] *vi* rebotar.

rictus ['riktəs] *n* rictus *m*, gesto *m*.

rid* [rid] *vt* librar; *to rid a country of bandits* librar de bandidos un país || — *to be rid of* estar libre de || *to get rid of s.o. of sth.* deshacerse de alguien, de algo || *to rid s.o. of* librarse de; *to rid o.s. of an obligation* librarse de una obligación || *to rid o.s. of an idea* quitarse una idea de la cabeza.

— OBSERV Pret y pp *rid, ridded*.

ridable ['raidəbəl] *adj* → **rideable**.

riddance ['ridəns] *n* liberación *f* || *good riddance!* ¡vete con viento fresco! (go to blazes!), ¡menudo alivio!, ¡qué bien! (what a relief!).

ridden ['ridn] *pp* acosado, da; abobiado, da || infestado, da (invaded) || → **ride**.

riddle ['ridl] *n* acertijo *m*, adivinanza *f*; *to ask s.o. a riddle* poner un acertijo a alguien || FIG enigma *m* (puzzling person, situation) || criba *f* (sieve) || *to speak in riddles* hablar en clave.

riddle ['ridl] *vt* cribar (to sieve) || acribillar (with holes, with bullets, etc.) || criticar (an argument) || infestar (to corrupt) || resolver *or* adivinar [un acertijo] (to solve a riddle).

◆ *vi* hablar en clave.

riddled [-d] *adj* acribillado, da (with holes) || plagado, da (plagued by).

ride [raid] *n* paseo *m* a caballo (on a horse) || paseo *m* en coche (in a car) || paseo *m* en bicicleta (on a bicycle) || viaje *m* en tren (in a train) || viaje *m* en barco (on a ship) || viaje en avión (in a plane) || camino *m* de herradura, vereda *f* (path) || trayecto *m*, viaje *m* (journey) || vuelta *f*, paseo *m*; *the children had a ride on a camel* los niños dieron una vuelta en un camello || precio *m* del viaje *or* del paseo (price) || — *he gave me a ride from London to Blackpool* me llevó de Londres a Blackpool || *it's a ten penny ride on the bus* cuesta diez peniques en autobús || *it's only a short ride by bus* no se tarda mucho en autobús || *to give a child a ride on one's back* llevar a un niño a cuestas || *to go for a ride* dar un paseo [en coche, a caballo, etc.] || FAM *to take s.o. for a ride* dar gato por liebre a uno (to deceive s.o.), dar el paseo a uno (to kill).

ride* [raid] *vt* montar, ir montado en; *he was riding a black horse* montaba un caballo negro || montar a; *I can't ride a horse* no sé montar a caballo || montar en (a bicycle, a donkey) || ir en; *to ride a bus* ir en autobús || conducir, guiar [AMER manejar] (to drive a bicycle, etc.) || recorrer (to cover a distance) || cruzar *or* atravesar a caballo (a country, a town); *to ride the deserts* atravesar los desiertos a caballo || surcar, hender; *to ride the waves* surcar las olas || llevar; *to ride a baby on one's back* llevar a un niño a cuestas || SP correr, participar en (a race) || montar, acaballar (to mate) || FIG dominar, tiranizar (to dominate) | acosar, agobiar; *ridden by doubts* acosado por las dudas || US FAM meterse con (to tease) || — *I rode my horse down to the river* llevé el caballo al río, fui a caballo al río || *I rode my horse up the hill* subí la colina a caballo || *the motorcycle was ridden by* la motocicleta iba conducida por || *to ride to death* agotar (a horse), repetir hasta la saciedad (an idea, a theory).

◆ *vi* montar, ir montado; *he was riding on a donkey* iba montado en un burro || montar; *to ride sidesaddle* montar a la amazona || ir [a caballo, en bicicleta, etc.]; *to ride to a place* ir a un sitio; *to ride a good pace* ir a buen paso; *I rode by bicycle to London* fui a Londres en bicicleta || viajar (to travel) || montar a caballo; *we rode* o *we went riding all morning* montamos *or* estuvimos montando a caballo toda la mañana || cabalgar; *I rode hard all morning* cabalgué toda la mañana sin parar || viajar en coche (in a car) || viajar en tren (in a train) || montar en bicicleta (on a bicycle) || ser llevado a cuestas (on s.o.'s back) || recorrer; *to ride fifty miles* recorrer cincuenta millas || moverse; *to ride on an axis* moverse en un eje || MAR flotar || flotar (sun or moon) || FIG seguir su curso; *let the problem ride* deja que el problema siga su curso || — *I rode all the way* hice todo el camino a caballo || *the ground rides hard* el terreno es muy duro para ir a caballo || *the moon was riding high in the heavens* la luna estaba alta en el cielo || FIG *to be riding high* estar en plena forma || *to ride astride* montar a horcajadas || MAR *to ride at anchor* estar fondeado *or* anclado || FIG *to ride for a fall* ir a la ruina.

◆ *phr v* **to ride along** pasar || **to ride away** irse [a caballo, etc.] || **to ride back** volver [a caballo, etc.] || **to ride behind** montar a la grupa (on same horse) | ir en el asiento trasero (in carriage) | ir detrás (to follow) || **to ride by** pasar [a caballo, etc.] || **to ride down** adelantar a caballo (to overtake on a horse) | atropellar (to run over) || **to ride in** entrar [a caballo, etc.] | ir en [en vehículo] || **to ride off** irse [a caballo, etc.] || **to ride on** seguir adelante [a caballo, etc.] || **to ride out** salir [a caballo, etc.] | *to ride out the storm* capear el temporal || **to ride up** llegar [a caballo, etc.] | subirse; *this pullover always rides up* este jersey siempre se sube.

— OBSERV Pret ***rode***; pp ***ridden***.

rideable; ridable [-əbl] *adj* que se puede montar (horse) || transitable (path).

rider [-ə*] *n* jinete *m*, caballista *m* (on horse) || ciclista *m* & *f* (on a bicycle) || motociclista *m* (on a moped) || motorista *m* & *f* (on a motorbike) || caballista *m* & *f* (in a circus) || SP jockey *m* || JUR cláusula *f* adicional || MATH ejercicio *m* de aplicación.

ridge [ridʒ] *n* GEOGR cadena *f*, cordillera *f* (of hills) | cumbre *f*, cresta *f* (crest) | loma *f* (hillock) | arista *f*, estría *f* (on a rock) | ondulación *f* (on sand) | escollo *m* (of reefs, etc.) || AGR caballón *m* (between furrows) || ANAT caballete *m* (of nose) || ARCH caballete *m* (of a roof) || cordoncillo *m* (in cloth).

ridge [ridʒ] *vt* surcar || ARCH cubrir con un caballete.

◆ *vi* rizarse (sea).

ridgepiece [-pi:s] *n* ARCH caballete *m*, cumbrera *f*, parhilera *f* (of a roof).

ridgepole [-pəul] *n* caballete *m*, cumbrera *f*, parhilera *f* (of a roof).

ridge tile [-tail] *n* teja *f* de caballete *or* de cumbrera.

ridgy [-i] *adj* surcado de estrías, estriado, da || con aristas || ARCH a dos aguas (roof).

ridicule ['ridikju:l] *n* irrisión *f*, burla *f* (mockery) || — *to expose s.o. to ridicule* poner a uno en ridículo || *to hold s.o. up to ridicule* ridiculizar a uno || *to invite ridicule* hacer reír, causar la risa || *to lay o.s. open to ridicule* exponerse al ridículo.

ridicule ['ridikju:l] *vt* ridiculizar, poner en ridículo.

ridiculous [ri'dikjuləs] *adj* ridículo, la; *to say ridiculous things* decir cosas ridículas || *to make s.o. ridiculous* poner en ridículo a alguien.

ridiculously [-li] *adv* ridículamente || *at a ridiculously low price* a un precio de risa.

riding ['raidiŋ] *adj* de montar; *riding habit* traje de montar; *riding breeches* pantalones de montar || de silla (horse) || — *riding crop* fusta *f* || *riding light* luz *f* de posición (ship, planes) || *riding master* profesor *m* de equitación || *riding school* escuela *f* de equitación, picadero *m* || *riding whip* fusta *f*.

◆ *n* camino *m* de herradura (path) || AUT suspensión *f* || MAR anclaje *m* || SP equitación *f* || TECH imbricación *f* || *riding is easy* es fácil montar a caballo.

Rif [rif] *pr n* GEOGR Rif *m*.

rife [raif] *adj* abundante (*with* en) || *to be rife* abundar, ser muy corriente.

riffle ['rifl] *n* US ranura *f* de una artesa (for catching gold particles) | rápido *m*, rabión *m* (in a river) | peinado *m* (of cards).

riffle ['rifl] *vt* US hacer pasar por la ranura de una artesa (in gold mining) | pasar rápidamente [las hojas de un libro] | hojear (book) | peinar (cards).

riffraff ['rifræf] *n* FAM canalla *f*, chusma *f*, gentuza *f* (disreputable persons).

rifle ['raifl] *n* rifle *m* (for hunting) || fusil *m* (soldier's) || raya *f*, estría *f* (groove).

◆ *pl* fusileros *m* (soldiers).

rifle ['raifl] *vt* saquear, desvalijar (to steal everything of value from) || saquear (to plunder) || vaciar (the pockets) || rayar (to cut grooves in) || disparar a (to shoot).

rifleman [-mən] *n* MIL fusilero *m*.

— OBSERV El plural de la palabra inglesa es *riflemen*.

rifle range [-reindʒ] *n* campo *m* de tiro, polígono *m* de tiro (for target practice) || alcance *m* del fusil *or* del rifle (distance) || barraca *f* de tiro al blanco (in fairground).

rifle shot [-ʃɔt] *n* disparo *m*, tiro *m* || *within rifle shot* a tiro de fusil.

rifling [-iŋ] *n* rayado *m*.

rift [rift] *n* grieta *f*, fisura *f* (crack, fissure) || claro *m* (opening in clouds, mist) || GEOL falla *f* (a fault) || FIG ruptura *f* (in friendship, etc.) | escisión *f* (in a political party, etc.) || FIG *a rift in the lute* una desavenencia.

rift saw [-sɔ:] *n* sierra *f* para cortar madera.

rig [rig] *n* MAR aparejo *m* || equipo *m* (equipment) || instalación *f* || FAM traje *m*, vestimenta *f*, indumentaria *f*; *the rig of an Englishman* la vestimenta de un inglés || broma *f* (joke) || mala pasada *f* (trick) || artimaña *f*, engañifa *f* (pieces of trickery) || especulación *f* en la Bolsa.

rig [rig] *vt* MAR aparejar (a ship) | enjarciar (a mast) || armar (a plane) || montar, armar, instalar (machines) || equipar (to provide with equipment) || preparar; *the fire was rigged to throw blame on the caretaker* el incendio fue preparado para que se le achacara la culpa al portero || arreglar (to arrange) || amañar; *to rig an election* amañar una elección || especular en (on the stock exchange) || hacer trampas con (cards) || — *the fight was rigged* hubo tongo en el combate || *to rig out* ataviar, vestir || *to rig up* improvisar.

Riga ['riɑgə] *pr n* GEOGR Riga.

rigadoon [rigə'du:n] *n* rigodón *m* (dance).

rigamarole ['rigəməˌrəul] *n* → **rigmarole**.

rigger ['rigə*] *n* MAR aparejador, ra || AVIAT montador *m* || ARCH andamio *m* protector (in construction) || especulador, ra (in the stock exchange).

rigging ['rigiŋ] *n* MAR aparejo *m*, jarcia *f* || TECH montaje *m* (of a machine) || equipo *m* (equipment).

right [rait] *adj* bueno, na (obeying moral law); *right conduct* buena conducta || bien; *to know what is right and what is wrong* saber lo que está bien y lo que está mal || justo, ta; equitativo, va (fair); *God is right* Dios es justo || correcto, ta; exacto, ta (correct); *the right answer* la respuesta correcta || exacto, ta; *the bill is not right* la cuenta no es exacta; *have you got the right time?* ¿tiene la hora exacta? || exacto, ta; justo, ta; *the right conclusion* la conclusión exacta; *I can't find the right word* no puedo encontrar la palabra exacta || exacto, ta; verdadero, ra (true) || fundado, da (justified); *our suspicions were right* las sospechas eran fundadas || oportuno, na; bueno, na (opportune); *at the right moment* en el momento oportuno || apropiado, da; conveniente (most appropiate); *I thought it right to tell you* pensé que era conveniente decírselo || adecuado, da; conveniente (suitable); *the right word in this context* la palabra adecuada en este contexto || que hace falta; *this painting is just right for the bedroom* este cuadro es exactamente lo que hace falta para el dormitorio || decente; *it is not the right film for a young girl* no es una película decente para una chica || respetable (respectable) || bien (physically and mentally sound); *I don't feel right* no me encuentro bien; *he is not rigth in the head* no está bien de la cabeza || bueno, na; *we'll leave tomorrow if the weather is right* nos iremos mañana si hace buen tiempo || en orden, ordenado, da (in order) || FAM verdadero, ra (complete); *he is a right idiot* es un verdadero idiota; *this is a right mess!* ¡es un verdadero lío! || derecho, cha; *the right leg* la pierna derecha; *the right bank of a river* la orilla derecha de un río || SP derecha; *the right winger* el extremo derecha | de derecha; *a right hook* un gancho de derecha || de derecha, derechista (politics) || MATH recto, ta; *a right angle* un ángulo recto; *right line* línea recta || — *all right* bien (well); *I am all right* estoy bien; bastante bien (well enough), de confianza (trustworthy) || *all right!* ¡bueno!, ¡bien! (now then), ¡de acuerdo!, ¡muy bien!, ¡vale! (agreed), ¡está bien! (enough!) || *all right?* ¿de acuerdo? || *are you all right?* ¿te encuentras bien? || *everything will be all right* todo saldrá bien || *is it all right for me to go?* ¿puedo ir? || *is that right?* ¿de verdad? || *is this the right house?* ¿es ésta la casa que buscamos? || *is this the right road for...?* ¿es ésta la carretera de...?, ¿vamos bien para...? || *it is all right* no importa, déjalo (it doesn't matter) || *it is all right for some* los hay con suerte || *it is all right for you* Ud. no tiene problemas || *it is right that* es justo que || *it's not right!* ¡no hay derecho! || *my watch is right* mi reloj va bien || *quite right!* ¡perfectamente! || *right?* ¿vale? || *right!, right you are!, right ho!* ¡bueno!, ¡de acuerdo! || *right side up* en posición vertical || FAM *she's a bit of all right* está muy bien, es para comérsela || *that's right* eso es || *the right side of a fabric* el derecho de una tela || FAM *to be as right as rain* estar perfectamente bien || *to be in one's right mind* estar en su sano juicio *or* en sus cabales || *to be right* tener razón || *to be right to* hacer bien en || FIG *to be s.o.'s right hand* ser el brazo derecho de alguien || *to come out* o *to turn out right* salir bien || *to do the right thing* hacer bien || *to put* o *to set right* poner en el buen camino (to put on the right road), desengañar (to show the truth), corregir (to correct), curar (to cure), ordenar, poner en orden, arreglar (to put in order), arreglar (to repair), poner bien (to put in the right position), poner en hora (watch) || *to get sth. right* hacer algo bien || *to say the right thing* decir lo que se debe.

◆ *n* bien *m*; *right and wrong* el bien y el mal || justicia *f*; *to fight for the right* luchar por la justicia; *to do s.o. right* hacerle justicia a alguien || equidad *f* (equity) || derecho *m*; *divine right* derecho divino; *the rights of man* los derechos del hombre; *right to the throne* derecho al trono; *what right have you to enter?* ¿de qué derecho se vale para entrar? || derecha *f* (the right hand side); *to turn to the right* torcer a la derecha; *it's on your right* está a su derecha || SP derechazo *m* (a blow with the right hand) || derecha *f* (the right hand) || pie *m* derecho (in dancing); *to lead with the right* empezar con el pie derecho || — *by right, by rights* de derecho; *it is yours by right* te corresponde de derecho || MIL *by the right* ¡derecha! || *by what right do you arrest me?* ¿con qué derecho me detiene usted? || *in one's own right* por derecho propio || *keep to the right* circulen por la derecha || *member as of right* miembro *m* por derecho propio || *might and right* la fuerza y el derecho || *on the right* a la derecha || *right of pardon* derecho de gracia || *right of way* servidumbre *m* de paso, derecho de paso (land), preferencia *f* de paso, prioridad *f* (roads) || COMM *sole right* exclusiva *f* || *the Right* la derecha (politics) || *to be in the right* tener razón || *to have a right to* tener derecho a (sth.), tener derecho de *or* a (to do sth.) || *to waive one's right to speak* renunciar al uso de la palabra || *with a right to vote* con voz y voto || *without a right to vote* con voz pero sin voto.

◆ *pl* derechos *m*; *civil rights* derechos civiles; *feudal rights* derechos señoriales || — *all rights reserved* reservados todos los derechos, es propiedad || *the rights and wrongs of* lo bueno y lo malo de || *to be within one's rights* estar en su derecho || *to know the rights of a case* conocer todos los pormenores de un asunto || *to put* o *to set things to rights* arreglar las cosas || *to put to rights* poner en orden, ordenar (to put in order), deshacer, enderezar (a wrong).

◆ *adv* bien, como es debido (well); *I think you did right* creo que obraste bien || correctamente, bien; *add the figures right* suma bien las cifras || a la derecha; *turn right* tuerza a la derecha || exactamente, justo (exactly); *right where you are now* exactamente donde estás tú ahora || de lleno; *he ran right into the tree* dio de lleno contra el árbol || inmediatamente, justo; *right after dinner* justo después de la cena; *right by the church* justo al lado de la iglesia || directamente, derecho; *go right home* vete directamente a casa || muy (very); *I was right glad to see him* estuve muy contento de verlo || — MIL *eyes right!* ¡vista a la derecha! || *go right ahead* siga, continúe || *he owed money right and left* debía dinero a diestro y siniestro || *he's coming right enough* va a venir por supuesto || *he put his finger right into the cake* metió todo el dedo en el pastel || *if I remember right* si mal no recuerdo || *I knew he was coming all right!* sabía perfectamente que venía || *it serves you right!* ¡bien merecido lo tienes!, ¡te está bien empleado! || *right against the wall* muy pegado a la pared (sin que haya movimiento), de lleno contra la pared (dar, arrojar algo, etc.) || *right and left* a diestro y siniestro || *right at the top* en todo lo alto || *right away* en seguida, inmediatamente || *right here* aquí mismo || *right in the middle* en pleno centro || *right now* en este momento, ahora mismo || *right off* inmediatamente, en seguida (at once), de un tirón (in one go), seguidos, das (one after the other) || US *right on!* ¡adelante! || *right Reverend* reverendísimo || *right to the end* hasta el final || MIL *right turn!* ¡media vuelta a la derecha! || *to do right* obrar bien || *to do right by s.o.* tratar bien a alguien || *to get right away* escaparse sin dejar rastro || *to go right* salir bien || *to go right on* seguir adelante || *to speak right out* hablar sin rodeos || *we had to pass right through the town centre* tuvimos que pasar por el centro mismo de la ciudad.

— OBSERV A veces la palabra *right* en su uso adverbial tiene un carácter enfático y no se traduce: *he threw the ball right over the wall* echó el balón por encima del muro.

right [rait] *vt* enderezar (to put in an upright position) || MAR enderezar, adrizar; *to right a boat* enderezar un barco || enderezar (a wrong) || hacer justicia a (a person) || corregir, rectificar (to correct); *to right an error* corregir un error.

◆ *vi* enderezarse.

right about; right-about [-əˌbaut] *adj* MIL *right-about turn* media vuelta a la derecha.

◆ *n* MIL media vuelta *f* a la derecha.

◆ *adv* *to turn right about* dar media vuelta.

right-about-face [-əˌbautˈfeis] *n* US MIL media vuelta *f* a la derecha || US cambio *m* completo (of opinion).

right-about-face [-əˌbautˈfeis] *vi* US dar media vuelta a la derecha || cambiar completamente.

right angle [-æŋgl] *n* MATH ángulo *m* recto || *at right angles* en ángulo recto.

right-angled [-ˈæŋgld] *adj* MATH rectángulo, la (triangle) | rectangular; *right-angled figure* figura rectangular || en ángulo recto (bend).

right ascension [-əˈsenʃən] *n* ASTR ascensión *f* recta.

right-down [-ˌdaun] *adj* FAM completo, ta.

◆ *adv* FAM muy.

righteous [-ʃəs] *adj* recto, ta; honrado, da; *a righteous ruler* un gobernante honrado || justo, ta; *righteous anger* cólera justa || justificado, da (act).

righteousness [-ʃəsnis] *n* rectitud *f* (uprightness) || justicia *f* (fairness).

righter [-ə*] *n* enderezador *m* de entuertos.

right field [-fiːld] *n* US SP parte *f* derecha del campo (in baseball).

rightful [-ful] *adj* legítimo, ma; *rightful owner* propietario legítimo || equitativo, va; justo, ta (fair).

rightfully [-i] *adv* legítimamente.

right-hand [-hænd] *adj* de la derecha; *right-hand door* puerta de la derecha || a la derecha; *a right-hand turn* una vuelta a la derecha || por la derecha; *right-hand drive* conducción por la derecha || — FIG *right-hand man* brazo derecho || *right-hand side* derecha *f*, lado derecho.

right-handed [-ˈhændid] *adj* que usa la mano derecha (person) || para la mano derecha (tools, etc.) || TECH dextrógiro, ra (dextrorotatory) || torcido de izquierda a derecha (rope) || con la mano derecha (boxing).

right hander [-hændə*] *n* persona *f* que usa la mano derecha || derechazo *m* (in boxing).

rightist [-ist] *adj* de derechas, derechista.

◆ *n* derechista *m* & *f*.

reghtly [-li] *adv* como es debido, debidamente, correctamente (correctly) || exactamente (exactly) || justamente, con justicia (fairly, justly) || con derecho, con razón (reasonably) || prudentemente, cuerdamente (wisely) || — *and rightly so* y con razón || *rightly or wrongly* con razón o sin ella.

right-minded [-maindid] *adj* honrado, da; recto, ta.

rightness [-nis] *n* exactitud *f*, precisión *f* (accuracy) || rectitud *f*, honradez *f* (honesty) || justicia *f* (fairness) || JUR lo bien fundado, legitimidad *f*.

right-thinking [-ˈθiŋkiŋ] *adj* honrado, da; recto, ta.

righto [ˈraitəu] *interj* FAM vale.

right wing [-ˈwiŋ] *n* derecha *f* (in politics) || SP extremo *m* derecha, ala *m* derecha.

right-wing [-ˈwiŋ] *adj* de derecha, derechista.

right winger [-ˈwiŋə*] *n* derechista *m* & *f* (in politics) || SP extremo *m* derecha, ala *m* derecha (in rugby).

rigid [ˈridʒid] *adj* rígido, da; *his arm went rigid with cold* su brazo se puso rígido con el frío || fijo, ja; *a rigid stare* una mirada fija || severo, ra; riguroso, sa; inflexible; *rigid discipline* disciplina rigurosa || riguroso, sa; rígido, da; *a rigid regard for rules* un concepto rígido del reglamento || preciso, sa; exacto, ta; riguroso, sa (precise) || AVIAT rígido, da.

rigidity [riˈdʒiditi] *n* rigidez *f* || fijeza *f* (of glance) || rigor *m*, severidad *f*, inflexibilidad *f* (of discipline, etc.).

rigidly [-li] *adv* rígidamente || rigurosamente, al pie de la letra.

rigmarole ['rigmərəul]; **rigamarole** ['rigəmə,rəul] *n* galimatías *m*, sarta *f* de disparates.

rigor ['rigə*] *n* MED escalofríos *m pl* (shivering fit) | rigidez *f* (stiffness) ‖ US ⟶ **rigour** ‖ MED *rigor mortis* rigidez cadavérica.

rigorist ['rigərist] *n* rigorista *m* & *f*.

rigorous ['rigərəs] *adj* riguroso, sa.

rigorousness [-nis] *n* rigurosidad *f*.

rigour ['rigə*] *n* rigor *m*, severidad *f* (strictness); *the rigour of the law* el rigor de la ley ‖ rigor *m*, austeridad *f* (austerity) ‖ MATH & PHIL exactitud *f* ‖ rigor *m* (of weather).

rile [rail]; **roil** [rɔil] *vt* FAM irritar, poner nervioso, sacar de quicio (to exasperate).

rill [ril] *n* riachuelo *m*.

rillet ['rilet] *n* arroyuelo *m*.

rim [rim] *n* llanta *f* (of a wheel) ‖ borde *m* (of cup, of vase) ‖ canto *m* (of a coin) ‖ montura *f* (of spectacles) ‖ ASTR cerco *m*.

rime [raim] *n* escarcha *f* (frost) ‖ ⟶ **rhyme.**

rimer [raimə*]; **rimester** ['raimstə*] *n* rimador, ra.

Rimini ['rimini] *pr n* GEOGR Rimini.

rimmed ['rimd] *adj* bordeado de, con un borde de (cup, vase) ‖ con una montura de (spectacles).

rimose; rimous [rai'məus] *adj* BOT agrietado, da.

rimy ['raimi] *adj* escarchado, da.

rind [raind] *n* cáscara *f* (of fruits) ‖ corteza *f* (of bacon) ‖ corteza *f*, costra *f* (of cheese).

rinderpest ['rindəpest] *n* VET peste *f* bovina.

ring [riŋ] *n* sonido *m* (sound) ‖ tañido *m*, repique *m*, campaneo *m* (of a large bell) ‖ toque *m* (act of sounding a bell) ‖ toque *m*, timbrazo *m*, toque *m* de timbre (of an electric bell) ‖ campanilleo *m*, toque *m* de la campanilla (of handbell) ‖ timbre *m* (of the alarm clock) ‖ llamada *f*, timbre *m* (of phone) ‖ sonido *m* metálico (metallic sound) ‖ resonancia *f* (resonance) ‖ tintineo *m*, retintín *m* (tinkle) ‖ timbre *m* (of the voice) ‖ tono *m*, entonación *f* (tone) ‖ cascabeleo *m* (of laughter) ‖ círculo *m* (circle) ‖ anillo *m*, sortija *f* (on finger) ‖ aro *m* (rim, ornament) ‖ arete *m* (earring) ‖ aro *m*, servilletero *m* (for napkins) ‖ llavero *m* (for keys) ‖ anillo *m* (of smoke, tree, fire) ‖ anilla *f* (for birds, for curtains) ‖ corte *m* circular (on tree trunks) ‖ anilla *f* (in gymnastics) ‖ pista *f* (circus) ‖ SP ring *m*, cuadrilátero *m* (in boxing) ‖ ruedo *m*, redondel *m* (in bullring) ‖ aro *m*, segmento *m* (of a piston) ‖ recinto *m*, cercado *m* para apuestas (racecourse) ‖ corro *m* (of children); *sitting in a ring* sentados en corro ‖ círculo *m*, grupo *m* (of people) ‖ camarilla *f* (coterie) ‖ banda *f* (of thieves, etc.) ‖ COMM cártel *m* ‖ red *f*, organización *f* (of spies) ‖ ASTR anillo *m* (of a planet) | halo *m* (of moon) | cerco *m* (of sun) ‖ BOT cerco *m* ‖ MAR arganeo *m* (of the anchor) ‖ CHEM cadena *f* ‖ — *a ring of bells* un juego de campanas ‖ *there is a ring at the door* llaman a la puerta, tocan el timbre ‖ SP *the ring* los corredores de apuestas (bookmakers), el boxeo (boxing), los boxeadores (boxers) ‖ *to give s.o. a ring* llamar por teléfono a alguien, dar un telefonazo a alguien, telefonear a alguien ‖ *to have rings round the eyes* tener ojeras, estar ojeroso ‖ FIG *to make* o *to run rings round s.o.* dar cien vueltas a alguien | *to throw one's hat in the ring* echarse al ruedo ‖ *wedding ring* alianza *f*, anillo *m* de boda ‖ *with a ring of defiance* en son de reto.

ring* [riŋ] *vt* tocar; *to ring a bell* tocar una campana ‖ hacer sonar (coins) ‖ FIG cantar (s.o.'s praises) ‖ rodear, circundar; *trees ring the lake* unos árboles rodean el lago ‖ anillar (bird, animal) ‖ acorralar (to ride round) ‖ AGR hacer un corte circular en la corteza de [un árbol] ‖ — *that rings a bell* eso me suena ‖ FIG *to ring the bell* dar en el blanco.

◆ *vi* sonar (to sound) ‖ repicar, tañer, sonar; *the bell rang* sonó la campana ‖ llamar [con una campana *or* con un timbre]; *s.o. rang at the door* alguien llamó a la puerta ‖ tocar la campanilla (the altar boy) | resonar; *the room rang with laughter* la sala resonó con risas ‖ tintinear (coins) ‖ zumbar, pitar; *the noise made my ears ring* el ruido me hizo zumbar los oídos ‖ llamar (por teléfono), telefonear; *I'll ring tomorrow* llamaré mañana ‖ llamar; *to ring for the lift* llamar el ascensor ‖ formar círculo *or* corro (to form a circle) ‖ moverse en círculo (to move in a circle) ‖ subir en espiral (smoke) ‖ — *to ring false* sonar a falso ‖ *to ring true* parecer verdad ‖ *to set all the bells ringing* echar las campanas al vuelo.

◆ *phr v* ***to ring back*** volver a llamar (telephone) ‖ ***to ring down*** bajar (the curtain) | *to ring the curtain down on* acabar con ‖ ***to ring in*** tocar las campanas por la llegada de, anunciar; *to ring in the New Year* anunciar el Año Nuevo ‖ ***to ring off*** colgar ‖ ***to ring out*** oírse; *a shot rang out* se oyó un tiro | tocar las campanas por la ida de ‖ ***to ring up*** llamar (por teléfono), telefonear (to telephone) | subir (cortain).

— OBSERV Este verbo es irregular en todos los sentidos referentes a sonido (pret ***rang***; pp ***rung***) y regular en las demás acepciones.

ring-a-ring-a-roses [-ə'riŋə'rəuziz] *n* corro *m*.

ring binder [-,baində*] *n* carpeta *f* de anillas.

ringbolt [-bəult] *n* TECH cáncamo *m*, armella *f*.

ringdove [-dʌv] *n* ZOOL paloma *f* torcaz.

ringed [-d] *adj* anillado, da (finger, birds) ‖ en anillo (circular) ‖ ASTR rodeado por un anillo (planet).

ringer [-ə*] *n* campanero, ra (person who rings a bell) ‖ timbre *m* (doorbell) ‖ badajo *m* (bell clapper) ‖ SP aro *m* que da en el blanco (quoits) ‖ FIG & FAM intruso, sa (illegal entry in a race) ‖ US FIG *he's a ringer for his brother* es la viva imagen de su hermano.

ring fence [-fens] *n* cercado *m* ‖ FIG barrera *f*.

ring finger [-,fiŋgə*] *n* anular *m*.

ringing [-iŋ] *adj* que suena (bell) ‖ resonante, sonoro, ra (cry) ‖ estruendoso, sa (laughter) ‖ clamoroso, sa (applause).

◆ *n* tañido *m* (of bells) ‖ toque *m* de timbre (of an electric bell) ‖ sonido *m* (sound) ‖ zumbido *m*, pitido *m* (in one's ears).

ringing tone [-təun] *n* señal *f* de llamada (telephone).

ringleader [-,li:də*] *n* cabecilla *m*.

ringlet [-lit] *n* arillo *m*, anillito *m* ‖ bucle *m*, rizo *m* (of hair).

ringmaster [-,ma:stə*] *n* maestro *m* de ceremonias.

ring road [-rəud] *n* carretera *f* de circunvalación.

ringside [-said] *n* cercanías *f pl* del cuadrilátero (boxing) ‖ FIG primera fila *f*.

◆ *adj* de primera fila.

ringworm [-wə:m] *n* MED tiña *f*.

rink [riŋk] *n* SP pista *f* de hielo (ice skating) | pista *f* de patinaje (roller skating) | terreno *m* (bowling) | equipo *m* de cuatro (bowling or curling team).

rinse [rins] *n* enjuague *m* (of dishes) ‖ aclarado *m* (of clothes, of hair) ‖ reflejo *m* (hair colouring).

rinse [rins] *vt* enjuagar (dishes) ‖ aclarar (clothes) ‖ dar reflejos a (to dye).

rinsing [-iŋ] *n* enjuague *m* (of dishes) ‖ aclarado *m* (of clothes, of hair) ‖ reflejo *m* (hair colouring).

◆ *pl* agua *f sing* de aclarado ‖ heces *f* (dregs).

Rio de Janeiro [,ri:əudədʒə'niərəu] *pr n* GEOGR Río de Janeiro.

riot ['raiət] *n* disturbio *m*; *race riots* disturbios raciales ‖ motín *m* (uprising) ‖ FIG derroche *m* (of colours) | exuberancia *f* (of plants) ‖ — FAM *he's a riot* es divertidísimo ‖ *Riot Act* ley *f* de orden público ‖ US *riot policeman* guardia *m* de asalto ‖ FIG *to be a riot* tener mucho éxito, tener un éxito clamoroso (a theatre play) ‖ FAM *to read the riot act to s.o.* echar un rapapolvo a alguien, leerle la cartilla a alguien ‖ *to run riot* desmandarse, desenfrenarse (people), proliferar, pulular (plants).

riot ['raiət] *vt* *to riot away* perder (time), derrochar, despilfarrar (money).

◆ *vi* alborotarse, amotinarse; *the people rioted in the streets* la gente se amotinó en las calles ‖ causar alboroto, armar jaleo (to make a row) ‖ FIG *to riot in* entregarse a.

rioter [-ə*] *n* alborotador, ra; amotinado, da; revoltoso, sa ‖ juerguista *m* & *f* (reveller).

rioting [-iŋ] *n* disturbios *m pl*.

riotous [-əs] *adj* alborotado, da; sedicioso, sa; amotinado, da (engaging in riots) ‖ ruidoso, sa; bullicioso, sa (noisy) ‖ desenfrenado, da; *riotous living* vida desenfrenada ‖ juerguista, jaranero, ra (revelling) ‖ FIG *a riotous success* un éxito clamoroso.

rip [rip] *n* rasgón *m*, desgarrón *m* (a tear) ‖ descosido *m* (split seam) ‖ aguas *f pl* revueltas (rough water) ‖ FAM tunante *m*, bribón *m* (child) | mal bicho *m*, mala persona *f* (rogue) | calavera *m* (rotter) ‖ matalón *m*, rocín *m* (horse).

rip [rip] *vt* rasgar, desgarrar (to tear); *I ripped my trousers* me rasgué el pantalón ‖ descoser (to tear a seam); *rip the hem* descosa el dobladillo ‖ serrar al hilo (in carpentry) ‖ quitar las tejas de, destejar (a roof) ‖ *to rip open* abrir de un tirón *or* desgarrando.

◆ *vi* rasgarse, desgarrarse (to tear) ‖ FAM volar (to move fast) ‖ FAM *let her rip!* ¡a todo gas!, ¡pisa el acelerador! (car).

◆ *phr v* ***to rip along*** ir a todo gas, ir a toda mecha (quickly) ‖ ***to rip away*** o ***off*** arrancar, quitar (to remove) ‖ FAM ***to rip into*** atacar ‖ ***to rip out*** arrancar (to tear out) | soltar (to utter) ‖ ***to rip up*** desgarrar (to tear to pieces) | romper (to break) | destrozar (to destroy) | deshacer, descoser (a seam) | abrir (to open up) | rajar, partir, hender (wood) | destripar, despanzurrar (s.o.) | reavivar (old grievances).

riparian [rai'pɛəriən] *adj* ribereño, ña.

rip cord ['ripkɔ:d] *n* cuerda *f* de desgarre (of a balloon) ‖ cuerda *f* de abertura (of a parachute).

ripe [raip] *adj* maduro, ra; *a ripe apple* una manzana madura; *a ripe plan* un proyecto maduro ‖ hecho, cha; *a ripe cheese* un queso hecho ‖ listo, ta; preparado, da (ready) ‖ oportuno, na (suitable); *when the time is ripe* cuando llegue el momento oportuno ‖ sensato, ta; maduro, ra; *a ripe judgement* un juicio sensato ‖ MED maduro, ra (abscess) ‖ encarnado, da; rojo, ja (lips) ‖ — *the ripe old age of ninety* la avanzada edad de noventa años ‖ *the time is ripe for action* ha llegado el momento de hacer algo.

ripen ['raipən] *vt/vi* madurar.

ripeness ['raipnis] *n* madurez *f*.

ripening ['raipniŋ] *adj* que madura.

◆ *n* madurez *f*, maduración *f*.

rip-off ['ripɔf] *n* FAM timo *m* (swindle) ‖ FAM *this place is a real rip-off* en este sitio le clavan a uno.

riposte; ripost [ri'pəust] *n* SP respuesta *f* (in fencing) || respuesta *f*, réplica *f* (a retort).

riposte; ripost [ri'pəust] *vi* SP parar atacando (in fencing) || replicar, responder (to retort).

ripper ['ripə*] *n* TECH sierra *f* de cortar al hilo *or* de hender (ripsaw) || destripador *m*; *Jack the Ripper* Jack el Destripador || FAM persona *f or* cosa *f* estupenda.

ripping ['ripiŋ] *adj* FAM formidable, estupendo, da.

ripple ['ripl] *n* onda *f*, rizo *m* (on water) || chapoteo *m* (sound of water, of waves) || murmullo *m* (of a river) || ondulación *f* (of hair) || murmullo *m* (of a conversation) || ondulación *f* dejada por la marea en la arena (ripple mark) || TECH desgranadora *f* (textiles) || *ripple mark* ondulación dejada por la marea en la arena.

ripple [ripl] *vt* ondular, rizar (water) || TECH desgranar (textiles).
◆ *vi* rizarse (to form waves) || murmurar (a stream) || ondular (corn, hair).

ripplet ['riplit] *n* onda *f or* ola *f* pequeña.

riprap ['ripræp] *n* US fondo *m* de roca (foundation) | escollera *f*, muro *m* de rocas (wall).

riprap ['ripræp] *vt* US echar cimientos de roca a.

rip-roaring ['rip'rɔːriŋ] *adj* FAM clamoroso, sa (success) | muy animado, da (party).

ripsaw ['ripsɔː] *n* TECH sierra *f* de cortar al hilo *or* de hender.

rise [raiz] *n* elevación *f*, altura *f* (hill) || cuesta *f*, pendiente *f*, subida *f* (slope) || subida *f*, ascensión *f* (of a hill, of a slope, etc.) || subida *f* (in social status) || ascenso *m* (in rank) || subida *f*, ascensión *f* (to power) || salida *f* (of sun, of moon) || desarrollo *m* (development); *the rise of industry* el desarrollo de la industria || crecimiento *m* (of town) || subida *f*, alza *f*, aumento *m* (price); *rise in prices* aumento de los precios || aumento *m*, elevación *f* (in rate) || aumento *m* (in value, in salary, etc.) || alza *f* (in the stock exchange) || PHYS aumento *m* (of pressure) || aumento *m*, elevación *f*, subida *f* (of temperature) || subida *f* (in a thermometer, etc.) || crecida *f* (in water level) || flujo *m* (of the tide) || aparición *f* (of an empire) || elevación *f* (in the voice) || THEATR subida *f* (of the curtain) || manantial *m*, fuente *f* (source of a river) || FIG fuente *f*, origen *m* (source) || — FIG *I haven't had a rise all day* no han picado en todo el día (in fishing) || *rise and fall* grandeza *f* y decadencia (of an empire), flujo y reflujo (of the sea) || *to ask for a rise* pedir un aumento de sueldo || *to be on the rise* estar subiendo || FIG *to get* o *to take a rise out of s.o.* tomarle el pelo a alguien || *to give rise to* provocar, causar, ocasionar, dar origen a || *to shoot a bird on the rise* disparar a un pájaro al levantar el vuelo.

rise* [raiz] *vt* espantar, hacer que levanten el vuelo (birds) || atraer, hacer picar al anzuelo (fish).
◆ *vi* levantarse; *he rose from the chair* se levantó de la silla; *I rise early in the morning* me levanto por la mañana temprano; *to rise from one's bed* levantarse de la cama; *a strong wind rose* se levantó un viento fuerte || levantarse, ponerse de pie; *the men all rose as she came in* todos los hombres se pusieron de pie cuando ella entró || levantarse, alzarse; *mountains rose in the distance* los montes se levantaban a lo lejos || elevarse; *the balloon rose in the air* el globo se elevó en el aire || subir, ascender (to slope up) || subir (ground) || levantar *or* alzar el vuelo (birds) || picar, morder (fish) || subir, aumentar (temperature) || mejorar de posición, subir, medrar; *to rise in society* mejorar de posición en la sociedad || ascender (in rank); *he rose to an important post* ascendió a un cargo importante || subir (to power) || subir, aumentar (prices, salary); *prices rose by ten per cent* los precios aumentaron en un diez por ciento || estar en alza (stock exchange) || aumentar (the pressure) || desarrollarse (to develop) || alzarse, levantarse; *her voice rose in anger* su voz se alzó con ira || crecer (river); *the Seine is rising fast* el Sena está creciendo rápidamente || subir (tide) || salir (sun, moon, stars) || THEATR subir (the curtain) || FIG crecer, aumentar (anger, hopes) | surgir, aparecer, presentarse (to appear) | surgir, armarse, haber (a quarrel) || nacer; *the river rises in the mountains* el río nace en las montañas || tener su origen, originarse (*from* en) (to originate) || levantarse, sublevarse (to revolt) || arreciar (to get stronger) || levantarse (to adjourn a meeting) || levantar la sesión (to end a meeting) || erizarse; *fear made his hair rise* el pelo se le erizó de miedo || CULIN leudarse (bread, cakes) || brotar (plants) || hincharse (to swell) || MED salir (blister, bruise, etc.) || — *tears rose to her eyes* se le subieron las lágrimas a los ojos || FIG *to rise above* sobreponerse a || *to rise early* madrugar, levantarse temprano || *to rise from nothing* haber empezado con nada, salir de la nada || REL *to rise from the dead* resucitar de entre los muertos || *to rise on a point of order* plantear *or* formular una cuestión de orden (during a meeting) || FIG *to rise to* ser capaz de hacer, poder hacer | *to rise to a challenge* aceptar un reto || *to rise to one's feet* ponerse de pie, levantarse || *to rise to the occasion* ponerse a la altura de las circunstancias || *to rise to the surface* salir a la superficie || *to rise up in arms* alzarse en armas.
— OBSERV Pret ***rose***; pp ***risen***.

risen ['rizn] *pp* → **rise.**

riser ['raizə*] *n* contrahuella *f* (of stair) || tubo *m* de subida (pipe) || columna *f* ascendente (of gas, of water, etc.) || — *early riser* madrugador, ra || *late riser* dormilón, ona.

risibility [,rizi'biliti] *n* risibilidad *f*.

risible ['rizibl] *adj* risible (causing laughter) || risueño, ña (inclined to laugh).

rising ['raiziŋ] *adj* naciente; *the rising sun* el sol naciente || que se levanta (wind) || ascendente (quantity) || creciente (number, tide, anger, importance) || que sube, que aumenta, creciente (price) || en cuesta, pendiente (sloping) || nuevo, va; joven; *the rising generation* la nueva generación || que tiene casi, que raya en; *rising forty five* que raya en los cuarenta y cinco años || prometedor, ra (promising); *rising man* hombre prometedor || *rising damp* humedad *f* || *rising vote* votación *f* por levantados y sentados.
◆ *n* salida *f*; *the rising of the sun* la salida del sol || REL resurrección *f*; *the rising of Jesús from the dead* la resurrección de Cristo de entre los muertos || levantamiento *m*, alzamiento *m* (rebellion) || JUR clausura *f* || levantamiento *m* (of a meeting) || THEATR subida *f* (curtain) || subida *f*, ascensión *f* (of a slope, etc.) || elevación *f* (of ground) || aumento *m*, subida *f* (of prices, of salary) || ascenso *m* (in rank) || subida *f* (of fever, of thermometer) || crecida *f* (of river) || nacimiento *m* (source of river) || *on the rising of the meeting* al levantarse la sesión.

risk [risk] *n* riesgo *m*, peligro *m* || riesgo *m* (in insurance) || — *at one's own risk* bajo su propia responsabilidad, por su cuenta y riesgo || *at the risk of* a *or* con riesgo de || *at the risk of one's life* con peligro de su vida || *at your own risk* por su cuenta y riesgo || *to run the risk of* correr el riesgo de || *to take risks* arriesgarse.

risk [risk] *vt* arriesgar; *to risk one's life* arriesgar la vida || exponerse a; *to risk a defeat* exponerse a una derrota || arriesgarse a, correr el riesgo de; *you can't risk doing it* no puede arriesgarse a hacerlo; *he risked breaking his arm* corrió el riesgo de romperse el brazo || — FIG *to risk everything on one throw* jugarse el todo por el todo || FAM *to risk one's neck* jugarse el tipo.

riskiness [-inis] *n* riesgo *m*, peligro *m*, lo arriesgado.

risk-taking [-teikiŋ] *n* asunción *f* de riesgos || *our success is based on risk-taking* si nos va bien es porque nos arriesgamos.

risky [-i] *adj* arriesgado, da; peligroso, sa; aventurado, da.

risorius [ri'sɔriəs] *n* risorio *m* (muscle).
— OBSERV El plural de la palabra inglesa es *risorii*.

risotto [ri'zɔtəu] *n* CULIN risotto *m*.

risqué ['riskei] *adj* escabroso, sa; de color subido, subido de color; *a risqué joke* un chiste de color subido.

rissole ['risəul] *n* CULIN empanadilla *f* rellena.

rite [rait] *n* rito *m* || — *the Rite of Spring* la Consagración de la Primavera (work by Stravinsky) || REL *the Roman Rite* el rito romano.

ritornello [ritɔː'neləu] *n* MUS ritornelo *m*, retornelo *m*.
— OBSERV El plural de *ritornello* es *ritornelli*.

ritual ['ritjuəl] *adj* ritual; *ritual dances* danzas rituales.
◆ *n* ritual *m*, ceremonial *m* (rites) || ritual *m* (book).

ritualism [-izəm] *n* ritualismo *m* || ritualidad *f*.

ritualist ['ritjuəlist] *n* ritualista *m* & *f*.

ritualistic [,ritjuə'listik] *adj* ritualista.

ritzy ['ritsi] *adj* US lujoso, sa.

rival ['raivəl] *n* rival *m* & *f*, competidor, ra.
◆ *adj* rival, competidor, ra.

rival ['raivəl] *vt* competir con, rivalizar con (to be in competition with); *her beauty rivalled that of the queen* su belleza competía con la de la reina || poder rivalizar con (to equal).
◆ *vi* rivalizar, competir (*with* con).

rivalize ['raivəlaiz] *vi* rivalizar.

rivalry ['raivəlri] *n* rivalidad *f*, competencia *f*.

rive* [raiv] *vt* rajar, hender, partir || *to rive sth. from s.o.* arrancar algo a alguien.
◆ *vi* rajarse, henderse.
— OBSERV Pret ***rived***; pp ***riven, rived***.

riven ['rivən] *pp* → **rive.**

river ['rivə*] *n* río *m* || FIG río *m* || — *down the river* río abajo || FIG *to be up the river* estar en chirona, estar en la cárcel | *to sell s.o. down the river* traicionar a alguien || *up the river* río arriba.
◆ *adj* de río, del río; *river fish* pez de río; *river diversion* desviación del río || fluvial; *river harbour* puerto fluvial.
— OBSERV La palabra *river* precede el nombre en Gran Bretaña: *the River Thames* y lo sigue en los Estados Unidos: *the Hudson River*.

riverain ['rivərein] *adj/n* ribereño, ña.

riverbank ['rivə'bæŋk] *n* orilla *f*, ribera *f*.

river basin ['rivə,beisn] *n* cuenca *f* de río.

riverbed ['rivə'bed] *n* lecho *m* del río, cauce *m* del río.

riverhead ['rivə,hed] *n* fuente *f or* nacimiento *m* de un río.

river horse ['rivə,hɔːs] *n* hipopótamo *m* (animal).

riverine ['rivərain] *adj* ribereño, ña (situated or living by a river) || fluvial (relating to a river).

river lamprey ['rivə'læmpri] *n* ZOOL lampreílla *f*, lamprehuela *f*.

riverman ['rivəmən] *n* barquero *m*.
— OBSERV El plural de la palabra inglesa es *rivermen*.

River Plate ['rivə,pleit] *pr n* GEOGR Río *m* de la Plata.

riverside ['rivəsaid] *n* ribera *f*, orilla *f*.
◆ *adj* ribereño, ña.

rivet ['rivit] *n* TECH remache *m*, roblón *m*; *flat-head rivet* roblón de cabeza plana.

rivet ['rivit] *vt* TECH remachar, roblonar || FIG captar (the attention) | sellar, cimentar (a friendship) | fijar (one's eyes).

riveter [-ə*] *n* remachador *m* (person) || remachadora *f* (machine).

riveting; rivetting [-iŋ] *n* remachado *m*, remache *m* (operation) || *riveting hammer* martillo *m* de remachar, remachadora *f*.

Riviera [,rivi'ɛərə] *n* Riviera *f* (in Italy) || Costa *f* Azul (in France).

rivière [rivi'ɛə*] *n* collar *m* de brillantes.

rivulet ['rivjulit] *n* arroyo *m*.

rix-dollar ['riks'dɔlə*] *n* rixdal *m*.

Riyadh ['riːæd] *pr n* GEOGR Riad.

roach [rəutʃ] *n* ZOOL cucaracha *f* (cockroach) | gobio *m* (European freshwater fish) || MAR borde *m* curvo de la parte inferior de la vela.

road [rəud] *n* carretera *f*; *the road to London* la carretera de Londres || calle *f* (in a town) || calzada *f* (roadway) || camino *m* (way) || FIG camino *m*, vías *f pl*; *the road to success* el camino de la gloria; *he's well on the road to recovery* está en vías de recuperación || US FAM vía *f* férrea (track) | ferrocarril *m* (railway) || — *«A» road* carretera nacional *or* general || *arterial* o *trunk road* carretera nacional || *«B» road* carretera secundaria *or* comarcal || *country road* camino vecinal || *main road* carretera general (highway), calle mayor (high street) || THEATR *on the road* de gira || *road accidents* accidentes *m* de tráfico || US *road agent* bandolero *m*, salteador *m* de caminos || *road narrows* estrechamiento *m* de carretera (traffic sign) || *road network* red *f* de carreteras || *road safety* seguridad *f* en carretera || *road tax* impuesto *m* de circulación || *road transport* transporte *m* por carretera || *road up* obras *f pl* || FIG *to be on the right road* ir por buen camino | *to be on the road* estar de gira (actors), estar de viaje (salesman) || *to have road sense* saber circular (driver, pedestrian) || FIG & FAM *to hit the road* largarse, irse || AUT *to hold the road* agarrarse, tener buena adherencia *or* estabilidad.
◆ *pl* rada *f sing* fondeadero *m sing* (roadsted).

road atlas [-'ætləs] *n* mapas *m pl* de carreteras, atlas *m* de carreteras.

roadbed [-bed] *n* US infraestructura *f* (foundation of a road) | firme *m* (surface of a road) | terraplén *m* (of a railway).

roadblock [-blɔk] *n* MIL barricada *f*.

road hog [-hɔg] *n* conductor *m* imprudente.

roadhouse [-haus] *n* parador *m*, albergue *m* de carretera (inn) || US sala *f* de fiestas en las afueras de una ciudad.

roadie ['rəudi] *n* FAM pipa *m* & *f*.

road labourer [-'leibərə*] *n* peón *m* caminero.

road making [-'meikiŋ] *n* construcción *f* de carreteras.

roadman [-mən]; **roadmender** [-,mendə*] *n* peón *m* caminero.
— OBSERV El plural de *roadman* es *roadmen*.

road map [-mæp] *n* mapa *m* de carreteras.

road metal [-,metl] *n* grava *f*.

road race [-reis] *n* carrera *f* en carretera.

road roller [-'rəulə*] *n* apisonadora *f*.

road show [-ʃəu] *n* espectáculo *m* callejero.

roadside [-said] *n* borde *m* de la carretera.
◆ *adj* situado al borde de la carretera || *roadside hotel* albergue *m* de carretera.

road sign [-sain] *n* señal *f* de tráfico.

roadstead [-sted] *n* fondeadero *m*, rada *f*.

roadster [-stə*] *n* dos plazas *m inv* (car).

road sweeper [-,swiːpə*] *n* barrendero *m*.

road trial [-,traiəl] *n* prueba *f or* carrera *f* en carretera.

roadway [-wei] *n* calzada *f* (of a road) || tablero *m* (of a bridge).

roadworks [-wəːks] *pl n* obras *f pl* de carretera.

roadworthy [-wəːði] *adj* en buen estado (vehicle).

roam [rəum] *n* paseo *m* (ramble); *I went for a roam in the forest* di un paseo por el bosque || vagabundeo *m* (wandering).

roam [rəum] *vt* rondar, vagar por || *to roam the seas* surcar los mares.
◆ *vi* vagar, errar.

roamer [-ə*] *n* azotacalles *m inv* (loafer) || vagabundo *m*.

roaming [-iŋ] *n* vagabundeo *m* || paseos *m pl*.

roan [rəun] *n* caballo *m* ruano (horse) || marrón *m* rojizo (colour) || badana *f* (in bookbinding).
◆ *adj* ruano, na (horse).

roar [rɔʁ*] *n* rugido *m* (of lion); *the lion let out a roar* el león lanzó un rugido || mugido *m* (of cow) || bramido *m* (of bull) || estruendo *m* (noise) || fragor *m* (of thunder) || bramido *m* (of wind, sea) || zumbido *m* (of an engine) || rugido *m*, berrido *m*, vociferaciones *f pl* (of a man) || clamor *m* (of crowd) || *roars of laughter* carcajadas *f*.

roar [rɔː*] *vt* vociferar (an order) || berrear (a song) || *to roar s.o. down* callar a alguien a gritos.
◆ *vi* rugir (lion) || mugir (cow) || bramar (bull) || vociferar, berrear (to shout) || bramar (sea, wind) || zumbar (an engine) || retumbar (to resound) || respirar trabajosamente, padecer huélfago (horses) || — *the cars roared by* los coches pasaban zumbando || *to road with anger* rugir de cólera || *to roar with laughter* reírse a carcajadas || *to roar with pain* rugir de dolor.

roaring [-riŋ] *adj* rugiente (lion) || bramante (bull) || vociferante (people) || FAM clamoroso, sa; *roaring success* éxito clamoroso | formidable, estupendo, da; *a roaring trade* negocios formidables || — FIG *the roaring twenties* los felices años veinte | *we had a roaring night* pasamos una noche estupenda.
◆ *n* ⟶ **roar.**

roast [rəust] *adj* asado, da; *roast chicken* pollo asado || tostado, da; torrefacto, ta (coffee) || FIG asado, da; achicharrado, da (very hot) || *roast beef* rosbif *m*, carne de vaca asada.
◆ *n* asado *m* || US barbacoa *f* (barbecue).

roast [rəust] *vt* asar (meat) || tostar, torrefactar (coffee) || FIG achicharrar, asar; *the sun was roasting us* el sol nos achicharraba || TECH tostar, calcinar (minerals) || FAM meterse con, burlarse de (to banter) || US FAM poner como los trapos a, desollar vivo a, vapulear a (to criticize) || — FIG *to roast o.s.* asarse, achicharrarse | *to roast o.s. before a fire* tostarse al fuego.
◆ *vi* asarse (meat) || tostarse, torrefactarse (coffee) || FIG achicharrarse, asarse (to feel hot).

roasted [-id] *adj* tostado, da; torrefacto, ta (coffee).

roaster [-ə*] *n* animal *m* para asar (animal) || pollo *m* para asar (chicken) || asador *m* (oven) || TECH horno *m* de calcinación (for minerals) || torrefactor *m*, tostador *m* de café (for coffee).

roasting [-iŋ] *adj* achicharrante, abrasador, ra (fire).
◆ *n* asado *m* (of meat) || torrefacción *f*, tostado *m* (of coffee) || TECH calcinación *f* (of minerals) || FAM burla *f*, tomadura *f* de pelo (mockery) || US FAM rapapolvo *m*, sermón *m* (ticking off); *he gave me a roasting* me echó un rapapolvo | crítica *f*, vapuleo *m* (slander) || *roasting jack*, *roasting spit* asador *m* || CULIN *roasting tin* fuente *f* metálica para el horno.

rob [rɔb] *vt* robar (to steal); *to rob a thousand pesetas* robar mil pesetas; *in this shop they rob you* en esta tienda te roban; *he robbed me of my handbag* me robó el bolso || asaltar, atracar; *to rob a bank* asaltar un banco || FIG quitar; *fear robbed him of speech* el miedo le quitó el habla || FIG *to rob Peter to pay Paul* desnudar un santo para vestir a otro.
◆ *vi* robar.

robalo [rəu'bɑːləu] *n* róbalo *m*, robalo *m* (fish).
— OBSERV El plural de la palabra inglesa es *robalos* o *robalo*.

roband ['rəubənd] *n* MAR envergue *m*.

robber ['rɔbə*] *n* ladrón, ona (thief) || atracador, ra (of a bank) || salteador *m* (highwayman) || bandido *m* (brigand) || *robber baron* señor *m* feudal que vivía del robo (feudal noble), capitalista enriquecido por la explotación (capitalist).

robbery ['rɔbəri] *n* robo *m*; *to commit a robbery* cometer un robo; *armed robbery* robo a mano armada || *highway robbery* atraco *m*, asalto *m*.

robe [rəub] *n* toga *f*; *a judge's robe* la toga de un juez || bata *f* (dressing gown) || traje *m* (dress, costume) || traje *m* de noche (evening gown) || hábito *m* (of a monk) || sotana *f* (of a priest) || albornoz *m* (after bathing) || mantillas *f pl* (in the baptism) || US manta *f* de viaje (rug) || *gentlemen of the robe* togados *m*.

robe [rəub] *vt* vestir.
◆ *vi* vestirse.

robin ['rɔbin] *n* ZOOL petirrojo *m* (bird) || *Robin Hood* Robín *m* de los Bosques.

robinia [rə'biniə] *n* BOT robinia *f*.

robot ['rəubɔt] *n* robot *m*, autómata *m*.

robotics [rəu'bɔtiks] *n* INFORM robótica *f*.

robust [rəu'bʌst] *adj* robusto, ta; vigoroso, sa; fuerte (person) || duro, ra; *a robust job* un trabajo duro || resistente (plants).

robustness [rəu'bʌstnis] *n* robustez *f*, fuerza *f*, vigor *m*.

rochet [rɔtʃit] *n* REL roquete *m*.

rock [rɔk] *n* GEOL roca *f*; *igneous rock* roca ígnea || GEOGR roca *f*, peña *f* || MAR escollo *m* (reef) || FIG base *f* (foundation) | escollo *m* (obstacle) || US piedra *f* (stone) || POP diamante *m* (diamond) || pirulí *m* (sweet) || balanceo *m* (swaying movement) || cuneo *m*, mecedura *f* (of a cradle) || — FIG & FAM *a business on the rocks* un negocio que va a la ruina, un negocio en bancarrota || *bare rock* roca viva || FIG *built on rock* sólido, da || FAM *on the rocks* con cubitos de hielo || REL *Rock of Ages* Jesucristo *m* || *the Rock of Gibraltar* el Peñón de Gibraltar || FAM *to be on the rocks* no tener un céntimo, estar sin blanca, no tener una perra (penniless), ir a la ruina (to go to ruin) || *to give the child a rock* mecer *or* acunar al niño.
◆ *adj* rupestre; *rock drawings* pinturas rupestres || rocoso, sa; *rock face* vertiente rocosa || de roca; *rock water* agua de roca || de rocas; *rock garden* jardín de rocas; *rock fall* corrimiento de rocas.

rock [rɔk] *vt* mecer; *to rock a baby's cradle* mecer la cuna de un niño || acunar, mecer; *to rock a baby to sleep* acunar a un niño para que se duerma || balancear, mover (to move) || zarandear (a ship) || sacudir, hacer temblar (to shake) || mover, dar a (a lever) || MIN lavar || FIG mecer.
◆ *vi* mecerse, balancearse; *stop rocking in that chair* deja de mecerte en la silla || temblar, vibrar (to vibrate); *the earthquake made the*

whole house rock el terremoto hizo que toda la casa vibrase || sacudirse (to shake violently) || FAM *to rock with laughter* partirse de risa, desternillarse de risa.

rock and roll [-ənd'rəul] *n* MUS «rock and roll» *m*.

rock bottom [-'bɔtəm] *n* fondo *m* rocoso (of the sea) || FIG fondo *m*.

rock-bottom [-'bɔtəm] *adj* mínimo, ma; bajísimo, ma; *rock-bottom prices* precios mínimos || FIG *to hit rock-bottom* tocar fondo.

rockbound [-baund] *adj* rocoso, sa.

rock candy [-,kændi] *n* azúcar *m* candi.

rock-climber [-'klaimə*] *n* escalador *m* de rocas.

rock-climbing [-'klaimiŋ] *n* escalada *f*.

rock crystal [-,kristl] *n* MIN cristal *m* de roca.

rock dove [-dʌv] *n* paloma *f* zorita, paloma *f* zurita (bird).

rock drill [-drill] *n* perforadora *f*.

rocker ['rɔkə*] *n* arco *m* (leg of rocking chair or cradle) || mecedora *f* (rocking chair) || MIN criba *f* || AUT balancín *m* || US SP patín *m* de cuchilla curva || — FAM *to go off one's rocker* perder la chaveta | *Michael is off his rocker* Miguel está mal del coco *or* está chalado.

rocker arm [-rɑːm] *n* AUT balancín *m*.

rockery [-ri] *n* jardín *m* de rocas.

rocket ['rɔkit] *n* cohete *m* (projectile); *space rocket* cohete espacial || BOT jaramago *m*, oruga *f* (plant) || FAM bronca *f*, rapapolvo *m* (reprimand) || — *rocket bomb* proyectil teledirigido || *rocket launcher* lanzacohetes *m inv* || *rocket ship* nave *f* espacial.

rocket ['rɔkit] *vi* subir vertiginosamente; *prices rocketed* los precios subieron vertiginosamente || levantar el vuelo (birds) || — *he rocketed into the room* entró como un cohete en la habitación || *he rocketed to stardom* tuvo una ascensión vertiginosa.

rocketry [-ri] *n* estudio *m* y uso *m* de los cohetes.

rockfish ['rɔkfiʃ] *n* rescaza *f*, escorpina *f* (fish).

rock-hard ['rɔkhɑːd] *adj* duro, ra como una piedra.

Rockies ['rɔkiz] *pl n* GEOGR Montañas Rocosas *f*.

rocking ['rɔkiŋ] *adj* oscilante (oscillating) || basculante (tilting, tipping) || — *rocking chair* mecedora *f* || *rocking horse* caballito *m* de balancín || *rocking shaft* eje *m* de balancín.

rock music [-'mjuːzik] *n* música *f* rock.

rock'n'roll [-ən'rəul] *n* MUS «rock and roll» *m*.

rock oil [-ɔil] *n* petróleo *m*.

rock pigeon ['rɔk,pidʒin] *n* paloma *f* zorita *or* zurita (bird).

rock-ribbed ['rɔk'ribd] *adj* rocoso, sa.

rockrose ['rɔk'rəuz] *n* BOT jara *f*.

rock salt ['rɔk'sɔːlt] *n* sal *f* gema.

rockshaft ['rɔk'ʃɑːft] *n* eje *m* de balancín.

rock wool ['rɔk'wul] *n* lana *f* mineral.

rocky ['rɔki] *adj* rocoso, sa (full of or made of rocks) || duro como una piedra (hard as a rock) || FAM bamboleante (shaky) | poco firme, débil (government).

Rocky Mountains [-'mauntinz] *pl n* GEOGR Montañas *f* Rocosas.

rococo [rəu'kəukəu] *n* rococó *m*.
◆ *adj* rococó.

rod [rɔd] *n* barra *f* (bar, pole) || jalón *m* (topography) || caña *f* (for fishing) || AUT biela *f* || cetro *m* (of a king) || vara *f*, bastón *m* de mando (symbol of authority) || varilla *f* (of fasces) || varilla *f*, barra *f* (for curtains) || medida *f* de longitud equivalente a 5, 029 m (measure) || vara *f* de medir (measuring stick) || ANAT & BIOL bastoncillo *m* || US FAM pistolón *m* (gun) || — FIG *spare the rod and spoil the child* quien bien te quiere te hará llorar || *the rod* castigo *m* corporal, varas *f pl*, azotes *m pl*, disciplinas *f pl* || FAM *to make a rod for one's own back* hacer algo contraproducente | *to rule s.o. with a rod of iron* mandar a alguien a la baqueta.

rode [rəud] *pret* → **ride.**

rodent ['rəudənt] *n* ZOOL roedor *m*.
◆ *adj* roedor, ra.

rodeo [rəu'deiəu] *n* US rodeo *m*.

rodomontade [,rɔdəmɔn'teid] *n* fanfarronada *f*.
◆ *adj* fanfarrón, ona; jactancioso, sa (bragging).

roe [rəu] *n* ZOOL hueva *f* (fish eggs) | freza *f* (eggs of shellfish) | corzo, za (deer).

roebuck ['rəubʌk] *n* ZOOL corzo *m*.

roe deer ['rəudiə*] *n* ZOOL corzo, za.

roentgen; röntgen ['rɔntjən] *n* PHYS Roentgen *m* || *Roentgen rays* rayos *m* X.

roentgenogram ['rɔntjənəgræm] *n* PHYS radiografía *f*.

roentgenotherapy [,rɔntgənə'θerəpi] *n* roentgenoterapia *f*.

rogation [rəu'geiʃən] *n* REL rogativa *f*.

rogatory ['rɔgətəri] *adj* US JUR rogatorio, ria; *rogatory commission* comisión rogatoria.

Roger ['rɔdʒə*] *pr n* Rogelio *m*, Roger *m* || — RAD *Roger!* ¡recibido! || *the Jolly Roger* el pabellón negro (of pirates).

rogue [rəug] *n* granuja *m*, pícaro *m* (crook) || pillo, lla (mischievous person or child) || animal *m* solitario y bravo || elefante *m* solitario (elephant) || *rogue's gallery* registro *m* central de delincuentes.

roguery [-əri] *n* granujada *f*, picardía *f* (of a person) || pillería *f*, travesura *f*, diablura *f* (of a child).

roguish [-iʃ] *adj* de granuja, picaresco, ca (relating to a rogue) || pillo, lla; travieso, sa (mischievous) || picaruelo, la (glance, smile).

roguishness [-iʃnis] *n* tunantería *f*, picardía *f* || travesura *f*.

roil [rɔil] *vt* → **rile.**

roily [-i] *adj* US turbio, bia.

roister ['rɔistə*] *vi* andar de jarana, estar de juerga.

roisterer [-rə*] *n* jaranero, ra; juerguista *m* & *f*.

role; rôle [rəul] *n* THEATR & CINEM papel *m*; *leading role* papel principal; *supporting role* papel secundario || FIG papel *m*, función *f*; *the role of concrete in modern building* el papel del hormigón en la arquitectura moderna || *role model* modelo *m* a imitar || *role playing* juego *m* de roles || *to play* o *to take a role* hacer un papel, desempeñar un papel.

roll [rəul] *n* rollo *m* (of paper) || carrete *m*, rollo *m* (of camera film) || rollo *m*, bobina *f* (of cinema film) || bucle *m* (of hair) || rosca *f*, michelín *m* (of fat) || panecillo *m*, bollo *m* (piece of baked dough) || rollo *m* de mantequilla (of butter) || rollo *m* (of tobacco) || pieza *f* (of cloth) || rollo *m* de pergamino (scroll) || nómina *f* (list of names) || lista *f* (list of things) || registro *m*, estado *m* (register) || relación *f* (record) || censo *m*, lista *f*; *electoral roll* censo electoral || catálogo *m* (catalogue) || PRINT rodillo *m* (tool) || ARCH junquillo *m* (curved moulding) | voluta *f* (of an ionic capital) || MAR oleaje *m* (of the sea) | balanceo *m* (of a ship) | rol *m* (list) || balanceo *m* (a swaying movement) || contoneo *m* (gait) || AVIAT balanceo *m* | tonel *m* (aerobatics) || redoble *m* (of a drum) || fragor *m*, retumbo *m* (of thunder) || gorjeo *m* (trill) || FIG ritmo *m*, cadencia *f* (of a sentence) || TECH rodillo *m* (of a steel mill) | maza *f* (of a drop hammer) | pisón *m* (for roads) || US FAM fajo *m* (of paper money); *a big roll of bills* un gran fajo de billetes || — MAR & AVIAT *angle of roll* ángulo *m* de balanceo || CULIN *French roll* panecillo *m* || *roll collar* cuello vuelto || *roll shutter* persiana *f* enrollable || CULIN *Swiss roll* brazo *m* de gitano || *the roll of honour* la lista de los caídos por la patria || *to call the roll* pasar lista.
◆ *pl* escalafón *m sing* de abogados (solicitors) || archivos *m* (archives) || TECH tren *m sing* laminador || — FIG *on the rolls of fame* en los anales de la gloria | *on the rolls of saints* entre los santos || MIL *to enter* o *to put a man on the rolls* incluir a un hombre en las listas || MIL & JUR *to strike s.o. off the rolls* excluir a alguien de la lista, tachar a uno de la lista.

roll [rəul] *vt* hacer rodar; *to roll a marble* hacer rodar una canica || liar (cigarette); *I roll my own cigarettes* yo lío mis cigarrillos || envolver, enrollar (to envelop) || mover (to move) || empujar (to push) || balancear (one's body) || arrastrar; *the waves rolled the bathers towards the shore* las olas arrastraban a los bañistas hacia la playa || allanar con un rodillo, pasar el rodillo pora (to level with a roller) || apisonar (with a steamroller) || CULIN pasar el rodillo por (dough) | dar vueltas, girar (roast) || laminar (metals) || tocar redobles en (drums) || PRINT entintar con el rodillo || US FAM desplumar (to rob s.o.) || — CULIN *to roll and fold* hojaldrar || *to roll one's eyes* poner los ojos en blanco (to show the white of one's eyes), hacer juegos de ojos (to rotate the eyes) || *to roll one's r's* pronunciar fuerte las erres.
◆ *vi* rodar; *the marble rolled across the floor* la canica rodó por el suelo; *the car rolled down the slope* el coche rodó cuesta abajo || revolcarse; *to roll in the mud* revolcarse en el barro || ondular (to have an ondulating surface) || retumbar (thunder) || tronar (cannons) || redoblar (the drum) || trinar (to trill) || MAR & AVIAT balancearse (a ship, a plane) || andar bamboleándose *or* balanceándose *or* contoneándose (to walk) || enrollarse (to curl up) || desenvolverse normalmente (to proceed smoothly) || TECH laminarse (metals).
◆ *phr v* ***to roll about*** vagar, ir de acá para allá (to wander) | llevar de acá para allá (to make s.o. go to and fro) || ***to roll along*** rodar por | andar; *the car was rolling along nicely* el coche andaba perfectamente | hacer rodar por; *they rolled the barrel along the corridor* hicieron rodar el barril por el pasillo || ***to roll away*** alejarse (to go away) | apartar (to push sth. away) || ***to roll back*** hacer retroceder (to cause to retreat) | poner en blanco (eyes) | US bajar, reducir (prices) || ***to roll by*** pasar; *as the months roll by* a medida que pasan los meses || ***to roll down*** caerse rodando por; *he rolled down the stairs* se cayó rodando por las escaleras | bajar sin motor (a car) | hacer rodar por; *they rolled the barrel down the stairs* hicieron rodar el barril por las escaleras | correr por; *tears were rolling down his face* las lágrimas le corrían por la cara || ***to roll in*** llegar en abundancia *or* a raudales (to arrive in large quantity) | FAM acostarse (to go to bed) | FAM *he is rolling in money* o *in plenty* nada en dinero *or* en la abundancia, apalea oro || ***to roll off*** caer rodando | PRINT tirar, imprimir || ***to roll on*** seguir rodando (to continue to roll) | pasar (time) | correr, seguir su curso (river) | extender con el rodillo (to spread on) || ***to roll out*** extender con el rodillo (pastry) | desenrollar (to unroll) || ***to roll over*** derribar (s.o.) | dar una vuelta (to turn over) || ***to roll up*** enrollar; *to roll up a newspaper, a map* enrollar un periódico, un mapa | envolver (to wrap) | remangar, arremangar (sleeves) | MIL arrollar | elevarse formando espirales (smoke) | en-

rollarse (blind, paper, etc.) | encogerse, enroscarse (a dying insect) | FAM presentarse, aparecer (to arrive) || — *to roll o.s. up in* envolverse en | *to roll o.s. up into a ball* acurrucarse, hacerse una bola *or* un ovillo.

rollaway bed [-əwei'bed] *n* US cama *f* plegable.

rollback [-bæk] *n* US reducción *f* de precios.

roll bar [-bɑː] *n* AUT barra *f* antivuelco.

roll call [-kɔːl] *n* lista *f*, el pasar lista || *vote by roll call* votación *f* nominal.

rolled [rəuld] *adj* enrollado, da (in a roll) || *rolled into one* todo en uno.

rolled-gold [-dgəuld] *adj* chapado, da en oro.

roller [rəulə*] *n* rodillo *m* (cylinder) || ruedecilla *f* (small wheel) || TECH rodillo *m* (for flattening metal) | apisonadora *f* (for road) || ola *f* larga, ola *f* grande (wave) || ZOOL pichón *m* volteador (pigeon) || rulo *m* (for the hair).

roller bearing [-,bɛəriŋ] *n* TECH cojinete *m* de rodillos.

roller blind [-blaind] *n* persiana *f* enrollable.

roller coaster [-'kəustə*] *n* US montaña *f* rusa.

roller skate [-skeit] *n* patín *m* de ruedas.

roller-skate [-skeit] *vi* patinar sobre ruedas.

roller skating [-,skeitiŋ] *n* patinaje *m* sobre ruedas.

roller towel [-,tauəl] *n* toalla *f* de rodillo.

rollick ['rɔlik] *vi* juguetear, retozar || divertirse.

rollicking [-iŋ] *adj* jovial, alegre (gay) || ajetreado, da (life) || animado, da (lively) || divertido, da (funny) || *to have a rollicking time* pasarlo bomba.

rolling ['rəuliŋ] *adj* que rueda, rodante (stone) || ondulado, da (ground) || MAR agitado, da; encrespado, da (sea) | que se balancea (ship) || oscilante.
◆ *n* rodamiento *m* || MAR balanceo *m* (of ship) || redoble *m* (of drum) || TECH apisonamiento *m* (of ground) | laminado *m* (of metal).

rolling mill [-mil] *n* TECH taller *m* de laminación (workshop) | tren *m* de laminación, laminador *m*, laminadora *f* (machine).

rolling pin [-pin] *n* rodillo *m*.

rolling stock [-stɔk] *n* material *m* móvil *or* rodante (railway).

rolling stone [-'stəun] *n* canto *m* rodado || — FIG *rolling stone gathers no moss* piedra movediza nunca moho la cobija, agua pasada no mueve molino | *to be a rolling stone* rodar por el mundo.

roll-neck ['rəulnek] *adj* de cuello cisne (jumper).

roll neck ['rəulnek] *n* jersey *m* de cuello cisne.

roll-on ['rəulɔn] *n* faja *f* elástica.

roll-on roll-off ship [-'rəulɔfʃip] *n* buque *m* de transbordo horizontal.

rolltop ['rəultɔp] *adj* de tapa corrediza (desk).

roly-poly ['rəuli'pəuli] *adj* rechoncho, cha; regordete, ta.
◆ *n* persona *f* rechoncha (person) || CULIN brazo *m* de gitano (pudding).

ROM *abbr of* *[Read Only Memory]* memoria ROM *or* de sólo lectura.

romaine lettuce [rəu'mein'letis] *n* US lechuga *f* romana.

Roman ['rəumən] *adj* romano, na (of Rome) || REL romano, na || PRINT romano, na (type) || aguileño, ña (nose).
◆ *n* romano, na (native of rome) || REL católico, ca || PRINT letra *f* romana.

Roman arch [-'ɑːtʃ] *n* ARCH arco *m* de medio punto.

Roman Catholic [-'kæθəlik] *adj/n* REL católico romano, católica romana.

Roman Catholic Church [-'kæθəlik'tʃəːtʃ] *n* REL Iglesia *f* Católica Romana.

Roman Catholicism [-kə'θɔlisizəm] *n* REL catolicismo *m*.

romance [rəu'mæns] *n* romance *m* (medieval literary form, language) || novela *f* romántica (love story) || libro *m* de aventuras *or* de caballería || amores *m pl*, idilio *m*, amor *m*, aventura *f* amorosa, amorío *m* (love affair); *she was the one romance in my life* fue el único amor de mi vida || lo romántico (romantic character) || lo poético, poesía *f* (poetic character) || encanto *m* (charm) || fantasía *f* (exaggeration, falsehood) || MUS romanza *f*.
◆ *adj* románico, ca; neolatino, na; romance (language).

romance [rəu'mæns] *vt* novelar; *a romanced biography* una biografía novelada.
◆ *vi* exagerar, fantasear (to exaggerate).

romancer [-ə*] *n* fantaseador, ra.

Romanesque [,rəumə'nesk] *n* ARCH románico *m*, arte *m* románico.
◆ *adj* románico, ca.

Romania [ru'meinjə] *pr n* GEOGR Rumania *f*.

Romanian [ru'meinjən] *adj/n* rumano, na.

Romanic [rəu'mænik] *adj* románico, ca; romance.
◆ *n* romance *m*.

Romanism ['rəumənizəm] *n* REL romanismo *m*.

Romanist ['rəumənist] *adj* REL romanista, católico, ca.

Romanize ['rəumənaiz] *vt* romanizar.

Roman numerals ['rəumən'njuːmərəlz] *pl n* números *m* romanos.

Romansh; Romansch [rəu'mænʃ] *n* retorromano *m*, rético *m*.

romantic [rəu'mæntik] *adj* romántico, ca; *a romantic novel* una novela romántica; *a romantic person* una persona romántica.
◆ *n* romántico, ca.

romanticism [rəu'mæntisizəm] *n* romanticismo *m*.

romanticize [rəu'mæntisaiz] *vt* hacer romántico.
◆ *vi* obrar de modo romántico || fantasear (to dream).

Romany ['rɔməni] *n* gitano, na (gipsy) || lengua *f* de los gitanos (gipsy language), caló *m* (in Spain).
◆ *adj* gitano, na.

Rome [rəum] *pr n* GEOGR Roma || — FIG *all roads lead to Rome* por todas partes se va a Roma, todos los caminos llevan a Roma | *Rome was not built in a day* no se ganó Zamora en una hora | *when in Rome do as the Romans do* cuando a Roma fueres, haz lo que vieres.

Romeo ['rəumiəu] *pr n* Romeo *m*.

Romish ['rəumiʃ] *adj* papista, católico, ca.

romp [rɔmp] *n* jugueteo *m*, retozo *m* (playing) || niño *m* travieso (child) || marimacho *m* (tomboy).

romp [rɔmp] *vi* juguetear, retozar || — FAM *to romp home* ganar con facilidad | *to romp through sth.* hacer algo con facilidad.

rompers [-əz] *pl n* pelele *m sing* (child's one-piece garment).

Romulus ['rɔjuləs] *pr n* MYTH Rómulo *m*.

rondeau ['rɔndəu] *n* letrilla *f* (poem).
— OBSERV El plural de la palabra inglesa es *rondeaux*.

rondel ['rɔndl] *n* POET rondel *m*.

rondo ['rɔndəu] *n* MUS rondó *m*.

Roneo ['rəuniəu] *n* multicopista *f*.

Roneo ['rəuniəu] *vt* reproducir con multicopista.

röntgen ['rɔntjən] *n* PHYS ⟶ **roentgen**.

rood [ruːd] *n* REL crucifijo *m* (crucifix) || cuarta parte *f* de un acre (measure) || — *rood loft* galería *f* encima de la reja de separación entre el coro y la nave || *rood screen* reja *f* que separa el coro de la nave.

roof [ruːf] *n* ARCH tejado *m* (of a building) || techo *m*; *the roof of a cave* el techo de una cueva; *thatched roof* techo de paja; *the roof of a car* el techo de un coche || capota *f* (of a convertible car) || cielo *m* (of mouth) || FIG techo *m*; *I have no roof to cover me* no tengo un techo donde cobijarme; *to live under the same roof* vivir bajo el mismo techo || bóveda *f* celeste (sky) || AVIAT altura *f* máxima, techo *m* || — *flat roof* azotea *f* || *roof light* luz *f* cenital *or* del techo (in cars) || *sliding* o *sun roof* techo corredizo || *tiled roof* tejado *m* || FIG *to have a roof over one's head* dormir bajo techo || FAM *to raise* o *to hit the roof* poner el grito en el cielo (with anger), armar un alboroto (with enthusiasm).

roof [ruːf] *vt* techar || FIG alojar, cobijar (s.o.) || *to be roofed with* tener tejado *or* techo de.

roofer [-ə*] *n* techador *m*.

roof garden [-gɑːdn] *n* jardín *m* en una azotea || US restaurante *m* en la azotea de un edificio (terrace restaurant).

roofing [-iŋ] *n* material *m* para techar || techumbre *f*, techado *m* (roof).

roofless [-lis] *adj* sin techo (house) || sin hogar (people).

rooftop ['ruːf,tɔp] *n* tejado *m*.

rooftree [-triː] *n* ARCH cumbrera *f*, parhilera *f*.

rook [ruk] *n* grajo *m* (bird) || FAM timador *m*, estafador *m* (swindler) | fullero *m* (in gambling) || torre *f* (in chess).

rook [ruk] *vt* FAM estafar, timar (to swindle).
◆ *vi* enrocar (in chess) || FAM hacer trampas (to cheat) | fullear (in gambling).

rookery [-əri] *n* colonia *f* de grajos (of rooks) || colonia *f* [de animales gregarios] (of gregarious animals) || FAM tugurio *m*.

rookie [-i] *n* MIL & FAM quinto *m*, recluta *m* || FAM novato *m* (novice).

room [ruːm] *n* habitación *f*, cuarto *m*; *hotel room* habitación de hotel; *single room* habitación individual || sala *f* (public room); *committee room* sala de comisiones; *conference room* sala de conferencias || sitio *m*; *is there room for me in your car?* ¿queda sitio para mí en su coche? || espacio *m*; *leave room at the beginning of this page* deja espacio al principio de esta página; *there was hardly any room to breathe* casi no había espacio para respirar || sala *f* (people) || — *room and board* cama y comida, pensión completa || *there is no room for doubt* no cabe duda || *there is room for improvement* podría mejorarse || *to make room for* hacer *or* dejar sitio *or* espacio.
◆ *pl* alojamiento *m sing* (accommodation) || piso *m sing* (flat); *bachelor's rooms* piso de soltero || *allocation of rooms* distribución *f* de las salas.

room [ruːm] *vi* alojarse; *where is he rooming?* ¿dónde se aloja? || compartir la habitación (*with* con).
◆ *vt* alojar.

roomer [-ə*] *n* US inquilino, na (tenant) | huésped, da (lodger).

roomful [-ful] *n* habitación *f* llena, cuarto *m* lleno (*of* de).

roominess [-inis] *n* dimensiones *f pl* espaciosas, amplitud *f*.

rooming house [-iŋ,haus] *n* US pensión *f*, casa *f* de huéspedes.

roommate [-eit] *n* compañero *m* de habitación, compañera *f* de habitación.

room service [-'sə:vis] *n* servicio *m* de habitaciones.

room temperature [-'tempritʃə*] *n* temperatura *f* ambiente.

roomy [-i] *adj* espacioso, sa; amplio, plia (place) || holgado, da (garment).

roost [ru:st] *n* varilla *f*, percha *f*, palo *m* (in a cage) || palo *m* (for domestic fowls) || gallinero *m* || — FAM *chickens and curses come home to roost* si escupes al cielo, en la cara te caerá | *to come home to roost* ser contraproducente, volverse en contra de uno | *to go to roost* irse a dormir | *to rule the roost* llevar la voz cantante, llevar la batuta, dirigir el cotarro.

roost [ru:st] *vi* posarse [para dormir] (birds) || FIG pasar la noche.

rooster [-ə*] *n* ZOOL gallo *m* (cock).

root [ru:t] *n* BOT raíz *f* (underground part of a plant) | tubérculo *m* (vegetable) || ANAT raíz *f* (of hair, of teeth) || FIG raíz *f*, origen *m* (origin, source) | fundamento *m*, base *f* (base) || MATH & GRAMM raíz *f*; *square root* raíz cuadrada || — FIG *to get to the root of* ir a la raíz de || *to pull up by the roots* extirpar, arrancar, cortar *or* arrancar de raíz || FIG *to put down one's roots in a country* radicarse *or* establecerse en un país || *to strike* o *to take root* echar raíces, arraigar, enraizar.

root [ru:t] *vt* FIG arraigar (to fix firmly); *a rooted idea* una idea arraigada || — *to root out, to root up* desarraigar, arrancar de raíz (a plant), extirpar, arrancar *or* cortar de raíz (to remove completely) || FAM *to root s.o. to the spot* paralizar *or* dejar inmovilizado a alguien.
◆ *vi* echar raíces (to grow roots) || FIG arraigar, echar raíces (to become firmly fixed) || hurgar con el hocico, hozar (swine) || hurgar (to search about) || US FAM *to root for* animar, alentar; *to root for one's team* animar a su equipo.

root beer [-'biə*] *n* cerveza *f* de raíces.

root cap [-kæp] *n* BOT pilorriza *f*, cofia *f*.

rooter [-ə*] *n* US FAM hincha *m*, partidario, ria.

root hair [-hεə*] *n* BOT pelos *m pl* absorbentes.

rootless ['ru:tlis] *adj* desarraigado, da.

rootlet ['ru:tlet] *n* BOT radícula *f*, raicilla *f*.

rootstalk ['ru:tstɔ:k] *n* BOT rizoma *m*.

rootstock ['ru:tstɔk] *n* BOT rizoma *m*.

rope [rəup] *n* cuerda *f*; *I slid down the rope* me deslicé por la cuerda || soga *f* (of hemp, of flax) || cable *m* (of wire) || tirador *m* (of a handbell) || sarta *f*, hilo *m* (of pearl) || ristra *f* (of garlic, of onions) || MAR maroma *f*, cabo *m* || lazo *m* (a lasso) || SP cordada *f* (of mountaineers); *first on the rope, head of the rope* primero *or* cabeza *or* jefe de cordada || — FIG *at the end of one's rope* en un aprieto (in a desperate situation) || *hangman's rope* dogal *m* || FIG *to give s.o. enough rope to hang himself* dar completa libertad a alguien con la esperanza de que vaya a enredarse | *to give s.o. plenty of rope* dar rienda suelta a alguien, dar completa libertad a alguien.
◆ *pl* cuerdas *f* (in boxing) || — FIG *to know the ropes* estar al tanto | *to learn the ropes* ponerse al tanto.

rope [rəup] *vt* amarrar, atar (to fasten) || coger con lazo (to lasso) || encordar (climbers) || MAR relingar (sails) || sujetar con las riendas (a horse) || — *to rope off* acordonar || FIG *to rope s.o. in* conseguir que alguien participe en algo.
◆ *vi* ahilarse (wine, beer) || *to rope up* encordarse (mountaineers).

ropedancer [-,dɑn:sə*] *n* funámbulo, la.

rope ladder [-'lædə*] *n* escala *f* de cuerda.

ropemaker [-,meikə*] *n* cordelero *m*.

ropewalk [-wɔ:k] *n* cordelería *f*.

ropewalker [-,wɔ:kə*] *n* funámbulo, la.

ropeway [-wei] *n* teleférico *m*.

ropiness [-inis] *n* viscosidad *f* (of beer).

ropy [-i] *adj* viscoso, sa (viscous) || fibroso, sa (stringy) || ahilado, da (wine, beer) || FAM malo, la (unsatisfactory).

Roquefort ['rɔkfɔ:*] *n* queso *m* de Roquefort (cheese).

rorqual ['rɔ:kwəl] *n* rorcual *m* (cetacean).

rosaceous [rə'zeiʃəs] *adj* BOT rosáceo, a.

rosarium [rəu'zεəriəm] *n* rosaleda *f*.

rosary ['rəuzəri] *n* rosaleda *f* (rose garden) || REL rosario *m*; *to say the rosary* rezar el rosario.

rose [rəuz] *n* BOT rosal *m* (plant) | rosa *f* (flower) || rosa *f* (emblem) || rosa *m*, color *m* de rosa (colour) || diamante *m* rosa, rosa *f* (diamond) || alcachofa *f* (sprinkler) || rosa *f* náutica, rosa *f* de los vientos || ARCH rosetón *m* (window) | roseta *f* (decoration) || MED roseta *f* || — FIG *every rose has its thorn* no hay rosa sin espinas | *life is not a bed of roses* la vida no es un camino de rosas || *Rose of Jericho* rosa de Jericó || *tea rose* rosa de té || *the Wars of the Roses* la guerra de las Dos Rosas || FIG *to be in a bed of roses* estar en un lecho de rosas.
◆ *adj* de rosa; *rose petals* pétalos de rosa; *rose perfume* perfume de rosa || rosa, rosado, da; color de rosa (colour).

rose [rəuz] *pret* → **rise.**

rosé [rəu'zei] *n* rosado *m*, clarete *m* (wine).

roseate ['rəuziit] *adj* róseo, a; rosado, da || FIG optimista.

rosebay ['rəuzbei] *n* BOT adelfa *f*.

rose bed ['rəuzbed] *n* rosaleda *f*.

rosebud ['rəuzbʌd] *n* BOT capullo *m* || FIG pimpollo *m*.

rosebush ['rəuzbuʃ] *n* BOT rosal *m*.

rose-coloured; US **rose-colored** ['rəuz,kʌləd] *adj* rosa, rosado, da (pink) || FIG optimista (optimistic) || FIG *to see everything through rose-coloured spectacles* o *rose-coloured glasses* verlo todo color de rosa.

rose garden ['rəuz,gɑ:dn] *n* rosaleda *f*.

rose hip ['rəuz'hip] *n* escaramujo *m*.

rose honey ['rəuz,hʌni] *n* rodomiel *m*.

rose mallow ['rəuz'mæləu] *n* US BOT malvarrosa *f*, malva *f* loca *or* real *or* rósea.

rosemary ['rəuzməri] *n* BOT romero *m*.

roseola [rəu'zi:ələ] *n* MED roséola *f*.

rose-red ['rəuz'red] *adj* (de) color de rosa.

rose tree ['rəuztri:] *n* rosal *m*.

rosette [rəu'zet] *n* escarapela *f* (of ribbons) || ARCH florón *m* (representation of the wild rose) | rosetón *m* (rose window) || BOT roseta *f*.

rose water ['rəuz,wɔ:tə*] *n* agua *f* de rosas.

rose window ['rəuz'windəu] *n* ARCH rosetón *m*.

rosewood ['rəuzwud] *n* BOT palisandro *m* | palo *m* de rosa.

rosily ['rəuzili] *adv* de color de rosa (with rose colour) || FIG alegremente (cheerfully).

rosin ['rɔzin] *n* colofonia *f*.

rosin ['rɔzin] *vt* frotar con colofonia.

rosiness ['rəuzinis] *n* color *m* de rosa (of flowers) || aspecto *m* prometedor (of future).

roster ['rəustə*] *n* lista *f*, rol *m* || *promotion roster* escalafón *m*.

rostral ['rɔstrəl] *adj* rostrado, da; rostral.

rostrate ['rɔstreit] *adj* rostrado, da; rostral.

rostrum ['rɔstrəm] *n* tribuna *f* (platform); *to go up to the rostrum* subir a la tribuna || ZOOL rostro *m*, pico *m* || MAR espolón *m*, rostro *m*.
— OBSERV El plural de *rostrum* es *rostrums* o *rostra*.

rosy ['rəuzi] *adj* sonrosado, da (complexion) || de color de rosa, rosado, da; rosa (rose-coloured) || FIG de color de rosa, prometedor, ra (future) | optimista (view, outlook).

rot [rɔt] *n* putrefacción *f* (action of rotting) || podredumbre *f* (rotten substance) || VET comalia *f* || FAM bobadas *f pl*, tonterías *f pl*, sandeces *f pl*, majaderías *f pl*; *don't talk rot!* ¡no digas tonterías! || FIG desmoralización *f* (of a team, of an army) | decadencia *f* (decline).
◆ *interj* ¡tonterías!, ¡sandeces!

rot [rɔt] *vt* pudrir, podrir; *rain rotted the wood* la lluvia pudrió la madera || descomponer (to decompose) || FAM tomar el pelo a (to tease) || enriar (hemp, flax).
◆ *vi* pudrirse, podrirse, descomponerse (to decay) || degenerar (to degenerate) || FAM bromear (to joke) | pudrirse || *to rot away* pudrirse, descomponerse.

rota ['rəutə] *n* lista *f*, rol *m* (list).

Rota ['rəutə] *pr n* REL Rota *f*.

Rotarian [rəu'tεəriən] *n* rotario, ria.

rotary ['rəutəri] *adj* rotatorio, ria; giratorio, ria; rotativo, va.
◆ *n* rotativa *f* (press) || US plaza *f* circular, glorieta *f* (roundabout, intersection) || *Rotary Club* Club *m* Rotario.

rotary press [-'pres] *n* PRINT rotativa *f*.

rotate [rəu'teit] *adj* BOT rotáceo, a.

rotate [rəu'teit] *vt* (hacer) girar, dar vueltas a (to cause to revolve) || AGR alternar (crops) || alternar (work).
◆ *vi* girar, dar vueltas (to revolve) || alternar; *the seasons rotate* las estaciones alternan || turnarse (in a job).

rotating [-iŋ] *adj* giratorio, ria || AGR alternativo, va (crops).

rotation [rəu'teiʃən] *n* giro *m*, rotación *f* (turning) || revolución *f* (turn) || turno *m*; *by* o *in rotation* por turno || AGR *rotation of crops* rotación de cultivos.

rotational [-əl] *adj* giratorio, ria (rotating).

rotative ['rəutətiv] *adj* rotarorio, ria; giratorio, ria; rotativo, va (which revolves) || rotativo, va (of rotation).

rotator [rəu'teitə*] *n* ANAT músculo *m* rotatorio || MAR hélice *f* (of a ship's log).
— OBSERV El plural de la palabra *rotator* en el sentido anatómico es *rotatores*.

rotatory ['rəutətəri] *adj* rotatorio, ria; giratorio, ria; rotativo, va (rotary) || alternativo, va (alternate).

rote [rəut] *n* rutina *f* || *by rote* de memoria (by heart), maquinalmente, por rutina.

rotgut ['rɔtgʌt] *n* FAM matarratas *m inv* (spirits).

rotifer ['rəutifə*] *n* ZOOL rotífero *m*.

rotogravure [,rəutəugrə'vjuə*] *n* rotograbado *m*.

rotor ['rəutə*] *n* TECH rotor *m*.

rotproof ['rɔt'pru:f] *adj* imputrescible.

rotten ['rɔtn] *adj* podrido, da (decayed) || estropeado, da; echado a perder (fruit) || cariado, da; picado, da (tooth) || carcomido, da (worm-eaten) || VET infectado de comalia (sheep) || desmenuzable, friable (rocks) || FIG corrompido, da (corrupt) || FAM malísimo, ma; pésimo, ma; infame; *rotten weather* tiempo infame | malo, la; *that was a rotten trick* fue una mala jugada || asqueroso, sa (dirty) || — FIG & FAM *I feel rotten today* hoy me encuentro fatal

| *to be rotten with money* estar podrido de dinero || *to smell rotten* oler a podrido || FAM *what rotten luck!* ¡qué suerte más negra!, ¡qué mala pata!

rottenness [-nis] *n* podredumbre *f*, putrefacción *f* || FIG corrupción *f*.

rotter ['rɔtə*] *n* FAM sinvergüenza *m* & *f*.

Rotterdam ['rɔtə'dæm] *pr n* GEOGR Rotterdam.

rotulian [rɔ'tju:liən] *adj* ANAT rotuliano, na; rotular.

rotund [rəu'tʌnd] *adj* corpulento, ta (person) || redondo, da (round) || FIG rimbombante, ampuloso, sa; grandilocuente (bombastic).

rotunda [-ə] *n* ARCH rotonda *f*.

rotundity [-iti] *n* grandilocuencia *f*, ampulosidad *f* (of bombastic speech) || rotundidad *f* (of language) || corpulencia *f* (corpulence) || redondez *f* (of a person's figure).

rouble ['ru:bl] *n* rublo *m* (Russian currency).

roué ['ru:ei] *n* libertino *m*.

rouge [ru:ʒ] *n* colorete *m*, arrebol *m* (cosmetic in powder) || lápiz *m* de labios (lipstick) || colcótar *m* (jewellers' rouge).

rouge [ru:ʒ] *vt* poner colorete a, pintar || *to rouge o.s.* ponerse colorete.

◆ *vi* ponerse colorete, pintarse.

rouge et noir ['ru:ʒein'wɑ:*] *n* treinta y cuarenta *m* (card game).

rough [rʌf] *adj* áspero, ra (surface, skin, etc.) || calloso, sa (hands) || tosco, ca; chapucero, ra (hastily or badly made) || accidentado, da; fragoso, sa; desigual (ground) || pedregoso, sa (path) || accidentado, da; desigual (road) || basto, ta; burdo, da (cloth) || áspero, ra (sound, touch, taste) || bronco, ca (voice) || desgreñado, da (hair) || inculto, ta; tosco, ca (person) || tosco, ca; grosero, ra (character, manner) || rudo, da; ordinario, ria; grosero, ra (language) || tosco, ca (style) || difícil, duro, ra (work) || duro, ra; brutal; *he was very rough with me* fue muy brutal conmigo || severo, ra; duro, ra (severe); *rough punishment* castigo severo || duro, ra; malo, la (life, journey, etc.); *they had a rough time of it* pasaron una temporada muy mala || tempestuoso, sa; borrascoso, sa (weather) || encrespado, da; alborotado, da; agitado, da (sea) || movido, da; agitado, da (sea crossing) || violento, ta; *children play rough games* los niños tienen juegos violentos || alborotador, ra (rowdy) || violento, ta (wind) || aspirado, da (in phonetics) || sumario, ria (justice) || preliminar (not elaborated) || aproximado, da (approximate); *this will give you a rough idea* esto le dará una idea aproximada || SP duro, ra (play) | TECH bruto, ta; en bruto (diamond) | sin desbastar (timber) || — *at a rough guess* o *estimate* haciendo un cálculo aproximado, a ojo de buen cubero || *it's rough on him!* ¡qué mala suerte tiene! || *rough draft* borrador *m* || *rough justice* justicia *f* sumaria || *rough notes* o *copy* borrador *m* || *rough sketch* esbozo *m*, boceto *m*, bosquejo *m* || *rough stuff* violencia *f* || *to be rough on s.o.* tratar brutalmente a alguien (to treat harshly), ser una mala suerte para alguien (to be bad luck) || *to give s.o. a rough time* hacer pasar a alguien un mal rato.

◆ *adv* duro; *to play rough* jugar duro || brutalmente || ásperamente || chapuceramente, toscamente (manual work) || — FAM *to cut up rough* ponerse hecho una fiera || *to sleep rough* dormir en el suelo (inside), dormir al raso (outside).

◆ *n* terreno *m* accidentado *or* desigual (uneven ground) || aspereza *f* (of a surface) || boceto *m* (sketch) || borrador *m* (first draft) || estado *m* bruto || estado *m* basto *or* burdo || ramplón *m* (of horseshoe) || FAM matón *m*, duro *m* (tough) || FIG lado *m* malo de las cosas || SP terreno *m* apenas cuidado (in golf) || — *in the rough* en bruto (in the crude state), en líneas generales (project, etc.), en la hierba alta (in golf) || FIG *to take the rough with the smooth* tomar la vida como es, estar a las duras y a las maduras.

rough [rʌf] *vt* poner ramplones a (a horseshoe) || desgreñar, despeluznar (the hair) || maltratar (to ill-treat) || — *to rough down* desbastar || *to rough in* bosquejar || *to rough it* vivir sin comodidades, pasar muchas dificultades || *to rough out* bosquejar (a map, a statue), esbozar (a plan) || *to rough up* erizar, poner de punta (hair, fur, etc.), pegarle una paliza a (a person).

roughage [-idʒ] *n* AGR forraje *m* duro (fodder) || alimento *m* poco digerible.

rough-and-ready [-ən'redi] *adj* tosco, ca (not well finished); *a rough-and-ready piece of work* un trabajo tosco || improvisado, da (makeshift) || tosco pero eficaz (crude, but efficient).

rough-and-tumble [-ən'tʌmbl] *adj* agitado, da; movido, da; *a rough-and-tumble life* una vida agitada || desordenado, da (fight).

◆ *n* pelea *f* (fight) || agitación *f* (of life).

rough breathing [-'bri:ðiŋ] *n* GRAMM aspiración *f*.

roughcast [-kɑ:st] *n* mezcla *f* gruesa, revoque *m* (for covering a wall) || modelo *m* tosco (rough model) || boceto *m*, esbozo *m* (sketch).

roughcast [-kɑ:st] *vt* revocar (wall) || esbozar, bosquejar (to sketch).

roughen [-ən] *vt* poner áspero *or* tosco.

◆ *vi* ponerse áspero *or* tosco || volverse calloso (hands) || volverse accidentado (a road) || encresparse (the sea).

roughhew [-'hju:] *vt* desbastar (to cut roughly into shape) || labrar toscamente (to make a rough model of).

roughhewn [-'hju:n] *adj* desbastado, da (wood) || toscamente labrado (statue) || FIG esbozado, da; bosquejado, da (sketched).

roughhouse [-haus] *n* jaleo *m*, trapatiesta *f*, trifulca *f* (row).

roughhouse [-haus] *vi* armar jaleo, armar una trapatiesta *or* una trifulca.

◆ *vt* zarandear.

roughly [-li] *adv* toscamente (manual work); *roughly made* toscamente hecho || ásperamente || brutalmente (brutally) || aproximadamente, más o menos (approximately) || *to treat s.o. roughly* maltratar a alguien.

roughneck [-nek] *n* US FAM duro *m*, matón *m* (tough) | palurdo *m*, rústico *m* (rustic).

roughness [-nis] *n* aspereza *f*, rugosidad *f* (of surface, of skin) || aspereza *f* (of taste, sound, touch) || callosidad *f* (of hands) || tosquedad *f* (crudeness) || desigualdad *f* (of the land, of a road) || brusquedad *f* (of character, of manner) || brutalidad *f* (of treatment) || severidad *f* (severity) || ordinariez *f*, grosería *f* (of language) || agitación *f*, encrespamiento *m* (of the sea) || violencia *f* (of wind) || inclemencia *f* (of weather) || incultura *f* (lack of culture) || falta *f* de educación (impoliteness) || chapucería *f* (of sth. badly made) || SP dureza *f* (of playing).

roughrider [-ˌraidə*] *n* domador *m* de caballos.

roughshod [-ʃɔd] *adj* herrado con ramplones (horse).

◆ *adv* FIG *to ride roughshod over* pisotear (to ill-treat), hacer caso omiso de (to ignore).

rough-spoken [-'spəukən] *adj* malhablado, da.

roulade [ru:'lɑ:d] *n* MUS trino *m*, gorgorito *m*.

rouleau [ru'ləu] *n* cartucho *m*.

roulette [ru'let] *n* ruleta *f* (game); *Russian roulette* ruleta rusa || ruleta *f* (toothed wheel) || perforación *f* (of a postage stamp).

Roumania [ru'meinjə] *pr n* GEOGR Rumania *f*.

Roumanian [-n] *adj* rumano, na.

◆ *n* rumano, na (person) || rumano *m* (language).

round [raund] *adj* redondo, da; *a round table* una mesa redonda; *round cheeks* mejillas redondas; *a round hole* un agujero redondo; *round handwriting* letra redonda || arqueado, da (shoulders) || sonoro, ra (voice, sound) || redondo, da; *in round figures* en números redondos || completo, ta; bueno, na; *a round dozen* una docena completa || rotundo, da; categórico, ca; terminante (refusal) || pronunciada con los labios redondeados (a vowel) || — *round trip* viaje *m* de ida y vuelta (return), viaje *m* circular (circular) || *to be round with s.o.* ser franco *or* sincero con alguien || *to go at a good round pace* ir a buen paso.

◆ *adv* por todas partes (everywhere); *leaves scattered round* hojas esparcidas por todas partes || de un lado para otro (to and fro); *people walking round* la gente que anda de un lado para otro || de perímetro, de circunferencia (in circumference); *a tower sixty feet round* una torre de sesenta pies de perímetro || a la redonda (in a circle); *the sound could be heard a mile round* el ruido se podía oír a una milla a la redonda || alrededor (around); *the people standing round* el ruido se podía oír a una milla a la redonda || alrededor (around); *the people standing round* la gente que está de pie alrededor || a *or* por casa [de alguien]; *come round when you like* pasa por casa cuando quieras; *to invite s.o. round* invitar a alguien a casa || — *all round* para todos (for everybody) || *all the year round* durante todo el año || *an orchard with a wall all round* una huerta rodeada por un muro || *is there enough to go round?* ¿hay para todos? || *it's a long way round* hay que dar un gran rodeo || *round about* en los alrededores || *round and round* dando vueltas a la redonda (in circles); *birds flying round and round* pájaros dando vueltas a la redonda || *taken all round* en conjunto || *to gather round* apiñarse || *to go the long way round* ir por el camino más largo || *to pass* o *to hand round* pasar de mano en mano, hacer circular || *to send s.o. round for* mandar a alguien a buscar *or* a traer || *to show s.o. round the town* hacer visitar la ciudad a alguien || *to spin round* girar, dar vueltas || *to whirl round* girar, dar vueltas || *to win s.o. round* convencer a uno.

◆ *prep* alrededor de; *the wind blew round the house* el viento soplaba alrededor de la casa; *round the world* alrededor del mundo; *sitting round the table* sentados alrededor de la mesa; *the earth turns round its axis* la tierra gira alrededor de su eje; *round 1830* alrededor de 1830 || que rodea; *the wall round the garden* la tapia que rodea el jardín || a la vuelta de; *the bar round the corner* el bar a la vuelta de la esquina || en; *to wear a scarf round one's neck* llevar una bufanda en el cuello || cerca de, por (near); *somewhere round the High Road* cerca de la calle Mayor; *it's round here somewhere* está por aquí cerca || por; *to walk round the town singing* andar cantando por la ciudad || a eso de; *round (about) five o'clock* a eso de las cinco || acerca de; *to write a book round an incident* escribir un libro acerca de un incidente || de; *to measure twenty inches round the neck* medir veinte pulgadas de cuello || — *just round the corner* a la vuelta de la esquina || *to go round an obstacle* dar la vuelta a un obstáculo || MAR *to sail round* doblar un cabo || *to swim, to run round the island* dar la vuelta a la isla a nado, corriendo || FAM *to talk round a subject* andar con rodeos, andarse por las ramas.

◆ *n* círculo *m* (circle) || curva *f* (curve) || esfera *f* (sphere) || rodaja *f* (slice) || vuelta *f* (in knitting) || escalón *m*, peldaño *m* (of a ladder) || vuelta *f* (circular movement) || revolución *f* (of earth) || recorrido *m* (of a salesman) || viaje *m* de negocios (of a tradesman) || visita *f* (of a doctor); *to go the rounds* hacer visitas || serie *f*, sucesión *f*; *a round of parties* una serie de fiestas || ronda *f* (of drinks); *to stand a round of drinks* invitar a una ronda || ronda *f* (of negotiations) || vuelta *f* (of elections) || salva *f* (of applause) || rutina *f*; *the daily round* la rutina cotidiana || MIL ronda *f* (patrol) | visita *f* de inspección | tiro *m* (shot) | cartucho *m* (of ammunition) | descarga *f*, salva *f* (salvo) || SP asalto *m*, «round» *m* (in boxing) | vuelta *f* (stage of a competition) | circuito *m* (lap) | partido *m*; *to play a round of golf* jugar un partido de golf || partida *f* (game) || MUS canon *m* || — *in the round* en alto relieve (a sculpture) || *to go the round* o *the rounds* ir de boca en boca (a story, a rumour) || *to go the round of the pubs looking for s.o.* ir por todas las tabernas en busca de alguien.

round [raund] *vt* redondear (to make round) || dar la vuelta a, doblar, torcer (a corner) || doblar (a cape) || costear (an island) || dar la vuelta a (an obstacle) || pulir (written work, style).
◆ *vi* redondearse (to become round).
◆ *phr v* *to round off* redondear (a sharp end, a number, etc.) | acabar, rematar (to end, to close) | pulir (one's sentences) || *to round on* denunciar (to betray) | volverse en contra de (to turn on) | *to round on one's heels* dar media vuelta || *to round out* acabar (to end) | ponerse rellenito (to become plump) || MAR *to round to* ponerse al pairo || *to round up* acorralar, rodear (cattle, etc.) | reunir (people).

roundabout [-abaut] *adj* indirecto, ta (indirect) || tortuoso, sa (tortuous) || — *roundabout means* rodeos *m* || *roundabout phrase* circunloquio *m*, rodeo *m*.
◆ *n* tiovivo *m* (merry-go-round) || plaza *f* circular, glorieta *f* (at the intersection of crossroads) || rodeo *m* (circumlocution) || rodeo *m*, vuelta *f* (detour).

rounded [-id] *adj* redondeado, da.

roundel [-l] *n* ventana *f* circular (window) || letrilla *f*, rondel *m* (poetry) || HERALD roel *m*.

roundelay [-ilei] *n* MUS rondó *m* | baile *m* en corro | canción *f* cantada en corro.

rounder [-ə*] *n* TECH herramienta *f* para redondear || US FAM calavera *m* (gay dog).

rounders [-əz] *n* SP juego *m* parecido al béisbol.

round-eyed [-aid] *adj* con los ojos desorbitados; *to gaze round-eyed at* mirar con los ojos desorbitados.

Roundhead [-hed] *n* HIST cabeza *f* redonda.

roundhouse [-haus] *n* MAR toldilla *f*, chupeta *f* || depósito *m* de locomotoras (circular building for railway engines).

roundish [-iʃ] *adj* regordete, ta (plump) || casi redondo, da.

roundly [-li] *adv* completamente (completely) || abiertamente (openly) || francamente (frankly) || FIG rotundamente, categóricamente, terminantemente.

roundness [-nis] *n* redondez *f*.

round robin [-'rɔbin] *n* petición *f* [hecha de modo que ningún nombre encabece la lista] || torneo *m* (contest).

round-shouldered [-'ʃəuldəd] *adj* cargado de espaldas.

roundsman [-zmən] *n* repartidor *m* (delivery man) || US cabo *m* de policía.
— OBSERV El plural de *roundsman* es *roundsmen*.

Round Table [-'teibl] *n* Tabla *f* Redonda (in the Arthurian legend).

round table conference [-'teibl'kɔnfərəns] *n* mesa *f* redonda.

round-the-clock ['raundðə'klɔk] *adj* que dura veinticuatro horas.

roundtop [-tɔp] *n* MAR gavia *f*, cofa *f*.

roundup [-ʌp] *n* rodeo *m* (of cattle) || FIG redada *f* (of suspects) | resumen *m* (summary).

roundworm [-wəːm] *n* ZOOL ascáride *f*.

roup [rup] *n* VET moquillo *m*.

rouse [rauz] *vt* despertar (to wake up) || animar (to make active) || despertar (a feeling, an indignation) || suscitar, provocar (admiration) || sacudir (from indifference) || irritar, enfadar (to make angry) || MAR halar (to haul) || avivar (the fire) || levantar (the game) || — *to rouse o.s.* animarse || *to rouse s.o. to action* hacer que alguien haga algo.
◆ *vi* despertarse, despertar.

rouser [-ə*] *n* agitador *m* || estimulante *m* (stimulus) || FAM bola *f*, mentira *f* (lie).

rousing [-iŋ] *adj* conmovedor, ra (moving) || caluroso, sa (applause) || vigorizante, estimulante (invigorating) || FAM descomunal, enorme; *rousing lie* mentira enorme.

Roussillon ['ruːsij˜ɔn] *n* GEOGR Rosellón *m*.

roustabout ['raustəbaut] *n* estibador *m* (in a dock) || US peón *m* (labourer).

rout [raut] *n* derrota *f* completa, desbandada *f* (defeat) || fuga *f* desordenada (flight) || canalla *f*, chusma *f* (rabble) || pandilla *f* (of revellers) || alboroto *m*, tumulto *m* (uproar).

rout [raut] *vt* derrotar (to defeat) || poner en fuga (to put to flight) || hacer salir (to make s.o. come out) || descubrir (to discover).
◆ *vi* hozar, hocicar (swine) || hurgar (to search about).

route [ruːt] *n* ruta *f*, itinerario *m* (for a journey); *to map out a route* trazar un itinerario || camino *m* (path) || línea *f*, recorrido *m* (bus route) || MAR rumbo *m*, derrota *f* (of a ship); *to change route* cambiar de rumbo || ruta *f* aérea (airway) || MIL itinerario *m* || US recorrido *m* (round) || — *route map* mapa *m* de carreteras || MIL *route march* marcha *f* de entrenamiento | *route order* orden *m* de marcha || *sea route* vía marítima.

router ['rautə*] *n* TECH guimbarda *f* (plane) | fresa *f*, fresadora *f* (milling machine).

routine [ruː'tiːn] *n* rutina *f*; *the daily routine* la rutina cotidiana; *as a matter of routine* por rutina || MIL *routine orders* órdenes *f* de servicio.
◆ *adj* rutinario, ria; *a routine job* un trabajo rutinario.

rove [rəuv] *n* arandela *f* (washer) || madeja *f* (of cotton, of wool) || torzal *m* (of silk) || FAM *to be on the rove* errar, vagar.

rove [rəuv] *vt* torcer (thread) || recorrer (to travel round) || errar por, vagar por (to roam).
◆ *vi* andar errante, vagar, errar || *his eyes roved over the landscap* recorría el paisaje con la mirada.

rove [rəuv] *pret/pp* ⟶ **reeve.**

rover [-ə*] *n* vagabundo *m* (vagabond) || explorador *m* (senior boy scout) || blanco *m* (target) || MAR pirata *m*, corsario *m* (pirate).

roving [-iŋ] *adj* errante (wandering) || ambulante (salesman) || itinerante (ambassador).

row [rəu] *n* fila *f*, hilera *f*; *a row of houses* una hilera de casas || fila *f* (of seats, of persons) || vuelta *f* (of knitting) || paseo *m* en bote (trip in a rowboat) || — *in a row* en fila (in a line), seguidos, das (one after the other) || *in rows* en filas || *to go for a row* pasearse en bote.

row [rəu] *vt* hacer avanzar con el remo (a boat) || remar en (a race) || competir con (to compete against) || llevar a remo (a person) || ser movido por; *a boat which rows ten oars* una barca que es movida por diez remos.
◆ *vi* remar || *to row across the river* cruzar el río a remo *or* remando.

row [rau] *n* alboroto *m*, estrépito *m*, jaleo *m*, escándalo *m* (noise, disturbance) || jaleo *m*, escándalo *m* (fuss) || bronca *f*, pelea *f* (quarrel) || riña *f*, regañuza *f* (scolding) || INFORM línea (of characters) || — *family rows* peleas *or* riñas familiares || FAM *hold your row!* ¡cállate! || FIG *if they catch you, you will get into a row* si te cogen, cobrarás || *to kick up* o *to make a row* armar jaleo (to make a lot of noise), armar un escándalo (to protest strongly).

row [rau] *vi* reñir, pelearse.
◆ *vt* FAM echar una regañuza a, reñir.

rowan ['rauən] *n* BOT serbal *m* (tree) | serba *f* (fruit).

rowboat ['rəubəut] *n* bote *m* de remos.

rowdiness ['raudinis] *n* carácter *m* pendenciero (quarrelsomeness) || alboroto *m* (disturbance) || ruido *m* (noise).

rowdy ['raudi] *adj* ruidoso, sa (noisy) || camorrista, pendenciero, ra (loud and quarrelsome).
◆ *n* camorrista *m* & *f*, pendenciero, ra.

rowdyism [-izəm] *n* disturbios *m pl*, pendencias *f pl*, alboroto *m* (disturbance).

rowel ['rauəl] *n* rodaja *f* (of a spur).

rowel ['rauəl] *vt* espolear.

rower [rəuə*] *n* remador, ra; remero, ra.

rowing ['rəuiŋ] *n* remo *m*.

rowing boat [-bəut] *n* bote *m* de remos.

rowlock ['rɔlək] *n* MAR escálamo *m*, tolete *m* || ARCH sardinel *m*.

royal ['rɔiəl] *adj* real; *the royal family* la familia real || principesco, ca (princely) || grandioso, sa; magnífico, ca; espléndido, da; regio, gia (splendid); *they gave her a royal send-off* le hicieron una despedida magnífica || MAR de sobrejuanete || BOT real || — *royal blue* azul marino || *royal flush* escalera real (in card games) || *The Royal Academy of Music* La Real Academia de Música || FIG *to have a royal time* pasarlo en grande.
◆ *n* ZOOL ciervo *m* de doce cuernos || MAR sobrejuanete *m* || miembro *m* de la familia real.

Royal Air Force [-εə*,fɔːs] *n* MIL Fuerzas *f pl* Aéreas británicas.

royalism [-izəm] *n* monarquismo *m*, realismo *m*.

royalist [-ist] *adj/n* monárquico, ca; realista.

royally [-i] *adv* FIG regiamente, magníficamente.

Royal Marines [-mə'riːns] *n* MIL regimiento *m* de infantería de marina en el Reino Unido.

Royal Navy [-'neivi] *n* MIL cuerpo *m* de marina del Reino Unido.

royal palm [-'pɑːm] *n* BOT palma *f* real, palmiche *m* (ornamental palm).

royalty [-ti] *n* realeza *f* || miembro *m* de la familia real | familia *f* real (royal family).
◆ *pl* derechos *m* de autor *or* de inventor, regalías *f*.

RPI *abbr of [retail price index]* IPC, índice de precios al consumo.

rub [rʌb] *n* fricción *f*, frotamiento *m*, frote *m* (voluntary) || roce *m* (accidental, unwanted) || desigualdad *f* del terreno (in bowls) || dificultad *f*, obstáculo *m* (hindrance) || — FIG *there's the rub* allí está el busilis, ésa es la dificultad, ahí está el quid || *to give one's shoes a rub* sacar brillo a los zapatos || *to give the silver a rub* limpiar la plata.

rub [rʌb] *vt* friccionar; *to rub one's leg with ointment* friccionar la pierna con una pomada || limpiar, dar brillo a; *to rub the silverware* dar

brillo a la plata || lustrar, encerar (floors) || limpiar frotando (to clean) || rozar; *my shoes rub my heels* los zapatos me rozan los talones || rozar contra; *to rub the kerb with one's ankle* rozar con el tobillo contra el borde de la acera || frotar, restregar; *to make fire by rubbing two pieces of wood together* hacer fuego frotando dos trozos de madera || frotarse; *to rub one's hands together* frotarse las manos || lijar (with sandpaper) || estarcir (a drawing) || — FIG *to rub elbows* o *shoulders with* codearse con | *to rub noses with* ser amigo íntimo de || FIG & FAM *to rub (up) the wrong way* coger a contrapelo.
◆ *vi* rozar; *the wheel rubs against the mudguard* la rueda roza contra el guardabarros || friccionarse (a person) || desviarse (a ball in bowls) || desgastarse (to wear out).
◆ *phr v* ***to rub along*** ir tirando, ganar justo lo suficiente para vivir (to get by) | evitar fricciones (to avoid frictions) | *to rub along in a language* defenderse en una lengua | *to rub along very well together* llevarse bien || ***to rub away*** quitar frotando (to remove by rubbing) | desgastar (to wear out) | hacer desaparecer (to make disappear) || ***to rub down*** almohazar (a horse) | friccionar (s.o.) | raspar (a surface) | lijar (with sandpaper) || ***to rub in*** frotar (una parte del cuerpo) con (ointment) | FIG *don't rub it in!* ¡no insista! || ***to rub off*** quitar frotando (to remove) | quitarse frotando (to be removable); *that stain will rub off* esa mancha se quitará frotando | desaparecer (to disappear) | FIG *to rub off on s.o.* pegársele a uno (bad habits), transmitírsele a uno (another's intelligence, etc.) || ***to rub out*** borrar (to erase) | borrarse (to be erased) | FAM liquidar (to kill) || ***to rub through*** salir adelante || ***to rub up*** limpiar, dar brillo a (to polish) | refrescar (memory).

rub-a-dub ['rʌbə'dʌb]; **rub-a-dub-dub** [-dʌb] *n* râtaplán *m* (of drums).

rubber ['rʌbə*] *n* BOT caucho *m* || goma *f*, caucho *m* (synthetic substance) || goma *f* de borrar (eraser) || masajista *m* & *f* (person) || chanclo *m* (overshoe) || FAM goma *f*, condón *m* (contraceptive sheath) || «rubber» *m* (bridge).
◆ *adj* de goma; *rubber ball* pelota de goma || sin fondos (cheque) || — *rubber band* goma *f* || *rubber* industry *f* del caucho.

rubberize ['rʌbəraiz] *vt* cauchutar.

rubberneck ['rʌbənek] *n* US FAM curioso, sa (inquisitive person) | mirón, ona (sightseer) | turista *m* & *f* (tourist).

rubberneck ['rʌbənek] *vi* US FAM curiosear, meter las narices.

rubber plant ['rʌbəplɑ:nt] *n* BOT árbol *m* del caucho, gomero *m*.

rubber ring ['rʌbə'riŋ] *n* goma *f* (rubber band) || flotador *m* (for swimming).

rubber stamp ['rʌbə'stæmp] *n* tampón *m*, sello *m* de goma || FIG aprobación *f* maquinal.

rubber-stamp ['rʌbə'stæmp] *vt* marcar con un sello de goma (to put a stamp on) || FIG aprobar maquinalmente (to give one's approval).

rubber tree ['rʌbə'tri:] *n* gomero *m*, árbol *m* del caucho.

rubbery ['rʌbəri] *adj* parecido a la goma || elástico, ca (elastic).

rubbing ['rʌbiŋ] *n* frotamiento *m* (voluntary) || roce *m* (undesirable); *the rubbing of one's shoes* el roce de los zapatos || MED fricción *f*.

rubbish ['rʌbiʃ] *n* basura *f* (refuse) || desperdicios *m pl* (waste) || escombros *m pl* (from building) || FIG & FAM birria *f*, porquería *f*, asquerosidad *f*; *these photographs are rubbish* estas fotos son una birria | tonterías *f pl*, disparates *m pl*, sandeces *f pl*; *to talk rubbish* decir tonterías.

rubbish bin [-bin] *n* cubo *m* de la basura.

rubbish chute [-ʃu:t] *n* vertedero *m* de basuras, colector *m* de basuras.

rubbish dump [-dʌmp]; **rubbish heap** [-hi:p] *n* basurero *m*, muladar *m*, vertedero *m*.

rubbishy ['rʌbiʃi] *adj* sin valor, de pacotilla || lleno de sandeces (book, speech, etc.).

rubble ['rʌbl] *n* escombros *m pl* (loose bricks, debris, etc.) || cascotes *m pl*, ripios *m pl* (for foundations, for roadbuilding) || morrillo *m* (masonry).

rubblework [-wə:k] *n* morrillo *m*.

rubdown [-daun] *n* masaje *m* || secado *m* con una toalla || *to give a horse a rubdown* almohazar un caballo.

rube [ru:b] *n* US FAM paleto *m*, palurdo *m* (bumpkin).

rubefacient [ˌru:bi'feiʃjənt] *adj* MED rubefaciente.
◆ *n* MED rubefaciente *m*.

rubefaction [ˌru:bi'fækʃən] *n* MED rubefacción *f*.

rubefy [ˌru:bifai] *vt* MED rubificar.

rubella [ru:'belə] *n* MED rubéola *f* (German measles).

rubeola [ru:'bi:ələ] *n* MED sarampión *m* (measles) | rubéola *f* (German measles).

rubescent [ru:'besənt] *adj* rubescente.

rubiaceae [rubi'eisii] *pl n* BOT rubiáceas *f*.

rubicelle ['ru:bisel] *n* MIN rubicela *f*.

Rubicon ['ru:bikən] *pr n* GEOGR Rubicón *m*; *to cross the Rubicon* pasar el Rubicón.

rubicund ['ru:bikənd] *adj* rubicundo, da.

rubidium [ru'bidiəm] *n* rubidio *m* (metal).

rubied ['ru:bid] *adj* del color del rubí.

ruble ['ru:bl] *n* rublo *m* (Russian currency).

rubric ['ru:brik] *n* rúbrica *f*.

ruby ['ru:bi] *n* rubí *m* (stone) || PRINT tipo *m* de 5, 5 puntos || color *m* de rubí.
◆ *adj* de color de rubí.

ruche [ru:ʃ] *n* encañonado *m* de encaje (lace frills).

ruck [rʌk] *n* vulgo *m* (ordinary people) || pelotón *m* (in racing) || «melée» *f* (in rugby) || arruga *f* (wrinkle).

ruck [rʌk]; **ruckle** [-l] *vt* arrugar.
◆ *vi* arrugarse.

rucksack [-sæk] *n* mochila *f*.

ruckus [-əs]; **ruction** [-ʃən] *n* FAM jaleo *m*, cisco *m*, jollín *m* (noisy disturbance) || FAM *there will be ructions* se va a armar la de San Quintín *or* la gorda.

rudder ['rʌdə*] *n* MAR & AVIAT timón *m* || *rudder bar* caña *f* del timón, timón *m* (of a ship), palanca *f* de mando (of a plane).

rudderless [-lis] *adj* sin timón.

rudderpost [-ˌpəust] *n* MAR codaste *m*.

ruddiness [-inis] *n* color *m* rubicundo *or* rojizo, rubicundez *f*.

ruddle ['rʌdl] *n* almagre *m*.

ruddy [-i] *adj* rubicundo, da; rojizo, za || FAM maldito, ta; condenado, da (damned).

rude [ru:d] *adj* grosero, ra; ordinario, ria (coarse); *rude behaviour* comportamiento grosero || descortés, mal educado, da; grosero, ra (impolite); *don't be rude* no sea mal educado; *he was very rude to me* estuvo muy descortés conmigo || tosco, ca; *a rude table* una mesa tosca; *a rude plough* un arado tosco || duro, ra; *a rude blow* un golpe duro || penoso, sa; desagradable (painful); *a rude surprise* una sorpresa penosa || escabroso, sa; verde, indecente, grosero, ra; *rude story* historia indecente || inculto, ta (uneducated) || crudo, da; riguroso, sa (weather) || violento, ta (sea, wind) || brusco, ca; repentino, na (sudden) || aproximado, da (estimation) || fuerte, robusto, ta (health) || — *it's rude* es de mala educación, es descortés || *to make rude remarks* decir groserías.

rudely [-li] *adv* groseramente (impolitely) || toscamente (coarsely) || bruscamente (suddenly).

rudeness [-nis] *n* grosería *f*, descortesía *f* (impoliteness, vulgarity) || mala educación *f* (bad breeding) || indecencia *f*, lo verde, escabrosidad *f*, grosería *f* (obscenity) || tosquedad *f*, lo basto (roughness) || dureza *f*, rudeza *f* (of a blow, of a shock) || incultura *f* (lack of education) || rigor *m*, lo crudo (of weather) || violencia *f* (of wind, of sea).

rudiment ['ru:dimənt] *n* BIOL rudimento *m*.
◆ *pl* rudimentos *m*; *the rudiments of grammar* los rudimentos de la gramática.

rudimentary [ˌru:di'mentəri] *adj* rudimentario, ria.

rue [ru:] *n* ruda *f* (plant) || arrepentimiento *m* (regret).

rue [ru:] *vt* arrepentirse de, lamentar, sentir mucho || *you'll live to rue the day you left him* un día lamentarás haberle dejado.

rueful [-ful] *adj* pesaroso, sa; arrepentido, da (regretful) || triste (sad); *the Knight of the Rueful Countenance* el Caballero de la Triste Figura || lastimoso, sa; lamentable (deplorable).

ruefulness [-fulnis] *n* tristeza *f*, pesar *m*.

rufescent [ru:'fesənt] *adj* rojizo, za.

ruff [rʌf] *n* collarín *m* (on animals and birds) || gorguera *f*, gola *f* (starched collar) || fallo *m* (in cards) || paloma *f* moñuda (bird).

ruff [rʌf] *vt/vi* fallar (in card games).

ruffian [-jən] *n* rufián *m*, canalla *m*.

ruffle ['rʌfl] *n* chorrera *f* (on the chest); *a blouse with a ruffle* una blusa con chorrera || volante *m* (at the wrists, etc.) || gorguera *f*, gola *f* (around the neck) || collarín *m* (of a bird, etc.) || rizo *m* (ripple of water) || redoble *m* (of drums) || agitación *f* (disturbance) || FIG enfado *m*, enojo *m*, disgusto *m* (anger).

ruffle ['rʌfl] *vt* agitar (to disturb) || desgreñar (hair) || agitar, rizar (water) || erizar (bird's feathers) || arrugar (to wrinkle) || fruncir (to gather cloth) || FIG enojar, disgustar (to offend) | perturbar (to perturb) || barajar (cards).
◆ *vi* agitarse, rizarse (water, etc.) || encresparse (with waves) || erizarse (feathers) || desgreñarse (hair).

rufous ['ru:fəs] *adj* rojizo, za.

rug [rʌg] *n* alfombra *f* (carpet) || alfombrilla *f* de cama (bedside rug) || alfombrilla *f*, tapete *m* (small carpet) || piel *f*; *a tiger skin rug* una piel de tigre || manta *f* de viaje (travelling rug).

rugby ['rʌgbi] *n* SP rugby *m* || *Rugby League* rugby a trece || *Rugby Union* rugby a quince.

rugby football [-'futbɔ:l] *n* SP rugby *m*.

rugged ['rʌgid] *adj* accidentado, da; desigual (ground, road) || escarpado, da (mountain, rock) || rugoso, sa (bark) || duro, ra (features) || desabrido, da (character) || desigual, tosco, ca (style) || duro, ra (way of life) || riguroso, sa (climate) || basto, ta; tosco, ca (manners) || US robusto, ta; fuerte (strong).

ruggedness [-nis] *n* lo accidentado, desigualdad *f* (of the ground) || lo escarpado (of mountains, of rocks) || dureza *f* (of lace, features, way of life) || desabrimiento *m* (of character) || tosquedad *f* (of manners) || US robustez *f*.

rugger ['rʌgə*] *n* FAM rugby *m*.

rugose ['ru:gəus]; **rugous** ['ru:gəus] *adj* rugoso, sa.

rugosity [ru'gɔsiti] *n* rugosidad *f*.

Ruhr [ruə] *pr n* GEOGR Ruhr *m*.

ruin [ruin] *n* ruina *f*; *drink led to his ruin* la bebida le llevó a la ruina; *the palace is now a ruin* el palacio es ahora una ruina ‖ ruina *f*, perdición *f*; *the flood will be the ruin of the crops* la inundación será la ruina de las cosechas; *she will be the ruin of me* será mi perdición ‖ ruina *f* (financial disaster) ‖ — FIG *he is but the ruin of what he was* no es ni sombra de lo que fue, está hecho una ruina ‖ FAM *mother's ruin* matarratas *m inv*, ginebra muy mala ‖ *to be on the road to ruin* ir a la ruina ‖ *to bring to ruin* arruinar ‖ FIG *to go to rack and ruin* venirse abajo ‖ *to go to ruin* caer en ruinas (building), venirse abajo (project) ‖ *to lie in ruin* estar en ruinas.
◆ *pl* ruinas *f*; *the ruins of a castle* las ruinas de un castillo ‖ *to be in ruins* estar en ruinas.

ruin [ruin] *vt* arruinar (financially); *inflation ruined the firm* la inflación arruinó la empresa ‖ asolar (to destroy); *the earthquake ruined the city* el terremoto asoló la ciudad ‖ estropear (to spoil); *to ruin s.o.'s hairdo* estropear el peinado de alguien ‖ echar abajo; *bad weather ruined my plans* el mal tiempo echó abajo mis planes ‖ arruinar, echar a perder (health) ‖ arruinar, estropear (one's life) ‖ arruinar, echar por tierra (one's reputation) ‖ estragar (one's taste) ‖ desacreditar (to disparage) ‖ perder (to cause moral downfall, to seduce).

ruination [rui'neiʃən] *n* arruinamiento *m*, ruina *f*, perdición *f* (cause of ruin).

ruined [ruind] *adj* arruinado, da (financially) ‖ en ruinas (in ruins).

ruinous ['ruinəs] *adj* ruinoso, sa; *ruinous expenses* gastos ruinosos; *ruinous houses* casas ruinosas.

rule [ru:l] *n* regla *f*, norma *f*; *rules of conduct* normas de conducta ‖ regla *f*; *rules of arithmetic* reglas aritméticas; *rule of three* regla de tres; *rule of an order* regla de una orden; *an exception to the rule* una excepción a la regla ‖ dominio *m*, mando *m*; *country under British rule* país bajo dominio británico ‖ imperio *m*; *the rule of law* el imperio de la ley ‖ reinado *m*; *England under the rule of Elizabeth I* Inglaterra bajo el reinado de Isabel I ‖ regla *f* graduada (ruler) ‖ metro *m* (metre) ‖ PRINT filete *m* ‖ JUR fallo *m*, decisión *f* ‖ — MATH *alligation rule* regla de aligación ‖ *as a rule* generalmente, por regla general ‖ *by rule* de acuerdo con las reglas ‖ *by rule of thumb* de modo empírico ‖ *folding rule* metro plegable ‖ *home rule* autonomía *f* ‖ *slide rule* regla de cálculo ‖ *the exception proves the rule* la excepción confirma la regla ‖ *to make it a rule to* ser un deber para uno ‖ *to work to rule* ceñirse al reglamento, negarse a hacer horas extraordinarias.
◆ *pl* reglas *f*, normas *f* (in sports, etc.) ‖ reglamento *m sing* (regulations); *to abide by the rules* respetar el reglamento ‖ — *rules and regulations* reglamento ‖ *rules of the game* reglas del juego ‖ *rules of the road* reglamento del tráfico ‖ *to act according to the rules* obrar según las reglas ‖ FIG *to play by the rules* obrar como es debido *or* como Dios manda.

rule [ru:l] *vt* mandar, gobernar (to govern); *he ruled the country for ten years* gobernó el país durante diez años ‖ dirigir (a firm) ‖ aconsejar, guiar (to advise) ‖ llevar (a household, one's life, etc.) ‖ decretar (to decree) ‖ decidir (to decide); *the chairman ruled that the question was out of order* el presidente decidió que no se podía discutir la cuestión ‖ dominar (one's passions, s.o.); *is it true that she rules her husband?* ¿es verdad que domina a su marido? ‖ trazar, tirar (a line) ‖ rayar, reglar, pautar (paper) ‖ JUR fallar ‖ — *to rule off* trazar una línea debajo de (a paragraph, etc.), cerrar (an account) ‖ *to rule out* excluir (s.o.), excluir, descartar (sth.) ‖ *to rule over* dominar, regir ‖ *to rule the waves* dominar los mares.
◆ *vi* gobernar (to govern) ‖ reinar (to reign) ‖ reinar, imperar; *silence ruled* reinaba el silencio ‖ regir (prices) ‖ JUR fallar, decidir ‖ — *to rule high* mantenerse a un nivel alto (prices) ‖ *to rule over* reinar en.

rule book [-buk] *n* reglamento *m*.

ruled [-d] *adj* rayado, da (paper).

ruler [-ə*] *n* gobernante *m* & *f* (person who governs) ‖ soberano, na (sovereign) ‖ regla *f* (for drawing lines).
◆ *pl* gobernantes *m*, dirigentes *m*.

ruling [-iŋ] *adj* dirigente; *ruling classes* clases dirigentes ‖ que rige, actual (price) ‖ dominante (passion).
◆ *n* JUR fallo *m*, decisión *f* ‖ gobierno *m* (action) ‖ *to give a ruling on* pronunciar un fallo sobre.

rum [rʌm] *adj* FAM extraño, ña; raro, ra (strange) ‖ FAM *he is a rum customer* es un tipo raro.
◆ *n* ron *m* (drink) ‖ US bebida *f* alcohólica.

Rumania [ru:'meinjə] *pr n* GEOGR Rumania *f*.

Rumanian [-n] *adj/n* rumano, na.

rumba ['rʌmbə] *n* rumba *f* (dance, music).

rumble ['rʌmbl] *n* ruido *m* sordo, el retumbar (sound) ‖ rodar *m* (of a vehicle) ‖ estruendo *m*, fragor *m* (of thunder) ‖ borborigmo *m* (of the stomach) ‖ AUT picado *m* de la biela.

rumble ['rʌmbl] *vt* decir con voz cavernosa (to say in a deep voice) ‖ FAM calar (s.o.) | olerse (sth.) ‖ *to rumble out a remark* hacer una observación con voz cavernosa.
◆ *vi* rodar con gran estrépito (vehicle) ‖ retumbar (thunder) ‖ hacer ruidos (stomach).

rumble seat [-si:t] *n* US asiento *m* trasero descubierto.

rumbling [-iŋ] *adj* retumbante.
◆ *n* ruido *m* sordo, estruendo *m*.

rumbustious [rʌm'bʌstʃəs] *adj* bullicioso, sa.

rumen ['ru:men] *n* herbario *m* (of a ruminant).
— OBSERV El plural de *rumen* es *rumina*.

ruminant ['ru:minənt] *adj* ZOOL rumiante.
◆ *n* ZOOL rumiante *m*.

ruminate ['ru:mineit] *vt/vi* rumiar (animals) ‖ FIG rumiar; *to ruminate a project* rumiar un proyecto.

rumination [,ru:mi'neiʃən] *n* rumia *f* ‖ FIG meditación *f*, reflexión *f*.

ruminative ['ru:minətiv] *adj* FIG meditabundo, da.

rummage ['rʌmidʒ] *vt* registrar; *to rummage a house from top to bottom* registrar una casa de arriba abajo.
◆ *vi* buscar desordenadamente, revolver; *to rummage in a drawer* revolver en un cajón.

rummage sale [-seil] *n* venta *f* de artículos con fines benéficos (for a church, etc.) ‖ liquidación *f* (clearance sale).

rummy ['rʌmi] *n* rami *m* (card game).
◆ *adj* FAM extraño, ña; raro, ra.

rumour; US **rumor** ['ru:mə*] *n* rumor *m*; *according to rumours* según los rumores ‖ *rumor has in that, there are rumours that* se rumorea que, se dice que, corre el rumor de que.

rumour; US **rumor** ['ru:mə*] *vt* rumorear ‖ *it is rumoured that* se rumorea que, se dice que, corre el rumor de que.

rump [rʌmp] *n* ancas *f pl*, grupa *f* (of a quadruped) ‖ rabadilla *f* (of birds) ‖ CULIN cuarto *m* trasero ‖ FAM trasero *m* (of person) ‖ CULIN *rump steak* filete *m*.

rumple ['rʌmpl] *vt* arrugar (to crease) ‖ FAM enfadar, molestar (to annoy) ‖ *to rumple s.o.'s hair* despeinar a uno.

rumpus ['rʌmpəs] *n* FAM jaleo *m* (shindy); *to kick up a rumpus* armar jaleo | agarrada *f*; *to have a rumpus with s.o.* tener una agarrada con alguien.

rumpus room [-ru:m] *n* cuarto *m* de juegos.

rumrunner ['rʌm,rʌnə*] *n* US contrabandista *m* de bebidas alcohólicas.

run [rʌn] *n* carrera *f* (race) ‖ serie *f*, racha *f*; *a run of mishaps* una serie de contratiempos ‖ período *m*; *a run of bad weather* un período de mal tiempo ‖ escalera *f* (in card games) ‖ gran demanda *f*; *there has been a run on sugar today* ha habido gran demanda de azúcar hoy ‖ libre uso *m*, libre disposición *f*; *to give s.o. the run of one's house* dar a alguien libre uso de su casa, dejar a alguien la libre disposición de su casa ‖ sendero *m* (habitual course of an animal) ‖ corral *m* (for farm animals) ‖ pasto *m* (pasture) ‖ migración *f* (of fish) ‖ vuelta *f*, paseo *m* (short journey); *to go for a run in the car* dar una vuelta en coche; *to go for a run over to the coast* darse una vuelta por la costa ‖ recorrido *m*, trayecto *m* (of a train, of a railway, etc.); *the run from Los Angeles to San Francisco is not very long* el trayecto de Los Ángeles a San Francisco no es muy largo ‖ tendencia *f* (general tendency); *the run of the market* la tendencia del mercado ‖ dirección *f* (direction) ‖ disposición *f*; *the run of the streets is perpendicular to the river* la disposición de las calles es perpendicular al río ‖ curso *m* (of a liquid) ‖ corriente *f* (of the tide) ‖ arroyo *m* (stream) ‖ curso *m*; *the present run of events* el curso actual de los acontecimientos ‖ funcionamiento *m* (of a machine) ‖ pasada *f* (of a machine tool) ‖ colada *f* (of a blast furnace) ‖ producción *f* (production) ‖ prueba *f* (trial) ‖ ritmo *m*, cadencia *f* (of a phrase) ‖ FIG hilo *m*; *to lose the run of the speech* perder el hilo de la conversación | boga *f*, moda *f* (popularity) | gran demanda *f* (demand) | carrera *f*, carrerilla *f* (in stockings) ‖ MUS carrerilla *f* ‖ SP carrerilla *f*; *to take a long run* coger mucha carrerilla | pista *f* (ski slope) | punto *m* (point scored) | carrera *f* (in baseball and cricket) ‖ PRINT tirada *f*; *a run of 10 000 copies* una tirada de diez mil ejemplares ‖ COMM categoría *f* (of goods) ‖ MIL pasada *f* (of bombers) ‖ MIN dirección *f* (of a vein) ‖ GEOL desprendimiento *m* (of ground) ‖ — *a run of bad luck* una mala racha ‖ *a run of luck* una buena racha ‖ *at a run* corriendo; *he came up at a run* llegó corriendo ‖ *Birmingham is two hour's run from London* Birmingham está a dos horas (de tren o de coche) de Londres ‖ MAR *day's run* singladura *f* ‖ CINEM *first run* período *m* de estreno (of a film) ‖ *I have a ten-minute run before breakfast* corro *or* echo una carrera de diez minutos antes del desayuno ‖ *in the long run* a la larga ‖ *it's only half an hour's run* está sólo a media hora de aquí ‖ *landing run* distancia recorrida al aterrizar ‖ *out of the common run* fuera de lo común ‖ *prices came down with a run* los precios experimentaron una caída vertical ‖ *the common run of men* el común de los mortales ‖ FIG *the play had a run of a year* la obra estuvo en cartel durante un año ‖ *there was a run on the bank* el banco sufrió el asedio de los cuentacorrentistas que querían retirar el dinero ‖ *to be always on the run* haberse fugado *or* escapado ‖ *to break into a run* echar a correr ‖ FIG *to give s.o. a run for his money* hacer pasar un mal rato a alguien (to give a bad time), permitir a alguien que le saque el jugo al dinero (to give good value) | *to have a good o a long run* estar mucho tiempo en cartel (play, show), ser popular durante mucho tiempo (person), estar de moda durante mucho tiempo (fashion) | *to have a good run for one's money* dar buena cuenta de sí (working for a long time), sacarle jugo al dinero (to have good value) ‖ *to keep the enemy on the run* hostigar al enemigo ‖ *to make a run for it* escaparse ‖ *trial run* prueba *f*.

run* [rʌn] *vi* correr (to move quickly); *he set off running* echó a correr; *the lions ran loose in* *the street* los leones corrían sueltos por la calle; *the rope runs in the pulley* la cuerda corre por la polea || echar a correr; *he grabbed the money and ran* cogió el dinero y echó a correr || ir corriendo; *to run for the doctor* ir corriendo en busca del médico || correr (rumour) || irse, huir; *to run from a place* irse de un sitio || resbalar, deslizarse (to slide); *sledges run on snow* los trineos se deslizan por la nieve || circular; *the traffic runs day and night* los coches circulan día y noche || circular, hacer el servicio; *trains running between London and the coast* trenes que circulan entre Londres y la costa || salir; *the train runs every two hours* el tren sale cada dos horas || MAR hacer, marchar a, navegar a; *the ship runs 12 knots* el barco marcha a doce nudos | navegar; *to run before the wind* navegar con el viento en popa || MED supurar (abscess) | llorar (eyes) | moquear (nose) || SP correr, participar; *to run in a race* participar en una carrera | llegar; *to run third in a race* llegar el tercero en una carrera | disputarse (a cup) || THEATR estar en cartel (a play, etc.) || TECH funcionar (machine); *the engine is still running* el motor funciona todavía | girar (wheel, spindle) | marchar; *this car runs very well* este coche marcha muy bien || derretirse; *the ice cream is beginning to run* el helado está empezando a derretirse || correrse; *the ink is running* la tinta se corre || desteñirse, correrse (colours) || salirse (to leak) || GEOGR tener un curso (*for* de); *river that runs for 100 miles* río que tiene un curso de cien millas || estar colocado; *the shelves run all round the room* los estantes están colocados alrededor de la habitación || extenderse; *the mountains run across the country* la cordillera se extiende a través del país || pasar; *the road runs quite close to the village* la carretera pasa bastante cerca del pueblo || decir, rezar (to say); *the poem runs like this* el poema dice así || girar (*on* sobre), tratar (*on* de); *the talk ran on this subject* la conversación giró sobre este tema || gotear (to drip) || correr (to flow) || manar, correr (blood) || hacerse una carrerilla (stockings) || JUR ser válido *or* estar vigente (decree) || COMM ser válido; *the contract has two years to run* el contrato es válido para dos años || BOT extenderse (roots) || emigrar (to migrate) || — *a heavy sea is running* el mar está encrespado || *his funds were running low* le quedaba poco dinero || *I can't run to that* no puedo comprar eso, no tengo bastante dinero para eso, no puedo permitirme eso || *it runs in the family* viene de familia || *money runs through his fingers like water* tiene un boquete en la mano, es un manirroto || *my pen runs* a mi pluma se le sale la tinta || *prices run from a pound to ten pounds* los precios oscilan entre una libra y diez libras || *run for your lives!* ¡sálvese quien pueda! || *the floor was running with water* el suelo estaba lleno de agua || *the gutters were running with water* el agua corría por los arroyos || *the money will not run to a car* no hay bastante dinero para comprar un coche || *the play ran for 200 nights* la obra estuvo en cartel doscientos días, la obra tuvo doscientas representaciones *or* se representó doscientas veces || *the river ran blood* el río estaba teñido de sangre || *the song kept running through his head* tenía esa canción metida en la cabeza || *the tap is running* el grifo está abierto || *the thought keeps running through my head* esta idea me está dando vueltas en la cabeza, no me puedo sacar esta idea de la cabeza || *the tide is running strongly* la marea sube *or* baja rápidamente || *this defect runs through all his work* esta falta se encuentra en todo su trabajo || MAR *to run aground* o *ashore* encallar, varar, embarrancarse || *to run cold* helarse (the blood) || *to run dry* secarse || *to run high* ser alto (precios), ser numerosos; *accidents are running high this year* son numerosos los accidentes este año; estar encrespado (the sea), estar crecido (river), estar acalorado (spirits), estar desencadenado (passions) || *to run like the devil* o *a hare* o *hell* correr como un descosido || *to run low* escasear || ELECTR *to run off the mains* funcionar con electricidad || *to run past s.o.* pasar delante de alguien corriendo (to pass by), adelantar (to overtake) || *to run short of money* andar escaso de dinero || *to run smoothly* transcurrir tranquilamente (life), marchar bien (engine), correr tranquilamente (river), ir bien (for s.o.); *things never run smoothly for me* nunca me van bien las cosas || *to run to* ascender a, alcanzar; *production runs to a million tons* la producción asciende a un millón de toneladas; durar; *our holidays ran to three weeks* nuestras vacaciones duraron tres semanas; tener; *this paper runs to twenty pages* este periódico tiene veinte páginas || *to run to fat* engordar || *to run to help s.o.* correr en ayuda de alguien || *to run to meet s.o.* correr al encuentro de alguien || AGR *to run to seed* granar || *to run upstairs* subir las escaleras corriendo || *to run with sweat* chorrear sudor || *we are running short of oranges* nos quedan pocas naranjas || *your bath is running* el baño se está llenando || *your nose is running, you are running at the nose* tienes mocos (fam).

◆ *vt* recorrer (a distance); *to run a mile* recorrer una milla || andar por; *to run the streets* andar por las calles || hincar (to drive in) || empujar (to push) || manejar, llevar (to operate); *to run a tractor* manejar un tractor || manejar, atender al funcionamiento de, ocuparse de (a machine) || dirigir, llevar; *to run a factory* dirigir una fábrica; *to run s.o.'s affairs* llevar los asuntos de alguien || llevar (a house) || organizar, dirigir (a campaign) || poner, meter; *he ran his car into the garage* puso el coche en el garaje || pasar; *you'll have to run the pipe through this wall* tendrá que pasar el tubo por esta pared || pasar de contrabando (to smuggle); *to run arms* pasar armas de contrabando || forzar, burlar (a blockade) || correr, exponerse a (risk) || publicar (a story in a newspaper, etc.) || exhibir, echar (a film) || presentar como candidato; *the Conservatives are running their best representative* los conservadores presentan a su mejor representante como candidato || SP correr en, participar en; *to run a race* correr una carrera | correr; *he ran a bad race* corrió muy mal; *to run a horse* correr un caballo || hacer correr; *to run a rope through a pulley* hacer correr una cuerda por una polea || deslizar, pasar; *to run one's fingers along a table* deslizar los dedos sobre la mesa || pasar; *he ran his hand through his hair* se pasó la mano por el pelo || tener (to possess); *it is very expensive to run a car these days* es muy caro tener coche actualmente || establecer un servicio de; *to run trains between two towns* establecer un servicio de trenes entre dos ciudades || poner; *airlines run extra flights in August* las compañías aéreas ponen vuelos extraordinarios en agosto || llevar; *could you run me to London in your car?* ¿me podría llevar a Londres en coche? || correr (in hunting); *to run a wild boar* correr un jabalí || AGR pacer (cattle) || COMM vender (goods) || TECH vaciar, colar; *to run molten metal into a mould* vaciar un metal fundido en un molde || — *cheap to run* económico, ca || *he ran a needle into his finger* se clavó una aguja en el dedo || *let the affair run its course* deja que el asunto siga su curso || *to be run* estar en servicio (planes, trains, etc.) || *to run a chance of being* tener la posibilidad de ser || *to run a line around sth.* rodear algo con una línea, trazar una línea alrededor de algo || *to run an errand* o *a message* hacer un recado || FIG *to run a parallel too far* llevar una comparación demasiado lejos || *to run a temperature* tener fiebre || *to run its course* seguir su curso || *to run one's pen through a word* tachar una palabra || *to run s.o. close* o *hard* seguir de cerca a uno, pisarle los talones a uno || *to run s.o. off his legs* hacer correr a alguien hasta agotarle || *to run s.o. through with a sword, to run a sword through s.o.* traspasar a uno con una espada || *to run the length of sth.* correr de un extremo a otro de algo.

◆ *phr v* **to run about** correr por todas partes || **to run across** cruzar corriendo; *he ran across the street* cruzó la calle corriendo | tropezar con (s.o., sth.); *I ran across him yesterday* tropecé con él ayer || **to run after** perseguir, ir detrás de (s.o., sth.) | solicitar; *she is very much run after* está muy solicitada || **to run against** chocar contra (to collide) | ir en contra de; *this runs against my interests* esto va en contra de mis intereses || **to run along** ir corriendo; *he was running along shouting* iba corriendo y gritando | correr a lo largo de; *the landing strip runs along the beach* la pista de aterrizaje corre a lo largo de la playa | MAR costear | FAM *run along!* ¡vete! || **to run around with** asociarse con || **to run at** abalanzarse sobre, arremeter contra || **to run away** escaparse, fugarse, evadirse; *the prisoner ran away from jail* el preso se escapó de la cárcel | huir (from one's responsibilities) | desbocarse (a horse) | *don't run away with the idea that* no te vayas a creer que | *his temper ran away with him* perdió el control de sí mismo | *that runs away with a lot of money* esto hace gastar mucho dinero | *to run away from home* escaparse *or* huir de casa | *to run away from the facts* negarse a reconocer los hechos | *to run away with* llevarse; *the thief ran away with five hundred pounds* el ladrón se llevó quinientas libras; ganar fácilmente (a race) || **to run back** volver corriendo || **to run by** pasar corriendo; *he has just run by* acaba de pasar corriendo || pasar corriendo delante de; *he ran by my house* pasó corriendo delante de mi casa | ser conocido por (a name) || **to run down** bajar corriendo; *he ran down the street* bajó la calle corriendo | correr (water) | pararse, quedarse sin cuerda (watch) | atropellar, pillar (to knock over); *the car ran down a child* el coche pilló a un niño | atropellar (to run over) | MAR hundir (a ship) | acorralar (a stag) | encontrar; *the police ran him down* la policía le encontró | FAM echar abajo (an argument), poner por los suelos (s.o.) || agotar (to exhaust) | TECH descargar | dejar de funcionar (an engine) || **to run for** presentar su candidatura a *or* para, presentarse a *or* para; *he ran for Parliament last year* presentó su candidatura al Parlamento el año pasado | *to run for it* darse a la fuga, fugarse || **to run in** detener (to arrest) | entrar corriendo (to enter at a run) | rodar, hacer funcionar (engine, car, etc.) | entrar un momento (to pay a quick call) | AUT *to be running in* estar en rodaje || **to run into** entrar corriendo en (to enter at a run) || chocar contra (to collide with); *the car ran into a tree* el coche chocó contra un árbol | tropezar con, encontrarse a (to meet by chance) | tropezar con; *to run into difficulties* tropezar con dificultades | enfrentarse con (danger) | desembocar en (rivers, streets) | llegar a; *the expenses run into hundreds of pounds* los gastos llegan a cientos de libras | *to run into debt* contraer deudas | *to run s.o. into debt* hacer que alguien contraiga deudas | MAR *to run into port* entrar en el puerto || **to run off** salirse (a liquid) | escaparse, fugarse (person) | salirse; *to run off the subject* salirse del tema | SP correr (a race) | dejar correr (water) | TECH colar, vaciar (metal) | PRINT tirar | redactar rápidamente (an article) | recitar de un tirón (a poem) | FAM *to run off at the mouth* irse de la boca, hablar más de la cuenta | *to run off the rails* descarrilarse | *to run off with* llevarse || **to run on** funcionar con; *this car runs on petrol* este coche funciona con gasolina | seguir corriendo (to continue running) | continuar, seguir (to continue) | transcurrir, pasar (time) | PRINT enlazar | FAM hablar sin parar (to talk without stopping) || **to run out** salirse (liquid) | desenrollarse (rope) | salir corriendo (to exit at a run) | acabarse, agotarse (to finish); *my patience is running out* se me está acabando la paciencia | agotarse (stocks) | expirar, vencer (contract, lease) | bajar (tide) | FAM echar, expulsar (of a club, etc.) | SP poner fuera de juego | *to run out of* quedarse sin; *we are running out of coal* nos estamos quedando sin carbón | *to run out on* dejar, abandonar; *Anthony has run out on Mary* Antonio ha abandonado a María || ***to run over*** pillar (to hit); *the car ran over a hedgehog* el coche pilló un erizo | atropellar; *he was run over* fue atropellado | echar un vistazo a (a text) | volver a ensayar (to rehearse) | rebosar (to overflow) | derramarse; *the milk ran over* la leche se derramó | desbordarse, salir de madre (a river) | *the meeting ran over by five minutes* la reunión duró cinco minutos más de lo previsto | *to run over to* pegar un salto a || *to run through* atravesar corriendo (a room, etc.) | pasar por (a river) | echar un vistazo a, leer por encima (a document) | hojear (a book) | despilfarrar (fortune) | despachar (an affair) | filtrar, colar (a liquid) | atravesar, traspasar (to transpierce) | tachar (to cross out) || ***to run to*** dar *or* alcanzar para (salary); *my salary won't run to a car* mi sueldo no da *or* alcanza para un coche || ***to run up*** izar (a flag) | hacer rápidamente (to make quickly) | construir (a house) | dejar que se acumule (debt) | hacer subir (prices) | llegar corriendo (to arrive at a run) | subir corriendo; *he ran up the stairs* subió corriendo las escaleras | crecer rápidamente (plant) | *to run up against* tropezar con | *to run up bills* endeudarse, contraer deudas.

— OBSERV Pret ***ran***; pp ***run***.

runabout [-əbaut] *n* coche *m* pequeño (car) | lancha *f* pequeña (boat) || *US* vagabundo *m* (tramp).

runaround [-əraund] *n* FAM *to give s.o. the runaround* dar largas a alguien.

runaway [-əwei] *adj* fugitivo, va (futigive) || clandestino, na; *runaway marriage* casamiento clandestino || fácilmente ganado, fácil (a race) || abrumador, ra; holgado, da; amplio, plia (victory) || desbocado, da (a horse) || incontrolado, da; *the runaway lorry hurtled into the crowd* el camión incontrolado se precipitó contra la muchedumbre || galopante; *runaway inflation* inflación galopante.

◆ *n* fugitivo *m* (fugitive) || MIL desertor *m* (deserter) || huida *f* (flight) || caballo *m* desbocado (horse).

run-down [-daun] *adj* agotado, da (exhausted) || parado, da; sin cuerda, que no tiene cuerda (clocks) || descargado, da (accumulator) || ruinoso, sa (houses, etc.).

rundown [-daun] *n* informe *m* detallado.

rune [ru:n] *n* runa *f* (ancient Scandinavian character).

rung [rʌŋ] *n* escalón *m*, peldaño *m* (of a ladder) || barrote *m* (of a chair).

rung [rʌŋ] *pp* ⟶ **ring.**

runic ['ru:nik] *adj* rúnico, ca.

run-in ['rʌnin] *n* PRINT palabras *f pl* insertadas || *US* FAM riña *f* (argument).

runlet ['rʌnlet]; **runnel** ['rʌnl] *n* arroyo *m*.

runner ['rʌnə*] *n* SP corredor, ra (athlete) | caballo *m* de carrera (horse) | cuchilla *f* (of skate) | patín *m* (of sledge) || mensajero *m*, recadero *m* (messenger) || MIL enlace *m* || contrabandista *m* & *f* (smuggler) || BOT estolón *m* | planta *f* trepadora (climbing plant) || tapete *m* (for a table) || alfombra *f* de un pasillo (long rug) || TECH carro *m* | guía *f*, cursor *m* (of a drawer, etc.) | polea *f* (pulley) | anillo *m* móvil (ring) | rueda *f* (wheel) | orificio *m* de colada (in metallurgy) || AVIAT patín *m* || rascón *m* (bird) || malla *f* suelta (in fabric) || carrerilla *f* (in stockings) || *US* mecánico *m* (of a railway engine) | cobrador *m* (of a bank) || *runner bean* judía *f* escarlata.

runner-up [-'ʌp] *n* subcampeón, ona; segundo, da.

— OBSERV El plural es *runners-up*.

running ['rʌniŋ] *adj* que está corriendo (that is running) || de carrera (horse, etc.) || MIL en retirada; *running fight* combate en retirada | graneado, da; *running fire* fuego graneado || corriente; *running water* agua corriente || corredizo, za; *running knot* nudo corredizo || movedizo, za (land) || en marcha; *running machine* máquina en marcha || MED supurante; *a running sore* una llaga supurante || COMM corriente (account, expenses) || TECH móvil; *running block* polea móvil || — *in running order* en buen estado || *running cold* constipado *m* muy fuerte || RAD *running commentary* reportaje *m* en directo || ECON *running costs* gastos *m pl* corrientes || *running handwriting* letra cursiva || SP *running kick* puntapié dado al correr || *running reading* lectura corrida || *running repairs* reparaciones *f pl* menores || SP *running start* salida lanzada || *three months running* tres meses seguidos || *twice running* dos veces seguidas.

◆ *n* carrera *f* (race) || derrame *m* (of a liquid) || chorro *m* (of water) || circulación *f* (of trains, etc.) || contrabando *m* (smuggling) || MED supuración *f* || COMM dirección *f* (of a firm) || TECH funcionamiento *m*, marcha *f* || — *to be in the running* tener posibilidades de ganar || *to be out of the running* no tener ninguna posibilidad de ganar || *to make the running* abrir el paso, marcar la pauta.

running aground [-ə'graund] *n* MAR varada *f*, encallamiento *m*.

running board [-bɔ:d] *n* AUT estribo *m*.

running head [-hed]; **running title** [-'taitl]; **running headline** [-'hedlain] *n* PRINT titulillo *m*.

running in [-'in] *n* rodaje *m*.

running light [-lait] *n* luz *f* de situación.

running mate [-meit] *n* *US* candidato *m* a la vicepresidencia.

running track [-træk] *n* SP pista *f*.

runny ['rʌni] *adj* blando, da (soft) || líquido, da (liquid) || que moquea (nose).

runoff ['rʌnɔf] *n* SP carrera *f* de desempate *or* final.

run-of-the-mill ['rʌnəvðə'mil] *adj* corriente y moliente.

runproof ['rʌnpru:f] *adj* indesmallable (stockings).

runt [rʌnt] *n* bóvido *m* de raza pequeña (cattle) || rocín *m* (horse) || FAM enano, na (small person).

run-through ['rʌnθru:] *n* ensayo *m* rápido || lectura *f* rápida.

runty [-i] *adj* *US* chiquitejo, ja; enano, na.

run-up ['rʌnʌp] *n* SP carrera *f* para tomar impulso || FIG período *m* preliminar.

runway ['rʌnwei] *n* AVIAT pista *f* [de aterrizaje o de despegue] || cauce *m* (of a river) || — *overhead runway* transportador aéreo || *runway light* baliza *f* (of an airport).

rupee [ru:'pi:] *n* rupia *f*.

rupestral [ru'pestrəl]; **rupestrian** [ru'pestriən] *adj* rupestre.

rupture ['rʌptʃə*] *n* ruptura *f* || MED hernia *f*.

rupture ['rʌptʃə*] *vt* romper || MED hacer una hernia en || *to rupture o.s.* herniarse, quebrarse, hacerse una hernia.

◆ *vi* MED quebrarse, hacerse una hernia, herniarse.

rural ['ruərəl] *adj* rural; *rural problems* problemas rurales; *rural farm* finca rural; *rural policeman* guarda rural || *rural dwellers* campesinos *m*.

ruralism ['ruərəlizəm] *n* rusticidad *f* || *US* regionalismo *m* (word).

ruse [ru:z] *n* astucia *f*, treta *f*, ardid *m*.

rush [rʌʃ] *adj* urgente; *a rush job* un trabajo urgente || *rush hour* hora *f* punta, hora *f* de mayor afluencia.

◆ *n* ímpetu *m* (impetus) || prisa *f*, precipitación *f* (haste); *what's your rush?* ¿por qué tiene prisa? || afluencia *f*, riada *f*, avalancha *f* (flow of people) || aglomeración *f* de gente (crowd) || bullicio *m*, confusión *f* (crush) || torrente *m*; *the rush of water* un torrente de agua; *a rush of words* un torrente de palabras || bullicio *m*, ajetreo *m*; *the rush of city life* el bullicio de la vida de la ciudad || agobio *m*; *a rush of work* un agobio de trabajo || MED aflujo *m*, agolpamiento *m*; *a rush of blood to the head* un agolpamiento de sangre en la cabeza || arrebato *m*; *a rush of tenderness* un arrebato de ternura || bocanada *f* (of air) || ráfaga *f* (of wind) || COMM gran demanda *f*; *there was a rush on oranges* hubo una gran demanda de naranjas || SP ataque *m* || MIL ataque *m*, acometida *f*, asalto *m* || ELECTR aumento *m* brusco de la corriente, sobrevoltaje *m* || primeras pruebas *f pl* (first proofs of a film) || BOT junco *m*; *the swamp was full of rushes* las marismas estaban llenas de juncos || — *in a rush* de prisa || *there is no rush* no corre prisa || *there was a rush to the emergency exit* la gente se precipitó hacia la salida de emergencia || *to be always in a rush* tener siempre prisa || *to do sth. in a rush* hacer algo precipitadamente || *to make a rush at* abalanzarse sobre, precipitarse sobre || *with a rush* de repente.

rush [rʌʃ] *vt* hacer precipitadamente *or* de prisa; *to rush a job* hacer precipitadamente una tarea || ejecutar urgentemente (an order) || dar *or* meter prisa; *don't rush me!* ¡no me metas prisa! || precipitarse, abalanzarse, lanzarse contra; *the crowd rushed the building* la muchedumbre se precipitó hacia el edificio || llevar de prisa, transportar de prisa *or* con urgencia; *they rushed the child to the doctor* llevaron de prisa al niño al médico || empujar a, forzar a; *to rush s.o. into marriage* forzar a alguien a casarse || MIL tomar por asalto (a position) || FAM sacar; *he rushed me 5 pounds for it* me sacó cinco libras para ello | ir tras de (to court assiduously) || — *I don't want to rush you* hágalo con tranquilidad || *to rush into print* publicar precipitadamente.

◆ *vi* precipitarse, abalanzarse (to haste); *everyone rushed to the doors* todos se precipitaron hacia las puertas || ir de prisa, correr (to go quickly) || darse prisa, apresurarse; *they rushed to help her* se apresuraron *or* se dieron prisa en ayudarle || irse corriendo, marcharse; *I simply must rush* me tengo que ir corriendo || — *tears rushed to her eyes* se le llenaron los ojos de lágrimas || *the blood rushed to his face* se puso colorado, se sonrojó || FIG *to be rushed off one's feet* estar muy liado, da || *to rush to conclusions* sacar conclusiones apresuradas.

◆ *phr v* *to rush about* correr de un lado a otro || ***to rush across*** atravesar rápidamente || ***to rush at*** abalanzarse sobre || ***to rush forward*** abalanzarse, precipitarse || ***to rush in*** o ***into*** meterse en (an affair) | surgir en, venir a (one's memory) | hacer irrupción en, entrar precipitadamente en (a room) || ***to rush off*** irse a toda velocidad || ***to rush out*** salir precipitadamente || ***to rush through*** leer de prisa (a book) | visitar precipitadamente (a museum) | atravesar a toda velocidad (a town) | despachar rápidamente (one's work) | hacer de prisa (to do quickly) | *to rush a bill through Parliament* hacer aprobar rápidamente un proyecto de ley.

rushing [-iŋ] *n* precipitación *f*, apresuramiento *m*.

◆ *adj* impetuoso, sa (torrent).

rushlight [-lait] *n* vela *f* de junco.

rushy [-i] *adj* de junco || cubierto de juncos.

rusk [rʌsk] *n* galleta *f* (biscuit) || bizcocho *m*.

russet ['rʌsit] *adj* rojizo, za.
◆ *n* color *m* rojizo.

Russia ['rʌʃə] *pr n* GEOGR Rusia *f*.

Russian [-n] *adj* ruso, sa.
◆ *n* ruso, sa (inhabitant of Russia) || ruso *m* (language).

Russianize ['rʌʃənaiz]; **Russify** ['rʌsifai] *vt* rusificar.

Russophil ['rʌsəufil]; **Russophile** ['rʌsəufail] *adj/n* rusófilo, la.

rust [rʌst] *n* oxidación *f*, corrosión *f* (action) || orín *m*, herrumbre *f*, moho *m* (on metal) || color *m* de orín (colour) || BOT roya *f*, añublo *m*, tizón *m*.

rust [rʌst] *vt* oxidar, enmohecer, poner mohoso.
◆ *vi* oxidarse, enmohecerse, ponerse mohoso || FIG entumecerse (a person).

rustic [-ik] *adj* campesino, na; campestre, rústico, ca (rural) || paleto, ta; palurdo, da (boorish).
◆ *n* rústico, ca; campesino, na (peasant) || palurdo, da; paleto, ta (bumpkin).

rusticate [-ikeit] *vi* (ir a) vivir en el campo.
◆ *vt* expulsar temporalmente (from a college).

rustication [ˌristi'keiʃən] *n* vida *f* en el campo || expulsión *f* temporal (from a college).

rusticity [rʌs'tisiti] *n* rusticidad *f*.

rustiness ['rʌstinis] *n* herrumbre *f*, moho *m*, oxidación *f* (of metals) || FIG enmohecimiento *m*.

rustle ['rʌsl] *n* susurro *m* (of leaves) || crujir (paper, material) || US robar ganado (to steal cattle) | moverse, agitarse (to move busily).
◆ *vt* hacer susurrar (sound) || hacer crujir (paper, material) || US robar [ganado] (to steal cattle).

rustler [-ə*] *n* US ladrón *m* de ganado | hombre *m* emprendedor.

rustless ['rʌstlis] *adj* inoxidable.

rustproof ['rʌstˌpru:f] *adj* inoxidable.

rusty ['rʌsti] *adj* oxidado, da; mohoso, sa; herrumbroso, sa (metal) || de color de orín, de color mohoso (colour) || ronco, ca (voice) || FIG desentrenado, da; falto de práctica; *I am a little rusty in French* estoy un poco falto de práctica en francés || FIG *my French is rusty* me falta práctica en francés, tengo que practicar el francés.

rut [rʌt] *n* surco *m* (furrow) || carril *m*, carrilada *f*, rodada *f* (of wheels) || ranura *f* (groove) || bache *m* (pothole); *a road full of ruts* una carretera llena de baches || FIG rutina *f*, camino *m* trillado (routine) || celo *m* (of animals) || FIG *to be in a rut* ser esclavo de la rutina.

rut [rʌt] *vt* surcar.
◆ *vi* estar en celo (animals).

rutabaga ['ru:təˌbeigə] *n* US BOT colinabo *m*, nabo sueco *m*.

rutaceae [ru'teisii:] *pl n* BOT rutáceas *f*.

ruth [ru:θ] *n* piedad *f*, compasión *f*.

Ruth [ru:θ] *pr n* Rut *f*.

ruthenium [ru:'θi:niəm] *n* CHEM rutenio *m*.

ruthless ['ru:θlis] *adj* despiadado, da; cruel || implacable.

ruthlessness [-nis] *n* crueldad *f*, falta *f* de piedad || implacabilidad *f*.

rutilant ['ru:tilənt] *adj* rutilante.

rutile ['ru:til] *n* MIN rutilo *m*.

rutty ['rʌti] *adj* lleno de baches.

rye [rai] *n* BOT centeno *m* || US whisky *m* de centeno (drink) || *rye bread* pan *m* de centeno.

ryegrass [-grɑ:s] *n* BOT ballico *m*.

ryot ['raiət] *n* campesino *m* indio.

S

s [es] *n* s *f* (letter).

's [-iz] *possessive ending* *the girl's handbag* el bolso de la chica; *the girls' handbags* los bolsos de las chicas.

Saar [saː*] *pr n* GEOGR Sarre *m*.
— OBSERV Esta palabra siempre lleva el artículo en español, lo mismo que en inglés.

Sabaean [sə'biən] *adj/n* sabeo, a.

sabbath ['sæbəθ] *n* REL domingo *m* (sunday) | sábado *m* (of the Jewish week) || aquelarre *m* (witches').

sabbatical [sə'bætikəl] *adj* sabático, ca || *sabbatical year* año *m* de permiso (granted to teachers).

sabbatine ['sæbətain] *adj* sabatino, na; *sabbatine bull* bula sabatina.

Sabean [sə'biːən] *adj/n* sabeo, a.

saber ['seibə*] *n* US sable *m*.

saber ['seibə*] *vt* US herir *or* matar a sablazos, acuchillar.

Sabine ['sæbain] *adj/n* sabino, na.

sable ['seibl] *n* ZOOL marta *f* cebellina, cebellina *f*, cibelina *f* || HERALD sable *m*.
◆ *pl* trajes *m* de luto (black clothing).
◆ *adj* negro, gra (black) || HERALD casquillo *m*.

sabot ['sæbəu] *n* zueco *m* (clog) || MIL casquillo *m*.

sabotage ['sæbətɑːʒ] *n* sabotaje *m*.

sabotage ['sæbətɑːʒ] *vt* sabotear.

saboteur [ˌsæbə'təː*] *n* saboteador, ra.

sabre ['seibə*] *n* sable *m* || FIG *saber rattling* amenazas *f pl*.

sabretache ['sæbətæʃ] *n* (ant) MIL portapliegos *m inv* (leather case).

sac [sæk] *n* ANAT bolsa *f*, saco *m*.

saccharification [sæˌkərifi'keiʃən] *n* CHEM sacarificación *f*.

saccharify [sæ'kærifai] *vt* CHEM sacarificar.

saccharin ['sækərin] *n* CHEM sacarina *f*.

saccharine ['sækərain] *adj* CHEM sacarino, na || FIG empalagoso, sa.

saccharoid ['sækərɔid] *adj* GEOL sacaroideo, a (granular in structure).

saccharometer [sækə'rɔmitə*] *n* sacarímetro *m*.

saccharomyces ['sækərə'maisiːz] *pl n* sacaromicetos *m* (yeasts).

saccharose ['sækərəus] *n* CHEM sacarosa *f*.

sacerdotal [ˌsæsə'dəutl] *adj* sacerdotal.

sachem ['seitʃəm] *n* sachem *m* (Indian chief) || US FIG & FAM pez *m* gordo.

sachet ['sæʃei] *n* saquito *m*, bolsita *f* (small bag) || almohadilla *f* perfumada (perfumed).

sack [sæk] *n* saco *m* (for goods) || costal *m* (for grains) || vestido *m* saco (dress) || FAM cama *f* (bed) || MIL saqueo *m*, saco *m* || — *sack race* carrera *f* de sacos || FIG & FAM *to get the sack* ser despedido | *to give s.o. the sack* poner a alguien de patitas en la calle, echar a alguien, despedir a alguien (to dismiss).

sack [sæk] *vt* ensacar (to put into sacks) || MIL saquear, entrar a saco en || FIG & FAM poner de patitas en la calle, echar, despedir (to dismiss).

sackbut [-bʌt] *n* MUS sacabuche *m*.

sackcloth [-klɔθ] *n* tela *f* de saco, arpillera *f* (coarse cloth) || sayal *m* (penitential clothing) || FIG *to wear sackcloth and ashes* arrepentirse.

sacker [-ə*] *n* saqueador, ra.

sackful [-ful] *n* saco *m* (content); *a sackful of coal* un saco de carbón.

sacking [-iŋ] *n* tela *f* de saco, arpillera *f* (coarse cloth) || FAM despido *m* (dismissal).

sacral ['seikrəl] *adj* ANAT sacro, cra || REL sagrado, da.

sacrament ['sækrəmənt] *n* REL sacramento *m*; *to administer the last sacraments* administrar los últimos sacramentos; *the Holy Sacrament* el Santísimo Sacramento || (ant) juramento *m* (solemn oath).

sacramental [ˌsækrə'mentl] *adj* sacramental.
◆ *n* sacramental *m*.

Sacramentarian [ˌsækrəmen'tɛəriən] *n* sacramentario *m*.

sacred ['seikrid] *adj* sacro, cra; sagrado, da; *sacred history* historia sacra *or* sagrada || religioso, sa (song, picture, procession) || consagrado, da; dedicado, da; *sacred to the memory of* consagrado a la memoria de || mayor (religious order) || de música religiosa (concert) || FIG sagrado, da; *the siesta is sacred in Spain* en España la siesta es sagrada || — FIG *nothing is sacred any more* ya no se respeta nada || *Sacred College* Sacro Colegio || *sacred cow* vaca sagrada || *sacred fire* fuego sacro || *Sacred Heart* Sagrado Corazón || *sacred music* música sacra || *the Sacred Way* la Vía Sacra.

sacredness [-nis] *n* santidad *f* || FIG lo sagrado.

sacrifice ['sækrifais] *n* sacrificio *m*; *to make a sacrifice to the gods* ofrecer un sacrificio a los dioses || ofrenda *f* (thing offered) || FIG sacrificio *m*; *to make sacrifices for one's children* hacer sacrificios por sus hijos || — COMM *at a sacrifice* con pérdida || FIG *at the sacrifice of* en detrimento de, sacrificando.

sacrifice ['sækrifais] *vt* sacrificar || COMM vender a un precio sacrificado, vender con pérdida || FIG sacrificar (one's interests, etc.) || FIG *to sacrifice o.s.* sacrificarse.
◆ *vi* ofrecer un sacrificio.

sacrificeable [-əbl] *adj* sacrificable.

sacrificer [-ə*] *n* sacrificador, ra.

sacrificial [ˌsækri'fiʃəl] *adj* sacrificatorio, ria || — COMM *sacrificial price* precio sacrificado | *sacrificial sale* venta *f* con pérdida.

sacrilege ['sækrilidʒ] *n* sacrilegio *m*.

sacrilegious [ˌsækri'lidʒəs] *adj* sacrílego, ga || *sacrilegious person* sacrílego, ga.

sacring bell ['seikriŋ'bel] *n* REL campanilla *f* de la Elevación.

sacrist ['sækrist] ; **sacristan** ['sækristən] *n* REL sacristán *m*.

sacristy ['sækristi] *n* REL sacristía *f*.

sacroiliac [seikrə'iliæk] *adj* ANAT sacroilíaco, ca.

sacrosanct ['sækrəusæŋkt] *adj* sacrosanto, ta.

sacrum ['seikrəm] *n* ANAT sacro *m*.
— OBSERV El plural de *sacrum* es *sacra* o *sacrums*.

sad [sæd] *adj* triste; *he is sad because his cat has died* está triste porque su gato ha muerto; *a sad place, book* un sitio, un libro triste || doloroso, sa; *a sad loss* una pérdida dolorosa || lamentable, deplorable, triste (deplorable); *a sad mistake* un error deplorable; *a sad lack of manners* una falta de educación lamentable || apagado, da; triste (colour) || FAM malísimo, ma (very bad) || — *a sadder and a wiser man* un hombre que ha escarmentado || *to be sad at heart* tener el corazón oprimido || *to make s.o. sad* entristecer a alguien.

sadden ['sædn] *vt* entristecer.
◆ *vi* entristecerse, ponerse triste.

saddle ['sædl] *n* silla *f* (of a horse); *riding saddle* silla de montar || sillín *m* (of a bicycle, a harness) || CULIN faldilla *f*, cuarto *m* trasero (of mutton) | rabadilla *f* (of hare) || GEOGR puerto *m*, paso *m* (between mountains) || TECH carro *m* de bancada (of a lathe) || — *English* o *hunting saddle* silla inglesa || *saddle horse* caballo *m* de silla || ARCH *saddle roof* tejado *m* de dos aguas || SP *the favourite is the Flying Dutchman with John Smith in the saddle* el favorito es el Flying Dutchman montado por John Smith || FIG *to be in the saddle* llevar las riendas || *to be thrown out of the saddle* perder los estribos.

saddle ['sædl] *vt* ensillar || — FIG & FAM *to get saddled with* o *to saddle o.s. with a responsibility* cargar con una responsabilidad || *to saddle s.o. with the blame* echar la culpa a alguien || *to saddle up* ensillar (a horse).

saddleback [-bæk] *n* ARCH tejado *m* de dos aguas (roof) || ensillada *f* (hill) || ZOOL animal *m* albardado (with a different-coloured back).

saddle-backed [-bækt] *adj* ARCH de dos aguas (roof) || ZOOL ensillado, da (with a hollow back).

saddlebag [-bæg] *n* alforja *f* (on a horse) || cartera *f* (on a bicycle).

saddlebow [-bəu] *n* arzón *m*.

saddlecloth [-klɔθ] *n* manta *f* sudadera, sudadero *m*.

saddler [-ə*] *n* guarnicionero *m*, talabartero *m*.

saddlery [-əri] *n* guarniciones *f pl*, arreos *m pl* (harness) || guarnicionería *f*, talabartería *f* (saddler's trade).

saddletree [-triː] *n* arzón *m* || US BOT tulipanero *m*.

Sadducee ['sædjusiː] *n* saduceo, a.

sadiron ['sædaiən] *n* plancha *f* (for pressing).

sadism ['seidizəm] *n* sadismo *m*.

sadist ['seidist] *n* sádico, ca.

sadistic [sə'distik] *adj* sádico, ca.

sadly ['sædli] *adv* con tristeza, tristemente (sorrowfully) || desgraciadamente (regrettably).

sadness ['sædnis] *n* tristeza *f*.

sad sack ['sædsæk] *n* FAM desgraciado, da.

safari [sə'fɑːri] *n* safari *m* || *safari park* safari, reserva *f*.

safe [seif] *adj* sano y salvo, ileso, sa; indemne (uninjured); *the car crashed but they were safe* el coche se estrelló pero salieron ilesos || intacto, ta; en buen estado (undamaged) || seguro, ra; en seguridad, a salvo (secure); *if we hide here, we shall be safe* si nos escondemos aquí, estaremos a salvo || seguro, ra; *a safe retreat* un retiro seguro; *a safe bridge* un puente seguro || prudente (cautious); *at a safe distance* a una distancia prudente; *safe policy* política prudente || de fiar, digno de confianza (trustworthy); *you must not tell him anything because he is not safe* no debe decirle nada porque no es de fiar || inofensivo, va (harmless) || salvado, da; *your honour is safe* su honor está salvado || seguro, ra (certain); *safe investment* inversión segura || — *as safe as houses* completamente seguro || *in order to be on the safe side* para mayor seguridad || FIG *in safe hands* en buenas manos || *it is safe to leave her alone?* ¿no es peligroso dejarla sola? || *it is safe to say that* se puede decir con seguridad que || *safe and sound* sano y salvo, ileso, sa || *safe from* a salvo de || *the safest course would be to go* lo más seguro sería marcharse || *this toy is not safe* este juguete es peligroso || *to be on the safe side* para mayor seguridad, para estar tranquilo (for safety's sake), ir sobre seguro, obrar sin riesgos || *to get safe into port* llegar a buen puerto.
◆ *n* caja *f* de caudales, caja *f* fuerte (strongbox) || fresquera *f* (for storing foods).

safeblower [-ˌbləuə*]; **safebreaker** ['seifˌbreikə*] *n* ladrón *m* de cajas de caudales.

safe-conduct [-'kɔndʌkt] *n* salvoconducto *m*.

safecracker [-ˌkrækə*] *n* ladrón *m* de cajas de caudales.

safe deposit [-diˌpɔzit] *n* sala *f* donde se guardan las cajas de seguridad en un banco.

safe-deposit box [-diˌpɔzitˌbɔks] *n* caja *f* de seguridad.

safeguard [-gɑːd] *n* salvaguardia *f*, salvaguarda *f*; *the law is the safeguard of freedom* las leyes son la salvaguardia de la libertad || protección *f* (protection) || garantía *f* (assurance); *I give you a safeguard that you will not suffer in any way* le doy la garantía de que no sufrirá ningún perjuicio || salvoconducto *m* (safe-conduct) || escolta *f* (convoy) || dispositivo *m* de seguridad (safety device) || — *as a safeguard against* para evitar || *to put money aside as a safeguard* poner dinero a un lado como reserva *or* por si acaso.

safeguard [-gɑːd] *vt* salvaguardar, proteger.

safekeeping [-'kiːpiŋ] *n* custodia *f* || *to put into safekeeping* poner a buen recaudo *or* a salvo.

safely [-li] *adv* a buen puerto, sin accidente; *we arrived safely* llegamos a buen puerto || sin peligro; *now you can cross the bridge safely* ahora puede cruzar el puente sin peligro || con toda seguridad, sin temor a equivocarse; *you can safely say that population is increasing* puedes decir con toda seguridad que la población está aumentando || por lo menos, fácilmente; *she is eighteen safely* tiene por lo menos diez y ocho años || — *put it away safely* póngalo en un sitio seguro || *safely and soundly* sano y salvo, ileso, sa || *safely invested money* dinero bien invertido.

safeness [-nis] *n* seguridad *f*.

safety [-ti] *n* seguridad *f*; *safety measures* medidas de seguridad; *public safety* seguridad pública || — *at safety* con el seguro puesto (a weapon) || *for safety's sake* para mayor seguridad || *in a place of safety* en un sitio seguro || *in safety* seguro, en seguridad, a salvo || *safety belt* cinturón *m* de seguridad || *safety bolt* cerrojo *m* de seguridad || *safety catch* seguro *m* (of firearms, of machinery), cadena *f* de seguridad (of bracelets, of brooches), retenedor *m*, cadena *f* de seguridad || *safety film* película *f* incombustible || *safety first!* ¡seguridad ante todo! || *safety first campaign* campaña *f* pro seguridad || *safety fuse* mecha lenta *or* de seguridad, espoleta *f* de seguridad (for detonators), fusible *m* (in an electric circuit) || *safety glass* vidrio *m* inastillable *or* de seguridad || *safety island* refugio *m* (in a street) || *safety lamp* lámpara *f* de seguridad || *safety lock* cerradura *f* de seguridad (on a door), seguro *m* (of firearms) || *safety match* fósforo *m* de seguridad || *safety net* red *f* (in a circus) || *safety pin* imperdible *m* || *safety razor* maquinilla *f* de afeitar || *safety valve* válvula *f* de seguridad || US *safety zone* zona *f* de seguridad || *to be able to do sth. with safety* poder hacer algo sin peligro || *to reach safety* llegar a buen puerto (s.o. who was travelling), llegar a un sitio seguro (s.o. who is hiding), ponerse a salvo (to avoid danger).

saffron ['sæfrən] *n* BOT & CULIN azafrán *m*.
◆ *adj* azafranado, da; de color de azafrán.

sag [sæg] *n* hundimiento *m* (sinking) || pandeo *m* (of a beam, of a wall) || comba *f*, pandeo *m* (of a plank) || caída *f* (of prices) || MAR deriva *f* || flexión *f* (in a rope).

sag [sæg] *vi* hundirse (to sink) || pandear (beam, wall) || combarse, pandear (plank) || aflojarse (rope, cable, etc.) || colgar (flesh, clothes) || caer, bajar (prices) || MAR ir a la deriva || FIG perder interés; *the programme began to sag towards the end* el programa empezó a perder interés hacia el final | decaer (one's spirits) || *his shoulders sagged* tenía los hombros caídos.
◆ *vt* hundir.

saga ['sɑːgə] *n* saga *f* || FIG epopeya *f* (epic) | novela *f* que relata la vida de una familia.

sagacious [sə'geiʃəs] *adj* sagaz.

sagacity [sə'gæsiti] *n* sagacidad *f*.

sagamore ['sægəmɔː*] *n* US sachem *m* (Indian chief).

sage [seidʒ] *adj* sabio, bia (wise) || sensato, ta; cuerdo, da (sensible).
◆ *n* sabio *m* (wise man) || BOT salvia *f*.

sagebrush [-brʌʃ] *n* BOT artemisa *f*.

sageness [-nis] *n* sabiduría *f* (wiseness) || sensatez *f*, cordura *f* (sensibleness).

saggar; US **sagger** ['sægə*] *n* TECH gaceta *f* refractaria (container) | arcilla *f* refractaria (fireclay).

sagging ['sægiŋ] *adj* hundido, da (sunken); *a sagging floor* un piso hundido || decreciente (prices) || flojo, ja (market) || decaído, da (one's spirits).
◆ *n* hundimiento *m* (of a roof, etc.) || baja *f* (of prices).

Sagittarius [ˌsædʒi'tɛəriəs] *n* ASTR Sagitario *m*.

saguntine [sæ'gʌntain] *adj/n* saguntino, na.

Sagunto [sæ'gʌntəu] *pr n* GEOGR Sagunto.

Sahara [sə'hɑːrə] *pr n* GEOGR Sáhara *m*, Sahara *m*.

Saharan [-ən]; **Saharian** [-iən] *adj* sahariano, na; sahárico, ca (place) || saharauí (people).
◆ *n* saharauí *m* & *f* (people).

said [sed] *pret/pp* ⟶ **say.**

sail [seil] *n* MAR vela *f* || velamen *m*, velas *f pl* (collectively) | velero *m*, barco *m* de vela; *not a sail in sight* ni un velero a la vista | viaje *m* [en barco]; *it is a five-day sail away* está a cinco días de viaje | travesía *f* (crossing) | paseo *m* [en barco]; *to go far a sail on the lake* ir de paseo por el lago | manga *f* de ventilación, manga *f* veleta (windsail) || brazo *m*, aspa *f* (of a windmill) || ZOOL aleta *f* (fin) || — *(at) full sail* a toda vela, a todo trapo || *sail ho!* ¡barco a la vista! || *to get under sail, to set sail* hacerse a la vela (sailing ship), hacerse a la mar, zarpar (any boat) || *to strike sail* arriar las velas || *to take in sail* arriar las velas (to haul down), apocar las velas (to reduce the number of sails), recoger velas (to curb one's ambitions) || FIG & FAM *to take the wind out of s.o.'s sails* bajarle los humos a alguien || *under full sail* a toda vela || *under sail* con las velas alzadas (sailing ship), en camino (any boat).

sail [seil] *vt* cruzar, atravesar [en barco]; *to sail the Atlantic* cruzar el Atlántico || gobernar (to manage a boat) || botar; *I sail my boat every Saturday* boto mi barco cada sábado || jugar con (toy boats) || *to sail the seas* surcar los mares.
◆ *vi* navegar; *a boat sailing to New York* un barco que navega rumbo a Nueva York || marchar, navegar; *to sail at 10 knots* marchar a diez nudos || ir en barco; *I sailed to America* fui a América en barco || zarpar, salir; *the ship sails tomorrow* el barco zarpa mañana || volar (to move through the air); *the book sailed through the air* el libro voló por los aires || cernerse (birds) || planear (a glider) || andar majestuosamente (to walk in a stately manner) || — FIG *I sailed through customs in two minutes* pasé por la aduana en dos minutos | *I sailed through the exam* hice el examen muy fácilmente, el examen no me planteó ningún problema || *to sail against the wind* hurtar el viento (a ship), actuar contra el viento y marea (person).
◆ *phr v* **to sail away** irse || **to sail in** entrar (a boat) | entrar majestuosamente (a person) || **to sail into** emprender, acometer (a task) | atacar (to eat greedily) | atacar, arremeter contra (to attack) | entrar majestuosamente en (a room) | tropezar con, topar con (to bump into) || **to sail out** salir || **to sail round** doblar (a headland) | dar la vuelta a (the world).

sail arm [-ɑːm] *n* brazo *m* (of windmill).

sailboat [-bəut] *n* US velero *m*, barco *m* de vela.

sailcloth [-klɔθ] *n* lona *f* (canvas cloth for sails, for tents, etc.).

sailer [-ə*] *n* velero *m* (sailing boat).

sailfish [-fiʃ] *n* ZOOL pez *m* vela (kind of sword-fish).

sailing [-iŋ] *n* MAR navegación *f* | salida *f* (departure); *sailings every half hour* salidas cada media hora | travesía *f* (voyage) || — MAR *plane sailing* navegación loxodrómica | *sailing boat* velero *m*, barco *m* de vela | *sailing orders* últimas instrucciones | *sailing ship* velero *m*, barco *m* de vela || FIG *to be plain sailing* ser coser y cantar, ser pan comido.

sailmaker [-ˌmeikə*] *n* velero *m*.

sailor ['seilə*] *n* marinero *m*, marino *m* || — *to be a bad sailor* marearse fácilmente || *to be a good sailor* no marearse || *sailor hat* sombrero *m* de paja || *sailor suit* traje *m* de marinero.

sailplane ['seilplein] *n* planeador *m* (glider).

sainfoin ['sænfɔin] *n* BOT pipirigallo *m*.

saint [seint] *n* santo, ta || FIG santo, ta (good person) || — *All Saint's Day* Fiesta *f* de Todos los Santos || *Saint John the Baptist* San Juan Bautista || FIG *to be with the Saints* estar con Dios.

— OBSERV The word *Santo* apocopates to *San* before all masculine names: *Saint Paul* San Pablo, except in the cases of *Domingo, Tomás, Tomé* and *Toribio*: *Saint Thomas* Santo Tomás.

saint [seint] *vt* canonizar.

Saint Bernard [snt'bɜːnəd] *n* perro *m* de San Bernardo.

sainted ['seintid] *adj* santo, ta; canonizado, da (canonized) || santo, ta; sagrado, da (holy) || piadoso, sa (pious, saintly) || FIG & FAM *my sainted aunt!* ¡Dios mío!

Saint Elmo's fire [snt'elməuz'faiə*] *n* fuego *m* de San Telmo.

Saint George's [snt'dʒɔːdʒiz] *pr n* GEOGR Saint George's.

sainthood ['seinthud] *n* santidad *f* || santos *m pl* (saints).

Saint John's [snt'dʒɔnz] *pr n* GEOGR Saint John's.

Saint-John's-wort [snt'dʒɔnz,wəːt] *n* BOT corazoncillo *m*, hipérico *m*, hierba *f* de San Juan.

saintliness ['seintlinis] *n* santidad *f*.

saintly ['seintli] *adj* santo, ta; piadoso, sa (holy, pious) || santo, ta (pertaining to a saint).

saint's day ['seints'dei] *n* fiesta *f or* día *m* del santo patrón (of a place) || santo *m*, día *m* onomástico (of a person); *today is my saint's day* hoy es mi santo.

Saint Simonian [sntsi'məunjən] *adj/n* sansimoniano, na.

Saint Valentine's day [snt'væləntains'dei] *n* día *m* de San Valentín, día *m* de los enamorados.

Saint Vitus's dance [snt'vaitəsiz'dɑːns] *n* MED baile *m* de San Vito.

saké; *US* **sake** ['sɑːki] *n* sakí *m*.

saith [seθ] archaic 3rd pers. sing. pres. ind. → **say.**

sake [seik] *n* *for brevity's sake* para ser breve || *for God's* o *for goodness' sake* por el amor de Dios || *for old times' sake* para recordar el pasado || *for pity's sake!* ¡por (el) amor de Dios! || *for the sake of, for... 's sake* por; *he did it for the sake of his children* o *for his children's sake* lo hizo por sus hijos; *for my sake* por mí; *he fought for the sake of his country* o *for his country's sake* luchó por su patria; *art for art's sake* el arte por el arte; *to argue for the sake of it* discutir por discutir; *to talk for talking's sake* hablar por hablar || *for your own sake* por tu propio bien.

saki ['sɑːki] *n* ZOOL sakí *m* (monkey) || sakí *m* (drink).

sal [sæl] *n* CHEM sal *f* || — *sal ammoniac* sal amoníaca, sal amoniaco || *sal volatile* sal volátil.

salaam [sə'lɑːm] *n* zalema *f*.

salaam [sə'lɑːm] *vt* hacer zalemas a.
◆ *vi* hacer zalemas.

salability ['seilə'biliti] *n* facilidad *f* de venta, posibilidad *f* de venta.

salable ['seiləbl] *adj* vendible, de fácil venta.

salacious [sə'leiʃəs] *adj* salaz.

salaciousness [-nis]; **salacity** [sə'læsiti] *n* salacidad *f*.

salad [sæləd] *n* CULIN ensalada *f*; *tomato salad* ensalada de tomates; *lobster salad* ensalada de langosta || lechuga *f* (lettuce) || — *fruit salad* macedonia *f* ensalada de frutas || *salad bowl* ensaladera *f* || *salad cream* salsa parecida a la mayonesa || *salad days* días *m* de juventud || *salad dressing* vinagreta *f*, aderezo *m*, aliño *m* || *salad oil* aceite *m* [para ensalada] || *vegetable salad* ensaladilla *f*.

Salamanca [,sælə'mæŋkə] *pr n* GEOGR Salamanca.

salamander ['sælə,mændə*] *n* ZOOL salamandra *f* || *salamander stove* salamandra *f* (heater).

salami [sə'lɑːmi] *n* CULIN especie *f* de salchichón [*AMER* salame *m*].

salaried ['sælərid] *adj* asalariado, da; *salaried employee, staff* empleado, personal asalariado || retribuido, da (position) || a sueldo (work) || *high-salaried officials* funcionarios bien pagados.

salary ['sæləri] *n* sueldo *m*, salario *m* || — *salary earner* persona *f* que cobra un sueldo || *salary scale* escala *f* salarial || *to be on a salary* estar a sueldo.

salary ['sæləri] *vt* pagar un sueldo a.

sale [seil] *n* venta *f*; *wine sales are rising* están aumentando las ventas de vino || saldo *m*, liquidación *f*, rebajas *f pl* (of old unwanted stock); *to hold a sale* hacer una liquidación; *to buy sth. at the sales* comprar algo en las rebajas || mercado *m*, salida *f* (market); *an object that has a good sale* un objeto que tiene un buen mercado || subasta *f* (by auction) || — *«car for sale»* «se vende coche» || *classing-down sale* liquidación || *credit sale* venta a crédito || *for* o *on sale* en venta || *it is not for sale* no se vende, no está en venta || *sale price* precio *m* de venta (selling price), precio *m* de saldo (reduced price) || *sale value* valor *m* comercial || *to put a piece of land up for sale* poner un terreno en venta || *to put a product on sale* poner un producto en venta || *white sale* quincena blanca.
◆ *pl* venta *f sing*; *sales department* servicio de venta || — *US sales check* factura *f* || *sales drive* promoción *f* de ventas || *sales goods* saldos *m* || *sales talk* cameleo *m* || *sales tax* impuesto *m* sobre las ventas || *sales team* equipo *m* de ventas.

saleability [seilə'biliti] *n* facilidad *f* de venta, posibilidad *f* de venta.

saleable ['seiləbl] *adj* vendible, de fácil venta.

saleratus [,sælə'reitəs] *n* *US* CHEM bicarbonato *m* de sosa.

saleroom ['seilrum] *n* sala *f* de subasta.

sales assistant ['seilzə,sistənt] *n* dependiente, ta.

salesclerk ['seilz,klɑːk] *n* dependiente *m*.

salesgirl ['seilzgəːl] *n* dependienta *f*.

Salesian [sə'liːʒən] *adj/n* REL salesiano, na.

saleslady ['seilz,leidi] *n* dependienta *f*.

salesman ['seilzmən] *n* dependiente *m* (in a shop) || vendedor *m* (seller) || representante *m* (representative) || *travelling salesman* viajante *m* de comercio (commercial traveller).
— OBSERV El plural de la palabra inglesa es *salesmen*.

salesmanship [-ʃip] *n* arte *m* de vender || *his salesmanship is good* es un buen vendedor.

sales representative [-,repri'zentətiv]; **sales rep** [-rep] *n* representante *m* & *f*.

salesroom ['seilzrum] *n* sala *f* de subasta (saleroom) || *US* sala *f* de exposición (showroom).

saleswoman ['seilz'wumən] *n* dependienta *f* (in a shop) || vendedora *f* (seller).
— OBSERV El plural de la palabra inglesa es *saleswomen*.

Salian ['seiljən] *n* HIST salio, lia.

Salic ['sælik] *adj* HIST sálico, ca; *Salic law* ley sálica.

salicylate [sæ'lisileit] *n* CHEM salicilato *m*.

salicylic [,sæli'silik] *adj* salicílico, ca.

salience ['seiliəns]; **saliency** [-i] *n* prominencia *f* (protruding part) || FIG rasgo *m* sobresaliente (striking feature) || *to give saliency to a fact* subrayar *or* destacar un hecho.

salient ['seiljənt] *adj* saliente (projecting); *salient angle* ángulo saliente || FIG sobresaliente, destacado, da; *the salient points of a speech* los puntos sobresalientes de un discurso.
◆ *n* saliente *m*.

salientian [,seili'entʃən] *n* ZOOL anuro *m*.
◆ *adj* ZOOL anuro, ra.

saliferous [sæ'lifərəs] *adj* GEOL salífero, ra.

salification [,sælifi'keiʃən] *n* CHEM salificación *f*.

salify ['sælifai] *vt* CHEM salificar.
◆ *vi* CHEM salificarse.

salina [sə'lainə] *n* salina *f* (salt marsh).

saline ['seilain] *adj* salino, na (containing salt) || salado, da (tasting of salt) || MED salino, na.
◆ *n* salina *f* (salina, deposit of salt) || solución *f* salina (solution) || sal *f* metálica (metallic salt).

salinity [sə'liniti] *n* salinidad *f*.

saliva [sə'laivə] *n* saliva *f*.

salivary ['sælivəri] *adj* salival; *salivary glands* glándulas salivales.

salivate ['sæliveit] *vt* hacer salivar.
◆ *vi* salivar.

salivation [,sæli'veiʃən] *n* salivación *f*.

sallet ['sælit] *n* celada *f* (helmet).

sallow ['sæləu] *adj* cetrino, na; *sallow complexion* tez cetrina.
◆ *n* BOT sauce *m* (willow) || BOT *goat sallow* sauce cabruno.

sallow ['sæləu] *vt* poner cetrino.

sallowness [-nis] *n* color *m* cetrino, palidez *f*.

Sallust ['sæləst] *pr n* Salustio.

sally ['sæli] *n* agudeza *f*, ocurrencia *f*, salida *f* (of wit) || arranque *m* (outburst); *sally of activity* arranque de energía || acceso *m* (of anger) || MIL salida *f*; *to make a sally* hacer una salida || paseo *m*, vuelta *f* (trip); *we made a sally into the woods* dimos un paseo por los bosques.

sally ['sæli] *vi* MIL hacer una salida || *to sally forth* o *out* salir, ponerse en marcha.

Sally Lunn [-'lʌn] *n* bollo *m* que se come caliente con mantequilla.

sally port [-pɔːt] *n* MIL poterna *f*.

salmagundi [,sælmə'gʌndi] *n* CULIN salpicón *m* || FIG revoltijo *m*.

salmi; *US* **salmis** ['sælmi] *n* CULIN guiso *m* de caza menor.

salmon ['sæmən] *n* ZOOL salmón *m*.
◆ *adj* color salmón || *salmon pink* rosa salmón.

salmonella [,sælmə'nelə] *n* MED salmonela *f*.

salmon trout [-traut] *n* ZOOL trucha *f* asalmonada.

salon ['sæl˜ɔːŋ] *n* salón *m* (drawing room) || tertulia *f*, salón *m* (group of writers, etc.) || exposición *f*, salón *m* (exhibition) || *beauty salon* instituto *m* de belleza.

saloon [sə'luːn] *n* salón *m*, sala *f* (hall); *billiard saloon* salón de billar || salón *m* (salon) || coche *m*, vagón *m* (on a train); *dining saloon* coche restaurante || AUT sedán *m* || salón *m* interior (of a public house) || *US* taberna *f*, bar *m* || *hairdressing saloon* peluquería *f*, salón de peluquería || *ice-cream saloon* heladería *f*.

saloon bar [-bɑː*] *n* salón *m* interior (of a public house).

saloon car [-kɑː*] *n* coche *m* salón (in a train).

saloon deck [-dek] *n* MAR cubierta *f* de primera clase.

saloonkeeper [-kiːpə*] *n* *US* tabernero *m*.

salsify ['sælsifi] *n* BOT salsifí *m*.

sal soda [sæl'səudə] *n* *US* CHEM sal *f* de sosa (crystallized sodium carbonate).

salt [sɔːlt] *n* sal *f*; *table salt* sal de mesa; *cooking* o *kitchen salt* sal de cocina; *sea salt* sal marina; *rock salt* sal gema || CHEM sal *f* || FIG salero *m*, sal *f* (piquancy, interest) || — FIG *not to be worth one's salt* no valer gran cosa, no mere cerse lo que se gana | *old salt* lobo *m* de mar (sailor) || FIG *the salt of the earth* la sal de la tierra | *to take sth. with a grain* o *a pinch of salt* admitir algo con reservas.

◆ *pl* sales *f*; *bath salts* sales de baño || — *fruit salts* sal *f sing* de frutas || *Liver* o *Epsom salts* sal de la Higuera || MIN *mineral salts* sales minerales || *smelling salts* sales aromáticas.

◆ *adj* salado, da; *salt water* agua salada || salinero, ra; *salt industry* industria salinera || para la sal; *salt spoon* cucharilla para la sal; *salt mill* molinillo para la sal || de sal; *salt mine* mina de sal.

salt [sɔːlt] *vt* salar (to treat with salt); *to salt beef* salar carne de vaca || echar sal a (to give flavour) || FIG salpicar (to sprinkle); *to salt a speech with jokes* salpicar un discurso con chistes | colocar mineral en (una mina) para darle valor (a mine) || — *to salt away* o *down* conservar en sal (to preserve in salt), ahorrar (money, etc.) || *to salt out* precipitar (una sustancia) añadiendo sal.

SALT *abbr of [Strategic Arms Limitation Talks]* SALT, conversaciones para la limitación de armas estratégicas.

saltation [sælˈteiʃən] *n* salto *m* (jump) || mutación *f* (evolution).

saltatory [ˈsæltətəri] *adj* ZOOL saltador, ra || FIG intermitente.

saltcellar [ˈsɔːltˌselə*] *n* salero *m*.

salted [sɔːltid] *adj* salado, da; *salted peanuts* cacahuetes salados.

salter [ˈsɔːltə*] *n* salinero *m* (person who makes or sells salt) || salador *m* (person who salts meat, fish, etc.).

saltern [ˈsɔːltəːn] *n* salina *f*.

saltiness [ˈsɔːltinis] *n* salinidad *f* (of the sea) || salobridad *f* (brackishness) || lo salado (of food) || FIG ingenio *m*, sal *f*, picante *m*.

salting [ˈsɔltiŋ] *n* salazón *f*, saladura *f*.

◆ *pl* saladar *m sing*.

salt lick [ˈsɔːltlik] *n* salegar *m*.

salt marsh [ˈsɔːltmɑːʃ] *n* salina *f*.

salt pan [ˈsɔːltpæn] *n* salina *f* (depression) || recipiente *m* utilizado para obtener sal, previa evaporación del agua (vessel).

saltpetre; *US* **salpeter** [ˈsɔːltˌpiːtə*] *n* salitre *m*, nitro *m* (potassium nitrate) || nitro *m* de Chile, caliche *m* (sodium nitrate) || *salpetre works* salitrería *f sing*, salitral *m sing*.

salt pit [ˈsɔːltpit] *n* salina *f*.

salt shaker [ˈsɔːltˌʃeikə*] *n* *US* salero *m*.

saltwater [ˈsɔːltˌwɔtə*] *adj* de agua salada.

saltworks [ˈsɔːltwəːks] *n* salinas *f pl* || refinería *f* de sal.

saltwort [ˈsɔːltwəːt] *n* BOT salicor *m*, barrilla *f*.

salty [ˈsɔːlti] *adj* salado, da (containing salt); *the soup is too salty* la sopa está demasiado salada || que huele a mar (smelling of the sea) || FIG picante; *salty joke* chiste picante.

salubrious [səˈluːbriəs] *adj* sano, na; salubre, saludable (good for the health); *a salubrious climate* un clima sano || sano, na (morally wholesome).

salubrity [səˈluːbriti] *n* salubridad *f*, sanidad *f* (of a climate, of a region, etc.) || lo sano (moral wholesomeness).

salutariness [ˈsæljutərinis] *n* salubridad *f*, sanidad *f* (of a climate) || lo saludable (of an example, of a punishment, etc.).

salutary [ˈsæljutəri] *adj* saludable; *a salutary climate* un clima saludable || benéfico, ca (beneficial).

salutation [ˌsæljuˈteiʃən] *n* saludo *m* (greeting or military salute) || encabezamiento *m* (of a letter) || REL *the Angelic Salutation* la Salutación angélica.

salutatorian [ˌsæljuːtəˈtɔːriən] *n* *US* estudiante *m* que pronuncia el discurso de apertura en la ceremonia de fin de curso.

salutatory [səˈljuːtətəri] *adj* de saludo (of salutation) || *US* de bienvenida.

◆ *n* discurso *m* de apertura.

salute [səˈluːt] *n* saludo *m* (greeting) || MIL saludo *m* | salva *f*; *to fire a salute of ten guns* disparar una salva de diez cañonazos.

salute [səˈluːt] *vt* saludar.

◆ *vi* hacer un saludo.

salvable [ˈsælvəbl] *adj* salvable.

Salvadoran [ˌsælvəˈdɔːrən]; **Salvadorian** [ˌsælvəˈdɔːriən] *adj/n* salvadoreño, ña.

salvage [ˈsælvidʒ] *n* objetos *m pl* salvados (things salvaged) || salvamento *m* (act of salvaging) || JUR derecho *m* de salvamento.

salvage [ˈsælvidʒ] *vt* salvar.

salvation [sælˈveiʃən] *n* salvación *f*.

Salvation Army [-ˈɑːmi] *n* Ejército *m* de Salvación.

Salvationist [sælˈveiʃənist] *n* salutista *m* & *f*.

salve [sɑːv] *n* MED ungüento *m*, pomada *f*, bálsamo *m* (ointment) || FIG bálsamo *m* (sth. that soothes) | halago *m* (flattery).

salve [sɑːv] *vt* MED poner pomada en || FIG tranquilizar, sosegar (to soothe) || *to salve one's conscience* descargar la conciencia.

salve [sælv] *vt* salvar (to rescue).

salver [ˈsælvə*] *n* salvilla *f*, bandeja *f*; *silver salver* bandeja de plata.

salvia [ˈsælviə] *n* BOT salvia *f*.

salvo [ˈsælvəu] *n* salva *f*; *salvo of shots, of applause* salva de cañonazos, de aplausos || reserva *f*, salvedad *f* (reservation).

Salzburg [ˈsæltsbəːg] *pr n* GEOGR Salzburgo.

Samaritan [səˈmæritn] *adj/n* samaritano, na.

samarium [səˈmærjəm] *n* samario *m* (metallic element).

samba [ˈsæmbə] *n* samba *f* (dance).

Sam Browne belt [ˈsæmˈbraunˈbelt] *n* MIL correaje *m* de oficial.

same [seim] *adj* mismo, ma; *I read the same newspaper every day* leo el mismo periódico todos los días; *several women had on the same dress at the party* varias mujeres llevaban el mismo traje en la fiesta; *it was hotter at the same time last year* hizo más calor el año pasado en la misma época; *you cannot write and eat at the same time* no se puede escribir y comer al mismo tiempo; *he is of the same age as you* tiene la misma edad que tú || igual, idéntico, ca; *the two buildings are the same* los dos edificios son iguales || — *in the same way* del mismo modo || *it amounts* o *it comes to the same thing* viene a ser lo mismo || *the same old story* la historia de siempre || *very same* mismísimo, ma; *at the very same moment* en ese mismísimo momento.

◆ *adv* de la misma forma, igual; *they both felt the same about it* los dos pensaban igual respecto a aquello || — *all the same* sin embargo || *if it's all the same to you* si no le importa, si le da lo mismo, si le da igual || *it's all the same to me* me da igual, me da lo mismo || *just the same* sin embargo (nevertheless), exactamente igual (exactly the same, in the same way) || *things go on much the same as ever* todo sigue más o menos como siempre.

◆ *pron* el mismo, la misma; *«Mr Smith?»... «the same»* «¿Sr Smith?»... «el mismo»; *I am the same as I have always been* soy el mismo de siempre || lo mismo; *the same applies to you* lo mismo vale por Ud || — *I'd do the same again* volvería a hacer lo mismo || *same here* yo también || *the Prime Minister and Foreign Minister are one and the same* el Primer Ministro y el ministro de Asuntos Exteriores son la misma persona || *the same to you!* ¡igualmente!

sameness [ˈseimnis] *n* igualdad *f*, identidad *f* (identity) || similaridad *f* (similarity) || monotonía *f*, uniformidad *f* (lack of variety).

samiel [səmˈjel] *n* simún *m* (wind).

samisen [ˈsæmisen] *n* MUS guitarra *f* japonesa.

samite [ˈsæmait] *n* HIST brocado *m* de seda.

samlet [ˈsæmlet] *n* ZOOL salmoncillo *m*.

Samnite [ˈsæmnait] *adj/n* HIST samnita.

samosa [səˈməusə] *n* CULIN empanadilla india rellena de carne o verduras.

Samothrace [ˈsæməuθreis] *n* GEOGR Samotracia.

samovar [ˌsæməuˈvɑː*] *n* samovar *m*.

samp [sæmp] *n* *US* sémola *f* gruesa de maíz (maize) | gachas *f pl* de sémola gruesa de maíz (porridge).

sampan [ˈsæmpæn] *n* MAR sampán *m*.

samphire [ˈsæmfaiə*] *n* BOT hinojo *m* marino.

sample [ˈsɑːmpl] *n* muestra *f*; *free sample* muestra gratuita; *a sample of the population* una muestra de la población.

sample [ˈsɑːmpl] *vt* probar; *to sample a dish* probar un plato || catar (drinks) || tomar una muestra *or* muestras de (to take samples).

sample book [-buk] *n* muestrario *m*.

sampler [-ə*] *n* dechado *m* (in sewing) || catador *m* (of drinks).

sampling [-iŋ] *n* catadura *f* (of food and drink) || toma *f* de muestras, muestreo *m* (sample taking) || muestra *f* (sample).

Samson [ˈsæmsn] *pr n* Sansón *m*.

samurai [ˈsæmurai] *inv n* HIST samurai *m*.

sanatarium [ˌsænəˈteriəm] *n* *US* sanatorio *m*.

— OBSERV El plural de la palabra americana es *sanatariums* o *sanataria*.

sanatorium [ˌsænəˈteriəm] *n* *US* sanatorio *m* (for patients undergoing treatment) || enfermería *f* (in a school, etc.).

— OBSERV El plural de la palabra inglesa es *sanatoriums* o *sanatoria*.

sanatory [ˈsænətəri] *adj* sanador, ra; curativo, va.

sanbenito [ˌsænbəˈniːtəu] *n* HIST sambenito *m* (robe).

sanctification [ˌsæŋktifiˈkeiʃən] *n* santificación *f*.

sanctifier [ˈsæŋktifaiə*] *n* santificador, ra.

sanctify [ˈsæŋktifai] *vt* santificar (to make holy) || venerar (to revere) || consagrar (to give authority to).

sanctimonious [ˌsæŋktiˈməunjəs] *adj* beato, ta; mojigato, ta.

sanctimoniousness [-nis]; **sanctimony** [ˈsæŋktiməni] *n* beatería *f*, mojigatería *f*.

sanction [ˈsæŋkʃən] *n* sanción *f* (punishment) || sanción *f*, aprobación *f* (approval) || autorización *f* (authorization) || consagración *f* (by usage) || decreto *m* (decree).

sanction [ˈsæŋkʃən] *vt* sancionar.

sanctity [ˈsæŋktiti] *n* santidad *f* (holiness) || inviolabilidad *f* (inviolability) || lo sagrado (of an oath, of a promise).

sanctuary [ˈsæŋktjuəri] *n* REL santuario *m* (a sacred place) | sagrario *m* (part of church) || refugio *m* (of birds) || JUR derecho *m* de asilo, inmunidad *f* de los lugares sagrados (immunity) | asilo *m* (place) || — *to seek sanctuary in* o *with* acogerse a || *to take sanctuary* acogerse a sagrado.

sanctum ['sæŋktəm] *n* santuario *m* (a sacred place) || FIG sanctasanctórum *m* (place of retreat).
— OBSERV El plural de *sanctum* es *sanctums* o *sancta*.

sanctum sanctorum [-sæŋk'tɔːrəm] *n* sanctasanctórum *m*.

sand [sænd] *n* arena *f* || MED arenilla *f* || — FIG *to build on sand* edificar sobre arena || US FAM *to have plenty of sand* tener agallas.
◆ *pl* playa *f sing* (beach) || banco *m sing* de arena (sandbank).

sand [sænd] *vt* lijar (to abrade) || enarenar (to cover with sand) || secar con arena (to dry with sand) || mezclar con arena (to falsify the weight).

sandal [-l] *n* sandalia *f* (shoe); *beach sandals* sandalias de playa || BOT sándalo *m* (sandalwood).

sandalwood [-lwud] *n* BOT sándalo *m*.

sandarac [-əræk] *n* BOT alerce *m* africano (tree) || sandáraca *f* (resin) || MIN sandáraca *f*, rejalgar *m* (realgar).

sandbag [-bæg] *n* saco *m* terrero || porra *f* (used as a weapon).

sandbag [-bæg] *vt* proteger con sacos terreros (to protect with sandbags) || golpear con una porra (to stun) || US FAM forzar, obligar (to coerce).

sandbank [-bæŋk] *n* banco *m* de arena.

sandbar [-bɑː*] *n* banco *m* de arena.

sandblast [-,blɑːst] *n* TECH chorro *m* de arena (jet of sand) | limpiadora *f* de chorro de arena (machine).

sandblast [-blɑːst] *vt* TECH pulir *or* limpiar con chorro de arena.

sandbox [-bɔːks] *n* arenero *m* (in a locomotive) || salvadera *f* (to dry ink) || US cajón *m* de arena para juegos infantiles (sandpit).

sand-cast [-kɑːst] *vt* vaciar en molde de arena (metal).

sandcastle [-'kɑːsl] *n* castillo *m* de arena.

sand dollar [-'dɔlə*] *n* ZOOL erizo *m* de mar poco grueso.

sand dune [-'djuːn] *n* duna *f*.

sand flea [-'fliː] *n* ZOOL pulga *f* de mar (beach flea) | nigua *f* (chigoe).

sand fly [-'flai] *n* jején *m*, mosquito *m*.

sandglass [-,glɑːs] *n* reloj *m* de arena.

sandgrouse [-graus] *n* ortega *m* (bird).

sandhog [-hɔg] *n* US trabajador *m* que efectúa obras subterráneas en una campana.

sandlot [-lɔt] *n* US solar *m*.

sandman [-,mæn] *n* ser *m* imaginario que adormece a los niños.

sandpaper [-,peipə*] *n* papel *m* de lija.

sandpaper [-,peipə*] *vt* lijar.

sand pie [-pai] *n* flan *m* de arena (for children).

sandpiper [-'paipə*] *n* ZOOL lavandera *f* (bird).

sandpit [-,pit] *n* cajón *m* de arena para juegos infantiles (for children) || mina *f* de arena (for extracting sand).

sandshoe [-ʃuː] *n* playera *f*.

sandstone [-stəun] *n* MIN arenisca *f*.

sandstorm [-stɔːm] *n* tempestad *f* de arena.

sandwich ['sænwidʒ] *n* bocadillo *m* (made with a roll) || sandwich *m*, emparedado *m* (made with squared sliced bread).

sandwich ['sænwidʒ] *vt* intercalar (to place between) || *to be sandwished between* estar entre.

sandwich board [-bɔːd] *n* carteles *m pl* que lleva el hombre anuncio.

sandwich course [-kɔːs] *n* curso *m* de formación superior con alternancia de prácticas.

sandwich man [-mæn] *n* hombre anuncio *m*.
— OBSERV El plural es *sandwich men*.

sandy ['sændi] *adj* cubierto de arena (full of sand) || arenoso, sa (covered with or like sand) || rubio rojizo (hair).

sane [sein] *adj* cuerdo, da; sensato, ta (sensible) || sano, na (mind) || *he is sane* está en sus cabales *or* en su sano juicio.

sanforized ['sænfəraizd] *adj* sanforizado, da (cotton, etc.).

sang [sæŋ] *pret* ⟶ **sing.**

sangaree ['sæŋgə'riː] *n* sangría *f*.

sangfroid ['sɑːŋ'frwɑː] *n* sangre *f* fría.

Sangrail [sæŋ'greil] *n* REL Santo Grial *m*.

sanguinary ['sæŋgwinəri] *adj* sangriento, ta (accompanied by much bloodshed) || sanguinario, ria (murderous); *a sanguinary tyrant* un tirano sanguinario.

sanguine ['sæŋgwin] *adj* sanguíneo, a (complexion) || optimista (optimistic) || sanguinario, ria (sanguinary).
◆ *n* sanguina *f* (drawing, pencil).

sanguineous [sæŋ'gwiniəs] *adj* sanguíneo, a (pertaining to blood) || sanguíneo, a; de color rojo sangre (bloodred) || sanguíneo, a (complexion) || sanguinario, ria (bloodthirsty).

sanguinolent ['sæŋgwinələnt] *adj* sanguinolento, ta.

Sanhedrim ['sænidrim]; **Sanhedrin** ['sænidrin] *n* HIST sanedrín *m*.

sanies ['seiniːz] *n* MED sanies *f*, sanie *f*.
— OBSERV La palabra inglesa es invariable.

sanitarian [,sæni'tɛəriən] *adj* sanitario, ria.

sanitarium [,sæni'tɛəriəm] *n* US sanatorio *m*.
— OBSERV El plural de la palabra americana es *sanitariums* o *sanitaria*.

sanitary ['sænitəri] *adj* sanitario, ria; higiénico, ca || MIL sanitario, ria || — *sanitary inspector* inspector *m* de sanidad || *sanitary napkin* o *towel* compresa *f*, paño higiénico.

sanitate ['sæniteit] *vt* sanear (to make sanitary).

sanitation [,sæni'teiʃən] *n* saneamiento *m* || higiene *f*.

sanity ['sæniti] *n* cordura *f*, juicio *m* (soundness of mind) || sensatez *f* (sensibleness) || — *to be restored to sanity* recobrar el juicio || *to lose one's sanity* perder el juicio, perder la razón || *to regain one's sanity* recobrar el juicio.

San José [,sænhəu'zei] *pr n* GEOGR San José.

sank [sæŋk] *pret* ⟶ **sink.**

San Marino [,sænmə'riːnəu] *pr n* GEOGR San Marino.

sansei [sæn'sei] *n* US ciudadano *m* americano descendiente de japoneses.
— OBSERV El plural de esta palabra es *sansei* o *sanseis*.

san serif [sæn'serif] *n* PRINT tipo *m* basto.

Sanskrit ['sænskrit] *adj* sánscrito, ta.
◆ *n* sánscrito *m*.

Santa Claus ['sæntə'kləuz] *n* San Nicolás *m*, Papá Noel *m*.

Santo Domingo [sæntəudə'miŋgəu] *pr n* GEOGR Santo Domingo.

Santo Tomé ['sæntəu'təumei] *pr n* GEOGR Santo Tomé.

São Paulo [saum'pauləu] *pr n* GEOGR São Paulo.

sap [sæp] *n* BOT savia *f* || FIG savia *f* || MIL zapa *f* (trench or tunnel) || FAM bobo, ba; memo, ma (fool).

sap [sæp] *vt* MIL zapar, socavar (to dig) | minar (to undermine) || FIG agotar (to weaken); *the heat saps your strength* el calor agota las fuerzas | socavar.

sapajou ['sæpədʒuː] *n* sapajú *m* (monkey).

sapanwood ['sæpənwud] *n* BOT sibucao *m*, sapan *m* (sappanwood).

saphead ['sæphed] *n* FAM bobo, ba; memo, ma.

saphena [sæ'fiːnə] *n* ANAT safena *f*.

saphenous [sæ'fiːnəs] *adj* safena (vein).

sapid ['sæpid] *adj* sabroso, sa; sápido, da.

sapidity [sæ'piditi] *n* sapidez *f*, sabor *m*.

sapience ['seipiəns] *n* sapiencia *f*.

sapient ['seipjənt] *adj* sapiente.

sapiential [,seipi'enʃəl] *adj* sapiencial || REL *sapiential books* libros sapienciales.

sapless ['sæplis] *adj* BOT sin savia (plant) || estéril (soil) || FIG débil (character) | insípido, da; trivial (idea).

sapling ['sæpliŋ] *n* BOT árbol *m* joven || ZOOL galgo *m* joven || FIG & FAM pimpollo *m*, jovenzuelo *m* (youth).

sapodilla [sæpə'dilə] *n* BOT zapote *m*.

saponaceous [,sæpəu'neiʃəs] *adj* saponáceo, a || FIG meloso, sa.

saponify [sə'pɔnifai] *vt* CHEM saponificar.
◆ *vi* CHEM saponificarse.

saponite ['sæpənait] *n* MIN saponita *f*.

sapor ['seipə*] *n* sabor *m*.

saporous ['seipərəs] *adj* sabroso, sa.

sappanwood ['sæpənwud] *n* BOT sibucao *m*, sapan *m*.

sapper ['sæpə*] *n* MIL zapador *m*.

Sapphic ['sæfik] *adj* sáfico, ca || lesbiano, na.
◆ *n* POET sáfico *m*, verso *m* sáfico (metre).
◆ *pl* POET poesía *f sing* sáfica.

sapphire ['sæfaiə*] *n* zafiro *m*.
◆ *adj* de color zafiro.

sapphirine ['sæfirain] *adj* zafirino, na.
◆ *n* MIN zafirina *f*.

sapphism ['sæfizəm] *n* safismo *m*.

Sappho ['sæfəu] *pr n* Safo *f*.

sappiness ['sæpinis] *n* jugosidad *f* || FIG & FAM sensiblería *f* (mawkishness) | tontería *f* (silliness).

sappy ['sæpi] *adj* BOT jugoso, sa; lleno de savia || FIG & FAM sensiblero, ra (mawkish) | tontuelo, la (silly).

saprophyte ['sæprəfait] *n* BIOL saprófito *m*.

sapsucker ['sæp,sʌkə*] *n* ZOOL pájaro *m* carpintero americano.

sapwood ['sæpwud] *n* albura *f*.

saraband; sarabande ['særəbænd] *n* MUS zarabanda *f*.

Saracen ['særəsn] *adj/n* HIST sarraceno, na.

Saragossa [,særə'gɔsə] *pr n* GEOGR Zaragoza.

Sarah ['sɛərə] *pr n* Sara *f*.

Saratoga trunk [,særə'təugə,trʌŋk] *n* baúl *m* mundo.

sarcasm ['sɑːkæzəm] *n* sarcasmo *m*.

sarcastic [sɑːkæstik] *adj* sarcástico, ca.

sarcastically [-əli] *adv* con sarcasmo, sarcásticamente.

sarcoma [sɑː'kəumə] *n* MED sarcoma *m*.
— OBSERV El plural de la palabra inglesa es *sarcomas* o *sarcomata*.

sarcomatous [-təs] *adj* MED sarcomatoso, sa.

sarcophagus [sɑː'kɔfəgəs] *n* sarcófago *m*.

— OBSERV El plural de *sarcophagus* es *sarcophagi* o *sarcophaguses.*

sardana [sɑː'dɑːnə] *n* sardana *f* (Catalan dance).

Sardanapalus [ˌsɑːdə'næpələs] *pr n* Sardanápalo *m.*

sardine [sɑː'diːn] *n* ZOOL sardina *f* || FIG *to be packed like sardines* estar como sardinas en banasta *or* en lata.

Sardinia [sɑː'dinjə] *pr n* GEOGR Cerdeña *f.*

Sardinian [-n] *n* sardo, da (person) || sardo *m* (language).
◆ *adj* sardo, da.

sardonic [sɑː'dɔnik] *adj* sardónico, ca.

sardonically [-əli] *adv* sardónicamente.

sargasso [sɑː'gæsəu] *n* BOT sargazo *m.*

Sargasso Sea [-siː] *pr n* GEOGR mar *m* de los Sargazos.

sarge [sɑːdʒ] *n* FAM sargento *m.*

sargo ['sɑːgəu] *n* ZOOL sargo *m* (fish).

sari ['sɑːri] *n* sari *m.*

sarmentose [sɑː'menˌtəus] *adj* BOT sarmentoso, sa.

sarong [sə'rɔŋ] *n* pareo *m* de Malasia.

sarsaparilla [ˌsɑːsəpə'rilə] *n* BOT zarzaparrilla *f.*

sartorial [sɑː'tɔːriəl] *adj* de sastre, de sastrería || *sartorial elegance* elegancia *f* en el vestir.

sartorius [sɑː'tɔːriəs] *n* ANAT sartorio *m*, músculo *m* sartorio.

sash [sæʃ] *n* marco *m* (frame) || hoja *f* móvil de la ventana de guillotina (of a sash window) || banda *f* (broad ribbon worn across the chest) || fajín *m* (worn around the waist by officers, by officials, etc.) || faja *f* (in local costume).

sashay [-'ei] *vi* US FAM andar pavoneándose (to swagger) | zigzaguear (to zigzag).

sash cord [-kɔːd] *n* cuerda *f* de ventana.

sash window [-'windəu] *n* ventana *f* de guillotina.

sasin ['seisin] *n* ZOOL antílope *m* indio.

sass [sæs] *n* US FAM descaro *m*, insolencia *f* (impudent talk).

sass [sæs] *vt* US FAM hablar con descaro a, insolentarse con.

sassafras ['sæsəfræs] *n* BOT sasafrás *m.*

Sassanian [sæ'seinjən]; **Sassanid** ['sæsənid] *adj/n* HIST sasánida.

Sassenach ['sæsənæk] *n* inglés, esa.

sassy ['sæsi] *adj* US FAM descarado, da.

sat [sæt] *pret/pp* ⟶ **sit.**

Satan ['seitən] *n* REL Satán *m*, Satanás *m.*

satanic [sə'tænik] *adj* satánico, ca.

Satanism [sə'tænizəm] *n* satanismo *m.*

satchel ['sætʃəl] *n* cartera *f*, cartapacio *m* (for schoolchildren) || morral *m* (for hunters) || cartera *f* (for bicycles).

sate [seit] *vt* saciar (one's appetite) || hartar (to surfeit).

sated [-id] *adj* sacio, cia; harto, ta.

sateen [sæ'tiːn] *n* satén *m.*

satellite ['sætəlait] *n* ASTR satélite *m*; *artificial satellite* satélite artificial || FIG acólito *m*, satélite *m* (servile follower) || *satellite country, town* país, ciudad satélite.

satiable ['seiʃəbl] *adj* saciable.

satiate ['seiʃieit] *vt* saciar (to satisfy) || hartar (to surfeit).

satiate ['seiʃieit] *adj* saciado, da; harto, ta.

satiation [ˌseiʃi'eiʃən]; **satiety** [sə'taiəti] *n* saciedad *f* (sufficiency) || hartura *f*, hartazgo *m* (excess).

satin ['sætin] *n* raso *m*, satén *m.*
◆ *adj* de raso; *a satin dress* un vestido de raso || satinado, da; *satin paper* papel satinado || *satin stitch* plumetís *m.*

satin ['sætin] *vt* satinar.

satinet; satinette ['sæti'neit] *n* rasete *m.*

satinwood ['sætinwud] *n* BOT satín *m.*

satiny ['sætini] *adj* satinado, da.

satire ['sætaiə*] *n* sátira *f.*

satiric [sə'tirik]; **satirical** [-əl] *adj* satírico, ca.

satirist ['sætərist] *n* satírico *m*, autor *m* de sátiras.

satirize ['sætəraiz] *vt/vi* satirizar.

satisfaction [ˌsætis'fækʃən] *n* satisfacción *f*; *to give complete satisfaction* dar entera satisfacción; *the satisfaction of one's appetite, of an ambition* la satisfacción del apetito, de una ambición || aplacamiento *m* (of one's thirst) || liquidación *f* (of a debt) || reembolso *m* (of a creditor) || compensación *f* (compensation) || cumplimiento *m* (of requirements, of promise) || FIG satisfacción *f*, reparación *f*; *to demand satisfaction for an offence* pedir satisfacción de una ofensa || — *to express one's satisfaction* declararse satisfecho, expresar su satisfacción || *to prove sth. to s.o.'s satisfaction* convencer a alguien de algo || *to the satisfaction of* a satisfacción de.

satisfactorily [ˌsætis'fæktərili] *adv* satisfactoriamente.

satisfactory [ˌsætis'fæktəri] *adj* satisfactorio, ria; *satisfactory answer* contestación satisfactoria.

satisfied ['sætisfaid] *adj* satisfecho, cha.

satisfy ['sætisfai] *vt* satisfacer; *to satisfy s.o.'s desires* satisfacer los deseos de alguien; *to satisfy one's appetite* satisfacer el apetito || aplacar (one's thirst) || cumplir con, satisfacer; *he satisfied the requirements* cumplió con los requisitos || cumplir con, cumplir (a promise) || pagar, liquidar (a debt) || pagar una deuda a, reembolsar (a creditor) || indemnizar (to compensate) || responder satisfactoriamente a (to counter); *to satisfy s.o.'s objections* responder satisfactoriamente a las objeciones de uno || convencer (to convince); *I am not absolutely satisfied that it is true* no estoy completamente convencido de que sea verdad || — *I am afraid you will have to be satisfied with that* lo siento, pero usted tendrá que contentarse con eso || *I have satisfied myself that he is telling the truth* estoy convencido de que dice la verdad.
◆ *vi* satisfacer.

satisfying [-iŋ] *adj* satisfactorio, ria; *a satisfying piece of news* una noticia satisfactoria || agradable; *driving a sports car is a satisfying experience* es una experiencia agradable conducir un coche deportivo || sustancioso, sa (food) || convincente (argument).

satrap ['sætrəp] *n* sátrapa *m.*

satrapy [-i] *n* satrapía *f.*

saturability [ˌsætjurə'biliti] *n* CHEM saturabilidad *f.*

saturable ['sætjurəbl] *adj* saturable.

saturate ['sætʃərit] *adj* saturado, da.

saturate ['sætʃəreit] *vt* saturar; *to saturate a market with a product* saturar un mercado con un producto || empapar (to soak); *the tablecloth is saturated with wine* el mantel está empapado en vino || PHYS & CHEM saturar.

saturated [-id] *adj* PHYS & CHEM saturado, da || FAM empapado, da (wet) || FIG *saturated with conceit* convencido de su propia importancia.

saturater; saturator [-ə*] *n* saturador *m.*

saturation [ˌsætʃə'reiʃən] *n* saturación *f* || *saturation point* punto *m* de saturación || *to reach saturation point* llegar a la saturación, saturarse.

Saturday ['sætədi] *n* sábado *m*; *on Saturday* el sábado; *on Saturdays* los sábados || *Easter Saturday* Sábado Santo *or* de Gloria.

Saturn ['sætən] *pr n* MYTH & ASTR Saturno *m.*

Saturnalia [ˌsætə:'neiljə] *n* HIST saturnales *f pl* || FIG bacanales *f pl* (orgy).
— OBSERV El plural de la palabra inglesa es *Saturnalias* o *Saturnalia* cuando tiene un sentido figurado.

Saturnian [sæ'təːnjən] *adj* saturnal, saturnio, nia || FIG *the Saturnian age* la edad de oro.

saturnic ['sætəːnik] *adj* MED saturnino, na.

saturnine ['sætənain] *adj* saturnino, na.

saturnism ['sætənizəm] *n* MED saturnismo *m.*

satyr ['sætə*] *n* MYTH & FIG sátiro *m* || ZOOL sátiro *m* (butterfly).

satyric [sə'tirik]; **satyrical** [-əl] *adj* satírico, ca.

sauce [sɔːs] *n* CULIN salsa *f*; *white sauce* salsa blanca; *tartare sauce* salsa tártara | compota *f* (stewed fruit) || FIG salsa *f* (appetizer); *hunger is the best sauce* no hay mejor salsa que el apetito | sal *f* (wit) || FAM descaro *m*, frescura *f*, insolencia *f* (impudence) || — *tomato sauce* salsa de tomate || *to thicken a sauce* trabar una salsa || *white cream sauce* salsa bechamel *or* besamel.

sauce [sɔːs] *vt* añadir salsa a, sazonar (to put sauce on) || FAM insolentarse con.

sauceboat [-bəut] *n* salsera *f.*

saucebox [-bɔks] *n* FAM fresco, ca (cheeky person).

saucepan [-pən] *n* cazo *m*, cacerola *f.*

saucer [-ə*] *n* platillo *m* || *flying saucer* platillo volante.

sauciness [-inis] *n* FAM descaro *m*, frescura *f*, insolencia *f* (impudence) || *that's enough of your sauciness!* ¡déjate de frescuras!, ¡no seas tan descarado!

saucy [-i] *adj* FAM descarado, da; insolente, fresco, ca (impudent) | pícaro, ra; *a saucy look* una mirada pícara || *a saucy little hat* un sombrerito coquetón.

Saudi Arabia ['sɔːdiə'reibjə] *pr n* GEOGR Arabia *f* Saudita *or* Saudí.

sauerkraut ['sauəkraut] *n* CULIN sauerkraut *m* (fermented cabbage).

sauna ['saunə] *n* sauna *f.*

saunter ['sɔːntə*] *n* paseo *m* (walk); *to go for a saunter* ir de paseo || paso *m* lento (gait).

saunter ['sɔːntə*] *vi* deambular, pasearse (to stroll) || *to saunter up to s.o.* acercarse lentamente a alguien.

saurel [sɔ'rel] *n* jurel *m* (fish).

saurian ['sɔːriən] *adj* ZOOL saurio, ria.
◆ *n* ZOOL saurio *m.*

sausage ['sɔsidʒ] *n* CULIN embutido *m*, salchicha *f* (for cooking); *pork sausage* salchicha de carne de cerdo || salchichón *m* (cured).

sausage meat [-miːt] *n* CULIN carne *f* de salchicha.

sausage roll [-rəul] *n* CULIN empanadilla *f* de salchicha.

sauté ['səutei] *adj* CULIN salteado, da.

sauté ['səutei] *vt* CULIN saltear.

savable [seivəbl] *adj* salvable.

savage ['sævidʒ] *adj* salvaje (primitive, wild); *savage tribe, land* tribu, tierra salvaje || feroz (ferocious); *savage animal* animal feroz || cruel (cruel) || violento, ta (attack) || violento, ta; acerbo, ba (criticism, etc.) || FAM rabioso, sa (angry).
◆ *n* salvaje *m* & *f.*

savage ['sævidʒ] *vt* embestir (to attack) || lacerar (to lacerate).

savageness [-nis]; **savagery** [-əri] *n* salvajismo *m*; *still in a state of complete savagery* todavía en un estado de completo salvajismo || salvajada *f* (savage act) || ferocidad *f* (of an animal) || crueldad *f* (of a tyrant) || violencia *f* (of an attack, of a criticism, etc.).

savanna; savannah [sə'vænə] *n* sabana *f*.

savant ['sævənt] *n* sabio *m*, erudito *m*.

save [seiv] *n* SP parada *f* (in football).
◆ *prep* salvo, excepto; *all his children save one are married* todos sus hijos, salvo uno, están casados || *save for* fuera de; *he is penniless save for a few shares* no tiene dinero fuera de unas cuantas acciones; si no fuese por; *he would do it save for his position* lo haría si no fuese por su posición.
◆ *conj* a no ser que || *save that* excepto que; *I know nothing about him save that he is a foreigner* no sé nada de él excepto que es extranjero.

save [seiv] *vt* salvar; *to save s.o. from danger* salvar a alguien del peligro; *to save s.o. from drowning* salvar a alguien que se está ahogando || evitar (to avoid); *we shall save a lot of trouble if we catch the bus* evitaremos muchas molestias si cogemos el autobús || ganar, ahorrarse (time, distance); *you can save ten minutes if you catch the underground* se puede ahorrar diez minutos si coge el metro || ahorrar (money, electricity, gas, etc.); *put out the fire to save coal* apaga el fuego para ahorrar carbón || proteger (to protect); *these covers will save the chairs* estas fundas protegerán los sillones || guardar (to keep for later); *to save the best till the end* guardar lo mejor para lo último; *I'll save you a seat* te guardaré un asiento || coleccionar (to collect) || INFORM salvaguardar (to store data) || SP parar (a goalkeeper) || — FIG *a stitch in time saves nine* no dejes para mañana lo que puedes hacer hoy || *God save the Queen!* ¡Dios guarde a la Reina! || FAM *save it!* ¡déjalo! || *to save appearances* o *face* salvar las apariencias || *to save one's soul* salvar el alma || *to save one's strength, to save o.s.* escatimar sus fuerzas, reservarse || *to save the day* o *the situation* salvar la situación || *you might as well save your breath, she isn't listening* no gastes saliva en balde ya que no está escuchando.
◆ *vi* ahorrar || *to save up* ahorrar; *I am saving up for a house* estoy ahorrando para comprar una casa.

saveable [-əbl] *adj* salvable.

save-all [-ɔːl] *n* apuracabos *m inv*.

saveloy ['sævəlɔi] *n* CULIN salchicha *f* seca sazonada.

saver [-'seivə*] *n* salvador, ra || ahorrador, ra (of money).

saving ['seiviŋ] *adj* atenuante; *saving circumstances* circunstancias atenuantes || económico, ca; ahorrador, ra; ahorrativo, va (not wasteful) || *saving clause* cláusula *f* de salvaguardia.
◆ *prep* salvo, excepto.
◆ *n* salvamento *m* (rescue) || ahorro *m*, economía *f*; *saving of time* ahorro de tiempo || REL salvación *f* || JUR salvedad *f*.
◆ *pl* ahorros *m* (money saved).

savings account ['seiviŋzə'kaunt] *n* US cuenta *f* de ahorros.

savings bank ['seiviŋz'bæŋk] *n* caja *f* de ahorros.

saviour; US savior ['seivjə*] *n* salvador, ra || REL *The Saviour* el Salvador.

savoir faire ['sævwaː'fɛə*] *n* tacto *m*, habilidad *f* (tact) || habilidad *f* (know-how) || don *m* de gente, mundo *m* (easy assurance).

savoir vivre ['sævwaː'viːvr] *n* mundología *f*.

savor ['seivə*] *n* US ⟶ **savour.**

savoriness [-rinis] *n* US ⟶ **savouriness.**

savorless [-lis] *adj* US ⟶ **savourless.**

savory ['seivəri] *n* BOT ajedrea *f*.
◆ *pl* US tapas *f*.
◆ *adj* US ⟶ **savoury.**

savour; US savor ['seivə*] *n* sabor *m*, gusto *m* (flavour, tastiness) || aroma *m* (smell) || FIG sabor *m* (*of* a); *it has a savour all of its own* tiene un sabor muy propio.

savour; US savor ['seivə*] *vt* dar sabor a (to give taste to) || saborear (to enjoy the taste of) || FIG saborear (to enjoy); *to savour a moment's rest* saborear un momento de descanso || FIG *I don't savour the idea of going alone* no me apetece la idea de ir solo.
◆ *vi* saber (*of* de) (to taste) || oler (*of* a) (to smell) || FIG oler (to smack); *this savours of subterfuge* esto huele a subterfugio.

savouriness; US savoriness [-rinis] *n* sabor *m* agradable (pleasant taste) || olor *m* agradable (pleasant smell).

savourless; US savorless [-lis] *adj* soso, sa; insípido, da.

savoury; US savory [-i] *adj* sabroso, sa (tasty) || salado, da (salted); *I prefer savoury things* me gustan más las cosas saladas || FIG *not very savoury* poco edificante (affair, film), malsano, na (district); sospechoso, sa (hotel).
◆ *n pl* tapas *f* (food eaten with an apéritif, etc.).

savoy [sə'vɔi] *n* BOT col *f* rizada, col *f* de Milán.

Savoy [sə'vɔi] *pr n* GEOGR Saboya *f*.

Savoyard [sə'vɔiaːd] *adj/n* saboyano, na.

savvy ['saevi] *n* FAM entendederas *f pl*.

savvy ['sævi] *vt* FAM chanelar, comprender.

saw [sɔː] *n* sierra *f* (cutting instrument); *band* o *belt* o *ribbon saw* sierra de cinta; *bow saw* sierra de arco; *circular saw* sierra circular; *compass saw* sierra de contornar; *pit saw* sierra abrazadera || serrucho *m* (handsaw) || ZOOL sierra *f* || máxima *f* (maxim) || refrán *m* (proverb) || dicho *m* (saying).

saw* [sɔː] *vt* serrar, aserrar (to cut) || FIG hender; *to saw the air* hender el aire || FAM rascar (a violin) | tocar rascando el violín (a tune) || dentar (in bookbinding).
◆ *vi* serrar, aserrar (to work with a saw) || cortarse (to be sawn); *this wood saws easily* esta madera se corta fácilmente || FAM *to saw on the fiddle* rascar el violín.
— OBSERV Pret ***sawed***; pp ***sawn, sawed***.

saw [sɔː] *pret* ⟶ **see.**

sawbones [-bəunz] *n* FAM matasanos *m inv*, cirujano *m*.

sawbuck [-bʌk] *n* US burro *m* (sawhorse) | billete *m* de diez dólares (bill).

sawdust [-dʌst] *n* serrín *m*, aserrín *m*.

sawed-off [-d'ɔf]; **sawn-off** [sɔːnɔf] *adj* US *sawed-off shotgun* escopeta *f* con los cañones cortados.

sawfish [-fiʃ] *n* ZOOL pez *m* sierra.

sawhorse [-hɔːs] *n* TECH burro *m*.

sawlike [-laik] *adj* en forma de sierra.

sawlog [-lɔg] *n* tronco *m* serradizo.

sawmill [-mil] *n* aserradero *m*, serrería *f*.

sawn [sɔːn] *pp* ⟶ **saw.**

sawn-off [-ɔf] *adj* ⟶ **sawed-off.**

saw set ['sɔːset] *n* TECH triscador *m*.

sawtooth ['sɔːtuːθ] *n* TECH diente *m* de sierra.
— OBSERV El plural de esta palabra es *sawteeth*.

sawtooth ['sɔːtuːθ]; **saw-toothed** [-t] *adj* serrado, da.

sawyer ['sɔːjə*] *n* aserrador *m*.

sax [sæks] *n* hacha *f* (axe) || MUS & FAM saxófono *m*.

Saxe [sæks] *pr n* Sajonia *f*.

saxhorn [-hɔːn] *n* MUS bombardino *m*.

saxifrage ['sæksifridʒ] *n* BOT saxifraga *f*.

Saxon ['sæksn] *adj/n* sajón, ona.

Saxony [-i] *pr n* GEOGR Sajonia *f*.

saxophone ['sæksəfəun] *n* MUS saxofón *m*, saxófono *m*.

saxophonist [sæk'sɔfənist] *n* MUS saxofón *m*, saxófono *m* (person).

say [sei] *n* *I had no say in it* no me pidieron mi opinión || *let him have his say* déjele hablar || *she is the one with the say* ella lleva la voz cantante || *we have no say in the matter* en este asunto no tenemos ni voz ni voto.

say* [sei] *vt* decir; *what did he say?* ¿qué dijo?; *he said she was coming* dijo que ella iba a venir; *do what he says* haz lo que él dice; *let us say X is the unknown quantity* digamos que X es la incógnita || expresar (to express) || afirmar, declarar, decir (to affirm); *he said that he would not do as I asked* declaró que no haría lo que yo le pedía || decir, rezar (a text, a proverb, a notice, etc.); *what does the sign say?* ¿cómo reza el rótulo? || decir (mass) || rezar (a prayer) || dar (a lesson) || marcar (a clock, an instrument); *the clock says half past six* el reloj marca las seis y media; *the thermometer says a hundred degrees* el termómetro marca cien grados || opinar, pensar (to think); *what do you say to this idea?* ¿qué piensa de esta idea? || poner, decir (as an example or an estimate); *let us say about ten metres* digamos unos diez metros; *half the population, say, will not vote* pongamos que la mitad de la población no votará || suponer (to imagine); *say the king were to die* supongamos que muriese el rey || — *as they say* como dicen || *enough said!* ¡basta! || *he doesn't have much to say for himself* es muy reservado || *I say!* ¡oiga!, ¡oye! (to draw attention), ¡ya lo creo! || *it goes without saying* por supuesto, ni que decir tiene, huelga decir (needless to say), eso cae de su peso (it is obvious) || *it is said that* dice que..., se dice que... || *it's easier said than done* es más fácil decirlo que hacerlo || *no sooner said than done* dicho y hecho || *not to say* por no decir; *it is difficult, not to say impossible* es difícil, por no decir imposible || US *say* oiga, oye; *say, what do you think of this?* oye, ¿qué piensas de esto? || US *say!* ¡vaya! (surprise) || *say no more!* ¡no me diga más! || *so to say* por decirlo así || *that is to say* es decir, o sea || *that film is said to be worth seeing* dicen que merece la pena ver esa película || *there is a lot to be said for not overeating* existen múltiples argumentos en contra del exceso de comida || *there is sth. to be said for his argument* su argumento tiene cierto valor || *there's no saying* es imposible decir || *they say that* dicen que..., se dice que... || *to say goodbye to s.o. ...* despedirse de alguien || *to say good morning to s.o.* dar los buenos días a alguien || *to say grace* bendecir la mesa || *to say no* decir que no || *to say nothing of* sin mencionar, sin hablar de, por no hablar de || *to say no to* rechazar (an offer, etc.) || *to say the word* dar la orden || *to say to o.s.* decir para sí || US FAM *to say uncle* rendirse || *to say yes to* aceptar (an offer, etc.) || *what say you?* ¿qué te parece? || *what would you say if we accepted?* ¿qué te parece si aceptamos? || *when all is said and done* al fin y al cabo || *you can say that again!* ¡dímelo a mí! || *you don't say!* ¡no me diga! || *you may well say so* tiene toda la razón || *you said it!* ¡dímelo a mí! || *their conduct says a lot about them* su conducta revela gran parte de su personalidad.
— OBSERV Pret y pp ***said***.

saying [-iŋ] *n* decir *m* (act of speaking); *saying and doing are two different things* una cosa es decir y otra es hacer || decir *m*, refrán *m*, dicho *m* (a maxim); *it's an old saying* es un viejo refrán ‖ rumor *m* (rumour) ‖ *as the saying goes* como dice *or* reza el refrán.

say-so [-səu] *n* FAM afirmación *f* (assertion) ‖ opinión *f* (judgment) ‖ autoridad *f* (authority) ‖ aprobación *f*, visto *m* bueno; *you need his say-so before you can go ahead* necesita su visto bueno para seguir adelante.

scab [skæb] *n* MED costra *f*, postilla *f* ‖ BOT & VET roña *f* (disease) ‖ FAM esquirol *m* (blackleg) | canalla *m* (scoundrel).

scab [skæb] *vi* MED formar costra ‖ FAM sustituir a un huelguista.

scabbard [-əd] *n* vaina *f* (of a weapon).

scabbiness [-inis] *n* MED estado *m* costroso ‖ FAM mezquindad *f*.

scabble [-l] *vt* desbastar.

scabby [-i] *adj* MED costroso, sa ‖ VET roñoso, sa ‖ FAM despreciable (contemptible) | mezquino, na.

scabies ['skeibii:z] *inv n* MED sarna *f*.

scabious ['skeibijəs] *adj* MED sarnoso, sa.
◆ *n* BOT escabiosa *f*.

scabrous ['skeibrəs] *adj* escabroso, sa.

scads [skædz] *pl n* US FAM montón *m sing*, montones *m*; *scads of money* un montón de dinero.

scaffold ['skæfəld] *n* andamio *m* (round a building, etc.) ‖ cadalso *m*, patíbulo *m* (for executing criminals) ‖ tarima *f* (platform) ‖ tribuna *f*.

scaffolding [-iŋ] *n* andamio *m*, andamiaje *m*.

scagliola [skæ'ljəulə] *n* escayola *f*.

scalage ['skeilidʒ] *n* US clasificación *f*.

scalar ['skeilə*] *adj* MATH & PHYS escalar.

scalawag ['skæləwæg] *n* FAM canalla *m* (rogue) | pícaro, ra (child).

scald [skɔ:ld] *n* escaldadura *f* (burn).

scald [skɔ:ld] *vt* escaldar (to burn); *to scald one's hand* escaldarse la mano ‖ CULIN escaldar | calentar (milk).

scalding [-iŋ] *adj* hirviendo, hirviente.
◆ *n* escaldado *m*.

scale [skeil] *n* escala *f*; *measuring scale* escala graduada; *centigrade scale* escala centígrada; *sliding wage scale* escala móvil salarial; *a large-scale map* un mapa a gran escala ‖ amplitud *f* (of a project, etc.) ‖ extensión *f* (of a disaster, of a damage, etc.) ‖ escala *f*, nivel *m*; *financial operations on an international scale* operaciones financieras a escala internacional ‖ platillo *m* (of a balance) ‖ MUS escala *f*, gama *f*; *the scale of F sharp* la escala de fa sostenido; *he is practising* o *running over his scales* está haciendo gamas ‖ escalafón *m* (hierarchy of employees) ‖ ZOOL escama *f* (of fish) ‖ MED escama *f* (on skin) | sarro *m* (on teeth) ‖ incrustaciones *f pl* (on a ship's hull, in a boiler, etc.) ‖ CHEM óxido *m* ‖ — *on a large scale* a gran escala ‖ *out of scale* desproporcionado, da ‖ *scale drawing* dibujo hecho a escala ‖ *scale model* modelo *m* a escala, maqueta *f* ‖ *social scale* jerarquía *f* social ‖ *to draw sth. to scale* dibujar algo a escala.
◆ *pl* balanza *f sing* (balance) ‖ báscula *f sing* (weighing machine) ‖ ASTR Libra *f sing* ‖ — *to tip the scales at* pesar más de; *it tips the scales at fifty kilogrammes* pesa más de cincuenta kilos ‖ FIG *to turn* o *to tip the scales* inclinar el fiel de la balanza, decidir; *his past record turned the scales in his favour* su historial decidió en su favor.

scale [skeil] *vt* escalar (to climb); *to scale a peak* escalar un pico ‖ subir (the stairs) ‖ trepar a (a tree) ‖ pesar (to weigh); *the fish scaled ten pounds* el pescado pesaba diez libras ‖ quitar las escamas a, escamar (fish) ‖ quitar el sarro a (teeth) ‖ depositar incrustaciones en (to cover with scales a boiler, etc.) ‖ TECH desincrustar (to remove the scales from a boiler, etc.) | decapar, desoxidar (a metal) ‖ clasificar (to classify) ‖ adaptar, ajustar (to adapt) ‖ dibujar a escala (a map) ‖ — *to scale a stone on water* lanzar una piedra para hacerla rebotar sobre el agua ‖ *to scale down* reducir proporcionalmente (to reduce proportionally), reducir a escala (a map) ‖ *to scale up* aumentar proporcionalmente (to increase proportionally), aumentar a escala (a map).
◆ *vi* desconcharse (to form or to shed scales); *the wall is beginning to scale* la pared está empezando a desconcharse ‖ ZOOL descamarse, perder las escamas (fish) ‖ descamarse (skin) ‖ cubrirse de sarro (teeth) ‖ pesar (to weigh) ‖ — *to scale off* desconcharse (paint), descamarse (skin) ‖ *to scale up* cubrirse de incrustaciones (the hull of a ship, etc.).

scaleboard [-bɔ:d] *n* tabla *f* delgada [de madera].

scaled [-d] *adj* escamoso, sa.

scalene ['skeili:n] *adj* MATH escaleno, na.

scaler ['skeilə*] *n* TECH contador *m* de impulsos ‖ escalador, ra (climber) ‖ escamador, ra (person who scales fish).

scaling ['skeiliŋ] *n* escalada *f* (climbing) ‖ TECH desincrustación *f* (of a boiler, etc.) | decapado *m*, desoxidación *f* (of metals) ‖ ajuste *m* (adjustment).

scallawag ['skæləwæg] *n* canalla *m* (rogue) ‖ pícaro, ra (child).

scallion ['skæljən] *n* BOT chalote *m*, escalonia *f* (shallot) | cebollino *m* (young onion).

scallop; scollop ['skɔləp] *n* ZOOL venera *f*, vieira *f* ‖ HERALD venera *f* ‖ festón *m* (as a decoration) ‖ CULIN escalope *m*.

scallop; scollop ['skɔləp] *vt* CULIN guisar al gratén ‖ festonear (to cut an edge into scallops).

scallywag ['skæliwæg] *n* canalla *m* (rogue) ‖ pícaro, ra (child).

scalp [skælp] *n* ANAT cuero *m* cabelludo ‖ escalpe *m*, escalpo *m* (Indian trophy) ‖ FIG *to clamour for s.o.'s scalp* pedir la cabeza de alguien.

scalp [skælp] *vt* escalpar, quitar el cuero cabelludo a (Indians) ‖ FAM pelar (barber) | dar un palo a (to defeat) ‖ US COMM especular en (shares, etc.) | dedicarse a la reventa de (theatre tickets, etc.).

scalpel ['skælpəl] *n* MED escalpelo *m*.

scalper ['skælpə*] *n* US COMM especulador *m* (on the stock market) ‖ revendedor *m* de billetes de teatro.

scaly ['skeili] *adj* escamoso, sa (skin, fish) ‖ sarroso, sa (teeth) ‖ TECH con incrustaciones (boiler, ship's hull, etc.) ‖ FAM vil, mezquino, na (mean).

scaly anteater [-'ænti:tə*] *n* ZOOL pangolín *m*.

scamp [skæmp] *n* pícaro, ra.

scamp [skæmp] *vt* chapucear (a piece of work).

scamper [-ə*] *n* correteo *m*.

scamper [-ə*] *vi* corretear ‖ precipitarse, correr (to make a dash); *to scamper for shelter* precipitarse hacia un refugio ‖ *to scamper away* o *off* irse corriendo.

scampi ['skæmpi] *n* CULIN gambas *f pl* rebozadas.

scan [skæn] *vt* escrutar, escudriñar (to scrutinize) ‖ recorrer con la mirada (to look round) ‖ echar un vistazo a (to glance at) ‖ hojear (a book) ‖ TECH explorar (television, radar) ‖ escandir (in poetry) ‖ *to scan the horizon* otear el horizonte.
◆ *vi* estar bien medido; *this line does not scan* este verso no está bien medido ‖ TECH explorar una superficie.

scandal ['skændl] *n* escándalo *m*; *political, financial scandal* escándalo político, financiero; *to create a scandal* formar un escándalo ‖ chismorreo *m*, habladurías *f pl* (gossiping) ‖ chismes *m pl* (pieces of gossip); *they do nothing but talk scandal all day* se pasan el día contando chismes ‖ JUR difamación *f* ‖ *it's a scandal!* ¡qué escándalo!, ¡qué vergüenza!

scandalize [-aiz] *vt* escandalizar; *his behaviour scandalized the local population* su conducta escandalizó a la gente del barrio ‖ *to be scandalized* escandalizarse.

scandalmonger [-ˌmʌŋgə*] *n* chismoso, sa.

scandalous ['skændələs] *adj* escandaloso, sa; vergonzoso, sa (conduct, happening) ‖ JUR difamatorio, ria.

Scandinavia [ˌskændi'neivjə] *pr n* Escandinavia *f*.

Scandinavian [-n] *adj/n* escandinavo, va.

scandium ['skændiəm] *n* CHEM escandio *m*.

scanner ['skænə*] *n* escudriñador, ra (s.o. who scans) ‖ TECH dispositivo *m* explorador (television) | antena *f* giratoria (radar) ‖ MED scanner *m*, tomógrafo *m* ‖ INFORM escáner *m*, analizador *m*.

scanning [-iŋ] *n* exploración *f* ‖ INFORM barrido *m*, exploración *f*.
◆ *adj* explorador, ra; *scanning beam* haz explorador.

scant [skænt] *adj* escaso, sa (measure, etc.) ‖ muy ligero (clothes) ‖ muy corto (dress) ‖ — *to be scant of* tener poco ‖ *to meet with scant success* tener poco éxito.

scant [skænt] *vt* escatimar.

scantily [-ili] *adv* escasamente ‖ muy ligeramente; *scantily dressed* muy ligeramente vestido.

scantiness [-inis] *n* escasez *f*.

scantlings [-liŋz] *pl n* escantillones *m*.

scanty [-i] *adj* escaso, sa; *a scanty knowledge of Latin* unos conocimientos escasos de latín ‖ escaso, sa; muy ligero, ra; *scanty clothes* ropa escasa ‖ muy corto, ta; *she was wearing a scanty skirt* llevaba una falda muy corta ‖ *scanty meal* comida parca.

scape [skeip] *n* BOT bohordo *m* (stem) ‖ ZOOL cañón *m* (of a feather) ‖ ARCH fuste *m*.

scapegoat [-gəut] *n* FIG cabeza *f* de turco, víctima *f* propiciatoria ‖ REL chivo *m* expiatorio.

scapegrace [-greis] *n* granuja *m*, canalla *m* (unprincipled person) ‖ pícaro, ra; granujilla *m* & *f* (child).

scape wheel [-wi:l] *n* rueda *f* dentada (of a clock).

scaphoid ['skæfɔid] *adj* ANAT escafoides.
◆ *n* ANAT escafoides *m inv*.

scapula ['skæpjulə] *n* ANAT omóplato *m*, escápula *f* (shoulder blade) ‖ ZOOL escápula *f*.
— OBSERV El plural de la palabra inglesa es *scapulae* o *scapulas*.

scapular ['skæpjulə*] *n* ANAT & ZOOL escápula *f* (scapula) | pluma *f* escapular (feather) ‖ REL escapulario *m*.
◆ *adj* ANAT & ZOOL escapular; *scapular feather* pluma escapular.

scapulary [-ri] *n* REL escapulario *m*.

scar [skɑ:*] *n* cicatriz *f*; *a scar on one's leg* una cicatriz en la pierna ‖ cicatriz *f*, señal *f*, chirlo *m*, costurón *m* (on the face) ‖ FIG cicatriz *f* ‖ GEOGR farallón *m*, roca *f* escarpada.

scar [skɑ:*] *vt* marcar con una cicatriz (to leave a scar on) ‖ marcar con un chirlo, señalar (the face) ‖ FIG marcar; *the experience scarred*

him for life aquella experiencia le marcó para toda la vida || *the doors are scarred with bullet marks* en las puertas se ven señales de balas.
◆ *vi* cicatrizar, cicatrizarse.

scarab ['skærəb] *n* ZOOL escarabajo *m.*

scarabaeus [ˌskærə'bi:əs] *n* ZOOL escarabajo *m.*

— OBSERV El plural de la palabra inglesa es *scarabeuses* o *scarabei.*

scarce [skεəs] *adj* escaso, sa (in short supply, barely sufficient); *medicines were scarce after the war* después de la guerra las medicinas eran escasas || raro, ra; poco común (rare); *a scarce species of plant* una especie de planta poco común ||— *blacksmiths are now scarce* los herreros escasean ahora, los herreros ya se ven muy poco || *to become scarce* escasear || FIG *to make o.s. scarce* esfumarse (to go away), no aparecer [por un sitio] (to stay away).
◆ *adv* apenas (scarcely).

scarcely [-li] *adv* apenas; *he is scarcely twenty-one* apenas tiene veintiún años; *I had scarcely arrived when they served me with a meal* apenas había llegado cuando me sirvieron una comida || seguramente no (certainly not) || — *he can scarcely have finished already* es muy difícil que haya terminado ya || *he will scarcely come at this hour* es poco probable que venga a estas horas || *I scarcely believe it* no lo creo || *scarcely anybody* casi nadie || *scarcely ever* casi nunca.

scarcement [-mənt] *n* saliente *m.*

scarceness [-nis]; **scarcity** [-iti] *n* escasez *f,* falta *f; scarcity of money* escasez de dinero; *scarcity of labour* falta de mano de obra || rareza *f,* poca frecuencia *f* (uncommonness).

scare [skεə*] *n* pánico *m; to create a scare* sembrar el pánico || susto *m; what a scare you gave me!* ¡qué susto me has dado! || alarma *f; the epidemic created a great scare* la epidemia produjo gran alarma || *the radioactive fallout scare produced by the explosion* el miedo a las lluvias radiactivas producido por la explosión.

scare [skεə*] *vt* asustar, espantar; *the sudden noise scared her* el ruido repentino le asustó || dar miedo; *old houses scare me* las casas viejas me dan miedo; *aircraft scare me to death* o *out of my wits* los aviones me dan un miedo espantoso || — FAM *to be scared stiff* estar muerto de miedo, tener un miedo espantoso || *to scare away* o *off* ahuyentar, espantar || *to scare s.o. into doing sth.* intimidar a alguien para que haga algo || US FAM *to scare up* juntar, reunir.
◆ *vi* asustarse.

scarecrow [-krəu] *n* espantapájaros *m inv,* espantajo *m* || FIG esperpento *m,* espantajo *m* (ugly person).

scarehead [-hed] *n* US FAM titulares *m pl* sensacionalistas.

scaremonger [-ˌmʌŋgə*] *n* alarmista *m* & *f.*

scarey ['skεəri] *adj* ⟶ **scary.**

scarf [skɑ:f] *n* bufanda *f* (woollen) || pañuelo *m* (light neckerchief or headwear) || fular *m* (of silk) || corte *m,* canal *f* (of a whale) || TECH empalme *m* || US tapete *m* (table cover) || US MIL banda *f* (sash).

— OBSERV El plural de *scarf,* cuando significa *bufanda, pañuelo, fular, tapete* o *banda,* es *scarves* o *scarfs.* En los demás casos es *scarfs* solamente.

scarf [skɑ:f] *vt* TECH empalmar, ensamblar || descuartizar (a whale).

scarfing [-iŋ] *n* TECH ensambladura *f.*

scarfskin [-ˌskin] *n* epidermis *f inv.*

scarification [ˌskεərifi'keiʃən] *n* escarificación *f.*

scarifier ['skεərifaiə*] *n* escarificador *m.*

scarify ['skεərifai] *vt* MED & AGR escarificar || FIG desollar (by criticism).

scarlatina [ˌskɑ:lə'ti:nə] *n* MED escarlatina *f.*

scarlet ['skɑ:lit] *adj* escarlata; *scarlet dress* vestido escarlata || colorado, da; *his face turned scarlet* su cara se puso colorada || — MED *scarlet fever* escarlatina *f* || *scarlet woman* prostituta *f* || BOT *scarlet pimpernel* murajes *m pl* | *scarlet runner* judía *f* escarlata.
◆ *n* escarlata *f* (colour, cloth) || REL púrpura *f.*

scarp [skɑ:p] *n* GEOL & MIL escarpa *f.*

scarp [skɑ:p] *vt* escarpar.

scarves [skɑ:vz] *pl n* ⟶ **scarf.**

scary; scarey ['skεəri] *adj* FAM asustadizo, za (easily frightened) | espantoso, sa; pavoroso, sa (frightening) || de miedo (film).

scat [skæt] *vi* largarse (to go away).

scathe [skeið] *vt* fustigar, vituperar (to criticize severely) || perjudicar (to harm).

scathing [-iŋ] *adj* mordaz, cáustico, ca.

scatological [ˌskætə'lɔdʒikəl] *adj* escatológico, ca.

scatology [skə'tɔlədʒi] *n* escatología *f.*

scatter ['skætə*] *n* PHYS dispersión *f* || *there was no more than a scatter of people there* había solamente unas pocas personas.

scatter [skætə*] *vt* esparcir, desparramar; *wreckage was scattered all over the field* los restos estaban esparcidos por todo el campo; *she slipped and scattered her shopping over the floor* resbaló y desparramó sus compras por el suelo || salpicar; *she scatters her novels with Spanish words* salpica sus novelas con palabras españolas || dispersar; *the dog scattered the sheep* el perro dispersó las ovejas || disipar (to dispel) || sembrar al voleo (seed) || PHYS dispersar.
◆ *vi* dispersarse; *the crowd scattered when the police charged* la multitud se dispersó cuando la policía atacó || desparramarse; *the family has scattered over the whole world* la familia se ha desparramado por el mundo entero.

scatterbrain [-brein] *n* cabeza *f* de chorlito.

scatterbrained [-breind] *adj* ligero de cascos, atolondrado, da.

scattered ['skætəd] *adj* disperso, sa; desparramado, da; *scattered villages* pueblos dispersos || intermitente; *scattered showers* chubascos intermitentes || diseminado, da; *scattered army* ejército diseminado || — *a meadow scattered with flowers* una pradera salpicada de flores || *the floor is scattered with toys* hay juguetes esparcidos por el suelo.

scattering ['skætəriŋ] *n* dispersión *f,* esparcimiento *m* || *a scattering of* un pequeño número de, unos pocos, unos cuantos (a few).

scatty ['skæti] *adj* FAM ligero, ra de cascos, atolondrado, da.

scavenge ['skævindʒ] *vt* recoger (rubbish) || barrer (streets) || buscar entre (to search amongst) || revolver; *the tramp scavenged the dustbin for food* el vagabundo revolvió el cubo de la basura buscando comida || TECH expulsar (gases) | limpiar (metal).
◆ *vi* recoger la basura (to remove waste) || buscar comida (to search for food).

scavenger [-ə*] *n* basurero *m* (refuse collector) || barrendero *m* (road sweeper) || ZOOL animal *m or* insecto *m* que se alimenta de carroña.

scavenger beetle [-əˌbi:tl] *n* ZOOL necróforo *m.*

scavengery [-ri]; **scavenging** [-iŋ] *n* recogida *f* de la basura (rubbish collection) || barrido *m* (of streets) || búsqueda *f* de comida (searching for food) || búsqueda *f* de objetos útiles (amongst rubbish) || TECH expulsión *f* (of gases).

scenario [si'nɑ:riəu] *n* THEATR argumento *m* || CINEM guión *m.*

scenarist ['si:nərist] *n* CINEM guionista *m* & *f.*

scene [si:n] *n* CINEM & THEATR escena *f* (division of a play, of a film); *Act 1, Scene 2* primer acto, segunda escena; *the big scene* la escena principal; *a love scene* una escena de amor | escena *f* (place where the action is set); *the scene is Venise* la escena representa Venecia; *the scene changes* cambia la escena | decorado *m* (scenery) || THEATR escenario *m* (stage) || panorama *m,* vista *f,* perspectiva *f* (view); *the scene from the window is magnificent* la vista desde la ventana es espléndida || paisaje *m* (landscape); *wooded scene* paisaje arbolado || FIG escenario *m,* lugar *m* (place where sth. takes place); *the scene of the disaster* el lugar del desastre; *the scene of the crime* el escenario del crimen | teatro *m; the scene of the war* el teatro de la guerra; *the scene of operations* el teatro de operaciones | panorama *m* (situation); *the present political scene* el panorama político actual || escándalo *m,* escena *f* (fuss); *he made an awful scene in the restaurant* armó un escándalo espantoso en el restaurante || riña *f,* pelea *f,* escena *f* (argument); *he had a scene with his wife in front of everybody* tuvo una riña con su mujer delante de todo el mundo || — FIG *behind the scenes* entre bastidores || FIG & FAM *it's not my scene* no me va || FIG *the scene was set for a tragedy* todo estaba preparado para la tragedia | *to come on the scene* aparecer | *to disappear from the scene* desaparecer | *to paint a scene of gloom* crear un mundo de tristeza (a writer) || RAD *to set the scene* describir el escenario (before an event) || FIG *you need a change of scene* necesita cambiar de aire.

scenery [-əri] *n* paisaje *m* (landscape); *a town set in mountain scenery* un pueblo situado en un paisaje montañoso || paisajes *m pl* (landscapes); *there is a lot of beautiful scenery in Spain* en España hay muchos paisajes hermosos || THEATR decorado *m* (painted background).

sceneshifter [-ʃiftə*] *n* THEATR tramoyista *m* (stagehand).

scenic ['si:nik]; **scenical** [-əl] *adj* escénico, ca (of stage scenery) || dramático, ca (dramatic) || del paisaje (of the countryside); *scenic beauty* belleza del paisaje || pintoresco, ca (picturesque) || FIG espectacular.

scenic railway [-reilwei] *n* montaña *f* rusa (big dipper) || tren *m* de recreo (miniature railway).

scenic route [-ru:t] *n* ruta *f* panorámica.

scenographer [si:'nɔgrəfə*] *n* escenógrafo, fa.

scenographic [ˌsi:nə'græfik]; **scenographical** [ˌsi:nə'græfikəl] *adj* escenográfico, ca.

scenography [si:'nɔgrəfi] *n* escenografía *f.*

scent [sent] *n* olor *m* (smell) || perfume *m,* fragancia *f* (pleasing smell); *the scent of violets* el perfume de las violetas || aroma *m* (of food) || perfume *m* (perfume); *a bottle of scent* un frasco de perfume || rastro *m* (in hunting) || FIG pista *f* (in crime detection) || olfato *m* (sense of smell); *to have no scent* carecer de olfato, no tener olfato || — FIG *to lose the scent* perder la pista | *to pick up the scent* encontrar la pista | *to throw off the scent* despistar.

scent [sent] *vt* olfatear, oler; *the dog scented the rabbit* el perro olfateó el conejo || FIG oler, presentir; *to scent danger* presentir el peligro || perfumar; *to scent soap* perfumar el jabón; *the roses scented the air* las rosas perfumaban el aire.
◆ *vi* olfatear.

scented [-id] *adj* fragante; *a scented garden, flower* un jardín, una flor fragante || perfumado, da; *she is always heavily scented* siempre va muy perfumada || — *a keen-scented dog* un perro con buen olfato || *the room was scented with lavender* el cuarto olía a lavanda.

scepsis ['skepsis] *n* PHIL escepticismo *m*.

scepter ['septə*] *n* US cetro *m*.

sceptic ['skeptik] *n* escéptico, ca.

sceptical [-əl] *adj* escéptico, ca; *to be sceptical about sth.* ser escéptico acerca de algo.

scepticism ['skeptisizəm] *n* escepticismo *m*.

sceptre ['septə*] *n* cetro *m*.

schedule ['ʃedju:l; US 'skedju:l] *n* lista *f*, inventario *m* (list) || apéndice *m* (appendix) || programa *m*; *my schedule for today* mi programa para hoy || calendario *m* (of meetings) || horario *m* (timetable); *train schedule* horario de trenes || — *the train arrived on schedule* el tren llegó a la hora || *the train is behind schedule* el tren tiene *or* lleva retraso || *the work is behind schedule* el trabajo está atrasado || *the work is up to schedule* o *is going according to schedule* el trabajo no tiene retraso, el trabajo se desarrolla como está previsto || *to be ahead of schedule* ir adelantado, da || *work schedule* plan *m* de trabajo.

schedule ['ʃedju:l; US 'skedju:l] *vt* catalogar (to make a list of) || registrar (to put on a register); *this building is scheduled as being of historic interest* este edificio está registrado como monumento histórico || programar (to plan) || fijar el horario de (trains, aeroplanes, etc.) || fijar; *their departure was scheduled for five o'clock* se fijó su salida para las cinco || *the concert is scheduled for eight o'clock* o *is scheduled to start at eight o'clock* el concierto está previsto para las ocho.

Scheldt [skelt] *pr n* GEOGR Escalda *m*.

schema ['ski:mə] *n* esquema *m* (outline, diagram) || proyecto *m*, plan *m* (plan) || PHIL esquema *m*.
— OBSERV El plural de esta palabra es *schemata*.

schematic [ski'mætik] *adj* esquemático, ca.

schematize ['skiməˌtaiz] *vt* esquematizar.

scheme [ski:m] *n* combinación *f*; *colour scheme* combinación de colores || esquema *m* (schema) || programa *m* (program) || proyecto *m* (plan); *the airport scheme* el proyecto de aeropuerto || idea *f*; *I've just thought of a marvellous scheme* acabo de tener una idea genial || intriga *f* (plot) || ardid *m*, estratagema *f* (ruse); *it is a scheme to get him here* es una estratagema para que venga || sistema *m*; *a marking scheme* un sistema de notas; *a firm's pension scheme* el sistema de pensión de una empresa || FIG *in one's scheme of things* en los esquemas de alguien.

scheme [ski:m] *vt* proyectar (to plan) || tramar (to plot).
◆ *vi* hacer planes *or* proyectos (to make plans) || intrigar, conspirar (to plot).

schemer [-ə*] *n* intrigante *m* & *f*, maquinador, ra (plotter).

scheming [-iŋ] *adj* intrigante.

scherzo ['skɛətsəu] *n* MUS scherzo *m*.

schilling ['ʃiliŋ] *n* schilling *m* (Austrian coin).

schism ['sizəm] *n* cisma *m*.

schismatic [siz'mætik] *adj/n* cismático, ca.

schismatical [-əl] *adj* cismático, ca.

schist [ʃist] *n* MIN esquisto *m*.

schistose ['ʃistəus]; **schistous** ['ʃistəs] *adj* MIN esquistoso, sa.

schizo ['skitsəu] *adj/n* FAM esquizofrénico, ca.

schizophrene [ˌskitsəu'fri:n] *n* MED esquizofrénico, ca.

schizophrenia [ˌskitsəu'fri:njə] *n* MED esquizofrenia *f*.

schizophrenic [ˌskitsəu'frenik] *adj/n* MED esquizofrénico, ca.

schmaltz [ʃmɔlts] *n* FAM música *f* sentimental (music) | sentimentalismo *m* excesivo, sensiblería *f* (extreme sentimentality).

schmaltzy [-i] *adj* FAM sentimentaloide.

schnapps [ʃnæps] *n* aguardiente *m*.

schnorkel ['ʃnɔ:kəl] *n* MAR esnórquel *m* (of a submarine) || tubo *m* de respiración (swimmer's).

scholar ['skɔlə*] *n* erudito, ta; sabio, bia (learned person) || becario, ria (scholarship holder) || alumno, na (pupil) || — *classical scholar* humanista *m* & *f* || *Greek scholar* helenista *m* & *f* || *Latin scholar* latinista *m* & *f*.

scholarly [-li] *adj* erudito, ta.

scholarship [-ʃip] *n* saber *m*, erudición *f* (learning) || beca *f* (grant); *to be on a scholarship* tener una beca; *to win a scholarship* conseguir una beca || *scholarship holder* becario, ria.

scholastic [skə'læstik] *adj* PHIL escolástico, ca (relative to scholasticism) || escolar; *scholastic year* año escolar || docente (profession) || FIG pedante.
◆ *n* PHIL escolástico *m*.

scholasticism [skə'læstisizəm] *n* PHIL escolástica *f*, escolasticismo *m* || FIG escolasticismo *m*.

scholium ['skəuljəm] *n* escolio *m*.
— OBSERV El plural de la palabra inglesa es *scholia*.

school [sku:l] *n* escuela *f* (in general) || escuela *f* (state primary) || colegio *m* (private primary or secondary) || instituto *m* (state secondary) || academia *f*, escuela *f* (specialized); *language school* academia de idiomas; *drama school* academia de arte dramático || clase *f*; *to miss school* faltar a clase; *to go to school* ir a clase; *there will be no school today* hoy no hay clase || alumnado *m*, alumnos *m pl*; *the school will have a holiday next week* los alumnos estarán de vacaciones la semana que viene || US universidad *f*; *to be in school* ir a la universidad || facultad *f* (of a university); *School of Medicine* facultad de medicina || escuela *f* (group); *the impressionist school* la escuela impresionista; *school of Aristotle* escuela aristotélica || educación *f*; *he was brought up in a hard school* recibió una educación severa || instrucción *f*, educación *f*, formación *f* (formal education); *he had only three years of school* tuvo una formación que sólo duró tres años || MUS método *m*, manual *m* || banco *m* (of fish) || — *Comprehensive school* instituto de segunda enseñanza || *driving school* autoescuela *f* || *Grammar school* instituto de segunda enseñanza (in Great Britain), escuela primaria (in the United States) || US *High school* instituto de segunda enseñanza || *Infant school* colegio *or* escuela de párvulos || US *Junior high school* instituto de bachillerato elemental || *Lower school* primero y segundo de bachillerato || *Middle school* tercero y cuarto de bachillerato || *Military school* academia militar || *night school* escuela nocturna || *of the old school* de la vieja escuela || *prep* o *preparatory school* escuela preparatoria || *primary school* escuela primaria *or* de primera enseñanza || *public school* colegio privado de segunda enseñanza (in Great Britain), instituto (in the United States) || *school leaving age* edad *f* en que se acaba la escolaridad obligatoria || *school of thought* escuela filosófica (in philosophy), opinión *f*, idea *f*; *there are several schools of thought as to how to make tea* existen varias opiniones sobre la manera de hacer el té || *Secondary modern school* instituto de segunda enseñanza [centrado en estudios prácticos] || *summer school* cursos *m pl* de verano || *Sunday school* catequesis *f* || *Technical school* instituto laboral || US *to teach school* ser profesor, dar clases.
◆ *adj* escolar; *school age* edad escolar; *school curriculum* programa escolar; *school year* año escolar.

school [sku:l] *vt* instruir, educar, formar (to educate s.o.) || enseñar; *to school s.o. to do sth.* enseñar a alguien a hacer algo || ejercitar (to train) || amaestrar (animal) || disciplinar (one's temper) || dominar (one's feelings) || *to school o.s. to patience* aprender a ser paciente.
◆ *vi* nadar en bancos.

schoolbook [-buk] *n* libro *m* escolar, libro *m* de texto.

schoolboy [-bɔi] *n* alumno *m*, colegial *m*.

schoolchild [-ˌtʃaild] *n* alumno *m*, alumna *f*.
— OBSERV El plural es *schoolchildren*.

schooldays [-deiz] *pl n* años *m or* tiempos *m* de colegio; *in my schooldays* en mis tiempos de colegio.

schoolfellow [-ˌfeləu] *n* compañero, ra (de clase).

schoolgirl [-gə:l] *n* alumna *f*, colegiala *f* || *schoolgirl complexion* tez *f* de colegiala.

schoolhouse [-haus] *n* colegio *m*, escuela *f*.

school-leaver [-li:və*] *n* joven *m* & *f* que está a punto de dejar la escuela *or* que acaba de dejar la escuela.

schooling [-iŋ] *n* instrucción *f*, educación *f*, enseñanza *f* (formal education) || estudios *m pl*; *she paid for her brother's schooling* pagó los estudios de su hermano || *compulsory schooling* escolaridad obligatoria.

schoolma'am [-'mæəm]; **schoolmarm** [-mɑ:m] *n* US profesora *f* (in a secondary school) | maestra *f* (in a primary school).

schoolman [-mən] *n* PHIL escolástico *m*.
— OBSERV El plural de esta palabra es *schoolmen*.

schoolmaster [-ˌmɑ:stə*] *n* profesor *m* (in a secondary school) || maestro *m* (in a primary school).

schoolmate [-meit] *n* compañero, ra (de clase).

schoolmistress [-ˌmistris] *n* profesora *f* (in a secondary school) || maestra *f* (in a primary school).

school report [-ri'pɔ:t] *n* boletín *m* de evaluación.

schoolroom [-rum] *n* clase *f*, aula *f*, sala *f* de clase.

school ship [-ʃip] *n* buque *m* escuela.

schoolteacher [-ˌti:tʃə*] *n* profesor, ra (in a secondary school) || maestro, tra (in a primary school).

schoolwork [-wə:k] *n* deberes *m pl*, trabajo *m* escolar.

schoolyard [-jɑ:d] *n* patio *m* de recreo.

schooner ['sku:nə*] *n* MAR goleta *f* || US jarra *f* (of beer).

schooner-rigged [-ˌrigd] *adj* MAR de velas cangrejas.

schorl [ʃɔ:l] *n* MIN turmalina *f* negra.

schottische [ʃɔ'ti:ʃ] *n* chotis *m*.

schuss [ʃus] *n* SP recta *f*.

schuss [ʃus] *vi* SP esquiar rápidamente en línea recta.

sciatic [sai'ætik] *adj* ciático, ca.

sciatica [-ə] *n* MED ciática *f*.

science ['saiəns] *n* ciencia *f*; *the advances of science* los adelantos de la ciencia; *the physical sciences* las ciencias físicas || arte *f*; *the science of fencing* el arte de la esgrima || — REL *Christian science* ciencia cristiana || *social science* sociología *f* || *to blind s.o. with science* deslumbrar a uno con sus conocimientos.

science fiction [-'fikʃən] *n* ciencia *f* ficción.

scientific [ˌsaiənˈtifik] *adj* científico, ca; *scientific principles* principios científicos; *scientific management* organización científica del trabajo || FIG estudiado, da (cruelty) || SP que tiene mucha técnica.

scientifically [-əli] *adv* científicamente.

scientist [ˈsaiəntist] *n* científico, ca.

sci-fi [ˈsɑiˈfɑi] *adj* FAM de ciencia ficción.
◆ *n* ciencia *f* ficción.

scilicet [ˈsailiset] *adv* a saber, es decir.

scilla [ˈsilə] *n* BOT cebolla *f* albarrana.

Scilly Isles [ˈsiliailz] *pl prn* GEOGR islas *f* Sorlingas.

scimitar [ˈsimitə*] *n* cimitarra *f*.

scintilla [sinˈtilə] *n* centella *f* (light trace) || chispa *f*, centella *f* (spark).

scintillant [ˈsintilənt] *adj* ⟶ **scintillating.**

scintillate [ˈsintileit] *vi* centellear (to twinkle) || titilar (stars) || destellar, chispear (to sparkle) || FIG brillar.

scintillating [-iŋ]; **scintillant** [ˈsintilənt] *adj* titilante (star) || centelleante, relumbrante (dazzling) || FIG chispeante (wit) | brillante (style, conversation, etc.).

scintillation [ˌsintiˈleiʃən] *n* centelleo *m* (twinkling) || titilación *f* (of stars) || FIG viveza *f* (wit) || PHYS centelleo *m*; *scintillation counter* contador de centelleo.

sciolist [ˈsaiəulist] *n* erudito *m* a la violeta, falso erudito *m*, falsa erudita *f*.

scion [ˈsaiən] *n* AGR retoño *m*, renuevo *m* (bud) | púa *f*, injerto *m*, esqueje *m* (shoot used for grafting) || FIG vástago *m*, descendiente *m* (descendant).

Scipio [ˈskipiəu] *pr n* HIST Escipión *m*; *Scipio Africanus* Escipión el Africano.

scissile [ˈsisil] *adj* hendible, escindible.

scission [ˈsiʒən] *n* escisión *f*, corte *m* (cut, cutting) || escisión *f*, división *f* (division).

scissor [ˈsizə] *vt* cortar con tijeras.

scissors [ˈsizəz] *pl n* tijeras *f* (tool) || SP salto *m* de tijera (in gymnastics) | tijera *f*, tijereta *f* (in wrestling) || *a pair of scissors* unas tijeras.

scissors jump [-dʒʌmp] *n* SP salto *m* de tijera.

scissors kick [-kik] *n* SP tijereta *f*.

sclera [ˈskliːərə] *n* ANAT esclerótica *f*.

sclerosed [skliːəˈrəust] *adj* MED escleroso, sa.

sclerosis [skliəˈrəusis] *n* MED esclerosis *f*.
— OBSERV El plural de *sclerosis* es *scleroses*.

sclerotic [skliəˈrɔtik] *adj* MED escleroso, sa.
◆ *n* ANAT esclerótica *f* (sclera).

sclerous [ˈskliːərəs] *adj* escleroso, sa.

scoff [skɔf] *n* mofa *f*, burla *f*; *he said it with a scoff* lo dijo con mofa || hazmerreír *m* (laughingstock) || FAM comida *f* (meal) || FAM *to have a good scoff* pegarse una comilona.

scoff [skɔf] *vt* FAM tragarse, zamparse (food).
◆ *vi* mofarse, burlarse; *to scoff at superstition* mofarse de la superstición || *that's not to be scoffed at* no es para tomarlo a broma.

scoffer [-ə*] *n* mofador, ra; burlón, ona.

scoffing [-iŋ] *n* mofa *f*, burla *f*, escarnio *m* || FAM comer *m*, jamancia *f* (eating).

scold [skəuld] *n* regañona *f*, gruñona *f* (woman) || reprensión *f*, regaño *m*, reprimenda *f* (scolding).

scold [skəuld] *vt* regañar, reñir; *to scold one's children* regañar a los niños.
◆ *vi* chillar, gritar.

scolding [-iŋ] *n* reprimenda *f*, regaño *m*, reprensión *f* || *to give s.o. a severe scolding* regañar severamente a alguien.

scoliosis [ˌskɔliˈəusis] *n* MED escoliosis *f*.

scollop [ˈskɔləp] *n* ⟶ **scallop.**

scollop [ˈskɔləp] *vt* ⟶ **scallop.**

scolopendra [ˌskɔləˈpendrə] *n* ZOOL escolopendra *f*.

sconce [skɔns] *n* candelabro *m* de pared (wall candle holder) || palmatoria *f* (handled candle stick) || MIL fortín *m*.

scone [skɔn] *n* torta *f*.

scoop [skuːp] *n* pala *f* (hollow utensil for serving flour, etc.) || cuchara *f* (spoon) || platillo *m* (of a balance) || pinzas *f pl* (for ice cream) || recogedor *m* (for dust, for rubbish) || cubo *m* para el carbón (for coal) || palada *f* (content of a scoop) || MAR achicador *m* (for bailing out) || TECH cuchara *f* (of an excavator) | gubia *f* (carpenter's tool) | cangilón *m* (of a dredge) || MED legra *f* (surgical instrument) || GEOL depresión *f* || FAM ganancia *f* grande (profit) || noticia *f* sensacional que se tiene en exclusiva (in journalism).

scoop [skuːp] *vt* sacar (profit) || — *to scoop in* sacar (money) || *to scoop out* sacar [con pala] (flour, etc.), achicar (water from a boat), cavar (to excavate), escotar (a neckline) || *to scoop the other newspapers* adelantarse a los otros periódicos en la publicación de una noticia || *to scoop up* sacar [con pala] (flour, etc.), achicar (water from a boat), sacar [del agua] (sth. from the water), recoger (dust, rubbish), coger; *to scoop s.o. up in one's arms* coger a uno en brazos.

scooper [-ə*] *n* gubia *f* (tool) || avoceta *f* (bird).

scoop net [-net] *n* red *f* barredera.

scoot [skuːt] *vi* FAM correr rápidamente (to go quickly) | largarse (to go away).

scooter [-ə*] *n* patineta *f* (child's toy) || scooter *m* (motor vehicle).

scope [skəup] *n* ámbito *m*; *such subjects are not within the scope of this book* temas de esa índole no están dentro del ámbito de este libro || esfera *f* or campo *m* de acción (person's field of action); *it does not come within my scope* no cae dentro de mi esfera de acción || incumbencia *f*, competencia *f* (person's responsibilities); *outside my scope* fuera de mi incumbencia || competencia *f* (ability); *his scope is fairly limited* su competencia es bastante limitada || alcance *m* (reach); *beyond the scope of his imagination* fuera del alcance de su imaginación; *a new car is quite beyond my scope* comprar un coche nuevo está completamente fuera de mi alcance || amplitud *f* (of a project) || campo *m* de aplicación (of a law) || — *he needs more scope to develop his talents* necesita más libertad para desarrollar sus capacidades || *to give s.o. full scope* dar carta blanca a alguien.

scops owl [ˈskɔpsaul] *n* ZOOL buharro *m*.

scorbutic [skɔːˈbjuːtik] *adj* MED escorbútico, ca.

scorch [skɔːtʃ] *n* quemadura *f*.

scorch [skɔːtʃ] *vt* quemar; *fields scorched by the summer sun* campos quemados por el sol de verano; *the iron scorched the sheet* la plancha quemó la sábana; *the cook has scorched the food* la cocinera ha quemado la comida || chamuscar (to singe) || FIG herir || MIL arrasar (to devastate).
◆ *vi* quemarse (to become burnt); *the grass scorched in the sun* con el sol se quemó la hierba || chamuscarse (to become singed) || FAM ir volando or a gran velocidad (to go very fast) || FAM *they scorched past at a hundred* pasaron (volando) a cien millas por hora.

scorched-earth policy [skɔːtʃtəːθˈpɔlisi] *n* MIL táctica *f* que consiste en arrasar todo lo que puede facilitar el avance del enemigo.

scorcher [ˈskɔːtʃə*] *n* FAM día *m* abrasador (hot day) | crítica *f* severa (criticism) | loco *m* del volante (driver) | ciclista *m* suicida (cyclist) | persona *f* or cosa estupenda.

scorching [ˈskɔːtʃiŋ] *adj* abrasador, ra (very hot) || FIG mordaz (comment, criticism).

score [skɔː*] *n* muesca *f*, incisión *f* (notch) || raya *f* (line) || arañazo *m* (on leather, on cardboard, etc.) || estría *f* (on rock) || TECH raya *f* (of a cylinder, bearing) || señal *f* (on a tree) || SP tanteo *m* (number of points, of goals, etc.); *the score at half time was two to one* al terminar el primer tiempo el tanteo era de dos a uno | resultado *m* (result); *what was the score?* ¿cuál fue el resultado? | tanto *m* (a point scored in a game) | puntuación *f* (in golf, shooting, cards, etc.) || calificación *f*, nota *f* (in a test, in an exam); *to get a score of nine out of ten* sacar una nota de nueve sobre diez || FAM cuenta *f* (debt) | observación *f* mordaz (well-directed remark) || veintena *f* (twenty); *a score of people* una veintena de personas || MUS partitura *f*; *full score* partitura de orquesta || — *on that score* por lo que se refiere a eso, a ese respecto || *on the score of* con motivo de, por causa de || SP *there was no score in the second half* no marcaron en el segundo tiempo || *three score years and ten* setenta años || SP *to keep the score* tantear || FIG *to know the score* conocer el percal (to know about sth.), ser muy despabilado (not to be easily deceived) | *to pay off old scores, to settle an old score with s.o.* ajustar cuentas con alguien.
◆ *pl* montones *m*; *scores of people* montones de gente.

score [skɔː*] *vt* hacer una muesca en (to notch) || rayar (to scratch a line on) || subrayar (to underline) || estriar (rock) || TECH rayar (a bearing, a piston, etc.) || apuntar [por medio de rayas or muescas] (to keep account of) || SP marcar (point, goal, etc.) | conseguir (a victory) || valer; *ace scores ten* el as vale diez || MUS orquestar (a composition) || sacar or obtener [una nota de] (in a test); *to score five* sacar un cinco || US calificar (to grade) | reprender, regañar (to scold) || *to score out* tachar (to cross out).
◆ *vi* SP tantear (to keep a score) | marcar un tanto (to win a point) | marcar un gol (in football) || aventajar; *to score over a rival* aventajar a un rival || FAM tener éxito (to have a success) || — FIG *that's where you score* es en eso donde llevas ventaja || *to score off s.o.* marcar un tanto a costa de alguien (to win at s.o.'s expense), reírse de uno (to make a joke about s.o.).

scoreboard [-bɔːd] *n* marcador *m*, tanteador *m*.

scorecard [-kɑːd] *n* SP tanteador *m*.

scorekeeper [-kiːpə*] *n* tanteador *m*.

scorer [-ə*] *n* SP goleador *m* (in football) || tanteador *m* (scorekeeper) || *the team's top scorer* el jugador que más goles ha marcado.

scoresheet [-ʃiːt] *n* SP tanteador *m*.

scoria [ˈskɔriə] *n* escoria *f*.
— OBSERV El plural de la palabra inglesa es *scoriae*.

scorify [ˈskɔriˌfai] *vt* escorificar.

scoring [ˈskɔːriŋ] *n* SP tanteo *m* || rayado *m* (scratching) || incisión *f* (cutting) || estriación *f* (of rock) || TECH rayado *m* (of bearing, of piston, etc.) || MUS orquestación *f* || US reprimenda *f*, reprensión *f* (reprimand).

scorn [skɔːn] *n* desprecio *m*, desdén *m*, menosprecio *m* || — *she is the scorn of her friends* sus amigas la desprecian || *to heap* o *pour scorn on sth., on s.o.* despreciar or ridiculizar algo, a alguien || *to laugh to scorn* ridiculizar.

scorn [skɔːn] *vt* despreciar, desdeñar, menospreciar || *to scorn to do sth.* no dignarse a hacer algo, negarse a hacer algo.

scornful [-ful] *adj* despreciativo, va; desdeñoso, sa.

Scorpio ['skɔːpiəu] *n* ASTR Escorpión *m*.

scorpion ['skɔːpjən] *n* ZOOL escorpión *m*, alacrán *m* || ASTR Escorpión *m* || *scorpion fish* rascacio *m*, rescaza *f*.

scorzonera [ˌskɔːzəˈniːərə] *n* BOT escorzonera *f*.

scot [skɔt] *n* parte *f*, escote *m* (share in joint expenses); *to pay one's scot* pagar su parte || HIST contribución *f* (money levied as a tax).

Scot [skɔt] *n* Escocés, esa.

scotch [skɔtʃ] *n* calza *f* (for wheel) || muesca *f* (notch) || herida *f* (wound) || whisky *m* escocés.

scotch [skɔtʃ] *vt* calzar (to prevent from rolling) || frustrar (to thwart); *to scotch s.o.'s plans* frustrar los proyectos de alguien || herir (to wound without killing) || suprimir (to suppress) || *to scotch a conspiracy* hacer fracasar una conspiración.

Scotch [skɔtʃ] *adj* escocés, esa; *Scotch terrier* terrier escocés; *Scotch whisky* whisky escocés; *Scotch broth* sopa escocesa || CULIN *Scotch egg* huevo cubierto de carne picada || *Scotch tape* cinta adhesiva.
◆ *n* escocés *m* (language) || *the Scotch* los escoceses.

Scotchman [-mən] *n* escocés *m*.
— OBSERV El plural de esta palabra es *Scotchmen*.

Scotchwoman [-ˌwumən] *n* escocesa *f*.
— OBSERV El plural de esta palabra es *Scotchwomen*.

scot-free ['skɔt'friː] *adj* sin castigo, impune (without punishment) || ileso, sa (unhurt) || sin pagar (without paying).

Scotland ['skɔtlənd] *pr n* GEOGR Escocia *f* || *Scotland Yard* sede *f* de la policía londinense.

Scots [skɔts] *adj* escocés, esa; *Scots Guards* Guardia escocesa.
◆ *n* escocés *m* (language).

Scotsman [-mən] *n* escocés *m*.
— OBSERV El plural de esta palabra es *Scotsmen*.

Scotswoman [-ˌwumən] *n* escocesa *f*.
— OBSERV El plural de esta palabra es *Scotswomen*.

scottie ['skɔti] *n* FAM terrier *m* escocés (dog).

Scottie ['skɔti] *n* FAM escocés, esa.

Scottish ['skɔtiʃ] *adj* escocés, esa; *Scottish terrier* terrier escocés.
◆ *n* escocés *m* (language) || *the Scottish* los escoceses.

scoundrel ['skaundrəl] *n* sinvergüenza *m*, canalla *m*.

scour ['skauə*] *n* restregón *m*, fregado *m* (act of scouring) || detergente *m* (cleansing agent) || lugar *m* derrubiado (eroded place).
◆ *pl* VET diarrea *f sing*.

scour ['skauə*] *vt* restregar, fregar (to clean by rubbing hard); *to scour a pan* restregar una cacerola || revocar (with high-pressure water) || limpiar (wool) || MED purgar (to purge) || derrubiar, erosionar (to erode) || FIG batir, registrar, recorrer; *police are scouring the district searching for the girl* la policía está batiendo el barrio en busca de la niña; *to scour the town* recorrer la ciudad.
◆ *vi* correr; *to scour after* correr en busca de.

scourer [-rə*] *n* estropajo *m* (abrasive pad).

scourge [skəːdʒ] *n* látigo *m* (whip) || FIG azote *m*, plaga *f* (cause of misery) | castigo *m* (divine punishment) || FIG *Attila, the Scourge of God* Atila, el Azote de Dios.

scourge [skəːdʒ] *vt* azotar, flagelar (to whip) || FIG azotar; *a country scourged by disease and famine* un país azotado por la enfermedad y el hambre | atormentar (to torment).

scouring ['skauəriŋ] *n* restregadura *f*, fregado *m* (of a cooking utensil, etc.) || revoque *m* (of a building's interior) || limpieza *f* (of wool) || derrubio *m* (erosion) || *scouring pad* estropajo *m* (scourer).
◆ *pl* basura *f sing* (refuse) || hez *f sing* (of society).

Scouse [skaus] *adj* FAM de Liverpool.
◆ *n* FAM habitante *m* & *f* de Liverpool || dialecto *m* de Liverpool.

scout [skaut] *n* MIL explorador *m* (soldier sent ahead) | escucha *m* (sent out to listen) | reconocimiento *m*, exploración *f* (scouting) || explorador *m* (boy scout) || criado *m* (at Oxford) || US observador *m* (person who observes rival sport team) | descubridor *m* de personas de talento (talent scout) | tipo *m* (fellow) || — MIL *scout plane* avión *m* de reconocimiento || *to be on the scout for* estar buscando.

scout [skaut] *vt* MIL explorar, batir, reconocer (to reconnoitre) || rechazar (to reject).
◆ *vi* hacer un reconocimiento (to reconnoitre) || hacer una batida (to search) || *to scout for* buscar.

scouting [-iŋ] *n* MIL exploración *f*, reconocimiento *m* || actividades *f pl* de los exploradores (boy scouts).

scoutmaster [-ˌmaːstə*] *n* jefe *m* de exploradores.

scow [skau] *n* MAR chalana *f* (boat).

scowl [skaul] *n* ceño *m* || *«no», he answered with a scowl* «no», contestó frunciendo el entrecejo.

scowl [skaul] *vi* fruncir el entrecejo || FIG tener un aspecto amenazador.
◆ *vt* *to scowl an answer* contestar frunciendo el entrecejo || *to scowl one's dissatisfaction* manifestar su descontento frunciendo el entrecejo.

scowling [-iŋ] *adj* ceñudo, da.

scrabble ['skræbl] *vi* escarbar (to make scratching movements) || garabatear, garrapatear (to scrawl) || subir gateando (to climb) || — *to be scrabbled in her bag for her matches* revolvió todo lo que tenía en el bolso para encontrar sus cerillas || *to scrabble on the floor for sth.* buscar algo en el suelo a gatas.
◆ *vt* garabatear (to write illegibly).

Scrabble ['skræbl] *n* (registered trademark) Scrabble *m* [juego *m* de palabras].

scrag [skræg] *n* persona *f* esquelética, animal *m* esquelético (scrawny person or animal) || CULIN pescuezo *m* (of mutton or veal) || pescuezo *m* (of a person).

scrag [skræg] *vt* FAM ahorcar (to kill by hanging) | torcer el pescuezo a (to kill by twisting the neck) | agarrar por el pescuezo, torcer el pescuezo a (to grab by the neck); *scrag him!* ¡tuércele el pescuezo!

scragginess [-inis] *n* flacura *f*, delgadez *f* (of the body) || aspereza *f* (of rocks).

scraggly [-li] *adj* US desaseado, da (unkempt) | ralo, la (of sparse growth).

scraggy [-i] *adj* flaco, ca; delgado, da (scrawny) || escabroso, sa; áspero, ra (rocks, etc.).

scram [skræm] *vi* FAM largarse.

scramble [-bl] *n* camino *m* difícil; *it is a scramble to get down the hillside* es un camino difícil para bajar la colina || lucha *f*, arrebatiña *f*, pelea *f*; *a scramble to get tickets* una lucha para conseguir entradas || SP carrera *f* de motocross.

scramble [-bl] *vt* revolver (to jumble) || mezclar (to mix) || RAD perturbar || CULIN revolver; *scrambled eggs* huevos revueltos.
◆ *vi* trepar, gatear (to climb with struggling movements) || pelearse; *they scrambled for the best seats* se pelearon por conseguir los mejores sitios || — *to scramble into one's clothes* vestirse rápidamente || *to scramble out* salir a gatas.

scrambler [-ə*] *n* RAD aparato *m* para perturbar las emisiones radiofónicas *or* telefónicas || SP motocicleta *f* de motocross.

scrambling [-bliŋ] *n* pelea *f*, arrebatiña *f*, lucha *f*; *I don't like all this scrambling for seats* no me gusta toda esta pelea para obtener asientos || trepa *f* (struggling uphill) || SP motocross *m*.

scrap [skræp] *n* trozo *m*, pedazo *m* (of paper, of food, etc.) || recorte *m* (piece of material, printed excerpt of book, speech, etc., newspaper cutting) || chatarra *f* (old metal); *scrap value* valor como chatarra; *to sell sth. for scrap* vender algo como chatarra || ápice *m*; *there is not a scrap of truth in it* no tiene un ápice de verdad || pizca *f* (very small piece); *not a scrap of food* ni una pizca de comida || FAM pelea *f* (fight) || — *it won't make a scrap of difference* no cambiará las cosas en absoluto, dará exactamente igual || FAM *to have a scrap with s.o.* pelearse con alguien.
◆ *pl* restos *m*, sobras *f* (leftovers); *table scraps* las sobras de la mesa || residuos *m*, desechos *m* (waste) || CULIN chicharrones *m* || — *a few scraps of knowledge* algunos conocimientos || *to catch scraps of conversation* poder oír algunas palabras de una conversación.

scrap [skræp] *vt* desechar (to discard) || desguazar (to break up) || desechar, descartar (idea).
◆ *vi* FAM pelearse (to fight).

scrapbook [-buk] *n* álbum *m* de recortes.

scrap dealer [-diːlə*] *n* chatarrero, ra.

scrape [skreip] *n* raspado *m* (act of scraping) || chirrido *m* (noise of scraping) || arañazo *m* (scraped mark on painwork, leather, etc.) || rasguño *m* (graze on skin) || FAM lío *m*, apuro *m* (awkward situation) | reverencia *f* obsequiosa (bow).

scrape [skreip] *vt* raspar; *to scrape a ship's hull* raspar el casco de un barco; *to scrape the paint off a door* raspar la pintura de una puerta || decapar, desoxidar (a metal) || limpiar (to clean) || arañar (to graze the skin, scratch paintwork, leather, etc.) || CULIN rallar || arrastrar (to drag); *to scrape furniture across the floor* arrastrar un mueble por el suelo; *to scrape one's feet along the ground* arrastrar los pies por el suelo || rozar; *to scrape the seabed* rozar el fondo del mar || rasgar (a violin) || hacer chirriar; *he scraped the chalk on the blackboard* hizo chirriar la tiza en la pizarra || MED legrar, raspar || — FIG *to scrape a living* vivir muy apretadamente || *to scrape off* o *away* quitar [raspando] || FIG FAM *to scrape one's plate* dejar el plato limpio || *to scrape out a tune on the violin* tocar la melodía rascando el violín || *to scrape together* o *up* reunir.
◆ *vi* rozar; *to scrape along the wall* pasar rozando la pared || chirriar; *the chalk scraped on the blackboard* la tiza chirrió en la pizarra || economizar (to live economically) || — FIG *to bow and scrape* hacer zalemas || FIG & FAM *to scrape along* o *by* ir tirando || *to scrape through* pasar muy justo por (a gap), aprobar por los pelos (an exam).

scraper ['skreipə*] *n* raspador *m*, rascador *m* (tool) || MAR rasqueta *f* || MED legra *f* || limpiabarros *m inv* (for scraping mud off one's shoes) || FAM rascatripas *m inv* (violinist).

scrap heap ['skræphiːp] *n* montón *m* de chatarra (pile of scrap) || cementerio *m* de coches (for old cars) || montón *m* de desechos (rubbish heap).

scraping ['skreipiŋ] *n* raspado *m* (act) || chirrido *m* (noise) || MED raspado *m*, legrado *m*.

◆ *pl* raspaduras *f.*

scrap iron [skræp'aiən]; **scrap metal** ['skræp'metl] *n* chatarra *f.*

scrap merchant [skræp'mə:tʃənt] *n* chatarrero *m.*

scrap paper ['skræp'peipə*] *n* papel *m* de borrador.

scrapper ['skræpə*] *n* FAM pendenciero *m*, peleón *m*, camorrista *m.*

scrappy ['skræpi] *adj* pobre, hecho con sobras *or* restos (meal) ‖ incompleto, ta (information, collection, education) ‖ deshilvanado, da (style, speech) ‖ FAM peleón, ona; pendenciero, ra ‖ *scrappy knowledge* unos conocimientos fragmentarios.

scrapyard ['skræpja:d] *n* cementerio *m* de coches.

scratch [skrætʃ] *n* arañazo *m*, rasguño *m* (on the skin); *to escape without a scratch* escapar sin un rasguño ‖ arañazo *m* (on paintwork, on wood, etc.) ‖ raya *f* (on a record, on a photograph) ‖ chirrido *m* (sound of scratching) ‖ rascadura *f* (to relieve itching) ‖ garabato *m* (meaningless mark made by pen, etc.) ‖ SP línea *f* de salida (in athletics) | chiripa *f* (in billiards) ‖ — INFORM *scratch pad memory* memoria *f* scratch *or* a corto plazo ‖ *to be o to come up to scratch* satisfacer los requisitos (to fulfil the requirements), ser tan bueno como siempre (to be as good as ever); *her performance was up to scratch* su actuación fue tan buena como siempre; estar a la altura de las circunstancias (to be good enough) ‖ *to feel up to scratch* sentirse en forma (fit) ‖ *to start from scratch* empezar sin nada (with nothing), empezar desde el principio (from the beginning).

◆ *adj* improvisado, da; *a scratch team* un equipo improvisado; *a scratch meal* una comida improvisada ‖ sin homogeneidad ‖ SP sin ventaja (who has no handicap).

scratch [skrætʃ] *vt* rayar; *to scratch the paintwork* rayar la pintura ‖ grabar; *I scratched my name on the tree* grabé mi nombre en el árbol ‖ rascar; *to scratch one's head* rascarse la cabeza ‖ arañar, rasguñar; *the dog scratched me* el perro me arañó; *I have scratched my hand* me he rasguñado la mano ‖ frotar (a match) ‖ escarbar; *hens scratch the ground* las gallinas escarban la tierra ‖ tachar, borrar (to cross out); *scratch his name from the list* tacha su nombre de la lista ‖ garabatear (to scrawl) ‖ SP cancelar (a match, a race, etc.) | retirar (a horse, a competitor, etc.) ‖ — *to scratch a hole in sth.* rascar algo hasta hacer un agujero ‖ *to scratch s.o.'s eyes out* sacar los ojos a alguien ‖ FIG *to scratch the surface* no profundizar ‖ FIG & FAM *to scratch together* o *up* reunir | *you scratch my back and I'll scratch yours* un favor con favor se paga.

◆ *vi* arañar; *a cat that scratches* un gato que araña ‖ rascarse (to relieve itching) ‖ escarbar (a hen) ‖ raspear (a pen) ‖ SP retirarse (to withdraw) ‖ FAM *to scratch along* o *by* ir tirando.

scratcher [-ə*] *n* raspador *m* (tool) ‖ raspador, ra (person).

scratch pad [-pæd] *n* bloc *m* [para apuntes].

scratch paper [-'peipə*] *n* papel *m* de borrador.

scratch test [-test] *n* cutirreacción *f* [para casos alérgicos].

scratchy [-i] *adj* arañado, da; rayado, da (covered with scratches) ‖ que pica (causing irritation or itching) ‖ que chirría, chirriante (making a harsh sound) ‖ que raspea (pen) ‖ garabatoso, sa (writing).

scrawl [skrɔ:l] *n* garabato *m*; *his signature is just a scrawl* su firma no es más que un garabato ‖ garabatos *m pl* (scrawling writing); *I can't read this scrawl* no consigo leer estos garabatos.

scrawl [skrɔ:l] *vt/vi* garabatear; *to scrawl a note* garabatear unas palabras ‖ *to scrawl over* cubrir de garabatos.

scrawny ['skrɔ:ni] *adj* flaco, ca; flacucho, cha.

screak [skrik] *n* chirrido *m.*

scream [skri:m] *n* grito *m*, chillido *m* (of pain, of fear) ‖ FAM persona *f or* cosa *f* divertidísima ‖ — FAM *he's an absolute scream* es divertidísimo, es mondante | *it was a scream* fue la monda ‖ *to give a scream of horror* dar un grito de horror.

◆ *pl* carcajadas *f* (of laughter).

scream [skri:m] *vt* vociferar; *to scream insults* vociferar insultos ‖ gritar; *yes!, he screamed* ¡sí!, gritó ‖ berrear; *the baby screamed itself to sleep* el niño berreó hasta dormirse.

◆ *vi* gritar, chillar (in fear, pain, anger, hysteria); *to scream with pain* gritar de dolor ‖ chillar, chirriar (bird) ‖ FIG ser muy llamativo; *posters screamed outside the theatre* los carteles del teatro eran muy llamativos ‖ FAM *to scream with laughter* partirse *or* mondarse de risa, reír a carcajadas.

screamer [-ə*] *n* chillón, ona; gritón, ona (person who screams) ‖ ave *f* chillona (bird) ‖ FAM chiste *m* graciosísimo (joke) | obra *f* divertidísima (play) | tipo *m* muy chistoso (person) | titulares *m pl* sensacionalistas (headlines) | punto *m* de exclamación (exclamation mark).

screaming [-iŋ] *adj* FIG mondante, graciosísimo, ma; divertidísimo, ma (funny) ‖ estridente (noise) ‖ llamativo, va; chillón, ona (colour); *painted in screaming red* pintado en rojo chillón ‖ FIG *screaming headlines* titulares *m* sensacionalistas.

screamingly [-iŋli] *adv* *screamingly funny* mondante, de morirse de risa.

scree [skri:] *n* GEOL piedra *f* (stone) | guijarro *m* (pebble) | acumulación *f* de piedras y rocas.

screech [skri:tʃ] *n* chillido *m.*

screech [skri:tʃ] *vi* chillar (to give a shrill scream) ‖ chirriar; *the brakes screeched* los frenos chirriaron.

◆ *vt* decir a gritos, gritar (to scream shrilly).

screech owl [-aul] *n* ZOOL lechuza *f.*

screed [skri:d] *n* discurso *m* largo y aburrido, perorata *f*, rollo *m* (fam), discurso *m* largo y aburrido, perorata *f*, rollo *m* (speech) ‖ escrito *m* largo y aburrido (piece of writing) ‖ sarta *f*, lista *f* larga (long list) ‖ TECH maestra *f* (used in plastering) | renglón *m* (in paving).

screen [skri:n] *n* biombo *m* (movable partition made of wood, of metal, etc.); *folding screen* biombo plegable ‖ ARCH tabique *m* (partition wall) ‖ reja *f* (of a window) ‖ AUT parabrisas *m inv* (windscreen) ‖ FIG cortina *f*; *a smoke screen* una cortina de humo ‖ MIL cobertura *f* (of men) ‖ MAR protección *f* (of vessels) ‖ tablón *m* de anuncios (notice board) ‖ PHYS & CINEM pantalla *f*; *cinema screen, television screen* pantalla de cine, de televisión; *the small screen* la pequeña pantalla ‖ cine *m*; *screen star* estrella de cine; *screen music* música de cine ‖ PRINT trama *f* ‖ criba *f* (sieve) ‖ SP pantalla *f* (cricket) ‖ — *fire screen* pantalla ‖ *safety screen* pantalla de seguridad ‖ *screen door* puerta *f* de tela metálica ‖ INFORM *screen mask* máscara *f* de pantalla ‖ *screen of trees* pantalla de árboles.

screen [skri:n] *vt* proteger, resguardar (to shelter); *to screen one's eyes from the light* protegerse los ojos de la luz ‖ tapar, ocultar (to conceal); *sun screened by clouds* sol tapado por las nubes; *to screen (off) a part of a room* tapar una parte de la habitación ‖ MIL & MAR cubrir, proteger ‖ cribar, tamizar (to sift) ‖ adaptar para el cine (to make into a film) ‖ proyectar (a film); *the film will be screened after the meal* proyectarán la película después de la comida ‖ FIG pasar por el tamiz *or* por la criba; *to screen candidates for a job* pasar por el tamiz los candidatos a un puesto ‖ FIG *to screen out* seleccionar (to select), eliminar (to eliminate).

◆ *vi* adaptarse para el cine; *this book will screen well* este libro se adaptará bien para el cine.

screening [-iŋ] *n* protección *f* (protection) ‖ ocultación *f* (hiding) ‖ cribado *m* (sifting) ‖ proyección *f* (of a film) ‖ FIG *to submit s.o. to a security screening* hacer una investigación sobre los antecedentes de alguien.

◆ *pl* cribaduras *f*, cerniduras *f* (refuse).

screenplay [-plei] *n* guión *m.*

screen test [-test] *n* prueba *f* cinematográfica.

screenwriter [-,raitə*] *n* guionista *m* & *f.*

screw [skru:] *n* tornillo *m*; *endless screw* tornillo sin fin ‖ tuerca *f* (female screw) ‖ vuelta *f* (one turn of a screw); *to give another screw* dar otra vuelta ‖ AVIAT & MAR hélice *f* (propeller) ‖ SP efecto *m* (of a ball) ‖ FAM tacaño, ña (miser) | sueldo *m* (salary); *to be on a good screw* ganar un buen sueldo | penco *m* (horse) | carcelero *m* (prison warder) ‖ POP polvo *m* (sexual intercourse) ‖ — *screwtop jar* tarro *m* con tapón de rosca ‖ FIG & FAM *to have a screw loose* tener flojos los tornillos, faltarle un tornillo a uno.

◆ *pl* empulgueras *f* (torture) | *to put the screws on s.o.* apretar las clavijas *or* los tornillos a uno.

screw [skru:] *vt* atornillar (to turn) ‖ apretar (to tighten) ‖ fijar con tornillos; *to screw sth. (on) to the wall* fijar algo en la pared con tornillos ‖ retorcer (to twist) ‖ FAM sacar; *to screw a dollar out of s.o.* sacarle un dólar a alguien ‖ POP joder (to make love to, to ruin things for) ‖ — *he screwed the letter into a ball* hizo una bola con la carta ‖ *to screw off* destornillar ‖ *to screw on* enroscar ‖ *to screw up* arrugar (paper), torcer (one's face), apretar (one's lips), fastidiar (to spoil); *to screw up the whole deal* fastidiar todo el negocio; armarse de; *to screw up one's courage* armarse de valor.

◆ *vi* enroscarse (to be joined or to turn like a screw); *the top screws on to the jar* la tapa se enrosca en el tarro ‖ estar atornillado, estar fijado con tornillos; *the shelf screws on to the wall* el estante está atornillado en la pared ‖ apretarse (to tighten).

screwball [-bɔ:l] *adj* US FAM chiflado, da; chalado, da; excéntrico, ca.

◆ *n* US SP pelota *f* lanzada con efecto (in baseball) ‖ US FAM excéntrico, ca.

screw bolt [-bəult] *n* TECH perno *m* roscado.

screw cap [-kæp] *n* tapón *m* de rosca *or* de tuerca.

screw coupling [-'kʌpliŋ] *n* TECH manguito *m* roscado.

screwdriver [-,draivə*] *n* TECH destornillador *m* ‖ cóctel *m* de vodka con naranja (drink).

screwed [-d] *adj* TECH roscado, da (bolt, etc.) ‖ torcido, da; retorcido, da (twisted) ‖ FAM achispado, da (drunk) ‖ US FAM fastidiado, da.

screwed-up [-dʌp] *adj* FAM fastidiado, da.

screw eye [-ai] *n* armella *f*, cáncamo *m.*

screwhead [-,hed] *n* cabeza *f* de tornillo.

screw propeller [-prə'pelə*] *n* hélice *f.*

screw tap [-tæp] *n* TECH macho *m* de aterrajar *or* de roscar.

screw thread [-θred] *n* rosca *f* de tornillo.

screw wrench [-rentʃ] *n* llave *f* inglesa.

screwy [-i] *adj* FAM chiflado, da; chalado, da (crazy) | absurdo, da (absurd).

scribble ['skribl] *n* garabato *m* (scrawl).

scribble ['skribl] *vt/vi* garabatear (to scrawl) || escribir de prisa y sin cuidado (to write hastily).

scribbler [-ə*] *n* emborronador *m* de cuartillas (s.o. who writes illegibly) || emborronador *m* de cuartillas, escritorzuelo, la (bad writer).

scribe [skraib] *n* HIST escriba *m* (of Jewish law) || amanuense *m*, escribiente *m* (copyist) || FAM emborronador *m* de cuartillas || TECH punta *f* de trazar (scriber).

scribe [skraib] *vt* trazar.
◆ *vi* desempeñar el trabajo de escribiente (to act as a copyist) || HIST actuar de escriba (of Jewish law).

scriber [-ə*] *n* TECH punta *f* de trazar.

scrimmage [-idʒ] *n* escaramuza *f* (skirmish) || SP melée *f* abierta (open scrum in American football) | entrenamiento *m* (practice).

scrimp [skrimp] *vt* escatimar; *to scrimp the servants' food* escatimar la comida a los criados.
◆ *vi* ahorrar, hacer economías || *to scrimp and save* apretarse el cinturón.

scrimpy [-i] *adj* escaso, sa; parco, ca; *a scrimpy meal* una comida escasa || mezquino, na; avaro, ra; cicatero, ra (person).

scrimshaw ['skrimʃɔː] *n* talla *f* en marfil *or* en concha *or* en barba de ballena.

scrip [skrip] *n* trozo *m* de papel (piece of paper) || vale *m* (certificate of indebtedness) || título *m* provisional de propiedad (of ownership of stock, property, etc.) || *US* HIST papel *m* moneda [que valía menos de un dólar].

script [skript] *n* escritura *f*, letra *f* (handwriting) || escritura; *phonetic script* escritura fonética || PRINT letra *f* cursiva || manuscrito *m* (manuscript) || THEATR argumento *m* || CINEM guión *m* || ejercicio *m* escrito (of an examination) || JUR original *m*.

scripted [-id] *adj* escrito, ta de antemano (speech, dialogue).

script girl [-gəːl] *n* secretaria *f* de rodaje, script-girl *f*.

scriptorium [skrip'tɔːriəm] *n* escritorio *m* (in a monastery).
— OBSERV El plural de *scriptorium* es *scriptoria*.

scriptural ['skriptʃərəl] *adj* bíblico, ca.

scripture ['skriptʃə*] *n* REL Sagrada Escritura *f*, Biblia *f* (the Bible) | pasaje *m* de la Sagrada Escritura (passage) | religión *f* (as a school subject) | libros *m pl* sagrados (of any religion).
◆ *pl* REL Sagradas Escrituras *f*.

scriptwriter ['skript‚raitə*] *n* guionista *m* & *f*.

scrivener ['skrivenə*] *n* HIST amanuense *m* (copyist) | notario *m* (notary).

scrod [skrɔd] *n* *US* bacalao *m* (cod).

scrofula ['skrɔfjulə] *n* MED escrófula *f*.

scrofulous ['skrɔfjuləs] *adj* MED escrofuloso, sa.

scroll [skrəul] *n* rollo *m* de papel *or* de pergamino || ARTS voluta *f* || rúbrica *f* (of a signature) || *Dead Sea Scrolls* manuscritos *m* del Mar Muerto.

scroll [skrəul] *vt* enrollar (to form into a scroll) || decorar con volutas (to decorate with scrolls).
◆ *vi* enrollarse.

scroll saw [-sɔː] *n* sierra *f* de marquetería.

scrollwork [-wəːk] *n* ARTS volutas *f pl*.

Scrooge [skruːdʒ] *n* avariento, ta; tacaño, ña (miser); *to be a real Scrooge* ser muy tacaño.
— OBSERV *Scrooge* es un personaje de Dickens que simboliza la avaricia.

scrotum ['skrəutəm] *n* ANAT escroto *m*.
— OBSERV El plural de *scrotum* es *scrota* o *scrotums*.

scrounge [skraundʒ] *vt* FAM conseguir gorroneando, sacar de gorra (to get by cadging) | birlar, robar (to pilfer).
◆ *vi* FAM gorronear (to eat, etc., at s.o.'s expenses) | dar sablazos (to borrow money) || — FAM *to scrounge around for* buscar | *to scrounge on s.o.* vivir a costa de alguien.

scrounger [-ə*] *n* FAM gorrón, ona; sablista *m* & *f* (cadger).

scrounging [-iŋ] *n* gorronería *f*.

scrub [skrʌb] *n* maleza *f*, monte *m* bajo (undergrowth) || matorral *m* (land covered with scrubby undergrowth) || árbol *m* achaparrado (stunted tree) || arbusto *m* achaparrado (shrub) || FAM aborto *m* (very small person) | don nadie *m* (insignificant person) || cepillo *m* de cerdas cortas (brush) || barba *f* corta (beard) || pequeño bigote *m* (moustache) || fregado *m* (act of scrubbing) || *US* SP jugador *m* suplente, reserva *m* (player) | equipo *m* de reservas (team) || *to give sth. a good scrub* fregar algo vigorosamente.
◆ *adj* achaparrado, da (tree, shrub) || FAM achaparrado, da; canijo, ja (small) | inferior.

scrub [skrʌb] *vt* fregar (the floor, the dishes) || restregar (clothes) || TECH depurar (gases) || FIG & FAM cancelar, anular; *to scrub a plan* cancelar un proyecto.
◆ *vi* fregar.

scrubber [-ə*] *n* fregón, ona (person who scrubs) || cepillo *m* de fregar (brush) || TECH depurador *m* (of gases).

scrubbing [-iŋ] *n* fregado *m* (of floor, of dishes) || TECH depuración *f* (of gases).

scrubbing brush [-brʌʃ] *n* cepillo *m* de fregar.

scrubby [-i] *adj* achaparrado, da (stunted) || cubierto de maleza (covered with scrub).

scrubwoman [-‚wumən] *n* *US* fregona *f*.
— OBSERV El plural de esta palabra es *scrubwomen*.

scruff [skrʌf] *n* cogote *m*, nuca *f* (of neck) || *to seize s.o. by the scruff of the neck* coger a alguien por el cogote.

scruffy ['skrʌfi] *adj* FAM desaliñado, da (neglected-looking); *a scruffy person, house* una persona, una casa desaliñada.

scrum [skrʌm] *n* SP melée *f* (rugby) || — SP *scrum half* medio *m* de melée | *open scrum* melée abierta.

scrummage [-idʒ] *n* SP melée *f* (rugby).

scrumptious ['skrʌmpʃəs] *adj* FAM de chuparse los dedos (food) || FAM *a scrumptious girl* un bombón.

scrunch [skrʌntʃ] *n* crujido *m*.

scrunch [skrʌntʃ] *vt/vi* → **crunch.**

scruple ['skruːpl] *n* escrúpulo *m* (weight) || escrúpulo *m*; *he has no scruples about thieving* no tiene ningún escrúpulo en robar.

scruple ['skruːpl] *vi* tener escrúpulos || *he does not scruple to betray his friends* no tiene escrúpulos *or* no vacila en traicionar a sus amigos.

scrupulous ['skruːpjuləs] *adj* escrupuloso, sa.

scrupulously [-li] *adv* escrupulosamente || *scrupulously careful* sumamente cuidadoso.

scrupulousness [-nis] *n* escrupulosidad *f* (uprightness, care) || escrúpulos *m pl* (scruples).

scrutator [skruː'teitə*]; **scrutineer** [‚skruːti'niə*] *n* escudriñador, ra || escrutador, ra (of votes).

scrutinize ['skruːtinaiz] *vt* hacer el recuento de, efectuar el escrutinio de (votes) || examinar a fondo, escudriñar (to examine); *to scrutinize a document* examinar un documento a fondo.

scrutinizer [-ə*] *n* escudriñador, ra || escrutador, ra (of votes).

scrutinizing [-iŋ] *n* examen *m* profundo (examination) || recuento *m* (of votes).

scrutiny ['skruːtini] *n* escrutinio *m*, recuento *m* (of votes) || examen *m* [profundo] (of a document, etc.); *this plan does not stand up to scrutiny* este proyecto no resiste al examen.

scuba ['skjubə] *n* escafandra *f* autónoma.

scud [skʌd] *n* carrera *f* (rush) || nubes *f pl* ligeras empujadas por el viento (clouds driven by the wind) || ráfaga *f* (gust of wind) || chaparrón *m* (brief shower of rain) || espuma *f* (ocean spray).

scud [skʌd] *vi* correr (to run) || — *to scud across the sky* pasar rápidamente por el cielo (clouds) || *to scud before the wind* ir viento en popa (a sailing ship).

scuff [skʌf] *n* arrastre *m* de los pies (dragging of the feet) || chancleta *f* (slipper) || parte *f* desgastada (worn spot).

scuff [skʌf] *vt* arrastrar (to drag); *to scuff one's feet* arrastrar los pies || estropear (to damage); *to scuff one's shoes* estropear los zapatos || rozar (to touch lightly) || rasguñar, arañar (to scratch).
◆ *vi* andar arrastrando los pies (to walk scraping the feet) || estropearse (to become worn).

scuffle [-l] *n* riña *f*, pelea *f* (struggle).

scuffle [-l] *vi* reñir, pelearse (to struggle) || arrastrar los pies (to scuff one's feet).

scull [skʌl] *n* remo *m* (oar) || espadilla *f* (used at the stern in propelling a boat) || *US* barco *m* de remo (boat).

scull [skʌl] *vt* impulsar con el remo *or* la espadilla.
◆ *vi* remar.

sculler [-ə*] *n* remero *m* (person who sculls) || barco *m* de remo (boat).

scullery [-əri] *n* oficio *m*, office *m*, trascocina *f*.

scullery maid ['skʌləri'meid] *n* fregona *f*.

scullion ['skʌljən] *n* pinche *m*, marmitón *m*.

sculpt [skʌlpt] *vt* esculpir.
◆ *vi* hacer esculturas, esculpir.

sculptor [-ə*] *n* escultor *m*.

sculptress [-tris] *n* escultora *f*.

sculptural ['skʌlptʃərəl] *adj* escultórico, ca; escultural.

sculpture ['skʌlptʃə*] *n* escultura *f*.

sculpture ['skʌlptʃə*] *vt* esculpir; *to sculpture a statue in stone* esculpir una estatua en piedra.
◆ *vi* hacer esculturas, esculpir.

sculpturesque [‚skʌlptʃə'resk] *adj* escultórico, ca.

scum [skʌm] *n* espuma *f* (froth, bubbles) || telilla *f* (skinlike mass) || nata *f* (on milk) || verdín *m* (on a pond) || TECH escoria *f* (of molten metals) || FIG hez *f*, escoria *f* (despicable people); *the scum of society* la escoria de la sociedad.

scum [skʌm] *vt* espumar (to skim) || desnatar (milk) || quitar la escoria de (molten metals).
◆ *vi* cubrirse de espuma.

scumble [-bl] *n* ARTS esfumado *m*, difuminado *m* (effect produced by scumbling) | difumino *m*, esfumino *m* (used for scumbling).

scummy [-i] *adj* espumoso, sa (a liquid) || cubierto de escoria (metals) || FIG canallesco, ca.

scupper ['skʌpə*] *n* MAR imbornal *m*.

scupper ['skʌpə*] *vt* MAR hundir || FAM frustrar, fastidiar (a plan, etc.).

scurf [skəːf] *n* caspa *f* (dandruff) || TECH incrustación *f* (in a boiler).

scurfy [-i] *adj* casposo, sa (full of dandruff) || TECH cubierto de incrustaciones.

scurrility [skʌ'riliti] *n* lo difamatorio, carácter *m* injurioso (of an accusation, etc.) || grosería *f* (coarseness).

scurrilous ['skʌriləs] *adj* injurioso, sa; calumnioso, sa; difamatorio, ria (insulting) || grosero, ra (coarse).

scurry ['skʌri] *n* carrera *f* (run) || huida *f* (flight).

scurry ['skʌri] *vi* correr (to run) || — *to scurry away* o *off* escabullirse || *to scurry by* o *past* pasar corriendo.

scurvy ['skə:vi] *adj* vil, ruin.
◆ *n* MED escorbuto *m*.

scut [skʌt] *n* rabo *m*, rabito *m* (short tail).

scutch [skʌtʃ] *n* agramadera *f*, agramador *m*.

scutch [skʌtʃ] *vt* agramar (flax, etc.).

scutcheon [-ən] *n* ⟶ **escutcheon.**

scutcher [-ə*] *n* agramadera *f*, agramador *m* (tool) || agramador, ra (person).

scute [skju:t] *n* ZOOL escudo *m* (of a reptile).

scutter ['skʌtə*] *n* carrera *f* (scurry).

scutter ['skʌtə*] *vi* correr (to scurry).

scuttle [skʌtl] *n* huida *f*, carrera *f* (scurry) || cubo *m* del carbón (small container holding coal) || cesta *f* (basket) || MAR escotilla *f* || trampa *f* (trapdoor) || US trampilla *f* (in the roof or floor of a building).

scuttle [skʌtl] *vt* MAR barrenar, dar barreno a || FIG barrenar, desbaratar (plans, etc.).
◆ *vi* correr (to run) || — *to scurry away* o *off* escabullirse || *to scurry by* o *past* pasar corriendo.

scuttlebutt [-,bʌt] *n* MAR barril *m* de agua fresca || FAM rumor *m* (rumour) | habladuría *f*, chisme *m* (gossip).

scutum ['skju:təm] *n* ZOOL escudo *m* || escudo *m* (shield) || ANAT rótula *f*.
— OBSERV El plural de *scutum* es *scuta*.

Scylla ['silə] *pr n* GEOGR Escila || FIG *to be between Scylla and Charybdis* estar entre Escila y Caribdis.

scyphus ['saifəs] *n* HIST copa *f* con dos asas (drinking cup).

scythe [saið] *n* AGR guadaña *f*.

scythe [saið] *vt* AGR guadañar, segar.

Scythia ['siðiə] *pr n* GEOGR Escitia *f*.

SDI *abbr of [Strategic Defense Initiative]* IDE, Iniciativa de Defensa Estratégica.

SDP *abbr of [Social Democratic Party]* SDP, Partido Social Demócrata [Reino Unido].

SDRs *abbr of [special drawing rights]* DEG, derechos especiales de giro.

sea [si:] *n* mar *m* or *f*; *rough sea* mar agitado; *angry* o *raging* o *stormy sea* mar enfurecido; *choppy sea* mar picado; *at sea* en el mar; *by the sea* a orillas del mar; *out at sea* en alta mar; *to travel by sea* viajar por mar; *to put to sea* hacerse a la mar || mar *m*, vía *f* marítima; *to send by sea* enviar por vía marítima || mar *m*; *Mediterranean Sea* mar Mediterráneo; *Caspian Sea* mar Caspio; *Black Sea* mar Negro; *Dead Sea* mar Muerto || lago *m*; *Sea of Galilee* o *of Tiberias* lago de Tiberíades || oleada *f*, ola *f* (wave) || FIG mar *m*; *to be swamped in a sea of doubt* estar sumido en un mar de dudas; *a sea of tears* un mar de lágrimas || — *beyond the sea* o *the seas* allende los mares || *heavy sea* marejada *f*, mar gruesa || *inland-sea* mar *m* interior || *on the high seas, on the open sea* en alta mar || *out to sea* mar adentro || *strong sea* marejada *f* || FIG *to be all at sea* estar en un mar de confusiones | *to be half seas over* estar achispado || *to follow the sea* ser marinero || *to go to sea* hacerse marinero || *to ship a sea* ser cubierto por una ola grande || *to stand out to sea* irse *or* hacerse mar adentro.
◆ *adj* del mar, marino, na; *sea air* aire marino || marítimo, ma; *sea transport* transporte marítimo || — *sea battle* batalla *f* naval || *sea chart* carta *f* de marear || *sea current* corriente marina || *sea voyage* viaje por mar *or* en barco, viaje marítimo.
— OBSERV *Mar* is generally masculine in everyday usage, but feminine when used by fishermen and seamen. It is also feminine in certain expressions (see MAR).

sea anchor [-'æŋkə*] *n* ancla *f* flotante.

sea anemone [-ə'neməni] *n* ZOOL anémona *f* de mar.

seabag [-bæg] *n* saco *m* de marinero.

seabed [-,bed] *n* fondo *m* del mar.

sea bird [-bə:d] *n* ave *f* marina.

sea biscuit [-'biskit] *n* galleta *f*.

seaboard [-bɔ:d] *n* costa *f*, litoral *m*.
◆ *adj* costanero, ra.

seaborne [-bɔ:n] *adj* transportado por mar (goods) || marítimo, ma (trade).

sea bream [-'bri:m] *n* ZOOL besugo *m*.

sea breeze [-'bri:z] *n* brisa *f* marina.

sea calf [-kɑ:f] *n* ZOOL foca *f*, becerro *m* marino (seal).

seacoast [-kəust] *n* litoral *m*, costa *f*.

sea cow [-'kau] *n* ZOOL manatí *m*, vaca *f* marina (manatee) | morsa *f* (walrus) | hipopótamo *m* (hippopotamus).

sea cucumber [-'kju:kʌmbə*] *n* ZOOL cohombro *m* de mar, holoturia *f*.

sea devil [-'devil] *n* raya *f* (devilfish).

sea dog [-dɔg] *n* lobo *m* de mar (experienced sailor) || pirata *m* (pirate) || ZOOL foca *f*, becerro *m* marino (sea calf) | cazón *m* (dogfish).

sea eagle [-'i:gl] *n* ZOOL águila *f* marina, águila *f* pescadora | quebrantahuesos *m inv* (osprey).

sea-ear [-'iə*] *n* ZOOL oreja *f* de mar.

sea elephant [-'elifənt] *n* ZOOL elefante *m* marino.

sea fan [-fæn] *n* ZOOL abanico *m* de mar (coral).

seafarer [-,fɛərə*] *n* marinero *m*, marino *m* (sailor) || navegante *m* & *f* (s.o. who travels by sea).

seafaring [-,fɛəriŋ] *n* oficio *m* de marinero, marinería *f* (occupation of a sailor) || viajes *m pl* por mar (sea travel).
◆ *adj* marinero, ra; *a seafaring people* un pueblo marinero || que viaja por mar (travelling by sea) || — *in my seafaring days* en mi época de marinero || *seafaring yarn* historia *f* de marinero.

seaflower [-'flauə*] *n* anémona *f* de mar.

sea foam [-fəum] *n* espuma *f* de mar (froth, meerschaum).

seafood [-fu:d] *n* mariscos *m pl* (shellfish) || pescado *m* (fish) || *seafood restaurant* marisquería *f*.

seafowl [-faul] *n* ave *f* marina.

seafront [-frʌnt] *n* paseo *m* marítimo.

seagirt [-gə:t] *adj* rodeado por el mar.

seagoing [-gəuiŋ] *adj* MAR de alta mar (vessel) | marinero, ra (people) | marítimo, ma (trade).

sea-green [-'gri:n] *adj* verdemar.

sea gull [-gʌl] *n* gaviota *f* (bird).

sea hare [-hɛə*] *n* liebre *f* de mar.

sea hog [-hɔg] *n* marsopa *f*, marsopla *f* (porpoise).

sea horse [-hɔ:s] *n* ZOOL caballo *m* de mar, hipocampo *m* | morsa *f* (walrus) || MYTH criatura *f* mitad caballo mitad pez.

sea kale [-keil] *n* BOT col *f* marina.

seal [si:l] *n* foca *f* (sea mammal) || piel *f* de foca (hide) || sello *m* (piece of wax, of lead, etc., stamped with a design); *wax seal* sello de lacre; *great seal* sello real || precinto *m* (paper sticker); *do not buy the bottle if the seal is broken* no compre la botella si el precinto está roto || junta *f*; *a watertight seal between the glass and the frame* una junta estanca entre el cristal y el marco || FIG sello *m* (hallmark); *his work bears the seal of genius* sus obras llevan el sello del genio | garantía *f*; *the seal of approval* la garantía de una aprobación || — FIG *to put* o *set the seal on sth.* sellar algo || *to set one's seal to* aprobar || *under the seal of secrecy* bajo secreto.
◆ *pl* sellos *m*; *breaking of seals* quebrantamiento *or* violación de sellos.

seal [si:l] *vt* sellar, marcar con un sello (a document, etc.); *signed and sealed* firmado y sellado || lacrar, sellar con lacre (with wax) || emplomar (with lead) || precintar (with a paper sticker); *the boxes of cigars are sealed before leaving the factory* las cajas de puros son precintadas antes de salir de la fábrica || cerrar (to close); *a sealed envelope* un sobre cerrado || JUR precintar || tapar (a crack) || cerrar herméticamente (two pipes, etc.) || impermeabilizar (to make waterproof) || FIG sellar (a friendship, an agreement, etc.) | decidir, determinar; *that sealed his fate* aquello decidió su destino || — *my lips are sealed* he prometido no decir nada, no puedo decir nada || TECH *sealed circuit* circuito sellado || *to seal off* cerrar (to close), acordonar; *the police sealed off the area* la policía acordonó el barrio.
◆ *vi* cazar focas.

sea-lane ['si:lein] *n* ruta *f or* vía *f* marítima.

sea lavender ['si:'lævində*] *n* BOT acelga *f* silvestre.

sea lawyer ['si:'lɔ:jə*] *n* FAM marinero *m* protestón.

sea legs ['si:'legz] *pl n* equilibrio *m sing* [para andar en un barco] || *to get one's sea legs* acostumbrarse a andar en un barco.

sealer ['si:lə*] *n* cazador *m* de focas (hunter) || barco *m* para cazar focas (boat) || US verificador *m* de pesas y medidas.

sea level ['si:'levl] *n* nivel *m* del mar; *the town is a thousand feet above sea level* la ciudad está a mil pies de altura sobre el nivel del mar.

sea lily ['si:'lili] *n* ZOOL crinoideo *m*.

sealing wax ['si:liŋwæks] *n* lacre *m*.

sea lion ['si:,laiən] *n* ZOOL león *m* marino, otaria *f* (large seal).

sea loch ['si:,lɔk] *n* ría *f*.

sea mist ['si:mist] *n* bruma *f*.

seal ring ['si:lriŋ] *n* sello *m* (signet ring).

sealskin ['si:lskin] *n* piel *f* de foca.

seam [si:m] *n* costura *f* (in sewing) || TECH juntura *f*, junta *f* (joint in a surface) || grieta *f* (in rock) || MIN veta *f*; *a coal seam* una veta de carbón || ANAT sutura *f* || arruga *f* (wrinkle) || cicatriz *f* (scar) || *to burst at the seams* estallar por las costuras (a garment), rebosar de gente (to overflow); *the hall was bursting at the seams* la sala rebosaba de gente.

seam [si:m] *vt* unir con una costura, coser (in needlework) || TECH juntar (to join) || arrugar (to wrinkle) || marcar; *scars seamed his face* tenía la cara marcada de cicatrices || agrietar (a rock).

sea-maid ['si:,meid] *n* sirena *f* (mermaid).

seaman ['si:mən] *n* MAR marinero *m*, marino *m*.
— OBSERV El plural de *seaman* es *seamen*.

seamanlike [-laik] *adj* MAR propio de un buen marinero.

seamanship [-ʃip] *n* MAR náutica *f*.

seamark ['siːmɑːk] *n* MAR marca *f*, baliza *f* (object on land which guides navigators) | línea que indica el límite de la altura de las mareas (high tide line).

sea mew ['siːmjuː] *n* ZOOL gaviota *f* (sea gull).

sea mile ['siːmail] *n* milla *f* marina.

seamless ['siːmlis] *adj* sin costura.

seamstress ['siːmstris] *n* costurera *f*.

seamy ['siːmi] *adj* que tiene costuras (in sewing) || arrugado, da (wrinkled) || que tiene cicatrices (covered with scars) || sórdido, da; *the seamy side of life* el lado sórdido de la vida || *the seamy side of a garment* el revés de un traje.

séance ['seiɑːns] *n* sesión *f* (session) || sesión *f* de espiritismo (spiritualist meeting).

sea needle ['siː'niːdl] *n* aguja *f* (fish).

sea onion ['siː'ʌnjən] *n* BOT cebolla *f* albarrana.

sea otter ['siː'ɔtə*] *n* ZOOL nutria *f* de mar.

sea pass ['siːpɑːs] *n* MAR pasavante *m*.

seaplane ['siːplein] *n* hidroavión *m*.

seaport ['siːpɔːt] *n* puerto *m* de mar, puerto marítimo.

sea power ['siːˌpauə*] *n* potencia *f* naval (country) || fuerza *f* naval (naval strength).

seaquake ['siːˌkweik] *n* maremoto *m*.

sear [siə*] *n* quemadura *f*.
◆ *adj* marchito, ta.

sear [siə*] *vt* marchitar (to wither) || abrasar, quemar (to scorch) || CULIN soasar || MED cauterizar (to cauterize) || FIG endurecer (the conscience) | endurecer, volver insensible (the heart).
◆ *vi* marchitarse (to wither).

search [səːtʃ] *n* búsqueda *f* (in order to find sth.) || registro *m* (of a house, of a car, etc.); *to carry out a search* efectuar un registro || cacheo *m* (of a person) || investigación *f* (in order to gain information) || MAR visita *f* (by customs) || — *in search of* en busca de || MAR *right of search* derecho *m* de visita.

search [səːtʃ] *vt* buscar en (in order to find sth., gain information, etc.); *to search the woods for a missing child* buscar en el bosque a un niño que se ha perdido; *to search the files* buscar en los archivos || registrar (police, customs, etc.); *to search a car for weapons* registrar un coche para ver si lleva armas || cachear (a person) || examinar (one's conscience) || MED sondar (a wound) || — *search me!* ¡yo qué sé!, ¡a mí que me registren! || *to search one's memory for sth.* intentar recordar algo || *to search out* descubrir.
◆ *vi* buscar (in order to find sth.) || indagar, investigar (in order to gain information) || hacer un registro (to find sth. concealed) || *to search after* o *for* buscar.

searcher [-ə*] *n* buscador, ra || vista *m* (customs officer) || investigador, ra (of information) || JUR indagador, ra; pesquisidor, ra || MED sonda *f*.

searching [-iŋ] *adj* minucioso, sa (thorough) || FIG penetrante (penetrating); *a searching look* una mirada penetrante.
◆ *n* búsqueda *f* || registro *m* (of luggage) || cacheo *m* (of people) || pesquisa *f* (of premises).

searchlight [-lait] *n* reflector *m*, proyector *m*.

search party [-ˌpɑːti] *n* equipo *m* de salvamento.

search warrant [-ˌwɔrənt] *n* mandamiento *m* de registro.

searing [siəriŋ] *adj* agudo, da, punzante (pain) || FIG mordaz, corrosivo, va (speech, article).

sea risk ['siːrisk] *n* peligro *m* de mar.

sea room ['siːruːm] *n* espacio *m* de maniobra.

sea rover ['siːˌrəuvə] *n* pirata *m* (pirate) || barco *m* pirata (ship).

seascape ['siːskeip] *n* ARTS marina *f* || vista *f* marina (view of the sea).

sea serpent ['siːˌsəːpənt] *n* ZOOL serpiente *f* de mar, serpiente *f* marina (sea snake) || serpiente *f* de mar (mythological sea monster).

sea shanty ['siːˌʃænti] *n* MAR saloma *f* (song).

seashell ['siːʃel] *n* concha *f* marina.

seashore ['siːʃɔː*] *n* playa *f*, orilla *f* del mar (beach) || costa *f*, litoral *m* (seacoast).

seasick ['siːsik] *adj* mareado, da || *to get seasick* marearse.

seasickness [-nis] *n* mareo *m*.

seaside ['siː'said] *n* playa *f*; *to spend a day at* o *by the seaside* pasar un día en la playa || costa *f*, litoral *m* (coast) || *to spend one's summer holiday at* o *by the seaside* veranear a orillas del mar *or* en el mar.
◆ *adj* costero, ra || *seaside resort* estación balnearia.

sea snail ['siː'sneil] *n* ZOOL caracola *f*.

sea snake ['siː'sneik] *n* ZOOL serpiente *f* de mar, serpiente *f* marina || serpiente *f* de mar (mythological sea monster).

season ['siːzn] *n* estación *f*; *the four seasons of the year* las cuatro estaciones del año || época *f*; *the mating season* la época del celo || temporada *f*; *football season* temporada de fútbol; *bullfighting season* temporada de toros; *tourist season* temporada turística; *strawberry season* temporada de las fresas; *concert season* temporada de conciertos || — *at the height of the season* en plena temporada || *in due season* a su debido tiempo || *in season* en sazón (fruit), en celo (on heat), oportuno (remark) || FIG *in season and out of season* a tiempo y a destiempo || *out of season* fuera de temporada *or* de sazón (fruit, etc.), inoportuno (remark) || *slack season* temporada baja *or* de poca venta *or* de venta reducida || *the close season* la veda (hunting and fishing) || *the off season* la temporada baja || *the open season* la temporada de caza *or* de pesca || *the summer season* el verano || *to last for a season* estar en cartel por una temporada (a play) || *with the compliments of the season* deseándoles felices Pascuas.

season ['siːzn] *vt* sazonar, condimentar (food) || madurar (wine) || secar (wood) || curar (pipe) || acostumbrar; *one gets seasoned to cold weather* uno se acostumbra al frío || madurar; *a man seasoned by many misfortunes* un hombre madurado por muchas desgracias || acostumbrar al mar (sailors) || aguerrir (troops) || moderar; *a judgment seasoned by goodwill* un fallo moderado por la benevolencia || sazonar, amenizar; *a letter seasoned with verse* una carta sazonada con versos || *a seasoned sailor* un marinero experimentado.
◆ *vi* secarse (wood) || madurar (wine) || acostumbrarse (to become accustomed) || acostumbrarse al mar (sailors) || aguerrirse (troops).

seasonable [-əbl] *adj* propio de la estación; *seasonable weather* tiempo propio de la estación || oportuno, na; *seasonable piece of advice* consejo oportuno.

seasonably [-əbli] *adv* oportunamente, a propósito.

seasonal ['siːzənl] *adj* estacional (characteristic of the season) || apropiado para la estación (suited to the season); *seasonal dress* ropa apropiada para la estación || temporal; *seasonal work* trabajo temporal || estacional (worker).

seasonally ['siːzənəli] *adv* según la temporada *or* estación.

seasoner ['siːzənə*] *n* persona *f* que sazona || condimento *m*.

seasoning ['siːzniŋ] *n* condimento *m*, aderezo *m* || TECH secado *m* (of wood) || maduramiento *m* (of wine) || endurecimiento *m* (hardening) || acostumbramiento *m*.

season ticket ['siːznˌtikit] *n* abono *m* (for football, theatre, trains, etc.).

seat [siːt] *n* asiento *m*; *front, rear seat* asiento delantero, trasero || silla *f* (chair) || asiento *m* (of a chair) || plaza *f* (when considering the number); *a car with four seats* un coche de cuatro plazas || CINEM & THEATR localidad *f*, entrada *f*; *to book seats* reservar localidades || centro *m*; *a seat of learning* un centro de estudios || sede *f*; *seat of government* sede del gobierno || fondo *m*; *the seat of the problem* el fondo del problema || escaño *m*, puesto *m* [*AMER* banco *m*] (in Parliament); *to lose one's seat* perder su escaño || sillín *m* (of a bicycle) || tabla *f* (of toilet) || trasero *m*, posaderas *f pl* (buttocks) || fondillos *m pl* (of trousers) || TECH asiento *m* || MED foco *m* (of an illness) || MIL teatro *m* (of operations) || — *to have a good seat* montar bien a caballo (in riding) || *to keep one's seat* permanecer sentado || *to take a seat* sentarse || *to take one's seat* colocarse || *to take one's seat in Parliament* tomar posesión de su cargo en el Parlamento.

seat [siːt] *vt* sentar; *he seated the child on the chair* sentó al niño en la silla || tener cabida para; *the theatre seats a hundred people* el teatro tiene cabida para cien personas || tener sitio para; *the table seats six easily* la mesa tiene sitio de sobra para seis personas || colocar (to allot a seat to s.o.); *the younger members were seated at the back of the room* los socios más jóvenes fueron colocados al fondo de la sala; *to seat the audience round the stage* colocar al público alrededor del escenario || poner asiento a (a chair) || TECH ajustar (an axle, a valve) | colocar (a machine) || ARCH asentar || — *to be seated* sentarse; *please be seated* siéntese, por favor; estar sentado (to be sitting), estar localizado (*in* en) (a disease) || *to remain seated* quedarse sentado || TECH *to seat on* descansar en || *to seat o.s.* sentarse.

seat belt [-belt] *n* cinturón *m* de seguridad.

seater [-ə*] *n* *a fifty-seater coach* un autocar de cincuenta plazas || *a three-seater settee* un sofá de tres plazas || *a two seated* un dos plazas (car, plane).

seating [-iŋ] *n* asientos *m pl* (seats); *the seating is rather poor* los asientos son bastante malos || distribución *f* de los asientos (arrangement of seats); *the man in charge of seating* el encargado de la distribución de los asientos || colocación *f*; *the seating of guests* la colocación de los invitados || tapicería *f* (material for covering seats) || TECH asiento *m* || *seating capacity* número *m* de plazas.

sea trout ['siːtraut] *n* ZOOL trucha *f* de mar.

sea urchin ['siː'əːtʃin] *n* ZOOL erizo *m* de mar.

sea wall ['siːwɔːl] *n* dique *m*, rompeolas *m inv*.

seaward ['siːwəd] *n* lado *m* del mar.
◆ *adj* que da al mar, del lado del mar.

seaward ['siːwəd]; **seawards** [-z] *adv* hacia el mar, mar adentro.

seaware ['siːwɛə*] *n* algas *f pl*.

seawater ['siːˌwɔːtə*] *n* agua *f* de mar.

seaway ['siːwei] *n* ruta *f or* vía *f* marítima (route) || canal *m* marítimo (ship canal) || MAR avance *m* (ship's progress) | estela *f* (trace) | mar *f* gruesa (heavy sea).

seaweed ['si:wi:d] *n* BOT alga *f*.

sea wolf [-,wulf] *n* lubina *f*, róbalo *m* (fish) || pirata *m* (pirate).

seaworthy ['si:,wə:ði] *adj* en buen estado para navegar, marinero, ra.

sea wrack ['si:ræk] *n* algas *f pl* (mass of seaweed).

sebaceous [si'beiʃəs] *adj* sebáceo, a; *sebaceous glands* glándulas sebáceas.

seborrhea; seborrhoea [,sebə'ri:ə] *n* MED seborrea *f*.

sebum ['si:bəm] *n* BIOL sebo *m*.

secant ['si:kənt] *adj* MATH secante.
◆ *n* MATH secante *f*.

secateurs [,sekə'tə:z] *pl n* podadera *f sing*.

secede [si'si:d] *vi* separarse; *to secede from a federation* separarse de una federación.

seceder [-ə*] *n* separatista *m* & *f*, secesionista *m* & *f*.

secession [si'seʃən] *n* secesión *f*, separación *f* || US *War of Secession* Guerra *f* de Secesión.

secessionism [si'seʃnizəm] *n* separatismo *m*.

secessionist [si'seʃnist] *n* secesionista *m* & *f*, separatista *m* & *f*.

seclude [si'klu:d] *vt* recluir (to keep apart) || aislar (to isolate) || *to seclude o.s. from* apartarse de, retirarse de.

secluded [-id] *adj* aislado, da (isolated) || retirado, da (withdrawn).

seclusion [si'klu:ʒən] *n* reclusión *f* (forceable keeping apart) || aislamiento *m*, retiro *m* (withdrawn existence) || *to live in seclusion* vivir aislado.

seclusive [si'klu:siv] *adj* que tiene tendencia a aislarse, solitario, ria.

second ['sekənd] *adj* segundo, da; *he married for the second time* se casó en segundas nupcias; *he came in the second place* llegó en segundo lugar || otro, otra; *you will need a second pair of shoes* le hará falta otro par de zapatos; *he seems to think he's a second Napoleon!* ¡parece que se cree otro Napoleón! || — *every second* uno de cada dos || *every second day* un día sí y otro no, cada dos días || *on second thoughts* pensándolo bien || REL *Second Advent* segundo advenimiento | *Second Adventist* adventista *m* & *f* || SP *second base* segunda base (in baseball) || *second chamber* cámara alta || *second childhood* segunda infancia || *second class* segunda clase, segunda (in a train) || *second cousin* primo segundo, prima segunda || *second cousin once removed* sobrino tercero, sobrina tercera || *second floor* segundo piso (in Great Britain and other countries), primer piso (in United States) || MIL *second lieutenant* alférez *m*, subteniente *m* || MAR *second mate* segundo *m* de a bordo || *second mortgage* segunda hipoteca || *second nature* segunda naturaleza || *second offence* reincidencia *f* || *second offender* reincidente *m* & *f* || GRAMM *second person* segunda persona || *second self* alter ego *m* || *second sight* clarividencia *f* || *second teeth* segunda dentición || *second wind* segundo aliento || *the second day of March* el dos de marzo || *the second largest city* la segunda ciudad en importancia || *to be second only to* estar en segundo lugar respecto a || *to be second to none* no ser inferior a nadie, no ir a la zaga de nadie || *to have a second helping* repetir de una cosa || *to have second thoughts about sth.* dudar de *or* sobre algo || *to play second fiddle* desempeñar un papel secundario.
◆ *n* segundo *m* (time) || segundo, da (in rank, in a series); *she came in second* llegó segunda || SP segundo *m*, cuidador *m* (in boxing) || padrino *m* (in a duel) || notable *m* (university degree); *to obtain a second* sacar un notable || segundo premio *m* (prize) || AUT segunda *f* (gear) || día *m* dos, dos *m* (of a month); *the second day of May* el dos de mayo || MUS segunda *f* (interval) | segunda parte *f* (of a composition) || MATH segundo *m* || — *just a second!* ¡un momento! || *in a split second* en un dos por tres || *Philip II (the Second)* Felipe II [segundo].
◆ *pl* artículos *m* de segunda clase (goods).
◆ *adv* en segundo lugar (in the second place) || en segunda, en segunda clase; *to travel second* viajar en segunda.

second ['sekənd] *vt* apoyar, secundar (to assist) || apoyar (a proposal, a speaker); *a few delegates seconded the motion* unos delegados apoyaron la moción.

second [si'kɔnd] *vt* MIL destinar, destacar.

secondary ['sekəndəri] *adj* secundario, ria || JUR indirecto, ta (evidence) || GRAMM derivado, da (meaning) || — ELECTR *secondary cell* acumulador *m* || *secondary colour* color secundario || *secondary education* enseñanza media, segunda enseñanza || PHYS *secondary emission* emisión secundaria || *secondary modern* centro de formación profesional || ASTR *secondary planet* planeta secundario, satélite *m* || *secondary school* instituto *m* de enseñanza media.
◆ *n* subalterno *m* (secondary person) || GEOL secundario *m*.

second best ['sekəndbest] *n* segundo, da (in quality) || — FIG *it's a second best* es una manera de salir del paso || *to come off second best* ser vencido, perder, llevar la peor parte.

second-best ['sekəndbest] *adj* mejor después del primero, segundo, da.

second born ['sekənd'bɔ:n] *adj/n* segundogénito, ta.

second-class ['sekənd'kla:s] *adj* de segunda clase, de segunda (trains, etc.) || de segunda categoría, de segunda clase (hotels, goods, etc.).
◆ *adv* en segunda, en segunda clase; *to travel second-class* viajar en segunda.

seconde [sə'kɔnd] *n* segunda *f* (in fencing).

seconder ['sekəndə*] *n* persona *f* que apoya [una moción, etc.].

second hand ['sekəndhænd] *n* segundero *m* (of a watch) || *at second hand* de segunda mano.

secondhand ['sekənd'hænd] *adj* de segunda mano, de ocasión; *secondhand books* libros de segunda mano || usado, da; viejo, ja; *secondhand clothes* ropa vieja || — *secondhand bookseller* librero *m* de lance || *secondhand bookshop* librería *f* de lance || *secondhand dealer* chamarilero, ra || *secondhand information* información conseguida indirectamente, información de segunda mano.
◆ *adv* de segunda mano || indirectamente, por terceros; *to hear sth. secondhand* enterarse de algo indirectamente *or* por terceros.

second-in-command [,sekəndinkə'mend] *n* MIL segundo jefe *m*.

secondly ['sekəndli] *adv* en segundo lugar.

secondment [si'kɔndmənt] *n* traslado *m* temporal (for work).

second-rate ['sekənd'reit] *adj* de segunda categoría.

secrecy ['si:krisi] *n* secreto *m*; *done in secrecy* hecho en secreto; *professional secrecy* secreto profesional || discreción *f*; *you can rely on Peter's secrecy* se puede confiar en la discreción de Pedro || *under pledge of secrecy* bajo secreto.

secret ['si:krit] *adj* secreto, ta; *a secret agreement* un acuerdo secreto; *there was a secret passage behind the fireplace* había un pasillo secreto detrás de la chimenea; *secret society* sociedad secreta; *secret agent, service* agente, servicio secreto || reservado, da; callado, da (secretive) || escondido, da; recóndito, ta (place) || — *secret partner* socio comanditario || FIG & ANAT *secret parts* partes pudendas || *secret police* policía *f* secreta || *to keep sth. secret* mantener algo secreto.
◆ *n* secreto *m*; *trade secret* secreto de fabricación || REL secreta *f* || — *an open secret* un secreto a voces || *as a secret* secretamente, de modo confidencial || *in secret* en secreto || *to be in on the secret* estar en el secreto || *to keep a secret* guardar un secreto || *to let s.o. into a secret* revelar un secreto a alguien || *to make no secret of sth.* no ocultar algo || *State secret* secreto de Estado.
◆ *pl* misterios *m* (of nature) || FIG & ANAT partes *f* pudendas.

secretaire [sekri'tɛə*] *n* secreter *m*.

secretarial [,sekrə'tɛəriəl] *adj* de secretario, de secretaria.

secretariat; secretariate [,sekrə'tɛəriət] *n* secretaría *f*, secretariado *m*.

secretary ['sekrətri] *n* secretario, ria (person); *general secretary* secretario general; *private secretary* secretario particular || secreter *m*, escritorio *m* (desk) || US ministro *m* (minister); *Secretary of the Treasury* ministro de Hacienda || — ZOOL *secretary bird* secretario *m*, serpentario *m* || *Secretary of State* ministro con cartera (in Britain), secretario de Estado, ministro de Asuntos Exteriores [AMER ministro de Relaciones Exteriores] (in United States).

secretary-general [-'dʒenərəl] *n* secretario *m* general.
— OBSERV El plural es *secretaries-general*.

secretaryship [-ʃip] *n* secretaría *f*, secretariado *m* || US ministerio *m*.

secrete [si'kri:t] *vt* secretar, segregar (to emit a substance) || ocultar (to hide) || JUR encubrir, ocultar.

secretin [si'kri:tin] *n* secretina *f* (hormone).

secretion [si'kri:ʃən] *n* secreción *f*; *the secretion of saliva* la secreción de la saliva || ocultación *f* (hiding) || JUR encubrimiento *m*, ocultación *f*.

secretive [si'kri:tiv] *adj* sigiloso, sa (disposed to secrecy) || reservado, da; callado, da (silent).

secretiveness [-nis] *n* sigilo *m*, discreción *f* (discretion) || reserva *f*.

secretory [si'kri:təri] *adj* secretor, ra; secretorio, ria.
◆ *n* ANAT órgano *m* secretorio.

sect [sekt] *n* secta *f*.

sectarian [sek'tɛəriən] *adj/n* sectario, ria.

sectarianism [-izəm] *n* sectarismo *m*.

sectary ['sektəri] *n* sectario, ria (sectarian) || cismático, ca.

section ['sekʃən] *n* sección *f*; *that section of the house over there belongs to the servants* aquella sección de la casa pertenece al servicio; *the string section of the orchestra* la sección de cuerdas de la orquesta || parte *f* (part) || parte *f*, distrito *m* (of a town) || parte *f*, región *f* (of a country) || sector *m* (of population) || JUR artículo *m* (of a law) || párrafo *m* (of book, of document) || página *f*, sección *f* (in a newspaper) || trozo *m* (of cheese, of cake) || gajo *m* (of orange) || casilla *f* (of a drawer) || MIL sección *f* || AVIAT patrulla *f* || TECH tramo *m* (of a tube) | perfil *m* (of metal) || tramo *m* (of a tube) | perfil *m* (of metal) || tramo *m*, ramal *m* (of railway track) || departamento *m*, compartimiento *m* (of a sleeper) || MATH sección *f* || ARTS & ARCH corte *m*, sección *f* || pliego *m* (in bookbinding) || *cross section* sección transversal.

section ['sekʃən] *vt* seccionar, cortar (to cut) || dividir en secciones (to divide).

sectional [-l] *adj* particular, local, regional; *sectional interests* intereses particulares || en corte (plans, designs) || cuadriculado, da (paper) || en compartimentos (bookcase) ||

TECH en perfil (metal) | desmontable (dismountable).

sectionalize ['sekʃənənˌlaiz] *vt* dividir en regiones.

sectioning ['sekʃəniŋ] *n* seccionamiento *m*.

sector ['sektə*] *n* MATH sector *m* (area) | compás *m* de proporciones (instrument) || MIL & COMM sector *m*; *public, private sector* sector público, privado || zona *f* (of a town) || INFORM sector *m* (of a disk).

sectorial [sek'tɔːriəl] *adj* sectorial (of a sector).

secular ['sekjulə*] *adj* profano, na; *secular music* música profana || REL secular, seglar (clergy) | seglar; *the secular apostolate* el apostolado seglar || laico, ca; *secular school* escuela laica || mundano, na; *a very secular life* una vida muy mundana || secular (occurring once a century) || JUR secular (justice) || FIG secular (very ancient) | duradero, ra (renown).
◆ *n* REL seglar *m*, secular *m*.

secularism ['sekjulərizəm] *n* laicismo *m* (in education) || PHIL materialismo *m*.

secularist ['sekjulərist] *n* partidario *m* del laicismo || PHIL materialista *m* & *f*, libre pensador, ra.

secularization ['sekjuləraiˈzeiʃən] *n* secularización *f*.

secularize ['sekjuləraiz] *vt* secularizar.

secure [si'kjuə*] *adj* seguro, ra (certain, free from anxiety, safe); *our victory is secure* nuestra victoria es segura; *do you feel secure about your future?* ¿se siente seguro en cuanto a su porvenir? || seguro, ra; firme, sólido, da; *is this ladder secure?* ¿está segura esta escalera? || COMM seguro, ra (investment) || — *secure from attack* protegido contra los ataques || *to make secure* fijar, sujetar, afianzar, asegurar (door, beam, etc.).

secure [si'kjuə*] *vt* asegurar, afianzar (to make firm) || poner a buen recaudo (to put in a safe place) || cerrar firmemente (a door, a window) || garantizar (a loan, a creditor); *secured by mortgage* garantizado por una hipoteca || conseguir, obtener (to obtain) || reservar; *to secure seats at the theatre* reservar entradas en el teatro || asegurar (to procure); *to secure employment* asegurar el empleo || proteger (to protect) || consolidar, reforzar, asegurar; *to secure one's positions* consolidar sus posiciones || TECH bloquear (a screw) || JUR detener, encarcelar (to take into custody) || MAR amarrar (a boat) || AGR recoger (crop) || *to secure o.s. against* protegerse contra.

security [si'kjuəriti] *n* seguridad *f*; *the security of the home* la seguridad del hogar; *national security* la seguridad nacional; *security measures to protect a secret weapon* medidas de seguridad para proteger un arma secreta || fianza *f*, garantía *f* (guarantee); *on security* bajo fianza; *in security for* en garantía de; *to lodge a security* dejar una fianza || fiador, ra (guarantor) || FIG salvaguardia *f*, defensa *f*; *the family is the security of society* la familia es la salvaguardia de la sociedad || — *Security Council* Consejo *m* de Seguridad (of UN) || *security guard* guardia *m* & *f* de seguridad || COMM *security market* la Bolsa || *Social Security* seguridad social || *security risk* peligro *m* para la seguridad (action, person) || *to stand security for* salir *or* ser fiador de, garantizar a.
◆ *pl* COMM valores *m*, títulos *m*; *public securities* valores públicos; *gilt-edged securities* valores de máxima garantía; *securities in hand* valores en cartera || COMM *government securities* fondos *m* del Estado || *security forces* fuerzas *f* de seguridad.

sedan [si'dæn] *n* AUT sedán *m*, automóvil *m* de carrocería cerrada || silla *f* de manos (portable chair) || *sedan chair* silla *f* de manos.

sedate [si'deit] *adj* sosegado, da; tranquilo, la (conduct, person) || sentado, da; serio, ria; formal (temperament).

sedateness [-nis] *n* tranquilidad *f*, sosiego *m* (calmness) || seriedad *f*, formalidad *f* (seriousness).

sedation [si'deiʃən] *n* MED sedación *f*.

sedative ['sedətiv] *adj* sedativo, va; sedante, calmante.
◆ *n* MED sedante *m*, sedativo *m*, calmante *m*.

sedentary ['sedntəri] *adj* sedentario, ria; *a sedentary occupation* un trabajo sedentario || ZOOL sedentario, ria || ARTS sedente.

sedge [sedʒ] *n* BOT juncia *f*.

sedge warbler [-ˌwɔːblə*] *n* curruca *f* (bird).

sediment ['sedimənt] *n* sedimento *m* || poso *m* (of a liquid) || borra *f* (of ink) || poso *m*, heces *f pl* (of wine) || GEOL sedimento *m*.

sedimentary [ˌsedi'mentəri] *adj* sedimentario, ria; *sedimentary rock* roca sedimentaria.

sedimentation ['sedimen'teiʃən] *n* sedimentación *f*.

sedition [si'diʃən] *n* sedición *f*.

seditious [si'diʃəs] *adj* sedicioso, sa.

seduce [si'djuːs] *vt* seducir || *to seduce a man from his duty* apartar a un hombre de su deber.

seducer [-ə*] *n* seductor, ra.

seduction [si'dʌkʃən] *n* seducción *f* || FIG atractivo *m* (attractiveness); *the seductions of wealth* los atractivos de la riqueza.

seductive [si'dʌktiv] *adj* seductor, ra; seductivo, va || seductor, ra; atractivo, va; tentador, ra (offer) || provocativo, va (smile).

seductiveness [-nis] *n* seducción *f*, atractivo *m* (of a woman) || atractivo *m* (of an offer).

sedulity [si'djuːliti] *n* diligencia *f*.

sedulous ['sedjuləs] *adj* diligente.

see [siː] *n* REL sede *f*; *the Holy See* la Santa Sede | arzobispado *m* (of an archbishop) | obispado *m* (of a bishop).

see* [siː] *vt* ver; *I see you* te veo; *I'm going to see a bullfight* voy a ver una corrida; *I'd like to see more of you* me gustaría verle más a menudo; *let me see your papers* déjame ver tus papeles; *I saw him running* le he visto correr; *I saw it done* lo vi hacer; *monument that can be seen from afar* monumento que se ve desde lejos || visitar; *to see the town* visitar la ciudad || mirar; *see if this coat suits you* mire si le sienta bien este abrigo || ver (friends); *when shall I see you again?* ¿cuándo le volveré a ver?; *can I see her for a minute?* ¿puedo verla un momento? || comprender, entender, ver; *I don't see what you mean* no comprendo lo que quiere decir || comprender, entender; *I don't see that joke* no entiendo ese chiste || ver; *I can't see the advantage of* no veo el interés de; *I see that you have changed your mind* veo que ha cambiado de parecer || imaginarse, figurarse, ver; *I just can't see them married* no me los imagino casados || ver; *go and see what he wants* vaya a ver lo que quiere || tener una entrevista con, entrevistarse con, ver (to have an interview); *I'll see the Prime Minister tomorrow* tendré una entrevista mañana con el Primer Ministro || recibir (visitors); *the doctor will see you in a moment* el doctor le recibirá dentro de un momento || ir a ver, consultar; *Mary, you must see the dentist* María, tienes que ir a ver al dentista || asegurarse de; *see that you take all your papers with you* asegúrese de que se lleva todos los papeles || procurar; *see that we are housed* procure encontrarnos alojamiento || tener cuidado de; *see that you don't fall down the stairs* ten cuidado de no caerte por las escaleras || acompañar; *to see s.o. home* acompañar a alguien a casa; *I'll see you to the door* le acompaño hasta la puerta || llevar (to carry); *to see s.o. to bed* llevar a alguien a la cama || conocer (changes, life, etc.); *we have seen better days* hemos conocido tiempos mejores || aceptar (a bet, a challenge) || — *as I see it* por lo que veo, por lo visto || *he has seen a good deal of the world* ha corrido mucho mundo || FIG *he will never see fifty again* tiene cincuenta años cumplidos, tiene más de cincuenta años | *I don't know what you see in him* no sé lo que encuentra en él | *I don't see it* no creo que sea posible || *I fail to see how he did it* no consigo ver cómo pudo hacerlo || FIG & FAM *I have to see a man about a dog* tengo que ir a llamar por teléfono (to go to the toilet) || FAM *I'll see him damned first!* ¡que le parta un rayo! || *I saw it with my own eyes* lo vi con mis propios ojos || *I shall be seing you for lunch* ya nos veremos en el almuerzo || *it's not fit to be seen* no se puede ver || *it's worth seing* merece la pena verlo || *I wanted to see you on business* quería verle para hablar de negocios || *let's see* vamos a ver, a ver; *let's see what film they're showing* vamos a ver qué película echan || FIG *nothing could be seen of him* no se le veía nada, no se le veía en ninguna parte || *seeing is believing* ver para creer || *see page 20* véase página veinte || *see you!* ¡hasta luego! || *see you later!, see you soon!* ¡hasta luego!, ¡hasta pronto! || *see you on Thursday!* ¡hasta el jueves! || *that remains to be seen* eso está por ver || *there's nothing to see* no hay nada que merezca la pena verse || *this is how I see it* esta es mi manera de verlo *or* de enfocarlo || *to go and see s.o., to call and see s.o., to call to see s.o.* ir a ver a alguien || *to make s.o. see sth.* hacer ver algo a alguien || *to see no one* no ver a nadie || *to see o.s. in one's children* verse (retratado) en sus hijos || *to see one's way clear* ver claramente la manera de hacer las cosas || FIG & FAM *to see red* ponerse furioso || FAM *to see stars* ver las estrellas || FIG *to see the light* o *the light of day* nacer, ver la luz (to be born), salir a la luz (work) || *we can't see to read* no vemos lo suficiente para leer || *you have to see it to believe it* hay que verlo para creerlo || FIG *you're seeing things!* ¡está usted viendo visiones! || *you see...* es que...; *you see I haven't got any money* es que no tengo dinero.
◆ *vi* ver; *I can see very well* veo muy bien; *to see poorly* ver mal; *let me see* vamos a ver || comprender, entender, ver (to understand) || — *as far as I can see* por lo visto, por lo que veo || *as far as the eye can see* hasta donde alcanza la vista || *do as you see fit* haz como te parezca || *I see!* ¡ya veo! || *let's see* a ver, veamos, vamos a ver || FAM *not to see further than the end of one's nose* no ver más allá de sus narices || *see for yourself* vea usted mismo || FAM *see here!* ¡oiga!, ¡mire! || *you see?* ¿me entiendes?, ¿comprendes?
◆ *phr v* ***to see about*** encargarse de, ocuparse de (to attend to); *don't worry, I'll see about it* no se preocupe, me encargaré de ello | pensar; *you'd better see about it* sería mejor que usted lo pensara || ***to see after*** o ***to see to*** ocuparse de; *to see to the children* ocuparse de los niños | encargarse de; *I'll see to the tickets* me encargaré de las entradas || — *to see to it that* procurar que; *see to it that all is ready* procure que todo esté listo || ***to see in*** celebrar (the New Year) || ***to see into*** investigar, examinar (to investigate); *we must see into this matter* tenemos que examinar este asunto | penetrar (secret, etc.) | ver (the future) || ***to see off*** ir a despedir (to say good-bye) || — *to see s.o. off the premises* acompañar a alguien hasta la puerta || ***to see out*** acompañar hasta la puerta (to say good-bye) | quedarse hasta el final de (to stay till the end); *I saw the film out* me quedé hasta el final de la película | llevar a cabo (to carry out) || — FIG *he will see us all out!* ¡nos enterrará a todos! || ***to see over*** visitar || ***to see through*** ver a través de; *I saw him through the curtains* le vi a través de los visillos | calar, ver claramente las in-

tenciones de (not to be deceived by) | penetrar (a mystery) | ayudar a salir de un apuro (to help) | llevar a cabo (to carry out); *to see a business through* llevar a cabo una empresa.

— OBSERV *Pret* **saw**; *pp* **seen**.

seeable ['siəbəl] *adj* visible.

seed [si:d] *n* BOT semilla *f* (in general) | pepita *f* (of fruit) || AGR simiente *f*, semilla *f* (for sowing) || ANAT semen *m* (sperm) || FIG semilla *f*, germen *m*, origen *m*; *the seeds of revolution* las semillas de la revolución | descendencia *f* (descendants) || freza *f* (of an oyster) || — FIG *to broadcast seed* sembrar a los cuatro vientos || *to go* o *to run to seed* granar, dar grana (a plant), ajarse (a person), echarse a perder (to deteriorate) || FIG *to sow the seeds of discord* sembrar la discordia.

seed [si:d] *vt* despepitar (to take the seed out) || AGR sembrar (to sow); *when did you seed the lawn?* ¿cuándo sembró usted el césped? || fumigar (clouds) || SP preseleccionar (players).
◆ *vi* AGR granar, dar grana (to go to seed) || desgranarse (to shed seed) || sembrar (to sow).

seedbed [-bed] *n* AGR semillero *m* || FIG semillero *m*, foco *m*; *a seedbed of subversion* un foco de subversión.

seedcake [-keik] *n* CULIN torta *f* de alcaravea.

seedcase [-keis] *n* BOT vaina *f* (pod).

seed corn [-kɔ:n] *n* BOT trigo *m* de siembra || US maíz *m* de siembra.

seed drill [-dril] *n* AGR sembradora *f*, sembradera *f*.

seeder [-ə*] *n* AGR sembradora *f*, sembradera *f* (sowing machine) | máquina *f* de despepitar (seed removing machine).

seediness [-inis] *n* aspecto *m* raído (of a garment) || lo desastrado (of appearance, of dress) || FAM indisposición *f*, malestar *m*.

seed leaf [-ˌli:f] *n* BOT cotiledón *m*.

seedless [-lis] *adj* BOT sin semillas | sin pepitas (fruit).

seedling [-liŋ] *n* BOT planta *f* de semillero | plantón *m* (young plant).

seed pearl [-'pə:l] *n* aljófar *m*.

seedsman [-zmən] *n* vendedor *m* de semillas.

— OBSERV El plural de esta palabra es *seedsmen*.

seedtime [-taim] *n* siembra *f*.

seed vessel [-vesl] *n* BOT pericarpio *m*.

seedy [-i] *adj* BOT granado, da || FAM raído, da (clothing) | desastrado, da (appearance, person) | sórdido, da (place) | pachucho, cha (in poor health).

seeing ['si:iŋ] *adj* vidente.
◆ *n* vista *f* (sense of sight) || visión *f* (act of perceiving) || *seeing is believing* ver para creer.
◆ *conj seeing that* en vista de que, visto que; *seeing that it is so late you can stay* en vista de que es tan tarde te puedes quedar.

seek* [si:k] *vt* buscar; *he sought shelter* buscaba abrigo; *to go and seek s.o.* ir a buscar a alguien; *he seeking employment* está buscando trabajo || tratar, procurar; *he seeks to persuade everybody* trata de convencer a todo el mundo || pedir; *to seek advice* pedir consejo || solicitar (a post) || *to seek s.o.'s life* atentar contra la vida de alguien.
◆ *vi* buscar || — *to be much sought after* ser muy solicitado (person), ser muy cotizado (thing) || *to seek after* o *for* buscar; *to seek for information* buscar información.

— OBSERV Pret y pp ***sought***.

seeker [-ə*] *n* buscador, ra.

seem [si:m] *vi* parecer; *it seems to me that* me parece que; *it seems interesting* parece interesante; *he seems to be working* parece que está trabajando || — *I seem to remember that* me parece recordar que || *it seems not* parece que no || *so it seems* así parece, eso parece || *what seems to be the trouble?* ¿qué pasa?

seeming [-iŋ] *adj* aparente, supuesto, ta.
◆ *n* apariencia *f*.

seemingly [-iŋli] *adv* al parecer, por lo visto, aparentemente || *he was seemingly content* parecía satisfecho.

seemliness [-linis] *n* decoro *m*, decencia *f* (correctness) || atractivo *m* (attractiveness).

seemly [-li] *adj* decente, decoroso, sa; correcto, ta (correct) || atractivo, va (attractive).

seen [si:n] *pp* ⟶ **see.**

seep [si:p] *vi* rezumarse.

seepage [-idʒ] *n* filtración *f*.

seer [siə*] *n* vidente *m* & *f*, adivino, na.

seesaw ['si:sɔ:] *n* subibaja *m*, columpio *m* (for children) || FIG vaivén *m*; *the seesaw of prices* el vaivén de los precios.
◆ *adj* de vaivén; *seesaw motion* movimiento de vaivén.

seesaw ['si:sɔ:] *vi* columpiarse || TECH oscilar || FIG vacilar, oscilar; *to seesaw between two opinions* vacilar entre dos opiniones.

seethe [si:ð] *vi* borbotar, hervir (liquid) || FIG hervir; *the streets were seething with people* las calles hervían de gente || FIG *to be seething with anger* estar bufando de cólera.

seething [-iŋ] *adj* hirviente || agitado, da (waters) || FIG hormigueante (mass) | agitado, da (country).

see-through ['si:θru:] *adj* transparente.

segment ['segmənt] *n* MATH & ZOOL segmento *m* || gajo *m* (of orange).

segment [seg'ment] *vt* dividir en segmentos, segmentar.
◆ *vi* segmentarse, dividirse en segmentos.

segmental [-əl] *adj* segmentario, ria || ARCH rebajado, da (arch) || parcial, fragmentario, ria (part).

segmentation [ˌsegmən'teiʃən] *n* segmentación *f*, división *f* en segmentos.

segmented [seg'mentid] *adj* segmentario, ria || *segmented mirror* espejo *m* de varios cuerpos.

Segovian [se'gəuviən] *adj/n* segoviano, na.

segregate ['segrigit] *adj* aislado, da; separado, da.

segregate ['segrigeit] *vt* segregar, separar, aislar.
◆ *vi* dividirse, separarse.

segregation [ˌsegri'geiʃən] *n* segregación *f*; *racial segregation* segregación racial.

segregationist [ˌsegri'geiʃnist] *n* segregacionista *m* & *f*.

seguidilla [segi'di:liə] *n* MUS seguidilla *f*.

seignior ['seinjə*] *n* señor *m* feudal.

seigniory [-ri] *n* señorío *m*.

seine [sein] *n* jábega *f* (fishing net).

seine [sein] *vt/vi* pescar con jábega.

Seine [sein] *pr n* GEOGR Sena *m*.

seism ['saizəm] *n* seísmo *m* [*AMER* sismo *m*].

seismic ['saizmik] *adj* sísmico, ca.

seismogram ['saizməgræm] *n* sismograma *m*.

seismograph ['saizməgrɑ:f] *n* sismógrafo *m*.

seismologic [ˌsaizmə'lɔdʒik]; **seismological** [-əl] *adj* sismológico, ca.

seismology [saiz'mɔlədʒi] *n* sismología *f*.

seismometer [saiz'mɔmitə*] *n* sismómetro *m*.

seizable ['si:zəbl] *adj* asible || JUR embargable.

seize [si:z] *vt* agarrar, asir, coger (to grab firmly); *to seize s.o. by the collar* agarrar a alguien por el cuello || tomar (to take hold of) || JUR embargar, incautarse de (property) | incautarse de; *the police seized fifty kilograms of drugs on the border* la policía se incautó de cincuenta kilos de drogas en la frontera | secuestrar, retirar de la circulación (newspapers) | detener, arrestar (a person) || MIL apoderarse de, tomar (fortress, etc.) || FIG apoderarse de; *panic seized him* el pánico se apoderó de él | captar, comprender (to understand); *to seize the meaning of sth.* comprender el sentido de algo | no dejar escapar, aprovechar (an opportunity) || MAR amarrar || *to be seized with* estar sobrecogido por; *to be seized with fear* estar sobrecogido por el miedo; darle (a uno); *he was seized with apoplexy* le dio un ataque de apoplejía; entrarle (a uno); *to be seized with a desire to do sth.* entrarle a uno el deseo de hacer algo.
◆ *vi to seize on* o *upon* valerse de (a pretext), echar mano de (to take hold of) || TECH *to seize up* agarrotarse (an engine), atorarse, atascarse (to become clogged).

seizin ['si:zin] *n* JUR toma *f* de posesión.

seizure ['si:ʒə*] *n* asimiento *m* || JUR detención *f* (of a person) | incautación *f*, embargo *m* (of property) | secuestro *m* (of newspapers) || MIL toma *f* (of fortress, of ship) || MED ataque *m* || TECH agarrotamiento *m* (of an engine) | atoramiento *m*, atascamiento *m* (clogging).

sejant; sejeant ['si:dʒənt] *adj* HERALD sentado, da.

selachian [si'lækiən] *n* ZOOL selacio *m*.

seldom ['seldəm] *adv* raramente, rara vez, muy pocas veces; *to be seldom seen* verse raramente.

select [si'lekt] *adj* selecto, ta; escogido, da; *select society* sociedad selecta || selecto, ta; exclusivo, va (club, etc.) || escogido, da; *select passages from* trozos escogidos de || COMM de primera calidad.

select [si'lekt] *vt* escoger, elegir || SP seleccionar || COMM clasificar.

selected [-id] *adj* SP seleccionado, da || selecto, ta; escogido, da; *selected poems* poesías selectas.

selection [si'lekʃən] *n* selección *f*; *natural selection* selección natural; *a selection of books* una selección de libros || elección *f* (choice) || surtido *m*; *a large selection of wines* un gran surtido de vinos.
◆ *pl* trozos *m* escogidos (of a writer, of a musician) || SP pronósticos *m* (in horse racing).

selective [si'lektiv] *adj* selectivo, va.

selectivity [silek'tiviti] *n* selectividad *f*.

selectman [si'lektmən] *n* US concejal *m*.

— OBSERV El plural de esta palabra es *selectmen*.

selector [si'lektə*] *n* SP seleccionador, ra || TECH selector *m*.

selenite ['sel'nait] *n* MIN selenita *f*.

selenium [si'li:njəm] *n* CHEM selenio *m*.

selenographer [selə'nɔgrəfə*] *n* ASTR selenógrafo *m*.

selenography [ˌselə'nɔgrəfi] *n* ASTR selenografía *f*.

Seleucid [si'lju:sid] *n* HIST seleúcida *m* & *f*.

self [self] *n* personalidad *f*; *he showed his true self* mostró su verdadera personalidad || sí mismo, sí misma; *to think of others before self* pensar en los demás antes que en sí mismo || egoísmo *m*, interés *m* personal (selfishness) || COMM al portador (en cheques) || PHIL yo *m*; *my other self* mi otro yo || BOT flor *f* unicolor || — *all by one's very self* completamente solo || *he is his old self again* se ha recuperado completamente, vuelve a ser el mismo de siempre || *he is only a shadow of his former self* es sólo

una sombra de lo que fue || *his better self* su lado bueno || *my humble self* ese servidor || *my second self* mi alter ego || *our noble selves* nosotros || *your good selves* ustedes.
◆ *adj* BOT unicolor || idéntico, ca; igual (of same kind, material, etc.) || puro, ra (whisky).
— OBSERV El plural de *self* es *selves*.

self-abandonment [-ə'bændənmənt] *n* olvido *m* de sí mismo || falta *f* de moderación.

self-abasement [-ə'beismənt] *n* autodegradación *f*, rebajamiento *m* de sí mismo.

self-absorption [-əb'sɔːpʃən] *n* ensimismamiento *m*.

self-abuse [-ə'bjuːs] *n* masturbación *f*, onanismo *m* (masturbation) || autocrítica *f* (reproach of o.s.).

self-accusation [-ˌækju'zeiʃən] *n* autoacusación *f*.

self-acting [-'æktiŋ] *adj* automático, ca.

self-addressed [-ə'drest] *adj* con su propia dirección, con la dirección de uno mismo; *a self-addressed envelope* un sobre con su propia dirección || dirigido a sí mismo.

self-adhesive [-əd'hiːsiv] *adj* autoadhesivo, va.

self-advertisement [əd'vəːtismənt] *n* autobombo *m*.

self-analysis [-ə'nælisis] *n* autoanálisis *m inv*.

self-apparent [-ə'pærənt] *adj* evidente.

self-appointed [-ə'pɔintid] *adj* nombrado por sí mismo.

self-approving [-ə'pruːviŋ] *adj* suficiente.

self-assertion [-ə'səːʃən] *n* presunción *f* (presumption) || agresividad *f*.

self-assertive [-ə'səːtiv] *adj* presumido, da (conceited) || agresivo, va.

self-assurance [-ə'ʃuərəns] *n* seguridad *f or* confianza *f* en sí mismo.

self-assured [-ə'ʃuəd] *adj* seguro de sí mismo.

self-binder [-'baində*] *adj* AGR segadora *f* agavilladora.

self-catering [-'keitəriːŋ] *adj* con cocina individual (flat).

self-centred; *US* **self-centered** [-'sentəd] *adj* egocéntrico, ca.

self-closing [-'kləuziŋ] *adj* de cierre automático.

self-coloured; *US* **self-colored** [-'kʌləd] *adj* de color natural (having the natural colour) || unicolor (having one colour) || liso, sa; de un solo color (a fabric).

self-command [-kə'mɑːnd] *n* dominio *m* de sí mismo.

self-communion [-kə'mjuːnjən] *n* recogimiento *m*.

self-complacent [-kəm'pleisnt] *adj* suficiente, pagado *or* creído de sí mismo, engreído, da.

self-composed [-kɔm'pəuzd] *adj* dueño de sí mismo.

self-conceit [-kən'siːt] *n* suficiencia *f*, vanidad *f*, engreimiento *m*.

self-conceited [-kən'siːtid] *adj* suficiente, vanidoso, sa; engreído, da.

self-confessed [-kən'fest] *adj* confeso, sa.

self-confidence [-'kɔnfidəns] *n* seguridad *f or* confianza *f* en sí mismo.

self-confident [-'kɔnfidənt] *adj* seguro de sí mismo.

self-conscious [-'kɔnʃəs] *adj* cohibido, da; tímido, da || *to make s.o. self-conscious* cohibir a alguien.

self-consciousness [-'kɔnʃəsnis] *n* timidez *f*.

self-contained [-kən'teind] *adj* autónomo, ma (complete) || independiente, con entrada particular (a flat, a house) || autosuficiente, independiente (independant) || reservado, da (reserved).

self-contempt [-kən'tempt] *n* desprecio *m* de sí mismo.

self-contradiction [-ˌkɔntrə'dikʃən] *n* contradicción *f*.

self-contradictory [-ˌkɔntrə'diktəri] *adj* contradictorio, ria; que lleva implícita una contradicción.

self-control [-kən'trəul] *n* dominio *m* de sí mismo, sangre *f* fría.

self-controlled [-d] *adj* con dominio de sí mismo.

self-cooker [-'kukə*] *n* olla *f* de presión.

self-criticism [-'kritisizəm] *n* autocrítica *f*.

self-deception [-di'sepʃən] *n* engaño *m* de sí mismo, ilusión *f*.

self-defeating [-di'fiːtiŋ] *adj* contraproducente.

self-defence; *US* **self-defense** [-di'fens] *n* autodefensa *f* (physical) || JUR legítima defensa *f*, defensa *f* propia.

self-delusion [-di'luːʒən] *n* engaño *m* de sí mismo, ilusión *f*.

self-denial [-di'naiəl] *n* abnegación *f*.

self-denying [-di'naiiŋ] *adj* abnegado, da.

self-dependent [-di'pendənt] *adj* independiente.

self-destruction [-dis'trʌkʃən] *n* suicidio *m*, autodestrucción *f*.

self-determination [-diˌtəːmineiʃən] *n* autodeterminación *f*.

self-discipline [-'disiplin] *n* autodisciplina *f*.

self-distrust [-dis'trʌst] *n* inseguridad *f*, falta *f* de seguridad en sí mismo.

self-driven [-'drivn] *adj* automotor, ra; automóvil.

self-educated [-'edjukeitid] *adj* autodidacto, ta.
— OBSERV Although the form *autodidacto, autodidacta* is the only one the Real Academia de la Lengua accepts as correct, the form *autodidacta* is most generally used for both the masculine and feminine.

self-effacement [-i'feismənt] *n* modestia *f*, humildad *f*.

self-effacing [-i'feisiŋ] *adj* modesto, ta; humilde.

self-employed [-im'plɔid] *adj* que trabaja por cuenta propia.

self-esteem [-is'tiːm] *n* amor *m* propio.

self-evident [-'evidənt] *adj* evidente, patente, manifiesto, ta.

self-examination [-igˌzæmi'neiʃən] *n* examen *m* de conciencia.

self-excitation [-ˌeksi'teiʃən] *n* ELECTR autoexcitación *f*.

self-explanatory [-iks'plænətəri] *adj* que se explica por sí mismo.

self-expression [-iks'preʃən] *n* expresión *f* de la propia personalidad.

self-feeding [-'fiːdiŋ] *adj* TECH de alimentación automática.

self-fertilization [-ˌfəːtilai'zeiʃən] *n* BIOL autofecundación *f* || BOT polinización *f* directa.

self-fulfilment; *US* **self-fulfillment** [-ful'filmənt] *n* realización *f* de las ambiciones de uno.

self-governed [-'gʌvənd]; **self-governing** [-'gʌvəniŋ] *adj* autónomo, ma.

self-government [-'gʌvnmənt] *n* gobierno *m* autónomo, autonomía *f* (of a country) || dominio *m* de sí mismo (self-control).

self-help [-'help] *n* esfuerzo *m* personal.

selfhood [-ˌhud] *n* individualidad *f*, personalidad *f* || egoísmo *m* (selfishness).

self-ignition [-ig'niʃən] *n* autoencendido *m*.

self-importance [-im'pɔːtəns] *n* presunción *f*, vanidad *f*.

self-important [-im'pɔːtənt] *adj* presumido, da; vanidoso, sa.

self-imposed [im'pəuzd] *adj* que uno se impone a sí mismo (penalty).

self-induction [-in'dʌkʃən] *n* ELECTR autoinducción *f*, selfinducción *f* || *self-induction coil* self *f*.

self-indulgence [-in'dʌldʒəns] *n* satisfacción *f* inmoderada de sus deseos.

self-indulgent [-in'dʌldʒənt] *adj* inmoderado, da; que satisface todos sus deseos.

self-inflicted [in'fliktid] *adj* que uno se inflinge a sí mismo (penance) || voluntario, ria (wound).

self-interest [-'intrist] *n* interés *m* propio (one's own interest) || egoísmo *m* (selfishness).

selfish [-iʃ] *adj* egoísta || interesado, da (having an ulterior motive).

selfishness [-iʃnis] *n* egoísmo *m*.

self-knowledge [-'nɔlidʒ] *n* conocimiento *m* de sí mismo.

selfless [-lis] *adj* desinteresado, da.

self-locking [-'lɔkiŋ] *adj* de cierre automático.

self-love [-'lʌv] *n* egoísmo *m* (selfishness) || egolatría *f* (self-worship) || PHIL narcisismo *m*.

self-made man [-'meidmən] *n* hombre *m* que ha triunfado por su propio esfuerzo.

self-moving [-'muːviŋ] *adj* automotor, ra.

self-opinionated [-ə'pinjəneitid] *adj* obstinado, da; testarudo, da; terco, ca.

self-pity [-'piti] *n* lástima *f* de sí mismo.

self-pollinated [-'pɔlineitid] *adj* fecundado por polinización directa.

self-pollution [-pə'luːʃən] *n* masturbación *f*.

self-portrait [-'pɔːtrit] *n* autorretrato *m*.

self-possessed [-pə'zest] *adj* sereno, na; dueño de sí mismo.

self-possession [-pə'zeʃən] *n* dominio *m* de sí mismo, serenidad *f*, sangre *f* fría.

self-praise [-'preiz] *n* autobombo *m*.

self-preservation [-ˌprezə'veiʃən] *n* instinto *m* de conservación.

self-proclaimed [-prə'kleimd] *adj* autoproclamado, da.

self-propelled [-prə'peld] *adj* autopropulsado, da; *self-propelled rocket* cohete autopropulsado.

self-propelling [-prə'peliŋ] *adj* autopropulsor, ra.

self-raising [-'reisiŋ] *n* CULIN *self-raising flour* harina *f* con levadura incorporada.

self-recording [-ri'kɔːdiŋ] *adj* registrador, ra.

self-regard [-ri'gɑːd] *n* dignidad *f*, amor *m* propio.

self-regulating [-'regjuleitiŋ] *adj* TECH autorregulador, ra.

self-reliance [-ri'laiəns] *n* confianza *f or* seguridad *f* en sí mismo || independencia *f*.

self-reliant [-ri'laiənt] *adj* seguro de sí mismo || independiente.

self-renunciation [-riˌnʌnsi'eiʃən] *n* abnegación *f*.

self-reproach [-ri'prəutʃ] *n* remordimiento *m*.

self-respect [-ris'pekt] *n* dignidad *f*, amor *m* propio.

self-respecting [-ris'pektiŋ] *adj* que se precie, que tiene amor propio; *as every self-respecting man should know* como debería de saber todo hombre que se precie.

self-restraint [-ris'treint] *n* dominio *m* de sí mismo.

self-rewarding [-ri'wɔːdiŋ] *adj* que compensa.

self-righteous [-'raitʃəs] *adj* farisaico, ca.

self-righteousness [-'raitʃəsnis] *n* fariseísmo *m*, farisaísmo *m*.

self-sacrifice [-'sækrifais] *n* sacrificio *m* de sí mismo, abnegación *f*.

self-sacrificing [-'sækrifaisiŋ] *adj* sacrificado, da; abnegado, da.

selfsame [-seim] *adj* mismísimo, ma; *at that selfsame moment* en ese mismísimo momento.

self-satisfaction [-,sætis'fækʃən] *n* suficiencia *f*, satisfacción *f* de sí mismo.

self-satisfied [-'sætisfaid] *adj* suficiente, satisfecho de sí mismo.

self-sealing [-'siːliŋ] *adj* que se cierra automáticamente ‖ autoadhesivo, va (envelopes, etc.).

self-seeking [-'siːkiŋ] *adj* egoísta.
◆ *n* egoísmo *m*.

self-service [-'səːvis] *adj* de autoservicio.
◆ *n* autoservicio *m*.

self-starter [-'stɑːtə*] *n* TECH arranque *m* automático.

self-starting [-'stɑːtiŋ] *adj* TECH de arranque automático (motor).

self-styled [-'staild] *adj* supuesto, ta.

self-sufficiency [-sə'fiʃənsi] *n* independencia *f*, autosuficiencia *f* (independence) ‖ seguridad *f or* confianza *f* en sí mismo.

self-sufficient [-sə'fiʃənt] *adj* independiente, autosuficiente ‖ seguro de sí mismo (self-conceited).

self-suggestion [-sə'dʒestʃən] *n* autosugestión *f*.

self-support [-sə'pɔːt] *n* independencia *f* económica.

self-supporting [-sə'pɔːtiŋ] *adj* económicamente independiente, que vive con sus propios recursos ‖ *he is self-supporting* se mantiene a sí mismo, vive con sus propios recursos.

self-surrender [-sə'rendə*] *n* abandono *m* de sí mismo.

self-taught [-'tɔːt] *adj* autodidacto, ta ‖ *self-taught person* autodidacto, ta.
— OBSERV Although the form *autodidacto, ta* is the only one the Real Academia de la Lengua accepts as correct, the form *autodidacta* is most generally used for both the masculine and feminine.

self-willed [-'wild] *adj* obstinado, da; terco, ca (obstinate).

self-winding [-'waindiŋ] *adj* de cuerda automática (watch).

self-worship [-'wəːʃip] *n* egolatría *f*.

self-worshipping [-'wəːʃipiŋ] *adj* ególatra.

sell [sel] *n* FAM engaño *m*, camelo *m* (trick) ‖ decepción *f* (disappointment) ‖ venta *f* (selling) ‖ — *hard sell* publicidad agresiva ‖ *soft sell* publicidad discreta.

sell* [sel] *vt* vender; *he sold his car* vendió su coche; *to sell a painting for ten thousand pesetas* vender un cuadro en *or* por diez mil pesetas; *to sell wholesale* vender al por mayor; *to sell on credit* vender a plazos [AMER vender a cuota] ‖ hacer vender; *television sells many products* la televisión hace vender muchos productos ‖ FIG vender; *to sell one's soul* vender su alma; *he sold his friend to the police* vendió su amigo a la policía | hacer aceptar, convencer (scheme, idea) ‖ — FIG *to be sold on* estar entusiasmado por (to be enthusiastic about), convencerle a uno; *I am sold on this idea* esta idea me convence ‖ *to sell at a loss* vender con pérdida ‖ FIG & FAM *to sell down the river* traicionar | *to sell for a song* vender en cuatro cuartos ‖ *to sell for cash* vender al contado ‖ *to sell off* liquidar ‖ FIG *to sell one's life dearly* vender cara su vida | *to sell o.s.* venderse ‖ *to sell out* liquidar (to get rid of), realizar (shares), agotarse, estar agotado; *the edition sold out overnight* la edición se agotó en una noche; traicionar, vender (to betray) ‖ *to sell short, to sell a bear* vender al descubierto (Stock Exchange) ‖ JUR *to sell up* hacer embargar ‖ *we are sold out of this article* se nos ha agotado este artículo ‖ FIG & FAM *you've been sold!* ¡le han dado gato por liebre!
◆ *vi* venderse; *these books sell well* estos libros se venden bien; *eggs are selling at o for twenty pesetas a dozen* los huevos se venden a veinte pesetas la docena ‖ FIG ser aceptado (scheme, idea) ‖ — FIG *to sell like hot cakes* venderse como rosquillas ‖ *to sell out* liquidar todas las existencias; traicionar (to betray).
— OBSERV Pret y pp ***sold***.

sell-by-date ['selbɑi'deit] *n* fecha *f* de caducidad.

seller [-ə*] *n* vendedor, ra (person who sells) ‖ comerciante *m* (dealer) ‖ — *quick seller* artículo que se vende fácilmente ‖ *seller's market* mercado *m* favorable al vendedor (in the Stock Exchange).

selling [-iŋ] *adj* de venta; *selling price* precio de venta ‖ de fácil venta (product).

sell-off [-'ɔf] *n* baja *f* de valores (in the Stock Exchange).

Sellotape ['seləteip] *n* (registered trademark) celo *m*, cinta *f* adhesiva.

sellout [-aut] *n* traición *f* (betrayal) ‖ lleno *m*, función *f* para la que se han vendido todas las localidades, éxito *m* de taquilla (in a theatre, in a stadium, etc.) ‖ COMM agotamiento *m* de todas las existencias.

Seltzer ['seltsə*]; **Seltzer water** [-'wɔːtə*] *n* agua *f* de Seltz.

selvage; selvedge ['selvidʒ] *n* orillo *m* (edge of cloth).

selves [selvz] *pl n* ⟶ **self.**

semantic [si'mæntik]; **semantical** [-əl] *adj* semántico, ca.

semantics [-s] *n* GRAMM semántica *f*.

semaphore ['seməfɔː*] *n* MAR semáforo *m*.

semaphore ['seməfɔː*] *vt* transmitir por semáforo.
◆ *vi* hacer señales con semáforo.

semasiology [si'meisi'ɔlədʒi] *n* GRAMM semasiología *f*.

semblance ['sembləns] *n* apariencia *f*; *under a semblance of friendship* bajo una apariencia de amistad; *in semblance* en apariencia ‖ *to put on a semblance of gaiety* fingir alegría.

semeiologist [,siːmai'ɔlədʒist] *n* semiólogo *m*.

semeiology [,siːmai'ɔlədʒi] *n* semiología *f*.

semeiotic [siːmai'ɔtik] *adj* semiótico, ca.

semeiotics [-s] *n* semiótica *f*.

semen ['siːmən] *n* semen *m*.
— OBSERV El plural de la palabra inglesa es *semina* o *semens*.

semester [simestə*] *n* US semestre *m* (academic half year).

semi ['semi] *n* FAM casa *f* unida a otra por una pared medianera.

semiannual [-'ænjuəl] *adj* semestral.

semiarid [-'ærid] *adj* semiárido, da.

semiautomatic [-,ɔːtə'mætik] *adj* semiautomático, ca.

semiaxis [-'æksis] *n* semieje *m*.

semibreve [-briːv] *n* MUS semibreve *f*.

semichromatic [-krəu'mætik] *adj* MUS semicromático, ca.

semicircle [-,səːkl] *n* MATH semicírculo *m*.

semicircular [-'səːkjulə*] *adj* semicircular ‖ ARCH de medio punto (arch).

semicircumference [-sə'kʌmfərəns] *n* MATH semicircunferencia *f*.

semicolon [-'kəulən] *n* GRAMM punto y coma *m*.

semiconductor [-kən'dʌktə*] *n* ELECTR semiconductor *m*.

semiconscious [-'kɔnʃəs] *adj* semiconsciente.

semiconsonant [-'kɔnsənənt] *n* GRAMM semiconsonante *f*.

semiconsonantal [-,kɔnsə'næntl] *adj* GRAMM semiconsonante.

semidarkness [-'dɑːknis] *n* media luz *f*, penumbra *f*.

semidetached [-di'tætʃt] *adj* *semidetached houses* casas separadas por una pared medianera.

semidiameter [-dai'æmitə*] *n* MATH semidiámetro *m*.

semidirect [-di'rekt] *adj* semidirecto, ta.

semidouble [-'dʌbl] *adj* BOT semidoble.

semifinal [-'fainl] *n* SP semifinal *f*.
◆ *adj* SP semifinalista; *the two semifinal teams* los dos equipos semifinalistas.

semifinalist [-'fainəlist] *n* semifinalista *m* & *f*.

semifine [-fain] *adj* semifino, na.

semilunar [-'luːnə*] *adj* semilunar.

semi-manufactured [-,mænju'fæktʃəd] *adj* semimanufacturado, da.

seminal ['siːminl] *adj* seminal; *seminal fluid* líquido seminal.

seminar ['seminɑː*] *n* seminario *m* (of students, of experts).

seminarian [semi'nɛəriən]; **seminarist** ['seminərist] *n* estudiante *m* & *f or* experto *m* que asiste a un seminario ‖ REL seminarista *m*.

seminary ['seminəri] *n* REL seminario *m*.

seminiferous [,semi'nifərəs] *adj* seminífero, ra.

seminomadic ['seminəu'mædik] *adj* seminómada.

semiofficial ['semiə'fiʃəl] *adj* semioficial.

semiologist [,semi'ɔlədʒist] *n* US semiólogo *m*.

semiology [,semi'ɔlədʒi] *n* US MED semiología *f*.

semiotic [,semi'ɔtik] *adj* US semiótico, ca.

semiotics [-s] *n* US semiótica *f*.

semiprecious ['semi,preʃəs] *adj* fino, na; semiprecioso, sa; *semiprecious stone* piedra fina.

semiquaver ['semi,kweivə*] *n* MUS semicorchea *f*; *semiquaver rest* silencio de semicorchea.

semi-refined ['semiri'faind] *adj* semirrefinado, da.

semirigid ['semi'ridʒid] *adj* semirrígido, da.

semiskilled ['semi'skild] *adj* semicualificado, da.

semisolid ['semi'sɔlid] *adj* semisólido, da.
◆ *n* semisólido *m*.

Semite ['siːmait] *n* semita *m* & *f*.

Semitic [si'mitik] *adj* semítico, ca; semita.

Semitism ['semitizəm] *n* semitismo *m*.

semitone ['semitəun] *n* MUS semitono *m*.

semitrailer ['semi'treilə*] *n* semirremolque *m*.

semitransparent ['semitræns'pɛərənt] *adj* semitransparente.

semitropic ['semi'trɔpik]; **semitropical** [-əl] *adj* subtropical.

semivocalic ['semivəu'kælik] *adj* GRAMM semivocal.

semivowel ['semi,vauəl] *n* GRAMM semivocal *f*.

semiweekly ['semi'wi:kli] *adj* bisemanal.
◆ *n* publicación *f* bisemanal.

semolina [,semə'li:nə] *n* CULIN sémola *f*.

sempiternal [,sempi'tə:nl] *adj* sempiterno, na (everlasting).

sempstress ['sempstris] *n* costurera *f*.

senate ['senit] *n* senado *m* || consejo *m* (in a university) || US POL *the Senate* el Senado.

senator ['senətə*] *n* senador *m*.

senatorial [,senə'tɔ:riəl] *adj* senatorial.

senatorship ['senətəʃip] *n* senaduría *f*.

send* [send] *vt* mandar; *she sent him to his grandmother's* lo mandó a casa de su abuela; *I shall send him for her* le mandaré buscarla; *did he send any message?* ¿mandó algún recado? || mandar, enviar; *to send a postcard* mandar una postal || poner, mandar (telegram); *I have a telegram to send* tengo que poner un telegrama || echar; *she wrote the letter but she forgot to send it* escribió la carta pero se le olvidó echarla || adjuntar, mandar adjunto, enviar adjunto (to enclose); *with this letter I'm sending you a price list* en esta carta le adjunto una lista de precios || enviar; *the prophets were sent from God* los profetas fueron enviados por Dios || lanzar (to throw) || volver; *the noise sent him crazy* el ruido le volvió loco || RAD transmitir || FAM chiflar; *this record sends me* este disco me chifla || — *God sent him victorious* Dios le dé la victoria || *he sent the book flying at me* me tiró el libro a la cabeza || *it sent a shiver down my spine* me dio escalofríos || *to be sent into the world* venir al mundo || *to send one's love to s.o.* mandar *or* enviar cariñosos saludos a alguien || *to send s.o. sprawling* hacer que uno se caiga || FIG *to send s.o. to Coventry* hacer el vacío a alguien.
◆ *vi* mandar a alguien; *she sent to inquire after you* mandó a alguien a preguntar por ti; *I shall send for it* mandaré a alguien a buscarlo || mandar un recado; *send to me in the morning* mándeme un recado por la mañana || RAD emitir, transmitir || *to send for the doctor* llamar al médico, enviar a alguien a buscar al médico.
◆ *phr v* ***to send along*** mandar; *send him along!* ¡mándemelo! || ***to send away*** echar, despedir (an employee) | escribir pidiendo; *I have sent away for the latest catalogue* he escrito pidiendo el último catálogo | enviar, mandar, expedir (a package) || ***to send back*** devolver; *he sent the ball back with a magnificent backhand stroke* devolvió la pelota con un magnífico revés; *I have sent back the umbrella* devolví el paraguas | hacer volver, enviar *or* mandar de nuevo (to make s.o. return) || ***to send down*** hacer bajar; *to send down prices* hacer bajar los precios | expulsar (a student) | encarcelar (a thief) | MAR desaparejar || ***to send forth*** echar (odour, leaves, etc.) || ***to send in*** devolver (to return); *you have to send the form in after you have filled it in* tiene que devolver el formulario después de haberlo rellenado | mandar; *send in your suggestions on a postcard* mándenos sus sugerencias en una postal; *he has sent in his bill* ha mandado su factura | presentar (a calling card, a resignation) | hacer entrar, hacer pasar (s.o.) | *send her in!* ¡que pase! | *to send in one's name* dar su nombre para ser recibido || ***to send off*** mandar, echar al correo (a letter) | escribir pidiendo; *I have sent off for the latest catalogue* he escrito pidiendo el último catálogo | mandar, enviar; *they sent soldiers off on an important mission* mandaron soldados con una importante misión | despedir (to see s.o. off) | SP expulsar; *the player was sent off in the sixth minute* el jugador fue expulsado en el minuto seis *or* a los seis minutos || ***to send on*** mandar, reexpedir; *if you write to me at home, mummy will send the letter on to me* si me escribe a casa, mamá me mandará la carta | transmitir (orders) || ***to send out*** echar (s.o.) | echar, despedir (an odour) | echar (smoke, leaves) | mandar (a circular letter) | emitir (to emit) | dar (a shout) || ***to send round*** hacer circular; *word was sent round that* se hizo circular la noticia de que | mandar; *I sent him round to the butcher's* le mandé a la carnicería || ***to send up*** satirizar (to caricature) | hacer subir (to make s.o. come up) | mandar arriba (to make s.o. go up) | hacer subir (prices, temperature) | lanzar (balloon, ball) | presentar (a calling card) | meter en la cárcel (to put in a jail).
— OBSERV Pret y pp ***sent***.

sendal ['sendəl] *n* cendal *m* (fabric).

sender [-ə*] *n* remitente *m* & *f* (of a letter, etc.) || RAD transmisor *m*.

send-off [-'ɔf] *n* despedida *f* (farewell) || *the press has given the play a good send-off* la prensa ha acogido muy favorablemente la obra.

send-up [-ʌp] *n* FAM sátira *f*, parodia *f*.

Seneca ['senikə] *pr n* Séneca *m*.

Senegal [,seni'gɔ:l] *pr n* GEOGR Senegal *m*.

Senegalese ['senigə'li:z] *adj/n* senegalés, esa || *the Senegalese* los senegaleses.

senescence [se'nesəns] *n* senectud *f*.

senescent [se'nesənt] *adj* senescente.

seneschal ['seniʃəl] *n* senescal *m*.

senile ['si:nail] *adj* senil.

senility [si'niliti] *n* senilidad *f*.

senior ['si:njə*] *adj* padre; *John Brown senior* John Brown padre || mayor (in age) || superior (in rank, in grade) || más antiguo, gua (of prior enrolment); *senior members* los socios más antiguos || SP senior || — US *senior citizen* jubilado, da | *senior college* colegio universitario para los dos últimos años || *the senior partner* el socio mayoritario || *the senior Service* la marina || *to be senior to s.o.* ser mayor que alguien || *to be three years senior to s.o.* tener tres años más que alguien, llevarle tres años a alguien.
◆ *n* mayor *m* & *f* (in age) || mayor *m* & *f* (at school) || miembro *m* más antiguo (member) || socio *m* principal *or* mayoritario (partner) || US estudiante *m* & *f* de último año || — *she is his senior* es mayor que él || *she is his senior by three years* le lleva tres años, tiene tres años más que él.

seniority [,si:ni'ɔriti] *n* antigüedad *f*.

sensation [sen'seiʃən] *n* sensación *f*; *I have a slight sensation of dizziness* tengo una ligera sensación de mareo; *this act was the sensation of the evening* este número fue la sensación de la noche || — *she was a great sensation as Cleopatra* estuvo sensacional en el papel de Cleopatra || *to create* o *to make* o *to cause a sensation* causar sensación.

sensational [sen'seiʃənl] *adj* sensacional (excellent) || sensacionalista (writer, novel) || sensacional (event).

sensationalism [sen'seiʃnəlizəm] *n* sensacionalismo *m* (in journalism, in philosophy).

sensationalist [sen'seiʃnəlist] *n* sensacionalista *m* & *f* (in journalism, in philosophy).

sense [sens] *n* sentido *m*; *the five senses* los cinco sentidos; *the sense of sight, of smell* el sentido de la vista, del olfato; *sense of direction, honour, humour* sentido de la orientación, del honor, del humor || sentido *m*, significado *m* (meaning); *the sense of a word* el sentido de una palabra; *figurative sense* sentido figurado; *in the literal sense* en sentido propio || sentido *m* común, juicio *m* (intelligence) || sensación *f* (sensation); *sense of pain* sensación de dolor; *sense of insecurity* sensación de inseguridad || sentimiento *m* (of injustice, etc.) || sentir *m* general, parecer *m*, opinión *f* (consensus); *the sense of the assembly* la opinión de la asamblea || — *against common sense, in defiance of common sense* en contra del sentido común || *common sense* sentido común || *good sense* buen sentido, juicio *m*, sentido común, sensatez *f* || *I can't make any sense of it* no le encuentro sentido alguno || *in a sense* en cierto sentido || *in every sense* en todos los sentidos || *in no sense* de ninguna forma || *in the best sense of the word* en el buen sentido de la palabra || *in the broad sense* o *in all senses of the word* en el sentido amplio de la palabra, en toda la extensión de la palabra || *person of sense* persona sensata || *sixth sense* sexto sentido || *there is no sense in that* eso no tiene sentido || *this doesn't make sense* esto no tiene sentido || *to have the sense to* tener la inteligencia *or* la cordura de || *to make sense* tener sentido || *to make sense of sth.* comprender el sentido de algo, entender algo || *to take the sense of the meeting* consultar a la asamblea, pedir el parecer de la asamblea || *to talk sense* hablar razonablemente *or* con sentido común || *to talk sense into* meter en razón || *what is the sense of talking like that?* ¿de qué sirve hablar así?
◆ *pl* MED juicio *m sing* (reason); *to be out of one's senses* haber perdido el juicio | sentido *m sing* (consciousness); *to regain one's senses* recobrar el sentido || — *to be in one's senses* estar en su sano juicio || *to bring s.o. to his senses* hacer sentar la cabeza a alguien, hacer entrar en razón a alguien (to bring s.o. to reason), hacer volver a alguien en sí (s.o. who is unconscious) || *to come to one's senses* recobrar el juicio, sentar la cabeza (to become sensible), volver en sí (after unconsciousness) || FIG *to lose one's senses* perder el sentido, volverse loco || FIG *to make s.o. lose his senses* hacerle perder el sentido a uno, volverle loco a uno | *to take leave of one's senses* perder el juicio, volverse loco.

sense [sens] *vt* sentir || PHIL percibir.

senseless [-lis] *adj* inconsciente, sin conocimiento, sin sentido (unconscious); *the blow knocked him senseless* el golpe le dejó sin sentido || insensato, ta (foolish); *a senseless act* una acción insensata; *senseless person* persona insensata.

senselessness [-lisnis] *n* insensatez *f* (foolishness).

sense organ [-'ɔ:gən] *n* ANAT órgano *m* sensorio.

sensibility [,sensi'biliti] *n* sensibilidad *f*.
◆ *pl* susceptibilidad *f sing*.

sensible ['sensəbl] *adj* sensato, ta (showing good sense); *sensible decision* decisión sensata || sensato, ta; cuerdo, da; razonable; *sensible person* persona razonable || acertado, da (choice) || cómodo, da; práctico, ca (clothing) || sensible (perceivable) || sensible, apreciable, notable; *sensible difference* diferencia notable || *to be sensible of* darse cuenta de.

sensibleness [-nis] *n* sensatez *f*, juicio *m*, cordura *f* || inteligencia *f* || *the sensibleness of a choice* lo acertado de una elección.

sensitive ['sensitiv] *adj* sensible; *sensitive to light* sensible a la luz; *sensitive scales* balanza sensible; *the scar is still very sensitive* la cicatriz está todavía muy sensible || PHOT sensible (film) || susceptible (easily offended); *he is very sensitive on questions of honour* es muy susceptible para las cuestiones de honor || COMM inestable; *a sensitive market* un mercado inestable || — *to be sensitive to cold* ser friolero || *to have a sensitive ear* ser fino de oídos, tener un oído fino.

sensitiveness ['sensitivnis]; **sensitivity** [sensi'tiviti] *n* susceptibilidad *f* (susceptibility) || sensibilidad *f* (responsiveness).

sensitive plant ['sensitiv'plɑ:nt] *n* BOT sensitiva *f*.

sensitization [sensitai'zeiʃən] *n* sensibilización *f*.

sensitize ['sensitaiz] *vt* sensibilizar.

sensor ['sensə*] *n* sensor *m*.

sensorial [sen'sɔ:riəl]; **sensory** ['sensəri] *adj* sensorio, ria.

sensual ['sensjuəl] *adj* sensual; *sensual pleasures* placeres sensuales; *a sensual woman* una mujer sensual; *a sensual mouth* una boca sensual.

sensualism [-izəm] *n* sensualismo *m*.

sensualist [-ist] *n* sensualista *m* & *f*.

sensuality [ˌsensju'æliti] *n* sensualidad *f*.

sensualize ['sensjuəlaiz] *vt* volver sensual.

sensuous ['sensjuəs] *adj* sensual.

sensuousness [-nis] *n* sensualidad *f*.

sent [sent] *pret/pp* ⟶ **send.**

sentence ['sentəns] *n* GRAMM oración *f* (grammatical term), frase *f* (common term) || JUR sentencia *f* || — *death sentence* pena *f* de muerte || *life sentence* condena perpetua || *suspended sentence* condena condicional, sentencia suspendida || *to be under sentence of death* estar condenado a muerte || *to pass sentence on* sentenciar, condenar || *to serve one's sentence* cumplir la sentencia.

sentence ['sentəns] *vt* JUR sentenciar, condenar; *to sentence s.o. to five years' imprisonment* sentenciar a alguien a cinco años de prisión.

sententious [sen'tenʃəs] *adj* sentencioso, sa.

sententiousness [-nis] *n* tono *m* sentencioso.

sentient ['senʃənt] *adj* sensible.

sentiment ['sentimənt] *n* sentimiento *m*; *to have noble sentiments* tener sentimientos nobles || sentimiento *m*, sensibilidad *f*; *to play a tune with sentiment* tocar una melodía con sentimiento || sentimentalismo *m*, sensiblería *f* (sentimentality) || parecer *m*, opinión *f* (opinion) || *those are my sentiments* es mi opinión.

sentimental [ˌsenti'mentl] *adj* sentimental || sentimental, sensiblero, ra (mawkish) || sentimental, romántico, ca (romantic).

sentimentalism [-izəm] *n* sentimentalismo *m*.

sentimentalist [-ist] *n* sentimental *m* & *f*.

sentimentality [ˌsentimen'tæliti] *n* sentimentalismo *m* || sentimentalismo *m*, sensiblería *f* (mawkishness).

sentimentalize [ˌsenti'mentəlaiz] *vt* hablar con sentimentalismo de.

◆ *vi* ponerse sentimental.

sentinel ['sentinl] *n* MIL centinela *m* || *to stand sentinel* hacer guardia.

sentry ['sentri] *n* MIL centinela *m* || *to be on sentry, to stand sentry* estar de guardia, hacer guardia.

sentry box [-bɔks] *n* garita *f* [de centinela].

sentry go [-gəu] *n* guardia *f*; *to be on sentry go* estar de guardia.

sepal ['sepəl] *n* BOT sépalo *m*.

separability [ˌsepərə'biliti] *n* posibilidad *f* de separación.

separable ['sepərəbl] *adj* separable.

separate ['seprit] *adj* separado, da || particular (entrance, room) || distinto, ta; *cut into three separate parts* córtelo en tres partes distintas || suelto, ta; *there are several separate sheets of instructions* hay varias hojas sueltas de instrucciones || otro, otra; *please give details of former employment on a separate sheet* se ruega den informes sobre su empleo anterior en otra hoja || aislado, da (existence) || independiente (interests) || *under separate cover* por separado.

◆ *n* PRINT separata *f*.

◆ *pl n* prendas *f pl* de vestir que se combinan.

separate ['sepəreit] *vt* separar; *to separate two boxers* separar a dos boxeadores; *the border separates France and Spain* la frontera separa Francia y España; *different cultures separate these countries* distintas culturas separan estos dos países || dividir; *to separate sth. into several parts* dividir algo en varias partes || distinguir entre; *I find it hard to separate good from evil* me es difícil distinguir entre el bien y el mal || clasificar (to sort out); *to separate mail* clasificar el correo || CULIN desnatar (milk).

◆ *vi* separarse; *they separated when they reached the crossroads* se separaron al llegar a la encrucijada; *my husband and I have decided to separate* mi marido y yo hemos decidido separarnos.

separately ['sepritli] *adv* separadamente, por separado.

separation [ˌsepə'reiʃən] *n* separación *f* || clasificación *f* || CULIN desnatado *m* (of milk) || JUR *legal separation* separación matrimonial.

separatism ['sepərətizəm] *n* separatismo *m*.

separatist ['sepərətist] *adj/n* separatista.

separator ['sepəreitə*] *n* TECH separador *m*.

Sephardi [se'fɑ:di] *n* sefardí *m* & *f*, sefardita *m* & *f*.

— OBSERV El plural de la palabra inglesa es *Sephardim*.

Sephardic [-k] *adj* sefardí, sefardita.

sepia ['si:pjə] *n* sepia *f*.

sepoy ['si:pɔi] *n* cipayo *m*.

seps [seps] *n* ZOOL sepedón *m*, seps *m*.

sepsis [-is] *n* MED septicemia *f*.

septangular [sep'tæŋgjulə*] *adj* heptagonal.

September [sep'tembə*] *n* septiembre *m*, setiembre *m*; *I went on the 29th of September* fui el 29 de septiembre.

— OBSERV See ***Septiembre*** in the other part.

septemvir [sep'temvə*] *n* septenviro *m*.

septennate [sep'tenət] *n* septenado *m*, septenato *m*, septenio *m*.

septennium [sep'teniəm] *n* septenio *m*.

— OBSERV El plural de *septennium* es *septenniums* o *septennia*.

septet; septette [sep'tet] *n* MUS septeto *m*.

septic ['septik] *adj* MED séptico, ca; *septik tank* fosa séptica.

septicaemia; *US* **septicemia** [septi'si:miə] *n* MED septicemia *f*.

septicaemic; *US* **septicemic** [septi'si:mik] *adj* MED septicémico, ca.

septime ['septi:m] *n* séptima *f* (in fencing).

septimole ['septiməul] *n* MUS septillo *m*.

septuagenarian [ˌseptjuədʒi'nɛəriən] *adj/n* septuagenario, ria.

Septuagesima [ˌseptjuə'dʒesimə] *n* REL Septuagésima *f*.

septuple ['septjupl] *adj* séptuplo, pla.

◆ *n* séptuplo *m*.

sepulcher ['sepəlkə*] *n/vt* *US* ⟶ **sepulchre.**

sepulchral [si'pʌlkrəl] *adj* sepulcral; *sepulchral stone* lápida sepulcral; *sepulchral voice* voz sepulcral || *sepulchral vault* panteón *m*.

sepulchre; *US* **sepulcher** ['sepəlkə*] *n* sepulcro *m*; *the Holy Sepulchre* el Santo Sepulcro || *whited sepulchre* sepulcro blanqueado.

sepulture ['sepəltʃə*] *n* sepultura *f*.

sequacious [se'kweiʃəs] *adj* coherente (argument) || servil (imitator).

sequel ['si:kwəl] *n* continuación *f* (of speech, narrative) || consecuencia *f*, resultado *m* (consequence).

sequela [si'kwi:lə] *n* secuela *f*.

— OBSERV El plural de *sequela* es *sequelae*.

sequence ['si:kwəns] *n* sucesión *f*; *the sequence of events that led to his downfall* la sucesión de acontecimientos que lo llevaron a la caída || serie *f*; *a sequence of sonnets* una serie de sonetos || orden *m* (historical) || resultado *m*, consecuencia *f* (result) || escalera *f* (of cards) || CINEM secuencia *f* || REL secuencia *f* || GRAMM concordancia *f* (of tenses).

sequent [si'kwent]; **sequential** [si'kwenʃəl] *adj* sucesivo, va (successive) || consecutivo, va (consecutive) || consecuente, subsecuente (consequent).

sequential [si'kwenʃəl] *adj* ⟶ **sequent** || INFORM secuencial; *sequential access* acceso secuencial; *sequential processing* tratamiento secuencial.

sequester [si'kwestə*] *vt* JUR embargar, confiscar, secuestrar (property) | secuestrar (a person) || apoderarse de (to seize) || aislar (to isolate) || *to sequester o.s.* retirarse, confinarse.

sequestered [-əd] *adj* retirado, da; aislado, da (isolated) || JUR embargado, da; confiscado, da; secuestrado, da.

sequestrate ['sikwestreit] *vt* JUR embargar, confiscar, secuestrar (to sequester).

sequestration [ˌsi:kwes'treiʃən] *n* JUR embargo *m*, confiscación *f*, secuestro *m* (of a property) | secuestro *m*, secuestración *f* (of a person) || aislamiento *m*, retiro *m* (isolation).

sequestrator [si'kwestreitə*] *n* JUR embargador, ra; secuestrador, ra.

sequestrum [se'kwestrəm] *n* MED secuestro *m*.

— OBSERV El plural de *sequestrum* es *sequestra* o *sequestrums*.

sequin ['si:kwin] *n* lentejuela *f* (spangle) || cequí *m* (old coin).

sequoia [si'kwɔiə] *n* secoya *f* (tree).

sera ['siərə] *pl n* ⟶ **serum.**

serac ['seræk] *n* GEOL sérac *m*.

seraglio [se'rɑ:liəu] *n* serrallo *m*, harén *m*.

— OBSERV El plural de *seraglio* es *seraglios* o *seragli*.

serai [se'rai] *n* caravanserallo *m* (caravansary).

serape [se'rɑ:pei] *n* sarape *m*.

seraph ['serəf] *n* REL serafín *m*.

— OBSERV El plural de *seraph* es *seraphs* o *seraphim*.

seraphic [se'ræfik]; **seraphical** [-əl] *adj* seráfico, ca || *Seraphic Doctor* Doctor Seráfico [San Buenaventura].

seraphim ['serəfim] *pl n* serafines *m*.

Serb [sə:b] *adj/n* ⟶ **Serbian.**

Serbia [-jə] *pr n* GEOGR Serbia *f*, Servia *f*.

Serbian [-jən]; **Serb** [sə:b] *adj* serbio, bia; servio, via.

◆ *n* serbio, bia; servio, via (inhabitant of Serbia) || serbio *m*, servio *m* (language).

Serbo-Croat ['sə:bəu'krəuæt] *n* serbocroata *m*, servocroata *m*.

Serbo-Croatian [ˌsəːbəukrəu'eiʃən] *adj* serbocroata, servocroata.
◆ *n* serbocroata *m*, servocroata *m* (language).
sere [siə*] *adj* marchito, ta (whitered).
serenade [ˌseri'neid] *n* MUS serenata *f*.
serenade [ˌseri'neid] *vt* MUS dar una serenata a.
◆ *vi* MUS dar una serenata.
serene [si'riːn] *adj* sereno, na (person, sea, sky) || *His Serene Highness* Su Alteza Serenísima.
◆ *n* mar *m* en bonanza (sea) || cielo *m* sereno (sky).
serenely [-li] *adv* tranquilamente, con tranquilidad, serenamente.
serenity [si'reniti] *n* serenidad *f* || *Your Serenity* Su Serenidad.
serf [səːf] *n* siervo, va.
serfage [-idʒ]; **serfdom** [-dəm]; **serfhood** [-hud] *n* servidumbre *f*.
serge [səːdʒ] *n* sarga *f* (textile).
sergeant ['sɑːdʒənt]; **serjeant** *n* MIL sargento *m* || cabo *m* (of police) || ujier *m* (sergeant at arms).
sergeant at arms [-ət'ɑːmz] *n* ujier *m*.
sergeant-at-law [-ət'lɔː] *n* JUR abogado *m*.
sergeant major [-'meidʒə*] *n* MIL sargento *m* mayor.
serial ['siəriəl] *adj* consecutivo, va (consecutive) || de serie; *serial number* número de serie || INFORM serial; *serial port* puerto serial || *serial processing* tratamiento *m or* procesamiento secuencial || seriado, da (radio, television programme, etc.) || por entregas (novel) || de publicación por entregas; *serial rights* derechos de publicación por entregas.
◆ *n* serial *m*, novela *f* por entregas, folletín *m* (in a magazine) || serial *m* (on television, on radio).
serialization [ˌsiəriəlai'zeiʃən] *n* publicación *f* por entregas.
serialize ['siːəriəlaiz] *vt* publicar por fascículos *or* por entregas *or* como serial (a novel) || TECH fabricar en serie.
serial killer ['siəriəl'kilə*] *n* asesino, na múltiple.
serially ['siːəriəli] *adv* en serie || por entregas, por fascículos (novel).
seriate ['siːərieit] *vt* seriar.
seriatim [ˌsiəri'eitim] *adv* sucesivamente, por separado.
sericeous [si'riʃəs] *adj* sedoso, sa.
sericulture [ˌseri'kʌltʃə*] *n* sericultura *f*, sericicultura *f*.
sericulturist [-rist] *n* sericultor *m*, sericicultor *m* (who raises silkworms).
series ['siəriːz] *n* serie *f* || ELECTR *in series* en serie.
— OBSERV El plural de la palabra inglesa es *series*.
series-wound [-waund] *adj* arrollado en serie.
serigraphy [sə'rigrəfi] *n* serigrafía *f*.
serin ['serin] *n* canario *m* (bird).
seringa [si'riŋgə] *n* siringa *f* (rubber tree).
seriocomic ['siəriəu'kɔmik] *adj* tragicómico, ca; jocoserio, ria.
serious ['siəriəs] *adj* serio, ria; *a serious decision* una decisión seria; *a serious book* un libro serio; *a serious promise* una promesa seria || serio, ria; formal (earnest) || grave, serio, ria; *serious illness* enfermedad grave; *a serious situation* una situación grave; *a serious mistake* un grave error || grave, de gravedad (wound) || serio, ria; importante (damage, loss, etc.) || — *I am serious* estoy hablando en serio || *to make a serious attempt to* esforzarse realmente por.
seriously [-li] *adv* seriamente || seriamente, gravemente, de gravedad (ill, wounded) || en serio; *don't take things so seriously* no tome las cosas tan en serio.
serious-minded [-'maindid] *adj* serio, ria.
seriousness [-nis] *n* seriedad *f* || gravedad *f*, seriedad *f* (of illness, of situation, etc.) || *in all seriousness* en serio, con toda seriedad.
serjeant ['sɑːdʒənt] *n* ⟶ **sergeant**.
serjeant at arms [-ət'ɑːmz] *n* ujier *m*.
serjeant-at-law [-ət'lɔː] *n* JUR abogado *m*.
sermon ['səːmən] *n* REL & FIG sermón *m* || *the Sermon on the Mount* el Sermón de la Montaña.
sermonize ['səːmənaiz] *vt/vi* sermonear.
sermonizer [-ə*] *n* sermoneador, ra.
serology [siə'rɔlədʒi] *n* serología *f*.
serosity [si'rɔsiti] *n* serosidad *f*.
serotherapy [siərə'θerəpi] *n* MED sueroterapia *f*, seroterapia *f*.
serous ['siərəs] *adj* seroso, sa || ANAT *serous membrane* membrana serosa.
Serpens ['səːpenz] *pr n* ASTR Serpentario *m*.
serpent ['səːpənt] *n* ZOOL serpiente *f* || FIG víbora *f*, serpiente *f* (person) || buscapiés *m inv* (firework).
Serpentarium [ˌsəːpən'tɛəriəm] *pr n* ASTR Serpentario *m*.
— OBSERV El plural de *serpentarium* es *serpentariums* o *serpentaria*.
serpent charmer ['səːpənt'tʃɑːmə*] *n* encantador *m* de serpientes.
serpentine ['səːpəntain] *adj* serpentino, na || FIG sinuoso, sa (road) | viperino, na; pérfido, da (person).
◆ *n* MIN serpentina *f*.
serrate ['serit] *adj* BOT dentado, da; serrado, da || TECH dentado, da.
serrated [se'reitid] *adj* BOT dentado, da; serrado, da || serrato (muscle) || — *serrated edge* dientes *m pl* || *serrated suture* juntura *f* serrátil.
serration [se'reiʃən] *n* borde *m* dentado.
serratus [sə'rætəs] *n* ANAT serrato *m* (muscle).
— OBSERV El plural de *serratus* es *serrati*.
serried ['serid] *adj* apretado, da.
serum ['siərəm] *n* MED suero *m* || — *protective serum* suero inmunizador || *serum therapy* sueroterapia *f*, seroterapia *f* || *serum vaccination* vacuna *f* con suero.
— OBSERV El plural de *serum* es *serums* o *sera*.
serval ['səːvəl] *n* ZOOL gato *m* cerval.
servant ['səːvənt] *n* criado, da; sirviente, ta (domestic help, valet, maid, etc.) || empleado, da (in industry) || funcionario, ria (of a government); *public servant* funcionario público || servidor, ra (epistolary form); *your humble servant* su seguro servidor || — *civil servant* funcionario, ria || *servant of the Lord* siervo de Dios || *your servant, Sir!* ¡un servidor!
◆ *pl* servicio *m sing*, servidumbre *f sing*.
serve [səːv] *n* SP saque *m*, servicio *m* (in tennis); *to break the serve* romper el saque.
serve [səːv] *vt* servir; *to serve God, one's country* servir a Dios, a la patria; *to serve lunch* servir la comida; *to serve o.s. with soup* servir sopa a alguien; *fish served with tomato sauce* pescado servido con salsa de tomate || servir, estar al servicio de; *I served Lord Fotheringale for twenty years* serví a lord Fotheringale durante veinte años || ser útil, servir; *his old car served him very well* su antiguo coche le fue muy útil || despachar (in a shop); *to serve s.o. with a pound of butter* despachar a alguien una libra de mantequilla || atender; *are you being served?* ¿le atienden? || ejercer, desempeñar (a function); *he served an office* desempeñó un cargo || cumplir (an assignment) || ser suficiente, bastar; *this amount serves him for two months* esta cantidad le basta para dos meses || JUR entregar (a writ, a summons) | entregar a (to a person) | cumplir (a term of punishment); *to serve one's sentence* cumplir la sentencia || REL ayudar a (mass) || abastecer (to supply) || tratar; *fate served her badly* el destino le trató mal || ZOOL cubrir, montar (to mount the female) || MIL servir (a gun) || MAR forrar (a rope) || TECH ocuparse de, manejar (a machine) || — *if my memory serves me right* si la memoria no me falla, si mal no recuerdo || FAM *I'll serve him out!* ¡me las pagará! || *it serves you right!* ¡te está bien empleado!, ¡bien merecido lo tienes! || *it will serve you nothing to* no le servirá para nada || *localities served by a railway line* localidades por donde pasa una vía férrea *or* donde hay una vía férrea || *lunch is served, madam* la señora está servida || *to serve one's apprenticeship* hacer el aprendizaje || *to serve out* repartir (to distribute), servir (food) || SP *to serve the ball* hacer el saque, sacar, servir (in tennis) || *to serve the purpose* servir para el caso; *this example will serve the purpose* este ejemplo servirá para el caso || *to serve the purpose of* utilizarse como || *to serve up* servir.
◆ *vi* servir; *I served in the residence of Lord Fotheringale as a butler* serví en la casa de lord Fotheringale de mayordomo; *to serve in the army* servir en el ejército; *this cushion will serve* este cojín servirá; *this box will serve as a table* esta caja servirá de mesa; *to serve at the table* servir la mesa || SP sacar, hacer *or* tener el saque, servir (in tennis) || REL ayudar (at mass) || despachar (in a shop) || — *as occasion serves* cuando se presente la ocasión || *that serves to show that he is honest* eso demuestra que es honrado || *to serve as a waiter in a restaurant* ser camarero *or* servir de camarero en un restaurante || *to serve for* servir para || *to serve on the jury* ser miembro del jurado.
server [-ə*] *n* monaguillo *m*, acólito *m* (at mass) || SP saque *m* (in tennis) || cubierto *m* (utensil for salad, etc.) || pala *f* (for fish) || bandeja *f* (tray) || criado *m* (servant) || camarero *m* [AMER mozo *m*] (waiter) || INFORM servidor *m*.
service ['səːvis] *n* servicio *m*; *I was in the service of Lord Fotheringale* estuve al servicio de lord Fotheringale; *military service* servicio militar; *the service in this restaurant is bad* el servicio en este restaurante es malo; *after-sales service* servicio postventa; *bus service* servicio de autobuses; *public service* servicio público; *social service* servicio social; *repair service* servicio de reparaciones || MIL servicio *m* militar; *compulsory service* servicio militar obligatorio | servicio *m*; *he saw service on several fronts* prestó servicio en varios frentes; *active service* servicio activo || favor *m*, servicio *m*; *you have rendered me a great service* me has hecho un gran favor, me has prestado un gran servicio || utilidad *f*; *to be of great service* ser de gran utilidad || uso *m* (use) || REL oficio *m*, servicio *m* || JUR entrega *f* (of a writ, of a summons, etc.) || SP saque *m*, servicio *m* (in tennis); *to break the service* romper el saque || juego *m*, servicio *m*; *tea service* juego de té || vajilla *f* (crockery) || ZOOL cubrición *f*, monta *f* (mating) || BOT serbal *m* (tree) || MAR funda *f*, forro *m* (of gear) || revisión *f* (of a car, etc.) || — *at your service* a su disposición, a sus órdenes || *at your service, sir* para servirle, señor || *civil service* administración pública || *diplomatic service* cuerpo diplomático, diplomacia *f*, carrera diplomática || *how can I be of service to you?* ¿en qué puedo ayudarle? || *in service* en funcionamiento || *intelligence service* servicio de información || *National Health*

Service Seguridad *f* Social || *secret service* servicio secreto || MIL *the senior Service* la marina || *to be in the civil service* ser funcionario || *to be of service, to do service* ser útil, servir || MIL *to be on active service* estar en (servicio) activo || *to be out of service* no funcionar || *to bring into service* poner en servicio || *to come into service* empezar a utilizarse (machine), aplicarse (timetable) || MIL *to go into service* entrar a servir || FAM *to have seen long service* haberse utilizado mucho tiempo || *what good service this pen has done me!* ¡lo que me ha servido esta pluma!
◆ *pl* servicios *m*; *to dispense with s.o.'s services* prescindir de los servicios de alguien | servicios *m* (third sector of the economy) || *the three services* el ejército, la marina y la aviación, las fuerzas armadas.
◆ *adj* de servicio; *service staircase* escalera de servicio || MIL militar (military) | de diario (uniform) || — *service area* área *f* de servicio || REL *service book* misal *m* || *service brake* freno *m* de pedal || *service charge* servicio *m*; *service charge included* servicio incluido || *service families* familias *f* de militares || SP *service line* línea *f* de saque (in tennis) || MIL *service record* hoja *f* de servicios || *service road* vía *f* de acceso || *service station* estación *f* de servicio || MIL *service stripe* galón *m* de servicio || BOT *service tree* serbal *m* || *service workshop* taller *m* de reparaciones.

service ['sə:vis] *vt* mantener (to maintain) || revisar (to check); *to service a car* revisar un coche || atender a (to treat) || cubrir (a mare).

serviceability ['sə:visə'biliti] *n* utilidad *f*.

serviceable ['sə:visəbl] *adj* utilizable, servible (that can be used) || práctico, ca; útil (practical) || resistente, duradero, ra (lasting) || servicial (obliging).

serviceableness ['sə:visəblnis] *n* utilidad *f* (usefulness) || solidez *f*, resistencia *f* (of clothing) || solicitud *f* (of a person).

serviceman ['sə:vismən] *n* MIL militar *m* || TECH reparador *m*.
— OBSERV El plural de esta palabra es *servicemen*.

serviette [,sə:vi'et] *n* servilleta *f*.

servile ['sə:vail] *adj* servil.

servility [sə:'viliti] *n* servilismo *m*.

serving ['sə:viŋ] *n* servicio *m* (of a master) || CULIN porción *f* (helping) | servicio *m* (of a meal) || SP saque *m*, servicio *m* || JUR entrega *f* || MAR funda *f*, forro *m* || ZOOL cubrición *f*, monta *f* (mating).
◆ *adj* de servir.

Servite ['sə:vait] *n* REL servita *m*.

servitude ['sə:vitju:d] *n* servidumbre *f* || JUR *penal servitude* trabajos forzados.

servo brake ['sə:vəu'breik] *n* TECH servofreno *m*.

servo control ['sə:vəukən'trəul] *n* servomando *m*.

servomechanism ['sə:vəu,mekənizəm] *n* TECH servomecanismo *m*.

servomotor ['sə:vəu,məutə*] *n* servomotor *m*.

sesame ['sesəmi] *n* BOT sésamo *m*, ajonjolí *m*, alegría *f* || *open sesame!* ¡ábrete, sésamo!

sesamoid ['sesəmɔid] *adj* ANAT sesamoideo, a (bone, cartilage).
◆ *n* ANAT hueso *m* sesamoideo (bone) | cartílago *m* sesamoideo (cartilage).

sesquicentennial ['seskwisen,tenjəl] *adj* sesquicentenario, ria.
◆ *n* sesquicentenario *m*.

sesquioxide ['seskwi,ɔksaid] *n* CHEM sesquióxido *m*.

sesquipedalian ['seskwipi'deiljən] *adj* FIG larguísimo, ma; que no acaba nunca (word) | pesado, da (style).

session ['seʃən] *n* sesión *f* (meeting); *opening, plenary, closed session* sesión de apertura, plenaria, a puerta cerrada; *closing* o *final session* sesión de clausura || período *m* de sesiones, reunión *f* (series of meetings) || JUR audiencia *f* || CINEM sesión *f* || curso *m* académico (academic period) || *to be in session* celebrar una sesión (parliament, law court).

sessional [-l] *adj* de una sesión (in Parliament, court, cinema) || de fin de curso (exam).

sesterce ['sestə:s] *n* HIST sestercio *m* (ancient Roman coin).

sestet [ses'tet] *n* POET dos últimos tercetos *m pl* de un soneto || MUS sexteto *m*.

sestina [ses'ti:nə] *n* POET sextina *f*.

set [set] *adj* fijado, da; señalado, da (date, time) || establecido, da (form, manner); *a set practice* una práctica establecida || determinado, da; *a set intention* una intención determinada || inmóvil (immovable) || rígido, da (stiff) || firme (opinion) || fijo, ja; *set gaze* mirada fija; *set price* precio fijo || estable (weather) || cuajado, da (jelly, blancmange, etc.) || fraguado, da (cement) || montado, da; armado, da (a machine) || engastado, da (a jewel) || arraigado, da (habits) || preparado, da (prepared); *a set speech* un discurso preparado || estereotipado, da (stereotyped); *set smile* sonrisa estereotipada || dispuesto, ta; *set for trouble* dispuesto a la lucha || listo, ta; *set to go* listo para salir || campal (battle) || apretado, da (teeth) || — *everyone has his own set task* cada uno tiene un trabajo determinado || *set menu* menú *m* del día || *set phrase* frase hecha *or* estereotipada || *the set books* los libros que hay que estudiar durante el curso || *to be all set* estar completamente listo || *to be dead set against* estar resueltamente opuesto a || *to be set in one's ways* tener costumbres arraigadas || *to be set on* estar empeñado en; *she was set on being an actress* estaba empeñada en ser actriz || *to be set on an idea* aferrarse a una idea.
◆ *n* conjunto *m*; *a set of laws* un conjunto de leyes || serie *f*; *a set of measures* una serie de medidas || juego *m*; *tea set* juego de té || batería *f* (of kitchen implements) || tiro *m*, tronco *m* (of horses) || juego *m*, aderezo *m* (of jewelry) || colección *f* (of volumes, etc.); *a set of poems* una colección de poemas || juego *m*, surtido *m* (of buttons) || grupo *m* (group) || clase *f*; *ask any set of people* pregunte a cualquier clase de personas || pandilla *f* (of friends); *he is a member of Antonio's set* es un miembro de la pandilla de Antonio || banda *f* (of thieves) || círculo *m*; *we don't move in the same set* no pertenecemos al mismo círculo || camarilla *f* (political) || categoría *f* (of thinkers, of writers) || caída *f* (of clothes, of drapery) || marcado *m* (of hair) || forma *f*, porte *m*; *I recognized him by the set of his head* lo reconocí por su porte de cabeza || tendencia *f* (of opinion) || aparato *m* (radio, television) || TECH tren *m* (of wheels) | grupo *m*, equipo *m* (of turbines, etc.); *generating set* grupo electrógeno | dispositivo *m* (device) | estuche *m* (of tools) | entibado *m* (of a mine) | bastidor *m* (of timber) || SP set *m* (in tennis) || BOT esqueje *m* || MAR dirección *f* (of wind, of current) | juego *m* (of oars) || ARCH asiento *m* (of a beam) | alabeo *m* (under pressure) || puesta *f* (of sun) || PRINT ojo *m*, anchura *f* (of type) || puesta *f* (of eggs) || muestra *f* (of hunting dog) || CINEM plató *m* || THEATR decorado *m* || — *dinner set* servicio *m* de mesa, vajilla *f* || *on the set* en el escenario || INFORM *set of characters* juego *m* de caracteres || *set of false teeth* dentadura postiza || *set of features* fisonomía *f* || *set of furniture* muebles *m pl*, mobiliario *m* || *set of mind* manera *f* de ser, mentalidad *f* || *set of points* agujas *f pl*, cambio *m* de agujas || *set of teeth* dentadura *f* || *the smart set* la gente elegante || FIG *to make a dead set at* meterse con (to attack vigorously), intentar conquistar a (a woman).

set* [set] *vt* colocar, poner (to put) || poner; *to set sentries at the gate* poner centinelas en la entrada; *to set s.o. to work* poner a alguien a trabajar; *to set the table* poner la mesa; *to set an examination* poner un examen; *I set my alarm clock for 8 o'clock* puse el despertador para las ocho; *to set s.o. amongst the great writers* poner a alguien entre los grandes escritores || poner en hora (watch, clock); *I want to set my clock* quiero poner mi reloj en hora || fijar, señalar (date); *the time and date of the meeting have not yet been set* no se ha fijado todavía ni la hora ni la fecha de la reunión || fijar, señalar (colour, price, etc.) || dar, citar; *to set an example* dar un ejemplo || sentar (a precedent) || establecer (a record, a standard) || dar (to assign work); *he set me seven pages to do* me dio siete páginas para que las hiciese || señalar; *to set books for an exam* señalar libros para un examen | hacer (a question) || plantear (a problem) || imponer (a fashion) || cuajar (jelly, milk, etc.) || coagular (blood) || fraguar (cement) || marcar (hair) || situar; *to set a novel in Spain* situar una novela en España; *town set in the mountains* pueblo situado en las montañas || dirigir (to direct) || armar, preparar (a trap) || hacer; *the smoke set him coughing* el humo le hizo toser || MUS afinar (to tune) | poner; *Peter set words to the music I had composed* Pedro le puso la letra a la música que yo había compuesto; *Michael set the words to music* Miguel le puso música a la letra || afilar (a blade); *to set a razor* afilar una cuchilla de afeitar || MED reducir, encajar (a bone) | reducir (a fracture) || desarrollar; *too much exercises sets a boy's muscles prematurely* demasiado ejercicio desarrolla prematuramente los músculos de los chicos || THEATR & CINEM montar (scenery) || MAR desplegar (the sails) || CULIN dejar reposar (dough) || TECH ajustar (to adjust) | triscar (a saw) | engastar, montar (gem) || PRINT componer || poner a empollar (hen, eggs) || — FIG *he is setting his career on this interview* de esta entrevista depende su carrera || *set your mind at ease* tranquilícese || *to set a glass to one's lips* llevarse un vaso a la boca || *to set a match to, to set fire to* prenderle fuego a || *to set an engine going* poner un motor en marcha || *to set a price on s.o.'s head* poner precio a la cabeza de alguien || FIG *to set a trap* tender un lazo, poner una trampa || *to set a watch* poner un reloj en hora (time), poner guardia *or* centinela (a guard) || *to set eyes on* poner el ojo *or* los ojos en || *to set foot on* pisar || *to set free* liberar (a person), libertar (a slave), libertar, poner en libertad, liberar (a prisoner), soltar (a bird, etc.) || *to set great store by* valorar en mucho || *to set limits to* poner límites a || *to set one's hand to* firmar || *to set one's jaw* o *one's teeth* apretar los dientes || *to set on fire* prender fuego || *to set sail* hacerse a la vela || *to set s.o. a problem* poner a alguien un problema || *to set s.o.'s teeth on edge* darle dentera a uno || *to set the fashion* dictar la moda || *to set thinking* dar que pensar a.
◆ *vi* cuajarse (jelly) || coagularse (blood) || fraguarse (cement) || fijarse (colours) || ponerse fijo (eyes) || seguir con la misma expresión (face) || ponerse rígido (corpse) || empollar (fowl) || ponerse (moon, sun) || dirigirse (to go in a specified direction) || soplar (wind) || MED encajarse (a bone) || caer (clothes); *the jacket sets badly* la chaqueta cae mal || BOT formarse || mermar, declinar (reputation) || formarse (character) || estar completamente desarrollado (body) || parar (a hunting dog).
◆ *phr v* *to set about* ponerse a (to begin); *I must set about my packing* tengo que ponerme a hacer las maletas | emprender (to undertake) | difundir, propagar, propalar (to spread); *to set a rumour about* propagar un rumor | atacar (to attack) | *they set about each*

other at once en seguida llegaron a las manos || ***to set above*** o ***before*** anteponer; *he sets honour before glory* antepone el honor a la gloria || ***to set after*** seguir la pista de, perseguir (to pursue) | echar tras; *to set a dog after s.o.* echar un perro tras alguien || ***to set against*** enemistar con (to turn against); *he is trying to set you against me* está intentando enemistarte conmigo | comparar con; *to set advantages against disadvantages* comparar las ventajas con los inconvenientes | oponerse a; *public opinion is setting against the proposal* la opinión pública se opone a la propuesta || ***to set apart*** poner aparte, apartar; *to set the women apart from the men* apartar a las mujeres de los hombres | reservar (money, time) || ***to set aside*** apartar, poner aparte; *set the best apples aside* aparta las mejores manzanas | dejar de lado (to pay no attention to); *to set aside one's own feelings* dejar de lado sus sentimientos | desechar, rechazar (a claim) || ***to set at*** lanzar contra | *to set at liberty* poner en libertad || ***to set back*** detener, frenar (to halt progress) | retrasar (to delay); *this accident set me back three weeks* este accidente me ha retrasado tres semanas | atrasar (a watch, a clock) | FAM costar, salir por (to cost); *my car set me back six thousand dollars* mi coche me ha costado seis mil dólares | *house set back from the road* casa que no está al borde de la carretera | *house set back from the street* casa que no está alineada con las demás de una calle || ***to set by*** ahorrar (money) || ***to set down*** poner por escrito (to write down); *set down the main arguments* ponga por escrito los principales argumentos | apuntar; *set me down for ten pounds* apúnteme para diez libras | dejar *or* poner en el suelo (to lay down); *he set the parcel down* dejó el paquete en el suelo | dejar; *I'll set you down at your door* le dejaré en su casa | dejar bajar, dejar apearse; *the train stopped at the station to set down three passengers* el tren se detuvo en la estación para dejar bajar a tres viajeros | hacer aterrizar (a plane) | considerar, tomar por (to consider) | fijar, prever; *the meeting is set down for Tuesday* la reunión está prevista para el martes | establecer, fijar (to prescribe); *rules have been set down and must be obeyed* las reglas han sido establecidas para ser respetadas | *to set down to* atribuir a; *to set one's success down to hard work* atribuir su éxito a un trabajo intenso || ***to set forth*** enunciar | desarrollar (an argument) | exponer; *to set forth one's views* exponer sus opiniones | salir, ponerse en camino (to begin a journey) || ***to set forward*** adelantar | exponer (a theory) | salir (to start) || ***to set in*** engastar (a stone) | encajar (to insert) | empezar, llegar; *the rainy season has set in* la época de las lluvias ha empezado | cerrar (night) | levantarse (wind) | subir (tide) | montar (in dressmaking) | *it is setting in for a wet day* parece que va a llover | *this fashion is setting in* esto se está poniendo de moda || ***to set off*** ponerse en camino, salir (to begin a journey) | hacer resaltar, realzar, poner de relieve; *the red scarf sets off the dark jacket* el pañuelo rojo hace resaltar la chaqueta oscura | adornar, embellecer (to adorn) | volar (a mine) | hacer; *the joke set him off laughing* el chiste lo hizo reír | compensar (a debt, a loss) | *to set off running* salir corriendo | *to set s.o. off* hacer hablar a alguien || ***to set on*** atacar (to attack) | instigar contra (to provoke) | azuzar contra; *he set the dog on me* azuzó el perro contra mí | seguir adelante (to go on) || ***to set out*** ponerse en camino, salir (to begin a journey) | declarar (to state) | exponer, explicar; *he set out his reasons for his behaviour* expuso las razones por las cuales había actuado así | proponerse; *he set out to prove that Shakespeare was a woman* se propuso demostrar que Shakespeare era una mujer | disponer (to arrange) | exponer (to display); *to set out goods* exponer mercancías | adornar (to adorn) | presentar (one's work) | MAR bajar (tide) | PRINT espaciar | *to set out the table* poner la mesa || *to set out to do* empezar a hacer || ***to set over*** poner por encima de || ***to set to*** ponerse a trabajar | empezar a, ponerse a; *to set to work* empezar a trabajar | FAM pelearse || ***to set up*** establecerse; *to set up as a butcher* establecerse de carnicero | abrir, poner (a business) | levantar (a statue) | construir, edificar (a house) | instalar (an exhibition) | fundar, crear; *this school was set up in 1927* esta escuela fue creada en 1927 | crear, constituir; *to set up a committee* crear una comisión | colocar (a person) | TECH montar, armar (a piece of machinery) | establecer (a record) | instaurar, establecer (a government); *to set up a monarchy* instaurar una monarquía | planear, proyectar (to plan) | exponer (theory) | lanzar, dar, soltar, pegar (a yell) | convidar, invitar (to invite) | abastecer, proveer (to supply with) | provocar, causar (to be the cause of) | restablecer, reponer; *a fortnight in the country will set him up* unos quince días en el campo le restablecerán | PRINT componer | INFORM inicializar || — *to be set up for life* tener el porvenir asegurado | *to set up as a model* dar como ejemplo | *to set up for, to set o.s. up as* dárselas de, presumir de (to pretend to be); *although he's such an ignorant fellow he sets up for an expert* aunque sea tan ignorante se las da de experto || ***to set upon*** atacar; *to set upon the enemy* atacar al enemigo | emprender (a task) | instigar contra (to provoke).

— OBSERV Pret y pp ***set***.

setaceous [si'teiʃəs] *adj* cerdoso, sa.

setback ['setbæk] *n* revés *m* (misfortune); *he met with many setbacks* sufrió muchos reveses || contratiempo *m* (sth. which stops progress) || baja *f*, caída *f* (of prices) || regresión *f* (of trade) || MED recaída *f*.

setdown ['setdaun] *n* repulsa *f*.

set-in ['setin] *adj* empotrado, da.

setoff ['set'ɔf] *n* contrapeso *m* (sth. that counterbalances) || compensación *f* (of a debt) || contrapartida *f* (counterpart) || realce *m*, relieve *m* (bringing out) || ARCH saliente *m*.

seton ['si:tn] *n* MED sedal *m*.

setout [set'aut] *n* principio *m* (beginning) || salida *f* (departure) || preparativos *m pl* (preparations) || exposición *f*, presentación *f* (display).

set piece [setpi:s] *n* THEATR escena *f* de gran efecto dramático || MIL estrategia *f* || SP jugada *f* planeada de antemano.

setscrew ['set'skru:] *n* TECH tornillo *m* de fijación.

set square ['setskwɛə*] *n* cartabón *m*, escuadra *f*.

settee [se'ti:] *n* sofá *m*.

settee-bed [-bed] *n* sofá cama *m*.

setter ['setə*] *n* setter *m*, perro *m* de muestra (dog) || engastador, ra (of gems).

setting ['setiŋ] *n* colocación *f* || engaste *m*, montura *f* (of a gem) || puesta *f* (of sun) || FIG marco *m* (background) | escenario *m*, teatro *m*: *the setting of the battle* el escenario de la batalla | declinación *f*, disminución *f* (of fame) || escenario *m*, escena *f* (of a play, of a film) || MUS música *f*: *I prefer Handel's setting of the twenty third psalm to Haydn's* prefiero la música que Haendel ha puesto al salmo veintitrés a la de Haydn | arreglo *m* (arrangement) || puesta *f* (of eggs) || TECH ajuste *m* (of a machine) | afilado *m* (of a tool) | fraguado *m* (of cement) || PRINT composición *f* || MED reducción *f* (of bone, fracture).

◆ *adj* poniente (sun).

setting lotion [-'ləuʃən] *n* fijador *m* [para el pelo].

setting-up [-ʌp] *n* instalación *f* || establecimiento *m*: *setting-up of a new order* establecimiento de un nuevo régimen || creación *f*, fundación *f* (of an organization, institution, etc.) || construcción *f* (of a house) || PRINT composición *f*.

settle ['setl] *n* banco *m* (wooden seat).

settle ['setl] *vt* establecer, instalar (people) || colonizar, poblar (land, country) || estabilizar (to stabilize): *a good thunderstorm would settle the weather* una buena tempestad estabilizaría el tiempo || colocar (to put) || asentar (to put firmly) || colocar, establecer (one's children) || clarificar, dejar asentarse (a liquid) || hacer caer: *the rain settled the dust* la lluvia hizo caer el polvo || disipar (a doubt) || calmar (nerves) || arreglar (stomach) || fijar (date) || acordar, decidir (to agree on): *to settle to do sth.* acordar hacer algo || resolver, solucionar (problem): *to settle a question once and for all* resolver definitivamente una cuestión || resolver, arreglar, dirimir (a dispute) || arreglar: *to settle a matter amicably* arreglar una cuestión amistosamente || arbitrar (an arbitrator) || satisfacer (a claim) || terminar *or* acabar con (to put an end to) || saldar, liquidar (an account) || pagar (a debt) || JUR asignar (an annuity, an inheritance) || poner en orden, ordenar, arreglar (to put in order) || — FAM *I'll settle accounts with him!* ¡voy a ajustarle las cuentas! | *it's as good as settled* está prácticamente resuelto, está prácticamente en el bote (fam.) || *question not yet settled* cuestiones pendientes || *that settles it!* ¡eso resuelve el problema! (that solves the problem), ¡no hay más que hablar! (let's say no more about it) || *to settle an affair out of court* llegar a un arreglo amistoso sobre un asunto || *to settle o.s.* instalarse.

◆ *vi* posarse: *the bird settled on a branch* el pájaro se posó en una rama || domiciliarse, instalarse, establecerse: *to settle in London* domiciliarse en Londres || fijar la residencia, afincarse (to take up residence) || arrellanarse (in an armchair) || estabilizarse, serenarse (weather) || localizarse (a disease): *the inflammation settled on his lungs* la inflamación se localizó en los pulmones || depositarse, asentarse (sediment): *the dregs settled and the wine was clear* se depositaron las heces y el vino quedó claro || asentarse, clarificarse (liquid) || depositarse, caer: *the dust settled on everything* el polvo se depositó por todas partes || asentarse (building) || calmarse (excitement) || arreglarse, resolverse (business matters) || espesarse (fog) || caer, venir (the night) || cuajar (snow) || volver a la normalidad, normalizarse: *the situation has settled* la situación ha vuelto a la normalidad || pagar: *please settle as quickly as possible* haga el favor de pagar cuanto antes || MAR hundirse poco a poco (ship) || — *he can't settle down anywhere* no puede estarse quieto || *he can't settle to anything* no consigue decidirse por nada || *the wind is settling in the north* el viento sopla del norte || *to settle down* domiciliarse, establecerse, instalarse (to take up permanent residence), calmarse (to calm), sentar cabeza (to lead a more serious life), casarse (to get married), normalizarse, volver a la normalidad: *since the war things have settled down* desde la guerra las cosas se han normalizado; acostumbrarse: *he is settling down to his new job* se está acostumbrando a su nuevo trabajo || *to settle down to work* ponerse seriamente a trabajar || *to settle for* contentarse con || *to settle in* instalarse || *to settle on* o *upon* decidirse por, escoger (to choose), ponerse de acuerdo sobre: *they settled on the terms of the treaty* se pusieron de acuerdo sobre los términos del tratado || *to settle o.s. down in an armchair* arrellanarse en un sillón || *to settle to work* ponerse seriamente a trabajar || *to settle up* ajustar cuentas, saldar cuentas (to adjust accounts).

settlement [-mənt] **; settling** [-iŋ] *n* establecimiento *m* (of people) || colonización *f*, población *f* (of land, of country) || colonia *f* (colony) || poblado *m*, pueblo *m* (little village) || acuerdo *m* (agreement): *the terms of the settlement are quite just* los términos del acuerdo son completamente justos || arreglo *m* (of an argument): *a friendly settlement* un arreglo amistoso || solución *f* (of a problem) || liquidación *f* (of an account) || pago *m* (of a debt) || asentamiento *m*, hundimiento *m* (of a building) || JUR pensión *f*, renta *f* (pension) | dote *f* (dowry) | asignación *f* (of an annuity, an endowment) | domicilio *m* (residence) || — *act of settlement* ley *f* de sucesión al trono (in England) || *marriage settlement* capitulaciones *f pl* || *penal settlement* penal *m*.

settler [-ə*] *n* colonizador, ra; colono *m*, poblador, ra.

settling [-iŋ] *n* ⟶ **settlement.**

set-to ['set'tu:] *n* FAM lucha *f*, refriega *f* (fight) | agarrada *f* (verbal) || SP asalto *m* (in fencing).

setup ['setʌp] *n* porte *m* (of the body) || organización *f* || disposición *f* (of the parts of a machine) || plan *m*, proyecto *m* (plan) || situación *f* || FAM combate *m* amañado.

seven ['sevn] *adj* siete || — *the seven deadly sins* los siete pecados capitales || *the seven wise men* los siete sabios de Grecia.
◆ *n* siete *m* (number, card) || *it's seven o'clock* son las siete.

sevenfold [-fəuld] *adj* séptuplo, pla.
◆ *adv* siete veces.

seven hundred [-'hʌndrəd] *n* setecientos *m*.

seven hundredth [-'hʌndrədθ] *adj/n* septingentésimo, ma.

seventeen [-ti:n] *adj* diecisiete, diez y siete.
◆ *n* diecisiete *m*, diez y siete *m*.

seventeenth [-ti:nθ] *adj* decimoséptimo, ma || *the seventeenth century* el siglo diecisiete.
◆ *n* decimoséptimo, ma; diecisiete *m* & *f*, diez y siete *m* & *f* (in a series) || diecisieteava parte *f*, decimoséptima parte *f*, diecisieteavo *m* (fraction) || día *m* diecisiete, diecisiete *m* (day of month) || diecisiete, diez y siete: *John XVII* (the seventeenth) Juan XVII [diecisiete].

seventh [-θ] *adj* séptimo, ma || en séptima posición: *he came seventh* llegó en séptima posición || — *seventh century* siglo *m* siete || FIG *seventh heaven* séptimo cielo.
◆ *n* séptimo, ma (person or thing in seventh position) || séptima parte *f* (fraction) || MUS séptima *f* (interval) || día *m* siete, siete *m* (day of month) || *Charles VII* (the Seventh) Carlos VII [Séptimo].

seventieth [-iəθ] *adj* septuagésimo, ma.
◆ *n* septuagésimo, ma; setenta *m* & *f* (in seventieth position) || setentavo *m*, septuagésima parte *f* (one of seventy parts).

seventy [-ti] *adj* setenta.
◆ *n* setenta *m* (number) || *the seventies* los años setenta (years), los setenta grados (temperature), los setenta (age).

seventy-one [-ti'wʌn] *adj* setenta y uno.
◆ *n* setenta y uno *m* (number).

seventy-two [-ti'tu:] *adj* setenta y dos.
◆ *n* setenta y dos *m* (number).

sever ['sevə*] *vt* cortar: *to sever a rope with a knife* cortar una cuerda con un cuchillo || separar (*from* de) || FIG romper (connections, etc.): *to sever a friendship* romper una amistad.
◆ *vi* romperse (things) || separarse (persons).

several ['sevrəl] *adj* varios, rias: *I have seen him several times* lo he visto varias veces; *he and several others* él y varios más || distinto, ta: *the several members of the committee* los distintos miembros de la comisión || respectivo, va: *our several rights* nuestros derechos respectivos || JUR individual || — JUR *joint and several bond* obligación solidaria || *they went their several ways* cada uno se fue por su lado.
◆ *pron* varios, rias: *several were in the garden* varios estaban en el jardín; *several of the team were absent* faltaban varios del equipo.

severally [-i] *adj* separadamente, individualmente, por separado (one by one) || respectivamente.

severalty [-ti] *n* JUR propiedad *f* individual || *in severalty* en propiedad exclusiva.

severance ['sevərəns] *n* división *f* (division in two parts) || separación *f* (breaking away from main body) || interrupción *f* (of communications) | FIG ruptura *f* (of relations) || *severance pay* indemnización *f* por despido.

severe [si'viə*] *adj* severo, ra: *a severe critic* un crítico severo; *a severe punishment* un castigo severo; *he is very severe with his children* es muy severo con sus hijos || duro, ra; fuerte (blow) || riguroso, sa: *to take severe measures* tomar medidas rigurosas || fuerte, severo, ra (reprimand) || grave, serio, ria; grande (loss) || violento, ta (fight) || intenso, sa (bombardment) || duro, ra: *a severe trial* una dura prueba || austero, ra; severo, ra: *severe architecture* arquitectura austera || duro, ra; riguroso, sa (climate) || intenso, sa (heat) || MED grave, serio, ria (illness) | agudo, da (pain) || minucioso, sa; serio, ria: *my car will have to undergo a severe test* habrá que someter mi coche a una revisión minuciosa || *to be severe on* tratar con severidad, tratar severamente.

severely [-li] *adv* severamente, con severidad || MED de gravedad (ill, wounded) || austeramente (built) || — *he has suffered severely* ha sufrido mucho || *severely plain* muy austero, de lo más austero || *to leave severely alone* dejar completamente de lado.

severity [si'veriti] *n* severidad *f* (of character, of punishment) || rigor *m* (of climate) || dificultad *f* (of an ordeal) || gravedad *f*, importancia *f* (of a loss) || austeridad *f*, severidad *f* (of style) || MED gravedad *f*, seriedad *f* (of an illness) | agudeza *f* (of a pain).

Seville [sə'vil] *pr n* GEOGR Sevilla.

Sevilian [-jən] *adj/n* sevillano, na.

sew* [səu] *vt/vi* coser: *I make my living by sewing* me gano la vida cosiendo || MED coser || encuadernar, coser (in bookbinding) || — *to sew on* coser; *to sew a button on* coser un botón || *to sew up* coser, remendar (a tear), cerrar con una costura (tear, wound, etc.), monopolizar (to monopolize), arreglar (to settle).
— OBSERV Pret ***sewed***; pp ***sewn, sewed***.

sewage ['sju:idʒ] *n* aguas *f pl* residuales || — *sewage disposal* depuración *f* de las aguas residuales || *sewage farm* huerta abonada con aguas residuales || *sewage system* alcantarillado *m*.

sewer ['sjuə*] *n* alcantarilla *f*, cloaca *f*, albañal *m* || FIG cloaca *f* || — *main sewer* colector *m* || *sewer gas* gas mefítico || *sewer man* alcantarillero *m* || *sewer rat* rata *f* de alcantarilla.

sewerage ['sjuəridʒ] *n* alcantarillado *m* (system) || aguas *f pl* residuales (sewage).

sewing ['səuiŋ] *n* costura *f* || encuadernación *f* (in bookbinding).
◆ *adj* de coser: *sewing machine* máquina de coser || *sewing basket* cesto *m* de la costura.

sewn [səun] *pp* ⟶ **sew.**

sex [seks] *n* sexo *m* || — *fair sex* bello sexo || *gentle* o *weaker sex* sexo débil || *stronger sex* sexo fuerte || *to have sex with* tener relaciones sexuales con.
◆ *adj* sexual: *sex education* educación sexual; *sex life* vida sexual; *sex organs* órganos sexuales.

sex [seks] *vt* determinar el sexo de.

sexagenarian [,seksədʒi'nɛəriən] *adj/n* sexagenario, ria.

Sexagesima [,seksə'dʒesimə] *n* REL sexagésima *f*.

sexagesimal [-l] *adj* sexagesimal.

sex appeal ['seksə,pi:l] *n* atractivo *m* sexual, «sex appeal» *m*.

sexed [sekst] *adj* sexuado, da || FAM *to be highly sexed* tener mucho temperamento.

sexiness ['seksinis] *n* FAM atractivo *m* sexual.

sexless ['sekslis] *adj* asexuado, da; asexual || FAM sin atractivo.

sex-linked ['seks'liŋkt] *adj* ligado al sexo.

sex object ['seks,ɔbdʒekt] *n* hombre *m or* mujer *f* objeto.

sexologist [seks'ɔlədʒist] *n* sexólogo *m*.

sexology [seks'ɔlədʒi] *n* sexología *f*.

sex shop ['seksʃɔp] *n* sex shop *m*.

sext [sekst] *n* REL Sexta *f*.

sextant ['sekstənt] *n* MAR sextante *m*.

sextet or **sextette** [seks tet] *n* MUS sexteto *m* (musical composition, group).

sextodecimo ['sekstəu'desiməu] *adj* PRINT en dieciseisavo.
◆ *n* PRINT libro *m* en dieciseisavo, tamaño *m* en dieciseisavo.

sexton ['sekstən] *n* REL sacristán *m* || FAM sepulturero *m* (gravedigger).

sextuple ['sekstjupl] *adj* séxtuplo, pla.
◆ *n* séxtuplo *m*.

sextuplet [-et] *n* seisillo *m*, sextillo *m*.

sexual ['seksjuəl] *adj* sexual || — *sexual intercourse* relaciones *f pl* sexuales || *sexual organs* órganos *m* genitales *or* sexuales.

sexuality [,seksju'æliti] *n* sexualidad *f* || vida *f* sexual.

sexy ['seksi] *adj* atractivo, va (woman) || erótico, ca; verde (film, book, etc.) || provocativo, va (dress).

Seychelles (the) Seychelles (islas).

sh [ʃ] *interj* ¡chitón!

shabbiness ['ʃæbinis] *n* aspecto *m* andrajoso *or* desharrapado (of a person) || lo raído (of clothing) || pobreza *f*, aspecto *m* lastimoso (of furniture, of house, of district) || mezquindad *f* (of behaviour).

shabby ['ʃæbi] *adj* andrajoso, sa; desharrapado, da (poorly dressed) || raído, da (clothing) || lamentable, de aspecto lastimoso, pobre (furniture, house, district) || mezquino, na (behaviour) || *to play a shabby trick* hacer una mala jugada.

shabby-looking [-'lukiŋ] *adj* de aspecto lastimoso.

shack [ʃæk] *n* choza *f*.

schack [ʃæk] *vi* US FAM *to shack up with* vivir con, juntarse con.

shackle [-l] *n* argolla *f* (of a chain).
◆ *pl* grilletes *m*, grillos *m* (for prisoners) || trabas *f* (for animals) || FIG trabas *f* (hindrance).

shackle [-l] *vt* poner grilletes a (a prisoner) || poner trabas a (animals) || FIG atar, poner trabas a (to restrict the freedom of).

shad [ʃæd] *n* sábalo *m* (fish).

shaddock ['ʃædɔk] *n* pomelo *m* (fruit).

shade [ʃeid] *n* sombra *f*: *he was sitting in the shade* estaba sentado a la sombra; *light and shade* luz y sombra; *temperature in the shade* temperatura a la sombra; *to give shade* dar sombra || visera *f* (eye-shade) || pantalla *f*

(lampshade) || persiana *f* (window blind) || fanal *m* de cristal (for clocks) || tono *m*, matiz *m*: *a different shade of pink* un tono diferente de rosa || tono *m*: *I don't like the shade of this dress* no me gusta el tono de este traje || matiz *m* (of a meaning, an opinion) || tendencia *f*: *newspapers of every shade* periódicos de todas las tendencias || FIG poquito *m*, pizca *f*: *he is a shade better* está un poquito mejor | fantasma *m*, sombra *f* (ghost) || — ARTS *light and shade* claroscuro *m* (of a painting) || FAM *of every shade and hue* de toda calaña, de todas clases || FIG *to put s.o. o sth. in the shade* hacer sombra a alguien *or* a algo, eclipsar a alguien *or* algo.
◆ *pl* sombras *f*: *the shades of the evening* las sombras del crepúsculo || tinieblas *f* (of night) || MYTH averno *m sing* || FIG *shades of Wagner!* ¿qué diría Wagner si lo oyera?

shade [ʃeid] *vt* dar sombra a: *trees that shade the house* árboles que dan sombra a la casa || proteger contra el sol, resguardar: *a hat that shades one's eyes* un sombrero que protege los ojos contra el sol || tamizar (light) || poner una pantalla a (lamp) || ARTS sombrear || COMM reducir progresivamente (prices) || FIG matizar (a meaning) | entristecer (face) || *to shade off* degradar.
◆ *vi* oscurecerse || *to shade into* o *to shade off into* fundirse en.

shadeless [-lis] *adj* sin sombra.

shadiness [ˈʃeidinis] *n* sombra *f* || FAM lo turbio, aspecto *m* turbio (of a deal) | honradez *f* dudosa (of a person).

shading [ˈʃeidiŋ] *n* protección *f* contra la luz *or* contra el sol || sombra *f* (shadow) || ARTS degradación *f* (colours) | sombreado *m* (of a drawing).

shadow [ˈʃædəu] *n* sombra *f*: *I could see your shadow on the wall* veía su sombra en la pared; *he was sitting in the shadow* estaba sentado a la sombra; *he is only a shadow of his former self* es sólo una sombra de lo que fue; *not a shadow of doubt* ni sombra de duda; *that friend is your shadow* ese amigo es tu sombra || oscuridad *f* (darkness) || FIG policía *m* (policeman) || sombra *f*, fantasma *m* (ghost) || sombreado *m*, sombra *f* (of a drawing) || sombreador *m* (for eyelids) || sombra *f* (in television) || poquito *m*, pizca *f* (a little) || — MATH *cast shadow* sombra proyectada || FIG *not to even trust one's own shadow* desconfiar hasta de su sombra, no fiarse ni de su sombra || *shadow play* o *theatre* sombras chinescas || FIG *to be afraid even of one's own shadow* tener miedo hasta de su sombra | *to be under the shadow of misfortune* tener muchas desgracias || *to cast a shadow* hacer sombra || FIG *to cast a shadow over the festivities* aguar la fiesta | *to run after a shadow* soñar con quimeras | *to wear o.s. to a shadow* agotarse.
◆ *pl* oscuridad *f* || *to have shadows under the eyes* tener ojeras.

shadow [ˈʃædəu] *vt* sombrear (to throw into shadow) || oscurecer (to darken) || FIG seguir (la pista a) (a follow in secret): *the spy was shadowed by detectives* el espía era seguido por detectives || *to shadow forth* anunciar.

shadowbox [-bɔks] *vi* SP entrenarse con un adversario imaginario (in boxing).

shadow cabinet [-ˈkæbinit] *n* gabinete *m* fantasma.

shadowy [ˈʃædəui] *adj* oscuro, ra (dark) || sombrío, a (a place) || sombreado, da (shaded) || FIG quimérico, ca (dream) | vago, ga; indistinto, ta (outline) | vago, ga (plan) | oscuro, ra (mysterious).

shady [ˈʃeidi] *adj* sombreado, da: *a shady place* un sitio sombreado || que da sombra (tree) || FAM turbio, bia (dealings): *there is sth. shady in the business* hay algo turbio en el asunto | dudoso, sa; sospechoso, sa (person): *shady character* persona dudosa || FIG *to be on the shady side of fifty* tener más de cincuenta años.

shaft [ʃɑːft] *n* mango *m* (handle) || flecha *f* (arrow) || asta *f* (of a lance) || TECH árbol *m*, eje *m* (for transmitting motion): *driving shaft* árbol motor | varal *m* (of carriage) || ARCH hueco *m*, caja *f* (of a lift) | fuste *m*, caña *f* (of a column) | aguja *f* (of a tower) || pozo *m* (of mines, wells, etc.): *ventilation shaft* pozo de ventilación || conducto *m* (duct) || ANAT caña *f* (of bone) || ZOOL cañón *m* (of feather) || BOT tallo *m* (of plants) || rayo *m* (of light, of lightning) || FIG pullazo *m*, pulla *f* (remark) || FIG *Cupid's shafts* flechas de Cupido.

shag [ʃæg] *n* cormorán *m* moñudo (bird) || picadura *f* (tobacco) || greñas *f pl* (hair) || pelusa *f* (of textiles) || borra *f* (of wool).

shagginess [ˈʃæginis] *n* aspecto *m* desgreñado (of hair) || *the shagginess of his beard* su barba enmarañada.

shaggy [ˈʃægi] *adj* peludo, da (with long hair) || desgreñado, da (hair) || enmarañado, da (beard, eyebrows) || lanudo, da (with long wool) || con pelusa (textiles) || BOT cubierto de maleza (field) | tupido, da (hedge) | velludo, da; velloso, sa (leaf) || FAM *shaggy dog story* chiste largo y pesado.

shagreen [ʃæˈgriːn] *n* zapa *f*.

shah [ʃɑː] *n* sha *m*, chah *m*, cha *m*.

shake [ʃeik] *n* sacudida *f* (a shaking or being shaken) || temblor *m*, estremecimiento *m* (tremble) || movimiento *m*, meneo *m* (of the head) || apretón *m* de manos (of hands) || grieta *f* (crack) || FAM batido *m* (milkshake) || MUS trino *m* (trill) || — FAM *in two shakes* en un momento, en un periquete, en un dos por tres || *shake of hands* apretón *m* de manos || *to be all of a shake* estar todo tembloroso, estar temblequeando || FIG *to be no great shakes* no valer gran cosa || *to give sth. a good shake* sacudir bien algo || FIG *to have the shakes* temblar como un azogado (of fear), tener escalofríos (of fever) || *with a shake in his voice* con la voz temblorosa.

shake* [ʃeik] *vt* sacudir (to agitate): *to shake a carpet* sacudir una alfombra || agitar (bottle) || hacer temblar (a table, etc.) || esgrimir (to brandish) || mover, menear (head) || zarandear, sacudir (s.o.) || mover (dice) || FIG hacer vacilar (s.o.'s faith, courage, etc.) | librarse de (a habit) | conmocionar, trastornar (to upset) | desconcertar (to disconcert) | mermar, hacer mella en (s.o.'s reputation) | quebrantar (health) | estremecer: *new ideas which shake the foundations of society* nuevas ideas que estremecen los cimientos de la sociedad || — FIG & FAM *to shake a leg* darse prisa, volar (to hurry up), mover el esqueleto, bailar (to dance) || *to shake hands* darse la mano, estrecharse la mano || *to shake hands with* dar la mano a, estrechar la mano a || *to shake one's finger at* decir que no con el dedo a || *to shake one's head* negar con la cabeza (in dissent), dar muestras de desaprobación (disapproval).
◆ *vi* temblar (to tremble, to quiver): *the earth was shaking* la tierra estaba temblando; *he was shaking with cold* estaba temblando de frío || vibrar (to vibrate) || agitarse, moverse, menearse (to move rapidly) || MUS trinar || — US FAM *shake!* ¡enhorabuena! (congratulations), ¡chócala! (to seal bargain) || FIG *to shake like a leaf* temblar como un azogado || *to shake with* temblar de, estremecerse de (fear), tiritar de, temblar de (cold) || *to shake with laughter* desternillarse de risa.
◆ *phr v* *to shake down* hacer caer sacudiendo: *to shake fruit down from a tree* hacer caer las frutas sacudiendo un árbol | esparcir (straw) | echar en el suelo (blanket) | acostarse (to lie down) | acostumbrarse (to become accustomed) | instalarse (to settle down) | US FAM sacar dinero a || *to shake off* deshacerse de, quitarse de encima, librarse de: *to shake off a bad habit* librarse de una mala costumbre || — FIG *to shake off the yoke* sacudir el yugo || *to shake out* sacudir | desplegar (flag, sail) || *to shake up* agitar, mover: *to shake up a bottle* agitar una botella | sacudir (a pillow, etc.) | conmocionar, trastornar (to shock) | estimular (to stimulate) | reorganizar (to reorganize).
— OBSERV Pret ***shook***; pp ***shaken***.

shakedown [-ˈdaun] *n* FAM cama *f* improvisada (bed) || US FAM exacción *f* de dinero (by a racketeer).

shaken [-ən] *pp* ⟶ **shake.**

shaker [-ə*] *n* criba *f* vibradora (sieve) || — *cocktail shaker* coctelera *f* || REL *the Shakers* los cuáqueros *m*, los tembladores *m*.

Shakespearean or **Shakespearian** [ʃeiksˈpiəriən] *adj* shakesperiano, na.

shake-up [ˈʃeikˈʌp] *n* reorganización *f* (reorganization): *government shake-up* reorganización ministerial || sacudida *f* (shake).

shakily [ˈʃeikili] *adv* con voz temblorosa (speaking) || con paso inseguro (walking) || con mano temblorosa (writing) || de modo poco estable (built).

shakiness [ˈʃeikinis] *n* inestabilidad *f* (unsteadiness) || temblor *m* (of the hand) || debilidad *f* (of health).

shaking [ˈʃeikiŋ] *adj* tembloroso, sa: *shaking voice* voz temblorosa || desconcertante (disconcerting) || que conmociona (upsetting).
◆ *n* sacudida *f*.

shako [ˈʃækəu] *n* MIL chacó *m*.

shaky [ˈʃeiki] *adj* inestable (situation, etc.): *a shaky table* una mesa inestable || tembloroso, sa (hand, voice) || temblón, ona (handwriting) || vacilante, inseguro, ra (step) || delicado, da (health) || cortado, da (style) || sin ilación (speech) || tambaleante (building) || poco sólido, da: *a shaky argument* un argumento poco sólido || — *he got off to a shaky start* tuvo un comienzo incierto || *his English is shaky* no domina el inglés, no tiene conocimientos muy seguros en inglés || *to be shaky on one's legs* tener las piernas poco firmes.

shale [ʃeil] *n* GEOL esquisto *m* || *shale oil* aceite *m* de esquisto bituminoso.

shall [ʃæl] *v aux* se usa para expresar el futuro de indicativo [primera persona del singular y del plural]: *I shall go tomorrow* iré mañana; *shall we be back in time?* ¿estaremos de vuelta a tiempo?; *he said I was not to go but I certainly shall* dijo que yo no iba a ir pero seguramente iré || se utiliza para expresar una promesa, una amenaza, una intención o una obligación [segundas y terceras personas]: *they shall be set free* serán liberados; *he should not have gone if I could have stopped him* no se hubiera ido si hubiese podido impedírselo; *you say you will not do it, but I say you shall (do it)* usted dice que no lo hará pero yo digo que usted lo va a hacer || expresa el deber, un mandato o una obligación [todas las personas]: *shall I close the door?* ¿cierro la puerta?; *you should have been more careful* tenía que haber sido más prudente || equivale al subjuntivo [todas las personas]: *I'm anxious that it shall be done at once* deseo que se haga en seguida; *it is surprising that he should be so foolish* es extraño que sea tan estúpido || *let's go, shall we?* vamos, ¿os parece?
— OBSERV El verbo auxiliar *shall* puede contraerse cuando le antecede un pronombre personal *(I'll, you'll, he'll, we'll, they'll)*. Si va seguido por la negación *not* puede formar con ella la palabra *shan't*: *you shan't do it* no lo hará; *shan't I go?* ¿no puedo ir?

— OBSERV El pretérito de *shall* es *should*. *Should* se emplea también para expresar la probabilidad: *they should be there by now* ya deben de estar allí.

shallop [-əp] *n* MAR chalupa *f*.

shallot [ʃə'lɔt] *n* BOT chalote *m*.

shallow ['ʃæləu] *adj* poco profundo, da: *shallow water* agua poco profunda || llano, na: *a shallow plate* un plato llano || AGR superficial (soil) || MAR poco, ca (ship's draught) || FIG superficial (person, knowledge, etc.).
◆ *pl n* MAR bajío *m sing*, bajos *m*.

shallow-minded [-'maindid] *adj* superficial.

shallowness ['ʃæləunis] *n* poca profundidad *f* (of water) || FIG superficialidad *f* (of knowledge, etc.).

shalt [ʃælt] *2nd pers. sing. of shall* (ant) *thou shalt not steal* no robarás.

shaly ['ʃeili] *adj* esquistoso, sa.

sham [ʃæm] *adj* fingido, da; simulado, da: *a sham illness* una enfermedad fingida || de imitación, de bisutería (jewelry) || falso, sa (title, knowledge) || COMM ficticio, cia (dividend) || adulterado, da (food) || MIL *a sham battle* un simulacro de combate.
◆ *n* impostor, ra (person) || impostura *f*, engaño *m*, farsa *f* (thing, act) || joya *f* de imitación, bisutería *f* (jewelry).

sham [ʃæm] *vt* fingir, simular: *he shams illness* simula que está enfermo.
◆ *vi* fingir, fingirse, simular: *to sham dead* fingirse muerto; *he is not ill, he is not shamming* no está enfermo, sólo está simulando.

shamble ['ʃæmbl] *vi* andar arrastrando los pies.

shambles [-z] *n* matadero *m* (slaughterhouse) || FIG ruinas *f pl* (great destruction) | carnicería *f*, matanza *f* (carnage) | follón *m* (extreme disorder) | confusión *f*.

shame [ʃeim] *n* vergüenza *f*: *the shame of having to admit defeat* la vergüenza de tener que admitir la derrota; *to flush with shame* ruborizarse de vergüenza; *you are a shame to your country* eres una vergüenza para tu país; *red with shame* colorado de vergüenza || deshonra *f* (dishonour) || FAM pena *f*, lástima *f*: *it's a shame the rain spoiled our holidays* es una lástima que la lluvia nos haya estropeado las vacaciones; *what a shame!* ¡qué lástima! || — *for shame!* ¡qué vergüenza! || *shame on you!* ¡qué vergüenza! || *to be without shame, to be lost to all sense of shame* no tener vergüenza alguna || *to bring shame upon s.o.* deshonrar a alguien || *to cry shame* poner el grito en el cielo || *to feel shame at having done sth.* avergonzarse de haber hecho algo || *to my shame* con gran vergüenza mía || *to put to shame* avergonzar.

shame [ʃeim] *vt* avergonzar (to cause to feel shame) || deshonrar (to bring shame upon) || *to shame s.o. into doing sth.* avergonzar a alguien de tal manera que se sienta obligado a hacer algo.

shamefaced [-feist] *adj* avergonzado, da (showing shame) || vergonzoso, sa; tímido, da (shy).

shamefacedly [-fesitli] *adv* con vergüenza.

shamefacedness [-feistnis] *n* vergüenza *f* (shame) || vergüenza *f*, timidez *f* (shyness).

shameful [-ful] *adj* vergonzoso, sa: *shameful behaviour* comportamiento vergonzoso || *how shameful!* ¡qué vergüenza!, ¡es vergonzoso!

shamefully [-fuli] *adv* vergonzosamente.

shamefulness [-fulnis] *n* vergüenza *f*.

shameless [-lis] *adj* desvergonzado, da; descarado, da (behaviour) || sinvergüenza, descarado, da; desvergonzado, da (person) || vergonzoso, sa (action).

shamelessness [-lisnis] *n* desvergüenza *f*, falta *f* de vergüenza, descaro *m*.

shammer ['ʃæmə*] *n* impostor, ra; simulador, ra.

shammy ['ʃæmi] *n* gamuza *f* (chamois).

shampoo [ʃæm'pu:] *n* champú *m* || *to give s.o. a shampoo* lavar la cabeza a alguien, dar un champú a alguien.

shampoo [ʃæm'pu:] *vt* dar un champú a, lavar la cabeza a (person) || lavar (hair).

shamrock ['ʃæmrɔk] *n* BOT trébol *m*.

shandy ['ʃændi] or **shandygaff** [-gæf] *n* cerveza *f* con gaseosa.

shanghai ['ʃæŋ'hai] *vt* emborrachar *or* drogar (a alguien) para llevarlo como marinero.

Shanghai ['ʃæŋ'hai] *pr n* GEOGR Shangai.

Shangri-la ['ʃæŋgri'la:] *n* Jauja *f*, tierra *f* de Jauja.

shank [ʃæŋk] *n* ANAT pierna *f* (leg) | espinilla *f* (part of leg) || caña *f* (of a horse) || CULIN pierna *f* || TECH mango *m* (of a tool) | pierna *f* (of scissors, pliers) | tija *f* (of a key, of a pin) || MAR caña *f* (of an anchor) || BOT peciolo *m* (of a leaf) | rabillo *m* (of flowers) | tallo *m* (of a plant) || ARCH fuste *m*, caña *f* || PRINT cuerpo *m* || FIG & FAM *to ride Shanks' mare* o *on Shanks' pony* ir en el coche de San Fernando.

shank [ʃæŋk] *vi* BOT *to shank off* caerse (fruit), pudrirse por el tallo (plant).

shan't [ʃa:nt] contracción de «shall not».

shantung [ʃæn'tʌŋ] *n* shantung *m*.

shanty ['ʃænti] *n* MUS saloma *f* (sailor's song) || chabola *f* (poor dwelling).

shantytown [-taun] *n* barrio *m* de las latas [*AMER* villa *f* miseria].

shape [ʃeip] *n* forma *f*; *what shape is his hat?* ¿de qué forma es su sombrero? || figura *f* (figure) || aspecto *m*, apariencia *f* (aspect) || tipo *m*; *what shape was the man you saw?* ¿qué tipo tenía el hombre que viste? || silueta *f*, bulto *m*; *two shapes came up to me in the darkness* dos siluetas vinieron hacia mí en la oscuridad || aparición *f* (ghost) || condición *f*, estado *m*; *my business is in bad shape* mis negocios están en mal estado || SP forma *f*; *this athlete is in bad shape* este atleta está en baja forma; *he kept in shape* se mantuvo en forma || CULIN molde *m* || horma *f* (for hats) || hechura *f*, corte *m* (of a garment) || TECH perfil *m* (of iron) || — FIG *an enemy in the shape of a friend* un enemigo que se las da de amigo *or* que finge ser amigo || *in shape* en orden, arreglado, da || *in the shape of* en forma de || *out of shape* deformado, da || *something in the shape of* una especie de || *to get into shape* ordenar, poner en orden || *to lick into shape* pulir, poner a punto (an article), formar; *travel licks a young man into shape* los viajes forman a los jóvenes; pulir, desbastar (an uncouth person) || *to put an idea into shape* dar forma a una idea || *to put into shape* arreglar, preparar, poner a punto || *to put out of shape* deformar || *to take shape* tomar forma, concretarse; *our plans are taking shape* nuestros proyectos se están concretando || *you are in no shape to go on* no estás en condiciones de continuar.

shape [ʃeip] *vt* dar forma a; *to shape the rock into a statue* dar a la piedra la forma de una estatua || labrar, tallar; *to shape a statue out of stone* labrar una estatua en piedra || tallar (wood) || modelar (clay) || cortar; *to shape a coat* cortar un abrigo || formar; *to shape s.o.'s character* formar el carácter de alguien || determinar; *to shape the destiny of men* determinar el destino de los hombres || amoldar, conformar, ajustar; *to shape one's life to certain principles* ajustar su vida a ciertos principios || concebir (an idea, a plan) || formular (an idea) || construir (an essay) || — *to shape one's course towards* dirigirse hacia || MAR *to shape the course* determinar el rumbo.
◆ *vi* tomar forma, formarse (to acquire a particular shape) || formarse; *clouds shaping on the horizon* nubes formándose en el horizonte || suceder, ocurrir (to arrive) || desarrollarse (to develop) || — *as things are shaping* tal y como van las cosas || *he is shaping well at Latin* se le da bien el latín, hace progresos en latín || *shaped like* en forma de || *to shape up to s.o.* prepararse a luchar contra alguien || *to shape well* tomar buen cariz, prometer, ser prometedor.

shaped [-t] *adj* en forma de; *pear-shaped* en forma de pera.

shapeless [-lis] *adj* informe (formless) || deforme (not shapely).

shapelessness [-lisnis] *n* falta *f* de forma || deformidad *f*.

shapeliness [-linis] *n* formas *f pl* bien proporcionadas.

shapely [-li] *adj* bien proporcionado, da.

shaper [-ə*] *n* TECH moldeador *m* (workman) | embutidora *f* (machine) || FIG autor, ra.

shard [ʃa:d] *n* casco *m* (of broken earthenware) || élitro *m* (of a beetle).

share [ʃɛə*] *n* parte *f*; *to get one's share of the booty* recibir su parte del botín; *he did his share of the work* hizo su parte del trabajo; *what share had he in their success?* ¿qué parte tuvo en su éxito? || contribución *f* (contribution) || COMM acción *f* (of stock); *bearer, registered share* acción al portador, nominal | aportación *f* (of capital) | participación *f*; *share in profits* participación en los beneficios | cupo *m* (quota) | cuota *f* (part) || AGR reja *f* (of a plough) || — *everyone will pay his own share* pagaremos a escote || *I have had my share of worries* ya tuve mi parte de preocupaciones || *share and share alike* por partes iguales || FIG *the lion's share* la parte del león, la mejor parte, la mejor tajada || *to come in for one's full share of* recibir la parte que le corresponde a uno de || *to do one's share* hacer de su parte || *to fall to s.o.'s share* tocar a uno, corresponder a uno || *to go half shares with s.o.* ir a medias con alguien || *to go shares in* compartir || *to have a share in* participar en || *to pay share and share alike* pagar a escote, compartir los gastos || *you had a share in this* ha tenido algo que ver en esto.

share [ʃɛə*] *vt* compartir; *he will share the prize with you* compartirá el premio con usted; *I share your opinion* comparto su opinión; *two children who share a bedroom* dos niños que comparten un dormitorio || partir, dividir (to divide); *he shared the cake among us* dividió el pastel entre nosotros || *to share out* repartir, distribuir.
◆ *vi* *to share and share alike* participar por igual, participar por partes iguales || *to share in* participar en, tener parte en.

share certificate [-sə'tifikeit] *n* acción *f*.

sharecropper [-'krɔpə*] *n* US AGR aparcero *m*.

shareholder [-'həuldə*] *n* COMM accionista *m* & *f*.

share-out [-aut] *n* reparto *m*.

sharer [-ə*] *n* partícipe *m* & *f*.

sharif ['ʃerif] *n* jerife *m*.

shark [ʃa:k] *n* tiburón *m* (fish) || FIG estafador *m* (swindler) || US FAM as *m* (expert).

sharkskin [-skin] *n* zapa *f* (skin of a shark).

sharp [ʃa:p] *adj* afilado, da; aguzado, da (able to cut or pierce); *sharp knife* cuchillo afilado || puntiagudo, da (sharp-pointed) || cerrado, da (bend); *a sharp bend in the road* una curva cerrada en la carretera || agudo, da (angle) || anguloso, sa (feature) || puntiagudo, da (roof) || definido, da (outline) || nítido, da (photograph) || marcado, da (contrast, opposition) || empinado, da (slope) || fuerte (incline) || brusco, ca; repentino, na (change) || agudo, da (pain, eyesight, cry) || seco, ca (noise) || chillón, ona (voice) || acre (taste) || ácido, da (fruit) || penetrante (cold, wind) || frío, a (air) || fuerte (frost) || mordaz (criticism) || violento, ta (argument) || arisco, ca (temper) || acerbo, ba; áspero, ra (tone) || severo, ra (reproof) || áspero, ra (answer) || encarnizado, da; feroz (struggle) || aplastante (defeat) || profundo, da; intenso, sa (feeling, regret, remorse) || intenso, sa (attention) || fino, na (hearing, sense of smell) || rápido, da (pace) || perspicaz, penetrante, agudo, da (mind) || listo, ta; inteligente (clever); *a sharp child* un chico inteligente || astuto, ta; vivo, va; despabilado, da (quick-witted) || deshonesto, ta; poco honrado (practice, procedure) || MUS sostenido, da || — *sharp edge* filo *m* || *sharp words* palabras *f* mayores || FIG *that was sharp work* lo has hecho muy rápido *or* en un dos por tres | *to be as sharp as a needle* ser un lince || *to be sharp at arithmetic* ser muy bueno en matemáticas || *to have a sharp appetite* tener un apetito feroz || *to have a sharp tongue* tener una lengua viperina || *we must be sharp if we are to catch the train* tenemos que darnos prisa si queremos coger el tren.

◆ *n* MUS sostenido *m* || aguja *f* afilada (needle) || FAM estafador, ra (swindler) | fullero, ra (cardsharper) || US FAM experto *m*.

◆ *adv* en punto; *at ten o'clock sharp* a las diez en punto || de pronto, repentinamente; *he turned sharp right* torció repentinamente a la derecha || en seco; *he stopped sharp* se paró en seco || MUS demasiado alto, desafinadamente || *look sharp!* ¡pronto!, ¡rápido!

sharp [ʃɑːp] *vt* MUS marcar con un sostenido || FAM estafar (to cheat).

◆ *vi* hacer fullerías en el juego (in cards) || MUS dar un agudo.

sharp-edged [-ˈedʒd] *adj* afilado, da; aguzado, da.

sharpen [-ən] *vt* afilar (blade) || sacar punta a (pencil) || FIG aguzar, abrir (appetite) | aguzar (intelligence) | avivar, acentuar, agudizar (desire, enmity) | despabilar (s.o.) | hacer más severo (a law) | hacer más encarnizado (a struggle) | hacer más agudo (a pain).

◆ *vi* volverse más agudo (noise) || afilarse (features) || FIG agudizarse (faculties).

sharpener [-nə*] *n* sacapuntas *m inv*, afilalápices *m inv* (for pencil) || TECH afiladora *f* (machine).

sharpening [-niŋ] *n* afilado *m* (of tools, etc.) || FIG agudizamiento *m* (of faculties).

sharper [-ə*] *n* FAM fullero, ra (cardsharper) | estafador, ra (swindler).

sharp-eyed [-aid]; **sharp-sighted** [-ˈsaitid] *adj* de vista aguda, de mirada penetrante, que tiene ojos de lince (having good sight) || perspicaz (perspicacious) || observador, ra (observant).

sharply [-li] *adv* bruscamente, repentinamente; *he turned sharply* torció repentinamente || con aspereza, abruptamente; *she answered him sharply* le contestó con aspereza || de modo incisivo (remark) || claramente; *sharply divided* dividido claramente || severamente, con severidad; *he spoke sharply to her* le habló severamente || rápidamente; *he walked sharply* andaba rápidamente || pronunciadamente (sloping) || fuerte (freezing, hitting) || atentamente (listening) || con un ruido seco (sounding) || mucho (suffering) || — *sharply edged* afilado, da || *sharply pointed* puntiagudo, da.

sharpness [-nis] *n* lo afilado (of edge) || agudeza *f* (of noise, senses, pain) || lo cerrado (of a bend) || nitidez *f* (clarity) || lo empinado (of a slope) || brusquedad *f* (of a change, of a gesture) || acritud *f* (of taste) || violencia *f* (of an argument) || acritud *f*, lo arisco (of temper) || aspereza *f* (of tone) || mordacidad *f* (of criticism) || severidad *f* (of a reprimand) || rigor *m* (of the weather) || agudeza *f*, perspicacia *f* (of mind) || inteligencia *f* (intelligence) || lo profundo, intensidad *f* (of feeling, of remorse) || CULIN acidez *f* (of a fruit) | lo picante (of a sauce).

sharp-pointed [-ˈpɔintid] *adj* puntiagudo, da.

sharpshooter [-ʃuːtə*] *n* MIL tirador *m* de primera.

sharpshooting [-ʃuːtiŋ] *n* puntería *f* certera.

sharp-sighted [-ˈsaitid] *adj* ⟶ **sharp-eyed.**

sharp-sightedness [-ˈsaitidnis] *n* vista *f* aguda (keen eyesight) || perspicacia *f*, sagacidad *f*.

sharp-tongued [-ˈtʌŋd] *adj* de lengua viperina.

sharp-witted [-ˈwitid] *adj* listo, ta (clever) || agudo, da; ingenioso, sa (witty) || perspicaz (shrewd).

shatter [ˈʃætə*] *vt* hacer añicos, hacer pedazos, romper, destrozar; *he shattered the window* rompió la ventana; *the explosion shattered the house* la explosión destrozó la casa || FIG echar por tierra; *this objection shatters your theory* esta objeción echa por tierra su teoría | destruir, echar por tierra, frustrar; *to shatter s.o.'s hopes* destruir las esperanzas de alguien | dejar pasmado (to stun) || MED quebrantar (health) | destrozar (nerves).

◆ *vi* hacerse pedazos, hacerse añicos, romperse.

shattering [-iŋ] *adj* agotador, ra, aplastante (exhausting) || FIG conmovedor, ra (shocking).

shatterproof [-pruːf] *adj* inastillable (glass).

shave [ʃeiv] *n* afeitado *m* (act of shaving) || roce *m* (act of passing very near) || TECH cepillo *m* (plane) | viruta *f* (slice of wood) || — *to get a shave* afeitarse || *to give s.o. a shave* afeitar a alguien || FIG *to have a close shave* librarse por los pelos || *to have a shave* afeitarse.

shave [ʃeiv] *vt* afeitar || rapar; *to shave s.o.'s head* rapar la cabeza a alguien || TECH cepillar (wood) || FIG cercenar (to reduce); *to shave the budget estimates* cercenar las previsiones presupuestarias | pasar rozando (to pass very close); *the car shaved a wall* el coche pasó rozando un muro || — *to shave off one's moustache* afeitarse el bigote | *to shave one's legs* afeitarse las piernas.

◆ *vi* afeitarse.

shaveling [-liŋ] *n* US chaval *m*.

shaven [ˈʃeivn] *adj* afeitado, da (face) || rapado, da (head) || tonsurado, da (monk) || TECH cepillado, da (wood).

shaver [ˈʃeivə*] *n* maquinilla *f* de afeitar eléctrica, afeitadora *f* (electric razor) || barbero *m* (barber) || FAM *little* o *young shaver* chaval *m* (young boy).

shaving [ˈʃeiviŋ] *n* afeitado *m* || TECH cepillado *m* (act of shaving wood) | viruta *f* (slice of wood or metal) || — *shaving bowl* bacía *f* || *shaving brush* brocha *f* de afeitar || *shaving cream* crema *f* de afeitar || *shaving horse* banco *m* de carpintero || *shaving is obligatory in the army* es obligatorio afeitarse en el ejército || *shaving soap, shaving stick* jabón *m* de afeitar.

shawl [ʃɔːl] *n* chal *m*.

shawm [ʃɔːm] *n* MUS caramillo *m* (instrument).

she [ʃiː] *n* ZOOL hembra *f*; *is it a he or a she?* ¿es macho o hembra?

◆ *pron* ella; *she didn't speak* ella no habló; *it is she* es ella || — *if I were she* si fuera ella, si estuviera en su lugar || MAR *isn't she a beautiful boat?* es un barco precioso ¿verdad? || *she who* la que, aquella que, quien.

◆ *adj* *she-ass* burra *f* || *she-bear* osa *f* || *she-cat* gata *f* || *she-devil* diabla *f*, diablesa *f* || *she-elephant* elefante *m* hembra || *she-monkey* mona *f*.

sheaf [ʃiːf] *n* AGR gavilla *f* || haz *m* (of arrows) || fajo *m* (of papers, of tickets).

— OBSERV El plural de esta palabra es *sheaves*.

shear* [ʃiə*] *vt* esquilar (sheep) || cortar (a branch) || rapar (hair) || FIG privar, despojar; *shorn of his power* privado de su poder || FIG & FAM pelar, desplumar (of money) || TECH cizallar (metal) || tundir (cloth) || — *shorn of* sin || *to shear off* o *through* cortar.

◆ *vi* esquilar ovejas (to clip sheep) || TECH romperse por cizallamiento || FIG abrirse camino.

— OBSERV Pret ***sheared***; pp ***shorn, sheared***.

shearer [-rə*] *n* esquilador, ra.

shearing [-riŋ] *n* esquileo *m* (of sheep) || TECH cizallamiento *m* (of metals).

◆ *pl* lana *f sing* esquilada.

shearing machine [-iŋməˈʃiːn] *n* esquiladora *f*.

shear legs [-legz] *n* TECH cabria *f* (for hoisting).

shearling [-liŋ] *n* añal *m*, cordero *m* esquilado una vez.

shears [-z] *pl n* tijeras *f* (for hedging) || TECH cizalla *f sing* (for cutting metal) | cabria *f sing* (for hoisting).

sheatfish [ˈʃiːtfiʃ] *n* siluro *m* (catfish).

sheath [ʃiːθ] *n* funda *f* (for knife, scissors, umbrella) || vaina *f* (of sword) || BOT vaina *f* || vaina *f* (of an organ, an artery) || MED preservativo *m* (contraceptive).

sheath dress [-dres] *n* vestido *m* tubo *or* tubular.

sheathe [ʃiːð] *vt* envainar (a sword) || enfundar (a knife) || cubrir (a boat, a roof, etc.) || retraer (claws) || TECH forrar (a cable) || hundir en la carne (a dagger, a fang, etc.).

sheathing [-iŋ] *n* enfundadura *f* (of a knife) || acción *f* de envainar (of a sword) || revestimiento *m* (covering) || TECH forro *m* (of a cable, of metal).

sheath knife [-naif] *n* cuchillo *m* de monte.

sheave [ʃiːv] *n* roldana *f* (of a pulley) || escudo *m* (of a keyhole).

sheaves [-z] *pl n* ⟶ **sheaf.**

Sheba [ˈʃiːbə] *pr n* GEOGR Saba; *the Queen of Sheba* la reina de Saba.

shebang [ʃiˈbæŋ] *n* US FAM *the whole shebang* todo el asunto (affair), todos los bártulos (things).

shed [ʃed] *n* cobertizo *m* (lean-to) || hangar *m* (for engines) || nave *f* (workshop) || barraca *f* (for workmen) || almacén *m* (warehouse) || AGR establo *m* (for cattle).

shed* [ʃed] *vt* quitarse, despojarse de (clothes) || deshacerse de (to get rid of) || ZOOL mudar (skin) || BOT despojarse de (leaves) || derramar (tears) || verter, derramar (blood) || despedir (a smell) || dar (light) || verter (water) || FIG traer; *to shed happiness* traer la felicidad | perder (weight) || FIG *to shed light on a subject* aclarar un asunto.

◆ *vi* ZOOL pelechar, mudar.

— OBSERV Pret y pp ***shed***.

she'd [ʃiːd] contración de «she had», «she would».

shedding [-iŋ] *n* muda *f* (of skin, of plumage) || derramamiento *m* (of blood, of tears).

sheen [ʃiːn] *n* brillo *m* (brightness) || viso *m* (of silk) || brillo *m*, espejeo *m* (of water).

sheeny [-i] *adj* brillante.

sheep [ʃiːp] *inv n* ZOOL oveja *f* || FIG corderito, ta; cordero, ra (easily led person) || REL grey *f* || AGR ganado *m* lanar, ovinos *m pl* || — FIG *a wolf in sheep's clothing* un lobo con piel de oveja | *the black sheep of the family* la oveja negra de la familia | *to be like sheep* ser como borregos | *to cast sheep's eyes at s.o.* mirar a alguien con ternura | *to feel like a lost sheep* sentirse perdido | *to separate the sheep from the goats* separar la cizaña del buen grano.

sheep bot [-bɔt] *n* rezno *m*.

sheepdip [-dip] *n* desinfectante *m* (liquid) || baño *m* desinfectante (bath).

sheep dog [-dɔg] *n* perro *m* pastor (dog).

sheep farming [-ˈfɑːmiŋ] *n* AGR cría *f* de las ovejas para la lana.

sheepfold [-ˌfəuld] *n* aprisco *m*, majada *f*, redil *m*.

sheepherder [-ˌhəːdə*] *n* US pastor *m*.

sheepherding [-ˌhəːdiŋ] *adj* pastoril.
◆ *n* pastoreo *m*.

sheephook [-huk] *n* cayado *m*.

sheepish [-iʃ] *adj* tímido, da; vergonzoso, sa (bashful).

sheepishness [-iʃnis] *n* timidez *f*, vergüenza *f*.

sheepman [-mən] *n* propietario *m* de ganado lanar, ganadero *m*.
— OBSERV El plural de esta palabra es *sheepmen*.

sheep run [rʌn] *n* redil *m*, aprisco *m*.

sheepshearer [-ʃiərə*] *n* esquilador, ra (person) || esquiladora *f* (machine).

sheepshearing [-ʃiəriŋ] *n* esquileo *m*.

sheepskin [-skin] *n* piel *f* de carnero *or* de oveja, zamarra *f* (hide) || badana *f* (leather) || pergamino *m* (parchment) || US FAM diploma *m*, pergamino *m* (diploma) || *sheepskin jacket* o *coat* zamarra *f*, pelliza *f*.

sheepwalk [-wɔːk] *n* pasto *m*, dehesa *f*.

sheer [ʃiə*] *adj* completo, ta; total, absoluto, ta (impossibility) || total; *a sheer waste of time* una pérdida total de tiempo || puro, ra [AMER mero, ra] (kindness, etc.); *out of sheer malice* por pura maldad; *it is sheer nonsense* es pura necedad || verdadero, ra; *it is sheer robbery* es un verdadero robo || escarpado, da; cortado a pico (cliff) || acantilado, da (coast) || vertical (drop, fall) || fino, na; transparente (cloth) || — *by sheer force* a viva fuerza || *in sheer desperation* en último extremo.
◆ *adv* perpendicularmente, a pico (perpendicularly) || completamente; *the tree was torn sheer out by the roots* el árbol fue completamente desarraigado.
◆ *n* MAR arrufadura *f*, arrufo *m* (curve of ship) | desviación *f* (deviation from a course) | guiñada *f* (yaw).

sheer [ʃiə*] *vi* MAR guiñar, desviarse || caer a pico (rock, etc.) || *to sheer off* desviarse (ship), desviarse (from a subject), largarse (to go away).

sheerlegs [-legz] *n* MAR cabria *f* (hoist).

sheet [ʃiːt] *n* sábana *f* (of bed); *bottom, top sheet* sábana bajera, encimera || hoja *f* (of paper, of tin) || lámina *f* (of glass) || chapa *f*, lámina *f* (of metal, etc.) || capa *f* (of water, snow, ice) || cortina *f* (of fog, smoke, rain) || COMM hoja *f* (for orders) || MAR escota *f* (rope) || FAM periodicucho *m* (newspaper) || — FIG *as white as a sheet* blanco como el papel || *balance sheet* balance *m* || *in sheets* en pliegos, sin encuadernar (book) || *loose sheet* hoja suelta || PRINT *proof sheet* prueba *f* || *sheet anchor* ancla *f* de la esperanza (of a ship), tabla *f* de salvación (last resort) || *sheet brass* chapa de latón || *sheet glass* vidrio plano, vidrio laminado || *sheet iron* chapa || *sheet lightning* fucilazo *m* || *sheet metal* chapa de metal, metal *m* en chapa || *sheet music* música *f* en hojas de partitura || *sheet pile* tablestaca *f* || *sheet shop* hojalatería *f* || *sheet steel* chapa de acero, acero *m* en chapa || FAM *to be three sheets in the wind* estar como una cuba | *to get between the sheets* meterse entre sábanas *or* en la cama || *winding sheet* mortaja *f* (shroud).

sheet [ʃiːt] *vt* cubrir con una sábana (to cover with a sheet) || cubrir con una capa (of tar, of mist, etc.) || cubrir; *river sheeted with ice* río cubierto de hielo || amortajar (in a winding sheet).

sheeting [-iŋ] *n* tela *f* de sábana (fabric) || chapas *f pl* (sheets of metal).

sheik; sheikh [ʃeik] *n* jeque *m* (Arab chief) || FAM seductor *m*, conquistador *m*.

shekel [ˈʃekl] *n* siclo *m* (Hebrew coin).
◆ *pl* FAM pasta *f sing* [AMER plata *f sing*] (money).

shelf [ʃelf] *n* anaquel *m*, estante *m* (in a library) || estante *m*, repisa *f* (in a room, in a kitchen, etc.) || tabla *f*, anaquel *m* (in a cupboard, in a closet) || parrilla *f* (in oven, in fridge) || GEOL saliente *m* (projecting rock) | graderío *m*, escalón *m*, rellano *m* (of a cliff) || MAR banco *m* (of sand) | arrecife *m* (of rock, of coral) || — *continental shelf* plataforma *f* continental || *shelf ice* plataforma *f* de hielo || *shelf life* tiempo de conservación de un producto en venta || FAM *to be left on the shelf* quedarse para vestir santos.
◆ *pl* estantería *f sing*.
— OBSERV El plural de esta palabra es *shelves*.

shell [ʃel] *n* concha *f* (of molluscs); *I have a lovely collection of shells* tengo una colección de conchas preciosa || caparazón *m* (of crustacean) || concha *f*, caparazón *m* (of tortoise) || concha *f*, carey *m* (for making combs, etc.) || cáscara *f*, cascarón *m* (of eggs) || cáscara *f* (of nuts) || vaina *f* (of peas) || armazón *f*, esqueleto *m* (of a building) || caja *f* (of a car) || MIL proyectil *m*, granada *f* (cannon projectile) | casquillo *m* (of a bullet) || taza *f* (of a sword) || MAR casco *m* (hull) | yola *f* (boat) || TECH revestimiento *m* (of a furnace, etc.) | soporte *m* (of pulley) || capa *f* (of an atom) || FIG líneas *f pl* generales (plan) | apariencia *f* (outward appearance) || — *sea shell* concha || FIG *to come out of one's shell* salir de su concha | *to retire into one's shell* meterse en su concha.

shell [ʃel] *vt* pelar, desvainar (peas) || quitar la cáscara de (eggs) || descascarar (nuts) || sacar de la concha *or* del caparazón (molluscs, crustaceans) || abrir, desbullar (oysters) || pelar (shrimps) || MIL bombardear || FAM *to shell out* soltar, aflojar (money).
◆ *vi* *to shell off* desconcharse (paint) || FAM *to shell out* cascar, aflojar (money).

she'll [ʃiːl] contracción de «she will», «she shall».

shellac; US **shellack** [ʃəˈlæk] *n* laca *f*, goma *f* laca.

shellac; US **shellack** [ʃəˈlæk] *vt* dar laca, laquear || US FAM dar una paliza (to beat).

shellfire [-ˈfaiə*] *n* MIL bombardeo *m*, cañoneo *m*.

shellfish [-fiʃ] *n* ZOOL marisco *m* (cockles, mussels, etc.) | crustáceo *m* (crabs, lobsters, etc.) || CULIN mariscos *m pl*.

shelling [-iŋ] *n* pelado *m* (of peas) || descascarillado *m* (of nuts) || desbulla *f* (of oysters) || pelado *m* (of shrimps) || MIL bombardeo *m*.

shellproof [-pruːf] *adj* MIL a prueba de bombas.

shell shock [-ʃɔk] *n* MED trauma *m* causado por la guerra, conmoción *f* debida a los bombardeos.

shelter [ˈʃeltə*] *n* refugio *m*, abrigo *m* (place of safety) || asilo *m* (for the old, for the homeless); *night shelter* asilo nocturno || cobertizo *m* (against the rain) || albergue *m* (for mountaineers) || FIG amparo *m* (protection) | albergue *m*, refugio *m*; *to find shelter with a friend* encontrar albergue en casa de un amigo || MIL garita *f* (for a sentry) || — *fallout shelter* refugio atómico || *shelter tent* tienda *f* de campaña || *to take shelter* ponerse a cubierto, refugiarse || FIG *to take s.o. under one's shelter* amparar a alguien || *under shelter* al abrigo, a cubierto || *under the shelter of* al abrigo de.

shelter [ˈʃeltə*] *vt* abrigar, proteger; *to shelter sth. from the rain* abrigar algo de la lluvia || proteger, resguardar; *the trenches sheltered the soldiers from the enemy's fire* las trincheras protegían a los soldados del fuego enemigo || dar hospitalidad, recoger, acoger, dar asilo (poor people, etc.) || FIG amparar, proteger || *to shelter o.s.* refugiarse.
◆ *vi* resguardarse; *to shelter from the wind* resguardarse del viento || ponerse a cubierto, refugiarse; *to shelter under a tree* ponerse a cubierto debajo de un árbol.

sheltered [-d] *adj* protegido, da.

shelterless [-lis] *adj* sin hogar, desamparado, da.

shelve [ʃelv] *vt* poner en un estante (to put on a shelf); *to shelve some books* poner unos libros en un estante || poner estantes en (to fit with shelves) || FAM dar carpetazo a (a matter) | dejar de lado (a discussion) | arrinconar (s.o., sth.).
◆ *vi* estar en declive.

shelves [-z] *pl n* ⟶ **shelf.**

shelving [-iŋ] *n* estantería *f* (shelves) || disposición *f* de los estantes (of books) || FIG aplazamiento *m* indefinido (of a matter) | arrinconamiento *m* (of s.o.).

shenanigans [ʃiˈnænigənz] *pl n* US FAM engaños *m*, trampas *f* (trickery).

shepherd [ˈʃepəd] *n* pastor *m* || — *shepherd boy* zagal *m* || *shepherd's pie* pastel *m* de carne y patatas || REL *the Good Shepherd* el Buen Pastor.

shepherd [ˈʃepəd] *vt* cuidar de (animals).

shepherdess [-is] *n* pastora *f*.

sherbet [ˈʃəːbət] *n* sorbete *m*.

sherd [ʃəːd] *n* casco *m* (of broken earthenware) || ZOOL élitro *m*.

shereef; sherif [ʃeˈriːf] *n* jerife *m*.

sheriff [ˈʃerif] *n* JUR gobernador *m* civil (in England) | primer presidente *m* del tribunal de un condado (in Scotland) || US "sheriff" *m* (law officer).

sherry [ˈʃeri] *n* jerez *m* (wine).

she's [ʃiːz] contracción de «she is», «she has».

Shetland Islands [ˈʃetləndˌailəndz] *pr n* GEOGR islas Shetland.

shibboleth [ˈʃibəleθ] *n* contraseña *f*, santo y seña *m* (password).

shield [ʃiːld] *n* MIL, ZOOL & HERALD escudo *m* || TECH capa *f* protectora (coating) | blindaje *m* (of an atomic reactor, etc.) | pantalla *f* protectora (on a machine, for welding, etc.) | careta *f* (for workers) || BOT escudete *m*, escudo *m* || FIG escudo *m*, protección *f* || sobaquera *f* (for a garment) || US placa *f* (of a policeman).

shield [ʃiːld] *vt* proteger (to protect) || tapar (to mask) || TECH blindar || FIG proteger, escudar.

shield bearer [-ˈbɛərə*] *n* escudero *m*.

shield budding [-ˈbʌdiŋ]; **shield grafting** [-ˈgrɑːftiŋ] *n* AGR injerto *m* de escudete.

shift [ʃift] *n* cambio *m*; *a shift in position* un cambio de posición || salto *m* (of wind) || movimiento *m* (moving) || cambio *m*; *a shift in public opinion* un cambio en la opinión pública || turno *m*, tanda *f*; *to work in shifts* trabajar por turnos; *the night shift was going to work* el turno de noche iba a trabajar || expediente *m*, recurso *m* (expedient) || subterfugio *m*, artificio *m* (trick) || escapatoria *f* (evasion) || traje *m* recto (frock) || GEOL falla *f* || MUS cambio *m* de posición (in violin playing) || GRAMM cambio *m* || variación *f* (in the Stock Exchange) || SP desplazamiento *m* lateral || — AGR *shift of crops* rotación *f* de cultivos || *to make a shift* cambiar de sitio || *to make a shift to* arreglárselas para || *to make shift with* arreglárselas con || *to make shift without* prescindir de.
◆ *adj* por turno (work) || — *shift key* tecla *f* de mayúsculas || *shift pedal* pedal *m* de sordina (of a piano).

shift [ʃift] *vt* cambiar; *the river shifts its course* el río cambia su curso; *to shift the scenery* cambiar los decorados || cambiar de sitio, trasladar, desplazar; *he shifted his chair* cambió su silla de sitio || mover; *I can't shift it* no lo puedo mover || pasar; *to shift a burden from one shoulder to the other* pasar una carga de un hombro al otro || cambiar de, mudar de; *to shift one's opinion* cambiar de opinión || retrasar (to put back a train schedule) || adelantar (to put forward a train schedule) || FIG echar; *to shift the blame upon s.o.* echar la culpa a alguien | quitarse de encima (to get rid of) || — US *to shift gears* cambiar de velocidad || FIG *to shift one's ground* cambiar de táctica.
◆ *vi* cambiar de sitio (to change place) || moverse (to move) || MAR desplazarse (cargo) || cambiar (wind, scenery, opinion) || FAM tergiversar || US AUT cambiar de velocidad (gears) || — *to shift about* cambiar constantemente de sitio || FIG *to shift for o.s.* arreglárselas solo, valerse por sí mismo.

shiftiness [-inis] *n* falsedad *f* (falsehood) || astucia *f* (cunning).

shifting [-iŋ] *adj* movedizo, za (sand).

shiftless [-lis] *adj* vago, ga; perezoso, sa (lazy) || indolente (indolent) || torpe, inútil (incapable).

shiftlessness [-lisnis] *n* pereza *f* (laziness) || inutilidad *f*, incapacidad *f* (incapacity).

shifty [-i] *adj* falso, sa (untrustworthy) || astuto, ta; taimado, da (wily) || sospechoso, sa (behaviour) || *to have shifty eyes* no mirar nunca a los ojos *or* a la cara.

shifty-eyed [ʃiftiaid] *adj* *to be shifty-eyed* no mirar nunca a los ojos *or* a la cara.

Shiite [ʃi:ait] *n* REL chiíta *m* & *f*.

shill [ʃil] *n* US FAM cómplice *m* (of a gambler).

shillalah [ʃi'leilə]; **shillelagh** [ʃi'leilə] *n* porra *f* (cudgel).

shilling [ʃiliŋ] *n* chelín *m* (coin) || — FIG *to cut s.o. off with a shilling* desheredar a alguien | *to take the King's shilling* alistarse en el ejército.

shilly-shally [ʃili,ʃæli] *n* titubeo *m*, vacilación *f*, indecisión *f*, irresolución *f*.
◆ *adj* titubeante, vacilante, indeciso, sa.

shilly-shally [ʃili,ʃæli] *vi* titubear, vacilar, no decidirse.

shim [ʃim] *n* TECH calce *m*.

shimmer [-ə*] *n* luz *f* trémula, resplandor *m* tenue (wavering shine) || brillo *m* (of pearls, of jewelry) || *the shimmer of the moon in the sea* el reflejo de la luna en el mar, la luna que riela en el mar.

shimmer [ʃimə*] *vi* rielar, relucir, brillar.

shimmering [-riŋ]; **shimmery** [-ri] *adj* trémulo, la (light) || reluciente (glittering) || tornasolado, da (tints).

shimmy [ʃimi] *n* "shimmy" *m* (dance) || AUT "shimmy" *m*, abaniqueo *m*, trepidación *f* oscilante (of wheels) || US camisa *f* (chemise).

shimmy [ʃimi] *vi* bailar el shimmy (to dance) || AUT abaniquear, oscilar (the wheels).

shin [ʃin] *n* ANAT espinilla *f* (of the leg) || caña *f* (of a horse) || CULIN jarrete *m*, corva *f*, corvejón *m* (of beef, etc.) || TECH eclisa *f*, mordaza *f*.

shin [ʃin] *vi* *to shin down* bajar como por una cuerda || *to shin up* trepar; *to shin up a tree* trepar a un árbol.
◆ *vt* dar una patada *or* patadas en las espinillas a (s.o.).

shinbone [-bəun] *n* ANAT tibia *f* (bone).

shinding [ʃindig]; **shindy** [ʃindi] *n* FAM jaleo *m* (noise); *to kick up a shindy* armar un jaleo | pelea *f* (row); *to have a shindy with s.o.* tener una pelea con alguien || US FAM fiesta *f* (party).

shine [ʃain] *n* brillo *m*, lustre *m* || buen tiempo *m* (good weather) || — *give my shoes a shine* límpieme los zapatos, sáqueme brillo a los zapatos [AMER lústreme los zapatos] || *rain or shine* llueva o truene, aunque llueva, independientemente del tiempo que haga || FAM *to take a shine to* coger cariño a, aficionarse a || *to take the shine off sth.* quitarle el brillo a algo, deslustrar algo (a surface), quitar a algo su encanto (sth. attractive) || FIG *to take the shine out of* eclipsar.

shine* [ʃain] *vt* sacar brillo a (by polishing) || hacer brillar || dirigir (a light) || limpiar [AMER lustrar] (shoes).
◆ *vi* brillar, relucir; *the sun shines* el sol brilla || brillar, relucir (polished article) || FIG rebosar de (with health) | resplandecer de, rebosar de; *his face shone with happiness* su cara resplandecía de felicidad | brillar, sobresalir, lucirse (to excel at) || — *the moon is shining* hay un claro de luna || *to shine on* iluminar || FAM *to shine up* intentar caer en gracia a.
— OBSERV El pretérito y participio pasivo de *to shine* son irregulares: ***shone.*** En Estados Unidos se usa también la forma ***shined*** en el participio pasivo.

shiner [-ə*] *n* limpiabotas *m inv* [AMER lustrabotas] (of shoes) || moneda *f* de oro (gold coin) || US FAM ojo *m* a la funerala (black eye).
◆ *pl* FAM pasta *f sing* [AMER plata *f sing*] (money).

shingle [ʃiŋgl] *n* tablilla *f* (in roofing) || corte *m* a lo "garçon" (hairstyle) || guijarros *m pl* (mass of pebbles) || playa *f* de guijarros (beach) || US FAM placa *f* (signboard) || US FAM *to hang out one's shingle* abrir consulta (doctor), abrir un bufete (lawyer).
◆ *pl* MED zona *f sing*.

shingle [ʃiŋgl] *vt* cortar a lo "garçon" (hair) || cubrir con tablillas (roof).

shingly [-i] *adj* de guijarros, guijarroso, sa (covered with pebbles).

shin guard [ʃingɑ:d] *n* espinillera *f*.

shininess [ʃaininis] *n* brillo *m*.

shining [ʃainiŋ] *adj* brillante, reluciente (things) || radiante (face) || excelente (remarkable).

shinny [ʃini] *vt* US FAM *to shinny up* trepar a.

shin pad [ʃinpæd] *n* espinillera *f*.

Shinto [ʃintəu]; **Shintoism** [-izəm] *n* REL sintoísmo *m*.

shiny [ʃaini] *adj* brillante (bright) || radiante (face) || con brillo (through wear).

ship [ʃip] *n* MAR barco *m*, buque *m*, navío *m* (vessel) | tripulación *f* (crew) || US FAM avión *m* (aircraft) | dirigible *m* || — MAR *capital ship* acorazado *m* || *Her* o *His Majesty's Ship (H M S)* buque de la marina británica || *hospital ship* buque hospital || *merchant ship* buque mercante || *mother ship* buque nodriza || *on board ship* a bordo || *passenger ship* buque de pasajeros || *ship biscuit* galleta *f* || *ship of the line* buque de línea || *ship's boat* lancha *f* [que permite bajar a tierra], bote *m* salvavidas || *ship's company* tripulación || *ship's papers* documentación *f* del barco || FIG *the ship of the desert* el camello || *to take ship* embarcarse || FIG *when one's ship comes home* cuando lleguen las vacas gordas.

ship [ʃip] *vt* MAR embarcar (a cargo, passengers, water) | armar (a mast) | montar (a rudder) | desarmar (oars) | enrolar (crew) || transportar (to transport) || enviar, mandar, expedir (to send); *I'll ship my car to New York* mandaré mi coche a Nueva York || FAM *to ship off* echar, despedir.
◆ *vi* MAR embarcarse (to go on board ship) || soportar el transporte; *fruit ships badly* la fruta soporta mal el transporte || enrolarse (sailors).

shipboard [-,bɔ:d] *n* MAR *on shipboard* a bordo.

shipboy [-,bɔi] *n* grumete *m*.

shipbreaker [-,breikə*] *n* MAR desguazador *m*.

ship broker [-'brəukə*] *n* agente *m* marítimo, consignatario *m* de buques.

shipbuilder [-,bildə*] *n* MAR constructor *m* de buques.

shipbuilding [-,bildiŋ] *n* MAR construcción *f* naval.

ship canal [-kə'næl] *n* canal *m* navegable.

ship chandler [-'tʃɑ:ndlə*] *n* abastecedor *m* de buques.

shipload [-ləud] *n* MAR cargamento *m*, carga *f*.

shipmaster [-,mɑ:stə*] *n* MAR capitán *m* de un buque mercante (captain) | patrón *m* (owner).

shipmate [-meit] *n* MAR compañero *m* de a bordo *or* de tripulación.

shipment [-mənt] *n* MAR embarque *m* (loading) | enrolamiento *m* (of a crew) | transporte *m* (transporting) | envío *m* (goods to be delivered); *this shipment is for Spain* este envío es para España | carga *f*, cargamento *m* (goods shipped); *a boat with a shipment of bananas* un barco con una carga de plátanos.

shipowner [-,əunə*] *n* naviero *m*, armador *m*.

shipper [-ə*] *n* MAR expedidor *m*, cargador *m* || AVIAT transportista *m*.

shipping [-iŋ] *n* MAR embarque *m* (loading on board ship); *shipping port* puerto de embarque | transporte *m* (transporting) | envío *m*, expedición *f* (sending); *shipping expenses* gastos de envío | barcos *m pl*, buques *m pl* (ships of a port) | flota *f* (of a country) | navegación *f*; *dangerous for shipping* peligroso para la navegación | montaje *m* (of rudder, etc.).

shipping agent [-iŋ'deidʒənt] *n* agente *m* marítimo, consignatario *m* de buques (ship broker) || expedidor *m* (shipper).

shipping bill [-iŋbil] *n* MAR conocimiento *m*.

shipping clerk [-iŋ'klɑ:k] *n* COMM expedidor *m*.

shipping company [-iŋ'kʌmpəni] *n* compañía *f* naviera.

shipping line [-iŋlain] *n* MAR compañía *f* naviera.

shipping master [-iŋ'mɑ:stə*] *n* MAR persona *f* encargada de enrolar a la tripulación.

shipping office [-iŋ'ɔfis] *n* MAR oficina *f* de enrolamiento de marineros | agencia *f* marítima.

shipping room [-iŋru:m] *n* US COMM despacho *m* de envíos.

shipshape [-ʃeip] *adj* en orden, ordenado, da.

shipside [-said] *n* dársena *f*.

ship's log [lɔg] *n* diario *m* de a bordo, cuaderno *m* de bitácora.

shipway [-wei] *n* MAR grada *f* (support for launching) | canal *m* navegable (ship canal).

shipwreck [-rek] *n* MAR naufragio *m* ‖ FIG catástrofe *f*, ruina *f*.

shipwreck [-rek] *vt* MAR hacer naufragar ‖ *to be shipwrecked* naufragar.

shipwright [-rait] *n* MAR carpintero *m* de barcos (carpenter).

shipyard [-jɑ:d] *n* MAR astillero *m*.

shire [ˈʃaiə*] *n* condado *m* ‖ *the Shires* los condados de Leicestershire, Northamptonshire y Rutland.

shire horse [-hɔ:s] *n* percherón.

shire town [-taun] *n* capital *f* de condado.

shirk [ʃə:k] *vt* eludir (a question) ‖ esquivar, eludir, zafarse de (a duty) ‖ rehuir (a task) ‖ esquivar, evitar (danger, difficulties) ‖ FAM fumarse (school).

◆ *vi* esquivarse (to practice evasion) ‖ no cumplir con el deber (to neglect one's duty) ‖ MIL escurrir el bulto ‖ hacer el vago, gandulear (to idle).

shirker [-ə*] *n* gandul, la.

shirr [ʃə:*] *vt* fruncir (in dressmaking) ‖ US CULIN cocer en el horno (eggs).

shirt [ʃə:t] *n* camisa *f* (for men); *stiff shirt* camisa almidonada ‖ blusa *f* (for women) ‖ (ant) cota *f* (of mail) ‖ — *in shirt sleeves* en mangas de camisa ‖ FIG *keep your shirt on!* ¡no te sulfures! | *stiff shirt* persona envarada *or* estirada | *to lose one's shirt* perder hasta la camisa | *to put one's shirt on a horse* apostar todo lo que se tiene a un caballo.

shirtband [-bænd] *n* tirilla *f* de la camisa.

shirtfront [-frʌnt] *n* pechera *f*.

shirting [-iŋ] *n* tela *f* de camisa.

shirtless [-lis] *adj* sin camisa, descamisado, da.

shirtmaker [-ˈmeikə*] *n* camisero, ra.

shirt-sleeve [-ˌsli:v]; **shirt-sleeves** [-ˌsli:vz]; **shirt-sleeved** [-sli:vd] *adj* en mangas de camisa; *to be in one's shirt-sleeves* estar en mangas de camisa ‖ US sencillo, lla (informal) | casero, ra (homespun) | elemental.

shirttail [-teil] *n* faldón *m*.

shirtwaist [-weist] *n* US blusa *f* (of women) ‖ *shirtwaist dress* vestido camisero.

shirty [-i] *adj* FAM furioso, sa; enfadado, da (angry).

shit [ʃit] *n* POP mierda *f*.

shit [ʃit] *vt/vi* POP cagar ‖ POP *to shit bricks* cagarse de miedo.

shiver [ˈʃivə*] *n* escalofrío *m* (with cold) ‖ temblor *m*, escalofrío *m*, estremecimiento *m* (with fear) ‖ astilla *f* (of wood) ‖ fragmento *m*, pedazo *m* (fragment) ‖ piedra *f* esquistosa (stone) ‖ — *a shiver went down his back* le dio un escalofrío ‖ *it gives me the shivers to think of it* cuando lo pienso me echo a temblar ‖ *to have the shivers* estar temblando.

shiver [ˈʃivə*] *vt* hacer añicos *or* astillas (to break) ‖ MAR hacer flamear (sails).

◆ *vi* tiritar (with cold) ‖ temblar, estremecerse (with fear) ‖ hacerse añicos *or* astillas (to break).

shivery [-ri] *adj* estremecido, da (shivering) ‖ estremecedor, ra (causing shivers) ‖ friolero, ra (sensitive to the cold) ‖ destemplado, da (feverish).

shoal [ʃəul] *n* banco *m* de arena, bajío *m* (sandbank) ‖ banco *m*, cardumen *m* (of fish) ‖ FIG multitud *f* (of people); *a shoal of tourists* una multitud de turistas | montón *m* (of things) | peligro *m* oculto (hidden danger) ‖ FIG *in shoals* a montones.

◆ *adj* poco profundo (water).

shoal [ʃəul] *vi* disminuir en profundidad, hacerse menos profundo (to become shallow) ‖ desplazarse *or* ir en bancos (fish) ‖ FIG agruparse (people).

shoat [ʃəut] *n* US ZOOL cochinillo *m*, lechón *m*.

shock [ʃɔk] *n* sacudida *f* (violent shaking) ‖ seísmo *m*, sacudida *f* (of an earthquake) ‖ choque *m* (of a collision, of an explosion, etc.); *when the cars collided there was a terrible shock* al entrar en colisión los coches se produjo un choque terrible ‖ MED «shock» *m*, choque *m*, conmoción *f* ‖ FIG conmoción *f* (commotion) | sobresalto *m*, susto *m* (start, scare); *he died of the shock* se murió del susto | golpe *m*; *his marriage was a great shock to her* su casamiento fue un golpe muy duro para ella ‖ MIL choque *m*, refriega *f* ‖ AGR tresnal *m* ‖ greñas *f pl*, melena *f* (mass of hair) ‖ *electric shock* descarga *or* sacudida eléctrica; *to get an electric shock* sentir una sacudida eléctrica; electrochoque *m* (treatment).

shock [ʃɔk] *vt* producir una conmoción a, conmocionar a (to cause an emotional or physical shock) ‖ escandalizar, chocar (to give offence); *book that is shocking everybody* libro que escandaliza a todos ‖ indignar, dar un disgusto (to anger) ‖ sobresaltar, dar un susto (to startle) ‖ lastimar (the ear) ‖ AGR hacinar ‖ *to be shocked at* escandalizarse por.

◆ *vi* chocar.

shock absorber [-əbˌzɔ:bə*] *n* amortiguador *m*.

shocker [-ə*] *n* FAM sinvergüenza *m* & *f*, horror *m* (person) | cosa *f* horrible, horror *m* (thing) | novela *f* escandalosa (novel) | obra *f* de teatro escandalosa (play) ‖ sorpresa *f* desagradable.

shock-headed [-ˈhedid] *adj* desgreñado, da.

shocking [-iŋ] *adj* escandaloso, sa; vergonzoso, sa; chocante (morally incorrect); *shocking behaviour* comportamiento escandaloso ‖ espantoso, sa; horroroso, sa; horrible (causing horror); *shocking spectacle* espectáculo horrible ‖ aterrador, ra; *the shocking news of his death* la noticia aterradora de su muerte ‖ FAM espantoso, sa; horrible, horroroso, sa; malísimo, ma (very bad); *shocking weather* tiempo espantoso.

◆ *adv* → **shockingly.**

shockingly [-iŋli] *adv* de manera chocante *or* escandalosa (incorrectly) ‖ muy mal, horrorosamente, espantosamente; *he writes shockingly* escribe muy mal ‖ muy, sumamente, espantosamente; *shockingly dear, difficult* sumamente caro, difícil.

shockproof [-pru:f] *adj* a prueba de choques ‖ FIG inquebrantable.

shock tactics [-ˈtæktiks] *pl n* MIL táctica *f sing* de choque.

shock therapy [-ˈθerəpi]; **shock treatment** [-ˈtri:tmənt] *n* MED tratamiento *m* por electrochoques.

shock troops [-tru:ps] *pl n* MIL tropas *f* de choque *or* de asalto.

shock wave [-weiv] *n* PHYS onda *f* de choque *or* expansiva.

shod [ʃɔd] *pret/pp* → **shoe.**

shoddy [-i] *n* lana *f* regenerada (cloth) ‖ FIG mercancía *f* de mala calidad (goods) | pacotilla *f* (anything of poor quality).

◆ *adj* regenerado, da (cloth) ‖ FIG de mala calidad, de pacotilla (goods, etc.) | mal hecho (work).

shoe [ʃu:] *n* zapato *m*; *to put on one's shoes* ponerse los zapatos; *to take off one's shoes* quitarse los zapatos; *brown shoes* zapatos marrones ‖ herradura *f* (for a horse); *to cast a shoe* perder una herradura ‖ AUT zapata *f* (of brake) | cubierta *f* (of tyre) ‖ regatón *m* (metal end) ‖ TECH patín *m* (of sledge, etc.) | calzo *m* (chock) ‖ ELECTR frotador *m* ‖ MAR zapata *f* (of anchor) ‖ carrito *m* (in baccarat) ‖ — FIG & FAM *as hard as shoe leather* como suela de zapato (very hard) ‖ FIG *I should not like to be in his shoes* no me gustaría estar en su pellejo *or* en su lugar ‖ *shoe industry* industria *f* del calzado ‖ FIG *to be waiting for dead men's shoes* esperar que se muera alguien para ocupar su puesto | *to know where the shoe pinches* saber dónde le aprieta el zapato | *to put the shoe on the right foot* echar la culpa al que la tiene | *to step into s.o.'s shoes* ocupar el puesto de alguien.

shoe* [ʃu:] *vt* calzar (a person); *to be well shod* ir bien calzado ‖ herrar (a horse) ‖ poner un regatón a (a stick, etc.) ‖ poner una cubierta a (a wheel) ‖ TECH poner un patín *or* un calzo a.

— OBSERV Pret y pp ***shod***.

shoeblack [-blæk] *n* limpiabotas *m inv* [*AMER* lustrabotas *m inv*].

shoeblacking [-ˈblækiŋ] *n* US betún *m* [*AMER* bola *f*, lustre *m*].

shoe brush [-brʌʃ] *n* cepillo *m* para los zapatos.

shoe cream [-kri:m] *n* betún *m*, crema *f* para el calzado [*AMER* bola *f*, lustre *m*].

shoehorn [-hɔ:n] *n* calzador *m*.

shoelace [-leis] *n* cordón *m*.

shoe leather [-ˌleðə*] *n* cuero *m* para zapatos ‖ FIG zapatos *m pl* (shoes).

shoemaker [-ˌmeikə*] *n* zapatero *m* ‖ *shoemaker's* zapatería *f*.

shoe mender [-ˌmendə*] *n* zapatero *m* remendón.

shoe polish [-ˈpɔliʃ] *n* betún *m*, crema *f* para el calzado [*AMER* bola *f*, lustre *m*].

shoer [-ə*] *n* herrador *m*.

shoe repairer [-riˈpɛərə*] *n* zapatero *m* remendón, zapatero *m* de viejo.

shoeshine [-ʃain] *n* US betún *m*, crema *f* para el calzado [*AMER* bola *f*, lustre *m*] (polish) ‖ limpieza *f* de los zapatos [*AMER* lustrada *f*] (polishing) ‖ *shoeshine boy* limpiabotas *m inv* [*AMER* lustrabotas *m inv*] (shoeblack).

shoe shop [-ʃɔp]; US **shoe store** [stɔ:] *n* zapatería *f*, tienda *f* de zapatos, tienda *f* de calzado.

shoestring [-striŋ] *n* cordón *m* (shoelace) ‖ — FAM *on a shoestring* con muy poco dinero ‖ US CULIN *shoestring potatoes* patatas *f* paja.

shone [ʃɔn] *pret/pp* → **shine.**

shoo [ʃu:] *interj* ¡fuera! (to children) ‖ ¡zape! (to animals).

shoo [ʃu:] *vt* espantar, ahuyentar (animals) ‖ FIG mandar a otra parte (children).

shook [ʃuk] *pret* → **shake.**

shoot [ʃu:t] *n* BOT brote *m*, retoño *m*, renuevo *m* ‖ rápido *m* (river) ‖ plano *m* inclinado (a slope down) ‖ tobogán *m* (in swimming pool) ‖ vertedero *m* (for rubbish) ‖ aliviadero *m*, vertedero *m* (for overflow) ‖ punzada *f* (of pain) ‖ carrera *f* rápida [de algo lanzado] ‖ rebote *m* hacia adelante (of a ball) ‖ coto *m* de caza (land for hunting) ‖ cacería *f* (hunting party) ‖ caza *f* (the game shot) ‖ MIL ejercicio *m* de tiro, tiro *m* ‖ concurso *m* de tiro al blanco (shooting contest) ‖ lanzamiento *m* (of a rocket) ‖ FAM *the whole shoot* todos los bártulos, toda la pesca.

shoot* [ʃu:t] *vt* lanzar, tirar (a projectile) ‖ arrojar (by violent motion) ‖ disparar (arrow, bullet, gun) || herir (to wound); *he shot him in the leg* le hirió en la pierna || matar (to kill); *to shoot a rabbit* matar un conejo || pegar un tiro (to fire on); *he shot his father* le pegó un tiro a su padre || fusilar (to execute) || cazar; *he is in Africa shooting lions* está cazando leones en África || echar, tender (fishing net) || salvar; *to shoot a rapid* salvar un rápido || pasar rápidamente por debajo de (a bridge) || soltar, espetar (question) || echar (glance) || verter (coal, rubbish) || echar (beams, rays) || SP marcar (a goal) | tirar (the ball) || lanzar, tirar (a marble) || CINEM rodar, filmar || fotografiar, tomar, sacar (photograph) || MAR tomar la altura de (the sun) || echar (dice) || correr (a bolt) || BOT echar || MED & FAM poner una inyección || — *he was shot through the arm* una bala le atravesó el brazo || FIG *I'll be shot if...!* ¡que me ahorquen si...! || *to shoot a match* participar en un concurso de tiro || *to shoot craps* jugar a los dados || FIG *to shoot one's bolt* quemar su último cartucho || *to shoot s.o. dead* matar a alguien de un tiro *or* a tiros || FIG & FAM *to shoot the bull* charlar; *we spent the afternoon shooting the bull* hemos pasado la tarde charlando; decir tonterías (to talk nonsense) || *to shoot to death* matar a tiros.

◆ *vi* precipitarse, lanzarse (to move swiftly) || cazar (to hunt); *he is out shooting* se ha ido a cazar || disparar (with a bow, with a gun); *he shot at me* disparó contra mí || tirar; *to shoot at a target* tirar al blanco || tirar a, tener un alcance de (to reach) || CINEM rodar, filmar || fotografiar (photograph) || sobresalir, proyectarse (to project) || SP chutar (in football) | tirar (to attempt to score); *to shoot at goal* tirar a gol || correrse, echarse, cerrarse (a bolt) || pasar rápidamente *or* fugazmente (a star) || dar punzadas (a pain) || BOT brotar (bud) | crecer (plant) | echar brotes (tree) || — FAM *shoot!* ¡suéltalo!, ¡habla! || *to shoot past* o *by* pasar como un rayo || *to shoot through* cruzar rápidamente.

◆ *phr v* ***to shoot ahead*** tomar rápidamente la delantera (in a race) || ***to shoot away*** arrancar de un tiro | quemar (all one's ammunition) | disparar sin parar (to shoot incessantly) || ***to shoot down*** derribar (an aeroplane) | matar de un tiro (s.o.) | echar abajo (an argument) || ***to shoot forth*** echar (buds) || ***to shoot in*** entrar como un torbellino || ***to shoot off*** salir disparado (to rush out) | arrancar de un tiro | *she had a food shot off* una bala le arrancó el pie || ***to shoot out*** salir disparado (to rush out) | brotar (water) | salir (flames) | sobresalir, proyectarse (to project) | sacar (to stick out); *the snake shot out its tongue* la serpiente sacó la lengua | echar (sparks, buds, etc.) | *to shoot it out* resolverlo a tiros || ***to shoot up*** subir rápidamente (aeroplane, ball, etc.) | subir vertiginosamente (prices) | BOT crecer | FIG crecer, espigar (children) | salir (flames); *flames shot up from the house* las llamas salían de la casa || US aterrorizar, atemorizar [pegando tiros] (village, district).

— OBSERV Pret y pp ***shot***..

shooter [-ə*] *n* tirador, ra || cazador, ra (hunter) || SP goleador *m* || FIG estrella *f* fugaz || US arma *f* de fuego (firearm) || *six-shooter rifle* rifle *m* de seis tiros.

shooting [-iŋ] *n* disparo *m*, tiro *m* (of an arrow, a bullet, a gun) || herida *f* mortal (wound) || asesinato *m* (murder) || fusilamiento *m* (execution) || tiros *m pl*, disparos *m pl* (shots) || tiroteo *m* (exchange of shots) || MIL cañoneo *m*, bombardeo *m* (bombing) || tiro *m* al blanco; *shooting competition* concurso *m* de tiro al blanco || caza *f* (of animals) || paso *m* (of rapids) || BOT brote *m* (of buds) | salida *f* (of branches) || punzadas *f pl* (of pain) || CINEM toma *f* de vistas, rodaje *m*, filmación *f* || foto *f* (photograph).

◆ *adj* punzante, lancinante (pain).

shooting box [-iŋbɔks] *n* pabellón *m* de caza.

shooting brake [-iŋbreik] *n* AUT furgoneta *f*, rubia *f* (fam).

shooting gallery [-iŋgæləri] *n* barraca *f* de tiro al blanco (at the fair) || MIL galería *f* de tiro.

shooting jacket [-iŋdʒækit] *n* chaquetón *m*.

shooting licence [-iŋˌlaisəns] *n* licencia *f* de caza.

shooting lodge [-iŋˌlɔdʒ] *n* pabellón *m* de caza.

shooting match [-iŋˌmætʃ] *n* concurso *m* de tiro al blanco.

shooting party [-iŋˌpɑːti] *n* cacería *f*.

shooting range [-iŋˌreindʒ] *n* MIL campo *m* de tiro (for rifles) | polígono *m* de tiro (for artillery) || CINEM distancia *f* de toma de vistas || *within shooting range* a tiro.

shooting script [-iŋˌskript] *n* CINEM guión *m*.

shooting star [-iŋˌstɑː*] *n* estrella *f* fugaz.

shooting stick [-iŋˌstik] *n* bastón *m* que sirve de asiento.

shop [ʃɔp] *n* tienda *f*; *grocer's shop* tienda de ultramarinos || almacén *m* (large store) || departamento *m*, sección *f* (of a department store) || despacho *m* (for wine) || expendeduría *f* (for tobacco) || FAM negocios *m pl* (business) | oficina *f* (office) || US taller *m* (workshop) || — *baker's shop* panadería *f* || *shop!* ¿quién despacha? (when entering a shop) || FAM *to be all over the shop* estar en desorden, estar patas arriba || *to keep a shop* tener una tienda || *to set up shop* abrir *or* poner una tienda (to open a shop), poner un negocio (to open business) || *to shut up shop* cerrar una tienda (to close a shop), dejar los negocios, dejar su trabajo (to go out of business) || *to talk shop* hablar de negocios, hablar de asuntos profesionales.

shop [ʃɔp] *vi* hacer compras; *I spent the whole afternoon shopping* pasé toda la tarde haciendo compras || — *to go shopping* ir de compras || *to shop for* ir a buscar, ir a comprar.

◆ *vt* FAM denunciar, delatar.

shop assistant [-əˌsistənt] *n* dependiente, ta.

shop boy [-bɔi] *n* recadero *m*, chico *m* de los recados.

shop front [-frʌnt] *n* escaparate *m* [*AMER* vidriera *f*, vitrina *f*].

shopgirl [-gəːl] *n* dependienta *f*.

shop hours [-ˌauəz] *pl n* horas *f* de apertura y cierre [durante las cuales están abiertas las tiendas].

shopkeeper [-ˌkiːpə*] *n* tendero, ra; comerciante *m* & *f*.

shoplifter [-ˌliftə*] *n* ladrón *m* que roba en las tiendas, mechero, ra; ratero, ra.

shoplifting [-ˌliftiŋ] *n* ratería *f*, hurto *m*.

shopman [-mən] *n* dependiente *m* (employee) || tendero *m* (shopkeeper).

— OBSERV El plural de esta palabra es *shopmen*.

shopper [-ə*] *n* comprador, ra.

shopping [-iŋ] *n* compras *f pl*; *she is doing her shopping* está de compras.

shopping bag [-iŋˌbæg] *n* bolsa *f* de la compra.

shopping basket [-iŋˌbɑːskit] *n* cesta *f* de la compra.

shopping cart [-iŋˌkɑːt] *n* carrito *m*.

shopping centre; US **shopping center** [-iŋˌsentə*] *n* centro *m* comercial.

shopping list [-iŋˌlist] *n* lista *f* de compras.

shop-soiled [-sɔild] *adj* estropeado, da.

shop steward [-stjuəd] *n* enlace *m* sindical.

shoptalk [-tɔːk] *n* argot *m* (specialized vocabulary) || conversación *f* sobre asuntos profesionales (conversation).

shopwalker [-ˈwɔːkə*] *n* jefe *m* de sección *or* de departamento (person who supervises clerks).

shopwindow [-ˈwindəu] *n* escaparate *m* [*AMER* vidriera *f*, vitrina *f*].

shopworn [-wɔːn] *adj* estropeado, da (damaged) || FIG trasnochado, da; *shopworn ideas* ideas trasnochadas.

shore [ʃɔː*] *n* orilla *f* (sea or river edge); *how far is it to the other shore?* ¿qué distancia hay a la otra orilla? || playa *f* (beach) || costa *f* (coast) || tierra *f* (land); *on shore* en tierra || ARCH puntal *m* || MAR escora *f*, puntal *m* || — *in shore* cerca de la costa || *off shore* ⟶ **offshore.**

shore [ʃɔː*] *vt* desembarcar (a cargo) || escorar (to prop a ship) || ARCH apuntalar || *to shore up* apuntalar.

shore battery [-ˈbætəri] *n* batería *f* costera.

shore leave [-liːv] *n* MAR permiso *m* para bajar a tierra.

shoreless [-lis] *adj* sin límites.

shoreline [-lain] *n* orilla *f* (lake), litoral *m*, costa *f* (sea).

shore patrol [-pəˈtrəul] *n* US MAR patrulla *f* guardacostas.

shoreward [-wəd]; **shorewards** [-wədz] *adv* hacia la costa.

shoring [-iŋ] *n* puntales *m pl* (shores).

shorn [ʃɔːn] *pp* ⟶ **shear.**

short [ʃɔːt] *adj* corto, ta (of little length); *a short skirt* una falda corta; *to go by the shortest road* ir por el camino más corto; *the rope is too short* la cuerda es demasiado corta || bajo, ja (not tall); *person of short nature* persona de baja estatura || pequeño, ña; corto, ta; *short distance* distancia pequeña; *a short stick* un bastón corto; *short steps* pasos pequeños || escaso, sa (insufficient); *short crops* cosechas escasas; *I was short of money* andaba escaso de dinero || corto, ta; breve (not long in time) || poco, ca; *of short duration* de poca duración || conciso, sa (style) || seco, ca (brusque) || tajante (tone, answer) || vivo, va; *very short temper* carácter muy vivo || CULIN curruscante, crujiente (pastry) || GRAMM breve || COMM a corto plazo (bill, payment, loan) | al descubierto; *short sale* venta al descubierto || rápido, da (pulse) || cerrado, da (turn) || RAD corto, ta (wave) || TECH quebradizo, za (iron) || — *a short distance from* a poca distancia de || *a short eight kilometres* unos ocho kilómetros escasos || *a short time ago* hace poco tiempo || *a short way off* a poca distancia, cerca || *a short while ago* hace un momento || *Dick is short for Richard* Dick es el diminutivo de Richard || *for a short time* durante *or* por poco tiempo || *for short* para abreviar || *I am twenty pounds short* me faltan veinte libras || *in a short time* dentro de poco || *in short order* en seguida || *in short supply* escaso, sa || *it is one pound short* falta una libra || *not far short of* no lejos de, casi; *he is not far short of a masterpiece* casi una obra maestra || *nothing short of* nada menos que, nada fuera de, nada excepto, sólo; *nothing short of an operation can save you* sólo una operación le salvará || *on short notice* en poco tiempo || *pram is short for perambulator* "pram" es la abreviatura de «perambulator» || FIG *short and sweet* corto y bueno || *short drink* bebida corta, bebida alcohólica servida sin agua || CINEM *short film* cortometraje *m* || SP *short head* media cabeza (in horse racing) || *short list* lista *f* de seleccionados || *short sight* vista corta, miopía *f* || *short story* novela corta || *short time* jornada reducida || *short ton* tonelada corta || FAM *something short* una copita || *to be short in one's payments* quedarse corto en el pago || *to be short* *in the arms* tener los brazos cortos (person), tener las mangas demasiado cortas (garment) || *to be short of* andar escaso de, tener poco; *to be short of money* tener poco dinero || *to be short on* tener poco || *to be short with s.o.* hablar a alguien con tono tajante || *to get the short end of the stick* llevarse la peor parte || *to give short measure* dar de menos || *to give short weight* dar menos que el peso exacto || *to go short of* privarse de || *to grow short* menguar (days) || *to make short work of* despachar rápidamente || *to run short* agotarse; *our supplies run short* nuestras provisiones se agotan || *to run short of* acabársele (a uno), agotársele (a uno); *we ran short of oil* se nos acabó el aceite || *to take shorter steps* aminorar el paso || *we are still a mile short of our destination* nos falta todavía una milla para llegar a nuestro destino.

◆ *adv* en seco; *to stop short* pararse en seco || bruscamente (in a brusque manner) || cerca (near) || COMM a corto plazo (borrowing) | al descubierto; *to sell short* vender al descubierto || — *short of* excepto, menos; *he would do anything short of murder* haría cualquier cosa excepto matar || *to be taken up short* cogerle a uno desprevenido || *to come* o *to fall short of* no cumplir (one's duty), no alcanzar (one's mark), no corresponder a (one's expectations), no satisfacer (requisites), estar muy por debajo de (a model) || *to cut s.o. short* interrumpir bruscamente *or* cortar en seco a uno (to interrupt), dejarle cortado a uno (to silence) || *to stop short of doing sth.* quedarse a un paso de hacer algo.

◆ *n* abreviatura *f* (abbreviation) || diminutivo *m* (of a name) || apodo *m*, mote *m* (nickname) || CINEM cortometraje *m* || COMM vendedor *m* al descubierto (person) | venta *f* al descubierto (sale) | déficit *m* || GRAMM sílaba *f* breve (syllable) | vocal *f* breve (vowel) || ELECTR cortocircuito *m* || FAM bebida *f* corta, bebida *f* alcohólica servida sin agua || *in short* en resumen.

◆ *pl* "shorts" *m*, pantalones *m* cortos || US calzoncillos *m* (underpants).

short [ʃɔːt] *vt* ELECTR poner en cortocircuito.

◆ *vi* ELECTR ponerse en cortocircuito.

shortage [-idʒ] *n* falta *f*, escasez *f*, insuficiencia *f*; *labour shortage* falta de mano de obra || crisis *f*; *housing shortage* crisis de la vivienda || COMM déficit *m*; *to make up the shortage* enjugar el déficit.

short back and sides [ˈʃɔːtækənˌsaidz] cuello hecho y corto a los lados (at mens' hairdresser).

shortbread [-bed] *n* especie *f* de mantecada.

shortcake [-keik] *n* CULIN especie *f* de mantecada (shortbread) || US CULIN torta *f* de frutas.

shortchange [-tʃeindʒ] *vt* FAM dar de menos en la vuelta, devolver menos de lo debido en el cambio || FIG estafar (to cheat).

short circuit [-ˈsəːkit] *n* ELECTR cortocircuito *m*.

short-circuit [-ˈsəːkit] *vt* ELECTR poner en cortocircuito || FIG saltarse, hacer caso omiso de.

◆ *vi* ELECTR ponerse en cortocircuito.

shortcoming [-ˈkʌmiŋ] *n* defecto *m*, punto *m* flaco (defect) || falta *f* (shortage).

shortcut [-ˌkʌt] *n* atajo *m*.

shorten [-n] *vt* acortar (to maker shorter); *I'm going to shorten my skirt* voy a acortar mi falda; *I had to shorten my holiday* tuve que acortar mis vacaciones || compendiar, resumir (a text) || reducir (a task) || disminuir, reducir (rations) || abreviar (to abbreviate).

◆ *vi* acortarse (to become shorter) || menguar (days) || disminuir, reducirse (to diminish) || abreviarse; *Member of Parliament shortens to MP* "Member of Parliament" se abrevia en MP.

shortening [-niŋ] *n* acortamiento *m* (of garment, of holiday, etc.) || compendio *m*, resumen *m* (of a text) || reducción *f*, disminución *f* (decrease) || abreviación *f* (abbreviation) || CULIN materia *f* grasa.

shortfall [-fɔːl] *n* COMM déficit *m*.

shorthand [-hænd] *n* taquigrafía *f* || — *shorthand typewriter* estenotipo *m*; máquina *f* de taquigrafía || *shorthand typist* taquimecanógrafo, fa || *shorthand writer* taquígrafo, fa; estenógrafo, fa || *to take down in shorthand* tomar taquigráficamente.

◆ *adj* taquigráfico, ca (system, symbol) || tomado en taquigrafía (report, etc.).

shorthanded [-ˈhændid] *adj* falto de mano de obra.

short-haul [-hɔːl] *adj* de corto recorrido (transport).

shorthead [-hed] *n* braquicéfalo, la.

shortish [-iʃ] *adj* bastante corto || bajito, ta (person).

short-lived [-ˈlivd] *adj* efímero, ra.

shortly [-li] *adv* en pocas palabras (in a few words) || dentro de poco (soon) || secamente (discourteously) || — *shortly after* poco después || *shortly before four o'clock* poco antes de las cuatro.

shortness [-nis] *n* brevedad *f* (duration) || pequeñez *f* (length, size) || falta *f*, escasez *f* (of money, of provisions) || sequedad *f* (of manner) || falta *f* (of breath, of memory) || *shortness of sight* miopía *f*.

short-range [-ˈreindʒ] *adj* MIL de corto alcance || AVIAT de autonomía limitada.

shortsighted [-ˈsaitid] *adj* miope, corto de vista (myopic) || FIG corto de vista, miope (without foresight).

shortsightedness [-saitidnis] *n* miopía *f* || FIG cortedad *f* de vista, miopía *f*, falta *f* de perspicacia, imprevisión *f*.

short-spoken [-ˈspəukən] *adj* tajante, seco, ca.

short-staffed [-stɑft] *adj* falto de personal.

short-tempered [-ˈtempəd] *adj* de mal genio.

short-term [-təːm] *adj* a corto plazo; *short-term loan* préstamo a corto plazo.

shortwave [-weiv] *n* onda *f* corta.

◆ *adj* de onda corta.

short-winded [-windid] *adj* de respiración corta, corto de resuello.

shorty [-i] *n* FAM retaco *m*, tapón *m* de alberca (small person).

shot [ʃɔt] *n* bala *f* (of a gun) || bala *f* de cañón (of a cannon) || perdigones *m pl* (for hunting) || tiro *m*, disparo *m* (act of shooting, detonation, wound); *at a shot* de un tiro || cañonazo *m* (of cannon) || alcance *m* (range of shoot); *out of shot* fuera de su alcance || tirador, ra (person who shoots); *he is a good shot* es un buen tirador || FIG indirecta *f* (hinting criticism); *that was a shot at you* eso fue una indirecta dirigida a ti | oportunidad *f* (chance) | conjetura *f* (guess) | tentativa *f* (intent) || CINEM toma *f* | plano *m*; *close shot* primer plano; *long shot* plano largo || PHOT foto *f*, instantánea *f* (photograph) || SP peso *m* [AMER pesa *f*, bala *f*] (weight); *to put the shot* lanzar el peso | tiro *m* (at goal) | chut *m* (at goal in football) || golpe *m*, jugada *f* (in billiards) || redada *f* (in fishing) || FAM trago *m* (of drinks) || MED inyección *f* (injection) | dosis *f* (dose) || — FIG *at the first shot* a la primera || FAM *big shot* pez gordo || *exchange of shots* tiroteo *m* || CINEM *exterior shots* exteriores *m pl* || FIG *good shot!* ¡muy bien! || *it's your shot* te toca a ti || FIG *like a shot* como movido por un resorte; *he was out of the chair like a shot* saltó del sillón como movido por un resorte || *Moon shot* lanzamiento *m* de un cohete hacia la Luna || FIG *not by a long shot* ni mucho menos || CINEM *three-quarter shot* plano americano || FIG *to be off like a shot* hacer algo sin vacilar || *to have a flying shot at* tirar al vuelo || FIG *to have a shot at sth.* probar suerte con algo, intentar hacer algo | *to have sth. within shot* tener algo a tiro | *to make a shot at an answer* contestar a la buena de Dios *or* al azar | *to pay one's shot* pagar su parte || *without firing a shot* sin pegar un tiro.

◆ *adj* tornasolado, da (fabric) || FAM gastado, da (worn-out) | agotado, da (completely exhausted) | destrozado, da (ruined); *his nerves are shot* tiene los nervios destrozados || FAM *to get shot of* quitarse de encima (to get rid of).

shot [ʃɔt] *pret/pp* → **shoot.**

shote [ʃəut] *n* US ZOOL cochinillo *m*, lechón *m*.

shotgun [ˈʃɔtgʌn] *n* escopeta *f*; *double-barrelled shotgun* escopeta de dos cañones || FAM *it was a shotgun marriage* se casaron de prisa y corriendo.

shot put [ˈʃɔtput] *n* US SP lanzamiento *m* de peso.

shot-putter [-ə*] *n* lanzador *m* de peso.

should [ʃud] *v aux* se emplea para formar el potencial [primera persona del singular y del plural]; *I should have arrived earlier if the train had not been late* hubiera llegado más temprano si el tren no hubiese tenido retraso || deber, tener que (suggestion); *you should walk faster if you want to arrive in time* deberías andar más de prisa si quieres llegar a tiempo || tener que (obligation); *all doors should be locked by ten* todas las puertas tienen que estar cerradas a las diez || deber de (probability); *they should be there by now* ya deben de estar allí || — *how should I know?* ¿cómo iba yo a saber? || *I should if I were you* lo haría si estuviese en tu lugar, yo que tú lo haría || *I should think so* supongo que sí || *it should rain tonight if the wind drops* lloverá probablemente esta noche si amaina el viento.

— OBSERV *Should* es el pretérito de *shall* (see SHALL). El verbo auxiliar *should* puede contraerse cuando le antecede un pronombre personal: *I'd, we'd.* Si va seguido por la negación *not* puede formar con ella la palabra *shouldn't: I shouldn't do it, shouldn't we go?*

— OBSERV En la primera persona del potencial *would* sustituye frecuentemente a *should: I would have arrived earlier if....*

— OBSERV Cuando *should* se encuentra en una oración que expresa una condición o una finalidad, el verbo que acompaña tiene que ir en subjuntivo en español: *should he come, he would be welcome* si viniera sería bienvenido; *he gave me an umbrella so that I should not get wet* me dio un paraguas para que no me mojara. Lo mismo ocurre en los casos en que se halla en una oración subordinada precedida por la expresión de un sentimiento: *I am astonished that he should say that* me extraña que diga eso.

shoulder [ˈʃəuldə*] *n* ANAT hombro *m* || espaldilla *f*, codillo *m*, paletilla *f* (of meat) || hombro *m* (of a garment) || desnivel *m* (of ground) || rellano *m* (of hill) || estribación *f* (of mountain) || andén *m* (of road) || *shoulder to shoulder* hombro a hombro, hombro con hombro || FIG *straight from the shoulder* francamente, con toda sinceridad, sin rodeos | *to be s.o.'s shoulder to cry on* ser el paño de lágrimas de alguien | *to give s.o. the cold shoulder* tratar a alguien con frialdad, volver la espalda a alguien || *to look over one's shoulder* mirar hacia atrás || FIG *to put one's shoulder to the wheel* arrimar el hombro || *to sling sth. over one's shoulders* echarse algo al hombro.

◆ *pl* hombros *m*, espalda *f sing* || — *on the shoulder a or* en hombros || FIG *to have one's head squarely on one's shoulders* tener la cabeza en su sitio ‖ *to have round shoulders* ser cargado de espaldas | FIG *to put the blame on s.o.'s shoulders* echarle la culpa a alguien | *to rub shoulders with s.o.* codearse con alguien ‖ *to shrug one's shoulders* encogerse de hombros ‖ *to stand head and shoulders above s.o.* llevarle la cabeza a uno, sacarle la cabeza a uno ‖ *to take a responsibility on one's shoulders* cargar con una responsabilidad.

shoulder [ˈʃəuldə*] *vt* empujar con el hombro (to push) ‖ echarse al hombro (to put on one's shoulder) ‖ llevar en hombros (to carry on the shoulders) ‖ cargar con (task, responsibility) ‖ — MIL *shoulder arms!* ¡arma al hombro! ‖ *to shoulder one's way through a crowd* abrirse paso a codazos entre la muchedumbre ‖ *to shoulder s.o. out of the way* apartar a alguien con el hombro.

shoulder bag [-bæg] *n* bolso *m* de bandolera.

shoulder belt [-belt] *n* tahalí *m* (baldric) ‖ bandolera *f* (bandoleer).

shoulder blade [-bleid] *n* ANAT omóplato *m*, omoplato *m* ‖ paletilla *f* (of an animal).

shoulder braid [-breid] *n* MIL forrajera *f*.

shoulder-high [-ˈhai] *adv* a hombros; *to carry shoulder-high* llevar *or* sacar a hombros.

shoulder knot [-nɔt] *n* cordones *m pl*, charretera *f* (insignia, decoration).

shoulder-length [-leŋθ] *adj* hasta los hombros (hair).

shoulder pad [-pæd] *n* hombrera *f*.

shoulder plate [-pleit] *n* hombrera *f* (of armour).

shoulder strap [-stræp] *n* bandolera *f*, correa *f* (of bag, of knapsack) ‖ tirante *m* (on underwear) ‖ MIL dragona *f*.

shouldn't [ˈʃudənt] contracción de «should not».

should've [ˈʃudəv] contracción de «should have».

shout [ʃaut] *n* grito *m* (cry, call) ‖ — *shout of laughter* carcajada *f* ‖ *shouts of applause* aclamaciones *f*.

shout [ʃaut] *vt* gritar; *he shouted to me that it was not safe* me gritó que era peligroso ‖ vociferar, soltar a voz en grito (an insult) ‖ expresar en alta voz *or* a voz en grito (an opinion) ‖ — *to shout o.s. hoarse* volverse ronco a fuerza de gritar, desgañitarse gritando ‖ *to shout out* gritar ‖ *to shout s.o. down* callar a alguien a gritos ‖ *to shout sth. down* abuchear algo.

◆ *vi* gritar; *to shout at the top of one's voice* gritar a voz en cuello; *to shout for joy* gritar de alegría ‖ — *to shout at s.o.* gritarle a uno ‖ *to shout for s.o.* llamar a alguien a gritos ‖ *to shout like mad* gritar como un desaforado ‖ *to shout with laughter* reírse a carcajadas.

shouting [-iŋ] *n* gritos *m pl* ‖ *within shouting distance* al alcance de la voz.

◆ *adj* que grita.

shove [ʃʌv] *n* empujón *m* ‖ *to give a shove* empujar, dar un empujón.

shove [ʃʌv] *vt* empujar (by pushing) ‖ meter, meterse (to put); *shove it in your pocket* métaselo en el bolsillo ‖ FIG *to shove the responsibility on to s.o.* cargar uno con la responsabilidad de.

◆ *vi* empujar ‖ — FAM *to shove along* o *off* largarse ‖ *to shove by* o *past s.o.* empujar *or* dar un empujón a alguien al pasar ‖ MAR *to shove off* desatracar (a boat) ‖ *to shove through* abrirse paso a codazos entre (a crowd).

shovel [ˈʃʌvl] *n* pala *f*; *coal shovel* pala para el carbón ‖ TECH pala *f* mecánica *or* cargadora, excavadora *f*.

shovel [ˈʃʌvl] *vt* mover con la pala (to move with a shovel) ‖ echar con la pala (to put with a shovel) ‖ sacar con la pala (to clear with a shovel) ‖ FIG & FAM echar una gran cantidad de; *he shoveled sugar into his coffee* echó una gran cantidad de azúcar en el café ‖ — *to shovel a path through the snow* despejar un camino quitando la nieve con la pala ‖ FAM *to shovel food into one's mouth* zamparse la comida.

shovelboard [-bɔːd] *n* juego *m* de tejo.

shoveler [-ə*] *n* ⟶ **shoveller.**

shovel hat [-hæt] *n* REL sombrero *m* de teja.

shoveller; shoveler [-ə*] *n* paleador *m* (worker) ‖ espátula *f* común (bird).

show [ʃəu] *n* demostración *f* (showing); *a show of strength* una demostración de fuerza ‖ exposición *f* (exhibition); *flower show* exposición de horticultura ‖ apariencia *f* (appearance) ‖ feria *f*; *agricultural show* feria del campo ‖ concurso *m*; *horse show* concurso hípico ‖ salón *m*; *motor show* salón del automóvil ‖ función *f* (performance) ‖ espectáculo *m* (entertainment); *to go to a show* ir a ver un espectáculo ‖ RAD programa *m* ‖ sombra *f*, traza *f*, vestigio *m* (trace) ‖ indicación *f*, señal *f* (sign) ‖ vista *f* (view) ‖ oportunidad *f* (chance) ‖ alarde *m* (pretence); *to make a show of wealth* hacer alarde de riqueza ‖ ostentación *f* (display) ‖ aparato *m* (pomp) ‖ actuación *f*, papel *m*; *he put up a good show* tuvo una buena actuación, hizo un buen papel ‖ FAM negocio *m* (undertaking); *he wrecked the whole show* estropeó todo el negocio ‖ US FAM tercer lugar *m* (in horse racing) ‖ — FAM *bad show!* ¡malo! ‖ *by show of hands* a mano alzada (vote) ‖ *dumb show* pantomima *f* ‖ *fashion show* desfile *m* de modelos ‖ *for show* para impresionar a los demás ‖ FAM *good show!* ¡muy bien! ‖ *Lord Mayor's show* desfile organizado en honor del alcalde de Londres ‖ *one-man show* recital *m* ‖ COMM *on show* expuesto, ta ‖ *show of hands* votación *f* a mano alzada ‖ *to deceive s.o. under a show of friendship* engañar a alguien fingiendo amistad ‖ FAM *to give the show away* descubrir el pastel | *to make a show of* hacer gala de, alardear de | *to make a show of o.s.* hacer el ridículo ‖ *to put up a show of resistance* hacer el paripé de resistir, fingir resistencia ‖ FAM *to run* o *to boss the show* llevar la voz cantante, ser el que manda, tener la sartén por el mango | *to steal the show* llevarse todos los aplausos.

show* [ʃəu] *vt* enseñar, mostrar; *he showed his books to me* me enseñó sus libros; *show me your hands* enséñeme las manos ‖ dejar ver; *this dress shows your slip* este traje deja ver tu combinación ‖ llevar, conducir; *she showed me to my seat* me condujo a mi asiento ‖ explicar; *this letter shows why she could not come* esta carta explica por qué no pudo venir ‖ exponer; *to show one's reasons* exponer sus razones ‖ demostrar, mostrar, probar (to demonstrate); *the evidence shows that he was right* las pruebas demuestran que tenía razón ‖ manifestar, mostrar (to manifest); *she showed her displeasure* manifestó su descontento ‖ demostrar, mostrar; *his attempt shows courage* su intento demuestra valor ‖ tener; *they showed no reaction* no tuvieron reacción alguna ‖ conceder, hacer (to grant); *he showed me a favour* me hizo un favor ‖ tener (mercy) ‖ registrar, arrojar; *the firm showed a profit* la empresa registró un beneficio ‖ experimentar; *exports showed an important increase last year* las exportaciones experimentaron un gran aumento el año pasado ‖ indicar, señalar, mostrar, enseñar (the way) ‖ indicar, señalar, mostrar (time, a place, etc.); *the traffic lights show that we must stop* los semáforos indican que tenemos que pararnos ‖ marcar, indicar (temperature) ‖ indicar, revelar (to reveal) ‖ indicar; *place shown in a map* sitio indicado en un mapa ‖ presentar; *the account shows him as a rascal* el relato lo presenta como un bribón ‖ ARTS representar ‖ COMM presentar (to present); *the firm showed its new designs* la empresa presentó sus nuevos diseños | exponer, presentar, exhibir (in a display window) ‖ representar, dar (a play) ‖ poner, echar, proyectar, exhibir (film) ‖ proyectar, enseñar (slides) ‖ exponer (in an exhibition); *he won prizes for all the roses he showed* ganó premios por todas las rosas que expuso ‖ JUR alegar, hacer constar (one's right) ‖ — *as shown in the illustration* como se ve en el grabado ‖ FIG *he has been working all day and has nothing to show for it* ha estado trabajando todo el día para nada ‖ *he is beginning to show his age* ya empieza a notarse la edad que tiene ‖ FAM *he will never show his face here again* nunca más aparecerá *or* se dejará ver por aquí | *I'll show you!* ¡te vas a enterar!, ¡ya me las pagarás! ‖ FIG *to have nothing to show for it* no sacar ningún provecho | *to show one's hand* poner las cartas boca arriba, descubrir su juego ‖ *to show o.s.* dejarse ver ‖ *to show o.s. a coward* mostrarse cobarde, demostrar ser un cobarde ‖ *to show s.o. a light* iluminar a alguien ‖ *to show s.o. how to read* enseñar a alguien a leer ‖ *to show s.o. into a room* hacer pasar *or* entrar a alguien en una habitación ‖ *to show s.o. round the town* hacer visitar la ciudad a alguien ‖ FAM *to show s.o. the door* echar a alguien con cajas destempladas ‖ *what can I show you, Madam?* ¿qué desea la señora?

◆ *vi* verse, notarse (to be noticeable); *the parts that do not show* las partes que no se ven; *does the mark of the wound still show?* ¿se ve todavía la marca de la herida?; *your petticoat is showing* se te ven las enaguas; *it doesn't show that you are tired* no se nota que estás cansado ‖ aparecer, salir; *the buds are beginning to show* los retoños empiezan a salir ‖ THEATR dar una función ‖ CINEM exhibirse, proyectarse (a film) ‖ US FAM llegar en tercer lugar (in horse racing) ‖ — *it just goes to show!* ¡hay que ver! ‖ *to show to advantage* apreciarse mejor; *his talent shows to advantage when he plays a Stradivarius* su talento se aprecia mejor cuando toca con un Stradivarius ‖ *what is showing at the cinema?* ¿qué ponen en el cine?, ¿qué echan en el cine?, ¿qué dan en el cine?

◆ *phr v* **to show in** hacer pasar (a visitor) ‖ **to show off** hacer alarde de; *he likes to show off his strength* le gusta hacer alarde de su fuerza | realzar, hacer resaltar; *setting that shows off a stone* engaste que hace resaltar una piedra | presumir, darse pisto (to boast) ‖ **to show out** acompañar a la puerta ‖ **to show through** transparentarse ‖ **to show up** hacer subir (a guest) | poner en evidencia, sacar a luz (a thing); *to show up s.o.'s faults* poner en evidencia los defectos de alguien | poner de manifiesto; *when he plays on a Stradivarius his talent is shown up* cuando toca con un Stradivarius su talento se pone de manifiesto | revelar, descubrir; *to show up a fraud* revelar un fraude | desenmascarar (an impostor) | hacer resaltar, realzar; *this dress shows up her figure* este traje hace resaltar su figura | entregar (one's work) | destacarse, sobresalir, resaltar (against a background) | perfilarse (on the horizon) | FAM venir, aparecer (to be present at); *he didn't show up at the meeting* no vino a la reunión.

— OBSERV Pret ***showed***; pp ***shown, showed***.

show bill [-bil] *n* cartel *m* (poster).

show biz [-biz] *n* FAM mundo *m* del espectáculo, espectáculos *m pl*.

showboat [-bəut] *n* US barco *m* donde se dan representaciones teatrales.

show business [-ˈbiznis] *n* mundo *m* del espectáculo, espectáculos *m pl*.

show card [-kaːd] *n* rótulo *m*, letrero *m* (in a shopwindow) ‖ muestrario *m*, colección *f* de muestras (samples).

showcase [-keis] *n* vitrina *f* (in a museum) || escaparate *m* [*AMER* vidriera *f*, vitrina *f*] (in a shop).

showdown [-daun] *n* momento *m* decisivo, hora *f* de la verdad (decisive moment) || confrontación *f* (of two persons).

shower [ˈʃauə*] *n* chubasco *m*, aguacero *m*, chaparrón *m* (of rain) || granizada *f* (of hail) || nevada *f* (of snow) || FIG lluvia *f* (of blows, of stones) | avalancha *f* (of insults) | diluvio *m*, lluvia *f* (of letters) | haz *m* (of sparks) || ducha *f* (bath) || FAM panda *f* de imbéciles (stupid people) || *US* fiesta *f* en que todos traen un regalo (gathering) || — *showers of* montones de || *to take a shower* ducharse, tomar una ducha, darse una ducha.

shower [ˈʃauə*] *vt* derramar (to pour) || FIG colmar; *to shower attentions on s.o.* colmar a alguien de atenciones | inundar; *my friends showered me with presents* mis amigos me inundaron de regalos || — FIG *I was showered with invitations* me llegaron las invitaciones de todas partes | *questions were showered on him* le acosaron con preguntas.
◆ *vi* llover (to rain) || ducharse (to take a shower) || FIG *congratulations showered on her* todos la felicitaban.

shower bath [-bɑːθ] *n* ducha *f*.

showerproof [-pruːf] *adj* impermeable.

showery [-ri] *adj* lluvioso, sa (weather).

show flat [ˈʃəuflæt] *n* piso *m* de muestra, piso *m* piloto.

show girl [ˈʃəugəːl] *n* THEATR corista *f*.

showily [ˈʃəuili] *adv* con ostentación (displayed) || vistosamente, de una manera llamativa (dressed) || lujosamente pero con mal gusto (furnished).

showiness [ˈʃəuinis] *n* ostentación *f* (ostentation); *dressed without showiness* vestido sin ostentación || lo aparatoso (of a ceremony) || lo llamativo, lo vistoso (of a dress) || lujo *m* que revela mal gusto (of furniture).

showing [ˈʃəuiŋ] *n* exposición *f* (exhibition) || actuación *f* (performance) || proyección *f* (of film) || manifestación *f* (of one's feelings) || demostración *f* (of evidence) || presentación *f* (of facts) || resultados *m pl* (results) || — *on this showing* mirando así las cosas || *on your own showing* según lo que usted mismo dice, según sus propias palabras || *to make a good showing* hacer un buen papel, quedar bien.

show jumping [ˈʃəuˈdʒʌmpiŋ] *n* SP concurso *m* hípico.

showman [ˈʃəumən] *n* organizador *m* *or* empresario *m* de espectáculos || feriante *m* (in a fair) || director *m* de circo (of a circus) || FIG exhibicionista *m* | comediante *m*.
— OBSERV El plural de esta palabra es *showmen*.

showmanship [-ʃip] *n* talento *m* para organizar espectáculos || FIG exhibicionismo *m* | teatralidad *f* (theatricality).

shown [ʃəun] *pp* ⟶ **show.**

show-off [ˈʃəuˈɔf] *n* FAM presumido, da (conceited person) | alarde *m*, ostentación *f* (ostentation).

showpiece [ˈʃəupiːs] *n* obra *f* maestra || FIG modelo *m*.

showplace [ˈʃəupleis] *n* sitio *m* de interés turístico.

showroom [ˈʃəurum] *n* sala *f* de muestras || ARTS sala *f* de exposición.

show window [ˈʃəuˈwindəu] *n* escaparate *m* [*AMER* vidriera *f*, vitrina *f*].

showy [ˈʃəui] *adj* ostentoso, sa (people) || aparatoso, sa (ceremony) || llamativo, va; vistoso, sa; *a showy dress* un traje llamativo.

shrank [ʃræŋk] *pret* ⟶ **shrink.**

shrapnel [ˈʃræpnl] *n* MIL "shrapnel" *m* (projectile) | metralla *f* (shell fragment).

shred [ʃred] *n* fragmento *m*, trozo *m* (fragment) || jirón *m* (of cloth); *in shreds* hecho jirones || tira *f* (strip); *to cut sth. into shreds* cortar algo en tiras || FIG chispa *f*, pizca *f*, átomo *m*; *there is not a shred of truth in what he says* no hay ni chispa de verdad en lo que dice || — *there isn't a shred of evidence* no hay la menor prueba de ello || *to tear to shreds* hacer trizas, destrozar (sth.), echar abajo *or* por tierra (an argument).

shred [ʃred] *vt* hacer trizas, destrozar || CULIN despedazar (meat) | cortar en tiras (vegetables) || TECH desfibrar (paper, rags).

shredder [-ə*] *n* TECH desfibradora *f*.

shrew [ʃruː] *n* ZOOL musaraña *f* || FIG arpía *f* (brawling woman) || *the Taming of the Shrew* La fierecilla domada, La doma de la bravía (Shakespeare's play).

shrewd [-d] *adj* perspicaz (perspicacious) || sagaz, listo, ta (clever) || astuto, ta (astute) || juicioso, sa; atinado, da (reasoning) || hábil (answer) || fino, na (wit) || (ant) duro, ra (blow) || penetrante (cold) || — *I can make a shrewd guess as to who is the author* me es muy fácil adivinar quién es el autor || *I have a shrewd idea that* me parece que.

shrewdly [-dli] *adv* con perspicacia.

shrewdness [-dnis] *n* perspicacia *f* (perspicacity) || sagacidad *f*, inteligencia *f* (cleverness) || astucia *f* (astuteness).

shrewish [-iʃ] *adj* de mal genio, regañón, ona (ill-tempered).

shrewmouse [-maus] *n* ZOOL musaraña *f*.

shriek [friːk] *n* chillido *m* (piercing cry) || grito *m* (scream) || *shrieks of laughter* carcajadas *f*.

shriek [friːk] *vi* chillar (to utter a piercing cry) || gritar (to scream) || FIG & FAM darse patadas (two colours) || — *to shriek at the top of one's voice* gritar a voz en cuello || *to shriek with laughter* reírse a carcajadas.
◆ *vt* gritar || *to shriek out a cry for help* pedir socorro a voz en grito.

shrieking [-iŋ] *adj* chillón, ona (colour).
◆ *n* chillidos *m pl*, gritos *m pl*.

shrift [ʃrift] *n* (ant) confesión *f* (confession) || absolución *f* (remission) || FIG *to give s.o. short shrift* despachar a alguien.

shrike [ʃraik] *n* alcaudón *m* (bird).

shrill [ʃril] *adj* chillón, ona; agudo, da (voice, tone) || agudo, da; estridente (cry, sound) || estridente (whistle).

shrill [ʃril] *vi* tener un sonido agudo *or* estridente.
◆ *vt* chillar || *to shrill out* gritar (insults), cantar con voz aguda (a song).

shrillness [-nis] *n* lo chillón, lo agudo (of a voice, of a tone) || lo estridente, lo agudo, estridencia *f* (of a sound).

shrilly [-i] *adv* con tono agudo || con un sonido estridente.

shrimp [ʃrimp] *n* ZOOL camarón *m* || FAM renacuajo *m* (small person).

shrimp [ʃrimp] *vi* pescar camarones.

shrine [ʃrain] *n* REL relicario *m* (reliquary) | capilla *f* (chapel) | altar *m* (altar) | mausoleo *m*, sepulcro *m* (tomb) | lugar *m* santo (place) | santuario *m* (sanctuary) || FIG santuario *m*.

shrink* [ʃriŋk] *vt* encoger (clothes, etc.); *this soap won't shrink woolen goods* este jabón no encogerá los artículos de lana || TECH contraer (metal) | montar en caliente || reducir (heads, value); *shrunken head* cabeza reducida.
◆ *vi* encoger (to become smaller); *woolen clothes often shrink when they are washed* la ropa de lana encoge a menudo cuando se lava || disminuir (value) || TECH contraerse (metal) || FIG encogerse || — FIG *to shrink away* o *back* echarse atrás (to draw back) | *to shrink from doing sth.* horrorizarle a uno hacer algo | *to shrink into o.s.* recogerse en sí mismo, meterse en el caparazón.
— OBSERV Pret ***shrank***; pp ***shrunk.*** En Estados Unidos también existe el pretérito ***shrunk.*** El participio pasivo ***shrunken*** sólo se usa como adjetivo.

shrink [ʃriŋk] *n* encogimiento *m* || FAM psiquiatra *m* (psychiatrist).

shrinkable [-əbl] *adj* que puede encoger.

shrinkage [-idʒ] *n* encogimiento *m* (of cloth) || contracción *f* (of metal); *shrinkage factor* coeficiente de contracción || FIG disminución *f*, reducción *f*.

shrink-wrap [-ræp] *vt* envolver en plástico transparente.

shrive* [ʃraiv] *vt* (ant) REL confesar.
◆ *vi* (ant) REL confesarse.
— OBSERV Pret ***shrove***; pp ***shriven***.

shrivel [ˈʃrivl] *vt* encoger (to shrink) || apergaminar, arrugar (to wrinkle) || marchitar, secar (plants) || quemar (to burn) || consumir (to waste away).
◆ *vi* *to shrivel up* encogerse (to shrink), apergaminarse, arrugarse, consumirse (people), marchitarse, consumirse, secarse (plants), quemarse (to burn up).

shriven [ˈʃrivn] *pp* ⟶ **shrive.**

shroud [ʃraud] *n* sudario *m*, mortaja *f* (for corpses) || FIG velo *m*; *a shroud of mystery* un velo de misterio | manto *m*; *the shroud of night* el manto de la noche || MAR obenque *m* || REL *the Holy Shroud* el Santo Sudario.

shroud [ʃraud] *vt* amortajar (a corpse) || FIG ocultar, tapar (to hide) | envolver (to surround); *shrouded in mist* envuelto en la niebla || FIG *shrouded in mystery* misterioso, sa; envuelto en el misterio.

shroud-laid [-leid] *adj* MAR de cuatro cabos (rope).

shrove [ʃrəuv] *pret* ⟶ **shrive.**

Shrovetide [-taid] *n* Carnestolendas *f pl*.

Shrove Tuesday [-ˈtjuːzdi] *n* martes *m* de carnaval.

shrub [ʃrʌb] *n* arbusto *m* (small tree) || matorral *m* (bush) || zumo *m* de frutas con ron *or* con coñac.

shrubbery [-əri] *n* arbustos *m pl*, matorrales *m pl* (shrubs).

shrubby [-i] *adj* lleno de arbustos (full of shrubs) || parecido a un arbusto (like a shrub) || arbustivo, va (plantation).

shrug [ʃrʌg] *n* encogimiento *m* de hombros || *he answered with a shrug* contestó encogiéndose de hombros *or* con un encogimiento de hombros.

shrug [ʃrʌg] *vt* encoger, encogerse de; *to shrug one's shoulders* encogerse de hombros || FIG *to shrug off the difficulties* no dejarse impresionar por las dificultades, minimizar las dificultades.
◆ *vi* encogerse de hombros.

shrunk [ʃrʌŋk] *pret/pp* ⟶ **shrink.**

shrunken [-ən] *adj* encogido, da (material) || reducido, da (head) || apergaminado, da; arrugado, da (skin).

shuck [ʃʌk] *n* *US* cáscara *f* (of nuts) | vaina *f* (of peas) | espata *f* (of corn) | concha *f* (of oysters, etc.) || *US* FAM *not worth shucks* que no vale un pimiento *or* un comino.

shuck [ʃʌk] *vt* *US* desvainar (peas) | descascarillar (cereals) | pelar (fruits, nuts) | desbullar (oysters) || *US* FAM *to shuck off* desechar, arrumbar.

shucks! [-s] *interj* ¡cáscaras!

shudder [ˈʃʌdə*] *n* repeluzno *m*, escalofrío *m*, estremecimiento *m* (of fear, etc.) ‖ vibración *f* (of machines, of motor, etc.).

shudder [ˈʃʌdə*] *vi* estremecerse; *he shuddered at the news* se estremeció ante la noticia ‖ sentir un escalofrío, darle a uno un escalofrío, estremecerse; *we shuddered with fear* nos dio un escalofrío de miedo.

shuffle [ˈʃʌfl] *n* arrastramiento *m* de los pies (of feet) ‖ barajada *f* (of cards) ‖ FIG evasiva *f* (evasion) ‖ *whose shuffle is it?* ¿a quién le toca barajar?

shuffle [ˈʃʌfl] *vt* revolver, mezclar (to stir) ‖ barajar (cards) ‖ arrastrar (feet) ‖ — *to shuffle off* quitarse, despojarse de (clothes), quitarse de encima (responsibilities) ‖ *to shuffle on* ponerse rápidamente (clothes).
◆ *vi* andar arrastrando los pies (to walk) ‖ bailar arrastrando los pies (to dance) ‖ moverse de un lado para otro (to move nervously) ‖ barajar (in cards) ‖ FIG andar con rodeos ‖ — *he came shuffling towards me* se acercó a mí arrastrando los pies ‖ *to shuffle in* o *into* entrar arrastrando los pies en ‖ FIG *to shuffle into a job* conseguir un trabajo por medios poco recomendables ‖ *to shuffle off* irse arrastrando los pies ‖ FIG *to shuffle out of a tricky situation* conseguir salir de una situación difícil ‖ *to shuffle through* hacer sin cuidado, hacer con los pies (a task).

shuffleboard [-bɔːd] *n* juego *m* de tejo (game).

shuffler [-ə*] *n* persona *f* que baraja (in cards) ‖ US pato *m* marino (duck).

shuffling [-iŋ] *adj* lento, ta (gait) ‖ que arrastra los pies (person) ‖ FIG evasivo, va.
◆ *n* arrastramiento *m* de los pies.

shun [ʃʌn] *vt* rehuir, huir de, evitar (people, responsibilities, etc.).

shunt [ʃʌnt] *n* maniobras *f pl* (of trains) ‖ agujas *f pl* (railway points) ‖ ELECTR derivación *f*, shunt *m* ‖ ELECTR *shunt circuit* circuito derivado.

shunt [ʃʌnt] *vt* desviar ‖ cambiar de vía (train) ‖ ELECTR derivar ‖ FIG desviar (conversation) ‖ — *to shunt s.o. aside* apartar a alguien ‖ *to shunt s.o. backwards and forwards* mandar a uno de acá para allá ‖ *to shunt s.o. off* o *out of the way* dejar de lado a uno (to leave aside).
◆ *vi* cambiar de vía (trains) ‖ ELECTR derivarse.

shunter [-ə*] *n* guardagujas *m inv.*

shunting [-iŋ] *n* maniobras *f pl* ‖ *shunting engine* locomotora *f* de maniobras.

shunt-wound [-waund] *adj* ELECTR devanado en derivación.

shush [ʃʌʃ] *interj* ¡chitón!

shut [ʃʌt] *adj* cerrado, da; *the door is shut* la puerta está cerrada ‖ FAM *to get shut of sth.* deshacerse de algo, quitarse algo de encima.

shut* [ʃʌt] *vt* cerrar (door, shop, eyes, mouth, etc.) ‖ encerrar; *to shut a dog in the kitchen* encerrar un perro en la cocina ‖ — FAM *shut your mouth* o *face!* ¡cierra el pico!, ¡cállate la boca! ‖ *to shut one's ears to sth.* hacer oídos sordos a algo ‖ *to shut one's eyes to sth.* cerrar los ojos ante algo ‖ *to shut one's finger in the door* pillarse el dedo en la puerta ‖ *to shut the door in s.o.'s face* dar a alguien con la puerta en las narices.
◆ *vi* cerrarse.
◆ *phr v* ***to shut away*** guardar bajo llave (to keep under lock and key) | encerrar (to imprison) ‖ ***to shut down*** cerrar (curtain, etc.) | cerrar (factory, etc.) | cerrarse (to close) ‖ encerrar (to imprison) | rodear, cercar (to surround) ‖ ***to shut off*** cortar (gas, electricity, water) | desconectar (machine) | aislar (to isolate) | apartar; *to shut o.s. off from society* apartarse de la sociedad | *to be shut off from* estar apartado *or* aislado de ‖ ***to shut out*** no admitir (not to admit) | dejar fuera (to leave outside); *they shut me out of the house* me dejaron fuera de la casa | excluir (to exclude) | evitar; *to shut out all risk of fire* evitar todo peligro de incendio | tapar (the light, a view) | *to be shut out* quedarse fuera ‖ ***to shut up*** guardar bajo llave (to keep under lock and key) | encerrar (to imprison, to enclose) | cerrar; *to shut up a shop* cerrar una tienda; *the shop is shutting up* la tienda está cerrando | obstruir (to block) | callar, hacer callar (to cause to be quiet) | callarse; *shut up!* ¡cállate! | *he spends the whole day shut up in his workshop* se pasa el día entero encerrado en su taller | FIG *to shut up shop* liquidar el negocio.
— OBSERV Pret y pp ***shut***.

shutdown [-daun] *n* cierre *m*.

shut-eye [-ai] *n* FAM *to get some shut-eye* echar un sueño.

shut-in [-in] *n* US enfermo *m* que tiene que guardar cama *or* quedarse en su casa.
◆ *adj* US encerrado, da ‖ introvertido, da.

shutoff [-ɔf] *n* válvula *f* (valve) ‖ interrupción *f*, cierre *m*.

shutout [-aut] *n* US cierre *m* patronal (lockout) ‖ US SP victoria *f* ganada sin que el adversario marque un tanto.

shutter [-ə*] *n* postigo *m*, contraventana *f* (on window) ‖ PHOT obturador *m* ‖ — PHOT *shutter speed* tiempo *m* de exposición ‖ FIG *to put up the shutters* cerrar definitivamente (to close down), desistir (to give up).

shutter [-ə*] *vt* poner postigos a (to provide with shutters) ‖ cerrar los postigos de (to close).

shuttle [ʃʌtl] *n* lanzadera *f* (in sewing and weaving) ‖ US vehículo *m* que hace trayectos cortos y regulares entre dos puntos (vehicle) ‖ trayecto *m* corto y regular entre dos puntos (journey) ‖ SP volante *m* (shuttlecock) ‖ *space shuttle* transbordador *m* espacial.

shuttle [ʃʌtl] *vt* transportar [en trayectos cortos y regulares] (to transport in a shuttle service) ‖ *to shuttle s.o. about* mandar a alguien de acá para allá.
◆ *vi* hacer trayectos cortos y regulares (a shuttle service) ‖ FIG ir y venir, ir de acá para allá (to go back and forth).

shuttlecock [-kɔk] *n* SP volante *m*.

shuttle service [-ˈsəːvis] *n* servicio *m* regular de ida y vuelta entre dos puntos.

shy [ʃai] *adj* tímido, da; *a shy person, smile* una persona, una sonrisa tímida ‖ vergonzoso, sa (bashful) ‖ asustadizo, za (animals) ‖ cauteloso, sa (cautious) ‖ US escaso, sa; *shy of money* escaso de dinero ‖ — *come on, don't be shy!* ¡venga, no tengas vergüenza! ‖ *I can't, I'm shy* no puedo, me da vergüenza ‖ FIG *I'm ten pounds shy* me faltan *or* he perdido diez libras | *to be shy of* desconfiar de (to distrust) | *to be shy of doing sth.* no atreverse a hacer algo | *to fight shy of* evitar.
◆ *n* tiro *m*, lanzamiento *m* (a throw) ‖ respingo *m*, espantada *f* (of a horse) ‖ FIG tentativa *f*, intento *m* (try) ‖ FIG *to have a shy at doing sth.* intentar hacer algo.

shy [ʃai] *vt* tirar, lanzar (to throw).
◆ *vi* asustarse, sobresaltarse; *I shied at the noise* me sobresalté al oír el ruido ‖ negarse a saltar; *to shy at a fence* negarse a saltar una valla ‖ — *to shy away* espantarse (to be frightened) ‖ *to shy away from* huir; *he shies away from reporters* huye de los periodistas; negarse a, rehusar; *to shy away from doing sth.* negarse a hacer algo.

Shylock [-lɔk] *n* FIG usurero *m*.

shyly [-li] *adv* tímidamente, con vergüenza.

shyness [-nis] *n* timidez *f* (bashfulness) ‖ cautela *f* (caution).

shyster [ˈʃaistə*] *n* US FAM picapleitos *m inv.*

si [siː] *n* MUS si *m*.

sial [ˈsaiəl] *n* GEOGR sial *m*.

Siam [ˈsaiæm] *pr n* GEOGR Siam *m*.

Siamese [ˌsaiəˈmiːz] *adj* siamés, esa; *Siamese twins* hermanos siameses ‖ *Siamese cat* gato siamés.
◆ *n* siamés, esa (inhabitant of Thailand) ‖ siamés *m* (language) ‖ *the Siamese* los siameses.

sib [sib] *n* hermano, na (sibling) ‖ pariente *m* (relative) ‖ parientes *m pl* (kinfolk).

Siberia [saiˈbiəriə] *pr n* GEOGR Siberia *f*.

Siberian [-n] *adj/n* siberiano, na.

sibilance [ˈsibiləns]; **sibilancy** [-i] *n* carácter *m* sibilante.

sibilant [ˈsibilənt] *adj* sibilante ‖ MED silbante.
◆ *n* GRAMM sibilante *f*.

sibilate [ˈsibileit] *vt* pronunciar con sibilante.
◆ *vi* silbar (to hiss).

sibling [ˈsibliŋ] *n* hermano, na (brother, sister) ‖ medio hermano, media hermana (half brother, half sister).

sibyl [ˈsibil] *n* sibila *f*.

sibylline [siˈbilain] *adj* sibilino, na ‖ *Sibylline Books* libros sibilinos.

sic [sik] *adv* sic.

sic [sik] *vt* ⟶ **sick.**

siccative [ˈsikətiv] *adj* secante.
◆ *n* secante *m*, aceite *m* secante.

Sicilian [siˈsiljən] *adj* siciliano, na.
◆ *n* siciliano, na (native of Sicily) ‖ siciliano *m* (Italian dialect).

Sicily [ˈsisili] *pr n* GEOGR Sicilia *f*.

sick [sik] *adj* enfermo, ma (ill, unhealthy); *how long has he been sick?* ¿desde cuándo está enfermo? ‖ enfermizo, za (sickly) ‖ FIG enfermo, ma; *he was sick with envy* se puso enfermo de envidia ‖ FIG & FAM enfermo, ma; malo, la; *his bad manners make me sick* su mala educación me pone enfermo; *you make me sick!* ¡me pones malo! | morboso, sa; negro, gra; *sick humour* humor negro | morboso, sa (joke) ‖ (ant) ansioso, sa; anhelante (longing) ‖ — *I feel sick when you go this fast* me mareo cuando vas tan de prisa ‖ FIG *I get sick of it* me cansa | *it makes me sick to think that* me pone malo pensar que | *my car looks pretty sick next to yours* mi coche es muy poca cosa al lado del suyo | *our economy is sick at present* actualmente nuestra economía va mal ‖ *sick person* enfermo, ma ‖ *to be off sick* estar ausente por enfermedad ‖ *to be sick* estar enfermo (to be ill), vomitar (to vomit) ‖ FIG *to be sick for* anhelar | *to be sick of* estar harto de ‖ *to be sick with flu* estar con gripe ‖ FAM *to be worried sick* estar preocupadísimo, ma ‖ *to fall* o *to go* o *to take sick* caer *or* ponerse enfermo ‖ *to feel sick* tener náuseas, estar mareado ‖ FIG *to feel sick at heart* estar desesperado | *to feel* o *to be sick and tired of* estar harto de, estar hasta las narices de ‖ *to get sick* marearse (seasick, airsick, etc.), caer *or* ponerse enfermo (to take sick) ‖ *to report sick* darse de baja por enfermedad.
◆ *n* *the sick* los enfermos.

sick; sic [sik] *vt* atacar, coger (to attack) ‖ echar (*on* a) (a dog on s.o.) ‖ — *sick!* ¡a por él! ‖ FAM *to sick up* vomitar.

sick bay [-bei] *n* enfermería *f*.

sickbed [-bed] *n* lecho *m* de enfermo.

sick benefit [-ˈbenifit] *n* subsidio *m* de enfermedad.

sicken [ˈsikn] *vt* poner enfermo (to make ill) ‖ empalagar; *sweet things sicken me* las cosas dulces me empalagan ‖ dar náuseas, marear

(to cause nausea) || FIG hartar (to bore) || FIG *it sickens me that there is so much violence* me pone enfermo que haya tanta violencia.
◆ *vi* enfermar, ponerse *or* caer enfermo (to get ill) || marearse (to become nauseated) || — *to sicken for* echar de menos (to miss), anhelar (to yearn for), incubar (an illness) || FIG *to sicken of* hartarse de.

sickening [-iŋ] *adj* nauseabundo, da; repugnante (revolting) || deprimente (distressing).

sickeningly [-iŋli] *adv* repugnantemente || *sickeningly dirty* tan sucio que da asco.

sick headache [-'hedeik] *n* US MED jaqueca *f*; *to have a sick headache* tener jaqueca.

sickish ['sikiʃ] *adj* enfermizo, za (person) || empalagoso, sa (taste, smell).

sickle ['sikl] *n* hoz *f*.

sick leave ['sikli:v] *n* baja *f* por enfermedad.

sickliness ['siklinis] *n* mala salud *f*, salud *f* delicada (of a person) || palidez *f* (of complexion) || lo empalagoso (of cakes, etc.).

sickly ['sikli] *adj* enfermo, ma (ill) || enfermizo, za (prone to sickness, weak) || pálido, da (pale) || forzado, da; *a sickly smile* una sonrisa forzada || nauseabundo, da (nauseating) || empalagoso, sa (taste) || macilento, ta (light) || malsano, na (climate) || *sickly sweet* empalagoso, sa; dulzón, ona.

sickness ['siknis] *n* enfermedad *f* (illness); *absence through sickness* ausencia por enfermedad; *sleeping sickness* enfermedad del sueño || ganas *f pl* de vomitar, náuseas *f pl* (desire to vomit) || mareo *m* (seasickness, airsickness).

sick pay ['sikpei]; **sickness benefit** ['siknis'benifit] *n* subsidio *m* de enfermedad.

sickroom ['sikrum] *n* cuarto *m* de un enfermo.

side [said] *n* lado *m*; *the right, the left side* el lado derecho, izquierdo || lado *m*, costado *m* (of the body) || ijar *m*, ijada *f* (of an animal) || lonja *f*; *a side of bacon* una lonja de tocino || ladera *f*, falda *f* (of a hill, of a mountain) || cara *f*, lado *m* (of a paper, of a record) || lado *m* (of a tape) || borde *m* (edge) || orilla *f* (shore) || banda *f*, costado *m* (of a boat) || lado *m*, parte *f*; *whose side are you on?* ¿de qué lado estás?, ¿de parte de quién estás?; *I'm on your side* estoy de tu lado; *on the side of* del lado de || lado *m*, parte *f*, línea *f*; *an uncle on my mother's side* un tío por parte de mi madre *or* por el lado materno || aspecto *m*, lado *m*; *a new side to the matter* un nuevo aspecto del asunto; *the many sides of his character* los múltiples aspectos de su carácter; *to consider a problem from all sides* examinar todos los aspectos de un problema || MIL flanco *m*, lado *m* (flank) || MATH lado *m*; *a triangle has three sides* un triángulo tiene tres lados | cara *f* (face) || SP equipo *m* (team); *to field a good side* sacar un buen equipo | efecto *m* (spin on a ball) || JUR parte *f*; *the other side* la parte adversa || RAD canal *m* (on television); *what's on the other side?* ¿qué hay en el otro canal? || — *at o by the side of* al lado de || COMM *credit side* haber *m* | *debit side* debe *m* || *from all sides* de todos lados, de todas partes || *from side to side* de un lado para otro (with movement), de ancho; *the room measures four metres side to side* el cuarto mide cuatro metros de ancho || *God is in our side* Dios está de nuestro lado || *it's best to be on the safe side* más vale estar seguro || *it's on the other side of the forest* está del otro lado del bosque || *it's on this side of the forest* está antes del bosque *or* de este lado del bosque || *on all sides* por todos lados, por todas partes || *on both sides* por ambas partes, por ambos lados || *on either side* de cada lado || *on one's blind side* fuera de la vista de uno || *on one side... on the other...* por una parte... por otra... || *on the French side of the border* en el lado francés de la frontera || *on the large, the cold, the sweet side* bastante grande, frío, dulce || *on the left-hand side* a la izquierda || *on the right-hand side* a la derecha || US *on the side* por añadidura || *on this side* por este lado || *side by side* juntos, uno al lado del otro, lado a lado || FIG *the other side of the picture* el reverso de la medalla || *there are two sides to the problem* el problema se divide en dos partes *or* presenta dos aspectos || *the right side* el derecho (of cloth), el lado derecho, la derecha (right-hand side), el lado bueno (the correct side) || *the under, the upper side* la parte inferior, superior || *to be on the safe side* para mayor seguridad, para estar tranquilo (for safety's sake), ir sobre seguro, obrar sin riesgos || FIG *to be on the wrong side of forty* tener cuarenta años bien cumplidos, tener más de cuarenta años || *to be sitting side by side* estar sentados uno al lado del otro || FIG *to change sides* cambiar de partido | *to get on the right side of s.o.* congraciarse con alguien, granjearse la simpatía de alguien | *to get on the wrong side of s.o.* tomar a alguien a contrapelo || *to go side by side* ir juntos, ir lado a lado || FIG *to keep on the good o on the right side of s.o.* tratar de llevarse bien con alguien | *to keep on the right side of the law* mantenerse dentro de la ley | *to let the side down* dejar mal a los suyos [a su equipo, a su regimiento, etc.] | *to look on the bright side* ver el lado bueno de las cosas || FAM *to make a bit on the side* ganar algún dinero fuera de su trabajo normal || *to move to one side* apartarse, hacerse a un lado || FIG *to put on side* tener muchos humos || *to put o to leave on o to one side* poner a un lado, poner aparte || *to sleep on one's side* dormir de costado || FIG *to split one's sides laughing* partirse *or* desternillarse de risa || *to take sides* tomar partido || *to take sides with s.o.* ponerse del lado *or* de parte de alguien || *to turn over on one's side* ponerse de costado (a person), volcar (a car, etc.) || *wrong side out* al revés, del revés.
◆ *adj* lateral; *a side wall* un muro lateral; *a side street* una calle lateral || secundario, ria (secondary); *side issue* cuestión secundaria; *side effects* efectos secundarios; *side road* carretera secundaria || adicional (supplementary) || indirecto, ta; *a side comment* un comentario indirecto || — *side door* puerta *f* lateral (secondary), entrada *f* de servicio (tradesmen's entrance) || *side view* vista *f* de perfil.

side [said] *vt* poner lados a.
◆ *vi* *to side with* ponerse del lado *or* de parte de || *to side with nobody* no tomar partido.

side arms [-ɑ:mz] *pl n* MIL armas *f* de mano, armas *f* blancas.

sideboard [-bɔ:d] *n* aparador *m* (furniture).
◆ *pl* patillas *f* (of hair).

sideburns [-bə:nz] *pl n* patillas *f* (of hair).

sidecar [-kɑ:*] *n* sidecar *m* (of motorcycle) || cóctel *m* de coñac, licor de naranja y zumo de limón (drink).

side dish [-diʃ] *n* plato *m* que acompaña el principal.

side drum [-drʌm] *n* MUS tambor *m*.

side face [-feis] *n* perfil *m*.
◆ *adj/adv* de perfil.

side-glance [-glɑ:ns] *n* mirada *f* de reojo *or* de soslayo.

sidehead [-hed] *n* título *m* al margen.

sidekick [-kik] *n* US FAM compañero *m*, amigo *m* (friend) | socio *m* (partner).

sidelight [-lait] *n* luz *f* lateral || piloto *m*, luz *f* de posición (of a car) || MAR luz *f* de situación (of ship) || FIG aclaración *f* (enlightening comment).

sideline [-lain] *n* negocio *m* suplementario (supplementary trade) || empleo *m* suplementario, actividad *f* suplementaria (second job) || vía *f* secundaria (of railway) || SP línea *f* de banda.
◆ *pl* SP banquillo *m sing*; *to sit on the sidelines* quedarse en el banquillo || FIG *from the sidelines* desde la barrera, desde fuera.

sidelong [-lɔŋ] *adj* de reojo, de soslayo; *a sidelong glance* una mirada de reojo || lateral (lateral) || oblicuo, cua (oblique) || de costado, lateral (fall, dive, etc.).
◆ *adv* de reojo, de soslayo; *to glance sidelong* mirar de reojo || lateralmente || oblicuamente || de costado (to dive, etc.).

sidenote [-nəut] *n* nota *f* al margen.

sidepiece [-pi:s] *n* pieza *f* lateral.

sidereal [sai'diəriəl] *adj* sideral, sidéreo, a || — *sidereal day* día *m* sideral || *sidereal year* año sideral.

siderite ['saidərait] *n* MIN siderita *f*, siderosa *f*.

siderosis [sidə'rəusis] *n* MED siderosis *f*.

siderurgy ['sidə,rə:dʒi] *n* siderurgia *f*.

sidesaddle ['said,sædl] *n* silla *f* de amazona || *to ride sidesaddle* montar a mujeriegas, montar a la amazona.

sideshow ['saidʃəu] *n* atracción *f* secundaria (supporting act) || caseta *f* (stall) || FIG acontecimiento *m* secundario (event) || MIL diversión *f*.

sideslip ['saidslip] *vi* deslizarse lateralmente (to slip sideways) || patinar, resbalar (a car) || AVIAT resbalar.

sidesman [saidzmən] *n* mayordomo *m* (of Anglican church).
— OBSERV El plural de esta palabra es *sidesmen*.

sidesplitting ['said'splitiŋ] *adj* FAM divertidísimo, ma; mondante, de partirse de risa (funny).

side step ['saidstep] *n* paso *m* lateral || SP quiebro *m* || MIL paso *m* de lado *or* lateral.

side-step ['saidstep] *vt* esquivar, evitar (to avoid, to dodge) || evitar (a problem, an issue).
◆ *vi* dar un paso lateral || SP dar un quiebro.

sidestroke ['saidstrəuk] *n* *to swim sidestroke* nadar de costado.

sideswipe ['saidswaip] *vt* chocar de refilón contra.

sidetrack ['saidtræk] *n* apartadero *m*, vía *f* muerta (siding) || FIG cuestión *f* de interés secundario.

sidetrack ['saidtræk] *vt* poner en vía muerta, apartar (a train) || FIG despistar (a person) | dejar de lado (an issue) | desviar (from a course).

sidewalk ['saidwɔ:k] *n* US acera *f* || US *sidewalk artist* artista callejero.

sideward ['saidwə:d]; **sidewards** [-z]; **sidewise** [saidwaiz] *adj* lateral, de lado, a un lado (to one side); *a sideward step, movement* un paso, un movimiento lateral || de reojo, de soslayo; *a sideward glance* una mirada de soslayo || de costado, de lado; *a sideward dive* un salto de costado || oblicuo, cua (oblique).
◆ *adv* de lado, lateralmente, de costado; *it goes in sidewards* entra de lado; *to walk sidewards* andar de lado || de lado, de costado (to dive, to fall) || a un lado, hacia un lado; *to step sidewards* dar un paso hacia un lado || oblicuamente (obliquely) || de reojo, de soslayo (to look, to glance).

sideways ['saidweiz]; US **sideway** ['saidwei] *adj/adv* → **sideward.**

side-wheeler ['said,wilə*] *n* vapor *m* de ruedas (paddle steamer).

side-whiskers ['said'wiskəz] *pl n* patillas *f*.

sidewise ['saidwaiz] *adj/adv* → **sideward.**

siding ['saidiŋ] *n* apartadero *m*, vía *f* muerta.

sidle ['saidl] *n* movimiento *m* furtivo (furtive movement) || movimiento *m* lateral (sideways movement).

sidle ['saidl] *vi* avanzar *or* moverse furtivamente (to move furtively) || FAM *to sidle up to s.o.* acercarse furtivamente a alguien.

siege [siːdʒ] *n* MIL sitio *m*, cerco *m* || FIG acoso *m* (insistence) || US calvario *m* (exhausting period) || — *to lay* o *to stand siege to* sitiar, poner sitio a, asediar, cercar || *to raise the siege* levantar el sitio.

sienna [si'enə] *n* tierra *f* de siena, siena *f*.

sierra ['siərə] *n* GEOGR sierra *f*.

Sierra Leone [si,erəli'əun] *pr n* GEOGR Sierra Leona.

siesta [si'estə] *n* siesta *f*; *to have a siesta* dormir *or* echar una siesta.

sieve [siv] *n* cedazo *m*, cernedor *m*, tamiz *m*, criba *f* || FIG indiscreto, ta || FIG *to have a memory like a sieve* tener una memoria como un colador.

sieve [siv] *vt* cerner, tamizar, cribar.

sift [sift] *vt* tamizar, cerner, cribar (to sieve) || espolvorear (to sprinkle) || FIG examinar cuidadosamente (to examine) || — FIG *to sift out* encontrar (to find), seleccionar (to choose), separar (to separate) | *to sift through* examinar cuidadosamente.
◆ *vi* filtrarse; *light sifted through the curtains* la luz se filtraba a través de las cortinas.

sifter [-ə*] *n* cedazo *m*, cernedor *m*, tamiz *m*.

sifting [-iŋ] *n* cernido *m*.
◆ *pl* cerniduras *f* (residue).

sigh [sai] *n* suspiro *m*; *to heave* o *to breathe a sigh of relief* dar un suspiro de alivio || FIG susurro *m*, gemido *m* (of the wind).

sigh [sai] *vt* decir suspirando.
◆ *vi* suspirar (to emit a sigh) || FIG susurrar, gemir; *the wind sighs in the trees* el viento susurra entre los árboles || FIG *to sigh for* suspirar por.

sight [sait] *n* vista *f*; *the gift of sight* el don de la vista; *within sight* a la vista || visión *f* (vision) || examen *m* (examination) || mira *f* (of a gun) || — FAM *a sight more, better, worse* mucho más, mejor, peor || *at* o *on first sight* a primera vista || *guilty in the sight of the law* culpable a los ojos de la ley || *I hate the sight of him* no le puedo ver (ni en pintura) || *it was a sight to see!* ¡era una cosa digna de verse! || *it was love at first sight* fue un flechazo || *not to let s.o. out of one's sight* no perder de vista a alguien || *not to lose sight of* no perder de vista (a person, an object), tener presente (a fact, etc.) || *on sight* a primera vista, nada más verlo; *I recognized them on sight* los reconocí nada más verlos || *out of sight, out of mind* ojos que no ven, corazón que no siente || COMM *payable on* o *at sight* pagadero a la vista || *people on the streets after curfew will be shot on sight* se disparará inmediatamente contra toda persona que circule por la calle después del toque de queda || *short sight* miopía *f* || *sight translation* traducción *f* a libro abierto *or* a la vista || *sight unseen* sin haberlo visto || *the accident was not a pretty sight* el accidente fue un espectáculo bastante desagradable || *the end is in sight* el final está a la vista *or* está cerca || *the oasis was a sight for sore eyes* la vista del oasis era un verdadero alivio || *the sight of blood makes me faint* me desmayo cuando veo sangre || *to be a sight* o *a long sight* o *a darned sight bigger* ser muchísimo más grande || *to be in sight of land* divisar tierra || *to be out of sight* estar fuera de la vista, no poder verse || *to catch sight of* divisar || *to come into sight* aparecer || *to drop out of sight* desaparecer || *to find favour in the sight of s.o.* ser acogido favorablemente por alguien (an idea, etc.), caerle en gracia a alguien (a person) || *to get a sight of* conseguir *or* lograr ver (to get a look at) || MAR *to heave into sight* aparecer || *to keep out of sight* no dejarse ver || *to keep sth. in sight* no perder de vista (an object, a person), tener presente (a fact, etc.) || *to know by sight* conocer de vista || *to lose one's sight* perder la vista, quedar ciego || *to lose sight of* perder de vista || *to make a sight of o.s.* ir hecho una facha, estar hecho un adefesio || *to play music at sight* repentizar || *to regain one's sight* recobrar la vista || *to take sight* apuntar (to aim) || *victory was in sight* la victoria estaba cerca || *what a sight he looked!* ¡había que verlo!, ¡menuda pinta tenía! || *you look a real sight in that cap!* ¡menuda pinta tienes con esa gorra! || *you're a sight for sore eyes!* ¡qué gusto verte!, ¡cuánto me alegro de verte!, ¡felices los ojos que te ven!
◆ *pl* cosas *f* dignas de verse (things worth seeing) || monumentos *m* (monuments) || — *to see the sights (of the city)* visitar la ciudad || *to set one's sights on sth.* echar el ojo a algo || *to set one's sights very high* apuntar muy alto.

sight [sait] *vt* divisar, avistar, ver; *to sight land* divisar tierra || observar (to observe); *to sight a star* observar una estrella || descubrir (to discover) || apuntar, apuntar con [un arma] (to aim); *to sight a gun at s.o.* apuntar a alguien con un fusil || poner una mira a [un arma] (to provide with a sight).
◆ *vi* apuntar (to take aim) || mirar detenidamente (to look carefully).

sight draft [-draːft] *n* US letra *f* a la vista.

sighted [-id] *adj* que ve, de vista normal.

sighthole [-həul] *n* mirilla *f* (peephole).

sighting [-iŋ] *n* observación *f*.

sightless [-lis] *adj* ciego, ga (blind) || invisible.

sightliness [-linis] *n* hermosura *f*.

sightly [-li] *adj* agradable a la vista, hermoso, sa.

sight-read [-riːd] *vt* leer a primera vista || MUS repentizar.

sight reading [-,riːdiŋ] *n* MUS acción *f* de repentizar, ejecución *f* a primera vista.

sight-seeing [-,siːiŋ] *n* turismo *m*; *I don't like sight-seeing* no me gusta hacer turismo || *to go sight-seeing* visitar la ciudad, hacer turismo.

sightseer [-,siːə*] *n* turista *m* & *f*.

sigillography [sidʒi'lɔgrəfi] *n* sigilografía *f*.

Sigismund ['sigismənd] *pr n* Segismundo *m*.

sigma ['sigmə] *n* sigma *f* (Greek letter).

sigmate ['sigmeit] *adj* en forma de S.

sigmoid ['sigmɔid] *adj* sigmoideo, a; sigmoides || ANAT *sigmoid flexure* flexura sigmoidea.

sign [sain] *n* MATH, MUS & ASTR signo *m*; *the sign of the Bull* el signo del Tauro || símbolo *m* (symbol) || seña *f*; *to converse in signs* conversar por señas || señal *f*; *to make a sign with one's hand* hacer una señal con la mano || gesto *m*, ademán *m* (gesture) || muestra *f*; *he is showing signs of weakness* da muestras de debilidad || rastro *m*, huella *f* (trace); *they left no sign of their passage* no dejaron ningún rastro de su paso || señal *f*; *good, bad sign* buena, mala señal || presagio *m* (omen); *a sign of doom* un presagio de catástrofe || señal *f*, indicio *m* (of rain, etc.) || anuncio *m* (notice); *put a sign in the window* pon un anuncio en la ventana || cartel *m* (poster) || letrero *m* (board); *the sign says it is forbidden to walk on the grass* el letrero dice que está prohibido pisar la hierba || letrero *m*, rótulo *m* (over shop, over doorway, etc.) || MED síntoma *m* (symptom) || huella *f*, rastro *m* (track of animal) || — *as a sign of good faith* como prueba de buena fe || *at the slightest sign of* al menor signo de || *he made a sign for me to come* me hizo una señal para que viniese || *"no parking" sign* señal de prohibición de estacionamiento || *not to show any signs of life* no dar señales de vida || *road sign* señal de tráfico || *sign of the times* signo del tiempo en que vivimos || *there was no sign of them anywhere* no se les veía por ninguna parte || *the sign of the Cross* la señal de la Cruz.

sign [sain] *vt* firmar (name, document, treaty) || hacer la señal de la cruz sobre, santiguar (to bless) || indicar (to express) || — *to sign and seal* firmar y sellar || REL *to sign o.s.* persignarse.
◆ *vi* firmar || hacer señas (to make signs).
◆ *phr v* ***to sign away*** o ***over*** ceder (a property) || *to sign in* registrarse, firmar en el registro de entrada (at hotel, club), fichar (at work) || ***to sign off*** acabar el programa (on the radio) | terminar (to finish) || ***to sign on*** o ***up*** alistarse (to join the army, navy, etc.) | MAR enrolar (to take on) | MAR enrolarse (to enrol) | SP fichar (a player); *to sign on a player* fichar a un jugador | COMM contratar (to take on) | firmar un contrato (to engage o.s.) || — *to sign up for* matricularse en (a class).

signal ['signəl] *n* señal *f* (agreed sign); *to give the signal for* dar la señal de *or* para || RAD sintonía *f* || señal *f* (traffic, railway, etc.) || — *alarm signal* señal de alarma || US *busy signal* señal de ocupado (telephone) || *distress signals* señales de socorro.
◆ *adj* señalado, da; notable.

signal ['signəl] *vt* dar la señal de *or* para (to order by signal); *he signalled them to stop* les dio la señal de pararse || indicar (to convey by signals) || — *he signalled that he was turning left* indicó *or* avisó que iba a torcer a la izquierda || *he signalled them on* les indicó que avanzaran || *to signal before overtaking* indicar que se va a adelantar.
◆ *vi* hacer señales, avisar.

signal book [-buk] *n* código *m* de señales.

signal box [-bɔks] *n* cabina *f* del cambio de agujas.

signal code [-kəud] *n* código *m* de señales.

Signal Corps [-kɔː] *n* MIL Servicio *m* de Transmisiones.

signal flag [-flæg] *n* bandera *f* de señales.

signal flare [-flɛə*] *n* bengala *f* de señales.

signaling [-iŋ] *n* US señalización *f*.

signalize ['signəlaiz] *vt* señalar, distinguir (to distinguish) || señalar (to point out).

signalling ['signəliŋ] *n* señalización *f*.

signally ['signəli] *adv* ostensiblemente, notablemente (to fail, to triumph).

signalman ['signəlmən] *n* guardavía *m* (on a railway).
— OBSERV El plural de esta palabra es *signalmen*.

signalment ['signəlmənt] *n* descripción *f*, filiación *f* (of a person).

signal tower ['signəl'tauə*] *n* US cabina *f* del cambio de agujas.

signatory ['signətəri] *adj/n* signatario, ria; firmante; *the signatory countries* los países firmantes; *the signatories to an agreement* los firmantes de un acuerdo.

signature ['signitʃə*] *n* firma *f* (of name, document, treaty); *blank signature* firma en blanco || RAD sintonía *f* || MUS armadura *f* (of key) || signatura *f* (in bookbinding) || US MED parte *f* de una receta en que se indica la posología.

signature tune [-tjuːn] *n* sintonía *f* (on radio, etc.).

signboard ['sainbɔːd] *n* letrero *m* (sign) || cartel *m* (poster) || tablón *m* de anuncios (notice board).

signer ['sainə*] *n* firmante *m* & *f*, signatario, ria.

signet ['signit] *n* sello *m*.

signet ring [-riŋ] *n* sortija *f* de sello, sello *m*.

significance [sig'nifikəns]; **significancy** [-i] *n* significado *m* (meaning) ‖ significación *f*, importancia *f* (importance).

significant [sig'nifikənt] *adj* significativo, va (meaningful) ‖ importante; *a significant increase* un aumento importante ‖ mucho, cha (a lot of); *to place significant emphasis on* dar mucho énfasis a ‖ MATH *significant figures* cifras significativas.

significantly [-li] *adv* de modo significativo ‖ *to smile significantly* dirigir una sonrisa de entendimiento.

signification [,signifi'keiʃən] *n* significado *m* (meaning) ‖ significación *f* (act of signifying).

signify ['signifai] *vt* indicar (to indicate) ‖ significar (to mean) ‖ dar a conocer (an opinion).
◆ *vi* tener importancia (to be significant) ‖ *please signify* le ruego tenga a bien dar su opinión.

signing ['sainiŋ] *n* firma *f*.

sign language ['sain'læŋgwidʒ] *n* lenguaje *m* por señas ‖ *to speak to each other in sign language* hablarse por señas.

sign manual ['sain'mænjuəl] *n* firma *f*.

signpost ['sainpəust] *n* señal *f* de tráfico, poste *m* indicador (traffic sign) ‖ letrero *m* (notice).

signpost ['sainpəust] *vt* señalizar ‖ *the way is well signposted* el camino está bien indicado.

signposting [-iŋ] *n* señalización *f*.

signwriter ['sain'raitə*] *n* rotulista *m* & *f*.

Sikh [si:k] *adj* sij.
◆ *n* sij *m* & *f*.

silage ['sailidʒ] *n* ensilaje *m*.

silence ['sailəns] *n* silencio *m*; *deadly silence* silencio sepulcral; *to suffer in silence* sufrir en silencio ‖ — *silence!* ¡silencio! ‖ FIG *silence gives consent* quien calla otorga | *silence is golden* el silencio es oro ‖ *to break the silence* romper el silencio ‖ *to call for silence* pedir *or* imponer silencio ‖ *to pass over sth. in silence* silenciar algo, callar algo, pasar algo por alto.

silence ['sailəns] *vt* hacer callar (to cause to be quiet) ‖ silenciar, callar (to quieten) ‖ amortiguar (a sound) ‖ TECH silenciar (a motor) ‖ FIG reducir al silencio (guns, s.o. who knows too much).

silencer [-ə*] *n* silenciador *m* (of gun, of engine).

silent ['sailənt] *adj* silencioso, sa (making no sound); *a silent audience, motor* un público, un motor silencioso ‖ callado, da; silencioso, sa (person) ‖ mudo, da; *a silent letter, film* una letra, una película muda ‖ — *be silent!* ¡cállate!, ¡cállese! ‖ COMM *silent partner* socio comanditario ‖ *the house was deathly silent* en la casa había un silencio sepulcral ‖ *the silent majority* la mayoría silenciosa ‖ *to keep silent about sth.* guardar silencio respecto a algo.

silently [-li] *adv* silenciosamente, en silencio.

silex ['saileks] *n* silex *m*, pedernal *m*.

silhouette [,silu'et] *n* silueta *f*.

silhouette [,silu'et] *vt* siluetear (to represent as an outline) ‖ *the firemen were silhouetted against the burning building* la silueta de los bomberos se perfilaba *or* se destacaba en el edificio en llamas.

silica ['silikə] *n* CHEM sílice *f*.

silicate ['silikit] *n* CHEM silicato *m*.

siliceous [si'liʃəs] *adj* CHEM silíceo, a.

silicic [si'lisik] *adj* CHEM silícico, ca (acid).

silicify [si'lisifai] *vt* CHEM impregnar de sílice (to impregnate) | convertir en sílice (to turn into silica).
◆ *vi* CHEM impregnarse de sílice (to become impregnated) | convertirse en sílice (to turn into silica).

silicon ['silikən] *n* MIN silicio *m* ‖ INFORM *silicon chip* chip *m or* pastilla *f* de silicio.

silicone ['silikəun] *n* CHEM silicona *f*.

silicosis [,sili'kəusis] *n* MED silicosis *f*.

silk [silk] *n* seda *f* (fabric, fibre) ‖ FAM toga *f* (of lawyer) ‖ BOT estigma *m* del maíz (of maize) ‖ — *as smooth as silk* suave como la seda ‖ *to take silk* tomar la toga, hacerse abogado.
◆ *pl* US gorra *f sing* y chaquetilla *f sing* de jockey.
◆ *adj* de seda; *a silk dress* un vestido de seda; *silk paper* papel de seda ‖ sedero, ra; *silk industry* industria sedera.

silk [silk] *vi* madurar (maize).

silk cotton [-'kɔtn] *n* seda *f* vegetal.

silk culture [-'kʌltʃə*] *n* sericultura *f*, sericicultura *f* (sericulture).

silken ['silkən] *adj* sedoso, sa (lustrous) ‖ suave, sedoso, sa (smooth) ‖ suave (suave) ‖ de seda (made of silk).

silk hat [hæt] *n* sombrero *m* de copa, chistera *f*.

silkiness ['silkinis] *n* suavidad *f* ‖ aspecto *m* sedoso (of fabric).

silk-screen ['silkskri:n] *adj* PRINT *silk-screen process* o *print* serigrafía *f*.

silk stocking ['silk'stɔkiŋ] *n* US FIG aristócrata *m* & *f*.

silk-stocking ['silk'stɔkiŋ] *adj* US FIG elegante | aristocrático, ca.

silkworm ['silkwə:m] *n* ZOOL gusano *m* de seda.

silky ['silki] *adj* sedoso, sa (fabric, etc.) ‖ suave (voice).

sill [sil] *n* alféizar *m* (of window) ‖ umbral *m* (of a door) ‖ ARCH solera *f* ‖ GEOL capa *f*.

sillabub ['siləbʌb] *n* batido *m* de leche, azúcar y licores.

silliness ['silinis] *n* necedad *f*, estupidez *f* (quality of being silly) ‖ tontería *f* (silly act) ‖ *such silliness does not become your age* esas tonterías no son propias de tu edad.

silly ['sili] *adj* tonto, ta; bobo, ba; *don't be silly!* ¡no seas tonto! ‖ ridículo, la (ridiculous) ‖ absurdo, da (absurd) ‖ — *that was a silly thing to do* eso fue una tontería, hiciste una tontería ‖ FAM *to knock s.o. silly* pegar una paliza a alguien (to beat s.o. up), dejar atontado a alguien (to leave s.o. senseless) ‖ *to make s.o. look silly* poner a alguien en ridículo.
◆ *n* tonto, ta; bobo, ba.

silo ['sailəu] *n* silo *m*.

silt [silt] *n* cieno *m*, limo *m*, légamo *m* (mud).

silt [silt] *vt* *to silt up* encenagar (canal), enarenar (port).
◆ *vi* *to silt up* cegarse (canal), enarenarse (port).

Silurian [sai'ljuəriən] *adj/n* siluriano, na; silúrico, ca.

silvan ['silvən] *n adj/n* ⟶ **sylvan.**

silver ['silvə*] *n* MIN plata *f* (metal); *silver foil* hoja de plata ‖ color *m* plateado (colour) ‖ FIG monedas *f pl* de plata (silver coins) | suelto *m* (change) ‖ plata *f* (silverware) ‖ *German silver* plata alemana.
◆ *adj* de plata (made of silver); *a silver tray* una bandeja de plata; *silver coin* moneda de plata ‖ plateado, da (like silver) ‖ argentino, na (voice) ‖ argentífero, ra (mineral) ‖ — *silver gilt* plata dorada ‖ *silver nitrate* nitrato *m* de plata.

silver ['silvə*] *vt* platear (to silver-plate) ‖ azogar (a mirror) ‖ volver cano (hair).

silver age [-reidʒ] *n* edad *f* de plata.

silver anniversary [-,ræni'və:səri] *n* bodas *f pl* de plata.

silver fir [-'fə:*] *n* BOT abeto *m* blanco, pinabete *m*.

silverfish [-fiʃ] *n* ZOOL lepisma *f* (insect) | pez *m* plateado (fish).

silver fox [-fɔks] *n* ZOOL zorro *m* plateado.

silvering [-riŋ] *n* plateado *m*.

silver lining [-'lainiŋ] *n* FIG resquicio *m* de esperanza, perspectiva *f* esperanzadora ‖ *every cloud has a silver lining* no hay mal que por bien no venga.

silver paper ['peipə*] *n* papel *m* de plata *or* de estaño.

silver plate [-'pleit] *n* baño *m* de plata, plateado *m* (thin coating of silver) ‖ plata *f*, vajilla *f* de plata (silverware).

silver-plate [-'pleit] *vt* platear, dar un baño de plata a.

silver-plating [-'pleitiŋ] *n* plateado *m*.

silver screen [-,skri:n] *n* industria *f* del cine.

silversmith [-,smiθ] *n* platero *m* ‖ *silversmith's* platería *f*.

silver-tongued [-'tʌŋd] *adj* elocuente, con pico de oro.

silverware [-wεə*] *n* plata *f*, vajilla *f* de plata.

silver wedding [-'wediŋ] *n* bodas *f pl* de plata.

silvery ['silvəri] *adj* plateado, da (of or like silver) ‖ argentino, na (tone, voice).

silviculture ['silvikʌltʃə*] *n* silvicultura *f*.

simian ['simiən] *adj* ZOOL símico, ca; simiesco, ca.
◆ *n* ZOOL simio *m*.

similar ['similə*] *adj* similar, parecido, da; semejante ‖ MATH semejante ‖ — *it is very similar to the one you have* se parece mucho al que tiene Ud ‖ *they are quite similar* se parecen bastante.

similarity [,simi'læriti] *n* similitud *f*, semejanza *f*, parecido *m*.

similarly [-li] *adv* del mismo modo.

simile ['simili] *n* símil *m*.

similitude [si'militju:d] *n* similitud *f*, parecido *m*, semejanza *f* (similarity) ‖ imagen *f* (image) ‖ forma *f* (form).

simmer ['simə*] *n* *to be* o *to keep on the simmer* hervir a fuego lento.

simmer ['simə*] *vt* hervir a fuego lento.
◆ *vi* hervir a fuego lento (to be boiling gently) ‖ estar a punto de hervir (to be almost boiling) ‖ FIG fermentar, estar a punto de estallar (revolt, etc.) ‖ — FIG *he was simmering with rage* estaba a punto de estallar | *to simmer down* calmarse.

simnel cake ['simnlkeik] *n* torta *f* de frutas que se prepara para Pascuas.

simoniac [sai'məuniæk] *adj/n* simoniaco, ca; simoniático, ca.

simonist ['saimənist] *n* simoniaco, ca; simoniático, ca.

simon-pure ['saimən'pjuə*] *adj* auténtico, ca.

simony ['saiməni] *n* simonía *f*.

simoom; simoon [si'mu:m] *n* simún *m* (wind).

simp [simp] *n* US FAM tonto, ta; bobo, ba.

simper ['simpə*] *n* sonrisa *f* afectada (affected smile) ‖ sonrisa *f* boba *or* tonta (silly smile).

simper ['simpə*] *vt* decir con una sonrisa afectada *or* tonta.

◆ *vi* sonreír con afectación *or* tontamente.

simple ['simpl] *adj* sencillo, lla; simple; *a simple dress* un vestido sencillo; *he is a simple man* es un hombre sencillo; *the simple life* la vida sencilla || natural; *simple beauty* belleza natural || fácil, sencillo, lla; simple (easy) || inocente, ingenuo, nua (guileless); *he is simple enough to believe anything* es tan inocente que se lo cree todo || simple (half-witted) || simple (mere); *he is a simple herdsman* es un simple pastor || JUR, CHEM & MED simple || — *a simple soul* un alma de Dios || ZOOL *simple eye* ojo *m* simple || MATH *simple equation* ecuación *f* de primer grado | *simple fraction* fracción ordinaria || COMM *simple interest* interés *m* simple || BOT *simple leaf* hoja *f* simple || GRAMM *simple sentence* oración *f* simple.

◆ *n* simple *m* & *f* (silly person) || simple *m* (plant).

simplehearted [-'hɑːtid] *adj* sencillo, lla (unsophisticated) || inocente, ingenuo, nua (artless).

simpleminded [-'maindid] *adj* sencillo, lla (unsophisticated) || ingenuo, nua (guileless) || simple (of subnormal intelligence) || tonto, ta (silly).

simplemindedness [-'maindidnis] *n* simpleza *f* (silliness) || ingenuidad *f* (ingenuousness).

simpleness [-nis] *n* ⟶ **simplicity.**

Simple Simon [-'saimən] *n* bobo *m*, simplón *m*.

simpleton ['simpltən] *n* simplón, ona; tontuelo, la; bobalicón, ona.

simplicity [sim'plisiti]**; simpleness** [simplnis] *n* sencillez *f* (lack of affectation or complexity) || naturalidad *f* (naturalness) || ingenuidad *f* (guilelessness) || simpleza *f* (silliness).

simplifiable ['simplifaiəbl] *adj* simplificable.

simplification [ˌsimplifi'keiʃən] *n* simplificación *f*.

simplifier ['simplifaiə*] *n* simplificador, ra.

simplify ['simplifai] *vt* simplificar.

simplistic [sim'plistik] *adj* simplista.

simply ['simpli] *adv* simplemente, sencillamente, con sencillez (in a simple way); *I simply left* me fui sencillamente; *simply dressed* vestido sencillamente || meramente, simplemente, solamente (merely) || realmente, francamente; *the play was simply awful* la obra era francamente horrible || *you simply must see it* tienes que verlo, no puedes dejar de verlo.

simulacrum [ˌsimju'leikrəm] *n* simulacro *m*.
— OBSERV El plural de la palabra *simulacrum* es *simulacra* o *simulacrums*.

simulate ['simjuleit] *vt* simular, fingir || — *a simulated attack* un simulacro de ataque || AVIAT *simulated flight* vuelo simulado.

simulation [ˌsimju'leiʃən] *n* simulación *f*, fingimiento *m* (pretence) || simulacro *m* (simulacrum).

simulator ['simjuleitə*] *n* TECH simulador *m*.

simulcast ['simʌlˌkɑːst] *n* transmisión *f* simultánea por radio y televisión (of programme, of event, etc.).

simultaneity [ˌsiməltə'niəti] *n* simultaneidad *f*.

simultaneous [ˌsiməl'teinjəs] *adj* simultáneo, a; *simultaneous translation* traducción simultánea || MATH *simultaneous equations* sistema *m sing* de ecuaciones.

simultaneously [-li] *adv* simultáneamente.

simultaneousness [-nis] *n* simultaneidad *f*.

sin [sin] *n* pecado *m*; *mortal, venial, original sin* pecado mortal, venial, original; *the seven deadly sins* los siete pecados capitales || — FIG & FAM *as ugly as sin* más feo que un pecado || *every sin carries its down punishment* en el pecado va la penitencia || *for my sins* por mis pecados || FIG *it would be a sin to miss this chance* sería un pecado no aprovechar esta oportunidad || *there is forgiveness for every sin* todo pecado merece perdón || *to be in sin* estar en pecado || FIG *to live in sin* vivir en el pecado.

sin [sin] *vi* pecar.

Sinai ['sainiai] *pr n* GEOGR Sinaí *m*.

sinapism ['sinəpizəm] *n* MED sinapismo *m*.

sin bin [-bin] *n* FAM prostíbulo *m*.

since [sins] *adv* desde entonces; *he moved away three years ago but she has seen him since* hace tres años que se marchó pero ella le ha visto desde entonces || — *a short time since* hace poco || *ever since* desde entonces || *he has married long since* hace tiempo *or* hace mucho tiempo que se ha casado, se ha casado desde hace tiempo *or* desde hace mucho tiempo || *how long since?* ¿cuánto tiempo hace?, ¿desde cuándo? || *not long since* hace poco.

◆ *prep* desde; *since childhood* desde la niñez || *since that time* desde entonces, a partir de entonces.

◆ *conj* desde que; *much has happened since they last met* muchas cosas han pasado desde que se vieron por última vez || ya que; *since you have come you can do the washing up* ya que has venido puedes fregar los platos || — *how long is it since he left?* ¿cuánto tiempo hace que se fue? || *how long is it since you've seen him?* ¿cuánto tiempo hace que no le ves? || *it's just a month since he left* sólo hace un mes que se fue || *since he was a child* desde niño.

sincere [sin'siə*] *adj* sincero, ra.

sincerely [-li] *adv* sinceramente || *yours sincerely* le saluda atentamente (in a letter).

sincerity [sin'seriti] *n* sinceridad *f*; *in all sincerity* con toda sinceridad.

sine [sain] *n* MATH seno *m* || *sine curve* sinuoside *f*.

sine die ['saini'daiiː] *adv phr* sine die.

sinecure ['sainikjuə*] *n* sinecura *f*, canonjía *f*.

sinew ['sinjuː] *n* ANAT tendón *m* || nervio *m* (in meat) || FIG nervio *m*, vigor *m* (strength).

◆ *pl* recursos *m* (means) || *the sinews of war* el nervio de la guerra.

sinewy [-i] *adj* nervudo, da (hands, body) || estropajoso, sa (meat) || FIG vigoroso, sa; enérgico, ca (vigorous).

sinfonia [ˌsinfə'niːə] *n* MUS sinfonía *f*.
— OBSERV El plural de la palabra inglesa *sinfonia* es *sinfonie*.

sinful ['sinful] *adj* pecaminoso, sa (deed, thought) || pecador, ra (person) || de perdición (place) || FIG escandaloso, sa (scandalous).

sinfulness [-nis] *n* maldad *f* (wickedness) || culpabilidad *f* (guilt) || pecado *m* (sin).

sing [siŋ] *n* silbido *m*, zumbido *m* (shrill sound); *the sing of a bullet* el silbido de una bala || canto *m* (singing).

sing* [siŋ] *vt* cantar || — *to sing a baby to sleep* arrullar a un niño || FIG *to sing a different tune* cambiar de tono || *to sing out* gritar (to shout), celebrar cantando (the old year) || FIG *to sing the praises of* cantar las alabanzas de.

◆ *vi* cantar (music, poetry, birds) || silbar, zumbar (bullets, etc.) || zumbar (insects, ears) || silbar (kettle) || FIG & FAM cantar (to confess) || — *to sing out* gritar || *to sing out of tune* desafinar || FIG *to sing small* achantarse || *to sing up* cantar más fuerte (louder).
— OBSERV Pret ***sang***; pp ***sung***.

Singapore [ˌsingə'pɔː*] *pr n* GEOGR Singapur.

Singaporean [ˌsingəpɔː'riən] *adj/n* singapurés, esa.

singe [sindʒ] *n* chamusquina *f*.

singe [sindʒ] *vt* chamuscar, socarrar || quemar las puntas de (hair).

singer [siŋə*] *n* cantante *m* & *f*, cantor, ra (s.o. who sings) || cantor, ra (in a choir) || cantante *m* & *f*, cantor *m*, cantatriz *f* (of opera) || cantante *m* & *f* (pop singer, folk singer, etc.) || ave *f* canora (a bird that sings) || *flamenco singer* cantaor *m* de flamenco.

Singhalese [ˌsiŋhə'liːz] *adj/n* cingalés, esa.

singing ['siŋiŋ] *n* MUS canto *m* (operatic, etc.) || canción *f* (pop singing) || zumbido *m*, silbido *m* (buzz) || silbido *m* (whistle) || — *I can hear singing* oigo a alguien que canta || *I enjoyed their singing* me gustó mucho como cantaron.

single ['siŋgl] *adj* solo, la; *a single spectator remained* un solo espectador se quedó; *there wasn't a single seat left* no quedaba ni un solo asiento || único, ca (sole, only) || suelto; *a single copy of a magazine* un número suelto de una revista || individual (for one person); *a single room, bed* una habitación, una cama individual || soltero, ra (unmarried); *to stay single* quedarse soltero || de soltero; *single life is very difficult* la vida de soltero es muy difícil || simple (not compound) || BOT simple || de ida; *one single ticket* un billete de ida || — *every single person* todos (y cada uno) || *not a single* ninguno, na || *not a single one* ni uno, ni una || *not a single person* ninguno, na; nadie || *not a single thing* nada || INFORM *single channel* monocanal || *single file* fila india || SP *single game* partido *m* individual *or* simple.

◆ *n* individuo *m*, persona *f* (person) || objeto *m*, cosa *f* (thing) || billete *m* de ida (ticket) || SP golpe *m* que marca un tanto (in cricket) | primera base *f* (in baseball).

◆ *pl* SP individual *m sing*, simple *m sing* (in tennis, in golf); *men's singles* individual caballeros.

single [siŋgl] *vt* *to single out* separar (to isolate), escoger, seleccionar, elegir (to choose), distinguir, singularizar (to distinguish).

◆ *vi* US SP pasar a la primera base (baseball).

single-acting [-'æktiŋ] *adj* de efecto simple.

single-barrelled; US **single-barreled** [-'bærəld] *adj* de un cañón (rifle).

single-breasted [-'brestid] *adj* recto, ta; sin cruzar; *a single-breasted jacket* una chaqueta recta.

single-cell [-sel] *adj* unicelular.

single combat [-'kɔmbət] *n* combate *m* singular || *to engage the enemy in single combat* luchar cuerpo a cuerpo con el enemigo.

single cream [-kriːm] *n* nata *f* ligera.

single-cylinder [-'silində*] *adj* monocilíndrico, ca.

single-engined [-'endʒind] *adj* monomotor.

single entry [-'entri] *n* COMM partida *f* simple.

single-foot [-fut] *vi* US amblar.

single-handed [-'hændid] *adj* sin ayuda (done without assistance) || manco, ca (having only one hand) || que se emplea con una sola mano (used with one hand).

◆ *adv* sin ayuda, solo, la.

single-hearted [-'hɑːtid] *adj* leal (loyal).

single-minded [-'maindid] *adj* que tiene un solo objetivo, resuelto, ta (with one purpose) || leal (single-hearted).

single-mindedness [-'maindidnis] *n* perseverancia *f* || franqueza *f* (frankness).

singleness [-nis] *n* lealtad *f*, honradez *f* (sincerity) || unidad *f* (unity) || soltería *f* (unmarried state) || *with singleness of purpose* con un solo objetivo, con determinación.

single-parent [-'pɛərənt] *adj* monoparental; *single-parent family* familia monoparental.

single-phase [-feiz] *adj* ELECTR monofásico, ca.

single-pole [-'pəul] *adj* unipolar.

singles bar [-z bɑː*] *n* US bar *m* de solteros.

single-seater [-'siːtə*] *n* monoplaza *m* (plane).

single-stage [-steidʒ] *adj* de un solo cuerpo (rocket).

singlestick [-stik] *n* bastón *m* (in fencing).

singlet ['siŋglit] *n* camiseta *f*.

singleton ['siŋgltən] *n* semifallo *m* (in cards).

single-track [-træk] *adj* de vía única (railway) || FIG limitado, da; de pocos alcances (mind).

singletree ['siŋgltriː] *n* US balancín *m*.

singly ['siŋgli] *adv* individualmente, por separado, separadamente (separately) || uno a uno (one by one) || sin ayuda, solo, la (single-handed).

singsong ['siŋsɔŋ] *n* tono *m* monótono, sonsonete *m*, canto *m* monótono (tone of voice) || *we had a little singsong after the meal* cantamos un poco después de la comida.
◆ *adj* monótono, na.

singular ['siŋgjulə*] *adj* GRAMM singular || singular, excepcional; *singular beauty* belleza singular || singular, raro, ra; extraño, ña (strange) || individual || solo, la; único, ca (single).
◆ *n* GRAMM singular *m*; *in the singular* en singular.

singularity [ˌsiŋgju'læriti] *n* singularidad *f* (strangeness, distinctiveness) || peculiaridad *f* (peculiarity).

singularize ['siŋgjuləraiz] *vt* singularizar.

singularly ['siŋgjuləli] *adv* particularmente.

sinister ['sinistə*] *adj* siniestro, tra (evil) || HERALD siniestrado, da (left).

sink [siŋk] *n* lavabo *m* (in bedroom, in bathroom) || fregadero *m*, pila *f* (in kitchen) || sumidero *m* (drain) || pozo *m* negro (cesspool) || depresión *f* (depressed land) || FIG cloaca *f* (place of vice).

sink* [siŋk] *vt* hundir, sumergir; *to sink one's hand in boiling water* sumergir la mano en agua hirviendo || echar al fondo del mar *or* de un río; *to sink a hundred tons of explosives* echar cien toneladas de explosivos al fondo del mar || hundir, echar a pique; *the torpedo sank the ship* el torpedo echó el barco a pique || hincar; *to sink a post in the ground* hincar un poste en el suelo; *to sink one's teeth into an apple* hincar los dientes en una manzana || meter; *I sank my hand in my pocket* metí la mano en el bolsillo || clavar, hundir; *to sink a knife into the ground* clavar un cuchillo en el suelo || cavar, excavar (a well, a mine, etc.) || TECH avellanar (to countersink) | grabar en hueco (in engraving) || bajar (to reduce in intensity, in volume); *to sink one's voice* bajar la voz || COMM invertir (to invest) | enterrar, gastar (one's fortune) || meter (la bola) en el agujero (billiards) || meter (la pelota en el hoyo) (in golf) || FIG acabar con; *to sink s.o.'s hopes* acabar con las esperanzas de uno | echar abajo; *to sink s.o.'s plans* echar abajo los planes de uno; *to sink a theory* echar abajo una teoría | hundir (person) | bajar (one's head, one's eyes) | beberse (a drink) | echar tierra sobre, olvidar (to cover up, to hush up) || — FIG & FAM *now we're sunk!* ¡estamos perdidos! || FIG *to be sunk in* estar sumido en (thought, despair, melancholy, etc.).
◆ *vi* hundirse; *the cart sunk into the mud* el carro se hundió en el barro; *sinking into the cushions* hundiéndose en los cojines; *land that is sinking* tierra que se está hundiendo || hundirse, irse a pique (boat, drowning man) || ponerse, bajar, ocultarse (heavenly body); *the sun was sinking behind the hills* el sol estaba bajando detrás de las colinas || desaparecer; *to sink into the distance* desaparecer en la lejanía || arrellanarse; *he sank back into the chair* se arrellanó en la silla || dejarse caer (to drop); *he sank heavily into the chair* se dejó caer pesadamente en la silla || descender, bajar, estar en declive; *hills that sink to the sea* colinas que bajan hacia el mar || disminuir, bajar; *over the years sales figures have sunk* a través de los años las ventas han bajado || bajar (opinion, etc.); *he has sunk in my esteem* ha bajado en mi estima || amainar (the wind) || hundirse (the cheeks) || bajar (voice) || FIG caer; *night sank upon the town* la noche cayó sobre la ciudad | venirse abajo; *his hopes sunk* sus esperanzas se vinieron abajo | doblarse; *to sink under a heavy load* doblarse bajo una carga pesada | debilitarse, consumirse (a sick person); *he is sinking fast* se está debilitando rápidamente || COMM bajar (values, shares) || — FIG *his heart sank* se le cayó el alma a los pies | *his legs sank under him* le flaquearon las piernas | *to leave s.o. sink or swim* abandonar a alguien a su suerte || *to sink in* o *into* hundirse en; *the knife sank into his flesh* el cuchillo se le hundió en la carne; penetrar; *the rain sank into the dry ground* la lluvia penetró en la tierra seca; fijarse (dye), caer en; *to sink into oblivion* caer en el olvido; *to sink into decay* caer en la decadencia; grabarse en; *to sink into the memory* grabarse en la memoria; causar impresión (words) || *to sink into a deep sleep* caer *or* sumirse en un profundo sueño || *to sink to one's knees* hincarse de rodillas || FIG *when the importance of the news finally sank in* cuando por fin nos dimos cuenta de la importancia de la noticia.

— OBSERV Pret ***sank***; pp ***sunk***.

sinkage [-idʒ] *n* hundimiento *m*.

sinker [-ə*] *n* plomo *m* (to sink a fishing line, a net, etc.) || pocero *m* (well digger) || excavador *m* (shaft sinker) || US FAM buñuelo *m* (doughnut).

sinkhole [-həul] *n* sumidero *m* (drain) || pozo *m* negro (cesspool).

sinking [-iŋ] *n* hundimiento *m* (of boat, road, building, etc.) || excavación *f* (excavation) || amortización *f* (of debt) || debilitación *f*, disminución *f* (of debt) || debilitación *f*, disminución *f* (of strength) || bajada *f* (of voice) || FIG *to have that sinking feeling* tener el sentimiento de que todo se acaba.

sinking fund [-iŋfʌnd] *n* fondo *m* de amortización.

sinless ['sinlis] *adj* inmaculado, da; puro, ra; sin pecado.

sinner ['sinə*] *n* pecador, ra.

Sinn Fein ['ʃinfein] *n* Sinn Fein *m* [movimiento nacionalista irlandés].

Sino-Japanese ['sainəudʒæpə'niːz] *adj* sinojaponés, esa.

Sinologist [sai'nɔlədʒist]; **Sinologue** ['sainəlɔg] *n* sinólogo, ga.

Sinology [si'nɔlədʒi] *n* sinología *f*.

sinter ['sintə*] *n* GEOL toba *f* caliza || TECH frita *f* (product of sintering).

sinter ['sintə*] *vt* TECH sinterizar.

sinuate ['sinjuet] *adj* BOT ondeado, da; sinuoso, sa.

sinuosity [ˌsinju'ɔsiti] *n* sinuosidad *f*.

sinuous ['sinjuəs] *adj* sinuoso, sa (winding, having many curves) || BOT ondeado, da; sinuoso, sa.

sinus ['sainəs] *n* ANAT, MED & BOT seno *m*.

sinusitis [ˌsainə'saitis] *n* MED sinusitis *f*.

sinusoid ['sainəsɔid] *n* sinusoide *f*.

sinusoidal [sainəs'ɔidəl] *adj* sinusoidal.

Sioux [suː] *adj/n* siux.

— OBSERV El plural de la palabra *Sioux* es *Sioux* [su: z].

sip [sip] *n* sorbo *m*; *let me have a sip from your glass* déjame tomar un sorbo de tu vaso.

sip [sip] *vt/vi* sorber, beber a sorbos (to drink) || probar (to taste).

siphon; syphon ['saifən] *n* sifón *m* || *siphon bottle* sifón *m*.

siphon ['saifən] *vt* trasegar con sifón || *to siphon off* o *out* sacar con sifón.
◆ *vi* pasar por un sifón.

sippet ['sipit] *n* picatoste *m* (for soaking in soup, for garnishing) || FIG trozo *m*, fragmento *m* (morsel).

sir [səː*] *n* señor *m*, caballero *m*; *excuse me, Sir* perdone usted, señor || sir *m* (title) || — *Dear Sir* Muy Señor mío || *my dear sir!* ¡amigo mío! || MIL *Yes, Sir!* ¡Sí, mi General! [mi Capitán, etc.!], ¡a sus órdenes, mi General [mi Capitán, etc.!].

— OBSERV En plural se emplean las formas *Sirs* o *Gentlemen*. El título *Sir* va siempre seguido del nombre de pila de la persona considerada.

sire ['saiə*] *n* (ant) mi Señor *m*, Majestad *f* (form of address to a king) || ZOOL padre *m* (of a quadruped) | semental *m* (stud animal).

sire ['saiə*] *vt* ser el padre de, engendrar || — *he sired eleven children* fue el padre de once hijos || *this horse was sired by...* el padre de este caballo es *or* fue...

siren ['saiərən] *n* MYTH, MAR & TECH sirena *f* || FIG mujer *f* fatal, sirena *f*.

sirenian [sai'riːniən] *n* ZOOL sirenio *m*.

sirloin ['səːlɔin] *n* CULIN solomillo *m*.

sirocco [si'rɔkəu] *n* siroco *m* (wind).

sirup ['sirəp] *n* ⟶ **syrup.**

sisal ['saisəl] *n* sisal *m*, pita *f*, henequén *m*.

siskin ['siskin] *n* chamariz *m* (bird).

sissy; cissie; cissy ['sisi] *n* FAM blandengue *m* (softy) | gallina *f* (coward) | afeminado *m*, mariquita *f* (effeminate man).

sister ['sistə*] *n* hermana *f* || enfermera *f* jefe (in hospital) || REL hermana *f*, monja *f* (nun) || FIG mujer *f* (woman) || — *Sister Mary* Sor María || *sister nations* naciones hermanas || *sister ships* barcos gemelos.

sister-german [-'dʒəːmən] *n* hermana *f* carnal.

— OBSERV El plural de *sister-german* es *sisters-german*.

sisterhood [-hud] *n* hermandad *f* || REL comunidad *f* religiosa.

sister-in-law [-rinlɔː] *n* cuñada *f*, hermana *f* política.

— OBSERV El plural de *sister-in-law* es *sisters-in-law*.

sisterly [-li] *adj* fraternal, de hermana.

Sistine ['sistain] *adj* sixtino, na; *the Sistine Chapel* la Capilla Sixtina.

sit [sit] *vt* sentar; *sit him on her left* siéntale a su izquierda || montar (a horse) || presentarse a; *to sit an exam* presentarse a un examen || tener cabida para (to accommodate); *it sits fifty people* tiene cabida para cincuenta personas || — *to sit o.s.* sentarse || *to sit out* no bailar; *do you mind if we sit this one out?* ¿te importa que no bailemos esta vez?; quedarse hasta el final de, aguantar hasta el final de (a meeting, a film, etc.) || *to sit s.o. up* incorporar a alguien.
◆ *vi* sentarse; *sit on my left* siéntese a mi izquierda; *tables are not meant for sitting on* las mesas no están hechas para que uno se siente encima || estar sentado; *when everyone was sitting* cuando todos estuvieron sentados; *they were sitting round the fire* estaban sentados alrededor del fuego || posarse (bird, insect) || empollar; *the hen sits on the eggs* la gallina empolla

los huevos || posar (to pose); *to sit for a portrait* posar para un retrato || sentar (clothes); *to sit very well on one* sentarle bien a uno || yacer, estar situado (to lie, to be situated) || quedarse, estar, permanecer; *the car sits there all day long* el coche se queda allí todo el día || ser miembro; *to sit on a committee* ser miembro de una comisión || ocupar un escaño; *to sit in Parliament* ocupar un escaño en el parlamento || reunirse, celebrar sesión (an assembly, a court, etc.); *the committee is sitting* la comisión está reunida || actuar; *the assembly will sit as a general committee* la asamblea actuará como comité || cuidar niños (to look after children) || FIG corresponder; *conduct that sits badly on a young lady* conducta que no corresponde a una señorita | pesar (to weigh); *the responsability sits heavily on him* la responsabilidad le pesa mucho || soplar (wind) || — FIG *now we just have to sit back and wait* ahora sólo tenemos que esperar || *they sat looking at each other* estaban sentados mirándose el uno al otro || *to be sitting at breakfast, at dinner* estar desayunando, cenando || *to be sitting at table* sorprender a alguien (to surprise), despertarle el interés a alguien (to arouse s.o.'s interest) || *to shoot a pheasant sitting* disparar un faisán en tierra || *to sit at home doing nothing* quedarse en casa sin hacer nada || *to sit back in one's chair* recostarse sin hacer nada || *to sit back in one's chair* recostarse en la silla || *to sit down* sentarse; *please sit down* siéntese por favor; *they sat down to a meal of chicken* se sentaron para comer un pollo; *to sit down to a game of cards* sentarse a jugar a las cartas || FIG *to sit about* o *around* estar cruzado de brazos | *to sit down on* suprimir (to suppress), reprimir (to repress), oponerse firmemente a (to oppose) | *to sit down under* aguantar (to accept) || *to sit for a constituency* representar un distrito electoral || *to sit for an examination* presentarse a un examen || FIG *to sit in for s.o.* sustituir a alguien | *to sit in on* asistir sin participar (a meeting, a discussion) | *to sit on* o *over a matter* discutir un asunto, examinar un asunto | *to sit on s.o.* poner a alguien en su sitio, bajarle los humos a alguien | *to sit over a book* estar leyendo un libro | *to sit over a glass of brandy* estar sentado con una copa de coñac || *to sit still* no moverse || FIG *to sit through* aguantar hasta el final (a concert, a lecture) || *to sit up* incorporarse (from a lying position); *to sit up in bed* incorporarse en la cama; ponerse derecho (to straighten one's back), quedarse levantado, no acostarse; *I sat up all night* no me acosté en toda la noche; quedar asombrado; *everybody sat up at the news* todos quedaron asombrados con la noticia || *to sit and take notice* aguzar el oído, prestar atención || *to sit up for s.o.* quedarse esperando a alguien || *to sit up with s.o.* hacer compañía a alguien (to keep s.o. company), cuidar a alguien (to look after) || FIG *we can't just sit back and let them get away* no podemos cruzarnos de brazos y dejar que se escapen.

— OBSERV Pret y pp ***sat***.

sitcom ['sitkɔm] *n* FAM RAD comedia *f* de enredo (situation comedy).

sit-down strike [-daun'straik] *n* huelga *f* de brazos caídos *or* de brazos cruzados, sentada *f*.

site [sait] *n* situación *f*, emplazamiento *m*; *the site of ancient Carthage* la situación de la antigua Cartago || solar *m*; *the site for the new factory* el solar para la nueva fábrica || lugar *m*, escenario *m*, sitio *m*; *the exact site of the battle* el lugar exacto de la batalla || — *building site* obra *f* (under construction); *I work on that building site* trabajo en esa obra; solar *m* (for sale, etc.) || *on site* en el sitio.

site [sait] *vt* situar; *where will it be sited?* ¿dónde estará situado?

sit-in ['sitin] *n* ocupación *f* || *to stage a sit-in in a building* ocupar un edificio.

siting ['saitiŋ] *n* emplazamiento *m*, localización *f*, situación *f*.

sitter ['sitə*] *n* modelo *m* & *f* (painter's model) || persona *f* que cuida a los niños (babysitter) || FAM gol *m* facilísimo (easy goal) | blanco *f* facilísimo (easy target); *to miss a sitter* errar un blanco facilísimo || gallina *f* clueca (broody hen).

sitting ['sitiŋ] *n* sentada *f*, tirón *m*; *she read the novel at one sitting* leyó la novela de un tirón || sesión *f*; *a portrait painted in two sittings* un retrato pintado en dos sesiones || sesión *f* (of an assembly); *the sitting is open* o *is called to order* queda abierta la sesión; *to hold a sitting* celebrar (una) sesión || servicio *m* (in a restaurant) || asiento *m* reservado (in a church) || incubación *f* (brooding of a hen) || nidada *f* (of eggs) || — *final sitting* sesión de clausura || *opening sitting* sesión de apertura || *to resume a sitting* reanudar la sesión.

◆ *adj* sentado, da || — FIG & FAM *sitting duck* blanco facilísimo || *sitting hen* gallina clueca.

sitting room [-rum] *n* cuarto *m* de estar, sala *f* de estar.

sitting tenant [-'tenənt] *n* inquilino, na.

situate ['sitjueit] *vt* situar [AMER ubicar].

situated [-id] *adj* situado, da; *to be well situated* estar bien situado.

situation [,sitju'eiʃən] *n* situación *f* [AMER ubicación *f*] (location) || situación *f*; *an embarrassing situation* una situación embarazosa || colocación *f* (paid occupation) || — *situations vacant* ofertas *f* de trabajo || *situations wanted* solicitudes *f* de trabajo || *to save the situation* salvar la situación.

sitz bath ['sitsbɑːə] *n* baño *m* de asiento.

six [siks] *adj* seis || — *six hundred* seiscientos, tas || *six hundredth* sexcentésimo, ma.

◆ *n* seis *m* (number, card, figure) || SP equipo *m* de seis (team) || — *half past six* las seis y media || *he is six* tiene seis años || *he is six today* cumple seis años hoy || FIG *it's six of one and half a dozen of the other* olivo y aceituno todo es uno || *six o'clock* las seis || *to be at sixes and sevens* estar en desorden (to be in disorder), estar reñidos (at loggerheads).

sixfold [-fəuld] *adj* séxtuplo, pla.

◆ *adv* seis veces.

sixpence [-pɛs] *n* seis peniques *m pl* (value) || moneda *f* de seis peniques (coin).

sixpenny [-pəni] *adj* de seis peniques || FIG de tres al cuarto (cheap).

six-shooter [-'ʃuːtə*] *n* revólver *m* de seis tiros.

sixteen ['siks'tiːn] *adj* dieciséis, diez y seis.

◆ *n* dieciséis *m*, diez y seis *m*.

sixteenmo [siks'tiːnməu] *n* libro *m* en dieciseisavo (book).

sixteenth ['sikst'tiːnθ] *adj* decimosexto, ta (in a series) || dieciseisavo, va (one of sixteen parts).

◆ *n* decimosexto, ta || dieciséis, diez y seis; *John XVI (the sixteenth)* Juan XVI [dieciséis] || dieciseisavo *m* (one of sixteen equal parts) || — *on the sixteenth of May* el día dieciséis de mayo || US MUS *sixteenth note* semicorchea *f*.

sixth [siksθ] *adj* sexto, ta.

◆ *n* sexto, ta (of a series); *John VI (the sixth)* Juan VI [sexto] || MUS sexta *f* || seis *m* (in dates) || *on the sixth of July* el (día) seis de julio || *sixth form* último curso *m* de enseñanza secundaria en Gran Bretaña.

sixtieth ['sikstiiθ] *adj* sexagésimo, ma (in a series) || sexagésimo, ma; sesentavo, va (being one of sixty equal parts).

◆ *n* sexagésima parte *f*, sesentavo *m* (one of sixty equal parts) || sexagésimo, ma (of a series).

Sixtus ['sikstəs] *pr n* Sixto *m*.

sixty ['siksti] *adj* sesenta.

◆ *n* sesenta *m* || *the sixties* los años sesenta.

sixty-fourth note [-fɔːθnəut] *n* US MUS semifusa *f*.

sizable; sizeable ['saizəbl] *adj* grande; *a sizable majority* una gran mayoría || considerable, importante (quantity).

sizar ['saizə*] *n* becario, ria.

size [saiz] *n* tamaño *m*; *it is about the size of a football* tiene aproximadamente el tamaño de un balón de fútbol; *medium size* tamaño mediano; *life size* tamaño natural || talla *f*, estatura *f* (of a person) || número *m* (of shoes, of gloves) || talla *f* (of garments); *what is your size?* ¿cuál es su talla? || formato *m*, tamaño *m* (of a book) || FIG talla *f* (capacity); *it is not a job for a man of his size* no es un trabajo para un hombre de su talla | magnitud *f* (magnitude) | alcance *m* (scope) || apresto *m*, cola *f* (for paper, for textile, etc.) || calibre *m* (of a cartridge) || — *a bump the size of an egg* un bulto del tamaño de un huevo || *of a size* igual del mismo tamaño || FAM *that's about the size of it* es más o menos eso || *this is a size too small* esta talla me está un poco pequeña || FIG *to be quite a size* ser muy grande | *to cut s.o. down to size* bajarle los humos a alguien, ponerle en su sitio a alguien || *to cut sth. to size* cortar algo del tamaño que se necesita || *to take the size of* medir || *what size collar do you take?* ¿qué cuello tiene? || *what size shoes do you take?* ¿qué número calza usted?

size [saiz] *vt* clasificar según el tamaño (to arrange according to size) || calibrar (to gauge) || aprestar (paper, textiles, etc.) || *to size up* evaluar (to estimate), medir con la vista, evaluar el tamaño de (to estimate the size of), juzgar (the character or qualities of); *it's difficult to size him up* es difícil juzgarle; comparar (to compare).

— OBSERV Muy frecuentemente el participio *sized* se combina con un sustantivo o con un adjetivo para formar una palabra compuesta (*egg-sized* del tamaño de un huevo; *average-sized* de tamaño mediano).

sizeable [-əbl] *adj* → **sizable.**

sizing [-iŋ] *n* apresto *m*.

sizzle ['sizl] *vi* chisporrotear.

sizzling [-iŋ] *adj* muy caliente (very hot) || candente (issue).

◆ *n* chisporroteo *m* (sizzle).

skate [skeit] *n* patín *m* (ice or roller skate) || raya *f* (fish) || FAM matalón *m*, rocín *m* (old horse) | desgraciado *m* (despicable person).

skate [skeit] *vi* patinar || FIG *to skate on thin ice* pisar un terreno peligroso.

skateboard [-bɔːd] *n* monopatín *m*.

skater [-ə*] *n* patinador, ra.

skating [-iŋ] *n* patinaje *m*; *ice skating* patinaje sobre hielo; *roller skating* patinaje sobre ruedas.

skating rink [-iŋriŋk] *n* pista *f* de patinaje.

skedaddle [ski'dædl] *vi* FAM salir pitando.

skeet [skiːt] *n* US tiro *m* al plato.

skein [skein] *n* madeja *f*, ovillo *m* (of thread, wool, silk, etc.) || bandada *f* (of birds) || FIG enredo *m*, maraña *f*.

skeletal ['skelətəl] *adj* esquelético, ca.

skeleton ['skelətəl] *n* ANAT esqueleto *m* || TECH armazón *f*, armadura *f* (of a building) || FIG estructura *f*; *the skeleton of the organization* la estructura de la organización | mínimo *m*; *to reduce sth. to a skeleton* reducir algo al mínimo | esqueleto *m* (thin person) | esquema *m*, bosquejo *m* (outline) || — FIG *skeleton at the feast* aguafiestas *m inv* | *skeleton in the cupboard* o *in the closet* vergüenza *f* de la familia, secreto *m* de la familia || *skeleton key* llave *f* maestra (master key), ganzúa *f* (for picking locks) || *skeleton staff* personal *m* mínimo || FIG *to work with a skeleton team* trabajar con un equipo muy reducido.

skene [ski:n] *n* puñal *m*, daga *f*.

skep [skep] *n* cesta *f* (basket, basketful) || colmena *f* de paja (straw beehive).

skeptic [-tik] *adj/n* US escéptico, ca.

skeptical [-tikəl] *adj* US escéptico, ca.

skepticism ['skeptisizəm] *n* US escepticismo *m*.

sketch [sketʃ] *n* croquis *m*, apunte *m* (quick drawing) || bosquejo *m*, esbozo *m* (preliminary drawing) || dibujo *m* (drawing) || descripción *f*; *character sketch* descripción de un personaje || esquema *m* (outline) || THEATR sketch *m*, obra *f* corta || MUS pieza *f* corta.

sketch [sketʃ] *vt* hacer un croquis de (rough drawing) || bosquejar, esbozar (preliminary drawing); *to sketch in pencil* esbozar a lápiz || dibujar (to draw) || FIG *to sketch in the details for s.o.* resumirle los detalles a alguien | *to sketch out* trazar las líneas generales (to give the main points).
◆ *vi* dibujar.

sketchbook [-buk] *n* bloc *m* de dibujo (of drawings) || colección *f* de obras cortas (of literary sketches).

sketchiness [-inis] *n* superficialidad *f*, falta *f* de detalles, imprecisión *f*.

sketchpad [-pæd] *n* bloc *m* de dibujo.

sketchy [-i] *adj* incompleto, ta (incomplete) || sin detalles, impreciso, sa; superficial (not detailed) || vago, va; impreciso, sa (idea).

skew [skju:] *adj* oblicuo, cua; sesgado, da (not straight) || asimétrico, ca (lacking symmetry) || ARCH esviado, da (wall, arch, etc.).
◆ *n* oblicuidad *f*, sesgo *m* || sesgo *m* (in cloth) || esviaje *m* (of wall, of arch, etc.).

skew [skju:] *vt* sesgar (to cut or set slantingly) || tergiversar, desvirtuar (to distort).
◆ *vi* torcerse.

skewback [-bæk] *n* ARCH salmer *m*.

skewbald [-bɔ:ld] *adj* pío, a (horse).

skewer [-ə*] *n* pincho *m*, broqueta *f*, brocheta *f* (for meat, for cooked food, etc.) || espetón *m* (for sardines) || FAM espada *f* (sword).

skewer [-ə*] *vt* ensartar, espetar.

skew-eyed [-aid] *adj* bizco, ca.

skewness [-nis] *n* oblicuidad *f* (obliquity) || falta *f* de simetría (lack of symmetry).

skewwhiff [-'wif] *adj/adv* FAM → **askew.**

ski [ski:] *n* esquí *m* || — *ski boots* botas *f* de esquiar || *ski jump* salto *m* con esquís (action), pista *f* de salto (course) || *ski lift* telesquí *m* || *ski run* o *slope* pista *f* de esquí || *ski stick, ski pole* bastón *m* || *ski tow* telesquí *m*.
— OBSERV El plural de la palabra inglesa es *ski* o *skis*.

ski [ski:] *vi* esquiar.

skid [skid] *n* patinazo *m* (of a wheel, of a car) || calzo *m* (block of wood, of metal) || rampa *f* de descarga (for unloading) || AVIAT patín *m* || MAR varadera *f* (for protection) || — FIG *to be on the skids* estar *or* andar de capa caída | *to put the skids under s.o.* poner chinas en el camino de uno.

skid [skid] *vt* hacer deslizar [sobre maderos, etc.] (to slide down a ramp) || poner en calzo a, calzar (to block) || hacer patinar (a car) || MAR poner varaderas a.
◆ *vi* patinar (car, wheel, etc.).

skiddoo [ski'du:] *vi* US FAM largarse.

skid row ['skid'rəu] *n* US barrio *m* bajo.

skier ['ski:ə*] *n* esquiador, ra.

skiff [skif] *n* esquife *m*.

skiing ['ski:iŋ] *n* esquí *m* || *to go skiing* ir a esquiar.

skilful; US **skillful** ['skilful] *adj* hábil, diestro, tra.

skilfully [-li] *adv* hábilmente, diestramente.

skilfulness; US **skillfulness** [-nis] *n* habilidad *f*, destreza *f*.

skill [skil] *n* habilidad *f*, destreza *f* (ability to do sth. well) || técnica *f*, arte *f* (particular technique); *a difficult skill to acquire* una técnica difícil de adquirir || oficio *m* (trade); *one learns several skills in the army* se aprenden varios oficios en el ejército || experiencia *f* (experience).

skilled [-d] *adj* hábil, habilidoso, sa; diestro, tra (having skill) || cualificado, da; especializado, da; *skilled workman* obrero cualificado || especializado, da; *skilled work* trabajo especializado || experto, ta; *to be skilled in a craft* ser experto en un arte.

skillet ['skilət] *n* cacerola *f* [con patas y mango largo] || US sartén *f* (frying pan).

skillful ['skilful] *adj* US → **skilful.**

skillfully [-li] *adv* hábilmente, diestramente.

skillfulness [-nis] *n* US → **skilfulness.**

skim [skim] *n* espumado *m* (act of skimming) || leche *f* desnatada (milk) || capa *f* fina (thin covering) || *skim milk* leche desnatada.

skim [skim] *vt* espumar (a liquid) || desnatar (milk) || hacer cabrillas con (a stone) || rozar (a surface); *to skim the ground* rozar el suelo || FIG echar una ojeada a; *to skim the headlines* echar una ojeada a los títulos | tocar, tratar superficialmente (a subject).
◆ *vi* pasar rozando (to go smoothly over); *to skim along at treetop height* pasar rozando los árboles || US cubrirse con una capa fina (to become coated) || — AVIAT *to skim along the ground, the water* volar a ras de tierra, a ras del agua, volar rozando el suelo, el agua || *to skim over* pasar rozando (a surface), volar rozando, volar a ras de (an aeroplane), tocar, tratar superficialmente (a subject) || *to skim through* hojear (to flick through), echar una ojeada a (to read quickly).

skimmer [-ə*] *n* espumadera *f* (for skimming liquids) || desnatadora *f* (for milk).

skimp [skimp] *vt* escatimar; *to skimp material in making a curtain* escatimar tela para hacer una cortina; *to skimp s.o. in money* escatimarle dinero a alguien || chapucear; *to skimp a piece of work* chapucear un trabajo.
◆ *vi* escatimar los gastos, vivir con estrechez.

skimpily [-ili] *adv* insuficientemente, escasamente || — *to be skimpily dressed* ir ligero de ropa || *to feed s.o. skimpily* darle poco de comer a alguien.

skimpiness [-inis] *n* insuficiencia *f* (insufficiency) || tacañería *f* (stinginess).

skimpy [-i] *adj* escaso, sa (scarce, scanty, poor) || pequeño, ña (too small) || mezquino, na (mean) || tacaño, ña (stingy) || corto, ta (dress).

skin [skin] *n* piel *f* (membrane of body, animal hide) || cutis *m* (of face) || tez *f* (complexion) || pellejo *m*, odre *m* (container) || pellejo *m* (of sausage) || piel *f* (of drum) || piel *f* (of fruit) || cáscara *f*, piel *f* (of orange, of banana) || nata *f* (of boiled milk, of custard, etc.) || MAR & AVIAT forro *m* || — FIG *he has a thick skin* es poco sensible | *he has a thin skin* es muy susceptible | *he is nothing but skin and bone* está en los huesos, está hecho un esqueleto | *it's no skin off my back* esto no me va ni me viene || *soaked to the skin* calado hasta los huesos || FIG *to escape by the skin of one's teeth* escapar *or* librarse por los pelos || FIG & FAM *to get under one's skin* irritarle a uno | *to have s.o. under one's skin* tener a alguien en la masa de la sangre | FIG & FAM *to jump out of one's skin* llevarse un susto tremendo || *to save one's skin* salvar el pellejo || *to strip to the skin* desnudarse completamente.
◆ *pl* FAM batería *f sing*, tambores *m* (drums) || *to play the skins* tocar la batería.

skin [skin] *vt* despellejarse, desollar; *to skin a rabbit* despellejar un conejo || pelar (fruit, vegetables) || desollar, arañar (to graze, to scrape); *I skinned my knuckles* me desollé los nudillos || quitarse (clothes) || FIG & FAM despojar (to take from); *he skinned me of all I had* me despojó de todo lo que tenía || MAR & AVIAT proveer de forro || — *dark skinned* de piel morena || *to skin s.o. alive* desollar vivo a alguien.
◆ *vi* cubrirse de nata (custard, etc.) || MED *to skin over* cicatrizarse.

skin-deep [-'di:p] *adj* superficial; *skin-deep wound* herida superficial; *skin-deep feelings* sentimientos superficiales.

skin disease [-di'zi:z] *n* MED dermatosis *f*, enfermedad *f* de la piel.

skin diver [-daivə*] *n* SP buceador, ra.

skin diving [-'daiviŋ] *n* SP buceo *m*, natación *f* submarina (swimming) | pesca *f* submarina (fishing).

skin effect [-i'fekt] *n* ELECTR efecto *m* superficial.

skinflint [-flint] *n* tacaño, ña; roñoso, sa.

skinful [-ful] *n* odre *m*, pellejo *m* || FAM *he's got a good skinful* está como una cuba.

skin game [-geim] *n* FAM estafa *f*, timo *m*.

skin graft [-grɑ:ft] *n* injerto *m* de piel (tissue).

skin grafting [-'grɑ:ftiŋ] *n* injerto *m* de piel.

skinhead [-hed] *n* skinhead *m* & *f*, cabeza rapada *m* & *f*.

skink [skiŋk] *n* escinco *m* (lizard).

skinner [θkinə*] *n* desollador, ra (s.o. who strips skin) || FAM estafador, ra (swindler) || peletero *m* (furrier).

skinniness ['skininis] *n* delgadez *f*, flacura *f*.

skinny ['skini] *adj* flaco, ca; enjuto, ta (person) || trasijado, da; flaco, ca (horse).

skint [skint] *adj* FAM sin un duro, pelado, da.

skin test ['skintest] *n* MED cutirreacción *f*, dermorreacción *f*.

skintight ['skintait] *adj* muy ajustado, da; muy ceñido, da.

skip [skip] *n* salto *m*, brinco *m* (jump) || rebote *m* (rebound) || FIG salto *m*, omisión *f* || capitán, ana (in games) || MIN montacargas *m inv* (lift).

skip [skip] *vt* saltarse; *to skip a year at school* saltarse un curso en el colegio || saltarse, saltar, omitir; *to skip a passage in a book* saltarse un párrafo en un libro || hacer rebotar (to skim a stone, etc.) || FAM fumarse; *to skip a lecture* fumarse una clase || *skip it!* ¡déjalo!
◆ *vi* ir dando saltos; *to skip along the street* ir dando saltos por la calle || saltar, brincar (to jump) || saltar (over a skipping rope, over a fence, etc.) || saltar a la comba; *the girls were in the garden skipping* las niñas estaban saltando a la comba en el jardín || saltar, pasar; *to skip to another subject* saltar a otro tema || rebotar (to rebound) || US FAM largarse (to leave hurriedly) || FIG *to skip over* saltar, saltarse.

skip-bomb ['skip,bɔm] *vt* MIL bombardear de rebote.

skipper [-ə*] *n* saltador, ra || capitán *m*, patrón *m* (of a small vessel) || AVIAT capitán *m* || SP & FAM capitán, ana.

skipper [-ə*] *vt* capitanear (games).

skipping rope [-iŋrəup] *n* comba *f*, saltador *m*.

skirl [skəːl] *n* sonido *m* agudo || *the skirl of the pipes* el sonido de las gaitas.

skirl [skəːl] *vi* tener un sonido agudo || sonar; *the bagpipes skirl* suenan las gaitas.

skirmish ['skəːmiʃ] *n* MIL escaramuza *f* || pelea *f* (fight) || agarrada *f* (slight conflict).

skirmish ['skəːmiʃ] *vi* MIL escaramuzar, escaramucear, tener una escaramuza *or* escaramuzas || pelear (to fight).

skirmisher [-ə*] *n* MIL tirador *m*.

skirr [skəː] *vi* aletear.

skirt [skəːt] *n* falda *f*; *bell, straight skirt* falda acampanada, estrecha || faldones *m pl* (of a coat) || FAM gachí *f* (girl, woman) || *divided* o *split skirt* falda pantalón.
◆ *pl* afueras *f* (of a city).

skirt [skəːt] *vt/vi* rodear (to surround) || rodear, dar la vuelta a (a hill, a mountain, etc.) || bordear (a lake, a coast).

skirting board [-iŋbɔːd] *n* zócalo *m*, cenefa *f*.

skit [skit] *n* relato *m* corto y satírico (story) || THEATR sketch *m* satírico || escarnio *m*, burla *f* (gibe).

skiting [-iŋ] *n* borde *m* (edge) || zócalo *m*, cenefa *f* (of a wall).

skitter [-ə*] *vi* pasar rozando el agua (to skim the surface of water).

skittish [-iʃ] *adj* frívolo, la (fickle) || caprichoso, sa (whimsical) || asustadizo, za (horse).

skittishness [-iʃnis] *n* frivolidad *f* (fickleness) || inconstancia *f*.

skittle [-l] *n* bolo *m* (pin, in bowling) || *skittle alley* bolera *f*.
◆ *pl* juego *m sing* de bolos, bolos *m* (game); *to play skittles* jugar a los bolos || FIG *it's not all beer and skittles* no todo es coser y cantar.

skive [skaiv] *vt* chiflar (to pare leather) || cortar en capas finas (rubber) || pulir (a diamond) || FAM fumarse; *to skive a lecture* fumarse una clase | remolonear (to slack).

skiver [-ə*] *n* chifla *f* (knife for cutting leather) || cuero *m* fino y blando [para encuadernar, etc.] (leather).

skivvy ['skivi] *n* criada *f* (maid).
◆ *pl* FAM ropa *f sing* interior (underwear).

skulduggery [skʌl'dʌgəri] *n* trampas *f pl*, engaños *m pl* (trickery).

skulk [skʌlk] *n* FAM remolón, ona.

skulk [skʌlk] *vi* esconderse (to hide) || FAM escurrir el bulto, zafarse.

skull [skʌl] *n* calavera *f* (lay term) || ANAT cráneo *m* (scientific term); *to break one's skull* romperse el cráneo || FAM caletre *m* (mind) || *skull and crossbones* calavera (danger sign, pirate flag).

skullcap [-kæp] *n* solideo *m* (of a priest) || gorro *m* (of jews).

skunk [skʌŋk] *n* mofeta *f* (mammal) || FAM canalla *m*.

skunk [skʌŋk] *vt* FAM dar una paliza a (to defeat).

sky [skai] *n* cielo *m* || clima *m* (weather) || — *sky blue* azul *m* celeste || FIG *out of a clear blue sky* de repente | *under the open sky* al aire libre.
◆ *pl* cielo *m sing*; *a week of blue skies* una semana con cielo azul || FIG *to praise to the skies* poner por las nubes.

sky [skai] *vt* FAM bombear (a ball) || colgar muy alto (to hang up high).

sky-blue [-'bluː] *adj* azul celeste, celeste.

sky diver [-'daivə*] *n* SP paracaidista *m* & *f*.

skydiving [-'daiviŋ] *n* SP paracaidismo *m*.

sky-high [-'hai] *adj* muy alto, ta || — *prices are sky-high* los precios están por las nubes || *sky-high prices* precios astronómicos.
◆ *adv* hasta las nubes, por las nubes (very high) || — *to blow sky-high* destruir completamente (to blow up), echar por tierra (arguments) || *to praise s.o. sky-high* poner a alguien por las nubes.

skyjack [-,dʒæk] *vt* secuestrar en vuelo (an aircraft).

skylark [-laːk] *n* alondra *f* (bird).

skylark [-laːk] *vi* hacer travesuras (to be mischievous) || divertirse, estar de juerga (to have fun) || — *stop skylarking about!* ¡déjate de tonterías! || *to skylark about* hacer el tonto.

skylight [-lait] *n* claraboya *f*, tragaluz *m* (window in a roof) || luz *f* cenital.

skyline [-lain] *n* horizonte *m* (horizon) || perfil *m*, silueta *f* (of a building) || contorno *m*, perfil *m* (of a city).

sky pilot [-'pailət] *n* FAM sacerdote *m* (priest) | capellán *m* (chaplain).

skyrocket [-,rɔkit] *n* cohete *m* (fireworks).

skyrocket [-,rɔkit] *vi* subir un cohete (to shoot up) || subir vertiginosamente (prices).

skyscraper [-,skreipə*] *n* rascacielos *m inv*.

skyward [-wəd] *adj/adv* hacia el cielo.

skywards [-wədz] *adv* hacia el cielo.

sky wave [-weiv] *n* onda *f* ionosférica.

skyway [-,wei] *n* ruta *f* aérea.

skywriting [-,raitiŋ] *n* publicidad *f* aérea [formando palabras en el cielo con humo].

slab [slæb] *n* trozo *m* (piece) || porción *f* (of cake, etc.) || losa *f* (of stone, of marble) || plancha *f*, lámina *f* (of metal) || tableta *f* (of chocolate) || rodaja *f* (of fish) || tajada *f* (of meat) || costero *m* (of a log) || bloque *m* (block); *a slab of ice* un bloque de hielo.

slab [slæb] *vt* cortar los costeros de (to cut slabs from wood) || aplicar una capa espesa de; *to slab paint on canvas* aplicar una capa espesa de pintura al lienzo || enlosar (to pave with slabs).

slabber [-ə*] *n* —> **slobber.**

slabber [-ə*] *vt/vi* —> **slobber.**

slack [slæk] *adj* flojo, ja; *a slack rope* una cuerda floja; *a slack screw* un tornillo flojo || descuidado, da; negligente (careless); *a slack workman* un trabajador negligente || tranquilo, la; descansado, da; *a slack job* un trabajo tranquilo || vago, ga; perezoso, sa (lazy) || bajo, ja; *the slack season* la temporada baja || de poco trabajo, de poca actividad; *to go through a slack period* atravesar un período de poca actividad || quieto, ta; tranquilo, la; *slack sea* mar quieta || — *business is slack* hay poco trabajo || *slack demand* poca demanda || *slack hours* horas *f* de poca actividad || *slack lime* cal muerta || *slack water* aguas muertas || *the market is slack* el mercado está flojo, hay poca actividad en el mercado || *they are very slack about whom they let in* son muy tolerantes con respecto a quienes dejan entrar.
◆ *n* período *m* de poca actividad (dull period) || baja temporada *f* (season) || aguas *f pl* muertas (slack water) || cisco *m* (coal particles) || parte *f* floja (of a rope) || — *there is a lot of slack in the rope* la cuerda está muy floja || *to take up the slack in a rope* tensar una cuerda.
◆ *pl* pantalones *m* (trousers).

slack [slæk] *vt* aflojar (rope, screw) || aminorar (pace) || disminuir (activity) || apagar (lime) || *to slack off* disminuir.
◆ *vi* aflojarse (rope, etc.) || apagarse (lime) || aflojar; *he has slacked in his work* ha aflojado en su trabajo || FAM gandulear, holgazanear (to be lazy) || — *to slack off* disminuir || *to slack up* ir más despacio, reducir la velocidad.

slacken [-ən] *vt* disminuir, reducir (to lessen); *the driver slackned his speed* el conductor disminuyó la velocidad; *to slacken the rhythm* disminuir el ritmo || aminorar (one's pace) || aflojar (rope, effort, etc.) || FIG *to slacken the reins* soltar las riendas.
◆ *vi* aflojarse (rope, etc.) || disminuir (rhythm, speed) || aflojar (to reduce one's efforts) || amainar (wind) || *business is slackening* los negocios están aflojando.

slacker [-ə*] *n* FAM gandul, la; holgazán, ana (lazybones) || MIL prófugo *m*.

slackness [-nis] *n* flojedad *f* (looseness) || estancamiento *m* (of business) || inactividad *f* (inactivity) || relajamiento *m*, relajación *f* (of discipline) || pereza *f*, gandulería *f* (laziness) || descuido *m*, negligencia *f* (carelessness).

slag [slæg] *n* escoria *f* (from metals and mines) || escoria *f*, lava *f* (from a volcano) || *slag heap* escorial *m*.

slag [slæg] *vi* escorificar.

slagging [-iŋ] *n* escorificación *f*.

slain [slein] *pp* —> **slay.**

slake [sleik] *vt* apagar, aplacar (thirst) || satisfacer, saciar (passions) || apagar (lime) || *slaked lime* cal apagada *or* muerta.

slalom ['sleiləm] *n* SP slalom *m*, prueba *f* de habilidad (in skiing).

slam [slæm] *n* portazo *m* (of a door) || golpe *m* (blow) || FAM vapuleo *m* (harsh criticism) || slam *m* (in card games); *grand slam* gran slam.

slam [slæm] *vt* cerrar de un golpe (to shut noisily) || hacer golpear; *the wind slammed the shutters against the window* el viento hacía golpear las persianas contra la ventana || FAM disparar; *to slam a ball* disparar una pelota | vapulear (to criticize harshly); *the critics slammed the play* los críticos vapulearon la obra || — SP *to slam in a goal* marcar un gol || *to slam sth. down on a table* poner algo violentamente en la mesa || *to slam sth. down on the ground* tirar algo al suelo || *to slam the brakes on* dar un frenazo || *to slam the door* dar un portazo || *to slam the door in s.o.'s face* dar con la puerta en las narices de alguien || FIG *to slam the door on* cerrar la puerta a || SP & FAM *to slam the opposing team* darle una paliza al equipo contrario || US *to slam through* hacer aprobar (a proposal).
◆ *vi* cerrarse de golpe (to shut violently) || — *I was kept awake all night by slamming doors* no dormí en toda la noche a causa de los portazos que se oían || *she slammed down the corridor* se fue corriendo por el pasillo.

slander ['slaːndə*] *n* calumnia *f* (false statement) || JUR difamación *f* [oral]; *to sue s.o. for slander* demandar a alguien por difamación.

slander ['slaːndə*] *vt* calumniar || JUR difamar.

slanderer [-rə*] *n* calumniador, ra || JUR difamador, ra.

slanderous [-rəs] *adj* calumnioso, sa || JUR difamatorio, ria.

slang [slæŋ] *n* germanía *f*, argot *m* (of criminals, etc.) || jerga *f* (jargon); *student's slang* jerga estudiantil || argot *m* (colloquial language).
◆ *adj* de germanía || de jerga || de argot.

slang [slæŋ] *vt* FAM poner verde, insultar.

slanginess [-inis] *n* vulgaridad *f* (of language).

slangy [-i] *adj* vulgar.

slant [slaːnt] *n* inclinación *f*; *a slant of ten degrees* una inclinación de diez grados || pendiente *f*, declive *m* (slope) || FIG giro *m*; *the affair took on a new slant* el asunto tomó un nuevo giro | punto *m* de vista, parecer *m* (opinion) || *to be on a slant* o *on the slant* estar inclinado; *the ground is on a slant* el terreno está incli-

nado; estar sesgado, estar al bies (a picture, etc.).
◆ *adj* inclinado, da (inclined) || *slant eyes* ojos achinados.

slant [slɑːnt] *vi* estar inclinado; *the table slants* la mesa está inclinada.
◆ *vt* inclinar (to incline) || poner al sesgo *or* al bies, sesgar (to put out of line) || FIG enfocar de modo parcial (a problem, etc.).

slanted [-id] *adj* FIG parcial.

slanting [-iŋ] *adj* inclinado, da (roof, handwriting, etc.) || que cae en sentido oblicuo (rain, snow) || al sesgo, sesgado, da (not straight) || oblicuo, cua (oblique) || *slanting eyes* ojos achinados.

slantingly [-iŋli]; **slantways** [-weiz]; **slantwise** [-waiz] *adv* oblicuamente.

slap [slæp] *n* bofetada *f* (blow on the face) || palmada *f* (on thigh, on back, etc.) || azote *m* (on child's bottom) || — FIG *a slap in the face* un bofetón, una bofetada, un feo, una afrenta, un desaire (affront) | *to give s.o. a slap on the back* dar una palmada en la espalda a alguien (in greeting, etc.), dar a alguien la enhorabuena (to congratulate s.o.) || FAM *to have a slap at* intentar (hacer) (to try sth.), dar un bofetón a (to attack in criticism).
◆ *adv* de lleno; *he ran slap into the lamppost* dio de lleno contra el farol || justo; *slap in the middle of the pond* justo en medio de la charca.

slap [slæp] *vt* abofetear (to hit) || dar una palmada; *to slap s.o. on the back* dar a alguien una palmada en la espalda || poner violentamente, tirar; *he slapped the book on the table* tiró el libro en la mesa || — *to slap a new wing on a building* ponerle un anexo a un edificio || *to slap paint on a wall* pintar una pared a brochazos || *to slap s.o.'s face, to slap s.o. on the face* darle una bofetada *or* un tortazo a alguien.
◆ *vi* romper; *the waves slapped against the boat* las olas rompían contra el barco.

slap-bang [-'bæŋ] *adv* de sopetón, de golpe y porrazo (with suddenness) || violentamente (violently).

slapdash [-dæʃ] *adj* descuidado, da; chapucero, ra.
◆ *adv* descuidadamente.

slap-happy [-'hæpi] *adj* aturdido, da (dazed) || inconsciente (carefree).

slapjack [-ʒæk] *n* US torta *f* (flapjack).

slapstick [-stik] *n* payasada *f*, bufonada *f* (farcical comedy).
◆ *adj* bufonesco, ca.

slap-up [-ʌp] *adj* FAM elegante (elegant) | excelente, de primera categoría (first-rate) || FAM *slap-up meal* comilona *f*, banquete *m*.

slash [slæʃ] *n* cuchillada *f*, tajo *m* (with a knife) || cuchillada *f* (slit in clothing) || latigazo *m* (with a whip) || reducción *f* (of costs, of prices, etc.) || tala *f* (in a forest) || US pantano *m* (bog).

slash [slæʃ] *vt* acuchillar (with a knife) || azotar (with a whip) || dar un tajo a (with the edge of a sword) || acuchillar (to put a slit in clothes) || FIG poner por los suelos, vapulear (to criticize) | sacrificar (prices) | reducir (wages, etc.) | cortar (a speech) || talar (trees).
◆ *vi* tirar tajos y estocadas.

slashing [-iŋ] *adj* mordaz, áspero, ra (criticism) || extraordinario, ria (sucess).
◆ *n* → **slash**.

slat [slæt] *n* tablilla *f* (short, thin piece of wood) || listón *m* (long, thin piece of wood).

slat [slæt] *vt* hacer con listones (to lath) || poner listones a (to furnish with laths) || tirar (to throw) || pegar (to beat).
◆ *vi* MAR gualdrapear (sails).

slate [sleit] *n* pizarra *f* (rock, roofing, writing surface) || color *m* pizarra (colour) || US lista *f* de candidatos || — *slate pencil* pizarrín *m* || *slate quarry* pizarral *m* || FIG *to clean the slate, to wipe the slate clean* hacer borrón y cuenta nueva | *to start with a clean slate* empezar una nueva vida.
◆ *adj* de color pizarra (colour) || de pizarra (made of slate).

slate [sleit] *vt* empizarrar (to cover with slates) || FIG vapulear (to criticize) | echar una bronca a (to scold) | castigar (to punish) || US inscribir (on a list) | designar (to appoint).

slating [-iŋ] *n* FIG vapuleo *m* (criticism) | bronca *f* (scolding) | reprimenda *f* (reprimand) || empizarrado *m* (work, material).

slatted ['slætid] *adj* de tablillas (blind, door).

slattern ['slætəːn] *n* mujer *f* desaseada.

slatternly [-li] *adj* desaseado, da; dejado, da.
◆ *adv* desaseadamente.

slaty ['sleiti] *adj* pizarroso, sa (like slate) || de color pizarra (slate-coloured).

slaughter ['slɔːtə*] *n* matanza *f*, sacrificio *m* (of animals) || matanza *f*, degollina *f* (massacre) || *the Slaughter of the Innocents* la Degollación de los Inocentes.

slaughter ['slɔːtə*] *vt* matar, sacrificar (animals for food) || matar brutalmente (to kill brutally) || exterminar (to kill in large numbers) || FIG dar una paliza a (an opponent).

slaughterer [-rə*] *n* jifero *m*, matarife *m* (of animals) || asesino, na (of people).

slaughterhouse [-haus] *n* matadero *m*.

Slav [slɑːv] *adj/n* eslavo, va.

slave [sleiv] *n* esclavo, va || FIG esclavo, va; *a slave to work* un esclavo del trabajo || *to make a slave of* esclavizar.

slave [sleiv] *vi* trabajar como un negro (*at* en).

slave driver [-ˌdraivə*] *n* negrero *m*.

slaveholder [-ˌhəuldə*] *n* negrero *m*.

slave labour; US **slave labor** [-ˌleibə*] *n* trabajo *m* de negros (job) || esclavos *m pl* (people).

slaver [-ə*] *n* negrero *m* (person) || barco *m* negrero (ship) || *white slaver* tratante *m* de blancas.

slaver ['slævə*] *n* baba *f* (dribble) || US tonterías *f pl* (nonsense).

slaver [-ə*] *vt* babosear (to cover with spittle).
◆ *vi* babear.

slavery [-əri] *n* esclavitud *f*; *to live in slavery* vivir en la esclavitud; *slavery is forbidden in most countries* la esclavitud está prohibida en la mayoría de los países; *this job is pure slavery* este trabajo es una esclavitud || — *to sell s.o. into slavery* vender a alguien como esclavo || *white slavery* trata *f* de blancas.

slavery ['slævi] *n* FAM criada *f* (servant).

slave ship [-ʃip] *n* barco *m* negrero.

slave trade [-treid] *n* trata *f* de esclavos || *white slave trade* trata de blancas.

slave trader [-ˌtreidə*] *n* negrero *m*.

Slavic [-k] *adj* eslavo, va.
◆ *n* eslavo *m* (language).

slavish ['sleiviʃ] *adj* de esclavo (life, etc.) || servil; *slavish person* persona servil; *slavish imitation* imitación servil.

slavishness [-nis] *n* servilismo *m*.

Slavonic [slə'vɔnik] *adj* eslavo, va.
◆ *n* eslavo *m* (language).

slaw [slɔː] *n* ensalada *f* de col.

slay* [slei] *vt* matar, asesinar (to kill) || US FAM encantar, chiflar (to be immensely pleasing); *he slays me* me chifla | hacer mucha gracia (to be funny).

— OBSERV Pret ***slew***; pp ***slain***.

slayer [-ə*] *n* asesino *m*.

sleaziness ['sliːzinis] *n* mala calidad *f* (poor quality) || sordidez *f* (shabbiness).

sleazy ['sliːzi] *adj* de mala calidad (of poor quality) || sórdido, da (shabby); *a sleazy joint* un lugar sórdido.

sled [sled] *n* trineo *m*.

sled [sled] *vt* transportar *or* llevar en trineo.
◆ *vi* ir en trineo.

sledding [-iŋ] *n* transporte *m* por trineo || FIG *it was hard sledding* fue muy difícil.

sledge [sledʒ] *n* trineo *m* (sled) || TECH almádana *f*, almádena *f* (sledgehammer).

sledge [sledʒ] *vt* transportar *or* llevar en trineo.
◆ *vi* ir en trineo (to sled) || US golpear con la almádena (to use a sledgehammer).

sledgehammer [-ˌhæmə*] *n* almádana *f*, almádena *f* (heavy hammer).

sleek [sliːk] *adj* liso y brillante, lustroso, sa (smooth and shiny) || impecable; *a sleek appearance* un aspecto impecable || elegante (elegant) || FAM meloso, sa; empalagoso, sa (manners).

sleekness [-nis] *n* lustre *m*, brillo *m* || elegancia *f* || FAM melosidad *f* (of manners).

sleep [sliːp] *n* sueño *m*; *deep sleep* sueño profundo; *lack of sleep* falta de sueño || — FIG *eternal sleep* sueño eterno || *hypnotic sleep* sueño hipnótico || FIG *last sleep* último sueño (death) || *not to have a wink of sleep all night* no pegar ojo en toda la noche || FIG *to abandon o.s. to sleep* entregarse al sueño || *to cry o.s. to sleep* llorar hasta dormirse || *to drop off to sleep* quedarse dormido || *to fall into a deep sleep* caer en un sueño profundo || *to get some sleep* dormir un poco || *to get to sleep* conciliar el sueño || *to go for an after-dinner sleep* ir a dormir la siesta || *to go to sleep* dormirse; *he went to sleep* se durmió; *my leg has gone to sleep* la pierna se me ha dormido || *to have a sleep* echar un sueñecito || *to lose sleep* perder el sueño || FIG *to put an animal to sleep* sacrificar un animal || *to put o to send somebody to sleep* dormir a alguien || FIG *to sleep the sleep of the just* dormir el sueño de los justos || *to walk in one's sleep* ser sonámbulo || FIG *to ward off sleep* espantar el sueño.

sleep* [sliːp] *vt* dormir; *he slept five hours before leaving* durmió cinco horas antes de marcharse || tener cabida para, poder alojar; *this hotel sleeps fifty guests* este hotel tiene cabida para cincuenta personas || — *to sleep away* pasa las horas durmiendo || FAM *to sleep it off* dormir la mona || *to sleep off* dormir para que desaparezca (fatigue, headache, etc.) || *to sleep through a film* pasarse toda la película durmiendo.
◆ *vi* dormir; *to sleep like a log* dormir como un tronco; *he was sleeping soundly* o *deeply* dormía profundamente || pasar la noche, dormir; *we slept at a very good hotel* pasamos la noche en un hotel muy bueno || — FAM *to sleep around* acostarse con todos || *to sleep in* dormir en casa (a domestic servant) || *to sleep on* o *over sth.* consultar algo con la almohada || *to sleep out* dormir fuera || *to sleep with, together* acostarse con, juntos.

— OBSERV Pret y pp ***slept***.

sleeper [-ə*] *n* persona *f* que duerme (s.o. who sleeps) || traviesa *f*, durmiente *m* (on railway lines) || coche *m* cama (sleeping car) || US pelele *m* (child's sleeping garment) | éxito *m* inesperado (success) || *to be a heavy, a light sleeper* tener el sueño pesado, ligero.

sleepily [-ili] *adv* soñolientamente; *he walked sleepily up the stairs* subió soñolientamente la escalera || *she replied sleepily* contestó soñolienta *or* entre sueños.

sleepiness [-inis] *n* somnolencia *f* ‖ *to try to hide one's sleepiness* intentar disimular el sueño.

sleeping [-iŋ] *adj* durmiente, dormido, da.
◆ *n* sueño *m*.

sleeping bag [-iŋbæg] *n* saco *m* de dormir.

Sleeping Beauty [-iŋ'bjuːti] *n* Bella *f* durmiente del bosque.

sleeping car [-iŋkɑː*] *n* coche *m* cama.

sleeping partner [-iŋ'pɑːtnə*] *n* COMM socio *m* comanditario.

sleeping pill [-iŋpil] *n* somnífero *m*.

sleeping policeman [-pə'liːs] *n* rompecoches *m inv*.

sleeping sickness [-iŋˌsiknis] *n* MED enfermedad *f* del sueño, tripanosomiasis *f* (transmitted by the tsetse fly) | encefalitis *f* letárgica (inflammation of the brain).

sleepless [-lis] *adj* en blanco (with no sleep); *a sleepless night* una noche en blanco ‖ insomne, desvelado, da (insomnious) ‖ incansable (unceasingly active).

sleeplessness [-lisnis] *n* insomnio *m*.

sleepwalker [-ˌwɔːkə*] *n* sonámbulo, la; somnámbulo, la.

sleepwalking [-ˌwɔːkiŋ] *n* sonambulismo *m*, somnambulismo *m*.

sleepy [-i] *adj* soñoliento, ta (tired); *sleepy eyes* ojos soñolientos ‖ FIG dormido, da; *a sleepy village* un pueblo dormido | soporífero, ra; *a sleepy atmosphere* un ambiente soporífero | letárgico, ca (lethargic) | pasado, da (fruit) ‖ — *sleepy face* cara dormida ‖ *to be awfully sleepy* caerse de sueño ‖ *to be sleepy* tener sueño ‖ *to make sleepy* dar sueño.

sleepyhead [-ihed] *n* dormilón, ona.

sleepy sickness [-iˌsiknis] *n* MED encefalitis *f* letárgica.

sleet [sliːt] *n* aguanieve *f* (snow mixed with rain).

sleet [sliːt] *vi* cellisquear, caer aguanieve (to rain snow and water).

sleeve [sliːv] *n* manga *f* (of a garment) ‖ funda *f* (of record) ‖ TECH manguito *m* (of shaft, etc.) | camisa *f* (of cylinder) ‖ — FIG *to have sth. up one's sleeve* tener algo en reserva, traer algo en la manga | *to laugh up one's sleeve* reírse para su capote ‖ *to roll up one's sleeves* arremangarse.

sleeved [-d] *adj* con mangas ‖ — *long-sleeved* de manga larga ‖ *short-sleeved* de manga corta.

sleeveless [-lis] *adj* sin mangas.

sleigh [slei] *n* trineo *m* (sledge).

sleight [slait] *n* habilidad *f*, destreza *f* (skill) ‖ FIG artimañas *f pl* (trickery).

sleight of hand ['slaitəv'hænd] *n* prestidigitación *f*, juego *m* de manos (of conjurers).

slender ['slendə*] *adj* delgado, da; fino, na (thin) ‖ esbelto, ta (thin and graceful) ‖ FIG ligero, ra; *slender hopes* ligeras esperanzas; *slender chance* ligera posibilidad | bajo, ja; *slender income* sueldo bajo | escaso, sa (resources) | malo, la; pobre (excuse).

slenderize ['slendəraiz] *vt* adelgazar.

slenderness ['slendənis] *n* delgadez *f* (thinness) ‖ esbeltez *f* (gracefulness) ‖ FIG ligereza *f* (slightness) | escasez *f* (scarcity).

slept [slept] *pret/pp* ⟶ **sleep.**

sleuth [sluːθ] *n* detective *m* (detective).

sleuthhound [-'haund] *n* sabueso *m* (dog, man).

slew; slue [sluː] *n* giro *m* (turn) ‖ US FAM gran cantidad *f* (a lot) ‖ US lodazal *m*, cenagal *m* (slough).

slew [sluː] *pret* ⟶ **slay.**

slew; slue [sluː] *vt* hacer girar a (to turn round).
◆ *vi* girar (to turn) ‖ MAR virar.

slice [slais] *n* rebanada *f* (of bread) ‖ lonja *f*, loncha *f* (of ham) ‖ tajada *f* (of meat) ‖ rodaja *f*, raja *f* (of salami) ‖ raja *f* (of fish, of cheese) ‖ raja *f*, tajada *f* (of melon) ‖ pala *f*, paleta *f* (for serving fish) ‖ FIG parte *f* (part); *a large slice of my income* una gran parte de mis ingresos ‖ FAM tajada *f* (benefit) ‖ SP golpe *m* que da efecto a la pelota *or* al balón.

slice [slais] *vt* partir en rodajas [o rajas, rebanadas, lonjas, etc.] (to cut into slices) ‖ cortar (to cut) ‖ SP dar efecto a (a ball) | cortar (a ball in tennis) ‖ *to slice off* cortar.
◆ *vi* dar efecto a la pelota.

slicer [-ə*] *n* máquina *f* de cortar.

slick [slik] *adj* diestro, tra; hábil (skilful) ‖ astuto, ta (astute) ‖ liso, sa (hair) ‖ elegante (elegant) ‖ US resbaladizo, za (slippery).
◆ *adv* hábilmente (skilfully) ‖ rápidamente (quickly).
◆ *n* US superficie *f* resbaladiza (smooth surface) | capa *f* de aceite (oil slick) | herramienta *f* para alisar (tool for smoothing).

slick [slik] *vt* alisar; *to slick one's hair* alisarse el pelo ‖ acicalar (to spruce up) ‖ *to slick o.s. up* acicalarse.

slicker [-ə*] *n* US FAM estafador, ra (swindler) | impermeable *m* (raincoat).

slid [slid] *pret/pp* ⟶ **slide.**

slide [slaid] *n* deslizamiento *m*, desliz *m* (the act of sliding) ‖ superficie *f* resbaladiza (smooth surface) ‖ tobogán *m* (for children, parcels, etc.) ‖ resbaladero *m* (for logs) ‖ tapa *f* corrediza (lid) ‖ cursor *m* (of mathematical instrument) ‖ PHOT diapositiva *f*, transparencia *f*; *colour slide* diapositiva en color ‖ portaobjeto *m* (of a microscope) ‖ desprendimiento *m* (of rock, of earth, etc.) ‖ pasador *m* (for hair) ‖ FIG baja *f* (drop) ‖ MUS vara *f* corredera (of an instrument).

slide* [slaid] *vt* hacer resbalar ‖ deslizar; *to slide a letter under the door, into s.o.'s hand* deslizar una carta por debajo de la puerta, en la mano de alguien ‖ correr; *slide your chair nearer* corre la silla más cerca ‖ arrastrar (to drag) ‖ añadir; *he slid a clause into the contract* añadió una cláusula al contrato ‖ — *slide it down* o *over to me* échamelo ‖ *to slide a box across to s.o.* mandar una caja a alguien de un empujón ‖ *to slide a glance at s.o.* mirar a alguien de reojo ‖ *to slide a ring on s.o.'s finger* ponerle a alguien un anillo en el dedo.
◆ *vi* resbalar (to slip); *he slid over and broke an arm* resbaló y se rompió un brazo ‖ deslizarse; *children sliding in the snow* niños deslizándose por la nieve ‖ — *the rain slid down the windows* la lluvia corría por las ventanas ‖ FIG *to let things slide* desatenderse de lo que pasa, dejar que ruede la bola | *to slide by* o *away* pasar (time, procession) ‖ *to slide down* bajar deslizándose (por) ‖ *to slide into* introducirse en (a place), caer imperceptiblemente en (a habit) ‖ FIG *to slide over* pasar por alto (a subject) ‖ — *to slide up to s.o.* acercarse furtivamente a alguien.
— OBSERV Pret y pp ***slid***.

slide fastener [-'fɑːsnə*] *n* US cremallera *f* (zip fastener).

slider [-ə*] *n* guía *f*, cursor *m*, corredera *f*.

slide rule [-ruːl] *n* regla *f* de cálculo.

slide projector [-prə'dʒektə*] *n* proyector *m* de diapositivas *or* de transparencias.

slide trombone [-trɔm'bəun] *n* MUS trombón *m* de varas.

slide valve [-vælv] *n* TECH corredera *f*.

sliding [-iŋ] *adj* corredizo, za (roof) ‖ corredera, de corredera (door) ‖ móvil (scale).
◆ *n* deslizamiento *m* de una corredera.

slight [slait] *adj* ligero, ra; pequeño, ña; *a slight difference, improvement* una ligera diferencia, mejora; *slight error, pause* pequeño error, pequeña pausa ‖ menudo, da (small); *a slight person* una persona menuda ‖ delgado, da (slim) ‖ esbelto, ta (slender) ‖ leve (not serious) ‖ insignificante ‖ — *a slight amount of difficulty* cierta dificultad ‖ *a slight wound* una pequeña herida, una herida superficial ‖ *I have a slight headache* me duele un poco la cabeza, tengo un ligero dolor de cabeza ‖ *I haven't the slightest idea* no tengo la más remota *or* la más mínima *or* la menor idea ‖ *not in the slightest* en absoluto ‖ *of slight intelligence* de corta inteligencia, corto de inteligencia ‖ *there is not the slightest hope* no queda ninguna esperanza, no queda ni la más remota esperanza.
◆ *n* desaire *m*, feo *m* (affront); *a slight on the family* un desaire a la familia.

slight [slait] *vt* despreciar, menospreciar; *he slighted my efforts* despreció mis esfuerzos ‖ desairar (to treat with rudeness) ‖ ofender, insultar (to offend, to insult) ‖ US desatender, descuidar; *to slight one's work* descuidar el trabajo.

slighting [-iŋ] *adj* despreciativo, va; menospreciativo (scornful) ‖ ofensivo, va (offensive).

slightly [-li] *adv* ligeramente ‖ un poco; *the patient is slightly better today* hoy el enfermo está un poco mejor ‖ *slightly built* menudo, da (small), esbelto, ta (slender), delgado, da (slim).

slightness [-nis] *n* pequeñez *f* (smallness) ‖ delgadez *f* (slimness) ‖ insignificancia *f* (insignificance) ‖ superficialidad *f*, levedad *f*, poca gravedad *f* (of wound, etc.).

slim [slim] *adj* delgado, da (thin); *a slim person* una persona delgada ‖ esbelto, ta (slender) ‖ delgado, da; fino, na (thing) ‖ FIG pequeño, ña; ligero, ra; *a slim chance* una ligera posibilidad | escaso, sa; poco, ca (public) | escaso, sa (resources) ‖ *to get slim* o *slimmer* adelgazar (a person), disminuir (hopes, etc.).

slim [slim] *vt/vi* adelgazar.

slime [slaim] *n* limo *m*, cieno *m*, fango *m*, lodo *m* (mud) ‖ baba *f*, babaza *f* (of slugs, of snails, etc.).

sliminess [-inis] *n* fangosidad *f* (of mud) ‖ lo baboso (of snails) ‖ viscosidad *f* (viscosity) ‖ FIG obsequiosidad *f*.

slimming ['slimiŋ] *adj* que no engordan (foods) ‖ que adelgaza (dress) ‖ *to be on slimming diet* seguir un régimen para adelgazar.

slimness ['slimnis] *n* delgadez *f* (of s.o.) ‖ FIG escasez *f* (of chances, etc.).

slimy ['slaimi] *adj* fangoso, sa (covered with mud) ‖ baboso, sa; *the snail left a slimy trail* el caracol dejó un rastro baboso ‖ viscoso, sa (sticky) ‖ FIG rastrero, ra; adulón, ona (obsequious) ‖ US asqueroso, sa (filthy) ‖ FIG *a slimy trick* una mala jugada.

sling [sliŋ] *n* honda *f* (for throwing stones) ‖ tirador *m* (toy) ‖ portafusil *m* (for rifle) ‖ MAR eslinga *f* (rope) ‖ MED cabestrillo *m* (for injured arm) ‖ US cóctel *m* [hecho con ginebra, agua, azúcar y limón].

sling* [sliŋ] *vt* colgar (to hang) ‖ tirar con honda; *he slung a stone at it* le tiró una piedra con honda ‖ tirar, arrojar (to throw) ‖ MED poner en cabestrillo (an arm) ‖ FIG & FAM *to sling one's hook* irse con la música a otra parte.
— OBSERV Pret y pp ***slung***.

slingback [-bæk] *n* zapato *m* abierto por detrás.

slingshot [-ʃɔt] *n* tirador *m* (catapult) ‖ honda *f* (sling).

slink* [sliŋk] *vi* *to slink in* entrar furtivamente ‖ *to slink off* o *away* escabullirse.

◆ *vt* malparir (an animal).
— OBSERV Pret y pp ***slunk***.

slinky [-i] *adj* sigiloso, sa (stealthy) || ceñido, da (women's clothes) || esbelto, ta (woman's figure) || provocativo, va (provocative).

slip [slip] *n* resbalón *m* (a slipping) || traspiés *m*, paso *m* en falso (trip); *one slip and he'll fall to his death* un traspiés y se mata || equivocación *f*, error *m* (mistake in writing, in calculating, etc.) || desliz *m*, descuido *m* (mistake in one's actions, in one's words, etc.) || funda *f*; *pillow slip* funda de la almohada || combinación *f* (long petticoat) || combinación *f* de medio cuerpo (short petticoat) || correa *f* (dog's leash) || esqueje *m* (plant cutting) || tira *f* (strip) || trozo *m*; *a slip of paper* un trozo de papel || papel *m* (with a note) || ficha *f* (filing card) || desprendimiento *m* (of land, of stones, etc.) || ARTS barbotina *f* (liquid clay) || PRINT galerada *f*, galera *f* (galley proof) || MAR grada *f* (shipway) || — FAM *a slip of a girl* una chiquilla || *gym slip* traje *m* de gimnasia || *slip of the pen* lapsus *m* cálami || *slip of the tongue* lapsus *m* linguae || *there's many a slip' twixt the cup and the lip* de la mano a la boca se pierde la sopa || *to give s.o. the slip* dar esquinazo a alguien.
◆ *pl* THEATR bastidores *m*.

slip [slip] *vt* pasar; *to slip a rope round s.o.'s neck* pasarle una cuerda por el cuello a alguien; *he slipped his hand round her waist* le pasó la mano por la cintura || poner, meter (to put); *he slipped his biro back into his pocket* volvió a meter el bolígrafo en el bolsillo || poner disimuladamente (to put furtively) || escaparse de, librarse de; *she slipped her pursuers* se escapó de sus perseguidores || soltar (to let loose) || descorrer (to slide open); *to slip the catch* descorrer el cerrojo || correr (to slide shut) || dejar (un punto) sin hacer (in knitting) || mudar (snakes, etc.) || parir antes de tiempo (animals) || MAR soltar, largar (a cable, an anchor) || MED dislocar (to dislocate) || — *the dog slipped its leash* el perro se soltó de la correa || *to slip in* introducir || *to slip off* quitarse [rápidamente] (clothes) || *to slip on* ponerse [rápidamente] (clothes) || FIG & FAM *to slip one over on s.o.* engañar a alguien || FIG *to slip one's memory* o *one's mind* írsele de la memoria *or* de la cabeza, olvidársele | *to slip s.o.'s notice* pasarle desapercibido a uno || FAM *to slip s.o. a pound* deslizar *or* poner en la mano *or* darle una libra a alguien (de propina, etc.) || *try to slip in a good word for me* a ver si me recomiendas, a ver si hablas bien de mí.
◆ *vi* resbalar; *he slipped on the ice* resbaló en el hielo || escurrirse, escabullirse; *he slipped out of the room* se escabulló de la habitación || ir un momento (to go); *slip round to the baker's, please* ve un momento a la panadería, por favor || equivocarse (to be wrong) || dislocarse (bone) || desprenderse (rocks) || desatarse, soltarse (a knot) || FIG ir para atrás, empeorar (to drop from previous standards) || AUT patinar (clutch) || AVIAT resbalar || — *my foot slipped* se me fue el pie || *to let an opportunity slip* perder *or* dejar pasar una oportunidad || FIG *to let sth. slip (out)* escapársele algo a uno, decir algo sin querer (to disclose inadvertently).
◆ *phr v* ***to slip away*** correr (time) | escabullirse (to go stealthily) | desaparecer (to disappear) || ***to slip back*** volver sigilosamente || ***to slip by*** correr (time) | pasar inadvertido (to pass unnoticed) || ***to slip down*** dejarse caer || ***to slip in*** meterse, introducirse || ***to slip into*** ponerse rápidamente (clothes) | introducirse | *to slip into bad habits* coger malas costumbres || ***to slip off*** escabullirse (to go stealthily) | caerse (to fall off) || ***to slip out*** salir | escapársele a uno (a secret) || ***to slip through*** escabullirse por | *to slip through one's fingers* escapársele de las manos || FAM ***to slip up*** meter la pata (to make a mistake) | salir mal (a plan, etc.).

slipcase [-keis]; **slipcover** [-'kʌvə*] *n* funda *f* (for records) || estuche *m* (for books).

slipknot [-nɔt] *n* nudo *m* corredizo.

slip-on [-ɔn] *adj* sin cordones (shoes) || de quitaipón (garment).

slippage ['slipidʒ] *n* resbalón *m* (slipping) || retraso *m* (failure to meet a deadline).

slipper [-ə*] *n* zapatilla *f*, babucha *f* (shoe) || TECH zapata *f*, patín *m* (of a brake).

slipperiness [-ərinis] *n* lo resbaladizo || *the accident was caused by the slipperiness of the road* el accidente tuvo lugar porque la carretera estaba resbaladiza.

slippery [-əri] *adj* resbaladizo, za; escurridizo, za; *a slippery ball, surface* un balón escurridizo, una superficie resbaladiza || FIG evasivo, va; escurridizo, za (evasive); *a slippery customer* un tipo escurridizo | delicado, da; *a slippery problem* un problema delicado | que no es de fiar (untrustworthy) || FIG *to be on a slippery slope* estar en un terreno resbaladizo.

slippy [-i] *adj* FAM escurridizo, za; resbaladizo, za (slippery) || FAM *to be* o *to look slippy* darse prisa; *look slippy!* ¡date prisa!

slip road [-rəud] *n* ramal *m* de conexión (motorway).

slipshod [-ʃɔd] *adj* descuidado, da; negligente (careless) || gastado, da (shoe heel) || con zapatos gastados (person).

slipslop [-slɔp] *n* aguachirle *f* (watery food) || FIG disparate *m*.

slipstream [-striːm] *n* estela *f*.

slipup [-ə] FAM metedura *f* de pata, error *m* (mistake in writing, in calculating, etc.) || desliz *m* descuido *m* (mistake) || desliz *m*, descuido *m* (neglect, carelessness).

slipway [-wei] *n* MAR grada *f*.

slit [slit] *n* raja *f*, abertura *f* (in a long dress) || corte *m* (cut) || abertura *f*, rendija *f*, hendidura *f* (long, thin opening).
◆ *adj* con una abertura, con una raja (skirt, etc.) || achinado, da; rasgado, da (eyes).

slit* [slit] *vt* partir *or* cortar a lo largo (to cut lengthwise) || rasgar, cortar en tiras (to tear into strips) || hacer una abertura *or* abrir una rendija en (to make a long opening in) || hender (to split) || cortar (to cut) || *to slit s.o.'s throat* cortarle el cuello a alguien.
— OBSERV Pret y pp ***slit***.

slither ['sliðə*] *vt* hacer resbalar (to cause to slide).
◆ *vi* resbalar (to slide) || arrastrarse (to crawl) || deslizarse; *to slither from a tree* bajar deslizándose por un árbol.

slit trench [slittrentʃ] *n* trinchera *f*.

sliver ['slivə*] *n* astilla *f* (of wood) || pequeña lonja *f* (of ham) || pequeña tajada *f* (of meat) || pequeña rodaja *f* (of salami) || pedacito *m*, trocito *m* (bit) || cebo *m* (bait) || torzal *m* (of cotton, etc.).

sliver ['slivə*] *vt* astillar (wood) || cortar en tiras (to cut into very thin pieces).
◆ *vi* astillarse (wood).

slob [slɔb] *n* US FAM palurdo *m*, patán *m* (boor).

slobber [-ə*]; **slabber** [slæbə*] *n* baba *f*, baboseo *m* (dribbling saliva) || FAM sensiblería *f* (sentimentality).

slobber [-ə*]; **slabber** [slæbə*] *vt* babosear.
◆ *vi* babear (to dribble) || decir sensiblerías (to gush sentimentality).

sloe [sləu] *n* BOT endrino *m* (shrub) | endrina *f* (fruit).

sloe-eyed [-aid] *adj* de ojos endrinos (dark-blue eyed) || de ojos achinados (slant eyed).

sloe gin [-dʒin] *n* ginebra *f* de endrinas.

slog [slɔg] *n* gopetazo *m* (hard blow) || FAM pesadez *f* (drag) || FIG & FAM *it was a hard slog, but we made it* nos costó trabajo, pero lo conseguimos.

slog [slɔg] *vt* golpear (a ball).
◆ *vi* avanzar *or* caminar con dificultad (to walk) || FAM *to slog away* sudar tinta, trabajar como un negro.

slogan ['sləugən] *n* «slogan» *m*, lema *m* publicitario (in sales promotion) || lema *m* (in politics).

slogger ['slɔgə*] *n* SP pegador *m* (boxer) || FAM trabajador, ra.

sloop [sluːp] *n* MAR balandro *m* || MAR *sloop of war* corbeta *f*.

slop [slɔp] *n* aguachirle *f* (watery food) || bazofia *f* (leftover food, bad food, pigswill) || fango *m*, barro *m* (mud) || FIG sensiblería *f* (sentimental rubbish).
◆ *pl* lavazas *f*, agua *f sing* sucia (dirty water) || posos *m* de té (of tea) || ropa *f sing* barata (cheap clothes).

slop [slɔp] *vt* derramar, verter (to pour) || salpicar (to splash) || servir con brusquedad (to serve clumsily) || comer con torpeza (to eat).
◆ *vi* derramarse, verterse (a liquid) || chapotear, avanzar chapoteando (to plod through mud, etc.) || chapotear (to make a slapping sound) || *to slop over* derramarse.

slop basin [-,beisn] *n* recipiente *m* para echar los posos de té.

slope [sləup] *n* cuesta *f*, pendiente *f*, declive *m* (incline); *a steep slope* una cuestión empinada || vertiente *f* (of roof) || vertiente *f*, ladera *f*, falda *f* (of mountain); *we camped on the western slope* acampamos en la vertiente oeste || — *degree of slope* inclinación *f* || *the ground is on a slope* la tierra está en declive.

slope [sləup] *vt* inclinar || *slope arms!* ¡armas al hombro!
◆ *vi* inclinarse; *the roof slopes* el tejado se inclina || FAM andar (to walk) || — *to slope down* descender, bajar || FIG & FAM *to slope off* largarse || *to slope up* ascender, subir.

sloping [-iŋ] *adj* inclinado, da; en pendiente; *sloping roof, ground* tejado inclinado, tierra en pendiente || al bies, al sesgo, oblicuo, cua (slanted, crooked) || inclinado, da (handwriting).

slop pail ['slɔppeil] *n* cubo *m* para el agua sucia.

sloppiness ['slɔpinis] *n* estado *m* fangoso (of the ground) || estado *m* líquido (of food) || descuido *m*, mala presentación *f* (of work); *the sloppiness of his work* su descuido en el trabajo, la mala presentación de su trabajo || desaseo *m* (slovenliness) || suciedad *f* (dirtiness) || sensiblería *f* (sentimental rubbish) || blandura *f* (of character) || descuido *m* (of style).

sloppy ['slɔpi] *adj* mojado, da (wet) || aguado, da (food) || fangoso, sa; cenagoso, sa (ground) || encharcado, da (with puddles) || sensiblero, ra; empalagoso, sa (sentimental) || desaliñado, da (slovenly) || muy ancho, cha (garment) || chapucero, ra (careless) || sucio, cia (dirty) || flojo, ja; poco enérgico, ca (unenergetic).

slops [slɔps] *pl n* ⟶ **slop.**

slop shop ['slɔp,ʃɔp] *n* US FAM tienda *f* de ropa barata.

slopwork ['slɔpwəːk] *n* confección *f* de ropa barata || FAM chapucería *f* (bad work).

slosh [slɔʃ]; **slush** [slʌʃ] *n* ⟶ **slush.**

slosh [slɔʃ]; **slush** [slʌʃ] *vt* aplicar a brochazos (paint) || salpicar (to splash) || FAM pegar (to beat) || FAM *to get sloshed* coger una tajada (to get drunk).
◆ *vi* andar chapoteando (to walk splashing); *to slosh along a wet path* andar chapo-

teando por un camino mojado || chapotear (water in a bucket, etc.) || *to slosh about in the bath* chapotear en el baño.

slot [slɔt] *n* ranura *f*, muesca *f* (groove) || abertura *f*, rendija *f* (narrow opening) || ranura *f* (for coins) || rastro *m*, huella *f* (of an animal).

slot [slɔt] *vt* hacer una ranura *or* muesca en (to cut a groove in) || encajar (one part into another).
◆ *vi* encajarse.

sloth [sləuθ] *n* pereza *f*, indolencia *f* (laziness) || apatía *f* (spiritual apathy) || ZOOL perezoso *m* || ZOOL *sloth bear* oso *m* bezudo.

slothful [-ful] *adj* perezoso, sa; indolente (lazy) || apático, ca (spiritually apathetic).

slot machine ['slɔtməʃi:n] *n* distribuidor *m* automático (vending machine) || máquina *f* tragaperras (for games of chance).

slouch [slautʃ] *n* andar *m* desgarbado (bad posture) || US holgazán, ana; perezoso, sa (lazy person) || *to walk with a slouch* andar con los hombros caídos y arrastrando los pies.

slouch [slautʃ] *vt* bajar (shoulders) || echar hacia adelante (a hat).
◆ *vi* andar con los hombros caídos y arrastrando los pies (walking) || bajar (the brim of a hat) || — *to slouch about* holgazanear, gandulear (to loaf) || *to slouch in a chair* estar repantigado en un sillón || *to slouch on a table* apoyarse con dejadez en una mesa.

slouch hat [-hæt] *n* flexible *m*, sombrero *m* flexible.

slough [slʌf] *n* camisa *f*, piel *f* (of snake, etc.) || MED costra *f*, postilla *f*, escara *f*.

slough [slau] *n* ciénaga *f*, lodazal *m*, fangal *m*, cenagal *m* (swamp) || US estero *m* || FIG abismo *m* (abyss) || *in the slough of despair* en la desesperación más profunda.

slough [slʌf] *vt* mudar (to shed) || descartar (cards) || — FIG *to slough off* deshacerse de | *to slough over* quitar importancia a.
◆ *vi* caerse (the skin).

sloven ['slʌvn] *n* persona *f* desaseada (untidy) || vago, ga (idle person).

slovenliness ['slʌvnlinis] *n* lo desaseado, desaliño *m* (of appearance) || dejadez *f* (of habits) || suciedad *f* (dirtiness) || descuido *m* (*of* en) (work).

slovenly ['slʌvnli] *adj* desaseado, da; desaliñado, da (in appearance) || dejado, da (in character) || descuidado, da; chapucero, ra (work) || sucio, cia (dirty).

slow [sləu] *adj* lento, ta; *slow response* respuesta lenta; *slow worker* trabajador lento; *slow recovery* recuperación lenta; *a rather slow boy* un chico bastante lento; *in a slow oven* a fuego lento; *slow to grasp an opportunity* lento en aprovechar una oportunidad || frío, a; *a slow audience* un público frío || atrasado, da; *my watch is slow* mi reloj está atrasado || difícil; *slow to take offence* difícil de ofender || aburrido, da (boring); *slow conversation* conversación aburrida || MED perezoso, sa (liver, etc.) || SP pesado, da (pitch, field, track, etc.) || — *business is slow* hay poca actividad *or* poco trabajo || *life was too slow for me there* allí la vida era muy aburrida *or* lenta para mi gusto || *my watch is always slow* mi reloj atrasa siempre || *my watch is ten minutes slow* mi reloj tiene diez minutos de retraso *or* está diez minutos atrasado || *slow fire* fuego lento || *slow match* mecha *f* de combustión lenta || *slow train* tren *m* ómnibus || *to be slow to* tardar en; *he was slow to answer* tardó en contestar.
◆ *adv* lentamente, despacio || FIG *to go slow* trabajar a ritmo lento [con fines reivindicativos].

slow [sləu] *vt* *to slow down* o *up* aminorar la velocidad de, reducir la marcha de (machine, car, etc.), retrasar (to hold up).
◆ *vi* *to slow down* o *up* aminorar la velocidad, reducir la marcha (in a car, etc.), aminorar el paso (walking), ir más despacio (to go slower), disminuir (to decrease) || *slow down!* ¡más despacio!

slow coach [-kəutʃ] *n* FIG & FAM tortuga *f* (slow person) | torpe *m* & *f* (stupid person).

slowdown [-daun] *n* retraso *m* || US tipo *m* de huelga que consiste en trabajar con excesiva meticulosidad y lentitud.

slowish [-iʃ] *adj* algo lento, ta.

slowly [-li] *adv* lentamente, despacio || — *slowly but surely* lenta pero seguramente || *slowly does it!* ¡despacito!

slow motion [-'meuʃən] *n* cámara *f* lenta; *in slow motion* a cámara lenta.

slow-motion [-'məuʃən] *adj* a cámara lenta; *a slow-motion picture* una película a cámara lenta.

slowness [-nis] *n* lentitud *f* || torpeza *f* (stupidity) || FIG pesadez *f*, aburrimiento *m* (boredom) || retraso *m* (of watch).

slowpoke [-pəuk] *n* US tortuga *f* (slow person) | torpe *m* & *f* (stupid person).

slow-witted [-'witid] *adj* lento, ta (person).

slowworm [-wə:m] *n* lución *m*.

slub [slʌb] *vt* torcer [el hilo].

sludge [slʌdʒ] *n* fango *m*, cieno *m*, lodo *m* (mud) || lodo *m* (in drilling) || sedimento *m*, residuos *m pl* (sediment) || fango *m* de alcantarillado (sewage) || capa *f* de hielo flotante (of sea ice).

slue [slu:] *n* ⟶ **slew.**

slue [slu:] *vt/vi* ⟶ **slew.**

slug [slʌg] *n* posta *f* (bullet) || trozo *m* de metal (roughly shaped piece of metal) || PRINT lingote *m* (for spacing type) | línea *f* de linotipia || ZOOL babosa *f* || porrazo *m* (heavy blow) || US ficha *f* (for telephone, for slot machine, etc.) | moneda *f* falsa (coin used in machines).

slug [slʌg] *vt* FAM pegar un porrazo a (to hit); *he slugged him* le pegó un porrazo.

sluggard [-əd] *n* holgazán, ana; vago, ga (loafer).

sluggish [-iʃ] *adj* lento, ta (slow) || COMM flojo, ja; inactivo, va; encalmado, da (trade) || perezoso, sa; holgazán, ana (lazy) || MED perezoso, sa (liver, etc.) || *the market is sluggish* hay poca actividad en el mercado.

sluggishness [-nəs] *n* lentitud *f* || pereza *f* (of s.o., of liver) || COMM inactividad *f*.

sluice [slu:s] *n* canal *m* (artificial waterway) || compuerta *f*, esclusa *f* (gate to control water level) || canal *m* de desagüe (drainage channel) || saetín *m* (of a water mill) || — *to give sth. a sluice down* lavar algo con mucha agua || FAM *to have a quick sluice* lavarse rápidamente.

sluice [slu:s] *vt* regar; *to sluice the floor* regar el suelo || transportar por un canal (logs) || lavar [en lavadero] (ores) || *to sluice sth. down* regar algo con agua.

sluice gate [-'geit] *n* compuerta *f*.

sluiceway [-wei] *n* canal *m* (artificial channel) || aliviadero *m* (of reservoir).

slum [slʌm] *n* barrio *m* bajo, tugurios *m pl* (area) || tugurio *m* (house) || *slum clearance* demolición *f* y reconstrucción de los barrios bajos.
◆ *pl* barrio *m sing* bajo, tugurios *m* (slum area).

slum [slʌm] *vi* visitar los barrios bajos.

slumber ['slʌmbə*] *n* sopor *m*, sueño *m* ligero (light sleep) || sueño *m* (sleep).

slumber ['slʌmbə*] *vt* *to slumber away* pasar durmiendo; *to slumber away the afternoon* pasar la tarde durmiendo.
◆ *vi* dormir (to sleep) || dormitar (to sleep lightly) || FIG estar inactivo (to lie inactive).

slumberous; slumbrous [-rəs] *adj* dormido, da (asleep) || soñoliento, ta (sleepy) || FIG inactivo, va (inactive) | adormecedor, ra (soporific).

slummy ['slʌmi] *adj* sórdido, da (sordid) || de tugurios (area).

slump [slɔp] *n* COMM caída *f* vertical, baja *f* repentina (*in* de) (prices) | depresión *f* económica, crisis *f* económica (economic depression) | disminución *f* brusca (of production, etc.) || FIG *a slump in morale* una depresión.

slump [slʌmp] *vi* hundirse (to fall into water, through ice, etc.) || desplomarse; *he slumped to the floor* se desplomó en el suelo || desplomarse, dejarse caer pesadamente (into a chair, etc.) || COMM caer verticalmente, bajar de pronto (prices) | disminuir bruscamente (production, demand) || *the country's economy slumped* hubo una depresión económica en el país.

slung [slʌŋ] *pret/pp* ⟶ **sling.**

slunk [slʌŋk] *pret/pp* ⟶ **slink.**

slur [slə:*] *n* calumnia *f*, difamación *f* (slanderous remark, etc.) || FIG mancha *f*, borrón *m* (stain) || afrenta *f*, ofensa *f*, insulto *m* (affront) || pronunciación *f* incomprensible (indistinct pronunciation) || MUS ligado *m* || PRINT maculatura *f* || *to cast a slur on s.o.'s reputation* manchar la reputación de alguien.

slur [slə:*] *vt* calumniar, difamar (to slander) || pronunciar mal (words) || MUS ligar || FIG manchar, mancillar (one's reputation) || PRINT macular (to mackle).
◆ *vi* articular mal (to speak indistinctly) || borrarse (to blur, to fade) || *to slur over* pasar por alto (not to mention), ocultar (to hide).

slurp [slə:p] *n* sorbo *m* ruidoso.

slurred [-d] *adj* MUS ligado, da.

slurry [-ri] *n* lechada *f*.

slush; slosh [slʌʃ; slɔʃ] *n* nieve *f* medio derretida, aguanieve *f* (melting snow) || lodo *m*, fango *m*, cieno *m* (mud) || grasa *f* (for lubricating) || FAM sentimentalismo *m* exagerado, sensiblería *f* || US *slush fund* dinero utilizado con fines deshonestos.

slush [slʌʃ] *vt/vi* ⟶ **slosh.**

slushy [-i] *adj* medio derretida (snow) || lodoso, sa; fangoso, sa (muddy) || FAM sensiblero, ra; sentimentaloide.

slut [slʌt] *n* marrana *f*, puerca *f* (slovenly woman) || mujerzuela *f* (loose woman).

sluttish [-iʃ] *adj* puerco, ca; marrano, na (dirty) || de mujerzuela (of a loose woman).

sly [slai] *adj* astuto, ta (artful) || furtivo, va; sigiloso, sa (furtive) || malicioso, sa (showing underhandedness) || — *he's a sly old devil* o *fox* es muy zorro || *to do sth. on the sly* hacer algo a hurtadillas *or* a escondidas.

slyness [-nis] *n* astucia *f* (artfulness) || disimulo *m* (feigning) || malicia *f* (wickedness).

smack [smæk] *n* tortazo *m*, bofetada, *f* (slap on the face) || palmada *f* (soft blow) || chasquido *m* (of a whip) || azote *m* (to punish a child) || golpe *m* (blow, stroke) || sabor *m*, gusto *m* (flavour) || poco *m* (small quantity) || FAM beso *m* sonoro (loud kiss) || MAR barco *m* de pesca con velas áuricas || FIG & FAM *to have a smack at* probar (to have a try at).
◆ *adv* de lleno; *the ball hit him smack in the face* la pelota le dio de lleno en la cara || *smack in the middle* justo en medio.

smack [smæk] *vt* dar una bofetada *or* un tortazo, abofetear (to slap); *she smacked him on*

the face le dio una bofetada || dar una palmada; *he smacked him on the back* le dio una palmada en la espalda || dar un azote; *she smacked his bottom* le dio un azote en el trasero || chasquear; *to smack a whip* chasquear un látigo || hacer un chasquido con; *to smack one's tongue* hacer un chasquido con la lengua || pegar (to hit) || FAM besar sonoramente (to kiss).
◆ *vi* saber (to taste); *it smacks of almonds* sabe a almendras || FIG oler a; *his stories smack of the sea* sus historias huelen a mar || chasquear, restallar (whip) || resonar (a kiss).

smacker [-ə*] *n* FAM beso *m* sonoro (loud kiss) | bofetón *m* (heavy blow) | dólar *m* (dollar) | maravilla *f* (wonder).

small [smɔːl] *adj* pequeño, ña; *a small garden* un jardín pequeño || pequeño, ña; bajo, ja (person) || sin importancia, pequeño, ña; insignificante (unimportant); *a small matter* un asunto sin importancia || escaso, sa; *a small spoonful of sugar* una cucharilla escasa de azúcar || humilde, modesto, ta (modest); *small people* gente modesta; *to live in a small way* vivir de manera modesta || pequeño, ña; exiguo, gua; bajo, ja; *a small salary* un sueldo pequeño || mezquino, na (petty); *it's small of her* es mezquino de su parte || débil (voice) || flojo, ja (liqueur) || ligero, ra (meal) || — *a small time* un tiempo corto, poco tiempo || *four times smaller* cuatro veces más pequeño || *he is smaller than you* es más pequeño *or* más bajo que tú || *how much smaller is it?* ¿cómo es de pequeño? || *in small numbers* poco numerosos, pocos || *it was small recompense for all his efforts* era poca recompensa para todos los esfuerzos que había hecho || *my smaller brother* mi hermano menor || *small arms* armas *f* portátiles || *small beer* cerveza floja (weak bear), persona *f or* cosa *f* sin importancia (s.o. or sth.) || *small calorie* pequeña caloría || PRINT *small capital* versalita *f* || *small change* cambio *m*, dinero suelto || *small craft* pequeña embarcación || *small fry* fritura *f sing* (fish), gente *f sing* menuda (children), gente *f sing* de poca monta (people) || *small game* caza *f* menor || *small holding* pequeña propiedad, minifundio *m* || ANAT *small intestine* intestino delgado || *small letters* minúsculas *f* || FIG *small potatoes* don nadie *m* (person), cosa *f* sin importancia (thing) || *small print* letra pequeña || *small shopkeeper* pequeño comerciante || *small shot* perdigones *m pl* (ammunition) || *small talk* charla *f*, charloteo *m* || FIG *to feel small* sentirse pequeño, sentirse poca cosa || *to make o.s. small* achicarse || *to make s.o. look o feel small* achicar a alguien || *when I was small* cuando era pequeño.
◆ *n* parte *f* pequeña (small part of sth.) || *small of the back* región *f* lumbar.
◆ *pl* paños *m* menores, ropa *f sing* interior (underclothes) || examen *m sing* preliminar de ingreso (in Oxford).
◆ *adv* en trozos pequeños (to cut) || finalmente (to grind) || FIG desdeñosamente (to look, to treat).
— OBSERV In everyday spoken Spanish the diminutive is sometimes used to convey the idea of smallness: *a small house* una casita.

small ads [-æds] *n* anuncios *m pl* por palabras, clasificados *m pl*.

smallholder [-'həuldə*] *n* propietario *m* de un minufundio.

smallish [-iʃ] *adj* más bien pequeño, más bien pequeña, bastante pequeño, ña.

small-minded [-'maindid] *adj* mezquino, na (petty) || de miras estrechas (narrow-minded).

small-mindedness [-'maindidnis] *n* mezquindad *f* (pettiness) || estrechez *f* de miras (narrow-mindedness).

smallness [-nis] *n* pequeñez *f* (in size) || escasez *f* (scantiness) || exigüedad *f* (of salary) || mezquindad *f* (meanness) || insignificancia *f* (insignificance).

smallpox [-pɔks] *n* MED viruela *f*.

small-scale [-skeil] *adj* en pequeña escala.

smallsword [-sɔːd] *n* espada *f* de esgrima corta.

small-time [-taim] *adj* US FAM de poca categoría, de poca monta.

small-town [-taun] *adj* US provinciano, na; pueblerino, na.

smalt [smɔːlt] *n* esmalte *m* (colour).

smarm [smɑːm] *vt* *to smarm one's hair down* alisarse el pelo.

smarmy [-i] *adj* zalamero, ra; cobista.

smart [smɑːt] *adj* elegante; *a smart hat* un sombrero elegante; *she looks very smart* está muy elegante || de moda (fashionable) || ligero, ra; rápido, da; *smart pace* paso ligero || rápido, da; *his smart action prevented a disaster* su acción rápida evitó un desastre || inteligente, listo, ta (intelligent) || espabilado, da (alert) || vivo, va (lively) || sagaz; *a smart politician* un político sagaz || ingenioso, sa (ingenious) || punzante, agudo, da (pain) || que escuece *or* pica (itching) || FAM listo, ta (in the bad sense); *don't get smart with me* no te hagas el listo conmigo || — FIG *he was too smart for me* era demasiado listo para mí || *look smart about it!* ¡date prisa! || INFORM *smart card* tarjeta *f* inteligente || FIG *the smart set of Madrid* la gente más selecta *or* distinguida de Madrid.
◆ *n* punzada *f* (sharp pain) || escozor *m* (sting) || FIG resquemor *m* (mental pain).

smart [smɑːt] *vi* escocer, picar (to sting); *my eyes are smarting* me pican *or* me escuecen los ojos || dar punzadas (to cause a sharp pain) || — FIG *to smart under* sufrir con || *you shall smart for this!* ¡lo vas a pagar!, ¡te va a escocer!

smart aleck; smart alec [-'ælik] *n* sabihondo *m*, sabelotodo *m*.

smarten [-n] *vt* arreglar, acicalar (a person) || arreglar (a house) || FAM espabilar (to wake up).
◆ *vi* arreglarse (a person).
— OBSERV Este verbo va generalmente seguido por *up* sin que cambie el sentido.

smarting [-iŋ] *adj* punzante (pain) || que pica, que escuece (itching).
◆ *n* punzada *f* (sharp pain) || escozor *m* (sting).

smartly [-li] *adv* elegantemente, con elegancia (elegantly) || a la moda (fashionably) || inteligentemente || astutamente (cunningly) || ingeniosamente (wittily) || de repente (suddenly) || secamente, bruscamente (to answer, etc.) || rápidamente (quickly) || violentamente (violently).

smartness [-nis] *n* elegancia *f* (elegance) || inteligencia *f* (intelligence) || astucia *f* (cunning) || ingeniosidad *f*, ingenio *m* (wit) || sequedad *f*, brusquedad *f* (sharpness) || rapidez *f* (speed) || violencia *f* (of a slap, etc.).

smarty [-i] *n* FAM sabelotodo *m* & *f*, sabihondo, da (know-all).

smash [smæʃ] *n* rotura *f* (the act of breaking) || estrépito *m* (loud crash) || puñetazo *m* (heavy blow) || choque *m* (collision) || accidente *m* (accident); *a rail smash* un accidente ferroviario || COMM crisis *f* económica (crisis) | quiebra *f* (bankruptcy) || ruina *f* (ruin) || SP mate *m*, "smash" *m* (tennis).
◆ *adj* descomunal, enorme || *smash hit* exitazo *m*, gran éxito *m*.
◆ *adv* violentamente; *to go smash into a tree* chocar violentamente contra un árbol || con gran estrépito (noisily).

smash [smæʃ] *vt* romper (to break); *to smash a window* romper un cristal || destrozar, hacer pedazos (to shatter) || aplastar (to crush) || estrellar; *he smashed the car into a tree* estrelló el coche contra un árbol; *she smashed the glass against the wall* estrelló el vaso contra la pared; *to smash a boat against the rocks* estrellar un barco contra las rocas || FIG arruinar (to ruin) || destruir (to destroy); *to smash s.o.'s hopes* destruir las esperanzas de alguien; *the police smashed the spy ring* la policía destruyó la red de espías || aplastar (to defeat resoundingly) || — FAM *his face was badly smashed up* tenía la cara destrozada || *to smash a place up* destrozar un local || *to smash s.o.'s face in* romper la cara a uno || *to smash sth. through a window* arrojar algo por una ventana || SP *to smash the ball* dar un mate (tennis).
◆ *vi* chocar (to come into collision) || estrellarse; *he smashed into the door* se estrelló contra la puerta; *the car smashed into the tree* el coche se estrelló contra el árbol || hacerse pedazos (to shatter) || romperse (to break) || quebrar, arruinarse (to go bankrupt) || abrirse paso; *to smash through the forest* abrirse paso a través del bosque || SP dar un mate (tennis).

smash-and-grab [-əndˌgræb] *n* robo *m* relámpago.

smasher [-ə*] *n* FAM maravilla *f* (wonder) | golpe *m* demoledor (blow) | destructor, ra (destructive person).

smashing [-iŋ] *adj* aplastante; *smashing victory* victoria aplastante || demoledor, ra; *smashing blow* golpe demoledor || FAM estupendo, da; extraordinario, ria (marvellous) || FAM *I had a smashing time* me lo pasé en grande, lo pasé estupendamente.

smashup [-ʌp] *n* choque *m* violento (violent collision) || accidente *m* (accident) || quiebra *f*, ruina *f* (brankruptcy) || MED colapso *m*.

smattering ['smætəriŋ] *n* ligero conocimiento *m*, nociones *f pl*; *to have a smattering of French* tener un ligero conocimiento del francés.

smear [smiə*] *n* mancha *f* (stain, mark) || FIG calumnia *f*, mancha *f* (slur) || MED frotis *m* (for microscopic examination) || *smear campaign* campaña *f* de desprestigio || *to cast a smear on s.o.* manchar la reputación de alguien.

smear [smiə*] *vt* untar; *to smear butter on bread* untar mantequilla en el pan; *to smear bread with butter* untar pan con mantequilla || estropear (a freshly painted surface) || manchar (to soil or stain sth.); *the baby's face was smeared with chocolate* la cara del niño estaba manchada de chocolate || FIG manchar (s.o.'s reputation) | calumniar (to defame) || MED preparar un frotis de (for microscopic examination) || US FAM aplastar (to defeat overwhelmingly).

smeary [-ri] *adj* manchado, da || grasiento, ta (greasy).

smell [smel] *n* olor *m*; *a strong smell of gas* un olor fuerte a gas; *the smell of freshly cut grass* el olor de la hierba recién cortada || olor *m*, perfume *m*; *a wonderful smell of roses* un perfume agradable de rosas || olfato *m* (sense); *to have a keen sense of smell* tener buen olfato || — *have a smell* huélelo || FIG *there is a smell of treason in all this* todo esto huele a traición || *this room has a funny smell in it* esta habitación huele raro *or* tiene un olor extraño.

smell* [smell] *vt* oler || olfatear (animals) || FIG olfatear, olerse, husmear (to detect); *he smelt danger* olfateó el peligro || — FIG *I smell a rat* hay gato encerrado || *to smell out* olfatear, husmear (a dog), descubrir (to discover).
◆ *vi* oler; *the cake smells good* el pastel huele bien; *the old man smelt of whisky* el anciano olía a whisky; *it smells musty* huele a cerrado || tener olfato (to have a sense of smell) || apestar (to stink) || — *it doesn't smell of anything* no

huele a nada, no tiene olor || FIG *it smells fishy to me* me huele a chamusquina.
— OBSERV Pret y pp ***smelt, smelled.***

smeller [-ə*] *n* husmeador, ra || FAM napias *f pl*, nariz *f* (nose).

smelling salts [-iŋsɔːlts] *pl n* sales *f* aromáticas.

smelly [-i] *adj* maloliente, apestoso, sa.

smelt [smelt] *pret/pp* ⟶ **smell.**

smelt [smelt] *n* eperlano *m* (fish).
— OBSERV El plural de *smelt* es *smelts* o *smelt.*

smelt [smelt] *vt* fundir (ores).

smelter [-ə*] *n* fundidor *m* (person) || fundición *f* (smelting works).

smelting [-iŋ] *n* fundición *f* || — *smelting furnace* horno *m* de fundición || *smelting works* fundición.

smew [smjuː] *n* mergo *m* (duck).

smilax ['smailæks] *n* BOT zarzaparrilla *f*.

smile [smail] *n* sonrisa *f* || — *bitter smile* sonrisa amarga || *broad smile* sonrisa abierta || *forced smile* sonrisa forzada || *stereotyped smile* sonrisa estereotipada || *to give s.o. a smile* sonreír a alguien, dirigir una sonrisa a alguien || FIG *to knock* o *to take* o *to wipe the smile off s.o.'s face* quitarle a uno las ganas de sonreír *or* de reír.

smile [smail] *vi* sonreír, sonreírse || FIG sonreír, favorecer; *if fortune smiles on me* si la fortuna me sonríe || FIG *to smile at* reírse de (to regard with amusement, to contempt, etc.).
◆ *vt* dirigir una sonrisa de; *to smile a welcome* dirigir una sonrisa de bienvenida || — *to smile a sad smile* sonreír tristemente || *to smile one's thanks one's encouragement* dar las gracias, animar con una sonrisa.

smiling [-iŋ] *adj* sonriente, risueño, ña || *a smiling landscape* un paisaje risueño.

smirch [sməːtʃ] *n* mancha *f* (stain) || FIG mancha *f*, mancilla *f*, tacha *f*.

smirch [sməːtʃ] *vt* manchar (to stain) || FIG manchar, mancillar.

smirk [sməːk] *n* sonrisa *f* afectada.

smirk [sməːk] *vi* sonreír afectadamente.

smite* [smait] *vt* golpear con violencia (to hit) || aplastar (to inflict a crushing defeat on) || castigar (to punish) || FIG remorder (conscience) | ocurrírsele (a uno) (an idea) || — *to be smitten with* estar aquejado de (an illness), estar lleno de (fear), estar encaprichado por (a girl, an idea) || *to be smitten with remorse* remorderle a uno la conciencia.
— OBSERV Pret ***smote***; pp ***smitten.***

smith [smiθ] *n* herrero *m* (blacksmith).

smithereens ['smiθə'riːnz]; **smithers** ['smiðəz] *pl n* FAM añicos *m*; *to break sth. to smithereens* hacer algo añicos.

smithy ['smiði] *n* herrería *f*.

smitten ['smitn] *pp* ⟶ **smite.**

smock [smɔk] *n* bata *f* corta (woman's garment) || babero *m* (for very small children) || delantal *m* (for children) || guardapolvo *m* (of artist, etc.).

smock [smɔk] *vt* adornar con pliegues fruncidos y bordados, adornar con punto de nido de abeja.

smocking [-iŋ] *n* nido *m* de abeja (stitch).

smockmill [-mil] *n* molino *m* de viento holandés.

smog [smɔg] *n* niebla *f* espesa con humo [*AMER* "smog" *m*].

smokable ['sməukəbəl] *adj* fumable.

smoke [sməuk] *n* humo *m* || FAM cigarrillo *m*, pitillo *m* (cigarette) || — *smoke bomb* bomba *f* de humo, bomba fumígena || *smoke screen* cortina *f* de humo || FIG *there's no smoke without fire* cuando el río suena, agua lleva || *to go up in smoke* ser destruido por un incendio (house, etc.), esfumarse, evaporarse, irse en humo (money), quedar en agua de borrajas, irse en humo (plans) || FAM *to have a smoke* fumar un cigarrillo, echar un pitillo, fumar (cigarette), fumarse una pipa (pipe).

smoke [sməuk] *vt* ahumar; *to smoke glass, meat* ahumar cristal, carne || fumar; *I never smoke cigars* no fumo nunca puros || fumar, fumarse; *I must smoke a cigarette* tengo que fumar un cigarrillo; *she smokes twenty cigarettes a day* se fuma veinte cigarrillos diarios || fumigar (to fumigate) || — *to smoke a pipe* fumar en pipa || *to smoke out* desalojar con bombas fumígenas (people, animals), ahuyentar con humo (insects), llenar de humo (a room).
◆ *vi* fumar; *he smokes too much* fuma demasiado || echar humo (chimney, fire, etc.) || — *do you mind if I smoke?* ¿le molesta que fume? || FAM *to smoke like a chimney* fumar como una chimenea.

smokebox [-bɔks] *n* caja *f* de humos (in a steam boiler).

smoked [-t] *adj* ahumado, da (food, glass, etc.); *smoked salmon* salmón ahumado.

smoke-dried [-'draid] *adj* ahumado, da.

smokehouse [-haus] *n* lugar *m* donde se ahuma [carne, pescado, pieles, etc.].

smokeless [-lis] *adj* sin humo, libre de humos; *smokeless fuel* combustible sin humo; *smokeless zone* zona libre de humos.

smoker [-ə*] *n* fumador, ra (of cigarettes, etc.) || compartimiento *m* de fumadores (train compartment) || *US* tertulia *f* de hombres (meeting for men only) || *to be a heavy smoker* fumar mucho, ser un fumador empedernido.

smokeroom [-rum] *n* salón *m* de fumar.

smokestack [-stæk] *n* chimenea *f* || conducto *m* de humos (flue).

smoking [-iŋ] *adj* que echa humo, humeante || — *smoking car* coche *m* de fumadores || *smoking jacket* batín *m* || *smoking room* salón *m* de fumar.
◆ *n* el fumar || fumigación *f* (against insects) || CULIN ahumado *m* || *no smoking* se prohibe fumar, prohibido fumar.

smoking-room [-rum] *adj* FIG atrevido, da.

smoky [-i] *adj* humeante (giving off smoke) || que huele a humo (smelling of smoke) || ahumado, da (colour) || ennegrecido por el humo (sooty) || ahumado, da (tasting of smoke) || lleno de humo (filled with smoke) || *smoky quartz* cuarzo ahumado.

smolder ['sməuldə*] *vi* *US* ⟶ **smoulder.**

smolt [sməult] *n* esguín *m*, murgón *m* (fish).

smooch ['smuːtʃ] *vi* FAM besuquearse (to kiss) | acariciarse, abrazarse (to hug).
◆ *vt* manchar.

smooth [smuːð] *adj* liso, sa (having an even surface) || llano, na (flat) || sin grumos; *smooth paste* masa sin grumos || suave; *smooth wine* vino suave; *smooth voice* voz suave || liso, sa (hair) || terso, sa; suave (skin) || sin arrugas (brow) || pulido, da (glass) || imberbe, lampiño, ña (beardless) || tranquilo, la (day, journey) || sin novedad (uneventful) || en calma, tranquilo, la (the sea) || gastado, da (worn); *a smooth tyre* un neumático gastado || grato, ta; agradable (pleasant) || afable (affable) || suelto, ta; fluido, da (style) || fácil (easy) || FAM refinado, da (refined) | zalamero, ra; meloso, sa (ingratiating) || GRAMM suave (not aspirated) || — FIG *as smooth as silk* suave como la seda || *smooth talk* zalamerías *f pl*.
◆ *n* alisado *m* (act of smoothing) || parte *f* lisa (smooth side) || llano *m* (ground) || zona *f* de calma (smooth patch of sea).

smooth [smuːð] *vt* alisar (hair) || igualar, alisar (a surface) || cepillar (wood) || pulir (metals) || esmerilar (glass) || suavizar (an angle) || desarrugar, hacer desfruncir (one's brow) || hacer desaparecer (wrinkles) || FIG calmar (to soothe); *to smooth s.o. down* calmar a alguien | aliviar, hacer llevadero (grief) | refinar, pulir (to polish, to refine) || — FIG *to smooth the way for* allanar el camino para, preparar el terreno para | *to smooth things over* limar asperezas (to settle differences, etc.).

smoothbore [-bɔː*] *adj* de ánima lisa (firearm).
◆ *n* ánima *f* lisa.

smooth-chinned [-'tʃind] *adj* barbilampiño, ña; imberbe (young) || bien afeitado (clean-shaven).

smooth-faced [-feist] *adj* barbilampiño, ña; imberbe (young) || bien afeitado, da (clean-shaven) || zalamero, ra; meloso, sa (flattering) || liso, sa (surface).

smoothie [-i] *n* *US* FAM zalamero, ra.

smoothing ['smuːðiŋ] *adj* suavizador, ra || allanador, ra.
◆ *n* allanamiento *m*, igualación *f* (of a surface) || cepillado *m* (of wood) || pulido *m* (of metals) || esmerilado *m* (of glass) || desaparición *f* (of wrinkles).

smoothing iron [-,aiən] *n* plancha *f*.

smoothing plane [-plein] *n* TECH cepillo *m*.

smoothness ['smuːðnis] *n* suavidad *f* (softness) || uniformidad *f* (of surface) || tranquilidad *f* (peacefulness) || fluidez *f* (of style) || afabilidad *f* (affability) || zalamería *f* (flattery).

smooth-running ['smuːð'rʌniŋ] *adj* que funciona normalmente.

smooth-shaven ['smuːð'ʃeivn] *adj* bien afeitado.

smooth-spoken ['smuːð'spəukən] *adj* afable || zalamero, ra (flattering).

smooth-tongued ['smuːðtʌŋd] *adj* zalamero, ra (flattering).

smorgasbord ['smɔːgəsbɔːd] *n* buffet *m* sueco.

smote [sməut] *pret* ⟶ **smite.**

smother ['smʌðə*] *vt* sofocar (to stifle, to suffocate) || asfixiar (to asphyxiate, to kill) || sofocar, apagar (a fire) || contener (yawn, anger, laughter) || cubrir; *to smother s.o. with a blanket* cubrir a alguien con una manta; *to smother s.o. with kisses* cubrir a alguien de besos || colmar, abrumar; *to smother with attentions* colmar de atenciones || echar tierra a, enterrar (a scandal).
◆ *vi* asfixiarse (to die of suffocation) || sofocarse (to be unable to breathe).

smoulder ['sməuldə*]; *US* **smolder** *vi* arder sin llama || FIG arder; *eyes smouldering with indignation* ojos que arden de indignación | latir; *smouldering hatred* odio latente.

smudge [smʌdʒ] *n* mancha *f* (stain) || borrón *m* (of ink) || humo *m* para fumigar (used to repel insects).

smudge [smʌdʒ] *vt* correr (ink, paint, etc.) || emborronar (a piece of writing) || manchar (by touching with sth. dirty); *to smudge paint on one's shirt* mancharse la camisa de pintura || *US* fumigar (an orchard) || FIG manchar, mancillar (a reputation).
◆ *vi* correrse (ink, paint, etc.) || emborronarse (a piece of writing) || mancharse (to stain).

smudginess [-inis] *n* suciedad *f* (dirtiness).

smudgy [-i] *adj* emborronado, da (a piece of writing) || manchado, da (stained).

smug [smʌg] *adj* pagado de sí mismo.

smuggle ['smʌgl] *vt* pasar de contrabando (goods liable to customs duty); *to smuggle sth. through customs* pasar algo de contrabando por

la aduana || pasar clandestinamente (to pass secretly) || — *to smuggle sth. into the country* pasar algo de contrabando al país, meter algo de contrabando en el país || *to smuggle sth. out* sacar algo de contrabando (through customs), sacar algo clandestinamente (secretly).
◆ *vi* hacer contrabando, contrabandear.

smuggled [-d] *adj* de contrabando.

smuggler [-ə*] *n* contrabandista *m* & *f*.

smuggling [-iŋ] *n* contrabando *m*.

smugly [-i] *adv* con aire satisfecho, con suficiencia.

smugness ['smʌgnis] *n* presunción *f*, suficiencia *f*.

smut [smʌt] *n* carbonilla *f*, hollín *m* (in the air) || mancha *f* de tizne (mark) || AGR tizón *m*, añublo *m* (fungus and disease) || FIG & FAM verdulerías *f pl* (indecent talk, picture, etc.).

smut [smʌt] *vt* tiznar (to mark with smuts) || manchar, ensuciar (to dirty) || AGR atizonar, añublar; *smutted corn* maíz atizonado.
◆ *vi* tiznarse (to stain) || AGR atizonarse, añublarse (plants).

smuttiness [-inis] *n* suciedad *f*, negrura *f* (dirtiness) || FIG obscenidad *f*, escabrosidad *f*.

smutty [-i] *adj* tiznado, da; manchado, da (soiled with smut) || AGR atizonado, da || FIG & FAM verde, obsceno, na (indencent) || negruzco, ca (colour).

Smyrna ['smə:nə] *pr n* GEOGR Esmirna.

snack [snæk] *n* bocado *m*, piscolabis *m inv*, tentempié *m*; *to have a snack* tomarse un tentempié || *snack bar* cafetería *f*, bar *m*.

snaffle ['snæfl] *n* filete *m*, bridón *m* (of horse's harness).

snaffle ['snæfl] *vt* poner filete a (a horse) || sujetar con filete (to control with a snaffle) || FIG controlar || FAM mangar, birlar (to filch).

snafu [snæ'fu:] *adj* US FAM liado, da; embrollado, da (mixed up).
◆ *n* US FAM lío *m*, embrollo *m* (mess) | confusión *f*.
— OBSERV Esta palabra es la abreviatura de *Situation Normal, All Fouled Up*.

snag [snæg] *n* gancho *m* (of a branch) || tocón *m* (of a tree) || raigón *m* (of a tooth) || tronco *m* sumergido (wood in a river) || FIG pega *f*, obstáculo *m* (difficulty); *there's just one snag* hay una pega; *the only snag is that* la única pega es que || protuberancia *f* (protuberance) || — FIG *that's the snag* ahí está la pega | *to come across* o *to run into* o *to strike* o *to hit a snag* encontrarse con una pega *or* un obstáculo.

snag [snæg] *vt* enganchar (a jumper, material) || encallar (a boat on a snag) || FIG estorbar, obstaculizar.

snaggletooth ['snægltu:θ] *n* US raigón *m* (broken stump of tooth) | diente *m* salido.

snaggy ['snægi] *adj* FIG sembrado de obstáculos.

snail [sneil] *n* ZOOL caracol *m* || FIG tortuga *f* (slow person) || FIG *to walk at a snail's pace* andar a paso de tortuga.

snake [sneik] *n* ZOOL serpiente *f* (in general) | culebra *f* (harmless) || FIG víbora *f*, bicho *m* (malevolent person) || — FIG *snakes and ladders* juego *m* de la oca | *there is a snake in the grass* hay gato encerrado (sth.), hay un traidor (s.o.) | *to cherish a snake in one's bosom* criar cuervos.

snake [sneik] *vi* serpentear; *the river snaked across the valley* el río serpenteaba a través del valle || *to snake out* extenderse (a tentacle).
◆ *vt* hacer serpentear || US arrastrar (to haul logs) | hacer deslizar (to skid logs).

snakebite [-bait] *n* mordedura *f* de serpiente.

snake charmer [-,tʃɑ:mə*] *n* encantador *m* de serpientes.

snakelike [-laik] *adj* serpentino, na; en forma de serpiente.

snaky [-i] *adj* sinuoso, sa; serpentino, na (winding) || lleno de serpientes (snake infested) || traidor, ra (treacherous).

snap [snæp] *adj* instantáneo, a; rápido, da; *a snap decision* una decisión instantánea || rápido, da; *a snap vote* una votación rápida || US FAM tirado, da (simple, easy).
◆ *n* chasquido *m* (of wood breaking, of whip, etc.) || crujido *m*, ruido *m* seco (of the teeth, mouth, joints) || mordisco *m*, dentellada *f* (bite); *to make a snap at* dar un mordisco en || castañeteo *m* (of the fingers) || PHOT instantánea *f*, foto *f* (snapshot) || ola *f* (of bad weather); *a cold snap* una ola de frío || galleta *f* (thin hard biscuit) || FAM energía *f*, vigor *m* (vigour) | réplica *f* mordaz (answer) || US automático *m* (snap fastener) | cosa *f* tirada *or* fácil (easy task) || — *he shut the book with a snap* cerró el libro de golpe || FAM *put some snap into it!* ¡venga!
◆ *adv* con un chasquido, con un crujido || *to go snap* romperse con un chasquido (to break), crujir (joints).

snap [snæp] *vt* partir; *to snap a branch in two* partir una rama en dos || romper (bones) || hacer crujir (joints) || intentar morder (to try to bite) || agarrar (to seize) || castañetear; *to snap one's fingers* castañetear los dedos || chasquear; *to snap a whip* chasquear los dedos || chasquear; *to snap a whip* chasquear un látigo || tomar una instantánea de, sacar una foto a (to take a snapshot of) || — FIG *to snap one's fingers at* burlarse de || *to snap open* abrir de golpe || *to snap out* soltar, decir con brusquedad (words), espetar (order) || *to snap shut* cerrar de golpe || FIG & FAM *to snap s.o.'s head off* poner verde a alguien, echar un rapapolvo a alguien || FIG *to snap up* agarrar; *to snap up an offer* agarrar una oportunidad; llevarse; *to snap up the last tickets* llevarse las últimas entradas.
◆ *vi* partirse, romperse; *the rope snapped* la cuerda se rompió || regañar; *don't snap at the boy* no regañes al niño || intentar morder (to make as if to bite) || morder; *to snap at the bait* morder el anzuelo || crujir; *a twig snapped* una rama crujió || chasquear (a whip) || castañetear, crujir (fingers) || dar un estampido (gun) || ponerse; *to snap into action* ponerse en acción || — FIG *snap out of it!* ¡anímate! | *to snap at* agarrarse a; *he snapped at the chance to go* se agarró a la oportunidad de marcharse; intentar morder (a dog), hablar con brusquedad a (to speak harshly to) || *to snap off* desprenderse, caerse || *to snap open* abrirse de golpe || FIG & FAM *to snap out of it* recuperarse (to recover), olvidarlo (to forget it) || *to snap shut* cerrarse de golpe.

snap bean [-bi:n] *n* judía *f* verde.

snapdragon [-,drægən] *n* dragón *m* (flower).

snap fastener [-'fɑ:snə*] *n* automático *m*.

snappish [-iʃ] *adj* irritable (irritable) || mordedor, ra (dog).

snappy [-i] *adj* irritable, irascible (short-tempered) || mordedor, ra (dog) || animado, da (lively) || rápido, da (fast) || FAM elegante (stylish) || *be snappy about it!*, *make it snappy!* ¡date prisa!

snapshot [-ʃɔt] *n* PHOT instantánea *f*, foto *f*.

snare [snεə*] *n* trampa *f*, cepo *m*, lazo *m* (for catching animals) || FIG trampa *f*, lazo *m*, celada *f* (trap, trick) || MUS cuerda *f* (of a drum) || *snare drum* tambor *m*.

snare [snεə*] *vt* cazar con trampa, coger con lazo || FIG hacer caer en la trampa (to trick).

snarl [snɑ:l] *n* gruñido *m* (of a dog, of a person, etc.) || maraña *f*, enredo *m*; *a snarl of hair* una maraña de pelo || — *to say sth. with a snarl* decir algo gruñendo || US FAM *traffic snarl* embotellamiento *m*, atasco *m* (traffic jam).

snarl [snɑ:l] *vt* enredar, enmarañarse (to entangle).
◆ *vi* enredarse, enmarañarse (to become entangled) || gruñir (to growl).

snarl-up [-ʌp] *n* enredo *m*, maraña *f* (muddle) || atasco *m*, embotellamiento (traffic jam).

snatch [snætʃ] *n* arrebatamiento *m* (snatching) || fragmento *m* (portion of talk, of song, etc.) || FAM robo *m* (robbery) | secuestro *m* (kidnapping) || rato *m*; *in snatches* a ratos; *to work in snatches* trabajar a ratos || SP arrancada *f* (weight lifting) || *to make a snatch at sth.* intentar arrebatar algo (to take it from s.o.), intentar agarrar algo (to grab at).

snatch [snætʃ] *vt* arrebatar (to seize from s.o.); *he snatched it from my hands* me lo arrebató de las manos || agarrar, coger (to pick up) || sacar tiempo para; *to snatch a meal, a sleep* sacar tiempo para comer, para dormir || sacar; *they snatched the drowning man from the river* sacaron al ahogado del río || FAM robar (to steal) | secuestrar (to kidnap) || — FIG *to snatch an opportunity* agarrar una oportunidad al vuelo || *to snatch up* agarrar rápidamente.
◆ *vi* agarrar || — *don't snatch!* ¡no me lo quites así de las manos! || *to snatch at an opportunity* agarrar una oportunidad al vuelo || *to snatch at sth.* intentar agarrar algo.

snatch block [-blɔk] *n* MAR pasteca *f*.

snatchy [-i] *adj* irregular.

snazzy ['snæzi] *adj* FAM bonito, ta (pretty) | llamativo, va (flashy).

sneak [sni:k] *n* FAM chivato, ta; soplón, ona (s.o. who betrays one) || ladronzuelo, la (thief) || salida *f* disimulada (exit).
◆ *pl* zapatos *m* de lona (sneakers).

sneak [sni:k] *vt* hacer furtivamente (to do stealthily) || meter a escondidas; *he sneaked the papers into his desk* metió los papeles a escondidas en su escritorio || FAM mangar, birlar (to steal) || *to sneak a look at* mirar furtivamente.
◆ *vi* *to sneak away* o *off* escabullirse || *to sneak in, out* entrar, salir furtivamente *or* a hurtadillas || *to sneak off with sth.* llevarse algo furtivamente || *to sneak on s.o.* traicionar *or* acusar a alguien.

sneakers [-əz] *pl n* US zapatos *m* de lona.

sneaking [-iŋ] *adj* furtivo, va (furtive) || ligero, ra (slight) || secreto, ta (secret).

sneak preview [-'pri:'vju:] *n* US proyección *f* anterior al estreno para conocer la opinión del público (of a film).

sneak thief [-θi:f] *n* ratero *m*.

sneaky [-i] *adj* vil, bajo, ja; rastrero, ra (low, despicable) || secreto, ta (secret) || furtivo, va (furtive); *to have a sneaky look at* echar un vistazo furtivo a || solapado, da (sly).

sneer [sniə*] *n* desprecio *m* (scorn) || burla *f*, chifla *f*, escarnio *m* (mockery) || sonrisa *f* de desprecio (scornful smile) || sonrisa *f* burlona (mocking smile) || sarcasmo *m* (sarcasm).

sneer [sniə*] *vt* decir con desprecio.
◆ *vi* reír burlonamente *or* sarcásticamente || *to sneer at* despreciar (an offer), mofarse *or* burlarse de (to mock).

sneerer [-rə*] *n* burlón, ona; socarrón, ona.

sneering [-riŋ] *adj* burlón, ona; socarrón, ona.

sneeze [sni:z] *n* estornudo *m*.

sneeze [sni:z] *vi* estornudar || FIG *it is not to be sneezed at* no es de despreciar.

sneezewort [-wə:t] *n* BOT milenrama *f*.

snell [snel] *n* hilo *m* para atar el anzuelo.

snick [snik] *n* muesca *f* (small cut in wood, etc.) || tijeretada *f* (in paper, in cloth) || SP golpe *m* con el borde del bate (in cricket).

snick [snik] *vt* hacer una muesca en (wood) || cortar un poco (to cut slightly) || SP golpear con el borde del bate (in cricket).

snicker [-ə*] *n/vi* → **snigger.**

snide [snaid] *adj* FAM bajo, ja; vil (mean, cheap) | sarcástico, ca; *to make snide remarks* hacer comentarios sarcásticos || FAM *what a snide thing to do!* ¡qué cochinada!

sniff [snif] *n* aspiración *f* (of air) || olfateo *m* (of dogs) || inhalación *f*; *one sniff is enought to kill* una inhalación basta para matar || — FIG & FAM *I didn't even get a sniff of the champagne* ni siquiera olí el champán || *to open the window and take a sniff of fresh air* abrir la ventana y aspirar el aire fresco || *to take a sniff at* oler || *with a scornful sniff* con un gesto de desprecio.

sniff [snif] *vt* oler (to smell); *to sniff a rose* oler una rosa || olfatear, husmear (a dog); *to sniff the ground* olfatear la tierra || aspirar (smelling salts, etc.) || FIG oler, olfatear; *to sniff danger* oler el peligro || — FIG *to sniff out* oler, olfatear || *to sniff up* sorber (liquids), aspirar (snuff, smelling salts, powder, etc.).
◆ *vi* aspirar por la nariz, sorber || — FIG *it's not to be sniffed at* no es de despreciar || *to sniff at* oler (to smell), olfatear, husmear (a dog), despreciar (to scorn).

sniffer dog [-ə* dɔg] *n* perro *m* antidroga.

sniffle [-l] *n* sorbo *m* || *to have the sniffles* estar resfriado.

sniffle [-l] *vi* sorberse los mocos (because of catarrh) || sorberse las lágrimas (when weeping).

sniffy [-i] *adj* FAM desdeñoso, sa; despreciativo, va (scornful) | maloliente (bad-smelling) || *to be sniffy about sth.* tratar algo con desdén *or* desprecio.

snifter ['sniftə*] *n* US FAM copa *f*, trago *m* (drink); *to have a snifter* echarse un trago.

snigger ['snigə*]; **snicker** [snikə*] *n* risa *f* disimulada, risita *f*.

snigger; snicker [snikə*] ['snigə*] *vi* reír disimuladamente.

snip [snip] *n* tijereteo *m* (action and noise); *the snip of the barber's scissors* el tijereteo del peluquero || tijeretazo *m*, tijeretada *f* (cut made with scissors) || recorte *m* (piece snipped off) || FAM ganga *f* (bargain) | ganga *f*, cosa *f* fácil (easy task) | sastre *m* (tailor) || US FAM joven *m* impertinente.

snip [snip] *vt* tijeretear || *to snip off* cortar con tijeras.

snipe [snaip] *n* agachadiza *f* (bird).

snipe [snaip] *vi* cazar agachadizas (to shoot snipe) || MIL tirar desde una posición emboscada (to fire shots from a hiding place).

sniper [-ə*] *n* MIL tirador *m* emboscado, francotirador *m*.

snippet ['snipit] *n* recorte *m* (fragment cut off) || FIG retazo *m*, fragmento *m*, trozo *m* (fragment) || FIG *snippets of news* noticias sueltas.

snitch [snitʃ] *vt* FAM chivarse (to inform).

snivel ['snivl] *n* lloriqueo *m*, gimoteo *m* (whimpering) || moco *m* (in the nose).

snivel ['snivl] *vi* caérsele a uno los mocos (to have a runny nose) || lloriquear, gimotear (to whine).

sniveller; US **sniveler** [-ə*] *n* llorón, ona (whiner).

snivelling; US **sniveling** [-iŋ] *adj* llorón, ona (whining).
◆ *n* lloriqueo *m*, gimoteo *m*.

snob [snɔb] *n* snob *m*, esnob *m*.

snobbery [-əri] *n* snobismo *m*, esnobismo *m*.

snobbish [-iʃ] *adj* snob, esnob.

snobbishness [-iʃnis] *n* snobismo *m*, esnobismo *m*.

snobby [-i] *adj* snob, esnob.

snood [snu:d] *n* redecilla *f* (hair net) || cintillo *m* (ribbon) || hilo *m* para atar el anzuelo (in fishing).

snook [snu:k] *n* robalo *m*, róbalo *m* (fish) || FIG *to cock a snook at* hacer un palmo de narices a, hacer burla con la mano a (to thumb one's nose at), mofarse de, burlarse de, reírse de (to laugh at).

snooker [-ə*] *n* billar *m* ruso.

snooker [-ə*] *vt* imposibilitar el tiro directo a (the opponent in snooker) || FIG fastidiar (to hinder s.o.).

snoop; snooper [-ə*] *n* entrometido, da; fisgón, ona (nosey person) || FAM detective *m* (detective) || *I had a snoop around, but found nothing* estuve husmeando *or* fisgando, pero no encontré nada.

snoop [snu:p] *vi* entrometerse (to pry) || *to snoop around* husmear, fisgonear, curiosear.

snoopy ['snu:pi] *adj* US FAM entrometido, da; curioso, sa.

snootiness ['snu:tinis] *n* FAM snobismo *m*, esnobismo *m*, presunción *f*.

snooty ['snu:ti] *adj* FAM snob, esnob, presumido, da.

snooze [snu:z] *n* cabezada *f* (short light sleep); *to have a snooze* dar una cabezada.

snooze [snu:z] *vi* dar una cabezada, dormitar.

snore [snɔ:*] *n* ronquido *m*.

snore [snɔ:*] *vi* roncar.

snoring [-riŋ] *n* ronquidos *m pl*.

snorkel ['snɔ:kəl] *n* tubo *m* de respiración (swimmer's) || esnórquel *m* (of a submarine).

snort [snɔ:t] *n* resoplido *m*; *the snorts of the horses* los resoplidos de los caballos || FIG zumbido *m*, ronquido *m* (of an engine) | resoplido *m*, bufido *m* (of a person); *a snort of rage* un bufido de rabia || US FAM trago *m* (drink).

snort [snɔ:t] *vt* decir con un bufido.
◆ *vi* bufar, resoplar || zumbar (an engine) || *to be snorting with rage* estar bufando de rabia.

snorter [-ə*] *n* ventarrón *m* (violent gale) || FAM cosa *f* impresionante || — FAM *a snorter of a letter* una carta impresionante | *his new car is a snorter* su nuevo coche es impresionante.

snot [snɔt] *n* moco *m* (in the nose) || FAM mocoso, sa (person) || POP *snot rag* pañuelo *m*.

snotty [-i] *adj* mocoso, sa (dirty with snot) || FAM despreciable (contemptible) | snob, esnob, presumido, da (snooty) || de mal humor (angry).
◆ *n* FAM guardiamarina *m*.

snout [snaut] *n* hocico *m* (of a pig, bull, boar, dog, etc.) || FAM napias *f pl* (nose) | hocico *m*, jeta *f* (face) | pitillo *m* (cigarette) || FIG morro *m* (of a plane) | pitorro *m* (of a teapot, of a hosepipe).

snow [snəu] *n* nieve *f* || nevada *f* (a fall of snow) || FAM mandanga *f* (cocaine) || — *a heavy fall of snow* una fuerte nevada || *as white as snow* blanco como la nieve.

snow [snəu] *vt* hacer caer como copos (like flakes) || bloquear; *to be snowed in* o *up* estar bloqueado por la nieve || FIG *to be snowed under with work, with debts* estar abrumado *or* agobiado de trabajo, de deudas.
◆ *vi* nevar.

snowball [-bɔ:l] *n* bola *f* de nieve (snow pressed into a ball) || BOT mundillo *m*, bola *f* de nieve.

snowball [-bɔ:l] *vt* tirar bolas de nieve a.
◆ *vi* aumentar rápidamente (to grow rapidly) || acumularse (to accumulate) || tirar bolas de nieve (to throw snowballs).

snowbird [-bə:b] *n* pinzón *m* de las nieves.

snow-blind [-'blaind] *adj* cegado por el reflejo de la nieve.

snow-blindness [-'blaindnis] *n* ceguera *f* producida por el reflejo de la nieve.

snowbound [-baund] *adj* bloqueado por la nieve.

snow-capped [-kæpt]; **snow-covered** [-'kʌvəd] *adj* cubierto de nieve, nevado, da.

snowdrift [-drift] *n* acumulación *f* de nieve, ventisquero *m* [producida por el viento].

snowdrop [-drɔp] *n* BOT campanilla *f* de invierno.

snowfall [-fɔ:l] *n* nevada *f*.

snowfield [-fi:ld] *n* campo *m* de nieve.

snowflake [-fleik] *n* copo *m* de nieve.

snow leopard [-'lepəd] *n* ZOOL onza *f*.

snow line [-lain] *n* límite *m* de las nieves perpetuas.

snowman [-mæn] *n* muñeco *m* de nieve || *the abominable snowman* el abominable hombre de las nieves.
— OBSERV El plural de *snowman* es *snowmen*.

snowplough; US **snowplow** [-plau] *n* quitanieves *m inv* (device for cleaning snow) || cuña *f* (in skiing).

snowshoe [-ʃu:] *n* raqueta *f*.

snowslide [-slaid] *n* alud *m* de nieve (avalancha).

snowstorm [-stɔ:m] *n* tormenta *f* de nieve.

snow-white [-'wait] *adj* blanco como la nieve.

Snow White [-'wait] *n* *Snow White and the Seven Dwarfs* Blancanieves y los siete enanitos.

snowy [-i] *adj* nevado, da (snow-covered) || blanco como la nieve (white) || de las nieves (season) || de mucha nieve, nevoso, sa (region, climate) || *it was very snowy last week* la semana pasada nevó mucho, hubo mucha nieve la semana pasada.

SNP *abbr of [Scottish National Party]* Partido Nacionalista Escocés.

snub [snʌb] *n* desaire *m* (of a person) || rechazo *m* (of an offer).

snub [snʌb] *vt* desairar, despreciar (to slight or to ignore s.o.) || despreciar (an offer) || parar con brusquedad (to stop abruptly) || *to snub out* apagar (a cigarette).

snubber [-ə*] *n* US TECH amortiguador *m* (shock absorber) | tambor *m* del freno (of the brake).

snub nose [-nəuz] *n* nariz *f* chata y respingona.

snub-nosed [-'nəuzd] *adj* de nariz chata y respingona.

snuff [snʌf] *n* inhalación *f* (act of snuffing) || rapé *m* (powdered tobacco); *pinch of snuff* toma de rapé || pabilo *m* (of a candle) || — FIG *to be up to snuff* ser muy despabilado || *to take snuff* tomar rapé.

snuff [snʌf] *vt* inhalar, aspirar (to inhale) || oler, olfatear (to sniff) || despabilar (to cut the wick off) || — FIG & FAM *to snuff it* estirar la pata || *to snuff out* apagar (a candle), terminar con (conspiracy, etc.).
◆ *vi* tomar rapé.

snuffbox [-bɔks] *n* caja *f* de rapé, tabaquera *f*.

snuffer [-ə*] *n* apagavelas *m inv* || tomador *m* de rapé.
◆ *pl* despabiladeras *f* (scissors).

snuffle [-l] *n* resuello *m* (sniff) || obstrucción *f* nasal, respiración *f* ruidosa (noisy breathing) || tono *m* gangoso.
◆ *pl* romadizo *m sing* (cold) || *to have the snuffles* estar resfriado *or* constipado *or* acatarrado.

snuffle [-l] *vi* respirar ruidosamente || ganguear (to speak with a twang).

snug [snʌg] *adj* cómodo, da; confortable; *a snug room* una habitación confortable || calentito, ta (nice and warm) || ajustado, da; ceñido, da (tightfitting); *a snug jacket* una chaqueta ajustada || MAR bien aparejado (ship) || abrigado, da (sheltered) || FIG bueno, na; *a snug income* un buen sueldo | agradable (job) || FIG *to be as snug as a bug in a rug* estar muy cómodo.

snug [snʌg] *vt* MAR *to snug down* preparar [para hacer frente a la tempestad] || abrigar (to shelter) || ajustar, ceñir (a garment).

snuggery [-əri] *n* habitación *f* cómoda.

snuggle [-l] *vt* acurrucar, apretar.
◆ *vi* arrimarse; *she snuggled up to him* se arrimó a él || acurrucarse (to curl up); *he snuggled up in the hay, in bed* se acurrucó en el heno, en la cama; *the cat snuggled up on her lap* el gato se acurrucó en sus rodillas || *to snuggle up with a book* ponerse cómodo para leer un libro.

snugly [-li] *adv* cómodamente (comfortably) || al abrigo (under shelter) || *to fit snugly* ajustar perfectamente (clothes), caber perfectamente (one object inside another).

snugness [-nis] *n* comodidad *f* (comfort) || ajuste *m*, ajustamiento *m* (of a garment).

so [səu] *adv* así, de esta manera; *it must be done so* debe hacerse así; *she wrapped up well and so was warm* se arropó bien y así consiguió tener calor || tan; *he was so ill that we thought he would die* estaba tan enfermo que creíamos que se iba a morir; *it's not so difficult* no es tan difícil; *it won't be so bad as you think* no será tan malo como crees; *so happy* tan feliz; *he is so kind* es tan amable || también; *he wants to go and so do I* él quiere ir y yo también; *so did she* ella también || tanto; *she misses him so* le echa tanto de menos; *why do you protest so?* ¿por qué protesta usted tanto? || — *and in doing so* y al hacer eso || *and so forth* y así sucesivamente, etcétera || *and so it was that...* y ocurrió que... (and it happened that), y así fue como... (and that was how...) || *and so on* y así sucesivamente, etcétera || *and so to bed* y después a la cama || *be so kind as to* tenga la bondad de || *ever so* muy, infinitamente (grateful) || *ever so little* muy pequeño, pequeñísimo; *he is ever so little* es muy pequeño; muy poco; *give me ever so little* dame muy poco || *how so?* ¿cómo es eso? || *if so* en ese caso, si es así (in that case) || *I hope so* eso espero, espero que sí || *in so far as* en la medida en que || *in so many words* palabra por palabra, textualmente; *I can't tell you what he said in so many words* no puedo decirle lo que dijo textualmente; explícitamente, claramente; *he didn't say so in so many words* no lo dijo explícitamente || *is that so?* ¿es verdad?, ¿de verdad? || *I think so* creo que sí || *I told you so* ya te lo dije || *it so happens that* resulta que, da la casualidad de que || *just so, quite so* ni más ni menos, así es || *not so* no es así || *not so much as* ni siquiera || *not so much... as* no... sino más bien || *only more so* pero más aún || *or so* o poco más o menos || *so as to* para; *so as not to be heard* para no ser oído || *so... as* tan... como; *he is not so kind as his wife* no es tan amable como su mujer || *so... as to* tan... como para, tantos... que; *cars so numerous as to block the traffic* coches tan numerosos como para bloquear el tráfico, tantos coches que bloquearon el tráfico || *so be it* así sea || *so far* hasta aquí *or* allí; *you can go so far in the car, but eventually you'll have to get out and walk* se puede ir hasta allí en coche, pero luego hay que bajar e ir andando; hasta ahora (until now) || *so far as* hasta || *so far as I am concerned* por lo que a mí respecta *or* se refiere || *so far as I can make out* por lo que veo || *so far as I know* que yo sepa || *so far so good* hasta ahora todo va bien || *so forth and so on* y así sucesivamente || *so he says* eso dice él, según dice él || *so it is!* ¡es verdad!, ¡así es! || *so it seems* eso parece || *so long* tanto tiempo; *they did not stay so long* no se quedaron tanto tiempo; hasta luego, hasta pronto (good-bye) || *so long as* mientras que || *so many* tanto, ta; *so many people* tanta gente; *so many guests* tantos invitados || *so much* tanto, ta; *so much money* tanto dinero; tanto; *so much has been said that* tanto se ha dicho que || *so much for that* ¿qué le vamos hacer? || *so much so that* tanto que || *so much the better* tanto mejor || *so so* así, así || *so that* para que, de manera que (in order that); *I helped him so that he might finish earlier* le ayudé para que terminase antes; de modo que, de manera que (with the result that) || *so that's that* así son las cosas || *so then* así pues || *so to speak* por decirlo así || *so what?* ¿y qué? || *they are just so many thieves* no son más que unos ladrones || *they did not so much as answer* ni siquiera contestaron || *they get so much per day* ganan tanto por día || *very much so* mucho || *what he said was so much nonsense* lo que dijo no fueron más que tonterías || *why so?* ¿por qué? || *without so much as a by your leave* sin decir nada a nadie, sin pedirle siquiera permiso a nadie.
◆ *conj* así que, por lo tanto; *you are not listening so I'll shut up* no me estás escuchando, así que me callaré || así que, conque, entonces, de modo que; *so you are not coming* ¿así que no vienes?; *so it was you who did it* conque fuiste tú el que lo hiciste || US para que; *I'll show you so you can see how it is done* te lo voy a enseñar para que veas cómo se hace; *I only said it so you'd stay* sólo lo dije para que te quedases || de manera que, de modo que (whit the result that).

soak [səuk] *n* remojo *m* (washing, food) || empapamiento *m* (of soil, etc.) || remojón *m*, empapamiento *m* (of a person) || FAM borrachín, ina (drunkard) | borrachera *f* (spree).

soak [səuk] *vt* remojar, poner en remojo (washing, food); *to soak a shirt before washing it* poner una camisa en remojo antes de lavarla || empapar, calar; *we got absolutely soaked* nos empapamos *or* nos calamos completamente || empapar, mojar (to wet); *soak the cotton wool in antiseptic* empapa el algodón en un antiséptico || — *soaked to the skin* calado hasta los huesos || *to soak in* o *up* absorber (a liquid) || *to soak o.s.* calarse hasta los huesos (to get soaked) || FIG *to soak o.s. in* empaparse de || *to soak out* quitar *or* sacar remojando; *to soak the stains out of sth.* quitar las manchas de algo remojándolo || FIG & FAM *to soak s.o. for twenty pounds* clavarle veinte libras a alguien.
◆ *vi* estar en remojo, remojarse (clothes, food) || FIG & FAM pimplar, soplar (to drink a lot) || — *to leave sth. to soak* dejar algo en remojo || *to soak in* penetrar || *to soak through* penetrar (to penetrate), calar; *the rain has soaked through his overcoat* la lluvia le ha calado el abrigo.

soaking [-iŋ] *n* remojón *m* (accidental) || — *to get a soaking* empaparse || *to give sth. a soaking* poner algo en remojo.
◆ *adj* *soaking (wet)* empapado, da; calado hasta los huesos.

so-and-so ['səuənsəu] *n* fulano, na || — FAM *he's a useless so-and-so* es un inútil || *Mr. So-and-so* don Fulano de Tal.

soap [səup] *n* jabón *m* || — *soap bubble* pompa *f* de jabón || *soap dish* jabonera *f* || US FAM *soap opera* serial *m*.

soap [səup] *vt* jabonar, enjabonar.

soapbark [-bɑːk] *n* BOT quillay *m*.

soapberry [-'beri] *n* BOT jaboncillo *m*.

soapbox [-bɔks] *n* tribuna *f* improvisada (of open-air speaker).
◆ *adj* *soapbox orators* oradores *m* callejeros.

soap flakes [-fleiks] *pl n* jabón *m sing* en escamas.

soap plant [-plɑːnt] *n* BOT jabonera *f*.

soap powder [-'paudə*] *n* jabón *m* en polvo.

soapstone [-stəun] *n* MIN esteatita *f* || jaboncillo *m* (in dressmaking).

soapsuds [-sʌdz] *pl n* espuma *f sing*, jabonaduras *f* (lather).

soapwort [-wəːt] *n* BOT jabonera *f*.

soapy [-i] *adj* jabonoso, sa; *soapy water, hands* agua jabonosa, manos jabonosas || FIG meloso, sa.

soar [sɔː*] *vi* elevarse, remontarse (up into the air); *the plane soared to ten thousand metres* el avión se elevó a diez mil metros || volar, planear; *the birds were soaring high above us* los pájaros volaban muy alto por encima de nosotros || FIG elevarse; *the tower soared above the town* la torre se elevaba por encima de la ciudad | subir vertiginosamente (prices) || FIG *our hopes soared* cobramos nuevas esperanzas.

soaring [-riŋ] *n* vuelo *m* (flight) || subida *f* vertiginosa (of prices).
◆ *adj* que planea en las alturas (bird, plane, etc.) || altísimo, ma (very high) || *to check soaring prices* controlar la subida excesiva de los precios.

sob [sɔb] *n* sollozo *m*.

sob [sɔb] *vt* decir sollozando *or* con sollozos || — *she sobbed herself to sleep* se durmió sollozando || *to sob one's heart out* llorar a lágrima viva.
◆ *vi* sollozar.

sobbing [-iŋ] *n* sollozos *m pl*.

sober ['səubə*] *adj* sobrio, bria (not drunk) || moderado, da; sobrio, bria (temperate); *sober habits* costumbres moderadas || sensato, ta; *a sober opinion* una opinión sensata || equilibrado, da (showing discretion) || grave, serio, ria (serious, grave); *his expression was very sober* tenía una expresión muy seria || sobrio, bria (not ornamented); *a sober style, dress* un estilo, un vestido sobrio || discreto, ta; *sober colours* colores discretos || puro, ra; *the sober truth* la pura verdad || — *as sober as a judge, stone-cold sober* completamente sobrio || *in sober fact* en realidad || *we'll have to wait until he's sober* tendremos que esperar hasta que se le pasen los efectos de la bebida.

sober ['səubə*] *vt* desembriagar (a drunken person) || FIG calmar (to calm).
◆ *vi* *to sober down* calmarse (to calm down) || *to sober up* pasársele a uno la embriaguez.

sobering [-riŋ] *adj* que da que pensar (action, words).

sober-minded [-'maindid] *adj* sensato, ta.

sobersides [-saidz] *n* persona *f* muy seria.

sobriety [səu'braiəti] *n* sobriedad *f* || moderación *f* (moderation) || serenidad *f* (sedateness) || seriedad *f* (seriousness) || sensatez *f* (good sense) || discreción *f* (discretion).

sobriquet ['səubrikei] *n* apodo *m*, mote *m* (nickname).

sob sister ['sɔb,sistə*] *n* US FAM periodista *f* que escribe artículos sentimentales.

sob story ['sɔb,stɔːri] *n* FAM historia *f* sentimental.

socage; soccage ['sɔkidʒ] *n* HIST arriendo *m.*

so-called ['səu'kɔ:ld] *adj* llamado, da; supuesto, ta; *a so-called liberal* un llamado liberal.

soccer ['sɔkə*] *n* SP fútbol *m.*

sociability [,səuʃə'biliti] *n* sociabilidad *f,* carácter *m* sociable.

sociable ['səuʃəbl] *adj* sociable; *he is a very sociable person* es una persona muy sociable ‖ amistoso, sa; afable (friendly).

social ['səuʃəl] *adj* social; *social legislation* legislación social; *social rank* rango *or* posición social; *social life* vida social; *social events* acontecimientos sociales ‖ amistoso, sa (friendly) ‖ sociable (sociable); *man is a social being* el hombre es un ser sociable ‖ — *social climber* arribista *m* & *f,* advenedizo, za ‖ *social column* ecos *m pl* de sociedad (in a newspaper) ‖ *Social Democracy* democracia *f* social, socialdemocracia *f* ‖ *Social Democrat* socialdemócrata *m* & *f* ‖ *social disease* enfermedad causada por condiciones precarias de vida (disease related to social conditions), enfermedad venérea (venereal disease) ‖ *social insurance* seguro *m* social ‖ *social order* orden *m* social ‖ *social reformer* reformador *m* de la sociedad ‖ *social science* sociología *f* ‖ *social scientist* sociólogo, ga ‖ *social security* seguridad *f* social ‖ *social order* orden *m* social ‖ *social service* servicio *m* social ‖ *social settlement* centro *m* de asistencia social ‖ *social welfare* asistencia *f* social ‖ *social work* asistencia *f* social ‖ *social worker* asistente *m* social, asistenta *f* social ‖ *to be a social outcast* vivir rechazado por la sociedad.
◆ *n* reunión *f,* tertulia *f.*

socialism [-izəm] *n* socialismo *m.*

socialist [-ist] *adj/n* socialista.

socialistic [,səuʃə'listik] *adj* socialista.

socialite ['səuʃəlait] *n* FAM mundano, na.

socialization [,səuʃəlai'zeiʃən] *n* socialización *f.*

socialize ['səuʃəlaiz] *vt* socializar.

socialized medicine [-d'medsin] *n* medicina *f* estatal.

socially ['səuʃəli] *adv* socialmente ‖ para la sociedad; *socially unacceptable* inaceptable para la sociedad ‖ por la sociedad (accepted, etc.) ‖ — *I never meet my colleagues socially* nunca me reúno con mis colegas fuera del trabajo ‖ *socially inferior* de condición social inferior.

society [sə'saiəti] *n* sociedad *f; feudal society* sociedad feudal; *American society* la sociedad americana; *high society* alta sociedad ‖ alta sociedad *f* (upper class) ‖ asociación *f* (organized group) ‖ compañía *f* (company) ‖ ZOOL sociedad *f* ‖ — *cooperative society* sociedad cooperativa ‖ *friendly* o *provident society* sociedad de socorro mutuo, mutualidad *f* ‖ *society column* o *news* ecos *m pl* de sociedad ‖ *society woman* mujer mundana ‖ *to go into society* ponerse de largo, ser presentada en sociedad.

Society of Friends [-əv,frendz] *n* REL sociedad *f* de los amigos.

Society of Jesus [-əv,dʒi:zəs] *n* REL Compañía *f* de Jesús.

socioeconomic ['səusjəu,i:kə'nɔmik] *adj* socioeconómico, ca.

sociologic [,səusjə'lɔdʒik]; **sociological** [-əl] *adj* sociológico, ca.

sociologist ['səusi'ɔlədʒist] *n* sociólogo, ga.

sociology [,səusi'ɔlədʒi] *n* sociología *f.*

sociopolitical ['səusjəupə'litikəl] *adj* sociopolítico, ca.

sock [sɔk] *n* calcetín *m* (foot garment) ‖ plantilla *f* (inner sole of a shoe) ‖ manga *f* (showing wind direction) ‖ (ant) coturno *m* (for actors) ‖ FAM puñetazo *m* (blow) ‖ — FAM *put a sock in it!* ¡cierra la boca!, ¡cállate! ‖ FIG *to pull up one's socks* hacer un esfuerzo.

sock [sɔk] *vt* pegar.

socket ['sɔkit] *n* hueco *m,* cubo *m* (for holding sth.) ‖ ELECTR enchufe *m,* enchufe *m* hembra (electrical connection) | casquillo *m* (of a bulb) ‖ arandela *f* (of a candlestick) ‖ ANAT cuenca *f* (of the eye) | alveolo *m* (of teeth) | glena *f* (of bones).

socket wrench [-rentʃ] *n* US TECH llave *f* de tubo.

sockeye ['sɔkai] *n* salmón *m* rojo.

socle ['sɔkəl] *n* ARCH zócalo *m* (for a wall) | pedestal *m,* peana *f* (for a statue).

Socrates ['sɔkrəti:z] *pr n* Sócrates *m.*

Socratic [sɔ'krætik] *adj/n* socrático, ca.

sod [sɔd] *n* césped *m* (surface soil with grass growing) ‖ tepe *m* (piece of turf) ‖ POP cabrón *m* (term of abuse) ‖ FAM *under the sod* debajo de tierra.

sod [sɔd] *vt* cubrir de césped.

soda ['səudə] *n* CHEM sosa *f; caustic soda* sosa cáustica ‖ soda *f,* sifón *m,* agua *f* de Seltz (soda water); *a whisky and soda* un whisky con soda ‖ — *soda ash* carbonato sódico ‖ *soda biscuit* (US *soda cracker*) galleta ligeramente salada ‖ US *soda fountain* bar *m* donde sólo se venden bebidas sin alcohol (bar), sifón (siphon) ‖ US FAM *soda jerk* camarero *m* ‖ *soda water* agua de Seltz, soda, sifón.

sodality [səu'dæliti] *n* asociación *f* (organized society) ‖ REL cofradía *f,* hermandad *f.*

sodden ['sɔdn] *adj* empapado, da (saturated) ‖ mal cocido, da (bread) ‖ embrutecido por el alcohol (from frequent drunkenness).

sodium ['səudjəm] *n* CHEM sodio *m* ‖ — *sodium bicarbonate* bicarbonato sódico *or* de sosa ‖ *sodium carbonate* carbonato sódico ‖ *sodium chloride* cloruro sódico *or* de sodio ‖ *sodium hydroxide* hidróxido sódico ‖ *sodium nitrate* nitrato sódico *or* de sodio.

sodium-vapour-lamp [-'veipə,læmp] *n* lámpara *f* de vapor de sodio.

Sodom ['sɔdəm] *pr n* HIST Sodoma.

sodomite ['sɔdəmait] *n* sodomita *m.*

sodomy ['sɔdəmi] *n* sodomía *f.*

sofa ['səufə] *n* sofá *m.*

sofa bed [-bed] *n* US sofá *m* cama.

soffit ['sɔfit] *n* ARCH sofito *m.*

Sofia ['səufjə] *pr n* GEOGR Sofía.

soft [sɔft] *adj* blando, da; *soft bed* cama blanda ‖ suave; *soft hair* pelo suave; *soft skin* cutis suave; *soft colours* colores suaves ‖ confuso, sa; borroso, sa (outline) ‖ silencioso, sa (silent) ‖ bajo, ja (low); *in a soft voice* en voz baja ‖ dulce (sweet); *soft words* palabras dulces ‖ débil (weak) ‖ benigno, na; templado, da; suave (climate) ‖ no alcohólico, ca (drinks) ‖ blando, da; suave (diet) ‖ blando, da (water) ‖ flexible (hat) ‖ FAM fácil (easy) | blando, da; tolerante (tolerant) | tonto, ta; lelo, la (silly) ‖ PHOT borroso, sa; desenfocado, da ‖ PHYS blando, da; poco penetrante (rays) ‖ GRAMM suave (consonant) ‖ — FAM *a soft job* un chollo ‖ *as soft as silk* suave como la seda ‖ *soft answer* respuesta suave ‖ *soft coal* hulla grasa, carbón bituminoso ‖ *soft currency* moneda *or* divisa débil *or* blanda ‖ *soft drugs* drogas *f pl* blandas ‖ FIG & FAM *soft in the head* bobo, ba; lelo, la; tonto, ta ‖ *soft iron* hierro *m* dulce ‖ *soft palate* velo *m* del paladar ‖ *soft sell* publicidad discreta ‖ *soft solder* soldadura *f* de estaño ‖ *soft spot* debilidad *f* (weakness); *to have a soft spot for s.o., for sth.* tener una debilidad por alguien, por algo ‖ *soft to the touch* blando *or* suave al tacto ‖ FAM *to be soft on s.o.* ser poco servero con alguien (to be too lenient), estar encaprichado por *or* enamoriscado de alguien (to be fond of) ‖ *to go soft* ponerse blando (butter, etc.), perder la cabeza (to go mad) ‖ FAM *to go soft in the head* perder la cabeza.
◆ *n* parte *f* blanda *or* suave.

softball [-bɔ:l] *n* variedad *f* de béisbol que se juega con pelota blanda.

soft-boiled [-bɔild] *adj* pasado por agua (egg).

soften ['sɔfn] *vt* ablandar; *to soften the heart* ablandar el corazón; *to soften leather* ablandar el cuero ‖ amortiguar (to deaden); *to soften a blow* amortiguar un golpe ‖ atenuar; *to soften the light* atenuar la luz ‖ suavizar (contours, the skin, etc.) ‖ bajar, templar (the voice) ‖ MED reblandecer (the brain) ‖ destemplar, adulzar (steel) ‖ templar (the temperature) ‖ *to soften up* debilitar (to weaken), ablandar (leather, etc.).
◆ *vi* ablandarse; *he softened* se ablandó; *the leather softens with time* el cuero se ablanda con el tiempo ‖ templarse (weather) ‖ debilitarse (to weaken) ‖ MED reblandecerse (the brain) ‖ — *to soften up on s.o.* ablandarse con alguien ‖ *to soften up on the rules* aplicar las reglas con más flexibilidad.

softener [-ə*] *n* suavizador *m.*

softening [-iŋ] *n* ablandamiento *m* (of leather, etc.) ‖ amortiguamiento *m* (deadening) ‖ debilitación *f* (weakening) ‖ reblandecimiento *m* (of the brain) ‖ adulzado *m* (of steel) ‖ suavización *f* (of design, skin, character).

soft focus ['sɔft,fəukəs] *n* PHOT degradado *m.*

soft-footed ['sɔft,futid] *adj* que anda sin hacer ruido.

softheaded [-id] *adj* bobo, ba; tonto, ta.

softhearted ['sɔft'hɑ:tid] *adj* bondadoso, sa.

softly ['sɔftli] *adv* suavemente, con delicadeza.

softness ['sɔftnis] *n* blandura *f* (of bed) ‖ suavidad *f* (of hair, of colours) ‖ dulzura *f* (sweetness) ‖ tolerancia *f,* indulgencia *f* (tolerance) ‖ debilidad *f,* falta *f* de energía (weakness) ‖ estupidez *f.*

soft pedal [sɔft'pedl] *n* sordina *f* (of a piano).

soft-pedal ['sɔft'pedl] *vt* tocar con sordina (piano) ‖ FIG suavizar, moderar.

soft soap ['sɔftsəup] *n* jabon *m* líquido ‖ FAM jabón *m,* pelotilla *f,* coba *f* (flattery).

soft-soap ['sɔftsəup] *vt* FAM dar jabón a, hacer la pelotilla a, dar coba a (to flatter).

soft-spoken ['sɔft,spəukən] *adj* de voz baja *or* dulce.

software ['sɔftwɛə*] *n* INFORM software *m,* programa *m* ‖ *software package* paquete *m* de programas.

softwood ['sɔftwud] *n* madera *f* blanda.

softy ['sɔfti] *n* FAM blando, da (indulgent person) | sensiblero, ra (sentimental) | bobo, ba (idiot).

soggy ['sɔgi] *adj* empapado, da (soaked) ‖ pesado, da (atmosphere) ‖ pastoso, sa (bread).

soh [səu] *n* MUS sol *m.*

soi-disant [swɑ:dizɑ:n] *adj* supuesto, ta.

soigné ['swænjei] *ajd* elegante (carefully dressed) ‖ cuidadoso, sa (attentive to detail).

soil [sɔil] *n* suelo *m,* tierra *f; he came home covered in soil* vino a casa cubierto de tierra; *when Colombus first stepped on American soil* cuando Colón pisó tierra americana por primera vez ‖ mancha *f* (dirty mark) ‖ estiércol *m* (excrement) ‖ basura *f* (refuse) ‖ *one's native soil* su tierra natal, su país.

soil [sɔil] *vt* ensuciar, manchar; *to soil a dress* manchar un traje ‖ FIG manchar, mancillar; *to*

soil s.o.'s reputation manchar la reputación de alguien || alimentar con forraje verde (cattle).
◆ *vi* ensuciarse, mancharse.

soiled [-d] *adj* sucio, cia; manchado, da.

soil pipe [-paip] *n* tubo *m* de desagüe sanitario.

soirée ['swɑːrei] *n* sarao *m*, velada *f*.

soja bean ['sɔiəbiːn] *n* BOT soja *f*.

sojourn ['sɔdʒəːn] *n* residencia *f*, estancia *f*, permanencia *f* [AMER estada *f*] (stay).

sojourn ['sɔdʒəːn] *vi* residir, permanecer.

soke [səuk] *n* HIST derecho *m* de jurisdicción.

sol [sɔl] *n* MUS & CHEM sol *m* || sol *m* (monetary unit).

solace ['sɔləs] *n* consuelo *m*, alivio *m*.

solace ['sɔləs] *vt* consolar, aliviar.

solanaceae [sɔlə'neisiiː] *pl n* BOT solanáceas *f*.

solan goose ['səulənguːs] *n* ZOOL alcatraz *m*.

solanum [səu'leinəm] *n* BOT solanácea *f*.

solar ['səulə*] *adj* solar || — *solar battery, flare, month, plexus, prominence, system, year* batería, erupción, mes, plexo, protuberancia, sistema, año solar || *solar panel* placa *f* solar.

solarium [səu'lɛəriəm] *n* solario *m*.
— OBSERV El plural de *solarium* es *solaria* o *solariums*.

sold [səuld] *pret/pp* ⟶ **sell.**

solder [-ə*] *n* soldadura *f*.

solder [-ə*] *vt* soldar.
◆ *vi* soldarse.

soldering [-əriŋ] *n* soldadura *f* || *soldering iron* soldador *m*.

soldier ['səuldʒə*] *n* MIL soldado *m* (non officer); *raw soldier* soldado bisoño; *discharged soldier* soldado licenciado; *volunteer soldier* soldado voluntario | militar *m* (a man serving in an army) || — *old soldier* veterano *m* || *private soldier* soldado raso || *soldier ant* hormiga *f* soldado || *tin* o *toy soldier* soldadito *m* de plomo || *to become a soldier* hacerse soldado.

soldier ['səuldʒə*] *vi* servir como soldado || FIG *to soldier on* seguir adelante a pesar de todo.

soldierly [-li] *adj* militar, marcial.

soldier of fortune [-əv'fɔːtʃən] *n* MIL mercenario *m* || FIG aventurero *m*.

soldiery [-ri] *n* MIL tropa *f*, soldadesca *f* || arte *f* militar (military science).

sole [səul] *adj* único, ca; *the sole survivor* el único superviviente || exclusivo, va; *sole agent, right* agente, derecho exclusivo || JUR *sole legatee* legatario *m* universal.
◆ *n* planta *f* (of a foot) || suela *f* (of a shoe); *half soles* medias suelas || base *f* (lower part of sth.) || AGR cama *f* (of ploughshare) || lenguado *m* (fish).

sole [səul] *vt* poner suela a (to provide with a sole).

solecism ['sɔlisizəm] *n* GRAMM solecismo *m* || FIG incorrección *f* (bad social manners).

solely ['səulli] *adv* únicamente, solamente.

solemn ['sɔləm] *adj* solemne; *solemn ceremony* ceremonia solemne; *a solemn mass* una misa solemne || serio, ria; *don't look so solemn!* ¡no te pongas tan serio! || estirado, da (pompous).

solemnity [sə'lemniti] **; solemness** ['sɔləmnis] *n* solemnidad *f*, seriedad *f* (of behaviour) || solemnidad *f*, ceremonia *f* solemne (solemn rite) || JUR requisito *m* (formality).

solemnization ['sɔləmnai'zeiʃən] *n* solemnización *f* || celebración *f*.

solemnize ['sɔləmnaiz] *vt* solemnizar (to perform with ceremony) || celebrar (a marriage).

solenoid ['səulinɔid] *n* PHYS solenoide *m*.

soleus [sə'liːəs] *n* ANAT sóleo *m* (muscle).

sol-fa [sɔl'fɑː] *n* MUS solfeo *m*.

solfatara [sɔlfə'tɑːrə] *n* GEOL solfatara *f*.

solfège [sɔl'feʒ] *n* solfeo *m*.

solfeggio [sɔl'fedʒiəu] *n* MUS solfeo *m*.
— OBSERV El plural de *solfeggio* es *solfeggi* o *solfeggios*.

solicit [sə'lisit] *vt* solicitar (to request); *to solicit s.o. for sth.* solicitar algo a alguien || importunar (to importune) || abordar (a prostitute) || FIG requerir (to require) | incitar (to incite) | inducir (to induce).
◆ *vi* hacer de buscona (a prostitute).

solicitation [səˌlisi'teiʃən] *n* solicitación *f* (request) || provocación *f* (of a prostitute).

solicitor [sə'lisitə*] *n* JUR procurador *m* (lawyer who prepares a case) | notario *m* (for will, for deeds, etc.) | abogado *m* (in lower courts) || US agente *m*, representante *m* (agent).
— OBSERV El *solicitor* acumula las funciones de procurador, notario, asesor y, en algunos casos, de abogado defensor.

solicitor general [-'dʒenərəl] *n* procurador *m* de la Corona || US subsecretario *m* de Justicia.

solicitous [sə'lisitəs] *adj* solícito, ta; atento, ta (attentive) || preocupado, da; ansioso, sa (*to* de) (eager).

solicitude [sə'lisitjuːd] *n* solicitud *f*, cuidado *m* (care, attention) || preocupación *f*, afán *m*, ansiedad *f* (eagerness).

solid ['sɔlid] *adj* sólido, da; *solid body, state* cuerpo, estado sólido; *solid foods* alimentos sólidos || firme; *solid conviction* convicción firme || continuo, nua; *a solid line* una línea continua || denso, sa (fog, smoke) || espeso, sa (jungle) || entero, ra; *a solid day's work* un día entero de trabajo || consistente, sólido, da; sustancial (arguments) || bien fundado, da; poderoso, sa; *solid reasons* razones poderosas || serio, ria (serious) || fuerte, resistente (building, structure) || sin interlíneas (typography) || compacto, ta; *a solid mass* una masa compacta || macizo, za (gold, silver, ebony, tyre); *a solid gold watch* un reloj de oro macizo || sustancioso, sa (meal) || duro, ra; *solid snow* nieve dura || uniforme, unido, da (colour) || cúbico, ca; *solid yard* yarda cúbica || unánime (unanimous); *solid vote, support* votación, apoyo unánime || incondicional (friends) || atestado, da (full); *the room was solid with people* el cuarto estaba atestado de gente || — *as solid as a rock* tan firme como una roca || *person of solid build* persona *f* fuerte || MATH *solid angle* ángulo sólido || *solid fuel* combustible *m* sólido || MATH *solid geometry* geometría *f* del espacio || *solid measure* medida *f* de volumen || *to become solid* solidificarse || *to be* o *to go solid for* estar unánimemente en favor de || *to rain for three solid weeks* o *for three weeks solid* llover durante tres semanas enteras, llover sin parar durante tres semanas.
◆ *n* sólido *m*.

solidarity [ˌsɔli'dæriti] *n* solidaridad *f*; *out of* o *in solidarity with* por solidaridad con.

solidification [səˌlidifi'keiʃən] *n* solidificación *f*.

solidify [sə'lidifai] *vt* solidificar.
◆ *vi* solidificarse.

solidity [sə'liditi] *n* solidez *f*.

solidly ['sɔlidli] *adv* unánimemente, por unanimidad (unanimously) || sin parar (non-stop) || *solidly built* sólidamente construido, de construcción sólida.

solidness ['sɔlidnis] *n* solidez *f* || unanimidad *f* (of a vote).

solidungulate [sɔlid'ʌŋgjulət] *adj/n* ⟶ **soliped.**

soliloquize [sə'liləkwaiz] *vi* soliloquiar, hablar a solas, monologar.

soliloquy [sə'liləkwi] *n* soliloquio *m*, monólogo *m*.

soliped ['sɔliped] **; solidungulate** [sɔlid'ʌŋgjulət] *adj* ZOOL solípedo *m*.
◆ *n* ZOOL solípedo *m*.

solipsism ['səulipsizəm] *n* solipsismo *m*.

solitaire [sɔli'tɛə*] *n* solitario *m* (card game, diamond).

solitariness ['sɔlitərinis] *n* soledad *f*.

solitary ['sɔlitəri] *adj* solitario, ria (alone, lonely) || único, ca; solo, la (only) || — *I didn't see a solitary soul* no había ni un alma || *solitary confinement* incomunicación *f* || *to be in solitary confinement* estar incomunicado.
◆ *n* solitario, ria (person who lives alone) || US FAM incomunicación *f* || US FAM *to put s.o. in solitary* dejar a alguien incomunicado.

solitude ['sɔlitjuːd] *n* soledad *f* (loneliness) || aislamiento *m* (isolation) || lugar *m* solitario (lonely place).

solleret [sɔlə'ret] *n* HIST escarpe *m*.

solmization [sɔlmi'zeiʃən] *n* MUS solfeo *m*.

solo ['səuləu] *n* MUS solo *m*; *a drum solo* un solo de tambor; *a soprano solo* un solo para soprano || solo *m* (in cards).
◆ *adj* MUS solo, la || *my first solo flight* la primera vez que vuelo solo.
◆ *adv* a solas || *to fly solo* volar solo.

soloist ['səuləuist] *n* solista *m* & *f*.

Solomon ['sɔləmən] *pr n* Salomón *m*.

Solomonic [ˌsɔlə'mɔnik] *adj* salomónico, ca.

solstice ['sɔlstis] *n* solsticio *m*; *winter, summer solstice* solsticio de invierno, de verano.

solubility [sɔlju'biliti] *n* solubilidad *f*.

soluble ['sɔljubl] *adj* soluble.

solution [sə'luːʃən] *n* solución *f*; *to find the solution to a problem* encontrar la solución de un problema || resolución *f* (act of solving) || CHEM solución *f* || MED *physiological salt solution, physiological saline solution* suero fisiológico.

solvability [sɔlvə'biliti] *n* solubilidad *f*.

solvable ['sɔlvəbl] *adj* soluble.

solve [sɔlv] *vt* resolver, solucionar.

solvency ['sɔlvənsi] *n* solvencia *f*.

solvent ['sɔlvənt] *adj* solvente (able to pay debts) || soluble (able to dissolve).
◆ *n* disolvente *m*, solvente *m* (chemical which dissolves).

soma ['səumə] *n* BIOL soma *m*.
— OBSERV El plural de la palabra inglesa *soma* es *somata* o *somas*.

Somali [səu'mɑːli] *adj/n* somalí.

Somalia [-ə] *pr n* GEOGR Somalia *f*.

Somaliland [-lænd] *pr n* GEOGR Somalia *f*.

somatic [sə'mætik] *adj* somático, ca.

somatology [səumə'tɔlədʒi] *n* BIOL somatología *f*.

sombre; US somber ['sɔmbə*] *adj* sombrío, a (dark and shadowy) || melancólico, ca (melancholic) || pesimista (pessimistic).

sombreness; US somberness [-nis] *n* aspecto *m* sombrío || melancolía *f* || pesimismo *m*.

sombrero [sɔm'brɛərəu] *n* sombrero *m* de ala ancha.

some [sʌm] *adj* algunos, nas; *some poeple can't take decisions* algunas personas no pueden tomar decisiones; *leave us some oranges* déjanos algunas naranjas || alguno, na; *some fool left the light on* algún idiota ha dejado la luz encendida || unos, unas; varios, rias; *some* *weeks ago* hace unas semanas; *there are some men waiting for you* hay unos hombres que te esperan ‖ unos, unas, algo como; *some ten hours* unas diez horas ‖ cierto, ta; *some distance away* a cierta distancia; *that might take some time* podría tardar cierto tiempo ‖ FAM menudo, da; valiente (with irony); *some friend you are* menudo amigo eres; *some help you were* menuda ayuda me diste | extraordinario, ria (very good); *it was some game* fue un partido extraordinario ‖ — *do you want some tea?* ¿quieres té? ¿quieres un poco de té? ‖ *for some reason or other* por alguna razón, por una razón o por otra ‖ *I gave him some money* le di un poco de *or* algo de dinero ‖ *I have some money* tengo dinero, tengo un poco *or* algo de dinero ‖ *I'll give it some thought* lo pensaré ‖ *in some regulation or other* en algún reglamento, en algún que otro reglamento ‖ *some day* algún día, algún día de éstos, un día de éstos ‖ *some hopes!* ¡espérate sentado! ‖ *some luck!* ¡vaya suerte! ‖ *some meal!* ¡vaya comida! ‖ *some people I could mention* algunos a quienes podría nombrar ‖ *some other time* o *day* otro día ‖ *some way or other* de una manera o de otra, de cualquier manera ‖ *that was some party!* ¡eso sí que fue una buena fiesta!, ¡menuda fiesta! ‖ *they must have found some other way* han debido encontrar algún otro medio ‖ *they only finished some of the food* sólo terminaron una parte de la comida ‖ *try to get some sleep* intenta dormir un poco.

◆ *pron* algunos, nas; unos, unas; *some left and some stayed* algunos se fueron y otros se quedaron ‖ un poco; *some of that paper* un poco de ese papel; *this cake is nice, do you want some?* este pastel está muy rico, ¿quieres un poco? ‖ algunos, nas; *some of my friends* algunos de mis amigos ‖ parte *f*; *some of the time* parte del tiempo; *I liked some of the film* me gustó parte de la película, la película me gustó en parte; *some of what he said* parte de lo que dijo ‖ — *and then some* y algunos más ‖ *I already have some, thank you* ya tengo, gracias ‖ *I've no money I have some* no tengo dinero. yo sí tengo ‖ *please take some* tome un poco (a little), tome unos cuantos (a few) ‖ *there are some who would disagree* los hay *or* hay algunos que no estarían de acuerdo, hay quienes no estarían de acuerdo.

◆ *adv* unos, unas; *some six months* unos seis meses; *some 500 people* unas quinientas personas; *some few* unos pocos, unos cuantos ‖ US FAM un poco, algo (a little); *we chatted some* charlamos un poco | bastante (quite a lot).

somebody [-bədi]; **someone** [sʌmwʌn] *pron* alguien; *somebody is calling you* alguien te está llamando ‖ alguien, alguno, na; *somebody probably picked it up* lo habrá cogido alguno *or* alguien ‖ — *somebody was asking for you* alguien estaba preguntando por ti, han estado preguntando por ti ‖ *somebody else* otro, otra; algún otro, alguna otra.

◆ *n* personaje *m*, alguien; *he must be somebody to receive a welcome like that* debe ser alguien *or* un personaje para que le hagan tal recibimiento; *he thinks he is somebody* se cree alguien.

someday [-dei] *adv* algún día.

somehow [-hau] *adv* de algún modo, de una forma o de otra; *we shall manage somehow* nos las arreglaremos de algún modo ‖ por alguna razón (for some unknown reason) ‖ *this doesn't seem right to me somehow* no sé por qué, pero no me parece bien.

someone [-wʌn] *pron/n* ⟶ **somebody.**

someplace [-pleis] *adv* US ⟶ **somewhere.**

somersault; summersault [ˈsʌməsɔːlt] *n* salto *m* mortal; *back somersault* salto mortal hacia atrás; *to turn a somersault* dar un salto mortal ‖ vuelta *f* de campana (of a car, etc.); *to turn a somersault* dar una vuelta de campana ‖ FIG cambio *m* total.

somersault; summersault [ˈsʌməsɔːlt] *vi* dar un salto mortal (a person) ‖ dar una vuelta de campana, volcar (a car, etc.).

something [ˈsʌmθiŋ] *pron/n* algo; *there must be something we can do* debe de haber algo que podamos hacer; *something to eat* algo de comer; *I need something to eat* necesito comer algo; *something of a problem* algo problemático ‖ — *a hundred and something* ciento y pico ‖ *her name is Mary something* se llama Mary algo *or* Mary y no sé qué más ‖ *her name is Mary Trotter or something* se llama Mary Trotter o algo así *or* algo por el estilo, se llama algo así como Mary Trotter ‖ *his new book is quite something* su nuevo libro es algo extraordinario ‖ *is something the matter?* ¿le pasa algo?, ¿pasa algo? ‖ *it's quite something to be able to speak six languages* no es cualquier cosa hablar seis idiomas ‖ *she has a certain something* tiene un no sé qué ‖ *something else* otra cosa; *and there's something else* y hay otra cosa; algo extraordinario; *that film was something else!* ¡esa película fue algo extraordinario! ‖ *something like* algo como ‖ *something of a coward* algo cobarde ‖ *something of the kind* algo por el estilo ‖ *something or other* una cosa u otra, alguna cosa ‖ *that certain something was missing* faltaba un no sé qué ‖ *the figure represents something of an increase* la cifra demuestra cierto aumento ‖ *there's something in his theory* su teoría tiene cierto valor ‖ *to be something of an artist* tener algo de artista ‖ *to see something of s.o.* ver a alguien de vez en cuando ‖ *well, that's something* ya es algo.

◆ *adv* algo; *something over fifty* algo más de cincuenta; *something like fifty pounds* algo así como cincuenta libras; *something like yours* algo parecido al tuyo ‖ — FAM *it hurts something shocking* duele una barbaridad | *now that's something like it!* ¡eso sí que es!

sometime [ˈsʌmtaim] *adv* algún día, alguna vez ‖ — *sometime before Saturday* antes del sábado ‖ *sometime last week* (un día de) la semana pasada ‖ *sometime next week* (un día de) la semana que viene ‖ *sometime or other* tarde o temprano (sooner or later) ‖ *sometime soon* pronto, algún día de estos.

◆ *adj* ex, antiguo, gua; *the sometime chairman* el ex presidente.

sometimes [-z] *adv* de vez en cuando, a veces, unas veces ‖ *sometimes... sometimes...* unas veces... y otras...; ya... ya; *sometimes sad sometimes gay* ya triste, ya alegre.

someway [ˈsʌmwei]; **someways** [-z] *adv* de alguna manera.

somewhat [ˈsʌmwɔt] *adv* algo, un poco; *to be somewhat surprised* estar algo sorprendido.

◆ *n* algo *m*; *he was somewhat of a coward, of an athlete* tenía algo de cobarde, de atleta ‖ *this is somewhat of a relief* en cierto modo es un alivio.

somewhere [ˈsʌmwɛə*] *adv* en alguna parte; *somewhere in the world* en alguna parte del mundo ‖ a alguna parte (with motion) ‖ — *somewhere between* entre; *somewhere between two and three o'clock* entre las dos y las tres; de; *somewhere between two and three weeks* de dos a tres semanas ‖ *somewhere else* en otra parte (without motion), a otra parte (with motion) ‖ *somewhere in the region of twenty pounds* unas veinte libras poco más o menos ‖ *somewhere near here* cerca de aquí, por aquí.

◆ *n* sitio *m*, lugar *m*.

somnambulate [sɔmˈnæmbjuleit] *vi* andar dormido.

somnambulism [sɔmˈnæmbjulizəm] *n* sonambulismo *m*, somnambulismo *m*.

somnambulist [sɔmˈnæmbjulist] *n* sonámbulo, la; somnámbulo, la.

somniferous [sɔmˈnifərəs] *adj* somnífero, ra.

somniloquist [sɔmˈniləkwist] *n* persona que habla dormida, somnílocuo, cua.

somnolence [ˈsɔmnələns]; **somnolency** [-i] *n* somnolencia *f*.

somnolent [ˈsɔmnələnt] *adj* soñoliento, ta; somnoliento, ta; somnolento, ta.

son [sʌn] *n* hijo *m*; *eldest, youngest son* hijo mayor, menor ‖ FIG hijo *m*; *the sons of Spain* los hijos de España ‖ — FAM *every mother's son* todo quisque, todo hijo de vecino ‖ *prodigal son* hijo pródigo ‖ *second son* segundogénito *m*, segundón *m* ‖ POP *son of a bitch!* ¡hijo de puta! ‖ REL *the Son* el Hijo (second person of the Trinity).

sonance [ˈsəunəns] *n* sonoridad *f*.

sonant [ˈsəunənt] *adj* sonoro, ra.

◆ *n* GRAMM sonora *f* (consonant).

sonar [ˈsəunɑː*] *n* TECH sonar *m*.

sonata [səˈnɑːtə] *n* MUS sonata *f*.

sonatina [ˈsɔnəˈtiːnə] *n* MUS sonatina *f*.

sonde [sɔnd] *n* sonda *f*.

son et lumière [ˌsɔ̃eluːˈmjeːr] *n* espectáculo *m* de luz y sonido.

song [sɔŋ] *n* canto *m* (art of singing) ‖ canción *f* (musical composition); *to sing a romantic song* cantar una canción romántica ‖ canto *m* (of birds) ‖ FIG rumor *m* (of waves) | poesía *f*, canto *m* (poetry) ‖ REL cántico *m* ‖ — *drinking song* canción báquica ‖ *hit song* éxito *m* ‖ *song festival* festival *m* de la canción ‖ FIG & FAM *there's no need to make such a song and dance about it* no es para tanto ‖ REL *the Song of Songs* el Cantar de los Cantares ‖ *to burst into song* empezar a cantar ‖ FIG & FAM *to buy sth. for a song* comprar algo por una bicoca *or* por cuatro cuartos ‖ US FAM *to give s.o. a song and dance* contarle toda una historia a alguien, colocarle un rollo a alguien ‖ FIG *to make a song and dance* armar un follón | *to sing the same old song* volver a la misma cantilena.

songbird [-bəːd] *n* ave *f* canora, pájaro *m* cantor.

songbook [-buk] *n* cancionero *m*.

songster [-stə*] *n* ave *f* canora, pájaro *m* cantor (bird) ‖ MUS cantor *m*, cantante *m*.

songstress [-stris] *n* cantante *f*, cantora *f*.

songwriter [-ˈraitə*] *n* compositor, ra (who composes the music) ‖ autor *m* de la letra (lyrics writer) ‖ autor *m* de canciones (who composes the lyrics and music).

sonic [ˈsɔnik] *adj* acústico, ca; *sonic depth finder* sonda acústica ‖ sónico, ca (of the speed of sound) ‖ — *sonic bang* o *boom* estampido supersónico ‖ *sonic barrier* barrera *f* del sonido.

son-in-law [ˈsʌninlɔː] *n* yerno *m*, hijo *m* político.

— OBSERV El plural de *son-in-law* es *sons-in-law*.

sonnet [ˈsɔnit] *n* POET soneto *m*.

sonneteer [ˈsɔniˈtiə*] *n* sonetista *m*.

sonny [ˈsʌni] *n* FAM hijito *m*, hijo *m*.

sonometer [səuˈnɔmitə*] *n* sonómetro *m*.

sonority [səˈnɔriti] *n* sonoridad *f*.

sonorous [səˈnɔːrəs] *adj* sonoro, ra.

sonorousness [-nis] *n* sonoridad *f*.

soon [suːn] *adv* pronto, dentro de poco (within a short time); *it will soon be dinner time* pronto será la hora de cenar ‖ pronto; *write to me soon* escríbeme pronto ‖ rápidamente, en seguida (quickly); *he will soon solve the problem* en seguida resolverá el problema ‖ pronto, temprano (early); *you needn't go so soon* no necesitas marcharte tan pronto; *to arrive too soon* llegar demasiado temprano ‖ — *as soon as* o *so soon as* en cuanto, nada más; *as soon as she saw him she remembered him* en cuanto lo vio se acordó de él ‖ *as soon as possible* en cuanto pueda, cuanto antes, lo más pronto posible;

he came as soon as possible vino en cuanto pudo; *we will come as soon as possible* vendremos en cuanto podamos || *how soon can you send it?* ¿cuándo me lo puede mandar? || *how soon will it be ready?* ¿para cuándo estará listo? || *it's still too soon to ask him* todavía es muy pronto *or* es demasiado pronto todavía para preguntárselo || *I would as soon* o *I had sooner do it by myself* me gustaría más *or* preferiría hacerlo yo solo || *my holidays ended all too soon* mis vacaciones acabaron demasiado pronto || *no sooner... than* en cuanto, nada más; *no sooner had he arrived than he began to complain* en cuanto llegó *or* nada más llegar empezó a quejarse; *no sooner had he arrived than they interrupted the concert* nada más llegar él *or* en cuanto llegó interrumpieron el concierto || *no sooner said than done* dicho y hecho || *soon after* poco después; *soon after twelve* poco después de las doce || *sooner or later* tarde o temprano || *sooner than* antes que || *the reinforcements arrived none too soon* los refuerzos llegaron justo en el momento oportuno || *the sooner... the better* cuanto más pronto... mejor; *the sooner you do it, the better it will be for you* cuanto más pronto lo hagas, mejor será para ti || *the sooner the better* cuanto antes mejor.

soot [sut] *n* hollín *m*.

sooth [su:θ] *n* realidad *f*; *in sooth* en realidad.

soothe [su:ð] *vt* apaciguar, calmar, tranquilizar, sosegar (to calm) || aplacar (temper, anger, etc.) || aliviar, calmar (pain).

soothing [-iŋ] *adj* MED calmante, sedante || tranquilizador, ra (calming) || dulce (sweet).

soothsayer ['su:θ'seiə*] *n* adivino, na.

soothsaying ['su:θ'seiiŋ] *n* adivinación *f*.

sootiness ['sutinis] *n* fuliginosidad *f* (resemblance to soot) || suciedad *f* (dirtiness).

sooty ['suti] *adj* fuliginoso, sa (like soot) || cubierto de hollín (soot covered) || negro como el hollín (as black as soot).

sop [sɔp] *n* sopa *f* (bread soaked in liquid) || soborno *m*, regalo *m* (bribe) || compensación *f* (compensation).

sop [sɔp] *vt* remojar || *to sop up* absorber.

sophism ['sɔfizəm] *n* sofisma *m*.

sophist ['sɔfist] *n* sofista *m*.

sophistic [sə'fistik]; **sophistical** [-əl] *adj* sofístico, ca; sofista.

sophisticate [sə'fistikeit] *vt* sofisticar (to make complex or affected) || falsificar (a text) || adulterar (wine) || perfeccionar (system, method, mechanism, etc.).

sophisticated [-id] *adj* sofisticado, da; complejo, ja; complicado, da (made complex) || falsificado, da (text) || adulterado, da (wine) || perfeccionado, da (system, method, etc.) || sofisticado, da; carente de naturalidad (person).

sophistication [səˌfisti'keiʃən] *n* sofisticación *f*, complejidad *f* (complexity) || perfección *f* (perfection) || sofisticación *f*, falta *f* de naturalidad (affectation).

sophistry ['sɔfistri] *n* sofistería *f* (the use of sophisms) || sofisma *m* (sophism).

Sophocles ['sɔfəkli:z] *pr n* Sofocles *m*.

sophomore ['sɔfəmɔ:*] *n* US estudiante *m* & *f* de segundo año.

sophomoric [sɔfə'mɔ:rik] *adj* US de estudiante de segundo año || FIG carente de madurez (immature).

soporific [sɔpə'rifik] *adj* soporífico, ca; soporífero, ra.
◆ *n* somnífero *m* (sleep pill).

sopping ['sɔpiŋ] *adj* empapado, da || *sopping wet* calado hasta los huesos (person), empapado, da (thing).

soppy ['sɔpi] *adj* empapado, da (soaked) || FAM bobo, ba; tonto, ta (silly) | sensiblero, ra (foolishly sentimental).

soprano [sə'prɑ:nəu] *n* MUS soprano *m* & *f*.
◆ *adj* de soprano.

sorb [sɔ:b] *n* BOT serbal *m* (tree) | serba *f* (fruit) || *sorb apple* serba *f*.

sorbet ['sɔ:bət] *n* sorbete *m*.

sorcerer ['sɔ:sərə*] *n* brujo *m*, hechicero *m*.

sorceress ['sɔ:səris] *n* bruja *f*, hechicera *f*.

sorcery ['sɔ:səri] *n* brujería *f*, hechicería *f*.

sordid ['sɔ:did] *adj* sórdido, da; *sordid dwellings* viviendas sórdidas || sucio, cia; *a sordid affair* un asunto sucio; *a sordid story* una historia sucia || sórdido, da (mean, contemptible).

sordidness [-nis] *n* sordidez *f* || suciedad *f*.

sordino [sɔ:'di:nəu] *n* MUS sordina *f*.
— OBSERV El plural de *sordino* es *sordini*.

sore [sɔ:*] *adj* malo, la (bad); *a sore foot* un pie malo || dolorido, da; que duele, doloroso, sa (which hurts) || FIG doloroso, sa; *a sore memory* un recuerdo doloroso || grande; *a sore disappointment* una gran decepción; *sore need* gran necesidad | penoso, sa (work, etc.) || US FAM molesto, ta; resentido, da; *to feel sore about not being promoted* sentirse molesto *or* estar resentido por no haber sido ascendido || — FIG *a sore point* o *subject* un tema delicado, un asunto espinoso || *his wound is still very sore* todavía le duele mucho la herida || *my eyes are sore* me pican *or* me duelen los ojos || *my nose is sore* me duele la nariz || FIG *to be sore at heart* tener el corazón dolorido || US FAM *to be sore at s.o.* estar enfadado con alguien | *to get sore* ofenderse (to take offence), enfadarse (*at* con) (to get angry) || *to have a sore throat* dolerle a uno la garganta, tener dolor de garganta.
◆ *n* llaga *f*, úlcera *f* (on people) || FIG dolor *m*, pena *f* || FIG *to reopen an old sore* renovar la herida.
◆ *adv* → **sorely.**

sorehead [-hed] *n* US FAM cascarrabias *m* & *f inv*, resentido, da.

sorely [-li] *adv* muy (very) || mucho (a lot) || profundamente (deeply); *sorely offended* profundamente ofendido || gravemente (seriously) || — *to be sorely afraid* tener mucho miedo || *to be sorely tempted to* sentir una gran tentación de || *when the sorely needed supplies arrived* cuando llegaron las provisiones que tanta falta hacían.

soreness [-nis] *n* dolor *m* (pain) || US resentimiento *m* (resentment).

sorghum ['sɔ:gəm] *n* BOT zahína *f*, sorgo *m*.

sorites [sə'raiti:z] *inv n* PHIL sorites *m*.

sorority [sə'rɔriti] *n* US club *m* femenino de estudiantes.

sorption ['sɔ:pʃən] *n* absorción *f*, adsorción *f*.

sorrel ['sɔrəl] *adj* alazán, ana.
◆ *n* alazán *m* (colour) || alazán *m* (horse) || BOT acedera *f*.

sorrow ['sɔrəu] *n* tristeza *f*, pesar *m*, dolor *m*, pena *f* (sadness) || — *more in sorrow than in anger* con más pesar que enojo || *much to my sorrow* con gran pesar mío || FIG *to drown one's sorrows* ahogar sus penas.

sorrow ['sɔrəu] *vi* entristecerse (to become sad) || sentir pesar *or* pena, sentirse afligido (to feel sorrow); *to sorrow over sth.* sentir pesar *or* pena por algo || *to sorrow for* añorar.

sorrowful [-ful] *adj* afligido, da; triste, pesaroso, sa (air, person) || entristecedor, ra; triste, lastimoso, sa; doloroso, sa (news, sight, etc.).

sorrow-stricken [-'strikən] *adj* muy afligido, da.

sorry ['sɔri] *adj* triste; *a sorry sight* un triste espectáculo; *the sorry truth* la triste verdad *or* realidad || — *a sorry fellow* un infeliz, un desgraciado || *I can't say I'm sorry to hear it* no puedo decir que lo sienta || *I don't want you to feel sorry for me* no quiero que me tengas lástima *or* que tengas pena por mí || *I'm not at all sorry for what I did* no me arrepiento en absoluto de *or* no me pesa nada lo que hice || *I'm sorry about the other night* siento lo que ocurrió la otra noche, me disculpo por lo de la otra noche || *to be in a sorry plight* estar en una situación lamentable || *to be in a sorry state* estar en un estado lamentable *or* lastimoso || *to be sorry* sentir; *I'm very sorry* lo siento mucho; *to be sorry about not having done sth.* sentir no haber hecho algo; *I was sorry not to be there* sentí mucho no estar allí; *I am sorry to have to tell you* siento tener que decirle; arrepentirse, sentir; *you'll be sorry!* ¡te arrepentirás! || *to feel sorry for* compadecer; *I feel sorry for him* le compadezco; sentir (to regret) || *to feel sorry for o.s.* sentirse desgraciado.
◆ *interj* ¡perdone!, ¡perdóneme!, ¡disculpe!, ¡perdón!, ¡lo siento!

sort [sɔ:t] *n* clase *f*, tipo *m*; *all sorts of flowers* toda clase de flores; *and all that sort of thing* y todo ese tipo de cosas || especie *f*; *it formed a sort of arch* formaba una especie de arco || modo *m*, forma *f*, manera *f* (manner) || tipo *m* (type of person); *to be a strange sort* ser un tipo extraño || persona *f* (person); *to be a good sort* ser buena persona || INFORM ordenación *f* || — *after a sort* en cierta manera || *an unusual sort of film* una película extraña || *a sort of big black ball* una especie de bola grande y negra || *did you tell him? sort of* ¿se lo has dicho? en cierto modo || *he has bought some sort of sports car* ha comprado no sé qué clase de coche deportivo || *he sort of smiled* esbozó una especie de sonrisa || *he's some sort of officer* es oficial, pero no sé qué graduación tiene || *he's the sort that will take advantage* es de los que se aprovechan || *I know his sort* sé la clase de persona que es || *I'm sort of lost* estoy como perdido || *is this the sort of thing you had in mind?* ¿es eso *or* es algo así lo que busca usted? || *it's sort of big* es más bien grande || *it's sort of presentable* está más o menos presentable || *it takes all sorts to make a world* de todo hay en el mundo *or* en la viña del Señor || *nothing of the sort!* ¡nada de eso!, ¡ni hablar! || *of a sort, of sorts* una especie de; *there is a cupboard of sorts* hay una especie de aparador || *out of sorts* pachucho, cha (unwell), de mal humor, enfadado, da (cross) || *she's not that sort of woman* no es de ésas || *something of the sort* algo por el estilo || *to have a sort of idea that* tener una ligera idea de que.

sort [sɔ:t] *vt* seleccionar (to select) || clasificar (to classify) || ordenar, arreglar (to put in order) || — *to sort goods into lots* distribuir mercancías en lotes || *to sort out* separar; *to sort out the good from the bad* separar lo bueno de lo malo; apartar; *to sort out the bad ones* apartar los malos; resolver (problems, difficulties), ordenar, arreglar (to put in order), seleccionar (to select), clasificar (to classify) || FAM *to sort s.o. out* ajustarle a uno las cuentas.

sorter [-ə*] *n* clasificador, ra (person) || clasificadora *f* (machine).

sortie ['sɔ:ti] *n* MIL salida *f*.

sortilege ['sɔ:tilidʒ] *n* sortilegio *m*.

sorting ['sɔ:tiŋ] *n* clasificación *f* || INFORM clasificación *f* || *sorting office* sala *f* de batalla (in post office).

sort-out ['sɔ:taut] *n* FAM *to have a sort-out* ordenar, arreglar.

SOS [esəu'es] *n* SOS *m*; *to pick up an SOS* recibir un SOS.

so-so ['səusəu] *adj/adv* regular.

sot [sɔt] *n* borracho, cha.

sottish ['sɔtiʃ] *adj* borracho, cha; embrutecido por la bebida.

sotto voce ['sɔtəu'vəutʃi] *adv* en voz baja.

sou [su:] *n* (ant) moneda *f* francesa de cinco *or* diez céntimos ‖ FAM gorda *f*, perra *f*, céntimo *m* [AMER centavo *m*]; *they haven't a sou* no tienen una gorda.

soubrette [su:'bret] *n* THEATR confidenta *f*.

soubriquet ['su:brikei] *n* apodo *m*, mote *m* (nickname).

Soudan [su'dɑ:n] *pr n* GEOGR Sudán *m*.

Soudanese [ˌsu:də'ni:z] *adj/n* sudanés, esa.

souffle [su:fl] *n* MED soplo *m*.

soufflé ['su:flei] *n* CULIN "soufflé" *m*.

sough [sau] *n* murmullo *m*, susurro *m*.

sough [sau] *vi* murmurar, susurrar.

sought [sɔ:t] *pret/pp* → **seek.**

sought-after [-'ɑ:ftə*] *adj* solicitado, da (job, person, etc.) ‖ deseado, da (desired) ‖ codiciado, da (coveted).

soul [səul] *n* alma *f*; *to commend one's soul to God* encomendar su alma a Dios; *with all one's soul* con toda el alma ‖ FIG imagen *f*, personificación *f*, mismo, ma; *to be the soul of honour* ser la personificación del honor, ser el honor mismo ‖ FAM garra *f*; *his performance lacks soul* su actuación carece de garra ‖ — *a good* o *a simple soul* un alma de Dios ‖ REL *All Souls' Day* Día *m* de Difuntos ‖ *bless my soul!* ¡Dios mío! ‖ *every living soul* todo ser viviente ‖ *God rest his soul* que Dios le tenga en su gloria ‖ *like a lost soul* como un alma en pena ‖ *not a soul was in sight* no se veía ni un alma ‖ *poor little soul* pobre criatura *f* ‖ *poor soul* pobre *m* & *f*, pobrecito, ta ‖ *put some soul into it!* ¡venga, un poco de ánimo! ‖ *the ship went down with all souls* el barco se hundió con todos los que iban a bordo ‖ FIG *to be the life and soul of the party* ser el alma de la fiesta | *to be the soul of discretion* ser la discreción personificada | *to throw o.s. life and soul* o *body and soul into sth.* darse de lleno a algo, entregarse cuerpo y alma a algo | *unable to call one's soul one's own* completamente esclavizado ‖ *upon my soul!* ¡por mi vida!, ¡vaya por Dios!

soul-destroying [-dis'trɔiiŋ] *adj* embrutecedor, ra.

soul-felt [-felt] *adj* sincero, ra; sentido, da (sincere).

soulful [-ful] *adj* lleno de sentimiento (showing feeling) ‖ expresivo, va (expressive) ‖ sentimental ‖ conmovedor, ra (moving).

soulless [-lis] *adj* sin alma (having no soul) ‖ inexpresivo, va (unexpressive) ‖ monótono, na; sin interés (dull, boring).

soul mate [-meit] *n* amigo *m* del alma, amiga *f* del alma.

soul music [-ˌmju:zik] *n* soul *m*, música *f* soul.

soul-searching [] *n* reflexión *f*, examen *m* de conciencia; *after much soul-searching* después de una profunda reflexión.

soul-stirring [-stə:riŋ] *adj* emocionante (exciting) ‖ conmovedor, ra (moving).

sound [saund] *adj* sano, na (healthy) ‖ bueno, na; *sound character* buen carácter; *sound health* buena salud; *sound investment* buena inversión; *sound piece of advice, argument* buen consejo, argumento ‖ profundo, da (sleep) ‖ válido, da (valid) ‖ bien fundado, da (well-founded) ‖ razonado, da; lógico, ca (reasoned) ‖ acertado, da (propitious); *a sound policy considering the situation* una política acertada dada la situación ‖ competente (competent) ‖ sólido, da (strong) ‖ seguro, ra (trustworthy) ‖ ortodoxo, xa (orthodox) ‖ COMM solvente (solvent) | seguro, ra (business) ‖ MAR en buen estado, en buenas condiciones (goods, ship) ‖ — *safe and sound* sano y salvo ‖ FIG *to be sound as a bell* ser muy seguro (to be very solid), estar más sano que una manzana (to be healthy) ‖ *to be sound asleep* estar profundamente dormido ‖ *to be sound in body and mind* ser sano de cuerpo y alma ‖ *to be sound in wind and limb* estar más sano que una manzana ‖ *to be sound of mind* o *of sound mind* estar en su sano juicio.
◆ *n* sonido *m*; *the sound of her voice* el sonido de su voz ‖ ruido *m* (noise); *the sound of wheels* el ruido de las ruedas ‖ MAR estrecho *m* (channel connecting two seas) | brazo *m* de mar (ocean inlet) ‖ MED sonda *f* ‖ ZOOL vejiga *f* natatoria ‖ — FIG & FAM *I don't like the sound of it* no me huele bien ‖ *light and sound* luz y sonido ‖ *the speed of sound* la velocidad del sonido ‖ *to live within the sound of the sea* vivir a orilas del mar *or* donde todavía se oye el romper de las olas ‖ *to the sound of* al son de ‖ *we camped within the sound of the battle* desde donde acampamos se oían los cañonazos ‖ *within, out of sound* al alcance, fuera del oído.
◆ *adv* *to sleep sound* dormir profundamente.

sound [saund] *vt* tocar; *to sound the trumpets* tocar las trompetas; *to sound the bells* tocar las campanas; *to sound the retreat* tocar retreta ‖ pronunciar; *sound your consonants clearly* pronuncia bien las consonantes ‖ MED auscultar (with a stethoscope) | sondar (with a sound) ‖ MAR sondar, sondear, escandallar (to measure the depth of) | estudiar, examinar (the ocean floor, seabed, etc.) ‖ FIG sondear, tantear (s.o.'s opinion) ‖ — FIG *to sound s.o. out* tantear *or* sondear a alguien ‖ *to sound the horn* tocar el claxon.
◆ *vi* sonar; *the alarm, a gun, a bell sounded* sonó la alarma, un tiro, una campana; *piano note that is not sounding* una nota de piano que no suena; *it sounds like an aircraft* suena como un avión; *it sounds hollow, full* suena a hueco, a lleno ‖ FIG sonar; *it sounds wrong, funny* suena mal, raro | parecer; *it sounds marvellous, silly* parece estupendo, tonto | sonar; *it sounds like a lie to me* me suena a mentira ‖ sumergirse (a whale) ‖ MAR hacer sondeos, sondear (to measure the depth of water) ‖ US FAM *to sound off about sth.* protestar a voz en grito sobre algo.

sound absorber [-əb'sɔ:bə*] *n* amortiguador *m* del sonido.

sound barrier [-ˌbæriə*] *n* barrera *f* del sonido.

soundboard [-bɔ:d] *n* MUS tabla *f* de armonía (of piano) | secreto *m* (of organ) ‖ tornavoz *m* (to reflect the voice).

sound box [-bɔks] *n* captador *m* acústico (of gramophone) ‖ caja *f* de resonancia (of musical instrument).

sound effects [-iˌfekts] *pl n* efectos *m* sonoros.

sound film [-film] *n* película *f* sonora.

sound head [-hed] *n* cabeza *f* sonora.

sound hole [-həul] *n* ese *f* (of a violin).

sounding [-iŋ] *adj* resonante, sonoro, ra (resonant) ‖ sonoro, ra (making a sound) ‖ altisonante (highsounding) ‖ — *sounding balloon* globo *m* sonda ‖ *sounding board* tabla *f* de armonía (of a piano), secreto *m* (of an organ), tornavoz *m* (to reflect the voice), portavoz *m*; *the government uses the press as a sounding board* el gobierno emplea la prensa como portavoz ‖ *sounding line* o *lead* sonda *f*, escandallo *m*, sondaleza *f*.
◆ *n* MAR & GEOL sondeo *m* ‖ FIG sondeo *m* (of opinion).

soundless [-lis] *adj* mudo, da (silent) ‖ silencioso, sa; sin ruido (noiseless) ‖ insondable, sin fondo (bottomless).

soundlessly [-lisli] *adv* sin sonido, silenciosamente, sin ruido (silently).

soundly [-li] *adv* sólidamente (firmly) ‖ sensatamente; *he advised them soundly* les aconsejó sensatamente ‖ profundamente; *he slept soundly all through the journey* durmió profundamente durante todo el viaje ‖ *to thrash s.o. soundly* dar una buena paliza a alguien (to punish, to defeat).

soundness [-nis] *n* validez *f* (validity) ‖ seguridad *f* (of an investment) ‖ firmeza *f*, solidez *f* (firmness) ‖ acierto *m*, sensatez *f* (good sense) ‖ solvencia *f* (solvency) ‖ *soundness of health* buena salud.

sound post [-pəust] *n* alma *f* (of a violin).

soundproof [-pru:f] *adj* a prueba de sonido, insonoro, ra.

soundproof [-pru:f] *vt* insonorizar.

soundproofing [-'pru:fiŋ] *n* aislante *m* acústico (material) ‖ insonorización *f* (action).

sound track [-træk] *n* banda *f* sonora, pista *f* sonora.

sound wave [-weiv] *n* onda *f* sonora *or* acústica.

soup [su:p] *n* sopa *f*; *tomato soup* sopa de tomate; *vegetable soup* sopa de verduras *or* de legumbres ‖ FAM niebla *f* espesa (fog) ‖ — US FAM *from soup to nuts* de cabo a rabo ‖ FIG & FAM *to be in the soup* estar en un apuro *or* en un aprieto.
◆ *adj* sopero, ra; *soup dish* plato sopero ‖ — *soup kitchen* comedor *m* de beneficencia ‖ *soup ladle* cucharón *m* ‖ *soup tureen* sopera *f*.

soup [su:p] *vt* FAM *to soup up* aumentar la potencia de (a car).

soupçon ['su:psˉɔ:ŋ] *n* pizca *f*, algo *m*; *a soupçon of irony* una pizca de ironía.

soup spoon ['su:pspu:n] *n* cuchara *f* sopera.

soupy ['su:pi] *adj* espeso, sa.

sour ['sauə*] *adj* ácido, da; agrio, gria; amargo, ga; *sour taste* sabor agrio ‖ acre (smell) ‖ cortado, da; *sour milk* leche cortada ‖ rancio, cia (bread) ‖ FIG amargo, ga; *a sour smile* una sonrisa amarga | acre, desabrido, da (character) | agrio, gria; amargado, da; *a sour person* una persona agria ‖ — CULIN *sour cream* nata *f* *or* crema *f* agria ‖ FIG *sour grapes* ¡están verdes! ‖ *to turn sour* cortarse (milk), agriarse (wine, etc.), agriarse (character, situation, etc.).

sour [sauə*] *vt* agriar ‖ cortar (milk) ‖ poner rancio (bread) ‖ FIG amargar; *her death soured his caracter* su muerte le amargó el carácter.
◆ *vi* agriarse ‖ cortarse (milk) ‖ ponerse rancio (bread) ‖ FIG amargarse (to furn britter).

source [sɔ:s] *n* nacimiento *m*, manantial *m* (of a river) ‖ FIG fuente *f*, origen *m*; *the source of the trouble* el origen del problema | fuente *f* (of supply, of information); *well-informed sources* fuentes bien informadas ‖ MED foco *m* (of infection) ‖ — *reliable source* fuente fidedigna ‖ *source book* libro *m* de consulta ‖ INFORM *source program* programa *m* fuente.

sourdine [suə'di:n] *n* MUS sordina *f*.

sour-faced ['sauəfeist] *adj* arisco, ca.

sourly ['sauəli] *adv* agriamente.

sourness ['sauənis] *n* amargura *f*, acidez *f* (of taste) ‖ FIG acritud *f*, desabrimiento *m* (of character).

sourpuss ['sauəpus] *n* FAM persona *f* desabrida.

soursop ['sauəsɔp] *n* BOT guanábano *m* (tree) | guanábana *f* (fruit).

sousaphone ['su:zəfəun] *n* US MUS instrumento *m* de cobre parecido a la tuba.

souse [saus] *n* conserva *f* en vinagre (pickled food) ‖ adobo *m* (preparation for pickling meat) ‖ escabeche *m* (for pickling fish) ‖ remojón *m* (soaking) || FAM borracho, cha (drunkard).

souse [saus] *vt* adobar (meat) || escabechar (fish) || empapar (to soak) || sumergir (to plunge) || — FAM *to be soused* estar trompa (drunk) | *to get soused* empaparse, calarse (to get soaked), entromparse, coger una trompa (to get drunk).

soutache ['sutæʃ] *n* trencilla *f*.

soutane ['su:tæn] *n* sotana *f*.

south [sauθ] *n* sur *m* (direction) || sur *m*, mediodía *m* (region).
◆ *adj* del sur; *south wind* viento del sur || — *South Pole* Polo *m* Sur || *South Seas* mares *m* del Sur.
◆ *adv* hacia el sur; *to travel south* viajar hacia el sur || al sur; *my house lies south of London* mi casa está al sur de Londres; *my window looks south* mi ventana da al sur.

south [sauθ] *vi* MAR ir rumbo al sur.

South Africa [-'æfrikə] *pr n* GEOGR África *f* del Sur (the South of Africa) | República *f* Sudafricana, África *f* del Sur (South African Republic).

South African [-'æfrikən] *adj/n* sudafricano, na.

South America [-ə'merikə] *pr n* GEOGR Sudamérica *f*, Suramérica *f*, América *f* del Sur.

South American [-ə'merikən] *adj/n* sudamericano, na; suramericano, na.

southbound [-baund] *adj* con rumbo al sur.

south by east [-bai'i:st] *n* sur *m* cuarta al sudeste.

south by west [-bai'west] *n* sur *m* cuarta al suroeste.

South Carolina [sauθ,kærə'laina] *pr n* GEOGR Carolina del Sur.

South Dakota [sauθdə'kautə] *pr n* GEOGR Dakota del Sur.

southeast [-'i:st] *n* sudeste *m*.
◆ *adj* del sudeste (of the southeast) || sudeste (direction, part).
◆ *adv* hacia el sudeste.

southeast by east [-i:stbai'i:st] *n* sudeste *m* cuarta al este.

southeast by south [-i:stbai'sauθ] *n* sudeste *m* cuarta al sur.

southeaster [-'i:stə*] *n* viento *m* del sudeste.

southeasterly [-'i:stəli] *adj* sudeste (direction) || del sudeste (wind).
◆ *adv* hacia el sudeste.

southeastern [-'i:stən] *adj* del sudeste (of the southeast) || sudeste (direction, part).

southeastward [-'i:stwəd]; **southeastwards** [-'i:stwədz] *adv* hacia el sudeste || MAR rumbo al sudeste.

southerly ['sʌðəli] *adj* en el sur (in the south) || del sur (wind) || sur (part, direction) || *the most southerly part* la parte más meridional.
◆ *adv* hacia el sur.

southern ['sʌðən] *adj* sur, meridional; *the southern part of the country* la parte sur del país || del sur; *the southern region* la región del sur || hacia el sur, sur; *in a southern direction* en dirección sur *or* hacia el sur || HIST sudista || — *southern Asia* el sur de Asia || *Southern Cross* Cruz *f* del Sur || *southern hemisphere* hemisferio *m* sur *or* austral.

southerner [-ə*] *n* habitante *m* del sur, meridional *m* & *f* (person) || HIST sudista *m* & *f* || — *he's a southerner* es del sur || *the southerners are friendlier* la gente del sur es más abierta, los del sur *or* los meridionales son más abiertos.

southern lights [-laits] *pl n* aurora *f sing* austral.

southernmost [-məust] *adj* del extremo sur.

southernwood [-,wud] *n* BOT abrótano *m*.

South Korea ['sauθkə'riə] *pr n* GEOGR Corea *f* del Sur.

South Korean [-n] *adj/s* surcoreano, na.

southpaw ['sauθpɔ:] *adj/s* US FAM zurdo, da.

south-southeast ['sauθsauθi:st] *n* sudsudeste *m*.
◆ *adj* sudsudeste || del sudsudeste (winds).
◆ *adv* hacia el sudsudeste.

south-southwest ['sauθsauθ'west] *n* sudsudoeste *m*.
◆ *adj* sudsudoeste || del sudsudoeste (winds).
◆ *adv* hacia el sudsudoeste.

South Vietnam ['sauθ'vjet'næm] *pr n* Vietnam *m* del Sur.

South Vietnamese ['sauθ'vjetnə'mi:z] *adj/n* survietnamita.

southward ['sauθwəd] *adj* sur (direction).
◆ *adv* hacia el sur.
◆ *n* sur *m*; *to the southward* hacia el sur.

southwards [-z] *adv* hacia el sur.

southwest ['sauθ'west] *n* sudoeste *m*, suroeste *m*.
◆ *adj* del sudoeste (wind) || sudoeste (direction, part).
◆ *adv* hacia el sudoeste.

southwest by south [-bai'sauθ] *n* sudoeste *m* cuarta al sur.

southwest by west [-bai'west] *n* sudoeste *m* cuarta al oeste.

southwester [-'westə*] *n* viento *m* del sudoeste (wind) || sueste *m* (sailor's waterproof hat).

southwesterly [-'westəli] *adj* del sudoeste (wind) || sudoeste (direction).

southwestern [-'westən] *adj* del sudoeste.

southwestward [-'westwəd] *adj* sudoeste.
◆ *adv* hacia el sudoeste.

southwestwards [-'westwədz] *adv* hacia el sudoeste.

souvenir ['su:vəniə*] *n* recuerdo *m*.

sou'wester [sau'westə*] *n* sueste *m* (sailor's waterproof hat).

sovereign ['sɔvrin] *adj* soberano, na; *sovereign power, state* poder, estado soberano || eficaz (effective) || FIG soberano, na (absolute, supreme, unmitigated); *sovereign contempt* soberano desprecio.
◆ *n* soberano, na (king, etc.) || soberano *m* (coin).

sovereignty ['sɔvrənti] *n* soberanía *f* || estado *m* soberano (state).

soviet ['səuviət] *n* soviet *m*.
◆ *adj* soviético, ca; *Soviet Russia* la Rusia Soviética; *the Soviet Union* la Unión Soviética.

sovietization ['səuviəti'zeiʃən] *n* sovietización *f*.

sow [sau] *n* cerda *f* (female pig) || tejón *m* hembra (female badger) || hembra *f* (female animal) || TECH reguera *f* (ditch) | galápago *m*, lingote *m* (ingot).

sow* [səu] *vt* sembrar; *to sow wheat* sembrar trigo; *to sow a field with wheat* sembrar un campo de trigo; *to sow discontent, panic* sembrar el descontento, el pánico || FIG colocar, sembrar (mines) || introducir (ostras, anchoas, etc.) en un criadero (oysters, etc.) || — FIG *to sow on stony ground* sembrar en el desierto | *to sow the seeds of discord* sembrar la discordia.
◆ *vi* sembrar.
— OBSERV Pret. ***sowed***; pp ***sowed, sown***.

sowbread ['səu,bred] *n* BOT pamporcino *m*.

sow bug ['saubʌg] *n* cochinilla *f* (wood louse).

sower ['səuə*] *n* sembrador, ra.

sowing ['səuiŋ] *n* siembra *f* (action) || — *sowing machine* sembradora *f* || *sowing time* sementera *f*, siembra *f*.

sown [səun] *pp* → **sow.**

sow thistle ['sau,θisl] *n* BOT cerraja *f*.

soy [sɔi] *n* CULIN salsa *f* picante de soja (sauce) || soja *f* (soya bean).

soya bean ['sɔiəbi:n] *n* soja *f*.

soybean ['sɔibi:n] *n* US soja *f*.

sozzled [sɔzld] *adj* FAM trompa (drunk); *he is sozzled* está trompa || FAM *to get sozzled* coger una trompa.

spa [spɑ:] *n* balneario *m* (resort) || manantial *m* de agua mineral (spring).

space [speis] *n* espacio *m*; *a space of six metres* un espacio de seis metros; *in the space of half an hour* en el espacio de media hora; *a journey into space* un viaje al espacio; *write your name in the blank space* ponga su nombre en el espacio en blanco || sitio *m*, espacio *m* (room); *to take up a lot of space* ocupar mucho sitio || MUS & PRINT espacio *m*; *double space* doble espacio || — *space age* era *f* espacial || PRINT *space band* espaciador *m* | *space bar* barra *f* espaciadora || *space capsule* cápsula *f* espacial || PHYS *space charge* carga *f* espacial || *space flight* vuelo *m* espacial || PHYS *space lattice* red *f* cristalina || PRINT *space line* interlínea *f* || *space programme* o *program* programa *m* de vuelos espaciales || *space shot* lanzamiento *m* de un cohete espacial || *space shuttle* transbordador *m* espacial || *space station* estación *f* espacial || *space suit* traje *m* espacial || *space travel* viaje *m* espacial, viajes *m pl* espaciales || *space vehicle* vehículo *m* espacial || *space writer* escritor pagado por líneas || *to stare into space* tener la mirada perdida.

space [speis] *vt* espaciar, separar; *to space (out) posts at ten metre intervals* espaciar los postes a intervalos de diez metros || espaciar; *to space payments* espaciar los pagos; *to space lines of type* espaciar los renglones || distanciar (to move apart) || distribuir (to distribute) || MIL escalonar (to stagger) || *well spaced out* bastante separados *or* distanciados.

spacecraft [-krɑ:ft] *n* nave *f* espacial, astronave *f*, vehículo *m* espacial.

spaceman [-mən] *n* astronauta *m*, cosmonauta *m*.
— OBSERV El plural de *spaceman* es *spacemen*.

spacer [-ə*] *n* espaciador *m* (of a typewriter).

spaceship [-ʃip] *n* nave *f* espacial, astronave *f*.

space-time [-taim] *n* espacio tiempo *m*.

spaceward [-wəd] *adv* en dirección al espacio, hacia el espacio.

spacial ['speiʃəl] *adj* espacial, del espacio.

spacing ['speisiŋ] *n* espaciamiento *m* (arrangement of spaces) || espacio *m* (space, room) || PRINT espacio *m*; *double spacing* doble espacio.

spacious ['speiʃəs] *adj* espacioso, sa; amplio, plia (roomy) || amplio, plia (wide) || *to live a spacious life* vivir holgadamente.

spaciousness [-nis] *n* espaciosidad *f*, amplitud *f*.

spade [speid] *n* pala *f* (for digging) || laya *f* (for cutting turf) || MIL arado *m* (of a gun carriage) || pico *m* (card or mark) || FIG *to call a spade a spade* llamar al pan pan y al vino vino.
◆ *pl* picos *m* (in international cards) || espadas *f* (in spanish cards) || *the ace of spades* el as de picos.

spadeful [-ful] *n* pala *f*, paletada *f*.

spader [-ə*] *n* pala *f* mecánica.

spadework [-wəːk] *n* FIG trabajo *m* preparatorio.

spaghetti [spəˈgeti] *n* CULIN espaguetis *m pl.*

Spain [spein] *pr n* GEOGR España *f.*

spake [speik] *pret* (ant) ⟶ **speak.**

spall [spɔːl] *n* astilla *f* (of wood) ‖ laja *f* (of stone).

spall [spɔːl] *vt* descantillar (to chip) ‖ astillar (wood) ‖ labrar (stone) ‖ machacar (ore).
◆ *vi* descantillarse (to get chipped) ‖ astillarse (wood) ‖ desprenderse (rock).

span [spæn] *n* envergadura *f* (of wings) ‖ lapso *m*, espacio *m* (of time); *over a span of ten years* en un lapso de diez años ‖ duración *f*; *life span* duración de la vida ‖ período *m* (period) ‖ distancia *f* (of space) ‖ pareja *f* (of horses) ‖ yunta *f* (of oxen) ‖ palmo *m*, cuarta *f* (measurement) ‖ FIG esfera *f* (sphere) ‖ ARCH tramo *m* (part of a bridge); *a bridge consisting of two fifty metre spans* un puente con dos tramos de cincuenta metros | luz *f*, ojo *m* (distance between supports); *an arch with a fifty metre span* un arco con una luz de cincuenta metros ‖ MAR envergadura *f* (of sails) ‖ AVIAT envergadura *f* (of wings).

span [spæn] *vt* MAR amarrar (to fasten with ropes) ‖ atravesar; *the bridge spans the river* el puente atraviesa el río ‖ tender sobre; *to span a river with a bridge* tender un puente sobre un río ‖ salvar, atravesar, pasar por encima (to jump over) ‖ durar; *his life spanned fifty years* su vida duró cincuenta años ‖ medir en palmos (to measure) ‖ abarcar, comprender (to include); *this theme spans many subjects* este tema abarca muchas materias.

span [spæn] *pret* ⟶ **spin.**

spandrel [ˈspændrəl] *n* ARCH tímpano *m*, enjuta *f.*

spangle [ˈspæŋgl] *n* lentejuela *f.*

spangle [ˈspæŋgl] *vt* adornar con lentejuelas (clothes); *a spangled dress* un vestido adornado con lentejuelas ‖ FIG salpicar; *the sky was spangled with stars* el cielo estaba salpicado de estrellas.
◆ *vi* brillar.

Spaniard [ˈspænjəd] *n* español, la.

spaniel [ˈspænjəl] *n* perro *m* de aguas (dog).

Spanish [ˈspæniʃ] *adj* español, la.
◆ *n* español *m*, castellano *m* (language) ‖ *the Spanish* los españoles.

Spanish America [-əˈmerikə] *pr n* GEOGR Hispanoamérica *f.*

Spanish American [-əˈmerikən] *n* hispanoamericano, na.

Spanish American [-əˈmerikən] *adj* hispanoamericano, na.
— OBSERV See OBSERV at LATIN-AMERICAN.

Spanish Armada [-ɑːˈmɑːdə] *n* HIST Armada *f* Invencible.

Spanish bayonet [-ˈbejənit] *n* BOT yuca *f.*

Spanish fir [-fəː*] *n* BOT pinsapo *m.*

Spanish fly [-flai] *n* cantárida *f* (insect).

Spanish leather [-ˈleðə*] *n* cordobán *m.*

Spanish Main [-mein] *n* MAR Caribe *m* ‖ tierra *f* firme (terra firma).

Spanish moss [-mɔs] *n* BOT liquen *m.*

Spanishness [-nis] *n* españolismo *m*, carácter *m* español.

Spanish-speaking [-ˈspiːkiŋ] *adj* de habla española *or* castellana, hispanohablante, hispanoparlante.

Spanish white [-wait] *n* blanco *m* de España, albayalde *m.*

spank [spæŋk] *n* azote *m* (single smack) ‖ zurra *f*, azotaina *f* (beating).

spank [spæŋk] *vt* dar un azote a, dar una zurra a.
◆ *vi* ir volando, ir a toda mecha; *they were spanking along* iban a toda mecha.

spanker [-ə*] *n* caballo *m* veloz (fast horse) ‖ azotador, ra (person) ‖ MAR cangreja *f* ‖ — MAR *spanker boom* botavara *f* ‖ FIG & FAM *to be a spanker* ser fenomenal (a flat, a car, etc.).

spanking [-iŋ] *adj* rápido, da; veloz; *spanking pace* paso veloz ‖ estupendo, da; fenomenal (impressive) ‖ fuerte (breeze).
◆ *n* zurra *f*, azotaina *f* (beating).

spanner [ˈspænə*] *n* TECH llave *f* ‖ — TECH *adjustable spanner* llave inglesa | *box spanner* llave de tubo | *double-ended spanner* llave plana de doble boca ‖ FAM *to throw a spanner in the works* poner chinitas en el camino.

span-new [ˈspænˈnjuː] *adj* flamante.

span roof [spænruːf] *n* cubierta *f* de dos aguas.

spanworm [ˈspænwəːm] *n* ZOOL oruga *f.*

spar [spɑː*] *n* MAR palo *m* ‖ AVIAT larguero *m* ‖ MIN espato *m*; *Iceland spar* espato de Islandia ‖ SP combate *m* de entrenamiento, entrenamiento *m* (in boxing) | amago *m*, finta *f* (feint) | pelea *f* con espolones (in cockfight).

spar [spɑː*] *vt* MAR poner palos a ‖ AVIAT poner largueros a.
◆ *vi* SP entrenarse (in boxing) | hacer fintas, fintar (to feint) | pelear con espelones (cocks) ‖ FIG discutir (to argue).

sparable [ˈspærəbl] *n* puntilla *f* (nail).

spare [spɛə*] *adj* disponible (available); *I'm afraid we have no men spare* lo siento, pero no tenemos a nadie disponible ‖ sobrante, que sobra (left over, remaining); *are there any spare apples?* ¿hay manzanas sobrantes? ‖ delgado, da (thin) ‖ frugal (frugal); *a spare meal* una comida frugal ‖ mezquino, na (mean) ‖ de repuesto, de recambio (part); *a spare wheel* una rueda de repuesto ‖ libre; *if you have a spare moment* si tiene un momento libre; *in my spare time* en mis ratos libres ‖ — *have you any spare glasses you could lend me?* ¿tienes algún vaso de sobra que me podrías prestar? ‖ *spare of speech* parco en palabras ‖ *spare room* cuarto *m* de los invitados ‖ *there was some cheese spare* sobraba un poco de queso ‖ *this one seems to be going spare* parece que sobra éste.
◆ *n* pieza *f* de recambio, repuesto *m* (spare part) ‖ *you can have it, it is a spare* cógelo, está de sobra.

spare [spɛə*] *vt* reservar (to conserve); *to spare one's strength* conservar las fuerzas ‖ perdonar la vida a; *they only spared the women and children* sólo perdonaron la vida a las mujeres y a los niños ‖ salvar [de la destrucción]; *Paris has been spared* París ha sido salvado ‖ no herir, tener en consideración; *to spare s.o.'s feelings* no herir los sentimientos de alguien ‖ escatimar; *no effort was spared to save him* ningún esfuerzo fue escatimado para salvarle; *to spare no expense* no escatimar gastos; *don't spare the wine* no escatimes el vino ‖ ahorrar (to save); *spare me the details* ahórrate los detalles; *you can spare yourself the trouble* te puedes ahorrar el esfuerzo ‖ prescindir de (to do without); *I can't spare him right now* no puedo prescindir de él en este momento ‖ dar, dejar; *can you spare me five hundred dollars?* ¿puedes darme quinientos dólares? ‖ dispensar; *he was spared answering* fue dispensado de responder ‖ disponer de, tener; *can you spare two minutes?* ¿puedes disponer de *or* tienes dos minutos? ‖ conceder, dedicar; *I can only spare you two minutes* le puedo conceder dos minutos solamente ‖ — *are you sure you can spare it?* ¿está seguro de que no le hace falta? ‖ *have you any to spare?* ¿le sobra alguno *or* algo? ‖ *he spares neither himself nor his employees* es muy exigente *or* duro tanto consigo mismo como con sus empleados ‖ *it fits in the box with room to spare* cabe holgadamente en la caja ‖ *nothing was spared for his comfort* se hizo todo lo posible para su comodidad ‖ *spare me* tenga piedad de mí ‖ *the flood spared nothing* la inundación no respetó *or* no perdonó nada ‖ *there is room and to spare* hay sitio de sobra ‖ *to be spared a horrible fate* librarse de un terrible destino ‖ *very few lives were spared by the flood* la inundación dejó a muy pocas personas con vida ‖ *we arrived with time to spare* llegamos con tiempo de sobra ‖ *we have no time to spare* no tenemos tiempo que perder.
◆ *vi* ser frugal ‖ tener piedad (to have mercy).

spareness [-nis] *n* escasez *f* ‖ frugalidad *f.*

spare part [-pɑːt] *n* recambio *m*, pieza *f* de recambio *or* de repuesto, repuesto *m.*

spareribs [-ribs] *pl n* CULIN costillas *f* de cerdo.

spare tyre [-ˈtaiə*] *n* neumático *m* de repuesto ‖ FIG michelín *m.*

sparing [-riŋ] *adj* frugal (frugal) ‖ escaso, sa (scarce, sparse) ‖ limitado, da (limited) ‖ económico, ca (economical) ‖ parco, ca; *to be sparing of words* ser parco en el hablar *or* en palabras; *sparing of compliments* parco en cumplidos ‖ — *he is sparing in his use of adjectives* emplea los adjetivos con parquedad ‖ *his sparing use of adjectives* su parquedad en el empleo de los adjetivos.

sparingly [-riŋli] *adv* con moderación (with moderation) ‖ poco (little) ‖ frugalmente (frugally) ‖ en pequeñas cantidades (in small amounts).

spark [spɑːk] *n* chispa *f*; *to give off sparks* echar chispas ‖ ELECTR chispa *f* ‖ AUT encendido *m* ‖ FIG destello *m*, chispa *f*; *not a spark of life* ni un destello de vida ‖ FIG & FAM galán *m* (dandy) ‖ — FIG & FAM *bright spark* listillo *m* (person) | *sparks* radiotelegrafista *m* ‖ FIG & FAM *sparks are going to fly when he finds out* echará chispas cuando se entere | *sparks flew* se armó la gorda.

spark [spɑːk] *vi* chispear, echar chispas.
◆ *vt* encender ‖ FIG *to spark off* provocar, causar.

spark arrester [-əˈrestə*] *n* parachispas *m inv.*

spark coil [-kɔil] *n* ELECTR bobina *f* de inducción.

spark gap [-gæp] *n* ELECTR distancia *f* explosiva, entrehierro *m.*

sparking plug [ˈspɑːkiŋplʌg] *n* AUT bujía *f.*

sparkle [ˈspɑːkl] *n* destello *m*, centelleo *m*; *sparkle of the diamond* centelleo del diamante ‖ FIG viveza *f*, vivacidad *f* (liveliness).

sparkle [ˈspɑːkl] *vi* centellear, destellar; *a diamond sparkles in the sun* un diamante centellea al sol ‖ echar chispas, chispear (to spark) ‖ FIG ser muy animado (to be vivacious) ‖ brillar, chispear; *eyes that sparkle with happiness* ojos que brillan de alegría ‖ burbujear, ser espumoso (wine) ‖ FIG & FAM lucirse, brillar (to perform brilliantly) ‖ FIG *to sparkle with wit* tener un ingenio chispeante.

sparkler [-ə*] *n* fuego *m* de artificio [que desprende chispas blancas] (firework) ‖ US FAM diamante *m* (diamond).

sparkling [-iŋ] *adj* centelleante, brillante (stars, jewels, etc.) ‖ FIG chispeante, brillante (wit, eyes) | vivaz (vivacious) | espumoso, sa (liquid); *sparkling wine* vino espumoso ‖ US *sparkling water* soda *f* (soda water).

spark plug [ˈspɑːkplʌg] *n* US AUT bujía *f.*

sparling [ˈspaliŋ] *n* ZOOL eperlano *m* (fish).

sparring partner ['spɑːriŋ'pɑːtnə*] *n* SP "sparring-partner" *m*, boxeador *m* que entrena a otro antes de un combate.

sparrow ['spærəu] gorrión *m* (bird).

sparrow hawk [-hɔːk] *n* gavilán *m* (bird).

sparry ['spɑːri] *adj* MIN espático, ca.

sparse [spɑːs] *adj* escaso, sa; disperso, sa; *sparse vegetation* vegetación escasa || poco denso, sa (not dense) || ralo, la (hair).

sparsely [-li] *adv* escasamente; *sparsely forested* escasamente poblado de árboles; *sparsely populated* escasamente poblado || *sparsely scattered* esparcidos.

Sparta ['spɑːtə] *pr n* GEOGR Esparta *f*.

Spartan ['spɑːtən] *adj/n* espartano, na.

spasm ['spæzəm] *n* MED espasmo *m* (contraction) | acceso *m*, ataque *m* (of fever, of coughing, etc.) || FIG arrebato *m* (surge of anger, of enthusiasm) | arranque *m* (of humour, of gaiety) || *to work in spasms* trabajar irregularmente.

spasmodic [spæz'mɔdik] *adj* MED espasmódico, ca | involuntario, ria (movement) || FIG irregular, intermitente (not continuous).

spastic ['spæstik] *adj* MED espástico, ca.
◆ *n* MED espástico, ca.

spat [spæt] *pret/pp* → **spit.**

spat [spæt] *n* polaina *f* (gaiter) || ZOOL freza *f*, hueva *f* (spawn) | ostra *f* joven (young oyster) || *US* FAM riña *f*.
— OBSERV En el sentido zoológico el plural de *spat* es *spat* o *spats*.

spat [spæt] *vi* *US* FAM reñir (to quarrel) || ZOOL frezar (to spawn).

spate [speit] *n* avenida *f*, crecida *f* (of a river) || FIG torrente *m*; *a spate of words* un torrente de palabras || *in spate* crecido, da (a river).

spathe [speiːð] *n* BOT espata *f*.

spathic ['spæθik]; **spathose** [spæ'θəus] *adj* MIN espático, ca.

spatial ['speiʃəl] *adj* espacial, del espacio.

spatter ['spætə*] *n* salpicón *m*, salpicadura *f* (splash) || — *spatter of applause* unos cuantos aplausos || *spatter of rain* un poco de lluvia.

spatter ['spætə*] *vt* salpicar, rociar; *to spatter with mud* salpicar de barro || FIG mancillar, manchar.
◆ *vi* salpicar.

spatterdash [-dæʃ] *n* polaina *f* (gaiter).

spatula ['spætjulə] *n* espátula *f*.

spatulate ['spætjulit] *adj* espatulado, da.

spavin ['spævin] *n* VET esparaván *m*.

spawn [spɔːn] *n* freza *f*, hueva *f* (of fish) || huevos *m pl* (of a frog) || BOT micelio *m* (of mushrooms) || FIG resultado *m*; *the spawn of my research* el resultado de mi investigación | semilla *f*, germen *m* (origin) | engendro *m* (offspring).

spawn [spɔːn] *vt* depositar (eggs) || producir, engendrar (to produce).
◆ *vi* frezar, desovar (fishes) || multiplicarse, reproducirse (to reproduce).

spawning [-iŋ] *n* desove *m*, freza *f*.

spay [spei] *vt* quitar los ovarios.

speak* [spiːk] *vt* decir; *to speak the truth* decir la verdad; *to speak nonsense* decir tonterías || hablar; *do you speak Spanish?* ¿habla usted español?; *English spoken* se habla inglés || FIG expresar; *her eyes spoke a warm welcome* sus ojos expresaban una cordial bienvenida | cantar, hablar de; *his deeds speak his bravery* sus hazañas cantan su valor | indicar (indicate) || MAR comunicar con || — *he didn't speak a word* no dijo ni una palabra, no habló || *to speak one's mind, to speak straight from the shoulder* decir lo que uno piensa, hablar sin rodeos || *to speak pidgin English* hablar un inglés macarrónico, hablar como los indios || *to speak volumes; her look spoke volumes* su mirada era muy elocuente || *it speaks volumes for his attitude* indica claramente su actitud.
◆ *vi* hablar; *he speaks clearly* habla claramente; *he was too sad to speak* estaba demasiado triste para hablar; *he is going to speak at the meeting* va a hablar en la reunión; *to speak about sth.* hablar de algo; *to speak to s.o.* hablar con alguien; *you must speak to John about the noise he makes* tienes que hablar con Juan del ruido que hace || hablarse (to each other); *they aren't speaking* no se hablan || tomar la palabra (to take the floor) || pronunciar un discurso (to give a speech) || FIG sonar; *the organ spoke* el órgano sonó || — *did s.o. speak?* ¿ha hablado alguien?, ¿alguien ha dicho algo? || *generally speaking* hablando en general || *I don't know him to speak to* no he hablado nunca con él || *I'll never speak to you again* no te volveré a dirigir la palabra || FIG *it almost speaks* sólo le falta hablar (portrait, animal) || *roughly speaking* aproximadamente || *so to speak* por así decirlo, como quien dice || *speaking* al aparato (on the telephone) || *this is Elena speaking* soy Elena (on the telephone) || *to speak behind s.o.'s back* hablar a espaldas de alguien || *to speak cryptically* hablar a medias palabras || *to speak like a book* hablar como un libro || *to speak like a fishwife* hablar como una verdulera || *to speak through one's nose* hablar con *or* por la nariz, hablar con voz gangosa.
◆ *phr v* ***to speak for*** recomendar (to recommend) | hablar en nombre de (on behalf of) | hablar en favor de (a motion) | FAM coger, comprometer; *I am spoken for* estoy cogido (engaged, married, etc.), coger, reservar; *this table is spoken for* esta mesa está cogida | *it speaks for itself* es evidente, habla por sí mismo | *speaking for myself* personalmente | *speak for yourself!* ¡eso lo dirás tú! | *the evidence speaks for itself* las pruebas hablan por sí solas | FIG *to speak well for s.o.* decir mucho en favor de uno || ***to speak of*** hablar de (to talk about) | revelar (to indicate) || — *speaking of marriage* hablando de matrimonio | *to be nothing to speak of* no ser nada especial | *to speak ill of* hablar mal de | *to speak well of* hablar bien de || ***to speak out*** hablar claro | hablar más fuerte || ***to speak to*** garantizar, confirmar | *to speak to the point* ceñirse al tema, ir al grano || ***to speak up*** hablar más fuerte; *speak up, he's deaf* habla más fuerte, que es sordo | *to speak up for* intervenir en favor de.
— OBSERV Pret ***spoke***; pp ***spoken***.

speakeasy [-'iːzi] *n* *US* FAM despacho *m* de bebidas clandestino.

speaker [-ə*] *n* orador, ra; *a good speaker* un buen orador; *to interrupt the speaker* interrumpir al orador || persona *f* que habla (person speaking) || presidente *m* (in Parliament) || portavoz *m* [*AMER* vocero *m*] (spokesman) || ELECTR altavoz *m* [*AMER* altoparlante *m*] (loudspeaker) || *speakers of English* los que hablan inglés.

speakership [-əʃip] *n* presidencia *f* (of Parliament).

speaking [-iŋ] *adj* hablante, parlante (who is speaking) || de habla; *English-speaking people* personas de habla inglesa || manifiesto, ta; *a speaking resemblance* un parecido manifiesto || fiel (likeness) || elocuente; *a speaking glance* una mirada elocuente || expresivo, va (face) || elocuente (proof) || cuando habla; *his speaking voice is better than his singing voice* su voz cuando habla es mejor que cuando canta || hablado, da; *he was a speaking part in the play* tiene una parte hablada en la obra de teatro || — *to be on speaking terms* hablarse; *I am not on speaking terms with him* no me hablo con él; *they are not on speaking terms* no se hablan || *within speaking distance* al alcance de la voz.
◆ *n* habla *f* (speech, use of voice) || — *public speaking* arte *m* de la oratoria || *speaking acquaintance* conocido, da || *speaking clock* servicio *m* telefónico de información horaria || *speaking trumpet* megáfono *m*, bocina *f*.

spear [spiə*] *n* lanza *f* (weapon) || arpón *m* (harpoon) || SP jabalina *f* (javelin) || *with a thrust of his spear* de una lanzada.

spear [spiə*] *vt* traspasar, atravesar [con una lanza]; *to spear s.o. through the heart* traspasarle el corazón a alguien || arponear (to harpoon).

spearhead [-hed] *n* punta *f* de lanza || FIG vanguardia *f*; *the cavalry was the spearhead of the attack* la caballería constituyó la vanguardia del ataque.

spearhead [-hed] *vt* encabezar.

spearmint [-mint] *n* BOT menta *f* verde.

spec [spek] *n* COMM especulación *f* || FIG *on spec* por si acaso.

special ['speʃəl] *adj* especial, particular; *each spice imparts a special flavour* cada especia da un sabor particular; *it requires special knowledge* requiere un conocimiento especial || superior; *special brand* marca superior || íntimo, ma; *special friends* amigos íntimos || especial; *special licence* autorización especial || extraordinario, ria (edition) || — *nothing special* nada especial, nada extraordinario || *special constable* guardia *m* auxiliar || *special delivery* carta *f* or correo *m* urgente (letter), entrega inmediata (delivery) || *this week's special offer* la oferta especial de esta semana || *what's so special about it?* ¿qué tiene de particular?
◆ *n* tren *m* especial (train) || guardia *m* auxiliar (policeman) || número *m* extraordinario (edition).

specialist [-ist] *n* especialista *m* & *f*.

speciality ['speʃi'æliti] *n* especialidad *f* || *speciality of the house, our speciality* especialidad de la casa.

specialization ['speʃəlai'zeiʃən] *n* especialización *f*.

specialize ['speʃəlaiz] *vi* especializarse; *to specialize in French* especializarse en francés || BIOL diferenciarse.
◆ *vt* especializar; *to specialize one's studies* especializar los estudios || BIOL adaptar.

specially ['speʃəli] *adv* especialmente.

specialty ['speʃəlti] *n* especialidad *f* (speciality) || JUR contrato *m* formal.

speciation [spiʃi'eiʃən] *n* evolución *f* de las especies.

specie ['spiːʃiː] *n* metálico *m*, efectivo *m* || *in specie* en metálico.

species ['spiːʃiːz] *n* especie *f*, clase *f*; *a species of cherry* una clase de cereza || BIOL especie *f*; *the human species* la especie humana || REL especies *f pl* sacramentales.
— OBSERV El plural de *species* es *species*.

specific [spi'sifik] *adj* específico, ca || *he wasn't very specific* no especificó, no concretó, no fue muy explícito.
◆ *n* MED específico *m*.
◆ *pl* datos *m* específicos.

specifically [-li] *adv* específicamente, propiamente.

specification ['spesifi'keiʃən] *n* especificación *f* || estipulación *f* (of a contract, etc.) || requisito *m* (requirement).
◆ *pl* descripción *f sing* detallada (detailed description) || pliego *m sing* de condiciones (list of requirements).

specific gravity [-'græviti] *n* PHYS peso *m* específico.

specific heat [-hiːt] *n* PHYS calor *m* específico.

specify ['spesifai] *vt* especificar, precisar, concretar || *unless otherwise specified* salvo indicación contraria.

specimen ['spesimin] *n* modelo *m* (model) || muestra *f* (sample) || ejemplar *m* (example) || BIOL espécimen *m* || FAM individuo *m*, tipo *m*; *he is a queer specimen* es un tipo extraño || — MED *blood specimen* muestra de sangre || PRINT *specimen page* o *copy* espécimen.

speciosity [ˌspiːʃi'ɔsiti] *n* especiosidad *f*.

specious ['spiːʃəs] *adj* especioso, sa.

speciousness [-nis] *n* especiosidad *f*.

speck [spek] *n* partícula *f*, mota *f* (small particle) || mota *f* (small defect) || FIG punto *m*; *he was a speck on the horizon* era un punto en el horizonte | pizca *f*; *there's not a speck of kindness in him* no tiene ni pizca de generosidad.

speck [spek] *vt* motear, salpicar de manchas.

speckle ['spekl] *n* mancha *f*, mota *f* (small spot) || peca *f* (freckle).

speckle [spekl] *vt* motear, salpicar de manchas.

specs [speks] *pl n* FAM gafas *f* [AMER lentes *m*, anteojos *m*].

spectacle ['spektəkl] *n* espectáculo *m* (display) || — FAM *to make a spectacle of o.s.* dar el espectáculo, ponerse en ridículo.
◆ *pl* gafas *f* [AMER lentes *m*, anteojos *m*] (glasses); *spectacle case* estuche de las gafas || FIG *to see life through rose-coloured spectacles* ver la vida color de rosa.

spectacled [-d] *adj* que lleva gafas, con gafas || ZOOL *spectacled snake* serpiente *f* de anteojos.

spectacular [spek'tækjulə*] *adj* espectacular.
◆ *n* espectáculo *m* grandioso.

spectate [spek'teit] *vi* ser espectador, ra, ver; *to spectate at a match* ser espectador de *or* ver un partido.

spectator [spek'teitə*] *n* espectador, ra.

spectator sport [-spɔːt] *n* deporte *m* de masas.

specter ['spektə*] *n* US espectro *m*.

spectra ['spektrə] *pl n* ⟶ **spectrum.**

spectral ['spektrəl] *adj* espectral.

spectre ['spektə*] *n* espectro *m*.

spectrogram ['spektrəugræm] *n* espectrograma *m*.

spectrograph ['spektrəugrɑːf] *n* espectrógrafo *m*.

spectrometer [spek'trɔmitə*] *n* espectrómetro *m*.

spectroscope ['spektrəskəup] *n* espectroscopio *m*.

spectroscopic ['spektrəs'kɔpik] *adj* espectroscópico, ca.

spectrum ['spektrəm] *n* espectro *m*.
— OBSERV El plural de la palabra inglesa *spectrum* es *spectra* o *spectrums*.

specula ['spekjulə] *pl n* ⟶ **speculum.**

speculate ['spekjuleit] *vi* especular; *to speculate on the Stock Exchange, in cereals* especular en la Bolsa, en cereales; *to speculate about what might have happened* especular sobre lo que hubiera podido acontecer.

speculation [ˌspekju'leiʃən] *n* especulación *f*.

speculative ['spekjulətiv] *adj* especulativo, va.

speculator ['spekjuleitə*] *n* especulador, ra.

speculum ['spekjuləm] *n* MED espéculo *m* || ZOOL espéculo *m*, espejo *m*.
— OBSERV El plural de la palabra *speculum* es *specula* o *speculums*.

sped [sped] *pret/pp* ⟶ **speed.**

speech [spiːtʃ] *n* habla *f* (capacity to speak); *he lost his speech* perdió el habla || conferencia *f* (lecture); *he gave a speech on Spanish gypsies* dio una conferencia sobre los gitanos españoles || discurso *m*; *to deliver a speech in Parliament* pronunciar un discurso en el parlamento || conversación *f* (talk) || palabras *f pl* (words) || pronunciación *f*; *speech defect* o *impediment* defecto de pronunciación || diálogo *m* (dialogue in play, in film) || habla *f*; *the speech of the Incas* el habla de los incas || MUS sonoridad *f* (of an instrument) || GRAMM oración *f*; *direct, indirect speech* oración directa, indirecta; *part of speech* parte de la oración; *reported speech* estilo indirecto || — *figure of speech* tropo *m*, figura *f* retórica (rethoric), manera *f* de hablar || *free speech* libertad *f* de expresión || *opening, closing speech* discurso inaugural *or* de apertura, de clausura || INFORM *speech recognition* reconocimiento *m* de la voz.

speech area [-'ɛəriə] *n* área *f* lingüística.

speech community [-kə'mjuːniti] *n* US comunidad *f* lingüística.

speech day [-dei*] *n* día *m* del reparto de premios.

speechify [-ifai] *vi* perorar.

speechless [-lis] *adj* sin habla, mudo, da (dumb); *I was speechless* me quedé mudo.

speech therapist [-'θerəpist] *n* logopeda *m* & *f*.

speech therapy [-'θerəpi] *n* logopedia *f*.

speed [spiːd] *n* velocidad *f*; *the speed of a car* la velocidad de un coche || PHYS velocidad *f* || rapidez *f*, velocidad *f*; *the speed at which one works* la rapidez con la que se trabaja || PHOT velocidad *f* || US TECH velocidad *f* (gear) || FAM droga *f* estimulante || INFORM velocidad *f* || — *at full* o *top speed* a toda velocidad || MAR *full speed ahead!* ¡adelante a toda máquina! || *its top* o *maximum speed is* su velocidad máxima es de || *they were doing quite a speed* llevaban mucha velocidad || *to make good speed* llevar buena velocidad || *to pick up* o *to gain speed* coger velocidad || *to put on speed* acelerar.

speed* [spiːd] *vi* ir corriendo, correr, ir de prisa (a person) || ir a toda velocidad (a car, etc.) || apresurarse (to hurry) || JUR conducir con exceso de velocidad (to break the speed limit) || — *he sped round the corner* dio la vuelta a la esquina a toda velocidad || *to speed up* acelerar.
◆ *vt* despedir (to say good-bye to) || disparar (an arrow) || acelerar (an engine) || — *God speed you!* ¡que Dios le ampare! || *to speed up* acelerar (car, process, matters), dar prisa a (a person).
— OBSERV Pret y pp ***sped, speeded***.

speedboat [-bəut] *n* lancha *f* motora.

speedily [-ili] *adv* rápidamente.

speed indicator [-'indikeitə*] *n* indicador *m* de velocidad, velocímetro *m*.

speediness [-inis] *n* rapidez *f*, velocidad *f*.

speeding [-iŋ] *n* exceso *m* de velocidad.

speed limit [-'limit] *n* límite *m* de velocidad (restriction) || velocidad *f* máxima (on road signs).

speedometer [spi'dɔmitə*] *n* velocímetro *m*, indicador *m* de velocidad.

speedup ['spiːdʌp] *n* US aceleración *f* | aumento *m* de productividad (increase in productivity).

speedway ['spiːdwei] *n* pista *f* de carreras (for racing) || US autopista *f* (motorway).

speedwell ['spiːdwel] *n* BOT verónica *f*.

speedy ['spiːdi] *adj* veloz, rápido, da || FAM drogado, da.

speleologist [ˌspiːli'ɔlədʒist] *n* espeleólogo *m*.

speleology; spelaeology [ˌspiːli'ɔlədʒi] *n* espeleología *f*.

spell [spel] *n* turno *m* (shift); *a spell on watch* un turno de vigilancia || temporada *f*; *I am going to the country for a spell* me voy al campo por una temporada || rato *m*; *we chatted for a spell* charlamos un rato || descanso *m* (a rest) || racha *f*; *he is going through a good, a bad spell* está atravesando una buena, una mala racha || acceso *m* (of bad temper) || ataque *m* (of disease) || sortilegio *m*, maleficio *m* (evil spell) || encanto *m*; *the spell of Ireland* el encanto de Irlanda; *the light broke the spell* la luz rompió el encanto || — *cold, warm spell* racha *or* ola *f* de frío, de calor || *to be under a spell* estar hechizado || *to cast* o *to put a spell on s.o.* hechizar a alguien.

spell* [spel] *vt* escribir; *he spells my name wrong* escribe mal mi nombre || deletrear (letter by letter) || FIG significar, representar, equivaler a; *the flood spelled disaster for many people* la inundación significó un desastre para mucha gente || encantar, hechizar (to bewitch) || US remplazar, reemplazar, relevar (to take over from) || — *c-a-t spells cat* g-a-t-o significa gato || *how do you spell his name?* ¿cómo se escribe su nombre? || *to spell backward* escribir *or* deletrear al revés || *to spell out* deletrear (to read letter by letter), explicar (to explain), captar (to understand), entrever (to see).
◆ *vi* escribir || US tomarse un descanso (to rest) | tomar su turno (to shift) || *he spells well* su ortografía es buena, tiene buena ortografía.
— OBSERV Pret y pp ***spelled, spelt***.

spellbind* [-baind] *vt* hechizar, encantar.
— OBSERV Pret y pp ***spellbound***.

spellbinder [-'baində*] *n* orador *m* arrebatador.

spellbound [-baund] *adj* hechizado, da; embrujado, da (bewitched) || FIG fascinado, da; hechizado, da; *he held his audience spellbound* tenía fascinado al auditorio.

speller [-ə*] *n* abecedario *m* (spelling book) || *to be a bad, a good speller* tener mala, buena ortografía.

spelling [-iŋ] *n* ortografía *f* || deletreo *m* (letter by letter).

spelling bee [-iŋbiː] *n* concurso *m* de ortografía.

spelling book [-iŋbuk] *n* abecedario *m*.

spelt [spelt] *pret/pp* ⟶ **spell.**

spelter [-ə*] *n* CHEM cinc *m*.

spelunker [spi'lʌŋkə*] *n* US FAM espeleólogo *m*.

spelunking [spi'lʌŋkiŋ] *n* US FAM espeleología *f*.

spencer ['spensə*] *n* MAR vela *f* cangreja || chaqueta *f* corta (jacket).

spend* [spend] *vt* gastar, gastarse (money); *he spent a lot on cigarettes* gastó mucho en cigarrillos || pasar; *to spend a week in bed* pasar una semana en la cama; *to spend one's holidays abroad* pasar las vacaciones en el extranjero || emplear, usar (to use) || dedicar; *you must spend more time on your homework* tiene que dedicar más tiempo a los deberes || agotar (to exhaust).
◆ *vi* gastar dinero.
— OBSERV Pret y pp ***spent***.

spender [-ə*] *n* gastador, ra; derrochador, ra.

spending [-iŋ] *n* gasto *m* || — *spending money* dinero para gastos menudos || *spending power* poder adquisitivo.

spendthrift [-θrift] *adj/n* manirroto, ta; gastador, ra; derrochador, ra; despilfarrador, ra.

spent [spent] *pret/pp* ⟶ **spend.**
◆ *adj* agotado, da (exhausted) || gastado, da; acabado, da (worn-out) || — *spent bullet* bala

muerta || *the storm was spent* la tormenta se había calmado.

sperm [spəːm] *n* esperma *f*, esmerma *m*.

spermaceti [ˌspəːməˈseti] *n* espermaceti *m*, esperma *f* de ballena.

spermatic [spəːˈmætik] *adj* espermático, ca.

spermatocyte [ˌspəːˈmətəsait] *n* espermatocito *m*.

spermatogenesis [ˈspəːmætəˈdʒenəsis] *n* espermatogénesis *f*.

spermatophyte [ˈspəːmətəfait] *n* BOT espermatofita *f*.

spermatozoid [ˈspəːmətəˈzəuid] *n* espermatozoide *m* (of a plant).

spermatozoon [ˈspəːmətəuˈzəuən] *n* espermatozoo *m*, espermatozoide *m*.
— OBSERV El plural de *spermatozoon* es *spermatozoa*.

sperm oil [ˈspəːmɔil] *n* aceite *m* de ballena.

sperm whale [ˈspəːmweil] *n* ZOOL cachalote *m*.

spew [spjuː] *n* vómito *m*.

spew [spjuː] *vt* vomitar, devolver, arrojar (to vomit) || FIG vomitar, arrojar (smoke, flames, etc.).
◆ *vi* vomitar, devolver, arrojar.

Speyer [ˈʃpaiə*] *pr n* GEOGR Espira.

sphenoid [ˈsfiːnɔid] *adj* ANAT esfenoideo, a; esfenoidal, esfenoides.
◆ *n* ANAT esfenoides *m inv*.

sphenoidal [-əl] *adj* ANAT esfenoidal.

sphere [sfiə*] *n* MATH esfera *f* || FIG esfera *f*; *sphere of activity* esfera de actividad; *sphere of influence* esfera de influencia | competencia *f* (province).

spheric [ˈsferik]; **spherical** [-əl] *adj* esférico, ca || *spherical trigonometry* trigonometría esférica.

spherics [ˈsferiks] *n* MATH trigonometría *f* esférica.

spheroid [ˈsfiərɔid] *n* MATH esferoide *m*.

spheroidal [sfiəˈrɔidl] *adj* MATH esferoidal.

spherometer [sfiəˈrɔmitə*] *n* esferómetro *m*.

sphincter [ˈsfiŋktə*] *n* ANAT esfínter *m*.

sphinx [sfiŋks] *n* MYTH esfinge *f* || FIG esfinge *f* || ZOOL esfinge *f* (hawkmoth).

spice [spais] *n* especia *f* || FIG picante *m*, sabor *m*, sal *f*; *to give spice to a book* dar sabor a un libro || — *spice of life* lo sabroso de la vida, sal de la vida | *variety is the spice of life* en la variedad está el gusto.

spice [spais] *vt* condimentar, sazonar || FIG sazonar, salpimentar.

spice box [-bɔks] *n* especiero *m*, caja *f* de especias.

spicery [-əri] *n* especias *f pl*.

spiciness [-inis] *n* picante *m*, sabor *m* || FIG picante *m*.

spick-and-span [ˈspikəndˈspæn] *adj* flamante, impecable (cleaned up) || nuevo, va (new) || impecable (person).

spicule [ˈspaikjuːl] *n* espícula *f*.

spicy [ˈspaisi] *adj* picante, sazonado con especias (food) || FIG picante.

spider [ˈspaidə*] *n* ZOOL & TECH araña *f* || US trébedes *f pl* (frying pan) || — ZOOL *spider crab, sea spider* centollo *m*, centolla *f*, araña *f* de mar || *spider's web* telaraña *f*, tela *f* de araña.

spidery [ˈspaidəri] *adj* de alambre; *John has spidery legs* Juan tiene patas de alambre || que tiene forma de telaraña (like spider's web) || lleno de arañas (full of spiders) || *spidery handwriting* patas *f pl* de mosca, garabatos *m pl*.

spiegeleisen [ˈspiːgəlaizən] *n* arrabio *m* (pig iron).

spiel [spiːl] *n* US FAM perorata *f* (speech) | charlatanería *f* (sales patter) | camelo *m*, cuento *m* (story) | publicidad *f* (publicity).

spiel [spiːl] *vt* US FAM *to spiel off* soltar (a speech, a list, etc.).
◆ *vi* US FAM perorar.

spiffing [ˈspifiŋ]; **spiffy** [ˈspifi] *adj* FAM estupendo, da.

spigot [ˈspigət] *n* espita *f*, bitoque *m* (of a barrel) || macho *m*, enchufe *m* (of a tube) || macho *m*, espiga *f* (tenon) || US grifo *m*, espita *f* (tap).

spike [spaik] *n* punta *f*, púa *f*, pincho *m* (sharp-pointed object) || estaca *f* (pointed rod or bar) || barrote *m* (on a railing) || bastón *m* con pincho (for picking up litter) || pincho *m*, clavo *m* (for filing bills) || clavo *m* (of running shoes) || ZOOL pitón *m* (a single antler) || BOT espiga *f*.
◆ *pl* zapatillas *f* con clavos (running shoes).

spike [spaik] *vt* clavar (to fix with a spike) || empalar, atravesar (to impale) || FIG frustrar (s.o.'s plans) || acabar con, poner fin a (a rumour) || MIL clavar (a cannon) || US añadir alcohol a (a drink).
◆ *vi* formar espigas.

spiked [-t] *adj* claveteado, da (shoes).

spikelet [ˈspaiklət] *n* BOT espiguilla *f*.

spikenard [ˈspaiknɑːd] *n* BOT nardo *m*.

spiky [ˈspaiki] *adj* erizado, da (with many sharp points) || puntiagudo, da (sharp-pointed).

spile [spail] *n* tarugo *m* (wedge) || espita *f* (plug) || estaca *f*, pilote *m* (stake, pile) || US gotera *f* para sangrar un árbol.

spile [spail] *vt* poner una espita a (to put a spile on) || asegurar con pilotes (to pile) || US sangrar con gotera (trees).

spill [spil] *n* espita *f* (spile) || clavija *f* (peg) || tarugo *m* (wedge) || astilla *f* (splinter) || pajuela *f* (for lighting fire) || derramamiento *m*, derrame *m* (of a liquid) || caída *f* (from a horse) || *to take a spill* caerse (to fall).

spill* [spil] *vt* derramar; *he spilled the water on the table* derramó el agua sobre la mesa || volcar (to knock over) || verter (to pour) || hacer caer; *the horse spilled the rider to the ground* el caballo hizo que el jinete cayese al suelo || FIG derramar; *a lot of blood has been spilt* ha sido derramada mucha sangre || FAM soltar (to divulge) || FIG & FAM *to spill the beans* descubrir el pastel.
◆ *vi* derramarse, verterse (a liquid); *mind your coffee doesn't spill* cuidado que no se derrame el café || salirse; *as he walked petrol spilled from the can* al andar se le salía la gasolina de la lata || romper (waves) || caer; *the wine spilt over her dress* el vino le cayó en el vestido || — *to spill out* salir; *as the crowd spilled out of the football ground* mientras los espectadores salían del campo de fútbol; desparramarse (objects) || *to spill over* salirse; *the bathwater was spilling over* el agua del baño se salía; rebosar, estar rebosante (to be full to overflowing).
— OBSERV Pret y pp ***spilled, spilt***.

spillage [ˈspilidʒ] *n* vertido *m*, derrame *m*, escape *m* (accidental loss).

spillikin [ˈspilikin] *n* palillo *m*.
◆ *pl* juego *m sing* de los palillos.

spillway [ˈspilwei] *n* aliviadero *m*, derramadero *m*.

spilt [spilt] *pret/pp* ⟶ **spill.**

spin [spin] *n* giro *m*, vuelta *f* (act of revolving) || efecto *m*; *to put spin on a ball* dar efecto a una pelota || vuelta *f*, paseo *m*; *to go for a spin on a motorbike* dar un paseo en moto || aturdimiento *m*, confusión *f* (confusion) || AVIAT barrena *f*; *to go into a spin* entrar en barrena || PHYS espín *m*, «spin» *m*, giro *m* (of electrons) || — FIG *my head is in a spin* estoy aturdido || *to give sth. a spin* hacer girar algo || *to risk a fortune on the spin of a coin* jugarse una fortuna a cara o cruz.

spin* [spin] *vt* hacer girar, dar vueltas a; *to spin a wheel, a top* hacer girar una rueda, una peonza || hilar; *to spin cotton* hilar algodón || tejer; *the spider spins his web* la araña teje su tela || fabricar, hacer (a cocoon) || hacer girar (a dancing partner) || contar; *to spin a tale* contar un cuento || suspender; *to spin a candidate* suspender a un candidato || SP dar efecto a (a ball) || TECH tornear (metal on a lathe) || — *to spin a coin for sth.* echar algo a cara o cruz || *to spin out* estirar, hacer dar de sí (time, money), alargar (holiday), prolongar (trial), alargar, prolongar (speech) || FIG *to spin s.o. a yarn* contarle a uno una historia.
◆ *vi* girar, dar vueltas; *the top was spinning* la peonza estaba dando vueltas || perturbarse, volverse loco (a compass) || hilar (cotton, silk, etc.) || tejer la tela (spiders) || FIG dar vueltas (ideas, thoughts) || AUT patinar (wheels) || AVIAT entrar *or* descender en barrena (a plane) || — *my head was spinning* me daba vueltas la cabeza, estaba mareado || *the blow sent him spinning* el golpe le hizo rodar || *to send sth. spinning* echar algo a rodar || *to spin along* ir volando (to speed along) || *to spin round* dar una vuelta, girar en redondo (to turn round), girar, dar vueltas (a top, a wheel, etc.).
— OBSERV Pret y pp ***spun***.

spina bifida [ˈspɑinəˌbifidɑ] *n* MED espina *f* bífida.

spinach [ˈspinidʒ] *n* BOT espinaca *f* || CULIN espinacas *f pl*.

spinal [ˈspainl] *adj* ANAT espinal, vertebral || — ANAT *spinal column* columna *f* vertebral, espina *f* dorsal | *spinal cord* médula *f* espinal || MED *spinal curvature* desviación *f* de la columna vertebral, escoliosis *f inv*.

spindle [ˈspindl] *n* TECH eje *m* (axle, shaft) | mandril *m* (of a lathe) | vástago *m* (of a valve) | huso *m* (of a spinning wheel or spinning machine) | espiga *f* (of gramophone) || MAR mecha *f* (of a capstan) || AUT mangueta *f* || US pincho *m*, clavo *m* (filing device) || BOT *spindle tree* bonetero *m* (shrub).

spindle [spindl] *vi* crecer alto y delgado, espigar.

spindleshanks [-ʃæŋks] *n* FAM zanquilargo, ga (person).
◆ *pl* FIG & FAM palillos *m* (long legs).

spindly [ˈspindli] *adj* FAM larguirucho, cha.

spindrift [ˈspindrift] *n* rocío *m* del mar, salpicaduras *f pl* de las olas.

spin-dry [ˈspinˌdrɑi] *vt* centrifugar.

spin dryer [ˈspinˈdraiə*] *n* secador *m* centrífugo.

spine [spain] *n* ANAT espina *f* dorsal, columna *f* vertebral (backbone) || ZOOL púa *f* || BOT espina *f* || GEOL cresta *f* || PRINT lomo *m* (back of a book) || FIG temple *m*.

spineless [-lis] *adj* invertebrado, da (invertebrate) || sin espinas (having no spines or thorns) || sin púas (a hedgehog) || FIG sin carácter, blando, da; débil (characterless).

spinet [spiˈnet] *n* MUS espineta *f*.

spinnaker [ˈspinəkə*] *n* MAR "spinnaker" *m*, vela *f* balón, velón *m* (sail).

spinner [ˈspinə*] *n* máquina *f* de hilar (spinning machine) || rueca *f* (spinning wheel) || hilandero, ra; hilador, ra (person who spins) || SP cebo *m* artificial de cuchara (in fishing) | pelota *f* con efecto (in cricket) || AVIAT cono *m*, ojiva *f* (of a propeller).

spinneret [ˈspinəret] *n* hilera *f*.

spinney ['spini] *n* soto *m.*

spinning ['spiniŋ] *n* hilado *m* (production of thread) || rotación *f* (circular motion) || MAR perturbación *f* de la brújula || AUT patinazo *m* (of wheels) || AVIAT barrena *f* || — *spinning factory* o *mill* hilandería *f,* fábrica *f* de hilados || *spinning frame* o *machine* máquina *f* de hilar || *spinning jenny* "jenny" *f,* máquina *f* de hilar algodón || *spinning top* peonza *f,* trompo *m* || *spinning wheel* rueca *f.*

spinose ['spainəus]; **spinous** ['spainəs] *adj* espinoso, sa.

spinster ['spinstə*] *n* soltera *f* (unmarried woman) || solterona *f* (old maid).

spinsterhood [-hud] *n* soltería *f.*

spiny ['spaini] *adj* espinoso, sa || FIG peliagudo, da; espinoso, sa (problem, etc.) || *spiny lobster* langosta *f.*

spiral ['spaiərəl] *adj* espiral; *spiral curve* curva espiral || de caracol, en espiral; *spiral staircase* escalera de caracol || helicoidal (helical) || — *spiral ascent* ascenso *m* en espiral || *spiral descent* descenso *m* en espiral.
◆ *n* MATH espiral *f* || FIG espiral *f; spiral of smoke* espiral de humo || COMM espiral *f* (of prices) || AVIAT espiral *f* || US SP pase *m* de la pelota con efecto (in American football).

spiral ['spaiərəl] *vt* aumentar, hacer subir (prices).
◆ *vi* moverse en espiral, dar vueltas || — *to spiral down* descender en espiral || *to spiral up* ascender en espiral (to rise upwards), subir vertiginosamente (prices).

spirally [-i] *adv* en espiral.

spirant ['spaiərənt] *n* espirante *f,* fricativa *f* (consonant).

spire [spaiə*] *n* ARCH aguja *f* || BOT brizna *f* || MATH espiral *f* (spiral) || vuelta *f,* rosca *f* (single turn).

spirit ['spirit] *n* espíritu *m,* alma *f* (soul); *the spirit leaves the body at the moment of death* el espíritu *or* el alma se separa del cuerpo en el momento de la muerte || espíritu *m* (ghost, etc.); *to summon the spirits* llamar a los espíritus; *evil spirit* espíritu maligno; *to believe in spirits* creer en los espíritus || ser *m,* alma *f* (person) || persona *f,* ser *m; she was one of the weaker spirits among us* era una de las personas más débiles entre nosotros || carácter *m* (strong character); *a man of spirit* un hombre de carácter; *he lacks spirit* no tiene carácter || ánimo *m,* energía *f* (liveliness); *to be full of spirit* estar lleno de ánimo || vigor *m* (vigour) || vitalidad *f* (vitality) || valor *m* (courage) || espíritu *m; the spirit of the law* el espíritu de la ley || temple *m,* humor *m* (mood); *in good spirit* de buen humor || espíritu *m; team, fighting spirit* espíritu de equipo, de lucha || alcohol *m* || — *community* o *public spirit* civismo *m* || *familiar spirit* demonio *m* familiar || *I'll do it when the spirit moves me* lo haré cuando me dé la gana || *in a friendly spirit* de manera amistosa || *in spirit* para sus adentros, en su fuero interno || *leading* o *moving spirit* alma || *poor in spirit* pobre de espíritu || *spirit lamp* lámpara *f* de alcohol || *spirit level* nivel *m* de burbuja || *spirit of turpentine* esencia *f* de trementina || *spirit rapping* comunicación *f* con los espíritus || *that's the spirit!* ¡así me gusta! || REL *the Holy Spirit* el Espíritu Santo || *the spirit world* el mundo de los espíritus || *to come in the spirit of peace* venir en son de paz || *to do sth. in a spirit of mischief* hacer algo para gastar una broma || *to enter into the spirit of sth.* meterse *or* entrar en el espíritu de algo, entrar *or* meterse en el ambiente de algo || *to take sth. in good spirit* o *in the right spirit* tomar algo a bien, tomar algo como es debido.
◆ *pl* humor *m sing* (mood) || ánimos *m,* ánimo *m sing* (liveliness); *to dampen s.o.'s spirits* rebajarle los ánimos a alguien || alcohol *m sing* (drink); *I never touch spirits* no bebo nunca alcohol || CHEM espíritu *m sing; spirits of salt, of wine* espíritu de sal, de vino | alcohol *m sing; methylated spirits* alcohol metílico *or* de quemar || — *to be full of spirits* estar muy animado *or* muy alegre || *to be in high spirits* estar muy animado *or* alegre || *to be in low spirits* estar desanimado || *to keep up one's spirits* no desanimarse || *to raise s.o.'s spirits* animarle *or* levantarle el ánimo a alguien.

spirit ['spirit] *vt* alentar, animar (to cheer up) || *to spirit away* o *off* hacer desaparecer.

spirited [-id] *adj* animado, da; *a spirited argument* una discusión animada || vigoroso, sa; enérgico, ca (vigorous, energetic) || fogoso, sa (horse) || alegre (music).

spiritist [-ist] *n* espiritista *m* & *f.*

spiritless [-lis] *adj* desanimado, da (downhearted) || sin vigor *or* energía (flabby) || irresoluto, ta; indeciso, sa (irresolute).

spiritual ['spiritjuəl] *adj* espiritual; *spiritual life* vida espiritual || REL eclesiástico, ca; *spiritual court* tribunal eclesiástico || *spiritual adviser, director, father, home* consejero *m,* director *m,* padre *m,* patria *f* espiritual.
◆ *n* "negro spiritual" *m* (song).

spiritualism ['spiritjuəlizəm] *n* PHIL espiritualismo *m* || espiritismo *m.*

spiritualist ['spiritjuəlist] *adj/n* PHIL espiritualista || espiritista; *spiritualist séance* sesión espiritista.

spiritualistic [ˌspiritjuə'listik] *adj* PHIL espiritualista || espiritista.

spirituality ['spiritju'æliti] *n* espiritualidad *f.*
◆ *pl* REL bienes *m* eclesiásticos.

spiritualization [spiritjuəlai'zeiʃən] *n* espiritualización *f.*

spiritualize ['spiritjuəlaiz] *vt* espiritualizar.

spiritually ['spiritjuəli] *adv* espiritualmente.

spirituous ['spiritjuəs] *adj* espirituoso, sa (drink).

spirochaete; *US* **spirochete** [spairə'kiːtiː] *n* BIOL espiroqueta *f.*

spiroid ['spairɔid] *adj* espiroidal.

spirometer ['spaiə'rɔmitə*] *n* MED espirómetro *m.*

spirt [spəːt] *n/vt/vi* ⟶ **spurt.**

spit [spit] *n* escupitajo *m,* gargajo *m,* salivazo *m* (saliva expelled from the mouth) || saliva *f* (in the mouth) || MED esputo *m; a spit of blood* un esputo de sangre || bufido *m* (of a cat) || espuma *f* (of insects) || rocío *m* (of rain) || CULIN asador *m,* espetón *m* || GEOL banco *m* (of sand) | punta *f* (of land) || paletada *f* (spadeful) || — FIG *he is the spit and image* o *the very spit of his father* es el vivo retrato de su padre || *spit and polish* limpieza *f* (clean, cleanliness), preocupación exagerada por la limpieza (exaggerated cleanliness), material *m* de limpieza (tools).

spit* [spit] *vt* escupir; *I spat in his face* le escupí en la cara; *to spit blood* escupir sangre || FIG echar, escupir, arrojar; *the guns spat fire* los cañones escupían fuego | soltar, proferir; *to spit insults* proferir insultos || encender (a fuse, a match) || espetar, atravesar, ensartar (to pierce) || — FAM *spit it out!* ¡suéltalo!, ¡desembucha! || *to spit sth. out* escupir algo.
◆ *vi* escupir (to emit saliva); *it is rude to spit* escupir es de mala educación || FIG chisporrotear; *the fire, the frying pan was spitting* el fuego, la sartén chisporroteaba || dar un bufido (cat) || gotear, chispear (to rain lightly) || FIG *to spit at* o *on* o *upon* despreciar (to scorn).
— OBSERV Pret y pp *spat, spit.*

spitball [-bɔːl] *n* pelotilla *f* de papel mascado.

spite [spait] *n* rencor *m,* ojeriza *f* (animosity); *to have a spite against s.o.* tener ojeriza a alguien || — *in spite of* a pesar de, pese a; *in spite of everyone, of everything* a pesar de todos, de todo || *to do sth. out of spite* hacer algo por despecho.

spite [spait] *vt* molestar, fastidiar (to annoy) || *to cut off one's nose to spite one's face* fastidiarse a sí mismo por querer fastidiar a los demás.

spiteful [-ful] *adj* rencoroso, sa (person) || viperino, na (tongue) || malévolo, la (remark, etc.).

spitefulness [-fulnis] *n* rencor *m* || malevolencia *f.*

spitfire ['spitfaiə*] *n* colérico, ca.

spitting ['spitiŋ] *n* MED expectoración *f.*

spitting image [-'imidʒ] *n* vivo retrato *m.*

spittle ['spitl] *n* escupitajo *m,* salivazo *m,* gargajo *m* (spit) || espuma *f* (of insects) || MED esputo *m.*

spittoon [spi'tuːn] *n* escupidera *f.*

spitz [spits] *n* lulú *m,* perro *m* de Pomerania (dog).

spiv [spiv] *n* FAM gandul *m* (layabout) | caballero *m* de industria (well-dressed trickster) | estraperlista *m* (blackmarketeer).

splash [splæʃ] *n* salpicadura *f; splashes of paint* salpicaduras de pintura || chapoteo *m* (lapping, slopping sound) || mancha *f* (of colour) || chorro *m; a whisky with a splash of soda, please!* un whisky con un chorro de soda, por favor || FIG grandes titulares *m pl* (of news) || — *the splash of the waves against the rocks* el golpe de las olas contra las rocas, las olas que rompen contra las rocas || FIG *to make a splash* causar sensación || *to fall into the water with a splash* caer ruidosamente al agua.

splash [splæʃ] *vt* salpicar; *a car splashed him with mud* un coche le salpicó de barro; *I splashed ink on the wall* salpiqué la pared de tinta || chapotear, agitar; *to splash one's feet in the water* chapotear los pies en el agua || rociar (to spray) || FIG derrochar; *to splash one's money about* derrochar el dinero | salpicar (the sky with stars) | poner en primera plana; *to splash a piece of news* poner una noticia en primera plana.
◆ *vi* chapotear; *we splashed about in the water* chapoteamos en el agua || salpicar; *the water splashed all around* el agua lo salpicó todo || ir chapoteando; *we splashed through the waves* fuimos chapoteando entre las olas || — *to splash down* amerizar (spaceship) || FIG *to splash out* derrochar *or* tirar el dinero (to spend a lot) || *to splash over* saltar por encima; *the waves splashed over the breakwater* las olas saltaban por encima del rompeolas.

splashboard [-bɔːd] *n* AUT guardabarros *m inv* [*AMER* guardafango *m*] (mudguard) || *US* alza *f* (of a dam).

splashdown [-daun] *n* amerizaje *m.*

splasher [-ə*] *n* guardabarros *m inv* [*AMER* guardafango *m*] (car's splashboard).

splash guard [-gɑːd] *n* guardabarros *m inv* [*AMER* guardafango *m*].

splashing [-iŋ] *n* salpicadura *f.*

splashy [-i] *adj* fangoso, sa (muddy) || salpicado, da (of water, etc.) || ARTS pintarrajeado, da || FAM llamativo, va (people, clothes).

splat [splæt] *n* listón *m* del espaldar (of a chair).

splatter [-ə*] *n* salpicadura *f.*

splatter [-ə*] *vt* salpicar; *the car splattered him with mud* el coche le salpicó de barro || aplastar; *he splattered an egg against the wall* aplastó un huevo contra la pared.

splay [splei] *n* ARCH derrame *m*, alféizar *m* (of a window) | chaflán *m* (bevelled edge) ‖ extensión *f* (a spreading).

splay [splei] *vt* extender ‖ ARCH hacer un derrame en (a window) | abocinar (an arch) | achaflanar (to bevel).
◆ *vi* ensancharse, extenderse.

splayfoot [-fut] *n* pie *m* plano y torcido.

splayfooted [-'futid] *adj* de pies planos.

spleen [spli:n] *n* ANAT bazo *m* ‖ esplín *m* (depression) ‖ melancolía *f* (melancholy) ‖ mal humor *m* (ill-temper) ‖ capricho *m* (whim).

splendent ['splendənt] *adj* brillante.

splendid ['splendid] *adj* espléndido, da; magnífico, ca; *splendid palaces* palacios magníficos ‖ espléndido, da; estupendo, da; *a splendid performance* una actuación espléndida.

splendidly [-li] *adv* espléndidamente, magníficamente.

splendiferous [splen'difərəs] *adj* FAM espléndido, da.

splendour; *US* **splendor** ['splendə*] *n* esplendor *m*, esplendidez *f*; *the splendour of the Golden Age* el esplendor del Siglo de Oro ‖ brillantez *f*, resplandor *m* (brilliance) ‖ magnificencia *f*, esplendor *m* (magnificence).

splenetic [spli'netik] *adj* MED esplénico, ca ‖ FIG malhumorado, da.
◆ *n* persona *f* malhumorada.

splenic ['splenik] *adj* MED esplénico, ca.

splenius ['spli:niəs] *n* ANAT esplenio *m* (muscle).

splice [splais] *n* empalme *m* ‖ FIG & FAM casorio *m*.

splice [splais] *vt* empalmar (ropes, wood) ‖ FIG & FAM unir, casar ‖ encolar, pegar (a film) ‖ FIG & FAM *to get spliced* pasar por la vicaría (to get married).

splicer [-ə*] *n* encoladora *f*.

splicing [-iŋ] *n* empalme *m* (of wood, of ropes) ‖ encolado *m* (of films).

spline [splain] *n* tira *f* (thin strip of wood, of plastic, etc.) ‖ TECH lengüeta *f* ‖ ranura *f* (slot).

splint [splint] *n* MED tablilla *f* ‖ VET sobrecaña *f* ‖ MED *in a splint* entablillado, da | *to put in splints* entablillar (an arm, etc.).

splint [splint] *vt* MED entablillar.

splinter ['splintə*] *n* astilla *f* (of wood) ‖ fragmento *m*, pedazo *m* (small piece) ‖ MED esquirla *f* (of bone) ‖ casco *m*, metralla *f* (of a bomb).
◆ *adj* disidente; *splinter group* grupo disidente.

splinter ['splintə*] *vt* astillar, rajar, hender.
◆ *vi* astillarse, rajarse.

splinter bone [-bəun] *n* ANAT peroné *m*.

splintering [-riŋ] *n* MED entablillado *m*.

splinterless [-lis] *adj* inastillable.

splinterproof [-pruf] *adj* inastillable (glass).

splintery [-ri] *adj* astilloso, sa.

split [split] *adj* partido, da; hendido, da (wood) ‖ agrietado, da (a rock, etc.) ‖ desgarrado, da (clothes) ‖ reventado, da (burst); *the sack is split* el saco se ha reventado ‖ dividido, da; *the party is split on this issue* el partido está dividido sobre este asunto; *I am split between love and hate* mis sentimientos están divididos entre el amor y el odio ‖ — *split pea* guisante seco ‖ MED *split personality* desdoblamiento *m* de la personalidad ‖ *split pin* pasador *m* ‖ *split screen* pantalla *f* partida (in films, computers) ‖ *split second* fracción *f* de segundo.
◆ *n* raja *f*, desgarrón *m*; *I had a split in my shirt* tenía un desgarrón en la camisa ‖ grieta *f*, hendidura *f* (fissure); *a split in the table, in the rock* una grieta en la mesa, en la roca ‖ escisión *f*, división *f*, ruptura *f* (of a group) ‖ CULIN helado *m*; *banana split* helado de plátano ‖ media botella *f* (half bottle) ‖ diente *m* (of a comb) ‖ claro *m* (space between teeth) ‖ tira *f* de piel (of leather) ‖ SP disposición *f* separada de los bolos (in bowling) ‖ MED grieta *f* (in the skin).
◆ *pl* "ecart" *m*, despatarrada *f sing* (in ballet).

split* [split] *vt* agrietar, hender; *the pressure split the rock* la presión agrietó la roca ‖ partir (into two parts); *the lightning split the tree* el rayo partió el árbol ‖ desgarrar, rajar; *I split my dress* me desgarré el vestido ‖ resquebrajar, cuartear, agrietar; *the earthquake split all the walls of the house* el terremoto resquebrajó todas las paredes de la casa ‖ repartir, dividir; *they split the prize between the two winners* repartieron el premio entre los dos vencedores ‖ dividir; *the abdication split the country* la abdicación dividió al país ‖ MED agrietar (the skin) ‖ GRAMM separar (an infinitive) ‖ CHEM descomponer (a compound) ‖ PHYS descomponer (a molecule) | desintegrar (the atom) ‖ — FIG *to split hairs* hilar muy fino ‖ *to split off* separar ‖ FIG *to split one's sides laughing* partirse de risa ‖ *to split one's vote* dividir el voto ‖ *to split the difference* partir la diferencia ‖ *to split up* dividir (to divide), dispersar (a meeting), compartir (to share), descomponer (a fraction, a compound), desintegrar (the atom), separar (friends, lovers).
◆ *vi* partirse; *the piece of wood split* la madera se partió ‖ agrietarse, henderse (rock) ‖ desgarrarse, rajarse (cloth) ‖ reventarse (shoes) ‖ cuartearse, resquebrajarse; *the wall split with the earthquake* la pared se resquebrajó con el terremoto ‖ estrellarse, hacerse pedazos; *the boat split on a reef* el barco se estrelló contra un arrecife ‖ separarse, dividirse, fraccionarse (groups); *the party split into several factions* el partido se dividió en diversas facciones ‖ doler atrozmente; *my head is splitting* me duele atrozmente la cabeza ‖ MED agrietarse (skin) ‖ FAM delatar, vender; *he split on us to the police* nos vendió a la policía ‖ — FAM *let's split* vayámonos, larguémonos ‖ *to split off* separarse ‖ *to split open* abrirse ‖ *to split up* dividirse (to go different ways), separarse (a married couple).
— OBSERV Pret y pp ***split***.

split-level [-'levl] *adj* de pisos construidos a desnivel (house).

splitter [-ə*] *n* *atom splitter* ciclotrón *m*.

splitting [-iŋ] *adj* hendedor, ra (which splits) ‖ atroz, insoportable, horrible (headache) ‖ para partirse *or* desternillarse de risa (very funny).
◆ *n* hendimiento *m* ‖ cuarteo *m* (of a wall) ‖ PHYS desintegración *f*, fisión *f*, escisión *f* (of the atom) ‖ FIG división *f*.

splodge [splɔdʒ] *n* manchón *m*, mancha *f*.

splodge [splɔdʒ] *vt* ⟶ **splotch.**

splodgy [-i] *adj* manchado, da.

splotch [splɔtʃ] *n* mancha *f*, manchón *m*.

splotch [splɔtʃ]; **splodge** [splɔdʒ] *vt* manchar (to stain) ‖ *to splotch paint on a canvas* pintar a brochazos un lienzo.

splotchy [-i] *adj* manchado, da.

splurge ['splə:dʒ] *n* FAM faroleo *m*, fachenda *f*.

splurge ['splə:dʒ] *vi* FAM farolear, fachendear (to show off).
◆ *vt* FAM derrochar, gastar; *to splurge five hundred pounds on a fur coat* derrochar quinientas libras en un abrigo de piel.

splutter ['splʌtə*]; **sputter** ['spʌtə*] *n* farfulla *f* ‖ chisporroteo *m*.

splutter ['splʌtə*]; **sputter** ['spʌtə*] *vt* balbucear, farfullar.
◆ *vi* farfullar (a person) ‖ chisporrotear (candle) ‖ ELECTR chisporrotear (a collector).

splutterer [-rə*] *n* farfullador, ra.

spoil [spɔil] *n* MIN escombros *m pl* (waste) ‖ — *spoil heap* escorial *m*.
◆ *pl* botín *m sing*; *the burglar's spoils* el botín del ladrón; *the spoils of war* el botín de la guerra ‖ ventajas *f* (political privilege); *the spoils of office* las ventajas del oficio ‖ *US* FAM prebenda *f sing*, sinecura *f sing*, canonjía *f sing* (sinecure) ‖ *to have one's share of the spoils* sacar tajada, sacar su parte.

spoil* [spɔil] *vt* estropear, aguar; *the quarrel spoilt the party* la discusión estropeó la fiesta ‖ echar a perder, estropear (to damage); *the rain spoiled the crop* la lluvia estropeó la cosecha; *heat spoils food* el calor estropea los alimentos ‖ MED estropear; *reading in poor light spoils the eyes* leer con poca luz estropea la vista ‖ cortar (appetite) ‖ afear, estropear; *her hat spoiled her outfit* su sombrero afeaba su vestimenta; *the landscape has been spoiled by the new building* el paisaje ha sido afeado por el nuevo edificio ‖ consentir, mimar (a child) ‖ saquear (a town) ‖ despojar (to deprive) ‖ FAM despachar, liquidar (to kill) ‖ *to spoil s.o.'s fun* aguarle la fiesta a uno.
◆ *vi* estropearse, echarse a perder; *the fruit spoiled with the heat* la fruta se estropeó con el calor ‖ FAM *to be spoiling for a fight* tener ganas de pelearse.
— OBSERV Pret y pp ***spoilt, spoiled***.

spoilage [-idʒ] *n* desperdicios *m pl*, desechos *m pl* (waste) ‖ putrefacción *f* (process of decay).

spoiler [-ə*] *n* expoliador, ra (pillager) ‖ aguafiestas *m & f inv* (killjoy).

spoilsman [-zmən] *n* *US* FAM aprovechón *m*, oportunista *m* (opportunist).
— OBSERV El plural de *spoilsman* es *spoilsmen*.

spoilsport [-spɔ:t] *n* aguafiestas *m & f inv* (killjoy).

spoils system [-z'sistim] *n* acaparamiento *m* de los cargos públicos por el partido victorioso.

spoilt [spɔilt] *pret/pp* ⟶ **spoil.**
◆ *adj* estropeado, da ‖ mimado, da; consentido, da (child) ‖ COMM deteriorado, da; estropeado, da (merchandise).

spoke [spəuk] *n* radio *m* (of a wheel) ‖ escalón *m*, peldaño *m* (of a ladder) ‖ FAM *to put a spoke in s.o.'s wheel* poner trabas a alguien.

spoke [spəuk] *vt* enrayar.

spoke [spəuk] *pret* ⟶ **speak.**

spoken [-ən] *pp* ⟶ **speak.**
◆ *adj* hablado, da; *spoken English* inglés hablado ‖ *«English spoken»* "se habla inglés".

spokeshave [-ʃeiv] *n* TECH raedera *f*.

spokesman [-smən] *n* portavoz *m* [AMER vocero *m*] ‖ *to be spokesman for a group of people* ser portavoz de un grupo de personas, hablar en nombre de un grupo de personas.
— OBSERV El plural de *spokesman* es *spokesmen*.

spokesperson [-spə:sn] *n* portavoz *m & f*.

spoliate ['spəulieit] *vt* expoliar, despojar de.

spoliation [spəuli'eiʃən] *n* expoliación *f*, despojo *m* (pillage) ‖ JUR alteración *f* de documentos.

spondaic [spɔn'deiik] *adj* POET espondaico, ca.

spondee ['spɔndi:] *n* POET espondeo *m*.

spondulicks [spɔn'dju:liks] *n* FAM pasta *f* (money).

spondyl ['spɔndil]; **spondyle** ['spɔndail] *n* ANAT espóndilo *m*, vértebra *f*.

sponge [spʌndʒ] *n* ZOOL esponja *f* || esponja *f* (for domestic use) || CULIN bizcocho *m* esponjoso (cake) || MIL escobillón *m* (for cleaning a cannon) || FIG & FAM gorrón, ona (sponger) || — FIG & FAM *to drink like a sponge* beber como una esponja || FIG *to pass the sponge over* pasar la esponja por | *to throw in the sponge* tirar la esponja (in boxing, etc.).

sponge [spʌndʒ] *vt* limpiar con esponja (to clean) || pasar una esponja por (to wipe) || limpiar con un escobillón || FAM sacar de gorra, gorronear; *to sponge a meal* sacar una comida de gorra | dar un sablazo; *to sponge five pounds off s.o.* dar un sablazo de cinco libras a alguien || — *to sponge off* o *out* quitar con una esponja || *to sponge up* absorber.
◆ *vi* pescar esponjas || FAM sablear, dar sablazos (to borrow money) | vivir de gorra, gorrear, gorronear (to eat, etc., at s.o.'s expense) || — *the stain will sponge off easily* la mancha se quitará fácilmente con un trapo mojado || FAM *to sponge on s.o.* vivir a costa de alguien.

sponge bag [-bæg] *n* neceser *m*.

sponge bath [-bɑːθ] *n* lavado *m* con esponja.

sponge cake [-'keik] *n* CULIN bizcocho *m* esponjoso.

sponge pudding [-'pudiŋ] *n* CULIN pudín *m* de bizcocho.

sponger [-ə*] *n* pescador *m* de esponjas (who harvests sponges) || FAM gorrón, ona (person who lives parasitically) | sablista *m* & *f* (who borrows money).

sponge rubber [-'rʌbə*] *n* goma *f* esponjosa.

spongiae ['spʌndʒiiː] *pl n* espongiarios *m*.

sponginess ['spʌndʒinis] *n* esponjosidad *f*.

sponging ['spʌndʒiŋ] *n* limpieza *f* con esponja (cleaning) || FAM gorronería *f* (cadging).
◆ *adj* FAM gorrón, ona (cadging).

spongy ['spʌndʒi] *adj* esponjoso, sa.

sponsion ['spɔnʃən] *n* JUR garantía *f*.

sponson ['spɔnsn] *n* saliente *m* en un buque de guerra para colocar el cañón || AVIAT flotador *m* (of a hydroplane) || MAR cámara *f* de aire (of a canoe).

sponsor ['spɔnsə*] *n* patrocinador, ra (who gives financial support) || garante *m*, fiador, ra (warrantor) || padrino *m*, madrina *f* (of a child, club member) || RAD patrocinador, ra (of a program).

sponsor ['spɔnsə*] *vt* patrocinar (to support, to finance) || fiar, garantizar (to accept responsibility for) || apadrinar (to act as godparent to, to introduce to a society) || RAD *to sponsor a television programme* presentar *or* patrocinar un programa de televisión.

sponsorial [spɔn'sɔːriəl] *adj* del padrino || patrocinador, ra || garantizador, ra.

sponsorship ['spɔnsəʃip] *n* patrocinio *m* || *under the sponsorship of* bajo el patrocinio de, patrocinado por.

spontaneity ['spɔntə'niːiti] *n* espontaneidad *f*.

spontaneous [spɔn'teinjəs] *adj* espontáneo, a.

spoof [spuːf] *n* FAM engaño *m* (hoax) | broma *f* (parody).

spoof [spuːf] *vt* engañar.
◆ *vi* bromear, burlarse.

spook [spuːk] *n* FAM espectro *m*, aparición *f*.

spooky [-i] *adj* FAM fantasmal (like a ghost) | tétrico, ca (scary) | encantado, da; visitado por duendes (haunted).

spool [spuːl] *n* carrete *m*, bobina *f* (of sewing thread) || canilla *f* (of a sewing machine) || TECH devanadera *f* (in spinning) | enjulio *m* (in weaving) || carrete *m* (of a typewriter, fishing rod, still camera) || bobina *f* (of magnetic tape, cine film).

spool [spuːl] *vt* enrollar, encanillar (thread, etc.) || TECH devanar.

spoon [spuːn] *n* cuchara *f* || cucharada *f* (spoonful); *two spoons of flour* dos cucharadas de harina || SP «spoon» *m*, cuchara *f* (golf club) | cuchara *f* (in fishing) || — *basting spoon* cucharón *m* || *coffee spoon* cuchara *or* cucharilla *f* de café || *dessert spoon* cuchara de postre || *serving spoon* cuchara de servir || *soup spoon* cuchara sopera || FIG *to be born with a silver spoon in one's mouth* criarse en buenos pañales.

spoon [spuːn] *vt* sacar con cuchara || dar forma de cuchara || SP elevar (la pelota) de un golpe || *to spoon out the soup* servir la sopa con cuchara.
◆ *vi* pesca con cuchara (in fishing) || FAM hacerse carantoñas.

spoon bait [-beit] *n* cuchara *f* (in fishing).

spoonbill [-bil] *n* espátula *f* (bird).

spoonerism [-ərizəm] *n* lapsus *m* burlesco de trastrocamiento de letras.

spoon-fed [-fed] *adj* FIG mimado, da (spoilt) | subvencionado, da (enterprise) || que come con cuchara.
— OBSERV Pret y pp ⟶ **spoon-feed.**

spoon-feed* [-fiːd] *vt* dar de comer con cuchara (to feed with a spoon) || FIG mimar (to spoil) | subvencionar (an enterprise).
— OBSERV Pret y pp ***spoon-fed***.

spoonful [-ful] *n* cucharada *f*; *heaped spoonful of flour* cucharada colmada de harina || *small spoonful* cucharadita *f*.
— OBSERV El plural es *spoonfuls* o *spoonsful*.

spoony [-i] *adj* FAM acaramelado, da; enamorado, da (in love).

spoor [spuə*] *n* rastro *m*, pista *f*.

spoor [spuə*] *vt* rastrear, seguir el rastro de, seguir la pista de.
◆ *vi* seguir el rastro *or* la pista de un animal.

sporadic [spə'rædik] *adj* esporádico, ca.

sporangium [spə'rændʒiəm] *n* BOT esporangio *m*.

spore [spɔː*] *n* espora *f* || *spore case* esporangio *m*.

sporidium [spə'ridiəm] *n* BOT esporidio *m*.

sporozoan [ˌspɔrə'zəuən] *n* BIOL esporozoo *m*, esporozoario *m*.

sporran ['spɔrən] *n* bolsa *f* que llevan los escoceses sobre la falda.

sport [spɔːt] *n* deporte *m*; *winter sports* deportes de invierno; *to go in for sport* practicar deportes || caza *f* (hunting); *to have a good day's sport* pasar un buen día de caza || presa *f* (prey); *such people are easy sport for pickpockets* tales personas son presa fácil para los rateros || víctima *f* (victim); *the sport of fortune, of other people's jokes* la víctima del destino, de las bromas de los demás || juguete *m* (plaything) || burla *f*, diversión *f* (amusement); *a moment's sport* un momento de diversión || buen perdedor *m* (good loser) || BIOL mutación *f* || *be a sport!* ¡sé bueno!, ¡sé amable! || — *in sport* en broma || *to be a good sport* portarse como un caballero (to be a gentleman), ser buen chico (likeable) || *to make sport of* burlarse *or* mofarse de.
◆ *pl* competiciones *f*, campeonatos *m* (organized meetings for athletes) || *athletic sports* atletismo *m*.
◆ *adj* US deportivo, va; de sport (sports).

sport [spɔːt] *vi* jugar, divertirse (to play) || bromear (to joke) || juguetear (to frolic).
◆ *vt* lucir; *to sport a new dress* lucir un traje nuevo.

sporting [-iŋ] *adj* deportivo, va; *sporting event* encuentro deportivo; *sporting spirit* espíritu deportivo || aficionado a los deportes (fond of sport); *sporting man* hombre aficionado a los deportes || que juega (gambling) || — *sporting chance* buena posibilidad de éxito || *sporting offer* oferta interesante.

sportive [-iv] *adj* juguetón, ona.

sports [-s] *adj* deportivo, va; de sport || — *sports car* coche deportivo || *sports day* día dedicado a los deportes || *sports ground* campo deportivo || *sports jacket* chaqueta *f* de sport.

sportscast [-kɑːst] *n* retransmisión *f* deportiva.

sportsman [-smən] *n* deportista *m* (who practices a sport) || hombre *m* de espíritu deportivo, caballero *m* (gentleman) || buen perdedor *m* (good loser).
— OBSERV El plural de *sportsman* es *sportsmen*.

sportsmanlike [-smənlaik] *adj* de espíritu deportivo (person) || caballeroso, sa (attitude).

sportsmanship [-smənʃip] *n* deportividad *f* || caballerosidad *f*.

sportswear [-wɛə*] *n* ropa *f* de deporte (clothes for sport) || ropa *f* de sport (casual wear).

sportswoman [-s'wumən] *n* deportista *f* (who practices a sport) || señora *f* (real lady).
— OBSERV El plural de *sportswoman* es *sportswomen*.

sportswriter [-s'raitə*] *n* cronista *m* deportivo.

sporty [-i] *adj* de espíritu deportivo (sportsmanlike) || aficionado a los deportes (fond of sport) || deportivo, va (suitable for sport); *a sporty little boat* un pequeño bote deportivo || de sport (clothes) || alegre (gay) || US FAM ostentoso, sa (flashy).

sporulation [spɔrju'leiʃən] *n* esporulación *f*.

spot [spɔt] *n* mancha *f* (of dirt, on a leopard skin, on fruit, leaves, etc., on the sun, planets); *dog with a brown spot* perro con una mancha de color marrón || lunar *m* (pattern on material); *shirt with blue spots* camisa con lunares azules || MED grano *m* (on the body); *to come out in spots* salirle granos a uno | espinilla *f* (on the face) || sitio *m*, lugar *m* (place); *a quiet spot* un sitio tranquilo; *the spot where the accident ocurred* el sitio donde ocurrió el accidente || puesto *m*, sitio *m* (job) || parte *f*; *a wet spot on a painting* una parte mojada en un cuadro || punto *m* (on billiard table, on ball) || marca *f* (distinguishing mark) || RAD espacio *m*; *advertising spot* espacio publicitario || FIG mancha *f*, baldón *m*; *a spot on one's reputation* una mancha en la reputación de uno || gota *f* (of liquid); *a few spots of rain* unas gotas de lluvia || gota *f*, gotita *f* (of drink); *just a spot, please* sólo una gotita, por favor || FAM poco *m*, poquito *m*; *a spot of work* un poco de trabajo; *a spot to eat* un poquito de comida | foco *m*, proyector (spotlight) || — *accident black spot* lugar en que ocurren muchos accidentes || FAM *a spot of bother* cierta dificultad || *beauty spot* lunar *m* || *black spot* mancha *f* (on one's record) || *night spot* sala *f* de fiestas || *on the spot* en el lugar; *police were on the spot within five minutes* la policía se personó en el lugar en cinco minutos; en el momento; *he dealt with it on the spot* se ocupó de ello en el momento; en el acto; *killed on the spot* matado en el acto || *our man on the spot* nuestro representante (representative), nuestro corresponsal (correspondent) || FIG *sore spot* punto sensible | *tender spot* punto sensible | *to be in a tight spot* estar en un apuro, estar en un aprieto | *to have a soft spot for s.o., for sth.* tener una debilidad por alguien, por algo | *to hit the spot* venirle muy bien a uno, ser lo mejor | *to knock spots off* dar una paliza a (to triumph over), dejar muy atrás (to be better than) | *to put s.o. on the spot* poner a uno en un aprieto (in a difficult position) | *weak spot* punto flaco.

◆ *pl* COMM mercancías *f* disponibles.
◆ *adj* COMM contante; *spot cash* dinero contante | en existencia, disponible (goods) | con pago al contado (sell) || (hecho) al azar (at random); *spot check* inspección hecha al azar || RAD local (from a local station) | realizado entre programas (announcement, etc.).

spot [spɔt] *vt* cubrir con manchas (to mark with spots) || salpicar, motear (to speckle); *the passing car spotted me with mud* el coche me salpicó de barro al pasar || manchar (to dirty) || pronosticar, adivinar; *to spot the winner* pronosticar el ganador || escoger (to select) || reconocer (to recognize) || divisar; *she spotted him in the crowd* le divisó en medio de la multitud || notar, ver; *did you spot the errors?* ¿notaste los errores? || MIL localizar (to find the position of) | concentrar (artillery fire) | emplazar (to position) || US FAM dar como ventaja (to allow as a handicap).
◆ *vi* mancharse (to become stained) || manchar (to stain) || MIL observar el tiro || *to spot with rain* gotear.

spotless [-lis] *adj* sin tacha (character) || intachable (reputation) || inmaculado, da (clean).

spotlessly [-lisli] *adv* *spotlessly clean* limpísimo, ma; inmaculado, da.

spotlessness [-lisnis] *n* limpieza *f* perfecta.

spotlight [-lait] *n* THEATR proyector *m*, foco *m* || foco *m* (beam of light) || lámpara *f*, linterna *f* (torch) || AUT faro *m* auxiliar || FIG *to be in the spotlight* ser objeto de la atención pública, ser el blanco de las miradas.

spotlight [-lait] *vt* iluminar con un proyector (to light up) || FIG poner de relieve; *his speech spotlighted the difference between the two parties* en su discurso puso de relieve la diferencia que existe entre los dos partidos.

spot news [-nju:z] *n* noticias *f pl* de última hora.

spot-on ['spotɔn] *adj* FAM acertado, da, que da en el blanco.

spot-remover [-ri'mu:və*] *n* quitamanchas *m inv.*

spotted [-id] *adj* moteado, da (speckled) || de lunares; *spotted tie* corbata de lunares || con manchas; *spotted dog* perro con manchas || sucio, cia (dirty) || MED *spotted fever* tifus *or* tifo exantemático (typhus), meningitis *f* cerebroespinal.

spotter [-ə*] *n* coleccionista *m* & *f* (collector) || AVIAT avión *m* de observación || MIL observador *m* de tiro.

spotting [-iŋ] *n* MIL observación *f* del tiro.

spotty [-i] *adj* lleno de manchas (covered in spots) || MED con granos (skin) | espinilloso, sa (face) || FIG irregular, desigual (uneven in quality).

spot-welding [-,weldiŋ] *n* soldadura *f* por puntos.

spousals ['spauzəls] *pl n* desposorios *m.*

spouse [spauz] *n* esposo, sa; cónyuge *m* & *f.*

spout [spaut] *n* pico *m* (of a jug) || pitorro *m* (of a teapot) || ARCH canalón *m* (of roof) || caño *m*, conducto *m* (pipe for rainwater, etc.) || chorro *m* (jet) || alcachofa *f* (of watering can) || tromba *f* (waterspout) || FAM *up the spout* empeñado, da (in pawn), perdido, da (beyond remedy).

spout [spaut] *vt* echar, arrojar; *the well started to spout oil* el pozo empezó a echar petróleo || FAM soltar; *to spout nonsense* soltar tonterías.
◆ *vi* salir a chorro, chorrear (a fluid) || FAM declamar, perorar (to talk excessively).

sprag [spræg] *n* calce *m*, cuña *f.*

sprain [sprein] *n* MED torcedura *f*, esguince *m.*

sprain [sprein] *vt* MED torcer; *to sprain one's ankle* torcerse el tobillo.

sprang [spræŋ] *pret* ⟶ **spring.**

sprat [spræt] *n* espadín *m*, «sprat» *m* (fish).

sprawl [sprɔ:l] *n* postura *f* desgarbada || *urban sprawl* urbanización *f* irregular.

sprawl [sprɔ:l] *vt* extender.
◆ *vi* dejarse caer, tumbarse; *he sprawled on the sofa* se dejó caer en el sofá || extenderse; *London sprawls over a wide area* Londres se extiende sobre una gran zona || — *he went sprawling* cayó cuan largo era || *to send s.o. sprawling* tumbar *or* derribar a uno.

sprawling [-iŋ] *adj* de crecimiento desordenado (city, area).

spray [sprei] *n* rociada *f* (water) || MAR espuma *f* || esprai, pulverizador *m*, vaporizador *m* (device for spraying) || ramo *m*, ramillete *m* (of flowers) || barra *f* (of diamonds).

spray [sprei] *vt* pulverizar (to project a liquid); *to spray a plant with insecticide* pulverizar una planta con insecticida || rociar (to sprinkle) || AGR fumigar (crops) || *to spray paint on* pintar con pistola.
◆ *vi* vaporizarse.

spray can [-kæn] *n* esprai *or* espray, pulverizador *m* a presión.

sprayer [-ə*] *n* pulverizador *m*, vaporizador *m* (atomizer) || pistola *f* (for painting) || quemador *m* (for fuel oil).

spray gun [-gʌn] *n* pistola *f.*

spraying [-iŋ] *n* pulverización *f* (of a liquid) || AGR *crop spraying* fumigación *f* de los cultivos.

spray-paint [-peint] *vt* pintar con esprai *or* espray.

spread [spred] *n* propagación *f*, difusión *f*; *spread of a disease, of ideas* propagación de una enfermedad, de ideas || extensión *f* (of an area); *the spread of the city* la extensión de la ciudad; *the spread of one's arms* la extensión de los brazos; *the spread of a country, of a speech* la extensión de un país, de un discurso || envergadura *f* (of wings, of sails) || expansión *f*, desarrollo *m* (of an enterprise) || gama *f* (range); *a wide spread of prices, of books* una ancha gama de precios, de libros || CULIN pasta *f* (paste); *anchovy spread* pasta de anchoa || colcha *f* [AMER cubrecama *m*] (bedspread) || tapete *m* (for a table) || FAM comilona *f* (meal) || ARCH anchura *f* (of a vault) || PRINT anuncio *m* a doble página || — CULIN *cheese spread* queso *m* de untar || FAM *middle-age spread* la curva de la felicidad *or* del cincuentón.
◆ *pret/pp* ⟶ **spread.**

spread* [spred] *vt* extender; *to spread clothes to dry* extender ropa para secar; *to spread a newspaper on the ground* extender un periódico en el suelo; *to spread one's arms* extender los brazos; *to spread a privilege to more than one person* extender un privilegio a más de una persona; *to spread one's influence* extender su influencia || exponer; *the potter spread his wares* el alfarero expuso su mercancía || untar; *to spread marmalade on bread* untar mermelada en el pan; *to spread bread with marmalade* untas el pan con mermelada || cubrir; *to spread the floor with newspapers* cubrir el suelo con periódicos || poner (to set); *to spread the table* poner la mesa || llenar; *to spread the table with exquisite morsels* llenar la mesa con exquisitos manjares || PRINT imprimir a doble página | espaciar (lines) || propagar; *coughs and sneezes spread diseases* toses y estornudos propagan enfermedades || difundir; *to spread ideas* difundir ideas || propagar, hacer correr, difundir; *to spread a rumour* hacer correr un rumor || sembrar (panic, terror) || COMM espaciar (payment) || tender (a net) || aflojar (to distend) || desplegar (wings, sails, flags) || — *to spread its tail* hacer la rueda (peacock) || *to spread o.s.* ponerse a sus anchas (to have plenty of room), dedicarse a muchas actividades (to have many interests), superarse (in performing a task), darse aires, presumir (to give o.s. airs), extenderse, hablar extensamente (on a subject) || *to spread out* esparcir (to scatter), extender; *to spread out a newspaper* extender un periódico; exponer (goods), espaciar (to space out).
◆ *vi* esparcirse; *dust spread over the books* el polvo se esparció sobre los libros || extenderse; *the woods spread as far as the valley* el bosque se extendía hasta el valle; *the ink spread over the paper* la tinta se extendió sobre el papel; *the damp spread into the next room* la humedad se extendió hasta la habitación siguiente || ensancharse (a river) || untarse; *butter spreads more easily if warmed slightly* la mantequilla se unta más fácilmente si se calienta un poco || correr; *the rumour has spread* ha corrido el rumor || propagarse; *the disease quickly spread* la enfermedad se propagó rápidamente || difundirse, propagarse, diseminarse (news, ideas) || propagarse (fire) || desplegarse (flags, wings, sails) || separarse (to move apart) || FAM engordar (to grow stout) || *to spread out* esparcirse, desparramarse (to scatter), separarse (to separate), extenderse (to stretch), desarrollarse (to develop), ensancharse; *here the river spreads out* aquí se ensancha el río.
— OBSERV Pret y pp ***spread***.

spread-eagle [-'i:gl] *adj* con los miembros extendidos || US patriotero, ra (chauvinistic) | fanfarrón, ona (boasting).

spread-eagle [-'i:gl] *vt* extender los miembros de (as a punishment).

spreader [-ə*] *n* propagador, ra.

spreadsheet ['spredʃi:t] *n* INFORM hoja *f* de cálculo *or* electrónica.

spree [spri:] *n* juerga *f*, jarana *f* [AMER parranda *f*]; *to go on a spree* ir de juerga, andar de parranda || *to go on a shopping* o *a spending spree* hacer muchas compras.

sprig [sprig] *n* ramito *m*; *a sprig of holly* un ramito de acebo || TECH puntilla *f*, tachuela *f* (nail).

sprig [sprig] *vt* adornar con ramitos (to decorate) || TECH clavar con puntillas *or* con tachuelas.

sprightliness ['spraitlinis] *n* vivacidad *f* (liveliness) || energía *f* (energy) || agilidad *f* (in an old person).

sprightly ['spraitli] *adj* vivo, va (lively); *a sprightly style* un estilo vivo || enérgico, ca (energetic) || ágil; *he is very sprightly for his age* es muy ágil para la edad que tiene.

spring [spriŋ] *n* salto *m* (jump); *to take a spring* dar un salto || primavera *f* (season); *in spring* en la primavera; *spring is in the air* huele a primavera || manantial *m*, fuente *f* (of water); *hot spring* manantial de agua caliente || muelle *m*, resorte *m* (of watch, of mattress, etc.); *coil spring* muelle helicoidal || AUT ballesta *f* || FIG fuente *f*; *spring of life* fuente de vida || ARCH arranque *m* (of an arch, a vault) || elasticidad *f* (elasticity) || grieta *f* (crack) || FIG *to walk with a spring in one's step* andar con paso ligero.
◆ *adj* primaveral; *spring morning* mañana primaveral; *spring flowers* flores primaverales || resistente (resilient) || de muelles (a watch, a mattress, etc.) || montado sobre ballestas (carriage) || de manantial (water).

spring* [spriŋ] *vt* saltar; *the dog sprang the river* el perro saltó el río || hacer surgir *or* brotar (water, etc.) || soltar (to release) || poner muelles a (to put springs on) || hacer funcionar (a trap) || FAM soltar de repente; *he sprang a question on me* de repente me soltó una pregunta || volar, hacer explotar (to cause to explode) ||

torcer, combar (to warp) || hender (to split) || levantar [caza] (game) || FAM poner en libertad, soltar (prisoners) || — *to spring a leak* empezar a hacer agua || *to spring an ambush* tender una emboscada || *to spring a surprise on s.o.* coger de sorpresa a alguien.
◆ *vi* saltar (to jump); *to spring over a fence* saltar una valla || levantarse de un salto (to get up suddenly); *he sprang from his bed* de un salto se levantó de la cama || descender; *he springs from aristocratic stock* desciende de una familia aristocrática || surgir, derivarse; *the quarrel sprang from a misunderstanding* la riña surgió de un malentendido || brotar; *the point where the water springs from the rock* el lugar donde el agua brota de la roca; *the corn is springing* brota el maíz || salir a chorros; *the wine was springing from the hole in the barrel* el vino salía a chorros por el agujero en el tonel || torcerse, alabearse (to warp) || henderse (to split) || explotar (a mine) || ARCH arrancar; *several arches spring from the column* varios arcos arrancan de la columna || — *hope springs eternal* la esperanza es lo último que se pierde || *tears sprang to his eyes* se le llenaron los ojos de lágrimas || *to spring at s.o.* abalanzarse sobre alguien || *to spring back* volver a su posición original; *the branch sprang back* la rama volvió a su posición original; saltar para atrás, dar un salto para atrás (a person) || *to spring forth* brotar || *to spring forward* dar un salto hacia adelante || *to spring open* abrirse de un golpe || *to spring to one's feet* levantarse de un salto || *to spring to s.o.'s rescue* acudir rápidamente en ayuda de alguien || *to spring up* brotar, surgir, manar (a liquid), elevarse, levantarse (a building), levantarse de un salto (to get up quickly), levantarse (the wind), crecer rápidamente (to grow quickly), espigarse (a child), surgir (a problem), nacer (a friendship) || *where did you spring from?* ¿de dónde salió usted?
— OBSERV Pret ***sprang, sprung***; pp ***sprung***.

spring balance [-b'bæləns] *n* peso *m* de muelle.

spring bed [-'bed] *n* colchón *m* de muelles.

springboard [-bɔːd] *n* trampolín *m*.

spring bolt [-bɔlt] *n* pestillo *m* de golpe.

spring-clean [-kliːn] *vt* hacer una limpieza general.

spring-cleaning [-'kliːniŋ] *n* limpieza *f* general || *to do the spring-cleaning* hacer una limpieza general, limpiar toda la casa.

springe [sprindʒ] *n* lazo *m*.

springer [spriŋə*] *n* tipo de podenco *m* (dog) || sotabanco *m* (of an arch).

spring fever ['spriŋfiːvə*] *n* desasosiego *m* [debido a la llegada de la primavera].

springhead ['spriŋhed] *n* manantial *m*, fuente *f*.

springiness ['spriŋinis] *n* elasticidad *f*.

springing ['spriŋiŋ] *n* muelles *m pl* (strings) || ARCH arranque *m*.

spring leaf ['spriŋliːf] *n* hoja *f* de ballesta.

springlet ['spriŋlet] *n* manantial *m* pequeño.

springlike ['priŋlaik] *adj* elástico, ca (like a spring) || primaveral; *springlike weather* tiempo primaveral.

spring lock ['spriŋlɔk] *n* cerradura *f* de golpe.

spring mattress ['spriŋ'mætris] *n* colchón *m* de muelles.

spring onion ['spriŋ'ʌnjən] *n* cebolleta *f*, cebolla *f* tierna.

spring roll ['spriŋrəul] *n* CULIN rollo *m* de primavera.

spring tide ['spriŋtaid] *n* MAR marea *f* viva, aguas *f pl* vivas.

springtide ['spriŋtaid]; **springtime** ['spriŋtaim] *n* primavera *f*.

springwater ['pspriŋ'wɔːtə*] *n* agua *f* de manantial.

springy ['spriŋi] *adj* elástico, ca (resilient) || FIG ligero, ra; *springy step* paso ligero.

sprinkle ['spriŋkl] *n* rociada *f*, salpicadura *f* || *a sprinkle of grated cheese* un poquito de queso rallado; *a sprinkle of rain* unas gotas de lluvia.

sprinkle ['spriŋkl] *vt* rociar; *to sprinkle with water* rociar de agua || asperjar (with holy water) || salpicar; *to sprinkle with sugar* salpicar con azúcar; *a speech sprinkled with long words* un discurso salpicado de palabras largas || diseminar, desparramar; *he has relatives sprinkled all over the country* tiene parientes diseminados por todo el país || TECH jaspear (book).
◆ *vi* chispear, lloviznar (to drizzle) || rociar (to spray).

sprinkler [-ə*] *n* AGR regadera *f* || REL hisopo *m*, aspersorio *m* || extintor *m* (to estinguish fire) || *sprinkler system* sistema *m* de regadío (in agriculture), sistema *m* de aspersión automática (fire precaution).

sprinkling [-iŋ] *n* aspersión *f* (of a liquid) || REL aspersión *f* (of holy water) || FIG un poco, algo de; *a sprinkling of sugar* un poco de azúcar || — *a sprinkling of Latinisms in a letter* una carta salpicada de latinajos || *a sprinkling of rain* unas gotas de lluvia || *there was a sprinkling of peers at the reception* en la fiesta había unos cuantos aristócratas.

sprint [sprint] *n* SP «sprint» *m*, esprint *m* || FIG *it was quite a sprint for us to get the work finished on time* tuvimos que apresurarnos mucho para terminar a tiempo el trabajo.

sprint [sprint] *vt* SP sprintar en, esprintar en; *to sprint the last hundred metres* esprintar en los últimos cien metros.
◆ *vi* SP sprintar, esprintar || correr a toda velocidad (to run at full speed).

sprinter [-ə*] *n* SP sprinter *m* & *f*, esprinter *m* & *f*, corredor *m* de velocidad.

sprit [sprit] *n* MAR verga *f* (spar) | bauprés *m* (bowsprit).

sprite [sprait] *n* duende *m*, trasgo *m* (elf) || hada *f* (fairy).

spritsail ['spritseil] *n* MAR vela *f* de abanico, vela *f* tarquina, cebadera *f*.

spritzer ['spritzə*] *n* vino *m* con sifón.

sprocket [sprɔkit] *n* TECH diente *m* (of a chain, pinion) | rueda *f* dentada, rueda *f* catalina (wheel).

sprocket wheel [-wiːl] *n* TECH rueda *f* dentada, rueda *f* catalina.

sprout [spraut] *n* brote *m*, retoño *m* (shoot).
◆ *pl* *Brussels sprouts* coles *f* de Bruselas.

sprout [spraut] *vt* BOT echar; *the tree has sprouted leaves* el árbol ha echado hojas || echar, salirle [a un animal] (horns) || dejarse; *to sprout a moustache* dejarse bigote.
◆ *vi* BOT brotar; *after the rain the flowers sprouted* después de la lluvia brotaron las flores || echar brotes (branch) || FIG crecer rápidamente.

spruce [spruːs] *adj* cuidado, da (tidy) || pulcro, cra (neat) || elegante (smart) || acicalado, da (trim).
◆ *n* BOT picea *f* (tree).

spruce [spruːs] *vt* *to spruce o.s. up* acicalarse, ataviarse || *to spruce up* arreglar (sth.), acicalar, ataviar (s.o.).

spruceness [-nis] *n* pulcritud *f* (neatness) || elegancia *f* (smartness).

sprue [spruː] *n* TECH piquera *f*, orificio *m* de colada (hole) | mazarota *f* (waste metal).

sprung [sprʌŋ] *pret/pp* ⟶ **spring.**

spry ['sprai] *adj* vivo, va (lively) || activo, va (active).

spud [spʌd] *n* AGR escarda *f*, escardillo *m* (tool) || FAM patata *f* [AMER papa *f*] (potato).

spud [spʌd] *vt* escardar.

spue [spjuː] *n/vt/vi* ⟶ **spew.**

spume [spjuːm] *n* espuma *f*.

spume [spjuːm] *vi* espumar, hacer espuma.

spumous [-əs]; **spumy** [-i] *adj* espumoso, sa.

spun [spʌn] *pret/pp* ⟶ **spin.**
◆ *adj* hilado, da; *spun silk* seda hilada || — *spun glass* lana *f* de vidrio || MAR *spun yarn* meollar *m* (rope).

spunk [spʌŋk] *n* FAM valor *m*, arrojo *m*, agallas *f pl* (courage) || yesca *f* (tinder).

spunky [-i] *adj* FAM valiente, arrojado, da; que tiene agallas.

spur [spəː*] *n* espuela *f* (for horsemen) || ZOOL espolón *m* || BOT cornezuelo *m* || espolón *m* (of a gamecock) || trepador *m* (for climbing) || vía *f* muerta, apartadero *m* (in railways) || estribación *f* (of mountain) || ARCH riostra *f*, puntal *m* (strut) | contrafuerte *m* (buttress) || FIG estímulo *m*, espuela *f*, aguijón *m*, acicate *m* || MAR espolón *m*, tajamar *m* || — FIG *on the spur of the moment* sin pensarlo || *to dig one's spurs into one's horse* espolear un caballo, picar un caballo con las espuelas || FIG *to give a spur to s.o.'s efforts* estimular los esfuerzos de alguien | *to win one's spurs* dar pruebas de sus aptitudes.

spur [spə*] *vt* espolear, picar con las espuelas (a horse) || poner espuelas en (a horseman) || poner espolones a (a gamecock) || FIG *to spur on* estimular, incitar; *to spur s.o. on to do sth.* incitar a alguien a que haga algo; espolear, aguijonear; *spurred on by desire* aguijoneado por el deseo.
◆ *vi* *to spur on* o *forward* hincar las espuelas (to spur a horse), apresurarse (to hurry).

spur gear [-giə*] *n* TECH engranaje *m* cilíndrico.

spurious ['spjuəriəs] *adj* falso, sa (money, sentiments) || apócrifo, fa (document) || espúreo, a (child).

spuriousness [-nis] *n* falsedad *f* || carácter *m* espúreo, ilegitimidad *f* (of a child).

spurn [spəːn] *n* desprecio *m*, desdén *m*.

spurn [spəːn] *vt* despreciar, desdeñar (to disdain) || dar una patada a (to kick).

spurt [spəːt] *n* gran esfuerzo *m*, momento *m* de energía (sudden effort) || arrebato *m*, acceso *m* (sudden outburst); *a spurt of anger* un arrebato de cólera || chorro *m* (sudden gush) || — SP *final spurt* esfuerzo final || FAM *to put on a spurt* acelerar.

spurt [spəːt] *vi* hacer un gran esfuerzo (to make a big effort) || SP acelerar || chorrear, salir a chorros (to gush forth).
◆ *vt* echar (a liquid).

spur track ['spəːtræk] *n* apartadero *m*, vía *f* muerta.

spur wheel ['spəːwiːl] *n* TECH engranaje *m* cilíndrico.

sputnik ['sputnik] *n* «sputnik» *m* (satellite).

sputter ['spʌtə*] *n/vt/vi* ⟶ **splutter.**

sputum ['spjuːtəm] *n* MED esputo *m*.
— OBSERV El plural de esta palabra es *sputa*.

spy [spai] *n* espía *m* & *f* || — FAM *police spy* confidente *m*, soplón *m*, chivato *m* || *spy story* novela *f* de espionaje.

spy [spai] *vt* divisar (to catch sight of) || ver (to see) || conseguir ver (by careful observation) || espiar (to watch) || *to spy out* reconocer (the land), descubrir valiéndose de artimañas (a secret).

◆ *vi* ser espía || — *to spy into* mirar de cerca (to examine), intentar descubrir (a secret) || *to spy on* o *upon s.o.* espiar a alguien.

spyglass [-glɑ:s] *n* catalejo *m*.

spyhole [-həul] *n* mirilla *f* (in a door) || registro *m* (in machinery).

spying [-iŋ] *n* espionaje *m*.

squab [skwɔb] *adj* rechoncho, cha; regordete, ta (plump) || ZOOL sin plumas.
◆ *n* pichón *m* (young pigeon) || pollito *m* (young bird) || cojín *m*, almohadón *m* (cushion) || sofá *m* (couch) || FAM tapón *m* de alberca, persona *f* rechoncha *or* regordeta.

squabble [-l] *n* riña *f*, disputa *f*, pelea *f*.

squabble [-l] *vt* PRINT empastelar.
◆ *vi* reñir, pelearse, disputar.

squabbler [-lə*] *n* pendenciero, ra.

squabbling [-liŋ] *n* peleas *f pl*, riñas *f pl*.

squabby [-i] *adj* FAM rechoncho, cha; regordete, ta.

squad [skwɔd] *n* MIL pelotón *m*; *firing squad* pelotón de ejecución || brigada *f* (of police); *drug squad* brigada de estupefacientes || US equipo *m* (team).

squad car [-kɑ:*] *n* US coche *m* patrulla.

squadron ['skwɔdrən] *n* MIL escuadrón *m* || AVIAT escuadrilla *f* || MAR escuadra *f*.

squadron leader [-'li:də*] *n* comandante *m*.

squalid ['skwɔlid] *adj* mugriento, ta; asqueroso, sa; escuálido, da (very dirty) || sórdido, da (sordid) || miserable (poor).

squalidity [skwɔ'liditi]; **squalidness** ['skwɔlidnis] *n* asquerosidad *f*, escualidez *f* (dirtiness) || miseria *f* (poverty).

squall [skwɔ:l] *n* ráfaga *f*, racha *f* (sudden wind) || MAR turbonada *f* (sudden storm) || FAM tormenta *f*, borrasca *f* || chillido *m*, berrido *m* (harsh cry).

squall [skwɔ:l] *vi* chillar, berrear (to scream).

squalling [-iŋ] *n* chillidos *m pl*, berridos *m pl*.

squally [-i] *adj* tempestuoso, sa; borrascoso, sa.

squalor [-ə*] *n* mugre *f*, asquerosidad *f* (dirtiness) || miseria *f* (poverty).

squama ['skweimə] *n* escama *m*.
— OBSERV El plural de esta palabra es *squamae*.

squamate ['skweimət]; **squamosal** ['skwei'məusəl]; **squamose** ['skwei,məus]; **squamous** ['skweiməs] *adj* escamoso, sa.

squander ['skwɔndə*] *vt* malgastar, derrochar, despilfarrar (money) || desperdiciar (time).

squandering [-riŋ] *n* despilfarro *m*, derroche *m* (of money) || desperdicio *m* (of time).

square [skwɛə*] *adj* cuadrado, da (having four equal sides); *a square table* una mesa cuadrada || rectangular || en ángulo recto, a escuadra (sides of a box) || MATH cuadrado, da; *square mile* milla cuadrada; *square root* raíz cuadrada || de superficie (measure) || cuadrado, da (chin, shoulders) || FIG justo, ta; equitativo, va (fair); *square deal* trato justo || honrado, da (honest) || rotundo, da; categórico, ca; terminante; *square statement* afirmación categórica; *a square refusal* una negación rotunda || en orden (orderly); *to get things square* poner las cosas en orden || FAM satisfactorio, ria (meal) | anticuado, da; chapado a la antigua (old-fashioned) || SP empatado, da (tied) || — FIG *all square* en paz; *now we are all square* ahora estamos en paz; iguales, empatado, da (in sport) | *of square frame* fornido, da; cuadrado, da (person) || *square bracket* corchete *m* || *square dance* baile *m* de figuras || *square knot* nudo *m* de envergue *or* de rizo || *square meal* comida *f* decente || MAR *square sail* vela cangreja || FIG *to get square with s.o.* ajustarle las cuentas a uno.
◆ *adv* a escuadra, en ángulo recto (*to, with* con) (at right angles) || en forma cuadrada (in square shape) || FIG directamente (directly) | justo, exactamente; *the library is square in the middle of the town* la biblioteca está justo en medio de la ciudad || honradamente (honestly) || equitativamente, con justicia (fairly) | cara a cara (face to face).
◆ *n* cuadrado *m* (shape) || cuadro *m*; *decorated with black squares* decorado con cuadros negros || escuadra *f* (instrument) || MATH cuadrado *m* (figure, multiple); *nine is the square of three* nueve es el cuadrado de tres || casilla *f* (of a chessboard) || cristal *m* (of a window) || ARCH plaza *f* (in a town) | plaza *f* ajardinada, plazoleta *f* (with garden) || MIL cuadro *m* (of soldiers) || pañuelo *m* (handkerchief) || FAM anticuado, da; persona *f* chapada a la antigua (old-fashioned person) || US manzana *f* [AMER cuadra *f*] (block of houses) || — *on the square* en ángulo recto || FAM *to be back to square one* tener que empezar de cero *or* desde el principio || FIG *to be on the square* ser honrado.

square [skwɛə*] *vt* cuadrar (to make square) || TECH escuadrar, labrar a escuadra (stone) | escuadrar (timber) || cuadricular (paper, etc.) || MATH cuadrar, elevar al cuadrado *or* a la segunda potencia (a number) || FAM sobornar, untar la mano a (to bribe) || FIG adaptar (to adapt) | ajustar (accounts) | arreglar (to settle); *to square matters* arreglar las cosas || SP igualar, empatar (a score) || — FIG *to square accounts with* ajustarle las cuentas a || *to square one's shoulders* sacar el pecho || FIG *to square with* conformar con, ajustar a.
◆ *vi* cuadrar, estar de acuerdo; *his ideas do not square with mine* sus ideas no cuadran con las mías || *to square up* ponerse en guardia, disponerse a luchar (*to* contra) (to be ready to fight), saldar cuentas (*with* con) (to settle accounts), enfrentarse con (to face up to).

square-built [-bilt] *adj* de forma cuadrada (building) || fornido, da; cuadrado, da (person).

squared ['skwɛəd] *adj* cuadriculado, da (paper) || escuadrado, da (stone, timber) || MATH elevado al cuadrado, elevado a la segunda potencia.

squarely ['skwɛəli] *adv* en ángulo recto, a escuadra (forming a right angle) || con ángulos rectos (with right angles) || FIG honradamente (honestly) | justo, exactamente (exactly) | justo enfrente (directly opposite) | cara a cara, de frente (face to face) | firmemente (firmly).

square-necked ['skwɛə'nekt] *adj* con escote cuadrado (dress).

squareness ['skwɛənis] *n* forma *f* cuadrada || FIG honradez *f*.

square-shouldered ['skwɛə'ʃəuldəd] *adj* ancho de espaldas, con las espaldas cuadradas.

square-toed ['skwɛə'təud] *adj* con la punta cuadrada (shoe) || FAM anticuado, da; chapado a la antigua (old-fashioned).

squaring ['skwɛəriŋ] *n* corte *m* a escuadra (of a stone) || cuadriculado *m* || MATH cuadratura *f*; *squaring the circle* cuadratura del círculo.

squarish ['skwɛəriʃ] *adj* casi cuadrado, aproximadamente cuadrado.

squash [skwɔʃ] *n* zumo *m* (juice) || aplastamiento *m* (crushing) || tropel *m*, gentío *m* (closely packed crowd) || BOT calabaza *f* [AMER cidra *f*, chayote *m*] || chapoteo *m* (walking) || SP squash || — *lemon squash* limón *m* natural, zumo de limón || *squash hat* sombrero *m* flexible.

squash [skwɔʃ] *vt* aplastar (to crush); *I'm afraid I squashed the cake* temo haber aplastado el pastel || apretar (to squeeze) || meter (to put) || FAM aplastar, sofocar (to suppress); *to squash a rebellion* sofocar una rebelión | echar por tierra (an objection) | apabullar, callar (to silence a conceited person).
◆ *vi* aplastarse (to crush) || apretarse, apretujarse (to crowd together) || — *to squash into* conseguir meterse en, conseguir entrar en; *I squashed into the lift* conseguí meterme en el ascensor || *to squash through* entrar atropelladamente por.

squash rackets; **squash racquets** [-,rækits] *n* SP squash.

squashy [-i] *adj* blando, da (easily crushed) || cenagoso, sa (earth) || de pulpa blanda (fruit).

squat [skwɔt] *adj* en cuclillas (crouching) || agazapado, da (animals) || rechoncho, cha; achaparrado, da (person).
◆ *n* posición *f* en cuclillas.

squat [skwɔt] *vi* ponerse en cuclillas, agacharse (to crouch) || agazaparse (animals) || FAM sentarse (to sit) || JUR ocupar ilegalmente un sitio (to occupy property illegally).

squatter [-ə*] *n* JUR persona *f* que ocupa ilegalmente un sitio.

squaw [skwɔ:] *n* india *f* norteamericana.

squawk [skwɔ:k] *n* graznido *m*, chillido *m*.

squawk [skwɔ:k] *vi* graznar, chillar.

squeak [skwi:k] *n* chillido *m* (of mice, rats, rabbits) || chirrido *m*, rechinamiento *m* (of a hinge) || chirrido *m* (of certain birds) || crujido *m* (of shoes) || — FAM *I don't want to hear a squeak out of you* no quiero oírte, no quiero que rechistes | *to have a narrow squeak* librarse por los pelos.

squeak [skwi:k] *vt* decir con voz aguda.
◆ *vi* chillar (mice, rats, rabbits) || chirriar, rechinar (hinge) || rechinar (spring) || chirriar (certain birds) || crujir (shoes) || raspear (pen) || US FAM cantar, confesar (a secret) || — FIG *to squeak by* arreglárselas | *to squeak through* pasar dificultosamente.

squeaker [-ə*] *n* pichón *m* (pigeon) || pollito *m* (young bird) || FAM soplón *m*, chivato *m* (informer).

squeaky [-i] *adj* chirriador, ra; chirriante (birds) || que cruje (shoe) || chillón, ona (voice) || que rechina, chirriante (hinge).

squeal [skwi:l] *n* chillido *m* || FAM protesta *f*, queja *f* (complaint) | denuncia *f* (denunciation).

squeal [skwi:l] *vi* chillar (to make a shrill cry) || FAM protestar, quejarse (to complain) | cantar, confesar (to inform) || FAM *to squeal on* chivarse de (one's accomplices).
◆ *vt* *to squeal out sth.* decir algo chillando.

squeamish ['skwi:miʃ] *adj* remilgado, da (oversensitive) || delicado, da (excessively fastidious) || demasiado escrupuloso (excessively scrupulous) || pudibundo, da (prudish) || — *to be squeamish about* tener horror a || MED *to feel squeamish* estar mareado, sentir náuseas.

squeamishness [-nis] *n* remilgos *m pl* || delicadeza *f*.

squeegee ['skwi:'dʒi:] *n* enjugador *m*, rodillo *m* de goma.

squeeze [skwi:z] *n* apretón *m* (of the hand) || abrazo *m* (hug) || presión *f* (compression) || reducción *f*, disminución *f* || gentío *m*, bullicio *m* (crowd) || unas gotas; *a squeeze of lemon* unas gotas de limón || FIG aprieto *m* (difficulty); *if you are ever in a squeeze, come and see me* si alguna vez se encuentra en un aprieto, venga a verme || ARTS molde *m* || FAM exacción *f* || — *it was a tight squeeze* estábamos muy apretados || *to give s.o. a squeeze* abrazar a alguien || FIG *to put the squeeze on s.o.* apretarle las clavijas a uno.

squeeze [skwi:z] *vt* apretar, estrechar (to press); *to squeeze somebody's hand* apretar la mano a alguien || estrujar (to press very hard) || exprimir; *to squeeze an orange to extract the juice* exprimir una naranja para extraer el zumo; *to squeeze the juice out of an orange* exprimir el zumo de una naranja || FIG ejercer presión (to put pressure upon) || moldear (to mould) || abrazar (to hug) || FAM sacar, sonsacar; *to squeeze money from* sacar dinero a || — *the doctor managed to squeeze him in before lunch* el médico consiguió darle hora antes del almuerzo [aunque tenía muchos clientes] || *to squeeze in one's waist* ceñirse la cintura || *to squeeze into* meter (by force) || *to squeeze one's finger* pillarse *or* cogerse el dedo || *to squeeze o.s. into* meterse (con dificultad) en || *to squeeze o.s. through* abrirse paso (con dificultad) entre, conseguir pasar entre || *to squeeze out* sacar (water, money, a confession), derramar (a tear) || *to squeeze through* hacer pasar por.
◆ *vi* *to squeeze into* meterse (con dificultad) en || *to squeeze out* salir (con dificultad) de || *to squeeze through* abrirse paso (con dificultad), conseguir pasar entre (to force one's way) || *to squeeze together* o *up* apretarse, apretujarse, apiñarse.

squeeze-box [-bɔks] *n* FAM acordeón *m*.

squeezer [-ə*] *n* exprimidor *m*, exprimelimones *m inv* (for juice).

squelch [skweltʃ] *n* chapoteo *m* || FAM réplica *f* (retort).

squelch [skweltʃ] *vt* despachurrar, aplastar (to squash) || FIG aplastar, sofocar (a revolt) | callar, apabullar (s.o.).
◆ *vi* chapotear, ir chapoteando.

squib [skwib] *n* buscapiés *m inv* (firework) || detonador *m* (detonator) || FIG pasquín *m* (lampoon) || FIG *a damp squib* un fallo.

squid [skwid] *n* calamar *m* (fish).

squiffy ['skwifi] *adj* FAM achispado, da.

squiggle ['skwigl] *n* garabato *m*.

squill [skwil] *n* esquila *f*, cebolla *f* albarrana (onion) || esquila *f*, camarón *m* (prawn).

squilla [-ə] *n* esquila *f* camarón *m* (prawn).
— OBSERV El plural de esta palabra es *squillas* o *squillae*.

squint [skwint] *n* estrabismo *m*, bizquera *f* (strabismus) || mirada *f* bizca (cross-eyed look) || FAM ojeada *f*, vistazo *m* (quick look); *I had a squint at his paper* eché un vistazo a su periódico || mirada *f* de reojo (sidelong glance) || FIG inclinación *f* (tendency) || *to have a squint* ser bizco.
◆ *adj* bizco, ca (eyes) || que mira de reojo.

squint [skwint] *vt* cerrar casi, entrecerrar (eyes).
◆ *vi* bizquear, ser bizco (to be cross-eyed) || mirar de reojo (to look from the corner of the eye) || cerrar casi *or* entrecerrar los ojos (to keep the eyes partly closed) || *to squint at* echar un vistazo *or* una ojeada a (to have a look at), mirar de reojo (to look from the corner of the eye), mirar con los ojos entrecerrados.

squint-eyed [-aid] *adj* bizco, ca (s.o.) || FIG de reojo (look) || FIG avieso, sa (malicious).

squire ['skwaiə*] *n* HIST escudero *m* || propietario *m*, terrateniente *m* [AMER hacendado *m*, estanciero *m*] (landowner) || señor *m* (term of address) || FIG galán *m* (lady's escort) || *the squire* el señor (in a village).

squire ['skwaiə*] *vt* acompañar (a lady).

squirearchy [-rɑ:ki] *n* aristocracia *f* rural, terratenientes *m pl*.

squirm [skwə:m] *vi* retorcerse (to wriggle) || FIG estar violento (to be embarrassed).

squirrel ['skwirəl] *n* ZOOL ardilla *f*.

squirt [skwə:t] *n* chorro *m* (of liquid) || jeringa *f* (syringe) || atomizador *m* (atomizer) || FAM mequetrefe *m* (whippersnapper).

squirt [skwə:t] *vt* dejar salir a chorros; *the cracked pipe was squirting water* el tubo roto dejaba salir el agua a chorros || echar agua; *to squirt s.o. with a water pistol* echar agua a alguien con una pistola de agua || inyectar (with a syringe).
◆ *vi* salir a chorros; *beer squirted from the barrel* la cerveza salía a chorros del tonel.

squirter [-ə*] *n* FAM atomizador *m*.

squirt gun [-gʌn] *n* pistola *f* de agua (toy).

squirting [-iŋ] *n* salida *f* a chorros (of liquid) || inyección *f* (with a syringe).

Sri Lanka [ˌsri:'læŋkə] *pr n* GEOGR Sri Lanka.

Sri Lankan [ˌsri:'læŋkən] *adj/n* esrilanqués, esa.

St *abbr of* [street] c., c/., calle.

stab [stæb] *n* puñalada *f* (with a dagger) || navajazo *m* (with a knife) || herida *f* (wound) || FAM tentativa *f*, intento *m* (attempt) || FIG punzada *f* (of pain) || — FIG *stab in the back* puñalada trapera || FAM *taking a stab in the dark, I would say that...* a ojo de buen cubero diría que... || *to die of stab wounds* morir apuñalado || FAM *to have a stab at sth.* intentar (hacer) algo.

stab [stæb] *vt* apuñalar, dar una puñalada a (to pierce with a dagger) || dar un navajazo (with a knife) || FIG partir (s.o.'s heart) || — *to be stabbed to death* morir apuñalado || FIG *to stab s.o. in the back* darle a uno una puñalada por la espalda *or* una puñalada trapera || *to stab s.o. to death* matar a alguien a puñaladas.
◆ *vi* dar una puñalada || *to stab at* intentar apuñalar a (to try to wound), mancillar (s.o.'s reputation), señalar (sth. with one's finger).

stabbing [-iŋ] *adj* punzante (pain).
◆ *n* puñaladas *f pl* (stabs) || asesinato *m* a puñaladas (murder).

stability [stə'biliti] *n* estabilidad *f* || firmeza *f*, entereza *f* (firmness of character).

stabilization ['steibilai'zeiʃən] *n* estabilización *f*.

stabilize ['steibilaiz] *vt* estabilizar.
◆ *vi* estabilizarse.

stabilizer [-ə*] *n* estabilizador *m*.

stabilizing [-iŋ] *adj* estabilizador, ra.

stable ['steibl] *adj* estable; *a stable building, situation* un edificio, una situación estable || estable, fijo, ja (job) || firme (conviction) || estable (person) || *to become stable* estabilizarse.
◆ *n* cuadra *f*, caballeriza *f*, establo *m* (stall of horses) || cuadra *f* (group of race horses) || equipo *m* (of persons) || AUT escudería *f* (of race cars) || MYTH *Augean stables* establos *m* de Augias.

stable ['steibl] *vt* poner en una cuadra.
◆ *vi* estar en la cuadra.

stableboy [-bɔi]; **stableman** [-mən] *n* mozo *m* de cuadra.
— OBSERV El plural de *stableman* es *stablemen*.

stable lad [-læd] *n* mozo *m* de cuadras.

stableness [-nis] *n* estabilidad *f*.

staccato [stə'kɑ:təu] *adj* staccato || FIG entrecortado, da (style, voice).
◆ *n* MUS staccato *m* || FIG repiqueteo *m*; *a staccato of machine gun fire* el repiqueteo de una ametralladora.

stack [stæk] *n* AGR almiar *m*, hacina *f* || montón *m* (pile); *a stack of dishes* un montón de platos || MIL pabellón *m* (of rifles) || cañón *m* (of chimney) || chimenea *f* (of train, ship) || FAM montón *m* (large number) || US AUT tubo *m* de escape.
◆ *pl* biblioteca *f sing*, estantería *f sing*, estantes *m* (bookcase) || FAM montón *m sing*; *I have stacks of things to do* tengo un montón de cosas que hacer.

stack [stæk] *vt* amontonar, apilar (to pile) || AGR hacinar || llenar, atiborrar (to load); *the room is stacked with books* el cuarto está lleno de libros || — FIG *the cards are stacked against me* las circunstancias están en contra mía || MIL *to stack arms* armar pabellones || US *to stack the cards* hacer fullerías con las cartas (in card games), hacer trampas (to prearrange circumstances) || *to stack up* amontonar, apilar.

stadia ['steidjə] *n* estadía *f* || *stadia rod* estadía.

stadium ['steidjəm] *n* estadio *m*; *olympic stadium* estadio olímpico || FIG estadio *m*, fase *f*, etapa *f* (phase) || estadio *m* (ancient measure).
— OBSERV El plural de esta palabra es *stadiums* en los dos primeros sentidos y *stadia* en el tercero.

staff [stɑ:f] *n* personal *m*, empleados *m pl* (personnel) || palo *m* (stick) || bastón *m* (walking stick) || REL báculo *m* (of a bishop) || bordón *m* (of pilgrims) || cayado *m* (of shepherd) || bastón *m* de mando (rod) || asta *f* (flagpole) || mira *f* (measure) || estaf *m* (in construction) || MIL Estado *m* Mayor || servidumbre *f* (of a house) || MUS pentagrama *m* || FIG sostén *m*; *the staff of life* el sostén de la vida || — *editorial staff* redactores *m pl*, redacción *f* || *teaching staff* cuerpo *m* docente, profesorado *m* || *to be on the staff* estar en plantilla || FIG *to be the staff of s.o.'s old age* ser el báculo de la vejez de alguien || *to leave the staff* dimitir.
◆ *adj* del personal; *staff entrance* entrada del personal || MIL del Estado Mayor.
— OBSERV El plural de esta palabra es *staffs* cuando significa *personal, Estado Mayor, profesorado* y *estaf*, y *staffs* o *staves* en los demás casos.

staff [stɑ:f] *vt* proveer de personal.

staffing [-iŋ] *n* empleo *m* or contratación *f* de personal.

staff nurse [-nə:s] *n* enfermera *f* cualificada.

staff officer [-'ɔfisə*] *n* oficial *m* de Estado Mayor.

stag [stæg] *adj* FAM para hombres || *stag party* reunión *f* de hombres, despedida *f* de soltero.
◆ *n* ZOOL venado *m*, ciervo *m* (deer) | macho *m* (of certain animals) | animal *m* castrado (castrated animal) || COMM especulador *m* || FAM soltero *m* (bachelor) || *stag beetle* ciervo *m* volante.

stage [steidʒ] *n* THEATR escenario *m*, escena *f*, tablas *f pl* (raised platform); *I can't see the stage from this seat* no puedo ver el escenario desde este asiento | teatro *m*, tablas *f pl* (art, profession); *my sister is trying to get on the stage* mi hermana está intentando dedicarse al teatro *or* subir a las tablas || estrado *m*, tribuna *f*, plataforma *f* (platform) || andamio *m* (scaffold) || FIG escena *f*, escenario *m*; *England was the stage for one of the most important historical events of the century* Inglaterra fue escena de uno de los acontecimientos más importantes del siglo | campo *m* (area) || etapa *f* (step); *the first stage of the journey is the longest* la primera etapa del viaje es la más larga; *by easy stages* en pequeñas etapas; *it is necessary to learn Basque in several stages* es necesario aprender el vasco en varias etapas || etapa *f*, fase *f* (of development, of evolution); *this project is in the first stage of its development* este proyecto está en la primera etapa de su desarrollo || fase *f*, período *m* (phase); *the early stages of existence* el primer período de la existencia; *to reach a critical stage* llegar a una fase crítica || MAR desembarcadero *m* (landing stage) || portaobjeto *m*, platina *f* (of a microscope) || GEOL piso *m* || cuerpo *m* (of a rocket) || diligencia *f* (stagecoach) || relevo *m*; *horses were changed at every stage* se cambiaban los caballos en cada relevo || — *by stages* progresivamente || *fare stage* sección *f* (in a bus) || *front of the stage* proscenio *m* || *in stages* por etapas || *to come on the stage* salir a escena || *to go on the stage* hacerse actor, subir a las tablas || *to put a novel on the stage* llevar a la escena una novela || FIG *to set the stage for sth.* preparar el terreno para algo || *to write for the stage* escribir para el teatro.

stage [steidʒ] *vt* representar, poner en escena (a play); *the play was poorly staged* la obra estuvo mal representada || llevar a la escena (a novel) || efectuar; *to stage a counteroffensive* efectuar una contraofensiva || organizar (to arrange).

◆ *vi* representarse; *this play stages easily* esta obra se representa fácilmente.

stage box [-bɔks] *n* palco *m* de proscenio.

stagecoach [-kəutʃ] *n* diligencia *f*.

stagecraft [-krɑːft] *n* arte *m* escénico.

stage direction [-di'rekʃən] *n* THEATR acotación *f*.

stage door [-dɔː*] *n* THEATR entrada *f* de artistas.

stage effect [-i'fekt] *n* efecto *m* teatral *or* escénico.

stage fright [-frait] *n* miedo *m* al público, nerviosismo *m*.

stagehand [-hænd] *n* tramoyista *m*, maquinista *m*.

stage-manage [-'mænidʒ] *vt* dirigir la tramoya de (a play) || FIG manipular (to rig).

stage manager [-'mænidʒə*] *n* THEATR regidor *m* de escena || CINEM director *m* de producción, regidor *m*.

stage name [-neim] *n* nombre *m* de artista.

stage play [-plei] *n* obra *f* de teatro.

stage properties [-'prɔpətiz] *pl n* THEATR accesorios *m*.

stager [-ə] *n* FAM *old stager* perro viejo, hombre de gran experiencia.

stagestruck [-strʌk] *adj* apasionado por el teatro.

stage whisper [-'wispə*] *n* THEATR aparte *m*.

stagey ['steidʒi] *adj* teatral.

stagflation [stæg'fleiʃən] *n* inflación *f* acompañada por el estancamiento de la economía.

stagger ['stægə*] *n* tambaleo *m* (staggering movement).

stagger ['stægə*] *vt* hacer tambalearse, hacer titubear; *the blow staggered him* el golpe le hizo tambalearse || asombrar (to astonish) || escalonar; *to stagger the hours of the factories* escalonar las horas de las fábricas; *staggered holidays* vacaciones escalonadas || alternar (to alternate) || TECH colocar al tresbolillo.

◆ *vi* tambalearse, titubear || vacilar, titubear (to hesitate).

staggerer [-rə*] *n* FAM argumento *m* desconcertante (argument) | noticia *f* asombrosa (piece of news).

staggering [-riŋ] *adj* FIG asombroso, sa (amazing) || tambaleante (reeling).

◆ *n* escalonamiento *m*; *staggering of holidays* escalonamiento de las vacaciones.

staggers [-z] *n* VET modorra *f*.

staghound [-haund] *n* sabueso *m* (dog).

staging [steidʒiŋ] *n* puesta *f* en escena, escenificación *f* (in theatre) || andamio *m* (scaffold) || MIL estacionamiento *m*.

stagnant ['stægnənt] *adj* estancado, da (water) || FIG estancado, da; paralizado, da (paralysed) || COMM inactivo, va (market).

stagnate [stæg'neit] *vi* estancarse.

stagnation [stæg'neiʃən] *n* estancamiento *m* (of water) || FIG estancamiento *m*, paralización *f*.

stagy ['steidʒi] *adj* teatral.

staid [steid] *adj* serio, ria; formal.

staidness [-nis] *n* seriedad *f*, formalidad *f*.

stain [stein] *n* mancha *f*; *coffee stain* mancha de café; *to remove* o *to take out a stain* sacar *or* quitar una mancha || tinte *m*, tintura *f* (dye) || colorante *m* (for microscopic study) || FIG mancha *f*; *a stain on one's reputation* una mancha en la reputación de uno || *stain remover* quitamanchas *m inv*.

stain [stein] *vt* manchar, ensuciar; *the coffee stained her dress* el café le manchó el vestido; *to stain with ink* manchar con *or* de tinta || teñir (to dye) || colorar (to colour) || FIG manchar, mancillar; *to stain s.o.'s reputation* manchar la reputación de alguien.

◆ *vi* manchar, ensuciar; *be careful with the coffee, it stains* ten cuidado con el café, mancha || mancharse, ensuciarse (to become stained).

— OBSERV Muy frecuentemente el participio *stained* se combina con un sustantivo para formar una palabra compuesta (*blood-stained* manchado de sangre).

stainable [-əbl] *adj* que puede colorarse *or* teñirse.

stained glass [-d'glɑːs] *n* vidrio *m* de color.

stained-glass window [-d'glɑːs'windəu] *n* vidriera *f* (in churches, etc.).

stainer [-ə*] *n* tintorero, ra (person) || tinte *m* (substance).

stainless [-lis] *adj* que no se mancha (that cannot be stained) || inmaculado, da; sin mancha (immaculate) || *stainless steel* acero *m* inoxidable.

stair [stɛə*] *n* escalón *m*, peldaño *m* (single step).

◆ *pl* escaleras *f*, escalera *f sing*; *to go up, to go down the stairs* subir, bajar la escalera || — FIG *below stairs* sitio *m* donde se encuentra la servidumbre || *flight of stairs* tramo *m* de escalera.

staircase [-keis]; **stairway** [stɛəwei] *n* escalera *f*; *spiral staircase* escalera de caracol || *moving staircase* escalera mecánica.

stairhead [-hed] *n* rellano *m*, descansillo *m*.

stair rod [-rɔd] *n* varilla *f* para sujetar la alfombra de la escalera.

stairway [-wei] *n* ⟶ **staircase.**

stairwell [-wel] *n* caja *f* de la escalera.

stake [steik] *n* escala *f* (stick) || poste *m* (post) || AGR rodrigón *m*, tutor *m* || jalón *m* (in surveying) || hoguera *f*; *Joan of Arc was condemned to the stake* Juana de Arco fue condenada a la hoguera || intereses *m pl*; *I have a stake in the company* tengo intereses en la compañía || puesta *f*, apuesta *f* (bet) || tas *m* (small anvil) || — *at stake* en juego; *your honour is at stake* su honor está en juego; en peligro (in danger) || *the issue at stake* el asunto de que se trata.

◆ *pl* premio *m sing* || — US FAM *to pull up stakes* irse || *put down your stakes!* ¡hagan juego!

stake [steik] *vt* estacar, sujetar con estacas (to secure with stakes) || delimitar con estacas (to mark) || amarrar a un poste (to tether) || AGR rodrigar || apostar (to bet) || arriesgar, jugarse; *he has staked his life on this interview* se juega la vida en esta entrevista || presentar (a claim) || — *to stake off* o *out* jalonar (in surveying) || *to stake one's all* jugarse el todo por el todo.

stakeholder [-'həuldə*] *n* tenedor *m* de apuestas.

stakhanovite [stə'kænəvait] *n* stajanovista *m* & *f*.

stalactite ['stæləktait] *n* GEOL estalactita *f*.

stalagmite ['stæləgmait] *n* GEOL estalagmita *f*.

stale [steil] *adj* rancio, cia; pasado, da (food) || picado, da; echado a perder (wine, beer) || poco fresco (egg) || duro, ra (bread) || viciado, da (air) || a cerrado (smell) || averiado, da; echado a perder (goods) || viejo, ja (news) || trillado, da (joke) || decaído, da (run-down) || caducado, da (expired) || vencido, da (cheque) || desanimado, da (market) || SP entrenado en exceso, sobreentrenado, da.

stale [steil] *vi* echarse a perder (food) || perder novedad *or* interés (news, joke) || ZOOL orinar.

◆ *vt* echar a perder (food) || quitar novedad a, quitar interés a (news, joke).

stalemate ['steil'meit] *n* ahogado *m* (in chess) || FIG paralización *f* punto *m* muerto, estancamiento *m* (halt in progress) || FIG *to reach a stalemate* llegar a un punto muerto, estancar (to halt in progress of).

stalemate ['steil'meit] *vt* ahogar (in chess) || FIG paralizar, llevar a un punto muerto, estancar (to halt the progress of).

staleness [-nis] *n* ranciedad *f* (of food) || lo poco fresco (of egg) || dureza *f* (of bread) || olor *m* a cerrado (of a room) || lo viciado (of the air) || deterioro *m* (of goods) || vencimiento *m* (of a cheque) || caducidad *f* (of legal document) || SP sobreentrenamiento *m* || falta *f* de novedad (of news, of joke).

Stalinism ['stɑːlinizəm] *n* stalinismo *m*.

Stalinist ['stɑːlinist] *adj/n* staliniano, na; stalinista.

stalk [stɔːk] *n* BOT tallo *m* (stem) | pedúnculo *m* (of flower) | pecíolo *m* (of leaf) | caña *f* (of bamboo) | troncho *m* (of cabbages) || pie *m* (of a glass) || paso *m or* andar *m* majestuoso (majestic gait) || caza *f* al acecho (in hunting).

stalk [stɔːk] *vt* cazar al acecho *or* en puestos (to hunt) || acechar (animals) || seguir los pasos a, acechar a (s.o.) || cundir; *terror stalked the city* el terror cundía por la ciudad.

◆ *vi* andar con paso majestuoso || — *he stalked out of the room in anger* salió con paso airado de la habitación || *the plague stalked through the country* la peste se extendía por el país.

stalker [-ə*] *n* cazador *m* en puestos.

stalking-horse [-iŋhɔːs] *n* FIG tapadera *f*, pantalla *f* (screen) || candidato *m* presentado para engañar a la oposición (in politics).

stalky [-i] *n* talludo, da.

stall [stɔːl] *n* pesebre *m* (manger) || establo *m* (stable) || departamento *m* para un caballo en las cuadras (compartment in a stable) || jaula *f*, departamento *m* en un garaje (for cars) || COMM puesto *m* (in a market) || caseta *f* (in a fair, in an exhibition) || silla *f* de coro, sitial *m* (in church) || butaca *f* (in theatre, in cinema) || dedil *m* (for fingers) || AVIAT pérdida *f* de velocidad || FIG pretexto *m* || *newspaper stall* quiosco *m* de periódicos.

stall [stɔːl] *vt* poner en el establo (horses) || atascar (cart) || parar (a car, an engine) || AVIAT hacer perder velocidad || FIG *to stall s.o. off* quitarse a uno de encima con pretextos (to get rid of), evitar a alguien (to avoid).

◆ *vi* calarse, pararse (a car, an engine) || atascarse (a cart) || AVIAT entrar en pérdida de velocidad, perder velocidad || FIG andar con rodeos.

stall-feed [-fiːd] *vt* engordar en un establo.

stallholder [-həuldə*] *n* persona que tiene un puesto en el mercado.

stallion ['stæljən] *n* semental *m*.

stalwart ['stɔːlwət] *adj* robusto, ta; vigoroso, sa; fornido, da (sturdy) || leal (loyal) || firme, decidido, da; resuelto, ta (resolute) || incondicional (unconditional).

◆ *n* partidario *m* incondicional (supporter) || persona *f* fornida (sturdy person).

stamen ['steimen] *n* BOT estambre *m*.

stamina ['stæminə] *n* vigor *m*, energía *f*, nervio *m* (energy) || aguante *m*, resistencia *f* (endurance).

staminate ['stæmineit] *adj* BOT estaminífero, ra.

staminiferous [stæmi'nifərəs] *adj* BOT estaminífero, ra.

stammer ['stæmə*] *n* tartamudez *f*, tartamudeo *m* (stuttering).

stammer ['stæmə*] *vt* decir tartamudeando.
◆ *vi* tartamudear (to stutter).

stammerer [-rə*] *n* tartamudo, da.

stammering [-riŋ] *adj* tartamudo, da.
◆ *n* tartamudez *f*.

stamp [stæmp] *n* sello *m* [*AMER* estampilla *f*] (postage stamp) || timbre *m* (fiscal) || cupón *m* (of shares) || sello *m*, tampón *m* (mark left by rubber stamp, seal) || marca *f*, huella *f*, señal *f* (mark) || taconazo *m*, zapatazo *m* (with foot) || TECH estampa *f* (for forging) | cuño *m* (for metals) | troquel *m* (for coins) | punzón *m* (graver) | prensa *f* de estampar (for printing) | triturador *m*, machacadora *f* (for crushing ore) || FIG cuño *m*, marchamo *m*, sello *m*; *bearing the stamp of genius* marcado con el sello del genio | estampa *f*; *he has the stamp of a soldier* tiene la estampa de un soldado | clase *f*, calaña *f*, índole *f*; *of the same stamp* de la misma calaña || *rubber stamp* tampón *m*, sello *m*.

stamp [stæmp] *vt* estampar, imprimir; *to stamp one's foot in the sand* estampar el pie en la arena || sellar, poner el sello a [*AMER* estampillar] (letter, document) || timbrar (with fiscal stamp) || FIG señalar, catalogar; *his attitude stamped him as a revolutionary* su actitud le catalogaba como revolucionario | marcar, impresionar, afectar; *stamped by his experiences as a prisoner* marcado por sus experiencias de prisionero | estampar, grabar (to engrave); *he stamped it on his memory* lo grabó en su memoria || TECH poner el contraste a (gold) | acuñar (coins) | estampar, forjar (a metal) | triturar, machacar (ore) || — *paper stamped with one's name* papel con membrete || *stamped addressed envelope* sobre *m* impreso con franqueo pagado || *to stamp one's feet* patear (in anger), patalear (a child), golpear el suelo con los pies (to warm o.s., etc.), zapatear (in dancing) | *to stamp one's foot* golpear el suelo con el pie || *to stamp out* extirpar (to eliminate), acabar con, sofocar; *to stamp out a rebellion* acabar con una rebelión; apagar con el pie; *to stamp out a cigarette* apagar un cigarrillo con el pie; estampar (to punch out); *to stamp out washers* estampar arandelas.
◆ *vi* dar zapatazos, golpear con los pies (with feet) || patear (angrily) || piafar (a horse) || *to stamp on* pisar; *to stamp on s.o.'s foot* pisarle el pie a uno; pisotear (principles).

stamp album [-'ælbəm] *n* álbum *m* de sellos.

stamp collecting [-kə'lektiŋ] *n* colección *f* de sellos [*AMER* colección *f* de estampillas], filatelia *f*.

stamp collector [-kə'lektə*] *n* coleccionista *m* & *f* de sellos [*AMER* coleccionista *m* & *f* de estampillas], filatelista *m* & *f*.

stamp duty [-'dju:ti] *n* póliza *f*, timbre *m*, impuesto *m* del timbre.

stampede [stæm'pi:d] *n* espantada *f*, desbandada *f*, fuga *f* (flight) || desbocamiento *m* (of horses).

stampede [stæm'pi:d] *vt* provocar la espantada *or* la desbandada de; *the shot stampeded the elephants* el disparo provocó la desbandada de los elefantes || infundir terror a (to frighten).
◆ *vi* dar una espantada, salir en desbandada || abalanzarse, precipitarse (to rush).

stamper ['stæmpə*] *n* máquina *f* de estampar (machine) || troquel *m* (for coins) || triturador *m* (for ore) || estampador *m* (person).

stamping ['stæmpiŋ] *n* estampación *f*, estampado *m* (of design, of metal) || timbrado *m* (with fiscal stamp) || trituración *f* (of ore).

stamping ground [-graund] *n* US FAM lugar *m* predilecto *or* de elección; *this town was formerly the democrats' stamping ground* esta ciudad era antiguamente el lugar predilecto de los demócratas.

stamp machine ['stæmpmə:ʃi:n] *n* máquina *f* automática que distribuye sellos de correos.

stamp mill ['stæmpmil] *n* trapiche *m* (for pulverizing ore).

stance [stæns] *n* postura *f*; *he took up a stance* adoptó una postura.

stanch [sta:ntʃ] *vt* restañar (to staunch blood).

stanchion ['sta:nʃən] *n* puntal *m* (prop) || montante *m* (upright bar) || MAR candelero *m* || US yugo *m* (yoke).

stand [stænd] *n* parada *f* (stop) || posición *f*, situación *f*, sitio *m* (position) || posición *f*, postura *f* (stance) || plataforma *f* (platform) || tribuna *f* (in stadium) || MUS quiosco *m* de música (bandstand) | atril *m* (lectern) || puesto *m* (at market); *he has a vegetable stand* tiene un puesto de verduras || quiosco *m* (of newspapers) || caseta *f*, «stand» *m* (at an exhibition, etc.) || caseta *f*, barraca *f* (at fair) || parada *f* (of buses, of taxis, etc.) || pie *m*, pedestal *m* (of lamp) || velador *m* (table) || percha *f*, perchero *m* (for coats, for hats) || paragüero *m* (umbrella rest) || AGR cosecha *f* en pie || THEATR representación *f*, función *f* (performance); *one-night stand* representación única || FIG postura *f*, posición *f*; *the Government has taken a stand in favour of emigration* el Gobierno ha tomado una postura en favor de la emigración || TECH soporte *m* || US bosque *m*; *a stand of pines* un bosque de pinos || US JUR estrado *m*, tribuna *f* (witness box) || — *to come to a stand* pararse, detenerse || *liqueur stand* licorera *f* || FIG *to maintain one's stand* mantenerse firme en su postura | *to make a stand against* oponerse a, resistir a (s.o.), alzarse contra (an abuse) || MIL *to make a stand against the enemy* resistir al enemigo || *to take a firm stand* plantarse (standing), adoptar una actitud firme (decision) || *to take one's stand behind a tree* apostarse detrás de un árbol || *to take one's stand on a principle* basarse *or* fundarse en un principio || US JUR *to take the stand* subir al estrado, comparecer ante un tribunal || *to take up one's stand by the entrance* ponerse cerca de la entrada.

stand* [stænd] *vt* poner, colocar (to place); *to stand sth. upright* o *on end* poner algo de pie; *stand it over there* ponlo ahí || poner de pie (to set upright) || resistir; *it will stand heat up to 200 degrees* resistirá el calor hasta 200 grados; *this book won't stand criticism* este libro no resistirá a la crítica || someterse a; *to stand trial* someterse a juicio || soportar, aguantar (to endure); *I can't stand work* no puedo soportar el trabajo; *I can't stand him* no puedo aguantarle || FAM sufragar, pagar (to pay for); *to stand a round of drinks* pagar una ronda; *to stand the cost* sufragar los gastos | invitar, convidar; *to stand s.o. a drink, a dinner* invitar a alguien a tomar una copa, a cenar || — *I can't stand it any longer* ya no lo puedo aguantar, ya estoy harto || *to stand a chance* tener una posibilidad || MIL *to stand fire* aguantar el fuego del enemigo || FIG *to stand one's ground* mantener en sus trece, no ceder || MIL *to stand* o *to lay siege to* sitiar, poner sitio a, asediar, cercar.
◆ *vi* estar de pie; *he is standing near John* está de pie junto a Juan || estar de pie, quedarse de pie; *to stand waiting* estar de pie esperando || levantarse, ponerse de pie (to an upright position); *all stand!* ¡levántense todos! || ponerse, colocarse; *I'll stand under the clock and wait for you* me pondré debajo del reloj para esperarle || mantenerse en pie; *the house still stood after the earthquake* la casa se mantuvo en pie después del terremoto || andar; *how do you stand for money?* ¿cómo andas de dinero? || estar; *how do they stand in the matter of clothes?* ¿cómo están de ropa? || tener, medir; *he stands five feet tall* tiene cinco pies de altura || cotizarse (securities, commodities) || marcar (thermometer) || reposar; *let the dough stand an hour* deja la masa reposar una hora || mantenerse (a position, a point of view) || pararse (to stop); *the retreating army stood and fought* el ejército, que se batía en retirada, se paró y luchó || quedarse; *stand where you are!* ¡quédese donde está!; *I stood in the rain* me quedé bajo la lluvia; *I stood and looked at him* me quedé mirándole || quedarse; *this page must stand as it is* esta página tiene que quedarse tal cual || ponerse (hunting dog) || estancarse (water) || estar; *his house stands on the hill* su casa está en la colina; *she stood in the doorway* estaba en la puerta; *I stand opposed to that* estoy opuesto a esto || estar, encontrarse; *to stand in the front rank* encontrarse en primera fila || figurar; *this page must stand in the dictionary* esta página debe figurar en el diccionario || ser; *to stand first* ser el primero; *that's how it stands* así es || estar en condiciones; *he stands to win all* está en condiciones de ganarlo todo || presentarse; *he stood as a candidate for the election* se presentó como candidato a la elección || permanecer (to remain unchanged) || seguir siendo válido; *my offer still stands* mi oferta sigue siendo válida || durar (to last); *the house will stand another century* la casa durará todavía un siglo || regir, tener validez; *these rules still stand* estas reglas tienen validez todavía || MAR ir rumbo (*to* a) || — *as it stands, as things stand* tal y como están las cosas || *how does my account stand?* ¿qué tengo en la cuenta? || *I don't know where I stand* no sé cuál es mi situación || *I found the door standing open* encontré la puerta abierta || *it stands to reason* es lógico, es evidente || *it stands to reason that* ni que decir tiene que, es evidente que || *nothing stands between you and me* nada nos separa || *nothing stands between you and success* nada se opone a tu éxito || *stand and deliver!* ¡la bolsa o la vida! || MIL *stand at ease* en su lugar ¡descanso! || *stand out of the way!* ¡quítese de en medio! || *this is how I stand* ésta es mi posición || *to let stand* dejar; *don't let the car stand in the middle of the street* no dejes el coche en medio de la calle || *to stand alone* estar solo || MIL *to stand at attention* cuadrarse || *to stand fast* mantenerse firme (on one's opinion), resistir (to resist) || *to stand for nothing* no contar para nada || *to stand in need of* necesitar || *to stand in s.o.'s name* estar a nombre de alguien || *to stand in the way of* estorbar (to hinder), ser un obstáculo para (to be an obstacle), ser una desventaja para (to be a disadvantage) || *to stand on end* erizarse (hair) || FIG *to stand on one's own two feet* valerse por sí mismo, volar con sus propias alas || US *to stand pat* mantenerse en sus trece || *to stand ready to* estar dispuesto a || *to stand sentry* montar guardia, estar de guardia || *to stand still* no moverse, estarse quieto || *to stand together* mantenerse unidos || *to stand to it that* sostener que || *to stand to lose* tener las de perder || *to stand to lose a lot* tener mucho que perder || *to stand to lose nothing* no tener nada que perder || *to stand well with s.o.* llevarse bien con alguien, tener buenas relaciones con alguien || *your account stands at 100 pounds in your credit* tiene cien libras en su haber.
◆ *phr v* *to stand about* esperar de pie (to wait) | *we stood about watching the football match* miramos el partido de fútbol de pie || *to stand*

against resistir a, oponerse a ‖ ***to stand aside*** apartarse, echarse a un lado; *to stand aside to let s.o. pass* apartarse para dejar pasar a alguien | retirarse; *to stand aside in favour of s.o.* retirarse en favor de alguien ‖ ***to stand away*** apartarse ‖ ***to stand back*** retroceder; *to make the crowd stand back* hacer retroceder a la muchedumbre | ***house standing back from the road*** casa que no está al borde de la carretera ‖ ***to stand by*** estar preparado (to be ready to act) | MIL estar dispuesto para el combate ‖ estar dispuesto a prestar ayuda *or* a socorrer; *to stand by a sinking ship* estar dispuesto a socorrer a un barco en perdición | estar cerca (to be near) | estar al lado de; *I'll always stand by you in case of trouble* estaré siempre a su lado en caso de dificultad | estar atento; *stand by for the latest news* esté usted atento a las noticias de última hora | apoyar, sostener (to support) | atenerse a (a decision); *I stand by what I said* me atengo a lo que dije | cumplir (a promise, one's word) | quedarse sin hacer nada (to stand near as a onlooker); *please help instead of merely standing by* por favor ayude en vez de quedarse sin hacer nada | MAR *stand by!* ¡listo! ‖ ***to stand down*** retirarse ‖ ***to stand for*** significar (to mean) | representar (to represent); *in this code each number stands for a letter* en este código cada número representa una letra | ser las siglas de; *UN stands for United Nations* UN son las siglas de las Naciones Unidas | abogar por, ser partidario de; *to stand for free trade* abogar por el libre comercio | presentarse como candidato a (a post) | presentarse como candidato en, presentar su candidatura en; *I'm standing for Orpington* presento mi candidatura por Orpington | FAM aguantar, tolerar; *I won't stand for such behaviour* no toleraré semejante conducta | MAR ir rumbo a | *to stand for Parliament* presentarse como candidato a las elecciones parlamentarias ‖ ***to stand in*** unirse, asociarse (*with* a) | compartir los gastos; *let me stand in with you if it's too expensive* déjeme compartir los gastos con usted si es demasiado caro | estar en buenos términos (*with* con) (to be friendly) | MAR hacer rumbo (*for* a) | CINEM sustituir (*for* a) | costar ‖ ***to stand off*** apartarse | mantenerse apartado (to keep at a distance) | MAR apartarse de la costa | dejar sin trabajo (workers) | FIG evitar (to evade), rechazar (an assailant), aplazar (to put off) ‖ ***to stand on*** mantener el rumbo (ship) | FIG dar mucha importancia a | insistir en (to insist upon) | valerse de; *I'm going to stand on my rights* me valdré de mis derechos ‖ ***to stand out*** sobresalir; *his house stands out from the others* su casa sobresale de las demás | destacarse; *mountains that stand out on the horizon* montañas que se destacan en el horizonte | FIG descollar, destacarse, sobresalir; *the qualities that stand out in his work* las cualidades que sobresalen en su obra | *to stand out against* oponerse a, resistir a | FAM *to stand out a mile* verse a la legua | *to stand out for* insistir en | MAR *to stand out to sea* hacerse a la mar ‖ ***to stand over*** vigilar; *if I don't stand over him he does nothing* si no le vigilo no hace nada | quedar pendiente (to be postponed) | *to let sth. stand over* dejar algo pendiente ‖ ***to stand to*** estar alerta | MIL *stand to your arms!* ¡a las armas! ‖ ***to stand up*** levantarse, ponerse de pie (to rise) | resistir | US FAM dejar plantado; *he stood me up at the last minute* me dejó plantado en el último momento | *this soup is so thick you could stand a spoon up in it* esta sopa es tan espesa que una cuchara podría quedarse de pie | *to stand up for* defender, salir en defensa de, dar la cara por; *if we don't stand up for him nobody will* si no damos la cara por él nadie lo hará | *to stand up to* resistir a | *to stand up to a test* salir bien de una prueba ‖ ***to stand upon*** insistir en.

— OBSERV Pret y pp ***stood***.

standard [-əd] *adj* normal, corriente; *of standard size* de tamaño normal ‖ standard, tipo (model) ‖ clásico, ca (author, book) ‖ de ley (gold) ‖ oficial, legal (time) ‖ legal (weight) ‖ COMM standard, estándar, estandard, corriente; *standard model of a washing machine* modelo standard de una lavadora ‖ AUT de serie, standard, estándar, estandard ‖ CHEM reactivo, va (paper) ‖ BOT de tronco (tree) ‖ FIG clásico, ca (joke) ‖ — *a Standard Spanish Dictionary* un diccionario general de la lengua española ‖ *Standard English* el inglés correcto ‖ *Standard measure* medida *f* de tipo ‖ *the standard Spanish dictionary for schools is* el diccionario español que se utiliza generalmente en las escuelas es.

◆ *n* patrón *m* (money); *gold standard* patrón oro ‖ patrón *m* (of weight and length); *the metre is the standard of length* el metro es el patrón de longitud ‖ nivel *m*; *standard of living* nivel de vida; *the standard of wages* el nivel de los salarios; *standard of knowledge* nivel de conocimientos ‖ clase *f* (of products) ‖ modelo *m*, tipo *m* (model) ‖ regla *f*, norma *f* (norm); *standards of behaviour* normas de conducta ‖ criterio *m* (criterion); *judged by that standard* juzgado según ese criterio ‖ valor *m* moral (moral value) ‖ MIL estandarte *m*, bandera *f* (flag) ‖ MAR bandera *f*, pabellón *m* ‖ CHEM ley *f* (of a metal) | dosificación *f* (of a solution) ‖ pie *m* (of a lamp) ‖ poste *m* (of a streetlamp) ‖ TECH bancada *f* (of a machine) ‖ BOT árbol *m* de tronco (tree) ‖ clase *f*, grado *m* (in a primary school) ‖ — US *Bureau of standards* oficina *f* de pesas y medidas ‖ *not to come up to the standard* no satisfacer los requisitos ‖ *of low standard* de baja calidad ‖ FIG *to raise the standard of* ser el abanderado de.

standard-bearer [-əd'bɛərə*] *n* MIL abanderado *m*, portaestandarte *m* ‖ FIG jefe *m*, adalid *m*, abanderado *m* (of a movement, etc.).

standard gauge [-əd'geidʒ] *n* vía *f* normal.

standard-gauge [-əd'geidʒ] *adj* de vía normal.

standardization ['stændədai'zeiʃən] *n* COMM estandardización *f*, standardización *f*, producción *f* en serie ‖ TECH normalización *f*, tipificación *f* ‖ uniformación *f* (of methods).

standardize ['stændədaiz] *vt* COMM standardizar, estandardizar, producir en serie ‖ TECH normalizar, tipificar ‖ uniformar (methods).

standby ['stændbai] *n* recurso *m* (thing); *that story is an old standby of his* esa historia es un viejo recurso suyo ‖ persona *f* segura, persona *f* con quien siempre se puede contar (person) ‖ sustituto, ta (substitute) ‖ AVIAT persona *f* que está en la lista de espera ‖ *to be on standby* estar preparado para salir.

◆ *adj* de reserva (machine) ‖ *a stand-by passenger* un pasajero que está en la lista de espera.

standee ['stændi] *n* US espectador *m* que asiste de pie [a un espectáculo].

stand-in ['stænd'in] *n* CINEM doble *m* & *f* ‖ THEATR suplente *m* & *f* ‖ sustituto, ta (substitute) ‖ SP suplente *m* & *f*.

standing ['stændiŋ] *adj* de pie (upright) ‖ vertical (position) ‖ clásico, ca; *standing joke* broma clásica ‖ fijo, ja; *standing rule* regla fija ‖ arraigado, da (custom) ‖ permanente; *standing body, committee* órgano, comisión permanente ‖ MIL permanente (army, camp) ‖ AGR en pie (crops) ‖ parado, da (not in use) ‖ estancado, da (water) ‖ SP a pie juntillas (jump) | parado, da; *standing start* salida parada ‖ AUT estacionado, da ‖ — *standing expenses* gastos *m* generales ‖ *standing order* pedido regular ‖ *standing orders* reglamento *m* general (of committee, etc.) ‖ *standing wave* onda estacionaria ‖ FIG *to leave s.o. standing* dejar atrás a alguien.

◆ *n* posición *f* vertical (upright position) ‖ parada *f* (of a car) ‖ posición *f*, situación *f* (position); *social standing* posición social ‖ situación *f*; *financial standing of a firm* situación financiera de una empresa ‖ importancia *f*; *standing of a firm* importancia de una empresa ‖ reputación *f*; *firm of international standing* empresa de reputación internacional ‖ categoría *f*; *a man of high standing* un hombre que tiene mucha categoría ‖ duración *f* (duration) ‖ — *agreement of ten months' standing* acuerdo *m* vigente desde hace diez meses ‖ *employee of ten months' standing* empleado *m* que lleva diez meses en la empresa ‖ *friend of long standing* viejo amigo, amigo de toda la vida ‖ *habit of long standing* vieja costumbre.

standing rigging [-'rigiŋ] *n* MAR jarcia *f* muerta.

standing room [-ru:m] *n* sitio *m* donde la gente está de pie (in a bus, etc.) ‖ pasillo *m* (in a theatre) ‖ *standing room only* no quedan asientos.

standoff ['stænd'ɔf] *n* reserva *f*, distancia *f* ‖ empate *m* (in game or contest).

standoffish ['stænd'ɔfiʃ] *adj* distante, reservado, da.

standout ['stændaut] *n* US FAM original *m*.

standpat ['stændpæt] *adj* US FAM inmovilista, conservador, ra.

standpipe ['stændpaip] *n* tubo *m* vertical ‖ columna *f* de alimentación.

standpoint ['stændpɔint] *n* punto *m* de vista.

standstill ['stændstil] *n* parada *f* (stop) ‖ COMM estancamiento *m*, marasmo *m* (of economy) ‖ — *to be at a standstill* estar parado, estar estancado (economy) ‖ *to bring to a standstill* parar (a car), producir el estancamiento de (trade, etc.) ‖ *to come to a standstill* pararse (people, cars), estancarse (economy, etc.).

stand-up ['stændʌp] *adj* tomado de pie (lunch) ‖ vertical ‖ campal (battle) ‖ duro, ra (collar).

stank [stæŋk] *pret* ⟶ **stink.**

stannary ['stænəri] *n* MIN mina *f* de estaño (tin mine).

stannate ['stæneit] *n* CHEM estannato *m*.

stannic ['stænik] *adj* CHEM estánnico, ca.

stanniferous [stæ'nifərəs] *adj* CHEM estannífero, ra (tin-bearing).

stannous ['stænəs] *adj* CHEM estañoso, sa.

stanza ['stænzə] *n* POET estancia *f*, estrofa *f*.

stapedes [stə'pi:di:z] *pl n* ⟶ **stapes.**

stapes ['steipi:z] *n* ANAT estribo *m*.

— OBSERV El plural de *stapes* es *stapes* o *stapedes*.

staphylococcus [stæfilə'kɔkəs] *n* estafilococo *m*.

— OBSERV El plural de *staphylococcus* es *staphylococci*.

staple ['steipl] *adj* básico, ca; *staple food* alimento básico ‖ principal, básico, ca; *staple industry* industria básica ‖ FIG clásico, ca; principal; *staple topic of conversation* tema clásico de conversación ‖ *staple commodity* artículo *m* de primera necesidad.

◆ *n* producto *m* principal; *coffee is the staple of Brasil* el café es el producto principal del Brasil ‖ elemento *m* básico; *rice is the staple of their diet* el arroz es el elemento básico de su alimentación ‖ materia *f* prima (raw material) ‖ TECH grapa *f* (for fastening papers, etc.) | armella *f* (to hold a hook, etc.) ‖ fibra *f* (of wool, of cotton) ‖ calidad *f* (fineness) ‖ FIG tema *m* principal.

staple ['steipl] *vt* sujetar *or* coser con una grapa *or* grapas (to fasten with staples) ‖ clasificar según la longitud de las fibras (textiles).

stapler [-ə*]; **stapling machine** [-iŋməˈʃiːn] *n* grapadora *f*, máquina *f* de coser papeles con grapas.

star [stɑː*] *n* estrella *f* (luminous heavenly body); *the sky is full of stars tonight* el cielo está lleno de estrellas esta noche || astro *m* (heavenly body) || lucero *m*, estrella *f* (of a horse) || estrella *f*; *movie star* estrella de cine || THEATR primer actor *m*, primera actriz *f* (of a play) || figura *f* (in sports) || MIL estrella *f* || asterisco *m* (asterisk) || FIG estrella *f*; *he was born under a lucky star* nació con buena estrella || — *evening star* estrella vespertina || *morning star* estrella matutina, lucero del alba || *pole star* estrella polar || *shooting star* estrella fugaz || *star aniseed* anís estrellado || REL *star of David* estrella de David.
◆ *pl* astros *m* (in astrology) || — US HIST *Stars and Bars* primera bandera de los Estados Unidos || *Stars and Stripes* bandera estrellada (of the United States) || FIG *to see stars* ver las estrellas | *to sleep under the stars* dormir al raso *or* bajo las estrellas | *to thank one's lucky stars* dar las gracias a Dios.
◆ *adj* principal || más destacado, más brillante (outstanding) || estelar; *star bout* combate estelar || *star attraction* atracción *f* principal (thing), figura *f* estelar (person).

star [stɑː*] *vt* estrellar, sembrar de estrellas (to cover with stars) || señalar con un asterisco, poner un asterisco a (to put an asterisk on) || presentar como protagonista (to present in a leading role).
◆ *vi* ser protagonista, protagonizar; *Jimmy Neville stars in the film* Jimmy Neville es el protagonista de la película || destacarse, descollar (to be outstanding).

starboard [-bəd] *n* MAR estribor *m*; *land to starboard!* ¡tierra a estribor!
◆ *adj* MAR de estribor, a estribor.

starboard [-bəd] *vt* MAR poner a estribor.
◆ *vi* MAR ponerse a estribor.

starch [stɑːtʃ] *n* CHEM almidón *m* || fécula *f* (in food) || FIG rigidez *f* (unbending manners) | tiesura *f*, estiramiento *m* (stiffness).

starch [stɑːtʃ] *vt* almidonar.

Star Chamber [ˈstɑːˈtʃeimbə*] *n* antiguo tribunal *m* británico de inquisición.

starchiness [ˈstɑːtʃinis] *n* FIG rigidez *f* | tiesura *f*, estiramiento *m* (stiffness).

starchy [ˈstɑːtʃi] *n* almidonado, da (of or like starch) || amiláceo, a (containing starch) || feculento, ta (food) || FIG rígido, da (unbending) | tieso, sa; estirado, da (stiff).

star-crossed [ˈstɑːˈkrɔst] *adj* desgraciado, da; malhadado, da.

stardom [ˈstɑːdəm] *n* FAM estrellato *m*.

stardust [ˈstɑːdʌst] *n* ASTR polvo *m* de estrellas, enjambre *m* || FIG encanto *m*.

stare [stɛə*] *n* mirada *f* fija (steady look) || mirada *f* de extrañeza (with astonishment) || mirada *f* despavorida (with fear).

stare [stɛə*] *vt* mirar fijamente, fijar la mirada en || — *to stare s.o. down* hacer bajar los ojos a alguien mirándole fijamente || FIG *to stare s.o. in the face* saltar a la vista; *it's staring you in the face* salta a la vista || *to stare s.o. up and down* mirar a alguien de arriba abajo.
◆ *vi* mirar fijamente; *to stare in amazement* mirar fijamente con asombro; *he stared at me* me miró fijamente || abrir desmesuradamente los ojos, abrir los ojos de par en par, tener los ojos desorbitados (to gaze in wonder) || saltar a la vista (to be glaringly obvious) || FIG *to stare into space* mirar a las musarañas.

starfish [ˈstɑːfiʃ] *n* ZOOL estrella *f* de mar, estrellamar *f*.

stargaze [ˈstɑːgeiz] *vi* mirar las estrellas (to watch the stars) || FIG mirar a las musarañas (to indulge in dreamy thoughts).

stargazer [-ə*] *n* astrónomo *m* || FIG soñador, ra.

stargazing [-iŋ] *n* astronomía *f* || FIG distracción *f* (absentmindedness).

staring [ˈstɛəriŋ] *adj* que mira fijamente || llamativo, va; chillón, ona (colour) || *staring eyes* mirada fija (stare), ojos desorbitados (wide eyes).

stark [stɑːk] *adj* rígido, da; tieso, sa (stiff) || resuelto, ta; decidido, da (determined) || desolado, da; desierto, ta (bleak) || desnudo, da (unadorned) || puro, ra; absoluto, ta; completo, ta (utter).
◆ *adv* completamente || *stark mad* loco de atar.

stark-naked [-ˈneikid] *adj* en cueros.

starless [ˈstɑːlis] *adj* sin estrellas.

starlet [ˈstɑːlət] *n* actriz *f* principiante (young actress) || pequeña estrella *f* (small star).

starlight [ˈstɑːlait] *n* luz *f* de las estrellas; *by starlight* a la luz de las estrellas.

starlike [ˈstɑːlaik] *adj* estrellado, da (star-shaped) || brillante, radiante (brilliant).

starling [ˈstɑːliŋ] *n* estornino *m* (bird) || espolón *m*, tajamar *m* (of bridges).

starlit [ˈstɑːlit] *adj* iluminado por las estrellas.

starred [stɑːd] *adj* estrellado, da (full of stars) || presentado como protagonista (actor) || marcado con un asterisco.

starry [ˈstɑːri] *adj* estrellado, da; sembrado de estrellas (night, sky) || estelar (of the stars) || brillante, resplandeciente (shining).

starry-eyed [-aid] *adj* idealista (idealistic) || soñador, ra (daydreaming).

star shell [ˈstɑːʃel] *n* MIL cohete *m* luminoso, bengala *f*.

star shower [ˈstɑːʃauə*] *n* lluvia *f* de estrellas.

star-spangled [ˈstɑːˈspæŋgld] *adj* estrellado, da; salpicado *or* tachonado de estrellas || *Star-Spangled Banner* bandera estrellada (flag of the USA), himno *m* nacional de los Estados Unidos (anthem).

star-studded [ˈstɑːˈstʌdid] *adj* lleno de estrellas (sky) || *star-studded cast* reparto *m* estelar (in films, plays).

start [stɑːt] *n* principio *m*, comienzo *m* (of action, journey, course of events); *it was a failure from start to finish* fue un fracaso desde el principio hasta el final; *to get a good start in life* tener un buen principio en la vida || salida *f* (of a race); *false start* salida nula; *flying star* salida lanzada *f* || ventaja *f*; *I'll give you ten metres start* te daré diez metros de ventaja || sobresalto *m* (nervous jump) || respingo *m* (of a horse) || susto *m*; *what a start you gave me!* ¡qué susto me has dado! || — *at the start* al principio; *at the very start* muy al principio || *by fits and starts* a trompicones, a rachas || *for a start* para empezar || *odd* o *rum start* aventura peregrina, hecho extraño || FIG *the sales of his book got off to a good start* al principio su libro tenía buena venta | *to get off to a flying* o *a good start* empezar muy bien, empezar con buen pie || *to get one's start* empezar || *to give a sudden start* sobresaltarse || *to give s.o. a start in life* ayudar a uno en sus comienzos || *to make a fresh start* volver a empezar || *to make a start* empezar, comenzar || *to wake up with a start* despertarse sobresaltado.

start [stɑːt] *vt* empezar, comenzar, iniciar; *they started the meeting with questions* comenzaron la reunión con preguntas; *they started negotiations, a discussion* iniciaron las negociaciones, la discusión || entablar (conversation) || plantear (a question) || emitir (a doubt) || empezar a, comenzar a; *it's starting to rain* está empezando a llover; *she started feeling ill just after the dessert* empezó a sentirse enferma inmediatamente después del postre; *she started singing* empezó a cantar || poner en marcha, arrancar; *to start a car* poner un coche en marcha || poner en marcha, hacer funcionar (a clock) || cebar (a dynamo) || hacer salir, dar la salida a (a train) || dar la señal de salida a (a race) || fundar, crear (to establish) || emprender (a business) || FIG ayudar a emprender; *to start s.o. in a career* ayudar a alguien a emprender una carrera || levantar (an animal from its lair) || aflojar, soltar (mechanical parts) || FIG lanzar, hacer nacer (rumour); *who started the rumour?* ¿quién lanzó este rumor? | provocar, causar; *to start a fire* provocar un incendio | provocar, armar; *to start a row* provocar una riña | hacer; *he started everyone laughing* hizo reír a todo el mundo || verter (a liquid) || *to start s.o. learning Latin* iniciar a alguien en el aprendizaje del latín.
◆ *vi* empezar, comenzar (to begin); *to start by doing sth.* empezar por hacer algo; *to start in life* empezar en la vida; *don't start again!* ¡no empieces de nuevo! || salir (a train) || arrancar (car, etc.) || ponerse en marcha (a machine); *the engine started* la máquina se puso en marcha || salir, irse (to set off); *to start on a journey for* salir de viaje para || salir (in a race) || aflojarse, soltarse (a crew) || abrirse (seams) || salirse (eyes) || sobresaltarse (to jump) || — *starting from* a partir de; *starting from last month* a partir del mes pasado || *to start afresh* volver a empezar || *to start at the beginning* empezar desde el principio.
◆ *phr v* ***to start after*** ir *or* salir en busca de || ***to start aside*** echarse a un lado || ***to start back*** iniciar la vuelta (to return) | dar un salto atrás, retroceder || ***to start in*** empezar || ***to start off*** empezar, comenzar (to begin) | salir, ponerse en camino (on a journey) | salir (a train) | arrancar (a car) || ***to start on*** empezar || ***to start out*** salir, ponerse en camino (on a journey) | empezar (to begin) || — *to start out to* ponerse a || ***to start up*** empezar (to begin) | arrancar (engine) | levantarse de un golpe (to rise up) || ***to start with*** empezar con || — *to start with* para empezar (used as an adverbial phrase).

starter [-ə*] *n* SP juez *m* de salida (signal giver) | participante *m* & *f*, competidor, ra (competitor) || AUT arranque *m* || FIG promotor, ra (of a discussion) | autor, ra (of an objection) | iniciador, ra (of a project) || — *he is a fast runner but a slow starter* es un corredor rápido pero lento al salir || *to give as a starter* dar para empezar.

starting [-iŋ] *n* AUT arranque *m* || TECH puesta *f* en marcha (of a machine) || salida *f* (start) || comienzo *m*, principio *m* (beginning) || sobresalto *m*, susto *m* (fear).

starting block [-iŋblɔk] *n* SP taco *m* de salida.

starting gate [-iŋgeit] *n* SP barrera *f* en la línea de salida.

starting handle [-iŋˈhændl] *n* AUT manivela *f* [de arranque].

starting line [iŋˈlain] *n* SP línea *f* de salida.

starting motor [-iŋˈməutə*] *n* motor *m* de arranque.

starting point [-iŋpɔint] *n* punto *m* de partida.

starting post [-iŋpəust] *n* SP línea *f* de salida.

starting price [-iŋprais] *n* precio *m* inicial (in stock exchange) || SP última cotización antes de iniciarse una carrera de caballos.

starting switch [-iŋswitʃ] *n* AUT arranque *m*, botón *m* de arranque.

startle ['stɑːtl] *vt* asustar, sobresaltar.
◆ *vi* asustarse, sobresaltarse.

startling [-iŋ] *adj* sorprendente, asombroso, sa (amazing) || sobrecogedor, ra (frightening) || alarmante (alarming) || llamativo, va (colour, dress).

start turn ['stɑːtəːn] *n* atracción *f* principal (featured number).

starvation [stɑː'veiʃən] *n* hambre *f* || MED inanición *f*; *he died of starvation* murió de inanición || *starvation wages* sueldos *m* de hambre.

starve [stɑːv] *vt* hacer morir de hambre, matar de hambre (to cause to die of hunger) || privar de comida *or* de alimentos, hacer pasar hambre; *they starved him* le hicieron pasar hambre || FIG privar; *to starve s.o. of love* privar a alguien de amor || *to starve into surrender, to starve out* hacer rendirse por hambre.
◆ *vi* morir de hambre (to die of hunger) || pasar hambre (to suffer from hunger) || FAM morirse de hambre, estar muerto de hambre (to be hungry) | morirse de frío, estar helado (to be cold) || — FIG *to starve for* carecer de (to be in a great need of), anhelar (to have a strong desire for) || *to starve to death* morir de hambre.

starveling [-liŋ] *adj/n* muerto de hambre, muerta de hambre, hambriento, ta || *starveling wages* sueldos *m* de hambre.

starving [-iŋ] *adj* hambriento, ta; muerto de hambre.
◆ *n* hambre *f* || MED inanición *f*; *he died of starvation* murió de inanición || *starvation wages* sueldos *m* de hambre.

stash [stæʃ] *vt* US FAM esconder, guardar.

stasis ['steisis] *n* MED estasis *f*.
— OBSERV El plural de la palabra inglesa es *stases*.

state [steit] *n* estado *m* (in general); *in a bad state* en mal estado || estado *m*; *the United States* los Estados Unidos; *Church and State* la Iglesia y el Estado || condición *f*; *he lived in a style befitting his state* vivía de la forma que correspondía a su condición || lujo *m*; *to live in state* vivir en el lujo || gran pompa *f*, gran ceremonia *f* (pomp, display); *to escort s.o. in state* escoltar a alguien con gran pompa || PHYS & CHEM estado *m*; *the solid state* el estado sólido || — *he is not in a fit state to travel* no está en condiciones de viajar || *married state* estado matrimonial, matrimonio *m* || *reason of State* razón *f* de Estado || *single state* celibato *m*, soltería *f* || *state of affairs* situación *f* || *state of emergency* estado de emergencia (disaster), estado de excepción (political measure) || *state of grace* estado de gracia || *state of mind* estado de ánimo || REL *state of nature* estado de naturaleza || *state of siege* estado de sitio, estado de guerra || *States General* Estados Generales || *the States* los Estados Unidos || FAM *to be in a great state* estar fuera de sí | *to get into a state* ponerse nervioso || *to lie in state* estar de cuerpo presente.
◆ *adj* estatal, del Estado || público, ca; *state education* enseñanza pública; *state school* escuela pública || oficial || solemne; *a state occasion* una ocasión solemne || de gala (apartment, etc.) || *state secret* secreto *m* de Estado.

state [steit] *vt* declarar, afirmar (to declare); *I state that I heard it* afirmo haberlo oído || decir; *he did not state why* no dijo por qué || dar, expresar, manifestar; *I have stated my opinion* he dado mi opinion || escribir (to write down) || consignar; *as stated in the rules* como está consignado en el reglamento || JUR exponer, formular (a claim) || fijar, determinar (condition, date, time) || dar a conocer; *you must state full particulars* debe dar a conocer todos los detalles || plantear (a problem) || — *as stated below* como se indica a continuación || *to state one's name* dar su nombre || JUR *to state the case* exponer los hechos.

state bank [-bæŋk] banco *m* nacional (national), banco *m* del Estado (state's).

state capitalism [-'kæpitəlizəm] *n* capitalismo *m* de Estado.

statecraft [-krɑːft] *n* habilidad *f* política, diplomacia *f*, arte *m* de gobernar.

state-controlled [-kən'trəuld] *adj* controlado, da por el Estado || *state-controlled economy* economía dirigida.

stated [-id] *adj* dicho, cha; indicado, da.

State Department [-di'pɑːtmənt] *n* US Ministerio *m* de Asuntos Exteriores [AMER Ministerio *m* de Relaciones Exteriores].

statehouse [-haus] *n* US cámara *f* legislativa de un estado de los Estados Unidos.

stateless [-lis] *adj* apátrida.

stateliness [-linis] *n* majestad *f*, majestuosidad *f*.

stately [-li] *adj* majestuoso, sa (majestic) || impresionante (imposing) || *stately home* casa *f* solariega [abierta al público].

statement [-mənt] *n* declaración *f*; *a statement to the police* una declaración a la policía || informe *m*, relación *f* (report); *to draw up a statement* redactar un informe || afirmación *f*; *to contradict a statement* contradecir una afirmación || exposición *f*; *bare statement of the facts* simple exposición de los hechos || comunicado *m*; *an official statement to the press* un comunicado oficial a la prensa || planteamiento *m* (of a problem) || COMM extracto *m* de cuentas, estado *m* de cuentas || MUS exposición *f* || COMM *monthly statement* balance *m* mensual.

state-of-the-art [-əvðiɑːt] *adj* avanzado, da; moderno, na (equipment, technique).

stateroom [-ruːm] *n* camarote *m* (ship) || compartimento *m* privado (train).

State's attorney [-sə'təːni] *n* US fiscal *m*.

stateside [-said] *adj* FAM estadounidense.

statesman [-smən] *n* estadista *m*, hombre *m* de Estado.
— OBSERV El plural de *statesman* es *statesmen*.

statesmanlike [-smənlaik] *adj* propio de estadista.

statesmanship [-smənʃip] *n* habilidad *f* política, arte *m* de gobernar.

static ['stætik] *adj* estático, ca; *static electricity* electricidad estática || INFORM *static memory* o *storage* memoria *f* estática.
◆ *n* RAD parásitos *m pl*, interferencias *f pl*.

statics [-s] *n* estática *f*.

station ['steiʃən] *n* puesto *m*, lugar *m*; *the policeman took up his station near the door* el guardia ocupó su puesto junto a la puerta || sitio *m* (place) || estación *f*; *weather station* estación meteorológica; *tracking station* estación de seguimiento || estación *f* (train, etc.); *goods station* estación de mercancías; *railroad station* estación de ferrocarril || granja *f* de ganado lanar (sheep farm) || MIL puesto *m*; *action station* puesto de combate || posición *f* social, condición *f* (social standing) || RAD estación *f*; *radio, relay station* estación de radio, repetidora || REL estación *f* (of the cross) || — *bus station* término *m*, final *m* de línea || *first-aid station* casa *f* de socorro || MIL *military station* guarnición *f* || *naval station* puerto *m* militar || *petrol station* surtidor *m* de gasolina, gasolinera *f* || *police station* comisaría *f* || AUT *service station* estación de servicio || *to marry below one's station* malcasarse, casarse con una persona de posición social inferior.

station ['steiʃən] *vt* apostar; *to station sentries* apostar centinelas || estacionar; *to station troops abroad* estacionar tropas en el extranjero || colocar, situar (to place).

stationary ['steiʃnəri] *adj* fijo, ja; estacionario, ria (unchanging) || inmóvil (not moving) || PHYS *stationary wave* onda estacionaria.

stationer ['steiʃnə*] *n* librero, ra; papelero, ra || *stationer's* librería *f*, papelería *f*.

stationery ['steiʃnəri] *n* objetos *m pl* de escritorio (writing materials) || papel *m* de escribir y sobres.

station house ['steiʃnhaus] *n* comisaría *f* (of police) || cuartel *m* de bomberos (of firemen) || US estación *f* de ferrocarril.

stationmaster ['steiʃən'mɑːstə*] *n* jefe *m* de estación.

station wagon ['steiʃən'wægən] *n* break *m*.

statist ['steitist] *n* partidario *m* del estatismo.

statistic [stə'tistik] *n* estadística *f*.
◆ *adj* estadístico, ca.

statistical [-əl] *adj* estadístico, ca.

statistically [-əli] *adv* según las estadísticas, estadísticamente.

statistician ['stætis'tiʃən] *n* estadístico, ca.

statistics [stə'tistiks] *n* estadística *f* (science).
◆ *pl* estadísticas *f* (data).

stator ['steitə*] *n* TECH estator *m*.

statoscope ['steitəˌskəup] *n* PHYS estatoscopio *m* (aneroid barometer).

statuary ['stætjuəri] *adj* estatuario, ria; *statuary marble, art* mármol, arte estatuario.
◆ *n* estatuaria *f* (art of making statues) || estatuas *f pl* (statues collectively) || estatuario *m* (artist).

statue ['stætjuː] *n* estatua *f*; *equestrian statue* estatua ecuestre; *recumbent statue* estatua yacente.

statuesque ['stætju'esk] *adj* escultural.

statuette ['stætju'et] *n* figurina *f*, estatuilla *f*.

stature ['stætjə*] *n* estatura *f*, talla *f* (height) || FIG talla *f*, categoría *f*.

status ['steitəs] *n* condición *f*, estado *m* (state) || posición *f* social (position) || categoría *f* (standing) || JUR estado *m*; *marital* o *civil status* estado civil || *status symbol* símbolo *m* de posición social.

status quo [-'kwəu] *n* statu quo *m*.

statutable ['stætjuːtəbl] *adj* → **statutory.**

statute ['stætjuːt] *n* JUR estatuto *m*, decreto *m* (formally recorded law) || — *statute book* código *m* || *statute law* derecho escrito || *statute mile* milla *f* terrestre.
◆ *pl* estatutos *m* (of a chartered body); *in accordance with the statutes* según los estatutos.

statutory ['stætjutəri]; **statutable** ['stætjuːtəbl] *adj* establecido por la ley *or* los estatutos, estatutario, ria (established by a statute) || reglamentario, ria; estatutario, ria (conforming to a statute) || establecido por la ley (offence).

staunch [stɔːntʃ] *adj* fiel; seguro, ra; *a staunch friend* un amigo fiel || inquebrantable (courage) || MAR estanco, ca; hermético, ca (watertight).

staunch [stɔːntʃ] *vt* restañar (blood) || restañar la sangre a (a wound).

staunchness [-nis] *n* lealtad *f*, seguridad *f* (of friendship) || firmeza *f* (of courage) || estanquidad *f*, hermeticidad *f* (watertightness).

stave [steiv] *n* duela *f* (of barrel) || peldaño *m* (of a ladder) || barrote *m* (of a chair) || bastón *m* (stick) || MUS pentagrama *m* || estrofa *f* (of a poem).

stave* [steiv] *vt* poner duelas a (barrel) || — *to stave in* desfondar (a cask, a ship), romper (to break) || *to stave off* rechazar (an attack), apartar (to put aside), evitar; *to stave off a disaster* evitar un desastre; diferir, aplazar (to delay).

◆ *vi* desfondarse.
— OBSERV Pret y pp ***stove, staved***.

staves [-z] *pl n* ⟶ **staff.**

stay [stei] *n* estancia *f*, permanencia *f* [AMER estadía *f*]; *a stay of one week* una estancia de una semana; *during my stay in Cordoba* durante mi estancia en Córdoba || JUR aplazamiento *m* (postponement) | sobreseimiento *m* (of proceedings) || ARCH sostén *m*, soporte *m*, puntal *m* (prop) || apoyo *m*, sostén *m* (support) || ballena *f* (stiffener) || MAR estay *m*.
◆ *pl* corsé *m sing*.

stay [stei] *vt* JUR aplazar, diferir (to postpone) || quedarse, permanecer; *he stayed a month* se quedó un mes || resistir, aguantar (to endure); *to stay a race* resistir una carrera || detener, parar (to stop) || frenar (to check) || soportar, apoyar, sostener, apuntalar (to prop up, to secure) || FIG sostener, mantener (to support) || — *to stay one's hand* contenerse || *to stay one's hunger* engañar el hambre || *to stay out* quedarse hasta el final de; *he stayed the month, the film out* se quedó hasta el final del mes, de la película; terminar (a race).
◆ *vi* quedarse, permanecer; *to stay indoors* quedarse dentro || estar, vivir, alojarse, hospedarse; *I stayed in a very good hotel* estuve en un hotel muy bueno; *to stay with one's grandparents* estar en casa de sus abuelos || pararse, detenerse (to stop) || esperar, quedarse (to wait); *stay a little* espera un poco || resistir, aguantar; *the winner stayed well* el ganador resistió bien || MAR virar (to tack) || — *it has come to stay* se ha implantado || *to stay away* ausentarse (to absent o.s.),no venir (not to come) | *to stay away from* no acercarse a || *to stay in* quedarse en casa, no salir (not to go out), estar castigado sin salir (at school) || *to stay on* quedarse || *to stay out* quedarse fuera || *to stay over* pasar la noche || *to stay put* permanecer en el mismo sitio, no moverse (to remain in the same position), seguir igual (in the same condition) || *to stay to dinner* quedarse a cenar || *to stay up* no acostarse || *to stay up late* acostarse tarde.

stay-at-home [əthəum] *adj* casero, ra; hogareño, ña.
◆ *n* persona *f* casera *or* hogareña.

stayer [-ə*] *n* caballo *m* para carreras de fondo (horse) || corredor *m* de fondo (racer) || FIG persona *f* que tiene mucha resistencia.

staying power [iŋ'pˌuə*] *n* resistencia *f*, aguante *m*.

stay-in strike [-in'straik] *n* huelga *f* de brazos caídos *or* de brazos cruzados.

staysail [-seil] *n* MAR vela *f* de estay.

St Bernard [ˌseint'bəːnəd] *pr n* San Bernardo *m*.

STD *abbr of [sexually transmitted disease]* enfermedad de transmisión sexual.

stead [sted] *n* utilidad *f* || — *in s.o.'s, sth's stead* en lugar de alguien, de algo || *to stand s.o. in good stead* ser muy útil a alguien, ser de gran utilidad para alguien; *this will stand you in good stead* esto le será muy útil.

steadfast; stedfast [-fəst] *adj* constante, firme (constant) || inquebrantable (not wavering) || estable (not changing) || fijo, ja (gaze) || *steadfast in danger* impertérrito, ta.

steadfastness [-fəstnis] *n* constancia *f*, firmeza *f*, tenacidad *f* || estabilidad *f*.

steadily [-dili] *adv* firmemente || fijamente; *he looked at her steadily* la miró fijamente || a velocidad constante; *to drive steadily at 100* conducir a una velocidad constante de 100 || normalmente; *to walk steadily* andar normalmente || sin parar, continuamente (continuously); *he works steadily* trabaja sin parar || constantemente; *prices rise steadily* los precios aumentan constantemente || en equilibrio; *a table that stands steadily* una mesa que se mantiene en equilibrio || prudentemente, sensatamente (sensibly).

steadiness [-inis] *n* estabilidad *f*, equilibrio *m* (of person or object) || firmeza *f*, seguridad *f* (of hand, of mind) || regularidad *f* (in action) || constancia *f* (of demand, of faith, etc.) || estabilidad *f* (of prices) || continuidad *f* (continuity) || sensatez *f*, juicio *m* (good sense) || formalidad *f* (seriousness) || perseverancia *f* (perseverance) || fijeza *f*; *steadiness of gaze* fijeza en la mirada.

steady [-i] *adj* constante (constant) || firme, seguro, ra; *steady rest* sostén firme; *with a steady hand* con mano segura || en equilibrio; *to make a table steady* poner una mesa en equilibrio || tranquilo, la; manso, sa (horse) || regular; *to play a steady game* tener un juego regular; *steady pace* paso regular || ininterrumpido, da; continuo, nua; *steady progress* progresos continuos || estable; *steady weather* tiempo estable || continuo, nua; persistente; *steady downpour* lluvia continua || tenaz, firme (faith) || fiel, leal; *to be steady in one's principles* ser fiel a sus principios || sensato, ta; formal, equilibrado, da (sensible); *steady young man* joven sensato || asiduo, dua; aplicado, da (worker, student) || fijo, ja; seguro, ra; *he got a steady job* consiguió un empleo fijo || fijo, ja; *a steady gaze* una mirada fija || uniforme, regular; *steady heartbeat* pulso regular || estacionario, ria; *steady barometer* barómetro estacionario || sostenido, da (in the Stock Exchange) || COMM constante, continuo, nua; *steady demand for* pedido constante de | estable; *steady prices* precios estables || — *ship steady in a sea* barco *m* que navega bien || *steady!* ¡quieto! (remain calm), ¡despacio! (take it easy!), mantenga el rumbo (command to the helmsman) || *to go steady (with)* tener relaciones (con), salir (con) || *to keep steady* no moverse, quedarse quieto.
◆ *n* novio, via (sweetheart).

steady [-i] *vt* estabilizar (to stabilize) || hacer sentar cabeza (to make serious) || uniformar, regularizar (to make uniform) || calmar (nerves) || mantener firme, sostener (to hold) || — *to steady o.s.* recuperar el equilibrio || *to steady o.s. against sth.* apoyarse en algo.
◆ *vi* estabilizarse (to become stable) || sentar cabeza (a wild person) || uniformarse, regularizarse (to become uniform) || calmarse (to quieten down).

steak [steik] *n* filete *m* (slice of meat or fish) || bistec *m*, filete *m* (beefsteak).

steak house [-haus] *n* restaurante *m* especializado en bistecs.

steal [stiːl] *n* robo *m* (robbery) || plagio *m* (plagiarism) || US FAM ganga *f* (real bargain).

steal* [stiːl] *vt* robar, hurtar (to rob); *I didn't steal anything* no robé nada || FIG robar; *to steal a kiss* robar un beso || SP robar (in baseball) || — *to steal a glance at* echar una mirada furtiva a || *to steal a march on* adelantarse a, anticiparse a || *to steal the show* llevarse todos los aplausos.
◆ *vi* robar, hurtar || — *to steal away* escabullirse, marcharse sigilosamente || *to steal in, out* entrar, salir furtivamente *or* a hurtadillas.
— OBSERV Pret ***stole***; pp ***stolen***.

stealing [-iŋ] *n* robo *m*.

stealth [stelθ] *n* cautela *f*, sigilo *m* || *by stealth* a hurtadillas, furtivamente; *he did it by stealth* lo hizo a hurtadillas.

stealthily [-ili] *adv* a hurtadillas, furtivamente.

stealthiness [-inis] *n* cautela *f*, sigilo *m* (caution) || lo furtivo (of an action).

stealthy [-i] *adj* cauteloso, sa; sigiloso, sa (person) || furtivo, va (action) || *with stealthy step* con mucho sigilo.

steam [stiːm] *n* vapor *m* (from boiling water); *does it run on steam or electricity?* ¿funciona a vapor o con electricidad? || vaho *m* (from wet grass, from the mouth, etc.) || — *at full steam* a todo vapor || *to get up steam* dar presión (boiler), hacer acopio de energía (person) || FIG *to let off steam* desfogarse || FIG & FAM *to run out ot steam* quedarse sin pilas || FIG *under one's own steam* por sus propios medios, por sí mismo.
◆ *adj* de vapor; *steam launch* lancha de vapor; *steam locomotive* locomotora de vapor; *steam bath* baño de vapor.

steam [stiːm] *vt* CULIN cocer al vapor || limpiar con vapor (to clean) || tratar al vapor (to treat with steam) || arrojar, despedir (to emit) || empañar (window) || — *to steam open* abrir por medio de vapor || *to steam up* empañar.
◆ *vi* humear (to emit steam or vapour) || echar vapor; *the train streamed into the station* el tren entró en la estación echando vapor || evaporarse, salir en forma de vapor (to evaporate) || empañarse (windows, etc.) || funcionar con vapor (to work) || navegar, hacer, marchar a; *to steam at twelve knots* hacer doce nudos || — *to steam ahead* avanzar || MAR *to steam out* zarpar (a ship) || *to steam up* empañarse.

steamboat [-bəut] *n* vapor *m*, buque *m* de vapor.

steam boiler [-'bɔilə*] *n* caldera *f* de vapor.

steam box [-bɔks]; **steam chest** [-tʃest] *n* cámara *f* de vapor.

steam-driven [-ˌdrivn] *adj* a vapor, de vapor.

steam engine [-'endʒin] *n* máquina *f* de vapor.

steamer [-ə*] *n* vapor *m*, buque *m* de vapor (steamship) || máquina *f* de vapor (steam engine) || CULIN olla *f* de estofar.

steam fitter [-'fitə*] *n* montador *m* de calderas *or* de tuberías de vapor.

steam gauge; US **steam gage** [-geidʒ] *n* manómetro *m*.

steam hammer [-ˌhæmə*] *n* martillo *m* pilón.

steaminess [-inis] *n* humedad *f*.

steam iron [-'aiən] *n* plancha *f* de vapor.

steamroller [-'rəulə*] *n* TECH apisonadora *f* || FAM fuerza *f* arrolladora (overwhelming power).

steamroller [-'rəulə*] *vt* apisonar, allanar (to flatten with a steamroller) || FAM aplastar, arrollar; *to steamroller any opposition* aplastar toda oposición | imponer (idea, policy).

steam ship [-ʃip] *n* vapor *m*, buque *m* de vapor || *steamship company* compañía naviera.

steam shovel [-ʃʌvl] *n* excavadora *f*, pala *f* mecánica.

steamy [-i] *adj* húmedo, da (atmosphere) || empañado, da (glass) || humeante (giving off steam) || vaporoso, sa (of or like steam).

stearate ['stiəreit] *n* CHEM estearato *m*.

stearic [sti'ærik] *adj* esteárico, ca; *stearic acid* ácido esteárico.

stearin ['stiərin]; **stearine** ['stiəriːn] *n* CHEM estearina *f*.

steatite ['stiətait] *n* MIN esteatita *f*.

stedfast ['stedfəst] *adj* ⟶ **steadfast.**

steed [stiːd] *n* corcel *m* (horse).

steel [stiːl] *n* acero *m* (metal); *stainless steel* acero inoxidable; *cast steel* acero colado; *steel casting* fundición del acero || eslabón *m*, chaira *f* (for sharpening knives) || eslabón *m* (for making sparks) || acero *m* (sword) || ballena *f* (stiffener) || FIG resolución *f*, firmeza *f* (determination) | acero *m* (strength) || — *cold steel* arma

blanca || FIG *to be made of steel* ser de hierro || *to turn into steel* acerar; *to turn iron into steel* acerar el hierro.
◆ *adj* de acero.

steel [sti:l] *vt* acerar (to cover with steel) || FIG endurecer (one's heart) | fortalecer (to strengthen) || — FIG *to steel one's heart* endurecerse, volverse insensible | *to steel o.s.* fortalecerse (to strengthen), endurecerse, volverse insensible (to harden) | *to steel o.s. against* acorazarse contra.

steel-clad [-klæd] *adj* acorazado, da; cubierto de acero.

steel engraving [-in'greiviŋ] *n* grabado *m* en acero.

steel grey; US **steel gray** [-'grei] *n* gris *m* metálico.

steel industry [-'indəstri] *n* industria *f* siderúrgica.

steeliness [-inis] *n* dureza *f*, inflexibilidad *f*.

steel mill [-mil] *n* acería *f*, fábrica *f* de acero.

steel wool [-'wul] *n* estropajo *m*.

steelwork [-wə:k] *n* estructura *f* de acero.
◆ *pl* acería *f sing*, fundición *f sing* de acero.
— OBSERV *Steelworks* se construye con el singular o con el plural.

steely [-i] *adj* acerado, da (of or like steel) || FIG duro, ra (hard) | inflexible.

steelyard [-jɑ:d] *n* romana *f* (balance).

steep [sti:p] *adj* empinado, da; escarpado, da; abrupto, ta (slope); *steep hillside* ladera escarpada || cortado a pico (cliff) || FAM excesivo, va; exorbitante (price) | increíble, exagerado, da (story).
◆ *n* pendiente *f*, cuesta *f* empinada (steep slope) || remojo *m* (soaking).

steep [sti:p] *vt* remojar (to soak) || enriar (hemp) || FIG empapar, impregnar (to saturate); *to be steeped in* estar empapado de.
◆ *vi* estar en remojo || estar en infusión (tea).

steepen [-ən] *vt* volver más empinado (slope) || aumentar (prices).
◆ *vi* empinarse (slope) || aumentar (prices).

steeple [-l] *n* aguja *f* (spire) || campanario *m*, torre *f* (tower and spire).

steeplechase [-ltʃeis] *n* SP carrera *f* de obstáculos (horse racing, athletics).

steeplechaser [-l,tʃeisə*] *n* SP jockey *m or* caballo *m or* corredor *m* de obstáculos.

steeplechasing [-l,tʃeisiŋ] *n* carrera *f* de obstáculos.

steeplejack [-ldʒæk] *n* reparador *m* de chimeneas *or* de campanarios.

steeply [-li] *adv* en pendiente || — *prices rose steeply* los precios subieron vertiginosamente || *steeply inclined road* carretera muy empinada.

steepness [-nis] *n* pendiente *f*, inclinación *f*.

steer [stiə*] *n* novillo *m* (young bull) || US FAM consejo *m* (friendly suggestion).

steer [stiə*] *vt* dirigir, encaminar (one's steps) || dirigir, guiar (vehicle) || gobernar (a boat) || llevar (a bicycle) || conducir [AMER manejar] (a car) || seguir; *to steer a course* seguir un rumbo || FIG conducir, llevar, guiar (to lead) | orientar (to guide).
◆ *vi* llevar el timón (in a boat) || obedecer al timón (boat) || llevar el volante, conducir [AMER manejar] (in a car) || conducirse [AMER manejarse]; *a car that steers easily* un coche que se conduce fácilmente || — *to steer clear of* evitar || *to steer for* dirigirse a.

steerage [-ridʒ] *n* MAR entrepuente *m*, tercera clase *f* (cheapest quarters on a ship) | gobierno *m* (ship's reaction to the helm).

steerageway [-ridʒ'wei] *n* MAR velocidad *f* mínima para gobernar.

steering [-riŋ] *n* MAR gobierno *m* || AUT conducción *f* [AMER manejo *m*] (of a car).

steering column [-riŋ,kɔləm] *n* columna *f* de dirección.

steering committee [riŋkə'miti] *n* comité *m* de dirección *or* directivo.

steering gear [-riŋgiə*] *n* mecanismo *m* de dirección.

steering wheel [-riŋwi:l] *n* volante *m* (of a car) || rueda *f* del timón (of a ship).

steersman [-zmən] *n* MAR timonero *m*, timonel *m* (helmsman).
— OBSERV El plural de la palabra inglesa es *steersmen*.

steeve [sti:v] *n* MAR inclinación *f* (of bowsprit) | esteba *f* (for steeving cargo).

steeve [sti:v] *vt* MAR estibar (to stow) | inclinar (to angle a bowsprit).
◆ *vi* MAR inclinarse (bowsprit).

stein [stain] *n* US jarra *f* (beer mug).

steinbock [-bɔk] *n* ZOOL íbice *m* (ibex).

steinbok [-bɔk] *n* ZOOL antílope *m* africano.

stele ['sti:li:] *n* estela *f* (monument) || BOT estela *f*.

stellar ['stelə*] *adj* estelar (relating to the stars) || estrellado, da (stellate) || US principal, estelar; *a stellar role* un papel principal.

stellate ['steleit]; **stellated** ['steleitid] *adj* estrellado, da (shaped like a star) || radiado, da (leaves, cells, etc.).

stellionate ['steliəneit] *n* JUR estelionato *m*.

stem [stem] *n* tallo *m* (of a flower) || tronco *m* (of a tree) || rabo *m*, pedúnculo *m* (of a leaf) || rabo *m* (of fruit) || racimo *m* (of bananas) || pie *m* (of a glass) || tubo *m*, cañón *m* (of a pipe) || cañón *m* (of feathers) || TECH vástago *m* (rod) || tija *f* (of a key) || MUS rabo *m* (of a note) || grueso *m* (of a letter) || GRAMM radical *m* | tronco *m*, origen *m*, estirpe *f* (line of descent) || MAR tajamar *m*, roda *f* (vertical piece of bow) | proa *f* (bow) || SP cuña *f* (in skiing) || *from stem to stern* de proa a popa.

stem [stem] *vt* despalillar (to remove the stem from) || MAR hacer frente a, mantenerse contra (to make headway) || restañar (blood) || estancar, represar (to dam up) || detener, contener; *to stem an attack* detener un ataque || frenar (to stop).
◆ *vi* pararse en cuña (skiing) || *to stem from* derivarse de, ser el resultado de (to result).

stemless [-lis] *adj* sin tallo.

stench [stentʃ] *n* peste *f*, hedor *m* (foul smell).

stencil ['stensl] *n* plantilla *f* (for reproducing letters, designs, etc.) || cliché *m* de multicopista (for duplicator, for typewriter, etc.) || estarcido *m* (patterns or letters produced).

stencil ['stensl] *vt* estarcir || sacar con multicopista (documents).

stenocardia [,stenə'kɑ:diə] *n* MED estenocardia *f*.

stenograph ['stenəgrɑ:f] *n* taquigrafía *f* (symbols) || máquina *f* de taquigrafía (machine).

stenograph ['stenəgrɑ:f] *vt* taquigrafiar, estenografiar.

stenographer [ste'nɔgrəfə*] *n* taquígrafo, fa; estenógrafo, fa.

stenographic [ste'nɔgrəfik]; **stenographical** [-əl] *adj* taquigráfico, ca; estenográfico, ca.

stenography [ste'nɔgrəfi] *n* taquigrafía *f*, estenografía *f*.

stenotype ['tenətaip] *n* estenotipo *m*.

stenotypist ['stenətaipist] *n* estenotipista *m* & *f*.

stenotypy ['stenətaipi] *n* estenotipia *f*.

stentor ['stentɔ*] *n* esténtor *m*.

stentorian [sten'tɔ:riən] *adj* estentóreo, a.

step [step] *n* paso *m*; *to take three steps* dar tres pasos; *three steps away* a tres pasos; *to walk with a heavy step* andar con paso pesado; *to take a step backwards* dar un paso hacia atrás || paso *m*, huella *f* (footprint); *to follow in s.o.'s steps* seguir los pasos de alguien || paso *m*, pisada *f* (sound made by the foot); *steps were heard* se oían pasos || paso *m* (movement or sequence in dancing) || paso *m* (pace); *at a fast step* a paso rápido || peldaño *m*, escalón *m* (of stairs, of ladder); *I sat down on the top step* me senté en el último escalón || estribo *m* (of a vehicle) || umbral *m* (of doorway) || FIG escalón *m* (a degree in scale); *to go up a step in one's job* subir un escalón en su empleo | paso *m*, etapa *f* (stage in a process, in an activity); *the first step towards liberty* el primer paso hacia la libertad; *a process that is done in three steps* un proceso que se hace en tres etapas | medida *f* (measure); *to take steps to cut down inflation* tomar medidas para reducir la inflación | paso *m*, gestión *f*; *to take the necessary steps to get a passport* hacer las gestiones necesarias *or* dar los pasos necesarios para conseguir un pasaporte || MUS nota *f* (degree on a scale) | intervalo *m* (interval) || MAR carlinga *f* (socket) || MIN tajo *m* escalonado (shelf) || graderío *m* (in a stadium) || — *a great step forward* un gran paso adelante || FIG *at every step* a cada paso || *goose step* paso de la oca || *mind your step!* ¡tenga cuidado! || *step by step* paso a paso, poco a poco || *sure step* paso firme || *to be a step away* estar a dos pasos || *to be in step* llevar el paso || *to be out of step* no llevar el paso || *to break step* romper el paso || *to get o to fall into step* coger el paso || *to keep in step* llevar el compás (dancing), llevar el paso, ir con paso acompasado (marching) || FIG *to take a false step* dar un mal paso, dar un paso en falso || *to take a great step* dar un buen paso || FIG *to watch one's step* ir con cuidado.
◆ *pl* escalinata *f sing* (flight of outdoor stairs) || escaleras *f*, escalera *f sing* (staircase) || escalera *f sing* de tijera (stepladder) || escalerilla *f sing* (of a plane) || — *a few steps forward* a dos pasos || *first steps* primeros pasos (of children) || *flight of steps* tramo *m* (of a staircase), escalinata *f* (of an entrance) || *pair of steps* escalera *f* de tijera || *to retrace one's steps* desandar lo andado, volverse atrás || FIG *to take the first steps* dar los primeros pasos | *to turn one's steps towards* encaminarse hacia, dirigirse hacia | *with measured steps* a pasos contados.

step [step] *vt* dar; *to step three paces to the left* dar tres pasos a la izquierda || poner (the foot) || bailar (a dance) || MAR plantar (the mast into its socket) || escalonar (to construct in steps) || medir a pasos (a distance).
◆ *vi* dar un paso, dar pasos; *to step forward* dar un paso adelante || ir (to go) || — *step this way please* pase por aquí, por favor || *to step ashore* tomar tierra || FAM *to step round to the tobacconist's* darse una vuelta *or* pasarse por el estanco || *to step short* andar a paso corto.
◆ *phr v* *to step aside* apartarse, hacerse a un lado | FIG hacer una digresión || *to step back* retroceder, echarse atrás || *to step down* bajar; *to step down from the bus* bajar del autobús | renunciar a (from office) | ELECTR reducir (current) || *to step in* entrar | FIG intervenir || — *step in!* ¡adelante! || *to step into* poner el pie en; *to step into the road* poner el pie en la calzada | FIG heredar (a fortune) | ocupar (position) || *to step off* medir (a pasos) (to measure) | bajar de; *to step off the pavement* bajar de la acera || *to step on* pisar; *to step on s.o.'s foot* pisar el pie a alguien; *to step on the brake* pisar el freno; *to step on the grass* pisar la hierba || — *to step on board* subir a bordo | FAM *to step on it* darse prisa (to hurry), acelerar (to accelerate) || *to step out*

apretar el paso (to walk fast) | salir (to go out); *to step out for a while* salir un rato | apartarse (of one's way) | US irse de juerga (to have a good time) || *to step over* pasar por encima de (an obstacle) | darse una vuelta por, pasarse por (to go) || *to step up* subir; *to step up into the bus* subir al autobús | ascender (to promote) | aumentar; *to step up production* aumentar la producción | ELECTR aumentar (current) | acercarse (to approach).

stepbrother [-ˈbrʌðə*] *n* hermanastro *m*, medio hermano *m*.

step-by-step [-baiˈstep] *adj* progresivo, va; gradual; *a step-by-step method of learning English* un método progresivo para aprender inglés.

stepchild [-tʃaild] *n* hijastro, tra.
— OBSERV El plural es *stepchildren*.

stepdaughter [-ˈdɔːtə*] *n* hijastra *f*.

step-down [-daun] *adj* reductor, ra.

stepfather [-ˈfɑːðə*] *n* padrastro *m*.

stepladder [ˈstepˈlædə*] *n* escalera *f* de tijera.

stepmother [ˈstepˈmʌðə*] *n* madrastra *f*.

steppe [step] *n* estepa *f*.

stepped [-t] *adj* con escalones || escalonado, da || FIG gradual, progresivo, va.

stepped-up [-tʌp] *adj* aumentado, da || ascendido, da (promoted).

stepping-stone [-iŋ,stəun] *n* pasadera *f*, cada una de las piedras usadas para cruzar un río || FIG trampolín *m* (a means of advancement).

stepsister [ˈstepˈsistə*] *n* hermanastra *f*, media hermana *f*.

stepson [ˈstepsʌn] *n* hijastro *m*.

step-up [ˈstepʌp] *adj* ELECTR elevador, ra.

stere [ˈstiːə*] *n* estéreo *m* (cubic metre).

stereo [ˈstiəriəu] *adj* estereoscópico, ca || estereofónico, ca; estéreo, a; *a stereo record* un disco estéreo || PRINT estereotipado, da.
◆ *n* PRINT estereotipo *m* || estereoscopia *f* (stereoscopy) || estereofonía *f* (stereophony) || equipo *m* estereofónico (equipment).

stereobate [ˈstiəriəubeit] *n* ARCH estereóbato *m*.

stereochemistry [stiəriəuˈkemistri] *n* estereoquímica *f*.

stereogram [ˈstiəriəgræm] *n* estereograma *m*.

stereograph [ˈstiəriəugrɑːf] *n* estereograma *m*, estereografía *f*.

stereometer [,stiəriˈɔmitə*] *n* estereómetro *m*.

stereometry [stiəriˈɔmətri] *n* estereometría *f*.

stereophonic [stiəriəˈfɔnik] *adj* estereofónico, ca.

stereophony [steriˈɔfəni] *n* estereofonía *f*.

stereoscope [ˈstiəriəskəup] *n* estereoscopio *m*.

stereoscopic [stiəriəˈskɔpik]; **stereoscopical** [-əl] *adj* estereoscópico, ca.

stereoscopy [stiəriˈɔskəpi] *n* estereoscopia *f*.

stereotype [ˈstiəriətaip] *n* PRINT estereotipo *m* (plate) | estereotipia *f* (machine) || FIG estereotipo *m* (conventional idea, character, etc.).

stereotype [ˈstiəriətaip] *vt* estereotipar || FIG estereotipar; *stereotyped smile, attitude, phrase* sonrisa, actitud, expresión estereotipada.

stereotyping [-iŋ] *n* estereotipado *m*.

stereotypy [stiəriəˈtaipi] *n* estereotipia *f*.

sterile [ˈsterail] *adj* estéril.

sterility [steˈriliti] *n* esterilidad *f*.

sterilization [ˈsterilaiˈzeiʃən] *n* esterilización *f*.

sterilize [ˈsterilaiz] *vt* esterilizar.

sterilizing [-iŋ] *adj* esterilizador, ra.

sterling [ˈstəːliŋ] *adj* esterlina; *the pound sterling* la libra esterlina || de la libra esterlina; *sterling area* zona de la libra esterlina || FIG excelente, de buena ley, de buena calidad; *sterling fellow* persona excelente | verdadero, ra; auténtico, ca (genuine) || *sterling silver* plata *f* de ley.
◆ *n* libra *f* esterlina (money) || plata *f* de ley (sterling silver).

stern [stəːn] *adj* severo, ra; austero, ra; *stern discipline* disciplina severa || sombrío, a (air) || severo, ra; *stern judge* juez severo; *stern look* mirada severa || severo, ra; riguroso, sa (punishment) || austero, ra; *stern landscape* paisaje austero || triste (reality) || firme; *stern resolve* firme resolución.
◆ *n* MAR popa *f* || FAM parte *f* trasera, trasero *m* (of a person) || cuarto *m* trasero (of an animal).

sternforemost [-ˈfɔːməust] *adv* MAR con la popa hacia adelante.

sternmost [-məust] *adj* MAR más a popa.

sternness [-nis] *n* austeridad *f*, severidad *f* || severidad *f* (of judge, look, punishment) || austeridad *f* (of a landscape) || lo sombrío (of air) || tristeza *f* (sadness) || firmeza *f* (of resolve).

sternpost [-pəust] *n* MAR codaste *m*.

sternum [ˈstəːnəm] *n* ANAT esternón *m*.
— OBSERV El plural de *sternum* es *sternums* o *sterna*.

sternutation [ˈstəːnjuˈteiʃən] *n* estornudo *m*.

sternway [ˈstəːnwei] *n* MAR marcha *f* atrás, retroceso *m*.

steroid [ˈsterɔid] *n* CHEM esteroide *m*.

sterol [ˈsterɔl] *n* CHEM esterol *m*.

stertor [ˈstəːtɔː*] *n* MED estertor *m*.

stertorous [ˈstəːtərəs] *adj* MED estertoroso, sa.

stet [stet] *n* vale [lo tachado].

stet [stet] *vt* marcar como válido [lo tachado].

stethoscope [ˈsteθəskəup] *n* MED estetoscopio *m*.

stethoscopy [steˈθɔskəpi] *n* MED estetoscopia *f*.

Stetson [ˈstetsən] *pr n* (registered trademark) sombrero *m* tejano.

stevedore [ˈstiːvidɔː*] *n* MAR estibador *m*.

stew [stjuː] *n* CULIN estofado *m*, guisado *m* (of mutton, etc.) | encebollado *m* (of hare) | compota *f* (of fruit) || vivero *m*, criadero *m* (for fish, for oysters) || lupanar *m* (brothel) || FIG & FAM preocupación *f*, agitación *f* (worry) || FAM *to be in a stew* estar hecho un lío.

stew [stjuː] *vt* CULIN estofar, guisar, cocer a fuego lento (meat) || hacer una compota de, cocer (fruit) || FIG & FAM *to let s.o. stew* tener a alguien en ascuas.
◆ *vi* cocer a fuego lento || pasarse (tea) || FIG & FAM cocerse, ahogarse (to stifle) | empollar (to study hard) | estar en ascuas (to worry) || FIG & FAM *to stew in one's own juice* cocerse en su propia salsa.

steward [stjuəd] *n* mayoral *m* (of a farm) || administrador *m* (of an estate) || AVIAT auxiliar *m* de vuelo || camarero *m* (on a passenger ship) || mayordomo *m* (butler) || despensero *m*, administrador *m* de la cocina (in charge of serving and preparing meals on a boat) || organizador *m* (of public meetings) || *shop steward* enlace *m* sindical.

stewardess [-is] *n* camarera *f* (on a passenger ship) || AVIAT azafata *f* [AMER aeromoza *f*].

stewardship [-ʃip] *n* mayordomía *f* (catering) || administración *f*.

stewed [stjuːd] *adj* FAM bebido, da; como una cuba (drunk).

stewing steak [ˈstjuːiŋ,steik] *n* CULIN carne *f* para guisar.

stewpan [ˈstjuːpæn]; **stewpot** [ˈstjuːpɔt] *n* cazuela *f*, olla *f*.

sthene [ˈsθiːn] *n* estenio *m* (unit of force).

stibium [ˈstibiəm] *n* CHEM antimonio *m*.

stick [stik] *n* madero *m*, trozo *m* de madera (piece of wood) || estaca *f* (stake) || garrote *m*, porra *f* (club, weapon) || vara *f*, palo *m* (for hitting with); *I hit him with a stick* le golpeé con un palo || bastón *m* (for walking); *I knocked on the door with my stick* llamé a la puerta con el bastón || rodrigón *m* (for plants) || palo *m*, mango *m* (of a broom) || palillo *m* (drumstick, coctail stick) || MUS batuta *f* (of conductor) || MIL baqueta *f* (of guns) || barra *f* (of toffee, wax, chewing gum) || palo *m* (for lollipop) || SP palo *m*, «stick» *m* (hockey) || tallo *m* (of rhubarb) || rama *f* (of celery) || MAR mástil *m*, verga *f*, palo *m* (mast) || AVIAT palanca *f* [de mando] (control lever) || cartucho *m* (of dynamite) || ráfaga *f* (of machine gun) || haz *m* (of bombs) || PRINT componedor *m* (composing stick) || pinchazo *m*; *a stick in the ribs* un pinchazo en el costado || adhesión *f* (power of adhering) || — FIG *big stick policy* política *f* del gran garrote | *poor stick* desgraciado *m* | *odd* o *rum stick* tipo extraño || *stick of furniture* mueble *m* || FIG *to be in a cleft stick* estar entre la espada y la pared || FIG & FAM *to get the wrong end of the stick* tomar el rábano por las hojas || *to give s.o. the stick* dar a alguien una paliza.
◆ *pl* leña *f sing*, astillas *f* (to make a fire).

stick* [stik] *vt* clavar (to thrust); *to stick a pin into sth.* clavar un alfiler en algo || prender; *stuck with pins* prendido con alfileres || pinchar (to penetrate); *that pin is sticking me* este alfiler me está pinchando; *to stick a cushion with a pin* pinchar un cojín con un alfiler || fijar, sujetar (with tacks) || clavar, hincar (a knife, bayonet) || poner; *she stuck a flower in her hair* se puso una flor en la cabeza || picar (with a stick) || pegar; *to stick a postage stamp on a letter* pegar un sello de correos en una carta || FAM colocar, poner; *he stuck knicknacks all over the room* colocó cositas por toda la habitación | colocar, poner, clavar (on a spike) | meter; *he stuck the letter in his pocket* metió la carta en el bolsillo | timar, estafar; *to stick s.o. (for) five pounds* timar a alguien cinco libras | soportar, aguantar; *I can't stick him* no le puedo aguantar | meter; *don't stick your nose into other people's business* no meta la nariz en los asuntos ajenos | cargar; *they have stuck me with all the cooking* me han cargado toda la cocina | desconcertar (a problem) || degollar (a pig) || apuñalar (a person) || — FAM *I got stuck in geography* me cogieron en geografía | *to stick one's hat on one's head* calarse el sombrero | *you can stick it!* ¡aguántate!, ¡te aguantas! (telling s.o. to put up with sth.), ¡te lo puedes quedar! (keep it!).
◆ *vi* clavarse; *the pin stuck in the cushion* el alfiler se clavó en el cojín || estar prendido (pins) || clavarse, hincarse (a knife, a bayonet) || pegar; *this glue doesn't stick* esta goma no pega || pegarse (to adhere); *the paper sticks to my fingers* el papel se me pega a los dedos || atascarse, quedarse atascado (to become bogged down); *the car stuck in the mud* el coche se atascó en el barro || atascarse, atrancarse, bloquearse (a machine) || quedarse parado, pararse, detenerse (to come to a stop); *the car stuck on the hill* el coche se quedó parado en la colina || quedarse, permanecer (to stay) || pegarse (cooking) || FAM pegarse; *he sticks like a leech* se pega como una sanguijuela *or* como una lapa.
◆ *phr v* *to stick around* quedarse || *to stick at* tropezar con (a difficulty) | seguir (con); *he is*

sticking at the work he started sigue el trabajo que empezó | vacilar en (to hesitate at) || — FIG *he sticks at nothing* no se para en barras || *to stick by* ser fiel a (a friend) || *to stick down* poner (to put down) | apuntar (to write down) | pegar (to fasten with paste) || *to stick on* pegar (stamp) | pegarse (a person) || — FAM *to be stuck on* estar chalado por | FIG *to stick it on* exagerar || *to stick out* sacar; *to stick out one's tongue* sacar la lengua | asomar (one's head) | sobresalir; *the eaves are the part of the roof which sticks out* el alero es la parte del tejado que sobresale | aguantar (to endure) | FAM obstinarse (to be obstinate) || — *his tongue was sticking out* estaba con la lengua fuera, tenía la lengua fuera | FIG *it sticks out a mile* se ve a la legua | *to stick it out* aguantar hasta el final | *to stick out for* obstinarse en pedir || *to stick to* ser fiel a (a friend) | atenerse a, mantener; *I am sticking to what I said* me atengo a lo que he dicho, mantengo lo dicho | cumplir con (one's duty) | cumplir (a promise) | seguir (to continue, to follow) | ceñirse; *to stick to the truth, to the text* ceñirse a la verdad, al texto || — *stick to it!* ¡sigue! | *to stick to one's guns* mantenerse en sus trece || *to stick together* no separarse (persons) | pegar (to fasten) || *to stick up* fijar (posters) | aguzar (one's ears) | erizarse (hair, etc.) | salir, sobresalir (to project) | US FAM atracar (to rob) || — *stick 'em up!* ¡arriba las manos! | *to stick up for* defender, dar *or* sacar la cara por; *I would have been expelled if my friend had not stuck up for me* me habrían expulsado si mi amigo no me hubiera defendido | *to stick up to* resistir a || *to stick with* seguir con (sth.), no separarse de (s.o.).

— OBSERV Pret y pp **stuck**.

sticker [-ə*] *n* letrero *m* engomado, cartel *m*, pegatina *f* (poster) || etiqueta *f* adhesiva (label) || fijasellos *m inv* (for stamps) || matarife *m*, jifero *m* (in a slaughterhouse) || espina *f* (thorn) || FAM persona *f* tenaz (tenacious person) | lapa *f*, pelma *m* & *f* (tiresome person) | pega *f* (puzzling question).

stickiness [-inis] *n* pegajosidad *f* (viscosity) || humedad *f* (of climate) || pegajosidad *f* (of heat) || adherencia *f*, adhesividad *f* (power of adhering) || dificultad *f* (of a problem).

sticking [-iŋ] *adj* engomado, da || *sticking plaster* esparadrapo *m*.

◆ *n* adherencia *f*, adhesividad *f* (stickiness) || TECH agarrotamiento *m* (of pistons, etc.).

stick insect [-'insekt] *n* ZOOL insecto *m* palo.

stick-in-the-mud [-inðəmʌd] *n* persona *f* chapada a la antigua.

stickle [-l] *vi* ser rigorista.

stickleback [-lbæk] *n* picón *m* (fish).

stickler [-lə*] *n* rigorista *m* & *f* || FAM rompecabezas *m inv*, problema *m* peliagudo (puzzle) || — FIG *to be a stickler for* dar mucha importancia a | *to be a stickler for etiquette* ser muy etiquetero.

stick-on [-ɔn] *adj* adhesivo, va.

stickpin [-pin] *n* US alfiler *m* de corbata.

stickup [-ʌp] *n* US robo *m* a mano armada, atraco *m*.

sticky [-i] *adj* pegajoso, sa (viscous); *my fingers are sticky* tengo los dedos pegajosos || engomado, da (label, envelope, etc.) || resbaladizo, za (slippery) || húmedo, da (climate) || pegajoso, sa; bochornoso, sa (heat); *what a sticky day!* ¡qué día más pegajoso! || FAM quisquilloso, sa (touchy) | difícil, peliagudo, da (difficult) || *to come to a sticky end* acabar mal.

stiff [stif] *adj* rígido, da (rigid) || duro, ra; *stiff cardboard* cartón duro || tieso, sa (corpse) || almidonado, da; duro, ra (collar, cuffs, etc.) || empinado, da (slope, stairs) || espeso, sa (substance, paste, etc.) || MED anquilosado, da (joint) | tieso, sa (leg) | entumecido, da; embotado, da (numb) | con agujetas (after exercise) || AGR arcilloso, sa (soil) || duro, ra (hard to move) || TECH agarrotado, da (pistons, etc.) || FIG estirado, da; envarado, da (not natural) | ceremonioso, sa; etiquetero, ra; protocolario, ria (excessively formal) | inflexible (unyielding) | difícil, duro, ra (difficult); *stiff piece of work* trabajo difícil | reñido, da; *stiff battle* batalla reñida | fuerte (wind) || FAM fuerte, cargado, da (drink) | alto, ta; subido, da (prices) | firme (market) | severo, ra (punishment) | como una cuba, borracho, cha (drunk) || *stiff with cold* aterido *or* yerto de frío.

◆ *adv* *to be scared stiff* estar muerto de miedo.

◆ *n* FAM *big stiff* tonto *m* de capirote.

stiffen [-n] *vt* poner tieso *or* rígido, atiesar || endurecer (to harden) || espesar, hacer más espeso (substance, sauce, paste) || poner ballenas a (a bodice) || almidonar (a collar, cuffs, etc.) || MED anquilosar (a joint) | entumecer, embotar (limbs) | agarrotar (muscles) || FAM cargar (a drink).

◆ *vi* ponerse tieso *or* rígido || endurecerse (to harden) || hacerse más espeso (to become thicker) || MED anquilosarse (a joint) | entumecerse, embotarse (limbs) | agarrotarse (muscles) || FIG volverse más duro | ponerse más fuerte (wind).

stiffening [-niŋ] *n* almidonado *m* (of fabrics) || almidón *m* (starch) || endurecimiento *m* (hardening) || refuerzo *m*; *stiffening plate* chapa de refuerzo || rigidez *f* (stiffness).

stiff neck [-'nek] *n* tortícolis *f inv*.

stiff-necked [-'nekt] *adj* terco, ca; testarudo, da (stubborn) || FAM estirado, da; envarado, da (not natural) | ceremonioso, sa; etiquetero, ra; protocolario, ria (excessively formal).

stiffness [-nis] *n* rigidez *f* || dureza *f* || espesura *f* (of a sauce) || consistencia *f* || MED anquilosamiento *m* (of a joint) | embotamiento *m* (of limbs) | agarrotamiento *m* (of muscles) || FAM fuerza *f* (of a drink) || FIG dificultad *f*, lo difícil (difficulty) | obstinación *f*, testarudez *f* (stubborness) | envaramiento *m* (formality) | firmeza *f* (of market) || *stiffness of the legs* agujetas *f pl* en las piernas (after exercise).

stifle ['staifl] *n* ZOOL babilla *f* (of quadrupeds).

stifle ['staifl] *vt* ahogar, sofocar (to prevent from breathing) || contener (cough, yawn) || sofocar, reprimir (a revolt) || amortiguar, sofocar (sound).

◆ *vi* ahogarse, sofocarse.

stifling [-iŋ] *adj* sofocante || bochornoso, sa (atmosphere).

stigma ['stigmə] *pl n* estigma *m*.

— OBSERV El plural de *stigma* es *stigmata* o *stigmas*.

stigmata [-tə] *n* REL estigmas *m*.

stigmatism ['stigmətizəm] *n* PHYS estigmatismo *m*.

stigmatization ['stigmətai'zeiʃən] *n* estigmatización *f*.

stigmatize ['stigmətaiz] *vt* estigmatizar.

stile [stail] *n* escalera *f* para pasar por encima de una cerca (to cross a fence) || montante *m* (of a door).

stiletto [sti'letəu] *n* estilete *m* (dagger) || punzón *m* (tool) || *stiletto heels* tacones *m* de aguja.

— OBSERV El plural es *stilettos* o *stilettoes*.

still [stil] *adj* tranquilo, la (quiet, calm) || apacible, sosegado, da (peaceful) || suave, sordo, da (noise) || silencioso, sa (silent) || durmiente, estancado, da (water) || no espumoso (wine) || no gaseoso, sa (other drinks) || inmóvil (not moving) || — *keep still!* ¡estate quieto! || *keep still about this* no diga nada de esto || *the air is still* no corre aire || *to stand still* estarse quieto, no moverse (to stop fidgetting), no moverse (not to move), pararse (to stop).

◆ *adv* todavía, aún; *I am still in Paris* estoy todavía en París; *the green one is still bigger* el verde es todavía más grande || — *he is still here* está todavía aquí, aún está aquí, sigue aquí || *in spite of his faults she loved him still* a pesar de sus defectos le seguía queriendo || *still more* más aún.

◆ *conj* sin embargo, no obstante, con todo (y con eso) (nevertheless); *still, you did the right thing* no obstante, hizo lo que había que hacer.

◆ *n* calma *f*, quietud *f*, tranquilidad *f* (calm) || sosiego *m*, tranquilidad *f* (peacefulness) || silencio *m* (silence) || estancamiento *m* (of water) || alambique *m* (for distilling) || destilería *f* (distillery) || PHOT vista *f* fija, fotografía *f*.

still [stil] *vt* tranquilizar, calmar (to quieten) || calmar (fears) || callar, hacer callar (to make silent) || amortiguar (a noise) || aplacar (to allay) || CHEM destilar.

◆ *vi* calmarse, aplacarse.

stillbirth [-bə:θ] *n* alumbramiento *m* de un mortinato, nacimiento *m* de un niño muerto.

stillborn [-bɔ:n] *n* mortinato, ta; nacido muerto || FIG malogrado, da.

still life [-laif] *n* bodegón *m*, naturaleza *f* muerta.

— OBSERV El plural de *still life* es *still lives* o *still lifes*.

stillness [-nis] *n* calma *f*, quietud *f*, tranquilidad *f* (peacefulness) || silencio *m*, quietud *f* (silence).

stillson wrench [-sənrentʃ] *n* US llave *f* de tubos.

stilly [-i] *adj* tranquilo, la; silencioso, sa; quieto, ta.

◆ *adv* tranquilamente.

stilt [stilt] *n* zanco *m* (for walking) || zampa *f*, pilote *m* (for buildings) || AGR esteva *f* (plough handle) || *stilt walker* zancuda *f* (bird).

stilted [-id] *adj* construido sobre pilotes (building) || peraltado, da (arch, road) || FIG envarado, da (person) | pomposo, sa; afectado, da (style).

stimulant ['stimjulənt] *n* MED estimulante *m* || FIG bebida *f* alcohólica.

stimulate ['stimjuleit] *vt* MED estimular || FIG estimular, animar, incitar.

◆ *vi* actuar como estimulante || FIG servir de estímulo.

stimulating [-iŋ] *adj* estimulante || interesante (interesting) || alentador, ra (encouraging).

stimulation ['stimju'leiʃən] *n* estímulo *m*.

stimulative ['stimjulətiv] *adj* estimulante.

◆ *n* estimulante *m*.

stimulus ['stimjuləs] *n* estímulo *m*, incentivo *m*; *his words were a stimulus for me* sus palabras fueron un estímulo para mí || estímulo *m* (to activate the functioning of an organ, etc.).

— OBSERV El plural de *stimulus* es *stimuli*.

stimy; stymie ['staimi] *vt* obstruir (el hoyo) con una bola (in golf) || FIG obstaculizar (to hinder) || FAM *to be stimied* estar fastidiado.

sting [stiŋ] *n* ZOOL aguijón *m* (of bee, of wasp, etc.) | colmillo *m* (of a snake) || picadura *f* (wound) || escozor *m* (pain) || BOT pelo *m* urticante || FIG punzada *f*; *the sting of remorse* la punzada del remordimiento | mordacidad *f* (of an attack, of a remark) | herida *f*; *the sting of an insult* la herida provocada por un insulto | veneno *m*; *the sting of his words* el veneno de sus palabras || — FIG *to give a sting to* hacer mordaz | *to take the sting out of sth.* quitarle hierro a algo.

sting* [stiŋ] *vt* picar; *the wasp stung me* me picó la avispa || escocer, picar (a blow, etc.) || FIG herir, picar en lo vivo; *stung by an insult* herido por un insulto || FAM clavar (to overcharge) || — FIG *his conscience will sting him* le remorderá la conciencia | *to sting s.o. to do sth.* incitar a alguien a que haga algo.
◆ *vi* picar (bees, wasps, etc.) || escocer, picar; *my wound stings* me escuece la herida.
— OBSERV Pret y pp ***stung***.

stinger [-ə*] *n* US aguijón *m* (of bees, of wasps) || US FAM pulla *f* (painful remark) | cóctel *m* de coñac y licor | bofetada *f* (blow).

stingfish [-fiʃ] *n* peje *m* araña.

stingily ['stindʒili] *adv* tacañamente, mezquinamente.

stinginess ['stindʒinis] *n* tacañería *f*, mezquindad *f*, roñosería *f* (avarice).

stinging hair ['stiŋiŋhɛə*] *n* pelo *m* urticante.

stinging nettle ['stiŋiŋ'netl] *n* BOT ortiga *f*.

stingray ['stiŋrei] *n* pastinaca *f* (fish).

stingy ['stindʒi] *adj* FAM tacaño, ña; mezquino, na; roñoso, sa (avaricious) | escaso, sa; parco, ca (meagre).

stink [stiŋk] *n* peste *f*, hedor *m* (unpleasant smell) || FAM *to cause* o *to kick up* o *to raise a stink* armar un escándalo, organizar un follón.

stink* [stiŋk] *vi* apestar, oler mal, heder || FIG oler; *it stinks of corruption* huele a corrupción || FAM estar fatal; *his performance stank* su actuación estuvo fatal || FAM *he stinks of money* tiene tanto dinero que da asco.
◆ *vt* *to stink out* hacer salir *or* ahuyentar por el mal olor || US *to stink up* dar mal olor a.
— OBSERV Pret ***stank, stunk***; pp ***stunk***.

stink bomb [-bɔm] *n* bomba *f* fétida.

stinkbug [-bʌg] *n* US ZOOL chinche *f* hedionda.

stinker [-ə*] *n* FAM mala persona *f*, mal bicho *m* (person) | problema *m* peliagudo (problem) | examen *m* difícil (examination) || cosa *f* *or* persona *f* maloliente.

stinking [-iŋ] *adj* hediondo, da; apestoso, sa; fétido, da; pestilente (smelly) || FAM asqueroso, sa (disgusting) || BOT *stinking iris* lirio hediondo.
◆ *adv* FAM muy, enormemente, terriblemente || FAM *he is stinking rich* tiene tanto dinero que da asco.

stint [stint] *n* limitación *f*, restricción *f*, límite *m* (limit) || tarea *f*, trabajo *m* (work).

stint [stint] *vt* escatimar (expenses, efforts, etc.) || limitar, restringir (to limit) || privar; *to stint s.o. of sth.* privar a uno de algo || *to stint o.s.* privarse.

stipe [staip] *n* estípite *m*.

stipend ['staipənd] *n* estipendio *m*, remuneración *f*, salario *m*.

stipendiary [stai'pendjəri] *adj* remunerado, da; asalariado, da.
◆ *n* asalariado, da.

stipple ['stipl] *n* punteado *m*.

stipple ['stipl] *vt* puntear.

stipulate ['stipjuleit] *vt* estipular.
◆ *vi* *to stipulate for* estipular.

stipulation [ˌstipju'leiʃən] *n* estipulación *f*, condición *f* || JUR cláusula *f*, estipulación *f*.

stir [stə:*] *n* movimiento *m*; *he gave a stir* hizo un movimiento || FIG agitación *f* (disturbance) | murmullo *m*; *there was a stir among the audience* hubo un murmullo entre el público | emoción *f*, conmoción *f* (commotion) | sensación *f*, gran impresión *f* | escándalo *m*, revuelo *m*; *he raised quite a stir with his new novel* provocó un escándalo con su nueva novela || FAM chirona *f*, cárcel *f* (jail) || *give the tea a stir* mueve *or* remueve el té.

stir [stə:*] *vt* mover, remover, revolver; *to stir tea* mover el té || mezclar; *to stir water into paint* mezclar agua con pintura || mover, agitar; *the wind stirred the leaves* el viento movía las hojas || agitar; *stir before using* agítese antes de usarse || FIG incitar, animar; *he stirred me into doing my chores* me incitó a hacer mis quehaceres | conmover (to touch) | provocar (s.o.'s anger) | excitar; *to stir the imagination* excitar la imaginación || atizar, avivar (the fire) || — FIG *to stir o.s.* hacer un esfuerzo || *to stir s.o.'s pity* dar lástima a alguien || *to stir up* mover (a liquid), provocar, armar; *to stir up a trouble* provocar un escándalo; excitar (passions), fomentar (discord, revolt), despertar (curiosity), levantar (courage), atizar, avivar (hatred), aguijonear, espolear (s.o.), remover (the past), atizar, avivar (the fire).
◆ *vi* moverse; *nobody stirred* nadie se movía; *to stir in one's sleep* moverse durmiendo || levantarse (to get up).

stirabout [-ə'baut] *n* gachas *f pl* (of oatmeal) || FAM revuelo *m*.

stir-fry ['stə:frai] *vt* freír rápidamente y removiendo.

stirless [-lis] *adj* inmóvil.

stirps [-ps] *n* JUR estirpe *f* || raza *f* (of animals).
— OBSERV El plural de *stirps* es *stirpes*.

stirrer [-ə*] *n* CHEM agitador *m* || FIG fomentador, ra; promotor, ra (of trouble).

stirring [-iŋ] *adj* bullicioso, sa; revoltoso, sa (child) || FIG agitado, da; movido, da (life) | sensacional (event) | conmovedor, ra (speech, etc.) | que anima, animado, da (music).

stirrup ['stirʌp] *n* estribo *m* || TECH trepador *m* || — *stirrup bone* estribo *m* (in the ear) || FAM *stirrup cup* espuela *f* (drink) || *stirrup leather* ación *m* || *stirrup pump* bomba *f* de mano (for water).

stitch [stitʃ] *n* puntada *f* (in sewing) || punto *m* (in knitting) || punto *m* (style in sewing, embroidering, etc.); *chain stitch* punto de cadeneta || MED punto *m* de sutura || dolor *m* de costado, punzada *f* en el costado (pain in the side) || — FAM *he has not done a stitch of work all day* no ha dado puntada en todo el día | *not to have a dry stitch on* estar empapado | *not to have a stitch on* estar en cueros | *to be in stitches* desternillarse de risa.

stitch [stitʃ] *vt* coser || MED suturar || encuadernar en rústica (books) || *to stitch up* volver a coser, remendar.
◆ *vi* coser.

stitching ['stitʃiŋ] *n* puntos *m pl*, puntadas *f pl* (in sewing).

stiver ['staivə*] *n* FAM ochavo *m*.

stoa ['stəuə] *n* ARCH pórtico *m*.
— OBSERV El plural de *stoa* es *stoae* o *stoas*.

stoat [stəut] *n* armiño *m* (animal).

stock [stɔk] *n* COMM existencias *f pl*, reservas *f pl*, «stock» *m* (of tradesmen and manufacturers) | surtido *m*; *have you a good stock of men's wear?* ¿tiene un buen surtido de ropa de caballero? | reserva *f*, depósito *m* (of money) | capital *m* social (of a company) | acciones *f pl*, títulos *m pl*, valores *m pl* (in stock exchange); *I advise you not to buy those stocks* le aconsejo que no adquiera esas acciones || caudal *m* (of knowledge) || linaje *m*, familia *f*, estirpe *f*, cepa *f*; *he is of very ancient stock* es de una familia muy antigua || familia *f* (family of animals, of plants, etc.) || raza *f* (race); *are these animals of healthy stock?* ¿son estos animales de buena raza? || AGR ganado *m* (livestock) | alhelí *m* (flower) | tronco *m* (trunk) | cepa *f*, tocón *m* (tree stump) | cepa *f* (of vine) | patrón *m* (in grafting) || TECH materia *f* prima (raw material) | cepo *m* (of an anvil, of an anchor) | cabezal *m* (of a lathe) | caja *f* (of smoothing plane) | mango *m* (of a tool, of whip) | esteva *f*, mancera *f* (of plough) | caja *f*, culata *f* (of gun) | material *m* rodante *or* móvil (railways) || CULIN extracto *m* (of meat, etc.) | caldo *m* (of vegetables) || pechera *f* negra (worn over the chest by clergymen) || THEATR repertorio *m* (of plays) || — *government stock* papel *m* del Estado || *in stock* en existencia, en almacén, en reserva, en depósito || *joint stock* capital *m* social || *joint-stock company* sociedad anónima || *out of stock* agotado, da || *stock control* control *m* de existencias || *stock in hand* existencias disponibles || *surplus stock* excedentes *m pl* || *to have sth. in stock* tener existencias de algo || *to lay in a stock of* abastecerse de || FIG *to put* o *to take stock in* hacer poco caso de || *to take stock* hacer el inventario || FIG *to take stock of* examinar (to consider), evaluar (to appraise).
◆ *pl* picota *f sing*, cepo *m sing* (punishment) || MAR grada *f sing* de construcción, astillero *m sing* || — MAR *off the stocks* botado || *on the stocks* en los astilleros, en construcción (a boat), en el telar, en preparación; *he has two novels on the stocks* tiene dos novelas en el telar || COMM *stocks and shares* valores *m pl* mobiliarios.
◆ *adj* en existencia; *stock goods* mercancías en existencia || de las existencias; *stock clerk* encargado de las existencias || corriente, normal, de serie (size) || clásico, ca; *stock argument* argumento clásico || acuñado, da; estereotipado, da; *stock phrase* expresión acuñada || THEATR del repertorio || AGR reproductor, ra (animal) | ganadero, ra (farm).

stock [stɔk] *vt* surtir, abastecer (to provide); *he stocked his shop with tinned foods* abasteció su tienda con conservas || tener existencias de, tener en el almacén (to have in stock) || almacenar (to store) || tener (to have); *he does not stock that kind of food* no tiene esa clase de alimentos || poblar (with fishes, with trees) || AGR ensilar, entrojar (a crop) || MAR encepar (an anchor) || poner mango a (a whip) || poner culata a (a gun) || FIG enriquecer (one's memory).
◆ *vi* brotar (plants) || *to stock up with* o *on* abastecerse de.

stockade [stɔ'keid] *n* estacada *f*, empalizada *f*, vallado *m*.

stockade [stɔ'keid] *vt* empalizar, poner una estacada, vallar.

stock book ['stɔkbuk] *n* libro *m* de almacén.

stockbreeder ['stɔk'bri:də*] *n* ganadero, ra.

stockbreeding ['stɔkˌbri:diŋ] *n* ganadería *f*, cría *f* del ganado.

stockbroker ['stɔk'brəukə*] *n* corredor *m* de Bolsa, agente *m* de Bolsa.

stockbrokerage [-ridʒ]; **stockbroking** ['stɔkˌbrəukiŋ] *n* correduría *f* de Bolsa, corretaje *m* de Bolsa.

stockcar ['stɔkka:*] *n* US vagón *m* para el ganado.

stock car ['stɔkka:*] *n* «stock-car» *m*, automóvil *m* que participa en carreras donde se permiten choques y obstrucciones.

stock company ['stɔk'kʌmpəni] *n* COMM sociedad *f* anónima || THEATR compañía *f* de repertorio.

stock cube ['stɔkkju:b] *n* CULIN cubito *m* de caldo.

stock exchange ['stɔkiks'tʃeindʒ] *n* COMM Bolsa *f*.

stock farmer ['stɔkfa:mqp*] *n* ganadero *m*.

stock farming [-iŋ] *n* ganadería *f*.

stockfish ['stɔkfiʃ] *n* estocafís *m inv*, pejepalo *m*.

stockholder ['stɔk'həuldə*] *n* accionista *m* & *f*.

Stockholm ['stɔkhəum] *pr n* GEOGR Estocolmo.

stockiness ['stɔkinis] *n* robustez *f.*

stockinet; stockinette [ˌstɔki'net] *n* tejido *m* elástico de punto.

stocking ['stɔkiŋ] *n* media *f* (for ladies) || calcetín *m* (sock) || — *horse with white stockings* caballo calzado de blanco || *in one's stocking feet* con medias *or* calcetines pero sin zapatos, descalzo, za.

stock-in-trade ['stɔkin'treid] *n* existencias *f pl* || TECH herramientas *f pl*, instrumentos *m pl*, útiles *m pl* || FIG repertorio *m.*

stockist ['stɔkist] *n* distribuidor *m*, depositario *m.*

stockjobber ['stɔk'dʒɔbə*] *n* agiotista *m.*

stockjobbing ['stɔk'dʒɔbiŋ] *n* agiotaje *m.*

stock list ['stɔklist] *n* cotizaciones *f pl* de la Bolsa.

stockman ['stɔkmən] *n* ganadero *m* (of a stock farm) || almacenero *m* (of a stockroom).
— OBSERV El plural de *stockman* es *stockmen.*

stock market ['stɔk'mɑːkit] *n* COMM Bolsa *f or* mercado *m* de valores.

stockpile ['stɔkpail] *n* reservas *f pl.*

stockpile ['stɔkpail] *vt* almacenar, acumular.
◆ *vi* almacenarse, acumularse.

stockpot ['stɔkpɔt] *n* olla *f*, marmita *f.*

stock raising ['stɔk'reiziŋ] *n* ganadería *f*, cría *f* del ganado.

stockroom ['stɔkrum] *n* almacén *m*, depósito *m.*

stock-still ['stɔk'stil] *adj* completamente inmóvil.

stocktaking ['stɔkˌteikiŋ] *n* inventario *m*, balance *m* || *stocktaking sale* venta *f* postbalance.

stocky ['stɔki] *adj* rechoncho, cha; achaparrado, da (chubby) || robusto, ta (heavily built) || BOT achaparrado, da.

stockyard ['stɔkjɑːd] *n* corral *m* de ganado.

stodge [stɔdʒ] *n* FAM comida *f* indigesta.

stodge [stɔdʒ] *vt* FAM atiborrar (with food) | abarrotar (with facts) || FAM *to stodge o.s.* atiborrarse, hartarse.

stodgy [-i] *adj* FAM indigesto, ta; pesado, da (food) | abarrotado, da (crammed full) | pesado, da (dull) | rechoncho, cha (stocky).

stogie; stogy ['stəugi] *n* US puro *m* largo y barato.

stoic ['stəuik] *adj/n* estoico, ca; *the stoic doctrine* la doctrina estoica; *stoic in the face of misfortune* estoico ante la desgracia.

stoical [-əl] *adj* estoico, ca.

stoicism ['stəuisizəm] *n* PHIL estoicismo *m* || FIG estoicismo *m.*

stoke [stəuk] *vt* alimentar (fire, boiler).
◆ *vi* FAM *to stoke up* atiborrarse (to eat).

stokehold [-həuld] *n* MAR sala *f* de máquinas, sala *f* de fogoneros, cuarto *m* de calderas.

stokehole [-həul] *n* boca *f* del horno (mouth of furnace) || MAR sala *f* de máquinas, sala *f* de fogoneros, cuarto *m* de calderas.

stoker [-ə*] *n* fogonero *m* (person) || TECH cargador *m* mecánico (machine).

stole [stəul] *n* estola *f.*

stole [stəul] *pret* ⟶ **steal.**

stolen [-ən] *pp* ⟶ **steal.**

stolid ['stɔlid] *adj* impasible, imperturbable.

stolidity [stɔ'liditi]; **stolidness** ['stɔlidnis] *n* impasibilidad *f*, imperturbabilidad *f.*

stolon ['stəulən] *n* estolón *m*, latiguillo *m.*

stoma ['stəumə] *n* BOT & ANAT estoma *m.*
— OBSERV El plural de *stoma* es *stomata* o *stomas.*

stomach ['stʌmək] *n* ANAT estómago *m* || FAM vientre *m*, barriga *f* (belly) || FIG afición *f* (inclination); *I have no stomach for politics* no tengo ninguna afición a la política | ganas *f pl*, deseo *m* (desire) | valor *m*, estómago *m* (courage) || — *on an empty stomach* con el estómago vacío || *pit of the stomach* boca *f* del estómago || FIG *that turns my stomach* eso me revuelve el estómago | *to have a cast-iron stomach* tener un estómago de piedra || *to have an empty stomach* tener el estómago vacío || FIG *to put some stomach into s.o.* infundir ánimo a alguien.

stomach ['stʌmək] *vt* FIG soportar, aguantar, tragar (to bear).

stomachache [-eik] *n* dolor *m* de estómago.

stomacher ['stʌməkə*] *n* peto *m* (ornamental garment).

stomachic [stə'mækik] *adj* estomacal.
◆ *n* MED estomacal *m*, digestivo *m.*

stomach pump ['stʌmək'pʌmp] *n* MED bomba *f* gástrica.

stomach tooth ['stʌmək'tuːθ] *n* FAM colmillo *m*, canino *m.*

stomach upset ['stʌməkʌp'set] *n* trastorno *m* gástrico.

stomata ['stəumətə] *pl n* ⟶ **stoma.**

stomatitis [stɔmə'taitis] *n* MED estomatitis *f.*

stomatologist [stɔmə'tɔlədʒist] *n* MED estomatólogo, ga.

stomatology [stɔmə'tɔlədʒi] *n* MED estomatología *f.*

stomp [stɔmp] *vi* pisar fuerte.

stone [stəun] *n* piedra *f* (rock, piece of rock); *to throw a stone* tirar una piedra; *precious stone* piedra preciosa || lápida *f* (on graves) || MED cálculo *m*, piedra *f* (disease) || piedra *f*, muela *f* (of a mill) || granizo *m* (hailstone) || BOT hueso *m* (of fruit) || PRINT & ARTS piedra *f* || peso *m* que equivale a 6 kilos 350 gramos (weight) || — *meteoric stone* piedra meteórica || FIG *not to leave a stone standing* no dejar piedra sobre piedra || *philosopher's stone* piedra filosofal || *pumice stone* piedra pómez || *semiprecious stone* piedra fina || FIG *to cast the fist stone* tirar la primera piedra || *to lay the foundation stone* poner la primera piedra || FIG *to leave no stone unturned* no dejar piedra por mover, revolver Roma con Santiago | *to melt a heart of stone* ablandar las piedras | *to throw stones at s.o.* tirar piedras contra uno | *within a stone's throw* muy cerca, a tiro de piedra.
◆ *adj* de piedra.
— OBSERV Cuando tiene el sentido de *peso*, la palabra *stone* es invariable.

stone [stəun] *vt* apedrear, lapidar (to throw stones at) || quitar el hueso, deshuesar (a fruit) || empedrar, pavimentar (to face with stone) || FAM emborrachar (to make drunk) | drogar (to drug) || — FAM *to get stoned* coger una trompa (alcohol), fliparse (drugs) || *to stone s.o. to death* matar a alguien a pedradas.

Stone Age [-eidʒ] *n* Edad *f* de Piedra.

stone-blind [-'blaind] *adj* completamente ciego.

stone-broke [-'brəuk] *adj* FAM sin blanca, sin un centavo (without money).

stone coal [-kəul] *n* carbón *m* de piedra, antracita *f.*

stone-cold [-'kəuld] *adj* FAM helado, da; *the soup is stone-cold* la sopa está helada; *I am stone-cold* estoy helado.

stonecrop [-krɔp] *n* BOT uva *f* de gato.

stone crusher [-'krʌʃə*] *n* trituradora *f*, machacadora *f.*

stone curlew [-'kəːljuː] *n* ZOOL alcaraván *m* (bird).

stonecutter [-ˌkʌtə*] *n* cantero *m*, picapedrero *m.*

stone-dead [-'ded] *adj* FAM tieso, sa.

stone-deaf [-'def] *adj* FAM sordo como una tapia.

stone fruit [-fruːt] *n* BOT drupa *f*, fruta *m* con hueso.

stone marten [-'mɑːtin] *n* ZOOL garduña *f.*

stonemason [-'meisn] *n* albañil *m* (bricklayer) || cantero *m*, picapedrero *m* (in quarry).

stone pit [-pit]; **stone quarry** [-'kwɔri] *n* cantera *f* de piedras.

stoner [-ə*] *n* apedreador, ra (stone thrower) || deshuesadora *f* (for fruit).

stonewall [-'wɔːl] *vi* SP jugar a la defensiva || FIG practicar el obstruccionismo (in Parliament).

stoneware [-wɛə*] *n* gres *m*; *stoneware pot* vasija de gres || objetos *m pl* de barro.

stonewashed [-wɔʃt] *adj* lavado, da a la piedra (garment, fabric).

stonework [-wəːk] *n* ARCH construcción *f* de piedra (stone construction) | cantería *f*, sillería *f* (masonry).

stonily [-ili] *n* FIG glacialmente, fríamente.

stony [-i] *adj* pedregoso, sa (with many stones) || pétreo, a (like stone) || FIG de piedra, pétreo, a; *a stony heart* un corazón de piedra | frío, a; glacial; *a stony look* una mirada fría | sepulcral; *a stony silence* un silencio sepulcral.

stony-broke ['stəuni'brəuk] *adj* FAM sin blanca, sin un centavo (without money).

stonyhearted ['stəuni'hɑːtid] *adj* con el corazón de piedra, insensible.

stood [stud] *pret/pp* ⟶ **stand.**

stooge [stuːdʒ] *n* THEATR comparsa *m* || secuaz *m* (underling) || soplón, ona; chivato, ta (informer).

stook [stuk] *n* hacina *f*, fajina *f.*

stool [stuːl] *n* taburete *m*, banquillo *m* (seat without back or arms) || silla *f* de tijera (folding) || escabel *m* (footstool) || BOT planta *f* madre || alféizar *m* (of window) || reclamo *m* (decoy bird) || chivato, ta; soplón, ona (informer) || deposiciones *f pl*, deyecciones *f pl* (faeces) || *folding stool* silla *f* de tijera.

stool [stuːl] *vi* echar retoños (plants) || defecar.

stool pigeon [-'pidʒin] *n* reclamo *m* (decoy bird) || FAM chivato, ta; soplón, ona (informer).

stoop [stuːp] *n* inclinación *f* de hombros, espaldas *f pl* encorvadas (posture) || US pórtico *m* (porch) || REL pila *f* para el agua bendita || jarra *f* (drinking mug) || — *to have a stoop* ser cargado de espaldas || *to walk with a stoop* andar encorvado.

stoop [stuːp] *vt* inclinar, agachar (one's head) || encorvar (one's back).
◆ *vi* encorvarse, agacharse, inclinarse (to bend forwards) || ser cargado de espaldas (habitually) || FIG rebajarse; *to stoop to cheating* rebajarse a hacer trampas.

stooping [-iŋ] *adj* encorvado, da; cargado de espaldas || inclinado, da.

stop [stɔp] *n* parada *f* (act, halt); *it made a stop* hizo una parada; *five-minute stop* parada de cinco minutos || parada *f* (place where buses, etc., stop); *request stop* parada discrecional || escala *f* (of a ship, of a plane) || estancia *f* (stay) || pausa *f* (pause) || detención *f* (holdup) || interrupción *f* (interruption) || cesación *f* (cessation) || suspensión *f* (suspension) || tapón *m* (stopper of bottle, etc.) || TECH tope *m* (of a mechanism) || marginador *m* (of typewriter) || PHOT diafragma *m* || MAR boza *f* || MUS llave *f* (of clarinet, of saxophone) | agujero *m* (of flute, of wind instruments) | traste *m* (of guitar) | registro *m* (of organ) || FAM fin *m*, término *m* (end); *to put a stop to sth.* poner fin a algo || punto *m*, «stop» *m* (in telegrams) || «stop» *m*, señal *f* de parada (on road) || GRAMM punto *m* (full stop) | oclusión *f* (in phonetics) || — *full stop* punto *m* || *to be at a stop* estar parado || *to come to a stop* pararse || *to come to a sudden stop* pararse en seco || FIG & FAM *to pull out all the stops* tocar todos los registros || MUS *to pull out a stop* sacar un registro.

stop [stɔp] *vt* parar, detener; *he stopped his car near the house* paró su coche junto a la casa; *stop the bus* pare el autobús || interrumpir; *she stopped him in the middle of the speech* le interrumpió en medio del discurso; *the rain stopped the match* la lluvia interrumpió el partido || dejar de; *to stop crying* dejar de llorar || impedir; *he will not stop me from going* no me impedirá ir || evitar, parar (a danger) || tapar, taponar (a hole) || rellenar (a gap) || obturar, obstruir (a pipe) || empastar (a tooth) || restañar, detener (the flow of blood) || interceptar, cortar, cerrar (a road) || tapar; *to stop s.o.'s ears* tapar los oídos a alguien; *I stopped my ears* me tapé los oídos || cortar, interrumpir; *to stop supplies* cortar el suministro || cortar (electricity, gas, water) || parar, paralizar (production) || suprimir (s.o.'s holidays) || suspender; *they stopped my pay* me suspendieron el sueldo || deducir de, descontar de, retener de (to deduct) || anular, cancelar (a cheque) || oponerse a (payment of a cheque) || FAM parar; *to stop a blow* parar un golpe || rechazar, contener (an attack) || poner fin *or* término a, acabar con; *I am going to stop his nonsense* voy a poner fin a sus tonterías || GRAMM puntuar || MUS tapar los agujeros de (a flute) | pisar (a string) || — FAM *he stopped a bullet* recibió un balazo || *stop it!* ¡basta!, ¡ya está bien! || *stop thief!* ¡al ladrón!, ¡ladrones! || *what's stopping you?* ¿qué te impide continuar?, ¿qué te detiene?
◆ *vi* pararse, detenerse (to come to a halt, to cease to operate); *we stopped at the end of the road* nos paramos al final de la calle; *my watch has stopped* se ha parado mi reloj || parar, pararse (to cease to do sth.); *he was crying and then he stopped* estaba llorando y entonces se paró; *the rain has stopped* ha parado la lluvia || parar, pararse (buses, trains, etc.); *the bus stops near my house* el autobús para cerca de mi casa || cesar; *the noise stopped* el ruido cesó || terminarse, acabarse (to finish) || cortarse (electricity, gas, water) || suspenderse (to be suspended) || alojarse, vivir, parar; *I stop at my parents' place* vivo en casa de mis padres || quedarse (to stay) || — *to stop at nothing* no pararse en barras || *to stop dead* o *short* pararse en seco || *to stop to think* pararse a pensar, reflexionar || *without stopping* sin parar, sin cesar, sin interrupción.
◆ *phr v* *to stop away* no venir (not to come) | ausentarse (to go away) || *to stop behind* rezagarse, quedarse atrás (to lag behind) | quedarse (to stay) || *to stop by* pasar, hacer una visita corta (to visit) | pasar por || *to stop down* diafragmar (a lens) || *to stop in* quedarse en casa, no salir (to stay at home) | quedarse en el colegio, no salir (after school) || *to stop off* pararse (during a journey) | detenerse un rato; *let's stop off at the bar* detengámonos un rato en el bar || *to stop out* tapar una parte de (a surface to be printed) | quedarse fuera (to stay out) || *to stop over* pasar la noche (to spend the night) | quedarse; *stop over at my place for a few days* quédese unos días en casa || *to stop up* taponar, obturar, obstruir (a leak) | tapar (a hole) | velar, no acostarse (to stay awake) || *to stop with* vivir *or* alojarse *or* quedarse en casa de.

stopcock [-kɔk] *n* llave *f* de paso.

stope [stəup] *n* MIN bancada *f*.

stopgap ['stɔpgæp] *n* sustituto, ta (person) || recurso *m* (thing).

stoplight ['stɔplait] *n* AUT luz *f* de frenado || US disco *m* rojo, semáforo *m* rojo (of traffic lights).

stopover ['stɔp,əuvə*] *n* parada *f* [temporal] (during a journey) || escala *f* (of plane, of ship).

stoppage ['stɔpidʒ] *n* parada *f* (stop) || paro *m* (industrial) || huelga *f* (strike) || MED oclusión *f*, suspensión *f* (of payments) || detención *f*; *stoppage of play* dentención del juego || cesación *f* (ceasing) || interrupción *f* || deducción *f*, retención *f* (of wages) || obstrucción *f*, taponamiento *m* (blockage).

stopper ['stɔpə*] *n* tapón *m* (of bottle, etc.) || TECH tope *m* (in mechanics) | obturador *m* (of pipe) || MAR boza *f* || FAM coto *m*, término *m*, tope *m*; *to put a stopper on* poner tope a.

stopper ['stɔpə*] *vt* taponar, tapar.

stopping ['stɔpiŋ] *n* —→ **stop.**

stop press ['stɔp'pres] *n* noticias *f pl* de última hora.

stop-press ['stɔp'pres] *adj* de última hora; *stop-press news* noticias de última hora.

stop sign ['stɔpsain]; **stop signal** ['stɔp'signl] *n* stop *m*.

stop valve ['stɔpvælv] *n* TECH válvula *f* de retención.

stopwatch ['stɔpwɔtʃ] *n* cronómetro *m*.

storage ['stɔ:ridʒ] *n* almacenamiento *m*, almacenaje *m* (action) || almacenaje *m* (cost) || almacén *m*, depósito *m* (place) || guardamuebles *m inv* (for furniture) || INFORM almacenamiento *m*, memoria *f* || ELECTR acumulación *f* || — INFORM *storage device* dispositivo *m* de almacenamiento | *storage location* posición *f* de memoria.

storage battery [-'bætəri] *n* ELECTR acumulador *m*, batería *f*.

storage cell [-sel] *n* ELECTR acumulador *m*.

storage heater [-,hi:tə*] *n* placa *f* acumuladora.

storax ['stɔ:ræks] *n* BOT estoraque *m*.

store [stɔ:*] *n* provisión *f* (supply) || almacén *m*, depósito *m* (warehouse) || almacén *m* (large shop) || tienda *f* (any shop) || FIG reserva *f*; *I had sth. in store* tenía algo en reserva || INFORM almacenar (data) || — *department store* gran almacén || FIG *he has a large store of knowledge about history* tiene grandes conocimientos de historia || *in store* en almacén, en depósito || *store detective* guarda *m* & *f* de seguridad en una tienda || *store guide* indicador *m* || FIG *there was a surprise in store for him* le esperaba una gran sorpresa | *to hold in store for* reservar *or* guardar para | *to set great store by* valorar en mucho, estimar enormemente | *to set little store by* valorar *or* estimar en poco.
◆ *pl* provisiones *f* (supplies, provisions) || pertrechos *m* (equipment).
◆ *adj* de confección (clothes) || que viene de los grandes almacenes (furniture).

store [stɔ:*] *vt* almacenar (to put into storage) || guardar (to keep) || abastecer, suministrar (to supply) || AGR ensilar (crop) || archivar (documents) || — *to store away* guardar, tener en reserva || *to store up* almacenar, acumular.
◆ *vi* conservarse; *eggs do not store well* los huevos no se conservan bien.

storehouse [-haus] *n* almacén *m*, depósito *m* || FIG mina *f* (of information).

storekeeper [-,ki:pə*] *n* almacenero *m* (of a warehouse) || US tendero *m* (shopkeeper) || MAR pañolero *m*.

storeroom [-rum] *n* despensa *f* || MAR pañol *m* || AVIAT bodega *f*.

storey ['stɔ:ri] *n* —→ **story (2nd art.).**

storeyed ['stɔ:rid]; **storied** ['stɔrid] *adj* *a five-storied building* un edificio de cinco pisos.

storied ['stɔ:rid] *adj* celebrado por la historia || historiado, da (decorated).

stork [stɔ:k] *n* cigüeña *f* (bird).

storm [stɔ:m] *n* tormenta *f* (thunderstorm) || tempestad *f*, temporal *m* (at sea) || borrasca *f* (of wind) || vendaval *m* (gale) || FIG bombardeo *m*, lluvia *f* (of missiles) | arrebato *m* (of rage, of jealousy, etc.) | frenesí *m* (frenzy) | tormenta *f* (noisy argument) | torrente *m*, lluvia *f* (of protests, etc.) | salva *f* (of applause) || MIL asalto *m*; *to take by storm* tomar por asalto || — FIG *a storm in a teacup* una tempestad en un vaso de agua, mucho ruido y pocas nueces | *to raise a storm of laughter* provocar carcajadas || *to ride out* o *to weather the storm* capear el temporal.

storm [stɔ:m] *vt* MIL asaltar, tomar por asalto.
◆ *vi* haber tormenta; *it is storming* hay tormenta || ser tempestuoso (wind) || FIG echar pestes, vociferar (*at* contra) (with anger).

stormbound [-baund] *adj* detenido por la tormenta.

storm cellar [-'selə*] *n* US refugio *m* contra los ciclones.

storm centre; US **storm center** [-'sentə*] *n* centro *m* de la tormenta *or* del ciclón || FIG centro *m or* foco *m* de disturbios.

storm cloud [-klaud] *n* nubarrón *m*.

storm door [-dɔ:*] *n* contrapuerta *f*.

storminess [-inis] *n* estado *m* tempestuoso (of the weather) || FIG lo borrascoso (of a meeting).

storming [-iŋ] *n* MIL toma *f*, asalto *m*.

storm-tossed [-tɔst] *adj* zarandeado por la tempestad.

storm troops [-tru:ps] *pl n* tropas *f* de asalto.

storm window [-'windəu] *n* contraventana *f*.

stormy [-i] *adj* tempestuoso, sa (weather) || FIG borrascoso, sa; agitado, da; acalorado, da (meeting, etc.); *stormy discussion* discusión acalorada | agitado, da (life).

stormy petrel ['stɔ:mi'petrəl] *n* petrel *m* (bird) || FIG promotor *m* de disturbios (who brings trouble).

story ['stɔ:ri] *n* historia *f* (history); *the story of my life* la historia de mi vida; *true history* historia verídica || cuento *m*, relato *m* (tale); *he told me a story* me contó un cuento; *adventure story* cuento de aventuras || relato *m*, relación *f*, narración *f* (account) || argumento *m*, trama *f* (plot of book, play, film) || artículo *m* (in a newspaper) || chiste *m* (joke); *dirty story* chiste verde || rumor *m* (rumour) || mentira *f*, cuento *m*, embuste *m*, historia *f* (lie) || — *as the story goes* según lo que se cuenta || *funny story* chiste || *it's a long story* es muy largo de contar || FIG *it's always the same old story* es siempre la misma canción, es la historia de siempre || *short story* novela corta || *tall story* historia increíble || FAM *that's another story* esto es otro cantar || *that's not the whole story* no se lo ha dicho todo || *the full story has still to be told* no se ha contado todavía todo || *to be only part of the story* ser sólo una parte de la historia || *to cut a long story short* en pocas palabras, en resumidas cuentas || *your story is that* según lo que Ud. dice.

story; **storey** ['stɔ:ri] *n* piso *m* || FAM *to be weak in the upper story* estar majareta, estar mal de la azotea *or* del tejado, faltarle a uno un tornillo.

storybook [-buk] *n* libro *m* de cuentos.

storyteller [-'telə*] *n* cuentista *m* & *f*, autor *m* de cuentos (author) || narrador, ra (narrator) || FAM cuentista *m* & *f*, mentiroso, sa; embustero, ra (liar, fibber).

storytelling [-,teliŋ] *n* narración *f* || FAM cuentos *m pl* (lies) || *he is good at storytelling* sabe muy bien contar las historias.

stoup [stu:p] *n* REL pila *f* para el agua bendita || jarra *f* (drinking mug).

stout [staut] *adj* robusto, ta; corpulento, ta (corpulent) || fuerte (strong) || fuerte, resistente, sólido, da; *stout beams* vigas sólidas || valiente (brave) || firme, resuelto, ta; decidido, da (undaunted); *stout resistance* resistencia firme.
◆ *n* cerveza *f* de malta, cerveza *f* negra y fuerte (beer).

stouthearted [-'hɑ:tid] *adj* valiente (courageous).

stoutness [-nis] *n* corpulencia *f*, robustez *f* (of body) || vigor *m*, fuerza *f* (vigour) || solidez *f*, resistencia *f* (strength) || valor *m* (courage) || firmeza *f*, resolución *f*, decisión *f* (resoluteness).

stove [stəuv] *n* estufa *f* (for heating) || cocina *f* (cooker) || hornillo *m* (cooking ring) || horno *m* (oven).

stove [stəuv] *pret/pp* → **stave.**

stovepipe [-paip] *n* tubo *m* de cocina (of cooker) || tubo *m* de estufa (of heater) || FAM chistera *f* (hat).

stow [stəu] *vt* guardar (to put away); *to stow the books in a cupboard* guardar los libros en un armario || almacenar (to stock) || poder contener (to hold) || MAR estibar, arrumar (a cargo) | aferrar (sails) || — FAM *stow it!* ¡cierra el pico! || *to stow away* guardar (to put away), zamparse (food).
◆ *vi to stow away* viajar de polizón (to travel clandestinely).

stowage [-idʒ] *n* MAR estiba *f*, arrumaje *m* || depósito *m* (storage place) || almacenaje *m* (storage).

stowaway [-əwei] *n* polizón *m* (on board a ship).

stowing [-iŋ] *n* MAR estiba *f*, arrumaje *m*.

strabismal [strə'bizməl]; **strabismic** [strə'bizmik]; **strabismical** [strə'bizmikəl] *adj* estrábico, ca.

strabismus [strə'bizməs] *n* MED estrabismo *m*.

straddle ['strædl] *n* posición *f* a horcajadas (position) || MIL encuadramiento *m* (of target) || COMM operación *f* de Bolsa con opción de compra y venta || US FAM posición *f* ambigua.

straddle ['strædl] *vt* estar con una pierna a cada lado de (to stand over) || sentarse *or* montar a horcajadas sobre (to sit) || abrir [las piernas] (to spread the legs) || pasar por encima de, cruzar (a bridge) || encuadrar [el blanco] (target) || US FAM no tomar ningún partido en, no comprometerse acerca de (an issue).
◆ *vi* esparrancarse (to spread the legs) || sentarse a horcajadas (to sit astride sth.) || US FAM nadar entre dos aguas.

Stradivarius [strædi'vɑ:riəs] *n* estradivario *m* (violin).

strafe [strɑ:f] *vt* MIL bombardear, castigar.

straggle ['strægl] *vi* rezagarse (to lag behind) || extraviarse (to get lost) || dispersarse (to disperse) || desparramarse (to spread).

straggler [-ə*] *n* rezagado, da.

straggling [-iŋ]; **straggly** [-i] *adj* disperso, sa; diseminado, da (dispersed) || rezagado, da (left behind) || desordenado, da; en desorden (in disorder).

straight [streit] *adj* recto, ta; derecho, cha (not bent); *stand up straight* póngase derecho || recto, ta; *in a straight line* en línea recta || lacio, cia; liso, sa (hair) || erguido, da (erect) || seguido, da (continuous); *I work ten hours straight* trabajo diez horas seguidas || certero, ra (aim) || honrado, da (honest); *are you straight?* ¿eres honrado? || justo, ta; equitativo, va (fair) || serio, ria (serious) || sincero, ra; franco, ca (sincere) || claro, ra; preciso, sa (unqualified); *straight answer* contestación clara || auténtico, ca; *straight democrat* demócrata auténtico || seguro, ra; fidedigno, na (information) || incondicional (follower) || en orden (in order); *everything is straight now* todo está en orden ahora || arreglado, da (tidy) || bien puesto, ta; *is the picture straight?* ¿está bien puesto el cuadro? || en posición correcta (cricket bat) || correcto, ta (correct) || solo, la; sin mezcla, puro, ra (drinks) || fijo, ja (price) || TECH con los cilindros en línea recta (engine) || — *as straight as an arrow* derecho como una vela || *let me get this straight* a ver si me aclaro || *let's get the facts straight* pongamos las cosas claras || *straight face* cara seria *or* impávida || *straight fight* campaña *f* electoral de dos candidatos || *straight flush* escalera *f* de color (in cards) || *straight run* candidatura segura || *to get sth. straight* entender bien algo, aclararse || FIG *to have a straight eye* tener buena vista || *to keep a straight face* mantenerse impávido || *to put o to set straight* poner en el buen camino (to put on the right road), desengañar (to show the truth), corregir (to correct), curar (to cure), ordenar, poner en orden, arreglar (to put in order), arreglar (to repair), poner bien (to put in the right position), poner en hora (watch).
◆ *adv* en línea recta (in a straight line); *to fly straight* volar en línea recta || derecho, cha; *the book is standing up straight* el libro está derecho; *the house stands up straight* la casa está derecha || honradamente (honestly) || sinceramente, francamente, sin rodeos (sincerely); *to speak straight out* hablar sinceramente || derecho, directamente; *we will go straight to Salford* iremos directamente a Salford || correctamente; *to think straight* pensar correctamente || certeramente; *to shoot straight* tirar certeramente || — *he walked straight in* entró directamente || *I shall come straight back* vuelvo en seguida || *it is straight across the road* está justo enfrente || *straight ahead* todo recto, todo seguido (further on), en frente (in front) || *straight off* inmediatamente (at once), de un tirón, sin interrupción (in one go) || *straight on* todo recto, todo seguido || *straight out* sin rodeos, francamente, sinceramente || FIG *to go straight* enmendarse (a former criminal) || *to look s.o. straight in the face* mirar a alguien en los ojos || *to read a book straight through* leer un libro desde el principio hasta el final || FIG *to talk to s.o. straight from the shoulder* hablar francamente con alguien | *to tell s.o. sth. straight* decir algo a alguien francamente | *to tell s.o. straight, to let s.o. have it straight* decirle cuatro verdades a alguien.
◆ *n* línea *f* recta (straight line) || recta *f* (the straight part of sth.); *the last straight* la última recta || escalera *f* (in cards) || — FIG *to keep to the straight and narrow* ir por buen camino | *to stray from the straight and narrow* apartarse del buen camino.

straight angle [-'æŋgl] *n* MATH ángulo *m* plano.

straightaway [-ə'wei] *adv* en seguida, inmediatamente.
◆ *adj* recto, ta; derecho, cha.
◆ *n* recta *f*.

straightedge [-edʒ] *n* regla *f*.

straighten [-n] *vt* enderezar, poner derecho (sth.) || estirar (hair) || ordenar, arreglar (a room) | poner bien (one's tie) || — FIG *to straighten out* arreglar (one's affairs), resolver (a problem) || *to straighten up* enderezar.
◆ *vi* enderezarse, ponerse derecho || FIG arreglarse.

straight-faced [-'feist] *adj* imperturbable, impávido, da (showing no emotion) || serio, ria (showing no amusement).

straightforward [-'fɔ:wəd] *adj* sincero, ra; franco, ca (sincere) || honrado, da (honest) || abierto, ta (open) || claro, ra (clear); *a straightforward answer* una contestación clara || sencillo, lla (easy).

straightforwardness [-'fɔ:wədnis] *n* sinceridad *f*, franqueza *f* (sincerity) || sencillez *f* (easiness) || honradez *f* (honesty).

straightforwards [-'fɔ:wədz] *adv* sinceramente, francamente (sincerely) || abiertamente (openly) || honradamente (honestly).

straight-haired [-hɛəd] *adj* con el pelo lacio *or* liso.

straightjacket [-'dʒækit] *n* camisa *f* de fuerza.

straight-laced [-leist] *adj* mojigato, ta; gazmoño, ña.

straight-lined [-laind] *adj* rectilíneo, a.

straight man [-mən] *n* US THEATR actor *m* que da pie a un cómico.

straightness [-nis] *n* rectitud *f*.

straight-out [-aut] *adj* franco, ca; sincero, ra (sincere) || abierto, ta (open) || completo, ta.

straight razor [-'reizə*] *n* navaja *f*.

straightway [-wei] *adv* en seguida, inmediatamente (straightaway).

strain [strein] *n* tendencia *f* (tendency) || vena *f*; *a strain of madness* una vena de loco || tono *m*; *to speak in a cheerful strain* hablar con un tono alegre || tenor *m*, sentido *m*; *he said much more in the same strain* dijo muchas cosas del mismo tenor || tensión *f* (on an elastic body) || presión *f* (pressure) || TECH deformación *f* || FIG tensión *f*, tirantez *f* (of atmosphere) | esfuerzo *m*; *he put a great strain on him* le sometió a un gran esfuerzo; *it is a great strain to read by candlelight* requiere mucho esfuerzo leer a la luz de una vela | tensión *f* (nervous, mental) | agotamiento *m* (exhaustion) || MED torcedura *f* || torsión *f* (twisting) || raza *f* (race) || cepa *f* (descent) || *to bear the strain of sth.* llevar el peso de algo.
◆ *pl* sonidos *m* lejanos (sounds) || MUS son *m sing*, compases *m*, acordes *m*; *to the strains of the national anthem* a los acordes del himno nacional || acentos *m* (in poetry).

strain [strein] *vt* estirar, poner tirante, tensar (to stretch) || torcer (to twist) || encorvar (to bend) || estrechar (s.o.); *to strain s.o. to one's bosom* estrechar a alguien contra el pecho || agotar, cansar (to exhaust) || agotar los nervios (nervously) || forzar (one's voice) || cansar (the heart) || cansar; *to strain one's eyes* cansar la vista | aguzar; *to strain one's ears* aguzar el oído || MED torcer (a limb); *he strained his ankle* se torció el tobillo | dislocar; *I strained my shoulder* me disloqué el hombro | sufrir un tirón en (muscle) || FIG abusar de; *to strain s.o.'s generosity* abusar de la generosidad de alguien | sobrepasar, extralimitarse en (one's powers) | poner tirante, crear una tirantez en (a relationship) | forzar; *to strain a point* forzar las cosas | desnaturalizar (a meaning) || filtrar (to filter) || tamizar (to sieve) || colar (vegetables, etc.); *strain the tea* cuele el té || TECH deformar (to deform) || JUR violar (the law) || FIG sacar (money) || — *to strain one's back* derrengarse || *to strain o.s.* agotarse (to be exhausted), hacer un mal movimiento.
◆ *vi* esforzarse, hacer un gran esfuerzo (to make a great effort) || estar tirante (a rope) || filtrar, filtrarse (to filter) || TECH deformarse (to deform) || — *to strain after sth.* esforzarse por *or* hacer un gran esfuerzo para conseguir algo ||

to strain at tirar de (to pull hard) || *to strain under a burden* soportar un peso con gran dificultad.

strained [-d] *adj* muy tirante *or* tenso (rope) || dislocado, da (joint) || torcido, da (ankle) || cansado, da (heart, eyes) || tenso, sa (nerves) || FIG tirante, tenso, sa (relations) | forzado, da (voice, laugh) || colado, da (liquid).

strainer [-ə*] *n* colador *m* (kitchen utensil) || filtro *m* (filter) || tamiz *m* (sieve) || depurador *m* (of water, etc.).

strait [streit] *n* GEOGR estrecho *m* || FIG aprieto *m*, apuro *m*; *to be in desperate straits* estar en un gran aprieto, estar en grandes aprietos, estar en el mayor apuro || *the Strait of Gibraltar* el estrecho de Gibraltar.

— OBSERV La palabra inglesa se emplea sobre todo en plural.

straiten [-n] *vt* estrechar || FIG *to be in straitened circumstances* estar en un apuro, estar apurado de dinero.

straitjacket [-'dʒækit] *n* camisa *f* de fuerza.

straitlaced [-'leist] *adj* mojigato, ta; gazmoño, ña.

strait waistcoat [-'weiskəut] *n* camisa *f* de fuerza.

strake [streik] *n* MAR traca *f*.

stramonium [strə'məuniəm] *n* BOT estramonio *m* [AMER chamico *m*].

strand [strænd] *n* playa *f* (beach) || costa *f* (coast) || mechón *m* (tuft) || trenza *f* (plait) || pelo *m* (hair) || ramal *m* (of rope) || cable *m* (cable) || hebra *f*, hilo *m* (of thread) || sarta *f* (of beads, etc.) || BOT & ZOOL fibra *f* || FIG *to tie up the loose strands* atar cabos.

strand [strænd] *vt* varar, hacer encallar (a ship) || FIG dejar desamparado, dejar en la estacada (to leave helpless) || trenzar (to twist strands) || — MAR *to be stranded* estar encallado, da || FIG *to leave stranded* dejar desamparado, da; dejar en la estacada.

◆ *vi* MAR varar, encallar.

strange [streindʒ] *adj* desconocido, da (unknown); *the town was strange to him* la ciudad le era desconocida || inesperado, da; *a strange result* un resultado inesperado || extraño, ña; raro, ra (odd, bizarre, arousing wonder); *it is strange he has not come* es extraño que no haya venido || nuevo, va; recién llegado, da; *I am strange here* aquí soy nuevo || — *strangest of all* lo más curioso del caso es que || *strange to say* aunque parezca extraño || *to feel strange* sentirse extraño.

strangely [-li] *adv* extrañamente, de una manera extraña || *strangely enough* aunque parezca extraño.

strangeness [-nis] *n* lo extraño, lo raro, lo curioso || novedad *f*.

stranger [-ə*] *n* desconocido, da (unknown person); *he is a stranger to me* es un desconocido para mí || extranjero, ra (foreigner) || forastero, ra (outsider); *he is a stranger in this town* es un forastero en esta ciudad || — *he is no stranger here* es muy conocido aquí || *he is no stranger to fear* sabe perfectamente lo que es el miedo || *he is no stranger to London* conoce bien Londres || *hello, stranger!* ¡cuánto tiempo sin verte! || *I am stranger to the subject* soy profano en la materia, no conozco el tema || *to make a stranger of* tratar con frialdad a || *you are quite a stranger!* ¡hace siglos que no te vemos!

strangle ['strænɡl] *vt* estrangular || FIG ahogar (voice) | sofocar (rebellion) | amordazar (press).

◆ *vi* estrangularse || FIG ahogarse.

stranglehold [-həuld] *n* SP collar *m* de fuerza (in wrestling, etc.) || FIG dominio *m* completo (complete control) || FIG *to have a stranglehold on s.o.* dominar por completo a alguien.

strangler [-ə*] *n* estrangulador, ra.

strangling [-iŋ] *n* estrangulación *f*, estrangulamiento *m*.

◆ *adj* estrangulador, ra.

strangulate ['strænɡjuleit] *vt* MED estrangular (hernia, vein, etc.).

◆ *vi* estar estrangulado (hernia, vein, etc.).

strangulation ['strænɡju'leiʃən] *n* estrangulación *f* || MED estrangulación *f*, estrangulamiento *m* (of hernia, vein, blood circulation).

strangury ['strænɡjəri] *n* MED angurria *f*.

strap [stræp] *n* correa *f*, tira *f* (strip of leather) || tirante *m* (of a dress) || tira *f*, banda *f* (of material) || correa *f* (watch strap) || tirante *m* (on boots) || tira *f* (on shoes) || trabilla *f* (on trousers) || TECH collar *m*, abrazadera *f* (for pipes) | correa *f* (belt) || suavizador *m* (razor strop).

strap [stræp] *vt* atar con correa (to tie up) || azotar (to beat) || suavizar (a razor) || MED vendar.

straphang [-hæŋ] *vi* viajar de pie sujetándose a la correa.

straphanger [-'hæŋə*] *n* FAM pasajero de pie que se agarra a la correa (standing passenger).

strap iron [-'aiən] *n* fleje *m*.

strapless [-lis] *adj* sin tirantes (dress).

strappado [strə'peidəu] *n* estrapada *f*.

strapping ['stræpiŋ] *adj* FAM fornido, da; robusto, ta (very big and strong).

◆ *n* atadura *f* con correas || correas *f pl* (belts) || MED esparadrapo *m* || FAM azote *m*, paliza *f* (beating).

strass [stræs] *n* estrás *m* (glass).

strata ['strɑːtɑː] *pl n* ⟶ **stratum.**

stratagem ['strætidʒəm] *n* estratagema *f*.

strategic [strə'tiːdʒik]; **strategical** [-əl] *adj* estratégico, ca.

strategist ['strætidʒist] *n* estratega *m* || FAM *armchair strategist* estratega de café.

strategy ['strætidʒi] *n* estrategia *f*.

strath [stræθ] *n* valle *m*.

strathspey [-'spei] *n* danza *f* escocesa.

stratification ['strætifi'keiʃən] *n* estratificación *f*.

stratify ['strætifai] *vt* estratificar.

◆ *vi* estratificarse.

stratocumulus [ˌstreitəu'kjuːmjuləs] *n* estratocúmulo *m* (cloud formation).

stratosphere ['strætəusfiə*] *n* estratosfera *f* || *stratosphere balloon* globo estratosférico.

stratospheric ['strætəu'sferik] *adj* estratosférico, ca.

stratum ['strɑːtəm] *n* BIOL capa *f*, estrato *m* (layer of tissue) || capa *f* (in meteorology) || GEOL estrato *m* || FIG estrato *m*, capa *f*; *social stratum* estrato social.

— OBSERV El plural de *stratum* es *strata* o *stratums*.

stratus ['streitəs] *n* estrato *m* (cloud formation).

— OBSERV El plural de *stratus* es *strati*.

straw [strɔː] *n* paja *f* [AMER popote *m*] (of cereals and for drinking) || FIG & FAM ardite *m*, comino *m*; *she doesn't care a straw* (no) le importa un comino || — FIG *a straw in the wind* un indicio | *it's the last straw that breaks the camel's back* es la última gota que hace rebosar la copa | *man of straw* testaferro *m*, hombre *m* de paja | *that is the last straw* esto es el colmo | *to cling* o *to clutch at a straw* agarrarse a un clavo ardiendo || *to draw straws* echar pajas.

◆ *adj* de paja; *straw hat* sombrero de paja; *straw hut* choza de paja || pajizo, za (colour) || — *straw bed, straw mat* jergón *m* de paja || *straw loft* pajar *m* || *straw rick* almiar *m*.

strawberry [-bəri] *n* BOT fresa *f* [AMER frutilla *f*] (wild), fresón *m* (cultivated and larger) || color *m* de fresa (colour) || — *strawberry bed* fresal *m* || *strawberry blonde* pelirroja *f* || *strawberry jam* mermelada *f* de fresa || *strawberry mark* antojo *m* || *strawberry patch* fresal *m* || *strawberry tomato* alquequenje *m* || *strawberry tree* madroño *m*.

strawboard [-bɔːd] *n* cartón *m* (coarse cardboard).

straw-coloured; US **straw-colored** [-'kʌləd] *adj* pajizo, za; de color de paja.

straw man [-mæn] *n* testaferro *m*, hombre *m* de paja (man of straw) || don nadie *m*, pelele *m* (nonentity).

straw vote [-vəut] *n* US votación *f* de prueba.

straw wine [-wain] *n* vino *m* de paja.

stray [strei] *adj* perdido, da; extraviado, da (animal) || aislado, da; disperso, sa (houses) || perdido, da (bullet) || descarriado, da (morally) || — *stray child* niño abandonado || *stray dog* perro callejero.

◆ *n* animal *m* perdido *or* extraviado || perro *m* callejero (dog) || gato *m* callejero (cat) || niño *m* abandonado (child) || ELECTR dispersión *f*.

◆ *pl* RAD parásitos *m*, interferencias *f*.

stray [strei] *vi* desviarse, apartarse; *they strayed from the path and got lost* se desviaron del camino y se perdieron || extraviarse, perderse (to lose o.s.) || descarriarse (morally) || errar (to roam).

streak [striːk] *n* raya *f*, lista *f*, línea *f* (stripe) || señal *f*; *the tears have left streaks on her face* tiene señales de haber llorado || fondo *m*, lado *m*; *he has a serious streak you'd never suspect* tiene un fondo serio en el que nunca se pensaría || racha *f* (of luck, of good weather, etc.) || vena *f* (of madness, of genious) || haz *m*, rayo *m* (of light) || MIN veta *f* (in minerals) || — *a streak of irony* cierta ironía || *streak of lightning* rayo *m*.

streak [striːk] *vt* rayar (to stripe) || vetear; *white marble streaked with red* mármol blanco veteado de rojo.

◆ *vi* FIG pasar como un rayo.

streakiness [-inis] *n* rayado *m*, rayadura *f*, aspecto *m* rayado.

streaky [-i] *adj* rayado, da (streaked) || entreverado, da (bacon) || veteado, da (veined).

stream [striːm] *n* corriente *f* (current) || río *m* (river) || arroyo *m*, riachuelo *m* (small river) || torrente *m* (of lava) || chorro *m* (of water, of blood) || raudal *m* (of light) || serie *f*, sucesión *f* (of events) || torrente *m* (of tears) || sarta *f*; *a stream of oaths* una sarta de improperios || torrente *m*, flujo *m*; *a stream of words* un torrente de palabras || oleada *f*, riada *f*, flujo *m*; *stream of immigrants* oleada de inmigrantes || desfile *m* continuo; *a stream of cars* un desfile continuo de coches || grupo *m* (of pupils) || — *against the stream* a contracorriente || FIG *to go with the stream* ir con la corriente, seguir la corriente.

stream [striːm] *vt* hacer correr, derramar (liquid) || hacer ondear; *the wind streamed the flag* el viento hacía ondear la bandera || MAR echar, fondear (the anchor) || MIN lavar (minerals) || clasificar, poner en grupos (pupils in a school) || *her eyes streamed tears* estaba hecha un mar de lágrimas.

◆ *vi* correr, fluir (liquid) || manar, correr, chorrear (blood) || ondear, flotar (to wave in the wind); *the flags were streaming in the wind* flotaban las banderas en el viento || — *his eyes were streaming with tears* tenía la cara bañada en lágrimas || *to stream in* entrar a raudales (sunlight, people) || *to stream out* brotar (a liquid), salir en tropel; *people streamed out* la gente salía en tropel.

streamer [-ə*] *n* serpentina *f* (of paper) || MAR gallardete *m* || US titulares *m pl* (of newspaper).
◆ *pl* aurora *f sing* boreal.

streamlet [-lit] *n* riachuelo *m*, arroyuelo *m*.

streamline [-lain] *n* corriente *f* natural (of liquid, of gas) || línea *f or* forma *f* aerodinámica (of car, of plane).

streamline [-lain] *vt* carenar, dar línea aerodinámica a (cars, etc.) || FIG modernizar, simplificar, racionalizar (measure, system).

streamlined [-laind] *adj* de línea aerodinámica, aerodinámico, ca; carenado, da (cars, planes) || FIG moderno, na (modernized).

street [striːt] *n* calle *f*; *he walked down the street* bajaba la calle; *main* o *high street* calle mayor; *down the street* calle abajo; *up the street* calle arriba; *the whole street knew about it* toda la calle lo sabía || — FIG *he's streets above you* está muy por encima de ti | *not to be in the same street as s.o.* no estar a la altura de alguien, no llegarle a la suela del zapato || *one-way street* calle de dirección única || *street accident* accidente *m* de tráfico *or* de circulación || FIG *that's right up my street* eso es lo mío | *the man in the street* el hombre de la calle | *to be on easy street* llevar una vida acomodada || FIG & FAM *to be streets ahead of s.o.* darle cien vueltas a alguien || *to go out into the street* echarse a la calle || *to line the streets* hacer calle (soldiers) || *to roam the streets* callejear, azotar las calles || FAM *to turn s.o. out into the streets* poner a alguien de patitas en la calle || *to walk the streets* correr las calles, callejear (anyone), hacer la carrera (prostitute).

street arab [-'ærəb] *n* golfillo *m*, niño *m* de la calle, pilluelo *m*.

streetcar [-kɑː*] *n* US tranvía *m*.

street cleaner [-'kliːnə*] *n* barrendero *m*.

street credibility [-ˌkredi'biliti] *n* FAM imagen *f* [popularidad entre los jóvenes].

street cry [-krai] *n* pregón *m*, grito *m* de los vendedores ambulantes.

street door [-dɔ*] *n* puerta *f* principal, puerta *f* de la calle.

street floor [-flɔː*] *n* US planta *f* baja.

street guide [-gaid] *n* callejero *m*, guía *f* de la ciudad.

streetlamp [-læmp]; **streetlight** [-lait] *n* farol *m* (gas) || poste *m* de alumbrado (electric).

street lighting [-'laitiŋ] *n* alumbrado *m* público.

street map [-mæp]; **street plan** [-plæn] *n* callejero *m*.

street market [-'mɑːkit] *n* mercadillo *m*.

street musician [-mjuː'ziʃən] *n* músico *m* callejero.

street sweeper [-'swiːpə*] *n* barrendero *m* (person) || barredora *f* (lorry).

street urchin [-'əːtʃin] *n* golfillo *m*, niño *m* de la calle.

street value [-'væljuː] *n* precio *m* en la calle (of illegal drugs).

streetwalker [-'wɔːkə*] *n* carrerista *f*, buscona *f* (prostitute).

strength [streŋθ] *n* fuerza *f*; *a man of great strength* un hombre de gran fuerza || resistencia *f*, solidez *f*; *the strength of a wall* la resistencia de una muralla || intensidad *f*, fuerza *f* (of a colour) || fuerza *f* (of drugs, of drinks) || número *m*; *they came in full strength* vinieron en gran número || validez *f*, fuerza *f* (of an argument) || poder *m*, potencia *f*, fuerza *f* (power) || MIL efectivos *m pl*, fuerzas *f pl* || ELECTR intensidad *f* (of a current) || TECH resistencia *f*; *the strength of a metal under pressure* la resistencia de un metal a la presión || CHEM proporción *f*, cantidad *f*, graduación *f*; *alcoholic strength* graduación de alcohol || COMM firmeza *f* || — FIG *at full strength* con toda la plantilla || *by sheer strength* a viva fuerza || *on the strength of* teniendo como base, fundándose en || *strength of character* entereza *f*, firmeza *f* || *strength of mind* fortaleza *f* || *strength of will* fuerza de voluntad, resolución *f* || FIG *to be below strength* no tener la plantilla al completo || *to be present in great strength* estar en gran número || *to bring a battalion up to strength* completar un batallón || *to go from strength to strength* ir cada vez mejor || *to recover one's strength* recuperar *or* recobrar las fuerzas || *to reserve* o *to save one's strength* reservarse.

strengthen [-ən] *vt* fortalecer, consolidar; *to strengthen a house* consolidar una casa || reforzar; *to strengthen a wall* reforzar un muro || dar mayor intensidad a (colour, sound) || FIG intensificar (relations) | estrechar (links) | afianzar, consolidar (s.o.'s authority, etc.) | fortalecer, reforzar, consolidar (friendship) || MED fortificar, fortalecer || MIL reforzar.
◆ *vi* FIG reforzarse, fortalecerse, consolidarse; *their friendship strengthened* su amistad se consolidó | intensificarse (relations) | estrecharse (links) | afianzarse, consolidarse (s.o.'s authority, etc.).

strengthening [-əniŋ] *n* fortalecimiento *m* || refuerzo *m* || consolidación *f*.
◆ *adj* MED fortificante, tonificante.

strenuous ['strenjuəs] *adj* activo, va; vigoroso, sa; enérgico, ca; *a strenuous person* una persona activa || intenso, sa; activo, va; *a strenuous life* una vida intensa || fatigoso, sa; cansado, da; arduo, dua; *a strenuous occupation* un trabajo cansado || intenso, sa (effort) || tenaz, porfiado, da; firme (opposition) || encarnizado, da (fight) || — *through much strenuous work* a fuerza de mucho trabajo || *to offer strenuous opposition to* oponerse firmemente a.

strenuousness [-nis] *n* energía *f*.

streptococcosis ['streptəukɔ'kəusais] *n* MED estreptococia *f*.

streptococcus ['streptəu'kɔkəs] *n* MED estreptococo *m*.
— OBSERV El plural de la palabra inglesa es *streptococci*.

streptomycin ['streptəu'maisin] *n* MED estreptomicina *f*.

stress [stres] *n* MED tensión *f or* fatiga *f* nerviosa, estrés *m*; *I am under stress* sufro una tensión nerviosa || hincapié *m*; *he put the stress on the salary increase* hizo hincapié en el aumento de salarios || presión *f*, coacción *f*, fuerza *f* (compulsion) || GRAMM acento *m* tónico || TECH & PHYS esfuerzo *m* || — *by stress of weather* a causa del temporal || *the laws of stress in Spanish* las reglas de acentuación en español || *to lay stress on* insistir en, hacer hincapié en, subrayar (to emphasize), acentuar, poner el acento en (in linguistics) || *stress system* acentuación *f* || *times of stress* períodos *m pl* difíciles || *under the stress of a violent emotion* preso de una intensa emoción.

stress [stres] *vt* insistir en, recalcar, hacer hincapié en, subrayar (to emphasize); *he stressed the importance of the reform* recalcó la importancia de la reforma || GRAMM acentuar || TECH someter a un esfuerzo.

stressed [-t] *adj* GRAMM acentuado, da || estresado, da; con tensión *or* fatiga nerviosa.

stressful [-ful] *adj* estresante, que causa tensión *or* fatiga nerviosa.

stressless [-lis] *adj* GRAMM sin acento.

stretch [stretʃ] *n* alargamiento *m* (extension) || elasticidad *f* (of elastic fabric) || trozo *m*; *a stretch of rope* un trozo de cuerda || trecho *m*, tramo *m*; *this stretch of the road is dangerous* este tramo de carretera es peligroso || recta *f* (in a race track) || extensión *f*; *a stretch of land* una extensión de terreno || envergadura *f* (of wings) || extensión *f* (of arms) || intervalo *m*, tiempo *m*, período *m* (time) || vuelta *f* (short walk) || esfuerzo *m* (of imagination) || GRAMM extensión *f* (of meaning) || — FIG *at a stretch* de un tirón (in one go), seguido, da; *I can work for ten hours at a stretch* puedo trabajar durante diez horas seguidas | *at full stretch* a todo gas, a toda mecha | *home stretch* última etapa || FAM *to do a stretch* estar en chirona || *to give a stretch as one wakes up* estirarse al despertar.
◆ *adj* elástico, ca.

stretch [stretʃ] *vt* estirar, alargar; *he stretched the elastic* estiró la goma || tender; *they stretched the wires across the valley* tendieron los cables sobre el valle || alargar, extender; *he stretched his arm to reach the book* extendió el brazo para coger el libro || tender, alargar (the hand) || desentumecer, estirar; *to stretch one's legs* estirar las piernas || desplegar, extender, abrir (the wings) || distender (a tendon) || ensanchar; *he stretched his shoes* ensanchó sus zapatos || extender; *they stretched him on the operating table* le extendieron sobre la mesa de operaciones || FIG estirar; *they stretched their food over three days* estiraron la comida para tres días | forzar (meaning) | sobrepasar los límites de (law) | violar (one's principles) || MUS & TECH tensar || FAM derribar (to knock down) || — FIG *to stretch a point* hacer una excepción | *to stretch it* exagerar || *to stretch o.s.* estirarse || *to stretch out* alargar, extender (one's arm), estirar (one's legs), estirar (a speech, etc.).
◆ *vi* estirarse, alargarse (elastic) || estirarse; *he got up and stretched* se levantó y se estiró || extenderse; *the road stretched into the distance* la carretera se extendía a lo lejos || ensancharse, dar de sí (shoes) || FIG dar de sí (money) || *to stretch out* estirarse, desperezarse (one's limbs), tumbarse, echarse (to lie down), separarse (a line of runners, etc.), extenderse (a country), alargar la mano (to reach sth.), aligerar el paso (walking).

stretchable [-əbl] *adj* estirable.

stretcher [-ə*] *n* camilla *f*, parihuelas *f pl* (small portable bed) || horma *f* (for shoes) || ensanchador *m* (for gloves) || TECH tensor *m* || ARCH soga *f* || ARTS bastidor *m* (for canvas) || travesaño *m* (of a tent) || apoyo *m* (in a rowing boat) || FIG mentira *f*, exageración *f*.

stretcher-bearer [-ə'bɛərə*] *n* camillero *m*.

stretching [-iŋ] *n* estiramiento *m*.

stretchmark [-mɑːk] *n* estría *f*.

stretchy [-i] *adj* elástico, ca || que ensancha, que da de sí (shoes, etc.).

strew* [struː] *vt* regar, esparcir, derramar; *to strew sand* regar arena || salpicar, desparramar (to scatter) || cubrir, llenar; *a table strewn with books* una mesa cubierta de libros.
— OBSERV Pret ***strewed***; pp ***strewed, strewn***.

stria ['straiə] *n* GEOL estría *f* || ARCH estría *f*, ranura *f*, acanaladura *f*.
— OBSERV El plural de *stria* es *striae*.

striate ['straiit] *vt* estriar.

striated [strai'eitid] *adj* estriado, da || ANAT *striated muscle* músculo estriado.

striation [strai'eiʃən] *n* estriación *f*, estriado *m* (striated appearance) || GEOL estría *f* || ARCH estría *f*, ranura *f*, acanaladura *f*.

stricken ['strikən] *adj* afectado, da; *the stricken village* el pueblo afectado || destrozado, da (damaged) || afligido, da; *the stricken families* las familias afligidas; *he was stricken with* estaba afligido por || afectado, da; aquejado, da; atacado, da; *stricken with tuberculosis* aquejado de *or* atacado por la tuberculosis || herido, da (wounded).
◆ *pp* → **strike**.

strickle [strikl] *vt* dar forma con la plantilla *or* la terraja.

strickle [strikl] *n* rasero *m* (for removing surplus grain) || piedra *f* de afilar (sharpening stone) || plantilla *f*, terraja *f* (template).

strict [strikt] *adj* estricto, ta; preciso, sa; exacto, ta; *in the strict sense of the word* en el sentido estricto de la palabra || estricto, ta; severo, ra; riguroso, sa; *a strict headmaster* un director estricto; *strict discipline* disciplina severa || estricto, ta; riguroso, sa; *a strict Catholic* un católico estricto || terminante, estricto, ta (order) || absoluto, ta; completo, ta; *in strict seclusion* en un aislamiento absoluto.

strictly [-li] *adv* terminantemente; *smoking strictly forbidden* terminantemente prohibido fumar, se prohibe terminantemente fumar || exactamente; *it is not strictly true* no es exactamente cierto || con precisión; *to define a word strictly* definir una palabra con precisión || severamente, estrictamente; *I was brought up very strictly* fui educado muy severamente || *strictly speaking* hablando con propiedad (in the strict sense), en realidad; *strictly speaking it is not true* en realidad no es verdad.

strictness [-nis] *n* exactitud *f* (exactness) || severidad *f* (severity) || lo terminante (of an order).

stricture ['striktʃə*] *n* crítica *f* (criticism) || MED estrechamiento *m*.

stridden ['stridn] *pp* ⟶ **stride.**

stride [straid] *n* zancada *f* (long step); *with big strides* a grandes zancadas || paso *m* (step) || FIG progreso *m*, adelanto *m*; *making great strides in English* haciendo grandes progresos en inglés || — *to get into one's stride* coger el ritmo || *to take sth. in one's stride* tomarse las cosas con calma, hacer las cosas con tranquilidad || SP *to take the hurdles in one's stride* saltar las vallas sin perder el ritmo.

stride* [straid] *vt* pasar *or* saltar *or* salvar *or* franquear de una zancada (to cross over) || sentarse a horcajadas en (a branch, etc.) || montar a horcajadas (a horse).

◆ *vi* andar a zancadas *or* a grandes pasos || — *to stride away* alejarse a grandes zancadas || *to stride up to s.o.* acercarse a alguien a grandes zancadas.

— OBSERV Pret ***strode***; pp ***stridden***.

stridence [-əns]; **stridency** [-i] *n* estridencia *f*.

strident [-ənt] *adj* estridente.

stridor ['straidɔ:*] *n* MED estridor *m* (harsh vibrating sound).

stridulate ['stridjuleit] *vi* chirriar, estridular (p us), chirriar, estridular (cicadas, grasshoppers, etc.).

strife [straif] *n* disensión *f*, disputa *f* (enmity) || contienda *f*, lucha *f*, conflicto *m* (struggle) || disensiones *f pl*, discordias *f pl*; *internal strife* disensiones internas || querellas *f pl*, peleas *f pl*; *domestic strife* querellas domésticas.

strike [straik] *n* golpe *m* (blow) || huelga *f* (ceasing to work); *to go on strike* declararse en huelga; *to be on strike* estar en huelga || acuñación *f* (of coins) || descubrimiento *m* (of ore, of oil, etc.) || rasero *m* (for removing surplus grain) || piedra *f* de afilar (sharpening stone) || patrón *m*, plantilla *f* (template) || GEOL dirección *f* horizontal (of a stratum) || MIL ataque *m* || US SP golpe *m* (in baseball) || «strike» *m* (in bowling) || mordida *f*, picada *f* (in fishing) || FAM suerte *f*, chamba *f*, potra *f* (good luck) || — *hunger strike* huelga del hambre || *sit-down strike* sentada *f*, huelga de brazos caídos *or* de brazos cruzados || *staggered strike* huelga escalonada *or* alternativa *or* por turno || *strike pay* subsidio *m* de huelga || *sympathetic* o *sympathy strike* huelga por solidaridad.

strike* [straik] *vt* pegar, golpear; *he struck her on the face* le pegó en la cara || dar, asestar, pegar (a blow); *I struck a blow at him* le di un golpe || golpear, dar un golpe en; *he struck the table with his fist* golpeó la mesa con el puño || golpear (a ball) || herir (to wound) || alcanzar, dar (with a bullet) || tocar (the keys of an instrument) || dar, tocar; *the clock struck two* el reloj dio las dos || encender; *strike a match* encienda un fósforo || chocar contra, dar contra, dar un golpe contra (to collide with); *his head struck the wall* su cabeza chocó contra la pared || chocar con (a car) || atropellar; *he was struck by a car* fue atropellado por un coche || clavar, hundir, meter; *he struck the knife into her heart* le clavó el cuchillo en el corazón || llegar; *the news struck him to the heart* la noticia le llegó al alma; *the cold struck him to the bone* el frío le llegó hasta los huesos || acuñar (coins, medals) || batir (iron) || atravesar (fog); *the rays strike through the mist* los rayos atraviesan la neblina || hacer saltar (sparks) || caer en (lightning) || dar en; *the light strikes the wall* la luz da en la pared; *to strike the target* dar en el blanco || herir, lastimar; *a sound strikes my ear* un ruido me hiere el oído || impresionar; *we were struck by his intelligence* nos impresionó su inteligencia || hacer impresión; *how did it strike me?* ¿qué impresión me hizo? || sorprender (to astonish); *what struck me was* lo que me sorprendió fue || ocurrírsele a uno; *the thought struck me that* se me ocurrió la idea de que || parecer; *it strikes me as impossible* me parece imposible; *it struck me that* me pareció que || atraer (the eyes) || llamar (attention) || infundir (terror) || sobrecoger; *he was struck with panic* estaba sobrecogido por el pánico || aquejar; *struck with deafness* aquejado de sordera || abatirse sobre (disaster) || adoptar, tomar (a pose) || constituir, formar (a jury, a committee) || concertar (an agreement) || cerrar (a bargain) || liquidar, cerrar (an account) || hacer (a balance) || rasar (to level off) || MAR amainar, recoger (sails) | arriar (flags) || coger, enganchar con el anzuelo (to hook a fish) || arponear, arponar (a whale) || morder (a snake) || descubrir (oil, track); *they struck oil* descubrieron petróleo || dar con; *they struck the main road* dieron con la carretera principal || encontrar, dar con, topar con (difficulties, obstacles) || BOT echar (roots) || MIL levantar (camp) | desmontar (tents) | concertar (a truce) | atacar (to attack) || THEATR desmontar (scenery) || MATH hacer, calcular (an average) | trazar (a circle, a line) || — FIG *strike me dead if...!* ¡que me muera si...! | *strike when the iron is hot* al hierro caliente batir de repente || *the house was struck by lightning* cayó un rayo en la casa || *to be struck all of a heap* quedarse pasmado || *to be struck blind, dumb* quedarse ciego, sin habla *or* mudo || *to be struck by a stone* recibir una pedrada || FIG *to strike a balance* lograr un punto de equilibrio | *to strike a chord* sonar; *his name strikes a chord* su nombre me suena || *to strike fear, terror into s.o.* atemorizar, aterrorizar a alguien || *to strike it lucky* tener suerte || *to strike it rich* hacerse rico || FIG *to strike oil* encontrar una mina de oro || *to strike s.o. dead* matar a uno || *to strike s.o. deaf* dejarle sordo a uno, ensordecer a uno || *to strike s.o. dumb* dejarle a uno mudo *or* sin habla || MAR *to strike the bottom* dar con el fondo | *to strike the rocks* chocar contra las rocas || *to strike work* declararse en huelga.

◆ *vi* golpear, dar un golpe *or* golpes (to hit); *he struck at me* me dio un golpe || atacar; *the enemy struck at dawn* el enemigo atacó al amanecer || dirigirse hacia; *he struck south* se dirigió hacia el sur || sonar (a bell) || dar; *one o'clock struck* dio la una || dar la hora; *the clock struck* el reloj dio la hora || dar (*on, upon* en) (light) || penetrar (cold) || atravesar (sun) || dar, chocar (*against, on* contra) (to collide) || caer, tropezar (*on, upon* en, con) (a difficulty) || encenderse (match) || ocurrir (disaster) || declararse en huelga (to stop working) || morder (snake) || MAR encallar (to run aground) | arriar bandera (flag) || rendirse (town) || BOT echar raíces (to take root) | agarrar (cutting) || — FIG *his hour has struck* ha llegado su hora || *to strike home* dar en el blanco.

◆ *phr v* ***to strike aside*** apartar de un golpe || ***to strike back*** devolver un golpe *or* golpe por golpe *or* los golpes || ***to strike down*** derribar (to knock down) | hacer soltar de un golpe (firearm, etc.) | fulminar (disease) || ***to strike in*** clavar (a nail) | intervenir (to interrupt) || ***to strike into*** echarse a, empezar a; *he struck into song* empezó a cantar || ***to strike off*** cortar (to cut) | quitar de golpe (to remove) | borrar (to rub out) | tachar (to cross out) | deducir, rebajar (to deduct) | PRINT tirar || ***to strike on*** o ***upon*** ocurrírsele (a uno); *he struck on a good idea* se le ocurrió una buena idea || ***to strike out*** borrar (to rub out) | tachar (to cross out) | idear (a plan) | pegar, dar un golpe *or* golpes (to hit) | *to strike out for* ponerse en camino hacia (walking, etc.), ponerse a remar hacia (rowing), ponerse a nadar hacia (swimming) || — *to strike out for o.s.* volar con sus propias alas || ***to strike through*** tachar || ***to strike to*** torcer hacia *or* a; *the road strikes to the left* la carretera tuerce hacia la izquierda || ***to strike up*** empezar (to begin) | entablar, iniciar (conversation) | trabar, entablar (friendship) | entonar (a song) | atacar (a piece of music) | empezar a cantar (to start singing) | empezar a tocar (to start playing).

— OBSERV Pret ***struck***; pp ***struck, stricken***.

strikebound [-baund] *adj* paralizado por la huelga (industry, economy, etc.).

strikebreaker [-'breikə*] *n* esquirol *m*, rompehuelgas *m inv*.

striker [-ə*] *n* huelguista *m* & *f* (person) || badajo *m* (of a bell) || TECH percutor *m* || percusor *m* (of firearm) || US MIL ordenanza *m*.

striking [-iŋ] *adj* notable, grande, sorprendente; *striking difference* notable diferencia || llamativo, va; *a striking colour* un color llamativo || impresionante; *a striking spectacle* un espectáculo impresionante || (que está) en huelga (on strike) || que da las horas (clock) || *within striking distance* al alcance.

◆ *n* golpeteo *m*, golpes *m pl* || acuñación *f* (of coins) || campanada *f* (of clock).

string [striŋ] *n* cuerda *f*, bramante *m*, cordel *m* (for tying up) || cordón *m* (lace) || hilo *m* (of a puppet) || hebra *f* (of beans, of meat) || ristra *f* (of garlic, onions, sausages) || cuerda *f* (of tennis racket) || fila *f*, hilera *f* (of cars, of animals) || fila *f* (of barges) || reata *f* (of horses) || cadena *f*, sucesión *f* (of events) || cadena *f* (of hotels, etc.) || serie *f* (of questions, etc.) || sarta *f* (of lies) || retahíla *f* (of curses) || MUS cuerda *f*; *string instrument* instrumento de cuerda || ARCH zanca *f* (of a staircase) | hilada *f* volada (stringcourse) || GEOL veta *f* || SP cuadra *f* (in horse racing) | serie *f*; *first string athlete* atleta de primera serie | línea *f* de arranque (in billiards) || FIG condición *f*; *a loan with strings attached* un préstamo con ciertas condiciones || — *string of beads* rosario *m* (rosary), collar *m* (necklace) || *string orchestra* orquesta *f* de cuerdas || *string quartet* cuarteto *m* de cuerdas || FIG *to have s.o. on a string* tener a uno en un puño | *with no strings attached* sin condiciones | *to touch a string* tocar el punto sensible.

◆ *pl* MUS instrumentos *m* de cuerda || — FIG *to have two strings to one's bow* ser persona de recursos | *to pull all the strings one can* tocar todos los resortes | *to pull the strings* mover los hilos.

string* [striŋ] *vt* poner una cuerda a (to provide with a string) || atar con una cuerda (to fasten) || armar (a bow) || MUS poner cuer-

das a, encordar (to put strings on) | templar (to tune) || ensartar, enhebrar (pearls together) || enristrar (garlic, onions) || quitar las hebras de (beans) || estirar (to stretch) || tender; *to string a wire down the corridor* tender un cable a lo largo del pasillo || FIG ensartar (ideas) || — FIG *highly strung* tenso, sa (nerves), hipertenso, sa; muy nervioso, sa (person) || FIG & FAM *to string s.o. along* tomarle el pelo a alguien | *to string up* ahorcar (to hang).
◆ *vi* ahilarse, formar hilos (to form stringy fibres) || extenderse (to stretch out) || — *to string along with s.o.* acompañar a alguien || *to string out* extenderse a lo largo.
— OBSERV Pret y pp ***strung***.

string bean [-biːn] *n* US judía *f* verde.

stringboard [-bɔːd] *n* ARCH zanca *f*, limón *m*.

stringcourse [-kɔːs] *n* ARCH hilada *f* volada.

stringed [-d] *adj* MUS de cuerda.

stringency ['strindʒənsi] *n* rigor *m*, severidad *f* (of rules, of conditions) || fuerza *f* (of an argument) || COMM escasez *f* || *financial stringency* situación económica apurada.

stringent ['strindʒənt] *adj* estricto, ta; riguroso, sa; severo, ra; *stringent rules* reglas severas || convincente, fuerte (argument) || COMM escaso, sa (credit) | apurado, da (financial situation).

stringer ['striŋə*] *n* ARCH travesaño *m*, larguero *m* || AVIAT larguero *m* (of fuselage or wings) || US durmiente *m* (railway sleeper) || corresponsal *m* pagado por líneas (news correspondent).

stringiness ['striŋinis] *n* lo fibroso (of vegetables, etc.) || viscosidad *f* (viscosity).

stringpiece ['striŋpiːs] *n* ARCH riostra *f*.

string tie ['striŋtai] *n* lazo *m* (necktie).

stringy ['striŋi] *adj* fibroso, sa; filamentoso, sa (like a string) || lleno de hebras, fibroso, sa (vegetables) || correoso, sa; lleno de hebras (meat) || viscoso, sa (liquid) || enjuto, ta; flacucho, cha (person).

strip [strip] *n* banda *f*, faja *f* || franja *f*; *a strip of land* una franja de terreno || tira *f*, historieta *f* (comic strip) || pista *f* [de aterrizaje] (airstrip) || cinta *f* (of film) || tira *f* (of paper, of material) || listón *m* (of wood) || tira *f* (of leather) || fleje *m* (of metal) || FIG *to tear a strip off s.o.* echar una reprimenda *or* una bronca a alguien.

strip [strip] *vt* quitar (clothing) || desnudar (to undress) || quitar, sacar (to deprive sth. of its covering) || deshacer, quitar la ropa de (a bed) || desamueblar, quitar los muebles de (a room) || deshojar (to remove leaves from) || despalillar (tobacco leaves) || descortezar (a tree) || pelar (fruit) || descarnar (a bone) || quitar el pelo a (a dog) || TECH desmontar, desarmar (to dismantle) | estropear (a screw thread, the cogs of a gear) | quitar el forro a (a wire, a cable) || MAR desencapillar (a mast) | desaparejar (a ship) || FAM aligerar (to lighten a car for speed) || — *to strip down* raspar (to remove paint), desmontar (a motor) || *to strip of* despojar de (possessions, honours, etc.) || *to strip off* quitar.
◆ *vi* desnudarse, desvestirse (to undress); *strip to the waist* desnúdese hasta la cintura || hacer «strip-tease» (to perform striptease) || pasarse de rosca (a screw) || desconcharse, desprenderse (paint) || despegarse (paper, wood, etc.) || deshojarse (tree) || descortezarse (the trunk of a tree) || — *to strip off* desnudarse || *to strip to the skin* desnudarse completamente.

strip cartoon [-kɑː'tuːn] *n* tira *f* de periódico ilustrado, historieta *f*.

strip cropping [-'krɔpiŋ] *n* AGR cultivo *m* en fajas *or* en franjas.

stripe [straip] *n* azote *m*, latigazo *m* (stroke of the whip) || latigazo *m* (mark made by this) || raya *f*, lista *f* (band of colour, material) || raya *f* (on trousers) || tira *f* (of leather) || MIL galón *m* || US índole *f*, clase *f*, tipo *m* (kind).

stripe [straip] *vt* hacer rayas en, rayar.

striped [-t] *adj* a rayas, rayado, da.

strip lighting ['strip'laitiŋ] *n* alumbrado *m* con lámparas fluorescentes.

stripling ['stripliŋ] *n* mozalbete *m*, joven *m*.

strip mining ['strip'mainiŋ] *n* explotación *f* de una mina a cielo abierto.

stripper ['stripə*] *n* mujer *f* que hace «striptease».

strip-search ['stripsəːtʃ] *vt* registrar obligando a desnudarse.

striptease ['striptiːz] *n* «strip-tease» *m*.

stripy ['straipi] *adj* rayado, da.

strive* [straiv] *vi* esforzarse, procurar; *to strive to win the victory* esforzarse por conseguir la victoria, procurar conseguir la victoria || luchar (to fight) || rivalizar, competir (to rivalize) || *to strive for o after sth.* esforzarse por conseguir algo, procurar conseguir algo.
— OBSERV Pret ***strove***; pp ***striven***.

striven ['strivn] *pp* ⟶ **strive.**

strobe lighting ['strəub'laitiŋ] *n* luces *f pl* estroboscópicas.

stroboscope ['strəubəskəup] *n* estroboscopio *m*.

strode [strəud] *pret* ⟶ **stride.**

stroke [strəuk] *n* golpe *m* (blow, attempt to strike a ball) || campanada *f* (of bell, of clock) || latido *m* (heartbeat) || MED ataque *m* (fulminante), apoplejía *f* (attack of apoplexy) || rayo *m* (lightning) || caricia *f* (caress) || pincelada *f* (with a brush) || trazo *m* (with pencil, pen) || PRINT raya *f* (oblique line) || SP tacada *f* (in billiards) | brazada *f* (single movement when swimming) | estilo *m* (swimming style) | primer remero *m* (oarsman) | palada *f*, golpe *m* de remo (with an oar, style of rowing) | golpe *m*, jugada *f* (in tennis, golf, cricket, etc.) || TECH recorrido *m*, carrera *f* (of a piston) || — *at a o with one stroke of the pen* de un plumazo || *at one fell stroke* de un golpe || SP *butterfly stroke* estilo mariposa || FIG *by a stroke of luck* por suerte | *finishing stroke* golpe de gracia || *four-stroke engine* motor de cuatro tiempos || FAM *not to do a stroke of work* no dar golpe || *on the stroke of ten* al dar las diez || FIG *stroke of genius* rasgo *m* de genio, idea *f* genial || *to keep stroke* llevar el compás || FIG *to put the finishing strokes to* dar la última mano *or* el último toque a || *witty stroke* agudeza *f*.

stroke [strəuk] *vt* acariciar (with the hand); *he stroked the dog* acarició el perro || ser el primer remero en (to be stroke for a boat) || — FAM *to stroke s.o. down* ablandar a alguien | *to stroke s.o. the wrong way* tomar a alguien a contrapelo.

stroll [strəul] *n* paseo *m*, vuelta *f*; *to go for a stroll* (ir a) dar una vuelta.

stroll [strəul] *vt* dar un paseo por, dar una vuelta por, pasearse por || *strolling players* cómicos *m* de la legua.
◆ *vi* pasearse, vagar.

stroller [-ə*] *n* paseante *m* & *f* || cómico *m* de la legua (actor) || US cochecito *m* de niño (pram).

strong [strɔŋ] *adj* fuerte (cheese, drink, wind, current, light, smell, acid, tobacco) || fuerte, robusto, ta (person); *a strong man* un hombre fuerte || fuerte; *a very strong fabric* una tela muy fuerte || fuerte, sólido, da (object) || resistente; *is this ladder strong enough to hold me?* ¿es esta escalera de manos bastante resistente para aguantarme? || fuerte, potente (voice) || poderoso, sa (lenses) || fuerte (performed with physical strength); *a strong kick* una patada fuerte || fuerte (morally powerful); *a strong will* una voluntad fuerte || fuerte (morally powerful); *a strong nation* una nación poderosa || fuerte, enérgico, ca; decidido, da (resolute); *a strong character* un carácter enérgico || convincente (argument, evidence) || fuerte (proficient); *to be strong in Latin* estar fuerte en latín || acusado, da; fuerte (characteristic) || fuerte, marcado, da (accent) || bueno, na (sight) || drástico, ca; severo, ra; enérgico, ca; *strong measures* medidas drásticas || firme, profundo, da (conviction, devotion, faith) || fervoroso, sa (believer) || fuerte, profundo, da (impression) || fuerte, intenso, sa (emotion) || acérrimo, ma (supporter) || arraigado, da (habit) || fuerte; *strong currency* moneda fuerte || fuerte, intenso, sa; vivo, va (colours) || fuerte, marcado, da; notable (resemblance) || subido de tono, subido de color (language) || fuerte, violento, ta (terms) || rancio, cia (butter, bacon, etc.) || ELECTR intenso, sa (current) || GRAMM fuerte (verbs) || COMM firme || — *an army 2000 strong* un ejército de dos mil hombres || *as strong as an ox* fuerte como un toro *or* un roble || *strong man* hércules *m inv* (in circus) || *strong point* fuerte *m*; *politeness is not his strong point* la corrección no es su fuerte || *strong nerves* nervios bien templados || *strong reason* causa *f* mayor || FIG *that's too strong* eso es demasiado || *the strong and the weak* el fuerte y el débil || *to be strong in numbers* ser numerosos || *to be stronger* estar mejor (in health) || *to have a strong character* tener mucho carácter; *to have a strong head* aguantar mucho [alcohol] || *to have a strong stomach* tener un buen estómago || *to have strong feelings about sth.* tener ideas muy precisas *or* muy firmes sobre algo || *to use the strong arm* utilizar la fuerza.
◆ *adv* muy bien; *at 80 he is still going strong* tiene ochenta años y todavía se conserva muy bien; *the work is going strong* el trabajo marcha muy bien || fuertemente.

strong-arm [-ɑːm] *adj* severo, ra; de mano dura (policy, method, etc.) || — *strong-arm man* guardaespaldas *m inv* || *strong-arm tactics* fuerza *f*.

strong-arm [-ɑːm] *vt* pegar (to beat) || intimidar (to intimidate).

strongbox [-bɔks] *n* caja *f* fuerte *or* de caudales.

stronghold [-həuld] *n* MIL fortaleza *f*, plaza *f* fuerte (fortress) || FIG baluarte *m*; *conservative stronghold* baluarte del partido conservador.

strongly [-li] *adv* fuertemente, firmemente || — *strongly built* de construcción sólida || *to smell strongly of* tener un olor fuerte a.

strong-minded [-'maindid] *adj* resuelto, ta; decidido, da (resolute).

strong-mindedness [-'maindidnis] *n* resolución *f*, decisión *f*, carácter *m* (determination).

strongpoint [-pɔint] *n* plaza *f* fuerte, fuerte *m*.

strongroom [-rum] *n* cámara *f* acorazada (for storing money or valuables).

strong-willed ['strɔŋ'wild] *adj* resuelto, ta; decidido, da (resolute) || obstinado, da (obstinate).

strontian ['strɔnʃiən] *n* estroncio *m*.

strontium ['strɔntiəm] *n* estroncio *m*.

strop [strɔp] *n* suavizador *m* (of razors).

strop [strɔp] *vt* suavizar (a razor).

strophe ['strəufi] *n* estrofa *f*.

strove [strəuv] *pret* ⟶ **strive.**

struck [strʌk] *pret/pp* ⟶ **strike.**

struck jury [-'dʒuəri] *n* US JUR jurado *m* compuesto por 12 miembros escogidos entre 48 candidatos.

structural ['strʌktʃərəl] *adj* estructural || — *structural engineering* ingeniería *f* de construcción de pantanos, puentes y otras grandes obras || *structural steel* acero *m* para la construcción.

structuralism ['strʌktʃərəlizəm] *n* estructuralismo *m*.

structure ['strʌktʃə*] *n* estructura *f* || construcción *f* (building) || FIG base *f* (of arguments) | estructura *f* (of a play, etc.); *social structure* estructura social.

structure ['strʌktʃə*] *vt* estructurar || construir (to build).

structuring [-riŋ] *n* estructuración *f*.

struggle [strʌgl] *n* lucha *f*, combate *m*, contienda *f* (a contending); *desperate struggle* combate desesperado; *hand-to-hand struggle* lucha cuerpo a cuerpo || esfuerzo *m* (a great effort) || lucha *f*; *class struggle* lucha de clases; *struggle for survival* lucha por la vida || *without a struggle* sin resistencia, sin luchar; *he gave in without a struggle* se rindió sin resistencia.

struggle ['strʌgl] *vi* luchar; *to struggle to survive* luchar por la vida; *I am struggling with adversity* lucho contra la adversidad || forcejear; *he struggled to free himself* forcejeó para liberarse || esforzarse, luchar; *to struggle to succeed* esforzarse por triunfar || — *to struggle against* o *with* pelear contra, luchar contra || *to struggle along* avanzar penosamente || *to struggle for* luchar por conseguir || *to struggle on* continuar esforzándose *or* luchando || *to struggle to one's feet* levantarse con dificultad.

struggler [-ə*] *n* luchador, ra.

struggling [-iŋ] *adj* combativo, va.
◆ *n* lucha *f*.

strum [strʌm] *vt/vi* rasguear (the guitar) || rascar, tocar mal (an instrument).

struma [strumə] *n* MED escrófula *f* (scrofula) | bocio *m* (goitre).
— OBSERV El plural de *struma* es *strumae*.

strumming [strʌmiŋ] *n* rasgueo *m*, rasgueado *m*.

strumose ['struməus]; **strumous** ['struməs] *adj* MED escrofuloso, sa | que tiene bocio.

strumpet ['strʌmpit] *n* FAM fulana *f*, furcia *f* (prostitute).

strung [strʌŋ] *pret/pp* → **string.**

strut [strʌt] *n* pavoneo *m* (way of walking) || ARCH puntal *m*, riostra *f* || AVIAT montante *m*.

strut [strʌt] *vt* apuntalar (to fit struts to).
◆ *vi* pavonearse (to walk).

strychnia ['striknia]; **strychnine** ['strikni:n] *n* CHEM estricnina *f*.

Stuart ['stjuət] *pr n* Estuardo.

stub [stʌb] *n* tocón *m*, cepa *f* (of tree) || raigón *m* (of tooth) || cabo *m* (of pencil, crayon, candle, etc.) || colilla *f* (of cigarette) || talón *m*, matriz *f* (of a cheque) || resguardo *m* (of a ticket, of a receipt).

stub [stʌb] *vt* arrancar (to pull up by the roots) || rozar (to clear land) || — *to stub one's foot* o *one's toe against* tropezar con || *to stub out* apagar (a cigarette) || *to stub up* arrancar.

stubble [-l] *n* rastrojo *m* (stalks) || barba *f* incipiente (beard) || *stubble field* campo *m* de rastrojos.

stubbly [-li] *adj* cubierto de rastrojo (with stalks) || con una barba incipiente (chin) || al cepillo (hair) || *stubbl' beard* barba incipiente.

stubborn [-ən] *adj* obstinado, da; terco, ca; testarudo, da (obstinate); *a stubborn child* un niño testarudo || porfiado, da; tenaz; tesonero, ra (effort) || rebelde; *a stubborn illness* una enfermedad rebelde || terco, ca; testarudo, da (animals) || duro, ra; difícil de labrar (wood, stone) || ingrato, ta; poco fructífero, ra (soil) || difícil (problems, etc.) || rotundo, da (refusal).

stubbornness [-ənnis] *n* obstinación *f*, terquedad *f*, testarudez *f*.

stubby [-i] *adj* rechoncho, cha (person) || lleno de cepas *or* de tocones (land).

stucco ['stʌkəu] *n* estuco *m*.
◆ *adj* de estuco || *stucco plasterer, stucco worker* estucador *m*, estuquista *m*.
— OBSERV El plural de *stucco* es *stuccoes* o *stuccos*.

stuccowork [-wə:k] *n* estucado *m*.

stuck [stʌk] *pret/pp* → **stick.**

stuck-up [-ʌp] *adj* FAM presumido, da; engreído, da; pagado de sí mismo.

stud [stʌd] *n* cuadra *f* (collection of horses) || cuadra *f*, caballeriza *f* (place) || semental *m*, caballo *m* semental (studhorse) || tachón *m* (ornamental nail or rivet) || clavo *m* (of pedestrian crossing) || taco *m* (on football boots) || botón *m* de camisa (for shirt collar) || gemelo *m* (for shirt cuffs) || ELECTR contacto *m* || travesaño *m* (of chain) || espiga *f*, husillo *m* (spindle, pin) || ARCH montante *m* || *stud mare* yegua *f* de cría.

stud [stʌd] *vt* tachonar, adornar con clavos (to furnish with studs) || poner tacos a (boots) || FIG llenar de; *the piano was studded with ornaments* el piano estaba lleno de adornos | sembrar, cubrir, salpicar, tachonar (to scatter).

studbook [-buk] *n* registro *m* genealógico de caballos.

student ['stju:dənt] *n* estudiante *m* & *f* (who attends university, college, etc.) || alumno, na (pupil); *that's one of my best students* es uno de mis mejores alumnos || investigador, ra (researcher) || — *law student* estudiante de derecho || *student demonstrations* manifestaciones estudiantiles || *student* o *students' union* asociación *f* de estudiantes || *they are serious students of the subject* estudian el tema a fondo.

student body [-'bɔdi] *n* estudiantes *m pl*, estudiantado *m*.

studentship [-ʃip] *n* beca *f* (grant) || estudios *m pl* (time).

stud farm ['stʌdfɑ:m] *n* acalladero *m*.

studhorse ['stʌdhɔ:s] *n* caballo *m* semental, semental *m*.

studied ['stʌdid] *adj* premeditado, da; calculado, da (premeditated) || pensado, da; estudiado, da; *a well-studied plot* un argumento bien pensado || estudiado, da; afectado, da; *a studied gesture* un gesto estudiado.

studio ['stju:diəu] *n* estudio *m*, taller *m* (of an artist) || estudio *m*; *photographer's studio* estudio fotográfico; *television studio* estudio de televisión || CINEM estudios *m pl*, estudio *m* || *studio couch* sofá *m* cama.

studio flat [-flæt]; **studio appartment** [-ə'pɑ:tmənt] estudio *m*.

studious ['stju:djəs] *adj* estudioso, sa; aplicado, da (devoted to study) || solícito, ta; atento, ta (thoughtful) || → **studied.**

studiousness [-nis] *n* aplicación *f*.

study ['stʌdi] *n* estudio *m*; *a life devoted to study* una vida dedicada al estudio || estudio *m*, investigación *f*; *studies of animal behaviour* estudios de *or* investigaciones sobre el comportamiento de los animales || estudio *m*, examen *m* (consideration) || asignatura *f*; *my favourite study* mi asignatura preferida || estudio *m*; *he has published several studies in that field* ha publicado varios estudios sobre este tema || ARTS & MUS estudio *m* || estudio *m*; *Macbeth is a study of evil* Macbeth es un estudio de la maldad || despacho *m*, estudio *m*, escritorio *m* (room) || sala *f* de estudios (at school) || preocupación *f* (earnest effort) || — FIG *his face was a study!* ¡la cara que puso! || THEATR *to be a good, a slow study* aprender rápidamente, lentamente su papel (an actor) || FIG *to be in a brown study* estar en las nubes, estar meditando profundamente.
◆ *pl* estudios *m*; *to stop one's studies* dejar los estudios.

study ['stʌdi] *vt* estudiar; *to study Spanish* estudiar español || estudiar, examinar (to consider); *to study the possibilities* examinar las posibilidades || estudiar, observar; *to study the stars* observar las estrellas || estudiar, investigar, hacer un estudio sobre; *to study animal behaviour* hacer un estudio sobre el comportamiento de los animales || estudiar, meditar, pensar; *to study one's answer* meditar su respuesta || aprender [de memoria] (a part in a play) || *to study out* reflexionar *or* meditar en (a question), resolver (a problem).
◆ *vi* hacer estudios, estudiar (to be a student) || aplicarse, estudiar; *to study hard* estudiar mucho || — *to study for an exam* preparar un examen || *to study to be* de estudiar para; *he is studying to be a doctor* estudia para médico || *to study under* ser alumno de, estudiar con.

study hall [-hɔ:l] *n* sala *f* de estudios.

stuff [stʌf] *n* material *m*, materia *f*; *what stuff is it made of?* ¿de qué materia está hecho? || tejido *m*, tela *f*, paño *m*, género *m* (cloth) || cosas *f pl*; *the plumber went to collect his stuff* el fontanero fue a recoger sus cosas; *leave your stuff in the hall* deja tus cosas en la entrada; *they have produced a lot of new stuff* han producido muchas cosas nuevas; *there's good stuff in her* tiene cosas buenas; *there's some good stuff in your dictionary* hay cosas buenas en tu diccionario || eso; *does she call this stuff tobacco?* ¿llama a eso tabaco? || FIG tonterías *f pl* (worthless ideas, opinions) | madera *f*; *he has the stuff of a general, of an artist* tiene madera de general, de artista || FAM pasta *f*, moni *m* (money) || MAR galipote *m* || — FAM *a nice bit of stuff* un bombón, una monería | *did you bring the stuff?* ¿lo trajiste? | *give me the stuff* dámelo || *green stuff* verduras *f pl* (vegetables) || FAM *horrible stuff* porquería *f*, mejunje *m*, pócima *f* (bad tasting potion) || *stuff and nonsense!* ¡tonterías! || FIG *that's the stuff!* ¡eso es! | *the same old stuff* las tonterías de siempre | *to be good stuff* ser muy bueno || FAM *to be hot stuff* ser fenomenal *or* extraordinario *or* estupendo (to be fantastic), ser un as *or* un hacha (to be a champion, a wizard, etc.), ser sensacional (news), ser muy picante (spicy food), ser caliente (a woman) | *to do one's stuff* hacer lo que uno debe (to do one's duty), mostrar lo que uno sabe (to show one's worth) | *to know one's stuff* saber lo que uno se hace, conocer el percal.

stuff [stʌf] *vt* llenar, rellenar; *to stuff a jar with olives* llenar de aceitunas un tarro; *to stuff a cushion with feathers* rellenar un cojín con plumas || llenar completamente de; *to stuff olives into a jar* llenar completamente de olivas un tarro || meter; *I stuffed my things in a suitcase* metí mis cosas en una maleta || disecar (animals in taxidermy) || rellenar (toys, dolls) || CULIN rellenar || FAM atiborrar, llenar; *they stuffed us with food* nos atiborraron de comida | meter (en la cabeza), llenar (la cabeza) de (to cram into the mind) || impregnar con aceite (leather) || US poner votos falsos en (a ballot box) || — FAM *get stuffed!* ¡vete a paseo! || *to stuff o.s.* atiborrarse, hartarse, llenarse || *to stuff up* tapar, taponar (to block) || FIG *to stuff with* meter en la cabeza, llenar la cabeza de (ideas).
◆ *vi* atiborrarse, hartarse, llenarse.

stuffed [-t] *adj* CULIN relleno, na; *stuffed olives* aceitunas rellenas || FAM *stuffed shirt* persona envarada *or* estirada.

stuffiness [-inis] *n* falta *f* de ventilación, mala ventilación *f* (poor ventilation) || congesción *f* (in the nose) || FIG envaramiento *m* (pomposity) | pesadez *f* (dullness) | mal humor *m* (sulkiness).

stuffing [-iŋ] *n* relleno *m* (for food, cushions, animals, etc.) || disecación *f* (of animals) || FIG paja *f* (padding) || FIG *to knock the stuffing out of s.o.* quitarle los humos a uno (to deflate), pegarle una paliza a uno (to beat).

stuffing box [-iŋbɔks] *n* prensaestopas *m inv.*

stuffy [-i] *adj* mal ventilado, da (poorly ventilated) || cargado, da (air) || congestionado, da; taponado, da; *a stuffy nose* la nariz taponada || FAM estirado, da; envarado, da; pomposo, sa (pompous) | pesado, da (dull) | chapado a la antigua (old-fashioned) | malhumorado, da (sulky).

stultification ['stʌltifi'keiʃən] *n* ridiculización *f* (a ridiculing) || anulación *f*, aniquilamiento *m* (a making worthless) || JUR incapacitación *f*.

stultify ['stʌltifai] *vt* poner en ridículo, ridiculizar (to make ridiculous) || anular, aniquilar (to make worthless) || JUR alegar incapacidad mental.

stum [stʌm] *n* mosto *m* (unfermented grape juice).

stumble [-bl] *n* tropezón *m*, traspié *m* (trip) || lapsus *m* lingüe (in speech) || desliz *m* (error, sin).

stumble [-bl] *vi* tropezar (against an obstacle) || dar traspiés; *he stumbled along the road* iba por la calle dando traspiés || tropezar, topar (*over* con) (a difficulty) || cometer un desliz (to do wrong) || vacilar (to hesitate) || balbucear, decir torpemente; *to stumble through one's speech* decir torpemente un discurso || *to stumble across* o *on* o *upon* tropezar con, encontrar.

stumbling block [-bliŋblɔk] *n* FIG escollo *m*, tropiezo *m*.

stump [stʌmp] *n* tocón *m*, cepa *f* (of a tree) || troncho *m* (stalk of a cabbage) || raigón *m* (of tooth) || muñón *m* (of arm or leg) || cabo *m* (of pencil, of candle, etc.) || colilla *f* (of cigarette) || matriz *f*, talón *m* (of cheque, of ticket, etc.) || paso *m* pesado (heavy step) || pisada *f* (sound of footstep) || difumino *m* (in drawing) || SP estaca *f* (in cricket) || US tribuna *f* política (political rostrum) || FAM pata *f* de palo (wooden leg) || *to go on the stump* hacer una campaña electoral.

◆ *pl* FAM zancas *f*, patas *f* (legs) || FAM *to stir one's stumps* menearse, moverse.

stump [stʌmp] *vt* arrancar los tocones de (land) || SP expulsar (a un bateador) derribando la puerta antes de que llegue a ella (in cricket) || US recorrer haciendo propaganda electoral (to canvass an area) || FAM dejar perplejo *or* confuso (to baffle) | suspender (a candidate) || difuminar (to blur) || — *to be stumped* quedarse mudo || FAM *to stump up* apoquinar, cascar, aflojar; *to stump up twenty pounds* apoquinar veinte libras.

◆ *vi* renquear (to walk heavily) || US pronunciar discursos en una campaña electoral || FAM *to stump up* aflojar la mosca *or* los cuartos.

stumping [-iŋ] *n* difuminación *f*.

stump orator [-'ɔrətə*]; **stump speaker** [-'spi:kə*] *n* orador *m* callejero.

stumpy [-i] *adj* rechoncho, cha; achaparrado, da (people) || corto, ta (things) || lleno de tocones (land).

stun [stʌn] *n* aturdimiento *m*, atontamiento *m* || perplejidad *f* || choque *m* (shock).

stun [stʌn] *vt* aturdir, atontar (to make unconscious) || pasmar, dejar estupefacto *or* pasmado (to stupefy) || *stunned with surprise* pasmado, da.

stung [stʌŋ] *pret/pp* ⟶ **sting.**

stunk [stʌŋk] *pret/pp* ⟶ **stink.**

stunner ['stʌnə*] *n* FAM persona *f* estupenda, maravilla *f* (person) | cosa *f* estupenda, maravilla *f* (thing).

stunning ['stʌniŋ] *adj* imponente, bárbaro, ra; fenomenal (very attractive) || que aturde, aturdidor, ra; *a stuning blow* un golpe aturdidor || sorprendente; pasmoso, sa (astonishing).

stunt [stʌnt] *n* proeza *f*, hazaña *f* (exhibition of skill) || acrobacia *f* (acrobatics) || noticia *f* sensacional (in newspapers) || truco *m* publicitario (publicity) || recurso *m or* maniobra *f* sensacional (to attract attention) || engendro *m* (malformed animal or plant) || atrofia *f* (atrophy).

stunt [stʌnt] *vt* atrofiar, impedir el crecimiento *or* el desarrollo de (to stop the growth of).

◆ *vi* hacer acrobacias (in a plane).

stunted [-id] *adj* canijo, ja; encanijado, da || *to become stunted* encanijarse, ponerse canijo.

stunt flying [-'flaiiŋ] *n* vuelo *m* acrobático.

stunt man [-mæn] *n* doble *m* especial (in film).

stupa ['stju:pə] *n* REL stupa *f*.

stupe [stju:p] *n* compresa *f*.

stupefacient ['stju:pi'feiʃənt] *adj* estupefaciente.

◆ *n* estupefaciente *m*.

stupefaction ['stju:pi'fækʃən] *n* estupefacción *f*.

stupefy ['stju:pifai] *vt* dejar estupefacto, dejar pasmado (to amaze); *the news stupefied him* la noticia le dejó estupefacto || atontar (to make lethargic or dull).

stupefying [-iŋ] *adj* pasmoso, sa; asombroso, sa.

stupendous [stju'pendəs] *adj* estupendo, da; *she is a stupendous girl* es una chica estupenda || prodigioso, sa; formidable; *a stupendous effort* un esfuerzo formidable.

stupid ['stju:pid] *adj* estúpido, da; tonto, ta (slow-witted) || atontado, da (in a state of stupor) || — FIG *as stupid as a donkey* más tonto que una mata de habas || *that was stupid of me* fue una estupidez mía, fue una tontería de mi parte || *to drink o.s. stupid* atontarse bebiendo.

◆ *n* estúpido, da; tonto, ta.

stupidity [stju'piditi]; **stupidness** ['stju:pidnis] *n* estupidez *f*, tontería *f* (silliness) || atontamiento *m* (daze).

stupor ['stju:pə*] *n* estupor *m* || *in a drunken stupor* atontado por la bebida.

sturdiness ['stə:dinis] *n* robustez *f*, fuerza *f* (robustness) || energía *f* (energy) || firmeza *f*, determinación *f* (resolution).

sturdy ['stə:di] *adj* robusto, ta; fuerte (strong or healthy) || firme, resuelto, ta; decidido, da (resolute) || enérgico, ca (energetic).

◆ *n* VET modorra *f* (in sheep).

sturgeon ['stə:dʒən] *n* esturión *m* (fish).

stutter ['stʌtə*] *n* tartamudeo *m*.

stutter ['stʌtə*] *vt* tartamudear, farfullar.

◆ *vi* tartamudear.

stutterer [-rə*] *n* tartamudo, da.

stuttering [-riŋ] *adj* tartamudo, da.

◆ *n* tartamudeo *m*.

sty [stai] *n* pocilga *f* (for pigs) || FAM tugurio *m*, pocilga *f* (filthy place).

sty; stye [stai] *n* MED orzuelo *m* (in the eye).

Stygian ['stidʒiən] *adj* estigio, gia || FIG tenebroso, sa (night) | inviolable (oath).

style [stail] *n* estilo *m* (distinctive type, way of expression); *the Byzantine style* el estilo bizantino || manera *f*, estilo *m* (manner); *his style of playing the piano* su manera de tocar el piano || tipo *m* (kind); *an American-style comedy* una comedia de tipo americano || modelo *m*, tipo *m* (of manufactures) || moda *f* (fashion); *it's the latest style* es la última moda || hechura *f* (cut of clothes) || peinado *m* (of hair) || estilo *m*, elegancia *f*, clase *f*, distinción *f*; *that girl has style* esa chica tiene estilo || título *m* (title) || BOT estilo *m* || TECH buril *m* || estilete *m* (for writing on wax) || estilo *m*, gnomón *m* (of a dial) || aguja *f* (of gramophone) || COMM razón *f* social (name of a company) || — *a general in the old style* un general de la vieja escuela || *in the style of* al estilo de || *that's the style!* ¡muy bien! || *to do sth. in style* hacer algo como es debido || *to live in style* vivir con gran lujo || *to travel in style* viajar con la mayor comodidad || *to win in fine style* ganar limpiamente.

style [stail] *vt* llamar, dar el nombre de, titular (to give a name to) || hacer a la moda (clothes) || peinar a la moda (hair) || diseñar (to design).

stylet [-it] *n* MED estilete *m* || estilete *m* (stiletto) || ZOOL púa *f*, pincho *m*.

styling ['stailiŋ] *n* estilización *f*.

stylish ['stailiʃ] *adj* elegante (elegant) || a la moda (fashionable) || con estilo, que tiene estilo (behaviour).

stylishness [-nis] *n* elegancia *f*, estilo *m*.

stylist ['stailist] *n* estilista *m* & *f* (writer or fashion consultant) || diseñador, ra (of cars, etc.) || peluquero, ra (hairdresser).

stylistic [stai'listik]; **stylistical** [-əl] *adj* estilístico, ca.

stylistics [-s] *n* estilística *f*.

stylization ['stailai'zeiʃən] *n* estilización *f*.

stylize ['stailaiz] *vt* estilizar.

stylograph ['stailəgra:f] *n* estilográfica *f*.

stylographic ['stailə'græfik] *adj* estilográfico, ca.

stylus ['stailəs] *n* estilete *m* (for writing on wax) || punzón *m* (for writing Braille) || aguja *f* (of a record player).

— OBSERV El plural de *stylus* es *styluses* o *styli*.

stymie ['staimi] *vt* ⟶ **stimy.**

styptic ['stiptik] *adj* estíptico, ca; astringente.

◆ *n* MED estíptico *m*, astringente *m*.

styrax ['staiəræks] *n* BOT estoraque *m*.

styrene ['stairi:n] *n* CHEM estireno *m*, estiroleno *m*.

Styx [stiks] *n* MYTH laguna *f* Estigia.

suable ['sju:əbl] *adj* que puede ser citado ante la justicia, demandable.

suasion ['sweiʒən] *n* persuasión *f*.

suave [swa:v] *adj* suave || afable, amable (kind) || zalamero, ra (ingratiating).

suavity ['swa:viti] *n* suavidad *f* || afabilidad *f*, amabilidad *f* (kindness) || zalamería *f* (excessive politeness).

sub [sʌb] *n* FAM subalterno *m*, subordinado *m* (subordinate) | submarino *m* (submarine) | subteniente *m* (sublieutenant) | sustituto, ta (substitute) | suscripción *f* (subscription) | anticipo *m*, adelanto *m* (an advance).

sub [sʌb] *vi* *to sub for* sustituir a.

subacid ['sʌb'æsid] *adj* agridulce, ligeramente agrio (taste) || FIG agridulce (remarks).

subaltern ['sʌbltən] *adj* subordinado, da; subalterno, na.

◆ *n* subalterno *m*, subordinado *m* || MIL alférez *m* (subaltern officer) | subalterno *m*.

subaquatic [ˌsʌbə'kwætik] *adj* subacuático, ca.

subaqueous ['sʌb'eikwiəs] *adj* subacuático, ca.

subarctic [sʌb'ɑːktik] *adj* subártico, ca.

subastral [sʌb'æstrəl] *adj* sublunar, terrestre.

subbasement ['sʌb,beismənt] *n* segundo *m* sótano.

subcelestial ['sʌbsi'lestjəl] *adj* terrenal.

subclass ['sʌbklɑːs] *n* subclase *f.*

subclavian [,sʌb'kleiviən] *adj* subclavio, via; *subclavian vein* vena subclavia.

subcommittee ['sʌbkə'miti] *n* subcomisión *f,* subcomité *m.*

subconscious ['sʌb'kɔnʃəs] *adj* subconsciente.

◆ *n* subconsciente *m.*

subconsciously [-li] *adv* de manera subconsciente.

subconsciousness [-'sʌb'kɔnʃəsnis] *n* subconsciencia *f.*

subcontinent ['sʌb'kɔntinənt] *n* subcontinente *m.*

subcontract [sʌb'kɔntrækt] *n* subcontrato *m.*

subcontractor [-ə*] *n* subcontratista *m,* segundo contratista *m.*

subculture ['sʌb'kʌltʃə*] *n* subcultura *f.*

subcutaneous ['sʌbkju'teinjəs] *adj* subcutáneo, a.

subdeacon ['sʌb'diːkən] *n* REL subdiácono *m.*

subdeaconry [-ri] *n* REL subdiaconado *m,* subdiaconato *m.*

subdelegate ['sʌb'deligeit] *vt* subdelegar.

subdelegation ['sʌbdeli'geiʃən] *n* subdelegación *f.*

subdiaconate ['sʌbdai'ækənit] *n* REL subdiaconado *m,* subdiaconato *m.*

subdivide ['sʌbdi'vaid] *vt* subdividir.

◆ *vi* subdividirse.

subdivision ['sʌbdi'viʒən] *n* subdivisión *f.*

subdominant ['sʌb'dɔminənt] *n* MUS subdominante *f* (tone).

subdue [səb'djuː] *vt* sojuzgar, someter, dominar (a country, etc.) || atenuar, suavizar (sound, colour, light, etc.) || bajar (voice) || calmar, aliviar (pain) || reprimir, contener, sojuzgar, dominar (passion) || deprimir, abatir (s.o.'s spirits) || poner en cultivo (land).

subdued [-d] *adj* sojuzgado, da; sometido, da; dominado, da (a country, etc.) || sumiso, sa (docile) || suave, suavizado, da (colour, sound, light, etc.) || bajo, ja (voice) || aliviado, da (pain) || reprimido, da; contenido, da; sojuzgado, da; dominado, da (one's passion) || deprimido, da; abatido, da (depressed).

subedit ['sʌb'edit] *vt* corregir (an article).

subeditor [-ə*] *n* redactor *m* (of a newspaper).

suberose ['sjuːbərəus]**; suberous** ['sjuːbərəs] *adj* suberoso, sa.

subfamily ['sʌb'fæmili] *n* subfamilia *f.*

subfluvial ['sʌb'fluːvjəl] *adj* subfluvial, subálveo, a.

subfusc ['sʌbfʌsk] *adj* oscuro, ra.

subgenus ['sʌb,dʒiːnəs] *n* subgénero *m.*

subgroup ['sʌbgruːp] *n* subgrupo *m.*

subhead ['sʌbhed]**; subheading** [-iŋ] *n* subtítulo *m* (subtitle) || subdirector *m* (of a school).

subhuman ['sʌb'hjuːmən] *adj* infrahumano, na.

subindex [,sʌb'indeks] *n* MATH subíndice *m.*

— OBSERV El plural de la palabra inglesa es *subindices.*

subjacent [sʌb'dʒeisənt] *adj* subyacente.

subject ['sʌbdʒikt] *adj* sometido, da; dominado, da (people, race) || — *subject to* sujeto a (charge, fee, etc.); *we are subject to the laws of the country* estamos sujetos a las leyes del país || *subject to correction* que puede ser corregido || *subject to earthquakes* propenso a terremotos || *subject to government approval* previa aprobación del gobierno.

◆ *n* súbdito, ta (of a country); *British subject* súbdito británico || tema *m* (of conference, conversation, book); *let's change the subject* cambiemos de tema || sujeto *m* (of an experiment) || motivo *m* (of painting) || objeto *m* (of meditation, of gossip) || motivo *m* (reason) || GRAMM & PHIL sujeto *m* || MED paciente *m* & *f* || asignatura *f* (in school) || MUS tema *m* || — *enough on that subject* dejemos de hablar de esto || *on the subject of* a propósito de, referente al tema de || *to come to one's subject* entrar en materia || *to keep off a subject* no tocar un tema || *while we are on the subject* mientras hablamos del tema.

subject [səb'dʒekt] *vt* sojuzgar, dominar (to conquer) || supeditar (to subordinate) || someter (to an examination) || — *to subject o.s. to* sujetarse a, someterse a || *to subject to* someter a; *the thief was subjected to severe punishment* el ladrón fue sometido a un castigo severo; exponer a; *such behaviour will subject you to criticism* tal comportamiento le expondrá a críticas.

subjection [səb'dʒekʃən] *n* sojuzgamiento *m,* avasallamiento *m,* dominación *f* (domineering) || sujeción *f,* supeditación *f* (subordination) || sometimiento *m* (submission) || *to bring into subjection* sojuzgar, avasallar.

subjective [səb'dʒektiv] *adj* subjetivo, va || GRAMM nominativo, va.

subjectivism [səb'dʒektivizəm] *n* subjetivismo *m.*

subjectivity ['sʌbdʒek'tiviti] *n* subjetividad *f.*

subject matter ['sʌbdʒik'mætə] *n* tema *m,* materia *f* (theme, matter) || contenido *m* (contents).

subjoin ['sʌb'dʒɔin] *vt* adjuntar.

sub judice [sʌb'dʒuːdisi] *adj* JUR pendiente, por resolver, sub judice.

subjugate ['sʌbdʒugeit] *vt* sojuzgar.

subjugation ['sʌbdʒu'geiʃən] *n* dominación *f,* sometimiento *m,* sojuzgamiento *m.*

subjugator ['sʌbdʒugeitə*] *n* sojuzgador, ra.

subjunctive [səb'dʒʌŋktiv] *adj* GRAMM subjuntivo, va; *subjunctive mood* modo subjuntivo.

◆ *n* subjuntivo *m.*

subkingdom ['sʌb,kiŋdəm] *n* BIOL subreino *m.*

sublease ['sʌb'liːs] *vt* subarrendar.

sublessee ['sʌble'siː] *n* subarrendatario, ria.

sublessor ['sʌble'sɔː*] *n* subarrendador, ra.

sublet ['sʌb'let] *vt* subarrendar.

sublieutenant ['sʌble'tenənt] *n* MAR alférez *m* de navío || MIL alférez *m,* subteniente *m.*

sublimate ['sʌblimit] *n* CHEM sublimado *m.*

sublimate ['sʌblimeit] *vt* sublimar.

sublimation ['sʌbli'meiʃən] *n* CHEM sublimación *f* (process) | sublimado *m* (product) || FIG sublimación *f.*

sublime [sə'blaim] *adj* sublime (exalted, inspiring admiration) || supremo, ma (supreme, outstanding); *sublime indifference* indiferencia suprema || majestuoso, sa; sublime (scenery) || MED epidérmico, ca.

◆ *n* *the sublime* lo sublime || *to go from the sublime to the ridiculous* volverse cada vez más ridículo.

subliminal [sʌb'liminl] *adj* subconsciente.

◆ *n* subconsciente *m.*

sublimity [sə'blimiti] *n* sublimidad *f* || cosa *f* sublime.

sublunar [sʌb'luːnə*]**; sublunary** [-ri] *adj* sublunar || FIG terrenal (earthly).

submachine gun ['sʌbmə'ʃiːngʌn] *n* MIL pistola *f* ametralladora, metralleta *f.*

submarine ['sʌbmə'riːn] *adj* MIL submarino, na.

◆ *n* submarino *m* || *submarine chaser* cazasubmarinos *m inv.*

submariner [sʌb'mærinə*] *n* submarinista *m.*

submaxilla ['sʌbmæk'silə] *n* ANAT mandíbula *f* inferior.

— OBSERV El plural de *submaxilla* es *submaxillae.*

submaxillary ['sʌbmæk'siləri] *adj* submaxilar; *submaxillary gland* glándula submaxilar.

submediant [sʌb'miːdiənt] *n* MUS superdominante *f.*

submerge [səb'məːdʒ] *vt* sumergir || inundar (land).

◆ *vi* sumergirse.

submergence [-əns] *n* sumersión *f.*

submergible [-əbl] *adj* sumergible.

submerse [sʌb'məːs] *vt* sumergir.

submersed [-t] *adj* sumergido, da.

submergible [səb'məːsəbl] *adj* sumergible.

◆ *n* submarino *m,* sumergible *m.*

submersion [səb'məːʃən] *n* sumersión *f.*

submission [səb'miʃən] *n* sumisión *f* (act of submitting) || resignación *f,* conformidad *f* (resignation) || JUR sumisión *f* a la jurisdicción de un juez *or* tribunal | sumisión *f* (to arbitration) || sometimiento *m* (to an examination) || presentación *f* (of documents).

submissive [sʌb'misiv] *adj* sumiso, sa (willing to submit) || obediente (obedient).

submissiveness [-nis] *n* sumisión *f.*

submit [səb'mit] *vt* someter; *to submit s.o. to torture* someter a alguien a la tortura || presentar (a proposal) || proponer, exponer (a theory) || sugerir, proponer (to suggest) || señalar, indicar; *I submit that there is another point of view* señalo que existe otro punto de vista || someter (to refer for consideration); *to submit sth. for s.o.'s approval* someter algo a la aprobación de alguien.

◆ *vi* rendirse, someterse (to cease to resist) || someterse (to defer to s.o.'s wishes) || conformarse (to resign o.s.).

submittal [səb'mitəl] *n* sumisión *f.*

submultiple ['sʌb'mʌltipl] *n* MATH submúltiplo *m.*

subnormal ['sʌb'nɔːməl] *adj* MED subnormal.

◆ *n* MED subnormal *m* & *f* || MATH subnormal *f.*

suborbital [sʌb'ɔːbitəl] *adj* ANAT suborbitario, ria.

suborder ['sʌb,ɔːdə*] *n* suborden *m.*

subordinate [sə'bɔːdnit] *adj* subordinado, da; subalterno, na || GRAM subordinado, da; *subordinate clause* oración subordinada.

◆ *n* *subordinado, da; subalterno, na.*

subordinate [sə'bɔːdineit] *vt* subordinar.

subordination [sə'bɔːdi'neiʃən] *n* subordinación *f.*

suborn [sʌ'bɔːn] *vt* sobornar, cohechar.

suborner [sʌ'bɔːnə*] *n* sobornador, ra; cohechador, ra (briber).

subplot ['sʌbplɔt] *n* argumento *m* secundario (of novel, film, play, etc.).

subpoena [səb'piːnə] *n* JUR citación *f.*

subpoena [səb'piːnə] *vt* JUR citar, mandar comparecer.

sub-post office [,səb'pəust,ɔfis] *n* estafeta *f* de Correos.

subprefect ['sʌb'priːfekt] *n* subprefecto *m.*

subprefecture ['sʌbpriː'fektjə*] *n* subprefectura *f.*

subprincipal ['sʌb'prinsəpl] *n* subdirector *m* (of a school).

subprogram ['sʌb'prəugræm] *n* INFORM subprograma *m*.

subrent ['sʌb'rent] *vt* subarrendar.

subreption [səb'repʃən] *n* subrepción *f*.

subreptitious ['sʌbrep'tiʃəs] *adj* subrepticio, cia.

subrogate ['sʌbrəgeit] *vt* JUR subrogar.

subrogation ['sʌbrə'geiʃən] *n* JUR subrogación *f*.

sub rosa ['sʌb'rəuzə] *adv* en secreto, confidencialmente.

subroutine ['sʌbru:'ti:n] *n* INFORM subrutina *f*.

subscribe [səb'skraib] *vt* poner (one's name on a document) || firmar, suscribir (a document) || suscribir, aprobar, estar de acuerdo con (to support) || pagar (to pay) || suscribirse por (to promise to pay).
◆ *vi* suscribirse, abonarse (to make a subscription) || *to subscribe to* aprobar, estar de acuerdo con, suscribir (to agree with), abonarse a, suscribirse a (a newspaper, a magazine, etc.), suscribir, firmar (a document, etc.).
— OBSERV The verb *suscribir* may also be spelt *subscribir*.

subscribed [-d] *adj* suscrito, ta.

subscriber [-ə*] *n* suscriptor, ra; el que suscribe || suscriptor, ra; abonado, da (to a newspaper) || INFORM abonado *m*.

subscript ['sʌbskript] *adj* GRAMM escrito debajo de una letra.
◆ *n* signo *m* escrito debajo de una letra || MATH subíndice *m*.

subscription [səb'skripʃən] *n* suscripción *f* (act of subscribing) || firma *f* (on a document) || adhesión *f* (to a doctrine) || abono *m*, suscripción *f* (to a newspaper, to a magazine) || cuota *f or* cantidad *f* suscrita (sum subscribed) || cuota *f* (membership fees).
— OBSERV The word *suscripción* may also be spelt *subscripción*.

subsection ['sʌbˌsekʃən] *n* subdivisión *f* || apartado *m* (of a law).

subsequence ['sʌbsikwəns] *n* consecuencia *f* (happening) || posterioridad *f* (posteriority).

subsequent ['sʌbsikwənt] *adj* subsiguiente, consecutivo, va || posterior; *subsequent to* posterior a.

subsequently [-li] *adv* posteriormente, más tarde.

subserve [səb'sə:v] *vt* favorecer, ayudar.

subservience [səb'sə:vjəns]; **subserviency** [-i] *n* utilidad *f* (usefulness) || servilismo *m* (servility) || subordinación *f* (subordination) || sumisión *f* (submissiveness).

subservient [səb'sə:vjənt] *adj* servil (servile) || subordinado, da (subordinate) || sumiso, sa (submissive).

subside [səb'said] *vi* hundirse (ground, building) || bajar, descender (flood water, fever) || depositarse, asentarse (sediment) || calmarse, apaciguarse (the sea, anger, excitement) || amainar (storm, wind, etc.) || desplomarse, dejarse caer; *to subside into a chair* dejarse caer en una silla.

subsidence [-əns] *n* hundimiento *m* (of ground, of building) || bajada *f*, descenso *m* (of flood water, of fever) || depósito *m*, asentamiento *m* (of sediment) || apaciguamiento *m* (of sea, of anger, etc.) || amaine *m* (of storm, of wind).

subsidiary [səb'sidjəri] *adj* subsidiario, ria || secundario, ria || auxiliar || *subsidiary company* sucursal *f*, filial *f*.
◆ *n* auxiliar *m* & *f*, ayudante *m* & *f* (assistant) || sucursal *f*, filial *f* (company).

subsidize ['sʌbsidaiz] *vt* subvencionar (an enterprise) || dar subsidios a (a family).

subsidy ['sʌbsidi] *n* subvención *f* (to an enterprise, to a country) || subsidio *m* (to a family, to a person).

subsist [səb'sist] *vi* subsistir, perdurar (to continue to exist) || subsistir *m* (to continue to live) || *to subsist on* mantenerse con, sustentarse con.
◆ *vt* mantener.

subsistence [-əns] *n* subsistencia *f*, existencia *f* || mantenimiento *m*, subsistencia *f*, sustento *m* (livelihood) || PHIL subsistencia *f* || — *subsistence allowance* dietas *f pl* [AMER viático *m*] || *subsistence farming* agricultura *f* de subsistencia.

subsistent [-ənt] *adj* subsistente.

subsoil ['sʌbsɔil] *n* subsuelo *m*.

subsonic ['sʌb'sɔnik] *adj* subsónico, ca.

subspecies ['sʌb'spi:ʃi:z] *n* BOT & BIOL subespecie *f*.
— OBSERV El plural de *subspecies* es *subspecies*.

substance ['sʌbstəns] *n* sustancia *f*, substancia *f* (material) || esencia *f*; *the substance of an argument* la esencia de un argumento || sustancia *f*, substancia *f*; *his arguments have little substance* sus argumentos tienen poca sustancia || fondo *m*; *form and substance* forma y fondo || FIG caudal *m*, fortuna *f*, bienes *m pl* (wealth); *a man of substance* un hombre con fortuna || PHIL sustancia *f*, substancia *f* || consistencia *f*, cuerpo *m* (of a material, of cloth) || solidez *f* (solidity) || *in substance* en esencia, en sustancia.

substandard ['sʌb'stændəd] *adj* inferior (al nivel medio).

substantial [səb'stænʃəl] *adj* real, verdadero, ra (real) || sustancial, substancial; *a substantial argument* un argumento sustancial || considerable, sustancial, substancial; *substantial income* ingresos considerables || importante || abundante; *substantial meal* comida abundante || sustancioso, sa; substancioso, sa; nutritivo, va (food, drink) || consistente, fuerte, sólido, da (made to last) || FIG con fortuna, rico, ca; acaudalado, da; adinerado, da (wealthy).

substantiality [səbˌstænʃi'æliti] *n* realidad *f* (reality) || solidez *f* (solidity).

substantially [-i] *adv* sustancialmente, substancialmente (in a substantial manner) || considerablemente (considerably).

substantiate [səb'stænʃieit] *vt* establecer (a charge) || justificar (a claim) || *non-substantiated* sin pruebas que lo justifiquen.

substantiation [səb'stænʃi'eiʃən] *n* justificación *f*.

substantival ['sʌbstən'taivəl] *adj* GRAMM sustantivo, va; substantivo, va.

substantivate [səb'stæntiveit] *vt* sustantivar, substantivar.

substantive ['sʌbstəntiv] *adj* GRAMM sustantivo, va; substantivo, va || considerable (substantial) || real (actual) || esencial (essential) || autónomo, ma; independiente (not dependent) || JUR positivo, va; *substantive law* derecho positivo.
◆ *n* GRAMM sustantivo *m*, substantivo *m*.

substantivize [səb'stæntivaiz]; **substantize** ['sʌbstæntaiz] *vt* sustantivar, substantivar.

substation ['sʌbˌsteiʃən] *n* ELECTR subestación *f*.

substitutable ['sʌbstitju:əbl] *adj* sustituible, substituible.

substitute ['sʌbstitju:t] *n* sustituto, ta; substituto, ta; suplente *m* & *f* (person) || sucedáneo *m* (goods) || imitación *f* || SP suplente *m*, reserva *m* || *there is no substitute for fresh milk* no hay nada como la leche fresca.

substitute ['sʌbstitju:t] *vt* sustituir, substituir; *to substitute nylon for cotton, to substitute cotton by nylon* sustituir el algodón por el nylon.
◆ *vi* sustituir, substituir, suplir, reemplazar; *he is substituting for his brother* está sustituyendo a su hermano.

substitution ['sʌbsti'tju:ʃən] *n* sustitución *f*, substitución *f*.

substitutional [-l]; **substitutive** ['sʌbstitju:tiv] *adj* sustituidor, ra; substituidor, ra; sustitutivo, va; substitutivo, va.

substrata ['sʌb'stra:tə] *pl n* → **substratum.**

substratum ['sʌb'stra:təm] *n* sustrato *m*, substrato *m* || FIG fondo *m*; *a substratum of truth* un fondo de verdad || AGR & GEOL subsuelo *m*.
— OBSERV El plural de *substratum* es *substrata*.

substructure ['sʌb'strʌktʃə*] *n* infraestructura *f* || FIG base *f*.

subsume [səb'sju:m] *vt* PHIL incluir [en una categoría, en una clase, etc.].

subsurface ['sʌb'sə:fis] *adj* subterráneo, a.

subtangent ['sʌb'tændʒənt] *n* subtangente *f*.

subtenancy ['sʌb'tenənsi] *n* subarriendo *m*.

subtenant ['sʌb'tenənt] *n* subarrendatario, ria.

subtend [səb'tend] *vt* MATH subtender.

subterfuge ['sʌbtəfju:dʒ] *n* subterfugio *m*.

subterranean ['sʌbtə'reinjən]; **subterraneous** [sʌbtə'reinjəs] *adj* subterráneo, a.

subtilization [sʌtilai'zeiʃən] *n* sutilización *f*.

subtilize ['sʌtilaiz] *vt/vi* sutilizar.

subtitle ['sʌb'taitl] *n* subtítulo *m*.

subtitle ['sʌb'taitl] *vt* subtitular, poner subtítulos a.

subtle ['sʌtl] *adj* sutil (thin, not dense) || sutil; *a subtle difference* una diferencia sutil || agudo, da; sutil, perspicaz (keen); *a subtle mind* una menta aguda || ingenioso, sa; astuto, ta (clever); *a subtle argument* un argumento ingenioso || insidioso, sa (insidious) || misterioso, sa (charm) || delicado, da (perfume) || fino, na (irony, etc.).

subtleness [-nis] *n* → **subtlety.**

subtlety [-ti] *n* sutilidad *f*, sutileza *f* (of distinctions, of ideas, etc.) || astucia *f*, sutileza *f* (cunning).

subtly ['sʌtli] *adv* sutilmente.

subtonic ['sʌb'tɔnik] *n* MUS nota *f* sensible.

subtotal ['sʌb'təutl] *n* subtotal *m*.

subtract [səb'trækt] *vt* restar, sustraer, substraer; *to subtract 13 from 20* restar 13 a 20 || FIG sustraer, quitar.

subtraction [səb'trækʃən] *n* MATH resta *f*, sustracción *f*, substracción *f* || FIG sustracción *f*.

subtrahend ['sʌbtrəhend] *n* MATH sustraendo *m*, substraendo *m*.

subtropic ['sʌb'trɔpik]; **subtropical** [-əl] *adj* subtropical; *subtropical climate* clima subtropical.

subtropics [-s] *pl n* regiones *f* subtropicales.

subtype ['sʌbtaip] *n* BIOL subtipo *m*.

suburb ['sʌbə:b] *n* suburbio *m*, arrabal *m*.

suburban [sə'bə:bən] *adj* suburbano, na || *suburban train* tren *m* de cercanías.

suburbanite [sʌ'bə:bənait] *adj* de las afueras, suburbano, na.
◆ *n* persona *f* que vive en las afueras.

suburbia [sʌ'bəːbiə] *pl n* suburbios *m*, afueras *f*.

subvention [səb'venʃən] *n* subvención *f*, ayuda *f*, subsidio *m*.

subversion [səb'vəːʃən] *n* subversión *f*.

subversive [səb'vəːsiv] *adj* subversivo, va.
◆ *n* persona *f* subversiva.

subvert [sʌb'vəːt] *vt* derribar, derrocar (a government, etc.) ‖ derribar (sth. established) ‖ corromper, pervertir (a person).

subway ['sʌbwei] *n* paso *m* subterráneo (under street, etc.) ‖ conducto *m* subterráneo (underground conduit) ‖ US metro *m* [AMER subte *m*] (underground).

subzero ['sʌb'ziərəu] *adj* bajo cero.

succedaneous [sʌksi'deiniəs] *adj* sucedáneo, a.

succedaneum [sʌksi'deiniəm] *n* sucedáneo *m*, sustituto *m*.
— OBSERV El plural de *succedaneum* es *succedanea*.

succeed [sək'siːd] *vi* tener éxito (to be successful) ‖ salir bien; *the plan succeeded* el proyecto salió bien ‖ triunfar; *he succeeded in life* triunfó en la vida ‖ seguir, suceder; *a long peace succeeded* siguió un largo período de paz ‖ — *to succeed in doing sth.* conseguir *or* lograr hacer algo; *did you succeed in getting him on the phone?* ¿logró hablar con él por teléfono? ‖ *to succeed to a fortune* heredar una fortuna ‖ *to succeed to the throne* heredar el trono.
◆ *vt* suceder a; *he succeeded his father in the business* sucedió a su padre en el negocio ‖ seguir (to follow).

succeeding [-iŋ] *adj* siguiente (following) ‖ sucesivo, va (successive).

succentor [sək'sentə*] *n* REL sochantre *m*.

success [sək'ses] *n* éxito *m*, triunfo *m*; *he was a great success* tuvo un gran éxito; *to make a success of* tener éxito en ‖ — *box-office success* éxito de taquilla *or* taquillero ‖ *success story* historia *f* de un éxito ‖ *the portrait is a success* el retrato ha salido muy bien.

successful [-ful] *adj* que tiene éxito, de éxito [AMER exitoso, sa]; *a successful record* un disco de éxito ‖ afortunado, da (person) ‖ próspero, ra; venturoso, sa; *successful business* negocio próspero ‖ logrado, da; conseguido, da; *successful attempt* intento logrado ‖ elegido, da; afortunado, da (candidate) ‖ acertado, da; atinado, da; *successful union* unión acertada.

successfully [-fuli] *adv* con éxito.

succession [sʌk'seʃən] *n* sucesión *f*, serie *f*; *a succession of defeats* una serie de derrotas ‖ sucesión *f* (right to succeed to a position, to inherit); *succession duties* derechos de sucesión ‖ descendencia *f*, descendientes *m pl* (heirs) ‖ GEOL & BIOL serie *f* ‖ — *in close succession* a cortos intervalos ‖ *in succession* seguido, da; uno tras otro; *six shots in succession* seis tiros uno tras otro; consecutivo, va; seguido, da; *for three years in succession* durante tres años consecutivos ‖ *in succession to* como sucesor *or* heredero de ‖ *universal succession* sucesión universal.

successional [-əl] *adj* sucesorio, ria.

successive [sʌk'sesiv] *adj* sucesivo, va; consecutivo, va; *six successive months* seis meses seguidos.

successor [sʌk'sesə*] *n* sucesor, ra.

successory [-ri] *adj* sucesorio, ria.

succinct [sək'siŋkt] *adj* sucinto, ta (concise).

succinctness [-nis] *n* concisión *f*.

succinic ['sʌk'sinik] *adj* CHEM succínico, ca (acid).

succor ['sʌkə*] *n/vt* US → **succour.**

succory [-ri] *n* BOT achicoria *f*.

succour; US **succor** ['sʌkə*] *n* socorro *m*, auxilio *m*.

succour; US **succor** ['sʌkə*] *vt* socorrer, auxiliar.

succulence ['sʌkjuləns]; **succulency** [-i] *n* suculencia *f*.

succulent ['sʌkjulənt] *adj* suculento, ta ‖ BOT carnoso, sa (plant).
◆ *n* BOT planta *f* carnosa.

succumb [sə'kʌm] *vi* sucumbir; *to succumb to temptation* sucumbir a la tentación ‖ ceder, rendirse (to give up resistence) ‖ sucumbir (to die).

succursal [sʌ'kəːsəl] *adj* filial, sucursal.
◆ *n* filial *f*, sucursal *f*.

such [sʌtʃ] *adj* tal; *it gave me such a fright!* ¡me dio tal susto!; *the noise was such that I couldn't sleep* el ruido era tal que no podía dormir ‖ tal, semejante; *I had never seen such luxury* nunca había visto semejante lujo; *such luxury is a sin* semejante lujo es un pecado; *I can't afford such a price* no puedo pagar semejante precio; *such men as he and I* hombres tales como él y yo ‖ semejante, parecido, da; *is there such a book in English?* ¿hay un libro parecido en inglés? ‖ tan, tan grande; *he is such a liar!* ¡es tan mentiroso!, ¡es un mentiroso tan grande! ‖ de esta índole, de semejante índole, de este tipo; *any such reason* cualquier razón de esta índole ‖ en tales condiciones; *the road is such that it can be travelled only on foot* la carretera está en tales condiciones que sólo se puede recorrer a pie ‖ tanto, ta; *don't be in such a hurry* no tengas tanta prisa ‖ *in such a way that* de tal forma *or* de tal manera que ‖ *no such thing!* ¡no hay tal!, ¡nada de eso! ‖ *on just such a day* un día exactamente igual ‖ *such a lot* tanto ‖ *such a lot of things* tantas cosas ‖ *such and such* tal, tal o cual, tal y cual; *on such and such a day* en tal o cual día; *at such and such a time* a tal hora ‖ *such as* como; *a friend such as Peter* un amigo como Pedro; *books such as these* libros como éstos ‖ *such as it is* tal y como es, tal cual ‖ *such is life* así es la vida ‖ *until such time as* hasta que.
◆ *pron* los que, las que; *such as laugh today* los que se ríen hoy; *such as heard the news came* los que se enteraron de la noticia vinieron ‖ todo lo que; *I will give you such as I have* te daré todo lo que tenga ‖ lo que; *the castle, such of it as remained, was beautiful* lo que quedaba del castillo era muy bonito ‖ esto, éste, ésta; *such is my opinion* ésta es mi opinión ‖ (cosas, gente, etc.) de este tipo *or* clase, cosas similares, gente similar; *he plays football, hockey and such* juega al fútbol, hockey y deportes similares; *he knows bishops, priests and such* conoce obispos, curas y gente de este tipo ‖ *as such* en sí, de por sí, como tal; *the book as such was not bad* el libro de por sí no era malo; como tal; *he was a foreigner and they treated him as such* era un extranjero y le trataron como tal.
◆ *adv* tan; *such a pretty girl!* ¡una chica tan guapa!; *not such a happy person as I imagined* una persona no tan feliz como pensaba ‖ *such a long time ago* hace tanto tiempo.

suchlike [-laik] *adj* de este tipo, de esta clase, de esta índole, semejante, similar; *he plays football, rugby and suchlike games* juega al fútbol, al rugby y a deportes de este tipo.
◆ *n* cosas *f pl or* gente *f* de este tipo *or* de esta clase *or* de esta índole, cosas *f pl* similares, gente *f* similar; *tramps, beggars and suchlike* vagabundos, mendigos y gente de esta clase; *peas, beans and suchlike* guisantes, judías y cosas similares.

suck [sʌk] *n* succión *f* ‖ chupada *f*, sorbo *m* (action or noise) ‖ mamada *f* (of babies).

suck [sʌk] *vt* sorber (a liquid) ‖ aspirar (air, dust) ‖ absorber, chupar; *roots suck water from the earth* las raíces absorben el agua de la tierra ‖ chupar (orange, thumb, sweet, pipe, blood, etc.) ‖ chupar, mamar (babies) ‖ aspirar, sacar (with a pump) ‖ ZOOL libar (butterflies, bees, etc.) ‖ — *to suck one's fingers* chuparse los dedos ‖ FAM *to suck s.o. dry* chuparle a uno la sangre.
◆ *vi* chupar; *to suck at a sweet* chupar un caramelo ‖ dar chupadas ‖ mamar (babies) ‖ aspirar (pump, vacuum cleaner).
◆ *phr v* ***to suck down*** tragar (whirpool, sand) ‖ ***to suck in*** tragar (whirpool, sand) | aspirar (aire) | FIG absorber ‖ ***to suck out*** chupar; *to suck out poison from a wound* chupar el veneno de una herida ‖ ***to suck up*** absorber ‖ — FAM *to suck up to* hacer la pelotilla a, dar coba a.

sucker [-ə*] *n* chupador, ra; chupón, ona (person that sucks) ‖ ZOOL ventosa *f* (of leech, of octopus) | trompa *f* (of insects) | lechón *m* (sucking pig) ‖ BOT chupón *m*, mamón *m* (of plant roots) | retoño *m*, vástago *m* (shoot) ‖ TECH émbolo *m* (piston) | tubo *m* de aspiración (pipe) ‖ FAM primo *m* (simpleton) | novato *m*, primerizo *m* (beginner) ‖ US pirulí *m*, chupón *m* (lollipop).

suckfish [-fiʃ] *n* ZOOL rémora *f*.

sucking [-iŋ] *adj* de leche (animals) ‖ lechal (lamb) ‖ de pecho (child) ‖ *sucking pig* lechón *m*, cochinillo *m* de leche.

suckle ['sʌkl] *vt* amamantar a, dar de mamar a, dar el pecho a, criar a.

suckling ['sʌkliŋ] *n* cría *f* (animal) ‖ lactante *m* (child) ‖ lactancia *f*, crianza *f* (act).

sucre ['suːkrə] *n* sucre *m* (money of Ecuador).

sucrose ['sjuːkrəus] *n* sucrosa *f*, sacarosa *f*.

suction ['sʌkʃən] *n* succión *f*, aspiración *f* (of liquid) ‖ aspiración *f* (of hair) ‖ succión *f* (sucking force).
◆ *adj* de succión, aspirante, de aspiración.

suction pump [-pʌmp] *n* bomba *f* aspirante.

suction valve [-vælv] *n* válvula *f* de aspiración.

Sudan [su'dɑːn] *pr n* GEOGR Sudán *m*.

Sudanese [ˌsuːdə'niːz] *adj/n* sudanés, esa ‖ *the Sudanese* los sudaneses.

sudarium [sjuː'dɛəriəm] *n* REL sudario *m*.
— OBSERV El plural de *sudarium* es *sudaria*.

sudation [sjuː'deiʃən] *n* sudación *f*.

sudatorium [ˌsjuːdə'tɔːriəm] *n* sudadero *m*.
— OBSERV El plural de *sudatorium* es *sudatoria*.

sudatory ['sjuːdətəri] *adj* sudorífico, ca.
◆ *n* sudadero *m*.

sudden ['sʌdn] *adj* repentino, na; súbito, ta ‖ inesperado, da; imprevisto, ta (unexpected); *a sudden bend in the road* una curva inesperada en la carretera ‖ brusco, ca ‖ — *all of a sudden* de repente, de pronto; *all of a sudden he remembered* de repente se acordó ‖ *to die a sudden death* morir de repente, fallecer de muerte repentina.

suddenly [-li] *adv* repentinamente, súbitamente, de repente, de pronto.

suddenness [-nis] *n* lo repentino, lo súbito ‖ lo imprevisto ‖ brusquedad *f*.

Sudetes [su'dit,iz]; **Sudeten Mountains** [suː'deitn'mauntinz] *pl n* GEOGR Sudetes *m*, montes *m* de los Sudetes.

sudorific ['sjuːdə'rifik] *adj* sudorífico, ca.
◆ *n* sudorífico *m*.

sudoriparous ['sjuːdə'ripərəs] *adj* sudoríparo, ra.

suds [sʌdz] *pl n* espuma *f sing* de jabón, jabonaduras *f* (soapy water) ‖ FAM cerveza *f sing* (beer).

sudsy [-i] *adj* espumoso, sa; jabonoso, sa.

sue [sjuː] *vt* JUR demandar, poner pleito a (to bring legal action against); *to sue s.o. for damages* demandar a alguien por daños y perjui-

cios | presentar una demanda a [un tribunal] (to petition a court for justice) || cortejar (a young lady).
◆ *vi* JUR entablar acción judicial || hacer la corte (to woo) || — *to sue for* pedir; *to sue for peace* pedir la paz; suplicar; *to sue for mercy* suplicar misericordia || *to sue for divorce* solicitar el divorcio, presentar demanda de divorcio || *to sue to s.o. for sth.* pedir algo a alguien.

suède; *US* **suede** [sweid] *n* ante *m* (for shoes, for coats, etc.) || cabritilla *f* (for gloves).

suet [sjuit] *n* sebo *m*.

suety [-i] *adj* grasiento, ta; seboso, sa.

Suez ['suiz] *pr n* GEOGR Suez || *Suez canal* canal *m* de Suez.

suffer ['sʌfə*] *vt* sufrir; *to suffer punishment, injury* sufrir un castigo, una herida; *to suffer a loss, a defeat* sufrir una pérdida, una derrota || sentir, padecer; *are you suffering any pain?* ¿siente algún dolor? || tolerar, permitir; *he will suffer no insult* no tolera ningún insulto || soportar, aguantar; *I had to suffer her insults* tuve que soportar sus insultos || permitir, dejar; *suffer the little children to come unto me* dejad que los niños se acerquen a mí.
◆ *vi* sufrir; *to suffer acutely* sufrir mucho || ser dañado, da (to be damaged) || — *to suffer from* padecer de, padecer; *to suffer from neuralgia* padecer de neuralgia; adolecer de; *Madrid suffers from overcrowding* Madrid adolece de superpoblación || *you'll suffer for it!* ¡pagarás las consecuencias!

sufferable [-rəbl] *adj* soportable, tolerable.

sufferance [-rəns] *n* consentimiento *m* tácito || tolerancia *f*; *on sufferance* por tolerancia || *beyond sufferance* intolerable.

sufferer [-rə*] *n* víctima *f* (victim) || MED paciente *m* & *f*, enfermo, ma (patient).

suffering [-riŋ] *n* sufrimiento *m*, padecimiento *m* || dolor *m* (pain).
◆ *adj* que sufre, que padece || MED doliente, enfermo, ma.

suffice [sə'fais] *vt* ser suficiente (a alguien), bastar (a alguien); *a meal a day suffices him* una comida al día le basta || satisfacer; *to suffice s.o.'s needs* satisfacer las necesidades de uno.
◆ *vi* ser suficiente, bastar || *suffice it to say* basta con decir.

sufficiency [sə'fiʃənsi] *n* cantidad *f* suficiente; *a sufficiency of bread* la cantidad suficiente de pan || lo suficiente; *to eat a sufficiency* comer lo suficiente || eficacia *f*; *the sufficiency of the law* la eficacia de la ley || desahogo *m*, holgura *f*, buena posición *f* económica (wealth).

sufficient [sə'fiʃənt] *adj* suficiente, bastante.

suffix ['sʌfiks] *n* GRAMM sufijo *m* || MATH subíndice *m* (subindex).

suffix ['sʌfiks] *vt* GRAMM añadir como sufijo.

suffocate ['sʌfəkeit] *vt* asfixiar, ahogar (to kill) || sofocar, asfixiar, ahogar (to hinder the respiration of) || FIG ahogar (to oppress).
◆ *vi* asfixiarse, ahogarse || *the heat was suffocating* el calor era sofocante.

suffocation ['sʌfə'keiʃən] *n* asfixia *f*, ahogo *m*.

suffragan ['sʌfrəgən] *n* REL obispo *m* sufragáneo.
◆ *adj* sufragáneo, a.

suffrage ['sʌfridʒ] *n* sufragio *m* (vote); *election by universal suffrage* elección por sufragio universal || derecho *m* al voto (right to vote) || aprobación *f*, asentimiento *m* (vote of assent).

suffragette ['sʌfrə'dʒet] *n* sufragista *f*.

suffuse [sə'fju:z] *vt* cubrir (to cover); *a blush suffused her cheeks* el rubor cubría sus mejillas || bañar; *the room was suffused with light* la habitación estaba bañada de luz; *suffused with tears* bañado en lágrimas || difundirse por, extenderse por (to spread over).

suffusion [sə'fju:ʒən] *n* difusión *f* || rubor *m* (blush).

sugar ['ʃugə*] *n* azúcar *m* or *f*; *brown sugar* azúcar moreno; *to put sugar in* echar azúcar a; *a lump of sugar* un terrón de azúcar || terrón *m* (lump) || — *cane sugar* azúcar de caña || *castor sugar* azúcar extrafino || *icing sugar* azúcar en polvo || *loaf sugar* azúcar de pilón || *lump sugar* azúcar de cortadillo *or* en terrones || *refined sugar* azúcar refinado || FIG & FAM *to be all sugar* ser meloso.
◆ *adj* azucarero, ra; del azúcar; *sugar industry* industria azucarera.

sugar ['ʃugə*] *vt* azucarar, poner *or* echar azúcar a *or* en (to sweeten with sugar) || echar azúcar a (to sprinkle with sugar) || FIG endulzar, suavizar (to make more agreeable) || FIG *to sugar the pill* dorar la píldora.
◆ *vi* granularse (to become granular).

sugar almond [-'ɑ:mənd] *n* peladilla *f*.

sugar basin [-'beisn] *n* azucarero *m*.

sugar beet [-bi:t] *n* remolacha *f* azucarera.

sugar bowl [-bəul] *n* azucarero *m*.

sugar candy [-'kændi] *n* azúcar *m* candi, azúcar *m* cande.

sugarcane [-kein] *n* caña *f* de azúcar.

sugarcoat [-kəut] *vt* garapiñar (nuts) || cubrir con una capa de azúcar (food, sweets, etc.) || *US* FIG endulzar, suavizar (to make more agreeable) | dorar (the pill).

sugarcoated [-'kəutid] *adj* garapiñado, da (nuts) || cubierto con una capa de azúcar (food, sweets).

sugar crop [-krɔp] *n* zafra *f*.

sugar daddy [-'dædi] *n* FAM amigo *m* [viejo].

sugarhouse [-haus] *n* *US* azucarera *f*, fábrica *f* de azúcar.

sugariness [-rinis] *n* dulzura *f* (sweetness) || FIG melosidad *f*.

sugarloaf [-ləuf] *n* pilón *m*, pan *m* de azúcar.

sugar maple [-'meipl] *n* arce *m* azucarero.

sugar mill [-mil] *n* trapiche *m*, ingenio *m* de azúcar.

sugarplum [-plʌm] *n* confite *m*.

sugar refinery [-ri'fainəri] *n* refinería *f* de azúcar.

sugar tongs [-tɔŋz] *pl n* tenacillas *f* para el azúcar.

sugary [-ri] *adj* azucarado, da (like or containing sugar) || dulce (sweet) || granular (granular) || FIG meloso, sa (excessively sweet in manners).

suggest [sə'dʒest] *vt* sugerir, proponer; *to suggest a different plan* sugerir un proyecto distinto; *I suggest that you go now* sugiero que vayas ahora || proponer; *to suggest s.o. for a post* proponer a alguien para un puesto || sugerir, hacer pensar en, evocar; *the symphony suggests a sunrise* la sinfonía evoca una salida del sol || dar; *that suggested to me the idea of travelling* esto me dio la idea de viajar || inspirar; *my success suggested me further efforts* mi éxito me inspiró la continuación de mis esfuerzos || aconsejar (to advise) || indicar; *from Malaga as his accent suggests* malagueño como su acento indica || insinuar (to hint); *are you suggesting that I'm lying?* ¿estás insinuando que miento? || *a solution suggested itself to me* se me ocurrió una solución.

suggestibility [sʌdʒesti'biliti] *n* sugestibilidad *f*.

suggestible [sʌ'dʒestibl] *adj* sugestionable; *a suggestible person* una persona sugestionable || que puede proponerse (thing).

suggestion [sə'dʒestʃən] *n* sugerencia *f*; *to make a suggestion* hacer una sugerencia || sugestión *f* (a suggesting) || indicación *f*, indicaciones *f pl*; *you will follow my suggestion* seguirá mis indicaciones; *at the suggestion of you* por indicación suya || insinuación *f* (hint) || idea *f* (idea) || FIG tinte *m*, matiz *m* (nuance) | sombra *f*, traza *f* (trace) | poquitín *m*, pizca *f* (bit) || sugestión *f* (in psychology); *hypnotic suggestion* sugestión hipnótica || *your suggestion was that* usted proponía que.

suggestive [sə'dʒestiv] *adj* sugestivo, va (stimulating ideas) || evocador, ra; *suggestive of a sunrise* evocador de una salida del sol || sugestivo, va; insinuante (insinuating) || *to be suggestive of sth.* evocar algo, hacer pensar en algo.

suggestiveness [-nis] *n* lo sugestivo, lo insinuante.

suicidal [sjui'saidl] *adj* suicida; *suicidal tendencies* tendencias suicidas || FAM *it's suicidal to* es un suicidio.

suicide ['sjuisaid] *n* suicida *m* & *f* (person) || suicidio *m* (act) || — *to attempt suicide* atentar contra su vida || *to commit suicide* suicidarse.

suint [swint] *n* churre *m*, grasa *f* de la lana.

suit [sju:t] *n* traje *m* (clothes, uniform, etc.); *ready-made suit* traje de confección || traje *m* sastre (woman's) || conjunto *m*, juego *m* (set, series) || palo *m* (in cards) || JUR pleito *m*; *to bring a suit* entablar un pleito || petición *f* (petition, request); *at the suit of* a petición de || galanteo *m*, cortejo *m* (courtship) || MAR velamen *m* (sails) || — *bathing suit* bañador *m*, traje de baño || *suit of armour* armadura *f* [completa] || *suit of clothes* traje || *to follow suit* servir, jugar del mismo palo (in cards), seguir el ejemplo (to follow the example set) || *two-piece suit* conjunto.

suit [sju:t] *vt* convenir, venir bien a; *would it suit you to come tomorrow?* ¿te convendría venir mañana?; *that suits me best* eso me viene mejor || adaptarse a, ajustarse a, acomodarse a; *that suits my plans* esto se ajusta a mis planes || ir bien a, sentar bien a; *green suits you* el verde le sienta bien || satisfacer, agradar (to please); *does the program suit you?* ¿le agrada el programa? || adaptar al gusto; *try to suit the play to the audience* intente adaptar la comedia al gusto del público || — *he can be very cruel if it suits him* puede ser muy cruel cuando quiere || *he is not suited for engineering* no ha nacido para ingeniero || *he is suited for this job* es la persona adecuada para este trabajo || FIG *it suits me to a T* me viene de perlas || *to be suited with* haber encontrado (a servant, a situation) || *to be well suited* formar una buena pareja (two people) || *to suit o.s.* hacer lo que uno quiere || *with a hat to suit* con un sombrero haciendo juego.
◆ *vi* convenir, ir bien.

suitability [sju:tə'biliti] *n* conveniencia *f*, oportunidad *f*; *the suitability of a certain date* la conveniencia de cierta fecha || oportunidad *f* (of a remark, of an answer, etc.) || compatibilidad *f* (of two people) || aptitud *f*; *the suitability of a political candidate* la aptitud de un candidato político.

suitable ['sju:təbl] *adj* conveniente, oportuno, na; idóneo, a (convenient) || oportuno, na; adecuado, da; apropiado, da (appropriate) || compatible (two people) || apto, ta (apt) || satisfactorio, ria (satisfactory).

suitcase ['sju:tkeis] *n* maleta *f*.

suite [swi:t] *n* juego *m*; *a bedroom suite* un juego de dormitorio || «suite» *f*, apartamento *m* (in a hotel) || séquito *m*, cortejo *m* (of a king) || comitiva *f*, acompañantes *m pl* (of a minister, etc.) || serie *f*, sucesión *f* (series) || MUS «suite» *f*.

suiting ['sju:tiŋ] *n* tela *f* [para trajes] (material).

suitor ['sju:tə*] *n* JUR demandante *m* & *f* || galán *m*, pretendiente *m* (pretender, lover).

sulcate ['sʌlkeit]; **sulcated** [-id] *adj* ANAT surcado, da.

sulcus ['sʌlkəs] *n* ANAT surco *m*.
— OBSERV El plural de *sulcus* es *sulci*.

sulfa drug ['sʌlfə'drʌg] *n* US MED sulfamida *f*.

sulfate ['sʌlfeit] *n* US CHEM sulfato *m*.

sulfate ['sʌlfeit] *vt* US sulfatar.

sulfating [-iŋ] *n* US ⟶ **sulphating.**

sulfide ['sʌlfaid] *n* US CHEM sulfuro *m*.

sulfite ['sʌlfait] *n* US CHEM sulfito *m*.

sulfonamide [sʌl'fɔnəmaid] *n* US MED sulfamida *f*.

sulfur ['sʌlfə*] *n/vt* US ⟶ **sulphur.**

sulfurate ['sʌlfjurit] *adj* US CHEM sulfurado, da.

sulfurate ['sʌlfjureit] *vt* US ⟶ **sulphur.**

sulfuration [sʌlfju'reiʃən] *n* US ⟶ **sulphuration.**

sulfurator ['sʌlfjureitə*] *n* US AGR sulfatador *m*.

sulfureous [sʌl'fjuəriəs] *adj* US sulfuroso, sa.

sulfuretted ['sʌlfjuretid] *adj* US CHEM sulfurado, da.

sulfuric [sʌl'fjuərik] *adj* US sulfúrico, ca.

sulfurize ['sʌlfjəraiz] *vt* US ⟶ **sulphur.**

sulfurous ['sʌlfərəs] *adj* US ⟶ **sulphurous.**

sulfury ['sʌlfəri] *adj* US azufrado, da.

sulk [sʌlk] *n* enfado *m*, enfurruñamiento *m*, mal humor *m* || *to be in the sulks, to have the sulks* estar enfadado *or* enfurruñado, poner mala cara, poner cara larga.

sulk [sʌlk] *vi* estar malhumorado, enfurruñarse, poner mala cara, poner cara larga.

sulkily [-ili] *adv* con mal humor.

sulkiness [-inis] *n* mal humor *m*.

sulky [-i] *adj* malhumorado, da (cross) || resentido, da (resentful) || triste (gloomy) || *to be sulky with* poner mala cara a, poner cara larga a (s.o.).

sullage ['sʌlidʒ] *n* barro *m*, cieno *m* (mud) || escoria *f* (of molten metal) || aguas *f pl* residuales (sewage).

sullen ['sʌlən] *adj* hosco, ca; ceñudo, da; malhumorado, da (unsociable) || triste, taciturno, na (sad) || resentido, da (resentful) || triste, tétrico, ca; lúgubre, sombrío, a (place) || plomizo, za (sky) || amenazador, ra (cloud) || repropio, pia (horse) || lento, ta (slow); *sullen pace* paso lento.

sullenness [-nis] *n* malhumor *m* || tristeza *f* || taciturnidad *f* || resentimiento *m*.

sully ['sʌli] *vt* manchar, mancillar.

sulpha drug ['sʌlfə,drʌg] *n* MED sulfamida *f*.

sulphate ['sʌlfeit] *n* CHEM sulfato *m*.

sulphate ['sʌlfeit] *vt* sulfatar.

sulphating; US **sulfating** [-iŋ] *n* CHEM sulfatación *f*, sulfatado *m* || *sulphating machine* sulfatadora *f*.

sulphide ['sʌlfaid] *n* CHEM sulfuro *m*.

sulphite ['sʌlfait] *n* CHEM sulfito *m*.

sulphonamide [sʌl'fɔnəmaid] *n* MED sulfamida *f*.

sulphur; US **sulfur** ['sʌlfə*] *n* azufre *m* || *sulphur water* agua sulfurosa.

sulphur; US **sulfur** ['sʌlfə*]; **sulphurate**; US **sulfurate** ['sʌlfjureit]; **sulphurize**; US **sulfurize** ['sʌfəraiz] *vt* azufrar || CHEM sulfurar.

sulphurate ['sʌlfjurit] *adj* CHEM sulfurado, da.

sulphuration; US **sulfuration** [sʌlfju'reiʃən] *n* azufrado *m*, azuframiento *m* || CHEM sulfuración *f* || AGR sulfatado *m*, sulfurado *m*.

sulphurator ['sʌlfjureitə*] *n* AGR sulfatador *m*.

sulphureous [sʌlfjuəriəs] *adj* sulfuroso, sa.

sulphuretted ['sʌlfjuretid] *adj* CHEM sulfurado, da.

sulphuric [sʌl'fjuərik] *adj* sulfúrico, ca.

sulphurize ['sʌlfəraiz] *vt* ⟶ **sulphur.**

sulphurous; US **sulfurous** ['sʌlfərəs] *adj* sulfuroso, sa || FIG acalorado, da.

sulphury ['sʌlfəri] *adj* azufrado, da.

sultan ['sʌltən] *n* sultán *m*.

sultana [sʌl'tɑːnə] *n* sultana *f* (wife of a sultan) || pasa *f* de Esmirna (raisin).

sultanate ['sʌltənit] *n* sultanato *m*, sultanía *f*.

sultriness ['sʌltrinis] *n* bochorno *m*, calor *m* sofocante (of weather) || FIG sensualidad *f*.

sultry ['sʌltri] *adj* bochornoso, sa; de bochorno, sofocante (weather) || FIG sensual.

sum [sʌm] *n* suma *f*, cantidad *f*; *a sum of money* una cantidad de dinero || total *m*, suma *f* (the whole amount, entirety) || MATH suma *f*, adición *f* (addition) | cálculo *m*; *a quick mental sum* un cálculo mental rápido || — *in sum* en suma, en resumen, en resumidas cuentas || *the sum and substance of the matter* el fondo de la cuestión.
◆ *pl* aritmética *f sing* (arithmetic).

sum [sʌm] *vt* sumar || *to sum up* sumar (to add up), resumir, recapitular (to summarize), evaluar (to evaluate) || *to sum up I would say that* para resumir *or* en resumen yo diría que.
◆ *vi* *to sum to* sumar, ascender a (to total).

sumach; **sumac** ['suːmæk] *n* BOT zumaque *m* (shrub).

Sumerian [sju'miəriən] *adj/n* sumerio, ria.

summarily ['sʌmərili] *adv* sumariamente.

summarize ['sʌməraiz] *vt* resumir.

summary ['sʌməri] *adj* sumario, ria || US *summary court-martial* consejo de guerra sumarísimo.
◆ *n* resumen *m*.

summation [sʌ'meiʃən] *n* adición *f*, suma *f* || total *m*, suma *f* total || resumen *m* (summary) || recapitulación *f*.

summer ['sʌmə*] *n* verano *m*, estío *m* || ARCH viga *f* maestra || — FIG *a girl of twenty summers* una chica de veinte abriles || *Indian Summer* veranillo *m* de San Martín || *in summer* en verano, durante el verano.
◆ *adj* veraniego, ga; estival.

summer ['sʌmə*] *vt* pastar durante el verano (cattle).
◆ *vi* veranear, pasar el verano.

summer holidays [-'hɔlidiz] *pl n* vacaciones *f* de verano, veraneo *m sing*.

summerhouse [-haus] *n* cenador *m*, glorieta *f*.

summer house [-haus] *n* casa *f* de verano.

summer lightning [-'laitniŋ] *n* fucilazo *m*.

summer resort [-ri'zɔːt] *n* lugar *m* de veraneo.

summersault [-sɔːlt] *n/vi* ⟶ **somersault.**

summer solstice [-'sɔlstis] *n* solsticio *m* de verano.

summer stock [-stɔk] *n* US THEATR repertorio *m* de obras representadas en verano.

summer time [-'taim] *n* hora *f* de verano.

summertime [-taim] *n* verano *m*, estío *m*.

summery [-ri] *adj* veraniego, ga; estival.

summing-up ['sʌmiŋ'ʌp] *n* resumen *m*.
— OBSERV El plural de *summing-up* es *summings-up*.

summit ['sʌmit] *n* cima *f*, cumbre *f* (of a hill, of a mountain) || FIG cima *f*, apogeo *m*, cumbre *f*; *to reach the summit of honours* alcanzar la cima de los honores || conferencia *f* de alto nivel *or* en la cumbre (conference) || *summit conference* conferencia de alto nivel *or* en la cumbre.

summon ['sʌmən] *vt* convocar (a meeting); *to summon parliament* convocar el parlamento || pedir (aid) || JUR citar, emplazar || FIG evocar; *a picture that summons up many happy memories* un cuadro que evoca muchos recuerdos felices | reunir; *to summon one's strength* reunir sus fuerzas || llamar (to call a servant, s.o.) || MIL intimar (a town to surrender) || *to summon up one's courage* armarse de valor.

summons ['sʌmənz] *n* JUR citación *f* judicial, requerimiento *m* judicial, emplazamiento *m*, auto *m* de comparecencia || llamada *f*, llamamiento *m* (call) || convocatoria *f* (convocation) || *to take out a summons against s.o.* citar a uno ante la justicia.
— OBSERV El plural de *summons* es *summonses*.

summons ['sʌmənz] *vt* JUR citar ante la justicia.

sump [sʌmp] *n* AUT cárter *m* || MIN sumidero *m* (of mine) || letrina *f*, pozo *m* negro (cesspool) || FIG & FAM vertedero *m*, muladar *m*, estercolero *m*.

sumpter [-tə*] *n* bestia *f* de carga, acémila *f*.

sumptuary [-tjuəri] *adj* suntuario, ria; *sumptuary law* ley suntuaria.

sumptuous [-tjuəs] *adj* suntuoso, sa.

sumptuousness [-tjuəsnis] *n* suntuosidad *f*.

sum total ['sʌm'təutl] *n* suma *f* total, total *m* || FIG *and that is the sum total of his experience* y ésa es toda su experiencia.

sun [sʌn] *n* sol *m*; *setting, midnight sun* sol poniente, de medianoche; *in summertime the sun rises early and sets late* en verano el sol sale temprano y se pone tarde || — *from sun to sun* de sol a sol || FIG *there is everything under the sun* hay de todo como en botica | *there is nothing new under the sun* no hay nada nuevo bajo el sol || *the rising sun* el sol naciente || *the sun is shining today* hoy hace sol || *the Sun King* el Rey Sol || *to bask in the sun* tomar el sol || FIG *to have a place in the sun* tener una buena situación || *to sit in the sun* estar sentado al sol || *touch of the sun* quemadura *f* de sol || FIG *under the sun* en el mundo || MAR *with the sun* en el sentido de las agujas de un reloj.
◆ *adj* del sol, solar.

sun [sʌn] *vt* exponer al sol || *to sun o.s.* tomar el sol.

sunbaked [-beikt] *adj* curtido por el sol (person) || quemado por el sol (place) || secado al sol (brick).

sunbathe [-beið] *vi* tomar el sol.

sunbather [-'beiðə*] *n* persona *f* que toma el sol.

sunbathing [-'beiðiŋ] *n* baños *m pl* de sol.

sunbeam [-biːm] *n* rayo *m* de sol.

sunbed ['sʌnbed] *n* tumbona *f* || cabina *f* de rayos UVA.

sunblind [-blaind] *n* toldo *m* (awning) || persiana *f* (venetian blind).

sunbonnet [-'bɔnit] *n* sombrero *m* para protegerse del sol.

sunburn [-bəːn] *n* quemadura *f* de sol (burn) || bronceado *m* (tan).

sunburnt [-bəːnt] *adj* bronceado, da; tostado por el sol (tanned) || quemado por el sol (burnt).

sundae ['sʌndei] *n* helado *m* con frutas y nueces.

Sunda Islands ['sʌndə'ailəndz] *pl n* GEOGR islas *f* de la Sonda.

Sunday ['sʌndi] *n* domingo *m*; *Easter Sunday* Domingo de Resurrección; *Palm Sunday* Do-

mingo de Ramos; *Shrove Sunday* Domingo de Carnaval; *Low Sunday* Domingo de Cuasimodo || — FIG *never in a month of Sundays* nunca || *on Sunday* el domingo; *I shall come on Sunday* vendré el domingo.
◆ *adj* del domingo, dominical (rest, mass) || dominguero, ra (clothes, etc.).

Sunday best [-best] *n* traje *m* de los domingos, trapitos *m pl* de cristianar.

Sunday-go-to-meeting [-ˌgəutəˈmiːtiŋ] *adj* US dominguero, ra; del domingo.

Sunday school [-skuːl] *n* REL catequesis *f*.

sun deck [ˈsʌndek] *n* MAR cubierta *f* superior || terraza *f* donde se toma el sol (terrace).

sunder [ˈsʌndə*] *vt* partir (to tear apart) || separar (to separate).
◆ *vi* partirse.

sundial [ˈsʌndaiəl] *n* reloj *m* de sol.

sun dog [ˈsʌndɔg] *n* parhelio *m*.

sundown [ˈsʌndaun] *n* puesta *f* del sol, ocaso *m* || anochecer *m*; *at sundown* al anochecer.

sundress [ˈsʌndres] *n* traje *m* de playa.

sun-dried [ˈsʌndraid] *adj* secado al sol.

sundries [ˈsʌndriz] *pl n* miscelánea *f sing*, artículos *m* diversos || gastos *m* diversos (expenses).

sundry [ˈsʌndri] *adj* diversos, sas; varios, rias; *sundry objects* diversos objetos || *all and sundry* todos sin excepción.

sunfast [ˈsʌnfɑːst] *adj* resistente al sol.

sunfish [ˈsʌnfiʃ] *n* ZOOL pez *m* luna.

sunflower [ˈsʌnˈflauə*] *n* BOT girasol *m*.

sung [sʌŋ] *pp* → **sing.**

sunglasses [ˈsʌnˌglɑːsiz] *pl n* gafas *f* de sol [*AMER* anteojos *m* de sol].

sunglow [ˈsʌngləu] *n* arrebol *m*.

sun-god [ˈsʌngɔd] *n* dios *m* del Sol.

sunhat [ˈsʌnhæt] *n* pamela *f*, sombrero *m* para el sol.

sun helmet [ˈsʌnˈhelmit] *n* salacot *m*.

sunk [sʌŋk] *pp* → **sink.**

sunken [-ən] *adj* hundido, da (ships, ground, eyes, cheeks, etc.).

sunlamp [ˈsʌnlæmp] *n* lámpara *f* solar, lámpara *f* de rayos ultravioletas || CINEM foco *m*.

sunless [ˈsʌnlis] *adj* sin sol.

sunlight [ˈsʌnlait] *n* luz *f* del sol, sol *m*; *in the sunlight* al sol, a la luz del sol.

sunlit [ˈsʌnlit] *adj* iluminado por el sol.

Sunna; Sunnah [ˈsunə] *n* REL sunna *f*.

Sunni [ˈsuni]; **Sunnite** [ˈsunait] *n* REL sunnita *m*.

sunny [ˈsʌni] *adj* del sol; *a sunny day* un día de sol || soleado, da; *a sunny place* un lugar soleado || iluminado por el sol (sunlit) || expuesto al sol || FIG risueño, ña; sonriente; *a sunny future* un porvenir risueño || — FIG *a sunny smile* una sonrisa alegre || *it is sunny today* hoy hace sol || FIG *to see the sunny side of things* ver siempre el lado bueno de las cosas.

sun parlour; US **sun parlor** [ˈsʌnˈpɑːlə*] *n* solario *m*, solana *f*.

sunproof [ˈsʌnpruːf] *adj* inalterable a los rayos de sol, resistente al sol.

sunray [ˈsʌnrei] *n* rayo *m* de sol.
◆ *adj* *sunray lamp* lámpara *f* solar, lámpara *f* de rayos ultravioletas || *sunray treatment* helioterapia *f*.

sunrise [ˈsʌnraiz] *n* salida *f* del sol || *I work from sunrise to sunset* trabajo de sol a sol.

sun room [ˈsʌnrum] *n* solario *m*, solana *f*.

sunset [ˈsʌnset] *n* puesta *f* del sol, ocaso *m* || FIG ocaso *m* (of life).

sunshade [ˈsʌnʃeid] *n* sombrilla *f*, quitasol *m* (parasol) || toldo *m* (awning) || PHOT parasol *m*.

sunshine [ˈsʌnʃain] *n* sol *m*; *it is rather pleasant to be here in the sunshine* es muy agradable estar aquí al sol; *in the bright sunshine* en pleno sol || FIG alegría *f*; *bring a little sunshine into the life of an old man* da un poco de alegría a la vida de un anciano || *hours of sunshine* horas *f* de sol.

sunspot [ˈsʌnspɔt] *n* mancha *f* solar.

sunstroke [ˈsʌnstrəuk] *n* insolación *f* [*AMER* asoleada *f*].

sunsuit [ˈsʌnsjuːt] *n* traje *m* de playa.

suntan [ˈsʌntæn] *n* bronceado *m* || *to have a suntan* estar bronceado, estar moreno || *suntan cream, lotion, oil* crema *f*, loción *f* bronceadora, aceite *m* bronceador.

suntan [ˈsʌntæn] *vi* broncearse, ponerse muy moreno.

suntanned [-d] *adj* bronceado, da; moreno, na.

suntrap [ˈsʌntræp] *n* sitio *m* muy soleado.

sunup [ˈsʌnʌp] *n* salida *f* del sol.

sunwise [ˈsʌnwaiz] *adj/adv* en el sentido de las agujas de un reloj.

sup [sʌp] *n* sorbo *m* (sip).

sup [sʌp] *vt* sorber (to sip) || dar de cenar a, hacer cenar (to provide with supper).
◆ *vi* cenar (to have supper).

super [ˈsjuːpə*] *adj* FAM estupendo, da; formidable, de primera categoría.
◆ *n* FAM tamaño *m* muy grande (size) | calidad *f* extrafina (quality) | súper *f*, supercarburante *m*, plomo *m*, gasolina *f* súper (petrol) || parte *f* superior de una colmena (of beehive) || THEATR comparsa *m* & *f*, figurante *m* & *f* || CINEM extra *m* || superintendente *m* (superintendent) || segundo jefe *m*, subjefe *m* (of police).

superable [-rəbl] *adj* superable.

superabound [ˌsupərəˌbaund] *vi* superabundar, sobreabundar.

superabundance [ˈsjuːpərəˈbʌndəns] *n* superabundancia *f*, sobreabundancia *f*.

superabundant [ˈsjuːpərəˈbʌndənt] *adj* superabundante, sobreabundante.

superadd [ˈsjuːpərˈæd] *vt* sobreañadir.

superannuate [ˈsjuːpəˈrænjueit] *vt* jubilar (s.o.) || arrinconar, arrumbar (sth.).

superannuated [-id] *adj* jubilado, da (retired) || anticuado, da (out-of-date).

superannuation [ˈsjuːpəˈrænjuˈeiʃən] *n* jubilación *f* (retirement) || jubilación *f*, pensión *f* (pension).

superb [sjuˈpəːb] *adj* magnífico, ca; excelente, soberbio, bia.

supercargo [ˈsjuːpəˈkɑːgəu] *n* MAR sobrecargo *m*.
— OBSERV El plural de *supercargo* es *supercargoes* o *supercargos*.

supercharge [ˈsjuːpətʃɑːdʒ] *vt* TECH supercomprimir | sobrealimentar (motor).

supercharger [-ə*] *n* compresor *m*.

supercharging [-iŋ] *n* TECH supercompresión *f* | sobrealimentación *f* (of a motor).

superciliary [ˌsjuːpəˈsiliəri] *adj* superciliar; *superciliary arch* o *ridge* arco superciliar.

supercilious [ˈsjuːpəˈsiliəs] *adj* arrogante, desdeñoso, sa; altanero, ra.

superciliousness [-nis] *n* desdén *m*, arrogancia *f*, altanería *f*.

supercool [ˈsjuːpəkuːl] *vt* CHEM someter a la sobrefusión.

supercooling [-iŋ] *n* CHEM sobrefusión *f*.

superdominant [ˈsjuːpəˈdɔminənt] *n* MUS superdominante *f*.

supereminence [ˈsjuːpərˈeminəns] *n* supereminencia *f* (distinguished eminence).

supererogation [ˈsjuːpərˈerəˈgeiʃən] *n* supererogación *f*.

superexcellent [ˈsjuːpəerˈeksələnt] *adj* excelentísimo, ma.

superfetation [ˈsjuːpəfiːˈteiʃən] *n* superfetación *f*.

superficial [ˈsjuːpəˈfiʃəl] *adj* superficial; *superficial injury* herida superficial.

superficiality [ˌsjuːpəˈfiʃiˈæliti] *n* superficialidad *f*.

superficially [ˈsjuːpəˈfiʃəli] *adv* superficialmente.

superficies [ˈsjuːpəˈfiʃiːz] *inv n* superficie *f*.

superfine [ˈsjuːpəˈfain] *adj* superfino, na; extrafino, na || FIG refinado, da.

superfluity [ˈsjuːpəˈfluiti] *n* superfluidad *f* || exceso *m*, superabundancia *f* (excess).

superfluous [sjuˈpəːfluəs] *adj* superfluo, flua.

superfortress [ˈsjuːpəˌfɔːtris] *n* AVIAT superfortaleza *f*.

superheat [ˈsjuːpəhiːt] *n* sobrecalentamiento *m*, recalentamiento *m*.

superheat [ˈsjuːpəˈhit] *vt* sobrecalentar, recalentar.

superheater [-ə*] *n* sobrecalentador *m*, recalentador *m*.

superheterodyne [ˈsjuːpəˈhetərədain] *n* RAD superheterodino *m*.

superhighway [ˈsjuːpəˈhaiwei] *n* US autopista *f*.

superhuman [ˈsjuːpəˈhjuːmən] *adj* sobrehumano, na.

superhumeral [ˌsjupəˈhjuməral] *n* REL superhumeral *m*.

superimpose [ˈsjuːpərimˈpəuz] *vt* sobreponer, superponer.

superimposed [ˈsjuːpəimˈpəuzd] *adj* superpuesto, ta.

superimposition [ˈsjuːpərˌimpəˈziʃən] *n* superposición *f*.

superimpression [ˈsjuːpərimˈpreʃən] *n* PHOT & CINEM sobreimpresión *f*.

superincumbent [sjuːpərinˈkʌmbənt] *adj* superpuesto, ta; sobrepuesto, ta.

superintend [ˈsjuːpərinˈtend] *vt* supervisar (to supervise) || vigilar (to watch over).

superintendence [-əns]; **superintendency** [-i] *n* supervisión *f*, dirección *f* || superintendencia *f*.

superintendent [-ənt] *n* superintendente *m* || supervisor *m*, director *m* || vigilante *m* (custodian) || inspector *m*.

superior [sjuˈpriəriə*] *adj* superior; *he is superior to everybody* es superior a todos || superior, arrogante, altanero, ra (proud) || — GEOGR *Lake Superior* lago *m* Superior || *to be superior to flattery* estar muy por encima de la adulación.
◆ *n* superior *m* || REL superior *m*, superiora *f* || *mother superior* superiora *f*, madre *f* superiora.

superiority [sjuˈpiəriˈɔriti] *n* superioridad *f*; *superiority complex* complejo de superioridad.

superlative [sjuˈpəːlətiv] *adj* superlativo, va; supremo, ma || GRAMM superlativo, va || *to a superlative degree* en grado superlativo.
◆ *n* GRAMM superlativo *m* || *to speak in superlatives* deshacerse en elogios.

superlunary [ˌsjuːpəˈluːnəri] *adj* situado más allá de la luna || FIG celestial.

superman [ˈsjuːpəmæn] *n* superhombre *m*.
— OBSERV El plural de esta palabra es *supermen*.

supermarket [ˈsjuːpəˈmɑːkit] *n* supermercado *m*.

supernal [sju:'pə:nl] *adj* celestial || excelso, sa.

supernatant ['sju:pə'neitənt] *adj* sobrenadando, flotante.

supernatural ['sju:pə'nætʃrəl] *adj* sobrenatural; *supernatural force* fuerza sobrenatural || *the supernatural* lo sobrenatural.

supernumerary ['sju:pə'nju:mərəri] *adj* supernumerario, ria || superfluo, flua.

◆ *n* supernumerario, ria || THEATR figurante *m*, comparsa *m* & *f* || CINEM extra *m*.

superphosphate ['sju:pə'fɔsfeit] *n* CHEM superfosfato *m*.

superpose ['sju:pə'pəuz] *vt* superponer, sobreponer.

superposition ['sju:pəpə'ziʃən] *n* superposición *f*.

superpower ['sju:pə'pauə*] *n* superpotencia *f*.

supersaturate ['sju:pə'sætjureit] *vt* supersaturar, sobresaturar.

supersaturation ['sju:pə'sætju'reiʃən] *n* supersaturación *f*, sobresaturación *f*.

superscribe ['sju:pə'skraib] *vt* poner una indicación en (a parcel) || poner la dirección en (a letter).

superscription [,sju:pə'skripʃən] *n* inscripción *f*, indicación *f* || dirección *f* (on letter) || membrete *m* (on document).

supersede ['sju:pə'si:d] *vt* desbancar, suplantar; *buses have superseded trams* los autobuses han desbancado los tranvías || reemplazar, sustituir; *the written exam has been superseded by an oral exam* el examen escrito ha sido sustituido por un examen oral; *John has superseded Joseph as director* Juan ha sustituido a José como director.

supersensible ['sju:pə'sensibl] *adj* suprasensible.

supersensitive ['sju:pə'sensitiv] *adj* hipersensible (person) || PHOT muy sensible.

supersensory [,sju:pə'sensəri]; **supersensual** [,sju:pə'sensjəl] *adj* suprasensible.

supersession ['sju:pə:seʃən] *n* reemplazo *m*, sustitución *f* (replacement, substitution) || desbancamiento *m*, suplantación *f* (of a colleague, etc.).

supersonic ['sju:pə'sɔnik] *adj* supersónico, ca; *supersonic aircraft* avión supersónico.

supersonics [-s] *n* ciencia *f* que estudia los fenómenos supersónicos.

supersound ['sju:pə,saund] *n* ultrasonido *m*.

superstar ['sju:pəstɑ:*] *n* superestrella *f*, superstar *f*.

superstition ['sju:pə'stiʃən] *n* superstición *f*.

superstitious ['sju:pə'stiʃəs] *adj* supersticioso, sa.

superstratum ['sju:pə'strɑ:təm] *n* GEOL capa *f* superior.

— OBSERV El plural de esta palabra es *superstrata* o *superstratums*.

superstructure ['sju:pə'strʌktʃə*] *n* ARCH & MAR superestructura *f*.

supertanker ['sjupə,tæŋkə*] *n* petrolero *m* gigante.

supertax ['sju:pətæks] *n* sobretasa *f*, impuesto *m* adicional.

supervene ['sju:pə'vi:n] *vi* sobrevenir, ocurrir.

supervise ['sju:pəvaiz] *vt* supervisar.

supervision ['sju:pə'viʒən] *n* supervisión *f*.

supervisor ['sju:pəvaizə*] *n* supervisor, ra.

supervisory ['sju:pəvaizəri] *adj* de supervisión.

supervoltage ['sju:pə'vəultidʒ] *n* ELECTR sobretensión *f*, supervoltaje *m*.

supinating ['sjupineitiŋ] *adj* ANAT supinador.

supination [,sju:pi'neiʃən] *n* supinación *f*.

supinator ['sju:pineitə*] *n* ANAT supinador *m*.

supine [sju:pain] *adj* supino, na (face up) || FIG indolente, flojo, ja.

◆ *n* GRAMM supino *m* (in Latin).

supinely [-li] *adv* boca arriba, en posición supina || FIG indolentemente.

supineness [-nis] *n* indolencia *f*.

supper ['sʌpə*] *n* cena *f* || — REL *the Last Supper* la Última Cena | *the Lord's Supper* el pan eucarístico || *to have supper* cenar || *to have sth. for supper* cenar algo || *to stay to supper* quedarse a cenar.

suppertime [-taim] *n* hora *f* de cenar.

supplant [sə'plɑ:nt] *vt* suplantar (by cunning) || reemplazar, sustituir (to take the place of).

supplantation [səplɑ:n'teiʃən] *n* suplantación *f* || reemplazo *m*, sustitución *f*.

supplanter [sə'plɑ:ntə*] *n* suplantador, ra || sustituto, ta.

supple ['sʌpl] *adj* flexible; *supple stick* palo flexible || FIG flexible, adaptable | influenciable (easily influenced) | complaciente, obsequioso, sa (obsequious).

supplement ['sʌplimənt] *n* suplemento *m*, complemento *m* || MATH & PRINT suplemento *m*.

supplement ['sʌplimənt] *vt* suplir, completar (to add what lacks) || aumentar; *he has taken a second job to supplement his wages* ha tomado un segundo empleo para aumentar su sueldo.

supplementary ['sʌpli'mentəri] *adj* suplementario, ria; supletorio, ria; adicional || MATH *supplementary angles* ángulos suplementarios || *supplementary benefit* subsidio *m* estatal para gastos excepcionales [enfermedad, etc.].

suppleness ['sʌplnis] *n* flexibilidad *f* || FIG flexibilidad *f* | obsequiosidad *f*, complacencia *f*.

suppletory ['sʌplitəri] *adj* suplementario, ria; supletorio, ria.

suppliant ['sʌpliənt] *adj/n* suplicante.

supplicant ['sʌplikənt] *adj/n* suplicante.

supplicate ['sʌplikeit] *vt/vi* suplicar, rogar.

supplication ['sʌpli'keiʃən] *n* súplica *f*.

supplicatory ['sʌplikətəri] *adj* suplicante.

supplier [sə'plaiə*] *n* suministrador, ra; *the supplier of arms* el suministrador de armas || COMM proveedor, ra; abastecedor, ra.

supply [sə'plai] *n* oferta *f*; *the law of supply and demand* la ley de la oferta y la demanda || abastecimiento *m*, suministro *m* (act of supplying) || provisión *f*; *I need a supply of coal* necesito una provisión de carbón || suministro *m*; *electricity supply* suministro de electricidad || surtido *m* (stock); *we have a large supply of bathing costumes* tenemos un gran surtido de trajes de baño || — MIL *supply department* intendencia *f* || *supply teacher* profesor *m* suplente || *to be in short supply* escasear || *to lay in a supply of* hacer provisión de.

◆ *pl* suministros *m* || provisiones *f*, víveres *m* (stores, provisions) || MIL pertrechos *m*, municiones *f* (munitions) || material *m sing*, artículos *m* (for office, etc.) || créditos *m* (credits) || *Committee of Supplies* Comisión *f* del Presupuesto.

supply [sə'plai] *vt* proveer (to provide); *to supply s.o. with clothes* proveer a alguien de ropa || abastecer (*with* con), suministrar, aprovisionar (*with* con); *to supply a town with electricity* suministrar electricidad a una ciudad || COMM surtir || MIL avituallar, aprovisionar || alimentar (a machine) || dar, presentar; *to supply proof, an explanation* dar pruebas, una explicación || facilitar, proporcionar; *to supply a bus service* proporcionar un servicio de autobuses || proporcionarse (to procure); *when you go to university you must supply your own books* cuando uno va a la universidad tiene que proporcionarse sus propios libros || traer (to bring); *you will have to supply your own wine* tendrás que traer tu propio vino || poner; *I will supply the butter if you supply the cheese* yo pondré la mantequilla si tú pones el queso || satisfacer (a need) || reparar (an omission) || enjugar (a deficit) || corregir, remediar; *to supply a defect in manufacture* corregir un defecto de fabricación || cubrir (a vacancy) || suplir, sustituir (to supplement, to replace); *to supply a teacher who is ill* suplir a un profesor que está enfermo.

◆ *vi* sustituir (*for* a).

support [sə'pɔ:t] *n* apoyo *m*; *to give s.o. support* prestar apoyo a alguien || apoyo *m*, ayuda *f*; *he solicited my support* me pidió ayuda, pidió mi apoyo || apoyo *m* (base, sth. that supports, act of supporting); *a column which acts as a support* una columna que sirve de apoyo || TECH soporte *m* || ARCH soporte *m*, pilar *m* || FIG sostén *m* (of one's family) | mantenimiento *m*, sustento *m*; *several relatives depend on him for their support* varios parientes dependen de él para su mantenimiento || — *in support of* en apoyo de (an allegation, etc.), a favor de, en defensa de; *he spoke in support of my idea* habló en favor de mi idea; a beneficio de || *to lean on s.o. for support* apoyarse en uno.

support [sə'pɔ:t] *vt* sostener (to carry the weight of); *the beams support the roof* las vigas sostienen el tejado || apoyar (to lean) || apoyar (to back up); *I'll support your claims* apoyaré sus peticiones; *to support a motion, a candidature* apoyar una moción, una candidatura; *Mary does not agree with me, but John supports me* María no está de acuerdo conmigo, pero Juan me apoya || sustentar, respaldar; *this supports your theory* esto respalda su teoría || confirmar, corroborar (suspicions) || mantener (a family) || soportar, aguantar; *that bridge is not strong enough to support so much weight* este puente no es bastante fuerte para aguantar tanto peso || soportar; *Eskimoes can support intense cold* los esquimales pueden soportar un frío intenso || dar la entrada a (a leading actor) || — *supporting film* película secundaria || MIL *supporting fire* fuego *m* de apoyo || *supporting role* papel secundario || *to support o.s.* ganarse la vida, mantenerse (to earn one's living), apoyarse (to lean).

supportable [-əbl] *adj* sostenible || soportable.

supporter [-ə*] *n* partidario, ria; *a supporter of democracy* un partidario de la democracia || seguidor, ra; hincha *m* (of a team) || aficionado, da (of a sport); *football supporter* aficionado al fútbol || soporte *m*, apoyo *m* (support) || HERALD tenante *m* || *supporter's club* peña deportiva.

supportive [-iv] *adj* que ayuda, que apoya (friend, family).

supposable [sə'pəuzəbl] *adj* *it is supposable that* es de suponer que.

suppose [sə'pəuz] *vt* suponer; *let us suppose that what he says is true* supongamos que es verdad lo que dice; *he is not supposed to know it* se supone que no lo sabe || suponer, presuponer (to presuppose) || imaginarse (to imagine); *as you may suppose* como te puedes imaginar || creer (to think) || — *I suppose so* supongo que sí || *I suppose you are right* tendrás razón, debes de tener razón || *suppose* o *supposing she came back* y ¿si volviese? || *they are supposed to be at midday* tienen que estar aquí a las doce || *this tower is supposed to be the high-*

est in the world se considera que esta torre es la más alta del mundo || *we are not supposed to do it* no nos corresponde *or* no nos toca hacerlo (we have not to), no podemos *or* no debemos hacerlo (we are not allowed to) || *we are not supposed to tell you that* nos dijeron que no te lo contásemos || *you are supposed to be in London!* ¡creíamos que estabas en Londres!

supposed [-d] *adj* supuesto, ta; presunto, ta.

supposedly [sə'pəuzidli] *adv* según cabe suponer, probablemente.

supposition [ˌsʌpə'ziʃən] *n* suposición *f* || *on the supposition that* en la hipótesis de que, en el supuesto de que.

supposititious [sə'pɔzi'tiʃəs] *adj* hipotético, ca (suppositional) || falso, sa (counterfeit) || JUR supuesto, ta.

suppository [sə'pɔzitəri] *n* MED supositorio *m*.

suppress [sə'pres] *vt* suprimir || contener, reprimir (laughter, feeling, yawn, cough, etc.) || dominar (passions) || disimular (a fact) || callar, no revelar, ocultar (secret, name, news, etc.) || prohibir (a publication) || sofocar, reprimir (a revolt) || echar tierra a (a scandal) || contener (blood, etc.).

suppression [sə'preʃən] *n* supresión *f* || represión *f* (of anger, of revolt, etc.) || dominio *m* (of passions) || ocultación *f* (of facts, of truth, etc.) || prohibición *f* (of publications).

suppressive [sə'presiv] *adj* represivo, va.

suppressor [sə'presə*] *n* ELECTR supresor *m* || TECH silencioso *m* (muffler) || RAD antiparásito *m*.

suppurate ['sʌpjureit] *vi* MED supurar.

suppurating [-iŋ] *adj* MED supurante.

suppuration ['sʌpjuə'reiʃən] *n* MED supuración *f*.

suppurative ['sʌpjəˌreitiv] *adj* supurativo, va; supurante.

supranational [sju:prə'næʃənl] *adj* supranacional.

suprarenal ['sju:'prə'ri:nl] *adj* ANAT suprarrenal; *suprarenal gland* glándula suprarrenal.
◆ *n* glándula *f* suprarrenal.

supremacy [sju'preməsi] *n* supremacía *f*.

supreme [sju'pri:m] *adj* supremo, ma (highest) || supremo, ma; sumo, ma (greatest) || — *Supreme Being* Ser Supremo || *supreme commander* generalísimo *m*, jefe supremo || *supreme court* tribunal supremo.

supremo [su'pri:məu] *n* FAM mandamás, jefazo, za.

sura ['suərə] *n* REL sura *f*, surata *f*.

surah ['sjuərə] *n* surá *m* (material).

surbase ['sə:beis] *vt* ARCH rebajar.

surcharge ['sə:tʃɑ:dʒ] *n* sobrecarga *f* (load) || sobretasa *f* (surtax) || recargo *m* (of taxes) || sobrecarga *f* (on postage stamps).

surcharge [sə:'tʃɑ:dʒ] *vt* sobrecargar, recargar (to overcharge, to overload) || sobrellenar (to overfill) || poner sobretasa a (a letter) || sobrecargar, poner sobrecarga a (a postage stamp) || gravar con impuestos suplementarios *or* tasas suplementarias.

surcingle ['sə:siŋgl] *n* sobrecincha *f* (harness) || faja *f* (of a cassock).

surcoat ['sə:kəut] *n* sobretodo *m*.

surd [sə:d] *adj* GRAMM sordo, da || MATH irracional, sordo, da.
◆ *n* MATH número *m* sordo, número *m* irracional || GRAMM sonido *m* sordo.

sure [ʃuə*] *adj* seguro, ra; *a sure friend* un amigo seguro; *I'm sure he will come* estoy seguro de que vendrá; *it is by no means sure that* no es nada seguro que || seguro, ra; cierto, ta; *it's a sure sign of rain* es una señal segura de lluvia || seguro, ra; firme (hand) || certero, ra (shot) || — *be sure and wear* o *be sure to wear your overcoat* no deje de ponerse el abrigo || *be sure not to lose it* tenga cuidado en no perderlo || *be sure to come* venga sin falta, no deje de venir || *don't be too sure* no tenga tanta seguridad, no esté tan seguro || *he is sure to succeed* seguramente tendrá éxito || *I am sure he may go out if he wants to* por supuesto puede salir si así lo desea || *I'm sure I can't tell you* te aseguro que no puedo decírtelo || *sure thing!* ¡claro!, ¡seguro!, ¡por supuesto! || *to be sure!* ¡claro!, ¡por supuesto! || *to be sure of o.s.* estar seguro de sí mismo || *to be sure that* estar seguro de que, tener la seguridad de que || *to make s.o. sure of sth.* asegurar a uno algo || *to make sure* asegurarse; *I just want to make sure of the time* sólo quiero asegurarme de la hora.
◆ *adv* seguramente || realmente || claro, por supuesto; *sure, I'll do it* claro que lo haré || FAM sí que, vaya si; *he is very ugly but he sure sings well* es muy feo pero vaya si canta bien || — *for sure* seguramente (certainly), con seguridad; *do you know that for sure?* ¿lo sabe con seguridad? || *sure enough* efectivamente; *I said he would come, and sure enough he came* dije que vendría y efectivamente vino.

surefire [-'faiə*] *adj* US de éxito seguro, seguro, ra.

surefooted [-'futid] *adj* de pie firme.

surely [-li] *adv* sin duda, seguramente (without a doubt) || seguramente (in sure manner) || *surely!* ¡por supuesto!

sureness [-nis] *n* seguridad *f*, certeza *f* || firmeza *f* (of hand).

surety [-ti] *n* seguridad *f*, certeza *f* || fiador *m*, garante *m* & *f* (guarantor) || fianza *f*, garantía *f* (guarantee) || — *surety bond* fianza || *to go* o *to stand surety for* salir fiador *or* garante de.

surf [sə:f] *n* rompientes *m pl*, resaca *f* (breaking waves) || espuma *f* (foam).

surface ['sə:fis] *n* superficie *f*; *the surface of the water* la superficie del agua; *friction surface* superficie de rozamiento; *land surface* superficie terrestre || firme *m* (of road) || FIG aspecto *m* superficial, apariencia *f* || FIG *below* o *beneath the surface* en el fondo | *on the surface* superficialmente, en apariencia.
◆ *adj* de la superficie, superficial || de superficie; *surface transportation* transporte de superficie || a cielo abierto (mine) || PHYS superficial (tension) || *by surface mail* por vía terrestre *or* marítima.

surface ['sə:fis] *vt* pulir, alisar (to polish) || allanar (to flatten) || revestir (a road) || sacar a la superficie (a submarine).
◆ *vi* salir a la superficie (to come to the surface) || MIN trabajar a cielo abierto.

surface-to-air [-tu'εə*] *adj* *surface-to-air missile* proyectil tierra-aire.

surfboard ['sə:fbɔ:d] *n* tabla *f* hawaiana.

surfeit ['sə:fit] *n* exceso *m*; *there is a surfeit of apples* hay un exceso de manzanas || empacho *m* (indigestion) || saciedad *f*, hartura *f* (satiety).

surfeit ['sə:fit] *vt* colmar, saciar (to oversupply) || hartar, empachar (to overfeed) || saciar, hartar (to satiate).

surfing ['sə:fiŋ] *n* SP «surf» *m*.

surge [sə:dʒ] *n* oleada *f*, oleaje *m* (of waves) || mar *m* de fondo (enormous billow) || FIG oleada *f*, ola *f* (of indignation, etc.) | arranque *m*; *a surge of pity, anger* un arranque de compasión, de ira || ELECTR sobretensión *f*.

surge [sə:dʒ] *vt* MAR largar (a cable).
◆ *vi* encresparse, levantarse (the sea) || — FIG *people surged into the cinema* la gente entró a manadas en el cine || *rage surged up within him* la rabia se apoderó de él || *the blood surged to my cheeks* se me subió la sangre a la cara || ELECTR *the current surges* hay una sobretensión de corriente.

surgeon ['sə:dʒən] *n* MED cirujano *m* || — *dental surgeon* odontólogo *m*, dentista *m* || *veterinary surgeon* veterinario *m*.

surgery ['sə:dʒəri] *n* MED cirugía *f* (work of a surgeon) | consultorio *m* (consulting room) | clínica *f* (clinic) | dispensario *m* (dispensary) || US MED sala *f* de operaciones, quirófano *m* (operating theatre) || — *plastic surgery* cirugía estética *or* plástica || *surgery hours* horas *f* de consulta.

surgical ['sə:dʒikəl] *adj* MED quirúrgico, ca.

surgical spirit [-'spirit] *n* MED alcohol *m* de 90°

surging ['sə:dʒiŋ] *adj* agitado, da; encrespado, da.

Surinam [ˌsuəri'næm] *pr n* GEOGR Surinam.

surliness ['sə:linis] *n* malhumor *m*, mal genio *m* (bad temper) || hosquedad *f*, desabrimiento *m* (sullenness).

surly ['sə:li] *adj* malhumorado, da (bad-tempered) || hosco, ca; desabrido, da; arisco, ca (unfriendly).

surmise ['sə:maiz] *n* conjetura *f*, suposición *f*.

surmise [sə:'maiz] *vt* conjeturar, suponer.

surmount [sə:'maunt] *vt* superar; *to surmount a difficult situation* superar una situación difícil || coronar (to crown, to lie at the top of).

surmountabie [-əbl] *adj* superable.

surmullet [sə:'mʌlet] *n* salmonete *m* (fish).

surname ['sə:neim] *n* apellido *m* (family name) || apodo *m* (nickname).

surpass [sə:'pɑ:s] *vt* sobrepasar, superar, aventajar; *to surpass s.o. in intelligence* superar a alguien en inteligencia || rebasar, superar; *to surpass all expectations* rebasar todas las esperanzas.

surpassable [-əbl] *adj* superable.

surpassing [-iŋ] *adj* sobresaliente, incomparable, sin igual, sin par.

surplice ['sə:pləs] *n* REL sobrepelliz *f*.

surplus ['sə:pləs] *n* excelente *m* || COMM superávit *m* (of budget) | excedente *m* (of goods).
◆ *adj* excedente, sobrante || *sale of surplus stock* liquidación *f* de saldos.

surplusage [-idʒ] *n* excedente *m* (surplus) || JUR redundancia *f* (of words).

surprise [sə'praiz] *n* sorpresa *f*, asombro *m*; *much to my surprise* con gran asombro mío || sorpresa *f*; *he gave me a surprise* me dio una sorpresa || — FAM *surprise, surprise!* ¡vaya, vaya! || *to spring a surprise on s.o.* dar una sorpresa a alguien || *to take by surprise* coger desprevenido || *what a surprise!* ¡vaya sorpresa!
◆ *adj* inesperado, da; *a surprise visit* una visita inesperada || — *surprise attack* ataque *m* por sorpresa || *surprise party* asalto *m*, guateque *m*.

surprise [sə'praiz] *vt* sorprender, asombrar (to astonish); *his behaviour surprised me* me asombró su conducta || sorprender (a secret, a robber) || MIL coger por sorpresa || *to be surprised at* sorprenderle a uno; *I was surprised at his indifference* me sorprendió su indiferencia.

surprising [-iŋ] *adj* sorprendente, asombroso, sa.

surprisingly [-iŋli] *adv* terriblemente, asombrosamente || de modo sorprendente.

surrealism [sə'riəlizəm] *n* surrealismo *m*.

surrealist [sə'riəlist] *adj/n* surrealista.

surrealistic [səriə'listik] *adj* surrealista.

surrender [sə'rendə*] *n* rendición *f*; *their surrender meant the end of the war* su rendición significó el fin de la guerra || entrega *f* (handing over) || abandono *m* (abandoning) || JUR renuncia *f*, cesión *f* || rescate *m* (of insurance policy) || *in surrender* en señal de rendición.

surrender [sə'rendə*] *vt* rendir, entregar (to hand over); *to surrender the town* entregar la ciudad || ceder (to give up); *to surrender one's place to a lady* ceder el sitio a una señora || abandonar (hope) || JUR ceder, renunciar a || — *to surrender o.s.* rendirse || FIG *to surrender o.s. to vice* entregarse al vicio.
◆ *vi* rendirse; *I surrender!* ¡me rindo! || entregarse; *to surrender to justice* entregarse a la justicia; *to surrender to vice* entregarse al vicio.

surreptitious ['sʌrə'tiʃəs] *adj* subrepticio, cia.

surrey ['sʌri] *n* US coche *m* de punto, simón *m*.

surrogate ['sʌrəgit] *n* sustituto *m* || REL vicario *m* || *surrogate mother* madre *f* de alquiler *or* alquilada.

surround [sə'raund] *vt* cercar, rodear; *the sea surrounds the island* el mar rodea la isla; *surrounded by people* rodeado de gente || FIG rodear; *I am surrounded by friends* estoy rodeado de amigos || MIL sitiar, rodear, cercar.

surrounding [-iŋ] *adj* circundante.
◆ *pl n* alrededores *m* (environs) || medio *m sing*, ambiente *m sing*, medio *m* ambiente (environment).

surtax ['sə:tæks] *n* sobretasa *f*, recargo *m*.

surveillance [sə:'veiləns] *n* vigilancia *f*.

surveillant [sə:'veilənt] *n* vigilante *m* (watchman) || guardián *m* (of prison).

survey [sə:vei] *n* inspección *f* (inspection) || reconocimiento *m* (reconnaissance) || examen *m*, estudio *m* (of a question) || encuesta *f* (inquiry) || informe *m* (report) || panorama *m*, vista *f* de conjunto; *a survey of the economic situation* una vista de conjunto de la situación económica || idea *f* de conjunto || medición *f* (in topography) || alzado *m*, levantamiento *m* (of a map) || mapa *m* topográfico (map) || *market survey* estudio del mercado.

survey [sə:'vei] *vt* inspeccionar (to inspect) || reconocer (ground) || examinar (to examine) || estudiar (to study) || hacer una encuesta de (to make an inquiry into) || contemplar (to look at) || medir (to measure land) || levantar un plano de (to make a map) || hacer el catastro de (a parish).

surveying [-iŋ] *n* topografía *f*, agrimensura *f* (topography) || levantamiento *m* de planos (of maps) || inspección *f* (inspection) || *naval surveying* hidrografía *f*.

surveyor [-ə*] *n* agrimensor *m*, topógrafo *m* (of land) || inspector *m* || US vista *m*, inspector *m* de aduanas (in the customs) || — *surveyor's chain* cadena *f* de agrimensor || *surveyor's cross* escuadra *f* de agrimensor.

survival [sə'vaivəl] *n* supervivencia *f* || *survival of the fittest* selección *f* natural.

survive [sə'vaiv] *vt* sobrevivir a; *he survived his wife* sobrevivió a su mujer.
◆ *vi* sobrevivir (to continue to live) || subsistir; *we are trying to survive on 4 pounds a week* estamos intentando subsistir con cuatro libras a la semana || quedar, sobrevivir, subsistir; *only four houses have survived* no han quedado más que cuatro casas.

surviving [-iŋ] *adj* superviviente, sobreviviente.

survivor [-ə*] *n* superviviente *m* & *f*, sobreviviente *m* & *f*.

survivorship [-əʃip] *n* JUR supervivencia *f*.

susceptibility [sə'septə'biliti] *n* susceptibilidad *f* || sensibilidad *f* (sensitivity) || ELECTR susceptibilidad *f* || MED predisposición *f*, propensión *f*.

susceptible [sə'septəbl] *adj* susceptible || sensible (sensitive); *susceptible to beauty* sensible a la belleza || ELECTR susceptible || vulnerable, expuesto, ta (vulnerable) || MED predispuesto, ta; propenso, sa || — *to be susceptible of* estar expuesto a || *to be susceptible of proof* poder demostrarse || *to be susceptible to* ser propenso *or* predispuesto a; *to be susceptible to disease* ser propenso a enfermedades.

susceptive [sə'septiv] *adj* susceptible || sensible (sensitive).

suspect ['sʌspekt] *adj/n* sospechoso, sa.

suspect [səs'pekt] *vt* sospechar; *I would never had suspected him* nunca le hubiera sospechado || recelar de (to distrust) || sospechar, tener la impresión de; *we suspect he is a genius* tenemos la impresión de que es un genio || sospechar, tener la sospecha de; *I suspect him of being a thief* sospecho que es un ladrón.
◆ *vi* sospechar, tener sospechas || imaginarse, figurarse (to believe); *I suspected as much* ya me lo imaginaba.

suspend [səs'pend] *vt* suspender, colgar (to hang) || suspender, interrumpir (to interrupt) || suspender, privar temporalmente de sus funciones (to debar) || suspender (payment, newspaper) || reservar (one's judgment) || JUR suspender (proceedings) || *suspended animation* suspensión momentánea de las funciones vitales.

suspender [-ə*] *n* liga *f* (for socks or stockings) || *suspender belt* liguero *m*.
◆ *pl* US tirantes *m* (for trousers).

suspense [səs'pens] *n* ansiedad *f* (anxiety) || incertidumbre *f*, duda *f* (uncertainty); *to keep in suspense* mantener en la incertidumbre || tensión *f* || CINEM «suspense» *m* || JUR suspensión *f* (of proceedings) || *to remain in suspense* quedar pendiente.

suspension [səs'penʃən] *n* suspensión *f* || — *points of suspension, suspension points* puntos suspensivos || *suspension bridge* puente *m* colgante.

suspensive [səs'pensiv] *adj* suspensivo, va.

suspensory [-ri] *adj* suspensorio, ria.
◆ *n* MED suspensorio *m*.

suspicion [səs'piʃən] *n* sospecha *f*; *the police has suspicions about him* la policía tiene sospechas de él || recelo *m*, desconfianza *f* (mistrust); *to cast suspicion on s.o.'s good faith* tener recelo de la buena fe de alguien; *with suspicion* con desconfianza || ligera idea *f*; *he hadn't a suspicion of the truth* no tenía la más ligera idea de la verdad || pizca *f*, poco *m*; *a suspicion of garlic* una pizca de ajo || — *above suspicion* por encima *or* fuera de toda sospecha || *detention on suspicion* detención preventiva || *on suspicion* como sospechoso || *suspicion fell on me* se empezó a sospechar de mí, las sospechas recayeron sobre mí || *to arouse suspicion* despertar sospechas || *to hold s.o. in suspicion* sospechar de alguien || *to lay o.s. open to suspicion* hacerse sospechoso || *under suspicion* bajo sospecha || *without a shadow of a suspicion* sin la menor sospecha.

suspicion [səs'piʃən] *vt* US sospechar.

suspicious [səs'piʃəs] *adj* sospechoso, sa (suspected) || suspicaz, receloso, sa; desconfiado, da (suspecting).

suspiciousness [-nis] *n* suspicacia *f*, recelo *m*, desconfianza *f* (mistrust) || carácter *m* sospechoso.

suspiration [ˌsʌspi'reiʃən] *n* suspiro *m* (sigh).

suspire [sʌs'paiə*] *vi* suspirar; *to suspire for* suspirar por.

suss [sʌs] *vt* FAM *to suss s.o. out* calar a alguien || *to suss sth. out* descubrir el intríngulis de algo.

sustain [səs'tein] *vt* mantener; *to sustain a conversation* mantener una conversación || sostener, mantener, sustentar (a family) || sostener (weight, burden) || mantener, continuar, sostener (effort) || soportar, aguantar (to endure) || apoyar (an assertion, a theory) || MUS sostener (a note) || sufrir; *to sustain injuries, losses* sufrir heridas, pérdidas || sostener (an attack) || desempeñar (a rôle) || admitir; *to sustain an objection* admitir una objeción.

sustainable [-əbl] *adj* sostenible.

sustained [-d] *adj* ininterrumpido, da; sostenido, da; continuo, nua || MUS sostenido, da (note).

sustenance ['sʌstinəns] *n* sustento *m*, alimento *m* (food) || subsistencia *f*; *means of sustenance* medios de subsistencia.

sustentation ['sʌsten'teiʃən] *n* mantenimiento *m* || sustentación *f* (of the body).

sutler ['sʌtlə*] *n* MIL cantinero *m*.

sutra ['su:trə] *n* REL sutra *m*.

suttee ['sʌti] *n* REL inmolación *f* voluntaria de una viuda hindú.

suture ['sju:tʃə*] *n* MED sutura *f*.

suture ['sju:tʃə*] *vt* MED suturar, coser.

Suva ['su'və] *pr n* GEOGR Suva.

suzerain ['su:zərein] *n* HIST señor *m* feudal || JUR estado *m* protector.

suzerainty [-ti] *n* HIST soberanía *f* feudal, señorío *m* feudal || JUR soberanía *f*.

svelte [svelt] *adj* esbelto, ta.

swab [swɔb] *n* estropajo *m* (mop) || MAR lampazo *m* || MIL escobillón *m* (of gun) || MED tapón *m* || FAM patán *m* (loutish person).

swab [swɔb] *vt* fregar con estropajo (to mop) || MAR lampacear || MED limpiar con tapón.

Swabian ['sweibjən] *adj/n* suabo, ba.

swaddle ['swɔdl] *vt* poner los pañales a (a baby) || envolver (to wrap) || — *swaddling clothes* pañales *m*, pañal *m sing* || FIG *to be still in swaddling clothes* estar en pañales, estar en mantillas.

swag [swæg] *n* FAM botín *m* (booty) || festón *m* (festoon) || bulto *m* (bundle, in Australia).

swag [swæg] *vi* vagar, vagabundear.

swage [sweidʒ] *n* tas *m* de estampar.

swage [sweidʒ] *vt* forjar, embutir, estampar.

swagger ['swægə*] *n* contoneo *m*, pavoneo *m* (walking) || fanfarronada *f* (boast).
◆ *adj* FAM pera, elegante.

swagger ['swægə*] *vi* contonearse, pavonearse, andar pavoneándose (to walk) || fanfarronear, vanagloriarse (to boast).

swagger cane [-kein] *n* junco *m* (stick).

swaggering [-riŋ] *adj* jactancioso, sa.

swagger stick [-stik] *n* junco *m* (stick).

Swahili [swɑ:'hi:li] *adj* suajili.
◆ *n* suajili *m* & *f* (people) || suajili *m* (language).

swain [swein] *n* pretendiente *m*, galán *m* (suitor) || zagal *m* (boy, shepherd).

swallow ['swɔləu] *n* golondrina *f* (bird) || deglución *f* (swallowing) || gaznate *m* (throat) || trago *m* (of drink, etc.); *at o with one swallow* de un trago || bocado *m* (of food) || TECH garganta *f* de polea || FIG *one swallow doesn't make a summer* una golondrina no hace verano.

swallow [swɔləu] *vt* tragar (to take down food, etc.) || MED tomar (a pill) || FIG tragar, creer, tragarse (to believe); *he swallows everything he's told* se traga cuanto le dicen | tragar, tragarse, soportar; *he swallows all the insults* se traga todos los insultos | desdecirse de, retractarse de; *to swallow one's words* desdecirse de sus palabras | tragarse; *to swallow one's laughter* tragarse la risa | comerse, tragarse; *to swallow one's pride* tragarse el orgullo | comerse; *the Andalusians swallow many of their*

letters los andaluces comen muchas de las letras | tragarse; *the sea swallowed the boat* el mar se tragó el barco || *to swallow up* tragarse (to engulf), consumir; *to swallow up one's savings* consumir los ahorros.
◆ *vi* tragar.

swallow dive [-daiv] *n* salto *m* del ángel.

swallow fish [-fiʃ] *n* ZOOL golondrina *f* de mar.

swallowtail [-teil] *n* cola *f* de golondrina || macaón *m* (butterfly) || TECH cola *f* de milano.

swallow-tailed coat [-teild'kəut] *n* frac *m*.

swallowwort [-wəːt] *n* BOT vencetósigo *m*.

swam [swæm] *pret* → **swim.**

swamp ['swɔmp] *n* pantano *m*, terreno *m* pantanoso, ciénaga *f*.

swamp ['swɔmp] *vt* hundir (a boat) || encenagar, empantanar (in marsh, mud) || inundar, anegar, sumergir (with water) || FIG inundar (to inundate); *swamped with orders* inundado de pedidos | agobiar, abrumar (with work).
◆ *vi* hundirse (to sink) || inundarse (to become flooded) || empantanarse, encenagarse.

swamp fever [-'fiːvə*] *n* MED fiebre *f* de los pantanos, malaria *f*, paludismo *m*.

swampy [-i] *adj* pantanoso, sa.

swan [swɔn] *n* cisne *m* (bird).

swan dive [-daiv] *n* US salto *m* del ángel.

swank [swæŋk] *n* ostentación *f* || fanfarronada *f*.

swank [swæŋk] *vi* fanfarronear.

swanker [-ə*] *n* fanfarrón, ona.

swanky [-i] *adj* ostentoso, sa || fanfarrón, ona.

swannery ['swɔnəeri] *n* criadero *m* de cisnes.

swansdown ['swɔnzdaun] *n* muletón *m* (cotton flannel) || plumón *m* de cisne.

swan song ['swɔnsɔŋ] *n* canto *m* del cisne.

swap; swop [swɔp] *n* cambio *m*, canje *m*.

swap; swop [swɔp] *vt* cambiar, canjear.
◆ *vi* hacer un intercambio.

SWAPO *abbr of [South West Africa People's Organization]* SWAPO, Organización Popular del África del Suroeste.

sward [swɔːd] *n* césped *m*.

swarf [swɔːf] *n* limalla *f*, limaduras *f pl*.

swarm [swɔːm] *n* enjambre *m* (of bees) || FIG enjambre *m*, multitud *f* (of people, etc.).

swarm [swɔːm] *vi* salir en enjambre, enjambrar (bees) || FIG hormiguear, pulular; *the tourists swarmed all over the park* los turistas hormigueaban por todo el parque | rebosar, ser un hervidero, hervir; *the place was swarming with tourists* el lugar era un hervidero de turistas, el lugar rebosaba *or* hervía de turistas || escaparse [las zoosporas del zoosporangio] || *to swarm up* trepar.
◆ *vt* FIG invadir, inundar.

swart [swɔːt] *adj* moreno, na.

swarthiness ['swɔːðinis] *n* tez *f* morena, piel *f* atezada.

swarthy ['swɔːði] *adj* moreno, na; atezado, da.

swash [swɔʃ] *n* chapoteo *m*.

swash [swɔʃ] *vt* echar, arrojar (to splash).
◆ *vi* chapotear (water) || US FAM fanfarronear (to boast).

swashbuckler [-'bʌklə*] *n* espadachín *m*, bravucón *m*, matón *m*.

swashbuckling [-'bʌkliŋ] *n* bravuconería *f*.
◆ *adj* bravucón, ona.

swastika ['swɔstikə] *n* esvástica *f*, cruz *f* gamada.

swat [swɔt] *vt* aplastar (flies, etc.).

swath [swɔːθ] *n* AGR andana *f*, ringlera *f* (line of grass or grain).

swathe [sweið] *n* venda *f* (bandage) || banda *f* (of mummies).

swathe [sweið] *vt* envolver; *woman swathed in a shawl* mujer envuelta en un chal || vendar (with bandage).

swatter ['swɔtə*] *n* matamoscas *m inv*.

sway [swei] *n* vaivén *m*, balanceo *m*, oscilación *f* (oscillation) || movimiento *m*; *the sway of the train makes me sick* el movimiento del tren me marea || FIG dominio *m* (power, influence) || — FIG *to be under the sway of* estar dominado por | *to have o to hold sway over* dominar.

sway [swei] *vt* hacer oscilar (to move from side to side) || agitar, mover (trees, etc.) || inclinar (to cause to lean) || blandir, esgrimir (a cudgel, a sword) || llevar (a sceptre) || FIG gobernar, dirigir, dominar (to rule) | ejercer influencia en, influir en; *considerations that sway our opinions* consideraciones que influyen en nuestras opiniones | convencer, persuadir (to convince); *his advice swayed the whole assembly* su consejo convenció a toda la asamblea || — *to sway s.o. from* apartar *or* desviar a alguien de || MAR *to sway up* izar.
◆ *vi* oscilar, balancearse (to swing) || inclinarse (to lean) || tambalearse (to move unsteadily); *the drunken man was swaying along* el borracho iba tambaleándose || FIG vacilar (to hesitate) | gobernar, dirigir (to rule).

swaying [-iŋ] *adj* oscilante || *to walk with a swaying gait* andar tambaleándose.

swear [swɛə*] *n* blasfemia *f*, juramento *m*, voto *m*, reniego *m* (blasphemous word) || tacos *m pl*, palabrotas *f pl* (obscene words) || *to have a good swear* soltar una sarta de palabrotas.

swear* [swɛə*] *vt* jurar; *I swear that it is true* juro que es verdad; *to swear sth. on the Bible* jurar algo sobre la Biblia || JUR tomar juramento a (to put on oath) | declarar bajo juramento || jurar, prometer; *to swear to do sth.* prometer hacer algo || — *to be sworn in* prestar juramento, jurar || *to swear an oath* prestar juramento, jurar || *to swear away s.o.'s life* levantar un falso testimonio que hace condenar a alguien a muerte; *to swear in* tomar juramento a || *to swear s.o. to secrecy* hacer que uno jure guardar un secreto.
◆ *vi* jurar, prestar juramento (to make an oath) || jurar, blasfemar (to blaspheme) || soltar tacos, decir palabrotas, jurar (to use obscene language) || — FIG *he swears by castor oil* para él no hay nada como el aceite de ricino | *I would have sworn to him* hubiera jurado que era él || *to swear at* echar pestes de || *to swear by* jurar por; *to swear by all that one holds sacred* jurar por lo más sagrado; fiarse enteramente de, tener entera fe *or* confianza en (to have great confidence in) || *to swear off* prometer *or* jurar renunciar a || *to swear to* jurar; *I wouldn't swear to it* no lo juraría; declarar bajo juramento (a witness).
— OBSERV Pret ***swore***; pp ***sworn***.

swearer [-ə*] *n* el que presta juramento || blasfemador, ra.

swearword [-wəːd] *n* palabrota *f*, taco *m*.

sweat [swet] *n* sudor *m* (perspiration); *to be in a sweat* estar bañado en sudor || sudor *m*, sudación *f* (act of perspiring) || rezumamiento *m* (on a wall) || FIG trabajo *m* pesado (hard work) || — FIG *by the sweat of one's brow* con el sudor de su frente | *cold sweat* sudor frío || REL *in the sweat of thy face shalt thou eat bread* ganarás el pan con el sudor de tu frente || FAM *old sweat* veterano *m* || *running with sweat* sudando a chorros *or* a mares || FIG & FAM *to be dripping with sweat* sudar la gota gorda, sudar tinta | *to cause s.o. a lot of sweat* costarle a uno muchos sudores.

sweat* [swet] *vt* hacer sudar (to cause to perspire); *the doctor sweated his patient* el médico hizo sudar al enfermo || empapar de sudor (to make wet) || FIG explotar (workers) || estregar, cepillar (a horse) || hacer fermentar (tobacco) || TECH calentar (to heat) | soldar (to solder) || secar en la estufa (hides) || US FAM hacer cantar a (to get information from) || — FAM *to make s.o. sweat his guts out* hacer sudar a alguien la gota gorda | *to sweat blood* sudar sangre *or* tinta, sudar la gota gorda | *to sweat it out* pasar un mal rato, pasar muchos sudores || *to sweat out a cold* curar un resfriado sudando.
◆ *vi* sudar (people, plants) || fermentar (tobacco) || rezumar, sudar (wall) || FIG sudar (worker, etc.) || FAM tener sudores fríos.
— OBSERV Pret y pp ***sweat, sweated***.

sweatband [-bænd] *n* badana *f* de un sombrero.

sweat cloth [-klɔθ] *n* sudadero *m*.

sweated [-id] *adj* FIG explotado, da; mal pagado, da (labour).

sweater [-ə*] *n* suéter *m*, jersey *m* (pullover) || MED sudorífico *m* || FIG explotador *m* (employer).

sweat gland [-glænd] *n* ANAT glándula *f* sudorípara.

sweatiness [-inis] *n* sudor *m* (of body) || humedad *f* (of clothes).

sweating [-iŋ] *n* sudación *f* || FIG explotación *f*.
◆ *adj* sudoroso, sa.

sweating room [-iŋrum] *n* sudadero *m* || TECH estufa *f*.

sweating system [iŋ'sistim] *n* explotación *f* de los obreros.

sweat shirt [-ʃəːt] *n* chandal *m* (for athletes).

sweatshop [-ʃɔp] *n* fábrica *f* donde se explota al obrero.

sweaty [-i] *adj* sudoroso, sa; sudoso, sa (body, hand) || a sudor (odour) || empapado de sudor (clothes) || que hace sudar (causing sweat) || FIG agotador, ra; que hace sudar (work).

swede [swiːd] *n* BOT colinabo *m*, nabo *m* sueco.

Swede [swiːd] *n* sueco, ca.

Sweden [-n] *pr n* GEOGR Suecia *f*.

Swedish [-iʃ] *adj* sueco, ca.
◆ *n* sueco *m* (language) || *the Swedish* los suecos.

sweep [swiːp] *n* barrido *m*; *to give the room a sweep* dar un barrido a la habitación || deshollinador *m* (chimney cleaner) || curva *f* (of a river, of a road) || extensión *f* (of a plain) || movimiento *m* amplio (of the arm) || envergadura *f* (of wings) || lo aerodinámico (of motor car's lines) || MIL alcance *f* (of weapons); *within the sweep of the guns* al alcance de los cañones || giro *m* (of telescope, of a radar) || aspa *f* (of a mill) || FIG redada *f*; *the police made a sweep* la policía hizo una redada | alcance *m* (of an argument) || MAR remo *m* (oar) || draga *f* (for dredging sea beds) || cigoñal *m* (of a well) || ARCH curvatura *f* || SP «sweepstake» *m* || — FIG *at one sweep* de una vez | *to make a clean sweep* llevárselo todo (in gaming) | *to make a clean sweep of* hacer tabla rasa de (to get rid of), acaparar, llevarse todo (to get hold of); *the Russian team made a clean sweep of the awards* el equipo ruso se llevó todos los premios.

sweep* [swiːp] *vt* barrer (the dust, ground, room); *they haven't swept the streets* no han barrido las calles || deshollinar (a chimney) || dragar (a river bed) || arrasar, asolar; *the earthquake swept the town* el terremoto arrasó la

ciudad || arrastrarse por; *her dress swept the floor* su vestido se arrastraba por el suelo || barrer; *the bullets swept the beach* las balas barrieron la playa || arrastrar, llevarse; *a wave swept her overboard* una ola se la llevó por la borda || recorrer; *he swept the valley with his binoculars* recorrió el valle con los prismáticos; *he swept the map with his finger* recorrió el mapa con el dedo || explorar, barrer (the horizon); *the searchlight swept the sky* los proyectores barrían el cielo || pasar ligeramente por; *she swept her fingers over the strings of the harp* pasó ligeramente los dedos por las cuerdas del arpa || tocar, rozar; *she swept the strings of the guitar with her fingers* rozó las cuerdas de la guitarra con los dedos || pasar; *she swept her hand through her hair* pasó la mano por el pelo || explorar (radar, television) || rastrear (mines) || FIG limpiar, librar; *to sweep the seas of one's enemies* limpiar los mares de enemigos | llevarse, ganar de una manera aplastante (to win overwhelmingly) || — *to sweep a path through the snow* abrir un camino limpiando *or* quitando la nieve || *to sweep s.o. off his feet* entusiasmar a alguien, volverle loco a uno; *she swept him off his feet* le volvió loco; arrastrar; *the waves swept him off his feet* las olas le arrastraron; llevarse (a crowd) || FIG *to sweep sth. under the carpet* correr un velo sobre algo || FIG *to sweep the board* limpiar la mesa (in gambling), llevarse todas las medallas; *Spain swept the board in the championship* España se llevó todas las medallas en el campeonato; llevarse todos los puestos (in an election) || *to sweep the room with a glance* recorrer la habitación con la mirada || *to sweep the seas* ser dueño de los mares.
◆ *vi* extenderse, difundirse; *the news of his death swept over the country* la noticia de su muerte se extendió por todo el país; *a feeling of horror swept through the crowd* un sentimiento de horror se extendió por la multitud || extenderse; *the shore sweeps to the south* la costa se extiende hacia el sur || arrastrarse; *her dress swept along the floor* su vestido se arrastraba por el suelo || barrer; *you wash the window and I'll sweep* tú lavas las ventanas y yo barro || — *she swept into the room* entró en la sala con paso majestuoso || *the car swept past the house* el coche pasó rápidamente delante de la casa || *the car swept round the corner* el coche dobló rápidamente la esquina || *the crowd swept over the pitch* la multitud invadió el campo || *the road sweeps round the lake* la carretera rodea el lago.
◆ *phr v* *to sweep across* barrer || *to sweep along* arrastrar, llevarse; *the current swept him along* la corriente le arrastró | entusiasmar, arrebatar (to fill with enthusiasm) | andar con paso majestuoso (to move with dignity) | andar rápidamente (to go quickly) || *to sweep aside* apartar; *to sweep the curtains aside* apartar las cortinas | descartar (a suggestion) || *to sweep away* barrer | limpiar (snow) | llevar, arrastrar; *the current swept away the bridge* la corriente se llevó el puente | suprimir (to remove) || *to sweep by* pasar rápidamente (quickly) | pasar majestuosamente (majestically) || *to sweep down* arrastrar, llevarse (to carry) | caer sobre, echarse encima; *the storm swept down on us* la tormenta se nos echó encima | bajar suavemente (to descend); *hills sweeping down to the sea* colinas que bajan suavemente hacia el mar | bajar rápidamente (to go down quickly) | bajar majestuosamente; *she swept down the stairs* bajó la escalera majestuosamente || *to sweep in* estrecharse; *the hull sweeps in at the prow* el casco se estrecha en la proa | entrar rápidamente (quickly) | entrar majestuosamente (majestically) || *to sweep off* llevarse || *to sweep on* seguir avanzando || *to sweep out* barrer (a room) | limpiar, quitar (dust) || *to sweep up* barrer (a room) | recoger (dust, etc.); *to sweep up dead leaves* recoger las hojas muertas | llegar rápidamente (quickly) | llegar majestuosamente (majestically) | describir una curva (to curve) | emprender *or* alzar el vuelo (bird).
— OBSERV Pret y pp ***swept***.

sweeper [-ə*] *n* barrendero, ra (person) || barredora *f*, barredera *f* (machine) || deshollinador *m* (chimney sweep).

sweeping [-iŋ] *adj* aplastante; arrollador, ra; *sweeping victory* victoria aplastante || amplio, plia (gesture) || radical; *sweeping changes* cambios radicales || demasiado general; *a sweeping statement* una declaración demasiado general || profundo, da (bow) || COMM increíble, insuperable (reduction) || fuerte, violento, ta (blow) || aerodinámico, ca (car) || — *sweeping machine* barredora *f*, barredera *f* || *to give a sweeping glance* recorrer con la vista.
◆ *n* barrido *m*, barredura *f* (act of clearing away).
◆ *pl* barreduras *f*, basuras *f* (rubbish) || FIG heces *f* (of society, etc.).

sweep net [-net] *n* MAR jábega *f*.

sweep seine [-sein] *n* MAR jábega *f*.

sweepstake [-steik]; **sweepstakes** [-steiks] *n* «sweepstake» *m*.

sweet [swi:t] *adj* dulce (taste); *sweet oranges* naranjas dulces || azucarado, da; dulce (containing sugar); *this tea is very sweet* este té está muy azucarado || fresco, ca (milk, meat, fish, breath, air) || dulce (wine) || fértil (land) || suave (engine) || melodioso, sa; suave (music); *she has a very sweet voice* tiene una voz muy suave || fragante, bueno, na (smell) || potable (water) || mono, na; bonito, ta [AMER lindo, da] (facial features, dress, etc.) || amable, encantador, ra (friendly); *sweet old lady* viejecita encantadora || querido, da (dear) || amable; *that was very sweet of you* fue muy amable de su parte || afable, bondadoso, sa (kind); *he has a very sweet disposition* tiene un carácter muy afable || agradable; *it was sweet to be able to do it* fue agradable poder hacerlo || — *as sweet as honey* dulce como la miel || *at one's own sweet will* a su antojo || *isn't she sweet!* ¡es un encanto!, ¡es una monería! || *revenge is sweet* la venganza es un placer de dioses || BOT *sweet basil* albahaca *f* || *sweet cider* sidra *f* dulce || BOT *sweet corn* maíz tierno || *sweet oil* aceite *m* de oliva || BOT *sweet pea* guisante *m* de olor; *sweet pepper* pimiento *m* morrón | *sweet potato* batata *f*, boniato *m* [AMER camote *m*] || *sweet sixteen* quince abriles || *sweet stuff* golosinas *f pl*, dulces *m pl* || *to be sweet on s.o.* estar enamorado de alguien || *to have a sweet tooth* ser goloso, gustarle a uno los dulces *or* las golosinas || *to smell sweet* oler bien || *to taste sweet* estar dulce || *what a sweet little cat!* ¡qué gatito más mono!
◆ *n* caramelo *m* (toffee) || dulce *m* (candy) || postre *m* (dessert) || amor *m*, amor mío *m*, cielo *m*, cariño *m* (a beloved person).
◆ *pl* deleites *m*, delicias *f*, dulzura *f sing*; *the sweets of victory* los deleites de la victoria || US dulces *m*, golosinas *f* (sweet edible things).

sweet-and-sour [-ən'sauə*] *adj* agridulce.

sweetbread [-bred] *n* mollejas *f pl*, lechecillas *f pl*.

sweeten ['swi:tn] *vt* azucarar, endulzar (by adding sugar) || suavizar (a sound) || aplacar, calmar (a person) || purificar (air) || depurar (seawater) || sanear (soil) || FIG endulzar, dulcificar (to make more enjoyable) || CHEM neutralizar (an acid) || FIG *to sweeten the pill* dorar la píldora.
◆ *vi* endulzarse.

sweetener [-ə*] *n* dulcificante *m*.

sweetening [-iŋ] *n* endulzamiento *m*, dulcificación *f* || dulcificante *m* (sweetener) || FIG suavizamiento *m*.

sweetheart [-hɑ:t] *n* amor *m*, novio, via (loved one) || *my sweetheart* mi cielo, mi cariño, amor mío, mi amor.

sweetie [-i] *n* caramelo *m* (candy) || FIG amor *m* || *isn't she a sweetie?* ¡es un encanto!

sweetish [-iʃ] *adj* dulzón, ona.

sweetmeat [-mi:t] *n* caramelo *m* (candy).
◆ *pl* dulces *m* (a piece of confectionery).

sweetness [-nis] *n* dulzor *m*, lo dulce (of sugar) || suavidad *f* (to the touch) || dulzura *f*, suavidad *f* (of character) || buen olor *m* (smelling) || amabilidad *f* (kindness).

sweet-scented [-'sentid] *adj* perfumado, da; fragante.

sweetshop [-ʃɔp] *n* confitería *f*.

sweet-smelling [-'smeliŋ] *adj* perfumado, da; fragante.

sweet-tempered [-'tempəd] *adj* afable, amable, bondadoso, sa.

sweet-toothed [-tu:θt] *adj* goloso, sa.

swell [swel] *adj* elegantísimo, ma || US FAM fenomenal, bárbaro, ra (fabulous).
◆ *n* inflamiento *m*, inflado *m* (action) || hinchazón *f*; *the swell of her belly* la hinchazón de su vientre || curvatura *f*, redondez *f*; *the swell of a pot* la redondez de un puchero || abultamiento *m*; *the swell of a column* el abultamiento de una columna || alabeo *m* (through distortion) || GEOL ondulación *f* (of ground) || MAR elevación *f* (of seabed) | marejada *f*, oleaje *m* (of waves) || FAM ricachón, ona (wealthy person) | guapo, pa (handsome person) | pez *m* gordo, personaje *m* (important person) || *the swells* la gente bien.

swell* [swel] *vt* hinchar || hacer crecer (a river) || hacer aumentar, engrosar; *immigration swelled the population* la inmigración hizo aumentar la población || — *eyes swollen with tears* ojos hinchados de lágrimas || FIG *to get a swollen head* engreírse, envanecerse || *to swell the ranks* engrosar las filas del ejército.
◆ *vi* hincharse, inflamarse; *the boil began to swell* el divieso empezó a hincharse || inflarse, hincharse (to inflate) || subir, crecer; *the river swelled* el río creció || levantarse (the sea) || abombarse; *the barrel is swollen in the middle* el barril está abombado en el centro || hincharse; *chickpeas swell when cooked* los garbanzos se hinchan al cocer || CULIN subir (pastry) || MUS aumentar, subir (sound) || FIG crecer, aumentar (to increase) | hincharse, ensoberbecerse, engreírse; *to swell with pride* hincharse de orgullo || — *to swell out* hincharse, inflarse || *to swell up* hincharse (part of the body), crecer, aumentar (to increase).
— OBSERV Pret ***swelled***; pp ***swollen, swelled***.

swellhead [-hed] *n* vanidoso, sa; engreído, da.

swelling [-iŋ] *n* inflamiento *m*, inflado *m* (increase in size) || crecida *f* (of a river) || levantamiento *m* (of waves) || inflamiento *m* (of sails) || abultamiento *m* (of a column) || MED hinchazón *f*, tumefacción *f*; *the swelling of the belly* la hinchazón del vientre | ganglio *m* (ganglion) | chichón *m*, bulto *m* (bruise).
◆ *adj* inflado, da (in size) || crecido, da (a river) || levantado, da; encrespado, da (waves) || MED hinchado, da || FIG ampuloso, sa (speech) | exaltado, da (emotion).

swelter ['sweltə*] *vi* chorrear sudor, sudar a mares, sofocarse de calor.

sweltering [-riŋ]; **sweltry** [-ri] *adj* abrasador, ra; sofocante (day, office) || sudando a mares, chorreando sudor (person).

swept [swept] *pret/pp* → **sweep**.

swept-back [-bæk] *adj* en flecha (wing).

swerve [swə:v] *n* viraje *m; the car did a violent swerve* el coche dio un viraje brusco ‖ desviación *f* (deviation) ‖ SP regate *m* (of a player) | efecto *m* (of a ball).

swerve [swə:v] *vt* desviar; *to swerve s.o. from his duty* desviar a uno de su deber ‖ dar efecto a, cortar (a ball) ‖ *he swerved the car to the left* torció a la izquierda.
◆ *vi* dar un viraje; *the car swerved* el coche dio un viraje ‖ desviarse, apartarse; *I had to swerve to avoid him* tuve que apartarme para evitar chocar contra él; *he never swerves from his duty* nunca se desvía de su deber ‖ SP hacer un regate, dar un regate (a player) | tener efecto (a ball).

swift [swift] *adj* veloz, rápido, da; *a swift horse* un caballo veloz ‖ ligero, ra; rápido, da; *swiftstep* paso ligero ‖ pronto, ta; rápido, da; *he was very swift to act* fue muy pronto en obrar ‖ rápido, da; *a swift answer* una respuesta rápida.
◆ *n* vencejo *m* (bird) ‖ lagartija *f* (lizard) ‖ carrete *m* (reel) ‖ tambor *m* (cylinder in a carding machine).

swifter [-ə*] *n* MAR andarivel *m* del cabrestante (of a capstan).

swift-footed [-'futid] *adj* de pies ligeros.

swift-handed [-'hændid] *adj* hábil.

swiftness [-nis] *n* rapidez *f*, velocidad *f* (speed) ‖ prontitud *f* (promptness).

swig [swig] *n* FAM trago *m*.

swig [swig] *vt* FAM beber a tragos.

swill [swil] *n* desperdicios *m pl*, bazofia *f* (pig's food) ‖ basura *f* (rubbish) ‖ FAM bazofia *f*, basura *f*; *I can't eat that swill* no puedo comer esa bazofia | trago *m* (a swig) ‖ *give the bucket a swill* limpia el cubo con mucha agua.

swill [swil] *vt* enjuagar, lavar con mucha agua; *to swill the bucket* lavar el cubo con mucha agua ‖ beber a tragos (to drink).
◆ *vi* beber a tragos (to drink) ‖ emborracharse (to get drunk).

swim [swim] *n* baño *m; I am going for a swim* me voy a dar un baño ‖ natación *f* (swimming) ‖ parte *f* de un río en la que abundan los peces (part of river) ‖ MED & FAM vértigo *m*, mareo *m* ‖ — *in the swim* al tanto (informed), al día (up to date) ‖ *my head is in a swim* la cabeza me da vueltas ‖ *to go for a swim* ir a nadar, ir a bañarse, ir a darse un baño.

swim* [swim] *vt* cruzar *or* atravesar a nado; *to swim a river* cruzar a nado un río ‖ hacer nadar (an animal) ‖ nadar; *to swim the hundred metres* nadar los cien metros; *to swim the butterfly* nadar la braza mariposa.
◆ *vi* nadar; *he swims very well* nada muy bien ‖ flotar (to be afloat) ‖ dar vueltas; *my head is swimming* la cabeza me da vueltas ‖ dar vueltas, bailar; *the room is swimming before my eyes* la habitación está bailando ante mis ojos ‖ estar cubierto de, estar lleno de, estar inundado; *the floor is swimming with blood* el suelo está cubierto de sangre; *the yard is swimming with water* el patio está inundado de agua ‖ — *to go swimming* ir a bañarse, ir a nadar ‖ *to swim against the tide* nadar contra la corriente ‖ *to swim backstroke* o *on one's back* nadar de espalda ‖ *to swim for it* salvarse a nado ‖ *to swim like a brick* nadar como un plomo ‖ *to swim like a fish* nadar como un pez ‖ *to swim out to sea* alejarse a nado de la playa ‖ *to swim under water* bucear, nadar debajo del agua ‖ FIG *to swim with the tide* seguir la corriente.
— OBSERV Pret ***swam***; pp ***swum***.

swim bladder [-'blædə*] *n* ZOOL vejiga *f* natatoria.

swim fin [-fin] *n* aleta *f* (of swimmer).

swimmer [-ə*] *n* nadador, ra.

swimming [-iŋ] *n* natación *f*; *swimming is my favourite sport* la natación es mi deporte favorito ‖ mareo *m*, vértigo *m* (of the head) ‖ *synchronized swimming* natación sincronizada.
◆ *adj* inundado, da (eyes) ‖ que nada, nadador, ra ‖ que da vueltas (head).

swimming bath [-iŋbɑ:θ] *n* piscina *f* [AMER pileta *f*] (swimming pool).

swimming belt [-iŋbelt] *n* flotador *m*.

swimming cap [-iŋkæp] *n* gorro *m* de baño.

swimming costume [-iŋ'kɔstju:m] *n* traje *m* de baño, bañador *m*.

swimmingly [-iŋli] *adv* a las mil maravillas.

swimming pool [-iŋpu:l] *n* piscina *f* [AMER pileta *f*]; *indoor, outdoor swimming pool* piscina cubierta, al aire libre.

swimming suit [-iŋsju:t]; **swimsuit** [-sju:t] *n* traje *m* de baño, bañador *m* (bathing suit).

swimming trunks [-iŋtrʌŋks] *pl n* bañador *m sing* de hombre.

swindle ['swindl] *n* estafa *f*, timo *m*.

swindle ['swindl] *vt* estafar, timar (to cheat); *to swindle s.o. out of money* estafar dinero a alguien.
◆ *vi* estafar, timar.

swindler [-ə*] *n* estafador, ra; timador, ra.

swine [swain] *n* cerdo *m*, cochino *m*, puerco *m* [AMER chancho *m*] ‖ — *to eat like a swine* comer como un cerdo ‖ FAM *you swine!* ¡canalla!, ¡cerdo!
— OBSERV El plural de *swine* es *swine*.

swineherd [-hə:d] *n* porquero *m*, porquerizo *m*.

swinery [-əri] *n* pocilga *f*.

swing [swiŋ] *n* balanceo *m*, vaivén *m*, oscilación *f* (oscillation) ‖ columpio *m*, balancín *m* (plaything); *the child is sitting on the swing* el niño está sentado en el columpio ‖ oscilación *f* (of pendulum) ‖ recorrido *m* (distance) ‖ impulso *m*, ímpetu *m* (force) ‖ paso *m* rítmico (walk) ‖ golpe *m* (blow) ‖ FIG cambio *m* brusco, viraje *m*; *there has been a swing to the left in public opinion* ha habido un cambio brusco hacia la izquierda en la opinión pública ‖ COMM movimiento *m*, fluctuación *f* (in share prices) ‖ MUS ritmo *m* (of music) | «swing» *m* (jazz style) ‖ SP «swing» *m* (in boxing, in golf) ‖ — FIG *at full swing* con toda rapidez, a toda velocidad ‖ FIG *the party is in full swing* la fiesta está en pleno apogeo | *the plant is in full swing* la fábrica está en plena actividad | *to get into the swing of* ponerse al corriente de, coger el truco a ‖ *to give a swing* columpiar (a child), empujar (a hammock), girar (a starting handle) ‖ FIG *to give full swing to* dar libre curso a | *to go with a swing* ir sobre ruedas.
◆ *adj* giratorio, ria (bridge, etc.).

swing* [swiŋ] *vt* dar vueltas a, hacer virar; *to swing the cane* dar vueltas al bastón ‖ hacer oscilar, balancear (sth. suspended) ‖ mecer (in the arms) ‖ columpiar, balancear (on a swing) ‖ balancear, menear; *to swing one's hips* menear las caderas; *swinging his legs* balanceando las piernas ‖ colgar (to hang up); *to swing a hammock* colgar una hamaca ‖ blandir (sword, etc.) ‖ hacer girar; *to swing the wheels of a car* hacer girar las ruedas de un coche ‖ MUS tocar con ritmo ‖ — SP *to swing a blow* pegar un golpe ‖ *to swing a car round* dar un viraje brusco ‖ *to swing a jury* poner de su parte al jurado, ganar al jurado ‖ *to swing an election* ganar una elección ‖ AVIAT *to swing a propeller* hacer girar una hélice ‖ FAM *to swing it* fingirse enfermo | *to swing it on s.o.* engañar a uno ‖ *to swing the cargo ashore* descargar las mercancías ‖ *to swing the bells* echar las campanas a vuelo ‖ *to swing s.o. round and round* dar vueltas en volandas a uno ‖ *to swing sth. right round* dar una vuelta completa a algo ‖ *to swing up a load with a crane* levantar un peso con una grúa.
◆ *vi* oscilar; *the pendulum swung* el péndulo osciló ‖ girar; *the door swung on its hinges* la puerta giró sobre sus goznes ‖ columpiarse, balancearse; *she was swinging in the hammock* se estaba balanceando en la hamaca ‖ colgar (to hang) ‖ FIG dar un giro, volverse, virar; *public opinion swung in his favour* la opinión pública dio un giro en su favor ‖ contonearse; *she was swinging down the road* iba contoneándose por la calle ‖ bailar (to dance) ‖ intentar golpear, intentar dar un golpe; *he swung at me but missed* intentó darme un golpe pero falló ‖ montar de un salto; *to swing aboard a bus* montar de un salto en el autobús ‖ — FAM *he swung for murder* le colgaron por homicidio ‖ *the troops swung in through the gates* las tropas atravesaron la puerta a paso rápido ‖ *to swing clear* dar un viraje para evitar un choque ‖ *to swing open* abrirse de par en par (a door) ‖ *to swing round* dar media vuelta (person), girar (car) ‖ *to swing to* cerrarse (door) ‖ *to swing to and fro* balancearse; oscilar (pendulum).
— OBSERV Pret y pp ***swung***.

swing bridge [-'bridʒ] *n* puente *m* giratorio.

swing door [-dɔ:*] *n* puerta *f* de batiente.

swingeing ['swindʒiŋ] *adj* inmenso, sa.

swinging ['swiŋiŋ] *adj* oscilante ‖ MUS rítmico, ca ‖ FAM de vida alegre | muy moderno, na ‖ *swinging door* puerta *f* de batiente.
◆ *n* oscilación *f* ‖ balanceo *m* ‖ MUS ritmo *m*.

swingletree [-tri:] *n* balancín *m*.

swing shift ['swiŋʃift] *n* US turno *m* de la tarde.

swinish ['swainiʃ] *adj* cochino, na ‖ *a swinish eater* una persona glotona *or* tragona.

swipe [swaip] *n* golpetazo *m* (blow) ‖ tortazo *m* (slap).
◆ *pl* cerveza *f sing* floja.

swipe [swaip] *vt* FAM afanar, limpiar, birlar (to steal) ‖ golpear con fuerza (to hit) ‖ dar un tortazo a (to slap).

swirl [swə:l] *n* remolino *m*, torbellino *m* (of water, dust, air).

swirl [swə:l] *vt* formar remolinos con, formar torbellinos con.
◆ *vi* arremolinarse, hacer remolinos *or* torbellinos (water) ‖ dar vueltas (ideas, one's head).

swirling [-iŋ] *adj* turbulento, ta; revuelto, ta.

swish [swiʃ] *adj* elegante.
◆ *n* crujido *m*, silbido *m* (hissing sound) ‖ chasquido *m* (of a whip) ‖ susurro *m* (of receding waves) ‖ frufrú *m*, crujido *m* (of silk) ‖ latigazo *m* (lash).

swish; swoosh [swuʃ] [swiʃ] *vt* blandir (sword) ‖ hacer chasquear (a cane, a whip) ‖ sacudir, menear; *the bull swished its tail* el toro sacudió el rabo ‖ azotar (the air, s.o.).
◆ *vi* susurrar (water) ‖ dar un chasquido (a whip) ‖ hender el aire (a sword) ‖ crujir (silk).

Swiss [swis] *adj/n* suizo, za ‖ — *the Swiss* los suizos ‖ *the Swiss Guard* la Guardia Suiza.

switch [switʃ] *n* ELECTR interruptor *m*, conmutador *m* ‖ agujas *f pl* (railway points) ‖ desviación *f* (change of line) ‖ cambio *m*, paso *m*; *the switch from steam trains to electric trains* el paso de los trenes de vapor a los trenes eléctricos ‖ cambio *m*; *a switch in public opinion* un cambio de la opinión pública ‖ látigo *m* (whip) ‖ fusta *f* (riding whip) ‖ palmeta *f* (carpet beater) ‖ varilla *f* (for punishing) ‖ golpe *m* de fusta *or* de palmeta *or* de varilla (blow) ‖ trenza *f* postiza (tress of hair) ‖ mechón *m*, punta *f* de la cola (end of animal's tail).

switch [switʃ] *vt* desviar, cambiar de vía (a train) ‖ cambiar (places) ‖ cambiar de (policy) ‖ menear, agitar, sacudir; *the horse switched its*

tail el caballo meneó el rabo || blandir (the whip) || azotar, golpear, dar golpes (to beat) || FIG encaminar, orientar, encauzar (to guide).
◆ *vi* cambiar, pasar; *to switch from one to the other* pasar de uno a otro || desviarse.
◆ *phr v* *to switch off* desconectar | apagar (a light, radio, TV) | cortar (the current) | parar (car, engine) || *to switch on* encender (light) | encender, poner (radio, TV) | poner en marcha, arrancar (car, engine) || *to switch round* cambiar de sitio *or* de idea.

switchback [-bæk] *n* carretera *f* en zigzag (road) || vía *f* de tren en zigzag (railway) || montaña *f* rusa (scenic railway).

switchblade knife [-ˌbleidnaif] *n* US navaja *f* de muelle.

switchboard [-bɔːd] *n* ELECTR cuadro *m or* tablero *m* de distribución || centralita *f* de teléfonos (of phone) || *switchboard operator* telefonista *m* & *f*.

switchgear [-giə*] *n* dispositivos *m pl* de distribución.

switch knife [-naif] *n* navaja *f* de muelle.

switchman [-mən] *n* guardagujas *m inv*.
— OBSERV El plural de *switchman* es *switchmen*.

switchyard [ˈswitʃjɑːd] *n* patio *m* de maniobras.

Switzerland [ˈswitsələnd] *pr n* GEOGR Suiza *f*.

swivel [ˈswivl] *n* TECH eslabón *m* giratorio, pivote *m* || cabeza *f* de inyección de lodo (in oil wells).

swivel [ˈswivl] *vi* girar.
◆ *vt* hacer girar.

swivel chair [-tʃɛə*] *n* silla *f* giratoria.

swivel seat [-siːt] *n* asiento *m* giratorio.

swizzle [ˈswizl] *n* cóctel *m* (drink) || FAM estafa *f*, timo *m* || *swizzle stick* varilla *f* de cóctel.

swollen [ˈswəulən] *pp* → **swell.**

swoon [swuːn] *n* desmayo *m*, desvanecimiento *m*.

swoon [swuːn] *vi* desmayarse, desvanecerse.

swoop [swuːp] *n* descenso *m* en picado (of an aeroplane) || calada *f* (of a bird) || visita *f* de inspección sin previo aviso || redada *f* (by police) || FIG arremetida *f* (attack) || — *in* o *at one fell swoop* de un golpe || *to make a swoop on* abalanzarse sobre, precipitarse sobre.

swoop [swuːp] *vi* abatirse, abalanzarse, calarse (bird) || bajar en picado (aeroplane) || irrumpir; *the police swooped on the club* la policía irrumpió en el club || hacer una redada (to raid) || abalanzarse, precipitarse; *the children swooped on the cake* los niños se precipitaron sobre el pastel.

swoosh [swuʃ] *n/vt/vi* → **swish.**

swop [swɔp] *n/vt/vi* → **swap.**

sword [sɔːd] *n* espada *f*; *to sheathe one's sword* envainar la espada; *to plunge one's sword in up to the hilt* meter la espada hasta la guarnición || estoque *m* (in bullfighting) || — FIG *by fire and sword* a sangre y fuego | *he who lives by the sword will die by the sword* quienes matan con la espada por la espada morirán, quien a hierro mata a hierro muere | *to be at swords' point* estar a matar || *to cross swords with* cruzar la espada con (to fight), medir las armas con, habérselas con (to argue) || *to measure swords with s.o.* cruzar la espada con uno || *to put a country to fire and sword* entrar a sangre y fuego en un país || *to put to the sword* pasar a cuchillo || *to unsheathe* o *to draw one's sword* desenvainar la espada || *two-edged sword* espada de dos filos || FIG *with a sword at one's throat* con un puñal en el pecho.

sword belt [-belt] *n* talabarte *m*.

sword dance [-dɑːns] *n* danza *f* de las espadas.

swordfish [-fiʃ] *n* pez *m* espada (fish).

swordplay [-plei] *n* esgrima *f*.

swordsman [-zmən] *n* espadachín *m*, espada *f*; *to be a good swordsman* ser buena espada || esgrimidor *m* (fencer).
— OBSERV El plural de *swordsman* es *swordsmen*.

swordsmanship [-zmənʃip] *n* esgrima *f*, habilidad *f* con la espada.

sword stick [-stik] *n* bastón *m* de estoque.

sword-swallower [-ˈswɔləuə*] *n* tragasables *m*.

sword thrust [-θrʌst] *n* estocada *f*.

swore [swɔː*] *pret* → **swear.**

sworn [swɔːn] *pp* → **swear.**
◆ *adj* jurado, da; declarado, da; *sworn enemies* enemigos jurados || JUR bajo juramento (statement) | que ha jurado (witness) | juramentado, da (translator, etc.).

swot [swɔt] *n* FAM empollón, ona (person who studies excessively) | estudio *m* (study).

swot [swɔt] *vt/vi* FAM empollar (to study) || *to swot up* empollar.

swum [swʌm] *pp* → **swim.**

swung [swʌŋ] *pret/pp* → **swing.**

sybarite [ˈsibərait] *n* sibarita *m* & *f*.

sybaritic [ˌsibəˈritik]; **sybaritical** [-əl] *adj* sibarita, sibarítico, ca.

sycamore [ˈsikəmɔː*] *n* sicómoro *m*, sicomoro *m* (tree, wood).

sycophancy [ˈsikəfənsi] *n* adulación *f*, servilismo *m*.

sycophant [ˈsikəfənt] *n* sicofante *m*, sicofanta *m* (defamer) || adulador, ra (flatterer).

sycophantic [ˌsikəˈfæntik] *adj* adulatorio, ria; servil.

sycosis [saiˈkəusis] *n* MED sicosis *f inv*.

Sydney [ˈsidni] *pr n* GEOGR Sydney.

syllabary [ˈsiləbəri] *n* cartilla *f*, silabario *m*.

syllabic [siˈlæbik] *adj* silábico, ca.

syllabicate [siˈlæbikeit] *vt* silabear, dividir en sílabas.

syllabication [siˈlæbiˈkeiʃən]; **syllabification** [siˈlæbifiˈkeiʃən] *n* silabeo *m*, división *f* en sílabas.

syllabify [siˈlæbifai]; **syllabize** [ˈsiləbaiz] *vt* silabear.

syllable [ˈsiləbl] *n* sílaba *f*; *open, accentuated, closed syllable* sílaba abierta, aguda, cerrada || FIG palabra *f*; *there is not a syllable of truth in it* no hay una palabra de verdad en ello.

syllable [ˈsiləbl] *vt/vi* silabear.

syllabub [ˈsiləbʌb] *n* batido *m* de leche, azúcar y licores.

syllabus [ˈsiləbəs] *n* programa *m* de estudios || extracto *m*, resumen *m* (summary).
— OBSERV El plural de *syllabus* es *syllabuses* o *syllabi*.

syllepsis [siˈlepsis] *n* GRAMM silepsis *f inv*.
— OBSERV El plural de la palabra inglesa es *syllepses*.

syllogism [ˈsilədʒizəm] *n* silogismo *m*.

syllogistic [ˈsiləˈdʒistik]; **syllogistical** [-əl] *adj* silogístico, ca.

syllogize [ˈsilədʒaiz] *vi* hacer silogismos, silogizar.
◆ *vt* deducir por silogismos.

sylph [silf] *n* MYTH sílfide *f* (female spirit) | silfo *m* (male spirit) || FIG sílfide *f* (young woman).

sylphid [-id] *n* MYTH joven sílfide *f* (female spirit) | joven silfo *m* (male spirit).

sylphlike [-laik] *adj* de sílfide.

sylvan; silvan [ˈsilvən] *adj* selvático, ca; silvestre.
◆ *n* MYTH silvano *m*.

sylvanite [ˈsilvənait] *n* MIN silvanita *f*.

sylviculture [ˈsilvikʌltjə*] *n* AGR silvicultura *f*.

symbiosis [ˌsimbiˈəusis] *n* simbiosis *f inv*.

symbiotic [ˌsimbiˈɔtik] *adj* simbiótico, ca.

symbol [ˈsimbəl] *n* símbolo *m*.

symbolic [simˈbɔlik]; **symbolical** [-əl] *adj* simbólico, ca.

symbolism [ˈsimbəlizəm] *n* simbolismo *m*.

symbolist [ˈsimbəlist] *n* simbolista *m* & *f*.

symbolization [ˈsimbəlaiˈzeiʃən] *n* simbolización *f*.

symbolize [ˈsimbəlaiz] *vt* simbolizar.

symmetric [siˈmetrik]; **symmetrical** [-əl] *adj* simétrico, ca.

symmetrize [ˈsimitraiz] *vt* hacer simétrico.

symmetry [ˈsimitri] *n* simetría *f*.

sympathetic [ˈsimpəˈθetik] *adj* compasivo, va (*to* con) (compassionate); *a sympathetic person* una persona compasiva || comprensivo, va (understanding) || amable (kind) || que simpatiza (having an affinity of feeling) || favorable, en favor de (favourably disposed); *to be sympathetic to a plan* mostrarse favorable a un proyecto || ANAT simpático || PHYS simpático, ca || — *sympathetic ink* tinta simpática || ANAT *sympathetic nervous system* gran simpático *m* || *sympathetic strike* huelga *f* por solidaridad.

sympathetically [-əli] *adv* comprensivamente || con compasión.

sympathize [ˈsimpəθaiz] *vi* entender, comprender, compartir; *I sympathize with his point of view* entiendo su punto de vista || compadecerse, compadecer; *I sympathize with the poor* me compadezco de los pobres, compadezco a los pobres || dar el pésame (to express one's condolences) || *I sympathize with you* le acompaño en el sentimiento.

sympathizer [-ə*] *n* simpatizante *m* & *f*.

sympathy [ˈsimpəθi] *n* pésame *m*, condolencia *f*; *to send one's sympathy* dar el pésame || comprensión *f*; *sympathy for s.o.'s problems* comprensión de los problemas de alguien; *sympathy between two people* comprensión entre dos personas || compasión *f*, lástima *f*; *I have no sympathy for drunks* no tengo compasión por los borrachos || PHYS resonancia *f*; *a string which vibrates in sympathy* una cuerda que vibra por resonancia || MED simpatía *f*; *sympathy pains* dolores de simpatía || — *his sympathies lie with the anarchists* simpatiza con los anarquistas || *message of sympathy* pésame || *my deepest sympathy* le acompaño en el sentimiento, mi más sentido pésame || *prices rose in sympathy* subieron los precios a la par || *sympathy strike* huelga *f* por solidaridad || *to be in sympathy with* estar en favor de (to favour), estar de acuerdo con (to identify o.s. with) || *to strike in sympathy* declararse en huelga por solidaridad.

symphonic [simˈfɔnik] *adj* sinfónico, ca.

symphonist [ˈsimfənist] *n* sinfonista *m*.

symphony [ˈsimfəni] *n* sinfonía *f* || — *symphony concert* concierto sinfónico || *symphony orchestra* orquesta sinfónica.

symphysis [ˈsimfisis] *n* sínfisis *f inv*.
— OBSERV El plural de *symphysis* es *symphyses*.

symposium [simˈpəuzjəm] *n* simposio *m*.
— OBSERV El plural de la palabra inglesa es *symposia* o *symposiums*.

symptom [ˈsimptəm] *n* síntoma *m* | FIG señal *f*, síntoma *m*, indicio *m*.

symptomatic ['simptə'mætik] *adj* sintomático, ca.

symptomatology [ˌsimptəmə'tɔlədʒi] *n* sintomatología *f.*

synaeresis [ˌsi'niərəsis] *n* GRAMM sinéresis *f inv.*

synaestesia [ˌsinəs'θiːzjə] *n* MED sinestesia *f.*

synagogue; synagog ['sinəgɔg] *n* sinagoga *f.*

synalepha ['sinə'liːfə] *n* US GRAMM sinalefa *f.*

synallagmatic [ˌsinəlæg'mætik] *adj* JUR sinalagmático, ca.

synaloepha ['sinə'liːfə] *n* GRAMM sinalefa *f.*

synarthrosis [ˌsinɑː'θrəusis] *n* sinartrosis *f inv.*

sync; synch [siŋk] *n* FAM sincronización *f* || *to be out of sync* no estar sincronizados.

synchrocyclotron ['siŋkrəu'saiklətrɔn] *n* PHYS sincrociclotrón *m.*

synchromesh [siŋkrəu'meʃ] *n* AUT sincronizador *m*, cambio *m* sincronizado de velocidades.
◆ *adj* AUT sincronizado, da.

synchronic [siŋ'krɔnik] *adj* sincrónico, ca; síncrono, na.

synchronism ['siŋkrənizəm] *n* sincronismo *m.*

synchronization ['siŋkrənaiz'zeiʃən] *n* sincronización *f.*

synchronize ['siŋkrənaiz] *vt* sincronizar.
◆ *vi* ocurrir simultáneamente, coincidir (to occur simultaneously) || funcionar sincrónicamente, ser sincrónico (to work in unison).

synchronizer [-ə*] *n* sincronizador *m.*

synchronous ['siŋkrənəs] *adj* sincrónico, ca; síncrono, na.

synchrotron ['siŋkrəutrɔn] *n* PHYS sincrotrón *m.*

synclinal [sin'klainəl] *adj* sinclinal.

syncline ['siŋklain] *n* sinclinal *m.*

syncopate ['siŋkəpeit] *vt* GRAMM & MUS sincopar.

syncopation ['siŋkə'peiʃən] *n* GRAM & MUS síncopa *f.*

syncope ['siŋkəpi] *n* MED síncope *m* || MUS & GRAMM síncopa *f.*

syncretic [siŋ'kritik] *adj* sincrético, ca.

syncretism ['siŋkritizəm] *n* sincretismo *m.*

syncretist ['siŋkritist] *n* sincretista *m* & *f.*

syncretistic [θiŋkri'tistik] *adj* sincretista.

syndactyl; syndactyle [sin'dæktil] *adj* ZOOL sindáctilo, la.
◆ *n* ZOOL sindáctilo *m.*

syndic ['sindik] *n* síndico *m.*

syndical [-əl] *adj* sindical.

syndicalism [-əlizəm] *n* sindicalismo *m.*

syndicalist [-əlist] *adj/n* sindicalista.

syndicate ['sindikit] *n* sindicado *m* (of syndics) || sindicato *m* (group of persons or firms) || cadena *f* de periódicos (chain of newspapers) || agencia *f* de prensa (news agency).

syndicate ['sindikeit] *vt* sindicar.
◆ *vi* sindicarse.

syndrome ['sindrəum] *n* MED síndrome *m* (group of disease symptoms).

synecdoche [si'nekdəki] *n* sinécdoque *f.*

syneresis [si'niərəsis] *n* US sinéresis *f inv.*

synergetic [ˌsinəː'dʒetik] *adj* sinérgico, ca.

synergic [si'nəːdʒik] *adj* sinérgico, ca.

synergy [ˌsinəːdʒi] *n* sinergia *f.*

synesthesia [ˌsinəs'θiziə] *n* US sinestesia *f.*

synod ['sinəd] *n* REL sínodo *m*; *the Holy Synod* el Santo Sínodo.

synodal [-əl] *adj* sinodal.

synodic; synodical [si'nɔdik] *adj* REL sinódico, ca.

synonym ['sinənim] *n* sinónimo *m.*

synonymic [ˌsinə'nimik]; **synonymical** [-əl] *adj* sinonímico, ca.

synonymous [si'nɔniməs] *adj* sinónimo, ma (*with* de).

synonymy [si'nɔnimi] *n* sinonimia *f.*

synopsis [si'nəpsis] *n* sinopsis *f inv* || cuadro *m* sinóptico (diagram).
— OBSERV El plural de *synopsis* es *synopses.*

synoptic [si'nɔptik]; **synoptical** [-əl] *adj* sinóptico, ca.

synovia [si'nəuviə] *n* ANAT sinovia *f.*

synovial [-l] *adj* ANAT sinovial || *synovial capsule* cápsula *f* sinovial.

synovitis [ˌsinə'vaitis] *n* MED sinovitis *f inv.*

syntactic [sin'tæktik]; **syntactical** [-əl] *adj* GRAMM sintáctico, ca.

syntax ['sintæks] *n* GRAMM sintaxis *f inv.*

synthesis ['sinθisis] *n* síntesis *f inv.*
— OBSERV El plural de *synthesis* es *syntheses.*

synthesize ['sinθisaiz] *vt* sintetizar.

synthesizer [-ə*] *n* MUS sintetizador *m.*

synthetic [sin'θetik]; **synthetical** [-əl] *adj* sintético, ca; *synthetic rubber* caucho sintético.

synthetize ['sinθitaiz] *vt* sintetizar.

syntonic [sin'tɔnik] *adj* sintónico, ca.

syntonization ['sintənai'zeiʃən] *n* sintonización *f*, sintonía *f.*

syntonize [sintənaiz] *vt* sintonizar.

syntony ['sintəni] *n* sintonía *f.*

syphillis ['sifilis] *n* MED sífilis *f inv.*

syphilitic ['sifi'litik] *adj/n* MED sifilítico, ca.

syphon ['saifən] *n* ⟶ **siphon.**

Syracusan ['saiərə'kjuːzən] *adj/n* siracusano, na.

Syracuse ['saiərəkjuːz] *pr n* GEOGR Siracusa.

Syria ['siriə] *pr n* GEOGR Siria *f.*

Syrian ['siriən] *adj/n* sirio, ria; siriaco, ca.

syringa [si'riŋgə] *n* BOT jeringuilla *f.*

syringe ['sirindʒ] *n* jeringuilla *f*, jeringa *f* (for injections) || jeringa *f* (for cleansing).

syringe ['sirindʒ] *vt* jeringar (to clean) || inyectar con jeringuilla (to inject).

syrinx ['siriŋks] *n* siringe *m* (of birds) || siringa *f*, flauta *f* de Pan (panpipe) || MED trompa *f* de Eustaquio.
— OBSERV El plural de *syrinx* es *syrinxes* o *syringes.*

syrup; sirup ['sirəp] *n* jarabe *m* (drink) || MED jarabe *m*; *cough syrup* jarabe para la tos || almíbar *m*; *peaches in syrup* melocotones en almíbar.

syrupy [-i] *adj* almibarado, da.

system ['sistim] *n* sistema *m*; *administrative system* sistema administrativo; *public-address system* sistema de altavoces || PHIL & ASTR & GEOL & BIOL sistema *m* || régimen *m*; *feudal system* régimen feudal || red *f*; *railway system* red de ferrocarriles || método *m*; *to work with system* trabajar con método || MED sistema *m*; *nervous system* sistema nervioso | constitución *f*, organismo *m* (constitution) || — *centimetre-gram-second system* sistema cegesimal || *decimal system* sistema decimal || *it's bad for your system* es malo para el organismo || *metric system* sistema métrico || *number system* sistema de numeración || *planetary system* sistema planetario || *solar system* sistema solar || INFORM *systems analyst* analista *m* & *f* de sistemas | *systems engineer* ingeniero, ra de sistemas | *systems program* programa *m* del sistema || FIG & FAM *to get sth. out of one's system* desfogarse.

systematic ['sisti'mætik]; **systematical** [-əl] *adj* sistemático, ca.

systematically [-əli] *adv* sistemáticamente.

systematics [-s] *n* sistemática *f.*

systematization ['sistimətai'zeiʃən] *n* sistematización *f.*

systematize ['sistimətaiz] *vt* sistematizar.

systemization [ˌsistimai'zeiʃən] *n* sistematización *f.*

systemize ['sistimaiz] *vt* sistematizar.

systole ['sistəli] *n* ANAT sístole *f.*

syzygy ['sizidʒi] *n* ASTR sicigia *f.*

T

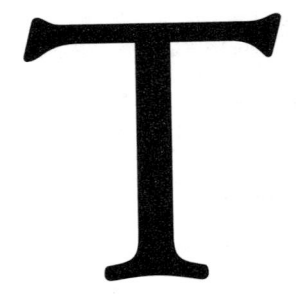

t [ti:] *n* t *f* (letter) || — FAM *to a T* como anillo al dedo; *this dress suits you to a T* este traje le sienta como anillo al dedo; de maravilla, de perlas; *this job suits me to a T* este trabajo me viene de perlas || FIG *to cross one's t's* poner los puntos sobre las íes.

ta [tɑ:] *interj* FAM ¡gracias!

tab [tæb] *n* etiqueta *f* (label) || MIL charretera *f*, hombrera *f* || herrete *m* (of shoelace) || oreja *f*, lengüeta *f* (of shoe) || orejera *f* (of cap) || presilla *f* (for hanging up coat) || uñero *m* (of book) || pestaña *f* (of a can) || AVIAT aleta *f* compensadora || US FAM cuenta *f* (bill) || FAM *to keep tabs on* no perder de vista.

tabard ['tæbəd] *n* tabardo *m*.

tabasco [tə'bæskəu] *n* CULIN tabasco *m*.

tabby ['tæbi] *n* gato *m* atigrado (cat with striped markings) || gata *f* (female cat) || falena *f* (butterfly) || muaré *m*, moaré *m* (fabric) || FAM chismosa *f* (old gossip).
◆ *adj* atigrado, da.

tabernacle ['tæbənækl] *n* REL sagrario *m*, tabernáculo *m* || ARCH templete *m* (niche with a canopy) | templo *m*, santuario *m* (place of worship).

tabes ['teibi:z] *n* MED tabes *f* || MED *tabes dorsalis* ataxia locomotora.

tablature ['tæblətʃə*] *n* MUS tabladura *f*.

table ['teibl] *n* mesa *f*; *to lay* o *to set the table* poner la mesa; *to rise from table* levantarse de la mesa; *to sit down at the table* sentarse a la mesa; *to wait* o *to help at table* servir la mesa; *the table consisted of many outstanding personalities* la mesa se componía de muchas personalidades eminentes; *draw* o *extension table* mesa con largueros; *table with flaps* mesa de alas; *gambling* o *gaming table* mesa de juego; *folding table* mesa de tijera *or* plegable; *operating table* mesa de operaciones || mesilla *f*, mesa *f*; *bedside table* mesilla de noche || bancada *f* (of machine tool) || mesa *f* (facet of a jewel) || GEOGR meseta *f* [*AMER* altiplano *m*] (tableland) || ARCH faja *f*, moldura *f* (stringcourse) | tablero *m* (panel) || ANAT tabla *f* (skull tissue) || lista *f*, tabla *f* (list) || lista *f* (of prices) || grúa *f* (railway) || cuadro *m* (for figures, for values, etc.) || MATH tabla *f*; *multiplication table* tabla de multiplicar; *logarithm table* tabla de logaritmos || ANAT palma *f* (of the hand) || — *at table* en la mesa || HIST *knights of the Round Table* caballeros de la Tabla Redonda || *nest of tables* mesas de nido || FIG *round table* mesa redonda || *sorting table* mesa de batalla (post office) || *table of contents* índice *m* || *table wine* vino *m* de mesa || FIG *the tables are turned* se volvieron las tornas || REL *the Tables of the Law* las tablas de la Ley || *to clear the table* quitar la mesa || *to keep a good table* tener buena mesa, dar bien de comer || *to leave the table* levantarse de la mesa || FIG *to turn the tables on s.o.* volverle a uno las tornas || FAM *under the table* por el suelo (drunk) || GEOL *water table* capa freática.

table ['teibl] *vt* presentar; *to table a motion* presentar una moción; *to table a motion of confidence* presentar la cuestión de confianza || MAR reforzar (the edge of a sail) || poner en un cuadro (to tabulate) || TECH encajar || US dar carpetazo a (to postpone indefinitely).

tableau ['tæbləu] *n* cuadro *m* || *tableau vivant* cuadro vivo.
— OBSERV El plural de *tableau* es *tableaux* o *tableaus*.

table centre ['teibl'sentə*] *n* centro *m* de mesa.

tablecloth ['teiblklɔθ] *n* mantel *m* (for meals) || tapete *m* (table cover).

table companion ['teiblkəm'pænjən] *n* convidado, da; comensal *m* & *f*.

table cover ['teibl,kʌvə*] *n* tapete *m*.

table d'hôte ['tɑ:bl'dəut] *n* menú *m*.
— OBSERV El plural es *tables d'hôte*.

table lamp ['teibl,læmp] *n* lámpara *f* de mesa.

tableland ['teibllænd] *n* GEOGR meseta *f* [*AMER* altiplano *m*].

talbe leaf ['teiblli:f] *n* larguero *m*.

table linen ['teibl,linin] *n* mantelería *f*.

table manners ['teibl,mænəz] *pl n* modales *m* en la mesa.

tablemat ['teiblmæt] *n* salvamanteles *m inv*.

table napkin ['teibl'næpkin] *n* servilleta *f*.

table service ['teibl,sə:vis] *n* servicio *m* de mesa, vajilla *f*.

tablespoon ['teiblspu:n] *n* cucharón *m*.

tablespoonful [-ful] *n* cucharada *f*.

tablet ['tæblit] *n* lápida *f* (memorial or commemorative stone) || tableta *f*, pastilla *f* (pastille, pill) || bloc *m*, taco *m* (of writing paper) || pastilla *f* (of soap) || tableta *f* (of chocolate) || HIST tablilla *f* (for writing on).

table talk ['teibltɔk] *n* conversación *f* de sobremesa.

table tennis ['teibl,tenis] *n* tenis *m* de mesa, ping-pong *m*.

tableware ['teiblwɛə*] *n* vajilla *f*, servicio *m* de mesa.

table water ['teibl,wɔ:tə*] *n* agua *f* mineral.

tabloid ['tæblɔid] *n* periódico *m* de pequeño formato || periódico *m* sensacionalista || MED tableta *f*.

taboo; tabu [tə'bu:] *adj* tabú.
◆ *n* tabú *m*.

tabor ['teibɔ:*] *n* MUS tamboril *m*.

taboret; tabouret ['tæbərit] *n* taburete *m* (stool) || bastidor *m*, tambor *m* (for embroidery).

tabu [tə'bu:] *adj/n* → **taboo.**

tabular ['tæbjulə*] *adj* tabular.

tabula rasa ['tæbjulə'rɑ:zə] *n* PHIL tábula rasa, tabla *f* rasa.

tabulate ['tæbjuleit] *vt* disponer en tablas (to put in tables) || clasificar (to arrange systematically).

tabulation [,tæbju'leiʃən] *n* disposición *f* en tablas.

tabulator ['tæbjuleitə*] *n* tabulador *m* (of a typewriter) || tabuladora *f* (machine).

tachometer [tæ'kɔmitə*] *n* tacómetro *m*.

tachycardia [,tæki'kɑ:djə] *n* MED taquicardia *f*.

tachymeter [tæ'kimitə*] *n* taquímetro *m*.

tachymetry [tæ'kimitri] *n* taquimetría *f*.

tacit ['tæsit] *adj* tácito, ta; *tacit understanding* acuerdo tácito.

taciturn ['tæsitə:n] *adj* taciturno, na.

taciturnity [,tæsi'tə:niti] *n* taciturnidad *f*.

Tacitus ['tæsitəs] *pr n* HIST Tácito *m*.

tack [tæk] *n* tachuela *f* (nail); *I need four tacks to fasten this photograph* me hacen falta cuatro tachuelas para fijar esta fotografía || hilván *m* (stitch) || MAR amura *f* (rope) | puño *m* de la amura (corner of a sail) | bordada *f* (distance sailed without changing direction) | virada *f* (act of changing direction) || FIG dirección *f*, línea *f* de conducta (course of action) | táctica *f* || — FIG *to be on the right tack* ir por buen camino | *to be on the wrong tack* estar equivocado | *to get down to brass tacks* ir al grano.

tack [tæk] *vt* fijar con tachuelas (to nail) || hilvanar (to stitch) || añadir (to append).
◆ *vi* MAR virar de bordo || cambiar de táctica *or* de dirección *or* de rumbo || FIG *to tack on to s.o.* juntarse con uno.

tack board [-bɔ:d] *n* tablón *m* de anuncios.

tackle ['tækl]; **tackling** [-iŋ] *n* MAR aparejo *m* (rigging) | jarcias *f pl* (ropes) || aparejo *m*; *fishing tackle* aparejo de pescar || aparejo *m*, polipasto *m* (system of ropes and pulleys) || arreos *m pl* (a horse's harness) || trastos *m pl*, avíos *m pl* (equipment) || FIG cosas *f pl*, trastos *m pl* (belongings) || SP placaje *m* (in rugby and American football).

tackle ['tækl] *vt* agarrar (to seize); *the policeman tackled the thief* el policía agarró al ladrón || hacer un placaje a (in rugby) || atajar (in American football) || FIG abordar; *to tackle a problem* abordar un problema | emprender (task) || *to tackle up* poner arreos a (a horse).
◆ *vi* SP placar (rugby) | atajar (American football).

tackling [-iŋ] *n* → **tackle.**

tacky ['tæki] *adj* pegajoso, sa (sticky) || US FAM desastrado, da (shabby) | vulgar, común (vulgar).

tact [tækt] *n* tacto *m*, discreción *f*.

tactful [-ful] *adj* discreto, ta; lleno de tacto (showing tact) || discreto, ta; que tiene tacto (possessing tact).

tactic ['tæktik] *adj* táctico, ca.

tactical [-əl] *adj* táctico, ca; *tactical voting* voto *m* útil *or* táctico || estratégico, ca; *tactical importance* importancia estratégica || FIG hábil.

tactician [tæk'tiʃən] *n* MIL táctico *m* || FIG persona *f* hábil (who acts cleverly).

tactics ['tæktiks] *n* MIL táctica *f* || FIG táctica *f*.

tactile ['tæktail] *adj* táctil || FIG tangible.

tactless ['tæktlis] *adj* falto de tacto, que carece de tacto.

tactlessness [-nis] *n* falta *f* de tacto.

tactual ['tæktjuəl] *adj* táctil, del tacto.

tadpole ['tædpəul] *n* ZOOL renacuajo *m*.

taenia ['ti:niə] *n* tenia *f*, solitaria *f* (tapeworm) || ARCH tenia *f*.
— OBSERV El plural de esta palabra es *taeniae* o *taenias*.

taeniafuge ['ti:nifju:dʒ] *adj* tenífugo, ga.
◆ *n* tenífugo *m*.

taffeta ['tæfitə] *n* tafetán *m* (cloth).

taffrail ['tæfreil] *n* MAR coronamiento *m*.

taffy ['tæfi] *n* US melcocha *f*, arropía *f* || US FAM coba *f*, adulación *f* (flattery).

tafia ['tæfiə] *n* tafia *f*.

tag [tæg] *n* etiqueta *f* (label for identification, classification, indicating price, etc.) || tirador *m* [de bota] (for pulling boots up) || herrete *m* (of shoelace) || cabo *m* (end) || tópico *m* (cliché) || cita *f* (quotation) || estribillo *m* (of a song) || pingajo *m* (hanging bit of cloth) || pillapilla *m* (children's game) || FIG etiqueta *f*; *to give s.o. the tag of a coward* colgarle a uno la etiqueta de cobarde | apodo *m* (nickname) || — US *tag day* día *m* de la banderita | *tag end* final *m*.

tag [tæg] *vt* poner una etiqueta a (to provide with a label) || denominar (to name) || seguir de cerca (to follow) || pillar (in the game of tag) || FIG salpicar; *to tag a speech with quotations* salpicar de citas un discurso || marcar (molecule) || INFORM etiqueta *f* || *to tag on* añadir, agregar.
◆ *vi* *to tag along* seguir, venir detrás; *he tagged along with us* vino detrás de nosotros || *to tag along behind* seguir a distancia || *to tag on to s.o.* pegarse a uno.

Tagalog [tə'gɑ:lɔg] *adj/n* tagalo, la.
◆ *n* tagalo *m* (language).
— OBSERV El plural es *Tagalog* o *Tagalogs*.

Tagus ['teigəs] *pr n* GEOGR Tajo *m* (river).

Tahiti [tɑ:hi:ti] *pr n* GEOGR Tahití.

Tahitian [tɑ:'hi:ʃən] *adj/n* tahitiano, na.

Tai [tai] *adj/n* tailandés, esa.

taiga ['taigə] *n* taiga *f* (coniferous forests).

tail [teil] *n* cola *f* (when part of the body, i. e. in birds, fishes, snakes) || rabo *m*, cola *f* (as an appendage, i. e. in bulls, monkeys, horses, dogs, cats) || cola *f* (of procession, aircraft, dress, kite, vehicle) || cola *f* (of people) || comitiva *f*, séquito *m* (retinue) || faldón *m* (of a shirt, of a jacket) || PRINT pie *m* (of a page) || cola *f* (of hair) || FIG final *m*; *the tail of a storm* el final de una tormenta || JUR vínculo *m*, vinculación *f* || ASTR cabellera *f*, cola *f* (of a comet) || rabillo *m*, ángulo *m* (of eyes) || — FIG *from head to tail* de pies a cabeza | *I can't make head or tail of this* esto no tiene pies ni cabeza | *to turn tail* poner pies en polvorosa | *with one's tail between one's legs* con el rabo entre las piernas.
◆ *pl* cruz *f sing* (of a coin); *heads or tails?* ¿cara o cruz? || frac *m sing* (tailcoat).
◆ *adj* final, último, ma || JUR vinculado, da.

tail [teil] *vt* quitar el rabo a (to remove the stalks from) || poner cola a (to provide with a tail) || cerrar; *to tail a procession* cerrar una procesión || añadir (to add on) || ARCH empotrar (*in, into* en) || FAM seguir (to follow).
◆ *vi* seguir de cerca (*after* a) || hacer cola (to queue) || ARCH estar empotrado (*in, into* en) || *to tail away* o *off* o *out* ir disminuyendo (noise), ir apagándose (voice), alargarse (marching column).

tailback ['teilbæk] *n* caravana *f* (on the road).

tailboard [-,bɔ:d] *n* tabla *f* posterior de la plataforma (of a lorry or cart).

tailcoat [-'kəut] *n* frac *m*.

tail end [-end] *n* cola *f* (of a line of people, etc.) || final *m* (of a storm, etc.); *they arrived at the tail end of the second act* llegaron al final del segundo acto || FAM trasero *m* (bottom).

tail fin [-fin] *n* aleta *f* caudal (of a fish) || plano *m* de deriva (of a plane).

tailgate [-geit] *vt* seguir muy de cerca.

tailing [-iŋ] *pl n* escorias *f* (refuse material) || ARCH parte *f sing* empotrada.

tail lamp [-'læmp] *n* → **taillight.**

tailless [-lis] *adj* sin cola, sin rabo.

taillight ['tail,lait] **; tail lamp** [teil'læmp] *n* AUT piloto *m*, luz *f* posterior || farol *m* de cola (of a train).

tailor ['teilə*] *vt* sastre *m* || — *tailor's* sastrería *f* || *tailor's chalk* jaboncillo *m* de sastre.

tailor ['teilə*] *vt* hacer a la medida (to make to measure) || cortar; *a well-tailored suit* un traje bien cortado || vestir; *well-tailored person* persona bien vestida || FIG adaptar; *tailored to the needs of the American airlines* adaptado a las necesidades de las compañías aéreas americanas.
◆ *vi* ser sastre.

tailored [-d] *adj* *tailored dress* traje *m* sastre.

tailoring [-riŋ] *n* profesión *f* de sastre, sastrería *f* || corte *m* y confección.

tailor-made [-meid] *adj* hecho a la medida || sastre; *tailor-made suit* traje sastre || FIG adaptado, da.

tailpiece ['teilpi:s] *n* MUS cordal *m* || PRINT colofón *m*, florón *m*, viñeta *f* al final del capítulo || apéndice *m* (part added to the end of sth.).

tail pipe ['teil'paip] *n* AUT tubo *m* de escape || AVIAT tobera *f*.

tail plane ['teil'plein] *n* AVIAT plano *m* de cola.

tail skid ['teil'skid] *n* AVIAT patín *m* de cola.

tailspin ['teilspin] *n* AVIAT barrena *f* || *tailspin fall* caída *f* en barrena.

tailstock ['teil,stɔk] *n* TECH contrapunta *f*.

tail unit ['teil'ju:nit] *n* AVIAT planos *m pl* de estabilización, empenaje *m*.

tail wind ['teil'wind] *n* viento *m* de cola *or* trasero.

tain [tein] *n* azogue *m* (for mirror).

Taino ['tainəu] *adj/n* taino, na.

taint [teint] *n* corrupción *f*, infección *f* || mancha *f*; *the taint of sin* la mancha del pecado || MED tara *f*.

taint [teint] *vt* echar a perder (food) || corromper (to corrupt morally) || contaminar (to cause to be spoiled).
◆ *vi* corromperse || estropearse (food).

tainted [-id] *adj* echado, da a perder (food) || contaminado, da (water, air) || manchado, da (family, blood).

taintless [-lis] *adj* sin mancha, inmaculado, da.

Taipeh [,tai'pei] *pr n* GEOGR Taipei.

Taiwan [,taiwɑ:n] *pr n* GEOGR Taiwán.

take [teik] *n* presa *f* (in hunting) || pesca *f* (in fishing) || captura *f* (act of capturing) || CINEM toma *f* || US ingresos *m pl* (receipts).

take* [teik] *vt* tomar; *the army took the town* el ejército tomó la ciudad; *to take medicines, sugar, nourishment* tomar medicinas, azúcar, alimento; *to take breakfast, lunch, dinner* tomar el desayuno, el almuerzo, la cena; *to take the waters, the sea air* tomar las aguas, el aire del mar; *to take notes, information, measurements, s.o.'s temperature* tomar notas, informes, medidas, la temperatura a alguien; *to take a resolution* tomar una decisión; *to take a corner* tomar una curva; *to take sth. seriously, as a joke* tomar algo en serio, a broma || coger, tomar; *he took the book and ran off* cogió el libro y salió corriendo; *to take sth. from the drawer* coger algo en el cajón; *to take a bus, the train* coger el autobús, el tren; *we took the Madrid road* cogimos la carretera de Madrid || coger; *take a chair* coja una silla; *to take s.o. by the hand* coger a alguien por la mano || llevarse; *take your umbrella with you* llévate el paraguas || cargarse; *to take sth. on one's back* cargarse algo a la espalda || llevar; *to take s.o. for a walk, to the station* llevar alguien a pasear, a la estación; *to take s.o. to dinner* llevar a alguien a cenar; *to take sth. to s.o.* llevar algo a alguien; *this road will take you to the station* esta carretera le llevará a la estación || llevar, conducir; *the yellow bus will take you* el autobús amarillo le llevará || llevarse, coger; *who has taken the book from the library?* ¿quién se ha llevado el libro de la biblioteca?; *who has taken my cigarettes?* ¿quién me ha cogido los cigarrillos?; *take the book for the journey* llévate el libro para el viaje || quitar, llevarse; *the thief took my watch* el ladrón me ha quitado el reloj *or* se ha llevado mi reloj || sacar; *to take a photo* sacar una foto; *to take a copy* sacar una copia; *to take a ticket* sacar un billete; *to take a degree in languages* sacar un título en lenguas || sacar; *to take a line from a poem* sacar un verso de un poema; *this illustration is taken from* este grabado está sacado de || capturar, coger, detener (to arrest); *the thief was taken by the police* el ladrón fue capturado por la policía || coger, capturar, pescar (fish) || coger (rabbit, etc.) || tomarse (holidays) || ganar, llevarse; *to take first prize* ganar el primer premio || ganar (to win) || ganar, cobrar (to earn); *he takes ten pounds a week* gana diez libras por semana || pedir; *what will you take for it?* ¿cuánto pide por esto? || alquilar, tomar (to rent); *to take a house by the sea* alquilar una casa a orillas del mar || tomar, coger; *to take a secretary* tomar un secretario || comprar (to buy); *to take the Times* comprar el Times || tomar; *I take two pints of milk daily* tomo dos pintas de leche diariamente || usar (size); *what size shirts do you take?* ¿qué talla de camisa usa? || calzar (of shoes); *what size shoes do you take?* ¿qué número de zapatos calzas? || reservar (to book); *all the seats are taken* todos los asientos están reservados || ocupar (to occupy); *is this seat taken?* ¿está ocupado este asiento? || coger; *the job is taken* el puesto está cogido || coger, contraer, agarrar (a disease); *he took a cold* agarró un resfriado || hacer; *to take a vow* hacer un voto; *to take exercise* hacer ejercicio; *to take a trip* hacer un viaje || coger, tomar; *take any example you like* coja el ejemplo que quiera || requerir; *big houses take a lot of cleaning* las casas grandes requieren mucha limpieza || costar; *it takes time and money* cuesta tiempo y dinero || necesitarse, hacer falta; *it takes intelligent people to do this* se necesita *or* hace falta gente inteligente para hacer esto; *it will take two weeks* harán falta dos semanas || tardar; *it takes us five minutes to get there* tardamos cinco minutos en llegar allí || tardarse; *it takes five minutes to get there* se tarda cinco minutos en llegar allí || requerir, tomar; *to take a long time* requerir mucho tiempo || durar (to last); *how long will the trip take?* ¿cuánto tiempo durará el viaje? || tener cabida para, poder contener; *the car only takes four* el coche sólo tiene cabida para cuatro personas || admitir; *this machine only takes small sheets of paper* esta máquina sólo admite hojas de papel pequeñas || aceptar; *take me as I am* acéptame como soy; *to take a bet* aceptar una apuesta; *to take an offer* aceptar una oferta; *will you take the call?* ¿acepta usted la llamada?; *to take no denial* no aceptar ninguna negativa || dar (a class); *I take Spanish lessons at the university* doy clases de español en la Universidad || estudiar; *I take Spanish at the university* estudio español en la Universidad || encargarse; *Miss Smith is taking the second form* la señorita

Smith se encarga del segundo año de bachillerato || asumir; *to take all the responsibility* asumir toda la responsabilidad || recibir; *to take a thrashing* recibir una paliza || aguantar, soportar; *I can't take any more* no puedo aguantar más; *to take heavy loads* soportar cargas pesadas || tomar; *to take s.o. for another* tomar una persona por otra || suponer, creer, juzgar, considerar (to suppose); *I take it that* supongo que || MATH restar, sustraer; *to take one number from another* restar una cifra de otra || tomar (to consider); *who do you take me for?* ¿por quién me toma usted? || llegar en; *to take third place* llegar en tercer lugar || saltar (fence, obstacle) || hacer, ganar (a trick) || comerse a (in games); *bishop takes pawn* el alfil se come al peón || echarse (a lover) || GRAMM llevar; *verb that takes a direct object* verbo que lleva complemento directo || — *as I take it* según creo, a mi parecer || *he took his friend's death badly* le afectó mucho la muerte de su amigo || *I take comfort from talking to you* hablar con usted me sirve de consuelo || MED *not to be taken* para uso externo || *take it from me!* ¡créame! || *take it or leave it* lo toma o lo deja || *take that!* ¡toma! || *take William, for example* toma como ejemplo a Guillermo || *take your pick* escoja *or* elija a su gusto || *to be taken ill* ponerse enfermo || *to be taken with* gustarle a uno; *he was very much taken with the idea* le gustó mucho la idea || *to be taken with a fit of laughter* entrarle a uno un ataque de risa || *to take a bath* bañarse, darse un baño || *to take a bite* comer un bocado, comer algo || *to take account of* tener en cuenta, tomar en consideración || *to take action against* tomar medidas contra || *to take a dislike to s.o.* cogerle antipatía a alguien || *to take a fright* llevarse un susto || *to take aim at* apuntar a || *to take a joke* soportar una broma || *to take a leap* dar un salto || *to take a liking to* tomar cariño a || *to take a look, a glance* echar una mirada, una ojeada || *to take a nap* descabezar un sueño || *to take an exam* examinarse || *to take an oath* prestar juramento, jurar || *to take an opportunity* o *a chance* aprovechar una oportunidad || *to take apart* desmontar (to dismantle), ser desmontable (able to be dismantled), tomar aparte (a person) || *to take a place in the queue* ponerse en la cola || *to take a seat* tomar asiento, sentarse || *to take a serious view of* considerar importante || *to take a shower* ducharse, darse *or* tomar una ducha || *to take a step* dar un paso || *to take a telephone call* coger el teléfono || *to take a turn* dar una vuelta || *to take a walk* dar un paseo || *to take a wife* casarse || *to take breath* tomar aliento || *to take care* tener cuidado || *to take charge of* encargarse de || *to take drugs* drogarse || *to take effect* surtir efecto (medicine, etc.), entrar en vigor, tener efecto (law, timetable, etc.) || *to take fright* asustarse || *to take leave of s.o., to take one's leave of s.o.* despedirse de alguien || *to take paying guests* alquilar habitaciones || *to take hold of* coger, agarrar (to catch, to pick up, etc.), agarrarse a (to hang on to), apoderarse de (to take control of), dominar (to control) || *to take holy orders* ordenarse de sacerdote || *to take it easy* descansar (to rest), ir despacio (to go slowly), tomárselo con calma, no preocuparse (not to worry); *take it easy!* ¡tómatelo con calma!; no ponerse nervioso (to remain calm), ir con cuidado (carefully), perder el tiempo (to idle) || *to take it for granted that* dar por supuesto *or* por sentado que || *to take it hard* tomarlo muy en serio *or* por la tremenda || *to take lodgings* alojarse, hospedarse || *to take notice of* hacer caso a; *he didn't take notice of him* no le hizo ningún caso; hacer caso de (advice) || *to take offence* ofenderse || *to take office* tomar posesión de su cargo, entrar en funciones || *to take one's advice* seguir el consejo de alguien || *to take pity on* tener lástima de || *to take one's time* tomarse el tiempo [necesario] (to use the time available), hacer las cosas con calma, no apresurarse (not to hurry), tardar mucho tiempo (to be very slow) || *to take place* suceder, ocurrir, tener lugar (to happen), tener lugar, celebrarse (a meeting, etc.) || *to take the place of* sustituir a || *to take prisoner* hacer prisionero || *to take pupils* alojar *or* hospedar alumnos (boarding), dar clases privadas *or* particulares (lessons) || *to take responsibility for* hacerse responsable de || *to take s.o. at his word* cogerle la palabra a uno || *to take s.o. in one's arms* abrazar a alguien, coger a alguien entre sus brazos || *to take s.o.'s hand* dar la mano a alguien, coger a alguien de la mano || *to take s.o.'s life* quitar la vida a alguien || *to take s.o. unawares* coger a alguien desprevenido || *to take sth. the right, the wrong way* tomar algo a bien, a mal || FIG *to take the field* entrar en campaña (sentido militar), salir a la palestra (sentido figurado) || *to take the floor* tomar la palabra || SP *to take the service* restar (in tennis) || *to take to be* echar; *I took him to be forty* le eché cuarenta años; tomar; *I took him to be German* le tomé por alemán || MAR *to take water* hacer agua (a boat) || FAM *what took him there?* ¿por qué se le ocurrió ir allí? || *you can take it from me that* puede estar seguro de que.

◆ *vi* prender, agarrar (vaccination) || arraigar (plant) || prender (graft) || prender (fire) || pegar (to stick) || gustar, tener éxito; *the play did not take well in the provinces* la obra no gustó mucho en provincias || salir (in photographs); *she takes well* sale bien.

◆ *phr v* **to take about** enseñar; *to take s.o. about London* enseñar Londres a alguien | sacar; *to take a girl about* sacar a una chica || **to take after** parecerse a; *he takes after his mother* se parece a su madre || **to take along** llevarse, llevar consigo || **to take away** llevarse (to carry off) | quitar la mesa (to clear the table) | quitar (to remove from s.o.'s possession); *to take s.o.'s job away* quitarle a uno el puesto | restar (to subtract) || **to take back** devolver (to return); *to take a book back to s.o.* devolverle un libro a uno | acompañar (a casa), llevar (a casa); *can you take us back?* ¿nos puede acompañar? | llevar de nuevo, volver a llevar; *he was taken back to prison* lo volvieron a llevar a la cárcel | recordar; *it takes me back to my youth* esto me recuerda mi juventud | retirar; *I take back what I just said* retiro lo que acabo de decir | volver a recibir (person) | aceptar la devolución de (object) | readmitir (employee) || **to take down** quitar (to remove) | descolgar (curtains, pictures) | bajar; *to take down a pot of jam from the shelf* bajar un tarro de mermelada del estante | llevar abajo (s.o.) | derribar (a wall, a building) | desmontar (a machine) | apuntar, tomar nota de (to write down); *I took down his name* apunté su nombre | FAM tragar (food) || — FIG *to take s.o. down* bajarle los humos a alguien || **to take from** reducir, disminuir (the value, the merit) || **to take in** recoger; *to take in a stray cat* recoger un gato abandonado; *to take in the harvest* recoger la cosecha | alojar, dar alojamiento; *can you take me in for a day?* ¿puede alojarme durante un día? | aceptar (work) | meter (a seam) | achicar (a dress) | menguar (in knitting) | abastecerse de (goods) | tomar, estar suscrito a (a newspaper) | hacer pasar (s.o.) | MAR cargar, aferrar (sails) | tomar (a reef) | entender (to understand) | darse cuenta de; *to take in the situation* darse cuenta de la situación | abarcar (to include); *the empire took in many countries* el imperio abarcaba muchos países | FAM tragarse (to believe), dar gato por liebre, engañar (to deceive) | ganar (to earn) || **to take into** meter en || — *to take it into one's head to do sth.* meterse en la cabeza la idea de hacer algo | *to take s.o. into one's confidence* depositar su confianza en alguien || **to take off** quitar; *to take a saucepan off the fire* quitar una cacerola del fuego | quitarse (clothes); *I took off my gloves* me quité los guantes | apartar de (one's attention, one's eye) | descolgar (the receiver) | recibir (a message) | quitar (an aftereffect) | suprimir (to suppress) | MED amputar (a leg) | MAR desembarcar (passengers) | descontar, hacer un descuento *or* una rebaja de (to deduct); *can you take twenty pence off the price?* ¿puede descontarme del precio veinte peniques? | llevarse; *they were taken off in the police van* se los llevaron en la furgoneta de la policía | FAM remedar, imitar (to mimic) | saltar (to leap) | despegar (an aircraft) | arrancar (a car) | irse (to go) | amainar (wind) | retirarse (tide) | *to take o.s. off* irse || **to take on** tomar (a form, a quality) | coger (an accent) | asumir (responsibility) | encargarse de (task) | contratar, coger, tomar (workman) | acompañar; *I'll take you on a bit* le voy a acompañar un poco | llevar [demasiado lejos]; *I was taken on to Lewes* me llevaron hasta Lewes | coger, tomar (passengers) | aceptar (a bet, a challenge) | jugar contra, medirse con; *I'll take him on at billiards* jugaré al billar contra él, me mediré con él jugando al billar | competir con; *I am ready to take on all comers* estoy dispuesto a competir con cualquiera | cuajar (theory, fashion) | FAM ponerse frenético || **to take out** sacar; *he took out his pipe from his pocket* sacó la pipa del bolsillo; *to take out a tooth* sacar una muela | quitar, sacar (a stain) | hacerse; *to take out an insurance policy* hacerse un seguro | sacar; *to take out a patent, money from the bank* sacar una patente, dinero del banco | sacar; *he is taking Mary out tonight* saca a María esta noche | FAM agotar; *it takes it out of you* te agota || — *to take it out in* pagarse en | *to take it out on s.o.* desquitarse con uno | *to take s.o. out for a walk* llevar a alguien a dar un paseo | *to take s.o. out to dinner* llevar a alguien a cenar | *to take the dog out for a walk* sacar al perro de paseo || **to take over** hacerse cargo de (business, debts, etc.) | tomar el poder, ocupar el poder (to assume control) | asumir (responsibility) | expropiar (a building) | sustituir; *to take over from s.o.* sustituir a alguien | recibir [dando la conformidad] (a car, a machine) | transportar (goods, people) | MAR *to take over the watch* entrar de guardia || **to take round** enseñar (to show round) | llevar (to transport) | pasar; *to take round the plate* pasar la bandeja || **to take to** aficionarse a (to become fond of); *to take to chemistry* aficionarse a la química | empezar a; *when did you take to writing?* ¿cuándo empezaste a escribir? | entregarse a; *to take to drinking* entregarse a la bebida | coger simpatía a, tener simpatía a; *I took to her at once* le tuve simpatía en seguida | irse a; *he took to his bed* se fue a la cama | tomar; *he took to the road again* volvió a tomar la carretera | refugiarse en; *the bandits took to the hills* los bandidos se refugiaron en las colinas | dirigirse hacia; *they took to the woods* se dirigieron hacia el bosque || — *to take to flight* huir, darse a la fuga | *to take to the open sea* hacerse mar adentro || **to take up** coger (to pick up) | acortar (to shorten) | tomar, coger (passengers) | subir; *take this up for me* súbeme esto | llevar arriba (s.o.) | levantar (pavement, rails) | quitar (carpet) | absorber (water); *a sponge takes up water* la esponja absorbe el agua | tomar posesión de (a post) | fijar, establecer (one's residence) | ocupar (space, time) | absorber (one's attention) || JUR detener (a thief) | COMM pagar (bill), suscribir (shares) | aceptar (challenge, bet) | seguir (idea, suggestion) | adoptar (motion, proposal) | proteger (to protect) | estudiar, examinar (a question) | empezar (a study) | dedicarse a (a career) | reanudar (conversation) | entender (to understand) | TECH amortiguar (bumps), compensar (wear) | criticar (to criticize) | reprender, censurar (to censure) | corregir; *his statement was false and I took him up at once* su declaración era errónea y le corregí en seguida | mejorar (weather) || — *to take s.o. up* *short* interrumpir a alguien | *to take up with* trabar amistad con (friends), juntarse con (bad people) || ***to take up on*** aceptar (an offer) | poner en duda (to challenge) || ***to take upon*** *o.s.* encargarse de.

— OBSERV Pret ***took***; pp ***taken***.

— OBSERV In some countries of Latin America the word *coger* is not in decent use and is usually replaced by *tomar* or *agarrar*: *to take the train* tomar el tren.

takeaway [-əwei]; US **takeout** [-aut] *n* establecimiento *m* de comida para llevar (shop, restaurant) || comida *f* para llevar (food).

takedown [-daun] *adj* desmontable (machine).

◆ *n* desmontaje *m* || FAM feo *m*, humillación *f*.

take-home pay [-'həum'pei] *n* US sueldo *m* neto.

take-in [-in] *n* FAM engaño *m*.

taken [-ən] *pp* → **take**.

takeoff [-ɔf] *n* AVIAT despegue *m* || salida *f* (of a rocket) || parodia *f* (mimicry) || caricatura *f* (caricature) || SP impulso *m* || *power takeoff* toma *f* de fuerza.

take-over [-,əuvə*] *n* toma *f* de posesión || toma *f* del poder || adquisición *f* (of a company).

taker [-ə*] *n* tomador, ra (s.o. who takes) || arrendador, ra (of a lease) | COMM comprador, ra || apostador, ra (of a bet).

taking ['teikiŋ] *adj* atractivo, va (attractive) || contagioso, sa (a disease).

◆ *n* toma *f* (of a town, etc.) || detención *f* (of a thief) || MED toma *f* (of blood).

◆ *pl* ingresos *m* (money earned) || recaudación *f sing*, taquilla *f sing* (of a show).

taking off [-ɔf] *n* AVIAT despegue *m*.

taking out [-aut] *n* MED & TECH extracción *f*.

talaria [tə'lɛəriə] *pl n* talares *m* (of mercury).

talayot [tə'læjət] *n* talayote *m*.

talc [tælk]; **talcum** [-əm] *n* talco *m*.

talcum powder ['tælkəm,paudə*] *n* talco *m*, polvos *m pl* de talco.

tale [teil] *n* cuento *m*; *fairy tales* cuentos de hadas || historia *f*, relato *m*, narración *f* (relation of events) || cotilleo *m*, chisme *m*, habladuría *f* (piece of gossip) || cuento *m* (lie) || — FIG *his tale is told* está perdido | *it tells its own tale* habla por sí mismo || *I've heard a fine tale about you!* ¡qué cosas me han contado de usted! || *old wives' tale* cuento de viejas || FAM *to tell tales* chivarse (to reveal secrets), venir con cuentos (to lie), contar chismes, cotillear (to gossip).

talebearer [-,bɛərə*] *n* soplón, ona; chivato, ta (informer) || cotilla *m* & *f*, chismoso, sa (gossip).

talent ['tælənt] *n* talento *m*; *a man of great talent* un hombre de mucho talento || aptitudes *f pl*, don *m*; *he has a talent for languages* tiene aptitudes para los idiomas, tiene don de lenguas || talento *m*, persona *f* de talento *or* de valor (person) || (ant) talento *m* (coin) || — *exhibition of local talent* exposición de las obras realizadas por los artistas de la región || *he has no talent for business* no sirve para los negocios.

talented [-id] *adj* talentudo, da; talentoso, sa.

talent scout [-skaut] *n* descubridor *m* de personas de talento *or* de valor.

tales ['teili:z] *n* JUR jurados *m pl* suplentes || *to pray a tales* pedir que se complete el jurado.

talesman ['teili:zmən] *n* JUR jurado *m* suplente.

— OBSERV El plural de *talesman* es *talesmen*.

tale-teller ['teil,telə*] *n* narrador, ra (who tells stories) || soplón, ona (informer) || chismoso, sa (gossipmonger).

talion ['tæliən] *n* talión *m*.

talisman ['tælizmən] *n* talismán *m*.

talk [tɔ:k] *n* conversación *f* [AMER plática *f*]; *to engage s.o. in talk* entablar conversación con alguien; *the Minister had a talk with his Spanish colleague* el ministro mantuvo una conversación con su colega español || charla *f*; *he gave a talk about Venezuela* dio una charla acerca de Venezuela || conferencia *f* (lecture) || discurso *m* (speech) || habladurías *f pl* (gossip); *it's all talk* no son más que habladurías || comidilla *f*, tema *m*; *he was the talk of the town* era la comidilla de la ciudad || palabras *f pl*; *we want actions not talk* queremos hechos no palabras || habla *f*, manera *f* de hablar; *baby talk* el habla de los niños || — *he is all talk* no hace más que hablar || *I'd like to have a talk with you* me gustaría hablar con usted || US FAM *that's the talk!* ¡muy bien! || *there is some talk of his returning* corre el rumor de que va a volver || *to keep the talk going* mantener la conversación.

◆ *pl* negociaciones *f*.

talk [tɔ:k] *vt* decir; *don't talk rubbish!* ¡no diga tonterías! || hablar; *I talk Spanish* hablo español || hablar de; *to talk politics, business* hablar de política, de negocios || INFORM dialogar || — *he talked himself hoarse* de tanto hablar se quedó ronco || *to be talked about* andar en boca de todo el mundo || FAM *to talk a blue streak* hablar por los codos || US *to talk (cold) turkey* no andarse con rodeos || *to talk dress* hablar de trapos || FIG *to talk o.s. blue in the face* hablar hasta que se le seque a uno la boca || *to talk sense* hablar razonablemente *or* sensatamente || *to talk shop* hablar de negocios || *to talk s.o. into doing sth.* convencer a alguien para que haga algo || *to talk s.o. out of doing sth.* disuadir a alguien de que haga algo || FIG *to talk the hind leg off a donkey* o *nineteen to the dozen* hablar por los codos *or* más que siete *or* como una cotorra.

◆ *vi* hablar; *to learn to talk* aprender a hablar; *what are you talking about?* ¿de qué hablas?; *to talk by signs* hablar por señas; *she has found s.o. to talk to* ha encontrado a alguien con quien hablar || charlar (to chatter) || hablar (to gossip); *people will talk* la gente hablará || — *he knows what he's talking about* sabe lo que se dice || *he likes to hear himself talk* se escucha cuando habla || FAM *I'll talk to him!* ¡me va a oír!, ¡le voy a echar una bronca! || *look who is talking!* ¡mira quién habla! || *now you're talking!* ¡así se habla!, ¡eso es hablar! || *talk about luck!* ¡Dios mío, qué suerte! || *talking of...* hablando de... || *talk of the devil and he will appear* hablando del rey de Roma por la puerta asoma || *that's no way to talk* ésa no es forma de hablar || *to get o.s. talked about* dar que hablar || *to talk about this, that and the other* hablar de todo un poco || *to talk behind s.o.'s back* criticar a alguien a sus espaldas || *to talk big* jactarse, fanfarronear || *to talk for the sake of talking* hablar por hablar || *to talk in riddles* hablar en clave || *to talk through one's hat* decir tonterías || *to talk to o.s.* hablar para su coleto *or* para sí || *to talk without rhyme or reason* hablar sin ton ni son || *who do you think you're talking to?* ¿con quién se cree usted que está hablando?

◆ *phr v* ***to talk at*** tirar indirectas a || — *are you talking at me?* ¿se dirige usted a mí? || ***to talk away*** pasar charlando; *to talk away the night* pasar la noche charlando | hablar sin parar (to speak a lot) || — *to talk s.o.'s fears away* demostrar a alguien con palabras que sus temores no tienen fundamento || ***to talk back*** contestar con impertinencia, replicar || ***to talk down*** callar, hacer callar (to silence) || — *I won't allow myself to be talked down* no permitiré que me callen | *to talk an aircraft down* dirigir un aterrizaje por radio | *to talk down to* ponerse al alcance *or* al nivel de (one's audience), hablar con altivez a | *to talk sth. down* quitar importancia a algo || ***to talk on*** seguir hablando || ***to talk out*** discutir a fondo; *I want to talk things out with you* quiero discutir las cosas a fondo con usted || — *to talk a bill out* prolongar los debates de tal manera que no se pueda votar un proyecto de ley || ***to talk over*** discutir, hablar de; *to talk a matter over* discutir un asunto | convencer (a person) || ***to talk round*** convencer; *to talk s.o. round* convencer a alguien || — *to talk round a question* tratar un tema superficialmente, andarse con rodeos || ***to talk up*** alabar, hacer mucho ruido en favor de; *to talk up a book* hacer mucho ruido en favor de un libro || — *to talk up to s.o.* hablar con alguien.

talkative [-ətiv] *adj* hablador, ra; charlatán, ana; parlanchín, ina; locuaz.

talkativeness [-ətivnis] *n* locuacidad *f*.

talker ['tɔ:kə*] *n* hablador, ra; parlanchín, ina || FAM jactancioso, sa || — *he is a good talker* habla muy bien || *he is a great talker* es muy parlanchín.

talkie ['tɔ:ki] *n* CINEM película *f* sonora.

talking ['tɔ:kiŋ] *adj* que habla (bird, doll) || sonoro, ra (picture) || expresivo, va (look).

◆ *n* conversación *f* || charloteo *m* (chatter) || — *I don't want to do all the talking* no quiero ser el único en hablar || *no talking please!* ¡silencio, por favor!

talking point [-pɔint] *n* tema *m* de conversación.

talking-to [-tu:] *n* bronca *f*; *to give s.o. a talking-to* echar una bronca a alguien.

talk show ['tɑ:kʃəu] *n* RAD programa *m* de entrevistas.

talky ['tɔ:ki] *adj* hablador, ra.

tall [tɔ:l] *adj* alto, ta; *he is tall for his age* es alto para su edad; *a tall oak* un roble alto || de alto, de altura; *to be six feet tall* tener seis pies de alto || FAM exagerado, da; increíble (incredible); *a tall story* una historia increíble || — *how tall are you?* ¿cuánto mide? || *she is growing tall* está creciendo || FAM *tall talk* jactancia *f*, fanfarronada *f*.

◆ *adv* *to talk tall* jactarse.

tallage ['tælidʒ] *n* HIST talla *f* (due).

tallboy ['tɔ:lbɔi] *n* cómoda *f* alta.

tallith ['tæliθ] *n* taled *m* (shawl).

tallness ['tɔ:lnis] *n* altura *f* (of building, etc.) || talla *f*, estatura *f* (of people).

tallow ['tæləu] *n* sebo *m*.

tallowy [-i] *adj* seboso, sa.

tally ['tæli] *n* tarja *f* (stick) || muesca *f* (notch) || total *m* (total figure) || cuenta *f* (account); *to keep tally of* llevar la cuenta de || lote *m*; *to buy sth. by the tally* comprar algo por lotes || resguardo *m* (receipt) || etiqueta *f* (label, tag) || contrapartida *f* (counterpart).

tally ['tæli] *vt* etiquetar (to put a label on) || puntear (on a list) || registrar (a number).

◆ *vi* corresponder, concordar (to agree, to match); *the stories of the two men tally* las historias de los dos hombres concuerdan.

tally clerk [-klɑ:k] *n* listero *m*, marcador *m*.

tallyho [-'həu] *interj* ¡hala! (call of huntsmen).

tallyman [-mən] *n* listero *m*, marcador *m* (who checks) || comerciante *m* que vende a plazos.

— OBSERV El plural de *tallyman* es *tallymen*.

Talmud ['tælmud] *pr n* Talmud *m*.

Talmudic [tæl'mudik]; **Talmudical** [-əl] *adj* talmúdico, ca.

talon ['tælən] *n* garra *f* (of bird of prey) || zarpa *f*, garra *f* (of tiger) || saliente *m*, uña *f* (of a lock) || montón *m* (of cards) || matriz *f* (of cheque-book) || ARCH talón *m* (moulding).

talus ['teiləs] *n* ANAT astrágalo *m* (astragalus) || GEOL talud *m* || MIL escarpa *f*.

tamable; tameable ['teiməbl] *adj* domesticable (animals) || domable (wild horse).

tamale [tə'mɑːli] *n* CULIN tamal *m.*

tamandua [tə'mændua] *n* ZOOL tamandúa *m.*

tamarack ['tæməræk] *n* BOT alerce *m* americano.

tamarau ['tæmərau] *n* tamarao *m* (Philippine buffalo).

tamarin ['tæmərin] *n* tití *m* (monkey).

tamarind ['tæmərind] *n* tamarindo *m* (fruit, tree).

tamarisk ['tæmərisk] *n* BOT taray *m,* tamarisco *m.*

tambour ['tæmbuə*] *n* MUS tambor *m* || bastidor *m,* tambor *m* (frame for embroidery) || ARCH tambor *m.*

tambourine [,tæmbə'riːn] *n* MUS pandereta *f,* pandero *m.*

tame [teim] *adj* domesticado, da (domesticated); *these animals are so tame that they eat out of your hand* estos animales están tan domesticados que comen en la mano || doméstico, ca (bred with human beings); *a tame monkey* un mono doméstico || domado, da (wild horses) || manso, sa (not wild) || FIG sumiso, sa (docile) || FAM aburrido, da (boring) | soso, sa; insípido, da (dull).

tame [teim] *vt* domesticar (animal) || domar, amansar (wild horse) || FIG domeñar, dominar (to bring under control).
◆ *vi* domesticarse.

tameable [-əbl] *adj* → **tamable.**

tamely ['teimli] *adv* dócilmente.

tameness [-nis] *n* mansedumbre *f* || FIG sumisión *f* | insipidez *f,* sosería *f* (of style).

tamer [-ə*] *n* domador, ra.

Tamil ['tæmil] *adj/n* tamul.
◆ *n* tamul *m* (language).

taming [-iŋ] *n* domesticación *f* (of animals) || doma *f,* domadura *f* (of wild horses) || *the Taming of the Shrew* La Fierecilla domada, La Doma de la bravía (Shakespeare's play).

tam-o'-shanter [,tæmə'ʃæntə*] *n* boina *f* escocesa.

tamp [tæmp] *vt* MIN atacar || apisonar (the ground).

tamper [-ə*] *n* pisón *m.*

tamper [-ə*] *vi* *to tamper with* sobornar (to bribe), desnaturalizar, amañar (a text), intentar forzar (a lock), estropear (to spoil), manosear; *don't tamper with what is not yours* no manosees lo que no es tuyo.

tamping [-iŋ] *n* apisonamiento *m.*

tampion ['tæmpiən] *n* MIL tapabocas *m inv* || MUS tapón *m* (of an organ pipe).

tampon ['tæmpən] *n* MED tapón *m.*

tampon ['tæmpən] *vt* MED taponar.

tamponade [,tæmpə'neid]; **tamponage** ['tæmpə,nidʒ] *n* MED taponamiento *m.*

tam-tam ['tæm,tæm] *n* MUS tantán *m* (drum) | batintín *m* (gong).

tan [tæn] *adj* de color marrón (shoes) || castaño, ña (animal) || bronceado, da; tostado, da (skin).
◆ *n* casca *f,* corteza *f* (tree bark) || tanino *m* (tanning substance) || bronceado *m,* color *m* tostado (colour of skin) || color *m* tabaco, marrón *m* (yellowish brown colour) || *to acquire a tan* broncearse, ponerse moreno.

tan [tæn] *vt* curtir (leather) || broncear, tostar (the skin) || FAM zurrar (to thrash) || FAM *to tan s.o.'s hide* zurrar la badana a alguien.
◆ *vi* broncearse, tostarse (the skin).

tanager ['tænədʒə*]; **tanagra** ['tænəgrə] *n* tanagra *f* (bird).

Tanagra ['tænəgrə] *n* tanagra *f* (statuette).

tanbark ['tænbɑːk] *n* casca *f.*

tandem ['tændəm] *n* tándem *m* (bicycle, etc.) || *in tandem with* junto con, en colaboración con.
◆ *adv* en fila, en tándem.

tang [tæŋ] *n* sabor *m* fuerte (taste) || olor *m* fuerte (smell) || frescor *m* (of air) || FIG sabor *m; the story has a romantic tang* el relato tiene un sabor romántico || espiga *f* (of knife, of tool) || tañido *m* (of a bell).

tang [tæŋ] *vt* tañer (a bell) || poner una espiga a (a knife, a tool).

Tanganica (Lake) [,tæŋgə'njiːkə] *pr n* GEOGR lago *m* Tanganica.

tangency ['tændʒənsi] *n* MATH tangencia *f.*

tangent ['tændʒənt] *adj* tangente.
◆ *n* tangente *f* || FIG *to fly off* o *to go off at a tangent* salirse por la tangente.

tangential [tæn'dʒenʃəl] *adj* tangencial.

tangerine [,tændʒə'riːn] *n* mandarina *f* (fruit).

Tangerine [,tændʒə'riːn] *adj/n* tangerino, na.

tangibility [,tændʒi'biliti] *n* carácter *m* tangible.

tangible ['tændʒəbl] *adj* tangible || FIG tangible, palpable || JUR material; *tangible assets* bienes materiales.

Tangier [tæn'dʒiə*] *pr n* GEOGR Tánger.

tangle ['tæŋgl] *n* maraña *f,* enredo *m; tangle of branches, of wires* maraña de ramas, de cables || nudo *m* (of hair) || FIG embrollo *m,* enredo *m* (affairs) | laberinto *m* (maze) || — *to be in a tangle* haberse enredado (ropes, a person) || *to get into a tangle* enredarse (wires, a person).

tangle ['tæŋgl] *vt* enredar, enmarañar (to form into a tangle) || enredar (to catch in a net) || FIG embrollar, enredar (affairs).
◆ *vi* enredarse, enmarañarse || FIG embrollarse, enredarse || FAM *to tangle with s.o.* meterse con alguien.

tangled [-d]; **tangly** [-i] *adj* enredado, da; enmarañado, da.

tanglement [-mənt] *n* enmarañamiento *m.*

tango ['tæŋgəu] *n* tango *m.*

tango ['tæŋgəu] *vi* bailar el tango.

tangy ['tæŋi] *adj* fuerte.

tank [tæŋk] *n* depósito *m* tanque *m; petrol tank* depósito de gasolina || depósito *m,* aljibe *m* (of water) || MIL carro *m* de combate, tanque *m.*

tank [tæŋk] *vt* guardar en un depósito.
◆ *vi* FAM *to tank up* beber mucho.

tankage [-idʒ] *n* almacenaje *m* en depósitos (storage in tanks) || capacidad *f* de un depósito (capacity) || gastos *m pl* de almacenaje (charge for storage) || AGR fertilizante *m* orgánico (animal residues).

tankard [-əd] *n* «bock» *m* (of beer).

tank car [-kɑː*] *n* US vagón *m* cisterna.

tank engine [-'endʒin] *n* locomotora *f* ténder.

tanker [-ə*] *n* MAR petrolero *m,* buque *m* aljibe (ship) || camión *m* cisterna (lorry) || MIL tanquista *m* || *rail tanker* vagón *m* cisterna.

tankful [-ful] *n* depósito *m* lleno (of petrol).

tank locomotive [-'ləukə,məutiv] *n* locomotora *f* ténder.

tank truck [-trʌk] *n* camión *m* cisterna.

tank wagon [-,wægən] *n* vagón *m* cisterna || AUT camión *m* cisterna.

tannage ['tænidʒ] *n* curtido *m.*

tanned ['tænd] *adj* curtido, da (leather) || bronceado, da; moreno, na (with the sun) || *to get tanned* ponerse moreno, broncearse.

tanner ['tænə*] *n* curtidor *m* (person) || FAM moneda *f* de seis peniques (sixpence).

tannery ['tænəri] *n* curtiduría *f,* tenería *f.*

tannic ['tænik] *adj* tánico, ca.

tannin ['tænin] *n* CHEM tanino *m.*

tanning ['tæniŋ] *n* curtido *m* || bronceado *m* (of the skin) || FAM zurra *f,* paliza *f* (thrashing); *to give s.o. a tanning* dar una zurra a alguien.

Tannoy ['tænɔi] *n* (registered trademark) sistema *m* de altavoces.

tanrec ['tænrek] *n* ZOOL tanrec *m,* tenrec *m.*

tantalize [,tæntəlaiz] *vt* torturar, atormentar, hacer sufrir el suplicio de Tántalo (to torment) || seducir (to tempt).

tantalizing [-iŋ] *adj* atormentador, ra; *it is tantalizing not being able to open our presents until Christmas Day* es atormentador el no poder abrir nuestros regalos hasta el día de Navidad || seductor, ra (attractive); *a tantalizing idea* una idea seductora.

tantalum ['tæntələm] *n* tantalio *m* (metal).

Tantalus ['tæntələs] *pr n* MYTH Tántalo *m.*

tantamount ['tæntəmaunt] *adj* equivalente || *to be tantamount to* equivaler a, ser equivalente a, venir a ser; *his threats are tantamount to blackmail* sus amenazas equivalen a un chantaje.

tantara ['tæntərə] *n* tarará *m.*

tantrum ['tæntrəm] *n* rabieta *f,* berrinche *m; to fly into a tantrum* coger una rabieta.

Tanzania [,tænzə'niɑ] *pr n* GEOGR Tanzania.

Taoism ['tɑːəuizəm] *n* REL taoísmo *m.*

Taoist ['tɑːəuist] *adj/n* REL taoísta.

tap [tæp] *n* grifo *m; to turn on the water tap* abrir el grifo de agua; *to turn off the tap* cerrar el grifo || canilla *f,* espita *f* (of a barrel) || macho *m* de aterrajar *or* de roscar (screw tap) || ELECTR derivación *f* || golpecito *m* (light blow); *a tap on the door* un golpecito en la puerta || cervecería *f* (taproom) || tapa *f* (for the heel of a shoe) || MED drenaje *m* || FAM sablazo *m* (of money) || *on tap* a mano (easily available), de barril (beer).

tap [tæp] *vt* golpear ligeramente, dar un golpecito en, dar un golpe ligero en; *to tap the door with one's knuckles, to tap one's knuckles on the door* dar un golpecito en la puerta con los nudillos || poner una espita a (a cask) || agujerear (to make a hole in) || sangrar (a tree) || sacar (wine from a barrel) || hacer una toma de (water, gas, etc.) || ELECTR hacer una derivación de, derivar || hacer una conexión en (to connect) || poner tapas a (shoes) || interceptar (to intercept communications); *to tap s.o.'s telephone* interceptar el teléfono de alguien || TECH roscar, aterrajar (to cut a thread on) | sangrar (a furnace) || FIG utilizar (to draw on) | aprovechar, explotar; *to tap a country's resources* explotar los recursos naturales de un país || MED drenar || FAM dar un sablazo de, sablear; *to tap s.o. for fifty pence* sablear cincuenta peniques a alguien || — *to tap in* clavar dando golpecitos (a nail) || *to tap out* enviar (a Morse message), escribir a máquina (on a typewriter), vaciar dando golpecitos (a pipe), sacar dando golpecitos (a split pin, etc.).
◆ *vi* tamborilear; *to tap with one's fingers* tamborilear con los dedos || taconear (to walk making a tapping sound) || zapatear (to dance making a tapping sound).

tap circuit ['səːkit] *n* ELECTR derivación *f.*

tap dance ['tæpdɑːns] *n* zapateado *m.*

tap-dance ['tæpdɑːns] *vi* zapatear.

tap dancer [-ə*] *n* bailarín *m* de zapateado, bailarina *f* de zapateado.

tape [teip] *n* cinta *f* (strip of cotton, of silk, etc.) || cinta *f* adhesiva (adhesive paper or plastic) || cinta *f* métrica (for measuring) || cinta *f* perforada (of teleprinter, of telex) || MED esparadrapo *m* || cinta *f* magnetofónica, cinta *f* (of a tape recorder) || FAM cinta *f* (a recording) || cinta *f* simbólica (at inauguration ceremony) || SP cinta *f* de llegada || tira *f* de gasa (in bookbinding) || — *adhesive tape* cinta adhesiva || *insulating tape* cinta aislante || INFORM *perforated tape* cinta *f* perforada || FAM *red tape* papeleo *m*, trámites *m pl* || *sticky tape* cinta adhesiva.

tape [teip] *vt* atar con cinta (to fasten) || medir con cinta métrica (to measure) || pegar con cinta adhesiva; *to tape a piece of paper to the wall* pegar un papel en la pared con cinta adhesiva || ribetear (in dressmaking) || grabar (to record) || FIG & FAM *to have s.o. taped* tener a alguien calado.
◆ *vi* medir.

tape deck [-dek] *n* platina *f* de casete.

tape measure [-ˌmeʒə*] *n* cinta *f* métrica.

taper [-ə*] *n* vela *f* (thin candle) || REL cirio *m*, vela *f* || estrechamiento *m* (narrowing).

taper [-ə*] *vt* estrechar (to make narrower) || afilar (to sharpen to a point).
◆ *vi* estrecharse (to become narrower) || afilarse (to narrow to a point) || *to taper off* disminuir; *demand usually tapers off in winter* la demanda suele disminuir en invierno.

tape reader [-riːdə*] *n* INFORM lector de cintas *or* de bandas.

tape-record [-riˌkɔːd] *vt* grabar [en cinta magnetofónica].

tape recorder [-riˌkɔːdə*] *n* magnetófono *m*, magnetofón *m* [*AMER* grabadora *f*] || TECH grabador *m* de cinta (part of an installation).

tape recording [-riˌkɔːdiŋ] *n* grabación *f* [en cinta magnetofónica].

tapered ['teipəd] *adj* afilado, da (finger) || *tapered trousers* pantalón *m* tubo.

tapestried ['tæpistrid] *adj* tapizado, da (covered with tapestry) || bordado en un tapiz (worked in tapestry).

tapestry ['tæpistri] *n* tapiz *m*; *Bayeux tapistry* tapiz de Bayeux || tapicería *f* (art, industry).

tapestry making [-'meikiŋ] *n* tapicería *f*.

tapeworm ['teipwəːm] *n* solitaria *f*, tenia *f*.

taphole ['tæphəul] *n* TECH bigotera *f* (for slag) | piquera *f* (for cast iron).

tapioca [ˌtæpi'əukə] *n* tapioca *f*.

tapir ['teipə*] *n* ZOOL tapir *m*.

tapper ['tæpə*] *n* ELECTR manipulador *m* || TECH aterrajadora *f*.

tappet ['tæpit] *n* varilla *f* de levantamiento.

tapping ['tæpiŋ] *n* golpecitos *m pl* || ELECTR derivación *f* || sangría *f* (of trees, of molten metal).

taproom ['tæprum] *n* cervecería *f* (bar).

taproot ['tæpruːt] *n* BOT raíz *f* primaria.

taps [tæps] *pl n* US MIL toque *m sing* de silencio.

tapster ['tæpstə*] *n* camarero *m* [*AMER* mozo *m*].

tapwater ['tæp'wɔːtə*] *n* agua *f* del grifo.

tar [tɑː*] *n* alquitrán *m*, brea *f* (in road making, etc.) || MED brea *f* || FAM marinero *m*.

tar [tɑː*] *vt* alquitranar (to cover with tar) || — FIG *to be tarred with the same brush* estar cortados por el mismo patrón | *to tar and feather* emplumar | *to tar on* incitar.

taradiddle ['tærədidl] *n* FAM sandez *f*, disparate *m*.

tarantella [ˌtærən'telə] *n* MUS tarantela *f*.

tarantula [tə'ræntjulə] *n* ZOOL tarántula *f*.
— OBSERV El plural de la palabra inglesa *tarantula* es *tarantula* o *tarantulae*.

tarboosh [tɑː'buːʃ] *n* fez *m* (felt cap).

tardigrada [ˌtɑːdi'greidə] *pl n* ZOOL tardígrados *m*.

tardigrade ['tɑːdiˌgreid] *adj* ZOOL tardígrado, da.
◆ *n* ZOOL tardígrado *m*.

tardily ['tɑːdili] *adv* tardíamente (too late) || lentamente (slowly).

tardiness ['tɑːdinis] *n* lentitud *f*, tardanza *f* (slowness) || retraso *m* (lateness).

tardy ['tɑːdi] *adj* tardío, a (late) || lento, ta; tardo, da (slow).

tare [tεə*] *n* tara *f* (weight) || BOT vicia *f*.
◆ *pl* REL cizaña *f sing*, mala semilla *f*.

target ['tɑːgit] *n* blanco *m*, diana *f* (in shooting, in archery) || puntuación *f* (score in shooting) || MIL objetivo *m* (of a missile attack) || FIG objeto *m*, blanco *m*; *to be the target for popular ridicule* ser el blanco de la mofa de todos | meta *f*, objetivo *m*; *his target was to succeed* su meta era triunfar || TECH anticátodo *m* (of an X-ray tube) || US disco *m* (signal) || mirilla *f* (in surveying) || HIST rodela *f* (small shield) || — *production target* objetivo *m* de producción || FIG *to be on target* seguir el rumbo previsto.

target day [-dei] *n* fecha *f* señalada.

target practice [-'præktis] *n* tiro *m* al blanco, prácticas *f pl* de tiro.

tariff ['tærif] *n* tarifa *f*, arancel *m* (on imports) || tarifa *f*, lista *f* de precios (in a hotel, etc.) || *tariff barrier* barrera arancelaria.

tariff ['tærif] *vt* tarifar (to fix a tariff for) || fijar los derechos arancelarios *or* los aranceles de (imports).

tarlatan ['tɑːlətən] *n* tarlatana *f* (fabric).

tarmac ['trɑːmæk] *n* superficie *f* alquitranada || *the aircraft is standing on the tarmac* el avión está en la pista de despegue.

tarn [tɑːn] *n* lago *m* pequeño de montaña.

tarnish [-iʃ] *n* empañadura *f*, deslustre *m* || FIG mancha *f*, deslustre *m* (of reputation).

tarnish [-iʃ] *vt* deslustrar (a surface) || FIG manchar, deslustrar, empañar; *to tarnish s.o.'s reputation* manchar la reputación de uno.
◆ *vi* deslustrarse, perder su brillo.

tarot ['tærəu] *n* naipe *m* [al que se atribuye un poder adivinatorio].

tarpaulin [tɑː'pɔːlin] *n* lona *f* alquitranada, alquitranado *m*.

Tarpeia [tɑː'piːə] *pr n* Tarpeya *f*.

Tarpeian [-n] *adj* *Tarpeian Rock* Roca Tarpeya.

Tarquin ['tɑːkwin] *pr n* HIST Tarquino *m*.

tarragon ['tærəgən] *n* BOT estragón *m*.

tarred [tɑːd]; **tarry** ['tɑːri] *adj* alquitranado, da || cubierto de alquitrán.

tarry ['tæri] *vi* quedarse atrás (to linger) || quedarse (to stay) || tardar (to be late).

tarsal ['tɑːsəl] *adj* ANAT tarsiano, na.
◆ *n* ANAT tarso *m*.

tarsus ['tɑːsəs] *n* ANAT tarso *m*.
— OBSERV El plural de *tarsus* es *tarsi*.

tart [tɑːt] *adj* agrio, gria; ácido, da (taste) || FIG áspero, ra; cáustico, ca; *a tart reply* una respuesta cáustica | desabrido, da (disposition).
◆ *n* CULIN tarta *f* [*AMER* torta *f*]; *apple tart* tarta de manzana || FAM fulana *f*, furcia *f* (prostitute).

tartan ['tɑːtən] *n* tartán *m*, tela *f* escocesa de cuadros (material) || MAR tartana *f* (boat).

tartar ['tɑːtə*] *n* CHEM tártaro *m* || sarro *m*, tártaro *m* (on the teeth).

Tartar ['tɑːtə*] *adj/n* tártaro, ra || FIG fiera *f*, persona *f* intratable (intractable person) || FIG *to catch a Tartar* dar con la horma de su zapato.

Tartarean [tɑː'tεəriən] *adj* tartáreo, a (infernal).

tartaric [tɑː'tærik] *adj* tartárico, ca; tártrico, ca.

tartar sauce; tartare sauce ['tɑːtə*sɔːs] *n* salsa *f* tártara.

Tartarus ['tɑːtərəs] *pr n* MYTH Tártaro *m*.

Tartary ['tɑːtəri] *pr n* HIST Tartaria *f*.

Tartessian [tɑː'tesiən] *adj/n* tartesio, sia.

tartlet ['tɑːtlit] *n* CULIN tartita *f*, pastelillo *m*.

tartness ['tɑːtnis] *n* acidez *f* (of taste) || FIG aspereza *f*, causticidad *f*.

tartrate ['tɑːtreit] *n* CHEM tartrato *m*.

tart up [ˌtɑːt'ʌp] *vt* arreglar (room, building) || *to tart o.s. up* emperifollarse (a woman).

tarty ['tɑːti] *adj* FAM provocativo, va; atrevido, da; *a tarty dress* un vestido provocativo.

task [tɑːsk] *n* tarea *f*, faena *f*, labor *f* (work) || misión *f*, cometido *m* (mission) || deber *m* (at school) || — *to set s.o. a task* encargar un trabajo a alguien || *to take to task* reprender, regañar, llamar la atención.

task [tɑːsk] *vt* imponer una tarea, encargar.

task force [-fɔːs] *n* MIL destacamento *m* de fuerzas [para una misión especial].

taskmaster [-ˌmɑːstə*] *n* capataz *m* || supervisor *m* || FIG *a hard taskmaster* un verdadero tirano.

taskwork [-ʃəːk] *n* trabajo *m* a destajo.

Tasmania [tæz'meinjə] *pr n* GEOGR Tasmania.

tassel ['tæsəl] *n* borla *f* (ornament).

taste [teist] *n* gusto *m* (sense) || sabor *m*, gusto *m*; *a sweet taste* un sabor dulce; *a meaty taste* un sabor a carne || degustación *f* (tasting) || gusto *m*, afición *f* (liking); *to acquire* o *to develop a taste for sth.* tomar gusto a algo, cobrar afición a algo || gusto *m* (discernment); *the house is decorated with taste* la casa está decorada con gusto || experiencia *f*, prueba *f*; *we had a taste of country life* tuvimos una experiencia de lo que es la vida en el campo || muestra *f*; *I have already had a taste of his bad manners* ya tuve una muestra de su falta de modales || pizca *f* (of food); *give me a taste* dame una pizca || sorbo *m* (sip) || — *add salt to taste* añádese sal a voluntad || *each to his own taste* sobre gustos no hay nada escrito || *give the horses a taste of the whip* haz probar el látigo a los caballos || *in bad taste* de mal gusto || *there is no accounting for tastes* sobre gustos no hay nada escrito || *to be to one's taste* gustar a uno, ser del gusto de uno; *spicy food is not to my taste* no me gusta la comida picante || *to find sth. to one's taste* encontrar algo al gusto de uno || *to give s.o. a taste of his own medicine* pagar a alguien con la misma moneda || *to have a taste for* gustarle a uno algo; *he has a taste for sports cars* le gustan los coches deportivos || FIG *to leave a nasty taste in one's mouth* dejarle a uno mal sabor de boca || *to lose one's taste for* perder el gusto por.

taste [teist] *vt* probar, saborear; *taste this, it's lovely* prueba esto, está estupendo || catar, probar (wine) || notar un sabor a; *you can taste garlic in this meat* se nota un sabor a ajo en esta carne || experimentar, saborear, conocer (to experience); *to taste the pleasures of riches* experimentar los placeres de la riqueza || sufrir (to suffer); *to taste s.o.'s temper* sufrir el mal genio de alguien || probar (to try); *to taste the good life* probar la buena vida.
◆ *vi* saber; *to taste of* saber a || — *to taste nice* estar bueno, estar rico, estar sabroso || *to taste strange* tener un sabor raro, saber raro, tener un gusto raro.

taste bud [-bʌd] *n* ANAT papila *f* gustativa.

tasteful [-ful] *adj* de buen gusto.

tastefully [-fuli] *adv* con (buen) gusto; *tastefully dressed* vestido con buen gusto.

tastefulness [-fulnis] *n* buen gusto *m*, elegancia *f*.

tasteless [-lis] *adj* insípido, da; soso, sa (food) || de mal gusto (in bad taste).

tastelessly [-lisli] *adv* con mal gusto, sin gusto; *a tastelessly decorated room* una habitación decorada sin gusto.

tastelessness [-lisnis] *n* insipidez *f* (of food) || mal gusto *m*, falta *f* de gusto (bad taste).

taster [-ə*] *n* catador *m* (person) || utensilio *m* para catar (instrument) || catavino *m* (glass for tasting wine).

tastiness [-inis] *n* sabor *m*, gusto *m* || buen gusto *m*.

tasting [-iŋ] *n* degustación *f*; *wine tasting* degustación de vino.

tasty [-i] *adj* sabroso, sa; apetitoso, sa || de buen gusto.

tat [tæt] *n* → **tit.**

tat [tæt] *vt* hacer bordados *or* encajes en.
◆ *vi* hacer bordados *or* encajes.

tata ['tæ'tɑː] *interj* FAM chao, hasta lueguito.

Tatar ['tɑːtə*] *n/adj* tártaro, ra; tátaro, ra.

Tatary ['tɑːtəri] *pr n* HIST Tartaria *f*.

tater ['teitə*] *n* FAM patata *f* [*AMER* papa *f*] (potato).

tatouay ['tætuei] *n* tatú *m* (armadillo).

tatter ['tætə*] *n* jirón *m*, pingajo *m*.
◆ *pl* andrajos *m*, harapos *m* (ragged clothing) || *to be in rags and tatters* ir con la ropa hecha jirones, ir desastrado.

tatterdemalion [,tætədə'meiljən] *n* zarrapastroso, sa; andrajoso, sa.

tattered [tætəd] *adj* hecho jirones, andrajoso, sa (clothes) || andrajoso, sa; harapiento, ta (person).

tatting ['tætiŋ] *n* encaje *m* de hilo.

tattle ['tætl] *n* palique *m*, cháchara *f* (idle talk) || chismorreo *m* (gossip).

tattle ['tætl] *vi* estar de palique *or* de cháchara (to engage in idle talk) || chismorrear (to gossip).

tattler [-ə*] *n* parlanchín, ina (talkative person) || chismoso, sa (gossip).

tattletale [-teil] *n* soplón, ona; acusica *m* & *f* (telltale) || chismoso, sa (gossip).

tattoo [tə'tuː] *n* MIL toque *m* de retreta, retreta *f* (signal) | desfile *m* militar, espectáculo *m* militar (entertainment) || repiqueteo *m* (succession of taps) || tatuaje *m* (on the skin) || *the hailstones beat a tattoo on the roof* el granizo tamborileaba en el tejado.

tattoo [tə'tuː] *vt* tatuar (the skin).
◆ *vi* tamborilear (to tap).

tattooing [-iŋ] *n* tatuaje *m*.

tattooist [-ist] *n* persona *f* que hace tatuajes.

tatty ['tæti] *adj* en mal estado (in poor condition) || pobre (house, street) || desaseado, da (person) || gastado, da; raído, da (clothes).

tau [tɔː] *n* tau *m*, tao *m* (cross) || tau *f* (Greek letter).

taught [tɔːt] *pret/pp* → **teach.**

taunt [tɔːnt] *adj* MAR alto, ta; de mucha guinda.
◆ *n* pulla *f*, sarcasmo *m* (provocation).

taunt [tɔːnt] *vt* mofarse de (to jeer at) || lanzar pullas a (to provoke) || *to taunt s.o. with sth.* echar algo en cara a uno.

taunting [-iŋ] *adj* burlón, ona (jeering) || provocate (provocative) || sarcástico, ca.

taupe [təup] *n* US gris *m* oscuro.

taurine ['tɔːrain] *adj* taurino, na.

Tauris ['tɔːris] *n* GEOGR Táuride.

tauromachian [tɔːrə'meikiən]; **tauromachic** [tɔː'rɔməkik] *adj* tauromáquico, ca.

tauromachy [tɔː'rɔməki] *n* tauromaquia *f*.

Taurus ['tɔːrəs] *n* ASTR Tauro *m* (constellation, sign of the zodiac) || GEOGR Tauro *m*.

taut [tɔːt] *adj* tenso, sa; *a taut rope* una cuerda tensa; *the situation is taut* la situación está tensa.

tauten ['tɔːtən] *vt* tensar (rope) || tesar (sails).
◆ *vi* tensarse.

tautness ['tɔːtnis] *n* tensión *f*.

tautological [,tɔːtəxlɔdʒikəl] *adj* tautológico, ca.

tautology [,tɔːtɔlədʒi] *n* tautología *f*.

tavern ['tævən] *n* taberna *f* (bar) || venta *f* (inn).

taw [tɔː] *n* canica *f or* bola *f* grande (large marble) || punto *m* de donde se empieza la jugada (starting point) || juego *m* de canicas *or* bolas (game).

taw [tɔː] *vt* curtir en blanco (hides).
◆ *vi* jugar a las canicas *or* bolas.

tawdriness ['tɔːdrinis] *n* oropel *m* relumbrón *m*.

tawdry ['tɔːdri] *adj* de oropel, de relumbrón.
◆ *n* oropel *m* relumbrón *m*.

tawniness ['tɔːninis] *n* color *m* rojizo *or* leonado || bronceado *m* (of skin).

tawny ['tɔːni] *adj* rojizo, za; leonado, da || bronceado, da (skin).

tax [tæks] *n* impuesto *m*, contribución *f* (on property, on income, etc.); *land tax* contribución territorial || impuesto *m* (on products); *tobacco tax* impuesto sobre el tabaco; *to levy* o *to impose a tax on sth.* gravar algo con un impuesto; *entertainment tax* impuesto sobre los espectáculos públicos || arancel *m* (at customs) || FIG esfuerzo *m* (effort) | carga *f* (burden); *to be a tax on s.o.* ser una carga para alguien | prueba *f* (test, trial) || — *airport tax* tasa *f* de aeropuerto || *capital gains tax* impuesto de plusvalía || *composition tax* impuesto concertado || *excise tax* impuesto indirecto || *free of tax* exento de impuesto || *income tax* impuesto sobre la renta de las personas físicas || *luxury tax* impuesto de lujo || *purchase tax* impuesto sobre la venta || *road tax, round fund tax* impuesto de circulación || *tax collector* recaudador *m* de contribuciones || *tax cut* recorte *m* de los impuestos || *tax disc* patente *f* del impuesto de circulación || *tax dodging* fraude *m* fiscal || *tax evasion* evasión *f* fiscal || *tax haven* paraíso *m* fiscal || *tax rate* imposición *f* || *tax relief* desgravación *f* fiscal || *tax return* declaración *f* de renta *or* de ingresos || *tax stamp* timbre *m* fiscal || *tax system* sistema tributario || *value added tax* tasa *f* al valor añadido *or* agregado.

tax [tæks] *vt* gravar con un impuesto (a product); *to tax petrol* gravar la gasolina con un impuesto || imponer contribuciones a (a person) || poner a prueba (to try); *his persistence taxed my patience* su persistencia puso a prueba mi paciencia || agotar (to exhaust) || tachar; *to tax s.o. with being idle* tachar a alguien de perezoso || JUR tasar (to fix the amount of costs, etc.) || *to be heavily taxed* estar sujeto a un impuesto elevado (a product), pagar muchos impuestos *or* contribuciones (a person).

taxable ['tæksəbl] *adj* imponible; *taxable income* renta imponible; *taxable profits* utilidades imponibles || impositivo, va; *taxable value* valor impositivo.

taxation [tæk'seiʃən] *n* impuestos *m pl*; *direct, indirect taxation* impuestos directos, indirectos; *heavy taxation* impuestos elevados || sistema *m* tributario (tax system).

tax-deductible ['tæksdi'dʌktəbl] *adj* deducible de los impuestos.

tax-exempt ['tæksig'zempt] *adj* exento de impuestos, libre de impuestos, exonerado de impuestos.

tax exile ['tæks'eksail] *n* persona *f* que vive fuera de su país para no pagar impuestos.

tax-free ['tæks'friː] *adj* exento de impuestos, libre de impuestos, exonerado de impuestos.

taxgatherer ['tæks,gæðərə*] *n* recaudador *m* de contribuciones.

taxi ['tæksi] *n* taxi *m*; *to go by taxi* ir en taxi.

taxi ['tæksi] *vt* llevar en taxi (to transport by taxi) || AVIAT hacer rodar por la pista (on the ground) | hacer deslizarse por el agua (on water).
◆ *vi* ir en taxi (to ride in a taxi) || AVIAT rodar por la pista (on the ground) | deslizarse por el agua (on water).

taxicab [-kæb] *n* taxi *m*.

taxi dancer [-,dgaːnsə*] *n* US cabaretera *f*.

taxidermal [-'dəːməl] *adj* taxidérmico, ca.

taxidermic [-'dəːmik] *adj* taxidérmico, ca.

taxidermist [-dəːmist] *n* taxidermista *m* & *f*.

taxidermy [-dəːmi] *n* taxidermia *f*.

taxi driver [-,draivə*] *n* taxista *m* & *f*.

taximan [-mæn] *n* taxista *m*.
— OBSERV El plural de *taximan* es *taximen*.

taximeter [-'miːtə*] *n* taxímetro *m*.

taxing ['tæksiŋ] *adj* agotador, ra (task) || difícil (problem).

taxiplane [-plein] *n* avión *m* de alquiler.

taxi rank [-'ræŋk] *n* parada *f* de taxis.

taxis [-s] *n* BIOL taxia *f*, taxis *f* || MED taxis *f*.

taxi stand [-'stænd] *n* parada *f* de taxis.

taxiway [-wei] *n* AVIAT pista *f* de rodaje.

taxonomic [,tæksə'nɔmik]; **taxonomical** [-əl] *adj* taxonómico, ca.

taxonomy [tæk'sɔnəmi] *n* taxonomía *f*.

taxpayer ['tæks,peiə*] *n* contribuyente *m* & *f*.

taylorism ['teilərizəm] *n* taylorismo *m*.

T-bone steak ['tiːbəun,steik] *n* CULIN chuletón *m* de buey.

TD *abbr of* [*Treasury Department*] departamento del Tesoro [United States].

tea [tiː] *n* té *m* (leaves, beverage); *a cup of tea* una taza de té; *lemon tea* té con limón || infusión *f*; *camomile tea* infusión de manzanilla || merienda *f*, té *m* (light afternoon snack) || merienda cena, *f* (meal replacing dinner) || — *afternoon tea* merienda || *high tea* merienda cena || FIG *it's not my cup of tea* no me gusta mayormente | *not for all the tea in China* por todo el oro del mundo.

tea bag [-bæg] *n* bolsita *f* de té, bolsa *f* de té.

tea break [-breik] *n* descanso *m* para el té.

tea caddy [-,kædi] *n* bote *m* del té.

tea cake [-keːk] *n* CULIN bollito *m*.

tea cart [-kaːt] *n* carrito *m* del té (tea trolley).

teach* [tiːtʃ] *vt* dar clases a; *to teach children* dar clases a los niños || dar clases de; *he teaches the guitar* da clases de guitarra || enseñar a; *to teach s.o. how to drive* enseñar a alguien a conducir; *that will teach him not to interfere!* ¡eso le enseñará a no entrometerse! || ser profesor de, dar clases de; *he teaches English* es profesor de inglés || — *to teach a lesson* dar una lección || US *to teach school* dar clases.
◆ *vi* ser profesor, dar clases (to be a teacher).
— OBSERV Pret/pp ***taught***.

teachable [-əbl] *adj* enseñable, fácil de enseñar (thing) || que aprende fácilmente (person).

teacher [-ə*] *n* profesor, ra (in a secondary school); *Spanish teacher* profesor de español ‖ maestro, tra (in a primary school).

teachers college [ˈtiːtʃəzˈkɔlidʒ] *n* escuela *f* normal.

teacher training [ˈtiːtʃəˈtreiniŋ] *n* formación *f* pedagógica.

tea chest [ˈtiːtʃest] *n* caja *f* grande para el té.

teach-in [ˈtiːtʃin] *n* seminario *m*.

teaching [ˈtiːtʃiŋ] *n* enseñanza *f* (act, profession); *English language teaching* la enseñanza de la lengua inglesa.
◆ *pl* enseñanzas *f*, doctrina *f sing; the teachings of Christ* las enseñanzas de Cristo.
◆ *adj* docente; *teaching body* o *staff* cuerpo docente ‖ pedagógico, ca; *teaching methods* métodos pedagógicos ‖ *teaching hospital* hospital *m* general con facultad de medicina ‖ *teaching practice* prácticas *f pl* de enseñanza.

tea cloth [ˈtiːklɔθ] *n* trapo *m* de cocina.

tea cosy; tea cozy [ˈtiːˈkəuzi] *n* cubretetera *m*.

teacup [ˈtiːkʌp] *n* taza *f* de té.

teacupful [-ful] *n* taza *f*.
— OBSERV El plural de la palabra *teacupful* es *teacupfuls* o *teacupsful*.

tea dance [ˈtiːdɑːns] *n* té *m* baile.

tea garden [ˈtiːˈɑːdn] *n* té *m* al aire libre ‖ AGR plantación *f* de té.

teahouse [ˈtiːhaus] *n* salón *m* de té.

teak [tiːk] *n* BOT teca *f*.

teakettle [ˈtiːˈketl] *n* tetera *f*.

teal [tiːl] *n* cerceta *f* (duck).

tea leaf [ˈtiːliːf] *n* hoja *f* de té (plant).
◆ *pl* poso *m sing* ‖ FIG *to read the tea leaves* ver el porvenir en el fondo de la taza.
— OBSERV El plural de *tea leaf* es *tea leaves*.

team [tiːm] *n* yunta *f* (animals yoked together) ‖ tronco *m*, tiro *m* (horses when pulling a carriage) ‖ equipo *m* (people working or playing together); *football team* equipo de fútbol; *rescue team* equipo de salvamento ‖ — SP *away team* equipo visitante | *home team* equipo casero | *team games* juegos *m pl* de equipo.

team [tiːm] *vt* hacer trabajar en equipo (to cause to work in a team) ‖ combinar, acompañar; *a knowledge of languages teamed with practical experience* un conocimiento de los idiomas acompañado por *or* combinado con una experiencia práctica ‖ enganchar (horses to a carriage) ‖ uncir (to yoke) ‖ transportar con yunta.
◆ *vi to team up* agruparse, unirse, asociarse.

teammate [-ˌmeit] *n* compañero *m* de equipo.

team spirit [-ˌspirit] *n* espíritu *m* de equipo.

teamster [-stə*] *n* cochero *m* (of a carriage) ‖ carretero *m* (of a cart) ‖ US camionero *m* (lorry driver).

teamwork [-wəːk] *n* trabajo *m* en equipo.

tea party [-ˈpɑːti] *n* té *m*.

teapot [ˈtiːpɔt] *n* tetera *f*.

tear [tiə*] *n* lágrima *f*; *a tear trickled down his cheek* una lágrima le bajaba por la mejilla ‖ FIG lágrima *f* (defect in glass).
◆ *pl* lágrimas *f*; *tears filled her eyes* tenía los ojos llenos de lágrimas ‖ llanto *m* (weeping) ‖ — FIG *crocodile tears* lágrimas de cocodrilo ‖ *in tears* llorando ‖ *to be bathed in tears* estar bañado en lágrimas ‖ FAM *to be bored to tears* aburrirse como una ostra ‖ *to bring tears to the eyes of the audience* arrancar lágrimas *or* hacer saltar las lágrimas al público ‖ *to burst* o *to dissolve into tears* deshacerse en lágrimas, echarse a llorar ‖ *to dry* o *to wipe away one's tears* tragarse las lágrimas ‖ FIG *to hold back one's tears* enjugarse las lágrimas ‖ *to move s.o. to tears* hacer llorar a alguien ‖ *to shed tears* derramar lágrimas ‖ *with tears in his eyes* con lágrimas en los ojos.

tear [tiə*] *vi* derramar lágrimas.

tear [tɛə*] *n* rasgón *m*, desgarrón *m* (split) ‖ prisa *f*, precipitación *f* (haste).

tear* [tɛə*] *vt* desgarrar, rasgar, romper; *to tear a piece of cloth, of paper* rasgar una tela, un papel ‖ arrancar, quitar violentamente; *he tore the poster from the wall* arrancó el cartel de la pared ‖ MED herir, lacerar (the flesh) | distender (a muscle, a ligament) ‖ FIG atormentar; *she was torn as to what she ought to do* estaba atormentada por lo que debía de hacer | dividir, desgarrar (to divide into opposing groups); *a country torn by interior strife* un país desgarrado por disensiones internas ‖ — *to tear a hole in* hacer un agujero en ‖ FIG *to tear one's hair* tirarse de los pelos ‖ *to tear sth. open* abrir algo rasgándolo *or* rompiéndolo violentamente ‖ *to tear to pieces* hacer pedazos (to break), echar abajo, echar por tierra (an argument), poner como un trapo, poner por los suelos (to criticize).
◆ *phr v* ***to tear along*** ir a toda velocidad ‖ ***to tear apart*** romper, rasgar | FIG desgarrar, dividir ‖ ***to tear around*** correr como un loco ‖ ***to tear at*** quitar precipitadamente ‖ — *to tear at s.o.'s eyes* intentar sacarlos los ojos a alguien ‖ ***to tear away*** arrancar (to remove) | salir disparado (to leave) ‖ — *he can't tear himself away from the television even for a minute* no deja de ver la televisión ni un solo minuto | *I couldn't tear myself away* no sabía cómo irme (from meeting, etc.), no podía deshacerme de él (from a person) ‖ ***to tear down*** arrancar (to pull down) | derribar, demoler (to demolish) | desmontar, desarmar (a machine) | US difamar, denigrar (to denigrate) ‖ ***to tear in*** entrar precipitadamente ‖ ***to tear into*** acometer ‖ ***to tear loose*** soltarse ‖ ***to tear off*** arrancar | cortar (a coupon) | salir disparado (to leave) ‖ ***to tear out*** arrancar (to rip) | salir disparado (to leave) ‖ ***to tear up*** hacer pedazos, despedazar (to destroy) | sacar de raíz, desarraigar (a plant) | anular; *to tear up a treaty* anular un tratado | llegar a toda velocidad (to arrive).
— OBSERV Pret ***tore***; pp ***torn***.

tearaway [ˈtɛərəwei] *n* gamberro, rra.

teardrop [ˈtiədrɔp] *n* lágrima *f* (tear).

tear duct [ˈtiədʌkt] *n* ANAT conducto *m* lacrimal.

tearful [ˈtiəful] *adj* lloroso, sa (shedding tears) ‖ lacrimoso, sa (causing or accompanied by tears) ‖ lastimoso, sa (event).

tear gas [ˈtiəgæs] *n* gas *m* lacrimógeno ‖ *tear-gas bomb* bomba lacrimógena.

tearing [ˈtɛəriŋ] *adj* desgarrador, ra ‖ violento, ta; *tearing rage* furia violenta ‖ *a tearing noise* el ruido de algo que se rasga.
◆ *n* desgarramiento *m*.

tearjerker [ˈtiəˌdʒəːkə*] *n* obra *f* sentimentaloide.

tearless [ˈtiəlis] *adj* sin lágrimas.

tear-off [ˈtɛərɔf] *adj* trepado, da; *complete the tear-off slip* rellénese el cupón trepado ‖ *tear-off calendar* calendario *m* de taco.

tearoom [ˈtiːrum] *n* salón *m* de té.

tea rose [ˈtiːrəuz] *n* BOT rosa *f* de té.

tearstain [ˈtiəˌstein] *n* mancha *f* de lágrima.

tease [tiːz] *n* broma *f*; *to do sth. for a tease* hacer algo en broma ‖ bromista *m* & *f* (joker); *to be sth. of a tease* ser un poco bromista ‖ FAM provocadora *f* (a woman).

tease [tiːz] *vt* molestar, fastidiar [*AMER* embromar] (to annoy) ‖ FAM provocar (to provoke) ‖ atormentar (to tantalize) ‖ tomar el pelo a (to make fun of); *to tease s.o. about his accent* tomarle el pelo a alguien a causa de su acento ‖ importunar (to pester) ‖ TECH cardar; *to tease wool* cardar lana; *to tease a cloth* cardar un paño.

teasel; teazel; teazle [-l] *n* BOT cardencha *f* ‖ carda *f* (wire device used to raise a nap).

teasel [-l] *vt* cardar.

teaser [-ə*] *n* bromista *m* & *f* (tease) ‖ TECH cardador, ra (of wool, etc.) ‖ rompecabezas *m inv* (puzzle) ‖ FAM provocadora *f* (woman).

tea service [ˈtiːˌsəːvis] *n* juego *m* de té.

tea set [ˈtiːset] *n* juego *m* de té.

tea shop [ˈtiːʃɔp] *n* salón *m* de té.

teasing [ˈtiːziŋ] *adj* burlón, ona (mocking) ‖ bromista (person) ‖ atormentador, ra (tantalizing).
◆ *n* bromas *f pl*, burlas *f pl* (jokes) ‖ tormentos *m pl* (torments).

Teasmaid [ˈtiːzmeid] *n* (registered trademark) tetera *f* automática.

teaspoon [ˈtiːspuːn] *n* cucharilla *f* (small spoon) ‖ cucharadita *f* (teaspoonful).

teaspoonful [-ful] *n* cucharadita *f*.
— OBSERV El plural de *teaspoonful* es *teaspoonfuls* o *teaspoonsful*.

tea strainer [ˈtiːstreinə*] *n* colador *m* para el té.

teat [tiːt] *n* ANAT pezón *m* ‖ teta *f* (of animals) ‖ tetina *f*, boquilla *f* (of a feeding bottle).

tea table [ˈtiːˈteibl] *n* mesita *f* de té.

teatime [ˈtiːtaim] *n* hora *f* del té.

tea towel [ˈtiːtauəl] *n* trapo *m* de cocina.

tea tray [ˈtiːtrei] *n* bandeja *f* del té.

tea trolley [ˈtiːtrɔli] *n* carrito *m* del té.

tea urn [ˈtiːəːn] *n* tetera *f* grande.

tea wagon [ˈtiːˈwægən] *n* carrito *m* del té.

teazel [ˈtiːzl]; **teazle** [ˈtiːzl] *n* ⟶ **teasel.**

technetium [tekˈniːʃiəm] *n* CHEM tecnecio *m*.

technic [ˈteknik] *adj* técnico, ca.
◆ *n* técnica *f*.

technical [-əl] *adj* técnico, ca; *technical books* libros técnicos; *technical terms* terminología técnica; *technical adviser* asesor *or* consejero técnico ‖ JUR en teoría, según la ley ‖ de forma, de terminología; *technical point* cuestión de forma ‖ — *technical college* instituto *m* de formación profesional ‖ *technical drawing* dibujo *m* técnico ‖ JUR *technical offence* cuasidelito *m* ‖ *technical school* instituto *m* laboral.

technicality [ˌtekniˈkæliti] *n* tecnicidad *f* ‖ tecnicismo *m* (word) ‖ detalle *m* técnico (detail).

technically [ˈteknikəli] *adv* técnicamente ‖ en términos técnicos; *expressed technically* dicho en términos técnicos ‖ en teoría; *you are technically guilty* en teoría usted es culpable.

technician [tekˈniʃən] *n* técnico, ca; especialista *m* & *f* ‖ *laboratory technician* ayudante *m* de laboratorio.

Technicolor [ˈtekniˌkʌlə*] *n* Tecnicolor *m*; *in Technicolor* en Tecnicolor.
◆ *adj* en Tecnicolor.

technics [ˈtekniks] *n* tecnología *f*.

technique [tekˈniːk] *n* técnica *f*.

technochemistry [teknəˈkemistri] *n* química *f* industrial.

technocracy [tekˈnɔkrəsi] *n* tecnocracia *f*.

technocrat [ˈteknəkræt] *n* tecnócrata *m* & *f*.

technocratic [teknəˈkrætik] *adj* tecnócrata.

technologic [ˌteknəˈlɔdʒik]; **technological** [-əl] *adj* tecnológico, ca.

technologist [tekˈnɔlədʒist] *n* tecnólogo, ga.

technology [tekˈnɔlədʒi] *n* tecnología *f*.

techy [ˈtetʃi] *adj* irritable, picajoso, sa.

tectonic [tekˈtɔnik] *adj* arquitectónico, ca ‖ GEOL tectónico, ca.

tectonics [-s] *n* arquitectura *f* (building) ‖ GEOL tectónica *f*.

tectrices [tek'traisi:z] *pl n* ZOOL tectrices *f*.

ted [ted] *vt* henificar.

tedder ['tedə*] *n* henificadora *f*.

teddy bear ['tedibεə*] *n* oso *m* de felpa.

teddy boy ['tedibɔi] *n* gamberro *m*.

Te Deum ['ti:'di:əm] *n* REL Tedéum *m*, Te Deum *m*.

tedious ['ti:djəs] *adj* aburrido, da; tedioso, sa; pesado, da.

tediousness [-nis]; **tedium** ['ti:djəm] *n* tedio *m*, aburrimiento *m*, pesadez *f*.

tee [ti:] *n* te *f* (letter) ‖ SP punto *m* de partida (in golf, the beginning of a hole) | «tee» *m*, soporte *m* donde se pone la pelota (in golf, object on which the ball is placed) ‖ FIG *to a tee* como anillo al dedo.

tee [ti:] *vt/vi* SP *to tee off* dar el primer golpe (in golf) | *to tee up* colocar en el «tee» (in golf).

tee-hee ['ti:'hi:] *n/interj* → **tehee.**

teem [ti:m] *vt* TECH verter.
◆ *vi* hormiguear, pulular; *refugees teemed in the streets* los refugiados hormigueaban por las calles ‖ hervir, rebosar; *the river teems with fish* el río hierve de peces ‖ *ideas teemed in his mind* tenía la cabeza llena de ideas.

teeming [-iŋ] *adj* abundante ‖ que hormiguea de gente; *teeming cities* ciudades que hormiguean de gente ‖ *teeming with mistakes* lleno de errores.

teen-age ['ti:n,eidʒ] *adj* adolescente ‖ *teen-age fashion* moda para jóvenes.

teen-ager [-ə*] *n* adolescente *m* & *f*, joven *m* & *f*.

teens [ti:nz] *pl n* adolescencia *f sing* ‖ *to be in one's teens* estar en la adolescencia, tener entre 13 y 19 años.

teeny ['ti:ni]; **teeny-weeny** [-'wi:ni] *adj* FAM pequeñito, ta; minúsculo, la; chiquitín, ina.

teepee ['ti:pi] *n* tepee *m*.

tee shirt ['ti:ʃə:t] *n* camiseta *f*.

teeter ['ti:tə*] *vi* balancearse (to move in a wobbly manner) ‖ FIG vacilar, titubear (to be indecise) ‖ US columpiarse (to seesaw).

teeter-totter [-'tɔtə*] *n* US columpio *m*, subibaja *m* (seesaw).

teeter-totter [-'tɔtə*] *vi* columpiarse.

teeth [ti:θ] *pl n* → **tooth.**

teethe [ti:ð] *vi* echar los dientes.

teething [-iŋ] *n* dentición *f*.

teething ring [-iŋriŋ] *n* chupador *m*.

teething troubles [-iŋtrʌblz] *pl n* FIG problemas *m pl* iniciales.

teetotal [ti:'təutl] *adj* abstemio, mia (abstaining from alcoholic drinks) ‖ US FAM total, completo, ta; *a teetotal failure* un fracaso total.

teetotalism [-izəm] *n* abstinencia *f*.

teetotaller; US **teetotaler** [-ə*]; **teetotalist** [-ist] *n* abstemio, mia.

teetotum ['ti:təu'tʌm] *n* perinola *f*.

TEFL *abbr of* *[Teaching of English as a Foreign Language]* enseñanza del inglés como lengua extranjera.

Teflón ['teflɔn] *n* (registered trademark) teflón *m*.

teg [teg] *n* oveja *f* de dos años (sheep).

tegmen [-mən] *n* tegmen *m*.
— OBSERV El plural de la palabra inglesa es *tegmina*.

Tegucigalpa [te,gu:tʃi'gælpə] *pr n* GEOGR Tegucigalpa.

tegument ['tegjumənt] *n* tegumento *m*.

tegumental [,tegju'mentəl] *adj* tegumentario, ria.

tehee ['ti:'hi:] *n* risa *f*, risita *f*.
◆ *interj* ¡ja ja!

Teheran; Tehran [tiə'rɑ:n] *pr n* GEOGR Teherán.

telaesthesia [,teles'θi:ʒjə] *n* telestesia *f*.

telamon ['teləmən] *n* ARCH telamón *m*, atlante *m*.
— OBSERV El plural de la palabra inglesa es *telamones*.

telecast ['telikɑ:st] *n* transmisión *f* por televisión, teledifusión *f* ‖ emisión *f or* programa *m* de televisión (programme).

telecine ['teli'sini] *n* telecine *m*, telecinematógrafo *m*.

telecommunication ['telikŋ'mjuni'keiʃən] *n* telecomunicación *f*.

telecourse ['telikɔ:s] *n* curso *m* televisado.

telefilm ['telifilm] *n* telefilm *m*.

telegenic [,teli'dʒenik] *adj* televisivo, va.

telegram ['teligræm] *n* telegrama *m*.

telegram ['teligræm] *vt* telegrafiar.

telegraph ['teligrɑ:f] *n* telégrafo *m*.
◆ *adj* telegráfico, ca; *telegraph pole, wire* poste, hilo telegráfico ‖ — *telegraph messenger* telegrafista *m* & *f* ‖ *telegraph operator* telegrafista *m* & *f*.

telegraph ['teligrɑ:f] *vt* telegrafiar (to wire).
◆ *vi* mandar un telegrama, telegrafiar.

telegrapher [ti'legrəfə*] *n* telegrafista *m* & *f*.

telegraphic [,teli'græfik] *adj* telegráfico, ca.

telegraphist [ti'legrəfist] *n* telegrafista *m* & *f*.

telegraphy [ti'legrəfi] *n* telegrafía *f*; *wireless telegraphy* telegrafía sin hilos.

telekinesis [,telikai'ni:sis] *n* telequinesia *f*.

telelens ['telilenz] *n* teleobjetivo *m*.

Telemachus [ti'leməkəs] *pr n* Telémaco *m*.

telemark ['telimɑ:k] *n* SP virage *m* (in skiing).

telematics [teli'mætiks] *n* INFORM telemática *f*.

telemechanic ['telimi'kænik] *adj* telemecánico, ca.

telemechanics [-s] *n* telemecánica *f*.

telemeter ['telimi:tə*] *n* telémetro *m*.

telemetric [teli'metrik] *adj* telemétrico, ca.

telemetry [ti'lemitri] *n* telemetría *f*.

telencephalon [,telin'sefəlɔn] *n* ANAT telencéfalo *m*.

teleologic [teli'ɔlədʒik]; **teleological** [-əl] *adj* teleológico, ca.

teleology [teli'ɔlədʒi] *n* teleología *f*.

teleost ['teliɔst]; **teleostean** [teli'ɔstiən] *adj* ZOOL teleósteo.
◆ *n* ZOOL teleósteo *m*.

telepathic [,teli'pæθik] *adj* telepático, ca.

telepathist [ti'lepəθist] *n* telépata *m* & *f*.

telepathy [ti'lepəθi] *n* telepatía *f*.

telephone ['telifəun] *n* teléfono *m* ‖ — *to be on the telephone* tener teléfono (to have a telephone), estar hablando por teléfono (to be speaking on the telephone) ‖ *you are wanted on the telephone* le llaman por teléfono.
◆ *adj* telefónico, ca; *telephone company* compañía telefónica.

telephone ['telifəun] *vt* decir *or* comunicar por teléfono (to transmit by telephone) ‖ hablar por teléfono con, telefonear a, llamar por teléfono a (to speak to on the telephone) ‖ *telephoned telegram* telefonema *m*.
◆ *vi* llamar por teléfono.

telephone book [-buk] *n* guía *f* de teléfonos.

telephone booth [-bu:ð]; **telephone box** [-bɔks] *n* cabina *f* telefónica, locutorio *m*.

telephone call [-kɔ:l] *n* llamada *f* telefónica.

telephone directory [-di'rektəri] *n* guía *f* de teléfonos.

telephone exchange [-iks'tʃeindʒ] *n* central *f* telefónica, central *f* de teléfonos.

telephone kiosk [-,kiɔsk] *n* cabina *f* telefónica, locutorio *m*.

telephone number [-'nʌmbə*] *n* número *m* de teléfono.

telephone operator [-'ɔpəreitə*] *n* telefonista *m* & *f*.

telephone receiver [-ri'si:və*] *n* microteléfono *m*.

telephone tapping [-'tæpiŋ] *n* escuchas *f pl* telefónicas.

telephonic [,teli'fɔnik] *adj* telefónico, ca.

telephonist [ti'lefənist] *n* telefonista *m* & *f*.

telephony [ti'lefəni] *n* telefonía *f*; *wireless telephony* telefonía sin hilos.

telephoto ['teli'fəutəu] *adj* PHOT telefotográfico, ca.
◆ *n* PHOT telefotografía *f*, telefoto *f* (photograph) | teleobjetivo *m* (lens).

telephotograph ['teli'fəutəgrɑ:f] *n* PHOT telefotografía *f*, telefoto *f*.

telephotographic [teli'fəutə'græfik] *adj* telefotográfico, ca.

telephotography ['telifə'tɔgrəfi] *n* PHOT telefotografía *f*.

telephoto lens ['teli'fəutəu,lenz] *n* PHOT teleobjetivo *m*.

teleprinter ['teli,printə*] *n* teleimpresor *m*, teletipo *m*.

teleprocess ['teli'prəuses] *vt* INFORM teleprocesar.

teleprocessing ['teli'prəusesiŋ] *n* INFORM teleprocesamiento *m*, teleproceso *m*, teletratamiento *m*.

teleprompter ['teli,prɔmptə*] *n* tablero *m* que se utiliza en televisión para recordar las palabras de un texto.

telescope ['teliskəup] *n* catalejo *m*; *to look at sth. through a telescope* mirar algo con un catalejo ‖ ASTR telescopio *m*.

telescope ['teliskəup] *vt* FIG hacer encastrar; *the collision telescoped four coaches of the train* el choque hizo que se encastrasen cuatro vagones del tren | resumir, abreviar (to shorten).
◆ *vi* plegarse como un telescopio (to fold up like a telescope) ‖ encajar; *this part telescopes into the other* esta parte encaja en la otra.

telescopic [telis'kɔpik] *adj* telescópico, ca ‖ que se meten unas en otras, que se encastran.

telesthesia [,teles'θi:ʒjə] *n* US telestesia *f*.

teletext ['telitekst] *n* teletexto *m*.

teletype ['telitaip] *n* teletipo *m* (teleprinter) ‖ despacho *m* (message).

teletypewriter [teli'taipraitə*] *n* US teletipo *m*, teleimpresor *m*.

televiewer ['telivju:ə*] *n* telespectador, ra; televidente *m* & *f*.

televise ['telivaiz] *vt* televisar.

television ['teliʌviʒən] *n* televisión *f* (system); *colour television* televisión en color ‖ televisor *m*, aparato *m* de televisión (set) ‖ — *to watch television* ver la televisión ‖ *what is on television?* ¿qué ponen en la televisión?

television broadcasting [-'brɔ:dkɑ:stiŋ] *n* teledifusión *f*.

television licence [-'laisəns] *n* impuesto *m* televisivo.

television screen [-skri:n] *n* pantalla *f* de televisión.

television set [-set] *n* televisor *m*, aparato *m* de televisión.

telex ['teleks] *n* télex *m*.

telex ['teleks] *vi* enviar un télex.

telfer ['telfə*] *n* US teleférico *m*.

telferage [-ridʒ] *n* US teleferaje *m*.

tell* [tel] *vt* decir; *to tell the truth* decir la verdad; *to tell s.o. the time* decir la hora a alguien; *promise you won't tell my mother?* ¿me promete que no se lo dirá a mi madre?; *I can't tell which is best* no puedo decir cuál es mejor; *I told him not to do it* le dije que no lo hiciera || comunicar (formally); *to tell s.o. a piece of news* comunicar una noticia a alguien || contar; *to tell a story, a joke* contar una historia, un chiste; *he told me everything that had happened* me contó todo lo que había pasado || divulgar, contar, revelar; *to tell a secret* divulgar un secreto || mandar, ordenar; *he was told to get his hair cut* le mandaron que se cortase el pelo || señalar, indicar; *the arrows tell you which route to follow* las flechas le indican el camino que hay que seguir || ver, notar; *one can tell she is not English* se nota que no es inglesa; *you can tell it's winter* se ve que estamos en invierno || reconocer, identificar; *you can tell him by his beard* se le puede reconocer por la barba || distinguir; *to tell margarine from butter* distinguir la margarina de la mantequilla; *to be able to tell right from wrong* saber distinguir el bien del mal || saber; *no one can tell what the future may bring* nadie sabe lo que el futuro nos deparará; *you never can tell* nunca se sabe || deducir; *I couldn't tell much from what he said* de lo que dijo no pude deducir gran cosa || contar (to count) || — *all told* en total (in total), mirándolo bien (all things considered) || *he won't be very pleased about it, I can tell you!* ¡te aseguro que no va a estar muy contento! || *I am glad* o *pleased to tell you that...* tengo el placer de comunicarle que... || *I can't begin to tell you* o *I can't tell you how grateful I am* no encuentro palabras para decirle lo agradecido que estoy || *I don't want to have to tell you twice* no quiero tener que repetírselo dos veces || *I have been told that* me han dicho que || *I hear tell that* dicen que || *I tell you what: let's drop the whole matter* mira, no hablemos más del asunto || *I tell you what: let's go out for dinner* se me ocurre una idea, ¿por qué no vamos a cenar? || *I told you so!* ¡ya te lo dije! || *tell me all about it* cuéntamelo todo || FAM *tell me another!, tell that to the marines!* ¡cuéntaselo a tu abuela!, ¡a otro perro con ese hueso! || *to tell one's beads* rezar el rosario || *to tell s.o.'s fortune* echar la buenaventura a alguien || FAM *to tell s.o. where to get off* poner a alguien en su sitio || *to tell the time* dar la hora (a clock), leer el reloj; *a child who is learning to tell the time* un niño que está aprendiendo a leer el reloj || *to tell you the truth* a decir verdad.

◆ *vi* relatar, contar (to relate) || notarse; *his age is beginning to tell* la edad se le está empezando a notar || influir; *the boxer's experience told in his favour* la experiencia del boxeador influyó en su favor || producir *or* tener su efecto; *every word told* cada palabra tuvo su efecto || — FAM *please don't tell* por favor no digas nada a nadie || *quality always tells* la calidad siempre se ve || *to hear tell of* oír hablar de || *you are telling me!* ¡a quién se lo vas a contar!, ¡a mí me lo vas a contar! || *you never can tell* nunca se puede decir.

◆ *phr v* *to tell against* perjudicar; *his record told against him* su historial le perjudicó || ***to tell of*** hablar de, contar; *he told me of his worries* me habló de sus preocupaciones | anunciar; *the dark clouds told of a rainstorm* las nubes oscuras anunciaban tormenta || ***to tell off*** designar; *to tell off four men for a duty* designar a cuatro hombres para un trabajo | FAM regañar, reñir (to rebuke, especially children) | echar una bronca a (to rebuke forcefully) || ***to tell on*** afectar a; *the fast pace began to tell on the runners* el paso rápido empezó a afectar a los corredores | delatar, denunciar (to report the misdeeds of).

— OBSERV Pret y pp ***told***.

teller [-ə*] *n* narrador, ra (who tells a story) || cajero, ra (in a bank) || escrutador, ra (who counts votes).

telling [-iŋ] *adj* eficaz, contundente; *a telling argument* un argumento eficaz || contundente; *a telling blow* un golpe contundente || expresivo, va; revelador, ra; *a telling look* una mirada expresiva.

◆ *n* narración *f*, relato *m* (of a story) || divulgación *f* (of a secret) || recuento *m* (of votes) || — *that's telling!* ¡es un secreto! || *there is no telling what will happen* es imposible saber lo que va a pasar.

telling off [-iŋɔf] *n* reprimenda *f*, bronca *f*.

telltale [-teil] *adj* revelador, ra || TECH *telltale light* indicador luminoso.

◆ *n* soplón, ona; chivato, ta (person who informs) || MAR axiómetro *m* (to show position of rudder) || TECH indicador *m*.

tellurian [te'ljuəriən] *adj* telúrico, ca.

◆ *n* terrícola *m* & *f*.

telluric [te'ljuərik] *adj* telúrico, ca.

tellurium [te'ljuəriəm] *n* CHEM telurio *m*.

telly ['teli] *n* FAM tele *f* (television).

telodynamic ['teləudai'næmik] *adj* teledinámico, ca.

telpher ['telfə*] *n* teleférico *m*.

telpherage [-ridʒ] *n* teleferaje *m*.

temblor ['temblə*] *n* US temblor *m* de tierra (earthquake).

temerarious [ˌteməˈrɛəriəs] *adj* temerario, ria.

temerity [ti'meriti] *n* temeridad *f*.

temp [temp] *n* FAM trabajador, ra temporal.

temper ['tempə*] *n* TECH temple *m* (of a metal, glass, clay, etc.) || cólera *f*, ira *f* (anger); *a fit of temper* un ataque de furia || genio *m*, mal genio *m* (tendency to become angry); *he has a temper* tiene genio || temperamento *m*, disposición *f* (disposition, character); *to have an equable temper* tener un temperamento ecuánime || humor *m* (mood); *to be in good temper* estar de buen humor || — *out of temper* de mal genio || *to get into* o *to fly into a temper* montar en cólera, ponerse furioso || *to get s.o.'s temper up* enfadar a alguien, poner furioso a alguien || *to keep one's temper* contenerse || *to lose one's temper* ponerse de malhumor, enfadarse, perder los estribos || *to show temper* estar de malhumor || *to try s.o.'s temper* probar la paciencia de uno.

temper ['tempə*] *vt* TECH templar (glass, steel, etc.) || amasar (mortar) || ARTS templar || FIG templar, suavizar (to make less harsh) || MUS afinar, templar.

◆ *vi* templarse.

tempera ['tempərə] *n* pintura *f* al temple.

temperament ['tempərəmənt] *n* temperamento *m*; *nervous, artistic temperament* temperamento nervioso, artístico || sensibilidad *f* (sensitivity) || genio *m* (temper) || MUS temperamento *m*.

temperamental [ˌtempərə'mentl] *adj* temperamental, del temperamento (of the temperament) || inestable, caprichoso, sa; inconstante (person) || *a temperamental machine* una máquina caprichosa.

temperance ['tempərəns] *n* templanza *f*, sobriedad *f*, moderación *f* || abstinencia *f* de bebidas alcohólicas (abstinence from alcohol).

temperate ['tempərit] *adj* templado, da; moderado, da || GEOGR *temperate zone* zona templada.

temperature ['tempritʃə*] *n* temperatura *f*; *maximum temperature* temperatura máxima || MED fiebre *f*, calentura *f*, temperatura *f*; *to have a temperature* tener fiebre || — *absolute temperature* temperatura absoluta || *critical temperature* temperatura crítica || MED *temperature chart* gráfico *m* de la temperatura || *temperature recorder* registrador *m* de temperatura || *to take s.o.'s temperature* tomar la temperatura a alguien.

tempered ['tempəd] *adj* dispuesto, ta (having a specified temper) || templado, da.

temperer ['tempərə*] *n* TECH templador *m* || mezcladora *f* (of mortar).

tempering ['tempəriŋ] *n* TECH templadura *f* || MUS temple *m*.

tempest ['tempist] *n* tempestad *f*.

tempestuous [tem'pestjuəs] *adj* tempestuoso, sa (weather) || FIG tempestuoso, sa; borrascoso, sa (meeting, etc.).

Templar ['templə*] *n* HIST templario *m* || abogado *m* del «Temple» (barrister).

template ['templet]; **templet** ['templit] *n* TECH plantilla *f* (metal or wooden pattern) || MAR gálibo *m*.

temple ['templ] *n* REL templo *m* || ANAT sien *f* (of the head) || — HIST *knights of the Temple* caballeros *m* del Temple, templarios *m* || JUR *the Temple* Colegio *m* de Abogados de Londres.

templet ['templit] *n* ⟶ **template.**

tempo ['tempəu] *n* MUS tempo *m*, compás *m* || FIG ritmo *m*; *the tempo of production decreases in winter* el ritmo de la producción disminuye en invierno.

— OBSERV El plural de la palabra inglesa *tempo* es *tempi* o *tempos*.

temporal ['tempərəl] *adj* ANAT, GRAMM & PHIL temporal || REL temporal, secular || — *temporal and spatial existence* existencia *f* en el tiempo y en el espacio || ANAT *temporal bone* temporal *m*.

temporality [ˌtempə'ræliti] *n* temporalidad *f*, carácter *m* temporal.

◆ *pl* REL temporalidades *f* (revenues).

temporarily ['tempərərili] *adv* temporalmente.

temporary ['tempərəri] *adj* temporal, provisional; *temporary job* trabajo temporal; *temporary arrangement* arreglo provisional || transitorio, ria; *temporary measures* medidas transitorias || temporero, ra (worker) || interino, na (officer).

temporization ['tempərai'zeiʃən] *n* contemporización *f*.

temporize ['tempəraiz] *vi* contemporizar, temporizar.

tempt [tempt] *vt* tentar, seducir; *to tempt s.o. with money* tentar a alguien con dinero || incitar, inducir, tentar; *to tempt s.o. into sth.* inducir a alguien a hacer algo, incitar a alguien para que haga algo || — *can I tempt you to a glass of wine?* ¿te puedo ofrecer un vaso de vino? || *I am sorely tempted to sell up and leave* tengo muchas ganas de venderlo todo y marcharme || *to be* o *feel tempted to do sth.* estar *or* sentirse tentado de hacer algo || *to let o.s. be tempted* ceder a la tentación || FIG *to tempt fate* tentar al destino | *to tempt providence* tentar a Dios | *to tempt the devil* tentar al diablo.

temptation [temp'teiʃən] *n* tentación *f*; *to fall into temptation* caer en la tentación; *to yield to temptation* caer en la tentación; *to yield to temptation* ceder a la tentación || — REL *lead us not into temptation* no nos dejes caer en la tentación || *there is always a temptation to do things* *quickly instead of well* se suele tener tendencia a hacer las cosas rápidamente en lugar de hacerlas bien || *to throw temptation in s.o.'s way* exponer a alguien a la tentación.

tempter ['temptə*] *n* tentador *m.*

tempting ['temptiŋ] *adj* tentador, ra; atractivo, va; *a tempting proposal* una propuesta tentadora || apetitoso, sa (food).

temptingly [-li] *adv* de modo tentador || atractivamente || *a temptingly prepared meal* una comida apetitosa.

temptress ['temptris] *n* tentadora *f.*

ten [ten] *adj* diez; *ten people* diez personas || REL *the Ten Commandments* los Diez Mandamientos.
◆ *n* diez *m* (number, card, figure).
◆ *pl* MATH columna *f sing* de las decenas (column of figures) || — *it's ten past ten* son las diez y diez || *ten o'clock* las diez || *tens of thousands of people* decenas de miles de personas || *to count in tens* contar de diez en diez.

tenability [,tenə'biliti] *n* valor *m*, validez *f* (of an argument) || *a post of limited tenability* un puesto que se puede ocupar sólo por cierto período de tiempo.

tenable ['tenəbl] *adj* defendible (against attack) || sostenible (opinions) || *post tenable for one year* puesto *m* que se puede ocupar durante un año.

tenacious [ti'neiʃəs] *adj* tenaz (obstinate) || firme; *tenacious beliefs* creencias firmes || adhesivo, va (adhesive) || retentivo, va; *a tenacious memory* una memoria retentiva || *to be tenacious of one's opinion* aferrarse a su opinión.

tenaciousness [-nis]; **tenacity** [ti'næsiti] *n* tenacidad *f.*

tenail; tenaille [ti'neil] *n* MIL tenallón *m.*

tenancy ['tenənsi] *n* tenencia *f* (holding) || arrendamiento *m*, arriendo *m* (lease of land) || alquiler *m*, arrendamiento *m* (lease of a house).

tenant ['tenənt] *n* arrendatario, ria (on renting land) || inquilino, na; arrendatario, ria (one renting property) || habitante *m* & *f*, ocupante *m* & *f* (inhabitant).

tenant ['tenənt] *vt* arrendar, tener en arriendo (land) || alquilar, arrendar (houses, etc.).

tenantable [-əbl] *adj* habitable || arrendable.

tenant farmer [-'fɑːmə*] *n* arrendatario *m.*

tenantry ['tenəntri] *n* arrendatarios *m pl* (tenants of land) || inquilinos *m pl* (tenants of a house) || tenencia *f* (holding) || arriendo *m*, arrendamiento *m* (lease).

tench [tenʃ] *n* tenca *f* (fish).

tend [tend] *vt* cuidar, atender, ocuparse de (a sick person, etc.) || cuidar, vigilar (stock) || cuidar, cultivar (a garden) || manejar, servir (a machine) || (ant) servir (to wait on) || MAR vigilar (a cable).
◆ *vi* tender, tener tendencia a; *she tends to eat too much* tiende a comer demasiado; *the car tends to stall* el coche tiene tendencia a calarse; *history tends to repeat itself* la historia tiende a repetirse || tender, encaminarse; *a situation tending towards anarchy* una situación que tiende hacia la anarquía || contribuir (to contribute) || tirar; *yellow tending to orange* amarillo que tira a naranja || dirigirse; *the road tends towards the coast* la carretera se dirige hacia la costa || — *I tend to agree* casi comparto su opinión || *I tend to disagree* no puedo compartir completamente su opinión || *it tends to rain in April* suele llover en abril || *to tend to* cuidar de *or* a; *to tend to the baby* cuidar al niño.

tendencious [ten'denʃəs] *adj* US tendencioso, sa.

tendency ['tendənsi] *n* tendencia *f* || *there is a tendency for prices to increase, prices have a tendency to increase* los precios tienden a subir, los precios tienen tendencia a subir.

tendentious [ten'denʃəs] *adj* tendencioso, sa.

tendentiousness [-nis] *n* lo tendencioso, carácter *m* tendencioso.

tender ['tendə*] *adj* frágil, delicado, da (easily damaged); *a tender plant* una planta delicada || tierno, na; *a tender steak* un filete tierno; *a tender age* una edad tierna || cariñoso, sa; dulce; *a tender smile* una sonrisa cariñosa || afectuoso, sa; cariñoso, sa; tierno, na; *tender work* palabras cariñosas || compasivo, va (quick to feel compassion) || delicado, da; *tender feet* pies delicados || sensible (sensitive); *a tender heart* un corazón sensible || sensible, susceptible; *a tender person is easily upset* una persona sensible se molesta fácilmente || delicado, da; *a tender subject* un asunto delicado || suave (colour) || dolorido, da (painful) || — *it is still tender* sigue doliéndome || *tender of* o *over* o *upon* solícito con.
◆ *n* vigilante *m* & *f* (person who tends) || MAR buque *m* nodriza (for fuel) | bote *m* (for general purposes) || ténder *m* (of a locomotive) || COMM oferta *f*, propuesta *f* (formal offer) || JUR oferta *f* de pago (to meet an obligation) || — *legal tender* curso *m* legal; *to be legal tender* tener curso legal || COMM *to put a piece of work out to tender, to invite tenders for a piece of work* sacar una obra a contrata *or* a licitación | *to put in a tender for a piece of work* hacer una oferta para realizar una obra.

tender ['tendə*] *vt* presentar, ofrecer; *to tender one's resignation* presentar la dimisión || JUR presentar (evidence) | ofrecer en pago (in order to meet an obligation) || enternecer (to soften) || — *please tender the exact fare* se ruega moneda fraccionaria || *to tender one's apologies* pedir disculpas || *to tender one's thanks* dar las gracias.
◆ *vi* hacer una oferta; *to tender for a piece of work* hacer una oferta para una obra || enternecerse (to soften).

tenderfoot [-fut] *n* novato *m* || recién llegado *m* (newcomer).
— OBSERV El plural es *tenderfeet* o *tenderfoots.*

tenderhearted [-'hɑːtid] *adj* compasivo, va (compassionate) || bondadoso, sa (kind) || susceptible.

tenderize ['tendəraiz] *vt* ablandar.

tenderloin ['tendəlɔin] *n* CULIN filete *m.*

tenderly ['tendəli] *adv* tiernamente, con ternura.

tenderness ['tendənis] *n* lo tierno (of meat) || ternura *f* (affection) || dulzura *f*, cariño *m* (of smile, of words, etc.) || sensibilidad *f* (sensitivity) || lo delicado (of a subject, etc.).

tending ['tendiŋ] *adj* tendente, tendiente, encaminado, da (*to* a).

tendinous ['tendinəs] *adj* tendinoso, sa.

tendon ['tendən] *n* ANAT tendón *m* || *Achilles' tendon* tendón de Aquiles.

tendril ['tendril] *n* zarcillo *m* (plant).

Tenebrae ['tenibriː] *pl n* REL Tinieblas *f.*

tenebrous ['tenibrəs] *adj* tenebroso, sa.

tenement ['tenimənt] *n* JUR propiedad *f* || casa *f* de vecindad (tenement house) || vivienda *f*, casa *f*, piso *m* (flat).

tenement house [-haus] *n* casa *f* de vecindad.

tenesmus [tə'nezməs] *n* MED pujo *m.*

tenet ['tiːnet] *n* principio *m* || dogma *m.*

tenfold ['tenfəuld] *adj* décuplo, pla.
◆ *adv* diez veces.

tenia ['tiːniə] *n* ZOOL tenia *f.*

teniafuge ['tinifjuːdʒ] *adj* tenífugo, ga.
◆ *n* tenífugo *m.*

tenner [tenə*] *n* FAM billete *m* de diez libras.

Tennessee [,teni'siː] *pr n* GEOGR Tennessee.

tennis ['tenis] *n* SP tenis *m* || *table tennis* tenis de mesa, ping-pong *m.*

tennis court [-kɔːt] *n* SP tenis *m*, campo *m* de tenis [*AMER* cancha *f* de tenis].

tennis elbow [-'elbəu] *n* MED calambre *m* en el codo.

tennis player [-,pleiə*] *n* SP tenista *m* & *f.*

tennis shoes [-ʃuːz] *n* zapatos *m* de lona *or* de tenis.

tenon ['tenən] *n* TECH espiga *f*, macho *m*, barbilla *f.*

tenon ['tenən] *vt* TECH espigar (to shape to fit in a mortise) | ensamblar a espiga (to join).

tenor ['tenə*] *n* curso *m*; *the tenor of events* el curso de los acontecimientos || contenido *m*, tenor *m* (of a document) || significado *m* (sense) || tono *m* (general drift); *the general tenor of the conversation* el tono general de la conversación || JUR copia *f* conforme (exact copy) || COMM plazo *m* (term) || MUS tenor *m.*
◆ *adj* MUS de tenor; *a tenor voice* una voz de tenor || tenor; *tenor saxophone* saxofón tenor.

tenpence ['tenpəns] *n* diez peniques *m pl.*

tenpin ['tenpin] *n* bolo *m* (skittle).
◆ *pl* bolos *m* (game) || *tenpin bowling* bolos *m pl.*

tenrec ['tenrek] *n* ZOOL tenrec *m*, tanrec *m.*

tense [tens] *adj* tenso, sa; *a tense situation* una situación tensa || nervioso, sa (nervous) || tenso, sa; tieso, sa; tirante; estirado, da (stretched tight).
◆ *n* GRAMM tiempo *m*; *past, future tense* tiempo pasado, futuro.

tense [tens] *vt* tensar, poner en tensión; *to tense one's muscles* tensar los músculos.

tensed up [-ʌp] *adj* tenso, sa; nervioso, sa.

tenseness [-nis] *n* tensión *f*, tirantez *f.*

tensible ['tensibl] *adj* extensible, capaz de tensión.

tensile ['tensail] *adj* extensible (able to be extended) || tensor, ra (exerting tension) || de tensión (pertaining to tension) || PHYS *tensile strength* resistencia *f* a la tracción.

tension ['tenʃən] *n* PHYS & ELECTR tensión *f*; *surface tension* tensión superficial; *high-tension cable* cable de alta tensión || tracción *f* (force causing extension of a body); *to subject a beam to tension* someter una viga a una tracción || tensión *f*, tirantez *f* (state of being tensed); *tension in a rope* tensión de una cuerda || tensión *f*; *nervous tension* tensión nerviosa || tensión *f*; *tension between two countries* tensión entre dos países || tirantez *f*, tensión *f* (between friends, etc.) || *racial tension* tensiones raciales.

tensor ['tensə*] *n* ANAT & MATH tensor *m.*

tent [tent] *n* tienda *f* de campaña, tienda *f* [*AMER* carpa *f*] (for camping, etc.); *to pitch a tent* armar una tienda de campaña || MED mecha *f* (for keeping wounds open) | tienda *f*, cámara *f*; *oxygen tent* tienda de oxígeno.

tent [tent] *vt* alojar en tiendas (to lodge in tents) || suministrar tiendas a (to supply with tents) || cubrir con un toldo || MED mantener abierto con una mecha (to keep open with a tent).
◆ *vi* vivir en tienda.

tentacle ['tentəkl] *n* tentáculo *m.*

tentacled [-d] *adj* tentaculado, da.

tentacular [ten'tækjulə*] *adj* tentacular.

tentative ['tentətiv] *adj* provisional [*AMER* provisorio, ria]; *a tentative arrangement* un arreglo provisional || de tanteo; *a tentative offer*

una oferta de tanteo || indeciso, sa; vacilante (hesitant).
◆ *n* tentativa *f.*

tentatively [-li] *adv* provisionalmente [AMER provisoriamente]; *an outing tentatively arranged for Saturday* una excursión que se ha previsto provisionalmente para el sábado || como tanteo || con indecisión (hesitantly).

tented ['tentid] *adj* con toldos, entoldado, da.

tenter ['tentə*] *n* bastidor *m* (for cloth).

tenterhook [-huk] *n* gancho *m* de bastidor || — FIG *to be on tenterhooks* estar sobre ascuas | *to have* o *to keep s.o. on tenterhooks* tener a alguien sobre ascuas.

tenth [tenθ] *adj* décimo, ma.
◆ *n* décimo, ma (in a series); *Louis X (the tenth)* Luis X [décimo] || décimo *m*, décima parte *f* (part) || diez *m*, día *m* diez; *he is coming on the tenth* viene el día diez.

tentmaker ['tent,meikə*] *n* tendero *m.*

tent peg ['tentpeg] *n* estaca *f.*

tent pole ['tentpəul] *n* mástil *m* de tienda.

tenuiroster [tenjui'rɔstə*] *n* tenuirrostro *m* (bird).

tenuirostres [tenjuirɔstri:z] *pl n* tenuirrostros *m.*

tenuity [te'njuiti]; **teneousness** ['tenjuəshis] *n* tenuidad *f* (flimsiness) || delgadez *f* (slenderness) || enrarecimiento *m* (of the air) || FIG pobreza *f* (meagreness); *the tenuity of his argument* la pobreza de su argumento | sutileza *f* (of a distinction, etc.) | sencillez *f* (of style).

tenuous ['tenjuəs] *adj* tenue, sutil (flimsy) || delgado, da (thin) || enrarecido, da; raro, ra (not dense) || FIG tenue, sutil (distinction) | poco convincente, poco sólido, da; flojo, ja (argument) | ligero, ra (connection) | sencillo, lla (style).

tenuousness [-nis] *n* → **tenuity.**

tenure ['tenjuə*] *n* arrendamiento *m* (tenancy) || posesión *f* (possession) || ocupación *f*, ejercicio *m* (of an office) || *land tenure* tenencia *f* de tierras.

teocalli [tiə'kɑ:li] *n* teocali *m.*

tepee ['ti:pi] *n* tepee *m.*

tepid ['tepid] *adj* tibio, bia (lukewarm) || FIG poco cálido, da; poco caluroso, sa (reception) | muy relativo, va (interest) | poco entusiasta (lacking enthusiasm).

tepidity [te'piditi]; **tepidness** ['tepidnis] *n* tibieza *f* (temperature) || FIG falta *f* de interés, falta *f* de entusiasmo.

teponaxtle [tepə'nɑ:stli] *n* teponascle *m* (Mexican drum).

tequila [ti'ki:lə] *n* tequila *m or f* (drink) || agave *m*, maguey *m* (plant).

teratology [terə'tɔlədʒi] *n* teratología *f.*

terbium ['tə:biəm] *n* CHEM terbio *m.*

terce [tə:s] *n* REL tercia *f* (hour).

tercentenary [,tə:sen'ti:nəri]; **tercentennial** [,tə:sen'ti:njəl] *adj* de tres siglos.
◆ *n* tricentenario *m.*

tercet ['tə:sit] *n* terceto *m.*

terebenthene [tere'benθi:n] *n* terebenteno *m.*

terebinth ['terəbinθ] *n* BOT terebinto *m.*

terebinthaceae [,terəbin'θɑ:sii] *pl n* BOT terebintáceas *f.*

terebinthine [,terə'binθain] *adj* de trementina.

Terence ['terəns] *pr n* Terencio *m.*

Teresian [tə'risiən] *n* REL teresiana *f.*

tergiversate ['tə:dʒivə:seit] *vi* cambiar de idea, cambiar de camisa (fam) (to change allegiance) || usar evasivas (to avoid decisions or firm action).

tergiversation [,tə:dʒivə:'seiʃən] *n* cambio *m* de idea, cambio *m* de camisa (fam) (change of allegiance) || evasión *f* (avoidance of decisions or firm action).

term [tə:m] *n* período *m*, plazo *m*, término *m* (period of time) || período *m* de validez (of an agreement, etc.) || COMM plazo *m* || mandato *m* (of a Prime Minister, etc.) || trimestre *m*; *the academic year has three terms* el año académico tiene tres trimestres || curso *m*; *term begins on the second* el curso empieza el día dos || término *m*, fin *m* (end); *to come to its term* llegar a su término || término *m*, voz *f*, vocablo *m* (word); *technical, medical term* término técnico, médico || JUR período *m* de sesiones (during which a court sits) || MATH, PHIL, GRAMM & ARCH término *m*; *to multiply two terms* multiplicar dos términos || — MED *born after term* tardío, a; nacido con retraso | *born before term* prematuro, ra || *in the long term* a la larga || *in the short term* en un futuro próximo || COMM *long-term transaction* operación *f* a largo plazo | *short-term transaction* operación *f* a corto plazo.
◆ *pl* condiciones *f* (conditions); *terms of payment* condiciones de pago; *terms of an issue* condiciones de una emisión; *you can name your own terms* usted puede fijar las condiciones; *what are your terms?* ¿cuáles son sus condiciones? || términos *m* (terminology, words); *vague terms* términos vagos; *terms of a contract, of a treaty* términos de un contrato, de un tratado || COMM tarifa *f sing*, precios *m*; *special terms for children* tarifa especial para niños || relaciones *f*, términos *m* (relationship); *to be on good terms with s.o.* estar en buenas relaciones con alguien || — *in international terms* a nivel internacional || *in no uncertain terms* claramente || *in terms of* por lo que se refiere a (as regards), en términos de; *to express X in terms of Y* expresar X en términos de Y; en función de, desde el punto de vista de; *he sees everything in terms of profit* ve todo en función del beneficio que pude producir || *in real terms* de hecho || *not on any terms* bajo ningún concepto || COMM *on easy terms* con facilidades de pago || *on equal* o *the same terms* en igualdad de condiciones || *terms of exchange* términos del intercambio || *terms of reference* mandato *m sing* || *terms of trade* términos del intercambio || *to be on intimate terms with s.o.* tener confianza con alguien || *to be on the best of terms* estar en muy buenos términos, ser muy amigos || *to choose one's terms with care* elegir sus palabras con cuidado || *to come to terms with a situation* aceptar una situación, adaptarse a una situación || *to come to terms with s.o.* llegar a un acuerdo con alguien, ponerse de acuerdo con alguien || *to think in terms of doing sth.* plantearse *or* pensar hacer algo.

term [tə:m] *vt* llamar, calificar de (to call); *he termed it a scandal* lo calificó de escándalo.

termagant ['tə:məgənt] *n* arpía *f*, fiera *f*, tarasca *f* (ferocious woman).

terminal ['tə:minl] *adj* terminal, final (of or forming the end) || de demarcación (forming a boundary) || trimestral; *terminal examinations* exámenes trimestrales || BOT terminal (bud, etc.) || *terminal station* estación *f* terminal.
◆ *n* extremidad *f*, extremo *m* (extremity) || ELECTR borne *m*, terminal *m* || final *m* de línea (of a bus, of a route) || estación *f* terminal, término *m* (of a railway) || AVIAT & MAR terminal *f*; *air terminal* terminal aérea || ARCH remate *m* (ornament) || INFORM terminal *m.*

terminate ['te:mineit] *vt* concluir, finalizar, terminar.
◆ *vi* concluirse, terminarse.

termination [,tə:mi'neiʃən] *n* terminación *f* || *to bring to a termination* poner término a.

terminological [,tə:minə'lɔdʒikəl] *adj* terminológico, ca.

terminology [,tə:mi'nɔlədʒi] *n* terminología *f.*

terminus ['tə:minəs] *n* final *m* de línea (of a bus, of a route) || estación *f* terminal, término *m* (railway) || AVIAT terminal *f* || ARCH término *m.*
— OBSERV El plural de la palabra *terminus* es *termini* o *terminuses.*

termite ['tə:mait] *n* comején *m*, termita *f*, termite *m*, termes *m.*

termor ['tə:mə*] *n* JUR poseedor *m* por un plazo determinado *or* vitalicio.

termtime ['tə:mtaim] *n* US trimestre *m* (at school) | período *m* de sesiones (of a court).

tern [tə:n] *n* golondrina *f* de mar (bird) || terno *m* (in lottery).

ternary ['tə:nəri] *adj* ternario, ria || tercero, ra (third) || MUS *ternary form* compás ternario.

ternate ['tə:neit] *adj* BOT trifoliado, da.

terpene ['tə:pi:n] *n* terpeno *m.*

Terpsichore [tə:p'sikəri] *pr n* MYTH Terpsícore *f.*

terpsichorean ['tə:psikə'riən] *adj* coreográfico, ca.

terrace ['terəs] *n* terraza *f* (balcony, open area) || azotea *f* (flat roof) || AGR terraza *f*, bancal *m* || terraplén *m* (raised embankment) || hilera *f* de casas (row of houses) || arriate *m* (of flowers).
◆ *pl* SP gradas *f.*

terrace ['terəs] *vt* formar terrazas en (to make terraces in) || poner terraza a (to add a terrace to) || terraplenar (to embank) || AGR disponer en bancales.

terraced [-t] *adj* colgante (garden) || *terraced house* casa *f* adosada.

terra-cotta ['terə'kɔtə] *n* terracota *f* (pottery and statue) || ladrillo *m* (colour).
◆ *adj* ladrillo (brownish-red) || de terracota (made of terra-cotta).

terra firma [terə'fə:mə] *n* tierra *f* firme.

terrain ['terein] *n* terreno *m.*

terramycin [,terəxmaisin] *n* MED terramicina *f.*

terrane [te'rein] *n* GEOL terreno *m.*

terrapin ['terəpin] *n* tortuga *f* acuática.

terraqueous [te'reikwiəs] *adj* terráqueo, a.

terrazzo [te'rætsəu] *n* terrazo *m.*

terrene [te'ri:n] *adj* terrenal.

terreplein ['tɛə:plein] *n* MIL terraplén *m.*

terrestrial [ti'restriəl] *adj* terrestre.
◆ *n* terrícola *m* & *f.*

terrible ['terəbl] *adj* terrible (terrifying) || atroz; *terrible vengeance, pain* venganza, dolor atroz || FAM terrible (excessive); *terrible heat* calor terrible; *terrible prices* precios terribles | fatal, malísimo, ma; horrible (bad); *an absolutely terrible book* un libro francamente fatal || FAM *we had a terrible time* lo pasamos fatal.

terribly [-i] *adv* terriblemente (terrifyingly) || FAM terriblemente, enormemente, tremendamente, extraordinariamente (extremely); *a terribly cold night* una noche terriblemente fría | malísimamente (badly); *he writes terribly* escribe malísimamente || — FAM *it really has been terribly nice of you to bring me home* ha sido realmente muy amable por su parte llevarme a casa | *terribly good* buenísimo.

terricolous [te'rikələs] *adj* terrícola.

terrier ['teriə*] *n* terrier *m* (dog).

terrific [tə'rifik] *adj* terrorífico, ca; terrífico, ca; terrible (terrifying) || FAM terrible (very bad); *a terrific scandal* un escándalo terrible | tremendo, da (great); *he does a terrific amount* *of work* hace una cantidad tremenda de trabajo | enorme (very big); *a terrific building* un edificio enorme | fenómeno, na; estupendo, da; fabuloso, sa; bárbaro, ra; extraordinario, ria (very good); *his new play is terrific* su nueva comedia es estupenda.

terrifically [-əli] *adv* terriblemente (terrifyingly) || FAM enormemente, tremendamente, terriblemente (extremely); *terrifically tired* terriblemente cansado | muy bien, maravillosamente (very well); *he sings terrifically* canta maravillosamente || — FAM *terrifically bad* malísimo, ma | *terrifically nice* simpatiquísimo, tremendamente simpático.

terrify ['terifai] *vt* aterrorizar, aterrar.

terrifying [-iŋ] *adj* espantoso, sa.

terrigenous [te'ridʒinəs] *adj* terrígeno, na.

terrine [tə'ri:n] *n* CULIN terrina *f*.

territorial [,teri'tɔ:riəl] *adj* territorial (of a territory) || regional (of a region) || jurisdiccional, territorial; *territorial waters* aguas jurisdiccionales || MIL *territorial army* segunda reserva.
◆ *n* soldado *m* de la segunda reserva.

territoriality [,teri'tɔ:ri'æliti] *n* territorialidad *f*.

territory [teritəri] *n* territorio *m*; *on Spanish territory* en territorio español; *overseas territories* territorios de ultramar || SP campo *m*, terreno *m* (either half of the playing area) || COMM zona *f*, región *f* (of a commercial traveller) || región *f*, territorio *m* (large tract of country) || FIG competencia *f*; *that's outside my territory* esto no es de mi competencia | sector *m*, esfera *f*, campo *m*.

terror ['terə*] *n* terror *m*, espanto *m*, pánico *m* (great fear); *to spread terror* sembrar el terror || terror *m* (person, thing) || — FAM *a terror of a child* un niño terrible || HIST *the Terror* el Terror (in the French Revolution).

terrorism [-rizəm] *n* terrorismo *m*.

terrorist [-rist] *n* terrorista *m* & *f*.

terrorize ['terəraiz] *vt* aterrorizar, aterrar.

terror-stricken ['terə'strikən] *adj* sobrecogido por el terror, aterrorizado, da.

terry ['teri] *n* felpa *f*, tela *f* de rizo, esponja *f*.

terry cloth [-klɔθ] *n* felpa *f*, tela *f* de rizo, esponja *f*.

terse [tə:s] *adj* conciso, sa; sucinto, ta.

tersely [-li] *adv* concisamente (concisely).

terseness [-nis] *n* concisión *f* (conciseness).

tertian ['tə:ʃiən] *adj* terciana (fever).
◆ *n* terciana *f*, fiebre *f* terciana.

tertiary ['tə:ʃiəri] *adj* tercero, ra (third) || GEOL terciario, ria || *tertiary education* enseñanza *f* superior.
◆ *n* REL terciario, ria || GEOL *the Tertiary* el Terciario.

Tertullian [tə:'tʌliən] *pr n* Tertuliano *m*.

tervalent [tə:'veilənt] *adj* CHEM trivalente.

Terylene ['terəlin] *n* Terylene *m*.

tessellate; *US* **tesselate** ['tesileit] *vt* hacer un mosaico de (to make into a mosaic) || decorar con mosaicos (to decorate with mosaic).

tessellated; *US* **tesselated** [-id] *adj* de mosaico.

tessellation; *US* **tesselation** [,tesi'leiʃən] *n* mosaico *m*.

tessitura [,tesi'tu:rə] *n* MUS tesitura *f*.

test [test] *n* prueba *f*; *a test of s.o.'s friendship* una prueba de la amistad de alguien; *test flight* vuelo de prueba; *to put to the test* poner a prueba; *to stand the test* pasar la prueba; *endurance test* prueba de resistencia; *nuclear tests* pruebas nucleares || «test» *m*, prueba *f*; *intelligence test* «test» de inteligencia || MED análisis *m*; *blood, urine test* análisis de sangre, de orina || examen *m*, prueba *f* (in school, in university); *end of term tests* exámenes trimestrales; *English test* examen de inglés || piedra *f* de toque (criterion) || CHEM prueba *f*, ensayo *m*, experimento *m* | reactivo *m* (reagent) || HIST copela *f* (cupel) || ZOOL caparazón *m*, concha *f* (shell or hard covering) || — FIG *acid test* prueba decisiva || *to stand the test of time* resistir al paso del tiempo.

test [test] *vt* probar, someter a una prueba, poner a prueba; *to test a prototype* probar un prototipo || examinar (to examine) || poner un examen a (in school, etc.); *to test pupils in history* poner un examen de historia a los alumnos || comprobar; *to test the weight of sth.* comprobar el peso de algo || analizar; *to test the water in a river* analizar el agua de un río || MED hacer un análisis de (blood, etc.) || CHEM probar, ensayar || graduar (sight) || *to test sth. for acidity* determinar el grado de acidez de algo.

testa ['testə] *n* BOT testa *f*.
— OBSERV El plural de la palabra inglesa es *testa* o *testae*.

testacean [tes'teiʃən]; **testaceous** [tes'teiʃəs] *adj* testáceo, a.

testament ['testəment] *n* testamento *m* (will) || — REL *the New Testament* el Nuevo Testamento | *the Old Testament* el Antiguo Testamento || *to make one's testament* testar, hacer testamento.

testamentary [,testə'mentəri] *adj* testamentario, ria.

testate ['testit] *adj* JUR testado, da.
◆ *n* JUR testador, ra.

testator [tes'teitə*] *n* JUR testador *m*.

testatrix [tes'teitriks] *n* JUR testadora *f*.
— OBSERV El plural de *testatrix* es *testatrices*.

test ban ['testbæn] *n* suspensión *f* de pruebas nucleares.

test bench ['testbentʃ] *n* banco *m* de pruebas.

test boring ['test'bɔ:riŋ] *n* sondeo *m*.

test card ['testkɑ:d] *n* carta *f* de ajuste (television).

test case ['testkeis] *n* JUR juicio *m* que hace jurisprudencia.

test chamber [test'tʃeimbə*] *n* cámara *f* de experimentos.

test-drive ['testdrɑiv] *vt* probar el funcionamiento de un coche.

tester ['testə*] *n* dosel *m* (of a four-poster bed) || baldaquín *m*, baldaquino *m* (over an altar or pulpit) || probador, ra; ensayador, ra (person).

testicle ['testikl] *n* ANAT testículo *m*.

testicular [tes'tikjulə*] *adj* ANAT testicular.

testification [,testifi'keiʃən] *n* testificación *f*.

testifier ['testifaiə*] *n* testigo *m* & *f*.

testify ['testifai] *vt* revelar, demostrar, atestiguar, testimoniar; *his look testified his guilt* su mirada revelaba su culpabilidad || declarar [bajo juramento], atestiguar; *he testified that he had not been there* declaró que no había estado allí.
◆ *vi* JUR declarar (to give evidence) || JUR *to testify to sth.* atestiguar algo.

testily ['testili] *adv* malhumoradamente.

testimonial [,testi'məunjəl] *n* testimonio *m* (testimony) || recomendación *f*, carta *f* de recomendación (character reference) || testimonio *m* de gratitud (tribute) || REL testimoniales *f pl*.
◆ *adj* testimonial.

testimony ['testiməni] *n* JUR testimonio *m*, atestación *f*, declaración *f* || — JUR *in testimony whereof* en fe de lo cual | *to bear testimony to sth.* atestiguar algo | *to be called in testimony* ser llamado como testigo.

testiness ['testinis] *n* irritabilidad *f*.

testing ['testiŋ] *adj* difícil (time, situation).

testing ground ['testiŋgraund] *n* zona *f* de pruebas.

testis ['testis] *n* ANAT testículo *m*.
— OBSERV El plural de *testis* es *testes*.

test match ['testmætʃ] *n* SP partido *m* internacional (in cricket).

testosterone [tes'tɔstərəun] *n* testosterona *f*.

test paper ['test'peipə*] *n* examen *m* (in school, etc.) || CHEM papel *m* indicador, papel *m* reactivo.

test pilot ['test'pailət] *n* AVIAT piloto *m* de pruebas.

test tube ['test'tju:b] *n* tubo *m* de ensayo.

test-tube [ðesttju:b] *adj* *test-tube baby* niño nacido por inseminación artificial.

testy ['testi] *adj* irritable || malhumorado, da.

tetanic [te'tænik] *adj* MED tetánico, ca.

tetanus ['tetənəs] *n* MED tétanos *m*.

tetany ['tetəni] *n* MED tetania *f*.

tetchy ['tetʃi] *adj* irritable, picajoso, sa.

tête-à-tête ['teitɑ:'teit] *adj* confidencial (conversation) || íntimo, ma (dinner).
◆ *n* conversación *f* a solas, conversación *f* confidencial || confidente *m* (sofa).
◆ *adv* a solas (to talk) || en la intimidad (to dine).
— OBSERV El plural del sustantivo *tête-à-tête* es *têtes-à-têtes*.

tether ['teðə*] *n* ronzal *m* (rope for animals) || FIG *at the end of one's tether* hartísimo, ma (at the end of one's endurance), en las últimas (at the end of one's financial resources).

tether ['teðə*] *vt* atar [con un ronzal].

tetragonal [te'trægənəl] *adj* MATH tetragonal.

tetrahedron ['tetrə'hedrən] *n* MATH tetraedro *m*.
— OBSERV El plural de tetrahedron es *tetrahedra* o *tetrahedrons*.

tetralogy [te'trælədʒi] *n* tetralogía *f*.

tetrameral [te'træmərəl]; **tetramerous** [te'træmərəs] *n* BOT & ZOOL tetrámero *m*.

tetrapod ['tetrəpɔd] *adj* ZOOL tetrápodo, da.
◆ *n* ZOOL tetrápodo *m*.

tetrarch ['ti:trɑ:k] *n* tetrarca *m*.

tetrarchy [-i] *n* tetrarquía *f*.

tetrasyllabic [,tetrəsi'læbik] *adj* tetrasílabo, ba.

tetrasyllable ['tetrə,siləbl] *n* tetrasílabo *m*.

tetravalent [tetrə'veilənt] *adj* CHEM tetravalente.

tetrode ['tetrəud] *n* ELECTR tetrodo *m*.

tetter ['tetə*] *n* MED herpes *m pl* || — MED *crusty tetter* impétigo *m* | *scaly tetter* psoriasis *f inv*.

Tetuan [tet'wɑ:n] *pr n* GEOGR Tetuán.

Teuton ['tju:tən] *adj/n* teutón, ona.

Teutonic [tju'tɔnik] *adj* teutónico, ca.
◆ *n* teutónico *m* (language).

Texan ['teksən] *adj/n* tejano, na; texano, na.

Texas ['teksəs] *pr n* GEOGR Tejas *m*, Texas *m*.

text [tekst] *n* texto *m* || tema *m*; *to keep to the text* ceñirse al tema || libro *m* de texto (textbook).

textbook [-buk] *n* libro *m* de texto.

text editor [-'editə*] *n* INFORM editor *m* de textos.

text hand [-hænd] *n* PRINT letra *f* gruesa.

textile ['tekstail] *adj* textil; *textile industry* industria textil || tejido, da (woven).
◆ *n* textil *m*, tejido *m*.

textual ['tekstjuəl] *adj* textual, literal (quotation, note) || en el texto, del texto (error).

textually [-i] *adv* textualmente.

textuary ['tekstjuəri] *adj* textual.

texture ['tekstʃə*] *n* textura *f* || FIG textura *f*, estructura *f*.

TGWU *abbr of [Transport and General Workers' Union]* sindicato interprofesional más importante [en Gran Bretaña].

Thai [tai] *adj/n* tailandés, esa.

Thailand ['tailænd] *pr n* GEOGR Tailandia *f*.

thalamus ['θæləməs] *n* BOT & ANAT tálamo *m*; *optic thalamus* tálamo óptico.
— OBSERV El plural de *thalamus* es *thalami*.

thalassotherapy ['θæləsə'θerəpi] *n* MED talasoterapia *f*.

Thales ['θeili:z] *pr n* Tales *m*.

Thalia [θə'laiə] *n* MYTH Talia *f*.

thalidomide [θə'lidəmaid] *n* MED talidomida *f*.

thallium ['θæliəm] *n* talio *m* (metal).

thallophites ['θæləfaits] *pl n* BOT talofitas *f*.

thallus ['θæləs] *n* BOT talo *m*.
— OBSERV El plural de *thallus* es *thalluses* o *thalli*.

Thames [temz] *pr n* GEOGR Támesis *m*.

than [ðæn] *conj* que (in comparison of inequality); *this house is bigger than that one* esta casa es más grande que aquélla; *I arrived earlier than he* llegué más pronto que él || de (with numbers); *more than twenty people* más de veinte personas; *she is more than thirty* tiene más de treinta años || cuando; *hardly had he arrived than the roof fell in* apenas había llegado cuando se cayó el tejado || del que, de la que, de lo que; *more persons than needed* más personas de las que se necesitaban; *it is more expensive than you thought* es más caro de lo que pensabas || — *any person other than himself* cualquier persona menos él, cualquier persona que no fuese él || *it was no other than the Emperor* era el mismo Emperador, era el Emperador en persona || *more than once* más de una vez || *no other than* nadie más que, nadie excepto; *no other than he can do it* nadie excepto él lo puede hacer || *other than* aparte de, fuera de; *other than that, I don't know what to say* aparte de eso, no sé qué decir || *rather than* antes que; *rather than walk home I would prefer to take the underground* antes que ir a casa andando prefiero coger el metro.

thank [θæŋk] *vt* agradecer, dar las gracias; *I thank you for coming* le doy las gracias por haber venido || — *I will thank you to close the door* le agradecería que cerrase la puerta || *she has you to thank for that* eso se lo tiene que agradecer a usted || *thank God!, thank heaven!, thank goodness!* ¡gracias a Dios!, ¡a Dios gracias! || *thank you* gracias || *thank you very much* muchas gracias || FIG *to have o.s. to thank* tener la culpa.

thankful [-ful] *adj* agradecido, da; *I am thankful to you for that* le estoy agradecido por ello || — *how thankful I am for the central heating!* ¡qué bien me viene la calefacción! || *to be thankful that* alegrase de que; *I am thankful that you could come* me alegro de que haya podido venir.

thankfully [-fuli] *adv* con agradecimiento, agradecidamente, con gratitud.

thankfulness [-fulnis] *n* agradecimiento *m*, gratitud *f*.

thankless [-lis] *adj* desagradecido, da; ingrato, ta (person) || ingrato, ta; ímprobo, ba; *a thankless task* una tarea ingrata.

thanklessness [-lisnis] *n* desagradecimiento *m*, ingratitud *f*.

thanks [-s] *pl n* gracias *f*; *to give thanks to God* dar gracias a Dios; *to give s.o. thanks* dar las gracias a alguien; *thanks for telling me* gracias por decírmelo || — FIG *I managed, but no thanks to you* o *small thanks to you* me las arreglé pero no fue gracias a ti || *many thanks, thanks very much, thanks a lot* muchas gracias || *no thanks are needed!* ¡de nada!, ¡no hay de qué! || FAM *thanks be!* ¡menos mal! || *thanks to* gracias a; *thanks to your help, we were successful* gracias a su ayuda, tuvimos éxito.

thanksgiving ['θæŋks,giviŋ] *n* acción *f* de gracias || US *Thanksgiving Day* día *m* de acción de gracias [cuarto jueves de noviembre].

thankworthy ['θæŋk,wə:ði] *adj* digno de agradecimiento.

that [ðæt] *dem adj* ese, esa (at a relatively near distance in space and time); *give me that book (that you have in your hand)* dame ese libro (que tienes en la mano); *those last five minutes were very unpleasant* esos cinco últimos minutos fueron muy desagradables || aquel, aquella (further away in space and time); *this book is more interesting than that newspaper on the table* este libro es más interesante que aquel periódico que está en la mesa; *at that time butter was cheap* en aquella época la mantequilla era barata; *that accident you saw the other day* aquel accidente que viste el otro día || el, la; aquel, aquella que; *the more simple way is that employed by me* la manera más sencilla es la empleada por mí *or* aquella que yo empleo || — *I hate that pride of hers* odio ese orgullo suyo || *that one* ése, ésa (at a relatively near distance in space and time), aquél, aquélla (further away in space and time) || *those people who* la gente que, aquella gente que.
◆ *dem pron* ése, ésa (relatively near in space and time); *that is my chair* ésa es mi silla || aquél, aquélla (further away in space and time); *this war is worse than that was* esta guerra es peor de lo que fue aquélla; *these hats are nicer than those* estos sombreros son más bonitos que aquéllos || eso (neuter, relatively near in time and space); *that is a lie* eso es mentira || aquello (neuter, further away in space and time); *of all that he said that was what annoyed me the most* de todo lo que dijo aquello fue lo que más me molestó || el, la, lo (followed by a relative pronoun or by «of»); *those who wish to go may do so* los que quieran irse pueden hacerlo; *that which I say to you* lo que os digo; *that of my friend* el de mi amigo || — *and all that* y cosas por el estilo || *and that's that!* ¡y eso es todo! || *at that* además; *he is a footballer and a good one at that* es futbolista y muy bueno además; sin más; *we have left it at that* lo hemos dejado sin más; en eso, en esa; *at that moment* en ese momento; ante eso (because of that); *he laughed and at that they all left* se rió y ante eso se marcharon todos || *for all that* a pesar de eso || *how do you like that?* ¿qué le parece? || *I am not one of those who* no soy de los que || *is that you, Peter?* ¿eres tú Pedro? || *like that* así; *he did it like that* lo hizo así || *that is, that is to say* es decir, o sea || *that is why I did it* por eso lo hice || *that I will!* ¡ya lo creo!, ¡naturalmente! || *that's a good boy!* ¡así me gusta! || *that's how I happened to be there* así fue como me encontré allí || *that's it!* ¡eso es! || *that's what I say!* ¡eso digo yo! || *there are those who think that* unos *or* algunos piensan que || *those who* los que, las que; aquellos que, aquellas que || *what do you mean by that?* ¿qué quieres decir con eso? || *with that* sin más.
◆ *rel pron* que (for things and people); *the man that I saw and the car that I bought* el hombre que vi y el coche que compré; *the man that came to see me lives in the house that is in this street* el hombre que vino a verme vive en la casa que está en esta calle || el que, la que; quien; el cual, la cual (people only, and when the relative is governed by a preposition); *he is the man that I was talking with* él es el hombre con quien estaba hablando; *the girls that I gave the books to* las chicas a las que *or* a quienes di los libros || el cual, la cual; el que, la que (things, when the pronoun is governed by a preposition); *the brooms that they were sweeping with* las escobas con las cuales estaban barriendo; *the fact that you are referring to* el hecho al cual *or* al que se refiere || lo que (neuter); *all that I know* todo lo que sé || en que (in expressions of time); *the day that he was born* el día en que nació || — *it is he that did it* fue él quien lo hizo, el que lo hizo fue él || *that I know of* que yo sepa; *no one has come that I know of* no ha venido nadie que yo sepa || *the one that* el que, la que; quien; *he is the one that killed my brother* él es quien mató a mi hermano.
◆ *adv* así de; *the bridge was that high* el puente era así de alto || tan; *he was that angry he could not speak* estaba tan enfadado que no pudo hablar; *I can't see that far ahead* no puedo ver tan lejos || — *that many* tantos, tas || *that much* tanto; *he sings that much that he has no time to work* canta tanto que no tiene tiempo para trabajar; *you should not have spent that much* o *that much money* no debías de haber gastado tanto *or* tanto dinero.
◆ *conj* que; *she said that she was ill* dijo que estaba enferma; *he went so fast that he had an accident* fue tan de prisa que tuvo un accidente; *I do not believe that you are French* no creo que seas francés || de que; *he is happy that you came* está contento de que hayas venido; *are you sure that you can do it?* ¿estás seguro de que lo puedes hacer? || para que (purpose); *I did it that you might be happy* lo hice para que te sintieras feliz || porque, que (because); *it is not that I love you less* no es porque te quiero menos, no es que te quiera menos || — *in that* ya que, en la medida en que; *these laws are bad in that they are unjust* estas leyes son malas ya que son injustas || *so that* para que; *let's finish this quickly so that we can go to the pictures* acabemos esto pronto para que podamos ir al cine || *that he should abandon us at a time like this!* ¡abandonarnos en un momento como éste!
— OBSERV El plural de *that* es *those*, el de *that one* es *those ones* o *those*.
— OBSERV There are cases when *aquel* and *ese*, *aquél* and *ése* and *aquello* and *eso* are interchangeable, especially when no position in relationship to the listener is emphasized: *give me that book* dame ese *or* aquel libro; *that one is better than this one* ésa *or* aquélla es mejor que ésta.
— OBSERV Es posible omitir el pronombre relativo y la conjunción *that* en la mayoría de los casos en inglés: *the man I saw* el hombre que vi; *the man I gave the cup to* el hombre al que di la taza; *he said he would do it* dijo que lo haría; *I am sure it is he* estoy seguro de que es él.
— OBSERV Although it is usually possible to omit the relative pronoun and the conjunction *that* in English, the relative pronoun and the conjunction in Spanish may never be omitted.

thatch [θætʃ] *n* paja *f* (straw) || techo *m* de paja (roof) || FAM pelo *m* (hair).

thatch [θætʃ] *vt* cubrir con paja (a roof) || cubrir con un tejado de paja (a house).

thatched [-t] *adj* de paja (roof).

thaumaturge ['θɔ:mətə:dʒ] *n* taumaturgo *m*.

thaumaturgy ['θɔ:mətə:dʒi] *n* taumaturgia *f*.

thaw [θɔ:] *n* deshielo *m* (melting) || derretimiento *m* (of snow).

thaw ['ɔ:] *vt* deshelar (to cause to thaw) || derretir (snow) || descongelar, deshelar (frozen food) || *to thaw out* deshelar.
◆ *vi* deshelarse, derretirse (ice) || derretirse (snow) || deshelarse, descongelarse (frozen food) || FIG cobrar confianza | ablandarse.
◆ *v impers* deshelarse.

the [ðə] before consonnants, [ði: or ði] before vowels, [ði:] when used emphatically *def art* el, la; los, las (masculine and feminine); *the boys are at home* los niños están en casa; *the soup is good* la sopa está buena; *the rich* los ricos; *on the other side* del otro lado; *give it to the child* dáselo al niño; *the Smiths* los Smiths ‖ lo (neuter); *I wish you all the best* le deseo todo lo mejor ‖ — *at the time* en aquel entonces, en aquel momento, entonces ‖ *Edward the Seventh* Eduardo Séptimo ‖ *eight tomatoes to the pound* ocho tomates por libra ‖ *he has the toothache* tiene dolor de muelas ‖ *he is not the man to do the job* no es el hombre adecuado para hacer este trabajo ‖ *it is «the restaurant» in town* es el mejor restaurante de la ciudad ‖ *the impudence of it!* ¡qué descaro!, ¡qué desfachatez! ‖ *the one* el, la; *the one with spectacles* el de las gafas; *the one who* el que.
◆ *adv the less said about it the better* cuanto menos se hable de esto mejor ‖ *the more he gets the more he wants* cuanto más tiene más quiere ‖ *the sooner the better* cuanto antes mejor ‖ *they were all the more anxious because* estaban tanto más preocupados cuanto que.

thearchy [ˈθi:ɑ:ki] *n* teocracia *f.*

theater [ˈθiətə*] *n* US → **theatre.**

theatergoer [-gəuə*] *n* US → **theatregoer.**

theatergoing [-gəuiŋ] *n* US → **theatregoing.**

Theatine [ˈθiətain] *n* REL teatino, na.

theatre; US **theater** [ˈθiətə*] *n* teatro *m; to go to the theatre* ir al teatro; *the theatre of Shakespeare* el teatro de Shakespeare; *to dedicate o.s. to the theatre* dedicarse al teatro ‖ MIL teatro *m*, escenario *m; the theatre of the battle* el teatro de la batalla ‖ aula *f* (for lectures) ‖ *operating theatre* quirófano *m*, sala *f* de operaciones.

theatregoer; US **theatergoer** [-gəuə*] *n* aficionado *m* al teatro.

theatregoing; US **theatergoing** [-ˈgəuiɛ] *n* afición *f* al teatro ‖ el ir al teatro.

theatrical [θiˈætrikəl] *adj* del teatro, teatral; *theatrical work* obra de teatro ‖ teatral; *in a theatrical tone* en tono teatral.

theatricalism [-izəm]; **theatricality** [θiˌætriˈkæliti] *n* teatralidad *f.*

theatrically [θiˈætrikəli] *adv* teatralmente.

theatricals [θiˈætrikəlz] *pl n* funciones *f* de teatro ‖ FIG maneras *f* teatrales ‖ *amateur theatricals* teatro *m sing* de aficionados.

Thebaid [ˈθi:beiid] *pr n* Tebaida *f.*

Theban [ˈθi:bən] *adj/n* tebano, na.

Thebes [θi:bz] *pr n* GEOGR Tebas.

theca [ˈθi:kə] *n* BOT & ANAT teca *f.*
— OBSERV El plural de *theca* es *thecae.*

thee [ði:orði] *pron* te ‖ ti (with preposition) ‖ *with thee* contigo.
— OBSERV Esta palabra es la antigua forma del pronombre correspondiente a la segunda persona del singular.

theft [θeft] *n* robo *m*, hurto *m* ‖ *aggravated theft* robo con agravante.

theine [ˈθiain] *n* CHEM teína *f.*

their [ðɛə*] *poss adj* su, sus; suyo, suya; *their car is red* su coche es rojo, el coche suyo es rojo; *their children* sus hijos, los hijos suyos.

theirs [ðɛəz] *poss pron* (el) suyo, (la) suya; (los) suyos, (las) suyas; *this is my house, that is theirs* ésta es mi casa, ésa es la suya *or* ésa es suya ‖ el suyo, la suya; los suyos, las suyas; *this is my car, where is theirs?* éste es mi coche, ¿dónde está el suyo?; *theirs are better* los suyos son mejores ‖ suyo, suya; suyos, suyas; *the fault is theirs* la culpa es suya ‖ los suyos (relatives); *them and theirs* ellos y los suyos ‖ — *is this car yours or theirs?* ¿es suyo este coche o es de ellos? ‖ *it is not theirs to ask questions* no son ellos quienes deben hacer preguntas ‖ *of theirs* suyo, suya; *a friend of theirs* un amigo suyo.

theism [ˈθi:izəm] *n* teísmo *m.*

theist [ˈθi:ist] *n* teísta *m* & *f.*

theistic [θi:ˈistik] *adj* teísta.

them [ðem], [ðəm] *pron* los, las (direct object); *I caught them* los cogí ‖ les (indirect object); *I told them* les dije ‖ ellos, ellas; *we are as clever as them* somos tan inteligentes como ellos; *one of them* uno de ellos; *let them decide* que decidan ellos.

thematic [θiˈmætik] *adj* temático, ca.

theme [θi:m] *n* tema *m* (matter) ‖ disertación *f* (essay) ‖ MUS tema *m.*

theme park [-pɑ:k] *n* parque *m* temático (in an amusement park).

theme song [-sɔŋ]; **theme tune** [-tju:n] *n* tema *m* musical (in a film) ‖ US sintonía *f* (signature tune).

Themis [-is] *pr n* MYTH Temis *f.*

Themistocles [θiˈmistəkli:z] *pr n* Temístocles *m.*

themselves [ðəmˈselvz] *pl refl pron* se; *they hurt themselves* se hirieron; *they are getting themselves a car* se van a comprar un coche ‖ ellos (mismos), ellas (mismas); *they bought it for themselves* lo compraron para ellos (mismos) ‖ ellos mismos, ellas mismas; *they couldn't believe it until they had seen it themselves* no pudieron creerlo hasta haberlo visto ellos mismos ‖ sí mismos, sí mismas; *they are always talking about themselves* están siempre hablando de sí mismos ‖ — *they did it all by themselves* lo hicieron ellos solos ‖ *with themselves* consigo mismos.

then [ðen] *adv* entonces, en aquel entonces (at that moment); *he was not there then* él no estaba allí entonces ‖ después, luego (afterwards); *they travelled in France and then in Spain* viajaron por Francia y luego por España; *first right then left* primero a la derecha luego a la izquierda ‖ además; *I haven't the time and then it isn't my business* no tengo tiempo y además no es asunto mío ‖ a pesar de eso (despite that); *he ate all the food and then he was still hungry* se comió toda la comida pero a pesar de eso todavía tenía hambre ‖ por lo tanto, por consiguiente (consequently) ‖ — *and what then?* y entonces ¿qué? ‖ *but then* pero entonces ‖ *now and then* de vez en cuando; *he goes to the pictures now and then* va al cine de vez en cuando ‖ *now... then* unas veces... otras veces ‖ *now then, what you could do is to read this book* ahora bien, lo que podría hacer es leer este libro ‖ *now then, where have you been?* ¡vamos a ver! ¿dónde has estado? ‖ *then and there, there and then* en seguida, inmediatamente; *he knew then and there that it was the house to buy* se dio cuenta en seguida de que era la casa que había que comprar ‖ *what then?* ¿y qué?
◆ *conj* entonces, en ese caso; *then you had better stay* en ese caso es mejor que te quedes ‖ entonces, así que; *then you decided not to come* así que has decidido no venir ‖ *he is very rich, but then he did inherit a fortune* es muy rico pero hay que tener en cuenta que heredó una fortuna.
◆ *adj* entonces, de entonces; *the then headmaster* el entonces director, el director de entonces.
◆ *n before then* antes de ese momento ‖ *between now and then* para entonces; *could you do it between now and then?* ¿puede hacerlo para entonces?; hasta entonces; *between now and then we have two weeks* nos quedan dos semanas hasta entonces ‖ *by then* para entonces ‖ *every now and then* de vez en cuando ‖ *from then on* desde entonces, a partir de entonces ‖ *until* o *till then* hasta entonces.

thenar [ˈθi:nɑ:] *n* ANAT palma *f* (of the hand) | planta *f* (of the foot) | tenar *m* (fleshy part of the thumb).
◆ *adj* tenar.

thence [ðens] *adv* (ant) de allí (from that place) ‖ por consiguiente, por lo tanto, por eso (for that reason).

thenceforth [ˈðensˈfɔ:θ]; **thenceforward** [ˈðensˈfɔ:wəd]; US **thenceforwards** [-z] *adv* desde entonces, a partir de entonces.

theocracy [θiˈɔkrəsi] *n* teocracia *f.*

theocratic [θiəˈkrætik] *adj* teocrático, ca.

Theocritus [θiˈɔkritəs] *pr n* Teócrito *m.*

theodicy [θiˈɔdisi] *n* teodicea *f.*

theodolite [θiˈɔdəlait] *n* teodolito *m.*

Theodoric [θiˈɔdərik] *pr n* Teodorico *m.*

Theodosian [θiəˈdəusjən] *adj* teodosiano, na; *the Theodosian Code* el código teodosiano.

Theodosius [θiəˈdəusjəs] *pr n* Teodosio *m.*

theogony [θiˈɔgəni] *n* teogonía *f.*

theologian [θiəˈləudʒjən] *n* teólogo, ga.

theologic [θiəˈlɔdʒik]; **theological** [-əl] *adj* teológico, ca; teologal ‖ *theological virtues* virtudes *f* teologales.

theologize [θiˈɔlədʒaiz] *vi* teologizar.

theology [θiˈɔlədʒi] *n* teología *f.*

theorem [ˈθiərəm] *n* MATH teorema *m; Pythagoras theorem* teorema de Pitágoras.

theoretic [θiəˈretik]; **theoretical** [-əl] *adj* teórico, ca.

theoretically [-əli] *adv* teóricamente, en teoría.

theoretician [ˌθiərəˈtiʃən] *n* teórico, ca.

theoretics [θiəˈretiks] *n* teoría *f.*

theorist [ˈθiərist] *n* teórico, ca.

theorize [ˈθiəraiz] *vi* teorizar.

theory [ˈθiəri] *n* teoría *f; quantum theory* teoría de los quanta ‖ FIG idea *f; have you any theory on who might have done it?* ¿tienes alguna idea de quién hubiera podido hacerlo? ‖ *in theory* en teoría, teóricamente.

theosophic [θiəˈsɔfik]; **theosophical** [-əl] *adj* teosófico, ca.

theosophist [θiˈɔsəfist] *n* teósofo, fa.

theosophy [θiˈɔsəfi] *n* teosofía *f.*

therapeutic [ˌθerəˈpju:tik]; **therapeutical** [-əl] *adj* terapéutico, ca.

therapeutics [ˌθerəˈpju:tiks] *n* terapéutica *f.*

therapist [ˈθerəpist] *n* terapeuta *m* & *f.*

therapy [ˈθepəpi] *n* terapia *f*, terapéutica *f.*

there [ðɛə*] *adv* allí [AMER allá] (away from listener or speaker); *she saw him there* lo vio allí; *he went there yesterday* fue allí ayer; *there he comes* allí viene ‖ allí, allá (less precise); *down there* allá abajo ‖ ahí (near to speaker or listener); *there it is!* ¡ahí está!; *you are sitting there* tú estás sentado ahí ‖ en eso, allí (on that point); *they agree with me there* ahí están de acuerdo conmigo ‖ — *can we go there and back before lunch?* ¿podemos ir y volver antes del almuerzo? ‖ FIG & FAM *he is not all there* le falta un tornillo ‖ *here and there* acá y allá ‖ *hurry up there* dése prisa ‖ FIG *I have been there* ya sé lo que es eso ‖ *there and then, then and there* en seguida, inmediatamente ‖ *there comes a time when* llega un momento en que ‖ *there is, there are* hay; *there are five million bicycles in the country* hay cinco millones de bicicletas en el país ‖ *there* o *thereabouts* más o menos ‖ *there he comes!* ¡ahí viene!, ¡ya viene! ‖ *there was, there were* había, hubo; *there was a lot of sugar in my tea* había mucho azúcar en el té; *there were thousands of people* hubo miles de personas ‖ *there were only two left* sólo quedaban dos ‖ *there will be* habrá ‖ *there you are* eso es ‖ *thirty*

miles there and back treinta millas ida y vuelta || FIG & FAM *to be all there* ser muy despabilado || *you there!* ¡usted!, ¡oiga!
◆ *interj* ¡vaya!; *there, it's finished!* ¡vaya!, ¡ya se acabó! || — *but there, what is the good of talking!* pero ¿de qué sirve hablar? || *there now!* ¡ya está! || *there!, there!* ¡ya!, ¡ya!

thereabout ['ðɛərə'baut]; **thereabouts** [-s] *adv* por ahí, por allí (place); *the theatre is in that district and the cinema is thereabouts as well* el teatro está en aquel barrio y el cine está tambien por ahí || más o menos, aproximadamente (amount, degree, weight); *it costs fifteen pounds or thereabouts* cuesta quince libras más o menos.

thereafter [ðɛər'ɑːftə] *adv* después, más tarde.

thereat [ðɛər'æt] *adv* por eso (for that reason) || en eso, sobre este punto (on that account) || ahí, allí (there).

thereby [ðɛə'bai] *adj* por eso, por ello || *thereby hangs a tale* sobre eso hay mucho que contar.

therefore ['ðɛəfɔː] *adv* por lo tanto, por consiguiente, por tanto; *living is dear, therefore we have to economize* la vida es cara, por consiguiente tenemos que ahorrar || *I think, therefore I am* pienso, luego existo.

therefrom [ðɛə'frɔm] *adv* de allí, de ahí || *it follows therefrom that* de eso resulta que.

therein [ðɛər'in] *adv* allí dentro (in that place) || en eso; *we don't know all the facts and therein lies our difficulty* no sabemos todos los hechos y en eso reside nuestra dificultad; *therein you are mistaken* en eso está usted equivocado.

thereinafter [,ðɛərin'ɑːftə] *adv* JUR más abajo, más adelante (later in the same document).

thereinbefore [,ðɛərinbi'fɔː] *adv* JUR más arriba.

thereof [ðɛər'ɔv] *adv* de eso (of this) || su, del mismo, de la misma; *this tin and the contents thereof* esta lata y el contenido de la misma *or* y su contenido.

thereon [ðɛər'ɔn] *adv* → **thereupon.**

Theresa [tə'riːzə] *pr n* Teresa *f.*

thereto [ðɛə'tuː] *adv* a eso, a ello || (ant) además.

thereunder [ðɛər'ʌndə] *adv* más abajo.

thereupon ['ðɛərə'pɔn]; **thereon** [ðɛər'ɔn] *adv* inmediatamente después (immediately afterwards) || por lo tanto, por consiguiente (therefore) || sobre eso (on that); *there is much to be spoken thereupon* hay mucho que hablar sobre eso.

therewith [ðɛə'wið]; **therewithal** [,ðɛəwi'ðɔːl] *adv* con eso (with that) || (ant) además (in addition to that).

theriaca [θi'riəkə] *n* triaca *f* (antidote).

therm [θəːm] *n* PHYS termia *f.*

thermae [-i] *pl n* termas *f.*

thermal [-əl] *adj* termal (hot springs) || PHYS térmico, ca; *thermal power* o *energy* energía térmica; *thermal diffusion* difusión térmica; *thermal reactor* reactor *m* térmico || calorífico, ca; *thermal capacity* capacidad calorífica || *thermal underwear* ropa *f* interior térmica.

thermic [-ik] *adj* térmico, ca.

thermionic [,θəːmi'ɔnik] *adj* PHYS termoiónico, ca; *thermionic valve* lámpara termoiónica.

thermocautery ['θəːməm'kɔːtəri] *n* termocauterio *m.*

termochemical ['θəːməu'kemikəl] *adj* termoquímico, ca.

thermochemistry ['θəːməu'kemistri] *n* termoquímica *f.*

thermocouple ['θəːməu,kʌpəl] *n* PHYS par *m* termoeléctrico, termopar *m*, pila *f* termoeléctrica.

thermodynamic ['θəːməudai'næmik] *adj* termodinámico, ca.

thermodynamics [-s] *n* termodinámica *f.*

thermoelectric ['θəːməui'lektrik] *adj* termoeléctrico, ca || *thermoelectric couple* par termoeléctrico, termopar *m.*

thermoelectricity ['θəːməuilek'trisiti] *n* termoelectricidad *f.*

thermoelement ['θəːməu'elimənt] *n* termoelemento *m.*

thermogenic ['θəːməu'dʒiːnik]; **thermogenous** [θəː'mɔdʒinəs] *adj* termógeno, na.

thermograph ['θəːməgrɑːf] *n* termógrafo *m.*

thermology [θəː'mɔlədʒi] *n* termología *f.*

thermometer [θə'mɔmitə] *n* termómetro *m*; *clinical thermometer* termómetro clínico; *maximum and minimum thermometer* termómetro de máxima y mínima.

thermometric [,θəːmə'metrik]; **thermometrical** [,θəːmə'metrikəl] *adj* termométrico, ca.

thermometry [θə'mɔmitri] *n* termometría *f.*

thermonuclear ['θəːməu'njuːkliə*] *adj* termonuclear.

thermopile ['θəːməupail] *n* PHYS termopila *f.*

thermoplastic ['θəːməu'plæstik] *adj* termoplástico, ca.

Thermopylae [θəː'mɔpiliː] *pl prn* Termópilas *f.*

thermoregulation ['θəːməuregju'leiʃən] *n* termorregulación *f.*

Thermos ['θəːmɔs] *n* termo *m*, termos *m* || *Thermos bottle* o *flask* termo, termos.

thermosetting ['θəːmou,setiŋ] *adj* termoestable, termoendurecible.

thermosiphon ['θəːməu'saifən] *n* termosifón *m.*

thermostat ['θəːməstæt] *n* termostato *m.*

thermotherapy ['θəːməu'θerəpi] *n* MED termoterapia *f.*

thesaurus [θi'sɔːrəs] *n* diccionario *m.*
— OBSERV El plural es *thesauri* o *thesauruses.*

these [ðiːz] *pl dem/adj pron* → **this.**

thesis ['θiːsis] *n* tesis *f*; *he and I maintain the same thesis* él y yo sostenemos la misma tesis; *I have already handed in my doctoral thesis* he entregado ya la tesis de doctorado || PHIL tesis *f.*
— OBSERV El plural de esta palabra es *theses.*

Thespian ['θespjən] *adj* dramático, ca; trágico, ca (of dramatic art) || de Tespis (of Thespis).
◆ *n* actor *m*, actriz *f.*

Thespis ['θespis] *pr n* Tespis *m.*

Thessalonica [,θesələ'naikə] *pr n* Tesalónica *f.*

Thessaly ['θesəli] *pr n* Tesalia *f.*

theta ['θiːtə] *n* theta *f* (of Greek alphabet).

Thetis ['θetis] *pr n* MYTH Tetis *f.*

theurgic [θi'əːdʒik]; **theurgical** [-əl] *adj* teúrgico, ca (magical).

theurgist ['θiːəːdʒist] *n* teúrgo *m.*

theurgy ['θiːəːdʒi] *n* teúrgia *f.*

thews [θjuːz] *pl n* músculos *m* (muscles) || nervios *m* (nerves) || fuerza *f sing* muscular (strength).

they [ðei] *pers pron* ellos, ellas; *it is they* son ellos, son ellas || — *they say it will be a hard winter* dicen *or* se dice que será un invierno duro || *they who* los que, quienes; *they who believe* los que creen.

they'd [ðeid] contracción de «they had», «they would».

they'll [ðeiəl] contracción de «they will», «they shall».

they're [ðeə] contracción de «they are».

they've [ðeiv] contracción de «they have».

thiamin ['θaiəmin]; **thiamine** ['θaiəmiːn] *n* tiamina *f.*

thick [θik] *adj* gordo, da; grueso, sa; *a thick fabric* una tela gruesa || grueso, sa (thread) || de espesor, de grosor, de grueso; *the ice is twenty centimetres thick* el hielo tiene veinte centímetros de espesor || ancho, cha; grueso, sa; *a thick wall* una pared ancha; *a thick line* una línea gruesa || abultado, da; grueso, sa (lips) || espeso, sa (liquid, hair) || poblado, da; tupido, da; espeso, sa (beard) || poblado, da; espeso, sa (eyebrows) || denso, sa; espeso, sa; tupido, da; *thick forest* bosque espeso || denso, sa (crowd) || turbio, bia (cloudy liquid) || profundo, da; intenso, sa (darkness) || cargado, da; viciado, da (stuffy); *thick atmosphere* atmósfera cargada; *air thick with smoke* aire cargado de humo || espeso, sa; denso, sa (fog) || nublado, da; cerrado, da; brumoso, sa (weather) || sofocante, bochornoso, sa (heat) || pesado, da (head) || poco claro, ra (voice) || borroso, sa (writing) || denso, sa (night) || fuerte, marcado, da; cerrado, da (accent) || FAM torpe, estúpido, da (slow to understand) | íntimo, ma; *thick friends* amigos íntimos || — FAM *it's a bit thick!* ¡es el colmo!, ¡eso pasa de castaño oscuro! || FAM *they are as thick as thieves* son uña y carne, están a partir un piñón || PRINT *thick stroke* lo grueso, trazo grueso (of a letter) | *thick type* negrilla *f* || *to be thick with* estar lleno de || FAM *to be very thick with s.o.* ser íntimo amigo de alguien.
◆ *adv* espesamente, densamente (thickly) || con voz poco clara (to speak) || — *don't spread the butter too thick* no untes demasiada mantequilla || FIG *his blows fell thick and fast* llovían los golpes || *snow lay thick on the ground* una capa espesa de nieve cubría el suelo || *the grass grew thick* la hierba crecía tupida || *to cut the bread thick* cortar el pan en gruesas rebanadas || FIG *to lay it on thick* ser demasiado efusivo.
◆ *n* parte *f* más gruesa (of the thumb, etc.) || grueso *m*, grosor *m*, espesor *m* || lo más denso (of a crowd) || lo más tupido (of a forest) || FAM torpe *m* & *f*, estúpido, da || — FIG *a friend through thick and thin* un amigo seguro | *in the thick of the fight* en lo más reñido *or* recio del combate || *in the thick of the forest* en pleno bosque || FIG *through thick and thin* contra viento y marea, pase lo que pase.

thicken [θikən] *vt* espesar; *to thicken a sauce* espesar una salsa || FIG hacer poco claro (speech) | complicar, embrollar (a plot).
◆ *vi* espesarse (to become thick) || volverse más grueso || volverse más denso || FIG embrollarse, complicarse; *the plot thickens* el asunto se complica.

thickening [-iŋ] *n* espesamiento *m* (of a wall, etc.) || aumento *m* (of waist).

thicket ['θikit] *n* matorral *m* (shrubs) || bosquecillo *m* (wood).

thickhead ['θikhed] *n* FAM estúpido, da; tonto, ta.

thickheaded ['θik'hedid] *adj* FAM estúpido, da; tonto, ta.

thickish ['θikiʃ] *adj* bastante espeso, sa || bastante denso, sa || bastante nublado, da (weather).

thick-lipped ['θik'lipt] *adj* de labios abultados *or* gruesos.

thickly ['θikli] *adv* espesamente, densamente || tupidamente (beard, wood) || con voz poco clara (to speak) || *snow fell thickly* la nieve caía muy fuerte, caía mucha nieve.

thickness ['θiknis] *n* espesor *m* (dimension); *this table is four centimetres in thickness* esta mesa tiene cuatro centímetros de espesor || espesor *m*, grueso *m*, grosor *m* (size) || espesura *f* (of forest) || espesor *m*, densidad *f* (of fog) || lo nublado, lo cerrado (of weather) || espesor *m*, densidad *f* (of a liquid).

thickset ['θikset] *adj* rechoncho, cha; achaparrado, da (person) || muy poblado, da; denso, sa (closely planted).

thick-skinned ['θik'skind] *adj* de piel gruesa (having a thick skin) || de pellejo grueso (grapes) || FIG insensible, duro, ra (insensitive).

thick-skulled ['θik'skʌld]; **thick-witted** ['θik'witid] *adj* estúpido, da; torpe.

thief [θi:f] *n* ladrón, ona || MAR ladrón *m* (of a sail) || — *den of thieves* cueva *f* de ladrones || FIG *opportunity makes the thief* la ocasión hace al ladrón || FIG *set a thief to catch a thief* a pillo, pillo y medio || *the penitent, the impenitent thief* el buen, el mal ladrón (in the gospel) || FAM *they are as thick as thieves* son uña y carne, están a partir un piñón.

— OBSERV El plural de *thief* es *thieves*.

thieve [θi:v] *vt/vi* robar, hurtar.

thievery ['θi:vəri] *n* robo *m*, hurto *m*.

thieving ['θi:viŋ] *adj* ladrón, ona.

◆ *n* robo *m*, hurto *m*.

thievish ['θi:viʃ] *adj* ladrón, ona.

thievishness [-nis] *n* propensión *f* a robar.

thigh [θai] *n* ANAT muslo *m*.

thighbone ['θaibəun] *n* ANAT fémur *m*.

thill [θil] *n* limonera *f* (shaft).

thimble ['θimbl] *n* dedal *m* (in sewing) || TECH abrazadera *f* || MAR guardacabo *m*.

thimbleful [-ful] *n* dedo *m*, poco *m*.

thimblerig [-rig] *n* juego *m* de manos que se efectúa con tres cubiletes.

thimblerigger [-'rigə*] *n* escamoteador *m* || FAM estafador *m* (swindler).

thin [θin] *adj* delgado, da; flaco, ca (person) || delgado, da (fingers) || fino, na (lips) || fino, na; delgado, da; *a thin sheet of paper* una hoja de papel delgada || fino, na; ligero, ra (cloth) || fino, na; *a thin rope* una cuerda fina || poco denso, sa; fino, na; *thin mist* niebla fina || ralo, la (hair) || poco, ca; escaso, sa (population, audience, etc.) || enrarecido, da (air) || claro, ra; poco denso, sa (liquid) || aguado, da (wine, beer, etc.) || débil (voice) || fino, na (steel sheet, etc.) || de poca consistencia, flojo, ja (excuse, argument) || con poco contraste (photo) || — *he has grown very thin* ha adelgazado mucho || *she is rather thin in the face* tiene la cara delgada || FAM *thin on top* calvo, va | *to be as thin as a rake* estar en los huesos | *to be wearing thin* estar pasado (joke), acabarse (patience) | *to disappear into thin air* desaparecer, esfumarse || *to get* o *to grow thinner* adelgazar (a person) || FIG *to have a thin time* pasar un mal rato, pasarlas moradas.

◆ *adv* *to cut bread thin* cortar el pan en rebanadas finas || *to spread the butter thin* untar una capa fina de mantequilla.

thin [θin] *vt* adelgazar, hacer adelgazar (s.o.) || diluir (to dilute) || entresacar (plants, hair) || reducir (to reduce) || diezmar (population) || despoblar (country, forest) || CULIN aclarar (a sauce) || *to thim down* diluir (paint) || *to thin out* hacer menos denso, entresacar.

◆ *vi* adelgazar (to get slim) || disminuir, dispersarse; *the crowd thinned* la muchedumbre se dispersó || disminuir, reducirse (to diminish) || disiparse; *the fog is thinning* la niebla se está disipando || *his hair has thinned a lot* ha perdido mucho pelo.

thine [ðain] *poss pron* (ant) (el) tuyo, (la) tuya; (los) tuyos, (las) tuyas; *my letter and thine* mi carta y la tuya; *this book is thine* este libro es tuyo || — *a friend of thine* un amigo tuyo || *for thee and thine* para ti y los tuyos.

◆ *poss adj* (ant) tu, tus; *thine eyes* tus ojos; *thine honour* tu honor.

thing [θiŋ] *n* cosa *f*; *what are those things you're carrying there?* ¿qué son esas cosas que lleva usted ahí? || objeto *m* (object) || artículo *m*; *expensive things* artículos costosos || FAM chisme *m*, cosa *f*; *what's that thing over there?* ¿qué es ese chisme que está allí? | criatura *f*, individuo *m* (person) | ser *m* (being) || cosa *f* (subject, action); *there's another thing I want to ask about* le quiero preguntar otra cosa; *you take things too seriously* se toma las cosas demasiado en serio; *how could you do such a thing?* ¿cómo ha podido hacer una cosa semejante? || FIG obsesión *f* (obsession); *to have a thing about sth.* tener obsesión con algo | manía *f* (dislike); *to have a thing about s.o.* tenerle manía a alguien || — *a dumb thing* un memo || *first thing* a primera hora; *he arrived first thing in the morning* llegó a primera hora de la mañana; lo primero; *I'll do it first thing in the morning* lo haré lo primero por la mañana || *for another thing* por otra parte || *for one thing* primero, en primer lugar; *he knows a thing or two about economics* sabe algo de economía || *I could tell you a thing or two about him* te podría decir alguna cosa que otra sobre él || *I don't know a thing about history* no sé nada de historia || *it's a good thing that* menos mal que || *it's just the thing* es precisamente lo que queremos || *it's not the (done) thing* esto no se hace || *it is the real thing* es auténtico || *it would be a good thing to* sería conveniente || *I've got the very thing for you* tengo exactamente lo que usted necesita *or* lo que usted busca || *last thing* a última hora || *no such thing* nada de eso || *not... a thing* no... nada; *he didn't hear a thing* no oyó nada || *not a thing has been overlooked* no se ha dejado de lado absolutamente nada || FAM *not to feel quite the thing* no encontrarse bien, encontrarse algo pachucho || *not to know the first thing about* no tener el menor conocimiento de, no tener la más mínima idea de || *old thing!* ¡hombre!, ¡viejo! || *one thing or the other* una de dos || FAM *poor thing* pobrecito, ta | *she's a lovely thing* es un encanto || *that's quite another thing* eso es otra cosa, eso es harina de otro costal || *that's the last thing to do* esto es lo último que hay que hacer || FIG *the latest thing* el último grito || *there's no such thing* no hay tal cosa || *the thing is that* el caso es que || *the thing is to succeed* lo importante es tener éxito || FIG *to be quite the thing* estar muy de moda | *to have not a thing* no tener nada | *to know a thing or two* saber cuántas son cinco | *to make a big thing of* dar mucha importancia a | *to make a good thing out of* sacar provecho de || *to say one thing and mean another* decir una cosa por otra || *to talk of one thing and another* hablar de todo un poco || FIG *to tell s.o. a thing or two* decirle a uno cuatro cosas *or* cuatro verdades || *what with one thing and another* entre unas cosas y otras || FAM *you silly thing!* ¡estúpido!

◆ *pl* ropa *f sing* (clothes) || cosas *f* (belongings); *I forbid you to touch my things* te prohibo tocar mis cosas || equipo *m sing*; *bring your tennis things* trae tu equipo de tenis || cosas *f* (affairs); *things are going badly* las cosas van mal || JUR bienes *m*; *things personal* bienes muebles || — *above all things* ante todo, antes que nada || *as things are* o *stand* tal y como están las cosas || *good things take time* las cosas de palacio van despacio || *how are things?* ¿qué tal van las cosas?, ¿cómo te va?, ¿qué tal? || *of all things!* ¡qué sorpresa! || *one of those things* una de esas cosas que pasan || *tea things* servicio *m* de té || *that's how* o *the way things are* así están las cosas || *to pack one's things* hacer las maletas || *to see things* ver visiones || *to take things easy* tomar las cosas con calma || *to wash up the dinner things* fregar los platos || *well of all things! what are you doing here?* ¿qué diablos está usted haciendo aquí?

— OBSERV In some cases *thing* cannot be translated literally into Spanish: *the extraordinary, the funny thing is that* lo extraordinario, lo gracioso es que; *the first thing to do is* lo primero que hay que hacer es; *what's this thing for?* ¿para qué sirve esto?

thingumabob ['θiŋəmibɔb]; **thingumajig** ['θiŋəmidʒig]; **thingummy** ['θiŋəmi] *n* FAM chisme *m*, cosa *f*, cacharro *m* (thing) || éste, ésta (person); *I saw thingumabob last night* anoche vi a éste.

think [θiŋk] *n* ejercicio *m* mental || idea *f*, pensamiento *m* || — *he had a good think about it* lo pensó mucho || *to have a quiet think* reflexionar.

think* [θiŋk] *vi* pensar; *are animals able to think?* ¿pensarán los animales? || pensar, reflexionar, meditar; *let me think a moment* déjeme reflexionar un momento; *I did it without thinking* lo hice sin pensar; *to think hard* pensar mucho || parecer, creer; *it is better, don't you think, to get it over?* ¿no le parece que es mejor acabar con ello? || — *as I think* a mi me parece, según creo || *I can't think why* no veo el porqué, no sé por qué || *I don't think so* no creo || *I should think so!* ¡ya lo creo! || *I think not* no creo || *I think so* creo que sí || *I think so too* yo lo creo también || *I think, therefore I am* pienso, luego existo || *just think!* ¡fíjese!, ¡piense un poco! || *so I thought!, I thought as much!* ¡ya me parecía!, ¡ya me lo figuraba!, ¡ya me lo imaginaba! || *to make one think* dar que pensar a uno || *to think aloud* pensar en voz alta || *to think for o.s.* pensar por sí mismo || *you should think twice before doing that* tendría que pensarlo dos veces antes de hacerlo.

◆ *vt* imaginarse, creer; *who would have thought it?* ¿quién se lo hubiera imaginado? || pensar; *and to think they have gone away!* ¡pensar que se han ido!; *I thought to myself that* pensaba para mis adentros que || acordarse; *did you think to bring your book?* ¿se acordó de traer su libro? || creer, parecerle (a uno); *I think he is honest* creo que es honrado, me parece honrado; *do you think it will rain?* ¿cree que va a llover? || creer, pensar, esperar (to expect); *I little thought to see you again* no esperaba volverle a ver || entender (to understand); *you can't think what I mean* no puede comprender lo que quiero decir || tener; *he thinks evil thoughts* tiene malos pensamientos || pensar, ocurrírsele (a uno) (to conceive the notion of); *I have been thinking that* se me ocurrió que || pensar, tener intención de; *I only thought to help you* sólo tenía intención de ayudarle; *the child thought no harm in doing it* el niño no tenía malas intenciones al hacerlo || encontrar; *I think she is pretty* la encuentro mona || considerar, creer, pensar, tener por; *everyone thought he was a fool* todos lo consideraban tonto || considerar, creer, parecerle (a uno); *if you think it necessary* si lo considera necesario, si le parece necesario || — *anybody would think...* cualquiera diría que... || *they were thought to be rich* la gente les consideraba ricos, se creía que eran ricos || *thinking to* con la intención de || *to think o.s. a hero* creerse un héroe || FAM *who does he think he is?* ¿quién se cree? || *who would have thought it?* ¿quién lo hubiera dicho *or* creído?

◆ *phr v* **to think about** pensar en; *what are you thinking about?* ¿en qué está usted pensando? | parecerle (a uno); *what do you think about it?* ¿qué le parece? | pensar; *without her thinking about it* sin que lo piense || — *just thinking about it* sólo con pensarlo || **to think away** pasar meditando; *he thinks his time away* se pasa el tiempo meditando || **to think back** recordar || **to think of** pensar en; *to think of everything* pensar en todo; *to think of one's neighbour* pensar en los demás | pensar; *when I think of it* cuando lo pienso | recordar, acordarse de (to remember); *I can't think of his name* no puedo acordarme de su nombre | ocurrírsele (a uno); *I never thought of telling you* nunca se me ocurrió decírselo; *we would not think of inviting them* no se nos ocurriría invitarlos | tener intención de, pensar; *he is thinking of going to Rome next week* tiene intención de ir a Roma la semana que viene | encontrar, acordarse de, recordar (to find); *to think of the right word* encontrar la palabra exacta | opinar de, tener opinión de, pensar de; *what do you think of him?* ¿qué opinión tiene de él? | figurarse, creer, imaginarse; *I thought of him as being tall* me lo figuraba alto || — *he is thought well of* se le aprecia mucho | *he won't think of it!* ¡en la vida lo haría! | *it isn't to be thought of!* ¡no hay ni que pensarlo!, ¡ni pensarlo! | *the best thing I can think of* lo mejor que se me ocurre | *to think a great deal of o.s.* ser muy creído | *to think badly of* pensar mal de, tener en poco a | *to think better of it* cambiar de opinión | *to think highly* o *much of s.o.* tener en mucho a alguien | *to think ill of* pensar mal de | *to think nothing of* no suponer nada para uno; *he thinks nothing of working sixteen hours a day* para él no supone nada trabajar dieciséis horas diarias; no encontrarle nada (not to like); *I'm afraid I think nothing of her* lo siento, pero yo no le encuentro nada | *to think well of* pensar bien de, tener buen concepto de | *we don't think much of the film* no nos gustó mucho la película || ***to think out*** elaborar, idear (a plan) | examinar, estudiar (a question) | encontrar (answer, solution) || — *that wants thinking out* eso requiere mucha reflexión, hay que pensarlo bien || ***to think over*** pensar bien, examinar detenidamente; *on* o *after thinking it over* pensándolo bien; *to think the matter over* examinar detenidamente la cuestión || — *to think it over well* pensarlo mucho, pensarlo bien || ***to think through*** estudiar *or* examinar a fondo || ***to think up*** elaborar, idear (plan) | inventar; *he thought up a good excuse* inventó una buena excusa.

— OBSERV Pret y pp ***thought***.

thinkable [-əbl] *adj* concebible.

thinker [-ə*] *n* pensador *m*.

thinking [-iŋ] *adj* que piensa, pensante; *any thinking man* cualquier hombre que piense || racional.

◆ *n* pensamiento *m*; *modern thinking* el pensamiento moderno || modo *m* de ver, opinión *f*, parecer *m*; *to my thinking* a mi modo de ver, en mi opinión, a mi parecer || pensar *m*; *thinking is a useful exercise* el pensar es un buen ejercicio || *wishful thinking* ilusiones *f pl*.

think tank [-tæŋk] *n* grupo *m or* reunión *f* de expertos.

thinly ['θinli] *adv* apenas; *a thinly veiled insult* un insulto apenas disimulado || poco; *country thinly populated* país poco poblado.

thinner [θinə*] *n* disolvente *m*.

thinness ['θinnis] *n* delgadez *f*, flaqueza *f* (of person) || delgadez *f* (of paper, of thread) || ligereza *f* (of wine, of material) || fluidez *f* (of liquid, of soup) || escasez *f* (of hair) || poca consistencia *f*, flojedad *f* (of an argument) || debilidad *f* (of the voice).

thin-skinned ['θin'skind] *adj* de piel fina (having a thin skin) || FIG susceptible, muy sensible (sensitive).

third [θə:d] *adj* tercero, ra; *third place* tercer lugar; *third part* tercera parte || — *by a third party* por tercera persona || *every third day* cada tres días || *third floor* tercer piso, tercero *m* || HIST *third estate* estado llano || *third gear* tercera *f*; *to change into third gear* poner la tercera || REL *third order* orden tercera || JUR *third party* tercero *m* || *third-party insurance* seguro *m* contra tercera persona || *third person* tercera persona (grammatical term), tercero *m* (legal term) || *Third World* Tercer Mundo || *third year* tercer curso, tercero *m* (at school).

◆ *n* tercero, ra; *he came in third* llegó tercero; *Henry III (the Third)* Enrique III [tercero] || tercio *m*, tercera parte *f*; *two thirds* dos tercios; *a third of the cake* un tercio del pastel, una tercera parte del pastel; *five is one third of fifteen* cinco es la tercera parte de quince || aprobado *m* (grade in an exam); *to get a third in history* sacar un aprobado en historia || AUT tercera *f* (third gear) || día *m* tres, tres *m*; *the third of the month* el día tres del mes || MUS tercera *f* || MATH tercero *m*.

◆ *adv* en tercer lugar (in third place) || en tercera (clase); *to travel third* viajar en tercera.

third class [-'klɑ:s] *n* tercera *f*, tercera clase *f* (of trains).

third-class [-klɑ:s] *adj* de tercera clase, de tercera (trains, etc.) || de tercera categoría (hotels, etc.) || de poca calidad (goods).

◆ *adv* en tercera, en tercera clase.

thirdly ['θə:dli] *adv* en tercer lugar.

third-rate ['θə:d'reit] *adj* de poca calidad (goods) || de poca categoría (people).

thirst [θə:st] *n* sed *f*; *an unquenchable thirst* una sed insaciable; *to quench one's thirst* apagar la sed || FIG afán *m*, sed *f*; *thirst for knowledge* sed de saber.

thirst [θə:st] *vi* tener sed (to feel thirsty) || FIG estar sediento, tener sed; *to be thirsting for revenge* estar sediento de venganza.

thirstily [-ili] *adv* con avidez; *to drink thirstily* beber con avidez.

thirstiness [-inis] *n* sed *f*.

thirsty [-i] *adj* sediento, ta || FIG sediento, ta; *thirsty soil* suelo sediento; *thirsty for adventure* sediento de aventuras; *thirsty for riches* sediento de riquezas || FAM que da sed (work) || — *to be thirsty for* tener sed de || *to make thirsty* dar sed.

thirteen ['θə:'ti:n] *adj* trece.

◆ *n* trece *m* (number).

thirteenth [-θ] *adj* decimotercero, ra; decimotercio, cia || trece (chapter, date); *the thirteenth century* el siglo trece.

◆ *n* decimotercero, ra; trece *m* & *f* (in thirteenth position) || trezavo *m*, decimotercera parte *f* (one of thirteen parts) || trece *m*, día *m* trece (day of month); *tomorrow, the thirteenth of February* mañana, trece de febrero || *Leo XIII (the Thirteenth)* León XIII [trece].

thirtieth ['θə:tiiθ] *adj* trigésimo, ma (in a series) || trigésimo, ma; treintavo, va (being one of 30 equal parts).

◆ *n* trigésima parte *f*, treintavo *m* (one of thirty parts) || trigésimo, ma; treinta *m* & *f* (in thirtieth position) || día *m* treinta, treinta *m* (of a month); *the thirtieth of May* el treinta de mayo.

thirty ['θə:ti] *adj* treinta; *thirty men* treinta hombres.

◆ *n* treinta *m* (number).

◆ *pl* treinta *m*; *to be in one's thirties* estar en los treinta || — *temperatures in the thirties* temperatura de más de treinta grados || *the thirties* los años treinta.

thirty-first ['θə:ti'fə:st] *adj/n* trigésimo primero, trigésima primera.

thirty-second ['θə:ti'seknd] *adj/n* trigésimo segundo, trigésima segunda.

this [ðis] *dem adj* este, esta; *this book* este libro; *these tables* estas mesas; *these men* estos hombres || — *he is one of these artist types* es uno de esos artistas || *I've been waiting these three weeks* hace tres semanas que estoy esperando, llevo tres semanas esperando, estuve esperando estas tres últimas semanas || *this day last year* hoy hace un año || *this one* éste, ésta || *to run this way and that* ir de un lado para otro.

◆ *dem pron* éste, ésta (masculine, feminine); *this is a pleasant country* éste es un país agradable; *who is this?* ¿quién es éste *or* ésta?; *who are these?* ¿quiénes son éstos *or* éstas? || esto (neuter); *this is what he told me* esto es lo que me dijo; *what is this?* ¿qué es esto?; *after this* después de esto || — *like this* así; *do it like this* hágalo así || *the thing is this* el problema es éste || *this and that* esto y lo otro || *this is how you do it* así es como se hace || *this is Mr. Smith* le presento al señor Smith || *this is where he lives* aquí es donde vive || *this or that?* ¿éste o aquél?, ¿esto o aquello? || *this, that and the other* esto, lo otro y lo de más allá || *with this* sin más; *with this he got up and went out* sin más se levantó y se fue.

◆ *adv* tan; *I didn't know that it could be this interesting* no sabía que podía ser tan interesante || tan, así de; *I didn't expect it to be this big* no esperaba que fuera así de grande || así de; *it was this big* era así de grande || — *I didn't expect to wait this long* no pensaba tener que esperar tanto || *this far it's been easy* hasta aquí *or* hasta ahora ha sido fácil || *this much* tanto; *he can't eat this much* no puede comer tanto.

— OBSERV El plural de esta palabra es *these*.

thistle ['θisl] *n* cardo *m*.

thistledown [-daun] *n* vilano *m* (of a thistle).

thistly [-i] *adj* lleno de cardos (full of thistles) || espinoso, sa (prickly) || FIG delicado, da; espinoso, sa; peliagudo, da.

thither ['ðiðə*] *adj* (ant) allá.

thitherward [-wəd] *adv* (ant) hacia allá.

tho [ðəu] *conj* US FAM aunque (though).

thole [θəul]; **tholepin** [-pin] *n* MAR escálamo *m*, tolete *m*.

Thomas ['tɔməs] *pr n* Tomás || — *Saint Thomas Aquinas* Santo Tomás de Aquino || *Thomas More* Tomás Moro.

Thomism ['təumizəm] *n* PHIL & REL tomismo *m*.

Thomist ['təumist] *adj/n* PHIL & REL tomista.

thong [θɔŋ] *n* correa *f*, tira *f* de cuero (strip of leather).

thoracic [θɔ'ræsik] *adj* ANAT torácico, ca; *thoracic cage* caja torácica.

thorax ['θɔ:ræks] *n* ANAT tórax *m*.

— OBSERV El plural de *thorax* es *thoraxes* o *thoraces*.

thorium ['θɔ:riəm] *n* CHEM torio *m*.

thorn [θɔ:n] *n* BOT espina *f* (of a plant, stem) | espino *m* (hawthorn) || FIG espina *f* (source of irritation) || — FIG *a thorn in one's side* o *in the flesh* una espina clavada || *crown of thorns* corona *f* de espinas || FIG *to be on thorns* estar sobre ascuas.

thornbush [-buʃ] *n* BOT espino *m*.

thornless [-lis] *adj* sin espinas.

thorny [-i] *adj* espinoso, sa || FIG espinoso, sa; peliagudo, da (question).

thorough ['θʌrə] *adj* minucioso, sa (search, investigation, etc.); *after a thorough study of the document* después de un estudio minucioso del documento || concienzudo, da (work, person); *he is thorough in his work* es concienzudo en su trabajo || profundo, da; *thorough knowledge* conocimiento profundo || completo, ta; *you must have a thorough change* necesita un cambio completo || a fondo; *a thorough cleaning* una limpieza a fondo || completo, ta; perfecto, ta; *a thorough command of Spanish* un dominio perfecto del español || perfecto, ta; cabal; *a thorough gentleman* un perfecto caballero || empedernido, da; redomado, da; *a thorough drunkard* un borracho empedernido.

thorough bass [-'beis] *n* MUS bajo *m* cifrado.

thoroughbred [-bred] *adj* de pura raza (dog, etc.) || (de) pura sangre (horse) || FIG con clase (person).
◆ *n* pura sangre *m* & *f*.

thoroughfare [-fɛə*] *n* carretera *f* (highway) || calle *f* (in a town) || vía *f* pública (road open to the public) || *no thoroughfare* calle sin salida (no through road), calle interceptada (road blocked), prohibido el paso (no entry).

thoroughgoing [-'gəuiŋ] *adj* minucioso, sa (thorough, conscientious) || completo, ta; perfecto, ta; cien por cien; *a thoroughgoing democrat* un perfecto demócrata.

thoroughly [-li] *adv* a fondo; *to investigate thoroughly* investigar a fondo; *to clean thoroughly* limpiar a fondo || perfectamente; *to understand thoroughly* entender perfectamente || de pies a cabeza; *to be thoroughly honest* ser honrado de pies a cabeza || completamente; *a thoroughly reliable machine* una máquina completamente segura || concienzudamente; *he does his work very thoroughly* hace su trabajo muy concienzudamente.

thoroughness [-nis] *n* minuciosidad *f*, lo minucioso; *the thoroughness of an investigation* la minuciosidad de una investigación || perfección *f*.

thorp [θɔːp] *n* caserío *m*.

those [ðəuz] *pl dem adj/pron* ⟶ **that.**

thou [ðau] *pers pron* (ant) tú, vos.
— OBSERV El pronombre *thou* actualmente se emplea casi únicamente para dirigirse a Dios.
— OBSERV Although the *tú* form is normally used when addressing God, *vos* can also be used, in which case the second person plural of the verb is required.

thou [ðau] *vt/vi* tratar de tú *or* vos.

though [ðəu] *conj* aunque; *though it was very late, he went on working* aunque era muy tarde siguió trabajando; *I will do it though it cost me my life* lo haré aunque me cueste la vida || — *as though* como si || *even though* aunque || *it looks as though he has gone* parece que se ha ido || *strange though it may seem* por extraño que parezca || *what though the way be long!* ¿qué importa que el camino sea largo?
◆ *adv* sin embargo; *the ground was muddy, it was a good game though* el suelo estaba lleno de barro, sin embargo el partido fue bueno || *did he though?* ¿de verdad?
— OBSERV The conjunction *aunque* is followed by the subjunctive when the clause it introduces expresses a hypothesis. It is used with the indicative when the clause expresses a fact.
— OBSERV Aunque en inglés con *though* se puede emplear el subjuntivo, se usa más frecuentemente el indicativo.

thought [θɔːt] *n* pensamiento *m*; *modern thought* pensamiento moderno; *to read s.o.'s thoughts* adivinar los pensamientos de alguien; *freedom of thought* libertad de pensamiento; *free thought* libre pensamiento; *nasty thought* mal pensamiento || idea *f*; *I've just had a thought* se me acaba de ocurrir una idea; *happy thought* idea afortunada || intención *f*; *he once had the thought of selling the house* una vez tuvo la intención de vender la casa; *he had no thought of offending you* no tenía intención de ofenderle || punto *m* de vista, opinión *f*; *man who keeps his thoughts to himself* hombre que no revela sus opiniones || consideración *f*, atenciones *f pl*; *he has no thought for his mother* no tiene consideración con su madre || — *after much thought* después de pensarlo mucho || *a penny for your thoughts* ¿en qué estás pensando? || FAM *a thought* un poquito; *he is a thought better* está un poquito mejor || *at the thought of* al pensar en || *don't give it a thought* no te preocupes por eso, no le des importancia || *his one thought is to earn money* su única idea es ganar dinero || *lost in thought* ensimismado, da || *my thoughts were elsewhere* estaba pensando en otra cosa || *on second thoughts* pensándolo bien || *our thoughts are with them* pensamos en ellos || *take thought for the morrow* piense en el día de mañana || *the mere thought of it* sólo el pensarlo || *to fall into deep thought* abstraerse, ensimismarse || *to give thought to* pensar en || *to have thoughts of doing sth.* tener la intención de hacer algo || *to take thought how to do sth.* pensar cómo hacer algo || *we wouldn't have given it another thought* no lo hubiéramos vuelto a pensar || *without a thought for* sin pensar en || *with the thought of* con la intención de, con la idea de.

thought [θɔːt] *pret/pp* ⟶ **think.**

thoughtful [-ful] *adj* pensativo, va; meditabundo, da (absorbed); *he was thoughtful a long time before he answered* se quedó pensativo mucho tiempo antes de contestar || serio, ria (serious); *a thoughtful book* un libro serio || cuidadoso, sa (mindful) || atento, ta; solícito, ta (considerate); *to be thoughtful of others* ser atento con los demás || *how thoughtful!* ¡qué detalle!

thoughtfully [-fuli] *adv* pensativamente, con aire pensativo *or* meditabundo || atentamente (with consideration).

thoughtfulness [-fulnis] *n* meditación *f* || seriedad *f* (seriousness) || atenciones *f pl*, solicitud *f* (consideration) || cuidado *m* (care).

thoughtless [-lis] *adj* irreflexivo, va; *a thoughtless action* una acción irreflexiva || desconsiderado, da; falto de consideración, poco atento, ta; *thoughtless of others* desconsiderado con los demás || descuidado, da (careless).

thoughtlessness [-lisnis] *n* irreflexión *f* || descuido *m* (carelessness) || desconsideración *f* (disregard).

thought-out [-'aut] *adj* bien pensado, da.

thought-read [-riːd] *vt* adivinar los pensamientos de.

thought reading [-'riːdiŋ] *n* adivinación *f* de los pensamientos.

thought transference [-'trænsfərəns] *n* telepatía *f*, transmisión *f* del pensamiento.

thousand ['θauzənd] *adj* mil; *a thousand men* mil hombres; *two thousand women* dos mil mujeres || *a thousand thanks* un millón de gracias, miles de gracias.
◆ *n* mil *m* || millar *m*; *they arrived in thousands o by the thousand* llegaban a millares || *thousands of* miles de, millares de.

thousandfold [-fəuld] *adj* multiplicado por mil.
◆ *adv* mil veces.

thousandth ['θauzəntθ] *adj* milésimo, ma.
◆ *n* milésima parte *f*, milésimo *m* (one of a thousand parts) || número *m* mil (in thousandth position); *she was the thousandth on the list* era el número mil de la lista.

Thrace [θreis] *pr n* GEOGR Tracia *f*.

Thracian ['θreisjən] *adj/n* tracio, cia.

thraldom ['θrɔːldəm] *n* esclavitud *f*.

thrall [θrɔːl] *n* esclavo, va (slave) || esclavitud *f* (slavery) || FIG *to hold in thrall* esclavizar.

thralldom [-dəm] *n* esclavitud *f*.

thrash [θræʃ] *n* movimiento *m* de piernas (swimming).

thrash [θræʃ] *vt* dar una paliza a, azotar a (to beat) || AGR trillar (to thresh) || FIG dar una paliza a (to defeat soundly) || — FIG *to thrash out* discutir a fondo (a matter), dar vueltas a (a question), descubrir (truth) | *to thrash over* machacar, estudiar a fondo.
◆ *vi* batir (waves) || SP mover las piernas (swimming) || *to thrash about* agitarse, revolverse.

thrashing [-iŋ] *n* paliza *f*, azotaina *f*; *I'll give you a thrashing* te voy a dar una paliza || AGR trilla *f* || FIG paliza *f* (a heavy defeat); *to give another team a thrashing* dar una paliza a otro equipo || AGR *thrashing floor* era *f*.

thrasonical [θrə'sɔnikəl] *adj* fanfarrón, ona; jactancioso, sa.

thread [θred] *n* hilo *m* (for sewing, for weaving, of a spider, of metal) || hebra *f* (of beans) || TECH rosca *f*, filete *m* (on a screw) || rayo *m* (of sun) || MIN filón *m*, veta *f* || FIG hilo *m* (of a conversation, life, story, etc.); *to lose the thread* perder el hilo || — *right hand, left hand thread* enroscado a la derecha, a la izquierda || FIG *to be hanging by a thread* estar pendiente de un hilo | *to gather up the threads* atar cabos.

thread [θred] *vt* ensartar, enhebrar (a needle) || ensartar (beads) || TECH roscar, filetear (screw) | aterrajar (a pipe) || pasar; *to thread an elastic through the hem of sth.* pasar una goma por el dobladillo de algo || PHOT cargar con (a film) || FIG entretejer; *hair threaded with silver* pelo entretejido de plata || *to thread one's way through* deslizarse por, colarse por.
◆ *vi* deslizarse, colarse (*through* por).

threadbare [-bɛə*] *adj* raído, da (cloth); *a threadbare suit* un traje raído || andrajoso, sa; desastrado, da (person) || FIG trillado, da (argument, opinion) | viejo, ja (joke) | flojo, ja (excuse).

thread counter [-'kauntə*] *n* cuentahilos *m inv.*

threader [-ə*] *n* TECH terraja *f*.

threadlike [-laik] *adj* filiforme.

thread mark [-mɑːk] *n* filigrana *f* (in banknotes).

thready [-di] *adj* fibroso, sa; filamentoso, sa || débil (voice, etc.).

threat [θret] *n* amenaza *f* || *there is a threat of rain* parece que va a llover.

threaten ['θretn] *vt/vi* amenazar; *he threatened me with a revolver* me amenazó con un revolver; *he threatened to kill me* amenazó (con) matarme; *race threatened with extinction* raza amenazada de desaparición || *it threatens to rain* parece que va a llover.

threatening ['θretniŋ] *adj* amenazador, ra; *threatening tone* tono amenazador.
◆ *n* amenazas *f pl*.

three ['θri] *adj* tres.
◆ *n* tres *m* (number, card, figure) || — *five past three* las tres y cinco || MATH *rule of three* regla *f* de tres || *the Big Three* los Tres Grandes || *three o'clock* las tres; *three o'clock in the afternoon* las tres de la tarde; *at three o'clock in the morning* a las tres de la mañana *or* de la madrugada; *it's three o'clock* son las tres.

three-act [-'ækt] *adj* de tres actos (play).

three-colour; *US* **three-color** [-'kʌlə*]; **three-coloured;** *US* **three-colored** [-'kʌləd] *adj* tricolor || PRINT tricromo, ma || *three-colour process* tricromía *f*.

three-cornered [-'kɔːnəd] *adj* triangular (having three angles) || *three-cornered hat* tricornio *m*, sombrero *m* de tres picos.

three-D [-dɑi] *adj* ⟶ **three-dimensional.**

three-day event [-deii'vent] *n* SP concurso *m* completo de equitación.

three-decker [-'dekə*] *n* MAR barco *m* de tres cubiertas || bocadillo *m* de tres pisos (sandwich).

three-dimensional [-dai'menʃənəl]; **three-D** [-dɑi] *adj* tridimensional.

three-engined [-'endʒind] *adj* trimotor.

threefold [-fəuld] *adj* triple; *a threefold rise* un aumento triple.
◆ *adv* tres veces; *to increase threefold* aumentar tres veces.

three hundred [-'hʌndrəd] *adj/n* trescientos, tas.

three hundredth [-'hʌndrətθ] *adj/n* tricentésimo, ma.

three-legged [-'legid] *adj* de tres patas *or* pies (stool, etc.).

three-master [-'mɑːstə*] *n* MAR barco *m* de tres palos.

threepence ['θrepəns] *n* tres peniques *m pl* (value) || moneda *f* de tres peniques (coin).

threepenny ['θrepəni] *adj* de tres peniques || FIG de tres al cuarto || *threepenny bit* moneda *f* de tres peniques.

three-phase ['θriːfeiz] *adj* trifásico, ca (current).

three-piece ['θriː'piːs] *adj* de tres piezas || *three-piece suite* tresillo *m* (furniture).
◆ *n* traje *m* de tres piezas.

three-ply ['θriːplai] *adj* contrachapado, da; contrachapeado, da (wood) || de tres hebras (rope) || de tres capas (of three layers).

three-point landing ['θriːpɔint'lændiŋ] *n* AVIAT aterrizaje *m* en tres puntos, aterrizaje *m* perfecto || FAM conclusión *f* brillante.

three-point turn ['θriːpoint'təːn] *n* maniobra *f* en L.

three-quarter ['θriː'kwɔːtə*] *adj* de tres cuartos; *a three-quarter coat* un abrigo de tres cuartos.
◆ *n* SP tres cuartos *m*.

threescore ['θriː'skɔː] *adj* sesenta.

three-sided ['θriːsaidid] *adj* trilátero, ra.

threesome ['θriːsəm] *n* grupo *m* de tres.

three-storied ['θriːstɔːrid] *adj* de tres pisos.

three-wheeler [θriːwiːlə*] *n* vehículo *m* de tres ruedas.

threnody ['θrenədi] *n* MUS treno *m*, canto *m* fúnebre.

thresh [θreʃ] *vt/vi* AGR trillar || FIG machacar.

thresher ['θreʃə*] *n* AGR trilladora *f*.

threshing ['θreʃiŋ] *n* AGR trilla *f*.

threshing floor [-flɔː*] *n* AGR era *f*.

threshing machine [-məʃiːn] *n* trilladora *f*.

threshold ['θreʃhəuld] *n* umbral *m* (of a door) || FIG umbral *m*; *to be on the threshold of life* estar en el umbral de la vida | puertas *f pl*; *we are at the threshold of a conflict* estamos a las puertas de un conflicto || *threshold visibility* visibilidad mínima.

threw [θruː] *pret* → **throw**.

thrice [θrais] *adv* tres veces.

thrift [θrift]; **thriftiness** [-inis] *n* economía *f*, ahorro *m*.

thriftless [-lis] *adj* gastoso, sa; despilfarrador, ra.

thriftlessness [-lisnis] *n* derroche *m*, despilfarro *m* (extravagance).

thrifty [-i] *adj* económico, ca; ahorrativo, va || US próspero, ra (thriving).

thrill [θril] *n* emoción *f* (excitement) || escalofrío *m*, estremecimiento *m* (quiver) || sensación *f* (sensation) || MED temblor *m*.

thrill [θril] *vt* estremecer (with horror, with pleasure) || emocionar, estremecer; *music that thrills one* música que emociona a uno || electrizar (an audience) || hacer mucha ilusión; *the idea of going to America thrills me* la idea de ir a América me hace mucha ilusión || *to be thrilled with horror* estremecerse de horror.
◆ *vi* estremecerse; *to thrill with fear* estremecerse de miedo || emocionarse.

thriller [-ə*] *n* novela *f or* película *f or* obra *f* de teatro escalofriante.

thrilling [-iŋ] *adj* emocionante; *it was a thrilling trip* fue un viaje emocionante || escalofriante (novel, film, play).

thrillingly [-iŋli] *adv* de manera emocionante.

thrive* [θraiv] *vi* crecer (child, plant); *plant that thrives in all soils* planta que crece en todos los terrenos || desarrollarse (to grow strong); *children thrive on good food* los niños se desarrollan con una buena alimentación || tener buena salud (to have good health) || FIG prosperar; *a business cannot thrive without good management* una empresa no puede prosperar sin una buena gestión | tener éxito (to be successful) | encantar; *he thrives on constructive criticism* le encantan las críticas constructivas.
— OBSERV Pret ***throve, thrived***; pp ***thriven, thrived***.

thriven ['θrivən] *pp* → **thrive.**

thriving ['θraiviŋ] *adj* lozano, na (plant, person) || FIG próspero, ra; floreciente.

throat [θrəut] *n* ANAT garganta *f*; *a fishbone has stuck in my throat* se me ha atragantado una espina en la garganta || cuello *m*; *to cut s.o.'s throat* cortarle el cuello a alguien || GEOGR paso *m*, desfiladero *m* || gollete *m*, cuello *m* (of a bottle) || TECH tragante *m* (of blast furnace) || ARCH goterón *m* || — *smell that catches one's throat* olor que se agarra a la garganta || MED *sore throat* dolor *m* de garganta || *the words stuck in my throat* no pude pronunciar una palabra || FIG *to be at each other's throat* andar a la greña || *to clear one's throat* aclararse la voz || FIG & FAM *to cut one's throat* labrar su propia ruina | *to jump down one's throat* echarle la bronca a uno | *to lie in one's throat* mentir desvergonzadamente | *to moisten one's throat* mojarse el gaznate | *to thrust sth. down s.o.'s throat* hacer tragar algo a alguien, meter a alguien algo por las narices || *whenever I hear that tune I get a lump in my throat* cada vez que oigo esta canción se me hace un nudo en la garganta.

throaty [-i] *adj* gutural.

throb [θrɔb] *n* latido *m*, palpitación *f* (of heart) || pulsación *f* (of pulse) || punzada *f* (of pain) || zumbido *m* (of engine) || FIG vibración *f* | estremecimiento *m* (of joy, etc.).

throb [θrɔb] *vi* latir, palpitar (heart) || latir (pulse) || dar punzadas (with pain); *my finger is throbbing* el dedo me da punzadas || zumbar (engine) || FIG estremecerse (with joy) | vibrar.

throbbing [-iŋ] *adj* palpitante (heart) || punzante (pain) || que zumba (engine) || FIG palpitante, vibrante || *throbbing centre of industry* centro *m* industrial que rebosa de actividad.
◆ *n* latido *m*, palpitación *f* (of heart) || pulsación *f* (of pulse) || punzadas *f pl* (of pain) || zumbido *m* (of engine) || FIG estremecimiento *m*.

throes [θrəuz] *pl n* dolores *m*; *throes of childbirth* dolores del parto || ansias *f*, angustias *f*; *throes of death* ansias de la muerte || FIG *the country was in the throes of a general election* el país estaba de lleno en las elecciones generales.

thrombin ['θrɔmbin] *n* trombina *f*.

thrombosis [θrɔm'bəusis] *n* MED trombosis *f inv*.

thrombus ['θrɔmbəs] *n* trombo *m*.
— OBSERV El plural de *thrombus* es *thrombi*.

throne [θxrəun] *n* trono *m*; *to come to the throne* subir al trono || *throne room* sala *f* del trono.
◆ *pl* tronos *m* (angels).

throne [θrəun] *vt* entronizar, elevar al trono.
◆ *vi* ocupar el trono.

throng [θrɔŋ] *n* multitud *f*, muchedumbre *f*, gentío *m* (crowd) || multitud *f* (large amount) || *they arrived in throngs* llegaron en tropel.

throng [θrɔŋ] *vt* atestar, llenar; *the shop was thronged with people* la tienda estaba atestada *or* llena de gente.
◆ *vi* afluir (to a place) || apiñarse, amontonarse; *they thronged round the speaker* se apiñaron alrededor del orador || llegar en tropel; *they thronged into the square* llegaron en tropel a la plaza.

thronging [-iŋ] *adj* apretado, da (crowd).

throstle ['θrɔsl] *n* zorzal *m*, tordo *m* (bird).

throttle ['θrɔtl] *n* FAM gaznate *m* (throat) || TECH válvula *f* de admisión (throttle valve) | acelerador *m* (for controlling the throttle valve) || — FAM *at full throttle* a todo gas || *to give it full throttle* acelerar a fondo.

throttle ['θrɔtl] *vt* estrangular, ahogar (s.o.) || TECH estrangular || FIG suprimir.
◆ *vi* asfixiarse, ahogarse.

through [θruː] *adj* directo, ta; *a through ticket* un billete directo; *through train* tren directo || que va hasta el término (passenger) || con preferencia de paso, con prioridad (a road, a street) || acabado, da (at the end of one's abilities); *he's through as a tennis player* está acabado como tenista || terminado, da; acabado, da; *when you are through with this* cuando haya terminado con esto || terminado, da; *he's through with her forever* ha terminado con ella para siempre || — *no through road* calle *f* sin salida || *through traffic* tránsito *m*.
◆ *adv* de parte a parte, de un lado a otro (from end to end) || enteramente, completamente; *wet through* completamente mojado || directamente; *this train goes through to London* este tren va directamente a Londres || hasta el final, desde el principio hasta el final; *to read a book through* leer un libro hasta el final || — *are you through?* ¿has aprobado? (in an exam) || *I'll be through with you in a second* termino con usted en seguida || *soaked through* calado hasta los huesos || *through and through* hasta la médula; *she is a gipsy through and through* es gitana hasta la médula; como la palma de la mano, de cabo a rabo; *he knows the town through and through* conoce la ciudad como la palma de la mano || *to carry sth. through* llevar algo a cabo || *to fall through* fracasar || *to let sth. through* dejar pasar algo || *would you put me through to?* póngame con (on the telephone) || *you are through!* ¡hablen! (on the telephone).
◆ *prep* a través de; *path through the fields* camino a través de los campos || por (via); *the Thames flows through London* el Támesis pasa por Londres; *to jump through the window* saltar por la ventana; *to send through the post* mandar por correo || durante; *to sleep through the storm* dormir durante la tormenta; *all through his life* durante toda su vida || entre; *the news spread through the crowd* la noticia se extendió entre la multitud || gracias a, por medio de, a través de (by means of); *I got the information through him* conseguí la información por medio de él || por, a causa de (by reason of); *it happened through no fault of mine* no ocurrió por culpa mía || US de... a, desde... hasta; *Monday through Friday* de lunes a viernes || — FIG *he's been through it* ha pasado por momentos muy malos || *to be through one's finals* haber aprobado los exámenes finales || *to go through* pasar por; *we went through Lima* pasamos por Lima; atravesar; *the arrow went right through him* la flecha lo atravesó.

throughout [θruː'aut] *adv* hasta el final; *to read a book throughout* leer un libro hasta el final || completamente; *to be wrong throughout* estar completamente equivocado || todo, da; por todas partes; *they decorated the house throughout* decoraron toda la casa || desde el

principio hasta el final; *the film is funny throughout* la película es divertida desde el principio hasta el final.
◆ *prep* por todo, en todo; *thoughout the country* por todo el país || durante todo; *throughout the year* durante todo el año || a lo largo de; *throughout the book* a lo largo del libro || *throughout the world* en el mundo entero.

throve [θrəuv] *pret* ⟶ **thrive.**

throw [θrəu] *n* lanzamiento *m*, tiro *m* (action of throwing) || lance *m* (of dice) || lanzado *m* (in fishing) || GEOGR dislocación *f* (in a strata) || TECH recorrido *m*, carrera *f*; *throw of the piston* carrera del émbolo || SP tumbado *m* (in wrestling) | lanzamiento *m* (of javelin, etc.) || *US* colcha *f* (ligh bedspread) || *at a stone's throw* a tiro de piedra.

throw* [θrəu] *vt* tirar, lanzar, arrojar; *he threw a stone at the dog* tiró una piedra al perro; *he threw the ball to me* me lanzó la pelota || lanzar; *to throw troops into battle* lanzar las tropas al combate || proyectar; *to throw light, shadows* proyectar luz, sombras || tender; *to throw a bridge over a river* tender un puente sobre un río || dar, asestar (a blow) || descartar (a card) || tirar, echar (dice) || sacar (at dice); *to throw a six* sacar seis || FIG echar; *to throw the blame on s.o.* echar la culpa a alguien; *to throw a glance* echar una mirada | hacer (a scene) | armar (a scandal) || FAM dar (a party) || TECH tornear, modelar en un torno (with a lathe) | torcer (silk) || SP derribar, tumbar (an opponent) | desmontar, derribar, desarzonar (a rider) | lanzar (javelin, disk, etc.) | hacer (hold in wrestling) || AUT poner (into a gear) || mudar; *a snake throws its skin* la serpiente muda la piel || producir, dar (a harvest) || parir (animals) || *US* perder adrede (a fight, etc.) | conectar (the lever of a machine, etc.) || — FIG *to be thrown upon* correr a cargo de | *to be thrown upon one's own resources* tener que valerse por sí solo | *to throw a fit* tener un ataque de nervios || *to throw a tale into verse* poner un cuento en verso || *to throw difficulties in s.o.'s way* ponerle obstáculos a alguien en el camino || *to throw light on a subject* arrojar luz sobre un asunto, aclarar un asunto || *to throw open the door* abrir la puerta de par en par || FIG *to throw o.s. at s.o.* o *at s.o.'s head* insinuarse || *to throw o.s. backwards* echarse hacia atrás || *to throw o.s. into* lanzarse en || *to throw o.s. on s.o.* echarse encima de alguien, abalanzarse sobre alguien || *to throw overboard* tirar por la borda || *to throw s.o. a kiss* tirar un beso a alguien || *to throw s.o. into confusion* desconcertar a alguien || *to throw s.o. into jail* meter a alguien en la cárcel || *to throw two rooms into one* reunir dos habitaciones.
◆ *vi* tirar, lanzar, arrojar || echar *or* tirar los dados (at dice).
◆ *phr v* ***to throw about*** esparcir, tirar; *to throw litter about* esparcir la basura | tirar, derrochar, despilfarrar (money) || — *to throw one's arms about* agitar mucho los brazos | *to throw o.s. about* moverse || ***to throw aside*** echar a un lado || ***to throw away*** tirar, arrojar; *he threw away his cigarette* tiró el cigarrillo; *throw these papers away* tira estos papeles | despilfarrar, malgastar (money) | desechar (to rid o.s. of) | MIL deponer (arms) | perder; *a kind action is never thrown away* una buena acción nunca está perdida | desaprovechar, desperdiciar (chance, opportunity) | ***to throw back*** reflejar (to reflect) | devolver (a ball) | rechazar (to reject) | echar hacia atrás; *he threw back his hat* echó su sombrero hacia atrás | retrasar; *this would throw me back two weeks* esto me retrasaría dos semanas | BIOL dar un salto atrás || ***to throw down*** tirar [de arriba abajo]; *they threw down stones on the besiegers* tiraban piedras sobre los sitiadores | tirar al suelo (to throw to the ground) | abatir (one's cards) | MIL deponer (arms) | derribar, echar abajo (building) | depositar (sediment) | lanzar (challenge) || — FIG *to throw down one's tools* declararse en huelga | arrojar el guante | *to throw o.s. down* tirarse al suelo || ***to throw in*** echar, tirar | dar de más, añadir (as an extra) | intercalar (to interject) | soltar (a quip) | sacar de banda (in football) || — *to throw in one's cards* tirar las cartas sobre la mesa | echar en cara a uno | *to throw in one's hand* tirar las cartas (at cards), renunciar (to renounce) | *to throw in one's lot with s.o.* compartir la suerte de alguien | *to throw in the clutch* embragar | FIG *to throw in the towel* tirar la esponja (in boxing), darse por vencido (to give up) || ***to throw off*** quitarse de encima (to get rid of) | quitarse (clothes) | quitarse de, renunciar a (a bad habit) | abandonar (disguise) | quitarse (mask) | despistar (to mislead); *to throw off one's pursuers* despistar a sus perseguidores | improvisar (a speech, a story, etc.) | soltar (remarks) | despedir (to emit) | desatraillar (hounds) | empezar (to start) || — *to throw a train off the rails* hacer descarrilar un tren | despistar los perros || ***to throw on*** ponerse rápidamente (one's clothes) | echarse encima (a coat) || ***to throw out*** expulsar, echar (to eject) | rechazar (to reject); *to throw out a bill* rechazar un proyecto de ley | despedir (heat, light, smell) | tirar (to throw away) | soltar (a suggestion) | sacar (one's chest) | echar (roots) | añadir (a new building) | hacer resaltar (to throw into relief) || MIL destacar || — FAM *to throw out on one's ear* poner de patitas en la calle | *to throw out the clutch* desembragar || ***to throw over*** abandonar, dejar (to abandon) | echar encima (a coat) || ***to throw together*** hacer sin cuidado (to assemble hastily) | reunir, unir (people) || ***to throw up*** lanzar al aire | levantar (to raise) | construir rápidamente (to build hastily) | dejar (a job) | renunciar a (claims) | devolver, arrojar, vomitar (to vomit) | arrojar; *thrown up by the sea* arrojado por el mar.
— OBSERV Pret ***threw***; pp ***thrown***.

throwaway ['θrəuəwei] *n* *US* prospecto *m* (handbill).
◆ *adj* para tirar (wrapping).

throwback ['θrəubæk] *n* BIOL salto *m* atrás, retroceso *m* || retroceso *m*.

thrower ['θrəuə*] *n* jugador, ra (of dice) || alfarero *m* (potter) || SP lanzador, ra.

throw-in ['θrəuin] *n* SP saque *m* de banda (in football).

thrown ['θrəun] *pp* ⟶ **throw.**

throw-out ['θrəuaut] *n* COMM desecho *m*, desperdicio *m* || ELECTR interruptor *m* automático || TECH desembrague *m* automático.

throwster ['θrəustə*] *n* torcedor, ra (of silk).

thru [θru:] *adv* *US* ⟶ **through.**

thrum [θrʌm] *n* cabo *m*.
◆ *pl* MAR cabos *m* cortos para hacer palletes.

thrum [θrʌm] *vt* tamborilear en (to drum on) || rasguear (a stringed instrument) || teclear en (a piano).
◆ *vi* tamborilear (with the fingers) || rasguear un instrumento de cuerda (on a stringed instrument) || teclear (on a piano).

thrush [θrʌʃ] *n* zorzal *m*, tordo *m* (bird) || MED afta *f* || VET arestín *m*.

thrust [θrʌst] *n* empujón *m* (push) || estocada *f* (stab) || ARCH & AVIAT empuje *m* || GEOL corrimiento *m*, deslizamiento *m* || MIL arremetida *f* || SP estocada *f* (in fencing) || pulla *f* (taunt) || *that was a thrust at you* esto iba por ti.

thrust* [θrʌst] *vt* empujar (to push with force) || clavar; *to thrust a dagger into s.o.'s side* clavar un puñal en el costado de alguien || meter; *to thrust one's hands into one's pockets* meter las manos en los bolsillos || poner; *he thrust the letter in front of me* me puso la carta delante || — *to be thrust into an unpleasant situation* meterse en una situación desagradable || *to thrust aside* o *away* rechazar || *to thrust back* hacer retroceder (people) || *to thrust down* bajar || *to thrust forward* empujar hacia adelante || FAM *to thrust one's nose into everything* meter las narices en todo || *to thrust one's way through the crowd* abrirse paso entre la multitud || FIG *to thrust o.s. forward* ponerse en evidencia | *to thrust o.s. upon* pegarse a; *she thrust herself upon us* se nos pegó || *to thrust out* sacar; *to thrust out one's head* sacar la cabeza; *to thrust out one's tongue* sacar la lengua; tender (hand), sacar (chest) || *to thrust sth. on s.o.* obligar a alguien a aceptar algo || *to thrust through* atravesar.
◆ *vi* dar un empujón, empujar (to make a sudden push) || abrirse paso; *he thrust through the crowd* se abrió paso entre la multitud || SP lanzar una estocada (in fencing) || — FIG *to thrust and parry* rivalizar en ingenio || *to thrust at* asestar un golpe a || *to thrust past s.o.* empujar a alguien para pasar.
— OBSERV Pret y pp ***thrust***.

thruster [-ə*] *n* FAM arribista *m* & *f*.

thruway ['θru:wei] *n* *US* autopista *f* de peaje.

thud [θʌd] *n* ruido *m* sordo.

thud [θʌd] *vt* *he thudded his fist down on the counter* dio un puñetazo fuerte en el mostrador || *he thudded the parcel down on the table* dejó caer pesadamente el paquete en la mesa.
◆ *vi* caer con un ruido sordo (to fall heavily) || — *the arrow thudded into the tree* la flecha se clavó en el árbol || *the guns thudded all around* se oía el disparo de los cañones alrededor || *to thud about* andar con pasos pesados.

thug [θʌg] *n* gamberro *m* (hooligan) || criminal *m* || secuaz *m* (hireling) || bruto *m* (brute).

thuggery ['θʌgəri] *n* gamberrismo *m* (hooliganism) || bandidaje *m* (crime).

thulium ['θju:liəm] *n* CHEM tulio *m*.

thumb [θʌm] *n* pulgar *m*, dedo *m* pulgar || — FAM *by rule of thumb* de modo empírico | *thumbs up!* ¡suerte! || FIG *to be all thumbs* ser un manazas | *to be thumbs down on* estar en contra de | *to be under s.o.'s thumb* estar dominado por alguien | *to twiddle one's thumbs* estar mano sobre mano.

thumb [θʌm] *vt* hojear; *to thumb the pages of a book* hojear las páginas de un libro || manosear; *a well-thumbed page* una página muy manoseada || tocar con el pulgar (to touch with the thumb) || — *to thumb a lift* o *a ride* hacer autostop, ir en autostop || *to thumb one's nose* hacer un palmo de narices || *to thumb through a book* hojear un libro.

thumb index [-indeks] *n* PRINT uñeros *m pl*.

thumbnail [-neil] *adj* minúsculo, la; pequeño, ña (small) || conciso, sa; breve (concise).
◆ *n* uña *f* del pulgar.

thumbnail sketch [-neilprint] *n* esquema *m*.

thumbprint [-print] *n* huella *f* digital *or* dactilar, huella *f* del pulgar.

thumbscrew [-scru:] *n* tornillo *m* de mariposa *or* de orejas (manual screw) || empulgueras *f pl* (instrument of torture).

thumbs-down [-z'daun] *n* señal *f* de desaprobación.

thumbstall [-stɔ:l] *n* dedil *m* [para el pulgar].

thumbs-up [-z'ʌp] *n* señal *f* de aprobación (approval) || luz *f* verde (go-ahead); *to give s.o. the thumbs-up* darle la luz verde a alguien.

thumbtack [-tæk] *n* chincheta *f*, chinche *f*.

thump [θʌmp] *n* porrazo *m* (heavy blow) || ruido *m* sordo (noise).

thump [θʌmp] *vt* golpear (to strike) || FAM dar una paliza a (to defeat heavily) || *to thump out a tune on the piano* tocar una melodía aporreando el piano.

◆ *vi* dar golpes (to hit out) ‖ latir con fuerza (the heart) ‖ *to thump about* andar pesadamente, andar haciendo mucho ruido.

thumping [-iŋ] *adj* FAM enorme, descomunal.

thunder ['θʌndə*] *n* trueno *m*; *thunder follows lightning* el trueno sigue al relámpago ‖ truenos *m pl*; *thunder and lightning* truenos y relámpagos ‖ FIG estruendo *m*, estrépito *m*, fragor *m*; *the thunder of the guns* el estruendo de los cañones | vociferaciones *f pl* (vehement rhetoric) ‖ — *clap of thunder* trueno, tronido *m* ‖ FIG *to seal s.o.'s thunder* quitarle el éxito a alguien.

thunder ['θʌndə*] *vi* tronar; *it is thundering* truena ‖ FIG tronar (to make a loud noise, to shout violently); *all around us cannons thundered* alrededor de nosotros tronaban los cañones; *to thunder against vice* tronar contra el vicio | retumbar (cannons, waterfall, etc.) ‖ — *to thunder into* caer *or* entrar con estruendo ‖ *to thunder past* pasar con un ruido infernal *or* estruendoso.

◆ *vt* vociferar (to utter loudly).

thunderbolt [-bəult] *n* rayo *m* (stroke of lightning) ‖ piedra *f* de rayo (imaginary missile that accompanies lightning) ‖ FIG bomba *f* (sth. destructive or surprising); *the news hit me like a thunderbolt* la noticia cayó como una bomba.

thunderclap [-klæp] *n* trueno *m*, tronido *m* ‖ FIG bomba *f* (sth. violent or shocking).

thundercloud [-klaud] *n* nube *f* de tormenta.

Thunderer [-ə*] *n* MYTH *the Thunderer* Júpiter *m* tonante.

thundering [-riŋ] *adj* estruendoso, sa; de trueno (very loud); *thundering voice* voz de trueno ‖ FAM enorme, tremendo, da (tremendous); *a thundering success* un éxito tremendo; *a thundering great hole* un agujero enorme | maldito, ta (damned).

thunderous [-rəs] *adj* estruendoso, sa; de trueno (noise, voice) ‖ ensordecedor, ra; atronador, ra (deafening); *thunderous applause* aplausos ensordecedores.

thunderstrom [-stɔːm] *n* tormenta *f*.

thunderstricken [-'strikən]; **thunderstruck** [-strʌk] *adj* atónito, ta; asombrado, da.

thundery [-ri] *adj* tormentoso, sa.

thurible ['θjuəribl] *n* incensario *m* (censer).

thurifer ['θjuərifə*] *n* REL turiferario *m* (incense bearer).

Thursday ['θəːrzdi] *n* jueves *m*; *on Thursday* el jueves; *next Thursday* el jueves que viene.

thus [ðʌs] *adv* así, de esta manera (in this way); *do it thus* hágalo así ‖ por eso, así que (for this reason); *he was not in and thus I could not speak to him* no estaba y por eso no pude hablar con él ‖ por ejemplo (as an example of sth. already said) ‖ — *thus far* hasta aquí ‖ *thus it is that* así es que.

thwack [θwæk] *n/vt* ⟶ **whack.**

thwart [θwɔːt] *adj* transversal.

◆ *adv* transversalmente, oblicuamente.

◆ *n* MAR bancada *f*.

thwart [θwɔːt] *vt* frustrar, desbaratar; *to thwart s.o.'s plans* frustrar los planes de alguien ‖ frustrar; *to thwart s.o.* frustrar a alguien.

thy [ðai] *poss adj* (ant) tu; *thy glory* tu gloria.

thyme [taim] *n* BOT tomillo *m* ‖ BOT *wild thyme* serpol *m*.

thymelaeaceous ['θiməli'eiʃəs] *adj* BOT timeleáceo, a.

thymus ['θaiməs] *n* ANAT timo *m*.

thyroid ['θairɔid] *adj* ANAT tiroideo, a ‖ — ANAT *thyroid cartilage* cartílago *m* tiroides | *thyroid gland* tiroides *f*, glándula *f* tiroides.

◆ *n* ANAT tiroides *f inv*.

thysanura ['θaisə'njuərə] *pl n* ZOOL tisanuros *m*.

thyself [ðai'self] *pron* (ant) te; *hast thou hurt thyself?* ¿te has hecho daño? ‖ ti, ti mismo; *for thyself* para ti ‖ tú mismo, tú mismo (emphatic).

ti [tiː] *n* MUS si *m*.

tiara [ti'ɑːrə] *n* tiara *f* (worn by the pope) ‖ diadema *f* (worn by women).

Tiber ['taibə*] *pr n* GEOGR Tíber *m*.

Tiberias [tai'biəriæs] *pr n* GEOGR Tiberíades.

Tiberius [tai'biəriəs] *pr n* HIST Tiberio *m*.

Tibet [ti'bet] *pr n* GEOGR el Tíbet *m*.

Tibetan [-ən] *adj/s* tibetano, na.

tibia ['tibiə] *n* ANAT tibia *f*.

— OBSERV El plural de la palabra inglesa *tibia* es *tibiae* o *tibias*.

Tibullus [ti'bʌləs] *pr n* HIST Tibulo *m*.

tic [tik] *n* tic *m*.

tick [tik] *n* tictac *m* (of a clock) ‖ marca *f*, señal *f* (mark) ‖ ZOOL garrapata *f* ‖ funda *f* de almohada *or* de colchón (case for mattress, for pillow) ‖ FAM crédito *m*; *to buy on tick* comprar a crédito | momento *m* (short time); *just a tick!* ¡un momento! ‖ FAM *I am coming in a tick* en seguida voy.

tick [tik] *vt* marcar [con una señal] (to mark) ‖ — *to tick off* reprender (to tell off), marcar; *to tick off the names of those present* marcar los nombres de los que están presentes ‖ *to tick out* registrar (a telegraph).

◆ *vi* hacer tictac (a clock) ‖ — *I could hear the bomb ticking* oía el tictac de la bomba ‖ *to tick away* pasar, transcurrir (time) ‖ *to tick over* funcionar al ralentí *or* a marcha lenta (engine).

ticker ['tikə] *n* teletipo *m* ‖ FAM reloj *m* (watch) | corazón *m* (heart) ‖ *ticker tape* cinta perforada.

ticket ['tikit] *n* etiqueta *f* (showing price, material, etc., of an article) ‖ billete *m* [AMER boleto *m*, boleta *f*] (for transport); *train ticket* billete de tren ‖ entrada *f* [AMER boleto *m*, boleta *f*] (for meetings, concerts, shows, etc.) ‖ pase *m* (permit) ‖ cupón *m* (of ration book) ‖ vale *m*; *meal ticket* vale de comida ‖ título *m* (licence); *pilot's ticket* título de piloto ‖ multa *f* (fine); *parking ticket* multa por aparcamiento indebido ‖ US candidatura *f* (candidates) | programa *m* (programme) | pasaporte *m*; *a good personality is a ticket to success* una gran personalidad es un pasaporte para el éxito ‖ — *cloakroom ticket* número *m* del guardarropa ‖ *complimentary ticket* billete *or* entrada de favor ‖ *platform ticket* billete de andén ‖ *return ticket* billete de ida y vuelta ‖ *single ticket* billete de ida, billete simple ‖ FIG *that's the ticket!* ¡está muy bien! ‖ *ticket agency* agencia *f* de venta de localidades *or* de billetes [AMER boletería *f*] ‖ *ticket agent* vendedor *m* de billetes ‖ *ticket collector* o *inspector* revisor *m* ‖ *ticket holder* poseedor *m* de billete *or* de entrada ‖ *ticket office* taquilla *f* [AMER boletería *f*] ‖ *ticket pinch* máquina *f* de picar billetes ‖ *ticket window* taquilla *f* [AMER boletería *f*].

ticket ['tikit] *vt* poner etiquetas, etiquetar (with prices, etc.) ‖ US vender billetes a.

ticket of leave [-əv'liːv] *n* libertad *f* condicional ‖ *ticket-of-leave man* hombre *m* en libertad condicional.

ticking ['tikiŋ] *n* terliz *m* (cotton material).

ticking off [-'ɔf] *n* reprimenda *f*, bronca *f*.

tickle ['tikl] *n* cosquilleo *m* ‖ picor *m* (in the throat) ‖ FIG *I didn't get a tickle* no picó nadie.

tickle [tikl] *vt* hacer cosquillas a; *to tickle s.o.'s foot* hacer cosquillas a alguien en el pie ‖ picar; *this shirt tickles me* esta camisa me pica ‖ FIG divertir (to amuse) | picar (one's curiosity) | regalar; *to tickle one's palate* regalar el paladar a uno ‖ coger con las manos (trout, etc.) ‖ FIG *to tickle (s.o.) pink* encantar, gustar mucho; *he was tickled pink by the present* le encantó el regalo; divertir mucho, hacer mucha gracia a (to amuse intensely).

◆ *vi* sentir cosquillas ‖ picar; *woolen clothes tickle* la ropa de lana pica ‖ *my hand tickles* siento cosquillas en la mano.

tickler ['tiklə*] *n* problema *m* difícil (poser) ‖ US agenda *f*, diario *m* (notebook).

tickling ['tikliŋ] *n* cosquilleo *m*, cosquillas *f pl*.

ticklish ['tikliʃ] *adj* cosquilloso, sa (sensitive to tickling) ‖ FIG delicado, da; espinoso, sa; peliagudo, da; *a ticklish situation* una situación delicada | picajoso, sa (irritable) ‖ *to be ticklish* tener cosquillas, ser cosquilloso, sa.

ticktacktoe [tik'tæk'təu]; **tit-tat-toe** [,ti,tæ'təu] *n* US tres en raya *m* (noughts-and-crosses).

ticktock ['tik'tɔk] *n* tictac *m*.

tidal ['taide] *adj* de la marea ‖ mareomotor, mareomotriz (activated by tides); *tidal power station* central mareomotriz ‖ — *tidal flood* maremoto *m* ‖ *tidal wave* maremoto *m*, marejada *f*, mar *m* de fondo (caused by an earthquake), mar *m* de fondo, marejada *f* (of indignation).

tidbit ['tidbit] *n* ⟶ **titbit.**

tiddler ['tidlə*] *n* FAM pececillo *m*.

tiddly ['tidli] *adj* FAM achispado, da; piripi (tipsy) | diminuto, ta; pequeñito, ta (titchy).

tiddlywinks ['tidliwiŋks] *n* pulga *f* (game).

tide [taid] *n* MAR marea *f*; *when the tide comes in* cuando sube la marea; *rising tide* marea creciente; *spring tide* marea viva ‖ FIG corriente *f*; *the tide of public opinion* la corriente de la opinión pública; *to go along with the tide* seguir la corriente ‖ — MAR *ebb* o *low tide* bajamar *f*, marea baja *or* menguante | *high* o *full* o *flood tide* pleamar *f*, marea alta ‖ FIG *high tide* apogeo *m* (high point) ‖ MAR *incoming tide* marea entrante *or* ascendente | *outgoing tide* marea saliente *or* descendente *or* menguante ‖ FIG *the tide has turned* han cambiado las cosas | *the tide of events* el curso de los acontecimientos | *time and tide wait for no man* la misma ocasión no se presenta dos veces | *to turn the tide of the war* cambiar el rumbo de la guerra.

tide [taid] *vt* arrastrar con la marea ‖ FIG *to tide over* sacar de apuro.

◆ *vi* crecer [la marea] ‖ navegar con la marea ‖ MAR *to tide in, out* entrar, salir con la marea.

tide gate [-geit] *n* compuerta *f*.

tideland [-lænd] *n* terreno *m* que se inunda con las mareas altas, marisma *f*.

tideless [-lis] *adj* sin mareas.

tidemark [-mɑːk] *n* línea *f* de la marea alta.

tide rip [-rip] *n* remolino *m* de la marea.

tidewater [-'wɔːtə*] *n* agua *f* de marea ‖ US tierras *f pl* bajas del litoral.

tideway [-wei] *n* canal *m* de marea.

tidily [-ili] *adv* bien; *tidily dressed* bien vestido ‖ *everything was tidily arranged* todo estaba perfectamente ordenado, todo estaba en su sitio.

tidiness [-inis] *n* orden *m* (orderliness) ‖ aseo *m*, limpieza *f*, pulcritud *f* (cleanliness).

tidings [-iŋz] *pl n* noticias *f*.

tidy ['taidi] *adj* ordenado, da; en orden; *the house was very tidy* la casa estaba muy ordenada; *tidy person* persona ordenada ‖ arreglado, da (in appearance); *tidy hair* pelo arreglado ‖ limpio, pia (clean); *the streets are tidier here than in London* aquí las calles están más limpias que en Londres ‖ FIG & FAM grande, bueno, na; *a tidy sum* una buena cantidad | ligero, ra; rápido, da; bueno, na (pace) | claro, ra; *tidy mind* espíritu claro, ideas claras || *it cost him a tidy penny* le costó bastante caro.

tidy ['taidi] *vt* ordenar, poner en orden; *to tidy one's room* ordenar la habitación de uno || limpiar (to clean) || — *to tidy away* quitar (dishes), poner en su sitio (to put back) || *to tidy o.s. up* arreglarse.
◆ *vi* *to tidy up* ordenar; *I always have to tidy up after you* siempre tengo que ir ordenando detrás de ti; limpiar (to clean up).

tie [tai] *n* corbata *f* (necktie); *tie knot* nudo de corbata || cuerda *f*, atadura *f* (cord) || MUS ligado *m* || ARCH tirante *m* || SP empate *m* (draw) | partido *m* (match); *cup tie* partido de copa || FIG lazo *m*, vínculo *m* (bond); *the ties of friendship* los lazos de la amistad | atadura *f*; *I don't like the ties of family life, of marriage* no me gustan las ataduras de la vida familiar, del matrimonio || US traviesa *f* (railway sleeper) || — *black tie* corbata negra de lazo (tie), traje *m* de etiqueta (dinner jacket) || FIG *children are a tie* los niños atan a uno || SP *tie breaker* saque *m* para desempatar (in tennis) | *to play off a tie* desempatar || *white tie* corbatín blanco (bow tie), frac *m* (formal evening dress).

tie [tai] *vt* atar; *tie the dog!* ¡ata al perro! || atar, liar (a package, etc.) || hacer; *to tie a knot* hacer un nudo || hacer un nudo a (a ribbon) || FIG atar; *tied by one's responsibilities* atado por sus obligaciones; *we are tied by previous contract* estamos atados por un contrato previo | vincular, ligar (to link); *the two facts are tied together* los dos hechos están vinculados | limitar, restringir || SP empatar (a match) || MUS ligar || — FIG *our hands are tied* tenemos atadas las manos, estamos atados de manos | *to be tied hand and foot* estar atado de pies y manos | *to be tied to one's bed* verse obligado a guardar cama | *to be tied to one's mother's apron strings* estar agarrado a las faldas de su madre || FAM *to tie the knot* echar las bendiciones (priest).
◆ *vi* atarse; *it ties easily* se ata con facilidad || SP empatar (to draw); *we tied 2-all* empatamos a dos.
◆ *phr v* *to tie down* atar, sujetar; *they tied him down to the bed* le ataron a la cama | someter a ciertas condiciones (capital) | FIG atar; *tied down by children* atado por los niños; *it's a promise which ties you down for the rest of your life* es una promesa que te ata para toda la vida | tener amarrado; *to tie s.o. down to a contract* tener amarrado a alguien por un contrato || *to tie in* unir (to integrate) | concordar (to be in agreement) || — *to tie in with* relacionar con; relacionarse con || *to tie into* arremeter (to rush) | regañar (to reprimand) || *to tie off* atar || *to tie together* atar || *to tie up* atar (to fasten) | obstruir, bloquear (traffic) | amarrar (a boat) | concluir; *to tie up a deal* concluir un negocio | COMM invertir (to invest) | inmovilizar (capital) | paralizar || FIG *I am tied up at the moment* estoy ocupado por el momento.

tie beam ['taibiːm] *n* ARCH tirante *m*.

tied cottage ['taid,kɔtidʒ] *n* vivienda *f* que un agricultor alquila a uno de sus braceros.

tie-in ['taiin] *n* relación *f* (connection).

tieless ['tailis] *adj* sin corbata.

tiepin ['taipin] *n* alfiler *m* de corbata.

tier [tiə*] *n* grada *f*; *seats arranged in tiers* asientos dispuestos en gradas || fila *f*, hilera *f* (row) || piso *m* (of a wedding cake).

tier [tiə*] *vt* disponer en gradas (auditorium) || poner en filas || *a tiered cake* un pastel de varios pisos.

tierce ['tiəs] *n* tercera *f*, tercia *f* (in card games) || tercera *f* (in fencing) || REL tercia *f*.

tierceron ['tiərsərən] *n* ARCH arco *m* tercelete.

Tierra del Fuego [ti,erədel'fweigəu] *pr n* GEOGR Tierra del Fuego.

tie-up ['taiʌp] *n* relación *f*, conexión *f*, enlace *m* (connection) || US paralización *f* (paralysis, stoppage) || *traffic tie-up* embotellamiento *m*, atasco *m*.

tiff [tif] *n* riña *f*, pelea *f* (quarrel) || *to have a tiff* reñir.

tiffany ['tifəni] *n* gasa *f* (material).

tiffin ['tifin] *n* comida *f*, almuerzo *m*.

tiger ['taigə*] *n* ZOOL tigre *m* || FIG & FAM fiera *f*, tigre *m* (aggresive person) || (ant) lacayo *m* (groom).

tiger cat [-kæt] *n* ZOOL ocelote *m* [AMER tigrillo *m*].

tigereye ['taigər,ai] *n* MIN ojo *m* de gato.

tigerish [-iʃ] *adj* de tigre; atigrado, da (like a tiger) || FIG feroz (ferocious).

tiger's-eye ['taigərz,ai] *n* MIN ojo *m* de gato.

tight [tait] *adj* apretado, da (nut, knot, etc.) || ajustado, da; ceñido, da (clothes) || apretado, da; estrecho, cha; pequeño, ña (fitting too closely) || apretado, da (embrace, hug) || estricto, ta; *tight control* control estricto || estrecho, cha (watch) || tirante (taut) || hermético, ca (shut, sealed) || cerrado, da (a bend) || FIG difícil (situation) | conciso, sa (style) | bien formado, da (comely) | COMM escaso, sa (money, goods) || FAM agarrado, da; tacaño, ña (mean) | borracho, cha (drunk) || callado, da (silent) || SP reñido, da (match) | cerrado, da (defence) || PRINT apretado, da || MAR estanco, ca (boat) || — *it's a tight fit* queda muy justo || FAM *to be in a tight spot* o *corner* estar en un aprieto *or* apuro || *to keep a tight hand* o *a tight hold over* controlar rigurosamente (to control strictly), ser muy severo con (people).
◆ *adv* bien; *shut tight* bien cerrado; *pull it tight* tira bien; *to screw a nut on tight* apretar bien una tuerca || herméticamente (sealed) || — *hold tight!* ¡agárrense bien! || *to hold sth. tight* agarrar algo fuertemente || FIG *to sit tight* cruzarse de brazos (to sit idle), estarse quieto (to keep still), mantenerse en su posición (not to submit).

tighten [-ən] *vt* apretar (a screw, a knot, etc.) || tensar (a rope, a string, etc.) || hacer estricto *or* riguroso, estrechar (control) || estrechar (bonds) || FIG *to tighten one's belt* apretarse el cinturón.
◆ *vi* apretarse (a screw, a knot, etc.) || tensarse (a rope, a string, etc.) || volverse más estricto *or* riguroso (control).

tightener [-ənə*] *n* TECH tensor *m*.

tightfisted [-'fistid] *adj* FAM agarrado, da; tacaño, ña; roñoso, sa (mean).

tight-fitting [-'fitiŋ] *adj* ceñido, da; ajustado, da.

tight-knit [-'nit] *adj* muy unido, da.

tight-lipped [-'lipt] *adj* con los labios apretados || FIG callado, da (silent).

tightly [-li] *adv* ⟶ **tight**.

tightness [-nis] *n* estrechez *f* (of clothing, of shoes, etc.) || tensión *f* (tension) || tirantez *f* (tautness) || lo apretado (of a screw) || FAM lo agarrado, tacañería *f*, roñosería *f* (meanness).

tightrope [-rəup] *n* cuerda *f* floja || *tightrope walker* funámbulo, la; equilibrista *m* & *f* || FIG *to be on* o *walking a tightrope* estar en la cuerda floja.

tights [-s] *pl n* leotardos *m* (women's wear) || mallas *f* (for actors, for dancers, etc.).

tightwad [-wɔd] *n* US FAM roñoso, sa; tacaño, ña; agarrado, da.

tigress ['taigris] *n* ZOOL tigre *m* hembra, tigresa *f* || FIG fiera *f* (ferocious woman).
— OBSERV The Spanish word *tigresa* is a Gallicism.

Tigris ['taigris] *pr n* GEOGR Tigris *m*.

tike [taik] *n* chucho *m* (dog) || niño *m* travieso (mischievous child) || pillo, lla; pícaro, ra (rascal).

tilbury ['tilbəri] *n* tílburi *m*.

tilde [tild] *n* tilde *f*.

tile [tail] *n* teja *f* (of a roof); *plain* o *flat tile* teja plana; *ridge tile* teja de cumbrera || baldosa *f* (on a floor) || azulejo *m* (coloured) || tubo *m* de desagüe (drainpipe) || FIG & FAM sombrero *m* de copa (top hat) || — FIG & FAM *to have a night on the tiles* pasar la noche fuera *or* de juerga | *to have a tile loose* faltarle a uno un tornillo, estar chalado, da.

tile [tail] *vt* tejar, poner tejas en (a roof) || embaldosar (a floor) || poner azulejos en, azulejar (with coloured tiles).

tiler [-ə*] *n* techador *m* (of roofs) || solador *m* (of floors) || tejero *m* (who makes tiles).

tiliaceae [tili'eisii] *pl n* BOT tiliáceas *f*.

tiling [tailiŋ] *n* colocación *f* de las tejas (on a roof) || embaldosado *m* (of a floor) || tejas *f pl* (roof tiles) || baldosas *f pl* (floor tiles) || azulejos *m pl* (wall tiles).

till [til] *prep* hasta; *he waited till ten o'clock* esperó hasta las diez.
◆ *conj* hasta que; *wait till he comes* espera hasta que venga.
◆ *n* caja *f* (cash register, money drawer and contents) || GEOL morrena *f*, morena *f*.
— OBSERV Las palabras *till* y *until* empleadas como preposición o conjunción son casi siempre intercambiables (véase UNTIL).

till [til] *vt* AGR labrar, cultivar.

tillable ['tiləbl] *adj* arable, cultivable.

tillage ['tilidʒ] *n* AGR labranza *f*, cultivo *m*.

tiller ['tilə*] *n* AGR labrador *m* || MAR caña *f* del timón || BOT retoño *m*, vástago *m* (shoot).

tilt [tilt] *n* toldo *m* (canvas cover) || inclinación *f* (slant) || justa *f*, torneo *m* (joust) || TECH martinete *m* de forja || — FIG *(at) full tilt* a toda mecha, a toda velocidad || *to be on a tilt* estar ladeado *or* inclinado || FIG *to have a tilt at s.o.* arremeter contra alguien | *to run full tilt into sth.* dar de lleno contra algo.

tilt [tilt] *vt* inclinar, ladear || arremeter contra (to charge) || TECH forjar (metal) || entoldar (with a canvas cover).
◆ *vi* inclinarse, ladearse (to slant) || participar en una justa *or* en un torneo (to joust) || *to tilt at* arremeter contra; *to tilt at windmills* arremeter contra los molinos de viento.

tilter ['tiltə*] *n* justador *m*, torneador *m*.

tilth [tilθ] *n* labranza *f*, cultivo *m* (cultivation) || tierra *f* cultivada *or* labrada (cultivated land).

tilt hammer ['tilt'hæmə*] *n* TECH martinete *m* de forja.

tiltyard ['tiltjɑːd] *n* palestra *f*.

timbal ['timbəl] *n* timbal *m*, atabal *m* (kettledrum).

timbale [tæm'bɑːl] *n* CULIN timbal *m*.

timber ['timbə*] *n* madera *f* [de construcción] (wood) || árboles *m pl* maderables *or* para madera (trees) || viga *f* (beam) || MAR cuaderna *f* || FIG madera *f* (character) || US bosque *m*.

timbered [-d] *adj* enmaderado, da (ceiling, wall) || entibado, da (a mine) || arbolado, da (land).

timber hitch [-hitʃ] *n* MAR vuelta *f* de braza.

timbering [-riŋ] *n* entibado *m*, entibación *f* (of a mine) || maderaje *m*, maderamen *m* (of any construction).

timberland [-lænd] *n* bosque *m* maderable.

timberline [-lain] *n* límite *m* de la vegetación arbórea.

timberman [-,mæn] *n* entibador *m*.

— OBSERV El plural es *timbermen.*

timber merchant [-'mə:tʃənt] *n* negociante *m* en madera.

timber wolf [-wulf] *n* ZOOL lobo *m* gris norteamericano.

timberwork [-wə:k] *n* maderaje *m,* maderamen *m.*

timbre ['tɛ̃mbr] *n* MUS & HERALD timbre *m.*

timbrel ['timbrəl] *n* pandereta *f.*

time [taim] *n* tiempo *m; I have no time to do it* no tengo tiempo para hacerlo; *it lasts a long time* dura mucho tiempo; *time is an important factor* el tiempo es un factor importante; *he spends his time reading* se pasa el tiempo leyendo || momento *m; he was not at home at that time* no estaba en casa en aquel momento || tiempos *m pl,* época *f; at the time of the Persian supremacy* en la época de la supremacía persa; *in my time* en mis tiempos; *in biblical times* en tiempo bíblicos || período *m,* periodo *m* (period) || época *f; during harvest time* durante la época de la cosecha || estación *f,* temporada *f; spring is the nicest time of year* la primavera es la estación más agradable del año || hora *f; time of departure* hora de salida; *lunch time* la hora del almuerzo; *it is time we went* era hora de que nos fuéramos; *it is time to go* es hora de que nos vayamos; *what time is it?, what is the time?* ¿qué hora es?; *have you got the time?* ¿tiene usted hora? || momento *m,* ocasión *f,* oportunidad *f; it is the time to buy* es la ocasión para comprar; *some other* o *another time* en otra ocasión, en otro momento || vez *f; that is the third time* es la tercera vez; *four times running* cuatro veces seguidas; *five times bigger* cinco veces mayor; *another time* otra vez || temporada *f; he is going to Paris for a short time* se va a pasar una temporada en París || rato *m,* tiempo *m; he woke up a short time after going to sleep* se despertó al poco rato de haberse dormido || plazo *m; within the required time* dentro del plazo fijado || servicio *m; he served his time in the Navy* hizo el servicio en la Marina || condena *f; he served his time in prison* cumplió la condena en la cárcel || vida *f* (lifetime) || horas *f pl* de trabajo (hours of work) || ASTR tiempo *m; true time* tiempo verdadero || MUS duración *f* (the length of a note) | compás *m* (rhythm, tempo); *4/8 time* compás de cuatro por ocho; *in time to the music* al compás de la música; *to beat time* llevar el compás; *to keep time* seguir el compás || SP final *m* (end of a match) | tiempo *m; his time was five seconds* hizo un tiempo de cinco segundos || — *against time* contra reloj; *race against time* carrera contra reloj || *all in good time* a su debido tiempo (in due time), luego (later) || *all the time* todo el tiempo; *I was listening all the time* estuve escuchando todo el tiempo; siempre, constantemente; *he says it all the time* lo dice siempre || *a long time ago* hace mucho tiempo || *a long time since* hace mucho tiempo (from now), hacía mucho tiempo (from then) || *a man of the times* un hombre de su época *or* de su tiempo || *any time* cuando quiera || *as time passes* o *goes by* andando el tiempo, con el tiempo || *at all times* en todo momento || *at any time* en cualquier momento; *he is likely to come at any time* puede llegar en cualquier momento; cuando quiera; *come at any time* ven cuando quieras || *at a time* a la vez, al mismo tiempo; *he works in six places at a time* trabaja en seis sitios a la vez; entero, ra; *for hours at a time* durante horas enteras || *at his time in life* con los años que tiene, a su edad || *at no time* nunca || *at one time* en cierta época, en un tiempo || *at some time or other* en un momento o en otro || *at the present time* actualmente || *at the same time* a la vez, al mismo tiempo; *I can wash six plates at the same time* puedo lavar seis platos a la vez; *I like it but at the same time it frightens me* me gusta pero al mismo tiempo me da miedo || *at the wrong time* en un mal momento || *at this time of day* en este momento, a estas alturas || *at times* a veces || *behind the times* anticuado, da; *my father is behind the times* mi padre es anticuado; atrasado de noticias (not well-informed) || *between times* en el intervalo || *by that time* para entonces; *by that time he had already gone* para entonces ya se había ido || *by the time we arrived he had already gone* cuando llegamos ya se había ido || *by this time next month* el mes que viene por estas fechas || *civil* o *standard* o *official time* hora legal *or* oficial || *each* o *every time* cada vez || *Father Time* el Tiempo || *for all time* para siempre || *for the first, for the last time* por primera vez, por última vez || *for the time being* de momento, por ahora || *four times three is twelve* cuatro por tres son doce || *from that time onwards* desde entonces || *from this time* a partir de ahora || *from time immemorial* desde tiempo inmemorial || *from time to time* de vez en cuando || *give it time* da tiempo al tiempo || *Greenwich mean time* hora según el meridiano de Greenwich || *have a good time!* ¡que lo pases bien!, ¡que lo paséis bien! || FIG *he wouldn't even give you the time of day* no da ni la hora (very stingy) || *his time had come* su hora había llegado || *his time was drawing near* se acercaba su hora || *how time flies!* ¡cómo pasa el tiempo! || *in due time* a su debido tiempo || *in five minutes' time* dentro de cinco minutos || *in former* o *in older times* en otros tiempos, en tiempos pasados *or* antiguos || *in good time* a tiempo (in time), a su debido tiempo (at the proper time), rápidamente (quickly) || *in no time (at all)* en un abrir y cerrar de ojos || *in one's own good time* cuando uno quiera, cuando le parezca bien a uno; *I'll do it in my own good time* lo haré cuando quiera || *in one's spare* o *free time* en el tiempo libre || *in the course of time* andando el tiempo, con el tiempo || FIG *in the nick of time* en el momento preciso *or* oportuno, a punto (at the right moment), justo a tiempo (just in time) || *in time* a tiempo; *were you in time for the train?* ¿llegaste a tiempo para coger el tren?; con el tiempo (with time); *we shall succeed in time* con el tiempo lo conseguiremos; con ritmo, al compás (in music) || *it is about time too!, and about time too!* ¡ya era hora! || *it is a long time since I saw him* hace mucho tiempo que no lo veo || *it is high time that* ya es hora de que; *it's high time you learnt the lesson* ya es hora de que aprendas la lección || *it takes time* toma *or* requiere tiempo || *many a time, many times* muchas veces || *near her time* a punto de dar a luz (a pregnant woman) || *on* o *in one's own time* fuera de las horas de trabajo || *on* o *in the firm's time* en las horas de trabajo || *on time* a la hora, puntualmente, a tiempo (in time), a plazos (on hire purchase) || MUS *out of time* fuera de compás || *overtime counts time and a half* cada hora extraordinaria cuenta como una hora y media || *right on time* a la hora en punto || *some time ago* hace algún tiempo || *there is a time and place for everything* cada cosa a su tiempo || *there is no time to lose* no hay tiempo que perder || *third time lucky* a la tercera va la vencida || *this time last year* el año pasado por estas fechas || *time after time, time and time again* repetidas veces, una y otra vez || *time and a half* la mitad más (rate of payment) || *time and tide wait for no man* la misma ocasión no se presenta dos veces || *time and words can never be recalled* lo dicho, dicho está || *time, gentlemen, please!* ¡caballeros, es la hora! || *time is money* el tiempo es oro || *time is on our side* el tiempo obra en nuestro favor || *time off* tiempo libre, horas libres || *times are hard* los tiempos son duros *or* difíciles || *time's up!* ¡es la hora! || *time will tell* el tiempo dirá || *to be ahead of one's time* estar por delante de su tiempo *or* época || *to be before one's time* no ser de la época de uno; *this song is before my time* esta canción no es de mi época || *to be behind time* llevar retraso; *we are an hour behind time* llevamos una hora de retraso || *to be in step with the times* ser de su tiempo || *to be on* o *to work short time* hacer jornada reducida || *to gain time* ganar tiempo; *they took a shortcut to gain time* cogieron un atajo para ganar tiempo; adelantar (a clock) || *to have a bad* o *a rough time* pasarlo mal || *to have a good time* pasarlo bien, divertirse || FAM *to have done time* haber cumplido su condena, haber estado a la sombra || FIG *to have no time for* no tener tiempo que perder con, no tener tiempo para || *to have the time of one's life, to have a whale of a time* pasarlo bomba, pasarlo en grande || *to have time on one's hands* o *time to kill* tener tiempo de sobra || *to keep bad time* andar mal (clock) || *to keep good time* andar bien (clock) || *to keep up with* o *abreast of the times* ser muy de su época || *to kill time* matar el tiempo || *to lose no time in* no tardar en || *to lose time* perder tiempo (s.o.), atrasarse (clock) || *to make good time* ganar tiempo || *to make time* ganar tiempo || *to mark time* marcar el paso (in a military march), no avanzar nada, estancarse (to stagnate), hacer tiempo (waiting) || *to pass the time* pasar el tiempo *or* el rato || FAM *to pass the time of day* charlar un rato || *to play for time* ganar tiempo || *to serve one's time* estar de aprendiz || MUS *to sing, to dance, to play in time* llevar el compás || *to take a long time to* tardar mucho (tiempo) en || *to take one's time* tomarse el tiempo [necesario] (to use the time available), hacer las cosas con calma, no apresurarse (not to hurry), tardar mucho tiempo (to be very slow) || *to waste time* perder el tiempo || *until such time as you comply* hasta que usted obedezca || *what a time we had!* ¡qué bien lo pasamos! || *what is the cooking time for an egg?* ¿cuánto tiempo tarda un huevo en cocerse? || *when my time comes* cuando llegue mi hora.

◆ *adj* del tiempo || a plazos (payment, etc.) || a plazo (deposit, draft).

time [taim] *vt* calcular, fijar la hora de; *he timed his arrival for nightfall* calculó su llegada para el anochecer || calcular el tiempo de (to evaluate the time) || cronometrar (a race, a runner, etc.) || regular (to set, to regulate); *the bomb is timed to explode in five minutes* la bomba está regulada para que explote dentro de cinco minutos || — *he timed his speech to last twenty minutes* calculó su discurso para que durara veinte minutos || *the queen's arrival was timed for one o'clock* la llegada de la reina estaba prevista para la una || *you timed your arrival just right* has llegado en el momento oportuno.

time and motion ['taimən,məuʃən] *adj time and motion study* estudio *m* de desplazamientos y tiempos.

time bomb [-bɔm] *n* MIL bomba *f* de efecto retardado *or* con mecanismo de relojería.

time card [-kɑ:d] *n* tarjeta *f* [para registrar la entrada y salida del trabajo].

time clock [-klɔk] *n* reloj *m* registrador.

time-consuming [-kən'sju:miŋ] *adj* que requiere mucho tiempo.

timed [-d] *adj* calculado, da || SP cronometrado, da || *a well-timed intervention* una intervención oportuna.

time exposure [-iks'pəuʒə*] *n* PHOT exposición *f,* pose *f.*

time fuse [-fju:z] *n* MIL espoleta *f* con mecanismo de relojería.

time-honoured; *US* **time-honored** [-'ɔnəd] *adj* tradicional, consagrado, da; *a time-honored custom* una costumbre consagrada.

timekeeper [-'ki:pə*] *n* cronómetro *m* (watch, clock) || cronometrador *m* (person).

timekeeping [-'ki:piŋ] *n* control *m* de entrada y salida del trabajo (in factories, in offices, etc.) || cronometraje *m* (of games, of matches).

time lag [-læg] *n* intervalo *m* (between two events) || retraso *m* (delay).

time-lapse [-læps] *adj* PHOT de lapso de tiempo; *time-lapse photography* fotografía de lapso de tiempo.

timeless [-lis] *adj* eterno, na || sin limitación de tiempo.

time limit [-'limit] *n* límite *m* de tiempo || plazo *m*, fecha *f* tope (for payment) || duración *f* (of a privilege) || *to impose a time limit on a speaker* limitar la intervención de un orador a cierto tiempo.

timeliness [-linis] *n* oportunidad *f*.

timely [-li] *adj* oportuno, na; *a timely arrival* una llegada oportuna.

time out [-'aut] *n* US descanso *m* (break) || SP interrupción *f* (of a match).

timepiece [-pi:s] *n* reloj *m*.

timer [-ə*] *n* cronometrador *m* (person) || cronómetro *m* (watch) || reloj *m* (clock) || AUT distribuidor *m* del encendido.

timesaving [-'seiviŋ] *adj* para ahorrar tiempo, que ahorra tiempo; *a timesaving tactic* una táctica para ahorrar tiempo.

time scale [-skeil] *n* lapso *m* de tiempo.

timeserver [-'sə:və*] *n* contemporizador, ra.

time-share [-ʃεə*] *n* multipropiedad *f*.

time sharing [-ʃεəriŋ] *n* INFORM tiempo *m* compartido.

time sheet [-ʃi:t] *n* hoja *f* de presencia.

time signal [-'signl] *n* señal *f* horaria.

time signature [-'signitʃə*] *n* MUS compás *m*.

time switch [-switʃ] *n* ELECTR interruptor *m* eléctrico automático.

timetable [-teibl] *n* horario *m* || guía *f* (for trains, etc.).

timework [-wə:k] *n* trabajo *m* por horas.

timeworn [-wɔ:n] *adj* trillado, da; gastado, da (hackneyed) || gastado, da; usado, da (showing signs of wear).

time zone [-zəun] *n* huso *m* horario.

timid ['timid] *adj* tímido, da (shy) || asustadizo, za; timorato, ta (easily frightened).

timidity [ti'miditi]**; timidness** ['timidnis] *n* timidez *f* (shyness).

timing ['taimiŋ] *n* cronometraje *m* (of races, etc.) || TECH reglaje *m*, regulación *f* || coordinación *f* (coordination); *the actor's timing was out* faltaba coordinación entre los artistas || oportunidad *f* (timeliness) || — *my timing was slightly out* no calculé muy bien || *the dancer's timing was all wrong* el bailador no llevaba el compás *or* el ritmo || AUT *the timing needs adjusting* hace falta regular el distribuidor || *timing gear* engranaje *m* de distribución || *what excellent timing!* ¡qué oportuno!

timorous ['timərəs] *adj* timorato, ta; asustadizo, za (easily frightened) || tímido, da (timid); *a timorous voice* una voz tímida.

timpani ['timpəni] *pl n* MUS timbales *m*.

tin [tin] *n* MIN estaño *m* || hojalata *f* (tinplate) || lata *f*, bote *m* (container) || CULIN molde *m* (for tarts, for cakes) || FAM parné *m*, pasta *f* [AMER plata *f*] (money).

◆ *adj* de estaño || de hojalata (of timplate) || *tin soldier* soldadito *m* de plomo.

— OBSERV Flat tins, such as those used in canning sardines, tend to be called *latas* rather than *botes*.

tin [tin] *vt* estañar (to coat with tin) || enlatar, envasar, conservar en lata; *to tin fruit* enlatar fruta || *tinned peaches* melocotones en lata *or* de lata *or* en conserva.

tinamou ['tinəmu:] *n* tinamú *m* (bird).

tin-bearing ['tin,bεəriŋ] *adj* estannífero, ra.

tin can ['tin'kæn] *n* bote *m*, lata *f* (container) || US FAM destructor *m* (destroyer).

tinctorial [tiŋk'tɔ:riəl] *adj* tintóreo, a.

tincture ['tiŋktʃə*] *n* color *m*, tinte *m* (hue) || MED tintura *f*; *tincture of iodine* tintura de yodo || FIG tinte *m*, matiz *m*; *to have a political tincture* tener un tinte político || HERALD esmalte *m*.

tincture ['tiŋktʃə*] *vt* teñir (*with* de) || FIG matizar.

tinder ['tində*] *n* yesca *f*.

tinderbox [-bɔks] *n* yesquero *m* (for striking a spark) || FIG polvorín *m*.

tinderfungus [-'fʌŋgəs] *n* BOT hongo *m* yesquero.

tine [tain] *n* punta *f*, púa *f* (of a pitchfork) || diente *m* (of a fork).

tinea ['tiniə] *n* MED tiña *f*.

tin fish ['tinfiʃ] *n* FAM torpedo *m*.

tinfoil ['tin'fɔil] *n* papel *m* de estaño.

ting [tiŋ] *vt* hacer tintinear.

◆ *vi* tintinear.

ting-a-ling ['tiŋəliŋ] *n* tilín *m*; *to go ting-a-ling* hacer tilín.

tinge [tindʒ] *n* tinte *m*, matiz *m* || *with a tinge of remorse* con cierto remordimiento.

tinge [tindʒ] *vt* teñir || FIG matizar || FIG *memories tinged with sadness* recuerdos impregnados de tristeza.

tingle ['tiŋgl] *n* escozor *m* (of a slight wound) || hormigueo *m* (sensation like pins and needles) || estremecimiento *m*, escalofrío *m* (shiver) || zumbido *m* (of ears).

tingle ['tiŋgl] *vi* sentir hormigueo || estremecerse (with pleasure) || zumbar (the ears) || *my whole body tingled* sentí hormigueo por todo el cuerpo.

tingling [-iŋ] *n* hormigueo *m*.

tin hat ['tin'hæt] *n* MIL & FAM casco *m* [de acero].

tininess ['taininis] *n* pequeñez *f*.

tinker [tiŋkə*] *n* calderero *m* (who mends pots and pans) || gitano, na (gipsy) || FAM pícaro, ra (child) || chapucero, ra (botcher) || — FIG & FAM *I couldn't give a tinker's cuss* o *a tinker's damn* me importa un bledo | *it's not worth a tinker's cuss* o *a tinker's damn* no vale un comino | *you little tinker!* ¡pícaro!, ¡malo!

tinker ['tiŋkə*] *vt* componer, arreglar (pots and pans) || arreglar, apañar (to mend) || *to tinker up* arreglar, apañar.

◆ *vi* enredar, jugar, entretenerse; *he loves to tinker with any kind of gadget* le encanta enredar *or* jugar con toda clase de aparatos || cambiar; *to tinker with the timetable* cambiar el horario || estropear (to put out of order); *s.o. tinkered with the alarm* alguien estropeó la alarma || arreglar (to mend); *is he still tinkering with the car?* ¿está todavía arreglando el coche? || tocar, enredar (*with* con); *who has been tinkering with the television?* ¿quién ha tocado el televisor? || — *to tinker with the house* hacer pequeños arreglos en la casa || *to tinker with words* jugar del vocablo.

tinkle ['tiŋkl] *n* tintineo *m* || FAM *to give s.o. a tinkle* llamar a alguien por teléfono (to telephone).

tinkle ['tiŋkl] *vt* hacer tintinear.

◆ *vi* tintinear.

tinkling [-iŋ] *n* tintineo *m*.

tinman ['tinmən] *n* hojalatero *m*.

— OBSERV El plural de esta palabra es *tinmen*.

tinned [tind] *adj* en lata, en conserva.

tinniness ['tininis] *n* sonido *m* metálico; *the tinniness of a piano, of a voice* el sonido metálico de un piano, de una voz.

tinnitus [ti'naitəs] *n* MED zumbido *m* (of ears).

tinny ['tini] *adj* de estaño, de hojalata (made of tin) || estañoso, sa (containing tin) || metálico, ca (sound, taste) || FAM de oropel (of inferior quality) | poco sólido, da (car, etc.).

tin opener ['tin,əupnə*] *n* abrelatas *m inv*.

Tin Pan Alley ['tinpæn'æli] *n* FIG & FAM mundo *m* de los compositores de música popular.

tinplate ['tin'pleit] *n* hojalata *f*.

tin-plating [-iŋ] *n* estañado *m*.

tin-pot ['tinpɔt] *adj* de pacotilla (cheap, inferior).

tinsel ['tinsəl] *n* oropel *m*.

◆ *adj* de oropel.

tin shop ['tinʃɔp] *n* hojalatería *f*.

tinsmith ['tinsmiθ] *n* hojalatero *m*, estañero *m*.

tinstone ['tinstəun] *n* MIN casiterita *f*.

tint [tint] *n* tinte *m* (hair dye) || tono *m*; *her hair has a reddish tint* su pelo tiene un tono rojizo || matiz *m*; *blue with a tint of green* azul con un matiz verde || FIG matiz *m* || ARTS plumeado *m*, sombreado *m* (shading) || PRINT fondo *m* de color claro (light background).

tint [tint] *vt* teñir; *to tint sth. red* teñir algo de rojo || matizar || ARTS plumear, sombrear (in engraving).

tin tack ['tintæk] *n* tachuela *f*.

tintinnabulation ['tinti,næbju'leiʃən] *n* tintineo *m* (tinkling sound).

tinware ['tinwεə*] *n* quincalla *f*.

tinwork ['tinwə:k] *n* hojalatería *f*.

tiny ['taini] *adj* diminuto, ta; pequeñísimo, ma; minúsculo, la || *a tiny drop* una gotita.

tip [tip] *n* punta *f*, extremidad *f* (of a stick, of fingers, etc.) || filtro *m* (of a cigarette) || contera *f*, regatón *m*, punta *f* (of umbrella, of walking stick) || vertedero *m* (for rubbish) || escorial *m* (for industrial waste) || inclinación *f* (slant) || consejo *m* (piece of advice); *let me give you a tip* déjame que te dé un consejo || información *f* (to the police, in horse racing, etc.); *I've got a hot tip for the 3:30* me han dado una buena información para la carrera de las tres y media || propina *f* (gratuity) || golpecito *m* (light blow) || SP golpe *m* con efecto (in criket) || — *filter tip* filtro || *filter tip cigarette* cigarrillo *m* con filtro || *from tip to toe* de pies a cabeza || *I had it on the tip of my tongue* lo tenía en la punta de la lengua || *rubbish tip* vertedero de escombros, escombrera *f* || *take my tip* sigue mi consejo || *to walk on the tips of one's toes* andar de puntillas.

tip [tip] *vt* poner una contera *or* un regatón a (a stick) || poner filtro a (a cigarette) || inclinar, ladear (to tilt); *to tip back one's chair* inclinar la silla hacia atrás || volcar (to upset, to turn over) || verter (to pour) || dar una información a (to give information) || pronosticar (a winner, etc.); *everyone is tipping X for the job* todos pronostican que se dará el puesto a X || dar una propina a (a waiter, etc.); *to tip s.o. heavily* dar una buena propina a alguien || dar un golpecito a (to strike lightly) || dar con efecto a [la pelota] (in cricket) || *to tip one's hat* saludar.

◆ *vi* volcar, volcarse (to turn over) || inclinarse, ladearse (to lean) || dar una propina (to give a gratuity).

◆ *phr v* *to tip off* dar una información a (the police, etc.) | hacer caer (to make fall) | caerse (to fall) || *to tip out* vaciar; *to tip out one's handbag* o *the contents of one's handbag* vaciar el bolso | verter (to pour) | hacer caer; *he tipped me out of the chair* me hizo caer de la silla || *to tip over* volcar | volcarse || *to tip up* inclinar, ladear (to tilt) | volcar (to overturn) | volcarse (to turn over) | hacer caer (to make fall) | levantar; levantarse (a seat).

tipcart [-kɑːt] *n* volquete *m*.

tip lorry [-ˌlɔri] *n* volquete *m*.

tip-off [-ɔf] *adj* con filtro, emboquillado, da (cigarette) || *tipped with steel* con contera de acero (walking stick).

tippet [ˈtipit] *n* esclavina *f* (short cape).

tipple [ˈtipl] *n* bebida *f* alcohólica (drink) || FAM traguito *m* (swig) || US vertedero *m* (tip).

tipple [ðipl] *vt* FAM soplar, pimplar.
◆ *vi* FAM empinar el codo.

tippler [ˈtiplə*] *n* FAM borrachín *m*.

tipsily [ˈtipsili] *adv* como un borracho.

tipsiness [ˈtipsinis] *n* FAM embriaguez *f*, borrachera *f*.

tipster [ˈtipstə*] *n* pronosticador *m*.

tipsy [ˈtipsi] *adj* achispado, da; piripi.

tiptoe [ˈtiptəu] *n* punta *f* del pie || *on tiptoe* de puntillas (on the tips of one's toes), ansioso, sa (eager), sigilosamente (stealthily).
◆ *adv* de puntillas.

tiptoe [ˈtiptəu] *vi* andar *or* ir de puntillas.

tip-top [ˈtipˈtɔp] *adj* FAM excelente, estupendo, da; de primera categoría; *a tip-top performance* una representación estupenda || FAM *on tip-top form* en plena forma.
◆ *n* cumbre *f*.

tip-up [ˈtipʌp] *adj* abatible (seat) || *tip-up truck* volquete *m*.

tirade [taiˈreid] *n* diatriba *f*, perorata *f*.

Tirana [tiˈrɑːnə] *pr n* GEOGR Tirana.

tire [ˈtaiə*] *n* calce *m*, llanta *f* (of cart wheel, etc.) || US neumático *m* [AMER llanta *f*] (tyre).

tire [taiə*] *vt* calzar (a cart wheel) || poner neumáticos *or* llantas a (the wheel of a car) || cansar (to fatigue) || *to tire out* agotar.
◆ *vi* cansarse (*of* de).

tired [-d] *adj* cansado, da; *to be very tired* estar muy cansado || — *I'm tired of you* estoy harto de ti || *tired out* agotado, da.

tiredly [-dli] *adv* cansadamente || *he said tiredly* dijo con voz cansada.

tiredness [-dnis] *n* cansancio *m*.

tireless [-lis] *adj* incansable, infatigable.

tiresome [-səm] *adj* cansado, da (tiring) || agotador, ra (exhausting) || pesado, da (boring).

tiresomeness [-səmnis] *n* pesadez *f*.

tirewoman [-ˌwumən] *n* (ant) doncella *f*.
— OBSERV El plural de esta palabra es *tirewomen*.

tiring [-riŋ] *adj* cansado, da.

tiro [ˈtaiərəu] *n* aprendiz *m*, principiante *m*.

Tirol [ˈtirəl] *pr n* GEOGR Tirol *m*.

Tirolean [tiˈrəuliən] *adj/n* tirolés, esa.

tisane [tiˈzæn] *n* tisana *f*.

tissue [ˈtiʃuː] *n* BIOL tejido *m*; *muscular tissue* tejido muscular || tisú *m* (cloth) || pañuelo *m* de papel (paper handkerchief) || FIG sarta *f*; *a tissue of lies* una sarta de mentiras || *tissue paper* papel *m* de seda.

tit [tit]; **tat** [tæt] *n* paro *m* (bird) || POP teta *f* (breast) | gilí *m* & *f*, jilí *m* & *f* (person) || FIG *to give tit for tat* devolver la pelota, devolver golpe por golpe.

Titan [ˈtaitən] *n* MYTH Titán *m*.

titanesque [ˌtaitəˈnesk] *adj* titánico, ca; colosal.

titanic [taiˈtænik] *adj* titánico, ca.

titanium [taiˈteinjəm] *n* CHEM titanio *m*.

titbit [ˈtidbit]; **tidbit** [ˈtidbit] *n* bocado *m* de cardenal.

titer [ˈtaitə*] *n* US ley *f* (of metal) | título *m*, dosificación *f* (of a solution).

tithe [taið] *n* (ant) diezmo *m* (tax) || décima parte *f*.

tithing [-iŋ] *n* (ant) diezmo *m* (tithe) || pago *m* del diezmo (payment) || recaudación *f* del diezmo (levying).

titi [tiˈti] *n* tití *m* (monkey).

titian [ˈtiʃiən] *adj* rojizo, za (colour).

Titian [ˈtiʃiən] *pr n* Ticiano.

titillate [ˈtitileit] *vt* excitar (to excite) || cosquillear (to tickle).

titillation [ˌtitiˈleiʃən] *n* excitación *f* || cosquilleo *m* (tickling).

titivate [ˈtitiveit] *vt* emperejilar, arreglar, acicalar.
◆ *vi* emperejilarse, acicalarse.

titivation; tittivation [ˌtitiˈveiʃən] *n* emperejilamiento *m*, acicalamiento *m*.

titlark [ˈtitlɑːk] *n* pitpit *m* (bird).

title [ˈtaitl] *n* título *m* (division, heading, page, name of book, etc.) || letrero *m* (of painting, of statue, etc.) || ley *f* (of metal) || título *m* (of nobility) || JUR título *m* (of legal text) | derecho *m* (right) | título *m* de propiedad (deed) || REL título *m* || SP campeonato *m* || calificativo *m* (epithet).

titled [-d] *adj* con título de nobleza (person) || titulado, da (book, etc.).

title deed [-diːd] *n* JUR título *m* de propiedad.

titleholder [-ˌhəuldə*] *n* SP campeón, ona; titular *m* & *f*.

title page [-peidʒ] *n* PRINT portada *f* (of a book).

title role [-rəul] *n* THEATR & CINEM papel *m* principal.

titmouse [ˈtitmaus] *n* paro *m* (bird).
— OBSERV El plural de *titmouse* es *titmice*.

titrate [ˈtaitreit] *vt* CHEM titular.

titration [taiˈtreiʃən] *n* CHEM titulación *f*.

titre [ˈtaiːtə*] *n* ley *f* (of a metal) || dosificación *f*, título *m* (of a solution).

tit-tat-toe [ˌtiˌtæˈtəu] *n* ⟶ **ticktacktoe.**

titter [ˈtitə*] *n* risa *f* disimulada.

titter [ˈtitə*] *vt* reírse disimuladamente *or* con disimulo.

tittivate [ðitiveit] *vt/vi* ⟶ **titivate.**

tittivation [ˌtitiˈveiʃən] *n* ⟶ **titivation.**

tittle [ˈtitl] *n* ápice *m*, pizca *f*.

tittle-tattle [-ˌtætl] *n* chismes *m pl*, chismorreo *m* (gossip).

tittup [ˈtitʌp] *vi* caracolear (horse).

titubation [ˌtitjuˈbeiʃən] *n* titubeo *m*.

titular [ˈtitjulə*] *adj/n* titular.

Titus [ˈtaitəs] *pr n* Tito *m*.

tizzy [ˈtizi] *n* FAM excitación *f* || moneda *f* de seis peniques (coin) || FAM *to get into a tizzy* ponerse nervioso.

T-junction [ˈtiːdʒʌŋkʃən] *n* cruce *m* en T.

TNT *abbr of [trinitrotolueno]* TNT, trinitrotolueno.

to [tuːtə] *prep* a (direction, motion, indirect object, etc.); *to the left* a la izquierda; *perpendicular to* perpendicular a; *I am going to school, to London, to Canada* voy a la escuela, a Londres, al Canadá; *then I went to the dentist's, to John's* luego fui al dentista, a casa de Juan; *to fall to the ground* caerse al suelo; *give it to me* dámelo (a mí); *give the book to Mary* dale el libro a María; *it seemed easy to John* a Juan le parecía fácil; *the score was 6 to 4* el resultado fue de 6 a 4; *open, closed to the public* abierto, cerrado al público; *to drink to s.o.'s health* beber a la salud de alguien; *inferior, superior to* inferior, superior a; *is the food to your taste?* ¿está la comida a su gusto?; *to write to the teacher's dictation* escribir al dictado del profesor; *to the strains of the wedding march* al son de *or* al compás de la marcha nupcial; *he was sentenced to life imprisonment* le condenaron a cadena perpetua; *to set words to music* poner música a la letra; *A is to B as C is to D* A es a B como C es a D; *to prefer A to B* preferir A a B; *to fight hand to hand* luchar mano a mano; *man to man* de hombre a hombre; *face to face* cara a cara || hacia, a (direction towards); *a little to the north* un poco hacia el norte || a, hasta; *he showed her to the door* le acompañó hasta la puerta || hasta (as far as); *count to fifty* cuenta hasta cincuenta; *to such an extent that* hasta tal punto que; *to this day* hasta el día de hoy || para, con destino a (train, plane, boat); *the train to London* el tren con destino a Londres || menos [AMER para] (telling the time); *it's ten to four* son las cuatro menos diez [AMER faltan diez minutos para las cuatro]; *it's a quarter to one* es la una menos cuarto; *at five to seven* a las siete menos cinco || de, para; *the road to Bogota* la carretera de Bogotá || de (of); *the key to the door* la llave de la puerta; *sth. to eat* algo de comer; *secretary to Mr. Jones* secretario del Sr. Jones || para (purpose); *to succeed one has to be hard* para tener éxito hace falta ser duro; *I called to see if she was in* llamé para ver si estaba en casa; *I got there only to find there were no tickets left* llegué allí par enterarme de que ya no quedaban entradas; *it's too cold to go out* hace demasiado frío para salir; *it's too big to go in the car* es demasiado grande para caber en el coche; *a threat to society* una amenaza para la sociedad; *he vanished, never to be seen again* desapareció para no volverse a ver nunca más; *who are you to give me orders?* ¿quién es usted para darme órdenes? || a, para (purpose with verbs of motion); *I've come to ask you a favour* vengo a pedirle un favor; *I only popped in to see how you were* sólo he entrado a *or* para ver cómo estás || con; *to be kind to* ser amable con; *to my great surprise* con gran sorpresa mía; *to this end* con este fin || según (according to); *made to his specifications* hecho según sus especificaciones || contra (against); *she clutched the letter to her heart* estrechó la carta contra el corazón; *the chances are two to one in his favour* tiene dos probabilidades contra una en su favor || en comparación con, comparando con (compared with); *that is nothing to what I saw* eso no es nada comparado con lo que he visto yo || por; *there are one hundred pence to the pound* hay cien peniques por libra; *ten people to a room* diez personas por habitación || en honor a *or* de (in honour of); *they erected a statue to him* erigieron una estatua en su honor || — *a year ago to this very day* hoy hace exactamente un año || *back to back* de espaldas || *back to the wall* de espaldas a la pared (facing away from the wall), con la espalda contra la pared (against the wall) || *do I have to?* ¿es necesario? || *don't work harder than you have to* no trabajes más de lo necesario || *down to* hasta || *do you want me to try?* ¿quiere que pruebe yo? || *from... to* de... en; *from door to door* de puerta en puerta; *from bad to worse* de mal en peor; de... a, de... hasta; *I stayed from three to five* me quedé desde las tres hasta las cinco; *from Washington to New York* de Washington a Nueva York || *greetings to you all* saludos a todos || *he had his back to me* me daba la espalda || *he has aspirations to the throne* aspira al trono || *he refused to* se negó || *here's to success!* ¡que tenga éxito! || *I didn't want to, but I had to* no quería, pero no tuve más remedio; no quería, pero tuve que hacerlo || *if you want to* si (usted)

quiere || *I have no objection to his coming* no tengo inconveniente en que venga || *it belongs to him* es suyo, le pertenece (a él) || *now is the time to buy* ahora es el mejor momento para comprar || *oh, to be in the United States!* ¡quién pudiera estar en Estados Unidos!, ¡ojalá estuviese en Estados Unidos! || *that has yet to be done* eso queda por hacer || *that's all there is to it* eso es todo || *there is much left to do* queda mucho por hacer || *the telephone is not to be used for personal calls* no se debe utilizar el teléfono para las llamadas personales || *to a man* todos (sin excepción) || *to be easy to solve* ser fácil de resolver, resolverse fácilmente || *to be or not to be* ser o no ser || *to be quick to answer* ser rápido en contestar, contestar rápidamente || *to be slow to learn* ser lento en aprender, aprender lentamente || *to be the first, the only one to do sth.* ser el primero, el único en hacer algo || *to one's face* en la cara; *he told me to my face* me lo dijo en la cara || *to see him you wouldn't think he was a genius* al verle *or* viéndole no pensaría que es un genio || *to the value of* por valor de || «to two new tyre» «(por) dos neumáticos nuevos» (on a bill) || *up to* hasta; *up to midnight* hasta la medianoche; *up to a point* hasta cierto punto || *welcome to you all* bienvenidos todos || *what did he say to that?* ¿qué te contestó (a eso)? || *what do you say to that?* ¿qué te parece? || *what is it to you?* ¿a usted qué le importa? || *you are like a brother to me* eres un hermano para mí.
◆ *adv* cerca (at hand) || MAR de bolina || — *the door, the window was fast to* la puerta, la ventana estaba cerrada || *to come to* volver en sí.

— OBSERV *To* in the infinitive form of English verbs is rendered in Spanish by the verbal suffixes *-ar, -ir* and *-er: to think* pensar.

— OBSERV Since the Spanish translation of *to* often depends on the accompanying verb or adjective, reference should be made to the verb or adjective in question for uses of *to* which are not treated in the above article.

toad [təud] *n* ZOOL sapo *m* || FAM asqueroso, sa (contemptible person).

toadfish [-ˌfiʃ] *n* ZOOL pejesapo *m*.

toadflax [-flæks] *n* BOT linaria *f*.

toadstone [-stəun] *n* MIN estelión *m*.

toadstool [-stu:l] *n* BOT seta *f* || FAM hongo *m* venenoso.

toady [-i] *n* adulador, ra; pelotillero, ra; cobista *m* & *f* (adulator).

toady [i] *vi* adular, hacer la pelotilla, dar coba (*to* a).

toadyism [-iizəm] *n* adulación *f*, pelotilla *f*, coba *f*.

to and fro ['tu:ən'frəu] *adv* *to go to and fro* ir de un lado para otro *or* de acá para allá, ir y venir.

to-and-fro ['tu:ən'frəu] *adj* *to-and-fro movement* vaivén *m*, movimiento *m* de vaivén.

toast [təust] *n* pan *m* tostado, tostada *f*; *marmalade on toast* pan tostado *or* tostada con mermelada || brindis *m inv* (of drink); *there followed several toasts* a continuación hubo varios brindis || FIG héroe *m*, heroína *f*; *he is the toast of the town* es el héroe de la ciudad || — *a piece of toast* una tostada || *to drink a toast to* brindar por || *to propose a toast* proponer un brindis.

toast [təust] *vt* tostar (bread, etc.) || FIG tostar (to make hot) || brindar por (to drink to).
◆ *vi* tostarse; *English bread toasts well* el pan inglés se tuesta bien || FIG tostarse, asarse (to warm thoroughly); *I am toasting in the sun* me estoy asando al sol.

toaster [-ə*] *n* tostadora *f* (for bread).

toasting fork [-iŋfɔ:k] *n* tenedor *m* largo para tostar.

toastmaster [-ˌmɑ:stə*] *n* maestro *m* de ceremonias.

toast rack [-ræk] *n* protatostadas *m inv*.

tobacco [tə'bækəu] *n* tabaco *m*; *black* o *dark tobacco* tabaco negro; *Virginia tobacco* tabaco rubio; *pipe tobacco* tabaco de pipa; *leaf tobacco* tabaco de hoja; *chewing tobacco* tabaco de mascar || tabaco *m* (colour).

tobacco box [-bɔks] *n* tabaquera *f*.

tobacco cut [-kʌt] *n* picadura *f*.

tobacco jar [-dʒɑ:*] *n* tabaquera *f*.

tobacconist [tə'bækənist] *n* estanquero, ra (person) || *tobacconist's* estanco *m*, expendeduría *f* de tabaco (shop).

tobacco plantation [tə'bækəuplænˌteiʃən] *n* tabacal *m*, plantación *f* de tabaco.

tobacco pouch [tə'bækəupautʃ] *n* petaca *f*, bolsa *f* para el tabaco [AMER tabaquera *f*].

to-be [tu:'bi] *adj* futuro, ra.
◆ *n* porvenir *m*, futuro *m*.

toboggan [tə'bɔgən] *n* tobogán *m*.

toboggan [tə'bɔgən] *vi* deslizarse por un tobogán || FIG ir deslizándose (to slide) | bajar verticalmente (prices).

Toby ['təubi] *n* bock *m* de cerveza.

toccata [tə'kɑ:tə] *n* MUS tocata *f*.

tocology [tə'kɔlədʒi] *n* tocología *f*.

tocsin ['tɔksin] *n* rebato *m*, señal *f* de alarma || *to sound the tocsin* tocar a rebato, dar la alarma.

today [tə'dei] *adj/n* hoy (the present day); *what did you do at school today?* ¿qué has hecho hoy en el colegio? || actualmente, hoy día, hoy en día (nowadays) || — *as from today* a partir de hoy || *a year ago today* hoy hace un año || *the young people of today* la juventud actual || *today is the tenth* hoy estamos a diez || *today's paper* el periódico de hoy || *today week, a week today* dentro de una semana || *what day is it today?* ¿qué día es hoy?, ¿a cuántos estamos hoy?

toddle [tɔdl] *vi* hacer pinitos (a child) || FAM ir *or* andar tambaleándose | marcharse (to leave); *I must be toddling* ya me tengo que marchar.

toddler [-ə*] *n* niño *m* [que empieza a andar].

toddy ['tɔdi] *n* ponche *m* (drink) || savia *f* de palma (sap).

to-do [tə'du:] *n* FAM follón *m*, jaleo *m*, lío *m*; *to make a great to-do about sth.* armar un jaleo por algo; *what's all the to-do about?* ¿por qué hay tanto jaleo?

toe [təu] *n* ANAT dedo *m* del pie; *big, little toe* dedo gordo, pequeño del pie || puntera *f* (reinforced part of shoe, of sock, etc.) || punta *f* (front of shoe, of sock, etc.) || punta *f* del pie (front of the foot) || TECH pestaña *f* || — *on one's toes* de puntillas (on tiptoe), alerta (alert) || FIG *to be on one's toes* estar atento *or* ojo avizor || *to dance on one's toes* bailar de puntas (in ballet) || FIG *to keep one's men on their toes* mantener alertos a sus hombres || *to step on s.o.'s toes* darle un pisotón a alguien, pisarle el pie a alguien (to tread on), pisotear a alguien (to offend) || FIG *to tread on s.o.'s toes* pisotear a alguien || FIG FAM *to turn up one's toes* estirar la pata (to die).

toe [təu] *vt* poner puntera a (shoe, sock) || tocar con el pie (to touch with foot) || clavar oblicuamente (a nail) || SP tirar con la punta del pie (a ball) || — *to toe a cigarette out* apagar un cigarrillo con la punta del pie || *to toe the line* pisar la línea (in a race), conformarse (to conform).
◆ *vi* ir, andar (to walk) || *to toe in, out* andar con los pies hacia adentro, hacia fuera.

toe cap [-kæp] *n* puntera *f*.

toed [-d] *adj* clavado oblicuamente (nails) || *man is a five-toed animal* el hombre tiene cinco dedos en el pie.

toe-dance [-dɑ:ns] *vi* bailar de puntas.

toehold [-həuld] *n* punto *m* de apoyo (in climbing) || FIG trampolín *m*; *the inheritance gave him a toehold in society* la herencia le sirvió de trampolín para entrar en la sociedad || FIG *to get a toehold on an island* asentarse en una isla.

toe-in [-in] *n* AUT convergencia *f* de las ruedas delanteras.

toenail [-neil] *n* uña *f* [del dedo del pie] || clavo *m* oblicuo.

toenail [-neil] *vt* sujetar con un clavo oblicuo.

toff [tɔf] *n* FAM ricachón *m* (rich man) | elegantón *m*, «dandy» *m*, currutaco *m* (elegant person).

toffee; toffy [-i] *n* toffee *m*, masticable *m* || caramelo *m* (any sweet).

toffee apple [-ˌæpl] *n* manzana *f* caramelizada.

toffee-nosed ['tɔfiˌnəuzd] *adj* presumido, da; engreído, da (person).

toffy ['tɔfi] *n* → **toffee.**

tofu ['tɔfu:] *n* CULIN tofu *m*, queso *m* de soja.

tog [tɔg] *vt* ataviar, vestir (*in* de) (to dress) || *to tog o.s. up* ataviarse, vestirse.

toga ['təugə] *n* toga *f*.

— OBSERV El plural de la palabra inglesa es *togas* o *togae*.

togaed [-d]; **togated** ['təugəitid] *adj* togado, da.

together [tə'geðə*] *adv* juntos, tas; *put the pages together* pon las páginas juntas; *they came together* vinieron juntos || a la vez, al mismo tiempo (at the same time); *to speak together* hablar a la vez || de acuerdo (in agreement); *we are together on this point* estamos de acuerdo en este punto || de común acuerdo; *to act together* actuar de común acuerdo || — *for days together* durante días y días, durante varios días seguidos || *to bring together* reunir || *to come together* reunirse, juntarse || *together with* junto con || *to get together* reunir | reunirse (to assemble) | ponerse de acuerdo (to agree) || *to go together* ir juntos; *let's go to the cinema together* vayamos juntos al cine; salir juntos; *John and Mary have been going together for two years* Juan y María salen juntos desde hace dos años; armonizar, ir juntos; *those colours don't go together* esos colores no van juntos || *to hang together* ser lógico (argument) || *to pull o.s. together* serenarse, tranquilizarse (to regain control) || *to put together* unir, reunir, juntar (to join) | comparar (facts) | MATH sumar | confeccionar (a dress) | TECH ensamblar, acoplar (pieces) | montar (a machine) | FIG *to put two and two together* atar cabos.

togetherness [-nis] *n* unión *f*, solidaridad *f*.

toggle ['tɔgl] *n* cabilla *f* (pin) || alamar *m* (button) || pasador *m* (for scarf) || tensor *m* (for tightening rope) || — *toggle joint* articulación *f*, rótula *f* (joint), eje acodado, palanca acodada (lever) || *toggle switch* interruptor eléctrico.

toggle [tɔgl] *vt* sujetar (to fix, to fasten) || MAR sujetar con cabilla.

Togo ['təugəu] *pr n* GEOGR Togo *m*.

togs [tɔgz] *pl n* FAM ropa *f sing*.

toil [tɔil] *n* trabajo *m*, esfuerzo *m* (effort) || trabajo *m* (work) || trabajo *m* agotador (hard work).

toil [tɔil] *vi* trabajar duro (to work hard) || ir *or* moverse con dificultad, avanzar *or* moverse penosamente; *the car toiled along* el coche avanzaba con dificultad; *the lady toiled through the corridor* la señora avanzaba penosamente por el pasillo || funcionar con dificultad (an en gine) || — *the peasants toiling at their daily round* los campesinos haciendo su dura labor cotidiana || *to toil away* trabajar de sol a sol || *to toil up a hill* subir penosamente una colina || *to toil with a problem* esforzarse por resolver un problema.

toilet ['tɔilit] *n* arreglo *m*, aseo *m* (dressing, washing, shaving, etc.) || traje *m*, vestido *m* (clothes) || tocador *m*, coqueta *f* (dressing table) || lavabo *m*, retrete *m* (lavatory) || *toilet requisites* artículos *m* de tocador.

toilet case [-keis]; **toilet bag** [-bæg] *n* neceser *m*.

toilet paper [-ˌpeipə*] *n* papel *m* higiénico *or* sánico.

toiletries [-riz] *pl n* artículos *m* de tocador.

toilet roll [-rəul] *n* rollo *m* de papel higiénico.

toilet set [-set] *n* juego *m* de tocador.

toilet soap [-səup] *n* jabón *m* de tocador.

toilette [twɑːˈlet] *n* arreglo *m*, aseo *m* (dressing, washing, etc.) || traje *m*, vestido *m* (clothes).

toilet tissue ['toilit'tiʃuː] *n* papel *m* higiénico *or* sánico.

toilet-trained ['tɔilit'freind] *adj* que no usa más pañales (child).

toilet water ['toilit'wɔːtə*] *n* agua *f* de Colonia.

toils [tɔilz] *pl n* redes *f*, lazos *m*.

toilsome ['tɔilsəm] *adj* penoso, sa; laborioso, sa; arduo, dua.

toilworn [-wɔːn] *adj* rendido, da; agotado, da; muy cansado, da (person) || cansado, da (face, expression) || estropeado, da (hands).

to-ing and fro-ing ['tuːiŋənˌfrəuiŋ] *n* idas y venidas *f pl*.

Tokay [təu'kei] *n* tocay *m* (wine).

token ['təukən] *n* prueba *f*, muestra *f*, señal *f* (sign); *a token of gratitude* una muestra de gratitud; *a token of friendship* una prueba de amistad || símbolo *m* (symbol) || recuerdo *m* (keepsake) || ficha *f* (disk) || vale *m*; *book token* vale para comprar libros; *gift token* vale para comprar un regalo; *record token* vale para comprar discos || — *by the same token* por la misma razón || *in token of* como prueba de, en señal de.
◆ *adj* simbólico, ca; *token resistance* resistencia simbólica; *a token strike* una huelga simbólica || *a token payment* una señal.

Tokyo [təukjəu] *pr n* GEOGR Tokio.

told [təuld] *pret/pp* → **tell.**

Toledan [tə'leidən] *adj/n* toledano, na.

tolerable ['tɔlərəbl] *adj* tolerable, soportable (bearable) || mediano, na; aceptable, regular (fair, reasonable); *a tolerable knowledge of Spanish* un conocimiento mediano del español.

tolerance ['tɔlərəns] *n* tolerancia *f* (readiness to accept opinions, behaviour, etc.) || TECH MED tolerancia *f* || *religious tolerance* tolerancia religiosa.

tolerant ['tɔlərənt] *adj* tolerante, indulgente || MED tolerante.

tolerate ['tɔləreit] *vt* tolerar, soportar, aguantar (to endure) || tolerar, permitir (to permit) || tolerar, admitir (people of other beliefs, opinions, etc.) || respetar (opinions, beliefs, etc.) || MED tolerar || *this kind of behaviour is not to be tolerated* este comportamiento es intolerable *or* inadmisible.

toleration [ˌtɔlə'reiʃən] *n* tolerancia *f*.

tolite ['tɔlait] *n* tolita *f*.

toll [təul] *n* peaje *m* (of road, of motorway) || pontaje *m*, pontazgo *m*, peaje *m* (of bridge) || tasa *f* (tax) || bajas *f pl*, número *m* de víctimas; *the battle took a terrible toll* la batalla hizo un gran número de víctimas *or* muchas bajas || tañido *m* (of bells) || — *but the plague had already taken its toll* pero la peste ya había hecho muchas víctimas || *the death toll on the roads* el número de muertos en la carretera || *to take toll of* infligir una pérdida *or* pérdidas a.

toll [təul] *vt/vi* tocar (a muerto), tañer (a muerto) || *for whom the bell tolls* por quién doblan las campanas.

toll bar [-bɑː*] *n* barrera *f* de peaje.

tollbooth [-buːð] *n* cabina *f* de peaje.

toll bridge [-bridʒ] *n* puente *m* de peaje *or* de pontazgo.

toll call [-kɔːl] *n* US conferencia *f* [interurbana] (long-distance call).

tollgate [-geit] *n* barrera *f* de peaje.

tollhouse [-haus] *n* casa *f* del peajero *or* del portazguero.

tolling [-iŋ] *n* doblar *m*, tañido *m* (of bells).

tollkeeper [-ˌkiːpə*] *n* peajero *m* || (ant) portazguero *m*.

toll road [-rəud]; **tollway** [-wei] *n* carretera *f* de peaje (road) || autopista *f* de peaje (motorway).

Toltec ['tɔltek] *adj/n* tolteca.

toluene ['tɔləwiːn] *n* CHEM tolueno *m*.

tom [tɔm] *n* macho *m* [de ciertos animales como el gato].

Tom [tɔm] *pr n* Tomás *m* || — *any Tom, Dick or Harry* cualquier hijo de vecino || *peeping Tom* mirón *m* || *Tom, Dick and Harry* Fulano, Mengano y Zutano || *Tom Thumb* Pulgarcito *m*.

tomahawk ['tɔməhɔːk] *n* tomahawk *m* || FIG *to bury the tomahawk* enterrar el hacha de la guerra, hacer las paces.

tomato [tə'mɑːtəu] *n* BOT tomate *m* (fruit) | tomatera *f*, tomate *m* (plant).
— OBSERV El plural de *tomato* es *tomatoes*.

tomb [tuːm] *n* tumba *f*, sepulcro *m*.

tombac; tombak ['tɔmbæk] *n* tumbaga *f* (alloy).

tombola ['tɔmbələ] *n* tómbola *f* (lottery with goods for prizes) || lotería *f* (bingo).

tomboy ['tɔmbɔi] *n* FAM marimacho *m* (girl).

tombstone ['tuːmstəun] *n* lápida *f* sepulcral, piedra *f* sepulcral.

tomcat ['tɔmkæt] *n* gato *m* [macho].

tome [təum] *n* libraco *m* (huge book) || volumen *m*, tomo *m* (volume).

tomfool ['tɔm'fuːl] *adj* necio, tonto, bobo.
◆ *n* necio *m*, tonto *m*, bobo *m*.

tomfoolery [tɔm'fuːləri] *n* estupidez *f*, tontería *f*, necedad *f* || *enough of this tomfoolery!* ¡basta de tonterías!

tommy ['tɔmi] *n* MIL soldado *m* raso (private) || US soldado *m* inglés (British soldier).

tommy gun [-gʌn] *n* MIL pistola *f* ametralladora, metralleta *f*.

tommyrot [-rɔt] *n* disparates *m pl*, tonterías *f pl*, bobadas *f pl*.

tomorrow [tə'mɔrəu] *n* mañana *m*; *tomorrow is Tuesday* mañana es martes; *tomorrow is another day* mañana será otro día; *to leave sth. until tomorrow* dejar algo para mañana || — *don't think about what tomorrow will bring* no pienses en lo que te traerá el día de mañana || *the day after tomorrow* pasado mañana || *the world of tomorrow* el mundo de mañana.
◆ *adv* mañana; *come back tomorrow* vuelva mañana; *tomorrow morning* mañana por la mañana || — *see you tomorrow* hasta mañana || *tomorrow week, a week tomorrow* de mañana en ocho días.

tompion ['tɔmpjən] *n* MIL tapabocas *m inv*.

tomtit ['tɔm'tit] *n* alionín *m* (bird).

tom-tom ['tɔmtɔm] *n* tantán *m*.

ton [tʌn] *n* tonelada *f* || — *long ton* tonelada larga || *metric ton* tonelada métrica || MAR *register ton* tonelada de arqueo || *short ton* tonelada corta || FIG *to weigh a ton* pesar una tonelada.
◆ *pl* FIG montones *m*; *he has got tons of money* tiene montones de dinero.

tonal ['təunl] *adj* tonal.

tonality [təu'næliti] *n* tonalidad *f*.

tone [təun] *n* tono *m*; *the tone of a letter, of his voice* el tono de una carta, de su voz; *in an angry tone* con tono enfadado; *decorated in pastel tones* decorado con tonos pastel; *out of tone* fuera de tono; *to lower, to change one's tone* bajar el tono, cambiar de tono || MUS & MED tono *m* || FIG tendencia *f* (of a market) | estilo *m*, carácter *m* (character).

tone [təun] *vt* entonar || matizar (a colour) || MUS afinar, templar (instruments) || PHOT virar || — *to tone down* atenuar, suavizar (to weaken), moderar (to moderate) || *to tone up* tonificar (the nervous system), entonar (s.o.), avivar, entonar (a colour, etc.).
◆ *vi* armonizar, ir juntos (colours) || armonizar (sounds) || PHOT virar || — *to tone down* atenuarse, suavizarse (volume, colours), moderarse (to be moderated) || *to tone in with* armonizar con, ir bien con || *to tone up* entonarse.

tone colour; US **tone color** [ˌkʌlə*] *n* MUS timbre *m*.

tone control [-kənˌtrəul] *n* RAD botón *m* de tonalidad.

tone-deaf ['-def] *adj* que no tiene buen oído.

toneless [-lis] *adj* apagado, da (colours) || inexpresivo, va; apagado, da (voice).

tonelessly [-lisli] *adv* con voz apagada.

tone poem ['təunˌpəuim] *n* MUS poema *m* sinfónico.

tong [tɔŋ] *n* sociedad *f* secreta china.

tonga ['tɔŋgə] *n* carruaje *m* ligero de dos ruedas.

tongs [tɔŋz] *pl n* tenacillas *f* (for sugar) || tenazas *f* (for coal) || TECH pinzas *f*, tenazas *f*.

tongue [tʌŋ] *n* ANAT & CULIN lengua *f*; *coated* o *furry tongue* lengua pastosa || lengua *f*, idioma *m* (language); *native, mother tongue* lengua nativa, materna || FIG lengua *f* (of flame, of land) || badajo *m* (of a bell) || lengüeta *f* (of wooden joint, shoe, musical instrument) || hebijón *m* (of a buckle) || aguja *f* (of railway line) || — FIG *evil tongue* mala lengua | *has a cat got your tongue?* ¿te has tragado la lengua? || FAM *I could have bitten my tongue when I said that* mejor hubiese sido callarme || *on the tip of one's tongue* en la punta de la lengua || FIG *poisonous* o *vicious* o *wicked tongue* lengua de víbora *or* viperina || *sister tongues* lenguas hermanas || *slip of the tongue* lapsus *m* linguae || FIG *to find one's tongue* recobrar el habla || *to give tongue* empezar a ladrar (dogs) || FIG *to hold* o *to bite one's tongue* callarse, morderse la lengua | *to keep a civil tongue in one's head* ser cortés | *to loosen s.o.'s tongue* soltarle la lengua a alguien || *tongue of fire* lengua de fuego || *to put out* o *to stick out one's tongue* sacar la lengua; *to put one's tongue at s.o.* sacarle la lengua a alguien || FIG *to speak with one's tongue in one's cheek* hablar irónicamente | *to wag one's tongue* darle a la lengua, hablar mucho || *with one's tongue hanging out* con la lengua fuera.

tongue [tʌŋ] *vt* machihembrar (to join) || lamer (to lick).
◆ *vi* sobresalir (to stick out).

tongue-and-groove joint [-ən'gruːvˌdʒɔint] *n* ensambladura *f* de ranura y lengüeta, machihembrado *m*.

tongue depressor [-di'presə*] *n* depresor *m*.

tongue-in-cheek [-intʃiːk] *adj* irónico, ca; dicho con sorna (remark).

tongue-lashing [-læʃiŋ] *n* FAM bronca *f* (telling off); *to give s.o. a tongue lashing* echar una bronca a alguien.

tongueless [-lis] *adj* sin lengua ‖ FAM mudo, da; sin habla.

tongue-tie [-tai] *n* MED frenillo *m* (speech defect).

tongue-tied [-taid] *adj* mudo, da (through shyness) ‖ MED que tiene frenillo ‖ *to get all tongue-tied* trabársele a uno la lengua.

tongue twister [-ˌtwistə*] *n* trabalenguas *m inv.*

tonic [ˈtɔnik] *adj* tónico, ca ‖ *tonic accent* acento tónico ‖ *tonic water* agua tónica.
◆ *n* MED tónico *m*; *hair tonic* tónico para el cabello ‖ tónica *f* (fizzy drink) ‖ GRAMM & MUS tónica *f* ‖ FIG *the news acted as a tonic on me* la noticia me entonó.

tonicity [təˈnisiti] *n* ANAT tonicidad *f.*

tonight [təˈnait] *adv/n* esta noche; *tonight is the première of the film* esta noche se estrena la película.

tonka bean [ˈtɔŋkəbiːn] *n* BOT haba *f* tonca.

Tonkin [ˈtɔnkin] *pr n* Tonkín *m*, Tonquín *m.*

Tonkinese [ˌtɔŋkəˈniːz] *adj/n* tonquinés, esa.

tonnage [ˈtʌnidʒ] *n* tonelaje *m*; *gross tonnage* tonelaje bruto.

tonne [tʌn] *n* tonelada *f* métrica.

tonner [ˈtʌnə*] *n* de... toneladas; *a thousand-tonner* un barco de mil toneladas.

tonsil [ˈtɔnsl] *n* ANAT amígdala *f*, tonsila *f.*

tonsillectomy [tɔnsiˈlektəmi] *n* tonsilectomía *f.*

tonsillitis [ˈtɔnsiˈlaitis] *n* MED amigdalitis *f*, tonsilitis *f.*

tonsure [ˈtɔnʃə*] *n* tonsura *f.*

tonsure [ˈtɔnʃə*] *vt* tonsurar.

tontine [tɔnˈtiːn] *n* COMM tontina *f.*

tonus [təunəs] *n* ANAT tonicidad *f*, tono *m.*

too [tuː] *adv* demasiado; *it's too far* está demasiado lejos ‖ también; *I hope you will come too* espero que tú también vengas ‖ además (as well as that); *and he called me a liar too* y además me trató de mentiroso ‖ muy; *I'm not too sure* no estoy muy seguro ‖ — *he's none too bright* no es muy listo, no es nada listo ‖ *it is too early yet* es muy temprano todavía ‖ *it is too hot to touch* está demasiado caliente para tocarlo ‖ *it is too kind of you* es usted muy amable ‖ *it looks none too good* no parece nada bueno, no parece muy bueno ‖ *it was just too delicious* estaba simplemente delicioso ‖ *so much rain! and in July too!* ¡qué manera de llover! y eso que estamos en julio ‖ *the car was too big for her to drive* el coche era demasiado grande para que lo condujera ella ‖ *the tea is too hot to drink* el té está demasiado caliente ‖ *to be too much for one* ser demasiado para uno ‖ FAM *too bad!* ¡qué pena! (what a shame!), ¿qué le vamos a hacer? (never mind) ‖ *to drink too heavily* beber demasiado ‖ *too little* muy poco, demasiado poco (amount), muy pequeño, demasiado pequeño (size) ‖ *too many* demasiados, das ‖ *too much* demasiado; *it costs too much* cuesta demasiado; de más; *she gave me ten pounds too much* me dio diez libras de más ‖ *to talk too much* hablar más de la cuenta *or* demasiado ‖ *we know him only too well* lo conocemos de sobra.

took [tuk] *pret* → **take.**

tool [tuːl] *n* herramienta *f*; *carpenter's tools* herramientas de carpintería ‖ útil *m*, utensilio *m*; *gardening tools* útiles de jardinería ‖ máquina herramienta *f* (machine tool) ‖ FIG instrumento *m*; *they used her as tool to get at the files* se sirvieron de ella como instrumento para tener acceso a los documentos | instrumento *m* (de trabajo); *the dictionary is a useful tool for the translator* el diccionario es un instrumento de trabajo muy útil para el traductor ‖ FIG *a bad workman always blames his tools* o *quarrel with his tools* no hay que buscar pretextos para un trabajo mal hecho ‖ *the tools of one's trade* los instrumentos *m* de trabajo.

tool [tuːl] *vt* labrar (to shape) ‖ mecanizar (to work with machine tools) ‖ estampar (to impress letters or designs) ‖ equipar con herramientas *or* maquinaria (to equip with tools, with machines) ‖ FAM conducir (a car).
◆ *vi* utilizar herramientas ‖ FAM *to tool along* ir en coche.

toolbag [-bæg] *n* bolsa *f* de herramientas.

toolbox [-bɔks] *n* caja *f* de herramientas.

toolhead [-hed] *n* TECH cabezal *m* (of a lathe).

toolholder [-ˌhəuldə*] *n* portaherramientas *m inv.*

tooling [-iŋ] *n* mecanizado *m* (with machine tools) ‖ estampación *f* (of a book cover).

tool kit [-kit] *n* juego *m* de herramientas (set of tools) ‖ AUT estuche *m* de herramientas.

toolmaker [-ˌmeikə*] *n* fabricante *m* de herramientas.

toot [tuːt] *n* bocinazo *m* (with a horn) ‖ silbido *m* (with a whistle) ‖ toque *m* (of trumpet).

toot [tuːt] *vt* tocar (to blow a horn, a trumpet).
◆ *vi* sonar (to sound) ‖ tocar el claxon *or* la bocina (s.o. in a car).

tooth [tuːθ] *n* diente *m* ‖ muela *f* (back tooth) ‖ púa *f* (of a comb) ‖ diente *m* (of a saw) ‖ — *an eye for an eye, a tooth for a tooth* ojo por ojo, diente por diente ‖ FIG *armed to the teeth* armado hasta los dientes ‖ *back tooth* muela *f* ‖ *false teeth* dentadura postiza ‖ *front teeth* incisivos *m* ‖ FIG *in the teeth of* en pleno; *in the teeth of the storm* en plena tormenta; a pesar de (despite); *in the teeth of criticism* a pesar de la crítica ‖ FAM *to be fed up* o *sick to the teeth of* estar hasta la coronilla de ‖ FIG *to be long in the tooth* tener ya muchos años ‖ *to clench one's teeth* apretar los dientes ‖ *to cut one's teeth* echar los dientes ‖ FIG *to cut one's teeth on* ejercitarse en | *to fight tooth and nail* luchar a brazo partido, defenderse como gato panza arriba | *to get one's teeth into* hincarle el diente a | *to have a sweet tooth* ser goloso ‖ *to have a tooth out* sacarse una muela *or* un diente ‖ FIG & FAM *to lie through one's teeth* mentir con toda la barba ‖ FIG *to put teeth into* dar mucha fuerza a ‖ *to say sth. between one's teeth* decir algo entre dientes ‖ *to set one's teeth on edge* darle dentera a uno ‖ *to show one's teeth* enseñar los dientes ‖ FIG *to throw* o *to cast sth. in s.o.'s teeth* echarle algo en cara a alguien ‖ *wisdom tooth* muela del juicio.
— OBSERV El plural de *tooth* es *teeth.*

tooth [tuːθ] *vt* dentar, endentar; *to tooth a saw* dentar una sierra.
◆ *vi* engranar.

toothache [-eik] *n* dolor *m* de muelas.

toothbrush [-brʌʃ] *n* cepillo *m* de dientes.

toothcomb [-kəum] *n* peine *m* de púa fina ‖ FIG *to go through sth. with a toothcomb* examinar algo detalladamente (to study), registrar algo minuciosamente (to search).

toothed [-t] *adj* dentado, da; *toothed wheel* rueda dentada ‖ con dientes, de dientes; *white-toothed* con dientes blancos; *fine-toothed* de dientes finos.

toothing [-iŋ] *n* ARCH adaraja *f* ‖ dientes *m pl* (teeth).

toothless [-lis] *adj* desdentado, da; sin dientes.

toothpaste [-peist] *n* pasta *f* dentrífica, crema *f* dental, dentífrico *m.*

toothpick [-pik] *n* palillo *m* de dientes, mondadientes *m inv.*

tooth powder [-ˌpaudə*] *n* polvo *m* dentífrico.

toothsome [-səm] *adj* sabroso, sa; apetitoso, sa.

toothy [-i] *adj* dentudo, da (having large teeth) ‖ enseñando los dientes (grin, etc.).

tootle [ˈtuːtl] *n* FAM toque *m* (on a musical instrument) ‖ *can I have a tootle?* ¿me dejas tocar un poco?

tootle [ˈtuːtl] *vi* tocar [la flauta, etc.] ‖ FAM ir; *to tootle along at thirty miles per hour* ir a treinta millas por hora ‖ FAM *to tootle off* irse.
◆ *vt* tocar (an instrument).

tootsie [ˈtuːtsi] *n* US FAM querida *f* (addressing a girl) | niña *f* (girl) ‖ FAM piececito *m* (foot).

tootsy [ˈtuːtsi] *n* FAM piececito *m* (foot).

top [tɔp] *n* peón *m*, peonza *f*, trompo *m* (child's toy) ‖ parte *f* de arriba, sostén *m* (of bikini, etc.) ‖ blusa *f* (blouse) ‖ chaqueta *f* (jacket) ‖ parte *f* de arriba, parte *f* superior, lo alto (upper part); *in the top of the bookshelf* en la parte de arriba de la estantería; *the top of a bus* la parte de arriba de un autobús; *at the top of the stairs* en lo alto de la escalera; *the top of the building is quite ugly* la parte de arriba del edificio es bastante fea ‖ parte *f* alta (higher part) ‖ parte *f* de encima *or* de arriba (upper side); *the top of the shoe is leather* la parte de encima del zapato es de cuero ‖ cima *f*, cumbre *f* (of a hill, of a mountain, etc.) ‖ copa *f* (highest tip of tree, of hat) ‖ tapa *f* (of saucepan, bottle, tin, etc.) ‖ capuchón *m* (of a pen) ‖ cabeza *f*, principio *m* (of page, etc.); *at the top of the list* al principio de la lista ‖ remate *m* (crest of a building) ‖ coronilla *f* (of the head) ‖ tejado *m* (outside roof of house) ‖ techo *m* (roof of bus, ceiling) ‖ capota *f* (of a car) ‖ baca *f* (of a stagecoach) ‖ tablero *m* (of table); *table with an oak, a glass, a formica top* mesa con tablero de roble, de cristal, de formica ‖ superficie *f* (surface); *the oil floated to the top* el aceite subió a la superficie ‖ cresta *f* (of a wave) ‖ BOT hojas *f pl* (of carrots, etc.) ‖ final *m*, extremo *m*; *let's go to the top of the street* vayamos hasta el final de la calle ‖ FIG los mejores *m pl*, los primeros *m pl*; *he is at the top of his profession* está entre los mejores de su profesión | cumbre *f* (height); *he reached the top of his career in 1970* llegó a la cumbre de su carrera en 1970 ‖ MAR cofa *f* (platform) ‖ AUT directa *f* (gear) ‖ — FIG *at the top of* a la cabeza de, el primero, la primera; *he is at the top of the class* es el primero de la clase | *at the top of one's form* en plena forma | *at the top of one's speed* a toda velocidad | *at the top of one's voice* a voz en grito *or* en cuello, a voces ‖ *don't drink beer on top of wine* no mezcles cerveza con vino ‖ *from top to bottom* de arriba abajo ‖ *from top to toe* de pies a cabeza ‖ FIG *he is headed for the top* está en el camino del éxito *or* de la fama | *he went straight to the top* alcanzó inmediatamente la fama *or* el éxito, se puso en seguida el primero | *it's just one thing on top of another* es una cosa tras otra ‖ *on top* encima; *put the best ones on top* pon los mejores arriba; encima de, sobre; *on top of the wardrobe* encima del armario ‖ FIG *on top of* además de | *on top of that, on top of it all* para colmo, por si fuera poco, por añadidura ‖ *sliding top* techo corredizo (of car), tapa corrediza (of box, etc.) ‖ FIG *to be on top* llevar ventaja, ir ganando (to be winning) ‖ FAM *to be over the top* ser una pasada ‖ FIG *to blow one's top* salir de sus casillas | *to come out on top* ganar, salir vencedor (to be the winner) | *to feel* o *to be on*

top of the world estar en el séptimo cielo, estar en la gloria (happy), sentirse muy bien (healthy) || *to fill up to the top* llenar completamente *or* hasta el borde || MIL *to go over the top* salir al ataque || FIG *to go to bed on top of one's supper* acostarse nada más cenar | *to go to the top of one's profession* hacer carrera | *top of the morning to you* muy buenos días || *to spin like a top* dar más vueltas que una peonza || *what is the position at the top of the league?* ¿quiénes van en cabeza de la liga? || *wipe the top of the table down* pasa la esponja por encima de la mesa.
◆ *adj* de arriba; *top sheet* sábana de arriba || máximo, ma; *top prices* precios máximos || máximo, ma; extremo, ma; *top security* seguridad máxima || último, ma (last); *top floor* último piso || más alto, ta (highest) || más importante (most important) || de la alta sociedad (high-society) || grande, muy bueno, na (great); *a top racing driver* un gran piloto de carreras || mejor, primero, ra (best) || — *he is top in the class* es el primero de la clase || *to earn top money* estar muy bien pagado || *top boy in his class, in history* el primero de la clase, el primero en historia || *top speed* velocidad máxima; *to have a top speed of* tener una velocidad máxima de || *top table* mesa *f* principal *or* de honor (in a banquet).

top [tɔp] *vt* coronar, rematar (to crown); *a spire tops the tower* una aguja remata la torre || rematar (to finish off) || estar a la cabeza de *or* al principio de (to be at the top of); *to top a list* estar a la cabeza de una lista || cubrir (to cover); *to top a cake with cream* cubrir un pastel con nata || superar (to be better or greater than) || superar, mejorar; *he topped his previous performance* superó su actuación anterior || medir más de; *he tops three feet* mide más de tres pies || medir más que; *he tops me by three centimetres* mide tres centímetros más que yo || llegar a la cumbre de (a mountain) || salvar, superar (an obstacle) || AGR descabezar, desmochar; *to top a tree* desmochar un árbol || MAR embicar || SP golpear en la parte superior para dar efecto (ball) || CHEM eliminar las fracciones más volátiles de || — *to top it all* para colmo, por si fuera poco || *to top off* terminar, rematar || *to top up* llenar completamente (to fill), volver a llenar (to fill again), recargar a fondo (a battery).

topaz ['təupæz] *n* MIN topacio *m*; *smoky topaz* topacio ahumado; *pink topaz* topacio quemado.

top boot ['tɔpbuːt] *n* bota *f* alta.

top brass ['tɔpbrɑːs] *n* FAM peces *m pl* gordos.

topcoat ['tɔpkəut] *n* abrigo *m* [AMER tapado *m*, sobretodo *m*] (overcoat) || última mano *f* (of paint).

top-drawer ['tɔp'drɔːə*] *adj* de la alta sociedad (people) || de primera (categoría) (first-class).

topdressing ['tɔp'dresiŋ] *n* AGR abono *m*, estiércol *m*.

tope [təup] *n* templete *m* budista.

tope [təup] *vi* beber con exceso.

topee ['təupi] *n* salacot *m* (helmet).

toper ['təupə*] *n* bebedor *m*, borrachín *m* (heavy drinker).

topflight ['tɔp'flait] *adj* de primera categoría, de primera clase.

topgallant [tɔp'gælənt] *n* MAR mastelerillo *m* de juanete (mast) | juanete *m* (sail).
◆ *adj* de juanete; *topgallant mast* mastelerillo de juanete.

top gear ['tɔpgiə*] *n* AUT directa *f*.

top-hamper ['tɔp'hæmpə*] *n* MAR superestructura *f*.

top hat ['tɔp'hæt] *n* sombrero *m* de copa, chistera *f*.

top-heavy ['tɔp'hevi] *adj* demasiado pesado en la parte superior, inestable || FIG con demasiado personal dirigente (having too many high-paid officials) | supercapitalizado, da (overcapitalized).

top-hole ['tɔp'həul] *adj* estupendo, da.

tophus ['təufəs] *n* GEOL toba *f* || MED nodo *m*, tofo *m*.
— OBSERV El plural de *tophus* es *tophi*.

topi ['təupi; US tə'pi] *n* salacot *m* (topee).

topiary ['təupjəri] *adj* de la jardinería.
◆ *n* jardinería *f* (art) || arbustos *m* recortados artísticamente.

topic ['tɔpik] *n* tema *m*, asunto *m*, tópico *m*.

topical [-əl] *adj* de actualidad; *highly topical* de gran *or* de mucha actualidad || sobre cuestiones de actualidad (conversation) || local || MED tópico, ca.

topicality [ˌtɔpi'kæliti] *n* actualidad *f* || carácter *m* local.

topknot ['tɔpnɔt] *n* moño *m* (of hair) || copete *m*, penacho *m* (of birds) || FAM coco *m* (head).

topless ['tɔplis] *adj* con el busto desnudo (person) || que deja el busto al descubierto (dress).

top-level ['tɔp'levl] *adj* de alto nivel, del más alto nivel.

topman ['tɔpmən] *n* minero *m* que trabaja en la superficie.
— OBSERV El plural de *topman* es *topmen*.

topmast ['tɔpmɑːst] *n* MAR mastelero *m*.

topmost ['tɔpməust] *adj* más alto.

top-notch ['tɔp'nɔtʃ] *adj* de primera calidad *or* categoría, de primera (first-rate).

topographer [tə'pɔgrəfə*] *n* topógrafo *m*.

topographic [ˌtɔpə'græfik]; **topographical** [-əl] *adj* topográfico, ca.

topography [tə'pɔgrəfi] *n* topografía *f*.

topology [tə'pɔlədʒi] *n* MATH topología *f*.

toponym ['tɔpənim] *n* topónimo *m*.

toponymic [ˌtɔpə'nimik]; **toponymical** [-əl] *adj* toponímico, ca.

toponymy [tə'pɔnimi] *n* toponimia *f*.

topper ['tɔpə*] *n* FAM sombrero *m* de copa, chistera *f* (top hat) | persona *f* extraordinaria (person) | cosa *f* extraordinaria (thing).

topping ['tɔpiŋ] *adj* estupendo, da; extraordinario, ria.
◆ *n* desmoche *m* (of a tree) || ⟶ **top**.

topple ['tɔpl] *vt* hacer caer, derribar (to cause to fall); *to topple a rider from his horse* derribar un jinete del caballo; *to topple a statue over* derribar una estatua || volcar (to knock over, to overturn) || FIG derribar (to cause to fall from power).
◆ *vi* venirse abajo, caerse (to fall) || volcarse; *the flower vase, the lorry toppled over* el florero, el camión se volcó || tambalearse (to be on the point of falling) || FIG venirse abajo, caer (government).

top-ranking ['tɔpræŋkiŋ] *adj* destacado, da || *a top-ranking official* un alto funcionario.

tops [tɔps] *n* FAM *it's the tops* es fantástico, es genial.

topsail ['tɔpsl] *n* MAR gavia *f*.

top-secret ['tɔp'siːkrit] *adj* confidencial, sumamente secreto, ta.

top sergeant ['tɔp'sɑːdʒənt] *n* MIL sargento *m*.

topside ['tɔp'said] *n*; **topsides** [-z] *pl n* MAR obra *f sing* muerta.
◆ *adv* MAR en cubierta (on deck).

topsoil ['tɔpˌsɔil] *n* capa *f* superficial del suelo, tierra *f* vegetal, mantillo *m*.

top spin ['tɔpspin] *n* SP efecto *m* liftado (in tennis) || efecto *m* de avance (in golf).

topsy-turvy ['tɔpsi'təːvi] *adj* revuelto, ta; desordenado, da; en desorden (in disorder) || al revés (upside down); *a topsy-turvy world* el mundo al revés.
◆ *adv* patas arriba, en desorden.

top ten ['tɔp'ten] *n* los diez mejores discos del momento.

top twenty ['tɔp'twenti] *n* los veinte mejores discos del momento.

toque [təuk] *n* toca *f* (woman's hat).

tor [tɔː*] *n* peñasco *m* (rock).

Torah; US **Tora** ['tɔːrə] *n* REL Tora *f*.

torch [tɔːtʃ] *n* antorcha *f*, hacha *f*, tea *f* (made of wood) || linterna *f* (electric) || soplete *m* (for welding) || FIG antorcha *f* (source of enlightenment) || FIG *to carry a torch for s.o.* estar enamorado de alguien [sin ser correspondido].

torchbearer [-ˌbɛərə*] *n* persona *f* que lleva una antorcha || nazareno *m* (in religious processions) || FIG abanderado *m* (person who brings enlightenment).

torchlight [-lait] *n* luz *f* de antorcha || *torchlight procession* procesión *f or* desfile *m* con antorchas.

torchon lace ['tɔːʃənleis] *n* encaje *m* de hilo basto.

torch singer ['tɔːtʃˌsiŋə*] *n* cantante *m* & *f* de canciones sentimentales.

torch song ['tɔːtʃsɔŋ] *n* canción *f* sentimental.

torchwood ['tɔːtʃwud] *n* madera *f* resinosa.

tore [tɔː*] *n* ARCH & MATH toro *m*.

tore [tɔː*] *pret* ⟶ **tear.**

toreador ['tɔriədɔː*]; **torero** [tɔ'rɛərəu] *n* torero *m* (bullfighter).

tori ['tɔri] *pl n* ⟶ **torus.**

toric ['tɔrik] *adj* tórico, ca.

torment ['tɔːment] *n* tormento *m*, suplicio *m*.

torment [tɔː'ment] *vt* atormentar, torturar; *he was tormented with remorse* le atormentaba el remordimiento || fastidiar (to annoy, to bother).

tormentor [tɔː'mentə*] *n* atormentador, ra (person who torments) || CINEM panel *m* de absorción acústica.
◆ *pl* THEATR alcahueta *f sing*, segunda embocadura *f sing*.

torn [tɔːn] *pp* ⟶ **tear.**

tornado [tɔː'neidəu] *n* tornado *m*.
— OBSERV El plural de la palabra inglesa es *tornadoes* o *tornados*.

torose [tə'rəus]; **torous** ['tɔːrəs] *adj* BOT nudoso, sa (with knobs).

torpedo [tɔː'piːdəu] *n* torpedo *m* (underwater missile) || US petardo *m* (rail detonator) | detonador *m* (used in oil wells) | petardo *m* (small firework) || torpedo *m* (fish).
— OBSERV El plural de la palabra inglesa es *torpedoes*.

torpedo [tɔː'piːdəu] *vt* torpedear (to attack) || poner detonadores en (an oil well) || FIG torpedear, hacer fracasar.

torpedo boat [-bəut] *n* torpedero *m*, lancha *f* torpedera || *torpedo-boat destroyer* cazatorpedero *m*, contratorpedero *m*.

torpedo body [-'bɔdi] *n* AUT torpedo *m*.

torpedo net [-net] *n* red *f* antitorpedo.

torpedo tube [-tjuːb] *n* tubo *m* lanzatorpedos, lanzatorpedos *m inv*.

torpid ['tɔːpid] *adj* letárgico, ca; aletargado, da (lethargic) || aletargado, da (animals) || FIG apático, ca.

torpidity [tɔː'piditi]; **torpor** ['tɔːpə*] *n* entorpecimiento *m*, torpor *m* || FIG apatía *f*.

torporific [,tɔːpə'rifik] *adj* soporífero, ra.

torque [tɔːk] *n* PHYS momento *m* de torsión || HIST torques *f* (necklace).

torrefaction [,tɔri'fækʃən] *n* torrefacción *f*.

torrefy ['tɔrifai] *vt* torrefactar.

torrent ['tɔrənt] *n* torrente *m* (fast stream) || FIG torrente *m*; *a torrent of light, of tears* un torrente de luz, de lágrimas || *to rain in torrents* llover a cántaros.

torrential [tɔ'renʃəl] *adj* torrencial.

torrid ['tɔrid] *adj* tórrido, da; *torrid zone* zona tórrida.

torrify ['tɔrifai] *vt* torrefactar.

torsion ['tɔːʃən] *n* torsión *f*.

torsional [-əl] *adj* de torsión || *torsional strength* resistencia *f* a la torsión.

torsion balance [-'bæləns] *n* PHYS balanza *f* de torsión.

torsion bar [-bɑː*] *n* AUT barra *f* de torsión.

torsk [tɔːsk] *n* bacalao *m* (fish).

torso ['tɔːsəu] *n* torso *m*.
— OBSERV El plural de la palabra inglesa es *torsos* o *torsi*.

tort [tɔːt] *n* JUR agravio *m* indemnizable en juicio civil.

torticollis [,tɔːtə'kɔlis] *n* MED tortícolis *m* o *f*.

tortilla [tɔː'tiːjæ] *n* tortilla *f* (pancake, omelet).

tortoise ['tɔːtəs] *n* ZOOL tortuga *f* [de tierra].

tortoiseshell [-ʃəl] *n* carey *m*, concha *f*.
◆ *adj* de carey, de concha.

tortuous ['tɔːtjuəs] *adj* tortuoso, sa; *a tortuous road* una carretera tortuosa; *tortuous means* métodos tortuosos || tortuoso, sa; retorcido, da; *tortuous mind* mentalidad retorcida.

torture ['tɔːtʃə*] *n* tortura *f*, tormento *m* || FIG FAM *it was torture at the dentist's!* ¡lo que sufrí con el dentista!

torture ['tɔːtʃə*] *vt* torturar, atormentar, dar tormento a (to inflict pain on) || FIG torcer, deformar (to twist, to deform) | atormentar (to torment).

torturer [-rə*] *n* torcionario *m*.

torus ['tɔːrəs] *n* ARCH & MATH toro *m* || BOT receptáculo *m* || ANAT torus *m*, protuberancia *f* redondeada.
— OBSERV El plural de la palabra inglesa es *tori*.

Tory ['tɔːri] *adj/n* conservador, ra (in England) || realista (in the War of American Independence) || FIG reaccionario, ria.

Toryism [-izəm] *n* conservadurismo *m*.

tosh [tɔʃ] *n* FAM bobadas *f pl*, tonterías *f pl*.

toss [tɔs] *n* lanzamiento *m* (throwing) || sacudida *f* (of the head) || sacudida *f* (buck) || movimiento *m* (of waves) || caída *f* (fall) || sorteo *m* a cara o cruz || cogida *f* (by a bull) || — *give the pancake a toss* dale la vuelta a la tortita || *give the salad a toss* dale vueltas a *or* mueve *or* revuelve la ensalada || *it's a toss between X and Y* se juega entre X e Y || *to argue the toss* seguir discutiendo, insistir (to keep arguing), andar en dimes y diretes, discutir (to argue) || *to take a toss* caerse del caballo || *to win the toss* ganar [a cara o cruz].

toss [tɔs] *vt* tirar, lanzar (to throw) || echar (la cabeza) para atrás (one's head) || sacudir; *the horse tossed its head* el caballo sacudió la cabeza || tirar (a horse its rider) || dar la vuelta a (a pancake, a hay, etc.) || revolver, mover, dar vueltas a; *to toss the salad* dar vueltas a la ensalada || sacudir; *the waves tossed the boat* las olas sacudían el barco || sacudir (a pillow) || echar a cara o cruz (a coin) || — *the bull tossed the bullfighter* el toro cogió al torero || *toss it over to me* tíramelo || *to toss aside* echar a un lado || *to toss back* echar para atrás (one's head, one's hair), devolver (a ball, etc.) || *to toss off* beber de un trago (a drink), escribir rápidamente (a letter), despachar (a task) || *to toss one's money about* tirar el dinero por la ventana || *to toss s.o. in a blanket* mantear a alguien || *to toss up* echar, lanzar al aire (a coin).
◆ *vi* agitarse (to move restlessly) || ondear (to wave) || dar vueltas, revolverse (when sleeping) || echar a cara o cruz; *let's toss for it* vamos a echarlo a cara o cruz || MAR cabecear (to pitch) | balancearse (to roll) || — *to toss and turn* dar vueltas (in bed) || *to toss up for sth.* echar algo a cara o cruz.

tosspot [-pɔt] *n* borracho *m* (drunkard).

toss-up [-ʌp] *n* *it's a toss-up between* se juega *or* se disputa entre || *it's a toss-up whether he'll come or not* no sabe si vendrá o no vendrá || *to decide sth. by a toss-up* decidir algo a cara o cruz.

tot [tɔt] *n* nene *m* (child) || trago *m* (drop); *we had a tot of whisky* nos tomamos un trago de whisky || poco *m* (little); *would you like a tot of rum?* ¿quieres un poco de ron?

tot [tɔt] *vt* *to tot up* sumar.
◆ *vi* acumularse, aumentar || *the bill tots up to ten pounds* la factura asciende a *or* suma diez libras.

total ['təutl] *adj* total; *total ignorance* ignorancia total; *total eclipse* eclipse total || *the total cost of the disaster in human lives was 3,560* la catástrofe costó la vida a 3.560 personas en total *or* a un total de 3.560 personas.
◆ *n* total *m*, totalidad *f* (the whole amount) || total *m*, suma *f* (sum) || *grand* o *sum total* total *m*.

total ['təutl] *vt* sumar (to find the total of) || totalizar, sumar, ascender a (to equal a total of).
◆ *vi* *to total up to* ascender a, sumar, totalizar.

totalisator ['təutəlaizeitə] *n* SP totalizador *m*.

totalitarian [,təutæli'tɛriən] *adj/n* totalitario, ria.

totalitarianism [-izəm] *n* totalitarismo *m*.

totality [təu'tæliti] *n* totalidad *f*.

totalizator ['təutəlaizeitə*] *n* SP totalizador *m*.

totalize ['təutəlaiz] *vt* totalizar.

totalizer [-ə*] *n* SP totalizador *m*.

totally ['təutəli] *adv* completamente, totalmente.

tote [təut] *n* US FAM totalizador *m* (totalizator) | carga *f*, peso *m* (weight).

tote [təut] *vt* US FAM llevar, cargar.

tote bag [-bæg] *n* bolso *m* grande.

totem ['təutəm] *n* tótem *m*.

totemic [təu'temik] *adj* totémico, ca.

totemism ['təutəmizəm] *n* totemismo *m*.

totem pole ['teutəm'pəul] *n* tótem *m*.

Totonac [təu'təunæk] *adj/n* totonaca, totoneca.

Totonaca [-ə] *n* totonaca *m* & *f*, totoneca *m* & *f*.

Totonaco [-əu] *n* totonaca *m* & *f*, totoneca *m* & *f*.

totter ['tɔtə*] *vi* tambalearse; *he was tottering along the street* iba tambaleándose por la calle || tambalearse (building, government) || *to totter on the brink of ruin* estar al borde de la ruina.

tottering; tottery [-riŋ] *adj* tambaleante || inseguro, ra; vacilante, titubeante (steps) || ruinoso, sa (wall).

toucan ['tuːkən] *n* tucán *m* (bird).

touch [tʌtʃ] *n* toque *m* (light stroke); *touch of the magic wand* toque de varita mágica; *give it a touch* dale un toque || roce *m* (slight contact) || tacto *m* (sense); *the sense of touch* el sentido del tacto; *smooth to the touch* suave al tacto || mano *f*; *the master's touch* la mano del maestro || contacto *m*; *to keep, to be in touch* mantenerse, estar en contacto; *to get in touch* ponerse en contacto; *to lose touch* perder contacto || FIG chispa *f*, pizca *f*, poquito *m* (small amount); *a touch of salt* una chispa de sal; *a touch too high* un poquito demasiado alto | sello *m*, estilo *m* (style of execution); *dress with an individual touch about it* traje con un sello personal | amago *m*; *the first touches of autumn* los primeros amagos del otoño | nota *f*; *there was a touch of humour in his speech* había una nota de humor en su discurso || toque *m*, piedra *f* de toque (touchstone) || MED amago *m*, acceso *m*; *a touch of fever* un amago de fiebre | punzada *f* (of pain) || pulsación *f* (of typist) || tecleo *m* (of pianist) || SP toque *m*, tocado *m* (in fencing) | banda *f*; *in touch* fuera de banda || ARTS pincelada *f*, toque *m*; *the finishing touches* los últimos toques || FAM sablazo *m* (sponging) || — *a clever touch* un acierto, un buen toque, un buen detalle || *at a touch* al primer roce || *a touch of irony* cierta ironía || *by touch* al tacto || FIG *final* o *finishing touch* último toque, última mano || *I felt a touch on my arm* sentí que me tocaban el brazo || *to add a finishing touch to, to give* o *to put the finishing touch to* dar el último toque *or* la última mano a || FIG *to be good for a touch* prestar *or* dar dinero con facilidad || *to be in touch with sth.* estar al tanto *or* al corriente de algo || *to be out of touch* estar aislado || *to be out of touch with* haber perdido el contacto con (s.o.), no estar al tanto de (sth.) || *to get a touch of the sun* coger una ligera insolación || FIG *to have a near touch* librarse por los pelos || *to keep in touch with events* mantenerse al corriente de los acontecimientos || *to put into touch* poner en relación *or* en contacto || *to put sth. to the touch* poner *or* someter algo a prueba.

touch [tʌtʃ] *vt* tocar; *she touched the iron to see if it was hot* tocó la plancha para ver si estaba caliente; *don't touch my radio* no toques mi radio; *you can't touch the money until you are 21* no puedes tocar el dinero antes de cumplir 21 años; *he touched me on the shoulder* me tocó el hombro || tocar, rozar; *the wheels touched the kerb* las ruedas rozaban el bordillo de la acera; *the mountains seemed to touch the clouds* las montañas parecían tocar las nubes || lindar con (to have a boundary in common); *the two estates touch each other* las dos propiedades lindan una con otra || llegar a, alcanzar (to reach); *the temperature touched 40 degrees* la temperatura llegó a 40 grados || afectar (to affect) || conmover (to move to pity); *her sad story touched us deeply* su triste historia nos conmovió profundamente || hacer mella; *his years in prison haven't touched him* sus años en la cárcel no le han hecho mella || estropear (to injure slightly); *the paintings were not touched by the fire* los cuadros no fueron estropeados por el incendio || trastornar (brain) || herir (to vex); *I touched his self-esteem* herí su amor propio || estar relacionado con (to concern); *what you say does not touch the point at issue* lo que está usted diciendo no está relacionado con el punto tratado || interesar, afectar; *the question touches you nearly* la cuestión le interesa particularmente || abordar, tocar; *he didn't touch the last point on the programme* no abordó el último punto del programa || tocar, probar (to taste); *he didn't touch his meal* no probó la comida || quitar (a stain) || tocar (to test gold or silver) || contrastar (to hallmark) || coger (to take); *he would never have touched your bicycle* nunca habría cogido tu bicicleta || utilizar (to use); *I never touch the typewriter now* ahora nunca utilizo la máquina de escribir || ocuparse de (to concern o.s. with); *don't touch the project* no te ocupes del proyecto || acercar; *he touched a match to the fire* acercó una cerilla al fuego || FAM dar un sablazo; *he touched us for 10 pounds* nos dio un sablazo de diez libras || (poder) compararse con, igualar a; *she can't touch him as a pianist* como pianista no se puede comparar con él; *there's nothing to touch mountain air for giving you an appetite* no hay nada que se pueda comparar con el aire de la sierra para abrir el apetito || imponer las manos sobre (a scrofulous person) || MAR tocar, hacer escala en; *to touch port* tocar puerto || MUS tocar (an instrument) || SP tocar (in fencing) || MATH ser tangente con || tocar (bell) || — *to touch bottom* tocar el fondo (boat), hacer pie (when swimming), llegar hasta lo más profundo *or* hasta el fondo (of misfortune, etc.) || SP *to touch down* depositar (el balón) detrás de la línea de gol (rugby) || *to touch in* esbozar (drawing, etc.) | *to touch off* desencadenar, provocar (to provoke), descargar (a gun), esbozar (a drawing) || *to touch one's hat to s.o.* saludar a alguien llevándose la mano al sombrero || FIG *to touch s.o. on a tender spot* o *to the quick* herir a alguien en lo vivo | *to touch the spot* venir como anillo al dedo || *to touch up* retocar (drawing, photograph, text), dar los últimos toques a (to finish off), dar latigazos a (a horse) || FIG *touch wood* toca madera.

◆ *vi* tocarse, rozarse; *the two ships touched* los dos barcos se tocaron || lindar (to have a common boundary) || — MAR *to touch at* tocar en, hacer escala en || *to touch down* tomar tierra, aterrizar (a plane), amerizar (space capsule), hacer un ensayo (in rugby) || *to touch on* o *upon* tratar superficialmente, tocar; *he touched on the economic problem* trató superficialmente el problema económico; aludir a, referirse a, tocar (to refer to).

touchable [-əbl] *adj* tangible, palpable.

touch and go [-ən'gəu] *n* *it was touch and go whether we should catch the train* era dudoso que pudiéramos coger el tren, corríamos el riesgo de perder el tren.

touch-and-go [-ən'gəu] *adj* arriesgado, da; aventurado, da; *a touch-and-go affair* un asunto arriesgado.

touchback [-bæk] *n* US SP balón *m* muerto.

touchdown [-daun] *n* aterrizaje *m* (of plane) || amerizaje *m* (of space capsule) || US SP ensayo *m*.

touched [-t] *adj* FAM tocado, da; chiflado, da; chalado, da (crazy) || FAM *touched in the head* tocado de la cabeza.

touchhole [-həul] *n* oído *m*, fogón *m* (of firearms).

touchiness [-inis] *n* susceptibilidad *f*.

touching [-iŋ] *adj* conmovedor, ra (moving).

◆ *prep* tocante a, relativo a, referente a.

touchingly [-iŋli] *adv* de manera conmovedora.

touch judge [-dʒʌdʒ] *n* SP juez *m* de línea *or* de banda (linesman).

touchline [-lain] *n* SP línea *f* de banda.

touch paper [-peipə*] *n* mecha *f* (of a firework).

touch screen [-skri:n] *n* INFORM pantalla *f* táctil.

touchstone [-stəun] *n* piedra *f* de toque.

touch-typing [-,taipiŋ] *n* mecanografía *f* al tacto.

touchwood [-wud] *n* yesca *f* (tinder).

touchy [-i] *adj* susceptible (easily offended) || delicado, da; *a touchy subject* un tema delicado.

tough [tʌf] *adj* duro, ra; fuerte, resistente (hard to break) || duro, ra; estropajoso, sa (meat) || correoso, sa (rubbery) || fuerte, resistente; *a tough fabric* una tela fuerte || duro, ra (metal) || fuerte, robusto, ta; *a tough constitution* una constitución robusta || FIG duro, ra; violento, ta (fight) | duro, ra; penoso, sa (work) | difícil (difficult) | severo, ra (harsh); *a tough fine* una multa severa | injusto, ta (unfair) | inflexible (unyielding) | bruto, ta (rough) || — FAM *he is a tough customer!* ¡es duro de pelar! || *they've been tough on him!* ¡han sido muy duros con él! || *tough guy* rufián *m* || *tough luck!* ¡mala suerte!

◆ *n* duro *m* (thug).

toughen [-n] *vt* endurecer.

◆ *vi* endurecerse.

toughish [-iʃ] *adj* ligeramente duro, ra (meat) || FIG poco flexible (person) | algo difícil (work).

toughness [-nis] *n* dureza *f* (hardness) || lo duro, lo correoso (of meat) || resistencia *f* (strength) || inflexibilidad *f* (unyielding nature) || dificultad *f* (of work) || carácter *m* desabrido (bad temper).

toupee ['tu:pei] *n* tupé *m* (curl) || postizo *m* (hairpiece).

tour [truə*] *n* excursión *f* (organized) || visita *f*; *a conducted tour of the castle* una visita acompañada al castillo || viaje *m*; *we are going on a tour of Scotland* vamos a ir de viaje por Escocia || gira *f*; *the theatre company is on tour* la compañía de teatro está de gira || viaje *m or* visita *f* de inspección (for inspection) || SP vuelta *f* ciclista; *the tour of France* la vuelta ciclista a Francia || — *circular tour* circuito *m* || *package tour* viaje todo comprendido || *to make a tour of* recorrer || *tour of duty* turno *m* de servicio.

tour [tuə*] *vt* viajar por, recorrer, hacer un viaje por; *we toured Spain* estuvimos viajando por España || THEATR ir de gira por | estar de gira por.

◆ *vi* ir de viaje *or* de excursión; *we are going touring in the car* nos vamos de viaje en coche || estar de viaje *or* de excursión; *my parents are touring in Canada* mis padres están de viaje en Canadá.

tour de force ['tuədə'fɔ:s] *n* proeza *f*, hazaña *f*.

tourer ['tuərə*] *n* ⟶ **touring car.**

touring ['tuəriŋ] *n* turismo *m*.

◆ *adj* de turismo || que se dedica a hacer giras, que está de gira (company) || *touring party* grupo *m* de turistas.

touring car [-kɑ:*]; **tourer** ['tuərə*] *n* descapotable *m*, coche *m* de turismo descapotable.

tourism ['tuərizəm] *n* turismo *m*.

tourist ['tuərist] *n* turista *m* & *f*.

◆ *adj* turista; *tourist class* clase turista || turístico, ca; *a tourist attraction* una atracción turística || de viajes; *tourist agency* agencia de viajes || *tourist trade* turismo *m*.

touristy [-i] *adj* FAM muy guiri.

tourmaline ['tuəməlin] *n* MIN turmalina *f*.

tournament ['tuənəmənt] *n* torneo *m*.

tourney ['tuəni] *n* torneo *m*.

tourniquet ['tuənikei] *n* MED torniquete *m*.

tour operator ['tuər,ɔpəreitə*] *n* agente *m* de viajes || agencia *f* de viajes.

tousle ['tauzl] *n* maraña *f* (of hair).

tousle ['tauzl] *vt* desgreñar, despeinar (hair) || arrugar, ajar (clothes, etc.).

tout [taut] *n* FAM gancho *m* (who solicits customers) || revendedor, ra (of tickets, etc.) || COMM corredor *m* || *on the tout* espiando.

tout [taut] *vt* acosar, importunar (to solicit) || vender (to sell) || revender (tickets) || SP seguir a escondidas el entrenamiento de (race horses).

◆ *vi* *to tout for* solicitar.

tow [təu] *n* remolque *m*; *on tow* a remolque || remolque *m*, sirga *f* (rope) || vehículo *m* remolcado (towed vehicle) || estopa *f* (fibre) || — FIG *he always has his family in tow* siempre lleva a su familia a cuestas || *to have* o *to take in tow* remolcar (car, etc.).

tow [təu] *vt* remolcar (car, boat) || sirgar, llevar a la sirga (from towpath) || FIG llevar a cuestas, arrastrar.

towage [-idʒ] *n* remolque *m* || sirga *f* (from towpath) || derechos *m pl* de remolque (tow fee).

toward ['təuəd] *adj* próximo, ma.

toward [tə'wɔ:d]; **towards** [-z] *prep* hacia (in the direction of); *as he came towards me* al venir hacia mí; *it was facing towards me* miraba hacia mí; *our country is rapidly moving towards prosperity* nuestro país se encamina rápidamente hacia la prosperidad || para (for); *to make a contribution towards charity* hacer un donativo para obras de caridad || con (with); *to feel angry towards s.o.* estar enfadado con alguien || para con (in respect of); *generosity towards others* generosidad para con los demás || con respecto a, respecto a (with regard to); *the attitude of Spain towards America* la actitud de España respecto a América || hacia, alrededor de (around); *towards midnight* alrededor de medianoche || próximo a, cerca de (near).

towbar ['təubɑ:*] *n* barra *f* de remolque.

towboat ['təubəut] *n* MAR remolcador *m*.

tow car ['təukɑ:*] *n* US grúa *f* remolque.

towel ['tauəl] *n* toalla *f*; *bath towel* toalla de baño || — *sanitary towel* paño higiénico, compresa *f* || FIG *to throw in the towel* tirar la esponja (in boxing), darse por vencido (to give up) || *Turkish towel* toalla de felpa.

towel ['tauəl] *vt* secar *or* frotar con toalla.

towel horse [-hɔ:s]; **towel rack** [-ræk]; **towel rail** [-reil]; **towel roller** [-,rəulə*] *n* toallero *m*.

towelling; toweling [-iŋ] *n* felpa *f* || *a towelling bathrobe* un albornoz.

tower ['tauə*] *n* torre *f*; *the Eiffel tower* la torre Eiffel; *the Tower of London, of Babel* la Torre de Londres, de Babel; *control tower* torre de control *or* de mando || fortaleza *f* (fortress) || — *church* o *bell tower* campanario *m*, torre de la iglesia || MAR *conning tower* torreta *f* (of a submarine), torre de mando (of a warship) || FIG *ivory tower* torre de marfil || *tower block* torre *f* || FIG *tower of strength* ayuda muy valiosa || *water tower* arca *f* de agua, depósito elevado de agua.

tower ['tauə*] *vi* elevarse, encumbrarse (to rise up) || *to tower above* o *over* dominar (building), descollar entre, destacarse de (person).

towered [-d] *adj* ARCH flanqueado por torres.

towering [-riŋ] *adj* elevado, da; encumbrado, da; altísimo, ma (very high) || grande; *a towering height* una gran altura || sobresaliente, destacado, da (rising above others) || violento, ta; intenso, sa (emotions) || ilimitado, da; desmedido, da (ambition).

towing ['təuiŋ] *n* remolque *m*.

towline ['təulain] *n* remolque *m*, sirga *f*.

town [taun] *n* ciudad *f* (large) || pueblo *m*, población *f* (small) || ciudad *f*, pueblo *m* (people); *the whole town was talking about it* la ciudad entera hablaba de ello || ciudad *f*; *to prefer the town to the country* preferir la ciudad al campo; *to live out of town* vivir fuera de la ciudad || centro *m*, ciudad *f*; *to go shopping in town* ir de compras al centro || capital *f*; *to go up to town* ir a la capital || US municipio *m* || — *boom town* ciudad hongo || *canvas town* ciudad de lona || *it's the talk of the town* es la comidilla del pueblo || *new town* pueblo nuevo || *satellite town* ciudad satélite || *to be out of town* estar fuera, estar de viaje || FIG *to go (out) on the town, to paint the town red* irse de juerga | *to go to town* no reparar en gastos | *to go to town on sth.* hacer una cosa con toda su alma (to put one's heart into sth.) || *town and gown* los estudiantes y la gente de la ciudad || *twin town* ciudad hermanada.

◆ *adj* de la ciudad, del pueblo; *town church* iglesia del pueblo || urbano, na; *town life* vida urbana || — *town clerk* secretario *m* del ayuntamiento || *town council* ayuntamiento *m*, concejo *m* municipal || *town councillor* concejal *m* || *town crier* pregonero *m* || *town hall* ayuntamiento *m* || *town planner* urbanista *m* || *town planning* urbanismo *m* || FIG *town talk* comidilla *f* del pueblo.

town house ['taunhaus] *n* casa *f* de ciudad de tres o más pisos (terraced house) || residencia *f* urbana (city residence).

townlet ['taunlet] *n* pueblecito *m*, aldea *f*.

townsfolk ['taunzfəuk] *pl n* ciudadanos *m*, habitantes *m* (of a particular town) || gente *f sing* de la ciudad, ciudadanos *m* (as opposed to country people).

township ['taunʃip] *n* municipio *m*, término *m* municipal.

townsman ['taunzmən] *n* habitante *m* de la ciudad, ciudadano *m*.

— OBSERV El plural de esta palabra es *townsmen*.

townspeople ['taunzˌpiːpl] *pl n* —> **townsfolk.**

towpath ['təupɑːθ] *n* camino *m* de sirga.

towrope ['təurəup] *n* remolque *m* || sirga *f* (of canal).

tow truck ['təutrʌk] *n* grúa *f* remolque.

toxic ['tɔksik] *adj* tóxico, ca.

toxicant [-ənt] *adj* tóxico, ca.

◆ *n* tóxico *m*.

toxicity [tɔk'sisiti] *n* toxicidad *f*.

toxicological ['tɔksikə'lɔdʒikəl] *adj* toxicológico, ca.

toxicologist [ˌtɔksi'kɔlədʒist] *n* toxicólogo *m*.

toxicology [ˌtɔksi'kɔlədʒi] *n* toxicología *f*.

toxicomania [ˌtɔksikə'meinjə] *n* toxicomanía *f* (drug addiction).

toxicosis [ˌtɔksi'kəusis] *n* MED toxicosis *f inv*.

toxin ['tɔksin] *n* toxina *f*.

toxophilite [tɔk'sɔfilait] *n* aficionado *m* al tiro al arco (man fond of archery).

toy [tɔi] *n* juguete *m*.

◆ *adj* de juguete; *a toy car* un coche de juguete || enano, na; *toy poodle* caniche enano || — FAM *toy boy* amiguito de una mujer mayor || *toy dog* perro faldero || *toy soldier* soldadito *m* de plomo || *toy theatre* teatro *m* de títeres, teatro *m* de marionetas.

toy [tɔi] *vi* *to toy with* acariciar (an idea), jugar con (to play with), juguetear con (to play around with), manosear, toquetear (to fiddle with), comisquear (food).

toyshop [-ʃɔp] *n* juguetería *f*, tienda *f* de juguetes.

trace [treis] *n* huella *f* (footprint) || rastro *m* (trail); *traces left by a snail* el rastro de un caracol || indicio *m* (indication); *there was no trace of his having been there* no había ningún indicio de que hubiera estado allí || vestigio *m* (remnant); *the Empire left no traces* el Imperio no dejó vestigio alguno || pizca *f* (slight amount); *not a trace of truth* ni pizca de verdad || tirante *m* (of horse's harness) || PHYS gráfico *m* (of seismograph, etc.) || MATH traza *f* (technical drawing) || MED indicio *m* (of albumen) || FIG *to kick over the traces* desmandarse || *without trace* sin dejar rastro.

trace [treis] *vt* trazar, dibujar (letters, plan) || calcar (with tracing paper) || seguir (a path, tracks, etc.) || rastrear, seguir la pista de (to follow the trail of); *the police traced the thief* la policía siguió la pista del ladrón || localizar, encontrar (to find s.o.) || encontrar (to find sth.) || — *the rumour was traced back to a shopkeeper* se descubrió que el rumor procedía de un tendero || *to trace back to* hacer remontar a (one's ancestry), remontarse a; *my family traces back to Henry VIII* mi familia se remonta a Enrique VIII; descubrir (to find out) || *to trace out* trazar (a plan), descubrir el rastro de (a thief), determinar (a date, an origin) || *to trace over* calcar.

traceable [-əbl] *adj* fácil de seguir (easily followed) || fácil de encontrar (easily found).

trace element [-ˌelimənt] *n* oligoelemento *m*.

tracer [-ə*] *n* diseñador, ra (person) || tiralíneas *m inv* (ruling pen) || patrón *m* (in sewing) || MIL bala *f* trazadora || CHEM indicador *m*.

◆ *adj* trazador, ra || MIL *tracer bullet* bala trazadora.

tracery [-əri] *n* ARCH tracería *f*.

trachea [trə'kiə] *n* tráquea *f*.

— OBSERV El plural de *trachea* es *tracheae* o *tracheas*.

tracheitis [ˌtræki'aitis] *n* MED traqueítis *f inv*.

tracheotomy [ˌtræki'ɔtəmi] *n* MED traqueotomía *f*.

trachoma [trə'kəumə] *n* MED tracoma *m*.

trachyte ['trækait] *n* MIN traquita *f*.

tracing ['treisiŋ] *n* calco *m* (copying of a drawing) || trazado *m* (drawing of a line) || rastreo *m* (trailing) || busca *f*, búsqueda *f* (search) || gráfico *m* (of a recording instrument) || — *tracing bullet* bala trazadora || *tracing paper* papel *m* de calcar || *tracing wheel* ruleta *f*, rodillo trazador (of tailors).

track [træk] *n* sendero *m*, camino *m* (path) || rodada *f*, carril *m* (of wheels) || rastro *m*, huella *f* (of persons, of animals) || vestigio *m*, rastro *m* (of things) || estela *f* (of a ship) || curso *m*, trayectoria *f*, recorrido *m* (course); *the track of a meteor* la trayectoria de un meteoro || vía *f* (railway); *single, double track* vía única, doble || distancia *f* entre ejes (width of a vehicle) || batalla *f* (of a car) || MAR & AVIAT rumbo *m* || oruga *f* (of a tank, of a tractor, etc.) || pista *f* (of tape recorder) || SP pista *f*; *dirt track* pista de ceniza || FIG pista *f*; *to be on s.o.'s track* seguir la pista de uno | camino *m*; *beaten track* camino trillado; *to be on the right track* ir por buen camino || — *dog-racing track* canódromo *m* || *forest track* camino forestal || *motor-racing track* autódromo *m* || *mule track* camino carretero || FIG *on the right, wrong track* en el buen, en el mal camino || *sheep track* cañada *f* || FIG *to be way off the track* estar completamente despistado (person), no tener nada que ver con el asunto (thing) || *to follow in s.o.'s track* seguir las huellas de alguien (to follow), seguir los pasos de alguien (to follow in s.o.'s footsteps) || *to go off the track* descarrilar (a train) || *to keep track of* seguir (to follow), vigilar, seguir de cerca (to keep an eye on) || *to leave the track* descarrilar (a train) || *to lose track of* perder la noción de (the time), perder el hilo de (a conversation), perder de vista, perder la pista de (people), no estar al tanto de (events) || FIG *to throw s.o. off the track* despistar a uno.

◆ *pl* huellas *f* (footprints) || — *in one's tracks* en seco; *to stop in one's tracks* pararse en seco; *to stop s.o. in his tracks* parar a alguien en seco || *to cover (up) one's tracks* no dejar rastro || FIG *to fall dead in one's tracks* caer muerto || FAM *to make tracks* largarse, marcharse (to leave), irse rápidamente (to go); *he made tracks for the station* se fue rápidamente a la estación || *to run off the tracks* descarrilar (a train).

track [træk] *vt* seguir las huellas de, seguir la pista de, rastrear (to hunt) || seguir la pista de (to pursue); *the police are tracking the criminal* la policía está siguiendo la pista del criminal || seguir; *to track an aeroplane by radar* seguir un avión con el radar || poner orugas a (tractors, tanks, etc.) || MAR remolcar a la sirga, sirgar (to tow) || — *to track down* acorralar (to corner), localizar (to locate), capturar (a thief), averiguar el origen de (to discover) || US *to track mud into the house* ensuciar la casa con barro || *to track out* encontrar.

◆ *vi* estar alineadas (wheels) || CINEM tomar vistas desplazándose (the camera) || US dejar huellas (to leave tracks).

trackage [-idʒ] *n* remolque *m* || red *f* de ferrocarriles (of railways) || derecho *m* a utilizar las vías de otra compañía.

tracker [-ə*] *n* perseguidor *m*.

track events [-i'vents] *pl n* SP atletismo *m sing* en pista.

track gauge; US **track gage** [-geidʒ] *n* ancho *m* de vía.

tracking [-iŋ] *n* seguimiento *m* (of a rocket) || rastreo *m* (of a dog) || *tracking station* estación *f* de seguimiento.

tracklayer [-ˌleiə*] *n* asentador *m* de vías.

trackless [-lis] *adj* sin huellas (without footprints) || sin caminos (without path) || sin rieles (without rails).

trackman [-mən] *n* US guardavía *m*.

— OBSERV El plural de esta palabra es *trackmen*.

track meet [-miːt] *n* US encuentro *m* de atletismo.

track record [-ˌrekɔːd] *n* historial *m*.

track shoe [-ʃuː] *n* zapatilla *f* deportiva claveteada.

tract [trækt] *n* octavilla *f* (propaganda sheet) || opúsculo *m* (pamphlet) || región *f*, zona *f* (area) || extensión *f* || ANAT aparato *m*; *digestive tract* aparato digestivo | vías *f pl*; *respiratory tract* vías respiratorias || REL tracto *m* || *tract of land* terreno *m*.

tractability [ˌtræktə'biliti] *n* docilidad *f* || maleabilidad *f*, ductilidad *f* (of materials).

tractable ['træktəbl] *adj* dócil, tratable (people) || dócil (animals) || manejable (device) || dúctil, maleable (materials).

tractate ['trækteit] *n* tratado *m* (treatise).

tractile ['træktail] *adj* dúctil, maleable.

traction ['trækʃən] *n* tracción *f* (act of hauling, pulling force) || fricción *f* adhesiva, adherencia *f* (friction) || MED tracción *f* || — *traction engine* locomotora tractora *or* de tracción || *traction wheel* rueda *f* de tracción.

tractive ['træktiv] *adj* de tracción.

tractor ['træktə*] *n* AGR tractor *m* || camión *m* tractor (lorry) || locomotora *f* de tracción (traction engine) || *caterpillar tractor* tractor oruga.

tractor-drawn [-drɔːn] *adj* arrastrado por un tractor.

tractor driver [-ˌdraivə*]; **tractor operator** [-ˌɔpəreitə*] *n* tractorista *m* & *f*.

tractor propeller [-prə'pelə*] *n* hélice *f* tractora.

trade [treid] *n* comercio *m*; *our trade with the Common Market* nuestro comercio con el

Mercado Común; *Board of Trade* Ministerio de Comercio; *foreign trade* comercio exterior || industria *f*; *the wood trade* la industria de la madera || artesanía *f* (craft) || ramo *m*; *I'm in the grocery trade* estoy en el ramo de la alimentación || oficio *m*, profesión *f*; *what's your trade?* ¿cuál es su oficio? || comerciantes *m pl* (tradespeople) || negociantes *m pl* (businessmen) || gremio *m* (people in the same profession) || transacción *f*, negocio *m* (a deal); *I did a good trade* hice un buen negocio || tráfico *m*, comercio *m* (of drugs) || cambio *m* (exchange) || US clientela *f*, clientes *m pl* (customers) || — *a baker by trade* de oficio panadero || *a doctor by trade* de profesión médico || *to be in trade* ser comerciante, tener un negocio || *to carry on a trade* ejercer un oficio *or* una profesión.
◆ *pl* vientos *m* alisios (winds).
◆ *adj* de comercio, comercial; *trade agreement* acuerdo comercial || industrial.

trade [treid] *vi* comerciar (*in* en) (as a business) || negociar (to have business dealings with s.o.) || ser cliente, comprar (to be a customer); *I don't trade at that store* no soy cliente de esta tienda, no compro en esta tienda || *to trade on* aprovecharse de.
◆ *vt* trocar, cambiar; *to trade skins for gold* cambiar pieles por oro || *to trade in* dar *or* tomar como entrada (a used car, etc.).

trade cycle [-saikl] *n* COMM ciclo *m* comercial.

trade discount [-ˌdiskaunt] *n* COMM descuento *m* comercial.

trade disputes [-dis'pjuːts] *pl n* conflictos *m* laborales.

trade gap [-gæp] *n* COMM déficit *m* [en la balanza comercial].

trade-in [-in] *n* US artículo *m* entregado como entrada para el pago de otro artículo.

trademark [-maːk] *n* marca *f* de fábrica || FIG sello *m*, marca *f* || *registered trademark* marca registrada.

trade name [-neim] *n* nombre *m* comercial (of an article) || marca *f* registrada (trademark) || razón *f* social (of a firm).

trade-off [-ɔf] *n* intercambio *m*, concesión *f* mutua.

trade price [-prais] *n* precio *m* al por mayor.

trader [-ə*] *n* comerciante *m* & *f* (merchant) || negociante *m* & *f* (dealer) || MAR barco *m* mercante.

trade route [-ruːt] *n* ruta *f* comercial.

trade school [-skuːl] *n* universidad *f* laboral.

tradesman [-zmən] *n* tendero *m*, comerciante *m* (shopkeeper) || *tradesmen's entrance* entrada *f* de proveedores, puerta *f* de servicio.
— OBSERV El plural de *tradesman* es *tradesmen*.

tradespeople [-zˌpiːpl] *pl n* comerciantes *m*.

trades union [-z'juːnjən] *n* sindicato *m*.

trades unionism [z'juːnjənizəm] *n* sindicalismo *m*.

trades unionist [-z'juːnjənist] *n* sindicalista *m* & *f*.

tradeswoman [-ˌwumən] *n* tendera *f*, comerciante *f*.
— OBSERV El plural de *tradeswoman* es *tradeswomen*.

trade union [-'juːnjən] *n* sindicato *m*; *member of a trade union* afiliado a un sindicato || (ant) gremio *m* || *Trades Union Congress* confederación *f* de los sindicatos británicos.

trade unionism [-'juːnjənizəm] *n* sindicalismo *m*.

trade unionist [-'juːnjənist] *n* sindicalista *m* & *f*, miembro *m* de un sindicato.

trade wind [-wind] *n* viento *m* alisio.

trading ['treidiŋ] *n* comercio *m*.
◆ *adj* comercial; *trading concern* empresa comercial.

trading post [-pəust] *n* (ant) factoría *f*.

trading stamps [-stæmps] *pl n* puntos *m*, cupones *m* [que se reúnen para conseguir un premio].

trading estate [-is'teit] *n* zona *f* industrial.

trading year [-jiə*] *n* ejercicio *m* económico, año *m* económico.

tradition [trə'diʃən] *n* tradición *f*.

traditional [-əl] *adj* tradicional.

traditionalism [-əlizəm] *n* tradicionalismo *m*.

traditionalist [-əlist] *adj/n* tradicionalista.

traditor ['trædità*] *n* traidor *m* [entre los primeros cristianos].

traduce [trə'djuːs] *n* difamar, calumniar.

traducement [-mənt] *n* difamación *f*, calumnia *f* (slander).

traducer [-ə*] *n* difamador, ra; calumniador, ra.

traffic ['træfik] *n* tráfico *m*, circulación *f* (of cars); *vehicular traffic* circulación rodada || tráfico *m* (of people, boats, planes, etc.) || tránsito *m* (of tourists, etc.) || tráfico *m* (illegal business) || comercio *m* (trade) || negocio *m* (dealings) || cambio *m* (exchange) || intercambio *m* (of ideas, etc.) || *white slave traffic* trata *f* de blancas.
◆ *adj* de la circulación, del tráfico.

traffic ['træfik] *vi* traficar, comerciar, negociar (*in* en).

trafficator [-eitə*] *n* AUT indicador *m* de dirección, flecha *f*.

traffic circle [-ˌsəːkl] *n* US encrucijada *f*, glorieta *f* (roundabout).

traffic controller [-kən'trəulə] *n* AVIAT controlador *m* del tráfico aéreo.

traffic island [-ˌailənd] *n* isleta *f*, refugio *m*.

traffic jam [-dʒæm] *n* embotellamiento *m*, atasco *m*.

trafficker [-ə*] *n* traficante *m* (of drugs, etc.) || tratante *m* (in white slaves) || negociante *m* & *f* (dealer).

traffic light [-lait] *n* semáforo *m*.

traffic police [-pəˌliːs] *n* policía *f* de tráfico.

traffic policeman [-pəˌliːsmən] *n* guardia *m*.
— OBSERV El plural es *traffic policemen*.

traffic sign [-sain] *n* señal *f* de tráfico.

traffic warden [-ˌwɔːdn] *n* guardia *m* urbano.

tragacanth ['trægəkænθ] *n* BOT tragacanto *m*.

tragedian [trə'dʒiːdjən] *n* trágico *m* (writer) || actor *m* trágico (actor).

tragedienne [trædʒe'djən] *n* actriz *f* trágica.

tragedy ['trædʒidi] *n* tragedia *f*.

tragic ['trædʒik]; **tragical** [-əl] *adj* trágico, ca; *don't be so tragic!* ¡no te pongas tan trágico!

tragically ['trædʒikli] *adv* trágicamente.

tragicomedy ['trædʒi'kɔmidi] *n* tragicomedia *f*.

tragicomic ['trædʒi'kɔmik]; **tragicomical** [-əl] *adj* tragicómico, ca.

tragus ['treigəs] *n* ANAT trago *m*.
— OBSERV El plural de la palabra inglesa es *tragi*.

trail [treil] *n* huellas *f pl*, rastro *m* (of an animal, of a person) || pista *f*; *false trail* pista falsa || camino *m*, sendero *m* (path) || estela *f* (of smoke, etc.) || nube *f* (of dust) || reguero *m* (of blood, of powder) || SP pista *f* || ASTR cola *f* (of a meteor) || MIL gualdera *f* (of a cannon) || FIG estela *f* || — *to be on the trail of* seguir la pista de || *to leave a trail of destruction* arrasar todo al pasar || *to lose, to pick up the trail* perder, encontrar la pista.

trail [treil] *vt* arrastrar (to drag) || llevar consigo (to bring with one) || perseguir (to pursue) || seguir el rastro de, rastrear (an animal) || seguir la pista de (a person) || localizar; *they trailed the jewels to a small shop* localizaron las joyas en una pequeña tienda || seguir a (to follow) || ir detrás de (to lag behind) || dejar un reguero de (to leave a trail of) || MIL suspender (arms) || MIL *trail arms!* suspendan ¡ar!
◆ *vi* arrastrarse (to drag); *his coat is trailing on the ground* su abrigo se arrastra por el suelo || colgar (to hang down) || ir lentamente (to go slowly) || BOT trepar (to climb) || — *to trail along* arrastrarse (to drag), avanzar lentamente (to walk slowly) || *to trail behind* quedarse atrás, rezagarse || *to trail off* desvanecerse (smoke), apagarse (sounds).

trailblazer [-ˌbleizə*] *n* pionero *m*.

trailblazing [-ˌbleiziŋ] *adj* precursor, ra.

trailer [-ə*] *n* remolque *m* (behind a car) || US remolque *m* habitable, caravana *f* (caravan) || CINEM trailer *m*, avance *m* || BOT planta *f* trepadora.

trailing [-iŋ] *adj* BOT trepador, ra; rastrero, ra || AVIAT *trailing edge* borde *m* de salida.

trail net [-net] *n* red *f* barredera.

train [trein] *n* tren *m* (railway); *express, fast, mail train* tren expreso, rápido, correo; *commuter* o *suburban train* tren de cercanías; *freight* o *goods train* tren de mercancías; *relief* o *extra train* tren suplementario; *slow* o *stopping train* tren ómnibus; *through train* tren directo; *up train* tren ascendente || serie *f*, sucesión *f* (series); *train of events* serie de acontecimientos; *in an unbroken train* en una serie ininterrumpida || procesión *f* (procession) || séquito *m*, comitiva *f* (retinue) || cortejo *m* (suite) || cola *f* (of a woman's dress) || cola *f* (of a comet, of the tail of a bird) || reguero *m* (of gunpowder) || TECH tren *m*; *train of gears* tren de engranajes || MIL tren *m* de campaña || recua *f* (of animals) || MAR convoy *m* (of ships) || rosario *m* (of bombs) || hilo *m* (of thought) || — *baggage train* tren de equipajes || *by train* en tren, por ferrocarril || FIG *in one's train* después | *to be in train* estar en curso || *to catch a train* tomar el tren || *to change trains* cambiar de tren, hacer transbordo || FIG *to set in train* poner en marcha.

train [trein] *vt* amaestrar (an animal) || domar (a horse) || formar, preparar, adiestrar, capacitar (a person to do a job) || educar (a child, one's voice) || hacer entrar en vereda, someter a una disciplina (to discipline) || enseñar (to teach) || guiar (plants) || apuntar (*on* a) (a gun) || enfocar (*on* a) (camera, telescope, etc.) || SP entrenar || MIL instruir || *to train o.s. in* ejercitarse en.
◆ *vi* entrenarse; *good sportsmen have to train a lot* los buenos deportistas tienen que entrenarse mucho || prepararse, formarse (to prepare o.s.) || estudiar, seguir un curso (to study) || ejercitarse (to practise) || MIL hacer la instrucción || FAM viajar *or* ir en tren (to go by rail).

trainbearer [-ˌbɛərə*] *n* persona *f* que lleva la cola a otra.

train dress [-dres] *n* traje *m* con cola.

trained [-d] *adj* diplomado, da (nurse, etc.) || especializado, da; cualificado, da (worker) || preparado, da (prepared) || amaestrado, da (an animal) || domado, da (a horse) || educado, da (a child) || disciplinado, da (an army) || entrenado, da (a sportsman) || experto, ta (eye).

trainee [trei'niː] *n* aprendiz, za (s.o. learning a job) || cursillista *m* & *f*, persona *f* que sigue un cursillo de formación profesional || persona *f* que está de prácticas || US MIL recluta *m*.

trainer ['treinə*] *n* SP entrenador, ra || amaestrador, ra (of animals) || domador, ra (of horses) || preparador, ra; cuidador, ra (of boxers, etc.) || MIL instructor *m*.
◆ *pl* zapatillas *f* deportivas (training shoes).

training ['treiniŋ] *n* entrenamiento *m* (in sports) || instrucción *f*, enseñanza *f* (teaching) || formación *f*, capacitación *f*; *vocational training* formación profesional || preparación *f*, adiestramiento *m* (instruction in a particular skill) || aprendizaje *m* (apprenticeship) || amaestramiento *m* (of animals) || doma *f* (of horses) || MIL puntería *f* (of gun) || instrucción *f* (of troops) || — *in training* haciendo un cursillo de formación *or* de preparación (doing a course of study), que está entrenando (sportsmen, etc.), en plena forma, entrenado, da (in form) || *out of training* desentrenado, da || *physical training* educación física, gimnasia *f*.

training camp [-kæmp] *n* MIL campo *m* de instrucción.

training center [-,sentə*] *n* centro *m* de formación profesional.

training college [-,kɔlidʒ] *n* escuela *f* normal (for teachers).

training school [-sku:l] *n* escuela *f* de formación profesional, centro *m* de capacitación || reformatorio *m* (correctional institution).

training ship [-ʃip] *n* MAR buque *m* escuela.

trainman ['treinmən] *n* US empleado *m* del ferrocarril, ferroviario *m*.
— OBSERV El plural de *trainman* es *trainmen*.

train oil ['treinɔil] *n* aceite *m* de ballena (from blubber) || aceite *m* de pescado (from codfish, etc.).

train spotter ['trein,spɔtə*] *n* coleccionista *m* & *f* de números de locomotora.

traipse; trapes [treips] *vi* FAM andar; *to traipse all over town* andar por toda la ciudad.

trait [trei] *n* rasgo *m*, característica *f*.

traitor ['treitə*] *n* traidor *m*.

traitorous [-rəs] *adj* traidor, ra; traicionero, ra.

traitress ['treitris] *n* traidora *f*.

Trajan ['treidʒən] *pr n* Trajano *m* || *Trajan's Column* Columna Trajana.

trajectory [trə'dʒektəri] *n* trayectoria *f*.

tram [træm] *n* tranvía *m* (vehicle) || vagoneta *f* (in mines) || vía *f* de tranvía (tramline) || trama *f* de seda (in textiles) || *tram system* red tranviaria.

tramcar [-ka:*] *n* tranvía *m*; *mule-drawn tramcar* tranvía de sangre *or* de mulas.

tramline [-lain] *n* vía *f* de tranvía (rails) || línea *f* de tranvía (route).
◆ *pl* líneas *f* laterales (in tennis).

trammel ['træməl] *n* trasmallo *m* (net) || traba *f* (for training a horse) || US llares *m pl* (pothook).
◆ *pl* compás *m sing* de varas (beam compass) || FIG trabas *f*, obstáculos *m* (impediments).

trammel ['træməl] *vt* pescar con trasmallo (to catch in a trammel) || poner trabas a (a horse) || FIG poner trabas a, obstaculizar.

tramontane [trəmɔn'teːnə] *n* tramontana *f* (wind).

tramp [træmp] *n* ruido *m* de pasos (footsteps) || paseo *m* largo, caminata *f* (walk) || vagabundo *m* (person with no fixed home) || MAR barco *m* mercante [de servicio irregular] (freight ship) || US FAM fulana *f* (prostitute).

tramp [træmp] *vi* andar pesadamente, andar con pasos pesados (to walk heavily) || ir a pie, caminar (to walk) || ser un vagabundo (to be a tramp).
◆ *vt* andar por, recorrer a pie; *to tramp the streets* andar por las calles || US pisotear (to trample).

trample [-l] *n* ruido *m* de pasos (sound) || pisoteo *m*.

trample [-l] *vt* pisar; *to trample grapes* pisar uvas || pisotear; *the crowd trampled him to death* la multitud le pisoteó hasta matarlo || — *to trample mud all over the floor* pisar el suelo con los zapatos llenos de barro || *to trample out* apagar de un pisotón.
◆ *vi* *to trample on* o *upon* o *over* pisotear; *to trample over the flower beds* pisotear las flores.

trampolin ['træmpəlin]; **trampoline** ['træmpəli:n] *n* cama *f* elástica.

tramway ['træmwei] *n* tranvía *m* (vehicle) || vía *f* de tranvía (line) || *tramway system* red tranviaria.

trance [trɑ:ns] *n* trance *m* (of medium) || MED catalepsia *f* || FIG éxtasis *m inv*.

tranquil ['træŋkwil] *adj* tranquilo, la.

tranquillity; US **tranquility** [træŋ'kwiliti] *n* tranquilidad *f*.

tranquillization; US **tranquilization** [,træŋkwilai'zeiʃən] *n* aplacamiento *m*, sosiego *m*.

tranquillize; US **tranquilize** ['træŋkwilaiz] *vt* tranquilizar.
◆ *vi* tranquilizarse.

tranquillizer; US **tranquilizer** [-ə*] *n* MED tranquilizante *m*.

tranquillizing; US **tranquilizing** [-iŋ] *adj* tranquilizador, ra || MED tranquilizante.

transact [træn'zækt] *vt* llevar a cabo, hacer (to perform) || tratar, negociar, tratar (to negotiate).
◆ *vi* negociar.

transaction [træn'zækʃən] *n* negociación *f*, tramitación *f* (of business) || transacción *f* (deal).
◆ *pl* actas *f*, memorias *f* (records).

transactional [-əl] *adj* INFORM transaccional.

transactor [træn'zæktə*] *n* negociador, ra.

transalpine ['trænz'ælpain] *adj* transalpino, na; trasalpino, na.

trans-Andean ['trænz'ændi:iən] *adj* transandino, na.

transatlantic ['trænzət'læntik] *adj* transatlántico, ca; trasatlántico, ca.

transcaspian ['trænz'kæspjən] *n* transcaspiano, na.

Transcaucasia ['trænzkɔ:'keizjə] *pr n* GEOGR Transcaucasia *f*.

Transcaucasian [-n] *adj/n* transcaucásico, ca.

transceiver [træn'si:və*] *n* transmisor-receptor *m*.

transcend [træn'send] *vt* ir más allá de, estar por encima de; *to transcend reason* estar por encima de la razón || exceder, superar, rebasar, sobrepasar; *to transcend one's hopes* sobrepasar las esperanzas de uno || PHIL & REL trascender, transcender.
◆ *vi* PHIL & REL trascender, transcender.

transcendence [træn'sendəns]; **transcendency** [-i] *n* PHIL & REL trascendencia *f*, transcendencia *f*.

transcendent [træn'sendənt] *adj* PHIL & REL trascendente || sobresaliente, extraordinario, ria.

transcendental [-əl] *adj* PHIL trascendental, transcendental || sobrenatural || *transcendental meditation* meditación *f* trascendental || *transcendental number* número trascendente *or* transcendente.

transcendentalism [,trænsen'dentəlizəm] *n* PHIL trascendentalismo *m*, transcendentalismo *m*.

transcoding [trænz'kəudiŋ] *n* INFORM transcodificación *f*.

transcontinental ['trænz,kɔnti'nentl] *adj* transcontinental.

transcribe [træn'skraib] *vt* transcribir, trascribir (shorthand, music, etc.) || RAD grabar (to record).

transcriber [-ə*] *n* transcriptor *m*.

transcript ['trænskript] *n* transcripción *f* || copia *f* (copy).

transcription [træn'skripʃən] *n* transcripción *f* || RAD emisión *f* diferida (program) | grabación *f* (recording) || *phonetic transcription* pronunciación figurada.

transducer [træns'dju:sə*] *n* PHYS transductor *m* (device for transferring power).

transect ['trænsekt] *vt* cortar transversalmente.

transection [træn'sekʃən] *n* corte *m* transversal.

transept ['trænsept] *n* crucero *m* (in a church).

transfer ['trænsfə:*]; **transferring** [træns'fə:riŋ] *n* traslado *m* (moving, displacement) || transbordo *m* (from one vehicle to another) || trasvase *m* (of rivers) || transferencia *f*, transmisión *f* (of property, of shares, etc.) || transporte *m* (transport) || traslado *m* (of employee, of corpse) || transmisión *f*; *transfer of power* transmisión de poder || transferencia *f* (of one's allegiance) || SP traspaso *m* (of a player) || ARTS reporte *m* || COMM transferencia *f* (of money) | traspaso *m* (of a shop) || calcomanía *f* (small picture) || US billete *m* de transbordo (ticket) || SP *transfer fee* traspaso *m* (for a player).

transfer [træns'fə:*] *vt* trasladar (from one place or job to another); *to transfer a prisoner* trasladar a un preso; *they transferred him to Barcelona* le trasladaron a Barcelona || transferir (one's allegiance) || transbordar (from one vehicle to another) || trasvasar (rivers) || transferir, transmitir (a right, a title) || ARTS reportar || calcar (a small picture) || SP traspasar (a player) || COMM transferir (money) | traspasar (a shop) || INFORM exportar (ficheros, archivos, documentos).
◆ *vi* trasladarse (from one place to another) || cambiar (to change) || hacer transbordo, transbordar (to change trains, buses, etc.).

transferable [-rəbl] *adj* transferible || transportable || trasladable || transmisible || *not transferable* intransferible (ticket), inalienable (right).

transferee [,trænsfə'ri:] *n* cesionario, ria.

transference ['trænsfərəns] *n* ⟶ **transfer** || **transferencia** *f*, trasferencia *f* (in psychology).

transferential [,trænsfə'renʃəl] *adj* de transferencia.

transfer paper ['trænsfə,peipə*] *n* papel *m* de calcar.

transferrer [træns'fə:rə*] *n* transferidor, ra.

transferring [træns'fə:riŋ] *n* ⟶ **transfer.**

transfiguration [,trænsfigju'reiʃən] *n* transfiguración *f*, trasfiguración *f*.

transfigure [træns'figə*] *vt* transfigurar, trasfigurar.

transfix [træns'fiks] *vt* traspasar, atravesar (to impale) || FIG traspasar; *transfixed with pain* traspasado de dolor | paralizar; *transfixed with* *fear* paralizado por el miedo || FIG *transfixed with horror* horrorizado, da.

transfixion [træns'fikʃən] *n* transfixión *f*.

transform [træns'fɔːm] *vt* transformar; *the experience transformed him* le transformó la experiencia || PHYS & ELECTR transformar.

transformation [ˌtrænsfə'meiʃən] *n* transformación *f* || (ant) postizo *m* (false hair) || THEATR *transformation scene* mutación *f*, cambio escénico.

transformer [træns'fɔːmə*] *n* transformador, ra || ELECTR transformador *m*.

transformism [træns'fɔːmizəm] *n* transformismo *m*.

transformist [træns'fɔːmist] *adj/n* transformista.

transfuse [træns'fjuːz] *vt* transfundir, trasegar, transvasar, trasvasar (a liquid) || infundir, comunicar; *to transfuse one's enthusiasm into the class* infundir su entusiasmo a la clase || MED hacer una transfusión de (blood) | hacer una transfusión a (a patient).

transfuser [-ə*] *n* transfusor *m*.

transfusion [træns'fjuːʒən] *n* MED transfusión *f*; *blood transfusion* transfusión de sangre || trasiego *m* (of liquids).

transgress [træns'gres] *vt* transgredir (a rule) || infringir, violar, quebrantar (a law) || traspasar (a limit).

◆ *vi* pecar (to sin) || cometer una infracción (to break a law).

transgression [træns'greʃən] *n* transgresión *f* (of a rule) || infracción *f* (of a law) || pecado *m* (sin).

transgressive [træns'gresiv] *adj* transgresivo, va.

transgressor [træns'gresə*] *n* transgresor, ra; infractor, ra || pecador, ra (sinner).

tranship [træn'ʃip] *vt* transbordar.

transhipment [-mənt] *n* transbordo *m*.

transhumance [trænzhjuːməns] *n* trashumancia *f*.

transience ['trænziəns]; **transiency** [-i] *n* transitoriedad *f*, corta duración *f*.

transient ['trænziənt] *adj* transitorio, ria; pasajero, ra (not permanent).

◆ *n* transeúnte *m* & *f*.

transilluminate [ˌtrænzi'ljumineit] *vt* MED explorar por medio de focos.

transistor [træn'zistə*] *n* transistor *m* || *transistor radio* transistor *m*, radio *f* de transistores.

transistorized [-raizd] *adj* transistorizado, da.

transit ['trænsit] *n* tránsito *m*, paso *m* (passage); *in transit* en tránsito, de paso || transición *f* (transition) || transporte *m* (transport) || ASTR culminación *f* || *country of transit* país *m* de tránsito || *transit lounge* sala *f* de tránsito.

transit ['trænsit] *vt* pasar por, transitar por || ASTR culminar por.

◆ *vi* transitar || ASTR culminar.

transit camp [-kæmp] *n* campamento *m* provisional (for soldiers, refugees).

transit compass [-'kʌmpəs] *n* teodolito *m* de brújula.

transit instrument [-'instrumənt] *n* ASTR anteojo *m* meridiano.

transition [træn'ziʃən] *n* transición *f* || MUS transición *f*.

transitional [-əl] *adj* de transición; *transitional government* gobierno de transición || transitorio, ria (period).

transitive ['trænzitiv] *adj* GRAMM transitivo, va.

◆ *n* GRAMM verbo *m* transitivo.

transitory ['trænzitəri] *adj* transitorio, ria.

Transjordan ['trænz'dʒɔrdən] *pr n* GEOGR Transjordania *f*.

translatable [træns'leitəbl] *adj* traducible.

translate [træns'leit] *vt* traducir; *how do you translate this word?* ¿cómo traduce esta palabra? || REL trasladar (a bishop to another see) || transferir, trasladar (relics, etc.) || retransmitir (a message) || arrebatar al cielo (to convey to heaven) || PHYS dar un movimiento de traslación a.

◆ *vi* traducir (to make a translation); *to translate from Spanish into English* traducir del español al inglés; *to translate at sight* traducir directamente *or* de corrido || traducirse; *this phrase translates well* esta expresión se traduce bien.

translation [træns'leiʃən] *n* traducción *f*; *translation into the foreign language* traducción inversa; *translation out of the foreign language* traducción directa || retransmisión *f* (of message) || PHYS traslación *f*; *movement of translation* movimiento de traslación || traslado *m* (transfer).

translative [træns'leitiv] *adj* traslativo, va.

translator [træns'leitə*] *n* traductor, ra.

transliterate [trænz'litəreit] *vt* transcribir.

transliteration [ˌtrænzlitə'reiʃən] *n* transcripción *f*.

translocate [trænz'ləukeit] *vt* desplazar.

translocation [trænzlə'keiʃən] *n* desplazamiento *m*.

translucence [trænz'luːsns]; **translucency** [-i] *n* translucidez *f*, traslucidez *f*.

translucent [trænz'luːsnt]; **translucid** [træns'luːsid] *adj* translúcido, da; traslúcido, da.

transmarine [trænzmə'riːn] *adj* ultramarino, na.

transmigrate ['trænzmai'greit] *vi* emigrar, transmigrar (people) || transmigrar (the soul).

transmigration [ˌtrænzmai'greiʃən] *n* transmigración *f*; *transmigration of souls* transmigración de las almas || emigración *f*, transmigración *f* (of people).

transmigratory [trænz'maigrətəri] *adj* emigrante || transmigratorio, ria (soul).

transmissibility [ˌtrænzmisə'biliti] *n* transmisibilidad *f*, trasmisibilidad *f*.

transmissible [trænz'misəbl] *adj* transmisible, trasmisible.

transmission [trænz'miʃən] *n* transmisión *f*, trasmisión *f* (a transmitting); *thought transmission* transmisión del pensamiento || transmisión *f*, trasmisión *f*; *the transmission of a match by radio* la transmisión de un partido por radio || AUT transmisión *f*, trasmisión *f*.

transmissive [trænz'misiv] *adj* transmisor, ra (transmitting) || transmisible (transmissible).

transmit [trænz'mit] *vt* transmitir, trasmitir.

transmitter [trænz'mitə*] *n* transmisor *m* (apparatus) || emisora *f* (station).

transmitting [trænz'mitiŋ] *adj* transmisor, ra || *transmitting station* estación transmisora *or* emisora.

transmogrify [trænz'mɔgrifai] *vt* transformar || metamorfosear.

transmutability [trænzˌmjuːtə'biliti] *n* transmutabilidad *f*.

transmutable [trænz'mjuːtə'bl] *adj* transmutable, trasmutable.

transmutation [ˌtrænzmjuː'teiʃən] *n* transmutación *f*, trasmutación *f* || MATH transformación *f*.

transmute [trænz'mjuːt] *vt* transmutar.

transoceanic ['trænzˌəuʃi'ænik] *adj* transoceánico, ca.

transom ['trænsəm] *n* ARCH dintel *m* (lintel) | travesaño *m* (crosspiece of a window) || travesaño *m* (of a cross) || MAR yugo *m* || telera *f* (of a cannon, of a cart) || US tragaluz *m* (skylight).

transonic [træn'sɔnik] *adj* transónico, ca.

transpacific [trænzpə'sifik] *adj* transpacífico, ca.

transparency [træns'pɛərənsi] *n* transparencia *f* (quality) || PHOT diapositiva *f*, transparencia *f* (slide) || transparente *m*.

transparent [træns'pɛərənt] *adj* transparente.

transpierce [trænz'piəs] *vt* traspasar (to pierce) || penetrar (to penetrate).

transpiration [ˌtrænspi'reiʃən] *n* transpiración *f* (perspiration) || BOT transpiración *f*.

transpire [træns'paiə*] *vt* transpirar.

◆ *vi* transpirar (to perspire, to exude) || FIG revelarse (to become known) | ocurrir, suceder (to happen); *it transpired that he didn't come* ocurrió que no vino.

transplant [træns'plɑːnt] *n* MED & AGR trasplante *m*; *heart transplant* trasplante de corazón.

transplant [træns'plɑːnt] *vt* MED & AGR trasplantar || FIG trasplantar (people).

transplantable [-əbl] *adj* trasplantable.

transplantation [ˌtrænsplɑːn'teiʃən] *n* trasplante *m*.

transport ['trænspɔːt] *n* transporte *m*; *the transport of goods* el transporte de mercancías || servicio *m* de transportes; *transport in this town is not very good* el servicio de transportes en esta ciudad no es muy bueno || deportado *m* (convict) || FIG transporte *m* (rapture) | arrebato *m* (of rage, etc.) || — *means of transport* medio *m* de transporte || *Ministry of Transport* Ministerio *m* de Transportes || *rail, road transport* transportes por ferrocarril, por carretera || *transport café* café *m* de carretera || *transport cost* gastos *m pl* de transporte || *transport plane* avión *m* de transporte || *transport ship* buque *m* de transporte.

transport [træns'pɔːt] *vt* transportar; *to transport goods* transportar mercancías || deportar (convicts) || FIG arrebatar.

transportability [træns,pɔːtə'biliti] *n* posibilidad *f* de ser transportado.

transportable [træns'pɔːtəbl] *adj* transportable || INFORM transportable.

transportation [ˌtrænspɔː'teiʃən] *n* → **transport** || **deportación** *f* (of a convict).

transporter [træns'pɔːtə*] *n* transportador *m*, transportista *m* (conveyor) || *transporter bridge* puente transbordador.

transporting [træns'pɔːtiŋ] *adj* transportador, ra; de transporte || FIG arrebatador, ra.

transpose [træns'pəuz] *vt* GRAMM & MATH transponer || MUS transportar || FIG transponer.

transposition [ˌtrænspə'siʃən] *n* GRAMM & MATH transposición *f* || MUS transporte *m*.

Trans-Pyrenean ['trænzˌpirə'niːən] *adj* transpirenaico, ca; traspirenaico, ca.

transsexual; **transexual** [ˌtrænz'seksjuəl] *adj* transexual.

◆ *n* transexual *m* & *f*.

transship [træns'ʃip] *vt* transbordar.

transshipment [-mənt] *n* transbordo *m*.

Trans-Siberian ['trænzsai'biəriən] *adj* transiberiano, na || *Trans-Siberian railway* transiberiano *m*.

transsonic [træn'sɔnik] *adj* transónico, ca.

transubstantiation ['trænsəbˌstænʃi'eiʃən] *n* REL transubstanciación *f*.

transudate ['trænsjudeit] *n* transudor *m*.

transudation [trænsju'deiʃən] *n* trasudación *f*.

transude [træn'sju:d] *vt/vi* trasudar.

transuranic [,trænzju'rænik] *adj* CHEM transuránico, ca.

transvase [træns'veiz] *vt* trasvasar.

transversal [trænz'vəːsəl] *adj* transversal.
◆ *n* transversal.

transverse ['trænzvəːs] *adj* transverso, sa; *transverse muscle* músculo transverso ‖ transversal ‖ *transverse wave* onda *f* transversal.
◆ *n* ANAT músculo *m* transverso.

transvestism [trænz'vestizəm] *n* travestismo *m*.

transvestite [trænz'vestait] *n* travestido *m*.

Transylvania [,trænsil'veinjə] *pr n* GEOGR Transilvania *f*.

Transylvanian [-n] *adj/n* transilvano, na.

trap [træp] *n* trampa *f* (to catch animals); *to set* o *to lay a trap* poner una trampa ‖ FIG trampa *f*, lazo *m*, celada *f*; *to set a trap* tender una trampa *or* un lazo, preparar una celada ‖ trampa *f* (trapdoor) ‖ THEATR escotillón *m* ‖ ratonera *f* (mousetrap) ‖ cabriolé *m* (carriage) ‖ TECH sifón *m*, bombillo *m* (in a pipe) ‖ SP lanzaplatos *m inv*, máquina *f* lanzaplatos (clay-pigeon shooting) | jaula *f* (greyhound racing) ‖ US SP hoyo *m* de arena (golf) ‖ — *gin trap, jaw trap* cepo *m* ‖ *police trap* ratonera, trampa ‖ POP *shut your trap!* ¡calla!, ¡cierra el pico!, ¡calla la boca! ‖ *speed trap* control *m* de velocidad ‖ *to bait a trap* poner el cebo en la trampa ‖ FIG *to be caught like a rat in a trap* caer en la ratonera | *to be caught in one's own trap* caer en su propia trampa | *to fall* o *to walk into the trap* caer en la trampa | *to lure s.o. into a trap* hacer que uno caiga en la trampa.
◆ *pl* cosas *f*, trastos *m*, chismes *m* (things) ‖ MUS instrumentos *m* de percusión.

trap [træp] *vt* poner trampas en (a place) ‖ coger en una trampa (to catch) ‖ poner un sifón *or* un bombillo a (a pipe) ‖ FIG hacer caer en el lazo *or* en la trampa ‖ coger, pillar; *I trapped my finger in the door* me cogí el dedo en la puerta ‖ bloquear (to place in a difficult position) ‖ rodear, cercar; *trapped by the flames* rodeado por las llamas ‖ atrapar, coger; *the police trapped the thief* la policía atrapó al ladrón ‖ retener, detener (gases, liquids) ‖ SP controlar, parar (a ball) ‖ — FIG *to trap s.o. into a confession* sacarle a uno mañosamente una confesión | *to trap s.o. into marriage* conseguir casarse con uno.
◆ *vi* poner trampas (to set traps for game).

trapdoor [-'dɔː*] *n* trampa *f* (in a floor) ‖ ventana *f* de ventilación ‖ THEATR escotillón *m*.

trapes [treips] *vi* → **traipse.**

trapeze [trə'piːz] *n* trapecio *m* ‖ *trapeze artist* trapecista *m* & *f*.

trapezium [trə'piːzjəm] *n* MATH & ANAT trapecio *m* ‖ US MATH trapezoide *m*.
— OBSERV El plural de *trapezium* es *trapeziums* o *trapezia*.

trapezius [trəxpiːzjəs] *n* ANAT trapecio *m*.

trapezohedron [,træpiːzəu'hiːdrən] *n* MATH trapezoedro *m*.
— OBSERV El plural de la palabra inglesa es *trapezohedrons* o *trapezohedra*.

trapezoid ['træpizɔid] *n* MATH & ANAT trapezoide *m* ‖ US MATH trapecio *m*.

trapezoid ['træpizɔid]; **trapezoidal** [-əl] *adj* MATH trapezoidal ‖ US MATH trapecial.

trapper ['træpə*] *n* trampero *m*.

trappings ['træpiŋz] *pl n* adornos *m*, atavíos *m* (ornamentation) ‖ arreos *m*, jaeces *m* (for a horse).

Trappist ['træpist] *adj* REL trapense; *Trappist monastery* monasterio trapense.
◆ *n* REL trapense *m*.

trapshooting ['træpʃuːtiŋ] *n* tiro *m* al plato.

trash [træʃ] *n* baratija *f* (trinket) ‖ deshechos *m pl*, desperdicios *m pl* (refuse) ‖ escamondadura *f* (cutting from trees) ‖ bagazo *m* (of sugar cane) ‖ tonterías *f pl* (worthless talk) ‖ basura *f* (worthless writing) ‖ gentuza *f* (disreputable people) ‖ US basura *f* (rubbish).

trash [træʃ] *vt* podar, mondar (trees) ‖ deshojar, desbrozar (sugar cane).

trash can [kæn] *n* US cubo *m* de la basura.

trashiness [-inis] *n* baja calidad *f*, mediocridad *f*.

trashy [-i] *adj* malo, la; de baja calidad.

trauma ['trɔːmə] *n* MED trauma *m*.
— OBSERV El plural de la palabra inglesa es *traumata* o *traumas*.

traumatic [trɔː'mætik] *adj* MED traumático, ca.

traumatism ['trɔːmətizəm] *n* traumatismo *m*.

traumatology [,trɔːmə'tɔlədʒi] *n* MED traumatología *f*.

travail ['træveil] *n* dolores *f pl* de parto (pains of childbirth) ‖ trabajo *m* duro (hard work) ‖ tormento *m* (intense pain).

travail ['træveil] *vi* estar de parto (to be in childbirth) ‖ afanarse, trabajar mucho (to work hard).

travel ['trævl] *n* viajar *m*; *the pleasures of travel* el placer de viajar ‖ viajes *m pl*; *I like travel* me gustan los viajes; *space travel* los viajes espaciales ‖ TECH recorrido *m* (of a machine part) ‖ US circulación *f*, tráfico *m*; *travel is heavy on the freeway* hay mucho tráfico en la autopista ‖ *travel broadens the mind* el viajar abre la mente.
◆ *pl* viajes *m*; *I met him on my travels* le conocí en mis viajes.

travel ['trævl] *vt* viajar por (a region, etc.) ‖ recorrer (a distance).
◆ *vi* viajar; *I travelled a lot when I was young* viajé mucho cuando era joven; *I travel by car* viajo en coche; *I travel round Spain* viajo por España ‖ circular; *to travel along the road* circular por una carretera ‖ extenderse; *the pain travelled down his arm* el dolor se extendió por el brazo ‖ recorrer; *her glance travelled over the crowd* su mirada recorrió la muchedumbre ‖ llegar (to reach); *do the BBC programs travel so far?* ¿llegan tan lejos los programas de la BBC? ‖ PHYS propagarse; *sound waves do not travel through a vacuum* las ondas sonoras no se propagan en el vacío ‖ correr, ir; *the electricity travels along his wire* la electricidad va por ese cable ‖ correr, propagarse, extenderse; *rumours travel fast* los rumores corren rápidamente ‖ hacer; *the train travels at sixty miles an hour* el tren hace sesenta millas por hora ‖ ir; *I was travelling too fast* iba demasiado rápido ‖ correr (to go fast); *your car really travels* su coche corre mucho ‖ ser viajante de; *he travels for Larousse* es viajante de la Editorial Larousse ‖ transportarse; *wine that does not travel* vino que no se transporta ‖ TECH correr, desplazarse ‖ — *he travels in encyclopedias* es un viajante que vende enciclopedias ‖ *to travel light* viajar con poco equipaje.

travel agency [-'eidʒənsi] *n* agencia *f* de viajes.

travel agent's [-'eidʒənts] *n* agencia *f* de viajes.

travelled; US **traveled** ['trævld] *adj* que ha viajado mucho (person) ‖ muy recorrido, da (route, path) ‖ GEOL errático, ca.

traveller; US **traveler** ['trævlə*] *n* viajero, ra (person who travels) ‖ viajante *m* de comercio (representative) ‖ TECH puente *m* grúa (crane) ‖ MAR racamento *m*, racamenta *f*.

traveller's cheque; US **traveler's check** [-ztʃek] *n* cheque *m* de viaje, cheque *m* de viajero.

traveller's-joy; US **traveler's-joy** [-z'dʒɔi] *n* BOT clemátide *f*, hierba *f* de los pordioseros.

travelling; US **traveling** ['trævliŋ] *adj* de viaje; *travelling companion* compañero de viaje ‖ ambulante (exhibition, street vendor, etc.) ‖ móvil (thing) ‖ — *travelling bag* bolsa *f* de viaje ‖ *travelling crane* puente *m* grúa ‖ *travelling expenses* gastos *m* de viaje ‖ *travelling pavement* o *platform* pasillo *m* rodante ‖ *travelling post office* ambulancia *f* de correos ‖ *travelling salesman* viajante *m* de comercio ‖ *travelling speed* velocidad *f* de marcha (of cars, etc.), velocidad *f* de traslación (of crane) ‖ *travelling staircase* escalera mecánica.
◆ *n* viajar *m*; *travelling is expensive* viajar es caro ‖ CINEM travelín *m*.

travelogue; US **travelog** ['trævəlɔg] *n* documental *m* sobre un viaje (film) ‖ conferencia *f* ilustrada sobre un viaje (lecture).

travel-sick ['trævl,sik] *adj* mareado, da.

travel sickness ['trævl,siknis] *n* mareo *m*.

traverse ['trævəːs] *n* travesía *f* (crossing); *the traverse of the forest took three days* la travesía del bosque duró tres días ‖ travesaño *m* (crossbar) ‖ travesía *f* (in mountaineering) ‖ MAR ruta *f* sinuosa ‖ zigzag *m* (a zigzag in skiing) ‖ descenso *m* en zigzag (zigzag descent) ‖ línea *f* quebrada (in surveying) ‖ MATH transversal *f* ‖ traslación *f*, desplazamiento *m* lateral ‖ MIL través *m* (fortification) ‖ TECH riostra *f*, tirante *m* (of a frame) ‖ JUR negación *f*, denegación *f*.
◆ *adj* transversal.

traverse ['trævəːs] *vt* atravesar, cruzar (to cross); *we traversed the wood* atravesamos el bosque ‖ recorrer (to move along) ‖ MIL apuntar (a cannon) ‖ trazar un itinerario de (in surveying) ‖ JUR negar (an allegation) | oponerse a (an indictment) ‖ FIG examinar detenidamente.
◆ *vi* girar sobre su eje (to pivot) ‖ trazar un itinerario (to make a survey) ‖ SP bajar en diagonal (skiing) | subir en diagonal (climbing).

travesty ['trævisti] *n* parodia *f*.

travesty ['trævisti] *vt* parodiar.

trawl [trɔːl] *n* MAR red *f* barredera, red *f* de arrastre ‖ US MAR palangre *m*.

trawl [trɔːl] *vt/vi* MAR pescar con red barredera.

trawler [-ə*] *n* MAR trainera *f* (with oars), bou *m* (ship).

trawling [-iŋ] *n* pesca *f* con red de arrastre.

tray [trei] *n* bandeja *f*; *silver tray* bandeja de plata ‖ PHOT cubeta *f* ‖ platillo *m* (of balance) ‖ cajón *m* (drawer).

treacherous ['tretʃərəs] *adj* traicionero, ra (action), traidor, ra (person) ‖ falso, sa (false) ‖ infiel (memory) ‖ movedizo, za (ground) ‖ poco firme (ice) ‖ FIG engañoso, sa.

treacherousness [-nis] *n* alevosía *f*.

treachery ['tretʃəri] *n* traición *f*.

treacle ['triːkl] *n* melaza *f*.

treacly [-i] *adj* parecido a la melaza ‖ FIG meloso, sa (sweet).

tread [tred] *n* paso *m* (step); *we heard his tread on the stairs* oímos su paso en la escalera ‖ andar *m*, andares *m pl* (gait) ‖ huella *f* (step of a staircase) ‖ anchura *f* de la huella (width of the step) ‖ pieza *f* de goma colocada sobre la huella para protegerla ‖ suela *f* (of a shoe) ‖ ancho *m* (of rails) ‖ distancia *f* (of car axle) ‖ banda *f* de rodadura (of a tyre) ‖ galladura *f*, chalaza *f* (of an egg).

tread* [tred] *vt* pisar; *to tread grapes* pisar la uva; *to tread dry land* pisar tierra firme ‖ pisotear; *to tread earth around a plant* pisotear la tierra alrededor de una planta ‖ andar por (to walk) ‖ ZOOL pisar (to mate) ‖ — *to tread down* pisotear ‖ *to tread out* sofocar (fire, revolt) ‖ *to tread sth. underfoot* pisotear algo ‖ THEATR *to tread the boards* pisar las tablas ‖ SP *to tread water* pedalear en el agua ‖ *trodden to death by elephants* aplastado bajo las patas de los elefantes ‖ FIG *well-trodden path* camino trillado.
◆ *vi* pisar ‖ andar (to walk); *to tread across the room* andar por la habitación ‖ meter el pie; *to tread in a puddle* meter el pie en el charco ‖ — FIG *to tread lightly* andar con tiento ‖ *to tread on* pisar ‖ FIG *to tread on s.o.'s heels* pisarle a uno los talones | *to tread on s.o.'s toes* pisotear a alguien.
— OBSERV Pret ***trod***; pp ***trodden, trod***.

treadle [tredl] *n* pedal *m* (of grindstone, lathe).

treadle ['tredl] *vi* pedalear.

treadmill ['tredmil] *n* rueda *f* de molino movida por hombres ‖ rueda *f* de ardilla (moved by animal) ‖ FIG rutina.

treason ['triːzn] *n* traición *f*; *high treason* alta traición.

treasonable [-əbl] or **treasonous** [-əs] *adj* traicionero, ra; traidor, ra.

treasure ['treʒə*] *n* tesoro *m* ‖ FIG tesoro *m*.

treasure ['treʒə*] *vt* valorar, estimar, apreciar; *I treasure his friendship* valoro su amistad ‖ guardar en la memoria; *to treasure s.o.'s words* guardar en la memoria las palabras de alguien ‖ *to treasure up* acumular, guardar, atesorar.

treasure hunt [-hʌnt] *n* caza *f* del tesoro.

treasurer [-rə*] *n* tesorero, ra.

treasure trove [-'trəuv] *n* tesoro *m* descubierto [*AMER* tapado *m*] ‖ FIG hallazgo *m*.

treasury [-ri] *n* tesoro *m* ‖ tesorería *f* (place, funds) ‖ antología *f*, florilegio *m* (of verse) ‖ FIG mina *f* ‖ *the Treasury* el Ministerio de Hacienda (department), el Tesoro, el Erario (funds).

Treasury Bench [-ribentʃ] *n* banco *m* azul [primera fila de escaños ocupada por los ministros del gobierno en la Cámara de Diputados].

treasury bond [-ribɔnd] *n* bono *m* del Tesoro.

Treasury Department [ridi'pɑːtmənt] *n* US Ministerio *m* de Hacienda.

treasury note [-rinəut] *n* bono *m* del Tesoro.

treat [triːt] *n* invitación *f* ‖ festín *m*, banquete *m* (feast) ‖ regalo *m* (present) ‖ placer *m*, delicia *f* (delight); *it was a treat to go to the cinema last night* fue un placer ir al cine ayer por la noche ‖ — *this is my treat* invito yo ‖ *to have a Dutch treat* pagar a escote.

treat [triːt] *vt* tratar; *I don't like the way he treats his dog* no me gusta la forma como trata a su perro ‖ tratar de; *the book treats an interesting subject* el libro trata de un tema interesante ‖ tratar; *he treats the problem objectively* trata el problema objetivamente; *to treat sth. apart* tratar algo por separado ‖ tomar; *he treats it as a joke* lo toma a broma ‖ invitar, convidar (to invite); *to treat s.o. to a good dinner* invitar a alguien a una buena cena ‖ comprar; *he treated his wife to a new coat* compró a su mujer un abrigo nuevo ‖ CHEM tratar ‖ MED tratar, curar (a disease) | atender (a patient) ‖ — *how has the world been treating you?* ¿cómo le van las cosas? ‖ *to treat badly* maltratar ‖ *to treat o.s. to sth.* permitirse el lujo de hacer algo ‖ *to treat s.o. as one's equal* tratar a alguien de igual a igual *or* en un pie de igualdad ‖ *to treat s.o. like a king* tratar a alguien a cuerpo de rey.
◆ *vi* negociar; *to treat with s.o. for peace* negociar la paz con alguien ‖ US invitar, convidar ‖ *to treat of* tratar de.

treatise ['triːtiz] *n* tratado *m*; *economic treatise* tratado de economía.

treatment ['triːtmənt] *n* trato *m*, tratamiento *m*; *the treatment of prisoners* el trato de los prisioneros ‖ trato *m*; *preferential treatment* trato preferente ‖ tratamiento *m* (title) ‖ CHEM & MED tratamiento *m* ‖ interpretación *f*; *the orchestra's treatment of Bach* la interpretación de Bach por la orquesta ‖ adaptación *f*; *the director's treatment of the script* la adaptación del texto por el director ‖ FIG *to give s.o. the treatment* dar a uno el tratamiento que merece.

treaty ['triːti] *n* tratado *m* (between nations) ‖ acuerdo *m* (agreement).

treble ['trebl] *adj* triple ‖ MUS de tiple, de soprano (voice) ‖ — MUS *treble clef* clave *f* de sol | *treble staff* pentagrama *m* de sol.
◆ *n* tiple *m*, soprano *m*.

treble ['trebl] *vt* triplicar, multiplicar por tres.
◆ *vi* triplicarse, multiplicarse por tres.

trebly ['trebli] *adv* tres veces.

tree [triː] *n* árbol *m*; *there are many trees in the garden* hay muchos árboles en el jardín; *fruit tree* árbol frutal ‖ horma *f* (shoe tree) ‖ CHEM árbol *m* ‖ — FAM *at the top of the tree* en la cúspide, en la cumbre ‖ FIG *a tree is known by its fruit* por el fruto se conoce el árbol ‖ *Christmas tree* árbol *m* de Navidad ‖ *family tree* árbol genealógico ‖ *the Tree* la Cruz ‖ FIG *to bark up the wrong tree* equivocarse | *to reach the top of the tree* llegar a la cúspide | *up a tree* entre la espada y la pared, en un apuro, en un aprieto.

tree [triː] *vt* obligar a refugiarse en un árbol ‖ poner en la horma (shoes) ‖ US FIG poner en un aprieto (to put in a difficult situation).

tree-covered [-ˌkʌvəd] *adj* cubierto de árboles, arbolado, da.

tree-dwelling [-ˌdweliŋ] *adj* arborícola.

tree fern [-fəːn] *n* BOT helecho *m* arborescente.

tree frog [-frʌg] *n* ZOOL rana *f* de zarzal, rubeta *f*.

treeless [-lis] *adj* sin árboles.

tree line [-lain] *n* límite *f* de la vegetación arbórea.

tree-lined [-laind] *adj* *tree-lined street* alameda *f*.

treenail [-neil] *n* MAR clavija *f*, cabilla *f*.

tree of heaven [-əv'hevn] *n* BOT ailanto *m*, árbol *m* del cielo.

tree of knowledge [-əv'nɔlidʒ] *n* árbol *m* de la ciencia del bien y del mal.

tree of life [-əv'laif] *n* árbol *m* de la vida.

tree toad [-təud] *n* ZOOL rana *f* de zarzal, rubeta *f*.

treetop [-tɔp] *n* copa *f*.

tree trunk [-trʌŋk] *n* tronco *m* de árbol.

trefoil ['trefɔil] *n* BOT trébol *m* ‖ ARCH trifolio *m*, trébol *m*.
◆ *adj* trebolado, da.

trek [trek] *n* viaje *m* largo y difícil (tedious journey) ‖ viaje *m* largo en carreta ‖ migración *f* ‖ FIG expedición *f* ‖ FIG FAM caminata *f*; *it's such a trek to get to the shops* hay una buena caminata para llegar hasta las tiendas.

trek [trek] *vi* viajar en carreta (to travel by ox wagon) ‖ hacer un viaje largo y difícil (to make a tedious journey) ‖ irse (to go) ‖ emigrar (to emigrate).

trellis ['trelis] *n* enrejado *m* ‖ espaldera *f* (for plants) ‖ emparrado *m*, parra *f* (for grapes).

trelliswork [-wəːk] *n* enrejado *m*.

trematode ['tremətəud] *n* ZOOL trematodo *m*.

tremble ['trembl] *n* temblor *m* ‖ — *he was all of a tremble* estaba todo tembloroso ‖ *they told me with a tremble* me dijeron temblando.

tremble ['trembl] *vi* temblar; *I am trembling all over* tiemblo de pies a cabeza.

trembler [-ə*] *n* ELECTR vibrador *m* ‖ miedoso, sa (coward).

trembling [-iŋ] *adj* tembloroso, sa.
◆ *n* temblor *m*.

trembly [-i] *adj* tembloroso, sa.

tremendous [tri'mendəs] *adj* enorme, tremendo, da (enormous); *a tremendous difference* una diferencia enorme ‖ extraordinario, ria; tremendo, da; asombroso, sa (amazing).

tremendously *adv* enormemente, tremendamente.

tremolant ['tremələnt] *n* MUS trémolo *m*.

tremolo ['trəmələu] *n* MUS trémolo *m*.

tremor ['tremə*] *n* temblor *m*; *earth tremor* temblor de tierra ‖ estremecimiento *m* (shiver).

tremulous ['tremjuləs] *adj* trémulo, la; tembloroso, sa; temblón, ona (trembling, quivering) ‖ tímido, da (timid) ‖ febril (excitement) ‖ tembloroso, sa; temblón, ona (voice, writing).

trench [trentʃ] *n* zanja *f* (for laying pipes, building foundations, etc.) ‖ MIL trinchera *f* ‖ AGR acequia *f* ‖ MIL *trench warfare* guerra *f* de trincheras.

trench [trentʃ] *vt* abrir zanjas en (to dig trenches in) ‖ AGR abrir acequias en ‖ MIL atrincherar, abrir trincheras en (to dig) | proteger con trincheras (to protect).
◆ *vi* abrir zanjas *or* trincheras ‖ *to trench on* o *upon* usurpar (s.o.'s rights, land), rayar en (to come close to).

trenchancy ['trentʃənsi] *n* agudeza *f*, mordacidad *f*, causticidad *f* (sharpness) ‖ fuerza *f* (vigour).

trenchant ['trentʃənt] *adj* agudo, da; mordaz, cáustico, ca (penetrating, incisive); *trenchant words* palabras mordaces ‖ enérgico, ca (vigorous).

trench coat ['trentʃkəut] *n* trinchera *f*.

trencher ['trentʃə*] *n* persona *f* que hace zanjas *or* acequias ‖ MIL persona *f* que hace trincheras ‖ tajo *m*, tajadero *m* (to carve meat).

trencherman [-mən] *n* *a good* o *a stout trencherman* un buen comilón (eater), un gorrón (sponger).
— OBSERV El plural de *trencherman* es *trenchermen*.

trend [trend] *n* tendencia *f*; *the trend of public opinion* la tendencia de la opinión pública; *the rising trend of the market* la tendencia al alza del mercado ‖ dirección *f* (direction) ‖ orientación *f*; *the trend of politics* la orientación de la política ‖ — *to set the trend* marcar la tónica ‖ *to show a trend towards* orientarse hacia, tender a.

trend [trend] *vi* tender; *modern thought is trending away from materialism* el pensamiento moderno tiende a apartarse del materialismo ‖ dirigirse, orientarse.

trendsetter *n* iniciador, ra de una moda *or* tendencia.

trendy *n* FAM moderno, na.

Trent [trent] or **Trento** [-əu] *pr n* GEOGR Trento.

trepan [tri'pæn] *n* TECH & MED trépano *m*.

trepan [tri'pæn] *vt* trepanar ‖ inducir (*into* a) (to lure) ‖ *to trepan s.o. out of* estafar (algo) a uno.

trepanation [ˌtripə'neiʃən] *n* MED trepanación *f*.

trephine [tri'fi:n] *vt* MED trepanar.

trepidation [,trepi'deiʃən] *n* agitación *f*, inquietud *f*, turbación *f* ‖ trepidación *f* (trembling movement).

treponema [,trepə'ni:mə] *n* treponema *m*.
— OBSERV El plural de la palabra inglesa es *treponemata* o *treponemas*.

trespass ['trespəs] *n* entrada *f* ilegal ‖ violación *f* (of property) ‖ ofensa *f* (offence) ‖ REL deuda *f*; *forgive us our trespasses* perdónanos nuestras deudas ‖ JUR delito *m* (an actionable wrong) | violación *f*, infracción *f* (a trespassing against the law) ‖ abuso *m* (*upon* de) (s.o.'s patience).

trespass ['trespəs] *vi* violar, entrar ilegalmente en [la propiedad de alguien] (to enter unlawfully) ‖ abusar; *to trespass on s.o.'s hospitality* abusar de la hospitalidad de alguien ‖ violar, invadir (s.o.'s privacy) ‖ JUR usurpar (s.o.'s rights) | infringir, violar; *to trespass against the law* violar la ley ‖ REL pecar (to sin) ‖ — *may I trespass upon your precious time* puedo abusar de su escaso tiempo ‖ *no trespassing!* ¡prohibido el paso!

trespasser [-ə*] *n* intruso, sa (on property) ‖ JUR delincuente *m* & *f*, violador, ra (lawbreaker) ‖ REL pecador, ra (sinner) ‖ *trespassers will be prosecuted* prohibido el paso, propiedad privada, los infractores serán sancionados por la ley.

tress [tres] *n* mechón *m* (lock) ‖ bucle *m* (curl) ‖ trenza *f* (plait).
◆ *pl* pelo *m sing*, melena *f sing*, cabellera *f sing* (mass of hair).

tressed [-t] *adj* trenzado, da.

trestle [tresl] *n* caballete *m* ‖ *trestle table* mesa *f* de caballete.

trews [tru:z] *pl n* pantalón *m sing* estrecho escocés.

trey [trei] *n* tres *m* (cards, dice, etc.).

triacid [trai'æsid] *adj* CHEM triácido, da.
◆ *n* CHEM triácido *m*.

triad ['traiəd] *n* trío *m*, tríada *f* (a group of three) ‖ CHEM elemento *m* trivalente ‖ REL Trinidad *f*.

trial ['traiəl] *n* prueba *f*, ensayo *m* (a testing by experiment) ‖ experimento *m* ‖ tentativa *f* (intent) ‖ prueba *f* (a test of character, of endurance) ‖ FIG molestia *f*, tormento *m* (source of annoyance) | sufrimiento *m* (suffering) | dificultad *f* (hardship) | prueba *f*; *in the hour of trial* en el momento de la prueba ‖ JUR juicio *m* (act of judging) | proceso *m*, juicio *m*, vista *f* (procedure); *during the trial* durante el proceso ‖ SP partido *m* de preselección (for choosing sports teams) ‖ — JUR *new trial* revisión *f* ‖ *on trial* procesado, da; sometido a juicio, enjuiciado, da; *he was on trial for murder* fue procesado por asesino; sometido a prueba; *aeroplane that is on trial* avión que está sometido a prueba; a prueba; *to have sth. for a week on trial* tener algo a prueba durante una semana ‖ *to bring s.o. to trial* someter a alguien a juicio, procesar *or* enjuiciar a uno ‖ *to commit s.o. for trial* citar a alguien ante los tribunales ‖ *to do sth. by trial and error* hacer algo por un método de tanteos ‖ *to give a trial* probar (sth.), poner a prueba (s.o.) ‖ JUR *to go on trial* ser procesado | *to put on trial* procesar, someter a juicio | *to stand one's trial* ser procesado ‖ *trial by ordeal* juicio de Dios.
◆ *pl* concurso *m sing*; *sheepdog trials* concurso de perros pastores.
◆ *adj* de prueba; *a trial period* un período de prueba.

trial balance [-'bæləns] *n* COMM balance *m* de comprobación.

trial balloon [-bə'lu:n] *n* globo *m* sonda.

trial jury [-'dʒuəri] *n* US JUR jurado *m*.

triangle ['traiæŋgl] *n* triángulo *m*; *equilateral, isosceles, scalene triangle* triángulo equilátero, isósceles, escaleno ‖ MUS triángulo *m* ‖ escuadra *f*, cartabón *m* (set square for drawing).

triangular [trai'æŋgjulə*] *adj* triangular; *triangular pyramid, muscle* pirámide, músculo triangular ‖ tripartito, ta; *triangular agreement* acuerdo tripartito.

triangulate [trai'æŋgjulit] *adj* triangulado, da.

triangulate [trai'æŋgjuleit] *vt* triangular.

triangulation [trai,æŋgju'leiʃən] *n* triangulación *f*.

Trias ['traiəs] *adj* GEOL triásico, ca.
◆ *n* GEOL triásico *m*, trías *m* (period).

Triassic [trai'æsik] *adj* GEOL triásico, ca.
◆ *n* GEOL triásico *m* (period).

triathlon [traiæθlən] *n* SP triatlón *m*.

triatomic ['traiə'tɔmik] *adj* triatómico, ca.

tribal ['traibl] *adj* tribal, de tribu.

tribalism [-izəm] *n* sistema *m* tribal, organización *f* en tribus (organization in tribes) ‖ amor *m* a la tribu (strong feeling for the tribe).

tribasic [trai'beisik] *adj* CHEM tribásico, ca.

tribe [traib] *n* tribu *f* ‖ FIG familia *f*.

tribesman [-zmən] *n* miembro *m* de una tribu.
— OBSERV El plural de esta palabra es *tribesmen*.

tribulation [,tribju'leiʃən] *n* tribulación *f*.

tribunal [trai'bju:nl] *n* tribunal *m*; *military tribunal* tribunal militar; *tribunal of God* tribunal de Dios.

tribunate ['tribjunit] *n* tribunado *m*.

tribune ['tribju:n] *n* tribuna *f* (platform) ‖ tribuno *m* (of Rome).

tributary ['tribjutəri] *adj* tributario, ria (person).
◆ *n* afluente *m* (of a river) ‖ tributario, ria (person).

tribute ['tribju:t] *n* tributo *m* (payment, tax) ‖ FIG tributo *m*, homenaje *m*; *to pay a tribute to* rendir homenaje a | tributo *m*; *respect is the tribute one pays to virtue* el respeto es el tributo debido a la virtud | ofrenda *f* (offering).

trice [trais] *n* FAM *in a trice* en un abrir y cerrar de ojos, en un dos por tres.

trice [trais] *vt* MAR *to trice (up)* izar (sails).

tricentennial [,traisen'tenjəl] *n* tricentenario *m*.
◆ *adj* de trescientos años.

tricephalous [trai'sefələs] *adj* tricéfalo, la.

triceps ['traiseps] *n* ANAT tríceps *m*.
— OBSERV El plural de la palabra inglesa es *tricepses* o *triceps*.

trichina [tri'kainə] *n* triquina *f*.
— OBSERV El plural de la palabra inglesa es trichinae.

trichinosis [,triki'nəusis] *n* triquinosis *f inv*.
— OBSERV El plural de *trichinosis* es *trichinoses*.

trichotomy [trai'kɔtəmi] *n* tricotomía *f*.

trichromatism [trai'krəumətizəm] *n* tricromía *f*.

trick [trik] *n* truco *m* (stratagem) ‖ astucia *f*, ardid *m* (ruse) ‖ maña *f*, habilidad *f* (skill) ‖ tranquillo *m* (knack); *he got the trick of it* le cogió el tranquillo ‖ triquiñuela *f*, treta *f*; *to resort to tricks* andar con triquiñuelas; *to use a trick* valerse de una treta ‖ truco *m*, juego *m* de manos (dextrous feat) ‖ broma *f* (practical joke); *to play a trick on s.o.* gastarle una broma a alguien ‖ jugada *f*, pasada *f*, trastada *f* (act of mischief or meanness); *a dirty trick* una mala pasada ‖ faena *f*; *my memory played a trick on me* la memoria me hizo una faena ‖ travesura *f*, diablura *f* (prank) ‖ estafa *f*, timo *m* (swindle) ‖ tic *m*, manía *f* (mannerism, peculiarity); *it's a trick of his* es una manía suya ‖ baza *f* (in card games); *he took all the tricks* ganó todas las bazas ‖ MAR turno *m* (turn of duty) ‖ gracia *f*, monería *f* (performed by a dog) ‖ — FIG *I don't miss a trick* no me pierdo una | *the whole bag of tricks* todo ‖ *to be up to one's old tricks again* (volver a) hacer de las suyas ‖ *to do the trick* servir (para el caso), resolver el problema; *that should do the trick* esto servirá.
◆ *adj* *trick photography* trucaje *m* ‖ *trick question* pega *f*.

trick [trik] *vt* engañar, embaucar ‖ — *to trick out of* estafar, timar; *he tricked fifty pounds out of me* me timó cincuenta libras ‖ *to trick s.o. into a confession* sacarle a uno mañosamente una confesión ‖ *to trick s.o. into marriage* conseguir casarse con uno ‖ *to trick up* o *out* ataviar (to dress up).

trickery [-əri] *n* engaño *m* (deceit) ‖ astucia *f* (cunning) ‖ *a piece of trickery* una superchería.

trickiness [-inis] *n* astucia *f* (cunning) ‖ dificultad *f* (difficult nature).

trickish [-iʃ] *adj* astuto, ta (cunning) ‖ difícil, complicado, da (difficult) ‖ engañoso, sa (deceitful).

trickle ['trikl] *n* hilillo *m*, hilo *m*, chorrito *m* (of liquid) ‖ FIG *a trickle of news* pocas noticias.

trickle ['trikl] *vt* chorrear un poco de, verter poco a poco; *the wound trickled blood* la herida chorreaba un poco de sangre.
◆ *vi* correr (tears) ‖ salir poco abundantemente, gotear (blood) ‖ gotear (drops, sweat) ‖ correr, discurrir; *the stream trickled through the fields* el arroyo discurría por los campos ‖ — *to trickle in* llegar en pequeñas cantidades (things), llegar en pequeños grupos (people) ‖ *to trickle out* gotear (liquid), difundirse poco a poco (news) ‖ *to trickle with* rezumar; *to trickle with moisture* rezumar humedad.

trickster ['trikstə*] *n* embaucador, ra; embustero, ra (who deceives) ‖ estafador, ra; timador, ra (who swindles).

tricksy ['triksi] *adj* travieso, sa.

tricktrack ['trik'træk] *n* chaquete *m* (backgammon).

tricky ['triki] *adj* difícil, complicado, da (difficult) ‖ delicado, da (delicate) ‖ hábil, mañoso, sa (artful) ‖ astuto, ta (cunning).

triclinic [trai'klinik] *adj* triclínico, ca (crystal).

triclinium [trai'kliniəm] *n* triclinio *m*.

tricolour; US **tricolor** [trikələ*] *adj* tricolor.
◆ *n* bandera *f* tricolor (flag).

tricorn ['traikɔ:n] *n* tricornio *m*.

tricot ['trikəu] *n* tejido *m* de punto.

tricuspid [trai'kʌspid] *adj* ANAT tricúspide; *tricuspid valve* válvula tricúspide.
◆ *n* ANAT tricúspide *m*.

tricycle ['traisikl] *n* triciclo *m*.

tridactyl [trai'dæktil] *adj* tridáctilo, la.

trident ['traidənt] *n* tridente *m*.

Tridentine [trai'dentain] *adj* tridentino, na (of the council of Trent).

tridimensional [,traidi'menʃnəl] *adj* tridimensional.

triduo ['tri:duəu]; **triduum** ['traidjuəm] *n* REL triduo *m*.

tried [traid] *adj* probado, da (proved, tested) ‖ seguro, ra (reliable).

triennial [trai'enjəl] *adj* trienal.
◆ *n* acontecimiento *m* trienal (event) ‖ tercer aniversario *m* (third anniversary).

triennium [trai'eniəm] *n* trienio *m*.
— OBSERV El plural de *triennium* es *triennia* o *trienniums*.

trier ['traiə*] *n* experimentador, ra || juez *m*, árbitro *m* (judge) || — *he is a trier* hace siempre todo lo posible, no escatima sus esfuerzos || *trier-on* probador, ra.

Trier ['triə*] *pr n* Tréveris.

trifle ['traifl] *n* nadería *f*, fruslería *f*, pequeñez *f* (insignificant fact) || baratija *f*, nadería *f*, fruslería *f* (insignificant thing) || poquito *m* (small amount) || miseria *f* (small amount of money) || peltre *m* (type of pewter) || CULIN bizcocho *m* borracho con gelatina, frutas y natillas (dessert) || *a trifle* un poquito, algo; *a trifle too big* un poquito grande.
◆ *pl* utensilios *m* de peltre (pewter utensils).

trifle ['traifl] *vt* *to trifle away* perder (time), malgastar (money).
◆ *vi* *to trifle with* jugar con; *to trifle with s.o.'s feelings* jugar con los sentimientos de alguien.

trifler [-ə*] *n* frívolo, la.

trifling [-iŋ] *adj* insignificante; *a trifling difference* una diferencia insignificante || sin importancia; *trifling incident* incidente sin importancia || ligero, ra; frívolo, la (person).
◆ *n* frivolidad *f*.

trifoliate [trai'fəuliet]; **trifoliated** [-id] *adj* BOT trifoliado, da (three-leaved).

triforium [trai'fɔːriəm] *n* ARCH triforio *m*.
— OBSERV El plural de *triforium* es *triforia*.

trig [trig] *adj* acicalado, da (trim and neat) || MATH trigonométrico, ca.
◆ *n* MATH trigonometría *f* || calzo *m* (wedge).

trig [trig] *vt* calzar.

trigeminal [trai'dʒeminəl] *adj* ANAT trigémino, na.
◆ *n* ANAT nervio *m* trigémino, trigémino *m*.

trigger ['trigə*] *n* gatillo *m* (of a gun) || disparador *m* (release) || *quick on the trigger* que no espera mucho para disparar (quick to fire), que no lo piensa dos veces (quick to act).

trigger ['trigə*] *vt* accionar, poner en funcionamiento; *opening the door triggers the alarm system* el abrir la puerta acciona el sistema de alarma || disparar, apretar el gatillo de (a gun) || *to trigger off* provocar, desencadenar; *the assassination triggered off the First World War* el asesinato provocó la primera guerra mundial.

triggerfish [-fiʃ] *n* ZOOL pez *m* ballesta.

trigger-happy [-,hæpi] *adj* pronto a disparar.

triglyph ['traiglif] *n* triglifo *m*, tríglifo *m*.

trigonal ['trigənəl] *adj* MATH trígono, na.

trigonometric [,trigənə'metrik]; **trigonometrical** [-əl] *adj* MATH trigonométrico, ca.

trigonometry [,trigə'nɔmitri] *n* MATH trigonometría *f*.

trihedral [trai'hiːdrəl] *adj* MATH triedro, dra.

trihedron [trai'hiːdrən] *n* MATH triedro *m*, ángulo *m* triedro.
— OBSERV El plural de *trihedron* es *trihedrons* o *trihedra*.

trike [traik] *n* FAM triciclo *m*.

trilateral [trai'lætərəl] *adj* trilátero, ra.

trilby ['trilby] *n* sombrero *m* flexible.

trilingual [trai'liŋgwəl] *adj* trilingüe.

trilithon ['traili,θɔn] *n* trilito *m*.

trill [tril] *n* trino *m*, gorjeo *m* (of a bird) || MUS trino *m* || GRAMM vibración *f* (action, sound) | vibrante *f* (letter).

trill [tril] *vt* GRAMM pronunciar con una vibración.
◆ *vi* trinar, gorjear (birds) || MUS trinar.

trillion ['triljən] *n* trillón *m* (10^{18}) || US billón *m* (10^{12}).

trilobate [trai'ləubit] *adj* BOT trilobulado, da.

trilobites ['trailəbaits] *pl n* trilobites *m*.

trilogy ['trilədʒi] *n* trilogía *f*.

trim [trim] *adj* aseado, da; arreglado, da (neat) || en buen estado (in good condition) || cuidado, da; *a trim lawn* un césped cuidado || elegante (smart) || apuesto, ta (well-proportioned).
◆ *n* estado *m* (state); *in perfect trim* en perfecto estado || orden *m* (order) || recorte *m* (light haircut) || adorno *m* (ornamental trimming) || recorte *m* (cutting) || MAR asiento *m*, equilibrio *m* (of a boat) | orientación *f* (of sails) | estiba *f* (of load) || AVIAT equilibrio *m* || US interior *m*, tapicería *f* (of a car) | marco *m* (of window, of door) || — *in fighting trim* listo para el combate || *out of trim* mal estibado (boat), en baja forma (people) || *to be in a good trim* estar en forma (people).

trim [trim] *vt* arreglar, poner en orden (to tidy) || adornar (a garment) || entresacar (hair) || recortar (nails, moustache, etc.) || desbarbar (moulding) || desbastar (timber) || cepillar (with a plane) || preparar (fire) || guillotinar (in bookbinding) || despabilar (a lamp) || podar (branches, hedge) || MAR orientar (sails) | equilibrar, asentar (to level) | estibar (load) || AVIAT equilibrar || cercenar, reducir (to reduce) || US FAM dar una paliza a (to thrash, to defeat) | desplumar (to swindle, to fleece, to rob) | echar una bronca a (to tick off) || — *to trim away* o *off* recortar || *to trim o.s. up* arreglarse, acicalarse || *to trim up* arreglar.
◆ *vi* zigzaguear, nadar entre dos aguas, ser oportunista (in politics).

trimester [trai'mestə*] *n* trimestre *m*.

trimestrial [trai'mestriəl] *adj* trimestral.

trimmed [trimd] *adj* adornado, da (garment).

trimmer ['trimə*] *n* desbastador *m* (person who trims) || máquina *f* desbastadora (machine) || guillotina *f* (for paper) || ARCH solera *f* || MAR estibador *m* (of cargo) || AVIAT aleta *f* compensadora || FIG & FAM oportunista *m* & *f* || US escaparatista *m* & *f* (of shopwindows).
◆ *pl* cizalla *f sing* (shears) || despabiladeras *f* (snuffers).

trimming ['trimiŋ] *n* arreglo *m*, orden *m* (arrangement) || adorno *m* (on a dress, etc.) || recorte *m* (of nails, of hair, etc.) || poda *f* (of branches, of hedge) || desbastado *m* (of timber, etc.) || cepillado *m* (with a plane) || desbarbadura *f* (of moulding) || MAR orientación *f* (of sails) | estiba *f* (of load) || FAM oportunismo *m* || US FAM paliza *f* (beating).
◆ *pl* CULIN guarnición *f sing* (garnishings) || adornos *m* (adornments) || recortes *m* (cuttings) || accesorios *m* (accessories).

trimness ['trimnis] *n* orden *m*, aspecto *m* ordenado (order) || elegancia *f*.

trimonthly [trai'mʌnθli] *adj* trimestral.

trimorphic [trai'mɔːfik] *adj* trimorfo, fa.

trimorphism [trai'mɔːfizəm] *n* trimorfismo *m*.

trimorphous [trai'mɔːfəs] *adj* trimorfo, fa.

trine [train] *adj* trino, na; triple || ASTR trino, na.
◆ *n* ASTR aspecto *m* trino || trío *m* (set of three) || REL *the Trine* la Trinidad.

Trinidad and Tobago ['trinidædəntə'beigəu] *pr n* GEOGR Trinidad y Tobago.

Trinitarian [,trini'tɛəriən] *adj/n* REL trinitario, ria.

trinotrotoluene [trai'naitrəu'tɔljuiːn] *n* trinitrotolueno *m*.

trinity ['triniti] *n* trío *m*, trinidad *f* (group of three).

Trinity ['triniti] *n* REL Trinidad *f*.

trinket ['triŋkit] *n* dije *m* (jewels, etc.) || baratija *f*, chuchería *f* (trifle).

trinomial [trai'nəumjəl] *n* MATH trinomio *m*.

trio ['triːəu] *n* trío *m*.

triode ['traiəud] *n* PHYS tríodo *m*.

triolet ['triəulet] *n* letrilla *f* (poem).

trioxide [trai'ɔksaid] *n* CHEM trióxido *m*.

trip [trip] *n* viaje *m* (journey); *to go on a trip to England* hacer un viaje a Inglaterra; *they are away on a trip* están de viaje; *pleasure trip* viaje de recreo; *boat trip* viaje en barco; *business trip* viaje de negocios; *tourist trip* viaje turístico; *we took a trip* hicimos un viaje; *round trip* viaje circular || excursión *f* (excursion) || tropezón *m*, traspié *m* (accidental stumble) || zancadilla *f* (intentional) || paso *m* ligero (light tread) || TECH disparador *m* (of a mechanism) | trinquete *m*, escape *m* (of a watch) || FIG desliz *m*, tropiezo *m*, error *m* (error) || FAM viaje *m* (effect of drugs).

trip [trip] *vi* dar un traspié; *he tripped and fell* dio un traspié y se cayó || tropezar; *he tripped over the kerb* tropezó con el borde de la acera || andar con paso ligero (to step lightly) || TECH soltarse (a catch) || FIG equivocarse, cometer un desliz (to make a mistake) | trabarse (the tongue) || *to trip in, out* entrar, salir con paso ligero.
◆ *vt* poner *or* echar la zancadilla a (to make s.o. fall over) || hacer tropezar *or* caer (a rope, a tree root, etc.) || FIG confundir; *the third question tripped me* la tercera pregunta me confundió | coger en falta (asking a trick question) || TECH soltar (a catch) || MAR levar (anchor) | izar (a topmast).

tripartite ['trai'pɑːtait] *adj* tripartito, ta; *tripartite agreement* acuerdo tripartito.

tripartition [,traipɑː'tiʃən] *n* tripartición *f*.

tripe [traip] *n* CULIN callos *m pl* || FAM bobadas *f pl*, tonterías *f pl*; *that's all tripe* no son más que tonterías || FAM *this play is tripe* esta obra de teatro no vale nada.

tripe butcher [-,butʃə*] *n* tripero, ra; casquero, ra.

tripe shop [-ʃɔp] *n* tripería *f*.

tripetalous [trai'petələs] *adj* tripétalo, la.

trip-hammer ['trip,hæmə*] *n* TECH martinete *m*.

triphase ['traifeiz] *adj* ELECTR trifásico, ca.

triphenylmethane [,trai,fenəl'meθein] *n* CHEM trifenilmetano *m*.

triphthong ['trifθɔn] *n* triptongo *m*.

triplane ['traiplein] *n* triplano *m*.

triple ['tripl] *adj* triple || MUS ternario, ria; *triple time* compás ternario || *triple the sum* el triple.
◆ *n* triple *m*; *nine is the triple of three* nueve es el triple de tres || US SP golpe *m* que permite al bateador llegar a la tercera base.

triple ['tripl] *vt* triplicar.
◆ *vi* triplicarse.

triple-expansion [-iks'pænʃən] *adj* de triple expansión.

triple jump [-dʒʌmp] *n* SP triple salto *m*.

triple play [-'plei] *n* US SP jugada *f* en que se elimina a tres jugadores (in baseball).

triplet ['triplit] *n* trío *m* (set of three) || trillizo, za (one of three babies) || POET terceto *m* || MUS tresillo *m*.

triplex ['tripleks] *adj* triple.

triplicate ['triplikit] *adj* triplicado, da (made in three copies) || triple.
◆ *n* triplicado *m*, copia *f* triplicada (one of three copies) || *in triplicate* por triplicado.

triplicate ['triplikeit] *vt* triplicar || hacer por triplicado (copy).

triplication [ˌtripli'keiʃən] *n* triplicación *f.*
tripod ['traipɔd] *n* trípode *m.*
tripodal ['tripədl]; **tripodic** [trai'pɔdik] *adj* de tres pies.
tripos ['traipɔs] *n* examen *m* para sacar el título (at Cambridge University).
— OBSERV El plural de esta palabra es *triposes.*
tripper ['tripə*] *n* turista *m* & *f* (tourist) ‖ excursionista *m* & *f* (on an excursion) ‖ TECH disparador *m.*
tripping ['tripiŋ] *adj* ligero, ra (pace).
triptych ['triptik] *n* ARTS tríptico *m.*
trip wire ['trip,waiə*] *n* MIL cable *m* trampa.
trirectangular [trairek'tæŋgjulə*] *adj* MATH trirrectángulo, la.
trireme ['trairi:m] *n* trirreme *m* (boat).
Trisagion [tri'sægiɔn] *n* REL Trisagio *m.*
— OBSERV El plural de la palabra inglesa es *Trisagia.*
trisect [trai'sekt] *vt* MATH trisecar.
trisection [trai'sekʃən] *n* MATH trisección *f.*
trisulphide; US **trisulfide** [trai'sʌlfaid] *n* CHEM trisulfuro *m.*
trisyllabic ['traisi'læbik] *adj* GRAMM trisílabo, ba.
trisyllable [trai'siləbl] *n* GRAMM trisílabo *m.*
trite [trait] *adj* trillado, da (hackneyed) ‖ trivial (commonplace).
triteness [-nis] *n* trivialidad *f* (triviality) ‖ lo trillado (of sth. well known).
tritium ['tritiəm] *n* CHEM tritio *m.*
triton ['traitn] *n* ZOOL tritón *m* (newt).
Triton ['traitn] *pr n* MYTH Tritón *m.*
triturate ['tritʃəreit] *vt* triturar.
trituration [ˌtritʃə'reiʃən] *n* trituración *f.*
triturator ['tritʃəreitə*] *n* trituradora *f.*
triumph ['traiəmf] *n* triunfo *m* (victory); *in triumph* en triunfo ‖ júbilo *m*, regocijo *m* (joy).
triumph ['traiəmf] *vi* alegrarse, congratularse, regocijarse; *they triumphed at the news* se congratularon al recibir la noticia ‖ triunfar; *to triumph over death, over the enemy* triunfar sobre la muerte, del enemigo ‖ vencer; *to triumph over one's difficulties* vencer sus dificultades.
triumphal [trai'ʌmfəl] *adj* triunfal ‖ *triumphal arch* arco *m* de triunfo.
triumphant [trai'ʌmfənt] *adj* triunfante.
triumphantly [-li] *adv* triunfalmente.
triumvir [tri'umvə*] *n* triunviro *m.*
— OBSERV El plural de *triumvir* es *triumvirs* o *triumviri.*
triumviral [-rəl] *adj* triunviral.
triumvirate [trai'ʌmvirit] *n* triunvirato *m.*
triune ['traiju:n] *adj* trino, na.
triunity [trai'ju:niti] *n* trinidad *f.*
trivalence ['trai'veiləns]; **trivalency** ['trai'veilənsi] *n* CHEM trivalencia *f.*
trivalent ['trai'veilənt] *adj* CHEM trivalente.
trivet ['trivit] *n* trébedes *m inv* (for cooking over fire) ‖ salvamantel *m* de tres pies (to protect table top).
trivia ['triviə] *pl n* trivialidades *f*, banalidades *f.*
trivial [-l] *adj* trivial, banal ‖ frívolo, la (frivolous) ‖ insignificante, poco importante (insignificant) ‖ superficial ‖ *trivial name* nombre *m* vulgar (vernacular name).
triviality [trivi'æliti] *n* trivialidad *f*, banalidad *f* ‖ frivolidad *f* ‖ insignificancia *f.*
trivialize ['triviəlaiz] *vt* trivializar.
trivium ['triviəm] *n* trivium *m*, trivio *m.*
— OBSERV El plural de la palabra inglesa es *trivia.*
triweekly ['trai'wi:kli] *adj* trisemanal.
◆ *adv* tres veces por semana ‖ cada tres semanas.
troat [trəut] *vi* bramar.
trocar ['trəuka:] *n* MED trocar *m.*
trochanter [trəu'kæntə*] *n* ANAT trocánter *m.*
trochilus ['trɔkələs] *n* troquilo *m* (bird).
— OBSERV El plural de *trochilus* es *trochili.*
trochlea [trɔk'liə] *n* ANAT tróclea *f.*
trochoid ['trəukɔid] *adj* ANAT trocoide ‖ MATH cicloidal.
◆ *n* ANAT articulación *f* trocoide ‖ MATH trocoide *f*, cicloide *f.*
trochoidal [trəu'kɔidəl] *adj* ⟶ **trochoid.**
trod [trɔd] *pret/pp* ⟶ **tread.**
trodden ['trɔdn] *pp* ⟶ **tread.**
troglodyte ['trɔglədait] *n* troglodita *m* & *f* (cave dweller) ‖ troglodita *m* (bird).
troglodytic [ˌtrɔglə'ditik]; **troglodytical** [-əl] *adj* troglodita, troglodítico, ca.
troika ['trɔikə] *n* troica *f.*
Trojan ['trəudʒən] *adj/n* troyano, na ‖ — FIG *to work like a Trojan* trabajar como un negro ‖ *Trojan horse* caballo *m* de Troya ‖ *Trojan war* guerra *f* de Troya.
troll [trəul] *n* cebo *m* de cuchara (lure) ‖ carrete *m* (reel) ‖ canon *m* (song) ‖ gnomo *m*, duendecillo *m* (supernatural being).
troll [trəul] *vt* cantar en canon (a song) ‖ pescar en (a lake) ‖ pescar con cebo de cuchara (fish).
◆ *vi* pescar con cebo de cuchara (to fish).
trolley; trolly ['trɔli] *n* carretilla *f* (for transporting goods) ‖ vagoneta *f* (in mines, on rails) ‖ mesita *f* de ruedas, carrito *m* (for serving tea, etc.) ‖ trole *m* (pole) ‖ teleférico *m* (cable car) ‖ US tranvía *m* (tram) ‖ US FAM *to be off one's trolley* desvariar, estar chalado.
trolleybus [-bʌs] *n* trolebús *m.*
trolley car [-ka:] *n* US tranvía *m.*
trolley line [-lain] *n* US línea *f* de tranvía.
trolley pole [-pəul] *n* trole *m.*
trolley wire [-waiə*] *n* cable *m* conductor.
trollop ['trɔləp] *n* ramera *f* (whore) ‖ puerca *f* (dirty woman).
trolly ['trɔli] *n* ⟶ **trolley.**
trombone [trɔm'bəun] *n* MUS trombón *m*; *slide trombone* trombón de varas; *valve trombone* trombón de pistones *or* de llaves.
trombonist [-ist] *n* MUS trombón *m.*
trommel ['trɔməl] *n* TECH tambor *m.*
trompe [trɔmp] *n* trompa *f.*
trompe l'oeil [tr˜ɔplə:j] *n* ARTS «trompe-l'oeil» *m*, efecto *m.*
troop [tru:p] *n* banda *f*, grupo *m* (of people) ‖ manada *f* (of animals) ‖ bandada *f* (of birds) ‖ grupo *m* (of boy scouts) ‖ MIL escuadrón *m* (company) ‖ tropa *f* (body) ‖ THEATR compañía *f* (of actors).
◆ *pl* MIL tropas *f*; *air-borne troops* tropas aerotransportadas; *line troops* tropas de línea ‖ *troops of tourists* cantidades de turistas.
troop [tru:p] *vi* ir en grupo *or* en grupos *or* juntos; *they all trooped off to the cinema* se fueron todos juntos al cine ‖ apiñarse (to gather) ‖ *to troop out* salir en tropel.
◆ *vt* MIL presentar (the colours).
troop carrier [-kæriə*] *n* MIL avión *m* de transporte de tropas.
trooper [-ə*] *n* MIL soldado *m* de caballería ‖ buque *m* de transporte (troopship) ‖ policía *m* montado (mounted policeman) ‖ *to swear like a trooper* blasfemar como un carretero.
trooping [-iŋ] *n* grupo *m* ‖ *trooping the colours* saludo *m* a la bandera.
troopship [-ʃip] *n* MIL buque *m* de transporte.
troop train [-trein] *n* tren *m* militar.
trope [trəup] *n* tropo *m* (figure of speech).
trophy ['trəufi] *n* trofeo *m.*
tropic ['trɔpik] *n* trópico *m*; *Tropic of Cancer, of Capricorn* Trópico de Cáncer, de Capricornio.
◆ *pl* Trópicos *m.*
◆ *adj* tropical.
tropical [-əl] *adj* tropical; *tropical climate* clima tropical ‖ trópico, ca (in rhetoric).
tropic bird [-bə:d] *n* ZOOL rabijunco *m.*
tropism ['trəupizəm] *n* BIOL tropismo *m.*
tropology [trɔ'pɔlədʒi] *n* tropología *f.*
troposphere ['trɔpəsfiə] *n* troposfera *f.*
trot [trɔt] *n* trote *m* (action, sound of a horse trotting); *at a trot* al trote; *at an easy o a slow trot* a trote corto ‖ palangre *m* (fishing line) ‖ US FAM chuleta *f* (crib) ‖ — *on the trot* seguidos, das (one after another); *for ten years on the trot* durante diez años seguidos ‖ *to break into a trot* empezar a trotar ‖ FIG *to keep s.o. on the trot* no dejarle parar a uno.
trot [trɔt] *vi* trotar, ir al trote (a horse) ‖ FIG correr (to run) ‖ FAM *to trot off* irse corriendo.
◆ *vt* hacer trotar (a horse) ‖ *to trot out* hacer trotar (a horse), sacar a relucir (arguments), hacer alarde de (to make a show of).
troth [trəuθ] *n* palabra *f*, promesa *f* ‖ fidelidad *f* (faithfulness) ‖ *to plight one's troth* dar palabra de matrimonio *or* de casamiento.
trotline ['trɔtlain] *n* palangre *m* (fishing line).
Trotskyist ['trɔtski:ist]; **Trotskyite** ['trɔtski:ait] *adj/n* trotskista.
trotter ['trɔtə*] *n* trotón *m* (horse) ‖ CULIN mano *f* (of a pig or other animal).
troubadour ['tru:bəduə*] *n* trovador *m.*
trouble ['trʌbl] *n* inquietud *f*, preocupación *f* (worry); *the trouble it gave me!* ¡las preocupaciones que me dio! ‖ apuro *m*; *to be in trouble* estar en un apuro; *he got out of trouble* salió de apuros ‖ pena *f*; *to tell s.o. one's troubles* contar a alguien sus penas ‖ desgracia *f* (misfortune) ‖ problema *m*, dificultad *f*; *the trouble is* el problema es; *we had trouble with the motor* tuvimos problemas con el motor; *money troubles* problemas de dinero; *with no little trouble* con cierta dificultad ‖ engorro *m* (person or thing that causes difficulty) ‖ disgusto *m*; *he caused trouble between them* causó un disgusto entre ellos ‖ camorra *f*; *to look for trouble* buscar camorra ‖ trastornos *m pl*, enfermedad *f* (illness); *the trouble started two years ago* los trastornos comenzaron hace dos años; *mental troubles* trastornos mentales ‖ disturbios *m pl* (disturbance); *trouble at a football match* disturbios en un partido de fútbol ‖ molestia *f*; *if it's no trouble for you* si no le sirve de molestia; *I saved myself the trouble* me ahorré la molestia; *to take the trouble to* tomarse la molestia de; *it is no trouble* no es ninguna molestia ‖ conflictos *m pl*; *labour trouble* conflictos laborales ‖ — *don't put yourself to any trouble* no se moleste Ud. ‖ *it did not give me much trouble to do it* no me costó mucho trabajo hacerlo ‖ *to be worth the trouble* valer *or* merecer la pena ‖ FIG *to get a girl into trouble* dejar embarazada a una chica ‖ *to get into trouble* meterse en líos ‖ *to get s.o. into trouble* meter a alguien en un lío ‖ *to go to great trouble over sth., to take trouble over sth.* hacer algo con mucho cuidado ‖ *to go to great trouble to do sth., to take great trouble in doing sth.* tomarse mucho trabajo haciendo algo ‖ *to go to the trouble of* tomarse la molestia de ‖ *to keep out of trouble* no meterse en líos ‖ *to make trou-*

ble, to stir up trouble armar lío, armar jaleo || *to put o.s. to great trouble* tomarse las mayores molestias || *to spare no trouble in order to* no escatimar esfuerzos para || *what's the trouble?* ¿qué pasa?

trouble ['trʌbl] *vt* preocupar (to cause worry); *he was deeply troubled* estaba sumamente preocupado || perturbar, trastornar (to disturb mentally) || afectar, afligir; *troubled by his friend's death* afectado por la muerte de su amigo || aquejar; *troubled by rheumatism* aquejado de reuma || molestar; *I don't want to trouble you with too many questions* no te quiero molestar con demasiadas preguntas; *my arm has been troubling me ever since the accident* me molesta este brazo desde el accidente || enturbiar (to make turbid) || — *may I trouble you for a cigarette?* ¿puedo pedirle un cigarrillo? || *to trouble o.s. about sth.* preocuparse por algo || *to trouble o.s. to do sth.* molestarse en hacer algo, tomarse la molestia de hacer algo.
◆ *vi* preocuparse, inquietarse (to be worried); *don't trouble about it* no se preocupe por eso || molestarse; *don't trouble to fetch it* no te molestes en ir a buscarlo.

troubled [-d] *adj* preocupado, da (worried); *a troubled countenance* una cara preocupada || agitado, da (sleep, period, life) || revuelto, ta; turbulento, ta (waters).

trouble-free [-fri:] *adj* sin preocupaciones || sin problemas, sin dificultades || sin disturbios.

troublemaker [-ˌmeikə*] *n* alborotador, ra; perturbador, ra.

troubleshooter [-ʃu:tə*] *n* US localizador *m* de averías (in power circuits, etc.) | mediador, ra (mediator).

troublesome [-səm] *adj* molesto, ta.

trouble spot [-spɔt] *n* zona *f* de conflicto.

troublous [-əs] *adj* molesto, ta (troublesome) || agitado, da; revuelto, ta (period).

trough [trɔf] *n* pesebre *m* (for animal food) || abrevadero *m* (for drinking) || comedero *m* (feeding for birds) || bebedero *m* (drinking for birds) || artesa *f*, amasadera *f* (for kneading) || CHEM cuba *f* || seno *m* (depression between waves) || depresión *f* (depression) || zona *f* de bajas presiones (in meteorology) || canalón *m* (water conduit) || mínimo *m* (in statistics) || MIN *washing trough* batea *f*.

trounce [trauns] *vt* FAM dar una paliza a, pegar (to thrash) | dar una paliza a, derrotar (to defeat).

trouncing [-iŋ] *n* paliza *f*.

troupe [tru:p] *n* THEATR compañía *f*.

trouper [-ə*] *n* actor *m* de una compañía.

trousers ['trauzəz] *pl n* pantalón *m sing*, pantalones *m* || FIG *to wear the trousers* llevar los pantalones.

trouser suit ['trauzə*ˌsju:t] *n* traje *m* pantalón (woman's suit).

trousseau ['tru:səu] *n* ajuar *m*.
— OBSERV El plural de *trousseau* es *trousseaux* o *trousseaus*.

trout [traut] *n* ZOOL trucha *f* (fish); *salmon trout* trucha asalmonada; *rainbow trout* trucha de arco iris || *trout river* río truchero.

trouvère [tru:vɛər] *n* trovador *m*, trovero *m*.

trove [trəuv] *n* tesoro *m* descubierto || FIG hallazgo *m*.

trowel ['trauəl] *n* palustre *m*, paleta *f*, llana *f* (for mortar, etc.) || desplantador *m* (for lifting plants) || FIG & FAM *to lay it on with a trowel* pasar la mano por el lomo.

trowel ['trəuəl] *vt* extender con el palustre.

Troy [trɔi] *pr n* Troya.

truancy ['tru:ənsi] *n* rabona *f*, falta *f* a clase.

truant ['tru:ənt] *n* persona *f* que hace novillos (from school) || haragán, ana (lazy person) || *to play truant* hacer novillos, hacer la rabona.
◆ *adj* que hace novillos *or* rabona || vago, ga; perezoso, sa (lazy).

truce [tru:s] *n* tregua *f*; *to declare a truce* acordar una tregua; *truce of God* tregua de Dios.

truck [trʌk] *n* trueque *m*, cambio *m* (barter) || FAM trato *m* (dealings); *to have no truck with* no tener trato con || baratijas *f pl* (articles of little value) || pago *m* de sueldos en especie (payment in kind) || batea *f* (open freight wagon) || vagoneta *f* (in mines) || carretón *m*, bogie *m* (bogie) || carretilla *f* de mano (handcart) || US camión *m* (lorry) | verduras *f pl* para el mercado (vegetables) | mesita *f* de ruedas, carrito *m* (small trolley).

truck [trʌk] *vt* trocar, cambiar (to exchange) || transportar en camión (to transport in a truck).
◆ *vi* hacer un trueque *or* un cambio.

truckage [-idʒ]; **trucking** [-iŋ] *n* camionaje *m*, transporte *m* por camión, acarreo *m*.

truck driver [-ˌdraivə*] *n* conductor *m* de camión, camionero *m*.

trucker [-ə*] *n* US transportista *m* (person engaged in trucking) | camionero *m* (truck driver) | hortelano *m* (truck farmer).

truck farm [-fɑ:m] *n* US huerto *m*.

truck farmer [-ˌfɑ:mə*] *n* US hortelano *m* (market gardener).

trucking [-iŋ] *n* ⟶ **truckage.**

truckle ['trʌkl] *n* ruedecilla *f*, rueda *f*.

truckle ['trʌkl] *vi* ser servil (*to* con).

truckle bed [-bed] *n* cama *f* baja con ruedas.

truckload ['trʌkləud] *n* camión *m* (load).

truckman ['trʌkmən] *n* camionero *m*.
— OBSERV El plural de esta palabra es *truckmen*.

truculence ['trʌkjuləns] *n* ferocidad *f*, crueldad *f*, salvajismo *m* || agresividad *f*, violencia *f* (in style).

truculent ['trʌkjulənt] *adj* feroz, salvaje, cruel (fierce) || agresivo, va.

trudge [trʌdʒ] *n* caminata *f*, paseo *m* largo y cansado.

trudge [trʌdʒ] *vt* recorrer (una distancia) con dificultad.
◆ *vi* andar con dificultad.

trudgen; trudgeon [-ən]; **trudgen stroke** [-ənstrəuk] *n* trudgeon *m* (in swimming).

true [tru:] *adj* verdadero, ra; de verdad; *a true friend* un verdadero amigo; *a true Christian* un verdadero cristiano || verídico, ca; verdadero, ra; auténtico, ca; *his story is true* su historia es auténtica || fiel, leal; *true to his principles* fiel a sus principios || legítimo, ma; *the true heir* el heredero legítimo || exacto, ta (accurate) || auténtico, ca (authentic, real) || seguro, ra; *these dark clouds are a true sign of rain* estos nubarrones son anuncio seguro de lluvia || MUS afinado, da (voice) || centrado, da (wheel) || a plomo (wall) || alineado, da (aligned) || — *to be out of true* no estar bien alineado *or* centrado *or* a plomo || *to be true to one's word* mantener su palabra || *to come true* realizarse, llegar a ser realidad, cumplirse || *to distinguish the true from the false* distinguir lo verdadero de lo falso || *too good to be true* demasiado bueno para ser cierto || *true copy* copia *f* fiel || *true to life* conforme a la realidad.
◆ *adv* verdaderamente (truly) || exactamente (accurately) || — *to aim true* apuntar bien || *to run true* estar centrada (wheel) || *to sign true* cantar afinadamente.

true [tru:] *vt* corregir, rectificar || centrar (a wheel).

true bill [-bil] *n* US JUR acta *f* de acusación.

true-blue [-'blu:] *adj* fiel, leal (utterly loyal).

trueborn [-bɔ:n] *adj* legítimo, ma; verdadero, ra.

truebred [-bred] *adj* de pura sangre (purebred).

truehearted [-'hɑ:tid] *adj* leal, fiel (faithful) || sincero, ra (sincere).

true-life ['tru:laif] *adj* verdadero, ra; de la vida real.

truelove [-lʌv] *n* amor *m* (loved one).

truelove knot [-lʌvnɔt] *n* nudo *m* difícil de desatar || FIG prueba *f* de amor eterno.

trueness [-nis] *n* fidelidad *f*, lealtad *f* (faithfulness) || sinceridad *f* (sincerity) || verdad *f* (truth) || timbre *m* perfecto (of voice).

truffle [trʌfl] *n* trufa *f*.

truism ['tru:izəm] *n* truismo *m*.

truly ['tru:li] *adv* verdaderamente (truthfully) || fielmente, lealmente (faithfully) || realmente, verdaderamente; *a truly lamentable performance* una actuación verdaderamente lamentable || sinceramente (sincerely) || — *really and truly?* ¿de verdad? || *yours truly* le saluda atentamente (in letters), su seguro servidor (me).

trump [trʌmp] *n* triunfo *m* (in cards) || FAM buena persona *f* (nice person) || (ant) trompeta *f* || — FIG *to hold all the trumps* tener todos los triunfos en la mano | *to turn up trumps* favorecerle (a uno) la suerte; *he always turns up trumps* siempre le favorece la suerte; resultar bien; *the idea turned up trumps* la idea resultó bien.

trump [trʌmp] *vt* fallar (in cards) || *to trump up* forjar, inventar (an excuse).
◆ *vi* jugar un triunfo.

trump card [-'kɑ:d] *n* triunfo *m* (in cards) || FIG triunfo *m*, baza *f*; *to hold all the trump cards* tener todos los triunfos en la mano.

trumped-up [-t'ʌp] *adj* forjado, da; inventado, da.

trumpery [-əri] *adj* sin valor (worthless) || de oropel (paltry and showy).
◆ *n* baratija *f* (worthless thing) || tonterías *f pl* (nonsense).

trumpet ['trʌmpit] *n* MUS trompeta *f* (wind instrument); *to play the trumpet* tocar la trompeta | trompeta *m* & *f* (musician) || trompetilla *f*; *ear trumpet* trompetilla acústica || FIG *to blow one's own trumpet* darse bombo, echarse flores.
◆ *pl* MUS trompetería *f sing* (of an organ).

trumpet ['trʌmpit] *vt* anunciar a son de trompeta (to announce).
◆ *vi* tocar la trompeta (to play the trumpet) || berrear, bramar, barritar (an elephant).

trumpet call [-kɔ:l] *n* toque *m* de trompeta.

trumpeter [-ə*] *n* MUS trompetista *m* & *f*, trompeta *m* & *f* || agamí *m* (bird).

trumpet player [-ˌpleiə*] *n* MUS ⟶ **trumpeter.**

truncate ['trʌŋkeit] *vt* truncar.

truncated [-id] *adj* truncado, da; *truncated cone* cono truncado.

truncation [trʌŋ'keiʃən] *n* truncamiento *m*.

truncheon ['trʌntʃən] *n* matraca *f* (cudgel) || porra *f* (policeman's).

trundle ['trʌndl] *n* ruedecilla *f* (small wheel) || cama *f* baja con ruedas (bed) || narria *f*, carretilla *f* (cart) || TECH linterna *f* (lantern pinion) | barra *f* de la linterna (bar).

trundle ['trʌndl] *vt* hacer rodar (a hoop) || empujar (a barrow).
◆ *vi* rodar.

trundle bed [-bed] *n* cama *f* baja con ruedas.

trunk [trʌŋk] *n* tronco *m* (of a tree or a body) || trompa *f* (of an elephant) || tórax *m* (of an

insect) || línea *f* interurbana (of telephone system) || línea *f* principal (of railway) || tronco *m* (main stem of a blood vessel) || ARCH fuste *m* (central shaft of a column) || baúl *m* (luggage) || TECH conducto *m* (shaft) | tubería *f* (pipe) || *US* maleta *f*, maletero *m*, portaequipaje *m* (of a car).
◆ *pl* bañador *m sing* (man's bathing costume) || pantalón *m sing* corto, «short» *m sing* (shorts).

trunk call [-kɔːl] *n* conferencia *f* [interurbana] (telephone).

trunk line [-lain] *n* línea *f* interurbana (of telephone system) || línea *f* principal (of railway).

trunk road [-rəud] *n* *US* carretera *f* nacional.

trunnion ['trʌnjən] *n* muñón *m*.

truss [trʌs] *n* braguero *m* (to support a hernia) || haz *m* (of hay or straw) || BOT racimo *m* (of flowers) || ARCH modillón *m* | armazón *m* (framework).

truss [trʌs] *vt* atar (to tie up) || CULIN sujetar con una brocheta || ARCH apuntalar.

truss bridge [-bridʒ] *n* puente *m* de celosía.

truss girder [-ˌgəːdə*] *n* viga *f* de celosía.

trust [trʌst] *n* confianza *f* (confidence in s.o. or sth.); *a position of trust* un puesto de confianza; *trust in the future* confianza en el futuro; *breach of trust* abuso de confianza; *he puts his trust in* tiene confianza en || esperanza *f* (hope) || deber *m*, obligación *f* (duty); *he deserted his trust* no cumplió con su obligación || depósito *m*; *shall I hold this money in trust for you?* ¿le guardo este dinero en depósito? || JUR fideicomiso *m*; *in trust* en fideicomiso || COMM trust *m* (association of companies) | crédito *m*, fiado *m*; *to sell on trust* vender a crédito *or* al fiado *or* fiado || *to take on trust* aceptar *or* creer a ojos cerrados.

trust [trʌst] *vt* confiar en, fiarse de, tener confianza en (to have faith in); *I trust him* confío en él || creer, dar crédito a (to believe) || esperar (to hope); *I trust so* espero que sí, eso espero || confiar (to a person's care) || encomendar (to commit to the responsible care of) || COMM dar crédito a || *he is not to be trusted* no es de fiar.
◆ *vi* confiar; *to trust in God* confiar en Dios || *to trust to* abandonarse a, confiar en.

trust company [-ˌkʌmpəni] *n* empresa *f* fideicomisaria || *US* banco *m* de depósito.

trustee [trʌs'tiː] *n* fideicomisario, ria || administrador *m* de una empresa (person managing the affairs of an institution) || síndico *m* (in bankruptcy) || país *m* fideicomisario (country responsible for a trust territory) || *board of trustees* consejo *m* de administración.

trusteeship [-ʃip] *n* cargo *m* de administrador (position as a trustee) || cargo *m* de síndico (in bankruptcy) || fideicomiso *m* (administration of a region, etc.).

trustful ['trʌstful] *adj* confiado, da.

trustiness ['trʌstinis] *n* fidelidad *f*, lealtad *f*.

trusting ['trʌstiŋ] *adj* confiado, da.

trust territory ['trʌstˌteritəri] *n* estado *m* en *or* bajo fideicomiso.

trustworthiness ['trʌstˌwəːðinis] *n* honradez *f* (of s.o.) || veracidad *f*, carácter *m* fidedigno, exactitud *f* (of a statement).

trustworthy ['trʌstˌwəːði] *adj* que merece confianza, digno de confianza, de fiar (person) || digno de crédito *or* de fe (statement) || fidedigno, na (news).

trusty ['trʌsti] *adj* que merece confianza, digno de confianza, de fiar || fiel, leal (servant).
◆ *n* *US* preso *m* a quien conceden algunos privilegios por su buena conducta.

truth [truːθ] *n* verdad *f*; *to tell the truth* decir la verdad; *if the truth were told* si se dijese la verdad; *it's the patent truth* eso es una verdad como un templo; *the honest truth is that* la pura verdad es que || veracidad *f*; *how can you test the truth of what he says?* ¿cómo puedes probar la veracidad de lo que dice? || sinceridad *f* (sincerity) || exactitud *f* (accuracy) || — *in truth, in all truth* honestamente || *moment of truth* hora *f* de la verdad || *nothing hurts like the truth* sólo la verdad ofende || *to swear to tell the truth, the whole truth, and nothing but the truth* jurar decir la verdad, toda la verdad y nada más que la verdad || *to tell s.o. a few home truths* decirle a uno cuatro verdades *or* las verdades del barquero || *to tell the truth* a decir verdad, la verdad sea dicha (actually) || *truth drug* droga *f* de la verdad || *truth value* valor *m* real.

truthful [-ful] *adj* veraz (telling the truth) || verídico, ca (true) || parecido, da (portrait).

truthfulness [-fulnis] *n* veracidad *f*, verdad *f* (of sth.) || veracidad *f* (of s.o.) || parecido *m* (of a portrait).

truthless [-lis] *adj* falso, sa.

try [trai] *n* prueba *f*, intento *m*, tentativa *f* (attempt); *to have a try* hacer una tentativa || ensayo *m* (in rugby) || *to have a try at doing sth.* intentar hacer algo.

try [trai] *vt* intentar; *he tried skiing but never liked it* intentó esquiar pero nunca le gustó || intentar, tratar de, procurar; *to try to open a door* intentar abrir una puerta || probar; *to try the brakes* probar los frenos; *try twice the quantity* prueba el doble de la cantidad; *to try an experiment* probar un experimento || poner a prueba; *she tries his patience* ella pone a prueba su paciencia || probar (to taste) || JUR juzgar, procesar, someter a juicio (a person) | someter a juicio, ver (a case) || fatigar, cansar; *small print tries the eyes* los caracteres pequeños cansan la vista || — *a people sorely tried* un pueblo que ha sufrido mucho || *to try it on with s.o.* intentar engañar a alguien || *to try on* probarse (clothes) || *to try one's best* hacer los mayores esfuerzos, hacer todo lo posible || *to try one's hand at* intentar, probar || *to try out* poner a prueba, probar (a thing, a person), derretir (fat), refinar (metal) || MUS *to try over* ensayar || *to try up* cepillar, acepillar (wood).
◆ *vi* esforzarse (to make an effort to do sth.) || intentar (to have a go) || — *to try and do sth.* intentar *or* procurar hacer algo, tratar de hacer algo || *to try for* intentar conseguir.

trying ['traiŋ] *adj* molesto, ta (causing annoyance) || penoso, sa (causing worry) || difícil (difficult) || cansado, da (tiring).

trying plane [-plein] *n* TECH garlopa *f*.

tryout ['traiaut] *n* prueba *f* de aptitud (aptitude test) || THEATR audición *f*.

trypanosome ['tripənəsəum] *n* ZOOL tripanosoma *m* (protozoan).

trypanosomiasis [ˌtripənəusəu'maiəsis] *n* MED tripanosomiasis *f inv*.

trysail ['traisəl] *n* MAR vela *f* triangular.

tryst [tryst] *n* cita *f*.

tsar [zɑː] *n* zar *m*.

tsarina [zɑː'riːnə] *n* zarina *f*.

tsetse ['tsetsi]; **tsetse fly** [-flai] *n* ZOOL mosca *f* tse-tsé, tse-tsé *f*.

T-shirt ['tiːʃəːt] *n* camiseta *f*.

T square ['tiːskwɛə*] *n* escuadra *f* en forma de T.

Tuareg ['tjuəreg] *n* tuareg *m*.

tub [tʌb] *n* tina *f* (made of wood, of metal, etc.) || cubo *m* (for carrying ore, etc.) || bote *m* (to practise rowing) || barreño *m*, tina *f* (old metal bath) || caja *f* (for flowers) || FAM carraca *f* (slow or clumpsy ship) | bañera *f* (bathtub) || (ant) baño *m* (bath).

tub [tʌb] *vt* lavar en una tina *or* barreño (to wash in a tub) || poner en una caja (plants).
◆ *vi* bañarse (to take a bath).

tuba ['tjuːbə] *n* MUS tuba *f* || tuba *f* (Philippine liquor).

tubate ['tjuːbeit] *adj* tubulado, da; tubular.

tubby ['tʌbi] *adj* rechoncho, cha.

tube [tjuːb] *n* tubo *m* (pipe, container); *toothpaste tube* tubo de pasta dentífrica; *test tube* tubo de ensayo || PHYS tubo *m*; *cathode-ray tube* tubo de rayos catódicos; *vacuum tube* tubo de vacío || metro *m* (underground railway) || BOT tubo *m* || ANAT trompa *f*; *Fallopian tube* trompa de Falopio | tubo *m*; *capillary tube* tubo capilar || *US* tunel *m* (for motor or rail traffic) | lámpara *f* (valve) | cámara *f* de aire (of a tyre) || *speaking tube* tubo acústico.

tube [tjuːb] *vt* entubar (to provide with tubes) || meter en tubos, entubar (to enclose in tubes).

tubeless [-lis] *adj* sin cámara (tyre).

tuber [-ə*] *n* BOT tubérculo *m* (modified underground stem) || ANAT tuberosidad *f* || MED tubérculo *m*.

tubercle ['tjuːbəːkl] *n* MED, ANAT & BOT tubérculo *m*.

tubercle bacillus [-bə'siləs] *n* bacilo *m* de Koch, bacilo *m* de la tuberculosis.

tubercular [tju'bəːkjulə*] *adj/n* tuberculoso, sa.

tuberculin [tju'bəːkjulin] *n* tuberculina *f* || *tuberculin test* prueba *f* de la tuberculina, tuberculino-diagnóstico *m*.

tuberculosis [tjuˌbəːkju'ləusis] *n* MED tuberculosis *f*.

tuberculous [tju'bəːkjuləs] *adj* tuberculoso, sa.

tuberose ['tjuːbərəuz] *n* BOT tuberosa *f*, nardo *m*.

tuberosity [ˌtjuːbə'rɔsiti] *n* tuberosidad *f*.

tuberous ['tjuːbərəs] *adj* BOT tuberoso, sa; *tuberous root* raíz tuberosa.

tube station ['tjuːbˌsteiʃən] *n* estación *f* de metro.

tubing ['tjuːbin] *n* tubería *f* || MED & TECH entubado *m*.

tub-thumper ['tʌbˌθʌmpə*] *n* arengador *m*.

tub-thumping ['tʌbˌθʌmpiŋ] *n* arenga *f*.

tubular ['tjuːbjulə*] *adj* tubular.

tubulate ['tjuːbjulit] *adj* tubulado, da.

TUC *abbr of* *[Trades Union Congress]* confederación de los sindicatos británicos.

tuck [tʌk] *n* alforza *f*, pliegue *m* (fold) || chucherías *f pl* (sweets, cakes, etc.) || comida *f* (food).

tuck [tʌk] *vt* meter; *he tucked his handkerchief in his pocket* metió el pañuelo en el bolsillo || remeter, meter; *to tuck one's sheets in* remeter las sábanas || meter; *to tuck one's shirt in one's trousers* meter la camisa dentro de los pantalones || hacer pliegues en, alforzar (to fold) || — *to tuck away* ocultar, esconder (to hide), tragar (to swallow) || *to tuck in* arropar (s.o. in bed) || *to tuck up* remangar (sleeves, trousers, etc.), arropar (s.o.).
◆ *vi* caber (to fit) || FAM *to tuck in* comer con mucho apetito.

tucker ['tʌkə*] *n* FAM comida *f*.

tucker ['tʌkə*] *vt* *US* FAM agotar.

tuck-in ['tʌkin] *n* FAM banquetazo *m*, comilona *f*.

tuck-shop ['tʌkʃɔp] *n* confitería *f*.

tuco-tuco ['tu:kəu'tu:kəu] *n* ZOOL tucutucu *m* (rodent).

Tudor ['tju:də*] *pr n* Tudor.

Tuesday ['tju:zdi] *n* martes *m*; *he will come on Tuesday* vendrá el martes.

tufa ['tju:fə] *n* toba *f* (stone).

tufaceous [tju:'feiʃəs] *adj* tobáceo, a.

tuff [tʌf] *n* toba *f* (stone).

tuffaceous [tʌ'feiʃəs] *adj* tobáceo, a.

tuft [tʌft] *n* penacho *m* (of feathers) ‖ mechón *m* (of hair) ‖ mata *f* (of plants) ‖ perilla *f* (beard) ‖ borla *f* (on a hat) ‖ copo *m* (of wool) ‖ nudo *m* de basta (of mattress) ‖ penacho *m*, copete *m* (of a bird).

tuft [tʌft] *vt* poner un penacho *or* una borla a (with feathers) ‖ acolchar (a mattress).

tufted ['tʌftid]; **tufty** ['tʌfti] *adj* copetudo, da.

tufting needle ['tʌftiŋ,ni:dl] *n* aguja *f* colchonera.

tug [tʌg] *n* tirón *m* (sharp pull); *give it a good tug* dale un tirón fuerte ‖ tracción *f* (pulling force) ‖ FIG lucha *f* (struggle) ‖ tirante *m* (of a harness) ‖ remolcador *m* (tugboat).

tug [tʌg] *vt* tirar de (to pull); *he was tugging the dog along* iba tirando del perro ‖ arrastrar (to drag) ‖ remolcar (to tow).
◆ *vi* tirar fuerte ‖ *to tug at* tirar de; *to tug at the oars* tirar de los remos.

tugboat ['tʌgbəut] *n* remolcador *m*.

tug-of-love ['tʌgəv,lʌv] *n* litigio *m* por la custodia de los hijos.

tug-of-war ['tʌgəv'wɔ:] *n* juego *m* de la cuerda ‖ FIG lucha *f* (hard struggle).
— OBSERV El plural es *tugs-of-war*.

tuition [tju'iʃən] *n* enseñanza *f*, educación *f* ‖ US matrícula *f* (enrolment fees) ‖ — *postal tuition* curso *m* por correspondencia ‖ *private tuition* clases *f pl* particulares.

tuitional [-əl] *adj* de enseñanza.

tulip ['tju:lip] *n* BOT tulipán *m* ‖ BOT *tulip tree* tulipero *m*, tulipanero *m*.

tulipwood ['tju:lipwud] *n* madera *f* de tulipero.

tulle [tju:l] *n* tul *m*.

tumble ['tʌmbl] *n* caída *f* (fall) ‖ voltereta *f* (handspring) ‖ FIG revoltijo *m* (jumble); *a tumble of books and papers* un revoltijo de libros y papeles ‖ — *in a tumble* en desorden, patas arriba ‖ *to take a tumble* caerse.

tumble ['tʌmbl] *vi* caerse (to fall); *they were tumbling over one another* se caían uno encima del otro ‖ dar volteretas (to do handsprings) ‖ agitarse, removerse (in bed) ‖ dar vueltas (a missile) ‖ tambalearse (to stagger) ‖ FIG caerse (price, government).
◆ *vt* derribar (to cause to fall) ‖ desordenar, desarreglar, revolver (to put in disorder) ‖ deshacer (a bed) ‖ despeinar (hair) ‖ arrugar (s.o.'s dress) ‖ FIG & FAM derrocar (a king, etc.) ‖ TECH desarenar (to clean castings) | pulir, limpiar (to polish).
◆ *phr v* ***to tumble down*** derribar (s.o.) | matar (game) | rodar, caerse; *to tumble down the stairs* rodar por las escaleras | venirse abajo, derrumbarse (to fall); *the walls tumbled down* las paredes se vinieron abajo | caer en ruinas, caerse (to fall into ruin); *this house is tumbling down* esta casa se está cayendo en ruinas ‖ ***to tumble into*** tropezar con | echarse en (bed) ‖ ***to tumble on*** dar con, encontrar (to find) ‖ ***to tumble to*** caer en (la cuenta de) (to understand suddenly) ‖ — FAM *he did not tumble to it* no cayó en la cuenta, no cayó en ello.

tumblebug ['tʌmblbʌg] *n* US ZOOL escarabajo *m* pelotero (dung beetle).

tumbledown ['tʌmbldaun] *adj* ruinoso, sa.

tumble-dry ['tʌmbldrai] *vt* secar en la secadora (clothes).

tumble drier; tumble dryer [-ə*] *n* secadora (for clothes).

tumbler ['tʌmblə*] *n* vaso *m* (glass) ‖ cubilete *m* (of a conjurer) ‖ vaso *m* graduado (in medicine) ‖ volatinero, ra; titiritero, ra (acrobat) ‖ ZOOL pichón *m* volteador ‖ dominguillo *m*, tentempié *m* (toy) ‖ TECH tambor *m* desarenador (for castings) | tambor *m* de limpieza (for other articles) | guarda *f* (of a lock) ‖ AUT balancín *m*.

tumbling ['tʌmbliŋ] *n* caída *f* (fall) ‖ acrobacia *f* (acrobatics) ‖ TECH desarenado *m*.

tumbling barrel [-,bærəl] *n* TECH tambor *m* desarenador (for castings) | tambor *m* de limpieza (for other articles).

tumbling box [-bɔks] *n* ⟶ **tumbling barrel.**

tumbling shaft [-ʃɑ:ft] *n* TECH árbol *m* de levas.

tumbrel; tumbril ['tʌmbrəl] *n* volquete *m* (farmer's cart) ‖ carreta *f* (for the condemned to the guillotine).

tumefaction [,tju:mi'fækʃən] *n* MED tumefacción *f*.

tumefy ['tju:mifai] *vt* MED hinchar, tumefacer.
◆ *vi* MED hincharse.

tumescence [tju:'mesns] *n* MED tumescencia *f*.

tumescent [tju:'mesnt] *adj* MED tumescente, tumefacto, ta.

tumid ['tju:mid] *adj* MED túmido, da; hinchado, da ‖ FIG ampuloso, sa; hinchado, da (style).

tumidity [tju:'miditi] *n* MED hinchazón *f* ‖ FIG ampulosidad *f* (of style).

tummy ['tʌmi] *n* FAM barriga *f*, tripa *f* (stomach).

tumour; US **tumor** ['tju:mə*] *n* MED tumor *m*; *malignant tumours* tumores malignos.

tumular ['tju:mjulə*] *adj* tumulario, ria; sepulcral.

tumult ['tju:mʌlt] *n* tumulto *m* ‖ FIG agitación *f*.

tumultuous [tju'mʌltjuəs] *adj* tumultuoso, sa ‖ FIG agitado, da; tumultuoso, sa.

tumulus [tju:mjuləs] *n* túmulo *m*.
— OBSERV El plural de tumulus es *tumuli*.

tun [tʌn] *n* cuba *f*, tonel *m* grande (cask) ‖ tina *f* de fermentación (fermenting vat).

tuna ['tu:nə] *n* ZOOL atún *m* (fish) ‖ BOT tunal *m*, tuna *f*, nopal *m*, chumbera *f* (plant) | tuna *f*, nopal *m*, higo *m* chumbo (fruit).
— OBSERV En el sentido zoológico se emplea frecuentemente también la forma *tuna fish*.

tundra ['tʌndrə] *n* GEOGR tundra *f*.

tune [tju:n] *n* MUS aire *m* (melody); *to play a tune on the piano* tocar un aire en el piano | tono *m* (correct pitch) ‖ RAD sintonización *f* ‖ FIG armonía *f* ‖ — MUS *in tune* afinado, da (instrument), afinadamente (to sing) | *out of tune* desafinado, da (instrument) ‖ FIG *to be in tune with* concordar con ‖ MUS *to be out of tune* desentonar, desafinar (a singer) ‖ FIG *to be out of tune with* desentonar con | *to be out of tune with the times* no andar con el tiempo | *to change one's tune, to sing a different tune* cambiar de tono ‖ MUS *to get out of tune* desafinar | *to sing out of tune* desentonar, desafinar ‖ FIG *to the tune of* por la friolera de, por la cantidad de (to the amount of).

tune [tju:n] *vt* MUS afinar (an instrument) ‖ RAD sintonizar (*to* con) ‖ FIG armonizar (to bring into harmony) | adaptar ‖ *to tune (up)* poner a punto (a motor).
◆ *vi* RAD *to tune in (on)* sintonizar ‖ *to tune up* afinar los instrumentos (a band).

tuneful ['tju:nful] *n* melodioso, sa; armonioso, sa (melodious) ‖ sonoro, ra.

tuneless ['tju:nlis] *adj* discordante (not melodious) ‖ mudo, da (silent).

tuner ['tju:nə*] *n* afinador *m* (of pianos, etc.) ‖ RAD sintonizador *m*, mando *m* de sintonización.

tune-up ['tju:nʌp] *n* TECH puesta *f* a punto, reglaje *m*.

tungstate ['tʌŋsteit] *n* CHEM tungstato *m*.

tungsten ['tʌŋstən] *n* CHEM tungsteno *m*.

tunic ['tju:nik] *n* túnica *f* (garment) ‖ MIL guerrera *f* ‖ ANAT & BOT túnica *f* ‖ REL tunicela *f* (tunicle).

tunica [-ə] *n* ANAT túnica *f*.
— OBSERV El plural de la palabra inglesa es *tunicae*.

tunicate [-ət] *adj* tunicado, da.
◆ *n* tunicado *m*.

tunicle [-l] *n* REL tunicela *f* ‖ ANAT túnica *f*.

tuning ['tju:niŋ] *n* MUS afinación *f*, afinamiento *m* ‖ RAD sintonización *f* ‖ TECH puesta *f* a punto, reglaje *m*.

tuning coil [-kɔil] *n* RAD bobina *f* de sintonización.

tuning eye [-ai] *n* RAD ojo *m* mágico.

tuning fork [-fɔ:k] *n* MUS diapasón *m*.

tuning hammer [-,hæmə*] *n* MUS afinador *m*.

tuning knob [-nɔb] *n* RAD botón *m* de sintonización.

Tunis ['tju:nis] *pr n* GEOGR Túnez (town).

Tunisia [tju'niziə] *pr n* GEOGR Túnez *m* (country).

Tunisian [-n] *adj/n* tunecino, na.

tunnage ['tʌnidʒ] *n* tonelaje *m* (tonnage).

tunnel ['tʌnəl] *n* túnel *m* ‖ MIN galería *f* ‖ túnel *m*, galería *f* (passage dug by an animal) ‖ — *tunnel of love* túnel de los enamorados (in a fairground) ‖ *wind tunnel* túnel aerodinámico.

tunnel ['tʌnəl] *vt* cavar (to dig); *to tunnel a passage* cavar un pasadizo ‖ construir *or* perforar *or* hacer un túnel en; *to tunnel a hill* construir un túnel en una colina ‖ hacer galerías en (animals) ‖ *to tunnel one's way through* abrirse paso a través de.
◆ *vi* construir *or* perforar *or* hacer un túnel ‖ hacer galerías (animals).

tunnel vision [-'viʒən] *n* MED falta *f* de visión lateral ‖ FIG estrechez *f* de miras.

tunny ['tʌni] *n* atún *m* (fish) ‖ *tunny fishery* almadraba *f*.

tup [tʌp] *n* ZOOL morueco *m*, carnero *m* padre (ram) ‖ TECH pilón *m*, mazo *m* (of a steam hammer) | pisón *m*, martinete *m* (pile driver).

tup [tʌp] *vt* cubrir (a ram).

tupaia [tju:'paiə] *n* ZOOL tupaya *f*.

Tupi ['tu:pi:] *n* Tupí *m* & *f*.
— OBSERV El plural de *Tupi* es *Tupi* o *Tupis*.

Tupian [-ən] *adj* Tupí.

tuppence ['tʌpəns] *n* dos peniques *m* (twopence).

tuppenny ['tʌpəni] *adj* de dos peniques (twopenny).

turban ['tə:bən] *n* turbante *m*.

turbary ['tə:bəri] *n* turbera *f* (peat bog).

turbellaria [,tə:bə'lɛəriə] *pl n* ZOOL turbelarios *m*.

turbid ['tə:bid] *adj* turbio, bia (liquid) ‖ denso, sa; espeso, sa (smoke, clouds) ‖ FIG confuso, sa (thought).

turbidity [tə:'biditi]; **turbidness** ['tə:bidnis] *n* turbiedad *f* ‖ FIG confusión *f*.

turbine ['tə:bain] *n* TECH turbina *f*; *hydraulic* o *water turbine* turbina hidráulica; *steam turbine* turbina de vapor.

turbo ['tə:bəu] *n* turbo *m*.

turboalternator [,tə:bəu'ɔ:ltəneitə*] *n* ELECTR turboalternador *m*.

turboblower ['tə:bəu,bləuə*] *n* TECH turbosoplante *f*.

turbocharged ['tə:bəutʃɑ:dʒd] *adj* TECH turbocargado, da.

turbocompressor [,tə:bəukəm'presə*] *n* TECH turbocompresor *m*.

turbodynamo [,tə:bəu'dainəməu] *n* ELECTR turbodinamo *m*.

turbogenerator [,tə:bəu'dʒenəreitə*] *n* ELECTR turbogenerador *m*.

turbojet ['tə:bəudʒet]; **turbojet engine** [-endʒin] *n* TECH turborreactor *m*.

turbomotor ['tə:bəu,məutə*] *n* TECH turbomotor *m*.

turboprop ['tə:bəuprɔp]; **turbo-propeller engine** [tə:bəuprə'pelə'endʒin] *n* TECH turbohélice *m*, turbopropulsor *m*.

turbopump ['tə:bəupʌmp] *n* TECH turbobomba *f*.

turbot ['tə:bət] *n* rodaballo *m* (fish).

turboventilator [,tə:bəu'ventileitə*] *n* TECH turboventilador *m*.

turbulence ['tə:bjuləns] *n* turbulencia *f*.

turbulent ['tə:bjulənt] *adj* turbulento, ta; *turbulent waters* aguas turbulentas.

Turcoman ['tə:kəmən] *n* turcomano, na.
— OBSERV El plural de *Turcoman* es *Turcomans*.

tureen [tə'ri:n] *n* sopera *f* (for soup) ‖ salsera *f* (for sauce).

turf [tə:f] *n* césped *m* (lawn) ‖ tepe *m* (square of earth) ‖ turba *f* (peat) ‖ SP «turf» *m*, hipódromo *m* (track for horse racing) | deporte *m* hípico, hipismo *m* (horse racing).
— OBSERV En el sentido de *hipismo* la palabra *turf* va generalmente precedida por el artículo *the*. El plural de *turf* es *turves* o *turfs*.

turf [tə:f] *vt* cubrir con césped, encespedar ‖ FAM *to turf out* echar (to throw out or away).

turf accountant [-ə'kauntənt] *n* corredor, ra de apuestas (bookmaker).

turfman [-mən] *n* turfista *m*.
— OBSERV El plural de *turfman* es *turfmen*.

turfy [-i] *adj* encespedado, da; cubierto por césped (covered with turf) ‖ turboso, sa (peaty) ‖ de carreras de caballos (of horse racing).

turgescence [tə:'dʒesns] *n* MED turgencia *f*, hinchazón *f* ‖ FIG ampulosidad *f* (bombast).

turgescent [tə:'dʒesnt] *adj* MED turgente, hinchado, da ‖ FIG ampuloso, sa; hinchado, da (bombastic).

turgid ['tə:dʒid] *adj* MED turgente, túrgido, da; hinchado, da ‖ FIG ampuloso, sa; hinchado, da (bombastic).

turgidity [tə:'dʒiditi] *n* MED turgencia *f* ‖ FIG ampulosidad *f* (bombast).

Turk [tə:k] *n* turco, ca (from Turkey) ‖ musulmán, ana (Moslem) ‖ FIG tirano *m* (cruel person).

Turkestan [,tə:kis'tɑ:n] *pr n* GEOGR Turquestán *m*.

turkey ['tə:ki] *n* ZOOL pavo, va ‖ CULIN pavo *m* ‖ US FIG fracaso *m*, fiasco *m* (failure) ‖ — FIG *to talk turkey* no andarse con rodeos, no tener pelos en la lengua (to talk candidly) ‖ ZOOL *young turkey* pavipollo *m*.

Turkey ['tə:ki] *pr n* GEOGR Turquía *f*.

turkey buzzard ['tə:ki,bʌzəd] *n* urubú *m*, zopilote *m*, aura *f* (bird).

turkey-cock ['tə:kikɔk] *n* pavo *m* (bird) ‖ FIG presumido *m*.

Turkey hen ['tə:kihen] *n* pava *f* (bird).

Turkish ['tə:kiʃ] *adj* turco, ca.
◆ *n* turco *m* (language).

Turkish bath [-bɑ:θ] *n* baño *m* turco.

Turkish delight [-di'lait] *n* «rahat lokum» *m* [especie de caramelo oriental].

Turkish towel [-'tauəl] *n* toalla *f* de felpa.

Turkmenistan [,tə:k'menis,tɑ:n] *pr n* GEOGR Turkmenistán *m*.

Turkoman ['tə:kəmən] *n* turcomano, na.
— OBSERV El plural de esta palabra es *Turkomans*.

turk's head ['tə:kshed] *n* escobón *m*, deshollinador *m* (large broom) ‖ MAR barrilete *m* (knot).

turmaline ['tuəməlin] *n* MIN turmalina *f*.

turmeric ['tə:mərik] *n* BOT cúrcuma *f*.

turmoil ['tə:mɔil] *n* confusión *f*, desorden *m* (great confusion); *the turmoil created by the revolution* la confusión creada por la revolución ‖ agitación *f* (agitation) ‖ alboroto *m*, tumulto *m* (tumult) ‖ trastorno *m*; *mental turmoil* trastorno mental ‖ *the crowd was in a turmoil* la muchedumbre estaba alborotada.

turn [tə:n] *n* vuelta *f*, revolución *f* (of a wheel) ‖ vuelta *f* (of key, of handle) ‖ vuelta *f* (change of direction) ‖ vuelta *f*, espira *f* (coil) ‖ vuelta *f* (of rope) ‖ curva *f* (of road, of river); *sharp turn* curva cerrada ‖ movimiento *m*; *with a turn of the hand* con un movimiento de la mano ‖ turno *m*, vez *f* (one of alternating opportunities); *wait your turn* espere su turno; *to give up one's turn* ceder la vez; *I missed my turn* perdí la vez ‖ turno *m* (shift of work); *a turn at the helm* un turno en el timón ‖ THEATR número *m* (short performance) ‖ vuelta *f* (short walk or drive); *to take a turn in the garden* dar una vuelta por el jardín ‖ curva *f* (shape); *the turn of an arm* la curva de un brazo ‖ FIG cambio *m* (change) | sesgo *m*, cariz *m*, aspecto *m* (change in condition); *this affair has taken a new turn* este asunto ha tomado un nuevo sesgo | carácter *m* (mental inclination); *he is of a humorous turn* tiene un carácter festivo | aptitudes *f pl* (capacities) | giro *m* (of a sentence) | viraje *m* decisivo (change in situation); *the Revolution was a turn in French history* la Revolución ha sido un viraje decisivo en la historia de Francia | final *m* (end); *at the turn of the century* al final del siglo | ataque *m* (fit); *I had another turn yesterday* tuve otro ataque ayer | vahído *m* (dizziness) ‖ FAM susto *m* (fright); *it gave him quite a turn* le dio un buen susto ‖ MAR cambio *m* (of tide) | giro *m* (of a ship) | salto *m* (of wind) ‖ MUS grupeto *m* ‖ — *a good turn of speed* una gran velocidad ‖ FIG *at every turn* a cada paso | *a turn of Fortune's wheel* un cambio de fortuna, un revés | *bad turn* mala jugada *f*, faena *f*, jugarreta *f* ‖ *by turns* por turno (one after the other), alternativamente, a ratos (alternately) ‖ FIG *good turn* favor *m*; *he did me a good turn* me hizo un favor; buena acción (among boy scouts) ‖ *in his turn* a su vez ‖ FIG *in the turn of a hand* en un abrir y cerrar de ojos, en un santiamén ‖ *in turn* cada uno a su vez, uno tras otro (one after another), alternativamente (alternately) ‖ FIG *it gave me a turn to hear such news* me dio un vuelco el corazón *or* se me encogió el corazón al oír la noticia ‖ AUT *no left turn* prohibido torcer a la izquierda ‖ FAM *not to do a turn of work* no dar golpe ‖ FIG *one good turn deserves another* amor con amor se paga ‖ *out of turn* cuando no le toca (a uno); *you mustn't speak out of turn* no tiene que hablar cuando no le toca; fuera de lugar (at the wrong time) ‖ MIL *right about turn!* ¡media vuelta a la derecha! ‖ *the star turn* la sensación, la atracción principal ‖ *the twists and turns of the road* las vueltas de la carretera ‖ FIG *to a turn* en su punto; *this turkey is done to a turn* el pavo está en su punto ‖ *to be one's turn to do sth.* tocarle a uno hacer algo; *whose turn is it?* ¿a quién le toca? ‖ FIG *to have a nasty turn* pasar un mal rato | *to have a serious turn of mind* ser serio, tener un carácter serio | *to have a turn for mathematics* dársele bien (a uno) las matemáticas, ser bueno para las matemáticas, tener aptitudes para las matemáticas ‖ *to make* o *to take a turn to port* virar a babor ‖ FIG *to serve s.o.'s turn* servirle a alguien (to be useful) ‖ AUT *to take a short turn* tomar una curva muy cerrada ‖ FIG *to take a turn for the better, for the worse* mejorar, empeorar ‖ *to take turns at* turnarse en, alternar en ‖ *turn and turn about* por turno ‖ FIG *turn of mind* manera de ver las cosas | *turn of phrase* expresión *f*, giro *m*.

turn [tə:n] *vt* hacer girar, dar vueltas a; *to turn a wheel* hacer girar una rueda ‖ dar la vuelta a; *to turn a key* dar la vuelta a una llave; *to turn an omelette* dar la vuelta a una tortilla ‖ dar vueltas a; *to turn a spit* dar vueltas a un asador ‖ volver; *he turned his head and looked back* volvió la cabeza y miró hacia atrás; *turn your eyes this way* vuelve la mirada hacia aquí; *turn your chair to the table* vuelve la silla hacia la mesa ‖ torcer, doblar, dar la vuelta a; *to turn a corner* doblar la esquina ‖ pasar, volver (a page) ‖ poner, volver; *the sun turned his face red* el sol le puso la cara colorada ‖ cambiar el color de; *frost turned the leaves very early* la escarcha ha cambiado el color de las hojas muy pronto ‖ cambiar de; *to turn colour* cambiar de color ‖ volver (to affect); *prison turned him bitter* la cárcel lo volvió más amargo ‖ poner; *it turned him sick* le puso enfermo ‖ trastornar (to derange) ‖ desviar (to deflect); *he managed to turn the blow* consiguió desviar el golpe ‖ desviar, hacer girar; *he turned the conversation to more cheerful topics* hizo girar la conversación hacia temas más alegres ‖ eludir, evitar, sortear (a difficulty) ‖ poner; *his speech turned the crowd in his favour* su discurso puso a la muchedumbre de su parte ‖ volver; *his own criticism was turned against him* volvieron su propia crítica en contra suya ‖ dirigir (one's steps, one's efforts, etc.); *to turn a hose on a fire* dirigir la manguera hacia el fuego ‖ dar (a somersault) ‖ dar la vuelta a, volver (in sewing); *to turn a collar* dar la vuelta a un cuello ‖ rechazar (to repel); *to turn an attack* rechazar un ataque ‖ pasar, pasar de (a certain age); *she has turned fourty* ha pasado los cuarenta años ‖ rebasar, superar, sobrepasar (an amount) ‖ echar a perder (to spoil); *the warmth has turned the meat* el calor ha echado a perder la carne ‖ agriar (wine) ‖ poner rancio (dairy products) ‖ cortar (milk) ‖ revolver; *it turned my stomach* me revolvió el estómago ‖ TECH tornear (on a lathe or pottery wheel) | labrar (metals) | desbarbar (to trim superfluous clay) | embotar (to blunt) ‖ FIG moldear, tornear (to give a graceful shape to) | construir (a phrase) | redactar (a letter) | formular (a request) ‖ AGR labrar, voltear (the soil) | voltear (hay) ‖ CULIN revolver, mover (a salad) ‖ MED torcer (an ankle) ‖ MIL envolver; *to turn the enemy's flank* envolver el flanco del enemigo | apuntar, dirigir (one's gun) ‖ SP dar efecto a (a ball in cricket) ‖ — FIG *he can turn his hand to almost anything* es muy mañoso ‖ *it has just turned half past two* acaban de dar las dos y media ‖ *it must have turned three o'clock* deben ser más de las tres ‖ *it turned my thoughts in another direction* esto cambió completamente mis ideas ‖ *to turn a heel* hacer el talón (in knitting) || FIG *to turn an honest penny* ganarse la vida honradamente || *to turn a screw* atornillar (to screw on), desatornillar (to unscrew) || *to turn inside out* volver del revés || *to turn loose* soltar (to free) || *to turn one's attention to* fijar la atención en || FIG *to turn one's coat* volver (la) casaca, chaquetear || *to turn s.o. adrift* abandonar a alguien a su suerte || *to turn s.o.'s brain* volverle loco a uno || *to turn s.o.'s head* subírsele a uno a la cabeza (success), volverle loco a uno; *she has turned his head* le ha vuelto loco || *to turn s.o. to different views* cambiar las ideas de alguien || *to turn sth. to account* sacar provecho de algo || *to turn the tap* abrir el grifo (to open), cerrar el grifo (to shut) || *to turn upside down* poner boca abajo, volver (in an inverted position), poner patas arriba (in disorder).

◆ *vi* girar; *the Earth turns round the Sun* la Tierra gira alrededor del Sol || girar, dar vueltas; *the wheels were turning slowly* las ruedas estaban girando lentamente || dar la vuelta; *shall we turn and go back now?* ¿damos la vuelta y regresamos ahora? || volver, regresar; *to turn home* volver a casa || volverse; *he turned towards me* se volvió hacia mí || doblarse (to become bent) || torcer; *the road turns after the village* la carretera tuerce después del pueblo || torcer a; *turn right* tuerza a la derecha || MAR & AVIAT virar || cambiar (tide, weather, wind) || cambiar de color (leaves) || cambiar (luck) || volverse, hacerse (to become); *he has turned stupid* se ha vuelto estúpido || hacerse; *to turn musician* hacerse músico || ponerse, volverse; *to turn red* ponerse colorado || transformarse, convertirse (to change into another form) || echarse a perder (to spoil) || ponerse rancio (butter, etc.) || cortarse (milk) || revolverse; *when I saw it my stomach almost turned* al verlo casi se me revolvió el estómago || TECH tornear (to use a lathe) | tornearse (wood) | labrarse (metals) || pasar; *let's turn to another subject* pasemos a otro tema || girar; *the conversation turned around this problem* la conversación giró alrededor de este problema || dedicarse; *when they turned to politics* cuando se dedicaron a la política || recurrir; *I have no one to turn to* no tengo a quién recurrir || — MIL *about turn!* media vuelta ¡ar! || *my head is turning* me da vueltas la cabeza, estoy mareado || *not to know which way to turn* no saber a quién recurrir *or* a quién acudir || MIL *right turn!* derecha ¡ar! || *their thoughts turned to the days of their youth* se pusieron a pensar en su época juvenil.

◆ *phr v* ***to turn about*** dar la vuelta a (sth.) | dar la vuelta (complete turn) | dar media vuelta (half turn) || ***to turn against*** poner en contra de, enemistar con (to antagonize) | volverse en contra de; *he turned against his mother* se volvió en contra de su madre || ***to turn around*** dar la vuelta | FIG desvirtuar (words); *you're just turning my words around* está usted desvirtuando mis palabras || ***to turn aside*** apartar; *to turn aside one's gaze* apartar la mirada | desviar; *to turn aside a blow* desviar un golpe | apartarse, hacerse a un lado; *he turned aside to let me pass* se hizo a un lado para dejarme paso || ***to turn away*** volver (face) | volver, apartar (eyes) | desviar (to divert) | rechazar; *we had to turn away five applicants* tuvimos que rechazar a cinco candidatos | despedir, echar (to dismiss) | alejarse (to go away) || — *to turn away from* volver la espalda a || ***to turn back*** volver; *he turned back to his work* volvió a su trabajo | retroceder (to go back) | volverse (to come back) | hacer retroceder; *bad weather turned him back* el mal tiempo le hizo retroceder | doblar (the edge of sth.) | arremangarse, remangarse (one's sleeves) | retrasar (the clock) || ***to turn down*** bajar (radio, television, fire) | mitigar (light) | rechazar (an offer, a person) | volver (a collar) | poner boca abajo (a card) | doblar (the edge of sth.) | abrir (a bed, sheets) | volverse hacia abajo; *the ends of his moustache turn down* las guías de su bigote se vuelven hacia abajo || — *turn down the noise!* ¡un poco de silencio! || ***to turn from*** apartarse de | apartar; *I turned him from his bad ways* le aparté de sus malas costumbres || — *to turn s.o. from his purpose* disuadir *or* hacer cambiar a alguien de propósito || ***to turn in*** estar vuelto hacia dentro (feet, toes) | presentar (to submit) | entregar (to hand in); *to turn in a report* entregar un informe; *to turn in a criminal, a weapon to the police* entregar un criminal, un arma a la policía | devolver (to give back) | meter (a hem, etc.) | FAM dejar (to leave); *to turn in a job* dejar un trabajo; recogerse, acostarse (to go to bed) || — *his eyes turn in* tiene los ojos torcidos hacia dentro || ***to turn into*** transformar en, convertir en; *he turned the play into a farce* transformó la obra en farsa; *Christ turned the water into wine* Jesucristo transformó el agua en vino | transformarse en, convertirse en; *the water turned into wine* el agua se transformó en vino; *tadpoles turn into frogs* los renacuajos se transforman en ranas | llegar a ser; *she has turned into a pretty little girl* ha llegado a ser una niña muy mona | ponerse; *it turned into a nice day* el día se puso bueno | meterse; *to turn into the park* meterse en el parque | soltar en; *to turn sheep into a field* soltar ovejas en un campo | poner en, vertir en; *turn the text into good English* póngase el texto en buen inglés | traducir a *or* en (to translate) || — *to turn a novel into a film* hacer una versión cinematográfica de una novela | *to turn ideas into deeds* pasar de las ideas a los hechos || ***to turn off*** cerrar, apagar, quitar (radio, television) | apagar (light, fire) | cerrar (a tap) | parar (engine, machine) | desconectar; *turn the current off before you go away* desconecte la corriente antes de irse | quitar del hornillo; *turn the soup off* quita la sopa del hornillo | salir de; *I turned off the road* salí de la carretera; *my street turns off the square* mi calle sale de la plaza | torcer; *I turned off to the left* torcí a la izquierda | despedir, echar (to dismiss) || — *it turned me off eating there* me quitó las ganas de comer allí || ***to turn on*** encender (light, fire) | poner, encender (radio, television) | abrir (a tap) | poner en marcha (engine, machine) | conectar (electric current) | FAM excitar | tratar de; *the discussion turned on politics* la discusión trataba de política | centrarse en; *the trial turns on your evidence* el proceso se centra en su testimonio | depender de (to depend upon); *everything turns on his decision* todo depende de su decisión | volverse en contra de (to become hostile towards, to attack); *I didn't expect you'd turn on me also* no me esperaba que se volviera también en contra mía || ***to turn out*** apagar (light, fire) | cerrar (to shut off) | volver hacia fuera (feet, toes) | sacar; *to turn s.o. out of bed* sacar a alguien de la cama | producir (to produce, to manufacture) | resultar, ser (to prove to be); *the battle turned out a disaster* la batalla resultó ser *or* fue una catástrofe | llegar a ser; *he will turn out (to be) a good pianist* llegará a ser un buen pianista | expulsar (to expel); *the police had to turn out several people* la policía tuvo que expulsar a varias personas | sacar (to remove from a container) | vaciar (to empty) | ordenar (to clear out) | vestir (to dress) | equipar (to equip) | salir (to go out) | formar (to assemble) | asistir a (to be present at); *to turn out for a practice* asistir a un ensayo | formar parte de; *to turn out for the school team* formar parte del equipo del colegio | FAM levantarse (to get up) || — *how are things turning out?* ¿cómo van las cosas? | *it turns out that* resulta que | *to turn out well, badly* salir bien, mal || ***to turn over*** dar la vuelta a; *to turn a steak over* dar la vuelta a un filete | volverse; *to turn over in bed* volverse en la cama | volcar, dar una vuelta de campana; *the car turned over* el coche volcó | capotar (aircraft) | poner al revés (to put upside down) | pasar (a page) | hojear (to glance at); *to turn over the pages of a book* hojear (las páginas de) un libro | ceder; *he turned the business over to his son* cedió el negocio a su hijo | considerar, dar vueltas a; *to turn a problem over* dar vueltas a un problema | COMM dar salida a (a stock of goods), sacar, tener un volumen de negocios de; *they turn over 800 pounds a week* sacan ochocientas libras por semana | AGR dar una vuelta a (soil) | entregar (to hand over); *to turn s.o. over to the police* entregar a alguien a la policía | convertir (to convert) || — *my stomach turned over* se me revolvió el estómago | *please turn over* véase al dorso || ***to turn round*** dar la vuelta a | dar la vuelta, volverse (to face the other way) | girar, dar vueltas (to rotate) | dar vueltas a (to cause to rotate) | cambiar de opinión (to change opinion) || — *to turn round and round* dar vueltas || ***to turn to*** empezar (to start) || ***to turn up*** poner más fuerte, subir (radio, television) | poner más fuerte (a fire) | aumentar (light, sound) | volverse hacia arriba; *the ends of his moustache turn up* las guías de su bigote se vuelven hacia arriba | levantar, subir; *to turn up a shirt collar* levantar el cuello de una camisa | arremangarse, remangarse (sleeves) | acortar (a dress) | meter (a hem) | subir (to change direction upwards) | poner boca arriba (to put face upwards) | AGR dar una vuelta a (soil) | desenterrar (to discover whilst digging) | encontrar (to find) | descubrir; *to turn up an old photo* descubrir una foto vieja | aparecer; *the missing watch turned up* el reloj perdido apareció | salir; *the five of spades turned up* el cinco de picos salió | salir, presentarse; *maybe sth. will turn up next week* puede que algo se presente la semana próxima | presentarse; *he turned up at my office at five o'clock* se presentó en mi despacho a las cinco | venir; *you must turn up for the practice* tienes que venir para el entrenamiento | ocurrir (to happen); *sth. will turn up* algo ocurrirá || — *his nose turns up* tiene la nariz respingona | FIG *to turn up one's nose at sth.* despreciar algo, hacer una mueca de desprecio ante algo.

turnabout ['tə:nəbaut] *n* vuelta *f* || cambio *m* completo (of opinion, of allegiance) || US tiovivo *m* (merry-go-round).

turnaround ['tə:nəraund] *n* → **turnabout.**

turnbuckle ['tə:nbʌkl] *n* tarabilla *f* (of shutters) || tensor *m* (of wire) || MAR acollador *m*.

turncap ['tə:nkæp] *n* sombrerete *m* (of chimney).

turncoat ['tə:nkəut] *n* renegado, da; veleta *m* & *f*.

turndown ['tə:n,daun] *adj* vuelto, ta (collar).

turned comma ['tə:nd,kɔmə] *n* comilla *f* (inverted comma).

turned-up ['tə:nd'ʌp] *adj* respingón, ona (nose).

turner ['tə:nə*] *n* TECH tornero *m*.

turnery [-ri] *n* torneado *m* (work, technique) || objetos *m pl* torneados (product) || tornería *f* (workshop).

turn indicator ['tə:n,indikeitə*] *n* AUT intermitente *m* || AVIAT indicador *m* de viraje.

turning ['tə:niŋ] *n* vuelta *f* (turn) || curva *f*, viraje *m* (of a road); *to take a turning at a high speed* tomar una curva a gran velocidad || bocacalle *f*; *take the first turning on the right* coja la primera bocacalle a la derecha || TECH torneado *m*, torneadura *f* || AVIAT viraje *m* || — *turning lathe* torno *m* || *turning point* viraje decisivo, momento *m* crucial, hito *m* || *turning radius* ángulo *m* de giro (of a car).

◆ *pl* virutas *f*, torneaduras *f*.

turnip ['təːnip] *n* BOT nabo *m* || reloj *m* de bolsillo (watch) || — BOT *Swedish turnip* colinabo *m* | *turnip top* grelos *m pl.*

turnkey ['təːnkiː] *n* llavero *m* (prison warder).

turnoff ['təːnɔf] *n* desvío *m* (on a motorway or main road) || *US* bocacalle *f* (side road in a town).

turnout ['təːnaut] *n* concurrencia *f* (gathering of people) || entrada *f*, público *m*, asistentes *m pl* (spectators) || presentación *f* (personal appearance) || atuendo *m* (outfit, array) || carroza *f*, carruaje *m* de lujo (coach, carriage) || huelga *f* (strike) || huelguista *m* & *f* (striker) || COMM producción *f* (output) || apartadero *m*, vía *f* muerta (railway siding) || limpieza *f*; *this drawer needs a good turnout* este cajón necesita una buena limpieza || *US* apartadero *m* (on a narrow road).

turnover ['təːn,əuvə*] *n* COMM volumen *m* de negocios, volumen *m* de ventas, facturación *f* (money received from sales) | movimiento *m* (purchase and sale of stock) | producción *f* | productividad *f* | rotación *f* (movement of people, of employees, etc.) || CULIN empanada *f* || vuelco *m* (a rolling over) || vuelta *f*; *a turnover on the horizontal bar* una vuelta en la barra fija || vuelta *f* (of socks) || embozo *m* (of sheets) || solapa *f* (of an envelope) || artículo *m* que continúa en la página siguiente (newspaper article).
◆ *adj* vuelto, ta.

turnpike ['təːnpaik] *n* barrera *f* de portazgo (toll gate) || *US* autopista *f* de peaje (toll highway) | autopista *f* (highway).

turnplate ['təːnpleit] *n* *US* ⟶ **turntable.**

turnscrew ['təːnskruː] *n* destornillador *m* (screw-driver).

turnsole ['təːnsəul] *n* girasol *m* (flower).

turnspit ['təːnspit] *n* asador *m*.

turnstile ['təːnstail] *n* torniquete *m* (at entrance).

turntable ['təːn,teibl]; *US* **turnplate** ['təːnpleit] *n* placa *f* or plataforma *f* giratoria (revolving platform for trains) || plato *m* giratorio (in a record player) || plataforma *f* giratoria (any revolving platform).

turnup ['təːnʌp] *n* vuelta *f* (on a trouser leg) || vuelta *f* (in card games) || FAM pelea *f* (quarrel) || *to be a turnup for the books* ser algo inesperado.
◆ *adj* respingona; *turnup nose* nariz respingona || alto, ta (collar).

turpentine ['təːpəntain] *n* trementina *f* || *oil of turpentine* esencia *f* de trementina, aguarrás *m*.

turpitude ['təːpitjuːd] *n* infamia *f*, bajeza *f*.

turps [təːps] *n* FAM trementina *f*, aguarrás *m*.

turquoise ['təːkwɔiz] *n* turquesa *f*.
◆ *adj* turquesa; *turquoise blue* azul turquesa.

turret ['tʌrit] *n* ARCH torreón *m* || MIL torreta *f* (gun platform on tank, on plane) | torre *f* (on a ship) || TECH portaherramientas *m inv.*

turreted [-id] *adj* con torreones (having turrets) || con torretas (tank, plane) || con torres (ship).

turret lathe [-leið] *n* TECH torno *m* de revólver.

turtle ['təːtl] *n* ZOOL tortuga *f* de mar || *US* tortuga *f* (tortoise) || *to turn turtle* volcar, dar una vuelta de campana (cars), zozobrar, volcar (boats).

turtledove [-dʌv] *n* tórtola *f* (bird).

turtleneck [-nek] *n* cuello *m* que sube ligeramente (collar) || *US* cuello *m* vuelto (poloneck).

turtle shell [-ʃel] *n* carey *m*.

turves [təːvz] *pl n* ⟶ **turf.**

Tuscan ['tʌskən] *adj/n* toscano, na.

Tuscany [-i] *pr n* GEOGR Toscana *f*.

tush [tʌʃ] *n* colmillo *m*, canino *m* (pointed tooth).
◆ *interj* ¡bah!

tusk [tʌsk] *n* defensa *f*, colmillo *m* (of elephant, walrus, rhinoceros) || colmillo *m* (of a boar) || TECH espiga *f* (in carpentry).

tusker [-ə*] *n* elefante *m* or jabalí *m* adulto que tiene defensas *or* colmillos.

tussah ['tʌsə] *n* *US* ⟶ **tussore.**

tussle ['tʌsl] *n* pelea *f* (scuffle) || FIG agarrada *f* (dispute) | lucha *f* (struggle).

tussle ['tʌsl] *vi* pelearse.

tussock ['tʌsək] *n* mata *f* de hierba.

tussore ['tʌsə*]; *US* **tussah** ['tʌsə] *n* tusor *m* (material) || gusano *m* de seda (silkworm).

tut [tʌt] *interj* ¡vaya!

tutelage ['tjuːtilidʒ] *n* tutela *f*.

tutelar ['tjuːtilə*] *adj* tutelar.

tutelary [-ri] *adj* tutelar.
◆ *n* divinidad *f* tutelar (deity) || santo *m* patrón (saint).

tutor ['tjuːtə*] *n* preceptor *m*, ayo *m* (in a family) || profesor *m* particular (private teacher) || tutor *m* (in a university) || método *m* (book); *a guitar tutor* un método para la guitarra || JUR tutor *m* (guardian).
— OBSERV El cargo de *tutor* no existe en las universidades de los países de lengua española. Lo desempeña un profesor que está encargado de un grupo pequeño de estudiantes.

tutor ['tjuːtə*] *vt* dar clases privadas a, enseñar; *to tutor s.o. in Latin* dar clases privadas de latín a alguien, enseñar latín a alguien || JUR ser tutor de.
◆ *vi* dar clases privadas.

tutorage [-ridʒ] *n* cargo *m* de preceptor (of a family tutor) || cargo *m* de tutor (of a university tutor) || enseñanza *f*, instrucción *f* (teaching) || JUR tutela *f*.

tutoress [-ris] *n* preceptora *f*, aya *f* (in a family) || JUR tutora *f* (guardian).

tutorial [tjuː'tɔːriəl] *adj* preceptoril (of a family tutor) || de tutor (of a university tutor) || basado en la dirección de estudios por un tutor (of a system of tutors) || JUR tutelar.
◆ *n* clases *f pl* prácticas || INFORM tutorial *m*.

tutti-frutti ['tuti'fruti] *n* tutti frutti *m*.

tutu ['tuːtuː] *n* tonelete *m*, faldilla *f* de bailarina, «tutú» *m*.

tuxedo [tʌk'siːdəu] *n* *US* smoking *m*, esmoquin *m*.

tuyère ['twiːjəː] *n* TECH tobera *f*.

TV *abbr of* [television] televisión.

twaddle ['twɔdl] *n* tonterías *f pl*.

twain [twein] *adj* dos.
◆ *n* dos *m*.

twang [twæŋ] *n* sonido *m* vibrante (sound) || tañido *m* (of harp, of guitar) || FAM gangueo *m* (of the voice).

twang [twæŋ] *vt* hacer vibrar (a stretched string) || tañer (an instrument) || pronunciar gangueando (to say with a twang) || disparar (an arrow).
◆ *vi* vibrar (string, etc.) || ganguear (voice) || *to twang on a guitar* tañer la guitarra.

twangy [-i] *adj* elástico, ca (string) || gangoso, sa (voice).

tweak [twiːk] *n* pellizco *m*.

tweak [twiːk] *vt* pellizcar.

twee [twiː] *adj* FAM cursi.

tweed [twiːd] *n* «tweed» *m*, tejido *m* de lana.
◆ *pl* traje *m sing* de «tweed».

Tweedledum [-l'dʌm] *pr n* FAM *it's Tweedledum and Tweedledee* olivo y aceituno todo es uno.

tweedy [-i] *adj* parecido al «tweed».

'tween [twiːn] *prep* ⟶ **between.**

tween deck ['twiːndek] *n* MAR entrepuente *m*, entrecubierta *f*.

tweet [twiːt] *n* pío pío *m* (of a bird) || TECH sonidos *m pl* agudos (in sound reproduction).

tweet [twiːt] *vi* piar (a bird).

tweeter [-ə*] *n* TECH altavoz *m* para los sonidos agudos.

tweezers ['twiːzəz] *pl n* pinzas *f* || *a pair of tweezers* unas pinzas.

twelfth [twelfθ] *adj* duodécimo, ma.
◆ *n* duodécimo, ma; doce *m* & *f* (in twelfth position) || duodécimo *m*, duodécima parte *f* (fraction) || doce; *Pius XII (the Twelfth)* Pío XII [doce] || doce *m*, día *m* doce (date); *I go on the twelfth* me voy el doce.

Twelfth Day [-'dei] *n* REL Día *m* de Reyes, Epifanía *f*.

Twelfth Night [-'nait] *n* REL Noche *f* de Reyes.

twelve [twelv] *adj* doce.
◆ *n* doce *m* || — REL *the Twelve* los doce apóstoles || *twelve o'clock* las doce.

twelvemo [-məu] *adj* PRINT en dozavo.
◆ *n* PRINT libro *m* en dozavo.

twelvemonth [-mʌnθ] *n* año *m* || *this day twelvemonth* de aquí a un año (future), hoy hace un año (past).

twelve-note [-nəut]; **twelve-tone** [təun] *adj* MUS dodecafónico, ca.

twentieth ['twentiiθ] *adj* vigésimo, ma.
◆ *n* vigésimo, ma; veinte *m* & *f* (in twentieth position) || vigésima parte *f*, vigésimo *m* (fraction) || veinte; *John XX (the Twentieth)* Juan XX [veinte] || veinte *m*, día *m* veinte (date); *today is the twentieth* hoy estamos a veinte.

twenty ['twenti] *adj* veinte.
◆ *n* veinte *m* || — *temperatures in the twenties* temperaturas de más de veinte grados || *the twenties* los años veinte || *to be in one's twenties* tener más de veinte años || *twenty twenty vision* visión *f* perfecta.

twenty-five [-'faiv] *adj* veinticinco, veinte y cinco.
◆ *n* veinticinco *m*, veinte y cinco *m* || SP *the twenty-five* la línea de veintidós metros (line), el área de veintidós metros (area).

twentyfold [-fəuld] *adv* veinte veces.
◆ *adj* veinte veces mayor.

twenty odd [-ɔd] *adj* veintitantos, tas.

twenty-one [-'wʌn] *adj* veintiuno, na.
◆ *n* veintiuno *m* (number, game).

twerp [twəːp] *n* FAM tío *m*, individuo *m*, tipo *m*; *stupid twerp* tío estúpido | idiota *m*, imbécil *m*.

twice [twais] *adv* dos veces; *think twice!* ¡piénsalo dos veces!; *he came twice* vino dos veces || dos veces, el doble; *I have to pay twice what he pays* tengo que pagar el doble de lo que paga || — *I feel twice the man I used to* me encuentro mucho mejor que antes (I feel better), me encuentro dos veces más hombre que antes || *twice as, twice as many, twice as much* dos veces más; *he is twice as big as you* es dos veces más grande que tú; *he earns twice as much as you* gana dos veces más que tú || *twice over* dos veces || *twice the amount* o *the sum* el doble.

twice-told [-'təuld] *adj* repetido, da || trillado, da (hackneyed) || *twice-told tale* cosa sabida, cosa archisabida.

twiddle ['twidl] *n* vuelta *f* || *to give a knob a twiddle* dar a un botón.

twiddle ['twidl] *vt* dar vueltas a; *to twiddle the ring on one's finger* dar vueltas al anillo en el dedo || FIG *to twiddle one's thumbs* estar mano sobre mano.
◆ *vi* *to twiddle with* jugar con, juguetear con (to toy with).

twig [twig] *n* ramita *f* (small branch) || rama *f* (branch); *a twig snapped under his foot* una rama crujió bajo su pie || ANAT vaso *m* capilar || varilla *f* de zahorí (divining rod).
◆ *pl* leña *f sing* menuda.

twig [twig] *vt* FAM fijarse en (to notice, to observe) || darse cuenta de, caer en la cuenta de (to understand).
◆ *vi* FAM caer en la cuenta.

twiggy ['twigi] *adj* ramoso, sa (full of twigs) || muy delgado (thin).

twilight ['twailait] *adj* crepuscular; *twilight sleep* sueño crepuscular.
◆ *n* crepúsculo *m* (dusk) || media luz *f* (dim light) || FIG crepúsculo *m*, ocaso *m* (decadence).

twill [twil] *n* tela *f* asargada *or* cruzada (fabric).

'twill [twil] contracción de «it will».

twin [twin] *adj* gemelo, la; mellizo, za; *a twin sister* una hermana gemela || FIG inseparable (which always go together) | doble (double) | parecido, da (similar) || TECH gemelo, la; *twin tyres* neumáticos gemelos || BOT geminado, da || MIN con maclas (crystals) || — *twin beds* camas separadas *or* gemelas || *twin cities* ciudades hermanadas (in separate countries).
◆ *n* gemelo, la; mellizo, za; *identical twins* gemelos homólogos || hermano *m* gemelo, hermana *f* gemela; *me and my twin* yo y mi hermano gemelo || MIN macla *f* || — *siamese twins* hermanos siameses || ASTR *the Twins* Géminis *m*.

twin [twin] *vt* ligar, vincular; *the projects are twinned in his plan* en su plan los proyectos están vinculados || hermanar; *to twin two cities* hermanar dos ciudades.
◆ *vi* dar a luz a mellizos *or* gemelos (a woman) || parir dos crías al mismo tiempo (an animal) || MIN maclarse (crystals) || *to twin with s.o.* ser gemelo *or* mellizo de alguien.

twinborn [-bɔːn] *adj* gemelo, la; mellizo, za.

twin-cylinder [-'silində*] *adj* de dos cilindros.

twine [twain] *n* bramante *m*, guita *f* (cord) || retorcimiento *m*, retorcedura *f* (twist) || enmarañamiento *m*, enredo *m* (tangle) || meandro *m* (of a river).

twine [twain] *vt* retorcer, torcer (to twist); *to twine strands* torcer hebras || trenzar, entretejer (to interlace); *to twine a garland* trenzar una guirnalda || rodear con; *she twined her arms round* o *about him* le rodeó con sus brazos || ceñir (to encircle) || enrollar (to wind).
◆ *vi* enroscarse; *the ivy twined around the tree trunk* la yedra se enroscaba en el tronco || serpentear (road, river) || enrollarse (to coil).

twin-engine ['twin'endʒin] *adj* AVIAT bimotor, ra.

twiner ['twainə*] *n* BOT planta *f* trepadora.

twinge [twindʒ] *n* punzada *f* (sudden sharp pain) || FIG arrebato *m*, acceso *m*; *a twinge of anger, of jealousy* un arrebato de ira, de celos || *a twinge of conscience* un remordimiento.

twinge [twindʒ] *vt/vi* dar punzadas; *my leg twinges* mi pierna me da punzadas || FIG remorder.

twining ['twainiŋ] *adj* BOT trepador, ra || sinuoso, sa (river).

twin-jet ['twin'dʒet] *adj* birreactor, ra || *twin-jet plane* birreactor *m*.

twinkle ['twiŋkl] *n* centelleo *m*, parpadeo *m* || guiño *m* (wink) || brillo *m* (brightness) || FIG *in a twinkle* en un abrir y cerrar de ojos.

twinkle [twiŋkl] *vi* centellear, parpadear (stars) || brillar (eyes) || moverse rápidamente (feet).
◆ *vt* despedir destellos de [luz] || hacer brillar (eyes).

twinkling ['twiŋkliŋ] *n* centelleo *m*, parpadeo *m* (of stars) || parpadeo *m* (of eyelids) || brillo *m* (of eyes) || FIG *in the twinkling of an eye* en un abrir y cerrar de ojos.
◆ *adj* centelleante (stars) || brillante (eyes).

twin-screw ['twin'scruː] *adj* MAR de dos hélices (ship).

twinset ['twinset] *n* conjunto *m*.

twirl [twəːl] *n* vuelta *f*, giro *m* (rotation) || rasgo *m* (with a pen) || voluta *f* (of smoke) || pirueta *f* (of dancers) || molinete *m* (in fencing).

twirl [twəːl] *vt* dar vueltas a (to cause to rotate); *to twirl a lasso* dar vueltas a un lazo || atusarse (a moustache) || retorcer (to twist) || US lanzar (in baseball) || FIG & FAM *to twirl one's thumbs* estar mano sobre mano.
◆ *vi* dar vueltas, girar (to rotate).

twist [twist] *n* torsión *f*, torcimiento *m* || torzal *m* (of yarn) || trenza *f* (tress) || cucurucho *m* (of paper) || andullo *m*, rollo *m* (of tobacco) || rosca *f* de pan (of bread) || vuelta *f*; *the twists of wire on a coil* las vueltas de alambre en una bobina || nudo *m* (knot) || contorsión *f* (of the face) || rasgo *m*, peculiaridad *f* (of s.o.'s character) || deformación *f*; *mental twist* deformación mental || inclinación *f*, tendencia *f* (tendency); *a criminal twist* una tendencia criminal || lance *m* imprevisto (in a story) || tergiversación *f*, desvirtuación *f* (distortion of meaning) || vuelta *f*, recodo *m* (of a road) || alabeo *m*, abarquillamiento *m* (warp) || efecto *m*; *to give a ball a twist* dar efecto a una pelota || tirabuzón *m* (in diving) || MED esguince *m*, torcedura *f* (of the ankle) || trampa *f* (cheat) || *to give one's ankle a twist* torcerse un tobillo.

twist [twist] *vt* torcer, retorcer; *to twist a wire* retorcer un alambre || retorcer; *to twist strands together* retorcer hilos || trenzar (a rope, hair) || estrujar, escurrir (washing) || enrollar; *to twist tobacco* enrollar tabaco; *to twist a rope around a post* enrollar una cuerda a un poste || entretejer (to intertwine) || retorcer; *he twisted my arm* me retorció el brazo || MED torcer; *to twist one's ankle* torcerse el tobillo | dislocar (one's knee) || dar efecto a (ball) || deformar (to deform) || tergiversar, desvirtuar (to distort); *to twist the meaning of s.o.'s words* tergiversar el sentido de lo que dice uno || combar, alabear, abarquillar (to warp) || FAM timar, estafar (to swindle) || — *to twist one's face* torcer el gesto || FIG *to twist s.o. round one's little finger* manejar a uno a su antojo.
◆ *vi* torcerse, retorcerse || dar vueltas (to rotate) || retorcerse, contorsionarse (to writhe) || enrollarse, enroscarse (to coil) || serpentear, dar vueltas a (a road) || escurrirse, colarse (*through* por) (to slip) || *to twist and turn* serpentear.

twist drill [-dril] *n* TECH broca *f* helicoidal.

twister ['twistə*] *n* torcedor, ra (person who twists) || torcedor *m* (machine) || FAM timador, ra; estafador, ra (cheat) || SP pelota *f* lanzada con efecto (ball) || rompecabezas *m inv* (baffling problem) || US ciclón *m*, tornado *m* (cyclone).

twisty ['twisti] *adj* torcido, da; retorcido, da (having many twists) || tortuoso, sa; *a twisty path* un camino tortuoso || retorcido, da (complicated).

twit [twit] *n* FAM imbécil *m* & *f*, majadero, ra (fool) || censura *f*, reprensión *f* (reproach) || mofa *f* (taunt).

twit [twit] *vt* echar en cara, censurar (to reproach); *to twit s.o. with sth.* echar algo en cara a alguien || ridiculizar, tomar el pelo a, mofarse de (to taunt).

twitch [twitʃ] *n* tirón *m* (tug) || tirón *m*, punzada *f* (pain); *his leg gave a twitch* le dio un tirón la pierna || tic *m*, contracción *f* nerviosa (nervous tic) || retortijón *m* (in the stomach) || BOT grama *f* || VET acial *m*.

twitch [twitʃ] *vt* tirar bruscamente de (to tug) || crispar (hands, etc.) || *to twitch sth. off s.o.* arrancar algo a alguien de un tirón.
◆ *vi* crisparse (with spasmodic jerks) || *to twitch at* dar un tirón a.

twitch grass ['twitʃgrɑːs] *n* BOT grama *f*.

twitter ['twitə*] *n* gorjeo *m* (of birds) || FIG & FAM agitación *f*, nerviosismo *m*.

twitter ['twitə*] *vi* gorjear (a bird) || ponerse nervioso, sa (to be nervous) || temblar, agitarse (to tremble).

'twixt [twikst] *prep* (ant) ⟶ **betwixt.**

two [tuː] *adj* dos.
◆ *n* dos *m* (number, card, figure) || — *by twos* de dos en dos || *in two* en dos || *in twos* de dos en dos || *they are two of a kind* son tal para cual || *to go two and two* ir de dos en dos || *to have two of everything* tener todo por duplicado || FIG *to put two and two together* atar cabos; *putting two and two together I concluded that* atando cabos llegué a la conclusión de que || *two by two* de dos en dos || *two o'clock* las dos.

two-barrelled ['tuː'bærəld] *adj* de dos cañones (gun).

two-bit ['tuː'bit] *adj* US FAM insignificante (insignificant) | barato, ta (cheap).

two-by-four ['tuːbai'fɔː] *adj* US FAM insignificante (insignificant) | estrecho, cha; angosto, ta (street, room, etc.).

two-chamber ['tuː'tʃeimbə*] *adj* bicameral.

two-cleft ['tuːkleft] *adj* bífido, da.

two-cycle ['tuː,saikl] *adj* de dos tiempos (engine).

two-decker ['tuːdekə*] *n* ⟶ **double-decker.**

two-dimensional ['tuːdai'menʃənəl] *adj* de dos dimensiones.

two-door ['tuːdɔː] *adj* de dos puertas.

two-edged ['tuː'edʒd] *adj* de dos filos.

two-engined ['tuː'endʒind] *adj* AVIAT bimotor.

two-faced ['tuː'feist] *adj* de dos caras (with two surfaces) || FIG falso, sa (deceitful).

two-fisted ['tuː'fistid] *adj* US fuerte.

twofold ['tuːfəuld] *adj* doble (double).
◆ *adv* dos veces.

two-handed ['tuː'hændid] *adj* de dos manos (used with both hands) || para dos manos (tool) || ambidextro, tra (ambidextrous) || para dos personas (card games).

two-headed ['tuː'hedid] *adj* bicéfalo, la.

two-legged ['tuː'legid] *adj* bípedo, da; de dos piernas.

two-master ['tuː'mɑːstə*] *n* barco *m* de dos palos (sailing ship).

twopence ['tʌpəns] *pl n* dos peniques *m*.

twopenny ['tʌpəni] *adj* de dos peniques, que cuesta dos peniques || FAM de cuatro perras, barato, ta (cheap).

twopenny-halfpenny [-'heipni] *adj* de dos peniques y medio || FAM de cuatro perras, barato ta (cheap) || insignificante.

two-phase ['tuː'feiz] *adj* ELECTR bifásico, ca; difásico, ca.

two-piece ['tuː'piːs] *adj* de dos piezas.

two-ply ['tu:plai] *adj* de dos cabos (wool, wire) ‖ de dos capas (wood) ‖ de dos tramas (carpet).

two-pole ['tu:pəul] *adj* bipolar.

two-seater ['tu:'sitə*] *n* dos plazas *m*, biplaza *m*.

two-sided ['tu:'saidid] *adj* bilateral ‖ FIG que tiene dos aspectos, doble (question) | falso, sa (person).

twosome ['tu:səm] *n* pareja *f* (couple, pair) ‖ SP simple *m*.

two-step ['tu:step] *n* «two-step» *m* (dance).

two-storey ['tu:'stɔ:ri] *adj* de dos pisos (house).

two-stroke ['tu:strəuk] *adj* de dos tiempos (engine).

two-time ['tu:'taim] *vt* US FAM engañar (to be unfaithful to) | traicionar (to double-cross).

two-timer ['tu:'taimə*] *n* US FAM infiel *m* & *f* (husband, wife, etc.) | traidor, ra (double-crosser).

two-tone ['tu:təun] *adj* de dos tonos, bicolor.

'twould [twud] contracción de «it would».

two-way ['tu:wei] *adj* de doble dirección (street) ‖ TECH de doble paso (valve) | de dos direcciones (switch) ‖ mutuo, tua (mutual) ‖ *two-way radio* aparato emisor y receptor.

tycoon [tai'ku:n] *n* magnate *m*.

tying ['taiiŋ] *pres part* → **tie**.

tyke ['taik] *n* FAM chucho *m* (dog) ‖ niño *m* travieso (mischievous child) ‖ pillo, lla; pícaro, ra (rascal).

tymbal ['timbal] *n* timbal *m* (kettledrum).

tympan ['timpən] *n* tímpano *m*.

tympani [-i] *pl n* MUS tímpanos *m*.

tympanist ['timpənist] *n* MUS timbalero *m*, atabalero *m*.

tympanites [,timpə'naiti:z] *n* MED timpanitis *f*, timpanismo *m*, timpanización *f*.

tympanum ['timpənəm] *n* ARCH & ANAT tímpano *m* ‖ MUS tímpano *m*, atabal *m*.
— OBSERV El plural de la palabra inglesa es *tympanums* o *tympana*.

Tyndall effect ['tindli,fekt] *n* tyndalización *f*.

typal ['taipl] *adj* típico, ca ‖ TECH tipográfico, ca.

type [taip] *n* tipo *m*, clase *f*, género *m* (kind, sort); *I like this type of music* me gusta esta clase de música ‖ tipo *m*, sujeto *m*, individuo *m* (person); *you are an odd type* eres un tipo raro ‖ tipo *m*, modelo *m*; *a new type of aircraft* un nuevo modelo de avión ‖ estilo *m* (person's character); *I don't like his type* no me gusta su estilo ‖ BIOL tipo *m* ‖ PRINT tipo *m*, carácter *m* | tipos *m pl*, caracteres *m pl*; *the type is too small to read* los caracteres son demasiado pequeños para que se puedan leer ‖ — PRINT *bold* o *heavy type* negrita *f* ‖ *she is the motherly type* es muy maternal.

type [taip] *vt* escribir a máquina, mecanografiar (using a typewriter) ‖ clasificar (to classify) ‖ representar el tipo de, tipificar, simbolizar (to represent, to symbolize) ‖ MED determinar el grupo sanguíneo de (blood) ‖ *to type up* pasar a máquina (notes).
◆ *vi* escribir a máquina; *can you type?* ¿sabe usted escribir a máquina?

typecast [-kɑ:st] *vt* encasillar (an actor).

typecast [-kɑ:st] *adj* encasillado, da (actor).

typeface [-feis] *n* PRINT tipografía *f* | tipo *m*, carácter *m* (type).

type founder [-,faundə*] *n* PRINT fundidor *m* de tipos de imprenta.

type gauge [-geiʃz] *n* PRINT tipómetro *m*.

type-high [-'hai] *adj* de la altura normal del tipo.

typescript [-skript] *n* texto *m* escrito a máquina *or* mecanografiado.

typeset [-,set] *vt* PRINT componer.

typesetter [-s,etə*] *n* PRINT cajista *m* & *f* (person) | máquina *f* para componer tipos (machine).

typesetting [-,setiŋ] *n* PRINT composición *f*.

typewrite* [-rait] *vt* mecanografiar, escribir a máquina.
◆ *vi* escribir a máquina.
— OBSERV Pret ***typewrote***; pp ***typewritten***.

typewriter [-,raitə*] *n* máquina *f* de escribir ‖ mecanógrafo, fa (person).

typewriting [-,raitiŋ] *n* mecanografía *f* (typing) ‖ texto *m* mecanografiado *or* escrito a máquina (piece of work).

typewritten [-,ritən] *adj* mecanografiado, da; escrito a máquina.

typhogenic [,taifə'dʒenik] *adj* MED tifogénico, ca.

typhoid ['taifɔid] *n* MED fiebre *f* tifoidea, tifoidea *f* (typhoid fever).
◆ *adj* MED tifoideo, a; *typhoid fever* fiebre tifoidea.

typhoon [tai'fu:n] *n* tifón *m*.

typhus ['taifəs] *n* MED tifus *m*.

typic ['tipik] *adj* BIOL característico, ca.

typical [-əl] *adj* típico, ca; característico, ca.

typically *adv* normalmente (normally) ‖ típicamente (characteristically) ‖ como era de esperar (predictably).

typification [,tipifi'keiʃən] *n* simbolización *f* ‖ tipo *m* (type).

typify ['tipifai] *vt* simbolizar; *the dove typifies peace* la paloma simboliza la paz ‖ representar el tipo de, tipificar, caracterizar (to exemplify) ‖ BIOL ser el tipo de.

typing ['taipiŋ] *n* mecanografía *f*.

typist ['tapist] *n* mecanógrafo, fa ‖ *shorthand typist* taquimecanógrafo, fa.

typographer [tai'pɔgrəfə*] *n* tipógrafo, fa.

typographic [,taipə'græfik]; **typographical** [-əl] *adj* tipográfico, ca ‖ PRINT *typographical error* errata *f*, error *m* de imprenta, gazapo *m* (*fam*).

typography [tai'pɔgrəfi] *n* tipografía *f*.

typology [tai'pɔlədʒi] *n* tipología *f*.

tyrannic [ti'rænik]; **tyrannical** [-əl] *adj* tiránico, ca.

tyrannicide [ti'rænisaid] *n* tiranicidio *m* (crime) ‖ tiranicida *m* & *f* (person).

tyrannize ['tirənaiz] *vt* tiranizar.
◆ *vi* ser un tirano (to be a tyrant) ‖ *to tyrannize over* tiranizar.

tyrannous ['tirənəs] *adj* tiránico, ca.

tyranny ['tirəni] *n* tiranía *f*.

tyrant ['tairənt] *n* tirano *m*.

tyre ['taiə*] *n* neumático *m* [AMER llanta *f*] (of rubber); *spare tyre* neumático de repuesto ‖ llanta *f* (of iron) ‖ — *non-skid tyre* neumático antideslizante ‖ *tyre burst* reventón *m* ‖ *tyre lever* desmontable *m* para neumáticos.

Tyre ['taiə*] *pr n* Tiro *m*.

Tyrian ['tiriən] *adj/n* tirio, ria.

tyro ['taiərəu] *n* aprendiz *m*, principiante *m* (beginner).

Tyrol ['tirəl] *pr n* GEOGR Tirol *m*.

Tyrolean [ti'rəuliən]; **Tyrolese** [,tirə'li:z] *adj/n* tirolés, esa.

tyrothricin [,taiərə'θraisin] *n* CHEM tirotricina *f*.

Tyrrhenian Sea [tai'ri:njən'si:] *pr n* GEOGR mar *m* Tirreno.

tzar [zɑ:] *n* zar *m*.

tzarina [zɑ:ri:na] *n* zarina *f*.

tzetze ['tsetsi] *n* ZOOL mosca *f* tse-tsé, tsetsé *f*.

tzigane [tsi'gɑ:n] *adj/n* cíngaro, ra; gitano, na.

U

u [juː] *n* u *f* (letter); *a capital u* una u mayúscula.

UB40 *abbr of [unemployment benefit form 40]* formulario de seguro de desempleo.

U-bend ['juːbend] *n* sifón *m* (in a pipe).

ubiquitous [juː'bikwitəs] *adj* ubicuo, cua; omnipresente (god) || que se encuentra por todas partes; *a ubiquitous species* una especie que se encuentra por todas partes.

ubiquity [juː'bikwiti] *n* ubicuidad *f* || REL ubicuidad *f*, omnipresencia *f*.

U-boat ['juːbəut] *n* MAR submarino *m* alemán.

udder ['ʌdə*] *n* ubre *f* (of cows, etc.).

UEFA *abbr of [Union of European Football Associations]* EUFA, Unión de Asociaciones Europeas de Fútbol.

UFO *abbr of [unidentified flying object]* OVNI, objeto *m* volador no identificado.

Uganda [juː'gændə] *pr n* GEOGR Uganda.

Ugandan [juː'gændən] *adj/n* ugandés, esa.

ugh! [uh] *interj* ¡uf! (of repugnance).

uglify ['ʌglifai] *vt* afear.

ugliness ['ʌglinis] *n* fealdad *f*.

ugly ['ʌgli] *adj* feo, a (unpleasant to look at); *he is ugly without his beard* está feo sin barba || FIG peligroso, sa; feo, a (dangerous); *an ugly situation* una situación peligrosa | feo, a (morally offensive); *an ugly habit* una costumbre fea | desagradable (unpleasant) | lamentable, deplorable; *an ugly incident* un incidente deplorable || — FIG *an ugly customer* un tipo de cuidado | *to be as ugly as sin* ser más feo que un pecado | *to be in an ugly mood* estar de un humor de perros | *to turn ugly* ponerse furioso (a person), ponerse feo (a situation, a wound, etc.).

ugly duckling [-'dʌkliŋ] *n* patito *m* feo.

uhlan [u'lɑːn] *n* MIL ulano *m*.

UHT *abbr of [ultra-heat treated]* UHT, uperizada [leche].

UK *abbr of [United Kingdom]* RU, Reino Unido.

ukase [juː'keiz] *n* ucase *m*, ukase *m*.

ukelele [ˌjuːkə'leili] *n* MUS ukelele *m*, ukulele *m*.

Ukraine [juː'krein] *pr n* GEOGR Ucrania *f*.

Ukrainian [-jən] *adj/n* ucraniano, na; ucranio, nia.

ukulele [ˌjuːkə'leili] *n* MUS ukulele *m*, ukelele *m*.

ulama ['uːləmə] *n* ulema *m*.
— OBSERV El plural de la palabra inglesa es *ulama* o *ulamas*.

Ulan-Bator [u'lɑːn'bɑːtɔː] *pr n* GEOGR Ulan-Bator.

ulcer ['ʌlsə*] *n* MED úlcera *f*; *stomach ulcer* úlcera de estómago || FIG cáncer *m* (corrupting force).

ulcerate ['ʌlsəreit] *vt* ulcerar.
◆ *vi* ulcerarse.

ulceration [ˌʌlsə'reiʃən] *n* MED ulceración *f*.

ulcerative ['ʌlsərətiv] *adj* MED ulcerativo, va; ulcerante.

ulcerous ['ʌlsərəs] *adj* MED ulceroso, sa.

ulema ['uːlimə] *n* ulema *m*.
— OBSERV El plural de la palabra inglesa es *ulema* o *ulemas*.

ullage ['ʌlidʒ] *n* merma *f* (loss) || *filling up of the ullage* atestadura *f* (of a barrel).

ulmaceae [ʌl'meisiiː] *pl n* BOT ulmáceas *f*.

ulna ['ʌlnə] *n* ANAT cúbito *m*.
— OBSERV El plural de *ulna* es *ulnae* o *ulnas*.

ulnar ['ʌlnə*] *adj* ANAT cubital.

ulster ['ʌlstə*] *n* abrigo *m* amplio y largo.

Ulster ['ʌlstə*] *pr n* GEOGR Ulster *m* (province) || FAM Irlanda *f* del Norte (Northern Ireland).

Ulsterman ['ʌlstəmən] *n* nativo *m* or habitante *m* del Ulster.

ulterior [ʌl'tiəriə*] *adj* ulterior || oculto, ta (undisclosed) || *ulterior motive* segunda intención.

ultimate ['ʌltimit] *adj* último, ma (last in order) || final; *ultimate purpose* objetivo final || definitivo, va; *ultimate decision* decisión definitiva || esencial, fundamental (fundamental, essential); *the ultimate truth* la verdad fundamental || máximo, ma (maximum) || CHEM elemental; *ultimate analysis* análisis elemental.
◆ *n* no va más *m*; *the ultimate in sports cars* el no va más en coches deportivos || lo absoluto.

ultimately [-li] *adv* finalmente, al final || en el fondo (basically) || *to ultimately do sth.* acabar por hacer algo *or* haciendo algo.

ultimatum [ˌʌlti'meitəm] *n* ultimátum *m*; *to give s.o. an ultimatum* dirigir a alguien un ultimátum.
— OBSERV El plural de la palabra inglesa es *ultimatums* o *ultimata*.

ultimo ['ʌltiməu] *adv* COMM el mes pasado || COMM *on the 10th ultimo* el pasado día 10, el 10 del mes pasado *or* próximo pasado, el 10 próximo pasado.

ultra ['ʌltrə] *adj* ultra (extreme in opinions) || extremo, ma; excesivo, va.
◆ *n* ultra *m* & *f*.

ultracentrifuge ['ʌltrə'sentrifjuːdʒ] *n* ultracentrifugadora *f*.

ultrafashionable ['ʌltrə'fæʃənəbl] *adj* muy de moda (clothes, etc.) || *to be ultrafashionable* ir a la última moda (person).

ultraism ['ʌltrəizəm] *n* extremismo *m*.

ultraist ['ʌltrəist] *adj/n* extremista.

ultramarine [ˌʌltrəmə'riːn] *n* azul *m* de ultramar *or* ultramarino (colour).
◆ *adj* ultramarino, na; de ultramar.

ultramicroscope ['ʌltrə'maikrəskəup] *n* ultramicroscopio *m*.

ultramodern ['ʌltrə'mɔdən] *adj* ultramoderno, na.

ultramontane [ˌʌltrə'mɔntein] *adj/n* ultramontano, na.

ultramontanism ['ʌltrə'mɔntinizəm] *n* ultramontanismo *m*.

ultramundane ['ʌltrə'mʌndein] *adj* ultramundano, na.

ultrared ['ʌltrə'red] *adj* PHYS ultrarrojo, ja; infrarrojo, ja.

ultrashort ['ʌltrə'ʃɔːt] *adj* PHYS ultracorto, ta (wave).

ultrasonic ['ʌltrə'sɔnik] *adj* ultrasónico, ca; supersónico, ca.

ultrasound ['ʌltrə'saund] *n* ultrasonido *m*.

ultraviolet ['ʌltrə'vaiəlit] *adj* ultravioleta, ultraviolado, da || *ultraviolet rays* rayos ultravioletas.

ultravirus ['ʌltrə'vaiərəs] *n* BIOL ultravirus *m*.

ululate ['juːljuleit] *vi* ulular, aullar.

ululation [juːlju'leiʃən] *n* ululación *f*, ululato *m*, aullido *m*.

ulva ['əlvə] *n* BOT ulva *f* (seaweed).

Ulysses [juː'lisiːz] *pr n* Ulises *m*.

umbellifer [ʌm'belifə*] *n* BOT umbelífera *f*.

umbelliferae [ˌʌmbe'lifəriː] *pl n* BOT umbelíferas *f*.

umbelliferous [ˌʌmbe'lifərəs] *adj* BOT umbelífero, ra.

umbelliform [ʌm'belifɔːm] *adj* umbeliforme.

umber ['ʌmbə*] *n* tierra *f* de sombra.
◆ *adj* ocre oscuro.

umbilical [ʌm'bilikəl] *adj* ANAT umbilical; *umbilical cord* cordón umbilical.

umbilicate [ʌm'bilikit] *adj* umbilicado, da.

umbilicus [ʌm'bilikəs] *n* ANAT & BOT ombligo *m*.
— OBSERV El plural de *umbilicus* es *umbilici* o *umbilicuses*.

umbrage ['ʌmbridʒ] *n* resentimiento *m* (resentment) || sombra *f* (shade) || *to take umbrage at* ofenderse por, quedar resentido por.

umbrageous [ʌm'breidʒəs] *adj* sombrío, a (shady) || resentido, da (resentful).

umbrella [ʌm'brelə] *n* paraguas *m inv* (against rain) || sombrilla *f* (for shade) || ZOOL umbrela *f* || AVIAT cobertura *f* aérea || — *beach umbrella* quitasol *m* || *umbrella stand* paragüero *m*.

umbrella tree [-triː] *n* BOT magnolia *f*.

Umbria ['ʌmbriə] *pr n* GEOGR Umbría *f*.

umlaut ['umlaut] *n* GRAMM metafonía *f* (phenomenon) | diéresis *f* (symbol).

umpirage ['ʌmpairidʒ] *n* arbitraje *m*.

umpire ['ʌmpaiə*] *n* árbitro *m* || JUR tercer árbitro *m*.

umpire ['ʌmpaiə*] *vt* arbitrar.
◆ *vi* actuar de árbitro, ser árbitro.

umpteen ['ʌmptiːn] *adj* FAM muchísimos, mas; no sé cuantos, tas; *umpteen times* muchísimas veces, no sé cuántas veces.

umpteenth [-θ] *adj* FAM enésimo, ma; *for the umpteenth time* por enésima vez.

UN *abbr of [United Nations]* ONU, Organización de las Naciones Unidas; *the UN headquarters* la sede de la ONU.

'un [ən] *pron* FAM *a bad 'un* un tiparraco, un bicho malo | *a little 'un* un pequeñín, un chiquitín (baby, small child) | *a rum 'un* un tipo curioso, un tipo raro.
— OBSERV *'Un* es un barbarismo empleado en lugar del pronombre *one*.

unabashed ['ʌnə'bæʃt] *adj* imperturbable || descarado, da (shameless).

unabated ['ʌnə'beitid] *adj* constante, que no disminuye; *with unabated interest* con un interés constante.

unabbreviated ['ʌnə'bri:vieitid] *adj* sin abreviar, entero, ra; con todas las letras (name) || completo, ta; íntegro, gra (text).

unabetted ['ʌnə'betid] *adj* sin ayuda, solo, la.

unabiding ['ʌnə'baidiŋ] *adj* efímero, ra.

unable ['ʌn'eibl] *adj* incapaz || *to be unable to do sth.* no poder hacer algo, ser incapaz de hacer algo (physical inability), no poder hacer algo, verse en la imposibilidad de hacer algo (because of circumstances).

unabridged ['ʌnə'bridʒd] *adj* íntegro, gra; completo, ta; *unabridged text* texto íntegro.

unaccented ['ʌnæk'sentid]; **unaccentuated** [ˌʌnæk'sentueitid] *adj* átono, na; sin acento, inacentuado, da (syllable, etc.).

unacceptable ['ʌnək'septəbl] *adj* inaceptable; *unacceptable to me* inaceptable para mí.

unaccommodating ['ʌnə'kɔmədeitiŋ] *adj* poco complaciente || poco sociable, poco tratable.

unaccompanied ['ʌnə'kʌmpənid] *adj* solo, la; que no está acompañado || MUS sin acompañamiento, solo, la.

unaccomplished ['ʌnə'kɔmpliʃt] *adj* incompleto, ta; sin acabar (not finished) || sin talento (having no talent) || no realizado, da; sin realizar (ambitions, etc.).

unaccountable ['ʌnə'kauntəbl] *adj* inexplicable (inexplicable) || extraño, ña (strange) || irresponsable, libre (responsible to no one).

unaccounted ['ʌnə'kauntid] *adj* *twelve passengers are unaccounted for* no se tiene noticia de doce pasajeros, han desaparecido doce pasajeros || *unaccounted for* inexplicado, da (unexplained) || *unaccounted for in the balance sheet* que no figura en el balance.

unaccredited ['ʌnə'kreditid] *adj* no acreditado, da (person) || que no es fidedigno (source of information).

unaccustomed ['ʌnə'kʌstəmd] *adj* inacostumbrado, da; inhabitual, desacostumbrado, da; insólito, ta (unusual) || no *or* poco acostumbrado, da (not accustomed); *she is unaccustomed to cooking* no está acostumbrada a guisar.

unachievable ['ʌnə'tʃi:vəbl] *adj* irrealizable.

unacknowledged ['ʌnək'nɔlidʒd] *adj* no reconocido, da (not recognized) || sin contestar (a letter).

unacquainted ['ʌnə'kweintid] *adj* *to be unacquainted with* no conocer a (a person), desconocer, ignorar, no conocer (sth.).

unacquired ['ʌnə'kwaiəd] *adj* no adquirido, da; innato, ta; natural.

unadaptable ['ʌnə'dæptəbl] *adj* inadaptable, incapaz de adaptarse.

unadapted ['ʌnə'dæptid] *adj* inadaptado, da.

unadmired ['ʌnəd'maiəd] *adj* desconocido, da; ignorado, da.

unadmiring ['ʌnəd'maiəriŋ] *adj* poco admirativo, va.

unadoptable ['ʌnə'dɔptəbl] *adj* inadoptable.

unadopted ['ʌnə'dɔptid] *adj* rechazado, da; no adoptado, da (measures) || sin mantener (roads).

unadorned ['ʌnə'dɔ:nd] *adj* sin adorno, sencillo, lla || FIG escueto, ta (style, truth).

unadulterated ['ʌnə'dʌltəreitid] *adj* sin mezcla (not mixed) || puro, ra (pure).

unadventurous ['ʌnəd'ventʃərəs] *adj* poco atrevido, da; poco arriesgado, da.

unadvisable ['ʌnəd'vaizəbl] *adj* poco aconsejable, imprudente (action) || terco, ca (person).

unadvised ['ʌnəd'vaizd] *adj* imprudente, irreflexivo, va (ill-considered) || *to do sth. unadvised* hacer algo sin pedir consejo.

unaesthetic ['ʌni:s'θetik] *adj* antiestético, ca.

unaffected ['ʌnə'fektid] *adj* no afectado, da (*by* por) || insensible (*by* a), indiferente (*by* a) (indifferent) || sin afectación, natural, sencillo, lla (without affectation) || sincero, ra (sincere).

unaffectedness [-nis] *n* naturalidad *f*, sencillez *f* (simplicity) || sinceridad *f* (sincerity).

unafraid ['ʌnə'freid] *adj* sin miedo (*of* a).

unaggressive ['ʌnə'gresiv] *adj* poco agresivo, va || pacífico, ca.

unaided ['ʌn'eidid] *adv* sin ayuda, solo, la.

unalarmed ['ʌnə'lɑ:md] *adj* tranquilo, la || *to be unalarmed about sth.* no preocuparse por algo.

unalienable ['ʌn'eiljənəbl] *adj* inalienable, no enajenable.

unallowable ['ʌnə'lauəbl] *adj* inadmisible.

unallowed ['ʌnə'laud] *adj* prohibido, da.

unalloyed ['ʌnə'lɔid] *adj* sin mezcla, puro, ra || puro, ra (metal).

unalterable ['ʌn'ɔltərəbl] *adj* inalterable, invariable.

unaltered ['ʌn'ɔ:ltəd] *adj* inalterado, da.

unambiguous ['ʌnæm'bigjuəs] *adj* inequívoco, ca; sin ambigüedad.

unambitious ['ʌnæm'biʃəs] *adj* poco ambicioso, sa; sin ambiciones.

un-American ['ʌnə'merikən] *adj* antiamericano, na (anti-American) || poco americano, na (unlike an American).

unamiable [ʌn'eimjəbl] *adj* poco amable.

unanimated ['ʌn'ænimeitid] *adj* inanimado, da (inanimate) || poco animado, da (dull) || *unanimated by any ambition* sin ambición alguna.

unanimity [ˌju:nə'nimiti] *n* unanimidad *f*.

unanimous [ju:'næniməs] *adj* unánime.

unanimously [-li] *adv* por unanimidad; *to approve a decision unanimously* aprobar una decisión por unanimidad || de común acuerdo (with one accord).

unannounced ['ʌnə'naunst] *adj* sin ser anunciado.

unanswerable [ʌn'ɑ:nsərəbl] *adj* que no tiene contestación *or* respuesta (question) || irrebatible, irrefutable (criticism, attack).

unanswered ['ʌn'ɑ:nsəd] *adj* no contestado, da; sin contestar (letter) || no correspondido, da (love) || *he left the question unanswered* dejó la pregunta sin contestación.

unanticipated ['ʌnæn'tisipeitid] *adj* imprevisto, ta (unexpected).

unappalled ['ʌnə'pɔ:ld] *adj* impasible, impávido, da (unfrightened).

unapparent ['ʌnə'pærənt] *adj* no evidente; *the answer was unapparent* la respuesta no era evidente.

unappealable ['ʌnə'pi:ləbl] *adj* JUR inapelable.

unappeasable ['ʌnə'pi:zəbl] *adj* imposible de aplacar || insaciable (hunger) || implacable (hatred).

unappealing ['ʌnə'pi:liŋ] *adj* poco atractivo, va.

unappetizing ['ʌn'æpitaiziŋ] *adj* poco apetecible (idea, etc.) || poco apetitoso, sa (food, person, etc.).

unapplied ['ʌnə'plaid] *adj* inaplicado, da (system) || inutilizado, da (energy) || *post unapplied for* puesto para el cual no se ha presentado ningún candidato.

unappreciated ['ʌnə'pri:ʃieitid] *adj* no preciado, da || ignorado, da; *unappreciated writer* escritor ignorado || incomprendido, da (misunderstood).

unappreciative ['ʌnə'pri:'ʃiətiv] *adj* desagradecido, da (ungrateful) || *to be unappreciative of* no apreciar.

unapprehensive ['ʌnæpri'hensiv] *adj* torpe (mind) || *to be unapprehensive of danger* no temer al peligro.

unapproachability [ˌʌnəˌprəutʃə'biləti] *n* inaccesibilidad *f*.

unapproachable ['ʌnə'prəutʃəbl] *adj* inaccesible (not accessible) || inabordable, inaccesible (a person) || sin par, sin igual (unrivalled).

unappropriated ['ʌnə'prəuprieitid] *adj* no asignado, da (funds) || libre, disponible (available).

unapproved ['ʌnə'pru:vd] *adj* desaprobado, da || *unapproved of* desaprobado, da.

unapproving ['ʌnə'pru:viŋ] *adj* desaprobador, ra.

unapt [ʌn'æpt] *adj* inadecuado, da (inadequate) || impropio, pia (word) || no apto; *unapt for business* no apto para los negocios.

unaptness [-nis] *n* falta *f* de oportunidad (of a remark) || impropiedad *f* (of a word) || inaptitud *f* (*for* para).

unarm ['ʌn'ɑ:m] *vt* desarmar (to disarm).

unarmed [-d] *adj* desarmado, da; sin armas (person) || BOT & ZOOL inerme || FIG desarmado, da || *unarmed combat* lucha *f or* combate *m* sin armas.

unartistic ['ʌnɑ:'tistik] *adj* poco artístico, ca.

unascertainable ['ʌnæsə'teinəbl] *adj* inaveriguable.

unascertained ['ʌnæsə'teind] *adj* sin averiguar, no comprobado, da.

unashamed ['ʌnə'ʃeimid] *adj* desvergonzado, da; que no tiene vergüenza; descarado, da (shameless) || *he was unashamed of what he had done* no estaba avergonzado de lo que había hecho, no se avergonzaba de lo que había hecho.

unashamedy [-li] *adv* descaradamente, desvergonzadamente (shamelessly).

unasked ['ʌn'ɑ:skt] *adj* sin ser invitado; *he came unasked* vino sin ser invitado || sin formular (a question) || no solicitado, da (advice) || *unasked for* espontáneo, a (spontaneous), no solicitado, da (advice, opinion).

unassailable [ˌʌnə'seiləbl] *adj* inatacable.

unassertive ['ʌnə'sə:tiv] *adj* tímido, da; modesto, ta.

unassimilable ['ʌnə'similəbl] *adj* inasimilable.

unassimilated ['ʌnə'simileitid] *adj* no asimilado, da.

unassisted ['ʌnə'sistid] *adj* solo, la; sin ayuda.

unassuming ['ʌnə'sju:miŋ] *adj* modesto, ta; sin pretensiones.

unattached ['ʌnə'tætʃt] *adj* sin atar, suelto, ta (not fastened) || suelto, ta (loose); *unattached* *leaf* hoja suelta || independiente (independent) || disponible (available) || libre (without any commitment) || en disponibilidad, disponible (employee) || soltero, ra (not married) || libre (no engaged) || MIL de reemplazo || JUR no embargado, da.

unattackable [ˈʌnəˈtækəbl] *adj* inatacable.

unattainable [ˈʌnəˈteinəbl] *adj* inalcanzable (out of reach); *an unattainable goal* un objetivo inalcanzable || inaccesible, inasequible (*by* para) (inaccessible).

unattended [ˈʌnəˈtendid] *adj* desatendido, da; *the reception desk was unattended* la recepción estaba desatendida || descuidado, da (neglected) || solo, la (lacking escort, etc.).

unattested [ˈʌnəˈtestid] *adj* no atestiguado, da.

unattired [ˈʌnəˈtaiəd] *adj* desnudo, da (undressed) || sin adorno (unadorned).

unattractive [ˌʌnəˈtræktiv] *adj* poco atractivo, va.

unattractiveness [-nis] *n* falta *f* de atractivo.

unauthenticated [ˈʌnɔːˈθentiˌkeitid] *adj* no autentizado, da; no autentificado, da || JUR no legalizado, da || anónimo, ma; de autor desconocido.

unauthorized [ˈʌnˈɔːθəraizd] *adj* no autorizado, da; desautorizado, da || ilícito, ta (trade, etc.).

unavailability [ˈʌnəˌveiləˈbiliti] *n* indisponibilidad *f* || inutilidad *f* (uselessness).

unavailable [ˈʌnəˈveiləbl] *adj* indisponible, no disponible || ocupado, da (busy) || PRINT agotado, da (out of print) || inutilizable (unusable).

unavailing [ˈʌnəˈveiliŋ] *adj* infructuoso, sa; inútil, vano, na.

unavenged [ˈʌnəˈvendʒd] *adj* no vengado, da; sin vengar.

unavoidable [ˌʌnəˈvɔidəbl] *adj* inevitable.

unavoidably [-li] *adv* inevitablemente || *unavoidably absent* ausente por causas ajenas a su voluntad.

unavowable [ˈʌnəˈvauəbl] *adj* inconfesable.

unaware [ˈʌnəˈwɛə*] *adj* ignorante (*of, that* de, de que) || inconsciente; *unaware of the danger* inconsciente del peligro || — *to be unaware of* ignorar || *to be unaware that* ignorar que || *unaware that they were waiting for him* ignorando que le esperaban.

unawareness [-nis] *n* ignorancia *f* || inconsciencia *f*; *unawareness of the risk* inconsciencia del peligro.

unawares [-z] *adv* desprevenido, da (unexpectedly); *we caught them unawares* les cogimos desprevenidos || sin darse cuenta (unintentionally).

unbacked [ˈʌnˈbækt] *adj* sin apoyo, sin ayuda (not helped, not supported) || sin domar (never mounted by a rider) || SP al cual nadie ha apostado (horse).

unbaked [ˈʌnˈbeikt] *adj* crudo, da.

unbalance [ˈʌnˈbæləns] *n* desequilibrio *m*.

unbalance [ˈʌnˈbæləns] *vt* desequilibrar || hacer perder el equilibrio (to make s.o. lose his balance) || trastornar (s.o.'s mind).

unbalanced [-t] *adj* desequilibrado, da || FIG desequilibrado, da; trastornado, da (mentally) || COMM que no está en equilibrio.

unballast [ʌnˈbæləst] *vt* MAR deslastrar, quitar el lastre de.

unbandage [ʌnˈbændidʒ] *vt* desvendar, quitar las vendas a.

unbaptized [ˈʌnbæpˈtaizd] *adj* sin bautizar.

unbar [ˈʌnˈbɑː*] *vt* desatrancar (a door) || FIG abrir.

unbearable [ʌnˈbɛərəbl] *adj* inaguantable, insoportable, intolerable.

unbearably [-i] *adv* inaguantablemente, insoportablemente, intolerablemente || *it was unbearably cold* hacía un frío inaguantable.

unbeatable [ʌnˈbiːtəbl] *adj* invencible || insuperable, inmejorable (price).

unbeaten [ˈʌnˈbiːtn] *adj* no pisado, da (track) || inexplorado, da; virgen (unexplored) || invicto, ta (team, champion, etc.) || FIG *unbeaten path* camino nuevo.

unbecoming [ˈʌnbiˈkʌmiŋ] *adj* que no sienta bien, que sienta mal (clothes) || impropio, pia (unseembly); *behaviour unbecoming of you* o *unbecoming you* comportamiento impropio de ti || indecoroso, sa (not decent).

unbecomingly [-li] *adv* mal; *unbecomingly dressed* mal vestido.

unbecomingness [-nis] *n* impropiedad *f*, lo impropio (unseemliness) || falta *f* de decoro (indecency).

unbefitting [ˈʌnbiˈfitiŋ] *adj* impropio, pia.

unbegotten [ˈʌnbiˈgɔtn] *adj* REL no engendrado, da.

unbeknown [ˈʌnbiˈnəun] *adj* desconocido, da.

◆ *adv* *unbeknown to me* sin saberlo yo, sin que yo lo supiera.

unbelief [ˈʌnbiˈliːf] *n* incredulidad *f* || escepticismo *m* (scepticism).

unbelievable [ˌʌnbiˈliːvəbl] *adj* increíble.

unbeliever [ˈʌnbiˈliːvə*] *n* incrédulo, la; descreído, da.

unbelieving [ˈʌnbiˈliːviŋ] *adj* incrédulo, la; descreído, da (incredulous) || escéptico, ca (sceptical).

unbend* [ˈʌnˈbend] *vt* desencorvar, enderezar (to straighten) || aflojar (a bow) || MAR soltar (cables) | desenvergar (sails) || FIG relajar.

◆ *vi* desencorvarse, enderezarse (to straighten out) || FIG relajarse (to become less stiff).

— OBSERV Pret y pp ***unbent***.

unbending [-iŋ] *adj* inflexible || firme (resolute).

unbeneficial [ˈʌnˌbeniˈfiʃəl] *adj* poco ventajoso, sa; poco provechoso, sa || ineficaz (inefficacious).

unbent [ˈʌnˈbent] *pret/pp* —→ **unbend.**

unbiased; unbiassed [ˈʌnˈbaiəst] *adj* imparcial.

unbidden [ˈʌnˈbidn] *adj* espontáneo, a (spontaneous) || sin ser invitado (without being invited) || *to do sth. unbidden* hacer algo espontáneamente.

unbind* [ˈʌnˈbaind] *vt* desatar (to untie) || desencuadernar (a book) || MED desvendar (a wound).

— OBSERV Pret y pp ***unbound***.

unblamable; unblameable [ˈʌnˈbleiməbl] *adj* irreprochable.

unbleached [ˈʌnˈbliːtʃt] *adj* sin blanquear, crudo, da (cloth).

unblemished [ʌnˈblemiʃt] *adj* sin mancha, sin tacha.

unblessed; unblest [ˈʌnˈblest] *adj* REL sin bendecir, que no ha sido bendecido || FIG desafortunado, da (unfortunate).

unblock [ˈʌnˈblɔk] *vt* desatascar (sink, pipe, etc.) || despejar (passage, road, etc.) || descalzar (wheel) || COMM desbloquear, descongelar (credit, etc.).

unblocking [-iŋ] *n* COMM descongelación *f*, desbloqueo *m*.

unblushing [ʌnˈblʌʃiŋ] *adj* desvergonzado, da; sinvergüenza (shameless) || que no se ruboriza.

unbolt [ˈʌnˈbəult] *vt* desatrancar, descorrer el cerrojo de (a door).

unborn [ˈʌnˈbɔːn] *dj* aún no nacido, da; nonato, ta (not yet born) || venidero, ra; futuro, ra (future).

unbosom [ʌnˈbuzəm] *vt* descubrir, revelar || *to unbosom o.s.* desahogarse, abrir su corazón; *to unbosom o.s. to s.o.* desahogarse con alguien, abrir su corazón a alguien.

unbound [ˈʌnˈbaund] *pret/pp* —→ **unbind.**

◆ *adj* desatado, da (untied) || PRINT sin encuadernar, sin tapa (without cover) | en rústica (paperback).

unbounded [-id] *adj* ilimitado, da; sin límites.

unbowed [ˈʌnˈbaud] *adj* derecho, cha; erguido, da.

unbrace [ʌnˈbreis] *vt* aflojar, soltar (to loosen) || debilitar (to weaken).

unbreakable [ˈʌnˈbreikəbl] *adj* irrompible || indomable (horse) || FIG inquebrantable.

unbreathable [ˈʌnˈbriːðəbl] *adj* irrespirable.

unbred [ˈʌnˈbred] *adj* mal educado, da.

unbribable [ˈʌnˈbraibəbl] *adj* incorruptible, insobornable.

unbridle [ʌnˈbraidl] *vt* desembridar, desbridar (horse) || FIG dar rienda suelta a (to give free rein to).

unbridled [-d] *adj* FIG desenfrenado, da; *unbridled passions* pasiones desenfrenadas.

un-British [ˈʌnˈbritiʃ] *adj* poco inglés, esa.

unbroached [ˈʌnˈbrəutʃt] *adj* sin empezar (barrel) || sin tratar (question).

unbroken [ˈʌnˈbrəukən] *adj* intacto, ta; sin romper || no domado, da; indomado, da (horse) || ininterrumpido, da (silence, peace) || continuo, nua (continuous) || que no ha sido batido (record) || indómito, ta (spirit) || JUR inviolado, da || AGR sin labrar (ground).

unbuckle [ˈʌnˈbʌkl] *vt* desabrochar (a belt) || desabrochar *or* desatar la hebilla de (shoes, etc.).

unbuilt [ˈʌnˈbilt] *adj* sin construir || *unbuilt ground* solar *m*.

unburden [ʌnˈbəːdn] *vt* descargar (to unload) || FIG confiar (one's worries, etc.) | abrir (one's heart) | aliviar (to relieve) || — *porters unburdened them of their luggage* los mozos les cogieron el equipaje || FIG *to unburden o.s.* desahogarse (*to* con), abrir el corazón (*to* a) | *to unburden o.s. of* desahogarse de.

unburied [ˈʌnˈberid] *adj* insepulto, ta.

unbury [ʌnˈberi] *vt* desenterrar.

unbusinesslike [ʌnˈbiznislaik] *adj* que carece de método, poco metódico, ca (unmethodical) || ineficaz (not efficient) || incorrecto, ta; *unbusinesslike proceeding* procedimiento incorrecto.

unbutton [ˈʌnˈbʌtn] *vt* desabrochar, desabotonar.

◆ *vi* desabrocharse (a shirt, etc.) || FIG desahogarse.

uncalled [ʌnˈkɔːld] *ad* sin ser llamado.

uncalled-for [-fɔː*] *adj* innecesario, ria; inútil (unnecessary) || fuera de lugar, inapropiado, da (out of place) || impertinente (impertinent) || injustificado, da (unjustified).

uncannily [ʌnˈkænili] *adv* extrañamente, misteriosamente || *it was uncannily silent* había un silencio extraño.

uncanny [ʌnˈkæni] *adj* extraño, ña; misterioso, sa (strange).

uncap [ʌn'kæp] *vt* destapar.
◆ *vi* descubrirse, quitarse el sombrero.

uncared-for ['ʌn'kɛədfɔː*] *adj* descuidado, da (garden, appearance) ‖ abandonado, da; desamparado, da (person).

uncaring ['ʌn'kɛəriŋ] *adj* insensible, poco caritativo, va.

uncarpeted ['ʌn'kɑːpitid] *adj* sin alfombra.

uncaught ['ʌn'kɔːt] *adj* libre, en libertad.

unceasing [ʌn'siːsiŋ] *adj* incesante, continuo, nua (incessant).

unceasingly [-li] *adv* incesantemente, sin cesar.

uncensored ['ʌn'sensəd]; **uncensured** ['ʌn'senʃəd] *adj* no censurado, da.

unceremonious ['ʌn,seri'məunjəs] *adj* poco ceremonioso, sa (without ceremony) ‖ descortés (lacking courtesy).

unceremoniously [-li] *adv* sin cumplidos (without ceremony) ‖ sin miramientos, descortésmente (without courtesy).

uncertain [ʌn'səːtn] *adj* incierto, ta; dudoso, sa (not certain) ‖ poco seguro, ra (not sure or reliable) ‖ indeterminado, da (not calculated) ‖ vacilante, indeciso, sa (hesitant) ‖ inconstante, variable (variable) ‖ — *to be uncertain of sth.* no estar seguro de algo ‖ *to be uncertain what to do* no saber qué hacer ‖ *to be uncertain whether* no saber si ‖ *uncertain health* salud precaria.

uncertainty [-ti] *n* incertidumbre *f* (lack of certainty) ‖ duda *f* (doubt) ‖ poca seguridad *f* (lack of security).

unchain ['ʌn'tʃein] *vt* desencadenar ‖ FIG dar rienda suelta a.

unchaining [-iŋ] *n* desencadenamiento *m*.

unchallengeable ['ʌn'tʃælindʒəbl] *adj* indiscutible, incontrovertible.

unchallenged ['ʌn'tʃælindʒd] *adj* indiscutido, da; incontrovertido, da (undisputed) ‖ MIL sin ser detenido; *to pass unchallenged* pasar sin ser detenido ‖ JUR no recusado, da ‖ único, ca (candidate).

unchangeable [ʌn'tʃeindʒəbl] *adj* inmutable, inalterable.

unchanged ['ʌn'tʃeindʒd] *adj* igual.

unchanging [ʌn'tʃeindʒiŋ] *adj* invariable, constante, inalterable.

uncharacteristic ['ʌnkærəktə'ristik] *adj* poco característico.

uncharged ['ʌn'tʃɑːdʒd] *adj* JUR no acusado, da ‖ no cargado, da (firearm) ‖ COMM *uncharged for* gratuito, ta.

uncharitable [ʌn'tʃæritəbl] *adj* poco caritativo, va.

uncharitably [-i] *adv* sin caridad.

uncharted ['ʌn'tʃɑːtid] *adj* que no figura en el mapa (not on the map) ‖ desconocido, da (unknown) ‖ inexplorado, da (unexplored).

unchaste ['ʌn'tʃeist] *adj* impúdico, ca (lewd) ‖ incontinente (incontinent).

unchastised [ʌntʃæs'taizd] *adj* impune.

unchastity ['ʌn'tʃæstiti] *n* impudicicia *f*, impudicia *f* (lewdness) ‖ incontinencia *f*, falta *f* de castidad (incontinence) ‖ infidelidad *f* (unfaithfulness).

uncheckable ['ʌn'tʃekəbl] *adj* incontenible (emotions, rush, etc.) ‖ que no se puede comprobar (figure, etc.).

unchecked ['ʌn'tʃekt] *adj* sin obstáculos; *unchecked advance* avance sin obstáculos ‖ desenfrenado, da (passions) ‖ mimado, da (child) ‖ COMM no comprobado, da; sin comprobar.

unchivalrous ['ʌn'ʃivəlrəs] *adj* poco caballeroso, sa.

unchock ['ʌn'tʃɔk] *vt* desengalgar (a wheel).

unchristened ['ʌn'krisənd] *adj* REL sin bautizar.

unchristian ['ʌn'kristjən] *adj* REL infiel ‖ poco cristiano, na ‖ FIG indecente.

uncircumcised ['ʌn'səːkəmsaizd] *adj* incircunciso, sa.

uncircumscribed ['ʌn'səːkəmskraibd] *adj* incircunscrito, ta.

uncivil ['ʌn'sivl] *adj* incorrecto, ta; descortés, incivil (impolite); *he was quite uncivil to her* fue muy descortés con ella.

uncivilizable ['ʌn'sivilaizəbl] *adj* incivilizable.

uncivilized ['ʌn'sivilaizd] *adj* incivilizado, da; salvaje.

unclad ['ʌn'klæd] *adj* desnudo, da.

unclaimed ['ʌn'kleimd] *adj* sin reclamar.

unclasp ['ʌn'klɑːsp] *vt* desabrochar (to undo) ‖ aflojar (to loosen).

unclassical ['ʌn'klæsikəl] *adj* no clásico, ca.

unclassifiable ['ʌn'klæsifaiəbl] *adj* imposible de clasificar, inclasificable.

uncle ['ʌŋkl] *n* tío *m* ‖ — FIG & FAM *at my uncle's* en peñaranda (in pawn) | *say uncle!* ¡ríndete! | *Uncle Sam* el Tío Sam.

unclean ['ʌn'kliːn] *adj* sucio, cia (dirty) ‖ desaseado, da (untidy) ‖ REL impuro, ra.

uncleanliness ['ʌn'klenlinis] *n* ⟶ **uncleanness**.

uncleanly ['ʌn'klenli] *adj* sucio, cia (dirty) ‖ desaseado, da (untidy) ‖ impuro, ra (impure).
◆ *adv* suciamente ‖ desaseadamente ‖ impuramente.

uncleanness [-nis]; **uncleanliness** ['ʌn'klenlinis] *n* suciedad *f* (dirtiness) ‖ desaseo *m* (untidiness) ‖ impureza *f* (impurity).

uncleansed ['ʌn'klenzd] *adj* sucio, cia.

unclear ['ʌn'kliə*] *adj* poco claro, ra ‖ confuso, sa; poco claro, ra (confused) ‖ *I am unclear as to* no estoy seguro de.

uncleared ['ʌn'kliəd] *adj* sin quitar (table) ‖ sin desbrozar (ground) ‖ COMM que no han pasado por la aduana (goods) | sin pagar (debt) ‖ JUR no declarado inocente ‖ FIG que no ha sido aclarado (mystery) | que no ha sido disipado (doubt).

unclench ['ʌn'klentʃ] *vt* aflojar.

uncloak ['ʌn'kləuk] *vt* quitar el abrigo a (to take s.o.'s coat) ‖ desencapotar (to remove s.o.'s cloak) ‖ FIG desenmascarar.

unclog ['ʌn'klɔg] *vt* desatascar.

unclothe ['ʌn'kləuð] *vt* desnudar.
◆ *vi* desnudarse.

unclothed [-d] *adj* desnudo, da.

unclouded ['ʌn'klaudid] *adj* despedado, da; sin nubes (sky) ‖ FIG sin nubes, sereno, na (future).

uncock ['ʌn'kɔk] *vt* desmontar (a rifle).

uncoil ['ʌn'kɔil] *vt* desenrollar.
◆ *vi* desenroscarse (a snake) ‖ desenrollarse (a rope, etc.).

uncollected ['ʌnkə'lektid] *adj* disperso, sa; no reunido, da (scattered) ‖ agitado, da (person) ‖ no recaudado, da; sin cobrar (taxes).

uncoloured; US **uncolored** ['ʌn'kʌləd] *adj* incoloro, ra; sin color ‖ FIG sin color (style) | imparcial (unbiassed) ‖ FIG *to remain uncoloured by* no ser influenciado por.

uncombed ['ʌn'kəumd] *adj* despeinado, da.

uncomeliness [ʌn'kʌmlinis] *n* falta *f* de gracia *or* de garbo.

uncomely ['ʌn'kʌmli] *adj* falto de gracia *or* de garbo.

uncomfortable [ʌn'kʌmfətəbl] *adj* incómodo, da; poco confortable (not comfortable); *an uncomfortable bed* una cama incómoda; *to feel uncomfortable in a chair* encontrarse incómodo en una silla ‖ desagradable (unpleasant) ‖ incómodo, da; molesto, ta (awkward) ‖ inquietante (worrying) ‖ — *to feel uncomfortable* no estar a gusto (not at ease), estar molesto *or* incómodo (awkward), estar preocupado (worried) ‖ *we can make things uncomfortable for you* le podemos crear dificultades, le podemos complicar la vida.

uncomfortableness [-nis] *n* incomodidad *f*.

uncommercial ['ʌnkə'məːʃəl] *adj* poco comercial ‖ con pocos comercios (town).

uncommitted ['ʌnkə'mitid] *adj* no comprometido, da (person, country).

uncommon [ʌn'kɔmən] *adj* raro, ra; poco común, poco corriente (rare) ‖ fuera de lo común, extraordinario, ria (unusual).

uncommonly [-li] *adv* extraordinariamente, particularmente ‖ *not uncommonly* con cierta frecuencia, bastantes veces.

uncommunicative ['ʌnkə'mjuːnikətiv] *adj* poco comunicativo, va; reservado, da.

uncompanionable ['ʌnkəm'pænjənəbl] *adj* insociable.

uncomplaining ['ʌnkəm'pleiniŋ] *adj* que no protesta, resignado, da.

uncomplainingly [-li] *adv* con resignación, sin protestar.

uncompleted ['ʌnkəm'pliːtid] *adj* incompleto, ta; inacabado, da; sin acabar.

uncomplicated ['ʌn'kɔmplikeitid] *adj* sencillo, lla.

uncomplimentary ['ʌn,kɔmpli'mentəri] *adj* poco halagüeño, ña.

uncomplying ['ʌnkəm'plaiiŋ] *adj* inflexible, intransigente.

uncomprehending ['ʌnkɔmpri'hendiŋ] *adj* desconcertado, da; confundido, da.

uncomprehensive [ʌn,kɔmpri'hensiv] *adj* incompleto, ta.

uncompromising [ʌn'kɔmprəmaiziŋ] *adj* inflexible, intransigente (making no concessions) ‖ absoluto, ta; *uncompromising integrity* integridad absoluta.

unconcealed ['ʌnkən'siːld] *n* evidente, abierto, ta; no disimulado, da.

unconcern ['ʌnkən'səːn] *n* indiferencia *f*, despreocupación *f* ‖ tranquilidad *f* (calm).

unconcerned [-d] *adj* despreocupado, da (not worried) ‖ indiferente; *unconcerned about his brother's troubles* indiferente a las dificultades de su hermano; *unconcerned about the danger* indiferente al peligro ‖ no interesado, da (not concerned).

unconcernedly ['ʌnkən'səːnidli] *adv* con indiferencia (indifferently) ‖ tranquilamente, sin preocuparse.

unconditional ['ʌnkən'diʃənl] *adj* incondicional ‖ terminante (refusal).

unconditioned ['ʌnkən'diʃənd] *adj* incondicional ‖ no condicionado, da; espontáneo, a (reflex).

unconfessable ['ʌnkən'fesəbl] *adj* inconfesable.

unconfessed ['ʌnkən'fest] *adj* no confesado, da (sin) ‖ sin confesar (person).

unconfined ['ʌnkən'faind] *adj* libre (free) ‖ ilimitado, da; sin límites (boundless).

unconfirmed ['ʌnkən'fəːmd] *adj* no confirmado, da; sin confirmar.

unconformable ['ʌnkən'fɔːməbl] *adj* disconforme (which does not conform) ‖ incompatible || GEOL discordante || no conformista (person).

unconformity ['ʌnkənfɔːmiti] *n* disconformidad *f* || GEOL discordancia *f*.

uncongealable ['ʌnkən'dʒiələbl] *adj* incongelable.

uncongenial ['ʌnkən'dʒiːniəl] *adj* antipático, ca (person) || desagradable (unpleasant); *uncongenial job* trabajo desagradable.

unconnected ['ʌnkə'nektid] *adj* no relacionado, da (*with* con) || sin hilación, inconexo, xa (ideas).

unconquerable [ʌn'kɔŋkərəbl] *adj* invencible (army) || inconquistable (heart, region) || insuperable (difficulty) || incorregible (defect) || irresistible (curiosity, etc.).

unconquered ['ʌn'kɔŋkəd] *adj* invicto, ta (not defeated) || no conquistado, da (not conquered) || indómito, ta (not subjugated) || incontenible (passion) || insuperable (difficulty).

unconscientious ['ʌn,kɔnʃi'enʃəs] *adj* poco concienzudo, da.

unconscionable [ʌn'kɔnʃnəbl] *adj* poco escrupuloso, sa (unscrupulous) || desmedido, da; excesivo, va; desmesurado, da (excessive).

unconscious [ʌn'kɔnʃəs] *adj* inconsciente || — *the blow knocked him unconscious* el golpe le dejó inconsciente *or* sin conocimiento *or* sin sentido || *to be unconscious of* estar inconsciente de, no darse cuenta de.
◆ *n* PHIL inconsciente *m*.

unconsciousness [-nis] *n* inconsciencia *f*.

unconsenting ['ʌnkən'sentiŋ] *adj* que no consiente.

unconsidered ['ʌnkən'sidəd] *adj* inconsiderado, da; irreflexivo, va || insignificante.

unconsolable ['ʌnkən'səuləbl] *adj* inconsolable.

unconsoled ['ʌnkən'səuld] *adj* desconsolado, da.

unconstitutional ['ʌn,kɔnsti'tjuːʃənl] *adj* anticonstitucional, inconstitucional.

unconstitutionality ['ʌn,kɔnstitjuːʃə'næliti] *n* inconstitucionalidad *f*.

unconstrained ['ʌnkən'streind] *adj* libre || franco, ca (laughter) || espontáneo, a (spontaneous).

unconstricted ['ʌnkən'striktid] *adj* libre || sin restricción || desenvuelto, ta (person).

unconsumed ['ʌnkən'sjuːmd] *adj* sin consumir.

uncontainable ['ʌnkən'teinəbl] *adj* incontenible.

uncontaminated ['ʌnkən'tæmineitid] *adj* incontaminado, da.

uncontemplated ['ʌn'kɔntəmpleitid] *adj* imprevisto, ta (unexpected).

uncontested ['ʌnkən'testid] *adj* incontestado, da || ganado sin oposición (parliamentary seat).

uncontinuous ['ʌnkən'tinjuəs] *adj* discontinuo, nua.

uncontradictable ['ʌn,kɔntrə'diktəbl] *adj* irrefutable, indiscutible.

uncontrite ['ʌn'kɔntrait] *adj* incontrito, ta.

uncontrollable [,ʌnkən'trəuləbl] *adj* incontrolable || irresistible, incontrolable (wish, laughter) || ingobernable (people) || indisciplinado, da (child) || *she burst into uncontrollable laughter* le dio un ataque de risa.

uncontrolled ['ʌnkən'trəuld] *adj* no dominado, da; no controlado, da || desenfrenado, da (passion) || irresponsable || absoluto, ta; completo, ta (liberty).

uncontroverted ['ʌn,kɔntrəu'vəːtid] *adj* indiscutido, da; no controvertido, da; incontrovertido, da.

uncontrovertible ['ʌn'kɔntrəvəːtəbl] *adj* incontrovertible, indiscutible.

unconventional ['ʌnkən'venʃənl] *adj* poco convencional || original; *unconventional dress* traje original.

unconventionality [,ʌnkənvenʃə'næliti] *n* originalidad *f*.

unconversant ['ʌnkən'vəːsənt] *adj* *to be unconversant with* no estar al tanto de (not to be informed of), estar poco versado en, no saber mucho de (not to know much about).

unconverted ['ʌnkən'vəːtid] *adj* no convertido, da.

unconvertible ['ʌnkən'vəːtəbl] *adj* inconvertible.

unconvinced ['ʌnkən'vinst] *adj* poco convencido, da; escéptico, ca.

unconvincing ['ʌnkən'vinsiŋ] *adj* poco convincente.

uncooked ['ʌn'kukt] *adj* CULIN crudo, da; sin cocer.

uncooperative ['ʌnkəu'ɔpərətiv] *adj* poco cooperativo, va.

uncoordinated ['ʌnkəu'ɔːdineitid] *adj* no coordinado, da.

uncork ['ʌn'kɔːk] *vt* descorchar, destaponar, destapar || FIG dar rienda suelta a (one's feelings).

uncorrected ['ʌnkə'rektid] *adj* no corregido, da; sin corregir.

uncorroborated ['ʌnkə'rɔbəreitid] *adj* sin corroborar, no confirmado, da.

uncorrupted ['ʌnkə'rʌptid] *adj* incorrupto, ta.

uncountable ['ʌn'kauntəbl] *adj* incontable, innumerable.

uncounted ['ʌn'kauntid] *adj* sin contar (not counted) || innumerable, incalculable (innumerable).

uncouple ['ʌn'kʌpl] *vt* desacoplar (wheels, etc.) || desenganchar (railway trucks) || desconectar (to disconnect) || soltar (hounds).

uncoupling [-iŋ] *n* desacoplamiento *m* (of wheels) || desenganche *m* (of railway trucks).

uncourteous ['ʌn'kəːtjəs] *adj* descortés.

uncourtly ['ʌn'kɔːtli] *adj* descortés.

uncouth [ʌn'kuːθ] *adj* grosero, ra (vulgar) || tosco, ca; rústico, ca (rough) || torpe (awkward).

uncouthness [-nis] *n* grosería *f* (vulgarity) || tosquedad *f*, rusticidad *f* (roughness) || torpeza *f* (awkwardness).

uncover [ʌn'kʌvə*] *vt* descubrir || revelar (to reveal) || destapar (to take the lid off) || desfundar (furniture) || dejar al descubierto (to leave exposed) || quitarse el sombrero de (one's head) || *to uncover o.s.* destaparse (in bed).
◆ *vi* (ant) descubrirse (to take one's hat off).

uncovered [-d] *adj* descubierto, ta (not covered) || desnudo, da (bare) || descubierto, ta (bareheaded) || destapado, da (in bed).

uncreated ['ʌnkri'eitid] *adj* increado, da.

uncritical ['ʌn'kritikəl] *adj* falto de sentido crítico (undiscerning) || que no es criticón, ona (not very critical).

uncriticizable ['ʌn'kritisaizəbl] *adj* incensurable.

uncross ['ʌn'krɔs] *vt* descruzar; *to uncross one's arms* descruzar los brazos.

uncrossed [-t] *adj* descruzado, da || que no ha sido cruzado, da (land) || sin cruzar (a cheque).

uncrowded ['ʌn'kraudid] *adj* con poca gente (street) || poco apretado, da (people) || poco denso, sa (population).

uncrown ['ʌn'kraun] *vt* descoronar, destronar.

uncrowned [-d] *adj* sin corona.

unction ['ʌŋkʃən] *n* unción *f* (ointment) || ungüento *m* (balm) || FIG unción *f*, fervor *m* (religious fervour) | deleite *m*, fruición *f* (relish) | zalamería *f* (cajoling) || REL *extreme unction* extremaunción *f*.

unctuous ['ʌŋktjuəs] *adj* untuoso, sa; grasiento, ta (oil, fat) || ubérrimo, ma (soil) || plástico, ca || FIG lleno de unción (speech, manner) | zalamero, ra; meloso, sa (cajoling).

unctuousness [-nis] *n* untuosidad *f* || FIG unción *f* (of manners).

uncultivable ['ʌn'kʌltivəbl]; **uncultivatable** ['ʌn'kʌltiveitəbl] *adj* incultivable.

uncultivated ['ʌn'kʌltiveitid] *adj* sin cultivar, inculto, ta; baldío, a (land) || inculto, ta (person).

uncultured ['ʌn'kʌltʃəd] *adj* inculto, ta.

uncurbed ['ʌn'kəːbd] *adj* desenfrenado, da (unchecked) || libre (free) || sin barbada (horse).

uncured ['ʌn'kjuəd] *adj* CULIN fresco, ca (fresh) || MED sin curar.

uncurl ['ʌn'kəːl] *vt* desenroscar (rope, etc.) || desrizar, estirar (hair).
◆ *vi* desenroscarse (rope, snake) || desrizarse (hair).

uncurtailed ['ʌnkəː'teild] *adj* entero, ra; completo, ta (not abridged) || sin restricción.

uncustomary ['ʌn'kʌstəməri] *adj* desacostumbrado, da (uncommon).

uncut ['ʌn'kʌt] *adj* sin cortar (not cut) || en bruto, sin tallar (diamond) || sin tallar (stone) || PRINT intonso, sa (book) || sin cortes, entero, ra (film, etc.).

undamaged ['ʌn'dæmidʒd] *adj* en buen estado, no estropeado, da (goods, etc.) || intacto, ta (intact) || indemne; ileso, sa (people) || FIG intacto, ta.

undamped ['ʌn'dæmpt] *adj* no mojado, seco, ca (not wet) || no amortiguado, da (sounds, etc.) || no disminuido, da (feelings).

undated ['ʌn'deitid] *adj* sin fecha.

undaunted [ʌn'dɔːntid] *adj* intrépido, da (intrepid) || impávido, da (*by* ante) (dauntless).

undebatable [,ʌndi'beitəbl] *adj* indiscutible.

undecagon ['ʌn'dekəgən] *n* MATH undecágono *m*, endecágono *m*.

undeceive ['ʌndi'siːv] *vt* desengañar.

undecided ['ʌndi'saidid] *adj* indeciso, sa; *the election results are still undecided* los resultados de la elección son todavía indecisos || no resuelto, ta; *undecided affair* asunto no resuelto || indeciso, sa; irresoluto, ta (person) || *she was undecided whether she would go or not* no sabía si iría o no.

undecipherable ['ʌndi'saifərəbl] *adj* indescifrable.

undeclarable ['ʌndi'klɛərəbl] *adj* indeclarable.

undeclared ['ʌndi'klɛərd] *adj* no declarado, da.

undeclinable ['ʌndi'klainəbl] *adj* indeclinable.

undefeated ['ʌndi'fiːtid] *adj* invicto, ta.

undefended ['ʌndi'fendid] *adj* indefenso, sa.

undeferable; undeferrable ['ʌndi'fəːrəbl] *adj* inaplazable.

undefiled ['ʌndi'faild] *adj* impoluto, ta; inmaculado, da || — *English undefiled* inglés puro || *undefiled by* no corrompido por.

undefinable [ˌʌndiˈfainəbl] *adj* indefinible ‖ indeterminable.

undefined [ˌʌndiˈfaind] *adj* indefinido, da ‖ indeterminado, da.

undelivered [ˈʌndiˈlivəd] *adj* sin entregar, no entregado, da (goods) ‖ no entregado al destinatario (letters) ‖ no pronunciado, da (speech) ‖ JUR no fallado, da (verdict).

undemanding [ˈʌndiˈmɑːndiŋ] *adj* poco exigente (person) ‖ poco absorbente (job).

undemonstrable [ˈʌnˈdemənstrəbl] *adj* indemostrable.

undemonstrated [ˈʌnˈdemənstreitid] *adj* no demostrado, da.

undemonstrative [ˈʌndiˈmɔnstrətiv] *adj* reservado, da; poco expresivo, va.

undeniable [ˌʌndiˈnaiəbl] *adj* innegable, irrefutable.

undenominational [ˈʌndiˌnɔmiˈneiʃənl] *adj* no confesional ‖ *undenominational school* escuela laica.

undependable [ˈʌndiˈpendəbl] *adj* poco seguro, ra; que no es de fiar.

under [ˈʌndə*] *adj* inferior; *the under jaw* la mandíbula inferior ‖ insuficiente (insufficient) ‖ subalterno, na (subordinate).
◆ *adv* más abajo (below); *see under* véase más abajo ‖ debajo; *she wears a girdle under* lleva una faja debajo; *quick, get under* venga, métete debajo ‖ menos (less); *ten dollars or under* diez dólares o menos ‖ — *buried under* enterrado, da ‖ *children ten years old or under* menores de once años.
◆ *prep* debajo de, bajo (véase OBSERV); *under the bed* debajo de la cama; *under a clear blue sky* bajo un cielo azul despejado ‖ por debajo de, debajo de (movement); *the boat passed under the bridge* el barco pasó por debajo del puente ‖ debajo; *hide under here* escóndete aquí debajo ‖ menos de (less than); *in under two minutes* en menos de dos minutos; *it cost under ten dollars* costó menos de diez dólares ‖ menor de; *he is under ten (years old)* es menor de diez años ‖ por debajo de (lower in rank); *a sergeant is under a captain* un sargento está por debajo de un capitán ‖ bajo (during); *under the Roman Empire* bajo el Imperio Romano ‖ durante el reinado de; *under Charles II* durante el reinado de Carlos II ‖ según, conforme a, de conformidad con (according to); *under the terms of the contract* según los términos del contrato ‖ bajo (subject to); *under government control* bajo el control del gobierno ‖ con (instructed by); *to study under Mr. X* estudiar con el señor X ‖ a; *under the care of* al cuidado de; *under full steam* a todo vapor ‖ en; *under repair, construction, cultivation* en reparación, construcción, cultivo; *the article should come under international news* el artículo debería figurar en las noticias internacionales ‖ bajo *or* a las órdenes de; *we work under Peter* trabajamos bajo las órdenes de Pedro ‖ AGR sembrado de; *a field under wheat* un campo sembrado de trigo ‖ — FIG *right under one's nose* delante de las narices de uno ‖ *to be under the doctor* estar bajo tratamiento médico ‖ *to come o to get out from under* salir de debajo de ‖ *under arrest* bajo arresto, detenido, da ‖ *under bail* bajo fianza ‖ *under examination* sometido a examen ‖ MAR *under full sail* a toda vela, con las velas desplegadas ‖ *under lock and key* bajo llave, bajo siete llaves ‖ *under oath* bajo juramento ‖ *under one's breath* en voz baja ‖ *under our very eyes* delante de nuestros propios ojos ‖ *under pain o under penalty of* bajo *or* so pena de ‖ *under pretence of* bajo *or* so pretexto de ‖ *under separate cover* por separado (letter) ‖ *under the authority of* bajo la autoridad de ‖ *under the circumstances* en tales circunstancias, dadas las circunstancias ‖ *under the name of* con *or* bajo el nombre de ‖ *under these conditions* en estas condiciones.
— OBSERV In general the preposition *under* is translated in Spanish by *debajo de* in its concrete sense: *under the table* debajo de la mesa, and by *bajo* in its figurative and abstract senses: *under the Republic* bajo la República.

underact [-rˈækt] *vt* THEATR representar mal (one's part).
◆ *vi* THEATR representar mal su papel.

underage [-rˈeidʒ] *adj* menor de edad.

underarm [-rɑːm] *adj* por debajo del brazo ‖ ANAT de la axila.
◆ *adv* manteniendo la mano a un nivel inferior a la altura del hombro, sin levantar la mano.
◆ *n* axila *f*, sobaco *m*.

underbelly [-ˌbeli] *n* parte *f* inferior ‖ FIG parte *f* más vulnerable.

underbid* [-ˈbid] *vt* ofrecer menos que (to offer less than) ‖ ofrecer condiciones más ventajosas que (to offer better conditions than) ‖ *to underbid one's hand* declarar menos de lo que se tiene (in cards).
— OBSERV Pret y pp ***underbid***.

underbrush [-brʌʃ] *n* maleza *f*, monte *m* bajo.

undercarriage [-ˌkæridʒ] *n* AVIAT tren *m* de aterrizaje ‖ TECH bastidor *m* (framework).

undercharge [-ˈtʃɑːdʒ] *vt* cobrar *or* hacer pagar menos de lo debido (money) ‖ cargar insuficientemente (a gun) ‖ *to undercharge s.o. by ten pounds* cobrar diez libras de menos a alguien.

underclassman [-ˈklɑːsmən] *n* US estudiante *m* de primer año *or* de segundo año.
— OBSERV El plural de esta palabra es *underclassmen*.

underclothes [-kləuðz] *pl n* ropa *f sing* interior.

underclothing [-ˈkləuðiŋ] *n* ropa *f* interior.

undercoat [-kəut] *n* primera mano *f* (of paint) ‖ ZOOL pelaje *m* corto (short hair).

undercover [-ˌkʌvə*] *adj* secreto, ta; clandestino, na.

undercroft [-krɔft] *n* ARCH cripta *f*.

undercurrent [-ˌkʌrənt] *n* corriente *f* submarina ‖ FIG fondo *m* (underlying tendency) | corriente *f* oculta (hidden tendency) ‖ *an undercurrent of discontent* un mar de fondo.

undercut [-ˈkʌt] *n* solomillo *m* (meat) ‖ SP corte *m* (in tennis).

undercut* [-kʌt] *vt* socavar (to undermine) ‖ ARTS tallar en relieve (to cut in relief) ‖ COMM vender más barato que (to sell cheaper) | trabajar a menor precio que (to work for a lower wage than) ‖ SP cortar (a ball).
— OBSERV Pret y pp ***undercut***.

undercutting [-ˈkʌtiŋ] *n* COMM competencia *f* desleal.

underdevelopped [-diˈveləpt] *adj* subdesarrollado, da (country, industry, etc.) ‖ poco *or* insuficientemente desarrollado, da (body, etc.) ‖ PHOT insuficientemente revelado, da.

underdevelopment [-diˈveləpmənt] *n* subdesarrollo *m* (of a country, of an industry) ‖ desarrollo *m* insuficiente (of body) ‖ PHOT revelado *m* insuficiente.

underdo* [-ˈduː] *vt* CULIN soasar.
— OBSERV Pret ***underdid***; pp ***underdone***.

underdog [-dɔg] *n* desvalido, da; el *or* la más débil (in the struggle for life) ‖ perdedor, ra (in a struggle).

underdone [-ˈdʌn] *adj* CULIN poco hecho, cha.

underdrawers [-ˌdrɔːəz] *pl n* US calzoncillos *m*.

underdress [-ˈdres] *vi* no vestirse de forma apropiada.

underemployment [-imˈplɔimənt] *n* subempleo *m*.

underestimate [-ˈestimit] ; **underestimation** [-estiˈmeiʃən] *n* infravaloración *f*, apreciación *f* errónea (of the value) ‖ estimación *f* demasiado baja (of forecasts) ‖ desestimación *f*, menosprecio *m* (of a person).

underestimate [-ˈestimeit] *vt* subestimar, infravalorar ‖ menospreciar.

underestimation [-estiˈmeiʃən] *n* → **underestimate.**

underexpose [-iksˈpəuz] *vt* PHOT subexponer, exponer insuficientemente.

underexposure [-iksˈpəuʒə*] *n* PHOT subexposición *f*, exposición *f* insuficiente.

underfed [-ˈfed] *pret/pp* → **underfeed.**
◆ *adj* desnutrido, da; subalimentado, da.

underfeed* [-ˈfiːd] *vt* subalimentar, alimentar insuficientemente (to feed insufficiently) ‖ alimentar por la parte inferior (a fire).
— OBSERV Pret y pp ***underfed***.

underfeeding [-ˈfiːdiŋ] *n* subalimentación *f*, desnutrición *f*.

underfelt [-felt] *n* arpillera *f*.

underfoot [-ˈfut] *adv* bajo los pies, debajo de los pies (beneath one's feet) ‖ — US *his toys are always getting underfoot* sus juguetes estorban siempre el paso ‖ *to trample underfoot* pisotear.

undergarment [-gɑːmənt] *n* prenda *f* interior.
◆ *pl* ropa *f sing* interior.

underglaze [-gleiz] *adj* aplicado antes del vidriado.

undergo* [-ˈgəu] *vt* sufrir, aguantar (to endure) ‖ experimentar (to experience) ‖ MED sufrir (an operation).
— OBSERV Pret ***underwent***; pp ***undergone***.

undergone [-ˈgɔn] *pp* → **undergo.**

undergraduate [-ˈgrædjuit] *adj* no licenciado, da.
◆ *n* estudiante *m* & *f* [no licenciado].

underground [-graund] *adj* subterráneo, a; *an underground pipeline* un oleoducto subterráneo ‖ FIG secreto, ta | clandestino, na; *an underground magazine* una revista clandestina | para aficionados, no tradicional, no comercial (films, music, etc.) ‖ MIL de la Resistencia (movement).
◆ *adv* bajo tierra (under the ground) ‖ FIG clandestinamente, secretamente (secretly).
◆ *n* metro *m*, metropolitano *m* [AMER subterráneo *m*] (railway) ‖ FIG movimiento *m* clandestino ‖ MIL resistencia *f*.

underground railroad [-graundˈreilrəud] *n* US metro *m*, metropolitano *m* [AMER subterráneo *m*].

Underground Railroad [-graundˈreilrəud] *n* US organización *f* clandestina para liberar a los esclavos antes de la Guerra de la Secesión.

underground railway [-graundˈreilwei] *n* metro *m*, metropolitano *m* [AMER subterráneo *m*].

undergrown [-ˈgrəun] *adj* enclenque, poco desarrollado, da (child) ‖ poco desarrollado, da (plant) ‖ lleno de maleza (forest, land).

undergrowth [-grəuθ] *n* maleza *f*, monte *m* bajo.

underhand [-hænd] *adj* secreto, ta; clandestino, na (secret) ‖ poco limpio, pia (dirty) ‖ bajo cuerda, bajo mano (by stealth) ‖ socarrón, ona (not straightforward) ‖ SP ejecutado sin levantar la mano.
◆ *adv* bajo cuerda, bajo mano (by stealth) ‖ secretamente, clandestinamente (secretly) ‖ SP sin levantar la mano.

underhanded [-ˈhændid] *adj* US secreto, ta; clandestino, na (secret) | poco limpio, pia (dirty) | bajo cuerda, bajo mano (by stealth) | falto de mano de obra (shorthanded).

underhandedness [-ˈhændidnis] *n* disimulo *m*.

underhung [-ˈhʌŋ] *adj* ANAT prognato, ta (with a projecting jaw) || saliente (jaw) || corredizo, za; corredero, ra (moving on a rail).

underlaid [-ˈleid] *pret/pp* ⟶ **underlay.**

underlain [-ˈlein] *pp* ⟶ **underlie.**

underlay [-lei] *n* arpillera *f* (under a carpet) || PRINT alza *f* || MIN buzamiento *m*.

underlay* [-ˈlei] *vt* reforzar por debajo (a carpet) || poner debajo de (to put under) || sostener, apoyar (to support) || PRINT calzar, realzar.
◆ *vi* MIN buzar.
— OBSERV Pret y pp ***underlaid***.

underlay [-ˈlei] *pret* ⟶ **underlie.**

underlease [-liːs] *n* subarriendo *m*.

underlet* [-ˈlet] *vt* subarrendar, realquilar (to sublet) || alquilar por debajo del precio normal.
— OBSERV Pret y pp ***underlet***.

underlie* [-ˈlai] *vt* estar debajo de (to lie under) || FIG servir de base (to be the basis of) | ser el fundamento de, ser la base de (to be the foundation of) | ocultarse tras; *the jealousy which underlies his indifference* los celos que se ocultan tras su indiferencia || COMM tener prioridad sobre.
◆ *vi* MIN buzar.
— OBSERV Pret ***underlay***; pp ***underlain***.

underline [-lain] *n* raya *f* (under a word, etc.).
◆ *pl* falsilla *f sing*.

underline [-ˈlain] *vt* subrayar (to draw a line under) || FIG subrayar, hacer hincapié en, recalcar (to stress).

underling [-liŋ] *n* subordinado *m*, subalterno *m* (inferior) || seguidor *m*, secuaz *m* (follower).

underlining [-ˈlainiŋ] *n* subrayado *m*.

underlip [-lip] *n* labio *m* inferior.

underlying [-ˈlaiiŋ] *adj* subyacente, oculto, ta (lying or placed underneath) || fundamental.

undermanned [-ˈmænd] *adj* falto de mano de obra, falto de personal || MAR con una tripulación insuficiente.

undermentioned [-ˈmenʃənd] *adj* abajo mencionado, da; abajo citado, da.

undermine [-ˈmain] *vt* socavar, minar; *foundations undermined by water* cimientos socavados por el agua || FIG socavar (to weaken gradually) | minar; *drugs undermined his health* las drogas le minaron la salud.

undermost [-məust] *adj* más bajo, ja; inferior || último, ma (in a pile).

underneath [-ˈniːθ] *adj* inferior, de abajo.
◆ *adv* debajo, por debajo; *and iron underneath* y hierro por debajo.
◆ *prep* debajo de, bajo; *the garage is underneath my room* el garaje está debajo de mi habitación.
◆ *n* fondo *m*, parte *f* inferior.

undernourish [-ˈnʌriʃ] *vt* subalimentar, desnutrir.

undernourished [-ˈnʌriʃt] *adj* desnutrido, da; subalimentado, da.

undernourishment [-ˈnʌriʃmənt] *n* desnutrición *f*, subalimentación *f*.

underpaid [-ˈpeid] *pret/pp* ⟶ **underpay.**

underpants [-pænts] *pl n* calzoncillos *m*.

underpass [-pɑːs] *n* paso *m* subterráneo.

underpay* [-ˈpei] *vt/vi* pagar mal *or* poco || *underpaid workers* obreros mal pagados.
— OBSERV Pret y pp ***underpaid***.

underpin [-ˈpin] *vt* apuntalar || FIG sostener.

underpinning [-ˈpiniŋ] *n* apuntalamiento *m*.

underplay [-ˈplei] *vt* representar mal (to underact) || jugar una carta más baja que (a card).
◆ *vi* representar mal su papel.

underplot [-plɔt] *n* intriga *f* secundaria (of a story, of a play, etc.).

underpopulated [-ˈpɔpjuleitid] *adj* poco poblado, da.

underpraise [-ˈpreiz] *vt* no encomiar suficientemente.

underprice [-ˈprais] *vt* poner un precio demasiado bajo a.

underprivileged [-ˈprivilidʒd] *adj* desvalido, da.
◆ *n* *the underprivileged* los desvalidos.

underproduction [-prəˈdʌkʃən] *n* subproducción *f*, producción *f* insuficiente.

underprop [-ˈprɔp] *vt* apuntalar.

underrate [-ˈreit] *vt* subestimar, infravalorar (sth.) || menospreciar (s.o., the importance of sth.).

underripe [-ˈraip] *adj* insuficientemente maduro, ra.

underscore [-ˈskɔː*] *vt* subrayar || FIG subrayar, hacer hincapié en, recalcar (to stress).

undersea [-siː] *adj* submarino, na.
◆ *adv* bajo la superficie del mar.

underseas [-siːz] *adv* bajo la superficie del mar.

undersecretary [-ˈsekrətəri] *n* subsecretario, ria; *undersecretary of State* subsecretario de Estado || *undersecretary's office* subsecretaría *f*.

unsersecretaryship [-ˈsekrətəriʃip] *n* subsecretaría *f*.

undersell* [-ˈsel] *vt* vender más barato que (to sell at a lower price than) || malvender, malbaratar (to sell at a low price).
— OBSERV Pret y pp ***undersold***.

underset [-set] *n* MIN vena *f* subyacente || corriente *f* submarina (undercurrent).

undershirt [-ʃəːt] *n* US camiseta *f*.

undershoot [-ˈʃuːt] *vt* no alcanzar (el blanco) por haber disparado corto || AVIAT no alcanzar (the runway).
◆ *vi* disparar corto.

undershot [-ʃɔt] *adj* ANAT prognato, ta (with a projecting jaw) || *undershot wheel* rueda hidráulica impulsada por el agua en su parte inferior.

underside [-said] *n* cara *f* inferior, parte *f* inferior.

undersigned [-saind] *adj* abajo firmante, infrascrito, ta; *I, the undersigned, bequeath* el abajo firmante deja en herencia.

undersize [-ˈsaiz]; **undersized** [-ˈsaizd] *adj* pequeño, ña; de tamaño reducido (small) || demasiado pequeño, ña (too small) || achaparrado, da (person).

underskirt [-skəːt] *n* enaguas *f pl*.

underslung [-slʌŋ] *adj* AUT colgante (chassis).

undersold [-ˈsəuld] *pret/pp* ⟶ **undersell.**

undersong [-sɔŋ] *n* MUS estribillo *m*, melodía *f* de acompañamiento.

understaffed [-ˈstɑːft] *adj* falto de personal.

understand* [-ˈstænd] *vt* entender, comprender; *I don't understand this sentence* no entiendo esta frase; *nobody understands me* no me comprende nadie; *I make myself understood* yo me hago comprender; *I understand English, but I don't speak it* entiendo el inglés, pero no lo hablo || entender de, ser entendido en; *to understand business* ser entendido en negocios || tener entendido que; *I understand they went to Mexico* tengo entendido que fueron a México || creer (to think, to believe) || sobreentender, sobrentender (not to state) || — *am I given to understand that?* ¿debo entender que?, ¿me quiere usted decir que? || *I can understand your being angry* comprendo que estés enfadado || *I don't quite understand why* no acabo de entender por qué || *it being understood that* con tal que || *it is understood that* tenemos entendido que, se supone que, se sobreentiende que || *it must be clearly understood that* que quede claramente sentado que || *I wish it to be understood* o *let it be understood that* que quede bien claro que, que conste que || *now I understand!* ¡ahora caigo!, ¡ahora entiendo! || *that's understood* eso se entiende, por supuesto || *to give to understand that* dar a entender que || *to understand each other* comprenderse, entenderse || *to understand how to do sth.* saber hacer algo || *understood?* ¿entendido?, ¿comprendido?
◆ *vi* comprender.
— OBSERV Pret y pp ***understood***.

understandable [-ˈstændəbl] *adj* comprensible.

understanding [-ˈstændiŋ] *adj* comprensivo, va.
◆ *n* comprensión *f*; *lacking in understanding* falto de comprensión || entendimiento *m*; *problems beyond my understanding* problemas que están más allá de mi entendimiento || razón *f*, juicio *m*; *to reach the age of understanding* llegar a la edad de la razón || compenetración *f*, comprensión *f* mutua; *there is perfect understanding between them* tienen una compenetración perfecta || interpretación *f*; *what is your understanding of this paragraph?* ¿cuál es su interpretación de este párrafo? || manera *f* de entender (way of looking at sth.) || inteligencia *f*, entendimiento *m*; *the good understanding between nations* la buena inteligencia entre las naciones || acuerdo *m*, arreglo *m* (agreement, arrangement); *to arrive at an understanding* llegar a un acuerdo || conocimientos *m pl* (knowledge); *I have a good understanding of mathematics* tengo buenos conocimientos de matemáticas || — *on the understanding that* a condición de que, con tal que || *to arrive at an understanding of* llegar a comprender.

understate [-ˈsteit] *vt* quitar importancia a (to make seem less important) || subestimar (to underestimate) || exponer incompletamente (not to give all the facts).

understatement [-ˈsteitmənt] *n* eufemismo *m* (euphemism) || subestimación *f* (underestimation) || exposición *f* incompleta (incomplete statement).

understock [-ˈstɔk] *vt* suministrar existencias insuficientes.

understood [-ˈstud] *pret/pp* ⟶ **understand.**
◆ *adj* GRAMM sobrentendido, da; sobreentendido, da; implícito, ta || entendido, da (agreed upon).

understrapper [-ˌstræpə*] *n* subalterno *m*.

understudy [-ˌstʌdi] *n* THEATR suplente *m* & *f*, sobresaliente *m* & *f*.

understudy [-ˌstʌdi] *vt* THEATR aprender un papel para poder suplir a.

undersurface [-ˌsəːfis] *n* superficie *f* inferior.

undertake* [-ˈteik] *vt* emprender; *to undertake a journey, a task* emprender un viaje, una tarea || encargarse de; *he undertook to go and fetch the doctor* se encargó de ir a buscar al médico || prometer, comprometerse (to promise); *I made him undertake to deliver the letter* le hice prometer que entregaría la carta, hice

que se comprometiese a entregar la carta || *to undertake that* prometer que.
— OBSERV Pret ***undertook***; pp ***undertaken***.

undertaken [-'teikən] *pp* → **undertake.**

undertaker [-,teikə*] *n* empresario *m* de pompas fúnebres || *undertaker's* funeraria *f*, pompas *f pl* fúnebres.

undertaking [-'teikiŋ] *n* tarea *f*, empresa *f* (task); *that's quite an undertaking!* ¡vaya tarea! || empresa *f*; *a daring undertaking* una empresa atrevida || COMM empresa *f* || compromiso *m*, garantía *f* (pledge) || promesa *f* (promise); *I gave an undertaking that* hice la promesa de que || funeraria *f*, pompas *f pl* fúnebres (business of an undertaker).

undertenant [-,tenənt] *n* subarrendatario, ria.

under-the-counter [-ðə'kauntə*] *adj* bajo mano.

undertone [-təun] *n* voz *f* baja (low voice); *in an undertone* en voz baja || murmullo *m* (murmur) || color *m* apagado *or* de fondo, fondo *m* (colour) || FIG fondo *m* (underlying element) | corriente *f* (tendency).

undertook [-'tuk] *pret* → **undertake.**

undertow [-təu] *n* MAR contracorriente *f*, resaca *f*.

undervaluation [-,vælju'eiʃən] *n* infravaloración *f*, subestimación *f*.

undervalue [-'vælju:] *vt* infravalorar, subestimar (sth.) || menospreciar (s.o.'s merit, etc.).

underwater [-'wɔ:tə*] *adj* submarino, na; *underwater fishing* pesca submarina || bajo la línea de flotación (part of a boat).

underwear [-wεə*] *n* ropa *f* interior.

underweight [-'weit] *adj* de peso insuficiente || *to be underweight* no pesar bastante.
◆ *n* peso *m* insuficiente.

underwent [-'went] *pret* → **undergo.**

underwing [-wiŋ] *n* ala *f* posterior (of insects).

underwood [-wud] *n* maleza *f*, monte *m* bajo.

underworld [-wə:ld] *n* mundo *m* terrenal (earth) || mundo *m* de los muertos (of the dead) || infierno *m* (hell) || antípodas *f pl* (antipodes) || hampa *f*, gente *f* maleante (criminal world).

underwrite* [-rait] *vt* subscribir, suscribir (to sign) || asegurar (to insure) || garantizar (to guarantee) || subscribir, suscribir (bonds).
— OBSERV Pret ***underwrote***; pp ***underwritten***.

underwriter [-raitə*] *n* asegurador *m* (insurer) || suscriptor *m* (of bonds).

underwriting [-raitiŋ] *n* seguro *m*.

underwritten [-'ritn] *pp* → **underwrite.**

underwrote [-rəut] *pret* → **underwrite.**

undescribable ['ʌndis'kraibəbl] *adj* indescriptible.

undeserved ['ʌndi'zə:vd] *adj* inmerecido, da.

undeserving ['ʌndi'zə:viŋ] *adj* de poco mérito (not meritorious) || indigno, na (*of* de) || *undeserving of attention* que no merece atención.

undesigned ['ʌndi'zaind] *adj* involuntario, ria (act) || imprevisto, ta (result).

undesigning ['ʌndi'zainiŋ] *adj* cándido, da; sin malicia.

undesirable ['ʌndi'zaiərəbl] *adj/n* indeseable.

undesirous ['ʌndi'zaiərəs] *adj* *to be undesirous of doing sth.* tener pocas ganas de hacer algo, no querer hacer algo.

undetachable [,ʌndi'tætʃəbl] *adj* inamovible.

undetected ['ʌndi'tektid] *adj* sin ser visto *or* descubierto || *to pass undetected* pasar desapercibido.

undeterminable ['ʌndi'tə:minəbl] *adj* indeterminable.

undetermined ['ʌndi'tə:mind] *adj* indeterminado, da (question, number, date, etc.) || irresoluto, ta (irresolute).

undeterred ['ʌndi'tə:d] *adj* sin dejarse intimidar *or* impresionar (*by* por).

undeveloped ['ʌndi'veləpt] *adj* sin desarrollar || inexplotado, da; sin explotar (land) || subdesarrollado, da (underdeveloped) || PHOT sin revelar (film) || inculto, ta (mind).

undeviating [ʌn'di:vieitiŋ] *adj* recto, ta (straight) || directo, ta (direct) || constante (constant).

undid ['ʌn'did] *pret* → **undo.**

undies ['ʌndiz] *pl n* FAM ropa *f sing* interior.

undigested ['ʌndi'dʒestid] *adj* MED no digerido, da || FIG mal digerido, da; mal asimilado, da.

undignified [ʌn'dignifaid] *adj* poco digno, na; poco decoroso, sa; indecoroso, sa.

undiluted ['ʌndai'lju:tid] *adj* no diluido, da || FAM puro, ra; *undiluted nonsense* pura tontería.

undiminished ['ʌndi'miniʃt] *adj* no disminuido, da.

undine ['ʌndi:n] *n* MYTH ondina *f*.

undiplomatic ['ʌn,diplə'mætik] *adj* poco diplomático, ca.

undirected ['ʌndi'rektid] *adj* sin dirección, sin señas (letter).

undiscernible ['ʌndi'sə:nəbl] *adj* imperceptible, indiscernible.

undiscerning ['ʌndi'sə:niŋ] *adj* sin discernimiento.

undischarged ['ʌndis'tʃɑ:dʒd] *adj* sin descargar (rifle, electric battery) || no rehabilitado, da (bankrupt) || sin liquidar (debt) || no cumplido, da; incumplido, da (duty) || no licenciado (soldier) || *undischarged of* no liberado de.

undisciplined [ʌn'disiplind] *adj* indisciplinado, da.

undisclosed ['ʌndis'kləuzd] *adj* sin revelar.

undiscovered ['ʌndis'kʌvəd] *adj* sin descubrir, no descubierto, ta || desconocido, da (place).

undiscriminating ['ʌndis'krimineitiŋ] *adj* sin discernimiento, poco juicioso, sa (without discernment) || sin discriminación (not preferential).

undisguised ['ʌndis'gaizd] *adj* sin disfraz (not in fancy dress) || franco, ca; sincero, ra; no disfrazado, da (feeling).

undismayed ['ʌndis'meid] *adj* impávido, da (unmoved) || sin desanimarse (without losing heart).

undisposed ['ʌndis'pəuzd] *adj* *undisposed of* sin utilizar (unused), no vendido, da (unsold), no invertido, da (not invested).

undisputed ['ʌndis'pju:tid] *adj* incontestable (unchallenged) || indiscutido, da; indiscutible (unquestioned); *undisputed truth* verdad indiscutible.

undissolvable ['ʌndi'zɔlvəbl] *adj* indisoluble.

undistinguished ['ʌndis'tiŋgwiʃt] *adj* mediocre.

undistorted ['ʌndis'tɔ:tid] *adj* ELECTR sin distorsión.

undisturbed ['ʌndis'tə:bd] *adj* tranquilo, la; sereno, na (still, peaceful, untroubled) || no perturbado, da (peace, sleep) || sin tocar (untouched) || sin desordenar (papers).

undiversified ['ʌndai'və:sifaid] *adj* uniforme.

undivided ['ʌndi'vaidid] *adj* indiviso, sa; *undivided property* propiedad indivisa || entero, ra; íntegro, gra (complete) || no distribuido, da (profits) || unánime (opinion) || *give me your undivided attention* préstenme ustedes toda su atención.

undo* ['ʌn'du:] *vt* desatar, deshacer (a knot) || deshacer el nudo de, desanudar (a tie) || deshacer, desatar, abrir (a parcel) || desabrochar, desabotonar (a clasp, a button) || bajar (a zip) || abrir (to open) || deshacer; *to undo the work of another* deshacer el trabajo de otro || reparar (to put right); *to undo the damage* reparar el daño || perder, arruinar; *his overconfidence undid him* le perdió la confianza excesiva en sí mismo.
— OBSERV Pret ***undid***; pp ***undone***.

undoing [-iŋ] *n* perdición *f*, ruina *f* (ruin); *drink will be his undoing* la bebida será su perdición || deshacer *m*, desatar *m* (of a parcel, of a knot, etc.) || desabrochar *m* (of buttons, etc.) || bajada *f* (of a zip) || reparación *f* (of a damage).

undomesticated ['ʌndə'mestikeitid] *adj* indomesticado, da; no domesticado, da.

undone ['ʌn'dʌn] *pp* → **undo.**
◆ *adj* inacabado, da (not finished) || sin hacer, por hacer, no hecho, cha (not done) || deshecho, cha; desatado, da (parcel, knot, etc.) || desabrochado, da (buttons) || bajado, da (zip) || suelto, ta (hair) || desatado, da (shoes) || reparado, da (damage) || — FIG *to be undone* estar perdido (a person) || *to come undone* desatarse, soltarse (laces) || *to leave undone* dejar sin hacer *or* sin acabar (work).

undoubted [ʌn'dautid] *adj* indudable, indubitable.

undoubtedly [ʌn'dautidli] *adv* sin duda alguna, indudablemente.

undoubting [ʌn'dautiŋ] *adj* convencido, da; seguro, ra.

undraw* ['ʌn'drɔ:] *vt* descorrer, correr, abrir (curtains).
— OBSERV Pret ***undrew***; pp ***undrawn***.

undrawn [-n] *pp* → **undraw.**

undreamed [ʌn'dri:md]; **undreamt** [ʌn'dremt] *adj* *undreamed of* no soñado, da; nunca soñado, da; inimaginable.

undress ['ʌn'dres] *n* bata *f* (informal dress) || MIL uniforme *m* de cuartel.

undress ['ʌn'dres] *vt* desnudar (to take off the clothes of) || MED quitar el vendaje *or* la venda de.
◆ *vi* desnudarse.

undressed [-t] *adj* desnudo, da (naked) || en bata (with an informal dress) || sin labrar (stone) || sin desbastar (timber) || sin aliñar, sin aderezar (salad, food) || sin adobar (leather) || *to get undressed* desnudarse.

undrew ['ʌn'dru:] *pret* → **undraw.**

undrinkable ['ʌn'driŋkəbl] *adj* imbebible (foul tasting) || no potable (water).

undriveable ['ʌn'draivəbl] *adj* imposible de conducir [*AMER* inmanejable].

undue ['ʌn'dju:] *adj* excesivo, va; indebido, da (excessive) || impropio, pia (improper) || inmerecido, da (undeserved) || JUR ilegítimo, ma (unlawful) | no vencido, da (bill of exchange).

undulant ['ʌndjulənt] *adj* ondulante || MED *undulant fever* fiebre *f* de Malta.

undulate ['ʌndjuleit] *adj* ondulado, da.

undulate ['ʌndjuleit] *vt* hacer ondear (to cause to move in a wavy manner) || ondular (to give wavelike form to).
◆ *vi* ondear, ondular.

undulated [-id] *adj* ondulado, da.

undulating [-iŋ] *adj* ondulado, da (country) || ondeante, ondulante (corn).

undulation [ˌʌndju'leiʃən] *n* ondulación *f* (motion, form) || pulsación *f* || onda *f* (wave).

undulatory ['ʌndjulətəri] *adj* ondulante || PHYS ondulatorio, ria; *undulatory theory* teoría ondulatoria.

unduly ['ʌn'djuːli] *adv* excesivamente, indebidamente (excessively) || impropiamente (improperly) || injustamente (unjustly).

undying [ʌn'daiiŋ] *adj* imperecedero, ra.

unearned ['ʌn'əːnd] *adj* inmerecido, da (undeserved) || no ganado, da (not earned by working) || — *unearned income* renta *f* [que no se gana trabajando] || *unearned increment* plusvalía *f*.

unearth ['ʌn'əːθ] *vt* desenterrar (to dig up) || FIG descubrir (a conspiracy) | desenterrar (to bring to light).

unearthing [-iŋ] *n* desenterramiento *m*.

unearthly [-li] *adj* sobrenatural; extraterreno, na (not earthly) || misterioso, sa; fantástico, ca (mysterious) || FAM horrible, infernal, espantoso, sa; *an unearthly din* un barullo espantoso | intempestivo, va; *what an unearthly time to get up!* ¡qué hora más intempestiva para levantarse!

uneasiness [ʌn'iːzinis] *n* intranquilidad *f*, desasosiego *m*, inquietud *f* (worry) || incomodidad *f*, molestia *f*, malestar *m*.

uneasy [ʌn'iːzi] *adj* molesto, ta; incómodo, da (ill at ease) || inquieto, ta; desasosegado, da (disturbed, troubled) || preocupado, da (worried) || molesto, ta (annoying) || MED agitado, da (patient, sleep) || *to make uneasy* inquietar, preocupar.

uneatable ['ʌn'iːtəbl] *adj* incomible, incomestible.

uneaten ['ʌn'iːtən] *adj* no tocado, da; no comido, da.

uneconomic ['ʌnˌiːkə'nɔmik]; **uneconomical** ['ʌnˌiːkə'nɔmikl] *adj* poco económico, ca; antieconómico, ca (method) || poco rentable (work).

uneducated ['ʌn'edjukeitid] *adj* inculto, ta; ignorante (uncultured).

uneffected ['ʌni'fektid] *adj* sin realizar, no efectuado, da.

unembodied ['ʌnim'bɔdid] *adj* incorpóreo, a.

unemotional ['ʌni'məuʃənəl] *adj* poco emotivo, va || poco impresionable || impasible (character) || objetivo, va (report, etc.).

unemployable ['ʌnim'plɔiəbl] *adj* incapacitado para tener un empleo.
◆ *n* persona *f* incapacitada para tener un empleo.

unemployed ['ʌnim'plɔid] *adj* parado, da; desempleado, da; sin trabajo [AMER desocupado, da] (not in paid employment); *to be unemployed* estar parado || sin utilizar, inutilizado, da (not being used) || sin invertir, no invertido, da; improductivo, va (capital, funds).
◆ *n the unemployed* los parados, los desempleados [AMER los desocupados].

unemployment ['ʌnim'plɔimənt] *n* paro *m*, desempleo *m* [AMER desocupación *f*]; *seasonal unemployment* paro estacional || *unemployment benefit*, US *unemployment compensation* subsidio *m* de paro.

unencumbered ['ʌnim'kʌmbəd] *adj* sin gravámenes (estate) || *unemcumbered by* sin las trabas de.

unending ['ʌn'endiŋ] *adj* interminable (endless).

unendurable ['ʌnin'djuərəbl] *adj* intolerable, insoportable.

unengaged ['ʌniŋ'geidʒd] *adj* libre (person, room, seat).

un-English ['ʌn'iŋgliʃ] *adj* poco inglés, esa.

unenlightened ['ʌnin'laitnd] *adj* ignorante, poco ilustrado, da (person).

unenterprising ['ʌn'entəpraiziŋ] *adj* poco emprendedor, ra; sin iniciativa, poco dinámico, ca; tímido, da.

unentertaining [ʌnˌentə'teiniŋ] *adj* poco entretenido, da; aburrido, da.

unenthusiastic ['ʌninˌθjuːzi'æstik] *adj* poco entusiasta.

unenviable ['ʌn'enviəbl] *adj* poco envidiable.

unequal ['ʌn'iːkwəl] *adj* desigual, distinto, ta; *unequal lengths* largos desiguales || MED irregular; *unequal pulse* pulso irregular || inadecuado, da (not adequate) || — *to be unequal to a mission* no estar a la altura de una misión, ser incapaz de cumplir una misión || *to be unequal to doing sth.* no ser capaz de hacer algo, no tener talla para hacer algo.

unequalled; US **unequaled** ['ʌn'iːkwəld] *adj* sin igual, sin par.

unequivocal ['ʌni'kwivəkəl] *adj* inequívoco, ca; claro, ra.

unerring ['ʌn'əːriŋ] *adj* infalible, seguro, ra.

unescapable [ˌʌnis'keipəbl] *adj* inevitable, ineludible.

UNESCO *abbr of [United Nations Educational, Scientific and Cultural Organization]* Unesco.

unessential ['ʌni'senʃəl] *adj* no esencial, accesorio, ria; secundario, ria.
◆ *n* lo accesorio, lo secundario.

unestimated ['ʌn'estimeitid] *adj* inestimado, da.

unethical [ʌn'eθikəl] *adj* poco ético, ca; inmoral.

uneven ['ʌn'iːvən] *adj* accidentado, da; desigual; *an uneven surface* una superficie accidentada || desigual (unequal); *an uneven match* un combate desigual || MATH impar (numbers) || irregular; *uneven progress* progresos irregulares.

unevenness [-nis] *n* desigualdad *f* (of a surface) || irregularidad *f* (irregularity) || desigualdad *f* (inequality).

uneventful ['ʌni'ventful] *adj* sin acontecimientos, sin incidentes.

unexampled ['ʌnig'zaːmpld] *adj* sin par, sin igual, sin precedente.

unexceptionable [ˌʌnik'sepʃənəbl] *adj* irreprochable, intachable || JUR irrecusable.

unexceptional ['ʌnik'sepʃənəl] *adj* ordinario, ria; corriente (ordinary) || irreprochable, intachable (unexceptionable) || sin excepción (without exception).

unexchangeable ['ʌniks'tʃeindʒəbl] *adj* incambiable.

unexciting ['ʌnik'saitiŋ] *adj* sin interés.

unexecuted ['ʌn'eksikjuːtid] *adj* no ejecutado, da.

unexpected ['ʌniks'pektid] *adj* inesperado, da; imprevisto, ta; *unexpected event* suceso imprevisto; *if anything unexpected turns up* o *happens* si ocurre algo imprevisto || *the unexpected* lo imprevisto.

unexpectedly [-li] *adv* de improviso, inesperadamente.

unexperienced ['ʌniks'piəriənsd] *adj* inexperto, ta; inexperimentado, da; sin experiencia (inexperienced) || nunca experimentado, da (never felt).

unexpiated ['ʌn'ekspieitid] *adj* inexpiado, da.

unexpired ['ʌniks'paiəd] *adj* no vencido, da (bill) || no caducado, da; válido, da (tickets, etc.).

unexplained ['ʌniks'pleind] *adj* inexplicado, da.

unexploitable ['ʌniks'plɔitəbl] *adj* inexplotable.

unexploited ['ʌniks'plɔitid] *adj* inexplotado, da.

unexplorable ['ʌniks'plɔːrəbl] *adj* inexplorable.

unexplored ['ʌniks'plɔːd] *adj* inexplorado, da.

unexposed ['ʌniks'pəuzd] *adj* no expuesto, ta || FIG no descubierto, ta (crime).

unexpressed ['ʌniks'prest] *adj* no expresado, da; inexpresado, da || tácito, ta (tacit) || GRAMM sobreentendido, da; sobrentendido, da.

unexpressive ['ʌniks'presiv] *adj* inexpresivo, va.

unexpurgated ['ʌn'ekspəːgeitid] *adj* no expurgado, da; íntegro, gra.

unextended ['ʌniks'tendid] *adj* inextenso, sa.

unextinguishable ['ʌniks'tiŋgwiʃəbl] *adj* inextinguible.

unfading ['ʌn'feidiŋ] *adj* inmarcesible, inmarchitable || FIG imperecedero, ra; imborrable.

unfailing ['ʌn'feiliŋ] *adj* inagotable (inexhaustible) || constante (never ceasing) || infalible (infallible) || seguro, ra; infalible, indefectible (certain); *we were awaiting his unfailing twelve-o'clock arrival* esperábamos su indefectible llegada a las doce.

unfair ['ʌn'fɛə*] *adj* injusto, ta (not just) || desleal (competition) || sucio, cia (play) || excesivo, va; exagerado, da (price) || no equitativo, va (wages) || *unfair dismissal* despido *m* improcedente.

unfairness [-nis] *n* injusticia *f* || deslealtad *f* (in competition) || suciedad *f* (in play) || exceso *m*, exageración *f* (in prices) || falta *f* de equidad (in wages).

unfaithful ['ʌn'feiθful] *adj* infiel; *his wife is unfaithful to him* su mujer le es infiel || desleal (disloyal).

unfaithfulness [-nis] *n* infidelidad *f* || deslealtad *f* (disloyalty).

unfalsifiable ['ʌn'fɔːlsifaiəbl] *adj* infalsificable.

unfaltering ['ʌn'fɔːltəriŋ] *adj* resuelto, ta; decidido, da; firme.

unfamiliar ['ʌnfə'miljə*] *adj* no familiarizado, da; *unfamiliar with firearms* no familiarizado con las armas de fuego || desconocido, da; *an unfamiliar face* una cara desconocida || poco corriente; *unfamiliar phrase* expresión poco corriente || extraño, ña (strange) || *to be unfamiliar with the customs* no conocer las costumbres, desconocer las costumbres.

unfashionable ['ʌn'fæʃənəbl] *adj* pasado de moda (out of date) || poco elegante (not very smart).

unfasten ['ʌn'faːsən] *vt* desabrochar (one's dress) || abrir (a door) || desatar (a knot, a rope, etc.) || soltar, desatar (a dog) || soltar (to set free) || aflojar (to loosen).

unfathered ['ʌn'faːðəd] *adj* sin padre, ilegítimo, ma (child) || FIG de fuente desconocida (news) | de autor desconocido (theory).

unfathomable ['ʌn'fæðəməbl] *adj* insondable.

unfavourable; US **unfavorable** ['ʌn'feivərəbl] *adj* desfavorable.

unfeasible ['ʌn'fiːzibl] *adj* irrealizable, impracticable.

unfeeling [ʌn'fiːliŋ] *adj* insensible.

unfeelingness [-nis] *n* insensibilidad *f*.

unfeigned [ʌn'feind] *adj* sincero, ra; no fingido, da; verdadero, ra.

unfelt [ʌn'felt] *adj* no percibido, da; no sentido, da; insensible.

unfermented ['ʌnfə'mentid] *adj* no fermentado, da; sin fermentar (liquor) || ácimo (bread).

unfetter ['ʌn'fetə*] *vt* desencadenar (a prisoner) || destrabar (a horse) || FIG liberar, libertar.

unfilial ['ʌn'filjəl] *adj* indigno de un hijo.

unfilmed ['ʌn'filmd] *adj* que no ha sido llevado a la pantalla (novel, etc.).

unfinished ['ʌn'finiʃt] *adj* inacabado, da; sin acabar || incompleto, ta (not complete) || TECH bruto, ta || *the Unfinished Symphony* la Sinfonía incompleta *or* inconclusa.

unfit [ʌn'fit] *adj* incapaz (*to* de), no apto, ta (*to* para) (not suitable); *unfit for business* no apto para los negocios; *unfit to govern* incapaz de gobernar || inadecuado, da (*to* para) (not adequate) || impropio, pia; *unfit to eat* impropio para el consumo || incompetente || inútil (for military service) || MIL *to be discharged as unfit* ser declarado inútil, ser dado de baja.

unfit ['ʌn'fit] *vt* inhabilitar, incapacitar.

unfitness [-nis] *n* incapacidad *f* (inability) || falta *f* de aptitud, incompetencia *f* (incompetence) || inoportunidad *f* (of a remark) || debilidad *f* física, mala salud *f*.

unfitted [-id] *adj* impropio, pia (*for* para) || incapacitado, da; *unfitted for the job* incapacitado para el trabajo || *unfitted with* sin.

unfitting [-iŋ] *adj* impropio, pia; *unfitting behaviour for his age* comportamiento impropio de su edad.

unfix ['ʌn'fiks] *vt* separar (to separate) || quitar (to remove) || soltar (to disengage) || desarmar, desmontar (to take apart) || desequilibrar (to unsettle).

unfixed [-t] *adj* suelto, ta (disengaged) || indeterminado, da (date) || irresoluto, ta; indeciso, sa (person).

unflagging [ʌn'flægiŋ] *adj* infatigable, incansable (courage) || constante (interest).

unflappable ['ʌn'flæpəbəl] *adj* FAM imperturbable.

unflattering ['ʌn'flætəriŋ] *adj* poco halagüeño, ña.

unfledged ['ʌn'fledʒd] *adj* implume, sin plumas (not fledged) || inexperto, ta; inexperimentado, da (immature).

unflinching [ʌn'flintʃiŋ] *adj* resuelto, ta (resolute) || impávido, da (dauntless).

unflyable ['ʌn'flaiəbl] *adj* que impide el despegue de los aviones (weather).

unfold ['ʌn'fəuld] *vt* desdoblar, desplegar, abrir (to open) || extender (sth. on the table) || revelar, descubrir (to reveal) || exponer (a theory, a plan, etc.).

◆ *vi* abrirse, desplegarse, desdoblarse (to open out) || extenderse; *the landscape unfolds before us* el paisaje se extiende ante nosotros || revelarse, descubrirse (a secret) || desarrollarse (one's thoughts, action).

unfolding ['ʌn'fəuldiŋ] *n* desdoblamiento *m*, despliegue *m*.

unforbidden ['ʌnfə'bidn] *adj* no prohibido, da; permitido, da.

unforced ['ʌn'fɔːst] *adj* no forzado, da; no obligado, da (not obliged) || espontáneo, a; franco, ca; *unforced laugh* risa espontánea.

unforeseeable ['ʌnfɔː'siːəbl] *adj* imprevisible.

unforeseeing ['ʌnfɔː'siːiŋ] *adj* imprevisor, ra.

unforeseen ['ʌnfɔː'siːn] *adj* imprevisto, ta || *the unforeseen* lo imprevisto.

unforgeable ['ʌn'fɔːdʒəbl] *adj* infalsificable (money).

unforgettable ['ʌnfə'getəbl] *adj* inolvidable.

unforgivable ['ʌnfə'givəbl] *adj* imperdonable, indisculpable.

unforgiven ['ʌnfə'givən] *adj* no perdonado, da.

unforgiving ['ʌnfə'giviŋ] *adj* que no perdona, implacable.

unforgotten ['ʌnfə'gɔtn] *adj* no olvidado, da || *he remains unforgotten* su recuerdo permanece vivo.

unformatted ['ʌnfɔː'mætid] *adj* INFORM sin formatear, no formateado, da.

unformed ['ʌn'fɔːmd] *adj* no formado, da || informe, sin forma (shapeless) || poco maduro, ra (immature).

unfortified ['ʌn'fɔːtifaid] *adj* sin fortificaciones || abierto, ta (town).

unfortunate ['ʌn'fɔːtjunit] *adj* desafortunado, da; desgraciado, da (person) || desgraciado, da; *unfortunate event* suceso desgraciado || poco afortunado, da; desacertado, da (remark) || malogrado, da (lately dead).

◆ *n* infortunado, da; desgraciado, da.

unfounded ['ʌn'faundid] *adj* infundado, da; sin fundamento.

unframed ['ʌn'freimd] *adj* sin marco.

unfreezable ['ʌn'friːzəbl] *adj* incongelable.

unfreeze* ['ʌn'friːz] *vt* descongelar || desbloquear, descongelar (money, prices, credits, wages) || desbloquear (an account).

— OBSERV Pret ***unfroze***; pp ***unfrozen***.

unfreezing ['ʌn'friːziŋ] *n* descongelación *f* || descongelación *f*, desbloqueo *m* (of money, prices, wages, credits) || desbloqueo *m* (of an account).

unfrequented ['ʌnfri'kwentid] *adj* poco frecuentado, da.

unfriendliness ['ʌn'frendlinis] *n* hostilidad *f*, enemistad *f*.

unfriendly ['ʌn'frendli] *adj* hostil, poco amistoso, sa (hostile) || desfavorable (unfavourable).

unfrock ['ʌn'frɔk] *vt* obligar a colgar los hábitos (a priest).

unfroze ['ʌn'frəuz] *pret* → **unfreeze.**

unfrozen ['ʌn'frəuzn] *pp* → **unfreeze.**

unfruitful ['ʌn'fruːtful] *adj* estéril (not producing offspring) || AGR estéril, improductivo, va; infecundo, da || FIG infructuoso, sa (labour, etc.); *unfruitful efforts* esfuerzos infructuosos | poco lucrativo, va (unprofitable).

unfruitfulness [-nis] *n* esterilidad *f* || FIG infructuosidad *f*.

unfulfilled ['ʌnful'fild] *adj* incumplido, da; no cumplido, da (desire, duty) || no cumplido, da (prophecy, promise) || no satisfecho, cha; insatisfecho, cha; *an unfulfilled petition* una súplica insatisfecha.

unfunded [ʌn'fʌndid] *adj* flotante, no consolidado, da (debt).

unfurl [ʌn'fəːl] *vt* desplegar.

◆ *vi* desplegarse.

unfurnished ['ʌn'fəːniʃt] *adj* desamueblado, da; sin amueblar (room) || *unfurnished with* desprovisto de, sin.

ungainliness [ʌn'geinlinis] *n* torpeza *f* (clumsiness) || desgarbo *m* (in one's gait).

ungainly [ʌn'geinly] *adj* torpe (clumsy) || desgarbado, da (in one's gait).

ungallant ['ʌn'gælənt] *adj* poco galante.

ungarnished ['ʌn'gɑːniʃt] *adj* sin adornos, sencillo, lla.

ungather ['ʌn'gæðə*] *vt* desfruncir.

ungenerous ['ʌn'dʒenərəs] *adj* poco generoso, sa.

ungentle ['ʌn'dʒentl] *adj* brusco, ca; poco amable.

ungentlemanlike [ʌn'dʒentlmənlaik]; **ungentlemanly** [ʌn'dʒentlmənli] *adj* indigno de un caballero, poco caballeroso, sa (behaviour) || incorrecto, mal educado (man).

un-get-at-able ['ʌnget'ætəbl] *adj* inaccesible.

ungird* ['ʌn'gəːd] *vt* desatar, desceñir (belt, girdle) || quitar el cinturón a (s.o.).

— OBSERV Pret y pp ***ungirded, ungirt***.

ungirt ['ʌn'gəːt] *pret/pp* → **ungird.**

ungirth ['ʌn'gəːθ] *vt* descinchar, quitar la cincha a.

unglazed ['ʌn'gleizd] *adj* sin cristales (window) || sin satinar, mate (paper) || mate (photograph) || ARTS no vidriado, da (ceramics).

unglue ['ʌn'gluː] *vt* despegar.

◆ *vi* despegarse.

ungodliness [ʌn'gɔdlinis] *n* impiedad *f* (impiety) || maldad *f* (wickedness).

ungodly [ʌn'gɔdli] *adj* impío, a || malvado, da (wicked) || FAM atroz (outrageous).

ungovernable [ʌn'gʌvənəbl] *adj* ingobernable (country, person) || irreprimible, irrefrenable (desire) || incontenible (passion).

ungoverned ['ʌn'gʌvənd] *adj* no gobernado, da; sin gobernar (country) || desenfrenado, da (passion).

ungraceful ['ʌn'greisful] *adj* desgarbado, da; falto de gracia || torpe (clumsy).

ungracefully [-li] *adv* desgarbadamente, sin garbo *or* gracia || torpemente (clumsily).

ungracefulness [-nis] *n* falta *f* de garbo *or* de gracia || torpeza *f* (clumsiness).

ungracious ['ʌn'greiʃəs] *adj* brusco, ca; poco amable, descortés (discourteous) || desagradable (unpleasant).

ungrammatical ['ʌngrə'mætikəl] *adj* incorrecto, ta; contrario a la gramática.

ungrateful [ʌn'greitful] *adj* ingrato, ta; desagradecido, da (*to, towards* con, para con) (person); *ungrateful child* hijo ingrato || ingrato, ta (work).

ungratefulness [-nis] *n* ingratitud *f*, desagradecimiento *m*.

ungratified ['ʌn'grætifaid] *adj* insatisfecho, cha.

ungrudging ['ʌn'grʌdʒiŋ] *adj* generoso, sa (generous) || incondicional (support) || dado de buena gana (gift).

ungrudgingly [-li] *adv* de buena gana.

ungual ['ʌŋgwəl] *adj* ZOOL ungular.

unguarded ['ʌn'gɑːdid] *adj* indefenso, sa (unprotected) || desprevenido, da; descuidado, da (careless) || imprudente; *unguarded speech* discurso imprudente || de descuido (moment).

unguent ['ʌŋgwənt] *n* ungüento *m*.

unguiculate ['ʌŋ'gwikjulit] *adj* ZOOL unguiculado, da.

◆ *n* ZOOL unguiculado *m*.

unguis ['ʌŋgwis] *n* ZOOL pezuña *f* (hoof) | garra *f* (claw) || ANAT unguis *m* (bone).

— OBSERV El plural de la palabra inglesa es *ungues*.

ungula ['ʌŋgjulə] *n* MATH cono *m* truncado || ZOOL pezuña *f* (hoof) | garra *f* (claw).

— OBSERV El plural de *ungula* es *ungulae*.

ungular ['ʌŋgjulə*] *adj* ungular.

ungulate ['ʌŋgjuleit] *adj* ungulado, da.
◆ *n* ungulado *m*.

unhackneyed [ʌn'hæknid] *adj* nuevo, va; original; no trillado, da.

unhallowed [ʌn'hæləud] *adj* no consagrado, da (unconsecrated) || impío, a (impious) || profano, na (profane).

unhampered ['ʌn'hæmpəd] *adj* libre.

unhand [ʌn'hænd] *vt* soltar.

unhandsome [-səm] *adj* sin atractivo (not attractive) || feo, fea (ugly) || mezquino, na (mean, stingy) || descortés (discourteous) || impropio, pia; indecoroso, sa (unbecoming).

unhandy [-i] *adj* torpe, desmañado, da (clumsy) || incómodo, da; poco manejable (difficult to use).

unhang* ['ʌn'hæŋ] *vt* descolgar.
— OBSERV Pret y pp ***unhung***.

unhappiness [ʌn'hæpinis] *n* desdicha *f*, infortunio *m*, infelicidad *f*, desgracia *f*.

unhappy [ʌn'hæpi] *adj* desdichado, da; infeliz (not happy) || triste (sad); *that unhappy year* aquel triste año || desgraciado, da; desventurado, da; desdichado, da (unfortunate); *unhappy in one's marriage* desgraciado en el matrimonio || infausto, ta (event) || poco afortunado, da (translation, choice, remark) || *I am unhappy about your decision* no me agrada su decisión.

unharmed ['ʌn'hɑːmd] *adj* ileso, sa; indemne, incólume, sano y salvo, sana y salva (safe and sound) || intacto, ta (intact).

unharmonious ['ʌnhɑː'məunjəs] *adj* inarmónico, ca; poco armonioso, sa.

unharness ['ʌn'hɑːnis] *vt* desenjaezar, desguarnecer, desaparejar (a horse) || despojar de la armadura (a knight).

unhealthiness [ʌn'helθinis] *adj* mala salud *f* (bad health) || insalubridad *f* (of a place) || FIG *unhealthiness of mind* espíritu malsano, mentalidad morbosa.

unhealthy [ʌn'helθi] *adj* enfermo, ma; enfermizo, za (person) || malsano, na; insalubre (place) || FIG malsano, na; morboso, sa.

unheard ['ʌn'həːd] *adj* no oído, da || *to condemn a prisoner unheard* condenar a un preso sin haberle oído.

unheard-of [ʌn'həːdɔv] *adj* inaudito, ta; sin precedente (unprecedented) || desconocido, da (unknown).

unheeded ['ʌn'hiːdid] *adj* desatendido, da || *his warning went unheeded* su advertencia no fue escuchada.

unheeding ['ʌn'hiːdiŋ] *adj* poco atento (*of* a) || despreocupado, da (*of* por).

unhelpful ['ʌn'helpful] *adj* inútil, vano, na (advice) || poco servicial (person).

unhesitating [ʌn'heziteitiŋ] *adj* inmediato, ta (answer) || decidido, da; resuelto, ta (person).

unhesitatingly [-li] *adv* sin vacilar.

unhindered [ʌn'hindəd] *adj* libre, sin estorbos.

unhinge [ʌn'hindʒ] *vt* desquiciar (door) || FIG desquiciar, trastornar (mind).

unhitch ['ʌn'hitʃ] *vt* soltar, descolgar (sth.) || desenganchar (a horse).

unhitching [-iŋ] *n* desenganche *m*.

unholiness [ʌn'həulinis] *n* carácter *m* profano || impiedad *f* (impiety).

unholy [ʌn'həuli] *adj* impío, a (person) || profano, na (thing) || FIG & FAM infernal, terrible; *an unholy mess* un desorden infernal.

unhonoured; *US* **unhonored** ['ʌn'ɔnəd] *adj* no honrado, da; desdeñado, da || rechazado, da (a cheque).

unhood ['ʌn'hud] *vt* descaperuzar, descapirotar (bird) || desenmascarar (to unmask).

unhook ['ʌn'huk] *vt* desenganchar (sth. which is caught or hooked) || descolgar (to unhang) || desabrochar (dress).

unhooking [-iŋ] *n* desenganche *m*.

unhoped-for [ʌn'həuptfɔː*] *adj* inesperado, da.

unhopeful [ʌn'həupful] *adj* desesperante || poco alentador, ra (prospect) || pesimista (person).

unhorse ['ʌn'hɔːs] *vt* desmontar, desarzonar (from a horse) || desenganchar (a vehicle).

unhung ['ʌn'hʌŋ] *pret/pp* ⟶ **unhang**.

unhurried ['ʌn'hʌrid] *adj* pausado, da; lento, ta.

unhurt ['ʌn'həːt] *adj* indemne, ileso, sa (unharmed); *the driver was unhurt* el conductor resultó ileso *or* salió ileso.

unhygienic ['ʌnhai'dʒiːnik] *adj* antihigiénico, ca.

unicameral [ˌjuːni'kæmərəl] *adj* unicameral.

UNICEF *abbr of [United Nations International Children's Emergency]* UNICEF, Fondo de las Naciones Unidas para la Infancia.

unicellular [ˌjuːni'seljulə*] *adj* unicelular.

unicity [juː'nisiti] *n* unicidad *f*.

unicorn ['juːnikɔːn] *n* MYTH & ASTR unicornio *m* || *unicorn fish* narval *m*, unicornio marino.

unicycle ['juːnisaikl] *n* monociclo *m*.

unidentified ['ʌnai'dentifaid] *adj* sin identificar, no identificado, da || *unidentified flying object (UFO)* ovni *m*, objeto volador no identificado.

unidirectional [ˌjuːnidi'rekʃənl] *adj* RAD unidireccional.

unification [ˌjuːnifi'keiʃən] *n* unificación *f*.

unifier ['juːnifaiə*] *n* unificador, ra.

uniform ['juːnifɔːm] *adj* uniforme; *uniform velocity, density* velocidad, densidad uniforme || *to make uniform* hacer uniforme, uniformizar.
◆ *n* uniforme *m*; *school uniform* uniforme del colegio || MIL uniforme *m*; *full-dress uniform* uniforme de gala.

uniform ['juːnifɔːm] *vt* poner un uniforme a (to supply with a uniform) || uniformizar (to make uniform).

uniformed [-d] *adj* con uniforme.

uniformity [ˌjuːni'fɔːmiti] *n* uniformidad *f*.

uniformize ['juːnifɔːmaiz] *vt* uniformar, uniformizar.

uniformly [ˌjuːni'fɔːmli] *adv* uniformemente.

unify ['juːnifai] *vt* unificar.

unifying ['juːnifaiiŋ] *adj* unificador, ra.

unilateral ['juːnilætərəl] *adj* unilateral.

unilocular ['juːni'lɔkjulə] *adj* BOT unilocular.

unimaginable ['ʌni'mædʒinəbl] *adj* inimaginable.

unimaginative ['ʌni'mædʒinətiv] *adj* poco imaginativo, va; falto de imaginación.

unimpaired ['ʌnim'pεəd] *adj* intacto, ta (unharmed) || inalterado, da (unaltered) || no disminuido, da (not lessened).

unimpeachable ['ʌnim'piːtʃəbl] *adj* irrecusable (unquestionable) || irreprochable, irreprensible (unreproachable).

unimpeached ['ʌnim'piːtʃt] *adj* inatacado, da; no controvertido, da (unquestioned) || no acusado, da (not accused).

unimpeded ['ʌnim'piːdid] *adj* continuo, nua; ininterrumpido, da.

unimportance ['ʌnim'pɔːtəns] *n* poca importancia *f*, insignificancia *f*.

unimportant ['ʌnim'pɔːtənt] *adj* poco importante, sin importancia, insignificante.

unimposing ['ʌnim'pəuziŋ] *adj* poco impresionante.

unimpressed ['ʌnim'prest] *adj* no acuñado, da (medal) || FIG no impresionado, da (person) || *to be unimpressed by* no quedar impresionado por.

unimpressionable ['ʌnim'preʃnəbl] *adj* poco impresionable || impasible (impassive).

unimpressive ['ʌnim'presiv] *adj* poco impresionante || poco conmovedor, ra (not moving) || sin relieve (speech).

unimprovable ['ʌnim'pruːvəbl] *adj* inmejorable.

unimproved ['ʌnim'pruːvd] *adj* no mejorado, da (not improved) || no aprovechado, da (not made use of) || sin construir (not built on) || sin cultivar (not cultivated) || no pavimentado, da (road).

uninflammable ['ʌnin'flæməbl] *adj* no inflamable, ininflamable.

uninflated ['ʌnin'fleitid] *adj* desinflado, da (tyre).

uninfluenced ['ʌn'influənst] *adj* no influenciado, da; no influido, da.

uninfluential ['ʌninflu'enʃəl] *adj* poco influyente, sin gran influencia.

uninformed ['ʌnin'fɔːmd] *adj* mal informado, da (badly informed) || ignorante (ignorant) || inculto, ta (uneducated).

uninhabitable ['ʌnin'hæbitəbl] *adj* inhabitable.

uninhabited ['ʌnin'hæbitid] *adj* inhabitado, da; deshabitado, da || despoblado, da (deserted).

uninhibited ['ʌnin'hibitid] *adj* sin inhibición.

uninitiated ['ʌni'niʃieitid] *adj* no iniciado, da.

uninjured ['ʌn'indʒəd] *adj* ileso, sa; indemne.

uninominal ['juːni'nɔminl] *adj* uninominal.

uninspired ['ʌnin'spaiəd] *adj* sin inspiración, falto de inspiración.

uninspiring ['ʌnin'spaiəriŋ] *adj* aburrido, da; sin interés (unexciting).

uninstructed ['ʌnins'trʌktid] *adj* sin haber recibido instrucciones || sin instrucción *or* cultura (uncultured).

uninsured ['ʌnin'ʃuəd] *adj* no asegurado, da; sin asegurar, sin seguro.

unintelligent ['ʌnin'telidʒənt] *adj* ininteligente, poco inteligente, falto de inteligencia.

unintelligibility ['ʌninˌtelidʒə'biliti] *n* incomprensibilidad *f*.

unintelligible ['ʌnin'telidʒəbl] *adj* ininteligible, incomprensible.

unintentional ['ʌnin'tenʃənl] *adj* involuntario, ria; no intencionado, da.

unintentionally [-li] *adv* sin querer, involuntariamente, no intencionadamente.

uninterested ['ʌn'intristid] *adj* no interesado, da; indiferente || desinteresado, da (disinterested).

uninteresting ['ʌn'intristiŋ] *adj* poco interesante, sin interés, falto de interés.

uninterpretable ['ʌnin'təːpritəbl] *adj* MUS inejecutable.

uninterrupted ['ʌnˌintə'rətid] *adj* ininterrumpido, da; sin interrupción, continuo, nua.

uninterruption ['ʌnˌintə'rʌpʃən] *n* ininterrupción *f*.

uninvited ['ʌnin'vaitid] *adj* no convidado, da; no invitado, da (guest) || gratuito, ta; no solicitado, da (comment) || *to come uninvited* venir sin ser invitado *or* convidado.

uninviting [ʌnin'vaitiŋ] *adj* poco atractivo, va ‖ poco apetitoso, sa (food).

union ['juːnjən] *n* unión *f* (uniting) ‖ armonía *f*, unión *f* (harmony) ‖ enlace *m*, unión *f* (marriage) ‖ unión *f*, confederación *f* (political) ‖ sindicato *m* (trade union) ‖ emblema *m* de unión (on a flag) ‖ TECH unión *f* ‖ — *customs union* unión aduanera ‖ *union is strength* la unión hace la fuerza ‖ *Universal Postal Union* Unión Postal Universal.
◆ *adj* del sindicato; *union members* miembros del sindicato ‖ sindical; *union affairs* asuntos sindicales.

Union ['juːnjən] *n* Estados *m pl* Unidos ‖ *Soviet Union* Unión Soviética.

unionism [-izəm] *n* sindicalismo *m* (trade unionism) ‖ unionismo *m* (loyalty to any kind of union).

unionist [-ist] *n* sindicalista *m* & *f* (trade unionist) ‖ unionista *m* & *f* (of any union).

unionization [-ai'zeiʃən] *n* sindicación *f*, sindicalización *f*.

unionize [-aiz] *vt* sindicar.

Union Jack [-'dʒæk] *n* bandera *f* del Reino Unido.

union shop [-ʃɔp] *n* empresa *f* que contrata sólo a obreros sindicados.

union suit [-suːt] *n* US ropa *f* interior de cuerpo entero.

uniparous [juː'nipərəs] *adj* uníparo, ra.

unipersonal [juːni'pəːsənəl] *adj* unipersonal.

unipolar [juːni'pəulə*] *adj* unipolar.

unique [juː'niːk] *adj* único, ca ‖ FIG único, ca; incomparable | extraño, ña; extraordinario, ria; raro, ra (unusual).

uniqueness [-nis] *n* unicidad *f*.

unisex ['juːniseks] *adj* unisexo *inv*; *unisex fashions* modas unisexo.

unisexual [ˌjuːni'seksjuəl] *adj* unisexual.

unison ['juːnizn] *n* MUS unisonancia *f* ‖ FIG armonía *f* (harmony) ‖ *in unison* al unísono.

unisonous [ju'nisənəs] *adj* MUS unísono, na.

unit ['juːnit] *n* unidad *f*; *metric units* unidades métricas; *monetary unit* unidad monetaria ‖ elemento *m*; *bookshelves in separate units* estantería en elementos separados; *kitchen unit* elemento de cocina; *the family is the basic unit of society* la familia es el elemento básico de la sociedad ‖ MATH & MIL unidad *f*; *units column* columna de las unidades; *combat unit* unidad de combate ‖ conjunto *m*; *the engine forms a unit with the transmission* el motor forma un conjunto con la transmisión ‖ TECH grupo *m*; *compressor unit* grupo compresor; *generator unit* grupo electrógeno ‖ centro *m*; *research unit* centro de investigaciones ‖ servicio *m* (department); *accident unit* servicio de urgencia ‖ fábrica *f* (plant) ‖ aparato *m* (device) ‖ máquina *f* (machine) ‖ equipo *m* (of several machines) ‖ equipo *m* (team); *film unit* equipo de rodaje ‖ — RAD *mobile unit* unidad móvil ‖ TECH *motor unit* bloque *m* del motor ‖ *production unit* fábrica ‖ *unit cost* coste *m* por unidad ‖ *unit furniture* muebles *m pl* por elementos ‖ *unit price* precio unitario, precio por unidad ‖ *unit trust* sociedad *f* inversora por obligaciones.

unitable; uniteable [juː'naitəbl] *adj* unible.

Unitarian [juːni'tɛəriən] *adj/n* REL unitario, ria.

Unitarianism [-izəm] *n* REL unitarismo *m*.

unitary ['juːnitəri] *adj* unitario, ria.

unite [juː'nait] *vt* unir (to bring together, to attach, to join); *to unite in matrimony* unir en matrimonio; *s.o. is needed to unite the people* se necesita alguien que una al pueblo; *to unite bricks with mortar* unir ladrillos con argamasa ‖ reunir (to assemble); *to unite an army* reunir un ejército; *she unites beauty with brains* reúne la belleza con la inteligencia.
◆ *vi* unirse, juntarse; *to unite in fighting poverty* unirse para luchar contra la pobreza.

united [juː'naitid] *adj* unido, da; *a united front* un frente unido; *a very united family* una familia muy unida ‖ *united we stand, divided we fall* la unión hace la fuerza, unidos venceremos.

United Arab Emirates [juː'naitid'ærəbsteits] *pr n* GEOGR Emiratos Árabes Unidos.

United Kingdom [-'kiŋdəm] *pr n* Reino *m* Unido.

United Nations [-'neiʃəns] *pl prn* Naciones *f* Unidas.

United States of America [-'steitsəvə'merikə] *pl prn* Estados *m* Unidos de América.

unity ['juːniti] *n* unidad *f*; *unity of purpose* unidad de propósitos; *there is no unity about his plans* no hay unidad en sus proyectos ‖ armonía *f* (harmony); *to live together in unity* vivir en armonía ‖ unión *f* (union); *unity is strength* la unión hace la fuerza; *European unity* unión europea ‖ MATH unidad *f* ‖ THEATR unidad *f*; *the three unities* las tres unidades.

universal [ˌjuːni'vəːsəl] *adj* universal; *universal suffrage* sufragio universal ‖ mundial (worldwide) ‖ PHIL universal ‖ — *by universal request* a petición general ‖ *to make universal* generalizar ‖ TECH *universal coupling* acoplamiento *m* universal *or* de cardán | *universal joint* junta *f* universal *or* de cardán ‖ *universal remedy* panacea *f*.
◆ *n* PHIL proposición *f* universal.

universality [ˌjuːnivəː'sæliti] *n* universalidad *f*; *the universality of the English and Spanish languages* la universalidad de las lenguas inglesa y española.

universalization ['juːniˌvəːsəlai'zeiʃən] *n* universalización *f*.

universalize [ˌjuːni'vəːsəlaiz] *vt* universalizar, generalizar.

universally [ˌjuːni'vəːsəli] *adv* universalmente, por todos (by everyone); *he is universally recognized as an expert* es reconocido por todos como un experto ‖ universalmente, por todas partes (everywhere); *a language which is spoken universally* un idioma que se habla por todas partes ‖ mundialmente (throughout the world) ‖ siempre (always); *a universally applicable rule* una regla que se puede aplicar siempre.

universe ['juːnivəːs] *n* universo *m*.

university [ˌjuːni'vəːsiti] *n* universidad *f* ‖ — *a man with a university education* un hombre con estudios universitarios ‖ *to be at university, to go to university* ser estudiante universitario, ir a la facultad *or* a la universidad ‖ *university degree* título universitario ‖ *university town* ciudad universitaria, ciudad *f* que tiene una universidad.

univocal ['juːni'vəukəl] *n* unívoco, ca.

unjust ['ʌn'dʒʌst] *adj* injusto, ta (*to, with* para, con).

unjustifiable [ʌn'dʒʌstifaiəbl] *adj* injustificable.

unjustifiably [-i] *adv* sin justificación, injustificadamente.

unjustified [ʌn'dʒʌstifaid] *adj* injustificado, da.

unkempt ['ʌn'kempt] *adj* despeinado, da (hair, person) ‖ FIG descuidado, da (untidy).

unkind [ʌn'kaind] *adj* poco amable; *she is very unkind to her servants* es muy poco amable con sus criados; *that was unkind of him* eso fue poco amable de su parte ‖ severo, ra (harsh) ‖ cruel, despiadado, da (cruel); *unkind criticism* crítica despiadada ‖ riguroso, sa (weather).

unkindly [-li] *adj* poco amable (unkind) ‖ riguroso, sa (weather).
◆ *adv* poco amablemente, de manera poco amable, con poca amabilidad; *to treat s.o. unkindly* tratar a alguien de manera poco amable ‖ cruelmente (cruelly) ‖ severamente (harshly) ‖ a mal; *don't take it unkindly* no lo tomes a mal.

unkindness [-nis] *n* falta *f* de amabilidad ‖ crueldad *f* (cruelty) ‖ severidad *f* (harshness) ‖ rigor *m* (of weather).

unkingly ['ʌn'kiŋli] *adj* indigno de un rey.

unknit* ['ʌnnit] *vt* destejer ‖ *to unknit one's brow* desfruncir el ceño.
— OBSERV Pret y pp ***unknit, unknitted***.

unknot ['ʌn'nɔt] *vt* desanudar, desatar.

unknowable ['ʌn'kəuəbl] *adj* incognoscible.

unknowing ['ʌn'nəuiŋ] *adj* ignorante (ignorant) ‖ inconsciente (without realizing).

unknowingly [-li] *adv* sin darse cuenta, inconscientemente.

unknown ['ʌn'nəun] *adj* desconocido, da (region, author, etc.); *for some unknown reason* por una razón desconocida ‖ — *a person unknown to me* una persona desconocida por mí, una persona que yo no conozco *or* que yo desconozco ‖ *the unknown soldier* el soldado desconocido ‖ FIG & MATH *unknown quantity* incógnita *f*; *to isolate the unknown quantity* despejar la incógnita ‖ *unknown to David, they had gone* sin que lo supiera David se habían ido.
◆ *n* desconocido, da (person) ‖ lo desconocido (that which is not known); *to fear the unknown* temer lo desconocido ‖ MATH incógnita *f*.

unlabelled; unlabeled ['ʌn'leibld] *adj* sin etiqueta.

unlace ['ʌn'leis] *vt* desatar.

unladderable ['ʌn'lædərəbl] *adj* indesmallable.

unlade* ['ʌn'leid] *vt* descargar.
— OBSERV Pret ***unladed***; pp ***unladen***.

unladen [-ən] *adj* sin cargamento, vacío, a.

unladylike ['ʌn'leidilaik] *adj* poco señora, poco distinguida (a woman) ‖ impropio de una señora (behaviour).

unlamented ['ʌn'lə'mentid] *adj* no lamentado, da ‖ *to die unlamented* morir sin ser llorado.

unlash ['ʌn'læʃ] *vt* desamarrar.

unlatch ['ʌn'lætʃ] *vt* levantar el picaporte de, abrir (a door).

unlawful ['ʌn'lɔːful] *adj* ilegal (illegal) ‖ ilegítimo, ma (illegitimate).

unlawfulness [-nis] *n* ilegalidad *f* (illegality) ‖ ilegitimidad *f* (illegitimacy).

unleaded ['ʌn'ledid] *adj* sin plomo (petrol) ‖ PRINT sin regletear *or* espaciar.

unlearn* ['ʌn'ləːn] *vt* olvidar, desaprender ‖ quitarse (a habit).
— OBSERV Pret y pp ***unlearnt, unlearned***.

unlearned [-d]; **unlearnt** [-t] *adj* indocto, ta; inculto, ta; ignorante (lacking learning) ‖ sin aprender (not learnt) ‖ poco ejercitado (*in* en) (unskilled).

unleash ['ʌn'liːʃ] *vt* soltar (a dog) ‖ FIG liberar (to free) | dar rienda suelta a, desatar (one's passions) | provocar (s.o.'s anger).

unleavened ['ʌn'levnd] *adj* ácimo, ázimo, sin levadura; *unleavened bread* pan ácimo.

unless [ən'les] *conj* a no ser que, a menos que (with subjunctive), si no (with indicative); *they never go out unless forced to* nunca salen a no ser que se les obligue; *unless I am mistaken*

a no ser que me equivoque, si no me equivoco.
◆ *prep* salvo, excepto; *no one, unless John* nadie, excepto Juan.

unlettered ['ʌn'letəd] *adj* iletrado, da.

unlicensed ['ʌn'laisenst] *adj* ilícito, ta; no autorizado, da; sin permiso; *unlicensed sale of alcohol* venta ilícita de alcohol.

unlike ['ʌn'laik] *adj* diferente, distinto, ta; *two unlike quantities* dos cantidades diferentes ‖ diferente a, diferente de, distinto de; *people quite unlike ourselves* gente muy distinta de nosotros ‖ a diferencia de; *Peter, unlike his father, is rather shy* Pedro, a diferencia de su padre, es algo tímido ‖ impropio de; poco característico de; *it's unlike me to be so worried* es impropio de mí preocuparme tanto ‖ PHYS opuesto, ta; *unlike poles* polos opuestos.

unlikeable [-əbl] *adj* antipático, ca.

unlikelihood [-lihud]; **unlikeliness** [-linis] *n* improbabilidad *f*.

unlikely [-li] *adj* improbable, poco probable (improbable); *it is unlikely that anything will happen* es poco probable que ocurra algo ‖ inverosímil (unexpected); *he always visits the most unlikely places* siempre visita los lugares más inverosímiles ‖ poco prometedor, ra (unpromising) ‖ — *he was unlikely to win* tenía pocas probabilidades de ganar ‖ *it is not at all unlikely* es muy probable, es muy posible.

unlikeness ['ʌn'laiknis] *n* diferencia *f*.

unlimber [ʌn'limbə*] *vt* quitar el armón a (a gun).

unlimitable [ʌn'limitəbl] *adj* ilimitable.

unlimited [ʌn'limitid] *adj* ilimitado, da.

unlined [ʌn'laind] *adj* sin rayar (paper) ‖ sin forro, sin forrar (coat, etc.) ‖ sin arrugas (face).

unlink ['ʌn'liŋk] *vt* quitar los eslabones de (a chain) ‖ desatar (to unfasten).

unliquidated ['ʌn'likwideitid] *adj* sin liquidar, sin saldar (a debt).

unlisted [ʌn'listid] *adj* que no figura en la lista (not on the list) ‖ no cotizado, da (securities).

unlit ['ʌn'lit] *adj* sin luz, no iluminado, da ‖ *unlit street* calle *f* sin alumbrado.

unlivable; unliveable [ʌn'livəbl] *adj* inaguantable (unbearable) ‖ inhabitable (uninhabitable).

unload ['ʌn'ləud] *vt* descargar (transport vehicles, goods, a gun); *to unload the sugar from a boat* descargar el azúcar de un barco ‖ FIG abrir, desahogar (one's heart) | deshacerse de (to get rid of) ‖ FIG *to unload one's responsibilities on a colleague* descargarse de sus obligaciones en un colega.
◆ *vi* descargar.

unloaded [-id] *adj* descargado, da.

unloader [-ə*] *n* descargador *m*.

unloading [-iŋ] *n* descarga *f*; *unloading of a boat* descarga de un barco.

unlock [ʌn'lɔk] *vt* abrir [con llave] (a door) ‖ FIG revelar (a secret) | resolver (a puzzle) ‖ desbloquear (to unblock).

unlooked-for [ʌn'luktfɔː*] *adj* imprevisto, ta; inesperado, da.

unloose ['ʌn'luːs]; **unloosen** [ʌn'luːsn] *vt* soltar (to loosen, to let go) ‖ desatar (a shoelace).

unlosable [ʌn'luːzəbl] *adj* imperdible.

unloveable; unlovable [ʌn'lʌvəbl] *adj* poco amable, antipático, ca.

unloved [ʌn'lʌvd] *adj* no querido, da.

unlovely ['ʌn'lʌvli] *adj* desgarbado, da; sin atractivo (person) ‖ feo, a (thing).

unloving ['ʌn'lʌviŋ] *adj* poco cariñoso, sa.

unluckily [ʌn'lʌkili] *adv* desafortunadamente, desgraciadamente.

unluckiness [ʌn'lʌkinis] *n* desgracia *f* ‖ mala suerte *f*.

unlucky [ʌn'lʌki] *adj* desgraciado, da; desafortunado, da; desdichado, da; *how unlucky I am!* ¡qué desgraciado soy!; *unlucky in gambling* desgraciado en el juego ‖ aciago, ga; nefasto, ta; funesto, ta; de mala suerte; *an unlucky day* un día de mala suerte ‖ gafe (who brings bad luck) ‖ — *how unlucky!* ¡qué mala suerte! ‖ *it is unlucky to break a mirror* trae mala suerte romper un espejo ‖ *to be born unlucky* haber nacido con mala estrella ‖ *to be unlucky* tener mala suerte (a person) ‖ *unlucky devil* pobre diablo *m* ‖ *unlucky omen* cosa *f* de mal agüero.

unmade [ʌn'meid] *adj* sin hacer.
◆ *pret/pp* → **unmake.**

unmaidenly [ʌn'meidnli] *adj* poco señorita (girl) ‖ impropio de una señorita (behaviour).

unmaintainable [ʌnmein'teinəbl] *adj* insostenible.

unmake* ['ʌn'meik] *vt* deshacer.
— OBSERV Pret y pp ***unmade***.

unman ['ʌn'mæn] *vt* acobardar (to make cowardly) ‖ desanimar, abatir (to dishearten) ‖ castrar (to castrate) ‖ MIL desguarnecer (a gun) ‖ — *unmanned aeroplane* avión *m* sin piloto ‖ *unmanned device* aparato automático ‖ *unmanned flight* vuelo no tripulado ‖ *unmanned spacecraft* nave *f* espacial no tripulada *or* sin tripulación.

unmanageable [ʌn'mænidʒəbl] *adj* inmanejable, poco manejable (a large book, etc.) ‖ poco dócil (person, horse).

unmanliness ['ʌn'mænlinis] *n* poca virilidad *f*, afeminamiento *m* (effeminacy) ‖ cobardía *f* (cowardice) ‖ falta *f* de caballerosidad.

unmanly ['ʌn'mænli] *adj* poco viril, afeminado, da (effeminate) ‖ impropio de un hombre (behaviour) ‖ cobarde (cowardly).

unmannered [ʌn'mænəd] *adj* descortés, mal educado, da (impolite) ‖ sencillo, lla (not affected).

unmannerly [ʌn'mænəli] *adj* descortés, mal educado, da (impolite).

unmarked ['ʌn'mɑːkt] *adj* sin marcar ‖ sin letrero (a street) ‖ ileso, sa; indemne (uninjured) ‖ en perfecto estado (as new) ‖ desapercibido, da (unnoticed); *to go unmarked* pasar desapercibido ‖ SP desmarcado, da (player).

unmarketable [ʌn'mɑːkitəbl] *adj* invendible.

unmarriable [ʌn'mæriəbl]; **unmarriageable** [ʌn'mæridʒəbl] *adj* incasable ‖ no casadero, ra (too young to be married).

unmarried [ʌn'mærid] *adj* soltero, ra.

unmask ['ʌn'mɑːsk] *vt* desenmascarar (to remove the mask from) ‖ MIL descubrir (a battery) ‖ FIG *to unmask a plot* descubrir un complot.
◆ *vi* quitarse la máscara.

unmast [ʌn'mɑːst] *vt* MAR desarbolar.

unmatchable ['ʌn'mætʃəbl] *adj* incomparable ‖ imposible de emparejar (impossible to pair).

unmatched ['ʌn'mætʃt] *adj* sin par, incomparable, único, ca (unique) ‖ sin pareja, no emparejado, da (not paired).

unmeaning [ʌn'miːniŋ] *adj* sin sentido (words) ‖ inexpresivo, va (expressionless).

unmeant [ʌn'ment] *adj* involuntario, ria.

unmeasured [ʌn'meʒəd] *adj* ilimitado, da (boundless) ‖ no medido, da.

unmeet [ˌʌn'miːt] *adj* impropio, pia.

unmendable [ʌn'mendəbl] *adj* irreparable.

unmentionable [ʌn'menʃnəbl] *adj* indecible, que no se debe mencionar.
◆ *pl n* FAM ropa *f sing* interior (underwear).

unmerciful [ʌn'məːsiful] *adj* despiadado, da.

unmerited ['ʌn'meritid] *adj* inmerecido, da.

unmethodical [ʌnmi'θɔdikəl] *adj* poco metódico, ca.

unmindful [ʌn'maindful] *adj* descuidado, da (careless) ‖ — *not unmindful of* no olvidando, teniendo presente ‖ *to be unmindful of* no pensar en (to forget), hacer caso omiso de (to pass over).

unmistakable ['ʌnmis'teikəbl] *adj* inconfundible; *written in his own unmistakable style* escrito en su inconfundible estilo ‖ inequívoco, ca; *unmistakable signs of inebriation* señales inequívocas de embriaguez.

unmistakably ['ʌnmis'teikəbli] *adv* sin lugar a dudas, con toda evidencia.

unmitigated ['ʌn'mitigeitid] *adj* profundo, da (grief) ‖ implacable (hatred, heat) ‖ desenfrenado, da (anger) ‖ FIG rematado, da; redomado, da; de tomo y lomo (arrant); *an unmitigated liar* un mentiroso rematado.

unmixed ['ʌn'mikst] *adj* puro, ra; sin mezcla.

unmodified ['ʌn'mɔdifaid] *adj* sin modificar.

unmolested ['ʌnmə'lestid] *adj* tranquilo, la ‖ *to leave unmolested* no molestar, dejar en paz.

unmoor ['ʌn'muə*] *vi* MAR soltar las amarras.
◆ *vt* MAR desamarrar.

unmotivated ['ʌn'məutiveitid] *adj* inmotivado, da; sin motivo.

unmounted ['ʌn'mauntid] *adj* desmontado, da (rider) ‖ MIL de a pie (soldier) ‖ sin engastar, sin montar (jewel) ‖ sin marco (picture).

unmovable ['ʌn'muːvəbl] *adj* inamovible.

unmoved ['ʌn'muːvd] *adj* en su sitio, sin mover (in its place) ‖ impasible, indiferente (indifferent); *to be unmoved by sth.* permanecer impasible ante algo ‖ impávido, da (unflinching) ‖ insensible; *unmoved by all our pleas* insensible a todas nuestras súplicas.

unmuffle ['ʌn'mʌfl] *vt* destapar, descubrir (one's face) ‖ quitar la sordina a (a drum, a bell, etc.).

unmusical ['ʌn'mjuːzikəl] *adj* poco armonioso, sa (not harmonious) ‖ que tiene mal oído (without musical skill) ‖ poco aficionado a la música (uninterested in music).

unmuzzle ['ʌn'mʌzl] *vt* quitar el bozal a (a dog) ‖ FIG *to unmuzzle the press* dejar de amordazar la prensa.

unnail ['ʌn'neil] *vt* desclavar.

unnamable; unnameable ['ʌn'neiməbl] *adj* que no tiene nombre, vergonzoso, sa; innominable.

unnamed ['ʌn'neimd] *adj* sin nombre, innominado, da (having no name) ‖ anónimo, ma (anonymous) ‖ *I prefer to remain unnamed* prefiero conservar el anónimo.

unnatural ['ʌn'nætʃrəl] *adj* antinatural, no natural; *his appetite is unnatural* su apetito no es natural ‖ contra natura (vice) ‖ anormal (abnormal) ‖ afectado, da; sofisticado, da; poco natural (affected); *he has a rather unnatural manner* tiene una manera de ser algo sofisticada ‖ artificial (artificial).

unnaturally [-li] *adv* de manera poco natural (in an unnatural way) ‖ anormalmente (abnormally) ‖ con afectación, de una manera sofisticada (affectedly) ‖ *I not unnaturally thought that* pensé naturalmente que.

unnavigable ['ʌn'nævigəbl] *adj* innavegable.

unnecessarily [ʌn'nesisərili] *adv* sin necesidad, innecesariamente, inútilmente.

unnecessary [ʌn'nesisəri] *adv* innecesario, ria; inútil.

unneighbourly; US **unneighborly** ['ʌn'neibəli] *adj* poco amistoso, sa (unfriendly) || poco amable (unpleasant).

unnerve ['ʌn'nəːv] *vt* desconcertar, turbar (to disturb, to worry) || desanimar (to dishearten) || acobardar (to make lose courage).

unnerving ['ʌn'nəːviŋ] *adj* desconcertante, turbador, ra.

unnoticeable ['ʌn'nəutisəbl] *adj* imperceptible.

unnoticed ['ʌn'nəutist] *adj* inadvertido, da; desapercibido, da; *to go o to pass unnoticed* pasar desapercibido || — *to leave a fact unnoticed* pasar un hecho por alto || *to let sth. pass unnoticed* no reparar en algo.

unnumbered ['ʌn'nʌmbəd] *adj* sin numerar (pages, etc.) || innumerable (countless).

UNO *abbr of [United Nations Organization]* ONU, Organización de las Naciones Unidas.

unobjectionable ['ʌnəb'dʒekʃənəbl] *adj* irreprochable.

unobservable ['ʌnəb'zəːvəbl] *adj* inobservable.

unobservant ['ʌnəb'zəːvənt] *adj* poco observador, ra || *to be unobservant of the law* no respetar *or* acatar la ley.

unobserved ['ʌnəb'zəːvd] *adj* desapercibido, da; inadvertido, da.

unobserving ['ʌnəb'zəːviŋ] *adj* desatento, ta.

unobstructed ['ʌnəb'strʌktid] *adj* no obstruido, da; sin obstáculos, despejado, da; *the way is unobstructed* el camino está despejado || *unobstructed view* vista despejada.

unobtainable ['ʌnəb'teinəbl] *adj* inalcanzable.

unobtrusive ['ʌnəb'truːsiv] *adj* discreto, ta.

unoccupied ['ʌn'ɔkjupaid] *adj* desocupado, da; *unoccupied person* persona desocupada; *unoccupied flat* piso desocupado || libre (seat, time, etc.) || vacante (job) || despoblado, da (region) || no ocupado, da (not occupied by troops).

unoffending ['ʌnə'fendiŋ] *adj* inofensivo, va.

unofficial ['ʌnəfiʃəl] *adj* extraoficial, no oficial || oficioso, sa; *unofficial information* información oficiosa.

unopened ['ʌn'əupənd] *adj* sin abrir.

unopposed ['ʌnə'pəuzd] *adj* sin oposición; *to be elected unopposed* ser elegido sin oposición || *unopposed candidate* candidato único.

unordinary ['ʌn'ɔːdinəri] *adj* que se sale de lo corriente, poco corriente, fuera de lo común.

unorganized ['ʌn'ɔːgənaizd] *adj* no organizado, da.

unoriginal ['ʌnə'ridʒinəl] *adj* poco original.

unorthodox ['ʌn'ɔːθədɔks] *adj* poco ortodoxo, xa || REL heterodoxo, xa; no ortodoxo, xa.

unostentatious ['ʌn,ɔsten'teiʃəs] *adj* sin ostentación.

unpack ['ʌn'pæk] *vt* desembalar (packing case, etc.) || desempaquetar (a parcel) || deshacer [*AMER* desempacar] (a suitcase).
◆ *vi* deshacer las maletas [*AMER* desempacar].

unpacking [-iŋ] *n* desembalaje *m* || desempaquetado *m* (of a parcel) || *to do one's unpacking* deshacer las maletas [*AMER* desempacar] (suitcases).

unpaid ['ʌn'peid] *adj* impagado, da; sin pagar, por pagar (bill, debt) || no retribuido, da (work, person).

unpaired ['ʌn'pɛəd] *adj* desparejado, da (glove, etc.) || ANAT impar; *unpaired organ* órgano impar.

unpalatable [ʌn'pælətəbl] *adj* desagradable al gusto, de mal sabor (food) || FIG difícil de tragar *or* de aceptar, desagradable (unpleasant).

unparalleled [ʌɛ'pærəleld] *adj* sin par, incomparable, sin pararelo || sin precedente (unprecedented).

unpardonable [ʌn'pɑːdənəbl] *adj* imperdonable, indisculpable.

unparliamentary ['ʌn,pɑːlə'mentəri] *adj* antiparlamentario, ria.

unpatriotic ['ʌn,pætri'ɔtik] *adj* antipatriótico, ca (action) || poco patriota (person).

unpave ['ʌn'peiv] *vt* desempedrar.

unpaved [-d] *adj* sin pavimentar || desempedrado, da.

unpayable ['ʌn'peiəbl] *adj* impagable.

unperceivable ['ʌnpə'siːvəbl] *adj* imperceptible.

unperceived ['ʌnpə'siːvd] *adj* desapercibido, da; inadvertido, da.

unperformable ['ʌnpə'fɔːməbl] *adj* MUS inejecutable || THEATR irrepresentable.

unpersuasive ['ʌnpə'sweisiv] *adj* poco convincente.

unperturbed ['ʌnpə'təːbd] *adj* impasible, impávido, da || no perturbado, da (*by* por).

unpick ['ʌn'pik] *vt* descoser (in sewing).

unpile ['ʌn'pail] *vt* desamontonar.

unpin ['ʌn'pin] *vt* quitar alfileres a (in sewing) || desprender (to take off) || TECH quitar la clavija a.

unplaced ['ʌn'pleist] *adj* SP no colocado, da.

unplait ['ʌn'plæt] *vt* destrenzar.

unplanned ['ʌn'plænd] *adj* imprevisto, ta; *unplanned journey* viaje imprevisto.

unplayable ['ʌn'pleiəbl] *adj* MUS inejecutable.

unpleasant ['ʌn'pleznt] *adj* desagradable; *unpleasant weather* tiempo desagradable || antipático, ca; desagradable (unfriendly); *to be unpleasant to o with s.o.* ser antipático con alguien || molesto, ta (annoying).

unpleasantly [-li] *adv* desagradablemente, de manera desagradable; *to treat s.o. unpleasantly* tratar a alguien de manera desagradable || *the music is unpleasantly loud* la música es tan fuerte que resulta desagradable *or* molesta.

unpleasantness [-nis] *n* lo desagradable; *the unpleasantness of his position* lo desagradable de su situación || antipatía *f* (person's unfriendliness) || disgusto *m*, desagrado *m*, molestia *f*; *to cause unpleasantness* causar desagrado *or* un disgusto *or* una molestia || FAM desavenencia *f* (disagreement); *there was some unpleasantness between them* hubo una desavenencia entre ellos.

unpleasing ['ʌn'pliːziŋ] *adj* desagradable (unpleasant) || poco atractivo, va (unattractive).

unpliable ['ʌn'plaiəbl] *adj* poco flexible.

unploughed; US **unplowed** ['ʌn'plaud] *adj* sin arar, sin labrar.

unplug ['ʌn'plʌg] *vt* desenchufar (to disconnect).

unplugging [-iŋ] *n* desenchufado *m*.

unplumbed ['ʌn'plʌmd] *adj* no sondado, da; no sondeado, da || FIG insondable (mystery).

unpoetical ['ʌnpəu'etikəl] *adj* poco poético, ca; prosaico, ca.

unpolished ['ʌn'pɔliʃt] *adj* sin pulir || en bruto (precious stones); *an unpolished diamond* un diamante en bruto || no encerado, da (floor) || no embetunado, da [*AMER* no lustrado, da] (shoes) || FIG tosco, ca; poco pulido, da (style, manners, etc.).

unpolite ['ʌnpə'lait] *adj* descortés, mal educado, da.

unpolitic ['ʌn'pɔlitik] *adj* imprudente, impolítico, ca.

unpolitical ['ʌnpə'litikəl] *adj* apolítico, ca.

unpolluted ['ʌnpə'ljuːtid] *adj* no contaminado, da; incontaminado, da; puro, ra; *unpolluted water* agua no contaminada.

unpopular ['ʌn'pɔpjulə*] *adj* impopular.

unpopularity ['ʌn,pɔpju'læriti] *n* impopularidad *f*.

unpostponable ['ʌnpəust'pəunəbl] *adj* inaplazable.

unpractical ['ʌn'præktikəl] *adj* poco práctico, ca.

unpractised; US **unpracticed** ['ʌn'præktist] *adj* inexperto, ta (inexpert) || falto de práctica, sin práctica (needing practice).

unprecedented [ʌn'presidəntid] *adj* inaudito, ta; sin precedente.

unprecise ['ʌnpri'sais] *adj* impreciso, sa.

unpredictable ['ʌnpri'diktəbl] *adj* que no se puede prever, imprevisible (occurrence) || de reacciones imprevisibles (person) || antojadizo, za (capricious).

unprejudiced [ʌn'predʒudist] *adj* imparcial || sin prejuicios.

unpremeditated ['ʌnpri'mediteitid] *adj* impremeditado, da || improvisado, da (speech).

unprepared ['ʌnpri'pɛəd] *adj* desprevenido, da (unready); *it caught me unprepared* me cogió desprevenido || hecho sin preparación, improvisado, da (recital, etc.) || *to be unprepared for sth.* no estar preparado para algo (not ready), no esperar algo (not to be expecting sth.).

unpreparedness [-nis] *n* falta *f* de preparación (lack of preparation) || imprevisión *f* (of s.o. caught unawares).

unprepossessing ['ʌn,priːpə'zesiŋ] *adj* poco atractivo, va.

unpresentable ['ʌnpri'zentəbl] *adj* impresentable.

unpretending ['ʌnpri'tendiŋ]; **unpretentious** ['ʌnpri'tenʃəs] *adj* modesto, ta; sin pretensiones, sencillo, lla.

unprime ['ʌn'praim] *vt* descebar (a firearm).

unprincipled ['ʌn'prinsəpld] *adj* falto de principios, sin principios.

unprintable [ʌn'printəbəl] *adj* impublicable.

unprized ['ʌn'praizd] *adj* poco apreciado, da.

unproductive ['ʌnprə'dʌktiv] *adj* improductivo, va.

unproductiveness [-nis] *n* improductividad *f*.

unprofessional ['ʌnprə'feʃənəl] *adj* impropio, pia; contrario a la ética profesional (conduct) || inexperto, ta; poco experto, ta (incompetent) || sin título; *unprofessional lawyer* abogado sin título || SP aficionado, da.

unprofitable [ʌn'prɔfitəbl] *adj* poco provechoso, sa; poco lucrativo, va (business, etc.) || improductivo, va (unproductive) || inútil (useless) || infructuoso, sa (fruitless).

unpromising ['ʌn'prɔmisiŋ] *adj* poco prometedor, ra.

unprompted ['ʌn'prɔptid] *adj* espontáneo, a.

unpronounceable ['ʌnprə'naunsəbl] *adj* impronunciable.

unpropitious ['ʌnprə'piʃəs] *adj* impropicio, cia; poco propicio, cia; desfavorable.

unprosperous ['ʌn'prɔspərəs] *adj* poco próspero, ra || desafortunado, da (unlucky) || poco propicio, cia; desfavorable (winds).

unprotected ['ʌnprə'tektid] *adj* sin protección, indefenso, sa (defenceless) || sin ayuda, sin apoyo (unsupported) || TECH sin protección (moving parts).

unprovable [ʌn'pru:vəbl] *adj* indemostrable, imposible de demostrar *or* de probar.

unproved ['ʌn'pru:vd]; **unproven** ['ʌn'pru:vn] *adj* no probado, da; no demostrado, da; sin probar, sin demostrar || no comprobado, da; no puesto a prueba; *his loyalty is as yet unproved* su fidelidad no ha sido comprobada todavía.

unprovided ['ʌnprə'vaidid] *adj* desprovisto, ta (*with* de) (not supplied) || desprevenido, da (unprepared) || *unprovided for* desvalido, da (child), imprevisto, ta; no previsto, ta (contingencies), sin recursos.

unprovoked ['ʌnprə'vəukt] *adj* no provocado, da (attack, etc.) || tranquilo, la; sereno, na (person); *to remain unprovoked* quedarse tranquilo.

unpublishable [ʌn'pʌbliʃəbl] *adj* impublicable.

unpublished ['ʌn'pʌbliʃt] *adj* inédito, ta; no publicado, da; sin publicar (book) || FIG no revelado al público.

unpunctual ['ʌn'pʌŋktjuəl] *adj* poco puntual.

unpunished ['ʌn'pʌniʃt] *adj* impune, sin castigar; *unpunished crimes* delitos impunes || *to go unpunished* no ser castigado, quedar impune.

unqualifiable ['ʌn'kwɔlifaiəbl] *adj* incalificable.

unqualified ['ʌn'kwɔlifaid] *adj* incompetente (incompetent) || sin título (without qualifications) || sin autorización || sin reserva, incondicional, total (without reservation); *unqualified endorsement* aprobación sin reserva || inhabilitado, da || *unqualified statement* declaración *f* general.

unquenchable [ʌn'kwentʃəbl] *adj* inextinguible (fire) || insaciable (thirst).

unquenched [ʌn'kwentʃt] *adj* sin extinguir (fire) || no saciado, da; sin saciar (thirst).

unquestionable [ʌn'kwestʃənəbl] *adj* indiscutible, incuestionable.

unquestioned [ʌn'kwestʃənd] *adj* no interrogado, da (person) || indiscutido, da; incontrovertido, da (a right, etc.).

unquestioning [ʌn'kwestʃəniŋ] *adj* incondicional.

unquiet ['ʌn'kwaiət] *adj* agitado, da || ruidoso, sa (noisy).

unquote ['ʌnkwəut] *vi* *unquote* fin de la cita.

unquoted ['ʌn'kwəutid] *adj* no citado, da || COMM no cotizado, da (securities).

unravel [ʌn'rævəl] *vt* desenredar, desenmarañar (to untangle) || deshacer (a knitted garment) || FIG desenmarañar, desembrollar (a problem, a mystery).
◆ *vi* desenredarse, desenmarañarse (to become untangled) || deshacerse (a knitted garment) || FIG desenmarañarse, desembrollarse.

unreachable ['ʌn'ri:tʃəbl] *adj* inalcanzable.

unread ['ʌn'red] *adj* sin leer, no leído, da (book) || poco leído, da; inculto, ta; *unread person* persona inculta.

unreadable ['ʌn'ri:dəbl] *adj* ilegible (handwriting, figure, etc.) || imposible de leer (book) || incomprensible || que no merece la pena leerse (not worth reading).

unreadiness ['ʌn'redinis] *n* falta *f* de preparación.

unready ['ʌn'redi] *adj* no listo, ta; no preparado, da; *they were unready for war* no estaban listos para la guerra || desprevenido, da (unprepared).

unreal ['ʌn'riəl] *adj* irreal.

unrealistic ['ʌnriə'listik] *adj* poco realista.

unreality ['ʌnri'æliti] *n* irrealidad *f*.

unrealizable ['ʌn'riəlaizəbl] *adj* irrealizable.

unreason ['ʌn'ri:zən] *n* insensatez *f*.

unreasonable [ʌn'ri:zənəbl] *adj* irracional (irrational) || irrazonable, desrazonable (not reasonable) || — *at an unreasonable hour* a deshora || *unreasonable demands* pretensiones desmedidas *or* exageradas || *unreasonable prices* precios exorbitantes.

unreasonableness [-nis] *n* irracionalidad *f* (irrationality) || inmoderación *f*, falta *f* de moderación (of demands) || lo exorbitante (of prices).

unreasoning [ʌn'ri:zəniŋ] *adj* irracional.

unreclaimed ['ʌnri'kleimd] *adj* sin reclamar || sin aprovechar (land).

unrecognizable ['ʌn'rekəgnaizəbl] *adj* imposible de reconocer, irreconocible || desconocido, da; *since his illness he is unrecognizable* desde su enfermedad está desconocido.

unrecognized ['ʌn'rekəgnaizd] *adj* desconocido, da (genius, etc.); *unrecognized merits* méritos desconocidos || no reconocido, da (leader, etc.) || *to go unrecognized* pasar sin ser reconocido.

unrecorded ['ʌnri'kɔ:did] *adj* sin grabar (music, etc.) || sin registrar (event, etc.).

unrecoverable ['ʌnri'kʌvərəbl] *adj* irrecuperable.

unredeemable ['ʌnri'di:məbl] *adj* irredimible, sin remisión.

unredeemed ['ʌnri'di:md] *adj* sin redimir (sin) || sin cumplir (promise) || sin desempeñar (pawned article) || COMM sin amortizar (loan) || irredento, ta (territory) || FIG *unredeemed by* no compensado por.

unreel ['ʌn'ri:l] *vt* desenrollar.

unrefined ['ʌnri'faind] *adj* sin refinar, no refinado, da || FIG basto, ta; poco fino, na; tosco, ca.

unreflecting ['ʌnri'flektiŋ] *adj* irreflexivo, va.

unregarded ['ʌnri'gɑ:did] *adj* desatendido, da; descuidado, da.

unregardful ['ʌnri'gɑ:dful] *adj* poco atento, ta (*of* a) (unmindful) || poco cuidadoso, sa (*of* con) (lacking care) || *unregardful of his duties* sin tener en cuenta sus obligaciones.

unregenerate ['ʌnri'dʒenərit] *adj* no regenerado, da || impenitente (unrepentant, inveterate).

unrehearsed ['ʌnri'hə:st] *adj* sin preparar, improvisado, da; *an unrehearsed speech* un discurso improvisado || imprevisto, ta (unexpected); *an unrehearsed incident* un incidente imprevisto || THEATR sin ensayar.

unrelated ['ʌnri'leitid] *adj* inconexo, xa; no relacionado, da (not related) || *they are entirely unrelated* no son de la misma familia.

unrelenting ['ʌnri'lentiŋ] *adj* implacable.

unreliability ['ʌnri,laiə'biliti] *n* inestabilidad *f* (of character) || poca formalidad *f* (of a person) || poca seguridad *f* (of information).

unreliable ['ʌnri'laiəbl] *adj* inconstante, inestable (character) || de poca confianza, que no es de fiar, poco formal, poco seguro, ra (person) || poco fiable (machine) || poco seguro, ra; que no es de fiar (information, service).

unrelieved ['ʌnri'li:vd] *adj* no aliviado, da (pain) || monótono, na (landscape) || MIL no relevado, da || *unrelieved poverty* miseria profunda, miseria total.

unreligious ['ʌnri'lidʒəs] *adj* no religioso, sa || irreligioso, sa (impious).

unremarkable ['ʌnri'mɑ:kəbl] *adj* corriente, que no tiene nada de particular.

unremembered ['ʌnri'membəd] *adj* olvidado, da.

unremitting [,ʌnri'mitiŋ] *adj* incesante, continuo, nua (kept up without interruption) || incansable (persevering).

unremunerative ['ʌnri'mju:nərətiv] *adj* poco remunerador, ra.

unrenewable ['ʌnri'nju:əbl] *adj* improrrogable.

unrented ['ʌn'rentid] *adj* desalquilado, da.

unrepealable ['ʌnri'pi:ləbl] *adj* inabrogable.

unrepealed ['ʌnri'pi:ld] *adj* JUR no revocado, da.

unrepeatable ['ʌnri'pi:təbl] *adj* que no se puede repetir.

unrepentant ['ʌnri'pentənt] *adj* impertinente.

unrepresentative ['ʌn,repri'zentətiv] *adj* poco representativo, va.

unrepresented ['ʌn,repri'zentid] *adj* sin representación.

unrequested ['ʌnri'kwestid] *adj* no solicitado, da || espontáneo, a.

unrequired ['ʌnri'kwaiəd] *adj* no exigido, da; no requerido, da || innecesario, ria; inútil (unnecessary).

unrequited ['ʌnri'kwaitid] *adj* no correspondido, da (love) || no recompensado, da (service).

unreserved ['ʌnri'zə:vd] *adj* sin reserva (approval) || expansivo, va; abierto, ta (frank) || sin reservar, libre (seat).

unreservedly [-li] *adv* sin reserva.

unresisting ['ʌnri'zistiŋ] *adj* que no ofrece resistencia.

unresolved ['ʌnri'zɔlvd] *adj* sin resolver, no resuelto, ta (problem) || irresoluto, ta (person).

unresponsive ['ʌnri'spɔnsiv] *adj* insensible.

unrest [ʌn'rest] *n* inquietud *f* (restlessness) || malestar *m* (uneasiness); *social unrest* malestar social || agitación *f*, disturbios *m pl* (state of disturbance); *labour unrest* agitación obrera.

unrestrainable ['ʌnris'treinəbl] *adj* incontenible (anger, laughter).

unrestrained ['ʌnris'treind] *adj* no contenido, da || libre (free).

unrestricted ['ʌnris'triktid] *adj* sin restricción.

unrevealed ['ʌnri'vi:ld] *adj* no revelado, da.

unrewarded ['ʌnri'wɔ:did] *adj* no recompensado, da || sin recompensa.

unrewarding ['ʌnri'wɔ:diŋ] *adj* ingrato, ta; *an unrewarding task* una labor ingrata || infructuoso, sa (useless).

unriddle ['ʌn'ridl] *vt* explicar (a dream) || descifrar, aclarar, resolver (a mystery).

unrig ['ʌn'rig] *vt* MAR desaparejar.

unrighteous [ʌn'raitʃəs] *adj* inicuo, cua; injusto, ta (unjust) || malo, la; perverso, sa (wicked).

unripe ['ʌn'raip] *adj* verde, inmaduro, ra (fruit) || FIG inmaduro, ra; verde, insuficientemente maduro, ra.

unrivalled; US **unrivaled** [ʌn'raivəld] *adj* sin rival || sin par, sin igual, incomparable.

unrobe ['ʌn'rəub] *vt* desnudar, desvestir.
◆ *vi* desnudarse, desvestirse.

unroll ['ʌn'rəul] *vt* desenrollar.
◆ *vi* desenrollarse.

unroof ['ʌn'ruːf] *vt* destechar, quitar el techo de (a house).

unrope ['ʌn'rəup] *vt* desatar.
◆ *vi* desatarse.

unruffled ['ʌn'rʌfld] *adj* liso, sa (hair) ‖ sereno, na; tranquilo, la (water) ‖ imperturbable (person).

unruled [ʌn'ruːld] *adj* sin rayar (paper) ‖ no gobernado, da (country) ‖ no reprimido, da; no contenido, da (passion).

unruliness [ʌn'ruːlinis] *n* indocilidad *f*, insumisión *f*.

unruly [ʌn'ruːli] *adj* revoltoso, sa; indisciplinado, da (child, etc.) ‖ ingobernable (country) ‖ fogoso, sa (horse) ‖ desenfrenado, da (passions) ‖ despeinado, da (hair).

unsaddle ['ʌn'sædl] *vt* desensillar (a horse) ‖ desarzonar, desmontar (a horseman).

unsafe ['ʌn'seif] *adj* peligroso, sa (dangerous) ‖ malo, la (bad) ‖ inseguro, ra (uncertain) ‖ inhospitalario, ria (a place, etc.).

unsafety [-ti] *n* inseguridad *f* ‖ peligro *m* (danger).

unsaid ['ʌn'sed] *pret/pp* ⟶ **unsay.**
◆ *adj* sin decir ‖ *to leave sth. unsaid* dejar de decir algo.

unsalable; unsaleable ['ʌn'seiləbl] *adj* COMM invendible.

unsalaried ['ʌn'sælərid] *adj* no asalariado, da; sin sueldo.

unsanitary ['ʌn'sænitəri] *adj* antihigiénico, ca; falto de higiene.

unsatisfactory ['ʌnˌsætis'fæktəri] *adj* poco satisfactorio, ria.

unsatisfied ['ʌn'sætisfaid] *adj* insatisfecho, cha (not satisfied) ‖ poco convencido, da (*about* de) ‖ insatisfecho, cha (appetite, etc.) ‖ no saldado, da; no liquidado, da (debts).

unsatisfying ['ʌn'sætisfaiiŋ] *adj* poco satisfactorio, ria ‖ insuficiente (insufficient).

unsaturated ['ʌn'sætʃəreitid] *adj* no saturado, da.

unsavoury; US **unsavory** ['ʌn'seivəri] *adj* desagradable (in smell or taste) ‖ insípido, da (tasteless) ‖ infame, deshonroso, sa (morally offensive) ‖ indeseable (person) ‖ sospechoso, sa; dudoso, sa (business).

unsay* ['ʌn'sei] *vt* desdecirse de (what one has said).
— OBSERV Pret y pp ***unsaid***.

unscathed ['ʌn'skeiðd] *adj* ileso, sa; indemne, sano y salvo; *to come out of an accident unscathed* salir ileso de un accidente.

unscheduled ['ʌn'ʃedjuːl] *adj* imprevisto, ta (event).

unscholarly ['ʌn'skɔləli] *adj* poco erudito, ta ‖ impropio de un erudito.

unschooled ['ʌn'skuːld] *adj* ignorante ‖ natural, innato, ta (feeling) ‖ no instruido, da (not schooled).

unscientific ['ʌnˌsaiən'tifik] *adj* poco científico, ca.

unscramble ['ʌn'skræmbl] *vt* descifrar (a message).

unscreened ['ʌn'skriːnd] *adj* no protegido, da (unprotected) ‖ descubierto, ta (uncovered) ‖ sin cribar (coal) ‖ sin interrogar (refugees) ‖ sin adaptar para el cine.

unscrew ['ʌn'skruː] *vt* destornillar, desatornillar.

unscripted ['ʌn'skriptid] *adj* improvisado, da (talk, speech).

unscrupulous [ʌn'skruːpjuləs] *adj* poco escrupuloso, sa; sin escrúpulos.

unscrupulously [-li] *adv* sin escrúpulos.

unscrupulousness [-nis] *n* falta *f* de escrúpulos.

unseal ['ʌn'siːl] *vt* abrir (a letter) ‖ FIG abrir (eyes).

unsearched [ʌn'səːtʃt] *adj* sin registrar (ship, luggage, etc.).

unseasonable [ʌn'siːznəbl] *adj* impropio de la estación (weather) ‖ que no es del tiempo (fruit) ‖ FIG inoportuno, na; poco a propósito (act, comment).

unseasoned [ʌn'siːznd] *adj* CULIN sin sazonar (not seasoned) ‖ no maduro, ra, inmaduro, ra (immature, unripe) ‖ verde (timber, wine) ‖ FIG inexperimentado, da; poco maduro, ra (inexperienced) ‖ MIL no aguerrido, da.

unseat ['ʌn'siːt] *vt* desarzonar, derribar (a rider) ‖ quitar el puesto a (from a job) ‖ destituir (an official) ‖ derribar, echar abajo (a government) ‖ quitar el escaño a (a Member of Parliament).

unseaworthy ['ʌn'siːˌwəːði] *adj* que no se puede navegar, innavegable (boat).

unseconded ['ʌn'sekəndid] *adj* no apoyado, da (motion) ‖ no secundado, da; no asistido, da (person).

unsecured ['ʌnsi'kjuəd] *adj* mal fijado, da (badly secured) ‖ COMM no respaldado, da (loan).

unseeded ['ʌn'siːdid] *adj* SP no preseleccionado, da (player).

unseeing ['ʌn'siːiŋ] *adj* ciego, ga; que no ve ‖ vago, ga (look).

unseemliness [ʌn'siːmlinis] *n* impropiedad *f*.

unseemly [ʌn'siːmli] *adj* indecoroso, sa (indecorous) ‖ impropio, pia (*in* de) (unsuitable).

unseen ['ʌn'siːn] *adj* sin ser visto; *he entered unseen* entró sin ser visto ‖ inadvertido, da; *several mistakes passed unseen* varios errores pasaron inadvertidos ‖ no visto, ta (not seen) ‖ oculto, ta (hidden) ‖ invisible (invisible) ‖ a libro abierto (translation).
◆ *n* traducción *f* a libro abierto (translation) ‖ lo invisible.

unselfish ['ʌn'selfiʃ] *adj* desinteresado, da; falto de egoísmo, generoso, sa.

unselfishly ['ʌn'selfiʃli] *adv* desinteresadamente.

unselfishness [-nis] *n* desinterés *m*, falta *f* de egoísmo, generosidad *f*.

unsellable ['ʌn'seləbl] *adj* invendible.

unserviceable ['ʌn'səːvisəbl] *adj* inservible, inutilizable (thing) ‖ poco servicial (person).

unset ['ʌn'set] *adj* no cuajado, da (jelly) ‖ no fraguado, da (concrete) ‖ no fijado, da (not fixed) ‖ no engastado, da; no engarzado, da; sin montar (precious stone).

unsettle ['ʌn'setl] *vt* perturbar (a person, plans, weather) ‖ desequilibrar (a person's mind) ‖ desquiciar, trastornar (institutions) ‖ *to unsettle one's stomach* sentarle mal a uno.

unsettled [-d] *adj* perturbado, da (perturbed) ‖ intranquilo, la (worried) ‖ agitado, da (country) ‖ desequilibrado, da (unbalanced) ‖ inestable (not stable) ‖ irresoluto, ta; indeciso, sa (irresolute) ‖ molesto, ta (uncomfortable); *to feel unsettled* sentirse molesto ‖ inseguro, ra; incierto, ta (weather) ‖ pendiente (question, matter) ‖ sin colonizar (uninhabited) ‖ sin domicilio fijo ‖ COMM por pagar, pendiente, sin saldar (account).

unsettling [-iŋ] *adj* inquietante.

unsew* ['ʌn'səu] *vt* descoser.
— OBSERV Pret ***unsewed***; pp ***unsewn, unsewed***.

unsewn ['ʌn'səun] *pp* ⟶ **unsew.**

unsex ['ʌn'seks] *vt* quitar el instinto sexual a.

unshackle ['ʌn'ʃækl] *vt* desencadenar (a prisoner) ‖ destrabar (a horse).

unshakable; unshakeable [ʌn'ʃeikəbl] *adj* firme, inquebrantable.

unshaken ['ʌn'ʃeikən] *adj* firme, impertérrito, ta (person) ‖ que no vacila, firme (faith).

unshaped ['ʌn'ʃeipt] *adj* sin forma, informe.

unshapely ['ʌn'ʃeipli] *adj* feo, a (ugly) ‖ deforme, mal proporcionado, da (badly proportioned).

unsharable; unshareable ['ʌn'ʃɛərəbl] *adj* incompartible.

unshaven ['ʌn'ʃeivn] *adj* sin afeitar.

unsheathe ['ʌn'ʃiːð] *vt* desenvainar (a sword, etc.).

unshell ['ʌn'ʃel] *adj* descascarar.

unsheltered ['ʌn'ʃeltəd] *adj* sin protección ‖ expuesto, ta (*from* a) (exposed).

unship ['ʌn'ʃip] *vt* MAR desembarcar, descargar (to unload) | desmontar (rudder) | quitar (mast) | desarmar (oars).

unshod ['ʌn'ʃɔd] *adj* descalzo, za (person) ‖ desherrado, da (a horse).
◆ *pret/pp* ⟶ **unshoe.**

unshoe* ['ʌn'ʃuː] *vt* desherrar (a horse).
— OBSERV Pret y pp ***unshod***.

unshorn ['ʌn'ʃɔːn] *adj* intonso, sa (person) ‖ no esquilado, da (sheep).

unshrinkable ['ʌn'ʃriŋkəbl] *adj* inencogible, que no puede encogerse.

unshrinking [ʌn'ʃriŋkiŋ] *adj* impávido, da (fearless).

unshroud ['ʌn'ʃraud] *vt* quitar la mortaja a (a dead person) ‖ FIG descubrir, revelar (sth.).

unsighted ['ʌn'saitid] *adj* que no puede ver, que no ve; *the referee was unsighted* el árbitro no podía ver ‖ que no está a la vista (ship) ‖ sin mira (gun).

unsightliness [ʌn'saitlinis] *n* fealdad *f*.

unsightly [ʌn'saitli] *adj* feo, a; desagradable a la vista, antiestético, ca.

unsigned ['ʌn'saind] *adj* sin firmar, no firmado, da.

unsingable ['ʌn'siŋəbl] *adj* incantable.

unsized ['ʌn'saizd] *adj* desencolado, da; sin apresto (paper).

unskilful; US **unskillful** ['ʌn'skilful] *adj* torpe, desmañado, da; poco hábil, inhábil.

unskilled ['ʌn'skild] *adj* no cualificado, da; no especializado, da; *unskilled worker* obrero no cualificado ‖ no especializado, da; *unskilled work* trabajo no especializado ‖ inexperto, ta (not skilled).

unskimmed ['ʌn'skimd] *adj* sin desnatar; *unskimmed milk* leche sin desnatar.

unsling* ['ʌn'sliŋ] *vt* descolgar ‖ MAR quitar de la eslinga.
— OBSERV Pret y pp ***unslung***.

unslung ['ʌn'slʌŋ] *pret/pp* ⟶ **unsling.**

unsmokable ['ʌn'sməukəbəl] *adj* infumable.

unsmooth ['ʌn'smuːð] *adj* desigual (road) ‖ rugoso, sa; áspero, ra (surface).

unsociability ['ʌnˌsəuʃə'biliti] *n* insociabilidad *f*.

unsociable [ʌn'səuʃəbl] *adj* insociable.

unsocial [ʌn'səuʃəl] *adj* insociable, insocial.

unsold ['ʌn'səuld] *adj* no vendido, invendido, da; sin vender ‖ *unsold copies* remanente *m* de ejemplares sin vender (books, magazines, etc.).

unsolder ['ʌn'sɔldə*] *vt* desoldar.

unsolicited ['ʌnsə'lisitid] *adj* no solicitado, da (not solicited) ‖ espontáneo, a (spontaneous).

unsolvable [ʌn'sɔevəbl] *adj* insoluble, irresoluble.

unsolved ['ʌn'sɔlvd] *adj* sin resolver, no resuelto, ta (problem).

unsophisticated ['ʌnsə'fistikeitid] *adj* sencillo, lla; no sofisticado, da (not sophisticated) || COMM puro, ra; no adulterado, da (unadulterated) || FIG ingenuo, nua (naïve).

unsought ['ʌn'sɔːt] *adj* espontáneo, a (spontaneous) || sin solicitar, no solicitado (unsolicited) || no buscado, da (not looked for).

unsound ['ʌn'saund] *adj* enfermizo, za (not physically sound) || demente (not mentally sound) || corrompido, da (not morally sound) || defectuoso, sa; imperfecto, ta (goods) || podrido, da (fruit) || poco sólido, da; *the foundations are unsound* los cimientos son poco sólidos; *the ice is unsound* el hielo es poco sólido || ligero, ra (sleep) || COMM poco seguro, ra (business) || FIG falso, sa; equivocado, da; erróneo, a (ideas, opinions).

unsoundable [-əbl] *adj* insondable.

unsoundness [-nis] *n* lo defectuoso || falta *f* de solidez || falsedad *f*, equivocación *f*.

unsparing [ʌn'spɛəriŋ] *adj* pródigo, ga; generoso, sa (without reserve); *unsparing in his praise* pródigo de *or* en alabanzas || incansable (tireless) || sin piedad, despiadado, da (*of* para) (without mercy) || — *to be unsparing in one's efforts to* no regatear ningún esfuerzo para || *to be unsparing of, to make unsparing use of* no escatimar.

unspeakable [ʌn'spiːkəbl] *adj* indecible, inexpresable, inenarrable (ineffable) || incalificable (very bad).

unspecialized ['ʌn'speʃəlaizd] *adj* sin especializar, no especializado, da.

unspecified ['ʌn'spesifaid] *adj* no especificado, da; sin especificar.

unspent ['ʌn'spent] *adj* no gastado, da.

unsplinterable ['ʌn'splintərəbl] *adj* inastillable.

unspoiled ['ʌn'spɔild]; **unspoilt** ['ʌn'spɔilt] *adj* sin estropear (not marred or damaged) || no mimado, da (a child) || no podrido, da (food).

unspoken ['ʌn'spəukən] *adj* tácito, ta; *an unspoken agreement* un acuerdo tácito || *unspoken word* palabra sobreentendida.

unsporting ['ʌn'spɔːtiŋ]; **unsportsmanlike** ['ʌn'spɔːtsmənlaik] *adj* antideportivo, va.

unspotted ['ʌn'spɔtid] *adj* sin mancha, inmaculado, da; sin tacha (free from moral stain) || ZOOL sin mancha.

unstable ['ʌn'steibl] *adj* inestable.

unstained ['ʌn'steind] *adj* sin manchas.

unstamped ['ʌn'stæmpt] *adj* sin franqueo, sin franquear, sin sello (a letter) || no acuñado, da (a coin) || sin sellar (a document) || no contrastado, da (gold).

unstated ['ʌn'steitid] *adj* no manifestado, da abiertamente.

unstatesmanlike ['ʌn'steitsmənlaik] *adj* indigno de un estadista.

unsteadiness ['ʌn'stedinis] *n* inestabilidad *f* (of furniture, the mind, prices) || inseguridad *f* (of footsteps, of position) || temblor *m* (of hand) || irregularidad *f* (of heartbeat) || FIG irresolución *f*, indecisión *f* (irresolution) | disipación *f* (of a young man).

unsteady ['ʌn'stedi] *adj* inestable (furniture) || inseguro, ra; vacilante (footsteps) || inseguro, ra; incierto, ta (position) || tembloroso, sa (light) || poco firme (hand) || inestable (mentally unstable) || COMM fluctuante (the stock market) || irregular (not constant); *an unsteady pulse* un pulso irregular || variable (barometer) || variable, cambiante (wind) || FIG irresoluto, ta; indeciso, sa (irresolute) | inconstante (affection) | poco serio, ria (conduct) || *to be unsteady on one's feet* titubear.

unstick* ['ʌn'stik] *vt* despegar || *to come unstuck* despegarse, desprenderse (sth.), venirse abajo (plans).

— OBSERV Pret y pp ***unstuck***.

unstinted [ʌn'stintid] *adj* sin límites, ilimitado, da.

unstinting [ʌn'stintiŋ] *adj* pródigo, ga || — *to be unstinting in one's praise* ser pródigo de alabanzas, no escatimar las alabanzas || *we were unstinting in our efforts to locate him* no regateamos ningún esfuerzo para dar con él.

unstitch [ʌn'stitʃ] *vt* descoser || *to come unstitched* descoserse.

unstop ['ʌn'stɔp] *vt* destaponar (to take a stopper from) || desatascar (to free from obstruction).

unstoppable [-əbl] *adj* incontenible || SP imparable (a shot).

unstrap ['ʌn'stræp] *vt* desatar la correa.

unstressed ['ʌn'strest] *adj* sin acentuar, átono, na; inacentuado, da.

unstring* ['ʌn'striŋ] *vt* desensartar (beads) || MUS aflojar las cuerdas de (to loosen) | desencordar, quitar las cuerdas de (to remove) || desatar las cuerdas de (to untie) || aflojar (a bow) || trastornar (s.o.'s nerves) || trastornar, desquiciar (s.o.).

— OBSERV Pret y pp ***unstrung***.

unstructured ['ʌn'strʌktʃəd] *adj* poco estructurado, da (activity).

unstrung ['ʌn'strʌŋ] *pret/pp* → **unstring.**

unstuck ['ʌn'stʌk] *pret/pp* → **unstick.**

unstudied ['ʌn'stʌdid] *adj* ignorante (unlearned) || natural, sin afectación (unaffected, not artificial) || sin estudiar (subject) || *unstudied in* sin conocimientos de.

unsubmissive ['ʌnsəb'misiv] *adj* insumiso, sa.

unsubstantial ['ʌnsəb'stænʃəl] *adj* insustancial || sin fundamento (unfounded) || imaginario, ria; irreal (unreal) || ligero, ra (light).

unsubstantiated ['ʌnsəb'stænʃieitid] *adj* no confirmado, da, sin confirmar (statement, story).

unsuccessful [-ful] *adj* sin éxito; *an unsuccessful song* una canción sin éxito || fracasado, da (a person, a negotiation, etc.) || fallido, da; infructuoso, sa; fracasado, da; sin éxito; *an unsucessful attempt* un intento fallido || vano, na; infructuoso, sa (effort) || suspendido, da (in an examination); *an unsuccessful candidate* un candidato suspendido || fracasado, da; vencido, da; derrotado, da (candidate in election) || *to be unsuccessful* fracasar, no tener éxito.

unsuccessfully [-fuli] *adv* sin éxito || en vano, infructuosamente.

unsuitability ['ʌn,sjuːtə'biliti] *n* impropiedad *f*, inadecuación *f* (of a thing) || inaptitud *f* (of a person) || inoportunidad *f* || inconveniencia *f*.

unsuitable ['ʌn'sjuːtəbl] *adj* incompetente, no apto, ta (person); *unsuitable for a position* no apto para un puesto || inadecuado, da; impropio, pia (thing); *it's an unsuitable place for the picture* es un sitio impropio para el cuadro || inconveniente (inconvenient); *an unsuitable time* una hora inconveniente || inoportuno, na (inopportune); *an unsuitable remark* una observación inoportuna.

unsuited ['ʌn'sjuːtid] *adj* no apto, ta (person); *unsuited for a position* no apto para un puesto || inadecuado, da; impropio, pia (thing); *unsuited for a job* inadecuado para un trabajo; *it's a place unsuited to the picture* es un sitio impropio para el cuadro || incompatible; *hobbies unsuited to his position in life* pasatiempos incompatibles con su situación || impropio, pia (unbecoming); *slovenliness unsuited to a man in his position* negligencia impropia de un hombre de su calidad.

unsullied ['ʌn'sʌlid] *adj* sin tacha, sin mancha.

unsung [ʌn'sʌŋ] *adj* no cantado || FIG no alabado, da; no celebrado, da (victory, etc.).

unsupported ['ʌnsə'pɔːtid] *adj* no apoyado, da; sin apoyo (person, amendment) || sin fundamento (statement).

unsure ['ʌn'ʃuə*] *adj* poco seguro, ra.

unsurmountable ['ʌnsə'mauntəbl] *adj* insuperable.

unsurpassable ['ʌnsə'pɑːsəbl] *adj* insuperable, inmejorable; *of unsurpassable quality* de calidad inmejorable.

unsurpassed ['ʌnsə'pɑːst] *adj* no superado, da; sin superar.

unsuspected ['ʌnsəs'pektid] *adj* insospechado, da || desconocido, da; ignorado, da || *the existence of this animal was unsuspected* se ignoraba la existencia de ese animal.

unsuspecting ['ʌnsəs'pektiŋ] *adj* confiado, da; poco suspicaz; *the unsuspecting victim was attacked from behind* la confiada víctima fue atacada por detrás || *to be unsuspecting of sth.* no sospechar algo.

unsustainable ['ʌnsəs'teinəbl] *adj* insostenible.

unswaddle ['ʌn'swɔdl] *vt* quitar los pañales a.

unsweetened ['ʌn'swiːtənd] *adj* no azucarado, da; sin azucarar.

unswerving ['ʌn'swəːviŋ] *adj* inquebrantable (faith, loyalty, etc.) || recto, ta (absolutely straight).

unsymmetrical ['ʌnsi'metrikəl] *adj* asimétrico, ca; disimétrico, ca.

unsympathetic ['ʌn,simpə'θetik] *adj* poco compasivo, va; sin compasión || indiferente; *he is not unsympathetic to your problem* su problema no le deja indiferente || falto de comprensión || — *he was unsympathetic to their appeal* no atendió su petición || *how can you be so unsympathetic?* ¿cómo puedes ser tan poco comprensivo?

unsystematic ['ʌn,sistə'mætik] *adj* sin sistema, poco metódico, ca.

untactful ['ʌn'tæktful] *adj* falto de tacto.

untainted ['ʌn'teintid] *adj* fresco, ca; no contaminado, da (food) || no corrompido, da (morally) || no mancillado, da (reputation).

untamable; untameable ['ʌn'teiməbl] *adj* indomable, indomesticable || FIG indomable.

untamed ['ʌn'teimd] *adj* indomado, da (animal).

untangle ['ʌn'tæŋgl] *vt* desenmarañar, desenredar.

untanned ['ʌn'tænd] *adj* sin curtir.

untapped ['ʌn'tæpt] *adj* sin explotar.

untarnished ['ʌn'tɑːniʃt] *adj* sin oxidar (a metal) || FIG sin mancha, no mancillado, da (reputation).

untasted ['ʌn'teistid] *adj* sin probar.

untaught ['ʌn'tɔːt] *pret/pp* → **unteach.**
◆ *adj* sin instrucción (person) || no enseñado, da (knowledge).

untaxed ['ʌn'tækst] *adj* libre *or* exonerado de impuestos.

unteach* ['ʌn'tiːtʃ] *vt* hacer olvidar.

— OBSERV Pret y pp ***untaught***.

unteachable ['ʌn'tiːtʃəbl] *adj* incapaz de aprender algo.

untellable ['ʌn'teləbl] *adj* incontable.

untempered [ʌn'tempəd] *adj* sin templar.

untenable [ʌn'tenəbl] *adj* insostenible, indefendible.

untenanted [ʌn'tenəntid] *adj* vacío, a; sin inquilino, desocupado, da.

untested [ʌn'testid] *adj* no probado, da (not tried out) || sin comprobar (not proved).

unthankful [ʌn'θæŋkful] *adj* ingrato, ta; desagradecido, da (not thankful) || ingrato, ta; *an unthankful task* una labor ingrata.

unthinkable [ʌn'θiŋkəbl] *adj* inimaginable, increíble, inconcebible (unimaginable) || inconcebible, impensable (out of the question).

unthinking [ʌn'θiŋkiŋ] *adj* irreflexivo, va.

unthought [ʌn'θɔːt] *adj* *unthought of* inesperado, da; imprevisto, ta.

unthread [ʌn'θred] *vt* desenhebrar, desensartar (a needle) || desensartar (beads) || deshebrar (cloth) || FIG desenmarañar.

unthrifty [ʌn'θrifti] *adj* despilfarrador, ra.

untidiness [ʌn'taidinis] *n* desorden *m* (disorder) || desaseo *m*, desaliño *m* (of dress, of appearance, etc.).

untidy [ʌn'taidi] *adj* desordenado, da; desarreglado, da; en desorden (room); *the house was untidy* la casa estaba desordenada || desaseado, da; desaliñado, da (dress, person's appearance) || desgreñado, da (hair) || desordenado, da (person).

untie [ʌn'tai] *vt* desatar; *to untie a knot, a parcel* desatar un nudo, un paquete || soltar; *to untie a dog* soltar un perro || MAR desamarrar; *to untie a boat* desamarrar un barco.
◆ *vi* desatarse.

until [ən'til] *prep* hasta; *we waited until Thursday* esperamos hasta el jueves || — *until now* hasta ahora || *until that time, until then* hasta entonces || *until when?* ¿hasta cuándo?
◆ *conj* hasta que; *wait until he has gone* espera hasta que se vaya; *he insisted until he got it* insistió hasta que lo consiguió.
— OBSERV Whilst *hasta que* may be used to translate all examples of the conjunction *until*, in cases where the subject of the two verbs is the same person the use of *hasta* with the infinitive is also possible: *keep looking until you find it* sigue buscando hasta encontrarlo *or* hasta que lo encuentres.

untile [ʌn'tail] *vt* quitar las tejas de.

untillable [ʌn'tiləbl] *adj* AGR incultivable.

untilled [ʌn'tild] *adj* AGR inculto, ta; no cultivado, da; sin cultivar.

untimeliness [ʌn'taimlinis] *n* inoportunidad *f*; *the untimeliness of their intervention* la inoportunidad de su intervención.

untimely [ʌn'taimli] *adj* inoportuno, na (inopportune); *untimely question* cuestión inoportuna || prematuro, ra (death, birth, etc.) || temprano, na (fruit) || impropio de la estación (weather) || *at an untimely hour* a deshora.
◆ *adv* inoportunamente (inopportunely) || prematuramente (prematurely).

untiring [ʌn'taiəriŋ] *adj* incansable, infatigable; *untiring in one's work* incansable en el trabajo.

unto ['ʌntu] *prep* (ant) a; *render unto Caesar* dale al César || hasta; *unto this day* hasta la fecha || hacia (towards).

untold [ʌn'təuld] *adj* fabuloso, sa; incalculable (incalculably great); *untold riches* riqueza fabulosa; *untold quantities* cantidades incalculables || inaudito, ta (very great); *untold suffering* sufrimiento inaudito || indecible, inefable (unspeakable) || *his story remains untold* no se ha contado todavía su historia.

untouchable [ʌn'tʌtʃəbl] *adj/n* intocable.

untouched [ʌn'tʌtʃt] *adj* no tocado, da || sin tocar; *he left his food untouched* dejó la comida sin tocar; *to leave a subject untouched* dejar un tema sin tocar || no afectado, da; *untouched by the scandal* no afectado por el escándalo || sin retocar (photos) || insensible (*by* a) (unmoved) || no mermado, da (reputation) || ileso, sa; indemne (unharmed) || *people untouched by modern civilization* gente hasta la cual no ha llegado la civilización moderna.

untoward [ʌn'təuəd] *adj* insumiso, sa (unruly) || difícil de labrar (a material) || adverso, sa; contrario, ria; *untoward circumstances* circunstancias adversas || desafortunado, da; *an untoward accident* un accidente desafortunado || desgraciado, da; *an untoward life* una vida desgraciada || funesto, ta (event) || poco propicio, cia; poco favorable (season, weather) || inconveniente.

untowardness [-nis] *n* insumisión *f*, indocilidad *f* || adversidad *f*.

untraceable [ʌn'treisəbl] *adj* que no se puede encontrar, imposible de encontrar.

untrained [ʌn'treind] *adj* no cualificado, da; sin formación profesional (worker) || no amaestrado, da (animals) || inexperimentado, da; inexperto, ta (inexpert) || SP falto de entrenamiento, sin preparar.

untrammeled; untrammelled [ʌn'træməld] *adj* sin límites (not limited) || libre (*by* de).

untransferable ['ʌntræns'fəːrəbl] *adj* intransferible.

untranslatable ['ʌntræns'leitəbl] *adj* intraducible.

untransportable ['ʌntræns'pɔːtəbl] *adj* intransportable.

untraveled; untravelled ['ʌn'trævld] *adj* poco frecuentado, da (road) || que no ha viajado (person) || inexplorado, da; poco conocido, da (country).

untreated [ʌn'triːtid] *adj* que no está en tratamiento (patient, injury) || sin tratar (harmful chemicals).

untried [ʌn'traid] *adj* inexperto, ta; inexperimentado, da (inexperienced) || no probado, da (not tested) || JUR no juzgado, da || *to leave nothing untried* intentarlo todo.

untrimmed [ʌn'trimd] *adj* sin podar (hedge) || descuidado, da (garden) || sin cortar (hair, nails) || sin debastar (wood) || sin labrar (stone) || sin adorno (hat) || sin aderezo (meat).

untrod [ʌn'trɔd]; **untrodden** [ʌn'trɔdn] *adj* inexplorado, da (country) || sin pisar (snow, sand) || no trillado, da (path) || *untrodden forest* selva *f* virgen.

untroubled [ʌn'trʌbld] *adj* tranquilo, la (calm) || no molestado, da (not disturbed) || *untroubled by worries* sin preocupaciones.

untrue [ʌn'truː] *adj* falso, sa (not true) || erróneo, a; inexacto, ta (statement) || infiel, desleal (unfaithful) || TECH inexacto, ta (inaccurate) | torcido, da (grindstone).

untrussed [ʌn'trʌst] *adj* ARCH sin entramado (bridge) | sin armazón (roof) || CULIN sin atar (chicken).

untrustworthy [ʌn'strʌst,wəːði] *adj* poco seguro, ra; que no es de fiar (unreliable); *untrustworthy person* persona que no es de fiar; *untrustworthy information* información poco segura.

untruth [ʌn'truːθ] *n* mentira *f* (falsehood) || falsedad *f* (lack of truthfulness).

untruthful [-ful] *adj* mentiroso, sa (inclined to lie) || falso, sa (untrue).

untruthfulness [-fulnis] *n* falsedad *f*.

untune [ʌn'tjuːn] *vt* MUS desafinar (an instrument).

unturned [ʌn'təːnd] *adj* no vuelto, ta || FIG *to leave no stone unturned* no dejar piedra por mover.

untutored [ʌn'tjuːtəd] *adj* sin instrucción, ignorante (person) || no formado, da (mind) || *to be untutored in* ignorar, desconocer.

untwine [ʌn'twain] *vt/vi* → **untwist.**

untwist [ʌn'twist] *vt* destorcer; *to untwist a cable* destorcer un cable.
◆ *vi* destorcerse.

unusable [ʌn'juːzəbl] *adj* inutilizable.

unused [ʌn'juːzd] *adj* sin emplear, sin usar, nuevo, va (never having been used); *some unused canvases* unos lienzos sin emplear || que no se utiliza (not currently in use); *an unused warehouse* un almacén que no se utiliza || libre; *my flat in Paris is unused at the moment* mi piso en París está libre ahora || insusitado, da; desusado, da (word, expression).

unused [ʌn'juːst] *adj* no acostumbrado, da; *I am unused to it* no estoy acostumbrado a ello.

unusual [ʌn'juːʒuəl] *adj* extraño, ña; raro, ra; insólito, ta (peculiar, strange) || original (different, unique) || desacostumbrado, da; inhabitual; *to work with unusual enthusiasm* trabajar con un entusiasmo desacostumbrado || poco común, que se sale de lo corriente; *unusual event* acontecimiento poco común || excepcional, extraordinario, ria; *a scene of unusual beauty* un panorama de una belleza excepcional || poco usado, da; poco empleado, da (word).

unusually [ʌn'juːʒuəli] *adv* extraordinariamente; *unusually tall* extraordinariamente alto || *he was unusually attentive* fue más atento que de costumbre.

unutterable [ʌn'ʌtərəbl] *adj* indecible.

unvalued [ʌn'væljuːd] *adj* no valorado, da || FIG poco apreciado, da.

unvanquished [ʌn'væŋkwiʃt] *adj* invicto, ta.

unvaried [ʌn'vɛərid] *adj* poco variado, da.

unvarnished [ʌn'vɑːniʃt] *adj* no barnizado, da; sin barnizar (not varnished) || FIG sencillo, lla; puro, ra (plain, unembellished) || *the unvarnished truth* la verdad escueta, la pura verdad.

unvarying [ʌn'vɛəriiŋ] *adj* invariable.

unveil [ʌn'veil] *vt* quitar el velo a (a person) || destapar (an object) || descubrir, inaugurar (a statue) || descubrir, revelar (a secret) || descubrir (sth. hidden).

unveiling [ʌn'veiliŋ] *n* inauguración *f*, descubrimiento *m* (of a statue).

unventilated [ʌn'ventileitid] *adj* sin ventilación.

unverifiable [ʌn'verifaiəbl] *adj* incomprobable.

unversed [ʌn'vəːst] *adj* poco versado, da [en algo].

unviolated [ʌn'vaiəleitid] *adj* inviolado, da.

unvisited [ʌn'vizitid] *adj* no visitado, da.

unvoiced [ʌn'vɔist] *adj* no expresado, da || sordo, da (consonant) || mudo, da (vowel).

unvouched [ʌn'vautʃt] *adj* *unvouched for* no garantizado, da.

unwaged [ʌn'weidʒd] *adj* que no recibe sueldo (unemployed, working at home).

unwanted [ʌnwɔntid] *adj* no deseado, da; *unwanted children* niños no deseados || no solicitado, da; no pedido, da; *unwanted advice* consejos no solicitados || superfluo, a (superfluous) || — *to feel unwanted* darse cuenta de que su presencia no es deseada || *to have some unwanted magazines* tener unas revistas que no se quieren conservar *or* que estorban.

unwarlike [ʌn'wɔːlaik] *adj* pacífico, ca.

unwarned [ʌn'wɔːnd] *adj* sin aviso.

unwarped [ʌn'wɔːpt] *adj* no alabeado, da (wood) || FIG torcido, da (mind).

unwarrantable [ʌn'wɔrəntəbl] *adj* injustificable.

unwarranted [ʌn'wɔrəntid] *adj* injustificable (unable to be justified) || injustificado, da (without justification) || sin garantía (not guaranteed).

unwary [ʌn'wɛəri] *adj* imprudente (rash, careless) || incauto, ta (incautious).

unwashed [ʌn'wɔʃt] *adj* sin lavar, sucio, cia || *the Great Unwashed* el populacho.

unwatered [ʌn'wɔːtəd] *adj* sin agua (a town) || sin regar (garden) || de secano (without rain or irrigation); *unwatered country* tierras de secano || no diluido, da (not diluted) || no aguado, da (wine) || sin abrevar (cattle) || sin aguas (silk).

unwavering [ʌn'weivəriŋ] *adj* constante, firme (steady) || inquebrantable; *unwavering fortitude* valor inquebrantable || fijo, ja; *unwavering gaze* mirada fija.

unwearable [ʌn'wɛərəbl] *adj* que no se puede llevar.

unwearied [ʌn'wiərid] *adj* incansable (tireless) || no cansado, da (not weary).

unweave* [ʌn'wiv] *vt* destejer.
— OBSERV Pret ***unwove***; pp ***unwoven***.

unwed [ʌn'wed] *adj* soltero, ra.

unwedge [ʌn'wedʒ] *vt* desencajar (a machine part).

unwelcome [ʌn'welkəm] *adj* importuno, na; molesto, ta; *an unwelcome guest* un invitado molesto || mal recibido, da (a visitor) || inoportuno, na; *an unwelcome visit* una visita inoportuna || desagradable; *unwelcome news* una noticia desagradable || incómodo, da; *to make s.o. feel unwelcome* hacer que alguien se sienta incómodo || *a little help wouldn't be unwelcome* no me (te, etc.) vendría mal un poco de ayuda.

unwell [ʌn'wel] *adj* malo, la (not well, sick).

unwept [ʌn'wept] *adj* no llorado, da (an event).

unwholesome [ʌn'həulsəm] *adj* malsano, na (climate, food, ideas).

unwieldy [ʌn'wiːldi] *adj* poco manejable, difícil de manejar (hard to handle) || voluminoso, sa; abultado, da (cumbersome) || pesado, da (heavy) || torpe (clumsy).

unwilled [ʌn'wild] *adj* involuntario, ria.

unwilling [ʌn'wiliŋ] *adj* no dispuesto, ta; *to be unwilling to do sth.* no estar dispuesto a hacer algo || (hecho, dicho, etc.) de mala gana; *an unwilling confession* una confesión hecha de mala gana || — *to be unwilling that* no estar dispuesto a que, no querer que (with subjunctive) || *we are unwilling for you to go* no queremos que vayas.

unwillingly [-li] *adv* de mala gana, a disgusto.

unwillingness [-nis] *n* desgana *f*, mala voluntad *f*.

unwind* [ʌn'waind] *vt* desenrollar (sth. that is wound up) || devanar (a skein) || FIG desenredar, desembrollar (to sort out).
◆ *vi* desenrollarse (to become unwound) || devanarse (a skein) || FIG relajarse (to relax).
— OBSERV Pret y pp ***unwound***.

unwinking [ʌn'wiŋkiŋ] *adj* que no parpadea (eyes, person) || fijo, ja (stare, attention).

unwisdom [ʌn'wizdəm] *n* imprudencia *f* || insensatez *f*, falta *f* de sensatez.

unwise [ʌn'waiz] *adj* imprudente (foolish) || insensato, ta (senseless) || poco aconsejable, desaconsejado, da (ill-advised); *it is unwise to go swimming after a meal* es poco aconsejable bañarse después de comer.

unwished [ʌn'wiʃt] *adj* *unwished for* no deseado, da (not wanted), no solicitado, da (unasked for).

unwithering [ʌn'wiðəriŋ] *adj* inmarcescible, inmarchitable.

unwitting [ʌn'witiŋ] *adj* hecho sin querer, involuntario, ria (not intentional) || *unwitting of* inconsciente de.

unwittingly [-li] *adv* inconscientemente, sin querer (unconsciously) || sin querer, involuntariamente (unintentionally).

unwomanly [ʌn'wumənli] *adj* poco femenino, na (not feminine) || impropio de una mujer (not befitting a woman).

unwonted [ʌn'wəuntid] *adj* extraño, ña; raro, ra; insólito, ta (unusual) || no acostumbrado, da; desacostumbrado, da (unaccostumed).

unwordable [ʌn'wəːdəbl] *adj* indecible, inexpresable.

unworkable [ʌn'wəːkəbl] *adj* inexplotable (a mine) || irrealizable (not possible); *an unworkable plan* un proyecto irrealizable.

unworldly [ʌn'wəːldli] *adj* no mundano, na; poco mundano, na (unconcerned with worldly values) || espiritual (spiritual) || celestial (heavenly) || ingenuo, nua (naïve).

unworn [ʌn'wɔːn] *adj* nuevo, va (clothes); *an unworn jacket* una chaqueta nueva || no usado, da (not worn out) || no trillado, da; original.

unworthiness [ʌn'wəːðinis] *n* falta *f* de mérito || indignidad *f*, lo indigno (of action, of thought).

unworthy [ʌn'wəːði] *adj* no digno, indigno, na; *unworthy of an honour* indigno de un honor; *conduct unworthy of a gentleman* conducta indigna de un caballero || de poco mérito (worthless) || despreciable (contemptible) || *unworthy of attention* que no merece atención.

unwound [ʌn'waund] *pret/pp* —→ **unwind.**

unwounded [ʌn'wuːndid] *adj* ileso, sa.

unwove [ʌn'wɔv] *pret* —→ **unweave.**

unwoven [ʌn'wɔvən] *pp* —→ **unweave.**

unwrap [ʌn'ræp] *vt* desenvolver || deshacer, desempaquetar (a parcel).

unwrinkle [ʌn'riŋkəl] *vt* desarrugar.

unwritten [ʌn'ritn] *adj* no escrito, ta (not written) || blanco, ca (paper) || oral; *unwritten tradition* tradición oral || JUR *unwritten law* derecho consuetudinario (common law).
— OBSERV En Gran Bretaña *unwritten law* se aplica a las conveniencias sociales, que no reconoce forzosamente la ley, mientras que en Estados Unidos indica más bien el derecho a vengar una ofensa con sangre.

unyielding [ʌn'jiːldiŋ] *adj* inflexible, inquebrantable.

unyoke [ʌn'jəuk] *vt* desuncir || FIG separar.

unzip [ʌn'zip] *vt* bajar la cremallera de.

up [ʌp] *adv* hacia arriba (upwards); *to look up* mirar hacia arriba || arriba; *all the way up* hasta arriba; *what are you doing up there?* ¿qué estás haciendo allá arriba?; *hands up!, up with your hands!* ¡manos arriba! || para arriba; *from fifty pesos up* de cincuenta pesos para arriba || en el aire (in the air) || al aire; *to throw sth. up* lanzar algo al aire || más fuerte, más alto; *speak up* habla más fuerte || levantado, da (out of bed) || crecido, da (river, corn, etc.) || alto, ta (tide) || entendido, da; competente; *to be well up in history* ser muy entendido en historia || fuerte; *he is up in chemistry* está fuerte en química || enterado, da; informado, da; *to be up on the news* estar enterado de las noticias || de pie, en pie (standing) || completamente; *to fill up a glass* llenar completamente un vaso || levantado, da; en obras; *the road is up* la carretera está levantada || hacia el norte (northwards) || en la universidad; *when he was up* cuando estaba en la universidad || — *close up to* muy cerca de || *face up* boca arriba || *from... up* a partir de *or* de... para arriba; *from three dollars up* a partir de tres dólares, de tres dólares para arriba; desde; *from my youth up* desde mi juventud || *halfway up* a la mitad del camino || *have you ever been up in an aeroplane?* ¿has subido ya en un avión? || *he is up at daybreak* se levanta al alba || *high up* muy arriba || FIG *his blood was up* se le subía la sangre a la cabeza || *his leave is up* acabó su permiso || *I am up for the day* he venido a pasar el día || *I'll play you fifty up* jugamos hasta cincuenta || *it is not up to much* no vale gran cosa || *it's all up* se acabó todo || *it's all up with him* está perdido, ya no le queda esperanza || *it's up to you* eres tú quien tienes que decidir, en tus manos está la decisión, depende de ti || *it's up to you to* eres tú quien tienes que, a ti te toca; *it's up to you to choose* eres tú quien tienes que escoger, a ti te toca escoger || *let us be up and doing* pongámonos a hacer algo || *meat is up again* la carne ha subido otra vez || *my room is four flights up* mi habitación está en el cuarto piso || *road up* (atención) obras (sign) || *the blinds are up* se han subido las persianas || *the curtain is up* se ha levantado el telón (in the theatre) || *the curtains are up* las cortinas están colgadas || FIG *the game is up!* ¡se acabó! || *the House is up* el Parlamento no celebra sesión *or* no se reúne || *the moon is up* ha salido la luna || *the plane is up* el avión está en vuelo || *there's sth. up* algo pasa || *the window is up* el cristal está cerrado (in carriage), la ventana está cerrada (sash window) || *this isn't up to standard* no satisface los requisitos || *this side up* este lado hacia arriba (on a parcel) || *time is up* es la hora (de acabar, cerrar, etc.), se acabó el tiempo reglamentario || FAM *to be hard up* no tener un céntimo || SP *to be one goal up* ir ganando por un gol || *to be up against* enfrentarse con || *to be up against it* tener mala suerte (unlucky), estar en un apuro (in trouble) || *to be up all night* no acostarse en toda la noche || *to be up for* presentarse para (approval), ser procesado por (at court) || *to be up in* ser un experto en || *to be up in arms* haberse levantado en armas (to fight), poner el grito en el cielo, sublevarse (against an abuse) || *to be up to anything* ser capaz de cualquier cosa || *to be up to s.o.* poder competir *or* rivalizar con uno || *to be up to* ser capaz *or* estar en condiciones de hacer (able), estar a la altura de (equal to); *he is not up to his job* no está a la altura de su trabajo; estar haciendo (busy); *what are you up to?* ¿qué está haciendo?; estar tramando; *the baby is quiet, I wonder what he is up to* el niño está callado, ¿qué estará tramando?; ir por; *where were we up to?* ¿por dónde íbamos? || *to come* o *to go up to* acercarse a || *to feel up to* sentirse capaz de, estar en condiciones de; *do you feel up to making this trip?* ¿se siente usted capaz de hacer este viaje? || *to go up to town* ir a la capital || *to hold o.s. up* mantenerse derecho || *to put an umbrella up* abrir un paraguas || *to stay up all night with a sick man* velar a un enfermo toda la noche || *to walk up and down* ir de un lado para otro, ir de acá para allá || *up!* ¡arriba! || *up above* arriba || *up against, up beside* al lado de, junto a (next to) || *up and about* haciendo vida normal, de nuevo en pie (after an illness) || *up and doing* activo, va; ocupado, da || *up and down* de arriba abajo || *up for president* candidato a la presidencia || JUR *up for trial* ante el tribunal || *up north* hacia *or* en el norte || *up to* hasta; *up to this day* hasta la fecha; *he earns anything up to twenty pounds a week* gana hasta veinte libras por semana || *up to date* hasta la fecha, hasta hoy || *up to now* hasta ahora || *up to one's*

old tricks haciendo de las suyas || *up went the flag* izaron la bandera || *up with X!* ¡viva X!, ¡arriba X! || *what's up?* ¿qué pasa? || *what's up with you?* ¿qué te pasa? || *we are well up in our work* vamos muy bien en nuestro trabajo.
◆ *prep* arriba; *up the river* río arriba; *up the street* calle arriba || en; *is there a restaurant up the Eiffel tower?* ¿hay un restaurante en la Torre Eiffel? || en lo alto de, arriba de (on the top of) || contra; *up the wind* contra el viento || en el fondo de; *up the yard* en el fondo del patio || — *further up the street* más allá en la calle || *halfway up the street* a la mitad de la calle || *to walk up and down the room* pasearse a lo largo y a lo ancho de la habitación.
◆ *adj* ascendente (train) || de subida (escalator).
◆ *n* *the ups and downs* los altibajos, las vicisitudes.
— OBSERV La palabra *up* acompaña frecuentemente un verbo cuyo sentido modifica o refuerza. Estos casos han sido tratados en el artículo correspondiente a cada uno de esos verbos. Por consiguiente *to stand up, to keep up with*, etc., se encontrarán en *stand, keep*, etc.

up [ʌp] *vt* levantar, alzar (to raise) || aumentar (to increase); *to up taxes* aumentar los impuestos.
◆ *vi* *to up and* coger y, de pronto; *he upped and left* cogió y se fue, de pronto se fue || *to up with* levantar; *to up with an axe* levantar un hacha.

up-anchor [-'æŋkə*] *vi* MAR levar anclas.

up-and-coming ['ʌpən'kʌmiŋ] *adj* joven y prometedor, joven y prometedora; *an up-and-coming artist* un artista joven y prometedor || que promete mucho; *the new mayor is an up-and-coming politician* el nuevo alcalde es un político que promete mucho.

up-and-down ['ʌpən'daun] *adj* vertical (motion) || variable (varying) || accidentado, da (uneven, eventful) || con altibajos (year) || fluctuante (prices).

up-and-up ['ʌpən'dʌp] *n* *to be on the up-and-up* ir cada vez mejor.

upbear* ['ʌp'bεə*] *vt* levantar (to raise up) || sostener (to support).
— OBSERV Pret ***upbore***; pp ***upborne***.

upbeat ['ʌpbi:t] *n* MUS tiempo *m* débil *or* no acentuado.
◆ *adj* FAM optimista, animado, da.

upbore ['ʌp'bɔ:*] *pret* → **upbear.**

upborne ['ʌp'bɔ:n] *pp* → **upbear.**

upbraid [ʌp'breid] *vt* regañar, reprender (to scold) || regañar, censurar, reprochar; *to upbraid s.o. for* o *with sth.* regañar a alguien por algo, reprochar *or* censurar algo a alguien.

upbraiding [-iŋ] *n* recriminación *f*, bronca *f* (*fam*); *to give s.o. an upbraiding* echarle una bronca a alguien, hacer recriminaciones a alguien.

upbringing ['ʌp,briŋiŋ] *n* educación *f*.

upcast ['ʌpkɑ:st] *adj* dirigido hacia arriba || *upcast eyes* ojos alzados al cielo.
◆ *n* MIN pozo *m* de ventilación (ventilation shaft) | corriente *f* de aire ascendente (current of air).

upcoming ['ʌp'kʌmiŋ] *adj* próximo, ma.

up-country ['ʌp'kʌntri] *adj* del interior.
◆ *adv* hacia el interior, tierra adentro.
◆ *n* interior *m*.

upcurrent ['ʌp'kʌrənt] *n* corriente *f* ascendente.

update ['ʌp'deit] *vt* US actualizar, poner al día (to bring up to date) | modernizar (to modernize).

upend ['ʌp'end] *vt* poner de pie.

up front ['ʌpfrʌnt] *adj* FAM directo, ta; franco, ca.
◆ *adv* por adelantado (payment).

upgrade ['ʌp'greid] *adj* ascendente (uphill).
◆ *n* cuesta *f*, pendiente *f* || FIG *to be on the upgrade* ir mejorando (getting better), aumentar (on the increase), prosperar (prospering), remontar la pendiente, recuperarse (after an illness).

upgrade ['ʌp'greid] *vt* ascender (to promote) || mejorar la calidad de (to improve the quality of).

upgrowing ['ʌp'grəuiŋ] *adj* que crece (child).

upgrowth ['ʌpgrəuθ] *n* desarrollo *m*.

upheaval ['ʌp'hi:vəl] *n* GEOL levantamiento *m* || FIG trastorno *m*, agitación *f*; *political upheaval* agitación política.

upheave [ʌp'hi:v] *vt* levantar.
◆ *vi* levantarse.

upheld [ʌp'held] *pret/pp* → **uphold.**

uphill ['ʌp'hil] *adj* ascendente (rising) || FIG penoso, sa; arduo, dua; duro, ra (task, struggle).
◆ *adv* cuesta arriba.
◆ *n* cuesta *f*, pendiente *f* (slope).

uphold* [ʌp'həuld] *vt* levantar (to lift up) || sostener, soportar (to keep from falling) || apoyar (to support); *the court upheld his claim* el tribunal apoyó su petición || sostener, mantener (an opinion) || mantener (one's position) || defender (to defend) || hacer respetar (the law).
— OBSERV Pret y pp ***upheld***.

upholder [-ə*] *n* defensor, ra (of an opinion) || partidario, ria (of a practice).

upholster [ʌp'həulstə*] *vt* tapizar (*in, with* con).

upholsterer [-rə*] *n* tapicero *m*.

upholstery [-ri] *n* tapicería *f* (material, work) || relleno *m* (padding).

upkeep ['ʌpki:p] *n* conservación *f*, mantenimiento *m*; *the upkeep of roads* la conservación de las carreteras || gastos *m pl* de mantenimiento (costs) || *in good upkeep* bien cuidado, da.

upland ['ʌplənd] *adj* elevado, da; alto, ta (region) || de la meseta, de la altiplanicie (people, vegetation).
◆ *n* meseta *f*, altiplanicie *f* [AMER altiplano *m*].

uplander [-ə*] *n* montañés, esa; persona *f* de la altiplanicie *or* de la meseta.

uplift ['ʌplift] *n* GEOL elevación *f* (rise) | levantamiento *m* (upheaval) | inspiración *f* | mejoramiento *m* (improvement) | reactivación *f* (of business) || *moral uplift* edificación *f*.

uplift [ʌp'lift] *vt* levantar (to lift up) | alzar, levantar (voice) | elevar (soul) | inspirar.

uplifting [-iŋ] *adj* edificante, enriquecedor, ra.

uploading ['ʌpləudiŋ] *n* INFORM telecarga *f*.

up-market ['ʌpmɑ:kit] *adj* de primera calidad (goods) || FAM elegante, distinguido, da (places, goods).

upmost ['ʌpməust] *adj* más alto, ta (in rank, in position, etc.) || predominante (in one's mind).

upon [ə'pɔn] *prep* → **on.**

upper ['ʌpə*] *adj* alto, ta; *the upper classes* las clases altas; *upper house* cámara alta || superior; *the upper jaw* la mandíbula superior || MUS agudo, da || GEOL superior || GEOGR alto, ta; *the Upper Amazon* el Alto Amazonas; *Upper Egypt* Alto Egipto; *Upper Volta* Alto Volta || — FIG *the upper crust* la flor y nata, la crema (the best of a social class) || *the upper end of the table* la cabecera de la mesa.
◆ *n* pala *f* (of a shoe) || US FAM litera *f* superior.
◆ *pl* US polainas *f* (gaiters) || FAM *on one's uppers* sin un céntimo, sin un cuarto.

uppercase [-keis] *n* PRINT caja *f* alta.
◆ *adj* mayúscula.

upper-class [-klɑ:s] *adj* de la clase alta.

uppercut [-kʌt] *n* SP «uppercut» *m*, gancho *m*.

upper hand [-'hænd] *n* dominio *m* || *to get* o *to have the upper hand* llevar ventaja, dominar.

uppermost [-məust] *adj* más alto, ta (in rank, in position, etc.); *the uppermost floor* el piso más alto || predominante (in one's mind).
◆ *adv* en primer lugar, en primer plano (in the first place) || — *face uppermost* boca arriba || *he said whatever came uppermost* dijo lo primero que le vino a la cabeza.

upperworks [-,wə:ks] *pl n* MAR obra *f sing* muerta.

uppish ['ʌpiʃ] *adj* FAM engreído, da; arrogante, presumido, da.

uppishness [-nis] *n* FAM engreimiento *m*, arrogancia *f*, presunción *f*.

uppity ['ʌpiti] *adj* FAM engreído, da; arrogante, presumido, da.

upraise [ʌp'reiz] *vt* levantar.

upright [ʌprait] *adj* vertical, derecho, cha (in a vertical position) || vertical, perpendicular (line) || FIG recto, ta; honrado, da (morally); *upright man* hombre honrado || de pie (on foot) || *upright piano* piano *m* vertical.
◆ *adv* en posición vertical || — *to hold o.s. upright* estar derecho, mantenerse derecho || *to sit upright on one's chair* mantenerse derecho en la silla.
◆ *n* pie *m* derecho, montante *m* (in carpentry) || piano *m* vertical (piano).
◆ *pl* SP postes *m* (in football).

uprightness [-nis] *n* verticalidad *f* || FIG rectitud *f*, honradez *f*.

uprisal [ʌp'raizəl] *n* levantamiento *m*.

uprise* [ʌp'raiz] *vi* levantarse || FIG sublevarse, alzarse.
— OBSERV Pret ***uprose***; pp ***uprisen***.

uprisen [ʌp'raizən] *pp* → **uprise.**

uprising [-iŋ] *n* levantamiento *m*, sublevación *f*, alzamiento *m*.

upriver ['ʌp'rivə] *adj/adv* río arriba.

uproar ['ʌprɔ:*] *n* alboroto *m*, tumulto *m* (dim) || alboroto *m* (disturbance) || — *the meeting ended in uproar* se armó mucho jaleo al final de la reunión, hubo protestas al final de la reunión || *the town is in an uproar* la ciudad está alborotada.

uproarious [ʌp'rɔ:riəs] *adj* tumultuoso, sa; ruidoso, sa || ruidoso, sa (laughter) || graciosísimo, ma; divertidísimo, ma (very funny) || *the class was getting uproarious* la clase empezaba a armar jaleo.

uproot [ʌp'ru:t] *vt* desarraigar; *the wind uprooted some trees* el viento desarraigó los árboles || FIG eliminar (to destroy utterly); *we must uproot poverty* tenemos que eliminar la pobreza | desarraigar (to remove from a place of residence).

uprose [ʌp'rəuz] *pret* → **uprise.**

uprush ['ʌprʌʃ] *n* subida *f* (upward movement) || arranque *m*; *an uprush of pity* un arranque de compasión.

upset [ʌp'set] *adj* trastornado, da (physically or mentally); *upset stomach* estómago trastornado || preocupado, da (worried) || enfadado, da; disgustado, da (*at* por) (angry) || indispuesto, ta (slightly sick) || desquiciado, da (nerves) || — *don't be so upset!* ¡no se preocupe tanto! || *upset price* precio mínimo, precio inicial.

upset ['ʌpset] *n* vuelco *m* (overturning) || indisposición *f*, malestar *m* (slight ailment) || trastorno *m* (of stomach) || trastorno *m* (emotional) || trastorno *m*, perturbación *f* (of plans, etc.) || molestia *f* (trouble) || dificultad *f* (difficulty) || resultado *m* inesperado (in sports).

upset* [ʌp'set] *vt* volcar (to tip over); *he upset the pitcher of water* volcó el jarro de agua || hacer zozobrar (a ship) || derramar (to spill) || desordenar, revolver, poner patas arriba; *he upset everything in the house* puso todo patas arriba en la casa || preocupar (to worry) || trastornar (physically or mentally) || desquiciar (s.o.'s nerves) || afectar; *his father's death upset him greatly* la muerte de su padre le afectó mucho || emocionar; *the least things upset him* cualquier cosa le emociona || disgustar, enfadar (to displease) || desconcertar (to disconcert) || desbaratar, trastornar; *to upset plans* desbaratar los planes || hacer fracasar (a plot) || derribar, derrocar, echar abajo (the government) || sentar mal; *beer upsets me* la cerveza me sienta mal || SP vencer inesperadamente || *to upset o.s.* preocuparse (to worry).
◆ *vi* volcar, volcarse.
— OBSERV Pret y pp ***upset***.

upsetting [ʌp'setiŋ] *adj* preocupante (worrying) || desconcertante (disconcerting).

upshot ['ʌpʃɔt] *n* resultado *m* || — *in the upshot* al fin y al cabo || *the upshot of it is that* total que.

upside ['ʌpsaid] *n* parte *f* superior.

upside down ['daun] *adv* al revés (in an inverted position); *you've put the tablecloth upside down* ha puesto el mantel al revés || FIG patas arriba (in great disorder); *the house was turned upside down* la casa estaba patas arriba || — *to turn everything upside down* revolverlo todo || *to turn upside down* poner boca abajo, volver (in an inverted position), poner patas arriba (in disorder).

upside-down [-'daun] *adj* al revés (in an inverted position) || FIG al revés; *an upside-down world* el mundo al revés || extraño, ña (strange).

upsilon [ju:p'sailən] *n* ypsilon *f*, ípsilon *f* (Greek letter).

upstage ['ʌpsteidʒ] *adv* en el fondo del escenario, hacia el fondo del escenario.
◆ *adj* FAM suficiente, presumido, da.

upstage ['ʌp'steidʒ] *vt* despreciar || THEATR *to upstage s.o.* atraer toda la atención del público a expensas de alguien.

upstairs ['ʌp'stɛəz] *adv* arriba, en el piso superior || — *to call s.o. upstairs* hacer subir a alguien || *to go upstairs* subir.
◆ *adj* de arriba, del piso superior || arriba de las escaleras.
◆ *n* piso *m* superior.

upstanding [ʌp'stændiŋ] *adj* honrado, da; recto, ta (honourable) || de pie (standing up straight) || robusto, ta (strong and healthy) || erizado, da; de punta (hairs) || fijo, ja (wages) || *to be upstanding* ponerse de pie, levantarse.

upstart ['ʌpstɑ:t] *adj/n* advenedizo, za; arribista.

upstate ['ʌpsteit] *adj* US interior.
◆ *n* US interior *m*.

upstream ['ʌpstri:m] *adv* río arriba, aguas arriba || más arriba; *I live upstream from the bridge* vivo más arriba del puente || a contracorriente (against the current).
◆ *adj* río arriba.

upstroke ['ʌpstrəuk] *n* trazo *m* ascendente (in writing) || TECH carrera *f* ascendente (an upward movement).

upsurge ['ʌpsə:dʒ] *n* arrebato *m*, acceso *m*; *an upsurge of anger* un arrebato de cólera || ola *f*; *an inflationary upsurge* una ola inflacionista || aumento *m* (increase).

upswept ['ʌpswept] *adj* alto, ta (hairdo).

upswing ['ʌpswiŋ] *n* movimiento *m* hacia arriba || FIG mejora *f* (improvement).

uptake ['ʌpteik] *n* cañón *m* de la chimenea || — FIG & FAM *to be quick on the uptake* ser rápido de comprensión | *to be slow on the uptake* ser duro de mollera *or* de entendederas.

upthrust ['ʌp'θrʌst] *n* GEOL levantamiento *m* || PHYS empuje *m* hacia arriba.

uptight ['ʌptait] *adj* FAM nervioso, sa; tenso, sa.

up-to-date ['ʌptə'deit] *adj* moderno, na; *an up-to-date house* una casa moderna || de moda (fashion); *it's an up-to-date dress* es un traje de moda || al día; *an up-to-date report* un informe al día || al tanto, al corriente; *to be up-to-date on the news* estar al tanto de las noticias.

up-to-the-minute ['ʌptu:θə'minit] *adj* de última hora; *up-to-the-minute news* noticias de última hora || muy al día; *an up-to-the-minute report* un informe muy al día || muy de moda (in fashion).

uptown ['ʌp'taun] *adv* US hacia *or* en la parte alta de la ciudad | hacia *or* en la parte residencial de la ciudad.
◆ *adj* US de la parte alta de la ciudad | de la parte residencial de la ciudad.

uptrend ['ʌp'trend] *n* tendencia *f* ascendente.

upturn [ʌp'tə:n] *n* mejora *f* (improvement) || aumento *m* (increase).

upturn [ʌp'tə:n] *vt* volcar (to turn over) || levantar, alzar; *to upturn one's eyes to the sky* levantar los ojos hacia el cielo || AGR voltear (ground).

upturned ['ʌptə:nd] *adj* *upturned nose* nariz respingona.

upward ['ʌpwəd] *adj* ascendente, hacia arriba; *an upward movement* un movimiento hacia arriba || COMM al alza (tendency).
◆ *adv* hacia arriba || — *and upward* y aún más || *face upward* boca arriba || *from the age of ten years upward* a partir de diez años || *the road runs upward* la carretera sube || *these shoes cost forty dollars and upward* estos zapatos cuestan a partir de cuarenta dólares *or* de cuarenta dólares para arriba || *to follow the river upward* ir río arriba || *upward of* más de; *upward of fifty pupils* más de cincuenta alumnos.

upwardly-mobile [-li,məubail] *adj* que escala posiciones socialmente.

upwards [-z] *adv* → **upward.**

upwind ['ʌpwind] *adj/adv* contra el viento.

uraemia [juə'ri:mjə] *n* MED uremia *f*.

Ural ['juərəl] *pr n* GEOGR Ural *m* (river).
◆ *pl* Urales *m* (mountains) || *Ural Mountains* montes *m* Urales.

Ural-Altaic [-æl'teiik] *adj* uraloaltaico, ca.

uranate ['juərəneit] *n* CHEM uranato *m*.

uranic [juə'rænik] *adj* CHEM uránico, ca || ASTR uranio, nia.

uraniferous [,juərə'nifərəs] *adj* uranífero, ra.

uranite ['juərənait] *n* CHEM uranita *f*.

uranium [juə'reinjəm] *n* CHEM uranio *m*.

Uranus ['juərənəs] *pr n* MYTH & ASTR Urano *m*.

urban ['ə:bən] *adj* urbano, na; *urban population* población urbana.

urbane [ə:'bein] *adj* urbano, na; cortés (polite).

urbanism ['ə:bənizəm] *n* urbanismo *m*.

urbanist ['ə:bənist] *n* urbanista *m* & *f*.

urbanity [ə:'bæniti] *n* urbanidad *f*, cortesía *f*.
◆ *pl* cumplidos *m*.

urbanization [,ə:bənai'zeiʃən] *n* urbanización *f*.

urbanize ['ə:bənaiz] *vt* urbanizar.

urchin ['ə:tʃin] *n* pilluelo *m*, golfillo *m* (mischievous boy) || chiquillo *m*, muchacho *m*, chaval *m*, rapaz *m* (young boy) || ZOOL erizo *m* de mar (sea urchin).

Urdu ['ə:du:] *n* urdu *m*.

urea ['juəriə] *n* urea *f*.

uremia [juə'ri:mjə] *n* MED uremia *f*.

uremic [juə'ri:mik] *adj* MED urémico, ca.

ureter [juə'ri:tə*] *n* ANAT uréter *m*.

ureteral [-əl] *adj* ANAT ureteral.

urethra [juə'ri:θrə] *n* ANAT uretra *f*.
— OBSERV El plural de *urethra* es *urethrae* o *urethras*.

urethral [-l] *adj* ANAT uretral.

urge [ə:dʒ] *n* impulso *m* (impulse) || vivo deseo *m* (persistent desire) || *to feel an urge to do sth.* tener muchas ganas de hacer algo, sentir un vivo deseo de hacer algo.

urge [ə:dʒ] *vt* exhortar (to exhort); *to urge s.o. to action* exhortar a alguien a la acción || incitar (to prompt); *to urge s.o. to spend* incitar a alguien al gasto; *hunger urged them to continue* el hambre les incitó a seguir || instar (to compel); *I urged him to stay* le insté a que se quedara || pedir con insistencia; *to urge reform* pedir una reforma con insistencia || requerir; *measures which urge attention* medidas que requieren atención || alegar (a reason) || recomendar (to recommend); *to urge sth. on s.o.* recomendar algo a alguien || preconizar, propugnar (to advocate); *the Minister urged a reform to stop inflation* el Ministro preconizó una reforma para frenar la inflación || — *to urge one's progress* apresurar el paso || *to urge s.o. on* animar a alguien.
◆ *vi* *to urge against* hacer objeciones contra || *to urge for* abogar por.

urgency ['ə:dʒənsi] *n* urgencia *f*; *the urgency of the matter* la urgencia del asunto; *this must be done with great urgency* esto se tiene que hacer con toda urgencia || petición *f* (demand) || *a matter of great urgency* un asunto muy urgente.

urgent ['ə:dʒənt] *adj* urgente, apremiante (pressing); *urgent need* necesidad apremiante || insistente (request) || porfiado, da; insistente; *an urgent creditor* un acreedor porfiado || importuno, na (importunate) || *it is urgent that I see him* me urge verle.

urgently ['ə:dʒəntli] *adv* urgentemente, con urgencia || *I need it urgently* me urge tenerlo.

uric ['juərik] *adj* MED úrico, ca.

urinal ['juərinəl] *n* urinario *m* (public lavatory) || orinal *m* (for bedridden people).

urinary ['juərinəri] *adj* ANAT urinario, ria; *urinary tract* vías urinarias.
◆ *n* urinario *m* (public lavatory).

urinate ['juərineit] *vi* orinar.

urination [,juəri'neiʃən] *n* MED micción *f*.

urine ['juərin] *n* MED orina *f*.

urinous ['juərinəs] *adj* urinario, ria.

urn [ə:n] *n* urna *f* (large vase) || recipiente *m* grande que sirve como tetera *or* cafetera.

urodela ['juərədi:lə] *pl n* ZOOL urodelos *m*.

urogenital [,juərəu'dʒenitəl] *adj* urogenital.

urography [juə'rɔgrəfi] *n* urografía *f*.

urologist [juə'rɔlədʒist] *n* urólogo, ga.

urology [juə'rɔlədʒi] *n* urología *f*.

uroscopy [juə'rɔskəpi] *n* MED uroscopia *f*.

Ursa Major ['ə:sə'meidʒə*] *pr n* ASTR Osa *f* Mayor.

Ursa Minor ['ə:sə'mainə*] *pr n* ASTR Osa *f* Menor.

ursine ['ə:sain] *adj* ZOOL osuno, na.

Ursuline ['ə:sjulain] *n* ursulina *f* (nun).

urtica ['ə:tikə] *n* BOT ortiga *f.*

urticaceae [ə:ti'keisii:] *pl n* BOT urticáceas *f.*

urticant ['ə:tikənt] *adj* urticante.

urticaria [,ə:ti'kɛəriə] *n* urticaria *f* (hives).

urubu [u:ru'bu:] *n* urubú *m* (black vulture).

Uruguay ['urugwai] *pr n* GEOGR Uruguay *m.*

Uruguayan [,uru'gwaiən] *adj/n* uruguayo, ya.

urunday ['urəndai] *n* urunday *m*, urundey *m.*

urus ['juərəs] *n* ZOOL uro *m* (aurochs).

us [ʌs] *pers pron* nos (direct object); *tell us what you did* dinos lo que hiciste; *they are calling us* nos están llamando ‖ nosotros, tras (after preposition); *he came with us* vino con nosotros; *three of us* tres de nosotros ‖ — *he could not believe that it was us* no podía creer que éramos nosotros ‖ *let us go, let's go* vámonos ‖ *pray for us* ruega por nos ‖ *there are three of us* somos tres ‖ *they are taller than us* son más altos que nosotros.

US ['ju:'es]; **USA** *abbr of [United States of America]* EE UU, Estados Unidos de América.

usability [,ju:zə'biliti] *n* utilidad *f.*

usable ['ju:zəbl] *adj* utilizable.

usage ['ju:sidʒ] *n* tratos *m pl*, tratamiento *m* (treatment); *ill usage* malos tratos ‖ usanza *f*, uso *m*, costumbre *f* (custom, established use) ‖ lenguaje *m* (parlance); *in fishermen's usage* en el lenguaje de los pescadores ‖ GRAMM uso *m.*

usance ['ju:zəns] *n* COMM plazo *m* concedido para pagar una letra de cambio.

use [ju:s] *n* uso *m*; *the good use of riches* el buen uso de las riquezas; *he lost the use of one arm* perdió el uso de un brazo; *to go wrong with use* estropearse con el uso ‖ empleo *m*, uso *m*; *the use of electricity to light our houses* el uso de la electricidad para iluminar nuestras casas ‖ manejo *m*, uso *m* (of a tool, etc.) ‖ empleo *m*, aplicación *f*; *the uses of plastics* las aplicaciones de los plásticos ‖ utilidad *f* (usefulness) ‖ derecho *m* al uso (the right to use) ‖ costumbre *f*, uso *m* (custom) ‖ REL rito *m* ‖ JUR usufructo *m*, disfrute *m* ‖ — *can I be of any use to you?* ¿puedo servirle en algo? ‖ *fit for use* en buen estado ‖ *for emergency use only* utilícese sólo en caso de emergencia ‖ *for external use* para uso externo ‖ *for use only in case of fire* utilícese sólo en caso de incendio ‖ *I have no further use for it* ya no me sirve para nada ‖ *I have the use of the bathroom only in the evening* sólo puedo usar el cuarto de baño por la noche ‖ *in common use, in current use, in everyday use* de uso corriente ‖ *instructions for use* instrucciones *f pl* para el uso, modo *m* de empleo ‖ *in use* en uso ‖ *it's no use your writing to me* es inútil que me escribas ‖ *machine that has been in use for ten years* máquina que se utiliza desde hace diez años ‖ *out of use* no funciona (lift) ‖ *to be in use* estar funcionando ‖ *to be of no use* no servir para nada ‖ *to be of use* servir ‖ *to be out of use* estar fuera de uso (machine, etc.), no utilizarse (not to be used), haber caído en desuso (word) ‖ *to come into use* empezar a utilizarse ‖ *to have no use for* no tener ocasión de emplear *or* usar *or* utilizar (to be useless), no necesitar (not to need), no soportar (to dislike); *I have no use for people who are always grumbling* no soporto a la gente que se queja constantemente ‖ *to have the use of* poder utilizar *or* usar ‖ *to make bad use of* usar *or* utilizar mal ‖ *to make good use of* hacer buen uso de, usar bien, aprovechar bien ‖ *to make great use of* emplear *or* utilizar mucho ‖ *to make use of* usar, utilizar, hacer uso de (to employ), aprovecharse de (to take advantage of), valerse de (one's rights, one's powers) ‖ *to put advice to use* seguir un consejo ‖ *to put into use* empezar a utilizar ‖ *to put to good use* sacar partido de ‖ *to put to use* utilizar (to employ), poner en servicio (to put into operation) ‖ *what's the use?* ¿para qué?; *what's the use of going?* ¿para qué ir? ‖ *with full use of all his faculties* en plena posesión de todas sus facultades ‖ *you are no use as a painter* usted no vale para pintor.

use [ju:z] *vt* emplear, utilizar, usar; *I use a knife to cut bread* utilizo un cuchillo para cortar el pan; *to use force* usar la fuerza; *we use this word* usamos esta palabra ‖ usar, utilizar; *ticket that cannot be used again* billete que ya no se puede usar ‖ utilizar; *can you use this tool?* ¿sabes utilizar esta herramienta? ‖ coger, tomar, utilizar; *those who use trains regularly* los que cogen el tren regularmente ‖ hacer uso de; *he has to use his special powers* tiene que hacer uso de sus poderes especiales ‖ consumir, gastar; *this fire uses one ton of coal a week* este fuego consume una tonelada de carbón por semana ‖ tomar (narcotics) ‖ utilizar, servirse de (to exploit) ‖ aprovechar; *he uses all his free time* aprovecha todo su tiempo libre; *he uses every opportunity* aprovecha todas sus oportunidades ‖ usar, hacer uso de, valerse de (one's right) ‖ tratar; *they have used me well* me han tratado bien ‖ — *book which is no longer used* libro que ya no se emplea ‖ FAM *I could use a holiday!* ¡qué bien me vendrían unas vacaciones! ‖ *to be used as* ser utilizado como, servir de; *a newspaper was used as a tablecloth* un periódico sirvió de mantel, se utilizó un periódico como mantel ‖ *to be used for* servir para; *what is this tool used for?* ¿para qué sirve esta herramienta? ‖ *to use badly* maltratar ‖ *to use up* agotar, consumir, gastar completamente; *to use up all one's provisions* agotar todas sus provisiones; acabar, terminar; *use up the milk* acabe la leche ‖ *to use up the scraps* sacar partido de los restos ‖ *use more care* tenga más cuidado ‖ *use your eyes* abra los ojos ‖ *word which is no longer used* palabra *f* que ha caído en desuso ‖ *you may use my name* puede dar mi nombre (as a reference).

◆ *v aux* acostumbrar, soler; *you used to go out at night* solías salir por la noche ‖ *things aren't what they used to be* las cosas han cambiado, las cosas ya no son lo que eran.

— OBSERV El verbo auxiliar se usa sólo en pretérito y tiene como equivalentes *soler* o *acostumbrar.* Pero en muchos casos no se traduce y se pone únicamente el verbo que sigue en imperfecto de indicativo: *I used to love him* le quería.

useable ['ju:zəbl] *adj* utilizable.

used [ju:zd] *adj* de segunda mano, usado, da; *used cars* coches de segunda mano ‖ usado, da; *hardly used* apenas usado ‖ *used up* agotado, da (supplies, person).

used [ju:st] *adj* acostumbrado, da ‖ — *to be used to* estar acostumbrado a ‖ *to get used to* acostumbrarse a (to become accustomed).

useful ['ju:sful] *adj* útil; *this book is very useful* este libro es muy útil ‖ provechoso, sa (beneficial) ‖ cómodo, da; práctico, ca; *a useful dress* un traje cómodo ‖ bueno, na; *he is a useful painter* es un buen pintor ‖ — *to be useful with* sabe valerse de; *he is useful with his fists* sabe valerse de sus puños ‖ *to come in useful* resultar útil ‖ *to make o.s. useful* ser útil, mostrarse útil ‖ *useful load* carga *f* útil (of a vehicle).

usefulness ['ju:sfulnis] *n* utilidad *f* ‖ *to have outlived one's* o *its usefulness* haber perdido su razón de ser (an institution), haberse vuelto inútil (person, object).

useless ['ju:slis] *adj* inútil; *he is useless* es inútil; *useless effort* esfuerzo inútil ‖ ineficaz; *a useless remedy* un remedio ineficaz ‖ — FAM *he is completely useless* es una nulidad *or* un inútil ‖ *it is useless to insist* es inútil insistir.

uselessly ['ju:slisli] *adv* inútilmente, en vano.

uselessness ['ju:slisnis] *n* inutilidad *f.*

user ['ju:zə*] *n* usuario, ria; *road users* usuarios de la carretera.

user-friendly [-,frendli] *adj* INFORM fácil de utilizar, amigable, asequible.

usher ['ʌʃə*] *n* acomodador *m* (in a theatre) ‖ ujier *m* (who introduces people) ‖ ujier *m*, portero *m* de estrados (in court).

usher ['ʌʃə*] *vt* llevar, acompañar; *to usher s.o. to his seat* llevar a alguien a su asiento ‖ acomodar (in theatre) ‖ anunciar (a guest), ‖ — *to usher in* anunciar; *the sun ushered in the spring* el sol anunció la primavera; hacer pasar; *they ushered him in* le hicieron pasar ‖ *to usher into* hacer pasar a, hacer entrar en; *the man ushered her into the room* el hombre le hizo entrar en la habitación ‖ *to usher out* acompañar hasta la puerta.

usherette [ʌʃə'ret] *n* acomodadora *f* (in theatre).

USSR *abbr of [Union of Soviet Socialist Republics]* URSS, Unión de las Repúblicas Socialistas Soviéticas.

usual ['ju:ʒuəl] *adj* usual, corriente (in use); *the usual word* la palabra corriente ‖ normal; *his usual state* su estado normal; *it is not usual for him to be so nasty* no es normal que sea tan antipático ‖ habitual, acostumbrado, da (habit); *my usual walk in the hills* mi paseo habitual por los cerros ‖ de todos los días, de diario; *his usual clothes* su ropa de todos los días ‖ — *as per usual* como de costumbre, como siempre ‖ *as is usual with women, she is* como todas las mujeres, es ‖ *as usual* como siempre, como de costumbre ‖ *he arrived later than usual* llegó más tarde que de costumbre *or* más tarde de lo normal ‖ *the usual thing* lo de siempre (the same as always).

◆ *n* *the usual* lo de siempre.

usually [-li] *adv* normalmente.

usucapion [ju:zju'keipiən]; **usucaption** [ju:zju'kæpʃən] *n* JUR usucapión *f.*

usucapt ['ju:zjukæpt] *vt* JUR usucapir.

usufruct ['ju:zjufrʌkt] *n* JUR usufructo *m.*

usufructuary [,ju:zju'frʌktʃəri] *adj/n* usufructuario, ria.

usurer ['ju:ʒərə*] *n* usurero, ra.

usurious [ju:'zjuəriəs] *adj* usurero, ra (person) ‖ de usurero, usurario, ria (rate of interest).

usurp [ju:'zə:p] *vt/vi* usurpar; *to usurp power* usurpar el poder ‖ *to usurp on* o *upon* usurpar.

usurpation [,ju:zə:'peiʃən] *n* usurpación *f.*

usurpative [ju:'zə:pətiv]; **usurpatory** [ju:'zə:pətəri] *adj* usurpatorio, ria.

usurper [,ju:'zə:pə*] *n* usurpador, ra.

usurping [,ju:'zə:piŋ] *adj* usurpador, ra.

usury ['ju:ʒuri] *n* usura *f.*

ut [ut; *US* ʌt] *n* MUS do *m.*

Utah ['ju:tɑ:] *pr n* GEOGR Utah.

utensil [ju'tensl] *n* utensilio *m* ‖ *kitchen utensils* batería *f sing* de cocina.

uterine ['ju:tərain] *adj* ANAT uterino, na ‖ *uterine brother* hermano uterino.

uterus ['ju:tərəs] *n* útero *m* (womb).

— OBSERV El plural de *uterus* es *uteri.*

utile ['ju:tail] *adj* útil.

utilitarian [,ju:tili'tɛəriən] *adj* utilitario, ria (relating to utility) ‖ utilitarista (relating to utilitarianism).

◆ *n* utilitarista *m* & *f.*

utilitarianism [-izəm] *n* utilitarismo *m.*

utility [ju:'tiliti] *n* utilidad *f* (usefulness) ‖ COMM utilidad *f*; *marginal utility* utilidad marginal ‖ empresa *f* de servicio público (company) ‖ acción *f* de una empresa de servicio público (share) ‖ *public utility* empresa *f* de servicio público.
◆ *adj* utilitario, ria; *utility goods, vehicles* artículos, coches utilitarios ‖ INFORM *utility program* programa *m* de utilidad ‖ *utility room* trastero *m*.

utilizable ['ju:tilaizəbl] *adj* utilizable (useable).

utilization [ˌju:tilai'zeiʃən] *n* utilización *f* (using).

utilize ['ju:tilaiz] *vt* utilizar (to use).

utmost ['ʌtməust]; **uttermost** ['ʌtəməust] *adj* supremo, ma; sumo, ma; extremo, ma; *utmost ignorance* suma ignorancia; *in the utmost degree of poverty* en grado extremo de pobreza ‖ mayor, más grande; *he made the utmost possible effort* hizo el mayor esfuerzo posible ‖ más lejano, na (farthest).
◆ *n* máximo *m* ‖ — *at the utmost* a lo más, a lo sumo ‖ *he did his utmost to help* hizo cuanto pudo *or* hizo todo lo posible para ayudar ‖ *that is the utmost that one can do* esto es todo lo que se puede hacer, esto es lo más que se puede hacer ‖ *to do one's utmost* hacer todo lo posible ‖ *to the utmost* hasta más no poder.

utopia [ju:'təupjə] *n* utopía *f*.

utopian [-n] *adj* utópico, ca.
◆ *n* utopista *m* & *f*.

utter ['ʌtə*] *adj* completo, ta; *an utter stranger* un completo desconocido; *an utter lack of* una falta completa de ‖ total, absoluto, ta; *utter surprise* sorpresa total ‖ empedernido, da; *an utter liar* un mentiroso empedernido ‖ rematado, da; *an utter fool* un loco rematado ‖ *utter nonsense!* ¡pura tontería!

utter ['ʌtə*] *vt* pronunciar, decir; *never utter his name* no diga nunca su nombre ‖ expresar (sentiments) ‖ soltar (lies, swearwords) ‖ lanzar, dar (shouts, cries) ‖ dar (sigh) ‖ proferir (threat) ‖ emitir (sound) ‖ poner en circulación (false documents, counterfeit money).

utterance ['ʌtərəns] *n* elocución *f*, pronunciación *f* (power of speech); *to have a clear utterance* tener una elocución clara; *defective utterance* defecto de pronunciación ‖ expresión *f* (of sentiments) ‖ emisión *f* (of a sound) ‖ pronunciación *f* (of a speech) ‖ emisión *f* (of counterfeit money) ‖ *to give utterance to* expresar, manifestar.
◆ *pl* palabras *f*.

utterly ['ʌtəli] *adv* completamente, totalmente, absolutamente.

uttermost ['ʌtəməust] *adj/n* → **utmost.**

uvula ['ju:vjulə] *n* ANAT úvula *f*, campanilla *f*.
— OBSERV El plural de la palabra inglesa *uvula* es *uvulas* o *uvulae*.

uvular ['ju:vjulə*] *adj* uvular.
◆ *n* sonido *m* uvular.

uxorious [ʌk'sɔ:riəs] *adj* locamente enamorado de su mujer ‖ dominado por su mujer.

V

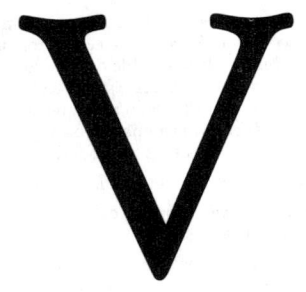

v [viː] *n* v *f* (letter); *a capital v* una v mayúscula || AUT *V-8 engine* motor *m* de ocho cilindros en V.

vac [væk] *n* FAM vacaciones *f pl* (vacation).

vacancy [ˈveikənsi] *n* vacío *m* (empty space) || lo vacío, vacuidad *f* (emptiness) || vacante *f*; *to fill a vacancy in the administration* cubrir una vacante en la administración; *should there be a vacancy* en caso de producirse una vacante || vaciedad *f* (of mind) || hueco *m*, espacio *m* vacío (gap) || habitación *f* libre (in a hotel) || — *«no vacancies»* completo (in a hotel) || *«vacancies»* se ofrece trabajo.

vacant [ˈveikənt] *adj* vacío, a (empty); *vacant house* casa vacía; *vacant space* sitio vacío || libre, disponible; *a vacant room in a hotel* una habitación libre en un hotel || libre (seat) || de ocio, libre; *it will fill your vacant hours* llenará sus horas libres || vacante; *vacant job* puesto vacante; *the vacant chair of philosophy* la cátedra vacante de filosofía || alelado, da; de bobo; *a vacant expression* una expresión alelada || vago, ga; perdido, da; *with a vacant stare* con la mirada perdida || inexpresivo, va (eyes) || vacío, a (mind) || JUR yacente; *vacant succession* herencia yacente.

vacantly [-li] *adv* distraídamente, con la mirada perdida.

vacate [vəˈkeit] *vt* dejar, dejar vacante (a post, a job) || desocupar; *to vacate the premises* desocupar los locales || dejar libre (a seat) || JUR anular (a contract).

vacation [vəˈkeiʃən] *n* vacaciones *f pl* (holidays, respite) || — *to be on vacation* estar de vacaciones || *vacation course* curso *m* de vacaciones, curso *m* de verano.

vacation [vəˈkeiʃən] *vi* US tomar las vacaciones.

vacationer [-ə*]; **vacationist** [-ist] *n* US persona *f* que está de vacaciones || veraneante *m* & *f* (in summer).

vaccinal [ˈvæksinəl] *adj* MED vaccíneo, a.

vaccinate [ˈvæksineit] *vt* MED vacunar || *to be vaccinated* vacunarse.

vaccination [ˌvæksiˈneiʃən] *n* MED vacunación *f*.

vaccinator [ˈvæksineitə*] *n* MED vaccinostilo *m* (instrument) | vacunador, ra (person).

vaccine [ˈvæksiːn] *adj* MED vaccíneo, a || *vaccine therapy* vaccinoterapia *f*.

◆ *n* MED vacuna *f*.

vaccinia [vækˈsiniə] *n* VET vacuna *f* (cowpox).

vacillate [ˈvæsileit] *vi* vacilar, titubear (to hesitate) || fluctuar (to fluctuate) || oscilar (to sway).

vacillating [-iŋ] *adj* vacilante, irresoluto, ta.

◆ *n* vacilación *f*.

vacillation [ˌvæsiˈleiʃən] *n* vacilación *f*, titubeo *m* (irresolution) || fluctuación *f* || oscilación *f* (swaying).

vacua [ˈvækjuə] *pl n* ⟶ **vacuum.**

vacuity [væˈkjuːiti]; **vacuousness** [ˈvækjuəsnis] *n* vacuidad *f*, lo vacío (emptiness) || vacío *m* (empty space) || vaciedad *f*; *to fill a speech with vacuities* llenar un discurso de vaciedades.

vacuolar [ˈvækjuələ*] *adj* BOT vacuolar.

vacuole [ˈvækjuəul] *n* vacuola *f*.

vacuous [ˈvækjuəs] *adj* vacuo, a; vacío, a (empty) || vago, ga; perdido, da (look) || FIG alelado, da; necio, cia (lacking intelligence).

vacuousness [-nis] *n* ⟶ **vacuity.**

vacuum [ˈvækjuəm] *n* PHYS vacío *m*; *to create a vacuum* dejar un vacío; *in a vacuum* en vacío || FIG vacío *m* (gap); *his death left a great vacuum* su muerte ha dejado un gran vacío.

◆ *adj* de vacío, neumático, ca; *vacuum brake* freno de vacío *or* neumático.

— OBSERV El plural de *vacuum* es *vacuums* o *vacua*.

vacuum [ˈvækjuəm] *vt* limpiar con aspiradora, pasar la aspiradora.

vacuum bottle [-ˌbɔtl] *n* termo *m*.

vacuum cleaner [-ˌkliːnə*] *n* aspiradora *f*.

vacuum flask [-flɑːsk] *n* termo *m*.

vacuum-packed [-pækt] *adj* envasado, da al vacío.

vacuum pump [-pʌmp] *n* bomba *f* neumática.

vacuum tube [-tjuːb] *n* tubo *m* de vacío.

vademecum [ˈveidiˈmiːkəm] *n* vademécum *m* (book).

Vaduz [fəˈduts] *pr n* GEOGR Vaduz.

vagabond [ˈvægəbɔnd] *adj/n* vagabundo, da; *a vagabond life* una vida vagabunda.

vagabond [ˈvægəbɔnd] *vi* vagabundear.

vagabondage [ˈvægəbɔndidʒ] *n* vagabundeo *m*, vagabundaje *m* (wandering) || vagabundos *m pl* (vagrants).

vagary [ˈveigəri] *n* capricho *m* (whim) || manía *f* (fad) || extravagancia *f* (excentricity).

vagina [vəˈdʒainə] *n* ANAT vagina *f* || BOT vaina *f*.

— OBSERV El plural de la palabra inglesa es vaginae o *vaginas*.

vaginal [-l] *adj* vaginal.

vaginitis [ˌvædʒiˈnaitis] *n* MED vaginitis *f inv*.

vagotomy [vəˈgɔtəmi] *n* MED vagotomía *f*.

vagotonia [ˌveigəˈtəuniə]; **vagotony** [veigəˈtəuni] *n* MED vagotonía *f*.

vagrancy [ˈveigrənsi] *n* vagabundeo *m*, vagancia *f* || *vagrancy act* ley *f* de vagos y maleantes.

vagrant [ˈveigrənt] *adj* vagabundo, da; *a vagrant life* una vida vagabunda || FIG errabundo, da; *vagrant imagination* imaginación errabunda || ambulante (musician).

◆ *n* vagabundo, da.

vague [veig] *adj* vago, ga; *vague desires* deseos vagos; *vague promise* promesa vaga || vago, ga; borroso, sa; *a vague outline* una silueta borrosa || impreciso, sa (imprecise) || indeciso, sa; dudoso, sa (uncertain) || mínimo, ma; remoto, ta; *I have not the vaguest idea* no tengo la más mínima idea || — *to be vague* andarse con vaguedades || *to make vague remarks* decir vaguedades.

vaguely [-li] *adv* vagamente || apenas; *do you know Paris? vaguely* ¿conoce usted París? apenas || — *he does vaguely resemble me* tiene cierto parecido conmigo || *he talks vaguely* habla en términos muy vagos, se anda con vaguedades.

vagueness [-nis] *n* vaguedad *f*; *the vagueness of his word* la vaguedad de sus palabras || lo borroso (of an outline) || lo impreciso, imprecisión *f*.

vagus [ˈveigəs] *n* ANAT nervio *m* vago.

◆ *adj* ANAT vago (nerve).

— OBSERV El plural de la palabra inglesa es *vagi*.

vain [vein] *adj* vano, na; *a vain attempt to escape* una tentativa vana de escapar; *vain promises, excuses, hopes* promesas, excusas, esperanzas vanas || vano, na; inútil; *it's vain to go* es inútil ir || presumido, a; vanidoso, sa (conceited); *she is very vain* es muy vanidosa || — *in vain* en vano, vanamente, infructuosamente || *thou shalt not take the name of the Lord thy God in vain* no tomarás el nombre de Dios en vano || FIG *to be as vain as a peacock* ser más orgulloso que un pavo real.

vainglorious [-ˈglɔːriəs] *adj* vanaglorioso, sa.

vainness [ˈveinnis] *n* vanidad *f* (vanity) || inutilidad *f* (uselessness).

vair [ˈvɛə*] *n* vero *m*, marta *f* cebellina (fur) || HERALD vero *m*.

valance [ˈvæləns] *n* guardamalleta *f* (of a window) || doselera *f* (of a bed) || THEATR bambalinón *m*.

vale [veil] *n* valle *m* || *vale of tears* valle de lágrimas.

valediction [ˌvæliˈdikʃən] *n* adiós *m*, despedida *f*.

valedictorian [ˌvælidikˈtɔːriən] *n* alumno *m* que da el discurso de despedida al final de curso.

valedictory [ˌvæliˈdiktəri] *adj* de despedida.

◆ *n* discurso *m* de despedida.

valence [ˈveiləns] *n* CHEM valencia *f*.

Valencian [vəˈlenʃiən] *adj/n* valenciano, na.

Valenciennes [ˌvælənsiˈen] *n* encaje *m* de Valenciennes.

valency [ˈveilənsi] *n* CHEM valencia *f*.

valentine [ˈvæləntain] *n* tarjeta *f or* carta *f* que se manda el Día de los Enamorados (card) || novio, via (person) || *Valentine* o *Valentine's Day* Día *m* de los Enamorados.

valerian [vəˈliəriən] *n* BOT valeriana *f*.

valet [ˈvælit] *n* ayuda *m* de cámara (personal servant) || camarero *m*, mozo *m* de habitación (in a hotel).

valet [ˈvælit] *vt* servir de ayuda de cámara a.

Valetta [vəˈletə] *pr n* GEOGR La Valeta.

valetudinarian [ˈvæliˌtjuːdiˈnɛəriən] *adj/n* valetudinario, ria; enfermizo, za.

valetudinary [vælɪ'tjuːdinəri] *adj* valetudinario, ria; enfermizo, za.

Valhalla [væl'hælə] *n* MYTH Walhalla *m.*

valiant ['væljənt] *adj* valiente, valeroso, sa; *a valiant soldier* un soldado valeroso.

valid ['vælid] *adj* válido, da; *a valid contract* un contrato válido; *valid arguments* argumentos válidos || valedero, ra (ticket) || vigente (law) || *no longer valid* caducado, da.

validate ['vælideit] *vt* validar, dar validez a.

validation [,væli'deiʃən] *n* validación *f.*

validity [və'liditi] *n* validez *f* || vigencia *f* (of a law).

valise [və'liːz] *n* maleta *f* (suitcase).

Valium ['væliəm] *n* (registered trademark) Valium *m.*

Valkyrie [væl'kiəri] *pr n* MYTH Valkiria *f,* Walkiria *f* (virgin goddess).

valley ['væli] *n* valle *m; a Swiss valley* un valle suizo || cuenca *f,* valle *m* (river basin) || TECH lima *f* hoya (of a roof).

valor ['vælə*] *n* US valor *m,* valentía *f.*

valorization [,vælərai'zeiʃən] *n* valorización *f.*

valorize ['væləraiz] *vt* valorizar.

valorous ['vælərəs] *adj* valiente, valeroso, sa (courageous).

valour ['vælə*] *n* valor *m,* valentía *f.*

valuable ['væljuəbl] *adj* valioso, sa; de valor (expensive, costly); *a valuable treasure* un tesoro valioso || valioso, sa; *your valuable help* su ayuda valiosa || — *is that valuable?* ¿vale mucho eso? || *this jewel is very valuable* esta joya vale mucho.

◆ *pl n* objetos *m* de valor.

valuation [,vælju'eiʃən] *n* valoración *f,* valuación *f,* valorización *f,* estimación *f,* tasación *f* (act) || valor *m* (estimated value).

valuator ['væljueitə*] *n* tasador *m.*

value ['væljuː] *n* valor *m; a thing of great value* una cosa de gran valor; *the value of the pound* el valor de la libra; *value in gold* valor en oro; *value received* valor recibido || valor *m,* monta *f* (importance); *a person of little value* una persona de poca monta || valor *m* (of colour) || GRAMM significado *m,* valor *m* (meaning) || MUS & MATH valor *m; absolute, relative value* disminución *f or* pérdida *f* de valor, depreciación *f* || — *increase in value* plusvalía *f* || *it is nothing of any value* no es nada de valor || *it is very good value for twenty pesetas* veinte pesetas es un buen precio || COMM *market* o *commercial value* valor comercial || *of no value* sin valor || *sense of values* sentido de los valores || *to attach little value to sth.* atribuir poco valor a algo (object), dar poca importancia a algo (event, news, etc.) || *to be of value* ser valioso, sa || *to get good value for one's money* sacarle jugo al dinero || *to lose value* desvalorizarse, perder valor || FIG *to place a high value on sth.* dar mucha importancia a algo || *to set a value on* poner precio a, estimar || *to set too much value on* sobreestimar || FIG *to take sth. at face value* creer algo a pies juntillas || *to the value of* por el valor de || *value judgement* juicio *m* de valor.

value ['væljuː] *vt* valorar, valorizar, tasar (to appraise) || estimar, apreciar, valuar, valorar; *I value him highly for his qualities* le estimo mucho por sus cualidades || — *to value one's life* apreciar la vida || *to value o.s. on* vanagloriarse de.

valued [-d] *adj* estimado, da; apreciado, da.

valueless [-lis] *adj* sin valor.

valuer [-ə*] *n* tasador *m.*

valvate ['vælvit] *adj* valvular.

valve [vælv] *n* ANAT válvula *f* (of heart) || TECH válvula *f* (in cars, in tyres, etc.); *safety valve* válvula de seguridad; *inlet valve* válvula de admisión; *rectifying valve* válvula rectificadora; *grinding of valves* esmerilado de válvulas; *butterfly, stem valve* válvula de mariposa, de vástago | chapaleta *f* (of a pump) | lámpara *f; valve set* radio de lámparas || ELECTR tubo *m* electrónico || llave *f* (of a trumpet) || ZOOL valva *f* || BOT ventalla *f,* valva *f* (of a capsule).

valve box [-bɔks] *n* caja *f* de válvulas || caja *f* de distribución (of steam).

valve cap [-kæp] *n* tapón *m.*

valve gear [-giə*] *n* mecanismo *m* de distribución.

valve holder [-,həuldə*] *n* RAD casquillo *m.*

valveless [-lis] *adj* sin válvulas.

valve rocker [-,rɔkə*] *n* TECH balancín *m.*

valve rod [-rɔd] *n* TECH vástago *m.*

valve seat [-siːt] *n* asiento *m* de la válvula.

valvula ['vælvjulə] *n* válvula *f.*

— OBSERV El plural de *valvula* es *valvulae.*

valvular ['vælvjulə*] *adj* valvular.

valvule ['vælvjul] *n* válvula *f.*

vamoose [və'muːs] *vi* FAM largarse.

vamp [væmp] *n* pala *f,* empeine *m* (of a shoe) || remiendo *m* (patch) || MUS acompañamiento *m* improvisado || FAM mujer *f* fatal, vampiresa *f* (woman).

vamp [væmp] *vt* poner la pala a (a shoe, boot) || remendar (to patch) || FAM engatusar (to seduce) || MUS improvisar un acompañamiento para.

◆ *vi* MUS improvisar un acompañamiento.

vamper [-ə*] *n* remendón *m.*

vampire ['væmpaiə*] *n* vampiro *m* (evil spirit) || THEATR escotillón *m* || ZOOL vampiro *m* || FIG vampiro *m* || FAM mujer *f* fatal, vampiresa *f* (woman).

vampire bat [-bæt] *n* ZOOL vampiro *m.*

vampirism [-rizəm] *n* vampirismo *m.*

van [væn] *n* furgoneta *f,* camioneta *f* (small lorry); *delivery van* furgoneta de reparto || capitoné *m,* camión *m* de mudanza (removal lorry) || furgón *m,* vagón *m* cerrado (goods car of a train) || tamiz *m* (sieve) || pala *f* (shovel) || vanguardia *f* (leading section); *to be in the van of* ir a la vanguardia de || ala *f* (wing) || — *guard's van* furgón de equipajes || *prison van* coche *m* celular.

vanadate ['vænədeit] *n* CHEM vanadato *m.*

vanadium [və'neidjəm] *n* CHEM vanadio *m.*

Vandal ['vændəl] *n* vándalo, la || FIG vándalo *m* (destructive person).

◆ *adj* vandálico, ca; vándalo, la.

vandalism [-izəm] *n* vandalismo *m; piece of vandalism* acto de vandalismo.

vandalize [-aiz] *vt* destruir, destrozar.

Vandyke [væn'daik] *n* perilla *f* (beard) || valona *f* (collar).

vane [vein] *n* paleta *f,* pala *f* (of propeller, electric fan) || álabe *m* (of waterwheel) || aspa *f* (of a windmill) || veleta *f* (weathercock) || cataviento *m* (on a boat) || barbas *f pl* (of a feather) || pluma *f* (of an arrow) || tablilla *f* de mira (of a quadrant).

vanguard ['vængɑːd] *n* vanguardia *f; of the vanguard* de vanguardia.

vanilla [və'nilə] *n* BOT vainilla *f* || mantecado *m,* vainilla *f; vanilla ice cream* helado de mantecado *or* de vainilla.

vanish ['væniʃ] *vi* desaparecer; *the man vanished* el hombre desapareció; *the pain vanished* el dolor desapareció || desvanecerse, esfumarse; *her hopes vanished* sus esperanzas se esfumaron || MATH tender hacia cero.

vanishing [-iŋ] *adj* que desaparece || que se desvanece, que se esfuma || de día (cream) || de fuga (point).

◆ *n* desaparición *f.*

vanity ['vænity] *n* vanidad *f; to leave the vanities of this world* dejar las vanidades de este mundo || vanidad *f,* orgullo *m* (self-satisfaction) || neceser *m* (vanity case) || US tocador *m* (dressing table) || — *out of sheer vanity* por pura vanidad || *vanity of vanities, all is vanity* vanidad de vanidades y todo es vanidad.

vanity case [-keis] *n* neceser *m.*

vanquish ['væŋkwiʃ] *vt* vencer, conquistar (to conquer) || dominar (one's feelings).

vanquished [-t] *pl n* vencidos, das.

vanquisher [-ə*] *n* vencedor *m.*

vanquishing [-iŋ] *adj* vencedor, ra.

◆ *n* conquista *f.*

vantage ['vɑːntidʒ] *n* ventaja *f* || — *from his vantage point he could see the whole valley* desde el lugar que ocupaba dominaba todo el valle || *vantage ground* o *point* posición ventajosa.

vapid ['væpid] *adj* insípido, da; soso, sa; insulso, sa.

vapidity [-iti]; **vapidness** [-nis] *n* insipidez *f,* insulsez *f.*

vapor ['veipə*] *n/vi* US → **vapour.**

vaporing ['veipəriŋ] *adj* US → **vapouring.**

vaporish ['veipəriʃ] *adj* US → **vapourish.**

vaporization [,veipərai'zeiʃən] *n* vaporización *f.*

vaporize ['veipəraiz] *vt* vaporizar.

◆ *vi* vaporizarse.

vaporizer [-ə*] *n* vaporizador *m* || pulverizador *m* (spray).

vaporizing [-iŋ] *adj* de vaporización.

◆ *n* vaporización *f.*

vaporous ['veipərəs] *adj* vaporoso, sa || FIG nebuloso, sa (style, etc.).

vapory ['veipəri] *adj* US → **vapoury.**

vapour; US vapor ['veipə*] *n* vapor *m; water vapour* vapor de agua || vaho *m* (on windowpanes) || vapor *m* (of alcohols) || — *vapour bath* baño *m* de vapor || *vapour density* densidad *f* del vapor || *vapour pressure* presión *f* del vapor || AVIAT *vapour trail* estela *f.*

◆ *pl* MED vapores *m.*

vapour; US vapor ['veipə*] *vi* vaporizarse, evaporarse (water) || FAM fanfarronear (to brag) | decir sandeces (to drivel).

vapouring; US vaporing ['veipəriŋ] *adj* FAM fanfarrón, ona.

vapourish; US vaporish [-riʃ] *adj* vaporoso, sa || MED hipocondríaco, ca.

vapoury; US vapory [-ri] *adj* vaporoso, sa.

vaquero [vɑː'kerəu] *n* vaquero *m.*

var [vɑː*] *n* ELECTR var *m.*

varec; varech ['værek] *n* varec *m* (kelp).

variability [,vɛəriə'biliti] *n* variabilidad *f* || FIG inconstancia *f,* variabilidad *f.*

variable ['vɛəriəbl] *adj* variable; *variable winds* vientos variables || MATH variable || FIG variable, cambiadizo, za || — ELECTR *variable condenser* condensador *m* variable || *variable time fuse* espoleta *f* de proximidad.

◆ *n* viento *m* variable (wind) || zona *f* de vientos variables (wind zone) || MATH variable *f.*

variance ['vɛəriəns] *n* desavenencia *f,* discrepancia *f* (between people) || discordancia *f,* desacuerdo *m* (between things) || variación *f* (change) || JUR divergencia *f* || — *at variance* en desacuerdo, en contradicción (opinion), reñido, da; desavenido, da (people, families) || *to be at variance with* estar en desacuerdo con ||

to set two people at variance sembrar la discordia entre dos personas.

variant ['vɛəriənt] *adj* variante, diferente (differing) ‖ variable (changeable).
◆ *n* variante *f*.

variate ['vɛəri,eit] *n* variable *f* (in statistics).

variation [,vɛəri'eiʃən] *n* variación *f* ‖ ASTR, BIOL, MATH & MUS variación *f* ‖ PHYS variación *f*, declinación *f*; *magnetic variation* declinación magnética.

varicella [,væri'selə] *n* MED varicela *f* (chickenpox).

varices ['værisi:z] *pl n* ⟶ **varix.**

varicocele ['værikəsi:l] *n* MED varicocele *m*.

varicoloured; *US* **varicolored** ['vɛərikʌləd] *adj* multicolor.

varicose ['værikəus] *adj* MED varicoso, sa ‖ *varicose veins* varices *f*; *stockings for varicose veins* medias para varices.

varied ['vɛərid] *adj* variado, da; vario, ria; diverso, sa (of different kinds) ‖ jaspeado, da; abigarrado, da (variegated).

variegate ['vɛərigeit] *vt* abigarrar, jaspear (to give various colours to) ‖ variar, diversificar (to vary).

variegated [-id] *adj* abigarrado, da; jaspeado, da (colour) ‖ variado, da; diversificado, da (full of variety).

variegation [,vɛəri'geiʃən] *n* abigarramiento *m*.

variety [və'raiəti] *n* diversidad *f*; *the variety of his occupations* la diversidad de sus ocupaciones ‖ variedad *f*; *a variety of opinions* una variedad de opiniones ‖ variedad *f*, surtido *m*; *a variety of cloths* un surtido de tejidos ‖ BIOL & BOT variedad *f* ‖ variedades *f pl*; *variety entertainment* o *show* espectáculo de variedades ‖ — *for a variety of reasons* por varias razones, por razones diversas ‖ *for variety* por variar ‖ *in a variety of colours* de diversos colores ‖ *in a variety of ways* de diversos modos ‖ *to lend variety to* variar, dar diversidad a ‖ FIG *variety is the spice of life* en la variedad está el gusto.

variety store [-'stɔ:*] *n* *US* bazar *m*.

variform ['vɛərifɔ:m] *adj* diversiforme.

variola [və'raiələ] *n* MED viruela *f*.

variolar [-:*] *adj* MED varioloso, sa.

various ['vɛəriəs] *adj* diverso, sa; diferente, vario, ria (differing); *various occupations* ocupaciones diversas; *in various ways* de diferentes modos ‖ variado, da (varied) ‖ vario, ria; *the various parts of the country* las varias partes del país; *for various reasons* por varios motivos.

varix ['vɛəriks] *n* MED varice *f*.
— OBSERV El plural de la palabra inglesa es *varices*.

varlet ['vɑ:lit] *n* paje *m* (page) ‖ FAM bribón *m*, granuja *m* (knave).

varmint ['vɑ:mint] *n* *US* FAM bicho *m* (animal) | bribón *m* (person).

varnish ['vɑ:niʃ] *n* barniz *m* (for wood, for metal) ‖ vidriado *m*, barniz *m* vítreo (for pottery) ‖ charol *m* (for leather) ‖ FIG barniz *m*, baño *m*, capa *f* (outward appearance) ‖ — *nail varnish* esmalte *m*, laca *f* [para uñas] ‖ *varnish remover* quitaesmalte *m* ‖ BOT *varnish tree* barniz *m* de Japón.

varnish ['vɑ:niʃ] *vt* barnizar (wood, paintings) ‖ charolar (leather) ‖ vidriar (pottery) ‖ pintar (nails) ‖ FIG disimular (to hide) | embellecer (to embellish).

varnisher [-ə*] *n* barnizador *m*.

varnishing [-iŋ] *n* barnizado *m* ‖ ARTS *varnishing day* inauguración *f* de una exposición de arte, apertura *f* de una exposición.

varsity ['vɑ:siti] *n* FAM universidad *f* ‖ SP equipo *m* universitario.

varus ['vɛərəs] *n* MED pie *m* contrahecho.

vary ['vɛəri] *vt* variar; *to vary one's food* variar la alimentación ‖ cambiar, variar (decision, methods) ‖ MUS hacer variaciones en.
◆ *vi* variar; *opinions vary* las opiniones varían ‖ cambiar, variar; *the temperature varies* la temperatura cambia ‖ diferir, variar, ser diferente; *customs vary from one country to another* las costumbres difieren de un país a otro ‖ diferir, no estar de acuerdo (to disagree) ‖ desviarse (to deviate) ‖ BOT variar ‖ MATH variar ‖ — *to vary from* diferenciarse de ‖ *X varies proportionately as* Y X varía proporcionalmente a Y.

varying [-iŋ] *adj* variante, variable ‖ — *varying prices* precios diversos ‖ *without varying* sin variación.

vascular ['væskjulə*] *adj* vascular ‖ *vascular tissue* tejido *m* vascular.

vascularity [væskju'læriti] *n* vascularidad *f*.

vas deferens ['vɑ:s'defərəns] *n* ANAT & BOT conducto *m* deferente.
— OBSERV El plural es *vasa deferentia*.

vase [vɑ:z] *n* vaso *m* (receptacle) ‖ jarrón *m* (artistic) ‖ florero *m* (for flowers) ‖ vasija *f*; *a pre-Columbian vase* una vasija precolombina.

vasectomy [væ'sektəmi] *n* MED vasectomía *f*.

Vaseline ['væsəli:n] *n* Vaselina *f*.

vasoconstrictor ['veizəukən'striktə*] *adj* vasoconstrictor, ra.
◆ *n* vasoconstrictor *m*.

vasodilator ['veizəudai'leitə*] *adj* vasodilatador, ra.
◆ *n* vasodilatador *m*.

vasomotor ['veizəu'məutə*] *adj* vasomotor, ra.
◆ *n* vasomotor *m*.

vassal ['væsəl] *adj/n* vasallo, lla.

vassalage [-idʒ] *n* vasallaje *m*.

vast [vɑ:st] *adj* inmenso, sa; vasto, ta; extenso, sa; *a vast region* una región inmensa ‖ enorme, considerable; *a vast difference* una enorme diferencia ‖ enorme; *a vast building* un edificio enorme ‖ abrumador, ra (majority).

vastitude [-itju:d]**; vasteness** [-nis] *n* inmensidad *f* (immensity).

vastly [-li] *adv* extensamente ‖ sumamente, muy (very); *he is vastly mistaken* está muy equivocado.

vat [væt] *n* cuba *f*, tina *f* (large tub).

VAT *abbr of* *[value added tax]* IVA, impuesto sobre el valor añadido.

Vatican ['vætikən] *pr n* REL Vaticano *m*.
◆ *adj* vaticano, na; del Vaticano ‖ — *Vatican City* Ciudad *f* del Vaticano ‖ *Vatican Council* Concilio vaticano.

vaticide ['vætisaid] *n* asesino *m* de un profeta.

vaticinal [væ'tisinəl] *adj* profético, ca.

vaticinate [væ'tisineit] *vt/vi* vaticinar.

vaticinator [væ'tisineitə*] *n* vaticinador *m*.

vatting ['vætiŋ] *n* encubamiento *m*.

vaudeville ['vəudəvil] *n* THEATR vodevil *m* (comedy) | variedades *f pl* (variety show).

vaudevillian [,vəudə'viljən]**; vaudevillist** ['vəudəvilist] *n* vodevilista *m*.

vault [vɔ:lt] *n* ARCH bóveda *f* ‖ sótano *m* (cellar) ‖ bodega *f* (wine cellar) ‖ panteón *m* [subterráneo] (burial chamber) ‖ cripta *f* (in church) ‖ cámara *f* acorazada (of a bank) ‖ ANAT bóveda *f* ‖ SP salto *m*; *pole vault* salto con pértiga; *at* o *with one vault* de un salto ‖ — ARCH *barrel vault* bóveda de cañón | *groined vault* bóveda por arista (not ribbed), bóveda de crucería (ribbed) | *ogival vault* bóveda ojival | *ribbed* o *cloister vault* bóveda de crucería *or* esquifada *or* claustral ‖ ASTR *vault of heaven* bóveda celeste.

vault [vɔ:lt] *vt* saltar (to jump); *to vault a gate* saltar una barrera ‖ ARCH abovedar; *vaulted dome* cúpula abovedada; *to vault a cellar* abovedar un sótano.
◆ *vi* saltar.

vaulted [-id] *adj* abovedado, da.

vaulter [-ə*] *n* SP saltador, ra.

vaulting [-iŋ] *n* construcción *f* de bóvedas (art of building) ‖ bóveda *f* (vaulted work) ‖ SP salto *m* ‖ SP *vaulting horse* potro *m*, potro *m* con arzón.

vaunt [vɔ:nt] *vt* alabar (to praise) ‖ jactarse de, vanagloriarse de (to boast of).
◆ *vi* jactarse, vanagloriarse (to boast).

vaunted [-id] *adj* alabado, da; encomiado, da.

vaunting [-iŋ] *adj* jactancioso, sa.
◆ *n* jactancia *f*.

V-Day ['vi:dei] *n* día *m* de la victoria.

VDU *abbr of* *[Visual Display Unit]* pantalla de visualización, visual.

veal [vi:l] *n* CULIN ternera *f* ‖ *veal chop* o *cutlet* chuleta *f* de ternera.

vector ['vektə*] *n* MATH vector *m* ‖ MED vector *m*, portador, ra (of a virus).
◆ *adj* MATH vectorial.

vectorial [vek'tɔ:riəl] *adj* MATH vectorial.

Veda ['veidə] *n* REL veda *m* (Hindu scripture).

vedette [vi'det] *n* MAR lancha *f* motora, motora *f* (boat).

Vedic ['veidik] *adj* védico, ca.

veep [vi:p] *n* *US* FAM vicepresidente *m*.

veer [viə*] *n* MAR virada *f* (of a ship) ‖ cambio *m* de dirección (of the wind) ‖ FIG cambio *m* brusco, viraje *m* (of opinion).

veer [viə*] *vt* MAR virar (a boat) ‖ cambiar de dirección, girar (to change direction) ‖ cambiar (wind) ‖ torcer; *the road veers left* la carretera tuerce a la izquierda ‖ FIG virar, girar, inclinarse; *public opinion veered to the left* la opinión pública viró hacia la izquierda ‖ — FIG *to veer round* cambiar de opinión | *to veer round to* adoptar, adherirse a (an opinion).

veg [vedʒ] *n* FAM verduras *f pl*.

vegetable ['vedʒitəbl] *adj* vegetal; *the vegetable kingdom* el reino vegetal ‖ de verduras; *vegetable market* mercado de verduras ‖ — *vegetable butter* vegetalina *f* ‖ *vegetable garden* huerta *f*, huerto *m* ‖ *vegetable ivory* corozo *m*, corojo *m*, marfil *m* vegetal ‖ *vegetable marrow* calabacín *m* ‖ *vegetable slicer* cortalegumbres *m inv*.
◆ *n* BOT vegetal *m*, planta *f* ‖ AGR hortaliza *f*, verdura *f*, legumbre *f* ‖ CULIN verdura *f*, legumbre *f* ‖ — *early vegetables* verduras tempranas ‖ *green vegetables* verduras *f*.

vegetal ['vedʒitl] *adj* BOT vegetal.

vegetarian [,vedʒi'tɛəriən] *adj/n* vegetariano, na.

vegetarianism [-izəm] *n* vegetarianismo *m*.

vegetate ['vedʒiteit] *vi* vegetar ‖ FIG vegetar.

vegetation [,vedʒi'teiʃən] *n* vegetación *f*.

vegetative ['vedʒitətiv] *adj* vegetativo, va.

veggie ['vedʒi] *n* FAM verduras *f pl* | vegetariano, na.

vehemence ['vi:iməns]**; vehemency** [-i] *n* vehemencia *f*; *we were surprised by the vehemence of his speech* nos sorprendió la vehemencia de su discurso ‖ violencia *f* (of an attack, etc.).

vehement ['vi:imənt] *adj* vehemente; *vehement speaker* orador vehemente ‖ violento, ta; *vehement opposition* oposición violenta.

vehemently [-li] *adv* con vehemencia; *to speak vehemently* hablar con vehemencia ‖

to be vehemently opposed to sth. estar completamente en contra de algo.

vehicle [ˈviːikl] *n* vehículo *m*; *motor vehicle* vehículo motorizado; *space vehicle* vehículo espacial; *air is the vehicle of sound* el aire es el vehículo del sonido ‖ MED excipiente *m* ‖ FIG vehículo *m*, medio *m*; *propaganda vehicle* un vehículo para la propaganda ‖ FIG *she is merely a vehicle for his ambition* para él ella no es nada más que un medio para realizar sus ambiciones.

vehicular [viˈhikjulə*] *adj* de vehículos ‖ *vehicular traffic* circulación rodada.

veil [veil] *n* velo *m*; *bride's veil* velo de novia ‖ REL velo *m*; *to take the veil* tomar el velo ‖ FIG capa *f*, pretexto *m*; *under the veil of* so capa de, con el pretexto de | velo *m*; *a veil of smoke* un velo de humo ‖ ANAT velo *m*; *humeral veil* velo humeral ‖ — FIG *beyond the veil* en el otro mundo | *to draw a veil over* correr un tupido velo sobre.

veil [veil] *vt* velar, cubrir con un velo; *a veiled face* un rostro cubierto con un velo ‖ FIG cubrir, velar; *clouds veiled the mountain* las nubes velaban la montaña | velar, disimular (to disguise); *thinly veiled disgust* repugnancia apenas disimulada; *veiled reference* alusión velada ‖ — *eyes veiled in* o *by tears* ojos velados por lágrimas ‖ *project veiled in secrecy* proyecto rodeado de secreto.

veiling [-iŋ] *n* tela *f* para hacer velos (material) ‖ acción *f* de velar (action) ‖ velo *m* (veil).

vein [vein] *n* ANAT vena *f*; *portal vein* vena porta ‖ GEOL vena *f*, veta *f*, filón *m* ‖ vena *f* (of water) ‖ ZOOL & BOT vena *f*, nervadura *f* ‖ vena *f*, veta *f* (streak in wood, in marble) ‖ FIG humor *m*, disposición *f* (mood) | vena *f* (streak); *a vein of madness* una vena de loco | estilo *m*; *other works in the same vein* otras obras del mismo estilo.

veined [-d] *adj* que tiene venas (having veins) ‖ veteado, da; jaspeado, da (marble, etc.).

veining [-iŋ] *n* jaspeado *m* ‖ ANAT red *f* de venas.

veinstone [-stəun] *n* MIN ganga *f*.

veiny [-i] *adj* venoso, sa ‖ veteado, da (marble, etc.).

velamen [viˈleimən] *n* ANAT velamen *m* ‖ BOT tegumento *m*.

— OBSERV El plural de la palabra inglesa *velamen* es *velamina*.

velar [ˈviːlə*] *adj* ANAT & GRAMM velar.

◆ *n* GRAMM velar *f*.

Velcro [ˈvelkrəu] *n* (registered trademark) velcro *m*.

velleity [veˈliːiti] *n* veleidad *f*.

vellum [ˈveləm] *n* vitela *f* ‖ *vellum paper* papel *m* vitela.

velocipede [viˈlɔsipiːd] *n* velocípedo *m*.

velocity [viˈlɔsiti] *n* PHYS velocidad *f* ‖ CHEM rapidez *f*, velocidad *f* ‖ *escape velocity* velocidad *f* de liberación (of a spacecraft).

velodrome [ˈveləudrəum] *n* velódromo *m*.

velour; velours [vəˈluə*] *n* velludillo *m*, veludillo *m*, terciopelo *m* (velvet).

velum [ˈviːləm] *n* ANAT velo *m*.

— OBSERV El plural de *velum* es *vela*.

velure [ˈveljə*] *n* (ant) terciopelo *m* (cloth).

velvet [ˈvelvit] *n* terciopelo *m*, velludillo *m* (cloth) ‖ ZOOL vello *m* (on antlers) ‖ — FIG *an iron hand in a velvet glove* una mano férrea con guante de seda ‖ *corduroy velvet* pana *f*, pana *f* de canutillo ‖ FIG *it's as smooth as velvet* es como una seda | *skin like velvet* piel de terciopelo *or* aterciopelada | *to be on velvet* estar en posición muy ventajosa.

◆ *adj* aterciopelado, da (like velvet) ‖ de terciopelo (made of velvet) ‖ FIG suave, aterciopelado, da (soft).

velveteen [velviˈtiːn] *n* pana *f*.

velvety [ˈvelviti] *adj* aterciopelado, da (like velvet); *velvety material* tejido aterciopelado; *velvety skin* piel aterciopelada.

vena cava [ˈviːnəˈkeivə] *n* ANAT vena *f* cava.

venal [ˈviːnl] *adj* venal.

venality [viːˈnæliti] *n* venalidad *f*.

venation [veˈneiʃən] *n* nervadura *f* (on leaves and insects' wings).

vend [vend] *vt* vender.

vendee [venˈdiː] *n* JUR comprador, ra.

vendetta [venˈdetə] *n* vendetta *f*.

vending machine [ˈvendiŋməʃiːn] *n* distribuidor *m* automático.

vendor [ˈvendə*] *n* vendedor, ra (seller) ‖ buhonero, ra; vendedor *m* ambulante, vendedora *f* ambulante (pedlar) ‖ *automatic vendor* distribuidor automático (machine).

veneer [viˈniə*] *n* chapa *f* (sheet of wood) ‖ enchapado *m*, chapeado *m* (wood surface) ‖ FIG máscara *f*, careta *f*, apariencia *f* (superficial appearance); *veneer of respectability* apariencia de respetabilidad | barniz *m* (of culture, etc.).

veneer [viˈniə*] *vt* chapear, enchapar; *to veneer a piece of furniture in mahogany* chapear un mueble con caoba ‖ FIG disfrazar, encubrir.

venerability [ˌvenərəˈbiliti] *n* carácter *m* venerable.

venerable [ˈvenərəbl] *adj* venerable.

venerate [ˈvenəreit] *vt* venerar.

veneration [ˈvenəreiʃən] *n* veneración *f*.

venerator [ˈvenəreitə*] *n* venerador, ra.

venereal [viˈniəriəl] *adj* venéreo, a; *venereal disease* enfermedad venérea.

venery [ˈvenəri] *n* deleite *m* sexual (sexual pleasure) ‖ montería *f* (hunting).

Venetian [viˈniːʃən] *adj/n* veneciano, na ‖ — *Venetian blind* persiana veneciana ‖ *Venetian glass* cristal *m* de Venecia.

Venezuela [ˌveneˈzweilə] *pr n* GEOGR Venezuela *f*.

Venezuelan [-n] *adj/n* venezolano, na.

vengeance [ˈvendʒəns] *n* venganza *f* ‖ — FIG *it was snowing with a vengeance* estaba nevando de verdad | *to punish s.o. with a vengeance* castigar muy severamente a uno ‖ *to take vengeance for sth.* vengarse de algo ‖ *to take vengeance on s.o.* vengarse de alguien.

vengeful [ˈvendʒful] *adj* vengativo, va.

venial [ˈviːnjəl] *adj* venial; *venial sin* pecado venial.

veniality [ˌviːniˈæliti] *n* venialidad *f*.

Venice [ˈvenis] *pr n* GEOGR Venecia.

venison [ˈvenzn] *n* carne *f* de venado.

venom [ˈvenəm] *n* veneno *m*.

venomous [-əs] *adj* venenoso, sa; *venomous snake* serpiente venenosa ‖ FIG venenoso, sa; malévolo, la; *venomous criticism* crítica venenosa ‖ FIG *venomous tongue* lengua viperina.

venose [ˈviːnəus] *adj* BOT venoso, sa.

venosity [viːˈnɔsiti] *n* ANAT & BOT venosidad *f*.

venous [ˈviːnəs] *adj* ANAT & BOT venoso, sa; *venous blood* sangre venosa.

vent [vent] *n* abertura *f*, agujero *m* (hole, passage) ‖ abertura *f*, raja *f* (of coat) ‖ cañón *m* de chimenea (chimney) ‖ respiradero *m*, agujero *m* de ventilación (air hole) ‖ tubo *m or* conducto *m* de ventilación (tube) ‖ rejilla *f* de ventilación (grille in a wall, etc.) ‖ MUS agujero *m* ‖ TECH válvula *f*; *safety vent* válvula de seguridad ‖ chimenea *f* (of volcano) ‖ piquera *f* (of barrel) ‖ MAR tronera *f* ‖ MIL oído *m*, fogón *m* (of a gun) ‖ ZOOL ano *m* ‖ FIG salida *f*, libre curso *m*, rienda *f* suelta; *to give vent to one's anger* dar libre curso a su cólera ‖ FIG *to give vent to one's feelings* desahogarse.

vent [vent] *vt* hacer un agujero en (to make an aperture in) ‖ descargar, emitir, dar salida a (to discharge) ‖ FIG desahogar, descargar; *to vent one's anger on s.o.* desahogar su ira contra alguien ‖ FIG *to vent one's feelings* desahogarse.

ventail [ˈventeil] *n* visera *f* (of helmet).

venter [ˈventə*] *n* ZOOL vientre *m*, abdomen *m* ‖ ANAT protuberancia *f* (protuberance) | cavidad *f* (bone cavity) ‖ JUR matriz *f* (womb).

venthole [ˈventhəul] *n* respiradero *m*.

ventilate [ˈventileit] *vt* ventilar, airear; *to ventilate a room* ventilar una habitación ‖ MED oxigenar (blood) ‖ FIG ventilar, discutir; *to ventilate a problem* ventilar un problema.

ventilating [-iŋ] *n* ventilación *f*, aireación *f* ‖ — *ventilating cowl* sombrerete *m* de ventilación ‖ *ventilating fan* ventilador *m* ‖ *ventilating shaft* pozo *m* de ventilación.

ventilation [ˌventiˈleiʃən] *n* ventilación *f*, aireación *f*; *the ventilation of a tunnel* la ventilación de un túnel ‖ MED oxigenación *f* (of blood) ‖ FIG discusión *f* ‖ — *pulmonary ventilation* ventilación pulmonar ‖ *ventilation duct* conducto *m* de ventilación ‖ *ventilation shaft* pozo *m* de ventilación.

ventilator [ˈventileitə*] *n* ventilador *m*.

ventral [ˈventrəl] *adj* ventral, abdominal.

ventricle [ˈventrikl] *n* ANAT ventrículo *m*.

ventricular [venˈtrikjulə*] *adj* ANAT ventricular.

ventriloquism [venˈtriləkwizəm] *n* ventriloquia *f*.

ventriloquist [venˈtriləkwist] *n* ventrílocuo, a.

ventriloquize [venˈtriləkwaiz] *vi* ser ventrílocuo, a.

ventriloquy [venˈtriləkwi] *n* ventriloquia *f*.

venture [ˈventʃə*] *n* aventura *f*, empresa *f* arriesgada; *a dangerous venture* una aventura peligrosa ‖ — *at a venture* al azar, a la ventura ‖ COMM *business venture* empresa comercial.

venture [ˈventʃə*] *vt* arriesgar, aventurar (life, fortune) ‖ aventurar (an opinion) ‖ jugar; *they ventured all* lo jugaron todo ‖ atreverse a, osar (to dare) ‖ permitirse; *may I venture to suggest...?* ¿puedo permitirme sugerir...? ‖ — *nothing ventured, nothing gained* quien no arriesga no pasa la mar ‖ *to venture a quick glance* echar una mirada furtiva.

◆ *vi* arriesgarse; *to venture out* o *abroad* arriesgarse fuera ‖ ir; *don't venture too far* no vayas muy lejos ‖ atreverse (to dare) ‖ *to venture on* o *upon* arriesgarse en.

venturer [-rə*] *n* aventurero *m*.

venturesome [-səm]; **venturous** [-rəs] *adj* aventurero, ra; atrevido, da (adventurous) ‖ emprendedor, ra (enterprising) ‖ atrevido, da; *venturesome towards women* atrevido con las mujeres ‖ aventurado, da; arriesgado, da; *a venturesome plan* un proyecto aventurado.

venue [ˈvenjuː] *n* lugar *m* (place); *the venue of the crime* el lugar del crimen ‖ lugar *m* de reunión, punto *m* de reunión (meeting place) ‖ SP campo *m* ‖ JUR jurisdicción *f* ‖ JUR *to change the venue* remitir la causa a otro tribunal.

Venus [ˈviːnəs] *pr n* Venus *f*.

veracious [vəˈreiʃəs] *adj* veraz, verídico, ca.

veracity [vəˈræsiti] *n* veracidad *f*.

veranda; verandah [vəˈrændə] *n* veranda *f*, mirador *m*, galería *f*.

verb [vəːb] *n* GRAMM verbo *m*; *transitive verb* verbo transitivo.

verbal [vəːbəl] *adj* verbal; *verbal message* mensaje verbal; *verbal agreement* acuerdo verbal; *verbal noun* sustantivo verbal ‖ literal (translation).

verbalism [-izəm] *n* expresión *f* verbal (an expression) ‖ PHIL verbalismo *m*.

verbalist [-ist] *n* verbalista *m* & *f*.

verbalization [-'eiʃən] *n* expresión *f* con palabras (of an idea) ‖ uso *m* como verbo (of a word).

verbalize ['vəːbəlaiz] *vt* convertir en verbo (to make into a verb) ‖ expresar con palabras.
◆ *vi* ser prolijo, ja (to speak verbosely).

verbascum [vəː'bæskʌm] *n* BOT gordolobo *m*.

verbatim [vəː'beitim] *adj* in extenso ‖ *verbatim record* actas taquigráficas.
◆ *adv* palabra por palabra, literalmente.

verbena [vəː'biːnə] *n* BOT verbena *f*.

verbenaceae [,vəːbi'neisiːi] *pl n* BOT verbenáceas *f*.

verbiage ['vəːbiidʒ] *n* palabrería *f*, verborrea *f*.

verbose [vəː'bəus] *adj* prolijo, ja; verboso, sa.

verbosity [vəː'bɔsiti] *n* verbosidad *f*, verborrea *f*.

verdancy ['vəːdənsi] *n* verdor *m* (greenness) ‖ FIG verdor *m*, ingenuidad *f*, inocencia *f*.

verdant ['vəːdənt] *adj* verde (green) ‖ FIG ingenuo, nua; inocente, verde (inexperienced).

verdict ['vəːdikt] *n* JUR veredicto *m*, fallo *m* (of jury) | juicio *m*, veredicto *m* (of coroner) ‖ fallo *m*, juicio *m* (of an arbitrator) ‖ opinión *f* ‖ — *open verdict* veredicto que no especifica ni el autor ni las circunstancias de un crimen ‖ *to bring in* o *to return a verdict of guilty* pronunciar un veredicto de culpabilidad.

verdigris ['vəːdigris] *n* verdín *m*, cardenillo *m*.

verdure ['vəːdjuə*] *n* verdor *m* (of vegetation) ‖ FIG verdor *m*, vigor *m* (vigour).

verge [vəːdʒ] *n* borde *m*, margen *m* (border, edge) ‖ arcén *m* (of a road) ‖ REL vara *f* ‖ eje *m* del áncora (of a watch) ‖ ARCH fuste *m* (of a column) | borde *m* (of tiling) ‖ HIST jurisdicción *f* ‖ — *on the verge of* al borde de, a dos dedos de; *on the verge of madness* al borde de la locura ‖ *on the verge of doing sth.* a punto de hacer algo ‖ *on the verge of tears* a punto de echarse a llorar.

verge [vəːdʒ] *vi* orientarse, inclinarse; *his policy is verging to the right* su política se inclina hacia la derecha ‖ torcer a; *the road verges to the east* la carretera tuerce al este ‖ *to verge on* rayar en; *courage verging on foolhardiness* valor que raya en la temeridad; *he is verging on forty* raya en los cuarenta años; tirar a; *blue verging on green* azul que tira a verde.

verger ['vəːdʒə*] *n* REL sacristán *m* ‖ macero *m* (mace bearer).

Vergil ['vəːdʒil] *pr n* Virgilio *m*.

Vergilian [vəː'dʒiliən] *adj* virgiliano, na.

verifiable ['verifaiəbl] *adj* comprobable.

verification [,verifi'keiʃən] *n* verificación *f*, comprobación *f* ‖ JUR confirmación *f*.

verify ['verifai] *vt* verificar, comprobar ‖ JUR confirmar.

verily ['verili] *adv* en verdad.

verisimilar [,veri'similə*] *adj* verosímil.

verisimilitude [,verisi'militjuːd] *n* verosimilitud *f*.

verism ['viərizəm] *n* verismo *m*.

veritable ['veritəbl] *adj* verdadero, ra; *a veritable idiot* un verdadero idiota.

verity ['veriti] *n* verdad *f*; *the eternal verities* las verdades eternas ‖ *unquestionable verities* hechos *m* indiscutibles.

verjuice ['vəːdʒuːs] *n* agraz *m*.

vermeil ['vəːmeil] *n* bermellón *m* (vermilion) ‖ color *m* bermejo.
◆ *adj* bermejo, ja.

vermicelli [,vəːmi'seli] *n* fideos *m pl*.

vermicide ['vəːmisaid] *n* vermicida *m*.

vermicular [vəː'mikjulə] *adj* vermicular.

vermiculate [vəː'mikjuleit]; **vermiculated** [-id] *adj* vermiculado, da.

vermiform ['vəːmifɔːm] *adj* vermiforme.

vermifuge ['vəːmifjuːdʒ] *adj* MED vermífugo, ga.
◆ *n* MED vermífugo *m*.

vermilion; vermillion [və'miljən] *adj* bermejo, ja.
◆ *n* bermellón *m*.

vermin ['vəːmin] *n* bichos *m pl* (rats, mice, etc.) ‖ sabandijas *f pl* (fleas, lice, etc.) ‖ FIG gentuza *f*, chusma *f*, canalla *f*, sabandijas *f pl*.

verminous [-əs] *adj* MED verminoso, sa (caused by vermin) ‖ piojoso, sa (lousy) ‖ lleno de bichos (infested with vermin).

vermivorous [vəː'mivərəs] *adj* ZOOL vermívoro, ra.

Vermont [vəː'mɔnt] *pr n* GEOGR Vermont.

vermouth ['vəːməθ] *n* vermut *m*, vermú *m*; *gin and vermouth* vermut con ginebra.

vernacular [və'nækjulə*] *adj* vernáculo, la; *the vernacular languages of Africa* los idiomas vernáculos de África ‖ vulgar; *in vernacular Spanish* en castellano vulgar.
◆ *n* lengua *f* vernácula (indigenous language) ‖ lenguaje *m* vulgar (everyday speech).

vernier ['vəːnjə*] *n* TECH nonio *m*, vernier *m*.

veronica [və'rɔnikə] *n* BOT & TAUR verónica *f*.

verruca [və'ruːkə] *n* MED verruga *f*.
— OBSERV El plural de la palabra *verruca* es *verrucae*.

Versailles [vɛə'sai] *pr n* GEOGR Versalles; *the Treaty of Versailles* el Tratado de Versalles.

versant ['vəːsənt] *n* vertiente *f*, ladera *f* (slope of mountain) ‖ vertiente *f* (inclination of a region).

versatile ['vəːsətail] *adj* de talentos variados, polifacético, ca; con muchas facetas (having various skills); *versatile artist* artista con muchas facetas ‖ ágil, flexible (mind) ‖ que tiene muchos usos (multipurpose); *versatile suit, table* traje, mesa que tiene muchos usos ‖ versátil (changeable) ‖ BOT & ZOOL versátil.

versatility [,vəːsə'tiliti] *n* diversos talentos *m pl*, carácter *m* polifacético, varias aptitudes *f pl* (many talents) ‖ agilidad *f*, flexibilidad *f* (of the mind) ‖ diversos usos *m pl* (many uses) ‖ versatilidad *f* (changeableness) ‖ BOT & ZOOL versatilidad *f*.

verse [vəːs] *n* verso *m* (poetry); *free verse* verso libre ‖ estrofa *f* (stanza) ‖ cuplé *m* (of a song) ‖ poesía *f*, versos *m pl*; *the verse of García Lorca* la poesía de García Lorca ‖ REL versículo *m* (of the Bible) ‖ *in verse* en verso.
◆ *adj* en verso; *a verse piece* una obra en verso.

verse [vəːs] *vt/vi* poner en verso, versificar ‖ *to verse o.s. in* familiarizarse con, dedicarse a.

versed [-t] *adj* versado, da; *to be versed in* estar versado en.

versicle ['vəːsikl] *n* versículo *m*.

versicolour; US **versicolor** ['vəːsi,kʌlə*]; **versicoloured;** US **versicolored** [-d] *adj* multicolor.

versification [,vəːsifi'keiʃən] *n* versificación *f*.

versifier ['vəːsifaiə*] *n* versificador, ra.

versify ['vəːsifai] *vt/vi* versificar.

version ['vəːʃən] *n* versión *f*; *each witness gave a different version of what happened* cada testigo dio una versión diferente de lo sucedido ‖ versión *f*, traducción *f* directa (translation) ‖ MED version *f* (of foetus) ‖ MUS interpretación *f*, versión *f* ‖ INFORM versión *f* ‖ — *according to his version* según su versión, según él ‖ *this is my version of what happened* así es como veo yo lo que pasó.

verso ['vəːsəu] *n* vuelta *f*, verso *m*, dorso *m* (of a page) ‖ reverso *m* (of a coin).

versus ['vəːsəs] *prep* contra; *Spain versus France* España contra Francia.

vertebra ['vəːtibrə] *n* ANAT vértebra *f*.
— OBSERV El plural de la palabra inglesa *vertebra* es *vertebrae* o *vertebras*.

vertebral [-l] *adj* ANAT vertebral; *vertebral discs* discos vertebrales; *vertebral column* columna vertebral.

vertebrate ['vəːtibrit] *adj* vertebrado, da.
◆ *n* vertebrado *m*.

vertex ['vəːteks] *n* MATH & ANAT vértice *m* ‖ ASTR cenit *m* ‖ FIG cumbre *f*, cúspide *f*, cima *f*.
— OBSERV El plural de *vertex* es *vertexes* o *vertices*.

vertical ['vəːtikəl] *adj* vertical; *vertical angle* ángulo vertical; *vertical circle* círculo vertical ‖ ANAT del vértice ‖ COMM vertical (organization).
◆ *n* vertical *f*.

verticality [,vəːtikæliti] *n* verticalidad *f*.

vertically ['vəːtikəli] *adv* verticalmente ‖ *vertically opposite angles* ángulos opuestos por el vértice.

vertices ['vəːtə,siz] *pl n* → **vertex.**

verticil ['vəːtisil] *n* BOT verticilo *m*.

vertiginous [vəː'tidʒinəs] *adj* vertiginoso, sa.

vertigo ['vəːtigəu] *n* MED vértigo *m*.
— OBSERV El plural de la palabra inglesa es *vertigoes* o *vertigines*.

vertu [vəː'tuː] *n* → **virtu.**

vervain ['vəːvein] *n* BOT verbena *f*.

verve [vəːv] *n* entusiasmo *m*, vigor *m*, brío *m*, ánimo *m* ‖ THEATR vis *f* cómica.

very ['veri] *adj* mismo, ma; *the very day* el día mismo; *in this very house* en esta misma casa; *at that very moment* en ese mismo momento ‖ propio, pia; *he knew our very thoughts* conocía nuestros propios pensamientos ‖ verdadero, ra (real) ‖ puro, ra; *the very truth* la pura verdad ‖ — *at the very beginning* al principio de todo ‖ *come here this very minute!* ¡ven aquí ahora mismo! ‖ *for that very reason* por eso mismo ‖ *from this very day* a partir de ahora mismo, a partir de hoy mismo ‖ *he arrived a year ago this very day* hoy mismo hace un año que llegó, hoy hace justo un año que llegó ‖ *in the very middle* en el mismísimo centro, justo en medio ‖ *it is the very thing I was looking for* es justo *or* exactamente lo que buscaba ‖ *I shudder at the very thought of it* con sólo *or* nada más pensarlo me echo a temblar ‖ *I was told by the very President himself* me lo dijo el mismísimo *or* el propio Presidente ‖ *she is the very image of her mother* es el vivo retrato *or* la viva imagen de su madre ‖ *the veriest ignorant knows it* hasta el más ignorante lo sabe ‖ *the very air we breathe is polluted* hasta el mismo aire que respiramos está contaminado ‖ *the very idea!* ¡vaya idea!, ¡ni soñarlo! ‖ *the very man I need* exactamente el hombre que necesito.
◆ *adv* muy (extremely); *a very tall building* un edificio muy alto; *very well* muy bien ‖ mucho; *isn't she beautiful? yes, very* es muy guapa ¿verdad? sí, mucho ‖ — *are you hungry? very* ¿tienes hambre? mucha ‖ *at the very latest* a

más tardar || *at the very least* por lo menos || *at the very most* a lo sumo, como máximo, a lo más || *a very little* muy poco; *he only gave me a very little* sólo me dio muy poco || *do your very best!* ¡haz todo lo que puedas!, ¡haz todo lo posible! || *I am so very hungry* tengo tanta hambre || *it's not so very far* no está tan lejos || *it's very cold* está muy frío (thing), hace mucho frío (weather) || *I can't very well do that* no estaría bien que yo lo haga || *of one's very own* de la propiedad exclusiva de uno || *the very best* el mejor de todos, la mejor de todas; *we have many excellent wines but this one is the very best* tenemos muchos vinos excelentes pero éste es el mejor de todos; lo mejor; *he insists on the very best* exige lo mejor || *the very last* el último de todos || *the very next day* el día siguiente || *the very same* el mismísimo, la mismísima || *very good* muy bueno (extremely good), muy bien (all right) || *very many* muchísimos || *very much* mucho, muchísimo; *very much better* mucho mejor; *I love you very much* te quiero mucho || *very much so* muchísimo || *very very few* muy pocos, muy pocas, poquísimos, poquísimas.

— OBSERV The prefixes *requete-* and *archi-* may sometimes be used to translate the idea of *very* or *very very*: *very good* requetebueno, archibueno.

Very light [ˈviərilait] *n* MIL bengala *f* Very.

vesica [ˈvesikə] *n* ANAT vejiga *f* || *vesica natatoria* vejiga natatoria.

— OBSERV El plural de *vesica* es *vesicae*.

vesical [-l] *adj* de la vejiga, vesical.

vesicant [-nt] *adj* MED vesicante.

◆ *n* MED vesicante *m*.

vesicate [ˈvesikeit] *vt* levantar ampollas.

vesicatory [ˈvesikətəri] *adj* MED vejigatorio, ria; vesicatorio, ria.

◆ *n* MED vejigatorio *m*, vesicatorio *m*.

vesicle [ˈvesikl] *n* ANAT vesícula *f*.

vesicula [vəˈsikjulə] *n* ANAT vesícula *f*.

vesicular [-*] *adj* ANAT vesicular.

vesper [ˈvespə*] *n* POET tarde *f* || ASTR estrella *f* vespertina (evening star).

◆ *pl* REL vísperas *f*.

◆ *adj* vespertino, na (of evening).

vesperal [-rəl] *n* REL vesperal *m* (book).

vespiary [ˈvespjəri] *n* avispero *m*.

Vespucci [vesˈputʃi] *pr n* Vespucio *m*.

vessel [ˈvesəl] *n* vasija *f*, vaso *m*, recipiente *m* (receptacle) || MAR nave *f*, navío *m*, buque *m*, barco *m* || BOT & ANAT vaso *m*; *blood vessel* vasos sanguíneos || — REL *sacred vessels* vasos sagrados || FIG *the weaker vessel* el sexo débil | *to be a weak vessel* no tener carácter, ser débil.

vest [vest] *n* camiseta *f* (underwear) || US chaleco *m* (waistcoat) || SP *running vest* camiseta *f*.

vest [vest] *vt* investir; *to vest s.o. with sth.* investir a alguien de algo || conferir, conceder; *to vest s.o. with authority* conferir autoridad a alguien || (ant) vestir (to clad) || — *the power vested in the State* el poder atribuido al Estado || *to vest in* conceder a, conferir a; *to vest rights in s.o.* conceder derechos a alguien; dar a, ceder a (property).

◆ *vi* *to vest in s.o.* ser atribuido a alguien, corresponder por derecho a alguien.

vesta [ˈvestə] *n* cerilla *f* (wax match).

vestal [ˈvəstal] *adj* vestal (related to vesta) || *vestal virgin* vestal *f*.

◆ *n* vestal *f*.

vested [ˈvestid] *adj* concedido, da || *vested interest* derecho adquirido (legal term), interés *m* personal; *many vested interest are involved in this affair* muchos intereses personales entran en juego en este asunto; intereses *m pl*; *to have a vested interest in a concern* tener intereses en una empresa.

vestibular [vesˈtibjulə*] *adj* ANAT vestibular.

vestibule [ˈvestibjuːl] *n* ARCH vestíbulo *m* (of a building) | zaguán *m*, vestíbulo *m* (of a house) || ANAT vestíbulo *m* || US fuelle *m* (in a railway carriage).

vestige [ˈvestidʒ] *n* vestigio *m*, rastro *m*; *not a vestige could be found* ni un rastro se podía encontrar || BIOL rudimento *m* || FIG *without a vestige of doubt* sin la menor duda.

vestigial [vesˈtidʒiəl] *adj* rudimentario, ria.

vestment [ˈvestmənt] *n* vestidura *f*.

vest-pocket [ˈvestˈpɔkit] *adj* de bolsillo.

vestry [ˈvestri] *n* REL sacristía *f* (sacristy) | junta *f* parroquial (administrative body).

vestryman [-mən] *n* REL miembro *m* de la junta parroquial.

— OBSERV El plural de esta palabra es *vestrymen*.

vesture [ˈvestʃə*] *n* (ant) vestidura *f*.

vesturer [-rə*] *n* REL sacristán *m* (sexton).

Vesuvius [viˈsuːvjəs] *pr n* GEOGR Vesubio *m*.

vet [vet] *n* FAM veterinario *m* || veterano *m*.

vet [vet] *vt* FAM reconocer (to examine an animal) | castrar (to castrate an animal) | corregir, revisar (an article) | someter a una investigación [hecha por los servicios de Seguridad] (person).

vetch [vetʃ] *n* BOT arveja *f*.

vetchling [-liŋ] *n* BOT almorta *f*.

veteran [ˈvetərən] *adj* veterano, na; *a veteran soldier* un soldado veterano || experimentado, da (experienced) || US excombatiente || *veteran car* coche *m* de época || *veteran troops* tropas aguerridas.

◆ *n* veterano *m* (old soldier) || US excombatiente *m* (ex-serviceman).

veterinarian [ˌvetəriˈnɛərjən] *n* US veterinario *m*.

veterinary [ˈvetərinəri] *adj* veterinario, ria || — *veterinary medecine* o *science* veterinaria *f* || *veterinary surgeon* veterinario *m*.

◆ *n* veterinario *m*.

veto [ˈviːtəu] *n* veto *m*; *to put a veto on sth.* ponerle el veto a algo; *power* o *righ of veto* derecho de veto; *suspensory, absolute veto* veto suspensivo, absoluto.

— OBSERV El plural de la palabra inglesa *veto* es *vetoes*.

veto [ˈviːtəu] *vt* vetar, poner el veto a (to use one's veto) || vedar, prohibir (to forbid); *the police vetoed the demonstration* la policía prohibió la manifestación.

vex [veks] *vt* molestar, fastidiar (to annoy); *his continuous chatter vexes me* su charla continua me molesta || disgustar; *her behaviour severely vexed her father* su comportamiento disgustó mucho a su padre || enfadar (to make angry) || afligir (to afflict) || agitar (the sea).

◆ *vi* *to vex over* preocuparse por.

vexation [vekˈseiʃən] *n* molestia *f*, fastidio *m* (irritation) || disgusto *m*; *the vexations one has to support* los disgustos que uno tiene que aguantar || aflicción *f*.

vexatious [vekˈseiʃəs] *adj* molesto, ta; fastidioso, sa (annoying) || JUR vejatorio, ria.

vexed [vekst] *adj* enfadado, da; *to be vexed about* estar enfadado con *or* por; *he is vexed with me* está enfadado conmigo || batallón, ona; controvertido, da (question) || *to get* o *to become vexed* enfadarse.

vexing [ˈveksiŋ] *adj* molesto, ta; fastidioso, sa.

VHF *abbr of* *[very high frequency]* VHF, frecuencia muy alta.

via [ˈvaiə] *prep* por, vía; *Madrid-London via Paris* Madrid Londres vía París; *I came home via Rome* volví a casa por Roma.

viability [ˌvaiəˈbiliti] *n* viabilidad *f*.

viable [ˈvaiəbl] *adj* viable.

viaduct [ˈvaiədʌkt] *n* viaducto *m*.

vial [ˈvaiəl] *n* frasco *m* (phial).

viands [ˈvaiəndz] *pl n* manjares *m*, viandas *f*.

viaticum [vaiˈætikəm] *n* viático *m*.

— OBSERV El plural de *viaticum* es *viaticums* o *viatica*.

vibrancy [ˈvaibrənsi] *n* vibración *f*.

vibrant [ˈvaibrənt] *adj* vibrante (which vibrates) || FIG lleno de vitalidad, enérgico, ca (person); *vibrant woman* mujer enérgica | animado, da (place); *vibrant streets* calles animadas || GRAMM vibrante (sound).

◆ *n* GRAMM vibrante *f*.

vibraphone [ˈvaibrəfəun] *n* MUS vibráfono *m*.

vibrate [vaiˈbreit] *vi* vibrar; *the house vibrates when a train passes* la casa vibra cuando pasa un tren || oscilar (to swing to and fro) || FIG vibrar (*with* de).

◆ *vt* hacer vibrar.

vibratile [ˈvaibrətail] *adj* vibrátil.

vibrating [vaiˈbreitiŋ] *adj* vibrante || vibratorio, ria; *vibrating movement* movimiento vibratorio || FIG vibrante; *voice vibrating with emotion* voz vibrante de emoción.

vibration [vaiˈbreiʃən] *n* vibración *f* || oscilación *f* (of a pendulum).

vibrato [viˈbrɑːtəu] *n* MUS vibrato *m*.

vibrator [vaiˈbreitə*] *n* vibrador *m* || MUS lengüeta *f*.

vibratory [-ri] *adj* vibratorio, ria.

vibrio [ˈvibriəu] *n* MED vibrión *m*.

vibromassage [ˈvaibrəuˌmæsɑːʒ] *n* MED vibromasaje *m*.

vicar [ˈvikə*] *n* REL vicario *m*; *the Pope is the Vicar of Christ* el Papa es el Vicario de Jesucristo | cura *m*, párroco *m* (of a parish) | vicario *m* (bishop's assistant).

— OBSERV El *vicar* es un pastor de la Iglesia anglicana titular de un beneficio eclesiástico.

vicarage [-ridʒ] *n* casa *f* del párroco.

vicar-general [-ˈdʒenərəl] *n* vicario *m* general.

vicariate [vaiˈkɛəriit] *n* vicariato *m*, vicaría *f*.

vicarious [vaiˈkɛəriəs] *adj* delegado, da (authority) || sustituto, ta (agent) || hecho por otro (work) || sufrido por otro (punishment) || indirecto, ta (pleasure, thrill).

vicariously [-li] *adv* por otro, indirectamente.

vice [vais] *n* vicio *m* (depravity) || vicio *m*, defecto *m* (fault) || resabio *m* (of a horse) || TECH torno *m* de banco, tornillo *m* de banco.

vice [vaisi] *prep* en lugar de, sustituyendo a, en vez de.

vice admiral [ˈvaisˈædmərəl] *n* vicealmirante *m*.

vice admiralty [-ti] *n* vicealmirantazgo *m*.

vice-chairman [ˈvaisˈtʃɛəmən] *n* vicepresidente *m*.

— OBSERV El plural de esta palabra es *vice-chairmen*.

vice-chairmanship [-ʃip] *n* vicepresidencia *f*.

vice-chancellor [ˈvaisˈtʃɑːnsələ*] *n* vicecanciller *m* (of a country) || rector *m* (of a university) || *vicechancellor's office* vicecancillería *f*, rectoría *f*.

vice-chancellorship [-ʃip] *n* vicecancillería *f* (in a country) || rectorado *m* (in a university).

vice-clamp [vaisˌklæmp] *n* TECH mordaza *f*, tenaza *f*.

vice-consul [ˈvaisˈkɔnsəl] *n* vicecónsul *m*.

vice-consulate [ˈvaisˈkɔnsjulit] *n* viceconsulado *m*.

vicegerent [ˈvaisˈdʒerənt] *n* representante *m*.

vice-governor [ˈvaisˈgʌvənə*] *n* vicegobernador *m*.

vicenary [ˈvisənəri] *adj* vigesimal.

vice-presidency [ˈvaisˈprezidənsi] *n* vicepresidencia *f*.

vice-president [ˈvaisˈprezidənt] *n* vicepresidente *m*.

vice-rector [ˈvaisˈrektə*] *n* vicerrector *m*.

vicereine [ˈvaisˈrein] *n* virreina *f*.

viceroy [ˈvaisrɔi] *n* virrey *m*.

viceroyalty [ˈvaisrɔiəlti] *n* virreinato *m*.

vice squad [ˈvaisskwəd] *n* brigada *f* contra el vicio.

vice versa [ˈvaisiˈvəːsə] *adv* viceversa.

vicinage [ˈvisinidʒ] *n* vecindad *f* (neighbourhood) || vecinos *m pl* (persons).

vicinal [ˈvisinəl] *adj* vecinal; *vicinal roads* caminos vecinales.

vicinity [ˈvisiniti] *n* vecindad *f*, proximidad *f* (nearness) || vecindad *f* inmediaciones *f pl* (neighbourhood) || región *f*; *the roads in the vicinity* las carreteras de la región || — *in the vicinity of a large town* cerca de una gran ciudad || *in the vicinity of twenty* alrededor de unos veinte.

vicious [ˈviʃəs] *adj* vicioso, sa (given to vice, characterized by vice) || depravado, da; pervertido, da (depraved) || disoluto, ta (life) || corrompido, da (taste) || incorrecto, ta; vicioso, sa (reasoning) || resabiado, da (horse) || malo, la (bad); *vicious style* estilo malo || malintencionado, da (with evil intent) || rencoroso, sa (rancorous) || atroz, horrible (crime) || fuerte; *a vicious pull* un tirón fuerte || violento, ta (violent) || FIG *vicious circle* círculo vicioso.

viciously [-li] *adj* viciosamente (depravedly) || con mala intención (spitefully) || furiosamente, con rabia (angrily) || incorrectamente (incorrectly).

viciousness [-nis] *n* lo vicioso || perversidad *f*, depravación *f* (depravation) || maldad *f* (evil) || resabios *m pl* (of a horse).

vicissitude [viˈsisitjuːd] *n* vicisitud *f*.

vicissitudinous [viˌsisiˈtjuːdinəs] *adj* agitado, da; lleno de vicisitudes.

victim [ˈviktim] *n* víctima *f*; *he was the victim of an accident* fue víctima de un accidente; *she was the victim of dishonest shopkeepers* fue víctima de tenderos poco honrados || — *many fell a victim to the plague* muchos murieron víctimas de la peste || *to fall a victim to a heavy cold* coger un resfriado muy fuerte || *to fall a victim to a woman's charm* sucumbir ante el atractivo de una mujer.

victimization [ˌviktimaiˈzeiʃən] *n* persecución *f* (persecution) || represalias *f pl* (in strike settlement); *there shall be no victimization* no habrá represalias || *a case of victimization* un engaño.

victimize [ˈviktimaiz] *vt* tomar como víctima (to make a victim of); *I don't know why you are victimizing me* no sé por qué me ha tomado como víctima || perseguir (to persecute) || tomar represalias contra (strikers, etc.) || engañar (to trick).

victor [ˈviktə*] *n* vencedor, ra; triunfador, ra.

victoria [vikˈtɔːriə] *n* victoria *f* (carriage) || BOT victoria *f* regia.

Victoria [vikˈtɔːriə] *pr n* Victoria *f*.

Victoria Cross [-krɔs] *n* MIL Cruz *f* Victoria [condecoración al valor militar].

Victoria Lake [-leik] *pr n* GEOGR lago *m* Victoria.

Victorian [-n] *adj/n* victoriano, na.

Victoriana [vikˌtɔːriˈɑːnə] *n* antigüedades *f pl* del período victoriano.

victorious [vikˈtɔːriəs] *adj* victorioso, sa; *victorious action* acción victoriosa || vencedor, ra; triunfante; *the victorious army* el ejército vencedor || de victoria (day) || *to be victorious over s.o.* vencer a alguien, triunfar de alguien.

victoriously [-li] *adv* victoriosamente || triunfalmente; *to receive victoriously* recibir triunfalmente.

victory [ˈviktəri] *n* victoria *f*; *overwhelming victory* victoria aplastante; *to gain* o *to win a victory over s.o.* obtener una victoria sobre uno || triunfo *m* || FIG triunfo *m* (success) || *pyrrhic victory* victoria pírrica.

victress [ˈviktris] *n* triunfadora *f*, vencedora *f*.

victual [ˈvitəl] *vt* abastecer, aprovisionar || MIL avituallar, aprovisionar.

◆ *vi* abastecerse, tomar provisiones || MIL avituallarse, tomar provisiones || comer (to eat).

victualer; victualler [-ə*] *n* proveedor, ra; abastecedor, ra (supplier) || MAR buque *m* abastecedor || *licenced victualler* vendedor *m* de bebidas alcohólicas.

victualing; victualling [-iŋ] *n* abastecimiento *m* || MIL avituallamiento *m*, aprovisionamiento *m*.

victuals [-z] *pl n* vituallas *f* (food) || provisiones *f*, víveres *m*.

vicuna; vicuña; vicugna [viˈkjuːnə] *n* vicuña *f*.

vide [ˈvaidi] *vt* véase; *vide ante* véase lo anterior; *vide infra* véase más adelante; *vide supra* véase más arriba.

— OBSERV *Vide* es la segunda persona del singular del imperativo del verbo latino *videre*. Tiene dos abreviaturas: *v.* y *vid.*

videlicet [viˈdiːliset] *adv* a saber, es decir.

— OBSERV La abreviatura de este adverbio es *viz.*

video [ˈvideiəu] *n* RAD video *m* | televisión *f*.

◆ *adj* video; *video signal* señal video || *video tape* cinta magnética para grabar programas de televisión || INFORM *video terminal* terminal *m* vídeo.

videocassette [-kəˌset] *n* videocasete *m*.

video game [-geim] *n* videojuego *m*.

videotext [-tekst] *n* INFORM videotexto *m* || *videotex terminal* terminal videotex.

vie [vai] *vi* competir, rivalizar; *I refuse to vie with him over sth. so silly* me niego a competir con él por una cosa tan tonta || — *they vie with one another for the first place* se disputan el primer puesto || *to vie in civilities with* rivalizar en cortesía con.

Vienna [viˈenə] *pr n* GEOGR Viena *f*.

Viennese [ˌviəˈniːz] *adj/n* vienés, esa.

Vietnam [ˈvjetˈnæm] *pr n* GEOGR Vietnam *m*.

Vietnamese [ˌvjetnəˈmiːz] *adj/n* vietnamita.

view [vjuː] *n* vista *f*, panorama *m*; *you get a lovely view from the castle* tiene un panorama magnífico desde el castillo || vista *f*; *your room has a fine view of the park* tu habitación tiene una bonita vista del parque || vista *f* (photo); *views of London* vistas de Londres || ARTS vista *f* (scene) | paisaje *m* (landscape) || inspección *f*; *they asked for a view of the boat* pidieron una inspección del barco || idea *f*; *he holds extremist views* tiene ideas extremistas || visión *f* de conjunto, panorama *m* (survey); *he gave us a view of contemporary literature* nos dio un panorama de la literatura contemporánea || opinión *f*, parecer *m* (opinion); *in my view* a mi parecer, en mi opinión || enfoque *m* (approach) || — *a first view* a primera vista || *exchange of views* cambio *m* de impresiones || *exposed to view* expuesto a las miradas || *field of view* campo *m* de visión || *from my point of view* desde mi punto de vista || *front view of a house* casa vista de frente || *hidden from view* tapado, da || *house with a sea view* casa *f* con vistas al mar || *I have nothing in view tonight* no tengo ningún plan para esta noche || *in full view of the crowd* ante la multitud, a la vista de la multitud || *in view of* dado, considerando, en vista de, a la vista de; *in view of the problems* considerando los problemas || FIG *overall view* visión de conjunto, vista de conjunto || *panoramic view* vista panorámica || *point of view* punto *m* de vista || *private view* inauguración *f* de una exposición de arte || *to be in view* estar a la vista || *to be on view* estar expuesto || *to be on view to the public* estar abierto al público || *to come into view* aparecer || *to get a better view of* ver mejor || *to get a bird's eye view of the town* tener una vista panorámica de la ciudad || *to get a side view of sth.* ver algo de lado || *to go out of view* desaparecer || *to have a closer view of* ver más de cerca || *to have sth. in view* tener algo a la vista; *I have a project in view* tengo un proyecto a la vista; tener en cuenta, tener presente (to keep in mind) || *to keep sth. in view* no perder algo de vista || *to take a dim view of* ver con malos ojos || *to take a favourable view of* ver con buenos ojos || *to take the view that* pensar que, tener la impresión de que || *what are your views of this?* ¿cuáles son tus opiniones acerca de esto?, ¿cuál es su parecer acerca de esto?, ¿qué opina de esto? || *with a view* con buena vista || *with a view to* con miras a, con vistas a, con objeto de; *negotiations with a view to an alliance* negociaciones con vistas a una alianza || *with this in view* con este objetivo, con este fin.

view [vjuː] *vt* mirar, ver (to look at) || ver, visitar; *they are coming to view the room* vienen a ver la habitación || inspeccionar (to inspect) || considerar, ver (to consider); *he views the matter from the taxpayer's standpoint* considera el asunto desde el punto de vista del contribuyente || enfocar, considerar; *the subject may be viewed in various ways* el tema se puede enfocar de varias maneras.

viewdata [-deitə] *n* servicio *m* británico de videotex interactivo.

viewer [-ə*] *n* telespectador, ra; televidente *m* & *f* (television watcher) || espectador, ra (onlooker) || inspector, ra || PHOT visionadora *f* (for slides).

viewfinder [-ˌfaində*] *n* PHOT visor *m*.

viewing [-iŋ] *n* visita *f*; *show flat open for viewing from 9 till 12* visita del piso modelo de 9 a 12 || inspección *f*.

viewless [-lis] *adj* sin vista (house) || invisible || sin opinión.

viewpoint [-pɔint] *n* punto *m* de vista; *from my viewpoint* desde mi punto de vista || mirador *m*.

viewy [-i] *adj* US visionario, ria.

vigesimal [vaiˈdʒesiməl] *adj* vigesimal.

vigil [ˈvidʒil] *n* vigilia *f*, vela *f* || vela *f*; *the vigil of a corpse* la vela de un cadáver || REL vigilia *f* || *to keep vigil* velar.

vigilance [-əns] *n* vigilancia *f*; *they scaped the police's vigilance* burlaron la vigilancia de la policía || MED insomnio *m* || *vigilance committee* vigilancia.

vigilant [-ənt] *adj* vigilante.

vigilante [ˌvidʒiˈlænti] *n* US vigilante *m*.

vignette [vi'njet] *n* PRINT viñeta *f* (ornamentation) || retrato *m* de medio cuerpo con bordes desvanecidos (portrait, photo) || THEATR sainete *m*.

vigor ['vigə*] *n* US ⟶ **vigour.**

vigorous [-rəs] *adj* vigoroso, sa; *a vigorous man* un hombre vigoroso || enérgico, ca; *a vigorous massage* un masaje enérgico.

vigour; US **vigor** ['vigə*] *n* vigor *m*, energía *f* || FIG vigor *m*, fuerza *f* (of style) || — *in vigour* en vigor, vigente (law) || *man of vigour* hombre enérgico.

Viking ['vaikiŋ] *n* vikingo *m*.

vilayet [vi'lɑːjet] *n* vilayato *m* (Turkish province).

vile [vail] *adj* vil, ruin (morally base); *the vilest of men* el hombre más ruin || infame; *a vile calumny* una calumnia infame || malísimo, ma (very bad) || asqueroso, sa; repugnante; *a vile smell* un olor repugnante || pésimo, ma; horrible, espantoso, sa; de perros (weather) || muy malo, la; de perros (temper); *he is in a vile temper* está de muy mal humor, está de un humor de perros || sin valor (worthless).

vilely [-li] *adv* vilmente || de una manera infame || malísimamente (very badly) || horriblemente.

vileness [-nis] *n* vileza *f* (baseness) || infamia *f* (infamy) || bajeza *f* (of a sentiment) || *the vileness of the weather* el tiempo pésimo que hace.

vilification [ˌvilifi'keiʃən] *n* denigración *f*, difamación *f*.

vilifier ['vilifaiə*] *n* difamador, ra; denigrador, ra.

vilify ['vilifai] *vt* denigrar, difamar.

vilipend ['vilipend] *vt* vilipendiar.

vilipender [-ə*] *n* vilipendiador, ra.

villa ['vilə] *n* casa *f* de campo, quinta *f* (country house) || chalet *m* (suburban residence).

village ['vilidʒ] *n* pueblo *m* (large) || aldea *f*, pueblecito *m* (small).
◆ *adj* pueblerino, na; *village life* vida pueblerina || del pueblo; *the village idiot* el tonto del pueblo.

villager [-ə*] *n* aldeano, na.

villain ['vilən] *n* canalla *m*, maleante *m* (s.o. wicked); *some villain robbed the widow of her savings* un canalla robó a la viuda sus ahorros || FAM bribón, ona; *this child is a villain* este niño es un bribón || THEATR malo *m* | (ant) siervo *m* de la gleba, villano, na (villein) || FIG *the villain of the piece* el responsable.

villainous [-əs] *adj* vil, infame; *a villainous deed* una acción infame || horrible, espantoso, sa; pésimo, ma; de perros; *villainous weather* tiempo de perros || malísimo, ma; espantoso, sa; pésimo, ma; *villainous handwriting* letra malísima.

villainy [-i] *n* villanía *f*, maldad *f*, vileza *f* (villainous act) || infamia *f*, maldad *f*, vileza *f* (of an action).

villein ['vilin] *n* siervo *m* de la gleba, villano, na.

villeinage [-idʒ] *n* villanía *f*, villanaje *m*.

villosity [vi'lɔsiti] *n* vellosidad *f*.

Vilnius ['vilniəs] *pr n* GEOGR Vilna.

vim [vim] *n* FAM energía *f*; *full of vim* lleno de energía || — *put some vim into it!* ¡dale fuerte! || *put some vim into your work!* ¡dale fuerte al trabajo!

vinaceous [vi'neiʃəs] *adj* vinoso, sa (colour).

vinaigrette [vini'gret] *n* vinagrera *f* (container) || vinagreta *f* (sauce) || frasco *m* de sales (for smelling salts).

Vincent ['vinsənt] *pr n* Vicente *m*.

vindicable ['vindikəbl] *adj* justificable.

vindicate ['vindikeit] *vt* justificar (one's behaviour) || defender (one's faith) || mantener, sostener (one's opinion) || reivindicar (one's rights) || *to vindicate o.s.* justificarse.

vindication [ˌvindi'keiʃən] *n* justificación *f* || reivindicación *f* (of one's rights).

vindicative [vin'dikətiv] *adj* justificativo, va.

vindicator ['vindikeitə*] *n* defensor *m*.

vindicatory [-ri] *adj* justificativo, va (vindicative) || vindicativo, va (vindictive).

vindictive [vin'diktiv] *adj* vindicativo, va; vengativo, va || impuesto como venganza (punishment) || *there is no need to feel vindictive towards him* no hay por qué guardarle rencor.

vindictiveness [-nis] *n* carácter *m* vengativo || rencor (resentment).

vine [vain] *n* BOT vid *f* (grapevine) | sarmiento *m* (stem) || parra *f*; *to sit under the vine* sentarse bajo la parra || US BOT enredadera *f*, planta *f* trepadora (climbing plant).

vine arbour; US **vine arbor** [-ˌɑːbə*] *n* parra *f*.

vinedresser [-ˌdresə*] *n* viñador *m*, viñatero *m*.

vinegar ['vinigə*] *n* vinagre *m* || — *vinegar bottle* vinagrera *f* || *vinegar cruet* vinagreras *f pl* || *vinegar maker* vinagrero *m* || *vinegar sauce* vinagreta *f*.

vinegary [-ri] *adj* avinagrado, da.

vine grower ['vainˌgrəuə*] *n* viticultor *m*, viñador *m* (viticulturist).

vine growing ['vainˌgrəuiŋ] *n* viticultura *f*.

vine leaf ['vainliːf] *n* hoja *f* de parra *or* de vid.

vinery ['vainəri] *n* invernadero *m* para el cultivo de la vid (greenhouse).

vine shoot ['vainʃuːt] *n* sarmiento *m*.

vinestock ['vainstɔk] *n* cepa *f*.

vineyard ['vinjəd] *n* viña *f*, viñedo *m* || REL *to work in the Lord's vineyard* trabajar en la viña del Señor.

vinic ['vainik] *adj* vínico, ca.

vinicultural [ˌvini'kʌltʃərəd] *adj* vinícola, vitivinícola.

viniculture ['vinikʌltʃə*] *n* vinicultura *f*, viticultura *f*.

vinification [ˌvinifi'keiʃən] *n* vinificación *f*.

vinous ['vainəs] *adj* vinoso, sa || de color de vino || FIG borracho, cha (drunk).

vintage ['vintidʒ] *n* vendimia *f* (season, harvest) || cosecha *f* (crop); *the 1960 vintage* la cosecha de 1960.
◆ *adj* de calidad, añejo, ja (wine) || antiguo, gua (car) || muy bueno, na; excelente; *a vintage year for sport, wine* un año excelente para el deporte, el vino || antiguo, gua; *a vintage joke* un chiste antiguo.

vintner ['vintnə*] *n* vinatero *m*.

viny ['vaini] *adj* vinícola.

vinyl ['vainil] *n* CHEM vinilo *m*.
◆ *adj* vinílico, ca.

viol ['vaiəl] *n* MUS viola *f*.

viola [vi'əulə] *n* MUS viola *f* || BOT violeta *f*.

violaceous [vaiə'leiʃəs] *adj* violáceo, a.

viola da gamba [vi'əuləda'gæmbə] *n* MUS viola *f* de gamba.

violate ['vaiəleit] *vt* violar, infringir, quebrantar (a law) || no cumplir (promise) || violar (a woman) || violar, profanar (sacred place) || *to violate s.o.'s privacy* meterse en la vida privada de alguien.

violation [ˌvaiə'leiʃən] *n* violación *f* (of woman, of secret) || violación *f*, infracción *f* (of law) || profanación *f* (of sacred place).

violator ['vaiəleitə*] *n* violador, ra.

violence ['vaiələns] *n* violencia *f* || — JUR *acts of violence* vías *f* de hecho || *to die by violence* morir violentamente || *to do violence to* violentar (to use violence on), ir en contra de (one's principles) || *to resort to violence* recurrir a la violencia *or* a la fuerza || *to use violence* emplear la violencia.

violent ['vaiələnt] *adj* violento, ta; *a violent storm* una tormenta violenta || chillón, ona; *violent colours* colores chillones || intenso, sa; *violent pain* dolor intenso || profundo, da; *a violent dislike* una profunda antipatía || — *to become violent* mostrarse violento || *to be in a violent temper* estar furioso || *to lay violent hands on o.s.* atentar contra su vida || *to lay violent hands on s.o.* agredir a alguien.

violently [-li] *adv* violentamente; *to die violently* morir violentamente || terriblemente, extremadamente; *she was violently upset* estaba terriblemente disgustada || furiosamente, perdidamente; *to fall violently in love* enamorarse furiosamente || *to be violently sick* o *ill* vomitar mucho.

violet ['vaiəlit] *n* BOT violeta *f* (flower) || violado *m*, violeta *m* (colour) || — *violet seller* violetera *f* || *violet wood* palisandro *m*.
◆ *adj* violado, da; violeta.

violin [ˌvaiə'lin] *n* MUS violín *m* (instrument) | violín *m*, violinista *m* & *f*; *first violin* primer violín.

violinist [-ist] *n* MUS violinista *m* & *f*.

violoncellist [ˌvaiələn'tʃelist] *n* MUS violonchelista *m* & *f*, violoncelista *m* & *f*.

violoncello [ˌvaiələn'tʃeləu] *n* MUS violonchelo *m*, violoncelo *m*.

VIP [viːai'piː] *n* personalidad *f*.
— OBSERV VIP es la abreviatura de *Very Important Person* persona muy importante.

viper ['vaipə*] *n* ZOOL & FIG víbora *f*.

viperish [-riʃ] *adj* FIG viperino, na (tongue).

viperous [-rəs] *adj* viperino, na.

viper's grass [-s'grɑːs] *n* BOT escorzonera *f*.

virago [vi'rɑːgəu] *n* virago *m*, mujer *f* varonil (manlike) || fiera *f*, arpía *f* (quarrelsome).
— OBSERV El plural de la palabra inglesa es *viragoes* o *viragos*.

viral ['vairəl] *adj* vírico, ca; viral.

Virgil ['vəːdʒil] *pr n* Virgilio *m*.

virgin ['vəːdzin] *n* virgen *f* || ASTR Virgo *m* || — REL *the Blessed Virgin* la Virgen Santísima | *the Virgin* la Virgen | *the Virgin Mary* la Virgen María, María Santísima || GEOGR *Virgin Islands* islas *f* Vírgenes.
◆ *adj* virgen; *virgin forest* selva virgen; *virgin wax* cera virgen || *virgin birth* parto *m* virginal de María (of Jesus Christ), partenogénesis *f* (in zoology).

virginal [-əl] *adj* virginal.
◆ *n* MUS espineta *f*.

Virginia [və'dʒiniə] *pr n* GEOGR Virginia *f* || BOT *Virginia creeper* viña loca.

Virginian [-ən] *adj/n* virginiano, na.

virginity [vəː'dʒiniti] *n* virginidad *f*.

Virgo ['vəːgəu] *pr n* ASTR Virgo *m*.

virgule ['vəːgjuːl] *n* vírgula *f*.

viridescent [ˌviri'desnt] *adj* verdusco, ca; verdoso, sa (greenish).

viridity [vi'riditi] *n* verdor *m*.

virile ['virail] *adj* varonil, viril || FIG enérgico, ca; viril || ANAT *virile member* miembro viril.

virility [vi'riliti] *n* virilidad *f*.

virtu; vertu [vəːtuː] *n* afición *f* a los objetos de arte y a las antigüedades (knowledge, liking) || objetos *m pl* de arte, curiosidades *f pl*, antigüedades *f pl* (curios, etc.).

virtual [ˈvəːtjuəl] *adj* verdadero, ra; *he is the virtual head of the firm* es el verdadero jefe de la empresa; *it was a virtual confession* fue una verdadera confesión || PHYS virtual; *virtual focus* foco virtual; *virtual image* imagen virtual || INFORM *virtual address* dirección *f* virtual | *virtual memory* o *storage* memoria *f* virtual.

virtuality [ˌvəːtjuˈæliti] *n* virtualidad *f*.

virtually [ˈvəːtjuəli] *adv* prácticamente, casi; *I am virtually certain of it* estoy casi seguro de ello; *it's virtually impossible* es casi imposible.

virtue [ˈvəːtjuː] *n* virtud *f* (of a person) || virtud *f* (as a remedy) || ventaja *f*; *it has the virtue of being small* tiene la ventaja de ser pequeño; *I cannot see the virtue of it* no le veo la ventaja || castidad *f*, honra *f*, honestidad *f* (female chastity) || REL virtud *f* || — *by* o *in virtue of* debido a, en virtud de; *he can do it by virtue of his position* lo puede hacer debido a su posición || *to make a virtue of necessity* hacer de la necesidad virtud || *woman of easy virtue* mujer ligera || *woman of virtue* mujer honesta.

virtuosity [ˌvəːtjuˈɔsiti] *n* virtuosismo *m*, virtuosidad *f*.

virtuoso [ˌvəːtjuˈəuzəu] *n* virtuoso, sa (musician) || coleccionista *m* & *f*, aficionado a los objetos de arte.

— OBSERV El plural de la palabra inglesa *virtuoso* es *virtuosos* o *virtuosi*.

virtuous [ˈvəːtjuəs] *adj* virtuoso, sa.

virtuousness [-nis] *n* virtud *f*.

virulence [ˈvirulәns] *n* virulencia *f*.

virulent [ˈvirulənt] *adj* virulento, ta.

virus [ˈvaiərəs] *n* MED virus *m* || INFORM virus *m*.

visa [ˈviːzə]; **visé** [ˈviːzei] *n* visado *m* [AMER visa *f*].

visage [ˈvizidʒ] *n* rostro *m*, cara *f* (face) || semblante *m* (countenance) || aspecto *m*.

vis-à-vis [ˈviːzɑːviː] *n* persona *f* colocada enfrente de *or* frente a otra; *my vis-à-vis at table* la persona colocada frente a mí en la mesa || confidente *m* (sofa).

◆ *prep* respecto a, acerca de (about); *his opinion vis-à-vis the crisis* su opinión acerca de la crisis || comparado con, con relación a; *the situation vis-à-vis what it was yesterday* la situación comparada con lo que era ayer || enfrente de (opposite); *vis-à-vis the Town Hall* enfrente del Ayuntamiento.

◆ *adv* cara a cara, frente a frente.

viscacha [visˈkætʃæ] *n* vizcacha *f* (rodent).

viscera [ˈvisərə] *pl n* ANAT vísceras *f*.

visceral [-l] *adj* visceral.

viscid [ˈvisid] *adj* viscoso, sa; pegajoso, sa.

viscidity [viˈsiditi] *n* viscosidad *f*.

viscose [ˈviskəs] *n* viscosa *f*.

◆ *adj* viscoso, sa || de viscosa.

viscosity [visˈkɔsiti] *n* viscosidad *f*.

viscount [ˈvaikaunt] *n* vizconde *m*.

viscountcy [-si] *n* vizcondado *m*.

viscountess [-is] *n* vizcondesa *f*.

viscous [ˈviskəs] *adj* viscoso, sa.

vise [vais] *n* US TECH torno *m or* tornillo *m* de banco.

visé [ˈviːzei] *n* → **visa**.

visibility [ˌviziˈbiliti] *n* visibilidad *f*; *visibility is down to five metres* la visibilidad queda reducida a cinco metros.

visible [ˈvizəbl] *adj* visible || manifiesto, ta; evidente (obvious).

visibly [-i] *adv* visiblemente.

Visigoth [ˈvizigɔθ] *n* visigodo, da.

Visigothic [ˌviziˈgɔθik] *adj* visigodo, da; visigótico, ca.

vision [ˈviʒən] *n* visión *f*; *the eye is the organ of vision* el ojo es el órgano de la visión || vista *f*; *to have normal vision* tener la vista normal; *within the range of vision* al alcance de la vista || visión *f* (apparition) || sueño *m* (dream); *my vision of being a king* mi sueño de ser rey || clarividencia *f*, perspicacia *f* (foresight) || belleza *f* (beauty); *that woman is a vision* esa mujer es una belleza || — *a man of vision* un hombre clarividente || *field of vision* campo *m* visual || *I had visions of being behind bars* me veía ya encarcelado || *to have visions of fame* soñar con ser famoso.

visionary [-əri] *adj* visionario, ria (who sees visions) || soñador, ra (dreaming) || quimérico, ca; imaginario, ria (imaginary) || utópico, ca (impractical).

◆ *n* visionario, ria || soñador, ra (dreamer).

visit [ˈvizit] *n* visita *f*; *a brief visit to Rome* una corta visita a Roma || MAR visita *f* (of a ship) || — FIG *flying visit* visita relámpago *or* de médico || JUR *right of visit* derecho *m* de visita || *to be on a visit to* estar de visita en || FAM *to pay a visit* ir al excusado || *to pay s.o. a visit* visitar a alguien, hacer una visita a alguien || *to return a visit* devolver una visita.

visit [ˈvizit] *vt* visitar a, ir a (to go to) || visitar, hacer una visita a (to call on) || pasar una temporada en (to stay in) || visitar (a church, the sick) || visitar, inspeccionar; *the bishop visits his diocese* el obispo inspecciona su diócesis || REL infligir (punishment) | castigar por (s.o.'s sins) || FIG azotar (by a disease).

◆ *vi* hacer visitas || US FAM charlar.

Visitandine [ˌviziˈtændiːn] *n* REL visitandina *f*.

visitant [ˈvizitənt] *n* ZOOL ave *f* de paso || visitante *m* & *f* (visitor).

visitation [ˌviziˈteiʃən] *n* visita *f*; *pastoral visitation* visita pastoral || REL visitación *f* (feast) | castigo *m* (punishment) || MAR visita *f* (of a ship) || ZOOL migración *f* anormal || *sisters of the Visitation* visitandinas *f*.

visiting [ˈvizitiŋ] *adj* de visita; *visiting card* tarjeta de visita; *visiting hours* horas de visita || visitante; *visiting team* equipo visitante || *visiting lecturer* conferenciante venido de fuera.

visitor [ˈvizitə*] *n* visitante *m* & *f*, visita *f* || — *I'm expecting visitors tonight* tengo visitas esta noche || *visitors from Mars* seres venidos de Marte.

visor [ˈvaizə*] *n* visera *f* (of helmet, cap, windscreen).

vista [ˈvistə] *n* vista *f*, perspectiva *f* || FIG perspectiva *f*, horizonte *m*.

Vistula [ˈvistjulə] *pr n* GEOGR Vístula *m*.

visual [ˈvizjuəl] *adj* visual; *visual field* campo visual || visible || óptico, ca (nerve) || ocular; *visual inspection* inspección ocular; *visual proof* prueba ocular || *visual aids* medios *m* visuales || INFORM *visual display unit* pantalla *f* de visualización, visual *m*.

visualization [ˌvizjuəlaiˈzeiʃən] *n* imagen *m* mental (mental picture) || visualización *f* (action).

visualize [ˈvizjuəlaiz] *vt* imaginar, imaginarse; *I cannot visualize this room painted blue* no puedo imaginar esta habitación pintada de azul || prever, proyectar; *we visualize great changes in the company* prevemos grandes cambios en la sociedad.

visually [ˈvizjuəli] *adv* visualmente || *visually handicapped* invidente.

vital [ˈvaitəl] *adj* vital; *vital organs* órganos vitales || fundamental, esencial; *it is vital that we understand each other* es fundamental que nos entendamos || sumo, ma; capital; *of vital importance* de suma importancia || enérgico, ca; vivo, va (lively) || mortal (fatal) || crucial (moment) || — *vital force* impulso *m* vital, «elan» *m* vital || *vital statistics* mensuraciones *f* (of a woman), estadísticas demográficas (population figures).

◆ *pl n* órganos *m* vitales || MAR obras *f* vivas || FIG partes *f* esenciales.

vitalism [ˈvaitəlizəm] *n* vitalismo *m*.

vitalist [ˈvaitəlist] *n* vitalista *m* & *f*.

vitality [vaiˈtæliti] *n* vitalidad *f*.

vitalization [ˌvaitəlaiˈzeiʃən] *n* vitalización *f*.

vitalize [ˈvaitəlaiz] *vt* vitalizar, vivificar || FIG animar.

vitally [ˈvaitəli] *adv* *a vitally important document* un documento de suma importancia || *it is vitally important that* es fundamental *or* esencial que.

vitamin [ˈvitəmin] *n* vitamina *f* || — *enriched with vitamins* vitaminado, da || *vitamin deficiency* avitaminosis *f inv*.

vitaminized [ˈvitəminaizd] *adj* vitaminado, da.

vitelline [ˈvitəliːn] *adj* vitelino, na; *vitelline membrane* membrana vitelina.

vitellus [ˈviteləs] *n* vitelo *m*.

vitiate [ˈviʃieit] *vt* viciar, contaminar (blood, air) || viciar, corromper (to corrupt) || JUR viciar, invalidar.

vitiation [ˌviʃiˈeiʃən] *n* contaminación *f* || corrupción *f* || JUR invalidación *f*.

viticultural [ˌvitiˈkʌltʃərəl] *adj* vitícola.

viticulture [ˈvitikʌltʃə*] *n* viticultura *f*.

viticulturist [ˌvitiˈkʌltʃərist] *n* viticultor *m*.

vitiligo [ˌvitəˈlaigəu] *n* MED vitíligo *m*.

vitreous [ˈvitriəs] *adj* vítreo, a || — *vitreous body* o *humour* humor vítreo || *vitreous electricity* electricidad vítrea.

vitrifaction [ˌvitriˈfækʃən] *n* vitrificación *f*.

vitrifiable [ˈvitrifaiəbl] *adj* vitrificable.

vitrification [ˌvitrifiˈkeiʃən] *n* vitrificación *f*.

vitriform [ˈvitrifɔːm] *adj* vítreo, a.

vitrify [ˈvitrifai] *vt* vitrificar.

◆ *vi* vitrificarse.

vitriol [ˈvitriəl] *n* CHEM vitriolo *m* || FIG virulencia *f*, causticidad *f* (of s.o.'s words) | veneno *m* (caustic words).

vitriolic [ˌvitriˈɔlik] *adj* CHEM vitriólico, ca || FIG virulento, ta; mordaz.

vituperate [viˈtjuːpəreit] *vt* vituperar.

vituperation [viˌtjuːpəˈreiʃən] *n* vituperación *f*, vituperio *m*.

vituperative [viˈtjuːpərətiv] *adj* vituperioso, sa; vituperador, ra; vituperante.

vivacious [viˈveiʃəs] *adj* vivo, va (full of life) || vivaracho, cha (sprightly) || BOT vivaz.

vivaciousness [-nis]; **vivacity** [viˈvæsiti] *n* viveza *f*, vivacidad *f*.

vivarium [vaiˈvɛəriəm] *n* vivero *m*.

— OBSERV El plural de *vivarium* es *vivariums* o *vivaria*.

viva voce [ˈvaivəˈvəusi] *adj* oral; *a viva voce exam* un examen oral.

◆ *adv* de viva voz, de palabra.

◆ *n* examen *m* oral.

vivid [ˈvivid] *adj* vivo, va; intenso, sa (colour) || gráfico, ca; pintoresco, ca (description) || vivo, va; fuerte (impression, memory) || vivo, va (imagination).

vividness [-nis] *n* intensidad *f*, viveza *f* (of colours, etc.) || fuerza *f* (of style).

vivification [ˌvivifiˈkeiʃən] *n* vivificación *f*.

vivify [ˈvivifai] *vt* vivificar || animar.

vivifying [-iŋ] *adj* vivificador, ra; vivificante.

viviparity [ˌviviˈpæriti] *n* BOT & ZOOL viviparidad *f*.

viviparous [vi'vipərəs] *adj* BOT & ZOOL vivíparo, ra.

vivisect [ˌvivi'sekt] *vt* hacer la vivisección de (an animal, etc.).
◆ *vi* practicar la vivisección.

vivisection [ˌvivi'sekʃən] *n* vivisección *f.*

vixen ['viksən] *n* ZOOL zorra *f*, raposa *f* || FIG arpía *f.*

vizier; vizir [vi'ziə*] *n* visir *m* || *grand vizier* o *vizir* gran visir.

vizor ['vaizə*] *n* visera *f* (of helmet, cap, windscreen).

V-neck ['viːnek] *adj* de cuello de pico.
◆ *n* cuello *m* de pico.

vocable ['vəukəbl] *n* vocablo *m*, voz *f.*

vocabulary [və'kæbjuləri] *n* vocabulario *m.*

vocal ['vəukəl] *adj* ANAT & MUS vocal || GRAMM vocálico, ca (vocalic) | sonoro, ra (voiced) || FIG ruidoso, sa; gritón, ona; *the more vocal members of the audience* los miembros más ruidosos de la asistencia || *vocal cords* cuerdas *f pl* vocales.

vocalic [vəu'kælik] *n* GRAMM vocálico, ca.

vocalism ['vəukəlizəm] *n* GRAMM vocalismo *m* || MUS vocalización *f.*

vocalist ['vəukəlist] *n* vocalista *m* & *f* (in an orchestra) || cantante *m* & *f* (in a pop group).

vocalization [ˌvəukəlai'zeiʃən] *n* MUS & GRAMM vocalización *f.*

vocalize ['vəukəlaiz] *vt* GRAMM vocalizar || cantar (to sing) || articular (to utter) || poner las vocales en (a Hebrew text).
◆ *vi* vocalizar.

vocation [vəu'keiʃən] *n* REL vocación *f* || vocación *f*, inclinación *f*; *he has a vocation for the theatre* tiene vocación de artista || profesión *f*, carrera *f* (profession) || *to miss* o *to mistake one's vocation* errar la vocación.

vocational [-əl] *adj* profesional; *vocational training* formación *or* capacitación profesional; *vocational guidance* orientación profesional.

vocative ['vɔkətiv] *n* GRAMM vocativo *m* || *vocative case* vocativo *m.*

vociferance [vɔ'sifərəns] *n* vociferaciones *f pl.*

vociferate [vɔ'sifəreit] *vt* vociferar.
◆ *vi* vociferar, vocear.

vociferation [vɔˌsifə'reiʃən] *n* vociferación *f.*

vociferous [və'sifərəs] *adj* vociferante.

vociferously [-li] *adv* a gritos, ruidosamente.

vodka ['vɔdkə] *n* vodka *f* & *m.*

vogue [vəug] *n* moda *f*, boga *f*; *to be in vogue* estar en boga, estar de moda.

voice [vɔis] *n* voz *f*; *shrill voice* voz chillona || tono *m* (tone) || GRAMM voz *f*; *passive voice* voz pasiva; *active voice* voz activa || MUS voz *f* || — *at the top of one's voice* a voces, a voz en cuello, a voz en grito || FIG *he loves the sound of his own voice* le gusta escucharse cuando habla || *high-pitched voice* voz aguda || *in a loud voice* en voz alta || *in a low voice* a media voz, en voz baja || *in a soft voice* en voz baja || *loss of voice* afonía *f* || MUS *main* o *principal voice* voz cantante || *soft voice* voz baja, voz suave || *the voice of one's conscience* la voz de la conciencia || *thunderous voice* voz de trueno || *to be in good voice* estar en voz || *to give voice to* expresar || *to have a good voice* tener buena voz || *to have no voice in the matter* no tener voz ni voto en el asunto || *to keep one's voice down* no subir la voz, no levantar el tono || *to lose one's voice* perdèr la voz || *to put on a solemn voice* ahuecar la voz || *to raise one's voice* alzar *or* levantar la voz || *to strain one's voice* forzar la voz || *voice from the sky* voz del cielo || INFORM *voice input* entrada *f* vocal || *voice of the people* voz del pueblo || INFORM *voice recognition* reconocimiento *m* de la voz || *with one voice* a una voz, por unanimidad.

voice [vɔis] *vt* expresar, hacerse eco de (to express); *he voiced the common feeling* expresó la opinión de todos || articular (to articulate) || MUS afinar || GRAMM sonorizar (in phonetics).

voiced [-t] *adj* expresado, da (opinion, etc.) || GRAMM sonoro, ra || *low-voiced* con voz baja.

voiceless [-lis] *adj* mudo, da (dumb) || afónico, ca (from shouting too much) || GRAMM sordo, da.

voice-over [-ˌəuvə*] *n* RAD voz *f* en off.

void [vɔid] *adj* vacío, a (empty) || vacante (post, job) || JUR nulo, la; inválido, da || — *null and void* nulo y sin valor || *to be void of* estar desprovisto de, carecer de || JUR *to make sth. void* anular algo, invalidar algo.
◆ *n* vacío *m* || fallo *m* (cards); *to have a void in* tener fallo a || FIG vacío *m*; *his death left a great void* su muerte dejó un gran vacío.

void [vɔid] *vt* anular, invalidar (to annul) || evacuar (to evacuate) || desocupar, vaciar (to leave).

voidable [-əbl] *adj* JUR rescindible, anulable.

voidance [-əns] *n* REL vacante *f* || JUR anulación *f*, invalidación *f* || REL vacante *f* || JUR anulación *f*, invalidación *f* || evacuación *f* (emptying).

voidness [-nis] *n* vacío *m*, vacuidad *f* || JUR nulidad *f.*

voile [vɔil] *n* gasa *f* (material).

volant ['vəulənt] *adj* volante.

Volapük ['vɔləpuk] *n* volapuk *m* (language).

volar ['vəulə*] *adj* palmar (of the hand) || plantar (of the foot).

volatile ['vɔlətail] *adj* volátil; *volatile oil* aceite volátil || FIG voluble, inconstante (fickle).

volatileness [-nis]; **volatility** [ˌvɔlə'tiliti] *n* volatilidad *f* || FIG volubilidad *f*, inconstancia *f.*

volatilize [vɔ'lætilaiz] *vt* volatilizar.
◆ *vi* volatilizarse.

vol-au-vent ['vɔləu'vɑŋ] *n* CULIN volován *m.*

volcanic [vɔl'kænik] *adj* volcánico, ca || MIN *volcanic glass* obsidiana *f.*

volcanism ['vɔlkənizəm] *n* volcanismo *m*, vulcanismo *m.*

volcanist ['vɔlkənist] *n* volcanista *m*, vulcanista *m.*

volcanize [vɔlkənaiz] *vt* volcanizar.

volcano [vɔl'keinəu] *n* volcán *m.*
— OBSERV El plural de la palabra inglesa es *volcanoes* o *volcanos.*

volcanologist [ˌvɔlkə'nɔlədʒist] *n* vulcanólogo *m*, vulcanologista *m.*

volcanology [ˌvɔlkə'nɔlədʒi] *n* vulcanología *f.*

vole [vəul] *n* campañol *m*, ratón *m* de campo (rodent) || bolo *m*, bola *f* (in cards).

volet ['vɔlei] *n* hoja *f* (of a triptych).

Volga ['vɔlgə] *pr n* GEOGR Volga *m.*

volitant ['vɔlitənt] *adj* volante, volador, ra.

volition [vəu'liʃən] *n* volición *f* || *of one's own volition* de su propia voluntad.

volitional [-əl]; **volitive** ['vɔlitiv] *adj* volitivo, va.

volley ['vɔli] *n* andanada *f*, descarga *f* cerrada (of bullets) || lluvia *f* (of stones, of arrows) || salva *f* (of applause) || torrente *m* (of insults) || SP voleo *m* (in tennis).

volley ['vɔli] *vt* lanzar (missiles) || soltar, dirigir (insults) || SP volear.
◆ *vi* MIL lanzar una descarga || SP volear (in tennis).

volleyball [-bɔːl] *n* SP balonvolea *m* [AMER voleibol *m*].

volplane ['vɔlplein] *n* AVIAT vuelo *m* planeado, planeo *m.*

Volsci ['vɔlskiː] *pl n* Volscos *m.*

volt [vəult] *n* ELECTR voltio *m.*

volt [vɔlt] *n* esquiva *f*, parada *f* (in fencing) || vuelta *f* (of a horse).

Volta ['vɔltə] *pr n* GEOGR Volta *m.*

voltage ['vəultidʒ] *n* ELECTR voltaje *m*, tensión *f* || *high voltage* alta tensión.

voltaic [vɔl'teiik] *adj* voltaico, ca; *voltaic arc* arco voltaico.

voltameter [vɔl'tæmitə*] *n* ELECTR voltámetro *m.*

voltammeter ['vəult'æmitə*] *n* ELECTR voltamperímetro *m.*

volt-ampere ['vəult'æmpɛə*] *n* ELECTR voltamperio *m.*

volt-face ['vɔlt'fɑːs] *n* cambio *m* súbito de opinión (change of opinion).

voltmeter ['vəultˌmiːtə*] *n* voltímetro *m.*

volubility [ˌvɔlju'biliti] *n* locuacidad *f* || BOT volubilidad *f.*

voluble ['vɔljubl] *adj* locuaz (person) || suelto, ta (speech) || BOT voluble.

volubly [-i] *adv* con soltura, con facilidad.

volume ['vɔljuːm] *n* volumen *m* (space occupied) || tomo *m*, volumen *m*; *an encyclopedia in ten volumes* una enciclopedia en diez volúmenes || volumen *m* (of sound); *turn the volume down* baja el volumen || volumen *m*, cantidad *f*; *the volume of sales* el volumen de ventas; *the volume of water through a lock* el volumen de agua que pasa por una esclusa || *volume control* botón *m* del volumen (knob).
◆ *pl* gran cantidad *f sing* (of water, etc.) || — *her look spoke volumes* su mirada era muy elocuente | *he speaks volumes for his attitude* indica claramente su actitud.

volumeter [və'ljuːmitə*] *n* PHYS volúmetro *m.*

volumetric [ˌvɔlju'metrik]; **volumetrical** [-əl] *adj* PHYS volumétrico, ca.

volumetry [vɔ'ljuːmitri] *n* PHYS volumetría *f.*

voluminous [vɔ'ljuːminəs] *adj* voluminoso, sa (bulky) || abundante || FIG prolijo, ja (writer).

voluntarily ['vɔləntərili] *adv* voluntariamente.

voluntary ['vɔləntəri] *adj* voluntario, ria; *a voluntary action* un acto voluntario || espontáneo, a (spontaneous) || benévolo, la; voluntario, ria (benevolent) || JUR a título gratuito (without payment) || — *voluntary liquidation* liquidación *f* voluntaria || *voluntary redundancy* cese *m* voluntario.
◆ *n* MUS solo *m* de órgano.

volunteer [ˌvɔlən'tiə*] *adj* voluntario, ria (voluntary) || de voluntarios (army).
◆ *n* MIL voluntario *m* || JUR beneficiario, ria.

volunteer [ˌvɔlən'tiə*] *vt* ofrecer (services) || dar (information) || hacer (remark) || FIG designar (to designate s.o.); *I was volunteered* me designaron.
◆ *vi* ofrecerse || MIL alistarse como voluntario (to join up).

voluptuary [və'lʌptjuəri] *adj/n* voluptuoso, sa.

voluptuous [və'lʌptjuəs] *adj* voluptuoso, sa.

voluptuousness [-nis] *n* voluptuosidad *f.*

volute [və'ljuːt] *n* ARCH voluta *f* || ZOOL voluta *f* (of a mollusc) || espira *f* (of a shell).
◆ *adj* espiral, en espiral || TECH helicoidal.

volution [vɔ'ljuːʃən] *n* espira *f* (of a shell) || ANAT circunvolución *f.*

volvulus ['vɔlvjuləs] *n* MED vólvulo *m.*

vomer ['vɔmə*] *n* MED vómer *m.*

vomica [vɔmikə] *n* MED vómica *f.*

vomit [ˈvɔmit] *n* vómito *m* ‖ vomitivo *m* (emetic) ‖ MED *black vomit* vómito negro, fiebre amarilla.

vomit [ˈvɔmit] *vt* MED vomitar ‖ FIG vomitar, arrojar.
◆ *vi* vomitar, tener vómitos.

vomiting [ˈvɔmitiŋ] *n* MED vómito *m.*

vomitory [ˈvɔmitəri] *adj* vomitivo, va; vomitorio, ria.
◆ *n* vomitorio *m* (in Roman amphitheatres).

voodoo [ˈvuːduː] *n* vodú *m.*

voracious [vəˈreiʃəs] *adj* voraz; *a voracious appetite* un apetito voraz; *a voracious tiger* un tigre voraz ‖ insaciable, ávido, da; *a voracious reader* un lector ávido.

voraciousness [-nis]; **voracity** [vɔˈræsiti] *n* voracidad *f* (capacity to eat) ‖ avidez *f* (eagerness).

vortex [ˈvɔːteks] *n* vórtice *m,* torbellino *m.*
— OBSERV El plural de la palabra inglesa es *vortexes* o *vortices.*

vortical [ˈvɔːtikəl] *adj* vortiginoso, sa.

vorticella [ˌvɔːtiˈselə] *n* ZOOL vorticela *f.*
— OBSERV El plural de la palabra inglesa es *vorticellae* o *vorticellas.*

votaress [ˈvəutəris] *n* adoradora *f,* devota *f* (of a god) ‖ aficionada *f; a votaress of the arts* una aficionada a las artes ‖ partidaria *f* (supporter).

votary [ˈvəutəri] *n* adorador *m,* devoto *m* (of a god) ‖ aficionado *m* (fan) ‖ partidario *m* (supporter).

vote [vəut] *n* voto *m; vote of confidence* voto de confianza; *vote of censure* voto de censura; *to cast a vote* depositar un voto ‖ votación *f* (action); *the vote was taken today* la votación tuvo lugar hoy; *to move that a separate vote be taken* proponer la votación por separado ‖ derecho *m* de votar, derecho *m* de voto, voto *m; why did they give women the vote?* ¿por qué dieron el derecho de votar a las mujeres?, ¿por qué concedieron el voto a las mujeres? ‖ votos *m pl; the trade-union vote* los votos de los sindicatos ‖ créditos *m pl* votados (money granted) ‖ — *by a majority vote* por una mayoría de votos ‖ *by popular vote* por votación popular ‖ *casting vote* voto de calidad ‖ *floating votes* votos indecisos ‖ *secret vote* votación secreta ‖ *to count* o *to tell the votes* proceder al escrutinio ‖ *to give one's vote to* dar su voto a, votar por ‖ *to have* o *to take a vote on sth.* poner *or* someter algo a votación, votar algo ‖ *to have the vote* tener el derecho de votar ‖ *to proceed to a vote* proceder a votar ‖ *to put to the vote* poner *or* someter a votación ‖ *to record one's vote* votar ‖ *unanimous vote* votación unánime ‖ *unconclusive vote* votación nula ‖ *vote by proxy* voto por poderes ‖ *vote by roll call* votación nominal ‖ *vote by show of hands* votación a mano alzada ‖ *vote by sitting and standing,* US *rising vote* votación por «levantados» y «sentados» ‖ *vote of thanks* voto de gracias ‖ *votes cast* votos *or* sufragios emitidos.

vote [vəut] *vt* votar; *to vote the agricultural bill* votar la ley agrícola; *to vote ten thousand pounds for industry* votar diez mil libras para la industria ‖ elegir; *she was voted Miss England* fue elegida como Miss Inglaterra ‖ proponer; *I vote that we all go home* yo propongo que vayamos todos a casa ‖ declarar (to proclaim) ‖ — *to vote down* rechazar, votar en contra de (motion, etc.) ‖ *to vote in* elegir ‖ *to vote out* derrotar en las elecciones ‖ *with a right to vote* con voz y voto ‖ *without a right to vote* con voz pero sin voto.
◆ *vi* votar; *to vote for* votar por *or* a favor de; *to vote against* votar en contra (de) ‖ *to vote on* votar.

voter [-ə*] *n* votante *m* & *f* ‖ elector, ra; votante *m* & *f* (in a national election).

voting [ˈvəutiŋ] *n* votación *f* (action); *voting by a show of hands* votación a mano alzada.
◆ *adj* votante (member) ‖ electoral.

voting booth [-buːθ] *n* cabina *f* electoral.

voting machine [-məʃiːn] *n* US máquina *f* de votar, máquina registradora de votos.

voting paper [-ˌpeipə*] *n* papeleta *f* [AMER balota *f*].

votive [ˈvəutiv] *adj* votivo, va; *votive mass* misa votiva ‖ *votive offering* exvoto *m.*

vouch [vautʃ] *vt* atestiguar (to testify) ‖ confirmar (a statement) ‖ JUR citar ‖ *to vouch that* asegurar que.
◆ *vi* *to vouch for* responder de, garantizar (a thing), salir fiador de, responder por (a person).

voucher [-ə*] *n* JUR documento *m* justificativo | fiador, ra; garante *m* & *f* (person) ‖ COMM bono *m,* vale *m* ‖ prueba *f* (piece of evidence) ‖ contraseña *f* (in the theatre) ‖ — *cash voucher* vale [que representa cierta cantidad de dinero] ‖ *luncheon voucher* vale de comida.

vouchsafe [-seif] *vt* conceder, otorgar; *to vouchsafe s.o. sth.* conceder algo a alguien ‖ — *he vouchsafed no answer* no se dignó a contestar ‖ *to vouchsafe to do sth.* dignarse a hacer algo.

voussoir [vuːˈswɑːr] *n* ARCH dovela *f.*

vow [vau] *n* REL voto *m; to make a vow of chastity* hacer voto de castidad; *to take one's vows* pronunciar sus votos ‖ promesa *f* solemne; *lovers' vows* las promesas solemnes de los amantes ‖ *to make a vow to do sth.* prometer hacer algo, comprometerse a hacer algo.

vow [vau] *vt* jurar; *to vow obedience* jurar obediencia ‖ prometer; *he vowed not to drink any more* prometió no beber más ‖ — *to vow that* declarar que, afirmar que ‖ *to vow to* hacer voto de (religious vows), comprometerse a, prometer (to promise).
◆ *vi* jurar.

vowel [ˈvauəl] *n* GRAMM vocal *f.*
◆ *adj* GRAMM vocálico, ca.

vox [vɔks] *n* MUS voz *f; vox angelica* voz celeste; *vox humana* voz humana.

vox pop [ˈvɔkspɔp] *n* FAM vox populi *f.*

voyage [ˈvɔiidʒ] *n* viaje *m; a sea voyage* un viaje por mar, un viaje en barco ‖ travesía *f* (crossing) ‖ — *maiden voyage* primer viaje ‖ *the outward voyage* el viaje de ida, la ida ‖ *the voyage home* el viaje de regreso *or* de vuelta, la vuelta.

voyage [ˈvɔiidʒ] *vi* MAR viajar (por mar), navegar ‖ viajar por aire *or* en avión.
◆ *vt* viajar por (seas).

voyager [ˈvɔiədʒə*] *n* viajero, ra.

voyeur [vwɑːˈjəː*] *n* mirón, ona.

Vulcan [ˈvʌlkən] *pr n* MYTH Vulcano *m.*

vulcanism [ˈvʌlkənizəm] *n* vulcanismo *m.*

vulcanite [ˈvʌlkənait] *n* MIN vulcanita *f.*

vulcanization [ˌvʌlkənaiˈzeiʃən] *n* TECH vulcanización *f.*

vulcanize [ˈvʌlkənaiz] *vt* TECH vulcanizar.

vulcanized [-d] *adj* TECH vulcanizado, da; *vulcanized rubber* caucho vulcanizado.

vulcanologist [ˌvʌlkəˈnɔlədʒist] *n* vulcanólogo *m,* vulcanologista *m.*

vulcanology [ˌvʌlkəˈnɔlədʒi] *n* vulcanología *f.*

vulgar [ˈvʌlgə*] *adj* común, corriente; *a vulgar superstition* una superstición común ‖ vulgar, ordinario, ria (lacking refinement) ‖ de mal gusto (in bad taste) ‖ cursi (pretentious) ‖ grosero, ra; vulgar (rude); *don't be vulgar!* ¡no seas grosero! ‖ verde; *a vulgar joke* un chiste verde ‖ GRAMM vulgar, corriente; *to take a word in its vulgar sense* tomar una palabra en su sentido vulgar ‖ — *the vulgar era* la era vulgar *or* cristiana ‖ MATH *vulgar fraction* fracción *f* común ‖ GRAMM *vulgar Latin* latín *m* vulgar.
◆ *n* vulgo *m* (populace).

vulgarian [vʌlˈgɛəriən] *n* persona *f* vulgar, persona *f* ordinaria (vulgar person) ‖ nuevo rico *m* (rich person).

vulgarism [ˈvʌlgərizəm] *n* vulgarismo *m* (word, expression) ‖ vulgaridad *f* (lack of refinement) ‖ vulgaridad *f,* grosería *f,* ordinariez *f* (act).

vulgarity [vʌlˈgæriti] *n* vulgaridad *f* (lack of refinement) ‖ vulgaridad *f,* grosería *f,* ordinariez *f* (act).

vulgarization [ˌvʌlgəraiˈzeiʃən] *n* vulgarización *f.*

vulgarize [ˈvʌlgəraiz] *vt* vulgarizar.

vulgarizer [-ə*] *n* vulgarizador, ra.

Vulgate [ˈvʌlgit] *n* REL Vulgata *f* (Bible).

vulgus [ˈvʌlgəs] *n* vulgo *m.*

vulnerability [ˌvʌlnərəˈbiliti] *n* vulnerabilidad *f.*

vulnerable [ˈvʌlnərəbl] *adj* vulnerable.

vulnerary [ˈvʌlnərəri] *adj* MED vulnerario, ria (used in healing).
◆ *n* MED vulnerario *m.*

vulpine [ˈvʌlpain] *adj* vulpino, na ‖ FIG ladino, na (cunning).

vulture [ˈvʌltʃə*] *n* ZOOL buitre *m* ‖ FIG hombre *m* rapaz.

vulturous [ˈvʌltʃurəs] *adj* de buitre ‖ FIG rapaz.

vulva [ˈvʌlvə] *n* ANAT vulva.

vulval [-l]; **vulvar** [-*] *adj* vulvar.

vulvitis [vʌlˈvaitis] *n* MED vulvitis *f inv.*

vying [ˈvaiiŋ] *pres part* ⟶ **vie.**

W

w ['dʌbəlju:] *n* w *f* (letter).

wacke [wækə] *n* GEOL roca *f* parecida a la arenisca.

wacky [wæki] *adj* US FAM chiflado, da; chalado, da (person) | absurdo, da (thing).

wad [wɔd] *n* taco *m* (of a cartridge) || bolita *f* (of cotton wool) || tapón *m* (to stop an aperture) || fajo *m* (of banknotes) || lío *m* (of papers) || manojo *m* (of straw) || toma *f* (of chewing tobacco) || FAM dineral *m* (a lot of money) || FAM *to make wads of money* ganar el dinero a espuertas, ganar un dineral.

wad [wɔd] *vt* enguatar, forrar (to pad, to line) || acolchar (a wall) || tapar, obstruir (a hole) || rellenar (to fill) || atacar (a firearm) || apretar (to make into a wad).

wadding [-iŋ] *n* relleno *m* (filling or stuffing) || guata *f* (cotton wool) || taco *m* (of a cartridge) || acolchado *m* (of a wall).

waddle ['wɔdl] *n* anadeo *m*, manera *f* de andar de los patos || contoneo *m* (of people) || *to walk with a waddle* andar contoneandose (with a swaying gait), andar como un pato (like a duck).

waddle ['wɔdl] *vi* anadear (ducks) || contonearse (with a swaying gait) || andar como un pato (like a duck).

waddy ['wɔdi] *n* cachiporra *f* (thick club).

wade [weid] *vt* vadear (a river, a stream).
◆ *vi* andar con dificultad || — *to wade across a river* vadear un río || *to wade ashore* salir del agua || *to wade in* meterse en el agua (to go into the water), atacar, arremeter (to attack), ponerse a trabajar (to start working) || *to wade into* meterse en (water), sumergirse en (a crowd), arremeter contra, atacar (to attack physically), emprenderla con (verbally), echarse sobre (food) || *to wade through* abrirse paso entre (crowd, debris, undergrowth, etc.), vadear (water), leer con dificultad (to read).

wader [-ə*] *n* ZOOL ave *f* zancuda.
◆ *pl* botas *f* altas impermeables.

wadi ['wɔdi] *n* ued *m*.
— OBSERV El plural de *wadi* es *wadis* o *wadies*.

wading bird ['weidiŋbə:d] *n* ZOOL ave *f* zancuda.

wady ['wɔdi] *n* ued *m*.
— OBSERV El plural de wady es *wadies*.

wafer ['weifə*] *n* CULIN barquillo *m* || REL hostia *f* || oblea *f* (seal for documents).

wafer-thin [-θin] *n* finísimo, ma.

waffle ['wɔfl] *n* CULIN barquillo *m* || FAM paja *f*.

waffle ['wɔfl] *vi* FAM perorar (to talk at great length) | meter paja (in an essay or speech).

waffle iron ['wɔfl,aiən] *n* CULIN molde *m* para hacer barquillos.

waft [wa:ft] *n* ráfaga *f*, soplo *m* (of wind) || bocanada *f* (of smoke, etc.) || aletada *f* (of a bird) || MAR bandera *f* de señales.

waft [wa:ft] *vt* llevar por el aire (through the air) *or* por el agua (across water).
◆ *vi* FIG flotar (on the wind).

wag [wæg] *n* guasón, ona; bromista *m* & *f* (joker) || meneo *m*, movimiento *m* (movement) || coleada *f*, coletazo *m* (of tail).

wag [wæg] *vt* agitar, menear || mover (tail, head) || FAM *to wag one's tongue* darle a la lengua.
◆ *vi* agitarse, menearse, moverse || andar (to move along) || FAM *that should set tongues wagging* eso dará que hablar a la gente.

wage [weidʒ] *n* salario base *m* (of a workman) || sueldo *m* (of employees) || FIG pago *m* (reward) || — *basic wage* salario *or* básico || *collective wage* salario colectivo || *conventional wage* salario de convenio colectivo || *fixing of maximum wage* fijación de salarios máximos || *top or maximum wage* salario tope *or* máximo || *wage claim* reivindicación *f* salarial || *wage dividend* participación *f* en los beneficios || *wage earner* asalariado, da || *wage freeze* congelación *f* de salarios || *wage packet* sobre *m* de paga || *wage scale* escala *f* de salarios.
◆ *pl* COMM salarios *m* (industrial expenditure on labour) || salario *m sing* (workman's pay) || sueldo *m sing* (employee's pay) || *starvation wages* salario de hambre.

wage [weidʒ] *vt* hacer (war) || librar, dar, trabar (battle) || emprender (a campaign) || empeñar (to pledge).

wager [-ə*] *n* apuesta *f* || *to lay a wager* apostar, hacer una apuesta.

wager [-ə*] *vt/vi* apostar; *to wager five pounds that* apostar cinco libras a que.

wageworker [-,wə:kə*] *n* asalariado, da.

waggery [wægəri] *n* broma *f* (joke).

waggish [wægiʃ] *adj* bromista, guasón, ona (people) || en broma (action).

waggishly [-li] *adv* en broma, con guasa.

waggishness [-nis] *n* carácter *m* bromista.

waggle [wægl] *n* meneo *m* (wag).

waggle [wægl] *vt* agitar, menear (to shake).
◆ *vi* agitarse, menearse (to shake) || tambalearse (to totter).

waggly [-i] *adj* inseguro, ra; poco seguro, ra; tambaleante.

waggon; wagon [wægən] *n* carro *m* (horsedrawn) || vagón *m* (railway car) || furgón *m* (for freight) || TECH vagoneta *f* || carrito *m* para el té (tea trolley) || AUT furgoneta *f*, camioneta *f* || US furgoneta *f* de policía (for police) || — FIG & FAM *to be on the wagon* no beber | *to go on the wagon* tomar la decisión de no beber | *to hitch one's waggon to a star* picar muy alto (to be very ambitious).

waggonage; wagonage [-idʒ] *n* acarreo *m*, transporte *m* en vagones.

waggoner; wagoner [-ə*] *n* carretero *m*.

Waggoner; Wagoner [-ə*] *n* ASTR Cochero *m*, Auriga *m*.

waggonette; wagonette [,wægəu'net] *n* tartana *f*.

Wagnerian [va:g'niəriən] *adj/n* wagneriano, na.

wagon-lit ['væg˜ɔn'li:] *n* coche cama *m*.
— OBSERV El plural es *wagons-lits* o *wagon-lits*.

wagonload ['wægənləud] *n* carretada *f* (of a horsedrawn wagon) || vagón *m* (of railway car).

wagon train ['wægəntrein] *n* MIL tren *m* de equipajes.

wagtail ['wægteil] *n* aguzanieves *f inv* (bird).

Wahhabi; Wahabi [wə'ha:bi] *n* REL wahabita *m* & *f*.

wahoo ['wa:hu:] *n* BOT bonetero *m*.

waif [weif] *n* niño *m* abandonado, niña *f* abandonada (child) || animal *m* abandonado *or* extraviado (animal) || JUR bien *m* mostrenco || *waifs and strays* niños abandonados *or* desamparados.

wail [weil] *n* quejido *m*, lamento *m* (cry) || vagido *m* (of a new-born baby) || FIG gemido *m*; *the wail of the wind* el gemido del viento.

wail [weil] *vi* gemir, lamentarse || FIG gemir (wind) || FAM llorar (to complain); *don't come wailing to me* no me vengas a llorar a mí.
◆ *vt* lamentar.

wailing [-iŋ] *n* gemidos *m pl*, lamentos *m pl* || vagidos *m pl* (of a new-born baby).

Wailing Wall [weiliŋ'wɔ:l] *pr n* Muro *m* de las Lamentaciones.

wain [wein] *n* (ant) carro *m* || ASTR *the Wain* el Carro, la Osa Mayor.

wainscot [weinskət]; **wainscoting; wainscotting** [-iŋ] *n* ARCH entablado *m*, revestimiento *m* de madera (wooden panelling) || zócalo *m*, cenefa *f* (lower part of a wall, skirting board).

wainscoting; wainscotting [-iŋ] *n* → **wainscot.**

wainwright [weinrait] *n* carretero *m*.

waist [weist] *n* cintura *f*, talle *m* (of the body) || MAR combés *m* || estrechamiento *m* (narrow part) || US cuerpo *m* (bodice of woman's dress) | blusa *f* (blouse).

waistband [-bænd] *n* pretina *f*, cinturón *m*.

waistcloth [-klɔθ] *n* taparrabo *m*.

waistcoat [-kəut] *n* chaleco *m*.

waist-deep [-'di:p] *adv* hasta la cintura; *to be waist-deep in water* tener agua hasta la cintura.

waisted [-id] *adj* *high waisted* de cinturón alto (trousers) || *slim waisted* de cintura fina.

waist-high [-'hai] *adv/adj* hasta la cintura; *to be waist-high* llegar hasta la cintura.

waistline [-lain] *n* cintura *f*, talle *m*.

wait [weit] *n* espera *f*; *a long wait at the station* una larga espera en la estación || emboscada *f* (ambush) || — *to lie in wait for* estar al acecho de, acechar || *we have a long wait ahead of us* tendremos que esperar mucho tiempo.
◆ *pl* murga *f sing* de Nochebuena (carol singers).

wait [weit] *vt* esperar; *to wait one's turn* esperar su turno ‖ retrasar (to delay); *to wait a meal for s.o.* retrasar una comida por alguien ‖ atender, servir (a table) ‖ US *to wait out a storm* esperar a que acabe una tormenta.
◆ *vi* esperar; *he made me wait for three hours* me hizo esperar tres horas; *that decision can't wait* esta decisión no puede esperar ‖ ser camarero (to be a waiter) ‖ — *I couldn't wait to do it* estar ansioso, sa por hacerlo ‖ *just wait until I tell this to John!* ¡cuando se lo diga a Juan! ‖ *just wait until the teacher finds out!* ¡espera que se entere el profesor! ‖ *just you wait!* ¡me las pagarás! ‖ *repairs while you wait* reparaciones al minuto ‖ *to wait a minute* o *a second* o *a moment* esperar un minuto *or* un segundo *or* un momento ‖ *to keep s.o. waiting* hacer esperar a alguien ‖ *to wait about* o *around* esperar, pasarse el tiempo esperando ‖ *to wait at table* atender, servir ‖ *to wait for* esperar; *he was waiting for her* le estaba esperando ‖ *to wait on* servir a, atender a (s.o. at table), presentar sus respetos a (to pay a visit to), derivarse de (to result from), seguir de cerca (a competitor) ‖ FIG *to wait on s.o. hand and foot* ser el esclavo de alguien, desvivirse por alguien ‖ *to wait up for s.o.* esperar a alguien levantado ‖ *wait and see!* ¡espera a ver qué pasa! ‖ *wait for me to call* espera a que llame.

waiter [-ə*] *n* camarero *m* ‖ bandeja *f* (tray).

waiting [-iŋ] *adj* que espera (that waits) ‖ de espera; *waiting room* sala de espera ‖ de servicio (who is in attendance) ‖ *to play the waiting game* esperar, dejar pasar el tiempo.
◆ *n* espera *f* ‖ servicio *m* ‖ *after a good hour's waiting* después de haber esperado más de una hora.

waiting list [-iŋlist] *n* lista *f* de espera.

waitress [-ris] *n* camarera *f*.

waive [weiv] *vt* JUR renunciar a (right, objection) | desistir de (a claim) | aplazar, diferir (to postpone) | suspender (the rules) ‖ dejar de lado (one's own interests).

waiver [-ə*] *n* JUR renuncia *f* (of a right) | desistimiento *m* (of a claim).

wake [weik] *n* velatorio *m* (vigil of a corpse) ‖ MAR estela *f* (of a ship) ‖ FIG huella *f* ‖ fiesta *f* de la dedicación de una iglesia ‖ *in the wake of* después de, tras ‖ *to leave sth. in one's wake* dejar algo al paso de uno.
◆ *pl* fiesta *f sing* anual.

wake* [weik] *vt* despertar (to wake up, to arouse) ‖ resucitar (to revive) ‖ velar (a corpse) ‖ — *to make enough noise to wake the dead* hacer un ruido de todos los diablos ‖ *to wake to* hacer ver; *he woke his audience to the necessity of taking a decision* hizo ver al auditorio la necesidad de tomar una decisión ‖ *to wake s.o. up* despertar a alguien.
◆ *vi* despertarse (from sleep) ‖ estar despierto, ta (to be awake) ‖ FIG despertar; *he woke to the beauty of his country* despertó a la belleza de su país | amanecer; *to wake up a new man* amanecer como nuevo ‖ — *to wake up* despertarse (after sleep), despabilarse (to become alert) ‖ *to wake up to* darse cuenta de.
— OBSERV Pret ***woke, waked***; pp ***woken, waked***.

wakeful [-ful] *adj* alerta, vigilante (alert, watchful) ‖ despierto, ta (awake) ‖ desvelado, da (unable to sleep) ‖ en blanco; *a wakeful night* una noche en blanco.

wakefulness [-fulnis] *n* vigilancia *f* (watchfulness) ‖ insomnio *m* (sleeplessness).

waken [-ən] *vt* despertar; *he wakened the sleeping sentry* despertó al centinela dormido.
◆ *vi* despertarse.

waking [-iŋ] *adj* alerta, vigilante (watchful) ‖ *we spend ten out of sixteen waking hours at work* de las dieciséis horas en que estamos despiertos pasamos diez trabajando.
◆ *n* despertar *m*.

Walachia [wɔ'leikiə] *pr n* GEOGR Valaquia *f*.

Walachian [-n] *adj/n* valaco, ca.

wale [weil] *n* verdugón *m* (weal) ‖ canutillo *m* (in corduroy) ‖ TECH riostra *f* (brace).
◆ *pl* MAR cintas *f*.

Wales [weilz] *pr n* GEOGR Gales *f*, el País de Gales; *to Wales* a Gales, al País de Gales ‖ *South Wales* Gales del Sur.

Walhalla [væl'hælə] *n* Walhalla *m*.

walk [wɔ:k] *n* manera *f* de andar, andar *m* (way of walking) ‖ paso *m* (pace) ‖ paseo *m*; *to have* o *to take* o *to go for a walk* dar un paseo; *go through the wood, it is a pleasant walk* vaya por el bosque, es un paseo agradable ‖ camino *m*; *it is half and hour's walk from here* hay media hora de camino desde aquí ‖ avenida *f*, paseo *m* (avenue) ‖ sendero *m* (path) ‖ ronda *f* (of a postman, of a hawker, etc.) ‖ dehesa *f*, pasto *m* (sheepwalk) ‖ cordelería *f* (ropewalk) ‖ sector *m* de un bosque asignado a cada guarda (section of forest) ‖ plantación *f* ‖ SP marcha *f* (in athletics) ‖ — FIG *people from all walks of life* gente de toda condición ‖ *to fall into a walk* ponerse al paso (horse) ‖ *to take the dog for a walk* sacar al perro ‖ *to take s.o. for a walk* sacar a alguien de paseo ‖ SP *to win in a walk* ganar cómodamente ‖ FIG *walk of life* profesión *f* (profession), posición *f* social, clase *f* social, condición *f* (status).

walk [wɔ:k] *vt* recorrer a pie; *to walk the Lake District* recorrer a pie la región de Los Lagos ‖ andar, recorrer, hacer a pie (a distance); *to walk three miles* andar tres millas ‖ pasear; *to walk a child* pasear a un niño ‖ llevar al paso (horses) ‖ empujar (a bicycle, a motorcycle) ‖ acompañar [andando]; *I'll walk you home* te acompaño a casa ‖ — *to walk s.o. off his feet* agotar a alguien haciéndole andar mucho ‖ THEATR *to walk the boards* ser actor ‖ *to walk the streets* callejear (aimlessly), hacer la carrera (a prostitute) ‖ *you can walk it in ten minutes* se tarda diez minutos andando.
◆ *vi* andar; *children begin to walk at thirteen months* los niños empiezan a andar a los trece meses ‖ pasearse, dar un paseo (to stroll); *they are out walking* han salido a dar un paseo ‖ ir andando, ir a pie; *how did you go? I walked* ¿cómo fuiste? fui a pie; *I always walk to the office* siempre voy andando a la oficina ‖ moverse (to move) ‖ aparecer (a ghost) ‖ SP avanzar (in basketball) ‖ ir al paso (horse) ‖ — *to walk in one's sleep* ser sonámbulo, la ‖ *to walk in procession* desfilar, ir en procesión ‖ *to walk on all fours* andar a gatas ‖ *to walk with s.o.* acompañar a alguien.
◆ *phr v* ***to walk about*** pasearse, pasear ‖ ***to walk along*** andar, caminar ‖ ***to walk away*** irse, marcharse | US *to walk away from* dejar muy atrás a (a competitor), salir ileso de (from an accident) | *to walk away with* llevarse ‖ ***to walk back*** volver a pie, volver andando ‖ ***to walk down*** bajar andando *or* a pie; *you take the lift, I'll walk down* tome el ascensor, yo bajaré andando | bajar; *she walked slowly down the stairs* bajó lentamente la escalera ‖ ***to walk in*** entrar | *please, walk in* o *walk right in* pasen sin llamar ‖ ***to walk in on*** interrumpir sin querer ‖ ***to walk into*** entrar en (to enter) | encontrarse con; *to walk into a friend in the street* encontrarse con un amigo en la calle | tropezar con; *I turned round and I walked into a lamppost* di la vuelta y tropecé con un farol | caer en; *to walk into a trap* caer en una trampa | arremeter, atacar (to attack) ‖ ***to walk off*** irse, marcharse | *to walk off with* llevarse (to carry off) ‖ ***to walk on*** seguir su camino (to continue) | pisar (to tread on) | andar sobre; *to walk on the water* andar sobre el agua | THEATR hacer de comparsa (to have a non-speaking part), salir a escena (to come on stage) ‖ ***to walk out*** salir (to leave) | declararse en huelga (to go on strike) | sacar (to take out) | *to walk out on* abandonar, dejar | *to walk out with* salir con ‖ ***to walk over*** pisotear (rights, etc.) | FIG & FAM *to walk all over s.o.* tratar a patadas a alguien | *to walk over the course* ganar por ser el único participante ‖ ***to walk round*** dar la vuelta | *to walk round sth.* darle la vuelta a algo ‖ ***to walk through*** atravesar, pasar por ‖ ***to walk up*** subir (stairs) | *to walk up and down* ir de acá para allá | *to walk up to s.o.* acercarse a alguien | *walk up!* ¡acérquense!

walkaway [-əwei] *n* US pan *m* comido (easily won contest); *the game was a walkaway* el partido fue pan comido.

walker [-ə*] *n* paseante *m* & *f* ‖ peatón *m* (pedestrian) ‖ SP marchador *m* ‖ tacataca *m*, tacatá *m*, pollera *f* (for children) ‖ *to be a fast, a slow walker* andar de prisa, despacio.

walker-on [-ə'rɔn] *n* THEATR comparsa *m* & *f*, figurante *m* & *f* ‖ CINEM extra *m* & *f*.

walkie-talkie [-i'tɔ:ki] *n* RAD «talkie-walkie» *m*, radioteléfono *m* portátil.

walking [-iŋ] *n* andar *m*.
◆ *adj* ambulante ‖ a pie (tour) ‖ oscilante (oscillating) ‖ para andar (shoes) ‖ — *it is within walking distance* se puede ir a pie *or* andando ‖ FIG *walking dictionary* o *encyclopaedia* enciclopedia *f* ambulante.

walking cane [-iŋkein] *n* bastón *m*.

walking pace [-iŋpeis] *n* paso *m*; *at a walking pace* al paso.

walking papers [-iŋ,peipəz] *pl n* US FAM despido *m sing* ‖ *to get one's walking papers* ser despedido.

walking stick [-iŋstik] *n* bastón *m*.

Walkman [-mən] *n* (registered trademark) walkman *m*, cascos *m pl*.

walk-on [-ɔn] *n* THEATR papel *m* de comparsa *or* de figurante.

walkout [-aut] *n* huelga *f* (strike).

walkover [-,əuvə*] *n* victoria *f* fácil (easy win) ‖ FAM pan *m* comido (pushover); *it was a walkover* fue pan comido.

walk-up [-ʌp] *n* US casa *f or* piso *m* sin ascensor.

Walkyrie [væl'kjəri] *n* MYTH Walkiria *f*.

walky-talky [wɔ:ki'tɔ:ki] *n* RAD «talkie-walkie» *m*, radioteléfono *m* portátil.

wall [wɔ:l] *n* pared *f*; *the wall between two rooms* la pared entre dos habitaciones; *hang it on the wall* cuélgalo en la pared; *paintings on the walls of a cave* pinturas en las paredes de una cueva ‖ tapia *f*; *the garden wall* la tapia del jardín ‖ muro *m* (exterior wall of house, large garden wall, etc.) ‖ muralla *f*; *the city walls* las murallas de la ciudad ‖ FIG barrera *f*; *a wall of mountains* una barrera de montañas ‖ ANAT pared *f* ‖ AGR espaldera *f* (for fruit trees) ‖ — ARCH *blind wall* pared sin aberturas ‖ FIG *it's like talking to a brick wall* es como hablar a la pared ‖ ARCH *main wall* pared maestra ‖ FIG *to drive* o *to push to the wall* poner entre la espada y la pared, acorralar | *to go to the wall* fracasar (to fail), arruinarse (to be ruined), quebrar (to go bankrupt) | *we're banging our heads against a brick wall* con la Iglesia hemos topado ‖ *walls have ears* las paredes oyen | *with one's back to the wall* entre la espada y la pared, acorralado, da ‖ *within the walls* intramuros ‖ *without the walls* extramuros.
◆ *adj* de pared, mural.

wall [wɔ:l] *vt* poner una pared *or* un muro a (to furnish with a wall) ‖ — *to wall in* cercar con un muro *or* una tapia (a garden, an orchard, etc.), amurallar, fortificar (a town), emparedar, encerrar (a prisoner) || *to wall off* separar con una pared *or* un muro || *to wall up* tapiar.

wallaby [ˈwɔləbi] *n* ZOOL ualabi *m*, canguro *m* pequeño (kangaroo).

Wallachia [wɔˈleikiə] *pr n* GEOGR Valaquia *f*.

Wallachian [-n] *adj/n* valaco, ca.

wallah [ˈwɔlə] *n* FAM encargado *m*.

wallboard [ˈwɔːlbɔːd] *n* ARCH panel *m*, tablero *m*.

wall clock [ˈwɔːlklɔk] *n* reloj *m* de pared.

walled [wɔːld] *adj* amurallado, da (town) || cercado con una tapia (garden).

wallet [ˈwɔlit] *n* cartera *f* (for carrying papers, for bank notes, etc.) || morral *m* (knapsack).

walleye [ˈwɔːlai] *n* ojo *m* de color diferente || ojo *m* desviado hacia fuera || MED leucoma *m*.

wall fitting [ˈwɔːlˌfitiŋ] *n* aplique *m*.

wallflower [ˈwɔːlˌflauə*] *n* BOT alhelí *m* || FIG *to be a wallflower* quedarse en el poyete (not to dance).

wall lamp [ˈwɔːllæmp] *n* aplique *m*.

wall map [ˈwɔːlmæp] *n* mapa *m* mural.

Walloon [wɔˈluːn] *n* valón, ona.
◆ *n* valón *m* (language) || valón, ona (person).

wallop [ˈwɔlɔp] *n* FAM golpe *m* fuerte (blow) || FAM *to be going at a fair wallop* ir volando.

wallop [ˈwɔləp] *vt* FAM pegar fuerte (to hit hard) | dar una paliza (to thrash, to defeat).

walloping [-iŋ] *adj* FAM colosal, enorme.
◆ *n* FAM paliza *f* (thrashing, defeat).

wallow [ˈwɔləu] *vi* revolcarse (animals) || — *to wallow in vice* sumirse en el vicio || *to wallow in wealth* nadar en la abundancia.

wall painting [ˈwɔːlˌpeintiŋ] *n* pintura *f* mural.

wallpaper [ˈwɔːlˌpeipə*] *n* papel *m* pintado, papel *m* de empapelar.

wallpaper [ˈwɔːlˌpeipə*] *vt* empapelar.

wallpapering [-iŋ] *n* empapelado *m*.

wall plate [ˈwɔːlpleit] *n* ARCH carrera *f* || TECH placa *f* de apoyo.

wall seat [ˈwɔːlsiːt] *n* banqueta *f*.

wall tile [ˈwɔːltail] *n* ARCH azulejo *m*.

wall-to-wall [ˈwɔːltəˌwɔːl] *adj* de pared a pared.

wally [ˈwɔli] *n* POP majadero, ra.

walnut [ˈwɔːlnʌt] *n* nogal *m* (tree and timber) || nuez *f* (fruit) || nogalina *f* (colour).

walnut shell [-ʃel] *n* cáscara *f* de nuez.

walnut stain [-stein] *n* nogalina *f*.

walnut tree [-triː] *n* nogal *m*.

walrus [ˈwɔːlrəs] *n* ZOOL morsa *f*.

waltz [wɔːls] *n* MUS vals *m*.

waltz [wɔːls] *vt* MUS bailar el vals con.
◆ *vi* bailar el vals, valsar.

waltzer [-ə*] *n* valsador, ra; persona *f* que baila el vals.

wampum [ˈwɔmpəm] *n* cuentas *f pl* de concha usadas como adorno o dinero.

wan [wɔn] *adj* pálido, da; macilento, ta; lívido, da (unhealthily pale) || débil, macilento, ta (light) || triste (sad).

wand [wɔnd] *n* varita *f* (of magician) || varita *f* de las virtudes, varilla *f* mágica (of fairy) || vara *f* (symbol of authority) || US blanco *m* (in archery) || *Mercury's wand* caduceo *m*.

wander [-ə*] *vt* vagar por, errar por; *to wander the world* vagar por el mundo || *to wander the world over* recorrer el mundo entero.
◆ *vi* errar, vagar (to roam) || pasearse (to stroll); *to wander round a market* pasearse por un mercado || desvariar, delirar (the mind) || FIG desviarse, apartarse (from a subject) || serpentear (river, road) || — *his eyes wandered over the scene* observaba la escena || *to let one's thoughts wander* dejar vagar la imaginación || *to wander about* vagar, ir a la ventura || *to wander away from* apartarse de || *to wander off* alejarse || *to wander off the point* apartarse *or* salirse del tema.

wanderer [-ərə*] *n* vagabundo, da (vagabond) || viajero, ra (s.o. who travels) || nómada *m* & *f* (nomad) || FIG oveja *f* descarriada.

wandering [-əriŋ] *adj* errante; *The Wandering Jew* el Judío Errante || nómada; *wandering tribes* tribus nómadas || ambulante (salesman) || vagabundo, da (beggar) || sinuoso, sa (river) || incoherente (speech) || distraído, da (mind, eyes) || MED que delira, que desvaría (person) | flotante (kidney).
◆ *n* vagabundeo *m* (leisurely travelling about) || MED delirio *m*.
◆ *pl* vagabundeos *m* (leisury journeys) || divagaciones *f* (speech, thoughts).

wanderlust [-əlʌst] *n* pasión *f* por los viajes.

wane [wein] *n* ASTR cuarto *m* menguante (of the moon) || reflujo *m*, menguante *f* (of the tide) || FIG ocaso *m*, decadencia *f* (of life, of beauty, etc.) || *to be on the wane* estar menguando, menguar (the moon), bajar (the tide), estar en el ocaso, disminuir, declinar, decaer (to decrease, to decline).

wane [wein] *vi* ASTR menguar (the moon) || bajar (the tide) || FIG decaer, declinar, disminuir.

wangle [ˈwæŋgl] *vt* FAM agenciarse, conseguir (to get by cunning); *to wangle an invitation* agenciarse una invitación || falsificar (to falsify) || FAM *he wangled it so that he got the day off* se las arregló para tener el día libre.
◆ *vi* FAM arreglárselas.

wangler [-ə*] *n* trapacero, ra; tramposo, sa; trapisondista *m* & *f*.

wangling [-iŋ] *n* FAM trampas *f pl*, trucos *m pl*.

waning [ˈweiniŋ] *adj* menguante (moon, tide) || FIG decadente (declining).
◆ *n* → **wane.**

wanness [ˈwɔnnis] *n* palidez *f* (paleness) || tristeza *f* (sadness).

want [wɔnt] *n* falta *f* (lack); *want of tact* falta de tacto || necesidad *f* (need); *a man of few wants* un hombre de pocas necesidades || indigencia *f*, miseria *f* (poverty) || deseo *m* (wish) || laguna *f*, vacío *m* (gap); *this book answers a long-felt want* este libro llena una laguna que existía desde hacía mucho tiempo || — *for want of* por falta de; *they died for want of food* murieron por falta de alimento; a falta de; *for want of sth. better to do, he went to bed* a falta de algo mejor que hacer, se fue a la cama; por no tener; *for want of a nail the shoe is lost* por un clavo se pierde una herradura || *to be in want* estar necesitado, da || *to be in want of* necesitar, tener necesidad de; *I am in want of a dress* necesito un traje; estar falto de, carecer de; *millions of people are in want of food* millones de personas carecen de alimento.

want [wɔnt] *vt* querer; *they want to go to America* quieren ir a América; *I want a cup of coffee* quiero una taza de café; *I want him to come* quiero que venga || desear (to wish) || necesitar, hacer falta (to need); *the house wants a cleaning* la casa necesita limpieza; *he wants to rest* necesita descansar, le hace falta descansar; *what you want is a long holiday* lo que a ti te hace falta es tomarte unas vacaciones largas || faltarle a uno, carecer de (to lack); *he wants the stamina of a long-distance runner* le falta la resistencia *or* carece de la resistencia de un corredor de fondo || exigir, requerir (to demand, to require); *that work wants a lot of patience* ese trabajo requiere mucha paciencia || deber, necesitar; *you want to eat more* necesitas comer más || querer hablar con, querer ver, reclamar; *your father wants you* tu padre quiere hablar contigo *or* te reclama || buscar (to look for) || pedir (to ask); *how much does he want for it?* ¿cuánto pide por eso? || — *he is wanted by the police* lo busca la policía || *I don't want it known* no quiero que se sepa || *if you want to* si quieres || *it wants an hour till dinner time* falta una hora para la cena || FAM *it wants some doing* no es nada fácil, hay que tener valor para hacerlo || *the goods will be supplied as they are wanted* las mercancías serán suministradas a medida que se vayan necesitando || *wanted* se busca (criminals), se necesita (services) || *what does he want with me?* ¿qué quiere de mí? || *when you want to* cuando quieras || *you are not wanted here* aquí estás de más || *you are wanted in the office* te llaman *or* te reclaman en el despacho.
◆ *vi* querer || — *to want for* faltarle a uno, carecer de; *he never wanted for affection as a child* de niño nunca le faltó cariño, de niño nunca careció de cariño || *to want for nothing* tenerlo todo, no faltarle a uno nada.

want ad [-æd] *n* US anuncio *m* [en un periódico].

wanting [-iŋ] *adj* ausente (absent) || deficiente (deficient) || — *they are wanting in team spirit* les falta espíritu de equipo, carecen de espíritu de equipo || *wanting in* falto de, sin; *wanting in intelligence* sin inteligencia.
◆ *prep* sin; *a watch wanting its winder* un reloj sin cuerda.

wanton [-ən] *adj* lascivo, va; sensual (lewd) || libertino, na (promiscuous) || voluptuoso, sa (voluptuous) || desenfrenado, da (lacking moderation) || sin sentido (senseless) || sin motivo (without motive) || exuberante, lujuriante (luxuriant) || inhumano, na (inhumane) || juguetón, ona (playful) || desobediente (undisciplined) || extravagante (extravagant).
◆ *n* libertino, na.

wanton [-ən] *vi* juguetear.

wantonness [-ənnis] *n* libertinaje *m*, desenfreno *m* (licentiousness) || voluptuosidad *f* (voluptuousness) || desenfreno *m* (lack of moderation) || exuberancia *f* (luxuriance) || crueldad *f* (cruelty).

wapiti [ˈwɔpiti] *n* wapití *m* (deer).

war [wɔː*] *n* guerra *f* || — *at war* en guerra; *they are at war* están en guerra || *civil war* guerra civil || *lightning war* guerra relámpago || *the cold war* la guerra fría || *the Great War* la Primera Guerra Mundial || *the Trojan War* la Guerra de Troya || *the War of the Roses* la guerra de las Dos Rosas || *to be on a war footing* estar en pie de guerra || FIG *to be openly at war with s.o.* tenerle declarada la guerra a uno || *to declare war on* o *upon* declarar la guerra a || *to go to the wars* irse a la guerra || *to go to war* entrar en guerra (nations) || *to wage war* o *to make war on* hacer la guerra a || *war of nerves* guerra de nervios || *war of the knife* guerra a muerte || *World War* Guerra Mundial || FAM *you look as though you've been in the wars* parece que vuelves de la guerra.
◆ *adj* de guerra || — *war baby* niño nacido durante la guerra || *war chant* canto guerrero || FIG *war cloud* amenaza *f* de guerra || *war council* consejo *m* de guerra || *war crime* crimen *m* de guerra || *war criminal* criminal *m* de guerra || *war cry* grito *m* de guerra || *war dance* danza *f* de guerra || US *War Department* Ministerio *m* de la Guerra || *war fever* sicosis *f* de guerra || *war game* estudios tácticos sobre el mapa (tactical exercises), maniobras *f pl* (manœuvers) || *war*

memorial monumento *m* a los Caídos || *War Office* Ministerio *m* de la Guerra || *war paint* pinturas *f pl* de guerra (of primitive tribes), galas *f pl* (ceremonial dress), maquillaje *m* (cosmetics) || *war widow* viuda *f* de guerra.

war [wɔ:*] *vi* estar en guerra, guerrear (to be at war) || FIG luchar (*against* contra) (in order to exterminate sth.).

warble [wɔ:bl] *n* gorjeo *m*, trino *m* (sound) || VET tumor *m* producido por los reznos || rezno *m* (warble fly).

warble [wɔ:bl] *vt* cantar gorjeando *or* trinando.
◆ *vi* gorjear, trinar (birds) || cantar (to sing).

warble fly [-flai] *n* ZOOL rezno *m*.

warbler [-ə*] *n* curruca *f* (European bird).

warbling [-iŋ] *n* canoro, ra (bird).
◆ *n* gorjeo *m*.

ward [wɔ:d] *n* pupilo *m* (minor under legal care) || custodia *f*, tutela *f* (guardianship) || pabellón *m* (building in prison or hospital) || sala *f* (large room in hospital) || barrio *m*, distrito *m* (of a town) || guarda *f* (of a lock) || muesca *f* (of a key) || *the child was made a ward of Court* pusieron al niño bajo la protección del tribunal.

ward [wɔ:d] *vt* (ant) guardar, proteger || *to ward off* parar, desviar (a blow), prevenir, evitar (a danger), rechazar (an attack).

warden [-n] *n* guarda *m* (official) || vigilante *m* (keeper) || mayordomo *m* (churchwarden) || director *m* (of an institution) || US alcaide *m*, carcelero *m* (of a prison) || *game warden* guarda de caza, guardamonte *m*, guardabosque *m*.

wardenship [-ənʃip] *n* cargo *m* de guarda (of an official) *or* de director (of an institution) *or* de alcaide (of a prison).

warder [-ə*] *n* carcelero *m* (of a prison) || guardián *m*, vigilante *m* (watchman).

wardress [-ris] *n* carcelera *f* (of a prison) || guardiana *f*, vigilante *f*.

wardrobe [-rəub] *n* armario *m*, guardarropa *m*, ropero *m* (piece of furniture) || guardarropa *m*, vestuario *m* (a person's clothes) || THEATR vestuario *m* || THEATR *wardrobe keeper* guardarropa *m* & *f* | *wardrobe mistress* guardarropa *f*.

wardrobe trunk [-rəubtrʌnk] *n* baúl *m* armario *or* ropero.

wardroom [-rum] *n* MAR cámara *f* de oficiales (officer's living quarters).

wardship [-ʃip] *n* tutela *f*.

ware [wɛə*] *n* loza *f* (pottery) || objetos *m pl*, artículos *m pl* (things).
◆ *pl* mercancías *f* (goods for sale); *to shout one's wares* pregonar sus mercancías.

ware [wɛə*] *adj* ⟶ **aware.**

ware [wɛə*] *vt* tener cuidado con || *ware!* ¡cuidado!
— OBSERV El verbo *to ware* se utiliza sólo en la forma imperativa.

warehouse [wɛəhaus] *n* almacén *m* (storehouse) || guardamuebles *m inv* (for storing one's furniture) || depósito *m* de mercancías [en las aduanas] (customs storehouse).

warehouse [wɛəhaus] *vt* almacenar (goods, wares) || depositar (under bond) || guardar en el guardamuebles (one's furniture).

warehouseman [-mən] *n* almacenero *m*, guardalmacén *m*.
— OBSERV El plural de *warehouseman* es *warehousemen*.

warfare [wɔ:fɛə*] *n* guerra *f*; *atomic, germ, guerilla, trench, nuclear warfare* guerra atómica, bacteriológica, de guerrillas, de trincheras, nuclear.

warhead [wɔ:hed] *n* ojiva *f* (head of a projectile); *atomic warhead* ojiva atómica.

war-horse [wɔ:hɔ:s] *n* caballo *m* de batalla || FIG veterano *m*.

warily [wɛərili] *adv* con cautela, cautelosamente.

wariness [wɛərinis] *n* cautela *f*, precaución *f*.

warlike [wɔ:laik] *adj* belicoso, sa (inclined to favour war); *a warlike tribe* una tribu belicosa || guerrero, ra (feat) || militar, marcial (sound).

war loan [wɔ:ləun] *n* empréstito *m* de guerra.

warlock [wɔ:lɔk] *n* brujo *m* (male witch).

warlord [wɔ:lɔ:d] *n* jefe *m* militar.

warm [wɔ:m] *adj* tibio, bia (not very hot); *to bath a baby in warm water* bañar un niño en agua tibia || caliente; *the sea is warm today* el mar está caliente hoy || cálido, da; caluroso, sa (climate) || de calor, caluroso, sa (day) || caliente, de abrigo; *warm clothes* ropa caliente || acogedor, ra; agradable (fire) || acalorado, da; *a warm discussion* una discusión acalorada || FIG cariñoso, sa; afectuoso, sa (affectionate) | caluroso, sa (very cordial); *a warm welcome* una acogida calurosa; *warm applause* aplausos calurosos | cálido, da (colours) | fresco, ca (a scent) | caliente (in a guessing game) | ardiente, fervoroso, sa | entusiasta (enthusiastic) || FIG & FAM peligroso, sa (dangerous) | feo, a; desagradable (unpleasant) || — *the weather is warm* hace calor || *to be warm* hacer calor (weather), tener calor (person), estar caliente (thing) || *to get warm* entrar en calor (person), calentarse (thing), empezar a hacer calor (weather) || *to keep o.s. warm* abrigarse || *to keep warm* conservar caliente (food), abrigar (person) || *warm front* frente cálido (in meteorology) || FIG *you're getting warm* ¡caliente! (in guessing games).
◆ *n* calentamiento *m* || *to have a warm by the fire* calentarse junto al fuego.

warm [wɔ:m] *vt* calentar || FIG alegrar (the heart) | calentar (s.o.'s blood) | acalorar (s.o.) || — *to warm o.s. in the sun* calentarse al sol || *to warm over* recalentar (food) || FIG *to warm s.o.'s ears* calentarle a uno las orejas || *to warm up* calentar (to make sth. warm), recalentar (to reheat), hacer entrar en calor (to make s.o. warm), animar (to make more animated).
◆ *vi* calentarse || — *to warm to an idea* acoger *or* aceptar una idea con entusiasmo || *to warm to s.o.* tomarle simpatía a alguien || *to warm up* entrar en calor (to get warm), animarse (to liven up).

warm-blooded [-'blʌdid] *adj* de sangre caliente || FIG ardiente, apasionado, da.

warmer [-ə*] *n* calentador *m* || *foot warmer* calientapiés *m inv*.

warmhearted [-'ha:tid] *adj* afectuoso, sa; cariñoso, sa (loving) || bueno, na (kind).

warming [-iŋ] *n* FAM paliza *f*, tunda *f*.

warming pan [-iŋpæn] *n* calentador *m* de cama.

warming-up [-iŋ'ʌp] *adj* para entrar en calor (exercises).

warmly [-li] *adv* calurosamente (cordially) || afectuosamente, cariñosamente (affectionately) || con entusiasmo (enthusiastically).

warmonger [wɔ:,mʌŋgə*] *n* belicista *m* & *f*, agitador, ra.

warmongering [-riŋ] *n* belicismo *m*, incitación *f* a la guerra.

warmth [wɔ:mθ] *n* calor *m* (heat) || FIG ardor *m*, entusiasmo *m* (ardour) | cordialidad *f* || *the warmth of your welcome* su acogida calurosa.

warm-up [wɔ:mʌp] *n* SP ejercicios *m pl* para entrar en calor.

warn [wɔ:n] *vt* advertir, prevenir de, avisar de; *I warned you of the danger* le advertí del peligro || avisar (to inform); *somebody warned the police* alguien avisó a la policía || aconsejar; *I warned you not to go* le aconsejé que no fuese || amonestar (to rebuke) || — *be warned by me* que mi experiencia le sirva de ejemplo || *I have already warned you about your impoliteness* ya le dije que no fuera incorrecto || *the doctor warned him against smoking* el médico le dijo que tenía que dejar de fumar || *the public are warned that he is armed* se advierte al público que va armado || *to warn off* despedir (to send away); *her father warned the suitor off* su padre despidió al pretendiente || *to warn off the course* impedir que participe en las carreras (jockey, owner) || *to warn s.o. off the premises* expulsar a alguien (to order to leave), prohibir la entrada a alguien (to prevent from trespassing) || *we were warned of the risks involved* nos advirtieron los riesgos que corríamos || *we were warned to take warm clothing* nos advirtieron que lleváramos ropa de abrigo.

warner [-ə*] *n* TECH avisador *m*, aparato *m* de alarma (warning device).

warning [-iŋ] *n* advertencia *f*, aviso *m*; *they ignored his warning and jumped* no hicieron caso de su advertencia y saltaron || previo aviso *m* (notice) || amonestación *f* (rebuke) || señal *f* (signal) || alarma *f* (alarm) || lección *f* (lesson) || ejemplo *m* (example) || — *give me five minutes warning* avíseme cinco minutos antes || *let this be a warning to you* que esto le sirva de lección *or* de escarmiento || *take warming from it* que le sirva de lección || *to sound a note of warning* dar la alarma || *warning to leave* notificación *f* de despido || *without warning* sin avisar; *he came without warning* vino sin avisar; de repente (suddenly); *it happened without warning* ocurrió de repente.
◆ *adj* de aviso, de advertencia; *warning shot* disparo de advertencia || de alarma; *warning device* dispositivo de alarma || de amonestación (reprimanding) || — *warning light* lámpara indicadora, piloto *m*, señal luminosa || AUT *warning signs* señales *f* de peligro | *warning triangle* triángulo *m* de aviso de peligro.

warp [wɔ:p] *n* urdimbre *f* (in a fabric or loom) || alabeo *m* (of timber) || FIG deformación *f* (mental twist) | perversión *f* || MAR espía *f* (cable) || GEOL tierras *f pl* de aluvión.

warp [wɔ:p] *vt* alabear (timber, etc.) || FIG deformar, pervertir (the mind, the character, etc.) | tergiversar, desvirtuar (meaning) || urdir (yarn, etc.) || MAR halar, atoar.
◆ *vi* alabearse (to become twisted) || MAR ir a remolque.

warpath [wɔ:pa:θ] *n* *to be on the warpath* estar en pie de guerra (Indians), estar buscando guerra (to be looking for trouble).

warp beam [wɔ:pbi:m] *n* enjulio *m*, enjullo *m*.

warped [wɔ:pt] *adj* alabeado, da (timber) || FIG pervertido, da; retorcido, da (mind).

warper [wɔ:pə*] *n* urdidor, ra (person) || urdidor *m* (machine).

warping [wɔ:piŋ] *n* alabeo *m* (of timber, etc.) || urdidura *f* (of textiles) || MAR remolque *m*.

warplane [wa:plein] *n* avión *m* militar.

warrant [wɔrənt] *n* autorización *f* legal (legal authorization) || justificación *f* (justification) || garantía *f* (guarantee) || JUR orden *f*, mandamiento *m* judicial; *warrant of arrest* orden de detención | mandamiento *m* de pago (for a payment) || MIL patente *f* (patent) | nombramiento *m* de asimilado (certificate of appointment) || COMM recibo *m* de depósito.

warrant [ˈwɔrənt] *vt* justificar (to justify) ‖ garantizar (to guarantee) ‖ autorizar (to authorize).

warrantable [-əbl] *adj* garantizable (that can be guaranteed) ‖ justificable (justifiable).

warrantee [ˌwɔrənˈtiː] *n* JUR persona *f* que recibe una garantía.

warranter [ˈwɔrəntə*] *n* JUR fiador, ra; garante *m* & *f*.

warrant officer [ˈwɔrəntˌɔfisə*] *n* MIL suboficial *m*, oficial *m* asimilado ‖ *US* MAR contramaestre *m* (boatswain).

warrantor [ˈwɔrəntɔː*] *n* JUR fiador *m*, garante *m*.

warranty [ˈwɔrənti] *n* JUR garantía *f* ‖ autorización *f* (authorization) ‖ justificación *f* (justification) ‖ garantía *f* (guarantee).

warren [ˈwɔrin] *n* conejal *m*, conejar *m*, conejera *f* ‖ FIG colmena *f*, conejera *f* (overcrowded tenement house, etc.) | laberinto *m* (network of passages, etc.).

warring [ˈwɔriŋ] *adj* opuesto, ta (interest, etc.) ‖ en lucha (fighting) ‖ en guerra (at war).

warrior [ˈwɔriə*] *n* guerrero *m* ‖ *the Unknown Warrior* el Soldado Desconocido.

Warsaw [ˈwɔːsɔː] *pr n* GEOGR Varsovia.

warship [ˈwɔːʃip] *n* MAR buque *m* de guerra.

wart [wɔːt] *n* verruga *f*.

warthog [-hɔg] *n* ZOOL facoquero *m*, jabalí *m* verrugoso.

wartime [ˈwɔːtaim] *n* tiempo *m* de guerra.

warty [ˈwɔːti] *adj* verrugoso, sa.

war-weary [ˈwɔːˌwiəri] *adj* cansado de la guerra.

wary [ˈwɛəri] *adj* cauteloso, sa; precavido, da ‖ — *I was a bit wary at first* al principio estuve dudando ‖ *man to be wary of* hombre *m* de cuidado ‖ *to be wary of* tener cuidado con.

was [wɔz] *pret* ⟶ **be.**

wash [wɔʃ] *n* lavado *m* ‖ colada *f*, ropa *f* para lavar (clothes, linen, etc.) ‖ lavandería *f* (laundry); *I have sent all your clothes to the wash* he mandado toda su ropa a la lavandería ‖ GEOL aluvión *m* (debris) | erosión *f* | remolino *m* (of waves) ‖ MAR estela *f* (left by a ship) ‖ AVIAT perturbación *f* aerodinámica ‖ rumor *m*, murmullo *m* (sound made by water) ‖ MIN grava *f* aurífera (goldbearing earth) ‖ lavazas *f pl* (waste liquid) ‖ FAM aguachirle *f* (tasteless beverage) ‖ ARTS aguada *f* ‖ mano *f*, capa *f* (of whitewash, etc.) ‖ baño *m* (coat of gold, of silver, etc.) ‖ lavado *m* (of hair) ‖ loción *f* (cosmetic) ‖ enjuague *m* (mouthwash) ‖ — FIG *it will all come out in the wash* todo se arreglará ‖ *to give sth. a wash* lavar algo ‖ *to have a wash* lavarse ‖ *to have a wash and brush-up* lavarse y arreglarse.

wash [wɔʃ] *vt* lavar; *I have just washed all my shirts* acabo de lavar todas mis camisas ‖ quitar (dirt, stains) ‖ fregar; *to wash the dishes, the floor* fregar los platos, el suelo ‖ MIN & ARTS lavar ‖ bañar (the sea); *the Mediterranean washes the coast of Malaga* el Mediterráneo baña la costa de Málaga ‖ regar (a river) ‖ barrer; *the waves washed the deck* las olas barrieron la cubierta ‖ inundar, anegar; *heavy rains washed the roads* las fuertes lluvias inundaron las carreteras ‖ mojar, humedecer (to moisten) ‖ llevarse; *the waves washed the boat out to sea* las olas se llevaron el barco mar adentro ‖ arrojar; *a box washed ashore* una caja arrojada a la playa [por el mar] ‖ cavar (to excavate); *the rain washed a gulley in the hillside* las lluvias cavaron un barranco en la ladera de la colina ‖ erosionar (to erode) ‖ FIG purificar, limpiar (the soul) ‖ encalar, enjalbegar (walls) ‖ dar un baño a, bañar (a metal) ‖ depurar (gases) ‖ — *this detergent will not wash wollens* este detergente no es bueno para la lana ‖ *to wash one's face* lavarse la cara ‖ FIG *to wash one's hands of sth.* lavarse las manos de algo, desentenderse de algo ‖ *to wash o.s.* lavarse.

◆ *vi* lavarse (to cleanse o.s.) ‖ lavar la ropa, lavar (to clean clothes) ‖ lavarse; *material that washes well* tela que se lava muy bien ‖ lavar; *this detergent washes very well* este detergente lava muy bien ‖ barrer; *to wash over the deck* barrer la cubierta ‖ — *she washes for a living* es lavandera ‖ FAM *that excuse won't wash!* ¡esa excusa no cuela!

◆ *phr v* ***to wash away*** quitar [lavando] (stains) | derrubiar; *the river washed away its banks* el rió derrubió sus riberas | erosionar; *the waves washed away the cliff* las olas erosionaron el acantilado | llevarse; *the tide washed away his sunglasses* el mar se llevó sus gafas de sol | *to wash away one's sins* limpiar sus pecados ‖ ***to wash down*** lavar; *to wash the car down* lavar el coche | rociar; *a meal washed down with a good wine* una comida rociada con un buen vino | tragar; *to wash a pill down with water* tragar una pastilla con agua ‖ ***to wash off*** quitar *or* quitarse [lavando] ‖ ***to wash out*** lavar (clothes) | quitar [lavando] (stains) | quitarse (to be removed) | desteñirse (dye, colour) | lavar; *to wash a bottle out* lavar una botella | llevarse (to carry away) | ARTS degradar, rebajar (colours) | FIG abandonar (a plan, an idea, etc.), fracasar (to fail) | *the cricket match was washed out* se tuvo que cancelar el partido de cricket a causa de la lluvia | FIG *to wash out an insult in blood* lavar un insulto con sangre ‖ ***to wash up*** fregar | fregar los platos (to clean the dishes) | arrojar; *wreckage washed up by the sea* restos arrojados por el mar.

washable [ˈwɔʃəbl] *adj* lavable.

wash-and-wear [ˈwɔʃəndˈwɛə*] *adj* que no necesita plancha, de lava y pon.

washbasin [ˈwɔʃˌbeisn] *n* lavabo *m* (basin) ‖ palangana *f* (bowl).

washboard [ˈwɔʃbɔːd] *n* tabla *f* de lavar (for scrubbing clothes on) ‖ cenefa *f*, zócalo *m* (skirting board).

washbowl [ˈwɔʃbəul] *n* lavabo *m* (basin) ‖ palangana *f* (bowl).

washcloth [ˈwɔʃklɔθ]; **washrag** [ˈwɔʃræg] *n* *US* toallita *f* para lavarse la cara o el cuerpo.

washday [ˈwɔʃdei] *n* día *m* de la colada.

washed-out [ˈwɔʃtˈaut] *adj* descolorido, da; desteñido, da (faded in colour) ‖ FAM rendido, da; reventado, da (tired).

washed up [ˈwɔʃtˈʌp] *adj* FAM acabado, da; *he is completely washed up* está completamente acabado ‖ *their marriage is washed up* su matrimonio es un fracaso.

washer [ˈwɔʃə*] *n* TECH arandela *f* | depurador *m* de gas (for washing gases) ‖ lavador, ra (person) ‖ lavadora *f* (washing machine).

washerman [-mən] *n* lavandero *m* (laundryman).

— OBSERV El plural de *washerman* es *washermen*.

washer-up [-rˈʌp] *n* lavaplatos *m* & *f inv* (person).

— OBSERV El plural de *washer-up* es *washers-up*.

washerwoman [-ˌwumən] *n* lavandera *f*.

— OBSERV El plural de *washerwoman* es *washerwomen*.

washhouse [ˈwɔʃhaus] *n* lavadero *m*.

washing [ˈwɔʃiŋ] *n* lavado *m* ‖ colada *f* (of clothes) ‖ fregado *m* (of the floor, of the dishes) ‖ colada *f*, ropa *f* para lavar, ropa *f* sucia (clothes to wash) ‖ colada *f*, ropa *f* tendida (hung to dry) ‖ ARTS aguada *f*, lavado *m* ‖ encalado *m*, enjalbegado *m* (of walls) ‖ MIN lavado *m* ‖ TECH depuración *f* (of gas) ‖ COMM venta *f* ficticia ‖ — *colour that will not stand washing* color que se destiñe al ser lavado ‖ REL *the washing of feet* el lavatorio de los pies ‖ *to do the washing* lavar la ropa, hacer la colada ‖ *to take in washing* ser lavandera.

◆ *pl* lavazas *f* (dirty water) ‖ MIN mineral *m sing* obtenido tras el lavado (ore) | lavadero *m sing* (place).

washing day [-dei] *n* día *m* de la colada.

washing line [-lain] *n* tendedero *m*.

washing machine [-məʃiːn] *n* lavadora *f*.

washing powder [-ˌpaudə*] *n* jabón *m* en polvo.

washing soda [-ˌsəudə] *n* sosa *f*.

Washington [ˈwɔʃiŋtən] *pr n* GEOGR Washington.

Washington DC [ˈwɔʃiŋtəndiːsiː] *pr n* GEOGR Washington [capital federal].

washing-up [-ˈʌp] *n* fregado *m* de los platos (action) ‖ platos *m pl* para fregar (dirty dishes) ‖ platos *m pl* fregados (washed dishes) ‖ *to do the washing-up* fregar los platos.

washing-up bowl [-ˈʌpbəul] *n* barreño *m* [para fregar los platos].

washing-up liquid [-ʌpˈlikwid] *n* detergente *m* líquido.

washleather [ˈwɔʃˌleðə*] *n* gamuza *f*.

washout [ˈwɔʃaut] *n* derrubio *m* (erosion) ‖ lugar *m* derrubiado (eroded place) ‖ FAM desastre *m* (a complete failure); *he's a washout* es un desastre; *the film is a washout* la película es un desastre.

washrag [ˈwɔʃræg] *n* *US* ⟶ **washcloth.**

washroom [ˈwɔʃrum] *n* *US* servicios *m pl*.

wash sale [ˈwɔʃseil] *n* COMM venta *f* ficticia [de acciones].

washstand [ˈwɔʃstænd] *n* lavabo *m*.

washtub [ˈwɔʃtʌb] *n* tina *f* donde se lava la ropa.

washy [ˈwɔʃi] *adj* aguado, da (wine) ‖ soso, sa; insípido, da (food) ‖ deslavazado, da (colour, style).

wasp [wɔsp] *n* avispa *f* (insect).

waspish [-iʃ] *adj* mordaz (critical) ‖ irritable, enojadizo, za (irritable) ‖ esbelto, ta (slender).

waspishness [-iʃnis] *n* mordacidad *f* (of words) ‖ mal genio *m*, irritabilidad *f* (bad temper).

wasp waist [-ˈweist] *n* cintura *f* de avispa.

wasp-waisted [-ˈweistid] *adj* con cintura de avispa (person) ‖ ceñido, da (dress).

wassail [ˈwɔseil] *n* brindis *m* (toast) ‖ borrachera *f* (heavy drinking) ‖ cerveza *f* con especias y frutas (ale).

wastage [ˈweistidʒ] *n* pérdidas *f pl* (loss); *profit forecasts take into account a certain degree of wastage* las previsiones relativas a los beneficios toman en consideración cierta cantidad de pérdidas ‖ despilfarro *m*, derroche *m* (of money) ‖ desgaste *m* (wear) ‖ desperdicio *m*; *man's wastage of natural resources* el desperdicio por el hombre de los recursos naturales.

waste [weist] *adj* yermo, ma (barren) ‖ baldío, a (uncultivated) ‖ incultivable (not arable) ‖ de desecho (products) ‖ residual (water) ‖ desperdiciado, da (gas, heat, steam) ‖ sobrante (superfluous) ‖ de desagüe (pipe) ‖ — *to lay waste* asolar, devastar, arrasar ‖ *to lie waste* no cultivarse, quedar sin cultivar (land).

◆ *n* pérdida *f*; *a waste of energy* una pérdida de energía; *it's a waste of time* es una pérdida de tiempo ‖ desgaste *m*, deterioro *m* (by use) ‖ deterioro *m* (by lack of use) ‖ pérdidas *f pl* (wastage) ‖ CULIN desperdicios *m pl* (of food) ‖ residuos *m pl*, desechos *m pl* (from a manufacturing process) ‖ basura *f* (rubbish) ‖ desierto *m* (desert) || yermo *m* (barren land) || erial *m* (uncultivated land) || TECH borra *f* (remnants of cotton fibre) || GEOL erosión *f* || JUR deterioro *m* || — *radioactive waste* desechos radiactivos || *to go* o *to run to waste* desperdiciarse.

waste [weist] *vt* derrochar, despilfarrar, malgastar; *to waste one's fortune* derrochar su fortuna || desperdiciar (not to use) || perder (time); *you are wasting your time trying to convince him* pierdes el tiempo intentando convencerle || desaprovechar, perder (an opportunity) || agotar, consumir (to use up) || consumir; *the illness slowly wasted him* la enfermedad le fue consumiendo lentamente || debilitar (to weaken) || enflaquecer (to make thin) || devastar, asolar, arrasar (to devastate) || JUR deteriorar || — *don't waste your money on a new coat when you don't need one* no gastes tu dinero comprando un abrigo que no te hace falta || *he is wasted in that job* es un empleo muy por debajo de sus posibilidades || *I am wasted on you* no sabes apreciar lo que valgo || *my wit is wasted on you* no sabes apreciar mi ingenio || *nothing is wasted in this house* en esta casa no se desperdicia nada, en esta casa todo se aprovecha || *to waste words* gastar saliva en balde.

◆ *vi* desperdiciarse; *the water is wasting* el agua se está desperdiciando || desgastarse, gastarse (to wear away) || agotarse (to become used up); *they allowed their resources to waste rapidly* dejaron que se agotaran rápidamente sus recursos || disminuir (to diminish) || debilitarse (to become weak) || enflaquecer (to become thin) || JUR deteriorarse || — *time is wasting* estamos perdiendo tiempo || *to waste away* consumirse; *he was wasting away with fever* se estaba consumiendo con la fiebre.

wastebasket [-,bɑːskit] *n* US papelera *f*, cesto *m* de los papeles.

wastebin [-bin] *n* cubo *m* de la basura.

waste disposal unit [-dis'pəuzəl,juːnit] *n* triturador *m or* vertedero *m* de basuras.

wasteful [-ful] *adj* despilfarrador, ra; derrochador, ra (person) || ruinoso, sa; excesivo, va; *wasteful spending* gasto ruinoso || *the stove is wasteful of fuel* se gasta mucho combustible con la estufa.

wastefulness [-fulnis] *n* despilfarro *m*, derroche *m* (wasteful spending).

waste ground [-graund] *n* solar *m*.

waste heap [-hiːp] *n* vertedero *m* (rubbish dump) || escorial *m* (of a factory) || escombrera *f* (of a mine).

wasteland [-lænd] *n* yermo *m* (barren land) || erial *m* (uncultivated land).

waste matter [-,mætə*] *n* residuos *m pl*, desechos *m pl*.

wastepaper [-'peipə*] *n* papel *m* usado, papeles *m pl* viejos.

wastepaper basket [-'peipə,bɑːskit] *n* papelera *f*, cesto *m* de los papeles.

waste pipe [-paip] *n* tubo *m* de desagüe.

waste product [-,prɔdʌkt] *n* desecho *m*, producto *m* de desecho, residuo *m*; *industrial waste products* residuos industriales || *the body's waste products* los excrementos.

waster [-ə*] *n* derrochador, ra; despilfarrador, ra (ruinously extravagant) || TECH pieza *f* defectuosa.

wasting [-iŋ] *adj* devastador, ra || MED debilitante.

◆ *n* devastación *f*, asolamiento *m* || MED debilitación *f*.

wastrel [-rəl] *n* derrochador, ra; despilfarrador, ra (spendthrift) || FAM inútil *m* & *f*, golfo, fa.

watch [wɔtʃ] *n* reloj *m* de pulsera (wristwatch) || reloj *m* de bolsillo (pocket timepiece) || vigilancia *f* (vigilance) || vigilante *m* nocturno, guarda *m* nocturno (watchman) || MAR guardia *f* (period of duty); *to be on watch* estar de guardia | brigada *f* de guardia (crew on duty) | marinero *m* de guardia, vigía *m* (man on lookout) || HIST vigilante *m* (person) | ronda *f* (group of persons on guard) || — MAR *officer of the watch* oficial *m* de guardia || *on the watch* alerta, ojo avizor || *to be on the watch for s.o.* acechar a alguien, estar al acecho de alguien || *to keep watch* estar de guardia || *to keep watch on* o *over* vigilar || *to set a watch on s.o.* hacer vigilar a alguien.

watch [wɔtʃ] *vt* observar, mirar; *to watch s.o.'s reaction* observar la reacción de alguien; *to watch s.o. working* mirar a alguien que trabaja, observar cómo trabaja alguien || ver, mirar; *to watch a football match on television* ver un partido de fútbol en la televisión || fijarse en (to pay attention) || vigilar (to keep an eye on) || cuidar (to take care of); *to watch a child* cuidar a un niño || velar (a corpse, a sick person) || tener cuidado con (to be careful with); *watch the wet paint* tenga cuidado con la pintura; *I have to watch what I spend* tengo que tener cuidado con lo que gasto || seguir; *to watch a patient's progress* seguir los progresos de un enfermo || asistir; *hundreds of people watched the Wimbledon finals* cientos de personas asistieron a las finales de Wimbledon || — FIG *a watched pot* o *kettle never boils* quien espera desespera || *to watch one's chance* esperar el momento oportuno || *watch how you go!* ¡anda con cuidado! || *watch it!* ¡cuidado! || FIG *watch your step!* ¡tenga cuidado! || *we are being watched* nos están mirando.

◆ *vi* mirar, observar; *I don't like taking part, I prefer to watch* no me gusta tomar parte, prefiero observar || velar (to stay awake) || vigilar (to keep guard) || — *I watched all night* pasé toda la noche en vela || *to watch after* seguir con la mirada || *to watch by* velar (a sick person) || *to watch for* esperar; *I am watching for the postman* estoy esperando al cartero || *to watch out* estar atento, estar ojo avizor (to keep a lookout), tener cuidado (to be careful) || *to watch out for* estar al acecho de; *police are watching out for the criminals* la policía está al acecho de los criminales; tener cuidado con; *watch out for pick-pockets* tenga cuidado con los rateros || *to watch over* cuidar, vigilar (to look after), velar (a sick person), velar por (s.o.'s interests, welfare), guardar (a flock) || *watch out!* ¡cuidado!

watchband [-bænd] *n* correa *f* de reloj (leather, nylon) || cadena *f* de reloj (metal).

watchcase [-keis] *n* caja *f* de reloj.

watch chain [-tʃein] *n* cadena *f* de reloj, leontina *f*.

watchdog [-dɔg] *n* perro *m* guardián.

watcher [-ə*] *n* vigilante *m* (guard) || observador, ra (observer) || mirón, ona (onlooker).

watch fire [-faiə*] *n* hoguera *f*, fuego *m*.

watchful [-ful] *adj* atento, ta; vigilante, alerta (attentive) || desvelado, da (sleepless).

watchfulness [-fulnis] *n* vigilancia *f*, cuidado *m*.

watch glass [-glɑːs] *n* cristal *m* de reloj.

watching [-iŋ] *n* vigilancia *f* || observación *f*; *bird watching* observación de los pájaros || *he is a man who wants watching* es un hombre que hay que vigilar.

watchmaker [-,meikə*] *n* relojero *m* || *watchmaker's* relojería *f* (shop).

watchman [-mən] *n* vigilante *m* || *night watchman* vigilante nocturno (on a building site, in a factory, etc.), sereno *m* (in the street).

— OBSERV El plural de *watchman* es *watchmen*.

watch night [-nait] *n* nochevieja *f*.

watch pocket [-,pɔkit] *n* bolsillo *m* del reloj.

watch spring [-spriŋ] *n* muelle *m*, resorte *m*.

watch strap [-stræp] *n* correa *f* de reloj.

watchtower [-,tauə*] *n* atalaya *f*.

watchword [-wəːd] *n* contraseña *f*, santo y seña *m*; *to give the watchword* dar el santo y seña || consigna *f* (guiding principle); *to follow the party watchword* seguir la consigna del partido.

water [wɔːtə*] *n* agua *f*; *give me some water* dame agua; *ammonia water* agua amoniacal || marea *f*; *high, low water* marea alta, baja || MED orina *f* (urine) || aguas *f pl*; *the water of a diamond, of a material* las aguas de un diamante, de una tela || oriente *m* (of a pearl) || ARTS acuarela *f* || COMM acciones *f pl* emitidas sin aumento de capital equivalente || — *brackish* o *briny water* agua salobre || *by water* por mar, en barco || FIG *come hell or high water* pase lo que pase, contra viento y marea || MED *difficulty in passing water* retención de orina || *drinking water* agua potable || *fresh water* agua dulce || *hard water* agua gorda *or* dura || *heavy water* agua pesada || REL *holy water* agua bendita || *irrigation water* agua de regadío || *lavender water* agua de lavanda || *mineral water* agua mineral || *mother water* aguas madres || FIG *much water has flowed under the bridge since then* ha llovido mucho desde entonces | *of the first water* de primera categoría || *on the water* en barco (person), en el mar (a ship) || *orange-flower water* agua de azahar || *oxygenated water* agua oxigenada || *rain water* agua de lluvia || *running water* agua corriente || *salt water* agua salada || *stagnant water* agua estancada || MAR *the boat draws six feet of water* el barco tiene seis pies de calado || FIG *the sight of that cake brings water to my mouth* se me hace la boca agua al ver ese pastel | *the theory does not hold water* la teoría no tiene fundamento | *to be in hot water* estar en un apuro *or* en un aprieto | *to bring water to one's eyes* hacerle saltar las lágrimas a uno | *to dash cold water on* echar un jarro de agua fría sobre | *to fish in troubled waters* pescar en río revuelto | *to get into deep water, to get o.s. into hot water* meterse en dificultades, meterse en un aprieto *or* en un lío | *to keep one's head above water* mantenerse a flote || *to let in water* calarse; *these broken shoes let in water* estos zapatos rotos se calan; hacer agua (boat), || *to make water* hacer agua (to spring a leak), hacer aguas, orinar (to urinate) || *to pass water* hacer aguas, orinar || FIG *to pour* o *throw cold water on sth.* echar algo por tierra || MAR *to take on water* repostar agua || *to take the horses to water* llevar los caballos al abrevadero *or* a beber || FIG *to throw* o *to pour cold water on* echar un jarro de agua fría sobre (s.o.), desacreditar (a project) || CHEM *water of crystallization* agua de cristalización || MED *water of the brain* hidrocefalia *f* | *water on the knee* derrame *m* sinovial || FIG *to be water under the bridge* ser agua *f* pasada.

◆ *pl* aguas *f*; *to take the waters* tomar las aguas; *territorial waters* aguas jurisdiccionales; *in British waters* en aguas británicas || FIG *still waters ran deep* del agua mansa me libre Dios, que de la brava me libro yo *or* me guardaré yo.

◆ *adj* acuático, ca; *water bird* ave acuática; *water festival* festival acuático || acuático, ca; náutico, ca (sport) || TECH hidráulico, ca.

water [wɔːtə*] *vt* mojar (to soak) || humedecer (to wet) || regar; *to water the garden, the plants* regar el jardín, las plantas; *the Ganges waters a very large area* el Ganges riega un área muy extensa; *they have watered the road to settle the dust* han regado la carretera para asentar el polvo || dar a beber a, abrevar (animals) || abastecer de agua (to supply with water) || aguar, diluir, bautizar (*fam*); *this wine has been watered* este vino ha sido aguado || tornasolar

(a fabric) || — FIG *the pocket edition is a watered-down version of the original* la edición de bolsillo es una versión abreviada de la obra original || COMM *to water capital* emitir acciones sin aumento de capital || FIG *to water down* moderar, suavizar.
◆ *vi* llorar; *my right eye is watering* me llora el ojo derecho || hacerse agua; *my mouth is watering, it makes my mouth water* se me hace la boca agua || repostar agua (ship) || beber (animals).

waterage [-ridʒ] *n* transporte *m* por barco (service) || barcaje *m* (fare paid).

water bag [-bæg] *n* bolsa *f* para el agua || BIOL bolsa *f* de las aguas.

water ballast [-,bæləst] *n* MAR lastre *m* de agua.

water bath [-bɑːθ] *n* baño *m* de maría, baño *m* maría.

water-bearer [-,bɛərə*] *n* aguador *m* [AMER aguatero *m*] || ASTR *Water Bearer* Acuario *m*.

water-bearing [-,bɛəriŋ] *adj* acuífero, ra.

water bed [-bed] *n* colchón *m* de agua.

water biscuit [-,biskit] *n* CULIN galleta *f* de harina y agua.

water boat [-bəut] *n* barco *m* cisterna, buque *m* aljibe.

waterborne [-bɔːn] *adj* flotante (ship) || transportado por barco (goods) || por vía marítima *or* fluvial, marítimo, ma; fluvial (transport).

water bottle [-,bɔtl] *n* cantimplora *f* || *hot water bottle* bolsa *f* de agua caliente.

water brash [-bræʃ] *n* MED pirosis *f*.

water buffalo [-,bʌfələu] *n* ZOOL búfalo *m* de agua, búfalo *m*, carabao *m*.

water bug [-bʌg] *n* ZOOL chinche *f* de agua.

water cannon [-,kænən] *n* cañón *m* de agua.

water carriage [-,kæridʒ] *n* transporte *m* por barco, transporte *m* marítimo *or* fluvial.

water carrier [-,kæriə*] *n* aguador *m* [AMER aguatero *m*] || ASTR *Water Carrier* Acuario *m*.

water cart [-kɑːt]; **watering cart** [-riŋkɑːt] *n* carro *m* de riego (for irrigation, street sprinkling) || camión *m* de riego (motorized) || carro *m* aljibe (for distributing drinking water) || camión *m* aljibe (motorized).

water chestnut [-,tʃestnʌt] *n* castaña *f* de agua.

water chute [-ʃuːt] *n* tobogán *m*.

water clock [-klɔk] *n* clepsidra *f*, reloj *m* de agua.

water closet [-klɔzit] *n* wáter *m*, retrete *m*.

watercolour; *US* **watercolor** [-,kʌlə*] *n* ARTS acuarela *f*.

watercolourist; *US* **watercolorist** [-,kʌlərist] *n* ARTS acuarelista *m* & *f*.

water-cooling [-,kuːliŋ] *n* refrigeración *f* por agua.

watercourse [-kɔːs] *n* corriente *f* de agua (stream) || lecho *m*, cauce *m* (bed of stream) || canal *m*, conducto *m* (channel).

watercraft [-krɑːft] *n* barco *m*, embarcación *f* (boat) || buque *m* (ship).

water crane [-krein] *n* grúa *f* hidráulica.

watercress [-kres] *n* BOT berro *m*.

water cure [-kjuə*] *n* MED hidroterapia *f*.

water diviner [-di,vainə*] *n* zahorí *m*.

water dog [-dɔg] *n* perro *m* de aguas || FIG lobo *m* de mar (sailor) | buen nadador *m* (good swimmer).

watered [-d] *adj* regado, da; *a well-watered garden* un jardín bien regado || aguado, da (wine, milk, etc.) || tornasolado, da (fabrics).

watered-down [-ddaun] *adj* aguado, da (wine, milk) || FIG moderado, da; suavizado, da (speech, letter).

waterfall [-fɔːl] *n* cascada *f*, salto *m* de agua (small) || catarata *f* (large).

waterfinder [-,faində*] *n* zahorí *m*.

water flea [-fliː] *n* ZOOL pulga *f* de agua.

waterfowl [-faul] *n* ZOOL ave *f* acuática.

waterfront [-frʌnt] *n* parte *f* de la ciudad que da al mar (zone adjacent to the sea) || puerto *m*, muelles *m pl* (harbour).

water gage [-geidʒ] *n* *US* ⟶ **water gauge.**

water gap [-gæp] *n* GEOGR garganta *f*, desfiladero *m*.

water gas [-gæs] *n* gas *m* de agua.

water gate [-geit] *n* compuerta *f* (sluice).

water gauge; *US* **water gage** [-geidʒ] *n* TECH indicador *m* del nivel de agua (of a tank, etc.) | hidrómetro *m* (for a stream).

water glass [-glɑːs] *n* vaso *m* (for drinking water) || tubo *m* *or* caja *f* de vidrio (for examining objets under water) || CHEM silicato *m* sódico líquido, vidrio *m* soluble (silicate) || indicador *m* de nivel (water gauge) || clepsidra *f*, reloj *m* de agua (water clock).

water hammer [-,hæmə*] *n* PHYS martillo *m* de agua || golpe *m* de ariete (in a water pipe).

water-harden [-,hɑːdən] *vt* TECH templar [con agua].

water heater [-,hiːtə*] *n* calentador *m* de agua.

water hemlock [-,hemlɔk] *n* BOT cicuta *f* acuática.

water hen [-hen] *n* ZOOL polla *f* de agua (moorhen) | fúlica *f* (American coot).

water hole [-həul] *n* charca *f*, charco *m* (pond).

water hyacinth [-'haiəsinθ] *n* BOT jacinto *m* de agua.

water ice [-rais] *n* CULIN sorbete *m*.

wateriness [-rinis] *n* acuosidad *f* || FIG insipidez *f* (insipidity).

watering [-riŋ] *n* riego *m* (of garden, of plants, etc.) || AGR irrigación *f*, riego *m* (of fields) || aguado *m*, adición *f* de agua (of wine, of milk, etc.).
◆ *adj* de riego || lloroso, sa; *watering eyes* ojos llorosos.

watering can [-riŋkæn] *n* regadera *f*.

watering cart [-riŋkɑːt] *n* ⟶ **water cart.**

watering hole [-riŋhəu] *n* abrevadero *m* (for animals) || FAM pub.

watering place [-riŋpleis] *n* abrevadero *m* (for animals) || balneario *m* (spa) || estación *f* balnearia (seaside resort).

watering trough [-riŋtrɔf] *n* abrevadero *m*.

water jacket [-,dʒækit] *n* TECH camisa *f* de agua.

water jug [-dʒʌg] *n* aguamanil *m* (for toilet) || jarra *f* de agua (pitcher).

water jump [-dʒʌmp] *n* SP ría *f* (in steeplechase).

waterless [-lis] *adj* sin agua; *a waterless well* un pozo sin agua || árido, da (land).

water level [-,levəl] *n* nivel *m* del agua (height of water) || MAR línea *f* de flotación (of a ship) || TECH nivel *m* de agua (instrument).

water lily [-,lili] *n* BOT nenúfar *m*.

waterline [-lain] *n* MAR línea *f* de flotación; *the boat was holed below the waterline* se abrió una brecha en el barco por debajo de la línea de flotación || filigrana *f* (in papermaking) || nivel *m* del agua (height of water).

waterlogged [-lɔgd] *adj* saturado de agua (soaked with water) || inundado, da; anegado, da (ground) || empapado, da (wood).

water main [-mein] *n* cañería *f* principal.

waterman [-mən] *n* barquero *m*.
— OBSERV El plural de *waterman* es *watermen*.

watermark [-mɑːk] *n* marca *f* del nivel del agua (showing the water level) || filigrana *f* (in papermaking).

watermelon [-,melən] *n* BOT sandía *f*.

water meter [-'miːtə*] *n* contador *m* de agua.

water mill [-mil] *n* molino *m* de agua.

water motor [-,məutə*] *n* MYTH motor *m* hidráulico.

water nymph [-nimf] *n* MYTH náyade *f*.

water ouzel [-,uːzl] *n* tordo *m* de agua (bird).

water parting [-,pɑːtiŋ] *n* línea *f* divisoria de las aguas.

water pipe [-paip] *n* cañería *f* de agua, tubería *f* de agua || narguile *m* (narghile).

water pistol [-,pistl] *n* pistola *f* de agua.

water plane [-plein] *n* AVIAT hidroavión *m*.

water plant [-plɑːnt] *n* BOT planta *f* acuática.

water plantain [-,plæntin] *n* BOT llantén *m* de agua.

waterpolice [-pə,liːs] *n* policía *f* fluvial.

water polo [-,pəuləu] *n* SP water-polo *m*, polo *m* acuático.

waterpot [-pɔt] *n* jarra *f* de agua (jug) || regadera *f* (watering can).

waterpower [-,pauə*] *n* energía *f* hidráulica.

waterproof [-pruːf] *adj* impermeable (material) || sumergible (watch).
◆ *n* impermeable *m* (raincoat) || tela *f* impermeable (material).

waterproof [-pruːf] *vt* impermeabilizar.

waterproofing [-,pruːfiŋ] *n* impermeabilización *f*.

water pump [-pʌmp] *n* TECH bomba *f* de agua.

water ram [-ræm] *n* TECH ariete *m* hidráulico.

water rat [-ræt] *n* ZOOL rata *f* de agua (aquatic vole) | rata *f* almizclera (muskrat).

water rate [-reit] *n* impuesto *m* sobre el agua.

water-repellent [-ri'pelənt]; **water-resistant** [-ri'zistənt] *adj* hidrófugo, ga.

water rights [-raits] *pl n* derechos *m* de captación de agua.

water route [-ruːt] *n* vía *f* navegable.

water scorpion [-,skɔːpjən] *n* ZOOL escorpión *m* de agua.

water seal [-siːl] *n* TECH cierre *m* hidráulico.

watershed [-ʃed] *n* GEOGR línea *f* divisoria de las aguas (dividing line) || cuenca *f* (basin) || FIG momento *m* decisivo; *it was one of the watersheds of English history* fue un momento decisivo en la historia inglesa.

waterside [-said] *n* orilla *f*, ribera *f*.
◆ *adj* ribereño, ña.

water-ski [-skiː] *vi* SP hacer esquí *m* acuático, esquí *m* náutico.

water skiing [-,skiːiŋ] *n* SP esquí *m* acuático, esquí *m* náutico.

water skin [-skin] *n* odre *m*.

water snake [-sneik] *n* ZOOL serpiente *f* de agua.

water softener [-,sɔfnə*] *n* ablandador *m* del agua.

water-soluble [-ˌsɔljubl] *adj* hidrosoluble.

water spider [-ˌspaidə*] *n* ZOOL araña *f* de agua.

waterspout [-spaut] *n* canalón *m* (of a roof) || tromba *f* marina (meterological phenomenon).

water sprite [-sprait] *n* MYTH ondina *f*.

water-stained [-steind] *adj* con manchas de humedad.

water strider [-ˌstraidə*] *n* US tejedor *m* (insect).

water supply [-səˌplai] *n* abastecimiento *m* de agua (system) || reserva *f* de agua (stored water).

water system [-ˌsistəm] *n* red *f* fluvial (rivers) || abastecimiento *m* de agua (water supply).

water table [-ˌteibl] *n* ARCH retallo *m* de derrame || GEOL nivel *m* hidrostático, capa *f* freática.

water tank [-tæŋk] *n* aljibe *m*, tanque *m* (on a vehicle) || depósito *m* de agua, aljibe *m* (in a house or tower) || cisternilla *f* (of a lavatory).

water tap [-tæp] *n* grifo *m*.

watertight [-tait] *adj* estanco, ca; hermético, ca (impermeable to water) || FIG perfecto, ta; *a watertight alibi* una coartada perfecta | irrecusable, irrefutable (argument) || — MAR *watertight bulkhead* mamparo estanco | *watertight compartment* compartimiento estanco.

water tower [-ˌtauə*] *n* TECH arca *f* de agua, depósito *m* elevado de agua.

watertube [-tjuːb] *adj* acuotubular; *water-tube boiler* caldera acuotubular.

water vapour; US **water vapor** [-ˌveipə*] *n* vapor *m* de agua.

water vole [-vəul] *n* ZOOL rata *f* de agua.

water wall [-wɔːl] *n* dique *m* (dike) || TECH pantalla *f* de tubos de agua (in a boiler).

water wave [-weiv] *n* MAR ola *f* || ondulación *f* (of hair).

water-wave [-weiv] *vt* marcar (hair).

water-waving [-ˌweiviŋ] *n* aguas *f pl*, visos *m pl*, tornasolado *m* (of silk) || marcado *m* (of hair).

waterway [-wei] *n* vía *f* navegable, vía *f* fluvial (navigable channel) || MAR trancanil *m* (on a ship's deck) || *inland waterway* canal *m*.

waterweed [-wiːd] *n* BOT planta *f* acuática.

waterwheel [-wiːl] *n* rueda *f* hidráulica (of a mill) || rueda *f* de álabes (of a boat) || AGR noria *f* (in irrigation).

water wings [-wiŋz] *pl n* flotadores *m*.

waterworks [-wəːks] *n* sistema *m* or instalación *f* de abastecimiento de agua (water supply) || juegos *m pl* de agua (fountains) || FAM vías *f pl* urinarias || FAM *to turn on the waterworks* echarse a llorar.

waterworn [-wɔːn] *adj* desgastado por el agua.

watery [-ri] *adj* acuoso, sa (like water); *a watery fluid* un fluido acuoso || aguado, da; claro, ra (soup) || aguado, da (wine) || soso, sa; insípido, da (food) || húmedo, da (wet); *watery land* tierra húmeda || lloroso, sa (eyes) || pálido, da; desvaído, da (colours) || FIG deslavazado, da (style) | lluvioso, sa (weather) || *watery sunshine* sol pálido que anuncia lluvia.

watt [wɔt] *n* ELECTR vatio *m*.

wattage [-idʒ] *n* ELECTR potencia *f* en vatios.

watt-hour [-ˈauə*] *n* ELECTR vatio-hora *m*.

wattle [ˈwɔtl] *n* zarzo *m* (used to make walls, fences, etc.) || varas *f pl* (rods, twigs) || ZOOL barba *f* (of a bird) | barbilla *f* (of a fish) || BOT acacia *f*.

wattle [ˈwɔtl] *vt* entretejer, entrelazar (to make into wattle) || hacer con zarzos (walls, etc.) || unir entrelazando (fence posts).

wattmeter [ˈwɔtˌmiːtə*] *n* vatímetro *m*.

wave [weiv] *n* ola *f* (of sea) || ondulación *f* (on a surface, in the hair, etc.) || PHYS & RAD onda *f*; *short, medium, long wave* onda corta, media, larga || FIG racha *f*; *a wave of bad luck* una racha de mala suerte, una mala racha | oleada *f* (of people); *they came in waves* vinieron en oleadas | ola *f*, oleada *f*; *a crime wave* una ola de criminalidad, una oleada de crímenes | ola *f*; *a wave of cold weather* una ola de frío || señal *f*, ademán *m*, seña *f*, movimiento *m* (with the hand) || — FIG *new wave* nueva ola || *permanent wave* permanente *f*.
◆ *pl* POET piélago *m sing*, océano *m sing*, mar *m sing*.

wave [weiv] *vt* agitar; *to wave one's hand, a handkerchief, a flag* agitar una mano, un pañuelo, una banderita || blandir (a sword) || amenazar con (to threaten); *he waved his fist in my face* me amenazó con el puño || ondular; *to wave one's hair* ondularse el pelo || — *to wave a greeting to s.o.* saludar a alguien con la mano || *to wave a meal away* rechazar una comida con la mano || *to wave aside an objection* desechar una objeción || *to wave aside s.o.'s help* rechazar la ayuda de alguien || *to wave down a motorist* hacer señas a un automovilista para que se pare || *to wave one's arms about* agitar mucho los brazos || *to wave s.o. aside* apartar a alguien con la mano || *to wave s.o. good-bye* decir adiós a alguien con la mano *or* con un pañuelo || *to wave s.o. on* hacer una señal con la mano a alguien para que pase || *to wave the waiter over* llamar al camarero con la mano.
◆ *vi* ondear (fields of corn, etc.) || flotar (a flag) || ondular (hair) || hacer señales *or* señas con la mano; *to wave to s.o. to stop* hacer señas con la mano a alguien para que se pare || agitarse; *from the balcony I could see a sea of waving arms* desde el balcón veía un montón de brazos que se agitaban.

Wave [weiv] *n* US mujer *f* que forma parte de la marina americana.

wave band [-bænd] *n* RAD banda *f* de ondas.

waved [-d] *adj* ondulado, da; ondeado, da || tornasolado, da (fabric).

wave front [-frʌnt] *n* PHYS frente *m* de onda.

wave guide [-gaid] *n* PHYS guía *f* de ondas.

wavelength [-leŋθ] *n* PHYS longitud *f* de onda || FIG *to be on the same wavelength* estar en la misma onda.

waveless [-lis] *adj* tranquilo, la; sin olas.

wavelet [-lit] *n* ola *f* pequeña (of the sea) || pequeña ondulación *f* (on hair).

wave mechanics [-miˈkæniks] *n* PHYS mecánica *f* ondulatoria.

wave motion [-ˌməuʃən] *n* PHYS movimiento *m* ondulatorio.

waver [-ə*] *vi* dudar, vacilar, titubear; *she wavered between going and staying* dudó entre marcharse y quedarse || titubear, tambalearse (to totter) || flaquear (to falter) || vacilar (to flicker); *a light wavered in the distance* una luz vacilaba a lo lejos || temblar (voice).

waverer [-ərə*] *n* irresoluto, ta; indeciso, sa.

wavering [-əriŋ] *adj* vacilante, irresoluto, ta; indeciso, sa (indecisive) || vacilante (light) || tembloroso, sa (voice).
◆ *n* vacilación *f*, irresolución *f*, indecisión *f* (vacillation) || vacilación *f* (of light) || temblor *m* (of voice).

wave theory [-ˈθiəri] *n* PHYS teoría *f* ondulatoria.

wave train [-trein] *n* PHYS tren *m* de ondas.

waviness [-inis] *n* ondulación *f*.

wavy [-i] *adj* ondulado, da; *a wavy line* una línea ondulada; *wavy hair* pelo ondulado || ondulante (field) || onduloso, sa; sinuoso, sa (sinuous).

wax [wæks] *n* cera *f* || cerumen *m*, cerilla *f* (in the ear) || cerote *m* (used by shoemakers) || disco *m* (record) || lacre *m* (sealing wax) || FAM rabia *f* (anger).
◆ *adj* de cera.

wax [wæks] *vt* encerar (floor, etc.) || grabar en un disco (to record).
◆ *vi* crecer (the moon) || ponerse (to become); *to wax eloquent* ponerse elocuente || — FIG *to wax and wane* ir y venir, tener altibajos || *to wax indignant* indignarse || *to wax old* envejecer.

wax bean [-biːn] *n* US judía *f* de vaina amarilla.

waxberry [-ˌberi] *n* BOT árbol *m* de la cera.

wax candle [-ˈkændl] *n* vela *f* de cera || REL cirio *m*.

wax cloth [-klɔθ] *n* hule *m* (oilcloth).

wax doll [-ˈdɔl] *n* muñeca *f* de cera.

waxed [-t] *adj* encerado, da; *waxed paper* papel encerado.

waxen [-ən] *adj* ceroso, sa (resembling wax) || encerado, da (covered with wax) || céreo, a; de cera (made of wax) || ceroso, sa (complexion).

waxiness [-inis] *n* consistencia *f* cerosa.

waxing [-iŋ] *adj* creciente (moon).
◆ *n* crecimiento *m* (of the moon) || enceramiento *m* (polishing) || grabación *f* de un disco (recording) || disco *m* (record).

wax match [-ˈmætʃ] *n* cerilla *f*.

wax myrtle [-ˈməːtl] *n* BOT árbol *m* de la cera.

wax paper [-ˈpeipə*] *n* US papel *m* encerado.

wax taper [-ˈteipə*] *n* vela *f* alargada || REL cirio *m*.

waxwork [-wəːk] *n* figura *f* de cera (figure modelled in wax).
◆ *pl* museo *m sing* de figuras de cera.

waxy [ˈwæksi] *adj* → **waxen** || FAM rabioso, sa || MED *waxy liver* amilosis *f* del hígado.

way [wei] *n* camino *m*; *the way to the beach is rocky* el camino para ir a la playa es rocoso; *to go the wrong way* equivocarse de camino; *to go out of one's way* desviarse del camino; *the way of virtue* el camino de la virtud; *the right way* el buen camino || carretera *f* (road) || vía *f*; *the public way* la vía pública; *the Appian Way* la Vía Apia || distancia *f*, trecho *m*; *we have a long way to walk* tenemos que recorrer un gran trecho; *it's a long way to* hay mucha distancia a || recorrido *m*, trayecto *m*; *there were trees all the way* había árboles durante todo el trayecto || dirección *f*; *which way did he go?* ¿en qué dirección se fue?; *she didn't know which way to look* no sabía en qué dirección mirar || manera *f*, modo *m*; *he still hasn't found a way to make a living* todavía no había encontrado la manera de ganarse la vida; *the way of doing sth.* la manera de hacer algo; *in one way or another* de una manera o de otra; *in a friendly way* de modo amistoso; *in no way* de ninguna manera; *in such a way as to* de tal manera que || estilo *m*; *way of life, way of living* estilo de vida; *it is his way* es su estilo || escala *f*, medida *f*; *in a big way* en gran escala; *in a way* en cierta medida || ramo *m*; *he is in the grocery way* está en el ramo de la alimentación || asunto *m*; *it's not in my way* no es asunto mío || terreno *m*; *to prepare the way* preparar el terreno || estado *m*; *my car is in a bad way* mi coche está en mal estado || costumbre *f*; *I am out of the way of dancing* he perdido la costumbre de bailar; *it is not my way to do that* no es costumbre mía

hacer eso; *I got into the way of smoking* adquirí la costumbre de fumar || manera *f* de ser (behaviour); *don't take offence, it's only his way* no se ofenda, es simplemente su manera de ser || modal *m* (manner); *the ways of good society* los buenos modales || aspecto *m*, punto *m*; *in some ways you are mistaken* en algunos aspectos estás equivocado || MAR marcha *f* (movement of a boat) || JUR servidumbre *f* de paso || — *across* o *over the way* enfrente; *my house is just across the way from his* mi casa está justo enfrente de la suya || *a little way away* o *off* cerca, no muy lejos || *all the way* por todo el camino (the whole distance), hasta el final (making every effort) || *all the way down* a lo largo de || *all the way to* hasta || *a long way away* o *off* lejísimos, muy lejos || *a long way from* lejos de || *any way* de cualquier manera (in any manner), de todas maneras (in any case) || *by a long way* con mucho; *not by a long way* ni con mucho || *by the way* en el camino; *they stopped by the way* se detuvieron en el camino; entre paréntesis (incidental); *all this is by the way* todo eso está entre paréntesis; de paso; *be it said by the way* dicho sea de paso; a propósito, por cierto (incidentally); *by the way, are they coming for lunch?* a propósito, ¿vienen a almorzar? || *by the way of* por, pasando por (via); *we'll come back by the way of the Suez canal* volveremos por el canal de Suez; para (in order to); *they made inquiries by way of learning the truth* hicieron investigaciones para saber la verdad; como, a modo de (as); *by way of compliment* a modo de cumplido; *by way of introduction* como introducción || *can you find your way home?* ¿sabe usted por dónde se va a su casa? || *each way, both ways* a ganador y colocado (in horse racing) || *he is by way of being a liberal* pasa por ser un liberal, se le considera liberal || *I met him on my way here* lo encontré al venir aquí || *I met him on my way home* le encontré al volver a casa || *in a fair way of* o *to* en camino de, en vías de, en trance de (in process of) || *in a way* en cierta manera, en cierto modo, hasta cierto punto; *I like the work in a way* me gusta el trabajo hasta cierto punto || *in every way* en todos los aspectos || *in the ordinary* o *usual* o *general way* generalmente || *it's the wrong way up* está al revés || *I will do anything that comes in my way* estoy dispuesto a hacer cualquier cosa que se me presente || ASTR *Milky Way* Vía Láctea || *no way through* cerrado al paso || *once in a way* de vez en cuando || *on the way* en camino; *the parcel is on the way* el paquete está en camino; en el camino de, camino de; *it's on the way to Paris* está en el camino de París || *out of harm's way* a salvo || FAM *out of my way!* ¡quítese de en medio!, ¡fuera de aquí! || *out of the way* apartado, da; aislado, da; remoto, ta (place), extraordinario, ria; fuera de lo común; *nothing out of the way* nada extraordinario || *permanent way* vía férrea (railway) || *put it right way up* póngalo bien || *right of way* servidumbre *f* de paso, derecho de paso (land), preferencia *f* de paso, prioridad *f* (roads) || *that's the way* ¡así es!, ¡eso es! || *that way* por ahí, por allí (direction), así (manner) || *the other way round* al revés || *there's no way out* no hay ninguna salida, eso no tiene solución || *there's no way through* no se puede pasar || *the way of the world!* ¡así es la vida! || *the way things are* tal y como están las cosas || *they live somewhere London way* viven cerca de Londres, viven hacia Londres || *this way* por aquí, en esta dirección || *this way and that* en todas direcciones || *this way out!* ¡salgan por aquí! || FIG *to be a long way out* estar muy equivocado | *to be in the family way* estar en estado interesante (pregnant) || *to be* o *to get in the way* estorbar; *is my chair in the way?* ¿le estorba mi silla? || *to be on the way to* ir camino de; *he is on the way to do it* va camino de hacerlo || *to be out of one's way* no venirle *or* pillarle a uno de camino || *to be under way* estar en curso (affair), estar navegando (ship) || *to block the way* cerrar el paso || *to brush sth. the wrong way* cepillar algo a contrapelo || *to clear the way* despejar el camino || FIG *to come one's way* presentársele a uno || *to feel one's way* ir a tientas (to grope), andar con pies de plomo (to act cautiously), tantear el terreno (to explore) || *to find a way* encontrar una solución || *to find a way into* conseguir entrar en || *to find a way to* encontrar la forma de || *to find one's way to a place* conseguir llegar a un sitio || *to get in the way* ponerse en medio || MAR *to gather way* tomar velocidad (ship) || FIG *to get* o *to have one's (own) way* salirse con la suya || *to get out of the way* quitar a uno de en medio || *to get sth. out of the way* quitar algo de en medio (to remove), quitarse algo de encima; *I finally got that backlog out of the way* por fin me quité de encima se trabajo atrasado || *to get under the way* ponerse en camino (to set out), avanzar, progresar (to progress), zarpar (ship) || *to give the way* dejar paso || *to give way* ceder (to break), retroceder (to retire), ceder el paso (car) || *to give way to* ceder el paso a (to be replaced by), ceder ante (to make concessions to), dejarse llevar por, entregarse a (despair) || FIG *to go a long way* llegar muy lejos; *this boy will go a long way* este chico llegará muy lejos | *to go a long way towards* contribuir mucho a | *to go one's own way* seguir su camino (according to one's will), obrar a su antojo (according to one's fancy), hacer rancho aparte (by o.s.) | *to go one's way* seguir su camino || FIG *to go out of one's way to* tomarse la molestia de; *I wouldn't go out of my way to hear him* no me tomaría la molestia de ir a escucharle; desvivirse por, hacer todo lo posible por (to do one's utmost to) | *to go the way of all flesh* o *of all things* morir | *to have a way of doing sth.* tener la costumbre de hacer algo | *to have a way with* saber coger a | *to have a way with people* tener don de gentes || *to keep out of s.o.'s way* evitar encontrarse con alguien; *to keep out of the way* no estorbar el paso || FIG *to know one's way about* o *around* saber arreglárselas || *to know one's way about* o *around town* conocer muy bien la ciudad || *to lead the way* ir el primero, ir en cabeza (to go first), enseñar el camino (to show the way), dar el ejemplo (to set an example) || FIG *to leave the way open for* dejar una puerta abierta para | *to leave the way open to* abrir la puerta a || *to live in a small way* vivir modestamente || FIG *to look the other way* hacer la vista gorda || *to lose one's way* perderse, extraviarse || *to make one's way* abrirse paso (to open a path), salir bien (to come out all right), progresar, adelantar (to make progress) || *to make one's way home* volver a casa || FIG *to make one's way in the world* o *in life* abrirse camino en la vida || *to make* o *to work one's way through the crowd* abrirse paso entre la multitud || *to make one's way to* dirigirse hacia *or* a; *he made his way to the door* se dirigió hacia la puerta || *to make way* hacerse a un lado || FIG *to make way for* dejar paso a || *to my way of thinking* a mi modo de ver || FIG *to pave the way for* preparar el terreno para | *to pay one's way* pagar su parte (to pay one's share), ser solvente (to be solvent) | *to pay one's own way* satisfacer sus propias necesidades | *to put difficulties in s.o.'s way* crear dificultades a alguien, ponerle a uno obstáculos en el camino | *to put s.o. in a way to do sth.* dar a alguien la posibilidad de hacer algo || *to put s.o. out of the way* quitar a uno de en medio || FIG *to see one's way to* encontrar la manera de, ver la forma de || *to stand in the way of* estorbar (to hinder), ser un obstáculo para (to be an obstacle), ser una desventaja para (to be a disadvantage) || FIG *to start on one's way through college* trabajar para costearse los estudios | *to work one's way to* abrirse camino hacia | *to work one's way up* ascender por su trabajo || *way down* bajada *f* || *way in* entrada *f* || *way of business* negocios *m pl* || *way off* a lo lejos; *I see them way off* les veo a lo lejos || REL *Way of the Cross* Vía *m* Crucis || *way out* salida *f* || *way through* pasaje *m*, paso *m* || *way up* subida *f* || US FAM *we have skirts all the way from fifteen to fifty dollars* tenemos faldas de quince a cincuenta dólares || *what have you in the way of fruit?* ¿qué fruta tiene? || *where there's a will there's a way* querer es poder || *which way did you come?* ¿por dónde vino?
◆ *pl* TECH anguilas *f* || — *Committee of Ways and Means* Comisión *f* del Presupuesto | *to mend one's ways* enmendarse || *ways and customs* usos y costumbres || *ways and means* medios *m* || FIG *you can't have it both ways* no se puede estar en la misa y repicando.
◆ *adv* allá.

waybill [-bil] *n* MAR hoja *f* de ruta.

wayfarer [-ˌfɛərə*] *n* caminante *m*.

wayfaring [-ˌfɛəriŋ] *adj* que viaja a pie || BOT *wayfaring tree* viburno *m*.

waylay [weiˈlei] *vt* acechar, aguardar emboscado (in order to rob, etc.) || abordar (to accost by surprise).

way-out [ˈweiˈaut] *adj* muy moderno, na; ultramoderno, na.

wayside [ˈweisaid] *adj* al borde del camino.
◆ *n* borde *m* del camino || FIG *to fall by the wayside* quedarse en el camino.

way station [ˈweiˌsteiʃən] *n* US apeadero *m*.

way train [ˈweitrein] *n* US tren *m* carreta, ómnibus *m*.

wayward [ˈweiwəd] *adj* voluntarioso, sa (self-willed) || porfiado, da (obstinate) || díscolo, la; desobediente (not easily controlled) || caprichoso, sa (capricious).

waywardness [-nis] *n* capricho *m*, fantasía *f* (whim) || voluntariedad *f* (wilfulness) || porfía *f* (obstinacy) || desobediencia *f* (disobedience).

wayworn [ˈweiwɔːn] *adj* agotado por el camino.

WCC *abbr of [World Council of Churches]* COE, Consejo Ecuménico de las Iglesias.

we [wiː] *pers pron* nosotros, tras (oneself and others); *we two* nosotros dos || nos (used by a sovereign, by a judge, etc.).

weak [wiːk] *adj* débil; *too weak to climb higher* demasiado débil para subir más arriba; *a weak mind* una mente débil; *the weak point in a scheme* el punto débil de un proyecto || flojo, ja; *a weak blow* un golpe flojo; *weak in history* flojo en historia; *weak wine* vino flojo || flojo, ja; *a weak argument* un argumento flojo || poco enérgico, ca; *weak government* gobierno poco enérgico; *weak decision* decisión poco enérgica || claro, ra; *weak tea* té claro || poco sólido, da (easily broken) || MED débil; *a weak heart* un corazón débil || COMM flojo, ja (market) | poco, ca (demand) | GRAMM & MUS débil || — *s.o.'s weak side* el punto flaco *or* la debilidad de alguien || *the weaker sex* el sexo débil || *to grow weak* debilitarse || *to protect the weak* proteger a los débiles || *weak moment* momento *m* de debilidad.

weaken [-ən] *vt* debilitar || disminuir (to diminish).
◆ *vi* debilitarse || disminuir (to diminish).

weakening [-əniŋ] *n* debilitación *f*, debilitamiento *m*.
◆ *adj* debilitante.

weak-headed [-ˈhedid] *adj* mentecato, ta; tonto, ta.

weak-kneed [-ˈniːd] *adj* débil de rodillas || FIG sin carácter, sin personalidad.

weakling [-liŋ] *n* persona *f or* animal *m* débil *or* delicado || FIG persona *f* sin carácter *or* sin personalidad (person without character).
◆ *adj* débil.

weakly [-li] *adj* débil.
◆ *adv* débilmente.

weak-minded [-'maindid] *adj* mentecato, ta; tonto, ta (silly) || sin carácter, sin personalidad.

weakness [-nis] *n* MED debilidad *f* || punto *m* flaco *or* débil (weak point) || debilidad *f*, flaco *m*; *a weakness for olives* debilidad por las aceitunas.

weak-point [-pɔint] *n* FIG punto *m* flaco *or* débil.

weal [wi:l] *n* verdugón *m* (mark on the skin) || bienestar *m* (well-being) || — *for weal or woe* en la suerte y en la desgracia || *the general* o *the public weal* el bien público.

weald [wi:ld] *n* región *f* arbolada.

wealth [welθ] *n* riqueza *f* (riches) || abundancia *f*, profusión *f* (of details, of ideas, etc.) || riqueza *f* (valuable products); *the wealth of a country* la riqueza de un país || *man of wealth* hombre rico.

wealthiness [-inis] *n* riqueza *f*, opulencia *f*.

wealthy [-i] *adj* rico, ca.
◆ *n the wealthy* los ricos.

wean [wi:n] *vt* destetar (an infant or young animal) || FIG *to wean from* apartar de (object of affection), desacostumbrar de (a bad habit).

weaning [-iŋ] *n* destete *m*.

weanling [-liŋ] *n* niño *m or* animal *m* destetado.

weapon ['wepən] *n* MIL arma *f* || ZOOL & BOT defensa *f* || FIG arma *f* (any means of attack or defence).

weaponless [-lis] *adj* desarmado, da; sin armas.

weaponry [-ri] *n* armas *f pl*, armamento *m* (weapons) || fábrica *f* de armas (production).

wear [wɛə*] *n* uso *m*; *for everyday wear* para uso diario || desgaste *m*, deterioro *m* (damage due to use) || resistencia *f* (ability to resist damage) || ropa *f* (clothes); *men's wear* ropa para caballeros; *summer wear* ropa de verano || — *evening wear* traje *m* de noche || *for hard wear* resistente, duradero, ra || *of never-ending wear* que no se rompe con el uso, que no se desgasta || *there's still some good wear left in this suit* todavía está en buen estado este traje || *to be in (general) wear* estar de moda || *to look the worse for wear* estar desgastado, da (sth.), estar desmejorado, da (s.o.) || *wear and tear* desgaste *m*.

wear* [wɛə*] *vt* llevar; *to wear a coat* llevar un abrigo; *blue is being much worn at present* el azul se lleva mucho ahora; *to wear spectacles* llevar gafas; *to wear one's hair short* llevar el pelo corto || ponerse (to put on); *he wears the same suit every day* se pone todos los días el mismo traje; *what shall I wear?* ¿qué me voy a poner?; *he was wearing all his medals* se había puesto todas las medallas || usar; *to wear one's shirt to tatters* usar una camisa hasta hacerla jirones || tener (a look, a smile, etc.) || hacer; *to wear a hole in the carpet* hacer un agujero en la alfombra || MAR hacer virar || FIG consumir; *worn with care* consumido por las preocupaciones | agotar (to exhaust) || — *to have nothing fit to wear* no tener nada que ponerse || *to wear black* ir vestido de negro || *to wear one's age well* estar bien conservado, no representar la edad que se tiene || *to wear one's hair curled* tener el pelo rizado || *to wear o.s. to death* matarse [trabajando].
◆ *vi* gastarse, desgastarse (to deteriorate through use) || resistir, durar (to last); *material which wears well* tela que dura mucho || pasar, correr, transcurrir (time) || MAR virar || — *to wear thin* disminuir || *to wear well* conservarse bien, no representar la edad que se tiene.
◆ *phr v* *to wear away* gastar, desgastar; *rocks worn away by erosion* rocas desgastadas por la erosión | borrar (to erase) | pasar lentamente *or* tristemente (time) | gastarse, desgastarse (to deteriorate) | consumirse; *she was wearing away* se estaba consumiendo | borrarse (an inscription) | atenuarse, disminuir (a pain) | *the winter was wearing away* el invierno tocaba a su fin || *to wear down* gastar, desgastar; *to wear one's heels down* desgastar los tacones | agotar (to exhaust) || *to wear off* raer, gastar (one's clothes) | borrar (an inscription) | borrarse | desaparecer (to disappear) | disiparse (to diminish gradually) || *to wear on* pasar lentamente (time) | prolongarse; *the discussion wears on* la discusión se prolonga | *as the evening wore on...* a medida que avanzaba la noche || *to wear out* gastar (one's clothes) | pasar el resto de (one's life) | agotar (s.o.'s patience) | gastarse (to deteriorate) | acabarse lentamente (time) | *to wear o.s. out* agotarse, matarse.
— OBSERV Pret ***wore***; pp ***worn***.

wearable ['wɛərəbl] *adj* que se puede llevar *or* usar.

wear and tear ['wɛərənd'tɛə*] *n* desgaste *m*, deterioro *m* [por el uso].

wearer ['wɛərə*] *n* persona *f* que lleva || *straight from maker to wearer* directamente del fabricante al cliente.

wearied ['wiərid] *adj* cansado, da (tired).

weariless ['wiərilis] *adj* infatigable, incansable.

weariness ['wiərinis] *n* cansancio *m*, fatiga *f* || FIG aburrimiento *m*, hastío *m*.

wearing ['wɛəriŋ] *adj* cansado, da (tiring) || desgastador, ra (causing wear) || de vestir (apparel).

wearisome ['wiərisəm] *adj* cansado, da; fatigoso, sa (tiresome) || FIG fastidioso, sa; aburrido, da; pesado, da (boring).

weary ['wiəri] *adj* cansado, da; fatigado, da (tired) || agotador, ra (tiring); *weary work* trabajo agotador || cansado, da; aburrido, da; harto, ta; *weary of studying* harto de estudiar || fastidioso, sa; enojoso, sa (annoying).

weary ['wiəri] *vt* cansar, fatigar (to tire) || aburrir (to bore) || fastidiar (to annoy).
◆ *vi* cansarse, fatigarse (to become tired) || aburrirse (to become bored).

weasel ['wi:zəl] *n* comadreja *f* (animal) || vehículo *m* para andar sobre nieve *or* hielo (tracked motor vehicle) || *US* FAM chivato, ta (sneak) || *weasel words* palabras equívocas.

weather ['weðə*] *n* tiempo *m*; *what is the weather like?* ¿qué tiempo hace?; *the bad weather kept us in* el mal tiempo nos retuvo en casa; *weather permitting* si el tiempo no lo impide; *fine weather* buen tiempo; *in such weather* con semejante tiempo; *changeable weather* tiempo variable || boletín *m* meteorológico, el tiempo (in the newspaper) || — *heavy weather* temporal *m*, mar gruesa || FIG *to keep one's weather eye open* estar ojo avizor, estar alerta || MAR *to make bad weather of it* aguantar mal la tormenta | *to make good weather of it* aguantar bien la tormenta, capear el temporal || FIG *to make heavy weather of a job* complicar un trabajo || FAM *under the weather* borracho, cha (drunk), indispuesto, ta (not feeling well), en apuros (without money).
◆ *adj* meteorológico, ca; del tiempo || MAR de barlovento || *weather conditions* condiciones atmosféricas.

weather ['weðə*] *vt* exponer a la intemperie (to expose to the weather) || curtir (the skin) || patinar (bronze) || curar (wood) || FIG superar; *to weather a crisis* superar una crisis || MAR doblar (a cape) | pasar a barlovento de (a ship) | aguantar, capear (a storm).
◆ *vi* resistir; *the paint has weathered well* la pintura ha resistido bien || deteriorarse (con la acción del tiempo); *this paintwork will not weather* esta pintura no se deteriorará con la acción del tiempo || GEOL desgastarse, erosionarse || curtirse (skin) || patinarse (bronze) || FAM *to weather through* salir de apuros.

weather-beaten [-,bi:tn] *adj* deteriorado por la intemperie || azotado por el viento (by the wind) || curtido, da; *a weather-beaten face* una cara curtida.

weatherboard [-bɔ:d] *n* tabla *f* || MAR lado *m* del viento.

weatherboarding [-bɔ:diŋ] *n* tablazón *f*, tablas *f pl* (weatherboards).

weather-bound [-baund] *adj* detenido por el mal tiempo.

weather bureau [-,bjuərəu] *n* servicio *m* meteorológico.

weather chart [-tʃɑ:t] *n* mapa *m* meteorológico.

weathercock [-kɔk] *n* veleta *f* (to show wind direction) || FIG veleta *m* & *f*, persona *f* cambiadiza.

weather forecast [-,fɔ:kɑ:st] *n* boletín *m or* parte *m* meteorológico || previsión *f* del tiempo.

weather gauge [-geidʒ] *n* MAR posición *f* a barlovento || FIG ventaja *f*, posición *f* ventajosa.

weatherglass [-glɑ:s] *n* barómetro *m*.

weathering [-riŋ] *n* desgaste *m*, erosión *f* || intemperie *f* (forces of weather) || COMM pátina *f* || ARCH declive *m* de derrame.

weatherly [-li] *adj* MAR que puede navegar de bolina.

weatherman [-mən] *n* hombre *m* del tiempo, meteorólogo *m*.
— OBSERV El plural de esta palabra es *weathermen*.

weather map [-mæp] *n* mapa *m* meteorológico.

weatherproof [-pru:f] *adj* que resiste a la intemperie || impermeable (clothes).

weather report [-ri,pɔ:t] *n* boletín *m or* parte *m* meteorológico.

weather station [-,steiʃən] *n* estación *f* meteorológica.

weather strip [-strip] *n* burlete *m* (for windows).

weather vane [-vein] *n* veleta *f*.

weather-wise [-waiz] *adj* que pronostica el tiempo || FIG que pronostica los cambios de opinión.

weatherworn [-wɔ:n] *adj* deteriorado por la intemperie.

weave [wi:v] *n* tejido *m*; *a close weave* un tejido apretado.

weave* [wi:v] *vt* tejer (a thread, a fabric, etc.) || entrelazar (flowers, garlands, etc.) || FIG tramar, urdir (a plot, etc.) || tejer (a web) || FIG *to weave one's way through the crowd* abrirse paso entre la multitud.
◆ *vi* tejer (to engage in weaving) || entrelazarse (to become intertwined) || zigzaguear.
— OBSERV Pret ***wove***; pp ***woven***.

weaver [-ə*] *n* tejedor *m* (bird) || tejedor, ra (person).

weaverbird [-əbə:d] *n* tejedor *m* (bird).

weaving [-iŋ] *n* tejido *m* (weave) || tejeduría *f* (art).

web [web] *n* tejido *m*, tela *f* (fabric) || telaraña *f*, tela *f* de araña (of a spider) || FIG sarta *f*; *a web of lies* una sarta de mentiras | red *f* (network) | trampa *f* (snare) || ANAT membrana *f* || membrana *f* interdigital (of swimming birds) || barba *f* (of a feather) || ARCH alma *f* (of beam)

|| brazo *m* (of a crank) || bobina *f* de papel continuo (used on a rotary press) || paletón *m* (of a key) || hoja *f*, cuchilla *f* (of a saw).

webbed [-d] *adj* palmeado, da (bird).

webbing [-iŋ] *n* lona *f* (strong woven fabric) || correas *f pl*, cinchas *f pl* (strips).

weber ['veibə*] *n* PHYS weber *m*, weberio *m*.

webfoot ['webfut] *n* pata *f* palmeada (foot) || palmípedo *m* (bird).

web-footed ['web,futid] *adj* palmípedo, da.

wed [wed] *vt* casarse con; *he wedded Mary* se casó con María || casar (the priest, etc.); *he wedded the couple* casó a los novios; *he wedded his daughter to me* casó a su hija conmigo || FIG unir; *both things are happily wedded* ambas cosas están felizmente unidas.
◆ *vi* casarse.

wedded [wedid] *adj* casado, da (married) || conyugal (of marriage) || FIG unido, da || — *my wedded wife* mi legítima esposa || *the wedded pair* los novios || *to be wedded to* estar casado con (married), estar unido a (connected) || *to be wedded to an opinion* aferrarse a una opinión.

wedding ['wediŋ] *n* boda *f*, casamiento *m* (ceremony of marriage) || bodas *f pl*; *silver wedding* bodas de plata || FIG unión *f*, enlace *m* || — *civil wedding* matrimonio civil || *he had a civil, a church wedding* se casó por lo civil, por la iglesia || *to have a quiet wedding* casarse en la intimidad || *white wedding* boda *f* tradicional.
◆ *adj* de boda; *wedding anniversary* aniversario de boda; *wedding card* participación de boda; *wedding present* regalo de boda; *wedding night* noche de boda || nupcial; *wedding march* marcha nupcial || — *wedding breakfast* banquete *m* de bodas || *wedding cake* pastel *m* de boda || *wedding day* día *m* de la boda || *wedding dress* traje *m* de novia || *wedding party* boda *f* (guests) || *wedding reception* banquete *m* de bodas || *wedding ring* alianza *f*, anillo *m* de boda.

wedge [wedʒ] *n* cuña *f* (to split wood, etc.) || calce *m*, calzo *m* (for keeping in place) || cuña *f*, calzo *m* (for forcing sth. open) || cuña *f* (for shoes) || PRINT cuña *f* de fijación || cuña *f*, formación *f* en cuña (arrangement of troops) || trozo *m*, porción *f* [triangular]; *a wedge of cake* un trozo de pastel || — FIG *it is the thin end of the wedge* es un primer paso *or* un paso adelante || *to drive a wedge between two persons* romper los lazos que unen a dos personas.

wedge [wedʒ] *vt* poner cuñas a (to fix with wedges) || partir con cuña (to split) || abrir con cuña (to split open) || poner calces, calzar (wheels) || encajar (an object) || FIG apretar; *wedged into the bus like sardines* apretados en el autobús como sardinas || *to wedge a door open* dejar abierta una puerta poniéndole una cuña.

wedge-shaped [-ʃeipt] *adj* en forma de cuña || cuneiforme (handwriting).

wedgie [-i] *n* FAM zapato *m* tanque.

wedlock ['wedlɔk] *n* matrimonio *m*; *he was born out of wedlock* nació fuera del matrimonio || vida *f* conyugal (married life).

Wednesday ['wenzdi] *n* miércoles *m*; *I went on Wednesday* fui el miércoles.

wee [wiː] *adj* minúsculo, la; diminuto, ta; ínfimo, ma (very small) || *she is a wee bit jealous* es un poco celosa, es algo celosa.

weed [wiːd] *n* BOT hierba *f*, mala hierba *f*, maleza *f* | alga *f* (seaweed) || FAM animal *m* flaco (considered unfit for breeding) | rocín *m*, jamelgo *m* (hack) | tabaco *m* (tobacco) | puro *m* (cigar) | pitillo *m* (cigarette) | marihuana *f*.
◆ *pl* traje *m sing* de luto (mourning dress) || brazalete *m sing* negro (on sleeve) || gasa *f sing* (on hat).

weed [wiːd] *vt* desherbar (to remove weeds) || escardar (to hoe) || FIG *to weed out* suprimir (to eliminate), extirpar (to eradicate).
◆ *vi* quitar la maleza, desherbar.

weediness [-inis] *n* abundancia *f* de malas hierbas *or* de maleza.

weeding [-iŋ] *n* AGR escarda *f* || — *weeding hook* escarda *f*, escardillo *m* || *weeding machine* escardadora *f*.

weed killer [-,kilə*] *n* herbicida *m*.

weedy [-i] *adj* cubierto de maleza *or* de malas hierbas || flaco, ca; canijo, ja; enclenque (lanky).

week [wiːk] *n* semana *f*; *last week* la semana pasada; *next week* la semana que viene; *three times a week* tres veces por semana; *forty hour week* semana de cuarenta horas || — *a week from now, today week* de aquí a una semana, dentro de una semana, dentro de ocho días || FIG *a week of Sundays* una eternidad || *during* o *in the week* durante la semana, entre semana || *Holy Week* Semana Santa *or* Grande *or* Mayor || *monday week* el lunes que viene || *twice a week* dos veces por semana || *week after week* semana tras semana || *week by week* todas las semanas || *week in week out* semana tras semana || *working week* semana laborable || *yesterday week* ayer hizo una semana.

weekday [-dei] *n* día *m* laborable, día *m* de trabajo (working day) || día *m* de la semana (day of the week).

weekend [-'end] *n* fin *m* de semana, «weekend» *m* || *to take a long weekend* hacer puente.
◆ *adj* de fin de semana.

weekend [-'end] *vi* pasar el fin de semana.

weekly [-li] *adj* semanal, hebdomadario, ria; *a weekly newspaper* un periódico semanal.
◆ *n* semanario *m* (magazine).
◆ *adv* semanalmente, por semana.

ween [wiːn] *vt* suponer, creer, figurarse, imaginarse.

weeny [-i] *adj* FAM chiquito, ta; diminuto, ta.

weep [wiːp] *n* lágrimas *f pl* || *to have a good weep* llorar a lágrima viva.

weep* [wiːp] *vi* llorar (to cry); *to weep for joy* llorar de alegría; *I weep over my sins* lloro mis pecados; *she wept for her father* lloró a su padre || lamentarse (to mourn); *that's nothing to weep over* no hay por qué lamentarse || rezumar (wall).
◆ *vt* llorar, lamentar (to cry for) || derramar, verter (tears) || rezumar (walls) || MED supurar (sore) || — *to weep away the time* pasarse la vida llorando || *to weep o.s. to sleep* llorar hasta dormirse || *to weep one's eyes out* llorar a lágrima viva.

— OBSERV Pret y pp ***wept***.

weeper [-ə*] *n* llorón, ona (s.o. who weeps) || plañidera *f* (hired mourner) || brazalete *m* negro (on sleeve) || gasa *f* (on hat) || velo *m* negro (of a widow).

weep hole [-həul] *n* hendidura *f* de desagüe.

weeping [-iŋ] *adj* llorón, ona; lloroso, sa (person) || rezumante (wall) || MED supurador, ra; supurante (sore) || BOT llorón *m*; *weeping willow* sauce llorón.
◆ *n* llanto *m*.

weepy [-i] *adj* lloroso, sa; llorón, ona.

weever ['wiːvə*] *n* peje *m* araña (fish).

weevil ['wiːvil] *n* gorgojo *m* (beetle).

weevily; weevilly [-i] *adj* agorgojado, da.

wee-wee ['wiːwiː] *n* FAM pipí *m*.

wee-wee ['wiːwi] *vi* FAM hacer pipí.

weft [weft] *n* trama *f* (in weaving).

weigh [wei] *vt* pesar (to determine the weight of); *please weigh this package for me* haga el favor de pesarme este paquete || sopesar (in the hand) || FIG pesar (to consider the importance of); *to weigh one's words* pesar las palabras; *to weigh the pros and cons* pesar el pro y el contra || MAR levar (anchor).
◆ *vi* pesar; *it weighs thirty pounds* pesa treinta libras || FIG pesar; *the problem weighed on his mind* el problema le pesaba | tener importancia, pesar (to have importance) || MAR levar anclas.
◆ *phr v* ***to weigh down*** doblar bajo un peso (to cause to bend under a load) | inclinar (the scale) | pesar más que (sth. else) | FIG abrumar (s.o.) || ***to weigh in*** pesar (before a contest) | ser pesado, pesarse (to be weighed) | FIG *to weigh in with an argument* intervenir en una discusión con un argumento || ***to weigh out*** pesar (goods) | pesar después de una carrera (a jockey, etc.) | ser pesado *or* pesarse después de una carrera (a jockey, etc.) || ***to weigh up*** levantar por contrapeso | FIG pesar || ***to weigh with*** tener importancia para.

weighbeam ['weibiːm] *n* romana *f* (balance).

weighbridge ['weibridʒ] *n* puente *m* basculante.

weigher ['weiə*] *n* pesador, ra.

weighing ['weiiŋ] *n* peso *m*.

weighing-in [-in] *n* peso *m*, pesaje *m*.

weighing machine [-məʃiːn] *n* báscula *f*.

weight [weit] *n* peso *m* (heaviness); *to gain weight* ganar peso || pesa *f* (used for comparing other weights) || COMM peso *m*; *sold by (the) weight* vendido al peso || MED pesadez *f* (in the head or stomach) || ARCH carga *f* || FIG importancia *f*, peso *m*; *a matter of great weight* un asunto de mucho peso | influencia *f*, peso *m* (influence) | peso *m*; *you've just lift a weight off my mind* acaba de quitarme un peso de encima | peso *m*; *the weight of Justice* el peso de la Justicia || SP peso *m* (in boxing, in horse racing); *to put the weight* lanzar el peso || pesa *f* (in a clock) || — *atomic, molecular weight* peso atómico, molecular || *gross weight* peso bruto || FIG *it is worth its weight in gold* vale su peso en oro || *light weight* de poco peso || *live weight* peso en vivo || *net weight* peso neto || SP *putting the weight* lanzamiento *m* del peso || FIG *to carry weight* tener peso; *his argument will carry weight* su argumento tendrá peso || *to give good weight* dar buen peso, pesar corrido || *to lose weight* adelgazar || FIG *to pull one's weight* poner de su parte || *to put on weight* engordar || FIG *to throw one's weight about* darse importancia | *to try the weight of* sopesar || *weights and measures* pesas y medidas.

weight [weit] *vt* añadir peso a (to add weight to) || poner peso *or* pesas en; *make them balance by weighting this side* equilíbrelos poniendo peso en este lado || lastrar (a net) || dar valor a (in statistics) || FIG cargar.

weightiness [-inis] *n* peso *m*, pesadez *f* (heaviness) || FIG peso *m*, importancia *f*, fuerza *f* (of an argument).

weighting [-iŋ] *n* plus *m* por coste de vida.

weightless [-lis] *adj* ingrávido, da.

weightlessness [-lisnis] *n* ingravidez *f*.

weight lifter [-,liftə*] *n* halterófilo *m*, levantador *m* de pesos y halteras.

weight lifting [-liftiŋ] *n* SP levantamiento *m* de pesos y halteras, halterofilia *f*.

weight training [-,treiniŋ] *n* SP entrenamiento *m* con pesas.

weighty [-i] *adj* pesado, da; *a weighty load* una carga pesada || FIG de peso, importante (argument, people).

weir [wiə*] *n* presa *f* (built across a river) || vertedero *m* (in a dam) || encañizada *f* (to catch fish).

weird [wiəd] *adj* misterioso, sa; sobrenatural (supernatural) ‖ FAM extraño, ña; raro, ra (queer); *how weird!* ¡qué extraño! ‖ *the Weird Sisters* las Parcas (the Fates), las brujas (in Shakespeare's Macbeth).

weirdness [-nis] *n* lo misterioso ‖ FAM lo extraño, lo raro.

weirdo ['wiədəʊ] *n* FAM bicho *m* raro.

welch [welʃ] *vi* → **welsh.**

welcome ['welkəm] *adj* bienvenido, da (gladly received) ‖ grato, ta; agradable (agreeable) ‖ — *it was most welcome* fue muy oportuno ‖ *to be a welcome guest everywhere* ser siempre bien recibido en todas partes ‖ *to make s.o. welcome* recibir a alguien con los brazos abiertos ‖ *you are welcome* de nada, no hay de qué (in response to thanks) ‖ *you are welcome to use it* está a su disposición ‖ *you are welcome to try* puede probarlo cuando quiera ‖ *you will always be welcome here* están ustedes en su casa.
◆ *n* bienvenida *f*; *to give* o *to bid s.o. a warm welcome* dar a alguien una calurosa bienvenida ‖ recibimiento *m*, recepción *f*, acogida *f*; *they gave him a hearty welcome* le dispensaron un caluroso recibimiento ‖ — *to meet with a cold welcome* ser recibido fríamente ‖ FAM *to outstay* o *to wear out one's welcome* quedarse más tiempo de lo conveniente.
◆ *interj* ¡bienvenido!; *welcome home!* ¡bienvenido a casa! ‖ FAM con mucho gusto.

welcome ['welkəm] *vt* dar la bienvenida a (to bid welcome) ‖ recibir; *I went to the station to welcome her* fui a recibirla a la estación ‖ recibir bien; *they welcomed us to their house* nos recibieron bien en su casa ‖ alegrarse por; *to welcome s.o.'s return* alegrarse por la vuelta de alguien ‖ *we will welcome any useful suggestion* toda sugerencia será bien recibida.

welcoming [-iŋ] *adj* acogedor, ra.

weld [weld] *n* soldadura *f* (in metal) ‖ BOT gualda *f*.

weld [weld] *vt* soldar (metal) ‖ FIG unir (to unite).
◆ *vi* soldarse.

welder [-ə*] *n* soldador *m* (person) ‖ soldadora *f* (machine).

welding [-iŋ] *n* soldadura *f* ‖ — *butt welding* soldadura a tope ‖ *oxyacetylene welding* soldadura oxiacetilénica *or* autógena ‖ *spot welding* soldadura por puntos ‖ *welding torch* soplete *m* de soldar.

welfare ['welfεə*] *n* bienestar *m* (state of being healthy, happy, etc.) ‖ bien *m* (good) ‖ — *welfare centre* centro *m* de asistencia social ‖ *welfare institution* institución benéfica ‖ *welfare work* asistencia *f* social ‖ *welfare worker* asistenta *f* social.

welfare state [-'steit] *n* estado *m* benefactor, estado *m* basado en el principio de que el bienestar del individuo depende de la comunidad.

welkin ['welkin] *n* firmamento *m*, cielo *m*.

well [wel] *adv* bien; *he treats his staff well* trata bien a sus empleados; *he speaks English well* habla bien el inglés; *he sings well* canta bien; *well spoken* bien dicho; *he did it very well* lo hizo muy bien; *do you feel well?* ¿se encuentra bien?; *I know him well* le conozco bien; *to end well* acabar bien; *do the brothers get on well?* ¿se llevan bien los hermanos? ‖ completamente; *well up to the knees in mud* completamente metido en el barro hasta las rodillas ‖ bien; *it may well be true* bien puede ser verdad; *he can well save some money* bien puede ahorrar algún dinero ‖ — *all too well, only too well* de sobra, sobradamente ‖ *as well* también; *she sings and plays the piano as well* canta y también toca el piano ‖ *as well as* igual que, lo mismo que, así como; *his enemies as well as his friends respected him* sus enemigos lo mismo que sus amigos le respetaban; y además, también; *she bought a coat as well as a suit* compró un abrigo y además un traje ‖ *he accepted, as well he might* aceptó, y con razón ‖ *how well?* ¿qué tal? ‖ *I may* o *might as well do sth.* quizá debería *or* debiera hacer algo ‖ *it's just as well you were there* menos mal que estabas allí ‖ FAM *to be well in with s.o.* hacer buenas migas con alguien ‖ *to be well over forty* tener cuarenta años bien cumplidos ‖ *to be well up in a subject* conocer muy bien un tema, ser perito en un tema ‖ *to do well* ir bien (business), ir por buen camino, medrar (person), estar recuperándose (invalid), darse bien (plant), salir bien; *he did well in his exam* salió bien del examen; hacer bien; *he would do well to see the dentist* haría bien en ir al dentista ‖ *to do well by* portarse bien con ‖ *to stand well with s.o.* llevarse bien con alguien, tener buenas relaciones con alguien ‖ *well and truly over* acabado y bien acabado ‖ *well done!* ¡muy bien!, ¡bravo! ‖ *well over a million* mucho más de un millón ‖ *well now* ahora bien ‖ *you may well ask* puede perfectamente preguntar.
◆ *adj* bien (in good health); *to be well* estar bien ‖ bien; *things are well with you* las cosas le van bien; *it is well that he has come* está bien que haya venido ‖ — *to get well* reponerse, restablecerse ‖ *very well* muy bien ‖ *well and good* muy bien ‖ *well and good!* ¡tanto mejor!
◆ *n* *the well and the sick* los sanos y los enfermos ‖ *to wish s.o. well* desear todo lo mejor para alguien.
◆ *interj* bueno (aquiescence, hesitation, resignation, interrogation); *well, such is life* bueno, así es la vida ‖ ¡vaya! (surprise); *well! I never expected to see you here* ¡vaya!, no esperaba verte aquí.
— OBSERV El comparativo de *well* es *better* y el superlativo es *best*.

well [wel] *vi* manar, fluir (to flow) ‖ brotar (to gush) ‖ *the tears welled up in her eyes* se le llenaron los ojos de lágrimas.

well-adjusted ['welə'dʒʌstid] *adj* bien adaptado, da.

well-advised ['weləd'vaizd] *adj* sensato, ta; juicioso, sa.

well [wel] *n* pozo *m* (to obtain water, oil, gas, etc.); *they sank a well* perforaron un pozo ‖ caja *f* (containing the stairs or lift) ‖ depósito *m* (for holding a liquid) ‖ tintero *m* (inkwell) ‖ fuente *f*, manantial *m* (spring) ‖ FIG pozo *m*; *a well of knowledge* un pozo de ciencia ‖ MAR pozo *m* ‖ vivero *m* (of a fishing boat) ‖ JUR estrado *m* ‖ AVIAT carlinga *f*.

well-aimed ['wel'eimd] *adj* certero, ra.

well-appointed ['welə'pɔintid] *adj* bien amueblado, da.

well-balanced ['wel'bælənsd] *adj* bien equilibrado, da ‖ FIG equilibrado, da.

well-behaved ['welbi'heivd] *adj* bien educado, da (well-bred) ‖ formal, serio, ria (serious).

well-being ['wel'bi:iŋ] *n* bienestar *m* (of s.o.) ‖ buen estado *m* (of sth.).

well borer ['wel,bɔ:rə*] *n* pocero *m*.

wellborn ['wel'bɔ:n] *adj* bien nacido, da.

well-bred ['-wel'bred] *adj* bien educado, da (person) ‖ de raza (animal).

well-built ['wel'bilt] *adj* bien hecho, cha (person).

well-chosen ['wel'tʃəuzn] *adj* elegido cuidadosamente ‖ acertado, da (words, etc.).

well-content ['welkən'tent] *adj* satisfecho, cha; contento, ta.

well curb ['welkə:b] *n* brocal *m*.

well digger ['wel,digə*] *n* pocero *m*.

well-disposed ['weldis'pəuzd] *adj* bien dispuesto, ta ‖ favorable (*to, towards* a) ‖ bienintencionado, da (well-intentioned).

well-doer ['wel'duə*] *n* hombre *m* de bien (good man) ‖ bienhechor, ra (benefactor).

welldoing ['wel'duiŋ] *n* bien *m*.

well-done ['weld'dʌn] *adj* bien hecho, cha ‖ CULIN muy hecho, cha.

well-dressed ['wel'drest] *adj* bien vestido, da.

well-earned ['wel'ə:nd] *adj* merecido, da.

well-educated ['wel'edjukeitid] *adj* culto, ta.

well-established ['welis'tæbliʃt] *adj* arraigado, da (custom) ‖ de sólida reputación (company).

well-favoured; US **well-favored** ['wel'feivəd] *adj* bien parecido, da; agraciado, da.

well-fed ['wel'fed] *adj* bien alimentado, da.

well-fixed ['wel'fikst] *adj* US FAM rico, ca; adinerado, da.

well-founded ['wel'faundid] *adj* bien fundado, da; fundamentado, da.

well-groomed ['wel'gru:md] *adj* bien arreglado, da (person) ‖ bien cuidado, da (animal).

well-grounded ['wel'graundid] *adj* bien fundado, da.

well-handled ['wel'hændld] *adj* bien dirigido, da.

wellhead ['welhed] *n* manantial *m* (spring) ‖ FIG fuente *f*.

well-heeled ['wel'hi:ld] *adj* US FAM pudiente, rico, ca (rich).

well-informed ['welin'fɔ:md] *adj* muy documentado, da ‖ bien informado, da (*about* acerca de) ‖ *to be well-informed on a subject* conocer un tema a fondo.

wellies ['weliz] *pl n* FAM botas *f pl* de agua.

wellington ['weliŋtən] *n* bota *f* de agua.

well-intentioned ['welin'tenʃənd] *adj* bienintencionado, da ‖ piadoso, sa (lie).

well-judged ['wel'dʒʌdʒd] *adj* bien calculado, da.

well-kept ['wel'kept] *adj* bien cuidado, da (garden, etc.) ‖ bien guardado, da (secret).

well-knit ['wel'nit] *adj* robusto, ta; de buena estatura (person) ‖ bien construido, da; bien estructurado, da (speech, etc.).

well-known ['wel'nəun] *adj* muy conocido, da.

well-made ['wel'meid] *adj* bien hecho, cha.

well-mannered ['wel'mænəd] *adj* muy cortés, de buenos modales.

well-meaning ['wel'mi:niŋ] *adj* bienintencionado, da.

well-meant ['wel'ment] *adj* bienintencionado, da.

well-nigh ['welnai] *adv* casi.

well-off ['wel'ɔf] *adj* rico, ca; adinerado, da; acomodado, da (wealthy) ‖ *not to know when one is well-off* no saber lo afortunado que es uno.

well-ordered ['wel'ɔ:dəd] *adj* bien ordenado, da (orderly) ‖ bien organizado, da.

well-paid ['wel'peid] *adj* bien pagado, da; bien remunerado, da.

well-preserved ['welpri'zə:vd] *adj* bien conservado, da.

well-read ['wel'red] *adj* leído, da; instruido, da; culto, ta; *well-read people say so* la gente leída opina así.

well-spent ['wel'spent] *adj* bien empleado, da; bien gastado, da.

well-spoken ['wel'spəuken] *adj* bienhablado, da.

wellspring ['welspriŋ] *n* fuente *f*, manantial *m*.

well-stocked ['wel'stɔːkt] *adj* bien surtido, da.

well-thought-of ['wel'θɔːtɔv] *adj* bien considerado, da; de buena reputación.

well-timed ['wel'taimd] *adj* oportuno, na.

well-to-do ['weltə'duː] *adj* rico, ca; acaudalado, da.

well-trodden ['wel'trɔːdn] *adj* trillado, da.

well-turned ['wel'təːnd] *adj* bien construido, da (sentence) ‖ bien hecho, cha (body).

well-wisher ['wel'wiʃə*] *n* persona *f* que desea el bien de otro ‖ amigo *m* sincero (friend).

well-worn ['wel'wɔːn] *adj* gastado, da; desgastado, da ‖ FIG trillado, da.

welsh; welch [welʃ] *vi* FAM *to welsh on* no pagar una apuesta a (to fail to pay winning bets), no cumplir con (an obligation, etc.).

Welsh [welʃ] *adj* galés, esa.
◆ *n* galés, esa (person) ‖ galés *m* (language) ‖ *the Welsh* los galeses.

welsher [-ə*] *n* estafador *m*.

Welshman [-mən] *n* galés *m*.
— OBSERV El plural de esta palabra es *Welshmen*.

Welsh rabbit [-'ræbit]; **Welsh rarebit** [-'rɛəbit] *n* CULIN pan *m* tostado con queso derretido.

Welshwoman [-ˌwumən] *n* galesa *f*.
— OBSERV El plural de esta palabra es *Welshwomen*.

welt [welt] *n* vira *f* (in shoemaking) ‖ ribete *m*, vivo *m* (in sewing) ‖ verdugón *m* (weal).

welt [welt] *vt* poner vira a (a shoe) ‖ ribetear (in sewing) ‖ zurrar (to thrash).

welter ['weltə*] *adj* SP de peso welter.
◆ *n* welter *m*, semimedio *m*, boxeador *m* de peso welter (welterweight) ‖ confusión *f* (turmoil) ‖ revoltijo *m* (mess).

welter ['weltə*] *vi* revolcarse (to roll about) ‖ espumear, hacer espuma (the sea) ‖ FIG bañar (in blood) | encenagarse (in sin).

welterweight [-weit] *n* SP peso *m* welter (in horse racing) | welter *m*, semimedio *m*, boxeador *m* de peso welter (in boxing).

wen [wen] *n* runa *f* del inglés antiguo (rune) ‖ lobanillo *m*, quiste *m* sebáceo (cyst).

wench [wentʃ] *n* jovencita *f*, moza *f* (girl) ‖ FAM fulana *f* (prostitute).

wench [wentʃ] *vi* FAM ir de fulanas.

wend [wend] *vt* *to wend one's way to* dirigir sus pasos a, encaminarse a.

wendy house ['wendiˌhaus] *n* casa *f* a modelo reducido en la que juegan los niños.

went [went] *pret* ⟶ **go.**

wept [wept] *pret/pp* ⟶ **weep.**

were [wəː*] *pret* ⟶ **be.**

we're [wiə*] contracción de «we are».

weren't [wəːnt] contracción de «were not».

werewolf ['wəːwulf] *n* hombre *m* lobo.
— OBSERV El plural es *werewolves*.

west [west] *adv* al oeste, hacia el oeste ‖ — *east and west* del este al oeste ‖ FIG & FAM *to go west* irse al otro barrio (to die), fastidiarse (to break), estar perdido (to be wasted), fracasar (to fail) ‖ *west of* al oeste de.
◆ *adj* del oeste, occidental ‖ del oeste (wind) ‖ que da al oeste (window, door, etc.) ‖ — *West Berlin* Berlín *m* Occidental ‖ *West Germany* Alemania *f* Occidental.
◆ *n* oeste *m* (cardinal point) ‖ occidente *m*, poniente *m*, oeste *m* (direction of the setting sun) ‖ *the West* el Oeste (of United States), el Mundo Occidental (of the world).

westbound [-baund] *adj* con rumbo al oeste.

west by north [-bai'nɔːθ] *n* oeste *m* cuarta al noroeste.

west by south [-bai'sauθ] *n* oeste *m* cuarta al suroeste.

West Country [-ˌkʌntri] *n* suroeste *m* de Inglaterra.

West End [-end] *n* oeste *m* de Londres [barrio residencial de la capital inglesa].

wester [-ə*] *vi* moverse hacia el poniente (star, sun, moon) ‖ cambiar hacia el oeste (wind).

westerly [-əli] *adj/adv* en el oeste (in the west) ‖ hacia el oeste (towards the west) ‖ del oeste (wind).
◆ *n* viento *m* del oeste.

western [-ən] *adj* occidental, del oeste.
◆ *n* novela *f* del Oeste (story of life in the west of USA) ‖ película *f* del oeste, «western» *m* (film).

Western [-ən] *adj* del Oeste (relating to the west of USA) ‖ occidental (Europe, States) ‖ de Occidente (empire) ‖ REL latina (church).

Westerner [-ənə*] *n* occidental *m* & *f* ‖ US norteamericano *m* del Oeste.

western hemisphere [-ən'hemisfiə*] *n* hemisferio *m* occidental, mundo *m* occidental.

westernization [ˌwestənai'zeiʃən] *n* occidentalización *f*.

westernize ['westənaiz] *vt* occidentalizar.

westernized [-d] *adj* occidentalizado, da ‖ *to become westernized* occidentalizarse.

westernmost ['westənməust] *adj* más occidental, situado más al oeste.

West Indian ['west'indjən] *adj/n* antillano, na.

West Indies ['west'indiz] *pl prn* GEOGR Antillas *f*.

westing ['westiŋ] *n* MAR rumbo *m* hacia el oeste.

Westminster ['westminstə*] *n* Westminster [Parlamento británico].

west-northwest ['westnɔːθ'west] *adv* hacia el oesnorueste, hacia el oesnoroeste.
◆ *n* oesnorueste *m*, oesnoroeste *m*.

Westphalia [west'feiljə] *pr n* GEOGR Westfalia *f*.

West Point ['west'pɔint] *n* «West Point» [academia militar de Estados Unidos].

west-southwest ['westsauθ'west] *adv* hacia el oessudueste, hacia el oessudoeste.
◆ *n* oessudueste *m*, oessudoeste *m*.

West Virginia [westvə'dʒiniə] *pr n* GEOGR Virginia *f* Occidental.

westward ['westwəd] *adv/adj* hacia el oeste.
◆ *n* oeste *m*; *to westward* hacia el oeste.

westwards [-z] *adv* hacia el oeste.

wet [wet] *adj* mojado, da (soaked); *you'd better take off your wet clothes* es mejor que se quite la ropa mojada ‖ húmedo, da; *wet climate* clima húmedo; *the painting is still wet* el cuadro está todavía húmedo ‖ lluvioso, sa; de lluvia (day, season, weather) ‖ fresco, ca (paint) ‖ TECH por vía húmeda ‖ MED escarificado, da (cup) ‖ FIG soso, sa; tonto, ta; *don't be so wet!* ¡no seas tan tonto! ‖ US antiprohibicionista (person, town) ‖ US FAM erróneo, a; falso, sa ‖ — *to get one's hair wet* mojarse el pelo ‖ *to get wet* mojarse ‖ *wet through, wet to the skin* calado hasta los huesos ‖ *wringing wet* chorreando.
◆ *n* humedad *f* (state) ‖ lluvia *f* (rain) ‖ tiempo *m* lluvioso (weather) ‖ FAM copa *f* (drink) ‖ US antiprohibicionista *m* & *f*.

wet [wet] *vt* humedecer, mojar (to make wet) ‖ mojar (one's bed) ‖ FAM rociar, celebrar (an event) ‖ *to wet o.s.* mojarse.
◆ *vi* mojarse.

wet blanket [-'blæŋkit] *n* aguafiestas *m* & *f* *inv*.

wether ['weðə*] *n* carnero *m* castrado (ram).

wetness ['wetnis] *n* humedad *f* (dampness).

wet nurse ['wetnəːs] *n* nodriza *f*, ama *f* de leche.

wet-nurse ['wetnəːs] *vt* criar.

wet suit ['wet'sjuːt] *n* traje *m* de buzo.

wetting ['wetiŋ] *n* remojo *m* ‖ *to get a wetting* mojarse.

wettish ['wetiʃ] *adj* húmedo, da.

whack [wæk]; **thwack** *n* golpe *m* fuerte (resounding blow) ‖ FAM tentativa *f*, intento *m* (attempt) | parte *f* (share) ‖ — FAM *out of whack* fuera de servicio | *to take* o *to have a whack at* intentar (to attempt).

whack [wæk]; **thwack** *vt* golpear (to strike) ‖ FAM pegar una paliza a (to defeat) ‖ US FAM compartir (to share).

whacked [wækt] *adj* FAM hecho, cha polvo; molido, da.

whacker [-ə*] *n* FAM mastodonte *m* (person) | enormidad *f* (story, thing).

whacking [-iŋ] *adj* FAM enorme (very large) ‖ FAM *a whacking lie* una mentira como una casa.
◆ *adv* FAM extremadamente, sumamente ‖ FAM *whacking big* enorme.
◆ *n* paliza *f*, tunda *f* (thrashing).

whacky [-i] *adj* FAM chiflado, da; chalado, da (person) | absurdo, da (thing).

whale [weil] *n* ZOOL ballena *f* ‖ US FAM as *m*; *he's a whale at tennis* es un as del tenis ‖ — FAM *a whale of a* sensacional, extraordinario, ria (good in quality), enorme (huge) | *we had a whale of a time!* ¡lo pasamos bomba! ‖ *whale calf* ballenato *m*.

whale [weil] *vi* cazar ballenas.
◆ *vt* zurrar, dar una paliza a (to thrash) ‖ US FAM derrotar, pegar una paliza a.

whaleboat [-bəut] *n* ballenero *m*.

whalebone [-bəun] *n* barba *f* de ballena.

whale oil [-ɔil] *n* aceite *m* de ballena.

whaler [-ə*] *n* ballenero *m* (man, boat).

whaling [-iŋ] *n* pesca *f* or caza *f* de ballenas ‖ — *whaling gun* fusil *m* con arpón ‖ *whaling industry* industria ballenera ‖ *whaling ship* ballenero *m* (whaler).

wham [wæm] *n* golpe *m* ruidoso (noisy impact).
◆ *interj* ¡zas!

wham [wæm] *vt* golpear con fuerza.
◆ *vi* chocar ruidosamente.

whang [wæŋ] *n* golpe *m* resonante.
◆ *interj* ¡zas!

whang [wæŋ] *vt* azotar (to thrash) ‖ golpear con fuerza (to hit).
◆ *vi* resonar ‖ chocar ruidosamente.

wharf [wɔːf] *n* MAR muelle *m*, embarcadero *m*, desembarcadero *m*.
— OBSERV El plural de esta palabra es *wharfs* (empleado sobre todo en Gran Bretaña) o *wharves* (usado en los Estados Unidos).

wharf [wɔːf] *vt* MAR atracar en el muelle (a ship) | descargar en el muelle (goods).

wharfage [-idʒ] *n* MAR muellaje *m* (fee) ‖ muelles *m pl* (wharfs).

wharfinger [-indʒə*] *n* administrador *m* del muelle (manager) ‖ representante *m* de un armador en el muelle (representative).

what [wɔt] *rel pron* lo que; *he heard what I said* oyó lo que dije; *he told me what it would cost* me dijo lo que costaría; *I am sorry about what has happened* siento lo que ha ocurrido; *what I like is music* lo que me gusta es la música; *you know what he is busy with* sabes de lo que se ocupa; *I see what yhou are alluding to* veo a lo que te estás refiriendo || — *and what is more* y además || *come* o *happen what may* pase lo que pase || *do what I may* cualquier cosa que haga || *say what he will* diga lo que diga || FAM *to give s.o. what for* dar a alguien su merecido || *what with... and* entre... y; *what with one thing and another* entre una cosa y otra.

◆ *interr pron* qué; *what is the time?* ¿qué hora es?; *he did what?* ¿qué hizo?; *what is it?* ¿qué es?; *what gave you that idea?* ¿qué te hizo pensar eso?; *what are you talking about?* ¿de qué está hablando? || cuál; *what is her name?* ¿cuál es su nombre? || cuánto; *what is the rent?* ¿cuánto es el alquiler? || a cuánto; *what are potatoes today?* ¿a cuánto están hoy las patatas? || cómo; *what is he like?* ¿cómo es? || qué (indirect); *tell me what is happening* dime qué pasa; *I don't know what to do* no sé qué hacer || ¿cómo? (I beg your pardon) || — *and what not, and what have you* y tal y cual, y qué sé yo, y cosas por el estilo || *I'll show you what's what* te voy a poner al corriente (explanation), te voy a dar tu merecido (punishment) || *I tell you what: let's drop the whole matter* mira, no hablemos más del asunto || *I tell you what: let's go out for dinner* se me ocurre una idea, ¿por qué no vamos a cenar? || *see what courage can do!* ¡mira lo que puede conseguir el valor! || *so what?* ¿y qué? || *to know what's what* saber cuántas son cinco || *well, what about it?* bueno y ¿qué? || *what about?* ¿qué te parece?, ¿qué le parece?, etc.; *what about having dinner together?* ¿qué le parece si cenamos juntos?; *what about you?* y a ti ¿qué te parece?; ¿que es de?; *what about your mother?* ¿qué es de tu madre?; y; *what about the ten pounds I lent you?* ¿y las diez libras que te presté? || *what about it* ¿y qué? || *what does it matter?* ¿qué importa? || *what do seven and eight make?* ¿cuántos son siete con ocho? || *what else?* ¿qué más? || *what for?* ¿para qué? || *what if* y si; *what if he can't come after all?* ¿y si no puede venir después de todo? || *what is it to you?* y a ti, ¿qué te importa? || *what is it all about?* ¿de qué se trata? || *what is that all about?* ¿a qué viene todo eso? || *what is the Spanish for «table»?* ¿cómo se dice «table» en español? || *what next?* ¿y ahora qué?, ¿y entonces qué? || *what of it?* ¿y qué? || *what's the matter?* ¿qué pasa? || *what then?* ¿y qué? || *what though?* ¿qué importa?

◆ *interr adj* ¿qué?; *what time is it?* ¿qué hora es? || ¿de qué?; *what colour is your dress?* ¿de qué color es tu vestido? || *what good is it?* ¿para qué sirve?

◆ *exclamat adj* qué; *what silly fools we have been!* ¡qué tontos hemos sido!; *what an absurd question!* ¡qué pregunta más *or* tan absurda!; *what a pity!* ¡qué lástima!; *what a lot of people!* ¡qué cantidad de gente! || *what an idea!* ¡menuda idea!

◆ *rel adj* el que, la que, los que, las que, lo que; *lend me what money you can* déjame el dinero que puedas; *what few friends he has were on holiday* los pocos amigos que tenía estaban de vacaciones; *what little he said was interesting* lo poco que dijo fue interesante.

◆ *interj* ¡cómo!; *what!, another new dress!* ¡cómo!, ¡otro vestido nuevo! || ¡qué vergüenza!; *what!, fifty pounds for a chair!* ¡qué vergüenza!, ¡cincuenta libras por una silla! || — *nice little girl, what!* ¡qué chica más mona!, ¿verdad? || *what they have suffered!* ¡cuánto han sufrido!

what-d'ye-call-her [ˈwɔtdjuˌkɔːlhəˈ] *n* FAM fulana *f*, ésa *f* (woman).

what-d'ye-call-him [ˈwɔtdjuˌkɔːlhim] *n* FAM fulano *m*, ése *m* (man).

what-d'ye-call-it [ˈwɔtdjuˌkɔːlit] *n* FAM chisme *m*, cosa *f* (thing).

whatever [wɔtˈevəˈ]; **whatsoever** [ˌwɔtsəuˈevəˈ] *pron* todo lo que; *eat whatever you like* come todo lo que quieras || lo que; *I'll do it, whatever he says* lo haré diga lo que diga || cualquier cosa que, todo lo que; *whatever he wants he shall have* tendrá cualquier cosa que quiera || — FAM *or whatever* o lo que sea || *whatever happens* pase lo que pase || *whatever it may be* sea lo que sea.

◆ *adj* cualquiera... que; *whatever doubt I may have* cualquier duda que pueda tener || cualquiera que sea; *whatever difficulties you may encounter* cualesquiera que sean las dificultades que pueda encontrar || — *nothing whatever* absolutamente nada, nada en absoluto || *this will be no trouble whatever for us* no nos causará ninguna molestia.

what-ho! [ˈwɔtˈhəu] *interj* ¡vaya! (surprise) || ¡hola! (hello!).

whatnot [ˈwɔtnɔt] *n* estantería *f* (shelves) || chisme *m* (thingumajig).

what's-her-name [ˈwɔtsəneim] *n* FAM fulana *f*, ésa *f*.

what's-his-name [ˈwɔtsizneim] *n* FAM fulano *m*, ése *m*.

whatsoever [ˌwɔtsəuˈevəˈ] *adj/pron* → **whatever**.

wheal [wiːl] *n* verdugón *m* (weal).

wheat [wiːt] *n* trigo *m* (cereal).

wheatear [ˈwiːtiəˈ] *n* culiblanco *m* (bird).

wheaten [ˈwiːtən] *adj* de trigo (of wheat) || de color de trigo (of the colour of wheat).

wheat field [ˈwiːtfiːld] *n* trigal *m*.

wheat germ [ˈwiːtdʒəːm] *n* germen *m* de trigo.

wheedle [ˈwiːdl] *vi* engatusar (to coax); *she wheedled him into buying her a new coat* le engatusó para que le comprara un abrigo nuevo || conseguir (por medio de halagos); *she wheedled a new coat out of him* consiguió por medio de halagos que él le comprara un abrigo.

wheedling [ˈwiːdliŋ] *adj* zalamero, ra.

◆ *n* halagos *m pl*, engatusamiento *m*.

wheel [wiːl] *n* rueda *f* (of a vehicle); *the wheel of a car* la rueda de un coche; *back, front wheel* rueda trasera, delantera || volante *m* (for steering a car); *to take the wheel* coger el volante || rueda *f* (of torture); *to break on the wheel* atormentar en la rueda || MIL vuelta *f*, giro *m*; *left wheel* vuelta a la izquierda || MAR timón *m* (of a ship); *to be at the wheel* llevar el timón || torno *m* (potter's) || ruleta *f*, rodillo *m* trazador (in sewing) || US FAM bici *f* (bike) || — *big wheel* noria *f* (at fair), pez gordo (important person) || *fixed wheel* piñón fijo || FIG *fortune's wheel* rueda de la fortuna || MAR *the man at the wheel* el timonero || FIG *the wheel has come full circle* ¡qué de vueltas da la vida! | *to put one's shoulder to the wheel* arrimar el hombro.

◆ *pl* engranaje *m sing*, maquinaria *f sing*, mecanismo *m sing*; *the wheels of government* el mecanismo administrativo || — AVIAT *landing wheels* tren *m* de aterrizaje || FIG *there are wheels within wheels* es un asunto complicadísimo || *to go on wheels* ir sobre ruedas || *to turn wheels* dar volteretas.

wheel [wiːl] *vt* hacer rodar (to cause to roll) || hacer girar (to rotate) || llevar [sobre ruedas] (to carry on wheels); *to wheel sth. in a barrow* llevar algo en una carretilla; *to wheel a child in a pram* llevar a un niño en un cochecito || empujar (bicycle, motorcycle, etc.); *to wheel an invalid in a wheelchair* empujar a un inválido en un sillón de ruedas || marcar con el rodillo trazador (in sewing) || atormentar en la rueda (to torture).

◆ *vi* rodar (to move on wheels) || dar vueltas, girar (to turn, to spin) || revolotear; *the sea gulls were wheeling round me* las gaviotas estaban revoloteando alrededor mío || MIL dar una vuelta || US FAM ir en bicicleta || — *to wheel about* o *round* dar media vuelta || FIG *to wheel round* cambiar de opinión (to change one's mind).

wheelbarrow [-ˌbærəu] *n* carretilla *f*.

wheelbase [-beis] *n* AUT batalla *f*, distancia *f* entre ejes.

wheelchair [-tʃɛəˈ] *n* sillón *m* de ruedas.

wheel clamp [-klæmp] *n* cepo *m* [para vehículos].

wheeled [-d] *adj* de ruedas; *wheeled chair* sillón de ruedas || rodado, da; *wheeled traffic* tránsito rodado, circulación rodada || *two-wheeled* de dos ruedas.

wheeler [-əˈ] *n* caballo *m* de tronco (wheelhorse) || carretero *m* (man) || vapor *m* de ruedas (boat) || *two-wheeler* vehículo *m* de dos ruedas.

wheelhorse [-hɔːs] *n* caballo *m* de tronco || FIG colaborador *m* eficaz.

wheelhouse [-haus] *n* MAR timonera *f*, caseta *f or* cámara *f* del timón.

wheeling [-iŋ] *n* transporte *m* sobre ruedas || carácter *m* transitable.

wheeling and dealing [-iŋənˈdiːliŋ] *n* trejemaneje *m*.

wheelman [-mən] *n* MAR timonel *m*, timonero *m*.

— OBSERV El plural de *wheelman* es *wheelmen*.

wheel rope [-rəup] *n* MAR guardín *m*.

wheel window [-ˌwindəu] *n* ARCH rosetón *m*, rosa *f*.

wheelwright [-rait] *n* carretero *m* || *wheelwright's work* carretería *f*.

wheeze [wiːz] *n* MED respiración *f* jadeante *or* dificultosa, resuello *m* [ruidoso] || FAM idea *f* | gracia *f*, salida *f* (joke).

wheeze [wiːz] *vt* *to wheeze out* decir resollando.

◆ *vi* respirar con dificultad, resollar.

wheezing [-iŋ]; **wheezy** [-i] *adj* jadeante, dificultoso, sa (breath) || asmático, ca (person).

whelk [welk] *n* ZOOL buccino *m*.

whelm [welm] *vt* sumergir.

whelp [welp] *n* cachorro *m* (young animal) || bribón *m*, granuja *m* (a naughty boy).

whelp [welp] *vt/vi* parir (animals).

when [wen] *adv* cuándo, a qué hora (at what time); *¿when can you come?* ¿a qué hora puedes venir? || cuándo (on which occasion); *I don't know when I can do it* no sé cuándo lo podré hacer; *when did that happen?* ¿cuándo ocurrió? || *say when!* dime cuándo (tengo que pararme).

◆ *conj* cuando; *when spring came* cuando llegó la primavera || en cuanto, al (as soon as); *we'll have lunch when father comes* almorzaremos al llegar *or* en cuanto llegue papá || cuando (in spite of the fact that); *why does he live like a miser when he is so rich?* ¿por qué vive como un avaro cuando es tan rico? || en que; *at the very moment when* en el momento mismo en que; *the day when I met you* el día en que te conocí || cuando; *now is when I need him more* ahora es cuando más lo necesito || *when a child* de niño.

◆ *pron* cuándo; *since when?* ¿desde cuándo?; *till when?* ¿hasta cuándo?

◆ *n* cuándo *m*; *I can't remember the when or the why of it* no me puedo acordar ni del cuándo ni del porqué || momento *m*, fecha *f* (of an event).

whence [wens] *adv/conj* ¿de dónde? (from where); *whence are they?* ¿de dónde son? || *whence I conclude that* de lo cual deduzco que.

whencesoever [ˌwenssəu'evə*] *adv* de donde sea, de cualquier parte que sea.

whenever [wen'evə*]; **whensoever** [ˌwensəu'evə*] *adv/conj* cuando, en cualquier momento que; *come whenever you like* ven cuando quieras || cada vez que; *whenever I see it I think of you* cada vez que lo veo me acuerdo de ti; *I go whenever I can* voy cada vez que puedo.

where [wɛə*] *interj adv* dónde; *where are you?* ¿dónde estás? || adónde, a dónde; *where are you going?* ¿adónde vas? || de dónde; *where do you get your money?* ¿de dónde sacas el dinero? || por dónde; *where are you in your work?* ¿por dónde vas en tu trabajo?; *I don't know where to begin* no sé por dónde empezar || en qué (in what respect); *where am I wrong?* ¿en qué estoy equivocado? || — *where are you from?, where do you come from?* ¿de dónde es usted? || *where should I be if I had followed your advice?* ¿qué sería de mí si hubiese seguido su consejo?
◆ *rel adv* donde; *I shall stay where I am* me quedaré donde estoy || donde, en donde, en que, en el cual, en la cual, en los cuales, en las cuales; *the town where I was born* la ciudad en que nací || adonde, a donde; *they have gone where the police can't find them* han ido adonde la policía no los puede localizar || adonde, a donde, al que, al cual, a la cual, a los cuales, a las cuales; *the town where I am going* la ciudad a donde voy || — *that is where we have got to* a eso hemos llegado, aquí es a donde hemos llegado || *that is where you are mistaken* en eso está equivocado.
◆ *n* lugar *m*, sitio *m* (place).

whereabout ['wɛərə'baut] *adv* al respecto || donde, por donde; *whereabouts did you put it?* ¿dónde lo pusiste?

whereabouts [-s] *adv* dónde, por dónde; *wherabouts did you put it?* ¿dónde lo pusiste?

whereabouts ['wɛərəbauts] *n* paradero *m*; *her present whereabouts is unknown* no se conoce su paradero actual.

whereas [wɛər'æz] *conj* mientras (que), en tanto que; *some praise him whereas others condemn him* algunos le alaban mientras otros le condenan || JUR considerando que, visto que.
◆ *pl n* JUR *the whereases* los considerandos.

whereat [wɛər'æt] *adv* a lo cual; *whereat he replied* a lo cual contestó || — *he said sth. whereat everyone laughed* dijo algo de lo cual se rieron todos || *the words whereat he took offence* las palabras por las que se ofendió.

whereby [wɛə'bai] *adv* cómo; *whereby shall I know him?* ¿cómo podría conocerle? || por el que, por la que, por medio del cual *or* de la cual; *decision whereby...* decisión por la cual...

wherefore ['wɛəfɔː*] *adv* por qué (why); *wherefore comes he?* ¿por qué viene? || por lo que, por lo cual (for which).
◆ *n* porqué *m* || *the whys and wherefores* las causas y los motivos, todos los detalles, el cómo y el porqué.

wherefrom [wɛə'frɔm] *adv* de donde, de lo cual.

wherein [wɛər'in] *adv* en donde, en que, en el cual, en la cual; *the room wherein they were sleeping* la habitación en la cual estaban durmiendo || en qué; *wherein have we offended you?* ¿en qué le hemos ofendido?

whereof [wɛər'ɔv] *adv* de qué; *whereof is it made?* ¿de qué está hecho? || del que, de la que, de lo que; *wood whereof paper is made* madera de la que se hace el papel; *two sisters whereof one was a nun* dos hermanas de las que una era monja.

whereon [wɛər'ɔn] *adv* en qué; *whereon did he sit?* ¿en qué se sentó? || en el que, en la que; *the ground whereon he lies* el suelo en el que descansa || en que; *the day whereon he was assassinated* el día en que fue asesinado.

wheresoever [ˌwɛəsəu'evə*] *adv* ⟶ **wherever.**

whereto [wɛə'tuː] *adv* para qué || para lo cual (to which) || adonde, a donde (to which place).

whereupon [ˌwɛərə'pɔn] *adv* después de lo cual, con lo cual (after which) || ⟶ **whereon.**

wherever [wɛər'evə*]; **wheresoever** [wɛəsəu'evə*] *adv* dondequiera que; *you must find him, wherever he is* tienen que encontrarle dondequiera que esté || a dondequiera que; *I shall remember you wherever I go* me acordaré de ti a dondequiera que vaya || FAM ¿dónde diablos?, ¿dónde demonios?, ¿dónde? (where); *wherever did you get that cold?* ¿dónde demonios cogiste ese resfriado?

wherewith [wɛə'wiθ] *adv* con el que, con la que, con lo cual (with which) || ¿con qué? (with what?).
◆ *pron* lo necesario para.

wherewithal ['wɛəwiðɔːl] *n* medios *m pl*, recursos *m pl*, lo suficiente; *to have the wherewithal to pay* tener lo suficiente para pagar.

wherry ['weri] *n* esquife *m* (rowing boat) || barcaza *f*, chalana *f* (barge).

whet [wet] *n* afilado *m*, afiladura *f* (sharpening) || FIG estimulante *m* || FAM aperitivo *m*, copa *f* (drink).

whet [wet] *vt* afilar, sacar filo a (to sharpen) || FIG aguzar, despertar (the appetite) | estimular (courage, etc.).

whether ['weðə*] *conj* si; *he asked whether it was true* preguntó si era verdad; *it depends upon whether you are in a hurry or not* depende de si tiene prisa o no || — *the question arose whether...* la cuestión se planteó de saber si... || *to doubt whether* dudar que || *whether... or* sea... o (sea); *we'll take the next offer, whether good or bad* aceptaremos la próxima oferta sea buena o sea mala; que... o (que); *whether he drives or takes the train* que vaya en coche o que tome el tren || *whether or not* de todos modos || *whether she comes or not* venga o no venga.

whetstone ['wetstone] *n* amoladera *f*, piedra *f* de afilar, piedra *f* de amolar.

whew [hwuː] *interj* ¡vaya!

whey [wei] *n* suero *m* (of milk).

which [witʃ] *adj* qué; *which road should I take?* ¿qué carretera debo coger?; *deciding which candidate he is going to vote for* decidiendo por qué candidato va a votar || cuál, cuáles || cuyo, ya; *he stayed here six months, during which time...* se quedó aquí seis meses, durante cuyo tiempo... || — *look which way you will* mire por donde mire || *try which method you please* aplique el método que quiera || *which one?* ¿cuál? || *which ones?* ¿cuáles? || *which way?* ¿por dónde?; *which way do we go?* ¿por dónde vamos?; ¿de dónde?; *which way is the wind?* ¿de dónde viene el viento?; ¿cómo? (how); *which way shall we do it?* ¿cómo lo vamos a hacer?
◆ *interr pron* cuál; *which do you prefer?* ¿cuál prefieres?; *she did not know which were the best shops* no sabía cuáles eran las mejores tiendas; *which of you will go with me?* ¿cuál de vosotros vendrá conmigo? || qué; *which would you rather be, pretty or good?* qué preferirías ¿ser guapa o ser buena?; *which will you take, coffee or tea?* ¿qué tomas? ¿café o té? || *tell me which is which* dime cuál es cuál.
◆ *rel pron* que; *the book which you lent me* el libro que me dejaste || el cual, la cual, los cuales, las cuales, el que, la que, los que, las que; *the work to which she devoted all her time* el trabajo al cual dedicó todo su tiempo || lo cual, lo que; *he refused to come, which did not surprise me* se negó a venir, lo cual no me extrañó; *upon which she came out* con lo cual se fue || — *all which* todo lo cual || *of which* del que, de la que, de los que, de las que, del cual, de la cual, etc.; *the house of which I speak* la casa de la cual hablo; *the table one leg of which is broken* la mesa de la cual una pata está rota; cuyo, cuya; *the room the door of which is closed* la habitación cuya puerta está cerrada.

whichever [witʃ'evə*]; **whichsoever** [ˌwitʃsəu'evə*] *adj* cualquier, cualquiera [que sea]; *whichever party comes to power* cualquiera que sea el partido que *or* cualquier partido que llegue al poder || *take whichever book you like best* coja el libro que más le guste.
◆ *pron* el que, la que; *buy whichever is cheapest* compre el que sea más barato || cualquiera que; *whichever you choose you will have a good bargain* cualquiera que escoja, habrá hecho un buen negocio.

whiff [wif] *n* bocanada *f* (small volume of smoke, of air, etc.) || chupada *f*, calada *f* (of tobacco) || soplo *m* (of wind) || olorcillo *m* (odour) || MAR esquife *m* || FAM purito *m* (small cigar) || — *he went out for a whiff of fresh air* salió a tomar el fresco || *to get a whiff of ether* oler a éter.

whiff [wif] *vt* echar (smoke, scent, etc.).
◆ *vi* soplar (to blow) || echar bocanadas de humo (smoking, etc.) || *to whiff of* oler a (to smell of); *it whiffs of garlic* huele a ajo.

Whig [wig] *n* «Whig» *m*.
— OBSERV En Gran Bretaña, el *Whig party* es un partido político, creado en el siglo XVII, que ha sido sustituido por el partido liberal. En Estados Unidos, es un partido fundado en el siglo XIX que ha sido reemplazado por el partido republicano.

while [wail] *n* rato *m*, tiempo *m* (period of time); *a long while* largo rato, mucho tiempo || — *after a while* al poco rato, poco tiempo después || *a little while* un ratito || *a little while ago* hace poco tiempo, no hace mucho tiempo || *all the while* todo el tiempo || *a long while ago* hace mucho tiempo || *for a while* durante algún tiempo || *I'll make it worth your while* te recompensaré || *in a little while* dentro de poco || *in a while* dentro de un rato || *once in a while* de vez en cuando || *the while* mientras tanto, entre tanto; *I gave her a book to read the while* le di un libro para que leyera mientras tanto || *that will do for a while* esto le bastará de momento || *to be worth while* merecer *or* valer la pena; *I will come if it is worth while* vendré si merece la pena; *it is not worth while your going* no merece la pena que vayáis || *what a while you are!* ¡cuánto tardas!
◆ *conj* mientras; *she only saw him twice while he was staying there* le vio sólo dos veces mientras él estaba allí; *never while I live* nunca, mientras yo viva || mientras (que); *she was remained poor, while her friends have made a fortune* ha seguido siendo pobre mientras que sus amigas han ganado una fortuna || aunque (although); *while I admit it is difficult, I don't think it is impossible* aunque reconozco que es difícil no creo que sea imposible.

while [wail] *vt* *to while away* pasar; *she whiled away the hours of waiting by looking at the shops* pasó las horas de espera mirando los escaparates; disipar (cares).

whilom ['wailəm] *adv* antaño, en otro tiempo.
◆ *adj* de antaño, de antes.

whilst [wailst] *conj* ⟶ **while.**

whim [wim] *n* capricho *m*, antojo *m* (fancy) || TECH malacate *m* || — *passing whim* antojo || *to* *take a whim into one's head* antojársele a uno algo.

whimbrel [ˈwimbrəl] *n* zarapito *m* (bird).

whimper [ˈwimpə*] *n* gimoteo *m*, quejido *m* (complaint) || lloriqueo *m* (snivelling) || gañido *m* (of an animal).

whimper [ˈwimpə*] *vi* lloriquear (to snivel) || quejarse, gimotear (to complain) || gañir (a dog).
◆ *vt* decir lloriqueando.

whimpering [-riŋ] *adj* quejica.
◆ *n* gimoteo *m*, quejido *m* (complaint) || lloriqueo *m* (snivelling) || gañido *m* (of an animal).

whimsical [ˈwimzikəl] *adj* caprichoso, sa; antojadizo, za (person) || extraño, ña; peregrino, na (idea).

whimsicality [ˌwimziˈkæliti] *n* carácter *m* caprichoso (character) || rareza *f*, extravagancia *f* (oddity) || capricho *m* (caprice) || fantasía *f* (fancy).

whimsy [ˈwimzi] *n* capricho *m*, antojo *m* (whim) || extravagancia *f*, rareza *f* (oddity).

whin [win] *n* BOT tojo *m*, aulaga *f*.

whine [wain] *n* quejido *m*, gemido *m* (of pain) || queja *f* (complaint) || lloriqueo *m* (snivelling) || gañido *m* (of an animal) || zumbido *m* (of an engine, of a bullet).

whine [wain] *vt* decir lloriqueando.
◆ *vi* gimotear, quejarse (person) || lloriquear (child) || gañir (animal) || zumbar (engine, bullet).

whinge [windʒ] *vi* FAM gimotear, quejarse (to whine).

whining [-iŋ] *adj* quejica.
◆ *n* gimoteo *m*, quejidos *m pl*.

whinny [ˈwini] *n* relincho *m* (of a horse).

whinny [ˈwini] *vi* relinchar.

whiny [ˈwaini] *adj* llorón, ona; quejica.

whip [wip] *n* látigo *m* (long lash) || azote *m* (any beating instrument) || fusta *f* (for horses) || latigazo *m*, azote *m* (blow) || zumbel *m* (for a spinning top) || aspa *f* (of a windmill) || TECH aparejo *m* (hoisting apparatus) || montero *m* (in hunting party) || CULIN batidor *m* || cochero *m* (coachman) || miembro *m* de un partido político encargado de hacer observar las consignas de éste a los demás miembros (Member of Parliament) || llamada *f* a los miembros del partido para que presencien un debate (call) || — *the government have taken off the whips* el gobierno deja a los miembros del partido la libertad de votar como quieran | *three-line whip* llamada para que los diputados voten en un debate particularmente importante.

whip [wip] *vt* azotar, dar latigazos a; *to whip a horse* azotar un caballo || azotar (a child) || azotar, golpear; *the rain whipped our faces* la lluvia nos azotaba la cara || hacer bailar; *to whip a top* hacer bailar un trompo || FIG fustigar || MAR elevar con el aparejo (to hoist) || rebatir (in sewing) || CULIN batir (cream, eggs); *whipped cream* crema batida || FAM dar una paliza a (to defeat heavily) | mangar, birlar (to steal).
◆ *vi* azotar || restallar; *the flag whipped in the wind* la bandera restallaba en el viento || lanzarse (to move rapidly).
◆ *phr v* ***to whip away*** arrebatar; *he whipped the knife away from him* le arrebató el cuchillo | irse rápidamente (to leave) || ***to whip in*** reunir (hunting dogs, members of a political party) || ***to whip off*** quitar rápidamente (to remove) | quitarse rápidamente (clothes) | irse rápidamente (to leave) || ***to whip on*** dar latigazos para que avance (a horse) | ponerse rápidamente (clothes) || ***to whip out*** sacar de repente; *he whipped out a gun* de repente sacó una pistola | salir rápidamente (to go out) || ***to whip round*** volverse de repente (to turn around) | hacer una colecta (to ask for money) || ***to whip up*** avivar; *to whip up enthusiasm* avivar el entusiasmo | instar a que participen en una votación (Members of Parliament) | coger rápidamente (to take).

whipcord [-kɔːd] *n* tralla *f*, cuerda *f* de látigo (cord) || pana *f* (fabric).

whip hand [-ˈhænd] *n* *to have the whip hand of* o *over s.o.* tenerle dominado a alguien.

whiplash [-læʃ] *n* tralla *f* (whipcord) || latigazo *m* (blow).

whiplash injury [-læʃˌindʒəri] *n* desnucamiento *m*.

whipper-in [-ərˈin] *n* montero *m* (in hunting).
— OBSERV El plural es *whippers-in*.

whippersnapper [-əˌsnæpə*] *n* FAM chiquilicuatro *m*, mequetrefe *m*.

whippet [ˈwipit] *n* lebrel *m* (dog).

whipping [ˈwipiŋ] *n* azotamiento *m* (beating) || paliza *f* (flogging) || flagelación *f* (flagellation) || rebatido *m* (stitching) || CULIN batido *m* || FIG paliza *f*.

whipping boy [-bɔi] *n* FIG cabeza *f* de turco, víctima *f* propiciatoria, chivo *m* expiatorio (scapegoat) || (ant) niño *m* criado con un príncipe y que recibe los azotes en su lugar.

whipping top [-tɔp] *n* trompo *m*, peonza *f*.

whippoorwill [ˈwippuəˌwil] *n* chotacabras *m inv* (bird).

whippy [ˈwipi] *adj* elástico, ca; flexible.

whip-round [ˈwipraund] *n* colecta *f*; *to have a whip-round for* hacer una colecta por.

whipsaw [ˈwipsɔː] *n* sierra *f* abrazadera || US FIG arma *f* de dos filos.

whipsaw [ˈwipsɔː] *vt* aserrar || FIG & FAM pelar (in gambling) | hacer perder (in business).

whipstitch [ˈwipstitʃ] *n* sobrehilo *m*.

whip top [ˈwiptɔp] *n* trompo *m*, peonza *f* (toy).

whir [wəː*] *n/vi* ⟶ **whirr.**

whirl [wəːl] *n* giro *m*, rotación *f* (circular movement) || remolino *m*, torbellino *m* (of dust, of water) || FIG torbellino *m*, serie *f*; *a whirl of parties* un torbellino de fiestas || — FIG *my head is in a whirl* me está dando vueltas la cabeza || US FAM *to give sth. a whirl* probar algo.

whirl [wəːl] *vt* hacer girar, dar vueltas a (to cause to rotate) || hacer revolotear; *the wind whirled the dead leaves* el viento hacía revolotear las hojas muertas || lanzar con honda (to hurl) || *to whirl along* llevar a toda velocidad.
◆ *vi* girar, dar vueltas (to rotate rapidly); *the dancers whirled round the room* los bailarines daban vueltas por la sala || arremolinarse; *the leaves whirled round the garden* las hojas se arremolinaban por el jardín || pasar rápidamente; *the train whirled through the station* el tren pasó rápidamente por la estación || pasar; *the thoughts that whirl through my head* las ideas que me pasan por la cabeza || — FIG *my head was whirling down* me daba vueltas la cabeza || *to come whirling down* bajar dando vueltas || *to whirl along* pasar a toda velocidad, pasar como un rayo || *to whirl past sth.* pasar rápidamente delante de algo.

whirlbone [-bəun] *n* ANAT rótula *f*.

whirligig [-igig] *n* molinete *m* (toy) || tiovivo *m*, caballitos *m pl* (merry-go-round) || ZOOL girino *m* (beetle) || FIG torbellino *m* | cambios *m pl*, vaivenes *m pl*; *the whirligig of fortune* los cambios de la suerte.

whirlpool [-puːl] *n* remolino *m* (de agua) (eddy), vorágine *f* (vortex).

whirlwind [-wind] *n* torbellino *m*, remolino *m* (de aire).

whirlybird [-ibəːd] *n* US FAM helicóptero *m*.

whirr; whir [wəː*] *n* zumbido *m* (of engine, etc.) || batir *m*, aleteo *m* (of bird's wings).

whirr; whir [wəː*] *vi* zumbar (engine, etc.) || *the birds whirred past* se oía el ruido de las alas de los pájaros al pasar.

whish [wiʃ] *vi* zumbar, silbar.

whisk [wisk] *n* CULIN batidor *m* [de mano] || cepillo *m* (brush) || escobilla *f* (broom) || plumero *m* (feather duster) || matamoscas *m inv* (flyswatter) || movimiento *m* brusco; *with a whisk of the hand* con un movimiento brusco de la mano || *a whisk of the tail* un coletazo.

whisk [wisk] *vt* CULIN batir (cream, eggs, etc.) || sacudir, mover; *the horse whisked its tail* el caballo sacudió la cola || — *to whisk along* llevarse rápidamente *or* a toda velocidad || *to whisk away, to whisk off* espantar, ahuyentar (flies), cepillar (to brush), quitar (dust), enjugar discretamente (a tear), birlar, llevarse (to steal), llevarse rápidamente (to take away), llevar rápidamente (s.o.); *they whisked him off in a car* le llevaron rápidamente en un coche.
◆ *vi* ir como un rayo || — *to whisk away* o *off* irse a toda velocidad || *to whisk past* pasar a toda velocidad *or* como un rayo.

whisk broom [-brum] *n* US cepillo *m* de la ropa.

whisker [-ə*] *n* pelo *m* del bigote (of a cat, of a rabbit) || MAR arbotante *m* (of bowsprit).
◆ *pl* patillas *f* (sideboards) || pelos *m* de la barba (of a beard) || bigotes *m* (of an animal).

whiskered [-əd] *adj* barbudo, da (bearded) || bigotudo, da (with moustache) || patilludo, da (with sideboards).

whiskey; whisky [-i] *n* whisky *m*; *whisky and soda* whisky con sifón *or* con soda.

whisper [ˈwispə*] *n* cuchicheo *m* (low speech) || FIG susurro *m*, murmullo *m* (of leaves, of water) | rumor *m* (rumour) || — *there is a whisper that* se rumorea que, corre el rumor de que || *there wasn't a whisper of it* no se habló nada de ello en los periódicos || *to talk in a whisper* hablar bajo, hablar en voz baja.

whisper [ˈwispə*] *vt* decir en voz baja; *to whisper a word to s.o.* decir una palabra en voz baja a alguien || hacer correr (a rumour) || — *it is whispered that* corre la voz *or* el rumor de que, se rumorea que || *to whisper sth. in s.o.'s ear* decir algo al oído de alguien, decir algo bajito a alguien.
◆ *vi* cuchichear, hablar en voz baja; *they sat in the corner whispering* estaban sentados en el rincón cuchicheando || hablar al oído (secretly) || FIG susurrar; *the leaves whispered* las hojas susurraban.

whispering [-riŋ] *n* cuchicheo *m* || FIG rumor *m* (rumour) | murmuración *f* (gossip) | susurro *m*, murmullo *m* (of leaves, of water) || — US *whispering campaign* campaña *f* de difamación || ARCH *whispering gallery* galería *f* que tiene eco.

whist [wist] *n* «whist» *m* (card game).
◆ *interj* ¡chitón!

whistle [ˈwisl] *n* pito *m*, silbato *m* (instrument) || silbido *m*, pitido *m* (act, sound, signal) || canto *m* (of a bird) || — *to blow a whistle* tocar el pito, pitar || FAM *to wet one's whistle* echarse un trago al coleto, mojar la canal maestra, mojar el gaznate.

whistle [ˈwisl] *vt* silbar; *to whistle a tune* silbar una melodía; *to whistle a dog* silbar a un perro.
◆ *vi* silbar (with mouth) || pitar (with instrument) || silbar, zumbar (bullet, wind, etc.) || piar (birds) || — *to whistle for* silbar para llamar; *to whistle for a taxi* silbar para llamar un taxi || SP *to whistle for a foul* pitar una falta || *to whistle past* pasar silbando *or* zumbando || FAM *you can whistle for it* puedes esperar sentado.

whistle-stop ['wislstɔp] *n* US apeadero *m* (railway station) | breve parada *f* (on a political tour).

whistling ['wisliŋ] *n* silbido *m*, silbo *m*.

whit [wit] *n* pizca *f*, ápice *m*; *there's not a whit of truth* no hay un ápice de verdad || — *he is every whit as good as you* es tan bueno como tú || *I don't care a whit* me importa un comino.

Whit [wit] *n* Pentecostés *m*.
◆ *adj* de Pentecostés.

white [wait] *adj* blanco, ca; *white wine* vino blanco; *white bread* pan blanco; *the white race* la raza blanca; *white bear* oso blanco || cano, na; blanco, ca (hair) || blanco, ca (light); *white complexion* tez blanca || pálido, da (pale); *white with fear* pálido de miedo || REL blanco, ca (wearing white) || TECH blanco, ca; *white coal* hulla blanca; *white wood* madera blanca; *white gold* oro blanco || FIG blanco, ca (magic) | piadoso, sa (lie) | honrado, da (honest) | puro, ra; inocente (pure) || GEOGR blanco, ca; *White Nile* Nilo Blanco || — FIG *as white as a sheet, as white as a ghost* blanco como el papel || *a white man, woman* un blanco, una blanca || FIG *to bleed s.o. white* chuparle la sangre a alguien, esquilmar a alguien | *to turn white* ponerse blanco, palidecer, ponerse pálido || *white coffee* café con leche || *white lead* blanco *m* de plomo.
◆ *n* blanco *m*, color *m* blanco (colour) || blancura *f* (whiteness) || blanco, ca (person) || blanco *m* (of the eyes, of a target) || clara *f* (of an egg) || ropa *f* blanca (clothes) || — *dressed in white* vestido de blanco || *white sale* quincena blanca || *zinc white* blanco de cinc.
◆ *pl* MED flujo *m sing* blanco, leucorrea *f sing*.

white alloy [-'ælɔi] *n* metal *m* blanco.

white ant [-'ænt] *n* comején *m*, hormiga *f* blanca.

whitebait [-beit] *n* morralla *f* (small fishes).

white beet [-'bi:t] *n* BOT acelga *f*.

white blood cell [-'blʌdsel] *n* glóbulo *m* blanco.

whiteboard [-bɔ:d] *n* pizarra *f* para rotuladores.

white book [-buk] *n* libro *m* blanco.

whitecaps [-kæps] *pl n* MAR cabrillas *f*.

white-collar [-'kɔlə*] *adj* de oficina || *white-collar worker* empleado *m* de oficina, oficinista *m* & *f*.

white corpuscle [-'kɔ:pʌsl] *n* glóbulo *m* blanco.

white Christmas [-'krisməs] *n* Navidades *f pl* blancas.

whited [-id] *adj* blanqueado, da; *whited sepulchre*, US *sepulcher* sepulcro blanqueado.

white damp [-'dæmp] *n* CHEM óxido *m* de carbono.

white elephant [-'elifənt] *n* FIG gasto *m* inútil, despilfarro *m*.

whitefish [-fiʃ] *n* pescado *m* blanco.

white goods [-gudz] *pl n* ropa *f sing* blanca || US electrodomésticos *m pl*.

white-haired [-'hɛəd] *adj* de pelo cano.

Whitehall [-hɔ:l] *n* Whitehall [Gobierno británico].

white-headed [-'hedid] *adj* de pelo cano (with white hair) || de cabeza blanca (animal) || FIG mimado, da; *the white-headed boy* el niño mimado.

white heat [-'hi:t] *n* blanco *m*, rojo *m* blanco; *to bring to white heat* calentar al rojo blanco.

white hellebore [-'helibɔ:*] *n* BOT vedegambre *m*.

white horses [-'hɔ:siz] *pl n* MAR cabrillas *f*.

white-hot [-'hɔt] *adj* calentado al rojo blanco (at white heat) || FIG candente, al rojo vivo; *the situation is white-hot* la situación está candente.

White House [-haus] *n* *the White House* la Casa Blanca.

white lily [-'lili] *n* BOT azucena *f*.

white-livered [-,livəd] *adj* FAM cobarde (cowardly).

white meat [-mi:t] *n* CULIN carne *f* blanca.

whiten [-ən] *vt* blanquear (to make white) || encanecer (hair) || blanquecer (metals).
◆ *vi* blanquear || palidecer, ponerse blanco *or* pálido (face, person).

whitener [-ənə*] *n* blanqueador *m*.

whiteness [-nis] *n* blancura *f* || palidez *f* (paleness) || FIG pureza *f*, inocencia *f*.

whitening [-niŋ] *n* blanqueo *m* (of linen) || enlucido *m*, enjalbegado *m* (of walls) || blanquición *f* (of metals) || blanco *m* de España, albayalde *m* (whiting).

white paper [-'peipə*] *n* libro *m* blanco (government paper).

white slavery [-'sleivəri] *n* trata *f* de blancas.

whitesmith [-smiθ] *n* hojalatero *m* (tinsmith).

white spirit [-'spirit] *n* aguarrás *m*.

whitethorn [-θɔ:n] *n* BOT espino *m* blanco, majuelo *m*.

whitethroat [-θraut] *n* curruca *f* (bird).

whitewash [-wɔʃ] *n* cal *f*, lechada *f* de cal (for walls) || FIG encubrimiento *m* de faltas (concealing of faults) | disculpa *f* (excuse) | rehabilitación *f* (of a bankrupt) || US FAM paliza *f* (total defeat) || *to give a wall a coat of whitewash* encalar *or* enjalbegar *or* blanquear una pared.

whitewash [-wɔʃ] *vt* encalar, enjalbegar, blanquear (walls) || FIG encubrir (faults) | disculpar (s.o.) | rehabilitar (a bankrupt) || US FAM *to whitewash a team* impedir que un equipo marque, dar una paliza a un equipo.

whitewasher [-wɔʃə*] *n* blanqueador *m*, enjalbegador *m*, encalador *m*.

whitewashing [-wɔʃiŋ] *n* encalado *m*, blanqueo *m*, enjalbegado *m* (of walls) || FIG rehabilitación *f*.

white water [-'wɔ:tə*] *n* aguas *f pl* bravas.

whither ['wiðə*] *adv* ¿a dónde?, ¿adónde?; *whither do you go?* ¿adónde vas?; *whither will all this lead?* ¿a dónde nos llevará todo eso? || adonde, a donde.

whiting ['waitiŋ] *n* blanco *m* de España, albayalde *m* (finely powdered chalk) || pescadilla *f* (fish).

whitish ['waitiʃ] *adj* blanquecino, na; blancuzco, ca.

whitlow ['witləu] *n* MED panadizo *m*.

witlowwort [-wə:t] *n* BOT nevadilla *f*.

Whitmonday ['wit'mʌndi] *n* Lunes *m* de Pentecostés.

Whitsun ['witsn] *n* Pentecostés *m*.
◆ *adj* de Pentecostés.

Whitsunday ['wit'sʌndi] *n* Domingo *m* de Pentecostés.

Whitsuntide ['witsntaid] *n* Pentecostés *m*.

whittle ['witl] *n* cuchillo *m* grande.

whittle ['witl] *vt* cortar (to cut) || tallar [con cuchillo] (to carve) || FIG *to whittle away* o *down* reducir poco a poco, cercenar; *they are trying to whittle down our salaries* están intentando reducir poco a poco nuestros salarios.
◆ *vi* *to whittle at* cortar (to cut), tallar [con cuchillo] (to carve).

whittling ['witliŋ] *n* astilla *f* || FIG *whittling down* reducción progresiva.

whiz; whizz [wiz] *n* zumbido *m* (buzzing sound) || silbido *m* (hissing sound) || US FAM número *m* uno, as *m*; *he is a whizz at football* es el número uno en fútbol | trato *m* cerrado (deal).

whiz; whizz [wiz] *vi* silbar (to whistle) || zumbar (to hum) || — *to whizz along* ir a gran velocidad (fast) || *to whizz past* pasar silbando (bullet), pasar como un rayo (car).

whizz kid [-kid] *n* promesa *f*, joven *m* prometedor, joven *f* prometedora (promising person).

who [hu:] *interr pron* quién, quiénes; *who is that woman?* ¿quién es esa mujer?; *who are they?* ¿quiénes son?; *I didn't see who they were* me dijo quiénes eran; *he told me who they were* no vi quiénes eran || quién, quiénes (see OBSERV); *who do you think I got a letter from?* ¿de quién te crees que he recibido una carta?; *who did you give it to?* ¿a quién se lo diste? || — *Mrs who?* ¿la señora qué? || *tell me who's who* dígame quiénes son, dígame cuáles son los nombres de las personas aquí presentes || *who does he think he is?* ¿quién se cree que es? || *who on earth is it?* ¿quién diablos *or* quién demonios puede ser? || *who should I meet but Anthony?* ¿a quién te crees que me encontré? A Antonio || *Who's Who* quién es quién [anuario *m* que contiene los nombres y el historial de las personas más conocidas del mundo] || *you will soon find out who's who* pronto sabrás quién es cada cual.
◆ *rel pron* quien, quienes, el que, la que, los que, las que (the person who); *it was his father who said it* fue su padre quien lo dijo; *it is you who are responsible for it* son ustedes los que son responsables de ello; *who asks receives* quien pide recibe || que; *he likes women who dress well* le gustan las mujeres que visten bien || que, el cual, la cual, los cuales, las cuales; *his grandfather, who was a doctor* su abuelo, que era médico || que, a quien, a quienes (see OBSERV); *he likes the people who he employs* le gustan las personas que emplea; *the man who I saw* el hombre a quien vi || — *as who should say* como quien dice || *disagree who may, I think that* aunque habrá quien no esté de acuerdo, yo creo que || *those who* los que, las que; *those who want to, may leave* los que quieran pueden marcharse.

— OBSERV En muchos casos *who* se emplea en lugar de *whom* en la lengua hablada aunque sea incorrecto desde un punto de vista puramente gramatical. *Whom* es la forma correcta cuando es complemento directo o cuando se emplea después de una preposición.

whoa [wəu] *interj* ¡so!

whodunit ['hu:'dʌnit] *n* FAM novela *f or* película *f or* obra *f* de teatro policíaca.

whoever [hu:'evə*]; **whomever** [hu:m'evə*]; **whomsoever** [,hu:msəu'evə*]; **whoso** ['hu:səu]; **whosoever** [hu:səu'evə*] *pron* quienquiera que, cualquiera que, el que, la que, quien; *whoever wants it can have it* quienquiera que *or* el que *or* quien lo quiera puede guardarlo || el que, la que, quien; *whoever said that is a liar* el que lo dijo es un mentiroso || quienquiera que; *come out whoever you are!* ¡quienquiera que sea, salga de ahí! || FAM quién diablos; *whoever said that?* ¿quién diablos dijo eso? || *to everybody whoever he may be* a todos sin excepción alguna.

whole [həul] *adj* entero, ra; todo, da; *the whole night long* la noche entera, durante toda la noche; *the whole army* el ejército entero, todo el ejército; *don't swallow it whole* no te lo tragues entero; *I never saw him the whole evening* no le vi en toda la noche || entero, ra; *whole families disappeared* familias enteras desaparecieron; *to eat a whole chicken* comerse un pollo entero || total; *whole length* longitud total || sano, na (healthy) || ileso, sa (not injured) || intacto, ta; sano, na (undamaged); *there is not a plate that is whole* no queda un plato sano ||

íntegro, gra; completo, ta (containing all natural components) || único, ca; *the whole point of all this* la única razón de todo eso || carnal (having both parents in common); *whole sister* hermana carnal || MATH entero; *whole number* número entero || — FAM *a whole lot of* una gran cantidad de, muchísimo, ma || *the whole truth* toda la verdad.
◆ *n* todo *m*; *the parts of a whole* las partes de un todo || conjunto *m*; *the four parts made a pleasing whole* las cuatro partes formaban un conjunto agradable || total *m* (of a bill, etc.); *the whole amounts to* el total asciende a || — *as a whole* en conjunto, en su totalidad; *the play as a whole wasn't bad* la obra en conjunto no estaba mal || *on the whole* en general; *on the whole I agree with you* en general estoy de acuerdo con usted; considerándolo todo; *on the whole I am satisfied* considerándolo todo estoy satisfecho || *the whole of* todo, da; *the whole of the summer* todo el verano; *the whole of his works* todas sus obras; entero, ra; todo, da; *he smoked the whole of the packet* se fumó la cajetilla entera.

wholefood [-fu:d] *n* alimentos *m pl* integrales.
◆ *adj* a base de alimentos integrales (diet) || de comida integral (restaurant).

wholehearted [-ˈhɑ:tid] *adj* sincero, ra; franco, ca (frank) || sincero, ra; completo, ta; incondicional; *wholehearted support* completo apoyo || entusiasta (enthusiastic).

wholeheartedly [-ˈhɑ:tidli] *adv* sinceramente, de todo corazón || completamente, incondicionalmente || con entusiasmo.

wholeheartedness [-ˈhɑ:tidnis] *n* sinceridad *f* || entusiasmo *m*.

whole meal [-mi:l] *adj* integral (bread).

whole milk [-ˈmilk] *n* leche *f* sin desnatar.

wholeness [-nis] *n* integridad *f*.

whole note [-nəut] *n* US MUS semibreve *f*, redonda *f*.

whole number [-nʌmbə*] *n* número *m* entero.

wholesale [-seil] *adj* COMM al por mayor; *wholesale trade* comercio al por mayor || FIG en serie (manufacture) | general, en masa; *a wholesale slaughter* una matanza total || *wholesale dealer* mayorista *m* & *f*, comerciante *m* & *f* al por mayor.
◆ *n* COMM venta *f* al por mayor.
◆ *adv* al por mayor; *to sell sth. wholesale* vender algo al por mayor || FIG en serie (to manufacture) | en masa; *to kill wholesale* matar en masa.

wholesale [-seil] *vi* vender al por mayor (to trade in wholesale goods) || venderse al por mayor (to be sold wholesale).
◆ *vt* vender al por mayor.

wholesaler [-ˌseilə*] *n* comerciante *m* & *f* al por mayor, mayorista *m* & *f*.

wholesome [-səm] *n* sano, na (good for the health); *wholesome food* comida sana || sano, na; saludable (healthy); *a wholesome climate* un clima saludable || FIG saludable (advice, remedy) | sano, na (person, reading).

wholesomeness [-səmnis] *n* lo sano (of food) || lo sano, lo saludable (of climate) || FIG lo sano.

whole wheat [-wi:t] *n* US integral (bread).

who'll [hul] contracción de «who will» y «who shall».

wholly [ˈhəuli] *adv* completamente, totalmente, enteramente (entirely); *I don't wholly agree* no estoy completamente de acuerdo.

whom [hu:m] *interr pron* quién, quiénes, a quién, a quiénes; *from whom did you receive it?* ¿de quién lo recibiste?; *to whom are you speaking?* ¿a quién estás hablando?
◆ *rel pron* que, quien, quienes, a quien, a quienes; *he likes the people whom he employs* le gustan las personas que emplea; *the man whom I saw* el hombre a quien vi; *he wanted to find somebody to whom he might talk* quería encontrar a alguien con quien hablar || — *both of whom* ambos, ambas || *of whom* del cual, de la cual, de los cuales, de las cuales, de quien, de quienes; *the friend of whom I speak* el amigo de quien hablo.
— OBSERV Véase la observación situada al final del artículo «who».

whomever [hu:mˈevə*]; **whomsoever** [ˌhu:msəuˈevə*] *pron* → **whoever.**

whoop [wu:p] *n* grito *m* (cry, shout) || — *not to care a whoop* no importarle lo más mínimo a uno || *whoop!* ¡hurra!

whoop [wu:p] *vt* gritar (to shout) || — US FAM *to whoop it up* armar jaleo (to have a noisy time), pasarlo en grande (to have a gay time) | *to whoop it up for* aplaudir.
◆ *vi* gritar (to shout) || MED toser || US *to whoop for* aplaudir.

whoopee [ˈwuˈpi:ˈwupi] *interj* ¡hurra!, ¡viva!
◆ *n* FAM juerga *f*, parranda *f* (spree) || FAM *to make whoopee* pasarlo en grande (to have a gay time), armar jaleo (to have a noisy time).

whooping cough [ˈhu:piŋkɔf] *n* MED tos *f* ferina.

whoopla [ˈhuplɑ:] *n* FAM jarana *f*, jaleo *m*.

whoops [wups] *interj* ¡huy!

whoosh [wu:ʃ] *interj* ¡zas!

whoosh [wu:ʃ] *vi* FAM pasar disparado, da.

whop [wɔp] *n* FAM golpe *m* (blow) || *to fall with a whop* caer como un plomo.

whop [wɔp] *vt* FAM pegar una paliza a.

whopper [-ə*] *n* FAM cosa *f* enorme *or* gigantesca (big thing) | bola *f*, trola *f* (lie).

whopping [-iŋ] *adj* FAM enorme, gigantesco, ca.

whore [hɔ:*] *n* FAM puta *f*, furcia *f*.

whore [hɔ:*] *vi* prostituirse (a woman) || irse de putas (a man).

whorehouse [-haus] *n* US casa *f* de putas.

whoremonger [-ˌmʌŋgə*] *n* putero *m*, putañero *m* (lecher) || chulo *m* de putas (pimp).

whoreson [-sʌn] *n* FAM hijo *m* de puta | chulo *m* de putas (pimp).

whorish [-riʃ] *adj* putañero, ra.

whorl [wə:l] *n* espira *f* (of a shell) || BOT verticilio *m* (of leaves, of flowers, etc.) || espiral *f*.

whortleberry [ˈwə:tlˌberi] *n* BOT arándano *m*.

whose [hu:z] *interr pron* de quién, de quiénes; *whose are these books?* ¿de quiénes son estos libros?; *didn't you know whose shoes they were?* ¿no sabías de quién eran los zapatos?; *whose daughter are you?* ¿es usted hija de quién?; *he told me whose they were* me dijo de quién eran || — *whose book did you take?* ¿qué libro cogiste?, ¿de quién era el libro que cogiste? || *whose is this?* ¿de quién es esto?, ¿a quién pertenece esto?
◆ *rel pron* cuyo, cuya; *the man whose picture is in the paper* el hombre cuya foto está en el periódico; *the house whose windows are broken* la casa cuyas ventanas estaban rotas; *the woman from whose son I received it* la mujer de cuyo hijo lo recibí; *the person for whose sake he did it* la persona en cuyo nombre lo hizo.

whosesoever [ˌhu:zsəuˈevə*]; **whosever** [hu:zˈevə*] *pron* de quienquiera || *whosever it is* sea de quien sea.

whoso [ˈhu:səu]; **whosoever** [ˌhu:səuˈevə*] *pron* → **whoever.**

why [wai] *adv* ¿por qué?; *why didn't you come?* ¿por qué no viniste?; *why bother?* ¿por qué preocuparse? || por qué; *I don't see why you should worry* no veo por qué tienes que preocuparte || — *I can't see any reason why* no veo el porqué || *that is why I did it* por eso lo hice, ésa es la razón por la que lo hice || *why not?* ¿por qué no? || *why so?* ¿y eso por qué?
◆ *n* porqué *m* || *the whys and wherefores* el cómo y el porqué, las causas y los motivos, todos los detalles.
◆ *interj* ¡vaya!, ¡toma! (surprise); *why, it's Peter* ¡toma! ¡es Pedro! || ¡vamos! (protest); *why, you are not afraid, are you?* ¡vamos!, no tendrá usted miedo ¿verdad? || ¡pues bien!, ¡bueno! || *why, it's quite easy!* ¡si es muy fácil!

whydah [ˈwidə] *n* viuda *f* (bird).

whyever [wɑiˈevə*] *adv* ¿por qué diablos?; *whyever did you go there?* ¿por qué diablos fuiste allí?

wick [wik] *n* mecha *f* || FAM *it really gets on my wick* me saca de quicio *or* de mis casillas.

wicked [ˈwikid] *adj* malvado, da; malo, la (morally bad, malicious) || perverso, sa (depraved) || muy malo, la (temper) || travieso, sa; pícaro, ra (mischievous); *a wicked grin* una sonrisa traviesa || inicuo, cua; infame, inmundo, da (lie) || resabiado, da (horse) || feroz (animal) || FAM malísimo, ma; espantoso, sa; *a wicked winter* un invierno malísimo | terrible; *a wicked blow* un golpe terrible.
◆ *n* *the wicked* los malos.

wickedly [-li] *adv* muy mal; *to treat s.o. wickedly* tratar muy mal a alguien || con mala intención; *to say sth. wickedly* decir algo con mala intención || muy, terriblemente; *wickedly expensive* terriblemente caro || inicuamente; *to lie wickedly* mentir inicuamente.

wickedness [-nis] *n* maldad *f* || perversidad *f* (depravity) || resabio *m* (of a horse).

wicker [ˈwikə*] *n* mimbre *m* || artículos *m pl* de mimbre.
◆ *adj* de mimbre.

wickerwork [-wə:k] *n* artículos *m pl* de mimbre (objects) || cestería *f* (craft) || rejilla *f* (of a chair).

wicket [ˈwikit] *n* portillo *m* (small door) || ventanilla *f* (small window at a ticket office) || compuerta *f* pequeña (to regulate water flow) || SP puerta *f*, portería *f* (set of stumps) | terreno *m*, campo *m*; *a fast wicket* un campo rápido || US SP aro *m* (hoop in croquet) || FIG *to be on a sticky wicket* estar en un apuro.

wicketkeeper [-ˌki:pə*] *n* SP guardameta *m* (in cricket).

wide [waid] *adj* ancho, cha; *a wide river* un río ancho; *a wide road* una carretera ancha; *wide sleeves* mangas anchas; *wide trousers* pantalón ancho; *the wide world* el ancho mundo || de ancho; *five feet wide* de cinco pies de ancho || muy abierto, ta (eyes, mouth) || extenso, sa; vasto, ta; *a wide plain* una llanura extensa || amplio, plia; *a wide range of frequencies* una amplia gama de frecuencias || extenso, sa; *wide publicity* publicidad extensa || grande; *wide intervals* grandes intervalos; *wide experience, culture, influence* gran experiencia, cultura, influencia || grande, considerable; *the difference between us is wide* la diferencia entre nosotros es grande || amplio, plia; grande (knowledge) || SP fuera del alcance (ball) || — *how wide is the room?* ¿qué anchura tiene la habitación?, ¿cuál es el ancho de la habitación? || *in a wider sense* en un sentido más amplio || *to grow wider* ensancharse || *to have wide interests in life* tener muchos intereses en la vida || *to make wider* ensanchar || FIG *wide boy* chico muy vivo *or* muy despabilado || *wide of* lejos de; *wide of the truth* lejos de la verdad || *wide of the mark* lejos de la verdad *or* de la realidad

(false), lejos del blanco (off target) || *wide skirt* falda *f* de mucho vuelo || *wide views* amplitud *f* de miras, miras amplias.
◆ *adv* lejos || de par en par; *to open the window wide* abrir la ventana de par en par || mucho; *open your mouth wide* abre mucho la boca || — *far and wide* por todas partes; *to search far and wide* buscar por todas partes || *to be wide open* estar muy abierto (eyes, mouth), estar abierto de par en par (door, window) || *to fling the door open wide* abrir la puerta de par en par || *to go wide* no hacer efecto (a criticism, a remark), no dar en el blanco (blow) || FIG *to leave o.s. wide open to criticism* estar expuesto a muchas críticas || *to shoot wide* errar el tiro || *wide apart* muy separados.
◆ *n* SP bala *f* que pasa fuera del alcance del bateador (cricket).

wide-angle [-,æŋgl] *adj* PHOT gran angular; *wide-angle lens* objetivo gran angular.

wide-awake [-ə'weik] *adj* completamente despierto, ta || FIG despabilado, da.

wide-eyed [-'aid] *adj* con los ojos muy abiertos.

widely [-li] *adv* muy; *widely read newspaper* periódico muy leído || mucho; *he has travelled widely* ha viajado mucho || *it is widely known that* se sabe perfectamente que, todos saben que, por todas partes se sabe que.

widemouthed [-'mauðd] *adj* bocón, ona || boquiabierto, ta (agape).

widen [-ən] *vt* ensanchar || FIG extender, ampliar.
◆ *vi* ensancharse || FIG extenderse (influence) | aumentar (to increase).

wideness [-nis] *n* anchura *f*, ancho *m* (width) || extensión *f*.

widening [-əniŋ] *n* ensanchamiento *m* || FIG extensión *f*.

wide-open [-'əupən] *adj* abierto de par en par (open wide) || US muy tolerante, muy liberal (city).

wide-ranging [-'reindʒiŋ] *adj* de gran amplitud, amplio, plia.

widespread [-spred] *adj* extendido, da (stretched out) || general; *hunger is widespread* el hambre es general; *widespread fear* miedo general || muy difundido, da; *the rumour is widespread* el rumor está muy difundido.

widgeon ['widʒən] *n* ZOOL pato *m* silbador.

widow ['widəu] *n* viuda *f* || — *football widow* mujer *f* que se queda muchas veces sola porque su marido es muy aficionado al fútbol || *widow Smith* la viuda de Smith.

widow ['widəu] *vt* dejar viuda || *to be widowed* enviudar, quedar viuda.

widow bird [-bə:d] *n* ZOOL viuda *f*.

widowed [-d] *adj* viudo, da.

widower [-ə*] *n* viudo *m*.

widowhood [-hud] *n* viudez *f*.

width [widθ] *n* anchura *f*, ancho *m* (of an object) || distancia *f*; *the width between the window and the bed* la distancia entre la ventana y la cama || envergadura *f* (of wings) || FIG amplitud *f*; *width of views* amplitud de ideas || — *double width material* tela *f* de doble ancho || *two metres in width* dos metros de ancho.

widthways [-weiz] *adv* de lado, de costado (sideways) || de lado a lado (from side to side).

wield [wi:ld] *vt* manejar (tool) || blandir, esgrimir (weapon) || ejercer (control, influence, etc.); *to wield authority* ejercer la autoridad || empuñar (a scepter).

wiener ['wi:nə*] *n* US FAM salchicha *f* de Francfort.

wiener schnitzel [-ʃnitsəl] *n* CULIN escalope *m* de ternera, escalope *m* vienés.

wife [waif] *n* mujer *f*, esposa *f* || — *the Mery Wives of Windsor* Las alegres comadres de Windsor (Shakespeare's play) || *to take a wife* casarse || *to take s.o. to wife* casarse con alguien.
— OBSERV El plural de *wife* es *wives*.
— OBSERV When the word *wife* follows a noun indicating profession: *butcher's wife, ambassador's wife,* this is usually rendered in Spanish by the feminine form of the noun: *la carnicera, la embajadora.*

wifehood [-hud] *n* estado *m* de casada.

wifeless [-lis] *adj* sin mujer || viudo (widowed) || soltero *m* (unmarried).

wifely [-li] *adj* de mujer casada.

wig [wig] *n* peluca *f*.

wig [wig] *vt* poner peluca a || FAM dar un jabón, echar un rapapolvo *or* una bronca (to scold).

wigeon ['widʒən] *n* ZOOL pato *m* silbador.

wigged [wigd] *adj* que lleva peluca, con peluca.

wigging ['wigiŋ] *n* FAM rapapolvo *m*, bronca *f*, jabón *m*; *to give s.o. a wigging* echar un rapapolvo *or* una bronca a alguien, dar un jabón a alguien.

wiggle ['wigl] *n* meneo *m* || contoneo *m* (in walking).

wiggle ['wigl] *vt* menear.
◆ *vi* menearse || contonearse (in walking).

wight [wait] *n* individuo *m* || *sorry wight* pobre hombre *m*.

wigwag ['wigwæg] *vt/vi* comunicar por señales (a message).

wigwam ['wigwæm] *n* «wigwam» *m*, tienda *f* india.

wild [waild] *adj* silvestre (plant); *wild flowers* flores silvestres || salvaje (animal, person); *the pheasants are rather wild* los faisanes son bastante salvajes; *wild tribes* tribus salvajes || bravo, va (bull) || inculto, ta; no cultivado, da (field) || salvaje (country) || extraño, ña (gaze) || de loco, extraviado, da (eyes) || loco, ca; *wild laughter* risa loca || frenético, ca; desenfrenado, da; *a wild dance* un baile frenético || violento, ta (character); *a wild temperament* un temperamento violento || alocado, da; desordenado, da (conduct) || desordenado, da; *to lead a wild life* llevar una vida desordenada || disoluto, ta (dissolute) || de tormenta, tormentoso, sa; borrascoso, sa (weather) || enfurecido, da (sea) || impetuoso, sa (torrent) || furioso, sa; violento, ta (wind) || agitado, da; alborotado, da; *to live in wild times* vivir en una época agitada || revuelto, ta (hair) || frenético, ca; *wild applause* aplausos frenéticos || delirante; *wild enthusiasm* entusiasmo delirante || insensato, ta (rash, foolish); *a wild project* un proyecto insensato || absurdo, da; extravagante (rumour) || loco, ca; extravagante (ideas) || estrafalario, ria; extravagante (clothes) || espantoso, sa (disorder) || FAM hecho una fiera, furioso, sa (very cross); *to get wild* ponerse furioso || al azar (shot) || — *to be beyond one's wildest dreams* estar más allá de lo que uno pueda soñar || *to be wild about sth.* estar loco por algo || *to be wild to do sth.* estar loco por hacer algo || *to be wild with anger* estar furioso, estar hecho una fiera || *to be wild with joy* estar loco de alegría || *to be wild with s.o.* ponerse hecho una fiera con alguien || *to drive wild* volver loco, sacar de sus casillas || *to have a wild time* pasarlo en grande || *to let the children run wild* dejar que los niños hagan lo que les da la gana || *to make a wild guess* adivinar al azar || *to make a wild rash at* precipitarse como locos hacia || *to run o to grow wild* crecer en estado salvaje (plants), vivir como un salvaje (child) || *to run wild* desbocarse (horse) || *wild beast* fiera *f*, animal *m* salvaje || FIG *wild horses wouldn't draw o wouldn't drag it out of him* no se puede sacárselo ni con tenazas, no lo diría por todo el oro del mundo | *wild man* extremista *m* || *Wild West* Oeste *m* (western states of the United States).
◆ *n* naturaleza *f*; *the call of the wild* la llamada de la naturaleza.
◆ *pl* desierto *m sing* (desert) || regiones *f* salvajes *or* inexploradas; *the wilds of Africa* las regiones salvajes de África || regiones *f* incultas (uncultivated regions).
◆ *adv* violentamente || sin cultivo.

wild and wooly [-ənd'wuli] *adj* tosco, ca.

wild artichoke [-'ɑ:titʃəuk] *n* BOT alcaucí *m*, alcaucil *m*.

wildcat [-kæt] *n* ZOOL gato *m* montés || TECH sondeo *m* de exploración (oil well) || FIG fiera *f* (person).
◆ *adj* arriesgado, da; descabellado, da (risky); *wildcat scheme* proyecto arriesgado || *wildcat strike* huelga salvaje.

wildebeest ['wildi,bi:st] *n* ZOOL ñu *m*.

wilderness ['wildənis] *n* desierto *m* (desert) || soledad *f* (lonely place) || parte *f* dejada sin cultivar (of a garden) || FIG infinidad *f* (large mass) || FIG *to preach in the wilderness* predicar en el desierto.

wildfire ['waildfaiə*] *n* fuego *m* griego || FIG *to spread like wildfire* propagarse como un reguero de pólvora.

wildfowl ['waildfaul] *n* aves *f pl* de caza *or* salvajes.

wild goat ['waild'gəut] *n* cabra *f* montés.

wild goose ['waild'gu:s] *n* ZOOL ganso *m* salvaje.

wild-goose chase [-tʃeis] *n* búsqueda *f* inútil.

wilding ['waildiŋ] *n* BOT planta *f* silvestre (plant) | fruta *f* de una planta silvestre (fruit) || ZOOL animal *m* salvaje.

wild land ['waild'lænd] *n* yermo *m*, páramo *m*.

wildlife ['waildlaif] *n* fauna *f* (animals).

wildly ['waildli] *adv* de manera extravagante (to speak, to write) || desordenadamente (to live) || intensamente, sin reflexionar (to act) || sin disciplina (to behave) || violentamente, furiosamente (to blow) || frenéticamente; *to dance wildly* bailar frenéticamente || locamente; *to be wildly in love with* estar locamente enamorado de || en estado salvaje (to grow) || al azar (to shoot, to guess) || — *to be wildly happy* estar loco de alegría || *to look wildly* mirar con los ojos desorbitados || *to rush wildly* correr como un loco.

wildness ['waildnis] *n* estado *m* salvaje (of a country, of an animal) || estado *m* silvestre (of a plant) || furor *m*, furia *f* (of the wind) || lo salvaje, ferocidad *f*, fiereza *f* (ferocity) || desenfreno *m* (lack of moderation) || extravíos *m pl* (of behaviour) || locura *f* (madness) || insensatez *f* (foolishness) || extravagancia *f* (of ideas) || frenesí *m* (frenzy) || *the wildness of the applause* los aplausos frenéticos.

wile [wail] *n* artimaña *f*, ardid *m*, astucia *f*.

wile [wail] *vt* seducir, atraer || *to wile away the hours reading* pasarse las horas leyendo.

wilful; US **willful** [wilful] *adj* deliberado, da; intencionado, da (intentional) || JUR voluntario, ria; premeditado, da || obstinado, da; terco, ca (obstinate) || voluntarioso, sa (headstrong).

wilfully; US **willfully** [-i] *adv* intencionadamente, a propósito, deliberadamente (deliberately) || JUR voluntariamente, con premeditación || con obstinación (obstinately) || voluntariosamente.

wilfulness; US **willfulness** [-nis] *n* intención *f* || JUR premeditación *f* || obstinación *f*, terquedad *f* (obstinacy).

wiliness [wailinis] *n* astucia *f* (cunning, artfulness).

will [wil] *n* voluntad *f*; *to have a strong will* tener mucha voluntad; *the will to win* la voluntad de ganar; *ill will* mala voluntad; *will of iron, iron will* voluntad de hierro; *divine will* voluntad divina ‖ JUR testamento *m*; *to make one's will* hacer testamento ‖ — *against one's will* contra su voluntad, de mal grado ‖ *at will* a voluntad ‖ MIL *fire at will* fuego *m* a discreción ‖ *free will* libre albedrío *m* ‖ *he has a will of his own* sabe lo que quiere ‖ *it is his will that* quiere que ‖ REL *last will and testament* última voluntad ‖ *of one's own free will* por su propia voluntad ‖ REL *thy will be done* hágase tu voluntad ‖ *to bear s.o. ill will* tenerle manía a uno ‖ *to have one's will* salirse con la suya ‖ *to take the will for the deed* darse por contento con la intención ‖ (ant); *what is your will?* ¿cuál es su voluntad?, ¿qué desea? ‖ *where there's a will there's a way* querer es poder ‖ *will to power* ansias *f pl* de poder ‖ *with a will* de buena gana (willingly), con entusiasmo, con ilusión (enthusiastically); *to work with a will* trabajar con entusiasmo.

will [wil] *vt* JUR legar (to bequeath) ‖ disponer, ordenar, querer; *fate wills that is should be so* el destino dispone que sea así ‖ desear, querer; *the separation was willed, not forced* la separación era deseada, no forzada; *if you will* si quiere ‖ conseguir a fuerza de voluntad (to achieve by force of will); *when I will to move my arm* cuando consigo mover el brazo a fuerza de voluntad ‖ sugestionar (in hypnotism) ‖ *to will o.s. to* obligarse a.

will [wil] *v aux* se emplea para formar el futuro de indicativo; *tomorrow will be Monday* mañana será lunes; *you will do it!* ¡lo harás! ‖ se usa para expresar la voluntad o la intención; *we would have come, if you had invited us earlier* hubiéramos venido si nos hubiesen invitado más pronto ‖ ir a (immediate future); *I will explain the problem to you* le voy a explicar el problema ‖ querer (determination, consent, wish); *I will speak to her, whether she agrees or not* quiero hablarle que le guste o no; *I will not have it done no* quiero que se haga; *let him do what he will* déjele que haga lo que quiera; *I would have it understood that* quisiera que quedase bien sentado que ‖ gustar, querer; *where would you be?* ¿dónde le gustaría estar? ‖ poder (possibility); *this car will do 150* este coche puede alcanzar 150; *the hall will seat five hundred people* la sala puede contener quinientas personas ‖ soler, acostumbrar (habit); *she will sit there hour after hour* suele sentarse allí horas y horas; *she would go for a walk every morning* acostumbraba dar un paseo todas las mañanas ‖ empeñarse en, persistir en (obstinacy); *he will smoke although he knows it's bad for him* se empeña en fumar aunque sabe que le sienta mal ‖ deber (obligation); *the orders read: you will proceed at once to the next town* la orden dice: debe usted seguir inmediatamente hasta el próximo pueblo ‖ expresa la idea de probabilidad; *this battery will last another month yet* esta batería durará todavía un mes; *he will have arrived by now* habrá llegado ya, debe de haber llegado ya ‖ — *accidents will happen* siempre pueden ocurrir accidentes ‖ *boys will be boys* son cosas de chicos ‖ *he would never do that!* ¡es incapaz de hacer una cosa igual! ‖ *I will* sí quiero (marriage service) ‖ *just wait a moment, will you?* ¿quiere esperar un momento? ‖ *say what you will* diga lo que diga ‖ *sometimes he will talk, sometimes he won't* a veces habla, otras veces no dice nada ‖ *the door will not open* no se puede abrir la puerta ‖ *this street will take you there* esta calle le llevará allí ‖ *try as you will you won't open it* por mucho que lo intentes no lo abrirás ‖ *try as you would you couldn't open it* por mucho que lo hayas intentado no pudiste abrirlo ‖ *will you do it? I will* ¿lo harás? sí ‖ *would, would that, would to God that!* ¡ojalá!; *would I were rich!* ¡ojalá fuera rico!; *would that he were here!* ¡ojalá estuviera aquí! ‖ *you'll be there, won't you?* estarás allí, ¿verdad? ‖ *you won't be there, will you?* no estarás allí, ¿verdad?.

— OBSERV Este verbo es defectivo. No se emplea más que en presente de indicativo: ***will***, en pretérito y en potencial: ***would***.

— OBSERV El verbo auxiliar *will* puede contraerse cuando le antecede un pronombre personal: *I'll, you'll, he'll, we'll, they'll*. Si va seguido por una negación *not* puede formar con ella la palabra *won't*: *he won't come, won't you come?*

— OBSERV En una oración introducida por la conjunción *if* el verbo, que está en futuro en inglés, tiene que ponerse en presente en español: *if you will give me a gun, I will shoot* si me das una pistola tiraré.

Will [wil] *pr n* Guillermo *m* (diminutivo de *William*).

willed [-d] *adj* de voluntad, que tiene voluntad ‖ dispuesto, ta; decidido, da ‖ *weak-willed* que tiene poca voluntad.

willet [-it] *n* US chocha *f* (bird).

willful [-ful] *adj* US ⟶ **wilful.**

willfully [-fuli] *adv* US ⟶ **wilfully.**

willfulness [-fulnis] *n* US ⟶ **wilfulness.**

William [wiljəm] *pr n* Guillermo *m*; *William the Conqueror* Guillermo el Conquistador.

willies [wiliz] *pl n* FAM *he got the willies* se llevó un susto (he got a fright), le entró miedo (he go scared) | *it gives me the willies* me pone los pelos de punta.

willing [wiliŋ] *adj* de buena voluntad, que tiene buena voluntad (good-natured) ‖ complaciente, servicial (obliging) ‖ dispuesto, ta (ready); *he's quite willing to pay the price I asked* está completamente dispuesto a pagar el precio que he pedido ‖ espontáneo, a; hecho de buena gana (done voluntarily) ‖ — *God willing* si Dios quiere ‖ *I am quite willing to come with you* le acompaño con mucho gusto, le acompaño muy gustoso ‖ *I am willing that you should come, I am willing for you to come* consiento en que venga, le permito que venga ‖ *willing or not* de grado o por fuerza, que quiera que no quiera, quiera o no quiera.

willingly [-li] *adv* de buena gana; *to do sth. willingly* hacer algo de buena gana ‖ gustosamente, con (mucho) gusto (gladly); *to accept willingly* aceptar con gusto.

willingness [-nis] *n* buena voluntad *f* (good nature) ‖ consentimiento *m* (consent) ‖ *to declare one's willingness to do sth.* consentir en hacer algo.

will-o'-the-wisp [wiləðəwisp] *n* fuego *m* fatuo ‖ FIG quimera *f*.

willow [wiləu] *n* BOT sauce *m* ‖ TECH diablo *m* (machine for cleaning raw wool) ‖ SP bate *m* (in cricket) ‖ BOT *weeping willow* sauce llorón.

willow [wiləu] *vt* TECH tratar (la lana) con un diablo.

willow grove [-grəuv] *n* BOT salceda *f*, saucedal *m*.

willow pattern [-,pætən] *n* dibujos *m pl* de aspecto chinesco que representan sauces, ríos, pagodas, etc. [para la cerámica].

willowy [-i] *adj* esbelto, ta (slender) ‖ poblado de sauces (abounding in willows).

willpower [wil,pauə*] *n* fuerza *f* de voluntad, voluntad *f*; *she is very clever, but she lacks willpower* es muy inteligente pero le falta voluntad.

willy [wili] *n* FAM pito *m* (penis).

willy-nilly [wili'nili] *adv* de grado o por fuerza, quiera o no quiera.

wilt [wilt] *v aux* (ant) ⟶ **will.**

wilt [wilt] *vt* marchitar.

◆ *vi* marchitarse; *the plants have wilted in the sun* las plantas se han marchitado con el sol ‖ FIG languidecer, debilitarse (to lose strength) | desanimarse (to lose courage).

wily [waili] *adj* astuto, ta; taimado, da.

wimble [wimpl] *adj* TECH berbiquí *m* (brace) | barrena *f* de mano (gimlet) | taladro *m* (in mining).

wimple [wimbl] *adj* TECH griñón *m* (headdress).

wimp [wimp] *n* FAM canijo *m*, alfeñique *m*.

win [win] *n* victoria *f* (victory) ‖ ganancia *f* (amount won) ‖ *to have a win* ganar; *he had a win on the pools* ganó en las quinielas; *our team has had four wins this summer* nuestro equipo ha ganado cuatro veces este verano.

win* [win] *vt* ganar; *to win a fight, a case, a bet, a race* ganar un combate, un pleito, una apuesta, una carrera; *to win territory from the enemy* ganar tierras al enemigo; *to win one pound from s.o. at cards* ganarle una libra a uno jugando a las cartas ‖ ganar, llevarse (a prize); *he has won the first prize* se ha llevado el primer premio *or* el premio gordo ‖ granjearse, ganarse, captarse; *to win s.o.'s friendship* granjearse la amistad de alguien ‖ captar, ganarse, granjearse (s.o.'s confidence) ‖ ganarse; *to win friends* ganarse amigos ‖ ganar, hacerse; *to win a reputation* hacerse una reputación ‖ conseguir, lograr, obtener; *to win a victory* conseguir una victoria; *to win people's support* conseguir el apoyo de la gente ‖ hacer ganar, valer; *his picture won him the prize* su cuadro le valió el premio ‖ conquistar; *to win s.o.'s heart* conquistar el corazón de alguien ‖ ganar, alcanzar (to reach); *to win the summit* alcanzar la cumbre; *to win the shore* alcanzar la orilla ‖ MIN extraer, sacar (to extract) ‖ — FIG *slow and steady wins the race* con paciencia se gana el cielo ‖ *to win glory* cosechar laureles ‖ *to win one's bread* ganarse el pan ‖ *to win one's way to* conseguir llegar a ‖ *to win s.o.'s love* enamorar a alguien ‖ *to win s.o. to do sth.* conseguir que alguien haga algo ‖ *to win the favour of* ganarse el favor de ‖ *to win the field* ser dueño y señor del terreno ‖ *to win victory* ser victorioso, triunfar.

◆ *vi* ganar; *to win by a length* ganar por un largo ‖ *to win free* liberarse.

◆ *phr v* ***to win at*** ganar en ‖ ***to win away*** separar, apartar ‖ ***to win back*** reconquistar, volver a conquistar (territory) | recuperar (money, etc.) ‖ ***to win out*** ganar, salir victorioso, triunfar ‖ ***to win over*** o ***round*** ganarse, poner de su lado *or* de su parte; *to win round the audience* ganarse el auditorio | conseguir, obtener (supporters) | convencer (to convince); *to let o.s. be won over* dejase convencer | *to win s.o. over to a cause* conseguir que alguien se interese por una causa ‖ ***to win through*** superar los obstáculos, conseguir triunfar ‖ FAM *you can't win* tienes todas las de perder.

— OBSERV Pret y pp ***won***.

wince [wins] *n* mueca *f* de dolor (twisted expression of the face caused by pain).

wince [wins] *vt* hacer una mueca de dolor (with pain) ‖ poner mala cara (with disgust) ‖ *without wincing* sin pestañear.

winch [wintʃ] *n* torno *m* (for raising loads) ‖ manivela *f* (crank) ‖ carrete *m* (in fishing) ‖ MAR chigre *m*, maquinilla *f*.

Winchester [-istə*] *n* Winchester *m* (rifle).

wind [waind] *n* vuelta *f* (turn, bend).

wind* [waind] *vt* devanar; *to wind cotton* devanar algodón ‖ enrollar; *to wind sth. on a reel* enrollar algo en un carrete; *to wind a bandage* *round s.o.'s arm* enrollar una venda en el brazo de alguien || envolver; *to wind s.o. in a sheet* envolver algo en una sábana; *to wind sth. with wire* envolver algo con alambre || curvar, torcer (to bend) || dar cuerda a; *to wind a watch* dar cuerda a un reloj || TECH extraer, sacar (to extract) | subir con el torno (to hoist) || — *the stream winds its way through the country* el arroyo serpentea por el campo || *to wind itself* enroscarse, enrollarse (a snake) || *to wind one's arms round s.o.* rodear a alguien con los brazos, abrazar a alguien || FAM *to wind s.o. round one's little finger* manejar a alguien a su antojo || *to wind sth. into a ball* hacer un ovillo con algo.

◆ *vi* enrollarse (rope) || enroscarse, enrollarse (snake) || serpentear (road) || torcerse, encorvarse (to bend) || combarse, alabearse (to warp) || *the path winds round the lake* el camino rodea el lago.

◆ *phr v* ***to wind back*** rebobinar (a tape) || ***to wind down*** bajar (the window of a car) || ***to wind forward*** pasar hacia adelante (a tape) || ***to wind in*** enrollar || ***to wind off*** desenrollar (a rope, etc.) | desenrollarse || ***to wind on*** devanar, enrollar en un carrete || ***to wind up*** concluir, terminar (to conclude); *he wound up his speech with a quotation* concluyó el discurso con una cita; *how does it wind up?* ¿cómo termina? | concluir, cerrar (a debate) | clausurar (a meeting) | COMM liquidar; *to wind up a company* liquidar una compañía | resolver (affairs) | dar cuerda a (a watch, a clockwork mechanism, etc.) | MUS templar (strings) | enrollar (a rope) | levantar con un torno (to hoist) | acabar; *they'll wind up in goal* acabarán en la cárcel | poner nervioso (to make tense) | *to be wound up* estar nerviosísimo.

— OBSERV Pret y pp ***wound***.

wind [wind] *n* viento *m*; *west wind* viento del oeste; *stern wind* viento en popa; *wind ahead* con el viento en proa; *foul wind* viento en contra *or* contrario; *trade winds* vientos alisios; *a gust of wind* una ráfaga de viento; *the wind rises* se levanta el viento || aire *m*; *it made a wind rises* se levanta el viento || aire *m*; *it made a wind as it went past* hizo aire al pasar || MUS instrumentos *m pl* de viento || aliento *m* (breath); *to get one's second wind, to recover one's wind* recobrar el aliento || respiración *f* (ability to breathe) || gases *m pl* (produced in the stomach); *to have wind* tener gases || flato *m* (of a baby) || ANAT boca *f* del estómago (solar plexus) || olor *m* (in hunting) || FIG aire *m*, palabrería *f* (wordiness) || — FIG *against wind and tide* contra viento y marea | *as free as the wind* libre como el viento || MAR *before the wind* con el viento en popa, a favor del viento | *between wind and water* cerca de la línea de flotación | *down the wind* con el viento | *fair wind* viento favorable || FIG *gone with the wind* lo que el viento se llevó || MAR *head wind* viento en contra || FIG *he who sows the wind shall reap the whirlwind* quien siembra vientos recoge tempestades || MAR *in the teeth of the wind, in the wind's eye, up the wind, into the wind* contra el viento, con el viento en contra || FIG *it's an ill wind that blows nobody good* no hay mal que por bien no venga || MAR *off the wind* con viento en popa | *on a wind* de bolina || FIG *second wind* segundo aliento | *there's sth. in the wind* algo flota en el aire, algo se está preparando | *these promises are merely wind* estas promesas son palabras al aire | *the wind has changed o has turned* el viento ha cambiado || FAM *to break wind* ventosear || *to bring up wind* eructar || FIG *to catch o to get one's wind* recobrar el aliento | *to cast o to fling o to throw to the wind* dejar de lado | *to change with the wind, to be as fickle as the wind* moverse a todos los vientos, cambiar más que una veleta | *to find out how the wind blows o lies* ver de qué lado sopla el viento | *to get the wind up* pasar mucho miedo, asustarse | *to get wind of* enterarse de, descubrir (to find out); *I got wind of their plans yesterday* me enteré de sus proyectos ayer; olerse; *the authorities got wind of the escape plan* las autoridades se olieron el proyecto de fuga; revelar (to reveal) | *to go like the wind* ir más rápido que el viento, ir como un rayo | *to have one's wind taken* quedarse sin aliento | *to put the wind up s.o.* asustar a alguien, dar mucho miedo a alguien | *to run like the wind* correr como un gamo || MAR *to sail against the wind* hurtar el viento || *to sail close to the wind* navegar de bolina *or* contra el viento (ship), hacer *or* decir cosas arriesgadas (to border on foolhardiness) || MAR *to sail with the wind* navegar con el viento || FIG *to see how the wind blows, to see which way the wind is blowing* ver de qué lado sopla el viento | *to take the wind out of s.o.'s sails* tomar la delantera a alguien, ganar a alguien por la mano; *he was going to tell the joke but I took the wind out of his sails* iba a contar él el chiste pero le tomé la delantera; desanimar a uno (to dishearten); *that took all the wind out of my sails* eso me desanimó por completo; bajar los humos a alguien (to deflate s.o.) | *to the four winds* a los cuatro vientos.

wind [wind] *vt* dejar sin aliento, quitar el resuello (to leave breathless); *the run winded him* la carrera le dejó sin aliento || olfatear (to scent) || dejar recobrar el aliento a (to rest a horse, etc.) || airear, ventilar, orear (to air) || tocar (to sound).

— OBSERV Cuando el verbo *to wind* significa *tocar* tiene dos formas de pretérito y de participio pasivo: ***winded*** y ***wound***; en los demás casos es regular.

windage [-idʒ] *n* desvío *m* de un proyectil por efecto del viento || huelgo *m*, holgura *f* (between a bore of a firearm and the projectile) || resistencia *f* aerodinámica (of a ship, of an aircraft, etc.).

windbag [-bæg] *n* FAM charlatán, ana (person who talks a lot) || MUS odre *m*, fuelle *m* (in bagpipes, etc.).

windblown [-bləun] *adj* azotado por el viento; *windblown countryside* campo azotado por el viento || llevado por el viento || *windblown hair* pelo revuelto por el viento.

wind-borne [-bɔːn] *adj* llevado por el viento (pollen).

windbound [-baund] *adj* MAR detenido por el viento.

windbreak [-breik] *n* protección *f* contra el viento.

windbreaker [-ˌbreikə*]; **windcheater** [-ˌtʃiːtə*] *n* cazadora *f* (jacket).

wind cone [-kəun] *n* AVIAT manga *f* de aire.

winded [-id] *adj* jadeante (out of breath).

wind egg [-eg] *n* huevo *m* huero.

winder [ˈwaində*] *n* devanadera *f* (apparatus) || devanador, ra (person) || llave *f* (key) || BOT enredadera *f*.

windfall [ˈwindfɔːl] *n* fruta *f* caída (fallen fruit) || FIG ganancia *f* inesperada, ganga *f*, cosa *f* llovida del cielo (sth. received unexpectedly) | suerte *f* (stroke of luck).

windflaw [ˈwindflɔː] *n* ráfaga *f* de viento.

windflower [ˈwindˌflauə*] *n* BOT anémona *f*.

wind gauge [ˈwindgeidʒ] *n* anemómetro *m*.

windhover [ˈwindˌhɔvə*] *n* ZOOL cernícalo *m*.

windiness [ˈwindinis] *n* ventolera *f* (gust of wind) || MED flato *m* || FAM verbosidad *f* || *the windiness of these heights* el viento que sopla constantemente en estas cumbres.

winding [ˈwaindiŋ] *adj* tortuoso, sa; sinuoso, sa (road) || sinuoso, sa (river) || de caracol (staircase) || TECH en espiral.

◆ *n* serpenteo *m*, vueltas *f pl* (of road, of river) || enrollamiento *m* (of rope, of thread) || devanado *m* (of a reel) || cuerda *f* (of a clock) || TECH alabeo *m* (of a board) | extracción *f* (of ore).

winding frame [-freim] *n* devanadera *f*.

winding gear [-giə*] *n* torno *m*, cabrestante *m*.

winding key [-kiː] *n* llave *f* (of watch).

winding off [-ˈɔf] *n* devanado *m*.

winding on [-ˈɔn] *n* devanado *m*, enrollamiento *m*.

winding shaft [-ʃɑːft] *n* pozo *m* de extracción.

winding sheet [-ʃiːt] *n* mortaja *f*.

winding up [-ˈʌp] *n* conclusión *f* || COMM liquidación *f*.

wind instrument [ˈwindˌinstrumənt] *n* MUS instrumento *m* de viento.

windjammer [ˈwindˌdʒæmə*] *n* MAR velero *m* (sailing ship) | marinero *m* de un velero (sailor).

windlass [ˈwindləs] *n* torno *m* (for lifting) || MAR chigre *m*, maquinilla *f*, molinete *m*.

windless [ˈwindlis] *adj* sin viento.

windmill [ˈwindmil] *n* molino *m* de viento (a mill worked by sails) || molinillo *m*, molinete *m* (toy) || *to tilt at windmills* arremeter contra los molinos de viento.

window [ˈwindəu] *n* ventana *f*; *to lean out of the window* asomarse a la ventana || cristal *m* [de ventana] (windowpane) || ventanilla *f*, cristal *m* (of a car) || escaparate *m* [*AMER* vitrina *f*] (in a shop); *articles shown in the window* artículos que se ven en el escaparate || taquilla *f* (booking office) || ventanilla *f* (of booking office) || vidriera *f* (of stained glass) || ventanilla *f*, parte *f* transparente (of envelope, etc.) || INFORM ventana *f* || FAM *you make a better door than a window* la carne de burro no es transparente.

window bar [-bɑː] *n* barrote *m*.

window blind [-blaind] *n* persiana *f*.

window box [-bɔks] *n* jardinera *f* (for plants).

window cleaner [-ˌkliːnə*] *n* limpiacristales *m inv*.

window curtain [-ˌkəːtn] *n* cortina *f*.

window dresser [-ˌdresə*]; **window trimmer** [-trimə*] *n* escaparatista *m* & *f*, decorador *m* de escaparates.

window dressing [-ˌdresiŋ] *n* decoración *f* de escaparates (in a shopwindow) || FIG engaño *m* | fachada *f* (façade).

window envelope [-ˌenvələup] *n* sobre *m* con ventanilla.

window frame [-freim] *n* bastidor *m* de ventana, marco *m* de ventana.

window glass [-glɑːs] *n* cristal *m* de ventana.

window ledge [-ledʒ] *n* antepecho *m*, alféizar *m*.

windowpane [-pein] *n* cristal *m* de ventana.

window sash [-sæʃ] *n* bastidor *m* móvil, hoja *f* de la ventana de guillotina.

window screen [-skriːn] *n* tela *f* metálica adaptada al marco de una ventana.

window seat [-siːt] *n* asiento *m* junto a la ventana *or* ventanilla.

window shade [-ʃeid] *n* *US* persiana *f*.

window-shop [-ʃɔp] *vi* mirar los escaparates; *I like window-shopping* me gusta mirar los escaparates.

windowsill [-sil] *n* antepecho *m*, alféizar *m*.

window trimmer [-ˌtrimə*] *n* ⟶ **window dresser.**

windpipe [ˈwindpaip] *n* MED tráquea *f.*

wind-pollinated [ˈwindˌpɔlineitid] *adj* AGR fertilizado gracias al polen llevado por el viento.

windproof [ˈwindpruːf] *adj* a prueba de viento.

windrow [ˈwindrəu] *n* hilera *f* de trigo *or* hierba dejado al aire para que se seque || hojas *f pl or* polvo *m* amontonado por el viento (dust, leaves, piled up by the wind) || zanja *f* donde se planta la caña de azúcar (for sugar cane).

windsail [ˈwindseil] *n* MAR manguera *f*, manga *f* de ventilación.

windscale [ˈwindskeil] *n* escala *f* para medir la velocidad del viento.

windscreen [ˈwindskriːn]; **windshield** [ˈwindʃiːld] *n* parabrisas *m inv* || — *windscreen washer* lavaparabrisas *m inv* || *windscreen wiper* limpiaparabrisas *m inv*.

windshield [ˈwindʃiːld] *n* US ⟶ **windscreen.**

wind sleeve [ˈwindsliːv]; **wind sock** [ˈwindsɔk] *n* AVIAT manga *f* de aire.

windstorm [ˈwindstɔːm] *n* huracán *m*, vendaval *m*.

windswept [ˈwindswept] *adj* azotado por los vientos (place) || despeinado, da (hair).

wind tunnel [ˈwindˌtʌnəl] *n* túnel *m* aerodinámico.

windup [ˈwaindʌp] *n* final *m*, conclusión *f* || SP movimiento *m* previo al lanzamiento de la pelota (baseball).

windward [ˈwindwəd] *adj* de barlovento || *Windward Islands* islas *f* de Barlovento.
◆ *n* barlovento *m*.
◆ *adv* hacia barlovento, a barlovento

windy [ˈwindi] *adj* expuesto al viento; *a windy corner* una esquina expuesta al viento || ventoso, sa; de mucho viento; *a windy night* una noche ventosa || ventoso, sa; flatulento, ta (with stomach or intestinal gas) || FIG ampuloso, sa; *a windy speech* un discurso ampuloso || FAM miedoso, sa (frightened) || FAM *to get windy* tener mieditis.

wine [wain] *n* vino *m*; *red wine* vino tinto; *white wine* vino blanco; *sparkling wine* vino espumoso; *table wine* vino de mesa; *dry wine* vino seco; *local wine* vino del país || — FAM *Adam's wine* agua *f* | FIG *good wine needs no bush* el buen paño en el arca se vende || FAM *to be in wine* estar bebido, da || *wine from the barrel* vino a granel.

wine [wain] *vt* *to wine and dine s.o.* agasajar a alguien, festejar a alguien.
◆ *vi* beber vino.

wine bar [-bɑː*] *n* bar *m* donde se sirven vinos y comidas ligeras.

wine bibber [-ˌbibə*] *n* FAM bebedor *m*.

wine bottle [-ˌbɔtl] *n* botella *f* de vino.

wine box [-bɔks] *n* caja-barril *f* de vino.

wine butler [-ˌbʌtlə*] *n* escanciador *m*.

wine card [-kɑːd] *n* lista *f* de vinos.

wine cask [-kɑːsk] *n* barril *m* de vino.

wine cellar [-ˌselə*] *n* bodega *f.*

wine-coloured; US **wine colored** [-ˌkʌləd] *adj* color vino.

wine country [-ˌkʌntri] *n* región *f* vitícola.

wineglass [-glɑːs] *n* copa *f* [para vino].

winegrower [-ˌgrəuə*] *n* vinicultor, ra; viticultor, ra.

wine growing [-ˌgrəuiŋ] *adj* vitícola, vinícola.
◆ *n* vinicultura *f*, viticultura *f.*

wine merchant [-ˌməːtʃənt] *n* vinatero *m*, tratante *m* en vinos.

winepress [-pres] *n* lagar *m*.

winery [-əri] *n* lagar *m*.

wineskin [-skin] *n* odre *m*, pellejo *m*.

wine stone [-stəun] *n* tártaro *m*.

wine taster [-ˌteistə*] *n* catavinos *m inv*, catador *m* de vinos (person) || catavino *m* (flat bowl).

wine waiter [-ˌweitə*] *n* sumiller *m* (of a king) || sumiller *m* (p us), «sommelier» *m*, bodeguero *m*, botillero *m* (in a restaurant).

wing [wiŋ] *n* ZOOL, AVIAT & ARCH ala *f* || ANAT aleta *f*, ala *f* (of the nose) || ala *f*; *the left wing of the socialist party* el ala izquierda del partido socialista || FIG ala *f*; *on the wings of fantasy* en alas de la fantasía || SP extremo *m*, ala *m* (in football, in hockey); *to play on the wing* jugar de extremo | ala *m* (rugby); *the left wing* el ala izquierda || patilla *f* (of spectacles) || aspa *f* (of a mill) || pala *f*, paleta *f*, ala *f* (of ventilator, of airscrew) || orejera *f*, oreja *f*, cabecera *f* (of a chair) || AUT aleta *f* || MIL ala *f* (of the army) | aleta *f* (of missiles) | escuadrilla *f* (air force) || vuelo *m* (flight) || hoja *f*, batiente *m* (of a double door) || POP remo *m*, brazo *m* (arm) || — *on the wing* volando, al vuelo || FIG *to take under one's wing* acoger en su regazo, tomar bajo su protección || *to take wing* alzar el vuelo.
◆ *pl* THEATR bastidores *m* || MIL alas *f* (insignia) || — *my hat took wings* mi sombrero voló || FIG *to clip s.o.'s wings* cortarle las alas a alguien.

wing [wiŋ] *vt* hender, pasar volando por (the air) || emplumar (to put wings on) || lanzar, disparar (to let fly) || herir en el ala (to wound a bird) || tocar, herir, herir ligeramente (to wound a person) || ARCH añadir alas a || *to wing one's way* volar, ir volando.
◆ *vi* volar.

wingbeat [-biːt] *n* aletazo *m*.

wing case [-keis] *n* ZOOL élitro *m*.

wing chair [-tʃɛə*] *n* sillón *m* de orejas.

wing collar [-ˈkɔlə*] *n* cuello *m* de pajarita *or* de palomita.

wing commander [-kəˌmɑːndə*] *n* AVIAT teniente coronel *m*.

wing cover [-ˌkʌvə*] *n* ZOOL élitro *m*.

winged [-d] *adj* ZOOL alado, da (having wings) || con aletas (missiles) || BOT con alas || herido en el ala (wounded birds) || ligeramente herido, tocado, da (wounded people) || alígero, ra (god) || FIG veloz (swift).

winger [-ə*] *n* SP extremo *m*, ala *m* (in football, in hockey); *the right winger* el extremo derecha | ala *m* (in rugby).

wing flap [-flæp] *n* AVIAT alerón *m*.

wing-footed [-ˈfutid] *adj* alígero, ra.

wing game [-geim] *n* aves *f pl* de pluma.

wingless [-lis] *adj* sin alas, áptero, ra.

winglet [-lit] *n* alita *f* (small wing).

wing nut [-nʌt] *n* palometa *f*, tuerca *f* de mariposa, tuerca *f* de orejas *or* de aletas.

wingover [-ˌəuvə*] *n* AVIAT vuelta *f* sobre el ala.

wing-shaped [-ʃeipt] *adj* en forma de ala, aliforme.

wingspan [-spæn] *n* AVIAT & ZOOL envergadura *f.*

wingspread [-spred] *n* AVIAT & ZOOL envergadura *f.*

wink [wiŋk] *n* guiño *m*; *to give the wink to* hacer un guiño a || pestañeo *m* (blink) || centelleo *m*, parpadeo *m* (of light) || FAM momento *m* || — *he didn't get a wink of sleep all night, he didn't sleep a wink all night* no pegó el ojo en toda la noche, pasó la noche en vela || FIG *in a wink* en un abrir y cerrar de ojos || *to give* o *to tip s.o. the wink* guiñar a alguien || FIG *to snatch forty winks* echar un sueñecito.

wink [wiʃk] *vt* guiñar (the eye) || *to wink assent* guiñar el ojo en señal de asentimiento.
◆ *vi* guiñar el ojo; *she winked at me* me guiñó el ojo || pestañear (to blink) || centellear (stars) || vacilar, parpadear (light) || — FIG *like winking* en un abrir y cerrar de ojos | *to wink at* hacer la vista gorda a, cerrar los ojos a (to pretend not to see).

winker [ˈwiŋkə*] *n* AUT luz *f* intermitente, intermitente *m* || anteojera *f* (of a horse) || FAM lucero *m*, ojo *m* (eye) | pestaña *f* (eyelash).

winkle [ˈwiŋkl] *n* bígaro *m*, bigarro *m* (mollusc).

winkle [ˈwiŋkl] *vt* *to winkle out* eliminar (a person), sacar con dificultad (thing).

winkle-pickers [ˈwiŋklˌpikəz] *pl n* zapatos *m pl* de hombre puntiagudos.

winner [ˈwinə*] *n* ganador, ra; vencedor, ra || — *all the winners!* ¡todos los resultados! || *this record is a winner!* ¡este disco tendrá seguramente mucho éxito!

winning [ˈwiniŋ] *adj* vencedor, ra; victorioso, sa; *the winning team* el equipo victorioso || premiado, da (ticket, book) || decisivo, va (shot, play) || atractivo, va (attractive).
◆ *n* victoria *f* (victory) || adquisición *f* (acquisition) || MIN extracción *f* | pozo *m* de extracción (shaft).
◆ *pl* ganancias *f.*

winningly [-li] *adv* atractivamente.

winning post [-pəust] *n* SP meta *f*, poste *m* de llegada.

winnow [ˈwinəu] *vt* aventar (grain) || FIG escudriñar (to examine) | seleccionar, pasar por la criba (to select) | separar (to separate) | batir (the air, wings).

winnower [-ə*] *n* aventador, ra (person) || aventadora *f* (machine).

winnowing [-iŋ] *n* cribado *m*, aventamiento *m* (of grain) || FIG criba *f* (of persons, etc.) || — AGR *winnowing fork* bieldo *m* || *winnowing machine* aventadora *f.*

wino [ˈwainəu] *n* FAM borracho, cha.

winsome [ˈwinsəm] *adj* atractivo, va; encantador, ra.

winter [ˈwintə*] *n* invierno *m*.
◆ *adj* de invierno, invernal || — *winter pasture* invernadero *m* || *winter quarters* cuarteles *m* de invierno (of soldiers), residencia *f* de invierno || *winter season* temporada *f* de invierno || *winter solstice* solsticio *m* de invierno || *winter sports* deportes *m* de invierno.

winter [ˈwintə*] *vt* hacer invernar.
◆ *vi* invernar, pasar el invierno.

winter cherry [-ˈtʃeri] *n* BOT alquequenje *m*.

winterize [-raiz] *vt* preparar para el invierno, acondicionar para el invierno.

winterly [-li] *adj* ⟶ **wintry.**

wintertime [-taim]; **winterly** [-li] *n* invierno *m* (winter).

wintry [ˈwintri] *adj* de invierno, invernal || FIG frío, a; glacial.

winy [ˈwaini] *adj* vinoso, sa.

winze [winz] *n* MIN pozo *m* de comunicación.

wipe [waip] *n* limpieza *f* || TECH leva *f* || FAM mamporro *m* (blow) | bofetada *f* (swipe) || *to give sth. a wipe* limpiar algo.

wipe [waip] *vt* limpiar (to clean); *to wipe the table* limpiar la mesa || enjugar; *to wipe one's forehead* enjugarse la frente || secar; *to wipe one's hands* secarse las manos; *to wipe the dishes* secar los platos || — *to wipe one's nose* sonarse las narices || FIG *to wipe the floor with* pegar una paliza a alguien (to defeat).
◆ *vi* FAM *to wipe at* pegar.
◆ *phr v* *to wipe away* enjugar (tears) | quitar frotando (to remove) || *to wipe off* quitar frotando | borrar (a smile) | enjugar (a debt) || *to wipe out* limpiar (to clean) | secar (to dry) | borrar (to erase) | enjugar (a debt) | aniquilar, destruir (to destroy) | acabar con (a fortune) || *to wipe up* limpiar (to clean) | quitar (to remove) | secar (to dry).

wiper [-ə*] *n* trapo *m*, paño *m* (duster) || AUT limpiaparabrisas *m inv* || US leva *f* (of shaft).

wire [waiə*] *n* alambre *m* (of metal) || ELECTR cordón *m* (thin), cable *m* (thick) || hilo *m*; *silver wire* hilo de plata || tela *f* metálica (fence, mesh) || cuerda *f* (of a piano) || telegrama *m*; *to send off a wire* enviar un telegrama || telegrafía *f*, telégrafo *m* (telegraph system) || SP línea *f* de llegada (in horse racing) || — *barbed wire* alambrada *f*, alambre *m* de púas, alambre *m* de espino || *by wire* telegráficamente, por telégrafo || US FIG *under the wire* en el último momento.
◆ *pl* hilos *m* (for puppets) || FIG *to pull wires* tocar resortes.

wire [waiə*] *vt* poner el alambrado de (a house) || alambrar (to furnish with wire) || poner un telegrama a, telegrafiar (to telegraph) || coger en una trampa (an animal) || — *to wire in* alambrar || *to wire news to s.o.* enviar noticias a alguien por telegrama || *to wire up* poner el alambrado de (with barbed wire), poner la instalación eléctrica de (in a house), conectar (to connect).
◆ *vi* poner un telegrama, telegrafiar.

wire brush [-'brʌʃ] *n* cepillo *m* metálico, cepillo *m* de alambre.

wire cloth [-klɔθ] *n* tela *f* metálica.

wire cutter [-ˌkʌtə*] *n* cortaalambres *m inv*.

wired [-d] *adj* conectado, da a un sistema de alarma || con dispositivo de espionaje (bugged) || US FAM que está como una moto.

wiredancer [-ˌdɑːnsə*] *n* funámbulo, la (ropedancer).

wiredraw* [-drɔː] *vt* trefilar, estirar (metal) || FIG sutilizar.
— OBSERV Pret *wiredrew*; pp *wiredrawn*.

wiredrawing [-ˌdrɔːiŋ] *n* trefilado *m* || FIG sutileza *f* || *wiredrawing machine* trefiladora *f*.

wiredrew [-druː] *pret* → **wiredraw**.

wire fence [-fens] *n* alambrado *m*, alambrada *f*.

wire gauge [-geidʒ] *n* calibrador *m* para alambres.

wire gauze [-'gɔːz] *n* tela *f* metálica.

wireless [-lis] *adj* radiofónico, ca (association) || sin hilos (telegraphy) || — *wireless message* radiograma *m* || *wireless operator* radio *m*, radiotelegrafista *m* || *wireless set* radio *f*, aparato *m* de radio || *wireless telegraphy* radiotelegrafía *f*, telegrafía *f* sin hilos || *wireless telephony* radiotelefonía *f*.
◆ *n* radio *f* (system) || radio *f*, aparato *m* de radio, receptor *m* de radio (set) || — *by wireless* por radio || *to talk on the wireless* hablar por la radio.

wireless [-lis] *vt* radiotelegrafiar || radiar, transmitir por radio.
◆ *vi* comunicar por radio.

wire mesh [-'meʃ] *n* tela *f* metálica.

wire netting [-'netiŋ] *n* tela *f* metálica.

wirephoto [-ˌfəutəu] *n* US radiofotografía *f*, telefotografía *f*.

wirepull [-pul] *vi* FAM enchufarse, tocar todos los resortes.

wirepuller [-ˌpulə*] *n* FAM intrigante *m* & *f* | enchufado, da (who has got a post through influence).

wirepulling [-ˌpuliŋ] *n* FAM enchufe *m* (influence) | intrigas *f pl*.

wire recorder [-riˌkɔːdə*] *n* magnetófono *m*.

wire rope [-'rəup] *n* cable *m*.

wiretap [-tæp] *vi* interceptar las líneas telefónicas.

wiretapper [-ˌtæpə*] *n* persona *f* que intercepta las líneas telefónicas.

wiretapping [-ˌtæpiŋ] *n* instalación *f* de estaciones de escucha, interceptación *f* de líneas telefónicas.

wire wool [-wuːl] *n* estropajo *m* de aluminio.

wirework [-wəːk] *n* tela *f* metálica (netting constructed of wire).

wireworks [-wəːks] *n* trefilería *f*, fábrica *f* de alambre.

wiring [-riŋ] *n* instalación *f* eléctrica (electricity system) || colocación *f* de alambres || FAM envío *m* de un telegrama.

wiry [-ri] *adj* tieso, sa (hair) || enjuto y fuerte (person) || metálico, ca (sound).

Wisconsin [wis'kɔnsin] *pr n* GEOGR Wisconsin *m*.

wisdom [wizdəm] *n* sabiduría *f*, saber *m* (knowledge) || juicio *m*, cordura *f*, sensatez *f* (good judgment) || — REL *The Book of Wisdom, The Wisdom of Solomon* el Libro de la Sabiduría || FIG *to cut one's wisdom tooth* madurar || *wisdom tooth* muela *f* del juicio.

wise [waiz] *adj* sabio, bia (learned) || prudente, sensato, ta; juicioso, sa (cautions); *it does not seem wise to go* no parece prudente ir || atinado, da; acertado, da; prudente (move, step) || — *a wise man* un sabio || *he is none the wiser* sigue sin entender nada || *it would be wise to do it* sería aconsejable hacerlo || REL *the Three Wise Men* los Reyes Magos || FAM *to get wise to* darse cuenta de (to realize) | *to put s.o. wise to* poner a alguien al tanto de || US FAM *wise guy* sabelotodo *m* (know-all).
◆ *n* manera *f*, modo *m*; *in some wise* en cierta manera; *in no wise* de ningún modo.

wise [waiz] *vt/vi* FAM *to wise up* poner al tanto; ponerse al tanto.

wiseacre [-ˌeikə*] *n* sabihondo, da; sabelotodo *m* & *f* (know-all).

wisecrack [-kræk] *n* US FAM agudeza *f*, dicho *m* gracioso, salida *f*, ocurrencia *f*.

wisecrack [-kræk] *vi* US FAM ser gracioso, sa; tener salidas graciosas, ser ocurrente.

wisent [wiːzənt] *n* ZOOL bisonte *m* europeo.

wish [wiʃ] *n* deseo *m*; *it was my father's wish* fue el deseo de mi padre; *to go against s.o.'s wishes* ir en contra de los deseos de alguien; *the fairy grants you two wishes* la hada te concede dos deseos; *I shall have my wish* se cumplirá mi deseo || — *I have no great wish to see it* no tengo ganas de verlo || *it has long been my wish to do it* deseo hacerlo desde hace mucho tiempo || *to make a wish* pensar un deseo || *your wish is my command* sus deseos son órdenes para mí.
◆ *pl* votos *m*; *good wishes* votos de felicidad || — *give him my best wishes* dale recuerdos míos || *I gave him my best wishes* le felicité calurosamente || *my best wishes for the future* mis mejores votos para el futuro || *with best wishes* un fuerte abrazo (in a letter).

wish [wiʃ] *vt* querer; *I wish the month were over* quisiera que se hubiese acabado el mes; *I don't wish to go* no quiero ir; *what did you wish me to do?* ¿qué quería que hiciese?; *I wish I were a hundred miles away* quisiera estar muy lejos de aquí || desear; *I wish you every happiness* le deseo muchísima felicidad; *I don't wish you any harm* no le deseo ningún mal; *to wish s.o. well* desear todo lo mejor para alguien || gustar; *I wish I had a car* me gustaría tener un coche; *I wish you would go* me gustaría que fueras; *I wish I could stay here longer* me gustaría poder quedarme más tiempo aquí || — *it is to be wished that* es de desear que, es deseable que || *I wish I could!* ¡ojalá!, ¡ojalá pudiese! || *I wish you could understand it* me gustaría que pudiese comprenderlo || *I wouldn't wish it on anyone* no se lo desearía a nadie || *they wished it on me* me lo impusieron || *to wish s.o. a happy Christmas* desear a alguien felices Navidades || *to wish s.o. good-bye* decir adiós a alguien, despedirse de alguien || *to wish s.o. good luck* desear a uno mucha suerte || *to wish s.o. good morning* dar a alguien los buenos días.
◆ *vi* desear; *I have everything I could wish for* tengo todo lo que podría desear || *what more could you wish for?* ¿qué más quieres?

wishbone [-bəun] *n* espoleta *f* (of bird).

wisher [-ə*] *n* persona *f* que desea.

wishful [-ful] *adj* deseoso, sa (to do sth., of sth.) || *wishful thinking* ilusiones *f pl*.

wishing [-iŋ] *n* deseos *m pl* || *wishing bone* espoleta *f* (of birds).

wish-wash [-wɔʃ] *n* FAM calducho *m*, aguachirle *f* (weak drink).

wishy-washy [-iˌwɔʃi] *adj* insípido, da; soso, sa (insipid) || aguado, da (tea, etc.).

wisp [wisp] *n* manojo *m* (of straw, of hay) || mechón *m* (of hair) || vestigio *m* (small trace) || voluta *f*, espiral *f* (of smoke) || vuelo *m* (of snipe) || *a wisp of a man* un alfeñique.

wisp [wisp] *vt* hacer manojos de.

wispy [-i] *adj* fino, na.

wistaria [wis'tɛəriə]; **wisteria** [wis'tiəriə] *n* BOT glicina *f*.

wistful [wistful] *adj* triste, melancólico, ca (sad) || ansioso, sa (covetous) || pensativo, va; soñador, ra (dreamy) || desilusionado, da (unsatisfied).

wistfulness [-nis] *n* tristeza *f*, melancolía *f* (sadness) || lo soñador, lo pensativo (dream) || ansia *f* (covetousness) || desilusión *f* (disillusion).

wit [wit] *n* agudeza *f*, ingenio *m*; *a man of great wit* un hombre de gran agudeza || gracia *f* (humour) || dicho *m* agudo (remark, comment) || persona *f* aguda (funny person) || persona *f* ingeniosa (clever person) || inteligencia *f*; *he has not wit enough to see it* no tiene la inteligencia suficiente para darse cuenta de ello || — *flash of wit* rasgo *m* de ingenio || *to be at one's wit's end* no saber qué hacer || *to have a ready wit* tener ingenio, ser agudo, da.
◆ *pl* juicio *m sing*; *to have lost one's wits* haber perdido el juicio || — *it was a battle of wits between them* rivalizaron en ingenio || *to be out of one's wits* haber perdido la cabeza || *to be scared out of one's wits* estar muerto de miedo || *to collect one's wits* serenarse || *to frighten s.o. out of his wits* dar a alguien un susto mortal || *to keep one's wits about one* no perder la cabeza || *to live by one's wits* vivir de expedientes, vivir de su ingenio, ser caballero de industria || *to send s.o. out of his wits* volverle loco a alguien || *to set one's wits to a problem* atacar un problema || *to sharpen one's wits* aguzar el ingenio, despabilarse || *to use one's wits* valerse de su ingenio.

wit [wit] *vt/vi* saber || *to wit* a saber, es decir.

witan [witən] *n* consejero *m* de un rey glosajón.

witch [witʃ] *n* bruja *f*, hechicera *f* (sorceress) || FAM bruja *f* (old woman) | lagarta *f* (seductive young woman).

witch ball [-bɔːl] *n* bola *f* de cristal (to keep out witches).

witch broom [-brum] *n* escoba *f* de bruja.

witchcraft [-krɑːft] *n* brujería *f* (of sorceress) || FIG sortilegio *m*, hechizo *m*, encanto *m* (charm).

witch doctor [-ˌdɔktə*] *n* hechicero *m*.

witch elm [-'elm] *n* BOT → **wych elm.**

witchery [-əri] *n* brujería *f* (witchcraft) || FIG encanto *m*, hechizo *m* (charm).

witches' broom [-izbrum] *n* escoba *f* de bruja.

witches's sabbath [-iz'sæbəθ] *n* aquelarre *m*.

witch hazel [-'heizəl] *n* BOT olmo *m* escocés.

witch hunt [-hʌnt] *n* persecución *f* de brujas || FIG persecución *f* (political).

witching [-iŋ] *adj* hechicero, ra (charming) || mágico, ca.
◆ *n* brujería *f* || FIG hechizo *m* (charm).

witenagemot; witenagemote ['witinəgi'məut] *n* asamblea *f* de consejeros de un rey anglosajón.

with [wið] *prep* con; *to eat with a fork* comer con un tenedor; *to be angry with s.o.* estar enfadado con alguien; *the house with the green door* la casa con la puerta verde; *to fight with one's friends* luchar con los amigos; *to walk with difficulty* andar con dificultad; *to threaten with eviction* amenazar con el desahucio; *he walks with a stick* anda con un bastón; *to sail with the wind* navegar con el viento || con, en casa de; *to live with friends* vivir en casa de unos amigos || con, en compañía de; *I went with John to the cinema* fui con Juan al cine || de; *crowded with people* lleno de gente; *the man with the beard* el hombre de la barba; *to jump with joy* saltar de alegría; *in love with* enamorado de; *to fill with water* llenar de agua; *to be stiff with cold* estar yerto de frío || junto con; *with John he is the best player in the team* junto con Juan es el mejor jugador del equipo || más; *these chairs with those will be enough* estas sillas más aquellas bastarán || en manos de; *I left the book with Peter* dejé el libro en manos de Pedro || con, al cuidado de; *to leave a child with s.o.* dejar un niño al cuidado de alguien || con, a pesar de (in spite of); *with all his faults I love him* le quiero con todas sus faltas || con, según; *it changes with the weather* cambia con el tiempo || igual que; *he can swear with the others* sabe jurar igual que los otros || de acuerdo con; *I'm with you on that* estoy de acuerdo contigo en eso || — *bring it with you* tráelo || *down with the government!* ¡abajo el gobierno! || *he's down with cholera* tiene cólera || *he said this with a smile* lo dijo sonriendo, lo dijo con una sonrisa || *he was swimming with his hat on* iba nadando con el sombrero puesto || *it's a habit with him* es una costumbre en él || *it's pouring with rain* está lloviendo a cántaros || *she's good with children* es buena para *or* con los niños || *the decision lies* o *rests with you* a usted le corresponde tomar la decisión || *the problem is still with us* el problema sigue sin resolverse || *to vote with a party* votar por un partido || *up with Caesar!* ¡viva César! || *with all due respect* con el respeto debido || *with all my might* con todas mis fuerzas || *with all speed* a toda prisa, a toda velocidad || *with child* embarazada || FIG & FAM *with it* al corriente, al tanto, al día (person), a la moda, de moda (clothes) || *with me* conmigo || *with no difficulty* sin dificultad || *with one blow* de un solo golpe || *with open arms* con los brazos abiertos || *with pleasure* con gusto || *with that remark, he left* dicho eso, se marchó || *with you* contigo, con usted, con ustedes.

withal [wi'ðɔːl] *adv* además (moreover) || sin embargo, no obstante (nevertheless).

withdraw* [wið'drɔː] *vt* quitar, retirar, sacar (to remove) || apartar (to take aside) || retirar (troops, candidature, proposal) || sacar, retirar (money from a bank) || retirar, quitar (money from circulation) || desdecirse de (a promise, a statement) || retirar (one's words).
◆ *vi* retirarse (to leave) || apartarse (to move away) || retirarse (from a treaty) || retirar una moción || — *to withdraw in favour of s.o.* renunciar a favor de alguien || *to withdraw into o.s.* ensimismarse, abstraerse.
— OBSERV Pret *withdrew*; pp *withdrawn*.

withdrawal [-əl] *n* retirada *f* (of troops) || retirada *f* (from a bank) || salida *f* (on a bank statement) || retractación *f* (of a statement) || abandono *m* (abandonment) || renuncia *f* (renunciation).

withdrawal symptoms [-əl,simptəmz] *pl n* MED síntomas *m* sufridos por el toxicómano al carecer de la droga que solía tomar.

withdrawn [-n] *pp* → **withdraw.**
◆ *adj* aislado, da || reservado, da; introvertido, da.

withdrew [wið'druː] *pret* → **withdraw.**

withe [wiθ] *n* mimbre *m*.

wither ['wiðə*] *vt* marchitar, agostar (plants) || consumir, debilitar; *illness withered him* le consumió la enfermedad || FIG fulminar; *he withered him with a glance* le fulminó con la mirada.
◆ *vi* marchitarse (flowers) || debilitarse (to weaken) || secarse (to grow thin).

withered [-d] *adj* marchito, ta; seco, ca.

withering [-riŋ] *adj* que se marchita (flower) || abrasador, ra (heat) || FIG fulminante (look) | mordaz (biting).
◆ *n* marchitamiento *m*.

withers [-z] *pl n* cruz *f sing* (of horse).

withheld [wið'held] *pret/pp* → **withhold.**

withhold* [wið'həuld] *vt* negar, negarse a conceder (to refuse) || retener (to hold back) || ocultar, callar (not to reveal); *to withhold the truth from s.o.* ocultar la verdad a alguien || US *withholding tax* impuesto deducido del salario.
◆ *vi* *to withhold from* abstenerse de.
— OBSERV Pret y pp *withheld*.

within [wi'ðin] *adv* dentro; *enquire within* pregunten dentro; *within and without* dentro y fuera || en casa (at home) || FIG en su fuero interno (inside the mind) || — *from within* de dentro, del interior || FIG *to make pure within* purificar el alma.
◆ *prep* al alcance de; *within call* al alcance de la voz || dentro de; *within the house* dentro de la casa; *within the organization* dentro de la organización; *within a week* dentro de una semana; *within the law* dentro de la ley || en; *within a radius of* en un radio de || en un plazo de; *you must answer within five days* tiene que contestar en un plazo de cinco días || a menos de; *within two miles of* a menos de dos millas de || — FIG *a voice within* una voz interior | *to be within an inch of* estar a dos pasos de || *to be within s.o.'s jurisdiction* ser de la competencia de alguien || *to live within one's income* vivir con arreglo a sus recursos económicos || FIG *within o.s.* en su fuero interno || *within the frontier* fronteras adentro.

without [wi'ðaut] *prep* sin; *without money* sin dinero; *without work* sin trabajo; *without seeing anyone* sin ver a nadie || sin, sin que; *without my finding it* sin encontrarlo yo, sin que yo lo encontrase || fuera de; *without the city* fuera de la ciudad || — *it goes without saying* por supuesto, ni que decir tiene, huelga decir (needless to say), eso cae de su peso (it is obvious) || *not without difficulty* no sin dificultad || *to do* o *to go without* prescindir de.
◆ *adv* fuera; *from without* desde fuera.

withstand* [wið'stænd] *vt* resistir a (temptation, siege, blow) || resistir, aguantar (pain) || oponerse a (s.o.).
— OBSERV Pret y pp *withstood*.

withstood [wið'stud] *pret/pp* → **withstand.**

withy ['wiði] *n* mimbre *m*.

witless [witlis] *adj* estúpido, da; tonto, ta; idiota.

witloof ['witluːf] *n* BOT endibia *f* (endive).

witness ['witnis] *n* testigo *m* (of an incident) || prueba *f* (proof, evidence) || testimonio *m* (testimony) || JUR testigo *m*; *witness for the prosecution* testigo de cargo; *witness for the defence* testigo de descargo || — *in witness whereof* en fe de lo cual || *to bear witness to* atestiguar || *to be witness to sth.* ser testigo de algo || *to call as a witness* citar como testigo || *to call to witness* poner por testigo a.

witness ['witnis] *vt* asistir a, presenciar, ser testigo de (to be present at) || atestiguar (to bear witness to) || firmar como testigo (a document) || demostrar, dar prueba de; *a look which witnessed his surprise* una mirada que demostraba su sorpresa.
◆ *vi* declarar (*for* a favor; *against* en contra de) || *to witness to* atestiguar.

witness box [-bɔks] *n* JUR barra *f* de los testigos.

witness stand [-stænd] *n* US JUR barra *f* de los testigos.

witted ['witid] *adj* ingenioso, sa; agudo, da.

witter ['witə*] *vi* parlotear.

witticism ['witisizəm] *n* agudeza *f*, dicho *m* gracioso, salida *f* graciosa, ocurrencia *f*.

wittily ['witili] *adv* con agudeza.

wittiness ['witinis] *n* agudeza *f*.

witting ['witiŋ] *adj* deliberado, da; intencionado, da (deliberate) || consciente (aware, conscious).

wittingly [-li] *adv* a sabiendas.

witty ['witi] *adj* ingenioso, sa; agudo, da; gracioso, sa (person) || gracioso, sa; divertido, da (remark).

wivern ['waivəːn] *n* HERALD dragón *m*.

wives [waivz] *pl n* → **wife.**

wizard ['wizəd] *adj* FAM estupendo, da; formidable.
◆ *n* mago *m*, hechicero *m* || FIG genio *m*, as *m*; *a business wizard* un as de los negocios || *I am not a wizard* no soy un adivino.

wizardry [-ri] *n* magia *f*, hechicería *f*.

wizen ['wizən]; **wizened** [-d] *adj* marchito, ta; arrugado, da (skin) || hecho una pasa; *a wizened old man* un anciano hecho una pasa || marchito, ta (plants).

wo!; woa! [wəu] *interj* ¡so! (to stop a horse).

wobble ['wɔbl] *n* tambaleo *m*, bamboleo *m* || zigzag *m* (of a person) || temblor *m* (of voice, of jelly) || vacilación *f* (indecision) || fluctuación *f* || — *he walks with a wobble* anda tambaleándose, anda haciendo eses || *the table has a wobble* la mesa está coja.

wobble ['wɔbl] *vt* hacer tambalearse.
◆ *vi* tambalearse (to move unsteadily) || bambolearse, balancearse (to rock) || temblar (voice, jelly) || vacilar (to hesitate).

wobbly [-i] *adj* bamboleante, tambaleante (shaking, unstable) || haciendo eses, zigzagueando (a person) || tembloroso, sa (voice) || cojo, ja (chair, table).

wobbulator ['wɔbjuleitə*] *n* modulador *m* de frecuencia.

woe [wəu] *n* infortunio *m*, aflicción *f*.
◆ *pl* penas *f*; *to tell s.o. one's woes* contarle a alguien sus penas.
◆ *interj* ¡ay!; *woe is me!* ¡ay de mí! || *woe betide you!* ¡maldito seas!

woebegone [ˈwəubiˌgən] *adj* desconsolado, da (person) || desolado, da (place).

woeful [ˈwəuful] *adj* afligido, da, apenado, da (very sad) || lamentable, deplorable (deplorable) || infortunado, da; desgraciado, da (period).

woke [wəuk] *pret* → **wake.**

woken [-ən] *pp* → **wake.**

wold [wəuld] *n* región *f* ondulada.

wolf [wulf] *n* ZOOL lobo *m* || MUS sonido *m* discordante || US FAM tenorio *m*, don Juan *m*, conquistador *m* (woman chaser) || — FIG *a wolf in sheep's clothing* un lobo con piel de oveja | *lone wolf* persona solitaria | *to cry wolf* llamar al lobo, dar una falsa alarma | *to eat like a wolf* comer como una lima | *to hold the wolf by the ears* coger al lobo por las orejas | *to keep the wolf from the door* precaverse contra la miseria.
— OBSERV El plural de *wolf* es *wolves*.

wolf [wulf] *vt* zamparse, tragarse (one's food).

wolf call [-kɔːl]; **wolf whistle** [-wisl] *n* FAM silbido *m* de admiración.

wolf cub [-kʌb] *n* lobezno *m*, lobato *m*, cachorro *m* de lobo (animal) || «scout» *m* joven, joven explorador *m* (young boy scout).

wolf dog [-dɔg] *n* perro *m* lobo.

wolffish [-fiʃ] *n* lobo *m* de mar (fish).

wolfhound [-haund] *n* perro *m* lobo.

wolfish [-iʃ] *adj* ZOOL lobuno, na || FIG cruel, feroz || US FAM hambriento, ta || US FAM *to feel wolfish* tener un hambre canina.

wolf pack [-pæk] *n* manada *f* de lobos || MAR flotilla *f* de submarinos.

wolfram [-rəm] *n* volframio *m*, tungsteno *m* (tungsten) || volframita *f* (wolframite).

wolframine [-rəˌmin] *n* volframina *f*.

wolframite [-rəmait] *n* volframita *f*.

wolf whistle [-ˌwisl] *n* FAM → **wolf call.**

wolverene; wolverine [ˈwulvəriːn] *n* ZOOL glotón *m*.

wolves [wulvz] *pl n* → **wolf.**

woman [ˈwumən] *n* mujer *f* || — FAM *he is like an old woman* es una vieja histérica | *my old woman* la parienta, mi media naranja || *old woman* vieja *f*, anciana *f* || *the woman in her* su lado femenino, su feminidad *f* || FAM *there's a woman in it* es cuestión de mujeres *or* de faldas | *to make an honest woman of* casarse con, tomar por esposa a || *woman of the world* mujer de mundo || *woman's rights* derechos *m* de la mujer || *woman suffrage* sufragio femenino || *young woman* joven *f*; mujer joven.
— OBSERV El plural de *woman* es *women*.

woman chaser [-tʃeisə*] *n* mujeriego *m*.

woman doctor [-ˈdɔktə*] *n* médica *f*.

woman friend [-frend] *n* amiga *f*.

woman hater [-heitə*] *n* misógino *m*.

womanhood [-hud] *n* mujeres *f pl*, sexo *m* femenino; *the world's womanhood* las mujeres del mundo || condición *f* de mujer || feminidad *f* (femininity) || *to reach womanhood* hacerse mujer.

womanish [-iʃ] *adj* femenino, na; mujeril (of woman) || afeminado, da (men).

womanize [-aiz] *vi* ser mujeriego.
◆ *vt* afeminar.

womanizer [-aizə*] *n* mujeriego *m*.

womankind [-ˈkaind] *n* mujeres *f pl*, sexo *m* femenino || *my womankind* las mujeres de mi familia.

womanlike [-laik] *adj* de mujer, femenino, na.

womanliness [-linis] *n* feminidad *f*.

womanly [-li] *adj* femenino, na.

woman pilot [-ˈpailət] *n* mujer *f* piloto.

woman writer [-raitə*] *n* escritora *f*.

womb [wuːm] *n* ANAT matriz *f*, útero *m* || FIG cuna *f*; *the womb of the Renaissance* la cuna del Renacimiento; *from the womb to the tomb* desde la cuna hasta la sepultura | entrañas *f pl*.

wombat [ˈwɔmbæt] *n* ZOOL uombat *m*, oso *m* australiano.

women [ˈwimin] *pl n* → **woman.**

womenfolk [-fəuk] *pl n* mujeres *f*.

Women's institute [-sˈinstitjuːt] *n* Instituto *m* de la Mujer [en Gran Bretaña].

Women's Lib [-sˈlib] *n* movimiento *m* de Liberación de la Mujer.

women's page [-speidʒ] *n* sección *f* femenina.

won [wʌn] *pret/pp* → **win.**

wonder [ˈwʌndə*] *n* maravilla *f*, prodigio *m*; *a wonder of architecture* una maravilla de la arquitectura; *the wonders of science* los prodigios de la ciencia || maravilla *f*; *the seven wonders of the world* las siete maravillas del mundo || milagro *m*; *it is a wonder that he wasn't killed* es un milagro que no le hayan matado || admiración *f*, asombro *m* (sensation); *his skill is always a source of wonder to me* su destreza siempre me llena de admiración || — *for a wonder* por milagro || *it is a wonder that he ever got home* no sé cómo ha podido llegar a casa || *it is little* o *small wonder that...* no es de extrañar que || *my holidays did wonders for me* las vacaciones tuvieron un efecto maravilloso en mí || *no wonder!* ¡no me extraña!, ¡no es de extrañar! || *the wonder of it is that* lo asombroso es que || *to be a nine-days' wonder* durar muy poco, ser efímero, ra || *to fill with wonder* maravillar, dejar maravillado || *to promise wonders* prometer maravillas, prometer el oro y el moro || *to work* o *to do wonders* hacer maravillas.
◆ *adj* milagroso, sa; *wonder drug* remedio milagroso || *wonder child* niño prodigio.

wonder [ˈwʌndə*] *vt* preguntarse; *I wonder whether it is true* me pregunto si es verdad || pensar; *I was wondering what to do next* estaba pensando en lo que iba a hacer después || — *I wonder what time it is* ¿qué hora será? || *I wonder who will lend me 50 pounds* ¿quién me prestará 50 libras? || *I wonder why* ¿por qué será?; *Peter didn't come, I wonder why* Pedro no vino ¿por qué será? || *I wonder why he didn't go* me extraña que no fuese.
◆ *vi* admirarse, asombrarse; *I wonder at his foolhardiness* me admiro de su temeridad; *I wonder at nothing* no me asombro de nada || pensar; *I was wondering about what to do tonight* estaba pensando en lo que iba a hacer esta noche; *it made me wonder* me hizo pensar || — *I just wondered* sólo por curiosidad; *why did you ask? I just wondered* ¿por qué preguntaste? sólo por curiosidad || *I shouldn't wonder if it rained* no me extrañaría que lloviese || *it is all over now, I shouldn't wonder* supongo que ya se habrá terminado todo || *it is hardly to be wondered at* no tiene nada de extraño, no hay por qué extrañarse || *John will be there I wonder* Juan estará allí lo dudo.

wonderful [-ful] *adj* maravilloso, sa; estupendo, da (marvellous) || asombroso, sa; sorprendente (astonishing) || *wonderful!* ¡qué maravilla!, ¡estupendo!

wonderfully [-i] *adv* maravillosamente, estupendamente.

wondering [-riŋ] *adj* perplejo, ja (perplexed); *in a wondering tone* en un tono perplejo || asombrado, da (astonished).

wonderingly [-riŋli] *adv* perplejo, ja; con perplejidad; *he looked wonderingly at the statue* miró perplejo la estatua || con asombro, asombrado, da (in astonishment).

wonderland [-lænd] *n* mundo *m* maravilloso; *the wonderland of dreams* el mundo maravilloso de los sueños || *Alice in Wonderland* Alicia en el País de las Maravillas.

wonderment [-mənt] *n* admiración *f* (admiration) || asombro *m* (amazement).

wonderstruck [-strʌk] *adj* pasmado, da; asombrado, da.

wonderwork [-ˌwəːk] *n* prodigio *m*.

wondrous [ˈwʌndrəs] *adj* maravilloso, sa.

wondrously [-li] *adv* extraordinariamente; *wondrously big* extraordinariamente grande.

wonky [ˈwɔŋki] *adj* FAM torcido, da (out of position); *your tie is wonky* tu corbata está torcida | inclinado, da (a picture, etc.) | cojo, ja; *a wonky table* una mesa coja | poco sólido, da; poco seguro, ra (unsteady); *a wonky bridge* un puente poco seguro || FAM *the machine has gone a bit wonky* la máquina está algo estropeada.

wont [wəunt] *adj* *to be wont to* soler, acostumbrar; *he was wont to get up early* solía madrugar.
◆ *n* costumbre *f*; *as is his wont* como tiene por costumbre || *it is his wont to* acostumbra, suele, tiene por costumbre.

wonted [-id] *adj* acostumbrado, da; habitual.

woo [wuː] *vt* hacer la corte, cortejar (a young lady) || FIG solicitar (favour, support) | buscar (fame, fortune) | buscarse (defeat, trouble) | granjearse la amistad de (to win over s.o.) || FAM *a policy designed to woo the electors* una política encaminada a ganar votos *or* a conseguir el apoyo del electorado.
◆ *vi* cortejar a una mujer.

wood [wud] *n* bosque *m* (forest); *a walk in the wood* un paseo por el bosque || madera *f* (material); *a table made of wood* una mesa de madera || leña *f* (firewood) || palo *m* (stick, staff) || SP bola *f* (in bowls) | palo *m* de madera (golf club) || MUS instrumentos *m pl* de madera (woodwind section) || barril *m* (barrel); *wine from the wood* vino de barril || — FIG *to be out of the wood* estar a salvo, haber salido del apuro *or* del mal paso || *touch wood!* ¡toca madera! || *we'll succeed, touch wood* lo lograremos si Dios quiere || FIG *you can't see the wood for the trees* los árboles impiden ver el bosque.
◆ *pl* bosque *m sing* || *to take to the woods* echarse al monte.
◆ *adj* de los bosques, silvestres (plants, wildlife) || de madera; *a wood floor* un suelo de madera; *a wood table* una mesa de madera.

wood alcohol [-ˌælkəhɔl] *n* CHEM metanol *m*, alcohol *m* metílico.

wood anemone [-əˌneməni] *n* BOT anémona *f* silvestre.

woodbin [-bin] *n* US leñera *f*.

woodbine [-bain] *n* BOT madreselva *f* || US BOT viña *f* loca.

wood block [-blɔk] *n* tarugo *m* (in paving) || ARTS bloque *m* de madera.

wood-carver [-ˌkaːvə*] *n* tallista *m* en madera.

wood carving [-ˌkaːviŋ] *n* talla *f* de madera (object) || tallado *m* en madera (craft).

woodchat [-tʃæt] *n* alcaudón *m* (bird).

woodchuck [-tʃʌk] *n* ZOOL marmota *f* de América.

wood coal [-kəul] *n* carbón *m* vegetal.

woodcock [-kɔk] *n* chocha *f*, becada *f*

woodcraft [-kraːft] *n* conocimiento *m* del bosque (knowledge of forests) || artesanía *f* en madera (carving, etc.).

woodcut [-kʌt] *n* grabado *m* en madera.

woodcutter [-ˌkʌtə*] *n* leñador *m*.

wooded [-id] *adj* arbolado, da; poblado de árboles.

wooden [-ən] *adj* de madera (made of wood) || de palo; *wooden leg* pata de palo || FIG inexpresivo, va; *a wooden stare* una mirada inexpresiva | tieso, sa; rígido, da (rigid) | estirado, da (stiff) | inflexible (policy) | soso, sa (uninteresting) || FIG *wooden face* cara de palo.

wood engraving [-inˌgreiviŋ] *n* grabado *m* en madera.

wooden-headed [-ənˌhedid] *adj* mentecato, ta; estúpido, da (stupid).

woodenness [-ənnis] *n* FIG rigidez *f*.

wooden shoe [-ən'ʃuː] *n* zueco *m* (clog).

wooden spoon [-ən'spuːn] *n* cuchara *f* de palo || FIG premio *m* de consolación.

wood ibis [-'aibis] *n* ZOOL tántalo *m*.

woodiness [-inis] *n* carácter *m* arbolado (of a place) || carácter *m* leñoso (similarity to wood).

woodland [-lənd] *n* bosque *m*.
◆ *adj* de los bosques, silvestre.

wood louse [-laus] *n* ZOOL cochinilla *f*.
— OBSERV El plural de *wood louse* es *wood lice*.

woodman [-mən] *n* leñador *m* (woodcutter) || guardabosque *m* (forester).
— OBSERV El plural de esta palabra es *woodmen*.

wood nymph [-nimf] *n* ninfa *f* de los bosques.

wood paper [-ˌpeipə*] *n* papel *m* de celulosa.

woodpecker [-ˌpekə*] *n* pájaro *m* carpintero, pico *m*, picamaderos *m inv* (bird).

wood pigeon [-ˌpidʒin] *n* paloma *m* torcaz (bird).

woodpile [-pail] *n* montón *m* de leña.

wood pulp [-pʌlp] *n* pasta *f* de madera.

wood shavings [-ʃeiviŋz] *pl n* virutas *f*.

woodshed [-ʃed] *n* leñera *f*.

woodsman [-zmən] *n* US leñador *m* (woodcutter) || *to be an expert woodsman* conocer muy bien el bosque.
— OBSERV El plural de esta palabra es *woodsmen*.

wood sorrel [-ˌsɔrəl] *n* BOT acederilla *f*.

wood spirit [-'spirit] *n* CHEM metanol *m*, alcohol *m* metílico.

wood stork [-stɔːk] *n* ZOOL tántalo *m*.

woodsy [-zi] *adj* US poblado de árboles.

wood tar [-tɑː*] *n* alquitrán *m* vegetal.

wood tick [-tik] *n* ZOOL garrapata *f*.

woodturner [-ˌtəːnə*] *n* tornero *m* en madera.

wood turning [-ˌtəːniŋ] *n* torneado *m* en madera.

woodwaxen [-ˌwæksən] *n* BOT retama *f* de tintes, retama *f* de tintoreros.

woodwind [-wind] *n* MUS instrumentos *m pl* de viento de madera (section of orchestra) || US MUS instrumento *m* de viento de madera (instrument).

woodwork [-wəːk] *n* carpintería *f* (craft) || enmaderado *m*, maderaje *m* (in a construction) || artesanía *f* en madera; *Spanish woodwork is world famous* la artesanía en madera de España tiene fama mundial.

woodworker [-ˌwəːkə*] *n* carpintero *m* || tallista *m* en madera (wood-carver).

woodworking [-ˌwəːkiŋ] *n* carpintería *f* || talla *f* en madera (wood carving).

woodworm [-wəːm] *n* ZOOL carcoma *f*.

woody [-i] *adj* poblado de árboles, arbolado, da; *woody region* región arbolada || leñoso, sa (like wood); *a plant with a woody stem* una planta de tallo leñoso || — *woody sound* sonido sordo || *woody taste* sabor a madera.

wooer [wuːə*] *n* pretendiente *m*, galán *m*.

woof [wuf] *n* trama *f* (weft).

woofer [-ə*] *n* altavoz *m* para sonidos graves.

wooing ['wuːiŋ] *adj/n* galanteo *m*.

wool [wul] *n* lana *f*; *ball of wool* ovillo de lana || pelo *m*, lana *f* (of an animal) || — FIG *dyed-in-the-wood conservative* conservador acérrimo | *dyed-in-the wool Spaniard* español de pura cepa || *fibreglass wool* lana de vidrio || *knitting wool* lana para hacer punto || FIG *much cry and little wool* mucho ruido y pocas nueces || *shorn wool* lana de esquileo || *steel wool* fibra metálica || *steel wool pad* estropajo metálico || FIG *to go for wool and come home shorn* ir por lana y volver trasquilado || FIG & FAM *to pull the wool over s.o.'s eyes* dar a alguien gato por liebre.
◆ *adj* de lana; *a wool jersey* un jersey de lana || lanero, ra; de la lana; *the wool industry* la industria lanera; *wool trade* comercio de la lana.

wool-bearing [-ˌbɛəriŋ] *adj* lanar.

wool card [-kɑːd] *n* carda *f*.

wool clip [-klip] *n* producción *f* anual de lana.

wool comb [-kəum] *n* carda *f* de la lana.

woolen [-ən] *adj* US → **woollen.**

wool fat [-fæt] *n* grasa *f* de la lana.

woolgathering [-gæðəriŋ] *adj* FIG distraído, da || FIG *to be woolgathering* estar en las nubes, estar en Babia.
◆ *n* FIG distracción *f*.

wool grease [-griːs] *n* grasa *f* de la lana, churre *m* (wool fat).

woolgrowing [-ˌgrəuiŋ] *n* cría *f* de ganado lanar.

wool-hall [-hɔːl] *n* mercado *m* de lana.

woolies [-iz] *pl n* US ropa *f sing* de lana.

wooliness [-inis] *n* US → **woolliness.**

woollen; US woolen [-ən] *adj* de lana (made of wool) || lanero, ra; de la lana; *woollen industry* industria de la lana.
◆ *n* lana *f* (cloth).
◆ *pl* ropa *f sing* de lana.

woollies [-iz] *pl n* ropa *f sing* de lana.

woolliness; US wooliness [-inis] *n* carácter *m* lanoso || FIG poca claridad *f*, imprecisión *f* (of style, of thought) | lo borroso (of painting).

woolly; US wooly [-i] *adj* lanoso, sa (like wool); *woolly appearance* aspecto lanoso || de lana (made of wool); *woolly toy* juguete de lana || cubierto de lana (covered with wool) || aborregado, da (cloud) || crespo, pa (hair) || aterciopelado, da (leaf, peach, etc.) || FIG borroso, sa (blurred); *woolly outline* perfil borroso | confuso, sa; impreciso, sa; vago, ga (idea, reply, etc.) | empañado, da (voice).

woolly-headed [-iˌhedid] *adj* que no tiene las ideas claras.

woolman [-mən] *n* comerciante *m* en lanas (merchant) || fabricante *m* de productos de lana (manufacturer).
— OBSERV El plural de esta palabra es *woolmen*.

woolpack [-pæk] *n* bala *f* or paca *f* de lana (bale of wool) || nube *f* [aborregada] (cloud).

woolsack [-sæk] *n* saco *m* de lana || *the Woolsack* cojín *m* en que se sienta el «Lord Chancellor» (seat), cargo *m* del «Lord Chancellor» (office).

wool stapler [-ˌsteiplə*] *n* tratante *m* & *f* en lana.

wooly [-i] *adj* US → **woolly.**

woozy ['wuːzi] *adj* FAM indispuesto, ta; mareado, da.

Worcester sauce ['wustəˌsɔːs] *n* CULIN salsa *f* Worcester.

word [wəːd] *n* palabra *f*, vocablo *m*, voz *f*; *Spanish word* palabra española || noticia *f* (news); *word came that he was alive* llegó la noticia de que estaba vivo; *to bring word* traer noticias || recado *m* (message); *to send word* mandar recado || palabra *f* (promise); *to break one's word* faltar a su palabra; *to give one's word* dar su palabra || orden *f*; *to give the word to attack* dar la orden de atacar; *to pass the word round* transmitir la orden || santo y seña *m* (password); *to enter you must give the word* para entrar tiene que dar el santo y seña || — *a word of advice* un consejo || *a word to the wise is enough* al buen entendedor pocas palabras bastan || *by word or mouth* oralmente, verbalmente, de palabra || *clever isn't the word; I'd say he's a genius* inteligente no es la palabra; yo diría que es un genio || *don't breathe a word of this to anyone* de esto no digas ni una palabra a nadie || *he won't hear a word against her* no permite que se diga nada en contra de ella || *his word is law* su palabra es ley || *in a word* en una palabra || *in every sense of the word* en toda la extensión de la palabra || *in word* de palabra || *in word and deed* de palabra y obra || *it is his word against mine* su palabra contra la mía || *key word* palabra clave || *man of his word* hombre *m* de palabra || FAM *mum's the word!* ¡punto en boca!, ¡ni una palabra! || *my word!* ¡válgame Dios!, ¡Dios mío! || *nobody has a good word to say for him* no hay quien hable en su favor || FAM *not to be able to get a word in edgeways* no poder meter baza || *not to say a word* no decir ni una palabra *or* ni pío || *on my word* palabra, a fe mía || *take my word for it* se lo aseguro, le doy mi palabra || *the last word in* el último grito en || REL *the Word* el Verbo | *the Word of God* la palabra de Dios || *to be as good as one's word* cumplir con su palabra || *to be better than one's word* hacer más de lo prometido || *to hang on s.o.'s every word* estar pendiente de las palabras de alguien || *to have a word to say* tener algo que decir || *to have a word with s.o. about sth.* hablar de algo con alguien || *to have the last word* decir la última palabra || *to keep one's word* cumplir su palabra || *to leave word* dejar recado || *to leave word that* dejar dicho que || *to put in a good word for s.o.* decir unas palabras en favor de alguien || *to say the word* dar su aprobación || *to send s.o. word of sth.* avisar a alguien de algo || *to suit the action to the word* unir la acción a la palabra || *to take s.o. at his word* cogerle a uno la palabra || *to take s.o.'s word for it* creer lo que alguien dice, creer en la palabra de alguien || *upon my word* bajo palabra || *without a word* sin decir palabra || *word for word* palabra por palabra, literalmente || *word of honour* palabra de honor || *your word is good enough for me* me basta con su palabra.
◆ *pl* palabras *f*; *his words went unheeded* nadie prestó atención a sus palabras || MUS letra *f sing* (of a song) || papel *m sing* (of an actor); *to learn one's words* aprender el papel || — *actions speak louder than words* obras son amores, que no buenas razones || *a man of few words* un hombre de pocas palabras || *beyond words* hasta lo indecible; *it is ugly beyond words* es feo hasta lo indecible || *fine words* palabras elocuentes || *in my own words* con mis propias palabras || *in other words* en otros términos, en otras palabras (said in another way), es decir (that is to say) || *in so many words* palabra por

palabra, textualmente; *I can't tell you what he said in so many words* no puedo decirle lo que dijo textualmente; explícitamente, claramente; *he didn't say so in so many words* no lo dijo explícitamente || *in the words of Shakespeare* según las palabras de *or* como dice Shakespeare || *in words of one syllable* con palabras sencillas || *mark his words* toma nota de lo que dice || *more splendid than words can tell* mucho mejor de lo que se puede expresar con palabras || FAM *not to mince one's words* no andar con rodeos, no tener pelos en la lengua || *play on words* juego *m* de palabras || *time and words can never be recalled* lo dicho, dicho está || *to call on s.o. to say a few words* conceder la palabra a alguien || *to eat one's words* tragarse las palabras, retractarse || *to have no words* no tener palabras || *to have words with s.o.* tener unas palabras con alguien, reñir con alguien, discutir con alguien || *too beautiful, too stupid for words* de lo más hermoso que hay, de lo más estúpido que hay || *to play on words* hacer un juego de palabras, jugar del vocablo || *to take the words out of s.o.'s mouth* quitarle a uno la palabra de la boca || *to twist s.o.'s words* tergiversar las palabras de uno || *to waste words* gastar saliva en balde || *to weigh one's words* medir *or* sopesar las palabras || *with these words* dichas estas palabras, con estas palabras || *words fail me to express my gratitude* no encuentro palabras para expresar mi gratitud.

word [wəːd] *vt* expresar; *a well-worded protest* una protesta bien expresada || redactar; *a badly worded letter* una carta mal redactada.

word blindness [-ˌblaindnis] *n* MED alexia *f.*

wordbook [-buk] *n* vocabulario *m.*

word-for-word [-fəˌwəːd] *adj* literal, palabra por palabra, (hecho) al pie de la letra; *word-for-word translation* traducción literal.

word game [-geim] *n* juego *m* de formación de palabras (forming words) || juego *m* de adivinación de palabras (guessing words).

wordiness [-inis] *n* verbosidad *f,* palabrería *f.*

wording [-iŋ] *n* redacción *f* || texto *m,* términos *m pl* (text).

wordless [-lis] *adj* mudo, da.

word of command [-əvkəˈmaːnd] *n* orden *f,* voz *f* de mando.

word-of-mouth [-əvˌmauθ] *adj* verbal, oral.

word-painting [-ˌpeitiŋ] *n* descripción *f* gráfica.

word-perfect [-ˈpəːfint] *adj* *to be word-perfect* saber perfectamente (a role, a speech, etc.).

word picture [-ˌpintʃə*] *n* descripción *f* gráfica.

wordplay [-plei] *n* juego *m* de palabras.

word processing [-ˌprəusesiŋ] *n* INFORM procesamiento *m or* tratamiento *m* de textos.

word processor [-ˌprəusesə*] *n* INFORM procesador *m* de textos.

wordy [-i] *adj* prolijo, ja; verboso, sa (using too many words) || verbal (using words).

wore [wɔː*] *pret* → **wear.**

work [wəːk] *n* trabajo *m; manual work* trabajo manual; *a teacher's work* el trabajo de un profesor; *a week's work* el trabajo de una semana || trabajo *m,* empleo *m* (employment) || obra *f; the works of Shakespeare* las obras de Shakespeare; *collected* o *complete works* obras completas; *literary work* obra literaria; *work of genius* obra genial; *Newton's scientific work* la obra científica de Newton; *work of art, of charity* obra de arte, de caridad || obras *f pl; work has begun on the road* se han empezado las obras en la carretera || razón *f; he made it his life's work* hizo de ello la razón de su vida || PHYS trabajo *m* || TECH pieza *f* (piece being made) || — *all work and no play makes Jack a dull boy* trabajar sin descanso agota a cualquiera || *day's work* jornada *f* || *down to work* manos a la obra || FIG *do your own dirty work* sácate tú las castañas del fuego || *I had my work cut out to finish it* me costó muchísimo trabajo terminarlo || FIG *it's all in a day's work* es el pan nuestro de cada día; son gajes del oficio || *it's thirsty work* es un trabajo que da sed || *keep up the good work!* ¡que sigan así! || *let's get to work!* ¡manos a la obra! || *masonry work* obra de mampostería || «men at work», «obras» || *out of work* parado, da; sin trabajo [AMER desocupado, da] || *piece of work* trabajo || *the forces at work* las fuerzas que están en juego || *to be at work* estar trabajando || *to make short work of sth.* terminar algo rápidamente (to finish quickly), comerse algo rápidamente, zamparse algo (to eat quickly) || *to make work* dar trabajo || *to put s.o. out of work* despedir a alguien || *to set s.o. to work* poner a alguien a trabajar || *to set to work* ponerse a trabajar || *to throw s.o. out of work* despedir a alguien || *work of reference* libro *m* de consulta || *work sharing* reparto *m* del trabajo, distribución *f* del trabajo || INFORM *work station* estación *f* de trabajo || *work stoppage* paro *m.*

◆ *pl* fábrica *f sing; the car works* la fábrica de coches || MIL fortificaciones *f* || TECH mecanismo *m sing* (mechanism) || REL obras *f; good works* buenas obras, obras pías, obras de caridad || — *Ministry of Works* Ministerio *m* de Obras Públicas || «*Road Works*» «Obras» || FAM *to give s.o. the works* dar a uno una paliza, sacudir a uno el polvo (to beat), matar a uno (to murder) || FAM *to shoot the works* poner toda la carne en el asador || *works council* jurado *m* de empresa.

work [wəːk] *vt* hacer trabajar; *the company works us too hard* la empresa nos hace trabajar demasiado || producir (a change) || hacer (a miracle) || dirigir, manejar (a business) || tener a cargo (to be in charge of) || explotar; *to work a mine* explotar una mina || tallar (stone) || labrar (wood, metals) || forjar (iron) || CULIN amasar (to knead) || coser (to sew) || resolver (an equation) || manejar, hacer funcionar (a machine) || accionar, poner en funcionamiento, hacer funcionar (a moving part) || trabajar en; *he works the northern region* trabajar en la región del norte || causar (ruin) || realizar (a plan) || poner en práctica (a theory, a law) || cultivar (land) || — *to be worked by electricity* funcionar con electricidad (a machine, etc.) || *to work a cure* curar || FIG & FAM *to work it* arreglárselas; *he worked it so that he received five weeks' holidays* se las arregló para tener cinco semanas de vacaciones | *to work one's fingers to the bone* trabajar como un mulo *or* como un negro || *to work one's passage* costear su viaje trabajando || *to work one's way through* abrirse paso por (an obstacle) || *to work one's way through college* trabajar para costearse los estudios || *to work one's way to* abrirse camino hacia || *to work one's way up* subir poco a poco *or* a duras penas (to climb), ascender por su trabajo (in a company, etc.) || FIG *to work o.s. to death* matarse trabajando | *to work to death* matar trabajando (to overwork), abusar de (to use too often); *to work an expression to death* abusar de una expresión.

◆ *vi* trabajar; *he worked quickly* trabajó rápidamente; *she is too young to work* es demasiado joven para trabajar || tener trabajo, tener un empleo (to be employed) || funcionar (a machine); *it is not working, it won't work, it doesn't work* no funciona con electricidad || tener éxito, salir bien, tener resultados positivos; *your plan will not work* su plan no saldrá bien || surtir *or* tener efecto; *a medicine which works immediately* una medicina que tiene efecto enseguida || fermentar (to ferment) || torcerse (facial features) || moverse (one's hands) || hundirse (to sink) || obrar, ir; *it works against your plan* esto va en contra de tu plan || obra, proceder; *work with method* proceder con método || practicar mucho; *to work at one's piano playing* practicar mucho el piano || trabajar; *she works in metal and wood* trabaja metal y madera || — FIG *it works both ways* es un arma de dos filos || *to work for a living* trabajar para vivir || *to work free* soltarse (to come loose), deshacerse (knot) || FIG *to work like a Trojan* trabajar como un negro || *to work loose* desatarse, aflojarse (knot, rope), desprenderse (part).

◆ *phr v* **to work at** trabajar en || **to work away** trabajar, seguir trabajando || **to work down** bajar poco a poco || **to work in** introducir; *to work in a few quotations* introducir algunas citas | penetrar poco a poco | trabajar en || **to work into** introducir en, meter en (to put in); *to work a piece of furniture into a narrow space* meter un mueble en un espacio estrecho; *to work a reference into a speech* introducir una referencia en un discurso | *to work o.s. into* meterse en | *to work o.s. into a rage* montar poco a poco en cólera || **to work off** quitarse (excess weight) | desahogar (one's anger) | desprenderse (part) | *to work off one's feelings* desahogarse | FAM *to work off steam* desahogarse || **to work on** seguir trabajando (to continue working) | trabajar en; *I spent Sunday working on the shelves I am making* pasé el domingo trabajando en la estantería que estoy haciendo | estudiar (document) | investigar (a problem) | intentar persuadir, intentar convencer; *I've been working on him for days* llevo días y días intentando persuadirle | interrogar (to interrogate) | basarse, fundarse (to base o.s. on); *I have very little information to work on* tengo muy pocos datos en que basarme | afectar (to have an effect on) || **to work out** solucionar, resolver; *to work out a problem* resolver un problema | encontrar; *to work out a solution* encontrar una solución | elaborar; *to work out a plan* elaborar un proyecto | salir; *my plans worked out perfectly* mis planes salieron perfectamente | planificar (one's future) | sacar con dificultad (to remove) | agotar (a person) | MIN agotar | hacer; *to work out a sum* hacer un cálculo | sumar (to add up) | calcular; *work out how much it will cost* calcula cuánto costará | *that works out at 10 pounds* eso suma 10 libras, eso asciende a 10 libras | *their plans did not work out* sus proyectos fracasaron | *this addition doesn't work out* esta suma no me sale || **to work round** cambiar de dirección || **to work through** penetrar poco a poco | abrirse paso por (through the crowd) || **to work up** excitar; *to work s.o. up into a frenzy* excitar a alguien hasta el frenesí | desarrollar (business) | FAM *to get worked up, to work o.s. up* excitarse | *to work up to* preparar el terreno para; *he is working up to sth.* está preparando el terreno para algo; tender a (to tend to).

workability [-əˈbiləti] *n* viabilidad *f.*

workable [-əbl] *adj* que se puede trabajar; *a workable substance* una sustancia que se puede trabajar || explotable; *workable land* terreno explotable; *workable mine* mina explotable || realizable, factible, viable; *a workable plan* un proyecto factible || FIG influenciable, manejable.

workaday [-ədei] *adj* de cada día, de diario (clothes, etc.) || laborable (week, etc.) || FIG ordinario, ria (commonplace).

workaholic [-əhɔlik] *n* adicto, ta al trabajo.

workbag [-bæg] *n* bolsa *f* de labores (for sewing materials) || bolsa *f* de las herramientas (for tools).

workbasket [-ˌbaːskit] *n* costurero *m* (basket for sewing materials).

workbench [-bentʃ] *n* mesa *f or* banco *m* de trabajo.

workbook [-buk] *n* cuaderno *m* (exercise book) || libro *m* de texto || folleto *m* de instrucciones (instruction manual) || libro *m* de trabajo (book of work done).

workbox [-bɔks] *n* costurero *m* (for sewing materials) || caja *f* de herramientas (for tools).

work camp [-kæmp] *n* campo *m* de trabajo.

workday [-dei] *n* día *m* laborable (day of work) || jornada *f*; *an eight-hour workday* una jornada de ocho horas.
◆ *adj* → **workaday.**

worked-up [-t'ʌp] *adj* FAM excitado, da.

worker [-ə*] *n* trabajador, ra (in general); *country workers* trabajadores del campo || obrero, ra; operario, ria (industrial); *skilled worker* obrero cualificado *or* especializado || autor, ra; *worker or miracles* autor de milagros || ZOOL obrera *f* (ant, bee) || — *he is a hard worker* es muy trabajador || FIG *to be a fast worker* no perder el tiempo || *workers of the world unite!* trabajadores del mundo ¡uníos!

worker ant [-ərænt] *n* hormiga *f* obrera.

worker bee [-əbi:] *n* abeja *f* obrera *or* neutra.

work force [-fɔ:s] *n* mano *f* de obra.

workhorse [-hɔ:s] *n* US caballo *m* de tiro || US FIG fiera *f* para el trabajo (hard worker).

workhouse [-haus] *n* asilo *m* de pobres || US reformatorio *m*, correccional *m*.

working [-iŋ] *adj* obrero, ra; *the working class* la clase obrera || laborable, de trabajo; *working day* día laborable || activo, va; *the working population* la población activa || que funciona (machine, etc.) || básico, ca; suficiente; *a working knowledge* un conocimiento básico || que sirve, válido, da (valuable) || suficiente (majority) || de explotación (expenses) || de trabajo (clothes) || — *in working order* un estado de funcionamiento || *it is in working order* funciona || *working asset* activo *m* realizable || *working capital* fondo *m* de operaciones || *working drawing* plano *m* de construcción || MIN *working face* frente *m* de corte || *working group* grupo *m* de trabajo || *working hypothesis* hipótesis *f* de trabajo || *working language* idioma *m* de trabajo || *working paper* documento *m* de trabajo || US *working papers* permiso *m* de trabajo para un menor de edad || *working party* grupo *m* de trabajo || *working speed* velocidad *f* de funcionamiento.
◆ *n* trabajo *m* (work) || funcionamiento *m* (of a machine, of one's mind) || explotación *f* (of a mine) || manejo *m* (act of operating sth.) || labrado *m* (of metals) || forja *f* (of iron) || cultivo *m* (of fields) || efecto *m* (of a medicine) || fermentación *f* (of beer, of wine) || MAR maniobra *f*.
◆ *pl* MIN excavaciones *f* (excavations).

working-class [-iŋklɑ:s] *adj* de la clase obrera.

workingman [-iŋ'mæn] *n* obrero *m*.
— OBSERV El plural de *workingman* es *workingmen*.

working out [-iŋ'aut] *n* resolución *f* (of a problem) || elaboración *f* (of a plan) || MIN agotamiento *m* || FAM cálculo *m*.

workless [-lis] *adj/n* parado, da [*AMER* desocupado, da].

work load [-ləud] *n* cantidad *f* de trabajo.

workman [-mən] *n* trabajador *m* (worker) || obrero *m* (manual, industrial) || artesano *m* (craftsman) || FIG *a bad workman always blames his tools* o *quarrels with his tools* no hay que buscar pretextos para un trabajo mal hecho.
— OBSERV El plural de *workman* es *workmen*.

workmanlike [-mənlaik]; **workmanly** [-mənli] *adj* concienzudo, da (person) || bien hecho, cha (piece of work).

workmanship [-mənʃip] *n* habilidad *f*, destreza *f* (craft) || arte *f*, artesanía *f* (fine skill) || ejecución *f* habilidosa || fabricación *f*, confección *f*.

workmate [-meit] *n* compañero *m* de trabajo.

workmen's compensation [-menz,kɔmpən'seiʃən] *n* indemnización *f* por accidente *or* enfermedades del trabajo || *workmen's compensation insurance* seguro social obrero.

workout [-aut] *n* prueba *f* (test) || SP entrenamiento *m*.

workpeople [-,pi:pl] *pl n* obreros *m*.

work permit [-,pə:mit] *n* permiso *m* de trabajo.

workroom [-rum] *n* taller *m*.

work sheet [-ʃi:t] *n* ficha *f* de trabajo.

workshop [-ʃɔp] *n* taller *m* (workroom) || ARTS estudio *m* || US seminario *m* (seminar).

work-shy [-ʃai] *adj* perezoso, sa.

work surface [-,sə:fis]; **sork top** [-tɔp] *n* encimera *f*.

work-to-rule [-turu:l] *n* huelga *f* de celo.

worktable [-,teibl] *n* mesa *f* de trabajo.

workwoman [-,wumən] *n* trabajadora *f* (worker) || obrera *f* (manual, industrial) || artesana *f* (craftswoman).
— OBSERV El plural es *workwomen*.

world [wə:ld] *n* mundo *m*, tierra *f*; *the longest river in the world* el río más largo del mundo || universo *m* (universe) || mundo *m*; *the Old World* el Viejo Mundo; *half the world is starving* la mitad del mundo está muriéndose de hambre; *the world of sport* el mundo del deporte; *the world of dreams* el mundo de los sueños; *the business world* el mundo de los negocios; *the animal world* el mundo de los animales; *the whole world loves me* todo el mundo me quiere; *people from another world* gente de otro mundo || — *all the world over, all over the world* en el mundo entero || *around the world in 80 days* la vuelta al mundo en ochenta días || FIG *a world of difference between them* una diferencia enorme entre ellos | *half the world* medio mundo (people) | *he's not long for this world* medio mundo (people) | *he's not long for this world* le queda poco | *it's a small world* el mundo es un pañuelo | *it's the same the world over* en todas partes pasa lo mismo, en todas partes cuecen habas || *I would give anything in the world to know* daría cualquier cosa por saber || *I wouldn't do it for the world* no lo haría por nada del mundo || *man of the world* hombre de mundo || *she is for all the world like* es exactamente como || *the next* o *the other world* el otro mundo, la otra vida || *the world's worst painter* el peor pintor del mundo || FIG *to be dead to the world* estar durmiendo como un leño (asleep), estar borracho perdido (drunk) || *to bring into the world* traer al mundo || *to come down in the world* venir a menos || *to come into the world* venir al mundo || FIG *to feel* o *to be on top of the world* estar en el séptimo cielo, estar en la gloria (happy), sentirse muy bien (healthy) | *to go to a better world* pasar a un mundo mejor *or* a mejor vida || *to go up in the world* medrar || *to have the world at one's feet* tener el mundo a sus pies || *to know the best of both worlds* unir lo divino a lo humano || *to see the world* ver mundo || *to take the world as it is* aceptar la vida como es || FIG *to the world* completamente | *to think the world of s.o.* tener muy buena opinión *or* un alto concepto de alguien | *what in the world are you doing?* ¡qué demonios haces? || REL *world without end* por los siglos de los siglos || FIG *you are all the world to me* eres todo para mí | *you can't have the best of both worlds* no se puede nadar y guardar la ropa.
◆ *adj* mundial; *on a world scale* a escala mundial; *World Bank* Banco Mundial; *the First World War* la Primera Guerra Mundial || universal; *world history* historia universal.

world-class [-klɑ:s] *adj* SP de categoría mundial.

world-famous [-'feiməs] *adj* conocido mundialmente, de fama mundial.

worldliness [-linis] *n* mundanería *f*, mundanalidad *f* (devotion to worldly affairs).

worldling [-liŋ] *n* persona *f* mundana.

worldly [-li] *adj* mundano, na (devoted to this life) || del mundo, de este mundo || material; *wordly interests* intereses materiales.

worldly-minded [-li'maindid] *adj* mundano, na.

worldly-wisdom [-li'wizdəm] *n* experiencia *f* de la vida.

worldly-wise [-li'waiz] *adj* que tiene experiencia de la vida.

world map [-'mæp] *n* mapamundi *m*.

world music [-,mju:zik] *n* música *f* étnica.

world power [-'pauə*] *n* potencia *f* mundial.

world series [-'siəriz] *n* US SP serie *f* mundial.

world-weariness [-,wiərinis] *n* hastío *m* del mundo, cansancio *m* de la vida.

world-weary [-,wiəri] *adj* hastiado del mundo, cansado de la vida.

worldwide [-waid] *adj* mundial.

worm [wə:m] *n* ZOOL gusano *m* | lombriz *f* (earthworm) || TECH rosca *f*, filete *m* (thread of a screw) | tornillo *m* sin fin (endless screw) | serpentín *m* (of a still) | tubo *m* espiral (spiral pipe) || FAM canalla *m*, granuja *m* (vile person) | gusano *m* (insignificant person) || — FIG *the worm will turn* la paciencia tiene un límite | *worm of conscience* gusanillo *m* de la conciencia.
◆ *pl* MED lombrices *f*.

worm [wə:m] *vt* TECH roscar, filetear, aterrajar (a screw) || VET quitar las lombrices a || MAR reforzar con cuerda (a cable) || FAM sonsacar, sacar; *to worm a secret out of s.o.* sacar un secreto a alguien || — FIG *to worm one's way* deslizarse; *he wormed his way through the trees* se deslizó entre los árboles; colarse (to slip in) || *to worm one's way along* arrastrarse como un gusano || FIG *to worm o.s. into* insinuarse en.

worm drive [-draiv] *n* transmisión *f* por medio de un tornillo sin fin.

worm-eaten [-,it:tn] *adj* carcomido, da (wood) || apolillado, da (material) || picado por los gusanos (fruit).

worm gear [-giə*] *n* TECH engranaje *m* de tornillo sin fin | rueda *f* helicoidal (worm wheel).

wormhole [-həul] *n* agujero *m* de lombriz (in earth) || carcoma *f*, agujero *m* de carcoma (in wood) || picadura *f* de polilla (in cloth).

worm wheel [-wi:l] *n* TECH rueda *f* helicoidal.

wormwood [-wud] *n* BOT ajenjo *m* || FIG hiel *f*, amargura *f* (bitterness).

wormy [-i] *adj* agusanado, da (full of worms) || carcomido, da (wood) || apolillado, da (cloth).

worn [wɔ:n] *pp* → **wear.**

worn-out [-'aut] *adj* muy estropeado, da; gastado, da; *worn-out shoes* zapatos muy estropeados || agotado, da; rendido, da (exhausted) || FIG viejo, ja; anticuado, da (out of date).

worried ['wʌrid] *adj* preocupado, da; *a worried look* una mirada preocupada; *to be worried about* estar preocupado por.

worrier ['wʌriə*] *n* aprensivo, va.

worriment ['wʌrimənt] *n* US preocupación *f*.

worrisome [wʌrisəm] *adj* preocupante, inquietante (causing worry) || aprensivo, va (easily worried).

worry [ˈwʌri] *n* preocupación *f*, inquietud *f*; *the worry is killing me* la inquietud me mata || preocupación *f*, problema *m*; *this child is a worry to me* este niño es una preocupación para mí; *financial worries* problemas financieros; *the worry of having to* la preocupación de tener que || — *that's the least of my worries* eso es lo que menos me preocupa || *to be beside o.s. with worry* estar muy preocupado || *what's his worry?* ¿qué es lo que le preocupa?

worry [ˈwʌri] *vt* preocupar; *I am dreadfully worried* estoy enormemente preocupado; *this problem worries me* este problema me preocupa; *the event worried scholars for two hundred years* el hecho preocupó a los eruditos durante doscientos años || molestar (to bother); *don't worry me, I'm working* no me molestes, estoy trabajando; *the wound doesn't worry me when I walk* la herida no me molesta cuando ando || atacar; *wolves worry the sheep* los lobos atacan las ovejas || — *don't worry your head about me!* ¡no te preocupes por mí! || *to worry o.s.* preocuparse || *to worry sth. out* resolver algo [con dificultad].
◆ *vi* preocuparse (*about, over* por); *he worries so much* se preocupa tanto; *don't worry about me!* ¡no te preocupes por mí! || molestarse (to put o.s. out) || — FAM *I should worry!* ¿a mí qué me importa? || *to worry along* arreglárselas.

worrying [-iŋ] *adj* inquietante, preocupante; *a worrying problem* un problema inquietante.
◆ *n* preocupación *f*.

worse [wəːs] *adj* peor; *worse weather than yesterday* un tiempo peor que ayer; *he is worse than we feared* es peor de lo que temíamos; *worse than ever* peor que nunca || — *it could have been worse* podía haber sido peor || *it gets worse and worse* es cada vez peor || *I was none the worse for it* no por eso estaba peor || *so much the worse for him* tanto peor para él || *to get* o *to grow worse* empeorar || *to go from bad to worse* ir de mal en peor || *to look the worse for wear* estar desgastado, da (sth.), estar desmejorado, da (s.o.) || *to make things worse, he said* para empeorar las cosas, dijo || *worse and worse* cada vez peor, de mal en peor || *worse luck* (por) mala suerte || FIG *worse things happen at sea* más se perdió en Cuba.
◆ *adv* peor; *I am playing worse than last season* estoy jugando peor que la temporada pasada || más; *it hurts me worse* me duele más || — *to be worse off* estar peor || *worse still* peor aún.
◆ *n* lo peor; *worse was to come* quedaba todavía lo peor || — *he has been through worse* las ha visto peores || *I think none the worse of him* no ha variado mi opinión sobre él || *I have seen worse* he visto cosas peores || *to change for the worse* empeorar.
— OBSERV *Worse* es el comparativo de *bad* y *badly*.

worsen [-n] *vt* empeorar.
◆ *vi* empeorar, ponerse peor.

worsening [-niŋ] *n* agravación *f*, empeoramiento *m* (deterioration).

worship [ˈwəːʃip] *n* culto *m*; *the worship of idols* el culto a los ídolos || culto *m*, oficio *m* (ceremony) || FIG adoración *f*, culto *m* || — *freedom of worship* libertad *f* de cultos || *His Worship the Mayor* el señor alcalde || *Your Worship* su señoría, vuestra merced.

worship [ˈwəːʃip] *vt* venerar, rendir culto a (a god) || FIG adorar, idolatrar (to idolize).
— OBSERV En Gran Bretaña la *p* se duplica en el gerundio: *worshipping*, en el pretérito y en el participio pasivo: *worshipped*, lo que no ocurre en Estados Unidos: *worshiping* y *worshiped*.

worshiper [-ə*] *n* US adorador, ra.

worshipful [-ful] *adj* excelentísimo, ma (in titles) || venerable (freemason) || devoto, ta (adoring).

worshiping [-iŋ] *n* US ⟶ **worshipping.**

worshipper [-ə*] *n* adorador, ra.

worshipping; US **worshiping** [-iŋ] *n* culto; *the worshipping of a god* el culto a un dios || adoración *f*, veneración *f* (adoration).

worst [wəːst] *adj* peor; *the worst book I know* el peor libro que conozco; *my worst enemy* mi peor enemigo; *the worst two* los dos peores || más grave (most serious); *his worst mistake* su falta más grave; *the worst victims of the accident* las víctimas más graves del accidente.
◆ *adv* peor; *the worst educated people* la gente peor educada; *I ran worst of all* yo corrí peor que todos; *the worst treated animals* los animales peor tratados || *to come off worst* llevar la peor parte, salir vencido.
◆ *n* el peor, la peor; *John is the worst* Juan es el peor; *Mary is the worst in the school* María es la peor de la escuela || lo peor; *the worst of the storm has passed* ya ha pasado lo peor de la tormenta; *the worst of it is that* lo peor del caso es que || peor momento *m*; *when the epidemic was at its worst* en el peor momento de la epidemia || inconveniente *m*, lo malo; *the worst of buying cheap clothes is that they don't last long* el inconveniente *or* lo malo de comprar ropa barata es que dura poco || — *at worst, at the worst* en el peor de los casos || *do your worst* haga lo que quiera || *if the worst comes to the worst* en el peor de los casos || *the weather is at its worst* el tiempo está peor que nunca || *to assume the worst* imaginar lo peor || *to get the worst of it* llevar la peor parte, salir vencido || *to give s.o. the worst of it* hacerle pasar un mal rato a alguien || *when things are at their worst* cuando todo va muy mal.
— OBSERV *Worst* es el superlativo de *bad* y *badly*.

worst [wəːst] *vt* derrotar, vencer, superar.

worsted [ˈwustid] *n* estambre *m* (fabric).

wort [wəːt] *n* mosto *m* (of beer).

worth [wəːθ] *prep* digno de, merecedor de; *it is not worth attention* no es digno de atención || que vale, equivalente a; *it is not worth more than three pounds* no vale más de tres libras || — *for all one is worth* con todas sus fuerzas; *to swim for all one is worth* nadar con todas sus fuerzas || *for what it is worth* por si puede servir, por si sirve de algo; *I can give you his description for what it is worth* le puedo dar su descripción por si puede servirle || *friendship is sth. worth keeping* la amistad es algo que vale la pena conservar || *he is worth first prize* merece el primer premio || FAM *he is worth millions* es multimillonario, tiene un dineral || *he is worth three men* vale por tres hombres || *his offer is worth considering* su oferta es digna de consideración, su oferta merece ser considerada, su oferta es digna de ser considerada || *I have a company car, which is worth two hundred pounds a year to me* tengo un coche de la compañía, lo cual me ahorra doscientas libras al año || *is it worth my going?* ¿vale la pena que vaya? || *it is not worth it* no vale *or* no merece la pena || *it is not worth much* no vale gran cosa || *it is worth doing* vale *or* merece la pena hacerlo || *it is worth mentioning* es digno de mencionarse || *property worth a million pounds* propiedad que vale un millón de libras || *this book is worth reading* vale *or* merece la pena leer este libro, este libro es digno de leerse || *to be worth* valer; *this car is worth a thousand pounds* este coche vale mil libras; ser digno de, merecer (to merit), valer la pena; *it is worth trying* vale la pena intentarlo.
◆ *n* valor *m*; *a house of no worth* una casa sin valor; *her poetry is of little worth compared with her novels* su poesía tiene poco valor comparada con sus novelas || mérito *m*; *a man of great worth* un hombre de gran mérito || valía *f*, valor *m*; *her true worth was not appreciated until after her death* no se apreció su verdadera valía hasta después de su muerte || fortuna *f* (fortune); *his true worth must be millions of dollars* su verdadera fortuna debe ascender a millones de dólares || — *a hundred pounds' worth of clothes* ropa por valor de cien libras || *it's an expensive place, but you get your money's worth* es un sitio caro pero vale realmente lo que cuesta || *I've really had my money's worth out of these shoes* me han dado muy buen resultado estos zapatos || *moral worth* cualidades *f pl* morales, valor moral || *of great worth* de gran valor || *of little worth* de poco valor || *she knows where to shop to get her money's worth* sabe donde comprar para sacarle jugo al dinero || *two shillings' worth of sweets* dos chelines de caramelos.

worth [wəːθ] *vt* (ant) ser; *woe worth the day* maldito sea el día.

worthily [ˈwəːðili] *adv* dignamente.

worthiness [ˈwəːðinis] *n* mérito *m*.

worthless [ˈwəːθlis] *adj* sin valor (of no value) || inútil (useless) || despreciable (despicable) || — *to be quite worthless* no tener ningún valor, no valer nada || *to make sth. worthless* quitarle todo valor a algo.

worthlessness [-nis] *n* falta *f* de valor (lack of value) || inutilidad *f* (uselessness) || vileza *f* (lowness).

worthwhile [ˈwəːθwail] *adj* que vale la pena; *it was a worthwhile trip* fue un viaje que valió la pena || útil; *a worthwhile experience* una experiencia útil || digno de consideración (worth considering) || — *I never worry, it's not worthwhile* no me preocupo nunca, no vale la pena || *it's not worthwhile waiting* no vale *or* no merece la pena esperar || *to make it worthwhile* para que valga la pena.

worthy [ˈwəːði] *adj* noble, justo, ta; *a worthy cause* una causa noble || respetable (respectable) || digno, na (dignified); *worthy conduct* conducta digna || estimable (esteemed) || justo, ta (just); *a worthy reward* una recompensa justa || valioso, sa (good); *my worthy assistant* mi valioso asistente || meritorio, ria; *a worthy action* una acción meritoria || honesto, ta (motives, etc.) || — *it is worthy of note that* es digno de observar que, hay que señalar que || *other authors worthy of note* otros autores que merece la pena mencionar || *to be worthy of* ser digno de, merecer; *his crime is worthy of punishment* su crimen merece castigo || *worthy of* digno de; *an opponent worthy of him* un adversario digno de él; digno de, merecedor de; *an action worthy of reward* una acción digna de recompensa.
◆ *n* notabilidad *f*, prócer *m*.

would [wud] *v aux* se emplea para formar el potencial (2ª y 3ª persona del singular y del plural); *she would go if she could* iría si pudiese; *they said that they would go* me dijeron que irían || indica la probabilidad; *she would be about 50* debía de tener unos cincuenta años, tendría unos cincuenta años || expresa la duda; *that would appear to be the solution* eso parece ser la solución; *I would think so* supongo que sí || indica la voluntad; *would you get me my hat?* ¿quieres traerme el sombrero? || soler, acostumbrar (habit); *they would go for a walk before breakfast* solían dar un paseo antes del desayuno || — *it would be you!* ¡tú tenías que ser! || *of course it would rain!* ¡naturalmente tenía *or* tuvo que llover! || *that's just what you would do* ¡eso es muy tuyo! || *what would this be?* ¿qué será eso?
— OBSERV *Would* puede contraerse cuando le antecede un pronombre personal: *I'd, you'd, he'd, we'd, they'd*. Si va seguido por la

negación *not* puede formar con ella la palabra *wouldn't*: *he wouldn't come; wouldn't they come?*
— OBSERV Would es el pretérito y el potencial de *will*, por lo tanto está tratado en gran parte en el artículo *will* (véase WILL).
— OBSERV Después de *I wish* y de *if* el verbo introducido por *would* tiene que ponerse en imperfecto de subjuntivo en español: *I wish you would shut up* me gustaría que te callaras, ¡ojalá te callaras!; *if you would shut up, I would be able to hear* si tú te callaras, yo podría oír.
— OBSERV En la primera persona del potencial *would* sustituye a veces a *should*: *I would have arrived earlier if...*

would-be [-bi:] *adj* supuesto, ta (supposed, socalled); *a would-be painter* un supuesto pintor || *the would-be candidates* los aspirantes a la candidatura.

wouldn't [-nt] contracción de «would not».

wound [wu:nd] *n* herida *f*; *skin wound* herida superficial || FIG herida *f* (emotional hurt) || — REL *the five wounds of Christ* las cinco llagas de Cristo || FIG *to open up an old wound* renovar la herida | *to rub salt in the wound* hurgar en la herida, herir en carne viva.

wound [wu:nd] *vt/vi* herir; *he was slightly wounded* fue levemente herido; *the remark wounded her deeply* la observación le hirió profundamente; *to wound to the quick* herir en lo vivo.

wound [waund] *pret/pp* ⟶ **wind.**

wounded ['wu:ndid] *adj* herido, da; *a wounded soldier* un soldado herido || *a wounded man* un herido, un hombre herido.
◆ *pl n* heridos *m*; *the wounded* los heridos.

wounding ['wu:ndiŋ] *adj* hiriente.

wove [wəuv] *pret* ⟶ **weave.**

woven [-ən] *pp* ⟶ **weave.**

wove paper [-,peipə*] *n* papel *m* vitela.

wow [wau] *n* FAM *it was a wow!* ¡fue estupendo!, ¡fue formidable!

WP; wp *abbr of [word processing, word processor]* procesamiento de textos, procesador de textos.

WPC *abbr of [woman police constable]* mujer policía.

wrack [ræk] *n* varec *m* (seaweed) || ruina *f* (ruin) || *to go to wrack and ruin* venirse abajo.

wrack [ræk] *vt* destruir (to destroy) || ⟶ **rack.**

wraith [reiθ] *n* espectro *m*, fantasma *m*.

wrangle ['rŋŋgl] *n* disputa *f*, riña *f*, altercado *m* (quarrel).

wrangle ['ræŋgl] *vt* US rodear (to round up cattle).
◆ *vi* discutir (to argue) || reñir, pelearse (to quarrel) || regatear (to haggle).

wrangler [-ə*] *n* FAM pendenciero, ra; camorrista *m* & *f* (quarreller) || US vaquero *m*.

wrap [ræp] *n* chal *m* (shawl) || manta *f* [AMER frazada *f*] (blanket) || capa *f* (short cape) || bata *f* (dressing gown) || envoltura *f* (wrapping).
◆ *pl* FIG secreto *m sing* (secrecy) || FIG *to take the wraps off sth.* revelar algo (to reveal).

wrap [ræp] *vt* envolver; *he came in wrapped in a blanket* entró envuelto en una manta; *an affair wrapped in mystery* un asunto envuelto en el misterio || cubrir, envolver; *a mountain wrapped in mist* una montaña cubierta de *or* envuelta en niebla || absorber; *wrapped in thought* absorto en sus pensamientos || — *he wrapped a scarf round his neck* se puso una bufanda || *to be wrapped up in* estar envuelto en (paper, blanket, etc.), estar absorto en (to be absorbed in), dedicarse completamente a (to dedicate o.s. to) || *to wrap o.s.* envolverse || *to wrap up* envolver; *he wrapped her up in her coat* la envolvió en su abrigo; *shall I wrap it up for you?* ¿se lo envuelvo?; abrigar; *I always wrap up the children well* siempre abrigo bien a los niños; cubrir (to cover), concluir (a deal), resolver, terminar con (a case, a problem).
◆ *vi* enrollarse; *climbing plants wrap round trees* las plantas trepadoras se enrollan en los árboles || — *to wrap up* abrigarse; *wrap up well, it's cold today* abrígate bien, hace frío hoy || FAM *wrap up!* ¡cierra el pico!

wrapped-up ['ræptʌp] *adj* envuelto, ta (a parcel) || FIG liado, da (in work) | quedado, da (in s.o.).

wrapper ['ræpə*] *n* envoltura *f* (wrapping) || embalador, ra; empaquetador, ra (person) || sobrecubierta *f* (jacket of a book) || bata *f* (dressing gown) || faja *f* (for posting newspapers, etc.) || capa *f* (tobacco leaf round a cigar).

wrapping ['ræpiŋ] *n* embalaje *m* (action) || envoltura *f* (covering, material used) || *wrapping paper* papel *m* de envolver.

wrasse [ræs] *n* ZOOL budión *m* (fish).

wrath [rɔθ] *n* ira *f*; *the grapes of wrath* las uvas de la ira || FIG furia *f* (of the elements).

wrathful [-ful] *adj* colérico, ca; airado, da; iracundo, da.

wreak [ri:k] *vt* descargar (anger) || sembrar (destruction) || tomar (vengeance) || infligir (punishment) || gastar (to expend, to spend) || *to wreak havoc* hacer estragos.

wreath [ri:θ] *n* guirnalda *f*, corona *f* (circle of flowers) || corona *f* (for a funeral) || espiral *f* (of smoke).

wreathe [ri:ð] *vt* trenzar, hacer una guirnalda de; *to wreathe flowers* trenzar flores, hacer una guirnalda de flores || enguirnaldar (to garland) || enroscar (to wind); *the snake wreathed itself round the tree* la serpiente se enroscó en el árbol || enrollar; *he wreathed the rope round the stick* enrolló la cuerda en el palo || coronar (to cap, to crown) || cubrir (to cover) || envolver (to wrap) || coronar, ceñir (to crown with a wreath) || *a face wreathed in smiles* una cara muy risueña.
◆ *vi* subir en espirales (smoke) || serpentear (to wind, to twist).

wreck [rek] *n* MAR naufragio *m* (shipwreck) | barco *m* hundido *or* naufragado (wrecked ship) || restos *m pl* (remains of car, train, aeroplane) || colisión *f*, accidente *m* (accident) || escombros *m pl* (of a building) || FIG ruina *f* (person); *a human wreck* una ruina humana; *to be a wreck* estar hecho una ruina | hundimiento *m* (of a business) | fin *m* (of hopes) || — *the plane was a complete wreck* el avión estaba completamente destrozado || FIG *to be a nervous wreck* tener los nervios destrozados | *to look a wreck* estar hecho una pena || MAR *to suffer wreck* naufragar.

wreck [rek] *vt* hacer naufragar, hundir, echar a pique (a ship) || hacer descarrilar (a train) || destruir (a building) || destrozar (a car, a plane, etc.); *the vandals wrecked the premises* los gamberros destrozaron el local || estropear (a machine) || FIG destrozar, estropear, acabar con; *drugs wrecked his health* las drogas le destrozaron la salud | estropear, arruinar, desbaratar, destruir; *he wrecked their plans* estropeó sus planes | destrozar (one's life) | destrozar (the nerves) || MAR *to be wrecked* naufragar.
◆ *vi* naufragar, hundirse, irse a pique (a ship) || destrozarse || estropearse.

wreckage ['rekidʒ] *n* restos *m pl* (of a car, of an aeroplane) || escombros *m pl* (of a building) || MAR pecios *m pl*, pecio *m*, restos *m pl* de un naufragio.

wrecked ['rekt] *adj* naufragado, da (ship) || náufrago, ga (person) || destrozado, da (car, aeroplane, life) || destruido, da (building).

wrecker ['rekə*] *n* provocador *m* de naufragios (person who causes shipwrecks) || raquero *m* (plunderer) || persona *f* encargada de recoger los restos de un naufragio (person who recovers wrecked ships) || US demoledor *m* de casas (housebreaker) | grúa *f*, camión *m* grúa (breakdown lorry) || gamberro *m* (hooligan).

wrecking ['rekiŋ] *n* destrucción *f* || demolición *f* (of buildings) || descarrilamiento *m* (of a train) || pérdida *f* (of hopes) || US salvamento *m* (salvaging of ships).

wrecking service [-,sə:vis] *n* US AUT servicio *m* de auxilio en carretera.

wren [ren] *n* reyezuelo *m* (bird).

wrench [rentʃ] *n* tirón *m* (a sharp pull) || MED torcedura *f* || TECH llave *f* inglesa (adjustable spanner) || FIG dolor *m*, pena *f*; *the wrench of separation* el dolor de la separación || — TECH *elbowed wrench* llave de pipa para tuercas || *to give one's ankle a wrench* torcerse el tobillo || *to give sth. a wrench* torcer algo violentamente.

wrench [rentʃ] *vt* torcer; *to wrench s.o.'s arm* torcerle el brazo a alguien || FIG torcer, desvirtuar (a meaning, a statement) || — *to wrench a handle off a door* arrancar el picaporte de una puerta || *to wrench one's ankle* torcerse el tobillo || *to wrench out* arrancar || *to wrench sth. from s.o.* arrancarle algo a alguien || *to wrench sth. open* abrir algo de un tirón, abrir algo violentamente.

wrest [rest] *n* MUS llave *f* para afinar (for tuning).

wrest [rest] *vt* arrebatar; *he wrested the bag from the woman* arrebató el bolso a la mujer; *Real Madrid wrested the championship from Barcelona* el Real Madrid le arrebató el campeonato al Barcelona || FIG alterar, desvirtuar (to twist); *to wrest the truth* alterar la verdad | dar una falsa interpretación a (a law, etc.) | arrancar (a confession) || *to wrest o.s. free* soltarse.

wrestle [resl] *n* lucha *f* || *to have a wrestle with* luchar con.

wrestle ['resl] *vt* luchar con *or* contra; *to wrestle s.o.* luchar con *or* contra alguien || US derribar (a calf for branding).
◆ *vi* luchar; *the two men wrestled for the championship* los dos hombres lucharon por el campeonato || *to wrestle with* luchar con *or* contra; *to wrestle with adversity* luchar contra la adversidad; *to wrestle with s.o.* luchar con alguien.

wrestler [-ə*] *n* luchador, ra.

wrestling [-iŋ] *n* SP lucha *f*; *freestyle wrestling* lucha libre; *wrestling match* combate de lucha.

wrest pin ['restpin] *n* clavija *f* (in a piano).

wrest plank ['restplæŋk] *n* MUS clavijero *m*.

wretch [retʃ] *n* desgraciado, da (unfortunate person); *poor wretch* pobre desgraciado || miserable *m* & *f*, malvado, da (wicked person) || — *little wretch* pillo, lla (little rascal) || *poor little wretch* pobrecito, ta || *you wretch!* ¡desgraciado!

wretched ['retʃid] *adj* desgraciado, da; desdichado, da (unfortunate, unhappy) || espantoso, sa; horrible (horrible); *wretched weather* tiempo horrible || miserable (miserable); *to live in wretched conditions* vivir en condiciones miserables; *a wretched hovel* una casucha miserable || despreciable, miserable (contemptible) || lamentable (pitiful) || malísimo, ma (very bad) || maldito, ta; *this wretched zip is stuck* esta maldita cremallera no se cierra || — *to feel wretched* estar muy abatido (depressed), estar muy mal (ill) || *to feel wretched about doing sth.* sentir remordimientos por haber hecho algo || *what wretched luck!* ¡qué mala suerte! || *you see some wretched driving these days* hay que ver lo mal que conduce la gente hoy.

wretchedness [-nis] *n* tristeza *f* (sadness) || desgracia *f*, desdicha *f* (ill fortune) || miseria *f* (misery, poverty) || abatimiento *m* (depression) || lo despreciable, vileza *f* || *the wretchedness of the weather* el tiempo horrible.

wriggle ['rigl] *n* serpenteo *m*, culebreo *m* (snakelike movement) || meneo *m*, contoneo *m* (of hips).

wriggle ['rigl] *vt* mover, menear; *to wriggle one's hand* mover la mano || — *to wriggle one's way along* ir serpenteando || *to wriggle one's way through* deslizarse entre *or* por || *to wriggle o.s. free* lograr soltarse || *to wriggle o.s. into* introducirse con dificultad en, deslizarse en.
◆ *vi* agitarse, menearse; *the worm wriggled on the hook* el gusano se agitaba en el anzuelo || colear (fish) || moverse (people) || — *to wriggle along* serpentear, ir serpenteando, deslizarse || *to wriggle into* introducirse con dificultad en || *to wriggle out* escaparse mañosamente, librarse hábilmente (of a difficulty), salir con dificultad (from a hole, etc.), escaparse de; *the worm wriggled out of my hand* el gusano se escapó de mi mano || *to wriggle through* deslizarse entre *or* por.

wriggly [-i] *adj* sinuoso, sa.

wring [riŋ] *n* apretón *m* (of hands) || torsión *f* || *to give the clothes a wring* escurrir la ropa.

wring* [riŋ] *vt* retorcer, escurrir (wet clothes) || retorcer; *to wring a chicken's neck* retorcer el pescuezo de un pollo || FIG partir, oprimir (heart) || — FAM *I'll wring his neck!* ¡le retorceré el pescuezo! || *to wring one's hands* retorcerse las manos || *to wring out* escurrir; *to wring water out of clothes* escurrir el agua de la ropa; retorcer, escurrir; *to wring clothes out* retorcer la ropa; arrancar (truth, confession), sacar (money from s.o.) || *to wring s.o.'s hand* dar un apretón de manos a alguien.
— OBSERV Pret y pp ***wrung***.

wringer [-ə*] *n* escurridor *m* (machine).

wringing [-iŋ]; **wringing wet** [-iŋ'wet] *adj* chorreando, completamente mojado, da (clothes) || calado hasta los huesos (person).

wrinkle ['riŋkl] *n* arruga *f* (of skin) || rizo *m* (on water) || arruga *f* (in cloth, etc.) || GEOL pliegue *m* || FAM truco *m*, idea *f* (clever hint or suggestion).

wrinkle ['riŋkl] *vt* arrugar, chafar (clothes) || arrugar (skin) || *to wrinkle one's brow* fruncir el ceño *or* el entrecejo.
◆ *vi* arrugarse (dress, skin) || rizarse (water).

wrinkled [-d]; **wrinkly** [-i] *adj* arrugado, da.

wrist [rist] *n* ANAT muñeca *f* (of a person) || codillo *m* (of an animal) || puño *m* (of a garment) || TECH pasador *m* del émbolo.

wristband [-bænd] *n* puño *m* (of a shirt) || muñequera *f* (for gymnasts, etc.).

wristlet [-lit] *n* muñequera *f*.
◆ *pl* FAM esposas *f* (handcuffs).

wristlet watch [-litwɔtʃ] *n* reloj *m* de pulsera.

wristlock [-lɔk] *n* SP llave *f* de muñeca.

wrist pin [-pin] *n* TECH pasador *m* del émbolo.

wristwatch [-wɔtʃ] *n* reloj *m* de pulsera.

writ [rit] *n* REL escritura *f*; *the Holy Writ* la Sagrada Escritura || JUR orden *f*, mandato *m*, mandamiento *m*, auto *m* || — *to draw up a writ* extender un mandato judicial || *to serve a writ on* o *against* notificar un mandato judicial a || *to issue s.o. a writ* demandar a alguien en juicio, emplazar a alguien ante el juez || *writ of attachment* mandato de embargo || *writ of execution* ejecutoria *f* || *writ of summons* emplazamiento *m*.

write* [rait] *vt* escribir; *to write a letter* escribir una carta; *write your name here* escriba aquí su nombre; *proper names are written with capital letters* los nombres propios se escriben con mayúscula; *to write in ink* escribir con tinta || redactar, escribir (a dictionary, a book) || componer, escribir (music) || hacer, extender (a cheque) || rellenar, llenar (a form) || JUR redactar (to draw up in legal form) | suscribir (to underwrite) || — FIG *despair was written on every face* la desesperación estaba impresa *or* se reflejaba en todos los rostros | *hatred was written all over him* llevaba el odio escrito en la cara | *he had phoney written all over him* todo indicaba que era un farsante | *innocence is written on his face* se puede ver la inocencia en su rostro, la inocencia está impresa en su rostro | *nothing to write home about* nada del otro mundo || *to write a good hand* tener buena letra || *to write o.s.* titularse, calificarse.
◆ *vi* escribir; *to write legibly* escribir legiblemente || escribir (to be a writer) || escribirse (to each other); *we've been writing for years* nos escribimos desde hace años || — *he wrote for me to send it* me pidió por carta que se lo mandase || *I have written for information* he escrito pidiendo informaciones || *I wrote to them to come* les escribí para que viniesen.
◆ *phr v* ***to write back*** contestar [carta] || ***to write down*** apuntar, anotar; *they wrote down everything he said* apuntaron todo lo que dijo | poner por escrito (to put in writing) | rebajar (stocks, goods, etc.) | considerar (to regard) || ***to write in*** escribir; *thousands of people wrote in to complain* miles de personas escribieron quejándose | insertar (to insert) | *to write in for* solicitar por escrito || ***to write off*** escribir rápidamente (to compose rapidly) | cancelar, dar por perdido; *to write off a debt* cancelar una deuda | amortizar (capital) | solicitar por escrito; *to write off for a catalogue* solicitar un catálogo por escrito | destrozar; *to write off a car* destrozar un coche || ***to write out*** escribir | copiar (to copy) | transcribir (to transcribe) | pasar a limpio (to make a fair copy of) | escribir con todas las letras (to write in full) | hacer, extender (a cheque) || — *to write o.s. out* estar acabado (a writer) || ***to write up*** hacer un reportaje sobre, escribir un artículo sobre (in a newspaper) | poner por escrito (to put in writing) | redactar (a report, notes) | exagerar, hinchar (to exaggerate) | poner al día (diary, etc.) | sobrestimar (assets).
— OBSERV Pret ***wrote***; pp ***written***.

write-off [-ɔf] *n* cancelación *f* || amortización *f* (of capital).

writer [-ə*] *n* escritor, ra (s.o. who writes) || autor, ra (author) || escribano *m* (clerk) || — *the present writer* el que esto escribe, el abajo firmante || *to be a poor writer* escribir mal.

write-up [-ʌp] *n* crítica *f* (of a film, of a play, etc.) || relato *m* (of an event) || crónica *f* elogiosa (flattering report) || valoración *f* excesiva (in the assets).

writhe [raið] *vi* retorcerse; *I writhe with* o *in pain* me retuerzo de dolor || angustiarse (to suffer anguish) || — *I made him writhe* le torturé, le atormenté || *their attitude made him writhe with anger* su actitud le puso furioso.

writing [raitiŋ] *n* el escribir (act of s.o. who writes) || escritura *f*, letra *f* (handwriting) || escribir *m* (sth. written); *to put sth. in writing* poner algo por escrito || profesión *f* de escribir (occupation of an author) || obra *f*; *the writings of Borges* las obras de Borges || redacción *f*, estilo *m* (style) || — *at the time of writing* en el momento en que escribo estas líneas || *in one's own writing* de su puño y letra || FIG *the writing on the wall* un aviso del cielo || *writing case* o *set* estuche *m* de papel de escribir || *writing desk* escritorio *m* || COMM *writing off* amortización *f* (of capital) || *writing pad* bloc *m* de papel de escribir || *writing paper* papel *m* de escribir || *you are very bad about writing* te gusta muy poco escribir.

written [ritn] *pp* ⟶ **write.**
◆ *adj* escrito, ta || *written accent* acento ortográfico.

wrong [rɔŋ] *adj* malo, la (not morally right) || mal (not right); *it is wrong to lie* está mal mentir; *that is very wrong of you* has hecho muy mal || erróneo, a; equivocado, da; *you are wrong in thinking him intelligent* estás equivocado si le crees inteligente || inoportuno, na; impropio, pia; *they chose the wrong time to drop in* escogieron el momento inoportuno para venir || falso, sa; equivocado, da; erróneo, a; *wrong ideas* ideas falsas || MUS falso, sa; *wrong note* nota falsa || — *at the wrong time* en un mal momento, en un momento poco oportuno || *I hope there is nothing wrong* espero que no pasa nada || *in the wrong sense* en sentido equivocado || *is anything wrong?* ¿pasa algo? || *I was in the wrong plane* me equivoqué de avión || *not to be far wrong* no equivocarse en mucho, no ir muy descaminado || SP *on the wrong foot* a contrapié || *something is wrong* hay algo que no está bien || *sorry, wrong number* lo siento, se ha equivocado de número (on the telephone) || *that is wrong* eso no es cierto || *there is sth. wrong with me* no me encuentro bien || *there is sth. wrong with my lighter* le pasa algo a mi encendedor, mi encendedor está estropeado || *the wrong side of a material* el revés de un tela || *things are all wrong, everything is wrong* todo está mal || *things are going the wrong way* las cosas marchan mal || *to be in the wrong place* estar mal colocado || FIG *to be in the wrong road* ir por mal camino | *to be on the wrong side of forty* tener cuarenta años bien cumplidos, tener más de cuarenta años || *to be wrong* tener la culpa (to be blameworthy), no tener razón (to maintain sth. false), equivocarse, estar equivocado (to be mistaken), hacer mal en, no deber; *he is wrong to laugh* hace mal en reírse; *you were wrong to tell him the truth* hiciste mal en decirle la verdad; estar mal (thing), andar mal (a watch) || *to brush a hat the wrong way* cepillar un sombrero a contrapelo || *to buy the wrong clothes* comprar ropa que no le sienta bien a uno || *to do the wrong thing* hacer lo que no se debe || *to drive on the wrong side of the road* rodar por el lado de la carretera que está prohibido || *to get on the wrong side of s.o.* ponerse a malas con uno || FIG *to get out of bed on the wrong side* levantarse con el pie izquierdo || *to go to the wrong place* equivocarse de sitio || *to make a wrong choice* equivocarse al escoger, escoger mal || *to say the wrong thing* decir lo que no se debe || *to swallow the wrong way* atragantarse || *to take a word in the wrong sense* coger una palabra en mal sentido || *to take the wrong road* equivocarse de carretera || *what's wrong with going dancing?* ¿qué tiene de malo ir a bailar? || *what's wrong with you?* ¿qué te pasa? || *wrong side up* al revés || *what's wrong in drinking?* ¿qué tiene de malo beber?
◆ *n* mal *m*; *the difference between right and wrong* la diferencia entre el bien y el mal || error *m*; *to acknowledge one's wrongs* reconocer sus errores || injusticia *f* (act of injustice); *the wrongs that I have suffered* las injusticias que he sufrido || JUR daño *m*, perjuicio *m* || — *to be in the wrong* estar equivocado, da (to be mistaken), no tener razón (to maintain sth. false), ser culpable, tener la culpa (to be morally responsible for sth.) || *to do s.o. wrong, to do wrong to s.o.* ser injusto con alguien (to treat unjustly), perjudicar a alguien || *to do wrong* hacer mal || *to put s.o. in the wrong* echarle la culpa a alguien || *to right a wrong* enderezar un entuerto.
◆ *adv* mal; *to answer wrong* responder mal || injustamente (unjustly) || incorrectamente (incorrectly) || — *to get in wrong* comprender mal (to misunderstand) || *to get s.o. wrong* juzgar equivocadamente a alguien || *to go wrong* equi-

vocarse de dirección (to take the wrong direction), perderse, extraviarse (to loose one's way), darse a la mala vida, descarriarse (to start on a course of wrongdoing), equivocarse (to make a mistake), romperse, estropearse (to break down), fallar, fracasar (plants), ir mal (business).

wrong [rɔŋ] *vt* ser injusto con (to treat unjustly) || perjudicar, agraviar (to damage) || seducir (to seduce).

wrongdoer ['rɔŋ'duə*] *n* delincuente *m* & *f*, malhechor, ra.

wrongdoing ['rɔŋ'duiŋ] *n* mal *m* (wrong) || maldad *f* (evil) || pecado *m* (sin) || JUR infracción *f*, delito *m*.

wrong-foot ['rɔŋfut] *vt* SP desequilibrar.

wrongful ['rɔŋful] *adj* injusto, ta (no just) || ilegal (not lawful).

wrongfulness [-nis] *n* injusticia *f* (injustice) || ilegalidad *f* (illegality).

wrongheaded ['rɔŋ'hedid] *adj* obstinado, da; testarudo, da; terco, ca.

wrongheadedness [-nis] *n* obstinación *f*, testarudez *f*, terquedad *f*.

wrongly ['rɔŋli] *adv* mal || injustamente || equivocadamente, erróneamente || sin razón || *rightly or wrongly* con razón o sin ella.

wrongness ['rɔŋnis] *n* error *m*, equivocación *f* || inexactitud *f* || injusticia *f* || inoportunidad *f* || maldad *f*.

wrote [rəut] *pret* —→ **write.**

wroth [rəuθ] *adj* airado, da.

wrought [rɔːt] *pret/pp* (ant) —→ **work.**
◆ *adj* trabajado, da (worked) || labrado, da (metal) || forjado, da (iron).

wrought-up [rɔːt'ʌp] *adj* nervioso, sa.

wrung [rʌŋ] *pret/pp* —→ **wring.**

wry [rai] *adj* torcido, da; doblado, da; *wry neck* cuello torcido || retorcido, da (humour, remarks, etc.) || forzado, da (a smile) || irónico, ca (speech) || *to pull a wry face* torcer el gesto, poner mala cara.

wryneck [-nek] *n* MED tortícolis *m* & *f* || torcecuello *m* (bird).

wych elm; witch elm ['witʃelm] *n* BOT olmo *m* escocés.

wye [wai] *n* i griega *f* (letter).

Wyoming [wɑi'əumiŋ] *pr n* GEOGR Wyoming *m*.

WYSIWYG *abbr of [what you see is what you get]* tipo de presentación en pantalla de un procesador de textos.

wyvern ['waivən] *n* HERALD dragón *m* (two-legged winged dragon).

X

x [eks] *n* x *f* (letter) || MATH x *f*, incógnita *f* (unknown quantity) || — *Mr X* el señor X || CINEM *X film* película no apta para menores de 16 años.

xanthate ['zænθeit] *n* CHEM xantato *m*.

xanthene ['zæn,θin] *n* CHEM xanteno *m*.

xanthin ['zænθin]; **xanthine** ['zænθi:n] *n* CHEM xantina *f*.

xanthoma [zæn'θəumə] *n* MED xantoma *m*.
— OBSERV El plural es *xanthomas* o *xanthomata*.

xanthophyll ['zænθɔfil] *n* xantofila *f*.

xanthous ['zænθəs] *adj* amarillo, lla (yellow) || de pelo rubio (with yellowish hair) || de piel amarilla (yellow-skinned).

Xavier ['zæviə*] *pr n* Javier *m*.

x-axis ['eks,æksis] *n* MATH abscisa *f*.

xebec ['zi:bek] *n* jabeque *m* (small boat).

xenogenesis ['zenə'dʒenisis] *n* xenogénesis *f inv*.

xenon ['zenɔn] *n* CHEM xenón *m*.

xenophile ['zenəfail] *n* xenófilo, la.

xenophilia [,zenə'fi:ljə] *n* xenofilia *f*.

xenophobe ['zenəfəub] *n* xenófobo, ba.

xenophobia [,zenə'fəubjə] *n* xenofobia *f*.

xenophobic [,zenə'fəubik] *adj* xenófobo, ba.

Xenophon ['zenəfən] *pr n* Jenofonte *m*.

xeric ['ziərik] *adj* árido, da; seco, ca.

xerography [ze'rɔgrəfi] *n* xerografía *f*.

xerophilous [zi'rɔfiləs] *adj* xerófilo, la.

xerosis [zi'rəusis] *n* MED xerosis *f inv*.

Xerox ['zi:rɔks] *n* (registered trademark) xerocopia *f*.

Xerox ['zi:rɔks] *vt* hacer una xerocopia.

xerox copy ['ziərɔks,kɔpi] *n* xerografía *f*.

Xerxes ['zə:ksiz] *pr n* Jerjes *m*.

xi [sai] *n* xi *f* (Greek letter).

xiphoid ['zifɔid] *adj* ANAT xifoideo, a.
◆ *n* ANAT xifoides *m inv*.

xifosura [zifə'surə] *pl n* ZOOL xifosuros *m*.

xiphosuran [zifə'surən] *adj/n* ZOOL xifosuro.

Xmas ['krisməs] *n* Navidad *f*, Navidades *f pl* (Christmas) || — *Xmas card* crismas *m*, tarjeta *f* de Navidad || *Xmas tree* árbol *m* de Navidad.

X-ray ['eks'rei] *n* radiografía *f* (X-ray photograph).
◆ *pl* rayos *m* X.

X-ray ['eks'rei] *vt* tratar *or* examinar con rayos X (on a fluorescent screen) || radiografiar (to take an X-ray photograph of).

X-ray photograph [-'fəutəgrɑ:f]; **X-ray print** [-print] *n* radiografía *f*.

X-ray therapy [-'θerəpi] *n* radioterapia *f*.

X-ray tube [-tju:b] *n* tubo *m* de rayos X.

xylene ['zaili:n] *n* CHEM xileno *m*.

xylograph ['zailəgrɑ:f] *n* xilografía *f*.

xylographic [,zailə'græfik]; **xylographical** [-əl] *adj* xilográfico, ca.

xilography [zai'lɔgrəfi] *n* xilografía *f*.

xylophaga [zai'lɔfəgə] *pl n* ZOOL xilófagos *m*.

xylophone ['zailəfəun] *n* MUS xilófono *m*.

xylophonist [-ist] *n* MUS xilofonista *m* & *f*.

xyst [zist]; **xystus** [-əs] *n* (ant) galería *f* cubierta.

Y

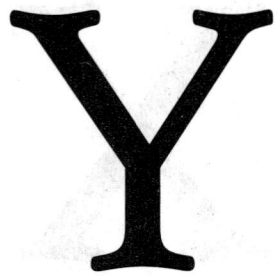

y [wai] *n* y *f* (letter).

yacht [jɔt] *n* MAR yate *m* || — *yacht club* club náutico || *yacht race* regata *f*.

yacht [jɔt] *vi* dedicarse a la navegación de recreo (to sail for pleasure) || participar en una regata (to race yachts).

yachting [-iŋ] *n* navegación *f* de recreo, navegación *f* a vela || *to go yachting* ir a pasear en yate (to go sailing), tomar parte en una regata (to race).

yachtsman [-smən] *n* aficionado *m* a la navegación de recreo, «yachtman» *m*, balandrista *m* (who sails a yacht) || dueño *m* de un yate (who owns a yacht).
— OBSERV El plural de *yachtsman* es *yachtsmen*.

yachtsmanship [-smənʃip] *n* arte *m* de manejar un yate, habilidad *f* en manejar un yate.

yackety-yack [ˈjækətiˈjæk] *n* charloteo *m*, cháchara *f* (chatter) || discusiones *f pl* (discussion) || machaqueo *m* (insistence).

yaguaza [jəˈgwɑːzə] *n* yaguasa *f*.

yahoo [jəˈhuː] *n* bruto *m*, patán *m*.

Yahweh; Yahveh [ˈjɑːwei] *pr n* Yahvé (Jehovah).

yak [jæk] *n* ZOOL yac *m*, yak *m*.

yak [jæk] *vi* US FAM parlotear, charlotear.

yam [jæm] *n* ñame *m* (plant) || US batata *f* [AMER camote *m*] (sweet potato).

yammer [-ə*] *vi* lloriquear (to whimper) || quejarse (to complain) || parlotear (to chatter).

yank [jæŋk] *n* tirón *m*; *to give sth. a yank* dar un tirón a algo.

yank [jæŋk] *vt* dar un tirón a.
◆ *vi* dar un tirón.

Yank [jæŋk] *n* FAM yanqui *m* & *f*.

Yankee [ˈjæŋki] *adj/n* yanqui.

Yankeeism [-izəm] *n* americanismo *m*.

Yaoundé [jæˈundei] *pr n* GEOGR Yaoundé.

yap [jæp] *n* ladrido *m* (of a dog) || FAM jeta *f*, hocico *m* (mouth) | patán *m*, palurdo *m* (person) | protesta *f* (protest) | charloteo *m* (chat).

yap [jæp] *vi* ladrar (a dog) || gañir, chillar (fox) || FAM charlotear, cotorrear (to chatter) | protestar (to protest).

yarborough [ˈjɑːbrə] *n* mano *f* en el juego de bridge en la que no figura ninguna carta que vale más de nueve.

yard [jɑːd] *n* patio *m* (of a building, of a school, etc.) || corral *m* (for animals) || almacén *m*, depósito *m*; *timber yard* depósito de madera || estación *f* (railways); *shunting* o *marshalling yard* estación de clasificación *or* de apartado || taller *m*; *repair yard* taller de reparaciones || yarda *f* [unidad de medida equivalente a 91, 44 cm] (measure) || MAR verga *f* (spar) | astillero *m* (dockyard) || — *the Yard* Scotland Yard, sede *f* de la policía londinense || FIG *yards long* muy largo | *with a face a yard long* con una cara muy larga.

yard [jɑːd] *vt* meter en el corral (cattle).

yardage [-idʒ] *n* encierro *m* (of cattle) || gastos *m pl* del encierro (cost) || maniobras *f pl* (railways) || longitud *f or* área *f or* volumen *m* en yardas, medida *f* en yardas.

yardarm [-ɑːm] *n* MAR penol *m*.

yardman [-mən] *n* empleado *m* en la estación de clasificación (railways) || empleado *m* de un depósito de madera.
— OBSERV El plural de *yardman* es *yardmen*.

yardmaster [-ˌmɑːstə*] *n* US encargado *m* de la estación de clasificación.

yardstick [-stik] *n* vara *f* que mide una yarda || FIG criterio *m*, patrón *m*, norma *f*.

yarn [jɑːn] *n* hilo *m*, hilado *m*, hilaza *f* (spun thread) || FIG historia *f*, cuento *m* (exaggerated story); *to spin a yarn* contar una historia.

yarn [jɑːn] *vi* contar una historia *or* un cuento.

yarrow [ˈjærəu] *n* BOT milenrama *f*.

yashmak [ˈjæʃmæk] *n* velo *m* (of Moslem women).

yataghan [ˈjætəgən] *n* yatagán *m* (short sword).

yaup [jɔːp] *n/vi* → **yawp.**

yaw [jɔː] *n* MAR guiñada *f* (of a ship) || bandazo *m*, despiste *m* (of a car).

yaw [jɔː] *vi* MAR guiñar, dar guiñadas (a ship) || dar un bandazo, despistarse (a car).

yawl [jɔːl] *n* MAR yola *f* (boat).

yawn [jɔːn] *n* bostezo *m* (made by a person) || abertura *f* (gaping hole).

yawn [jɔːn] *vi* bostezar (person) || abrirse; *the chasm yawned in front of him* el abismo se abría delante de él.
◆ *vt* decir bostezando || FAM *to yawn one's head off* bostezar hasta desencajarse las mandíbulas.

yawning [-iŋ] *adj* bostezando (person) || abierto, ta (thing) || profundo, da (chasm).
◆ *n* bostezo *m* (yawn).

yawp; yaup [jɔːp] *n* US grito *m*.

yawp; yaup [jɔːp] *vi* US gritar (to utter a cry) || US FAM cotorrear (to talk continually).

yaws [jɔːz] *n* MED pián *m*, frambesia *f*.

Y connection [waikəˈnekʃən] *n* montaje *m* en estrella.

ye [jiː] *pers pron* (ant) el, la; los, las.

yea [jei] *n* sí *m* || *the yeas and the nays* los votos a favor y los votos en contra.
◆ *adv* sí (yes) || incluso, y hasta (moreover).

yeah [jeː] *adv* FAM sí (yes).

year [jiə*] *n* año *m*; *last year* el año pasado; *the coming year* el año próximo; *next year* el año que viene; *the year before last* el año antepasado; *the year 2000* el año 2000; *the academic year* el año académico; *a lunar year* un año lunar; *to be 20 years old* tener 20 años; *500 pounds a year* 500 (quinientas) libras por año; *once a year* una vez al año; *every other year* cada dos años, un año sí y otro no; *every year* cada año, todos los años; *in my later years* en mis últimos años; *it will take years* tardará años y años || curso *m*, año *m*; *he was in my year at school* estaba en el mismo curso que yo en el colegio; *the first year boys* los niños del primer curso || — *all the year round* (durante) todo el año || *by the year* por año || *calendar year* año civil || FAM *donkey's years* siglos *m* || *financial year* año *or* ejercicio económico || *from year to year* cada año || *Happy New Year!* ¡Feliz Año Nuevo! || *in after years* en los años siguientes || FIG *in the year one, in the year dot* en el año de la nana, en tiempos de Mariacastaña || *in years* de edad || *in years to come* en años venideros || *leap year* año bisiesto || *light year* año luz || *New Year's Eve* Nochevieja *f* || *of late years* en los últimos años || *school year* año escolar || *to look young for one's years* parecer joven para la edad que uno tiene || *year after year, year by year* año tras año || *year in, year out* año tras año || *year of grace* año de gracia || *year of our Lord* año del Señor || *years ago* hace años.

yearbook [-buk] *n* anuario *m*.

yearling [-liŋ] *adj* de un año (one year old) || añal (calf, bullock, sheep, goat).
◆ *n* potro *m* de un año (year-old colt) || añal *m* (calf, bullock, sheep, goat).

yearlong [-ˈlɔŋ] *adj* que dura un año (which lasts a year) || que ha durado un año (which has lasted a year).

yearly [-li] *adj* anual.
◆ *adv* anualmente, cada año || *twice yearly* dos veces al año.

yearn [jəːn] *vi* *to yearn after* o *for* ansiar, anhelar, suspirar por (sth.), suspirar por (s.o.) || *to yearn to do sth.* ansiar *or* anhelar hacer algo.

yearning [-iŋ] *adj* anheloso, sa; ansioso, sa (longing) || tierno, na (tender).
◆ *n* anhelo *m*, ansia *f*.

yearningly [-iŋli] *adv* con ansia, ansiosamente (with longing) || con ternura, tiernamente (tenderly).

year-old [ˈjiərˈəuld] *adj* de un año de edad.

year-round [ˈjiərˈraund] *adj* abierto durante todo el año.

yeast [jiːst] *n* levadura *f* (leaven) || FIG fermento *m* || espuma *f* (of beer).

yeasty [-i] *adj* de levadura (of yeast) || espumoso, sa (frothy) || FIG turbulento, ta (unsettled) | frívolo, la (frivolous).

yegg [jeg] *n* US FAM ladrón *m* [de cajas fuertes].

yell [jel] *n* grito *m*; *to let out a yell* dar un grito.

yell [jel] *vt* gritar, vociferar, decir a gritos; *to yell insults* gritar insultos.
◆ *vi* gritar; *to yell with pain* gritar de dolor || *to yell for help* pedir auxilio a gritos.

yelling [-iŋ] *n* gritos *m pl*.

yellow [ˈjeləu] *adj* amarillo, lla; *yellow skin* piel amarilla; *to turn yellow with age* volverse amarillo con el tiempo || rubio, bia (hair) || de color avellana (gloves) || MED amarilla (fever) || FAM cobarde, miedoso, sa (cowardly) | sensacionalista; *a yellow newspaper* un periódico sensacionalista; *yellow press* prensa sensacionalista.

◆ *n* amarillo *m* (colour) || yema *f* (yolk of an egg).
◆ *pl* ictericia *f sing* (jaundice).

yellow ['jeləu] *vt* volver amarillo.
◆ *vi* volverse amarillo, ponerse amarillo, amarillear, amarillecer.

yellowback [-bæk] *n* (ant) novelucha *f*.

yellowbelly [-ˌbeli] *n* FAM cobarde *m* & *f*, cagueta *m* & *f* (*pop*).

yellow dog [-dɔg] *n* US canalla *m* || US *yellow-dog contract* contrato *m* de trabajo según el cual el contratado se compromete a no adherirse al sindicato.

yellow fever [-'fiːvə*] *n* MED fiebre *f* amarilla.

yellowhammer [-ˌhæmə*] *n* verderón *m* (bird).

yellowish [-iʃ] *adj* amarillento, ta.

yellow jack [-dʒæk] *n* fiebre *f* amarilla (yellow fever) || MAR bandera *f* amarilla || jurel *m* (fish).

yellow jacket [-ˌdʒækit] *n* US avispa *f*.

yellowness [-nis] *n* amarillez *f*, lo amarillo.

yellow ochre; US **yellow ocher** [-'əukə*] *n* ocre *m* amarillo.

Yellow Pages [-peidʒiz] *pl n* páginas *f pl* amarillas.

yellow spot [-'spɔt] *n* ANAT mancha *f* amarilla (in the eye).

Yellowstone National Park [-stən'næʃənlpɑːk] *pr n* GEOGR Parque Nacional de Yellowstone.

yelp [jelp] *n* gañido *m*.

yelp [jelp] *vi* gañir (an animal) || gritar (a person); *to yelp with pain* gritar de dolor.

Yemen ['jemən] *pr n* GEOGR Yemen *m*.

Yemenite [-ait] *adj/n* yemenita, yemení.

yen [jen] *n* yen *m* (monetary unit of Japan) || FAM deseo *m*, ganas *f pl* (desire); *I had a sudden yen to visit the East* de pronto me entraron ganas de visitar el Oriente.

yen [jen] *vi* tener ganas, desear ansiosamente.

yeoman ['jəumən] *n* pequeño terrateniente *m* (farmer who owns his land) || MIL soldado *m* de caballería || — FIG *to do yeoman service* prestar grandes servicios || MIL *yeoman of the guard* alabardeo *m* de la Casa Real.
— OBSERV El plural de *yeoman* es *yeomen*.

yeomanry [-ri] *n* pequeños terratenientes *m pl* (yeomen) || MIL cuerpo *m* voluntario de caballería para la defensa territorial.

yep [jep] *adv* FAM sí (yes).

yes [jes] *adv* sí; *say yes or no* diga sí o no || — *have you ever been to America? yes, I have* ¿ha estado alguna vez en América? sí || *I bet you haven't finished yes I have!* apuesto a que no has terminado ¡pues sí! || *to answer yes* contestar que sí || *yes?* ¿sí?, ¿dígame? (on telephone, etc.), ¿de verdad? (surprise), ¿quién es? (answering a knock on the door) || *yes!* ¡voy! (in answer to summons) || *yes indeed* por supuesto, claro que sí || *yes, of course!, yes rather!* ¡claro que sí!
◆ *n* sí *m*; *to answer with a yes* contestar con un sí.
— OBSERV El plural del sustantivo *yes* es *yeses* o *yesses*.

yes-man ['jesmæn] *n* FAM pelotillero *m*, cobista *m*.
— OBSERV El plural de *yes-man* es *yes-men*.

yesterday ['jestədi] *adv* ayer; *I only arrived yesterday* llegué solamente ayer || — *I saw him yesterday week* ayer hizo una semana que le vi || FIG *I was not born yesterday* no he nacido ayer || *late yesterday* ayer a última hora || *the day before yesterday* antes de ayer, anteayer || *yesterday morning, afternoon* ayer por la mañana, por la tarde.
◆ *n* ayer *m*, el día *m* de ayer || — *I spent all yesterday writting* ayer pasé todo el día escribiendo *or* pasé todo el día de ayer escribiendo || *yesterday's papers* los periódicos de ayer || *yesterday was rainy* ayer llovió.

yestereve ['jestəriːv]**; yesterevening** [-niŋ] *adv* (ant) ayer por la tarde.

yestermorn ['jestəmɔːm]**; yestermorning** [-iŋ] *adv* (ant) ayer por la mañana, en la mañana de ayer.

yesternight ['jestənait] *adv* (ant) ayer por la noche, en la noche de ayer, anoche.

yesteryear ['jestə'jiə*] *n* antaño *m*; *songs of yesteryear* canciones de antaño.

yet [jet] *adv* aún, todavía; *I have not seen him yet* aún no le he visto; *don't go yet* no te vayas aún; *he was not yet mayor* todavía no era alcalde; *there is yet light enough* todavía hay bastante luz; *not yet* todavía no; *yet more difficult* todavía más difícil || ya; *has your sister arrived yet?* ¿ha llegado tu hermana ya? || — *as yet* hasta ahora || *it has yet to be finished* todavía no está terminado || *no one had yet been there* nadie había estado allí antes, hasta entonces no había estado nadie allí || *we have yet to see the Eiffel Tower* todavía nos queda por ver la Torre Eiffel || *we'll manage yet* a pesar de todo lo lograremos || *yet again* otra vez || *yet more* todavía más, más aún || *you'll get to be famous yet!* un día serás famoso.
◆ *conj* sin embargo, no obstante (nevertheless); *and yet I enjoy it* y sin embargo me gusta || pero (but).

yeti [jeti] *n* abominable hombre *m* de las nieves.

yew [juː] *n* tejo *m* (tree and wood).

Y gun [waigʌn] *n* cañón *m* antisubmarino.

Yid [jid] *n* POP judío, a.

Yiddish [-iʃ] *n* yiddish *m*, judeoalemán *m* (language).

yield [jiːld] *n* producción *f*, rendimiento *m*; *yield per hectare* producción por hectárea; *the yield of a well* el rendimiento de un pozo || beneficio *m* (profit) || rédito *m*, interés *m* (interest); *a 4% yield* un rédito del cuatro por ciento || cosecha *f* (crop) || — *yield capacity* productividad *f* || *yield point* límite *m* de elasticidad || *yield strength* límite *m* de elasticidad || *yield temperature* temperatura *f* de fusión.

yield [jiːld] *vt* producir, dar; *these trees will yield good timber* estos árboles producirán buena madera; *to yield a good crop* dar una buena cosecha || dar, producir, proporcionar (profit); *the profit yielded by the investment* los beneficios proporcionados por la inversión || devengar, dar, producir (interest) || ceder; *to yield ground to the enemy* ceder terreno al enemigo || entregar (a town, etc., to the enemy) || dar; *to yield consent* dar su consentimiento || conceder (to concede) || — *he finally yielded the point* acabó por reconocer que no tenía razón || *the shares yielded ten per cent in a year* las acciones produjeron un beneficio del diez por ciento en un año || *to yield an argument to s.o.* darle la razón a alguien || FIG *to yield up the ghost* entregar el alma.
◆ *vi* producir, ser productivo, va (to be fruitful) || rendirse (to admit defeat) || ceder (to give in); *to yield to temptation* ceder a la tentación; *to yield to s.o.'s insistence* ceder ante la insistencia de alguien; *the ground yields when you tread on it* la tierra cede cuando la pisas || — *to yield in favour of* renunciar en favor de || US *to yield to* ceder la palabra a || FIG *to yield to nobody in enthusiasm* ser más entusiasta que nadie.

yielding ['jiːldiŋ] *adj* complaciente, condescendiente; *a yielding person* una persona complaciente || flexible (flexible, not rigid) || blando, da; *yielding ground* suelo blando || COMM productivo, va (fruitful).

yip [jip] *n* US ladrido *m* (bark of a dog) | protesta *f*, queja *f* (complaint).

yip [jip] *vi* US ladrar (a dog) | protestar, quejarse (to complaint).

yippee ['ji'piː] *interj* FAM ¡yupi!

YMCA *abbr of [Young Men's Christian Association]* albergue cristiano para chicos jóvenes.

yob [jɔb]**; yobbo** ['jɔbəu] *n* FAM gamberro, rra.

yod [jɔd] *n* yod *f* (in phonetics).

yodel [jəudl] *n* canción *f* tirolesa.

yodel ['jəudl] *vt/vi* cantar a la tirolesa.

yodeller; yodeler [-ə*] *n* cantante *m* & *f* tirolés.

yoga ['jəugə] *n* yoga *m*.

yoghourt; yoghurt ['jɔgəːt] *n* yogur *m*.

yogi ['jəugi] *n* yogi *m*, yogui *m*, yoghi *m*.

yogurt ['jɔgəːt] *n* yogur *m*.

yohimbine [jəu'himbiːn] *n* CHEM yohimbina *f*.

yoicks [jɔiks] *interj* ¡hala!

yoke [jəuk] *n* yugo *m* (for animals, crossbar for bells) || yunta *f* (pair of oxen) || balancín *m*, percha *f* (for carring loads) || canesú *m* (of garment) || ARCH cabecero *m* (of a window) || culata *f* (of electromagnet) || TECH brida *f*, estribo *m* (clamp) || MAR barra *f* (of rudder) || AVIAT palanca *f* de mando || FIG lazo *m*, vínculo *m* (bond) | yugo *m*, esclavitud *f* (slavery) | servidumbre *f* (servitude) || — FIG *to be under the yoke of* estar bajo el yugo de | *to pass under the yoke* pasar bajo el yugo | *to throw off the yoke* sacudir el yugo.

yoke [jəuk] *vt/vi* uncir (to put under a yoke) || atar (to attach) || FIG (to unite) || *to yoke together* trabajar juntos, estar uncidos al mismo carro.

yoke elm [-elm] *n* carpe *m* (tree).

yokefellow [-ˌfeləu] *n* compañero *m*.

yokel [-əl] *n* paleto *m*, cateto *m*, palurdo *m*, patán *m*.

yolk [jəuk] *n* yema *f* [de huevo] (of an egg) | churre *m* (found in the fleece of sheep).

yolk gland [-glænd] *n* glándula *f* vitelina.

yolk sac [-sæk] *n* membrana *f* vitelina.

yon [jɔn] *adj/adv* (ant) ⟶ **yonder.**

yonder ['jɔndə*] *adj* (ant) aquel, aquella, aquellos, aquellas; *yonder church tower* aquella torre de iglesia.
◆ *adv* a lo lejos, allá; *look yonder* mira allá.

yore [jɔː] *n* (ant); *in days of yore* antaño || *of yore* de otro tiempo, de antaño.

you [juː] *pers pron* tú (subjective case singular when addressing relatives, friends, children, etc.); *no, you must go* no, tienes que ir tú || te (direct and indirect object singular); *he heard you* te oyó; *he gave it to you* te lo dio || ti (after a preposition); *for you* para ti || vosotros, vosotras (subjective case plural and after a preposition when addressing relatives, friends, children, etc.); *you are the ones who saw it* vosotros sois los que los visteis; *this present is for you* este regalo es para vosotros || os (direct and indirect object plural); *I'm telling you* os digo; *he doesn't believe you* no os cree || usted, ustedes (subjective case and after a preposition when addressing a stranger or a person to whom respect is due); *how are you?* ¿cómo está usted?; *against you* contra ustedes || le, la, los, las (direct object); *I saw you, Mr. Smith* le vi, Sr. Smith || le, les (indirect object); *I asked you how you were; Mrs. Smith* le pregunté cómo estaba, señora Smith || se (indirect object singular and plural when accompanied by a direct pronoun); *I gave it to you* se lo di; *he asked* *you for it* se lo pidió || — *all of you* todos vosotros, todas vosotras, todos ustedes || *between you and me* dicho sea entre nosotros, entre nosotros dos || *can you swim here?* ¿se puede nadar aquí? || *I am older than you* soy mayor que tú *or* que usted || *if I were you* yo en tu lugar, yo que tú || *there's a lovely dress for you!* ¡mire que traje más bonito! || *with you* contigo, con vosotros, con vosotras, con usted, con ustedes || *you can't trust anyone* uno no se puede fiar de nadie, una no puede fiarse de nadie || *you Englishmen* vosotros los ingleses || *you idiot!* ¡idiota! || *you need to be young to succeed* hay que ser joven para triunfar || *you sit down and shut up!* ¡siéntate y calla!

— OBSERV In the subjective case, the personal pronoun is usually omitted in Spanish: *are you hungry?* ¿tienes hambre?; *you sold it* lo vendió, except in cases of emphasis or distinction: *no, you do it!* ¡no, hazlo tú!; *you are a doctor and he is an architect* usted es doctor y él es arquitecto.

— OBSERV See also the observation in «usted».

young [jʌŋ] *adj* joven; *a young country* un país joven; *the night is still young* todavía la noche es joven; *my brother married young* mi hermano se casó joven; *we are only young once* no somos jóvenes más que una vez en la vida; *he is young for his years* parece joven para la edad que tiene; *he is two years younger than I* es dos años más joven que yo || de juventud; *young love* amor de juventud || nuevo, va (new) || — *a young lady* una señorita || *a young man* un joven, un chico joven (youngster), un hombre joven; *to bring young men into the government* poner a hombres jóvenes en el gobierno || *a young woman* una joven, una chica joven (youngster), una mujer joven || *in his younger days* en su juventud || *his young lady* su novia *f* || *Pliny the Younger* Plinio el Joven || *the youngest of my children* el más joven de mis hijos || *to grow younger* rejuvenecer || *when I was five years younger* cuando tenía cinco años menos || *you are looking years younger* parece mucho más joven || *younger brother* hermano *m* menor || *young fellow* joven *m*, muchacho *m* || *young girl* joven *f*, muchacha *f* || *young people* los jóvenes, la gente joven, la juventud || *young person* persona joven, joven *m* & *f*.

◆ *pl n* cría *f sing* (of animals) || — *old and young* los mayores y los pequeños || *the young* los jóvenes, la gente joven, la juventud || *to bring forth young* parir || *with young* preñada (an animal).

youngish [-iʃ] *adj* FAM bastante joven, jovencito, ta.

young-looking [-ˌlukiŋ] *adj* que parece joven, de aspecto joven.

youngster [-stə*] *n* joven *m* & *f*, jovenzuelo, la; jovencito, ta.

your [jɔː*] *poss adj* tu, tus (singular when addressing friends, children, relatives, etc.); *your house* tu casa; *I like your shoes better than mine* me gustan más tus zapatos que los míos || vuestro, vuestra, vuestros, vuestras (plural when addressing friends, children, relatives, etc.); *your car is blue, ours is red* vuestro coche es azul, el nuestro rojo; *these are your tickets* éstas son vuestras entradas || su, sus; de usted, de ustedes (singular and plural when addressing strangers or people to whom respect is due); *your car is in the garage* el coche de usted está en el garaje; *your books are on the table* sus libros están encima de la mesa || su (preceding certain titles); *Your Majesty* Su majestad.

— OBSERV The English possessive adjective is often translated by the definite article in Spanish: *turn your head* vuelve la cabeza; *don't bite your nails* no te muerdas las uñas.

yours [jɔːz] *poss pron* (el) tuyo, (la) tuya, (el) vuestro, (la) vuestra (when addressing friends, children, relatives, etc.); *these are my books, those are yours* éstos son mis libros, ésos son tuyos *or* ésos son los tuyos; *my car is here, I don't know where yours is* mi coche está aquí, no sé dónde está el tuyo; *these are my letters, those are yours* éstas son mis cartas, ésas son las vuestras *or* ésas son vuestras; *my cigarettes are next to yours* mis cigarrillos están al lado de los vuestros || (el) suyo, (la) suya; (el) de usted, (la) de usted (when addressing strangers or people to whom respect is due); *this is my plate, that is yours* éste es mi plato, ése es el suyo *or* ése es suyo; *I like all these pictures, but yours are especially interesting* me gustan todos esos cuadros, pero los de usted tienen un interés especial || COMM su atenta (letter) || — *it is not yours to reason why* a usted no le corresponde preguntarse el porqué || *I would like to read sth. of yours* me gustaría leer algo tuyo || *of yours* tuyo, tuya; de usted, suyo, suya; *a friend of yours* un amigo suyo; *that is no business of yours* esto no es asunto suyo || *you and yours* tú y los tuyos, usted y los suyos || *yours is an interesting case* su caso es interesante || *Yours, J. Smith* reciba un cordial saludo de J. Smith (in letters) || *Yours truly* le saluda atentamente (in letters), su seguro servidor (me).

— OBSERV Téngase en cuenta que el pronombre posesivo *yours* se puede aplicar tanto a un objeto como a varios: *give me yours* dame el tuyo, dame los tuyos.

yourself [jɔːˈself] *pers pron* tú (mismo), tú (misma) (subjective case when addressing relatives, friends, children, etc.); *do it yourself* hazlo tú; *you said so yourself* lo dijiste tú mismo || ti (mismo) (after a preposition); *it is for yourself* es para ti mismo || usted (mismo), usted (misma) (subjective case and after a preposition when addressing a stranger or a person to whom respect is due); *you yourself came* usted mismo vino; *I'll go with yourself* iré con usted || — *by yourself* tú solo, usted solo; *did you do it by yourself?* ¿lo hiciste tú solo? || *you only think of yourself* sólo piensas en ti mismo, sólo piensa en sí mismo.

◆ *refl pron* te (when addressing relatives, friends, children, etc.); *have you hurt yourself?* ¿te has hecho daño? || se (when addressing a stranger or a person to whom respect is due); *you must ask yourself this* tiene que preguntase eso.

— OBSERV El plural de *yourself* es *yourselves.*

yourselves [jɔːˈselvz] *pers pron* vosotros (mismos), vosotras (mismas) (when addressing relatives, friends, children, etc.); *you yourselves were there* estabais allí vosotros mismos; *for yourselves* para vosotros || ustedes (mismos), ustedes (mismas) (when addressing strangers or people to whom respect is due); *yourselves, as members of the jury* ustedes, como miembros del jurado; *I'll go with yourselves* iré con ustedes || *you only think of yourselves* sólo pensáis en vosotros mismos, sólo piensan en sí mismos.

◆ *refl pron* os (when addressing relatives, friends, children, etc.); *have you washed yourselves?* ¿os habéis lavado? || se (when addressing strangers or people to whom respect is due); *you must ask yourselves this* tienen que preguntarse esto.

youth [juːθ] *n* juventud *f*; *during his early youth* durante su primera juventud || joven *m* (a young man) || juventud *f*, jóvenes *m pl* (young people); *the youth of today* la juventud actual || FIG *the campaing is still in its youth* la campaña está todavía en sus principios.

youth club [-klʌb] *n* club *m* juvenil.

youthful [-ful] *adj* joven, juvenil; *youthful appearance* aspecto juvenil || juvenil, de la juventud (error, enthusiasm) || *to look youthful* parecer joven.

youthfulness [-fulnis] *n* juventud *f*.

youth hostel [-ˌhɔstəl] *n* albergue *m* de juventud.

youth hosteller; *US* **youth hosteler** [-ˌhɔstələ*] *n* persona *f* que se aloja en un albergue de juventud.

youth hostelling [-ˌhɔstəliŋ] *n* hospedaje *m* en albergues juveniles || *to go youth hostelling* viajar hospedándose en albergues juveniles.

you've [juːv] contracción de «you have».

yowl [jaul] *n* aullido *m*.

yowl [jaul] *vi* aullar.

yo-yo [ˈjəujəu] *n* yoyo *m* (toy).

yperite [ˈipərait] *n* yperita *f*, iperita *f* (gas).

ytterbium [iˈtəːbjəm] *n* CHEM iterbio *m*, yterbio *m*.

yttria [ˈitriə] *n* CHEM itria *f*.

yttrium [ˈitriəm] *n* itrio *m* (metal).

Yucatan [ˌjuːkəˈtɑːn] *pr n* GEOGR Yucatán *m*.

Yucatec [ˈjuːkətek] *n* yucateco, ca.

Yucatecan [ˌjuːkəˈtekən] *adj* yucateco, ca.

yucca [ˈjʌkə] *n* BOT yuca *f*.

yuck [jʌk] *interj* ¡puaj!, ¡ugg!

Yugoslav [ˈjuːgəuˈslɑːv] *adj/n* yugoslavo, va.

Yugoslavia [-jə] *pr n* GEOGR Yugoslavia *f*.

Yugoslavian [-jən] *adj/n* yugoslavo, va.

Yule [juːl] *n* Pascuas *f pl*, Navidades *f pl*.

Yule log [-lɔg] *n* tronco *m* que se quema en Nochebuena (wood) || bizcocho *m* en forma de leño que se come en Nochebuena (confection).

Yuletide [-taid] *n* Pascuas *f pl*, Navidades *f pl*.

yummy [ˈjʌmi] *adj* FAM de chuparse los dedos, delicioso, sa.

yuppie; yuppy [ˈjʌpi] *n* yuppy *m* & *f*.

YWCA *abbr of* *[Young Women's Christian Association]* albergue cristiano para chicas jóvenes.

Z

z [zed] *n* z *f*; *a capital z* una z mayúscula.

zaffer; zaffre ['zæfə] *n* MIN zafre *m*.

Zaïre ['zaiːr] *pr n* GEOGR Zaire *m*.

Zairian ['zaiːrjən] *adj/n* zairense.

Zambezi [zæm'biːzi] *pr n* GEOGR Zambeze *m*.

Zambia ['zæmbjə] *pr n* GEOGR Zambia *f*.

zambo ['zæmbəu] *n* zambo, ba.

zany ['zeini] *adj* estrafalario, ria; absurdo, da.
◆ *n* bufón *m* (stage buffoon) || payaso *m* (joker) || tonto *m* (simpleton).

Zanzibar [zænzi'bɑ*] *pr n* GEOGR Zanzíbar *m*.

zeal [ziːl] *n* celo *m*, ardor *m*; *to show zeal* mostrar celo.

zealot ['zelət] *n* defensor, ra (defender of a cause) || fanático, ca (fanatic).

zealotry [-ri] *n* fanatismo *m*.

zealous ['zeləs] *adj* celoso, sa; entusiasta.

zealously [-li] *adv* celosamente, con entusiasmo.

zebra ['ziːbrə] *n* ZOOL cebra *f*.

zebra crossing [-'krɔsiŋ] *n* paso *m* de cebra, paso *m* de peatones.

zebu ['ziːbuː] *n* ZOOL cebú *m*.

zed [zed] *n* zeta *f*, zeda *f*, ceda *f* (the letter z).

zee [ziː] *n* US zeta *f*, zeda *f*, ceda *f* (the letter z).

Zeeland [-lənd] *pr n* GEOGR Zelanda *f*, Zelandia *f*.

Zeelander [-ləndə*] *n* zelandés, esa.

Zend [zend] *n* zendo *m* (language).
◆ *adj* zendo, da.

zenith ['zeniθ] *n* ASTR cenit *m* || FIG apogeo *m*; *he is at the zenith of his fame* está en el apogeo de la gloria.

Zeno ['ziːnəu] *pr n* Zenón *m*.

zeolite ['ziəulait] *n* MIN zeolita *f*.

zephyr ['zefə*] *n* céfiro *m*.

Zeppelin ['zepəlin] *n* AVIAT Zepelín *m*.

zero ['ziərəu] *adj* nulo, la; *zero visibility* visibilidad nula || cero; *zero altitude* altitud cero.
◆ *n* MATH & PHYS cero *m* || FIG cero *m* (lowest point) | cero *m* a la izquierda (nonentity) || — *absolute zero* cero absoluto || *it is ten degrees below zero* hace diez grados bajo cero.
— OBSERV El plural de la palabra inglesa *zero* es *zeros* o *zeroes*.

zero ['ziərəu] *vt/vi* poner en el cero (an instrument) || *to zero in on* apuntar hacia (artillery, etc.).

zero hour [-ˌauə*] *n* MIL hora *f* H (moment of attack) || hora *f* cero (in rocket launching) || FIG momento *m* decisivo, hora *f* H.

zest [zest] *n* ánimo *m*, entusiasmo *m* (enthusiasm) || brío *m*; *to fight with zest* luchar con brío || cáscara *f*; *a zest of orange* una cáscara de naranja || sabor *m* (piquancy) || sal *f*, gracia *f* (fun, wit) || *to eat with zest* comer con apetito.

zestful ['zestful] **; zesty** ['zesti] *adj* entusiasta, animado, da || sabroso, sa (piquant).

zestfully [-i] *adv* con entusiasmo.

zesty ['zesti] *adj* → **zestful.**

zeta ['ziːtə] *n* zeta *f* (Greek letter).

zeugma [zjuːgmə] *n* GRAMM zeugma *f*, zeuma *f*.

zibeline; zibelline ['zibiliːn] *n* marta *f* cebellina, cebellina *f*.

zibet; zibeth ['zibit] *n* civeta *f*, gato *m* de algalia (cat).

zigzag ['zigzæg] *adj* en zigzag, zigzagueante; *a zigzag road* una carretera en zigzag.
◆ *adv* *to go zigzag* zigzaguear, ir zigzagueando.
◆ *n* zigzag *m*.

zigzag ['zigzæg] *vt* poner en zigzag (to lay out).
◆ *vi* zigzaguear, ir zigzagueando || andar dando tumbos, andar haciendo eses, zigzaguear (a drunkard).

zigzagging [-iŋ] *n* zigzagueo *m*.

Zimbabwe [zim'bɑːbwi] *pr n* GEOGR Zimbabue.

zinc [ziŋk] *n* cinc *m*, zinc *m*.

zinc [ziŋk] *vt* galvanizar con cinc.
— OBSERV El gerundio y el participio pasivo de *to zinc* son *zincking* o *zincing* y *zincked* o *zinced*.

zinc carbonate [-'kɑːbənit] *n* MIN calamina *f*, carbonato *m* de cinc.

zincing; zincking [-iŋ] *n* TECH galvanización *f* con cinc.

zincograph [-əugrɑːf] *n* cincograbado *m*.

zincography [ziŋ'kɔgrəfi] *n* cincografía *f*.

zinc white ['ziŋk'wait] *n* blanco *m* de cinc.

zing [ziŋ] *n* FAM ánimo *m*, entusiasmo *m* (energy) | zumbido *m* (noise).

zing [ziŋ] *vi* FAM zumbar.

zingiberaceae [ˌzindʒibə'reisiiː] *pl n* BOT cingiberáceas *f*.

zinnia ['ziniə] *n* BOT zinnia *f*.

Zion ['zaiən] *n* REL Sión *m*.

Zionism [-izəm] *n* REL sionismo *m*.

Zionist [-ist] *adj/n* REL sionista.

zip [zip] *n* silbido *m* (whistle) || zumbido *m* (buzz) || cremallera *f* (fastener) || FAM nervio *m*, energía *f*, vigor *m*, brío *m* (vigour).

zip [zip] *vt* *to zip open* abrir la cremallera de || *to zip shut* cerrar con cremallera, cerrar la cremallera de || *to zip up* subir la cremallera de, cerrar (la cremallera de).
◆ *vi* silbar (to whizz like a bullet) || zumbar (to buzz) || ir como una bala (to move quickly) || cerrarse con cremallera (to fasten with a zip) || *to zip past* pasar silbando.

zip code [-kəud] *n* US código *m* postal.

zip fastener [-'fɑːsənə*] *n* cremallera *f*.

zipper [-ə*] *n* cremallera *f*.

zippy [-i] *adj* enérgico, ca (energetic) || veloz, rápido, da (fast) || pronto, ta (prompt).

zircon ['zəːkɔn] *n* MIN circón *m*, zircón *m*.

zirconia [zəː'kəunjə] *n* CHEM circona *f*.

zirconite ['zəːkənait] *n* circonita *f*.

zirconium [zəː'kəunjəm] *n* CHEM circonio *m*.

zither ['ziðə*] *n* MUS cítara *f*.

zloty ['zlɔti] *n* zloty *m* (Polish coin).

zoantharia [ˌzəuæn'θεəriə] *pl n* ZOOL zoantarios *m*.

zoanthropy [zəu'ænθrəri] *n* MED zoantropía *f*.

zodiac ['zəudiæk] *n* ASTR zodíaco *m*; *the signs of the zodiac* los signos del zodíaco.

zodiacal ['zəudiækəl] *adj* zodiacal.

zombi; zombie ['zɔmbi] *n* muerto *m* resucitado por magia negra || FIG & FAM autómata *m* & *f*.

zonal ['zəunəl] *adj* zonal, en zonas.

zonate ['zəuneit] *adj* dividido en zonas.

zonation [zəu'neiʃən] *n* división *f* en zonas.

zone [zəun] *n* zona *f* || US distrito *m*; *postal zone* distrito postal || — *demilitarized zone* zona desmilitarizada || *glacial zone* zona glacial || *industrial zone* zona industrial || *military zone* zona militar || *zone of influence* zona de influencia.

zone [zəun] *vt* dividir en zonas.

zoo [zuː] *n* zoo *m*, parque *m* zoológico.

zoogeography [ˌzəuədʒi'ɔgrəfi] *n* zoogeografía *f*.

zooid ['zəuɔid] *n* zooide *m*.

zooidal ['zəu'ɔidəl] *adj* zooide.

zoolater [zəu'ɔlətə*] *n* zoólatra *m* & *f*.

zoolatrous [zəu'ɔlətrəs] *adj* zoólatra.

zoolatry [zəu'ɔlətri] *n* zoolatría *f*.

zoological [ˌzəuə'lɔdʒikəl] *adj* zoológico, ca; *zoological garden* o *gardens* parque zoológico.

zoologist [zəu'ɔlədʒist] *n* zoólogo, ga.

zoology [zəu'ɔlədʒi] *n* zoología *f*.

zoom [zuːm] *n* zumbido *m* (buzz) || AVIAT subida *f* vertical || PHOT «zoom» *m*, objetivo *m* de distancia focal variable (of cameras).

zoom [zuːm] *vt* AVIAT hacer subir verticalmente (a plane) || PHOT enfocar con el «zoom».
◆ *vi* zumbar (to buzz) || ir zumbando (to whizz along) || AVIAT subir verticalmente || PHOT acercarse *or* alejarse rápidamente || — *to zoom away* o *off* salir zumbando || PHOT *to zoom in* enfocar en primer plano || *to zoom past* pasar zumbando.

zoom lens [-'lenz] *n* PHOT objetivo *m* de distancia focal variable, «zoom» *m*.

zoomorphism [ˌzəuə'mɔːfizəm] *n* zoomorfismo *m*.

zoophaga [zəu'ɔfəgə] *pl n* zoófagos *m*.

zoophagan [-n] *n* zoófago, ga.

zoophobia [ˌzəuə'fəubiə] *n* zoofobia *f*.

zoophorus [zəu'ɔfərəs] *n* ARCH zoóforo *m*.

zoophyta [zəuə'faitə] *pl n* zoófitos *m*.

zoophyte ['zəuəfait] *n* zoófito *m*.

zoosporangium [ˌzəuəspəˈrændʒiəm] *n* BOT zoosporagio *m*.
— OBSERV El plural de *zoosporagium* es *zoosporangia*.

zoospore [ˈzəuəspɔ*] *n* zoospora *f*.

zootechnic [ˌzəuəˈteknik] ; **zootechnical** [-əl] *adj* zootécnico, ca.

zootechnician [ˌzəuətekˈniʃən] *n* zootécnico, ca.

zootechny [ˈzəuəˌtekni] *n* zootecnia *f*.

zootherapy [ˌzəuəˈθerəpi] *n* zooterapia *f*.

zootrope [ˈzəuətrəup] *n* zoótropo *m*.

Zoroaster [ˌzɔrəuˈæstə*] *pr n* zoroastro *m*.

Zoroastrianism [-izəm] *n* zoroastrismo *m*.

zoster [ˈzɔstə*] *n* MED zona *f* (shingles).

Zouave [zuːˈɑːv] *n* zuavo *m*.

zucchetto [zuːˈketəu] *n* REL solideo *m* (skullcap).

zucchini [zuːˈkiːni] *n* *US* calabacín *m*.
— OBSERV El plural de *zucchini* es *zucchini* o *zucchinis*.

Zulu [ˈuːlu] *n* zulú *m* & *f*.
— OBSERV El plural de la palabra inglesa *Zulu* es *Zulu* o *Zulus*.

Zululand [-lænd] *pr n* GEOGR Zululandia *f*.

Zurich [ˈzjuərik] *pr n* GEOGR Zurich.

zwieback [ˈzwiːbæk] *n* *US* bizcocho *m* hecho con huevos.

Zwingli [ˈzwiŋli] *pr n* Zwinglio *m*.

zwitterion [ˈtsvitərˌaiən] *n* PHYS ion *m* con carga positiva y negativa.

zygoma [zaiˈgəumə] *n* ANAT cigoma *m*, zigoma *m*.
— OBSERV El plural de *zygoma* es *zygomata* o *zygomas*.

zygomatic [ˌzaigəˈmætik] *adj* ANAT cigomático, ca; zigomático, ca.

zygote [ˈzaigəut] *n* BIOL cigoto *m*, zigoto *m*.

ENGLISH GRAMMAR
GRAMÁTICA INGLESA

RESUMEN DE GRAMÁTICA INGLESA

El alfabeto inglés

El alfabeto inglés consta de 26 letras:

a	**b**	**c**	**d**	**e**	**f**	**g**	**h**	**i**	**j**	**k**
ei	bi:	si:	di:	i:	ef	dʒi:	eitʃ	ai	dʒei	kei
l	**m**	**n**	**o**	**p**	**q**	**r**	**s**	**t**	**u**	
el	em	en	əu	pi:	kju:	ɑ:*	es	ti:	ju:	
v	**w**	**x**	**y**	**z**						
vi:	dʌbəlju:	eks	wai	zed						

Pronunciación

Algunas de las letras inglesas representan más de un sonido y para poder reproducirlos oralmente de la manera más exacta posible se ha colocado entre corchetes, después de cada vocablo, simple o compuesto, la pronunciación figurada que le corresponde según el Alfabeto Fonético Internacional (véase pág. VI, 2.ª parte). La pronunciación varía mucho según las regiones y los países de habla inglesa. Este diccionario se limita a consignar la más empleada en Gran Bretaña, seguida por la norteamericana, señalada ésta por las letras US, cuando difiere de la primera.

El acento tónico principal queda indicado por una virgulilla colocada en el ángulo superior de la sílaba acentuada y el acento tónico secundario por otra situada en el ángulo inferior (*periodic* [ˌpiəriˈɔdik]). Se ha empleado el guión para reemplazar la parte común que tienen varias palabras seguidas.

Consonantes

1. **b.** Es semejante a la **b** inicial española (**b**all, ca**b**) y es muda en algunas palabras delante de *t* (de**b**t).

2. **c.** Se pronuncia como la **c** española en *casa* (**c**at, **c**olour, **c**luster).

Suena como una **s** ante *e, i* (**c**ertify, **c**ivilian).

El grupo **ch** tiene el mismo sonido que la **ch** española en vocablos como **ch**air, bea**ch**, ar**ch**bishop, etc., pero tiene el sonido de **k** en **Ch**ristmas, **ch**emist, **ch**iropodist, etc.

3. **d.** Tiene un sonido parecido a la **d** española en *caldo* (**d**o, pai**d**, ro**d**ent).

4. **f.** Es casi igual a la **f** española (**f**avour, i**f**), excepto en la preposición *of* en la cual se pronuncia como una v.

El grupo **ph** tiene el mismo sonido (**ph**ysics).

5. **g.** Ante *a, o, u,* precediendo otra consonante, excepto *n*, o al final de una palabra, se pronuncia como la **g** de *gato* (**g**ap, **g**o, **g**ust, **g**lance, bo**g**, pe**g**).

Cuando va seguida por *e, i,* además del sonido anterior (**g**et, **g**ive), puede tener el de la **y** argentina (**g**ender, **g**in).

Delante de *n* es muda (**g**narl).

6. **h.** Se asemeja a la jota, aunque su sonido es mucho más suave (**h**orse).

Es muda en *hour, honour, honest, heir.*

7. **j.** Suena como una **d** seguida por la **y** argentina (**j**ob, **j**ustice).

8. **k.** Es semejante a la **k** española (**k**ind, **k**eep).

Delante de *n* es muda (**k**nowledge, **k**nife).

9. **l.** Simple o doble, se pronuncia como la **l** española (**l**ife, ma**l**aria, be**ll**, fi**ll**).

En algunas palabras, como *calf, half, could,* etc., es muda.

10. **m.** Simple o doble, es igual a la **m** española (**m**other, co**mm**erce).

En posición final y precedida de una **m** la **n** es muda (*damn*).

11. **n.** Simple o doble, tiene el mismo sonido que la **n** española (**n**ever, co**nn**ect).

12. **p.** Es idéntica a la **p** española, pero más explosiva (**p**eo**p**le, lam**p**).

13. **q.** Combinada con la **u** da el sonido español de *cu* (**qu**ality, **qu**estion, **qu**ick).

14. **r.** Se parece a la **r** de *mero* (**r**un, p**r**ice).

Apenas se pronuncia ante una consonante o al final de una palabra (qua**r**te**r**).

15. **s.** Simple, se pronuncia como la **s** española en posición inicial (**s**ome), en el plural y en la tercera persona del presente de indicativo de los verbos cuando antecede una consonante sorda (map**s**, cut**s**) y en posición final después de *i, a, o, u, y* (thi**s**), con algunas excepciones (ha**s**, wa**s**, a**s**, hi**s**, flie**s**, etc.).

Simple, la **s** inglesa se articula apoyando suavemente la lengua entre los dientes y haciendo vibrar fuertemente las cuerdas vocales en los plurales cuyo singular termine en vocal o consonante sonora (house**s**, egg**s**), en la tercera persona del singular de los verbos, si éstos terminan en vocal o consonante sonora, y en otras palabras en posición final cuando sigue una *e* no muda.

Doble, equivale a la **s** española (le**ss**, ma**ss**ive).

Es muda en algunos vocablos como i**s**le.

Delante de *ia* e *io* la **s** se pronuncia como el grupo **sh** pero haciendo vibrar las cuerdas vocales (A**s**ian, le**s**ion).

El grupo **sh** tiene un sonido parecido a la **ch** española, aunque mucho más suave (**sh**ould, la**sh**).

16. **t.** Se asemeja a la **t** española, pero es ligeramente más aspirada (**t**ide, le**t**).

Tiene un sonido similar al de **sh** en términos como *conception, eredential,* etc.

El grupo **th** se pronuncia como la **z** española (**th**ing, sou**th**) o aproximadamente como la **d** española de *cada* (**th**en, wi**th**).

17. **v.** Es una consonante labiodental que se pronuncia apoyando los dientes superiores en el labio inferior (**v**isit, lo**v**e).

18. **w.** Suena como la **u** española (**w**ell, t**w**enty).

Es muda delante de *r* (**w**rap).

19. **x.** Equivale al sonido de **ks** (rela**x**) o de **kz** (e**x**act).

En posición inicial se pronuncia como la **z** inglesa (**x**ylophone).

20. **y.** Como consonante es parecida a la **y** española (**y**esterday).

21. **z.** Se articula apoyando suavemente la lengua entre los dientes y haciendo vibrar fuertemente las cuerdas vocales (**z**one, la**z**iness).

Vocales

1. **a.** Suene igual que la **a** española en palabras como f**a**ther, c**a**r, h**a**lf.

Tiene un sonido breve intermedio entre la **a** y la **e** españolas en vocablos del tipo **a**pple, m**a**n, gr**a**mmar.

Es parecida al diptongo en voces como t**a**ble, f**a**mous, b**a**by.

Equivale aproximadamente a **ea** en términos como **a**ir, d**a**re.

2. **e.** Se pronuncia como la **e** española de *nivel* en palabras como r**e**d, l**e**sson, m**e**mory, y con un sonido un poco más oscuro en voces como v**e**rb.

Suena como una **i** española larga al final de una sílaba al seguir una consonante (b**e**fore) o cuando es doble (tr**ee**).

Tiene el sonido de **ía** en h**e**re, f**e**ar, etc.

Generalmente es muda en posición final (lov**e**, glu**e**).

3. **i.** Es parecida a la **i** española en vocablos como b**i**t, f**i**sh, sh**i**p.

Tiene un sonido más oscuro que la **e** española en b**i**rd, f**i**rst, s**i**r, etc.

Se pronuncia como el diptongo **ai** en l**i**ke, r**i**de, arr**i**ve, etc.

4. **o.** Equivale a la **o** española (h**o**t, d**o**g).

Suena como la **u** española en d**o**, wh**o**, m**o**ve, etc., y cuando es doble (b**oo**k, t**oo**), aunque existen excepciones (d**oo**r, bl**oo**d, etc.).

Tiene el sonido de la **a** española en palabras como h**o**use.

En *women* se pronuncia **i**.

5. **u.** Es parecida a la **u** española en b**u**ll, p**u**t, etc.

Tiene un sonido intermedio entre la **o** y la **e** españolas en b**u**t, m**u**ch, **u**p, etc.

Se pronuncia como el diptongo **iu** en voces como mat**u**re, **u**se, etc.

6. **y.** Como vocal suena igual que la **i** española (ministr**y**).

Diptongos y triptongos

A diferencia de lo que ocurre en español, los **diptongos** y **triptongos** no corresponden siempre a la combinación de dos o tres vocales gráficas. Por ejemplo la **i** de *ice* representa por sí sola el sonido del diptongo español **ai**.

Variaciones ortográficas

Existen algunas diferencias entre la ortografía británica y la norteamericana.

— al inglés **-our** corresponde el americano **-or** (*labour* labor);

— al inglés **-re** corresponde el americano **-er** (*theatre* theater), con algunas excepciones como *ogre* y las palabras terminadas por *-cre* (*massacre, lucre*);

— al inglés **-ce** corresponde el americano **-se** (*licence* license);
— al inglés **-ould** corresponde el americano **-old** (*mould* mold);
— al inglés **-ae**, **-oe** de ciertas palabras cultas corresponde el americano **-e** (*haemoglobin* hemoglobin; *amoeba* ameba);
— en cierto número de casos se duplica una consonante en inglés mientras que no se hace en americano (*quarrelled* quarreled; *traveller* traveler; *waggon* wagon);
— en algunas palabras la **e**, que existe en inglés, desaparece en americano (*good-bye* good-by; *storey* story);
— en algunas voces tomadas del francés se conserva la ortografía francesa en Gran Bretaña, pero, en Estados Unidos, se suprime la terminación átona (*programme* program);
— ciertos términos no se escriben de la misma manera, sin que esto obedezca a determinadas normas precisas, en los dos países (*grey* gray; *tyre* tire; *fulfil* fulfill; *instalment* installment; *plough* plow).

Mayúsculas

El uso de las **mayúsculas** es mucho más frecuente en inglés que en español. En efecto, además de los casos en que así ocurre en Castellano, se emplean con los derivados de nombres propios (*Aritstotelian*), los sustantivos y adjetivos que indican la nacionalidad (*Englishman, English*), los idiomas (*Spanish*), los días de la semana (*Monday*), los meses (*February*), los títulos (*My Lord Duke*), los nombres de religiones, sectas o partidos y sus derivados (*Catholicism, Mormon, Labour*), el pronombre personal *I* y la interjección *O*.

Artículo

El **artículo definido** inglés es el mismo, **the**, en las formas masculina y femenina, singular o plural (*the boy, the girls, the animals*) y se emplea menos frecuentemente que en español.

No se debe emplear:
— con sustantivos en plural o nombres abstractos sin determinar (*he is very fond of tomatoes* le gustan mucho los tomates; *life is difficult* la vida es difícil);
— delante de *man* y *woman* usados en sentido abstracto o colectivo (*Man proposes, God disposes* el hombre propone y Dios dispone);
— con nombres de juegos, deportes, ocupaciones, artes, ciencias y enfermedades (*chess* el ajedrez; *to play tennis* jugar al tenis; *bookkeeping* la contabilidad; *architecture* la arquitectura; *chemistry* la química; *measles* el sarampión);
— con sustantivos que representan una materia líquida, sólida o gaseosa y con nombres de comidas en sentido general (*water is useful* el agua es útil; *to serve lunch* servir el almuerzo);
— con palabras como *school, church, hospital, prison* si éstas se refieren al uso que se hace de estos edificios (*to go to church* ir a la iglesia; *I was taken to hospital* me llevaron al hospital);
— con los días de la semana, las estaciones y ciertas expresiones de tiempo (*he will come on Tuesday* vendrá el martes; *when summer arrived* cuando llegó el verano; *last year* el año pasado; *I left at two o'clock* me fui a las dos);
— con idiomas y títulos (*Italian is not very difficult* el italiano no es difícil; *Doctor Burnet* el doctor Burnet; *Mr Brown* el señor Brown);
— con puntos cardinales en sentido absoluto y delante de un sustantivo seguido por un número cardinal (*to go south* ir al sur; *I am in room number seven* estoy en la habitación número siete).

Se debe emplear:
— delante de un sustantivo en singular al generalizar (*the dog is a faithful animal* el perro es un animal fiel);
— con un sustantivo determinado, en singular y en plural (*the woman (that) I saw* la mujer a quien vi; *the books (that) you read* los libros que usted leyó);
— con palabras que representan algo único (*the sun, the moon, the Bible, etc.*).

Se emplea asimismo:
— con ciertos adjetivos para sustantivarlos (*the rich* los ricos);
— delante de números ordinales en títulos y fechas (*Edward the Seventh* Eduardo Séptimo; *May the thirteenth* el trece de mayo);
— con función de adverbio (*the more he gets the more he wants* cuanto más tiene más quiere).

El **artículo indefinido** tiene la misma forma **a** en masculino y en femenino (*a man, a woman*) y sólo existe en singular. Se transforma en **an** delante de una palabra que empieza por vocal o *h* muda (*an artist, an hour*), excepto si se trata de *u* o del grupo *eu* con el sonido de *iu* (*a university, a European*). El plural español *unos, unas* se traduce por *some* (*some interesting books* unos libros interesantes). Es de uso más frecuente en inglés que en español.

Se debe emplear:
— antes de un sustantivo en singular al generalizar (*a dog is a faithful animal* el perro es un animal fiel);
— con un nombre que represente la nacionalidad, la profesión o la religión (*he is a Sppaniard* es español; *I am a teacher* soy profesor; *he was a naval officer* era oficial de marina; *she is a Moslem* es musulmana);
— delante de un sustantivo en aposición (*my friend, a teacher of languages* mi amigo, profesor de idiomas);
— después de las palabras *without, half, such, certain, other, as, what, hundred, thousand, million* (*without a jacket* sin chaqueta; *half an apple* media manzana; *it gave me such a fright!* ¡me dio tal susto!; *a certain day* cierto día; *another cup of tea* otra taza de té; *he came as an observer* vino en calidad de observador; *what a pity!* ¡qué lástima!; *a hundred houses* cien casas; *a thousand men* mil hombres; *a million pounds* un millón de libras);
— en expresiones de tiempo, de precio y de velocidad (*once a year* una vez al año; *two shillings a pound* dos chelines por libra, dos chelines la libra; *one hundred miles an hour* cien millas por hora).

Sustantivo

Género

Suelen ser **masculinos** los sustantivos que designan a varones o animales machos, profesiones, títulos o empleos desempeñados por hombres.

Son generalmente **femeninos** los sustantivos que representan a personas del sexo opuesto a las anteriores o animales hembras, profesiones, títulos o empleos desempeñados por mujeres.

Son **neutros** todos los demás, con la excepción de *ship, engine, aeroplane* and *car*, que se consideran femeninos la mayoría de las veces.

Hay que señalar que *parent* se aplica al padre y a la madre, *cousin* al primo y a la prima y que *child* y *baby* se clasifican muy frecuentemente entre los neutros.

Formación del femenino

El **femenino** se forma de las tres maneras siguientes:
— con la terminación **-ess** (*heir, heiress; lion, lioness*);
— con una palabra distinta (*boy, girl; cock, hen*);
— con un sustantivo compuesto (*milkman, milkmaid; manservant, maidservant; he-goat, she-goat*);
— con el adjetivo **female** (*male friend, female friend*).

Existe también el sufijo **-ine** (*hero, heroine*), pero su uso es menos frecuente.

Formación del plural

El **plural** se forma generalmente añadiendo **-s** al singular (*book, books; plate, plates*). Esta **s** es sorda después de *p, t, k, f, th* y sonora cuando sigue una vocal o una consonante distinta de las anteriormente mencionadas,
— los sustantivos terminados en *-s, -ss, -sh, -ch, -x, -z* añaden **-es**, en plural (*gases, classes, dishes, churches, boxes, topazes*);
— los que acaban en *-o* precedida de consonante añaden **-es** en plural (*potatoes*), con algunas excepciones (*pianos, photos, banjos, tobaccos*);
— los terminados en *-o* precedida de vocal toman sólo una **-s** en plural (*radios*);
— los acabados en *-y* cambian esta terminación en **-ies** cuando la letra anterior es una consonante (*skies*) y añaden simplemente una **-s** si es una vocal (*days*);
— algunas palabras terminadas en *-f* o *-fe* cambian su terminación en **-ves** (*leaves, knives*), mientras que otras, con las mismas características, sólo toman una **-s** (*roofs, safes*);
— ciertos sustantivos forman el plural añadiendo **-en** o **-ren** (*ox, oxen; child, children*). El plural de *brother* es *brothers* cuando significa «hermano de sangre» y *brethren* si tiene el sentido de «miembro de una comunidad»;
— otros sufren un cambio en la vocal interna (*man, men; woman, women; tooth, teeth; goose, geese; foot, feet; louse, lice; mouse, mice*);
— algunos conservan la misma forma en singular y en plural (*aircraft, deer, grouse, sheep, salmon, swine, trout*);
— ciertas palabras de origen extranjero se usan con el plural de origen (*datum, data; analysis, analyses*), aunque algunas pueden también tener un plural regular (*memorandum, memoranda* o *memorandums*);
— varios sustantivos compuestos de cantidad son invariables cuando se usan como adjetivos (*a five mile walk, a five-pound note*);

— algunos no tienen singular (*scissors, trousers, etc.*) y otros como *means, news* se emplean como si fueran singulares;

— los acabados en *-ics* pueden usarse en singular o en plural (*physics, politics, etc.*), aunque el empleo del singular sea más frecuente;

— los nombres compuestos añaden la terminación del plural solamente a la palabra principal (*son-in-law, sons-in-law*), excepto si están formados con *man* o *woman* como prefijo (*manservant, menservants*).

Caso posesivo

El **caso posesivo** o **genitivo** se emplea para expresar la posesión o la pertenencia, cuando el poseedor es un ser animado o capaz de ser personificado, y con algunos nombres que indican tiempo, medida, espacio o precio. Se forma invirtiendo los términos de la frase y añadiendo un apóstrofo y una **s** al poseedor seguidos de lo poseído sin artículo (*Peter's book* el libro de Pedro; *at a mile's distance* a una distancia de una milla; *an hour's walk* un paseo de una hora; *England's navy* la marina inglesa).

Si el poseedor está en plural, no se pone la *s* (*the girls' school* la escuela de las chicas), excepto si no acaba en *s* (*the children's bedroom* el dormitorio de los niños).

Cuando los poseedores son varios se aplica la forma del caso posesivo únicamente al último (*Peter and John's bedroom* el dormitorio de Pedro y Juan).

Se omiten frecuentemente las palabras *house, shop* y *church* después del caso posesivo (*I am at my brother's* estoy en casa de mi hermano; *have you been to the baker's?* ¿fuiste a la panadería?; *he goes to mass to St Peter's* va a misa a (la iglesia de) San Pedro).

Adjetivo

El **adjetivo** suele anteponerse al sustantivo. Tiene la misma forma en singular y plural y en masculino y femenino (*an expensive book* un libro caro; *expensive books* libros caros; *a tall boy* un chico alto; *a tall girl* una chica alta).

Los adjetivos demostrativos constituyen una excepción y varían en plural (*this woman* esta mujer; *these women* estas mujeres; *that man* ese hombre; *those men* esos hombres).

Adjetivo calificativo

El **adjetivo calificativo** con función de atributo se coloca siempre antes del sustantivo (*I have a blue pencil* tengo un lápiz azul).

En cambio, debe ir después del sustantivo que califica:

— cuando se usa como predicado (*my pencil is blue* mi lápiz es azul);

— si queda determinado por un complemento (*a glass full of water* un vaso lleno de agua);

— al calificar los pronombres terminados por *-thing* o *-body* (*something new* algo nuevo);

— cuando se trata de un adjetivo que empieza por *-a*, como *asleep, afraid, awake, aware, alive, ashamed, alone* (*the fastest man alive* el hombre más rápido del mundo);

— en algunos casos especiales como *court martial, heir apparent, from time immemorial.*

El adjetivo no se puede usar solo y requiere siempre la presencia de un sustantivo o del pronombre indefinido *one, ones* (*he has a black coat and a blue one* tiene un abrigo negro y otro blanco).

Se emplea como sustantivo al designar un idioma (*to teach Spanish* enseñar (el) español) y al representar una palabra abstracta o un grupo de personas, en cuyos casos va siempre precedido por el artículo definido *the* (*the ideal* lo ideal; *the rich* los ricos).

En inglés, un sustantivo califica a veces otro, teniendo así función de adjetivo (*house agent* agente inmobiliario).

Comparativos y superlativos

El **comparativo de igualdad** se forma con **as... as** en oraciones afirmativas (*she is as tall as her mother* es tan alta como su madre) y con **not as... as** o **not so... as** en frases negativas (*he is not as tall as his father* no es tan alto como su padre).

El **comparativo** y el **superlativo de superioridad** se forman con **more** y **most** respectivamente o con las terminaciones **-er** y **-est**:

— los adjetivos monosilábicos añaden **-er** y **-est** (*he is taller than his father* es más alto que su padre; *it is the highest building in Spain* es el edificio más alto de España);

— los de tres o más sílabas van precedidos por **more** y **most** (*he is more intelligent than his brother* es más inteligente que su hermano; *the most intelligent boy of the group* el chico más inteligente del grupo);

— Los de dos sílabas siguen una de las dos reglas anteriormente mencionadas. Los que acaban en *-er* o *-y* agregan **-er, -est** (*cleverer, prettiest*). Los terminados en **-ful** y **-re** suelen ir precedidos por **more, most** (*more careful, most obscure*);

— algunos son irregulares (véase el cuadro insertado a continuación).

El **comparativo** y el **superlativo de inferioridad** se forman con **less** y **least** respectivamente (*less interesting* menos interesante; *the least interesting* el menos interesante).

El **superlativo absoluto** se forma generalmente con los adverbios **very, much** y **most** (*very polite* muy cortés; *much loved* muy querido; *most helpful* muy útil).

El superlativo sólo se puede emplear en inglés cuando se trata de más de dos personas o cosas.

Comparativos y superlativos irregulares

Positivo	*Comparativo*	*Superlativo*
good	*better*	the best
bad	*worse*	the worst
little	*less*	the least
much	*more*	the most
many	*more*	the most
far	*farther* *further*	the farthest the furthest
old	*older* *elder*	the oldest the eldest
late	*later* *latter*	the latest the last

Much se usa con un sustantivo singular, *many* con un nombre plural.

Farther se refiere en general a una distancia y *further* a una progresión.

Elder y *eldest* indican el grado de antigüedad (*his eldest girl*), *older* y *oldest* el número de años (*she is older than her brother*).

Later, the latest tienen el sentido de «más reciente», mientras que *latter, the last* se aplican al último en una enumeración.

Adjetivos numerales

	Cardinales	*Ordinales*
0	nought	
1	one	first
2	two	second
3	three	third
4	four	fourth
5	five	fifth
6	six	sixth
7	seven	seventh
8	eight	eighth
9	nine	ninth
10	ten	tenth
11	eleven	eleventh
12	twelve	twelfth
13	thirteen	thirteenth
14	fourteen	fourteenth
15	fifteen	fifteenth
16	sixteen	sixteenth
17	seventeen	seventeenth
18	eighteen	eighteenth
19	nineteen	nineteenth
20	twenty	twentieth
21	twenty-one	twenty-first
22	twenty-two	twenty-second
30	thirty	thirtieth
31	thirty-one	thirty-first
40	forty	fortieth
50	fifty	fiftieth
60	sixty	sixtieth
70	seventy	seventieth
80	eighty	eightieth
90	ninety	ninetieth
100	a hundred, one hundred	hundredth

→

Cardinales		*Ordinales*
101	one hundred and one, a hundred and one	hundred and first
134	one hundred and thirty-four	hundred and thirty-fourth
200	two hundred	two hundredth
300	three hundred	three hundredth
400	four hundred	four hundredth
500	five hundred	five hundredth
600	six hundred	six hundredth
700	seven hundred	seven hundredth
800	eight hundred	eight hundredth
900	nine hundred	nine hundredth
1000	a thousand, one thousand	thousandth
1001	one thousand and one	thousand and first
2034	two thousand and thirty-four	two thousand and thirty-fourth
1 000 000	a million, one million	millionth
1 000 000 000	a milliard, one milliard [US a billion, one billion]	[US billionth]
1 000 000 000 000	a billion, one billion [US a trillion, one trillion]	billionth [US trillionth]

Numerales cardinales

Entre las decenas y las unidades no se usa nunca la conjunción *and*; a partir de 20 (*twenty*), los numerales se forman con el nombre de la decena correspondiente seguida de un guión y las unidades correlativas (*twenty-one; thirty-two*).

Después de *million, thousand* y *hundred*, los números inferiores a cien van siempre precedidos por la conjunción and (*one thousand two hundred and fifty-two; one thousand and one*).

Million, thousand y *hundred* son invariables, excepto cuando se usan como sustantivos con un sentido impreciso (*thousands of men were killed*). Lo mismo se aplica a *dozen* y *score* (*I saw him scores of times*).

Hundred, thousand, million, etc. van precedidos por **a** o **one**. *A* se emplea especialmente cuando se trata de una cifra redonda (*a hundred women*) y *one* si estos números van seguidos por otros (*one thousand and two*). Los números que indican el año suelen expresarse por centenas (*in seventeen hundred* en el año mil setecientos).

Numerales ordinales

En los números compuestos, el último elemento es el único en tomar la forma del ordinal (*twenty-fifth*). Los numerales ordinales se utilizan para expresar el orden (*he is the third* es el tercero; *chapter the second* el capítulo segundo), la cronología (*George the Fifth* Jorge Quinto; *the nineteenth century* el siglo diez y nueve) y las fechas (*May the 25th, the 25th of May* el veinticinco de mayo).

Adjetivos y pronombres

Pronombres personales

			Sujeto	*Complemento*	*Reflexivo*
Singular	1.ª pers		I	me	myself
	2.ª pers		you	you	yourself
	3.ª pers	masc	he	him	himself
		fem	she	her	herself
		neut	it	it	itself
Plural	1.ª pers		we	us	ourselves
	2.ª pers		you	you	yourselves
	3.ª pers		they	them	themselves

Los **pronombres personales** no han de omitirse nunca en inglés. En una oración afirmativa, los que tienen función de sujeto se colocan delante del verbo (*he bought a book* compró un libro) y los que se utilizan como complementos van detrás del verbo o de una preposición (*my brother took them* mi hermano los tomó; *he said to me that...* me dijo que...). El complemento indirecto no ha de colocarse nunca antes del complemento directo (*he gave it to me* me lo dio). Empleado con verbos seguidos de una partícula, el pronombre complemento directo se debe poner entre el verbo y la partícula (*give it up!* ¡déjalo!).

El pronombre sujeto de primera persona singular va siempre en mayúscula (*I am reading* estoy leyendo).

It se emplea en construcciones impersonales (*it is hot*).

You we, they e *it* sirven para traducir el pronombre impersonal español *se* (*it is rumoured that...* se rumorea que...; *we do not work on Sunday* no se trabaja el domingo).

Los pronombres reflexivos se usan para reforzar el pronombre (*he wrote it himself* lo escribió él mismo) o cuando la acción del verbo recae sobre el mismo sujeto (*he looks at himself in the mirror* se mira en el espejo). Conviene indicar que no todos los verbos reflexivos en español lo son en inglés (*quejarse* to complain; *equivocarse* to be mistaken; *sentarse* to sit down; *alegrarse* to be happy, *etc.*).

El pronombre personal indefinido **one** corresponde a «uno» (*one does not like to be beaten* a uno no le gusta que le peguen).

Pronombres y adjetivos posesivos

			Adjetivos	*Pronombres*
Singular	1.ª pers		my	mine
	2.ª pers		your	yours
	3.ª pers	masc	his	his
		fem	her	hers
		neut	its	its own
Plural	1.ª pers		our	ours
	2.ª pers		your	yours
	3.ª pers		their	theirs

Los **adjetivos** y **pronombres posesivos** varían con el poseedor y no con el objeto poseído (*my books* mis libros; *Jane plays with her brother and her sister* Juana juega con su hermano y su hermana; *this book is mine, it is not yours* este libro es mío, no es tuyo; *these pencils are his, they are not mine* estos lápices son suyos, no son míos).

Si el poseedor es indefinido, se usa **one's** (*it is sometimes hard to do one's duty* a veces es difícil cumplir con su deber).

El adjetivo posesivo se emplea con las partes del cuerpo y las prendas de vestir. En los mismos casos en castellano se utiliza el artículo definido (*he hurt his foot* se lastimó el pie; *put on your jacket* ponte la chaqueta). El pronombre posesivo precedido por **of** corresponde al adjetivo español *mío, mía, etc.* (*a friend of yours* un amigo tuyo).

Se puede reforzar la idea de posesión añadiendo **own** al adjetivo posesivo (*this is my own pen, not yours* esta pluma es mía y no suya).

Adjetivos y pronombres demostrativos

El **adjetivo demostrativo** es el único adjetivo que concuerda en número con el sustantivo que le sigue (*I like this book* me gusta este libro; *I like these books* me gustan estos libros).

La forma del pronombre sin que se pongan *one, ones* se emplea cuando el sujeto se expresa en la misma oración (*this is his coat* éste es el abrigo suyo; *that is my house* ésa es mi casa). En cambio, si se omite el nombre, es imprescindible utilizar el pronombre indefinido *one, ones* (*do you prefer this one or that one?* ¿le gusta más éste o ése?).

That y **those** seguidos por la preposición *of* se traducen por *el de, la de, los de, las de* (*this is not my book, it is that of my sister* éste no es mi libro, es el de mi hermana).

That y **those** seguidos por un relativo corresponden a *el que, la que, los que, las que* (*those who are tired may have a rest* los que están cansados pueden descansar).

Cuando se hace referencia a dos objetos ya mencionados, se suele emplear *the former* para el primero y *the latter* para el segundo (véase cuadro en la página siguiente).

Pronombres relativos

Los **pronombres relativos** tienen la misma forma en singular y en plural.

	Sujeto	*Complemento*	*Posesivo*
Personas	who, that	whom, that	whose
Cosas y animales	which, that	which, that	whose, of which

Adjetivos y pronombres demostrativos

Grado de lejanía (adverbios de lugar)		*Masculino y femenino*		*Neutro*
		Singular	*Plural*	*Singular*
here (aquí)	**adj**	**this** (este, esta)	**these** (estos, estas)	
	pron	**this, this one** (éste, ésta)	**these, these ones** (éstos, éstas)	**this** (esto)
there (ahí, allí, allá)	**adj**	**that** (ese, aquel; esa, aquella)	**those** (esos, aquellos; esas, aquellas)	
	pron	**that, that one** (ése, aquél; ésa, aquélla)	**those, those ones** (ésos, aquéllos; ésas, aquéllas)	**that** (eso, aquello)

No se puede omitir nunca el pronombre sujeto (*the man who comes* el hombre que viene). Sin embargo se prescinde frecuentemente del pronombre complemento (*the man I saw* el hombre a quien vi). Cuando éste es indirecto, la preposición se debe colocar después del verbo (*the man I spoke to yesterday* el hombre a quien hablé ayer).

El antecedente del pronombre relativo puede ser otro pronombre (*he who came yesterday* el que vino ayer).

— **That** tiene un sentido restrictivo (*bring me the pen that is on the table, and no other* tráeme la pluma que está en la mesa y no otra) y no ha de ser seguido por una preposición. Se emplea después de un superlativo, incluyendo *first* y *last* (*it is the finest city that I have ever seen* es la ciudad más bonita que jamás he visto), de un pronombre indefinido, de *only* y *very* o de un antecedente que incluye personas y cosas o animales (*the people, cattle and carts that went to market* la gente, el ganado y las carretas que iban al mercado).

— **Whose** se usa únicamente cuando existe una relación de posesión (*Peter, whose house we have visited, is American* Pedro, cuya casa hemos visitado, es americano).

— **What** se emplea cuando el antecedente no queda expresado (*tell me what you want to know* dígame lo que quiere saber).

Adjetivos y pronombres interrogativos

		Pronombres		
	Adjetivos	*Sujeto*	*Complemento*	*Posesivo*
Personas	what, which	who	who, whom	whose
Cosas y animales	what, which	what, which	what, which	whose

Para las personas **who** se refiere a la identidad (*who is this man?* ¿quién es este señor?), **what** a la función (*what is your brother?* ¿qué es tu hermano? y **which** a la elección (*which of these men did you see?* ¿a cuál de estos hombres viste?).

En la lengua hablada se usa frecuentemente la forma **who** para el complemento referente a personas en vez de *whom*.

Cuando el pronombre va acompañado por una preposición, ésta se suele poner al final de la oración (*whom did you play with?* ¿con quién jugaste?).

Si la pregunta es indirecta no hay inversión del verbo (*I asked him what he was doing* le pregunté lo que estaba haciendo).

What se emplea también en expresiones exclamativas (*what luck!* ¡qué suerte!).

Adjetivos y pronombres indefinidos

Los principales adjetivos y pronombres indefinidos son *each, either, neither, every, several, all, some, any, little, few, much, many, enough, no, not any, none, other, another.*

— **No** y **every** sólo son adjetivos y **none** pronombre.

— **Either** significa una de dos personas o cosas.

— Al igual que **either** y **neither, each** y **every** van siempre seguidos por un verbo en singular; *each* tiene un sentido individual, mientras que *every* expresa una idea de colectividad (*on each side* de cada lado; *on every side* por todos los lados).

— **Some** se emplea siempre en oraciones afirmativas (*leave us some oranges* déjanos algunas naranjas) y a veces en frases interrogativas cuya contestación será afirmativa.

— **Any** se usa en oraciones interrogativas y negativas (*do you take any sugar?* ¿tomas azúcar?; *I do not take any sugar* no tomo azúcar), después de *hardly, scarcely, barely* e *if.*

— Los pronombres compuestos derivados de SOME, ANY, NO y EVERY son respectivamente *something, somebody, someone, anything, anybody, anyone, nothing, nobody, no one* y *everything, everybody, everyone.*

— **Little** y **much** se aplican a cantidades que no se pueden contar (*he made little progress* hizo pocos progresos).

— **Few** y **many** se emplean con cantidades numerables (*he ate many cakes* comió muchos pasteles).

— **Other** es invariable cuando es adjetivo y variable como pronombre (*other examples* otros ejemplos; *show me the others* enséñeme los otros).

—**Each other** y **one another** se utilizan después de un verbo para expresar la reciprocidad. La primera forma si se habla de dos personas únicamente y la segunda si hay más de dos (*the two cousins love each other* las dos primas se quieren; *the three cousins love one another* las tres primas se quieren).

Preposición

El pronombre regido por una preposición tiene función de complemento (*he spoke to me* me habló). En las oraciones interrogativas y en las subordinadas introducidas por un pronombre relativo, la preposición antecede al pronombre o sigue al verbo (*this is the girl to whom I spoke yesterday, this is the girl whom I spoke to this morning*). Con «that» o cuando el relativo no queda expresado, la preposición se coloca siempre después del verbo (*this is the girl (that) I spoke to*).

Los sustantivos concretos usados en singular después de una preposición tienen que ir precedidos por el artículo indefinido (*she went out without an umbrella* salió sin paraguas).

El verbo que sigue a la preposición va siempre en gerundio (*she came in without knocking* entró sin llamar a la puerta).

La mayoría de las preposiciones existen como adverbios y muchas son también conjunciones (*after, before, since, till*).

Adverbio

Los **adverbios de modo** se forman generalmente añadiendo **-ly** al adjetivo (*slow, slowly*) y esto trae consigo las modificaciones ortográficas siguientes:

— los adjetivos terminados en *-le,* cambian la *-e* en *-y* (*comfortable, comfortably*);

— los acabados en *-ll* sólo añaden una *y* (*full, fully*);

— los terminados en *-y* sustituyen esta letra por una *i* antes del sufijo *-ly* (*noisy, noisily*);

— los acabados en *-ue* pierden la *-e* (*true, truly*).

Algunos adjetivos se usan como adverbios (*fast, straight, tight, etc.*).

Los principales **adverbios de cantidad** son *little, much, almost, rather, quite, very, too, enough, etc.*

Los **adverbios de lugar** más usados son *above, across, along, around, away, back, behind, below, down, far, here, in, near, off, out, there, up, where, etc.*

Los **adverbios de tiempo** más comúnmente empleados son *after, again, ago, already, always, before, early, ever, formerly, late, never, now, often, once, seldom, sometimes, soon, still, then, today, when, yesterday, yet, etc.*

Los **adverbios de negación** más frecuentemente utilizados son *no, not, never, not at all.*

Los comparativos y superlativos de los adverbios siguen la misma regla que los adjetivos. Algunos son irregulares.

Comparativos y superlativos irregulares

Positivo	*Comparativo*	*Superlativo*
well	*better*	best
badly	*worse*	worst
little	*less*	least
much	*more*	most
far	*farther* *further*	farthest furthest

El adverbio se pone antes del adjetivo, del participio pasivo o de otro adverbio, excepto en el caso de *enough* (*she is very clever; it is good enough*). Con un verbo transitivo suele colocarse después del complemento, excepto si éste es un infinitivo (*he banged the door noisily; they kindly asked her to stay at their house*). Cuando un verbo se construye con un auxiliar o un defectivo el adverbio debe seguir al primer auxiliar (*I shall probably have finished tomorrow* probablemente habré acabado mañana).

Verbo

División

Los verbos se dividen en:

— **transitivos,** cuando tienen complemento directo (*I open the window* abro la ventana);

— **intransitivos,** cuando no lo tienen (*the window opened* la ventana se abrió);

— **reflexivos,** cuando la acción recae en el mismo sujeto que la ejecuta. Se conjugan añadiendo un pronombre reflexivo de la misma persona que el sujeto (*he looked at himself* se miró);

— **recíprocos,** cuando representan una acción efectuada recíprocamente por dos o más personas. Si se trata sólo de dos personas, el verbo va seguido por *each other* (*Peter and Joan love each other* Pedro y Juana se quieren). En caso contrario se añade *one another* (*the four cousins love one another* los cuatro primos se quieren);

— **impersonales,** cuando sólo se emplean en la tercera persona del singular. En inglés van precedidos obligatoriamente por el pronombre neutro *it* y casi siempre se refieren a fenómenos meteorológicos (*it is raining* está lloviendo);

— **defectivos,** cuando se usan únicamente en algunos tiempos y se sustituyen por equivalentes para los demás. No llevan *s* en la tercera persona del singular del presente de indicativo, no van nunca precedidos por *do* u otro auxiliar, el verbo que les sigue está siempre en infinitivo sin «to» (excepto en el caso de *ought*) y el pretérito puede tener un significado de potencial (*we could not hear if we had no ears* no podríamos oír si no tuviéramos oídos). Tienen frecuentemente función de auxiliares.

Verbos defectivos	*Significado*	*Equivalentes*
I can, I could	*capacidad*	to be able
I may, I might	*permiso,* *probabilidad*	to be allowed futuro + perhaps
I must	*necesidad,* *obligación,* *probabilidad*	to have to
I will, I would	*consentimiento*	to want, to wish to
I shall, I should	*obligación* *moral*	to have to
I ought to	*obligación* *moral, consejo*	

Los verbos **need** y **dare** pueden tratarse como verbos normales o defectivos en las oraciones negativas e interrogativas:

— **auxiliares,** cuando sirven para conjugar los demás verbos (véase «verbos auxiliares» más adelante).

Es necesario observar que los verbos no se construyen siempre de la misma manera en ambos idiomas. Muchos verbos intransitivos en inglés son reflexivos o pronominales en español (*to sit down* sentarse), algunos son transitivos en una lengua e intransitivos en la otra (*to cross one's mind* pasar por la mente; *to ask for sth.* pedir algo), otros no van seguidos por la misma preposición en los dos idiomas (*to delight in something* deleitarse con algo; *he has profited by your advice* ha sacado provecho de su consejo).

Voces, modos y tiempos

Voz Pasiva

Los tiempos de la **voz pasiva** se forman con el auxiliar **to be** y el **participio pasivo** del verbo conjugado (*this picture was painted by Turner* este cuadro fue pintado por Turner).

En inglés se emplea mucho más la voz pasiva que en español, que la sustituye generalmente la forma pronominal (*the fire was seen from our house* se veía el incendio desde nuestra casa) o activa correspondiente (*this picture was painted by Turner* Turner pintó este cuadro).

Cuando un verbo, como *to teach, to tell, to show, to give, etc.*, tiene dos complementos, hay dos construcciones posibles para la forma pasiva (*Mary told me a story, I was told a story by Mary, a story was told me by Mary*).

Infinitivo

El **infinitivo** suele ir precedido por la preposición **to**. Se emplea como sujeto de una oración (*to err is human* errar es humano) o como complemento de la mayoría de los verbos (*I wish to see you soon* deseo verle pronto; *my mother wants me to write to my brother* mi madre quiere que escriba a mi hermano), después de adjetivos y sustantivos (*it is difficult to understand* es difícil de entender; *it was time to get up* era hora de levantarse), detrás de «to be» y «to have» para indicar la obligación (*do you have to go home?* ¿tienes que ir a casa?).

To se omite:

— después de auxiliares y defectivos, excepto OUGHT (*I shall go* iré; *I may go* puedo ir);

— después de los verbos de percepción (*we saw them come* les vimos venir);

— después de los verbos TO MAKE, TO LET, TO BID (*he made them listen* les hizo escuchar; *let me sit here* déjeme sentarme aquí; *he bade them be silent* les pidió que se callaran);

— después de las expresiones HAD BETTER, HAD RATHER y BUT (*I had better go* más vale que me vaya; *I cannot but admire it* no puedo dejar de admirarlo).

Gerundio y participio de presente

El gerundio y el participio de presente se forman de la misma manera, es decir añadiendo **-ing** al infinitivo sin *to*.

El **gerundio** ejerce la función de un sustantivo. Se usa como sujeto o complemento (*she loves reading poetry* le encanta leer poesía), después de todas las preposiciones, excepto TO (*she is tired of walking* está cansada de andar), detrás de algunos verbos que indican el principio, la continuación o la terminación de una acción (*to keep singing* seguir cantando) y de ciertas expresiones como *to be worth, I can't help, I don't mind, do you mind?, it is no use* y *it is no good* (*this book is worth reading* este libro es digno de leerse), cuando es precedido por un artículo, un adjetivo indefinido, un adjetivo o un caso posesivo (*I like his singing* me gusta su manera de cantar). También se emplea con verbos que expresan una intención o un gusto personal, aunque en este caso se puede utilizar también el infinitivo con *to*.

El **participio de presente** se usa en la forma progresiva (véase «Forma progresiva» en el apartado siguiente), como adjetivo (*an amusing story* una historia divertida) y en sustitución de una oración adverbial (*fearing that they would recognize him...* temiendo que le reconociesen...).

Forma progresiva

La forma progresiva se utiliza más frecuentemente en inglés que en español. Se forma con el verbo **to be** y el **participio de presente** del verbo (*I am reading* estoy leyendo). Se emplea para indicar que la acción se está realizando en el momento en que se habla o que se estaba efectuando en la época a la cual uno se refiere (*he was reading* estaba leyendo). Se usa también para expresar una acción que tendrá lugar en el futuro (*we are leaving tomorrow* nos iremos mañana), pero no puede hacerse cuando se trata de una acción de poca duración, habitual o instintiva.

Participio pasivo

El **participio pasivo** de los verbos regulares se forma añadiendo **-ed** al infinitivo.

Se emplea con *to be* para formar la voz pasiva y con *to have* para conjugar los tiempos compuestos del pasado. Cumple también las funciones de adjetivo.

Indicativo

El **presente**, que tiene la misma forma en todas las personas, excepto en la tercera del singular que toma **-s** o **-es** al final del infinitivo, indica que la acción se efectúa de una manera habitual (*he goes to school every day* va al colegio todos los días). Se emplea también para expresar una acción futura en proposiciones subordinadas que indican una condición o una idea de tiempo (*when the weather gets a bit better, we'll all go to the beach* cuando mejore un poco el tiempo, iremos todos a la playa).

El **pretérito indefinido** se forma en todas las personas añadiendo **-ed** al infinitivo. Se utiliza para una acción completamente terminada en el pasado (*my watch stopped yesterday* se me paró el reloj ayer). Empleado en la forma progresiva equivale al imperfecto español (*she was wearing a green skirt* llevaba una falda verde).

El **pretérito perfecto** se conjuga con el verbo auxiliar **to have** y el **participio pasivo** del verbo conjugado. Se usa para una acción que tuvo lugar en un pasado indeterminado (*I have seen this woman somewhere* he visto a esta mujer en alguna parte) o que se realizó en un período todavía sin concluir (*I haven't finished my work yet* aún no he acabado mi trabajo) o que no está terminada (*he has been ill for a month* hace un mes que está enfermo; *he has been ill since Saturday* está enfermo desde el sábado) o que acaba de realizarse (*he has just arrived* acaba de llegar).

El **futuro** se forma con el **infinitivo** sin *to* precedido por los auxiliares **shall** en la primera persona del singular y del plural y **will** en las otras. Actualmente *will* se suele aplicar a todas las personas. Sin embargo *shall* se emplea con la primera persona para pedir una opinión (*shall I make the tea?* ¿quiere que prepare el té?) y con las otras para ordenar o prometer algo (*you shall leave the room at once* les ordeno que salgan de la habitación inmediatamente).

El *futuro inmediato* se traduce por *to be going to* o *to be about to*, que significan «estar a punto de».

Potencial

El **potencial simple** se conjuga anteponiendo al **infinitivo** sin *to* los auxiliares **should** en la primera persona del singular y del plural y **would** en las otras. Actualmente *would* suele aplicarse a todas las personas.

Subjuntivo

En el inglés moderno este modo tiende a desaparecer. Tiene las mismas formas que el indicativo, excepto en el caso de la tercera persona del singular del presente que no lleva *s*. El auxiliar *to be* hace **be** en presente y **were** en pretérito para todas las personas.

Se emplea únicamente para expresar una hipótesis considerada ya como irrealizable (*if I were you* si estuviese en tu lugar) o un deseo (*God save the Queen!* ¡Dios guarde a la Reina!) y en algunas expresiones como *be that as it may, come what may, etc.*

El subjuntivo español se traduce generalmente por el infinitivo o el indicativo (véase THE SUBJUNCTIVE en SUMMARY OF SPANISH GRAMMAR) o mediante una forma compuesta con los auxiliares **may, might** y **should** (*if he should come* si él viniese).

Imperativo

El **imperativo** sólo tiene una forma propia, la segunda persona del singular y del plural, que corresponde al infinitivo sin *to*. Para las demás personas se usa «let» con los pronombres complementos (*let us go* vayámonos).

Forma frecuentativa

Se emplea para expresar una costumbre o una repetición. Se forma, en el presente, con **will** y el **infinitivo** y, en el pasado, con **would** o **used to** seguidos por el **infinitivo** (*she will sit there hour after hour* suele *or* acostumbra sentarse allí horas y horas; *she would go for a walk every morning* acostumbraba *or* solía dar un paseo todas las mañanas).

Forma enfática

La forma enfática se utiliza para insistir en la realidad del hecho que se afirma.

En presente y pasado, se forma añadiendo **do** conjugado, si no hay ningún auxiliar (*he did transmit your request to her* seguramente le transmitió tu petición), y se pronuncia con cierto énfasis el auxiliar en el caso contrario. En imperativo se construye siempre con **do** (*do come and see me* no deje de venir a verme; *do have a cup of tea* tome una taza de té, por favor).

Forma negativa

Para los auxiliares y defectivos se añade únicamente **not** (*you are not, they could not*).

En el caso de los demás verbos se coloca **not** entre el primer auxiliar y el verbo (*I have not seen*) en los tiempos compuestos y se pone **do not, does not, did not** delante del infinitivo sin *to* en los tiempos simples (*he does not go, we did not go*).

Los infinitivos y participios llevan la negación **not** antepuesta (*not seeing her, not to go*).

Sin embargo no se utiliza *do* con cualquier negación que no sea *not* (*I saw nobody*).

En la lengua familiar *not* se convierte en **n't** y se une al verbo (*he doesn't think so; you mustn't do that; don't go*).

Cuando *can* va seguido por *not* hace *cannot* o *can't* (*she cannot* o *she can't understand, she is too young* no puede entender, es demasiado joven).

Forma interrogativa

Para los auxiliares y defectivos se invierten el sujeto y el verbo en los tiempos simples (*is he a painter?; can he swim?*) y el sujeto y el primer auxiliar en los tiempos compuestos (*should he have been there?*).

En el caso de los demás verbos se pone el sujeto entre **do, does, did** y el infinitivo (*does he go?*) en los tiempos simples y se invierten el sujeto y el primer auxiliar en los tiempos compuestos (*would Peter have come?*).

No se emplea *do* si la oración empieza con un adjetivo o un pronombre interrogativo con función de sujeto (*who brought this letter?*).

La forma interrogativa en negaciones se construye con el auxiliar seguido por *not* y un sustantivo o pronombre indefinido o demostrativo (*is not John a good boy?; will not another do it?*). Con los pronombres personales *not* se pone al final (*is he not a good boy?*), excepto si se utiliza la contracción *n't* (*isn't he a good boy?*).

Para la traducción del español ¿«verdad»? véase la observación que hay al final de esta palabra en el cuerpo del diccionario.

Observaciones sobre la pronunciación

La terminación **-ed** del pretérito y del participio pasivo se pronuncia como una *d* cuando el radical del verbo acaba con una consonante sonora o un sonido vocálico (*filled, loved, moved, called, spared, sawed*), como una *t* cuando el radical del verbo termina por una consonante sorda (*brushed, scoffed, placed, remarked, passed, reached*) y como *id* después de una *t* o una *d* (*melted, glided*).

Los verbos cuyo infinitivo acaba en **-ce, -se** y **-ge** se pronuncian con una sílaba adicional que suena *-iz* en la tercera persona del singular del presente de indicativo (*dances, cleanses, changes*).

Los verbos cuyo infinitivo termina en **-ss, -x, -z, -sh** y **-ch** añaden, en la tercera persona del singular del presente de indicativo, las letras *-es* que tienen el sonido de *-iz* (*misses, fixes, fizzes, crushes, reaches*).

Modificaciones ortográficas

Se duplica la consonante final de un verbo monosilábico cuando va precedida por una sola vocal y seguida por una terminación que empieza con una vocal (*stopped*). La misma regla se aplica a los verbos de dos o más sílabas si éstos llevan el acento en la última sílaba (*preferred*), con excepción de los que acaban por vocal y *l* (*travelled*), salvo *parallel*.

Si un verbo termina en -y después de una consonante, se cambia ésta en *-i* antes de añadir la terminación *-es* para la tercera persona del singular del presente de indicativo (*he studies*) y *-ed* para el pretérito y el participio pasivo (*studied*).

En cambio, cuando la **-y** va precedida por una vocal en el infinitivo, se forma la tercera persona del singular del presente de indicativo agregando *-s* (*plays; says*) y el participio de presente añadiendo *-ing* (*playing; saying*).

Si un verbo monosilábico acaba en -ie, esta terminación se convierte en **-y** antes de añadir *-ing* para formar el participio de presente (*to die* hace *dying*).

El pretérito y el participio pasivo de los **verbos terminados en -o** se forman agregando *-ed* a la vocal final (*to halo* hace *haloed*).

Verbos auxiliares

Be. Este auxiliar se emplea, al igual que *ser*, para formar la voz pasiva y la forma progresiva.

Se usa también como impersonal, en cuyo caso va precedido de **there** y corresponde a *hay, había, hubo* (*there were twenty pupils* había veinte alumnos).

To be equivale a *tener* cuando indica una medida, una edad, una sensación o un estado (*the house is 100 feet high* la casa tiene cien pies de alto; *I am thirty* tengo treinta años; *they are hungry* tienen hambre) y a *estar* al referirse a la salud (*how are you?* ¿cómo estás?). Seguido por **to** expresa una obligación o una probabilidad (*we are to go to the theatre tonight* debemos ir al teatro esta noche).

Have. Este auxiliar, equivalente al *haber* castellano, se emplea para formar los tiempos compuestos de todos los verbos.

To have equivale a *tener* cuando indica posesión, en cuyo caso va frecuentemente acompañado por **got** (*his aunt has got a beautiful house* su tía tiene una casa preciosa) y a *tomar* al aplicarse a alimentos (*have a drink* tome una copa).

Con el infinitivo o el participio pasivo significa *mandar hacer* (*he had a new suit made* mandó hacer un traje nuevo; *he had the tailor make him a suit* mandó al sastre que le hiciera un traje).

Expresa una obligación cuando va seguido por **to** (*I have to go home* tengo que ir a casa) y una preferencia con **better** o **rather** (*I had better do it* más vale que lo haga; *I had rather do it* preferiría hacerlo).

Do. Este auxiliar se emplea en las formas negativa, interrogativa y enfática de los demás verbos. Se utiliza también para sustituir un verbo ya mencionado (*we did not take coffee, but she did* no tomamos café pero ella sí; *Peter came by train, so did John* Pedro vino en tren y Juan también).

Se conjuga como un verbo regular pero hace *does* en la tercera persona del singular del presente de indicativo, *did* en el pretérito indefinido y *done* en el participio pasivo.

Los **verbos defectivos** (*can, may, must, will, shall, ought to, dare, need*) se usan como auxiliares (*he will work* trabajará).

BE

Infinitivo: to be
Gerundio: being
Participio: been

INDICATIVO

presente

I	am
you	are
he / she / it	is
we	are
you	are
they	are

pret. indefinido

I	was
you	were
he / she / it	was
we	were
you	were
they	were

pret. perfecto

I	have been
you	have been
he / she / it	has been
we	have been
you	have been
they	have been

pluscuamperfecto

I	had been
you	had been
he / she / it	had been
we	had been
you	had been
they	had been

futuro

I	shall be
you	will be
he / she / it	will be
we	shall be
you	will be
they	will be

futuro perfecto

I	shall have been
you	will have been
he / she / it	will have been
we	shall have been
you	will have been
they	will have been

POTENCIAL

simple

I	should be
you	would be
he / she / it	would be
we	should be
you	would be
they	would be

compuesto

I	should have been
you	would have been
he / she / it	would have been
we	should have been
you	would have been
they	would have been

IMPERATIVO

let me be
be
let him / let her / let it be
let us be
be
let them be

SUBJUNTIVO

presente

be
(para todas las personas)

pretérito

were
(para todas las personas)

HAVE

Infinitivo: to have
Gerundio: having
Participio: had

INDICATIVO

presente

I	have
you	have
he / she / it	has
we	have
you	have
they	have

pret. indefinido

had
(para todas las personas)

pret. perfecto

I	have had
you	have had
he / she / it	has had
we	have had
you	have had
they	have had

pluscuamperfecto

had had
(para todas las personas)

futuro

I	shall have
you	will have
he / she / it	will have
we	shall have
you	will have
they	will have

futuro perfecto

I	shall have had
you	will have had
he / she / it	will have had
we	shall have had
you	will have had
they	will have had

POTENCIAL

simple

I	should have
you	would have
he / she / it	would have
we	should have
you	would have
they	would have

compuesto

I	should have had
you	would have had
he / she / it	would have had
we	should have had
you	would have had
they	would have had

IMPERATIVO

let me have
have
let him / let her / let it have
let us have
have
let them have

SUBJUNTIVO

presente

have
(para todas las personas)

pretérito

had
(para todas las personas)

VERBOS REGULARES

Sólo existe un grupo de verbos regulares.

OPEN

Infinitivo: to open
Gerundio: opening
Participio: opened

INDICATIVO

presente

I	open
you	open
he / she / it	opens
we	open
you	open
they	open

pret. indefinido

opened
(para todas las personas)

pret. perfecto

I	have opened
you	have opened
he / she / it	has opened
we	have opened
you	have opened
they	have opened

pluscuamperfecto

had opened
(para todas las personas)

futuro

I	shall open
you	will open
he / she / it	will open
we	shall open
you	will open
they	will open

futuro perfecto

I	shall have opened
you	will have opened
he / she / it	will have opened
we	shall have opened
you	will have opened
they	will have opened

POTENCIAL

simple

I	should open
you	would open
he / she / it	would open
we	should open
you	would open
they	would open

compuesto

I	should have opened
you	would have opened
he / she / it	would have opened
we	should have opened
you	would have opened
they	would have opened

IMPERATIVO

let me open
open
let him / let her / let it } open
let us open
open
let them open

SUBJUNTIVO

presente
open
(para todas las personas)

pretérito
opened
(para todas las personas)

Lista de verbos irregulares

Infinitivo	*Pretérito*	*Part. pasivo*
A		
abide	*abode, abided*	abode, abided
arise	*arose*	arisen
awake	*awoke*	awaked, awoke, awoken
B		
be	*was, were*	been
bear	*bore*	borne (llevado) born (nacido)
beat	*beat*	beaten, beat
become	*became*	become
befall	*befell*	befallen
beget	*begot, begat (ant.)*	begotten
begin	*began*	begun
behold	*beheld*	beheld
bend	*bent*	bent, bended *(ant.)*
bereave	*bereft, bereaved*	bereft, bereaved
beseech	*besought, beseeched*	besought, beseeched
beset	*beset*	beset
bespeak	*bespoke*	bespoken, bespoke *(ant.)*
bestrew	*bestrewed*	bestrewed, bestrewn
bestride	*bestrode*	bestridden
bet	*bet, betted*	bet, betted
betake	*betook*	betaken
bethink	*bethought*	bethought
bid (ordenar, rogar)	*bade*	bidden
(licitar)	*bid*	bid
bide	*bode*	bided
bind	*bound*	bound
bite	*bit*	bitten, bit
bleed	*bled*	bled
blow	*blew*	blown
break	*broke*	broken
breed	*bred*	bred
bring	*brought*	brought
broadcast	*boadcast*	broadcast
build	*built*	built
burn	*burnt, burned*	burnt, burned
burst	*burst*	burst
buy	*bought*	bought
C		
can	*could*	
cast	*cast*	cast
catch	*caught*	caught
chide	*chid, chided*	chid, chidden, chided
choose	*chose*	chosen
cleave		
(hender)	*cleaved, cleft, clove*	cleaved, cleft, cloven
(adherirse)	*cleaved*	cleaved
cling	*clung*	clung
clothe	*clothed, clad*	clothed, clad
cold-draw	*cold-drew*	cold-drawn
come	*came*	come
cost	*cost*	cost
countersink	*countersank*	countersunk
creep	*crept*	crept
crossbreed	*crossbred*	crossbred
crow	*crowed, crew*	crowed
cut	*cut*	cut
D		
deal	*dealt*	dealt
dig	*dug*	dug
dive	*dived, dove*	dived
do	*did*	done
draw	*drew*	drawn
dream	*dreamed, dreamt*	dreamed, dreamt
drink	*drank*	drunk
drive	*drove*	driven
dwell	*dwelt*	dwelt
E		
eat	*ate*	eaten
F		
fall	*fell*	fallen
feed	*fed*	fed
feel	*felt*	felt
fight	*fought*	fought
find	*found*	found
flee	*fled*	fled
fling	*flung*	flung
fly	*flew*	flown
forbear	*forbore*	forborne
borbid	*forbade, forbad*	forbidden
forego	*forewent*	foregone
foreknow	*foreknew*	foreknown
foresee	*foresaw*	foreseen
foretell	*foretold*	foretold
forget	*forgot*	forgotten
forgive	*forgave*	forgiven
forgo	*forwent*	forgone
forsake	*forsook*	forsaken
forswear	*forswore*	forsworn
freeze	*froze*	frozen
G		
get	*got*	got [US gotten]
gird	*girded, girt*	girded, girt
give	*gave*	given
gnaw	*gnawed*	gnawed, gnawn
go	*went*	gone
grind	*ground*	ground
grow	*grew*	grown
H		
hang (sentido general)	*hung*	hung
(ahorcar)	*hanged*	hanged
have	*had*	had
hear	*heard*	heard

Infinitivo	Pretérito	Part. pasivo
heave (sentido general)	*heaved*	heaved
(sentido marítimo)	*hove*	hove
hew	*hewed*	hewed, hewn
hide	*hid*	hidden, hid
hit	*hit*	hit
hold	*held*	held
hurt	*hurt*	hurt
I		
interweave	*interwove*	interwoven
inweave	*inwove*	inwoven
K		
keep	*kept*	kept
kneel	*knelt, kneeled*	knelt, kneeled
knit	*knit, knitted*	knit, knitted
know	*knew*	known
L		
lade	*laded*	laden
lay	*laid*	laid
lead	*led*	led
lean	*leant, leaned*	leant, leaned
leap	*leapt, leaped*	leapt, leaped
learn	*learnt, learned*	learnt, learned
leave	*left*	left
lend	*lent*	lent
let	*let*	let
lie	*lay*	lain
light	*lighted, lit*	lighted, lit
lip-read	*lip-read*	lip-read
lose	*lost*	lost
M		
make	*made*	made
may	*might*	
mean	*meant*	meant
meet	*met*	met
misbecome	*misbecame*	misbecome
miscast	*miscast*	miscast
misdeal	*misdealt*	misdealt
misgive	*misgave*	misgiven
mishear	*misheard*	misheard
mislay	*mislaid*	mislaid
mislead	*misled*	misled
misread	*misread*	misread
misspell	*misspelt*	misspelt
misspend	*misspent*	misspent
mistake	*mistook*	mistaken
misunderstand	*misunderstood*	misunderstood
mow	*mowed*	mowed, mown
O		
outbid	*outbid*	outbid
outbreed	*outbred*	outbred
outdo	*outdid*	outdone
outgo	*outwent*	outgone
outgrow	*outgrew*	outgrown
outride	*outrode*	outridden
outrun	*outran*	outrun
outsell	*outsold*	outsold
outshine	*outshone* [US outshined]	outshone [US outshined]
outwear	*outwore*	outworn
overbear	*overbore*	overborne
overbid	*overbid*	overbid
overbuild	*overbuilt*	overbuilt
overbuy	*overbought*	overbought
overcast	*overcast*	overcast
overcome	*overcame*	overcome
overdo	*overdid*	overdone
overdraw	*overdrew*	overdrawn
overdrink	*overdrank*	overdrunk
overdrive	*overdrove*	overdriven
overeat	*overate*	overeaten
overfeed	*overfed*	overfed
overfly	*overflew*	overflown
overgrow	*overgrew*	overgrown
overhang	*overhung*	overhung
overhear	*overheard*	overheard
overlay	*overlaid*	overlaid
overleap	*overleapt, overleaped*	overleapt, overleaped
overlie	*overlay*	overlain
overpay	*overpaid*	overpaid
override	*overrode*	overridden
overrun	*overran*	overrun
oversee	*oversaw*	overseen
oversell	*oversold*	oversold
overset	*overset*	overset
oversew	*oversewed*	oversewn, oversewed
overshoot	*overshot*	overshot
oversleep	*overslept*	overslept
overspend	*overspent*	overspent
overspread	*overspread*	overspread
overtake	*overtook*	overtaken
overthrow	*overthrew*	overthrown
overwind	*overwound*	overwound
P		
partake	*partook*	partaken
pay (sentido general)	*paid*	paid
(calafatear)	*payed, paid*	payed, paid
prepay	*prepaid*	prepaid
proofread	*proofread*	proofread
put	*put*	put
Q		
quit	*quit, quitted*	quit, quitted
R		
read	*read*	read
rebind	*rebound*	rebound
rebuild	*rebuilt*	rebuilt
recast	*recast*	recast
redo	*redid*	redone
redraw	*redrew*	redrawn
reeve	*rove, reeved*	*rove, reeved*
remake	*remade*	remade
rend	*rent*	rent
repay	*repaid*	repaid
rerun	*reran*	rerun
resell	*resold*	resold
reset	*reset*	reset
resew	*resewed*	resewn, resewed
respell	*respelt, respelled*	respelt, respelled
retake	*retook*	retaken
retell	*retold*	retold
rethink	*rethought*	rethought
re-tread	*re-trod*	re-trodden, re-trod
rewind	*rewound*	rewound
rewrite	*rewrote*	rewritten
rid	*rid, ridded*	rid, ridded
ride	*rode*	ridden
ring	*rang*	rung
rise	*rose*	risen
rive	*rived*	rived, riven
run	*ran*	run
S		
saw	*sawed*	sawed, sawn
say	*said*	said
see	*saw*	seen
seek	*sought*	sought
sell	*sold*	sold
send	*sent*	sent
set	*set*	set
sew	*sewed*	sewn, sewed

Infinitivo	Pretérito	Part. pasivo
shake	*shook*	shaken
shear	*sheared*	shorn, sheared
shed	*shed*	shed
shine	*shone*	shone [US shined]
shoe	*shod*	shod
shoot	*shot*	shot
show	*showed*	shown, showed
shrink	*shrank [US shrunk]*	shrunk
shrive	*shrove*	shriven
shut	*shut*	shut
sing	*sang*	sung
sink	*sank*	sunk
sit	*sat*	sat
slay	*slew*	slain
sleep	*slept*	slept
slide	*slid*	slid
sling	*slung*	slung
slink	*slunk*	slunk
slit	*slit*	slit
smell	*smelled, smelt*	smelled, smelt
smite	*smote*	smitten
sow	*sowed*	sown, sowed
speak	*spoke*	spoken
speed	*sped, speeded*	sped, speeded
spell	*spelled, spelt*	spelled, spelt
spellbind	*spellbound*	spellbound
spend	*spent*	spent
spill	*spilled, spilt*	spilled, spilt
spin	*spun*	spun
spit	*spat, spit*	spat, spit
split	*split*	split
spoil	*spoiled, spoilt*	spoiled, spoilt
spread	*spread*	spread
spring	*sprang, sprung*	sprung
stand	*stood*	stood
stave	*stove, staved*	stove, staved
steal	*stole*	stolen
stick	*stuck*	stuck
sting	*stung*	stung
stink	*stank, stunk*	stunk
strew	*strewed*	strewed, strewn
stride	*strode*	stridden
strike	*struck*	struck, stricken
string	*strung*	strung
strive	*strove*	striven
swear	*swore*	sworn
sweat	*sweat, sweated*	sweat, sweated
sweep	*swept*	swept
swell	*swelled*	swollen, swelled
swim	*swam*	swum
swing	*swung*	swung

T

Infinitivo	Pretérito	Part. pasivo
take	*took*	taken
teach	*taught*	taught
tear	*tore*	torn
tell	*told*	told
think	*thought*	thought
thrive	*throve, thrived*	thriven, thrived
throw	*threw*	thrown
thrust	*thrust*	thrust
tread	*trod*	trodden, trod
typewrite	*typewrote*	typewritten

U

Infinitivo	Pretérito	Part. pasivo
unbend	*unbent*	unbent
unbind	*unbound*	unbound
underbid	*underbid*	underbid
undercut	*undercut*	undercut
underdo	*underdid*	underdone
underfeed	*underfed*	underfed
undergo	*underwent*	undergone
underlay	*underlaid*	underlaid
underlet	*underlet*	underlet
underlie	*underlay*	underlain
underpay	*underpaid*	underpaid
undersell	*undersold*	undersold
understand	*understood*	understood
undertake	*undertook*	undertaken
underwrite	*underwrote*	underwritten
undo	*undid*	undone
undraw	*undrew*	undrawn
unfreeze	*unfroze*	unfrozen
ungird	*ungirded, ungirt*	ungirded, ungirt
unhang	*unhung*	unhung
unknit	*unknit, unknitted*	unknit, unknitted
unlade	*unladed*	unladen
unlearn	*unlearnt, unlearned*	unlearnt, unlearned
unmake	*unmade*	unmade
unsay	*unsaid*	unsaid
unsew	*unsewed*	unsewn, unsewed
unsling	*unslung*	unslung
unstick	*unstuck*	unstuck
unstring	*unstrung*	unstrung
unteach	*untaught*	untaught
unweave	*unwove*	unwoven
unwind	*unwound*	unwound
upbear	*upbore*	upborne
uphold	*upheld*	upheld
uprise	*uprose*	uprisen
upset	*upset*	upset

W

Infinitivo	Pretérito	Part. pasivo
wake	*waked, woke*	waked, woken
wear	*wore*	worn
weave	*wove*	woven
weep	*wept*	wept
win	*won*	won
wind	*wound*	wound
wiredraw	*wiredrew*	wiredrawn
withdraw	*withdrew*	withdrawn
withhold	*withheld*	withheld
withstand	*withstood*	withstood
wring	*wrung*	wrung
write	*wrote*	written

PESAS Y MEDIDAS
WEIGHTS AND MEASURES

Pesas y medidas en los países de lengua inglesa

Medidas de peso

— Sistema AVOIRDUPOIS

grain (grano)	[gr.]	1/7000 pound	0,0648 g
dram	[dr.]	27,34 grains	1,7718 g
ounce (onza)	[oz.]	16 drams	28,3495 g
pound (libra)	[lb.]	16 ounces	453,6 g
stone	[st.]	14 pounds	6,350 kg
quarter	[qr.]	2 stones	12,7 kg
cental (quintal)		100 pounds	45,360 kg
hundredweight	[cwt.]	112 pounds	50,802 kg
long ton (tonelada larga)	[l.t.]	20 hundred-weights	1016,044 kg
short ton (tonelada corta)		2000 pounds	907,18 kg

— Sistema TROY

Se utiliza únicamente para metales preciosos.

grain (grano)	[gr.]		0,0648 g
pennyweight	[dwt.]	24 grains	1,555 g
ounce (onza)	[oz.]	20 pennyweights	31,103 g
pound (libra)	[lb.]	12 ounces	373,242 g

Medidas de longitud

inch (pulgada)	[in.]		2,54 cm
foot (pie)	[ft.]	12 inches	30,48 cm
yard (yarda)	[yd.]	3 feet	91,44 cm
fathom	[fm.]	6 feet	1,8288 m
pole, rod, perch		5,5 yards	5,0292 m
chain		4 poles	20,116 m
furlong (estadio)		220 yards	201,16 m
mile (milla)	[m.]	1760 yards	1609 m
knot, nautical mile (milla marina)		2025 yards	1853 m

Medidas de superficie

square inch (pulgada cuadrada)	[sq. in.]	6,451 cm^2
square foot (pie cuadrado)	[sq. ft.]	929 cm^2
square yard (yarda cuadrada)	[sq. yd.]	0,836126 m^2
square mile (milla cuadrada)	[sq. m.]	2,58995 km^2
square pole		26,293 m^2
rood (= 40 square poles)		10,1169 áreas
acre (acre) [= 4 roods]		40,468 áreas

Medidas de volumen

cubic inch (pulgada cúbica)	[cu. in.]		16,387 cm^3
cubic foot (pie cúbico)	[cu. ft.]	1728 cubic inches	28,317 dm^3
cubic yard (yarda cúbica)	[cu. yd.]	27 cubic feet	764 dm^3
register ton (tonelada de arqueo)		100 cubic feet	2,8317 m^3

Medidas de capacidad

EN GRAN BRETAÑA Y CANADÁ

— *Para líquidos*

gill			0,142 l
pint (pinta)		4 gills	0,568 l
quart	[qt.]	2 pints	1,136 l
gallon (galón)	[gal.]	4 quarts	4,546 l

— *Para áridos*

peck	2 gallons	9,092 l
bushel	4 pecks	36,368 l
quarter	8 bushels	290,942 l

EN ESTADOS UNIDOS

— *Para líquidos*

liquid gill			0,118 l
liquid pint		4 gills	0,473 l
liquid quart		2 pints	0,946 l
gallon (galón)	[gal.]	4 quarts	3,785 l

— *Para áridos*

dry pint		0,550 l
dry quart	2 dry pints	1,1 l
peck	8 dry quarts	8,81 l
bushel	4 pecks	35,24 l

Metric system

Metric weights

miligramo (milligram)	[mg]	milésima de 1 gramo	0.015 grain
centigramo (centigram)	[cg]	centésima parte de 1 gramo	0.154 grain
decigramo (decigram)	[dg]	décima parte de 1 gramo	1.543 grain
gramo (gram, gramme)	[g, gr]		15.432 grains
decagramo (decagram)	[dag]	10 gramos	6.43 pennyweights
hectogramo (hectogram)	[hg]	100 gramos	3.527 ounces (avoirdupois)
kilogramo (kilogram)	[kg]	1000 gramos	2.2046 pounds
quintal métrico (quintal)	[q]	100 kilogramos	220.46 pounds
tonelada métrica (metric ton)	[t]	1000 kilogramos	2,204.6 pounds

Metric lineal measures

milímetro (millimetre)	[mm]	milésima parte de 1 metro	0.039 inch
centímetro (centimetre)	[cm]	centésima parte de 1 metro	0.393 inch
decímetro (decimetre)	[dm]	décima parte de 1 metro	3.937 inches
metro (metre)	[m]		1.0936 yard
decámetro (decametre)	[dam]	10 metros	10.9 yards
hectómetro (hectometre)	[hm]	100 metros	109.3 yards
kilómetro (kilometre)	[km]	1000 metros	1,093 yards *o* 0.6214 mile

Metric square and cubic measures

metro cuadrado (square metre)	[m^2]		1.196 square yard
área (are)	[a]	100 metros cuadrados	119.6 square yards
hectárea (hectare)	[ha]	100 áreas	2.471 acres
metro cúbico (cubic metre)	[m^3]		35.315 cubic feet

Liquid and dry measures

centilitro (centilitre)	[cl]	centésima parte de 1 litro	0.017 pint
decilitro (decilitre)	[dl]	décima parte de 1 litro	0.176 pint
litro (litre)	[l]		1.76 pint
decalitro (decalitre)	[dal]	10 litros	2.2 gallons
hectolitro (hectolitre)	[hl]	100 litros	22.01 gallons

UNIDADES MONETARIAS

MONETARY UNITS

La unidad monetaria de Gran Bretaña es la **libra** (pound) [£], dividida hasta el 15 de febrero de 1971, fecha en que se adoptó el sistema decimal, en veinte **chelines** (shillings) [s] o en doscientos cuarenta **peniques** (pence) [d] y actualmente en cien **peniques** [p]. Existe además la **guinea**, empleada únicamente para los artículos de lujo y honorarios, que tenía un valor de veintiún chelines y ahora corresponde a ciento cinco peniques.

La unidad monetaria de los Estados Unidos y Canadá es el **dólar** (dollar) [$], americano y canadiense, que se divide en cien **centavos** (cents).

Unidades monetarias en los países de habla española

País	*Unidad*	*Subdivisión*
Argentina	*peso*	= 100 centavos
Bolivia	*peso*	= 100 centavos
Chile	*peso*	= 100 centavos
Colombia	*peso*	= 100 centavos
Costa Rica	*colón*	= 100 céntimos
Cuba	*peso*	= 100 centavos
Ecuador	*sucre*	= 100 centavos
El Salvador	*colón*	= 100 centavos
España	*peseta*	= 100 céntimos
Filipinas	*peso*	= 100 centavos
Guatemala	*quetzal*	= 100 centavos
Honduras	*lempira*	= 100 centavos
México	*peso*	= 100 centavos
Nicaragua	*córdoba*	= 100 centavos
Panamá	*balboa*	= 100 centésimos
Paraguay	*guaraní*	= 100 céntimos
Perú	*sol*	= 100 centavos
Puerto Rico	*dólar americano*	= 100 centavos
República Dominicana	*peso*	= 100 centavos
Uruguay	*peso*	= 100 centésimos
Venezuela	*bolívar*	= 100 centavos

TEMPERATURA

TEMPERATURE

En los países de habla inglesa se utiliza la escala termométrica **Fahrenheit** en vez de la centígrada.

Para convertir los grados Fahrenheit en grados centígrados es preciso restar 32, multiplicar por 5 y dividir por 9. Así 212° Fahrenheit equivalen a 100° centígrados.

To convert centigrade degrees into Fahrenheit multiply by 9, divide by 5 and add 32.